S0-BDH-216

"Your work is a very sacred matter. God delights in it, and through it, He wants to best His blessings on you. This praise of work should be inscribed on all tools, on the forehead and the faces that sweat from toiling."

Martin Luther

The
1599
GENEVA
BIBLE

For: Pastor David
Christmas 2017
From: Judy Bullock

The
1599
GENEVA
BIBLE

500TH ANNIVERSARY OF THE REFORMATION

Luther Edition

THE HOLY SCRIPTURES
Contained in the
OLD AND NEW TESTAMENTS

Martin Luther

1483-1983 USA 20c

DALLAS, GEORGIA
UNITED STATES OF AMERICA

The 1599 Geneva Bible
500TH ANNIVERSARY OF THE REFORMATION
LUTHER EDITION

Copyright © 2010–2016 by Tolle Lege Press

First Printing September 2016

All Rights reserved. No part of this publication may be reproduced or transmitted in any form or by any means, electronic or mechanical, without written permission from the publisher, except in the case of brief quotations in articles, reviews, and broadcasts.

Published & Distributed by:

TOLLE LEGE PRESS
147 Ponderosa Trail
Dallas, Georgia 30132

www.TolleLegePress.com
www.GenevaBible.com

ISBN: 978-1-938139-35-2   Hardcover Edition

Printed in the United States of America.

Cover by Michael Minkoff, Jr. and Luis Lovelace

COVER ART: *Luther Posting the Ninety-five Theses* by Ferdinand Pauwels, 1872. This was one of seven Luther-themed wall panels Pauwels painted at Wartburg Castle, where Luther spent some time in hiding translating the Greek and Hebrew Bible into German.

Table of Contents

FOREWORD

As you hold this new edition of the venerated Geneva Bible, several realities converge in your heart, your mind, and your hands. What are these realities? They include:

History and Legacy It was the Geneva Bible that accompanied our forefathers to the new world. They made history in many ways, not the least of which was a legacy of Scriptural wisdom inspired by the Geneva Bible.

Power and Influence As Paul was not ashamed of the Gospel of Christ, knowing it to be the power of God, committed believers in Christ can, and have, changed the culture with powerful tools like the Geneva Bible's unique translation and wisdom. The Kingdom of Heaven is at hand.

Achievement and Celebration The restoration of the Geneva Bible to American life is both a remarkable achievement and an event that readers can best celebrate by reading and sharing with everyone possible.

Saving Knowledge and Jesus Christ The heart of the Bible is Christ and His glorious salvation. He is the central message of the entire Bible. The Geneva Bible leads you not only to know and love Him as the Sovereign Lord of grace but it also leads you to know and to love Him as the Sovereign Lord of history.

Joy and Hope There is joy because of the rich Biblical theology of God's sovereign grace. And there is thus hope for our fallen world because God's sovereignty can move mountains, bring down strongholds, and turn hearts of stone into hearts of flesh and faith.

Opportunity and Potential With this spiritual arsenal in your hands you are equipped to storm the strongholds with the spiritual wisdom that opened this continent to become the most blessed civilization in history. The restoration of spiritual glory—the potential to reassert our culture's values of freedom, prosperity, education, and truth—is before you.

Scholarship and Ideas The scholars of the past have been united in this edition with contemporary scholars. The Geneva Bible's timeless truths, revolutionary ideas, and spiritual renewal will enable you to renew your heart, inform your mind, and direct your hands. Love the Lord your God with all your heart and mind, and may the ancient and eternal truths in these pages be the pointers on your quest to plumb the treasures of wisdom hidden in Christ.

> "The Geneva Bible once changed the world. In your hands you hold something that is about to change the world—again."

Changing the World Simply put, nothing has ever really changed the world except God's power. In your hands you have been given the greatest source of the greatest ideas known to man. The Scriptures, and the wisdom of the theological minds who brought forth the Geneva Bible, will enable you to think God's thoughts after Him because the Bible is His special revelation. Herewith is a resource that you are sure to find indispensable for the study and interpretation of creation as God would have you see it.

The Geneva Bible once changed the world. In your hands you hold something that is about to change the world—again. So use this Bible with care. Use it faithfully with faith. Then watch God once more do above and beyond all that we can ask or imagine.

Dr. Peter A. Lillback
Advisory Board Chairman,
1599 Geneva Bible Restoration Project
President, Westminster Theological Seminary
President, The Providence Forum
Senior Pastor, Proclamation
Presbyterian Church

PREFACE

The God-given vision to restore this special edition of the 1599 Geneva Bible was announced in January of 2004. Soon thereafter a team was organized to reset every word, making no changes except these few: modern spelling; proofreading to ensure word-for-word accuracy with the original 1599 edition; and designing an easy-to-read format. Over the subsequent three years of meticulous work, the production/editorial team witnessed the Providence of God in the daily details. The Lord clearly has ordained this special project and brought it to completion. Our hope is that the Geneva Bible, restored to its rightful place among frequently referenced Scriptures, will remind Christians of their rich heritage in the Protestant Reformation and inspire them to continue advancing the Gospel and Christ's Kingdom with the same passion and conviction of the Reformers.

We would like to share with readers the editorial philosophy and restoration processes we employed as we prepared this edition of the 1599 Geneva Bible.

SOURCE TEXT

Unlike most contemporary Bible translations, which have unvarying contents because of copyright strictures, the Geneva Bible was never a uniform publication. Due to the relative novelty of publishing Bibles in English, as well as the sheer number of printings (approximately 150 in its first 75 years), its many editions often varied in content and presentation.

The Geneva Bible was first published in 1560, and then "in 1576 a revised form of the Geneva Bible was produced by Laurence Tomson, Secretary to Sir Francis Walsingham (then Elizabeth's Secretary of State) and formerly lecturer in Hebrew at Geneva. This contains a few changes in the translation, the most characteristic being Tomson's pedantic rendering of the Greek definite article by 'that'

(e.g., Matt. 16.16, 'Thou art that Christ'); but the chief difference is the introduction of an English translation of Theodore Beza's summaries of doctrine and exposition of phrases, in Beza's Latin Bible. In 1598, the annotations on the Book of Revelation by Francis Junius, a Huguenot divine, were introduced into the Geneva Bible" [Metzger, Bruce M., "Book Notes," Theology Today, Vol 46, no 4 (January 1990): 463].

The edition we have chosen as our source is a facsimile of the work of Tomson and Junius, dated 1599; however "in 1599 alone ten editions appeared" [Dr. Roger Nicole, "The Original Geneva Bible," Tabletalk Magazine, Vol. 19, no 4 (April 1995)]. Our source copy was published by L L Brown (The 1599 Geneva Bible. Ozark, MO: LL Brown Publishing, 7th printing, 2003), with an introduction by James W. Bennett, and back matter containing the (undated) Sternhold & Hopkins Psalms. The Apocrypha and metrical Psalms, included in that edition, are omitted here, as well as the brief introductions to the Old Testament books (since they were not available for the New Testament books, we elected to omit them consistently). A "Note to the Reader" in our source copy's front matter, lists errors that, "according to the Historical Catalogue of Printed Bibles," were in the original 1599 edition—indicating an edition printed early enough in 1599 to precede these corrections.

It has been our attempt faithfully to preserve this single source, rather than consult many editions that would risk producing an inauthentic pastiche. The only exceptions are rare indiscernible sections or words; in those cases we have consulted other editions, indicated by citations in brackets.

AUTHENTICITY

Every word, as well as exact sentence structure, of the source edition is retained. We carefully have preserved the use of italics, by which the original translators indicated that they had supplied words not found in the original manuscripts. We retained capitalization of words, even at the risk of presenting anomalies to contemporary eyes. We avoided editorial tinkering in the name of stylistic consistency. Original punctuation was retained except in cases of egregious mistakes or obvious typographical errors in the source edition.

David Norton, in A Textual History of the King James Bible (Cambridge: Cambridge University Press, 2005), describes his own editorial standards for a new edition of the KJB for Cambridge: "Very importantly, [to] not modernise wherever possible. Modernisation must not be at the expense of the text, even if the result is more difficult for the reader" (page 136). Similarly, we did not attempt to make the text readable from a modern standpoint—only to offer contemporary readers what the Geneva Bible said.

ACCESSIBILITY

"The Geneva Bible was written during a period where the English language was transforming from Middle English to Early Modern English.... English was also going through a shift in pronunciation that was caught in the printing press.... Grammar was also changing, due to influence from other languages, the printing press, and from natural simplification.... Sentence structure also changed...." [Bennett, introduction to The 1599 Geneva Bible, 2003, xv-xvii].

The English language evolved in major ways during the writing of the Geneva Bible, and since then has changed even more radically, especially in matters of typography and print. An exact facsimile reprint of the early Geneva Bible, therefore, would be largely inaccessible to the modern reader. We have therefore addressed and updated the spelling of some words, and the appearance of some old letters, for the sake of American readers' ease of comprehension. Many times this simply meant changing an apparent f to an s; a y to an i; a v to a u; an i to a j; and so forth. For example, instead of what contemporary eyes would read as "Iefus faid vnto him," we have typeset "Jesus said unto him."

However, some of the spelling decisions were not as clear-cut:

Possessives We added apostrophes for possessives (which were not used in the English of that day), because these were determined not to be changes in meaning. For instance, where the source text read "God his mercy," this edition reads "God's mercy."

Proper Names We have also changed the spelling of the proper names in the Bible to that of the NKJV, since this can greatly help the contemporary reader, and does not compromise the meaning of the original edition. If, however, the NKJV used a completely different word than the source text, we retained the word from the source text, since to change would be to make a different choice than the original translators made. For example, we did not substitute "Syria" for "Aram."

Changes in Meaning What seems like a spelling difference sometimes indicates a distinction in meaning that the original translators intended. If we were unable to discern whether that was the case, we retained the language of the source text. For example, we accepted both "bewray" and "betray," "shamefaced" and "shamefast," "astonied" and "astonished."

If, however, 16th-century spellings were freely interchanged with no distinction in meaning – and if that is not the case today – we adjusted the text based on current meaning. For example, the source uses "beside" and "besides" interchangeably, yet through the subsequent years of English usage there has developed a distinction in meaning between the two words; so we used "beside" for "by the side of," and "besides" for "in addition to." Other such examples include: "whiles" and "while," "other" and "others," "then" and "than." In such instances the original word no longer gives the original meaning.

We have referred above to philological challenges and typographical errors. Occasional words or passages in the original-source

Geneva Bible are beyond the realms of subtle ambiguity or theological debate. For example, in Matthew 3:16, the source Geneva reads that John saw the Spirit of God descending like a dove, and "lightning" upon Jesus. Because the intended word is so clearly "lighting," we made the change; but were yet concerned to place that word in brackets, indicating that it was a change from the source edition. Also, as has been noted above, if we have been unable to read our source book and have consulted another Geneva edition, we have enclosed that text in brackets. Withal, there are very few words in brackets in this edition.

Archaic Words If a word is archaic, obsolete, colloquial, such that the meaning is now inaccessible or completely changed, we were careful to retain the original word; to completely change one word to another supersedes a spelling correction and compromises authenticity. Instead we have provided a glossary with short definitions in the back of this edition to help the modern reader. Again, to quote Norton, "The English of the KJB has many archaic words that present... challenges to the understanding, but... it is obvious that changing them is translating them" [A Textual History of the King James Bible, 138]. The Geneva Bible of 1560, being even earlier than the King James Bible of 1611, has many archaic words. The purpose of this edition is to let the reader see what they are, not to see how we decided to translate them.

Indiscernible Text There have been occasions when we simply could not discern the meaning of a word, or the intent of the original translators, either from our original source or from any other resource available to us. In those few cases, we have used ellipses to indicate omitted text.

Study Notes Study notes from the source edition frequently employ wording like "Look afore, chap. 5,29" [found in Matthew 18:8] or "as God command Levit. 23.40" [at Matthew 21:9]. We have standardized all references to Scripture using the book name abbreviations listed on the Books of the Old and New Testaments page in this volume, and using contemporary practice of separating chapter and verse with a colon. In cases like the first one above we simply use, for these examples, "See Matt. 5:29" and "as God commanded, Lev. 23:40."

CONCLUSION

To God be the glory for allowing us to be used in the restoration of this historic work. The republication of this Bible is an indication that the Lord is a faithful, covenant-keeping God, "That thou mayest know, that the Lord thy God, he is God, the faithful God, which keepeth covenant and mercy unto them that love him and keep his commandments, even to a thousand generations." (Deut. 7:9)

Merciful Lord, we ask you to once again grant Repentance, Reformation, and Revival in your Church for the advancement of your Kingdom on earth as it is in heaven. Amen.

Tolle Lege Press
White Hall, WV
August 2006

The History and Impact of the
GENEVA BIBLE

The Bible you hold in your hands, known as "The Geneva Bible," has been the lost treasure of Christendom for almost four centuries. Nearly forgotten by the modern world, this version of the Holy Scriptures was researched, compiled, and translated into English by exiled Reformers in Geneva, Switzerland, between 1557 and 1560, and was destined to be the major component of the English-speaking people's rise from the backwaters of history to the center of civilization.

This edition of the Geneva Bible is the first completely new publication since the time of its first issue, and timed for release on the 400th anniversary of the settlement of Jamestown in what is now Virginia. The Geneva Bible surely was carried aboard their three ships that sailed from England in December of 1606. The New England Pilgrims likewise relied on the Geneva Bible for comfort and strength on their 66-day voyage aboard the Mayflower in 1620, and were even more dependent upon it as they wrote the Mayflower Compact, a document unique in world history and the first constitutional government in the western hemisphere.

SETTING THE STAGE

England of 1557 was a society beset by contradictions, oppression, even barbarity. More than 300 men had been burned at the stake by the Catholic tyrant, "Bloody Mary" Tudor, merely for promoting the English Reformation. Many clergymen, Catholic and Protestant both, exacerbated rather than soothed the distress; semi-literate as a class, most received their parish jobs as payoffs and often were unwilling to preach, or incapable of composing sermons. The impoverished and spiritually bereft masses found solace elsewhere—sloth, dissipation, or drink—while the gentry sought after wealth, social position, and favors of royal courts.

Into this seemingly hopeless culture of corruption and error, the light of God's written Word—in the newly translated, published, and distributed Geneva Bible—inexorably began to liberate the English-speaking people, penetrating hearts and transforming minds. It is no exaggeration to say that the Geneva Bible was the most significant catalyst of the transformation of England, Scotland, and America from slavish feudalism to the heights of Christian civilization.

As the first Bible to be read by the common people in English, the Geneva Bible inspired those who championed self-government, free enterprise, education, civic virtue, protection of women and children, and godly culture. John Knox preached with power from the Geneva Bible at St. Giles Cathedral in Edinburgh, mightily influencing Scotland's restoration from clan-dominated, semi-pagan barbarity to Christian faith and liberty. The legendary Soldier's Pocket Bible, famous as the spiritual companion to Oliver Cromwell's Christian soldiers in the English civil war, was composed of verses from the Geneva translation. And it was the Geneva Bible that was carried and read by the Pilgrims as they landed in the wilderness of America and extrapolated concepts of civic morality from its pages as they laid foundation-stones of the world's first constitutional republic.

For more than 1500 years, an unfettered spread of the Gospel in the world was stymied without a reliable, written version of God's Word in the common language of the people. Rome's missionaries and monasteries had played their roles in civilizing the pagan tribes of Europe and establishing Christian authority. But abuse of power and perversion of truth by prelates and kings were commonplace by the Renaissance.

The providential invention of movable type, enabling not just the publication but the practical distribution of the Geneva Bible, freed God's Book from the echoes of august cathedrals and the dead Latin language into the lives and homes, hearths and hearts, of everyday people in the English-speaking world.

History of The Geneva Bible

The Geneva translation's revolutionary impact can be better appreciated by the realization that the Bible has only been available to laymen for 400 years. Prior to the printing of Luther's German Bible in 1534, and the Geneva Bible in English, everyday believers, regardless of nationality, never had a Bible of their own to read, study, to "hide in their hearts." The Church and kings kept all but clergy and Latin scholars from reading Scripture; in England it even became, by royal edict, a capital crime even to read the Bible in the "vulgar tongue" (the English language). In 1526, the English scholar William Tyndale attempted to translate the Bible into English and was forced to flee to Germany, where he met Martin Luther, and then to Belgium, all in an effort to translate the Bible and to fulfill the commitment made to a clergyman who attempted to dissuade him from his mission: "[God's] version was to be made for all the people, even the humblest: if God spare my life, ere many years pass I will cause the boy that driveth the plow to know more of Scripture than thou [a theologian] dost."

Fulfilling his promise, Tyndale published the first-ever mechanically printed New Testament in the English language, in 1526. Six thousand first-edition copies were smuggled to England and lit a fire that could not be extinguished.

But Tyndale was hunted, captured, and imprisoned in the Belgian town of Vilvoorde. On March 6, 1536, he was strangled and burned at the stake, his last words "Lord, open the King of England's eyes." His prayers were answered. Tyndale's monumental work made its way to some English pulpits, and one had been paid for by the same king who persecuted him, Henry VIII, who became a supporter of Protestant reformers.

These first English passages of Scripture, however, were pulpit Bibles, for use by the clergy; still the people had no Bibles they could afford… nor, for the most part, that they could read.

In 1553, upon the death of Henry VIII's 16-year-old Protestant son Edward, Mary Tudor ascended the throne, soon married the Catholic King of Spain, and set about, often with violent cruelty, to stamp out the Reformation. Determined to force the English people back to Roman Catholicism, she ordered the burning of all copies of the Bible in English. She caused more than 300 reformers, pastors and Bible translators to be burned at the stake, well earning her for all of history the sobriquet Bloody Mary.

Queen Mary's vicious crusade drove approximately 800 English scholars to the Continent (the "Marian Exile") but God used this exodus to assemble, in Geneva, some of the finest theologians and Biblical scholars in history. Here, under the protection of John Calvin's "little republic," this special group of thinkers, led by William Whittingham (Calvin's brother-in-law) and assisted by Miles Coverdale, Christopher Goodman, Anthony Gilby, John Knox, and Thomas Sampson, produced a new English Bible not beholden to any king or prelate—The Geneva Bible,—the first English Translation from the original tongues since Tyndale's revised New Testament of 1534. The reformers sought to produce a Bible that was not based on the less-authentic Latin Vulgate promoted by Queen Mary. They researched the most recently collected Greek and Hebrew manuscripts. Whitingham's completed revision of William Tyndale's New Testament, including many annotations and commentaries, was published in 1557; and almost immediately work began on a revision of the entire Bible. Devoting more than two years of intense toil to the task, the result was the first Bible translation produced by a committee rather than by one individual. They drew upon painstaking translations from the original languages; Theodore Beza's work and other continental translations, such as Luther's; all overseen and supported by reformers like John Knox and John Calvin.

The completed Geneva Bible was published in 1560 and dedicated to Queen Elizabeth, who had succeeded her half-sister Bloody Mary to the throne and, at least for political reasons, supported a definitive break with the Church of Rome. The Geneva Bible was an instant success that captured the hearts of the people with its powerful, uncompromising prose and more than 300,000 words of annotations in the margins to aid in personal study and understanding.

This unique 2006 edition of the 1599 version of the Geneva Bible uses Tomson's revised New Testament (a later revision of Whitingham's New Testament of 1557) and Junius's annotated notes on "Revelation." The 1599 version has the most complete compilation of annotations of any of the Geneva editions. It also has a table of interpretations of proper names, which are chiefly found in the Old Testament, and a table of principle subjects contained in the Bible. The Books of Psalms were collected into English meters by Thomas Sternhold, John Hopkins, and others, to encourage their recitation in the manner of the early churches. Also included were prayers to be used by English congregations every morning and evening.

For generations after its first printing, the Geneva Bible remained the Bible of personal study in England, Scotland, and then in America. A 1579 Scottish edition of the Geneva version was the first Bible printed in Scotland; it soon became the standard of the Scottish Kirk. The Scottish Parliament required that every householder worth 300 marks, and every yeoman or burgess worth 500 pounds, have a Bible in the "vulgar tongue" in their homes, under penalty of 10 pounds.

The Geneva Bible came to be called affectionately the "Breeches Bible." The term derives from the reference in Genesis 3:7 to Adam and Eve clothing themselves in fig-leaf "breeches," a decidedly English term.

So popular was the Geneva Bible that between 1560 and 1644 at least 144 editions were published, compared to but five editions of another, inferior, translation known as The Bishops Bible. The Geneva Bible lost its prominence only after the King James Authorized Version of 1611 was widely promoted by the King and Bishop Laud (later Archbishop of Canterbury and persecutor of Presbyterians), who outlawed the printing of the Geneva Bible in the realm. When the Geneva Bible disappeared, there were widespread complaints that people "could not see into the sense of Scripture for lack of the spectacles of those Genevan annotations."

THE UNIQUENESS OF THE GENEVA BIBLE

The Geneva Bible stands as one of the great achievements of Biblical scholarship. It is the Bible of "firsts".

- It was the first English Bible to be fully translated from the original languages. The fall of Constantinople (1453) had a providential benefit, as previously unknown Greek and Hebrew manuscripts were carried to the West by Christians fleeing the Islamic onslaught. The Renaissance Period's interest in antiquity also brought authentic documents and historical details to the attention of the Geneva scholars.

- It was the first Bible translation to be printed in easy-to-read Roman type, rather than the older "Black Face" Gothic text. The 2006 edition of the 1599 Geneva version goes a step further; while keeping the Bible text and notes accurate word-for-word with the 16th-century edition, spelling has been updated and the type reset in an even easier-to-read form.

- It was the first Bible to qualify as a study Bible, providing readers with copious notes, annotations, and commentary about the original manuscripts, clarification of ambiguous meanings, and cross references. It is a tribute to the intellectual integrity of the translators that they also used italics for the interpolated words that were not in the original languages—helpful for the English vernacular, and the first-ever use of this tool in historical or literary analysis.

+ It was the first Bible to assign chapter demarcation, and to add verse numbers within chapters. These innovations facilitated the location of passages, memorization, and recitation… and the nurture of a nation of Bible readers.

+ It was the first Bible to be printed in a small quarto edition, portable and affordable. This made it suitable for family use without expensive folios. Every Pilgrim family, for example, had a Geneva Bible as the convenient center of its daily life.

IMPACT OF THE GENEVA BIBLE

The Geneva Bible significantly assisted the creation of the modern English language—the lingua franca of today's world. William Tyndale's linguistic genius and the poetic mastery of Miles Coverdale's earlier translation of the Poetic Books are widely credited with sparking the English literary excellence of the 17th and 18th centuries: the Geneva Bible was the Bible of William Shakespeare, John Milton, John Bunyan, the Puritans (considered history's greatest expositors), and the Pilgrims who sailed to America. It was the Bible that John Rolfe likely would have used in the conversion of Pocahontas at Jamestown in 1611.

The impact of the annotations and commentary in the Geneva Bible cannot be underestimated. The Calvinist notes of the Geneva Bible infuriated King James I at Hampton Court in 1604, prompting him to authorize a group of Puritan scholars to produce a version of the Bible without annotation for him; ironically, the excellent Authorized Version might never have been written were it not for King James's antipathy toward the Geneva Bible.

The marginal notes of the Geneva Bible present a systematic Biblical worldview centered on the Sovereignty of God over all of His creation including churches and kings. This unique Biblical emphasis, though fraught with dangers beyond spiritual debates (i.e., political and social pressure), was one of John Calvin's great contributions to the English Reformers. For example, the marginal note in the Geneva Bible for Exodus 1:19 indicated that the Hebrew midwives were correct to disobey the Egyptian rulers. King James called such interpretations "seditious." The tyrant knew that if the people could hold him accountable to God's Word, his days as a king ruling by "Divine Right" were numbered, but Calvin and the Reformers defended the clear meaning of Scripture against whims of king or popes. Thus did the Geneva Bible begin the unstoppable march to liberty in England, Scotland, and America.

The marginal notes of the Geneva Bible also served to liberate believers from the ignorance, heresy, and tyranny of the Middle Ages. Calvin, and the Reformers who followed in his footsteps, expounded the whole counsel of God concerning doctrines of Sola Scriptura—the Word of God alone, inspired and directional for our lives and culture; Sola Fide—faith alone as the only means of justification before God; Sola Christus—Christ alone as mankind's only mediator, lord, and king; Sola Gratia—grace alone as the only hope of salvation and sanctification; and Soli Deo Gloria—God alone, not king nor pope, to receive the glory He is due in heaven and on earth.

Today, these theological "marginalia" might seem rudimentary or innocuous, but when they were systematically taught from Scripture and applied to life, as was done in the commentary in the Geneva Bible, entire nations and societies were transformed. Ultimately, the knowledge of and obedience to God's written Word led to constitutional, limited government; the end of slavery and the caste system; free enterprise and the concept of private property; the so-called Puritan work ethic that fueled the scientific and industrial revolutions; wholesome, uplifting standards in the arts; and many other forms of progress.

The bold innovations of the Geneva Bible continue to have an impact in today's world. Because of its revolutionary format and features, the Geneva Bible became the foundation for what we call group Bible study, and was a catalyst for the acceptance of the liberating doctrine of the "priesthood of all believers." Puritan lay leaders expounded the Word and other congregants offered commentary and invited discussion—all of which, today, might be taken for granted; but such practices were previously and strictly proscribed.

THE GENEVA BIBLE'S APPLICATION FOR TODAY

The Geneva Bible providentially was unleashed upon a dark, discouraged, downtrodden English-speaking world, at a time when Christendom was in real danger of regressing to a form of Caesar-worship. A Bible appeared that created the conditions for a Christian reformation of life and culture, the likes of which the world had never seen—its hallmarks including the explosion of faith; an emphasis on integrity; a unique and vital missionary movement; creative literature, economic blessings; and political and religious freedom. By the time of the defeat of the Spanish Armada in 1588, just 28 years after the first printing of the Geneva Bible, it was already being said of the English that they were becoming a "people of the Book."

Almost 500 years later, our culture is once again desperate for the Truth. Many people have forgotten, abandoned, or rejected the great lessons of the Reformation and the Biblical theology that inspired the greatest accomplishments of Western Civilization. We fervently pray that the re-introduction of this powerful tool of Godly dominion, the Geneva Bible, will, with God's favor, light the fires for another powerful reformation. As we read this sacred volume, let us remember the sacrifice of the persecuted scholars on the shores of Lake Geneva.

John Calvin, in exile in Geneva, surrounded by pagan kings, wars, and a corrupt Roman church, said these optimistic words about the spread of God's Word:

"Whatever resistance we see today offered by almost all the world to the progress of the truth, we must not doubt that our Lord will come at last to break through all the undertakings of men and make a passage for His Word. Let us hope boldly, then, more than we can understand; He will still surpass our opinion and our hope."

May we be inspired from His Word, as our spiritual forbears were, to be fearlessly optimistic about the power of His Gospel and the furtherance of His Kingdom on earth.

"For unto us a Childe is borne, and unto us a sonne is given: and the government and peace shal have none end: he shall sit upon the throne of David, and upon his kingdome, to order it, and to establish it with judgement and with justice, from hence forthe, and for ever: the zeale of the Lorde of hostes wil performe this" (Isaiah 9: 6-7, 1599 Geneva Bible).

Dr. Marshall Foster
Advisory Board Member,
1599 Geneva Bible Restoration Project
Founder & President, The Mayflower Institute

The Legacy and Lessons of
LUTHER'S NINETY-FIVE THESES

Despite the undisputed reputation of Martin Luther's *Ninety-five Theses* as the inaugural document of the Protestant Reformation, it was neither the first document of its time attempting to address the severe abuses of papal authority, nor was it the most inflammatory.[1] In fact, many modern-day inheritors of Protestantism will likely find the *Ninety-five Theses* uncomfortably deferential toward papal authority and Catholic doctrines. Quite unexpectedly, thesis 73 states:

> . . . the pope justly thunders against those who by any means whatever contrive harm to the sale of indulgences.

The modest monk who nailed the *Ninety-five Theses* to the church door of Wittenberg had not yet begun to repudiate even the sale of indulgences (merely their abuses)—much less papal authority or canon law. One of Luther's aims with the *Theses* was actually to protect the pope's reputation from skeptics and detractors who exploited a few of the Catholic Church's more glaring abuses to condemn Christianity at large. For instance, thesis 81 remarks:

> This unbridled preaching of indulgences makes it difficult even for learned men to rescue the reverence which is due the pope from slander or from the shrewd questions of the laity.

He asked in 1517 to be instructed, even corrected, by his superiors in the faith. He had all confidence at first that the abuses of his beloved Church could be ameliorated if the pope and his men acted swiftly in the service of the faithful to restore the Gospel and God's Word to their rightfully primary positions.

HOW A DISCUSSION BECAME A DIVISION

So how did a rather polite invitation for discussion and clarification become the seed for Luther's eventual excommunication and exile and the spark that set the world on Reformational fire?

Unfortunately, the Pope, with the majority of his bishops and princes in the Holy Roman Empire, did not respond to the *Ninety-five Theses* in the spirit with which they were originally offered. Just a few months after their publication, the famous indulgence salesman Johann Tetzel called for Luther to be burned at the stake for heresy.[2] Luther's requests for disputation had been summarily stonewalled, by councils and by Pope Leo X himself.

The pope sanctioned no discussion. He and his emissaries gave Luther only one option: recant or be excommunicated. But,

---

[1] Jan Hus, John Wycliffe, and Johannes van Wesel all condemned the abuse of indulgences long before 1517. Andreas Karlstadt, a close acquaintance and one-time colleague of Luther's, wrote 151 theses in 1516 against the ecclesiastical abuses he had seen in Rome. Later, Luther attempted to distance himself from Karlstadt, whom Luther considered overly revolutionary, even calling him in one place "quite given over to the devil" [Martin Luther, *The Letters of Martin Luther*, Margaret A. Currie, ed. and trans. (London: Macmillan and Co., 1908), 133].

[2] Ironically, Tetzel himself later became an expedient scapegoat when the pope and his cardinals wanted to give evidence of "necessary reforms." He was summoned to a hearing to answer for both his "extravagant lifestyle" and reports that he had fathered illegitimate children. He then retired to a convent quite humiliated. Luther wrote to him, "Don't take it too hard. You didn't start this racket. The child had another father." His last reference (clearly implicating the Catholic church "Fathers") could also have been a mild gibe referencing Tetzel's allegedly bastard children. Cited in Roland H. Bainton, *Here I Stand: A Life of Martin Luther* (Nashville: Abingdon Press, [1950] 1978), 95.

as Luther pointed out often, to their great exasperation, they did not even make it clear *of what* he should recant, since they had endorsed various parts of his teaching at various times and refused to delineate which parts of his teaching were in error or in what ways:

> They show their ignorance and bad conscience by inventing the adverb "respectively." My articles are called "respectively some heretical, some erroneous, some scandalous," which is as much as to say, "We don't know which are which." Oh meticulous ignorance! I wish to be instructed, not respectively, but absolutely and certainly. I demand that they show absolutely, not respectively, distinctly and not confusedly, certainly and not probably, clearly and not obscurely, point by point and not in a lump, just what is heretical. Let them show where I am a heretic, or dry up their spittle.[3]

Whatever can be said against Luther, one thing is clear: from the beginning, he resolved to be unmoved from his convictions without being convinced from Scripture. When the Pope and his councils refused to convince Luther from Scripture, Luther began to think the worst: perhaps the Catholic church refused to draw her authority from the Word of God simply because her most prized doctrines *derived from elsewhere*. Eventually, Luther became convinced that the authority of Rome rested on little more than perhaps well-meaning human traditions which were now being manipulated by vicious men who, for personal advantage, postured as the mouthpieces of God though they had long forsaken his Christ.

So it was that in just three short years after the *Theses* were published, a resolute Luther could be found burning the entire canon law on a bonfire outside Wittenberg. By this time, he had become accustomed to calling Pope Leo X and his curiae Anti-Christ. Luther's pamphlets and tracts had become increasingly critical of Catholic doctrine and authority, and

in 1520, he told his friend George Spalatin that he had finished trying to be reconciled to the Roman Catholic church:

> For me the die is cast, and I despise Rome's displeasure as much as her favor. I shall never be reconciled to her, let her condemn or burn me as she will. But if I can get a fire I shall publicly burn the whole Papal code, this serpentine piece of treachery, and make an end of the humility I have hitherto displayed in vain, so that the enemies of the gospel may no longer vaunt themselves on account of it.[4]

Rome reciprocated Luther's attitude toward her, and at the Diet of Worms (in 1521), a secular council convened at the reluctant behest of Rome to outlaw Luther and sequester his "heretical" writings. Luther's excommunication from the church followed shortly after. The break was complete. The Reformation had begun in earnest.

The Ninety-five Theses and the Fullness of Time

One might rightly wonder why Luther's *Ninety-Five Theses* sparked a religious revolution whereas all the overtures toward reform that had come before 1517 fizzled into, at most, localized sectarian movements[5] that did not threaten the pope's authority or the solidarity of the Catholic church.

Part of the answer to this question lies in a few intersections of history and the fullness of time.

For one, the Renaissance Humanists, who had effectively taken over the most prestigious universities in Europe by Luther's time, by and large defended Luther's doctrines (or at least his right to formulate them) against the sophists of Rome. These Humanists cherished freedom of inquiry and personal

---

[3] From Martin Luther, *Against the Execrable Bull of the Anti-Christ.*

[4] Martin Luther, *The Letters of Martin Luther*, Margaret A. Currie, ed. and trans. (London: Macmillan and Co., 1908), 54–55.

[5] The Bohemian Hussites were the largest and most prominent of these proto-Protestant sects. Luther was regularly called the "Saxon Hus" by his papist opponents.

liberty, both of which were then suffering greatly at the hands of the unnecessarily authoritarian Catholic Church. The Humanists also decried the superstitions of the Catholic Church (especially concerning relics and the sacraments) which superstitions they believed had darkened the popular mind and hampered the progress of human knowledge. In other words, the best scholars who would have been available to the Roman Catholic church to debate Luther and "put him in his place" agreed with Luther on the principal points of contention.

The scholarly defense of Luther's teaching was nothing compared to the popular support he garnered across Europe, however. The common people, especially in Germany, viewed Luther as their champion and defender. At first, they considered him the "German Hercules" or even a German Prometheus. They knew all too well the hardships and deprivations they had endured to pay for Rome's interminable building projects and unimaginable opulence. They were sheep being fleeced by their princes and their pope, and they saw Luther as their good shepherd.

But most of them never would have heard Luther's encouraging words of evangelical fervor and simple truth had it not been for that veritable engine of the Reformation: the movable type printing press.

For centuries before Luther, theological disputation had been the exclusive province of scholars and scribes who had access to universities, libraries, and the precious few woodblock-printed books and hand-lettered manuscripts. In addition, most of the works of religious authorities would not have meant much to the common people anyway, since they were written above the common mind in the educated language of Latin. This is not unlike the plight of Isaiah's audience (Isa. 29:11–12):

> The entire vision will be to you like the words of a sealed book, which when they give it to the one who is literate, saying, "Please read this," he will say, "I cannot, for it is sealed." Then the book will be given to the one who is illiterate, saying, "Please read this." And he will say, "I cannot read."

Theological and political discourse had been limited in distribution both by necessity but also by design. The common people deferred to the wisdom of pundits from ignorance just as they obeyed the edicts of princes from fear.

Unlike most of the scholars before him, Luther wrote most of his pamphlets memorably and plainly in common German, and his writings were printed in bulk and distributed widely thanks to Gutenberg's invention. In this way, Luther struck first at the people's ignorance, and then, by his own willingness to suffer for his personal convictions, he inspired the people to courage against oppression—both political, scholastic, and ecclesiastical.

It is hard to tell whether a popular demand for access to education had expedited the advent of the printing press or if the printing press had driven a demand for private education. Either way, it would be hard to overstate the impact Gutenberg's press had on the Reformation.

Gutenberg had created the first movable type press in Mainz, Germany around 1450. By 1517, presses were common enough that a local printer in Wittenberg was able to have a translated version of the *Ninety-five Theses* in the hands of the common people of Germany long before a Latin version in Luther's hand had had time to reach the Vatican. By the time Leo X got around to responding to Luther, the common people were already on Luther's side. This popular tide likely incited the Pope to act with greater stridency than he would have if "the Luther question" had remained a limited scholarly debate.

Which brings us to perhaps the most important historical reality that precipitated the Reformation: the woefully corrupt state of the Catholic church in Luther's time. In a way, Pope Leo X and his successors, as well as the other "bad popes," are as much the fathers of the Reformation as Luther.

If not for their intractable unwillingness to address Luther's quite reasonable concerns, their infamous lack of piety and lavish life-styles, and their fear-driven over-reactions to losing political power in a rapidly changing international landscape, history could have turned out quite differently.

In fact, the concerns of the *Ninety-five Theses* (though not the more anti-papal objections of Luther's later writings) have all, at this point, been adequately addressed by the Roman Catholic church. It's odd to think that the Reformation might not have ever happened if Luther had been address-ing a conciliatory and compromising Pope Francis instead of an obdurate Pope Leo X. And if the Reformation had never happened, what about the Scientific Revolution, or the American War for Independence? As Solomon said, "The Lord has made everything for its own purpose, even the wicked for the day of evil" (Prov. 16:4).

LUTHER'S LEGACY AND THE MOD-ERN REFORMATION

Eventually, however, Luther lost the sup-port of the common people, especially after the disastrous Peasants' War of 1524–25. And the Humanists also deserted him, most notably the mild-mannered scholar Erasmus. Even the other Reformers, who later took up the cause he began, excluded him from the label "Reformed," thinking him too close in theology to the papists.[6] The papists, of course, did not accept him, blaming him for both the peasant uprisings which threatened the tranquility of the State as well as the Reformation which threatened the stability of the Church. In the end, it seems, most all sides were at odds with Luther, a rather cold thanks for his considerable sacrifices.

Was it a Protestant Reformation or a Protestant Revolution? Surely, Luther first published his objections in order to reform

and purify the church of his day, but his opponents claimed Luther had introduced a disastrous spirit of autonomy and divisive-ness that threatened the kingdom of God. Regularly, Luther's "friends" disappointed him by giving the papists ample cases in point. From the various peasant uprisings to the quick proliferation of radical Christian sects led by men who were entirely unwilling to submit to one another in the fear of Christ, Luther's spiritual progeny seemed determined to undermine his teaching in practice.

Yet God still used him. Whether you are Lutheran, Reformed, non-denominational, Baptist, or Catholic, you owe the complexion of your current church in some part to the work and legacy of Martin Luther. He was a real man, and prone to error like all humans are. Many would paint him as a monster for various reasons, mostly because of the earthy, even vulgar, countenance of his later writings, especially concerning the Jews. But God used him mightily to begin many good works we still have yet to complete. Furthermore, we have yet to correct in our own hearts many of the errors for which we censure him. By the time of his death, Luther had not been able to free himself from all of his forefather's inherited errors or his own unique peccadilloes, but Luther's modern-day critics must ask themselves: have any of us fought like Luther did for the purity and peace of the church against such wide-ranging opposition?

There is much we can still learn from Luther's life and letters. For all the fiery hyperbole and earthy vituperations that characterize much of his writing, Luther regularly mediated between extremes in personal and practical terms. He preached liberty and individual rights to princes while he preached to peasants about proper submission to authority. He re-emphasized the mystery of the incarnate Christ where the papists had exchanged mystery for magic and the Humanists had discarded mystery for materialism. Luther denied abstracted, "spiritualized" pietism and superstition-prone

---

[6] The somewhat humorous "revisionism" of printing a Luther Edition of the Geneva Bible does not escape us.

sacramentalism. He rejected formalism and legalism of all kinds, in fact. He refused to submit to either the authoritarianism of the papacy or the absolutism he sensed in the other Reformers.

Because of this, he often found himself marooned between the papists and the magisterial Reformers. He maintained a steadfast commitment to the orthodoxy of ecclesiastical diversity in practice and belief. *The Augsburg Confession* (included in the after-matter of this Geneva edition), written by Philip Melanchthon as a statement of Martin Luther's doctrine, cuts this line quite nicely:

> This is about the Sum of our Doctrine, in which, as can be seen, there is nothing that varies from the Scriptures, or from the Church Catholic, or from the Church of Rome as known from its writers. This being the case, they judge harshly who insist that our teachers be regarded as heretics. There is, however, disagreement on certain Abuses, which have crept into the Church without rightful authority. And even in these, if there were some difference, there should be proper lenity on the part of bishops to bear with us by reason of the Confession which we have now reviewed; because even the Canons are not so severe as to demand the same rites everywhere, neither, at any time, have the rites of all churches been the same; although, among us, in large part, the ancient rites are diligently observed. For it is a false and malicious charge that all the ceremonies, all the things instituted of old, are abolished in our churches. But it has been a common complaint that some abuses were connected with the ordinary rites. These, inasmuch as they could not be approved with a good conscience, have been to some extent corrected....[7]

Churches in our day, contrary to Luther's mild localism, generally have been "demanding the same rites everywhere." But, unable to achieve those "same rites" through confession and unwilling to maintain unity through force, the Protestant church has splintered into countless sects, all holding to their own exclusive versions of orthodoxy.

Look around at the Protestant church today. Do we not still shame Luther's legacy? The age-old debate between the papists and the Protestants has centered on one issue: authority. The Roman Catholics claimed that humans could not rightly apply an infallible document without an infallible interpreter. They forwarded the Pope to fill this need. Protestants, following Luther's lead, forwarded the living and active Holy Spirit.

But, as the papists asked Luther, anyone might rightly ask us: "How can you be sure that you alone are right, and that all the scholars and learned men who have come before you are wrong?" We reply, "Let God be true, though every man a liar." But in practice, we often use our appeal to God to avoid accountability to our brothers and sisters. Many pastors say, "These are not my opinions I'm preaching to you. They rest on the authority of the Bible, so they are God's opinions. If you don't like them, you are not disagreeing with me, but with God himself." Those words could have been spoken with little alteration by Pope Leo X. In many cases, Protestant preachers have done little more than replace *ex cathedra* with *Sola Scriptura*, and often with the same abusive consequences.

How can we claim to have the Holy Spirit as our infallible interpreter if the fruit of his presence cannot be found in our midst? Consider that seven out of fifteen (nearly half!) of the deeds of the flesh concern a lack of peace: "enmities, strife, jealousy, outbursts of anger, disputes, dissensions, factions" (Gal. 5:20) The one who separates himself from his fellow believers doesn't do so to protect the truth, no matter what he may say: "He who separates himself seeks his own desire; he quarrels against all sound wisdom" (Prov. 18:1). Jesus said: "By this all men will know that you are my disciples, if you have love for one another" (Jn. 13:35).

---

[7] *The Augsburg Confession*, Article XXI.

We can be sure the devil tends the fires of our doctrinal debates if they do no more than create dissensions, disputes, factions, jealousies, strife, and divisions. These are the deeds of the flesh, not the fruits of the infallible Spirit.

Indeed, the Spirit will lead us to all truth (Jn. 16:13). But if we do not display the fruits of the Spirit, how can we say the Spirit is with us? And if he is not with us, how can he lead us into the truth? And if he is not leading us into the truth, then all of our doctrine is the empty traditions of men, no matter how much we may tout our reliance on the Scriptures.

And this is where the Christian religion, both in Protestant and Catholic circles, has most regularly fallen short. Religion can easily become a merely human exercise, a merely external adherence to traditions. But in order for it to be *true* religion, it must produce works that transcend the corrupted capacities of men. It is not mere unity that God calls us to. Unity can be achieved by fear or mutual advantage. It is the unity achieved by love that God desires, for that is a work of his Spirit. And this unity will not manifest itself in some invisible abstraction, but in a reality as tangible as bread and wine. "Pure and undefiled religion" does not primarily produce untarnished creeds, but blameless lives (James 1:27).

With all that in mind, read and cherish this book. It is the Word of God translated into your mother tongue (though perhaps a more remote version of it than you speak in your kitchen). Recognize in this book one of the fruits of Luther's work: to bring the Word of God to bear on everyday life. He believed the Word of God had to be studied and known by every believer, not just "special" believers in monasteries and universities. His opponents said that the common mind would debase the lofty Word of God, just as their unwashed hands would defile the sacred elements of the Lord's Supper. Luther thought differently. His aim was not to debase the transcendent, but to elevate the lowly, and he knew that could only happen through the transforming presence of God. That presence is in this book, if through faith you hear Jesus speaking to you through the Spirit.

It has been nearly five hundred years since Luther nailed the *Ninety-five Theses* to the church door of Wittenberg. Much has changed since then. No pope or prince now restricts you from taking this book up and reading and understanding it for yourself. But then, not enough has changed, because in spite of the free access we have to the Scriptures, few people know it like Luther did. We cannot blame political tyranny or ecclesiastical oppression at this point. We have nothing to blame but our own apathy. So, *Tolle Lege*: take up and read. Find the promised Spirit here waiting for those with faith. With God's help, let us perfect and complete what Luther started.

Michael Minkoff, Jr.
Editor, Luther Edition
Co-Founder & President,
The Nehemiah Foundation for Cultural Renewal

THE
BIBLE,
THAT IS,
The holy Scriptures conteined
in the Olde and Newe Testament,

TRANSLATED ACCORDING
to the Ebrew and Greeke, and conferred with the
best translations in diuers languages.

With most profitable Annotations vpon all the hard
places, and other things of great importance.

FEARE YE NOT STAND STILL, AND
beholde the saluation of the Lord, which he will
shew to you this day, Exod. 14. 13.
But the Lord deliuereth him

THE LORD SHALL FIGHT FOR YOU:
Therefore hold you your peace. Exod. 14. 14.

IMPRINTED AT LONDON
by the Deputies of Christopher Barker, Printer to
the Queenes most excellent Maiestie.

1599.
Cum priuilegio.

Books of the Old and New
TESTAMENTS

THE OLD TESTAMENT

THE NEW TESTAMENT

The
Old Testament

THE FIRST BOOK OF MOSES,

CALLED

¹GENESIS

---

1 *1 God created the heaven and the earth.* *3 The light and the darkness,* *8 The firmament,* *9 He separateth the water from the earth.* *16 He createth the sun, the moon, and the stars.* *21 He createth the fish, birds, beasts,* *26 He createth man, and giveth him rule over all creatures,* *29 And provideth nurture for man and beast.*

1 In the ¹beginning ᵃGod created the heaven and the earth.

2 And the earth was ¹,²without form and void, and ³darkness *was* upon the ⁴deep, and the Spirit of God ⁵moved upon the ⁶waters.

3 Then God said, ᵇLet there be light: And there was ¹light.

4 And God saw the light that it was good, and God separated ¹the light from the darkness.

5 And God called the Light, Day, and the darkness he called Night. ¹So the evening and the morning were the first day.

6 ¶ Again God said, ᶜLet there be a ¹firmament in the midst of the waters, and let it separate the waters from the waters.

7 Then God made the firmament, and separated the waters, which were ¹under the firmament, from the waters which were ᵈabove the firmament: and it was so.

8 And God called the firmament, ¹Heaven. So the evening and the morning were the second day.

9 ¶ God said again, ᵉLet the waters under the heaven be gathered into one place, and let the dry land appear: and it was so.

10 And God called the dry land, Earth, and he called the gathering together of the waters, Seas: and God saw that it was good.

11 Then God said, ¹Let the earth bud forth the bud of the herb, that seedeth seed, the fruitful tree, which beareth fruit according to his kind, which hath his seed in itself upon the earth: and it was so.

12 And the earth brought forth the bud of the herb, that seedeth seed according to his kind, also the tree that beareth fruit, which hath his seed in itself according to his kind: and God ¹saw that it was good.

13 So the evening and the morning were the third day.

14 ¶ And God said, ᶠLet there be ¹lights in the firmament of the heaven, to ²separate the day from the night, and let them be for ³signs, and for seasons, and for days, and years.

15 And let them be for lights in the firmament of the heaven to give light upon the earth: and it was so.

16 God then made two great ¹lights: the greater light to ²rule the day, and the lesser light to rule the night: he *made* also the stars.

17 And God set them in the firmament of the heaven, to shine upon the earth,

CHAPTER 1
ᵃ Ps. 33:6
Ps. 136:5
Acts 14:15
Acts 17:24
ᵇ Heb. 11:3
ᶜ Ps. 33:6
Ps. 136:5
Jer. 10:12
Jer. 51:15
ᵈ Ps. 148:4
ᵉ Ps. 33:7
Ps. 89:11
Ps. 136:6
Job 38:4
ᶠ Ps. 136:7
Deut. 4:19

Title ¹ This word signifieth the beginning and generation of the creatures.

1:1 ¹ First of all, and before that any creature was, God made heaven and earth of nothing.

1:2 ¹ As a rude lump and without any creature in it: for the waters covered all.

² Or, waste.

³ Darkness covered the deep waters, for as yet the light was not created.

⁴ Hebrew, *face of the deep.*

⁵ He maintained this confused heap by his secret power.

⁶ Hebrew, *face of the waters.*

1:3 ¹ The light was made before either Sun or Moon was created: therefore we must not attribute that to the creatures that are God's instruments, which only appertaineth to God.

1:4 ¹ Hebrew, *between the light, and between the darkness.*

1:5 ¹ Hebrew, *so was the evening, so was the morning.*

1:6 ¹ Or, spreading over, and air.

1:7 ¹ As the sea and rivers, from those waters that are in the clouds, which are upheld by God's power, lest they should overwhelm the world.

1:8 ¹ That is, the region of the air, and all that is above us.

1:11 ¹ So that we see it is the only power of God's word that maketh the earth fruitful, which else naturally is barren.

1:12 ¹ This sentence is so oft repeated, to signify that God made all his creatures to serve to his glory, and to the profit of man: but for sin they were accursed, yet to the elect, by Christ they are restored, and serve to their wealth.

1:14 ¹ By the lights he meaneth the Sun, the Moon, and the Stars.

² Which is the artificial day, from the Sun rising, to the going down.

³ Of things appertaining to natural and political orders and seasons.

1:16 ¹ To wit, the Sun and the Moon, and here he speaketh, as man judgeth by his eye: for else the Moon is less than the planet Saturn.

² To give it sufficient light, as instruments appointed for the same, to serve to man's use.

18 And to ᵍrule in the day, and in the night, and to separate the light from the darkness: and God saw that it was good.

19 So the evening and the morning were the fourth day.

20 Afterward God said, Let the waters bring forth in abundance *every* ¹creeping thing that hath ²life: and let the fowl fly upon the earth in the ³open firmament of the heaven.

21 Then God created the great whales, and everything living and moving, which the ¹waters brought forth in abundance according to their kind, and every feathered fowl according to his kind: and God saw that it was good.

22 Then God ¹blessed them, saying, Bring forth fruit and multiply, and fill the waters in the seas, and let the fowl multiply in the earth.

23 So the evening and the morning were the fifth day.

24 ¶ Moreover God said, Let the earth bring forth the ¹living thing according to his kind, cattle, and that which creepeth, and the beast of the earth according to his kind, and it was so.

25 And God made the beast of the earth according to his kind, and the cattle according to his kind, and every creeping thing of the earth according to his kind: and God saw that it was good.

26 Furthermore God said, ʰ,ⁱLet us make man in our ²image according to our likeness, and let them rule over the fish of the sea, and over the fowl of the heaven, and over the beasts, and over all the earth, and over everything that creepeth and moveth on the earth.

27 Thus God created the man in his image: in the image of God created he him: he created them ⁱmale and female.

28 And God ¹blessed them, and God said to them, ʲBring forth fruit, and multiply, and fill the earth, and subdue it, and rule over the fish of the sea, and over the fowl of the heaven, and over every beast that

moveth upon the earth.

29 And God said, Behold, I have given unto you ¹every herb bearing seed, which is upon all the earth, and every tree, wherein is the fruit of a tree bearing seed: ᵏ*that* shall be to you for meat.

30 Likewise to every beast of the earth, and to every fowl of the heaven, and to everything that moveth upon the earth, which hath life in itself, every green herb *shall be* for meat, and it was so.

31 ˡAnd God saw all that he had made, and lo, it was very good. So the evening and the morning were the sixth day.

2

2 God resteth the seventh day, and sanctifieth it. 15 He setteth man in the garden. 22 He createth the woman. 24 Marriage is ordained.

1 Thus the heavens and the earth were finished, and all the ¹host of them.

2 For in the seventh day God ended his work which he had made, ᵃand the seventh day he ¹rested from all his work, which he had made.

3 So God blessed the seventh day, and ¹sanctified it, because that in it he had rested from all his work, which God created and made.

4 ¶ These are the ¹generations of the heavens and of the earth, when they were created, in the day, that the Lord God made the earth and the heavens,

5 And every ¹plant of the field, before it was in the earth, and every herb of the field, before it grew, for the Lord God had not caused it to ²rain upon the earth, neither *was there* a man to till the ground,

6 But a mist went up from the earth, and watered all the earth.

7 ¶ The Lord God also ¹made the man ²of the dust of the ground, and breathed in his face breath of life, ᵇand the man was a living soul.

8 And the Lord God planted a garden Eastward in ¹Eden, and there he put the man whom he had made.

9 (For out of the ground made the Lord God to

Cross-references (center column)

ᵍ Jer. 31:35
ʰ Gen. 5:1
  Gen. 9:6
  2 Cor. 11:7
  Col. 3:10
ⁱ Matt. 19:4
ʲ Gen. 8:17
  Gen. 9:1
ᵏ Gen. 9:3
ˡ Exod. 31:17
  Mark 7:37

CHAPTER 2
ᵃ Exod. 20:11
  Exod. 31:17
  Deut. 5:14
  Heb. 4:4
ᵇ 1 Cor. 15:45

Footnotes

1:20 ¹ As fish and worms which slide, swim, or creep.
  ² Hebrew, *the soul of life.*
  ³ Hebrew, *face of the firmament.*
1:21 ¹ The fish and fowls had both one beginning, wherein we see that nature giveth place to God's will, forasmuch as the one sort is made to fly about in the air, and the other to swim beneath in the water.
1:22 ¹ That is, by the virtue of his word he gave power to his creatures to engender.
1:24 ¹ Hebrew, *soul of life.*
1:26 ¹ God commanded the water and the earth to bring forth other creatures: but of man he saith, Let us make: signifying, that God taketh counsel with his wisdom and virtue, purposing to make an excellent work above all the rest of his creation.
  ² This image and likeness of God in man is expounded, Eph. 4:24, where it is written that man was created after God in righteousness and true holiness, meaning by these two words, all perfection, as wisdom, truth, innocence, power, etc.

1:28 ¹ The propagation of man is the blessing of God, Ps. 128.
1:29 ¹ God's great liberality to man, taketh away all excuse of his ingratitude.
2:1 ¹ That is, the innumerable abundance of creatures in heaven and earth.
2:2 ¹ For he had now finished his creation, but his providence still watcheth over his creatures, and governeth them.
2:3 ¹ Appointed it to be kept holy, that man might therein consider the excellency of his works and God's goodness toward him.
2:4 ¹ Or, the original and beginning.
2:5 ¹ Or, tree, as Gen. 21:15.
  ² God only openeth the heavens and shutteth them, he sendeth drought and rain according to his good pleasure.
2:7 ¹ Or, formed.
  ² He showeth whereof man's body was created, to the intent that man should not glory in the excellency of his own nature.
2:8 ¹ This was the name of a place, as some think in Mesopotamia, most pleasant and abundant in all things.

grow every tree pleasant to the sight, and good for meat: the [1]tree of life also in the midst of the garden, [2]and the tree of knowledge of good and of evil.

10 And out of Eden went a river to water the garden, and from thence it was divided, and became into four heads.

11 The name of one is Pishon: the same compasseth the whole land of [1]Havilah, where is gold.

12 And the gold of that land is good: there is [1]Bdellium, and the Onyx stone.

13 And the name of the second river is Gihon: the same compasseth the whole land of [1]Cush.

14 And the name of the [third] river is [1]Hiddekel: this goeth toward the East side of [2]Ashshur: and the fourth river is [3]Parah)

15 ¶ Then the Lord God took the man, and put him into the garden of Eden, that he might [1]dress it, and keep it.

16 And the Lord God [1]commanded the man, saying, [2]Thou shalt eat freely of every tree of the garden,

17 But of the tree of knowledge of good and evil, thou shalt not eat of it: for [1]in the day that thou eatest thereof, thou shalt die the [2]death.

18 Also the Lord God said, It is not good that the man should be himself alone: I will make him an help [1]meet for him.

19 So the Lord God formed of the earth every beast of the field, and every fowl of the heaven, and brought them unto the [1]man to see how he would call them: for howsoever the man named the living creature, so was the name thereof.

20 The man therefore gave names unto all cattle, and to the fowl of the heaven, and to every beast of the field: but for Adam found he not an helper meet for him.

21 ¶ Therefore the Lord God caused an heavy sleep to fall upon the man, and he slept: and he took one

of his ribs, and closed up the flesh in stead thereof.

22 And the rib which the Lord God had taken from the man, [1]made he a [2]woman, and brought her to the man.

23 Then the man said, 'This now is bone of my bones, and flesh of my flesh. She shall be called [1]woman, because she was taken out of the man.

24 [d]Therefore shall man leave [1]his father and his mother, and shall cleave to his wife, and they shall be one flesh.

25 And they were both naked, the man and his wife, and they were not [1]ashamed.

3 1 The woman seduced by the serpent, 6 enticeth her husband to sin. 8 They both flee from God. 14 They three are punished. 15 Christ is promised. 19 Man is dust. 22 Man is cast out of Paradise.

1 Now the serpent was more [1]subtle than any beast of the field, which the Lord God had made: and he [2]said to the woman, Yea, hath God indeed said, ye shall not eat of every tree of the garden?

2 And the woman said unto the serpent, We eat of the fruit of the trees of the garden.

3 But of the fruit of the tree which is in the midst of the garden, God hath said, Ye shall not eat of it, neither shall ye touch it, [1]lest ye die.

4 Then the [a]serpent said to the woman, Ye shall not [1,2]die at all,

5 But God doth know that when ye shall eat thereof, your eyes shall be opened, and ye shall be as gods, [1]knowing good and evil.

6 So the woman (seeing that the tree was good for meat, and that it was pleasant to the eyes, and a tree to be desired, to get knowledge) took of the fruit thereof, and did [b]eat, and gave also to her husband with her, and he [1]did eat.

Marginal refs: c 1 Cor. 11:8 / d Matt. 19:5, Mark 10:7, 1 Cor. 6:16, Eph. 5:31 / CHAPTER 3 / a 2 Cor. 11:3 / b 1 Tim. 2:14

2:9 [1] Which was a sign of the life received of God.
[2] That is, of miserable experience, which came by disobeying God.
2:11 [1] Which Havilah is a country joining to Persia Eastward, and inclineth toward the West.
2:12 [1] Or, precious stone, or pearl. Pliny saith it is the name of a tree.
2:13 [1] Or, Ethiopia.
2:14 [1] Or, Tigris.
[2] Or, Assyria.
[3] Or, Euphrates.
2:15 [1] God would not have man idle, though as yet there was no need to labor.
2:16 [1] So that man might know there was a sovereign Lord, to whom he owed obedience.
[2] Hebrew, eating thou shalt eat of.
2:17 [1] Or, whensoever.
[2] By this death he meaneth the separation of man from God, who is our life and chief felicity: and also that our disobedience is the cause thereof.
2:18 [1] Hebrew, before him.
2:19 [1] By moving them to come and submit themselves to Adam.
2:22 [1] Hebrew, built.

[2] Signifying that mankind was perfect, when the woman was created, which before was like an imperfect building.
2:23 [1] Or, Manness, because she cometh of man: for in Hebrew Ish is man, and Ishah the woman.
2:24 [1] So that marriage requireth a greater duty of us toward our wives, than otherwise we are bound to show to our parents.
2:25 [1] For before sin entered, all things were honest and comely.
3:1 [1] As Satan can change himself into an Angel of light, so did he abuse the wisdom of the serpent to deceive man.
[2] God suffered Satan to make the serpent his instrument and to speak in him.
3:3 [1] In doubting of God's threatenings she yielded to Satan.
3:4 [1] This is Satan's chiefest subtlety, to cause us not to fear God's threatenings.
[2] Hebrew, die the death.
3:5 [1] As though he should say, God doth not forbid you to eat of the fruit, save that he knoweth that if ye should eat thereof, ye should be like to him.
3:6 [1] Not so much to please his wife, as moved by ambition at her persuasion.

7 Then the eyes of them both were opened, and they [1]knew that they were naked, and they sewed fig tree leaves together, and made themselves [2]breeches.

8 ¶ Afterward they heard the voice of the Lord God walking in the garden in the [1]cool of the day, and the man and his wife [2]hid themselves from the presence of the Lord God among the trees of the garden.

9 But the Lord God called to the man, and said unto him, Where art thou?

10 Who said, I heard thy voice in the garden and was afraid: because I was [1]naked, therefore I hid myself.

11 And he said, Who told thee that thou wast naked? Hast thou eaten of the tree whereof I commanded thee that thou shouldest not eat?

12 Then the man said, The woman which thou [1]gavest *to be* with me, she gave me of the tree, and I did eat.

13 And the Lord God said to the woman, Why hast thou done this? And the woman said, [1]The serpent beguiled me, and I did eat.

14 ¶ Then the Lord God said to the serpent, [1]Because thou hast done this, thou art cursed above all cattle, and above every beast of the field: upon thy belly shalt thou go, and [2]dust shalt thou eat all the days of thy life.

15 I will also put enmity between [1]thee and the woman, and between thy seed and her seed. He shall break thine [2]head, and thou shalt [3]bruise his heel.

16 ¶ Unto the woman he said, I will greatly increase thy [1]sorrows, and thy conceptions. In sorrow shalt thou bring forth children, and thy desire *shall be subject* to thine husband, and he shall [c]rule over thee.

17 ¶ Also to Adam he said, Because thou hast

[c 1 Cor. 14:34]

obeyed the voice of thy wife, and hast eaten of the tree, (whereof I commanded thee, saying, Thou shalt not eat of it) [1]cursed *is* the earth for thy sake: in sorrow shalt thou eat of it all the days of thy life.

18 [1]Thorns also and thistles shall it bring forth to thee, and thou shalt eat the herb of the field.

19 In the sweat of thy face shalt thou eat bread till thou return to the earth: for out of it wast thou taken, because thou art dust, and to dust shalt thou return.

20 (And the man called his wife's name Eve, because she was the mother of all living)

21 Unto Adam also and to his wife did the Lord God [1]make coats of skins, and clothed them.

22 ¶ And the Lord God said, [1]Behold, the man is become as one of us, to know good and evil. And now lest he put forth his hand, and [2]take also of the tree of life, and eat, and live forever,

23 Therefore the Lord God sent him forth from the garden of Eden, to till the earth, whence he was taken.

24 Thus he cast out the man, and at the East side of the garden of Eden he set the Cherubims, and the blade of a sword shaken, to keep the way of the tree of life.

4

1 The generation of mankind.   3 Cain and Abel offer sacrifice.   8 Cain killeth Abel.   23 Lamech a tyrant encourageth his fearful wives.   26 True religion is restored.

1 Afterward the man knew Eve his wife which [1]conceived and bare Cain, and said, I have obtained a man [2]by the Lord.

2 And again she brought forth his brother Abel, and Abel was a keeper of sheep, and Cain was a tiller of the ground.

3 ¶ And in process of time it came to pass, that Cain brought an [1]oblation unto the Lord of the fruit

---

3:7 [1] They began to feel their misery, but they sought not to God for remedy.

  [2] Hebrew, *things to gird about them to hide their privities.*

3:8 [1] Or, wind.

  [2] The sinful conscience fleeth God's presence.

3:10 [1] His hypocrisy appeareth in that he hid the cause of his nakedness, which was the transgression of God's commandment.

3:12 [1] His wickedness and lack of true repentance appeareth in this that he burdeneth God with his fault, because he had given him a wife.

3:13 [1] Instead of confessing her sin, she increaseth it by accusing the serpent.

3:14 [1] He asked the reason of Adam and his wife, because he would bring them to repentance, but he asketh not the serpent, because he would show him no mercy.

  [2] As a vile and contemptible beast, Isa. 65:25.

3:15 [1] He chiefly meaneth Satan, by whose motion and craft the serpent deceived the woman.

  [2] That is, the power of sin and death.

  [3] Satan shall sting Christ and his members, but not overcome them.

3:16 [1] The Lord comforteth Adam by the promise of the blessed seed, and also punisheth the body for the sin which the soul should have been punished for; that the spirit having conceived hope of forgiveness, might live by faith.

3:17 [1] The transgression of God's commandment was the cause that both mankind and all other creatures were subject to the curse.

3:18 [1] These are not the natural fruits of the earth, but proceed of the corruption of sin.

3:21 [1] Or, gave them knowledge to make themselves coats.

3:22 [1] By this derision he reproacheth Adam's misery, whereinto he was fallen by ambition.

  [2] Adam deprived of life, lost also the sign thereof.

4:1 [1] Man's nature, the estate of marriage, and God's blessing were not utterly abolished through sin, but the quality or condition thereof was changed.

  [2] That is, according to the Lord's promise, as Gen. 3:15, some read, To the Lord, as rejoicing for the son which she had born, whom she would offer to the Lord as the firstfruits of her birth.

4:3 [1] This declareth that the father instructed his children in the knowledge of God, and also how God gave them sacrifices to signify their salvation, albeit they were destitute of the sacrament of the tree of life.

of the ground.

4 And Abel also himself brought of the firstfruits of his sheep, and of the fat of them, and the Lord had respect unto [a]Abel, and to his offering,

5 But unto Cain and to his offering he had no [1]regard: wherefore Cain was exceedingly wroth and his countenance fell down.

6 Then the Lord said unto Cain, Why art thou wroth? and why is thy countenance cast down?

7 If thou do well, shalt thou not be [1]accepted? and if thou doest not well, sin lieth at the [2]door: also unto thee his [3]desire *shall be subject*, and thou shalt rule over him.

8 ¶ Then Cain spake unto Abel his brother. And [b]when they were in the field, Cain rose up against Abel his brother, and slew him.

9 Then the Lord said unto Cain, Where is Abel thy brother? Who answered, I cannot tell. [1]Am I my brother's keeper?

10 Again he said, What hast thou done? the [1]voice of thy brother's blood crieth unto me, from the earth.

11 Now therefore thou art cursed [1]from the earth, which hath opened her mouth to receive thy brother's blood from thine hand.

12 When thou shalt till the ground, it shall not henceforth yield unto thee her strength: a [1]vagabond and a runagate shalt thou be in the earth.

13 Then Cain said to the Lord, [1,2]My punishment is greater than I can bear.

14 Behold, thou hast cast me out this day from [1]the earth, and from thy face shall I be hid, and shall be a vagabond, and a runagate in the earth, and whosoever findeth me shall slay me.

15 Then the Lord said unto him, Doubtless whosoever slayeth Cain, he shall be [1]punished seven fold. And the Lord set a [2]mark upon Cain, lest any man finding him, should kill him.

16 Then Cain went out from the presence of the

CHAPTER 4
[a] Heb. 11:4
[b] Matt. 23:35
1 John 3:11
Jude 11

Lord, and dwelt in the land of Nod toward the East side of Eden.

17 Cain also knew his wife, which conceived and bore Enoch: and he built a [1]city, and called the name of the city by the name of his son, Enoch.

18 And to Enoch was born Irad, and Irad begat Mehujael, and Mehujael begat Methushael, and Methushael begat Lamech.

19 ¶ And Lamech took to him [1]two wives: the name of the one *was* Adah, and the name of the other Zillah.

20 And Adah bare Jabal, who was the [1]father of such as dwell in the tents, and of such as have cattle.

21 And his brother's name *was* Jubal, who was the father of all that play on the harp and [1]organs.

22 And Zillah also bore Tubal-Cain, who wrought cunningly every craft of brass and of iron: and the sister of Tubal-Cain *was* Naamah.

23 Then Lamech said unto his wives, Adah and Zillah, Hear my voice, ye wives of Lamech; hearken unto my speech: [1]for I would slay a man in my wound, and a young man to mine hurt.

24 If Cain shall be avenged sevenfold, truly Lamech [1]seventy times sevenfold.

25 ¶ And Adam knew his wife again, and she bare a son, and she called his name Seth: for God, *said she*, hath appointed me another seed for Abel, because Cain slew him.

26 And to the same Seth also there was born a son, and he called his name Enosh. Then began men to [1]call upon the name of the Lord.

5 *The genealogy. 5 The age and death of Adam. 6 His succeession unto Noah and his children. 24 Enoch was taken away.*

1 This is the [1]book of the generations of Adam. In the day that God created Adam, in the [2]likeness

---

4:5 [1] Because he was an hypocrite, and offered only for an outward show without sincerity of heart.

4:7 [1] Both thou and thy sacrifice shall be acceptable to me.

  [2] Sin shall still torment thy conscience.

  [3] The dignity of the firstborn is given to Cain over Abel.

4:9 [1] This is the nature of the reprobate when they are reproved of their hypocrisy, even to neglect God and despite him.

4:10 [1] God revengeth the wrongs of his Saints, though none complain: for the iniquity itself crieth for vengeance.

4:11 [1] The earth shall be a witness against thee, which mercifully received that blood which thou most cruelly sheddest.

4:12 [1] Thou shalt never have rest: for thine heart shall be in continual fear and care.

4:13 [1] He burdeneth God as a cruel judge because he did punish him so sharply.

  [2] Or, my sin is greater than can be pardoned.

4:14 [1] Hebrew, *from off the face of.*

4:15 [1] Not for the love he bare to Cain, but to suppress murder.

[2] Which was some visible sign of God's judgment, that others should fear thereby.

4:17 [1] Thinking thereby to be sure, and to have less occasion to fear God's judgments against him.

4:19 [1] The lawful institution of marriage, which is, that two should be one flesh, was first corrupted in the house of Cain by Lamech.

4:20 [1] Or, first inventor.

4:21 [1] Or, flutes, and pipes.

4:23 [1] His wives seeing that all men hated him for his cruelty, were afraid, therefore he braggeth that there is none so lusty that were able to resist, although he were already wounded.

4:24 [1] He mocked at God's sufferance in Cain, jesting as though God would suffer none to punish him and yet give him license to murder others.

4:26 [1] In these days God began to move the hearts of the godly to restore religion, which a long time by the wicked had been suppressed.

5:1 [1] Or, rehearsal of the stock.

  [2] Read Gen. 1:26.

of God made he him,

2 Male and female created he them, and blessed them, and called their name ¹Adam in the day that they were created.

3 ¶ Now Adam lived an hundred and thirty years, and begat a child in his own ¹likeness after his image, and called his name Seth.

4 ᵃAnd the days of Adam, after he had begotten Seth, were eight hundred years, and he begat sons and daughters.

5 So all the days that Adam lived, were nine hundred and thirty years, and he died.

6 And ¹Seth lived an hundred and five years, and begat Enosh.

7 And Seth lived after he begat Enosh, eight hundred and seven years, and begat sons and daughters.

8 So all the days of Seth were ¹nine hundred and twelve years: and he died.

9 ¶ Also Enosh lived ninety years, and begat Cainan.

10 And Enosh lived after he begat Cainan, eight hundred and fifteen years, and begat sons and daughters.

11 So all the days of Enosh were nine hundred and five years: and he died.

12 ¶ Likewise Cainan lived seventy years, and begat Mahalalel.

13 And Cainan lived, after he begat Mahalalel, eight hundred and forty years, and begat sons and daughters.

14 So all the days of Cainan were nine hundred and ten years: and he died.

15 ¶ Mahalalel also lived sixty and five years, and begat Jared.

16 Also Mahalalel lived, after he begat Jared, eight hundred and thirty years, and begat sons and daughters.

17 So all the days of Mahalalel were eight hundred ninety and five years: and he died.

18 ¶ And Jared lived an hundred sixty and two years, and begat Enoch.

19 Then Jared lived, after he begat Enoch, eight hundred years, and begat sons and daughters.

CHAPTER 5
ᵃ 1 Chron. 1:1
ᵇ Heb. 11:5

20 So all the days of Jared were nine hundred sixty and two years: and he died.

21 ¶ ᵇAlso Enoch lived sixty and five years, and begat Methuselah.

22 And Enoch ¹walked with God, after he begat Methuselah, three hundred years, and begat sons and daughters.

23 So all the days of Enoch were three hundred sixty and five years.

24 And Enoch walked with God, and he was no more *seen*: for ¹God took him away.

25 Methuselah also lived an hundred eighty and seven years, and begat Lamech.

26 And Methuselah lived, after he begat Lamech, seven hundred eighty and two years, and begat sons and daughters.

27 So all the days of Methuselah were nine hundred sixty and nine years, and he died.

28 ¶ Then Lamech lived an hundred eighty and two years, and begat a son,

29 And called his name, Noah, saying, This same shall ¹comfort us concerning our work and sorrow of our hands, as touching the earth, which the Lord hath cursed.

30 And Lamech lived, after he begat Noah, five hundred ninety and five years, and begat sons and daughters.

31 So all the days of Lamech were seven hundred seventy and seven years: and he died.

32 And Noah was five hundred years old. And Noah begat Shem, Ham and Japheth.

6 *3 God threateneth to bring the flood. 5 Man altogether corrupt. 6 God repenteth that he made him. 18 Noah and his are preserved in the Ark, which he was commanded to make.*

1 So when men began to be multiplied upon the earth, and there were daughters born unto them,

2 Then the ¹sons of God saw the daughters ²of men that they were ³fair, and they took them wives of all that they ⁴liked.

3 Therefore the Lord said, My spirit shall not always ¹strive with man, because he is but flesh, and

---

5:2 ¹ By giving them both one name, he noteth the inseparable conjunction of man and wife.

5:3 ¹ As well concerning his creation, as his corruption.

5:6 ¹ He proveth Adam's generation by them which came of Seth, to show which is the true Church, and also what care God had over the same from the beginning, in that he continued ever his graces toward it by a continual succession.

5:8 ¹ The chief cause of long life in the first age, was the multiplication of mankind, that according to God's commandment at the beginning the world might be increased with people, which might universally praise him.

5:22 ¹ That is, he led an upright and godly life.

5:24 ¹ To show that there was a better life prepared, and to be a testimony of the immortality of souls and bodies. As to inquire where he

became, is mere curiosity.

5:29 ¹ Lamech had respect to the promise, Gen. 3:15, and desired to see the deliverer which should be sent, and yet saw but a figure thereof, he also spake this by the spirit of prophecy because Noah delivered the Church and preserved it by his obedience.

6:2 ¹ The children of the godly, which began to degenerate.

² Those that came of wicked parents, as of Cain.

³ Having more respect to their beauty and to worldly considerations, than to their manners and godliness.

⁴ Or, had chosen.

6:3 ¹ Because man could not be won by God's lenity and long sufferance whereby he strove to overcome him, he would no longer stay his vengeance.

his days shall be an ²hundred and twenty years.

4 There were ¹giants in the earth in those days: yea, and after that the sons of God came unto the daughters of men, and they had borne them children, these were mighty men, which in old time were men of ²renown.

5 ¶ When the Lord saw that the wickedness of man was great in the earth, and all the imaginations of the thoughts of his ᵃheart *were* only evil ¹continually,

6 Then it ¹repented the Lord, that he had made man in the earth, and he was sorry in his heart.

7 Therefore the Lord said, I will destroy from the earth the man, whom I have created, from man ¹to beast, to the creeping thing, and to the fowl of the heaven: for I repent that I have made them.

8 But Noah ¹found grace in the eyes of the Lord.

9 ¶ These are the ¹generations of Noah: Noah was a just and upright man in his time: *and* Noah walked with God.

10 And Noah begat three sons, Shem, Ham and Japheth.

11 The earth also was corrupt before God: for the earth was filled with ¹cruelty.

12 Then God looked upon the earth, and behold, it was corrupt: for all flesh had corrupted his way upon the earth.

13 And God said unto Noah, ¹An end of all flesh is come before me: for the earth is filled with ²cruelty ³through them: and behold, I will destroy them with the earth.

14 ¶ Make thee an Ark of ¹pine trees: thou shalt make ²cabins in the Ark, and shalt pitch it within and without with pitch.

15 And ¹thus shalt thou make it: the length of the Ark shall be three hundred cubits, the breadth of it fifty cubits, and the height of it thirty cubits.

16 A window shalt thou make in the Ark, and in a cubit shalt thou finish it above, and the door of the Ark shalt thou set in the side thereof: thou shalt make it with the ¹low, second, and third *room*.

CHAPTER 6
ᵃ Gen. 8:21
Matt. 15:19
ᵇ Heb. 11:7

CHAPTER 7
ᵃ 1 Pet. 2:5
ᵇ Matt. 24:37
Luke 27:26
1 Pet. 3:20

17 And, behold, I will bring a flood of waters upon the earth to destroy all flesh, wherein is the breath of life under heaven: all that is in the earth shall perish.

18 But with thee will I ¹establish my covenant, and thou shalt go into the Ark, thou, and thy sons, and thy wife, and thy sons' wives with thee.

19 And of every living thing of all flesh two of every sort shalt thou cause to come into the Ark, to keep *them* alive with thee: they shall be male and female.

20 Of the fowls, after their kind, and of the cattle after their kind, of every creeping thing of the earth after his kind, two of every sort shall come unto thee, that thou mayest keep *them* alive.

21 And take thou with thee of all meat that is eaten: and thou shalt gather it to thee, that it may be meat for thee and for them.

22 ᵇNoah therefore did according unto all that God commanded him: *even* ¹so did he.

7 *1 Noah and his enter into the Ark. 20 The flood destroyeth all the rest upon the earth.*

1 And the Lord said unto Noah, Enter thou and all thine house into the Ark: for thee have I seen ᵃ,¹righteous before me in this ²age.

2 Of every ¹clean beast thou shalt take to thee by sevens, the male and his female: but of unclean beasts by couples, the male and his female.

3 Of the fowls also of the heaven by sevens, male and female, to keep seed alive upon the whole earth.

4 For seven days hence I will cause it rain upon the earth forty days, and forty nights, and all the substance that I have made, will I destroy from off the earth.

5 ᵇNoah therefore did according to all that the Lord commanded him.

6 And Noah *was* six hundred years old, when the flood of waters was upon the earth.

7 ¶ So Noah entered and his sons, and his wife,

---

² Which term God gave man to repent before he would destroy the earth, 1 Pet. 3:20.
6:4 ¹ Or, tyrants.
² Which usurped authority over others, and did degenerate from that simplicity, wherein their fathers lived.
6:5 ¹ Hebrew, *every day.*
6:6 ¹ God doth never repent, but he speaketh after our capacity, because he did destroy him, and in that as it were did disavow him to be his creature.
6:7 ¹ God declareth how much he detesteth sin, seeing the punishment thereof extendeth to the brute beasts.
6:8 ¹ God was merciful unto him.
6:9 ¹ Or, history.
6:11 ¹ Meaning, that all were given to the contempt of God, and oppression of their neighbors.
6:13 ¹ Or, I will destroy mankind.

² Or, oppression and wickedness.
³ Hebrew, *from the face of them.*
6:14 ¹ Hebrew, *Gopher.*
² Hebrew, *nests.*
6:15 ¹ Or, of this measure.
6:16 ¹ That is, of three heights, as appeareth in the figure.
6:18 ¹ To the intent that in this great enterprise and mockings of the whole world, thou mayest be confirmed, that thy faith fail not.
6:22 ¹ That is, he obeyed God's commandment in all points without adding or diminishing.
7:1 ¹ In respect of the rest of the world, and because he had a desire to serve God and live uprightly.
² Or, generation.
7:2 ¹ Which might be offered in sacrifice, whereof six were for breed, and the seventh for sacrifice.

and his sons' wives with him into the Ark, because of the waters of the flood.

8 Of the clean beasts, and of the unclean beasts, and of the fowls, and of all that creepeth upon the earth,

9 There ¹came two *and* two unto Noah into the Ark, male and female, as God had commanded Noah.

10 And so after seven days, the waters of the flood were upon the earth.

11 ¶ In the six hundredth year of Noah's life, in the ¹second month, the seventeenth day of the month, in the same day were all the ²fountains of the great deep broken up, and the windows of heaven were opened,

12 And the rain was upon the earth forty days and forty nights.

13 In the selfsame day entered Noah with Shem, and Ham and Japheth, the sons of Noah, and Noah's wife, and the three wives of his sons with them into the Ark.

14 They and every beast after his kind, and all cattle after their kind, and everything that creepeth and moveth upon the earth after his kind, and every fowl after his kind, *even* every bird of every feather.

15 For they came to Noah into the Ark, two *and* two, ¹of all flesh wherein is the breath of life.

16 And they entering in, came male and female of all flesh, as God had commanded him: and the Lord ¹,²shut him in.

17 Then the flood was forty days upon the earth, and the waters were increased, and bare up the Ark, which was lifted up above the earth.

18 The waters also waxed strong, and were increased exceedingly upon the earth, and the Ark went upon the waters.

19 The waters ¹prevailed so exceedingly upon the earth, that all the high mountains, that are under the whole heaven, were covered.

20 Fifteen cubits upward did the waters prevail, when the mountains were covered.

21 Then all flesh perished that moved upon the earth, both fowl and cattle and beast, and everything that creepeth and moveth upon the earth, and every man.

22 Everything in whose nostrils the spirit of life did breathe, whatsoever they were in the dry land, they died.

23 So ¹he destroyed everything that was upon the earth, from man to beast, to the creeping thing, and to the fowl of the heaven: they were even destroyed from the earth. And Noah only ²remained, and they that were with him in the Ark.

24 And the waters prevailed upon the earth an hundred and fifty days.

8 *13 The flood ceaseth. 16 Noah is commanded to come forth of the Ark with his. 20 He sacrificeth to the Lord. 22 God promiseth that all things should continue in their first order.*

1 Now God ¹remembered Noah and ²every beast, and all the cattle that were with him in the Ark: therefore God made a wind to pass upon the earth, and the waters ceased.

2 The fountains also of the deep and the windows of heaven were stopped, and the rain from heaven was restrained.

3 And the waters returned from above the earth, going and returning: and after the end of the hundred and fiftieth day the waters abated.

4 And in the ¹seventh month, in the seventeenth day of the month, the Ark ²rested upon the mountains of ³Ararat.

5 And the waters were going and decreasing until the ¹tenth month: in the tenth month, and in the first day of the month, were the tops of the mountains seen.

6 ¶ So ¹after forty days, Noah opened the window of the Ark which he had made,

7 And sent forth a raven, which went out, going forth and returning, until the waters were dried up upon the earth.

8 Again he sent a dove from him, that he might see if the waters were diminished from off the earth.

9 But the dove found no rest for the sole of her foot: therefore she returned unto him into the Ark (for the waters *were* upon the whole earth) and he ¹put forth his hand, and received her, and took her

---

7:9 ¹ God compelled them to present themselves to Noah, as they did before to Adam, when he gave them names, Gen. 2:19.

7:11 ¹ Which was about the beginning of May, when all things did most flourish.

² Both the waters in the earth did overflow, and also the clouds poured down.

7:15 ¹ Every living thing that God would have to be preserved on earth, came into the Ark to Noah.

7:16 ¹ So that God's secret power defended him against the rage of the mighty waters.

² Or, shut it upon him.

7:19 ¹ Hebrew, *waxed very mighty.*

7:23 ¹ That is, God.

² Learn what it is to obey God only, and to forsake the multitude, 1 Pet. 3:20.

8:1 ¹ Not that God forgetteth his at any time, but when he sendeth succor then he showeth that he remembereth them.

² If God remember every brute beast, what ought to be the assurance of his children?

8:4 ¹ Which contained part of September, and part of October.

² Or, stayed.

³ Or, Armenia.

8:5 ¹ Which was the month of December.

8:6 ¹ Hebrew, *at the end of forty days.*

8:9 ¹ It is like that the raven did fly to and fro, resting on the Ark, but came not into it, as the dove that was taken in.

to him into the Ark.

10 And he abode yet another seven days, and again he sent forth the dove out of the Ark.

11 And the dove came to him in the evening, and lo in her ¹mouth *was* an ²olive leaf that she had plucked: whereby Noah knew that the waters were abated from off the earth.

12 Notwithstanding, he waited yet another seven days, and sent forth the dove, which returned not again unto him anymore.

13 ¶ And in the six hundred and one year, in the first *day* of the ¹first month, the waters were dried up from off the earth: and Noah removed the covering of the Ark, and looked, and behold, the upper part of the ground was dry.

14 And in the second month, in the seven and twentieth day of the month, was the earth dry.

15 ¶ Then God spake to Noah, saying,

16 ¹Go forth of the Ark, thou, and thy wife, and thy sons, and thy sons' wives with thee.

17 Bring forth with thee every beast that is with thee, of all flesh, *both* fowl and cattle, and everything that creepeth and moveth upon the earth, that they may breed abundantly in the earth, ᵃand bring forth fruit and increase upon the earth.

18 So Noah came forth, and his sons, and his wife, and his sons' wives with him.

19 Every beast, every creeping thing, and every fowl, all that moveth upon the earth, after their kinds, went out of the Ark.

20 ¶ Then Noah ¹built an altar to the Lord, and took of every clean beast, and of every clean fowl, and offered burnt offerings upon the altar.

21 And the Lord smelled a ¹,²savor of rest, and the Lord said in his heart, I will henceforth curse the ground no more for man's cause: for the ᵇimagination of man's heart *is* evil, *even* from his youth: neither will I smite anymore all things living, as I have done.

22 Hereafter ¹seed time and harvest, and cold and heat, and Summer and Winter, and day and night shall not cease, so long as the earth remaineth.

CHAPTER 8
ᵃ Gen. 1:22
Gen. 9:1
ᵇ Gen. 6:5
Matt. 15:12

CHAPTER 9
ᵃ Gen. 2:28
Gen. 8:17
ᵇ Gen. 1:29
ᶜ Lev. 17:14
ᵈ Matt. 26:52
Rev. 13:10
ᵉ Gen. 1:27
ᶠ Isa. 54:9

9 1 *The confirmation of marriage.* 2 *Man's authoritiy over all creatures.* 3 *Permission of meats.* 6 *The power of the sword.* 14 *The rainbow is the sign of God's promise.* 21 *Noah is drunk, and mocked of his son, whom he curseth.* 29 *The age and death of Noah.*

1 And God ¹blessed Noah and his sons, and said to them, ᵃBring forth fruit, and multiply, and replenish the earth.

2 Also the ¹fear of you, and the dread of you shall be upon every beast of the earth, and upon every fowl of the heaven, upon all that moveth on the earth, and upon all the fishes of the sea: into your hand are they delivered.

3 Everything ¹that moveth and liveth, shall be meat for you: as the ᵇgreen herb, have I given you all things.

4 ᶜ,¹But flesh with the life thereof, *I mean*, with the blood thereof, shall ye not eat.

5 ¹For surely I will require your blood, wherein your lives *are*: at the hands of every beast will I require it: and at the hand of man, *even* at the hand of a man's ²brother will I require the life of man.

6 Who so ᵈsheddeth man's blood, ¹by man shall his blood be shed: ᶜfor in the ²image of God hath he made man.

7 But bring ye forth fruit and multiply: grow plentifully in the earth, and increase therein.

8 ¶ God spake also to Noah and to his sons with him, saying,

9 Behold, I, even I establish my ¹covenant with you, and with your ²seed after you,

10 And with every living creature that is with you, with the fowl, with the cattle, and with every beast of the earth with you, from all that go out of the Ark, unto every beast of the earth.

11 ᶠAnd my covenant will I establish with you, that from henceforth all flesh shall not be rooted out by the waters of the flood, neither shall there be a flood to destroy the earth anymore.

12 Then God said, This is the token of the covenant

8:11 ¹ Or, bill.
² Which was a sign that the waters were much diminished: for the olives grow not on the high mountains.
8:13 ¹ Called in Hebrew *Abib*, containing part of March and part of April.
8:16 ¹ Noah declareth his obedience, in that he would not depart out of the Ark without God's express commandment, as he did not enter in without the same: the Ark being a figure of the Church, wherein nothing must be done without the word of God.
8:20 ¹ For sacrifices which were as an exercise of their faith, whereby they used to give thanks to God for his benefits.
8:21 ¹ Or, sweet savor.
² That is, thereby he showeth himself appeased and his anger to rest.
8:22 ¹ The order of nature destroyed by the flood, is restored by God's promise.
9:1 ¹ God increased them with fruit, and declared unto them his

counsel as touching the replenishing of the earth.
9:2 ¹ By the virtue of this commandment beasts rage not so much against man as they would, yea, and many serve to his use thereby.
9:3 ¹ By this permission man may with a good conscience use the creatures of God for his necessity.
9:4 ¹ That is, living creatures, and the flesh of beasts that are strangled: and hereby all cruelty is forbidden.
9:5 ¹ That is, I will take vengeance for your blood.
² Or, neighbor.
9:6 ¹ Not only by the magistrate, but oft times God raiseth up one murderer to kill another.
² Therefore to kill man is to deface God's image, and so injury is not only done to man, but also to God.
9:9 ¹ To assure you that the world shall be no more destroyed by a flood.
² The children which are not yet born, are comprehended in God's covenant made with their fathers.

which I make between me and you, and between every living thing that is with you unto perpetual generations.

13 I have set my ¹bow in the cloud, and it shall be for a sign of the covenant between me and the earth.

14 And when I shall cover the earth with a cloud, and the bow shall be seen in the cloud,

15 Then will I remember my ¹covenant which is between me and you, and between every living thing in all flesh, and there shall be no more waters of a flood to destroy all flesh.

16 Therefore the bow shall be in the cloud, that I may see it, and remember the everlasting covenant between God and every living thing, in all flesh that is upon the earth.

17 God said yet to Noah, ¹This is the sign of the covenant, which I have established between me and all flesh that is upon the earth.

18 ¶ Now the sons of Noah going forth of the Ark, were Shem and Ham and Japheth. And Ham is the father of Canaan.

19 These are the three sons of Noah, and of them was the whole earth ¹overspread.

20 ¹Noah also began *to be* an husbandman, and planted a vineyard.

21 And he drunk of the wine, and was ¹drunken, and was uncovered in the midst of his tent.

22 And when Ham the father of ¹Canaan saw the nakedness of his father, ²he told his two brethren without.

23 Then took Shem and Japheth a garment, and put it upon both their shoulders, and went backward and covered the nakedness of their father with their faces backward: so they saw not their father's nakedness.

24 Then Noah awoke from his wine, and knew what his younger son had done unto him,

25 And said, ¹Cursed *be* Canaan: a ²servant of servants shall he be unto his brethren.

26 He said moreover, Blessed *be* the Lord God of Shem, and let Canaan be his ¹servant.

27 God ¹,²persuade Japheth, that he may dwell in the tents of Shem, and let Canaan be his servant.

28 ¶ And Noah lived after the flood three hundred and fifty years.

29 So all the days of Noah were nine hundred and fifty years: and he died.

10

1 The increase of mankind by Noah and his sons. 10 The beginning of cities, countries, and nations.

1 Now these are the ¹generations of the sons of Noah, Shem, Ham and Japheth: unto whom sons were born after the flood.

2 The sons of Japheth *were* Gomer, and Magog, and ¹Madai, and Javan, and Tubal, and Meshech, and Tiras.

3 And the sons of Gomer, Ashkenaz, and Riphath, and Togarmah.

4 Also the sons of Javan, Elishah and Tarshish, Kittim, and Dodanim.

5 Of these were the ¹isles of the Gentiles divided in their lands, every man after his tongue, *and* after their families in their nations.

6 ¶ Moreover, the sons of Ham *were* ¹Cush, and Mizraim, and Put, and Canaan.

7 And the sons of Cush, Seba and Havilah, and Sabtah, and Raamah, and Sabtechah: also the sons of Raamah *were* Sheba and Dedan.

8 And Cush begat Nimrod, who began to be ¹mighty in the earth.

9 He was a mighty hunter before the Lord. Wherefore it is said, ¹As Nimrod the mighty hunter before the Lord.

10 And the beginning of his kingdom was Babel and Erech, and Accad, and Calneh, in the land of ¹Shinar.

9:13 ¹ Hereby we see that signs or sacraments ought not to be separate from the word.

9:15 ¹ When men shall see my bow in the heaven, they shall know that I have not forgotten my covenant with them.

9:17 ¹ God doth repeat this the oftener, to confirm Noah's faith so much the more.

9:19 ¹ This declareth what was the virtue of God's blessing, when he said, increase and bring forth, Gen. 1:28.

9:20 ¹ Or, Noah began again.

9:21 ¹ This is set before our eyes to show what an horrible thing drunkenness is.

9:22 ¹ Of whom came the Canaanites that wicked nation, who were also cursed of God.

² In derision and contempt of his father.

9:25 ¹ He pronounceth as a Prophet the curse of God against all them that honor not their parents: for Ham and his posterity were accursed.

² That is, a most vile slave.

9:26 ¹ Or, their.

9:27 ¹ Or, enlarge, or cause to return.

² He declareth that the Gentiles, which came of Japheth, and were separated from the Church, should be joined to the same by the persuasion of God's Spirit, and preaching of the Gospel.

10:1 ¹ These generations are here recited, partly to declare the marvelous increase in so small a time, and also to set forth their great forgetfulness of God's grace towards their fathers.

10:2 ¹ Of Madai and Javan came the Medes, and Greeks.

10:5 ¹ The Jews so call all countries which are separated from them by sea, as Greece, Italy, etc, which were given to the children of Japheth, of whom came the Gentiles.

10:6 ¹ Of Cush and Mizraim came the Ethiopians and Egyptians.

10:8 ¹ Meaning, a cruel oppressor and tyrant.

10:9 ¹ His tyranny came into a proverb as hated both of God and man: for he passed not to commit cruelty even in God's presence.

10:10 ¹ For there was another city in Egypt, called also Babel.

11 Out of that land came Assyria, and built Nineveh, and the [1]city Rehoboth, and Calah:

12 Resen also between Nineveh and Calah: this is a great city.

13 And Mizraim begat [1]Ludim, and Anamim, and Lehabim, and Naphtuhim.

14 Pathrusim also, and Casluhim (out of whom came the Philistines) and [1]Caphtorims.

15 Also Canaan begat Sidon his firstborn, and Heth,

16 And Jebusi, and Emori, and Girgashi,

17 And Hivi, and Arki, and Sini,

18 And Arvadi, and Zemari, and Hamathi: and afterward were the families of the Canaanites spread abroad.

19 Then the border of the Canaanites was from Sidon, as thou comest to Gerar until Gaza, and as thou goest unto Sodom and Gomorrah, and Admah, and Zeboiim, even unto Lasha.

20 These are the sons of Ham according to their families, according to their tongues in their countries, and in their nations.

21 ¶ Unto [1]Shem also the father of all the sons of [2]Eber, and elder brother of Japheth were children born.

22 [a]The sons of Shem were Elam and Asshur, and Arphaxad, and Lud, and Aram.

23 And the sons of Aram, Uz and Hul, and Gether, and Mash.

24 Also Arphaxad begat Salah, and Salah begat Eber.

25 Unto Eber also were born two sons: the name of the one was Peleg: for in his days was the earth [1]divided: and his brother's name was Joktan.

26 Then Joktan begat Almodad, and Sheleph, and Hazarmaveth, and Jerah,

27 And Hadoram, and Uzal, and Diklah,

28 And Obal, and Abimael, and Sheba,

29 And Ophir, and Havilah, and Jobab: all these were the sons of Joktan.

30 And their dwelling was from Mesha, as thou

CHAPTER 10
[a] 1 Chron. 1:17

CHAPTER 11
[a] 1 Chron. 1:17

goest up to Sephar, a mount of the East.

31 These are the sons of Shem, according to their families, according to their tongues in their countries and nations.

32 These are the families of the sons of Noah, after their generations among their people: and [1]out of these were the nations divided in the earth after the flood.

11

6 The building of Babel was the cause of the confusion of tongues. 10 The age and generation of Shem unto Abram. 31 Abram's departure from Ur with his father Terah, Sarai and Lot. 32 The age and death of Terah.

1 Then the whole earth was of one language and one speech.

2 And [1]as [2]they went from the [3]East, they found a plain in the land of [4]Shinar, and there they abode.

3 And they said one to another, Come, let us make brick and burn it in the fire, so they had brick for stone, and slime had they instead of mortar.

4 Also they said, Go to, let us [1]build us a city and a tower, whose top may reach unto the heaven, that we may get us a name, lest we be scattered upon the whole earth.

5 But the Lord [1]came down, to see the city and tower which the sons of men built.

6 And the Lord said, [1]Behold, the people is one, and they all have one language, and this they begin to do, neither can they now be stopped from whatsoever they have imagined to do.

7 Come on, [1]let us go down, and [2]there confound their language, that everyone perceive not another's speech.

8 So the Lord scattered them from thence upon all the earth, and they left off to build the city.

9 Therefore the name of it was called [1]Babel, because the Lord did there confound the language of all the earth: from thence then did the Lord scatter them upon all the earth.

10 ¶ [a]These are the generations [1]of Shem: Shem was an hundred years old, and begat Arphaxad two

---

10:11 [1] Or, the streets of the city.
10:13 [1] Of Lud came the Lydians.
10:14 [1] Or, the Cappadocians.
10:21 [1] In his stock the Church was preserved: therefore Moses leaveth off speaking of Japheth and Ham, and entreateth of Shem more at large.
 [2] Of whom came the Hebrews or Jews.
10:25 [1] This division came by the diversity of languages, as appeareth, Gen. 11:9.
10:32 [1] Or, of these came divers nations.
11:2 [1] In the year one hundred and thirty after the flood.
 [2] To wit, Nimrod and his company.
 [3] That is, from Armenia where the Ark stayed.
 [4] Which was afterward called Chaldea.
11:4 [1] They were moved with pride and ambition, thinking to prefer

their own glory to God's honor.
11:5 [1] Meaning, that he declared by effect, that he knew their wicked enterprise: for God's power is everywhere, and doth neither ascend nor descend.
11:6 [1] God speaketh this in derision, because of their foolish persuasion and enterprise.
11:7 [1] He speaketh as though he took counsel with his own wisdom and power: to wit, with the Son and holy Ghost: signifying the greatness and certainty of the punishment.
 [2] By this great plague of the confusion of tongues appeareth God's horrible judgment against man's pride and vain glory.
11:9 [1] Or, confusion.
11:10 [1] He returneth to the genealogy of Shem, to come to the history of Abram, wherein the Church of God is described, which is Moses' principle purpose.

years after the flood.

11 And Shem lived after he begat Arphaxad five hundred years, and begat sons and daughters.

12 Also Arphaxad lived five and thirty years, and begat Salah.

13 And Arphaxad lived after he begat Salah, four hundred and three years, and begat sons and daughters.

14 And Salah lived thirty years, and begat Eber.

15 So Salah lived after he begat Eber four hundred and three years, and begat sons and daughters.

16 Likewise Eber lived four and thirty years, and begat Peleg.

17 So Eber lived after he begat Peleg four hundred and thirty years, and begat sons and daughters.

18 And Peleg lived thirty years, and begat Reu.

19 [b]And Peleg lived after he begat Reu two hundred and nine years, and begat sons and daughters.

20 Also Reu lived two and thirty years, and begat Serug.

21 So Reu lived after he begat Serug two hundred and seven years, and begat sons and daughters.

22 Moreover Serug lived thirty years, and begat Nahor.

23 And Serug lived after he begat Nahor two hundred years, and begat sons and daughters.

24 And Nahor lived nine and twenty years, and begat Terah.

25 So Nahor lived after he begat Terah, an hundred and nineteen years, and begat sons and daughters.

26 [c]So Terah lived seventy years, and begat Abram, Nahor, and Haran.

27 ¶ Now these are the generations of Terah: Terah begat [1]Abram, Nahor, and Haran: and Haran begat Lot.

28 Then Haran died before Terah his father in the land of his nativity, in Ur of [1]the Chaldeans.

29 So Abram and Nahor took them wives. The name of Abram's wife was Sarai, and the name of Nahor's wife Milcah, the daughter of Haran, the father of Milcah, and the father of [1]Iscah.

30 But Sarai was barren, and had no child.

Side references:
[b] 1 Chron. 1:25
[c] 1 Chron. 1:26
Josh. 24:2
[d] Josh. 24:2
Neh. 9:7
Judg. 5:7
Acts 7:4

CHAPTER 12
[a] Acts 7:3

31 Then [1]Terah took Abram his son, and Lot the son of Haran his son's son, and Sarai his daughter-in-law, his son Abram's wife: and they departed together from Ur of the Chaldeans, to [d]go into the land of Canaan, and they came to [2]Haran, and dwelt there.

32 So the days of Terah were two hundred and five years, and Terah died in Haran.

12 *1 Abram by God's commandment goeth to Canaan. 3 Christ is promised. 7 Abram buildeth Altars for exercise and declaration of his faith among the infidels. 10 Because of the dearth he goeth into Egypt. 15 Pharaoh taketh his wife, and is punished.*

1 For the Lord had said unto Abram, [a,1]Get thee out of thy country, and from thy kindred, and from thy father's house unto [2]the land that I will show thee.

2 And I will make of thee a great nation, and will bless thee, and make thy name great, and thou shalt be a [1]blessing.

3 I will also bless them that bless thee, and curse them that curse thee, and in thee shall all families of the earth be blessed.

4 So Abram departed, even as the Lord spake unto him, and Lot went with him, (and Abram was seventy and five years old, when he departed out of Haran)

5 Then Abram took Sarai his wife, and Lot his brother's son, and all their substance that they possessed, and the [1]souls that they had gotten in Haran, and they departed to go to the land of Canaan, and to the land of Canaan they came.

6 ¶ So Abram [1]passed through the land unto the place of Shechem, and unto the [2]plain of Moreh (and the [3]Canaanite was then in the land)

7 And the Lord appeared unto Abram, and said, Unto thy seed will I give this land. And there built he [1]an altar unto the Lord, which appeared unto him.

8 Afterward removing [1]thence unto a mountain Eastward from Bethel, he pitched his tent having Bethel on the West side, and Ai on the East, and there he built an [2]altar unto the Lord, and called

---

11:27 [1] He maketh mention first of Abram, not because he was the firstborn, but for the history which properly appertaineth unto him. Also Abram at the confusion of tongues, was 48 years old, for in the destruction of Sodom he was 99. And it was destroyed 52 years after the confusion of tongues.

11:28 [1] Hebrew, *Casdim.*

11:29 [1] Some think that this Iscah was Sarai.

11:31 [1] Albeit the oracle of God came to Abram, yet the honor is given to Terah, because he was the father.
[2] Which was a city of Mesopotamia.

12:1 [1] From the flood to this time were four hundred twenty and three years.
[2] In appointed him no certain place, he proveth so much more his faith and obedience.

12:2 [1] The world shall recover by thy seed, which is Christ, the blessing which they lost in Adam.

12:5 [1] Meaning, as well servants as cattle.

12:6 [1] He wandered to and fro in the land before he could find a settling place: thus God exerciseth the faith of his children.
[2] Or, oak grove.
[3] Which was a cruel and rebellious nation, by whom God kept his in continual exercise.

12:7 [1] It was not enough for him to worship God in his heart, but it was expedient to declare by outward profession his faith before men, whereof this altar was a sign.

12:8 [1] Because of the troubles that he had among that wicked people.
[2] And so served the true God, and renounced all idolatry.

on the Name of the Lord.

9 ¹Again Abram went forth going and journeying toward the South.

10 ¶ Then there came a ¹famine in the land: therefore Abram went down into Egypt to sojourn there: for there was a great famine in the land.

11 And when he drew near to enter into Egypt, he said to Sarai his wife, Behold now, I know that thou art a fair woman to look upon:

12 Therefore it will come to pass that when the Egyptians see thee, they will say, She is his wife: so will they kill me, but they will keep thee alive.

13 Say, I pray thee, that thou art my ¹sister, that I may fare well for thy sake, and that my ²life may be preserved by thee.

14 ¶ Now when Abram was come into Egypt, the Egyptians beheld the woman: for she was very fair.

15 And the Princes of Pharaoh saw her, and commended her unto Pharaoh: so the woman was ¹taken into Pharaoh's house:

16 Who entreated Abram well for her sake, and he had sheep, and beeves, and he asses, and menservants, and maidservants, and she asses, and camels.

17 But the Lord ¹plagued Pharaoh and his house with great plagues, because of Sarai Abram's wife.

18 Then Pharaoh called Abram, and said, Why hast thou done this unto me? Wherefore diddest thou not tell me, that she was thy wife?

19 Why saidest thou, She is my sister, that I should take her to be my wife? Now therefore behold thy wife, take her and go thy way.

20 And Pharaoh gave men ¹commandment concerning him: and they conveyed him forth and his wife, and all that he had.

13 *1 Abram departeth out of Egypt. 4 He calleth upon the Name of the Lord. 11 Lot departeth from him. 13 The wickedness of the Sodomites. 14 The promise made to Abram is renewed. 18 Abram buildeth an altar to the Lord.*

CHAPTER 13
ᵃ Gen. 12:7
ᵇ Gen. 36:7

1 Then ¹Abram went up from Egypt, he and his wife, and all that he had, and Lot with him toward the South.

2 And Abram *was* very rich in cattle, in silver and in gold.

3 And he went on his journey from the South toward ¹Bethel, to the place where his tent had been at the beginning, between Bethel and Ai,

4 Unto the place of the ᵃaltar, which he had made there at the first: and there Abram called on the Name of the Lord.

5 ¶ And Lot also, who went with Abram, had sheep, and cattle and tents,

6 So that the land could not ¹bear them, that they might dwell together: for their ᵇsubstance was great, so that they could not dwell together.

7 Also there was debate between the herdsmen of Abram's cattle, and the herdsmen of Lot's cattle, (and the ¹Canaanites and the Perizzites dwelleth at that time in the land.)

8 Then said Abram unto Lot, Let there be no ¹strife, I pray thee, between thee and me, neither between mine herdsmen and thine herdsmen: for we be brethren.

9 Is not the whole land before thee? depart I pray thee from me: if thou wilt ¹take the left hand, then I will go to the right: or if thou go to the right hand, then I will take the left.

10 So when Lot lifted up his eyes, he saw that all the plain of Jordan was watered everywhere (*for* before the Lord destroyed Sodom and Gomorrah, it *was* as the ¹garden of the Lord like the land of Egypt, as thou goest unto Zoar.)

11 Then Lot chose unto him all the plain of Jordan, and took his journey from the East: and they departed the ¹one from the other.

12 Abram dwelled in the land of Canaan, and Lot abode in the cities of the plain, and pitched his tent even unto Sodom.

13 Now the men of Sodom *were* wicked and exceeding ¹sinners against the Lord.

12:9 ¹ Thus the children of God may look for no rest in this world, but must wait for the heavenly rest and quietness.

12:10 ¹ This was a new trial of Abram's faith: whereby we see that the end of one affliction is the beginning of another.

12:13 ¹ By this we may learn not to use unlawful means, nor to put others in danger to save ourselves, read verse 20, albeit it may appear that Abram feared not so much death, as that if he should die without issue, God's promise should not have taken place: wherein appeared a weak faith.

² Hebrew, *that my soul may live.*

12:15 ¹ To be his wife.

12:17 ¹ The Lord took the defense of this poor stranger against a mighty king: and as he is ever careful over his, so did he preserve Sarai.

12:20 ¹ To the intent that none should hurt him either in his person or goods.

13:1 ¹ His great riches gotten in Egypt, hindreth him not to follow his vocation.

13:3 ¹ He calleth the place by that name which was after given unto it, Gen. 28:19.

13:6 ¹ This incommodity came by their riches, which brake friendship and as it were the bound of nature.

13:7 ¹ Who seeing their contention, might blaspheme God and destroy them.

13:8 ¹ He cutteth off the occasion of contention: therefore the evil ceaseth.

13:9 ¹ Abram resigneth his own right to buy peace.

13:10 ¹ Which was in Eden, Gen. 2:10.

13:11 ¹ This was done by God's providence, that only Abram and his seed might dwell in the land of Canaan.

13:13 ¹ Lot thinking to get paradise, found hell.

14 ¶ Then the Lord said unto [1]Abram, (after that Lot was departed from him) Lift up thine eyes now, and look from the place where thou art, Northward, and Southward, and Eastward, and Westward:

15 For all 'the land which thou seest, will I give unto thee, and to thy seed [1]forever,

16 And I will make thy seed as the dust of the earth: so that if a man can number the dust of the earth, then shall thy seed be numbered.

17 Arise, walk through the land, in the length thereof, and breadth thereof: for I will give it unto thee.

18 Then Abram removed his tent, and came and dwelled in the plain of Mamre, which is in Hebron, and built there an altar unto the Lord.

14

12 In the overthrow of Sodom Lot is taken prisoner. 16 Abram delivereth him. 18 Melchizedek cometh to meet him. 23 Abram would not be enriched by the king of Sodom.

1 And in the days of Amraphel king of [1]Shinar, Arioch king of Ellasar, Chedorlaomer king of Elam, and Tidal king of the [2]nations:

2 *These men* made war with Bera king of Sodom, and with Birsha king of Gomorrah, Shinab king of Admah, and Shemeber king of Zeboiim, and the king of Bela, which is Zoar.

3 All these [1]joined together in the valley of [2]Siddim, which is the [3]salt Sea.

4 Twelve years were they subject to Chedorlaomer, but in the thirteenth year they rebelled.

5 And in the fourteenth year came Chedorlaomer, and the kings that were with him, and smote the [1]Rephaims in Ashteroth Karnaim, and the Zuzims in Ham, and the Emims in [2]Shaveh Kiriathaim,

6 And the Horites in their mount Seir, unto the plain of El Paran, which is by the wilderness.

7 And they returned and came to En Mishpat, which is Kadesh, and [1]smote all the country of the Amalekites, and also the Amorites that dwelled in Hazezon Tamar.

8 Then went out the king of Sodom, and the

[c] Gen. 12:7
Gen. 15:7,11
Gen. 26:4
Deut. 34:4

CHAPTER 14
[a] 2 Sam. 18:18
[b] Heb. 7:1
[c] Heb. 7:8

king of Gomorrah, and the king of Admah, and the king of Zeboiim, and the king of Bela, which is Zoar: and they joined battle with them in the valley of Siddim,

9 *To wit*, with Chedorlaomer king of Elam, and Tidal king of nations, and Amraphel king of Shinar, and Arioch king of Ellasar: four kings against five.

10 Now the [1]valley of Siddim was full of slime pits, and the kings of Sodom and Gomorrah fled and [2]fell there: and the residue fled to the mountain.

11 And they took all the substance of Sodom and Gomorrah, and all their vittles and went their way.

12 They [1]took Lot also Abram's brother's son and his substance (for he dwelt at Sodom) and departed.

13 ¶ Then came one that had escaped, and told Abram the Hebrew, which dwelt in the plain of Mamre the Amorite, brother of Eshcol, and brother of Aner, which were [1]confederate with Abram.

14 When Abram heard that his brother was taken, he [1]brought forth of them that were born and brought up in his house, three hundred and eighteen, and pursued them unto Dan.

15 Then he and his servants divided themselves against them by night, and smote them, and pursued them unto Hobah, which is on the left side of [1]Damascus,

16 And he recovered all the substance, and also brought again his brother Lot, and his goods, and the women also and the people.

17 ¶ After that he returned from the slaughter of Chedorlaomer and of the kings that were with him, came the King of Sodom forth to meet him in the valley of Shaveh, which is the [a]King's dale.

18 And [b]Melchizedek King of Salem [1]brought forth bread and wine: and he was a Priest of the most high God.

19 Therefore he [1]blessed him, saying, Blessed *art thou*, Abram, of God most high, Possessor of heaven and earth,

20 And blessed *be* the most high God, which hath delivered thine enemies into thine hand. [c]And *Abram* gave him tithes of all.

13:14 [1] The Lord comforted him, lest he should have taken thought for the departure of his nephew.

13:15 [1] Meaning, a long time, and till the coming of Christ as Exod. 12:14 and 21:6; Deut. 15:17, and spiritually this is referred to the true children of Abram, born according to the promise, and not according to the flesh, which are heirs of the true land of Canaan.

14:1 [1] That is, of Babylon: by kings here, meaning, them that were governors of cities.

  [2] Of a people gathered of divers countries.

14:3 [1] Ambition is the chief cause of wars among princes.

  [2] Or, of the labored fields.

  [3] Called also the dead sea, or the lake Asphaltite, near unto Sodom and Gomorrah.

14:5 [1] Or, giants.

  [2] Or, plain.

14:7 [1] Or, destroyed.

14:10 [1] And afterward was overwhelmed with water, and so was called the salt sea.

  [2] Or, were discomfited.

14:12 [1] The godly are plagued many times with the wicked: therefore their company is dangerous.

14:13 [1] God moved them to join with Abram, and preserveth him from their idolatry and superstitions.

14:14 [1] Or, armed.

14:15 [1] Hebrew, *Dammesck.*

14:18 [1] For Abram and his soldiers' refection, and not to offer sacrifice.

14:19 [1] In that Melchizedek fed Abram, he declared himself to represent a king, and in that he blessed him, the high Priest.

21 Then the king of Sodom said to Abram, Give me the ¹persons, and take the goods to thyself.

22 And Abram said to the king of Sodom, ¹I have lifted up mine hand unto the Lord the most high God possessor of heaven and earth,

23 ¹That I will not take of all that is thine, so much as a thread or shoe latchet, lest thou shouldest say, I have made Abram rich,

24 ¹Save only that, which the young men have eaten, and the parts of the men which went with me, Aner, Eshcol, and Mamre: let them take their parts.

15

1 The Lord is Abram's defense and reward.   6 He is justified by faith.   13 The servitude and deliverance out of Egypt is declared.   18 The land of Canaan is promised the fourth time.

1 After these things, the ¹word of the Lord came unto Abram in a ªvision, saying, Fear not, Abram, I am thy buckler, *and* thine exceeding ᵇgreat reward.

2 And Abram said, ¹O Lord God, what wilt thou give me, seeing I go childless, and the steward of mine house is this Eliezer of Damascus?

3 Again Abram said, Behold, to me thou hast given no seed: wherefore lo, a servant of mine house shall be mine heir.

4 Then behold, the word of the Lord came unto him, saying, This man shall not be thine heir, but one that shall come out of thine own bowels, he shall be thine heir.

5 Moreover he brought him forth and said, ᶜLook up now unto heaven, and tell the stars if thou be able to number them: and he said unto him, So shall thy seed be.

6 And *Abram* ᵈbelieved the Lord, and he counted that to him for righteousness.

7 Again he said unto him, I am the Lord, that brought thee out of ᵉUr, of the Chaldeans, to give thee this land to inherit it.

8 And he said, O Lord God, ¹Whereby shall I know that I shall inherit it?

9 Then he said unto him, Take me an heifer of three years old, and a she goat of three years old, and a ram of three years old, a turtle dove also and a pigeon.

CHAPTER 15
ª Num. 12:6
ᵇ Ps. 16:6
ᶜ Rom. 4:18
ᵈ Rom. 4:3
Gal. 3:6
James 2:23
ᵉ Gen. 11:28
ᶠ Acts 7:6
ᵍ Exod. 12:40
ʰ Gen. 12:7
Gen. 13:15
Gen. 26:4
Deut. 4:5
ⁱ 1 Kings 4:21
2 Chron. 9:26

10 So he took all these unto him, and ¹divided them in the midst, and laid every piece one against another: but the birds divided he not.

11 Then fowls fell on the carcasses, and Abram drove them away.

12 And when the sun went down, there fell an heavy sleep unto Abram: and lo, ¹a very fearful darkness fell upon him.

13 Then he said to Abram, ʲKnow for a surety, that thy seed shall be a stranger in a land that is not theirs, ᵍ¹four hundred years, and shall serve them: and they entreat them evil.

14 Notwithstanding, the nation whom they shall serve, will I judge: and afterward shall they come out with great substance.

15 But thou shalt go unto thy fathers in peace, *and* shalt be buried in a good age.

16 And in the ¹fourth generation they shall come hither again: for the ²wickedness of the Amorites is not yet full.

17 Also when the sun went down, there was a darkness: and behold, a smoking furnace, and a firebrand, which went between those pieces.

18 ʰIn that same day the Lord made a covenant with Abram, saying, Unto thy seed have I given this land: ⁱfrom the river of Egypt unto the great river ¹Euphrates.

19 Then Kenites, and the Kenezzites, and the Kadmonites,

20 And the Hittites, and the Perizzites, and the Rephaims,

21 The Amorites also, and the Canaanites, and the Girgashites, and the Jebusites.

16

3 Sarai being barren giveth Hagar to Abram.   4 Which conceiveth and despiseth her dame: 6 And being ill handled, fleeth.   7 The Angel comforteth her.   11, 12 The name and manners of her son.   13 She calleth upon the Lord, whom she findeth true.

1 Now ¹Sarai Abram's wife bore him no children, and she had a maid an Egyptian, Hagar by name.

2 And Sarai said unto Abram, Behold now, the Lord hath ¹restrained me from childbearing, I pray

14:21 ¹ Hebrew, *souls.*
14:22 ¹ Or, I have sworn.
14:23 ¹ Hebrew, *If I take from thee a thread,* etc. Read 1 Sam. 14:44.
14:24 ¹ He would not that his liberality should be hurtful to others.
15:1 ¹ Or, the Lord spake to Abram.
15:2 ¹ His fear was not only lest he should not have children, but lest the promise of the blessed seed should not be accomplished in him.
15:8 ¹ This is a particular motion of God's Spirit, which is not lawful for all to follow, in asking signs: but was permitted to some by a peculiar motion, as to Gideon and Hezekiah.
15:10 ¹ This was the old custom in making covenants, Jer. 34:18, to the which God added these conditions, that Abram's posterity should be as torn in pieces, but after they should be coupled together: also

that it should be assaulted, but yet delivered.
15:12 ¹ Hebrew, *a fear of great darkness.*
15:13 ¹ Counting from the birth of Isaac to their departure out of Egypt: Which declareth that God will suffer his to be afflicted in this world.
15:16 ¹ Or, after four hundred years.
² Though God suffer the wicked for a time, yet his vengeance falleth upon them, when the measure of their wickedness is full.
15:18 ¹ Hebrew, *Perath.*
16:1 ¹ It seemeth that she had respect to God's promise, which could not be accomplished without issue.
16:2 ¹ She faileth in binding God's power to the common order of nature, as though God could not give her children in her old age.

thee go in unto my maid: ²it may be that I shall ³receive a child by her. And Abram obeyed the voice of Sarai.

3 Then Sarai Abram's wife took Hagar her maid the Egyptian, after Abram had dwelled ten years in the land of Canaan, and gave her to her husband Abram for his wife.

4 ¶ And he went in unto Hagar, and she conceived: and when she saw that she had conceived, her dame was ¹despised in her eyes.

5 Then Sarai said to Abram, ¹Thou doest me wrong, I have given my maid into thy bosom, and she seeth that she hath conceived, and I am despised in her eyes: the Lord judge between me and thee.

6 Then Abram said to Sarai, Behold, thy maid *is* in thine ¹hand: do with her as it pleaseth thee. Then Sarai dealt roughly with her: wherefore she fled from her.

7 ¶ But the ¹Angel of the Lord found her beside a fountain in the way of Shur,

8 And he said, Hagar Sarai's maid, whence comest thou? and whither wilt thou go? And she said, I flee from my dame Sarai.

9 Then the Angel of the Lord said to her, ¹Return to thy dame, and humble thyself under her hands.

10 Again the Angel of the Lord said unto her, I will so greatly increase thy seed, that it shall not be numbered for multitude.

11 Also the Angel of the Lord said unto her, See, thou art with child, and shalt bear a son, and shalt call his name Ishmael: for the Lord hath heard thy tribulation.

12 And he shall be a ¹wild man: his hand *shall be* against every man, and every man's hand against him, ªand ²he shall dwell in the presence of all his brethren.

13 Then she called the name of the Lord that spake unto her, Thou God lookest on me: for she said, ¹Have I not also here looked after him that seeth me?

14 ᵇWherefore the Well was called, ¹Beer Lahai Roi: lo, *it is* between Kadesh and Bered.

15 ¶ And Hagar bare Abram a son, and Abram

CHAPTER 16
ª Gen. 25:18
ᵇ Gen. 24:62

CHAPTER 17
ª Gen. 5:22
ᵇ Rom. 4:17
ᶜ Gen. 13:16
ᵈ Acts 7:8
ᵉ Rom. 4:11

called his son's name which Hagar bare, Ishmael.

16 And Abram *was* four score and six years old when Hagar bare him Ishmael.

17

5 *Abram's name is changed to confirm him in the promise.* 8 *The land of Canaan is the fifth time promised.* 12 *Circumcision instituted.* 15 *Sarai is named Sarah.* 18 *Abraham prayeth for Ishmael.* 19 *Isaac is promised.* 23 *Abraham and his house are circumcised.*

1 When Abram was ninety years old and nine, the Lord appeared to Abram, and said unto him, I am God ¹all sufficient, ªwalk before me, and be thou ²upright,

2 And I will make my covenant between me and thee, and I will multiply thee exceedingly.

3 Then Abram fell on his face, and God talked with him, saying,

4 Behold, I *make* my covenant with thee, and thou shalt be a ¹father of many nations,

5 Neither shall thy name anymore be called Abram, but thy name shall be ¹Abraham: ᵇfor a father of many nations have I made thee.

6 Also I will make thee exceedingly fruitful, and will make nations of thee, yea, Kings shall proceed of thee.

7 Moreover, I will establish my covenant between me and thee, and thy seed after thee in their generations, for an ᶜeverlasting covenant, to be God unto thee, and to thy seed after thee.

8 And I will give thee and thy seed after thee the land, wherein thou art a stranger, *even* all the land of Canaan, for an everlasting possession, and I will be their God.

9 ¶ Again God said unto Abraham, Thou also shalt keep my covenant, thou, and thy seed after thee in their generations.

10 ¹This is my covenant which ye shall keep between me and you, and thy seed after thee, ᵈLet every man-child among you be circumcised:

11 That is, ye shall circumcise the ¹foreskin of your flesh, and it shall be a ᵉsign of the covenant between me and you.

12 And every man-child of eight days old among

16:2 ² Or, peradventure.
³ Hebrew, *be built by her.*
16:4 ¹ This punishment declareth what they gain that attempt anything against the word of God.
16:5 ¹ Hebrew, *mine injury is upon thee.*
16:6 ¹ Or, power.
16:7 ¹ Which was Christ, as appeareth verse 13 and Gen. 18:17.
16:9 ¹ God rejecteth none estate of people in their misery, but sendeth them comfort.
16:12 ¹ Or, fierce and cruel, or; as a wild ass.
² That is, the Ishmaelites shall be a peculiar people by themselves, and not a portion of another people.
16:13 ¹ She rebuketh her own dullness and acknowledgeth God's

graces, who was present with her everywhere.
16:14 ¹ Or, the well of the living, and seeing me.
17:1 ¹ Or, Almighty.
² Or, without hypocrisy.
17:4 ¹ Not only according to the flesh, but of a far greater multitude by faith, Rom. 4:17.
17:5 ¹ The changing of his name is a seal to confirm God's promise unto him.
17:10 ¹ Circumcision is called the covenant, because it signifieth the covenant, and hath the promise of grace joined unto it: which phrase is common to all Sacraments.
17:11 ¹ That privy part is circumcised, to show that all that is begotten of man is corrupt, and must be mortified.

you, shall be circumcised in your generations, as well he that is born in *thine* house, as he that is bought with money of any stranger, which is not of thy seed.

13 He that is born in thine house, and he that is bought with thy money, must needs be circumcised: so my covenant shall be in your flesh for an everlasting covenant.

14 But the uncircumcised ¹man-child, in whose flesh the foreskin is not circumcised, even that person shall be cut off from his people, *because* he hath broken my covenant.

15 ¶ Afterward God said unto Abraham, Sarai thy wife shalt thou not call Sarai, but ¹Sarah *shall be* her name.

16 And I will bless her, and will also give thee a son of her, yea, I will bless her, and she shall be *the mother* of nations: Kings *also* of people shall come of her.

17 Then Abraham fell upon his face, and ¹laughed, and said in his heart, Shall a child be born unto him, that is an hundred years old? and shall Sarah that is ninety years old, bear?

18 And Abraham said unto God, Oh, that Ishmael might live in thy sight.

19 Then God said, ⌐Sarah thy wife shall bear thee a son indeed, and thou shalt call his name Isaac: and I will establish my covenant with him for an ¹everlasting covenant, *and* with his seed after him.

20 And as concerning Ishmael, I have heard thee: lo, I have blessed him, and will make him fruitful, and will multiply him ¹exceedingly: twelve princes shall he beget, and I will make a great nation of him.

21 But my covenant will I establish with Isaac, which Sarah shall bear unto thee, the next ᵍyear at this season.

22 And he left off talking with him, and God went up from Abraham.

23 ¶ Then Abraham took Ishmael his son, and all that were born in his house, and all that was bought with his money, *that is*, every man-child among the men of Abraham's house, and ¹he circumcised the foreskin of their flesh in that selfsame day, as God had commanded him.

ᶠ Gen. 18:10
Gen. 21:2
ᵍ Gen. 21:2

CHAPTER 18

ᵃ Heb. 13:2
ᵇ Gen. 17:19,21
Gen. 21:2
Rom. 9:9

24 Abraham also himself was ninety years old and nine, when the foreskin of his flesh was circumcised.

25 And Ishmael his son was thirteen years old, when the foreskin of his flesh was circumcised.

26 The selfsame day was Abraham circumcised, and Ishmael his son:

27 And all the men of his house *both* born in his house, and bought with money of the stranger, were circumcised with him.

18 *2 Abraham receiveth three Angels into his house. 10 Isaac is promised again. 12 Sarah laugheth. 18 Christ is promised to all nations. 19 Abraham taught his family to know God. 21 The destruction of Sodom is declared unto Abraham. 23 Abraham prayeth for them.*

1 Again the Lord ᵃappeared unto him in the ¹plain of Mamre, as he sat in his tent door about the heat of the day.

2 And he lifted up his eyes, and looked: and lo, three ¹men stood by him, and when he saw *them*, he ran to meet them from the tent door, and bowed himself to the ground.

3 And he said, ¹Lord, if I have now found favor in thy sight, go not, I pray thee, from thy servant.

4 Let a little water, I pray you, be brought, and ¹wash your feet, and rest yourselves under the tree.

5 And I will bring a morsel of bread, that you may comfort your hearts, afterward ye shall go your ways: for therefore are ye ¹come to your servant. And they said, Do even as thou hast said.

6 Then Abraham made haste into the tent unto Sarah, and said, Make ready at once three ¹measures of fine meal, knead it, and make cakes upon the hearth.

7 And Abraham ran to the beasts, and took a tender and good calf, and gave it to the servant, who hasted to make it ready.

8 And he took butter and milk, and the calf which he had prepared, and set before them, and stood himself by them under the tree: and ¹they did eat.

9 ¶ Then they said unto him, Where is Sarah thy wife? And he answered, Behold, *she is* in the tent.

10 And he said, ᵇI will certainly come again unto

17:14 ¹ Albeit women were not circumcised, yet were they partakers of God's promise: for under the mankind all was consecrated, and here is declared, that whosoever contemneth the sign, despiseth also the promise.

17:15 ¹ Or, dame, or princess.

17:17 ¹ Which proceeded of a sudden joy, and not of infidelity.

17:19 ¹ The everlasting Covenant is made with the children of the Spirit: and with the children of the flesh is made the temporal promise, as was promised to Ishmael.

17:20 ¹ Hebrew, *greatly, greatly.*

17:23 ¹ They were well instructed which obeyed to be circumcised without resistance: which thing declareth that masters in their

houses ought to be as preachers to their families, that from the highest to the lowest they may obey the will of God.

18:1 ¹ Or, oak grove.

18:2 ¹ That is, three Angels in man's shape.

18:3 ¹ Speaking to one of them in whom appeared to be most majesty, for he thought they had been men.

18:4 ¹ For men used because of the great heat to go bare footed in those parts.

18:5 ¹ As sent of God, that I should do my duty to you.

18:6 ¹ Hebrew, *Seim.*

18:8 ¹ For as God gave them bodies for a time, so gave he them the faculties thereof, to walk, to eat and drink, and such like.

thee according to the time of [1]life: and lo, Sarah thy wife shall have a son: and Sarah heard in the tent door, which was behind him.

11 (Now Abraham and Sarah *were* old and stricken in age, *and* it ceased to be with Sarah after the manner of women.)

12 Therefore Sarah [1]laughed within herself, saying, After I am waxed old, [c]and my lord also, shall I have lust?

13 And the Lord said unto Abraham, Wherefore did Sarah thus laugh, saying, Shall I certainly bear a child, which am old?

14 (Shall anything be [1d]hard to the Lord? as the time appointed will I return unto thee, *even* according to the time of life, and Sarah shall have a son.)

15 But Sarah denied, saying, I laughed not: for she was afraid. And he said, [1]It is not so: for thou laughedst.

16 ¶ Afterward, the men did rise up from thence, and looked toward Sodom: and Abraham went with them to bring them on the way.

17 And the [1]Lord said, Shall I hide from Abraham that thing which I do,

18 Seeing that Abraham shall be indeed a great and a mighty nation, and [e]all the nations of the earth shall be blessed in him?

19 For I know him [1]that he will command his sons and his household after him, that they keep the way of the Lord to do righteousness and judgment, that the Lord may bring upon Abraham, that he hath spoken unto him.

20 Then the Lord said, Because the cry of Sodom and Gomorrah is great, and because their sin is exceedingly grievous,

21 I will [1]go down now, and see whether they have done altogether according to that [2]cry, which is come unto me: and if not, *that* I may know.

22 And the men turned thence, and went toward Sodom: but Abraham stood yet before the Lord.

23 Then Abraham drew near, and said, Wilt thou also destroy the righteous with the wicked?

24 If there be fifty righteous within the city, wilt thou destroy and not spare the place for the fifty

c 1 Pet. 3:6
d Zech. 8:6
e Gen. 12:3
  Gen. 22:18

CHAPTER 19
a Gen. 18:4

righteous that are therein?

25 Be it far from thee from doing this thing, to slay the righteous with the wicked: and that the righteous should be even as the wicked, be it far from thee. Shall not the Judge of all the world [1]do right?

26 And the Lord answered, If I shall find in Sodom [1]fifty righteous within the city, then will I spare all the place for their sakes.

27 Then Abraham answered and said, Behold now, I have begun to speak unto my Lord, and I am [1]but dust and ashes,

28 If there shall lack five of fifty righteous, wilt thou destroy all the city for five? And he said, If I find there five and forty, I will not destroy it.

29 And he yet spake to him again, and said, What if there shall be found forty there? Then he answered, I will not do it for forty's sake.

30 Again he said, Let not my Lord now be angry that I speak, What if thirty be found there? Then he said, I will not do it, if I find thirty there.

31 Moreover he said, Behold now, I have begun to speak unto my Lord, What if twenty be found there? And he answered, I will not destroy it for twenty's sake.

32 Then he said, Let not my Lord be now angry, and I will speak but this [1]once, What if ten be found there? And he answered, I will not destroy it for ten's sake.

33 ¶ And the Lord went his way, when he had left communing with Abraham, and Abraham returned unto his place.

19 3 *Lot recieveth two Angels into his house.* 4 *The filthy lusts of the Sodomites.* 16 *Lot is delivered.* 14 *Sodom is destroyed.* 26 *Lot's wife is made a pillar of salt.* 33 *Lot's daughters lie with their father, of whom came Moab and Ammon.*

1 And in the evening there came two [1]Angels to Sodom: and Lot sat at the gate of Sodom, and Lot saw *them*, and rose up to meet them, and he bowed himself with his face to the ground.

2 And he said, See my lords, I pray you turn in now into your servant's house, and tarry all night, and [a]wash your feet, and ye shall rise up early and

---

18:10 [1] That is, about this time when she shall be alive, or when the child shall come into this life.
18:12 [1] For she rather had respect to the order of nature, than believed the promise of God.
18:14 [1] Or, hid.
18:15 [1] Hebrew, *No.*
18:17 [1] Jehovah the Hebrew word which we call Lord, showeth that this Angel was Christ: for this word is only applied to God.
18:19 [1] He showeth that fathers ought both to know God's judgments, and to declare them to their children.
18:21 [1] God speaketh after the fashion of men: that is, I will enter into judgment with good advice.
 [2] For our sins cry for vengeance, though none accuse us.

18:25 [1] Hebrew, *do judgment.*
18:26 [1] God declareth that his judgments were done with great mercy, forasmuch as all were so corrupt, that not only fifty but ten righteous men could not be found there, and also that the wicked are spared for the righteous' sake.
18:27 [1] Hereby we learn, that the nearer we approach unto God, the more doth our miserable estate appear, and the more are we humbled.
18:32 [1] If God refused not the prayer for the wicked Sodomites, even to the sixth request, how much more will he grant the prayers of the godly for the afflicted Church?
19:1 [1] Wherein we see God's provident care in preserving his: albeit he revealeth not himself to all alike: for Lot had but two Angels, and Abraham three.

go your ways. Who said, Nay, but we will abide in the street all night.

3   Then [1]he pressed upon them earnestly, and they turned in to him, and came to his house, and he made them a feast, and did bake unleavened bread, and they [2]did eat.

4   But before they went to bed, the men of the city, *even* the men of Sodom compassed the house round about, from the young even to the old, [1]all the people from *all* quarters.

5   Who crying unto Lot said to him, Where are the men, which came to thee this night? bring them out unto us, that we may know them.

6   Then Lot went out at the door unto them, and shut the door after him,

7   And said, I pray you, my brethren, do not *so* wickedly.

8   Behold now, I have two [1]daughters, which have not known man: them will I bring out now unto you, and do them as seemeth you good: only unto these men do nothing: [2]for therefore are they come under the shadow of my roof.

9   Then they said, Away hence: and they said, He is come alone as a stranger, and shall he judge and rule? we will now deal worse with thee than with them. So they pressed sore upon Lot [b]himself, and came to break the door.

10   But the men put forth their hand, and pulled Lot into the house to them, and shut to the door.

11   Then they smote the men that were at the door of the house, with blindness, both small and great, so that they were weary in [1]seeking the door.

12   ¶ Then the men said unto Lot, Whom hast thou yet here? either son-in-law, or thy sons or thy daughters, or whatsoever thou hast in the city, bring it out of this place.

13   For [1]we will destroy this place, because the [c]cry of them is great before the Lord, and the Lord hath sent us to destroy it.

14   Then Lot went out and spake unto his sons-in-law, which [1]married his daughters, and said, Arise, get you out of this place: for the Lord will destroy the city, but he seemed to his sons-in-law, as though

[b] 2 Pet. 2:7
[c] Gen. 18:20
[d] Deut. 29:23
Isa. 13:19
Jer. 50:40
Ezek. 16:49
Hos. 11:8
Amos 4:11
Luke 17:29
Jude 7

he had mocked.

15   ¶ And when the morning arose, the Angels hasted Lot, saying, Arise, take thy wife and thy two daughters [1]which are here, lest thou be destroyed in the punishment of the city.

16   And *as* he [1]prolonged the time, the men caught both him and his wife, and his two daughters by the hands (the Lord being merciful unto him) and they brought him forth, and set him without the city.

17   ¶ And when they had brought them out, *the Angel* said, Escape for thy life: [1]look not behind thee, neither tarry thou in all the plain: escape into the mountain, lest thou be destroyed.

18   And Lot said unto them, Not so, I pray thee, my Lord.

19   Behold now, thy servant hath found grace in thy sight, and thou hast magnified thy mercy, which thou hast showed unto me in saving my life: and I cannot escape in the mountain, lest *some* evil take me, and I die.

20   See now this city hereby to flee unto, which is a little one: Oh let me escape thither: is it not a [1]little one, and my soul shall live?

21   Then he said unto him, Behold, I have received [1]thy request also concerning this thing, that I will not overthrow this city, for the which thou hast spoken.

22   Haste thee, save thee there: for I can do [1]nothing till thou come thither. Therefore the name of the city was called [2]Zoar.

23   ¶ The sun did rise upon the earth, when Lot entered into Zoar.

24   Then the Lord [d]rained upon Sodom and upon Gomorrah, brimstone and fire from the Lord out of heaven,

25   And overthrew those cities, and all the plain, and all the inhabitants of the cities, and that grew upon the earth.

26   ¶ Now his wife behind him looked back, and she became a [1]pillar of salt.

27   ¶ And Abraham rising up early in the morning *went* to the place, where he had stood before the Lord,

---

19:3 [1] That is, he prayed them so instantly.
  [2] Not for that they had necessity, but because the time was not yet come that they would reveal themselves.
19:4 [1] Nothing is more dangerous than to dwell where sin reigneth: for it corrupteth all.
19:8 [1] He deserveth praise in his guests, but he is to be blamed in seeking unlawful means.
  [2] That I should preserve them from all injury.
19:11 [1] Hebrew, *finding.*
19:13 [1] This proveth that the Angels are ministers, as well to execute God's wrath, as to declare his favor.
19:14 [1] Or, should marry.
19:15 [1] Hebrew, *which are found.*

19:16 [1] The mercy of God striveth to overcome man's slowness in following God's calling.
19:17 [1] He willed him to flee from God's judgments, and not to be sorry to depart from that rich country, and full of vain pleasures.
19:20 [1] Though it be little, yet it is great enough to save my life: wherein he offendeth in choosing another place than the Angel had appointed him.
19:21 [1] Hebrew, *thy face.*
19:22 [1] Because God's commandment was to destroy the city, and to save Lot.
  [2] Which before was called Bela, Gen. 14:2.
19:26 [1] As touching the body only: and this is a notable monument of God's vengeance to all them that passed that way.

28 And looking toward Sodom and Gomorrah, and toward all the land of the plain, behold, he saw the smoke of the land mounting up as the smoke of a furnace.

29 ¶ But yet when God destroyed the cities of the plain, God thought upon Abraham, and sent Lot out from the midst of the destruction, when he overthrew the cities, wherein Lot dwelled.

30 ¶ Then Lot went up out of Zoar, and dwelt in the mountain with his two daughters for he ¹feared to tarry in Zoar, but dwelt in a cave, he and his two daughters.

31 And the elder said unto the younger, Our father is old, and there is not a man in the ¹earth, to come in unto us after the manner of all the earth.

32 Come, we will make our father ¹drink wine, and lie with him, that we may preserve seed of our father.

33 So they made their father drink wine that night, and the elder went and lay with her father: but he perceived not, neither when she lay down, neither when she rose up.

34 And on the morrow the elder said to the younger, Behold, yester night lay I with my father: let us make him drink wine this night also, and go thou *and* lie with him, that we may ¹preserve seed of our father.

35 So they made their father drink wine that night also, and the younger arose, and lay with him: but he perceived it not, when she lay down, neither when she rose up.

36 Thus were ¹both the daughters of Lot with child by their father.

37 And the elder bare a son, and she called his name Moab: the same is the father of the ¹Moabites unto this day.

38 And the younger bare a son also, and she called his name ¹Ben-Ammi: the same is the father of the Ammonites unto this day.

20

1 Abraham dwelleth as a stranger in the land of Gerar. 2 Abimelech taketh away his wife. 3 God

reproveth the king, 9 and the king Abraham. 14 Sarah is restored with great gifts. 17 Abraham prayeth, and the king and his are healed.

1 Afterward Abraham departed thence toward the South country and dwelled between Kadesh and ¹Shur, and sojourned in Gerar.

2 And Abraham said of Sarah his wife, ¹She is my sister. Then Abimelech king of Gerar sent and took Sarah.

3 But God came to Abimelech in a dream by night, and said to him, Behold, ¹thou art but dead, because of the woman, which thou hast taken: for she is a man's wife.

4 (Notwithstanding Abimelech had not yet come near her) And he said, Lord, wilt thou slay even ¹the righteous nation?

5 Said not he unto me, She is my sister? yea, and she herself said, He is my brother: with an upright ¹mind, and ²innocent hands have I done this.

6 And God said unto him by a dream, I know that thou diddest this even with an upright mind, and I ¹kept thee also that thou shouldest not sin against me: therefore suffered I thee not to touch her.

7 Now then deliver the man his wife again: for he is a ¹Prophet, and he ²shall pray for thee, that thou mayest live: but if thou deliver her not again, be sure that thou shalt die the death, thou, and all that thou hast.

8 Then Abimelech rising up early in the morning, called all his servants, and told all these things ¹unto them, and the men were sore afraid.

9 Afterward Abimelech called Abraham, and said unto him, What hast thou done unto us? and what have I offended thee, that thou hast brought on me, and on my ¹kingdom *this* great sin? thou hast done things unto me that ought not to be done.

10 So Abimelech said unto Abraham, What sawest thou that thou hast done this thing?

11 Then Abraham answered, Because I thought *thus*, Surely the ¹fear of God *is* not in this place, and they will slay me for my wife's sake.

19:30 ¹ Having before felt God's mercy, he durst not provoke him again by continuing among the wicked.
19:31 ¹ Meaning in the country, which the Lord had now destroyed.
19:32 ¹ For except he had been overcome with wine, he would never have done that abominable act.
19:34 ¹ Hebrew, *keep alive.*
19:36 ¹ Thus God permitted him to fall most horribly in the solitary mountains, whom the wickedness of Sodom could not overcome.
19:37 ¹ Who as they were born in most horrible incest, so were they and their posterity vile and wicked.
19:38 ¹ That is, son of my people: signifying that they rather rejoiced in their sin, than repented for the same.
20:1 ¹ Which was toward Egypt.
20:2 ¹ Abraham had now twice fallen into this fault: such is man's frailty.

20:3 ¹ So greatly God detesteth the breach of marriage.
20:4 ¹ The infidels confessed that God would not punish but for just occasion: therefore, whensoever he punisheth, the occasion is just.
20:5 ¹ As one falling by ignorance, and not doing evil of purpose.
² Not thinking to do any man harm.
20:6 ¹ God by his holy Spirit retaineth them that offend by ignorance, that they fall not into greater inconvenience.
20:7 ¹ That is, one, to whom God revealeth himself familiarly.
² For the prayer of the godly is of force towards God.
20:8 ¹ Hebrew, *in their ears.*
20:9 ¹ The wickedness of the King bringeth God's wrath upon the whole realm.
20:11 ¹ He showeth that no honesty can be hoped for, where the fear of God is not.

12 Yet in very deed she is my [1]sister: for she is the daughter of my father, but not the daughter of my mother, and she is my wife.

13 Now when God caused me to wander out of my father's house, I said then to her, This is thy kindness that thou shalt show unto me in all places where we come, [a]Say thou of me, He is my brother.

14 Then took Abimelech sheep and beeves, and men servants, and women servants, and gave them unto Abraham, and restored him Sarah his wife.

15 And Abimelech said, Behold, my land is [1]before thee, dwell where it pleaseth thee.

16 Likewise to Sarah he said, Behold, I have given thy brother a thousand pieces of silver: behold, he is the [1]veil of thine eyes to all that are with thee, and to all others: and she was [2]thus reproved.

17 ¶ Then Abraham prayed unto God, and God healed Abimelech and his wife, and his women servants: and they bare children.

18 For the Lord [1]had shut up every womb of the house of Abimelech, because of Sarah Abraham's wife.

21

3 Isaac is born.   9 Ishmael mocketh Isaac.   14 Hagar is cast out with her son.   17 The Angel comforteth Hagar.   32 The covenant between Abimelech and Abraham.   33 Abraham called upon the Lord.

1 Now the Lord visited Sarah, as he had said, and did unto her [a]according as he had promised.

2 For [b]Sarah conceived, and bare Abraham a son in his [1]old age, at the same season that God told him.

3 And Abraham called his son's name that was born unto him, which Sarah bare him, Isaac.

4 Then Abraham circumcised Isaac his son, when he was eight days old, [c]as God had commanded him.

5 So Abraham was an hundred years old, when his son Isaac was born unto him.

6 ¶ Then Sarah said, God hath made me to rejoice: all that hear, will rejoice with me.

7 Again she said, [1]Who would have said to Abraham, that Sarah should have given children suck? for I have borne him a son in his old age.

8 Then the child grew and was weaned: and Abraham made a great feast the same day that Isaac

CHAPTER 20
[a] Gen. 12:13

CHAPTER 21
[a] Gen. 17:19
   Gen. 18:10
[b] Matt. 1:2
   Acts 7:8
   Gal. 4:23
   Heb. 11:11
[c] Gen. 17:12
[d] Gal. 4:30

was weaned.

9 ¶ And Sarah saw the son of Hagar the Egyptian (which she had borne unto Abraham) [1]mocking.

10 Wherefore she said unto Abraham, [d]Cast out this bondwoman and her son: for the son of this bondwoman shall not be heir with my son Isaac.

11 And this thing was very grievous in Abraham's sight, because of his son.

12 ¶ But God said unto Abraham, Let it not be grievous in thy sight for the child, and for thy bondwoman: in all that Sarah shall say unto thee, hear her voice: for in Isaac shall thy seed be [1]called.

13 As for the son of the bondwoman, I will make him [1]a nation also, because he is thy seed.

14 So Abraham arose up early in the morning and took bread, and a bottle of water, and gave it unto Hagar putting it on her shoulder, and the child also, and [1]sent her away: who departing, wandered in the wilderness of Beersheba.

15 And when the water of the bottle was spent, she cast the child under a certain tree.

16 Then she went and sat her over against him afar off about a bow shoot: for she said, I will not see the death of the child. And she sat down over against him, and lift up her voice, and wept.

17 Then God [1]heard the voice of the child, and the Angel of God called to Hagar from heaven, and said unto her, What aileth thee, Hagar? fear not, for God hath heard the voice of the child where he is.

18 Arise, take up the child, and hold him in thine hand: for I will make him a great people.

19 And God [1]opened her eyes, and she saw a well of water: so she went and filled the bottle with water, and gave the boy drink.

20 So God was [1]with the child, and he grew and dwelt in the wilderness, and was an [2]archer.

21 And he dwelt in the wilderness of Paran, and his mother took him a wife out of the land of Egypt.

22 ¶ And at the same time Abimelech and Phichol his chief captain spake unto Abraham, saying, God is with thee in all that thou doest.

23 Now therefore swear unto me here by God, that thou wilt not [1]hurt me, nor my children, nor my

---

20:12 [1] By sister, he meaneth his cousin germaine, and by daughter, Abraham's niece, Gen. 11:29, for so the Hebrews use these words.
20:15 [1] Or, is at thy commandment.
20:16 [1] Such an head, as with whom thou mayest be preserved from all dangers.
   [2] God caused this heathen King to reprove her because she dissembled, seeing that God had given her an husband as her veil and defense.
20:18 [1] Had taken away from them the gift of conceiving.
21:2 [1] Therefore the miracle was greater.
21:7 [1] She accuseth herself of ingratitude, that she did not believe the Angel.
21:9 [1] He derided God's promise made to Isaac, which the Apostle

calleth persecution, Gal. 4:29.
21:12 [1] The promised seed shall be counted from Isaac, and not from Ishmael, Rom. 9:7; Heb. 11:18.
21:13 [1] The Ishmaelites shall come of him.
21:14 [1] True faith renounceth all natural affections to obey God's commandment.
21:17 [1] For his promise sake made to Abraham; and not because the child had discretion and judgment to pray.
21:19 [1] Except God open our eyes, we can neither see, nor use the means which are before us.
21:20 [1] As touching outward things God caused him to prosper.
   [2] Or, shot in the bow, and was an hunter.
21:23 [1] Hebrew, *deal falsely with me*, or *lie*.

children's children: thou shalt deal with me, and with the country, where thou hast been a stranger, according unto the kindness that I have showed thee.

24 Then Abraham said, I will ¹swear.

25 And Abraham rebuked Abimelech for a well of water, which Abimelech's servants had violently taken away.

26 And Abimelech said, ¹I know not who hath done this thing: also thou toldest me not, neither heard I *of it* but this day.

27 Then Abraham took sheep and beeves, and gave them unto Abimelech: and they two made a covenant.

28 And Abraham set seven lambs of the flock by themselves.

29 Then Abimelech said unto Abraham, What mean these seven lambs, which thou hast set by themselves?

30 And he answered, Because thou shalt receive of mine hand *these* seven lambs, that it may be a witness unto me, that I have dug this well.

31 Wherefore the place is called ¹Beersheba, because there they both swear.

32 Thus made they a ¹covenant at Beersheba: afterward Abimelech and Phichol the chief captain rose up, and turned again unto the land of the Philistines.

33 ¶ And Abraham planted a grove in Beersheba, and ¹called there on the Name of the Lord, the everlasting God.

34 And Abraham was a stranger in the Philistine's land a long season.

22 1,2 *The faith of Abraham is proved in offering his son Isaac.* 3 *Isaac is a figure of Christ.* 20 *The generations of Nahor Abraham's brother of whom cometh Rebekah.*

1 And after these things God did ᵃprove Abraham, and said unto him, Abraham. Who answered, ¹Here am I.

2 And he said, Take now thine only son Isaac whom thou lovest, and get thee unto the land of ¹Moriah, and ²offer him there for a burnt offering upon one

CHAPTER 22
ᵃ Heb. 11:17
ᵇ James 2:21

of the mountains, which I will show thee.

3 Then Abraham rose up early in the morning, and saddled his ass, and took two of his servants with him, and Isaac his son, and clove wood for the burnt offering, and rose up and went to the place, which God had told him.

4 ¶ Then the third day Abraham lifted up his eyes, and saw the place afar off,

5 And said unto his servants, Abide you here with the ass: for I and the child will go yonder and worship, and ¹come again unto you.

6 Then Abraham took the wood of the burnt offering, and laid it upon Isaac his son, and he took the fire in his hand, and the knife: and they went both together.

7 Then spake Isaac unto Abraham his father, and said, My father. And he answered, Here am I, my son. And he said, Behold the fire and the wood, but where is the lamb for the burnt offering?

8 Then Abraham answered, My son, God will ¹provide him a lamb for a burnt offering: so they went both together.

9 And when they came to the place which God had showed him, Abraham built an altar there, and couched the wood, and ¹bound Isaac his son, ᵇand laid him on the altar upon the wood.

10 And Abraham stretching forth his hand, took the knife to kill his son.

11 But the Angel of the Lord called unto him from heaven, saying, Abraham, Abraham. And he answered, Here am I.

12 Then he said, Lay not thine hand upon the child, neither do anything unto him: for now I ¹know that thou fearest God, seeing for my sake ²thou hast not spared thine ³only son.

13 And Abraham lifting up his eyes, looked and behold, there was a ram behind *him* caught by the horns in a bush: then Abraham went and took the ram, and offered him up for a burnt offering in the stead of his son.

14 And Abraham called the name of that place ¹Jehovah Jireh: as it is said this day, In the mount will the Lord ²be seen.

21:24 ¹ So that it is a lawful thing to take an oath in matters of importance, for to justify the truth, and to assure others of our sincerity.
21:26 ¹ Wicked servants do many evils unknown to their masters.
21:31 ¹ Or, well of the oath, or of seven, meaning lambs.
21:32 ¹ Thus we see that the godly, as touching outward things may make peace with the wicked that know not the true God.
21:33 ¹ That is, he worshipped God in all points of true Religion.
22:1 ¹ Hebrew, *Lo, I.*
22:2 ¹ Which signifieth the fear of God, in the which place he was honored: and Solomon afterward built the Temple.
² Herein stood the chiefest point of his tentation, seeing he was commanded to offer up him in whom God had promised to bless all the nations of the world.

22:5 ¹ He doubted not, but God would accomplish his promise, though he should sacrifice his son.
22:8 ¹ The only way to overcome all tentation, is to rest upon God's providence.
22:9 ¹ For it is like that his father had declared to him God's commandment, whereunto he showed himself obedient.
22:12 ¹ That is, by thy true obedience thou hast declared thy lively faith.
² Or, and hast not withheld thine only son from me.
³ Hebrew, *thy son, thy only son.*
22:14 ¹ Or, the Lord will see or provide.
² The name is changed, to show that God doth both see and provide secretly for his, and also evidently is seen, and felt in time convenient.

15 ¶ And the Angel of the Lord cried unto Abraham from heaven the second time,

16 And said, ʿBy ¹myself have I sworn (saith the Lord) because thou hast done this thing, and hast not spared thine only son,

17 Therefore will I surely bless thee, and will greatly multiply thy seed, as the stars of the heaven, and as the sand which is upon the sea shore, and thy seed shall possess the ¹gate of his enemies.

18 ᵈAnd in thy seed shall all the nations of the earth be blessed, because thou hast obeyed my voice.

19 Then turned Abraham again unto his servants, and they rose up, and went together to Beersheba: and Abraham dwelt at Beersheba.

20 ¶ And after these things one told Abraham, saying, Behold Milcah, she hath also born children unto thy brother Nahor:

21 To wit, Huz his eldest son, and Buz his brother, and Kemuel the father of ¹Aram,

22 And Chesed, and Hazo, and Pildash, and Jidlaph, and Bethuel.

23 And Bethuel begat Rebekah: these eight did Milcah bear to Nahor, Abraham's brother.

24 And his ¹concubine called Reumah, she bare also Tebah, and Gaham, and Thahash and Maachah.

23 *2 Abraham laments the death of Sarah. 4 He buyeth a field to bury her, of the Hittites. 13 The equity of Abraham. 19 Sarah is buried in Machpelah.*

1 When Sarah was an hundred twenty and seven years old (¹so long lived she.)

2 Then Sarah died in Kirjath Arba: the same is Hebron in the land of Canaan. And Abraham came to mourn for Sarah and to weep for her.

3 ¶ Then Abraham ¹rose up from the sight of his corpse, and talked with the ²Hittites, saying,

4 I am a stranger, and a foreigner among you: give me a possession of burial with you, that I may bury my dead out of my sight.

5 Then the Hittites answered Abraham, saying unto him,

6 Hear us, my lord: thou art a prince ¹of God among us: in the chiefest of our sepulchers bury the dead: none of us shall forbid thee his sepulcher, but thou mayest bury thy dead *therein.*

7 Then Abraham stood up, and bowed himself before the people of the land of the Hittites.

8 And he communed with them, saying, If it be ¹your mind, that I shall bury my dead out of my sight, hear me, and entreat for me to Ephron the son of Zohar,

9 That he would give me the cave of ¹Machpelah, which he hath in the end of his field: that he would give it me for as much ²money as it is worth, for a possession to bury in among you.

10 (For Ephron dwelt among the Hittites) Then Ephron the Hittite answered Abraham in the audience of all the Hittites that ¹went in at the gates of his city, saying,

11 No, my Lord, hear me: the field give I thee and the cave that therein is, I give it thee: *even* in the presence of the sons of my people give I it thee to bury thy dead.

12 Then Abraham ¹bowed himself before the people of the land,

13 And spake unto Ephron in the audience of the people of the country, saying, Seeing thou *wilt give it,* I pray thee, hear me, I will give the price of the field: receive it of me, and I will bury my dead there.

14 Ephron then answered Abraham, saying unto him,

15 My lord, hearken unto me: the land *is worth* four hundred ¹shekels of silver: what *is* that between me and thee? bury therefore thy dead.

16 So Abraham hearkened unto Ephron, and Abraham weighed to Ephron the silver, which he had named, in the audience of the Hittites, *even* four hundred silver shekels of current money among merchants.

17 ¶ So the field of Ephron *which was* in Machpelah, and over against Mamre, *even* the field and the cave that was therein, and all the trees that were in the field, which were in all the borders round about, was made sure

18 Unto Abraham for a possession, in the sight of the Hittites, *even* of all that ¹went in at the gates of his city.

19 And after this, Abraham buried Sarah his wife in the cave of the field of Machpelah over against Mamre: the same is Hebron in the land of Canaan.

ᶜ Ps. 105:9
Luke 1:73
Heb. 6:13

ᵈ Gen. 12:3
Gen. 18:18
Acts 3:25
Gal. 3:8

22:16 ¹ Signifying, that there is no greater than he.

22:17 ¹ Or, holds.

22:21 ¹ Or, of the Syrians.

22:24 ¹ Concubine is oftentimes taken in the good part for those women which are inferior to the wives.

23:1 ¹ Hebrew, *the years of the life of Sarah.*

23:3 ¹ That is, when he had mourned: so the godly may mourn, if they pass not measure, and the natural affection is commendable.

² Hebrew, *sons of Heth.*

23:6 ¹ That is, godly or excellent: for the Hebrews so speak of all things that are notable, because all excellency cometh of God.

23:8 ¹ Hebrew, *in your soul.*

23:9 ¹ Or, double cave, because one was within another.

² Hebrew, *in full silver.*

23:10 ¹ Meaning, all the citizens and inhabitants.

23:12 ¹ To show that he had them in good estimation and reverence.

23:15 ¹ The common shekel is about 20 pence, so then 400 shekels mount to 33 pound 6 shillings and 8 pence after 5 shilling sterling the ounce.

23:18 ¹ Or, citizens.

20 Thus the field, and the cave that is therein, was made sure unto Abraham for a possession of burial [1]by the Hittites.

24

2 Abraham causeth his servant to swear to take a wife for Isaac in his own kindred. 12 The servant prayeth to God. 33 His fidelity toward his master. 50 The friends of Rebekah commit the matter to God. 58 They ask her consent, and she agreeth.

1 Now Abraham was old, and [1]stricken in years, and the Lord had blessed Abraham in all things.

2 Therefore Abraham said unto his eldest servant of his house, which had the rule over all that he had, [a,1]Put now thine hand under my thigh,

3 And I will make thee [1]swear by the Lord God of the heaven, and God of the earth, that thou shalt not take a wife unto my son of the daughters of the Canaanites among whom I dwell:

4 But thou shalt go unto my [1]country, and to my kindred, and take a wife unto my son Isaac.

5 And the servant said to him, What if the woman will not come with me to this land? shall I bring thy son again unto the land from whence thou camest?

6 To whom Abraham answered, Beware that thou bring not my son [1]thither again.

7 ¶ The Lord God of heaven, who took me from my father's house, and from the land where I was born, and that spake unto me, and that swear unto me, saying, [b]Unto thy seed will I give this land, he shall send his Angel before thee, and thou shalt take a wife unto my son from thence.

8 Nevertheless if the woman will not follow thee, then shalt thou be [1]discharged of this mine oath: only bring not my son thither again.

9 Then the servant put his hand under the thigh of Abraham his master, and sware to him for this matter.

10 ¶ So the servant took ten camels of the camels of his master, and departed: (for he had all his master's goods in his hand:) and so he arose, and went to [1]Aram Naharaim, unto the [2]city of Nahor.

CHAPTER 24
[a] Gen. 47:29
[b] Gen. 12:7
Gen. 13:15
Gen. 15:18
Gen. 26:4

11 And he made his camels to [1]lie down without the city by a well of water, at eventide about the time that the women come out to draw water.

12 And he said, O [1]Lord God of my master Abraham, I beseech thee, [2]send me good speed this day, and show mercy unto my master Abraham.

13 Lo, I stand by the well of water while the men's daughters of this city come out to draw water.

14 [1]Grant therefore that the maid, to whom I say: Bow down thy pitcher, I pray thee, that I may drink: if she say, Drink, and I will give thy camels drink also: may be she that thou hast ordained for thy servant Isaac: and thereby shall I know that thou hast showed mercy on my master.

15 ¶ And now yet he had left speaking, behold, [1]Rebekah came out, the daughter of Bethuel, son of Milcah the wife of Nahor Abraham's brother, and her Pitcher upon her shoulder.

16 (And the maid was very fair to look upon, a virgin and unknown of man) and she [1]went down to the well, and filled her pitcher and came up.

17 Then the servant ran to meet her, and said, Let me drink, I pray thee, a little water of thy pitcher.

18 And she said, Drink [1]sir: and she hasted, and let down her pitcher upon her hand and gave him drink.

19 And when she had given him drink, she said, I will draw water for thy camels also until they [1]have drunken enough.

20 And she poured out her pitcher into the trough speedily, and ran again unto the well to draw water, and she drew for all his camels.

21 So the man wondered at her, and held his peace, to know whether the Lord had made his journey prosperous or not.

22 And when the camels had left drinking, the man took a golden [1,2]abillement of [3]half a shekel weight, and two bracelets for her hands, of ten shekels weight of gold:

23 And he said, Whose daughter art thou? tell me, I pray thee, Is there room in thy father's house for us to lodge in?

23:20 [1] That is, all the people confirmed the sale.
24:1 [1] Hebrew, come into days.
24:2 [1] Which ceremony declared, the servant's obedience towards his master, and the master's power over the servant.
24:3 [1] This showeth that an oath may be required in a lawful cause.
24:4 [1] He would not that his son should marry out of the godly family: for the inconveniences that come by marrying with the ungodly are set forth in sundry places of the Scriptures.
24:6 [1] Lest he should lose the inheritance promised.
24:8 [1] Hebrew, innocent.
24:10 [1] Or, Mesopotamia, or, Syria of the two floods: to wit, of Tigris and Euphrates.
    [2] That is, to Haran.
24:11 [1] Hebrew, to bow their knees.

24:12 [1] He groundeth his prayer upon God's promise made to his master.
    [2] Or, cause me to meet.
24:14 [1] The servant moved by God's spirit desired to be assured by a sign, whether God prospered his journey or no.
24:15 [1] God giveth good success to all things that are undertaken for the glory of his name and according to his word.
24:16 [1] Here is declared that God ever heareth the prayers of his, and granteth their requests.
24:18 [1] Hebrew, my Lord.
24:19 [1] Hebrew, have made an end of drinking.
24:22 [1] Or, earring.
    [2] God permitted many things both in apparel and other things which are now forbid: specially when they appertain not to our mortification.
    [3] The golden shekel is here meant and not that of silver.

24 Then she said to him, I am the daughter of Bethuel the son of Milcah whom she bare unto Nahor.

25 Moreover she said unto him, We have litter also and provender enough, and room to lodge in.

26 And the man bowed himself and worshipped the Lord,

27 And said, Blessed be the Lord God of my master Abraham, which hath not withdrawn his mercy ¹and his truth from my master: *for* when I was in the way, the Lord brought me to my master's brethren's house.

28 And the maid ran and told them of her mother's house according to these words.

29 ¶ Now Rebekah had a brother called Laban, and Laban ran unto the man to the well.

30 For when he had seen the earrings and bracelets in his sister's hands, and when he heard the words of Rebekah his sister, saying, Thus said the man unto me, then he went to the man, and lo, ¹he stood by the camels at the well.

31 And he said, Come in thou blessed of the Lord: wherefore standest thou without, seeing I have prepared the house, and room for the camels?

32 ¶ Then the man came into the house, and ¹he unsaddled the ²camels, and brought litter and provender for the camels, and water to wash his feet, and the men's feet that were with him.

33 Afterward the meat was set before him: but he said, I ¹will not eat, until I have said my message. And he said: Speak on.

34 Then he said, I am Abraham's servant,

35 And the Lord hath ¹blessed my master wonderfully, that he is become great: for he hath given him sheep, and beeves, and silver, and gold, and men servants, and maid servants, and camels, and asses.

36 And Sarah my master's wife hath borne a son to my master, when she was old, and unto him hath he given all that he hath.

37 Now my master made me swear, saying, Thou shalt not take a wife to my son of the daughters of the ¹Canaanites, in whose land I dwell:

38 But thou shalt go unto my ¹father's house and

ᶜ Gen. 24:13

to my kindred, and take a wife unto my son.

39 Then I said unto my master, What if the woman will not follow me?

40 Who answered me, The Lord, before who I walk, will send his Angel with thee, and prosper thy journey, and thou shalt take a wife for my son of my kindred and my father's house.

41 Then shalt thou be discharged of ¹mine oath, when thou comest to my kindred: and if they give thee not one, thou shalt be free from mine oath.

42 So I came this day to the well, and said, O Lord, the God of my master Abraham, if thou now prosper my ¹journey which I go,

43 Behold, ᶜI stand by the well of water when a virgin cometh forth to draw water, and I say to her, Give me, I pray thee, a little water of thy pitcher to drink,

44 And she said to me, Drink thou, and I will also draw for thy camels, let her be the wife, which the Lord hath ¹prepared for thy master's son.

45 And before I had made an end of speaking in mine ¹heart, behold, Rebekah came forth and her pitcher on her shoulder, and she went down to the well, and drew water. Then I said unto her, Give me drink, I pray thee.

46 And she made haste, and took down her pitcher from her *shoulder*, and said, Drink, and I will give thy camels drink also. So I drank, and she gave the camels drink also.

47 Then I asked her, and said, Whose daughter art thou? And she answered, The daughter of Bethuel Nahor's son, whom Milcah bare unto him. Then I put the abillement upon her face, and the bracelets upon her hands:

48 ¹And I bowed down and worshipped the Lord, and blessed the Lord God of my master Abraham, which had brought me the ²right way to take my master's brother's daughter unto his son.

49 Now therefore, if ye will deal ¹mercifully and truly with my master, tell me: and if not, tell me, that I may turn me to the ²right hand or to the left.

50 Then answered Laban and Bethuel, and said, ¹This thing is proceeded of the Lord: we cannot

---

24:27 ¹ He boasteth not his good fortune (as do the wicked) but acknowledgeth that God hath dealt mercifully with his master in keeping promise.

24:30 ¹ For he waited on God's hand, who had now heard his prayer.

24:32 ¹ To wit, Laban.

² The gentle entertainment of strangers used among the godly fathers.

24:33 ¹ The fidelity that servants owe to their masters, causeth them to prefer their master's business to their own necessity.

24:35 ¹ To bless, signifieth here to enrich, or increase with substance, as the text in the same verse declareth.

24:37 ¹ The Canaanites were accursed, and therefore the godly could not join with them in marriage.

24:38 ¹ Meaning among his kinsfolk, as verse 40.

24:41 ¹ Which by mine authority I caused thee to make.

24:42 ¹ Or, way.

24:44 ¹ Or, showed.

24:45 ¹ Signifying that this prayer was not spoken by the mouth, but only meditated in his heart.

24:48 ¹ He showeth what is our duty, when we have received any benefit of the Lord.

² Hebrew, *in the way of truth*.

24:49 ¹ If you will freely and faithfully give your daughter to my master's son.

² That is, that I may provide elsewhere.

24:50 ¹ So soon as they perceive that it is God's ordinance they yield.

therefore say unto thee, *neither* evil nor good.

51 Behold, Rebekah *is* [1]before thee, take *her* and go, that she may be thy master's son's wife, even as the Lord hath [2]said.

52 And when Abraham's servant heard their words, he bowed himself toward the earth unto the Lord.

53 Then the servant took forth jewels of silver, and jewels of gold, and raiment, and gave to Rebekah: also unto her brother and to her mother he gave gifts.

54 Afterward they did eat and drink, *both* he, and the men that were with him, and tarried all night, and when they rose up in the morning, he said, [d]Let me depart unto my master.

55 Then her brother and her mother answered, Let the maid abide with us, at the least [1]ten days: then shall she go.

56 But he said unto them, Hinder you me not, seeing the Lord hath prospered my journey: send me away, that I may go to my master.

57 Then they said, We will call the maid, and ask [1]her consent.

58 And they called Rebekah, and said unto her: Wilt thou go with this man? And [1]she answered, I will go.

59 So they let Rebekah their sister go, and her nurse, with Abraham's servant and his men.

60 And they blessed Rebekah, and said unto her, Thou art our sister, grow into thousand thousand's, and thy seed possess the [1]gate of his enemies.

61 ¶ Then Rebekah arose, and her maids, and rode upon the camels, and followed the man, and the servant took Rebekah and departed.

62 Now Isaac came from the way of [e]Beer Lahai Roi, (for he dwelt in the South country.)

63 And Isaac went out to [1]pray in the field toward the evening: who lift up his eyes and looked, and behold, the camels came.

64 Also Rebekah lift up her eyes, and when she saw Isaac, she lighted down from the camel.

65 (For she had said to the servant, Who is yonder man, that cometh in the field to meet us? and the servant had said, It is my master.) So she took [1]a veil, and covered her.

66 And the servant told Isaac all things, that he had done.

67 Afterward Isaac brought her into the tent, of Sarah his mother, and he took Rebekah, and she was his wife, and he loved her: So Isaac was [1]comforted after his mother's *death*.

25

1 *Abraham taketh Keturah to wife, and getteth many children.* 5 *Abraham giveth all his goods to Isaac.* 8 *He dieth.* 12 *The genealogy of Ishmael.* 25 *The birth of Jacob and Esau.*

1 Now Abraham had taken [1]him another wife called Keturah,

2 Which bare him Zimran, and Jokshan, and Medan, and Midian, and Ishbak, and Shuah.

3 And Jokshan, begat Sheba, and Dedan: [a]And the sons of Dedan were Asshurim, and Letushim, and Leummim.

4 Also the sons of Midian *were* Ephah, and Epher, and Hanoch, and Abidah, and Eldaah, all these were the sons of Keturah.

5 ¶ And Abraham gave [1]all his goods to Isaac.

6 But unto the [1]sons of the [2]concubines, which Abraham had, Abraham [3]gave gifts, and sent them away from Isaac his son (while he yet lived) Eastward to the East country.

7 And this is the age of Abraham's life, which he lived, an hundred seventy and five years.

8 Then Abraham yielded the spirit, and died in a good age, an old man, and of great years, and was [1]gathered to his people.

9 And his sons Isaac and Ishmael buried him in the cave of Machpelah, in the field of Ephron son of Zohar the Hittite, before Mamre,

10 Which [b]field Abraham bought of the Hittites, where Abraham was buried with Sarah his wife.

11 ¶ And after the death of Abraham God blessed Isaac his son, [c]and Isaac dwelt by Beer Lahai Roi.

12 ¶ Now these are the [d]generations of Ishmael Abraham's son, whom Hagar the Egyptian Sarah's handmaid bare unto Abraham.

13 And these are the names of the sons of Ishmael, name by name, according to their kindreds: the [1]eldest son of Ishmael *was* Nebajoth then Kedar,

d Gen. 24:56,59
e Gen. 16:14
  Gen. 25:11

CHAPTER 25
a 1 Chron. 1:32
b Gen. 23:16
c Gen. 16:14
  Gen. 24:62
d 1 Chron. 1:20

24:51 [1] Or, at thy commandment.
   [2] Or, ordained.
24:55 [1] Hebrew, *days*, or *ten*.
24:57 [1] This showeth that parents have not authority to marry their children without consent of the parties.
24:58 [1] Hebrew, *her mouth*.
24:60 [1] That is, let it be victorious over his enemies: which blessing is fully accomplished in Jesus Christ.
24:63 [1] This was the exercise of the godly fathers to meditate God's promises, and to pray for the accomplishment thereof.
24:65 [1] The custom was that the spouse was brought to her husband, her head being covered, in token of shamefastness and chastity.

24:67 [1] Or, had left mourning for his mother.
25:1 [1] While Sarah was yet alive.
25:5 [1] Hebrew, *all that he had*.
25:6 [1] For by the virtue of God's word he had not only Isaac, but begat many more.
   [2] Read Gen. 22:24.
   [3] To avoid the dissention that else might have come because of the heritage.
25:8 [1] Hereby the ancients signified that man by death perished not wholly but as the souls of the godly lived after in perpetual joy, so the souls of the wicked [in] perpetual pain.
25:13 [1] Hebrew, *firstborn*.

and Adbeel, and Mibsam,

14 And Mishma, and Dumah, and Massa,

15 Hadar, and Tema, Jetur, Naphish, and Kedemah.

16 These are the sons of Ishmael, and these *are* their names, by their towns and by their castles: *to wit,* twelve princes of their nations.

17 (And these are the years of the life of Ishmael, an hundred thirty and seven years, and he yielded up the spirit, and died, and was gathered unto his ¹people.)

18 And they dwelt from Havilah unto Shur, that is towards Egypt, as thou goest to Asshur. *Ishmael* ¹dwelt ²in the presence of all his brethren.

19 ¶ Likewise these are the generations of Isaac Abraham's son. Abraham begat Isaac.

20 And Isaac was forty years old, when he took Rebekah to wife, the daughter of Bethuel the ¹Aramite of Padan Aram, *and* sister to Laban the Aramite.

21 And Isaac prayed unto the Lord for his wife, because she was barren: and the Lord was entreated of him, and Rebekah his wife conceived.

22 But the children ¹strove together within her: therefore she said, Seeing *it is* so, why am I ²thus? wherefore she went ³to ask the Lord.

23 And the Lord said to her, Two nations *are* in thy womb, and two manner of people shall be divided out of thy bowels, and the one people shall be mightier than the other, and the ᵉelder shall serve the younger.

24 ¶ Therefore when her time of deliverance was fulfilled, behold, twins *were* in her womb.

25 So he that came out first was red, and he was all over as rough as a garment, and they called his name Esau.

26 ᶠAnd afterward came his brother out, and his hand held Esau by the heel, therefore his name was called Jacob. Now Isaac was threescore years old when *Rebekah* bare them.

27 And the boys grew, and Esau *was* a cunning hunter, and ¹lived in the fields: but Jacob was a ²plain man, and dwelt in tents.

28 And Isaac loved Esau, for ¹venison *was* his

ᵉ Rom. 9:12
ᶠ Hos. 11:3
  Matt. 1:2
ᵍ Heb. 12:16

CHAPTER 26
ᵃ Gen. 13:15
  Gen. 15:18
ᵇ Gen. 12:3
  Gen. 15:18
  Gen. 18:18
  Gen. 22:18
  Gen. 28:14

meat, but Rebekah loved Jacob.

29 Now Jacob sod pottage, and Esau came from the field and was weary.

30 Then Esau said to Jacob, ¹Let me eat, I pray thee, of that *pottage* so red, for I am weary. Therefore was his name called Edom.

31 And Jacob said, Sell me even now thy birth-right.

32 And Esau said, Lo, I am almost dead, what *is* then this ¹birthright to me?

33 Jacob then said, Swear to me even now. And he swear to him, ᵍand ¹sold his birthright unto Jacob.

34 Then Jacob gave Esau bread and pottage of lentils: and he did eat and drink, and rose up, and went his way: So Esau contemned *his* birthright.

26 *1 God provideth for Isaac in the famine. 3 He reneweth his promise. 9 The King blameth him for denying his wife. 14 The Philistines hate him for his riches. 15 Stop his wells. 16 And drive him away. 24 God comforteth him.*

1 And there was a famine in the ¹land besides the first famine that was in the days of Abraham. Wherefore Isaac went to Abimelech King of the Philistines unto Gerar.

2 For the Lord appeared unto him, and said, ¹Go not down into Egypt, *but* abide in the land which I shall show thee.

3 Dwell in this land, and I will be with thee, and will bless thee: for to thee, and to thy seed I will give all these ᵃcountries, and I will perform the oath which I swear unto Abraham thy father.

4 Also I will cause thy seed to multiply as the stars of heaven, and will give unto thy seed all these countries: and in thy seed shall all the nations of the earth be ᵇblessed,

5 Because that Abraham ¹obeyed my voice and kept mine ²ordinance, my commandments, my statutes, and my laws.

6 ¶ So Isaac dwelt in Gerar.

7 And the men of the place asked *him* of his wife, and he said, She is my sister: for he ¹feared to say, she is my wife, lest, *said he,* the men of the place should

---

25:17 ¹ Which dwelt among the Arabians, and were separate from the blessed seed.
25:18 ¹ Or, his lot fell.
  ² He meaneth that his lot fell to dwell among his brethren as the Angel promised, Gen. 16:12.
25:20 ¹ Or, Syrian of Mesopotamia.
25:22 ¹ Or, hurt one another.
  ² That is, with child, seeing one shall destroy another.
  ³ For that is the only refuge in all our miseries.
25:27 ¹ Hebrew, *a man of the field.*
  ² Or, simple and innocent.
25:28 ¹ Hebrew, *venison in his mouth.*
25:30 ¹ Or, feed me quickly.

25:32 ¹ The reprobate esteem not God's benefits except they feel them presently, and therefore they prefer present pleasures.
25:33 ¹ Thus the wicked prefer their worldly commodities to God's spiritual graces: but the children of God do the contrary.
26:1 ¹ In the land of Canaan.
26:2 ¹ God's providence always watcheth to direct the ways of his children.
26:5 ¹ He commendeth Abraham's obedience, because Isaac should be the more ready to follow the like: for as God made this promise of his free mercy, so doth the confirmation thereof proceed of the same fountain.
  ² Hebrew, *my keeping.*
26:7 ¹ Whereby we see that fear and distrust is found in the most faithful.

kill me, because of Rebekah, for she was beautiful to the eye.

8 So after he had been there a long time, Abimelech King of the Philistines looked out at a window, and lo, he saw Isaac [1]sporting with Rebekah his wife.

9 Then Abimelech called Isaac, and said, Lo, she is of a surety thy wife, and why saidest thou, She is my sister? To whom Isaac answered, Because I thought *this*, It may be that I shall die for her.

10 Then Abimelech said, Why hast thou done this unto us? one of the people had almost lain by thy wife, so shouldest thou have brought [1]sin upon us.

11 Then Abimelech charged all his people, saying, He that toucheth this man, or his wife, shall die the death.

12 Afterward Isaac sowed in that land, and found in the same year an [1]hundredfold by estimation: and so the Lord blessed him.

13 And the man waxed mightily, and [1]still increased, till he was exceeding great.

14 For he had flocks of sheep, and herds of cattle, and a mighty household: therefore the Philistines had [1]envy at him,

15 Insomuch that the Philistines stopped, and filled up with earth all the wells, which his father's servants dug in his father Abraham's time.

16 Then Abimelech said unto Isaac, Get thee from us, for thou art mightier than we a great deal.

17 ¶ Therefore Isaac departed thence and pitched his tent in the [1]valley of Gerar, and dwelt there.

18 And Isaac returning, dug the wells of water, which they had dug in the days of Abraham his father, for the Philistines had stopped them after the death of Abraham, and he gave them the same names, that his father gave them.

19 Isaac's servants then dug in the valley and found there a well of [1]living water.

20 But the herdsmen of Gerar did strive with Isaac's herdsmen, saying, The water is ours, therefore called he the name of the well [1]Esek, because they were at strife with him.

21 Afterward they dug another well, and strove

c Gen. 27:46

for that also, and he called the name of it [1]Sitnah.

22 Then he removed thence, and dug another well, for which they strove not: therefore called he the name of it [1]Rehoboth, and said, Because the Lord hath now made us room, we shall increase upon the earth.

23 So he went up thence to Beersheba.

24 And the Lord appeared unto him the same night, and said, I am the God [1]of Abraham thy father: fear not, I am with thee, and will bless thee, and multiply thy seed for my servant Abraham's sake.

25 Then he built an [1]altar there, and called upon the Name of the Lord, and there spread his tent: where also Isaac's servants dug a well.

26 ¶ Then came Abimelech to him from Gerar, and Ahuzzath *one* of his friends, and Phichol the captain of his army.

27 To whom Isaac said, Wherefore come ye to me, seeing ye hate me and have put me away from you?

28 Who answered, We saw certainly that the Lord was with thee, and we thought *thus*, Let there be now an oath between us, *even* between us and thee, and let us make a covenant with thee.

29 [1]If thou shalt do us no hurt, as we have not touched thee, and as we have done unto thee nothing but good, and sent thee away in peace: thou now, the blessed of the Lord, *do this*.

30 Then he made them a feast, and they did eat and drink.

31 And they rose up betimes in the morning, and swear one to another: then Isaac let them go, and they departed from him in peace.

32 And that same day Isaac's servants came and told him of a well, which they had dug, and said unto him, We have found water.

33 So he called it [1]Shebah: therefore the name of the city is called [2]Beersheba unto this day.

34 ¶ Now when Esau was forty years old, he took to wife Judith, the daughter of Beeri an Hittite, and Basemath the daughter of Elon an Hittite *also*.

35 And they ʿwere [1]a grief of mind to Isaac and to Rebekah.

26:8 [1] Or showing some familiar sign of love, whereby it might be known that she was his wife.
26:10 [1] In all ages men were persuaded that God's vengeance should light upon wedlock breakers.
26:12 [1] Or, an hundred measures.
26:13 [1] Hebrew, *he went forth going and increasing.*
26:14 [1] The malicious envy always the graces of God in others.
26:17 [1] The Hebrew word signifieth a flood, or valley, where water at any time runneth.
26:19 [1] Or, springing.
26:20 [1] Or, contention, strife.
26:21 [1] Or, hatred.

26:22 [1] Or, largeness, room.
26:24 [1] God assureth Isaac against all fear by rehearsing the promise made to Abraham.
26:25 [1] To signify that he would serve none other God, but the God of his father Abraham.
26:29 [1] The Hebrews in swearing begin commonly with If, and understand the rest, that is, that God shall punish him that breaketh the oath: here the wicked show that they are afraid lest that come to them which they would do to others.
26:33 [1] Or, oath.
   [2] Or, the well of the oath.
26:35 [1] Or, disobedient and rebellious.

CHAPTER 27
a Heb. 11:20

27 *8 Jacob getteth the blessing from Esau by his mother's counsel.   38 Esau by weeping moveth his father to pity him.   41 Esau hateth Jacob and threateneth his death.   43 Rebekah sendeth Jacob away.*

1   And when Isaac was old, and his eyes were dim (so that he could not see) he called Esau his eldest son, and said unto him, My son. And he answered him, [1]I am here.

2   Then he said, Behold, I am now old, and know not the day of my death.

3   Wherefore now, I pray thee take thine instruments, thy quiver and thy bow, and get thee to the field, that thou mayest [1]take me some venison.

4   Then make me savory meat, such as I love, and bring it me that I may eat, *and* that my [1]soul may bless thee, before I die.

5   (Now Rebekah heard, when Isaac spake to Esau his son) and Esau went into the field to hunt for venison, and to bring it.

6   ¶ Then Rebekah spake unto Jacob her son, saying, Behold, I have heard thy father talking with Esau thy brother, saying,

7   Bring me venison, and make me savory meat, that I may eat and bless thee before the Lord, afore my death.

8   Now therefore, my son, hear my voice in that which I command thee.

9   [1]Get thee now to the flock, and bring me thence two good kids of the goats, that I may make pleasant meat of them for thy father, such as he loveth.

10   Then thou shalt bring it to thy father, and he shall eat, to the intent that he may bless thee before his death.

11   But Jacob said to Rebekah his mother, Behold, Esau my brother *is* rough, and I am smooth.

12   My father may possibly feel me, and I shall seem [1]to him as a [2]mocker: so shall I bring a curse upon me, and not a blessing.

13   But his mother said unto him, [1,2]Upon me *be* thy curse, my son: only hear my voice, and go and bring me *them*.

14   So he went and set *them*, and brought *them* to his mother: and his mother made pleasant meat, such as his father loved.

15   And Rebekah took fair clothes of her elder son Esau, which were in her house, and clothed Jacob her younger son:

16   And she covered his hands and the smooth of his neck with the skins of the kids of the goats.

17   Afterward she put the pleasant meat and bread, which she had prepared, in the hand of her son Jacob.

18   ¶ And when he came to his father, he said, My father. Who answered, I am here: who art thou, my son?

19   And Jacob said to his father, [1]I am Esau thy firstborn, I have done as thou badest me, arise, I pray thee: sit up and eat of my venison, that thy soul may bless me.

20   Then Isaac said unto his son, How hast thou found it so quickly my son? Who said, Because the Lord thy God brought it to mine hand.

21   Again said Isaac unto Jacob, Come near now, that I may feel thee, my son, whether thou be that my son Esau, or not.

22   Then Jacob came near to Isaac his father, and he felt him and said, The [1]voice *is* Jacob's voice, but the hands *are* the hands of Esau.

23   (For he knew him not, because his hands were rough as his brother Esau's hands: wherefore he blessed him.)

24   Again he said, Art thou that my son Esau? Who answered, [1]Yea.

25   Then said he, Bring it me hither, and I will eat of my son's venison, that my soul may bless thee. And he brought it to him, and he ate: also he brought him wine, and he drank.

26   Afterward his father Isaac said unto him, Come near now, and kiss me, my son.

27   And he came near and kissed him. Then he smelled the savor of his garments, and blessed him, and said, Behold, the smell of my son *is* as the smell of a field, which the Lord hath blessed.

28   [a]God give thee therefore of the dew of heaven, and the fatness of the earth, and plenty of wheat and wine.

29   Let people be thy servants, and nations bow down unto thee: be Lord over thy brethren, and let thy mother's children honor thee, cursed *be he* that curseth thee, and blessed *be he* that blesseth thee.

30   ¶ And when Isaac had made an end of blessing Jacob, and Jacob was scarce gone out from the presence of Isaac his father, then came Esau his brother from his hunting,

---

27:1 [1] Hebrew, *Lo, I.*
27:3 [1] Hebrew, *hunt.*
27:4 [1] The carnal affection, which he bare to his son made him forget that which God spake to his wife, Gen. 25:23.
27:9 [1] This subtlety is blameworthy because she should have tarried till God had performed his promise.
27:12 [1] Hebrew, *before his eyes.*
    [2] Or, as though I would deceive him.
27:13 [1] Or, I will take the danger on me.
    [2] The assurance of God's decree made her bold.
27:19 [1] Although Jacob was assured of this blessing by faith: yet he did evil to seek it by lies, and the more because he abuseth God's name thereunto.
27:22 [1] This declareth that he suspected something, yet God would not have his decree altered.
27:24 [1] Hebrew, *I am.*

31 And he also prepared savory meat, and brought it to his father, and said unto his father, Let my father arise, and eat of his son's venison, that thy soul may bless me.

32 But his father Isaac said unto him, Who art thou? And he answered, I am thy son, *even* thy firstborn Esau.

33 Then Isaac was ¹stricken with a marvelous great fear, and said, Who *and* where *is* he that hunted venison, and brought it me, and I have eaten ²of all before thou camest? and I have blessed him, therefore he shall be blessed.

34 When Esau heard the words of his father, he cried out with a great cry and bitter, out of measure, and said unto his father, Bless me, *even* me also, my father.

35 Who answered, Thy brother came with subtlety, and hath taken away thy blessing.

36 Then he said, Was he not justly called ¹Jacob? for he hath deceived me these two times: he took my birthright, and lo, now hath he taken my blessing. Also he said, Hast thou not reserved a blessing for me?

37 Then Isaac answered, and said unto Esau, Behold, I have made him ¹thy lord, and all his brethren have I made his servants: and with wheat and wine have I furnished him, and unto thee now what shall I do, my son?

38 Then Esau said unto his father, Hast thou but one blessing, my father? bless me, ¹*even* me, also my father: and Esau lifted up his voice, and *b*wept.

39 Then Isaac his father answered, and said unto him, Behold, the fatness of the earth shall be thy dwelling place, and *thou shalt have* of the dew of heaven from above.

40 And ¹by thy word shalt thou live, and shalt be thy brother's ²servant. But it shall come to pass, when thou shalt get the mastery, that thou shalt break his yoke from thy neck.

41 ¶ Therefore Esau hated Jacob, because of the blessing, wherewith his father blessed him. And Esau thought in his mind, 'The days of mourning for my father will come shortly, ¹then I will slay my brother Jacob.

42 And it was told to Rebekah of the words of Esau her elder son, and she sent and called Jacob her younger son, and said unto him, Behold, thy brother Esau ¹is comforted against thee, *meaning* to kill thee:

43 Now therefore my son, hear my voice: arise, and flee thou to Haran to my brother Laban,

44 And tarry with him a while until thy brother's fierceness be swaged,

45 And till thy brother's wrath turn away from thee, and he forget the things, which thou hast done to him: then will I send and take thee from thence: why should I be ¹deprived of you both in one day?

46 Also Rebekah said to Isaac, *d*I am weary of my life, for the daughters of Heth. If Jacob take a wife of the ¹daughters of Heth like these of the daughters of the land, ²what availeth it me to live?

28

1 Isaac forbiddeth Jacob to take a wife of the Canaanites. 6 Esau taketh a wife of the daughters of Ishmael against his father's will. 12 Jacob in the way to Haran seeth a ladder reaching to heaven. 14 Christ is promised.

1 Then Isaac called Jacob and ¹blessed him, and charged him, and said unto him, take not a wife of the daughters of Canaan.

2 Arise, *a*get thee to *b*Padan Aram to the house of Bethuel thy mother's father, and thence take thee a wife of the daughters of Laban thy mother's brother.

3 And God all ¹sufficient bless thee, and make thee to increase, and multiply thee, that thou mayest be a multitude of people,

4 And give thee the blessing of Abraham, *even* to thee and to thy seed with thee, that thou mayest inherit the land (wherein thou art a ¹stranger,) which God gave unto Abraham.

5 Thus Isaac sent forth Jacob, and he went to Padan Aram unto Laban son of Bethuel the Aramite, brother to Rebekah, Jacob's and Esau's mother.

6 ¶ When Esau saw that Isaac had blessed Jacob, and sent him to Padan Aram, to fetch him a wife thence, and given him a charge when he blessed him, saying, Thou shalt not take a wife of the daughters of Canaan,

7 And *that* Jacob had obeyed his father and his mother, and was gone to Padan Aram:

b Heb. 11:17
c Obad. 10
d Gen. 26:35

CHAPTER 28
a Hos. 12:12
b Gen. 24:10

27:33 ¹ In perceiving his error, by appointing his heir against God's sentence pronounced before.

² Or, sufficiently.

27:36 ¹ In Gen. 25, he was so called because he held his brother by the heel, as though he would overthrow him: and therefore he is here called an overthrower, or deceiver.

27:37 ¹ For Isaac did this as he was the minister and Prophet of God.

27:38 ¹ Or, I am also (thy son).

27:40 ¹ Because thine enemies shall be round about thee.

² Which was fulfilled in his posterity the Idumeans: who were tributaries for a time to Israel, and after came to liberty.

27:41 ¹ Hypocrites only abstain from doing evil for fear of men.

27:42 ¹ He hath good hope to recover his birthright by killing thee.

27:45 ¹ For the wicked son will kill the godly: and the plague of God will afterward light on the wicked son.

27:46 ¹ Which were Esau's wives.

² Hereby she persuaded Isaac to agree to Jacob's departing.

28:1 ¹ This second blessing was to confirm Jacob's faith, lest he should think that his father had given it without God's motion.

28:3 ¹ Or, almighty.

28:4 ¹ The godly fathers were put in mind continually, that they were but strangers in this world: to the intent they should lift up their eyes to the heavens where they should have a sure dwelling.

8   Also Esau seeing that the daughters of Canaan displeased Isaac his father,

9   Then went Esau to Ishmael, and took ¹unto the wives *which he had*, Mahalath the daughter of ²Ishmael Abraham's son, the sister of Nebajoth, to be his wife.

10   ¶ Now Jacob departed from Beersheba, and went to Haran,

11   And he came unto a *certain* place, and tarried there all night because the sun was down, and took of the stones of the place, and laid under his head and slept in the same place.

12   Then he dreamed, and behold, there stood a ¹ladder upon the earth, and the top of it reached up to heaven: and lo, the Angels of God went up and down by it.

13   ꞌAnd behold, the Lord stood above it, and said, I am the Lord God of Abraham thy father, and the God of Isaac: the land, upon the which thou sleepest, ¹will I give thee and thy seed.

14   And thy seed shall be as the dust of the earth, and thou shalt spread abroad ᵈto the West, and to the East, and to the North, and to the South, and in thee and in thy seed shall all the ᵉfamilies of the earth be blessed.

15   And lo, I am with thee, and will keep thee whithersoever thou goest, and will bring thee again into this land: for I will not forsake thee until I have performed that, that I have promised thee.

16   ¶ Then Jacob awoke out of his sleep and said, Surely the Lord is in this place, and I was not aware.

17   And he was ¹afraid, and said, How fearful is this place! this is none other but the house of God, and this is the gate of heaven.

18   Then Jacob rose up early in the morning, and took the stone that he had laid under his head, and ¹set it up *as* ᶠa pillar, and poured oil upon the top of it.

19   And he called the name of that place ¹Bethel: notwithstanding the name of that city was at the first called Luz.

20   Then Jacob vowed a vow, saying, If ¹God will be with me, and will keep me in this journey which I go, and will give me bread to eat, and clothes to put on:

21   So that I come again unto my father's house in safety, then shall the Lord be my God.

22   And this stone, which I have set up *as* a pillar, shall be God's house: and of all that thou shalt give me, I will give the tenth unto thee.

29   *13 Jacob cometh to Laban and serveth seven years for Rachel.   23 Leah brought to his bed instead of Rachel.   27 He serveth seven years more for Rachel.   31 Leah conceiveth and beareth four sons.*

1   Then Jacob ¹lift up his feet and came into the ²East country.

2   And as he looked about, behold, there was a well in the field, ¹and lo, three flocks of sheep lay thereby (for at that well were the flocks watered) and there was a great stone upon the well's mouth.

3   And thither were all the flocks gathered, and they rolled the stone from the well's mouth, and watered the sheep, and put the stone again upon the well's mouth in his place.

4   And Jacob said unto them, My ¹brethren, whence be ye? And they answered, We are of Haran.

5   Then he said unto them, Know ye Laban the son of Nahor? Who said, We know him.

6   Again he said unto them, ¹Is he in good health? And they answered, He *is* in good health, and behold, his daughter Rachel cometh with the sheep.

7   Then he said, Lo, *it is* yet high day, neither *is it* time that the cattle should be gathered together: water ye the sheep and go feed *them*.

8   But they said, We may not, until all the flocks be brought together, and *till men* roll the stone from the well's mouth, that we may water the sheep.

9   ¶ While he talked with them, Rachel also came with her father's sheep, for she kept them.

10   And as soon as Jacob saw Rachel the daughter of Laban his mother's brother, and the sheep of Laban his mother's brother, then came Jacob near, and rolled the stone from the well's mouth, and watered the flock of Laban his mother's brother.

11   And Jacob kissed Rachel, and lifted up his voice and wept.

12   (For Jacob told Rachel, that he was her father's ¹brother, and that he was Rebekah's son) then she

Cross references (center column):
ꞌ Gen. 35:1
Gen. 48:3
ᵈ Deut. 12:20
Deut. 19:14
ᵉ Gen. 12:8
Gen. 18:18
Gen. 22:18
Gen. 26:4
ᶠ Gen. 31:13

28:9 ¹ Or, beside his wives.
   ² Thinking hereby to have reconciled himself to his father, but all in vain: for he taketh not away the cause of the evil.
28:12 ¹ Christ is the ladder whereby God and man are joined together, and by whom the Angels minister unto us: all graces by him are given unto us, and we by him ascend into heaven.
28:13 ¹ He felt the force of this promise only by faith: for all his lifetime he was but a stranger in this land.
28:17 ¹ He was touched with a godly fear and reverence.
28:18 ¹ To be a remembrance only of the vision showed unto him.
28:19 ¹ Or, house of God.
28:20 ¹ He bindeth not God under this condition, but acknowledgeth his infirmity, and promiseth to be thankful.
29:1 ¹ That is, went forth on his journey.
   ² Hebrew, *to the land of the children of the East.*
29:2 ¹ Thus he was directed by the only providence of God, who brought him also to Laban's house.
29:4 ¹ It seemeth that in those days the custom was to call even strangers, brethren.
29:6 ¹ Or, he is in peace? by which word the Hebrews signify all prosperity.
29:12 ¹ Or, nephew.

ran and told her father.

13 And when Laban heard tell of Jacob his sister's son, he ran to meet him, and embraced him and kissed him, and brought him to his house: and he told Laban ¹all these things.

14 To whom Laban said, Well, thou art my ¹bone and my flesh, and he abode with him the space of a month.

15 ¶ For Laban said unto Jacob, Though thou be my brother, shouldest thou therefore serve me for nought? tell me, what *shall be* thy wages?

16 Now Laban had two daughters, the elder called Leah, and the younger called Rachel.

17 And Leah was ¹tender eyed, but Rachel was beautiful and fair.

18 And Jacob loved Rachel, and said, I will serve thee seven years for Rachel thy younger daughter.

19 Then Laban answered, It is better that I give her thee, than that I should give her to another man: abide with me.

20 And Jacob served seven years for Rachel, and they seemed unto him but a ¹few days, because he loved her.

21 ¶ Then Jacob said to Laban, Give *me* my wife, that I may go in to her: for my ¹term is ended.

22 Wherefore Laban gathered together all the men of the place, and made a feast.

23 But ¹when the evening was come, he took Leah his daughter, and brought her to him, and he went in unto her.

24 And Laban gave his maid Zilpah to his daughter Leah, *to be* her servant.

25 But when the morning was come, behold, it was Leah. Then said he to Laban, Wherefore hast thou done thus to me? did not I serve thee for Rachel? wherefore then hast thou beguiled me?

26 And Laban answered, It is not the ¹manner of this place, to give the younger before the elder.

27 Fulfill seven years for her, and we will also give thee this for the service, which thou shalt serve me yet seven years more.

28 Then Jacob did so, and fulfilled her seven years, so he gave him Rachel his daughter *to be* his wife.

29 Laban also gave to Rachel his daughter, Bilhah

CHAPTER 29
ª Matt. 1:2

his maid *to be* her servant.

30 So entered he in to Rachel also, and loved also Rachel more than Leah, and served him yet seven years more.

31 ¶ When the Lord saw that Leah was despised, he ¹made her ²fruitful: but Rachel *was* barren.

32 And Leah conceived and bare a son, and she called his name Reuben: for she said, Because the ¹Lord hath looked upon my tribulation, now therefore mine husband will ²love me.

33 And she conceived again and bare a son, and said, Because the Lord heard that I was hated, he hath therefore given me this *son* also, and she called his name Simeon.

34 And she conceived again and bare a son, and said, Now at this time will my husband keep me company, because I have borne him three sons: therefore was his name called Levi.

35 Moreover she conceived again and bare a son, saying, Now will I ¹praise the Lord: ªtherefore she called his name Judah, and ²left bearing.

30 *4,9 Rachel and Leah being both barren, give their maids unto their husband, and they bare him children.   15 Leah giveth mandrakes to Rachel that Jacob might lie with her.   27 Laban is enriched for Jacob's sake.   34 Jacob is made very rich.*

1 And when Rachel saw that she bare Jacob no children, Rachel envied her sister, and said unto Jacob, Give me children, or else I die.

2 Then Jacob's anger was kindled against Rachel, and he said, Am I in ¹God's stead, which hath withholden from thee the fruit of the womb?

3 And she said, Behold my maid Bilhah, go in to her, and she shall bear upon my ¹knees, and ²I shall have children also by her.

4 Then she gave him Bilhah her maid to wife, and Jacob went in to her.

5 So Bilhah conceived and bare Jacob a son.

6 Then said Rachel, God hath given sentence on my side, and hath also heard my voice, and hath given me a son: therefore called she his name, Dan.

7 And Bilhah Rachel's maid conceived again, and bare Jacob the second son.

29:13 ¹ That is, the cause why he departed from his father's house, and what he saw in the way.
29:14 ¹ That is, of my blood and kindred.
29:17 ¹ Or, blear-eyed.
29:20 ¹ Meaning, after that the years were accomplished.
29:21 ¹ Hebrew, *my days are full.*
29:23 ¹ The cause why Jacob was deceived was, that in old time the wife was covered with a veil, when she was brought to her husband in sign of chastity and shamefastness.
29:26 ¹ He esteemed more the profit that he had of Jacob's service, than either his promise of the manner of the country, though he alleged custom for his excuse.

29:31 ¹ Hebrew, *opened her womb.*
      ² This declareth that oft times they which are despised of men, are favored of God.
29:32 ¹ Hereby appeareth, that she had recourse to God in her affliction.
      ² For children are a great cause of mutual love between man and wife.
29:35 ¹ Or, confess.
      ² Hebrew, *stood from bearing.*
30:2 ¹ It is only God that maketh barren and fruitful, and therefore I am not in fault.
30:3 ¹ I will receive her children on my lap, as though they were mine own.
      ² Hebrew, *I shall be built.*

8 Then Rachel said, With [1]excellent wrestlings have I [2]wrestled with my sister, and have gotten the upper hand: and she called his name, Naphtali.

9 And when Leah saw that she had left bearing, she took Zilpah her maid, and gave her Jacob to wife.

10 And Zilpah Leah's maid bare Jacob a son.

11 Then said Leah, [1]A company cometh: and she called his name, Gad.

12 Again Zilpah Leah's maid bare Jacob another son.

13 Then said Leah, Ah, blessed am I, for the daughters will bless me, and she called his name Asher.

14 ¶ Now Reuben went in the days of the wheat harvest, and found [1]mandrakes in the field, and brought them unto his mother Leah. Then said Rachel to Leah, Give me, I pray thee, of thy son's mandrakes.

15 But she answered her, Is it a small matter for thee to take mine husband, except thou take my son's mandrakes also? Then said Rachel, Therefore he shall sleep with thee this night for thy son's mandrakes.

16 And Jacob came from the field in the evening, and Leah went out to meet him, and said, Come in to me, for I have [1]bought and paid for thee with my son's mandrakes: and he slept with her that night.

17 And God heard Leah and she conceived, and bare unto Jacob the fifth son.

18 Then said Leah, God hath given *me* my reward, because I gave my [1]maid to my husband, and she called his name Issachar.

19 After, Leah conceived again, and bare Jacob the sixth son.

20 Then Leah said, God hath endowed me with a good dowry: now will mine husband dwell with me, because I have borne him six sons: and she called his name Zebulun.

21 After that, she bare a daughter, and she called her name Dinah.

22 ¶ And God remembered Rachel, and God heard her, [1]and opened her womb.

23 So she conceived and bare a son, and said, God hath taken away my [1]rebuke.

24 And she called his name Joseph, saying, The Lord will give me yet another son.

25 ¶ And as soon as Rachel had borne Joseph, Jacob said to Laban, Send me away that I may go unto my place and to my country.

26 Give *me* my wives and my children, for whom I have served thee, and let me go: for thou knowest what service I have done thee.

27 To whom Laban answered, If I have now found favor in thy sight, *tarry*: I have [1]perceived that the Lord hath blessed me for thy sake.

28 Also he said, Appoint unto me thy wages, and I will give it *thee*.

29 But he said unto him, Thou knowest, what service I have done thee, and in what taking thy cattle hath been [1]under me.

30 For the little, that thou haddest before I came, is increased into a multitude: and the Lord hath blessed thee [1]by my coming: but now when shall [2]I travail for mine own house also?

31 Then he said, What shall I give thee? And Jacob answered, Thou shalt give me nothing at all: if thou wilt do this thing for me, I will return, feed, *and* keep thy sheep.

32 I will pass through all thy flocks this day, *and* [1]separate from them all the sheep with little spots and great spots, and all [2]black lambs among the sheep, and the great spotted, and little spotted among the goats: [3]and it shall be my wages.

33 So shall my [1]righteousness answer for me hereafter, when it shall come for my reward before thy face, *and* everyone that hath not little or great spots among the goats, and black among the sheep, the same shall be [2]theft with me.

34 Then Laban said, Go to, would God it might be according to thy saying.

35 Therefore [1]he took out the same day the he goats that were parti-colored and with great spots, and all the she goats with little and great spots, *and* all that had white in them, and all the [2]black among the sheep, and put them in the keeping of his sons.

36 And he set three days journey between himself

30:8 [1] Hebrew, *wrestlings of God*.
   [2] The arrogancy of man's nature appeareth in that she contemneth her sister, after she hath received this benefit of God to bear children.
30:11 [1] That is, God doth increase me with a multitude of children: for so Jacob doth expound this name Gad, Gen. 49:19.
30:14 [1] Which is a kind of herb whose root hath a certain likeness of the figure of a man.
30:16 [1] Hebrew, *buying I have bought*.
30:18 [1] Instead of acknowledging her fault, she boasteth as if God had rewarded her therefore.
30:22 [1] Or, made her fruitful.
30:23 [1] Because fruitfulness came of God's blessing, who said Increase and multiply: barrenness was counted as a curse.

30:27 [1] Or, tried by experience.
30:29 [1] Or, with me.
30:30 [1] Hebrew, *at my feet*.
   [2] The order of nature requireth that everyone provide for his own family.
30:32 [1] Or, separate thou.
   [2] Or, rid.
   [3] That which shall hereafter be thus spotted.
30:33 [1] God shall testify for my righteous dealing by rewarding my labors.
   [2] Or, counted theft.
30:35 [1] Or, Laban.
   [2] Or, red or brown.

and Jacob. And Jacob kept the rest of Laban's sheep.

37 ¶ Then Jacob [1]took rods of green poplar, and of hazel, and of the chestnut tree, and pilled white strakes in them, and made the white appear in the rods.

38 Then he put the rods, which he had pilled, in the gutters *and* watering troughs, when the sheep came to drink, before the sheep: (for they were in heat, when they came to drink.)

39 And the sheep [1]were in heat before the rods, and *afterward* brought forth young of parti-color, and with small and great spots.

40 And Jacob parted these lambs, and turned the faces of the flock towards *those lambs* parti-colored, and all manner of black, among the sheep of Laban: so he put his own flock by themselves, and put them not with Laban's flock.

41 And in every ramming time of the [1]stronger sheep, Jacob laid the rods before the eyes of the sheep in the gutters, that they might conceive before the rods.

42 But when the sheep were feeble, he put them not in: and so the feebler were Laban's, and the stronger Jacob's.

43 So the man increased exceedingly, and had many flocks, and maid servants, and men servants, and camels, and asses.

31

1 Laban's children murmur against Jacob. 3 God commandeth him to return to his country. 13, 14 The care of God for Jacob. 19 Rachel stealeth her father's idols. 23 Laban followeth Jacob. 44 The covenant between Laban and Jacob.

1 Now he heard the [1]words of Laban's sons, saying, Jacob hath taken away all that was our father's, and of our father's goods hath he gotten all this honor.

2 Also Jacob beheld the countenance of Laban, [1]that it was not towards him as in times past:

3 And the Lord had said unto Jacob, Turn again into the land of thy fathers, and to thy kindred, and I will be with thee.

4 Therefore Jacob sent and called Rachel and Leah to the field unto his flock.

5 Then said he unto them, I see your father's countenance, that it is not towards me [1]as it was wont, and the [2]God of my father hath been with me.

CHAPTER 31
ᵃ Gen. 28:18

6 And ye know that I have served your father with all my might,

7 But your father hath deceived me, and changed my wages [1]ten times: but God suffered him not to hurt me.

8 If he thus said, The spotted shall be thy wages, then all the sheep bare spotted: and if he said thus, The parti-colored shall be thy reward, then bare all the sheep parti-colored.

9 Thus hath [1]God taken away your father's [2]substance, and given it me.

10 ¶ For in ramming time I lifted up mine eyes and saw in a dream, and behold, the he goats leaped upon the she goats, that were parti-colored with little and great spots spotted.

11 And the Angel of God said to me in a dream, Jacob. And I answered, Lo, I am here.

12 And he said, Lift up now thine eyes, and see all the he goats leaping upon the she goats that are parti-colored, spotted with little and great spots: for I have seen all that Laban doeth unto thee.

13 [1]I am the God of Bethel, where thou ᵃanointedst the pillar, where thou vowedst a vow unto me. Now arise, get thee out of this country and return unto the land where thou wast born.

14 Then answered Rachel and Leah, and said unto him, Have we any more portion and inheritance in our father's house?

15 Doth not he count us as strangers? for he hath [1]sold us, and hath eaten up and consumed our money.

16 Therefore all the riches, which God hath taken from our father, is ours and our children's: now then whatsoever God hath said unto thee, do it.

17 ¶ Then Jacob rose up, and set his sons and his wives upon camels.

18 And he carried away all his flocks, and all his substance which he had gotten, *to wit*, his riches, which he had gotten in Padan Aram, to go to Isaac his father unto the land of Canaan.

19 When Laban was gone to sheer his sheep, then Rachel stole her father's [1]idols.

20 Thus Jacob [1]stole away the heart of Laban the Aramite: for he told him not that he fled.

30:37 [1] Jacob herein used no deceit: for it was God's commandment as he declareth in Gen. 31:9, 11.
30:39 [1] Or, received.
30:41 [1] As they which took the ram about September and brought forth about March: so the feebler in March, and lamb in September.
31:1 [1] The children uttered in words that which the father dissembled in heart, for the covetous think that whatsoever they cannot snatch, is plucked from them.
31:2 [1] Hebrew, *and lo, not be with him, as yesterday, and ere yesterday.*
31:5 [1] Hebrew, *as yesterday and before yesterday.*
   [2] The God whom my father worshipped.

31:7 [1] Or, many times.
31:9 [1] This declareth that the thing, which Jacob did before, was by God's commandment, and not through deceit.
   [2] Or, cattle.
31:13 [1] This Angel was Christ which appeared to Jacob in Bethel: and hereby appeareth he had taught his wives the fear of God: for he talketh as though they knew this thing.
31:15 [1] For they were given to Jacob in recompence of his service, which was a kind of sale.
31:19 [1] For so the word here signifieth, because Laban calleth them gods, verse 30.
31:20 [1] Or, went away privily from Laban.

21 So fled he with all that he had, and he rose up, and passed the ¹river, and set his face toward mount Gilead.

22 And the third day after was it told Laban, that Jacob fled.

23 Then he took his ¹brethren with him and followed after him seven days journey, and ²overtook him at mount Gilead.

24 And God came to Laban the Aramite in a dream by night, and said unto him, Take heed that thou speak not to Jacob ¹ought save good.

25 ¶ Then Laban overtook Jacob, and Jacob had pitched his tent in the mount: and Laban *also* with his brethren pitched upon mount Gilead.

26 Then Laban said to Jacob, What hast thou done? ¹thou hast even stolen away mine heart and carried away my daughters as though they had been taken captives with the sword.

27 Wherefore diddest thou flee so secretly and steal away from me, and diddest not tell me, that I might have sent thee forth with mirth and with songs, with timbrell and with harp?

28 But thou hast not suffered me to kiss my sons and my daughters: now thou hast done foolishly in doing *so*.

29 I am ¹able to do you evil: but the ²God of your father spake unto me yesternight, saying, Take heed that thou speak not to Jacob ought save good.

30 Now though thou wentest thy way, because thou greatly longedst after thy father's house, *yet* wherefore hast thou stolen my gods?

31 Then Jacob answered, and said to Laban, Because I was afraid, and thought that thou wouldest have taken thy daughters from me.

32 *But* with whom thou findest thy gods, ¹let him not live. Search thou before our brethren what I have *of thine*, and take it to thee, (but Jacob wist not that Rachel had stolen them.)

33 Then came Laban into Jacob's tent, and into Leah's tent, and into the two maid's tents, but found *them* not. So he went out of Leah's tent, and entered into Rachel's tent.

34 (Now Rachel had taken the idols, and put them in the camel's ¹litter and sat down upon them) and Laban searched all the tent, but found *them* not.

35 Then said she to her father, ¹My Lord, be

ᵇ Exod. 22:12

not angry that I cannot rise up before thee: for the custom of women *is* upon me: so he searched, but found not the idols.

36 ¶ Then Jacob was wroth, and chode with Laban: Jacob also answered and said to Laban, What have I trespassed? what have I offended, that thou hast pursued after me?

37 Seeing thou hast searched all my stuff, what hast thou found of all thine household stuff? put it here before my brethren and thy brethren, that they may judge between us both.

38 This twenty years I have been with thee: thine ewes and thy goats have not ¹cast their young, and the rams of thy flock have I not eaten.

39 ¹Whatsoever was torn *of beasts*, I brought it not unto thee, *but* made it good myself: ᵇof mine hand diddest thou require it, *were it* stolen by day, or stolen by night.

40 I was in the day consumed with heat, and with frost in the night, and my ¹sleep departed from mine eyes.

41 Thus have I been twenty years in thine house, and served thee fourteen years for thy two daughters, and six years for thy sheep, and thou hast changed my wages ten times.

42 Except the God of my father, the God of Abraham, and the ¹fear of Isaac had been with me, surely thou haddest sent me away now empty: *but* God beheld my tribulation, and the labor of mine hands, and rebuked *thee* yesternight.

43 Then Laban answered, and said unto Jacob, These daughters are my daughters, and these sons are my sons, and these sheep are my sheep, and all that thou seest, is mine, and what can I do this day unto these my daughters, or to their sons which they have borne?

44 Now therefore ¹come let us make a covenant, I and thou, which may be a witness between me and thee.

45 Then took Jacob a stone, and set it up *as* a pillar:

46 And Jacob said unto his brethren, Gather stones: who brought stones, and made a heap, and they did eat there upon the heap.

47 And Laban called it ¹Jegar Sahadutha, and Jacob called it ²Galeed.

31:21 ¹ Or, Euphrates.
31:23 ¹ Or, kinsfolks and friends.
   ² Or, joined with him.
31:24 ¹ Hebrew, *from good to evil.*
31:26 ¹ Or, conveyed thyself away privily.
31:29 ¹ Hebrew, *power is in mine hand.*
   ² He was an Idolater, and therefore would not acknowledge the God of Jacob for his God.
31:32 ¹ Or, let him die.
31:34 ¹ Or, straw, or saddle.

31:35 ¹ Hebrew, *let not anger be in the eyes of my Lord.*
31:38 ¹ Or, been barren.
31:39 ¹ Hebrew, *the torn,* or *taken by prey.*
31:40 ¹ Or, I slept not.
31:42 ¹ That is, the God whom Isaac did fear, and reverence.
31:44 ¹ His conscience reproved him of his misbehavior toward Jacob, and therefore moved him to seek peace.
31:47 ¹ Or, the heap of witness.
   ² The one named the place in the Syrian tongue, and the other in the Hebrew tongue.

48 For Laban said, This heap is witness between me and thee this day: therefore he called the name of it Galeed.

49 Also *he called it* ¹Mizpah, because he said, The Lord ²look between me and he, when we shall be ³departed one from another.

50 If thou shalt vex my daughters, or shalt take ¹wives beside my daughters: *there is* no man with us, behold, God *is* witness between me and thee.

51 Moreover Laban said to Jacob, Behold this heap, and behold the pillar, which I have set between me and thee.

52 This heap *shall be* witness, and the pillar *shall be* witness, that I will not come over this heap to thee, and that thou shalt not pass over this heap and this pillar unto me for evil.

53 The God of Abraham, and the God of ¹Nahor, *and* the God of their father be judge between us: but Jacob sware by the ²fear of his father Isaac.

54 Then Jacob did offer a sacrifice upon the mount, and called his brethren to eat ¹bread, and they did eat bread, and tarried all night in the mount.

55 And early in the morning Laban rose up and kissed his sons, and his daughters, and ¹blessed them, and Laban departing, went unto his place again.

32

1 God comforteth Jacob by his Angels.   9, 10 He prayeth unto God confessing his unworthiness.   13 He sendeth presents unto Esau.   24, 28 He wrestled with the Angel who nameth him Israel.

1 Now Jacob went forth on his journey, and ᵃthe Angels of God met him.

2 And when Jacob saw them, he said, ¹This is God's host: and he called the name of the same place ²Mahanaim.

3 Then Jacob sent messengers before him to Esau his brother, unto the land of Seir into the country of Edom.

4 To whom he gave commandment, saying, Thus shall ye speak to my ¹lord Esau: thy servant Jacob saith thus, I have been a stranger with Laban, and tarried unto this time.

5 I have beeves also and asses, sheep, and men servants, and women servants, and have sent to show

CHAPTER 32
ᵃ Gen. 48:16
ᵇ Gen. 31:13

my lord, that I may find grace in thy sight.

6 ¶ So the messengers came again to Jacob, saying, We came unto thy brother Esau, and he also cometh against thee and four hundred men with him.

7 Then Jacob was ¹greatly afraid, and was sore troubled, and divided the people that was with him, and the sheep, and the beeves, and the camels into two companies.

8 For he said, If Esau come to the one company and smite it, the other company shall escape.

9 ¶ Moreover Jacob said, O God of my father Abraham, and God of my father Isaac, Lord, which ᵇsaidst unto me, Return unto thy country, and to thy kindred, and I will do thee good.

10 I am not ¹worthy of the least of all the mercies, and all the truth, which thou hast showed unto thy servant: for with my ²staff came I over this Jordan, and now have I gotten two bands.

11 I pray thee, Deliver me from the hand of my brother, from the hand of Esau: for I fear him, lest he will come and smite me, *and* the ¹mother upon the children.

12 And thou saidest, I will surely do to thee good, and make thy seed as the sand of the sea, which cannot be numbered for multitude.

13 ¶ And he tarried there that same night and took of that which came to hand, a ¹present for Esau his brother:

14 Two hundred she goats, and twenty he goats, two hundred ewes and twenty rams:

15 Thirty milch camels with their colts, forty kine, and ten bullocks, twenty she asses, and ten foals.

16 So he delivered them into the hand of his servants, every drove by themselves, and said unto his servants, Pass before me, and put a space between drove and drove.

17 And he commanded the foremost, saying, If my brother Esau meet thee, and ask thee, saying, Whose *servant* art thou? And whither goest thou? and whose are these before thee?

18 Then thou shalt say, *They be* thy servant Jacob's: it is a present sent unto my lord Esau: and behold, he himself also is behind us.

19 So likewise commanded he the second and

31:49 ¹ Or, watch tower.
      ² To punish the trespasser.
      ³ Or, hid.
31:50 ¹ Nature compelleth him to condemn that vice, whereunto through covetousness he forced Jacob.
31:53 ¹ Behold, how the idolaters mingle the true God with their feigned gods.
      ² Meaning, by the true God whom Isaac worshipped.
31:54 ¹ Or, meat.
31:55 ¹ We see that there is ever some seed of the knowledge of God in the hearts of the wicked.
32:2 ¹ He acknowledgeth God's benefits: who for the preservation

of his, sendeth hosts of Angels.
      ² Or, tents.
32:4 ¹ He reverenced his brother in worldly things, because he chiefly looked to be preferred to the spiritual promise.
32:7 ¹ Albeit he was comforted by the Angels, yet the infirmity of the flesh doth appear.
32:10 ¹ Hebrew, *I am less than all thy mercies.*
      ² That is, poor and without all provision.
32:11 ¹ Meaning, he will put all to death. This proverb cometh of them which kill the bird together with his young ones.
32:13 ¹ Not distrusting God's assistance, but using such means as God had given him.

the third, and all that followed the droves, saying, After this manner, ye shall speak unto Esau, when ye find him.

20 And ye shall say moreover, Behold, thy servant Jacob *cometh* after us. (for he thought, I ¹will appease his wrath with the present that goeth before me, and afterward I will see his face: it may be that he will ²accept me.)

21 So went the present before him: but he tarried that night with the company.

22 And he rose up the same night, and took his two wives, and his two maids, and his eleven children, and went over the ford Jabbok.

23 And he took them, and sent them over the river, and sent over that he had.

24 ¶ Now when Jacob was left himself alone, there wrestled a ¹man with him unto the breaking of the day.

25 And he saw that he could not ¹prevail against him: therefore he touched the hollow of his thigh, and the hollow of Jacob's thigh was loosed, as he wrestled with him.

26 And he said, Let me go, for the morning appeareth. Who answered, ʿI will not let thee go, except thou bless me.

27 Then said he unto him, What is thy name? And he said, Jacob.

28 And said he, ᵈThy name shall be called Jacob no more, but Israel: because thou hast had ¹power with God, thou shalt also prevail with men.

29 And Jacob demanded, saying, Tell me, I pray thee, thy name. And he said, Wherefore now dost thou ask my name? and he blessed him there.

30 And Jacob called the name of the place, Peniel: for, *said he*, I have seen God face to face, and ¹my life is preserved.

31 And the sun rose up to him as he passed Peniel, and he ¹halted upon his thigh.

32 Therefore the children of Israel eat not of the sinew which shrank in the hollow of the thigh, unto this day: because he touched the sinew that shrank in the hollow of Jacob's thigh.

ᶜ Hos. 12:4
ᵈ Gen. 35:10

33

4 Esau and Jacob meet and are agreed. 11 Esau receiveth his gifts. 19 Jacob buyeth a possession, 20 And buildeth an altar.

1 And as Jacob lifted up his eyes, and looked, behold, Esau came, and with him four hundred men: and he ¹divided the children to Leah, and unto Rachel, and to the two maids.

2 And he put the maids, and their children foremost, and Leah, and her children after, and Rachel and Joseph hindermost.

3 So he went before them and ¹bowed himself to the ground seven times, until he came near to his brother.

4 And Esau ran to meet him, and embraced him, and fell on his neck, and kissed him, and they wept.

5 And he lifted up his eyes, and saw the women, and the children, and said, Who are these with thee? And he answered, *They are* the children whom God of his grace hath given thy servant.

6 Then came the maids near, they and their children, and ¹bowed themselves.

7 Leah also with her children came near and made obeisance: and after Joseph and Rachel drew near, and did reverence.

8 Then he said, What meanest thou by all this drove, which I met? Who answered, I *have sent it*, that I may find favor in the sight of my lord.

9 And Esau said, I have enough, my brother: keep that thou hast to thyself.

10 But Jacob answered, Nay, I pray thee, if I have found grace now in thy sight, then receive my present at my hand: for ¹I have seen thy face, as though I had seen the face of God, because thou hast accepted me.

11 I pray thee take my ¹blessing, that is brought thee: for God hath had mercy on me, and therefore I have all things: for he ²compelled him, and he took it.

12 And he said, Let us take our journey and go, and I will go before thee.

13 Then he answered him, My lord knoweth, that the children *are* tender, and the ewes and kine with young under mine hand: and if they should overdrive them one day, all the flock would die.

32:20 ¹ He thought it no loss to depart with these goods, to the intent he might follow the vocation whereunto God called him.
² Hebrew, *receive my face.*
32:24 ¹ That is, God in form of man.
32:25 ¹ For God assaileth his with the one hand, and upholdeth them with the other.
32:28 ¹ God gave Jacob both power to overcome, and also the praise of the victory.
32:30 ¹ Or, my soul is delivered.
32:31 ¹ The faithful to overcome their tentations, that they feel the smart thereof, to the intent that they should not glory, but in their humility.
33:1 ¹ That if the one part were assailed, the other might escape.
33:3 ¹ By this gesture he partly did reverence to his brother, and partly prayed to God to mitigate Esau's wrath.
33:6 ¹ Jacob and his family are the image of the Church under the yoke of tyrants which for fear are brought to subjection.
33:10 ¹ In that that his brother embraced him so lovingly, contrary to his expectation, he accepted it as a plain sign of God's presence.
33:11 ¹ Or, gift.
² By earnest entreaty.

14 Let now my lord go before his servant, and I will drive softly, according to the pace of the cattle, which is before me, and as the children be able to endure, until [1]I come to my lord unto Seir.

15 Then Esau said, I will leave then some of my folk with thee. And he answered, What *needeth* this? let me find grace in the sight of my lord.

16 ¶ So Esau returned, *and went* his way that same day unto Seir.

17 And Jacob went forward toward Succoth, and built him an house, and made booths for his cattle: therefore he called the name of the place [1]Succoth.

18 Afterward, Jacob came safe to Shechem a city, which is in the land of Canaan, when he came from [1]Padan Aram, and pitched before the city.

19 And there he bought a parcel of ground, where he pitched his tent, at the hand of the sons of Hamor Shechem's father, for an hundred [1]pieces of money.

20 And he set up there an altar, and called [1]it, The mighty God of Israel.

34

1 Dinah is ravished.   8 Hamor asketh her in marriage for his son.   22 The Shechemites are circumcised at the request of Jacob's sons and the persuasion of Hamor.   25 The whoredome is revenged.

1 Then Dinah the daughter of Leah, which she bare unto Jacob, [1]went out to see the daughters of that country.

2 Whom when Shechem the son of Hamor the Hivite lord of that country saw, he took her, and lay with her, and [1]defiled her.

3 So his heart clave unto Dinah the daughter of Jacob: and he loved the maid, and [1]spake kindly to the maid.

4 Then said Shechem to his father Hamor, saying, [1]Get me this maid to wife.

5 (Now Jacob heard that he had defiled Dinah his daughter, and his sons were with his cattle in the field: therefore Jacob held his peace, until they were come.)

6 ¶ Then Hamor the father of Shechem went out unto Jacob to commune with him.

7 And when the sons of Jacob were come out of the field and heard it, it grieved the men, and they were very angry, because he had wrought [1]villany in Israel, in that he had lain with Jacob's daughter: [2]which thing ought not to be done.

8 And Hamor communed with them, saying, The soul of my son: Shechem longeth for your daughter, [1]give her him to wife, I pray you.

9 So make affinity with us, give your daughters unto us, and take our daughters unto you.

10 And ye shall dwell with us, and the land shall be before you, dwell, and do your business in it, and have your possessions therein.

11 Shechem also said unto her father and unto her brethren, [1]Let me find favor in your eyes, and I will give whatsoever ye shall appoint me.

12 [1]Ask of me abundantly both dowry, and gifts, and I will give as ye appoint me, so that ye give me the maid to wife.

13 Then the sons of Jacob answered, Shechem and Hamor his father, talking deceitfully, because he had defiled their sister:

14 And they said unto them, [1]We cannot do this thing, to give our sister to an uncircumcised man: for that were a [2]reproof unto us.

15 But in this we will consent unto you, if ye will be as we *are*, that every man child among you be [1]circumcised,

16 Then will we give our daughters to you, and we will take your daughters to us, and will dwell with you, and be one people.

17 But if ye will not hearken unto us to be circumcised, then will we take our daughter and depart.

18 Now their words pleased Hamor, and Shechem Hamor's son.

19 And the young man deferred not to do the thing because he loved Jacob's daughter: he was also the [1]most set by of all his father's house.

20 ¶ Then Hamor and Shechem his Son went unto the [1]gate of their city, and communed with the men of their city, saying,

21 These men are [1]peaceable with us: and that they

33:14 [1] He promised that which (as seemeth) his mind was not to perform.

33:17 [1] Or, tent.

33:18 [1] Or, Mesopotamia.

33:19 [1] Or, lambs, or money so marked.

33:20 [1] He calleth the sign, the thing which it signifieth, in token that God had mightily delivered him.

34:1 [1] This example teacheth us that too much liberty is not to be given to youth.

34:2 [1] Hebrew, *humbled her.*

34:3 [1] Hebrew, *spake to the heart of the maid.*

34:4 [1] This proveth that the consent of parents is requisite in marriage, seeing the very Infidels did also observe it as a thing necessary.

34:7 [1] Or, folly.

[2] Hebrew, *and it shall not be so done.*

34:8 [1] Or, marriage.

34:11 [1] Or, grant my request.

34:12 [1] Hebrew, *multiply greatly the dowry.*

34:14 [1] They made the holy ordinance of God a means to compasse their wicked purpose.

[2] As it is abomination for them that are baptized to join with Infidels.

34:15 [1] Their fault is the greater in that they make religion a cloak for their craft.

34:19 [1] Or, most honorable.

34:20 [1] For the people used to assemble there, and justice was also ministered.

34:21 [1] Thus many pretend to speak for a public profit, when they only speak for their own private gain and commodity.

may dwell in the land, and do their affairs therein (for behold, the land hath room enough for them) let us take their daughters to wives, and give them our daughters.

22 Only herein will the men consent unto us for to dwell with us, and to be one people, if all the men children among us be circumcised as they are circumcised.

23 Shall not ¹their flocks and their substance and all their cattle be ours? only let us consent *herein* unto them and they will dwell with us.

24 And unto Hamor, and Shechem his son hearkened all that went out of the gate of his city: and all the men children were circumcised, *even* all that went out of the gate of his city.

25 And on the third day (when they were sore) two of the sons of Jacob, ¹Simeon and Levi, Dinah's brethren took either of them his sword and went into the city boldly, and ᵃslew ²every male.

26 They slew also Hamor and Shechem his son with the ¹edge of the sword, and took Dinah out of Shechem's house, and went their way.

27 *Again*, the *other* sons of Jacob came upon the dead, and spoiled the city, because they had defiled their sister.

28 They took their sheep and their beeves, and their asses, and whatsoever was in the city and in the fields.

29 Also they carried away captive and spoiled all their goods, and all their children and their wives, and all that was in the houses.

30 Then Jacob said to Simeon and Levi, Ye have troubled me, and made me ¹stink among the inhabitants of the land, *as well* the Canaanites, as the Perizzites, and I being few in number, they shall gather themselves together against me, and slay me, and so shall I, and my house be destroyed.

31 And they answered, Should he abuse our sister as a whore?

35 ¹*Jacob at God's commandment goeth up to Bethel built an altar.*   2 *He reformeth his household.*   5 *God maketh the enemies of Jacob afraid.*   8 *Deborah dieth.*   12 *The land of Canaan is promised him.*   18 *Rachel dieth in labor.*   22 *Reuben lieth with his father's concubine.*

1 Then ¹God said to Jacob, Arise, go up to Bethel and dwell there, and make there an altar unto God,

CHAPTER 34
ᵃ Gen. 49:6

CHAPTER 35
ᵃ Gen. 28:13
ᵇ Gen. 28:19
ᶜ Gen. 32:28

that appeared unto thee, ᵃwhen thou fleddest from Esau thy brother.

2 Then said Jacob unto his household and to all that were with him, Put away the strange gods that are among you, and ¹cleanse yourselves, and change your garments:

3 For we will rise and go up to Bethel, and I will make an altar there unto God, which heard me in the day of my tribulation, and was with me in the way which I went.

4 And they gave unto Jacob all the strange gods, which *were* in their hands, and all their ¹earrings which were in their ears, and Jacob hid them under an oak, which was by Shechem.

5 Then they went on their journey, and the ¹fear of God was upon the cities that were round about them: so that they did not follow after the sons of Jacob.

6 ¶ So came Jacob to Luz, which is in the land of Canaan: (the same is Bethel) he and all the people that were with him.

7 And he built there an altar, and ᵇhad called the place, The God of Bethel, because that God appeared unto him there, when he fled from his brother.

8 But Deborah Rebekah's nurse died, and was buried beneath Bethel under an oak: and he called the name of it ¹Allon Bachuth.

9 Again God appeared unto Jacob, after he came to Padan Aram, and blessed him.

10 Moreover God said unto him, Thy name is Jacob: thy name shall be no more called Jacob, but ᶜIsrael shall be thy name: and he called his name Israel.

11 And God said unto him, I am God ¹all-sufficient: grow, and multiply: a nation and a multitude of nations shall spring of thee, and kings shall come out of thy loins.

12 Also I will give the land, which I gave to Abraham and Isaac, unto thee: and unto thy seed after thee will I give that land.

13 So God ¹ascended from him in the place where he had talked with him.

14 And Jacob set up a pillar in the place where he talked with him, a pillar of stone, and poured drink offerings thereon: also he poured oil thereon.

15 And Jacob called the name of that place where God spake with him, Bethel.

16 ¶ Then they departed from Bethel, and when

34:23 ¹ Thus they lack no kind of persuasion, which prefer their own commodities before the commonwealth.
34:25 ¹ For they were the chief of the company.
     ² The people are punished with their wicked princes.
34:26 ¹ Hebrew, *mouth of the sword.*
34:30 ¹ Or, to be abhorred.
35:1 ¹ God is ever at hand to succor his in their troubles.
35:2 ¹ That by this outward act they should show their inward repentance.

35:4 ¹ For therein was some sign of superstition, as in tablets and Agnus deis.
35:5 ¹ Thus, notwithstanding the inconvenience that came before, God delivered Jacob.
35:8 ¹ Or, oak of lamentations.
35:11 ¹ Or, almighty.
35:13 ¹ As God is said to descend when he showeth some sign of his presence: so he is said to ascend when vision is ended.

there was [1]about half a day's journey of ground to come to Ephrath, Rachel travailed, and in travailing she was in peril.

17 And when she was in the pains of her labor, the midwife said unto her, Fear not, for thou *shalt have* this son also.

18 Then as she was about to yield up the ghost (for she died) she called his name Ben-Oni, but his father called him Benjamin.

19 Thus [d]died Rachel and was buried in the way to Ephrath, which is Bethlehem.

20 And Jacob set a [1]pillar upon her grave: This is the pillar of Rachel's grave unto this day.

21 ¶ Then Israel went forward, and pitched his tent beyond Migdal Eder.

22 Now when Israel dwelt in that land, Reuben went and [1]lay [c]*with* Bilhah his father's concubine, and it came to Israel's ear. And Jacob had twelve sons.

23 The sons of Leah: Reuben Jacob's eldest son, and Simeon, and Levi, and Judah, and Issachar, and Zebulun:

24 The sons of Rachel; Joseph, and Benjamin:

25 And the sons of Bilhah Rachel's maid: Dan and Naphtali:

26 And the sons of Zilpah Leah's maid: Gad and Asher. These are the sons of Jacob, which were born him in Padan Aram.

27 ¶ Then Jacob came unto Isaac his father unto Mamre a city of Kirjath Arbah: that is Hebron, where Abraham and Isaac were strangers.

28 And the days of Isaac were an hundred and fourscore years.

29 And Isaac gave up the ghost and died, and was [f]gathered unto his people, being old and full of days: and his sons Esau and Jacob buried him.

36

2 *The wives of Esau.*   7 *Jacob and Esau are rich.*   9 *The genealogy of Esau.*   24 *The finding of mules.*

1 Now these are [1]the generations of Esau, which is Edom.

2 Esau took his wives of the [1]daughters of Canaan: Adah the daughter of Elon an Hittite and Aholibamah the daughter of Anah, the daughter of Zibeon an Hivite.

Margin references:
[d] Gen. 48:7
[e] Gen. 49:4
[f] Gen. 23:8

CHAPTER 36
[a] 1 Chron. 1:35
[b] Josh. 24:4
[c] 1 Chron. 1:35

3 And *took* Basemath Ishmael's daughter, sister of Nebajoth.

4 And [a]Adah bare unto Esau, Eliphaz: and Basemath bare Reuel,

5 Also Aholibamah bare Jeush, and Jaalam, and Korah: these are the sons of Esau which were born to him in the land of Canaan.

6 So Esau took his wives and his sons, and his daughters, and all the souls of his house, and his flocks, and all his cattle, and all his substance, which he had gotten in the land of Canaan, and [1]went into *another* country from his brother Jacob.

7 For their riches were so great, that they could not dwell together, and the land, wherein they were strangers, could not receive them because of their flocks.

8 [b]Therefore dwelt Esau in mount Seir: this Esau is Edom.

9 ¶ So these are the generations of Esau father of [1]Edom in mount Seir:

10 These are the names of Esau's sons: [c]Eliphaz, the son of Adah, the wife of Esau, *and* Reuel the son of Basemath, the wife of Esau.

11 And the sons of Eliphaz were Teman, Omar, Zepho, and Gatam, and Kenaz.

12 And Timna was concubine to Eliphaz Esau's son, and bare unto Eliphaz, Amalek: these be the sons of Adah Esau's wife.

13 ¶ And these are the [1]sons of Reuel: Nahath, and Zerah, Shammah, and Mizzah: these be the sons of Basemath Esau's wife.

14 ¶ And these were the sons of Aholibamah the daughter of Anah, [1]daughter of Zibeon Esau's wife: for she bare unto Esau, Jeush, and Jaalam, and Korah.

15 ¶ These were [1,2]Dukes of the sons of Esau the sons of Eliphaz, the firstborn of Esau Duke Teman, Duke Omar, Duke Zepho, Duke Kenaz,

16 Duke Korah, Duke Gatam, and Duke Amalek: these are the Dukes *that came* of Eliphaz in the land of Edom: these were the [1]sons of Adah.

17 ¶ And these are the sons of Reuel Esau's son: Duke Nahath, Duke Zerah, Duke Shammah, Duke Mizzah: these are the Dukes *that came* of Reuel in the land of Edom: these are the [1]sons of Basemath Esau's wife.

35:16 [1] The Hebrew word signifieth as much ground as one may go from baite to baite, which is taken for half a day's journey.

35:20 [1] The ancient fathers used this ceremony to testify their hope of the resurrection to come, which was not generally revealed.

35:22 [1] This teacheth that the fathers were not chosen for their merits, but by God's only mercies, whose election by their faults was not changed.

36:1 [1] This genealogy declareth that Esau was blessed temporally, and that his father's blessing took place in worldly things.

36:2 [1] Besides those wives whereof is spoken, Gen. 26:34.

36:6 [1] Herein appeareth God's providence, which causeth the wicked to give place to the godly, that Jacob might enjoy Canaan according to God's promise.

36:9 [1] Or, the edomites.

36:13 [1] Or, nephews.

36:14 [1] Or, niece.

36:15 [1] Or, chief men.

[2] If God's promises be so sure towards them which are not of his household, how much more will he perform the same to us?

36:16 [1] Or, nephews.

36:17 [1] Or, nephews.

18 ¶ Likewise these were the sons of Aholibamah Esau's wife: Duke Jeush, Duke Jaalam, Duke Korah: these Dukes *came* of Aholibamah, the daughter of Anah Esau's wife.

19 These are the children of Esau, and these are the Dukes of them: This *Esau* is Edom.

20 ¶ ᵈThese are the sons of Seir the Horite, which ¹inhabited the land *before* Lotan, and Shobal, and Zibeon, and Anah,

21 And Dishon, and Ezer, and Dishan: these are the Dukes of the Horites, the sons of Seir in the land of Edom.

22 And the sons of Lotan were, Hori and Hemam, and Lotan's sister *was* Timna.

23 And the sons of Shobal were these: Alvan, and Manahath, and Ebal, Shepho, and Onam.

24 And these are the sons of Zibeon: Both Ajah, and Anah: this was Anah that found ¹mules in the wilderness, as he fed his father Zibeon's asses.

25 And the children of Anah were these: Dishon and Aholibamah, the daughter of Anah.

26 Also these are the sons of Dishon: Hemdan, and Eshban, and Ithran, and Cheran.

27 The sons of Ezer are these: Bilhan, and Zaavan, and Akan.

28 The sons of Dishan are these, Uz, and Aran.

29 These are the Dukes of the Horites: Duke Lotan, Duke Shobal, Duke Zibeon, Duke Anah,

30 Duke Dishon, Duke Ezer, Duke Dishan: these be the Dukes of the Horites, after their Dukedoms in the land of Seir.

31 ¶ And these are the ¹Kings that reigned in the land of Edom, before there reigned *any* King over the children of Israel.

32 Then Bela the son of Beor reigned in Edom, and the name of his city *was* Dinhabah.

33 And when Bela died, Jobab the son of Zerah of Bozrah reigned in his stead.

34 When Jobab also was dead, Husham of the land of Temani reigned in his stead.

35 And after the death of Husham, Hadad the son of Bedad, which slew Midian in the field of Moab, reigned in his stead, and the name of his city *was* Avith.

36 When Hadad was dead, then Samlah of Masrekah reigned in his stead.

ᵈ 1 Chron. 1:38

37 When Samlah was dead, Saul of ¹Rehoboth by the river, reigned in his stead.

38 When Saul died, Baal-Hanan the son of Achbor reigned in his stead.

39 And after the death of Baal-Hanan the son of Achbor, Hadar reigned in his stead, and the name of his city *was* Pau: and his wife's name Mehetabel the daughter of Matred, the ¹daughter of Mezahab.

40 Then these are the names of the Dukes of Esau according to their families, their places, *and* by their names: Duke Timnah, Duke Alvah, Duke Jetheth.

41 Duke Aholibamah, Duke Elah, Duke Pinon,

42 Duke Kenaz, Duke Teman, Duke Mibzar,

43 Duke Magdiel, Duke Iram: these be the Dukes of Edom, according to their habitations, in the land of their inheritance. This Esau is the father of ¹Edom.

37

2 *Joseph accuseth his brethren.* 5 *He dreameth and is hated of his brethren.* 28 *They sell him to the Ishmaelites.* 34 *Jacob bewaileth Joseph.*

1 Jacob now dwelt in the land, wherein his father was a stranger, in the land of Canaan.

2 These are the ¹generations of Jacob *when* Joseph was seventeen years old, he kept sheep with his brethren, and the child was with the sons of Bilhah, and with the sons of Zilpah, his father's wives, And Joseph brought unto their father their evil ²,³saying.

3 Now Israel loved Joseph more than all his sons, because he begat him in his old age and he made him a coat of many ¹colors.

4 So when his brethren saw that their father loved him more than all his brethren, then they hated him, and could not speak peaceably unto him.

5 ¶ And Joseph ¹dreamed a dream, and told his brethren, who hated him so much the more.

6 For he said unto them, Hear, I pray you this dream which I have dreamed.

7 Behold now, we were binding sheaves in the midst of the field: and lo, my sheaf arose and also stood upright, and behold, your sheaves compassed round about, and did reverence to my sheaf.

8 Then his brethren said to him, What, shalt thou reign over us, and rule us? or shalt thou have altogether dominion over us? And they ¹hated him so

---

36:20 ¹ Before that Esau did there inhabit.
36:24 ¹ Who not contented with those kinds of beasts, which God had created, found out the monstrous generation of mules between the Ass and the mare.
36:31 ¹ The wicked rise up suddenly to honor, and perish as quickly: but the inheritance of the children of God continueth ever, Ps. 102:28.
36:37 ¹ Which city is by the river Euphrates.
36:39 ¹ Or, niece.
36:43 ¹ Of Edom came the Idumeans.

37:2 ¹ That is, the story of such things as came to him and his family, as Gen. 5:1.
  ² Or, slander.
  ³ He complained of the evil words and injuries which they spake and did against him.
37:3 ¹ Or, pieces.
37:5 ¹ God revealed to him by a dream what should come to pass.
37:8 ¹ The more that God showed himself favorable to his, the more doth the malice of the wicked rage against them.

much the more, for his dreams, and for his words.

9 ¶ Again he dreamed another dream, and told it his brethren, and said, Behold, I have had one dream more, and behold, the Sun and the Moon and eleven stars did reverence to me.

10 Then he told it unto his father and to his brethren, and his father [1]rebuked him, and said unto him, What is this thy dream, which thou hast dreamed? shall I, and thy mother, and thy brethren come indeed and fall on the ground before thee?

11 And his brethren envied him, but his father [1,2]noted the saying.

12 ¶ Then his brethren went to keep their father's sheep in Shechem.

13 And Israel said unto Joseph, Do not thy brethren keep in Shechem? come and I will send thee to them.

14 And he answered him, I am here. Then he said unto him, Go now, see whether it be well with thy brethren, and how the flocks prosper, and bring me word again: so he sent him from the vale of Hebron, and he came to Shechem.

15 ¶ Then a man found him: for lo, he was wandering in the field, and the man asked him, saying, what seekest thou?

16 And he answered, I seek my brethren: tell me, I pray thee, where they keep *sheep*.

17 And the man said, they are departed hence: for I heard them say, Let us go unto Dothan. Then went Joseph after his brethren, and found them in Dothan.

18 And when they saw him afar off, even before he came at them, they [1]conspired against him for to slay him.

19 For they said one to another, Behold, this [1]dreamer cometh.

20 Come now therefore, and let us slay him, and cast him into some pit, and we will say, A wicked beast hath devoured him: then we shall see, what will come of his dreams.

21 [a]But when Reuben heard *that*, he delivered him out of their hands, and said, [1]Let us not kill him.

22 Also Reuben said unto them, Shed not blood, *but* cast him into this pit that is in the wilderness, and lay no hand upon him. *Thus he said*, that he might

CHAPTER 37
[a] Gen. 42:22
[b] Ps. 105:17
[c] Gen. 44:28

deliver him out of their hand, and restore him to his father.

23 ¶ Now when Joseph was come unto his brethren, they stripped Joseph out of his coat, his parti-colored coat that was upon him.

24 And they took him, and cast [1]him into a pit, and the pit *was* empty, without water in it.

25 Then they sat them down to eat bread: and lift up their eyes and looked, and behold, there came a company of Ishmaelites from Gilead, and their camels laden with spicery, and [1]balm, and myrrh, and were going to carry it down into Egypt.

26 Then Judah said to his brethren, What availeth it, if we slay our brother, though we keep his blood secret?

27 Come and let us [b]sell him to the Ishmaelites, and let not our hands be upon him: for he is our brother, *and* our flesh: and his brethren obeyed.

28 Then the [1]Midianites' merchant men passed by, and they drew forth, and lift Joseph out of the pit, and sold Joseph to the Ishmaelites for twenty *pieces* of silver: who brought Joseph into Egypt.

29 ¶ Afterward Reuben returned to the pit, and behold, Joseph *was* not in the pit: then he rent his clothes,

30 And returned to his brethren, and said, The child is not *yonder*, and I, whither shall I go?

31 And they took Joseph's coat, and killed a kid of the goats, and dipped the coat in the blood.

32 So they sent that parti-colored coat, [1]and they brought it unto their father, and said, This have we found: see now, whether it be thy son's coat, or no.

33 Then he knew it, and said, *It is* my son's coat: a wicked beast hath [c]devoured him: Joseph is surely torn in pieces.

34 And Jacob rent his clothes, and put sackcloth about his loins, and sorrowed for his son a long season.

35 Then all his sons and his daughters arose up to comfort him, but he would not be comforted, but said, [1]Surely I will go down into the grave unto my son mourning: so his father wept for him.

36 And the Midianites sold him into Egypt unto Potiphar [1]an Eunuch of Pharaoh's *and* his [2]chief steward.

37:10 [1] Not despising the vision, but seeking to appease his brethren.

37:11 [1] Or, kept diligently.
  [2] He knew that God was author of the dream, but he understood not the meaning.

37:18 [1] The holy Ghost covereth not men's faults, as do vain writers, which make vice virtue.

37:19 [1] Or, master of dreams.

37:21 [1] Hebrew, *let us not smite his life*.

37:24 [1] Their hypocrisy appeareth in this that they feared man more than God: and thought it was not murder, if they shed not his blood: or else had an excuse to cover their fault.

37:25 [1] Or, rosen, turpentine, or treacle.

37:28 [1] Moses writing according to the opinion of them which took the Midianites and Ishmaelites to be both one, doth here confound their names: as also appeareth, verse 36 and Gen. 39:1, or else he was first offered to the Midianites, but sold to the Ishmaelites.

37:32 [1] To wit, the messengers which were sent.

37:35 [1] Or, I will mourn for him so long as I live.

37:36 [1] Which word doth not always signify him that is gelded, but also him that is in some high dignity.
  [2] Or, captain of the guard.

38 2 *The marriage of Judah.* 7, 9 *The trespass of Er and Onan, and the vengeance of God that came thereupon.* 18 *Judah lieth with his daughter-in-law Tamar.* 24 *Tamar is judged to be burnt for whoredom.* 29, 30 *The birth of Perez and Zerah.*

CHAPTER 38
a 1 Chron. 2:3
b Num. 26:19
c Num. 26:19

1 And at that time [1]Judah went down from his brethren, and turned into a man called Hirah an Adullamite.

2 And Judah saw there a daughter of a man called *a*Shua a [1]Canaanite: and he took her *to wife*, and went into her.

3 So she conceived and bare a son, and he called his name Er.

4 *b*And she conceived again and bare a son, and she called his name Onan.

5 Moreover she bare yet a son, whom she called Shelah: and *Judah* was at Chezib when she bare him.

6 Then Judah took a wife to Er his firstborn *son*, whose name *was* Tamar.

7 'Now Er the firstborn of Judah was wicked in the sight of the Lord: therefore the Lord slew him.

8 And Judah said to Onan, Go in unto thy brother's wife, and do the office of a kinsman unto her, and raise [1]up seed unto thy brother.

9 And Onan knew that the seed should not be his: therefore when he went in unto his brother's wife, he spilled it on the ground, lest that he should give seed to his brother.

10 And it was wicked in the eyes of the Lord, which he did: wherefore he slew him also.

11 Then Judah said to Tamar his daughter-in-law, [1]Remain a widow in thy father's house, till Shelah my son grow up (for he thought *thus*, Lest he die as well as his brethren,) So Tamar went and dwelt in her father's house.

12 ¶ And in process of time also the daughter of Shua Judah's wife died. Then Judah, when he [1]had left mourning, went up to his sheepshearers to Timnah, he, and his neighbor Hirah the Adullamite.

13 And it was told Tamar, saying, Behold, thy father-in-law goeth up to Timnath, to shear his sheep.

14 Then she put her widow's garments off from her, and covered *her* with a veil, and wrapped herself,

and sat down in [1]Pethah-enam which is by the way to Timnah, because she saw that Shelah was grown, and she was not given unto him to wife.

15 When Judah saw her, he judged her an whore: for she had covered her face.

16 And he turned to the way towards her, and said, Come, I pray thee, let me lie with thee, (for he [1]knew not that she was his daughter-in-law.) And she answered, What wilt thou give me for to lie with me?

17 Then said he, I will send thee a kid of the goats from the flock, and she said, *Well*, if thou wilt give me a pledge, till thou send it.

18 Then he said, What is the pledge that I shall give thee? And she answered, Thy signet and thy [1]cloak and thy staff that is in thine hand. So he gave it her, and lay by her, and she was with child by him.

19 Then she rose, and went and put her veil from her and put on her widow's raiment.

20 Afterward Judah sent a kid of the goats by the hand of his [1]neighbor the Adullamite, for to receive his pledge from the woman's hand: but he found her not.

21 Then asked he the men of the place, saying, Where is the whore, *that sat* in Enaim by the wayside? and they answered, There was no whore there.

22 He came therefore to Judah again, and said, I cannot find her, and also the men of the place said, There was no whore there.

23 Then Judah said, Let her take it to her, lest we be [1,2]shamed: behold, I sent this kid, and thou hast not found her.

24 ¶ Now after three months, one told Judah, saying, Tamar thy daughter-in-law hath played the whore, and lo, with playing the whore, she is great with child. Then Judah said, Bring ye her forth and let her be [1]burnt.

25 When she was brought forth, she sent to her father-in-law, saying, By the man, unto whom these things *pertain*, am I with child: and said also, Look I pray thee, whose these are, the seal, and the cloak, and the staff.

26 Then Judah knew *them*, and said, She is [1]more righteous than I: for *she hath done it* because I gave her not to Shelah my son. So he lay with her [2]no more.

38:1 [1] Moses describeth the genealogy of Judah, because the Messiah should come of him.
38:2 [1] Which affinity notwithstanding was condemned of God.
38:8 [1] This order was for the preservation of the stock, that the child begotten by the second brother should have the name and inheritance of the first: which in the new Testament abolished.
38:11 [1] For she could not marry in any other family so long as Judah would retain her in his.
38:12 [1] Hebrew, *was comforted.*
38:14 [1] Or, in the door of the fountain, or, where were two ways.

38:16 [1] God had wonderfully blinded him that he could not know her by her talk.
38:18 [1] Or, tyre of thine head.
38:20 [1] That his wickedness might not be known to others.
38:23 [1] Hebrew, *in contempt.*
   [2] He feareth man more than God.
38:24 [1] We see that the Law, which was written in man's heart, taught them that whoredom should be punished with death: albeit no law, as yet was given.
38:26 [1] That is, she ought rather to accuse me than I her.
   [2] For the horror of the sin condemned him.

27 ¶ Now, when the time was come that she should be delivered, behold, there *were* twins in her womb.

28 And when she was in travail, *the one* put out his hand: and the midwife took and bound a red *thread* about his hand, saying, this is come out first.

29 But when he [1]plucked his hand back again, lo, his brother came out, and *the midwife* said, How hast [2]thou broken the breach upon thee? and his name was called [d]Perez.

30 And afterward came out his brother that *had* the red *thread* about his hand, and his name was called Zerah.

39

1 *Joseph sold to Potiphar.* 2 *God prospereth him.* 7 *Potiphar's wife tempteth him.* 13, 20 *He is accused and cast in prison.* 23 *God showeth him favor.*

1 Now Joseph was brought down into Egypt: and Potiphar [1]an Eunuch of Pharaoh's (*and his* chief steward an Egyptian) bought him at the hand of the Ishmaelites, which had brought him thither.

2 And the [1]Lord was with Joseph, and he was a man that prospered and was in the house of his master the Egyptian.

3 And his master saw that the Lord *was* with him, and that the Lord made all that he did to prosper in his hand.

4 So Joseph found favor in his sight, and served him: and made him [1]ruler of his house, and put all that he had in his hand.

5 And from that time that he had made him ruler over his house and over all that he had, the Lord [1]blessed the Egyptian's house for Joseph's sake: and the blessing of the Lord was upon all that he had in the house, and in the field.

6 Therefore he left all that he had in Joseph's hand, [1]and took account of nothing, *that was* with him, save only of the bread, which he did eat. And Joseph was a fair person, and well favored.

7 Now therefore after these things, his master's wife cast her eyes upon Joseph, and said, [1]Lie with me.

8 But he refused and said to his master's wife, Behold, my master knoweth not what *he hath* in

[d] 1 Chron. 2:4
Matt. 1:3

the house with me, but hath committed all that he had to mine hand.

9 There is no man greater in this house than I: neither hath he kept anything from me, but only thee, because thou art his wife: how then can I do this great wickedness and *so* sin against [1]God?

10 And albeit she spake to Joseph day by day, yet he hearkened not unto her, to lie with her, *or* to be in her company.

11 Then on a certain day *Joseph* entered into the house to do his business: and there was no man of the household in the house.

12 Therefore she caught him by his garment, saying, Sleep with me: but he left his garment in her hand and fled, and got him out.

13 Now when she saw that he had left his garment in her hand, and was fled out,

14 She called unto the men of her house, and told them, saying, Behold, he hath brought in an Hebrew unto us [1]to mock us: who came in to me for to have slept with me: but I [2]cried with a loud voice.

15 And when he heard that I lift up my voice and cried, he left his garments with me, and fled away, and got him out.

16 So she laid up his garment by her, until her lord came home.

17 Then she told him [1]according to these words, saying, The Hebrew servant, which thou hast brought unto us, came into me, to mock me.

18 But as soon as I lift up my voice and cried, he left his garment with me, and fled out.

19 Then when his master heard the words of his wife, which she told him, saying, After this manner did thy servant to me, his anger was kindled.

20 And Joseph's master took him and put him in [1,2]prison, in the place, where the king's prisoners lay bound: and there he was in prison.

21 ¶ But the Lord was with Joseph, and [1]showed him mercy, and got him favor in the sight of the [2]master of the prison.

22 And the keeper of the prison committed to Joseph's hand all the prisoners that were in the prison, and [1]whatsoever they did there, that did he.

23 And the keeper of the prison looked unto nothing that was under his hand, seeing that the

---

38:29 [1] Their heinous sin was signified by this monstrous birth.
   [2] Or the separation between thee and thy brother.
39:1 [1] Read Gen. 37:36.
39:2 [1] The favor of God is the fountain of all prosperity.
39:4 [1] Because God prospered him: and so he made religion to serve his profit.
39:5 [1] The wicked are blessed by the company of the godly.
39:6 [1] For he was assured that all things should prosper well: therefore he ate and drank and took no care.
39:7 [1] In this word he declareth the sum whereunto all her flatteries did tend.

39:9 [1] The fear of God preserved him against her continual tentations.
39:14 [1] Or, to do us villainy and shame.
   [2] This declareth that where incontinence is, thereunto is joined extreme impudency and craft.
39:17 [1] Or, after this manner.
39:20 [1] Hebrew, *in the prison house.*
   [2] His evil intreatment in the prison may be gathered of Ps. 105:18.
39:21 [1] Hebrew, *inclined mercy unto him.*
   [2] Or, lord.
39:22 [1] That is, nothing was done without his commandment.

Lord *was* with him: for whatsoever he did, the Lord made it to prosper.

40

8 The interpretation of dreams is of God. 12, 19 Joseph expoundeth the dreams of the two prisoners. 23 The ingratitude of the butler.

1   And after these things, the butler of the King of Egypt and his baker offended their Lord the King of Egypt.

2   And Pharaoh was angry against his two [1]Officers, against the chief butler, and against the chief baker.

3   Therefore he put them in ward in his chief steward's house, in the prison *and* place where [1]Joseph was bound.

4   And the chief steward gave Joseph charge over them, and he served them: and they continued a season in ward.

5   ¶ And they both dreamed a dream, either of them his dream in one night, [1]each one according to the interpretation of his dream, *both* the butler and the baker of the King of Egypt, which were bound in the prison.

6   And when Joseph came in unto them in the morning, and looked upon them, behold, they were sad.

7   And he asked Pharaoh's officers, that were with him in his master's ward, saying, Wherefore [1]look ye so sadly today?

8   Who answered him, We have dreamed *each one* a dream, and there is none to interpret the same. Then Joseph said unto them, [1]Are not interpretations of God? tell them me now.

9   So the chief butler told his dream to Joseph, and said unto him, In my dream, behold, a vine *was* before me,

10   And in the vine *were* three branches, and as it budded, her flower came forth: and the clusters of grapes waxed ripe.

11   And *I had* Pharaoh's cup in mine hand, and I took the grapes, and wrung them into Pharaoh's cup, and I gave the cup into Pharaoh's hand.

12   Then Joseph said unto him, This [1]is the interpretation of it: the three branches are three days:

13   Within three days shall Pharaoh lift up thine head, and restore thee unto thine [1]office, and thou shalt give Pharaoh's cup into his hand after the old manner, when thou wast his butler,

14   But have me in remembrance with thee, when thou art in good case, and show mercy, I pray thee unto me, and [1]make mention of me to Pharaoh, that thou mayest bring me out of this house.

15   For I was stolen away by theft out of the land of the Hebrews, and here also have I done nothing, wherefore they should put me [1]in the dungeon.

16   And when the chief baker saw that the interpretation was good, he said unto Joseph, Also me thought in my dream that I had three [1]white baskets on mine head.

17   And in the uppermost basket there *was* of all manner bakemeats for Pharaoh: and the birds did eat them out of the basket upon mine head.

18   Then Joseph answered, and said, [1]This is the interpretation thereof: The three baskets are three days:

19   Within three days shall Pharaoh take thine head from thee, and shall hang thee on a tree and the birds shall eat thy flesh from off thee.

20   ¶ And so the third day, *which was* Pharaoh's [1]birthday, he made a feast unto all his servants: and he lifted up the head of the chief butler, and the chief baker among his servants.

21   And he restored the chief butler unto his butlership, who gave the cup into Pharaoh's hand.

22   But he hanged the chief baker, as Joseph had interpreted unto them.

23   Yet the chief butler did not remember Joseph, but forgot him.

41

26 Pharaoh's dreams are expounded by Joseph.   40 He is made ruler over all Egypt.   45 Joseph's name is changed.   50 He hath two sons Manasseh and Ephraim.

1   And [1]two years after, Pharaoh also [2]dreamed, and behold, he stood by a river.

2   And lo, there came out of the river seven [1]goodly kine and fat-fleshed, and they fed in a [2]meadow.

3   And lo, seven other kine came up after them out of the river, evil favored and lean fleshed, and

---

40:2 [1] Or, eunuchs, the word signifieth them, that were in high estate, or them that were gelded.
40:3 [1] God worketh many wonderful means to deliver his.
40:5 [1] That is, every dream had his interpretation, as the thing afterward declared.
40:7 [1] Hebrew, *why are your faces evil?*
40:8 [1] Cannot God raise up such as shall interpret such things?
40:12 [1] He was assured by the spirit of God, that his interpretation was true.
40:13 [1] Hebrew, *place.*
40:14 [1] He refused not the means to be delivered, which he thought God had appointed.

40:15 [1] Or, in the pit.
40:16 [1] That is made of white twigs, or as some read, baskets full of holes.
40:18 [1] He showeth that the ministers of God ought not to conceal that, which God revealeth unto them.
40:20 [1] Which was an occasion to appoint his officers, and so to examine them that were in prison.
41:1 [1] Hebrew, *at the end of two years of days.*
        [2] This dream was not so much for Pharaoh, as to be a means to deliver Joseph, and to provide for God's Church.
41:2 [1] Or, fair to behold.
        [2] Or, staggie place.

stood by the *other* kine upon the brink of the river.

4   And the evil favored and lean fleshed kine did eat up the seven well favored and fat kine: so Pharaoh awoke.

5   Again he slept, and dreamed the [1]second time: and behold, seven ears of corn grew upon one stalk, rank and goodly.

6   And lo, seven thin ears, and blasted with the East wind, sprang up after them.

7   And the thin ears devoured the seven rank and full ears, then Pharaoh awaked, and lo *it was* a dream.

8   Now when the morning came, his spirit was [1]troubled: therefore he sent and called all the soothsayers of Egypt, and all the wise men thereof, and Pharaoh told them his dreams: but [2]none could interpret them to Pharaoh.

9   Then spake the chief butler unto Pharaoh, saying, I [1]call to mind my faults this day.

10   Pharaoh being angry with his servants, put me in ward in the chief steward's house, *both* me, and the chief baker.

11   Then we dreamed a dream in one night *both* I, and he: we dreamed each man according to the interpretation of his dream.

12   And there *was* with us a young man, an Hebrew, servant unto the chief steward, whom when we told, he declared our dreams to [1]us, to everyone he declared according to his dream.

13   And as he declared unto us, so it came to pass: *for* he restored me to mine office, and hanged him.

14   *a*Then sent Pharaoh, and called [1]Joseph and they brought him hastily out of prison, and he shaved him, and changed his raiment, and came to Pharaoh.

15   Then Pharaoh said to Joseph, I have dreamed a dream, and no man can interpret it, and I have heard say of thee, *that when* thou hearest a dream, thou canst interpret it.

16   And Joseph answered Pharaoh, saying, [1]Without me God shall [2]answer for the wealth of Pharaoh.

17   And Pharaoh said unto Joseph: In my dream, behold, I stood by the bank of the river:

18   And lo, there came up out of the river seven fat fleshed, and well favored kine. and they fed in the meadow.

19   Also lo, seven other kine came up after them

CHAPTER 41
a Ps. 105:20

poor and very [1]evil favored kine, and lean fleshed: I never saw the like in all the land of Egypt, for evil favored.

20   And the lean and the evil favored kine did eat up the first seven fat kine.

21   And when they [1]had eaten them up: it could not be known that they had eaten them, but they were still as evil favored, as they were at the beginning: so did I awake.

22   Moreover I saw in my dream, and behold, seven ears sprang out of one stalk, full and fair.

23   And lo, seven ears withered, thin, *and* blasted with the East wind, sprang up after them.

24   And the thin ears devoured the seven good ears. Now I have told the soothsayers, and none can declare it unto me.

25   ¶ Then Joseph answered Pharaoh, [1]*Both* Pharaoh's dreams are one. God hath showed Pharaoh what he is about to do.

26   The seven good Kine are seven years, and the seven good ears are seven years: this is one dream.

27   Likewise the seven thin and evil favored kine, that came out after them, are seven years: and the seven empty ears blasted with the East wind, are seven years of famine.

28   This is the thing which I have said unto Pharaoh, that God hath showed unto Pharaoh, what he is about to do.

29   Behold, there come seven years of great [1]plenty in all the land of Egypt.

30   Again, there shall arise after them seven years of famine, so that all the plenty shall be forgotten in the land of Egypt, and the famine shall consume the land:

31   Neither shall the plenty [1]be known in the land, by reason of this famine that *shall come* after, for it shall be exceeding great.

32   And therefore the dream was doubled unto Pharaoh the second time, because the thing is established by God, and God hasteth to perform it.

33   Now therefore let Pharaoh [1]provide for a man of understanding and wisdom, and set him over the land of Egypt.

34   Let Pharaoh make and appoint officers over the land, and take up the fifth part of the land of Egypt in the seven plenteous years.

41:5 [1] All these means God used to deliver his servant, and to bring him into favor and authority.

41:8 [1] This fear was enough to teach him that this vision was sent of God.

[2] The wise of the world understand not God's secrets, but to his servants his will is revealed.

41:9 [1] He confesseth his fault against the king before he speak of Joseph.

41:12 [1] Read Gen. 40:5.

41:14 [1] The wicked seek to the Prophets of God in their necessity, whom in their prosperity they abhor.

41:16 [1] As though he would say, if I interpret thy dream it cometh of God, and not of me.

[2] Hebrew, *answer peace*.

41:19 [1] Hebrew, *naught*.

41:21 [1] Hebrew, *were gone into their inward parts*.

41:25 [1] Both his dreams tend to one end.

41:29 [1] Or, abundance and saturity.

41:31 [1] Or, they shall remember no more the plenty.

41:33 [1] The office of a true Prophet is not only to show the evils to come, but also the remedies for the same.

35 Also let them gather all the food of these good years that come, and lay up corn under the hand of Pharaoh for food, in the cities, and let them keep *it*.

36 So the food shall be for the provision of the land, against the seven years of famine, which shall be in the land of Egypt, that the land perish not by famine.

37 ¶ And the saying pleased Pharaoh and all his servants.

38 Then said Pharaoh unto his servants, Can we find *such* a man as this, in whom *is* the [1]Spirit of God?

39 Then Pharaoh said to Joseph, Forasmuch as God hath showed thee all this, there is no man of understanding, or wisdom like unto thee.

40 [b]Thou shalt be over mine house, and at thy [1,2]word shall all my people be armed, only in the king's throne will I be above thee.

41 Moreover Pharaoh said to Joseph, Behold, I have set thee over all the land of Egypt.

42 And Pharaoh took off his [1]ring from his hand, and put it upon Joseph's hand, and arrayed him in garments of fine linen, and put a golden chain about his neck.

43 So he sat him upon the [1]best chariot that he had, save one: and they cried before him, [2]Abrech, and placed him over all the land of Egypt.

44 Again Pharaoh said unto Joseph, I am Pharaoh, and without thee shall no man lift up his hand or his foot in the land of Egypt.

45 And Pharaoh called Joseph's name [1]Zaph-nath-Paaneah: and he gave him to wife Asenath the daughter of Poti-Pherah [2]Prince of On: then went Joseph abroad in the land of Egypt.

46 ¶ And Joseph *was* [1]thirty years old when he stood before Pharaoh King of Egypt: and Joseph departing from the presence of Pharaoh, went throughout all the land of Egypt.

47 And in the seven plenteous years the earth [1]brought forth store.

48 And he gathered up all the food of the seven plenteous years, which were in the land of Egypt, and laid up the food in the cities: the food of the

field, that was round about *every* city, laid he up in the same.

49 So Joseph gathered wheat, like unto the sand of the sea in multitude out of measure, until he left numbering: for *it was* without number.

50 Now unto Joseph were born [c]two sons (before the year of famine came) which Asenath the daughter of Poti-Pherah prince of On bare unto him.

51 And Joseph called the name of the firstborn Manasseh: for God, *said he*, hath made me forget all my labor and all my [1]father's household.

52 Also he called the name of the second, Ephraim: For God, *said he*, hath made me fruitful in the land of my affliction.

53 ¶ So the seven years of the plenty that was in the land of Egypt were ended.

54 [d]Then began the seven years of famine to come, according as Joseph had said: and the famine was in all lands, but in all the land of Egypt was [1]bread.

55 At the length all the land of Egypt was famished, and the people cried unto Pharaoh for bread. And Pharaoh said unto all the Egyptians, Go to Joseph: what he saith to you, do ye.

56 When the famine was upon all the land, Joseph opened all *places*, wherein *the store was*, and sold unto the Egyptians: for the famine waxed sore in the land of Egypt.

57 And all the countries [1]came to Egypt to buy corn of Joseph, because the famine was sore in all lands.

42

3 Joseph's brethren come into Egypt to buy corn. 7 He knoweth them, and trieth them. 24 Simeon is put in prison. 34 The others go to fetch Benjamin.

1 Then [1]Jacob saw that there was [2]food in Egypt, and Jacob said unto his sons, Why [3]gaze ye one upon another?

2 And he said, Behold, I have heard that there is food in Egypt, [a]Get you down thither, and buy us food thence, that we may live and not die.

3 ¶ So went Joseph's ten brethren down to buy corn of the Egyptians.

4 But Benjamin Joseph's brother, would not Jacob

Margin references:

[b] Ps. 105:21
Acts 7:10
[c] Gen. 46:20
Gen. 48:5
[d] Ps. 105:16

CHAPTER 42
[a] Acts 7:12

41:38 [1] None should be preferred to honor that have not gifts of God meet for the same.

41:40 [1] Hebrew, *mouth.*

[2] Some read, the people shall kiss thy mouth, that is shall obey thee in all things.

41:42 [1] Or, his signet.

41:43 [1] Hebrew, *second chariot.*

[2] In sign of honor: which word some expound, tender father, or father of the king, or kneel down.

41:45 [1] Or, the expounder of secrets.

[2] Or, priest.

41:46 [1] His age is mentioned both to show that his authority came

of God, and also that he suffered imprisonment and exile twelve years and more.

41:47 [1] Hebrew, *made for gatherings.*

41:51 [1] Notwithstanding that his father's house was the true Church of God: yet the company of the wicked and prosperity caused him to forget it.

41:54 [1] Or, food.

41:57 [1] Or, came to Egypt to Joseph.

42:1 [1] This story showeth plainly that all things are governed by God's providence for the profit of his Church.

[2] Or, corn.

[3] As men destitute of counsel.

send with his brethren: for he said, Lest death should ¹befall him.

5 And the sons of Israel came to buy food among them that came: for there was famine in the land of Canaan.

6 Now Joseph was governor of the land, who sold to all the people of the land: then Joseph's brethren came, and bowed their faces to the ground before him.

7 And when Joseph saw his brethren, he knew them, and ¹made himself strange toward them, and spake to them roughly, and said unto them, Whence come ye? Who answered, Out of the land of Canaan, to buy vittles.

8 (Now Joseph knew his brethren, but they knew not him.

9 And Joseph remembered the ᵇdreams, which he dreamed of them) and he said unto them, Ye are spies, *and* are come to see the ¹weakness of the land.

10 But they said unto him, Nay, my lord, but to buy vittles thy servants are come.

11 We are all one man's sons: we mean truly, and thy servants are no spies.

12 But he said unto them, Nay, but ye are come to see the weakness of the land.

13 And they said, We thy servants, are twelve brethren, the sons of one man in the land of Canaan: and behold, the youngest *is* this day with our father, and one ¹is not.

14 Again Joseph said unto them, This is it that I spake unto you, saying, Ye are spies.

15 Hereby ye shall be proved: ¹by the life of Pharaoh, ye shall not go hence, except your youngest brother come hither.

16 Send one of you which may fetch your brother, and ye shall be kept in prison, that your words may be proved, whether there be truth in you, or else *by* the life of Pharaoh ye are but spies.

17 So he put them in ward three days.

18 Then Joseph said unto them the third day, This do, and live: *for* I ¹fear God.

19 If ye be true men, let one of your brethren be bound in your prison house, and go ye, carry food *for* the famine of your houses:

20 ᶜBut bring your younger brother unto me, that your words may be tried, and that ye die not: and

ᵇ Gen. 37:5
ᶜ Gen. 35:5
ᵈ Gen. 37:21

they did so.

21 ¶ And they said one to another, ¹We have verily sinned against our brother, in that we saw the anguish of his soul, when he besought us, and we would not hear *him*: therefore is this trouble come upon us.

22 And Reuben answered them, saying, Warned I not you, saying, ᵈSin not against the child, and ye would not hear? and lo, his ¹blood is now required.

23 (And they were not aware that Joseph understood them: for he ¹spake unto them by an interpreter.)

24 Then he turned from them, and ¹wept, and turned to them again, and communed with them, and took Simeon from among them, and bound him before their eyes.

25 ¶ So Joseph commanded that they should fill their sacks with wheat, and put every man's money again in his sack, and give them vittles for the journey: and thus did he unto them.

26 And they laid their vittles upon their asses, and departed thence.

27 And as one of them opened his sack for to give his ass provender in the Inn, he espied his money: for lo, it was in his sack's mouth.

28 Then he said unto his brethren, My money is restored: for lo, it is even in my sack. And their heart ¹failed them, and they were ²astonished, and said one to another, What is this, *that* God hath done unto us?

29 ¶ And they came unto Jacob their father unto the land of Canaan, and told him all that had befallen them, saying,

30 The man *who is* lord of the land, spake roughly to us, and put us *in prison* as spies of the country.

31 And we said unto him, We are true men, *and* are no spies.

32 We be twelve brethren, sons of our father: one ¹is not, and the youngest *is* this day with our father in the land of Canaan.

33 Then the lord of the country said unto us, Hereby shall I know if ye be true men: Leave one of your brethren with me, and take *food* for the famine of your houses, and depart,

34 And bring your youngest brother unto me, that I may know that ye are no spies, but true men: *so* will I deliver you your brother, and ye shall occupy in the land.

35 ¶ And as they emptied their sacks, behold,

42:4 ¹ Hebrew, *should meet him.*
42:7 ¹ This dissembling is not to be followed, nor any particular facts of the fathers not approved by God's word.
42:9 ¹ Hebrew, *nakedness,* or, *filthiness.*
42:13 ¹ Or, is dead.
42:15 ¹ The Egyptians which were idolaters, used to swear by their king's life: but God forbiddeth to swear by any but him: yet Joseph dwelling among the wicked smelleth of their corruptions.
42:18 ¹ And therefore am true and just.
42:21 ¹ Affliction maketh men to acknowledge their faults, which otherwise they would dissemble.
42:22 ¹ God will take vengeance upon us, and measure us with our own measure.
42:23 ¹ Hebrew, *an interpreter between them.*
42:24 ¹ Though he showed himself rigorous, yet his brotherly affection remained.
42:28 ¹ Hebrew, *went out.*
² Because their conscience accused them of their sin, they thought God would have brought them to trouble by this money.
42:32 ¹ Or, cannot be found.

every man's bundle of money was in his sack: and when they and their father saw the bundles of their money, they were afraid.

36 Then Jacob their father said to them, Ye have robbed me of my children: Joseph is not, and Simeon is not, and ye will take Benjamin: all these things [1]are against [2]me.

37 Then Reuben answered his father, saying, Slay my two sons, if I bring him not to thee again: deliver him to mine hand, and I will bring him to thee again.

38 But he said, My son shall not go down with you: for his brother is dead, and he is left alone: if death come unto him by the way which ye go, then ye shall bring my gray head with sorrow unto the grave.

43

13 Jacob suffereth Benjamin to depart with his children. 14 Simeon is delivered out of prison. 30 Joseph goeth aside and weepeth.

1 Now great [1]famine *was* in the land.

2 And when they had eaten up the vittles, which they had brought from Egypt, their father said unto them, Turn again and buy us a little food.

3 And Judah answered him, saying, The man charged us by an oath, saying, [a]Never see my face, except your brother *be* with you.

4 If thou wilt send our brother with us, we will go down, and buy thee food.

5 But if thou wilt not send *him*, we will not go down: for the man said unto us, [b]Look me not in the face, except your brother *be* with you.

6 And Israel said, Wherefore dealt ye so evil with me, as to tell the man, whether ye had yet a brother or no?

7 And they answered, The man asked straightly of [1]ourselves and of our kindred, saying, Is your father yet alive? have ye *any* brother? And we told him according to [2]these words: could we know certainly that he would say, Bring your brother down?

8 Then said Judah to Israel his father, Send the boy with me, that we may rise and go, and that we may live, and not die, both we, and thou, and our children.

9 I will be surety for him: of mine hand shalt thou

CHAPTER 43
[a] Gen. 42:20
[b] Gen. 42:20
[c] Gen. 44:32
[d] Gen. 42:3

require him. [1]If I bring him not to thee, and set him before thee, [1]then let me bear the blame forever.

10 For except we had made this tarrying, doubtless by this we had returned the second time.

11 Then their father Israel said unto them, If *it must needs be* so now, do thus: take of the best fruits of the land in your vessels, and bring the man a present, a little rosin, and a little honey, [1]spices and myrrh, nuts, and almonds:

12 And take [1]double money in your hand, and the money, that was brought again in your sacks' mouths carry it again in your hand, lest it were some oversight.

13 Take also your brother and arise, *and* go again to the man.

14 And [1]God Almighty give you mercy in the sight of the man, that he may deliver you your other brother, and Benjamin: but I shall be [2]robbed of my child, as I have been.

15 Thus the men took this present, and took twice so much money in their hand with Benjamin, and rose up, and went down to Egypt, and stood before Joseph.

16 And when Joseph saw Benjamin with them, he said [1]to his steward, Bring these men home and kill meat, and make ready: for the men shall eat with me at noon.

17 And the men did as Joseph bade, and brought the men unto Joseph's house.

18 Now when the men were brought into Joseph's house, they were [1]afraid, and said, Because of the money, that came in our sack's mouths at the first time, are we brought, that he may [2]pick a quarrel against us, and [3]lay something to our charge, and bring us in bondage and our asses.

19 Therefore came they to Joseph's steward, and communed with him at the door of his house,

20 And said, O sir, [d]we came indeed down hither at the first time to buy food,

21 And as we came to an Inn and opened our sacks, behold, every man's money was in his sack's mouth, *even* our money in full weight, but we have brought it in our hands.

22 Also other money have we brought in our hands to buy food, *but* we cannot tell, who put our

---

42:36 [1] Or, light upon me.
  [2] For they seemed not to be touched with any love toward their brethren which increased his sorrow: and partly as appeareth he suspected them for Joseph.
43:1 [1] This was a great tentation to Jacob to suffer so great famine in that land where God had promised to bless him.
43:7 [1] Or, of our estate and condition.
  [2] Hebrew, *to the mouth of these words*: that is, that thing which he asked us.
43:9 [1] Hebrew, *I will sin to thee.*

43:11 [1] Or, sweet smells.
43:12 [1] When we are in necessity or danger, God forbiddeth not to use all honest means to better our estate and condition.
43:14 [1] Our chief trust ought to be in God, and not in worldly means.
  [2] He speaketh these words not so much of despair, as to make his sons more careful to bring again their brother.
43:16 [1] Or, to the ruler of his house.
43:18 [1] So the judgment of God pressed their conscience.
  [2] Hebrew, *roll himself upon us.*
  [3] Hebrew, *cast himself upon us.*

money in our sacks.

23 And he said, ¹Peace be to you, fear not: ²your God, and the God of your father hath given you that treasure in your sacks, I had your money: and he brought forth Simeon to them.

24 So the man led them into Joseph's house, and gave them water to wash their feet, and gave their asses provender.

25 And they made ready their present against Joseph came at noon, (for they heard say, that they should eat bread there.)

26 When Joseph came home, they brought the present into the house to him, which was in their hands, and bowed down to the ground before him.

27 And he asked them of *their* ¹prosperity, and said, Is your father the old man, of whom ye told me, in good health? is he yet alive?

28 Who answered, Thy servant our father is in good health, he is yet alive: and they bowed down, and made obeisance.

29 And he lifting up his eyes, beheld his brother Benjamin, his ¹mother's son, and said, Is this your younger brother of whom ye told me? And he said, God be merciful unto thee, my son.

30 And Joseph made haste (for his ¹affection was inflamed toward his brother, and sought *where* to weep) and entered into his chamber and wept there.

31 Afterward he washed his face, and came out, and refrained himself, and said, Set on ¹meat.

32 And they ¹prepared for him by himself, and for them by themselves, and for the Egyptians, which did eat with him, by themselves, because the Egyptians might not eat bread with the Hebrews: for that was an ²abomination unto the Egyptians.

33 So they sat before him: the eldest according unto his age, and the youngest according unto his youth: and the men marveled among themselves.

34 And they took meats from before him, *and* sent to them: but Benjamin's meat was five times so much as any of theirs: and they drank, ¹and had of the best drink with him.

44 15 Joseph accuseth his brother of theft.   33 Judah offereth himself to be servant for Benjamin.

1 Afterward he commanded his steward, saying, Fill the men's sacks with food, as much as they can carry, and put every man's money in his sack's mouth.

2 And ¹put my cup, *I mean*, the silver cup, in the sack's mouth of the youngest, and his corn money. And he did according to the commandment that Joseph gave *him*.

3 And in the ¹morning the men were sent away, they, and their asses.

4 And when they went out of the city not far off, Joseph said to his steward, Up, follow after the men: and when thou dost overtake them, say unto them, Wherefore have ye rewarded evil for good?

5 Is not that *the cup* wherein my lord drinketh? ¹and in the which he doth divine and prophesy? ye have done evil in so doing.

6 ¶ And when he overtook them, he said these words unto them.

7 And they answered him, Wherefore saith my lord such words? God forbid that thy servants should do such a thing.

8 Behold, the money which we found in our sacks' mouths, we brought again unto thee out of the land of Canaan: how then should we steal out of thy lord's house silver or gold?

9 With whomsoever of thy servants it be found, let him die, and we also will be my lord's bondmen.

10 And he said, Now then let it be according unto your words: he with whom it is found, shall be my servant, and ye shall be ¹blameless.

11 Then at once every man took down his sack to the ground, and everyone opened his sack.

12 And he searched, and began at the eldest, and left at the youngest: and the cup was found in Benjamin's sack.

13 Then they ¹rent their clothes, and laded every man his ass, and went again into the city.

14 ¶ So Judah and his brethren came to Joseph's house (for he *was* yet there) and they fell before him on the ground.

15 Then Joseph said unto them, What act is this, which ye have done? know ye not that such a man as I, can divine and prophesy?

16 Then said Judah, What shall we say unto my

43:23 ¹ Or, you are well.
² Notwithstanding the corruptions of Egypt, yet Joseph taught his family to fear God.
43:27 ¹ Hebrew, *peace*.
43:29 ¹ For they two only were born of Rachel.
43:30 ¹ Hebrew, *bowels*.
43:31 ¹ Hebrew, *bread*.
43:32 ¹ To signify his dignity.
² The nature of the superstitious is to condemn all others in respect of themselves.
43:34 ¹ Sometimes this word signifieth to be drunken, but here it is

meant, that they had enough, and drank of the best wine.
44:2 ¹ We may not by this example use any unlawful practices, seeing God hath commanded us to walk in simplicity.
44:3 ¹ Hebrew, *the morning shone*.
44:5 ¹ Because the people thought he could divine, he attributeth to himself that knowledge: or else he feigneth that he consulted with soothsayers for it: Which simulation is worthy to be reproved.
44:10 ¹ Hebrew, *innocent*.
44:13 ¹ To signify how greatly the thing displeased them, and how sorry they were for it.

lord? what shall we speak? and how can we justify ourselves? ¹God hath found out the wickedness of thy servants: behold, we *are* servants to my lord, both we, and he, with whom the cup is found.

17 But he answered, God forbid, that I should do so, *but* the man, with whom the cup is found, he shall be my servant, and go ye in peace unto your father.

18 ¶ Then Judah drew near unto him, and said, Oh my lord, let thy servant now speak a word in my lord's ears, and let not thy wrath be kindled against thy servant: for thou art even ¹as Pharaoh.

19 My lord asked his servants, saying, ªHave ye a father, or a brother?

20 And we answered my lord, We have a father that is old, and a young ¹child, *which he begat* in his age: and his brother is dead, and he alone is left of his mother, and his father loveth him.

21 Now thou saidest unto thy servants, Bring him unto me, that I may ¹set mine eye upon him.

22 And we answered my lord, The child cannot depart his father: for if he leave his father, *his father* would die.

23 Then saidest thou unto thy servants, ᵇExcept your younger brother come down with you, look in my face no more.

24 So when we came unto thy servant our father, and showed him what my lord had said,

25 And our father said unto us, Go again, buy us a little food.

26 Then we answered, We cannot go down, *but* if our youngest brother ¹go with us, then will we go down: for we may not see the man's face, except our youngest brother be with us.

27 Then thy servant my father said unto us, Ye know that my ¹wife bare me two *sons.*

28 And the one went out from me, and I said, Of a surety he is torn in ᶜpieces, and I saw him not since.

29 Now ye take this also away from me: if death take him, then ¹ye shall bring my gray head in sorrow to the grave.

30 Now therefore, when I come to thy servant my father, and the child be not with us (seeing that his ¹life dependeth on the *child's* life,)

31 Then when he shall see that the child *is* not *come,* he will die: so shall thy servants bring down

CHAPTER 44
ª Gen. 42:13,16
ᵇ Gen. 43:3
ᶜ Gen. 37:33
ᵈ Gen. 43:9

CHAPTER 45
ª Acts 7:13
ᵇ Gen. 50:20

the gray head of thy servant our father with sorrow to the grave.

32 Doubtless thy servant became surety for the child to my father, and, ᵈIf I bring him not unto thee again, then I will bear the blame unto my father forever.

33 Now therefore, I pray thee, let me thy servant abide for the child, *as* a servant to my lord, and let the child go up with his brethren.

34 For ¹how can I go up to my father: if the child *be* not with me, unless I would see the evil that shall come on my father.

45

1 *Joseph maketh himself known to his brethren.* 8 *He showeth that all was done by God's providence.* 18 *Pharaoh commandeth him to send for his father.* 24 *Joseph exhorteth his brethren to concord.*

1 Then Joseph could not refrain himself before all that stood by him, but he cried, ¹Have forth every man from me. And there tarried not one with him, while Joseph uttered himself unto his brethren.

2 And he wept, and cried, *so* that the Egyptians heard: the house of Pharaoh heard also.

3 Then Joseph said unto his brethren, I am Joseph: doth my father yet live? But his brethren could not answer him, for they were astonished at his presence.

4 Again, Joseph said to his brethren, Come near, I pray you, to me. And they came near. And he said, ªI am Joseph your brother, whom ye sold into Egypt.

5 Now therefore be not ¹sad, neither grieved with yourselves, that ye sold me hither: ᵇFor God did send me before you for your preservation.

6 For now two years of famine *have been* through the land, and five years *are* behind, wherein neither *shall be* earing nor harvest.

7 Wherefore God sent me before you to preserve your posterity in this land, and to save you alive by a great deliverance.

8 Now then you sent not me hither, but ¹God, who hath made me a father unto Pharaoh, and lord of all his house, and ruler throughout all the land of Egypt.

9 Haste you and go up to my father, and tell him, Thus saith thy son Joseph, God hath made me lord

44:16 ¹ If we see no evident cause of our affliction, let us look to the secret counsel of God, who punisheth us justly for our sins.
44:18 ¹ Equal in authority or, next unto the king.
44:20 ¹ Hebrew, *child of his old age.*
44:21 ¹ Or, that I may see him.
44:26 ¹ Hebrew, *be with us.*
44:27 ¹ Rachel bare to Jacob, Joseph and Benjamin.
44:29 ¹ Ye shall cause me to die for sorrow.

44:30 ¹ Hebrew, *his soul is bound to his soul.*
44:34 ¹ Meaning, he had rather remain their prisoner, than to return and see his father in heaviness.
45:1 ¹ Not that he was ashamed of his kindred, but that he would cover his brethren's fault.
45:5 ¹ This example teacheth that we must by all means comfort them, which are truly humbled and wounded for their sins.
45:8 ¹ Albeit God detest sin, yet he turneth man's wickedness to serve to his glory.

of all Egypt: come down to me, tarry not.

10　And thou shalt dwell in the land of Goshen, and shalt be near me, thou and thy children, and thy children's children, and thy sheep, and thy beasts, and all that thou hast.

11　Also I will nourish thee there (for yet *remain* five years of famine) lest thou perish through poverty, thou and thy household, and all that thou hast.

12　And behold, your eyes do see, and the eyes of my brother Benjamin, that [1]my mouth speaketh to you.

13　Therefore tell my father of all mine honor in Egypt, and of all that ye have seen, and make haste, and bring my father hither.

14　Then he fell on his brother Benjamin's neck, and wept, and Benjamin wept on his neck.

15　Moreover, he kissed all his brethren, and wept upon them: and afterward his brethren talked with him.

16　¶ And the [1]tidings came to Pharaoh's house, so that they said, Joseph's brethren are come: and it pleased Pharaoh well, and his servants.

17　Then Pharaoh said to Joseph, Say to thy brethren, This do ye, laid your beasts and depart, go to the land of Canaan,

18　And take your father, and your household, and come to me, and I will give you the [1]best of the land of Egypt, and ye shall eat of the [2]fat of the land.

19　And I command thee, Thus do ye, take you chariots out of the land of Egypt for your children, and for your wives, and bring your father and come.

20　Also [1]regard not your stuff: for the best of all the land of Egypt is yours.

21　And the children of Israel did so: and Joseph gave them chariots according to the commandment of Pharaoh: he gave them vittles also for the journey.

22　He gave them all, none except, change of raiment: but unto Benjamin he gave three hundred pieces of silver, and five suits of raiment.

23　And unto his father [1]likewise he sent ten he asses laden with the best things of Egypt, and ten she asses laden with wheat, and bread and meat for his father by the way.

24　So sent he his brethren away, and they departed: and he said unto them, [1]Fall not out by the way.

25　Then they went up from Egypt, and came unto the land of Canaan, unto Jacob their father,

CHAPTER 46
a Josh. 24:4
Ps. 105:23
Isa. 52:4
b Exod. 1:2
Exod. 6:24
Num. 26:5
1 Chron. 5:1
c Exod. 6:15
1 Chron. 4:24
d 1 Chron. 6:1

26　And told him, saying, Joseph *is* yet alive, and he also is governor over all the land of Egypt, and *Jacob's* heart [1]failed: for he believed them not.

27　And they told him all the words of Joseph, which he had said unto them: but when he saw the chariots, which Joseph had sent to carry him, then the spirit of Jacob their father revived.

28　And Israel said, *I have* enough: Joseph my son *is* yet alive: I will go and see him yet I die.

46

2 God assureth Jacob of his journey into Egypt.　27 The number of his family when he went into Egypt.　29 Joseph meeteth his father.　34 He teacheth his brethren what to answer to Pharaoh.

1　Then Israel took his journey with all that he had, and came to Beersheba, and [1]offered sacrifice unto the God of his father Isaac.

2　And God spake unto Israel in a vision by night, saying, Jacob, Jacob. Who answered, I am here.

3　Then he said, I am God, the God of thy father, fear not to go down into Egypt: for I will there make of thee a great nation.

4　I will [1]go down with thee into Egypt, and I will also [2]bring thee up again, and Joseph shall [3]put his hand upon thine eyes.

5　Then Jacob rose up from Beersheba: and the sons of Israel carried Jacob their father, and their children, and their wives in the chariots, which Pharaoh had sent to carry him.

6　And they took their cattle, and their goods, which they had gotten in the land of Canaan, and came into Egypt, *both* *a*Jacob and all his seed with him.

7　His sons and his sons' sons with him, his daughters, and his sons' daughters, and all his seed brought he with him into Egypt.

8　¶ And these are the names of the children of Israel, which came into Egypt, *even* Jacob and his sons: *b*Reuben, Jacob's firstborn.

9　And the sons of Reuben: Hanoch, and Pallu, and Hezron, and Carmi.

10　¶ And the sons of *c*Simeon: Jemuel, and Jamin, and Ohad, and Jachin, and Zohar, and Shaul the son of a Canaanitish woman.

11　¶ Also the sons of *d*Levi: Gershon, Kohath, and Merari.

45:12　[1] That is, that I speak in your own language, and have none interpreter.

45:16　[1] Hebrew, *voice.*

45:18　[1] The most plentiful ground.

　　[2] The chiefest fruits and commodities.

45:20　[1] Hebrew, *let not your eyes spare your vessel.*

45:23　[1] Or, he sent as much, to wit, silver as verse 22, and ten asses.

45:24　[1] Seeing he had remitted the fault done toward him, he would

not that they should accuse one another.

45:26　[1] As one between hope and fear.

46:1　[1] Whereby he both signifieth, that he worshipped the true God, and also that he kept in his heart the possession of that land from whence present necessity drove him.

46:4　[1] Conducting thee by my power.

　　[2] In thy posterity.

　　[3] Shall shut thine eyes when thou diest: which appertained to him that was most dearest, or chief of the kindred.

12 ¶ Also the sons of ᵉJudah: Er, and Onan, and Shelah, and Perez, and Zerah: (but Er and Onan died in the land of Canaan.) And the sons of Perez *were* Hezron and Hamul.

13 ¶ Also the sons of ᶠIssachar: Tola, and Puvah, and Job, and Shimron.

14 ¶ Also the sons of Zebulun: Sered, and Elon, and Jahleel.

15 These be the sons of Leah, which she bare unto Jacob in Padan Aram, with his daughter Dinah. All the ¹souls of his sons and his daughters *were* thirty and three.

16 Also the sons of Gad: Ziphion, and Haggi, Shuni, and Ezbon, Eri, and Arodi, and Areli.

17 ¶ Also the sons of ᵍAsher: Jimnah, and Ishuah, and Isui, and Beriah, and Serah their sister. And the sons of Beriah: and Heber, Malchiel.

18 These are the children of Zilpah, whom Laban gave to Leah his daughter: and these she bare unto Jacob, *even* sixteen souls.

19 The sons of Rachel Jacob's wife *were* Joseph, and Benjamin.

20 ¶ And unto Joseph in the land of Egypt were born Manasseh, and Ephraim, which ʰAsenath the daughter of Poti-Pherah prince of On bare unto him.

21 ¶ Also the sons of ᶦBenjamin: Belah, and Becher, and Ashbel, and Gera, Naaman, Ehi, and Rosh, Muppim, and Huppim, and Ard.

22 These are the sons of Rachel, which were born unto Jacob, fourteen souls in all.

23 ¶ Also the sons of Dan: Hushim.

24 ¶ Also the sons of Naphtali: Jahzeel, and Guni, and Jezer, and Shillem.

25 These are the sons of Bilhah, which Laban gave unto Rachel his daughter, and she bare these unto Jacob, in all seven souls.

26 All the ʲsouls, that came with Jacob into Egypt, which came out of his ¹loins (besides Jacob's sons' wives) *were* in the whole, threescore and six souls.

27 Also the sons of Joseph, which were born him in Egypt, *were* two souls: *so that* all the souls of the house of Jacob, which came into Egypt, *are* seventy.

28 ¶ Then he sent Judah before him unto Joseph, to ¹direct his way unto Goshen, and they came into the land of Goshen.

29 Then Joseph ¹made ready his chariot, and went

up to Goshen to meet Israel his father, and presented himself unto him, and fell on his neck and wept upon his neck a ²good while.

30 And Israel said unto Joseph, Now let me die since I have seen thy face, and that thou art yet alive.

31 Then Joseph said to his brethren, and to his father's house, I will go up and show Pharaoh, and tell him, My brethren and my father's house, which were in the land of Canaan, are come unto me.

32 And the men are ¹sheepherders, and because they are sheepherders, they have brought their sheep and their cattle, and all that they have.

33 And if Pharaoh call you, and ask you, What is your trade?

34 That ye shall say, Thy servants are men occupied about cattle, from our childhood even unto this time, both we and our fathers: that ye may dwell in the land of Goshen: for every sheep keeper is an ¹abomination unto the Egyptians.

47 7 *Jacob cometh before Pharaoh, and telleth him his age.* 11 *The land of Goshen is given him.* 22 *The idolatrous priests have living of the King.* 28 *Jacob's age when he dieth.*

1 Then came Joseph and told Pharaoh, and said, My father, and my brethren, and their sheep, and their cattle, and all that they have, are come out of the land of Canaan, and behold, they are in the land of Goshen.

2 And Joseph took part of his brethren, *even* ¹five men, and presented them unto Pharaoh.

3 When Pharaoh said unto his brethren, What is your trade? And they answered Pharaoh, Thy servants *are* shepherds, both we and our fathers.

4 They said moreover unto Pharaoh, For to sojourn in the land are we come: for thy servants have no pasture for *their* sheep, so sore is the famine in the land of Canaan, Now therefore, we pray thee: let thy servants dwell in the land of Goshen.

5 Then spake Pharaoh to Joseph, saying, Thy father and thy brethren are come unto thee.

6 The ¹land of Egypt is before thee: in the best place of the land make thy father and thy brethren to dwell: let them dwell in the land of Goshen: and if thou knowest that there be men of activity among them, make them rulers over my cattle.

7 Joseph also brought Jacob his father, and set him before Pharaoh. And Jacob ¹saluted Pharaoh.

ᵉ 1 Chron. 2:3 / 1 Chron. 9:21 / Gen. 38:3
ᶠ 1 Chron. 7:1
ᵍ 2 Chron. 7:30
ʰ Gen. 41:50
ᶦ 1 Chron. 7:6 / 1 Chron. 8:1
ʲ Deut. 10:25

46:15 ¹ Or, persons.
46:26 ¹ Hebrew, *thighs*.
46:28 ¹ Or, to prepare him a place.
46:29 ¹ Hebrew, *bound his chariot*.
  ² Hebrew, *yet*, or *still*.
46:32 ¹ He was not ashamed of his father and kindred, though they were of base condition.

46:34 ¹ God suffereth the world to hate his, that they may forsake the filth of the world, and cleave to him.
47:2 ¹ That the king might be assured they were come, and see what manner of people they were.
47:6 ¹ Joseph's great modesty appeareth in that he would enterprise nothing without the king's commandment.
47:7 ¹ Hebrew, *blessed*.

8 Then Pharaoh said unto Jacob, ¹How old art thou?

9 And Jacob said unto Pharaoh, The whole time of my ªpilgrimage *is* an hundred and thirty years: few and evil have the days of my life been, and I have not attained unto the years of the life of my fathers, in the days of their pilgrimages.

10 And Jacob ¹took leave of Pharaoh, and departed from the presence of Pharaoh.

11 ¶ And Joseph placed his father, and his brethren, and gave them possession in the land of Egypt, in the best of the land, *even* in the land of ¹Rameses, as Pharaoh had commanded.

12 ¶ And Joseph nourished his father, and his brethren, and all his father's household with bread ¹even to the young children.

13 ¶ Now there was no bread in all the land; for the famine *was* exceeding sore: so that the land of Egypt, and the land of Canaan were ¹famished by reason of the famine.

14 And Joseph gathered all the money, that was found in the land of Egypt, and in the land of Canaan, for the corn which they bought: and ¹Joseph laid up the money in Pharaoh's house.

15 So when money failed in the land of Egypt, and in the land of Canaan, then all the Egyptians came unto Joseph and said, Give us bread: for why should we die before thee? for *our* money is spent.

16 Then said Joseph, Bring your cattle, and I will give you for your cattle, if *your* money be spent.

17 So they brought their cattle unto Joseph, and Joseph gave them bread for the horses, and for the flocks of sheep, and for the herds of cattle, and for the asses: so he fed them with bread for all their cattle that year.

18 But when the year was ended, they came unto him the second year, and said unto him, We will not hide from my lord, that since our money is spent; my lord hath the herds of the cattle; there is nothing left in the sight of my lord, but our bodies and our ground.

19 Why shall we perish in thy sight, both we and our ¹land? buy us and our land for bread, and we and our land will be bound to Pharaoh: therefore give us seed, that we may live and not die, and that the land go not to waste.

CHAPTER 47
ª Heb. 11:9,13
ᵇ Gen. 24:2

20 So Joseph bought all the land of Egypt for Pharaoh: for the Egyptians sold every man his ground, because the famine was sore upon them: so the land became Pharaoh's.

21 And he ¹removed the people unto the cities, ²from one side of Egypt even to the other.

22 Only the land of the Priests bought he not: for the Priests had an ordinary of Pharaoh, and they did eat their ordinary, which Pharaoh gave them: wherefore they sold not their ground.

23 Then Joseph said unto the people, Behold, I have bought you this day, and your land for Pharaoh: lo, *here is* seed for you: sow therefore the ground.

24 And of the increase ye shall give the fifth part unto Pharaoh, and four parts shall be yours for seed of the field, and for your meat, and for them of your households, and for your children to eat.

25 And they answered, Thou hast saved our lives: let us find grace in the sight of my lord, and we will be Pharaoh's servants.

26 And Joseph made it a law over the land of Egypt unto this day, *that* Pharaoh should have the fifth *part*, ¹except the land of the Priests only, which was not Pharaoh's.

27 ¶ And Israel dwelt in the land of Egypt, in the country of Goshen; and they had their possessions therein, and grew, and multiplied exceedingly.

28 Moreover, Jacob lived in the land of Egypt seventeen years: so the whole age of Jacob *was* an hundred forty and seven years.

29 Now when the time drew near that Israel must die, he called his son Joseph, and said unto him, If I have now found grace in thy sight, ᵇput thine hand now under my thigh, and deal mercifully and truly with me: bury me not, I pray thee, in Egypt.

30 But when I shall ¹sleep with my fathers, thou shalt carry me out of Egypt, and bury me in their burial. And he answered, I will do as thou hast said.

31 Then he said, swear unto me. And he sware unto him. And Israel ¹worshipped towards the bed's head.

48 *1 Joseph with his two sons visiteth his sick father. 3 Jacob rehearseth God's promise. 5 He receiveth Joseph's sons as his. 19 He preferreth the younger.*

1 Again after this, one said to Joseph, Lo, thy

47:8 ¹ Hebrew, *how many days are the years of thy life?*
47:10 ¹ Hebrew, *blessed.*
47:11 ¹ Which was a city in the country of Goshen, Exod. 1:11.
47:12 ¹ Some read, that he fed them as little babes, because they could not provide for themselves against that famine.
47:13 ¹ Hebrew, *brought to an extremity,* or *at their wit's end.*
47:14 ¹ Wherein he both declareth his fidelity toward the King, and his mind free from covetousness.
47:19 ¹ For except the ground be tilled and sown, it perisheth, and is as it were dead.

47:21 ¹ By this changing they signified that they had nothing of their own, but received all of the king's liberality.
       ² Hebrew, *end of the border.*
47:26 ¹ Pharaoh in providing for Idolatrous priests, shall be a condemnation to all them which neglect the true ministers of God's word.
47:30 ¹ Hereby he protested that he died in the faith of his fathers, teaching his children to hope for the promised land.
47:31 ¹ He rejoiced that Joseph had promised him, and setting himself up upon his pillow, praised God. Read 1 Chron. 29:10.

father is sick: then he took with him his ¹two sons, Manasseh and Ephraim.

2 Also one told Jacob, and said, Behold thy son Joseph is come to thee, and Israel took his strength unto him and sat upon the bed.

3 Then Jacob said unto Joseph, God ¹almighty appeared unto me at ªLuz in the land of Canaan, and blessed me,

4 And said unto me, Behold, I will make thee fruitful, and will multiply thee, and will make a great number of people of thee, and will give this land unto thy seed after thee for an ¹everlasting possession.

5 ¶ And now thy ᵇtwo sons, Manasseh and Ephraim, which are born unto thee in the land of Egypt before I came to thee into Egypt, shall be mine, as Reuben and Simeon are mine.

6 But thy lineage, which thou hast begotten after them, shall be thine: they shall be called after the names of their brethren in their inheritance.

7 Now when I came from Padan, Rachel ᶜdied upon mine hand in the land of Canaan, by the way when *there was* but half a day's journey of ground to come to Ephrath: and I buried her there in the way to Ephrath: the same *is* Bethlehem.

8 Then Israel beheld Joseph's sons and said, Whose are these?

9 And Joseph said unto his father, They are my sons, which ¹God hath given me here. Then he said, I pray thee, bring them to me, that I may bless them:

10 (For the eyes of Israel were dim for age, so that he could not *well* see) Then he caused them to come to him, and he kissed them and embraced them.

11 And Israel said unto Joseph, I had not thought to have seen thy face: yet lo, God hath showed me also thy seed.

12 And Joseph took them away from his knees, and did reverence ¹down to the ground.

13 Then took Joseph them both, Ephraim in his right hand toward Israel's left hand, and Manasseh in his left hand toward Israel's right hand, so he brought *them* unto him.

14 But Israel stretched out his right hand, and laid it on ¹Ephraim's head which was the younger, and his left hand upon Manasseh's head (directing his hands of purpose) for Manasseh *was* the elder.

CHAPTER 48
ª Gen. 28:13
ᵇ Gen. 41:50
ᶜ Gen. 35:19
ᵈ Heb. 11:21
ᵉ Gen. 34:25

CHAPTER 49
ª Gen. 32:22
1 Chron. 5:1

15 ¶ ᵈAlso he blesseth Joseph, and said, The God, before whom my fathers, Abraham and Isaac did walk, the God which hath fed me all my life long, unto this day, *bless thee.*

16 The ¹Angel, which hath delivered me from all evil, bless the children, and let my ²name be named upon them, and the name of my fathers Abraham and Isaac, that they may grow as fish into a multitude in the midst of the earth.

17 But when Joseph saw that his father laid his right hand upon the head of Ephraim, it ¹displeased him: and he stayed his father's hand to remove it from Ephraim's head to Manasseh's head.

18 And Joseph said unto his father, Not so, my father: for this is the eldest: put thy right hand upon his head.

19 But his father refused, and said, I know well, my son, I know well: he shall be also a people, and he shall be great likewise: but his younger brother shall be greater than he, and his seed shall be full of nations.

20 So he blessed them that day, and said, In thee Israel shall bless, and say, God make thee as ¹Ephraim and as Manasseh, and he set Ephraim before Manasseh.

21 Then Israel said unto Joseph, Behold, I die, and God shall be with you, and bring you again unto the land of ¹your fathers.

22 Moreover, I have given unto thee one portion above thy brethren, which ¹I got out of the hand of the Amorite by my ᶜsword and by my bow.

49 *1 Jacob blesseth all his sons by name. 10 He telleth them that Christ shall come out of Judah. 29 He will be buried with his fathers. 33 He dieth.*

1 Then Jacob called his sons, and said, Gather yourselves together, that I may tell you what shall come to you in the ¹last days.

2 Gather yourselves together, and hear, ye sons of Jacob, and hearken unto Israel your father.

3 ¶ Reuben mine eldest son, thou art my ¹might, and the beginning of my strength, ²the excellency of dignity, and the excellency of power:

4 *Thou wast* light as water: thou shalt not be excellent, because ªthou wentest up to thy father's

---

48:1 ¹ Joseph more esteemeth that his children should be received into Jacob's family, which was the Church of God, than to enjoy all the treasures of Egypt.
48:3 ¹ Or, all sufficient.
48:4 ¹ Which is true in the carnal Israel unto the coming of Christ, and in the spiritual forever.
48:9 ¹ The faithful acknowledge all benefits come of God's free mercies.
48:12 ¹ Hebrew, *his face to the ground.*
48:14 ¹ God's judgments is oft times contrary to man's, and he preferreth that, which man despiseth.

48:16 ¹ This Angel must be understood of Christ, as Gen. 31:13 and 32:1.
  ² Let them be taken as my children.
48:17 ¹ Joseph faileth in binding God's grace to the order of nature.
48:20 ¹ In whom God's graces should manifestly appear.
48:21 ¹ Which they had by faith in the promise.
48:22 ¹ By my children whom God spared for my sake.
49:1 ¹ When God shall bring you out of Egypt, and because that he speaketh of the Messiah, he nameth it the last days.
49:3 ¹ Begotten in my youth.
  ² If thou hadst not lost thy birthright by thine offense.

bed: [1]then diddest thou defile my bed, *thy dignity* is gone.

5 ¶ Simeon and Levi, brethren *in evil,* [1]the instruments of cruelty *are* in their habitations.

6 Into their secret let not my soul come: my [1]glory be not thou joined with their assembly: for in their wrath they slew a [2]man, and in their self-will they dug down a wall.

7 Cursed be their wrath, for it was fierce, and their rage, for it was cruel: I will [1]divide them in Jacob, and scatter them in Israel.

8 ¶ Thou Judah, thy brethren shall praise thee: thy hand *shall be* in the neck of thine enemies: thy father's son shall [1]bow down before unto thee.

9 Judah *as* a Lion's whelp shalt thou come up from the spoil, my son. He shall lie down *and* couch a Lion, and as a Lioness: [1]Who shall stir him up?

10 The [1]Sceptre shall not depart from Judah, nor a Lawgiver from between his feet, until [2]Shiloh come, and the people *shall be* gathered unto him.

11 He shall bind his Ass foal unto the [1]vine, and his ass's colt unto the best vine. He shall wash his garment in wine, and his cloak in the blood of grapes.

12 His eyes *shall be* red with wine, and his teeth white with milk.

13 ¶ Zebulun shall dwell by the seaside, and he *shall be* an haven for ships: and his border *shall be* unto Sidon.

14 ¶ Issachar *shall be* [1,2]a strong ass, couching down between two burdens:

15 And he shall see that rest is good, and that the land is pleasant, and he shall bow his shoulder to bear, and shall be subject unto tribute.

16 ¶ Dan [1]shall judge his people as one of the tribes of Israel.

17 Dan shall be a [1]serpent by the way, an adder by the path, biting the horse heels, so that his rider shall fall backward.

18 [1]O Lord, I have waited for thy salvation.

19 ¶ Gad, a host of men shall overcome him, but

[b] Gen. 47:30

he shall overcome at the last.

20 ¶ Concerning Asher, his [1]bread *shall be* fat, and he shall give pleasures for a king.

21 ¶ Naphtali *shall be* a hind let go, giving [1]goodly words.

22 ¶ Joseph *shall be* [1]a fruitful bough, *even* a fruitful bough by the well side: the [2]small boughs shall turn upon the wall:

23 [1]And the archers grieved him, and shot *against him,* and hated him.

24 But his bow abode strong, and the hands of his arms were strengthened, by the hands of the mighty God of Jacob, of whom *was* the feeder *appointed* by the [1]stone of Israel,

25 *Even* by the God of thy father, who shall help thee, and by the almighty, who shall bless thee with heavenly blessings from above, with blessings of the deep that lieth beneath, with blessings of the breasts, and of the womb.

26 The blessings of thy father shall be [1]stronger than the blessings of mine elders: unto the end of the hills of the world they shall be on the head of Joseph, and on the top of the head of him that was [2]separated from his brethren.

27 ¶ Benjamin shall raven *as* a wolf: in the morning he shall devour the prey, and at night he shall divide the spoil.

28 ¶ All these are the twelve tribes of Israel, and thus their father spake unto them, and blessed them: every one of them blessed he with a several blessing.

29 And he charged them and said unto them, I am ready to be gathered unto my people: [b]bury me with my fathers in the cave, that is in the field of Ephron the Hittite,

30 In the cave that is in the field of Machpelah, besides Mamre in the land of Canaan: which *cave* Abraham bought with the field of Ephron the Hittite for a possession to bury in.

31 There they buried Abraham and Sarah his wife: there they buried Isaac and Rebekah his wife:

49:4 [1] Or, it ceased to be my bed.

49:5 [1] Or, their swords were instruments of violence.

49:6 [1] Or, tongue: meaning that he neither consented to them in word nor thought.

[2] The Shechemites, Gen. 34:26.

49:7 [1] For Levi had no part, and Simeon was under Judah, Josh. 19:1, till God gave them the place of the Amalekites, 1 Chron. 4:43.

49:8 [1] As was verified in David and Christ.

49:9 [1] His enemies shall so fear him.

49:10 [1] Or, Kingdom.

[2] Which is Christ the Messiah, the giver of prosperity who shall call the Gentiles to salvation.

49:11 [1] A country most abundant with vines and pastures is promised him.

49:14 [1] Hebrew, *an ass of great bones.*

[2] His force shall be great, but he shall want courage to resist his enemies.

49:16 [1] Shall have the honor of a tribe.

49:17 [1] That is, full of subtlety.

49:18 [1] Seeing the miseries that his posterity should fall into, he bursteth out in prayer to God to remedy it.

49:20 [1] He shall abound in corn and pleasant fruits.

49:21 [1] Overcoming more by fair words than by force.

49:22 [1] Hebrew, *a son of increase.*

[2] Hebrew, *daughters.*

49:23 [1] As his brethren when they were his enemies, Potiphar and others.

49:24 [1] That is God.

49:26 [1] Inasmuch as he was more near to the accomplishment of the promise, and it had been more often confirmed.

[2] Either in dignity, or when he was sold from his brethren.

and there I buried Leah.

32 The purchase of the field and the cave that is therein, *was bought* of the children of Heth.

33 Thus Jacob made an end of giving charge to his sons, and [1]plucked his feet into the bed, and gave up the ghost, and was gathered to his people.

50

1 Jacob is buried.   19 Joseph forgiveth his brethren.   23 He seeth his children's children.   26 He dieth.

1 Then Joseph fell upon his father's face and wept upon him, and kissed him.

2 And Joseph commanded his servants the [1]physicians to embalm his father, and the physicians embalmed Israel.

3 So forty days were accomplished (for so long did the days of them that were embalmed last) and the Egyptians bewailed him [1]seventy days.

4 And when the days of his mourning were past, Joseph spake to the house of Pharaoh, saying, If I have now found favor in your eyes, speak, I pray you, in the ears, of Pharaoh, and say,

5 My father made me *a*swear saying, Lo, I die, bury me in my grave, which I have made me in the land of Canaan: now therefore let me go, I pray thee, and bury my father, and I will come again.

6 Then Pharaoh said, Go up and bury thy father, [1]as he made thee to swear.

7 ¶ So Joseph went up to bury his father, and with him went all the servants of Pharaoh, *both* the elders of his house, and all the elders of the land of Egypt,

8 Likewise all the house of Joseph, and his brethren, and his father's house: only their children, and their sheep, and their cattle left they in the land of Goshen.

9 And there went up with him both chariots and horsemen: and they were an exceeding great company.

10 And they came to [1]Goren Atad, which is beyond Jordan, and there they made a great and exceeding sore lamentation: and he mourned for his father seven days.

11 And when the Canaanites the inhabitants of the land saw the mourning in Goren Atad, they said, This is a great mourning unto the Egyptians: wherefore the name thereof was called [1]Abel Mizraim, which is beyond Jordan.

12 So his sons did unto him, according as he had

CHAPTER 50
a Gen. 47:29
b Acts 7:26
c Gen. 23:16
d Gen. 45:5
e Num. 32:39
f Heb. 11:22
g Exod. 13:19

commanded them:

13 [b]For his sons carried him into the land of Canaan, and buried him in the cave of the field of Machpelah, which *cave* [c]Abraham bought with the field, to be a [1]place to bury in, of Ephron the Hittite beside Mamre.

14 ¶ Then Joseph returned into Egypt, he and his brethren, and all that went up with him to bury his father, after that he had buried his father.

15 And when Joseph's brethren saw that their father was dead, they said, [1]It may be that Joseph will hate us, and will pay us again all the evil which we did unto him.

16 Therefore they sent unto Joseph, saying, Thy father commanded before his death, saying,

17 Thus shall ye say unto Joseph, Forgive now, I pray thee, the trespass of thy brethren, and their sin: for they rewarded thee evil. And now, we pray thee, forgive the trespass of the servants of thy father's [1]God. And Joseph wept, when [2]they spake unto him.

18 Also his brethren came unto him, and fell down before his face, and said, Behold, we be thy servants.

19 To whom Joseph said, [d]Fear not: for [1]am not I under [2]God?

20 When ye thought evil against me, God disposed it to good, that he might bring to pass, as it is this day, and save much people alive.

21 Fear not now therefore, I will nourish you, and your children: and he comforted them, and spake [1]kindly unto them.

22 ¶ So Joseph dwelt in Egypt, he, and his father's house: and Joseph lived an [1]hundred and ten years.

23 [e]And Joseph saw Ephraim's children, even unto the third generation: also the sons of Machir the son of Manasseh were brought upon Joseph's knees.

24 And Joseph said unto his brethren, [f]I am ready to die, and God will surely visit you, and bring you out of this land, unto the land which he sware unto Abraham, unto Isaac, and unto Jacob.

25 And Joseph took an oath of the children of Israel, saying, [g,1]God will surely visit you, and ye shall carry my bones hence.

26 So Joseph died, when he was an hundred and ten years old: and they embalmed him, and put him in a chest in Egypt.

49:33 [1] Whereby is signified how quietly he died.
50:2 [1] He meaneth them that embalmed the dead and buried them.
50:3 [1] They were more excessive in lamenting than the faithful.
50:6 [1] The very infidels would have oaths performed.
50:10 [1] Or, the corn floor of Atad.
50:11 [1] Or, the lamentation of the Egyptians.
50:13 [1] Or, a possession.
50:15 [1] An evil conscience is never fully at rest.
50:17 [1] Meaning, that they which have one God should be joined

in most sure love.
[2] Or, the messenger.
50:19 [1] Or, am I in God's stead, meaning to take vengeance.
[2] Who by the good success seemeth to remit it, and therefore it ought not to be revenged by me.
50:21 [1] Hebrew, *to their heart.*
50:22 [1] Who, notwithstanding he bare rule in Egypt about fourscore years, yet was joined with the church of God in faith and religion.
50:25 [1] He speaketh this by the spirit of prophecy, exhorting his brethren to have full trust in God's promise for their deliverance.

THE SECOND BOOK OF MOSES,

CALLED

EXODUS

1 *2 The children of Jacob that came into Egypt.   8 The new Pharaoh oppresseth them.   12 The providence of God toward them.   15 The King's commandment to the midwives.   22 The sons of the Hebrews are commanded to be cast into the river.*

1 Now [a,1]these are the names of the children of Israel, which came into Egypt (every man and his household came *thither* with Jacob)

2 Reuben, Simeon, Levi, and Judah,

3 Issachar, Zebulun, and Benjamin,

4 Dan, and Naphtali, Gad, and Asher.

5 So all the [1]souls, that came out of the loins of Jacob, were [b]seventy souls: Joseph was in Egypt already.

6 Now Joseph died and all his brethren, and that whole generation.

7 ¶ And the [c]children of Israel [1]brought forth fruit and increased in abundance, and were multiplied, and were exceeding mighty, so that the [2]land was full of them.

8 Then there rose up a new King in Egypt, who [1]knew not Joseph.

9 And he said unto his people, Behold, the people of the children of Israel *are* greater, and mightier than we.

10 Come, let us work wisely with them, lest they multiply, and it come to pass, that if there be war, they join themselves also unto our enemies, and fight against us, and [1,2]get them out of the land.

11 Therefore did they set taskmasters over them, to keep them under with burdens: and they built the cities Pithom and Raamses for the [1]treasures of Pharaoh.

12 But the more they vexed them, the more they multiplied and grew: therefore [1]they were more

grieved against the children of Israel.

13 Wherefore the Egyptians by cruelty caused the children of Israel to serve.

14 Thus they made them weary of their lives by sore labor in clay and in brick, and in all work in the field, with all manner of bondage, [1]which they laid upon them most cruelly.

15 ¶ Moreover the King of Egypt commanded the midwives of the Hebrew women (of which the one's name was [1]Shiphrah, and the name of the other Puah)

16 And said, When ye do the office of a midwife to the women of the Hebrews, and see them on their [1]stools, if it be a son, then ye shall kill him: but if it be a daughter, then let her live.

17 Notwithstanding the midwives feared God, and did not as the King of Egypt commanded them, but preserved alive the men children.

18 Then the King of Egypt called for the midwives, and said unto them, Why have ye done thus, and have preserved alive the men children?

19 And the midwives answered Pharaoh, Because the Hebrew [1]women *are* not as the women of Egypt: for they are lively, and are delivered ere the midwives come at them.

20 God therefore prospered the midwives, and the people multiplied, and were very mighty.

21 And because the midwives feared God, therefore he [1]made them houses.

22 Then Pharaoh charged all his people, saying, Every man-child that is born, [1]cast ye into the river, but reserve every maid-child alive.

2 *2 Moses is born and cast into the flags.   5 He is taken up of Pharaoh's daughter and kept.   12 He killeth*

1:1 [1] Moses describeth the wonderful order that God observeth in performing his promise to Abraham, Gen. 15:14.

1:5 [1] Or, persons.

1:7 [1] Or, did grow.

[2] He meaneth the country of Goshen.

1:8 [1] He considered not how God had preserved Egypt for Joseph's sake.

1:10 [1] Into Canaan, and so we shall lose our commodity.

[2] Or, go up out of the land.

1:11 [1] Or, corn and provision.

1:12 [1] The more that God blesseth his, the more doth the wicked envy them.

1:14 [1] Hebrew, *wherewith they served themselves of them by cruelty.*

1:15 [1] These seem to have been the chief of the rest.

1:16 [1] Or, seats whereupon they sat in travail.

1:19 [1] Their disobedience herein was lawful, but their dissembling evil.

1:21 [1] That is, God increased the families of the Israelites by their means.

1:22 [1] When tyrants cannot prevail by craft, they burst forth into open rage.

the Egyptian.   15 *He fleeth and marrieth a wife.*   23 *The Israelites cry unto the Lord.*

1 Then there went a [1]man of the house of Levi, and took *to wife* a daughter of Levi.

2 And the woman conceived and bare a son: and when she saw that he was fair, [a]she hid him three months.

3 But when she could no longer hide him, she took for him an ark *made* of reed, and daubed it with slime and with pitch, and [1]laid the child therein, and put *it* among the bulrushes by the river's brink.

4 Now his sister stood afar off, to wit what would come of him.

5 ¶ Then the daughter of Pharaoh came down to wash her in the river, and her maidens walked by the river's side: and when she saw the ark among the bulrushes, she sent her maid to fetch it.

6 Then she opened it, and saw it was a child, and behold, the babe wept: so she had compassion on it, and said, This is one of the Hebrews' children.

7 Then said his sister unto Pharaoh's daughter, Shall I go and call unto thee a nurse of the Hebrew women to nurse thee the child?

8 And Pharaoh's daughter said to her, Go. So the maid went and called the [1]child's mother.

9 To whom Pharaoh's daughter said, Take this child away, and nurse it for me, and I will reward thee. Then the woman took the child, and nursed him.

10 Now the child grew, and she brought him unto Pharaoh's daughter, and he was as her son, and she called his name Moses, because, said she, I drew him out of the water.

11 ¶ And in those days, when Moses was [1]grown, he went forth unto his brethren, and looked on their burdens: also he saw an Egyptian smiting an Hebrew one of his brethren.

12 And he looked [1]round about, and when he saw no man, he [2]slew the Egyptian, and hid him in the sand.

13 Again he came forth the second day, and behold two Hebrews strove: and he said unto him that did the wrong, Wherefore smitest thou thy fellow?

14 And he answered, Who made thee a man of authority, and a judge over us? Thinkest thou to kill me, as thou killedst the Egyptian? Then Moses

CHAPTER 2
[a] Num. 26:59
1 Chron. 23:13
Acts 7:20
Heb. 11:23
[b] Exod. 18:3

CHAPTER 3
[a] Acts 7:30

[1]feared and said, Certainly this thing is known.

15 Now Pharaoh heard this matter, and sought to slay Moses: therefore Moses fled from Pharaoh, and dwelt in the land of Midian, and he sat down by a well.

16 And the [1]Priest of Midian had seven daughters, which came and drew *water*, and filled the troughs, for to water their father's sheep.

17 Then the shepherds came and drove them away: but Moses rose up, and [1]defended them, and watered their sheep.

18 And when they came to Reuel their [1]father, he said, How are ye come so soon today?

19 And they said, A man of Egypt delivered us from the hand of the shepherds, and also drew us water enough, and watered the sheep.

20 Then he said unto his daughters, And where is he? why have ye so left the man? [1]call him that he may eat bread.

21 And Moses agreed to dwell with the man: who gave unto Moses Zipporah his daughter:

22 And she bare a son, [b]whose name he called Gershom: for he said, I have been a stranger in a strange land.

23 ¶ Then in process of time, the King of Egypt died, and the children of Israel sighed for the bondage and [1]cried: and their cry for the bondage came up unto God.

24 Then God heard their moan, and God remembered his covenant with Abraham, Isaac, and Jacob.

25 So God looked upon the children of Israel, and God [1]had respect unto them.

3 *1 Moses keepeth sheep, and God appeareth unto him in a bush.   10 He sendeth him to deliver the children of Israel.   14 The name of God.*

1 When Moses kept the sheep of Jethro his father-in-law, Priest of Midian, and drove the flock to the [1]back side of the desert, and came to the [2]Mountain of God, [3]Horeb,

2 Then the Angel of the Lord appeared unto him [a]in a flame of fire out of the midst of a [1]bush, and he looked, and behold, the bush burned with fire, and the bush was not consumed.

2:1 [1] This Levite was called Amram, who married Jochebed, Exod. 6:20.
2:3 [1] Committing him to the providence of God, whom she could not keep from the rage of the tyrant.
2:8 [1] Man's counsel cannot hinder that, which God hath determined shall come to pass.
2:11 [1] That is, was forty years old, Acts 7:23.
2:12 [1] Hebrew, *thus and thus.*
   [2] Being assured that God had appointed him to deliver the Israelites, Acts 7:25.
2:14 [1] Though by his fear he showed his infirmity, yet faith covered it, Heb. 11:27.
2:16 [1] Or, prince.

2:17 [1] Hebrew, *saved them.*
2:18 [1] Or, grandfather.
2:20 [1] Wherein he declared a thankful mind, which would recompense the benefit done unto his.
2:23 [1] God humbleth his by afflictions, that they should cry unto him, and receive the fruit of his promise.
2:25 [1] He judgeth their causes or acknowledged them to be his.
3:1 [1] Or, far within the desert.
   [2] It was so called after the law was given.
   [3] Called also Sinai.
3:2 [1] This signifieth that the Church is not consumed by the fire of affliction, because God is in the midst thereof.

3   Therefore Moses said, I will turn aside now, and see this great sight, why the bush burneth not.

4   And when the ¹Lord saw that he turned aside to see, God called unto him out of the midst of the bush, and said, Moses, Moses. And he answered, I am here.

5   Then he said, Come not hither, ¹put thy shoes off thy feet: for the place whereon thou standest is ²holy ground.

6   Moreover he said, ᵇI am the God of thy father, the God of Abraham, the God of Isaac, and the God of Jacob. Then Moses hid his face: for he was ¹afraid to look upon God.

7   ¶ Then the Lord said, I have surely seen the trouble of my people, which are in Egypt, and have heard their cry, because of their ¹taskmasters: for I know their sorrows.

8   Therefore I am come down to deliver them out of the hand of the Egyptians, and to bring them out of that land into a good land and a large, into a land that ¹floweth with milk and honey, even into the place of the Canaanites, and the Hittites, and the Amorites, and the Perizzites, and the Hivites, and the Jebusites.

9   ¹And now lo, the cry of the children of Israel is come unto me, and I have also seen the oppression wherewith the Egyptians oppress them.

10   Come now therefore, and I will send thee unto Pharaoh, that thou mayest bring my people the children of Israel out of Egypt.

11   ¶ But Moses said unto God, Who am ¹I, that I should go unto Pharaoh, and that I should bring the children of Israel out of Egypt?

12   And he answered, ¹Certainly I will be with thee: and this shall be a token unto thee, that I have sent thee, After that thou hast brought the people out of Egypt, ye shall serve God upon this mountain.

13   Then Moses said unto God, Behold, when I shall come unto the children of Israel, and shall say unto them, The God of your fathers hath sent me unto you: if they say unto me, What is his Name? what shall I say unto them?

14   And God answered Moses, I ¹AM THAT I AM. Also he said, Thus shalt thou say unto the children of Israel, I AM hath sent me unto you.

ᵇ Matt. 22:32
Acts 7:32

ᶜ Exod. 11:2
Exod. 12:35

15   And God spake further unto Moses, Thus shalt thou say unto the children of Israel, The Lord God of your fathers, the God of Abraham, the God of Isaac, and the God of Jacob hath sent me unto you: this is my Name forever, and this is my memorial unto all ages.

16   Go and gather the Elders of Israel together, and thou shalt say unto them, The Lord God of your fathers, the God of Abraham, Isaac, and Jacob appeared unto me, and said, ¹I have surely remembered you, and that which is done to you in Egypt.

17   Therefore I did say, I will bring you out of the affliction of Egypt unto the land of the Canaanites, and the Hittites, and the Amorites, and the Perizzites, and the Hivites, and the Jebusites, unto a land that floweth with milk and honey.

18   Then shall they obey my voice, and thou and the Elders of Israel shall go unto the King of Egypt, and say unto him, The Lord God of the Hebrews hath ¹met with us: we pray thee now therefore, let us go three days' journey in the wilderness, that we may ²sacrifice unto the Lord our God.

19   ¶ But I know, that the King of Egypt will not let you go, but by strong hand.

20   Therefore will I stretch out mine hand and smite Egypt with all my wonders, which I will do in the midst thereof: and after that shall he let you go.

21   And I will make this people to be favored of the Egyptians: so that when ye go, ye shall not go empty.

22   ¹ᵃFor every woman shall ask of her neighbor, and of her ²that sojourneth in her house, jewels of silver and jewels of gold and raiment, and ye shall put them on your sons, and on your daughters, and shall spoil the Egyptians.

4   3 Moses' rod is turned into a serpent.   6 His hand is leprous.   9 The water of the river is turned into blood.   14 Aaron is given to help Moses.   21 God hardeneth Pharaoh.   25 Moses' wife circumciseth her son.

1   Then Moses answered, and said, ¹But lo, they will not believe me, nor hearken unto my voice: for they will say, The Lord hath not appeared unto thee.

2   And the Lord said unto him, What is that in

3:4 ¹ Whom he calleth the Angel, verse 2.
3:5 ¹ Resign thyself up to me, Ruth 4:7; Josh. 5:15.
   ² Because of my presence.
3:6 ¹ For sin causeth man to fear God's justice.
3:7 ¹ Whose cruelty was intolerable.
3:8 ¹ Most plentiful of all things.
3:9 ¹ He heard before, but now he would revenge it.
3:11 ¹ He doth not fully disobey God, but acknowledgeth his own weakness.
3:12 ¹ Neither fear thine own weakness, nor Pharaoh's tyranny.
3:14 ¹ The God which ever have been, am, and shall be: the God

almighty, by whom all things have their being, and the God of mercy, mindful of my promise, Rev. 1:8.
3:16 ¹ Hebrew, in visiting have visited.
3:18 ¹ Or, appeared unto us.
   ² Because Egypt was full of idolatry, God would appoint them a place where they should serve him purely.
3:22 ¹ This example may not be followed generally: though at God's commandment they did it justly, receiving some recompense of their labors.
   ² Or, in whose house she sojourneth.
4:1 ¹ God beareth with Moses' doubting, because he was not altogether without faith.

thine hand? And he answered, A rod.

3 Then said he, Cast it on the ground. So he cast it on the ground, and it was *turned* into a serpent: and Moses fled from it.

4 Again the Lord said unto Moses, Put forth thine hand, and take it by the tail. Then he put forth his hand and caught it, and it was *turned* into a rod in his hand.

5 *Do this* [1]that they may believe, that the Lord God of their fathers, the God of Abraham, the God of Isaac, and the God of Jacob hath appeared unto thee.

6 ¶ And the Lord said furthermore unto him, Thrust now thine hand into thy bosom. And he thrust his hand into his bosom, and when he took it out *again*, behold his hand was [1]leprous as snow.

7 Moreover he said, Put thine hand into thy bosom again. So he put his hand into his bosom again, and plucked it out of his bosom, and behold, it was turned again as his *other* flesh.

8 So shall it be, if they will not believe thee, neither obey [1]the voice of the first sign, yet shall they believe for the voice of the second sign.

9 But if they will not yet believe these two signs, neither obey unto thy voice, then shalt thou take of the [1]water of the river, and pour it upon the dry land: so the water which thou shalt take out of the river, shall be *turned* to blood upon the dry land.

10 ¶ But Moses said unto the Lord, Oh my Lord, I am not eloquent, [1]neither at any time *have been*, nor yet since thou hast spoken unto thy servant: but I am [2]slow of speech and slow of tongue.

11 Then the Lord said unto him, Who hath given the mouth to man? or who hath made the dumb, or the deaf, or him that seeth, or the blind? have not I the Lord?

12 Therefore go now, and [a]I will be with thy mouth, and will teach thee what thou shalt say.

13 But he said, Oh my Lord, send, I pray thee, by the [1]hand *of him*, whom thou [2]shouldest send.

14 Then the Lord was [1]very angry with Moses, and said, Do not I know Aaron thy brother the Levite,

CHAPTER 4
[a] Matt. 10:19
Matt. 12:22
[b] Exod. 7:1

that he himself shall speak? for lo, he cometh also forth to meet thee, and when he seeth thee, he will be glad in his heart.

15 Therefore thou shalt speak unto him, and [1]put the words in his mouth, and I will be with thy mouth, and with his mouth, and will teach you what ye ought to do.

16 And he shall be thy spokesman unto the people: and he shall be, *even* he shall be as thy mouth, and thou shalt be to him as [b,1]God.

17 Moreover thou shalt take this rod in thine hand, wherewith thou shalt do miracles.

18 ¶ Therefore Moses went and returned to Jethro his father-in-law, and said unto him, I pray thee, let me go, and return to my [1]brethren, which are in Egypt, and see whether they be yet alive. Then Jethro said to Moses, Go in peace.

19 (For the Lord had said unto Moses in Midian, Go, return to Egypt: for they are all dead which [1]went about to kill thee.)

20 Then Moses took his wife and his sons, and [1]put them on an ass, and returned toward the land of Egypt, and Moses took the [2]rod of God in his hand.

21 And the Lord said unto Moses, When thou art entered and come into Egypt again, see that thou do all the wonders before Pharaoh, which I have put in thine hand: but I will [1]harden his heart, and he shall not let the people go.

22 Then thou shalt say to Pharaoh, Thus saith the Lord, Israel *is* my son, *even* my [1]firstborn.

23 Wherefore I say to thee, Let my son go, that he may serve me: if thou refuse to let him go, behold, I will slay thy son, *even* thy firstborn.

24 ¶ And as he was by the way in the Inn, the Lord met him, and [1]would have killed him.

25 Then Zipporah took a sharp knife, and [1]cut away the foreskin of her son, and cast it at his feet, and said, Thou *art* indeed a bloody husband unto me.

26 So [1]he departed from him. Then she said, O bloody husband (because of the circumcision).

27 ¶ Then the Lord said unto Aaron, Go meet

4:5 [1] This power to work miracles was to confirm his doctrine, and to assure him of his vocation.
4:6 [1] Or, white as snow.
4:8 [1] Or, the words confirmed by the first sign.
4:9 [1] Because these three signs should be sufficient witnesses to prove that Moses should deliver God's people.
4:10 [1] Hebrew, *from yesterday, and ere yesterday.*
[2] Hebrew, *heavy of mouth.*
4:13 [1] Or, ministry.
[2] That is, the Messiah: or some other, that is more meet than I.
4:14 [1] Though we provoke God justly to anger, yet he will never reject his.
4:15 [1] Thou shalt instruct him what to say.

4:16 [1] Meaning, as a wise counselor and full of God's spirit.
4:18 [1] Or, kinsfolk, and lineage.
4:19 [1] Hebrew, *sought thy soul.*
4:20 [1] Hebrew, *caused them to ride.*
[2] Whereby he wrought the miracles.
4:21 [1] By receiving my spirit and delivering him unto Satan to increase his malice.
4:22 [1] Meaning, most dear unto him.
4:24 [1] God punished him with sickness for neglecting his Sacrament.
4:25 [1] This act was extraordinary: for Moses was sore sick, and God even then required it.
4:26 [1] Or, the Angel.

Moses in the wilderness. And he went and met him in the ¹Mount of God, and kissed him.

28 Then Moses told Aaron all the words of the Lord, who had sent him, and all the signs wherewith he had charged him.

29 ¶ So went Moses and Aaron, and gathered all the elders of the children of Israel.

30 And Aaron told all the words, which the Lord had spoken unto Moses, and he did the miracles in the sight of the people.

31 And the ¹people believed, and when they heard that the Lord had visited the children of Israel, and had looked upon their tribulation, they bowed down, and worshipped.

5 *1 Moses and Aaron do their message unto Pharaoh, who oppresseth the people of Israel more and more. 20 They cry out upon Moses and Aaron therefore, and Moses complaineth unto God.*

1 Then afterward Moses and Aaron went and said to ¹Pharaoh, Thus saith the Lord God of Israel, Let my people go, that they may ²celebrate a feast unto me in the wilderness.

2 And Pharaoh said, Who is the Lord, that I should hear his voice, and let Israel go? I know not the Lord, neither will I let Israel go.

3 And they said, ¹We worship the God of the Hebrews: we pray thee, let us go three days' journey in the desert, and sacrifice unto the Lord our God, lest ²he bring upon us the pestilence or sword.

4 Then said the King of Egypt unto them, Moses and Aaron, why cause ye the people to cease from their works? get you to your burdens.

5 Pharaoh said furthermore, Behold, much people *is* now in the land, and ye ¹make them leave their burdens.

6 Therefore Pharaoh gave commandment the same day unto the taskmasters of the people, and to their ¹officers, saying,

7 Ye shall give the people no more straw, to make brick (¹as in time past) *but* let them go and gather them straw themselves.

8 Notwithstanding lay upon them the number of brick, which they made in *time* past, diminish nothing thereof: for they be idle, therefore they cry,

saying, Let us go to offer sacrifice unto our God.

9 ¹Lay more work upon the men, and cause them to do it, and let them not regard ²vain words.

10 ¶ Then went the taskmasters of the people and their officers out, and told the people, saying, Thus saith Pharaoh, I will give you no more straw.

11 Go yourselves, get ye straw where ye can find it, yet shall nothing of your labor be diminished.

12 Then were the people scattered abroad throughout all the land of Egypt, for to gather stubble instead of straw.

13 And the taskmasters hasted them, saying, Finish your day's work ¹every day's task, as *ye did* when ye had straw.

14 And the Officers of the children of Israel, which Pharaoh's taskmasters had set over them, were beaten, and demanded, Wherefore have ye not fulfilled your [task] in making brick yesterday and today, as in times past?

15 ¶ Then the officers of the children of Israel came and cried unto Pharaoh, saying, Wherefore dealest thou thus thy servants?

16 There is no straw given to thy servants, and they say unto us, Make brick: and lo, thy servants are beaten, and ¹thy people is blamed.

17 But he said, ¹Ye are too much idle: therefore ye say, Let us go to offer sacrifice to the Lord.

18 Go therefore now *and* work: for there shall no straw be given you, yet shall ye deliver the whole tale of brick.

19 Then the officers of the children of Israel ¹saw themselves in an evil case, because it was said, Ye shall diminish nothing of your brick, *nor* of every day's task.

20 ¶ And they met Moses and Aaron, which stood in their way as they came out from Pharaoh.

21 To whom they said, The Lord look upon you and judge: for ye have made our savor to ¹stink before Pharaoh and before his servants, in that ye have ²put a sword in their hand to slay us.

22 Wherefore Moses returned to the Lord, and said, Lord, why hast thou afflicted this people? wherefore hast thou thus sent me?

23 For since I came to Pharaoh to speak in thy name, he hath vexed this people, and yet thou hast not delivered thy people.

4:27 ¹ Or, Horeb.

4:31 ¹ So that Moses had now experience of God's promise that he should have good success.

5:1 ¹ Faith overcometh fear, and maketh men bold in their vocation.
  ² And offer sacrifice.

5:3 ¹ Or, God hath met us.
  ² Hebrew, *Lest he meet us with pestilence.*

5:5 ¹ As though ye would rebel.

5:6 ¹ Which were of the Israelites, and had charge to see them do their work.

5:7 ¹ Hebrew, *yesterday and ere yesterday.*

5:9 ¹ The more cruelly that tyrants rage, the nearer is God's help.
  ² Of Moses and Aaron.

5:13 ¹ Hebrew, *the work of a day in his day.*

5:16 ¹ Or, thy people the Egyptians are in fault.

5:17 ¹ Hebrew, *idle, ye are idle.*

5:19 ¹ Or, looked sad on them, which said.

5:21 ¹ Read Gen. 34:30.
  ² It is a grievous thing to the servants of God to be accused of evil, specially of their brethren, when they do as their duty requireth.

6 *8 God reneweth his promise of deliverance of the Is-raelites.   9 Moses speaketh to the Israelites, but they believe him not.   10 Moses and Aaron are sent again unto Pharaoh.*

CHAPTER 6
a Gen. 46:9
Num. 26:5
1 Chron. 5:8
b 1 Chron. 4:24
c Num. 3:17
1 Chron. 6:1
1 Chron. 23:6
d Num. 26:57
1 Chron. 6:1
1 Chron. 23:6
e Exod. 2:2
Num. 26:59
f Num. 25:18

1   Then the Lord said unto Moses, Now shalt thou see, what I will do unto Pharaoh: for by a strong hand shall he let them go, and even [1]be constrained to drive them out of his land.

2   Moreover God spake unto Moses, and said unto him, I am the Lord,

3   And I appeared unto Abraham, to Isaac, and to Jacob by *the* Name of [1]Almighty God, but by my Name [2]Jehovah was I not known unto them.

4   Furthermore as I made my covenant with them to give them the land of Canaan, the land of their pilgrimage, wherein they were strangers:

5   So I have also heard the groaning of the children of Israel, whom the Egyptians keep in bondage, and have remembered my covenant.

6   Wherefore say thou unto the children of Israel, I am the Lord, and I will bring you out from the burdens of the Egyptians, and will deliver you out of their bondage, and will redeem you in a stretched out arm, and in great [1]judgments.

7   Also I will [1]take you for my people, and will be your God: then ye shall know that I the Lord your God bring you out from the burdens of the Egyptians.

8   And I will bring you into the land which I [1]sware that I would give to Abraham, and to Isaac, and to Jacob, and I will give it unto you for a possession: I am the Lord.

9   ¶ So Moses told the children of Israel thus: but they hearkened [1]not unto Moses, for anguish of spirit and for cruel bondage.

10   Then the Lord spake unto Moses, saying,

11   Go speak to Pharaoh King of Egypt, that he let the children of Israel go out of his land.

12   But Moses spake before the Lord, saying, Behold, the children of Israel hearken not unto me, how then shall Pharaoh hear me, which am of [1]uncircumcised lips?

13   Then the Lord spake unto Moses and unto Aaron, and charged them *to* go to the children of Israel and to Pharaoh King of Egypt, to bring the children of Israel out of the land of Egypt.

14   ¶ These be the heads [1]of their father's houses:

the [a]sons of Reuben the firstborn of Israel *are* Hanoch and Pallu, Hezron and Carmi: these are the families of Reuben.

15   [b]Also the sons of Simeon: Jemuel and Jamin, and Ohad, and Jachin, and Zohar, and Shaul the son of a Canaanitish woman: these are the families of Simeon.

16   ¶ [c]These also are the names of the sons of Levi in their generations: Gershon and Kohath and Merari (and the years of the life of Levi *were* an hundred [1]thirty and seven years).

17   The sons of Gershon *were* Libni and Shimi by their families.

18   [d]And the sons of Kohath, Amram and Izhar, and Hebron, and Uzziel (and Kohath lived an hundred thirty and three years).

19   Also the sons of Merari *were* Mahli and Mushi: these are the families of Levi their kindreds.

20   And Amram took Jochebed his [1]father's sister to his wife, and she bare him Aaron and [e]Moses (and Amram lived an hundred thirty and seven years).

21   ¶ Also the sons of Izhar: [1]Korah, and Nepheg, and Zichri.

22   And the sons of Uzziel: Mishael, and Elzaphan, and Zithri.

23   And Aaron took Elisheba daughter of Amminadab, sister of [1]Nahshon to his wife, which bare him Nadab, and Abihu, Eleazar and Ithamar.

24   Also the sons of Korah: Assir, and Elkanah and Abiasaph: these are the families of the Korahites.

25   And Eleazar Aaron's son took him *one* of the daughters of Putiel to his wife, which bare him [f]Phinehas: these are the principal fathers of the Levites throughout their families.

26   These are Aaron and Moses to whom the Lord said, Bring the children of Israel out of the land of Egypt, according to their [1]armies.

27   These are that Moses, and Aaron, which spake to Pharaoh King of Egypt, that they might bring the children of Israel out of Egypt.

28   ¶ And at that time when the Lord spake unto Moses in the land of Egypt,

29   When the Lord, *I say*, spake unto Moses, saying, I am the Lord, speak thou unto Pharaoh the King of Egypt all that I say unto thee.

6:1 [1] Hebrew, *in a strong hand.*
6:3 [1] Or, all sufficient.
    [2] Whereby he signifieth that he will perform indeed that which he promised to their fathers: for this name declareth that he is constant and will perform his promise.
6:6 [1] Or, plagues.
6:7 [1] He meaneth, as touching the outward vocation, the dignity whereof they lost afterward by their rebellion: but as for election to life everlasting, it is immutable.
6:8 [1] Hebrew, *Lift up mine hand.*
6:9 [1] So hard a thing it is to show true obedience under the cross.

6:12 [1] Or barbarous and rude in speech: and by this word (uncircumcised) is signified the whole corruption of man's nature.
6:14 [1] This genealogy showeth of whom Moses and Aaron came.
6:16 [1] For he was 42 years old, when he came into Egypt, and there lived 94.
6:20 [1] Which kind of marriage was after in the law forbidden, Lev. 18:12.
6:21 [1] Moses and he were brothers' children, whose rebellion was punished, Num. 16:1.
6:23 [1] Who was a prince of Judah, Num. 1:7.
6:26 [1] For their families were so great, that they might be compared to armies.

30 Then Moses said before the Lord, Behold, I am of [1]uncircumcised lips, and how shall Pharaoh hear me?

CHAPTER 7
a Exod. 17:5
b Ps. 78:44

7 *3 God hardeneth Pharaoh's heart. 10 Moses and Aaron do the miracles of the serpent, and the blood: and Pharaoh's sorcerers do the like.*

1 Then the Lord said to Moses, Behold, I have made thee [1]Pharaoh's [2]God, and Aaron thy brother shall [3]be thy Prophet.

2 Thou shalt speak all that I commanded thee: and Aaron thy brother shall speak unto Pharaoh, that he suffer the children of Israel to go out of his land.

3 But I will harden Pharaoh's heart, and multiply my miracles, and my wonders in the land of Egypt.

4 And Pharaoh shall not hearken unto you, that I may lay mine hand upon Egypt, and bring out mine armies, *even* my people, the children of Israel out of the land of Egypt, by great [1]judgments.

5 Then the Egyptians shall know that I am the Lord, when I stretch forth mine hand upon Egypt, and bring out the children of Israel from among them.

6 So Moses and Aaron did as the Lord commanded them, *even* so did they.

7 (Now Moses was [1]fourscore years old, and Aaron fourscore and three, when they spake unto Pharaoh.)

8 ¶ And the Lord had spoken unto Moses and Aaron, saying,

9 If Pharaoh speak unto you, saying, Show a miracle for you, then thou shalt say unto Aaron, Take thy rod, and cast it before Pharaoh, *and* it shall be *turned* into a [1]serpent.

10 ¶ Then went Moses and Aaron unto Pharaoh, and did even as the Lord had commanded, and Aaron cast forth his rod before Pharaoh and before his servants, and it was *turned* into a serpent.

11 Then Pharaoh also called for the wise men and [1]sorcerers: and those charmers also of Egypt did in like manner with their enchantments.

12 For they cast down every man his rod, and they were *turned* into serpents: but Aaron's rod devoured their rods.

13 So Pharaoh's heart was hardened, and he hearkened not to them, as the Lord had said.

14 ¶ The Lord then said unto Moses, Pharaoh's heart is [1]obstinate, he refuseth to let the people go.

15 Go unto Pharaoh in the morning, (lo, he will come forth unto the water) and thou shalt stand and meet him by [1]the river's brink, and the rod, which was turned into a serpent, shalt thou take in thine hand.

16 And thou shalt say unto him, The Lord God of the Hebrews hath sent me unto thee, saying, Let my people go that they may serve me in the wilderness: and behold, hitherto thou wouldest not hear.

17 Thus saith the Lord, In this thou shalt know that I am the Lord: behold, I will smite with the rod that is in mine hand upon the water that is in the river, and it shall be turned into blood.

18 And the fish that is in the river shall die, and the river shall stink, and it shall [1]grieve the Egyptians to drink of the water of the river.

19 ¶ The Lord then spake to Moses, Say unto Aaron, Take thy rod, and stretch out thine hand over the waters of Egypt, over their streams, over their rivers, and over their ponds, and over all pools of their waters, and they shall be [1]blood, and there shall be blood throughout the land of Egypt, both in *vessels* of wood, and of stone.

20 So Moses and Aaron did even as the Lord commanded: *a*and he lift up the rod, and smote the water that was in the river in the sight of Pharaoh, and in the sight of his servants: and *b*all the water that was in the river, was turned into blood.

21 And the [1]fish that was in the river died, and the river stank: so that the Egyptians could not drink of the water of the river: and there was blood throughout the land of Egypt.

22 And the enchanters of Egypt did [1]likewise with their sorceries: and the heart of Pharaoh was [2]hardened: so that he did not hearken unto them, as the Lord hath said.

23 Then Pharaoh returned, and went again into his house, [1]neither did this yet enter into his heart.

24 All the Egyptians then dug round about the river *for* waters to drink: for they could not drink of the water of the river.

6:30 [1] The disobedience both of Moses and of the people, showeth that their deliverance came only of God's free mercy.

7:1 [1] Or, a God to Pharaoh.

[2] I have given thee power and authority to speak in my name and to execute my judgments upon him.

[3] Or, shall speak for thee (before Pharaoh.)

7:4 [1] To strengthen Moses' faith, God promiseth again to punish most sharply the oppression of his Church.

7:7 [1] Moses lived in affliction and banishment forty years before he enjoined his office to deliver God's people.

7:9 [1] Or, dragon.

7:11 [1] It seemeth that these were Jannes and Jambres: read 2 Tim. 3:8, so ever the wicked maliciously resist the truth of God.

7:14 [1] Or, heavy and dull.

7:15 [1] To wit, the river Nile.

7:18 [1] Or, they shall be weary, and abhor to drink.

7:19 [1] The first plague.

7:21 [1] To signify that it was a true miracle, and that God plagued them in that which was most necessary for the preservation of life.

7:22 [1] In outward appearance, and after that the seven days were ended.

[2] Hebrew, *was made strong.*

7:23 [1] Hebrew, *he set not his heart at all thereunto.*

25 And *this* [1]continued fully seven days after the Lord had smitten the river.

8

6 *Frogs are sent.*   13 *Moses prayeth, and they die.* 17 *Lice are sent, whereby the sorcerers acknowledge God's power.*   24 *Egypt is plagued with noisome flies.* 30 *Moses prayeth again.*

1 Afterward the Lord said unto Moses, Go unto Pharaoh, and tell him, Thus saith the Lord, Let my people go, that they may serve me.

2 And if thou wilt not let them go, behold, I will smite all thy country with [1]frogs:

3 And the river shall crawl full of frogs, which shall go up and come into thine house, and into thy chamber, where thou sleepest, and upon thy bed, and into the house of thy servants, and upon thy people, and into thy ovens, and [1]into thy kneading troughs.

4 Yea, the frogs shall climb up upon thee, and on thy people, and upon all thy servants.

5 ¶ Also the Lord said to Moses, Say thou unto Aaron, Stretch out thine hand with thy rod upon the streams, upon the rivers, and upon the ponds, and cause frogs to come up upon the land of Egypt.

6 Then Aaron stretched out his hand upon the waters of Egypt, and the [1]frogs came up and covered the land of [2]Egypt.

7 And the sorcerers did likewise with their sorceries, and brought frogs up upon the land of Egypt.

8 Then Pharaoh called for Moses and Aaron, and said, [1]Pray ye unto the Lord, that he may take away the frogs from me, and from my people, and I will let the people go, that they may do sacrifice unto the Lord.

9 And Moses said unto Pharaoh, [1]Concerning me, *even* [2]command when I shall pray for thee, and for thy servants, and for thy people, to destroy the frogs from thee and from thine houses, that they may remain in the river only.

10 Then he said, Tomorrow. And he answered, Be it [1]as thou hast said, that thou mayest know, that there is none like unto the Lord our God.

11 So the frogs shall depart from thee, and from thine houses, and from thy servants, and from thy people: only they shall remain in the river.

12 Then Moses and Aaron went out from Pharaoh: and Moses cried unto the Lord concerning the frogs, which he had [1]sent unto Pharaoh.

13 And the Lord did according to the saying of Moses: So the frogs [1]died in the houses, in the towns, and the fields.

14 And they gathered them together by heaps, and the land stank *of them*.

15 But when Pharaoh saw that he had rest *given him*, he [1]hardened his heart, and hearkened not unto them, as the Lord had said.

16 ¶ Again the Lord said unto Moses, Say unto Aaron, Stretch out thy rod, and smite the dust of the earth, that it may be *turned* to [1]lice throughout all the land of Egypt.

17 And they did so: for Aaron stretched out his hand with his rod, and smote the dust of the earth: and lice came upon man and upon beast: all the dust of the earth was lice throughout all the land of Egypt.

18 Now the enchanters assayed likewise with their enchantments to bring forth lice, but they [1]could not. So the lice were upon man and upon beast.

19 Then said the enchanters unto Pharaoh, This is [1]the finger of God. But Pharaoh's heart remained obstinate, and he hearkened not unto them, as the Lord had said.

20 ¶ Moreover the Lord said to Moses, Rise up early in the morning, and stand before Pharaoh (lo, he will come forth unto the water) and say unto him, Thus saith the Lord, Let my people go, that they may serve me.

21 Else, if thou wilt not let my people go, behold, I will send [1]swarms of flies both upon thee, and upon thy servants, and upon thy people, and into thine houses: and the houses of the Egyptians shall be full of swarms of flies, and the ground also whereon they are.

22 But the land of Goshen, where my people are, will I cause to be [1]wonderful in that day, so that no swarms of flies shall be there, that thou mayest know that I am the Lord in the midst of the [2]earth.

23 And I will make a deliverance of my people from thy people: tomorrow shall this miracle be.

24 And the Lord did so: for there came [1]great swarms of flies into the house of Pharaoh, and *into* his servants' houses, so that through all the land of

---

7:25 [1] Or seven days accomplished.

8:2 [1] There is nothing so weak, that God cannot cause to overcome the greatest power of man.

8:3 [1] Or, upon thy dough, or into thine ambries.

8:6 [1] The second plague.

    [2] But Goshen, where God's people dwelt, was excepted.

8:8 [1] Not love, but fear causeth the very Infidels to seek unto God.

8:9 [1] Hebrew, *have this honor over me.*

    [2] Or, speak plain unto me.

8:10 [1] Hebrew, *according to thy word.*

8:12 [1] Or, laid upon.

8:13 [1] In things of this life God oft times heareth the prayers of the just for the ungodly.

8:15 [1] Or, made his heart heavy.

8:16 [1] The third plague.

8:18 [1] God confounded their wisdom and authority in a thing most vile.

8:19 [1] They acknowledged that this was done by God's power and not by sorcery, Luke 11:20.

8:21 [1] Or, a multitude of venomous beasts as serpents, etc.

8:22 [1] Or, I will separate.

    [2] Or, land of Egypt.

8:24 [1] The fourth plague.

Egypt, the earth was corrupt by the swarms of flies.

25 Then Pharaoh called for Moses and Aaron, and said, Go, do sacrifice unto your God in this land.

26 And Moses answered, It is not meet to do so: for *then* we should offer unto the Lord our God *that, which is* an [1]abomination unto the Egyptians. Lo, can we sacrifice the abomination of the Egyptians before their eyes, and they not stone us?

27 Let us go three days' journey in the desert, and sacrifice unto the Lord our God, [a]as he hath commanded us.

28 And Pharaoh said, I will let you go, that ye may sacrifice unto the Lord your God in the wilderness: but [1]go not far away, pray for me.

29 And Moses said, Behold, I will go out from thee, and pray unto the Lord, that the swarms of flies may depart from Pharaoh, from his servants, and from his people tomorrow: but let Pharaoh from henceforth [1]deceive no more, in not suffering the people to sacrifice unto the Lord.

30 So Moses went out from Pharaoh and prayed unto the Lord.

31 And the Lord did according to the saying of Moses, and the swarms of flies departed from Pharaoh, from his servants, and from his people, *and* there remained not one.

32 Yet Pharaoh [1]hardened his heart at this time also, and did not let the people go.

9 3 *The moraine of beasts.*   10 *The plague of botches and sores.*   23 *The horrible hail, thunder, and lightning.*   26 *The land of Goshen ever is excepted.*   27 *Pharaoh confesseth his wickedness.*   33 *Moses prayeth for him.* 35 *Yet he is obstinate.*

1 Then the Lord said unto Moses, Go to Pharaoh, and tell him, Thus saith the Lord God of the Hebrews, Let my people go, that they may serve me.

2 But if thou refuse to let *them* go, and wilt yet hold them still,

3 Behold, the hand of the Lord is upon thy flock which is in the field: *for* upon the horses, upon the asses, upon the camels, upon the cattle, and upon the sheep *shall be* a [1]mighty great moraine.

4 And the Lord shall do [1]wonderfully between the beasts of Israel, and the beasts of Egypt: so that

CHAPTER 8
[a] Exod. 3:18

CHAPTER 9
[a] Exod. 4:21
[b] Rom. 9:17

there shall nothing die at all, that *pertaineth* to the children of Israel.

5 And the Lord appointed a time, saying, Tomorrow the Lord shall finish this thing in this land.

6 So the Lord did this thing on the morrow, and all the cattle of Egypt died: but of the cattle of the children of Israel died not one.

7 Then Pharaoh [1]sent, and behold, there was not one of the cattle of the Israelites dead: and the heart of Pharaoh was obstinate, and he did not let the people go.

8 ¶ And the Lord said to Moses and to Aaron, Take your handful of [1]ashes of the furnace, and Moses shall sprinkle them toward the heaven in the sight of Pharaoh,

9 And they shall be *turned* to dust in all the land of Egypt: and it shall be as a scab breaking out into blisters upon man, and upon beast throughout all the land of Egypt.

10 Then they took ashes of the furnace, and stood before Pharaoh: and Moses sprinkled them toward the heaven, and there came [a] [1]scab breaking out into blisters upon man, and upon beast.

11 And the sorcerers could not stand before Moses, because of the scab: for the scab was upon the enchanters and upon all the Egyptians.

12 And the Lord hardened the heart of Pharaoh, and he hearkened not unto them, [a]as the Lord had said unto Moses.

13 ¶ Also the Lord said unto Moses, Rise up early in the morning, and stand before Pharaoh, and tell him, Thus saith the Lord God of the Hebrews, Let my people go that they may serve me.

14 For I will at this time send my plagues upon [1]thine heart, and upon thy servants, and upon thy people, that thou mayest know that there is none like me in all the earth.

15 For now I will stretch out mine hand, that I may smite thee and thy people with the pestilence: and thou shalt perish from the earth.

16 And indeed, [b]for this cause have [1]I appointed thee, to [2]show my power in thee, and to declare my [3]name throughout all the world.

17 Yet thou exaltest thyself against my people, and lettest them not go.

18 Behold, tomorrow this time I will cause to rain

8:26 [1] For the Egyptians worshipped divers beasts, as the ox, the sheep and such like which the Israelites offered in sacrifice, which thing the Egyptians abhorred to see.

8:28 [1] So the wicked prescribe unto God's messengers how far they shall go.

8:29 [1] He could not judge his heart, but yet he charged him to do this unfeignedly.

8:32 [1] Where God giveth not faith, no miracles can prevail.

9:3 [1] The fifth plague.

9:4 [1] He shall declare his heavenly judgment against his enemies,

and his favor toward his children.

9:7 [1] Into the land of Goshen, where the Israelites dwelled.

9:8 [1] Or, embers.

9:10 [1] The sixth plague.

9:14 [1] So that thine own conscience shall condemn thee of ingratitude and malice.

9:16 [1] Or, set thee up.

[2] Or, to show thee.

[3] That is, that all the world may magnify my power in overcoming thee.

a mighty great hail, such as was not in Egypt since the foundation thereof was laid unto this time.

19 Send therefore now, *and* ¹gather the cattle, and all that thou hast in the field: *for* upon all the men, and the beasts, which are found in the field, and not brought home, the hail shall fall upon them, and they shall die.

20 Such *then* as feared the word of the Lord among the servants of Pharaoh, made his servants and his cattle flee into the houses.

21 But such as ¹regarded not the ²word of the Lord, left his servants, and his cattle in the field.

22 ¶ And the Lord said to Moses, Stretch forth thine hand toward heaven, that there may be hail in all the land of Egypt, upon man, and upon beast, and upon all the herbs of the field in the land of Egypt.

23 Then Moses stretched out his rod toward heaven, and the Lord sent thunder and ¹hail, and ²lightning upon the ground: and the Lord caused hail to rain upon the land of Egypt.

24 So there was hail, and fire mingled with the hail, so grievous, as there was none throughout all the land of Egypt, since ¹it was a nation.

25 And the hail smote throughout all the land of Egypt all that was in the field, both man and beast: also the hail smote all the trees of the field and brake to pieces all the trees of the field.

26 Only in the land of Goshen (where the children of Israel were) was no hail.

27 Then Pharaoh sent and called for Moses and Aaron, and said unto them, I ¹have now sinned: the Lord is righteous, but I and my people are wicked.

28 Pray ye unto the Lord (for it is enough) that there be no more ¹mighty thunders, and hail, and I will let you go, and ye shall tarry no longer.

29 Then Moses said unto him, As soon as I am out of the city, I will spread mine hands unto the Lord, *and* the thunder shall cease, neither shall there be any more hail, that thou mayest know that ʿthe earth is the Lord's.

30 As for thee and thy servants, I know ¹afore *I pray*, ye will fear before the face of the Lord God.

31 (And the flax, and the barley were smitten: for

the margin: ᶜ Ps. 24:1

CHAPTER 10
ᵃ Exod. 4:2

the barley was eared, and the flax was bolled.

32 But the wheat and the rye were not smitten, for they were ¹hid in the ground.)

33 Then Moses went out of the city from Pharaoh, and spread his hands to the Lord, and the thunder and the hail ceased, neither rained it upon the earth.

34 And when Pharaoh saw that the rain and the hail and the thunder were ceased, he sinned again, and hardened his heart, *both* he, and his servants.

35 So the heart of Pharaoh was hardened: neither would he let the children of Israel go, as the Lord had said ¹by Moses.

10

7 Pharoah's servants counsel him to let the Israelites depart. 13 Grasshoppers destroy the country. 16 Pharaoh confesseth his sin. 22 Darkness is sent.

1 Again the Lord said unto Moses, Go to Pharaoh, ᵃfor I have hardened his heart, and the heart of his servants, that I might work these ¹my miracles in the midst of his *realm,*

2 And that thou mayest declare in the ¹ears of thy son, and of thy son's son, what things I have done in Egypt, and my miracles, which I have done among them: that ye may know that I am the Lord.

3 Then came Moses and Aaron unto Pharaoh, and they said unto him, Thus saith the Lord God of the Hebrews, How long wilt thou refuse ¹to humble thyself before me? Let my people go, that they may serve me.

4 But if thou refuse to let my people go, behold, tomorrow will I bring ¹grasshoppers into thy coasts.

5 And they shall cover the face of the earth, that a man cannot see the earth: and they shall eat the residue which remaineth unto you, and hath escaped from the hail: and they shall eat all your trees that bud in the field.

6 And they shall fill thine houses, and all thy servants' houses, and the houses of all the Egyptians, as neither thy fathers, nor thy fathers' fathers have seen, since the time they were upon the earth unto this day. So he returned, and went out from Pharaoh.

7 Then Pharaoh's servants said unto him, How

9:19 ¹ Here we see though God's wrath be kindled, yet there is a certain mercy showed even to his enemies.
9:21 ¹ Hebrew, *set not his heart to.*
     ² The word of the minister is called the word of God.
9:23 ¹ The seventh plague.
     ² Hebrew, *fire walked.*
9:24 ¹ Or, since it was inhabited.
9:27 ¹ The wicked confess their sins to their condemnation, but they cannot believe to obtain remission.
9:28 ¹ Hebrew, *voice of God.*
9:30 ¹ Meaning, that when they have their request, they are never

the better, though they make many fair promises, wherein we see the practices of the wicked.
9:32 ¹ Or, late sown.
9:35 ¹ Hebrew, *by the hand of Moses.*
10:1 ¹ Or, in his presence, or among them.
10:2 ¹ The miracles should be so great, that they should be spoken of for ever: where also we see the duty of parents toward their children.
10:3 ¹ The end of affliction is, to humble ourselves with true repentance under the hand of God.
10:4 ¹ Or, locusts.

long shall he be [1]an [2]offence unto us? let the men go, that they may serve the Lord their God: wilt thou first know that Egypt is destroyed?

8 So Moses and Aaron were brought again unto Pharaoh, and he said unto them, Go, serve the Lord your God, but who are they that shall go?

9 And Moses answered, We will go with our young, and with our old, with our sons, and with our daughters, with our sheep, and with our cattle will we go: for we *must celebrate* a feast unto the Lord.

10 And he said unto them, Let [1]the Lord so be with you, as I will let you go and your children: [2]behold, for evil is before your face.

11 *It shall* not *be* so: now go ye *that are* men, and serve the Lord: for that was your desire. Then they were thrust out from Pharaoh's presence.

12 ¶ After, the Lord said unto Moses, Stretch out thine hand upon the land of Egypt for the grasshoppers, that they may come upon the land of Egypt, and eat all the herbs of the land, *even* all that the hail had left.

13 Then Moses stretched forth his rod upon the land of Egypt: and the Lord brought an East wind upon the land all that day, and all that night: and in the morning the East wind brought the [1]grasshoppers.

14 So the grasshoppers went up upon all the land of Egypt, and [1]remained in all quarters of Egypt: so grievous Grasshoppers, like to these were never before, neither after them shall be such.

15 For they covered all the face of the earth, so that the land was dark: and they did eat all the herbs of the land, and all the fruits of the trees, which the hail had left, so that there was no green thing left upon the trees, nor among the herbs of the field throughout all the land of Egypt.

16 Therefore Pharaoh called for [1]Moses and Aaron in haste, and said, I have sinned against the Lord your God, and against you.

17 And now forgive me my sin only this once, and pray unto the Lord your God, that he may take away from me this death only.

18 *Moses* then went out from Pharaoh, and prayed unto the Lord.

19 And the Lord turned a mighty strong West wind, and took away the grasshoppers, and violently

CHAPTER 11
a Exod. 3:32
Exod. 3:35

cast them into the [1]red Sea, *so that* there remained not one grasshopper in all the land of Egypt.

20 But the Lord hardened Pharaoh's heart, and he did not let the children of Israel go.

21 ¶ Again the Lord said unto Moses, Stretch out thine hand toward heaven, that there may be upon the land of Egypt darkness, even darkness that may be [1]felt.

22 Then Moses stretched forth his hand toward heaven, and there was a [1]black darkness in all the land of Egypt three days.

23 No man saw another, neither rose up from the place where he was *for* three days: but all the children of Israel had light where they dwelt.

24 Then Pharaoh called for Moses, and said, Go serve the Lord: only your sheep and your cattle shall abide, and your children shall go with you.

25 And Moses said, Thou must give us also sacrifices, and burnt offerings that we may do *sacrifice* unto the Lord our God.

26 Therefore our cattle also shall go with us: there shall not an [1]hoof be left, for thereof must we take to serve the Lord our God: neither do we know [2]how we shall serve the Lord, until we come thither.

27 (But the Lord hardened Pharaoh's heart, and he would not let them go.)

28 And Pharaoh said unto him, Get thee from me: look thou see my face no more: for whensoever thou comest in my sight, thou shalt [1]die.

29 Then Moses said, Thou hast said well: from henceforth will I see thy face no more.

11 1 *God promiseth their departure.* 2 *He willeth them to borrow their neighbors' jewels.* 3 *Moses was esteemed of all save Pharaoh.*

1 Now the Lord had said unto Moses, yet will I bring one plague more upon Pharaoh, and upon Egypt, after that, he will let you go hence: when he letteth you go, he shall [1]at once chase you hence.

2 Speak thou now to the people, that every man [1]require of his neighbor, and every woman of her neighbor, *a*jewels of silver, and jewels of gold.

3 And the Lord gave the people favor in the sight of the Egyptians: also Moses *was* very great in the

---

10:7 [1] Or, snare.
  [2] Meaning, the occasion of all these evils: so are the godly ever charged as Elijah was by Ahab.
10:10 [1] That is, I would the Lord were no more affectioned toward you, than I am minded to let you go.
  [2] Punishment is prepared for you. Some read, Ye intend some mischief.
10:13 [1] The eighth plague.
10:14 [1] Or, he caused them to remain.
10:16 [1] The wicked in their miseries seek to God's ministers for help, albeit they hate and detest them.

10:19 [1] The water seemed red, because the sand or gravel is red: the Hebrews called it the Sea of bulrushes.
10:21 [1] Because it was so thick.
10:22 [1] The ninth plague.
10:26 [1] The ministers of God ought not to yield one iota to the wicked, as touching their charge.
  [2] That is, with what beasts, or how many.
10:28 [1] Though before he confessed Moses just, yet again his own conscience he threateneth to put him to death.
11:1 [1] Without any condition, but with haste and violence.
11:2 [1] Or, borrow.

land of Egypt, in the sight of Pharaoh's servants, and in the sight of the people.

4 And Moses said, Thus saith the Lord, [b]About midnight will I go out into the midst of Egypt.

5 And all the firstborn in the land of Egypt shall die, from the firstborn of Pharaoh that sitteth on his throne, unto the firstborn of the maid servant, that is at [1]the mill, and all the firstborn of beasts.

6 Then there shall be a great cry throughout all the land of Egypt, such as was never none like, nor shall be.

7 But against none of the children of Israel shall a dog move his tongue, neither against man nor beast, that ye may know that the Lord putteth a difference between the Egyptians and Israel.

8 And all these thy servants shall come down unto me, and fall before me, saying, Get thee out, and all the people that [1]are at thy feet, and after this will I depart. So he went out from Pharaoh very angry.

9 And the Lord said unto Moses, Pharaoh shall not hear you, [1]that my wonders may be multiplied in the land of Egypt.

10 So Moses and Aaron did all these wonders before Pharaoh: but the Lord hardened Pharaoh's heart, and he suffered not the children of Israel to go out of his land.

12

1 The Lord instituteth the passover. 26 The fathers must teach their children the mystery thereof. 29 The firstborn are slain. 31 The Israelites are driven out of the land. 35 The Egyptians are spoiled. 37 The number that departeth out of Egypt.

1 Then the Lord spake to Moses and to Aaron in the land of Egypt, saying,

2 This [1]month *shall be* unto you the beginning of months: it *shall be* to you the first [2]month of the year.

3 Speak ye unto all the congregation of Israel, saying, In the tenth of this month let every man take unto him a lamb, according to the house of the [1]fathers, a lamb for an house.

4 And if the household be too little for the lamb, he shall take his neighbor, which is next unto his house, according to the number of the persons: every one of you, according to his [1]eating shall make your count for the lamb.

[b] Exod. 12:29

5 Your lamb shall be without blemish, a male of a year old: ye shall take it of the lambs, or of the kids.

6 And ye shall keep *it* until the fourteenth day of this month: then [1]all the multitude of the congregation of Israel shall kill it [2]at even.

7 After, they shall take of the blood, and strike it on the two posts, and on the upper doorpost of the houses where they shall eat it.

8 And they shall eat the flesh that same night, roast with fire, and unleavened bread: with sour *herbs* they shall eat it.

9 Eat not thereof raw, boiled nor sodden in water, but roast with fire, both his [1]head, his feet, and his purtenance.

10 And ye shall reserve nothing of it unto the morning: but that, which remaineth of it unto the morrow shall ye burn with fire.

11 ¶ And thus shall ye eat it, Your loins girded, your shoes on your feet, and your staves in your hands, and ye shall eat it in haste: *for* [1]it is the Lord's Passover.

12 For I will pass through the land of Egypt the same night, and will smite all the firstborn in the land of Egypt, both man and beast, and I will execute judgment upon all the [1]gods of Egypt, I *am* the Lord.

13 And the blood shall be a token for you upon the houses where ye are: so when I see the blood, I will pass over you, and the plague shall not be upon you to destruction, when I smite the land of Egypt.

14 And this day shall be unto you a [1]remembrance: and ye shall keep it an holy feast unto the Lord, throughout your generations: ye shall keep it holy by an ordinance [2]forever.

15 Seven days shall ye eat unleavened bread, and in any case ye shall put away leaven the first day out of your houses: for whosoever eateth leavened bread from the first day until the seventh day, that person shall be cut off from Israel.

16 And in the first day *shall be* an holy [1]assembly: also in the seventh day shall be an holy assembly unto you: no work shall be done in them, save about that which every man must eat: that only may ye do.

17 Ye shall keep also *the feast* of unleavened bread: for that same day I will bring your armies out of the land of Egypt: therefore ye shall observe this day, throughout your posterity, by an ordinance forever.

11:5 [1] From the highest to the lowest.
11:8 [1] That is, under thy power and government.
11:9 [1] God hardeneth the hearts of the reprobate, that his glory thereby might be the more set forth, Rom. 9:17.
12:2 [1] Called Nisan, containing part of March, and part of April.
  [2] As touching the observation of feasts: as for other policies, they reckoned from September.
12:3 [1] As the fathers of the household had great or small families.
12:4 [1] He shall take so many as are sufficient to eat the lamb.

12:6 [1] Everyone his house.
  [2] Hebrew, *between the two evenings, or twilight.*
12:9 [1] That is, all that may be eaten.
12:11 [1] The lamb was not the Passover, but signified it, as sacraments are not the thing itself, which they do represent, but signify it.
12:12 [1] Or, princes, or Idols.
12:14 [1] Of the benefit received for your deliverance.
  [2] That is, until Christ's coming: for then ceremonies had an end.
12:16 [1] Or, calling together of the people to serve God.

18 ¶ ªIn the first *month* and the fourteenth day of the month at ¹even, ye shall eat unleavened bread unto the one and twentieth day of the month at even.

19 Seven days shall no leaven be found in your houses: for whosoever eateth leavened bread, that person shall be cut off from the Congregation of Israel: whether he be a stranger, or born in the land.

20 Ye shall eat no leavened bread: *but* in all your habitations shall ye eat unleavened bread.

21 ¶ Then Moses called all the Elders of Israel, and said unto them, Choose out and take you for *every* of your households a lamb, and kill the Passover.

22 And take ᵇa bunch of hyssop, and dip it in the blood that is in the basin, and strike the ¹lintel, and the ²door cheeks with the blood that is in the basin, and let none of you go out at the door of the house, until the morning.

23 For the Lord will pass by to smite the Egyptians: and when he seeth the blood upon the lintel and on the two door cheeks, the Lord will pass over the door, and will not suffer the ¹destroyer to come into your houses to plague *you.*

24 Therefore shall ye observe this thing as an ordinance, *both* for thee and thy sons forever.

25 And when ye shall come into the ¹land, which the Lord will give you, as he hath promised, then ye shall keep this ²service.

26 ᶜAnd when your children ask you, What service is this ye *keep?*

27 Then ye shall say, It is the sacrifice of the Lord's Passover, which passed over the houses of the children of Israel in Egypt, when he smote the Egyptians, and preserved our houses. Then the people ¹bowed themselves and worshipped.

28 So the children of Israel went, and did as the Lord had commanded Moses and Aaron: so did they.

29 ¶ Now at ᵈmidnight, the Lord ¹smote all the firstborn in the land of Egypt, from the firstborn of Pharaoh that sat on his throne, unto the firstborn of the captive that was in prison, and all the firstborn of beasts.

30 And Pharaoh rose up in the night, he, and all his servants, and all the Egyptians: and there was a great cry in Egypt: for there *was* ¹no house where there *was* not one dead.

31 And he called to Moses and to Aaron by night,

CHAPTER 12
ª Lev. 23:5
Num. 28:16
ᵇ Heb. 21:28
ᶜ Josh. 4:6
ᵈ Exod. 11:4
ᵉ Exod. 3:12
Exod. 11:2
ᶠ Num. 32:3
Josh. 24:6
ᵍ Gen. 15:13
Acts 7:6
Gal. 3:17
ʰ Num. 9:12

and said, Rise up, get you out from among my people, both ye, and the children of Israel, and go serve the Lord as ye have said.

32 Take also your sheep and your cattle as ye have said, and depart, and ¹bless me also.

33 And the Egyptians did force the people, because they would send them out of the land in haste: for they said, We die all.

34 Therefore the people took their dough before it was leavened, *even* their dough bound in clothes upon their shoulders.

35 And the children of Israel did according to the saying of Moses, and they asked of the Egyptians ᶜjewels of silver and jewels of gold, and raiment.

36 And the Lord gave the people favor in the sight of the Egyptians: and they ¹granted their request: so they spoiled the Egyptians.

37 Then the ᶠchildren of Israel took their journey from ¹Rameses to Succoth about six hundred thousand men of foot, besides children.

38 And ¹a great multitude of sundry sorts of people went out with them, and sheep, and beeves, *and* cattle in great abundance.

39 And they baked the dough which they brought out of Egypt, *and* made unleavened cakes: for it was not leavened, because they were thrust out of Egypt, neither could they tarry, nor yet prepare themselves vittles.

40 ¶ So the dwelling of the children of Israel, while they dwelled in Egypt, *was* ᵍfour hundred and thirty years.

41 And when the ¹four hundred and thirty years were expired, even the selfsame day departed all the hosts of the Lord out of the land of Egypt.

42 It *is* a night to be kept *holy* to the Lord, because he brought them out of the land of Egypt: this is that night of the Lord, which all the children of Israel must keep throughout their generations.

43 Also the Lord said unto Moses and Aaron, This is the Law of the Passover: ¹no stranger shall eat thereof.

44 But every servant that is bought for money, when thou hast circumcised him, then shall he eat thereof.

45 A stranger or an hired servant shall not eat thereof.

46 ᵇIn one house shall it be eaten: thou shalt carry

12:18   ¹ For in old time so they counted, beginning the day at Sunset till the next day at the same time.
12:22   ¹ Or, transom, or upper door post.
    ² Or, two side posts.
12:23   ¹ The Angel sent of God to kill the firstborn.
12:25   ¹ The land of Canaan.
    ² Or, ceremony.
12:27   ¹ They gave God thanks for so great a benefit.
12:29   ¹ The tenth plague.

12:30   ¹ Of those houses, wherein any firstborn was, either of men or beasts.
12:32   ¹ Pray for me.
12:36   ¹ Or, lent them.
12:37   ¹ Which was a city in Goshen, Gen. 47:11.
12:38   ¹ Which were strangers, and not born of the Israelites.
12:41   ¹ From Abraham's departing from Ur in Chaldea unto the departing of the children of Israel from Egypt are 430 years.
12:43   ¹ Except he be circumcised, and only profess your religion.

none of the flesh out of the house, ʲneither shall ye break a bone thereof.

47 All the Congregation of Israel shall observe it.

48 But if a stranger dwell with thee, and will observe the passover of the Lord, let him circumcise all the males, that belong unto him, and then let him come and observe it, and he shall be as one that is born in the land: for none uncircumcised person shall eat thereof.

49 One ¹law shall be to him that is born in the land, and to the stranger that dwelleth among you.

50 Then all the children of Israel did as the Lord commanded Moses and Aaron: so did they.

51 And the selfsame day did the Lord bring the children of Israel out of the land of Egypt by their armies.

13

The firstborn are offered to God.   3 The memorial of their deliverance.   6 The institution of the Passover.   8, 14 An exhortation to teach their children to remember this deliverance.   17 Why they are led by the wilderness.   19 The bones of Joseph.   21 The pillar of the cloud and of the fire.

1 And the Lord spake unto Moses, saying,

2 ᵃSanctify unto me all the firstborn: that is, every one that first openeth the womb among the children of Israel, as well of man as of beast: for it is mine.

3 ¶ Then Moses said unto the people, ᵇRemember this day in the which ye came out of Egypt, out of the ¹house of ²bondage: for by a mighty hand the Lord brought you out from thence: therefore no leavened bread shall be ³eaten.

4 This day come ye out in the month of ¹Abib.

5 ¶ Now when the Lord hath brought thee into the land of the Canaanites, and Hittites, and Amorites, and Hivites, and Jebusites, (which he sware unto thy fathers, that he would give thee, a land flowing with milk and honey) then thou shalt keep this service in this month.

6 Seven days shalt thou eat unleavened bread, and the ¹seventh day shall be the feast of the Lord.

7 Unleavened bread shall be eaten seven days, and there shall no leavened bread be seen with thee, nor yet leaven be seen with thee in all thy quarters.

8 ¶ And thou shalt show thy son ¹in that day,

ʲ John 29:36

CHAPTER 13
ᵃ Exod. 22:29
Exod. 34:19
Lev. 27:26
Num. 3:13
Num. 8:16
Luke 2:23
ᵇ Exod. 23:23
ᶜ Exod. 22:29
Exod. 34:19
Ezek. 44:30
ᵈ Gen. 50:22
Josh. 24:30
ᵉ Num. 33:6

saying, This is done, because of that which the Lord did unto me, when I came out of Egypt.

9 And it shall be a sign unto thee ¹upon thine hand, and for a remembrance between thine eyes, that the Law of the Lord may be in thy mouth: for by a strong hand the Lord brought thee out of Egypt.

10 Keep therefore this ordinance in his season appointed from year to year.

11 ¶ And when the Lord shall bring thee into the land of the Canaanites, as he sware unto thee and to thy fathers, and shall give it thee,

12 ᶜThen shalt thou set apart unto the Lord all that first openeth the womb: also everything that first doth open the womb, and cometh forth of thy beast: the males shall be the Lord's.

13 But every ¹first foal of an ²ass, thou shalt redeem with a lamb: and if thou redeem him not, then shalt thou break his neck: likewise also the firstborn of man among thy sons shalt thou ³buy out.

14 ¶ And when thy son shall ask thee ¹tomorrow, saying, What is this? thou shalt then say unto him, With a mighty hand the Lord brought us out of Egypt, out of the house of bondage.

15 For when Pharaoh was hard hearted against our departing, the Lord then slew all the firstborn in the land of Egypt, from the firstborn of man even to the firstborn of beast: therefore I sacrifice unto the Lord all the males that first open the womb, but all the firstborn of my sons I redeem.

16 And it shall be as a token upon thine hand, and as ¹frontlets between thine eyes, that the Lord brought us out of Egypt by a mighty hand.

17 ¶ Now when Pharaoh had let the people go, God carried them not by the way of the Philistines' country, ¹though it were nearer: (for God said, Lest the people repent when they ²see war, and turn again to Egypt).

18 But God made the people to go about by the way of the wilderness of the red sea: and the children of Israel went up ¹armed out of the land of Egypt.

19 (And Moses took the bones of Joseph with him: for he had made the children of Israel swear, saying, ᵈGod will surely visit you, and ye shall take my bones away hence with you.)

20 ¶ ᵉSo they took their journey from Succoth, and

12:49 ¹ They that are of the household of God, must be all joined in one faith and religion.

13:3 ¹ Hebrew, house of servants.
    ² Where they were in most cruel slavery.
    ³ To signify that they had not leisure to leaven their bread.

13:4 ¹ Containing part of March and part of April, when corn began to ripe in that country.

13:6 ¹ Both the seventh and the first day were holy, as Exod. 12:16.

13:8 ¹ When thou dost celebrate the feast of unleavened bread.

13:9 ¹ Thou shalt have continual remembrance thereof, as thou wouldest of a thing that is in thine hand, or before thine eyes.

13:13 ¹ Hebrew, that first cometh forth.
    ² This is also understood of the horse and other beasts which were not offered in sacrifice.
    ³ By offering a clean beast in sacrifice, Lev. 12:6.

13:14 ¹ Or, hereafterwards.

13:16 ¹ Or, signs of remembrance.

13:17 ¹ Or, because.
    ² Which the Philistines would have made against them by stopping them the passage.

13:18 ¹ That is, not privily, but openly and as the word doth signify, set in order by five and five.

camped in Etham in the edge of the wilderness.

21 *f*And the Lord went before them by day in a pillar of a [1]cloud to lead them the way, and by night in a pillar of fire to give them light, that they might go both by day and by night.

22 *g*He took not away the pillar of the cloud by day, nor the pillar of fire by night from before the people.

f Num. 14:14
Deut. 1:33
Ps. 78:14
1 Cor. 10:1
g Neh. 9:19

CHAPTER 14

a Num. 33:7
b Josh. 24:6
c Josh. 4:23
Ps. 114:3
d Ps. 78:13
1 Cor. 10:1
Heb. 11:29

14

4, 8 Pharaoh's heart is hardened, and pursueth the Israelites.   11 The Israelites stricken with fear, murmur against Moses.   13 Moses doth encourage them.   21 He divideth the Sea.   23, 27 The Egyptians follow and are drowned.

1 Then the Lord spake unto Moses, saying,

2 Speak to the children of Israel, that they [1]return and camp before [2]Pi Hahiroth, between Migdol and the Sea, over against *a*Baal Zephon: about it shall ye camp by the Sea.

3 For Pharaoh will say of the children of Israel, They are tangled in the land: the wilderness hath shut them in.

4 And I will harden Pharaoh's heart that he shall follow after you: so I will [1]get me honor upon Pharaoh, and upon all his host: the Egyptians also shall know that I am the Lord: and they did so.

5 ¶ Then it was told the king of Egypt, that the people fled: and the heart of Pharaoh and of his servants was turned against the people, and they said, Why have we this done, and have let Israel go out of our service?

6 And he made ready his chariots, and took his people with him,

7 And took six hundred chosen chariots, and [1]all the chariots of Egypt, and captains over every one of them.

8 (For the Lord had hardened the heart of Pharaoh king of Egypt, and he followed after the children of Israel: but the children of Israel went out with an [1]high hand.)

9 *b*And the Egyptians pursued after them, and all the horses *and* chariots of Pharaoh, and his horsemen and his host overtook them camping by the Sea, beside Pi Hahiroth, before Baal Zephon.

10 And when Pharaoh drew nigh, the children of Israel lift up their eyes, and behold, the Egyptians marched after them, and they were sore [1]afraid: wherefore the children of Israel cried unto the Lord.

11 And they said unto Moses, Hast thou brought us to die in the wilderness, because there were no graves in Egypt? wherefore hast thou served us thus, to carry us out of Egypt?

12 Did not we tell thee this thing in Egypt, saying, Let [1]us be in rest, that we may serve the Egyptians? for it had been better for us to serve the Egyptians, than that we should die in the wilderness.

13 Then Moses said to the people, Fear ye not, stand still, and behold [1]the salvation of the Lord which he will show to you this day. For the Egyptians whom ye have seen this day, ye shall never see them again.

14 The Lord shall fight for you: therefore [1]hold you your peace.

15 ¶ And the Lord said unto Moses, Wherefore [1]cryest thou unto me? speak unto the children of Israel, that they go forward:

16 And lift thou up thy rod, and stretch out thine hand upon the Sea and divide it, and let the children of Israel go on dry ground through the midst of the Sea.

17 And I, behold, I will harden the heart of the Egyptians, that they may follow them, and I will get me honor upon Pharaoh, and upon all his host, upon his chariots, and upon his horsemen.

18 Then the Egyptians shall know that I am the Lord, when I have gotten me honor upon Pharaoh, upon his chariots, and upon his horsemen.

19 (And the Angel of God, which went before the host of Israel, removed, and went behind them: also the pillar of the cloud went from before them, and stood behind them,

20 And came between the camp of the Egyptians and the camp of Israel: it was both a cloud and darkness, yet gave it [1]light by night, so that all the night long the one came not at the other.)

21 And Moses stretched forth his hand upon the Sea, and the Lord caused the Sea to run back by a strong East wind all the night, and made the Sea dry land: for the waters were *c*divided.

22 Then the *d*children of Israel went through the midst of the Sea upon the dry ground, and the waters *were* a wall unto them on their right hand, and on their left hand.

13:21 [1] To defend them from the heat of the sun.
14:2 [1] From toward the country of the Philistines.
 [2] So the Sea was before them, mountains on either side, and the enemies at their back: yet they obeyed God, and were delivered.
14:4 [1] By punishing his obstinate rebellion.
14:7 [1] Josephus writeth, that besides those chariots there were 50,000 horsemen, and 80,000 footmen.
14:8 [1] With great joy and boldness.
14:10 [1] They which a little before in their deliverance rejoiced, being now in danger, are afraid and …
14:12 [1] Such is the impatience of the flesh, that it cannot abide God's appointed time.
14:13 [1] Or, deliverance.
14:14 [1] Only put your trust in God without grudging or doubting.
14:15 [1] Thus in tentations faith fighteth against the flesh, and crieth with inward groanings to the Lord.
14:20 [1] The cloud showeth light to the Israelites, but to the Egyptians it was darkness, so that their two hosts could not join together.

23 And the Egyptians pursued and went after them to the midst of the Sea, *even* all Pharaoh's horses, his chariots, and his horsemen.

24 Now, in the morning [1]watch, when the Lord looked unto the host of the Egyptians, out of the fiery and cloudy pillar, he struck the host of the Egyptians with fear.

25 For he took off their chariot wheels, and they drove them with [1]much ado: so that the Egyptians *every* one said, I will flee from the face of Israel: for the Lord fighteth for them against the Egyptians.

26 ¶ Then the Lord said to Moses, Stretch thine hand upon the Sea, that the waters may return upon the Egyptians, upon their chariots and upon their horsemen.

27 Then Moses stretched forth his hand upon the Sea, and the Sea returned to his force early in the morning, and the Egyptians fled against it: but the Lord [1]overthrew the Egyptians in the midst of the Sea.

28 So the water returned and covered the chariots, and the horsemen, *even* all the host of Pharaoh that came into the Sea after them: there remained not one of them.

29 But the children of Israel walked upon dry land through the midst of the Sea, and the waters *were* a wall unto them on their right hand, and on their left.

30 Thus the Lord saved Israel the same day out of the hand of the Egyptians, and Israel saw the Egyptians dead upon the Sea bank.

31 And Israel saw the mighty [1]power, which the Lord showed upon the Egyptians: so the people feared the Lord, and believed the Lord, and his [2]servant Moses.

15

1, 20 Moses with the men and women sing praises unto God for their deliverance. 23 The people murmur. 25 At the prayer of Moses the bitter waters are sweet. 26 God teacheth the people obedience.

1 Then [1]sang Moses and the children of Israel this song unto the Lord, and said in this manner, I will sing unto the Lord: for he hath triumphed gloriously: the horse and him that rode upon him hath he overthrown in the Sea.

CHAPTER 15
a Deut. 2:25
Josh. 2:9

2 The Lord *is* my strength, and [1]praise, and he is become my salvation. He is my God, and I will [2]prepare him a tabernacle: *he is* my father's God, and I will exalt him.

3 The Lord *is* a [1]man of war, his [2]Name *is* Jehovah.

4 Pharaoh's chariots and his host hath he cast into the sea: his chosen captains also were drowned in the red Sea.

5 The depths have covered them, they sank to the bottom as a stone.

6 Thy [1]right hand, O Lord, is glorious in power: thy right hand, O Lord, hath bruised the enemy.

7 And in thy great glory thou hast overthrown them that rose against [1]thee: thou sentest forth thy wrath, *which* consumed them as the stubble.

8 And by the blast of thy nostrils the waters were gathered, the floods stood still as an heap, the depths congealed together in the [1]heart of the Sea.

9 The enemy said, I will pursue, I will overtake *them*, I will divide the spoil, [1]my lust shall be satisfied upon them, I will draw my sword, mine hand shall destroy them.

10 Thou blewest with thy wind, the sea covered them, they sank as lead in the mighty waters.

11 Who is like unto thee, O Lord, among the [1]gods! Who is like thee *so* glorious in holiness, [2]fearful in praises, doing wonders!

12 Thou stretchedst out thy right hand, the earth swallowed them.

13 Thou wilt by thy mercy carry this people, *which* thou deliveredst, thou wilt bring *them* in thy strength unto thine holy [1]habitation.

14 The people shall hear *and* be afraid: sorrow shall come upon the inhabitants of Philistia.

15 Then the dukes of Edom shall be amazed, and trembling shall come upon the great men of Moab: all the inhabitants of Canaan shall wax faint hearted.

16 [a]Fear and dread shall fall upon them: because of the [1]greatness of thine arm, they shall be still as a stone, till thy people pass, O Lord: till this people pass, *which* thou hast purchased.

17 Thou shalt bring them in, and plant them in the mountain of thine [1]inheritance, *which is* the

---

14:24 [1] Which was about the three last hours of the night.
14:25 [1] Or, heavily.
14:27 [1] So the Lord by the water saved his, and by the water drowned his enemies.
14:31 [1] Hebrew, *hand*.
   [2] That is, the doctrine which he taught them in the Name of the Lord.
15:1 [1] Praising God for the overthrow of his enemies, and their deliverance.
15:2 [1] Or, the occasion of my song of praise.
   [2] To worship him therein.
15:3 [1] In battle he overcometh ever.

[2] Ever constant in his promise.
15:6 [1] Or, power.
15:7 [1] Those, that are enemies to God's people, are his enemies.
15:8 [1] Or, in the depth of the sea.
15:9 [1] Hebrew, *my soul shall be filled.*
15:11 [1] For so oftentimes the Scripture calleth the mighty men of the world.
   [2] Which oughtest to be praised with all fear and reverence.
15:13 [1] That is, into the land of Canaan: or into mount Zion.
15:16 [1] Or, for thy great power.
15:17 [1] Which was mount Zion, where afterward the Temple was built.

place *that* thou hast prepared, O Lord, for to dwell in, *even* the sanctuary, O Lord, *which* thine hands shall establish.

18 The Lord shall reign forever and ever.

19 For Pharaoh's horses went with his chariots and horsemen into the sea, and the Lord brought the waters of the sea upon them: but the children of Israel went on dry land in the midst of the sea.

20 ¶ And Miriam the Prophetess, sister of Aaron, took a timbrel in her hand, and all the women came out after her with timbrels and [1]dances.

21 And Miriam [1]answered the men, Sing ye unto the Lord: for he hath triumphed gloriously: the horse and his rider hath he overthrown in the sea.

22 Then Moses brought Israel from the red sea, and they went out into the wilderness of [1]Shur: and they went three days in the wilderness, and found no waters.

23 And when they came to Marah, they could not drink of the waters of Marah, for they were bitter: therefore the name of the place was called [1]Marah.

24 Then the people murmured against Moses, saying, What shall we drink?

25 And he cried unto the Lord, and the Lord showed him a tree, *which* when he had cast into the waters, the waters were sweet: there he made them an ordinance and a law, and there [1]he proved them,

26 And said, If thou wilt diligently hearken, *O Israel*, unto the voice of the Lord thy God, and wilt do that which is [1]right in his sight, and wilt give ear unto his commandments, and keep all his ordinances, then will I put none of these diseases upon thee, which I brought upon the Egyptians: for I *am* the Lord that healeth thee.

27 ¶ [b]And they came to Elim, where *were* twelve fountains of water, and seventy [1]palm trees, and they camped there by the waters.

16

1 The Israelites come to the desert of Sin, and murmur against Moses and Aaron. 13 The Lord sendeth Quails and Manna. 23 The Sabbath is sanctified unto the Lord. 27 The seventh day Manna could not be found. 32 It is kept for a remembrance to the posterity.

1 Afterward all the Congregation of the children of Israel departed from Elim, and came to the wil-

[b] Num. 33:9

CHAPTER 16

[a] Exod. 13:21

derness of [1]Sin, (which is between Elim and Sinai) the fifteenth day of the second month after their departing out of the land of Egypt.

2 And the whole Congregation of the children of Israel murmured against Moses, and against Aaron in the wilderness.

3 For the children of Israel said to them, Oh that we had died by the hand of the Lord in the land of Egypt, when we sat by the flesh [1]pots, when we ate bread *our* bellies full: for ye have brought us out into this wilderness, to kill this whole company with famine.

4 ¶ Then said the Lord unto Moses, Behold, I will cause bread to rain from heaven to you, and the people shall go out, and gather [1]that that is sufficient for every [2]day, that I may prove them, whether they will walk in my law or no.

5 But the sixth day they shall prepare that, which they shall bring *home*, and it shall be twice as much as they gather daily.

6 Then Moses and Aaron said unto all the children of Israel, At even ye shall know, that the Lord brought you out of the land of Egypt:

7 And in the morning ye shall see the glory of the Lord: [1]for he hath heard your grudgings against the Lord: and what are we that ye have murmured against us?

8 Again, Moses said, At even shall the Lord give you flesh to eat, and in the morning your fill of bread: for the Lord hath heard your murmurings, which ye murmur against him: for what are we? your murmurings are not against us, but against the [1]Lord.

9 ¶ And Moses said to Aaron, Say unto all the Congregation of the children of Israel, Draw near before the Lord: for he hath heard your murmurings.

10 Now as Aaron spake unto the whole Congregation of the children of Israel, they looked toward the wilderness, and behold, the glory of the Lord appeared [a]in a cloud.

11 (For the Lord had spoken unto Moses, saying,

12 I have heard the murmurings of the children of Israel: tell them *therefore*, and say, [1]At even ye shall eat flesh, and in the morning ye shall be filled with bread,

---

15:20 [1] Signifying their great joy: which custom the Jews observed in certain solemnities, Judg. 11:34 and 11:21, but it ought not to be a cloak to cover our wanton dances.

15:21 [1] By singing the like song of thanksgiving.

15:22 [1] Which was called Etham, Num. 33:8.

15:23 [1] Or, bitterness.

15:25 [1] That is, God, or Moses in God's name.

15:26 [1] Which is, to do that only that God commanded.

15:27 [1] Or, date trees.

16:1 [1] This is the eighth place wherein they had camped, there is another place called Zin, which was the 33rd place wherein they

camped: and is also called Kadesh, Num. 33:36.

16:3 [1] So hard a thing is it to the flesh not to murmur against God when the belly is pinched.

16:4 [1] Hebrew, *the portion of a day in his day.*

[2] To signify, that they should patiently depend upon God's providence from day to day.

16:7 [1] He gave them not Manna because they murmured, but for his promise sake.

16:8 [1] He that contemneth God's ministers, contemneth God himself.

16:12 [1] Or, in the twilight.

and ye shall know that I am the Lord your God.)

13 And so at even the [b]quails came and covered the camp: and in the morning the dew lay round about the host.

14 [c]And when the dew that was fallen was ascended, behold, a small round thing *was* upon the face of the wilderness, small as the hoary frost upon the earth.

15 And when the children of Israel saw it, they said one to another, It is [1]Manna, for they wist not what it was. And Moses said unto them, [d]This is the bread which the Lord hath given you to eat.

16 ¶ This is the thing which the Lord hath commanded: gather of it every man according to his eating, [1]an omer for [2]a man *according* to the number of your persons: every man shall take for them which are in his tent.

17 And the children of Israel did so, and gathered, some more, some less.

18 And when they did measure it with an omer, [e]he that had gathered much, had nothing over, and he that had gathered little, had no [1]lack: *so* every man gathered according to his eating.

19 Moses then said unto them, Let no man reserve thereof till morning.

20 Notwithstanding, they obeyed not Moses: but some of them reserved of it till morning, and it was full of worms, and [1]stank: therefore Moses was angry with them.

21 And they gathered it every morning, every man according to his eating: for when the heat of the sun came, it was melted.

22 ¶ And the sixth day they gathered [1]twice so much bread, two omers for one man: then all the rulers of the Congregation came and told Moses.

23 And he answered them, This is that which the Lord hath said, Tomorrow *is* the rest of the holy Sabbath unto the Lord: bake that *today* which ye will bake, and seethe that which ye will seethe, and all that remaineth, lay it up to be kept till the morning for you.

24 And they laid it up till the morning, as Moses bade, and it stank not, neither was there any worm therein.

25 Then Moses said, Eat that today: for today *is* the Sabbath unto the Lord: today ye shall not [1]find

[b] Num. 11:31
[c] Num. 11:7
    Ps. 78:24
[d] John 6:30
    1 Cor. 10:3
[e] 2 Cor. 8:15
[f] Josh. 5:12
    Neh. 5:15

CHAPTER 17
[a] Num. 20:4

it in the field.

26 Six days shall ye gather it, but in the seventh day *is* the Sabbath: in it there shall be none.

27 ¶ Notwithstanding, there [1]went out *some* of the people in the seventh day for to gather, and they found none.

28 And the Lord said unto Moses, How long refuse ye to keep my commandments, and my laws?

29 Behold, how the Lord hath given you the Sabbath: therefore he giveth you the sixth day bread for two days: tarry *therefore* every man in his place: let no man go out of his place the seventh day.

30 So the people rested the seventh day.

31 And the house of Israel called the name of it Manna, and it was like [1]to coriander seed, *but* white: and the taste of it was like unto wafers *made* with honey.

32 And Moses said, This is that which the Lord had commanded, Fill an omer of it, to keep it for your posterity: that they may see the bread wherewith I have fed you in wilderness, when I brought you out of the land of Egypt.

33 Moses also said to Aaron, Take a [1]pot and put an omer full of Manna therein, and set it before the Lord to be kept for your posterity.

34 As the Lord commanded Moses, so Aaron laid it up before the [1]Testimony to be kept.

35 And the children of Israel did eat Manna [f]forty years, until they came unto a land inhabited: they did eat Manna until they came to the borders of the land of Canaan.

36 The omer *is* the tenth part of the [1]Ephah.

17

1 The Israelites come into Rephidim, and grudge for water. 6 Water is given them out of the rock. 11 Moses holdeth up his hands, and they overcome the Amalekites. 15 Moses buildeth an altar to the Lord.

1 And all the Congregation of the children of Israel departed from the wilderness of Sin, by their journeys at the [1]commandment of the Lord, and camped in [2]Rephidim, where *was* no water for the people to drink.

2 [a]Wherefore the people contended with Moses, and said, Give us water, that we may drink. And Moses said unto them, Why contend ye with me? wherefore do ye [1]tempt the Lord?

16:15 [1] Which signifieth a part, portion, or gift: also meat prepared.
16:16 [1] Which containeth about a pottle of our measure.
       [2] Hebrew, *for an head.*
16:18 [1] God is a rich feeder of all, and none can justly complain.
16:20 [1] No creature is so pure, but being abused it turneth to our destruction.
16:22 [1] Which portion should serve for the Sabbath and the day before.
16:25 [1] God took away the occasion from their labor, to signify how holy he would have the Sabbath kept.
16:27 [1] Their infidelity was so great, that they did expressly against God's commandment.
16:31 [1] In form and figure, but not in color, Num.11:7.
16:33 [1] Of this vessel, read Heb. 9:4.
16:34 [1] That is, the Ark of the covenant, to wit, after that the Ark was made.
16:36 [1] Which measure contained about ten pottels.
17:1 [1] Hebrew, *at the mouth.*
     [2] Moses here noteth not every place where they camped, as Num. 33, but only those places, where some notable thing was done.
17:2 [1] Why distrust you God? why look ye not for succor of him without murmuring against us?

3   So the people thirsted there for water, and the people murmured against Moses, and said, Wherefore hast thou thus brought us out of Egypt, to kill us, and our children, and our cattle with thirst?

4   And Moses cried unto the Lord, saying, What shall I do to this people? for they be almost ready to [1]stone me.

5   And the Lord answered to Moses, Go before the people, and take with thee of the Elders of Israel: and thy rod wherewith thou [b]smotest the river, take in thine hand, and go:

6   [c]Behold, I will stand there before thee upon the rock in Horeb, and thou shalt smite on the rock, and water shall come out of it, that the people may drink. And Moses did so in the sight of the Elders of Israel.

7   And he called the name of the place [1]Massah and [2]Meribah, because of the contention of the children of Israel, and because they had tempted the Lord, saying, Is the [3]Lord among us, or no?

8   ¶ [d]Then came [1]Amalek and fought with Israel in Rephidim.

9   And Moses said to Joshua, Choose us out men, and go fight with Amalek: tomorrow I will stand on the top of the [1]hill with the rod of God in mine hand.

10   So Joshua did as Moses bade him, and fought with Amalek: and Moses, Aaron, and Hur, went up to the top of the hill.

11   And when Moses held up his hand, Israel prevailed: but when he let his hand [1]down, Amalek prevailed.

12   Now Moses' hands were heavy: therefore they took a stone and put it under him, and he sat upon it: and Aaron and Hur stayed up his hands, the one on the one side, and the other on the other side: so his hands were steady until the going down of the sun.

13   And Joshua discomfited Amalek and his people with the edge of the sword.

14   ¶ And the Lord said to Moses, Write this for a remembrance [1]in the book, and [2]rehearse it to Joshua: for [e]I will utterly put out the remembrance

Marginal references:
[b] Exod. 7:20
[c] Num. 2:9
  Ps. 78:15
  Ps. 105:41
  1 Cor. 10:4
[d] Deut. 25:17
[e] Num. 24:20
  1 Sam. 15:3

CHAPTER 18
[a] Exod. 2:16
[b] Exod. 2:22

of Amalek from under heaven.

15   (And Moses built an altar, and called the name of it [1]Jehovah Nissi.)

16   Also he said, [1]The Lord hath sworn, that he will have war with Amalek from generation to generation.

18

1 Jethro cometh to see Moses his son-in-law. 8 Moses telleth him of the wonders of Egypt. 9 Jethro rejoiceth and offereth sacrifice to God. 21 What manner of men officers and judges ought to be. 24 Moses obeyeth Jethro's counsel in appointing officers.

1   When Jethro the [a]Priest of Midian, Moses' father-in-law, heard all that God had done for Moses, and for Israel his people, and how the Lord had brought Israel out of Egypt,

2   Then Jethro the father-in-law of Moses, took Zipporah Moses' wife, (after he had [1]sent her away)

3   And her two sons, (whereof the one was called [b]Gershom: for he said, I have been an alien in a strange land:

4   And the name of the other was Eliezer: for the God of my father, said he, was mine help, and delivered me from the sword of Pharaoh).

5   And Jethro Moses' father-in-law came with his two sons, and his wife unto Moses into the wilderness, where he camped by the [1]mount of God.

6   And he [1]said to Moses, I thy father-in-law Jethro am come to thee, and thy wife and her two sons with her.

7   ¶ And Moses went out to meet his father-in-law, and did obeisance, and kissed him, and each asked other of his [1]welfare: and they came into the tent.

8   Then Moses told his father-in-law all that the Lord had done unto Pharaoh, and to the Egyptians for Israel's sake, and all the travail that had come unto them by the way, and how the Lord delivered them.

9   And Jethro rejoiced at all the goodness, which the Lord had showed to Israel, and because he had delivered them out of the hand of the Egyptians.

10   Therefore Jethro said, [1]Blessed be the Lord who hath delivered you out of the hand of the

---

17:4 [1] How ready the people are for their own matters to slay the true Prophets, and how slow they are to revenge God's cause against his enemies and false Prophets.

17:7 [1] Or, tentation.
  [2] Or, strife.
  [3] When in adversity we think God to be absent, then we neglect his promise, and make him a liar.

17:8 [1] Who came of Eliphaz, son of Esau, Gen. 36:12.

17:9 [1] That is, Horeb, which is also called Sinai.

17:11 [1] So that we see how dangerous a thing it is to faint in prayer.

17:14 [1] In the book of the Law.
  [2] Hebrew, put it in the ears of Joshua.

17:15 [1] That is, the Lord is my banner as he declared by holding up

his rod and his hands.

17:16 [1] Hebrew, the hand of the Lord upon the throne.

18:2 [1] It may seem that he sent her back for a time to her father for her impatience, lest she should be a let to his vocation, which was so dangerous, Exod. 4:25.

18:5 [1] Horeb is called the mount of God, because God wrought many miracles there. So Peter calleth the mount where Christ was transfigured, the holy mount: for by Christ's presence it was holy for a time, 2 Pet. 1:18.

18:6 [1] That is, he sent messengers to say unto him.

18:7 [1] Hebrew, of peace.

18:10 [1] Whereby it is evident that he worshipped the true God, and therefore Moses refused not to marry his daughter.

Egyptians, and out of the hand of Pharaoh: who hath *also* delivered the people from under the hand of the Egyptians.

11 Now I know that the Lord is greater than all the gods: for as they have dealt ᶜproudly with them, *so are they* ¹*recompensed*.

12 Then Jethro Moses' father-in-law took burnt offerings and sacrifices, *to offer* unto God. And Aaron and all the Elders of Israel came to eat bread with Moses' father-in-law ¹before God.

13 ¶ Now on the morrow, when Moses sat to judge the people, the people stood about Moses from morning unto even.

14 And when Moses' father-in-law saw all that he did to the people, he said, What is this that thou doest to the people? why sittest thou thyself alone, and all the people stand about thee from morning unto even?

15 And Moses said unto his father-in-law, Because the people come unto me to seek ¹God.

16 When they have a matter, they come unto me, and I judge between one and another, and declare the ordinances of God, and his laws.

17 But Moses' father-in-law said unto him, The thing which thou doest, is not well.

18 Thou both ¹weariest thyself greatly, and this people that is with thee: for the thing *is* too heavy for thee: ᵈthou art not able to do it thyself alone.

19 Hear now my ¹voice, (I will give thee counsel, and God shall be with thee) be thou for the people to ²Godward, and report thou the causes unto God,

20 And admonish them of the ordinances, and of the laws, and show them the way, wherein they must walk, and the work that they must do.

21 Moreover, provide thou among all the people ¹men of courage, fearing God, men dealing truly, hating covetousness: and appoint *such* over them *to be* rulers over thousands, rulers over hundreds, rulers over fifties, and rulers over tens.

22 And let them judge the people at all seasons: but every great matter let them bring unto thee, and let them judge all small causes: so shall it be easier for thee, when they shall bear *the burden* with thee.

23 If thou do this thing, (and God *so* command

thee) both thou shalt be able to endure, and all this people shall also go quietly to their place.

24 So Moses ¹obeyed the voice of his father-in-law, and did all that he had said:

25 And Moses chose men of courage out of all Israel, and made them heads over the people, rulers over thousands, rulers over hundreds, rulers over fifties, and rulers over tens.

26 And they judged the people at all seasons, *but* they brought the hard causes to Moses: for they judged all small matters themselves.

27 Afterward Moses ¹let his father-in-law depart, and he went into his country.

19 1 *The Israelites come to Sinai.* 5 *Israel is chosen from among all other nations.* 8 *The people promise to obey God.* 12 *He that toucheth the hill, dieth.* 16 *God appeareth unto Moses upon the mount in thunder and lightning.*

1 In the ¹third month, after the children of Israel were gone out of the land of Egypt, the same ²day came they into the wilderness of Sinai.

2 For they departed from Rephidim, and came to the desert of Sinai, and camped in the wilderness, even there Israel camped before the mount.

3 ᵃBut Moses went up unto God, for the Lord had called out of the mount unto him, saying, Thus shalt thou say to the house of ¹Jacob, and tell the children of Israel.

4 ᵇYe have seen what I did unto the Egyptians, and *how* I carried you upon ¹eagle's wings, and have brought you unto me.

5 Now therefore ᶜif ye will hear my voice indeed, and keep my covenant, then ye shall be my chief treasure above all people, ᵈthough all the earth be mine.

6 Ye shall be unto me also a kingdom of ᵉPriests, and an holy nation. These *are* the words which thou shalt speak unto the children of Israel.

7 ¶ Moses then came and called for the Elders of the people, and proposed unto them all these things, which the Lord commanded him.

8 And the people answered all together, and said, ᶠAll that the Lord hath commanded, we will do. And Moses reported the words of the people unto the Lord.

9 And the Lord said unto Moses, Lo, I come unto

Cross references

ᶜ Exod. 1:10, 16, 22
Exod. 5:7
Exod. 14:8
ᵈ Deut. 1:9

CHAPTER 19
ᵃ Acts 7:38
ᵇ Deut. 29:2
ᶜ Deut. 5:2
ᵈ Deut. 10:14
Ps. 24:1
ᵉ 1 Pet. 2:9
Rev. 1:6
ᶠ Exod. 24:3
Deut. 5:27
Deut. 26:17
Josh. 21:16

18:11 ¹ For they that drowned the children of the Israelites, perished themselves by water.
18:12 ¹ They ate in that place, where the sacrifice was offered: for part was burnt, and the rest eaten.
18:15 ¹ That is, to know God's will, and to have justice executed.
18:18 ¹ Hebrew, *thou wilt faint and fall.*
18:19 ¹ Or, counsel.
² Judge thou in hard causes, which cannot be decided but by consulting with God.
18:21 ¹ What manner of men ought to be chosen to bear office.
18:24 ¹ Godly counsel ought ever to be obeyed, though it come of

our inferiors, for to such God oftentimes giveth wisdom to humble them that are exalted, and to declare that one member hath need of another.
18:27 ¹ Read the occasion, Num. 10:29.
19:1 ¹ Which was in the beginning of the month Sivan, containing part of May, and part of June.
² That they departed from Rephidim.
19:3 ¹ God called Jacob, Israel: therefore the house of Jacob and the people of Israel signify only God's people.
19:4 ¹ For the Eagle by flying high, is out of danger, and by carrying her birds rather on her wings than in her talons declareth her love.

thee in a thick cloud, that the people may hear while I talk with thee, and that they may also believe thee forever. (For Moses had told the words of the people unto the Lord.)

10 Moreover the Lord said unto Moses, Go to the people, and ¹sanctify them today and tomorrow, and let them wash their clothes.

11 And let them be ready on the third day: for the third day the Lord will come down in the sight of all the people upon mount Sinai:

12 And thou shalt set marks unto the people round about, saying, Take heed to yourselves, that ye go not up to the mount, nor touch the border of it, whosoever toucheth the ᵍmount, shall surely die.

13 No hand shall touch it, but he shall be stoned to death, or stricken through with darts: whether it be beast or man, he shall not live: when the ¹horn bloweth long, they shall come up ²into the mountain.

14 ¶ Then Moses went down from the mount unto the people, and sanctified the people, and they washed their clothes.

15 And he said unto the people, Be ready on the third day, *and* come not at *your* ¹wives.

16 And the third day, when it was morning, there was thunders and lightnings, and a thick cloud upon the mount, and the sound of the trumpet exceeding loud, so that all the people that was in the camp was afraid.

17 Then Moses brought the people out of the tents to meet with God, and they stood in the nether part of the mount.

18 ᵇAnd mount Sinai *was* all on smoke, because the Lord came down upon it in fire, and the smoke thereof ascended, as the smoke of a furnace, and all the mount ¹trembled exceedingly.

19 And when the sound of the trumpet blew long, and waxed louder and louder, Moses spake, and God answered him by ¹voice.

20 (For the Lord came down upon mount Sinai on the top of the mount) and when the Lord called Moses up into the top of the mount, Moses went up.

ᵍ Heb. 12:20
ᵇ Deut. 4:11

CHAPTER 20
ᵃ Deut. 5:6
Ps. 81:10
ᵇ Lev. 26:1
Ps. 97:7
ᶜ Lev. 19:12
Deut. 5:11
Matt. 5:33
ᵈ Exod. 23:12
Ezek. 20:12

21 Then the Lord said unto Moses, Go down, charge the people, that they break not *their bounds, to go up* to the Lord to gaze, lest many of them perish.

22 And let the ¹Priests also which come to the Lord be sanctified, lest the Lord ²destroy them.

23 And Moses said unto the Lord, The people cannot come up into the mount Sinai: for thou hast charged us, saying, Set marks on the mountain, and sanctify it.

24 And the Lord said unto him, Go, get thee down, and come up thou, and Aaron with thee: but let not the ¹Priests and the people break *their bounds* to come up unto the Lord, lest he destroy them.

25 So Moses went down unto the people, and told them.

20 *2 The Commandments of the first Table.   13 The Commandments of the second.   18 The people afraid are comforted by Moses.   23 Gods of silver and gold are again forbidden.   24 Of what sort the altar ought to be.*

1 Then God ¹spake all these words, saying,

2 ᵃI am the Lord thy God, which have brought thee out of the land of Egypt, out of the house of ¹bondage.

3 Thou shalt have none other gods ¹before me.

4 ᵇThou shalt make thee no graven image, neither any similitude *of things* that are in heaven above, neither that are in the earth beneath, nor that are in the waters under the earth.

5 Thou shalt not ¹bow down to them, neither serve them: for I am the Lord thy God, a ²jealous God, visiting the iniquity of the fathers upon the children, upon the third *generation* and upon the fourth of them that hate me:

6 And showing mercy unto ¹thousands to them that love me, and keep my commandments.

7 ᶜThou shalt not take the Name of the Lord thy God in ¹vain: for the Lord will not hold him guiltless that taketh his Name in vain.

8 Remember the Sabbath day, ¹to keep it holy.

9 ᵈSix days shalt thou labor, and do all thy work,

19:10 ¹ Teach them to be pure in heart, as they show themselves outwardly clean by washing.

19:13 ¹ Or, trumpet.

   ² Or, toward.

19:15 ¹ But give yourselves to prayer and abstinence, that you may at this time attend only upon the Lord, 1 Cor. 7:5.

19:18 ¹ God used these fearful signs, that his law should be had in greater reverence, and his majesty the more feared.

19:19 ¹ He gave authority to Moses by plain words, that the people might understand him.

19:22 ¹ Or, rulers.

   ² Or, break out upon them.

19:24 ¹ Neither dignity nor multitude have authority to pass the bounds that God's word prescribeth.

20:1 ¹ When Moses and Aaron were gone up, or had passed the bounds of the people, God spake thus out of the mount Horeb, that all the people heard.

20:2 ¹ Or, servants.

20:3 ¹ To whose eyes all things are open.

20:5 ¹ By this outward gesture, all kinds of service and worship to idols is forbidden.

   ² And will be revenged on the contemners of mine honor.

20:6 ¹ So ready is he rather to show mercy than to punish.

20:7 ¹ Either by swearing falsely or rashly by his Name, or by contemning it.

20:8 ¹ Which is by meditating the spiritual rest, by hearing God's word, and resting from worldly travails.

10 But the seventh day *is* the Sabbath of the Lord thy God: *in it* thou shalt not do any work, thou, nor thy son, nor thy daughter, thy manservant, nor thy maid, nor thy beast, nor thy stranger that is within thy [1]gates.

11 [e]For in six days the Lord made the heaven and the earth, the sea, and all that in them is, and rested the seventh day: therefore the Lord blessed the seventh day, and hallowed it.

12 ¶[f]Honor thy [1]father and thy mother, that thy days may be prolonged upon the land, which the Lord thy God giveth thee.

13 ¶[g]Thou shalt not [1]kill.

14 Thou shalt not [1]commit adultery.

15 Thou shalt not [1]steal.

16 Thou shalt not bear false [1]witness against thy neighbor.

17 [h]Thou shalt not [1]covet thy neighbor's house, neither shalt thou covet thy neighbor's wife, nor his manservant, nor his maid, nor his ox, nor his ass, neither anything that is thy neighbor's.

18 ¶ And all the people [1]saw the thunders: and the [2]lightnings, and the sound of the trumpet, and the mountain smoking, and when the people saw it, they fled and stood afar off,

19 And said unto Moses, [i]Talk thou with us, and we will hear: but let not God talk with us, lest we die.

20 Then Moses said unto the people, Fear not: for God is come to [1]prove you, and that his fear may be before you, that ye sin not.

21 So the people stood afar off, but Moses drew near unto the darkness where God *was*.

22 ¶ And the Lord said unto Moses, Thus thou shalt say unto the children of Israel, Ye have seen that I have talked with you from heaven.

23 Ye shall not make *therefore* with me gods of silver, nor gods of gold: you shall make you none.

24 [j]An altar of earth thou shalt make unto me, and thereon shalt offer thy burnt offerings, and thy [k]peace offerings, thy sheep, and thine oxen: in all places, where I shall put the remembrance of my Name, I will come unto thee, and bless thee.

25 [l]But if thou wilt make me an altar of stone, thou shalt not build it of hewn stones: for *if* thou lift up thy tool upon them, thou hast polluted [1]them.

26 Neither shalt thou go up by steps unto mine altar, that thy [1]filthiness be not discovered thereon.

21

Temporal and civil ordinances appointed by God touching servitude, murders, and wrongs: the observation whereof doth not justify a man, but are given to bridle our corrupt nature, which else would break out into all mischief and cruelty.

1 Now these are the laws, which thou shalt set before them:

2 [a]If thou buy an Hebrew servant, he shall serve six years, and in the seventh he shall go out free for [1]nothing.

3 If he [1]came himself alone, he shall go out himself alone: if he *were* married, then his wife shall go out with him.

4 If his master hath given him a wife and she hath borne him sons or daughters, the wife and her children shall be her [1]master's, but he shall go out himself alone.

5 But if the servant say thus, I love my master, my wife and my children, I will not go out free,

6 Then his master shall bring him unto the [1]Judges, and set him to the [2]door, or to the post, and his master shall bore his ear through with an awl, and he shall serve him [3]forever.

7 Likewise if a man [1]sell his daughter to be a servant, she shall not go out as the menservants do.

8 If she please not her master, who hath betrothed her to himself, then shall [1]he cause to buy her: he shall have no power to sell her to a strange people, seeing he [2]despised her.

9 But if he hath betrothed her unto his son, he shall deal with her [1]according to the custom of the daughters.

10 If he take [1]him another *wife*, he shall not diminish her food, her raiment, and recompense of her virginity.

11 And if he do not these [1]three unto her, then

Cross references (center column):

[e] Gen. 2:2
[f] Deut. 5:16
   Matt. 15:4
   Eph. 6:2
[g] Matt. 5:21
[h] Rom. 7:7
[i] Deut. 5:24
   Deut. 18:16
   Heb. 12:18
[j] Exod. 27:8
   Exod. 38:7
[k] Lev. 3:1
[l] Deut. 27:5
   Josh. 8:31

CHAPTER 21
[a] Lev. 25:39
   Deut. 15:12
   Jer. 34:14

20:10 [1] Or, city.
20:12 [1] By the parents also is meant all that have authority over us.
20:13 [1] But love and preserve thy brother's life.
20:14 [1] But be pure in heart, word and deed.
20:15 [1] But study to save his goods.
20:16 [1] But further his good name, and speak truth.
20:17 [1] Thou mayst not so much as wish his hinderance in anything.
20:18 [1] Or, heard.
   [2] Hebrew, *fire brands*.
20:20 [1] Whether you will obey his precepts as you promised, Exod. 19:8.
20:25 [1] Hebrew, *it*, that is, *the stone*.
20:26 [1] Which might be by his stooping or flying abroad of his clothes.
21:2 [1] Paying no money for his liberty.

21:3 [1] Not having wife nor children.
21:4 [1] Till her time of servitude was expired which might be the seventh year or the fiftieth.
21:6 [1] Hebrew, *gods*.
   [2] Where the judges sat.
   [3] That is, to the year of Jubilee, which was every fiftieth year.
21:7 [1] Constrained either by poverty, or else to the intent that the master should marry her.
21:8 [1] By giving another money to buy her of him.
   [2] Or, deflowered her.
21:9 [1] That is, he shall give his dowry.
21:10 [1] For his son.
21:11 [1] Neither marry her himself, nor give another money to buy her, nor bestow her upon his son.

shall she go out free, paying no money.

12 ¶ [b]He that smiteth a man, and he die, shall die the death.

13 And if a man hath not laid wait, but [1]God hath offered *him* into his hand, then I will appoint thee a place whither he shall flee.

14 But if a man come presumptuously upon his neighbor to slay him with guile, 'thou shalt take him from mine [1]altar, that he may die.

15 ¶ Also he that smiteth his father or his mother, shall die the death.

16 ¶ And he that stealeth a man, and selleth him, if it be found with him, shall die the death.

17 ¶ [d]And he that curseth his father or his mother, shall die the death.

18 When men also strive together, and one smite another with a [1]stone, or with the fist, and he die not but lieth in bed.

19 If he rise again and walk without upon his staff, then shall he that smote him go [1]quit, save only he shall bear his charges [2]for his resting, and shall pay for his healing.

20 ¶ And if a man smite his servant, or his maid with a rod, and he die under his hand, he shall be surely punished.

21 But if he continue a day or two days, he shall not [1]be punished: for he *is* his money.

22 ¶ Also if men strive and hurt a woman with child, so that her child depart from her and [1]death follow not, he shall be surely punished, according as the woman's husband shall appoint him, or he shall pay as the [2]Judges determine.

23 But if death follow, then thou shalt pay life for life.

24 [c,1]Eye for eye, tooth for tooth, hand for hand, foot for foot,

25 Burning for burning, wound for wound, stripe for stripe.

26 ¶ And if a man smite his servant in the eye, or his maid in the eye, and hath perished it, he shall let him go free for his eye.

27 Also if he smite [1]out his servant's tooth, or his maid's tooth, he shall let him go out free for his tooth.

Margin references:
[b] Lev. 24:17
[c] Deut. 12:3
[d] Lev. 22:9
Prov. 20:20
Matt. 15:4
Mark 7:10
[e] Lev. 24:20
Deut. 19:21
Matt. 5:38
[f] Gen. 9:5

CHAPTER 22
[a] 2 Sam. 12:6

28 ¶ If an ox gore a man or a woman that he die, the [f]ox shall be [1]stoned to death, and his flesh shall not be eaten, but the owner of the ox *shall go quite.*

29 If the ox were wont to push in times past, and it hath been [1]told his master, and he hath not kept him, and after he killeth a man or a woman, the ox shall be stoned, and his owner shall die also.

30 If there be set to him a [1]sum of money, then he shall pay the ransom of his life, whatsoever shall be laid upon him.

31 Whether he hath gored a son, or gored a daughter, he shall be judged after the same manner.

32 If the ox gore a servant or a maid, he shall give unto their master thirty [1]shekels of silver, and the ox shall be stoned.

33 ¶ And when a man shall open a well, or when he shall dig a pit and cover it not, and an ox or an ass fall therein,

34 The owner of the pit shall [1]make it good, *and* give money to the owner thereof, but the dead *beast* shall be his.

35 ¶ And if a man's ox hurt his neighbor's ox that he die, then they shall sell the live ox, and divide the money thereof, and the dead *ox* also they shall divide.

36 Or if it be known that the ox hath used to push in times past, and his master hath not kept him, he shall pay ox for ox, but the dead shall be his own.

22

1 *Of theft.* 5 *Damage.* 7 *Lending.* 14 *Borrowing.* 16 *Enticing of maids.* 18 *Witchcraft.* 20 *Idolatry.* 21 *Support of strangers, widows, and fatherless.* 25 *Usury.* 28 *Reverence to Magistrates.*

1 If a man steal an [1]ox or a sheep, and kill it or sell it, he shall restore five oxen for the ox, [a]and four sheep for the sheep.

2 ¶ If a thief be found [1]breaking up, and be smitten that he die, no blood *shall be shed* for him.

3 *But if it be* [1]in the daylight, [2]blood *shall be shed* for him: *for* he should [1]make full restitution: if he had not *wherewith*, then should he be sold for his theft.

21:13 [1] Though a man be killed at unawares, yet it is God's providence that it should be so.
21:14 [1] The holiness of the place ought not to defend the murderer.
21:18 [1] Either far off him or near.
21:19 [1] By the civil Justice.
  [2] Or, losing of his time.
21:21 [1] By the civil magistrate, but before God he is a murderer.
21:22 [1] Of the mother or child.
  [2] Or, arbiters.
21:24 [1] The execution of this law only belonged to the magistrate, Matt. 5:38.

21:27 [1] So God revengeth cruelty in the most least things.
21:28 [1] If the beast be punished, much more shall the murderer.
21:29 [1] Or, testified to his.
21:30 [1] By the next of the kindred of him that is so slain.
21:32 [1] Read Gen. 23:15.
21:34 [1] This law forbiddeth not only not to hurt, but to beware lest any be hurt.
22:1 [1] Either [a] great beast of the herd, or a small beast of the flock.
22:2 [1] Breaking an house to enter in, or undermining.
22:3 [1] Hebrew, *when the sun riseth upon him.*
  [2] He shall be put to death that killeth him.

4 If the theft be found ¹with him alive, (whether it be ox, ass, or sheep) he shall restore the double.

5 ¶ If a man do hurt field, or vineyard, and put in his beast to feed in another man's field, he shall recompense of the best of his own field, and of the best of his own vineyard.

6 ¶ If fire break out, and catch in the thorns, and the stacks of corn, or the standing corn, or the field be consumed, he that kindled the fire shall make full restitution.

7 ¶ If a man deliver his neighbor money or stuff to keep, and it be stolen out of his house, if the thief be found, he shall pay the double.

8 If the thief be not found, then the master of the house shall be brought unto the ¹Judges *to swear*, whether he hath ²put his hand unto his neighbor's good, or no.

9 In all manner of trespass, whether it be for oxen, for ass, for sheep, for raiment, or for any manner of lost thing which another challengeth to be his, the cause of both *parties* shall come before the judges, *and* whom the Judges condemn, he shall pay the double unto the neighbor.

10 If a man deliver unto his neighbor to keep ass, or ox, or sheep, or any beast, and it die, or be ¹hurt, or taken away by enemies, *and* no man see it,

11 ¹An oath of the Lord shall be between them twain, that he hath not put his hand unto his neighbor's good, and the owner of it shall take the *oath*, and he shall not make it good:

12 ᵇBut if it be stolen from him, he shall make restitution unto the owner thereof.

13 If it be torn in pieces, he shall bring ¹record, *and* shall not make that good, *which is* devoured.

14 ¶ And if a man borrow *ought* of his neighbor, and it be hurt, or else die, the owner thereof not being by, he shall surely make it good.

15 If the owner thereof be by, he shall not make it good: *for if it be* an hired thing, it ¹came for his hire.

16 ¶ ᶜAnd if a man entice a maid that is not betrothed, and lie with her, he shall endow her, and take her to his wife.

17 If her father refuse to give her to him, he shall pay money according to the dowry of virgins.

18 ¶ Thou shalt not suffer a witch to live.

19 Whosoever lieth with a beast, shall die the death.

ᵇ Gen. 31:39
ᶜ Deut. 12:28
ᵈ Deut. 13:13-15
ᵉ Lev. 19:33
ᶠ Zech. 7:10
ᵍ Lev. 25:37
Deut. 23:19
Ps. 15:5
ʰ Acts 25:5
ⁱ Exod. 13:2-12
Exod. 34:19
ʲ Lev. 22:8
Ezek. 44:31

20 ¶ ᵈHe that offereth unto *any* gods, save unto the Lord only, shall be slain.

21 ¶ ᵉMoreover, thou shalt not do injury to a stranger, neither oppress him: for ye were strangers in the land of Egypt.

22 ¶ ᶠYe shall not trouble any widow, nor fatherless child.

23 If thou vex or trouble such, and so he call and cry unto me, I will surely hear his cry.

24 Then shall my wrath be kindled, and I will kill you with the sword, and your ¹wives shall be widows, and your children fatherless.

25 ¶ ᵍIf thou lend money to my people, *that is*, to the poor with thee, thou shalt not be as an usurer unto him: ye shall not oppress him with usury.

26 If thou take thy neighbor's raiment to pledge, thou shalt restore it unto him before the sun go down.

27 For that is his covering only, *and* this is his garment for his skin: wherein shall he sleep? therefore when he ¹crieth unto me, I will hear him: for I am merciful.

28 ¶ ʰThou shalt not rail upon the Judges, neither speak evil of the ruler of thy people.

29 ¶ Thine ¹abundance and thy liquor shalt thou not keep back. ⁱThe firstborn of thy sons shalt thou give me.

30 Likewise shalt thou do with thine oxen and with thy sheep: seven days it shall be with his dam, *and* the eighth day thou shalt give it me.

31 ¶ Ye shall be an holy people unto me, ʲneither shall ye eat any flesh that is torn *of beasts* in the field: ye shall cast it ¹to the dog.

23 2 *Not to follow the multitude.* 13 *Not to make mention of the strange gods.* 14 *The three solemn feasts.* 20, 23 *The Angel is promised to lead his people.* 25 *What God promiseth if they obey him.* 29 *God will cast out the Canaanites by little and little, and why.*

1 Thou shalt not ¹receive a false tale, neither shalt thou put thine hand with the wicked, to be a ²false witness.

2 ¶ Thou shalt not follow a multitude to do evil, neither ¹agree in a controversy ²to decline after many and overthrow *the truth*.

3 ¶ Thou shalt not esteem a poor man in his cause.

22:4 ¹ Hebrew, *in his hand.*
22:8 ¹ Hebrew, *gods.*
     ² That is, whether he hath stolen.
22:10 ¹ Hebrew, *broken.*
22:11 ¹ They should swear by the Name of the Lord.
22:13 ¹ He shall show some part of the beast, or bring in witnesses.
22:15 ¹ He that hired it shall be free by paying the hire.
22:24 ¹ The just plague of God upon the oppressors.

22:27 ¹ For cold and necessity.
22:29 ¹ Thine abundance of thy corn, oil and wine.
22:31 ¹ And so have nothing to do with it.
23:1 ¹ Or, report a false tale.
     ² Or, cruel.
23:2 ¹ Hebrew, *answer.*
     ² Do that which is godly, though few do favor it.

4 ¶ If thou meet thine enemy's ox, or his ass going astray, thou shalt ¹bring him to him again.

5 If thou see thine enemy's ¹ass lying under his burden, wilt thou cease to help him? thou shalt help him up again with it.

6 Thou shalt not overthrow the right of the poor in his suit.

7 Thou shalt keep thee far from a false matter, thou shalt not slay the ¹innocent and the righteous: for I will not justify a wicked man.

8 ¶ ᵃThou shalt take no gift: for the gift blindeth the ¹wise, and perverteth the words of the righteous.

9 ¶ Thou shalt not oppress a stranger: for ye know the ¹heart of a stranger, seeing ye were strangers in the land of Egypt.

10 ᵇMoreover, six years thou shalt sow thy land, and gather the fruits thereof.

11 But the seventh year thou shalt let it rest and lie still, that the poor of thy people may eat, and what they leave, the beasts of the field shall eat. In like manner thou shalt do with thy vineyard, *and* with thine olive trees.

12 ᶜSix days thou shalt do thy work, and in the seventh day thou shalt rest, that thine ox, and thine ass may rest, and the son of thy maid, and the stranger may be refreshed.

13 And ye shall take heed to all things that I have said unto you: and ye shall make ¹no mention of the name of other gods, neither shall it be heard out of thy mouth.

14 ¶ Three times shalt thou keep a feast unto me in the year.

15 Thou ᵈshalt keep the feast of ¹unleavened bread: thou shalt eat unleavened bread seven days, as I commanded thee, in the season of the month of Abib: for in it thou camest out of Egypt: and ᵉnone shall appear before me empty.

16 The ¹feast also of the harvest of the first fruits of thy labors, which thou hast sown in the field: and the ²feast of gathering *fruits* in the end of the year, when thou hast gathered in thy labors out of the field.

CHAPTER 23
ᵃ Deut. 16:19
ᵇ Lev. 25:3
Lev. 26:43
Deut. 15:1
ᶜ Exod. 20:8
Deut. 5:13
ᵈ Exod. 13:3
Exod. 34:18
ᵉ Exod. 16:16
ᶠ Exod. 34:26
Deut. 14:22
ᵍ Exod. 33:2
Deut. 7:22
ʰ Exod. 33:2
Deut. 7:21
Josh. 24:12
ⁱ Deut. 7:25
ʲ Deut. 7:14
ᵏ Josh. 24:12

17 *These* three times in the year shall all thy men children appear before the Lord Jehovah.

18 Thou shalt not offer the blood of my sacrifice with ¹leavened bread: neither shall the fat of my sacrifice remain until the morning.

19 ᶠThe first of the firstfruits of thy land, thou shalt bring into the house of the Lord thy God: *yet* shalt thou not seethe a kid in his ¹mother's milk.

20 ¶ ᵍBehold, I send an Angel before thee, to keep thee in thy way, and to bring thee to the place which I have prepared.

21 Beware of him, and hear his voice, *and* provoke him not: for he will not spare your misdeeds, because my ¹name is in him.

22 But if thou hearken unto his voice, and do all that I speak, then I will be an enemy unto thine enemies, and will afflict them that afflict thee.

23 For mine Angel ʰshall go before thee, and bring thee unto the Amorites, and the Hittites, and the Perizzites, and the Canaanites, the Hivites, and the Jebusites, and I will destroy them.

24 Thou shalt not bow down to their gods, neither serve them, nor do after the works of them: but ⁱ˒¹utterly overthrow them, and break in pieces their images.

25 For ye shall serve the Lord your God, and he shall bless thy ¹bread and thy water, and I will take all sickness away from the midst of thee.

26 ¶ ʲThere shall none cast their fruit, nor be barren in thy land, the number of thy days will I fulfill.

27 I will send my ¹fear before thee, and will destroy all the people among whom thou shalt go: and I will make all thine enemies *turn* their backs unto thee:

28 And I will send ᵏhornets before thee, which shall drive out the Hivites, the Canaanites, and the Hittites from thy face.

29 I will not cast them out from thy face in one year, lest the land grow to a wilderness, and the beasts of the field multiply against thee.

30 By little and little I will drive them out from thy face, until thou increase, and inherit the land.

31 And I will make thy coasts from the red sea unto the sea ¹of the Philistines, and from

---

23:4 ¹ If we be bound to do good to our enemy's beast, much more to our enemy himself, Matt. 5:44.
23:5 ¹ If God command to help up our enemy's ass under his burden, will he suffer us to cast down our brethren with heavy burdens?
23:7 ¹ Whether thou be magistrate or art commanded by the magistrate.
23:8 ¹ Hebrew, *seeing*.
23:9 ¹ For in that that he is a stranger, his heart is sorrowful enough.
23:13 ¹ Neither by swearing by them nor speaking of them, Ps. 16:4; Eph. 5:3.
23:15 ¹ That is, Easter, in remembrance that the Angel passed over and spared the Israelites, when he slew the firstborn of the Egyptians.
23:16 ¹ Which is Whitsuntide, in token that the Law was given 50

days after they departed from Egypt.
² This is the feast of Tabernacles, signifying that they dwelled 40 years under the tents or the Tabernacles in wilderness.
23:18 ¹ No leavened bread shall be there in thine house.
23:19 ¹ Meaning, that no fruits should be taken before just time: and hereby are bridled all cruel and wanton appetites.
23:21 ¹ I will give him mine authority, and he shall govern you in my name.
23:24 ¹ God commandeth his not only not to worship idols, but to destroy them.
23:25 ¹ That is, all things necessary for this present life.
23:27 ¹ I will make them afraid at thy coming and send mine Angel to destroy them, as Exod. 35:2.
23:31 ¹ Called the Sea of Syria.

the [2]desert unto the [3]River: for I will deliver the inhabitants of the land into your hand, and thou shalt drive them out from thy face.

32 [l]Thou shalt make no covenant with them, nor with their gods:

33 Neither shall they dwell in the land, lest they make thee sin against me: for if thou serve their gods, surely it shall be thy [1,m]destruction.

24

3 The people promise to obey God.   4 Moses writeth the civil Laws.   9, 13 Moses returneth into the mountain.   14 Aaron and Hur have the charge of the people. 18 Moses was forty days and forty nights in the mountain.

1 Now he had [1]said unto Moses, Come up to the Lord, thou, and Aaron, Nadab, and Abihu, and seventy of the Elders of Israel, and ye shall worship afar off.

2 And Moses himself alone shall come near to the Lord, but they shall not come near, neither shall the people go up with him.

3 ¶ [1]Afterward Moses came and told the people all the words of the Lord, and all the [2]Laws: and all the people answered with one voice, and said, [a]All the things which the Lord hath said, will we do.

4 And Moses wrote all the words of the Lord and rose up early, and set up an [b]altar [1]under the mountain, and twelve pillars according to the twelve tribes of Israel.

5 And he sent young [1]men of the children of Israel, which offered burnt offerings of beeves, and sacrificed peace offerings unto the Lord.

6 Then Moses took half of the blood, and put it in basins, and half of the blood he sprinkled on the altar.

7 After, he took the [1]book of the covenant, and read it in the audience of the people: who said, All that the Lord hath said, we will do, and be obedient.

8 Then Moses took the [c]blood, and sprinkled it on the people, and said, Behold the [1]blood of the covenant, which the Lord hath made with you concerning all these things.

9 ¶ Then went up Moses, and Aaron, Nadab, and Abihu, and seventy of the Elders of Israel.

10 And they [1]saw the God of Israel, and under his feet *was* as it were a [2]work of a Sapphire stone, and as the very heaven when it is clear.

11 And upon the nobles of the children of Israel he [1]laid not his hand: also they saw God, and [2]did eat and drink.

12 ¶ And the Lord [1]said unto Moses, Come up to me into the mountain, and be there, and I will give thee [2]tables of stone, and the Law, and the Commandment, which I have written, for to teach [3]them.

13 Then Moses rose up, and his minister Joshua, and Moses went up into the mountain of God,

14 And said unto the Elders, Tarry us here until we come again unto you: and behold, Aaron and Hur *are* with you: whosoever hath any matters, let him come to them.

15 Then Moses went up to the mount, and the cloud covered the mountain,

16 And the glory of the Lord abode upon mount Sinai, and the cloud covered [1]it six days: and the seventh day he called unto Moses out of the midst of the cloud.

17 And the sight of the glory of the Lord *was* like [1]consuming fire on the top of the mountain, in the eyes of the children of Israel.

18 And Moses entered into the midst of the cloud, and went up to the mountain and Moses was in the [d]mount forty days and forty nights.

25

2 The voluntary gifts for the making of the Tabernacle.   10 The form of the Ark.   17 The Mercy seat.   23 The Table.   31 The Candlestick.   40 All must be done according to the pattern.

1 Then the Lord spake unto Moses, saying,

2 [1]Speak unto the children of Israel that they receive an offering for me: of [a]every man, whose heart giveth it freely, ye shall take the offering for me.

3 And this is the offering which ye shall [1]take of them, gold and silver, and brass,

4 And [1]blue silk, and purple, and scarlet, and fine linen and goat's *hair*,

5 And ram's skins colored red, and the skins of

Marginal references:

l Exod. 34:15
Deut. 7:2

m Deut. 7:16
Josh. 23:13

CHAPTER 24
a Exod. 19:8
b Exod. 20:24
c 1 Pet. 1:2
Heb. 9:20
d Exod. 34:28
Deut. 9:9

CHAPTER 25
a Exod. 35:5

---

[2] Of Arabia called desert.

[3] To wit, Ephraim.

23:33 [1] Hebrew, *offense or snare.*

24:1 [1] When he called him up to the mountain to give him the Laws, beginning at Exod. 20, hitherto.

24:3 [1] When he had received these laws in mount Sinai.

[2] Hebrew, *judgments.*

24:4 [1] Or, at the foot of the mountain.

24:5 [1] For as yet the Priesthood was not given to Levi.

24:7 [1] Or, the book of the Law.

24:8 [1] Which blood signifieth that the covenant broken cannot be satisfied without blood shedding.

24:10 [1] As perfectly as their infirmities could behold his majesty.

[2] Hebrew, *brick work.*

24:11 [1] He made them not afraid, nor punished them.

[2] That is, rejoiced.

24:12 [1] The second time.

[2] Signifying the hardness of our hearts, except God do write his laws therein by his Spirit, Jer. 31:33; Ezek. 11:19; 2 Cor. 3:3; Heb. 8:10 and 10:16.

[3] To wit, the people.

24:16 [1] Or, him.

24:17 [1] The Lord appeareth like devouring fire to carnal men: but to them that he draweth with his Spirit, he is like pleasant Sapphire.

25:2 [1] After the moral and judicial law he giveth them the ceremonial law that nothing should be left to man's invention.

25:3 [1] For the building and use of the Tabernacle.

25:4 [1] Or, yellow.

badgers, and the wood [1]Shittim,

6 Oil for the light, spices for [1]anointing oil, and for the perfume of sweet savor.

7 Onyx stones, and stones to be set in the [b]Ephod, and in the [c]breastplate.

8 Also they shall make me a [1]Sanctuary, that I may dwell among them.

9 According to all that I show thee, even so shall ye make the form of the Tabernacle, and the fashion of all the instruments thereof.

10 ¶ They shall make also an [d]Ark of Shittim wood, two cubits and an half long, and a cubit and an half broad, and a cubit and an half high.

11 And thou shalt overlay it with pure gold, within and without shalt thou overlay it, and shalt make upon it a [1]crown of gold round about.

12 And thou shalt cast four rings of gold for it, and put them in the four [1]corners thereof: that is, two rings *shall be* on the one side of it, and two rings on the other side thereof.

13 And thou shalt make bars of Shittim wood, and cover them with gold.

14 Then thou shalt put the bars in the rings by the sides of the Ark, to bear the Ark with them.

15 The bars shall be in the rings of the Ark: they shall not be taken away from it.

16 So thou shalt put in the Ark the [1]Testimony, which I shall give thee.

17 Also thou shalt make a [1,2]Mercy seat of pure gold, two cubits and an half long and a cubit and an half broad.

18 And thou shalt make two Cherubims of gold: of work beaten out with the hammer shalt thou make them at the two ends of the Mercy seat.

19 And the one Cherub shalt thou make at the one end, and the other Cherub at the other end: of *the matter* of the Mercy seat shall ye make the Cherubims, on the two ends thereof.

20 And the Cherubims shall stretch their wings on high, covering the Mercy seat with their wings and their faces one to another: to the Mercy seatward shall the faces of the Cherubims be.

21 And thou shalt put the Mercy seat above upon the Ark, and in the Ark thou shalt put the Testimony, which I will give thee.

22 And there I will [1]declare myself unto thee, and from above the Mercy seat [c]between the two

[b] Exod. 28:4
[c] Exod. 28:15
[d] Exod. 37:1
[e] Num. 7:89
[f] Exod. 37:10
[g] Exod. 37:17

Cherubims, which are upon the Ark of the Testimony, I will tell thee all things which I will give thee in commandment unto the children of Israel.

23 ¶ [f]Thou shalt also make a Table of Shittim wood, of two cubits long, and one cubit broad, and a cubit and a half high:

24 And thou shalt cover it with pure gold, and make thereto a crown of gold round about.

25 Thou shalt also make unto it a border of [1]four fingers round about: and thou shalt make a golden crown round about the border thereof:

26 After, thou shalt make for it four rings of gold, and shalt put the rings in the four corners that are in the four feet thereof.

27 Over against the border shall the rings be for places for bars to bear the Table.

28 And thou shalt make the bars of Shittim wood, and shalt overlay them with gold, that the Table may be borne with them.

29 Thou shalt make also [1]dishes for it, and *incense* cups for it, and coverings for it, and goblets, wherewith it shall be covered, *even* of fine gold shalt thou make them.

30 And thou shalt set upon the Table Showbread before me continually.

31 ¶ [g]Also thou shalt make a candlestick of pure gold: of [1]work beaten out with the hammer shall the Candlestick be made, his shaft, and his branches, his bowls, his knops: and his flowers shall be of the same.

32 Six branches also shall come out of the sides of it: three branches of the candlestick out of the one side of it, and three branches of the Candlestick out of the other side of it.

33 Three bowls like unto almonds, one knop and *one* flower in one branch: and three bowls like almonds in the *other* branch, one knop and *one* flower: so throughout the six branches that come out of the Candlestick.

34 And in the *shaft* of the Candlestick *shall be* four bowls like unto almonds, his knops and his flowers.

35 And *there shall be* a knop under two branches *made* thereof: and a knop under two branches *made* thereof: and a knop under two branches *made* thereof, according to the six branches coming out of the Candlestick.

25:5 [1] Which is thought to be a kindle of Cedar, which will not rot.
25:6 [1] Ordained for the Priests.
25:8 [1] A place both to offer sacrifice, and to hear the Law.
25:11 [1] Or, a circle and a border.
25:12 [1] Or, feet.
25:16 [1] The stone tables, the rod of Aaron and Manna which were a testimony of God's presence.
25:17 [1] Or, covering: or propitiatory.

[2] There God appeared mercifully unto them: and this was a figure of Christ.
25:22 [1] Or, will appoint with thee.
25:25 [1] Or, an hand broad.
25:29 [1] To set the bread upon.
25:31 [1] It shall not be molten, but beaten out of the lump of gold with the hammer.

36 Their knops and their branches shall be thereof: all this shall be one beaten work of pure gold.

37 And thou shalt make the seven lamps thereof: and the lamps thereof shalt thou put thereon, to give light toward that that is before it.

38 Also the snuffers and snuffdishes thereof *shall be* of pure gold.

39 Of a [1]talent of fine gold shalt thou make it with all these instruments.

40 [b]Look therefore that thou make *them* after their fashion, that was showed thee in the mountain.

[b] Heb. 8:5
Acts 7:44

26

1 The form of the Tabernacle and the appertinences. 33 The places of the Ark, of the Mercy seat, of the Table, and of the Candlestick.

1 Afterward thou shalt make the Tabernacle with ten curtains of fine twined linen and blue silk, and purple, and scarlet: and in them thou shalt make Cherubims of [1]broidered work.

2 The length of one curtain *shall be* eight and twenty cubits, and the breadth of one curtain four cubits: every one of the curtains shall have one measure.

3 Five curtains shall be coupled one to another: and the *other* five curtains shall be coupled one to another.

4 And thou shalt make strings of blue silk upon the edge of the one curtain, *which is* in the selvedge [1]of the coupling: and likewise shall thou make in the edge of the *other* curtain in the selvedge, in the second coupling.

5 Fifty strings shalt thou make in one curtain, and fifty strings shalt thou make in the edge of the curtain, which is in the [1]second coupling: the strings *shall be* one right against another.

6 Thou shalt make also fifty [1]taches of gold, and couple the curtains one to another with the taches, and it shall be one [2]Tabernacle.

7 ¶ Also thou shalt make curtains of goats' *hair*, to be a [1]covering upon the Tabernacle, thou shalt make them *to the number* of eleven curtains.

8 The length of a curtain *shall be* thirty cubits, and the breadth of a curtain four cubits: the eleven curtains *shall be* of one measure.

9 And thou shalt couple five curtains by themselves, and the six curtains by themselves: but thou shalt double the [1]sixth curtain upon the forefront of the covering.

10 And thou shalt make fifty strings in the edge of one curtain in the selvedge of the coupling, and fifty strings in the edge of the *other* curtain in the second coupling.

11 Likewise thou shalt make fifty [1]taches of brass, and fasten them on the strings, and shalt couple the covering together that it may be one.

12 And the [1]remnant that resteth in the curtains of the covering, *even* the half curtain that resteth, shall be left at the backside of the Tabernacle.

13 That the cubit on the one side, and the cubit on the other side of that which is left in the length of the curtains of the covering may remain on either side of the Tabernacle to cover it.

14 Moreover, for that covering thou shalt make a [1]covering of rams' skins dyed red, and a covering of [2]badgers' skins above.

15 ¶ Also thou shalt make boards for the Tabernacle of Shittim wood to stand up.

16 Ten cubits *shall be* the length of a board, and a cubit and an half cubit the breadth of one board.

17 Two tenons *shall be* in one board set in order as the feet of a Ladder, one against another: thus shalt thou make for all the boards of the Tabernacle.

18 And thou shalt make boards for the Tabernacle, *even* twenty boards on the South side, even full South.

19 And thou shalt make forty [1]sockets of silver under the twenty boards, two sockets under one board for his two tenons, and two sockets under another board for his two tenons.

20 In like manner on the other side of the Tabernacle toward the North side *shall be* twenty boards,

21 And their forty sockets of silver, two sockets under one board, and two sockets under another board.

22 And on the side of the Tabernacle, toward the West, shalt thou make six boards.

23 Also two boards shalt thou make in the corners of the Tabernacle in the two sides.

24 Also they shall be [1]joined beneath, and likewise they shall be joined above to a ring: thus shall it be for them two: they shall be for the two corners.

25 So they shall be eight boards having sockets of

25:39 [1] This was the talent weight of the Temple, and weighed 120 pounds.
26:1 [1] That is, of most cunning or fine work.
26:4 [1] On the side that the curtains might be tied together.
26:5 [1] In tying together both the sides.
25:6 [1] Or, hooks.
　　[2] Or, partition.
26:7 [1] Lest rain and weather should mar it.
26:9 [1] That is, five on the one side, and five on the other, and the

sixth should hang over the door of the Tabernacle.
26:11 [1] Or, hooks.
26:12 [1] For these curtains were two cubits longer than the curtains of the Tabernacle so that they were wider by a cubit on both sides.
26:14 [1] To be put upon the covering that was made of goats' hair.
　　[2] This was the third covering of the Tabernacle.
26:19 [1] Or, brass pieces, wherein were the mortises for the tenons.
26:24 [1] The Hebrew word signifieth twins: declaring that they should be so perfect and well joined as was possible.

silver, *even* sixteen sockets, *that is*, two sockets under one board, and two sockets under another board.

26 ¶ Then thou shalt make five bars of Shittim wood for the boards of one side of the Tabernacle.

27 And five bars for the boards of the other side of the Tabernacle: also five bars for the boards of the side of the Tabernacle toward the West side.

28 And the middle bar shall go through the midst of the boards, from end to end.

29 And thou shalt cover the boards with gold, and make their rings of gold, for places for the bars, and thou shalt cover the bars with gold.

30 So thou shalt rear up the Tabernacle, [a]according to the fashion thereof, which was showed thee in the Mount.

31 ¶ Moreover, thou shalt make a veil of blue silk, and purple, and scarlet, and fine twined linen, thou shalt make it of broidered work with Cherubims.

32 And thou shalt hang it upon four pillars of Shittim wood covered with gold, (whose [1]hooks shall be of gold) *standing* upon four sockets of silver.

33 ¶ Afterward thou shalt hang the veil [1]on the hooks, that thou mayest bring in thither, *that is*, within the veil, the Ark of the Testimony: and the veil shall make you a separation between the Holy place and the [2]most holy place.

34 Also thou shalt put the Mercy seat upon the Ark of the Testimony in the most Holy place.

35 And thou shalt set the Table [1]without the veil, and the Candlestick over against the Table on the South side of the Tabernacle, and thou shalt set the Table on the North side.

36 Also thou shalt make an [1]hanging for the door of the Tabernacle of blue silk, and purple, and scarlet, and fine twined linen wrought with needle.

37 And thou shalt make for the hanging five pillars of Shittim, and cover them with gold: their heads *shall be* of gold, and thou shalt cast five sockets of brass for them.

27

1 *The Altar of the burnt offering.* 9 *The courts of the Tabernacle.* 20 *The lamps continually burning.*

1 Moreover thou shalt make the [1]Altar of Shittim wood, five cubits long and five cubits broad (the altar shall be four square) and the height thereof three cubits.

2 And thou shalt make it horns in the four corners

CHAPTER 26
[a] Exod. 25:9,40
Heb. 8:5
Acts 7:44

thereof: the horns shall be of [1]itself, and thou shalt cover it with brass.

3 Also thou shalt make his ash pans for his ashes, and his besoms, and his basins, and his flesh-hooks, and his [1]censers: thou shalt make all the instruments thereof of brass.

4 And thou shalt make unto it a grate, *like* network of brass: also upon that [1]grate shalt thou make four brazen rings upon the four corners thereof.

5 And thou shalt put it under the compass of the altar beneath, that the grate may be in the midst of the altar.

6 Also thou shalt make bars for the altar, bars, *I say*, of Shittim wood, and shalt cover them with brass.

7 And the bars thereof shall be put in the rings, the which bars shall be upon the two sides of the altar to bear it.

8 Thou shalt make the *altar* hollow *between* the boards: as *God* showeth thee in the mount, so shall they make it.

9 ¶ Also thou shalt make the [1]court of the Tabernacle in the South side, even full South: the court shall have curtains of fine twined linen, of an hundred cubits long, for one side,

10 And it shall have twenty pillars, with their twenty sockets of brass: the heads of the pillars, and their [1]fillets *shall be* silver.

11 Likewise on the North side in length *there shall be* hangings of an hundred *cubits* long, and the twenty pillars thereof with their twenty sockets of brass: the heads of the pillars and the fillets *shall be* silver.

12 ¶ And the breadth of the court, on the West side *shall have* curtains of fifty cubits, *with* their ten pillars, and their ten sockets.

13 And the breadth of the court, Eastward full East, *shall have* [1]fifty cubits.

14 Also hangings of fifteen cubits *shall be* on the one [1]side *with* their three pillars and their three sockets.

15 Likewise on the other side *shall be* hangings of fifteen cubits, *with* their three pillars and their three sockets.

16 ¶ And in the gate of the court *shall be* a veil of twenty cubits of blue silk, and purple, and scarlet, and fine twined linen wrought with needle, *with* the

---

26:32 [1] Some read, heads of the pillars.
26:33 [1] Hebrew, *Under the hooks:* meaning that it should hang downward from the hooks.
  [2] Whereinto the high Priest only entered once a year.
26:35 [1] Meaning, in the holy place.
26:36 [1] This hanging or veil was between the holy place, and there where the people were.
27:1 [1] For the burnt offering.

27:2 [1] Of the same wood and matter not fastened unto it.
27:3 [1] Or, fire pans.
27:4 [1] Hebrew, *net.*
27:9 [1] This was the first entry into the Tabernacle, where the people abode.
27:10 [1] They were certain hoops or circles for to beautify the pillar.
27:13 [1] Meaning, curtains of fifty cubits.
27:14 [1] Of the door of the court.

four pillars thereof and their four sockets.

17 All the pillars of the court shall have fillets of silver round about, *with* their heads of silver, and their sockets of brass.

18 ¶ The length of the court *shall be* an hundred cubits, and the breadth fifty [1]at either end, and the height five cubits, *and the hangings* of fine twined linen, and their sockets of brass.

19 All the vessels of the Tabernacle for all manner service thereof, and all the [1]pins thereof, and all the pins of the court *shall be* brass.

20 ¶ And thou shalt command the children of Israel, that they bring unto thee pure oil olive [1]beaten for the light, that the lamps may always [2]burn.

21 In the Tabernacle of the Congregation without the veil, which is before the Testimony, shall Aaron and his sons dress them from evening to morning before the Lord, for a statute forever unto their generations, *to be observed* by the children of Israel.

28

1 The Lord calleth Aaron and his sons to the Priesthood. 4 Their garments. 13, 29 Aaron entereth into the Sanctuary in the name of the children of Israel. 30 Urim and Thummim. 38 Aaron beareth the iniquity of the Israelites' offerings.

1 And cause thou thy brother Aaron to come unto thee, and his sons with him, from among the children of Israel, that he may serve me in the Priest's office: *I mean*, Aaron, Nadab, and Abihu, Eleazar, and Ithamar Aaron's sons.

2 Also thou shalt make holy garments for Aaron thy brother, [1]glorious and beautiful.

3 Therefore thou shalt speak unto all [1]cunning men, whom I have filled with the spirit of wisdom, that they make Aaron's garments to [2]consecrate him, that he may serve me in the Priest's office.

4 Now these shall be the garments, which they shall make, a breastplate, and an [1]Ephod, and a robe, and a broidered coat, a mitre, and a girdle: so *these* holy garments shall they make for Aaron thy brother, and for his sons, that he may serve me in the Priest's office.

5 Therefore they shall take gold, and blue silk, and purple, and scarlet, and fine linen.

6 ¶ And they shall make the Ephod of gold, blue silk, and purple, scarlet, and fine twined linen of broidered work.

7 The two shoulders thereof shall be joined together by their two edges: so shall it be closed.

8 And the [1]embroidered girdle of the same Ephod, which shall be upon him, shall be of the selfsame work and stuff, *even* of gold, blue silk, and purple, and scarlet, and fine twined linen.

9 And thou shalt take two Onyx stones, and grave upon them the names of the children of Israel.

10 Six names of them upon the one stone, and the six names that remain, upon the second stone, according to [1]their generations.

11 Thou shalt cause to grave the two stones according to the names of the children of Israel, by a graver of signets that worketh and graveth in stone, and shalt make them to be set and embossed in gold.

12 And thou shalt put the two stones upon the shoulders of the Ephod, *as* stones of [1]remembrance of the children of Israel: for Aaron shall bear their names before the Lord upon his two shoulders for a remembrance.

13 So thou shalt make bosses of gold,

14 ¶ And two chains of fine gold [1]at the end, of wreathen work shalt thou make them, and shalt fasten the wreathen chains upon the bosses.

15 ¶ Also thou shalt make the breastplate of [1]judgment with broidered work: like the work of the Ephod shalt thou make it: of gold, blue silk, and purple, and scarlet, and fine twined linen shalt thou make it.

16 [1]Foursquare it shall be *and* double, an hand breadth long and an hand breadth broad.

17 Then thou shalt set it full of places for stones, *even* four rows of stones: the order *shall be this*, a [1]ruby, a topaz, and a [2]carbuncle in the first row.

18 And in the second row *thou shalt set* an [1]emerald, a sapphire, and a [2]diamond.

19 And in the third row a turquoise, an agate, and an Hematite.

20 And in the fourth row [1]a chrysolite, an onyx, and a jasper: and they shall be set in gold in their embossments.

27:18 [1] Hebrew, *fifty in fifty.*
27:19 [1] Or, stakes, wherewith the curtains were fastened to the ground.
27:20 [1] Such as cometh from the olive, when it is first pressed or beaten.
   [2] Or, ascend up.
28:2 [1] Whereby his office may be known to be glorious and excellent.
28:3 [1] Hebrew, *wise in heart.*
   [2] Which is to separate him from the rest.
28:4 [1] A short and straight coat without sleeves, put upmost upon his garments to keep them close unto him.
28:8 [1] Which went about his upmost coat.
28:10 [1] As they were in age, so should they be graven in order.
28:12 [1] That Aaron might remember the Israelites to Godward.
28:14 [1] Of the bosses.
28:15 [1] It was so called, because the high Priest could not give sentence in judgment without that on his breast.
28:16 [1] The description of the breastplate.
28:17 [1] Or, Sardius.
   [2] Or, Emerald.
28:18 [1] Or, Carbuncle.
   [2] Or, Jasper.
28:20 [1] Hebrew, *Tarshish.*

21 And the stones shall be according to the names of the children of Israel, twelve, according to their names, graven as signets, every one after his name, *and* they shall be for the twelve tribes.

22 ¶ Then thou shalt make upon the breastplate two chains at the ends, of wreathen work of pure gold.

23 Thou shalt make also upon the breastplate two rings of gold, and put the two rings on [1]the two ends of the breastplate.

24 And thou shalt put the two wreathen chains of gold in the two rings in the ends of the breastplate.

25 And the *other* two ends of the two wreathen *chains*, thou shalt fasten in the two embossments, and shalt put *them* upon the shoulders of the Ephod upon the foreside of it.

26 ¶ Also thou shalt make two rings of gold, which thou shalt put in the [1]two *other* ends of the breastplate, upon the border thereof, toward the inside of the Ephod.

27 And two *other* rings of gold thou shalt make, and put them on the two sides of the Ephod, beneath in the forepart of it over against the coupling of it upon the broidered girdle of the Ephod.

28 Thus shall they bind the breastplate by his rings unto the rings of the Ephod, with a lace of blue silk, that it may be *fast* upon the broidered girdle of the Ephod, and that the breastplate be not loosed from the Ephod.

29 So Aaron shall [1]bear the names of the children of Israel in the breastplate of judgment upon his heart, when he goeth into the holy place for a remembrance continually before the Lord.

30 ¶ Also thou shalt put in the breastplate of judgment, the [1]Urim and the Thummim, which shall be upon Aaron's heart, when he goeth in before the Lord, and Aaron shall bear the judgment of the children of Israel upon his heart before the Lord continually.

31 ¶ And thou shalt make the robe of the Ephod altogether of blue silk.

32 And the hole for his head shall be in the midst of it, having an edge of woven work round about the collar of it: so shall it be as the collar of an habergeon, that it rent not.

33 ¶ And beneath upon the skirts thereof, thou

CHAPTER 29
[d] Lev. 9:2

shalt make pomegranates of blue silk, and purple, and scarlet round about the skirts thereof, and bells of gold between them round about:

34 *That is*, a golden bell and a pomegranate, a golden bell and a pomegranate round about upon the skirts of the robe.

35 So shall it be upon Aaron, when he ministereth, and his sound shall be heard when he goeth into the holy place before the Lord, and when he cometh out, and he shall not die.

36 ¶ Also thou shalt make a plate of pure gold, and grave thereon, as signets are graven, [1]HOLINESS TO THE LORD.

37 And thou shalt put it on a blue silk lace, and it shall be upon the mitre, *even* upon the forefront of the mitre shall it be.

38 So shall it be upon Aaron's forehead, that Aaron may [1]bear the iniquity of the offerings, which the children of Israel shall offer in all their holy offerings: and it shall be always upon his forehead, to make them acceptable before the Lord.

39 Likewise thou shalt embroider the fine linen coat, and thou shalt make a mitre of fine linen, but thou shalt make a girdle of needle work.

40 Also thou shalt make for Aaron's sons coats, and thou shalt make them girdles, and bonnets shalt thou make for them, for glory and comeliness.

41 And thou shalt put them upon Aaron thy brother, and on his sons with him, and shalt anoint them, and [1]fill their hands, and sanctify them, that they may minister unto me in the Priest's office.

42 Thou shalt also make them linen breeches to cover their privities: from the loins unto the thighs shall they reach.

43 And they shall be for Aaron and his sons, when they come into the Tabernacle [1]of the Congregation, or when they come unto the altar to minister in the holy place, that they [2]commit not iniquity, and so die. *This shall be* a law forever unto him, and to his seed after him.

29

1 *The manner of consecrating the Priests.*   38 *The continual sacrifice.*   45 *The Lord promiseth to dwell among the children of Israel.*

1 This thing also shalt thou do unto them, when thou consecratest them to be my Priests, [a]Take a young calf, and two rams without blemish,

---

28:23 [1] Which are upmost toward the shoulder.
28:26 [1] Which are beneath.
28:29 [1] Aaron shall not enter into the holy place in his own name, but in the name of all the children of Israel.
28:30 [1] Urim signifieth light, and Thummim perfection: declaring that the stones of the breastplate were most clear, and of perfect beauty: by Urim also is meant knowledge, and Thummim holiness, showing what virtues are required in the Priests.

28:36 [1] Holiness appertaineth to the Lord: for he is most holy, and nothing unholy may appear before him.
28:38 [1] Their offerings could not be so perfect, but some fault would be therein: which sin the high Priest bare, and pacified God.
28:41 [1] That is, consecrate them, by giving them things to offer and thereby admit them to their office.
28:43 [1] Or, of witness.
    [2] In not hiding their nakedness.

2 And unleavened bread, and cakes unleavened tempered with oil, and wafers unleavened anointed with oil: (of fine wheat flour shalt thou make them).

3 Then thou shalt put them in one basket, and ¹present them in the basket with the calf and the two rams,

4 And shalt bring Aaron and his sons unto the door of the Tabernacle of the Congregation, and wash them with water.

5 Also thou shalt take the garments, and put upon Aaron the tunicle, and the ¹robe of the Ephod, and the Ephod, and the breastplate, and shalt close *them* to him with the broidered girdle of the Ephod.

6 Then thou shalt put the mitre upon his head, and shalt put the holy ᵇcrown upon the mitre.

7 And thou shalt take the anointing ᶜoil, and shalt pour upon his head and anoint him.

8 And thou shalt bring his sons, and put coats upon them.

9 And shalt gird them with girdles, *both* Aaron and his sons: and shalt put the bonnets on them, and the Priest's office shall be theirs for a perpetual law: thou ᵈshalt also ¹fill the hands of Aaron, and the hands of his sons.

10 After, thou shalt present the calf before the Tabernacle of the congregation, ᶜand Aaron and his sons shall ¹put their hands upon the head of the calf.

11 So shalt thou kill the calf before the Lord, at the door of the Tabernacle of the Congregation.

12 Then thou shalt take of the blood of the calf, and put it upon the horns of the Altar with thy finger, and shalt pour all *the rest* of the blood at the foot of the Altar.

13 ᶠAlso thou shalt take all the fat that covereth the inwards, and the caul, *that is* on the liver, and the two kidneys, and the fat that is upon them, and shalt burn them upon the Altar.

14 But the flesh of the calf, and his skin, and his dung shalt thou burn with fire without the host: it is a ¹sin offering.

15 ¶ Thou shalt also take one ram, and Aaron and his sons shall put their hands upon the head of the ram.

16 Then thou shalt kill the ram, and take his blood, and sprinkle it round about upon the Altar,

17 And thou shalt cut the ram in pieces, and wash the inwards of him and his legs, and shalt put them

ᵇ Exod. 28:36
ᶜ Exod. 30:25
ᵈ Exod. 28:41
ᵉ Lev. 1:4
ᶠ Lev. 3:3

upon the pieces thereof, and upon his head.

18 So thou shalt burn the whole ram upon the Altar: *for* it is a burnt offering unto the Lord ¹for a sweet savor: it is an offering made by fire unto the Lord.

19 And shalt thou take the other ram, and Aaron and his sons shall put their hands upon the head of the ram.

20 Then shalt thou kill the ram, and take of his blood, and put it ¹upon the lap of Aaron's ear, and upon the lap of the right ear of his sons, and upon the thumb of their right hand, and upon the great toe of their right foot, and shalt sprinkle the blood upon the altar round about.

21 And thou shalt take of the blood that is ¹upon the Altar, and of the anointing oil, and shalt sprinkle it upon Aaron, and upon his garments, and upon his sons, and upon the garments of his sons with him: so he shall be hallowed, and his clothes, and his sons, and the garments of his sons with him.

22 Also thou shalt take of the rams the fat and the rump, even the fat that covereth the inwards, and the caul of the liver, and the two kidneys, and the fat that is upon them, and the right shoulder, (for it is the ¹ram of consecration).

23 And one loaf of bread, and one cake of bread *tempered* with oil, and one wafer, out of the basket of the unleavened *bread* that is before the Lord:

24 And thou shalt put all this in the hands of Aaron, and in the hands of his sons, and shalt shake them to and fro before the Lord.

25 Again, thou shalt receive them of their hands, and burn them upon the altar besides the burnt offering for a sweet savor before the Lord: *for* this is an offering made by fire unto the Lord.

26 Likewise thou shalt take the breast of the ram of the consecration, which is for Aaron, and shalt shake it to ¹and fro before the Lord, and it shall be thy part.

27 And thou shalt sanctify the breast of the shaken offering, and the shoulder of the ¹heave offering, which was shaken to and fro, and which was heaved up of the ram of the consecration which *was* for Aaron, and which *was* for his sons.

28 And Aaron and his sons shall have it by a statute forever, of the children of Israel: for it is an heave offering, and it shall be an heave offering of the children of Israel, of their ¹peace offerings, *even* their heave offering to the Lord.

29:3 ¹ To offer them in sacrifice.
29:5 ¹ Which was next under the Ephod.
29:9 ¹ Or, consecrate them.
29:10 ¹ Signifying that the sacrifice was also offered for them, and that they did approve it.
29:14 ¹ Hebrew, *sin*, 2 Cor. 5:21.
29:18 ¹ Or, savor of rest, which causeth the wrath of God to cease.
29:20 ¹ Meaning the soft and nether part of the ear.
29:21 ¹ Wherewith the Altar must be sprinkled.
29:22 ¹ Which is offered for the consecration of the high Priest.
29:26 ¹ This sacrifice the Priest did move toward the East, West, North, and South.
29:27 ¹ So called because it was not only shaken to and fro, but also lifted up.
29:28 ¹ Which were offerings of thanksgiving to God for his benefits.

29 ¶ And the holy garments which *appertain* to Aaron, shall be his sons' after him, to be anointed therein, and to be consecrated therein.

30 That son that shall be Priest in his stead, shall put them on seven days, when he cometh into the Tabernacle of the Congregation to minister in the holy place.

31 ¶ So thou shalt take the ram of the consecration, and seethe his flesh in the holy place.

32 *g*And Aaron and his sons shall eat the flesh of the ram, and the bread that is in the basket, at the door of the Tabernacle of the Congregation.

33 So they shall eat these things, [1]whereby their atonement was made, to consecrate them, *and* to sanctify them: but a stranger shall not eat *thereof*, because they are holy things.

34 Now if ought of the flesh of the consecration, or of the bread remain unto the morning, then thou shalt burn the rest with fire: it shall not be eaten, because it is an holy thing.

35 Therefore shalt thou do thus unto Aaron and unto his sons, according to all things which I have commanded thee: seven days shalt thou [1]consecrate them.

36 And shalt offer every day a calf for a sin offering, for [1]reconciliation: and thou shalt cleanse the Altar, when thou hast offered upon it for reconciliation, and shalt anoint it to sanctify it.

37 Seven days shalt thou cleanse the Altar and sanctify it, so the Altar shall be most holy: *and* whatsoever toucheth the Altar, shall be holy.

38 ¶ *b*Now this is that which thou shalt present upon the altar: *even* two lambs of one year old, day by day continually.

39 The one lamb thou shalt present in the morning, and the other lamb thou shalt present at even.

40 And with the one lamb, a [1]tenth part of fine flour mingled with the fourth part of an [2]Hin of beaten oil, and the fourth part of an Hin of wine for a drink offering.

41 And the other lamb thou shalt present at even: thou shalt do thereto according to the offering of the morning, and according to the drink offering thereof, *to be* a burnt offering for a sweet savor unto the Lord.

42 *This shall be* a continually burnt offering in your generations at the door of the Tabernacle of the Congregation before the Lord, where I will

g Lev. 8:31
Lev. 24:9
Matt. 12:4

b Num. 28:3

i Lev. 26:12
2 Cor. 6:16

[1]make appointment with you, to speak there unto thee.

43 There I will appoint with the children of Israel, and *the place* shall be sanctified by my [1]glory.

44 And I will sanctify the Tabernacle of the Congregation and the Altar: I will sanctify also Aaron and his sons to be my Priests,

45 And I will [i]dwell among the children of Israel, and will be their God.

46 Then shall they know that I am the Lord their God, that brought them out of the land of Egypt, that I might dwell among them: [1]I am the Lord their God.

30

The Altar of incense.   13 The sum that the Israelites should pay to the Tabernacle.   28 The brazen laver.   33 The anointing oil.   34 The making of the perfume.

1 Furthermore thou shalt make an Altar [1]for sweet perfume, of Shittim wood thou shalt make it.

2 The length thereof a cubit, and the breadth thereof a cubit, (it shall be foursquare) and the height thereof two cubits: the horns thereof *shall be* [1]of the same.

3 And thou shalt overlay it with fine gold, *both* the top thereof, and the sides thereof round about, and his horns: also thou shalt make unto it [1]a crown of gold round about.

4 Besides this thou shalt make under this crown two golden rings on either side: *even* on every side shalt thou make *them*, that they may be as places for the bars to bear it withal.

5 The which bars thou shalt make of Shittim wood, and shalt cover them with gold.

6 After thou shalt set it [1]before the veil, that is near the Ark of the Testimony, before the Mercy seat that is upon the Testimony, where I will appoint with thee.

7 And Aaron shall burn thereon sweet incense every morning: when he [1]dresseth the lamps thereof, shall he burn it.

8 Likewise at even, when Aaron setteth up the lamps thereof, he shall burn incense: *this* perfume *shall be* perpetually before the Lord, throughout your generations.

9 Ye shall offer no [1]strange incense thereon, nor burnt sacrifice, nor offering, neither pour any drink

---

29:33 [1] That is, by the sacrifices.
29:35 [1] Hebrew, *fill their hands.*
29:36 [1] To appease God's wrath that sin may be pardoned.
29:40 [1] That is, an Omer, read Exod. 16:16.
    [2] Which is about a pint.
29:42 [1] Or, declare myself to you.
29:43 [1] Because of my glorious presence.

29:46 [1] It is I the Lord, that am their God.
30:1 [1] Upon the which the sweet perfume was burnt, verse 34.
30:2 [1] Of the same wood and matter.
30:3 [1] Or, a circle and border.
30:6 [1] That is, in the Sanctuary, and not in the holiest of all.
30:7 [1] Meaning, when he trimmeth them, and refresheth the oil.
30:9 [1] Otherwise made them this, which is described.

offering [2]thereon.

10 And Aaron shall make reconciliation upon the horns of it once in a year with the blood of the sin offering *in the day* of reconciliation: once in the year shall he make reconciliation upon it throughout your generations: this is most holy unto the Lord.

11 ¶ Afterward the Lord spake unto Moses, saying,

12 [a]When thou takest the sum of the children of Israel after their number, then they shall give every man [1]a redemption of his life unto the Lord, when thou tellest them, that there be no plague among them when thou countest them.

13 This shall every man give, that goeth into the number, half a shekel, after the [1]shekel of the Sanctuary: ([b]a shekel *is* twenty gerahs) the half shekel *shall be* an offering to the Lord.

14 All that are numbered from twenty years old and above, shall give an offering to the Lord.

15 The rich shall not pass, and the poor shall not diminish from half a shekel, when ye shall give an offering unto the Lord, [1]for the redemption of your lives.

16 So thou shalt take the money of the redemption of the children of Israel, and shalt put it unto the use of the Tabernacle of the Congregation, that it may be a memorial unto the children of Israel before the Lord, for the redemption of your lives.

17 ¶ Also the Lord spake unto Moses, saying,

18 Thou shalt also make a Laver of brass, and his foot of brass to wash, and shalt put it between the Tabernacle of the Congregation and the Altar, and shalt put water therein.

19 For Aaron and his sons shall [1]wash their hands, and their feet thereat.

20 When they go into the Tabernacle of the Congregation, or when they go unto the Altar to minister, *and* to make the perfume of the burnt offering to the Lord, they shall wash themselves with water, lest they die.

21 So they shall wash their hands and their feet that they die not: and *this* shall be to them an ordinance [1]forever, *both* unto him and to his seed throughout their generations.

22 ¶ Also the Lord spake unto Moses, saying,

23 Take thou also unto thee principal spices: of the most pure myrrh five hundred [1]shekels, of sweet cinnamon half so much, *that is,* two hundred and fifty,

CHAPTER 30
[a] Num. 1:2,5
[b] Lev. 27:25
Num. 3:47
Ezek. 45:12
[c] Exod. 29:40

and of sweet [2]calamus, two hundred, and fifty:

24 Also of Cassia five hundred, after the shekel of the Sanctuary, and of oil olive an [c]Hin.

25 So thou shalt make of it the oil of holy ointment, *even* a most precious ointment after the art of the Apothecary: this shall be the oil of holy ointment.

26 And thou shalt anoint the [1]Tabernacle of the Congregation therewith, and the Ark of the Testimony:

27 Also the Table, and all the instruments thereof, and the Candlestick, with all the instruments thereof, and the altar of incense:

28 Also the altar of burnt offering with all his instruments, and the laver and his foot.

29 So thou shalt sanctify them, and they shall be most holy: all that shall touch them, shall be holy.

30 Thou shalt also anoint Aaron and his sons, and shalt consecrate them, that they may minister unto me in the Priest's office.

31 Moreover thou shalt speak unto the children of Israel, saying, This shall be an holy anointing oil unto me, throughout your generations.

32 None shall anoint [1]man's flesh therewith, neither shall ye make any composition like unto it: *for* it is holy, and shall be holy unto you.

33 Whosoever shall make the like ointment, or whosoever shall put any of it upon [1]a stranger, even he shall be cut off from his people.

34 And the Lord said unto Moses, Take unto thee *these* spices, pure myrrh and [1]clear gum and galbanum, *these* odors with pure frankincense of each like weight:

35 Then thou shalt make of them perfume composed after the art of the apothecary, mingled together, pure *and* holy.

36 And thou shalt beat it to powder, and shalt put it before *the Ark* of the Testimony in the tabernacle of the congregation, where I will make appointment with thee: it shall be unto you most holy.

37 And ye shall not make unto you any composition like this perfume, which thou shalt make: it shall be unto thee holy for the [1]Lord.

38 Whosoever shall make like unto that to smell thereto, even he shall be cut off from his people.

31

2 God maketh Bezalel and Aholiab meet for his work.   13 The Sabbath day is the sign of our sanc-

---

[2] But it must only serve to burn perfume.

30:12 [1] Whereby he testified that he redeemed his life which he had forfeit, as is declared by David, 2 Sam. 24:1.

30:13 [1] This shekel valued two common shekels: and the gerah valued about 12 pence after five shillings sterling the ounce of silver.

30:15 [1] That God should be merciful unto you.

30:19 [1] Signifying, that he that cometh to God, must be washed from all sin and corruption.

30:21 [1] So long as the Priesthood shall last.

30:23 [1] Weighing so much.

[2] It is a kind of reed of a very sweet savor within, and it is used in powders and odors.

30:26 [1] All things which appertain to the Tabernacle.

30:32 [1] Neither at their burials nor otherwise.

30:33 [1] Either a stranger or an Israelite, save only the Priests.

30:34 [1] In Hebrew, *Sheheleth*: which is a sweet kind of gum and shineth as the nail.

30:37 [1] Only dedicated to the use of the Tabernacle.

tification.   18 The Tables written by the finger of God.

1   And the Lord spake unto Moses, saying,

2   Behold, I [1]have called by name Bezalel the son of Uri, the son of Hur, of the tribe of Judah,

3   Whom I have filled with the Spirit of God, in wisdom, and in understanding, and in knowledge, and in all [1]workmanship:

4   To find out curious works to work in gold, and in silver, and in brass,

5   Also in the art to set stones, and to carve in timber, and to work in all manner of workmanship.

6   And behold, I have joined him with Aholiab the son of Ahisamach of the tribe of Dan, and in the hearts of all that are [1]wise hearted, have I put wisdom to make all that I have commanded thee:

7   *That is*, the Tabernacle of the Congregation, and the Ark of the Testimony, and the Mercy seat that shall be thereupon, with all instruments of the Tabernacle:

8   Also the Table and the instruments thereof, and the [1]pure Candlestick with all his instruments, and the Altar of perfume:

9   Likewise the Altar of burnt offering with all his instruments, and the Laver with his foot:

10   Also the garments of the ministration, and the holy garment for Aaron the Priest, and the garments of his sons, to minister in the Priest's office,

11   And the [1]anointing oil, and sweet perfume for the Sanctuary according to all that I have commanded thee, shall they do.

12   ¶ Afterward the Lord spake unto Moses, saying,

13   Speak thou also unto the children of Israel, and say, [1]Notwithstanding keep ye my Sabbaths: for it is a sign between me and you in your generations, that ye may know that I the Lord do sanctify you.

14   [a]Ye shall therefore keep the [1]Sabbath: for it is holy unto you: he that defileth it, shall die the death: therefore whosoever worketh therein, the same person shall be even cut off from among his people.

15   Six days shall men work, but in the seventh day is the Sabbath of the holy rest to the Lord:

CHAPTER 31
[a] Exod. 20:8
Ezek. 20:12
[b] Gen. 31
Gen. 22
[c] Deut. 9:10

CHAPTER 32
[a] Ps. 106:19
[b] 1 Kings 12:28
[c] 1 Cor. 10:7
[d] Deut. 9:12

whosoever doeth any work in the Sabbath day, shall die the death.

16   Wherefore the children of Israel shall keep the Sabbath, that they may observe the [1]rest throughout their generations for an everlasting Covenant.

17   It is a sign between me and the children of Israel forever: [b]for in six days the Lord made the heaven and the earth, and in the seventh day [1]he ceased and rested.

18   Thus (when the Lord had made an end of communing with Moses upon mount Sinai) [c]he gave him two Tables [1]of the Testimony, *even* tables of stone, written with the finger of God.

32

4 The Israelites impute their deliverance to the calf.   14 God is appeased by Moses' prayer. 19 Moses breaketh the Tables.

1   But when the people saw, that Moses tarried long ere he came down from the mountain, the people gathered themselves together against Aaron, and said unto him, Up, [1]make us gods to go before us: for of this Moses (the man that brought us out of the land of Egypt) we know not what is become of him.

2   And Aaron said unto them, [1]Pluck off the golden earrings, which are in the ears of your wives, of your sons, and of your daughters, and bring them unto me.

3   Then all the people plucked from [1]themselves the golden earrings, which were in their ears, and they brought *them* unto Aaron.

4   [a]Who received them at their hands, and fashioned it with the graving tool, and made of it a [1]molten calf: then they said, [b]These be thy gods, O Israel, which brought thee out of the land of Egypt.

5   When Aaron saw *that*, he made an Altar before it: and Aaron proclaimed, saying, Tomorrow *shall be* the holy day of the Lord.

6   So they rose up the next day in the morning, and offered burnt offerings, and brought peace offerings: also [c]the people sat them down to eat and drink, and rose up to play.

7   ¶ Then the Lord said unto Moses, [d]Go get thee down: for thy people which thou hast brought out

---

31:2 [1] I have chosen and made meet, Exod. 35:30.
31:3 [1] This showeth that handicrafts are the gifts of God's spirit, and therefore ought to be esteemed.
31:6 [1] I have instructed them, and increased their knowledge.
31:8 [1] So called, because of the cunning and art used therein, or because the whole was beaten out of the piece.
31:11 [1] Which only was to anoint the Priests and the instruments of the tabernacle, and not to burn.
31:13 [1] Though I command these works to be done, yet will I not that you break my Sabbath days.
31:14 [1] God repeateth this point because the whole keeping of the law standeth in the true use of the Sabbath, which is to cease from our works, and to obey the will of God.

31:16 [1] Or, Sabbath.
31:17 [1] From creating his creatures, but not from governing and preserving them.
31:18 [1] Whereby he declared his will to his people.
32:1 [1] The root of Idolatry is, when men think that God is not at hand, except they see him carnally.
32:2 [1] Thinking that they would rather forego idolatry, than to resign their most precious jewels.
32:3 [1] Such is the rage of idolaters, that they spare no cost to satisfy their wicked desires.
32:4 [1] They smelled of their leaven of Egypt, where they saw calves, oxen and serpents worshipped.

of the land of Egypt, hath corrupted *their ways.*

8 They ¹are soon turned out of the way, which I commanded them: *for* they have made them a molten calf, and have worshipped it, and have offered thereto, saying, *ᵉ*These be thy gods, O Israel, which have brought thee out of the land of Egypt.

9 Again the Lord said unto Moses, ᶠI have seen this people, and behold, it is a stiff-necked people.

10 Now ¹therefore let me alone, that my wrath may wax hot against them, for I will consume them: but I will make of thee a mighty people

11 ᵍBut Moses prayed unto the Lord his God, and said, O Lord, why doth thy wrath wax hot against thy people, which thou hast brought out of the land of Egypt, with great power and with a mighty hand?

12 ʰWherefore shall the Egyptians ¹speak, and say, He hath brought them out maliciously for to slay them in the mountains, and to consume them from the earth? turn from thy fierce wrath, and ²change thy mind from this evil toward thy people.

13 Remember ¹Abraham, Isaac, and Israel thy servants, to whom thou swarest by thine own self, and saidest unto them, ⁱI will multiply your seed, as the stars of heaven, and all this land, that I have spoken of, will I give unto your seed, and they shall inherit it forever.

14 Then the Lord changed his mind from the evil, which he threatened to do unto his people.

15 So Moses returned and went down from the mountain with the two Tables of the Testimony in his hand: the tables *were* written on both their sides, even on the one side and on the other were they written.

16 And these Tables were the work of God, and ¹this writing was the writing of God graven in the Tables.

17 And when Joshua heard the noise of the people, as they shouted, he said unto Moses, *There is* a noise of war in the host.

18 Who answered, It is not the noise of them that have the victory, nor the noise of them that are overcome: *but* I do hear the noise of singing.

19 Now, as soon as he came near unto the host, he saw the calf and the dancing: so Moses' wrath waxed hot, and he cast the Tables out of his hands, and brake them in pieces beneath the mountain.

20 ʲAfter, he took the calf, which they had made,

and burned it in the fire, and ground it unto powder, and strowed it upon the water, and made the children of Israel ¹drink of it.

21 Also Moses said unto Aaron, What did this people unto thee, that thou hast brought so great a sin upon them?

22 Then Aaron answered, Let not the wrath of my Lord wax fierce: Thou knowest this people, that they are *even set* on mischief.

23 And they said unto me, Make us gods to go before us: for we know not what is become of this Moses (the man that brought us out of the land of Egypt).

24 Then I said to them, Ye that have gold, pluck it off: and they brought it me, and I did cast it into the fire, and *thereof* came this calf.

25 Moses therefore saw that the people were ¹naked (for Aaron had made them naked unto *their* shame among their enemies)

26 And Moses stood in the gate of the camp, and said, Who *pertaineth* to the Lord? *let them come* to me. And all the sons of Levi gathered themselves unto him.

27 Then he said unto them, Thus saith the Lord God of Israel: Put every man his sword by his side, go to and fro, from gate to gate, through the host, and ¹slay every man his brother, and every man his companion, and every man his neighbor.

28 So the children of Levi did as Moses had commanded: and there fell of the people the same day about three thousand men.

29 (For Moses had said, Consecrate your hands unto the Lord this day, even every man upon his ¹son, and upon his brother, that there may be given you a blessing this day.)

30 And when the morning came, Moses said unto the people, Ye have committed a grievous crime: but now I will go up to the Lord, if I may pacify *him* for your sin.

31 Moses therefore went again unto the Lord, and said, Oh, this people have sinned a great sin, and have made them gods of gold.

32 Therefore now if thou pardon their sin, *thy mercy shall appear*: but if thou wilt not, I pray thee, raise me ¹out of thy book, which thou hast written.

33 Then the Lord said to Moses, Whosoever hath sinned against me, I will put him out of my ¹book.

ᵉ 1 Kings 12:28
ᶠ Exod. 33:3
  Deut. 9:13
ᵍ Ps. 106:23
ʰ Num. 14:13
ⁱ Gen. 12:7
  Gen. 15:7
  Gen. 48:16
ʲ Deut. 9:21

32:8 ¹ Whereby we see what necessity we have to pray earnestly to God, to keep us in his true obedience, and to send us good guides.
32:10 ¹ God showeth that the prayers of the godly stay his punishment.
32:12 ¹ Or, blaspheme.
     ² Or, repent.
32:13 ¹ That is, thy promise made to Abraham.
32:16 ¹ All these repetitions show how excellent a thing they defrauded themselves of by their idolatry.
32:20 ¹ Partly to despite them of their idolatry, and partly that they should have none occasion to remember it afterward.

32:25 ¹ Both destitute of God's favor, and an occasion to their enemies to speak evil of their God.
32:27 ¹ This fact did so please God, that he turned the curse of Jacob against Levi to a blessing, Deut. 33:9.
32:29 ¹ In revenging God's glory we must have no respect to person, but put off all carnal affection.
32:32 ¹ So much he esteemed the glory of God, that he preferred it even to his own salvation.
32:33 ¹ I will make it known that he was never predestinated in mine eternal counsel to life everlasting.

34 Go now therefore, bring the people unto the place which I commanded thee: behold, mine Angel shall go before thee, but yet in the day of my visitation I will visit their sin upon them.

35 ¹So the Lord plagued the people, because they caused Aaron to make the calf which he made.

33

2 God promiseth to send an Angel before his people. 4 They are sad because the Lord denieth to go up with them. 9 Moses talketh familiarly with God. 13 He prayeth for the people.

1 Afterward the Lord said unto Moses, Depart, ¹go up from hence, thou, and the people (which thou hast brought up out of the land of Egypt) unto the land which I sware unto Abraham, to Isaac, and to Jacob, saying, ªUnto thy seed will I give it.

2 And ᵇI will send an Angel before thee, and will cast out the Canaanites, the Amorites, and the Hittites, and the Perizzites, the Hivites, and the Jebusites,

3 To a land, I say, that floweth with milk and honey: for I will not go up with thee, ᶜbecause thou art a stiff-necked people, lest I consume thee in the way.

4 And when the people heard this evil tidings, they sorrowed, and no man put on his best raiment.

5 (For the Lord had said unto Moses, Say unto the children of Israel, Ye are a stiff-necked people, I will come suddenly upon thee and consume thee: therefore now put thy costly raiment from thee, that I may know ¹what to do unto thee.)

6 So the children of Israel laid their good raiment from them, after Moses came down from the mount Horeb.

7 Then Moses took his tabernacle, and pitched it without the host far off from the host, and called it ¹Ohel-moed. And when any did seek to the Lord, he went out unto the Tabernacle of the Congregation, which was without the host.

8 And when Moses went out unto the Tabernacle, all the people rose up, and stood every man at his tent door, and looked after Moses, until he was gone into the Tabernacle.

9 And as soon as Moses was entered into the

CHAPTER 33
ª Gen. 12:7
ᵇ Exod. 23:27
Josh. 24:11
Deut. 7:22
ᶜ Exod. 31:9
Deut. 9:13
ᵈ Rom. 9:15

Tabernacle, the cloudy pillar descended and stood at the door of the Tabernacle, and the Lord talked with Moses.

10 Now when all the people saw the cloudy pillar stand at the Tabernacle door, all the people rose up, and worshipped every man in his tent door.

11 And the Lord spake unto Moses, ¹face to face, as a man speaketh unto his friend. After he turned again into the host, but his servant Joshua the son of Nun a young man, departed not out of the Tabernacle.

12 ¶ Then Moses said unto the Lord, See, thou sayest unto me, Lead this people forth, and thou hast not showed me whom thou wilt send with me: thou hast said moreover, I know thee by ¹name, and thou hast also found grace in my sight.

13 Now therefore, I pray thee, if I have found favor in thy sight, show me now thy way, that I may know thee, and that I may find grace in thy sight: consider also that this nation is thy people.

14 And he answered, My ¹,²presence shall go with thee, and I will give thee rest.

15 Then he said unto him, If thy presence go not with us, carry us not hence.

16 And wherein now shall it be known, that I and thy people have found favor in thy sight? shall it not be when thou goest with us? so I, and thy people shall have preeminence before all the people that are upon the earth.

17 And the Lord said unto Moses, I will do this also that thou hast said: for thou hast found grace in my sight, and I know thee by name.

18 Again he said, I beseech thee, show me thy ¹glory.

19 And he answered, I will make all my ¹good go before thee, and I will ²proclaim the Name of the Lord before thee: ᵈfor I will show ³mercy to whom I will show mercy, and will have compassion on whom I will have compassion.

20 Furthermore he said, Thou canst not see my face, for there shall no man see me, and ¹live.

21 Also the Lord said, Behold, there is a place by ¹me, and thou shalt stand upon the rock:

22 And while my glory passeth by, I will put thee in a cleft of the rock, and will cover thee with mine

---

32:35 ¹ This declareth how grievous a sin idolatry is, seeing that at Moses' prayer God would not fully remit it.
33:1 ¹ The land of Canaan was compassed with hills: so they that entered into it, must pass up by the hills.
33:5 ¹ That either I may show mercy, if thou repent, or else punish thy rebellion.
33:7 ¹ That is, the Tabernacle of the Congregation: so called, because the people resorted thither, when they should be instructed of the Lord's will.
33:11 ¹ Most plainly and familiarly of all others, Num. 12:7,8; Deut. 34:10.
33:12 ¹ I care for thee and will preserve thee in this thy vocation.

33:14 ¹ Hebrew, face.
² Signifying that the Israelites should excel through God's favor all other people, verse 16.
33:18 ¹ Thy face, thy substance, and thy majesty.
33:19 ¹ My mercy and fatherly care.
² Read Exod. 34:6,7.
³ For finding nothing in man that can deserve mercy, he will freely save his.
33:20 ¹ For Moses saw not his face in full majesty, but as man's weakness could bear.
33:21 ¹ In mount Horeb.

hand while I pass by.

23 After I will take away mine hand, and thou shalt see my ¹back parts: but my face shall not be seen.

34

1 The Tables are renewed.   6 The description of God.   12 All fellowship with idolaters is forbidden.   18 The feasts.   28 Moses is 40 days in the mount. 30 His face shineth, and he covereth it with a veil.

1   And the Lord said unto Moses, ªHew thee two Tables of stone, like unto the first, and I will write upon the Tables the words that were in the first Tables, which thou brakest in pieces.

2   And be ready in the morning, that thou mayest come up early unto the mount of Sinai, and ¹wait there for me in the top of the mount.

3   But let no man come up with thee, neither let any man be seen throughout all the mount; neither let the sheep nor cattle feed ¹before this mount.

4   Then Moses hewed ¹two Tables of stone like unto the first, and rose up early in the morning, and went up unto the mount of Sinai, as the Lord had commanded him, and took in his hand two Tables of stone.

5   And the Lord descended in the cloud, and stood with him there, and proclaimed the name of the Lord.

6   So the Lord passed before his face, and ¹cried, The Lord, the Lord, strong, merciful, and gracious, slow to anger, and abundant in goodness and truth.

7   Reserving mercy for thousands, forgiving iniquity, and transgression and sin, and not ¹making the *wicked* innocent, ᵇvisiting the iniquity of the fathers upon the children, and upon children's children, unto the third and fourth *generation*.

8   Then Moses made haste and bowed himself to the earth, and worshipped,

9   And said, O Lord, I pray thee, If I have found grace in thy sight, that the Lord would now go with us (¹for it is a stiff-necked people) and pardon our iniquity and our sin, and take us for thine inheritance.

10   And he answered, Behold, ᶜI will make a covenant before all thy people, *and* will do marvels, such as have not been done in all the world, neither

CHAPTER 34
ª Deut. 10:1
ᵇ Deut. 5:9
Jer. 32:18
ᶜ Deut. 5:2
ᵈ Deut. 7:2
ᵉ Exod. 20:5
ᶠ 1 Cor. 8:10
ᵍ Exod. 23:32
Deut. 7:2,3
ʰ 1 Kings 11:2
ⁱ Exod. 23:15
ʲ Exod. 23:15
ᵏ Exod. 13:2
Exod. 22:29
Ezek. 44:30
ˡ Exod. 23:25
ᵐ Exod. 23:12
ⁿ Exod. 23:15
ᵒ Deut. 16:16
Exod. 23:14,17

in all nations: and all the people among whom thou art, shall see the work of the Lord: for it is a terrible thing that I will do with thee.

11   Keep diligently that which I command thee this day: Behold, I will cast out before thee the Amorites, and the Canaanites, and the Hittites, and the Perizzites, and the Hivites, and the Jebusites.

12   ᵈTake heed to thyself, that thou make no compact with the inhabitants of the land whither thou goest, lest they be the cause of ¹ruin among you:

13   But ye shall overthrow their altars, and break their images in pieces, and cut down their ¹groves,

14   (For thou shalt bow down to none other god, because the Lord, whose Name *is* ᵉJealous, is a jealous God.)

15   Lest thou make a ᶠcompact with the inhabitants of the land, and when they go a whoring after their gods, and do sacrifice unto their gods, *some man* call thee, and thou ᵍeat of his sacrifice.

16   And *lest* thou take of their ʰdaughters unto thy sons, and their daughters go a whoring after their gods, and make thy sons go a whoring after their gods.

17   Thou shalt make thee no gods of ¹metal.

18   The feast of ⁱunleavened bread shalt thou keep: seven days shalt thou eat unleavened bread, as I commanded thee, in the time of the ʲmonth of Abib: for in the month of Abib thou camest out of Egypt.

19   ᵏEvery *male* that *first* openeth the womb, *shall be* mine: also all the firstborn of thy flock shall be reckoned *mine, both* of beeves and sheep.

20   But the first of the ass thou shalt buy out with a lamb: and if thou redeem *him* not, then thou shalt break his neck: all the firstborn of thy sons shalt thou redeem, and none shall appear before me ¹·¹empty.

21   ¶ ᵐSix days shalt thou work, and in the seventh day thou shalt rest: both in earing time, and in the harvest thou shalt rest.

22   ¶ ⁿThou shalt also observe the feast of weeks *in the time* of the firstfruits, of wheat harvest, and the feast of gathering *fruits* in ¹the end of the year.

23   ¶ ᵒThrice in a year shall all your men children appear before the Lord Jehovah God of Israel.

24   For I will cast out the nations before thee and enlarge thy coasts, so that no man shall ¹desire thy land, when thou shalt come up to appear before the

---

3:23 ¹ So much of my glory as in this mortal life thou art able to see.
34:2 ¹ Hebrew, *stand to me.*
34:3 ¹ Or, about.
34:4 ¹ Or, polished.
34:6 ¹ This ought to be referred to the Lord, and not to Moses proclaiming: as Exod. 33:19.
34:7 ¹ Hebrew, *not making innocent.*
34:9 ¹ Seeing the people are thus of nature, the rulers have need to call upon God that he would always be present with his Spirit.

34:12 ¹ If thou follow their wickedness, and pollute thyself with their idolatry.
34:13 ¹ Which pleasant places they chose for their idols.
34:17 ¹ As gold, silver, brass, or anything that is molten: And herein is condemned all manner of idols, whatsoever they be made of.
34:20 ¹ Without offering something.
34:22 ¹ Which was in September, when the sun declined which in the count of political things they called the end of the year.
34:24 ¹ God promiseth to defend them and theirs, which obey his commandment.

Lord thy God thrice in the year.

25 *Thou shall not offer the blood of my sacrifice with leaven, neither shall ought of the sacrifice of the feast of Passover be left unto the morning.

26 The first ripe fruits of thy land thou shalt bring unto the house of the Lord thy God: *yet* shalt thou not ¹seethe a kid in his mother's milk.

27 And the Lord said unto Moses, Write thou these words: for after the tenor of ⁴these words I have made a covenant with thee and with Israel.

28 So he was there with the Lord ¹forty days and forty nights, *and* did neither eat bread nor drink water, and he wrote in the Tables ʳthe words of the covenant, *even* the ²Ten commandments.

29 ¶ So when Moses came down from mount Sinai, the two Tables of the Testimony *were* in Moses' hand, as he descended from the mount: (now Moses wist not that the skin of his face shone bright, after that *God* had talked with him).

30 And Aaron and all the children of Israel looked upon Moses, and behold, the skin of his face shone bright, and they were ¹afraid to come near him.

31 But Moses called them: and Aaron and all the chief of the congregation returned unto him: and Moses talked with them.

32 And afterward all the children of Israel came near, and he charged them with all that the Lord had said unto him in mount Sinai.

33 So Moses made an end of communing with them, ˢand had put a covering upon his face.

34 But, when Moses came ¹before the Lord to speak with him, he took off the covering until he came out: then he came out, and spake unto the children of Israel that which he was commanded.

35 And the children of Israel saw the face of Moses, how the skin of Moses' face shone bright: therefore Moses put the covering upon his face, until he went to speak with *God*.

35

2 *The Sabbath.*   5 *The free gifts are required.*
21 *The readiness of the people to offer.*   30 *Bezalel and Aholiab are praised of Moses.*

1 Then Moses assembled all the Congregation of the children of Israel, and said unto them, These are the words which the Lord hath commanded, that ye should do them:

2 ªSix days thou shalt work, but the seventh day shall be unto you the holy ¹Sabbath of rest unto the Lord: whosoever doeth *any* work therein,

Marginal references

p Exod. 23:18
q Exod. 24:18
   Deut. 9:9
r Deut. 4:23
s 2 Cor. 3:13

CHAPTER 35
a Exod. 20:9
b Exod. 25:2
c Exod. 26:31
d Exod. 30:1
e Exod. 27:1

shall die.

3 Ye shall kindle no fire throughout all your habitations upon the Sabbath day.

4 ¶ Again, Moses spake unto all the Congregation of the children of Israel, saying, This is the thing which the Lord commandeth, saying,

5 Take from among you an offering unto the Lord: whosoever is of a ᵇwilling heart, let him bring this offering to the Lord, *namely* gold, and silver and brass:

6 Also blue silk, and purple, and scarlet, and fine linen, and goats' *hair*,

7 And rams' skins dyed red, and badgers' skins with Shittim wood:

8 Also oil for light, and spices for the anointing oil, and for the sweet incense,

9 And onyx stones, and stones to be set in the Ephod, and in the breastplate.

10 And all the wise ¹hearted among you, shall come and make all that the Lord hath commanded:

11 *That is,* the ᶜTabernacle, the pavilion thereof, and his covering, and his taches, and his boards, his bars, his pillars, and his sockets,

12 The Ark, and the bars thereof: the Mercy seat, and the veil that ¹covereth *it*,

13 The Table, and the bars of it, and all the instruments thereof, and the showbread:

14 Also the Candlestick of light and his instruments, and his lamps with the oil for the light:

15 ᵈLikewise the Altar of perfume and his bars, and the anointing oil, and the sweet incense, and the veil of the door at the entering in of the Tabernacle,

16 The ᵉAltar of burnt offering with his brazen grate, his bars and all his instruments, the laver and his foot,

17 The hangings of the court, his pillars and his sockets, and the veil of the gate of the court,

18 The pins of the Tabernacle, and the pins of the court with their cords,

19 The ¹ministering garments to minister in the holy place, *and* the holy garments of Aaron the Priest, and the garments of his sons, that they may minister in the Priest's office.

20 ¶ Then all the Congregation of the children of Israel departed from the presence of Moses.

21 And every one, whose heart ¹encouraged him, and every one, whose spirit made him willing, came *and* brought an offering to the Lord, for the work of the Tabernacle of the Congregation, and for all his uses, and for the holy garments.

34:26 ¹ Read Exod. 23:1; Deut. 14:21.
34:28 ¹ This miracle was to confirm the authority of the law, and ought no more to be followed than other miracles.
  ² Or, words.
34:30 ¹ Read 2 Cor. 3:7.
34:34 ¹ Which was in the Tabernacle of the congregation.

35:2 ¹ Wherein ye shall rest from all bodily work.
35:10 ¹ Read Exod. 28:3.
35:12 ¹ Which hanged before the Mercy seat that it could not be seen.
35:19 ¹ Such as appertain to the service of the Tabernacle.
35:21 ¹ Hebrew, *lifted him up.*

22 Both men and women, as many as were free hearted, came *and* brought [1]taches and earrings, and rings, and bracelets, all *were* jewels of gold: and every one that offered an offering of gold unto the Lord:

23 Every man also, which had blue silk, and purple, and scarlet, and fine linen and goats' *hair*, and rams' skins dyed red, and badgers' skins, brought *them*.

24 All that offered an oblation of silver and of brass, brought the offering unto the Lord: and every one, that [1]had Shittim wood for any manner work of the ministration, brought it.

25 And all the women that were [1]wise-hearted, did spin with their hands, and brought the spun work, *even* the blue silk, and the purple, the scarlet, and fine linen.

26 Likewise all the women, [1]whose hearts were moved with knowledge, spun goats' *hair*.

27 And the rulers brought onyx stones, and stones to be set in the Ephod, and in the breastplate:

28 Also spice, and oil for light, and for the [f]anointing oil, and for the sweet perfume.

29 Every man and woman of the children of Israel, whose hearts moved them willingly to bring for all the work which the Lord had commanded them to make [1]by the hand of Moses, brought a free offering unto the Lord.

30 ¶ Then Moses said unto the children of Israel, Behold, [g]the Lord hath called by name Bezalel the son of Uri, the son of Hur of the tribe of Judah,

31 And hath filled him [1]with an excellent spirit of wisdom, of understanding, and of knowledge, and in all manner work,

32 To find out curious works, to work in gold, and in silver, and in brass,

33 And in graving stones to set them, and in carving of wood, *even* to make any manner of fine work.

34 And he hath put in his heart that he may teach *other*: both he, and Aholiab the son of Ahisamach of the tribe of Dan:

35 Them hath he filled with wisdom of heart to work all manner [1]of cunning [h]and broidered, and needle work: in blue silk, and in purple, in scarlet, and in fine linen and weaving, *even* to do all manner of work and subtle inventions.

36 5 *The great readiness of the people.* 8 *The curtains made.* 19 *The coverings.* 20 *The boards.* 31 *The bars,* 35 *and the veil.*

Side notes:
[f] Exod. 30:23
[g] Exod. 31:2
[h] Exod. 26:1

CHAPTER 36
[a] Exod. 26:3,4
[b] Exod. 26:10

1 Then wrought Bezalel, and Aholiab, and all [1]cunning men, to whom the Lord gave wisdom, and understanding, to know how to work all manner work for the service of the [2]Sanctuary, according to all that the Lord had commanded.

2 For Moses had called Bezalel, and Aholiab, and all the wise-hearted men, in whose hearts the Lord had given wisdom, *even* as many as their hearts encouraged to come unto that work to work it.

3 And they received of Moses all the offering which the children of Israel had brought for the work of the service of the Sanctuary, to make it: also [1]they brought still unto him free gifts every morning.

4 So all the wise men, that wrought all the holy work, came every man from his work which they wrought,

5 And spake to Moses, saying, The people bring too [1]much, *and* more than enough for the use of the work, which the Lord hath commanded to be made.

6 Then Moses gave a commandment, and they caused it to be proclaimed throughout the host, saying, Let neither man nor woman prepare any more work for the oblations of the Sanctuary. So the people were stayed from offering.

7 For the stuff they had, was sufficient for all the work to make it, and too much.

8 [a]All the cunning men therefore among the workmen, made *for* the Tabernacle ten curtains of fine twined linen, and of blue silk, and purple, and scarlet: [1]Cherubims of broidered work made they *upon* them.

9 The length of one curtain *was* twenty and eight cubits, and the breadth of one curtain four cubits: *and* the curtains were all of one size.

10 And he coupled five curtains together, and another five coupled he together.

11 And he made strings of blue silk by the edge of one curtain, in the selvedge of the coupling: likewise he made on the side of the *other* curtain in the selvedge in the second coupling.

12 [b]Fifty strings made he in the one curtain, and fifty strings made he in the edge of the *other* curtain, which was in the second coupling: the strings were set one against another.

13 After, he made fifty [1]taches of gold, and coupled the curtains one to another with the taches: *so* was it one Tabernacle.

35:22 [1] Or, hooks.
35:24 [1] Hebrew, *with whom was found.*
35:25 [1] Which were witty and expert.
35:26 [1] That is, which were good spinners.
35:29 [1] Using Moses as a minister thereof.
35:31 [1] Or, with the spirit of God.
35:35 [1] Pertaining to graving, or carving, or such like.

36:1 [1] Hebrew, *wise in heart.*
    [2] By the Sanctuary he meaneth all the Tabernacle.
36:3 [1] Meaning, the Israelites.
36:5 [1] A rare example and notable to see the people so ready to serve God with their goods.
36:8 [1] Which were little pictures with wings in the form of children.
36:13 [1] Or, hooks.

14 ¶ Also he made curtains of goats' *hair* for the [1]covering upon the Tabernacle: he made them *to the number* of eleven curtains.

15 The length of one curtain *had* thirty cubits, and the breadth of one curtain four cubits: the eleven curtains *were* of one size.

16 And he coupled five curtains by themselves, and six curtains by themselves.

17 Also he made fifty strings upon the edge of *one* curtain in the selvedge in the coupling, and fifty strings made he upon the edge of the *other* curtain in the second coupling.

18 He made also fifty taches of brass to couple the covering that it might be one.

19 And he made a [1]covering upon the pavilion of rams' skins dyed red, and a covering of badgers' skins above.

20 ¶ Likewise he made the boards for the Tabernacle, of Shittim wood to [1]stand up.

21 The length of a board *was* ten cubits, and the breadth of one board *was* a cubit and an half.

22 One board had two tenons, set in order as the feet of a ladder, one against another: thus made he for all the boards of the Tabernacle.

23 So he made twenty boards for the South side of the Tabernacle, even full South.

24 And forty sockets of silver made he under the twenty boards, two sockets under one board for his two tenons, and two sockets under another board for his two tenons.

25 Also for the other side of the Tabernacle toward the North, he made twenty boards.

26 And their forty sockets of silver, two sockets under one board, and two sockets under another board.

27 Likewise toward [1]the West side of the Tabernacle he made six boards.

28 And two boards made he in the corners of the Tabernacle for either side,

29 And they were [*c*]joined beneath, and likewise were made sure above with a ring: thus he did to both in both corners.

30 So there were eight boards, and their sixteen sockets of silver, under every board two sockets.

31 ¶ After, he made [*d*]bars of Shittim wood, five for the boards in the one side of the Tabernacle,

32 And five bars for the boards in the other side of the Tabernacle, and five bars for the boards of the Tabernacle on the side toward the West.

c Exod. 26:24
d Exod. 25:28
Exod. 30:4,5

CHAPTER 37
a Exod. 25:10
b Exod. 25:17

33 And he made the middle bar to shoot through the boards, from the one end to the other.

34 He overlaid also the boards with gold, and made their rings of gold for places for the bars, and covered the bars with gold.

35 ¶ Moreover he made a [1]veil of blue silk and purple, and of scarlet, and of fine twined linen: with Cherubims of broidered work made he it:

36 And made thereunto four pillars of Shittim, and overlaid them with gold: whose [1]hooks were *also* of gold, and he cast for them four sockets of silver.

37 And he made an [1]hanging for the Tabernacle door, of blue silk, and purple, and scarlet, and fine twined linen, *and* needle work,

38 And the five pillars of it with their hooks, and overlaid their chapiters, and their [1]fillets with gold, but their five sockets *were* of brass.

37
1 The Ark.   6 The Mercy seat.   10 The Table.   17 The Candlestick.   25 The altar of incense.

1 After this, Bezalel made the [*a*]Ark of Shittim wood, two cubits and an half long, and a cubit and an half broad, and a cubit and an half high:

2 And overlaid it with fine gold within and without, and made a [1]crown of gold to it round about,

3 And cast for it four rings of gold for the four corners of it: that is, two rings for the one side of it, and two rings for the other side thereof.

4 Also he made bars of Shittim wood, and covered them with gold,

5 And put the bars in the rings by the sides of the Ark, to bear the Ark.

6 ¶ And he made the [*b*]Mercy seat of pure gold: two cubits and an half *was* the length thereof, and one cubit and an half the breadth thereof.

7 And he made two Cherubims of gold, upon the two ends of the Mercy seat: *even* of work beaten with the hammer made he them.

8 One Cherub on the one end, and another Cherub on the other end: [1]of the Mercy seat made he the Cherubims, at the two ends thereof.

9 And the Cherubims spread out their wings on high, and covered the Mercy seat with their wings and their faces *were* one towards another: toward the Mercy seat were the faces of the Cherubims.

10 ¶ Also he made the Table of Shittim wood: two cubits *was* the length thereof and a cubit the breadth thereof, and a cubit and an half the height of it.

36:14 [1] Or, pavilion.
36:19 [1] These two were about the covering of goats' hair.
36:20 [1] And to bear up the curtains of the Tabernacle.
36:27 [1] Or, toward the Sea, which was the Sea called Mediterranean, Westward from Jerusalem.
36:35 [1] Which was between the Sanctuary and the Holiest of all.

36:36 [1] Or, heads.
36:37 [1] Which was between the court and the Sanctuary.
36:38 [1] Or, graven borders.
37:2 [1] Like battlements.
37:8 [1] Of the selfsame matter that the Mercy seat was.

11 And he overlaid it with fine gold, and made thereto a crown of gold round about.

12 Also he made thereto a border of an [1]hand breadth round about, and made upon the border a crown of gold round about.

13 And he cast for it four rings of gold, and put the rings in the four corners that *were* in the four feet thereof.

14 Against the border were the rings, as places for the bars to bear the Table.

15 And he made the bars of Shittim wood, and covered them with gold to bear the Table.

16 ‘Also he made the instruments for the Table of pure gold: dishes for it, and *incense* cups for it, and goblets for it, and coverings for it, wherewith it should be covered.

17 ¶ Likewise he made the Candlestick of pure gold: of work beaten out with the hammer made he the Candlestick: *and* his shaft, and his branch, his bowls, his knops, and his flowers were of one piece.

18 And six branches came out of the sides thereof: three branches of the Candlestick out of the one side of it, and three branches of the Candlestick out of the other side of it.

19 In one branch three bowls made like almonds, a knop and a flower: and in another branch three bowls made like almonds, a knop and a flower: *and* so throughout the six branches that proceeded out of the Candlestick.

20 And upon the Candlestick *were* four bowls after the fashion of almonds, the knops thereof and the flowers thereof.

21 That is, under every two branches a knop *made* thereof, and a knop under the second branch thereof, and a knop under the third branch thereof, according to the six branches coming out of it.

22 Their knops and their branches were of the same: it was all one [d]beaten work of pure gold.

23 And he made for it seven lamps with the snuffers, and snuffdishes thereof of pure gold.

24 Of a [1]talent of pure gold made he it with all the instruments thereof.

25 ¶ Furthermore he made the [e]perfume altar of Shittim wood: the length of it *was* a cubit, and the breadth of it a cubit (it was square) and two cubits high, *and* the horns thereof were of the same.

26 And he covered it with pure gold, both the top and the sides thereof round about, and the horns of it, and made unto it a crown of gold round about.

27 And he made two rings of gold for it, under the crown thereof in the two corners of the two sides

thereof, to put bars in for to bear it therewith.

28 Also he made the bars of Shittim wood, and overlaid them with gold.

29 And he made the holy [f]anointing oil, and the sweet pure incense after the apothecary's art.

1 Also he made the altar of the burnt offering of [a]Shittim wood: five cubits *was* the length thereof, and five cubits the breadth thereof: *it was* square and three cubits high.

2 And he made unto it horns in the four corners thereof: the horns thereof were of the same, and he overlaid it with brass.

3 Also he made all the instruments of the altar: the [1]ashpans, and the besoms and the basins, the fleshhooks, and the [b]censers: all the instruments thereof made he of brass.

4 Moreover, he made a brazen grate wrought like a net to the Altar, under the compass of it beneath in the [1]midst of it.

5 And cast four rings of brass for the four ends of the grate to put bars in.

6 And he made the bars of Shittim wood, and covered them with brass.

7 The which bars he put into the rings on the sides of the altar to bear it withal, and made it [c]hollow *within* the boards.

8 ¶ Also he made the laver of brass, and the foot of it of brass of the [1]glasses of the women that did assemble and came together at the door of the Tabernacle of the Congregation.

9 ¶ Finally, he made the court on the South side full South: the hangings of the court *were* of fine twined linen, having an hundred cubits.

10 Their pillars *were* twenty, and their brazen sockets twenty: the hooks of the pillars and their fillets *were* of silver.

11 And on the North side *the hangings were* an hundred cubits: their pillars twenty, and their sockets of brass twenty, the hooks of the pillars, and their fillets of silver.

12 On the west side also *were* hangings of fifty cubits, their ten pillars with their ten sockets: the hooks of the pillars, and their fillets of silver.

13 And toward the East side, full East *were* hangings of fifty cubits.

14 The hangings of the one side *were* fifteen cubits, their three pillars, and their three sockets:

c Exod. 25:29
d Exod. 25:31
e Exod. 30:1-4
f Exod. 30:33-39

CHAPTER 38
a Exod. 27:1
b Exod. 27:3
c Exod. 27:8

37:12 [1] Or, four fingers.
37:24 [1] Read Exod. 25:39.
38:3 [1] Or, fire pans.
38:4 [1] So that the gridiron or grate was half so high as the altar, and

stood within it.
38:8 [1] R. Kimbi saith, that the women brought their looking glasses, which were of brass or fine metal, and offered them freely unto the use of the Tabernacle: which was a bright thing and of great majesty.

15 ᵈAnd of the other side of the court gate on both sides *were* hangings of fifteen cubits, *with* their three pillars and their three sockets.

16 All the hangings of the court round about *were* of fine twined linen.

17 But the sockets of the pillars *were* of brass: the hooks of the pillars and their fillets of silver, and the covering of their chapiters of silver: and all the pillars of the court were hooped about with silver.

18 He *made* also the hanging of the gate of the court of needle work, blue silk, and purple, and scarlet, and fine twined linen even twenty cubits long, and five cubits in height and breadth, ¹like the hangings of the court.

19 And their pillars *were* four with their four sockets of brass: their hooks of silver, and the covering of the chapiters, and their fillets of silver.

20 But all the ᶜpins of the Tabernacle and of the court round about were of brass.

21 ¶ These are the parts of the Tabernacle, *I mean*, of the Tabernacle of the Testimony, which was appointed by the commandment of Moses for the office of the ¹Levites, by the hand of Ithamar son to Aaron the Priest.

22 So Bezalel the son of Uri, the son of Hur of the tribe of Judah, made all that the Lord commanded Moses.

23 And with him Aholiab son of Ahisamach of the tribe of Dan, a ¹cunning workman and an embroiderer, and a worker of needle work in blue silk, and in purple, and in scarlet, and in fine linen.

24 All the gold that was occupied in all the work wrought for the holy place (which was the gold of the offering) was nine and twenty talents and seven hundred and thirty shekels, according to the shekel of the Sanctuary.

25 But the silver of them that were numbered in the Congregation, *was* an hundred talents, and a thousand seven hundred seventy and five shekels, after the shekel of the Sanctuary.

26 A ¹portion for a man, *that is*, half a shekel after the shekel of the Sanctuary, for all them that were numbered from twenty years old and above, among six hundred thousand, and three thousand, and five hundred and fifty men.

27 Moreover there were an hundred talents of silver, to cast the sockets of the Sanctuary, and the sockets of the veil: an hundred sockets of an hundred talents, a talent for a socket.

28 But he made the hooks for the pillars of a

d Exod. 27:14
e Exod. 29:17
f Exod. 17:15

a Exod. 31:10
Exod. 35:29
b Exod. 28:9
c Exod. 28:12

thousand seven hundred and seventy and five *shekels*, and overlaid their chapiters, and made fillets about them.

29 Also the brass of the offering *was* seventy ¹talents, and two thousand, and four hundred shekels.

30 Whereof he made the sockets to the door of the Tabernacle of the Congregation, and the brazen altar, and the brazen grate which was for it, with all the instruments of the Altar.

31 And the sockets of the court round about, and the sockets for the court gate, and all the ʲpins of the Tabernacle, and all the pins of the court round about.

39

1 *The apparel of Aaron and his sons.* 32 *All that the Lord commanded was made, and finished.* 43 *Moses blesseth the people.*

1 Moreover they made ¹garments of ministration to minister in the Sanctuary of blue silk, and purple, and scarlet: they ᵃmade also the holy garments for Aaron, as the Lord had commanded Moses.

2 So he made the Ephod of gold, blue silk, and purple, and scarlet, and fine twined linen.

3 And they did beat the gold into thin plates, and cut it into wires, to work it in the blue silk and in the purple, and in the scarlet, and in the fine linen, with broidered work.

4 For the which they made shoulders to couple together: *for* it was closed by the two edges thereof.

5 And the broidered girdle of his Ephod that was upon him, was of the same stuff, and of like work: *even* of gold, of blue silk, and purple, and scarlet, and fine twined linen, as the Lord had commanded Moses.

6 ¶ And they wrought ᵇtwo Onyx stones closed in ouches of gold, and graved, as ¹signets are graven, with the names of the children of Israel.

7 And put them on the shoulders of the Ephod, *as* stones for a ᶜremembrance of the children of Israel, as the Lord had commanded Moses.

8 ¶ Also he made the breastplate of broidered work like the work of the Ephod: to *wit*, of gold, blue silk, and purple, and scarlet, and fine twined linen.

9 They made the breast plate double, and it was square an hand breadth long, and an hand breadth broad: *it was also* double.

10 And they filled it with four rows of stones. The order *was thus*, a Ruby, a Topaz, and a Carbuncle in the first row.

11 And in the second row an Emerald, a Sapphire, and a Diamond:

12 Also in the third row ¹a Turquoise, an Agate,

38:18 ¹ Hebrew, *over against.*
38:21 ¹ That the Levites might have the charge thereof, and minister in the same, as did Eleazar and Ithamar, Num. 3:4.
38:23 ¹ Or, a graver, or carpenter, Exod. 36:4.
36:26 ¹ Or, half a shekel.

38:29 ¹ Read the weight of a talent, Exod. 25:39.
39:1 ¹ As coverings for the Ark, the Candlestick, the Altars and such like.
39:6 ¹ That is, of very fine and curious workmanship.
39:12 ¹ Or, a ligure, which stone authors write that it cometh of the urine of the beast called Lynx.

and an Hematite:

13 Likewise in the fourth row a Chrysolite, an Onyx, and a Jasper: closed and set in ouches of gold.

14 So the stones *were* according to the names of the children of Israel, *even* twelve [1]after their names, graven like signets, every one after his name, according to the twelve tribes.

15 After, they made upon the breastplate chains at the ends, of wreathen work *and* pure gold.

16 They made also two bosses of gold, and two gold rings, and put the two rings in the two corners of the breastplate.

17 And they put the two wreathen chains of gold in the two rings, in the corners of the breastplate.

18 Also the two *other* ends of the two wreathen chains they fastened in the two bosses, and put them on the shoulders of the Ephod, upon the forefront of it.

19 Likewise they made two rings of gold, and put them in the two *other* corners of the breastplate upon the edge of it, which was on the inside of the Ephod.

20 They made also two *other* golden rings, and put them on the two sides of the Ephod, beneath on the foreside of it, and over against his coupling above the broidered girdle of the Ephod.

21 Then they fastened the breastplate by his rings unto the rings of the Ephod, with a lace of blue silk that it might be *fast* upon the broidered girdle of the Ephod, and that the breastplate should not be loosed from the Ephod, as the Lord had commanded Moses.

22 ¶ Moreover, he made the robe of the [1]Ephod of woven work, altogether of blue silk.

23 And [1]the hole of the robe *was* in the midst of it, as the collar of an habergeon, with an edge about the collar, that it should not rent.

24 And they made upon the skirt of the robe pomegranates, of blue silk and purple, and scarlet, and *fine linen* twined.

25 They made also [d]bells of pure gold, and put the bells between the pomegranates upon the skirts of the robe round about between the pomegranates.

26 A bell and a pomegranate, a bell and a pomegranate round about the skirts of the robe to minister in, as the Lord had commanded Moses.

27 ¶ After, they made coats of fine linen, of woven work for Aaron and for his sons.

28 And the mitre of fine linen, and goodly bonnets of fine linen, and linen [e]breeches of fine twined

[d] Exod. 28:33
[e] Exod. 28:41
[f] Exod. 28:36
[g] Exod. 27:21

linen.

29 ¶ And the girdle of fine twined linen, and of blue silk, and purple, and scarlet, *even* of needle work, as the Lord had commanded Moses.

30 ¶ Finally, they made the plate for the holy crown of fine gold, and wrote upon it a superscription *like* to the graving of a signet, [f]HOLINESS TO THE LORD.

31 And they tied unto it a lace of blue silk to fasten it on high upon the mitre, as the Lord had commanded Moses.

32 ¶ Thus was all the work of the Tabernacle, *even* of the [g]Tabernacle of the Congregation finished: and the children of Israel did according to all that the Lord had commanded Moses: so did they.

33 ¶ Afterward they brought the Tabernacle unto Moses, the Tabernacle and all his instruments, his taches, his boards, his bars, and his pillars, and his sockets,

34 And the covering of rams' skins, dyed red, and the coverings of badgers' skins, and the [1]covering veil.

35 The Ark of the testimony, and the bars thereof, and the Mercy seat.

36 The Table, with all the instruments thereof, and the showbread.

37 The pure Candlestick, the lamps thereof, *even* the Lamps [1]set in order, and all the instruments thereof, and the oil for light:

38 Also the golden Altar and the anointing oil, and the sweet incense, and the hanging of the Tabernacle door,

39 The brazen Altar with his grate of brass, his bars and all his instruments, the Laver and his foot.

40 The curtains of the court with his pillars, and his sockets, and the hanging to the court gate, *and* his cords, and his pins, and all the instruments of the service of the Tabernacle, *called* the Tabernacle of the Congregation.

41 *Finally*, the ministering garments to serve in the Sanctuary, *and* the holy garments for Aaron the Priest, and his sons' garments to minister in the Priest's office.

42 According to every point that the Lord had [1]commanded Moses, so the children of Israel made all the work.

43 And Moses beheld all the work, and behold they had done it as the Lord had commanded: so had they done: and Moses [1]blessed them.

39:14 [1] That is, every tribe had his name written on a stone.
39:22 [1] Which was next under the Ephod.
39:23 [1] Where he should put through his head.
39:34 [1] So called, because it hanged before the mercy seat and covered it from sight, Exod. 35:12.

39:37 [1] Or, which Aaron dressed and refreshed with oil every morning, Exod. 30:7.
39:42 [1] Signifying that in God's matters man may neither add, nor diminish.
39:43 [1] Praised God for the people's diligence, and prayed for them.

40

The Tabernacle with the appertinences is reared up. 34 The glory of the Lord appeareth in the cloud covering the Tabernacle.

CHAPTER 40
a Num. 7:1
b Exod. 35:12
c Num. 9:15
1 Kings 8:20

1 Then the Lord spake unto Moses, saying,

2 In the ¹*first* day of the first month in the *very first of the same* month shalt thou set up the Tabernacle, *called* the Tabernacle of the Congregation:

3 And thou shalt put therein the Ark of the Testimony, and cover the Ark with the veil.

4 Also thou shalt bring in the ¹Table, and set it in order as it doth require: thou shalt also bring in the Candlestick, and light his lamps.

5 And thou shalt set the incense Altar ¹of gold before the Ark of the Testimony; and put the ²hanging at the door of the Tabernacle.

6 Moreover, thou shalt set the burnt offering Altar before the door of the Tabernacle, *called* the Tabernacle of the Congregation.

7 And thou shalt set the Laver between the Tabernacle of the Congregation and the Altar, and put water therein.

8 Then thou shalt appoint the court round about, and hang up the hanging at the court gate.

9 After, thou shalt take the anointing oil, and anoint the Tabernacle, and all that is therein, and hallow it with all the instruments thereof, that it may be holy.

10 And thou shalt anoint the Altar of the burnt offering, and all his instruments, and shalt sanctify the Altar, that it may be an altar most holy.

11 Also thou shalt anoint the Laver, and his foot, and shalt sanctify it.

12 Then thou shalt bring Aaron and his sons unto the door of the Tabernacle of the Congregation, and wash them with water.

13 And thou shalt put upon Aaron the holy garments, and shalt anoint him, and sanctify him, that he may minister unto me in the Priest's office.

14 Thou shalt also bring his sons and clothe them with garments.

15 And shalt anoint them as thou didst anoint their father, that they may minister unto me in the Priest's office: for their anointing shall be *a sign*, that the Priesthood ¹shall be everlasting unto them throughout their generations.

16 So Moses did according to all that the Lord had commanded him; so did he.

17 ¶ *a*Thus was the Tabernacle reared up the first day of the first month in ¹the second year.

18 Then Moses reared up the Tabernacle and fastened his sockets, and set up the boards thereof, and put in the bars of it, and reared up his pillars.

19 And he spread the covering over the Tabernacle, and put the covering of that covering on high above it, as the Lord had commanded Moses.

20 ¶ And he took and put the ¹Testimony in the Ark, and put the bars in *the rings* of the Ark, and set the Mercy seat on high upon the Ark.

21 He brought also the Ark into the Tabernacle, and hanged up the *b*covering veil, and covered the Ark of the Testimony, as the Lord had commanded Moses.

22 ¶ Furthermore he put the Table in the Tabernacle of the Congregation in the North side of the Tabernacle, without the veil,

23 And set the bread in order before the Lord, as the Lord had commanded Moses.

24 ¶ Also he put the Candlestick in the Tabernacle of the Congregation, over against the Table toward the South side of the Tabernacle.

25 And he ¹lighted the lamps before the Lord, as the Lord had commanded Moses.

26 ¶ Moreover, he set the golden Altar in the Tabernacle of the Congregation before the veil,

27 And burnt sweet incense thereon, as the Lord had commanded Moses.

28 ¶ Also he hanged up the veil at the ¹door of the Tabernacle.

29 After, he set the burnt offering Altar *without* the door of the Tabernacle, *called* the Tabernacle of the Congregation, and offered the burnt offering and the sacrifice thereon, as the Lord had commanded Moses.

30 ¶ Likewise he set the Laver between the Tabernacle of the Congregation and the Altar, and poured water therein to wash with.

31 So Moses and Aaron, and his sons washed their hands and their feet thereat.

32 When they went into the Tabernacle of the Congregation, and when they approached to the Altar, they washed, as the Lord had commanded Moses.

33 Finally, he reared up the court round about the Tabernacle and the Altar, and hanged up the veil at the court gate: so Moses finished the work.

34 ¶ Then the cloud covered the Tabernacle of

40:2 ¹ After that Moses had been 40 days, and 40 nights in the mount, that is, from the beginning of August to the tenth of September, he came down, and caused this work to be done: which being finished, was set up in Abib, which month containeth half March and half April.

40:4 ¹ Read Exod. 26:35.

40:5 ¹ That is, the altar of perfume, or to burn incense on.

² This hanging or veil was between the Sanctuary and the court.

40:15 ¹ Till both the Priesthood and the ceremonies should end, which was at Christ's coming.

40:17 ¹ After they came out of Egypt, Num. 7:1.

40:20 ¹ That is, the Tables of the law, Exod. 31:18 and 34:29.

40:25 ¹ Or, set up.

40:28 ¹ Between the Sanctuary and the court.

the Congregation, and the glory of the Lord filled the Tabernacle.

35 So Moses could not enter into the Tabernacle of the Congregation, because the cloud abode thereon, and the glory of the Lord filled the Tabernacle.

36 Now when the cloud ascended up from the Tabernacle, the children of Israel went forward in all their journeys.

37 But if the cloud ascended not, then they journeyed not till the day that it ascended.

38 For [1]the cloud of the Lord was upon the Tabernacle by day, and fire was in it by night in the sight of all the house of Israel, throughout all their journeys.

40:38 [1] Thus the presence of God preserved and guided them night and day, till they came to the land promised.

THE THIRD BOOK OF MOSES,

CALLED

¹LEVITICUS

1

1 Of burnt offerings for particular persons.   3, 10, and 14 The manner to offer burnt offerings as well of bullocks, as of sheep and birds.

CHAPTER 1
a Exod. 29:10

1   Now the ¹Lord called Moses, and spake unto him out of the Tabernacle of the Congregation, saying,

2   Speak unto the children of Israel, and thou shalt say unto them, If any of you offer a sacrifice unto the Lord, ye shall offer your sacrifice of ¹cattle, *as* of beeves and of the sheep.

3   *a*If his sacrifice *be* a burnt offering of the herd, he shall offer a male without blemish, presenting him of his own voluntary will at the door of the ¹Tabernacle of the Congregation before the Lord.

4   And he shall put his hand upon the head of the burnt offering, and it shall be accepted ¹to *the Lord*, to be his atonement.

5   And ¹he shall kill the bullock before the Lord, and the Priests Aaron's sons shall offer the blood, and shall sprinkle it round about upon the ²altar, that is by the door of the Tabernacle of the Congregation.

6   Then shall he slay the burnt offering, and cut it in pieces.

7   So the sons of Aaron the Priest shall put fire upon the altar, and lay the wood in order upon the fire.

8   Then the Priests Aaron's sons shall lay the parts in order, the head and the ¹caul upon the wood that is in the fire which is upon the altar.

9   But the inwards thereof and the legs thereof he shall wash in water, and the Priest shall burn all on the altar: *for* it is a burnt offering, an oblation made by fire, for a sweet savor ¹unto the Lord.

10   ¶ And if his sacrifice for the burnt offering be of the flocks (*as* of the sheep, or of the goats) he shall offer a male without blemish.

11   ¹And he shall kill it on the North side of the altar ²before the Lord, and the Priests Aaron's sons shall sprinkle the blood thereof round about upon the altar.

12   And he shall cut it in ¹pieces, *separating* his head and his ²caul, and the Priest shall lay them in order upon the wood that *lieth* in the fire which is on the altar:

13   But he shall wash the inwards, and the legs with water, and the Priest shall offer the whole and burn it upon the altar: *for* it is a burnt offering, an oblation made by fire for a sweet savor unto the Lord.

14   ¶ And if his sacrifice *be* a burnt offering to the Lord of the fowls, then shall he offer his sacrifice of the turtledoves, or of the young pigeons.

15   And the Priest shall bring it unto the altar, and ¹wring the neck of it asunder, and burn it on the altar: and the blood thereof shall be ²shed upon the side of the altar.

16   And he shall pluck out his maw with his feathers, and cast them beside the altar on the ¹East part in the place of the ashes.

17   And he shall cleave it with his wings, *but* not divide it asunder: and the Priest shall burn it upon the altar upon the wood that is in the fire: *for* it is a burnt offering, an oblation made by fire for a sweet savor unto the Lord.

2

1 The meat offering is after three sorts of fine flour unbaked.   4 Of bread baked.

1   And when any will offer a ¹meat offering unto the Lord, his offering shall be of fine flour, and he

---

Title ¹ Because in this book is chiefly entreated of the Levites, and of things pertaining to their office.

1:1 ¹ Hereby Moses declareth that he taught nothing to the people but that which he received of God.

1:2 ¹ So they could offer of none other sort, but of those which were commanded.

1:3 ¹ Meaning, within the court of the Tabernacle.

1:4 ¹ Hebrew, *to him*.

1:5 ¹ The Priest or Levite.

  ² Of the burnt offering, Exod. 27:1.

1:8 ¹ Or, the body of the . . ., or the fat.

1:9 ¹ Or a savor of rest, which pacifieth the anger of the Lord.

1:11 ¹ Read verse 5.

  ² Before the altar of the Lord.

1:12 ¹ Hebrew, *into his pieces*.

  ² Or, fat.

1:15 ¹ The Hebrew word signifieth to pinch off with the nail.

  ² Or, strained or pressed.

1:16 ¹ On the side of the court gate in the pans which stood with ashes, Exod. 17:3.

2:1 ¹ Because the burnt offering could not be without the meat offering.

shall pour oil upon it, and put incense thereon.

2   And shall bring it unto Aaron's sons the Priests, and [1]he shall take thence his handful of the flour, and of the oil with all the incense, and the Priest shall burn it for a [2]memorial upon the altar: *for it is an offering made by fire for a sweet savor unto the Lord.*

3   But the remnant of the meat offering *shall be* Aaron's and his sons': *for it is* [1]most holy of the Lord's offerings made by fire.

4   ¶ If thou bring also a meat offering baked in the oven, *it shall be* an unleavened cake of fine flour mingled with oil, or an unleavened wafer anointed with oil.

5   ¶ But if thy [1]meat offering *be* an oblation of the frying pan, it shall be of fine flour unleavened, mingled with oil.

6   And thou shalt part it in pieces, and pour oil thereon: *for it is* a meat offering.

7   ¶ And if thy meat offering *be* an oblation *made* in the caldron, it shall be made of fine flour with oil.

8   After, thou shalt bring the meat offering (that is made of these things) unto the Lord, and shalt present it unto the Priest, and he shall bring it to the altar,

9   And the Priest shall take from the meat offering a [d]memorial of it, and shall burn it upon the altar: *for it is* an oblation [b]made by fire for a sweet savor unto the Lord.

10   But that which is left of the meat offering, *shall be* Aaron's and his sons': *for it is* most holy of the offerings of the Lord made by fire.

11   All the meat offerings which ye shall offer unto the Lord, shall be made without leaven: for ye shall neither burn leaven nor honey in any offering of the Lord made by fire.

12   ¶ *In* the oblation of the firstfruits ye shall offer [1]them unto the Lord, but they shall not be burnt [2]upon the altar for a sweet savor,

13   (All the meat offerings also shalt thou season with [c]salt, neither shalt thou suffer the salt of the [1]covenant of thy God to be lacking from thy meat offering, *but* upon all thine oblations thou shalt offer

CHAPTER 2
[a] Lev. 2:2
[b] Exod. 29:18
[c] Mark 9:49
[d] Lev. 23:14

CHAPTER 3
[a] Exod. 29:22

salt.)

14   If then thou offer a meat offering of thy firstfruits unto the Lord, thou shalt offer for thy meat offering of thy firstfruits [d]ears of corn dried by the fire, and wheat beaten out of [1]the green ears.

15   After, thou shalt put oil upon it, and lay incense thereon: *for it is* a meat offering.

16   And the Priest shall burn the memorial of it, *even* of that, that is beaten, and of the oil of it with all the incense thereof: *for it is* an offering unto the Lord made by fire.

3   *The manner of peace offerings, and beasts for the same.   17 The Israelites may not eat fat nor blood.*

1   Also if his oblation be a [1]peace offering, if he will offer of the drove (whether it be male or female) he shall offer such as is without blemish, before the Lord.

2   And shall put his hand upon the head of his offering, and kill it at the door of the Tabernacle of the Congregation: and Aaron's sons the Priests shall sprinkle the blood upon the altar round about.

3   So he shall offer [1]*part* of the peace offering, *as* a sacrifice made by fire unto the Lord, *even* the [a]fat that covereth the inwards, and all the fat that is upon the inwards.

4   He shall also take away the two kidneys, and the fat that is on them, and upon [1]the flanks, and the caul on the liver with the kidneys.

5   And Aaron's sons shall burn it on the altar, with the burnt offering, which is upon the wood, that is on the fire: *this is* a sacrifice made by fire for a sweet savor unto the Lord.

6   ¶ Also if his oblation *be* a peace offering unto the Lord out of the flock, whether it be [1]male or female, he shall offer it without blemish.

7   If he offer a Lamb for his oblation, then he shall bring it before the Lord.

8   And lay his hand upon the head of his offering, and shall kill it before the Tabernacle of the Congregation, and Aaron's sons shall sprinkle the blood thereof round about upon the altar.

9   After, of the peace offerings he shall offer [1]an offering made by fire unto the Lord: he shall take

---

2:2   [1] The Priest.
      [2] To signify that God remembereth him that offereth.
2:3   [1] Therefore none could eat of it but the Priest.
2:5   [1] Which is a gift offered to God to pacify him.
2:12 [1] That is, fruits, which were sweet as honey, ye may offer.
      [2] But reserved for the Priests.
2:13 [1] Which they were bound (as by covenant) to use all sacrifices, Num. 18:19; 2 Chron. 13:5; Ezek. 43:24, or it meaneth a sure and pure covenant.
2:14 [1] Or, full ears: for the word signifieth a fruitful field. Read 2 Chron. 26:10 in the note 2.
3:1   [1] A sacrifice of thanksgiving offered for peace and prosperity,

either generally or particularly.
3:3   [1] One part was burnt, another was to the Priests, and the third to him that offered.
3:4   [1] Or, the which kidneys are near the flank.
3:6   [1] In the peace offering it was indifferent to offer either male or female, but in the burnt offering only the male: so here can be offered no birds, but in the burnt offering they might: all there was consumed with fire, and in the peace offering put apart.
3:9   [1] The burnt offering was wholly consumed, and of the offering made by fire only the inwards, etc. were burnt: the shoulder and breast, with the two jaws and the maw were the Priest's, and the rest his that offered.

away the fat thereof, and the rump altogether, hard by the back bone, and the fat that covereth the inwards, and all the fat that is upon the inwards.

10 Also he shall take away the two kidneys, with the fat that is upon them, and upon the [b]flanks, and the caul upon the liver with the kidneys,

11 Then the Priest shall burn it upon the altar, *as* the meat of an offering made by fire unto the Lord.

12 ¶ Also if his offering *be* a goat, then shall he offer it before the Lord,

13 And shall put his hand upon the head of it, and kill it before [1]the Tabernacle of the Congregation, and the sons of Aaron shall sprinkle the blood thereof upon the altar round about.

14 Then he shall offer thereof his offering, *even* an offering made by fire unto the Lord, the fat that covereth the inwards, and all the fat that is upon the inwards.

15 Also he shall take away the two kidneys, and the fat that is upon them, and upon the flanks, and the caul upon the liver with the kidneys,

16 So the Priest shall burn them upon the altar, *as* the meat of an offering made by fire for a sweet savor: [c]all the fat *is* the Lord's.

17 *This shall be* a perpetual ordinance for your generations, throughout all your dwellings, *so that* ye shall eat neither [1]fat nor [d]blood.

4 [1] *The offering for sins done of ignorance.*   [3] *For the Priest, the Congregation, the ruler, and private man.*

1 Moreover, the Lord spake unto Moses, saying,

2 Speak unto the children of Israel, saying, If [1]any shall sin through [2]ignorance, in any of the commandments of the Lord, (which ought not to be done) but shall do *contrary* to any of them,

3 If [1]the Priest that is anointed do sin (according to the sin of the people) then shall he offer, for his sin which he hath sinned, a young bullock without blemish unto the Lord for a sin offering,

4 And he shall bring the bullock unto the door of the Tabernacle of the Congregation before the Lord, and shall put his hand upon the bullock's head, and [1]kill the bullock before the Lord.

5 And the Priest that is anointed, shall take of the bullock's blood, and bring it into the Tabernacle

of the Congregation.

6 Then the Priest shall dip his finger in the blood, and sprinkle of the blood seven times before the Lord, before the veil of the [1]Sanctuary.

7 The Priest also shall put *some* of the blood before the Lord, upon the horns of the altar of sweet incense, which is in the [1]Tabernacle of the Congregation, then shall he pour [a]all *the rest* of the blood of the bullock at the foot of the altar of burnt offering, which is at the door of the Tabernacle of the Congregation.

8 And he shall take away all the fat of the bullock for the sin offering: *to wit*, the fat that covereth the inwards, and all the fat that is about the inwards.

9 He shall take away also the two kidneys, and the fat that is upon them, and upon the flanks, and the caul upon the liver with the kidneys,

10 As it was taken away from the bullock of the peace offerings, and the Priest shall burn them upon the altar of burnt offering.

11 [b]But the skin of the bullock, and all his flesh, with his head, and his legs, and his inwards, and his dung *shall he bear out.*

12 So he shall carry the whole bullock out of the [c]host unto a clean place, where the ashes are poured, and shall burn him on the wood in the fire: where the ashes are cast out, shall he be burnt.

13 ¶ And if the [1]whole Congregation of Israel shall sin through ignorance, and the thing be [d]hid from the eyes of the multitude, and have done *against* any of the commandments of the Lord which should not be done, and have offended:

14 When the sin which they have committed shall be known, then the Congregation shall offer a young bullock for the sin, and bring him before the Tabernacle of the Congregation.

15 And the [1]Elders of the Congregation shall put their hands upon the head of the bullock before the Lord, and [2]he shall kill the bullock before the Lord.

16 Then the Priest that is anointed, shall bring of the bullock's blood into the Tabernacle of the Congregation,

17 And the Priest shall dip his finger in the blood, and sprinkle it seven times before the Lord, *even* before the veil.

18 Also he shall put *some* of the blood upon the

Marginal notes:

[b] Lev. 3:4
[c] Lev. 7:25
[d] Gen. 9:4
Lev. 17:4

CHAPTER 4
[a] Lev. 5:9
[b] Exod. 29:14
Num. 19:5
[c] Heb. 13:12
[d] Lev. 5:2-4

3:13 [1] Meaning, at the north side of the Altar, Lev. 1:1.

3:17 [1] By eating fat, was meant to be carnal, and by blood eating, was signified cruelty.

4:2 [1] Hebrew, *a soul.*

  [2] That is, of negligence or ignorance, specially in the ceremonial law: for otherwise the punishment for crime [is] appointed according to the transgression, Num. 15:22.

4:3 [1] Meaning, the high Priest.

4:4 [1] Hereby confessing that he deserved the same punishment which the beast suffered.

4:6 [1] Which was between the Holiest of all, and the Sanctuary.

4:7 [1] Which was in the court: meaning by the Tabernacle the Sanctuary: and in the end of this verse it is taken for the court.

4:13 [1] The multitude excuseth not the sin, but if all have sinned, they must all be punished.

4:15 [1] For all the people could not lay on their hands: therefore it was sufficient that the Ancients of the people did it in the name of all the Congregation.

  [2] Or, the Priest.

horns of the altar, which is before the Lord, that is in the Tabernacle of the Congregation: then shall he pour all the rest of the blood at the foot of the altar of burnt offering, which is at the door of the Tabernacle of the Congregation,

19 And he shall take all his fat from him, and ¹burn it upon the altar.

20 And the Priest shall do with his bullock, as he did with the bullock for his sin: so shall he do with this: so the Priest shall make an atonement for them, and it shall be forgiven them.

21 For he shall carry the bullock without the host, and burn him as he burned the first bullock: for it is an offering for the sin of the Congregation.

22 ¶ When a ruler shall sin, and do through ignorance against any of the commandments of the Lord his God, which should not be done, and shall offend,

23 If one show unto him his sin, which he hath committed, then shall he bring for his offering an ¹he goat without blemish,

24 And shall lay his hand upon the head of the he goat, and kill it in ¹the place where he should kill the burnt offering before the Lord: for it is a sin offering.

25 Then the Priest shall take of the blood of the sin offering with his finger, and put it upon the horns of the burnt offering altar, and shall pour the rest of his blood at the foot of the burnt offering altar,

26 And shall burn all his fat upon the altar, as the fat of the peace offering: so the Priest shall make ¹an atonement for him, concerning his sin, and it shall be forgiven him.

27 ¶ Likewise if any of the ¹people of the land shall sin through ignorance in doing against any of the commandments of the Lord, which should not be done, and shall offend,

28 If one show him his sin which he hath committed, then he shall bring for his offering, ¹a she goat without blemish for his sin which he hath committed.

29 ¹And he shall lay his hand upon the head of the sin offering, and slay the sin offering in the place of burnt offering.

30 Then the Priest shall take of the blood thereof with his finger, and put it upon the horns of the

Exod. 29:18

burnt offering altar, and pour all the rest of the blood thereof at the foot of the altar,

31 And shall take away all his fat, as the fat of the peace offerings is taken away, and the Priest shall burn it upon the altar for a ᶜsweet savor unto the Lord, and the Priest shall make an atonement for him, and it shall be forgiven him.

32 And if he bring a lamb for his sin offering, he shall bring a female without blemish.

33 And shall lay his ¹hand upon the head of the sin offering, and he shall slay it for a sin offering in the place where he should kill the burnt offering.

34 Then the Priest shall take of the blood of the sin offering with his finger, and put it upon the horns of the burnt offering altar, and shall pour all the rest of the blood thereof at the foot of the altar.

35 And he shall take away all the fat thereof, as the fat of the lamb of the peace offerings is taken away: then the Priest shall burn it upon the altar ¹with the oblations of the Lord made by fire, and the Priest shall make an atonement for him concerning his sin that he hath committed, and it shall be forgiven him.

5 1 Of him that testifieth the truth.   4 Of him that voweth rashly.   15 Of him that by ignorance withdraweth anything dedicated to the Lord.

1 Also if ¹any have sinned, that is, ²if he have heard the voice of an oath, and he can be a witness, whether he hath seen or ³known of it, if he do not utter it, he shall bear his iniquity:

2 Either if one touch any unclean thing, whether it be a carrion of an unclean beast, or a carrion of unclean cattle, or a carrion of unclean creeping things, and is not ware of it, yet he is unclean, and hath offended:

3 Either if he touch any uncleanness of man (whatsoever uncleanness it be, that he is defiled with) and is not ware of it, and after cometh to the knowledge of it, he hath sinned:

4 Either if any ¹swear and pronounce with his lips to do evil, or to do good (whatsoever it be that a man shall pronounce with an oath) and it be hid from him, and after knoweth that he hath offended in one of these points,

5 When he hath sinned in any of these ¹things,

4:19 ¹ Or, make a perfume with it.
4:23 ¹ Or, the male goat of the fold.
4:24 ¹ That is, the Priest shall kill it; for it was not lawful for any out of that office to kill the beast.
4:26 ¹ Wherein he represented Jesus Christ.
4:27 ¹ Or, private person.
4:28 ¹ Or, the female of the goats.
4:29 ¹ Read verse 24.
4:33 ¹ Meaning, that the punishment of his sin should be laid upon that beast, or, that he had received all things of God, and offered this

willingly.
4:35 ¹ Or, besides the burnt offerings, which were daily offered to the Lord.
5:1 ¹ Hebrew, a soul.
   ² Or, if the judge hath taken an oath of any other.
   ³ Whereby it is commanded to bear witness to the truth, and disclose the iniquity of the ungodly.
5:4 ¹ Or, vow rashly without just examination of the circumstances, and not knowing what shall be the issue of the same.
5:5 ¹ Which have been mentioned before in this Chapter.

then he shall confess that he hath sinned therein.

6 Therefore shall he bring his trespass offering unto the Lord for his sin which he hath committed, *even* a female from the flock, *be it* a lamb or a she goat for a sin offering, and the Priest shall make an atonement for him concerning his sin.

7 But ¹if he be not able to bring a sheep, he shall bring for his trespass which he hath committed, two turtledoves, or two young pigeons unto the Lord, one for a sin offering, and the other for a burnt offering.

8 So he shall bring them unto the Priest, who shall offer the sin offering first, and *a*wring the neck of it asunder, but not pluck it clean off.

9 After he shall sprinkle of the blood of the sin offering upon the side of the altar, and the rest of the blood shall be ¹shed at the foot of the altar: *for* it is a sin offering.

10 Also he shall offer the second for a burnt offering ¹as the manner is: so shall the Priest ²make an atonement for him (for his sin which he hath committed) and it shall be forgiven him.

11 ¶ But if he *b*be not able to bring two turtledoves, or two young pigeons, then he that hath sinned, shall bring for his offering the tenth part of an ¹Ephah of fine flour for a sin offering, he shall put none ²oil thereto, neither put any incense thereon: for it is a sin offering.

12 Then shall he bring it to the Priest, and the Priest shall take his handful of it for the *c*remembrance thereof, and burn it upon the altar *d*with the offerings of the Lord made by fire: *for* it is a sin offering.

13 So the Priest shall make an atonement for him, as touching his sin, that he hath committed in one of these *points*, and it shall be forgiven him: and *the remnant* shall be the Priest's, as the meat offering.

14 ¶ And the Lord spake unto Moses, saying,

15 If any person transgress and sin through ignorance ¹by *taking away* things consecrated unto the Lord, he shall then bring for his trespass offering unto the Lord a ram without blemish out of the flock, *worth* two shekels of silver ²by thy estimation after the shekel of the Sanctuary, for a trespass offering.

16 So he shall restore that wherein he hath offended, *in taking away* of the holy thing, and shall put the fifth part more thereto, and give it unto the Priest: so the Priest shall make an atonement for him

CHAPTER 5
a Lev. 1:16
b Lev. 5:7
c Lev. 2:2
d Lev. 4:35
e Lev. 4:2
f Exod. 30:13

CHAPTER 6
a Num. 5:6
b Num. 5:7
c Lev. 5:15

with the ram of the trespass offering, and it shall be forgiven him.

17 ¶ Also if any sin and *e*do *against* any of the Commandments of the Lord, which ought not to be done, and know not, and ¹sin and bear his iniquity,

18 Then shall he bring a ram without blemish out of the flock, in thy estimation *worth* *f*two shekels for a trespass offering unto the Priest: and the Priest shall make an atonement for him concerning his ¹ignorance wherein he erred, and was not ware: so it shall be forgiven him.

19 This is the trespass offering for the trespass committed against the Lord.

6 *6 The offering for sins which are done willingly.   9 The law of the burnt offerings.   13 The fire must abide evermore upon the altar.   14 The law of the meat offering.   20 The offerings of Aaron, and his sons.*

1 And the Lord spake unto Moses, saying,

2 If any sin and commit a trespass against the Lord, and deny unto his neighbor that which was taken him to keep, or that which was put to him¹of trust, or doth by ²robbery, or by violence oppress his neighbor,

3 Or hath found that which was lost, and denieth it, and sweareth falsely, *a*for any of *these* things that a man doeth, wherein he ¹sinneth:

4 When, I say, he thus sinneth and trespasseth, he shall then restore the robbery that he robbed, or the thing taken by violence which he took by force, or the thing which was delivered him to keep, or the lost thing which he found,

5 Or for whatsoever he hath sworn falsely, he shall both restore it in the whole *b*sum, and shall add the fifth part more thereto, *and* give it unto him to whom it pertaineth, the same day that he offereth for his trespass.

6 Also he shall bring for his trespass unto the Lord, a ram without blemish out of the *c*flock in thy estimation *worth two shekels* for a trespass offering unto the Priest.

7 And the Priest shall make an atonement for him before the Lord, and it shall be forgiven him, whatsoever thing he hath done, and trespassed therein.

8 ¶ Then the Lord spake unto Moses, saying,

9 Command Aaron and his sons, saying, This

5:7 ¹ Hebrew, *if his hand cannot touch*, meaning for his poverty.
5:9 ¹ Or, poured.
5:10 ¹ Or, according to the Law.
  ² Or, declare him to be purged of that sin.
5:11 ¹ Which was about a pottle.
  ² As in the meat offering, Lev. 2:1.
5:15 ¹ As touching the firstfruits or tithes, due to the Priests and Levites.

² By the estimation of the Priest, Lev. 27:12.
5:17 ¹ That is, afterward remembereth that he hath sinned when his conscience doth accuse him.
5:18 ¹ Else if his sin against God come of malice, he must die, Num. 15:30.
6:2 ¹ To bestow, and occupy for the use of him that gave it.
  ² By any guile, or unlawful means.
6:3 ¹ Wherein he cannot but sin: or, wherein a man accustometh to sin by perjury or such like thing.

is the [1]law of the burnt offering, (it is the burnt offering because it burneth upon the altar all the night unto the morning, and the fire burneth on the altar).

10 And the Priest shall put on his linen garment, and shall put on his linen breeches upon [1]his flesh, and take away the ashes when the fire hath consumed the burnt offering upon the altar, and he shall put them beside the [2]altar.

11 After, he shall put off his garments, and put on other raiment, and carry the ashes forth without the host unto a clean place.

12 But the fire upon the altar shall burn thereon *and* never be put out: wherefore the Priest shall burn wood on it every morning, and lay the burnt offering in order upon it, and he shall burn thereon the fat of the peace offerings.

13 The fire shall ever burn upon the altar, *and* never go out.

14 ¶ [d]Also this is the law of the meat offering, which Aaron's sons shall offer in the presence of the Lord, before the altar.

15 He shall even take thence his handful of fine flour of the meat offering and of the oil, and all the incense which *is* upon the meat offering, and shall burn it upon the altar for a sweet savor, *as* a [c]memorial therefore unto the Lord:

16 But the rest thereof shall Aaron and his sons eat: it shall be eaten without leaven in the holy place: in the court of the Tabernacle of the Congregation they shall eat it.

17 It shall not be [1]baked with leaven: I have given it for their portion of mine offering made by fire: *for* it is as the sin offering, and as the trespass offering.

18 All the males among the children of Aaron shall eat of it: It *shall be* a statute forever in your generations concerning the offerings of the Lord made by fire: [f]whatsoever toucheth them shall be holy:

19 ¶ Again the Lord spake unto Moses, saying,

20 This is the offering of Aaron and his sons, which they shall offer unto the Lord in the day when he is anointed: the tenth part of an [g]Ephah of fine flour, for a meat offering [1]perpetual: half of it in the morning, and half thereof at night.

21 In the frying pan it shall be made with oil: thou shalt bring it fried, *and* shalt offer the [1]baken

[d] Lev. 2:1
Num. 15:4
[e] Lev. 2:9
[f] Exod. 29:37
[g] Exod. 29:37
[h] Lev. 4:5
Heb. 13:11

pieces of the meat offering for a sweet savor unto the Lord.

22 And the Priest that is [1]anointed in his stead, among his sons shall offer it: *It is* the Lord's ordinance forever, it shall be burnt altogether.

23 For every meat offering of the Priest shall be *burnt* altogether, it shall not be eaten.

24 ¶ Furthermore, the Lord spake unto Moses, saying,

25 Speak unto Aaron, and unto his sons, and say, This is the Law of the sin offering, In the place where the burnt offering is killed, shall the sin offering be killed before the Lord, *for* it is most holy.

26 The Priest that offereth this sin offering, shall eat it: in the holy place shall it be eaten, in the court of the Tabernacle of the Congregation.

27 Whatsoever shall touch the flesh thereof shall be holy: and when there droppeth of the blood thereof upon a [1]garment, thou shalt wash that whereon it droppeth in the holy place.

28 Also the earthen pot that it is sodden in, shall be broken, but if it be sodden in a brazen pot, it shall both be scoured and washed with [1]water.

29 All the males among the Priests shall eat thereof, *for* it is most holy.

30 [h]But no sin offering, whose blood is brought into the Tabernacle of the Congregation, to make reconciliation in the holy place, shall be eaten, *but* shall be burnt with [1]fire.

7 1 *The law of the trespass offering.*   11 *Also of the peace offering.*   23 *The fat and the blood may not be eaten.*

1 Likewise this is the law of the [1]trespass offering, it is most holy.

2 In the place [1]where they kill the burnt offering, shall they kill the trespass offering, and the blood thereof shall he sprinkle round about upon the altar.

3 All the fat thereof also shall [1]he offer, the rump, and the fat that covered the inwards.

4 After, he shall take away the two kidneys, with the fat that is on them and upon the flanks, and the caul on the liver with the kidneys.

5 Then the Priest shall burn them upon the altar, for an offering made by fire unto the Lord: this is a trespass offering.

6 All the males among the Priests shall eat thereof, it shall be eaten in the holy place *for* it is most holy.

6:9 [1] That is, the ceremonies which ought to be observed therein.
6:10 [1] Upon his secret parts, Exod. 28:43.
         [2] In the ash pans appointed for that use.
6:17 [1] Or, kneaded with leaven and after baked.
6:20 [1] So oft as the high Priest shall be elected and anointed.
6:21 [1] Or, fried.
6:22 [1] His son that shall succeed him.

6:27 [1] Meaning, the garment of the Priest.
6:28 [1] Which was in the laver, Exod. 30:18.
6:30 [1] Out of the camp, Lev. 4:12.
7:1 [1] Which is for the smaller sins, and such as are committed by ignorance.
7:2 [1] At the court gate.
7:3 [1] The high Priest.

7 As the sin offering *is*, so *is* the trespass offering, one ¹law serveth for both: ²that wherewith the Priest shall make atonement, shall be his.

8 Also the Priest that offereth any man's burnt offering, shall have the skin of the burnt offering which he hath offered.

9 And all the meat offering that is baked in the oven, and that is dressed in the pan, and in the frying pan, shall be the Priest's that offereth it.

10 And every meat offering mingled with oil, and that is ¹dry, shall pertain unto all the sons of Aaron, to all alike.

11 Furthermore, this is the law of the peace offerings, which he shall offer unto the Lord.

12 If he offer it to ¹give thanks, then he shall offer for his thanks offering, unleavened cakes mingled with oil, and unleavened wafers anointed with oil, and fine flour fried *with* the cakes mingled with oil.

13 He shall offer *also* his offering with cakes of leavened bread, for his peace offerings, to give thanks.

14 And of all the sacrifice he shall offer one *cake* for an heave offering unto the Lord, *and* it shall be the Priest's that sprinkled the blood of the peace offerings.

15 Also the flesh of the peace offerings, for thanksgiving, shall be eaten the same day that it is offered: he shall leave nothing thereof until the morning.

16 But if the sacrifice of his offering *be* a ¹vow, or a free offering, it shall be eaten the same day that he offereth his sacrifice: and so in the morning the residue thereof shall be eaten.

17 But as much of the offered flesh as remaineth unto the third day, shall be burnt with fire.

18 For if any of the flesh of his peace offerings be eaten in the third day, he shall not be accepted that offereth it, neither shall it be reckoned unto him, *but* shall be an abomination: therefore the person that eateth of it shall ¹bear his iniquity.

19 The flesh also that toucheth any unclean ¹thing, shall not be eaten, *but* burnt with fire: but ²of this flesh all that be clean shall eat thereof.

20 But if any eat of the flesh of the peace offerings that pertaineth to the Lord, having his ᵃuncleanness upon him, even the same person shall be cut off from his people.

21 Moreover, when any toucheth any unclean thing, as the uncleanness of man, or of an unclean beast, or of any filthy abomination, and eat of the flesh of the peace offerings, which pertaineth unto the Lord, even that person shall be cut off from his people.

CHAPTER 7
ᵃ Lev. 15:3
ᵇ Lev. 3:17
ᶜ Gen. 9:4
Lev. 17:14
ᵈ Exod. 29:24

22 ¶ Again the Lord spake unto Moses, saying,

23 Speak unto the children of Israel, and say, ᵇYe shall eat no fat of beeves, nor of sheep, nor of goats.

24 Yet the fat of the dead beast, and the fat of that, which is torn *with beasts*, shall be occupied to any use, but ye shall not eat of it.

25 For whosoever eateth the fat of the beast, of the which ye shall offer an offering made by fire to the Lord, even the person that eateth, shall be cut off from his people.

26 Neither ᶜshall ye eat any blood, either of fowl, or of beast in all your dwellings.

27 Every person that eateth any blood, even the same person shall be cut off from his people.

28 ¶ And the Lord talked with Moses, saying,

29 Speak unto the children of Israel, and say, He that offereth his peace offerings unto the Lord, shall bring his gift unto the Lord of his peace offerings.

30 His ¹hands shall bring the offerings of the Lord made by fire: *even* the fat with the breast shall he bring, that the breast may be ᵈshaken to and fro before the Lord.

31 Then the Priest shall burn the fat upon the Altar, and the breast shall be Aaron's and his sons'.

32 And the right shoulder shall ye give unto the Priest for an heave offering, of your peace offerings.

33 The same that offereth the blood of the peace offerings, and the fat among the sons of Aaron, shall have the right shoulder for his part.

34 For the breast shaken to and fro, and the shoulder lifted up, have I taken of the children of Israel, *even* of their peace offerings, and have given them unto Aaron the Priest and unto his sons by a statute forever from among the children of Israel.

35 ¶ This is the ¹anointing of Aaron, and the anointing of his sons, concerning the offerings of the Lord made by fire, in the day when he presented them to serve in the Priest's office unto the Lord.

36 The which *portions* the Lord commanded to give them in the day that he anointed them from among the children of Israel, by a statute forever in their generations.

37 This is *also* the law of the burnt offering, of the meat offering, and of the sin offering, and of the trespass offering, and of the ¹consecrations, and of

---

7:7 ¹ The same ceremonies, notwithstanding that this word trespass signifieth less than sin.
² Meaning, the rest which is left and not burnt.
7:10 ¹ Because it had no oil nor liquor.
7:12 ¹ Peace offerings contain a confession and thanksgiving for a benefit received, and also a vow, and free offering to receive a benefit.
7:16 ¹ If he makes a vow to offer: for else the flesh of the peace offerings must be eaten the same day.

7:18 ¹ The sin wherefore he offered shall remain.
7:19 ¹ After it be sacrificed.
² Of the peace offering that is clean.
7:30 ¹ And should not send it by another.
7:35 ¹ That is, his privilege, reward and portion.
7:37 ¹ Which sacrifice was offered when the Priests were consecrated, Exod. 29:22.

the peace offerings,

38 Which the Lord commanded Moses in the mount Sinai, when he commanded the children of Israel to offer their gifts unto the Lord in the wilderness of Sinai.

8
12 The anointing of Aaron, and his sons, with the sacrifice concerning the same.

1 Afterward the Lord spake unto Moses, saying,

2 *a*Take Aaron and his sons with him, and the garments, and the *b*anointing oil, and a bullock for the sin offering, and two rams, and a basket of unleavened bread,

3 And assemble all the company at the door of the Tabernacle of the Congregation.

4 So Moses did as the Lord had commanded him, and the company was assembled at the door of the Tabernacle of the Congregation.

5 Then Moses said unto the company, *c*This is the thing which the Lord hath commanded to do.

6 And Moses brought Aaron and his sons, and washed them with water,

7 And put upon him the coat, and girded him with a girdle, and clothed him with the robe, and put the Ephod on him, which he girded with the broidered girdle of the Ephod, and bound it unto him therewith.

8 And he put the breastplate thereon, and put in the breastplate *d*the Urim and the Thummim.

9 Also he put the miter upon his head, and put upon the miter on the forefront the golden plate, *and* the [1]holy crown, as the Lord hath commanded Moses.

10 (Now Moses had taken the anointing oil, and anointed the [1]Tabernacle, and all that was therein, and sanctified them,

11 And sprinkled thereof upon the altar seven times, and anointed the altar and all his instruments, and the laver, and his foot, to sanctify them.)

12 *e*And he poured of the anointing oil upon Aaron's head, and anointed him to sanctify him.

13 After, Moses brought Aaron's sons, and put coats upon them, and girded them with girdles, and put bonnets upon their heads, as the Lord had commanded Moses.

14 *f*Then he brought the bullock for the sin offering, and Aaron and his sons put their hands upon the head of the bullock for the sin offering.

15 And Moses slew him, and took the blood, which he put upon the horn of the [1]Altar round about with

CHAPTER 8
a Exod. 28:1,4
b Exod. 30:24
c Exod. 29:30
d Exod. 28:30
e Ps. 33:2
f Exod. 29:1
    Lev. 9:2
g Exod. 29:31
h Exod. 29:24
i Exod. 29:26

his finger, and purified the altar, and poured *the rest* of the blood at the foot of the altar: so he sanctified [2]it, to make reconciliation upon it.

16 Then he took all the fat that was upon the inwards, and the caul of the liver, and the two kidneys with their fat, which Moses burned upon the altar.

17 But the bullock and his [1]hide, and his flesh, and his dung, he burnt with fire without the host as the Lord had commanded Moses.

18 ¶ Also he brought the ram for the burnt offering, and Aaron and his sons put their hands upon the head of the ram.

19 So Moses killed it, and sprinkled the blood upon the altar round about,

20 And Moses cut the ram in pieces, and burnt the head with the pieces, and the fat,

21 And washed the inwards and the legs in water: so Moses burnt the ram every whit upon the Altar: *for* it was a burnt offering for a sweet savor, which was made by fire unto the Lord, as the Lord had commanded Moses.

22 ¶ *g*After, he brought the other ram, the ram of consecrations, and Aaron and his sons laid their hands upon the head of the ram,

23 Which Moses [1]slew, and took of the blood of it, and put it upon the lap of Aaron's right ear, and upon the thumb of his right hand, and upon the great toe of his right foot.

24 Then Moses brought Aaron's sons, and put of the blood on the lap of their right ears, and upon the thumbs of their right hands, and upon the great toes of their right feet, and Moses sprinkled *the rest* of the blood upon the Altar round about.

25 And he took the fat and the rump, and all the fat that was upon the inwards, and the caul of the liver, and the two kidneys with their fat, and the right shoulder.

26 Also he took of the basket of the unleavened cake, and a cake of oiled bread, and one wafer, and put them on the fat, and upon the right shoulder.

27 So he put *h*all in Aaron's hands, and in his sons' hands, and shook it to and fro before the Lord.

28 After, Moses took them out of their hands, and burnt them upon the altar for a burnt offering: *for* these were consecrations for a sweet savor, which were made by fire unto the Lord.

29 Likewise Moses took the breast of the ram of consecrations, and shook it to and fro before the Lord: *for* it was Moses' [1]portion as the Lord had commanded Moses.

8:9 [1] So called, because this superscription, Holiness to the Lord, was graven in it.
8:10 [1] That is, the Holiest of all, the Sanctuary and the court.
8:15 [1] Of the burnt offering.
       [2] To offer for the sins of the people.

8:17 [1] In other burnt offerings, which are not of consecration, or offering for himself, the Priest hath the skin, Lev. 7:8.
8:23 [1] Moses did this because that the Priests were not yet established in their office.

30 Also Moses took of the anointing oil, and of the blood which was upon the Altar, and sprinkled it upon Aaron, upon his garments, and upon his sons, and on his sons' garments with him: so he sanctified Aaron, his garments, and his sons, and his sons' garments with him.

31 ¶ Afterward Moses said unto Aaron and his sons, Seethe the flesh at the door of the [1]Tabernacle of the Congregation, and there [j]eat it with the bread that is in the basket of consecrations, as I commanded, saying, Aaron and his sons shall eat it.

32 But that which remaineth of the flesh and of the bread, shall ye burn with fire.

33 And ye shall not depart from the door of the Tabernacle of the Congregation seven days, until the days of your consecrations be at an end: [k]for seven days, *said the Lord*, shall he [1]consecrate you,

34 As [1]he hath done this day: *so* the Lord hath commanded to do, to make an atonement for you.

35 Therefore shall ye abide at the door of the Tabernacle of the Congregation, day and night, seven days, and shall keep the watch of the Lord, that ye die not: for so I am commanded.

36 So Aaron and his sons did all things which the Lord had commanded by the[1]hand of Moses.

9 8 *The first offerings of Aaron.*   12 *Aaron blesseth the people.*   23 *The glory of the Lord is showed.*   24 *The fire cometh from the Lord.*

1 And in the [1]eighth day Moses called Aaron and his sons, and the Elders of Israel:

2 [a]Then he said unto Aaron, Take thee a young calf for a [1]sin offering, and a ram for a burnt offering, *both* without blemish, and bring *them* before the Lord.

3 And unto the children of Israel thou shalt speak, saying, Take ye an he goat for a sin offering, and a calf, and a lamb, both of a year old, without blemish for a burnt offering:

4 Also a bullock, and a ram for peace offerings, to offer before the Lord, and a meat offering mingled with oil: for today the Lord will appear unto you.

5 ¶ Then they brought that which Moses commanded before the Tabernacle of the Congregation, and all the assembly drew near, and stood before the [1]Lord.

6 (For Moses had said, This is the thing, which

the Lord commanded that ye should do, and the glory of the Lord shall appear unto you.)

7 Then Moses said unto Aaron, Draw near to the Altar, and offer thy sin offering, and thy burnt offering, and make an atonement for [1]thee and for the people: offer also the offering of the people, and make an atonement for them, as the Lord hath commanded.

8 ¶ Aaron therefore went unto the altar, and killed the calf of the sin offering, which was for himself.

9 And the sons of Aaron brought the blood unto him, and he dipped his finger in the blood, and put it upon the horns of the Altar, and poured *the rest* of the blood at the foot of the Altar.

10 But the fat and the kidneys, and the caul of the liver of the sin offering, he [1]burnt unto the Altar, as the Lord had commanded Moses.

11 The flesh also and the hide he burnt with fire without the host.

12 After, he slew the burnt offering, and Aaron's sons brought unto him the blood, which he sprinkled round about the Altar.

13 Also they brought the burnt offering unto him with the pieces thereof, and the head, and he burnt *them* upon the Altar.

14 Likewise he did wash the inwards and the legs, and [1]burnt *them* upon the burnt offering on the Altar.

15 ¶ Then he offered the people's offering and took a goat, which was the sin offering for the people, and slew it: and offered it for sin, as the first:

16 So he offered the burnt offering, and prepared it, according to the manner.

17 He presented also the meat offering, and filled his hand thereof, and [b]beside the burnt sacrifice of the morning he burnt *this* upon the altar.

18 He slew also the bullock, and the ram for peace offerings, that was for the people, and Aaron's sons brought unto him the blood, which he sprinkled upon the Altar round about.

19 With the fat of the bullock, and of the ram, the rump, and that which covereth the inwards, and the kidneys, and the caul of the liver.

20 So they laid the fat upon the breasts, and he burnt the fat upon the Altar.

21 But the [1]breasts and the right shoulder Aaron shook to and fro before the Lord, as the Lord had

Marginal notes (center column):
[j] Exod. 29:32 / Lev. 24:9
[k] Exod. 29:35

CHAPTER 9
[a] Exod. 29:1
[b] Exod. 29:38

8:31 [1] At the door of the court.
8:33 [1] Hebrew, *fill your hands.*
8:34 [1] Or, as I have done.
8:36 [1] By commission given to Moses.
9:1 [1] After their consecration: for the seven days before, the Priests were consecrated.
9:2 [1] Aaron entereth into the possession of the Priesthood: and offereth the four principal sacrifices, the burnt offering, the sin offer-

ing, the peace offerings, and the meat offering.
9:5 [1] Before the Altar where his glory appeared.
9:7 [1] Read for the understanding of this peace, Heb. 4:5 and 7:27.
9:10 [1] That is, he laid them in order, and so they were burnt when the Lord sent down fire.
9:14 [1] All this must be understood of the preparation of the sacrifices which were burnt after, verse 24.
9:21 [1] Of the bullock and the ram.

commanded Moses.

22 So Aaron lift up his hand toward the people, and blessed them, and [1]came down from offering of the sin offering, and the burnt offering, and the peace offerings.

23 After, Moses and Aaron went into the Tabernacle of the Congregation, and came out, and [1]blessed the people, and the glory of the Lord appeared to all the people.

24 [c]And there came a fire out from the Lord, and consumed upon the Altar the burnt offering and the fat: which when all the people saw, they [1]gave thanks, and fell on their faces.

10

2 Nadab and Abihu are burnt.   6 Israel mourneth for them.   9 The Priests are forbidden wine.

1 But [a]Nadab and Abihu, the sons of Aaron, took either of them his censor, and put fire therein, and put incense thereupon, and offered [1]strange fire before the Lord, which he had not commanded them.

2 Therefore a fire went out from the Lord, and devoured them: so they died before the Lord.

3 Then Moses said unto Aaron, This is it that the Lord spake, saying, I will be [1]sanctified in them that come near me, and before all the people I will be glorified: but Aaron held his peace.

4 And Moses called Mishael and Elzaphan the sons of Uzziel, the uncle of Aaron, and said unto them, Come near, carry your [1]brethren from before the Sanctuary out of the host.

5 Then they went, and carried them in their coats out of the host, as Moses had commanded.

6 After, Moses said unto Aaron and unto Eleazar, and Ithamar his sons, [1]Uncover not your heads, neither rent your clothes, lest ye die, and lest wrath come upon all the people: but let your brethren, all the house of Israel bewail the burning which the Lord hath [2]kindled.

7 And go not ye out from the door of the Tabernacle of the Congregation lest ye die: for the anointing oil of the Lord *is* upon you: and they did according to Moses' commandment.

Marginal references

[c] Gen. 4:4
1 Kings 18:38
2 Chron. 7:1

CHAPTER 10
[a] Num. 3:4
Num. 26:61
1 Chron. 24:2
[b] Exod. 29:24
[c] Lev. 6:26

8 ¶ And the Lord spake unto Aaron, saying,

9 Thou shalt not drink wine nor [1]strong drink, thou, nor thy sons with thee, when ye come into the Tabernacle of the Congregation, lest ye die: *this is* an ordinance forever throughout your generations,

10 That ye may put difference between the holy and the unholy, and between the clean and the unclean,

11 And that ye may teach the children of Israel all the statutes which the Lord hath commanded them by the [1]hand of Moses.

12 ¶ Then Moses said unto Aaron and unto Eleazar and to Ithamar his sons that were left, Take the meat offering that remaineth of the offerings of the Lord made by fire, and eat it without leaven beside the altar: for it is most holy:

13 And ye shall eat it in the holy place, because it is thy duty and thy son's duty of the offerings of the Lord made by fire: for so I am commanded.

14 Also the [b]shaken breast and the [heave] shoulder shall ye eat in a [1]clean place: thou, and thy sons, and thy [2]daughters with thee: for they are given as thy [3]duty and thy son's duty, of the peace offerings of the children of Israel.

15 The heave shoulder, and the shaken breast shall they bring with the offerings made by fire of the fat, to shake *it* to and fro before the Lord, and it shall be thine and thy sons with thee by a law forever, as the Lord hath commanded.

16 ¶ And Moses sought the goat that was offered for sin, and lo, it was burnt: therefore he was angry with Eleazar and Ithamar the sons of Aaron, which were [1]left *alive*, saying,

17 Wherefore have ye not eaten the sin offering in the holy place, seeing it is most Holy? and *God* hath given it you, to bear the iniquity of the Congregation, to make an atonement for them before the Lord.

18 Behold, the blood of it was not brought within the holy place: ye should have eaten *it* in the holy place, [c]as I commanded.

19 And Aaron said unto Moses, Behold, this day [1]have they offered their sin offering, and their burnt offering before the Lord, and such things *as*

9:22 [1] Because the altar was near the Sanctuary, which was the upper end, therefore he is said to come down.

9:23 [1] Or prayed for the people.

9:24 [1] Or, gave a shout for joy.

10:1 [1] Not taken of the altar, which was sent from heaven, and endured till the captivity of Babylon.

10:3 [1] I will punish them that serve me otherwise than I have commanded, not sparing the chief, that the people may fear and praise my judgments.

10:4 [1] Or, cousins.

10:6 [1] As though ye lamented for them, preferring your carnal affection to God's just judgment, Lev. 19:18; Deut. 14:1.

[2] In destroying Nadab and Abihu the chief, and menacing the rest, except they repent.

10:9 [1] Or, drink that maketh drunk.

10:11 [1] Or, commission.

10:14 [1] Or, where is no uncleanness.

[2] For the breast and shoulders of the peace offerings might be brought to their families, so that their daughters might eat of them, as also of the offerings of firstfruits, the firstborn, and the Easter lamb, Read Lev. 22:12,13.

[3] Or, right or portion.

10:16 [1] And not consumed as Nadab and Abihu.

10:19 [1] That is, Nadab and Abihu.

thou knowest are come unto me: If I had eaten the sin offering today, should it have been accepted in the sight of the Lord?

20　So when Moses heard *it*, he was ¹content.

11
1 *Of beasts, fishes and birds, which be clean, and which be unclean.*

1　After, the Lord spake to Moses and to Aaron, saying unto them,

2　Speak unto the children of Israel, and say, ᵃThese are the beasts which ye ¹shall eat, among all the beasts that are on the earth.

3　Whatsoever parteth the ¹hoof, and is cloven footed, and cheweth the cud, among the beasts, that shall ye eat:

4　But of them that chew the cud, or divide the hoof only, of them ye shall not eat: as the camel, because he cheweth the cud, and divideth not the hoof, he shall be unclean unto you.

5　Likewise the coney, because he cheweth the cud, and divideth not the hoof, he shall be unclean to you.

6　Also the hare, because he cheweth the cud, and divideth not the hoof, he shall be unclean to you.

7　And the swine, because he parteth the hoof, and is cloven footed, but cheweth not the cud, he shall be unclean to you.

8　Of their ¹flesh shall ye not eat, and their carcass shall ye not touch: *for* they shall be unclean to you.

9　¶ These shall ye eat, of all that are in the waters: whatsoever hath fins and scales in the waters, in the seas, or in the rivers, them shall ye eat.

10　But all that have not fins nor scales in the seas, or in the rivers, of all that ¹moveth in the waters, and of all ²living things that are in the waters, they shall be an abomination unto you.

11　They, I say, shall be an abomination to you: ye shall not eat of their flesh, but shall abhor their carcass.

12　Whatsoever hath not fins nor scales in the waters, that shall be abomination unto you.

13　¶ These shall ye have also in abomination among the fowls, they shall not be eaten, *for* they are an abomination, the eagle, and the ¹goshawk,

CHAPTER 11
ᵃ Gen. 7:2
Deut. 14:1
Acts 10:14

and the osprey:

14　Also the vulture, and the kite after his kind,

15　Also the ravens after their kind:

16　The ostrich also, and the night-crow, and the ¹seamew, and the hawk after his kind.

17　The little owl also, and the cormorant, and the great owl:

18　Also the ¹redshank, and the pelican, and the swan:

19　The stork also, the heron after his kind, and the lapwing and the [bat]:

20　Also every fowl that creepeth *and* goeth upon all four, such shall be an abomination unto you.

21　Yet these shall ye eat: of every fowl that creepeth, *and* goeth upon all four which ¹have their feet and legs all of one to leap withal upon the earth.

22　Of them ye shall eat these, the grasshopper after his kind, and the ¹solean after his kind, the hargol after his kind, and the hagab after his kind.

23　But all *other* fowls that creep *and* have four feet, they *shall be* abomination unto you.

24　For by such ye shall be polluted: whosoever toucheth the carcass, shall be unclean unto the evening.

25　Whosoever also ¹beareth of their carcass, shall wash his clothes, and be unclean until even.

26　Every beast that hath claws divided, and is ¹not cloven footed, nor cheweth the cud, such shall be unclean unto you: everyone that toucheth them, shall be unclean.

27　And whatsoever goeth upon his paws among all manner beasts that goeth on all four, such shall be unclean unto you: who so doth touch their carcass, shall be unclean until the even.

28　And he that beareth their carcass, shall wash his clothes, and be unclean until the even: *for* such shall be unclean unto you.

29　¶ Also these shall be unclean to you among the things that creep and move upon the earth, the weasel, and the mouse, and the ¹,²frog, after his kind:

30　Also the rat, and the lizard, and the chameleon, and the stellio, and the mole.

31　These shall be unclean to you among all that

10:20 ¹ Moses bare with his infirmity, considering his great sorrow, but doth not leave an example to forgive them that maliciously transgress the commandment of God.

11:2 ¹ Or, whereof ye may eat.

11:3 ¹ He noteth four sorts of beasts, some chew the cud only, and some have only the foot cleft: others neither chew the cud, nor have the hoof cleft: the fourth both chew the cud and have the hoof divided, which may be eaten.

11:8 ¹ God would that hereby for a time they should be discerned as his people from the Gentiles.

11:10 ¹ As little fish engendered of the slime.

² As they which come of generation.

11:13 ¹ Or, gryphon, as it is in the Greek.

11:16 ¹ Or, cuckoo.

11:18 ¹ Or, porphyrio.

11:21 ¹ Or, have no bowings on their feet.

11:22 ¹ These were certain kinds of grasshoppers, which are not now properly known.

11:25 ¹ Out of the camp.

11:26 ¹ Or, hath not his foot cloven in two.

11:29 ¹ The green frog that sitteth on the bushes.

² Or, crocodile.

creep: whosoever doth touch them when they be dead, shall be unclean until the even.

32 Also whatsoever any of the dead carcasses of them doth fall upon, shall be unclean, whether it be vessel of wood, or raiment, or [1]skin, or sack: whatsoever vessel it be that is occupied, it shall be put in the water as unclean until the even, and so be purified.

33 But every earthen vessel, wherein any of them falleth, whatsoever is within it shall be unclean, and [b]ye shall break it.

34 All meat also that shall be eaten, if any such water come upon it, shall be unclean: and all drink that shall be drunk in all such vessels shall be unclean.

35 And everything that their carcass fall upon, shall be unclean: the furnace or the pot shall be broken: for they are unclean, and shall be unclean unto you.

36 Yet the fountains and wells where there is plenty of water shall be clean: but that which [1]toucheth their carcasses, shall be unclean.

37 And if there fall of the dead carcass upon any seed, which useth to be sown, it shall be unclean.

38 But if any [1]water be poured upon the seed, and there fall of the dead carcass thereon, it shall be unclean unto you.

39 If also any beast, whereof ye may eat, die, he that toucheth the carcass thereof, shall be unclean until the even.

40 And he that eateth of the carcass of it, shall wash his clothes, and be unclean until the even: he also that beareth the carcass of it, shall wash his clothes, and be unclean until the even.

41 Every creeping thing therefore that creepeth upon the earth, shall be an abomination, and not be eaten.

42 Whatsoever goeth upon the breast, and whatsoever goeth upon all four, or that hath many feet among all creeping things that creep upon the earth, ye shall not eat of them, for they shall be abomination.

43 Ye shall not pollute yourselves with anything that creepeth, neither make yourselves unclean with them, neither defile yourselves thereby: ye shall not, I say, be defiled by them.

44 For I am the Lord your God: be sanctified therefore, and be [1]holy, for I am holy, and defile not yourselves with any creeping thing that creepeth upon the earth.

45 For I am the Lord that brought you out of the land of Egypt, to be your God, and that you should be holy, for I am holy.

[b] Lev. 6:28

CHAPTER 12
[a] Lev. 15:19
[b] Luke 1:21 John 7:22
[c] Luke 2:24

46 This is the law of beasts, and of fowls, and of every living thing that moveth in the waters, and of every thing that creepeth upon the earth:

47 That there may be a difference between the unclean and clean, and between the beast that may be eaten, and the beast that ought not to be eaten.

12 *2 A law how women should be purged after their deliverance.*

1 And the Lord spake unto Moses, saying,

2 Speak unto the children of Israel, and say, When a woman hath brought forth seed, and borne a man-child, she shall be unclean [1]seven days, like as she is unclean when she is put apart for her [2,a]disease.

3 ([b]And in the eighth day the foreskin of the children's flesh shall be circumcised.)

4 And she shall continue in the blood of her purifying three [1]and thirty days: she shall touch no [2]hallowed thing, nor come into the [3]Sanctuary, until the time of her purifying be out.

5 But if she bear a maid-child, then she shall be unclean two [1]weeks, as when she hath her disease: and she shall continue in the blood of her purifying threescore and six days.

6 Now when the days of her purifying are out (whether it be for a son or for a daughter) she shall bring to the Priest a lamb of one year old for a burnt offering, and a young pigeon or a turtledove for a sin offering, unto the door of the [1]Tabernacle of the Congregation,

7 Who shall offer it before the Lord, and make an atonement for her: so she shall be purged of the issue of her blood: this is the law for her that hath borne a male or female.

8 But if she [1]be not able to bring a lamb, she shall bring two [c]turtles, or two young pigeons: the one for a burnt offering, and the other for a sin offering: and the Priest shall make an atonement for her: so she shall be clean.

13 *2 What considerations the Priests ought to have in judging the leprosy, 29 the black spot, or scab, 47 and the leprosy of the garment.*

1 Moreover the Lord spake unto Moses and to Aaron, saying,

2 The man that shall have in the skin of his flesh a swelling or a scab, or a white spot, so that in the skin of his flesh [1]it be like the plague of leprosy, then

---

11:32 [1] As a bottle or bag.
11:36 [1] So much of the water as toucheth it.
11:38 [1] He speaketh of seed that is laid to sleep before it be sown.
11:44 [1] He showeth why God did choose them to be his people, 1 Pet. 1:15.
12:2 [1] So that her husband for that time could not resort to her.
  [2] Or, flowers.

12:4 [1] Besides the first seven days.
  [2] As sacrifice, or such like.
  [3] That is, into the court gate, till after forty days.
12:5 [1] Twice so long as if she bare a man-child.
12:6 [1] Where the burnt offerings were wont to be offered.
12:8 [1] Hebrew, if her hand find not the worth of a lamb.
13:2 [1] That it may be suspected to be the leprosy.

he shall be brought unto Aaron the Priest, or unto one of his sons the Priests,

3   And the Priest shall look on the sore in the skin of *his* flesh: if the hair in the sore be turned into white, and the sore seen to be ¹lower than the skin of his flesh, it is a plague of leprosy: therefore the Priest shall look on him, and ²pronounce him unclean.

4   But if the white spot be in the skin of his flesh, and seem not to be lower than the skin, nor the hair thereof be turned unto white, then the Priest shall shut up *him that hath* the plague, seven days.

5   After, the Priest shall look upon him the seventh day: and if the plague seem ¹to him to abide still, and the plague grow not in the skin, the Priest shall shut him up yet seven days more.

6   Then the Priest shall look on him again the seventh day, and if the plague ¹be dark, and the sore grow not in the skin, then the Priest shall ²pronounce him clean, *for* it is a scab: therefore he shall wash his clothes, and be clean.

7   But if the scab grow more in the skin, after that he is seen of the Priest for to be purged, he shall be seen of the Priest yet again.

8   Then the Priest shall consider, and if the scab ¹grow in the skin, then the Priest shall pronounce him ²unclean: *for* it is leprosy.

9   ¶ When the plague of leprosy is in a man, he shall be brought unto the Priest,

10   And the Priest shall see *him*: and if the swelling *be* white in the skin, and have made the hair white, and there be raw flesh in the swelling,

11   It is an old leprosy in the skin of his flesh: and the Priest shall pronounce him unclean, and shall not shut him up, for he is unclean.

12   Also if the leprosy ¹break out in the skin, and the leprosy cover all the skin of the plague, from his head even to his feet, wheresoever the Priest looketh,

13   Then the Priest shall consider: and if the leprosy cover all his flesh, he shall pronounce the plague to be ¹clean, because it is all turned into whiteness: *so* he shall be clean.

14   But if *there be* raw flesh on him when he is seen, he shall be unclean.

15   For the Priest shall see the raw flesh, and declare him to be unclean: *for* the raw flesh is ¹unclean,

therefore it is the leprosy.

16   Or if the raw flesh change and be turned into white, then he shall come to the Priest,

17   And the Priest shall behold him: and if the sore be changed into white, then the Priest shall pronounce the plague clean, *for* it is clean.

18   ¶ The flesh also in whose skin there is ¹a boil, and is healed

19   And in the place of the boil there be a white swelling, or a white spot somewhat reddish, it shall be seen of the Priest.

20   And when the Priest seeth it, if it appear lower than the skin, and the hair thereof be changed into white, the Priest then shall pronounce him ¹unclean: *for* it is a plague of leprosy, broken out in the boil.

21   But if the Priest look on it, and there be no white hairs therein, and if it be not lower than the skin, but be darker, then the Priest shall shut him up seven days.

22   And if it spread abroad in the flesh, the Priest shall pronounce him unclean, *for* it is a sore.

23   But if the spot continue in his place, and grow not, it is a burning boil: therefore the Priest shall declare him to be clean.

24   ¶ If there be any flesh, in whose skin there is an hot burning, and the quick flesh of the burning have a ¹white spot, somewhat reddish or pale,

25   Then the Priest shall look upon it: and if the hair in that spot be changed into white, and it appear lower than the skin, it is a leprosy broken out in the burning: therefore the Priest shall pronounce him unclean: *for* it is the plague of leprosy.

26   But if the Priest look on it, and there be no white hair in the spot, and be no lower than the *other* skin, but be darker, then the Priest shall shut him up seven days.

27   After, the Priest shall look on him the seventh day: if it be grown abroad in the skin, then the Priest shall pronounce him unclean: *for* it is the plague of leprosy.

28   And if the spot abide in his place, not growing in the skin, but is dark, it is a ¹rising of the burning: the Priest shall therefore declare him clean: for it is the drying up of the burning.

29   ¶ If also a man or a woman hath a sore on the head or in the beard,

---

13:3 ¹ That is, shrunken in, and be lower than the rest of the skin.
  ² Hebrew, *shall pollute him.*
13:5 ¹ Hebrew, *in his eyes.*
13:6 ¹ As having the skin drawn together, or blackish.
  ² Hebrew, *shall cleanse him.*
13:8 ¹ Or, be spread abroad.
  ² As touching his bodily disease: for his disease was not imputed to him for sin before God, though it were the punishment of sin.
13:12 ¹ Or, bud.
13:13 ¹ For it is not that contagious leprosy that infecteth, but a kind

of scurvy, which hath not the flesh raw as the leprosy.
13:15 ¹ That is, declareth that the flesh is not found, but is in danger to be leprous.
13:18 ¹ Or, impostume.
13:20 ¹ None were exempted, but if the Priest pronounced him unclean, he was put out from among the people: as appeareth by Mary the prophetess, Num. 12:14, and by king Uzziah, 2 Chron. 26:20.
13:24 ¹ If he have a white spot in the place where the burning was, and was after healed.
13:28 ¹ Or, swelling.

30 Then the Priest shall see the sore: and if it appears lower than the skin, and there be in it a small yellow ¹hair, then the Priest shall pronounce him unclean: *for* it is a black spot, and leprosy of the head or of the beard.

31 And if the Priest look on the sore of the black spot, and if it seem not lower than the skin, nor have any black hair in it, then the Priest shall shut up *him that hath* the sore of the black spot, seven days.

32 After, in the seventh day the Priest shall look on the sore: and if the black spot grow not, and there be in it no yellow hair, and the black spot seem not lower than the skin,

33 Then he shall be shaven, but *the place* of the black spot shall he not shave: but the Priest shall shut up *him that hath* black spot, seven days more.

34 And the seventh day the Priest shall look on the black spot: and if the black spot grow not in the skin, nor seem lower than the *other* skin, then the Priest shall cleanse him, and he shall wash his clothes, and be clean.

35 But if the black spot grow abroad in the flesh after his cleansing,

36 Then the Priest shall look on it, and if the black spot grow in the skin, the Priest shall not ¹seek for the yellow hair: *for* it is unclean.

37 But if the black spot seem to him to abide, and that black hair grow therein, the black spot is healed, he *is* clean, and the Priest shall declare him to be clean.

38 ¶ Furthermore if there be any white spots in the skin of the flesh of man or woman,

39 Then the Priest shall consider: and if the spots in the skin of their flesh be somewhat dark and white withal, it is but a white spot broken out in the skin: *therefore* he is clean.

40 And the man whose hair is fallen off his head, *and* is bald, is clean.

41 And if his head lose the ¹hair on the forepart, *and* be bald before, he is clean.

42 But if there be in the bald head, or in the bald forehead a white reddish sore, it is a leprosy springing in his bald head, or in his bald forehead.

43 Therefore the Priest shall look upon it, and if the rising of the sore be white reddish in his bald head, or in his bald forehead, appearing like leprosy in the skin of the flesh,

44 He is a leper and unclean: *therefore* the Priest shall pronounce him altogether unclean: *for* the sore *is* in his head.

CHAPTER 13
ᵃ Num. 5:2
2 Kings 15:5

45 The leper also in whom the plague is, shall have his clothes ¹rent, and his head bare, and shall put a covering upon his ²lips, and shall cry, *I am* unclean, *I am* unclean.

46 As long as the disease *shall be* upon him, he shall be polluted, *for* he is unclean: he shall dwell alone, ᵃwithout the camp *shall* his habitation *be.*

47 ¶ Also the garment that the plague of leprosy is in, whether it be a woolen garment or a linen garment,

48 Whether it be in the warp or in the woof of linen or of woolen, either in a skin, or in anything made of skin,

49 And if the sore be green or somewhat reddish in the garment or in the skin, or in the warp or in the woof, or in anything that is made of ¹skin, it is a plague of leprosy, and shall be showed unto the Priest.

50 Then the Priest shall see the plague, and shut up *it that hath* the plague, seven days,

51 And shall look on the plague the seventh day: if the plague grow in the garment or in the warp, or in the woof, or in the skin, or in anything that is made of skin, that plague *is* a fretting leprosy and unclean.

52 And he shall burn the garment, or the warp, or the woof, whether it be woolen or linen, or anything that is made of skin, wherein the plague is: for it is a fretting leprosy, *therefore* it shall be burnt in the fire.

53 If the Priest yet see that the plague ¹grow not in the garment, or in the woof, or in whatsoever thing of skin it be,

54 Then the Priest shall command them to wash the thing wherein the plague is, and he shall shut it up seven days more.

55 Again the Priest shall look on the plague, after it is washed: and if the plague have not changed his ¹color, though the plague spread no further, it is unclean: thou shalt burn it in the fire, *for* it is a fret inward, ²whether *the spot* be in the bare place of the whole, or in part thereof.

56 And if the Priest see that the plague be darker, after that it is washed, he shall cut it out of the garment, or out of the skin, or out of the warp, or out of the woof.

57 And if it appear still in the garment, or in the warp, or in the woof, or in anything made of skin, it is a spreading *leprosy*: thou shalt burn the thing wherein the plague is, in the fire.

13:30 ¹ Which was not wont to be there, or else smaller than in any other part of the body.
13:36 ¹ He shall not care whether the yellow hair be there or no.
13:41 ¹ By sickness, or any other inconvenience.
13:45 ¹ In sign of sorrow and lamentation.
² Either in token of mourning, or for fear of infecting others.
13:49 ¹ Whether it be garment, vessel, or instrument.
13:53 ¹ But abide still in one place, as verse 37.
13:55 ¹ But remain as it did before.
² Or, whether it be in any bare place before, or behind.

58 If thou hast washed the garment, or the warp, or the woof, or whatsoever thing of skin it be, if the plague be departed therefrom, then shall it be washed ¹the second time, and be clean.

59 This is the law of the plague of leprosy in a garment of woolen or linen, or in the warp, or in the woof, or in anything of skin, to make it clean or unclean.

14

1 *The cleansing of the leper,*   34 *And of the house that he is in.*

1 And the Lord spake unto Moses, saying,

2 ª This is the ¹law of the leper in the day of his cleansing: that is, he shall be brought unto the Priest,

3 And the Priest shall go out of the camp, and the Priest shall consider *him*: and if the plague of leprosy be healed in the leper,

4 Then shall the Priest command to take for *him* that is cleansed, two ¹sparrows alive and ²clean, and cedarwood and a scarlet *lace*, and hyssop.

5 And the Priest shall command to kill one of the birds over ¹pure water in an earthen vessel.

6 After, he shall take the live sparrow with the cedarwood, and the scarlet *lace*, and the hyssop, and shall dip them and the living sparrow in the blood of the sparrow slain, over the pure water.

7 And he shall sprinkle upon him, that must be cleansed of his leprosy, seven times, and cleanse him, and shall ¹let go the live sparrow into the broad field.

8 Then he that shall be cleansed, shall wash his clothes, and shave off all his hair, and wash himself in water, so he shall be clean: after that shall he come into the host, and shall tarry without his tent seven days.

9 So in the seventh day he shall shave off all his hair *both* his head and his beard, and his eyebrows: even all his hair shall be shaven, and shall wash his clothes, and shall wash his flesh in water: so he shall be clean.

10 Then in the eighth day he shall take two he lambs without ¹blemish, and an ewe lamb of a year old without blemish, and three-tenth deals of fine flour for a meat offering, mingled with oil, ²and a pint of oil.

11 And the Priest that maketh him clean shall bring the man which is to be made clean, and those things, before the Lord, at the door of the Tabernacle

CHAPTER 14
ª Matt. 8:2
Mark 1:40
Luke 5:12
ᵇ Exod. 29:24
ᶜ Lev. 7:17

of the Congregation.

12 Then the Priest shall take one lamb, and offer him for a trespass offering, and the pint of oil, and ᵇshake them to and fro before the Lord.

13 And he shall kill the lamb in the place where the sin offering and the burnt offering are slain, *even* in the holy place: for as the ᶜsin offering is the Priest's, *so* is the trespass offering: *for* it is most holy.

14 So the Priest shall take of the blood of the trespass offering, and put it upon the lap of the right ear of him that shall be cleansed, and upon the thumb of his right hand, and upon the great toe of his right foot:

15 The Priest shall also take of the pint of oil, and pour it into the palm of his left hand,

16 And the Priest shall dip his ¹right finger in the oil that is in his left hand, and sprinkle of the oil with his finger seven times before the Lord.

17 And of the rest of the oil that is in his hand, shall the Priest put upon the lap of the right ear of him that is to be cleansed, and upon the thumb of his right hand, and upon the great toe of his right foot, ¹where the blood of the trespass offering *was put*.

18 But the remnant of the oil that is in the Priest's hand, he shall pour upon the head of him that is to be cleansed: so the Priest shall make an atonement for him before the Lord.

19 And the Priest shall offer the burnt offering, and make an atonement for him that is to be cleansed of his uncleanness: then after shall he kill the burnt offering.

20 So the Priest shall offer the burnt offering and the meat offering upon the Altar: and the Priest shall make an atonement for him: so he shall be clean.

21 But if he be poor, and not ¹able, then he shall bring one lamb for a trespass offering to be shaken, for his reconciliation, and a ²tenth deal of fine flour mingled with oil, for a meat offering, with a pint of oil.

22 Also two turtledoves, or two young pigeons, as he is able, whereof the one shall be a sin offering, and the other a burnt offering,

23 And he shall bring them the eighth day for his cleansing unto the Priest at the door of the Tabernacle of the Congregation before the Lord.

24 Then the Priest shall take the lamb of the trespass offering, and the pint of oil, and the Priest shall ¹shake them to and fro before the Lord.

13:58 ¹ To the intent he might be sure that the leprosy was departed, and that all occasion of infection might be taken away.

14:2 ¹ Or, the ceremony which shall be used in his purgation.

14:4 ¹ Or, little birds.

     ² Of birds which were permitted to be eaten.

14:5 ¹ Running water, or of the fountains.

14:7 ¹ Signifying, that he that was made clean, was set at liberty, and restored to the company of others.

14:10 ¹ Which hath no imperfection in any member.

     ² This measure in Hebrew, is called *Log*, and contained six eggs in measure.

14:16 ¹ Hebrew, *the finger of his right hand*.

14:17 ¹ Hebrew, *upon the blood of the trespass offering*.

14:21 ¹ Hebrew, *his hand cannot take it*.

     ² Which is an Omer, read Exod. 16:16.

14:24 ¹ Or, shall offer them as the offering that is shaken to and fro.

25 And he shall kill the lamb of the trespass offering, and the Priest shall take of the blood of the trespass offering, and put it upon the lap of his right ear that is to be cleansed, and upon the thumb of his right hand, and upon the great toe of his right foot.

26 Also the Priest shall pour of the oil into the palm of his own [1]left hand.

27 So the Priest shall with his right finger sprinkle of the oil that is in his left hand, seven times before the Lord.

28 Then the Priest shall put of the oil that is in his hand, upon the lap of the right ear of him that is to be cleansed, and upon the thumb of his right hand, and upon the great toe of his right foot: upon the place [1]of the blood of the trespass offering.

29 But the rest of the oil that is in the Priest's hand, he shall put upon the head of him that is to be cleansed, to make an atonement for him before the Lord.

30 Also he shall present one of the turtledoves, or of the young pigeons, [1]as he is able.

31 Such, I say, as he is able, the one for a sin offering, and the other for a burnt offering, [1]with the meat offering: so the Priest shall make an atonement for him that is to be cleansed before the Lord.

32 This is the [1]Law of him which hath the plague of leprosy, who is not able in his cleansing *to offer the whole.*

33 ¶ The Lord also spake unto Moses and to Aaron, saying,

34 When ye be come unto the land of Canaan which I give you in possession, if I [1]send the plague of leprosy in an house of the land of your possession,

35 Then he that [owneth] the house shall come and tell the Priest, saying, Me think there is like a plague *of leprosy* in the house.

36 Then the Priest shall command them to empty the house before the Priest go into it to see the plague, that all that is in the house be not made unclean, and then shall the Priest go in to see the house.

37 And he shall mark the plague: and if the plague *be* in the walls of the house, and that there be [1]deep spots, greenish or reddish, which seem to be lower than the wall.

38 Then the Priest shall go out of the house to the door of the house, and shall cause to shut up the house seven days.

39 So the Priest shall come again the seventh day: and if he see that the plague be increased in the walls of the house,

40 Then the Priest shall command them to take away the stones wherein the plague *is*, and they shall cast them into a [1]foul place without the city.

41 Also he shall cause to scrape the house within round about, and pour the dust, that they have pared off, without the city in [1]an unclean place.

42 And they shall take other stones, and put them in the places of those stones, and shall take other mortar, to plaster the house with.

43 But if the plague come again and break out in the house, after that he hath taken away the stones, and after that he hath scraped and plastered the house,

44 Then the Priest shall come and see: and if the plague grow in the house, it is a fretting leprosy in the house: it is *therefore* unclean.

45 And he shall [1]break down the house, with the stones of it, and the timber thereof, and all the [2]mortar of the house, and he shall carry them out of the city unto an unclean place.

46 Moreover he that goeth into the house all the while that it is shut up, he shall be unclean until the even.

47 He also that sleepeth in the house shall wash his clothes: he likewise that eateth in the house, shall wash his clothes.

48 But if the Priest shall come and see, that the plague hath spread no further in the house, after the house be plastered, the Priest shall pronounce the house clean, for the plague is healed.

49 Then shall he take to purify the house, two sparrows, and cedarwood, and [1]scarlet *lace*, and hyssop.

50 And he shall kill one sparrow over pure water in an earthen vessel,

51 And shall take the cedarwood, and the hyssop, and the scarlet *lace* with the live Sparrow, and dip them in the blood of the slain Sparrow, and in the pure water, and sprinkle the house seven times:

52 So shall he cleanse the house with the blood of the sparrow, and with the pure water, and with the live sparrow, and with the cedarwood, and with the hyssop, and with the scarlet *lace.*

14:26 [1] Hebrew, *into the palm of the Priest's left hand.*
14:28 [1] Or, where the blood of the trespass offering was put, as verse 17.
14:30 [1] Whether of them he can get.
14:31 [1] Or, besides the meat offering.
14:32 [1] This order is appointed for the poor man.
14:34 [1] This declareth that no plague nor punishment cometh to man without God's providence and his sending.
14:37 [1] Or, blackness, or hollow streaks.
14:40 [1] Or, polluted.
14:41 [1] Where carrions were cast, and other filth, that the people might not be therewith infected.
14:45 [1] That is, he shall command it to be pulled down, as verse 40.
[2] Or, dust.
14:49 [1] It seemeth that this was a lace or string to bind the hyssop to the wood, and so was made a sprinkle: the Apostle to the Hebrews calleth it scarlet wool, Heb. 9:19.

53 Afterward he shall let go the live sparrow out of the ¹town into the ²broad fields: so shall he make atonement for the house, and it shall be clean.

54 This is the law for every plague of leprosy and ᵈblack spot,

55 And of the leprosy of the garment, and of the house,

56 And of the ¹swelling, and of the scab, and of the white spot.

57 This is the law of the leprosy, to teach ¹when *a thing* is unclean, and when it is clean.

ᵈ Lev. 13:30

CHAPTER 15
ᵃ Lev. 2:28

15

8, 19 *The manner of purging the unclean issues both of men and women.*   31 *The children of Israel must be separate from all uncleanness.*

1 Moreover the Lord spake unto Moses, and to Aaron, saying,

2 Speak unto the children of Israel, and say unto them, Whosoever hath an issue from his ¹flesh, is unclean, *because* of his issue.

3 And this shall be his uncleanness in his issue, *when* his flesh avoideth his issue, or if his flesh be stopped from his issue, this is ¹his uncleanness.

4 Every bed whereon he lieth that hath the issue, shall be unclean, and everything whereon he sitteth, shall be unclean.

5 Whosoever also toucheth his bed, shall wash his clothes, and wash himself in water, and shall be unclean until the even.

6 And he that sitteth on any thing, whereon he sat that hath the issue, shall wash his clothes, and wash himself in water, and shall be unclean until the even.

7 Also he that toucheth the flesh of him that hath the issue, shall wash his clothes, and wash himself in water, and shall be unclean until the even.

8 If he also that hath the issue, spit upon him that is clean, ¹he shall wash his clothes, and wash himself in water, and shall be unclean until the even.

9 And what ¹saddle soever he rideth upon, that hath the issue, shall be unclean,

10 And whosoever toucheth any thing that was under him, shall be unclean until the even: and he that beareth those *things*, shall wash his clothes, and wash himself in water, and shall be unclean until the even.

11 Likewise whomsoever he toucheth that hath the issue (and hath not washed his hands in water) shall wash his clothes, and wash himself in water, and shall be unclean until the even.

12 ᵃAnd the vessel of earth that he toucheth, which hath the issue, shall be broken: and every vessel of wood shall be rinsed in water.

13 But if he that hath an issue, be ¹cleansed of his issue, then shall he count him seven days for his cleansing, and wash his clothes, and wash his flesh in pure water: so shall he be clean.

14 Then the eighth day he shall take unto him two turtledoves, or two young pigeons, and come before the Lord at the door of the Tabernacle of the Congregation, and shall give them unto the Priest,

15 And the Priest shall make of the one of them a sin offering, and of the other a burnt offering: so the Priest shall make an atonement for him before the Lord for his issue.

16 Also if any man's issue of seed depart from him, he shall wash all his ¹flesh in water, and be unclean until the even.

17 And every garment, and every skin whereupon shall be issue of seed, shall be even washed with water, and be unclean unto the even.

18 If he that hath an issue of seed do lie with a woman, they shall both wash themselves with water, and be unclean until the even.

19 ¶ Also when a woman shall have an issue, *and* her issue in her ¹flesh shall be blood, she shall be put apart seven days: and whosoever toucheth her, shall be unclean until the even.

20 And whatsoever she lieth upon in ¹her separation, shall be unclean, and everything that she sitteth upon, shall be unclean.

21 Whosoever also toucheth her bed, shall wash his clothes, and wash himself with water, and shall be unclean unto the even.

22 And whosoever toucheth anything that she sat upon, shall wash his clothes, and wash himself in water, and shall be unclean until the even:

23 So that whether he toucheth her bed, or anything whereon she hath sat, he shall be unclean unto the even.

24 And if a man lie with her, and *the flowers* of her separation ¹touch him, he shall be unclean seven

---

14:53 ¹ Hebrew, *city.*
    ² Hebrew, *on the face of the field.*
14:56 ¹ Or, *rising.*
14:57 ¹ Hebrew, *in the day of the unclean, and in the day of the clean.*
15:2 ¹ Whose seed either in sleeping, or else of weakness of nature issueth at his secret part.
15:3 ¹ Of the thing wherefore he shall be unclean.
15:8 ¹ Of whom the unclean man did spit.
15:9 ¹ The word signifieth everything whereon a man rideth.

15:13 ¹ That is, be restored to his old state, and be healed thereof.
15:16 ¹ Meaning, all his body.
15:19 ¹ Or, secret part.
15:20 ¹ That is, when she hath her flowers, whereby she is separate from her husband, from the Tabernacle and from touching of any holy thing.
15:24 ¹ If any of her uncleanness did only touch him in the bed: for else the man that companied with such a woman, should die, Lev. 20:18.

days, and all the whole bed whereon he lieth, shall be unclean.

25 Also when a woman's issue of blood runneth long time besides the time of her [1]flowers, or when she hath an issue longer than her flowers, all the days of the issue of her uncleanness she shall be unclean, as in the time of her flowers.

26 Every bed whereon she lieth (as long as her issue lasteth) shall be to her as the [1]bed of her separation: and whatsoever she sitteth upon, shall be unclean, as her uncleanness when she is put apart.

27 And whosoever toucheth these *things*, shall be unclean, and shall wash his clothes, and wash himself in water, and shall be unclean unto the even.

28 But if she be cleansed of her issue, then she shall [1]count her seven days, and after, she shall be clean.

29 And in the eighth day she shall take unto her two turtles, or two young pigeons, and bring them unto the Priest at the door of the Tabernacle of the Congregation.

30 And the Priest shall make of the one a sin offering, and of the other a burnt offering, and the Priest shall make an atonement for her before the Lord, for the issue of her uncleanness.

31 Thus shall ye [1]separate the children of Israel from their uncleanness, that they die not in their uncleanness, if they defile my Tabernacle that is among them.

32 This is the law of him that hath an issue, and of him from whom goeth an issue of seed whereby he is defiled:

33 Also of her that is sick of her flowers, and of him that hath a running issue, whether it be man or woman, and of him that lieth with her which is unclean.

16

2 *The Priest might not at all times come into the most holy place.* 8 *The scapegoat.* 14 *The purging of the Sanctuary.* 17 *The cleansing of the Tabernacle.* 21 *The Priest confesseth the sins of the people.* 29 *The feast of cleansing sins.*

1 Furthermore the Lord spake unto [a]Moses, after the death of the two sons of Aaron, when they came *to offer* before the Lord, and died:

2 And the Lord said unto Moses, Speak unto

CHAPTER 16
[a] Lev. 10:1,2
[b] Exod. 30:10
   Heb. 9:7
[c] Heb. 9:7
[d] Heb. 9:13
   Heb. 10:4
[e] Lev. 1:5

Aaron thy brother, [b]that he come not at [1]all times into the holy place within the veil, before the Mercy seat, which is upon the Ark, that he die not, for I will appear in the cloud upon the Mercy seat.

3 After this *sort* shall Aaron come into the Holy place: *even* with a young bullock for a sin offering, and a ram for a burnt offering.

4 He shall put on the holy linen coat, and shall have linen breeches upon his [1]flesh, and shall be girded with a linen girdle, and shall cover his head with a linen miter, these are the holy garments: therefore shall he wash his flesh in water, when he doth put them on.

5 And he shall take of the Congregation of the children of Israel, two he goats for a sin offering, and a ram for a burnt offering.

6 Then Aaron shall offer the bullock for his sin offering, [c]and make an atonement for himself, and for his house.

7 And he shall take the two he goats, and present them before the Lord at the door of the Tabernacle of the Congregation.

8 Then Aaron shall cast lots over the two he goats: one lot for the Lord, and the other for the [1]Scapegoat.

9 And Aaron shall offer the goat, upon which the Lord's lot shall fall, and make him a sin offering.

10 But the goat, on which the lot shall fall to be the Scapegoat, shall be presented alive before the Lord, to make reconciliation by him, *and* to let him go (as a Scapegoat) into the wilderness.

11 Thus Aaron shall offer the bullock for his sin offering, and make a reconciliation for himself, and for his house, and shall kill the bullock for his sin offering.

12 And he shall take a censer full of burning coals from off the altar before the Lord, and his hand full of sweet incense beaten small, and bring *it* within the [1]veil,

13 And shall put the incense upon the fire before the Lord, that the [1]cloud of the incense may cover the Mercy seat that is upon [2]the Testimony: so he shall not die.

14 And he shall [d]take of the blood of the bullock, [e]and sprinkle it with his finger upon the Mercy seat [1]Eastward: and before the Mercy seat shall he sprinkle

---

15:25 [1] Hebrew, *separation*.
15:26 [1] Shall be unclean as the bed whereon she lay when she had her natural disease.
15:28 [1] After the time that she is recovered.
15:31 [1] Seeing that God required of his purity and cleanness: we cannot be his, except our filth and sins be purged with the blood of Jesus Christ, and so we learn to detest all sin.
16:2 [1] The high Priest entered into the Holiest of all but once a year even in the month of September.

16:4 [1] Or, privities.
16:8 [1] In Hebrew it is called *Azazel*, which some say, is a mountain near Sinai, whither this goat was sent, but rather it is called the Scapegoat, because it was not offered, but sent into the desert, as verse 11.
16:12 [1] The Holiest of all.
16:13 [1] Or, the smoke.
    [2] Or, the Ark.
16:14 [1] That is, on the side which was toward the people: for the head of the Sanctuary stood Westward.

of the blood with his finger seven times.

15 ¶ Then shall he kill the goat that is the people's sin offering, and bring his blood within the veil and do with that blood, as he did with the blood of the bullock, and sprinkle it upon the Mercy seat, and before the Mercy seat.

16 So he shall purge the Holy place from the uncleanness of the children of Israel, and from their trespasses of all their sins: so shall he do also for the Tabernacle of the Congregation [1]placed with them, in the midst of their uncleanness.

17 [f]And there shall be no man in the Tabernacle of the Congregation, when he goeth in to make an atonement in the Holy place, until he come out, and have made an atonement for himself, and for his household, and for all the Congregation of Israel.

18 After, he shall go out unto the [1]altar that is before the Lord, and make a reconciliation upon it, and shall take of the blood of the bullock, and of the blood of the goat, and put it upon the horns of the Altar round about.

19 So shall he sprinkle of the blood upon it with his finger seven times, and cleanse it, and hallow it from the uncleanness of the children of Israel.

20 ¶ When he hath made an end of purging the Holy place, and the Tabernacle of the Congregation, and the Altar, then he shall bring the live goat:

21 And Aaron shall put both his hands upon the head of the live goat, and confess over him all the iniquities of the children of Israel, and all their trespasses in all their sins, putting them [1]upon the head of the goat, and shall send *him* away (by the hand of a man appointed) into the wilderness.

22 So the goat shall bear upon him all their iniquities into [1]the land that is not inhabited, and he shall let the goat go into the wilderness.

23 After, Aaron shall come into the Tabernacle of the Congregation, and put off the linen clothes, which he put on when he went into the Holy place, and leave them there.

24 He shall wash also his flesh with water in [1]the holy place, and put on his own raiment, and come out, and make his burnt offering and the burnt offering of the people, and make an atonement for himself, and for the people.

25 Also the fat of the sin offering shall he burn upon the altar.

26 And he that carried forth the goat *called* the

[f] Luke 1:10
[g] Lev. 6:30 Heb. 15:11
[b] Lev. 23:7
[i] Exod. 30:10 Heb. 9:7

Scapegoat, shall wash his clothes, and wash his flesh in water, and after that shall come into the host.

27 Also the bullock for the burnt offering, and the goat for the sin offering (whose blood was brought to make a reconciliation in the Holy place) shall one [g]carry out without the host to be burnt in the fire, with their skins, and with their flesh, and with their dung.

28 And he that burneth them shall wash his clothes, and wash his flesh in water, and afterward come into the host.

29 ¶ So this shall be an ordinance forever unto you: the tenth *day* of the [1]seventh month, ye shall [2]humble your souls, and do no work at all, whether it be one of the same country, or a stranger that sojourneth among you.

30 For that [b]day shall the Priest make an atonement for you to cleanse you: ye shall be clean from all your sins before the Lord.

31 This shall be a [1]Sabbath of rest unto you, and you shall humble your souls by an ordinance forever.

32 And the Priest [1]whom he shall anoint, and whom he shall consecrate (to minister in his father's stead) shall make the atonement, and shall put on the linen clothes and holy vestments,

33 And shall purge the holy Sanctuary and the Tabernacle of the Congregation, and shall cleanse the altar, and make an atonement for the Priests and for all the people of the Congregation.

34 And this shall be an everlasting ordinance unto you to make an atonement for the children of Israel for all their sins [i]once a year: and as the Lord commanded Moses, he did.

17

All sacrifices must be brought to the door of the Tabernacle.   7 To devils they may not offer.   10 They may not eat blood.

1 And the Lord spake unto Moses, saying,

2 Speak unto Aaron, and to his sons, and to all the children of Israel, and say unto them, This is the thing which the Lord hath [1]commanded, saying,

3 Whosoever *he be* of the house of Israel that [1]killeth a bullock, or lamb, or goat in the host, or that killeth it out of the host,

4 And bringeth it not unto the door of the Tabernacle of the Congregation to offer an offering unto the Lord before the Tabernacle of the Lord, [1]blood

---

16:16 [1] Placed among them which are unclean.
16:18 [1] Whereupon the sweet incense and perfume was offered.
16:21 [1] Herein this goat is a true figure of Jesus Christ, who beareth the sins of the people, Isa. 53:9.
16:22 [1] Hebrew, *the land of separations*.
16:24 [1] In the court where was the Laver, Exod. 30:18.
16:29 [1] Which was Tishri, and answereth to part of September, and part of October.

[2] Meaning, by abstinence and fasting, Num. 25:7.
16:31 [1] Or a rest which ye shall keep most diligently.
16:32 [1] Whom the Priest shall anoint by God's commandment to succeed in his father's room.
17:2 [1] Lest they should practice that idolatry, which they had learned among the Egyptians.
17:3 [1] To make a sacrifice of offering thereof.
17:4 [1] I do as much abhor it as though he had killed a man, as Isa. 66:3.

shall be imputed unto that man: he hath shed blood, wherefore that man shall be cut off from among his people.

5 Therefore the children of Israel shall bring their offerings, which they would offer ¹abroad in the field, and present them unto the Lord at the door of the Tabernacle of the Congregation by the Priest, and offer them for peace offerings unto the Lord.

6 Then the Priest shall sprinkle the blood upon the Altar of the Lord before the door of the Tabernacle of the Congregation, and burn the fat for a ᵃsweet savor unto the Lord.

7 And they shall no more offer their offerings unto ¹devils, after whom they have gone a ²whoring: this shall be an ordinance forever unto them in their generations.

8 ¶ Also thou shalt say unto them, Whosoever he be of the house of Israel, or of the strangers which sojourn among them, that offereth a burnt offering or sacrifice,

9 And bringeth it not unto the door of the Tabernacle of the Congregation to offer it unto the Lord, even that man shall be cut off from his people.

10 ¶ Likewise whosoever he be of the house of Israel: or of the strangers that sojourn among them, that eateth any blood, I will even set ¹my face against that person that eateth blood, and will cut him off from among his people.

11 For the life of the flesh is in the blood, and I have given it unto you to offer upon the altar, to make an atonement for your souls: for this blood shall make an atonement for the soul.

12 Therefore I said unto the children of Israel, None of you shall eat blood: neither the stranger that sojourneth among you, shall eat blood.

13 Moreover whosoever he be of the children of Israel, or of the strangers that sojourn among them, which by hunting taketh any beast or fowl that may be ¹eaten, he shall pour out the blood thereof, and cover it with dust:

14 For the life of all flesh is his blood, it is joined with his life: therefore I said unto the children of Israel, ᵇYe shall eat the blood of no ¹flesh: for the life of all flesh is the blood thereof: whosoever eateth it, shall be cut off.

CHAPTER 17
ᵃ Exod. 29:18
Lev. 4:31
ᵇ Gen. 9:4

CHAPTER 18
ᵃ Ezek. 20:11
Rom. 10:5
Gal. 3:12
ᵇ Lev. 20:11
ᶜ Lev. 20:19
Lev. 20:20

15 And every person that eateth it which dieth alone, or that which is torn with beasts, whether it be one of the same country or a stranger, he shall both wash his clothes, and wash himself in water, and be unclean unto the even: after he shall be ¹clean.

16 But if he wash them not, nor wash his ¹flesh, then he shall bear ²his iniquity.

18 3 The Israelites ought not to follow the manners of the Egyptians and Canaanites. 6 The marriages that are unlawful.

1 And the Lord spake unto Moses, saying,

2 Speak unto the children of Israel, and say unto them, I am the Lord your God.

3 After the ¹doings of the land of Egypt, wherein ye dwelt, shall ye not do: and after the manner of the land of Canaan, whither I will bring you, shall ye not do, neither walk in their ordinances.

4 But do after my judgments, and keep mine ordinances, to walk therein: I am the Lord your God.

5 Ye shall keep therefore my statutes, and my judgments, ᵃwhich if a man do, he shall then live in them: ¹I am the Lord.

6 ¶ None shall come near to any of the kindred of his flesh to ¹uncover her shame: I am the Lord.

7 Thou shalt not uncover the shame of thy father, nor the shame of thy mother, for she is thy mother, thou shalt not discover her shame.

8 ᵇThe shame of thy father's ¹wife shalt thou not discover: for it is thy father's shame.

9 Thou shalt not discover the shame of thy ¹sister, the daughter of thy father, or the daughter of thy mother, whether she be born at home or born without: thou shalt not discover their shame.

10 The shame of thy son's daughter, or of thy daughter's daughter, thou shalt not, I say, uncover their shame: for it is thy ¹shame.

11 The shame of thy father's wife's daughter, begotten of thy father (for she is thy sister) thou shalt not, I say, discover her shame.

12 ᶜThou shalt not uncover the ¹shame of thy father's sister: for she is thy father's kinswoman.

13 Thou shalt not discover the shame of thy mother's sister: for she is thy mother's kinswoman.

14 Thou shalt not uncover the shame of thy ¹father's

17:5 ¹ Wheresoever they were moved with foolish devotion to offer it.
17:7 ¹ Meaning, whatsoever is not the true God, 1 Cor. 10:10; Ps. 95:5.
² For idolatry is spiritual whoredom, because faith toward God is broken.
17:10 ¹ I will declare my wrath by taking vengeance on him, as Lev. 20:3.
17:13 ¹ Which the law permitteth to be eaten, because it is clean.
17:14 ¹ Or, living creature.
17:15 ¹ Or, counted clean.

17:16 ¹ Or, himself.
² Or, the punishment of his sin.
18:3 ¹ Ye shall preserve yourselves from these abominations following, which the Egyptians and Canaanites use.
18:5 ¹ And therefore ye ought to serve me alone, as my people.
18:6 ¹ That is, to lie with her, though it be under title of marriage.
18:8 ¹ Which is thy stepmother.
18:9 ¹ Either by father or mother, born in marriage or otherwise.
18:10 ¹ They are her children whose shame thou hast uncovered.
18:12 ¹ Or, secrets.
18:14 ¹ Which thine uncle doth discover.

brother: *that is*, thou shalt not go in to his wife, *for* she is thine [2]aunt.

15 [d]Thou shalt not discover the shame of thy daughter-in-law: *for* she is thy son's wife: *therefore* shalt thou not uncover her shame.

16 [e]Thou shalt not discover the shame of thy [1]brother's wife: *for* it is thy brother's shame.

17 Thou shalt not discover the shame of the wife and of her daughter, neither shalt thou take her son's daughter, nor her daughter's daughter, to uncover her shame: *for* they are *thy* kinsfolks, *and* it were wickedness.

18 Also thou shalt not take a wife with her sister, during her life to [1]vex *her*, in uncovering her shame upon her.

19 [f] Thou shalt not also go unto a woman to uncover her shame, as long as she is put [1]apart for her disease.

20 Moreover, thou shalt not give *thy* self to thy neighbor's wife by carnal copulation, to be defiled with her.

21 [g]Also thou shalt not give thy [1]children to [2]offer *them* unto [3]Molech, neither shalt thou defile the Name of thy God: *for* I am the Lord.

22 Thou shalt not lie with the male as one lieth with a woman: *for* it is abomination.

23 [h]Thou shalt not also lie with any beast to be defiled therewith, neither shall any woman stand before a beast, to lie down thereto: *for* it is [1]abomination.

24 Ye shall not defile yourselves in any of these things: for in all these the Nations are defiled which I will cast out before you:

25 And the land is defiled: therefore I will [1]visit the wickedness thereof upon it, and the land [2]shall vomit out her inhabitants.

26 Ye shall keep therefore mine ordinances, and my judgments, and commit none of these abominations, *as well* he that is of the same country, as the stranger that sojourneth among you.

Marginal references:
[d] Lev. 20:12
[e] Lev. 20:21
[f] Lev. 20:18
[g] Lev. 20:2
2 Kings 23:10
[h] Lev. 20:15

CHAPTER 19
[a] Lev. 11:44
Lev. 20:7
1 Pet. 1:16
[b] Lev. 7:16
[c] Lev. 23:22

27 (For all these abominations have the men of the land done, which were before you, and the land is defiled:

28 And shall not the land spew you out if ye defile it, as it [1]spewed out the people that were before you?)

29 For whosoever shall commit any of these abominations, the persons that do *so*, shall [1]be cut off from among their people.

30 Therefore shall ye keep mine ordinances, that ye do not any of the abominable customs, which have been done before you, and that ye defile not yourselves therein: *for* I am the Lord your God.

19
A repetition of sundry Laws and Ordinances.

1 And the Lord spake unto Moses, saying,

2 Speak unto all the Congregation of the children of Israel, and say unto them, [a]Ye shall be [1]holy, for I the Lord your God *am* holy.

3 ¶ Ye shall fear every man his mother and his father, and shall keep my Sabbath: *for* I am the Lord your God.

4 ¶ Ye shall not turn unto idols, nor make you molten gods: I am the Lord your God.

5 ¶ And when ye shall offer a peace offering unto the Lord, ye shall offer it [1]freely.

6 [b]It shall be eaten the day ye offer it, or on the morrow: and that which remaineth until the third day, shall be burnt in the fire.

7 For if it be eaten the third day, it shall be unclean, it shall not be [1]accepted.

8 Therefore he that eateth it, shall bear his iniquity, because he hath defiled the hallowed thing of the Lord, and that person shall be cut off from his people.

9 ¶ [c]When ye reap the harvest of your land, ye shall not reap every corner of your field, neither shalt thou gather the [1]gleanings of thy harvest.

10 Thou shalt not gather the grapes of thy vineyard *clean*, neither gather every grape of thy vineyard, *but* thou shalt leave them for the poor and for the

---

[2] Hebrew, *thy father's brother's wife.*

18:16 [1] Because the idolaters, among whom God's people had dwelt and should dwell, were given to these horrible incests, God chargeth his to beware of the same.

18:18 [1] By seeing thine affliction more bent to her sister than to her.

18:19 [1] Or while she hath her flowers.

18:21 [1] Hebrew, *of thy seed.*

    [2] Or, to make them pass.

    [3] Which was an idol of the Ammonites, unto whom they burned and sacrificed their children, 2 Kings 23:10. This seemed to be the chief and principal of all idols: and as the Jews write, was of a great stature, and hollow within, having seven places or chambers within him: one was to receive meal that was offered: another turtle doves: the third, a sheep: the fourth, a ram: the fifth a calf: the sixth an ox: the seventh a child. This idol's face was like a calf: his hands were ever stretched out to receive gifts: his priests were called Chemarim,

2 Kings 23:5; Hos. 10:5; Zeph. 1:4.

18:23 [1] Or, confusion.

18:25 [1] I will punish the land where such incestuous marriages and pollutions are suffered.

    [2] He compareth the wicked to evil humors and surfeiting, which corrupt the stomach, and oppress nature, and therefore must be cast out by vomit.

18:28 [1] Both for their wicked marriages, unnatural copulations, idolatry or spiritual whoredom with Molech and such like abominations.

18:29 [1] Either by the civil sword or by some plague that God will send upon such.

19:2 [1] That is, void of all pollution, idolatry, and superstition both of soul and body.

19:5 [1] Of your own accord.

19:7 [1] To wit, of God.

19:9 [1] Or, gatherings and leavings.

stranger: I am the Lord your God.

11 ¶ Ye shall not steal, neither ¹deal falsely, neither lie one to another.

12 ¶ ᵈAlso ye shall not swear by my Name falsely, neither shalt thou defile the Name of thy God: I am the Lord.

13 ¶ Thou shalt not do thy neighbor ¹wrong, neither rob *him*. ᵉThe workman's hire shall not abide with thee until the morning.

14 ¶ Thou shalt not curse the deaf, ᶠneither put a stumbling block before the blind, but shalt fear thy God: I am the Lord.

15 ¶ Ye shall not do unjustly in judgment: ᵍThou shalt not favor the person of the poor, nor honor the person of the mighty, *but* thou shalt judge thy neighbor justly.

16 ¶ Thou shalt not ¹walk *about* with tales among thy people: Thou shalt not ²stand against the blood of thy neighbor: I am the Lord.

17 ¶ Thou shalt not hate thy brother in thine heart, *but* thou shalt plainly rebuke thy neighbor, ¹and suffer him not to sin.

18 ¶ Thou shalt not avenge, nor be mindful *of wrong* against the children of thy people, ᵇbut shalt love thy neighbor as thyself: I am the Lord.

19 ¶ Ye shall keep mine ordinances. Thou shalt not let thy cattle gender with ¹*others* of divers kinds. Thou shalt not sow thy field with mingled *seed*, neither shall a garment of divers things, *as* of linen and woolen come upon thee.

20 ¶ Whosoever also lieth and meddleth with a woman that is a bondmaid, affianced to a husband, and not redeemed, nor freedom given her, ¹she shall be scourged, *but* they shall not die, because she is not made free.

21 And he shall bring for his trespass offering unto the Lord, at the door of the Tabernacle of the Congregation, a ram for a trespass offering.

22 Then the Priest shall make an atonement for him with the ram of the trespass offering before the Lord, concerning his sin which he hath done, and pardon shall be given him for his sin which he hath committed.

23 ¶ Also when ye shall come into the land, and

ᵈ Exod. 20:7
Deut. 5:11
Matt. 5:34
ᵉ Deut. 24:14,15
Deut. 4:14
ᶠ Deut. 27:18
ᵍ Exod. 23:3
Deut. 1:17
Deut. 16:19
Prov. 24:23
James 2:2
ʰ Matt. 5:43
Rom. 13:9
Gal. 5:14
James 2:8
ⁱ Lev. 21:5
ʲ Deut. 14:1
ᵏ 1 Sam. 28:8
ˡ Exod. 22:21
ᵐ Prov. 11:1
Prov. 16:11
Prov. 20:10

have planted every tree for meat, ye ¹shall count the fruit thereof as uncircumcised: three years shall it be uncircumcised unto you: it shall not be eaten:

24 But in the fourth year all the fruit thereof shall be holy to the praise of the Lord.

25 And the fifth year shall ye eat of the fruit of it, that it may ¹yield to you the increase thereof: I am the Lord your God.

26 ¶ Ye shall not eat *the flesh* with the ¹blood: ye shall not use witchcraft, nor ²observe times.

27 ʲYe shall not ¹cut round the corners of your heads, neither shalt thou ²mar the tufts of thy beard.

28 ʲYe shall not cut your flesh for the ¹dead, nor make any print of a ²mark upon you: I am the Lord.

29 ¶ Thou shalt not make thy daughter common, to cause her to be a ¹whore, lest the land also fall to whoredom, and the land be full of wickedness.

30 ¶ Ye shall keep my Sabbaths, and reverence my Sanctuary: I am the Lord.

31 ¶ Ye shall not regard them that work with spirits, ᵏneither Soothsayers: ye shall not seek *to them* to be defiled by them, I am the Lord your God.

32 ¶ Thou shalt ¹rise up before the hoary head, and honor the person of the old man, and dread thy God: I am the Lord.

33 ¶ And if a stranger sojourn with thee in your land, ye shall not ¹vex him.

34 ˡBut the stranger that dwelleth with you, shall be as one of yourselves, and thou shalt love him as thyself: for ye were strangers in the land of Egypt: I am the Lord your God.

35 ¶ Ye shall not do unjustly in judgment, in ¹line, in weight, or in measure.

36 ᵐYou shall have just balances, true weights, a true ¹Ephah, and a true Hin, I am the Lord your God, which have brought you out of the land of Egypt.

37 Therefore shall ye observe all mine ordinances, and all my judgments, and do them: I am the Lord.

20

2 *They that give of their seed to Molech, must die.* 6 *They that have recourse to sorcerers.* 10 *The man that committeth adultery,* 11 *incest, or fornication with the kindred or affinity.* 24 *Israel a peculiar people to the Lord.*

19:11 ¹ In that which is committed to your credit.
19:13 ¹ Or, oppress him by violence.
19:16 ¹ As a slanderer, backbiter, or quarrel picker.
    ² By consenting to his death, or conspiring with the wicked.
19:17 ¹ Hebrew, *suffer not sin upon him.*
19:19 ¹ As a horse to leap an ass, or a mule a mare.
19:20 ¹ Hebrew, *a beating shall be,* some read, *they shall be beaten.*
19:23 ¹ It shall be unclean as that thing, which is not circumcised.
19:25 ¹ Or, that God may multiply.
19:26 ¹ Whether it be strangled, or otherwise.

² To measure lucky or unlucky days.
19:27 ¹ As did the Gentiles in sign of mourning.
    ² Or, cut, or tear.
19:28 ¹ Hebrew, *soul* or *person.*
    ² By whipping your bodies or burning marks therein.
19:29 ¹ As did the Cyprians, and Locrians.
19:32 ¹ In token of reverence.
19:33 ¹ Or, do him wrong.
19:35 ¹ As in measuring the ground.
19:36 ¹ By these two measures he meaneth all others. Of Ephah, read Exod. 16:36, and of Hin, Exod. 29:40.

1 And the Lord spake unto Moses, saying,

2 Thou shalt say also to the children of Israel, *Whosoever *he be* of the children of Israel, or of the strangers that dwell in Israel, that giveth his children unto [1]Molech, he shall die the death, the people of the land shall stone him to death.

3 And I will [1]set my face against that man and cut him off from among his people, because he hath given his children unto Molech, for to defile my Sanctuary, and to pollute mine holy Name.

4 And if the [1]people of the land hide their eyes, *and* wink at that man when he giveth his children unto Molech, and kill him not,

5 Then will I set my face against that man, and against his family, and will cut him off, and all that go a whoring after him to commit whoredom with Molech, from among their people.

6 ¶ If any turn after such as work with spirits, and after soothsayers to go a [1]whoring after them, then will I set my face against that person, and will cut him off from among his people.

7 ¶ Sanctify yourselves therefore, *b*and be holy, for I am the Lord your God.

8 Keep ye therefore mine ordinances, and do them: I am the Lord which doth sanctify you.

9 ¶ [1]If *there be* any that curseth his father or his mother he shall die the death, *seeing* he hath cursed his father and his mother, [1]his blood *shall be* upon him.

10 ¶ *d*And the man that committeth adultery with another man's wife, because he hath committed adultery with his neighbor's wife, the adulterer and the adulteress shall die the death.

11 And the man that lieth with his father's wife, *because* he hath uncovered his father's *c*shame, they shall both die: their blood *shall be* upon them.

12 Also the man that lieth with his daughter-in-law, they both shall die the death, they have wrought [1]abomination, their blood *shall be* upon them.

13 ¶ *f* The man also that lieth with the male, as one lieth with a woman, they have both committed abomination: they shall die the death, their blood *shall be* upon them.

14 Likewise he that taketh a wife and her mother, [1]committeth wickedness: they shall burn him and them with fire, that there be no wickedness among you.

15 *g*Also the man that lieth with a beast, shall die the death, and ye shall slay the beast.

16 And if a woman come to any beast, and lie therewith, then thou shalt kill the woman and the beast: they shall die the death, their blood *shall be* upon them.

17 Also the man that taketh his sister, his father's daughter, or his mother's daughter, and seeth her shame, and she seeth his shame, it is villainy: therefore they shall be cut off in the sight [1]of their people, *because* he that uncovered his sister's shame, he shall bear his iniquity.

18 *h*The man also that lieth with a woman having her [1]disease, and uncovereth her shame, *and* openeth her fountain, and she open the fountain of her blood, they shall be even both cut off from among their people.

19 Moreover, thou shalt not uncover the shame of thy mother's sister, [1]nor of thy father's sister: because he hath uncovered his [1]kin, they shall bear their iniquity.

20 Likewise the man that lieth with his father's brother's wife, and uncovereth his uncle's shame: they shall bear their iniquity, *and* shall die [1]childless.

21 So the man that taketh his brother's wife, committeth filthiness, *because* he hath uncovered his brother's [1]shame, they shall be childless.

22 ¶ Ye shall keep therefore all mine *j*ordinances and all my judgments, and do them, that the land whither I bring you to dwell therein, *k*spew you not out.

23 Wherefore ye shall not walk in the manners of this nation which I cast out before you: for they have committed all these things, *l*therefore I abhorred them.

24 But I have said unto you, Ye shall inherit their land, and I will give it unto you to possess it, *even* a land that [1]floweth with milk and honey: I am the Lord your God, which have separated you from *other* people.

25 *m*Therefore shall ye put difference between clean beasts and unclean, and between unclean fowls and clean, neither shall ye [1]defile your fowls with beasts and fowls, nor with any *creeping thing*, that the ground bringeth forth, which I have separated from you as unclean.

26 Therefore shall ye be *n*holy unto me: for I the

Cross references:

CHAPTER 20
a Lev. 18:21
b Lev. 11:44
1 Pet. 1:16
c Exod. 21:17
Prov. 20:20
Matt. 15:4
d Deut. 22:22
John 8:4,5
e Lev. 28:8
Deut. 22:30
f Lev. 18:22
g Lev. 18:23
h Lev. 18:19
i Lev. 18:12,13
j Lev. 18:26
k Lev. 18:25
l Deut. 9:5
m Lev. 11:2,3
Deut. 14:4
n Lev. 20:7

20:2 [1] By Molech he meaneth any kind of idol, Lev. 18:21.
20:3 [1] Read Lev. 17:10 and 18:21.
20:4 [1] Though the people be negligent to do their duty, and defend God's right, yet he will not suffer wickedness to go unpunished.
20:6 [1] To esteem sorcerers or conjurers is spiritual whoredom, or idolatry.
20:9 [1] He is worthy to die.
20:12 [1] Or, confusion.

20:14 [1] It is an execrable and detestable thing.
20:17 [1] Hebrew, *in the eyes of the children of their people.*
20:18 [1] Or, flowers.
20:19 [1] Hebrew, *flesh.*
20:20 [1] They shall be cut off from their people, and their children shall be taken as bastards, and not counted among the Israelites.
20:21 [1] Read Lev.18:16.
20:24 [1] Full of abundance of all things.
20:25 [1] By eating them contrary to my commandment.

Lord am holy, and I have separated you from *other* people that ye should be mine.

27 ¶ °And if a man or woman have a spirit of divination, or soothsaying in them, they shall die the death: they shall stone them to death, their blood *shall be* upon them.

21

2 For whom the Priests may lament.   6 How pure the Priests ought to be, both in themselves, and in their family.

1 And the Lord said unto Moses, Speak unto the Priests the sons of Aaron, and say unto them, Let none be ¹defiled by the dead among his people,

2 But by his kinsman that is near unto him: *to wit,* by his mother, or by his father, or by his son, or by his daughter, or by his brother,

3 Or by his sister a ¹maid, that is near unto him, which had not had an husband: for her ²he may lament.

4 He shall not lament for the ¹Prince among his people, to pollute himself.

5 They shall not make ᵃbald parts upon their head, nor shave off the locks of their beard, nor make any cuttings in their flesh.

6 They shall be holy unto their God, and not pollute the Name of their God: for the sacrifices of the Lord made by fire, *and* the bread of their God they do offer: therefore they shall be holy.

7 They shall not take to wife an whore, or ¹one polluted, neither shall they marry a woman divorced from her husband: for such one *is* holy unto his God.

8 Thou shalt ¹sanctify him therefore, for he offereth the ²bread of thy God: he shall be holy unto thee: for I the Lord which sanctify you, am holy.

9 ¶ If a Priest's daughter fall to play the whore, she polluteth her father: *therefore* shall she be burnt with fire.

10 ¶ Also the high Priest among his brethren, (upon whose head the anointing oil was poured, and hath consecrated his hand to put on the garments) shall not ¹uncover his head nor rent his clothes.

11 Neither shall he go to any ¹dead body, nor make himself unclean by his father or by his mother,

12 Neither shall he go out of the ¹Sanctuary, nor pollute the holy place of his God: for the ²crown of the anointing oil of his God *is* upon him: I am the Lord.

13 Also he shall take a maid unto his wife:

14 *But* a widow, or a divorced woman, or a polluted, *or* an harlot, these shall he not marry, but shall take a maid of his own ¹people to wife:

15 Neither shall he defile his ¹seed among his people: for I am the Lord which sanctify him.

16 ¶ And the Lord spake unto Moses, saying,

17 Speak unto Aaron, and say, Whosoever of thy seed in their generations hath any blemishes, shall not prease to offer the bread of his God:

18 For whosoever hath any blemish, shall not come near: *as* a man blind or lame, or that hath ¹a flat nose, or that hath any ²misshapen *member*,

19 Or, a man that hath a broken foot, or a broken hand,

20 Or, *is* crookbacked, or bleary-eyed, ¹or hath a blemish in his eye, or be scurvy, or scabbed, or hath *his* stones broken.

21 None of the seed of Aaron the Priest that hath a blemish, shall come near to offer the sacrifices of the Lord made by fire, having a blemish: he shall not prease to offer the ¹bread of his God.

22 The bread of his God, *even* of the ¹most holy, and ²of the holy shall he eat:

23 But he shall not go in unto the ¹veil, nor come near the altar, because he hath a blemish, lest he pollute my Sanctuaries: for I am the Lord that sanctify them.

24 Thus spake Moses unto Aaron, and to his sons, and to all the children of Israel.

22

3 Who ought to abstain from eating the things that were offered.   19 What oblation should be offered.

1 And the Lord spake unto Moses, saying,

2 Speak unto Aaron, and to his sons, that they be ¹separated from the holy things of the children of Israel, and that they pollute not mine holy name in those things, which they hallow unto me: I am the Lord.

° Deut. 18:11
1 Sam. 25:7

CHAPTER 21
ᵈ Lev. 19:27

21:1 ¹ By touching the dead, lamenting, or being at their burial.
21:3 ¹ For being married she seemed to be cut off from his family.
² Hebrew, *he may be defiled.*
21:4 ¹ The Priest was permitted to mourn for his next kindred only.
21:7 ¹ Which hath an evil name or is defamed.
21:8 ¹ Thou shalt count them holy and reverence them.
² The showbread.
21:10 ¹ He shall use no such ceremonies as the mourners observed.
21:11 ¹ Or, to the houses of the dead.
21:12 ¹ To go to the dead.
² For by his anointing he was preferred to the other Priests and therefore could not lament the dead, lest he should have polluted

his holy anointing.
21:14 ¹ Not only of his tribe, but of all Israel.
21:15 ¹ By marrying any unchaste or defamed woman.
21:18 ¹ Which is deformed or bruised.
² As not of equal proportion, or having in number more or less.
21:20 ¹ Or that hath a web or pearl.
21:21 ¹ As the showbread, and meat offerings.
21:22 ¹ As of sacrifice for sin.
² As of the tenths and firstfruits.
21:23 ¹ Into the Sanctuary.
22:2 ¹ Meaning, that the Priests abstain from eating, so long as they are polluted.

3 Say unto them, Whosoever *he be* of all your seed among your generations after you, that ¹toucheth the holy things which the children of Israel hallow unto the Lord, having his uncleanness upon him, even that person shall be cut off from my sight, I am the Lord.

4 ᵃWhosoever also of the seed of Aaron is a leper, or hath a running issue, he shall not eat of the holy things until he be clean: and who so toucheth any that is ¹unclean *by reason* of the dead, or a man whose issue of seed runneth from him,

5 Or the man that toucheth any creeping thing, whereby he may be made unclean, or a man by whom he may take uncleanness, ¹whatsoever uncleanness he hath,

6 The person that hath touched such, shall therefore be unclean until the even, and shall not eat of the holy things, ¹except he have washed his flesh with water.

7 But when the Sun is down, he shall be clean, and shall afterward eat of the holy things: for it is his ¹food.

8 ᵇOf a beast that dieth, or is rent *with beasts*, whereby he may be defiled, he shall not eat: I am the Lord.

9 Let them keep therefore mine ordinance, lest they bear *their* sin for it, and die for it, if they defile it: I the Lord sanctify them.

10 There shall no ¹stranger also eat of the holy thing, neither ²the guest of the Priest, neither shall an hired servant eat of the holy thing:

11 But if the Priest buy any with money, he shall eat of it, also he that is born in his house: they shall eat of his meat.

12 If the Priest's daughter also be married unto a ¹stranger, she may not eat of the holy offerings.

13 Notwithstanding if the Priest's daughter be a widow or divorced, and have no child, but is returned unto her father's house, she shall eat of her father's bread, as she did in her ᶜyouth: but there shall no stranger eat thereof.

14 ¶ If a man eat of the holy thing unwittingly, he shall put the ¹fifth part thereunto, and give it unto the Priest with the hallowed thing.

15 So shall they not defile the holy things of the children of Israel, which they offer unto the Lord,

16 Neither cause the *people* to bear the iniquity *of*

CHAPTER 22
ᵃ Lev. 15:2
ᵇ Exod. 12:21
Ezek. 45:31
ᶜ Lev. 10:14
ᵈ Deut. 15:21
ᵉ Lev. 21:12
ᶠ Deut. 22:6
ᵍ Lev. 7:15

their ¹trespass, while they eat their holy thing: for I the Lord do hallow them.

17 ¶ And the Lord spake unto Moses, saying,

18 Speak unto Aaron, and to his sons, and to all the children of Israel, and say unto them, Whosoever *he be* of the house of Israel, or of the strangers in Israel, that will offer his sacrifice for all their vows, and for all their free offerings, which they use to offer unto the Lord for a burnt offering,

19 *Ye shall offer* of your free mind a male without blemish of the beeves, of the sheep, or of the goats.

20 Ye shall not offer anything that hath a blemish: for that shall not be acceptable for you.

21 ᵈAnd whosoever bringeth a peace offering unto the Lord to accomplish his vow, or for a free offering of the beeves, or of the sheep, his free offering shall be perfect, no blemish shall be in it.

22 Blind, or broken, or maimed, or having a ¹wen, or scurvy, or scabbed: these shall ye not offer unto the Lord, nor make an offering by fire of these upon the Altar of the Lord.

23 Yet a bullock, or a sheep that hath *any* ᵉmember superfluous, or lacking, such mayest thou present for a free offering, but for a vow it shall not be accepted.

24 Ye shall not offer unto the Lord that which is bruised or crushed, or broken, or cut away, neither shall ye make *an offering thereof* in your land,

25 Neither ¹of the hand of a stranger shall ye offer the bread of your God of any of these, because their corruption is in them, there is a blemish in them: *therefore* shall they not be accepted for you.

26 ¶ And the Lord spake unto Moses, saying,

27 When a bullock, or a sheep, or a goat shall be brought forth, it shall be even seven days under his dam: and from the eighth day forth it shall be accepted for a sacrifice made by fire unto the Lord.

28 As for the cow or the ewe, ye shall not ᶠkill her, and her young *both* in one day.

29 So when ye will offer a thank offering unto the Lord, ye shall offer willingly.

30 The same day shall it be eaten, ye shall leave ᵍnone of it to the morrow: I am the Lord.

31 Therefore shall ye keep my Commandments and do them: *for* I am the Lord.

32 Neither shall ye ¹pollute my holy Name, but I will be hallowed among the children of Israel. I the

---

22:3 ¹ To eat thereof.
22:4 ¹ By touching any dead thing, or being at burial of the dead.
22:5 ¹ Hebrew, *according to all his uncleanness.*
22:6 ¹ Or, until.
22:7 ¹ Or, bread.
22:10 ¹ Which is not of the tribe of Levi.
  ² Some read, the servant which had his ear bored, and would not go free, Exod. 21:6.
22:12 ¹ Who is not of the Priest's kindred.

22:14 ¹ He shall give that and a fifth part over.
22:16 ¹ For if they did not offer for their error, the people by their example might commit the like offense.
22:22 ¹ Or, wart.
22:25 ¹ Ye shall not receive any imperfect thing of a stranger, to make it the Lord's offering: which he calleth the bread of the Lord.
22:32 ¹ For whosoever doth otherwise than God commandeth polluted his Name.

Lord sanctify you,

33 Which have brought you out of the land of Egypt, to be your God: I am the Lord.

23

2 *The feasts of the Lord.* 3 *The Sabbath.* 5 *The Passover.* 6 *The feast of unleavened bread.* 10 *The feast of firstfruits.* 16 *Whitsuntide.* 24 *The feast of blowing trumpets.* 34 *The feast of Tabernacles.*

CHAPTER 23
ᵃ Exod. 20:9,10
ᵇ Exod. 12:15
Num. 28:17
ᶜ Lev. 19:9
Deut. 24:19

1 And the Lord spake unto Moses, saying,

2 Speak unto the children of Israel, and say unto them, The feasts of the Lord which ye shall call the holy ¹assemblies, *even* these are my feasts.

3 ᵃSix days ¹shall work be done, but in the seventh day *shall be* the Sabbath of rest, an holy ²convocation: ye shall do no work *therein*, it is the Sabbath of the Lord, in all your dwellings.

4 ¶ These are the feasts of the Lord, *and* holy convocations, which ye shall proclaim in their ¹seasons.

5 In the first month *and* in the fourteenth *day* of the month at evening *shall be* the Passover of the Lord.

6 And on the fifteenth day of this month *shall be* the feast ᵇof unleavened bread unto the Lord: seven days ye shall eat unleavened bread.

7 In the first day ye shall have an holy convocation: ye shall do no ¹servile work *therein*.

8 Also ye shall offer sacrifice made by fire unto the Lord seven days, *and* in the ¹seventh day *shall be* an holy convocation: ye shall do no servile work *therein*.

9 ¶ And the Lord spake unto Moses, saying,

10 Speak unto the children of Israel, and say unto them, When ye be come into the land which I give unto you, and reap the harvest thereof, then ye shall bring ¹a sheaf of the firstfruits of your harvest unto the Priest,

11 And he shall shake the sheaf before the Lord, that it may be acceptable for you: the morrow after the ¹Sabbath, the Priest shall shake it.

12 And that day when ye shake the sheaf, shall ye prepare a lamb without blemish of a year old, for a burnt offering unto the Lord:

13 And the meat offering thereof *shall be* two ¹tenth deals of fine flour mingled with oil, for a sacrifice

made by fire unto the Lord of sweet savor: and the drink offering thereof the fourth part ²of an Hin of wine.

14 And ye shall eat neither bread nor parched corn, nor ¹green ears until the selfsame day that ye have brought an offering unto your God: *this shall be* a Law forever in your generations and in all your dwellings.

15 ¶ Ye shall count also to you from the morrow after the ¹Sabbath, *even* from the day that ye shall bring the sheaf of the shake offering, seven ²Sabbaths, they shall be complete.

16 Unto the morrow after the seventh Sabbath shall ye number fifty days: then ye shall bring a new meat offering unto the Lord.

17 Ye shall bring out of your habitations bread for the shake offering: they shall be two *loaves* of two tenth deals of fine flour, *which* shall be baken with ¹leaven for firstfruits unto the Lord.

18 Also ye shall offer with the bread seven lambs without blemish of one year old, and a young bullock and two rams: they shall be for a burnt offering unto the Lord, with their meat offerings and their drink offerings, for a sacrifice made by fire of a sweet savor unto the Lord.

19 Then ye shall prepare an he goat for a sin offering, and two lambs of one year old for peace offerings.

20 And the Priest shall shake them to and fro with the bread of the firstfruits before the Lord, *and* with the two lambs: they shall be holy to the Lord, for the ¹Priest.

21 So ye shall proclaim the same day, *that* it may be an holy convocation unto you: ye shall do no servile work *therein*: *it shall be* an ordinance forever in all your dwellings, throughout your generations.

22 ¶ ᶜAnd when you reap the harvest of your land, thou shalt not rid clean the corners of thy field when thou reapest, neither shalt thou make any aftergathering of thy harvest, *but* shalt leave them unto the poor and to the stranger, I am the Lord your God.

23 ¶ And the Lord spake unto Moses, saying,

24 Speak unto the children of Israel, and say, In the ¹seventh month, *and* in the first *day* of the month shall ye ²have a Sabbath, for the remembrance of

---

23:2 ¹ Or, convocations.

23:3 ¹ Or, ye may work.

   ² Or, assembly.

23:4 ¹ For the Sabbath was kept every week, and these others were kept but once every year.

23:7 ¹ Or, bodily labor, save about that which one must eat, Exod. 22:16.

23:8 ¹ The first day of the feast and the seventh were kept holy: in the rest they might work, except any feast were intermeddled, as the feast of unleavened bread, the fifteenth day, and the feast of sheaves the sixteenth day.

23:10 ¹ Or, an Omer, read Deut. 24:19; Ruth 2:15; Ps. 129:7.

23:11 ¹ That is, the second Sabbath of the Passover.

23:13 ¹ Which is, the fifth part of an Ephah, or two Omers: read Exod. 16:16.

   ² Read Exod. 29:40.

23:14 ¹ Or, full ears.

23:15 ¹ That is the seventh day after the first Sabbath of the Passover.

   ² Or, weeks.

23:17 ¹ Because the Priest should eat them, as Lev. 7:13, and they should not be offered to the Lord upon the altar.

23:20 ¹ That is, offered to the Lord, and the rest should be for the Priests.

23:24 ¹ That is, about the end of September.

   ² Or, an holy day to the Lord.

³blowing the trumpets, an holy convocation.

25 Ye shall do no servile work *therein*, but offer sacrifice made by fire unto the Lord.

26 ¶ And the Lord spake unto Moses, saying,

27 The ᵈtenth also of this seventh month, shall be a day of reconciliation: it shall be an holy convocation unto you, and ye shall ¹humble your souls, and offer sacrifice made by fire unto the Lord.

28 And ye shall do no work that same day: for it is a day of reconciliation, to make an atonement for you before the Lord your God.

29 For every person that humbleth not himself that same day, shall even be cut off from his people.

30 And every person that shall do any work that same day, the same person also will I destroy from among his people.

31 Ye shall do no manner work *therefore*: *this shall be* a law forever in your generations, *throughout* all your dwellings.

32 This shall be unto you a Sabbath of rest, and ye shall humble your souls: in the ninth *day* of the month at even, from ¹even to even shall ye ²celebrate your Sabbath.

33 ¶ And the Lord spake unto Moses, saying,

34 Speak unto the children of Israel, and say, 'In the fifteenth day of this seventh month *shall be* for seven days the feast of Tabernacles unto the Lord.

35 In the first day *shall be* an holy convocation: ye shall do no servile work *therein*.

36 Seven days ye shall offer ʲsacrifice made by fire unto the Lord, *and* in the eighth day shall be an holy convocation unto you, and ye shall offer sacrifices made by fire unto the Lord: it is the ¹solemn assembly, ye shall do no servile work *therein*.

37 These are the feasts of the Lord (which ye shall call holy convocations) to offer sacrifice made by fire unto the Lord, *as* burnt offering, and meat offering, ¹sacrifice, and drink offerings, every one upon his day,

38 Beside the Sabbaths of the Lord, and beside your gifts, and beside all your vows, and beside all your free offerings, which ye shall give unto the Lord.

39 But in the fifteenth day of the seventh month, when ye have gathered in the fruit of the land, ye shall keep an holy feast unto the Lord seven days:

ᵈ Lev. 19:29,30
Num. 29:7
ᵉ Num. 29:12
John 7:2,37
ʲ Exod. 29:18

CHAPTER 24
ᵃ Exod. 31:8
ᵇ Exod. 25:30
ᶜ Exod. 29:48
Lev. 8:31
Matt. 12:1,5

in the first day *shall be* a ¹Sabbath: likewise in the eighth day *shall be* a Sabbath.

40 And ye shall take you in the first day the fruit of goodly trees, branches of palm trees, and the boughs of ¹thick trees, and willows of the brook, and shall rejoice before the Lord your God seven days.

41 So ye shall keep this feast unto the Lord seven days in the year, by a perpetual ordinance through your generations: in the seventh month shall you keep it.

42 Ye shall dwell in booths seven days: all that are Israelites born, shall dwell in booths,

43 That your posterity may know that I have made the children of Israel to dwell in ¹booths, when I brought them out of the land of Egypt: I am the Lord your God.

44 So Moses declared unto the children of Israel the feasts of the Lord.

24 *The oil for the lamps.*   5 *The showbread.*   14 *The blasphemer shall be stoned.*   17 *He that killeth shall be killed.*

1 And the Lord spake unto Moses, saying,

2 ¹Command the children of Israel that they bring unto thee pure oil olive beaten, for the light, to cause the lamps to burn continually.

3 Without the veil ¹of the Testimony, in the Tabernacle of the Congregation, shall Aaron dress them, both even and morning before the Lord always: *this shall be* a law forever through your generations.

4 He shall dress the lamps upon the ᵃpure Candlestick before the Lord perpetually.

5 ¶ Also thou shalt take fine flour, and bake twelve ᵇcakes thereof: two ¹tenth deals shall be in one cake.

6 And thou shalt set them in two rows, six in a row upon the pure table before the Lord.

7 Thou shalt also put pure incense upon the rows, that ¹instead of the bread it may be for a remembrance, *and* an offering made by fire unto the Lord.

8 Every Sabbath he shall put them in rows before the Lord evermore, *receiving them* of the children of Israel for an everlasting Covenant.

9 'And the *bread* shall be Aaron's and his sons', and they shall eat it in the holy place: for it is most holy unto him of the offerings of the Lord made by

---

³ Which blowing was to put them in remembrance of the manifold feasts that were in that month, and of the Jubilee.
23:27 ¹ By fasting and prayer.
23:32 ¹ Which containeth a night and a day: yet they took it but for their natural day.
  ² Hebrew, *rest your Sabbath.*
23:36 ¹ Or, a day wherein the people are stayed from all work.
23:37 ¹ Or, peace offering.
23:39 ¹ Or, a solemn feast.

23:40 ¹ Or, of boughs thick with leaves.
23:43 ¹ In the wilderness, forasmuch as they would not credit Joshua and Caleb, when they returned from spying the land of Canaan.
24:2 ¹ Read Exod. 27:20.
24:3 ¹ Which veil separated the holiest of all, where was the Ark of the Testimony from the Sanctuary.
24:5 ¹ That is, two Omers, read Exod. 16:16.
24:7 ¹ For it was burnt every Sabbath, when the bread was taken away.

fire by a perpetual ordinance.

10 ¶ And there went [1]out among the children of Israel the son of an Israelitish woman, whose father was an Egyptian: and this son of the Israelitish woman, and a man of Israel strove together in the host.

11 So the Israelitish woman's son [1]blasphemed the Name *of the Lord*, and cursed, and they brought him unto Moses (his mother's name also was Shelomith, the daughter of Dibri of the tribe of Dan)

12 And they [d]put him in ward, till he told them the mind of the Lord.

13 Then the Lord spake unto Moses, saying,

14 Bring the blasphemer without the host, and let all that heard him, [e]put their hands upon his head, and let all the Congregation stone him.

15 And thou shalt speak unto the children of Israel, saying, Whosoever curseth his God, shall [1]bear his sin.

16 And he that blasphemeth the Name of the Lord, shall be put to death: all the Congregation shall stone him to death: as well the stranger, as he that is born in the land: when he blasphemeth the Name *of the Lord*, let him be slain.

17 ¶ [f]He also that [1]killeth any man, he shall be put to death.

18 And he that killeth a beast, he shall restore it, [1]beast for beast.

19 Also if a man cause *any* blemish in his neighbor: as he hath done, so shall it be done to him:

20 [g]Breach for breach, eye for eye, tooth for tooth: such a blemish as he hath made in any, such shall be repaid to him.

21 And he that killeth a beast, shall restore it: but he that killeth a man, shall be slain.

22 Ye shall have one [h]law: it shall be as well for the stranger as for one born in the country, for I am the Lord your God.

23 ¶ Then [1]Moses told the children of Israel, and they brought the blasphemer out of the host, and stoned him with stones: so the children of Israel did as the Lord had commanded Moses.

25

2 *The Sabbath of the seventh year.*   8 *The Jubilee in the fiftieth year.*   14 *Not to oppress their*

brethren.   23 *The sale and redeeming of lands, houses and persons.*

1 And the Lord spake unto Moses in mount Sinai, saying,

2 Speak unto the children of Israel, and say unto them, When ye shall come into the land which I give you, the [a]land shall [1]keep Sabbath unto the Lord.

3 [1]Six years thou shalt sow thy field, and six years thou shalt cut thy vineyard, and gather the fruit thereof.

4 But the seventh year shall be a Sabbath of rest unto the land: *it shall be* the Lord's Sabbath: thou shalt neither sow thy field nor cut thy vineyard.

5 That which groweth of its [1]own accord of thy harvest, thou shalt not reap, neither gather the grapes that thou hast left [2]unlabored: *for* it shall be a year of rest unto the land.

6 And the [1]rest of the land shall be meat for you, *even* for thee and for thy servant, and for thy maid, and for thy hired servant, and for the stranger that sojourneth with thee:

7 And for thy cattle, and for the beasts that are in thy land, shall all the increase thereof be meat.

8 ¶ Also thou shalt number seven [1]Sabbaths of years unto thee, *even* seven times seven years: and the space of the seven Sabbaths of years will be unto thee nine and forty years.

9 [1]Then thou shalt cause to blow the trumpet of the Jubilee in the tenth *day* of the seventh month: even in the day of the reconciliation shall ye make the trumpet blow throughout all your land.

10 And ye shall hallow that year, *even* the fiftieth year, and proclaim liberty in the land to all the [1]inhabitants thereof: it shall be the Jubilee unto you, and ye shall return every man unto his [2]possession, and every man shall return unto his family.

11 This fiftieth year shall be a year of Jubilee unto you: ye shall not sow, neither reap that which groweth of itself, neither gather *the grapes* thereof that are left unlabored.

12 For it is the Jubilee, it shall be holy unto you: ye shall eat of the increase thereof out of the field.

13 In the year of this Jubilee, ye shall return every man unto his possession.

[d] Num. 25:34
[e] Deut. 13:9
   Deut. 17:7
[f] Exod. 21:12
   Deut. 19:4,11
[g] Exod. 21:24
   Deut. 19:21
   Matt. 5:38
[h] Exod. 12:49

CHAPTER 25
[a] Exod. 23:10

24:10 [1] Meaning, out of his tent.
24:11 [1] By swearing or despiting God.
24:15 [1] Shall be punished.
24:17 [1] Hebrew, *smiteth the soul of any man.*
24:18 [1] Hebrew, *soul for soul.*
24:23 [1] Because the punishment was not yet appointed by the law for the blasphemer, Moses consulted with the Lord, and told the people what God commanded.
25:2 [1] Hebrew, *shall rest a rest.*
25:3 [1] The Jews began the count of this year in September: for then all the fruits were gathered.

25:5 [1] By reason of the corn that fell out of the ears the year past.
   [2] Or, which thou hast separated from thyself, and consecrated to God for the poor.
25:6 [1] That which the land bringeth forth in her rest.
25:8 [1] Or, weeks.
25:9 [1] In the beginning of the 50th year was the Jubilee, so called, because the joyful tidings of liberty [were] publicly proclaimed by the sound of a cornet.
25:10 [1] Which were in bondage.
   [2] Because the tribes should neither have their possessions or families diminished nor confounded.

14 And when thou sellest ought to thy neighbor, or buyest at thy neighbor's hand, ye shall ¹not oppress one another.

15 *But* according to the number of ¹years after the Jubilee, thou shalt buy of thy neighbor: *also* according to the number of the years of the revenues, he shall sell unto thee.

16 According to the multitude of years, thou shalt increase the price thereof, and according to the fewness of years thou shalt abate the price of it: for the number of ¹fruits doth he sell unto thee.

17 Oppress not ye therefore any man his neighbor, but thou shalt fear thy God: for I am the Lord your God.

18 ¶ Wherefore ye shall obey mine ordinances, and keep my laws, and do them, and ye shall dwell in the land ¹in safety.

19 And the land shall give her fruit, and ye shall eat your fill, and dwell therein in safety.

20 And if ye shall say, What shall we eat the seventh year, for we shall not sow, nor gather in our increase?

21 I will ¹send my blessing upon you in the sixth year, and it shall bring forth fruit for three years.

22 And ye shall sow the eighth year, and eat of the old fruit until the ninth year: until the fruit thereof come ye shall eat the old.

23 ¶ Also the land shall not be sold to be ¹cut off *from the family*: for the land is mine, *and* ye be but strangers and sojourners with me.

24 Therefore in all the land of your possession ye shall ¹grant a redemption of the land.

25 ¶ If thy brother be impoverished, and sell his possession, then his redeemer shall come, *even* his near kinsman, and buy out that, which his ¹brother sold.

26 And if he have no redeemer, but ¹hath gotten and found to buy it out,

27 Then shall he ¹count the years of his sale, and restore the overplus to the man, to whom he sold it: so shall he return to his possession.

28 But if he cannot get sufficient to restore to him, then that which is sold, shall remain in the hand of him that hath bought it, until the year of the Jubilee: and in the Jubilee it shall come ¹out, and he shall return unto his possession.

b Exod. 22:25
Deut. 23:19
Prov. 28:8
Ezek. 18:8
Ezek. 22:12

c Exod. 21:2
Deut. 15:12
Jer. 34:14

29 Likewise if a man sell a dwelling house in a walled city, he may buy it out again within a whole year after it is sold: within a year may he buy it out.

30 But if it be not bought out within the space of a full year, then the house that is in the walled city, shall be stablished, ¹as cut off *from the family*, to him that bought it, throughout his generations: it shall not go out in the Jubilee.

31 But the houses of villages which have no walls round about them, shall be esteemed as the field of the country: they may be bought out again, and shall ¹go out in the Jubilee.

32 Notwithstanding, the cities of the Levites, *and* the houses of the cities of their possession, may the Levites redeem ¹at all seasons.

33 And if a man purchase of the Levites, the house that was sold, and the city of their possession shall go out in the Jubilee: for the houses of the cities of the Levites are their possession among the children of Israel.

34 But the field of the ¹suburbs of their cities shall not be sold: for it is their perpetual possession.

35 ¶ Moreover, if thy brother be impoverished, and ¹fallen in decay with thee, thou shalt relieve him, and *as* a stranger and sojourner, so shall he live with thee.

36 *b*Thou shalt take no usury of him, nor vantage, but thou shalt fear thy God, that thy brother may live with thee.

37 Thou shalt not give him thy money to usury, nor lend him thy vittles for increase.

38 I am the Lord your God, which have brought you out of the land of Egypt, to give you the land of Canaan, *and* to be your God.

39 ¶ *c*If thy brother also *that dwelleth* by thee be impoverished, and be sold unto thee, thou shalt not compel him to serve as a bond servant,

40 *But* as an hired servant, and as a sojourner he shall be with thee: he shall serve thee unto the year of Jubilee.

41 Then shall he depart from thee, *both* he and his children with him, and shall return unto his family, and unto the possession of his fathers shall he return:

42 For they are my servants, whom I brought

25:14 ¹ By deceit, or otherwise.
25:15 ¹ If the Jubilee to come be near, thou shalt sell better cheap: if it be far off, dearer.
25:16 ¹ And not the full possession of the land.
25:18 ¹ Or, boldly without fear.
25:21 ¹ Hebrew, *I will command.*
25:23 ¹ It could not be sold forever, but must return to the family in the Jubilee.
25:24 ¹ Ye shall sell it on condition that it may be redeemed.
25:25 ¹ Or, kinsman.

25:26 ¹ Hebrew, *his hand hath gotten.*
25:27 ¹ Abating the money of the years past, and paying for the rest of the years to come.
25:28 ¹ From his hand that bought it.
25:30 ¹ That is, forever, read verse 23.
25:31 ¹ Or, return.
25:32 ¹ Hebrew, *forever.*
25:34 ¹ Where the Levites kept their cattle.
25:35 ¹ In Hebrew it is, *if his hand shake*: meaning, if he stretch forth his hand for help as one in misery.

out of the land of Egypt: they shall not [1]be sold as bondmen are sold.

43 [d]Thou shalt not rule over him cruelly, but shalt fear thy God.

44 Thy bond servant also, and thy bondmaid, which thou shalt have, *shall be* of the heathen that are round about you: of them shall ye buy servants and maids.

45 And moreover, of the children of the strangers that are sojourners among you, of them shall ye buy, and of their families that are with you which they begat in your land: these shall be your [1]possession.

46 So ye shall take them, as inheritance for your children after you to possess them by inheritance, ye shall use their labors forever: but over your brethren the children of Israel ye shall not rule one over another with cruelty.

47 ¶ If a sojourner or a stranger *dwelling* by thee [1]get *riches*, and thy brother by him be impoverished, and sell himself unto the stranger or sojourner *dwelling* by thee, or to the stock of the stranger's family,

48 After that he is sold, he may be bought out: one of his brethren may buy him out:

49 Or his uncle, or his uncle's son may buy him out, or *any* of the kindred of his flesh among his family, may redeem him: either if he can [1]get *so much*, he may buy himself out.

50 Then he shall reckon with his buyer from the year that he was sold to him, unto the year of Jubilee: and the money of his sale shall be according to the number of [1]years: according to the time of an hired servant shall he be with him.

51 If there be many years behind, according to them shall he give again for his deliverance, of the money that he was bought for.

52 If there remain but few years unto the year of Jubilee, then he shall count with him, and according to his years give again for his redemption.

53 He shall be with him year by year as an hired servant: he shall not rule cruelly over him in thy [1]sight.

54 And if he be not redeemed thus, he shall go out in the year of Jubilee, he, and his children with him.

55 For unto me the children of Israel *are* servants, they are my servants whom I have brought out of the land of Egypt: I am the Lord your God.

Cross-references
- *d* Eph. 6:9
  Col. 4:1

CHAPTER 26
- *a* Exod. 20:4
  Deut. 5:8
  Ps. 97:7
- *b* Lev. 19:30
- *c* Deut. 28:1
- *d* Job 11:19
- *e* Josh. 23:19
- *f* Ezek. 37:16
  2 Cor. 6:16
- *g* Deut. 28:15
  Lam. 2:17
  Mal. 2:2

26

1 *Idolatry forbidden.* 3 *A blessing to them that keep the commandments.* 14 *The curse to them that break them.* 42 *God promiseth to remember his covenant.*

1 Ye shall make you none idols nor graven image, neither rear you up any [a]pillar, neither shall ye set [1]any image of stone in your land to bow down to it: for I am the Lord your God.

2 Ye shall keep my Sabbaths, and [b]reverence my Sanctuary: I am the Lord.

3 ¶ [c]If ye walk in mine ordinances, and keep my commandments, and do them,

4 I will then send you [1]rain in due season, and the land shall yield her increase, and the trees of the field shall give their fruit.

5 And your threshing shall reach unto the vintage, and the vintage shall reach unto sowing time, and you shall eat your bread in plenteousness, and dwell in your land safely.

6 And I will send peace in the land, and ye shall sleep, and none [d]shall make you afraid: also I [1]will rid evil beasts out of the land, and the [2]sword shall not go through your land.

7 Also ye shall chase your enemies, and they shall fall before you upon the sword.

8 [e]And five of you shall chase an hundred, and an hundred of you shall put ten thousand to flight, and your enemies shall fall before you upon the sword.

9 For [1]I will have respect unto you, and make you increase, and multiply you, and [2]stablish my covenant with you.

10 Ye shall eat also old store, and carry out old because of the new.

11 [f]And I will set my [1]Tabernacle among you, and my soul shall not loathe you.

12 Also I will walk among you, and I will be your God, and ye shall be my people.

13 I am the Lord your God which have brought you out of the land of Egypt, that ye should not be their bondmen, and I have broken the [1]bonds of your yoke, and made you go upright.

14 ¶ [g]But if ye will not obey me, nor do all these commandments,

15 And if ye shall despise mine ordinances, either if your soul abhor my laws, so that ye will not do all my Commandments, but break my [1]Covenant,

16 Then will I also do this unto you, I will appoint

25:42 [1] Unto perpetual servitude.

25:45 [1] For they shall not be bought out at the Jubilee.

25:47 [1] Hebrew, *his hand take hold.*

25:49 [1] If he be able.

25:50 [1] Which remain yet to the Jubilee.

25:53 [1] Thou shalt not suffer him to entreat him rigorously, if thou know it.

26:1 [1] Or, stone having any imagery.

26:4 [1] By promising abundance of earthly things, he stirreth the mind to consider the rich treasures of the spiritual blessings.

26:6 [1] Hebrew, *will cause the evil beast to cease.*

 [2] Ye shall have no war.

26:9 [1] Hebrew, *I will turn unto you.*

 [2] Perform that which I have promised.

26:11 [1] I will be daily present with you.

26:13 [1] I have set you at full liberty, whereas before ye were as beasts tied in bands.

26:15 [1] Which I made with you in choosing you to be my people.

over you ¹fearfulness, a consumption, and the burning ague to consume the eyes, and make the heart heavy, and you shall sow your seed in vain: for your enemies shall eat it:

17 And I will set ¹my face against you, and ye shall fall before your enemies, and they that hate you, shall reign over you, ᵇand ye shall flee when none pursueth you.

18 And if ye will not for these *things* obey me, then will I punish you ¹seven times more, according to your sins,

19 And I will break the pride of your power, and I will make your heaven as ¹iron, and your earth as brass:

20 And your ¹strength shall be spent in vain: neither shall your land give her increase, neither shall the trees of the land give their fruit.

21 ¶ And if ye walk ¹stubbornly against me, and will not obey me, I will then bring seven times more plagues upon you, according to your sins.

22 I will also send wild beasts upon you, which shall ¹spoil you, and destroy your cattle, and make you few in number: so your ²highways shall be desolate.

23 Yet if by these ye will not be reformed by me, but walk stubbornly against me,

24 Then will I also walk ¹stubbornly against you, and I will smite you yet seven times for your sins:

25 And I will send a sword upon you, that shall avenge the quarrel of my Covenant: and when ye are gathered in your cities, I will send the pestilence among you, and ye shall be delivered into the hand of the enemy.

26 When I shall break the ¹staff of your bread, then ten women shall bake your bread in one ²oven, and they shall deliver your bread again by weight, and ye shall eat, but not be satisfied.

27 Yet if ye will not for this obey me, but walk against me stubbornly,

28 Then will I walk stubbornly in *mine* anger against you, and I will also chastise you seven times *more* according to your sins.

29 ʲAnd ye shall eat the flesh of your sons, and the flesh of your daughters shall ye devour.

30 I will also destroy your high places, and ᵏcut away your images, and cast your carcasses upon the

ᵇ Prov. 28:1
ⁱ 2 Sam. 22:37
   Ps. 8:16
ʲ Deut. 28:35
ᵏ 2 Chron. 34:7
ˡ Lev. 25:2

¹bodies of your idols, and my soul shall abhor you.

31 And I will make your cities desolate, and bring your Sanctuary unto naught, and ¹will not smell the savor of your sweet odors.

32 I will also bring the land unto a wilderness, and your enemies which dwell therein, shall be astonished thereat.

33 Also I will scatter you among the heathen, and ¹will draw out a sword after you, and your land shall be waste, and your cities shall be desolate.

34 Then shall the land enjoy her ˡSabbaths, as long as it lieth void, and ye shall be in your enemies' land: then shall the land rest, and enjoy her Sabbaths.

35 All the days that it lieth void, it shall rest, because it did not rest in your ¹Sabbaths, when ye dwelt upon it.

36 And upon them that are left of you, I will send even a ¹faintness into their hearts in the land of your enemies, and the sound of a leaf shaken shall chase them, and they shall ²flee as fleeing from a sword, and they shall fall, no man pursuing them.

37 They shall fall also one upon another, as before a sword, though none pursue them, and ye shall not be able to stand before your enemies:

38 And ye shall perish among the heathen, and the land of your enemies shall eat you up.

39 And they that are left of you, shall pine away for their iniquity, in your enemies' lands, and for the iniquities of their fathers shall they pine away with ¹them also.

40 Then they shall confess their iniquity, and the wickedness of their fathers for their trespass, which they have trespassed against me, and also because they have walked stubbornly against me.

41 Therefore I will walk stubbornly against them, and bring them into the land of their enemies: so then their uncircumcised hearts shall be humbled, and then they shall ¹willingly bear *the punishment of* their iniquity.

42 Then I will remember my Covenant with Jacob, and my Covenant also with Isaac, and also my Covenant with Abraham will I remember, and will remember the land.

43 ¹The land also *in the mean season* shall be left

26:16 ¹ Or, an hasty plague.
26:17 ¹ Read Lev.17:10.
26:18 ¹ That is, more extremely.
26:19 ¹ Ye shall have drought and barrenness, Hag. 1:10.
26:20 ¹ Or, labor.
26:21 ¹ Or as some read, by fortune, imputing my plagues to chance and fortune.
26:22 ¹ Of your children, 2 Kings 17:25.
    ² Because none dare pass thereby for fear of beasts.
26:26 ¹ That is, the strength, whereby the life is sustained, Ezek. 4:16 and 5:16.
² One oven shall be sufficient for ten families.
26:30 ¹ Or, carrions.
26:31 ¹ I will not accept your sacrifices.
26:33 ¹ Signifying that no enemy can come without God's sending.
26:35 ¹ Which I commanded you to keep.
26:36 ¹ Or, cowardness.
    ² As if their enemies did chase them.
26:39 ¹ Forasmuch as they are culpable of their fathers' faults, they shall be punished as well as their fathers.
26:41 ¹ Or, pray for their sin.
26:43 ¹ While they are captives, and without repentance.

of them, and shall enjoy her Sabbaths while she lieth waste without them, but they shall willingly suffer *the punishment of* their iniquity, because they despised my Laws, and because their soul abhorred mine ordinances.

44 Yet notwithstanding this, when they shall be in the land of their enemies, ᵐI will not cast them away, neither will I abhor them, to destroy them utterly, *nor* to break my Covenant with them: for I am the Lord their God:

45 But I will remember for them the ¹Covenant of old, when I brought them out of the land of Egypt in the sight of the heathen, that I might be their God: I am the Lord.

46 These are the Ordinances, and the Judgments, and the Laws, which the Lord made between him, and the children of Israel, in mount ¹Sinai by the hand of Moses.

27 *2 Of divers vows, and the redemption of the same. 28 A thing separate from the use of man, cannot be sold nor redeemed, but remained to the Lord.*

1 Moreover, the Lord spake unto Moses, saying,

2 Speak unto the children of Israel, and say unto them, If any man shall make a vow of ¹a person unto the Lord, by ²thy estimation,

3 Then thy estimation shall be *thus*: a male from twenty years old unto sixty years old shall be by thy estimation even fifty ¹shekels of silver, after the shekel of the Sanctuary.

4 But if it be a female, then thy valuation shall be thirty shekels.

5 And from five years old to twenty years old, thy valuation shall be for the male twenty shekels, and for the female ten shekels.

6 But from a ¹month old unto five years old, thy price of the male shall be five shekels of silver, and thy price of the female, three shekels of silver.

7 And from sixty years old and above, if *he be* a male, then thy price shall be fifteen shekels, and for the female ten shekels.

8 But if he be poorer ¹than thou hast esteemed *him*, then shall he present himself before the Priest, and the Priest shall value him, according to the ability of him that vowed, *so* shall the Priest value him.

9 And if *it be* a ¹beast, whereof men bring an offering unto the Lord, all that one giveth of such unto the Lord, shall be holy.

10 He shall not alter it nor change it, a good for a bad, nor a bad for a good: and if he change beast for beast, then *both* this and that, which was changed for it, shall be ¹holy.

11 And if *it be* any unclean beast, of which men do not offer a sacrifice unto the Lord, he shall then present the beast before the Priest.

12 And the Priest shall value it, whether it be good or bad: *and* as thou valuest it, *which art* the Priest, so shall it be.

13 But if he will buy it again, then he shall give the fifth part of it more above thy valuation.

14 ¶ Also when a man shall dedicate his house to be holy unto the Lord, then the Priest shall value it, whether it be good or bad, *and* as the Priest shall price it, ¹so shall the value be.

15 But if he that sanctified it, will redeem his house, then he shall give thereto the fifth part of money more than thy estimation, and it shall be his.

16 If also a man dedicate to the Lord any ground of his inheritance, then shalt thou esteem it according to the ¹seed thereof, an ²Homer of barley seed *shall be* at fifty shekels of silver.

17 If he dedicate his field *immediately* from the year of Jubilee, it shall be worth as thou dost esteem it.

18 But if he dedicate his field after the Jubilee, then the Priest shall reckon him the money according to the years that remain unto the year of Jubilee, and it shall be abated by thy estimation.

19 And if he that dedicateth it, will redeem the field, then he shall put the fifth part of the price, that thou esteemedst it at, thereunto, and it shall remain his.

20 And if he will not redeem the field, but *the* Priest ¹sell the field to another man, it shall be redeemed no more.

21 But the field shall be holy to the Lord, when it goeth out in the Jubilee, as a field ¹separate from common uses: the possession thereof shall be the Priest's.

22 If a man also dedicate unto the Lord a field which he hath bought, which is not of the ground of his inheritance,

23 Then the Priest shall set the price to him, as ᵃthou esteemest it, unto the year of Jubilee, and he shall give ¹thy price the same day, *as a thing* holy unto

---

ᵐ Deut. 4:31
Rom. 11:26

CHAPTER 27
ᵈ Lev. 27:11

26:45 ¹ Made to their forefathers.
26:46 ¹ Fifty days after they came out of Egypt.
27:2 ¹ As of his son or his daughter.
     ² Which art the Priest.
27:3 ¹ Read the value of the Shekel, Exod. 30:13.
27:6 ¹ He speaketh of those vows whereby the fathers dedicated their children to God which were not of such force; but they might be redeemed from them.
27:8 ¹ If he be not able to pay after thy valuation.
27:9 ¹ Which is clean, Lev. 11:2.

27:10 ¹ That is, consecrated to the Lord.
27:14 ¹ Hebrew, *so shall it stand.*
27:16 ¹ Valuing the price thereof according to the seed that is sown, or by the seed that it doth yield.
     ² Homer is a measure containing ten Ephahs, read of Ephah, Exod. 16:16, 36.
27:20 ¹ For their own necessity or godly uses.
27:21 ¹ That is, which dedicate to the Lord with a curse to him that doth turn it to his private use, Num. 21:2; Deut. 13:15; Josh. 9:17.
27:23 ¹ The Priest's valuation.

the Lord.

24 *But* in the year of Jubilee, the field shall return unto him, of whom it was bought: to him *I say*, whose inheritance the land was.

25 And all the valuation shall be according to the shekel of *b*the Sanctuary: a shekel containeth twenty gerahs.

26 ¶ *c*Notwithstanding the firstborn of the beasts, because it is the Lord's firstborn, none shall dedicate such, be it bullock, or sheep: *For* it is the [1]Lord's.

27 But if it be an unclean beast, then he shall redeem it by thy valuation, and give the fifth part more thereto: and if it be not redeemed, then it shall be sold, according to thy estimation.

28 *d*Notwithstanding, nothing separate from the common use that a man doth separate unto the Lord of all that he hath (whether it be man or beast, or land of his inheritance) may be sold nor redeemed: *for* everything separate from the common use is most

b Exod. 30:13
Num. 3:47
Ezek. 45:12

c Exod. 13:2
Exod. 22:19
Num. 3:23

d Josh. 6:19

holy unto the Lord.

29 Nothing separate from the common use, which shall be separate from man, shall be redeemed, *but* [1]die the death.

30 Also all the tithe of the land *both* of the seed of the ground, *and* of the fruit of the trees is the Lord's: *it is* holy to the Lord.

31 But if a man will redeem *any* of his tithe, he shall add the [1]fifth part thereto.

32 And every tithe of bullock, and of sheep, *and* of all that goeth under the [1]rod, the tenth shall be holy unto the Lord.

33 He shall not look if it be good or bad, neither shall he change it: else if he change it, both it, and that it was changed withal, shall be holy, *and* it shall not be redeemed.

34 These are the Commandments which the Lord commanded by Moses unto the children of Israel in Mount Sinai.

27:26 [1] It was the Lord's already.
27:29 [1] It shall remain without redemption.
27:31 [1] Besides the value of the thing itself.

27:32 [1] All that which is numbered: that is, every tenth as he falleth by tally without exception or respect.

THE FOURTH BOOK OF MOSES,

CALLED

¹NUMBERS

1 *2 Moses and Aaron with the twelve princes of the tribes are commanded of the Lord to number them that are able to go to war. 49 The Levites are exempted for the service of the Lord.*

CHAPTER 1
ᵃ Exod. 30:12

1 The Lord spake again unto Moses in the wilderness of ¹Sinai, in the Tabernacle of the Congregation, in the first *day* of the ²second month, in the second year after they were come out of the land of Egypt, saying,

2 ᵃTake ye the sum of all the Congregation of the children of Israel, after their families *and* households of their fathers, with the number of their names: *to wit*, all the males, ¹man by man:

3 From twenty years old and above, all that go forth to the war in Israel: thou and Aaron shall number them throughout their armies.

4 And with you shall be ¹men of every tribe, such *as are* the heads of the house of their fathers.

5 And these are the names of the men that shall ¹stand with you, of *the tribe of* Reuben, Elizur, the son of Shedeur:

6 Of Simeon, Shelumiel the son of Zurishaddai:

7 Of Judah, Nahshon the son of Amminadab:

8 Of Issachar, Nethanel the son of Zuar:

9 Of Zebulun, Eliab, the son of Helon:

10 Of the children of Joseph: of Ephraim, Elishama the son of Ammihud: of Manasseh, Gamaliel, the son of Pedahzur:

11 Of Benjamin, Abidan the son of Gideoni:

12 Of Dan, Ahiezer, the son of Ammishaddai:

13 Of Asher, Pagiel, the son of Ocran:

14 Of Gad, Eliasaph the son of Deuel:

15 Of Naphtali, Ahira the son of Enan.

16 These *were* famous in the Congregation, ¹princes of the tribes of their fathers, *and* heads over thousands in Israel.

17 ¶ Then Moses and Aaron took these men which are expressed by *their* names.

18 And they called all the Congregation together in the first *day* of the second month, who declared ¹their kindred by their families, *and* by the houses of their fathers according to the number of *their* names, from twenty years old and above, man by man.

19 As the Lord had commanded Moses, so he numbered them in the wilderness of Sinai.

20 So were the sons of ¹Reuben Israel's eldest son by their generations, by their families, *and* by the houses of their fathers according to the number of *their* names, man by man, every male from twenty years old and above, as many as ²went forth to war:

21 The number of them, *I say*, of the tribe of Reuben, *was* six and forty thousand, and five hundred.

22 Of the sons of Simeon by their generations, by their families, *and* by the houses of their fathers, the sum thereof by the number of *their* names, man by man, every male from twenty years old, and above, all that went forth to war:

23 The sum of them, *I say*, of the tribe of Simeon *was* nine and fifty thousand and three hundred.

24 ¶ Of the sons of Gad by their generations, by their families, *and* by the houses of their fathers, according to the number of *their* names, from twenty years old and above, all that went forth to war:

25 The number of them, *I say*, of the tribe of Gad *was* five and forty thousand, and six hundred and fifty.

26 ¶ Of the sons of Judah by their generations, by their families, *and* by the houses of their fathers, according to the number of *their* names, from twenty years old and above, all that went forth to war:

27 The number of them, *I say*, of the tribe of Judah, *was* three score and fourteen thousand, and six hundred.

28 ¶ Of the sons of Issachar by their generations, by their families, *and* by the houses of their fathers, according to the number of *their* names, from twenty

---

Title ¹ So called because of the diversity and multitude of numberings which are here chiefly contained, both of men's names and places.
1:1 ¹ In that place of the wilderness that was near to mount Sinai.
  ² Which contained part of April, and part of May.
1:2 ¹ Hebrew, *by their heads.*

1:4 ¹ That is, the chiefest man of every tribe.
1:5 ¹ And assist you when ye number the people.
1:16 ¹ Or captains, and governors.
1:18 ¹ In showing every man his tribe, and his ancestors.
1:20 ¹ These are the names of the twelve tribes, as first of Reuben.
  ² Or, as were able to bear weapons.

years old and above, all that went forth to war:

29 The number of them *also* of the tribe of Issachar *was* four and fifty thousand, and four hundred.

30 ¶ Of the sons of Zebulun by their generations, by their families, *and* by the houses of their fathers, according to the number of *their* names, from twenty years old and above: all that went forth to war:

31 The number of them *also* of the tribe of Zebulun *was* seven and fifty thousand and four hundred.

32 ¶ Of the sons of Joseph, *namely* of the sons of Ephraim by their generations, by their families, *and* by the houses of their fathers, according to the number of *their* names, from twenty years old and above, all that went forth to war:

33 The number of them *also* of the tribe of Ephraim *was* forty thousand and five hundred.

34 ¶ Of the sons of Manasseh by their generations, by their families *and* by the houses of their fathers, according to the number of *their* names, from twenty years old and above, all that went forth to war:

35 The number of them *also* of the tribe of Manasseh *was* two and thirty thousand and two hundred.

36 Of the sons of Benjamin by their generations, by their families, *and* by the houses of their fathers, according to the number of *their* names, from twenty years old and above, all that went forth to war:

37 The number of them *also* of the tribe of Benjamin *was* five and thirty thousand and four hundred.

38 Of the sons of Dan by their generations, by their families, *and* by the houses of their fathers, according to the number of *their* names, from twenty years old and above, all that went forth to war:

39 The number of them *also* of the tribe of Dan *was* three score and two thousand, and seven hundred.

40 ¶ Of the sons of Asher by their generations, by their families, *and* by the houses of their fathers, according to the number of *their* names, from twenty years old and above, all that went forth to war:

41 The number of them *also* of the tribe of Asher *was* one and forty thousand and five hundred.

42 ¶ Of the children of Naphtali, by their generations, by their families, *and* by the houses of their fathers, according to the number of *their* names, from twenty years old and above, all that went to the war:

43 The number of them *also* of the tribe of Naphtali *was* three and fifty thousand, and four hundred.

44 These are the [1]sums which Moses, and Aaron numbered, and the Princes of Israel, the twelve men *which* were every one for the house of their fathers.

45 So *this* was all the sum of the sons of Israel, by the houses of their fathers, from twenty years old and above, all that went to the war in Israel.

46 And all they were in number six hundred and three thousand five hundred and fifty.

47 But the Levites, after the tribes of their fathers were not numbered among [1]them.

48 For the Lord had spoken unto Moses, and said,

49 Only thou shalt not number the tribe of Levi, neither take the sum of them among the children of Israel.

50 But thou shalt appoint the Levites over the Tabernacle of the Testimony, and over all the instruments thereof, and over all things that belong to it: they shall bear the Tabernacle, and all the instruments thereof, and shall minister in it, and shall [1]dwell round about the Tabernacle.

51 And when the Tabernacle goeth forth, the Levites shall take it down: and when the Tabernacle is to be pitched, the Levites shall set it up: for the [1]stranger that cometh near, shall be slain.

52 Also the children of Israel shall pitch their tents every man in his camp, and every man under his standard throughout their armies.

53 But the Levites shall pitch round about the Tabernacle of the Testimony, lest vengeance [1]come upon the Congregation of the children of Israel, and the Levites shall take the charge of the Tabernacle of the Testimony.

54 So the children of Israel did according to all that the Lord had commanded Moses: so did they.

2 *2 The order of the tents, and the names of the Captains of the Israelites.*

1 And the Lord spake unto Moses, and to Aaron, saying,

2 [1]Every man of the children of Israel shall camp by his standard, *and* under the ensign of their father's house: far off, about the Tabernacle of the Congregation shall they pitch.

3 On the East side toward the rising of the sun, shall they of the standard of the host of Judah pitch according to their armies: and Nahshon the son of Amminadab *shall be* [1]captain of the sons of Judah.

4 And his host and the number of them *were* seventy and four thousand and six hundred.

1:44 [1] Or, full count.
1:47 [1] Which were warriors, but were appointed to the use of the Tabernacle.
1:50 [1] Hebrew, *camp.*
1:51 [1] Whosoever is not of the tribe of Levi.

1:53 [1] By not having due regard to the Tabernacle of the Lord.
2:2 [1] In the twelve tribes were four principle standards, so that every three tribes had their standard.
2:3 [1] Or, prince.

5 Next unto him shall they of the tribe [1]of Issachar pitch, and Nethanel the son of Zuar *shall be* the captain of the sons of Issachar:

6 And his host and the number thereof *were* four and fifty thousand, and four hundred.

7 *Then* the tribe of Zebulun, and Eliab the son of Helon captain over the sons of Zebulun:

8 And his host and the number thereof seven and fifty thousand and four hundred:

9 The whole number of the [1]host of Judah *are* an hundred fourscore and six thousand, and four hundred according to their armies: they shall first set forth.

10 ¶ On the South side *shall be* the standard of the host [1]of Reuben according to their armies: and the captain over the sons of Reuben *shall be* Elizur the son of Shedeur.

11 And his host and the number thereof, six and forty thousand and five hundred.

12 And by him shall the tribe of Simeon pitch, and the captain over the sons of Simeon *shall be* Shelumiel the son of Zurishaddai:

13 And his host, and the number of them, nine and fifty thousand and three hundred.

14 And the tribe of Gad, and the captain over the sons of Gad *shall be* Eliasaph the son of [1]Deuel:

15 And his host and the number of them *were* five and forty thousand, six hundred and fifty.

16 All the number of the camp of Reuben *were* an hundred and one and fifty thousand, and four hundred and fifty according to their armies, and they shall set forth in the second place.

17 ¶ Then the Tabernacle of the Congregation shall go *with* the host of the Levites, in the [1]midst of the camp as they have pitched, so shall they go forward, every man in his order, according to their standards.

18 ¶ [1]The standard of the camp of Ephraim *shall be* toward the West according to their armies: and the captain over the sons of Ephraim *shall be* Elishama the son of Ammihud:

19 And his host and the number of them *were* forty thousand and five hundred.

20 And by him *shall be* the tribe of Manasseh and the captain over the sons of Manasseh, *shall be* Gamaliel the son of Pedahzur:

21 And his host and the number of them *were* two and thirty thousand and two hundred.

22 And the tribe of Benjamin, and the captain over the sons of Benjamin *shall be* Abidan, the son of Gideoni:

23 And his host, and the number of them *were* five and thirty thousand and four hundred.

24 All the number of the camp of Ephraim *were* an hundred and eight thousand and one hundred according to their armies, and they shall go in the third place.

25 ¶ The standard of the host of [1]Dan *shall be* toward the North according to their armies: and the captain over the children of Dan *shall be* Ahiezer the son of Ammishaddai:

26 And his host and the number of them *were* two and threescore thousand and seven hundred.

27 And by him shall the tribe of Asher pitch, and the captain over the sons of Asher *shall be* Pagiel the son of Ocran.

28 And his host and the number of them *were* one and forty thousand, and five hundred.

29 ¶ Then the tribe of Naphtali, and the captain over the children of Naphtali *shall be* Ahira the son of Enan:

30 And his host and the number of them *were* three and fifty thousand and four hundred.

31 All the number of the host of Dan *was* an hundred and seven and fifty thousand and six hundred: they shall go hindmost with their standards.

32 ¶ These are the [1]sums of the children of Israel by the houses of their fathers, all the number of the host, according to their armies, six hundred and three thousand, five hundred and fifty.

33 But the Levites were not numbered among the children of Israel, as the Lord had commanded Moses.

34 And the children of Israel did according to all that the Lord had commanded Moses: so they pitched according to their [1]standards, and so they journeyed every one with his families, according to the houses of their fathers.

3 6 *The charge and office of the Levites.* 12, 35 *Why the Lord separated the Levites for himself.* 16 *Their number, families, and captains.* 40 *The firstborn of Israel is redeemed by the Levites.* 47 *The overplus is redeemed by money.*

1 These also were the [1]generations of Aaron and

2:5 [1] Judah, Issachar, and Zebulun the sons of Leah were of the first standard.

2:9 [1] Of them which were contained under that name.

2:10 [1] Reuben and Simeon, the sons of Leah, and Gad the son of Zilpah her maid, were of the second standard.

2:14 [1] Or, Reuel.

2:17 [1] Because it might be in equal distance from each one, and all indifferently have recourse thereunto.

2:18 [1] Because Ephraim and Manasseh supplied the place of Joseph

their father, they are taken to be Rachel's children, so they and Benjamin make the third standard.

2:25 [1] Dan and Naphtali the sons of Bilhah Rachel's maid with Asher the son of Zilpah make the fourth standard.

2:32 [1] Which were of twenty years and above.

2:34 [1] For under every one of the four principal standards were divers signs to keep every band.

3:1 [1] Or, families and kindreds.

Moses, in the day that the Lord spake with Moses in mount Sinai.

2 So these are the names of the sons of Aaron, [a]Nadab the firstborn, and Abihu, Eleazar, and Ithamar.

3 These are the names of the sons of Aaron the anointed Priests, whom *Moses* did [b]consecrate to minister in the Priest's office.

4 [c]And Nadab and Abihu died [1]before the Lord, when they offered [d]strange fire before the Lord in the wilderness of Sinai, and had no children: but Eleazar and Ithamar served in the Priest's office in the [2]sight of Aaron their father.

5 Then the Lord spake unto Moses, saying,

6 Bring the tribe of Levi, and [1]set them before Aaron the Priest that they may serve him,

7 And take the charge with him, even the charge of the whole Congregation, [1]before the Tabernacle of the Congregation to do the service of the Tabernacle.

8 They shall also keep all the instruments of the Tabernacle of the Congregation, and *have* the charge of the children of Israel to do the service of the Tabernacle.

9 And thou shalt give the Levites unto Aaron and to his [1]sons: *for* they are given him freely from among the children of Israel.

10 And thou shalt appoint Aaron and his sons to execute their Priest's office: and the [1]stranger that cometh near, shall be slain.

11 ¶ Also the Lord spake unto Moses, saying,

12 Behold, I have even taken the Levites from among the children of Israel: for all the firstborn that openeth the matrice among the children of Israel, and the Levites shall be mine,

13 Because all the firstborn are mine: for the same day, that I smote all the firstborn in the land of Egypt, [e]I sanctified unto me all the firstborn in Israel, both man and beast: mine they shall be: I am the Lord.

14 ¶ Moreover, the Lord spake unto Moses in the wilderness of Sinai, saying,

15 Number the children of Levi after the houses of their fathers, in their families: every male from a month old and above shalt thou number.

16 Then Moses numbered them according to the word of the Lord, as he was commanded.

17 And these were the sons of Levi by their names,

CHAPTER 3
[a] Exod. 6:23
[b] Exod. 28:3
[c] Lev. 10:1,2
Num. 26:61
1 Chron. 24:2
[d] Lev. 10:1,2
[e] Exod. 13:1
Exod. 34:19
Lev. 27:26
Num. 8:16
Luke 2:23
[f] Gen. 46:11
Exod. 6:66
Num. 26:57
1 Chron. 6:1
1 Chron. 23:6

[f]Gershon, and Kohath, and Merari.

18 Also these were the names of the sons of Gershon by their families: Libni and Shimei.

19 The sons also of Kohath by their families: Amram and Izehar, Hebron, and Uzziel.

20 And the sons of Merari by their families: Mahli and Mushi. These are the families of Levi, according to the houses of their fathers.

21 Of Gershon *came* the family of the Libnites and the family of the Shimites: these are the families of the Gershonites.

22 The sum whereof ([1]after the number of all the males from a month old and above) was counted seven thousand and five hundred.

23 ¶ The families of the Gershonites shall pitch behind the Tabernacle Westward.

24 The captain and [1]ancient of the house of the Gershonites *shall be* Eliasaph the son of Lael.

25 And the charge of the sons of Gershon in the Tabernacle of the Congregation, *shall be* the [1]Tabernacle, and the pavilion, the covering thereof, and the veil of the door of the Tabernacle of the Congregation,

26 And the hanging of the court, and the veil of the door of the court which is near the Tabernacle, and near the Altar round about, and the cords of it for all the service thereof.

27 And of Kohath *came* the family of the Amramites, and the family of the Izharites, and the family of the Hebronites, and the family of the Uzzielites: these are the families of the Kohathites.

28 The number of all the males from a month old and above, *was* eight thousand and six hundred, having the [1]charge of the Sanctuary.

29 The families of the sons of Kohath shall pitch on the South side of the Tabernacle.

30 The captain and ancient of the house *and* families of the Kohathites *shall be* Elizaphan the son of Uzziel:

31 And their charge *shall be* the [1]Ark, and the Table, and the Candlestick, and the altars, and the instruments of the Sanctuary that they minister with, and the veil, and all that serveth thereto.

32 And Eleazar the son of Aaron the Priest *shall be* [1]chief captain of the Levites, *having* the oversight of them that have the charge of the Sanctuary.

33 ¶ Of Merari *came* the family of the Mahlites,

3:4 [1] Or, before the Altar.
[2] Whiles their father lived.
3:6 [1] Offer them unto Aaron for the use of the Tabernacle.
3:7 [1] Which appertained to the executing of the high Priest's commandment, to the oversight of the people, and the service of the Tabernacle.
3:9 [1] Aaron's sons the Priests served in the Sanctuary in praying for the people and offering sacrifice: the Levites served for the inferior uses of the same.
3:10 [1] Any that would minister not being a Levite.
3:22 [1] Only numbering the male children.
3:24 [1] Or, father.
3:25 [1] Their charge was to carry the covering and hangings of the Tabernacle.
3:28 [1] Doing every one his duty in the Sanctuary.
3:31 [1] The chief things within the Sanctuary were committed to the Kohathites.
3:32 [1] Or, prince of princes.

and the family of the Mushites: these are the families of Merari.

34 And the sum of them, according to the number of all the males, from a month old and above *was* six thousand and two hundred.

35 The captain and the ancient of the house of the families of Merari *shall be* Zuriel the son of Abihail: they shall pitch on the Northside of the Tabernacle.

36 And in the charge and custody of the sons of Merari *shall be* [1]the boards of the Tabernacle, and the bars thereof, and his pillars, and his sockets, and all the instruments thereof, and all that serveth thereto,

37 With the pillars of the court round about, with their sockets, and their pins and their cords.

38 ¶ Also on the forefront of the Tabernacle toward the East, before the Tabernacle *I say,* of the Congregation Eastward shall Moses and Aaron and his sons pitch, having the charge of the Sanctuary, [1]and the charge of the children of Israel: but the stranger that cometh near shall be slain.

39 The whole sum of the Levites, which Moses and Aaron numbered at the commandment of the Lord throughout their families, *even* all the males from a month old and above, *was* two and twenty [1]thousand.

40 ¶ And the Lord said unto Moses, Number all the firstborn that are males among the children of Israel from a month old and above, and take the number of their names.

41 And thou shalt take the Levites to me [1]for all the firstborn of the children of Israel (I *am* the Lord) and the cattle of the Levites for all the firstborn of the cattle of the children of Israel.

42 And Moses numbered, as the Lord commanded him, all the firstborn of the children of Israel.

43 And all the firstborn males rehearsed by name (from a month old and above) according to their number were two and twenty thousand, two hundred seventy and three.

44 ¶ And the Lord spake unto Moses, saying,

45 Take the Levites for all the firstborn of the children of Israel, and the cattle of the Levites for their cattle, and the Levites shall be mine, (I am the Lord.)

46 And for the redeeming of the two hundred seventy and three, (which are more than the Levites) of the firstborn of the children of Israel,

g Exod. 30:13
Lev. 27:25
Num. 18:16
Ezek. 45:12

CHAPTER 4
a Exod. 25:15
Exod. 25:30
b Exod. 25:31

47 Thou shalt also take five shekels for every person: after the weight of the Sanctuary shalt thou take it: *g*the shekel *containeth* twenty gerahs.

48 And thou shalt give the money, wherewith the odd number of them is redeemed, unto Aaron and to his sons.

49 Thus Moses took the redemption of them that were redeemed, being more than the Levites:

50 Of the [1]firstborn of the children of Israel took he the money: *even* a thousand three hundred three score and five *shekels*, after the shekel of the Sanctuary.

51 And Moses gave the money of them that were redeemed, unto Aaron and to his sons according to the word of the Lord, as the Lord had commanded Moses.

4 5 *The offices of the Levites, when the host removed.* 6 *The number of the three families of Kohath, Gershon, and Merari.*

1 And the Lord spake unto Moses, and to Aaron, saying,

2 Take the sum of the sons of Kohath from among the sons of Levi, after their families, *and* houses of their fathers,

3 From [1]thirty years old and above, even until fifty years old all that enter into the assembly to do the work in the Tabernacle of the Congregation.

4 This shall be the office of the sons of Kohath in the Tabernacle of the Congregation *about* the holiest of all.

5 ¶ When the host removeth, then Aaron and his sons shall come and take down[1] the covering veil, and shall cover the Ark of the Testimony therewith.

6 And they shall put thereon a covering of badger's skins, and shall spread upon it a cloth altogether of blue silk, and put to [1]the bars thereof:

7 And upon the *a*table of show *bread*, they shall spread a cloth of blue silk, and put thereon the dishes, and the *incense* cups and goblets, and coverings to cover it [1]with, and the bread shall be thereon continually.

8 And they shall spread upon them a covering of scarlet, and cover the same with a covering of badger's skins, and put to the bars thereof.

9 Then they shall take a cloth of blue silk, and cover the *b*candlestick of light with his lamps, and his

3:36 [1] The woodwork and the rest of the instruments were committed to their charge.
3:38 [1] That none should enter into the Tabernacle contrary to God's appointment.
3:39 [1] So that the firstborn of the children of Israel were more by 273, as verse 43.
3:41 [1] So that now the Levites should satisfy unto the Lord for the firstborn of Israel, save for the 273 which were more than the Levites, for whom they paid money.
3:50 [1] Or the two hundred seventy and three, which were more than the Levites.
4:3 [1] The Levites were numbered after three sorts, first at a month old when they were consecrated to the Lord, next at 25 years old when they were appointed to serve in the Tabernacle, and 30 years old to bear the burdens of the Tabernacle.
4:5 [1] Which divided the Sanctuary from the holiest of all.
4:6 [1] That is, put them upon their shoulders to carry it: for the bars of the Ark could never be removed.
4:7 [1] Meaning, to cover the bread.

snuffers, 'and his snuffdishes, and all the oil vessels thereof, which they occupy about it.

10 So they shall put it, and all the instruments thereof in a covering of badger's skins, and put it upon the ¹bars.

11 Also upon the golden ¹altar they shall spread a cloth of blue silk, and cover it with a covering of badger's skins, and put to the bars thereof.

12 And they shall take all the instruments of the ministry, wherewith they minister in the Sanctuary, and put *them* in a cloth of blue silk, and cover them with a covering of badger's skins, and put them on the bars.

13 Also they shall take away the ashes from the ¹altar, and spread a purple cloth upon it,

14 And shall put upon it all the instruments thereof, which they occupy about it, the censers, the fleshhooks, and the besoms, and the basins, *even* all the instruments of the altar: and they shall spread upon it a covering of badger's skins, and put to the bars of it.

15 And when Aaron and his sons have made an end of covering the ¹Sanctuary, and all the instruments of the Sanctuary, at the removing of the host, afterward the sons of Kohath shall come to bear it, but they shall not ²touch *any* holy thing lest they die. This is the charge of the sons of Kohath in the Tabernacle of the Congregation.

16 ¶ And to the office of Eleazar the son of Aaron the Priest *pertaineth* the oil for the light, and the ᵈsweet incense, and the ¹daily meat offering, and the ᵉanointing oil *with* the oversight of all the Tabernacle, and of all that therein is, *both* in the Sanctuary, and in all the instruments thereof.

17 ¶ And the Lord spake unto Moses and to Aaron, saying,

18 Ye shall not ¹cut off the tribe of the families of the Kohathites from among the Levites:

19 But thus do unto them that they may live and not die, when they come near to the most holy things: let Aaron and his sons come and appoint ¹them, every one to his office, and to his charge.

20 But let them not go in, to see when the Sanctuary is folden up, lest they die.

21 ¶ And the Lord spake unto Moses, saying,

22 Take also the sum of the sons of Gershon, every one by the houses of their fathers, throughout their

ᶜ Exod. 25:38
ᵈ Exod. 30:34,35
ᵉ Exod. 30:23,25
ᶠ Exod. 26:25

families:

23 From thirty years old and above until fifty years old shalt thou number them, all that ¹enter into the assembly for to do service in the Tabernacle of the Congregation.

24 This shall be the service of the families of the Gershonites to serve and to bear.

25 They shall bear the curtains of the Tabernacle, and the Tabernacle of the Congregation, his covering, and the covering of badger's skins, that is on high upon it, and the veil of the ¹door of the Tabernacle of the Congregation.

26 The curtains also of the court, and the veil of the entering in of the gate of the court, ¹which is near the Tabernacle and near the altar round about, with their cords: and all the instruments for their service, and all that is made for them: so shall they serve.

27 At the commandment of Aaron and his sons shall all the service of the sons of the Gershonites be done, in all their charges and in all their service, and ye shall appoint them to keep all their charges.

28 This is the service of the families of the sons of the Gershonites in the Tabernacle of the Congregation, and their watch *shall be* under the ¹hand of Ithamar the son of Aaron the Priest.

29 ¶ Thou shalt number the sons of Merari by their families, *and* by the houses of their fathers.

30 From thirty years old and above, even unto fifty years old shalt thou number them, all that enter into the assembly, to do the service of the Tabernacle of the Congregation.

31 And this is their office *and* charge according to all their service in the Tabernacle of the Congregation: the ᶠboards of the Tabernacle with the bars thereof, and his pillars, and his sockets,

32 And the pillars round about the court, with their sockets and their pins, and their cords with all their instruments, even for all their service: and by ¹name ye shall reckon the instruments of their office *and* charge.

33 This is the service of the families of the sons of Merari, according to all their service in the Tabernacle of the Congregation under the hand of Ithamar the son of Aaron the Priest.

34 ¶ Then Moses and Aaron and the princes of the Congregation numbered the sons of the Kohathites, by their families and by the houses of their

---

4:10 ¹ The Hebrew word signifieth an instrument made of two staves or bars.
4:11 ¹ Which was to burn incense, read Exod. 30:1.
4:13 ¹ Of the burnt offering.
4:15 ¹ That is, in folding up the things of the Sanctuary, as the Ark, etc.
    ² Before it be covered.
4:16 ¹ Which was offered at morning and evening.
4:18 ¹ Committing by your negligence that the holy things be not well wrapped, and so they by touching thereof perish.

4:19 ¹ Showing what part every man shall bear.
4:23 ¹ Which were received into the company of them that ministered in the Tabernacle of the Congregation.
4:25 ¹ Which veil hanged between the Sanctuary and the court.
4:26 ¹ Which court compassed both the Tabernacle of the Congregation and the altar of burnt offering.
4:28 ¹ Under the charge and oversight.
4:32 ¹ Ye shall make an inventory of all the things, which ye commit to their charge.

fathers,

35 From thirty years old and above, even unto fifty years old, all that enter into the assembly for the service of the Tabernacle of the Congregation.

36 So the [1]numbers of them throughout their families were two thousand, seven hundred and fifty.

37 These are the numbers of the families of the Kohathites, all that serve in the Tabernacle of the Congregation, which Moses and Aaron did number according to the commandment of the Lord by the [1]hand of Moses.

38 Also the numbers of the sons of Gershon throughout their families and houses of their fathers,

39 From thirty years old and upward, even unto fifty years old: all that enter into the assembly for the service of the Tabernacle of the Congregation.

40 So the numbers of them by their families, and by the houses of their fathers were two thousand six hundred and thirty.

41 These are the numbers of the families of the sons of Gershon: of all that [1]did service in the Tabernacle of the Congregation, whom Moses and Aaron did number according to the commandment of the Lord.

42 ¶ The numbers also of the families of the sons of Merari by their families, and by the houses of their fathers,

43 From thirty years old and upward, even unto fifty years old: all that enter into the assembly for the service of the Tabernacle of the Congregation.

44 So the numbers of them by their families were three thousand, and two hundred.

45 These are the sums of the families of the sons of Merari, whom Moses and Aaron numbered according to the commandment of the Lord, by the hand of Moses.

46 So all the numbers of the Levites, which Moses, and Aaron, and the princes of Israel numbered by their families and by the houses of their fathers,

47 From thirty years old and upward, even to fifty years old, every one that came to do [1]his duty, office, service and charge in the Tabernacle of the Congregation.

48 So the number of them were eight thousand

CHAPTER 5
[a] Lev. 13:3
[b] Lev. 15:2
[c] Lev. 21:1
[d] Lev. 6:3
[e] Lev. 6:5
[f] Lev. 10:12

five hundred and four score.

49 According to the [1]commandment of the Lord by the hand of Moses did *Aaron* number them, every one according to his service, and according to his charge. Thus *were* they of that tribe numbered, as the Lord commanded [2]Moses.

5 *2 The leprous and the polluted shall be cast forth.   6 The purging of sin.   15 The trial of the suspect wife.*

1 And the Lord spake unto Moses, saying,

2 Command the children of Israel that they [a]put out of the host every leper, and every one that hath [b]an issue, and whosoever is defiled by [c]the dead.

3 Both male and female shall ye put out: [1]out of the host shall ye put them, that they defile not their [2]tents among whom I dwell.

4 And the children of Israel did so, and put them out of the host, even as the Lord had commanded Moses, so did the children of Israel.

5 And the Lord spake unto Moses, saying,

6 Speak unto the children of Israel, [d]When a man or woman shall commit any sin [1]that men commit, and transgress against the Lord, when that person shall trespass,

7 Then they shall confess their sin which they have done, and shall restore the damage thereof [e]with his principal, and put the fifth part of it more thereto, and shall give it unto him, against whom he hath trespassed.

8 But if the [1]man have no kinsman, to whom he should restore the damage, the damage shall be restored to the Lord for the Priest's use, besides the ram of the atonement, whereby he shall make atonement for him.

9 And every offering of all the [1]holy things of the children of Israel, which they bring unto the Priest, shall be [f]his.

10 And every man's hallowed things shall be his: *that is*, whatsoever any man giveth the Priest, it shall be his.

11 ¶ And the Lord spake unto Moses, saying,

12 Speak unto the children of Israel, and say unto them, If any man's wife [1]turn to evil, and commit a trespass against him,

13 So that another man lie with her fleshly, and it be hid from the eyes of her husband, and kept

---

4:36 [1] Hebrew, *the numbered of them.*
4:37 [1] God appointing Moses to be the minister and executor thereof.
4:41 [1] Which were of competent age to serve therein, that is between 30 and 50.
4:47 [1] Whosoever of the Levites that had any manner of charge in the Tabernacle.
4:49 [1] Hebrew, *according to the mouth,* or word.
     [2] So that Moses neither added, nor diminished, from that which

the Lord commanded him.
5:3 [1] Or, in a place out of the host.
     [2] There were three manner of tents: of the Lord, of the Levites, and of the Israelites.
5:6 [1] Commit any fault willingly.
5:8 [1] If he be dead to whom the wrong is done, and also have no kinsman.
5:9 [1] Or, things offered to the Lord, as firstfruits, etc.
5:12 [1] By breaking the band of marriage, and playing the harlot.

close, and yet she be defiled, and there be no witness against her, neither she taken with the manner,

14 ¹If he be moved with a jealous mind, so that he is jealous over his wife, which is defiled, or if he have a jealous mind, so that he is jealous over his wife, which is not defiled,

15 Then shall the man bring his wife to the Priest, and bring her offering with her, the tenth part of an Ephah of barley meal, *but* he shall not pour ¹oil upon it, nor put incense thereon: for it is an offering of jealousy, an offering for a remembrance, calling the sin to ²mind.

16 And the Priest shall bring her, and set her before the Lord.

17 Then the Priest shall take ¹the holy water in an earthen vessel, and of the dust that is in the floor of the Tabernacle, *even* the Priest shall take it and put it into the water.

18 After the Priest shall set the woman before the Lord, and uncover the woman's head, and put the offering of the memorial in her hands: it is the jealousy offering, and the Priest shall have bitter *and* ¹cursed water in his hand,

19 And the Priest shall charge her by an oath, and say unto the woman, If no man have lain with thee, neither thou hast turned to uncleanness from thine husband, be free from this bitter *and* cursed water.

20 But if thou hast turned from thine husband, and so art defiled, and some man hath lain with thee besides thine husband,

21 (Then the Priest shall charge the woman with an oath of cursing, and the Priest shall say unto the woman:) The Lord make thee to be ¹accursed, and detestable for the oath among the people, and the Lord cause thy thigh to ²rot, and thy belly to swell:

22 And that this cursed water may go into thy bowels, to cause thy belly to swell, and thy thigh to rot. Then the woman shall answer, ¹Amen, Amen.

23 After, the Priest shall write these curses in a book, and shall ¹blot them out with the bitter water,

24 And shall cause the woman to drink the bitter and cursed water, and the cursed water *turned* into bitterness shall enter into her.

CHAPTER 6
a Judg. 13:5
1 Sam. 1:11

25 Then the Priest shall take the jealousy offering out of the woman's hand, and shall shake the offering before the Lord, and offer it upon the altar.

26 And the Priest shall take *an handful* of the offering for a ¹memorial thereof, and burn it upon the ²altar, and afterward make the woman drink the water.

27 When he hath made her drink the water, if she be defiled and have trespassed against her husband, then shall the cursed water, *turned* into bitterness, enter into her, and her belly shall swell, and her thigh shall rot, and the woman shall be accursed among her people.

28 But if the woman be not defiled, but be ¹clean, she shall be free, and shall conceive and bear.

29 This is the law of jealousy, when a wife turneth from her husband and is defiled,

30 Or, when a man is moved with a jealous mind, being jealous over his wife, then shall he bring the woman before the Lord, and the Priest shall do to her according to all this law,

31 And the man shall be ¹free from sin, but this woman shall bear her iniquity.

6 2 *The law of the consecration of the Nazirites.* 24 *The manner to bless the people.*

1 And the Lord spake unto Moses, saying,

2 Speak unto the children of Israel, and say unto them, When a man or a woman doth separate themselves to vow a vow of a ¹Nazirite, to separate *himself* unto the Lord,

3 He shall abstain from wine and strong drink, and shall drink no sour wine nor sour drink, nor shall drink any liquor of grapes, neither shall eat fresh grapes nor dried.

4 As long as his abstinence endureth, shall he eat nothing that is made of the wine of the vine, neither the kernels nor the husk.

5 While he is separated by his vow, the *a*razor shall not come upon his head, until the days be out, in the which he separateth *himself* unto the Lord, he shall be holy, and shall let the locks of the hair of his head grow.

6 During the time that he separateth himself unto the Lord, he shall come at no ¹dead body:

5:14 ¹ Hebrew, *If the spirit of jealousy come upon him.*
5:15 ¹ Only in the sin offering, and so this offering of jealousy were neither oil nor incense offered.
   ² Or, making the sin known, and not purging it.
5:17 ¹ Which also is called the water of purification or sprinkling, read Num. 19:9.
5:18 ¹ It was so called by the effect, because it declared the woman to be accursed, and turned to her destruction.
5:21 ¹ Both because she had committed so heinous a fault, and forsware herself in denying the same.
   ² Hebrew, *to fall.*

5:22 ¹ That is, be it so, as thou wishest, as Ps. 41:23; Deut. 27:15.
5:23 ¹ Shall wash the curses, which are written, into the water in the vessel.
5:26 ¹ Or, perfume.
   ² Where the incense was offered.
5:28 ¹ Or, innocent.
5:31 ¹ The man might accuse his wife upon suspicion, and not be reproved.
6:2 ¹ Which separated themselves from the world, and dedicated themselves to God: which figure was accomplished in Christ.
6:6 ¹ As at burials, or mournings.

7   He shall not make himself unclean at the death of his father or mother, brother, or sister: for the consecration of his God is upon [1]his head.

8   All the days of his separation he shall be holy to the Lord.

9   And if any die suddenly by him, or he beware, then the [1]head of his consecration shall be defiled, and he shall shave his head in the day of his cleansing: in the seventh day he shall shave it.

10   And in the eighth day he shall bring two turtles, or two young pigeons to the Priest, at the door of the tabernacle of the Congregation.

11   Then the Priest shall prepare the one for a sin offering, and the other for a burnt offering, and shall make an atonement for him, because he sinned by [1]the dead: so shall he hallow his head the same day.

12   And he shall [1]consecrate unto the Lord the days of his separation, and shall bring a lamb of a year old for a trespass offering, and the first [2]days shall be void: for his consecration was defiled.

13   ¶ This then is the law of the Nazirite: when the time of his consecration is out, he shall come to the door of the tabernacle of the Congregation,

14   And he shall bring his offering unto the Lord, an he lamb of a year old without blemish, for a burnt offering, and a she lamb of a year old without blemish, for a sin offering, and a ram without blemish, for peace offerings,

15   And a basket of unleavened bread, of [b]Cakes of fine flour, mingled with oil, and wafers of unleavened bread anointed with oil, with their meat offering, and their drink offerings:

16   The which the Priest shall bring before the Lord, and make his sin offering and his burnt offering.

17   He shall prepare also the ram for a peace offering unto the Lord, with the basket of unleavened bread, and the Priest shall make his meat offering, and his drink offering.

18   And [c]the Nazirite shall shave the head [1]of his consecration at the door of the Tabernacle of the Congregation, and shall take the hair of the head of his consecration, and [2]put it in the fire which is under the peace offering.

19   Then the Priest shall take the sodden shoulder of the ram, and an unleavened cake out of the

[b] Lev. 2:15
[c] Acts 21:24
[d] Exod. 29:27

CHAPTER 7
[a] Exod. 40:18

basket, and a wafer unleavened, and put them upon the hands of the Nazirite, after he hath shaven his consecration.

20   And the Priest shall [d]shake them to and fro before the Lord: this is an holy thing for the Priest [1]besides the shaken breast, and besides the heave shoulder: so afterward the Nazirite may drink wine.

21   This is the law of the Nazirite, which he hath vowed, *and* of his offering unto the Lord for his consecration, [1]besides that that he is able to bring: according to the vow which he vowed, so shall he do after the law of his consecration.

22   ¶ And the Lord spake unto Moses, saying,

23   Speak unto Aaron and to his sons, saying, Thus shall ye [1]bless the children of Israel, and say unto them,

24   The Lord bless thee, and keep thee,

25   The Lord make his face shine upon thee, and be merciful unto thee,

26   The Lord lift up his countenance upon thee, and give thee peace.

27   So they shall put my [1]Name upon the children of Israel, and I will bless them.

7 *2 The heads or princes of Israel offer at the setting up of the Tabernacle.   10 And at the dedication of the Altar.   19 God speaketh to Moses from the Mercy seat.*

1   Now when Moses had finished the setting up of the Tabernacle, and [a]anointed it and sanctified it, and all the instruments thereof, and the altar with all the [1]instruments thereof, and had anointed them, and sanctified them,

2   Then the [1]princes of Israel, heads over the houses of their fathers, (they were the princes of the tribes, who were over them that were numbered) offered,

3   And brought their offering before the Lord, six [1]covered chariots, and twelve oxen: one chariot for two princes, and for every one an ox, and they offered them before the Tabernacle.

4   And the Lord spake unto Moses, saying,

5   Take *these* of them, that they may be to do the [1]service of the Tabernacle of the Congregation, and thou shalt give them unto the Levites, to every man according unto his office.

6   So Moses took the chariots and the oxen, and

6:7 [1] In that he suffered his hair to grow, he signified that he was consecrated to God.
6:9 [1] Which long hair is a sign that he is dedicated to God.
6:11 [1] By being present where the dead was.
6:12 [1] Beginning at the eighth day, when he is purified.
      [2] So that he shall begin his vow anew.
6:18 [1] In token that his vow is ended.
      [2] For the hair which was consecrated to the Lord, might not be cast into any profane place.

6:20 [1] Or, with the breast.
6:21 [1] At the least he shall do this, if he be able to offer no more.
6:23 [1] That is, pray for them.
6:27 [1] They shall pray in my Name for them.
7:1 [1] Or, vessels.
7:2 [1] Or, captains.
7:3 [1] Like horse litters, to keep the things that were carried in them from weather.
7:5 [1] That is, to carry things and stuff in.

gave them unto the Levites:

7 Two chariots and four oxen he gave to the sons of Gershon, according unto their [1]office.

8 And four chariots and eight oxen he gave to the sons of Merari, according unto their office, under the hand of Ithamar the son of Aaron the Priest.

9 But to the sons of Kohath he gave none, [1]because the charge of the Sanctuary belonged to them, *which* they did bear upon *their* shoulders.

10 ¶ The princes also offered in the [1]dedication for the altar in the day that it was anointed: then the princes offered their offering before the altar.

11 And the Lord said unto Moses, One prince one day, and another prince another day, shall offer their offering, for the dedication of the altar.

12 ¶ So then on the first day did Nahshon the son of Amminadab of the tribe of Judah offer his offering.

13 And his offering *was* a silver charger of an hundred and thirty *shekels* weight, a silver bowl of seventy shekels, after the shekel of the Sanctuary, both full of fine flour, mingled with oil, for a [b]meat offering,

14 An *incense* cup of gold of ten *shekels*, full of incense,

15 A young bullock, a ram, a lamb of a year old for a burnt offering,

16 An he goat for a sin offering,

17 And for peace offerings, two bullocks, five rams, five he goats, and five lambs of a year old: this was the offering of Nahshon the son of Amminadab.

18 ¶ The second day Nethanel, the son of Zuar, prince of *the tribe* of Issachar did offer.

19 Who offered for his offering a silver charger of an hundred and thirty *shekels* weight, a silver bowl of seventy shekels, after the shekel of the Sanctuary, both full of fine flour, mingled with oil, for a meat offering,

20 An *incense* cup of gold of ten *shekels*, full of incense,

21 A young bullock, a ram, a lamb of a year old for a burnt offering,

22 An he goat for a sin offering,

23 And for peace offerings two bullocks, five rams, five he goats, five lambs of a year old: this was the offering of Nethanel the son of Zuar.

24 ¶ The third day Eliab the son of Helon prince of the children of Zebulun *offered*.

25 His offering *was* a silver charger of an hundred and thirty *shekels* weight, a silver bowl of seventy shekels, after the shekel of the Sanctuary, both full of fine flour, mingled with oil, for a meat offering,

[b] Lev. 2:1

26 A golden *incense* cup of ten *shekels*, full of incense,

27 A young bullock, a ram, a lamb of a year old for a burnt offering,

28 An he goat for a sin offering,

29 And for peace offerings, two bullocks, five rams, five he goats, five lambs of a year old: this was the offering of Eliab the son of Helon.

30 ¶ The fourth day Elizur the son of Shedeur prince of the children of Reuben *offered*.

31 His offering *was* a silver charger of an hundred and thirty *shekels* weight, a silver bowl of seventy shekels, after the shekel of the Sanctuary, both full of fine flour, mingled with oil, for a meat offering,

32 A golden *incense* cup of ten *shekels*, full of incense,

33 A young bullock, a ram, a lamb of a year old for a burnt offering,

34 An he goat for a sin offering,

35 And for a peace offering, two bullocks, five rams, five he goats, and five lambs of a year old: this was the offering of Elizur the son of Shedeur.

36 ¶ The fifth day Shelumiel the son of Zurishaddai, prince of the children of Simeon *offered*.

37 His offering *was* a silver charger of an hundred and thirty *shekels* weight, a silver bowl of seventy shekels: after the shekel of the Sanctuary, both full of fine flour, mingled with oil, for a meat offering,

38 A golden *incense* cup of ten *shekels*, full of incense,

39 A young bullock, a ram, a lamb of a year old for a burnt offering,

40 An he goat for a sin offering,

41 And for a peace offering, two bullocks, five rams, five he goats, five lambs of a year old: this was the offering of Shelumiel the son of Zurishaddai.

42 ¶ The sixth day Eliasaph the son of Deuel prince of the children of Gad *offered*.

43 His offering *was* a silver charger of an hundred and thirty *shekels* weight, a silver bowl of seventy shekels, after the shekel of the Sanctuary, both full of fine flour, mingled with oil, for a meat offering,

44 A golden *incense* cup of ten *shekels*, full of incense,

45 A young bullock, a ram, a lamb of a year old for a burnt offering,

46 An he goat for a sin offering,

47 And for a peace offering, two bullocks, five rams, five he goats, five lambs of a year old: this was the offering of Eliasaph the son of Deuel.

48 ¶ The seventh day Elishama the son of Ammihud prince of the children of Ephraim *offered*.

7:7 [1] For their use to carry with.
7:9 [1] The holy thing of the Sanctuary must be carried upon their shoulders and not drawn with oxen, Num. 4:15.

7:10 [1] That is, when the first sacrifice was offered thereupon by Aaron, Lev. 9:1.

49 His offering was a silver charger of an hundred and thirty *shekels* weight, a silver bowl of seventy shekels, after the shekel of the Sanctuary, both full of fine flour, mingled with oil, for a meat offering,

50 A golden *incense* cup of ten *shekels*, full of incense,

51 A young bullock, a ram, a lamb of a year old for a burnt offering,

52 An he goat for a sin offering,

53 And for a peace offering, two bullocks, five rams, five he goats, five lambs of a year old: this was the offering of Elishama the son of Ammihud.

54 ¶ The eighth day *offered* Gamaliel the son of Pedahzur, prince of the children of Manasseh.

55 His offering *was* a silver charger of an hundred and thirty *shekels* weight, a silver bowl of seventy shekels, after the shekel of the Sanctuary, both full of fine flour, mingled with oil, for a meat offering,

56 A golden *incense* cup of ten *shekels*, full of incense,

57 A young bullock, a ram, a lamb of a year old for a burnt offering,

58 An he goat for a sin offering,

59 And for a peace offering, two bullocks, five rams, five he goats, five lambs of a year old: this was the offering of Gamaliel the son of Pedahzur.

60 ¶ The ninth day Abidan the son of Gideoni prince of the children of Benjamin *offered*.

61 His offering *was* a silver charger of an hundred and thirty *shekels* weight, a silver bowl of seventy shekels, after the shekel of the Sanctuary, both full of fine flour, mingled with oil, for a meat offering,

62 A golden *incense* cup of ten *shekels*, full of incense,

63 A young bullock, a ram, a lamb of a year old for a burnt offering,

64 An he goat for a sin offering,

65 And for a peace offering, two bullocks, five rams, five he goats, five lambs of a year old: this was the offering of Abidan the son of Gideoni.

66 ¶ The tenth day Ahiezer the son of Ammishaddai, prince of the children of Dan *offered*.

67 His offering *was* a silver charger of an hundred and thirty *shekels* weight, a silver bowl of seventy shekels, after the shekel of the Sanctuary, both full of fine flour, mingled with oil, for a meat offering,

68 A golden *incense* cup of ten *shekels*, full of incense,

69 A young bullock, a ram, a lamb of a year old for a burnt offering,

70 An he goat for a sin offering,

71 And for a peace offering, two bullocks, five

rams, five he goats, five lambs of a year old: this was the offering of Ahiezer the son of Ammishaddai.

72 ¶ The eleventh day Pagiel the son of Ocran, prince of the children of Asher *offered*.

73 His offering *was* a silver charger of an hundred and thirty *shekels* weight, a silver bowl of seventy shekels, after the shekel of the Sanctuary, both full of fine flour, mingled with oil, for a meat offering,

74 A golden *incense* cup of ten *shekels*, full of incense,

75 A young bullock, a ram, a lamb of a year old for a burnt offering,

76 An he goat for a sin offering,

77 And for a peace offering, two bullocks, five rams, five he goats, five lambs of a year old: this was the offering of Pagiel the son of Ocran.

78 ¶ The twelfth day Ahira the son of Enan, prince of the children of Naphtali *offered*.

79 His offering *was* a silver charger of an hundred and thirty *shekels* weight, a silver bowl of seventy shekels, after the shekel of the Sanctuary, both full of fine flour, mingled with oil, for a meat offering,

80 A golden *incense* cup of ten *shekels*, full of incense,

81 A young bullock, a ram, a lamb of a year old for a burnt offering,

82 An he goat for a sin offering,

83 And for peace offerings, two bullocks, five rams, five he goats, five lambs of a year old, this was the offering of Ahira the son of Enan.

84 This was the [1]dedication of the Altar by the princes of Israel, when it was anointed, twelve chargers of silver, twelve silver bowls: twelve *incense* cups of gold,

85 Every charger *containing* an hundred and thirty *shekels* of silver, and every bowl seventy: all the silver vessel *contained* two thousand and four hundred *shekels*, after the shekel of the Sanctuary.

86 Twelve *incense* cups of gold full of incense, *containing* ten shekels every cup, after the shekel of the Sanctuary: and the gold of the *incense* cups *was* an hundred and twenty *shekels*.

87 All the bullocks for the burnt offering *were* twelve bullocks, the rams twelve, the lambs of a year old twelve, with their meat offerings, and twelve he goats for a sin offering.

88 And all the bullocks for the peace offerings *were* four and twenty bullocks, the rams sixty, the he goats sixty, the lambs of a year old sixty: this was the dedication of the Altar, after that it was [1]anointed.

89 And when Moses went into the [1]tabernacle of the Congregation to speak with *God*, he heard the voice of one speaking unto him from the Mercy seat,

---

7:84 [1] This was the offering of the princes, when Aaron did dedicate the Altar.

7:88 [1] By Aaron.

7:89 [1] That is, the Sanctuary.

that was upon the Ark of the Testimony [2]between the two Cherubims, and he spake unto him.

CHAPTER 8
a Exod. 25:18
b Num. 3:45
c Num. 3:9
d Exod. 13:2
Luke 2:23

8 *2 The order of the lamps.   6 The purifying and offering of the Levites.   24 The age of the Levites when they are received to service, and when they are dismissed.*

1 And the Lord spake unto Moses, saying,

2 Speak unto Aaron, and say unto him, When thou lightest the lamps, the seven lamps shall give light toward the [1]forefront of the Candlestick.

3 And Aaron did so, lighting the lamps thereof toward the forefront of the Candlestick, as the Lord had commanded Moses.

4 And this was the work of the Candlestick, *even* of gold beaten out with the hammer, both the shaft, and the flower thereof *a*was beaten out with the hammer: [1]according to the pattern which the Lord had showed Moses, so made he the Candlestick.

5 ¶ And the Lord spake unto Moses, saying,

6 Take the Levites from among the children of Israel, and purify them.

7 And thus shalt thou do unto them, when thou purifiest them, Sprinkle [1]water of purification upon them, and let them shave all their flesh, and wash their clothes: so they shall be clean.

8 Then they shall take a young bullock with his meat offering of fine flour, mingled with oil, and another young bullock shalt thou take for a sin offering.

9 Then thou shalt bring the Levites before the Tabernacle of the Congregation, and assemble [1]all the Congregation of the children of Israel.

10 Thou shalt bring the Levites also before the Lord, and the [1]children of Israel shall put their hands upon the Levites.

11 And Aaron shall offer the Levites before the Lord, as a shake offering of the children of Israel, that they may execute the service of the Lord.

12 And the Levites shall put their hands upon the heads of the bullocks, and make thou the one a sin offering, and the other a burnt offering unto the Lord, that thou mayest make an atonement for the Levites.

13 And thou shalt set the Levites before Aaron and before his sons, and offer them as a shake offering to the Lord.

14 Thus thou shalt separate the Levites from among the children of Israel, and the Levites shall

be *b*mine.

15 And afterward shall the Levites go in, to serve in the Tabernacle of the Congregation, and thou shalt purify them, and offer them as a shake offering.

16 For they are freely given *c*unto me from among the children of Israel, for [1]such as open any womb: for all the firstborn of the children of Israel have I taken them unto me.

17 *d*For all the firstborn of the children of Israel are mine, both of man and beast: since the day that I smote every firstborn in the land of Egypt, I sanctified them for myself.

18 And I have taken the Levites for all the firstborn of the children of Israel,

19 And have given the Levites as a gift unto Aaron, and to his sons from among the children of Israel, to do the service of the [1]children of Israel in the Tabernacle of the Congregation, and to make an atonement for the children of Israel, that there be no plague among the children of Israel, when the children of Israel come near unto the [2]Sanctuary.

20 ¶ Then Moses and Aaron and all the Congregation of the children of Israel did with the Levites, according unto all that the Lord had commanded Moses concerning the Levites: so did the children of Israel unto them.

21 So the Levites were purified, and washed their clothes, and Aaron offered them as a shake offering before the Lord, and Aaron made an atonement for them, to purify them.

22 And after that, went the Levites in to do their service in the Tabernacle of the Congregation, [1]before Aaron and before his sons: as the Lord had commanded Moses concerning the Levites, so they did unto them.

23 ¶ And the Lord spake unto Moses, saying,

24 This also *belongeth* to the Levites: from five and twenty years old and upward, they shall go in, to execute *their* office in the service of the Tabernacle of the Congregation.

25 And after the age of fifty years, they shall cease from executing the [1]office, and shall serve no more.

26 But they shall minister [1]with their brethren in the Tabernacle of the Congregation, to keep things committed to their charge, but they shall do no service: thus shalt thou do unto the Levites touching their charge.

7:89 [2] According as he had promised, Exod. 25:22.
8:2 [1] To that part which is over against the Candlestick, Exod. 25:37.
8:4 [1] And not set together of divers pieces.
8:7 [1] In Hebrew it is called the water of sin, because it is made to purge sin, as Num. 19:9.
8:9 [1] That thou mayest do this in presence of them all.
8:10 [1] Meaning, certain of them in the name of the whole.

8:16 [1] That is, they that are the firstborn.
8:19 [1] Which service the Israelites should else do.
   [2] Because the Levites go into the Sanctuary in their name.
8:22 [1] In their presence, to serve them.
8:25 [1] Such office as was painful, as to bear burdens and such like.
8:26 [1] In singing Psalms, instructing, counseling and keeping the things in order.

9

2 The Passover is commanded again. 13 The punishment of him that keepeth not the Passover. 15 The cloud conducteth the Israelites through the wilderness.

1 And the Lord spake unto Moses in the wilderness of Sinai, in the first month of the second year, after they were come out of the land of Egypt, saying,

2 The children of Israel shall also celebrate the *a*Passover at the time appointed thereunto.

3 In the fourteenth day of this month at *b*even, ye shall keep it in his due season: according to *1*all the ordinances of it, and according to all the ceremonies thereof shall ye keep it.

4 Then Moses spake unto the children of Israel, to celebrate the Passover.

5 And they kept the Passover in the fourteenth day of the first month at even in the wilderness of Sinai: according to all that the Lord had commanded Moses, so did the children of Israel.

6 ¶ And certain men were defiled *1*by a dead man, that they might not keep the Passover the same day: and they came before Moses and before Aaron the same day.

7 And those men said unto him, We are defiled by a dead man: wherefore are we kept back that we may not *1*offer an offering unto the Lord in the time thereunto appointed among the children of Israel?

8 Then Moses said unto them, Stand still, and I will hear what the Lord will command concerning you.

9 And the Lord spake unto Moses, saying,

10 Speak unto the children of Israel, and say, If any among you, or of your posterity shall be unclean by the reason of a corpse, or be in a long journey, *1*he shall keep the Passover unto the Lord.

11 In the fourteenth day of the *1*second month at even they shall keep it: with unleavened bread, and sour herbs shall they eat it.

12 They shall leave none of it unto the morning, *c*nor break any bone of it: according to all the ordinance of the Passover shall they keep it.

13 But the man that is clean and is not in a *1*journey, and is negligent to keep the Passover, the same person shall be cut off from his people: because he brought not the offering of the Lord in his due season, that man shall bear his *2*sin.

CHAPTER 9
a Exod. 12:1
Lev. 23:5
Num. 28:16
Deut. 16:2
b Exod. 12:6
Deut. 16:6
c Exod. 12:46
John 19:36
d Exod. 12:49
e Exod. 40:34
f 1 Cor. 10:1
g Exod. 40:36,37
Num. 9:18

14 And if a stranger dwell among you, and will keep the Passover unto the Lord, as the ordinance of the Passover, and as the manner thereof *is*, so shall he do: *d*ye shall have one law both for the stranger, and for him that was born in the same land.

15 ¶ *e*And when the Tabernacle was reared up, a cloud covered the Tabernacle, *namely*, the Tabernacle of the Testimony: and at even there was upon the Tabernacle, as the *1*appearance of fire until morning.

16 So it was alway: the cloud covered it *by day*, and the appearance of fire by night.

17 And when the cloud was taken up from the Tabernacle, then afterward the children of Israel journeyed: and in the place where the cloud abode, there the children of Israel pitched their tents.

18 At the *1*commandment of the *2*Lord the children of Israel journeyed, and at the commandment of the Lord they pitched: as long as the cloud abode upon the Tabernacle, *f*they *3*lay still.

19 And when the cloud tarried still upon the Tabernacle a long time, the children of Israel kept the *1*watch of the Lord, and journeyed not.

20 So when the cloud abode *1*a few days upon the Tabernacle, they abode in their tents according to the commandment of the Lord: for they journeyed at the commandment of the Lord.

21 And though the cloud abode upon the Tabernacle from even unto the morning, yet *if* the cloud was taken up in the morning, then they journeyed: whether by day or by night the cloud was taken up, then they journeyed.

22 Or if the cloud tarried two days, or a month, or a year upon the Tabernacle, abiding thereon, the children of Israel *g*abode still, and journeyed not: but when it was taken up, they journeyed.

23 At the commandment of the Lord they pitched, and at the commandment of the Lord they journeyed, keeping the watch of the Lord at the commandment of the Lord by the *1*hand of Moses.

10

2 The use of the silver trumpets. 11 The Israelites depart from Sinai. 14 The captains of the host are numbered. 30 Hobab refuseth to go with Moses his son-in-law.

1 And the Lord spake unto Moses, saying,

9:3 *1* Even in all points as the Lord hath instituted it.
9:6 *1* By touching a corpse, or being at the burial.
9:7 *1* Or, celebrate the Passover the fourteenth day of the first month.
9:10 *1* And cannot come where the Tabernacle is, when others keep it.
9:11 *1* So that the unclean, and they that are not at home, have a month longer granted unto them.
9:13 *1* When the Passover is celebrated.
  2 Or, punishment of his sin.

9:15 *1* Like a pillar, read Exod. 13:22.
9:18 *1* Hebrew, *mouth*.
  2 Who taught them what to do by the cloud.
  3 Hebrew, *camped*.
9:19 *1* They waited when the Lord would signify either their departure, or their abode by the cloud.
9:20 *1* Hebrew, *days of number*.
9:23 *1* Under the charge and government of Moses.

2 Make thee two trumpets of silver: of an [1]whole piece shalt thou make them, that thou mayest use them for the assembling of the Congregation, and for the departure of the camp.

3 And when they shall blow with them, all the Congregation shall assemble to thee, before the door of the Tabernacle of the Congregation.

4 But if they blow with one, then the Princes, *or* heads over the thousands of Israel shall come unto thee.

5 But if ye blow an alarm, then the camp of them that pitch on the [1]East part, shall go forward.

6 If ye blow an alarm the second time, then the host of them that lie on the [1]South side, shall march: *for* they shall blow an alarm when they remove.

7 But in the assembling the Congregation, ye shall blow without an alarm.

8 And the sons of Aaron the Priest shall [1]blow the trumpets, and ye shall have them as a law forever in your generations.

9 And when ye go to war in your land against the enemy that vexeth you, ye shall blow an alarm with the trumpets, and ye shall be remembered before the Lord your God, and shall be saved from your enemies.

10 Also in the day of your [1]gladness, and in your feast days, and in the beginning of your months, ye shall also blow the trumpets [2]over your burnt sacrifices, and over your peace offerings, that they may be a remembrance for you before your God: I am the Lord your God.

11 ¶ And in the second year, in the second month, *and* in the twentieth *day* of the month, the cloud was taken up from the Tabernacle of the Testimony.

12 And the children of Israel departed on their [1]journeys out of the desert of Sinai, and the cloud rested in the wilderness of Paran.

13 So they [1]first took their journey at the commandment of the Lord by the hand of Moses.

14 ¶ [a]In the first place went the standard of the host of the children of Judah according to their armies: and [b]Nahshon the son of Amminadab *was* over his band.

15 And over the band of the tribe of the children of Issachar *was* Nethanel the son of Zuar.

16 And over the band of the tribe of the children

CHAPTER 10
[a] Num. 2:3
[b] Num. 1:7
[c] Num. 4:4

of Zebulun *was* Eliab the son of Helon.

17 When the Tabernacle was taken down, then the sons of Gershon and the sons of Merari went forward bearing [1]the Tabernacle.

18 ¶ After, departed the standard of the host of Reuben, according to their armies, and over his band *was* Elizur the son of Shedeur.

19 And over the band of the tribe of the children of Simeon *was* Shelumiel the son of Zurishaddai.

20 And over the band of the tribe of the children of Gad *was* Eliasaph the son of Deuel.

21 The Kohathites also went forward and [1]bare the [c]Sanctuary, and the [2]*former* did set up the Tabernacle against they came.

22 ¶ Then the standard of the host of the children of Ephraim went forward according to their armies, and over his band *was* Elishama the son of Ammihud.

23 And over the band of the tribe of the sons of Manasseh *was* Gamaliel the son of Pedahzur.

24 And over the band of the tribe of the sons of Benjamin *was* Abidan the son of Gideoni.

25 ¶ Last, the standard of the host of the children of Dan marched, [1]gathering all the hosts according to their armies: and over his band *was* Ahiezer the son of Ammishaddai.

26 And over the band of the tribe of the children of Asher *was* Pagiel the son of Ocran.

27 And over the band of the tribe of the children of Naphtali *was* Ahira the son of Enan.

28 [1]These were the removings of the children of Israel according to their armies, when they marched.

29 After, Moses said unto [1]Hobab the son of Reuel the Midianite, the father-in-law of Moses, We go into the place, of which the Lord said, I will give it you. Come thou with us, and we will do thee good: for the Lord hath promised good unto Israel.

30 And he answered him, I will not go: but I will depart to mine own country, and to my kindred.

31 Then he said, I pray thee, leave us not: for thou knowest our camping places in the wilderness: therefore thou mayest be [1]our guide.

32 And if thou go with us, what goodness the Lord shall show unto us, the same will we show unto thee.

33 ¶ So they departed from the [1]mount of the Lord,

10:2 [1] Or, of work beaten out with the hammer.
10:5 [1] That is, the host of Judah and they that are under his ensign.
10:6 [1] Meaning, the host of Reuben.
10:8 [1] So that only the Priests must blow the trumpets, so long as the Priesthood lasted.
10:10 [1] When ye rejoice that God hath removed any plague.
  [2] Or, when ye offer burnt offerings.
10:12 [1] Or, in keeping this order in their journeys.
10:13 [1] From Sinai to Paran, Num. 33:1.
10:17 [1] With all the appertainances thereof.

10:21 [1] Upon their shoulders.
  [2] The Merarites and Gershonites.
10:25 [1] Leaving none behind, nor any of the former that fainted in the way.
10:28 [1] This was the order of their host when they removed.
10:29 [1] Some think that Reuel, Jethro, Hobab, and Keni were all one: Kimhi saith, that Reuel was Jethro's father: so Hobab was Moses' father-in-law, see Exod. 2:18, 3:1, 4:18, 18:1, and Judg. 4:11.
10:31 [1] Hebrew, *eyes unto us.*
10:33 [1] Mount Sinai, or Horeb.

three days' journey: and the Ark of the covenant of the Lord went before them in the three days' journey, to search out a resting place for them.

34 And the cloud of the Lord *was* upon them by day, when they went out of the camp.

35 And when the Ark went forward, Moses said, [d][1]Rise up Lord, and let thine enemies be scattered, and let them that hate thee, flee before thee.

36 And when it rested, he said, Return, O Lord, to the [1]many thousands of Israel.

11

1 *The people murmureth, and is punished with fire.* 4 *The people lusteth after flesh.* 6 *They loathe Manna.* 11 *The weak faith of Moses.* 16 *The Lord divided the burden of Moses to seventy of the Ancients.* 31 *The Lord sendeth quails.* 33 *Their lust is punished.*

1 When the people became [1]murmurers, [2]it displeased the Lord: and the Lord heard it, therefore his wrath was kindled, and the fire of the Lord burnt among them, and [a]consumed the utmost part of the host.

2 Then the people cried unto Moses: and when Moses prayed unto the Lord, the fire was quenched.

3 And he called the name of the place [1]Taberah, because the fire of the Lord burnt among them.

4 ¶ And a number of [1]people that was among them, fell a lusting, and [2]turned away, and the children of Israel also wept, and said, Who shall give us flesh to eat?

5 We remember the fish which we did eat in Egypt for [1]nought, the cucumbers, and the pepons, and the leeks, and the onions, and the garlic.

6 But now our soul is [1]dried away, we can see nothing but this Manna.

7 (The Manna also was as [b]coriander seed, and his color like the color of [1]bdellium.

8 The people went about and gathered, and ground it in mills, or beat it in mortars, and baked it in a cauldron, and made cakes of it, and the taste of it was like unto the taste of fresh oil.

9 And when the dew fell down upon the host in night, the Manna fell with it.)

10 ¶ Then Moses heard the people weep throughout their families, every man in the door of his tent, and

[d] Ps. 68:1,2

CHAPTER 11
[a] Ps. 78:21
[b] Exod. 16:31
Ps. 78:24
John 6:31

the wrath of the Lord was grievously kindled: also Moses was grieved.

11 And Moses said unto the Lord, Wherefore hast thou [1]vexed thy servant? and why have I not found [2]favor in thy sight, seeing thou hast put the charge of all this people upon me?

12 Have I [1]conceived all this people? or have I begotten them, that thou shouldest say unto me, Carry them in thy bosom (as a nurse beareth the sucking child) unto the [2]land, for the which thou swarest unto their fathers?

13 Where should I have flesh to give unto all this people? for they weep unto me, saying, Give us flesh that we may eat.

14 I am not able to bear all this people alone, for it is too heavy for me.

15 Therefore if thou deal thus with me, I pray thee, if I have found favor in thy [1]sight, kill me, that I behold not my misery.

16 ¶ Then the Lord said unto Moses, Gather unto me seventy men of the Elders of Israel, whom thou knowest, that they are the Elders of the people, and governors over them, and bring them unto the Tabernacle of the Congregation, and let them stand there with thee.

17 And I will come down, and talk with thee there, [1]and take of the Spirit, which is upon thee, and put upon them, and they shall bear the burden of the people with thee: so thou shalt not bear it alone.

18 Furthermore thou shalt say unto the people, [1]Be sanctified against tomorrow, and ye shall eat flesh: for you have wept in the ears of the Lord, saying, Who shall give us flesh to eat? for we were better in Egypt: therefore the Lord will give you flesh, and ye shall eat.

19 Ye shall not eat one day nor two days, nor five days, neither ten days, nor twenty days,

20 But a whole month, until it come out at your nostrils, and be loathsome unto you, because ye have [1]contemned the Lord, which is [2]among you, and have wept before him, saying, Why came we hither out of Egypt?

21 And Moses said, Six hundred thousand footmen *are there* of the people, [1]among whom I am: and

---

10:35 [1] Declare thy might and power.
10:36 [1] Hebrew, *to the ten thousand thousands.*
11:1 [1] Hebrew, *as unjust complainers.*
   [2] Hebrew, *it was evil in the ears of the Lord.*
11:3 [1] Or, *burning.*
11:4 [1] Which were of those strangers that came out of Egypt with them, Exod. 12:38.
   [2] From God.
11:5 [1] For a small price, or good cheap.
11:6 [1] For the greedy lust of flesh.
11:7 [1] Which is a white pearl, or precious stone.
11:11 [1] Or, evil intreated.

[2] Or, wherein have I displeased thee?
11:12 [1] Am I their father, that none may have the charge of them but I?
   [2] Of Canaan promised by an oath to our fathers.
11:15 [1] I had rather die than to see my grief and misery thus daily increase by their rebellion.
11:17 [1] I will distribute my spirit among them, as I have done to thee.
11:18 [1] Prepare yourselves that ye be not unclean.
11:20 [1] Or, cast him off, because ye refused Manna, which he appointed as most meet for you.
   [2] Who leadeth and governeth you.
11:21 [1] Of whom I have the charge.

thou sayest, I will give them flesh, that they may eat a month long.

22 Shall the sheep and the beeves be slain for them to find them? either shall all the fish of the Sea be gathered together for them to suffice them?

23 And the Lord said unto Moses, Is 'the Lord's hand shortened? thou shalt see now whether my word shall come to pass unto thee, or no.

24 ¶ So Moses went out, and told the people the words of the Lord, and gathered seventy men of the Elders of the people, and set them round about the Tabernacle.

25 Then the Lord came down in a cloud, and spake unto him, and ¹took of the Spirit that was upon him, and put it upon the seventy Ancient men: and when the Spirit rested upon them, then they prophesied, and did not ²cease.

26 But there remained two of the men in the host: the name of the one was Eldad, and the name of the other Medad, and the Spirit rested upon them, (for they were of them that were written, and went not out unto the Tabernacle) and they prophesied in the host.

27 Then there ran a young man, and told Moses, and said, Eldad and Medad do prophesy in the host.

28 And Joshua the son of Nun the servant of Moses one of his ¹young men answered and said, My lord Moses, ²forbid them.

29 But Moses said unto him, Enviest thou for my sake? yea, would God that all the Lord's people were Prophets, and that the Lord would put his spirit upon them.

30 And Moses returned into the host, he and the Elders of Israel.

31 Then there went forth a wind from the Lord, and ᵈbrought quails from the sea, and let them fall upon the camp, a day's journey on this side, and a day's journey on the other side, round about the host, and they were about two cubits above the earth.

32 Then the people arose, all that day, and all the night, and all the next day, and gathered the quails: he that gathered the least, gathered ten ¹Homers full, and they spread them abroad for their use round about the host.

33 While the flesh was yet between their teeth,

before it was chewed, even the wrath of the Lord was kindled against the people, and the Lord ᶜsmote the people with an exceeding great plague.

34 So the name of the place was called, ¹Kibroth Hattaavah: for there they buried the people that fell a lusting.

35 From Kibroth Hattaavah the people took their journey to Hazeroth, and abode at Hazeroth.

12

1 Aaron and Miriam grudge against Moses. 10 Miriam is stricken with leprosy, and healed at the prayer of Moses.

1 Afterward Miriam and Aaron ¹spake against Moses, because of the woman of Ethiopia whom he had married (for he had married ²a woman of Ethiopia.)

2 And they said, What? hath the Lord spoken but only by Moses? hath he not spoken also by us? and the Lord heard *this*.

3 (But Moses *was* a very ¹meek man above all the men that were upon the earth.)

4 And by and by the Lord said unto Moses, and unto Aaron, and unto Miriam, come out ye three unto the Tabernacle of the Congregation: and they three came forth.

5 Then the Lord came down in the pillar of the cloud, and stood in the door of the Tabernacle, and called Aaron and Miriam, and they both came forth.

6 And he said, Hear now my words, If there be a Prophet of the Lord among you, I will be known to him by a ¹vision, *and* will speak unto him by dream.

7 My servant Moses *is* not so, who is faithful ¹in all mine house,

8 Unto him will I speak ᵃmouth to mouth, and by vision, and not in dark words, but he shall ¹see the similitude of the Lord. Wherefore then were ye not afraid to speak against my servant, *even* against Moses?

9 Thus the Lord was very angry with them, and departed.

10 Also the cloud departed from the ¹Tabernacle: and behold, Miriam *was* leprous like snow: and Aaron looked upon Miriam, and behold, *she was* leprous.

11 Then Aaron said unto Moses, Alas, my lord, I

ᵠIsa. 50:2
Isa. 59:1
ᵈ Exod. 16:13
Ps. 78:26,27
ᵉ Ps. 78:31

CHAPTER 12
ᵃ Exod. 33:11

11:25 ¹ Or, separated, verse 17.
   ² From that day the spirit of prophecy did not fail them.
11:28 ¹ Or, a young man whom he had chosen from his youth.
   ² Such blind zeal was in the Apostles, Mark 9:38; Luke 9:44.
11:32 ¹ Of Homer, read Lev. 27:16, also it signifieth an heap, as Exod. 8:14; Judg. 15:16.
11:34 ¹ Or, graves of lust.
12:1 ¹ Or, murmured.
   ² Zipporah Moses' wife was a Midianite, and because Midian bor-

dered on Ethiopia, it is sometimes in the Scriptures comprehended under this name.
12:3 ¹ And so bare with their grudging, although he knew them.
12:6 ¹ These were the two ordinary means.
12:7 ¹ In all Israel which was his Church.
12:8 ¹ So far as any man was able to comprehend, which he calleth his back parts, Exod. 33:23.
12:10 ¹ From the door of the Tabernacle.

beseech thee, lay not the sin upon us, which we have foolishly committed, and wherein we have sinned.

12 Let her not, I pray thee, be as one [1]dead, of whom the flesh is half consumed, when he cometh out of his mother's womb.

13 Then Moses cried unto the Lord, saying, O God, I beseech thee, heal her now.

14 ¶ And the Lord said unto Moses, If her father had [1]spit in her face, should she not have been ashamed seven days? let her be [b]shut out of the host seven days, and after she shall be received.

15 So Miriam was shut out of the host seven days, and the people removed not, till Miriam was brought in again.

13

4 Certain men are sent to search the land of Canaan. 24 They bring of the fruit of the land. 31 Caleb comforteth the people against the discouraging of the other spies.

1 Then afterward the people removed from Hazeroth, and pitched in the wilderness of [1]Paran.

2 ¶ And the Lord spake unto Moses, saying,

3 [1]Send thou men out to search the land of Canaan which I give unto the children of Israel: of every tribe of their fathers shall ye send a man, *such as are* all rulers among them.

4 Then Moses sent them out of the wilderness of Paran at the commandment of the Lord: all those men were [1]heads of the children of Israel.

5 Also their names are these: of the tribe of Reuben, Shammua the son of Zaccur:

6 Of the tribe of Simeon, Shaphat the son of Hori:

7 Of the tribe of Judah, Caleb the son of Jephunneh:

8 Of the tribe of Issachar, Igal the son of Joseph:

9 Of the tribe of Ephraim, [1]Hoshea the son of Nun:

10 Of the tribe of Benjamin, Palti the son of Raphu:

11 Of the tribe of Zebulun, Gaddiel the son of Sodi:

12 Of the tribe of Joseph, *to wit*, of the tribe of Manasseh, Gaddi the son of Susi:

13 Of the tribe of Dan, Ammiel the son of Gemalli:

[b] Lev. 13:46

CHAPTER 13
[a] Deut. 1:24
[b] Exod. 33:3

14 Of the tribe of Asher, Sethur the son of Michael:

15 Of the tribe of Naphtali, Nahbi the son of Vophsi:

16 Of the tribe of Gad, Geuel the son of Machi:

17 These are the names of the [1]men, which Moses sent to spy out the land: and Moses called the name of Hoshea the son of Nun, Joshua.

18 So Moses sent them to spy out the land of Canaan, and said to them, Go up this way toward the South, and go up into the [1]mountains.

19 And consider the land what it is, and the people that dwell therein, whether they be strong, or weak, either few or many.

20 Also what the land *is* that they dwell in, whether it be [1]good or bad: and what cities *they be*, that they dwell in, whether they dwell in tents, or in walled towns.

21 And what the land *is*: whether it be fat or lean, whether there be trees therein, or not. And be of good courage, and bring of the fruit of the land (for then *was* the time of the first ripe grapes.)

22 ¶ So they went up, and searched out the land, from the wilderness of [1]Zin unto Rehob, to go to Hamath.

23 And they ascended toward the South, and came unto Hebron, where were Ahiman, Sheshai, and Talmai, the sons of [1]Anak. And [2]Hebron was built seven years before Zoan in Egypt.

24 [a]Then they came to the river of Eshcol, and cut down thence a branch with one cluster of grapes, and they bare it upon a bar between two, and *brought* of the pomegranates and of the figs.

25 That place was called the [1]river Eshcol, because of the cluster of grapes, which the children of Israel cut down thence.

26 Then after forty days they turned again from searching of the land.

27 And they went and came to Moses and to Aaron, and unto all the Congregation of the children of Israel, in the wilderness of [1]Paran, to Kadesh, and brought to them, and to all the Congregation tidings, and showed them the fruit of the land.

28 And they told [1]him, and said, We came unto the land whither thou hast sent us, and surely it floweth with [b]milk and honey: and here is of the fruit of it.

29 Nevertheless the people be strong that dwell in

12:12 [1] As a child that cometh out of his mother's belly dead, having as it were but the skin.
12:14 [1] In his displeasure.
13:1 [1] That is, in Rithmah, which was in Paran, Num. 33:18.
13:3 [1] After the people had required it of Moses, as it is in Deut. 1:22, then the Lord spake to Moses so to do.
13:4 [1] Or, rulers.
13:9 [1] Or, Joshua.
13:17 [1] Which in number were twelve, according to the twelve tribes.

13:18 [1] Or, his country.
13:20 [1] Plentiful or barren.
13:22 [1] Which was in the wilderness of Paran.
13:23 [1] Which were a kind of giants.
    [2] Declaring the antiquity thereof: also Abraham, Sarah, Isaac and Jacob were buried there.
13:25 [1] Or, the valley of Eshcol, that is, of grapes.
13:27 [1] Called also Kadesh Barnea.
13:28 [1] That is, Moses.

the land, and the cities *are* walled and exceeding great: and moreover, we saw the [1]sons of Anak there.

30 The Amalekites dwell in the South country, and the Hittites, and the Jebusites, and the Amorites dwell in the mountains, and the Canaanites dwell by the sea, and by the coasts of Jordan.

31 Then Caleb stilled the people [1]before Moses, and said, Let us go up at once, and possess it: for undoubtedly we shall overcome it.

32 But the men that went up with him, said, We be not able to go up against the people: for they are stronger than we.

33 So they brought up an evil report of the land which they had searched for the children of Israel, saying, The land which we have gone through to search it out, is a land that [1]eateth up the inhabitants thereof: for all the people that we saw in it, are men of great stature.

34 For there we saw giants, the sons of Anak, *which come* of the giants, so that we seemed in our sight like grasshoppers: and so we were in their sight.

14 *2 The people murmur against Moses.   10 They would have stoned Caleb and Joshua.   23 Moses pacifieth God by his prayer.   45 The people that would enter into the land contrary to God's will, are slain.*

1 Then all the Congregation lifted up their voice, and cried: and the [1]people wept that night,

2 And all the children of Israel murmured against Moses and Aaron: and the whole assembly said unto them, Would God we had died in the land of Egypt, or in this wilderness: would God we were dead.

3 Wherefore now hath the Lord brought us into this land to fall upon the sword? our wives and our children shall be [1]a prey: were it not better for us to return into Egypt?

4 And they said one to another, Let us make a captain and return into Egypt.

5 Then Moses and Aaron [1]fell on their faces before all the assembly of the Congregation of the children of Israel.

6 And Joshua the son of Nun, and Caleb the son of Jephunneh *two* of them that searched the land, [1]rent their clothes,

7 And spake unto all the assembly of the children of Israel, saying, The land which we walked through to search it, is a very good land.

CHAPTER 14
a Exod. 32:12
b Exod. 13:21
c Deut. 9:28
d Exod. 34:6
   Ps. 103:8
e Ps. 10:3
f Exod. 20:5
   Exod. 34:7

8 If the Lord love us, he will bring us into this land, and give it us, which is a land that floweth with milk and honey.

9 But rebel not ye against the Lord, neither fear ye the people of the land: for they are *but* [1]bread for us: their shield is departed from them, and the Lord is with us, fear them not.

10 And all the multitude said, [1]Stone them with stones: but the glory of the Lord appeared in the Tabernacle of the Congregation before all the children of Israel.

11 And the Lord said unto Moses, How long will this people provoke me, and how long will it be ere they believe me, for all the signs which I have showed among them?

12 I will smite them with the pestilence and destroy them, and will make thee a greater nation and mightier than they.

13 But Moses said unto the Lord, [a]When the Egyptians shall hear it, (for thou broughtest this people by thy power from among them)

14 Then they shall say to the inhabitants of the land, (*for* they have heard, that thou Lord, art among this people, *and* that thou, Lord, art seen [1]face to face, and that thy cloud standeth over them, and that thou [b]goest before them, by daytime in a pillar of a cloud, and in a pillar of fire by night.)

15 That thou wilt kill this people as [1]one man: so the heathen which have heard the fame of thee, shall thus say,

16 Because the Lord was not [c]able to bring this people into the land which he sware unto them, therefore hath he slain them in the wilderness.

17 And now, I beseech thee, let the power of my Lord be great, according as thou hast spoken, saying,

18 The Lord is [d]slow to anger, and of great mercy, and [e]forgiving iniquity and sin, but not making *the wicked* innocent, and [f]visiting the wickedness of the fathers upon the children, in the third and fourth *generation*:

19 Be merciful, I beseech thee, unto the iniquity of this people, according to thy great mercy, and as thou hast forgiven this people from Egypt, even until now.

20 And the Lord said, I have forgiven [1]it, according to thy request.

21 Notwithstanding, as I live, all the earth, shall

13:29 [1] Ahiman, Sheshai, and Talmai, whom Caleb slew afterward, Josh. 11:21, 22.
13:31 [1] Or, murmuring against Moses.
13:33 [1] The giants were so cruel, that they spoiled and killed one another and those that came to them.
14:1 [1] Such as were afraid at the report of the ten spies.
14:3 [1] To our enemies the Canaanites.
14:5 [1] Lamenting the people, and praying for them.

14:6 [1] For sorrow, hearing their blasphemy.
14:9 [1] We shall easily overcome them.
14:10 [1] This is the condition of them that would persuade in God's cause, to be persecuted of the multitude.
14:14 [1] Hebrew, *eye to eye*.
14:15 [1] So that none shall escape.
14:20 [1] In that he destroyed not them utterly, but left their posterity and certain to enter.

be filled with the glory of the Lord.

22 For all those men which have seen my glory, and my miracles which I did in Egypt, and in the wilderness, and have tempted me this [1]ten times, and have not obeyed my voice,

23 Certainly they shall not see the land, whereof I sware unto their fathers: neither shall any that provoke me, see it.

24 But my servant [g]Caleb, because he had another [1]spirit, and hath followed me still, even him will I bring into the land, whither he went, and his seed shall inherit it.

25 Now the Amalekites and the Canaanites [1]remain in the valley: *wherefore* turn back tomorrow, and get you into the [2]wilderness, by the way of the red sea.

26 ¶ After, the Lord spake unto Moses and to Aaron, saying,

27 [h]How long *shall I suffer* this wicked multitude to murmur against me? I have heard the murmurings of the children of Israel, which they murmur against me.

28 Tell them, As I [i]live (saith the Lord) I will surely do unto you, even as ye have spoken in mine ears.

29 Your carcasses shall fall in this wilderness, and all you that were [j]counted through all your numbers, from twenty years old and above, which have murmured against me,

30 Ye shall not doubtless come into the land, for the which I [k]lifted up mine hand, to make you dwell therein, save Caleb the son of Jephunneh, and Joshua the son of Nun.

31 But your children (which ye said should be a prey) them will I bring in, and they shall know the land which ye have refused:

32 But even your carcasses shall fall in this wilderness.

33 And your children shall [1]wander in the wilderness forty years, and shall bear your [2]whoredoms, until your carcasses be wasted in the wilderness.

34 After the number of the days in the which ye searched out the land, *even* forty days, [l]every day for a year, shall you bear your iniquity, for [m]forty years, and ye [1]shall feel my breach of promise.

35 I the Lord have said, Certainly I will do so to all this wicked company that are gathered together against me: *for* in this wilderness they shall be consumed, and there they shall die.

36 And the men which Moses had sent to search

the land (which when they came again, made all the people to murmur against him, and brought up a slander upon the land.)

37 Even those men that did bring up that vile slander upon the land, [n]shall die by a plague before the Lord.

38 But Joshua the son of Nun, and Caleb the son of Jephunneh, of those men that went to search the land, shall live.

39 ¶ Then Moses told these sayings unto all the children of Israel, and the people sorrowed greatly.

40 [o]And they rose up early in the morning, and got them up into the top of the mountain, saying, Lo, we be ready to go up to the place which the Lord hath promised: for we have [1]sinned.

41 But Moses said, Wherefore transgress ye thus the commandment of the Lord? it will not so come well to pass.

42 Go not up, (for the Lord is not among you) lest ye be overthrown before your enemies.

43 For the Amalekites and the Canaanites *are* there before you, and ye shall fall by the sword: for inasmuch as ye are turned away from the Lord, the Lord also will not be with you.

44 Yet they presumed [1]obstinately to go up to the top of the mountain: but the Ark of the covenant of the Lord, and Moses departed not out of the camp.

45 Then the Amalekites and the Canaanites, which dwelt in that mountain, came down and smote them, [p]and consumed them unto Hormah.

15 2 *The offering which the Israelites should offer when they came into the land of Canaan.* 32 *The punishment of him that brake the Sabbath.*

1 And the Lord spake unto Moses, saying,

2 Speak unto the children of Israel, and say unto them, [a]When ye be come into the [1]land of your habitations which I give unto you,

3 And will make an offering by fire unto the Lord, a burnt offering or a sacrifice [b,1]to fulfill a vow, or a free offering, or in your feasts to make a [c]sweet savor unto the Lord, of the herd or of the flock,

4 Then [d]let him that offereth his offering unto the Lord, bring a meat offering of a tenth deal of fine flour, mingled with the fourth part of an [1]Hin of oil.

5 Also thou shalt prepare the fourth part of an

---

g Josh. 14:6
h Ps. 106:26
i Num. 26:65
Num. 32:10
j Deut. 1:35
k Gen. 14:22
l Ezek. 4:6
m Ps. 95:10
n 1 Cor. 10:10
Heb. 3:10,17
Jude 5
o Deut. 1:41
p Deut. 1:44

CHAPTER 15
a Lev. 23:10
b Lev. 22:21
c Lev. 2:1
d Exod. 29:18

14:22 [1] That is, sundry times and often.
14:24 [1] A meek and obedient spirit, and not rebellious.
14:25 [1] And lie in wait for you.
   [2] For I will not defend you.
14:33 [1] The word signifieth to be shepherds, or to wander like shepherds to and fro.
   [2] Your infidelity and disobedience against God.

14:34 [1] Whether my promise be true or no.
14:40 [1] They confess they sinned by rebelling against God, but consider not they offended in going up without God's commandment.
14:44 [1] They could not be stayed by any means.
15:2 [1] Into the land of Canaan.
15:3 [1] Or, separate.
15:4 [1] Read Exod. 29:40.

Hin of wine to be poured on a lamb *appointed* for the burnt offering, or *any* offering.

6 And for a ram thou shalt for a meat offering, prepare two tenth deals of fine flour, mingled with the third part of an Hin of oil.

7 And for a [1]drink offering thou shalt offer the third part of an Hin of wine, for a sweet savor unto the Lord.

8 And when thou preparest a bullock for a burnt offering, or for a sacrifice to fulfill a vow or a peace offering to the Lord,

9 Then let him offer with the bullock a meat offering of [1]three tenth deals of fine flour, mingled with half an Hin of oil.

10 And thou shalt bring for a drink offering half an Hin of wine, for an offering made by fire of a sweet savor unto the Lord.

11 Thus shall it be done for a bullock, or for a ram, or for a lamb, or for a kid.

12 According to the number [1]that ye prepare *to offer*, so shall ye do to everyone according to their number.

13 All that are born of the country, shall do these things thus, to offer an offering made by fire of sweet savor unto the Lord.

14 And if a stranger sojourn with you, or whosoever be among you in your generations, and will make an offering by fire of a sweet savor unto the Lord, as ye do, so he shall do.

15 *One ordinance *shall be* both for you of the Congregation, and also for the stranger that dwelleth *with you, even* an ordinance forever in your generations: as you are, so shall the stranger be before the Lord.

16 One law and one manner shall serve both for you and for the stranger that sojourneth with you.

17 ¶ And the Lord spake unto Moses, saying,

18 Speak unto the children of Israel, and say unto them, When ye be come into the land, to the which I bring you,

19 And when ye shall eat of the bread of the land, ye shall offer an heave offering unto the Lord.

20 Ye shall offer up a cake of the first of your [1]dough for an heave offering: *as the heave offering of the barn, so ye shall lift it up.

21 Of the first of your dough ye shall give unto the Lord an heave offering in your generations.

22 And if ye [1]have erred, and not observed all these commandments, which the Lord hath spoken unto Moses,

Exod. 12:49
Num. 9:14
Lev. 23:4
Lev. 4:1
Lev. 4:27
Lev. 24:12

23 *Even* all that the Lord hath commanded you by the hand of Moses, from the first day that the Lord commanded Moses, and hence forward among your generations:

24 And if so be that ought be committed ignorantly of the [1]Congregation, then all the Congregation shall give a bullock for a burnt offering, for a sweet savor unto the Lord, with the meat offering and drink offering thereto, according to the *manner, and an he goat for a sin offering.

25 And the Priest shall make an atonement for all the Congregation of the children of Israel, and it shall be forgiven them: for it is ignorance: and they shall bring their offering for an offering made by fire unto the Lord, and their sin offering before the Lord for their ignorance.

26 Then shall be forgiven all the Congregation of the children of Israel, and the stranger that dwelleth among them: for all the people *were* in ignorance.

27 ¶ *But if any one person sin through ignorance, then he shall bring a she goat of a year old for a sin offering.

28 And the Priest shall make an atonement for the ignorant person, when he sinneth by ignorance before the Lord, to make reconciliation for him: and it shall be forgiven him.

29 He that is born among the children of Israel, and the stranger that dwelleth among them, shall have both one law, who so doth sin by ignorance.

30 ¶ But the person that doeth ought [1]presumptuously, whether he be born in the land, or a stranger, the same blasphemeth the Lord: therefore that person shall be cut off from among his people,

31 Because he hath despised the word of the Lord, and hath broken his commandment: that person shall be utterly cut off: his [1]iniquity shall be upon him.

32 ¶ And while the children of Israel were in the wilderness, they found a man that gathered sticks upon the Sabbath day.

33 And they that found him gathering sticks, brought him unto Moses and to Aaron, and unto all the Congregation,

34 And they put him [1]ward: for it was not declared what should be done unto him.

35 Then the Lord said unto Moses, This man shall die the death: and let all the multitude stone him with stones without the host.

36 And all the Congregation brought him without

15:7 [1] The liquor was so called, because it was poured on the thing that was offered.

15:9 [1] Or, three Omers.

15:12 [1] Every sacrifice of beasts must have their meat offering and drink offering according to this proportion.

15:20 [1] Which is made of the first corn ye gather.

15:22 [1] As by oversight or ignorance, read Lev. 4:2, 13.

15:24 [1] Some read, from the eyes of the Congregation, that is, which is hid from the Congregation.

15:30 [1] Hebrew, *with an high hand,* that is, *in contempt of God.*

15:31 [1] He shall sustain the punishment of his sin.

the host, and stoned him with stones, and he died, as the Lord had commanded Moses.

37 ¶ And the Lord spake unto Moses, saying,

38 Speak unto the children of Israel, and bid them that they *make them fringes upon the borders of their garments throughout their generations, and put upon the fringes of the borders a ribbon of blue silk.

39 And ye shall have the fringes that when ye look upon them, ye may remember all the commandments of the Lord, and do them: and that ye seek not after your own heart, nor after your own eyes, after the which ye go a ¹whoring;

40 That ye may remember and do all my commandments, and be holy unto your God.

41 I am the Lord your God, which brought you out of the land of Egypt to be your God: I am the Lord your God.

16 1 *The rebellion of Korah, Dathan, and Abiram.* 31 *Korah and his company perisheth.* 41 *The people the next day murmur.* 49 *14,700 are slain for murmuring.*

1 Now ᵃKorah the son of Izhar, the son of Kohath, the son of Levi ¹went apart with Dathan, and Abiram the son of Eliab, and On the son of Peleth, the sons of Reuben:

2 And they rose up ¹against Moses, with certain of the children of Israel, two hundred and fifty captains of the assembly, ᵇfamous in the Congregation, and men of renown,

3 Who gathered themselves together against Moses, and against Aaron, and said unto them, ¹*Ye take* too much upon you, seeing all the Congregation is holy, ²every one of them, and the Lord *is* among them: wherefore then lift ye yourselves above the Congregation of the Lord?

4 But when Moses heard it, he fell upon his face,

5 And spake to Korah and unto all his company, saying, Tomorrow the Lord will show who is his, and who is holy, and who ought to approach near unto him: and whom he hath ¹chosen, he will cause to come near to him.

6 This do *therefore*, Take you censers, *both* Korah and all his company,

7 And put fire therein, and put incense in them

before the Lord tomorrow: and the man whom the Lord doth choose, the same shall be holy: ¹*ye take* too much upon you, ye sons of Levi.

8 Again Moses said unto Korah, Hear, I pray you, ye sons of Levi.

9 Seemeth it a small thing unto you, that the God of Israel hath separated you from the multitude of Israel, to take you near to himself, to do the service of the Tabernacle of the Lord, and to stand before the Congregation, and to minister unto them?

10 He hath also taken thee to ¹him, and all thy brethren, the sons of Levi with thee, and seek ye the office of the Priest also?

11 For which cause, thou, and all thy company are gathered together against the Lord: and what is Aaron, that ye murmur against him?

12 ¶ And Moses sent to call Dathan, and Abiram the sons of Eliab: who answered, We will not come up.

13 Is it a small thing that thou hast brought us out ¹of a land that floweth with milk and honey, to kill us in the wilderness, except thou make thyself lord and ruler over us also?

14 Also thou hast not brought us unto a land that floweth with milk and honey, neither given us inheritance of fields and vineyards: wilt thou ¹put out the eyes of these men? we will not come up.

15 Then Moses waxed very angry, and said unto the Lord, ᶜLook not unto their offering: I have not taken so much as an ass from them, neither have I hurt any of them.

16 And Moses said unto Korah, Be thou and all thy company ¹before the Lord: *both* thou, they, and Aaron tomorrow.

17 And take every man his censer, and put incense in them, and bring ye every man his censer before the Lord, two hundred and fifty censers: thou also and Aaron, every one his censer.

18 So they took every man his censer, and put fire in them, and laid incense thereon, and stood in the door of the Tabernacle of the Congregation with Moses and Aaron.

19 And Korah gathered all the ¹multitude against them unto the door of the Tabernacle of the Congregation: then the glory of the Lord appeared unto all the Congregation.

ʲ Deut. 22:12
Matt. 23:5

CHAPTER 16
ᵃ Num. 27:3
Jude 11
ᵇ Num. 26:9
ᶜ Gen. 44:3

15:39 ¹ By leaving God's commandments and following your own fantasies.
16:1 ¹ Or, took others with him.
16:2 ¹ Or, before Moses.
16:3 ¹ Or let it suffice you: meaning, to have abused them thus long.
² All are alike holy: therefore none ought to be preferred above others: thus the wicked reason against God's ordinance.
16:5 ¹ To be the Priest and to offer.

16:7 ¹ He layeth the same to their charge justly, wherewith they wrongfully charged him.
16:10 ¹ To serve in the Congregation, as in the verse before.
16:13 ¹ Thus they spake contemptuously, preferring Egypt to Canaan.
16:14 ¹ Wilt thou make them that searched the land, believe that they saw not that which they saw?
16:16 ¹ At the door of the Tabernacle.
16:19 ¹ All that were of their faction.

20 And the Lord spake unto Moses and to Aaron, saying,

21 Separate yourselves from among this Congregation, that I may consume them at once.

22 And they fell upon their faces and said, O God, the God of the spirits ¹of all flesh, hath not one man *only* sinned, and wilt thou be wroth with all the Congregation?

23 And the Lord spake unto Moses, saying,

24 Speak unto the Congregation, and say, Get you away from about the Tabernacle of Korah, Dathan, and Abiram.

25 Then Moses rose up, and went unto Dathan and Abiram, and the Elders of Israel followed him.

26 And he spake unto the Congregation, saying, Depart, I pray you, from the tents of these wicked men, and touch nothing of theirs, lest ye perish ¹in all their sins.

27 So they got them away from the Tabernacle of Korah, Dathan, and Abiram on every side: and Dathan and Abiram came out and stood in the door of their tents, with their wives, and their sons, and their little children.

28 And Moses said, Hereby ye shall know that the Lord hath sent me to do all these works: for *I have* not *done them* of mine own ¹mind.

29 If these men die the common death of all men, or if they be visited after the visitation of all men, the Lord hath not sent me.

30 But if the Lord make ¹a new thing, and the earth open her mouth, and swallow them up with all that they have, and they go down quick into ²,³the pit: then ye shall understand that these men have provoked the Lord.

31 ¶ And as soon as he had made an end of speaking all the words, even the ground clave asunder that was under them,

32 And the earth ᵈopened her mouth, and swallowed them up with their families, and all the men that were with Korah, and all their goods.

33 So they and all that they had, went down alive into the pit, and the earth covered them: so they perished from among the Congregation.

34 And all Israel that were about them, fled at the cry of them: for they said, *Let us flee,* lest the earth swallow us up.

35 But there came out a fire from the Lord, and consumed the two hundred and fifty men that of-

ᵈ Num. 17:3
Deut. 11:6
Ps. 106:17

fered the incense.

36 ¶ And the Lord spake unto Moses, saying,

37 Speak unto Eleazar the son of Aaron the Priest, that he take up the censers out of the burning, and scatter the fire beyond *the altar*: for they are hallowed,

38 The censers, *I say*, of these sinners, *that destroyed* ¹themselves: and let them make of them broad plates for a covering of the Altar: for they offered them before the Lord, therefore they shall be holy, and they shall be a ²sign unto the children of Israel.

39 Then Eleazar the Priest took the brazen censers, which they that were burnt had offered, and made broad plates of them for a covering of the Altar.

40 *It is* a remembrance unto the children of Israel, that no stranger which is not of the seed of Aaron, come near to offer incense before the Lord, that he be not like ¹Korah and his company, as the Lord said to him by the hand of Moses.

41 ¶ But on the morrow all the multitude of the children of Israel murmured against Moses and against Aaron, saying, Ye have killed the people of the Lord.

42 And when the Congregation was gathered against Moses and against Aaron, then they ¹turned their faces toward the tabernacle of the Congregation: and behold, the cloud covered it, and the glory of the Lord appeared.

43 Then Moses and Aaron were come before the Tabernacle of the Congregation.

44 ¶ And the Lord spake unto Moses, saying,

45 Get you up from among this Congregation: for I will consume them quickly: then they fell upon their faces.

46 And Moses said unto Aaron, Take the censer and put fire therein of the ¹Altar, and put *therein* incense, and go quickly unto the Congregation, and make an atonement for them: for there is wrath gone out from the Lord: the plague is begun.

47 Then Aaron took as Moses commanded him, and ran into the midst of the Congregation, and behold, the ¹plague was begun among the people, and he put incense, and made an atonement for the people.

48 And when he stood between the dead, and them that were alive, the ¹plague was stayed.

49 So they died of this plague fourteen thousand and seven hundred, beside them that died in the

---

16:22 ¹ Or, of every creature.
16:26 ¹ With them that have committed so many sins.
16:28 ¹ I have not forged them of mine own brain.
16:30 ¹ Or, show a strange sight.
  ² Or, hell.
  ³ Or, deep and dark places of the earth.
16:38 ¹ Which were the occasion of their own death.

² Of God's judgments against rebels.
16:40 ¹ Who presumed above his vocation.
16:42 ¹ Or fled, to wit, Moses and Aaron.
16:46 ¹ For it was not lawful to take any other fire, but of the altar of burnt offering, Lev. 10:1.
16:47 ¹ God had begun to punish the people.
16:48 ¹ God drew back his hand and ceased to punish them.

conspiracy of Korah.

50 And Aaron went again unto Moses before the door of the Tabernacle of the Congregation, and the plague was stayed.

CHAPTER 17
a Exod. 25:21
b Heb. 9:4

CHAPTER 18
a Num. 3:45

17

2 The twelve rods of the twelve princes of the tribes of Israel. 8 Aaron's rod buddeth, and beareth blossoms, 10 For a testimony against the rebellious people.

1 And the Lord spake unto [1]Moses, saying,

2 Speak unto the children of Israel, and take of every one of them a rod, after the house of their fathers, of all their princes according to the family of their fathers, *even* twelve rods: *and* thou shalt write every man's name upon his rod.

3 And write Aaron's name upon the rod of Levi: for every rod *shall be* for the head of the house of their fathers.

4 And thou shalt put them in the Tabernacle of the Congregation, before *the Ark* of the testimony, [a]where I will declare myself to you.

5 And the man's rod, whom I [1]choose, shall blossom: and I will make cease from me the grudgings of the children of Israel, which grudge against you.

6 ¶ Then Moses spake unto the children of Israel, and all their Princes gave him a rod, one rod for every prince, according to the houses of their fathers, *even* twelve rods, and the rod [1]of Aaron was among their rods.

7 And Moses laid the rods before the Lord in the Tabernacle of the Testimony.

8 And when Moses on the morrow went into the Tabernacle of the Testimony, behold, the rod of Aaron [1]for the house of Levi was budded, and brought forth buds, and brought forth blossoms, and bare ripe almonds.

9 Then Moses brought out all the rods from before the Lord unto all the children of Israel: and they looked upon them, and took every man his rod.

10 After, the Lord said unto Moses, [b]Bring Aaron's rod again before the Testimony to be kept for a token to the rebellious children, and thou shalt cause their [1]murmurings to cease from me, that they die not.

11 So Moses did as the Lord had commanded him: so did he.

12 ¶ And the children of Israel spake unto Moses, saying, Behold, [1]we are dead, we perish, we are all lost:

13 Whosoever cometh near or approacheth to the Tabernacle of the Lord, shall die: shall we be consumed and die?

18

1, 7 The office of Aaron and his sons, 2 With the Levites. 8 The Priest's part of the offerings. 20 God is their portion. 26 The Levites have their tithes, and offer the tenths thereof to the Lord.

1 And the Lord said unto Aaron, Thou, and thy sons, and thy father's house with thee, shall bear [1]the iniquity of the Sanctuary: both thou and thy sons with thee shall bear the iniquity of your Priest's office.

2 And bring also with thee thy brethren of the tribe of Levi of the family of thy father which shall be joined with thee, and minister unto thee: but thou and thy sons with thee *shall minister* before the Tabernacle of the Testimony:

3 And they shall [1]keep my charge, even the charge of all the Tabernacle: but they shall not come near the instruments of the Sanctuary, nor to the altar, lest they die, both they and you.

4 And they shall be joined with thee, and keep the charge of the Tabernacle of the Congregation for all the service of the Tabernacle: and no [1]stranger shall come near unto you:

5 Therefore shall ye keep the charge of the Sanctuary, and the charge of the Altar: so there shall fall no more wrath upon the children of Israel.

6 For lo, I have [a]taken your brethren the Levites from among the children of Israel, *which* as a gift of yours, are given unto the Lord, to do the service of the Tabernacle of the Congregation.

7 But thou, and thy sons with thee shall keep your Priest's office for all things of the Altar, and within the veil: therefore shall ye serve: *for* I have made your Priest's office [1]an office of service: therefore the stranger that cometh near shall be slain.

8 ¶ Again the Lord spake unto Aaron, Behold, I have given thee the keeping of mine [1]offerings, of all the hallowed things of the children of Israel: unto thee have I given them for the anointing's sake, and to thy sons for a perpetual ordinance.

9 This shall be thine of the most holy things, *reserved* from [1]the fire: all their offering of all their

---

17:1 [1] While he was in the door of the Tabernacle.
17:5 [1] To be the chief Priest.
17:6 [1] Though Joseph's tribe was divided into two in the distribution of the land, yet here it is but one and Levi maketh a tribe.
17:8 [1] To declare that God did choose the house of Levi to serve him in the Tabernacle.
17:10 [1] Grudging that Aaron should be high Priest.
17:12 [1] The Chaldea text describeth thus their murmuring: We die by the sword, the earth swalloweth us up, the pestilence doth con-

sume us.
18:1 [1] If you trespass in anything concerning the ceremonies of the Sanctuary of your office, you shall be punished.
18:3 [1] That is, the things which are committed to thee, or, which thou dost enjoin them.
18:4 [1] Which was not of the tribe of Levi.
18:7 [1] Or, gift.
18:8 [1] As the firstfruit, firstborn, and the tenths.
18:9 [1] That which was not burned should be the Priest's.

meat offering, and of all their sin offering, and of all their trespass offering, which they bring unto me, that shall be most holy unto thee, and to thy sons.

10 In the most [1]holy place shalt thou eat it: every male shall eat of it: it is holy unto thee.

11 This also shall be thine: the heave offering of their gift, with all the shake offerings of the children of Israel, I have given them unto thee, and to thy sons and to thy [1]daughters with thee, to be a duty forever: all the clean in thine house shall eat of it.

12 All the [1]fat of the oil, and all the fat of the wine, and of the wheat, which they shall offer unto the Lord for their firstfruits, I have given them unto thee.

13 And the first ripe of all that is in their land, which they shall bring unto Lord shall be thine: all the clean in thine house shall eat of it.

14 [b]Everything separate from the common use in Israel shall be thine.

15 All that *first* openeth the 'matrix of any flesh, which they shall offer unto the Lord of man or beast, shall be thine: but the firstborn of man shalt thou redeem, and the firstborn of the unclean beast shalt thou redeem.

16 And those that are to be redeemed, shalt thou redeem from the age of a month, according to thy estimation, for the money of five shekels, after the shekel of the Sanctuary, [d]which is twenty gerahs.

17 But the firstborn of a cow, or the firstborn of a sheep, or the firstborn of a goat shalt thou not [1]redeem: *for* they are holy: thou shalt sprinkle their blood at the altar, and thou shalt burn their fat: *it is* a sacrifice made by fire for a sweet savor unto the Lord.

18 And the flesh of them shall be thine, [e]as the shake breast, and as the right shoulder shall be thine.

19 All the heave offerings of the holy things which the children of Israel shall offer unto the Lord, have I given thee, and thy sons, and thy daughters with thee, to be a duty forever: *it is* a perpetual covenant [1]of salt before the Lord, to thee, and to thy seed with thee.

20 ¶ And the Lord said unto Aaron, Thou shalt have none inheritance in their [1]land: neither shalt thou have any part among them: [f]I am thy part and thine inheritance among the children of Israel.

21 For behold, I have given the children of Levi

[b] Lev. 27:28
[c] Exod. 13:2
Exod. 22:29
Lev. 27:26
Num. 3:13
[d] Exod. 30:13
Lev. 27:25
Num. 3:47
Ezek. 45:12
[e] Exod. 29:26
Lev. 7:30
[f] Deut. 10:9
Deut. 18:2
Josh. 13:14,33
Exod. 44:28

all the tenth in Israel for an inheritance, for their service which they serve in the Tabernacle of the Congregation.

22 Neither shall the children of Israel any more [1]come near the Tabernacle of the Congregation, lest they sustain sin, and die.

23 But the Levites shall do the service in the Tabernacle of the Congregation, and they shall bear [1]their sin: *it is* a law forever in your generations, that among the children of Israel they possess none inheritance.

24 For the tithes of the children of Israel, which they shall offer as an offering unto the Lord, I have given the Levites for an inheritance, therefore I have said unto them, Among the children of Israel ye shall possess none inheritance.

25 ¶ And the Lord spake unto Moses, saying,

26 Speak also unto the Levites, and say unto them, When ye shall take of the children of Israel the tithes, which I have given you of them for your inheritance, then shall ye take an heave offering of that same for the Lord, *even* the tenth part of the tithe.

27 And your heave offering shall be reckoned unto you, as the [1]corn of the barn, or as the abundance of the winepress.

28 So ye shall also offer an heave offering unto the Lord of all your tithes, which ye shall receive of the children of Israel, and ye shall give thereof the Lord's heave offering to Aaron the Priest.

29 Ye shall offer of all your [1]gifts all the Lord's heave offerings: of all the [2]fat of the same *shall ye offer* the holy things thereof.

30 Therefore thou shalt say unto them, When ye have offered the fat thereof, then it shall be counted unto the Levites, as the increase of the corn floor, or as the increase of the winepress.

31 And ye shall eat it in all [1]places, ye, and your households: for it is your wages for your service in the Tabernacle of the Congregation.

32 And ye shall [1]bear no sin by the reason of it, when ye have offered the fat of it: neither shall ye pollute the holy [2]things of the children of Israel, lest ye die.

19

2 *The sacrifice of the red cow.* 9 *The sprinkling water.* 11 *He that toucheth the dead.* 14 *The man that dieth in a tent.*

18:10 [1] That is, in the Sanctuary, between the court and the Holiest of all.
18:11 [1] Read Lev. 10:14.
18:12 [1] That is, the chiefest, or the best.
18:17 [1] Because they are appointed for sacrifice.
18:19 [1] That is, sure, stable, and incorruptible.
18:20 [1] Of Canaan.
18:22 [1] To serve therein: for the Levites are put in their place.

18:23 [1] If they fail in their office, they shall be punished.
18:27 [1] As acceptable as the fruit of your own ground or vineyard.
18:29 [1] Which ye have received of the children of Israel.
    [2] Read verse 12.
18:31 [1] As in verse 11.
18:32 [1] Ye shall not be punished therefore.
    [2] The offerings which the Israelites have offered to God.

1 And the Lord spake to Moses, and to Aaron, saying,

2 ¹This is the ordinance of the Law, which the Lord hath commanded, saying, Speak unto the children of Israel that they bring thee a red cow without blemish, wherein is no spot, upon the which never came yoke.

3 And ye shall give her unto Eleazar the Priest, that he may bring her ᵃwithout the host, and cause her to ¹be slain before his face.

4 Then shall Eleazar the Priest take of her blood with his ᵇfinger, and sprinkle it before the Tabernacle of the Congregation seven times,

5 And cause the cow to be burnt in his sight: with her ᶜskin, and her flesh, and her blood, and her dung shall he burn her.

6 Then shall the Priest take cedar wood, and hyssop, and scarlet lace, and cast them in the midst of the fire where the cow burneth.

7 Then shall the ¹Priest wash his clothes, and he shall wash his flesh in water, and then come into the host, and the Priest shall be unclean unto the even.

8 Also he that ¹burneth her, shall wash his clothes in water, and wash his flesh in water, and be unclean until even.

9 And a man, that is clean, shall take up the ashes of the cow, and put them without the host in a clean place: and it shall be kept for the Congregation of the children of Israel for ¹a sprinkling water: it is a sin offering.

10 Therefore he that gathereth the ashes of the cow, shall wash his clothes, and remain unclean until even: and it shall be unto the children of Israel, and unto the stranger that dwelleth among them, a statute forever.

11 He that toucheth the dead body of any man, shall be unclean even seven days.

12 He shall purify himself ¹therewith the third day, and the seventh day he shall be clean: but if he purify not himself the third day, then the seventh day he shall not be clean.

13 Whosoever toucheth the corpse of any man that is dead, and purgeth not himself, defileth the Tabernacle of the Lord, and that person shall be ¹cut off from Israel, because the sprinkling water was not sprinkled upon him: he shall be unclean,

and his uncleanness shall remain still upon him.

14 This is the law, When a man dieth in a tent, all that come into the tent, and all that is in the tent, shall be unclean seven days.

15 And all the vessels that be open, which have no ¹covering fastened upon them, shall be unclean.

16 Also whosoever toucheth one that is slain with a sword in the field, or a dead person, or a bone of a dead man, or a grave, shall be unclean seven days.

17 Therefore for an unclean person, they shall take of the burnt ashes of the ¹sin offering, and ²pure water shall be put thereto in a vessel.

18 And a ¹clean person shall take hyssop, and dip it in the water, and sprinkle it upon the tent, and upon all the vessels, and on the persons that were therein, and upon him that touched the bone, or the slain, or the dead, or the grave.

19 And the clean person shall sprinkle upon the unclean the third day, and the seventh day, and he shall purify himself the seventh day, and ¹wash his clothes, and wash himself in water, and shall be clean at even.

20 But the man that is unclean, and purifieth not himself, that person shall be cut off from among the Congregation, because he hath defiled the Sanctuary of the Lord: and the sprinkling water hath not been sprinkled upon him: therefore shall he be unclean.

21 And it shall be a perpetual law unto them, that he that sprinkleth the sprinkling water, shall wash his clothes: also he that toucheth the sprinkling water, shall be unclean until even.

22 And whatsoever the unclean person toucheth shall be unclean: and the person that toucheth ¹him, shall be unclean until the even.

20 1 Miriam dieth. 2 The people murmur. 8 They have water out of the rock. 14 Edom denieth the Israelites passage. 25, 28 The death of Aaron in whose room Eleazar succeedeth.

1 Then the children of Israel came with the whole Congregation to the desert of Zin in the first ¹month, and the people abode at Kadesh: where ²Miriam died, and was buried there.

2 But there was no water for the Congregation, and they ¹assembled themselves against Moses and

---

19:2 ¹ According to this law and ceremony ye shall sacrifice the red cow.
19:3 ¹ By another Priest.
19:7 ¹ Meaning, Eleazar.
19:8 ¹ The inferior Priest who killed her, and burned her.
19:9 ¹ Or, the water of separation because they that were separate for their uncleanness, were sprinkled therewith and made clean, Num. 8:7. It is also called holy water, because [it] was ordained to an holy use, Num. 1:17.
19:12 ¹ With the sprinkling water.
19:13 ¹ So that he should not be esteemed to be of the holy people. But as a polluted and excommunicated person.

19:15 ¹ Hebrew, a covering of cloth.
19:17 ¹ Of the red cow burnt for sin.
² Water of the fountain or river.
19:18 ¹ One of the priests which is clean.
19:19 ¹ Because he had been among them that were unclean: or, else had touched the water, as verse 21.
19:22 ¹ That is, unclean.
20:1 ¹ This was forty years after their departure from Egypt.
² Moses and Aaron's sister.
20:2 ¹ Another rebellion was in Raphidim, Exod. 17, and this was in Kadesh.

against Aaron.

3 And the people chode with Moses, and spake, saying, Would God we had perished *when our brethren died before the Lord.

4 *Why have ye thus brought the Congregation of the Lord unto this wilderness, that *both* we and our cattle should die there?

5 Wherefore now have ye made us to come up from Egypt, to bring us into this miserable place, *which is* no place of seed, nor figs, nor vines, nor pomegranates? neither is there any water to drink.

6 Then Moses and Aaron went from the assembly unto the door of the Tabernacle of the Congregation, and fell upon their faces: and the glory of the Lord appeared unto them.

7 And the Lord spake unto Moses, saying,

8 Take the ¹rod, and gather thou and thy brother Aaron the Congregation together, and speak ye unto the rock before their eyes, and it shall give forth his water, and thou shalt bring them water out of the rock: so thou shalt give the Congregation and the beasts drink.

9 Then Moses took the rod from before the Lord, as he had commanded him.

10 And Moses and Aaron gathered the Congregation together before the rock: and *Moses* said unto them, Hear now ye rebels: ¹shall we bring you water out of this rock?

11 Then Moses lift up his hand, and with his rod he smote the rock twice, and the water came out abundantly: so the Congregation, and their beasts drank.

12 ¶ Again, the Lord spake unto Moses, and to Aaron, Because ye believed me not, to ¹sanctify me in the presence of the children of Israel, therefore ye shall not bring this Congregation into the land which I have given them.

13 This is the water of ¹Meribah, because the children of Israel strove with the Lord, and he ²was sanctified in them.

14 ¶ Then Moses sent messengers from Kadesh unto the king of ¹Edom, *saying,* Thus saith thy brother Israel, Thou knowest all the travail that we have had,

15 How our fathers went down into Egypt, and we dwelt in Egypt a long time, where the Egyptians handled us evil and our fathers.

CHAPTER 20
a Num. 12:33
b Exod. 17:2
c Num. 33:35
d Num. 33:38
Deut. 32:50
e Deut. 10:6
Deut. 32:50

16 But when we cried unto the Lord, he heard our voice, and sent an Angel, and hath brought us out of Egypt, and behold, we are in the city Kadesh, in thine utmost border.

17 I pray thee that we may pass through thy country: we will not go through the fields nor the vineyards, neither will we drink of the water of the wells: we will go by the ¹king's way, and neither turn to the right hand nor to the left, until we be past thy borders.

18 And Edom answered him, ¹Thou shalt not pass by me, lest I come out against thee with the sword.

19 Then the children of Israel said unto him, We will go up by the highway: and if I and my cattle drink of thy water, I will then pay for it: I will only (without any harm) go through on my feet.

20 He answered again, Thou shalt not go through. Then ¹Edom came out against him with much people, and with a mighty power.

21 Thus Edom denied to give Israel passage through his country: wherefore Israel ¹turned away from him.

22 ¶ And when the children of Israel with all the Congregation departed from *c*Kadesh, they came unto mount Hor.

23 And the Lord spake unto Moses and to Aaron in the mount Hor near the coast of the land of Edom, saying,

24 Aaron shall be ¹gathered unto his people: for he shall not enter into the land, which I have given unto the children of Israel, because ye ²disobeyed my commandment at the water of ³Meribah.

25 Take *d*Aaron and Eleazar his son, and bring them up into the mount Hor,

26 And cause Aaron to put off his garments, and put them upon Eleazar his son: for Aaron shall be gathered *to his fathers,* and shall die there.

27 And Moses did as the Lord had commanded: and they went up into the mount Hor, in the sight of all the Congregation.

28 And Moses put off Aaron's clothes, and put them upon Eleazar his son: *e*so Aaron died there in the top of the mount: and Moses and Eleazar came down from off the mount.

29 When all the Congregation saw that Aaron was dead, all the house of Israel ¹wept for Aaron thirty days.

20:8 ¹ Wherewith thou diddest miracles in Egypt, and didst divide the sea.
20:10 ¹ The punishment which followed hereof, declared that Moses and Aaron believed not the Lord's promise, as appeareth, verse 12.
20:12 ¹ That the children of Israel should believe, and acknowledge my power, and so honor me.
20:13 ¹ Or, strife and contention, Num. 27:14.
 ² By showing himself almighty and maintaining his glory.
20:14 ¹ Because Jacob or Israel was Esau's brother, who was called Edom.
20:17 ¹ Or, highway.
20:18 ¹ Or, come not.
20:20 ¹ Or, the Edomites.
20:21 ¹ To pass by another way.
20:24 ¹ Read Gen. 25:8.
 ² Or, rebelled.
 ³ Or, strife.
20:29 ¹ Or, mourned.

21

3 Israel vanquisheth king Arad.   6 The fiery serpents are sent for the rebellion of the people.   24, 33 Sihon and Og are overcome in battle.

CHAPTER 21
a Num. 33:40
b Judg. 1:27
c Num. 11:6
d 1 Cor. 10:9
e 2 Kings 18:4
Job 3:14
f Num. 33:43
g Deut. 2:26
Judg. 11:19
h Deut. 29:7
i Josh. 12:2
Ps. 135:11
Amos 2:9

1   When *a*King Arad the Canaanite, which dwelt toward the South, heard tell that Israel came by the *1*way of the spies, then fought he against Israel, and took of them prisoners.

2   So Israel vowed a vow unto the Lord, and said, If thou wilt deliver *and* give this people into mine hand, then I will utterly destroy their cities.

3   And the Lord heard the voice of Israel, and delivered *them* the Canaanites: and they utterly destroyed them and their cities, and called the name of the place *1,b*Hormah.

4   ¶ After they departed from the mount Hor by the way of the Red Sea, to *1*compass the land of Edom: and the people were sore grieved because of the way.

5   And the people spake against God, and against Moses, *saying*, Wherefore have ye brought us out of Egypt, to die in the wilderness, for *here is* neither bread nor water, and our soul *c*loatheth this light *1*bread.

6   *d*Wherefore the Lord sent *1*fiery serpents among the people, which stung the people: so that many of the people of Israel died.

7   Therefore the people came to Moses, and said, We have sinned: for we have spoken against the Lord, and against thee: pray to the Lord, that he take away the serpents from us: and Moses prayed for the people.

8   And the Lord said unto Moses, Make thee a fiery serpent, and set it up for a *1*sign, that as many as are bitten, may look upon it, and live.

9   *e*So Moses made a serpent of brass, and set it up for a sign: and when a serpent had bitten a man, then he looked to the serpent of brass, and *1*lived.

10   *f*And the children of Israel departed thence, and pitched in Oboth.

11   ¶ And they departed from Oboth, and pitched *1*in Ije Abarim, in the wilderness, which is before Moab on the East side.

12   ¶ They removed thence, and pitched upon the river of Zared.

13   ¶ Thence they departed, and pitched on the other side of Arnon, which is in the wilderness, and cometh out of the coasts of the Amorites: (for Arnon *is* the border of Moab, between the Moabites and the Amorites),

14   Wherefore it shall be spoken in the *1*book of the battles of the Lord, *2*what thing he did in the red sea, and in the rivers of Arnon,

15   And *at* the stream of the rivers that goeth down to the dwelling of Ar, and lieth upon the border of Moab.

16   ¶ And from thence *they turned* to Beer: the same is the well where the Lord said unto Moses, Assemble the people, and I will give them water.

17   ¶ Then Israel sang this song, Rise up *1*well, *2*sing ye unto it.

18   The princes dug this well, the captains of the people dug it, even the *1*lawgiver, with their staves. And from the wilderness *they came* to Mattanah,

19   ¶ And from Mattanah to Nahaliel, and from Nahaliel to Bamoth,

20   ¶ And from Bamoth in the valley, that is in the plain of Moab, to the top of Pisgah, that looketh toward Jeshimon.

21   ¶ Then Israel sent messengers unto Sihon, king of the Amorites, saying,

22   *g*Let me go through thy land: we will not turn aside into the fields, nor into the vineyards, neither drink of the waters of the wells: we will go by the king's way, until we be past thy country.

23   *h*But Sihon gave Israel no license to pass through his country, but Sihon assembled all his people, and went out against Israel into the wilderness, and he came to Jahaz, and fought against Israel.

24   *i*But Israel smote him with the edge of the sword, and conquered his land, from Arnon unto *1*Jabbok, *even* unto the children of Ammon, for the border of the children of Ammon *was* *2*strong.

25   And Israel took all these cities, and dwelt in all the cities of the Amorites in Heshbon, and in all the *1*villages thereof.

26   For *1*Heshbon was the city of Sihon the king of the Amorites, which had fought beforetime against the king of the Moabites, and had taken all his land

---

21:1 *1* By that way which their spies, that searched the dangers found to be most safe.

21:3 *1* Or, destruction.

21:4 *1* For they were forbidden to destroy it, Deut. 2:5.

21:5 *1* Meaning, Manna, which they thought did not nourish.

21:6 *1* For they that were stung therewith, were so inflamed with the heat thereof, that they died.

21:8 *1* Or, upon a pole.

21:9 *1* Or, recovered.

21:11 *1* Or, in the heaps of Abarim, or hills.

21:14 *1* Which seemeth to be the book of the Judges, or as some think, a book which is lost.

2 Or, (How God destroyed) Waheb (the city) with a whirlwind and the valley of Arnon.

21:17 *1* Or, spring.

2 Ye that receive the commodity thereof, give praise for it.

21:18 *1* Moses and Aaron heads of the people only smote the rock with the rod or staff, which gave water as a well that were deep digged.

21:24 *1* The river.

2 For the people were tall and strong like giants, Deut. 2:20.

21:25 *1* Hebrew, *daughters*.

21:26 *1* For if it had been the Moabites, the Israelites might not have possessed it, Deut. 2:9.

out of his hand, *even* unto Arnon.

27 Wherefore they that speak in proverbs, say, Come to Heshbon, let the city of Sihon be built and repaired,

28 For ¹a fire is gone out of Heshbon, *and* a flame from the city of Sihon, and hath consumed Ar of the Moabites, *and* the lords of Bamoth in Arnon.

29 Woe be to thee, Moab: O people of ¹Chemosh, thou art undone: he hath suffered his sons to be pursued, and his daughters *to be* in captivity to Sihon the king of the Amorites.

30 Their ¹empire also is lost from Heshbon unto Dibon, and we have destroyed them unto Nophah, which *reacheth* unto Medeba.

31 ¶ Thus Israel dwelt in the land of the Amorites.

32 And Moses sent to search out Jazer, and they took the towns belonging thereto, and rooted out the Amorites that were there.

33 ¶ʲAnd they turned, and went up toward Bashan: and Og the king of Bashan came out against them, he, and all his people, to fight at Edrei.

34 Then the Lord said unto Moses, Fear him not: for I have delivered him into thine hand, and all his people, and his land: ᵏand thou shalt do to him as thou diddest unto Sihon the king of the Amorites, which dwelt at Heshbon.

35 They smote him therefore, and his sons, and all his people, until there was none left him: so they conquered his land.

22

5 *King Balak sendeth for Balaam to curse the Israelites.* 12 *The Lord forbiddeth him to go.* 22 *The Angel of the Lord meeteth him, and his ass speaketh.* 38 *Balaam protesteth that he will speak nothing, but that which the Lord putteth in his mouth.*

1 After, the children of Israel departed and pitched in the plain of Moab on the ¹other side of Jordan from Jericho.

2 ¶ Now Balak the son of Zippor saw all that Israel had done to the Amorites.

3 And the Moabites were sore afraid of the people, because they were many, and Moab ¹fretted against the children of Israel.

4 Therefore Moab said unto the ¹Elders of Midian, Now shall this multitude lick up all that are round about us, as an ox licketh up the grass of the

ʲ Deut. 3:1
Deut. 29:7
ᵏ Ps. 135:11

CHAPTER 22
ᵃ Josh. 24:9

field: and Balak the son of Zippor *was* King of the Moabites at that time.

5 ᵃHe sent messengers therefore unto Balaam the son of Beor to Pethor (which is by the ¹river of the land of the children of his folk) to call him, saying, Behold, there is a people come out of Egypt, which cover the face of the earth, and lie over against me.

6 Come now therefore, I pray thee, *and* curse me this people (for they are stronger than I) so it may be that I shall be able to smite them, and to drive them out of the land: for I know that he, whom thou blessest, is blessed, and he whom thou cursest, shall be cursed.

7 And the Elders of Moab, and the Elders of Midian departed, having ¹*the reward* of the soothsaying in their hand, and they came unto Balaam, and told him the words of Balak.

8 Who answered them, Tarry here this night, and I will give you an answer, as the Lord shall say unto me. So ¹the princes of Moab abode with Balaam.

9 Then God came unto Balaam, and said, What men are these with thee?

10 And Baalam said unto God, Balak the son of Zippor king of Moab hath sent unto me, *saying,*

11 Behold, *there is* a people come out of Egypt, and covereth the face of the earth: come now, curse them for my sake: so it may be that I shall be able to overcome them in battle, and to drive them out.

12 And God ¹said unto Balaam, Go not thou with them, neither curse the people, for they are blessed.

13 And Balaam rose up in the morning, and said unto the princes of Balak, Return unto your land: for the Lord hath refused to give ¹me leave to go with you.

14 So the princes of Moab rose up, and went unto Balak, and said, Balaam hath refused to come with us.

15 Balak yet sent again more princes, and more honorable than they,

16 Who came to Balaam, and said to him, Thus saith Balak the son of Zippor, ¹Be not thou stayed, I pray thee, from coming unto me.

17 For I will promote thee unto great honor, and will do whatsoever thou sayest unto me: come therefore, I pray thee, curse me this people.

21:28 ¹ Meaning, war.
21:29 ¹ Chemosh was the idol of the Moabites, 1 Kings 11:33, who was not able to defend his worshippers, which took the idol for their father.
21:30 ¹ Hebrew, *light.*
22:1 ¹ Being at Jericho, it was beyond Jordan: but where the Israelites were, it was on this side.
22:3 ¹ Or, was vexed.
22:4 ¹ Which were the heads and governors.
22:5 ¹ To wit, Euphrates, upon the which stood this city Pethor.

22:7 ¹ Thinking to bribe him with gifts to curse the Israelites.
22:8 ¹ Whom before he called Elders: meaning the governors, and after calleth them servants: that is, subjects to their king.
22:12 ¹ He warned him by a dream, that he should not consent to the king's wicked request.
22:13 ¹ Else he showed himself willing, covetousness had so blinded his heart.
22:16 ¹ The wicked seek by all means to further their naughty enterprises, though they know that God is against them.

18 And Balaam answered, and said unto the servants of Balak, [b]If Balak would give me his house full of silver and gold, I cannot go beyond the word of the Lord my God, to do less or more.

19 But now, I pray you, tarry here this night, that I may wit, what the Lord will say unto me [1]more.

20 And God came unto Balaam by night, and said unto him, If the men come to call thee, rise up, *and* go with them: but only what thing I say unto thee, that shalt thou do.

21 So Balaam rose up early, and saddled his ass, and went with the princes of Moab.

22 And the wrath of God was kindled, because he [1]went: and the Angel of the Lord stood in the way to be against him, as he rode upon his ass, and his two servants *were* with him.

23 And [c]when the ass saw the Angel of the Lord stand in the way, and his sword drawn in his hand, the ass turned out of the way, and went into the field, but Balaam smote the ass to turn her into the way.

24 [1]Again the Angel of the Lord stood in a path of the vineyards, *having* a wall on the one side, and a wall on the other.

25 And when the ass saw the Angel of the Lord, she thrust herself unto the wall, and dashed Balaam's foot against the wall: wherefore he smote her again.

26 Then the Angel of the Lord went further, and stood in a narrow place, where was no way to turn, *either* to the right hand, or to the left.

27 And when the ass saw the Angel of the Lord, she [1]lay down under Balaam: therefore Balaam was very wroth, and smote the ass with a staff.

28 Then the Lord [1]opened the mouth of the ass, and she said unto Balaam, What have I done unto thee, that thou hast smitten me now three times?

29 And Balaam said unto the ass, Because thou hast mocked me: I would there were a sword in mine hand, for now would I kill thee.

30 And the ass said unto Balaam, Am not I thine ass, which thou hast ridden upon [1]since thy first time unto this day? have I used at any time, to do thus unto thee? Who said, Nay.

31 And the Lord [1]opened the eyes of Balaam, and he saw the Angel of the Lord standing in the way

[b] Num. 24:13
[c] 2 Pet. 2:16
Jude 11

with his sword drawn in his hand: then he bowed himself, and fell flat on his face.

32 And the Angel of the Lord said unto him, Wherefore hast thou now smitten thine ass three times? behold, I came out to withstand thee, because *thy* [1]way is not straight before me.

33 But the ass saw me, and turned from me now three times: for else, if she had not turned from me, surely I had even now slain thee, and saved her alive.

34 Then Balaam said unto the Angel of the Lord, I have sinned: for I wist not that thou stoodest in the way [1]against me: now therefore if it displease thee, I will turn [2]home again.

35 But the Angel said unto Balaam, Go with the men: but [1]what I say unto thee, that shalt thou speak. So Balaam went with the princes of Balak.

36 And when Balak heard that Balaam came, he went out to meet him unto a city of Moab, which is in the [1]border of Arnon, even in the utmost coast.

37 Then Balak said unto Balaam, Did not I send for thee to call thee? Wherefore camest thou not unto me? am I not able indeed to promote thee unto honor?

38 And Balaam made answer unto Balak, Lo, I am come unto thee, and can I now say [1]anything at all? the word that God putteth in my mouth that shall I speak.

39 So Balaam went with Balak, and they came unto the city of [1]Huzoth.

40 Then Balak offered bullocks, and sheep, and sent *thereof* to Balaam, and to the princes that were with him.

41 And on the morrow Balak took Balaam and brought him up into the high places of [1]Baal, that thence he might see the utmost part of the people.

23 1 Balaam causeth seven altars to be built. 5 God teacheth him what to answer. 8 Instead of cursing he blesseth Israel. 19 God is not like man.

1 And Balaam said unto Balak, Build me here seven altars, and prepare me here seven bullocks, and seven rams.

2 And Balak did as Balaam said, and [1]Balak and

22:19 [1] Because he tempted God to require him contrary to his commandment, his petition was granted, but it turned to his own condemnation.
22:22 [1] Moved rather with covetousness than to obey God.
22:24 [1] The second time.
22:27 [1] Or, fell.
22:28 [1] Gave her power to speak.
22:30 [1] Since thou hast been my master.
22:31 [1] For whose eyes the Lord doth not open, they can neither see his anger, nor his love.
22:32 [1] Both thy heart is corrupt, and thine enterprise wicked.
22:34 [1] Or, before me, or to meet me.
[2] Hebrew, *I will return to me.*
22:35 [1] Because his heart was evil, his charge was renewed, that he should not pretend ignorance.
22:36 [1] Near the place where the Israelites camped.
22:38 [1] Of myself I can speak nothing: only what God revealeth, that will I utter, seem it good or bad.
22:39 [1] Or, of streets: or, a populous city.
22:41 [1] Where the idol Baal was worshipped.
23:2 [1] For among the Gentiles the kings oft times used to sacrifice, as did the Priests.

Balaam offered on *every* altar a bullock and a ram.

3 Then Balaam said unto Balak, Stand by thy burnt offering, and I will go, if so be that the Lord will come *and* meet me: and whatsoever he showeth me, I will tell thee: so he [1]went forth alone.

4 And God [1]met Balaam, and *Balaam* said unto him, I have prepared seven altars, and have offered upon *every* altar a bullock and a ram.

5 And the Lord [1]put an answer in Balaam's mouth, and said, Go again to Balak, and say on this wise.

6 So when he turned unto him, lo, he stood by his burnt offering, he, and all the princes of Moab.

7 Then he uttered his [1]parable, and said, Balak the king of Moab hath brought me from [2]Aram out of the mountains of the East, *saying*, Come, curse Jacob for my sake: come, and [3]detest Israel.

8 How shall I curse, where God hath not cursed? or how shall I detest, *where* the Lord hath not detested?

9 For from the top of the rocks I did see him, and from the hills I did behold him: lo, the people shall dwell by themselves, and shall not be reckoned among the [1]nations.

10 Who can tell the [1]dust of Jacob, and the number of the fourth part of Israel? Let me [2]die the death of the righteous, and let my last end be like his.

11 Then Balak said unto Balaam, What hast thou done unto me? I took thee to curse mine enemies, and behold, thou hast blessed them altogether.

12 And he answered, and said, Must I not take heed to speak that, which the Lord hath put in my mouth?

13 And Balak said unto him, Come, I pray thee, with me unto another place, whence thou mayest see them, and thou shalt see but the utmost part of them and shalt not see them all: therefore curse them out of that place for my sake.

14 ¶ And he brought him into [1]Zophim to the top of Pisgah, and built seven altars, and offered a bullock and a ram on *every* altar.

15 After, he said unto Balak, Stand here by thy burnt offering, and I will meet *the* Lord yonder.

16 And the Lord met Balaam, and [a]put an answer in his mouth, and said, Go again unto Balak, and say thus.

CHAPTER 23
[a] Num. 22:35

17 And when he came to him, behold, he stood by his burnt offering, and the princes of Moab with him: so Balak said unto him, What hath the Lord said?

18 And he uttered his parable, and said, Rise up Balak, and hear: hearken unto me, thou son of Zippor.

19 [1]God is not as man, that he should lie, neither as the son of man, that he should repent: hath he said, and shall he not do it? and hath he spoken, and shall he not accomplish it?

20 Behold, I have received *commandment* to bless: for he hath blessed, and I cannot alter it.

21 He seeth none iniquity in Jacob, nor seeth no transgression in Israel: the Lord his God *is* with him, and the [1]joyful shout of a King *is* among them.

22 God brought them out of Egypt: their strength *is* as an unicorn.

23 For *there is* no sorcery in Jacob, nor soothsaying in Israel, [1]according to this time it shall be said of Jacob and of Israel, What hath God wrought?

24 Behold, the people shall rise up as a lion, and lift up himself as a young lion: he shall not lie down, till he eat of the prey, and till he drink the blood of the slain.

25 Then Balak said unto Balaam, Neither curse, nor bless them at all.

26 But Balaam answered, and said unto Balak, Told not I thee, saying, All that the Lord speaketh, that must I do?

27 ¶ Again Balak said unto Balaam, Come, I pray thee, I will bring thee unto another [1]place, if so be it will please God, that thou mayest thence curse them for my sake.

28 So Balak brought Balaam unto the top of Peor, that looketh toward Jeshimon.

29 Then Balaam said unto Balak, Make me here seven altars, and prepare me here seven bullocks, and seven rams.

30 And Balak did as Balaam had said, and offered a bullock and a ram on *every* altar.

24
5 *Balaam prophesieth of the great prosperity that should come unto Israel.* 17 *Also of the coming of Christ.* 20 *The destruction of the Amalekites, and of the Kenites.*

23:3 [1] Or, went up higher.

23:4 [1] Appeared unto him.

23:5 [1] Taught him what to say.

23:7 [1] Or, prophecy.
   [2] Or, Syria.
   [3] Cause that all may hate and detest them.

23:9 [1] But shall have religion and laws apart.

23:10 [1] The infinite multitude, as the dust of the earth.
   [2] The fear of God's judgment caused him to wish to be joined to the household of Abraham: thus the wicked have their consciences

wounded when they consider God's judgments.

23:14 [1] Or, into the field of them that spied: to wit, lest the enemy should approach.

23:19 [1] God's enemies are compelled to confess that his government is just, constant, and without change or repentance.

23:21 [1] They triumph as victorious kings over their enemies.

23:23 [1] Considering what God shall work this time for the deliverance of his people, all the world shall wonder.

23:27 [1] Thus the wicked imagine of God, that that which he will not grant in one place, he will do it in another.

1 When Balaam saw that it pleased the Lord to bless Israel, then he went not, [a]as certain times before, to set divinations, but set his face toward the [1]wilderness.

2 And Balaam lift up his eyes, and looked upon Israel, which dwelt according to their tribes, and the Spirit of God came upon him,

3 [b]And he uttered his parable, and said, Balaam the son of Beor hath said, and the man whose eyes [1]were shut up, hath said,

4 He hath said which heard the words of God, and saw the vision of the Almighty, and [1]falling *in a trance* had his eyes opened:

5 ¶ How goodly are thy tents, O Jacob, *and* thine habitations, O Israel!

6 As the valleys are they stretched forth, as gardens by the river's side, as the [1]aloe trees, which the Lord hath planted, as the cedars beside the waters.

7 The [1]water droppeth out of his bucket, and his seed *shall be* in many waters, and his King shall be higher than [2]Agag, and his kingdom shall be exalted.

8 God brought him out of Egypt: his strength *shall be* as an unicorn: he shall eat the nations his enemies, and bruise their bones, and shoot them through with his arrows.

9 [c]He coucheth, *and* lieth down as a young Lion, and as a Lion: Who shall stir him up? blessed is he that blesseth thee, and cursed is he that curseth thee.

10 Then Balak was very angry with Balaam, and [1]smote his hands together: so Balak said unto Balaam, I sent for thee to curse mine enemies, and behold, thou hast blessed them now three times.

11 Therefore now flee unto thy place: I thought surely to promote thee unto honor, but lo, the [1]Lord hath kept thee back from honor.

12 Then Balaam answered Balak, Told I not also thy messengers, which thou sentest unto me, saying,

13 If Balak would give me his house full of silver and gold, I cannot pass the commandment of the Lord, to do *either* good or bad of mine own mind? what the Lord shall command, that same will I speak.

CHAPTER 24
[a] Num. 23:3,15
[b] Num. 23:7,18
[c] Gen. 49:9

CHAPTER 25
[a] Num. 35:49

14 And now behold, I go unto my people: come, I will [1,2]advertise thee what this people shall do to thy folk in the latter days.

15 And he uttered his parable, and said Balaam the son of Beor hath said, and the man whose eyes were shut up hath said,

16 He hath said that heard the words of God, and hath the knowledge of the most High, and saw the vision of the Almighty, and falling *in a trance* had his eyes opened:

17 I shall see him, but not now: I shall behold him, but not near: there shall come a [1]Star of Jacob, and a Scepter shall rise of Israel and shall smite the [2]coasts of Moab, and destroy all the sons of [3]Sheth.

18 And Edom shall be possessed, and Seir shall be a possession to their enemies: but Israel shall do valiantly.

19 He also that shall have dominion *shall be* of Jacob, and shall destroy the remnant of the [1]city.

20 ¶ And when he looked on Amalek, he uttered his parable, and said, Amalek *was* the [1]first of the nations: but his latter end *shall come* to destruction.

21 And he looked on the [1]Kenites, and uttered his parable, and said, Strong is thy dwelling place, and [2]put thy nest in the rock:

22 Nevertheless, [1]the Kenite shall be spoiled, until Asshur carry thee away captive.

23 Again he uttered his parable, and said, Alas, [1]who shall live when God doeth this?

24 The ships also shall *come* from the coasts of [1]Kittim, and subdue Asshur, and shall subdue Eber, and [2]he also *shall come* to destruction.

25 Then Balaam rose up, and went and returned to his place: and Balak also went his way.

25 *2 The people committeth fornication with the daughters of Moab. 9 Phinehas killeth Zimri and Cozbi. 11 God maketh his covenant with Phinehas. 17 God commandeth, to kill the Midianites.*

1 Now while Israel abode in [a]Shittim, the people began to commit whoredom with the [1]daughters of Moab:

24:1 [1] Where the Israelites camped.
24:3 [1] His eyes were shut up before in respect of the clear visions which he saw after: some read, were open.
24:4 [1] Though he lay as in a sleep, yet the eyes of his mind were open.
24:6 [1] Or, tents.
24:7 [1] His prosperity and posterity shall be very great.
  [2] Which name was common to the kings of Amalek.
24:10 [1] In token of anger.
24:11 [1] Thus the wicked burden God when they cannot compass their wicked enterprises.
24:14 [1] Hebrew, *counsel*.
  [2] He gave also wicked counsel to cause the Israelites to sin, that thereby God might forsake them, Num. 31:16.

24:17 [1] Meaning, Christ.
  [2] That is, the princes.
  [3] He shall subdue all that resist: for of Sheth came Noah, and of Noah all the world.
24:19 [1] Of the Edomites.
24:20 [1] The Amalekites first made war against Israel, as Num. 14:45.
24:21 [1] Or, Midianites.
  [2] Make thyself as strong as thou canst.
24:22 [1] Or, thou Kain shalt.
24:23 [1] Some read, Oh who shall not perish when the enemy *that is, Antichrist*, shall set himself up as God?
24:24 [1] The Grecians and Romans.
  [2] Meaning, Eber, or the Jews for rebelling against God.
25:1 [1] With the women.

2 Which called the people unto the sacrifice of their gods, and the people ate, and bowed down to their gods.

3 And Israel [1]coupled himself unto Baal of Peor: wherefore the wrath of the Lord was kindled against Israel:

4 And the Lord said unto Moses, [b]Take all the heads of the people and hang them up [1]before the Lord [2]against the Sun, that the indignation of the Lord's wrath may be turned from Israel.

5 Then Moses said unto the Judges of Israel, Everyone slay his [1]men that were joined unto Baal of Peor.

6 ¶ And behold, one of the children of Israel came and brought unto his brethren a Midianitish woman in the sight of Moses, and in the sight of all the Congregation of the children of Israel, [1]who wept before the door of the Tabernacle of the Congregation.

7 [c]And when Phinehas the son of Eleazar the son of Aaron the Priest saw it, he rose up from the midst of the Congregation, and took a [1]spear in his hand,

8 And followed the man of Israel into the tent, and thrust them both through: to wit, the man of Israel, and the woman, [1]through her belly: so the plague ceased from the children of Israel.

9 [d]And there died in that plague four and twenty thousand.

10 Then the Lord spake unto Moses, saying,

11 [e]Phinehas the son of Eleazar, the son of Aaron the Priest, hath turned mine anger away from the children of Israel, while he [1]was zealous for my sake among them: therefore I have not consumed the children of Israel in my jealousy.

12 Wherefore say to him, Behold, I give unto him my covenant of peace.

13 And he shall have it, and his seed after him, even the covenant of the Priest's office forever, because he was zealous for his God, and hath made an [1]atonement for the children of Israel.

14 And the name of the Israelite thus slain, which was killed with the Midianitish woman, was Zimri the son of Salu, prince [1]of the family of the Simeonites.

15 And the name of the Midianitish woman that was slain, was Cozbi the daughter of Zur, who was head over the people of his father's house in Midian.

b Deut. 4:3
Josh. 22:17
c Ps. 106:30
d 1 Cor. 10:8
e Ps. 106:30
f Num. 31:2

CHAPTER 26
a Num. 1:3
b Num. 1:1
c Gen. 46:8
Exod. 6:14
1 Chron. 5:1
d Num. 16:1

16 ¶ Again the Lord spake unto Moses, saying,

17 [f]Vex the Midianites, and smite them:

18 For they trouble you with their [1]wiles, wherewith they have beguiled you as concerning Peor, and as concerning their sister Cozbi daughter of a prince of Midian, which was slain in the day of the plague because of Peor.

26

2 The Lord commandeth to number the children of Israel in the plain of Moab, from twenty years old and above. 57 The Levites and their families. 64 None of them that were numbered in Sinai go into Canaan, save Caleb and Joshua.

1 And so after the [1]plague, the Lord spake unto Moses, and to Eleazar the son of Aaron the Priest, saying,

2 Take the number of all the Congregation of the children of Israel, [a]from twenty years old and above, throughout their father's houses, all that go forth to war in Israel.

3 So Moses and Eleazar the Priest spake unto them in the plain of Moab, by Jordan [1]toward Jericho, saying,

4 From twenty years old and above ye shall number the people, as the Lord [b]had commanded Moses, and the children of Israel, when they came out of the land of Egypt.

5 ¶ [c]Reuben the firstborn of Israel: the children of Reuben were: Hanoch, of whom came the family of the Hanochites, and of Pallu the family of the Palluites:

6 Of Hezron, the family of the Hezronites: of Carmi, the family of the Carmites.

7 These are the families of the Reubenites: and they were in number three and forty thousand, seven hundred and thirty.

8 And the sons of Pallu, Eliab.

9 And the sons of Eliab, Nemuel, and Dathan and Abiram: this Dathan and Abiram were famous in the Congregation, and [d]strove against Moses and against Aaron in the [1]assembly of Korah, when they strove against the Lord.

10 And the earth opened her mouth, and swallowed them up with Korah, when the Congregation died, what time the fire consumed two hundred and fifty men, who were [1]for a sign.

25:3 [1] Worshipped the idol of the Moabites, which was in the hill Peor.
25:4 [1] Or, to the Lord.
  [2] Openly in the sight of all.
25:5 [1] Let him see execution done of them that are under his charge.
25:6 [1] Repenting that they had offended God.
25:7 [1] Or, javelin.
25:8 [1] Or, in her tent. Chalde and Greek, in her secrets.
25:11 [1] He was zealous to maintain my glory.

25:13 [1] He hath pacified God's wrath.
25:14 [1] Hebrew, of the house of the father.
25:18 [1] Causing you to commit both corporal and spiritual fornication by Balaam's counsel, Num. 31:16; Rev. 2:14.
26:1 [1] Which came for their whoredom and idolatry.
26:3 [1] Where the river is near to Jericho.
26:9 [1] In that rebellion whereof Korah was head.
26:10 [1] That is, for an example that others should not murmur and rebel against God's ministers.

11 Notwithstanding, *all* the sons of Korah died not.

12 ¶ And the children of Simeon after their families *were*: Nemuel, *of whom came* the family of the Nemuelites: of Jamin, the family of the Jaminites: of Jachin the family of the Jachinites:

13 Of Zerah, the family of the Zarhites: of Shaul, the family of the Shaulites.

14 These are the families of the Simeonites: two and twenty thousand, and two hundred.

15 ¶ The sons of Gad after their families *were*: Zephon, *of whom came* the family of the Zephonites: of Haggi, the family of the Haggites: of Shuni, the family of the Shunites:

16 Of Ozni the family of the Oznites: of Eri, the family of the Erites:

17 Of Arod, the family of the Arodites: of Areli, the family of the Arelites.

18 These are the families of the sons of Gad, according to their numbers forty thousand and five hundred.

19 ¶ The sons of Judah, Er and Onan, but Er and Onan died in the land of ¹Canaan.

20 So were the sons of Judah after their families: of Shelah *came* the family of the Shelanites: of Perez, the family of the Parzites, of Zerah, the family of the Zarhites.

21 And the sons of ᶜPerez *were*: of Hezron, the family of the Hezronites: of Hamul the family of the Hamulites.

22 These are the families of Judah, after their numbers, seventy and six thousand and five hundred.

23 ¶ The sons of Issachar after their families *were*: Tola, *of whom came* the family of the Tolaites: of Puah, the family of the Punites:

24 Of Jashub the family of the Jashubites: of Shimron the family of the Shimronites.

25 These are the families of Issachar, after their numbers, threescore and four thousand and three hundred.

26 ¶ The sons of Zebulun, after their families *were*: of Sered, the family of the Sardites: of Elon, the family of the Elonites: of Jahleel, the family of the Jahleelites.

27 These are the families of the Zebulunites, after their numbers threescore thousand and five hundred.

28 ¶ The sons of Joseph after their families *were*: Manasseh and Ephraim.

29 The sons of Manasseh *were* of ᶠMachir, the family of the Machirites: and Machir begat Gilead: of Gilead *came* the family of the Gileadites.

30 These are the sons of Gilead: *of* Jeezer, the

ᵉ Gen. 46:12
ᶠ Josh. 17:2
ᵍ Num. 27:1

family of the Jeezerites, of Helek, the family of the Helekites.

31 Of Asriel the family of the Asrielites: of Shechem, the family of Shechemites.

32 Of Shemida, the family of the Shemidaites: of Hepher, the family of the Hepherites.

33 ¶ And ᵍZelophehad the son of Hepher had no sons but daughters: and the names of the daughters of Zelophehad *were* Mahlah, and Noah, Hoglah, Milcah and Tirzah.

34 These are the families of Manasseh, and the number of them, two and fifty thousand and seven hundred.

35 ¶ These are the sons of Ephraim after their families: of Shuthelah *came* the family of the Shuthalhites: of Becher, the family of the Bachrites: of Tahan, the family of the Tahanites.

36 And these are the sons of Shuthelah: of Eran, the family of the Eranites.

37 These are the families of the sons of Ephraim after their numbers two and forty thousand and five hundred: these are the sons of Joseph after their families.

38 ¶ *These are* the sons of Benjamin after their families: of Bela *came* the family of the Belaites: of Ashbel, the family of the Ashbelites: of Ahiram, the family of the Ahiramites:

39 Of Shupham, the family of the Shuphamites: of Hupham the family of the Huphamites.

40 And the sons of Bela, were Ard and Naaman; *of* Ard *came* the family of the Ardites, of Naaman the family of the Naamites.

41 These are the sons of Benjamin after their families, and their numbers, five and forty thousand and six hundred.

42 ¶ These are the sons of Dan after their families: of Shuham *came* the family of the Shuhamites: these are the families of Dan after their households.

43 All the families of the Shuhamites *were* after their numbers, threescore and four thousand, and four hundred.

44 ¶ The sons of Asher after their families *were* of Jimna, the families of the Jimnites: of Jesui, the family of the Jesuites: of Beriah, the family of the Beriites.

45 The sons of Beriah *were*: of Heber, the family of the Heberites: of Malchiel, the family of the Malchielites.

46 And the name of the daughter of Asher *was* Serah.

47 These are the families of the sons of Asher after their numbers three and fifty thousand and four hundred.

48 ¶ The sons of Naphtali, after their families

were: of Jahzeel, the families of the Jahzeelites: of Guni, the family of the Gunites.

49 Of Jezer, the family of the Jezerites: of Shillem, the family of the Shillemites.

50 These are the families of Naphtali according to their households, and their number, five and forty thousand and four hundred.

51 These are the [1]numbers of the children of Israel: six hundred and one thousand seven hundred and thirty.

52 ¶ And the Lord spake unto Moses, saying,

53 Unto these the land shall be divided for an inheritance, according to the number of [1]names.

54 [b]To many thou shalt give the more inheritance, and to few thou shalt give less inheritance: to every one according to his number shall be given his inheritance.

55 Notwithstanding, the land shall be [i]divided by lot: according to the names of the tribes of their fathers they shall inherit:

56 According to the lot shall the possession thereof be divided between many and few.

57 ¶ [j]These also *are* the numbers of the Levites, after their families: of Gershon *came* the family of the Gershonites: of Kohath, the family of the Kohathites: of Merari, the family of the Merarites.

58 These are the families of Levi, the family of the Libnites: the family of the Hebronites: the family of the Mahlites: the family of the Mushites: the family of the Korathites: and Kohath begat Amram.

59 And Amram's wife was called [k]Jochebed the daughter of Levi, which was born unto Levi in Egypt: and she bare unto Amram Aaron, and Moses, and Miriam their sister.

60 And unto Aaron were born Nadab, and Abihu, Eleazar, and Ithamar.

61 [l]And Nadab and Abihu died, because they offered strange fire before the Lord.

62 And their numbers were three and twenty thousand, all males from a month old and above, for they were not numbered among the children of Israel, because there was none inheritance given them among the children of Israel.

63 ¶ These are the numbers of Moses and Eleazar the Priest which numbered the children of Israel in the plain of Moab, near Jordan, *toward* Jericho.

64 And among these there was not a man of them, [1]whom Moses and Aaron the Priest numbered, when they told the children of Israel in the wilderness of Sinai.

65 For the Lord said unto them, [m]They shall die in the wilderness: so there was not left a man of them, save Caleb the son of Jephunneh, and Joshua the son of Nun.

h Num. 33:54
i Josh. 11:23
Josh. 14:2
j Exod. 6:16-19
k Exod. 2:2
Exod. 6:20
l Lev. 10:2
Num. 3:4
1 Chron. 24:2
m Num. 14:28,29
1 Cor. 20:5,6

CHAPTER 27
a Num. 26:33
Num. 36:11
Josh. 17:3
b Num. 14:35
Num. 26:64,65
c Deut. 32:40
d Num. 20:24

27

1 *The Law of the heritage of the daughters of Zelophehad.* 12 *The land of promise showed unto Moses.* 16 *Moses prayeth for a governor unto the people.* 18 *Joshua is appointed in his stead.*

1 Then came the daughters of [a]Zelophehad, the son of Hepher, the son of Gilead, the son of Machir, the son of Manasseh, of the family of Manasseh, the son of Joseph (and the names of his daughters were these, Mahlah, Noah, and Hoglah, and Milcah, and Tirzah)

2 And stood before Moses, and before Eleazar the Priest, and before the Princes, and all the assembly at the door of the Tabernacle of the Congregation, saying,

3 Our father [b]died in the wilderness, and he was not among the assembly of them that were assembled against the Lord in the company of Korah, but died in his [1]sin, and had no sons.

4 Wherefore should the name of our father be taken away from among his family, because he hath no son? give us a possession among the brethren of our father.

5 Then Moses brought their [1]cause before the Lord.

6 And the Lord spake unto Moses, saying,

7 The daughters of Zelophehad speak right: thou shalt give them a possession to inherit among their father's brethren, and shalt turn the inheritance of their father unto them.

8 Also thou shalt speak unto the children of Israel, saying, If a man die and have no son, then ye shall turn his inheritance unto his daughter.

9 And if he have no daughter, ye shall give his inheritance unto his brethren.

10 And if he have no brethren, ye shall give his inheritance unto his father's brethren.

11 And if his father have no brethren, ye shall give his inheritance unto his next kinsman of his family, and he shall possess it: and *this* shall be unto the children of Israel a law of [1]judgment, as the Lord hath commanded Moses.

12 ¶ Again the Lord said unto Moses, [c]Go up into this mount of Abarim, and behold the land which I have given unto the children of Israel.

13 And when thou hast seen it, thou shalt be gathered unto thy people also, [d]as Aaron thy brother was gathered.

26:51 [1] This is the third time that they are numbered.
26:53 [1] Or, persons.
26:64 [1] Wherein appeareth the great power of God, that so wonderfully increased his people.

27:3 [1] According as all men die, for as much as they are sinners.
27:5 [1] That is, their matter to be judged, to know what he should determine, as he did all hard matters.
27:11 [1] Meaning, an ordinance to judge by.

14 For ye were ᶜdisobedient unto my word in the desert of Zin, in the strife of the assembly to sanctify me in the waters before their eyes: ᶠThat is the water of ¹Meribah in Kadesh in the wilderness of Zin.

15 ¶ Then Moses spake unto the Lord, saying,

16 Let the Lord God of the ¹spirits of all flesh appoint a man over the Congregation,

17 Who may ¹go out and in before them, and lead them out and in, that the Congregation of the Lord be not as sheep, which have not a shepherd.

18 And the Lord said unto Moses, Take thee Joshua the son of Nun, in whom is the Spirit, and ¹put thine hands upon him,

19 And set him before Eleazar the Priest, and before all the Congregation, and give him a charge in their sight,

20 And ¹give him of thy glory, that all the Congregation of the children of Israel may obey.

21 And he shall stand before Eleazar the Priest, who shall ask counsel for him ᵍby the ¹judgment of Urim before the Lord: at his word they shall go out, and at his word they shall come in, *both* he, and all the children of Israel with him, and all the Congregation.

22 So Moses did as the Lord hath commanded him, and he took Joshua, and set him before Eleazar the Priest, and before all the Congregation.

23 Then he put his hands upon him, and gave him a ¹charge, as the Lord had spoken by the hand of Moses.

28

4 The daily sacrifice. 9 The sacrifice of Sabbath. 11 Of the Month, 16 Of the Passover, 26 Of the firstfruits.

1 And the Lord spake unto Moses, saying,

2 Command the children of Israel, and say unto them, Ye shall observe to offer unto me in their due season mine offering, *and* ¹my bread for my sacrifices made by fire for a sweet savor unto me.

3 Also thou shalt say unto them, ᵃThis is the offering made by fire which ye shall offer unto the Lord, two lambs of a year old, without spot daily, for a continual burnt offering.

4 One lamb shalt thou prepare in the morning, and the other lamb shalt thou prepare at even:

5 ᵇAnd the tenth part of an Ephah of fine flour for a ᶜmeat offering mingled with the fourth part of

ᵉ Num. 20:10
ᶠ Exod. 17:7
ᵍ Exod. 28:30

CHAPTER 28
ᵃ Exod. 29:38
ᵇ Exod. 16:36
ᶜ Lev. 2:1
ᵈ Exod. 29:40
ᵉ Exod. 12:18
　Exod. 23:15
　Lev. 23:5
ᶠ Lev. 23:7

an ᵈHin of beaten oil.

6 *This shall be* a daily burnt offering, as was made in the mount Sinai for a sweet savor: *it is* a sacrifice made by fire unto the Lord.

7 And the drink offering thereof the fourth part of an Hin for one lamb: in the holy place cause to pour the drink offering unto the Lord.

8 And the other lamb thou shalt prepare at even: as the meat offering of the morning, and as the drink offering thereof shalt thou prepare *this* ¹for an offering made by fire of sweet savor unto the Lord.

9 ¶ But on the Sabbath day *ye shall offer* two lambs of a year old, without spot, and two ¹tenth deals of fine flour for a meat offering mingled with oil, and the drink offering thereof.

10 *This is* the burnt offering of every Sabbath, beside the ¹continual burnt offering, and drink offering thereof.

11 ¶ And in the beginning of your months, ye shall offer a burnt offering unto the Lord, two young bullocks, and a ram, and seven lambs of a year old, without spot,

12 And three tenth deals of fine flour for a meat offering mingled with oil for one bullock, and two tenth deals of fine flour for a meat offering, mingled with oil for one ram,

13 And a tenth deal of fine flour mingled with oil for a meat offering unto one lamb, for a burnt offering of sweet savor: *it is* an offering made by fire unto the Lord.

14 And their ¹drink offerings shall be half an Hin of wine unto one bullock, and the third part of an Hin unto a ram, and the fourth part of an Hin unto a lamb: this is the burnt offering of every month, throughout the months of the year.

15 And one he goat for a sin offering unto the Lord shall be prepared, besides the continual burnt offering, and his drink offering.

16 ᶜAlso the fourteenth day of the first month *is* the Passover of the Lord.

17 And in the fifteenth day of the same month is the feast: seven days shall unleavened bread be eaten.

18 In the ᶠfirst day *shall be* an holy ¹convocation, ye shall do no servile work *therein*.

19 But ye shall offer a sacrifice made by fire for a burnt offering unto the Lord, two young bullocks, one ram, and seven lambs of a year old: see that they

---

27:14 ¹ Or, strife.
27:16 ¹ Who as he hath created, so he governeth the hearts of all men.
27:17 ¹ That is, govern them and do his duty, as 2 Chron. 1:10.
27:18 ¹ And so appoint him governor.
27:20 ¹ Commend him to the people as meet for the office and appointed by God.
27:21 ¹ According to his office: signifying that the civil magistrate could execute nothing but that which he knew to be the will of

God.
27:23 ¹ How he should govern himself in his office.
28:2 ¹ By bread he meaneth all manner of sacrifice.
28:8 ¹ The meat offering and drink offering of the evening sacrifice.
28:9 ¹ Of the measure Ephah.
28:10 ¹ Which was offered every day at morning and at evening.
28:14 ¹ That is, the wine that shall be poured upon the sacrifice.
28:18 ¹ Or, solemn assembly.

be without blemish.

20 And their meat offering *shall be* of fine flour mingled with oil: three tenth deals shall ye prepare for a bullock, and two tenth deals for a ram:

21 One tenth deal shalt thou prepare for every lamb, *even* for the seven lambs,

22 And an he goat for a sin offering, to make an atonement for you.

23 Ye shall prepare these beside the burnt offering in the morning, which is a continual burnt sacrifice.

24 After this manner ye shall prepare throughout all the seven days, for the ¹maintaining of the offering made by fire for a sweet savor unto the Lord: it shall be done beside the continual burnt offering and drink offering thereof.

25 And in the seventh day ye shall have an holy convocation, *wherein* ye shall do no servile work.

26 ¶ Also in the day of your firstfruits, when ye bring a new meat offering unto the Lord, according to your ¹weeks ye shall have an holy convocation: and ye shall do no servile work *in it*:

27 But ye shall offer a burnt offering for a sweet savor unto the Lord, two young bullocks, a ram, and seven lambs of a year old,

28 And their meat offering of fine flour mingled with oil, three tenth deals unto a bullock, two tenth deals to a ram,

29 And one tenth deal unto every lamb throughout the seven lambs,

30 And an he goat to make an atonement for you:

31 (Ye shall do *this* besides the continual burnt offering, and his meat offering:) ¹see they be without blemish, with their drink offerings.

29

1 Of the three principal feasts of the seventh month, to wit, the feast of trumpets, 7 The feast of reconciliation, 12 And the feast of Tabernacles.

1 Moreover, in the first *day* of the ¹seventh month ye shall have an holy convocation: ye shall do no servile work *therein*: ªit shall be a day of blowing the trumpets unto you.

2 And ye shall make a burnt offering for a sweet savor unto the Lord: one young bullock, one ram, *and* seven lambs of a year old, without blemish.

3 And their meat offering *shall be* of fine flour mingled with oil, three tenth deals unto the bullock, and two tenth deals unto the ram,

4 And one tenth deal unto the lamb, for the seven lambs,

CHAPTER 29
ª Lev. 23:24
ᵇ Lev. 16:30,31
Lev. 23:27
ᶜ Lev. 16:29

5 And an he goat for a sin offering to make an atonement for you,

6 Beside the burnt offering of the ¹month, and his meat offering, and the continual ²burnt offering, and his meat offering and the drink offerings of the same according to their manner, for a sweet savor: *it is* a sacrifice made by fire unto the Lord.

7 ¶ ᵇAnd ye shall have in the tenth *day* of the seventh month, an holy ¹convocation: and ye shall ᶜhumble yourselves, *and* shall not do any work *therein*.

8 But ye shall offer a burnt offering unto the Lord for a sweet savor: one young bullock, a ram, and seven lambs of a year old: see they be without blemish.

9 And their meat offering shall be of fine flour mingled with oil, three tenth deals to a bullock, *and* two tenth deals to a ram,

10 One tenth deal unto every lamb, throughout the seven lambs,

11 An he goat for a sin offering, (beside the sin offering to make the atonement, and the continual ¹burnt offering and the meat offering thereof) and their drink offerings.

12 ¶ And in the fifteenth day of the seventh month, ye shall have an holy ¹convocation: ye shall do no servile work *therein*, but ye shall keep a feast unto the Lord seven days.

13 And ye shall offer a burnt offering for a sacrifice made by fire of sweet savor unto the Lord, thirteen young bullocks, two rams, *and* fourteen lambs of a year old: they shall be without blemish.

14 And their meat offering shall be of fine flour mingled with oil, three tenth deals unto every bullock of the thirteen bullocks, two tenth deals to either of the two rams,

15 And one tenth deal unto each of the fourteen lambs,

16 And one he goat for a sin offering, beside the continual burnt offering, his meat offering, and his drink offering.

17 ¶ And the ¹second day *ye shall offer* twelve young bullocks, two rams, fourteen lambs of a year old without blemish,

18 With their meat offering and their drink offerings for the bullocks, for the rams and for the lambs according to their number, after the manner,

19 And an he goat for a sin offering, (beside the continual burnt offering and his meat offering) and their drink offerings.

20 ¶ Also the third day *ye shall offer* eleven bullocks,

28:24 ¹ Hebrew, *bread*.
28:26 ¹ In counting seven weeks from the Passover to Whitsuntide, as Lev. 23:15.
28:31 ¹ Hebrew, *they shall be to you*.
29:1 ¹ Which containeth part of September, and part of October.

29:6 ¹ Which must be offered in the beginning of every month.
   ² Which is for morning and evening.
29:7 ¹ Which is the feast of reconciliation.
29:11 ¹ That is, offered every morning and evening.
29:12 ¹ Meaning, the feast of the Tabernacles.
29:17 ¹ The second day of the feast of Tabernacles.

two rams and fourteen lambs of a year old without blemish,

21 With their meat offering and their drink offerings, for the bullocks, for the rams, and for the lambs, after their number, according to the ¹manner,

22 And an he goat for a sin offering, beside the continual burnt offering, and his meat offering, and his drink offering.

23 ¶ And the fourth day *ye shall offer* ten bullocks, two rams, *and* fourteen lambs of a year old without blemish.

24 Their meat offering and their drink offerings, for the bullocks, for the rams, and for the lambs according to their number after the manner,

25 And an he goat for a sin offering, beside the continual burnt offering, his meat offering and his drink offering.

26 ¶ In the fifth day also *ye shall offer* nine bullocks, two rams, *and* fourteen lambs of a year old without blemish,

27 And their meat offering, and their drink offerings for the bullocks, for the rams, and for the lambs according to their number, after the manner,

28 And an he goat for a sin offering, beside the continual burnt offering, and his meat offering and his drink offering.

29 ¶ And in the sixth day *ye shall offer* eight bullocks, two rams, *and* fourteen lambs of a year old without blemish,

30 And their meat offering, and their drink offerings for the bullocks, for the rams, and for the lambs according to their number, after the manner,

31 And an he goat for a sin offering, beside the continual burnt offering, his meat offering and his drink offerings.

32 ¶ In the seventh day also *ye shall offer* seven bullocks, two rams *and* fourteen lambs of a year old without blemish,

33 And their meat offering, and their drink offerings for the bullocks, for the rams, and for the lambs according to their number, after their manner,

34 And an he goat for a sin offering, beside the continual burnt offering, his meat offering and his drink offering.

35 ¶ In the eighth day, ye shall have ᵈa solemn assembly: ye shall do no servile work *therein*,

36 But ye shall offer a burnt offering, a sacrifice made by fire for a sweet savor unto the Lord, one bullock, one ram, *and* seven lambs of a year old

ᵈ Lev. 23:36

without blemish,

37 Their meat offering and their drink offerings for the bullock, for the ram, and for the lambs according to their number, after the manner,

38 And an he goat for a sin offering, beside the continual burnt offering, and his meat offering, and his drink offering.

39 These things ye shall do unto the Lord in your feasts, beside your ¹vows, and your free offerings, for your burnt offerings, and for your meat offerings, and for your drink offerings, and for your peace offerings.

30

3 *Concerning vows.*   4 *The vow of the maid,*   7 *Of the wife,*   10 *Of the widow or divorced.*

1 Then Moses spake unto the children of Israel according to all that the Lord had commanded ¹him.

2 Moses also spake unto the heads of the tribes ¹concerning the children of Israel, saying, This is the thing which the Lord hath commanded,

3 Whosoever voweth a vow unto the Lord, or sweareth an oath to bind ¹himself by a bond, he shall not ²break his promise, *but* shall do according to all that proceedeth out of his mouth.

4 If a woman also vow a vow unto the Lord, and bind herself by a bond, *being* in her father's house, in the time of her youth,

5 And her father hear her vow and bond, wherewith she hath bound herself, and her father hold his ¹peace concerning her, then all her vows shall stand and every bond, wherewith she hath bound herself, shall stand.

6 But if her ¹father disallow her the same day that he heareth all her vows and bonds, wherewith she hath bound herself, they shall not be of value, and the Lord will forgive her, because her father disallowed her.

7 And if she have an husband when she voweth or ¹pronounceth *ought* with her lips, wherewith she bindeth herself,

8 If her husband heard it, and holdeth his peace concerning her, the same day he heareth it, then her vow shall stand, and her bonds wherewith she bindeth herself shall stand in effect.

9 But if her husband disallow her the same day that he heareth it, then shall he make her vow which she hath made, and that that she hath pronounced with her lips, wherewith she bound ¹herself, of none effect: and the Lord will forgive her.

29:21 ¹ According to the ceremonies appointed thereunto.
29:39 ¹ Beside the sacrifices that you shall vow or offer of your own minds.
30:1 ¹ Hebrew, *Moses.*
30:2 ¹ Because they might declare them to the Israelites.
30:3 ¹ Hebrew, *his soul.*

² Hebrew, *violate his word.*
30:5 ¹ For in so doing he doth approve her.
30:6 ¹ By not approving or consenting to her vow.
30:7 ¹ Either by oath, or solemn promise.
30:9 ¹ For she is in subjection to her husband, and can perform nothing without his consent.

10 But every vow of a widow, and of her that is divorced (wherewith she hath bound herself) shall stand in ¹effect with her.

11 And if she vowed in her husband's ¹house, or bound herself straightly with an oath,

12 And her husband hath heard it, and held his peace concerning her, not disallowing her, then all her vows shall stand, and every bond, wherewith she bound herself, shall stand in effect.

13 But if her husband disannulled them the same day that he heard them, nothing that proceeded out of her lips concerning her vows or concerning ¹her bonds, shall stand in effect: *for* her husband hath disannulled them: and the Lord will forgive her.

14 So every vow, and every oath *or* bond, *made* to ¹humble the soul, her husband may stablish it, or her husband may break it.

15 But if her husband hold his peace concerning her from ¹day to day, then he stablisheth all her vows and all her bonds which she hath made: he hath confirmed them because he held his peace concerning her the same day that he heard *them*.

16 But if he ¹break them after that he hath heard them, then shall he bear her iniquity.

17 These are the ordinances which the Lord commanded Moses, between a man and his wife, *and* between the father and his daughter, *being* young in her father's house.

31 *8 Five Kings of Midian and Balaam are slain.   18 Only the maids are reserved alive.   27 The prey is equally divided.   50 A present given of Israel.*

1 And the Lord spake unto Moses, saying,

2 ᵃRevenge the children of Israel of the Midianites, *and* afterward shalt thou be ᵇgathered unto thy people.

3 And Moses spake to the people, saying, Harness some of you unto war, and let them go against Midian, to execute the vengeance of the Lord ¹against Midian.

4 A thousand of every tribe throughout all the tribes of Israel shall ye send to the war.

5 So there were taken out of the thousands of Israel, twelve thousand prepared unto war, of every tribe a thousand.

6 And Moses sent them to the war, *even* a thou-

CHAPTER 31
ᵃ Num. 25:17
ᵇ Num. 27:13
ᶜ Josh. 13:21
ᵈ Num. 25:2
ᵉ 2 Pet. 2:15
ᶠ Judg. 21:11
ᵍ Num. 19:11

sand of every tribe, and *sent* them with ¹Phinehas the son of Eleazar the Priest to the war: and the holy instruments, that is, the trumpets to blow *were* in his hand.

7 And they warred against Midian, as the Lord had commanded Moses, and slew all the males.

8 They slew also the kings of Midian among them that were slain: ᶜEvi, and Rekem, and Zur, and Hur, and Reba, five kings of Midian, and they slew ¹Balaam the son of Beor with the sword.

9 But the children of Israel took the women of Midian prisoners, and their children, and spoiled all their cattle, and all their flocks, and all their goods.

10 And they burnt all their cities, wherein they dwelt, and all their ¹villages with fire.

11 And they took all the spoil, and all the prey *both* of men and beasts.

12 And they brought the ¹captives and that which they had taken, and the spoil unto Moses and to Eleazar the Priest, and unto the Congregation of the children of Israel, into the camp in the plain of Moab, which was by Jordan *toward* Jericho.

13 ¶ Then Moses and Eleazar the Priest, and all the princes of the Congregation went out of the camp to meet them.

14 And Moses was angry with the captains of the host, with the captains over thousands, and captains over hundreds, which came from the war and battle.

15 And Moses said unto them, What? have ye saved all the ¹women?

16 Behold, ᵈthese caused the children of Israel through the ᶜcounsel of Balaam to commit a trespass against the Lord, ¹as concerning Peor, and there came a plague among the Congregation of the Lord.

17 Now therefore, ᶠslay all the males among the ¹children, and kill all the women that have known man by carnal copulation.

18 But all the women-children that have not known carnal copulation, keep alive for yourselves.

19 And ye shall remain without the host seven days, all that have killed any person, ᵍand all that have touched any dead, *and* purify both yourselves and your prisoners the third day and the seventh.

20 Also ye shall purify every garment and all that is made of skins, and all work of goats' hair, and all

---

30:10 ¹ For they are not under the authority of the man.
30:11 ¹ Her husband being alive.
30:13 ¹ Hebrew, *the bonds of her soul.*
30:14 ¹ To mortify herself by abstinence or other bodily exercise.
30:15 ¹ And warn her not the same day that he heareth it, as verse 9.
30:16 ¹ Not the same day he heard them, but some day after, the sin shall be imputed to him and not to her.
31:3 ¹ As he had commanded, Num. 25:17, declaring also that the

injury done against his people is done against him.
31:6 ¹ For his great zeal that he bare to the Lord, Num. 25:13.
31:8 ¹ The false prophet who gave counsel how to cause the Israelites to offend their God.
31:10 ¹ Or, palaces and gorgeous buildings.
31:12 ¹ As the women and little children.
31:15 ¹ As though he said, ye ought to have spared none.
31:16 ¹ For worshipping of Peor.
31:17 ¹ That is, all the men-children.

things made of wood.

21 ¶ And Eleazar the Priest said unto the men of war, which went to the battle, This is the ordinance ¹of the law which the Lord *ᵇ*commanded Moses.

22 As for gold, and silver, brass, iron, tin, and lead:

23 *Even* all that may abide the fire, ye shall make it go through the fire, and it shall be clean: yet, it shall be ¹purified with ʲthe water of purification: and all that suffereth not the fire, ye shall cause to pass by the ²water.

24 Ye shall wash also your clothes the seventh day, and ye shall be clean: and afterward ye shall come into the host.

25 ¶ And the Lord spake unto Moses, saying,

26 Take the sum of the prey that was taken, *both* of persons and of cattle, thou and Eleazar the Priest, and the chief fathers of the Congregation.

27 And divide the prey ¹between the soldiers that went to the war, and all the Congregation.

28 And thou shalt take a tribute unto the Lord of the ¹men of war, which went out to battle: one person of five hundred, *both* of the persons, and of the beeves, and of the asses, and of the sheep.

29 Ye shall take it of their half, and give it unto Eleazar the Priest, *as* an heave offering of the Lord.

30 But of the half of the children of Israel thou shalt take ¹one, taken out of fifty, *both* of the persons, of the beeves, of the asses, and of the sheep, *even* of all the cattle, and thou shalt give them unto the Levites, which have the charge of the Tabernacle of the Lord.

31 And Moses and Eleazar the Priest did as the Lord had commanded Moses.

32 And the booty, *to wit*, the rest of the prey which the men of war had spoiled, was six hundred seventy and five thousand sheep,

33 And seventy and two thousand beeves,

34 And threescore and one thousand asses,

35 And two and thirty thousand persons in all, of women that had ¹lain by no man.

36 And the half, *to wit*, the part of them that went out to war, touching the number of sheep, was three hundred seven and thirty thousand, and five hundred.

37 And the ¹Lord's tribute of the sheep was six hundred seventy and five.

38 And the beeves *were* six and thirty thousand,

ᵇ Num. 19:12
ʲ Num. 19:9

whereof the Lord's tribute *was* seventy and two.

39 And the asses *were* thirty thousand and five hundred, whereof the Lord's tribute *was* threescore and one:

40 And ¹of persons sixteen thousand, whereof the Lord's tribute *was* two and thirty persons.

41 And Moses gave the tribute of the Lord's offering unto Eleazar the Priest, as the Lord had commanded Moses.

42 And of the ¹half of the children of Israel, which Moses divided from the men of war,

43 (For the half that pertained unto the congregation, was three hundred thirty and seven thousand sheep and five hundred,

44 And six and thirty thousand beeves,

45 And thirty thousand asses, and five hundred,

46 And sixteen thousand persons.)

47 Moses, I say, took of the half that pertained unto the ¹children of Israel, one taken out of fifty, *both* of the persons, and of the cattle, and gave them unto the Levites, which have the charge of the Tabernacle of the Lord, as the Lord had commanded Moses.

48 ¶ Then the captains which were over thousands of the host, the captains over the thousands, and the captains over the hundreds came unto Moses:

49 And said to Moses, Thy servants have taken the sum of the men of war which are under ¹our authority, and there lacketh not one man of us.

50 ¹We have therefore brought a present unto the Lord, what every man found of Jewels of gold, bracelets, and chains, rings, earrings, and ornaments of the legs, to make an atonement for our souls before the Lord.

51 And Moses and Eleazar the Priest took the gold of them, *and* all wrought jewels,

52 And all the gold of the offering that they offered up to the Lord (of the captains over thousands and hundreds) *was* sixteen thousand seven hundred and fifty shekels.

53 (*For* the men of war had spoiled, every man for ¹himself.)

54 And Moses and Eleazar the Priest took the gold of the captains over the thousands, and over the hundreds, and brought it into the Tabernacle of the Congregation, for a ¹memorial of the children of Israel before the Lord.

31:21 ¹ Or, contained in the law.
31:23 ¹ The third day and before it be molten.
    ² It shall be washed.
31:27 ¹ The prey is first divided equally among all.
31:28 ¹ Of the prey that falleth to the soldiers.
31:30 ¹ The Israelites which had not been at war, of every fiftieth paid one to the Lord: and the soldiers one of every five hundredth.
31:35 ¹ Hebrew, *not known the bed of man.*
31:37 ¹ This is the portion that the soldiers gave to the Lord.

31:40 ¹ Meaning, of the maids, or virgins which had not companied with man.
31:42 ¹ Of that part which was given unto them in dividing the spoil.
31:47 ¹ Which had not been at war.
31:49 ¹ Hebrew, *under our hands.*
31:50 ¹ The captains by the free offering acknowledge the great benefit of God in preserving his people.
31:53 ¹ And gave no portion to their captains.
31:54 ¹ That the Lord might remember the children of Israel.

32

2 *The request of the Reubenites and Gadites,*   16 *and their promise unto Moses.*   20 *Moses granteth their request.*   33 *The Gadites, Reubenites, and half the tribe of Manasseh, conquer and build cities on this side Jordan.*

CHAPTER 32
a Num. 13:24
b Num. 14:28,29
c Josh. 1:13
d Josh. 4:12

1   Now the children of [1]Reuben, and the children of Gad had an exceeding great multitude of cattle: and they saw the land of Jazer, and the land of [2]Gilead, that it was an apt place for cattle.

2   Then the children of Gad, and the children of Reuben came, and spake unto Moses and to Eleazar the Priest, and unto the Princes of the Congregation, saying,

3   *The land of* Ataroth, and Dibon, and Jazer, and Nimrah, and Heshbon, and Elealeh, and Shebam, and Nebo, and Beon,

4   Which country the Lord smote before the Congregation of Israel; is a land *meet* for cattle, and thy servants have cattle:

5   Wherefore, said they, if we have found grace in thy sight, let this land be given unto thy servants for a possession, *and* bring us not over Jordan.

6   And Moses said unto the children of Gad, and to the children of Reuben, Shall your brethren go to war, and ye tarry here?

7   Wherefore now [1]discourage you the heart of the children of Israel to go over into the land, which the Lord hath given them?

8   Thus did your fathers, when I sent them from Kadesh Barnea to see the land.

9   For [a]when they went up even unto the [1]river of Eshcol, and saw the land, they discouraged the heart of the children of Israel, that they would not go into the land, which the Lord had given them.

10   And the Lord's wrath was kindled the same day, and he did swear, saying,

11   [1]None of the men that came out of Egypt, [b]from twenty years old and above, shall see the land for the which I sware unto Abraham, to Isaac, and to Jacob, because they have not [2]wholly followed me:

12   Except Caleb the son of Jephunneh the Kenizzite, and Joshua the son of Nun: for they have constantly followed the Lord.

13   And the Lord was very angry with Israel, and made [them] wander in the wilderness forty years, until all the generation that had done [1]evil in the sight of the Lord, was consumed.

14   And behold, ye are risen up in your father's stead *as* an increase of sinful men still to augment the fierce wrath of the Lord toward Israel.

15   For if ye turn away from following him, he will yet again leave *the people* in the wilderness, and [1]ye shall destroy all this folk.

16   And they went near to him, and said, We will build sheepfolds here for our sheep, *and* for our cattle, and cities for our children.

17   But we ourselves will be ready armed *to go* before the children of Israel, until we have brought them unto their [1]place: but our children shall dwell in the defensed cities, because of the inhabitants of the land.

18   We will not return unto our houses, until the children of Israel have inherited, every man his inheritance.

19   Neither will we inherit with them beyond Jordan and on that side, because our inheritance is fallen to us on this side Jordan Eastward.

20   ¶ [c]And Moses said unto them, If ye will do this thing, and go [1]armed before the Lord to war:

21   And will go every one of you in harness over Jordan before the Lord, until he have cast out his [1]enemies from his sight:

22   And until the land be subdued before the Lord, then ye shall return and be innocent toward the Lord, and toward Israel: and this land shall be your possession [1]before the Lord.

23   But if ye will not do so, behold, ye have sinned against the Lord, and be sure, that your sin [1]will find you out.

24   Build you *then* cities for your children, and folds for your sheep, and do that ye have spoken.

25   Then the children of Gad and the children of Reuben spake unto Moses, saying, Thy servants will do as my lord commandeth:

26   Our children, our wives, our sheep, and all our cattle shall remain there in the cities of Gilead,

27   But [d]thy servants will go every one armed to war before the Lord for to fight, as my lord saith.

28   So concerning them, Moses [1]commanded Eleazar the Priest, and Joshua the son of Nun, and the chief fathers of the tribes of the children of Israel.

29   And Moses said unto them, If the children of Gad and the children of Reuben will go with you over Jordan, all armed to fight before the Lord, then

---

32:1   [1] Reuben came of Leah, and Gad of Zilpah her handmaid.
   [2] Which mountain was so named of the heap of stones that Jacob made as a sign of the covenant between him and Laban, Gen. 31:47.
32:7   [1] Hebrew, *break.*
32:9   [1] Or, *valley.*
32:11   [1] Hebrew, *if any of the men.*
   [2] Or, persevered and continued.
32:13   [1] Because they murmured, neither would believe their report, which told the truth as concerning the land.

32:15   [1] By your occasion.
32:17   [1] In the land of Canaan.
32:20   [1] Before the Ark of the Lord.
32:21   [1] That is, the inhabitants of the land.
32:22   [1] The Lord will grant you this land which ye require, Josh. 1:15.
32:23   [1] Ye shall assuredly be punished for your sin.
32:28   [1] Moses gave charge that his promise made to the Reubenites, and others, should be performed after his death, so that they brake not theirs.

when the land is subdued before you, ye shall give them the land of Gilead for a possession:

30 But if they will not go over with you armed, then they shall have their possessions among you in the land of Canaan.

31 And the children of Gad, and the children of Reuben answered, saying, As the ¹Lord hath said unto thy servants, so will we do.

32 We will go armed before the Lord into the land of Canaan: that the possession of our inheritance may be to us on this side Jordan.

33 ᶜSo Moses gave unto them, even to the children of Gad, and to the children of Reuben, and to half the tribe of Manasseh the son of Joseph, the kingdom of Sihon king of the ¹Amorites, and the kingdom of Og king of Bashan, the land with the cities thereof and coasts, even the cities of the country round about.

34 ¶ Then the children of Gad built Dibon, and Ataroth, and Aroer,

35 And Atroth, Shophan, and Jazer, and Jogbehah,

36 And Beth Nimrah, and Beth Haran, defensed cities: also sheepfolds.

37 And the children of Reuben built Heshbon, and Elealeh, and Kirjathaim,

38 And Nebo, and Baal Meon, and turned their names, and Shibmah: and gave other names unto the cities which they built.

39 And the children ᶠof Machir the son of Manasseh went to Gilead, and took it, and put out the Amorites that dwelt therein.

40 Then Moses gave Gilead unto Machir the son of Manasseh, and he dwelt therein.

41 ᵍAnd Jair the son of Manasseh went and took the small towns thereof, and called them ¹Havoth Jair.

42 Also Nobah went and took Kenath, with the villages thereof, and called it Nobah after his own name.

33

8 Two and forty journeys of Israel are numbered. 52 They are commanded to kill the Canaanites.

1 These are the ¹journeys of the children of Israel, which went out of the land of Egypt, according to their bands under the hand of Moses and Aaron.

2 And Moses wrote their going out by their journeys, according to the commandment of the Lord: so these are the journeys of their going out.

3 Now they ᵃdeparted from Rameses the first month, even the fifteenth day of the first month, on the morrow after the Passover: and the children of Israel went out with an high hand in the sight of all the Egyptians.

4 (For the Egyptians buried all their firstborn, which the Lord had smitten among them: upon their ¹gods also the Lord did execution.)

5 And the children of Israel removed from Rameses, and pitched in Succoth.

6 And they departed from ᵇSuccoth, and pitched in Etham, which is in the edge of the wilderness.

7 And they removed from Etham, and turned again unto ¹Pi Hahiroth, which is before Baal Zephon, and pitched before Migdol.

8 And they departed from before Hahiroth, and ᶜwent through the midst of the Sea into the wilderness, and went three days' journey in the wilderness of Etham, and pitched in Marah.

9 And they removed from Marah, and came unto ᵈElim, and in Elim were twelve fountains of water, and seventy palm trees, and they pitched there.

10 And they removed from Elim, and camped by the red sea.

11 And they removed from the red Sea, and lay in the ᵉwilderness of Sin.

12 And they took their journey out of the wilderness of Sin, and set up their tents in Dophkah.

13 And they departed from Dophkah, and lay in Alush.

14 And they removed from Alush, and lay in ᶠRephidim, where was no water for the people to drink.

15 And they departed from Rephidim, and pitched in the ᵍwilderness of Sinai.

16 And they removed from the desert of Sinai, and pitched in ʰKibroth Hattaavah.

17 And they departed from Kibroth Hattaavah, and lay at ᶦHazeroth.

18 And they departed from Hazeroth, and pitched in Rithmah.

19 And they departed from ʲRithmah, and pitched at Rimmon Perez.

20 And they departed from Rimmon Perez, and pitched in Libnah.

21 And they removed from Libnah, and pitched in Rissah.

22 And they journeyed from Rissah, and pitched in Kehelathah.

23 And they went from Kehelathah, and pitched in mount Shepher.

24 And they removed from mount Shepher, and lay in Haradah.

25 And they removed from Haradah, and pitched

ᶜ Deut. 3:12
Josh. 13:8
Josh. 22:4
ᶠ Gen. 50:23
ᵍ Deut. 3:14

CHAPTER 33
ᵃ Exod. 12:37
ᵇ Exod. 13:19
ᶜ Exod. 15:22
ᵈ Exod. 16:27
ᵉ Exod. 15:1
ᶠ Exod. 17:1
ᵍ Exod. 19:1
ʰ Num. 11:34
ᶦ Num. 11:35
ʲ Num. 13:1

32:31 ¹ This is attributed to the Lord, which his messenger speaketh.
32:33 ¹ The Amorites dwelled on both sides of Jordan: but here he maketh mention of them that dwelt on this side: and Josh. 10:12, he speaketh of them that inhabited beyond Jordan.
32:41 ¹ That is, the villages of Jair.
33:1 ¹ From whence they departed, and whither they came.
33:4 ¹ Either meaning their idols, or their men of authority.
33:7 ¹ At the commandment of the Lord, Exod. 14:2.

in Makheloth.

26 And they removed from Makheloth, and lay in Tahath.

27 And they departed from Tahath, and pitched in Terah.

28 And they removed from Terah, and pitched in Mithkah.

29 And they went from Mithkah, and pitched in Hashmonah.

30 And they departed from Hashmonah, and lay in Moseroth.

31 And they departed from Moseroth, and pitched in Bene Jaakan.

32 And they removed from Bene Jaakan, and lay in Hor Hagidgad.

33 And they went from Hor Hagidgad, and pitched in Jotbathah.

34 And they removed from Jotbathah, and lay in Abronah.

35 And they departed from Abronah, and lay in Ezion Geber.

36 And they removed from Ezion Geber, and pitched in the [k]wilderness of Zin, which is Kadesh.

37 And they removed from Kadesh, and pitched in mount Hor, in the edge of the land of Edom.

38 ([l]And Aaron the Priest went up into mount Hor, at the commandment of the Lord and died there, in the fortieth year after the children of Israel were come out of the land of Egypt, in the first day of the [1]fifth month.

39 And Aaron was an hundred and three and twenty years old, when he died in mount Hor.)

40 And [m]King Arad the Canaanite, which dwelt in the South of the land of Canaan, heard of the coming of the children of Israel.

41 And they departed from mount [n]Hor, and pitched in Zalmonah.

42 And they departed from Zalmonah, and pitched in Punon.

43 And they departed from Punon, and pitched in Oboth.

44 [o]And they departed from Oboth, and pitched in Ije Abarim, in the borders of Moab.

45 And they departed from Ijim, and pitched in Dibon Gad.

46 And they removed from Dibon Gad, and lay in Almon Diblathaim.

47 And they removed from Almon Diblathaim, and pitched in the mountains of Abarim before Nebo.

48 And they departed from the mountains of Abarim, and pitched in the [1]plain of Moab by Jordan *toward* Jericho.

49 And they pitched by Jordan, from Beth Jesimoth unto [p]Abel Shittim, in the plain of Moab.

50 ¶ And the Lord spake unto Moses in the plain of Moab, by Jordan *toward* Jericho, saying,

51 ¶ Speak unto the children of Israel, and say unto them, [q]When ye are come over Jordan to enter into the land of Canaan,

52 Ye shall then drive out all the inhabitants of the land before you, and destroy all their [1]pictures, and break asunder all their images of metal, and pluck down all their high places,

53 And ye shall possess the land and dwell therein: for I have given you the land to possess it.

54 And ye shall inherit the land by lot, according to your families: [r]to the more ye shall give more inheritance, and to the fewer the less inheritance. Where the lot shall fall to any man, that shall be his: according to the tribes of your fathers shall ye inherit.

55 But if ye will not drive out the inhabitants of the land before you, then those which ye let remain of them, shall be [s,1]pricks in your eyes, and thorns in your sides, and shall vex you in the land wherein ye dwell.

56 Moreover, it shall come to pass, that I shall do unto you, as I thought to do unto them.

34

3 The coasts and borders of the land of Canaan. 17 Certain men are assigned to divide the land.

1 And the Lord spake unto Moses, saying,

2 Command the children of Israel, and say unto them, When ye come into the land of Canaan, this is the [1]land that shall fall unto your inheritance: *that is,* the land of Canaan with the coasts thereof.

3 [a]And your South quarter shall be from the wilderness of Zin to the borders of Edom: so that your South quarter shall be from the salt Sea coast Eastward

4 And the border shall compass you from the South to [1]Maaleh Akrabbim, and reach to Zin, and go out from the South to Kadesh Barnea: thence it shall stretch to Hazar Addar, and go along to Azmon.

5 And the border shall compass from Azmon unto the [1]river of Egypt, and shall go out to the sea.

6 And your West quarter shall be [1]the great sea: even that border shall be your West coast.

7 And this shall be your North quarter, ye shall

[k] Num. 20:22
[l] Num. 20:25 Deut. 32:50
[m] Num. 21:1
[n] Num. 11:4,10
[o] Num. 21:11
[p] Num. 25:1
[q] Deut. 7:2 Josh. 11:11,12
[r] Num. 26:53,54
[s] Josh. 23:13 Judg. 2:3

CHAPTER 34
[a] Josh. 15:1

33:38 [1] Which the Hebrews call Ab, and answereth to part of July and part of August.
33:48 [1] Or, field.
33:52 [1] Which were set up in their high places to worship.
33:55 [1] Or, knives.
34:2 [1] Meaning, the description of the land.
34:4 [1] Or, ascending up of scorpions.
34:5 [1] Which was Nilus, or as some think, Rhinocotura.
34:6 [1] Which is called Mediterranean.

mark out your border from the great sea *unto* mount ¹Hor.

8 From mount Hor ye shall point out till it come unto Hamath, and the end of the coast shall be at Zedad.

9 And the coast shall reach out to Ziphron, and go out at Hazar Enan, this shall be your North quarter.

10 And ye shall mark out your East quarter from Hazar Enan to Shepham.

11 And the coast shall go down from Shepham to Riblah, and from the East side of Ain: and the same border shall descend and go out at the side of the sea of ¹Chinnereth Eastward.

12 Also that border shall go down to Jordan, and leave at the salt sea: this shall be your land with the coasts thereof round about.

13 ¶ Then Moses commanded the children of Israel, saying, This is the land which ye shall inherit by lot, which the Lord commanded to give unto nine tribes, and half the tribe.

14 ᵇFor the tribe of the children of Reuben, according to the households of their fathers, and the tribe of the children of Gad, according to their fathers' households, and half the tribe of Manasseh have received their inheritance.

15 Two tribes and an half tribe have received their inheritance on this side of Jordan *toward* Jericho full East.

16 ¶ Again the Lord spake to Moses, saying,

17 These are the names of the men which shall divide the land unto you: ᶜEleazar the Priest, and Joshua the son of Nun.

18 And ye shall take also a ¹prince of every tribe to divide the land.

19 The names also of the men are these: Of the tribe of Judah, Caleb the son of Jephunneh.

20 And of the tribe of the sons of Simeon, Shemuel the son of Ammihud.

21 Of the tribe of Benjamin, Elidad the son of Chislon.

22 Also of the tribe of the sons of Dan, the prince Bukki, the son of Jogli.

23 Of the sons of Joseph: of the tribe of the sons of Manasseh, the prince Hanniel the son of Ephod.

24 And of the tribe of the sons of Ephraim, the prince Kemuel, the son of Shiphtan.

25 Of the tribe also of the sons of Zebulun, the

*ᵇ Num. 32:33
Josh. 14:2,3
ᶜ Josh. 19:51*

CHAPTER 35
*ᵃ Josh. 21:2
ᵇ Deut. 4:41
Josh. 20:2
Josh. 21:3
ᶜ Exod. 21:13
Deut. 19:2
Josh. 10:2*

prince Elizaphan, the son of Parnach.

26 So of the tribe of the sons of Issachar, the prince Paltiel, the son of Azzan.

27 Of the tribe also of the sons of Asher, the prince Ahihud, the son of Shelomi.

28 And of the tribe of the sons of Naphtali, the prince Pedahel, the son of Ammihud.

29 These are they, whom the Lord commanded to ¹divide the inheritance unto the children of Israel, in the land of Canaan.

35 *2 Unto the Levites are given cities and suburbs. 11 The cities of refuge. 16 The law of murder. 30 For one man's witness shall no man be condemned.*

1 And the Lord spake unto Moses in the plain of Moab by Jordan, *toward* Jericho, saying,

2 ᵃCommand the children of Israel, that they give unto the ¹Levites of the inheritance of their possession, ²cities to dwell in: ye shall give also unto the Levites the suburbs of the cities round about them.

3 So they shall have the cities to dwell in, and their suburbs shall be for their cattle, and for their substance, and for all their beasts.

4 And the suburbs of the cities, which ye shall give unto the Levites, from the wall of the city outward *shall be* a thousand cubits round about.

5 And ye shall measure without the city of the East side, ¹two thousand cubits: and of the South side, two thousand cubits: and of the West side, two thousand cubits: and of the North side, two thousand cubits: and the city *shall be* in the midst: this shall be *the measure* of the suburbs of their cities.

6 And of the cities which ye shall give unto the Levites, ᵇthere shall be six cities for refuge, which ye shall appoint, that he which killeth, may flee thither: and to them ye shall add two and forty cities more.

7 All the cities which ye shall give to the Levites, *shall be* eight and forty cities: them *shall ye give* with their suburbs.

8 And concerning the cities which ye shall give, of the possession of the children of Israel: of many ye shall take more, and of few ye shall take less: everyone shall give of his cities unto the Levites, according to his inheritance, which he inheriteth.

9 ¶ And the Lord spake unto Moses, saying,

10 Speak unto the children of Israel, and say unto them, ᶜWhen ye be come over Jordan into the land of Canaan,

34:7 ¹ Which is a mountain near Tyre and Sidon, and not that Hor in the wilderness where Aaron died.
34:11 ¹ Which in the Gospel is called the lake of Gennesaret.
34:18 ¹ One of the heads or chief men of every tribe.
34:29 ¹ And be judges over every piece of ground that should fall to any by lot, to the intent that all things might be done orderly and without contention.

35:2 ¹ Because they had no inheritance assigned them in the land of Canaan.
² God would have them scattered through all the land, because the people might be preserved by them in the obedience of God and his Law.
35:5 ¹ So that in all were three thousand, and in the compass of these two thousand, they might plant and sow.

11 Ye shall appoint you cities, to be cities of refuge for you, that the slayer, which slayeth any person unawares, may flee thither.

12 And these cities shall be for you a refuge from thy [1]avenger, that he which killeth, die not, until he stand before the Congregation in judgment.

13 And of the cities which ye shall give, six cities shall ye have for refuge.

14 Ye shall appoint three [1]on this side Jordan, and ye shall appoint three cities in the land of [d]Canaan which shall be cities of refuge.

15 These six cities shall be a refuge for the children of Israel, and for the stranger, and for him that dwelleth [1]among you, that everyone which killeth any person unawares, may flee thither.

16 [c]And if one [1]smite another with an instrument of iron that he die, he is a murderer, and the murderer shall die the death.

17 Also if he smite him by casting a [1]stone, wherewith he may be slain, and he die, he is a murderer, and the murderer shall die the death.

18 Or if he smite him with an hand weapon of wood, wherewith he may be slain, if he die, he is a murderer, and the murderer shall die the death.

19 The revenger of the blood himself shall slay the murderer: when he meeteth him, he shall slay him.

20 But if he thrust him [f]of hate, or hurl at him by laying of wait, that he die,

21 Or smite him through enmity with his hand, that he die, he that smote him shall die the death: for he is a murderer: the revenger of the blood shall slay the murderer when he meeteth him.

22 But if he pushed him [1]unadvisedly, and [g]not of hatred, or cast upon him [2]anything, without laying of wait,

23 Or any stone (whereby he might be slain), and saw him not, or caused it to fall upon him, and he die, and was not his enemy, neither sought him any harm,

24 Then the Congregation shall judge between the slayer and the [1]avenger of blood according to these laws.

25 And the Congregation shall deliver the slayer

[d] Josh. 20:7
[e] Exod. 21:14
[f] Deut. 19:11
[g] Exod. 21:13
[h] Deut. 17:6
Deut. 9:15
[i] Matt. 18:16
2 Cor. 13:1

CHAPTER 36
[a] Num. 27:1
Josh. 17:3

out of the hand of the avenger of blood, and the Congregation shall restore him unto the city of his refuge, whither he was fled: and he shall abide there unto the death of the [1]high Priest, which is anointed with the holy oil.

26 But if the slayer come without the borders of the city of his refuge, whither he was fled,

27 And the revenger of blood find him without the borders of the city of his refuge, and the revenger of blood slay the [1]murderer, he shall be guiltless,

28 Because he should have remained in the city of his refuge, until the death of the high Priest: and after the death of the high Priest, the slayer shall return unto the land of his possession.

29 So these things shall be a [1]law of judgment unto you, throughout your generations in all your dwellings.

30 Whosoever killeth any person, the Judge shall slay the murderer, through [h]witnesses: but [i]one witness shall not testify against a person to cause him to die.

31 Moreover ye shall take no recompense for the life of the murderer, which is [1]worthy to die: but he shall be put to death.

32 Also ye shall take no recompense for him that is fled to the city of his refuge, that he should come again, and dwell in the land, before the death of the high Priest.

33 So ye shall not pollute the land wherein ye shall dwell: for [1]blood defileth the land: and the land cannot be [2]cleansed of the blood that is shed therein, but by the blood of him that shed it.

34 Defile not therefore the land which ye shall inhabit, for I dwell in the midst thereof: For I the Lord dwell among the children of Israel.

36

6 An order for the marriage of the daughters of Zelophehad.

1 Then [1]the chief fathers of the family of the sons of Gilead, the son of Machir, the son of Manasseh, of the families of the sons of Joseph, came, and spake before Moses, and before the princes, the chief fathers of the children of Israel,

2 And said, [a]The Lord commanded [1]my lord

35:12 [1] Meaning, from the next of the kindred, who ought to pursue the cause.

35:14 [1] Among the Reubenites, Gadites, and half the tribe of Manasseh, Deut. 4:41.

35:15 [1] Hebrew, among them.

35:16 [1] Wittingly, and willingly.

35:17 [1] That is, with a big and dangerous stone: in Hebrew, with a stone of his hand.

35:22 [1] Or, suddenly.

[2] Hebrew, instrument.

35:24 [1] That is, his next kinsman.

35:25 [1] Under this figure is declared, that our sins could not be

remitted, but by the death of the high Priest Jesus Christ.

35:27 [1] By the sentence of the Judge.

35:29 [1] A law to judge murders done either of purpose, or unadvisedly.

35:31 [1] Which purposely hath committed murder.

35:33 [1] Or, murder.

[2] So God is mindful of the blood wrongfully shed, that he maketh his dumb creatures to demand vengeance thereof.

36:1 [1] It seemeth that the tribes contended who might marry these daughters to have their inheritance: and therefore the sons of Joseph proposed the matter to Moses.

36:2 [1] Meaning, Moses.

to give the land to inherit by lot to the children of Israel: and my lord was commanded by the Lord, to give the inheritance of Zelophehad our brother unto his daughters.

3 If they be married to any of the sons of the *other* tribes of the children of Israel, then shall their inheritance be taken away from the inheritance of our fathers, and shall be put unto the inheritance of the tribe whereof they shall be: so shall it be taken away from the lot of our inheritance.

4 Also when the ¹Jubilee of the children of Israel cometh, then shall their inheritance be put unto the inheritance of the tribe whereof they shall be: so shall their inheritance be taken away from the inheritance of the tribe of our fathers.

5 Then Moses commanded the children of Israel, according to the word of the Lord, saying, The tribe of the sons of Joseph have said ¹well.

6 This is the thing that the Lord hath commanded, concerning the daughters of Zelophehad, saying, They shall be wives, to whom they think best, only to the family of the tribe of their father shall they marry:

7 So shall not the inheritance of the children of

ᵇ Num. 27:1

Israel remove from tribe to tribe, for every one of the children of Israel shall join himself to the inheritance of the tribe of his fathers.

8 And every daughter that possesseth any ¹inheritance of the tribes of the children of Israel, shall be wife unto one of the family of the tribe of her father: that the children of Israel may enjoy every man the inheritance of their fathers.

9 Neither shall the inheritance go about from tribe to tribe: but every one of the tribes of the children of Israel shall stick to his own inheritance.

10 As the Lord commanded Moses, so did the daughters of Zelophehad.

11 For ᵇMahlah, Tirzah, and Hoglah, and Milcah, and Noah the daughters of Zelophehad were married unto their father's brother's sons,

12 They were wives *to certain* of the families of the sons of Manasseh the son of Joseph: so their inheritance remained in the tribe of the family of their father.

13 These are the ¹commandments and laws which the Lord commanded by the hand of Moses, unto the children of Israel in the plain of Moab, by Jordan *toward* Jericho.

36:4 ¹ Signifying that at no time it could return, for in the Jubilee all things returned to their own tribes.
36:5 ¹ For the tribe could not have continued, if the inheritance which

was the maintenance thereof should have been alienated to others.
36:8 ¹ When there is no male to inherit.
36:13 ¹ Touching the ceremonial and judicial laws.

THE FIFTH BOOK OF MOSES,

CALLED

¹DEUTERONOMY

CHAPTER 1

a Num. 21:24
b Gen. 15:18
Gen. 17:7,8
c John 7:24
d Lev. 19:15
Deut. 16:19
1 Sam. 16:7
Prov. 24:23
James 2:2

2 A brief rehearsal of things done before, from Horeb unto Kadesh Barnea. 32 Moses reproveth the people for their incredulity. 44 The Israelites are overcome by the Amorites because they fought against the commandment of the Lord.

1 These be the words which Moses spake unto all Israel, on ¹this side Jordan in the wilderness, in the plain, ²over against the red sea, between Paran and Tophel, and Laban, and Hazeroth, and Dizahab.

2 There *are* eleven days' journey from ¹Horeb unto Kadesh Barnea, by the way of mount Seir.

3 And it came to pass in the first day of the eleventh month, in the fortieth year that Moses spake unto the children of Israel according unto all that the Lord hath given him in commandment unto them.

4 After that he had slain ¹,ᵃSihon the King of the Amorites which dwelt in Heshbon, and Og king of Bashan, which dwelt at Ashtaroth in Edrei.

5 On this side Jordan at the land of Moab ¹began Moses to declare this law, saying,

6 The Lord our God spake unto us in ¹Horeb, saying, Ye have dwelt long enough in this mount,

7 Turn you and depart, and go unto the mountain of the Amorites, and unto all places near thereunto in the plain, in the mountain, or in the valley: both Southward, and to the Sea side to the land of the Canaanites, and unto Lebanon: *even* unto the great river, the river ¹Perah.

8 Behold, I have set the land before you: go in and ᵇpossess that land which the Lord sware, unto your fathers, Abraham, Isaac, and Jacob, to give unto them and unto their seed after them.

9 ¶And I spake ¹unto you the same time, saying, I am not able to bear you myself alone:

10 The Lord your God hath ¹multiplied you: and behold, ye are this day as the stars of heaven in number:

11 (The Lord God of your fathers make you a thousand times so many more as ye are, and bless you, as he hath promised you,)

12 How can I alone ¹bear your cumbrance and your charge, and your strife?

13 Bring you men of wisdom and of understanding, and ¹known among your tribes, and I will make them rulers over you:

14 Then he answered me and said, the thing is good that thou hast commanded *us* to do.

15 So I took the chief of your tribes, ¹wise and known men, and made them rulers over you, captains over thousands, and captains over hundreds, and captains over fifty, and captains over ten, and officers among your tribes.

16 And I charged your Judges that same time, saying, Hear the *controversies* between your brethren, and ᶜjudge righteously between every man and his brother, and the stranger that is with him.

17 Ye shall have no respect of person in judgment, ᵈbut shall hear the small as well as the great: ye shall not fear the face of man: for the judgment is ¹God's: and the cause that is too hard for you, bring unto me, and I will hear it.

18 Also I commanded you the same time all the things which ye should do.

19 ¶Then we departed from Horeb, and went through all that great and terrible wilderness (as ye have seen) by the way of the mountain of the Amorites, as the Lord our God commanded us: and we came to Kadesh Barnea.

Title ¹ That is, a second law: so called, because the Law which God gave in mount Sinai, is here repeated, as though it were a new Law: and this book is a commentary or exposition of the ten commandments.

1:1 ¹ In the country of Moab.
   ² So that the wilderness was between the Sea and this plain of Moab.

1:2 ¹ In Horeb, or Sinai, forty years before this the Law was given: but because all that were then of age and judgment were now dead, Moses repeateth the same to the youth which either then were not born, or had not judgment.

1:4 ¹ By these examples of God's favor, their minds are prepared to receive the Law.

1:5 ¹ The second time.

1:6 ¹ In the second year and second month, Num. 10:11.

1:7 ¹ Or, Euphrates.

1:9 ¹ By the counsel of Jethro my father-in-law, Exod. 18:19.

1:10 ¹ Not so much by the course of nature, as miraculously.

1:12 ¹ Signifying how great a burden it is, to govern the people.

1:13 ¹ Whose godliness and uprightness is known.

1:15 ¹ Declaring what sort of men ought to have a public charge, read Exod. 18:31.

1:17 ¹ And you are his Lieutenants.

20 And ¹I said unto you, Ye are come unto the mountain of the Amorites, which the Lord our God doth give unto us.

21 Behold, the Lord thy God hath laid the land before thee: go up *and* possess it, as the Lord the God of thy fathers hath said unto thee: fear not, neither be discouraged.

22 ¶ ¹Then ye came unto me everyone, and said, We will send men before us, to search us out the land, and to bring us word again, what way we must go up by, and unto what cities we shall come.

23 So the saying pleased me well, and I took twelve men of you, of every tribe one.

24 ᶜWho departed, and went up into the mountain, and came unto the ¹river Eshcol, and searched out the *land*.

25 And took of the fruit of the land in their hand, and brought it unto us, and brought us word again, and ¹said, It is a good land, which the Lord our God doth give us.

26 Notwithstanding, ye would not go up, but were disobedient unto the commandment of the Lord your God,

27 And murmured in your tents, and said, Because the Lord ¹hated us, therefore hath he brought us out of the land of Egypt, to deliver us into the hand of the Amorites, and to destroy us.

28 Whither shall we go up, our ¹brethren have discouraged our hearts, saying, The people *[are]* greater, and taller than we: the cities *are* great and walled up to heaven: and moreover we have seen the sons of the ᶠAnakims there.

29 But I said unto you, Dread not, nor be afraid of them.

30 The Lord your God, ¹who goeth before you, he shall fight for you, according to all that he did unto you in Egypt before your eyes,

31 And in the wilderness, where thou hast seen how the Lord thy God bare thee, as a man doth bear his son, in all the way which ye have gone, until ye came unto this place.

32 Yet for all this ye did not believe the Lord your God,

33 ᵍWho went in the way before you, to search you out a place to pitch your tents in, in fire by night, that

ᶜ Num. 13:24
ᶠ Num. 13:29
ᵍ Exod. 13:11
ʰ Num. 14:23
ⁱ Josh. 14:6
ʲ Num. 20:12
Num. 27:14
ᵏ Deut. 3:26
Deut. 4:21
Deut. 34:4

ye might see what way to go, and in a cloud by day.

34 Then the Lord heard the voice of your words, and was wroth, and sware, saying,

35 ʰSurely there shall not one of these men of this forward generation, see that good land, which I sware to give unto your fathers,

36 Save Caleb the son of Jephunneh: he shall see it, ⁱand to him will I give the land that he hath trodden upon, and to his children, because he hath constantly followed the Lord.

37 ʲAlso the Lord was angry with me for your sakes, saying, ᵏThou also shalt not go in thither,

38 But Joshua the son of Nun which standeth ¹before thee, he shall go in thither: encourage him: for he shall cause Israel to inherit it.

39 Moreover, your ¹children, which ye said should be a prey, and your sons, which in that day had no knowledge between good and evil, they shall go in thither, and unto them will I give it, and they shall possess it.

40 But as for you, turn back, and take your journey into the wilderness by the way of the red Sea.

41 Then ye answered and said unto me, We have sinned against the Lord, ¹we will go up, and fight, according to all that the Lord our God hath commanded us: and ye armed you every man to the war, and were ready to go up into the mountain.

42 But the Lord said unto me, Say unto them, Go not up, neither fight, (for I am ¹not among you) lest ye fall before your enemies.

43 And when I told you, ye would not hear, but rebelled against the commandment of the Lord, and were presumptuous, and went up into the mountain.

44 Then the Amorites which dwelt in that mountain came out against you, and chased you (as bees used to do) and destroyed you in Seir, *even* unto Hormah.

45 And when ye came again, ye wept before the Lord, but the Lord would not ¹hear your voice, nor incline his ears unto you.

46 So ye abode in Kadesh a long time, according to the time that ye had remained *before*.

2 *4 Israel is forbidden to fight with the Edomites, 9 Moabites, 19 and Ammonites. 23 Sihon King of Heshbon.*

1:20 ¹ So that the fault was in themselves, that they did not sooner possess the inheritance promised.
1:22 ¹ Read Num. 13:13
1:24 ¹ Or, valley of the cluster of grapes.
1:25 ¹ To wit, Caleb, and Joshua: Moses preferreth the better part to the greater, that is, two to ten.
1:27 ¹ Such was the Jews' unthankfulness, that they counted God's especial love, hatred.
1:28 ¹ The other ten, not Caleb and Joshua.
1:30 ¹ Declaring that to renounce our own force, and constantly to follow our vocation, and depend on the Lord, is the true boldness,

and agreeable to God.
1:38 ¹ Which ministreth unto thee.
1:39 ¹ Which were under twenty years old, as Num. 14:31.
1:41 ¹ This declareth man's nature, who will do that which God forbiddeth, and will not do that which he commendeth.
1:42 ¹ Signifying that man hath no strength, but when God is at hand to help him.
1:45 ¹ Because ye rather showed your hypocrisy, than true repentance: rather lamenting the loss of your brethren, than repenting for your sins.

1 Then ¹we turned, and took our journey into the wilderness, by the way of the red Sea, as the Lord spake unto me: and were compassed mount Seir [a] ²long time.

2 And the Lord spake unto me, saying,

3 Ye have compassed this mountain long enough: turn you Northward.

4 And warn thou the people, saying, Ye shall go through the ¹coast of your brethren the children of Esau, which dwell in Seir, and they shall be afraid of you: take ye good heed therefore.

5 Ye shall not provoke them: for I will not give you of their land so much as a foot breadth, ªbecause I have given mount Seir unto Esau for a possession.

6 Ye shall buy meat of them for money to eat, and ye shall also procure water of them for money to drink.

7 For the Lord thy God hath ¹blessed thee in all the works of thine hand: he knoweth thy walking through this great wilderness, and the Lord thy God hath been with thee this forty years, *and* thou hast lacked nothing.

8 And when we were departed from our brethren the children of Esau which dwelt in Seir: through the way of the ¹plain, from Elath, and from Ezion Geber, we turned and went by the way of the wilderness of Moab.

9 Then the Lord said unto me, Thou shalt not ¹vex Moab, neither provoke them to battle: for I will not give thee of their land for a possession, because I have given Ar unto the children ²of Lot for a possession.

10 The ¹Emims dwelt therein in times past, a people great and many, and tall, as the Anakims.

11 They also were taken for giants as the Anakims: whom the Moabites call Emims.

12 The ᵇHorites also dwelt in Seir before time, whom the children of Esau chased out and destroyed them before them, and dwelt in their stead: as Israel shall do unto the land of his possession, which the Lord hath given them.

13 Now rise up, *said I,* and get you over the river ᶜZered: and we went over the river Zered.

14 The ¹space also wherein we came from Kadesh Barnea, until we were come over the river Zered, *was*

CHAPTER 2
ª Gen. 36:3
ᵇ Gen. 36:29
ᶜ Num. 21:12
ᵈ Num. 21:21,22

eight and thirty years, until all the generation of the men of war were wasted out from among the host, as the Lord sware unto them.

15 For indeed the ¹hand of the Lord was against them, to destroy them from among the host, till they were consumed.

16 ¶ So when all the men of war were consumed and dead from among the people:

17 Then the Lord spake unto me, saying,

18 Thou shalt go through Ar the coast of Moab this day:

19 And thou shalt come near over against the children of Ammon: *but* shalt not lay siege unto them, nor move war against them: for I will not give thee of the land of the children of Ammon *any* possession: for I have given it unto the children of Lot for a possession.

20 That also was taken for a land ¹of giants: *for* giants dwelt therein afore time, whom the Ammonites called Zamzummims:

21 A people *that was* great, and many, and tall, as the Anakims: but the Lord destroyed them before them, and they succeeded them in their inheritance, and dwelt in their stead:

22 As he did to the children of Esau which dwell in Seir, when he destroyed the Horites before them, and they possessed them, and dwelt in their stead unto this day.

23 And the Avim which dwelt in Hazarim *even* unto ¹Azzah, the Caphtorims which came out of Caphtor destroyed them, and dwelt in their stead.

24 ¶ Rise up *therefore, said the Lord*: take your journey, and pass over the river Arnon: behold, I have given into thy hand Sihon, the ¹Amorite, King of Heshbon, and his land: begin to possess it, and provoke him to battle.

25 This day will I ¹begin to send thy fear and thy dread, upon all people under the whole heaven, which shall hear thy fame, and shall tremble and quake before thee.

26 Then I sent messengers out of the wilderness of Kedemoth unto Sihon King of Heshbon, with words of peace, saying,

27 ¶ ᵈLet me pass through thy land: I will go by the highway: I will neither turn unto the right hand

---

2:1 ¹ They obeyed, after that God had chastised them.
  ² Eight and thirty years, as verse 14.
2:4 ¹ This was the second time: for before they had caused the Israelites to return, Num. 20:21.
2:7 ¹ And given thee means, wherewith thou mayest make recompense: also God will direct thee by his providence, as he hath done.
2:8 ¹ Or, wilderness.
2:9 ¹ Or, besiege.
  ² Which were the Moabites and Ammonites.
2:10 ¹ Signifying that as these giants were driven out for their sins: so the wicked when their sins are ripe, cannot avoid God's plagues.

2:14 ¹ He showeth hereby, that as God is true in his promise, so his threatenings are not in vain.
2:15 ¹ His plague and punishment to destroy all that were twenty years old and above.
2:20 ¹ Who called themselves Rephaims: that is, preservers, or physicians to heal and reform vices: but were indeed Zamzummims, that is, wicked and abominable.
2:23 ¹ Or, Gaza.
2:24 ¹ According to his promise made to Abraham, Gen. 15:21.
2:25 ¹ This declareth that the hearts of men are in God's hands either to be made faint, or bold.

nor to the left.

28 Thou shalt sell me meat for money, for to eat, and shalt give me water for money for to drink: only I will go through on my foot,

29 (As the [1]children of Esau which dwell in Seir, and the Moabites which dwell in Ar, did unto me) until I be come over Jordan, into the land which the Lord our God giveth us.

30 But Sihon the King of Heshbon would not let us pass by him: for the Lord thy God had [1]hardened his spirit, and made his heart obstinate, because he would deliver him into thine hand, as *appeareth* this day.

31 And the Lord said unto me, Behold, I have begun to give Sihon and his land before thee: begin to possess and inherit his land.

32 *Then came out Sihon to meet us, himself with all his people to fight at Jahaz.

33 But the Lord our God delivered him [1]into our power, and we smote him, and his sons, and all his people.

34 And we took all his cities the same time, and destroyed every city, men, and [1]women, and children: we let nothing remain.

35 Only the cattle we took to ourselves, and the spoil of the cities which we took.

36 From Aroer, which is by the bank of the river of Arnon, and *from* the city that is upon the river, even unto Gilead: there was not one city that escaped us: *for* the Lord our God delivered up all [1]before us.

37 Only unto the land of the children of Ammon thou camest not, *nor* unto any place of the [1]river Jabbok, nor unto the cities in the mountains, nor unto whatsoever the Lord our God forbade us.

3 3 *Og King of Bashan is slain.* 11 *The bigness of his bed.* 18 *The Reubenites and Gadites are commanded to go over Jordan armed before their brethren.* 21 *Joshua is made captain.* 27 *Moses is permitted to see the land, but not to enter, albeit he desired it.*

1 Then we turned, and went up by the way of Bashan: *and Og King of Bashan [1]came out against us, he and all his people to fight at Edrei.

2 And the Lord said unto me, Fear him not, for I will deliver him, and all his people, and his land into thine hand, and thou shalt do unto him as thou

e Num. 21:23

CHAPTER 3
d Num. 21:35
Deut. 29:7
b Num. 21:24
c Num. 21:33
d Num. 32:33
e Num. 32:41

diddest unto [b]Sihon King of the Amorites, which dwelt at Heshbon.

3 So the Lord our God delivered also unto our hand, [c]Og the King of Bashan, and all his people: and we smote him, until none was left him *alive*.

4 And we took all his cities the same time, neither was there a city which we took not from them, *even* three score cities, *and* all the country of Argob, *even* the kingdom of Og in Bashan.

5 All these cities *were* fenced with high walls, gates and bars, beside [1]unwalled towns a great many.

6 And we overthrew them, as we did unto Sihon King of Heshbon, destroying every city, *with* men, [1]women, and children.

7 But all the cattle and the spoil of the cities we took for ourselves.

8 Thus we took at that time out of the hand of two Kings of the Amorites, the land that was on this side Jordan from the river of Arnon unto mount Hermon:

9 (Which Hermon the Sidonians call Sirion, but the Amorites call it Senir)

10 All the cities of the plain, and all Gilead, and all Bashan unto Salcah, and Edrei, cities of the kingdom of Og in Bashan.

11 For only Og King of Bashan remained of the remnant of the Giants, [1]whose bed *was* a bed of iron: is it not at Rabbath among the children of Ammon? the length thereof *is* nine cubits, and four cubits the breadth of it, after the cubit of a man.

12 And this land *which* we possessed at that time, from Aroer, which is by the river Arnon, and half mount Gilead, [d]and the cities thereof, gave I unto the Reubenites and Gadites.

13 And the rest of Gilead, and all Bashan, the kingdom of Og, gave I unto the half tribe of Manasseh: *even* all the country of Argob with all Bashan, which is called, The land of giants.

14 Jair the son of Manasseh took all the country of Argob, unto the coasts of Geshuri, and of Maachathi: and called them after his own name, Bashan, [e]Havoth Jair unto [1]this day.

15 And I gave *part* of Gilead unto Machir.

16 And unto the Reubenites and Gadites I gave *the rest* of Gilead, and unto the river of Arnon, half the river and the borders, even unto the river [1]Jabbok, *which is* the border of the children of Ammon:

2:29 [1] Because neither entreaty nor examples or others could move him, he could not complain of his just destruction.
2:30 [1] God in his election and reprobation doth not only appoint the ends, but the means tending to the same.
2:33 [1] Hebrew, *before us.*
2:34 [1] God had cursed Canaan, and therefore he would not that any of the wicked race should be preserved.
2:36 [1] Or, into our hand.
2:37 [1] Or, ford.

3:1 [1] Therefore beside the commandment of the Lord, they had just occasion of his part to fight against him.
3:5 [1] As villages and small towns.
3:6 [1] Because this was God's appointment, therefore it may not be judged cruel.
3:11 [1] The more terrible that this giant was, the greater occasion had they to glorify God for the victory.
3:14 [1] Meaning, when he wrote this history.
3:16 [1] Which separateth the Ammonites from the Amorites.

17 The plain also and Jordan, and the borders from Chinnereth even unto the sea of the plain, *to wit,* the salt Sea [1]under the springs of Pisgah Eastward.

18 ¶ And I commanded [1]you the same time, saying, The Lord your God hath given you this land to possess it: ye shall go over armed before your brethren the children of Israel, all men of war.

19 Your wives only, and your children, and your cattle (for I know that ye have much cattle) shall abide in your cities, which I have given you,

20 Until the Lord have given rest unto your brethren as unto you, and that they also possess the land, which the Lord your God hath given them beyond Jordan: then shall ye *f*return every man unto his possession, which I have given you.

21 ¶ *g*And I charged Joshua the same time, saying, Thine eyes have seen all that the [1]Lord your God hath done unto these two Kings: *h*so shall the Lord do unto all the kingdoms whither thou goest.

22 Ye shall not fear them: for the Lord your God, he shall fight for you.

23 And I besought the Lord the same time, saying,

24 O Lord God, thou hast begun to show thy servant thy greatness and thy mighty hand: for where is there a God in heaven or in earth, that can [1]do like thy works, and like thy [2]power?

25 I pray thee let me go over and see the good land that is beyond Jordan, that goodly [1]mountain, and Lebanon.

26 But the Lord was angry with me for your sakes, and would not hear me: and the Lord said unto me, Let it suffice thee, speak no more unto me of this matter.

27 Get thee up into the top of Pisgah, and [1]lift up thine eyes Westward, and Northward, and Southward, and Eastward, and behold it with thine eyes, for thou shalt not go over this Jordan:

28 But charge Joshua, and encourage him, and bolden him: for he shall go before this people, and he shall divide for inheritance unto them, the land which thou shalt see.

29 So we abode in the valley over against Beth Peor.

f Josh. 22:4
g Num. 27:18,19,23
h Josh. 15
Josh. 10:8,25

CHAPTER 4
a Deut. 12:32

1 Now therefore hearken, O Israel, unto the ordinances and to the laws which I teach you to [1]do, that ye may live and go in, and possess the land, which the Lord God of your fathers giveth you.

2 *a*Ye shall [1]put nothing unto the word which I command you, neither shall ye [2]take ought there from, that ye may keep the commandments of the Lord your God which I command you.

3 Your [1]eyes have seen what the Lord did because of Baal Peor, for all the men that followed Baal Peor, the Lord thy God hath destroyed every one from among you.

4 But ye that did [1]cleave unto the Lord your God, are alive every one of you this day.

5 Behold, I have taught you ordinances, and laws, as the Lord my God commanded me, that ye should do even so within the land whither ye go to possess it.

6 Keep them therefore, and do them: for that is your [1]wisdom, and your understanding in the sight of the people, which shall hear all these ordinances, and shall say, [2]Only this people *is* wise, and of understanding, *and* a great nation.

7 For what nation *is so* great, unto whom the gods come so near unto them, as the Lord our God *is*, [1]*near unto us*, in all that we call unto him for?

8 And what nation *is so* great, that hath ordinances and laws so righteous, as all this Law, which I set before you this day?

9 But take heed to thyself, and [1]keep thy soul diligently, that thou forget not the things which thine eyes have seen, and that they depart not out of thine heart, all the days of thy life: but teach them thy sons, and thy sons' sons:

10 *Forget not* the day that thou stoodest before the Lord thy God in Horeb, when the Lord said unto me, Gather me the people together, and I will cause

---

3:17 [1] Or, at Asdoth-Pisgah.

3:18 [1] That is, the Reubenites, Gadites, and half Manasseh, as Num. 32:28.

3:21 [1] So that the victories came not by your own wisdom, strength or multitude.

3:24 [1] He speaketh according to the common and corrupt speech of them which attribute that power unto idols that only appertaineth unto God.
[2] Or, wonders.

3:25 [1] He meaneth Zion, where the Temple should be built, and God honored.

3:27 [1] As before he saw by the spirits of prophecy the good mountain which was Zion: so here his eyes were lifted up above the order of nature to behold all the plentiful land of Canaan.

4:1 [1] For this doctrine standeth not in bare knowledge, but in practice of life.

4:2 [1] Think not to be more wise than I am.
[2] God will not be served by halves, but will have full obedience.

4:3 [1] God's judgments executed upon other idolaters ought to serve for our instruction, read Num. 25:3,4.

4:4 [1] And were not idolaters.

4:6 [1] Because all men naturally desire wisdom, he showeth how to attain unto it.
[2] Or, surely.

4:7 [1] Helping us, and delivering us out of all dangers, as 2 Sam. 7:23.

4:9 [1] He addeth all these words, to show that we can never be careful enough to keep the law of God and to teach it to our posterity.

them to hear my words, that they may learn to fear me all the days that they shall live upon the earth, and that they may teach their children:

11 Then came you near and [b]stood under the mountain, and the mountain [1]burnt with fire unto the midst of heaven, *and there was* darkness, clouds and mist.

12 And the Lord spake unto you out of the midst of the fire, *and* ye heard the voice of the words, but saw no similitude, save a voice.

13 Then he declared unto you his covenant which he commanded you to [1]do, *even* the ten [2]commandments, and wrote them upon two Tables of stone.

14 ¶ And the Lord commanded me that same time, that I should teach you ordinances and laws, which ye should observe in the land, whither ye go, to possess it.

15 Take therefore good heed unto your [1]selves: for ye saw no [2]image in the day that the Lord spake unto you in Horeb out of the midst of the fire:

16 That ye corrupt not yourselves, and make you a graven image, *or* representation of any figure: *whether it be* the likeness of male or female,

17 The likeness of any beast that is on earth, *or* the likeness of any feathered fowl that flieth in the air:

18 *Or* the likeness of anything that creepeth on the earth, *or* the likeness of any fish that is in the waters beneath the earth,

19 And lest thou lift up thine eyes unto heaven, and when thou seest the sun and the moon and the stars with all the host of heaven, shouldest be driven to worship them and serve them, which the Lord thy God hath [1]distributed to all people under the whole heaven.

20 But the Lord hath taken you and brought you out of the [1]iron furnace, out of Egypt to be unto him a people *and* inheritance, as *appeareth* this day.

21 And the Lord was angry with me for your words, and sware that I should not go over Jordan, and that I should not go in unto that good land, which the Lord thy God giveth thee for an inheritance.

22 For I must die in this land, and shall not go over Jordan: but [1]ye shall go over, and possess that

[b] Exod. 19:18

good land.

23 Take heed unto yourselves, lest ye forget the covenant of the Lord your God which he made with you, and *lest* ye make you any graven image, *or* likeness of anything, as the Lord thy God hath charged thee.

24 For the Lord thy God is a [1]consuming fire, *and* a jealous God.

25 ¶ When thou shalt beget children and children's children, and shalt have remained long in the land, if ye [1]corrupt yourselves, and make any graven image, *or* likeness of anything, and work evil in the sight of the Lord thy God, to provoke him to anger,

26 I [1]call heaven and earth to record against you this day, that ye shall shortly perish from the land, whereunto ye go over Jordan to possess it: ye shall not prolong your days therein, but shall utterly be destroyed.

27 And the Lord shall [1]scatter you among the people, and ye shall be left few in number among the nations, whither the Lord shall bring you:

28 And there ye shall serve gods: *even* the work of man's hand, wood, and stone, which neither see, nor hear, nor eat, nor smell.

29 But if from thence thou shalt seek the Lord thy God, thou shalt find him, if thou seek him with all thine [1]heart, and with all thy soul.

30 When thou art in tribulation, and all these things are come upon thee, [1]at the length, if thou return to the Lord thy God, and be obedient unto his voice,

31 (For the Lord thy God is a merciful God) he will not forsake thee, neither destroy thee, nor forget the covenant of thy fathers, which he [1]sware unto them.

32 For inquire now of the days that are past, which were before thee, since the day that God created man upon the earth, and [1]ask from the one end of heaven unto the other, if there came to pass such a great thing as this, or whether any such like thing hath been heard.

33 Did ever people hear the voice of God speaking out of the midst of a fire, as thou hast heard, and lived?

4:11 [1] The Law was given with fearful miracles, to declare both that God was the author thereof, and also that no flesh was able to abide the rigor of the same.

4:13 [1] God joineth this condition to his covenant.

[2] Or, words.

4:15 [1] Hebrew, *souls.*

[2] Signifying, that destruction is prepared for all them that make any image to represent God.

4:19 [1] He hath appointed them for to serve man.

4:20 [1] He hath delivered you out of most miserable slavery and freely chosen you for his.

4:22 [1] Moses' good affection appeareth in that he being deprived of such an excellent treasure, doth not envy them that must enjoy it.

4:24 [1] To those that come not unto him with love and reverence, but rebel against him, Heb. 12:29.

4:25 [1] Meaning hereby all superstition and corruption of the true service of God.

4:26 [1] Though men would absolve you, yet the insensible creatures shall be witnesses of your disobedience.

4:27 [1] So that his curse shall make his former blessings of none effect.

4:29 [1] Not with outward show or ceremony, but with a true confession of thy faults.

4:30 [1] Hebrew, *in the latter days.*

4:31 [1] To certify them the more of the assurance of their salvation.

4:32 [1] Man's negligence is partly cause, that he knoweth not God.

34 Or hath God assayed to go and take him a nation from among nations, by [1]tentations, by signs, and by wonders, and by war, and by a mighty hand, and by a stretched out arm, and by great fear, according unto all that the Lord your God did unto you in Egypt before your eyes?

35 Unto thee it was showed, that thou mightest [1]know that the Lord he is God, *and* that there is none but he alone.

36 Out of heaven he made thee hear his voice to instruct thee, and upon earth he showed thee his great fire, and thou heardest his voice out of the midst of the fire.

37 And because [1]he loved thy fathers, therefore he chose their seed after them, and hath brought thee out of Egypt in his sight by his mighty power,

38 To thrust out nations greater and mightier than thou, before thee, to bring thee in, *and* to give thee their land for inheritance: as *appeareth* this day.

39 Understand therefore this day, and consider in thine heart, that the Lord he is God in heaven above, and upon the earth beneath: there *is* none other.

40 Thou shalt keep therefore his ordinances, and his commandments which I command thee this day, that it may [1]go well with thee, and with thy children after thee, and that thou mayest prolong thy days upon the earth, which the Lord thy God giveth thee forever.

41 ¶ Then Moses separated three cities on this side of Jordan toward the sun rising:

42 That the slayer should flee thither, which had killed his neighbor at unawares, and hated him not in time past, might flee, I say, unto one of those cities, and live:

43 *That is,* [c]Bezer in the wilderness, in the plain country of the Reubenites: and Ramoth in Gilead among the Gadites: and Golan in Bashan among them of Manasseh.

44 ¶ So this is the law which Moses set before the children of Israel.

45 These are the [1]witnesses, and the ordinances, and the laws which Moses declared to the children of Israel after they came out of Egypt.

46 On this side Jordan, in the valley over against Beth Peor, in the land of Sihon King of the Amorites, which dwelt at Heshbon, whom Moses and the children of Israel [d]smote, after they were come out of Egypt:

47 And they possessed his land, and the land of [e]Og King of Bashan, two Kings of the Amorites, which were on this side Jordan toward the sun rising:

48 From Aroer, which is by the bank of the river Arnon, even unto mount Sion, which is Hermon,

49 And all the plain from Jordan Eastward, even unto [1]the Sea of the plain, under the [f]springs of Pisgah.

5

5 Moses is the mean between God and the people. 6 The Law is repeated. 23 The people are afraid at God's voice. 29 The Lord wisheth that the people would fear him. 32 They must neither decline to the right hand nor left.

1 Then Moses called all Israel, and said unto them, Hear, O Israel, the ordinances and the laws which [1]I propose to you this day, that ye may learn them, and take heed to observe them.

2 [a]The Lord our God made a covenant with us in Horeb.

3 The Lord [1]made not this covenant with our fathers *only*, but with us, *even* with us all here alive this day.

4 The Lord talked with you [1]face to face in the Mount, out of the midst of the fire.

5 (At that time I stood between the Lord and you, to declare unto you the word of the Lord: for ye were afraid at the sight of the fire, and went not up into the mount) and he said,

6 ¶ [b]I am the Lord thy God, which have brought thee out of the land of Egypt, from the house of [1]bondage.

7 Thou shalt have none [1]other gods before my face.

8 Thou shalt make thee no graven image *or* any likeness *of that* that is in heaven above, *or* which is in the earth beneath, or that is in the waters under the earth.

9 Thou shalt neither bow thyself unto them, nor serve them: for [c]I the Lord thy God am a [1]jealous God, visiting the iniquity of the fathers upon the children, even unto the third and fourth *generation* of them that hate me:

10 And showing mercy unto thousands of them that [1]love me, and keep my commandments.

11 Thou shalt not take the Name of the Lord thy God in vain: for the Lord will not hold him guiltless

c Josh. 20:8
d Num. 21:24
Deut. 1:4
e Num. 21:33
Deut. 3:3
f Deut. 3:17

CHAPTER 5
a Exod. 19:5,6
b Exod. 20:2
Lev. 26:1
Ps. 97:7,9
c Exod. 34:7
Jer. 32:18

4:34 [1] By so manifest proofs that none could doubt thereof.
4:35 [1] He showeth the cause why God wrought these miracles.
4:37 [1] Freely, and not of their deserts.
4:40 [1] God promiseth reward not for our merits, but to encourage us, and to assure us that our labor shall not be lost.
4:45 [1] The articles and points of the covenant.
4:49 [1] That is, the salt sea.
5:1 [1] Hebrew, *I speak in your ears.*

5:3 [1] Some read, God made not this covenant, that is, in such ample forth and with such signs and wonders.
5:4 [1] So plainly that ye need not to doubt thereof.
5:6 [1] Or, servant.
5:7 [1] God bindeth us to serve him only, without superstition and idolatry.
5:9 [1] That is, of his honor, not permitting it to be given to others.
5:10 [1] The first degree to keep the commandments, is to love God.

2

that taketh his Name in vain.

12 Keep the Sabbath day to sanctify it, as the Lord thy God hath commanded thee.

13 Six days [1]thou shalt labor, and shalt do all thy work:

14 But the seventh day *is* the Sabbath of the Lord thy God: thou shalt not do any work *therein*, thou, nor thy son, nor thy daughter, nor thy manservant, nor thy maid, nor thine ox, nor thine ass, neither any of thy cattle, nor the stranger that is within thy gates: that thy manservant and thy maid may rest as well as thou.

15 For, remember that thou wast a servant in the land of Egypt, and *that* the Lord thy God brought thee out thence by a mighty hand, and a stretched out arm: therefore the Lord thy God commanded thee to observe the Sabbath day.

16 ¶ [1]Honor thy father and thy mother, as the Lord thy God hath commanded thee, that thy days may be prolonged, and that it may go well with thee upon the land, which the Lord thy God giveth thee.

17 [d]Thou shalt not kill.

18 [e]Neither shalt thou commit adultery.

19 [f]Neither shalt thou steal.

20 Neither shalt thou bear false witness against thy neighbor.

21 [g]Neither shalt [1]thou covet thy neighbor's wife, neither shalt thou desire thy neighbor's house, his field, nor his manservant, nor his maid, his ox, nor his ass, nor ought that thy neighbor hath.

22 ¶ These words the Lord spake unto all your multitude in the mount of the midst of the fire, the cloud and the darkness, with a great voice, and [1]added no more *thereto*: and wrote them upon two tables of stone, and delivered them unto me.

23 And when ye heard the voice out of the midst of the darkness, (for the mountain did burn with fire) then ye came to me, all the chief of your tribes, and your Elders:

24 And ye said, Behold, the Lord our God hath showed us his glory and his greatness, and [h]we have heard his voice out of the midst of the fire: we have seen this day that God doth talk with man, and he [i]liveth.

25 Now therefore, why should we die? for this great fire will consume us: if we hear the voice of the Lord our God anymore, we shall die.

26 For what [1]flesh *was* there ever that heard the voice of the living God speaking out of the midst of the fire as *we have*, and lived?

27 Go thou near and hear all that the Lord our God saith: and declare thou unto us all that the Lord our God saith unto thee: [j]and we will hear it, and do it.

28 Then the Lord heard the voice of your words, when ye spake unto me: and the Lord said unto me, I have heard the voice of the words of this people, which they have spoken unto thee: they have well said, all that they have spoken.

29 Oh [1]that there were such an heart in them to fear me, and to keep all my commandments always: that it might go well with them, and with their children forever.

30 Go, say unto them, Return you into your tents.

31 But stand thou here with me, and I will tell thee all the commandments, and the ordinances, and the laws, which thou shalt teach them: that they may do them in the land which I give them to possess it.

32 Take heed therefore, that ye do as the Lord your God hath commanded you: [1]turn not aside to the right hand nor to the left.

33 *But* walk in all the ways which the Lord your God hath commanded you, that ye may [1]live, and that it may go well with you: and that ye may prolong *your* days in the land which ye shall possess.

6 1 *An exhortation to fear God, and keep his command-ments,* 5 *Which is, to love him with all thine heart.* 7 *The same must be taught to the posterity.* 16 *Not to tempt God.* 25 *Righteousness is contained in the Law.*

1 These now are the commandments, ordinances, and [1]laws, which the Lord your God commanded *me* to teach *you*, that ye might do them in the land whither ye go to possess it:

2 That thou mightest [1]fear the Lord thy God, and keep all his ordinances, and his commandments which I command thee, thou, and thy son, and thy son's son all the days of thy life, even that thy days may be prolonged:

3 Hear therefore, O Israel, and take heed to do it, that it may go well with thee, and that ye may increase mightily [1]in the land that floweth with

Marginal references:
[d] Matt. 5:21
[e] Luke 18:20
[f] Rom. 13:9
[g] Rom. 7:7
[h] Exod. 19:19
[i] Deut. 4:33
[j] Exod. 20:19

5:13 [1] Meaning, since God permitteth six days to our labors, that we ought willingly to dedicate the seventh to serve him wholly.

5:16 [1] Not for a show, but with true obedience, and due reverence.

5:21 [1] He speaketh not only of that resolute will, but that there be no motion or affection.

5:22 [1] Teaching us by his example to be content with his word, and add nothing thereto.

5:26 [1] Or, man.

5:29 [1] He requireth of us nothing but obedience, showing also that of ourselves we are unwilling thereunto.

5:32 [1] Ye shall neither add nor diminish, Deut. 4:2.

5:33 [1] As by obedience, God giveth us all felicity: so of disobeying God proceed all our miseries.

6:1 [1] Or, judgments.

6:2 [1] A reverent face and love of God is the first beginning to keep God's commandments.

6:3 [1] Which hath abundance of all things appertaining to man's life.

milk and honey, as the Lord God of thy fathers hath promised thee.

4   Hear, O Israel, The Lord our God is Lord only,

5   And *thou shalt love the Lord thy God with all thine heart, and with all thy soul, and with all thy might.

6   *And these words which I command thee this day, shall be in thine heart.

7   And thou shalt ¹rehearse them continually unto thy children, and shalt talk of them when thou tarriest in thine house, and as thou walkest by the way, and when thou liest down, and when thou risest up:

8   And thou shalt bind them for a sign upon thine hand, and they shall be ¹as frontlets between thine eyes.

9   Also thou shalt write them upon the ¹posts of thine house, and upon thy gates.

10   And when the Lord thy God hath brought thee into the land, which he sware unto thy fathers Abraham, Isaac, and Jacob, to give to thee, with great and goodly cities which thou buildedst not,

11   And houses full of all manner of goods which thou filledst not, and wells dug which thou dug not, vineyards and olive trees which thou plantedst not, and when thou hast eaten and art full,

12   ¹Beware lest thou forget the Lord, which brought thee out of the land of Egypt, from the house of bondage:

13   Thou shalt fear the Lord thy God, and serve him, and shalt ¹swear by his Name.

14   Ye shall not walk after other gods, *after any* of the gods of the people which are round about you.

15   (For the Lord thy God is a jealous God among you:) lest the wrath of the Lord thy God be kindled against thee, and destroy thee from the face of the earth.

16   ¶ Ye shall not ¹tempt the Lord your God, as ye did tempt him in Massah:

17   *But* ye shall keep diligently the commandments of the Lord your God, and his testimonies and his ordinances, which he hath commanded thee.

18   And thou shalt do that which is right and good in the ¹sight of the Lord: that thou mayest prosper, and that thou mayest go in, and possess that good land which the Lord sware unto thy fathers,

CHAPTER 6
ᵃ Matt. 22:37
Mark 12:29,34
Luke 13:27
ᵇ Deut. 11:18

CHAPTER 7
ᵃ Deut. 31:8
ᵇ Exod. 23:32
Exod. 34:12

19   To cast out all thine enemies before thee, as the Lord hath said.

20   When ¹thy son shall ask thee in time to come, saying, What mean these testimonies, and ordinances, and Laws, which the Lord our God hath commanded you?

21   Then shalt thou say unto thy son, We were Pharaoh's bondmen in Egypt: but the Lord brought us out of Egypt with a mighty hand.

22   And the Lord showed signs and wonders great and evil upon Egypt, upon Pharaoh, and upon all his household before our eyes,

23   And ¹brought us out from thence, to bring us in, and to give us the land which he sware unto our fathers.

24   Therefore the Lord hath commanded us, to do all these ordinances, *and* to fear the Lord our God, that it may go ever well with us, *and* that he may preserve us alive at this present.

25   Moreover, this shall be our ¹righteousness before the Lord our God, if we take heed to keep all these commandments, as he hath commanded us.

7   *1 The Israelites may make no covenant with the Gentiles. 5 They must destroy the idols. 8 The election dependeth on the free love of God. 19 The experience of the power of God ought to confirm us. 25 To avoid all occasion of idolatry.*

1   When the Lord thy God shall bring thee into the land whither thou goest to possess it, ᵃand shall root out many nations before thee: the Hittites, and the Girgashites, and the Amorites, and the Canaanites, and the Perizzites, and the Hivites, and the Jebusites, seven nations greater and mightier than thou,

2   And the Lord thy God shall give them ¹before thee, then thou shalt smite them: thou shalt utterly destroy them: thou shalt make no ᵇcovenant with them, nor have compassion on them,

3   Neither shalt thou make marriages with them, neither give thy daughter unto his son, nor take his daughter unto thy son.

4   For ¹they will cause thy son to turn away from me, and to serve other gods: then will the wrath of the Lord wax hot against you, and destroy thee suddenly.

5   But thus ye shall deal with them, ¹Ye shall

6:7 ¹ Some read, thou shalt whet them upon thy children: to wit, that they may print them more deeply in memory.
6:8 ¹ Or, signs of remembrance.
6:9 ¹ That when thou entrest in, thou mayest remember them.
6:12 ¹ Let not wealth and ease cause thee forget God's mercies, whereby thou wast delivered out of misery.
6:13 ¹ We must fear God, serve him only, and confess his Name, which is done by swearing lawfully.
6:16 ¹ By doubting of his power, refusing lawful means, and abusing his graces.
6:18 ¹ Here he condemneth all man's good intentions.

6:20 ¹ God requireth not only that we serve him all our life, but also that we take pains that our posterity may set forth his glory.
6:23 ¹ Nothing ought to move us more to true obedience than the great benefits which we have received of God.
6:25 ¹ But because none could fully obey the law, we must have our recourse to Christ to be justified by faith.
7:2 ¹ Into thy power.
7:4 ¹ Or, any of them.
7:5 ¹ God would have his service pure without all idolatrous ceremonies and superstitions, Deut. 22:3.

overthrow their altars, and break down their pillars, and ye shall cut down their groves, and burn their graven images with fire.

6 cFor thou art an holy people unto the Lord thy God, dthe Lord thy God hath chosen thee, to be a precious people unto himself, above all people that are upon the earth.

7 The Lord did not set his love upon you, nor chose you, because ye were more in number than any people: for ye were the fewest of all people:

8 But because the Lord 1loved you, and because he would keep the oath which he had sworn unto your fathers, the Lord hath brought you out by a mighty hand, and delivered you out of the house of bondage from the hand of Pharaoh King of Egypt.

9 That thou mayest know, 1that the Lord thy God, he is God, the faithful God, which keepeth covenant and mercy unto them that love him and keep his commandments, *even* to a thousand generations,

10 And rewardeth 1them to their face that hate him, to bring them to destruction: he will not defer to reward him that hateth him, to his face.

11 Keep thou therefore the commandments, and the ordinances, and the laws, which I command thee this day to do them.

12 ¶ For if ye hearken unto these laws, and observe and do them, then the Lord thy God shall keep with thee the covenant, and the 1mercy which he sware unto thy fathers.

13 And he will love thee, and bless thee, and multiply thee: he will also bless the fruit of thy womb, and the fruit of thy land, thy corn and thy wine, and thine oil, *and* the increase of thy kine, and the flocks of thy sheep in the land, which he sware unto thy fathers to give thee.

14 Thou shalt be blessed above all people: ethere shall be neither male nor female barren among you, nor among your cattle.

15 Moreover, the Lord will take away from thee all infirmities, and will put none of the evil diseases of fEgypt (which thou knowest) upon thee, but will send them upon all that hate thee.

16 Thou shalt therefore consume all people which the Lord thy God shall give thee: 1thine eye shall not spare them, neither shalt thou serve their gods, for that shall be thy gdestruction.

17 If thou say in thine heart, These nations are

Cross references (center column):
c Deut. 14:2
Deut. 26:18,19
d Exod. 19:5
2 Pet. 2:9
e Exod. 23:26
f Exod. 9:14
Exod. 15:26
g Exod. 23:33
h Exod. 23:28
i Deut. 12:3
Exod. 23:24
j Josh. 7:1,21
k Deut. 13:17

more than I, how can I cast them out?

18 Thou shalt not fear them, *but* remember what the Lord thy God did unto Pharaoh, and unto all Egypt:

19 The great 1tentations which thine eyes saw, and the signs and wonders, and the mighty hand and stretched out arm, whereby the Lord thy God brought thee out: so shall the Lord thy God do unto all the people, whose face thou fearest.

20 hMoreover, the Lord thy God will send 1hornets among them until they that are left, and hide themselves from thee, be destroyed.

21 Thou shalt not fear them: for the Lord thy God *is* among you, a God mighty and dreadful.

22 And the Lord thy God will root out these nations before thee by little and little: thou mayest not consume them at once, lest the 1beasts of the field increase upon thee.

23 But the Lord thy God shall give them before thee, and shall destroy them with a mighty destruction, until they be brought to naught.

24 And he shall deliver their Kings into thine hand, and thou shalt destroy their name from under heaven: there shall no man be able to stand before thee, until thou hast destroyed them.

25 The graven images of their gods shall ye iburn with fire, *and* jcovet not the silver and gold, *that is* on them, nor take it unto thee, lest thou 1be snared therewith: for it is an abomination *before* the Lord thy God.

26 Bring not therefore abomination into thine house, lest thou be accursed like it, *but* utterly abhor it, and count it most abominable: for it is kaccursed.

8

1 God humbleth the Israelites to try what they have in their heart. 5 God chastiseth them as his children. 14 The heart ought not to be proud of God's benefits. 19 The forgetfulness of God's benefits causeth destruction.

1 Ye shall keep all the commandments which I command thee this day, for 1to do them: that ye may live, and be multiplied, and go in, and possess the land which the Lord sware unto your fathers.

2 And thou shalt remember all the way which the Lord thy God led thee this forty years in the wilderness, for to humble thee, and to 1prove thee, to know what was in thine heart, whether thou

---

7:8 1 Freely, finding no cause in you more than in others so to do.

7:9 1 And so put difference between him and idols.

7:10 1 Meaning, manifestly, or in this life.

7:12 1 This covenant is grounded upon his free grace: therefore in recompensing their obedience, he hath respect to his mercy and not to their merits.

7:16 1 We ought not to be merciful, where God commandeth severity.

7:19 1 Or, plagues, or trials, Deut. 29:3; as Exod. 15:25 and Exod. 16:4.

7:20 1 There is not so small a creature, which I will not arm to fight on thy side against them.

7:22 1 So that it is your commodity that God accomplish not his promise so soon as you would wish.

7:25 1 And be enticed to idolatry.

8:1 1 Showing that it is not enough to hear the word, except we express it by example of life.

8:2 1 Which is declared in afflictions, either by patience, or by grudging against God's visitation.

wouldest keep his commandments or no.

3 Therefore he humbled thee, and made thee hungry, and fed thee with Manna, which thou knewest not, neither did thy fathers know it, that he might teach thee that man lived not by [1]bread only, but by every *word* that proceedeth out of the mouth of the Lord, doth a man live.

4 Thy raiment waxed not old upon thee, neither did thy foot [1]swell those forty years.

5 Know therefore in thine heart, that as a man nurtureth his son, so the Lord thy God [1]nurtureth thee.

6 Therefore shalt thou keep the commandments of the Lord thy God, that thou mayest walk in his ways, and fear him.

7 For the Lord thy God bringeth thee into a good land, a land in the which are rivers of water and fountains, and [1]depths that spring out of valleys and mountains:

8 A land of wheat and barley, and of vineyards, and fig trees, and pomegranates: a land of oil, olive and honey:

9 A land wherein thou shalt eat bread without scarcity, neither shalt thou lack anything therein: a land [1]whose stones *are* iron, and out of whose mountains thou shalt dig brass.

10 And when thou hast eaten and filled thyself, thou shalt [1]bless the Lord thy God for the good land, which he hath given thee.

11 Beware that thou forget not the Lord thy God, not keeping his commandments and his laws, and his ordinances, which I command thee this day:

12 Lest *when* thou hast eaten and filled thyself, and hast built goodly houses and dwelt *therein,*

13 And thy beasts, and the sheep are increased, and thy silver and gold is multiplied, and all that thou hast is increased;

14 Then thine heart [1]be lifted up and thou forget the Lord thy God, which brought thee out of the land of Egypt, from the house of bondage,

15 Who was thy guide in that great and terrible wilderness (*wherein were* fiery serpents, and scorpions and drought, where *was* no water, [a]who brought forth water for thee out of the rock of flint:

16 Who fed thee in the wilderness with [b]Manna, which thy fathers knew not) to humble thee, and to prove thee, that he might do thee good at the latter end.

CHAPTER 8
[a] Num. 20:11
[b] Exod. 16:15

17 *Beware* lest thou say in thine heart, My power, and the strength of mine own hand hath prepared me this abundance.

18 But remember the Lord thy God: for it is he which [1]giveth thee power to get substance to establish his covenant which he sware unto thy fathers, as *appeareth* this day.

19 And if thou forget the Lord thy God, and walk after other gods, and serve them, and worship them, I [1]testify unto you this day, that ye shall surely perish.

20 As the nations which the Lord destroyeth before you, so ye shall perish, because ye would not be obedient unto the voice of the Lord your God.

9 1 *God doth not them good for their own righteousness, but for his own sake.* 7 *Moses putteth them in remembrance of their sins.* 17 *The two Tables are broken.* 26 *Moses prayeth for the people.*

1 Hear, O Israel, Thou shalt pass over Jordan [1]this day, to go in *and* to possess nations greater and mightier than thyself, *and* cities great and walled up to heaven,

2 A people great and tall, *even* the children of the Anakims, whom thou knowest, and *of whom* thou hast [1]heard *say,* Who can stand before the children of Anak?

3 Understand therefore that this day the Lord thy God is he which [1]goeth over before thee *as* a consuming fire: he shall destroy them, and he shall bring them down before thy face: so thou shalt cast them out and destroy them suddenly, as the Lord hath said unto thee.

4 Speak not thou in thine heart (after that the Lord thy God hath cast them out before thee) saying, For my [1]righteousness the Lord hath brought me in, to possess this land: but for the wickedness of these nations, the Lord hath cast them out before thee.

5 For thou entrust not to inherit their land for thy righteousness, or for their upright heart, but for the wickedness of those nations, the Lord thy God doth cast them out before thee, and that he might perform the word which the Lord thy God sware unto thy fathers, Abraham, Isaac, and Jacob.

6 Understand therefore, that the Lord thy God giveth thee not this good land to possess it for thy

---

8:3 [1] Man liveth not by meat only, but by the power of God, which giveth it strength to nourish us.
8:4 [1] As they that go barefooted.
8:5 [1] So that his afflictions are signs of his fatherly love toward us.
8:7 [1] Or, meres.
8:9 [1] Where there are mines of metal.
8:10 [1] For to receive God's benefits, and not to be thankful, is to contemn God in them.
8:14 [1] By attributing God's benefits to thine own wisdom and labor,

or to good fortune.
8:18 [1] If things concerning this life, proceed only of God's mercy: much more spiritual gifts and life everlasting.
8:19 [1] Or, take to witness the heaven and the earth, as Deut. 4:26.
9:1 [1] Meaning, shortly.
9:2 [1] By the report of the spies, Num. 13:26.
9:3 [1] To guide thee and govern thee.
9:4 [1] Man of himself can deserve nothing but God's anger, and if God spare any it cometh of his great mercy.

righteousness: for thou art a ¹stiff-necked people.

7 ¶ Remember *and* forget not, how thou provokedst the Lord thy God to anger in the wilderness: ¹since the day that thou didst depart out of the land of Egypt, until ye came into this place, ye have rebelled against the Lord.

8 Also in Horeb ye provoked the Lord to anger, so that the Lord was wroth with you, *even* to destroy you.

9 When I was gone up into the mount, to receive the Tables of stone, the Tables, *I say*, of the Covenant, which the Lord made with you: and *ᵃ*I abode in the mount forty days and forty nights, *and* I neither ate bread nor yet drank water:

10 *ᵇ*Then the Lord delivered me two tables of stone, written with the ¹finger of God, and in them *was contained* according to all the words which the Lord had said unto you in the mount out of the midst of the fire, in the day of the assembly.

11 And when the forty days and forty nights were ended, the Lord gave me the two tables of stone, the tables, *I say*, of the covenant.

12 And the Lord said unto me, *ᶜ*Arise, get thee down quickly from hence: for thy people which thou hast brought out of Egypt, have ¹corrupt *their ways*: they are soon turned out of the way which I commanded them, they have made them a molten image.

13 Furthermore the Lord spake unto me, saying, I have seen this people, and behold, it is a stiff-necked people.

14 ¹Let me alone, that I may destroy them, and put out their name from under heaven, and I will make of thee a mighty nation and greater than they be.

15 So I returned, and came down from the mount (and the mount burnt with fire, and the two Tables of the Covenant *were* in my two hands.)

16 Then I looked, and behold, ye had sinned against the Lord your God: *for* ye had made you a molten calf, *and* had turned quickly out of the ¹way which the Lord had commanded you.

17 Therefore I took the two Tables, and cast them out of my two hands, and brake them before your eyes.

18 And I fell down before the Lord, forty days, and forty nights, as before: I neither ate bread nor drank water, because of all your sins which ye had committed, in doing wickedly in the sight of the Lord, in that ye provoked him unto wrath.

CHAPTER 9
ᵃ Exod. 24:18
Exod. 34:28
ᵇ Exod. 31:18
ᶜ Exod. 32:7
ᵈ Num. 11:1,3
ᵉ Exod. 17:7
ᶠ Num. 11:34
ᵍ Num. 14:16

CHAPTER 10
ᵃ Exod. 34:1

19 (For I was afraid of the wrath and indignation, wherewith the Lord was moved against you, *even* to destroy you) yet the Lord heard me at that time also.

20 Likewise the Lord was very angry with Aaron, *even* to ¹destroy him: but at that time I prayed also for Aaron.

21 And I took your sin, *I mean* the calf which ye had made, and burnt him with fire, and stamped him and ground him small, even unto very dust: and I cast the dust thereof into the river, that descended out of the ¹mount.

22 Also *ᵈ*in Taberah, and in *ᵉ*Massah, *ᶠ*and in Kibroth Hattaavah ye provoked the Lord to anger.

23 Likewise when the Lord sent you from Kadesh Barnea, saying, Go up, and possess the land which I have given you, then ye ¹rebelled against the commandment of the Lord your God, and believed him not, nor hearkened unto his voice.

24 Ye have been rebellious unto the Lord, since the day that I knew you.

25 Then I fell down before the Lord ¹forty days, and forty nights, as I fell down *before*, because the Lord had said that he would destroy you.

26 And I prayed unto the Lord, and said, O Lord God, destroy not thy people and thine inheritance, which thou hast redeemed through thy greatness, whom thou hast brought out of Egypt by a mighty hand.

27 ¹Remember thy servants Abraham, Isaac, and Jacob: look not to the stubbornness of this people, nor to their wickedness, nor to their sin,

28 Lest the country whence thou broughtest them, say, *ᵍ*Because the Lord was not able to bring them into the land which he promised them, or because he hated them, he carried them out to slay them in the wilderness.

29 Yet they are thy people, and thine inheritance, which thou broughtest out by thy mighty power, and by thy stretched out arm.

10

5 *The second Tables put in the Ark.* 8 *The tribe of Levi is dedicated to the service of the Tabernacle.* 12 *What the Lord requireth of his.* 16 *The circumcision of the heart.* 17 *God regardeth not the person.* 21 *The Lord is the praise of Israel.*

1 In the same time the Lord said unto me, *ᵃ*Hew

9:6 ¹ Like stubborn oxen which will not endure their master's yoke.
9:7 ¹ He proveth by the length of time, that their rebellion was most great and intolerable.
9:10 ¹ That is, miraculously, and not by the hand of men.
9:12 ¹ So soon as man declineth from the obedience of God, his ways are corrupt.
9:14 ¹ Signifying that the prayers of the faithful are a bar to stay God's anger that he consume not all.
9:16 ¹ That is, from the Law: wherein he declareth what is the cause

of our perdition.
9:20 ¹ Whereby he showeth what danger they are in, that have authority and resist not wickedness.
9:21 ¹ Horeb, or Sinai.
9:23 ¹ At the return of the spies.
9:25 ¹ Whereby is signified that God requireth earnest continuance in prayer.
9:27 ¹ The godly in their prayers ground on God's promise, and confess their sins.

thee two tables of stone like unto the first, and come up unto me into the mount, and make thee an Ark of wood,

2 And I will write upon the tables, the words that were upon the first Tables, which thou breakest, and thou shalt put them in the Ark.

3 And I made an Ark of ¹Shittim wood, and hewed two tables of stone like unto the first, and went up into the mountain, and the two Tables in mine hand.

4 Then he wrote upon the Tables according to the first writing, (the ten commandments, which the Lord spake unto you in the mount out of the midst of the fire, in the day of the ¹assembly) and the Lord gave them unto me.

5 And I departed and came down from the Mount, and put the Tables in the Ark which I had made: and there they be, as the Lord commanded me.

6 ¶ And the children of Israel took their journey from Beeroth of the children of Jaakan, to ¹Moserah, where Aaron died, and was buried, and Eleazar his son became Priest in his stead.

7 ¶ From thence they departed unto Gudgodah, and from Gudgodah to Jotbathah, a land of running waters.

8 ¶ The same time the Lord separated the tribe of Levi to bear the Ark of the Covenant of the Lord, *and* to stand before the Lord, to ¹minister unto him, and to bless in his Name unto this day.

9 Wherefore Levi hath no part nor inheritance with his brethren: *for* the Lord is his ¹inheritance, as the Lord thy God hath promised him.

10 And I tarried in the mount, as at the first time, forty days and forty nights, and the Lord heard me at that time also, *and* the Lord would not destroy thee.

11 But the Lord said unto me, Arise, go forth in the journey before the people, that they may go in and possess the land, which I sware unto their fathers to give unto them.

12 ¶ And now, Israel, what doth the Lord thy God ¹require of thee, but to fear the Lord thy God, to walk in all his ways, and to love him, and to serve the Lord thy God with all thine heart, and with all thy soul?

13 That thou keep the commandments of the Lord and his ordinances, which I command thee this day, for thy wealth?

14 Behold, heaven, and the heaven of heavens *is* the Lord's thy God, and the ᵇearth, with all that therein is.

ᵇ Ps. 24:1
ᶜ 2 Chron. 19:7
Rom. 2:11
ᵈ Deut. 6:13
Matt. 4:10
ᵉ Gen. 46:27
Exod. 1:5
ᶠ Gen. 15:5

15 ¹Notwithstanding, the Lord set his delight in thy fathers to love them, and did choose their seed after them, *even* you above all people, as *appeareth* this day.

16 ¹Circumcise therefore the foreskin of your heart, and harden your necks no more.

17 For the Lord your God is God of gods, and Lord of lords, a great God, mighty and terrible, which accepteth no ʿpersons, nor taketh reward:

18 Who doeth right unto the fatherless and widow, and loveth the stranger, giving him food and raiment.

19 Love ye therefore the stranger: for ye were strangers in the land of Egypt.

20 ᵈThou shalt fear the Lord thy God: thou shalt serve him, and thou shalt cleave unto him, and ¹shalt swear by his Name.

21 He is thy praise, and he is thy God, that hath done for thee these great and terrible things, which thine eyes have seen.

22 Thy fathers went down into Egypt ʿwith seventy persons, and now the Lord thy God hath made thee, as the ᶠstars of the heaven in multitude.

11 ¹ *An exhortation to love God, and keep his law.* 10 *The praises of Canaan.* 18 *To meditate continually the word of God.* 19 *To teach it unto the children.* 26 *Blessing and cursing.*

1 Therefore thou shalt love the Lord thy God and shalt keep that, which he commandeth to be kept: that is, his ordinances, and his laws and his commandments always.

2 And ¹consider this day (*for I speak not* to your children, which have neither known nor seen) the chastisements of the Lord your God, his greatness, his mighty hand, and his stretched out arm,

3 And his signs, and his acts, which he did in the midst of Egypt, unto Pharaoh the King of Egypt and unto all his land:

4 And what he did unto the host of the Egyptians, unto their horses, and to their chariots, when he caused the waters of the red Sea to overflow them, as they pursued after you, and the Lord destroyed them unto this day:

5 And ¹what he did unto you in the wilderness, until ye came unto this place:

6 And what he did unto Dathan and Abiram the sons of Eliab the son of Reuben, when the earth

---

10:3 ¹ Which wood is of long continuance.
10:4 ¹ When you were assembled to receive the Law.
10:6 ¹ This mountain was also called Hor, Num. 20:28.
10:8 ¹ That is, to offer sacrifice, and to declare the Law to the people.
10:9 ¹ So God turned the curse of Jacob, Gen. 49:7, unto blessing.
10:12 ¹ For all our sins and transgressions God requireth nothing but to turn to him and obey him.

10:15 ¹ Although he was Lord of heaven and earth, yet would he choose none but you.
10:16 ¹ Cut off all your evil affections, Jer 4:4.
10:20 ¹ Read Deut. 6:13.
11:2 ¹ Ye, which have seen God's graces with your eyes, ought rather to be moved, than your children, which have only heard of them.
11:5 ¹ As well concerning his benefits, as his corrections.

opened her mouth, and swallowed them with their households, and their tents, and all their substance that [1]they had in the midst of all Israel.

7 For your eyes have seen all the great acts of the Lord which he did.

8 Therefore shall ye keep [1]all the commandments, which I command you this day, that ye may be strong, and go in and possess the land whither ye go to possess it:

9 Also that ye may prolong *your* days in the land, which the Lord sware unto your fathers, to give unto them and to their seed, *even* a land that floweth with milk and honey.

10 ¶ For the land whither thou goest to possess it, is not as the land of Egypt, from whence ye came, where thou sowedst thy seed, and wateredst it with thy [1,2]feet as a garden of herbs:

11 But the land whither ye go to possess it, *is* a land of mountains and valleys, *and* drinketh water of the rain of heaven.

12 This land doth the Lord thy God care for: the eyes of the Lord thy God *are* always upon it, from the beginning of the year, even unto the end of the year.

13 ¶ If ye shall hearken therefore unto my commandments, which I command you this day, that ye love the Lord your God and serve him with all your heart, and with all your soul,

14 I also will give rain unto your land in due time, [1]the first rain and the latter, that thou mayest gather in thy wheat, and thy wine, and thine oil.

15 Also I will send grass in thy fields for thy cattle, that thou mayest eat, and have enough.

16 *But* beware lest your heart [1]deceive you, and lest ye turn aside, and serve other gods, and worship them.

17 And so the anger of the Lord be kindled against you, and he shut up the heaven, that there be no rain, and that your land yield not her fruit, and ye perish quickly from the good land, which the Lord giveth you.

18 ¶ Therefore shall ye lay up these my words in your heart and in your soul, and [a]bind them for a sign upon your hand, that they may be as a frontlet between your eyes,

19 And ye shall [b]teach them your children, speaking of them when thou sittest in thine house, and when thou walkest by the way, and when thou liest down, and when thou risest up.

20 And thou shalt write them upon the posts of thine house, and upon thy gates,

CHAPTER 11
[a] Deut. 6:6,8
[b] Deut. 4:10
   Deut. 6:7
[c] Josh. 1:3
[d] Deut. 28:2
   Deut. 30:1
[e] Deut. 28:15
[f] Deut. 27:13
   Josh. 8:33
[g] Deut. 5:32

21 That your days may be multiplied, and the days of your children, in the land which the Lord sware unto your fathers to give them, as long as [1]the heavens are above the earth.

22 ¶ For if ye keep diligently all these Commandments, which I command you to do: *that is,* to love the Lord your God, to walk in all his ways, and to cleave unto him,

23 Then will the Lord cast out all these nations before you, and ye shall possess great nations and mightier than you.

24 [c]All the places whereon the soles of [1]your feet shall tread, shall be yours: your coast shall be from the wilderness and from Lebanon, and from the River *even* the river Perath, unto the uttermost [2]Sea.

25 No man shall stand against you: *for* the Lord your God shall cast the fear and dread of you upon all the land that ye shall tread upon, as he hath said unto you.

26 ¶ Behold, I set before you this day a blessing and a curse:

27 [d]The blessing, if ye obey the commandments of the Lord your God, which I command you this day:

28 And the [e]curse, if ye will not obey the Commandments of the Lord your God, but turn out of the way, which I command you this day, to go after other gods which ye have not [1]known.

29 ¶ When the Lord thy God therefore hath brought thee into the land, whither thou goest to possess it, then thou shalt put the [f]blessing upon mount Gerizim, and the curse upon mount Ebal.

30 Are they not beyond Jordan on that part, [1]where the Sun goeth down in the land of the Canaanites, which dwell in the plain over against Gilgal, beside [2]the grove of Moreh?

31 For ye shall pass over Jordan, to go in to possess that land which the Lord your God giveth you, and ye shall possess it, and dwell therein.

32 Take heed therefore that ye [g]do all the commandments and the laws, which I set before you this day.

12 *3 To destroy the idolatrous places. 5, 8 To serve God where he commandeth, and as he commandeth, and not as men fantasize. 19 The Levites must be nourished. 31 Idolaters burnt their children to their gods, to add nothing to God's word.*

1 These are the ordinances and the laws, which ye shall observe and do in the land, (which the Lord God [1]of

---

11:6 [1] Hebrew, *was at their feet.*

11:8 [1] Because ye have felt both his chastisements and his benefits.

11:10 [1] Or, labor.
   [2] As by making gutters for the waters to come out of the river Nile to water the land.

11:14 [1] In the seed time, and toward harvest.

11:16 [1] By devising to yourselves foolish devotions according to your own fantasies.

11:21 [1] As long as the heavens endure, 2 Pet. 3:10,12.

11:24 [1] This was accomplished in David's and Solomon's time.
   [2] Called Mediterranean.

11:28 [1] He reproveth the malice of men which leave that which is certain to follow that which is uncertain.

11:30 [1] Meaning, in Samaria.
   [2] Or, plain.

12:1 [1] Whereby they are admonished to seek none other God.

thy fathers giveth thee to possess it) as long as ye live upon the earth.

2 ᵃYe shall utterly destroy all the places wherein the nations which ye shall possess, served their gods upon the high mountains, and upon the hills, and under every green tree.

3 ᵇAlso ye shall overthrow their altars, and break down their pillars, and burn their ¹groves with fire: and ye shall hew down the graven images of their gods, and abolish their names out of that place.

4 Ye shall ¹not do so unto the Lord your God,

5 But ye shall seek the place which the Lord your God shall ᶜchoose out of your tribes, to put his Name there, and there to dwell, and thither thou shalt come,

6 And ye shall bring thither your burnt offerings, and your sacrifices, and your tithes, and the ¹offering of your hands, and your vows, and your free offerings, and the firstborn of your kine and of your sheep.

7 And there ye shall eat ¹before the Lord your God, and ye shall rejoice in all that ye put your hand unto, both ye, and your households, because the Lord thy God hath blessed thee.

8 Ye shall not do after all these things that we do ¹here this day: that is, every man whatsoever seemeth him good in his own eyes.

9 For ye are not yet come to rest, and to the inheritance which the Lord thy God giveth thee.

10 But when ye go over Jordan, and dwell in the land, which the Lord your God hath given you to inherit, and when he hath given you ¹rest from all your enemies round about, and ye dwell in safety,

11 When there shall be a place which the Lord your God shall choose, to cause his name to dwell there, thither shall ye bring all that I command you: your burnt offerings, and your sacrifices, your tithes, and the offering of your hands, and all your ¹special vows which ye vow unto the Lord:

12 And ye shall rejoice before the Lord your God, ye, and your sons and your daughters, and your servants, and your maidens, and the Levite that is within your gates: ᵈfor he hath no part nor inheritance with you.

13 Take heed that thou offer not thy burnt offerings in every place that thou seest:

14 But in the place which the Lord shall ¹choose

CHAPTER 12
ᵃ Deut. 7:5
ᵇ Judg. 2:2
ᶜ 1 Kings 8:29
2 Chron. 6:5
2 Chron. 7:12,16
ᵈ Deut. 10:9
ᵉ Gen. 28:14
Deut. 19:8

in one of thy tribes, there thou shalt offer thy burnt offerings, and there thou shalt do all that I command thee.

15 Notwithstanding thou mayest kill and eat flesh in all thy gates, whatsoever thine heart desireth, according to the ¹blessing of the Lord thy God which he had given thee: both the unclean and the clean may eat thereof, ²as of the roebuck, and of the hart.

16 Only ye shall not eat the blood, but pour it upon the earth as water.

17 ¶ Thou mayest not eat within thy gates the ¹tithe of thy corn, nor of thy wine, nor of thine oil, nor the firstborn of thy kine, nor of thy sheep, neither any of thy vows which thou vowest, nor thy free offerings, nor the offering of thine hands,

18 But thou shalt eat it before the Lord thy God, in the place which the Lord thy God shall choose, thou and thy son, and thy daughter, and thy servant, and thy maid, and the Levite that is within thy gates: and thou shalt rejoice before the Lord thy God, in all that thou puttest thine hand to.

19 Beware, that thou forsake not the Levite, as long as thou livest upon the earth.

20 ¶ When the Lord thy God shall enlarge thy border, as ᵉhe hath promised thee, and thou shalt say, I will eat flesh (because thine heart longeth to eat flesh) thou mayest eat flesh, whatsoever thine heart desireth.

21 If the place which the Lord thy God hath chosen to put his Name there, be far from thee, then thou shalt kill of thy bullocks, and of thy sheep which the Lord hath given thee, as I have commanded thee, and thou shalt eat in thy gates, whatsoever thine heart desireth.

22 But as the roebuck, and the hart is eaten, so shalt thou eat them: both the unclean and the clean shall eat of them alike.

23 Only be ¹sure that thou eat not the blood: for the blood ²is the life, and thou mayest not eat the life with the flesh.

24 Therefore thou shalt not eat it, but pour it upon the earth as water.

25 Thou shalt not eat it, that it may go well with thee, and with thy children after thee, when thou shalt do that which is right in the sight of the Lord:

26 But thine ¹holy things which thou hast, and thy

12:3 ¹ Wherein they sacrificed to their idols.
12:4 ¹ Ye shall not serve the Lord with superstitions.
12:6 ¹ Meaning, the firstfruits.
12:7 ¹ Where his Ark shall be.
12:8 ¹ Not that they sacrificed after their fantasies, but that God would be served more purely in the land of Canaan.
12:10 ¹ It had not been enough to conquer, except God had maintained them in rest under his protection.
12:11 ¹ Or, that which ye choose out for your vows.
12:14 ¹ As was declared ever by the placing of the Ark, as in Shiloh

243 years, or as some write more than 300 years, and in other places till the temple was built.
12:15 ¹ As God hath given thee power and ability.
  ² Everyone might eat at home as well the beast appointed for sacrifice, as the other.
12:17 ¹ Meaning, whatsoever was offered to the Lord, might not be eaten, but where he had appointed.
12:23 ¹ Hebrew, be strong or constant.
  ² Because the life of beasts is in their blood.
12:26 ¹ That which thou wilt offer in sacrifice.

vows thou shalt take up, and come unto the place which the Lord shall choose.

27 And thou shalt make thy burnt offerings of the flesh, and of the blood upon the altar of the Lord thy God, and the blood of thine offerings shall be poured upon the altar of the Lord thy God, and thou shalt eat the flesh.

28 Take heed, and hear all these words which I command thee, that it may go [1]well with thee, and with thy children after thee forever, when thou doest that which is good and right in the sight of the Lord thy God.

29 ¶ When the Lord thy God shall destroy the nations before thee, whither thou goest to possess them, and thou shalt possess them and dwell in their land,

30 Beware, lest thou be taken in [1]snare after them, after that they be destroyed before thee, and lest thou ask after their gods, saying, How did these nations serve their gods, that I may do so likewise?

31 Thou shalt not do so unto the Lord thy God: for all abomination, which the Lord hateth, have they done unto their gods: for they have [1]burned both their sons and their daughters with fire to their gods.

32 Therefore whatsoever I command you, take heed you do it: /thou shalt put nothing thereto, nor take ought therefrom.

13

5 The enticers to idolatry must be slain, seem they never so holy.   6 So near of kindred or of friendship.   12 Or great in multitude or power.

1 If there arise among you a Prophet or a dreamer of [1]dreams, (and give thee a sign or wonder,

2 And the sign and the wonder, which he hath told thee, come to pass) saying, [1]Let us go after other gods, which thou hast not known, and let us serve them,

3 Thou shalt not hearken unto the words of the prophet, or unto that dreamer of dreams: for the Lord your God [1]proveth you, to know whether you love the Lord your God with all your heart, and with all your soul.

4 Ye shall walk after the Lord your God and fear him, and shall keep his commandments, and hearken unto his voice, and ye shall serve him, and cleave unto him.

f Deut. 4:2
Josh. 1:7
Prov. 30:6
Rev. 22:18

CHAPTER 13
a Deut. 17:13

5 But that Prophet, or that dreamer of dreams, he shall [1]be slain, because he hath spoken to turn you away from the Lord your God (which brought you out of the land of Egypt, and delivered you out of the house of bondage) to thrust thee out of the way, wherein the Lord thy God commanded thee to walk: so shalt thou take the evil away forth of the midst of thee.

6 ¶ If [1]thy brother, the son of thy mother, or thine own son, or thy daughter, or the wife, *that lieth* in thy bosom, or thy friend, which is as thine own [2]soul, entice thee secretly, saying, Let us go and serve other gods, (which thou hast not known, thou *I say*, nor thy fathers)

7 *Any* of the gods of the people which are round about you, near unto thee or far off from thee, from the one end of the earth unto the other:

8 Thou shalt not consent unto him, nor hear him, neither shall thine eye pity him, nor show mercy, nor keep him secret:

9 But thou shalt even kill him: [1]thine hand shall be first upon him to put him to death, and then the hands of the people.

10 And thou shalt stone him with stones, that he die (because he hath gone about to thrust thee away from the Lord thy God, which brought thee out of the land of Egypt: from the house of bondage)

11 *a*That all Israel may hear and fear, and do no more any such wickedness as this among you.

12 ¶ If thou shalt hear say (concerning any of thy cities, which the Lord thy God hath given thee to dwell in)

13 [1]Wicked men are gone out from among you, and have drawn away the inhabitants of their city, saying, Let us go and serve other gods, which ye have not known,

14 Then [1]thou shalt seek, and make search and inquire diligently: and if *it be* true, *and* the thing certain, that such abomination is wrought among you,

15 Thou shalt even slay the inhabitants of that city with the edge of the sword: destroy it utterly, and all that is therein, and the cattle thereof with the edge of the sword,

16 And [1]thou shalt gather all the spoil of it into the midst of the street thereof, and burn with fire the city and all the spoil thereof every whit, unto

---

12:28 [1] God by promise bindeth himself to do good to them that obey his word.
12:30 [1] By following their superstitions and idolatries, and thinking to serve me thereby.
12:31 [1] They thought nothing too dear to offer to their idols.
13:1 [1] Which sayeth that he hath things revealed unto him in dreams.
13:2 [1] He showeth whereunto the false prophets tend.
13:3 [1] God ordaineth all these things that his may be known.

13:5 [1] Being convicted by testimonies, and condemned by the judge.
13:6 [1] All natural affections must give place to God's honor.
    [2] Whom thou lovest as thy life.
13:9 [1] As the witness is charged, Deut. 17:7.
13:13 [1] Hebrew, *children of Belial*.
13:14 [1] Which art appointed to see faults punished.
13:16 [1] Signifying that no idolatry is so execrable, nor more grievously to be punished, than of them which once professed God.

the Lord thy God: and it shall be an heap forever, it shall not be built again.

17 And there shall cleave nothing of the [1]damned thing to thine hand, that the Lord may turn from the fierceness of his wrath, and show thee mercy, and have compassion on thee, and multiply thee as he hath sworn unto thy fathers:

18 When thou shalt obey the voice of the Lord thy God, and keep all his commandments which I command thee this day: that thou do that which is right in the eyes of the Lord thy God.

14 *1 The manners of the Gentiles in marking themselves for the dead, may not be followed. 4 What meats are clean to be eaten, and what not. 29 The tithes for the Levites, stranger, fatherless, and widow.*

1 Ye are the children of the Lord your God, [a]Ye shall not cut yourselves, nor make you *any* baldness between your eyes for the dead.

2 [b]For thou art an holy people unto the Lord thy God, and the Lord hath chosen thee to be a [1]precious people unto himself, above all the people that are upon the earth.

3 ¶ Thou shalt eat no manner of abomination.

4 [1]These are the beasts, which ye shall eat, the beef, the sheep, and the goat,

5 The hart, and the roebuck, and the bugle, and the wild goat, and the unicorn, and the wild ox, and the Chamois.

6 And every beast that parteth the hoof, and cleaveth the cleft into two claws, and *is* of the beasts that cheweth the cud, that shall ye eat.

7 But these ye shall not eat, of them that chew the cud, and of them that divide and cleave the hoof *only*: the camel, nor the hare, nor the coney: for they chew the cud, but divide not the hoof, *therefore* they shall be unclean unto you:

8 Also the swine, because he divideth the hoof: and cheweth not the cud, shall be unclean unto you: ye shall not eat of their flesh, nor touch their dead carcasses.

9 ¶ These ye shall eat, of all that are in the waters: all that have fins and scales shall ye eat.

10 And whatsoever hath no fins nor scales, ye shall not eat: it shall be unclean unto you.

11 ¶ Of all clean birds ye shall eat.

12 But these are they whereof ye shall not eat: the

CHAPTER 14
[a] Lev. 19:28
[b] Deut. 7:6
Deut. 26:18,19
[c] Lev. 11:9
[d] Lev. 11:19
[e] Exod. 23:19
Exod. 34:25

eagle nor the goshawk, nor the osprey,

13 Nor the glede, nor the kite, nor the vulture, after their kind,

14 Nor all kind of ravens,

15 Nor the ostrich, nor the night crow, nor the [1]seamew, nor the hawk after her kind,

16 Neither the little owl, nor the great owl, nor the redshank,

17 Nor the pelican, nor the swan, nor the cormorant:

18 The stork also, and the heron in his kind, nor the lapwing, nor [d]the [bat].

19 And every creeping thing that flieth, shall be unclean unto you: it shall not be eaten.

20 *But* of all clean fowls ye may eat.

21 Ye shall eat of nothing that [1]dieth alone, but thou shalt give it unto the [2]stranger that is within thy gates, that he may eat it: or thou mayest sell it unto a stranger: for thou art an holy people unto the Lord thy God. Thou shalt not [e]seethe a kid in his mother's milk.

22 Thou shalt [1]give the tithe of all the increase of thy seed, that cometh forth of the field year by year.

23 And thou shalt eat before the Lord thy God (in the place which he shall choose to cause his Name to dwell there) the tithe of thy corn, of thy wine, and of thine oil, and the firstborn of thy kine, and of thy sheep, that thou mayest learn to fear the Lord thy God always.

24 And if the way be too long for thee, so that thou art not able to carry it, because the place is far from thee, where the Lord thy God shall choose to set his name, [1]when the Lord thy God shall bless thee,

25 Then shalt thou make it in money, and [1]take the money in thine hand, and go unto the place which the Lord thy God shall choose.

26 And thou shalt bestow the money for whatsoever thine heart desireth: whether it be ox, or sheep, or wine, or strong drink, or whatsoever thine heart desireth: [1]and shalt eat it there before the Lord thy God, and rejoice, *both* thou, and thine household.

27 And the Levite that is within thy gates, shalt thou not forsake: for he hath neither part nor inheritance with thee.

28 At the end of three years thou shalt [1]bring forth all the tithes of thine increase of the same year, and

13:17 [1] Of the spoil of that idolatrous and cursed city, Read Deut. 7:26 and Josh. 7:11.
14:2 [1] Therefore thou oughtest not to follow the superstition of the Gentiles.
14:4 [1] This ceremonial Law instructed the Jews to seek a spiritual pureness, even in their meat and drink.
14:15 [1] Or, cuckoo
14:21 [1] Because their blood was not shed, but remaineth in them.

[2] Which is not of thy religion.
14:22 [1] The tithes were ordained for the maintenance of the Levites, which had none inheritance.
14:24 [1] When he shall give thee ability.
14:25 [1] Or, bind up.
14:26 [1] After the Priest hath received the Lord's part.
14:28 [1] Besides the yearly tithes that were given to the Levites, these were laid up in store for the poor.

lay it up within thy gates.

29 Then the Levite shall come, because he hath no part nor inheritance with thee, and the stranger, and the fatherless, and the widow, which are within thy gates, and shall eat, and be filled, that the Lord thy God may bless thee in all the work of thine hand which thou doest.

15 *1 The year of [releasing] of debts. 5 God blesseth them that keep his commandments. 7 To help the poor. 12 The freedom of servants. 19 The firstborn of the cattle must be offered to the Lord.*

1 At the term of seven years thou shalt make a freedom,

2 And this is the manner of the freedom: every [1]creditor shall quit the loan of his hand which he hath lent to his neighbor: he shall not ask it again of his neighbor, nor of his brother: for *the year* of the Lord's freedom is proclaimed.

3 Of a stranger thou mayest require it: but that which thou hast with thy brother, thine hand shall remit:

4 [1]Save when there shall be no poor with thee: for the Lord shall bless thee in the land, which the Lord thy God giveth thee, for an inheritance to possess it.

5 So that thou hearken unto the voice of the Lord thy God, to observe and do all these commandments, which I command thee this day.

6 For the Lord thy God hath blessed thee, as he hath promised thee: and [a]thou shalt lend unto many nations, but thou thyself shalt not borrow, and thou shalt reign over many nations, and they shall not reign over thee.

7 ¶ If one of thy brethren with thee be poor [1]within any of thy gates in thy land, which the Lord thy God giveth thee, thou shalt not harden thine heart, nor shut thine hand from thy poor brother:

8 [b]But thou shalt open thine hand unto him, and shalt lend him sufficient for his need which he hath.

9 Beware that there be not a wicked thought in thine heart, to say, The seventh year, the year of freedom is at hand: therefore [1]it grieveth thee to look on thy poor brother, and thou givest him nought, and he cry unto the Lord against thee, so that sin be in thee:

10 Thou shalt give him, and [1]let it not grieve thine heart to give unto him: for because of this the Lord thy God shall bless thee in all thy works, and in all

CHAPTER 15
[a] Deut. 28:12
[b] Matt. 5:42
Luke 6:24
[c] Exod. 21:2
Jer. 34:24
[d] Exod. 21:6
[e] Exod. 34:19
[f] Deut. 17:1

that thou puttest thine hand to.

11 [1]Because there shall be ever *some* poor in the land, therefore I command thee, saying, Thou shalt [2]open thine hand unto thy brother, to thy needy, and to thy poor in thy land.

12 ¶ [c]If thy brother an Hebrew sell himself to thee, or an Hebrewess, and serve thee six years, even in the seventh year thou shalt let him go free from thee:

13 And when thou sendest him out free from thee, thou shalt not let him go away empty,

14 *But* shalt [1]give him a liberal reward of thy sheep, and of thy corn, and of thy wine: thou shalt give him of that wherewith the Lord thy God hath blessed thee.

15 And remember that thou wast a servant in the land of Egypt, and the Lord thy God delivered thee: therefore I command thee this thing today.

16 And if he say unto thee, I will not go away from thee, because he loveth thee and thine house, and because he is well with thee,

17 [d]Then shalt thou take an awl, and pierce his ear through against the door, and he shall be thy servant [1]forever: and unto thy maid servant thou shall do likewise.

18 Let it not grieve thee, when thou lettest him go out free from thee: for he hath served thee six years, *which is* the double worth of [1]an hired servant: and the Lord thy God shall bless thee in all that thou doest.

19 ¶ [e]All the firstborn males that come of thy cattle, and of thy sheep, thou shalt sanctify unto the Lord thy God. [1]Thou shalt do no work with thy firstborn bullock, nor shear thy firstborn sheep.

20 Thou shalt eat it before the Lord thy God year by year, in the place which the Lord shall choose, *both* thou, and thine household.

21 [f]But if there be any blemish therein, *as if it be* lame, or blind, or have any evil fault, thou shalt not offer it unto the Lord thy God,

22 *But* shalt eat it within thy gates: the unclean, and the clean *shall eat it* alike, [1]as the roebuck, and as the hart.

23 Only thou shalt not eat the blood thereof, *but* [2]pour it upon the ground as water.

16 *1 Of Easter. 10 Whitsuntide, 13 And the feast of tabernacles. 18 What officers ought to be ordained. 21 Idolatry forbidden.*

15:2 [1] He shall only release his debtors, which are not able to pay for that year.
15:4 [1] For if thy debtor be rich, he may be constrained to pay.
15:7 [1] Or, any of thy cities.
15:9 [1] Hebrew, *thine eye is evil.*
15:10 [1] Hebrew, *let not thine heart be evil.*
15:11 [1] To try your charity, Matt. 26:11.

[2] Thou shalt be liberal.
15:14 [1] In token that thou dost acknowledge the benefit which God hath given thee by his labors.
15:17 [1] To the year of Jubilee, Lev. 25:40.
15:18 [1] For the hired servant served but three years, and he six.
15:19 [1] For they are the Lord's.
15:22 [1] Thou shalt as well eat them, as the roe buck, and other wild beasts.

1 Thou shalt keep the month of [1]Abib, and thou shalt celebrate the Passover unto the Lord thy God: for in the month of Abib the Lord thy God brought thee out of Egypt by night.

2 Thou shalt therefore [1]offer the Passover unto the Lord thy God, of sheep and bullocks [a]in the place where the Lord shall choose to cause his Name to dwell.

3 Thou [b]shalt eat no leavened bread with it: *but* seven days shalt thou eat unleavened bread therewith, *even* the bread of [1]tribulation: for thou camest out of the land of Egypt in haste: that thou mayest remember the day when thou camest out of the land of Egypt, all the days of thy life.

4 And there shall be no leaven seen with thee in all thy coasts seven days long: neither shall there remain the night any of the flesh until the morning which thou offeredst the first day at even.

5 Thou mayest [1]not offer the Passover within any of the gates, which the Lord thy God giveth thee:

6 But in the place which the Lord thy God shall choose to place his Name, there thou shalt offer the [1]Passover at even, about the going down of the sun, in the season that thou camest out of Egypt.

7 And thou shalt roast and eat it in the place which the Lord thy God shall choose, and shalt return on the morrow, and go unto thy tents.

8 Six days shalt thou eat unleavened bread, and the seventh day *shall be* a solemn assembly to the Lord thy God: thou shalt do no work *therein*.

9 ¶ Seven weeks shalt thou [1]number unto thee, and shalt begin to number the seven weeks, when thou beginnest to put the sickle to the corn:

10 And thou shalt keep the feast of weeks unto the Lord thy God, [1]*even* a free gift of thine hand, which thou shalt give unto the Lord thy God, as the Lord thy God hath blessed thee.

11 And thou shalt rejoice before the Lord thy God, thou and thy son, and thy daughter, and thy servant, and thy maid, and the Levite that is within thy gates, and the stranger, and the fatherless, and the widow, that are among you, in the place which the Lord thy God shall choose to place his Name there,

12 And thou shalt remember that thou wast a servant in Egypt: therefore thou shalt observe and do these ordinances.

13 ¶ Thou shalt [1]observe the feast of the Tabernacles seven days, when thou hast gathered in thy corn, and thy wine.

14 And thou shalt rejoice in thy feast, thou and thy son, and thy daughter, and thy servant, and thy maid, and the Levite, and the stranger, and the fatherless, and the widow, that are within thy gates.

15 Seven days shalt thou keep a feast unto the Lord thy God in the place which the Lord shall choose: when the Lord thy God shall bless thee in all thine increase, and in all the works of thine hands, thou shalt in any case be glad.

16 ¶ [c]Three times in the year shall all the males appear before the Lord thy God in the place which he shall choose: in the feast of the unleavened bread, and in the feast of the weeks, and in the feast of the Tabernacle: and they shall not appear before the Lord empty.

17 Every man *shall give* according to the gift of his [1]hand, and according to the blessing of the Lord thy God, which he hath given thee.

18 ¶ [1]Judges and officers shalt thou make thee in all thy cities, which the Lord thy God giveth thee, throughout the tribes: and they shall judge the people with righteous judgment.

19 Wrest not thou the Law, nor respect any person, neither take reward: for the reward blindeth the eyes of the wise, and perverteth the words of the just.

20 That which [1]is just and right shalt thou follow, that thou mayest live, and possess the land which the Lord thy God giveth thee.

21 ¶ Thou shalt plant thee no grove of any trees near unto the Altar of the Lord thy God, which thou shalt make thee.

22 Thou shalt set thee up no [1]pillar, which thing the Lord thy God hateth.

17

2 *The punishment of the idolater.* 9 *Hard controversies are brought to the Priest and the Judge.* 12 *The contemner must die.* 15 *The election of the King.* 16 *and* 17 *What things he ought to avoid, etc.*

1 Thou shalt offer unto the Lord thy God no bullock nor sheep wherein is [a,1]a blemish *or* any evil favored thing: for that is an abomination unto the Lord thy God.

CHAPTER 16
[a] Deut. 12:5
[b] Exod. 12:14,15
[c] Exod. 23:15
Exod. 34:23

CHAPTER 17
[a] Deut. 15:21

16:1 [1] Read Exod. 13:4.
16:2 [1] Thou shalt eat the Easter lamb.
16:3 [1] Which signified that affliction, which thou hadst in Egypt.
16:5 [1] This was chiefly accomplished, when the Temple was built.
16:6 [1] Which was instituted to put them in remembrance of their deliverance out of Egypt: and to continue them in the hope of Jesus Christ, of whom this lamb was a figure.
16:9 [1] Beginning at the next morning after the Passover, Lev. 23:15; Exod. 13:4.

16:10 [1] Or, as thou art able, willingly.
16:13 [1] That is, the 15th day of the seventh month, Lev. 23:34.
16:17 [1] According to the ability that God hath given him.
16:18 [1] He gave authority to that people for a time to choose themselves magistrates.
16:20 [1] The magistrate must constantly follow the tenor of the Law, and in nothing decline from justice.
16:22 [1] Or, image
17:1 [1] Thou shalt not serve God for fashion's sake, as hypocrites do.

2 ¶ If there be found among you in any of thy cities, which the Lord thy God giveth thee, man or [1]woman that hath wrought wickedness in the sight of the Lord thy God, in transgressing his covenant,

3 And hath gone and served other gods, and worshipped them: as the sun, or the moon, or any of the host of heaven, which I have not [1]commanded,

4 And it be told unto thee, and thou hast heard it, then shalt thou inquire diligently: and if *it be* true, *and* the thing certain, that such abomination is wrought in Israel,

5 Then shalt thou bring forth that man, or that woman (which hath committed that wicked thing) unto thy gates, *whether it be* man or woman, and shalt stone them with stones, till they die.

6 [b]At the mouth [1]of two or three witnesses shall he that is worthy of death, die: *but* at the mouth of one witness, he shall not die.

7 The hands of the [1]witnesses shall be first upon him, to kill him: and afterward the hands of all the [2]people: so thou shalt take the wicked away from among you.

8 ¶ If there rise a matter too hard for thee in judgment between blood and blood, between plea and plea, between plague and plague, in the matter of controversy within thy gates, then shalt thou arise, and go up unto the place which the Lord thy God shall choose,

9 And thou shalt come unto the Priests of the Levites, and unto the [1]Judge that shall be in those days, and ask, and they shall show thee the sentence of judgment,

10 And thou shalt do according to that thing, which they of that place (which the Lord hath chosen) show thee, and thou shalt observe to do according to all that they inform thee.

11 According to the Law, which they shall teach thee, and according to the judgment which they shall tell thee, shalt [1]thou do: thou shalt not decline from the thing which they shalt show thee, *neither* to the right hand, nor the left.

12 And that man that will do presumptuously, not hearkening unto the Priest (that standeth before the

Side references:
[b] Num. 35:30
Deut. 19:15
Matt. 18:16
1 Cor. 13:2

CHAPTER 18
[a] Num. 18:20
[b] Deut. 10:9
1 Cor. 9:13

Lord thy God to [1]minister there) or unto the Judge, that man shall die, and thou shalt take away evil from Israel.

13 So all the people shall hear and fear, and do no more presumptuously.

14 ¶ When thou shalt come unto the land which the Lord thy God giveth thee, and shalt possess it, and dwell therein, if thou say, I will set a king over me, like as all the nations that are about me,

15 *Then* thou shalt make him King over thee, whom the Lord thy God shall choose: from among thy brethren shalt thou make a King over thee: thou [1]shalt not set a [2]stranger over thee which is not thy brother.

16 In any wise he shall not prepare him many horses, nor bring the people again to [1]Egypt, for to increase the number of horses, seeing the Lord hath said unto you, Ye shall henceforth go no more again that way.

17 Neither shall he take him many wives, lest his heart [1]turn away, neither shall he gather him much silver and gold.

18 And when he shall sit upon the throne of his Kingdom, then shall he write him this [1]law repeated in a book, by the [2]Priest of the Levites.

19 And it shall be with him, and he shall read therein all days of his life, that he may learn to fear the Lord his God, *and* to keep all the words of this Law, and these ordinances to do them:

20 That his heart be not lifted up above his [1]brethren, and that he turn not from the commandment, to the right hand or to the left, *but* that he may prolong his days in his kingdom, he and his sons in the midst of Israel.

18

3 *The portion of the Levites.*   6 *Of the Levites coming from another place.*   9 *To avoid the abominations of the Gentiles.*   15 *God will not leave them without a true Prophet.*

1 The Priests of the Levites, *and* all the tribe of Levi [a]shall have no part nor inheritance with Israel, [b]but shall eat the offerings of the Lord made by fire, and his [1]inheritance.

2 Therefore shall they have no inheritance among their brethren: *for* the Lord is their inheritance, as

---

17:2 [1] Showing that the crime cannot be excused by the frailty of the person.

17:3 [1] Whereby he condemneth all religion and serving of God which God hath not commanded.

17:6 [1] Hebrew, *of two witnesses or three witnesses.*

17:7 [1] Whereby they declared that they testifieth the truth.
    [2] To signify a common consent to maintain God's honor and true religion.

17:9 [1] Who shall give sentence as the Priests counsel him by the Law of God.

17:11 [1] Thou shalt obey their sentence that the controversy may have an end.

17:12 [1] So long as he is the true minister of God, and pronounceth

according to his word.

17:15 [1] Or, mayest not.
    [2] Who is not of thy nation, lest he change true religion into idolatry, and bring thee to slavery.

17:16 [1] To revenge their injuries, and to take them of their best horses, 1 Kings 10:28.

17:17 [1] From the Law of God.

17:18 [1] Meaning, the Deuteronomy.
    [2] He shall cause it to be written by them, or he shall write it by their example.

17:20 [1] Whereby is meant, that Kings ought so to love their subjects as nature bindeth one brother to love another.

18:1 [1] That is, the Lord's part of his inheritance.

he hath said unto them.

3 ¶ And this shall be the Priest's duty of the people, that they which offer sacrifice, whether *it be* bullock or sheep, shall give unto the Priest the ¹shoulder, and the two cheeks, and the maw.

4 The firstfruits *also* of thy corn, of thy wine, and of thine oil, and the first of the fleece of thy sheep shalt thou give him.

5 For the Lord thy God hath chosen him out of all thy tribes, to stand and minister in the Name of the Lord, him, and his sons forever.

6 ¶ Also when a Levite shall come out of any of thy cities of all Israel, where he remained, and come with ¹all the desire of his heart unto the place, which the Lord shall choose,

7 He shall then minister in the Name of the Lord his God, as all his brethren the Levites, which remain there before the Lord.

8 They shall have like portions to eat ¹beside that which cometh of the sale of his patrimony.

9 When thou shalt come into the land which the Lord thy God giveth thee, thou shalt not learn to do after the abominations of those nations.

10 Let none be found among you that maketh his son or his daughter to ¹·ᶜgo thorough the fire, *or that* useth witchcraft, *or* a regarder of times, or a marker of the flying of fowls, or a sorcerer,

11 Or ᵈa charmer, or that counseleth with spirits, or a soothsayer, or that ᵉasketh counsel at the dead.

12 For all that do such things *are* abomination unto the Lord, and because of these abominations the Lord thy God doth cast them out before thee.

13 Thou shalt be ¹upright therefore with the Lord thy God.

14 For these nations which thou shalt possess, hearken unto those that regard the times, and unto sorcerers: ¹as for thee, the Lord thy God hath not ²suffered thee so.

15 ¶ ᶠThe Lord thy God will raise up unto thee a ¹Prophet like unto me, from among you, *even* of thy brethren: unto him ye shall hearken.

16 According to all that thou desiredst of the Lord thy God in Horeb, in the day of the assembly, when thou saidest, ᵍLet me hear the voice of my Lord God no more, nor see this great fire anymore, that I die not.

17 And the Lord said unto me, They have well

spoken.

18 ᵇI will raise them up a Prophet from among their brethren like unto thee, and will put my words in his ¹mouth, and he shall speak unto them all that I shall command him.

19 And whosoever will not hearken unto my words, which he shall speak in my Name, I will ¹require it of him.

20 But the Prophet that shall presume to speak a word in my name, which I have not commanded him to speak, or that speaketh in the name of other gods, even the same Prophet shall die.

21 And if thou think in thine heart, How shall we know the word which the Lord hath not spoken?

22 When a Prophet speaketh in the Name of the Lord, if the thing ¹follow not nor come to pass, that is the thing which the Lord hath not spoken, *but* the Prophet hath spoken it presumptuously: thou shalt not *therefore* be afraid of him.

19

2 *The franchised towns.* 14 *Not to remove thy neighbor's bounds.* 16 *The punishment of him that beareth false witness.*

1 When the Lord thy God ᵃshall root out the nations, whose land the Lord thy God giveth thee, and thou shalt possess them, and dwell in their cities, and in their houses,

2 ᵇThou shalt separate three cities for thee, in the midst of thy land which the Lord thy God giveth thee to possess it.

3 Thou shalt ¹prepare thee the way, and divide the coasts of the land, which the Lord thy God giveth thee to inherit, into three parts, that every ²manslayer may flee thither.

4 ¶ This also is the cause wherefore the manslayer shall flee thither, and live: who so killeth his neighbor ignorantly, and hated him not in time passed:

5 As he that goeth unto the wood with his neighbor to hew wood, and his hand striketh with the axe to cut down the tree, if the head slip from the helve, and hit his neighbor that he dieth, the same ¹shall flee unto one of the cities, and live,

6 Lest the ᶜavenger of the blood follow after the manslayer while his heart is chafed, and overtake him, because the way is long, and slay him, although he be not ¹worthy of death, because he hated him

---

Marginal references:
ᶜ Lev. 18:21
ᵈ Lev. 20:27
ᵉ 1 Sam. 28:7
ᶠ Acts 7:37
ᵍ Exod. 20:19
ᵇ Josh. 1:45
Acts 3:21

CHAPTER 19
ᵃ Deut. 12:29
ᵇ Exod. 21:13
Num. 35:9,11
Josh. 20:2
ᶜ Num. 35:12

18:3 ¹ The right shoulder, Num. 28:18.
18:6 ¹ Meaning, to serve God unfainedly, and not to seek ease.
18:8 ¹ Not constrained to live of himself.
18:10 ¹ Signifying they were purged by this ceremony of passing between two fires.
18:13 ¹ Without hypocrisy or mixture or false religion.
18:14 ¹ Hebrew, *but thou not so.*
² Hebrew, *given or appointed.*
18:15 ¹ Meaning, a continual succession of Prophets, till Christ the

end of all Prophets come.
18:18 ¹ Which promise is not only made to Christ, but to all that teach in his name, Isa. 59:21.
18:19 ¹ By executing punishment upon him.
18:22 ¹ Under this sure note he compriseth all the other tokens.
19:3 ¹ Make an open and ready way.
² Which killeth against his will, and bare no hatred in his heart.
19:5 ¹ That murder be not committed upon murder.
19:6 ¹ Or, cannot be judged to death.

not in time passed.

7 Wherefore I commanded thee, saying, Thou shalt appoint out three cities for thee.

8 And when the Lord thy God [1]enlargeth thy coasts (as he hath sworn unto thy fathers) and giveth thee all the land which he promised to give unto thy fathers.

9 (If thou keep all these commandments to do them, which I command thee this day: *to wit*, that thou love the Lord thy God, and walk in his ways forever) [d]then thou shalt add three cities more for thee besides those three,

10 That no innocent blood be shed within thy land, which the Lord thy God giveth thee to inherit, [1]lest blood be upon thee.

11 ¶ But if a man hate his neighbor, and lay wait for him, and rise against him, and smite any man that he die, and flee unto any of these cities,

12 Then the [1]Elders of his city shall send and fet him thence, and deliver him to the hands of the avenger of the blood, that he may die.

13 Thine [1]eye shall not spare him, but thou shalt put away the *cry* of innocent blood from Israel, that it may go well with thee.

14 ¶ Thou shalt not remove thy neighbor's mark, which they of old time have set in thine inheritance, that thou shalt inherit in the land, which the Lord thy God giveth thee to possess it.

15 ¶ [c]One witness shall not rise against a man for any trespass, or for any sin, or for any fault that he offendeth in, [f]but at the mouth of two witnesses, or at the mouth of three witnesses, shall the matter be stablished.

16 ¶ If a false witness rise up against a man to accuse him of trespass,

17 Then both the men which strive together, shall stand before the [1]Lord, *even* before the Priests and the Judges, which shall be in those days.

18 And the Judges shall make diligent inquisition: and if the witness be found false, *and* hath given false witness against his brother,

19 [g]Then shall ye do unto him as he had thought to do unto his brother: so thou shalt take evil away forth of the midst of thee.

20 And the rest shall hear *this*, and fear, and shall henceforth commit no more any such wickedness among you.

d Josh. 20:7
e Deut. 17:9
Matt. 18:6
John 8:17
f 2 Cor. 13:1
Heb. 13:21
g Prov. 19:5
h Exod. 21:13
Lev. 24:20
Matt. 5:38

CHAPTER 20
a Deut. 28:7
b Judg. 7:3
c Num. 21:21
Deut. 2:26

21 Therefore thine eye shall have no compassion, *but* [h]life for life, eye for eye, tooth for tooth, hand for hand, foot for foot.

20

3 The exhortation of the Priest when the Israelites go to battle. 5 The exhortation of the officers showing who should go to battle. 10 Peace must be first proclaimed. 19 The trees that bear fruit must not be destroyed.

1 When [1]thou shalt go forth to war against thine enemies, and shalt see horses and chariots, *and* people more than thou, be not afraid of them: for the Lord thy God *is* with thee, which brought thee out of the land of Egypt.

2 And when ye are come near unto the battle, then the Priest shall come forth to speak unto the people,

3 And shall say unto them, Hear, O Israel, ye are come this day unto battle against your enemies: [a]let not your hearts faint, neither fear, nor be amazed, nor a dread of them.

4 For the Lord your God [1]goeth with you, to fight for you against your enemies, *and* to save you.

5 ¶ And let the officers speak unto the people, saying, What man *is there* that hath built a new house, and hath not [1]dedicated it, let him go and return to his house, lest he die in the battle, and another man dedicate it.

6 ¶ And what man *is there* that hath planted a vineyard, and hath not [1]eaten of the fruit? let him go to return again unto his house, lest he die in the battle, and another eat the fruit.

7 And what man *is there* that hath betrothed a wife, and hath not taken her? let him go and return again unto his house, lest he die in battle, and another man take her.

8 And let the officers speak further unto the people, and say, [b]Whosoever is afraid and faint hearted, let him go and return unto his house, lest his brethren's heart faint like his heart.

9 And after that the officers have made an end of speaking unto the people, they shall make captains of the army to govern the people.

10 ¶ When thou comest near unto a city to fight against it, [c]thou shalt offer it peace.

11 And if it answer thee again [1]peaceably, and open unto thee, then let all the people that is found therein, be tributaries unto thee, and serve thee.

19:8 [1] When thou goest over Jordan to possess the whole land of Canaan.
19:10 [1] Lest thou be punished for innocent blood.
19:12 [1] The Magistrates.
19:13 [1] Then whosoever pardoneth murder, offendeth against the word of God.
19:17 [1] God's presence is where his true ministers are assembled.
20:1 [1] Meaning, upon just occasion: for God permitteth not his

people to fight when it seemeth good to them.
20:4 [1] Is present to defend you with his grace and power.
20:5 [1] For when they entered first to dwell in an house, they gave thanks to God, acknowledging that they had that benefit by his grace.
20:6 [1] The Hebrew word signifieth to make common or profane, Lev. 19:25.
20:11 [1] If it accept peace.

12 But if it will make no peace with thee, but make war against thee, then shalt thou besiege it.

13 And the Lord thy God shall deliver it into thine hands, and thou shalt smite all the males thereof with the edge of the sword.

14 Only the women, and the children, [d]and the cattle, and all that is in the city, *even* all the spoil thereof shalt thou take unto thyself, and shalt eat the spoil of thine enemies, which the Lord thy God hath given thee.

15 Thus shalt thou do unto all the cities, which are a great way off from thee, which are not of the cities of these [1]nations here.

16 But of the cities of this people, which the Lord thy God shall give thee to inherit, thou shalt save no person alive,

17 But shalt utterly destroy them, *to wit*, the Hittites, and the Amorites, the Canaanites, and the Perizzites, the Hivites, and the Jebusites: as the Lord thy God hath commanded thee,

18 That they teach you not to do after all their abominations, which they have done unto their gods, and *so* ye should sin against the Lord your God.

19 ¶ When thou hast besieged a city long time, and made war against it to take it, destroy not the trees thereof, by smiting an axe into them: for thou mayest eat of them: therefore thou shalt not cut them down to further thee in the siege, (for the [1]tree of the field is man's *life*).

20 Only those trees which thou knowest are not for meat, those shalt thou destroy and cut down, and make forts against the city that maketh war with thee until thou subdue it.

21

2 Inquisition for murder.   11 Of the woman taken in war.   15 The birthright cannot be changed for affection.   18 The disobedient child.   23 The body may not hang all night.

1 If one be found [1]slain in the land, which the Lord thy God giveth thee to possess it, lying in the field, *and* it is not known who hath slain him,

2 Then thine Elders and thy Judges shall come forth, and measure unto the cities that are round about him that is slain:

3 And let the Elders of that city, which is next

[d] Josh. 8:2

unto the slain man, take out of the drove an heifer that hath not been put to labor, nor hath drawn in the yoke.

4 And let the Elders of that city bring the heifer unto a [1]stony [2]valley, which is neither eared, nor sown, and strike off the heifer's neck there in the valley.

5 Also the Priests the sons of Levi (whom the Lord thy God hath chosen to minister, and to bless in the Name of the Lord) shall come forth, and by their word shall all strife and plague be tried.

6 And all the Elders of that city that came near to the slain man, shall wash their hands over the heifer that is beheaded in the valley:

7 And shall testify, and say, Our hands have not shed this blood, neither have our eyes seen it.

8 [1]O Lord, be merciful unto thy people Israel, whom thou hast redeemed, and lay no innocent blood to the charge of thy people Israel, and the blood shall be forgiven them.

9 So shalt thou take away the cry of innocent blood from thee, when thou shalt do that which is right in the sight of the Lord.

10 ¶ When thou shalt go to war against thine enemies, and the Lord thy God shall deliver them into thine hands, and thou shalt take them captives,

11 And shalt see among the captives a beautiful woman, and hast a desire unto her, and wouldest take her to thy wife,

12 Then thou shalt bring her home to thine house, [1]and she shall shave her head, and pare her nails,

13 And she shall put off the garment that she was taken in, and she shall remain in thine house, [1]and bewail her father and her mother a month long: and after that shalt thou go in unto her, and marry her, and she shall be thy [2]wife.

14 And if thou have no favor unto her, then thou mayest let her go whither she will, but thou shalt not sell her for money, nor make merchandise of her, because thou hast humbled her.

15 ¶ If a man have two wives, one loved and another [1]hated, and they have born him children, both the loved and also the hated: if the firstborn be the son of the hated,

16 Then when the time cometh, that he appointeth his sons to be heirs of that which he hath, he may not make the son of the beloved firstborn [1]before

---

20:15 [1] For God had appointed that the Canaanites should be destroyed, and made the Israelites executors of his will, Deut. 7:1.

20:19 [1] Some read, For man *shall be instead* of the tree of the field, to come out in the siege against thee.

21:1 [1] This law declareth how horrible a thing murder is, seeing that for one man whole country shall be punished, except remedy be found.

21:4 [1] Or, rough.
    [2] That the blood shed of the innocent beasts in a solitary place, might make them abhor the fact.

21:8 [1] This was the prayer, which the Priests made in the audience of the people.

21:12 [1] Signifying that her former life must be changed before she could be joined to the people of God.

21:13 [1] As having renounced parents and country.
    [2] This only was permitted in the wars, otherwise the Israelites could not marry strangers.

21:15 [1] This declareth that the plurality of wives came of a corrupt affection.

21:16 [1] Or, while the son of the hated liveth.

the son of the hated, which is the firstborn:

17 But he shall acknowledge the son of the hated for the firstborn, and give him ¹double portion for all that he hath: for he is the first of his strength, and to ²him belongeth the right of firstborn.

18 ¶ If any man have a son that is stubborn and disobedient, which will not hearken unto the voice of his father, nor the voice of his ¹mother, and they have chastened him, and he would not obey them,

19 Then shall his father and his mother take him, and bring him out unto the Elders of his city, and unto the gate of the place where he dwelleth,

20 And shall say unto the Elders of his city, This our son is stubborn and disobedient, and he will not obey our admonition: he is a rioter, and a drunkard.

21 Then all the men of his city shall ¹stone him with stones unto death: so thou shalt take away evil from among you, that all Israel may hear it, and fear.

22 ¶ If a man also have committed a trespass worthy of death, and is put to death, and thou hangest him on a tree,

23 His body shall not remain ¹all night upon the tree, but thou shalt bury him the same day: for the ªcurse of God is on him that is hanged. Defile not therefore thy land which the Lord thy God giveth thee to inherit.

22

2 He commandeth to have care of our neighbor's goods. 5 The woman may not wear man's apparel, nor man the woman's. 6 Of the dam and her young birds. 8 Why they should have battlements. 9 Not to mix divers kinds together. 13 Of the wife not being found a virgin. 23 The punishment of adultery.

1 Thou ªshalt not see thy brother's ox nor his sheep go astray, and ¹withdraw thyself from them, but shalt bring them again unto thy brother.

2 And if thy brother be not ¹near unto thee, or if thou know him not, then thou shalt bring it into thine house, and it shall remain with thee, until thy brother seek after it, then shalt thou deliver it to him again:

3 In like manner shalt thou do with his ¹ass, and so shalt thou do with his raiment, and shalt so do with all lost things of thy brother, which he hath lost: if thou hast found them, thou shalt not withdraw

CHAPTER 21
ª Gal. 3:13

CHAPTER 22
ª Exod. 23:4
ᵇ Num. 15:38

thyself from them.

4 ¶ Thou shalt not see thy brother's ass nor his ox fall down by the way, and withdraw thyself from them, but shalt lift them up with him.

5 The ¹woman shall not wear that which pertaineth unto the man, neither shalt a man put on woman's raiment: for all that do so, are abomination unto the Lord thy God.

6 ¶ If thou find a bird's nest in the way, in any tree, or on the ground whether they be young or eggs, and the dam sitting upon the young, or upon the eggs, ¹thou shalt not take the dam with the young,

7 But shalt in any wise let the dam go, and take the young to thee, that thou mayest prosper and prolong thy days.

8 ¶ When thou buildest a new house, thou shalt make a battlement on thy roof, that thou lay not blood upon thine house, if any man fall thence.

9 ¶ Thou shalt not ¹sow thy vineyard with divers kinds of seeds, lest thou defile the increase of the seed which thou hast sown, and the fruit of the vineyard.

10 ¶ Thou shalt not plow with an ox and an ass together.

11 ¶ Thou shalt not wear a garment of divers sorts, as of woolen and linen together.

12 ¶ ᵇThou shalt make thee fringes upon the four quarters of thy vesture, wherewith thou coverest thyself.

13 ¶ If a man take a wife, and when he hath lain with her, hate her,

14 And lay ¹slanderous things unto her charge, and bring up an evil name upon her, and say, I took this wife, and when I came to her, I found her not a maid,

15 Then shall the father of the maid and her mother take and bring the signs of the maid's virginity unto the Elders of the city to the gate.

16 And the maid's father shall say unto the Elders, I gave my daughter unto this man to wife and he hateth her:

17 And lo, he layeth slanderous things unto her charge, saying, I found not thy daughter a maid: lo, these are the tokens of my daughter's virginity: and they shall spread the ¹vesture before the Elders of the city.

18 Then the Elders of the city shall take that man and chastise him,

---

21:17 ¹ As much as to two of the others.
² Except he be unworthy, as was Reuben Jacob's son.
21:18 ¹ For it is the mother's duty also to instruct her children.
21:21 ¹ Which death was also appointed for blasphemers and idolaters: so that to disobey the parents is most horrible.
21:23 ¹ For God's Law by his death is satisfied, and nature abhorreth cruelty.
22:1 ¹ As though thou sawest it not.
22:2 ¹ Showing that brotherly affection must be showed, not only to

them that dwell near unto us, but also to them which are far off.
22:3 ¹ Much more art thou bound to do for thy neighbor's person.
22:5 ¹ For that were to alter the order of nature, and to despite God.
22:6 ¹ If God detests cruelty done to little birds, how much more to man, made according to his image?
22:9 ¹ The tenor of this Law, is to walk in simplicity, and not to be curious of new inventions.
22:14 ¹ That is, be an occasion that she is slandered.
22:17 ¹ Meaning, the sheet, wherein the signs of her virginity were.

19 And shall condemn him in an hundred *shekels* of silver, and give them unto the father [1]of the maid, because he hath brought up an evil name upon a maid of Israel: and she shall be his wife, and he may not put her away all his life.

20 But if this thing be true, that the maid be not found a virgin,

21 Then shall they bring forth the maid to the door of her father's house, and the men of her city shall stone her with stones to death: for she hath wrought folly in Israel, by playing the whore in her father's house: so thou shalt put evil away from among you.

22 ¶ [c]If a man be found lying with a woman married to a man, then they shall die even both twain: *to wit*, the man that lay with the wife, and the wife: so thou shalt put away evil from Israel.

23 ¶ If a maid be betrothed unto a husband, and a man find her in the town and lie with her,

24 Then shall ye bring them both out unto the gates of the same city, and shall stone them with stones to death: the maid because she cried not, *being* in the city, and the man, because he hath [1]humbled his neighbor's wife: so thou shalt put away evil from among you.

25 ¶ But if a man find a betrothed maid in the field and force her, and lie with her, then the man that lay with her, shall die alone:

26 And unto the maid thou shalt do nothing, because there is in the maid no [1]cause of death: for as when a man riseth against his neighbor and woundeth him to death, so [2]is this matter.

27 For he found her in the fields: the betrothed maid cried, and there was no man to succor her.

28 ¶ [d]If a man find a maid that is not betrothed, and take her, and lie with her, and they be found,

29 Then the man that lay with her, shall give unto the maid's father fifty *shekels* of silver: and she shall be his wife, because he hath humbled her: he can not put her away all his life.

30 ¶ No man shall [1]take his father's wife, nor shall uncover his father's skirt.

23
1 *What men ought not to be admitted to office.* 9 *What they ought to avoid when they go to war.* 15 *Of the fugitive servant.* 17 *To flee all kinds of whoredom.* 19 *Of usury.* 21 *Of vows.* 24 *Of the neighbor's vine and corn.*

1 None that is hurt by bursting, or that hath his privy member cut off, [1]shall enter into the Congregation of the Lord.

2 [1]A bastard shall not enter into the Congregation of the Lord: even to his tenth generation shall he not enter into the Congregation of the Lord.

3 [a]The Ammonites and the Moabites shall not enter into the Congregation of the Lord: even to their tenth generation shall they not enter into the Congregation of the Lord forever,

4 Because they [1]met you not with bread and water in the way, when ye came out of Egypt, and [b]because they hired against thee Balaam the son of Beor, of Pethor in Aram-naharaim, to curse thee.

5 Nevertheless, the Lord thy God would not hearken unto Balaam, but the Lord thy God turned the curse to a blessing unto thee, because the Lord thy God loved thee.

6 Thou [1]shall not seek their peace, nor their prosperity all thy days forever.

7 ¶ Thou shalt not abhor an Edomite: for he is thy brother, neither shalt thou abhor an Egyptian, because thou wast a stranger in his land.

8 The children that are begotten [1]of them in their third generation, shall enter into the Congregation of the Lord.

9 ¶ When thou goest out with the host against thine enemies, keep thee then from all wickedness.

10 ¶ If there be among you any that is unclean by that which cometh to him by night, he shall go out of the host, and shall not enter into the host,

11 But at even he shall wash *himself* with water, and when the sun is down, he shall enter into the host.

12 ¶ Thou shalt have a place also without the host, whither thou shalt [1]resort,

13 And thou shalt have a paddle among thy weapons, and when thou wouldest sit down without, thou shalt dig therewith, and returning, thou shalt [1]cover thine excrements.

14 For the Lord thy God walketh in the midst of thy camp to deliver thee, and to give *thee* thine enemies before thee: therefore thine host shall be holy, that he see no filthy thing in thee, and turn away from thee.

15 ¶ Thou shalt not [1]deliver the servant unto his master, which is escaped from his master unto thee.

c Lev. 20:20
d Exod. 22:16

CHAPTER 23
a Neh. 1:31
b Num. 22:5,6

22:19 [1] For the fault of the child redoundeth to the shame of the parents: therefore he was recompensed when she was faultless.
22:24 [1] Or, defiled.
22:26 [1] Or, no sin worthy of death.
  [2] Meaning, that the innocent cannot be punished.
22:30 [1] He shall not lie with his stepmother, meaning hereby all other degrees forbidden, Lev. 18.
23:1 [1] Either to bear office, or to marry a wife.
23:2 [1] This was to cause them to live chastely, that their posterity might not be rejected.

23:4 [1] Hereby he condemneth all that further not the children of God in their vocation.
23:6 [1] Thou shalt have nothing to do with them.
23:8 [1] If the fathers have renounced their idolatry, and received circumcision.
23:12 [1] For the necessities of nature.
23:13 [1] Meaning hereby that his people should be pure both in body and soul.
23:15 [1] This is meant of the heathen, who fled for their masters' cruelty, and embraced the true religion.

16 He shall dwell with thee, *even* among you, in what place he shall choose, in one of thy [1]cities where it liketh him best: thou shalt not vex him.

17 ¶ There shall be no whore of the daughters of Israel, neither shall there be a whore keeper of the sons of Israel.

18 ¶ Thou shalt neither bring the [1]hire of a whore, nor the price of a dog into the house of the Lord thy God for any vow: for even both these *are* abomination unto the Lord thy God.

19 ¶ ℂThou shalt not give to usury to thy brother: as usury of money, usury of meat, usury of anything that is put to usury.

20 Unto a [1]stranger thou mayest lend upon usury, but thou shalt not lend upon usury unto thy brother, that the Lord thy God may [2]bless thee in all that thou settest thine hand to, in the land whither thou goest to possess it.

21 ¶ When thou shalt vow a vow unto the Lord thy God, thou shalt not be slack to pay it: for the Lord thy God will surely require it of thee, and so it should be sin unto thee.

22 But when thou abstainest from vowing, it shall be no sin unto thee.

23 That which is gone out of thy lips, thou shalt [1]keep and perform, as thou hast vowed it willingly unto the Lord thy God: *for* thou hast spoken it with thy mouth.

24 ¶ When thou comest unto [1]thy neighbor's vineyard, then thou mayest eat grapes at thy pleasure, as much as thou wilt: but thou shalt put none in thy [2]vessel.

25 When thou comest unto thy neighbor's corn, [d]thou mayest pluck the ears with thine hand, but thou shalt not move a sickle to thy neighbor's corn.

24

1 *Divorcement is permitted.* 5 *He that is newly married is exempted from war.* 6 *Of the pledge.* 14 *Wages must not be retained.* 16 *The good must not be punished for the bad.* 17 *The care of the stranger, fatherless, and widow.*

1 When a man taketh a wife, and marrieth her, if so be she find no favor in his eyes, because he hath espied some filthiness in her, [1]then let him write her a bill of divorcement, and put it in her hand, and send her out of his house.

2 And when she is departed out of his house, and gone her way, and marry with another man,

3 And if the latter husband hate her, and write her a letter of divorcement, and put it in her hand, and send her out of his house, or if the latter man die which took her to wife:

4 *Then* her first husband, which sent her away, may not take her again to be his wife, after that she is [1]defiled: for that *is* abomination in the sight of the Lord, and thou shalt not cause the land to sin, which the Lord thy God doth give thee to inherit.

5 ¶ When a man taketh a new wife, he shall not go a warfare, [1]neither shall be charged with any business, but shall be free at home one year, and rejoice with his wife, which he hath taken.

6 ¶ No man shall take the nether nor the upper [1]millstone to pledge: for this gage is *his* living.

7 ¶ If any man be found stealing any of his brethren of the children of Israel, and maketh merchandise of him, or selleth him, that thief shall die: so shalt thou put evil away from among you.

8 ¶ Take heed of the [a]plague of leprosy, that thou observe diligently, and do according to all that the Priests of the Levites shall teach you: take heed ye do as I commanded them.

9 Remember what the Lord thy God did unto [b]Miriam by the way after that ye were come out of Egypt.

10 When thou shalt ask again of thy neighbor anything lent, thou shalt not go [1]into his house to fet his pledge.

11 But thou shalt stand without, and the man that borrowed it of thee, shall bring the pledge out of the doors unto thee.

12 Furthermore if it be a poor body, thou shalt not sleep with his pledge,

13 *But* shalt restore him the pledge when the sun goeth down, that he may sleep in his raiment, and bless thee: and it shall be righteousness unto thee [1]before the Lord thy God.

14 ¶ Thou shalt not oppress an hired servant that is needy and poor, *neither* of thy brethren nor of the stranger that is in thy land within thy gates.

15 ℂThou shalt give him his hire for his day, neither shall the sun go down upon it: for he is poor, and therewith sustaineth his life: lest he cry against thee

c Exod. 22:24
Lev. 25:36
d Matt. 12:1

CHAPTER 24
a Lev. 13:2
b Num. 12:20
c Lev. 10:13

23:16 [1] Hebrew, *gates.*

23:18 [1] Forbidding hereby that any gain gotten of evil things should be applied to the service of God, Mic. 2:7.

23:20 [1] This was permitted for a time for the hardness of their hearts.
  [2] If thou show thy charity to thy brother, God will declare his love toward thee.

23:23 [1] If the vow be lawful and godly.

23:24 [1] Being hired for to labor.
  [2] To bring home to thine house.

24:1 [1] Hereby God approveth not that light divorcement, but permitteth it to avoid further inconvenience, Matt. 19:7.

24:4 [1] Seeing that by dimitting her, he judged her to be unclean and defiled.

24:5 [1] That they might learn to know one another's conditions, and so afterward live in godly peace.

24:6 [1] Not anything whereby a man getteth his living.

24:10 [1] As though thou wouldest appoint what to have, but shalt receive what he may spare.

24:13 [1] Though he would be unthankful, yet God will not forget it.

unto the Lord, and it be sin unto thee.

16 ¶ [d]The fathers shall not be put to death for the children, nor the children put to death for the fathers, but every man shall be put to death for his own sin.

17 Thou shalt not pervert the right of the [1]stranger, *nor* of the fatherless, nor take a widow's raiment to pledge.

18 But remember that thou wast a servant in Egypt, and how the Lord thy God delivered thee thence. Therefore I command thee to do this thing.

19 ¶ [e]When thou cuttest down thine harvest in thy field, and hast forgotten a sheaf in the field, thou shalt not go again to fet it, *but* it shall be for the stranger, for the fatherless, and for the widow: that the Lord thy God may bless thee in all the works of thine hands.

20 When thou [1]beatest thine olive tree, thou shalt not go over the boughs again, *but* it shall be for the stranger, for the fatherless, and for the widow.

21 When thou gatherest thy [1]vineyard, thou shalt not gather the grapes clean after thee, *but* they shall be for the stranger, for the fatherless, and for the widow.

22 And remember that thou wast [1]a servant in the land of Egypt: therefore I command thee to do this thing.

25

3 *The beating of the offenders.*   5 *To raise up seed to the kinsmen.*   11 *In what case a woman's hand must be cut off.*   13 *Of just weights and measures.*   19 *To destroy the Amalekites.*

1 When there shall be strife between men, and they shall come unto judgment, [1]and sentence shall be given upon them, and the righteous shall be justified, and the wicked condemned:

2 Then if so be the wicked be worthy to be beaten, the judge shall cause him to lie down, [1]and to be beaten before his face, according to his trespass unto a certain number.

3 [1]Forty *stripes* shall he cause him to have, and not past, lest if he should exceed and beat him above that with many stripes, thy brother should appear despised in thy sight.

4 ¶ [a]Thou shalt not muzzle the ox that treadeth out the corn.

5 ¶ [b]If brethren dwell together, and one of them

die and have no son, the wife of the dead shall not marry without, *that is*, unto a stranger, but his [1]kinsman shall go in unto her, and take her to wife, and do the kinsman's office to her.

6 And the firstborn which she beareth, shall succeed in the name of his brother which is dead, that his name be not put out of Israel.

7 And if the man will not take his kinswoman, then let his kinswoman go up to the gate unto the Elders, and say, My kinsman refuseth to raise up unto his brother a name in Israel: he will not do the office of a kinsman unto me.

8 Then the Elders of the city shall call him, and commune with him: if he stand and say, I will not take her,

9 Then shall his kinswoman come unto him in the presence of the Elders, and loose his shoe from his foot, and spit in his face, and answer and say, So shall it be done unto that man that will not build up his brother's house.

10 And his name shall be called in Israel, The house of him whose shoe is put off.

11 ¶ [1]When men strive together, one with another, if the wife of the one come near, for to rid her husband out of the hands of him that smiteth him, and put forth her hand, and take him by his privities,

12 Then thou shalt cut off her hand: thine eye shall not spare her.

13 ¶ Thou shalt not have in thy bag two manner of [1]weights, a great and a small:

14 Neither shalt thou have in thine house divers [1]measures, a great and a small:

15 *But* thou shalt have a right and just weight: a perfect and a just measure shalt thou have, that thy days may be lengthened in the land, which the Lord thy God giveth thee.

16 For all that do such things, *and* all that do unrighteously, *are* abomination unto the Lord thy God.

17 [c]Remember what Amalek did unto thee by the way, when ye were come out of Egypt:

18 How he met thee by the way, and smote the hindmost of you, all that were feeble behind thee, when thou wast fainted and weary, and he feared not God.

19 Therefore, when the Lord thy God hath given thee rest from all thine enemies round about in the land which the Lord thy God giveth thee for an

---

[d] 2 Kings 14:6
2 Chron. 25:4
Jer. 31:29,30
Ezek. 18:20
[e] Lev. 19:9
Lev. 23:22

CHAPTER 25
[a] 1 Cor. 9:9
1 Tim. 5:18
[b] Ruth 4:3
Matt. 22:24
Mark 12:19
Luke 20:28
[c] Exod. 17:4

24:17 [1] Because the world did least esteem these sorts of people, therefore God hath most care over them.
24:20 [1] Or, gatherest thine olives.
24:21 [1] Or, the grapes of thy vineyard.
24:22 [1] God judged them not mindful of his benefit, except they were beneficial unto others.
25:1 [1] Whether there be a plaintiff or none, the magistrates ought to try our faults, and punish according to the crime.
25:2 [1] When the crime deserveth not death.
25:3 [1] The Jews of superstition afterward took one away, 2 Cor. 11:24.
25:5 [1] Because the Hebrew word signifieth not the natural brother, and the word that signifieth a brother, is taken also for a kinsman: it seemeth that it is not meant that the natural brother should marry his brother's wife, but some other of the kindred that was in that degree which might marry.
25:11 [1] This law importeth that godly shamefastness be preserved: for it is an horrible thing to see a woman past shame.
25:13 [1] Hebrew, *stone and stone*.
25:14 [1] Hebrew, *Ephah and Ephah*, read Exod. 12:6.

inheritance to possess it, *then* thou shalt put out the [1]remembrance of Amalek from under heaven: forget not.

26

3 The offering of the firstfruits.   5 What they must protest when they offer them.   12 The [tithe] of the first year.   13 Their protestation in offering it.   19 To what honor God preferreth them which acknowledge him to be their Lord.

1 Also when thou shalt come into the land which the Lord thy God giveth thee for inheritance, and shalt possess it, and dwell therein,

2 [1]Then shalt thou take of the first of all the fruit of the earth, and bring it out of the land that the Lord thy God giveth thee, and put it in a basket, and go unto the place which the Lord thy God shall choose, to [2]place his name there.

3 And thou shalt come unto the Priest, that shall be in those days, and say unto him, I acknowledge this day unto the Lord thy God, that I am come unto the country which the Lord sware unto our fathers for to give us.

4 Then the Priest shall take the basket out of thine hand, and set it down before the altar of the Lord thy God.

5 And thou shalt answer and say before the Lord thy God, A [1]Syrian *was* my father, who being ready to perish *for hunger*, went down into Egypt, and sojourned there with a small company and grew there unto a nation great, mighty [2]and full of people.

6 And the Egyptians vexed us, and troubled us, and laded us with cruel bondage.

7 But when we [1]cried unto the Lord God of our fathers, the Lord heard our voice, and looked on our adversity, and on our labor, and on our oppression:

8 And the Lord brought us out of Egypt in a mighty hand, and stretched out arm, with great terribleness, both in signs and wonders.

9 And he hath brought us into this place, and hath given us this land, *even* a land that floweth with milk and honey.

10 And now, lo, I have [1]brought the firstfruits of the land, which thou, O Lord, hast given me, and thou shalt set it before the Lord thy God, and worship before the Lord thy God:

CHAPTER 26
a Deut. 14:27
b Deut. 7:6
Deut. 14:2
c Deut. 4:7
Deut. 28:1
d Deut. 7:6
Deut. 14:2

11 And thou shalt rejoice in all the good things which the Lord thy God hath given unto thee, and to thine [1]household, thou and the Levite, and the stranger that is among you.

12 ¶ When thou hast made an end of tithing all the tithes of thine increase, the third year, *which is* the year of tithing, and hast given it unto the Levite, to the stranger, to the fatherless, and to the widow, that they may eat within thy gates, and be satisfied,

13 Then thou shalt [1]say before the Lord thy God, I have brought the hallowed thing out of mine house, and also have given it to the Levites and to the strangers, to the fatherless and to the widow, according to all thy *a*commandments which thou hast commanded me: I have [2]transgressed none of the commandments, nor forgotten *them*,

14 I have not eaten thereof in my [1]mourning, nor suffered ought to perish [2]through uncleanness, nor given ought thereof for the dead, *but* have hearkened unto the voice of the Lord my God: I have done [3]after all that thou hast commanded me.

15 Look down from thine holy habitation, *even* from heaven, and bless thy people Israel, and the land which thou hast given us (as thou swarest unto our fathers) the land that floweth with milk and honey.

16 ¶ This day the Lord thy God doth command thee to do these ordinances and laws: keep them therefore, and do them with [1]all thine heart, and with all thy soul.

17 Thou hast set up the Lord this day to be thy God, and to walk in his ways, and to keep his ordinances, and his commandments, and his laws, and to hearken unto his voice.

18 [1]And the Lord hath set thee up this day, to be a *b*precious people unto him (as he hath promised thee) and that thou shouldest keep all his commandments.

19 And to make thee *c*high above all nations (which he hath made) in praise, and in name, and in glory, *d*and that thou shouldest be an holy people unto the Lord thy God, as he hath said.

27

2 They are commanded to write the law upon stones for a remembrance.   5 Also to build an altar.   13 The cursings are given on mount Ebal.

25:19 [1] This was partly accomplished by Saul, about 450 years afterward.

26:2 [1] By this ceremony they acknowledged that they received the land of Canaan as a free gift of God.

[2] To be called upon, served and worshipped spiritually, Deut. 12:5.

26:5 [1] Meaning, Jacob, who served 20 years in Syria.

[2] Only by God's mercy, and not by their fathers' deservings.

26:7 [1] Alleging the promises made unto our fathers, Abraham, Isaac, and Jacob.

26:10 [1] In token of a thankful heart, and mindful of this benefit.

26:11 [1] Signifying that God giveth us not goods for ourselves only,

but for their uses also which are committed to our charge.

26:13 [1] Without hypocrisy.

[2] Of malice and contempt.

26:14 [1] Or, for any necessity.

[2] By putting them to any profane use.

[3] As far as my sinful nature would suffer: for else, as David and Paul say, there is not one just, Ps. 24:3; Rom. 3:10.

26:16 [1] With a good and simple conscience.

26:18 [1] Signifying that there is a mutual bond between God and his people.

1 Then Moses with the Elders of Israel [1]commanded the people, saying, Keep all the commandments, which I command you this day.

2 And when ye shall pass *over Jordan unto the land which the Lord thy God giveth thee, thou shalt set thee up great stones, and plaster them with plaster,

3 [1]And shalt write upon them all the words of this Law, when thou shalt come over, that thou mayest go into the land which the Lord thy God giveth thee: a land that floweth with milk and honey, as the Lord God of thy fathers hath promised thee.

4 Therefore when ye shall pass over Jordan, ye shall set up these stones, which I command you this day in mount Ebal, and thou shalt plaster them with plaster.

5 [b]And there shalt thou build unto the Lord thy God an altar, *even* an altar of stones: thou shalt lift none [1]iron *instrument* upon them.

6 Thou shalt make the altar of the Lord thy God of whole stones, and offer burnt offerings thereon unto the Lord thy God.

7 And thou shalt offer peace offerings, and shalt eat there and rejoice before the Lord thy God:

8 And thou shalt write upon the stones all the words of this Law, [1]well and plainly.

9 ¶ And Moses and the Priests of the Levites, spake unto all Israel, saying, Take heed and hear, O Israel: this day thou art become the people of the Lord thy God.

10 Thou [1]shalt hearken therefore unto the voice of the Lord thy God, and do his commandments and his ordinances, which I command thee this day.

11 ¶ And Moses charged the people the same day, saying,

12 These shall stand upon mount Gerizim, to bless the people when ye shall pass over Jordan: Simeon, and Levi, and Judah, and Issachar, and [1]Joseph, and Benjamin.

13 And these shall stand upon mount Ebal, to [1]curse: Reuben, Gad, and Asher, and Zebulun, Dan, and Naphtali.

14 And the Levites shall answer and say unto all the men of Israel with a loud voice,

CHAPTER 27
a Josh. 4:1
b Exod. 20:25
Josh. 8:31
c Ezek. 22:12
d Gal. 3:10

CHAPTER 28
a Lev. 26:3

15 ¶ Cursed be the man that shall make any carved or molten [1]image, *which is* an abomination unto the Lord, the work of the hands of the craftsman, and putteth it in a secret place: And all the people shall answer and say: So be it.

16 Cursed be he that [1]curseth his father and his mother: And all the people shall say: So be it.

17 Cursed be he that removeth his neighbor's [1]mark: And all the people shall say: So be it.

18 Cursed be he that maketh the [1]blind go out of the way: And all the people shall say: So be it.

19 Cursed be he that hindereth the right of the stranger, the fatherless, and the widow: And all the people say: So be it.

20 Cursed be he that lieth with his father's wife: for he hath uncovered his father's [1]skirt: And all the people say: So be it.

21 Cursed be he that lieth with any beast: And all the people shall say: So be it.

22 Cursed be he that lieth with his sister, the daughter of his father, or the daughter of his mother: And all the people shall say: So be it.

23 Cursed be he that lieth with his [1]mother-in-law: And all the people shall say: So be it.

24 Cursed be he that smiteth his neighbor [1]secretly: And all the people shall say: So be it.

25 [c]Cursed be he that taketh a reward to put to death innocent blood: And all the people shall say: So be it.

26 [d]Cursed be he that confirmeth not all the words of this Law, to do them: And all the people shall say: So be it.

28

1 *The promises to them that obey the Commandments.* 15 *The threatenings to the contrary.*

1 If [a]thou shalt obey diligently the voice of the Lord thy God, and observe and do all his commandments, which I command thee this day, then the Lord thy God will [1]set thee on high above all the nations of the earth.

2 And all these blessings shall come on thee, and [1]overtake thee, if thou shalt obey the voice of the Lord thy God.

3 Blessed shalt thou be in the [1]city, and blessed

27:1 [1] As God's minister and charged with the same.
27:3 [1] God would that his Law should be set up in the borders of the land of Canaan, that all that looked thereon might know that the land was dedicated to his service.
27:5 [1] The altar should not be curiously wrought, because it should continue but for a time: for God would have but one altar in Judah.
27:8 [1] That everyone may well read it, and understand it.
27:10 [1] This condition hath bound thee unto, that if thou wilt be his people, thou must keep his laws.
27:12 [1] Meaning, Ephraim and Manasseh.
27:13 [1] Signifying, that if they would not obey God for love, they should be made to obey for fear.

27:15 [1] Under this he containeth all the corruptions of God's service, and the transgression of the first Table.
27:16 [1] Or, contemneth: and this appertaineth to the second Table.
27:17 [1] He condemneth all injuries and extortions.
27:18 [1] Meaning, that helpeth not and counselleth not his neighbor.
27:20 [1] In committing villiany against him, Lev. 20:11; Deut. 22:30; Ezek. 22:10.
27:23 [1] Meaning, his wife's mother.
27:24 [1] For God that seeth in secret, will revenge it.
28:1 [1] He will make thee the most excellent of all people.
28:2 [1] When thou thinkest thyself forsaken.
28:3 [1] Thou shalt live wealthily.

also in the field.

4 Blessed shall be the fruit [1]of thy body, and the fruit of thy ground, and the fruit of thy cattle, the increase of thy kine, and the flocks of thy sheep.

5 Blessed shall be thy basket and thy dough.

6 Blessed shalt thou be when thou [1]comest in, and blessed also when thou goest out.

7 The Lord shall cause thine enemies that rise against thee, to fall before thy face: they shall come out against thee one way, and shall flee before thee [1]seven ways.

8 The Lord shall command the blessing to be with thee in thy store houses, and in all that thou settest thine [1]hand to, and will bless thee in the land which the Lord thy God giveth thee.

9 The Lord shall make thee an holy people unto himself, as he hath sworn unto thee, if thou shalt keep the commandments of the Lord thy God, and walk in his ways,

10 Then all people of the earth shall see that the Name of the Lord is [1]called upon over thee, and they shall be afraid of thee.

11 And the Lord shall make thee plenteous in goods, in the fruit of thy body, and in the fruit of thy cattle, and in the fruit of thy ground, in the land which the Lord swore unto thy fathers, to give thee.

12 The Lord shall open unto thee his good treasure, even the [1]heaven to give rain unto thy land in due season, and to bless all the work of thine hands: and [b]thou shalt lend unto many nations, but shalt not borrow thyself.

13 And the Lord shall make thee the head, and not the [1]tail, and thou shalt be above only, and shalt not be beneath, if thou obey the commandments of the Lord thy God which I command thee this day, to keep and to do them.

14 But thou shalt not decline from any of the words, which I command you this day, either to the ʿright hand or to the left, to go after other gods to serve them.

15 ¶ [d]But if thou wilt not obey the voice of the Lord thy God, to keep and to do all his commandments, and his ordinances, which I command thee this day, then all these curses shall come upon thee,

[b] Deut. 15:6
[c] Josh. 23:6
[d] Lev. 26:14
Lam. 2:17
Mal. 2:2
[e] Lev. 26:16

and overtake thee.

16 Cursed shalt thou be in the town, and cursed also in the field.

17 Cursed shall thy basket be, and thy [1]dough.

18 Cursed shall be the fruit of thy body, and the fruit of thy land, the increase of thy kine, and the flocks of thy sheep.

19 Cursed shalt thou be when thou comest in, and cursed also when thou goest out.

20 The Lord shall send upon thee cursing, trouble, and [1]shame, in all that which thou settest thine hand to do, until thou be destroyed, and perish quickly, because of the wickedness of thy works, whereby thou hast forsaken me.

21 The Lord shall make the pestilence cleave unto thee, until he hath consumed thee from the land, whither thou goest to possess it.

22 ʿThe Lord shall smite thee with a consumption, and with the fever, and with a burning ague, and with fervent heat, and with the sword, and with [1]blasting, and with the mildew, and they shall pursue thee until thou perish.

23 And thine heaven that is over thine head, shall be [1]brass, and the earth that is under thee, iron.

24 The Lord shall give thee for the rain of thy land, dust and ashes: even from [1]heaven shall it come down upon thee, until thou be destroyed.

25 And the Lord shall cause thee to fall before thine enemies: thou shalt come out one way against them, and shalt flee seven ways before them, and shalt be [1]scattered through all the kingdoms of the earth.

26 And thy [1]carcass shall be meat unto all fowls of the air, and unto the beasts of the earth, and none shall fray them away.

27 The Lord will smite thee with the botch of Egypt, and with the hemorrhoids, and with the scab, and with the itch, that thou canst not be healed.

28 And the Lord shall smite thee with madness, and with blindness, and with atoning of heart.

29 Thou shalt also grope at noon days, as the [1]blind gropeth in darkness, and shalt not prosper in thy ways: thou shalt never but be oppressed with wrong, and be powled evermore, and no man shall succor thee.

30 Thou shalt betroth a wife, and another man

28:4 [1] Thy children and succession.
28:6 [1] All thine enterprises shall have good success.
28:7 [1] Meaning, many ways.
28:8 [1] God will bless us, if we do our duty, and not be idle.
28:10 [1] In that he is thy God, and thou art his people.
28:12 [1] For nothing in the earth is profitable but when God sendeth his blessings from heaven.
28:13 [1] Or, the lowest
28:17 [1] Or, store.
28:20 [1] Or, rebuke.

28:22 [1] Or, drought.
28:23 [1] It shall give thee no more moisture than if it were of brass.
28:24 [1] Or, out of the air as dust raised with wind.
28:25 [1] Some read, thou shalt be a terror and fear, when they shall hear how God hath plagued thee.
28:26 [1] Thou shalt be cursed both in thy life and in thy death: for the burial is a testimony of the resurrection which sign for thy wickedness thou shalt lack.
28:29 [1] In things most evident and clear thou shalt lack discretion and judgment.

shall lie with her: thou shalt build an house, and shalt not dwell therein: thou shalt plant a vineyard, and shalt not [1]eat the fruit.

31 Thine ox shall be slain before thine eyes, and thou shalt not eat thereof: thine ass shall be violently taken away before thy face, and shall not be restored to thee: thy sheep shall be given unto thine enemies, and no man shall rescue *them* for thee.

32 Thy sons and thy daughters shall be given unto another people, and thine eyes [1]shall still look for them, even till they fall out, and there shall be no power in thine hand.

33 The fruit of thy land and all thy labors shall a people which thou knowest not, eat, and thou shalt never but suffer wrong, and violence always:

34 So that thou shalt be mad for the sight which thine eyes shall see.

35 The Lord shall smite thee in the knees, and in the thighs, with a sore botch, that thou canst not be healed: even from the sole of the foot unto the top of thine head.

36 The Lord shall bring thee and thy [1]King (which thou shalt set over thee) unto a nation, which neither thou nor thy fathers have known, and there thou shalt serve other gods: *even* wood and stone,

37 And thou shalt *f*be a wonder, a proverb and a common talk among all people, whither the Lord shall carry thee.

38 Thou shalt carry out much seed into the field, and shalt gather but little in: for the grasshoppers shall destroy it.

39 *g*Thou shalt plant a vineyard, and dress it, but shalt neither drink of the wine, nor gather *the grapes*: for the worms shall eat it.

40 Thou shalt have Olive trees in all thy coasts, but shalt not anoint thyself with the oil: for thine olives shall [1]fall.

41 Thou shalt beget sons and daughters, but shalt not have them: for they shall go into captivity.

42 All thy trees and fruit of thy land [1]shall the grasshopper consume.

43 The stranger that is among you, shall climb above thee up on high, and thou shalt come down beneath alow.

44 He shall lend thee, and thou shalt not lend him: he shall be the head, and thou shalt be the tail.

45 Moreover, all these curses shall come upon thee, and shall pursue thee and overtake thee, till thou be

f Jer. 24:9
Jer. 25:9
1 Kings 9:7
g Mic. 6:15
Hag. 1:6
h Lev. 26:29
2 Kings 6:29
Lam. 4:10
i Deut. 15:9

destroyed, because thou obeyedst not the voice of the Lord thy God, to keep his commandments, and his ordinances, which he commanded thee:

46 And they shall be upon [1]thee for signs and wonders, and upon thy seed forever,

47 Because thou servedst not the Lord thy God with joyfulness, and with a good heart, for the abundance of all things.

48 Therefore thou shalt serve thine enemies which the Lord shall send upon thee, in hunger and in thirst, and in nakedness, and in need of all things: and he shall put a yoke of iron upon thy neck until he have destroyed thee.

49 The Lord shall bring a nation upon thee from far, *even* from the end of the world, flying *swift* as an eagle: a nation whose tongue thou shalt not understand:

50 A nation of a [1]fierce countenance, which will not regard the person of the old, nor have compassion of the young.

51 The same shall eat the fruit of thy cattle, and the fruit of thy land, until thou be destroyed, and he shall leave thee neither wheat, wine, nor oil, *neither* the [1]increase of thy kine, nor the flocks of thy sheep, until he have brought thee to naught.

52 And he shall besiege thee in all thy cities, until thine high and strong walls fall down, wherein thou trustedst in all the land: and he shall besiege thee in all thy [1]cities throughout all thy land, which the Lord thy God hath given thee.

53 [h]And thou shalt eat the fruit of thy body, *even* the flesh of thy sons and thy daughters, which the Lord thy God hath given thee, during the siege and straitness wherein thine enemies shall enclose thee:

54 *So that* the man (that is tender and exceeding dainty among you,) [i]shall be grieved at his brother, and at his wife *that lieth* in his bosom, and at the remnant of his children, which he hath yet left,

55 For fear of giving unto any of them of the flesh of his children, whom he shall eat, because he hath nothing left him in that siege, and straitness, wherewith thine enemy shall besiege thee in all thy cities.

56 The tender and dainty [1]woman among you, which never would venture to set the sole of her foot upon the ground (for her softness and tenderness) shall be grieved at her husband *that lieth* in her bosom, and at her son, and at her daughter,

57 And at her [1]afterbirth (that shall come out

28:30 [1] Hebrew, *make it common.*
28:32 [1] When they shall return from their captivity.
28:36 [1] As he did Manasseh, Jehoiakim, Zedekiah and others.
28:40 [1] Or, be shaken before they be ripe.
28:42 [1] Under one kind he containeth all the vermin, which destroy the fruits of the land: and this is an evident token of God's curse.
28:46 [1] God's plagues be evident signs that he is offended with thee.

28:50 [1] Or, barbarous, cruel or impudent.
28:51 [1] Or, firstborn of thy bullock.
28:52 [1] Or, gates.
28:56 [1] As came to pass in the days of Joram king of Israel, 2 Kings 6:20, and when the Romans besieged Jerusalem.
28:57 [1] Hunger shall so bite her, that she shall be ready to eat her child before it be delivered.

from between her feet) and at her children, which she shall bear: for when all things lack, she shall eat them secretly, during the siege and straightness wherewith thine enemy shall besiege thee in thy cities.

58 ¶ If thou wilt not keep and do ¹all the words of the Law (that are written in this book) and fear this glorious and fearful Name, THE LORD THY GOD,

59 Then the Lord will make thy plagues wonderful, and the plagues of thy seed, *even* great plagues, and of long continuance, and sore diseases and of long durance.

60 Moreover, he will bring upon thee all the diseases of Egypt, whereof thou wast afraid, and they shall cleave unto thee.

61 And every sickness, and every plague, which is not ¹written in the book of this Law, will the Lord heap upon thee, until thou be destroyed.

62 And ye shall be left few in number, where ye were as the ʲstars of heaven in multitude, because thou wouldest not obey the voice of the Lord thy God.

63 And as the Lord hath rejoiced over you, to do you good, and to multiply you, so he will rejoice over you, to destroy you, and bring you to naught, and ye shall be rooted out of the land, whither thou goest to possess it.

64 And the Lord shall ¹scatter thee among all people from the one end of the world unto the other, and there thou shalt serve other gods, which thou hast not known, nor thy fathers, *even* wood and stone.

65 Also among these nations thou shalt find no rest, neither shall the sole of thy foot have rest: for the Lord shall give thee there a trembling heart, and *looking to return* till thine eyes fall out, and a sorrowful mind.

66 And thy life shall ¹hang before thee, and thou shalt fear both night and day, and shalt have none assurance of thy life.

67 In the morning thou shalt say, Would God it were evening, and at the evening thou shalt say, Would God it were morning, for the fear of thine heart, which thou shalt fear, and for the sight of thine eyes, which thou shalt see.

68 And the Lord shall bring thee into Egypt again

ʲ Deut. 10:22

CHAPTER 29
ᵃ Deut. 4:6
1 Kings 2:3

with ¹ships by the way, whereof I said unto thee, Thou shalt see it no more again: and there ye shall sell yourselves unto your enemies for bondmen and bondwomen, and there *shall be* no buyer.

29 2 *The people are exhorted to observe the commandments.* 10 *The whole people from the highest to the lowest are comprehended under God's covenant.* 19 *The punishment of him that flattereth himself in his wickedness.* 24 *The cause of God's wrath against his people.*

1 These are the ¹words of the covenant which the Lord commandeth Moses to make with the children of Israel, in the land of Moab, beside the covenant which he had made with them in ²Horeb.

2 ¶ And Moses called all Israel, and said unto them, Ye have seen all that the Lord did before your eyes in the land of Egypt unto Pharaoh and unto all his servants, and unto all his land,

3 The ¹great tentations which thine eyes have seen, those great miracles and wonders:

4 Yet the Lord hath not ¹given you an heart to perceive, and eyes to see, and ears to hear, unto this day.

5 And I have led you forty years in the wilderness: your clothes are not waxed old upon you, neither is thy shoe waxed old upon thy foot.

6 Ye have eaten no ¹bread, neither drunk wine, nor strong drink, that ye might know how that I am the Lord your God.

7 After, ye came unto this place, and Sihon King of Heshbon, and Og King of Bashan came out against us unto battle, and we slew them,

8 And took their land, and gave it for an inheritance unto the Reubenites, and to the Gadites, and to the half tribe of Manasseh.

9 ᵃKeep therefore the words of this covenant and do them, that ye may prosper in all that ye shall do.

10 Ye stand this day everyone of you before the Lord your ¹God: your heads of your tribes, your Elders and your officers, *even* all the men of Israel:

11 Your children, your wives, and thy stranger that is in thy camp, from the hewer of thy wood, unto the drawer of thy water,

12 That thou shouldest ¹pass into the covenant of the Lord thy God, and into his oath which the

28:58 ¹ For he that offendeth in one, is guilty of all, James 2:10.
28:61 ¹ Declaring, that God hath infinite means to plague the wicked, besides them that are ordinary or written.
28:64 ¹ Signifying that it is a singular gift of God to be in a place whereas we may worship God purely, and declare our faith and religion.
28:66 ¹ Or, thou shall be in doubt of thy life.
28:68 ¹ Because they were unmindful of that miracle, when the Sea gave place for them to pass through.
29:1 ¹ That is, the articles, or conditions.

² At the first giving of the law, which was forty years before.
29:3 ¹ The proofs of my power.
29:4 ¹ He showeth that it is not in man's power to understand the mysteries of God, if it be not given him from above.
29:6 ¹ Made by man's art, but Manna, which is called the bread of Angels.
29:10 ¹ Who knoweth your hearts, and therefore ye may not think to dissemble with him.
29:12 ¹ Alluding to them, that when they made a sure covenant, divided a beast in twain, and passed between the parts divided, Gen. 15:10.

Lord thy God maketh with thee this day,

13 For to establish thee this day a people unto himself, and that he may be unto thee a God, as he hath said unto thee, and as he hath sworn unto thy fathers, Abraham, Isaac, and Jacob.

14 Neither make I this covenant and this oath with you only,

15 But *as well* with him that standeth here with us this day before the Lord our God, as with him ¹that is not here with us this day.

16 For ye know, how we have dwelt in the land of Egypt, and how we passed through the midst of the nations, which ye passed by.

17 And ye have seen their abominations and their idols (wood and stone, silver and gold) which were among them,

18 That there should not be among you man nor woman, nor family, nor tribe, which should turn his heart away this day from the Lord our God, to go and serve the gods of these nations, *and* that there should not be among you ¹*any* root that bringeth forth ᵇgall and wormwood,

19 So that when he heareth the words of this curse, he ¹bless himself in his heart, saying, I shall have peace, although I walk according to the stubbornness of mine own heart, thus adding ²drunkenness to thirst.

20 The Lord will not be merciful unto him, but then the wrath of the Lord and his jealousy shall smoke against that man, and every curse that is written in this book, shall light upon him, and the Lord shall put out his name from under heaven.

21 And the Lord shall separate him unto evil out of all the tribes of Israel, according unto all the curses of the covenant, that is written in the book of this Law.

22 So that the ¹generation to come, *even* your children, that shall rise up after you, and the stranger that shall come from a far land, shall say, when they shall see the plagues of this land, and the diseases thereof, wherewith the Lord shall smite it:

23 (*For* all that land *shall* burn with brimstone and salt: it shall not be sown, nor bring forth, nor any grass shall grow therein, like as in the overthrowing of ᶜSodom and Gomorrah, Admah, and Zeboiim, which the Lord overthrew in his wrath and in his anger.)

24 Then shall all nations say, ᵈWherefore hath the

ᵇ Acts 8:23
ᶜ Gen. 19:24,25
ᵈ 1 Kings 9:8
Jer. 22:8

Lord done thus unto this land? how fierce is this great wrath?

25 And they shall answer, Because they have forsaken the covenant of the Lord God of their fathers, which he had made with them, when he brought them out of the land of Egypt,

26 And went and served other gods and worshipped them: *even* gods which they knew not, and ¹which had given them nothing,

27 Therefore the wrath of the Lord waxed hot against this land, to bring upon it every curse that is written in this book.

28 And the Lord hath rooted them out of their land in anger, and in wrath, and in great indignation, and hath cast them into another land, as *appeareth* this day.

29 The ¹secret things *belong* to the Lord our God, but the things revealed *belong* unto us, and to our children forever, that we may do all the words of this Law.

30 1 Mercy showed when they repent.   6 The Lord doth circumcise the heart.   11 All excuse of ignorance is taken away.   15, 19 Life and death is set before them.   20 The Lord is their life which obey him.

1 Now when all these things shall come upon thee, *either* the blessing or the curse which I have set before thee, and thou shalt ¹turn into thine heart, among all the nations whither the Lord thy God hath driven thee,

2 And shalt return unto the Lord thy God, and obey his voice in all that I command thee this day: thou, and thy children with all thine ¹heart and with all thy soul,

3 Then the Lord thy God will cause thy captives to return, and have compassion upon thee, and will return, to gather thee out of all the people where the Lord thy God hath scattered thee.

4 Though thou werest cast unto the utmost part of ¹heaven, from thence will the Lord thy God gather thee, and from thence will he ²take thee,

5 And the Lord thy God will bring thee into the land which thy fathers possessed, and thou shalt possess it, and he will show thee favor, and will multiply thee above thy fathers.

6 And the Lord thy God will ¹circumcise thine

29:15 ¹ Meaning, their posterity.
29:18 ¹ Such sin, as the bitter fruit thereof might choke and destroy you.
29:19 ¹ Or, flatter.
  ² For as he that is thirsty desireth to drink much, so he that followeth his appetites, seeketh by all means, and yet cannot be satisfied.
29:22 ¹ God's plagues upon them that rebel against him, shall be so strong, that all ages shall be astonished.
29:26 ¹ Or, which had not given them a land to possess.

29:29 ¹ Moses hereby proveth their curiosity, which seek those things that are only known to God: and their negligence that regard not that, which God hath revealed unto them, as the Law.
30:1 ¹ By calling to remembrance, both his mercies and plagues.
30:2 ¹ In true repentance is none hypocrisy.
30:4 ¹ Even to the world's end.
  ² And bring thee into thy country.
30:6 ¹ God will purge all thy wicked affections, which thing is not in thine own power to do.

heart, and the heart of thy seed, that thou mayest love the Lord thy God with all thine heart, and with all thy soul, that thou mayest live.

7 And the Lord thy God will lay all these curses upon thine enemies, and on them that hate thee, and that persecute thee.

8 ¹Return thou therefore, and obey the voice of the Lord, and do all his commandments, which I command thee this day.

9 And the Lord thy God will make thee plenteous in every work of thine hand, in the fruit of thy body, and in the fruit of thy cattle, and in the fruit of the land for thy wealth: for the Lord will turn again, and ¹rejoice over thee to do thee good, as he rejoiced over thy fathers,

10 Because thou shalt obey the voice of the Lord thy God, in keeping his commandments and his ordinances, which are written in the book of this law, when thou shalt return unto the Lord thy God with all thine heart and with all thy soul.

11 ¶ For this commandment which I command thee this day, is ¹not hid from thee, neither is it far off.

12 It is not in heaven, that thou shouldest say, ᵃWho shall go up for us to heaven, and bring it us, and cause us to hear it, that we may do it?

13 Neither is it beyond the ¹sea, that thou shouldest say, Who shall go over the sea for us, and bring it us, and cause us to hear it, that we may do it?

14 But the ¹word is very near unto thee: even in thy mouth, and in thine heart, for to ²do it.

15 Behold, I have set before thee this day life and good, death and evil,

16 In that I command thee this day, ¹to love the Lord thy God, to walk in his ways, and to keep his commandment, and his ordinances, and his laws, that thou mayest ²live, and be multiplied, and that the Lord thy God may bless thee in the land, whither thou goest to possess it.

17 But if thine heart turn away, so that thou wilt not obey, but shalt be seduced and worship other gods, and serve them,

18 I pronounce unto you this day, that ye shall surely perish, ye shall not prolong your days in the land, whither ye passest over Jordan to possess

CHAPTER 30
ᵃ Rom. 10:6
ᵇ Deut. 4:26

CHAPTER 31
ᵃ Num. 20:12
Deut. 3:26
ᵇ Num. 27:18
ᶜ Num. 21:24
ᵈ Deut. 7:2

it.

19 ᵇI call heaven and earth to record this day against you, *that* I have set before you life and death, blessing and cursing: therefore ¹choose life, that *both* thou and thy seed may live,

20 By loving the Lord thy God, by obeying his voice, and by cleaving unto him: for he is thy life, and the length of thy days, that thou mayest dwell in the land which the Lord sware unto thy fathers, Abraham, Isaac, and Jacob, to give them.

31

2, 7 Moses preparing himself to die, appointeth Joshua to rule the people. 9 He giveth the law to the Levites, that they should read it to the people. 19 God giveth them a song as a witness between him and them. 23 God confirmeth Joshua. 29 Moses showeth them that they will rebel after his death.

1 Then Moses went and spake these words unto all Israel,

2 And said unto them, I am an hundred and twenty years old this day: I ¹can no more go out and in: also the Lord hath said unto me, ᵃThou shalt not go over this Jordan.

3 The Lord thy God he will go over before thee: he will destroy these nations before thee, and thou shalt possess them. ᵇJoshua, he shall go before thee, as the Lord hath said.

4 And the Lord shall do unto them, as he did to ᶜSihon and to Og kings of the Amorites, and unto their land whom he destroyed.

5 And the Lord shall give them ¹before you, that ye may do unto them according unto every ᵈcommandment which I have commanded you.

6 Pluck ¹up your hearts therefore, and be strong: dread not, nor be afraid of them: for the Lord thy God himself doth go with thee: he will not fail thee, nor forsake thee.

7 ¶ And Moses called Joshua, and said unto him in the sight of all Israel, Be ¹of a good courage and strong: for thou shalt go with this people unto the land which the Lord hath sworn unto their fathers, to give them, and thou shalt give it them to inherit.

8 And the Lord himself doth ¹go before thee: he will be with thee: he will not fail thee, neither forsake thee: fear not *therefore*, nor be discomforted.

30:8 ¹ If we will have God to work in us with his holy Spirit, we must turn again to him by repentance.
30:9 ¹ He meaneth not that God is subject to these passions, to rejoice, or to be sad: but he useth this manner of speech to declare the love that he beareth unto us.
30:11 ¹ The Law is so evident that none can pretend ignorance.
30:13 ¹ By heaven and the sea he meaneth places most far distant.
30:14 ¹ Even the law and the Gospel.
² By faith in Christ.
30:16 ¹ So that to love and obey God, is only life and felicity.

² He addeth these promises to signify that it is for our profit that we love him, and not for his.
30:19 ¹ That is, love and obey God: which thing is not in man's power, but God's Spirit only worketh it in his elect.
31:2 ¹ I can no longer execute mine office.
31:5 ¹ Into your hands.
31:6 ¹ Or, be of good courage.
31:7 ¹ For he that must govern the people, hath need to be valiant to repress vice, and constant to maintain virtue.
31:8 ¹ Signifying that man can never be of good courage, except he be persuaded of God's favor and assistance.

9 ¶ And Moses wrote this Law, and delivered it unto the Priests the sons of Levi (which bare the Ark of the covenant of the Lord) and unto all the Elders of Israel.

10 And Moses commanded them, saying, 'Every seventh year *f*when the year of freedom *shall be* in the feast of the Tabernacles:

11 When all Israel shall come to appear [1]before the Lord thy God, and the place which he shall choose, thou shalt read this Law before all Israel that they may hear it.

12 Gather the people together: men, and women, and children, and thy stranger that is within thy gates, that they may hear, and that they may learn, and fear the Lord your God, and keep and observe all the words of this Law,

13 And that their children which [1]have not known it, may hear it, and learn to fear the Lord your God, as long as ye live in the land, whither ye go over Jordan to possess it.

14 ¶ Then the Lord said unto Moses, Behold, thy days are come, that thou must die: Call Joshua, and stand ye in the Tabernacle of the Congregation that I may give him a [1]charge. So Moses and Joshua went, and stood in the Tabernacle of the Congregation.

15 And the Lord appeared in the Tabernacle in the pillar of a [1]cloud: and the pillar of the cloud stood over the door of the Tabernacle.

16 ¶ And the Lord said unto Moses, Behold, thou shalt sleep with thy fathers, and this people will rise up, and go a whoring after the gods of a strange land (whither they go *to dwell* therein) and will forsake me: and break my covenant which I have made with them.

17 Wherefore my wrath will wax hot against them at that day, and I will forsake them, and will [1]hide my face from them: then they shall be consumed, and many adversities and tribulations shall come upon them: so then they will say, Are not these troubles come upon me, because God is not with me?

18 But I will surely hide my face in that day, because of all the evil which they shall commit, in that they are turned unto other gods.

19 Now therefore write ye this [1]song for you, and teach it the children of Israel: put it in their mouths, that this song may be my witness against the children of Israel.

20 For I will bring them into the land (which I

e Neh. 8:1
f Deut. 15:1
g Josh. 1:6

sware unto their fathers) that floweth with milk and honey: and they shall eat and fill themselves, and wax fat: [1]then shall they turn unto other gods, and serve them, and contemn me, and break my covenant.

21 And then when many adversities and tribulations shall come upon them, this song shall [1]answer them to their faces as a witness: for it shall not be forgotten out of the mouths of their posterity: for I know their imagination, which they go about even now, before I have brought them into the land which I sware.

22 ¶ Moses therefore wrote this song the same day, and taught it the children of Israel.

23 And *God* gave Joshua the son of Nun a charge, and said, *g*Be strong and of a good courage: for thou shalt bring the children of Israel into the land, which I sware unto them, and I will be with thee.

24 ¶ And when Moses had made an end of writing the words of this Law in a book until he had finished them,

25 Then Moses commanded the Levites, which bare the Ark of the covenant of the Lord, saying,

26 Take the book of this Law, and put ye it in the side of the Ark of the covenant of the Lord your God, that it may be there for a [1]witness against thee.

27 For I know thy rebellion and thy stiff neck: behold, I being yet alive with you this day, ye are rebellious against the Lord: how much more then after my death?

28 Gather unto me all the Elders of your tribes, and your [1]officers, that I may speak these words in their audience, and call heaven and earth to record against them.

29 For I am sure that after my death, ye will utterly be corrupt and turn from the way which I have commanded you: therefore evil will come upon you at the length, because ye will commit evil in the sight of the Lord, by provoking him to anger through the [1]work of your hands.

30 Thus Moses spake in the audience of all the Congregation of Israel the words of this song, until he had ended them.

32

The song of Moses containing   7 God's benefits toward the people,   15 and their ingratitude toward him.   20 God menaceth them,   21 and speaketh of the vocation of the Gentiles.   46 Moses commandeth to teach the Law to the children.   49 God forewarneth Moses of his death.

31:11 [1] Before the Ark of the covenant, which was the sign of God's presence, and the figure of Christ.

31:13 [1] Which were not born when the law was given.

31:14 [1] Or, commandment.

31:15 [1] In a cloud that was fashioned like a pillar.

31:17 [1] That is, I will take my favor from them: as to turn his face toward us, is to show us his favor.

31:19 [1] To preserve you and your children from idolatry, by remembering God's benefits.

31:20 [1] For this is the nature of flesh, no longer to obey God, than it is under the rod.

31:21 [1] That these evils are come upon them, because they forsook me.

31:26 [1] Of thine infidelity, when thou shalt turn away from the doctrine contained therein.

31:28 [1] As governors, judges and magistrates.

31:29 [1] By idolatry, and worshipping images, which are the work of your hands.

CHAPTER 32
ᵃ Rom. 10:19

1 Hearken, ye ¹heavens, and I will speak: and let the earth hear the words of my mouth.

2 My ¹doctrine shall drop as the rain, *and* my speech shall still as the dew, as the shower upon the herbs, and as the great rain upon the grass.

3 For I will publish the Name of the Lord: give ye glory unto our God.

4 Perfect is the work of the ¹mighty God: for all his ways *are* judgment. God is true, and without wickedness: just and righteous is he.

5 They have corrupted themselves toward him by their vice, not being his children, *but* a froward and crooked generation.

6 Do ye so reward the Lord, O foolish people and unwise? is not he thy father, that hath bought thee? he hath ¹made thee, and proportioned thee.

7 ¶ Remember the days of old: consider the years of so many generations: ask thy father, and he will show thee: thine Elders, and they will tell thee.

8 When the most high *God* divided to the nations their inheritance, when he separated the sons of Adam, he appointed the borders of the ¹people, according to the number of the children of Israel.

9 For the Lord's portion *is* his people: Jacob *is* the lot of his inheritance.

10 He found him in the land of the wilderness, in a waste and roaring wilderness: he led him about, he taught him, *and* kept him as the apple of his eye.

11 As an eagle stirreth up her nest, ¹fluttereth over her birds, stretcheth out her wings, taketh them *and* beareth them on her wings,

12 *So* the Lord alone led him, and there was no ¹strange god with him.

13 He carried him up to the high places of the ¹earth, that he might eat the fruits of the fields, and he caused him to suck ²honey out of the stone, and oil out of the hard rock:

14 Butter of kine, and milk of sheep with fat of the lambs, and rams fed in Bashan, and goats, with the fat of the grains of wheat: and the red ¹liquor of the grape hast thou drunk.

15 ¶ But *he that should have been* ¹upright, when he waxed fat, spurned with his heel: thou art fat, thou art gross, thou art laden with fatness: therefore he forsook God *that* made him, and regarded not the strong God of his salvation.

16 They provoked him with ¹strange *gods*: they provoked him to anger with abominations.

17 They offered unto devils, not to God, *but* to gods whom they knew not: ¹new *gods* that came newly up, whom their fathers feared not.

18 Thou hast forgotten the mighty God, *that* begat thee, and hast forgotten God that formed thee.

19 The Lord then saw it, and was angry, for the provocation of his ¹sons and of his daughters.

20 And he said, I will hide my face from them: I will see what their end shall be: for they are a froward generation, children in whom is no faith.

21 They have moved me to jealousy with *that which is* not God: they have provoked me to anger with their vanities: ᵃand I will move them to jealousy with *those which are* no ¹people: I will provoke them to anger with a foolish nation.

22 For fire is kindled in my wrath, and shall burn unto the bottom of hell, and shall consume the earth with her increase, and set on fire the foundations of the mountains.

23 I will spend plagues upon them: I will bestow mine arrows upon them.

24 *They shall be* burnt with hunger, and consumed with heat, and with bitter destruction: I will also send the teeth of beasts upon them, with the venom of serpents *creeping* in the dust.

25 The sword shall ¹kill them without, and in the chambers fear: both the young man and the young woman, the suckling with the man of gray hair.

26 I have said, I would scatter them abroad: I would make their remembrance to cease from among men,

27 Save that I feared the fury of the enemy, lest their adversaries should ¹wax proud, *and* lest they should say, Our high hand and not the Lord hath done all this.

28 For they are a nation void of counsel, neither is there *any* understanding in them.

29 Oh that they were wise, *then* they would under-

32:1 ¹ As witness of this people's ingratitude.

32:2 ¹ He desireth that he may speak to God's glory, and that the people, as the green grass, may receive the dew of his doctrine.

32:4 ¹ The Hebrew word is *rock*, noting that God only is mighty, faithful and constant in his promise.

32:6 ¹ Not according to the common creation, but he hath made thee a new creature by his Spirit.

32:8 ¹ When God by his providence divided the world, he lent for a time that portion to the Canaanites, which should after be an inheritance for all his people Israel.

32:11 ¹ To teach them to fly.

32:12 ¹ Or, god of strange nations.

32:13 ¹ Meaning, of the land of Canaan, which was high in respect of Egypt.

² That is, abundance of all things even in the very rocks.

32:14 ¹ Hebrew, *blood*.

32:15 ¹ He showeth what is the principal end of our vocation.

32:16 ¹ By changing his service for their superstitions.

32:17 ¹ Scripture calleth new, whatsoever man inventeth, be the error never so old.

32:19 ¹ He calleth them God's children, not to honor them, but to show them from what dignity they are fallen.

32:21 ¹ Which I have not favored, nor given my law unto them.

32:25 ¹ They shall be slain both in the field and at home.

32:27 ¹ Rejoicing to see the godly afflicted, and attributing that to themselves, which is wrought by God's hand.

stand this: they would [1]consider their latter end.

30 How should one chase a thousand, and two put ten thousand to flight, except their strong God had sold them, and the Lord had [1]shut them up?

31 For their god *is* not as our God, even our enemies being judges.

32 For their vine *is* of the vine of Sodom, and of the vines of Gomorrah: their grapes *are* grapes of gall, their clusters *be* bitter.

33 Their [1]wine *is* the poison of dragons, and the cruel gall of asps.

34 Is not this laid in store with me, *and* sealed up among my treasures?

35 [b]Vengeance and recompense are mine: their foot shall slide in due time: for the day of their destruction is at hand, and the things that shall come upon them, make haste.

36 For the Lord shall judge his people, and [1]repent toward his servants, when he seeth that their power is gone, and none [2]shut up *in hold* nor left *abroad*.

37 When men shall say, Where are their gods, their mighty God, in whom they trusted,

38 Which did eat the fat of their sacrifices, *and* did drink the wine of their drink offering? let them rise up, and help you: let him be your refuge.

39 Behold now, for I, I am he, and there is no gods with me: [c]I kill, and give life: I wound, and I make whole: neither is there *any* that can deliver out of mine hand.

40 For [1]I lift up mine hand to heaven, and say, I live forever.

41 If I whet my glittering sword, and mine hand take hold on judgment, I will execute vengeance on mine enemies, and will reward them that hate me.

42 I will make mine arrows drunk with blood, (and my sword shall eat flesh) for the blood of the slain, and of the captives, when I begin to take vengeance of the enemy.

43 [d]Ye nations, praise his people: for he will avenge the [1]blood of his servants, and will execute vengeance upon his adversaries, and will be merciful unto his land, *and* to his people.

44 ¶ Then Moses came and spake all the words of this song in the audience of the people, he and [1]Hoshea the son of Nun.

45 When Moses had made an end of speaking all these words to all Israel,

46 Then he said unto them, [e]Set your hearts unto all the words which I testify against you this day, that ye may command them unto your children, that they may observe and do all the words of this Law.

47 For it is no [1]vain word concerning you, but it is your life, and by this word ye shall prolong your days in the land, whither ye go over Jordan to possess it.

48 [f]And the Lord spake unto Moses the selfsame day, saying,

49 Go up into the mountain of Abarim, unto the mount Nebo, which is in the land of Moab, that is over against Jericho: and behold the land of Canaan, which I give unto the children of Israel for a possession,

50 And die in the mount which thou goest up unto, and thou shalt be [g]gathered unto thy people, [h]as Aaron thy brother died in mount Hor, and was gathered unto his people,

51 Because ye [i]trespassed against me among the children of Israel, at the waters [1]of Meribah, at Kadesh in the wilderness of Zin: for ye [2]sanctified me not among the children of Israel.

52 Thou shalt therefore see the land before thee, but shalt not go thither, *I mean*, into the land which I give the children of Israel.

33

1 *Moses before his death blesseth all the tribes of Israel.* 26 *There is no god like to the God of Israel:* 29 *Nor any people like unto his.*

1 Now this is the [1]blessing wherewith Moses the man of God blessed the children of Israel before his death, and said,

2 The Lord came from Sinai, and rose up from Seir unto them, *and* appeared clearly from mount Paran, and he came with ten [1]thousands of Saints, *and* at his right hand a fiery Law for them.

3 Though he love the people, *yet* [1]all thy Saints are in thine hands: and they are humbled at [2]thy feet, to receive thy words.

4 Moses commanded us a Law for an [1]inheritance of the Congregation of Jacob.

5 Then [1]he was among the [2]righteous *people, as* King, when the heads of the people, and the tribes of Israel were assembled.

Marginal references:
b Rom. 12:19 / Heb. 10:30
c 1 Sam. 2:6
d Rom. 15:10
e Deut. 6:6 / Deut. 11:18
f Num. 27:12
g Gen. 25:8
h Num. 20:25,28 / Num. 3:38
i Num. 20:12,13 / Num. 27:14

32:29 [1] They would consider the felicity, that was prepared for them, if they had obeyed God.
32:30 [1] Or, delivered them to their enemies.
32:33 [1] The fruits of the wicked are as poison, detestable to God, and dangerous for man.
32:36 [1] Or, change his mind.
  [2] When neither strong nor weak in a manner remain.
32:40 [1] That is, I swear, read Gen. 14:12.
32:43 [1] Whether the blood of God's people be shed for their sins or trial of their faith, he promiseth to revenge it.
32:44 [1] Or, Joshua.

32:47 [1] For I will perform my promise unto you, Isa. 55:10.
32:51 [1] Or, of strife.
  [2] Ye were not earnest and constant to maintain mine honor.
33:1 [1] This blessing containeth not only a simple prayer, but an assurance of the effect thereof.
33:2 [1] Meaning, infinite Angels.
33:3 [1] Hebrew, *his Saints*, that is, the children of Israel.
  [2] As thy disciples.
33:4 [1] To us and our successors.
33:5 [1] Or, Moses.
  [2] Or, Israel.

6 ¶ Let [1]Reuben live, and not die, though his men be a small number.

7 ¶ And thus *he blessed* Judah, and said, Hear, O Lord, the voice of Judah, and bring him unto his people: his hands shall be [1]sufficient for him, if thou help him against his enemies.

8 ¶ And of Levi he said, Let thy *a*Thummim and thine Urim be with thine Holy one, whom thou didst prove in Massah, *and* didst cause him to strive at the waters of Meribah.

9 Who said unto his father and to his mother, [1]I have not seen him, neither knew he his brethren, nor knew his own children: for they observed thy word, and kept thy Covenant.

10 They shall teach Jacob thy judgments, and Israel thy Law: they shall put incense before thy face, and the burnt offering upon thine Altar.

11 Bless, O Lord, his substance, and accept the work of his hands: [1]smite through the loins of them that rise against him, and of them that hate him, that they rise not again.

12 ¶ Of Benjamin he said, The beloved of the Lord shall [1]dwell in safety by him: *the Lord* shall cover him all the day long, and dwell between his shoulders.

13 ¶ And of Joseph he said, Blessed of the Lord is *his* land for the sweetness of heaven, for the dew, and for the [1]depth lying beneath,

14 And for the sweet increase of the Sun, and for the sweet increase of the Moon,

15 And for *thy sweetness* of the top of the ancient mountains, and for the sweetness of the old hills,

16 And for the sweetness of the earth, and abundance therefore: and the good will of him that dwelt in the [1]bush, shall come upon the head of Joseph, and upon the top of the head of him that was *b*separated *from* his brethren.

17 His beauty *shall be like* his firstborn bullock, and his [1]horns *as* the horns of an unicorn: with them he shall smite the people together, *even* the ends of the world: these are also the ten thousands of Ephraim, and these are the thousands of Manasseh.

18 ¶ And of Zebulun he said, Rejoice, Zebulun,

CHAPTER 33
a Exod. 28:30
b Gen. 49:26

in thy [1]going out, and *thou* Issachar in thy tents.

19 They shall call the people unto the [1]mountain: there they shall offer the sacrifices of righteousness: for [2]they shall suck of the abundance of the sea, and of the treasures hid in the sand.

20 ¶ Also of Gad he said, Blessed be he that enlargeth Gad: he dwelleth as a lion, that catcheth for his prey the arm with the head.

21 And he looked to himself at the beginning, because there was a portion of the [1]Law-giver hid: yet he shall come with the heads of the people, to execute the justice of the Lord, and his judgments with Israel.

22 ¶ And of Dan he said, Dan *is* a lion's whelp: he shall leap from Bashan.

23 ¶ Also of Naphtali he said, O Naphtali, satisfied with favor, and filled with the blessing of the Lord, possess [1]the West and the South.

24 ¶ And of Asher he said, Asher *shall be* blessed with children: he shall be acceptable unto his brethren, and shall dip his foot in oil.

25 Thy shoes *shall be* [1]iron and brass, and thy strength *shall continue* as long as thou livest.

26 ¶ There is none like God, O righteous *people*, which rideth upon the heavens for thine help, and on the clouds in his glory.

27 The eternal God *is thy* refuge, and under *his* arms thou art forever: he shall cast out the enemy before thee, and will say, Destroy *them*.

28 Then Israel [1]the fountain of Jacob shall dwell alone in safety in a land of wheat and wine: also his heavens shall drop the dew.

29 Blessed art thou, O Israel: who is like unto thee, O people saved by the Lord, the shield of thine help, and which is the sword of thy glory? therefore [1]thine enemies shall be in subjection to thee, and thou shalt tread upon their high places.

34

1 Moses seeth all the Land of Canaan.   5 He dieth.   8. Israel weepeth.   9 Joshua succeedeth in Moses' room.   10 The praise of Moses.

1 Then Moses went from the plain of Moab up into mount [1]Nebo unto the top of Pisgah that is

33:6 [1] Reuben shall be one of the tribes of God's people, though for his sin his honor be diminished, and his family but small.
33:7 [1] Signifying, that he should hardly obtain Jacob's promises, Gen. 49:8.
33:9 [1] He preferred God's glory to all natural affection, Exod. 32:29.
33:11 [1] He declareth that the ministers of God have many enemies, and therefore have need to be prayed for.
33:12 [1] Because the Temple should be built in Zion, which was in the tribe of Benjamin, he showeth that God should dwell with him there.
33:13 [1] Or, fountains.
33:16 [1] Which was God appearing unto Moses, Exod. 3:2.
33:17 [1] Or, strength.

33:18 [1] In thy prosperous voyages upon the Sea, Gen. 49:13.
33:19 [1] Or, mount Zion.
    [2] The tribe of Zebulun.
33:21 [1] So the portion of the Gadites, and others on this side Jordan was God's, though it was not so known.
33:23 [1] Meaning, near the sea.
33:25 [1] Thou shalt be strong, or thy country full of metal. It seemeth that Simeon is left out, because he was under Judah, and his portion of his inheritance, Josh. 19:9.
33:28 [1] Who was plentiful in issue as a fountain.
33:29 [1] Thine enemies for fear shall lie and fain to be in subjection.
34:1 [1] Which was a part of mount Abarim, Num. 27:12.

over against Jericho: and the Lord showed him [a]all the land of Gilead, unto Dan,

2   And all Naphtali and the land of Ephraim and Manasseh, and all the land of Judah, unto the utmost [1]sea:

3   And the South, and the plain of the valley of Jericho, the city of palm trees, unto Zoar.

4   And the Lord said unto him, [b]This is the land which I sware unto Abraham, to Isaac and to Jacob, saying, I will give it unto thy seed: I have caused thee to see it with thine eyes, but thou shalt not go over thither.

5   So Moses the servant of the Lord died there in the land of Moab, according to the word of the Lord.

6   And [1]he buried him in a valley in the land of Moab over against Beth Peor, but no man knoweth of his sepulcher unto [2]this day.

CHAPTER 34
[a] Deut. 3:27
[b] Gen. 12:7
Gen. 13:15

7   Moses was now an hundred and twenty years old when he died, his eye was not dim, nor his natural force abated:

8   And the children of Israel wept for Moses in the plain of Moab thirty days: so the days of weeping and mourning for Moses were ended.

9   And [1]Joshua the son of Nun was full of the spirit of wisdom: for Moses had put his hands upon him. And the children of Israel were obedient unto him, and did as the Lord had commanded Moses.

10   But there arose not a Prophet since in Israel like unto Moses (whom the Lord knew [1]face to face.)

11   In all the miracles and wonders which the Lord sent him to do in the land of Egypt before Pharaoh and before all his servants, and before all his land,

12   And in all that mighty [1]hand and all that great fear, which Moses wrought in the sight of all Israel.

34:2   [1] Called, Mediterranean.
34:6   [1] To wit, the Angel of the Lord, Jude 9.
       [2] That the Jews might not have occassion thereby to commit Idolatry.
34:9   [1] Hereby appeareth the favor of God, that leaveth not his

Church destitute of a governor.
34:10   [1] Unto whom the Lord did reveal himself so plainly, as Exod. 33:11.
34:12   [1] Meaning, the power of God working by Moses in the wilderness.

THE BOOK OF

JOSHUA

1
2 The Lord encourageth Joshua to invade the land.   4 The borders and limits of the land of the Israelites.   5 The Lord promiseth to assist Joshua, if he obey his word.   11 Joshua commandeth the people to prepare themselves to pass over Jordan,   12 and exhorteth the Reubenites to execute their charge.

1 Now after the ¹death of Moses the servant of the Lord, the Lord spake unto Joshua the son of Nun, Moses' minister, saying,

2 Moses my servant is dead: now therefore arise, go over this Jordan, thou, and all this people, unto the land which I give them, *that is*, to the children of Israel.

3 *ᵃ*Every place that the sole of your foot shall tread upon, have I given you, as I said unto Moses.

4 *ᵇ*From the ¹wilderness and this Lebanon even unto the great river, the river ²Perath: all the land of the ³Hittites, even unto the great ⁴Sea toward the going down of the sun, shall be your coast.

5 There shall not a man be able to withstand thee all the days of thy life: as I was with Moses, *so* will I be with thee: *ᶜ*I will not leave thee, nor forsake thee.

6 *ᵈ*Be strong and of a good courage: for unto this people shalt thou divide the land for an inheritance, which I swore unto their fathers to give them.

7 Only be thou strong, and ¹of a most valiant courage, that thou mayest observe and do according to all the Law which Moses my servant hath commanded thee: *ᵉ*thou shalt not turn away from it to the right hand, nor to the left, that thou mayest ²prosper whithersoever thou goest.

8 Let not this book of the Law depart out of thy mouth, but meditate therein day and ¹night, that thou mayest observe and do according to all that is written therein: for then shalt thou make thy way prosperous, and then shalt thou ²have good success.

9 Have not I commanded thee, saying, Be strong

CHAPTER 1
ᵃ Josh. 14:9
ᵇ Deut. 11:24
ᶜ Heb. 13:5
ᵈ Deut. 31:23
ᵉ Deut. 3:32
Deut. 28:14
ᶠ Num. 32:20

and of a good courage, fear not, nor be discouraged? for I the Lord thy God *will be* with thee whithersoever thou goest.

10 ¶ Then Joshua commanded the officers of the people, saying,

11 Pass through the host, and command the people, saying, Prepare you victuals: for ¹after three days ye shall pass over this Jordan, to go in to possess the land, which the Lord your God giveth you to possess it.

12 And unto the Reubenites, and to the Gadites, and to half the tribe of Manasseh spake Joshua, saying,

13 *ᶠ*Remember the word, which Moses the servant of the Lord commanded you, saying, The Lord your God hath given you rest, and hath given you this ¹land.

14 ¶ Your wives, your children, and your cattle shall remain in the land which Moses gave you ¹on this side Jordan: but ye shall go over before your brethren armed, all that be men of war, and shall help them,

15 Until the Lord have given your brethren rest as well as to you, and until they also shall possess the land, which the Lord your God giveth them: then shall ye return unto the land of your possession, and shall possess it, which *land* Moses the Lord's ¹servant gave you on this side Jordan toward the sun rising.

16 Then they answered Joshua, saying, All that thou hast commanded us, we will do, and whithersoever thou sendest us, we will go.

17 As we obeyed Moses in all things, ¹so will we obey thee: only the Lord thy God be with thee, as he was with Moses.

18 Whosoever shall rebel against thy commandment, and will not obey thy words in all that thou commandest him, let him be put to death: only be strong and of good courage.

2
1 Joshua sendeth men to spy Jericho, whom Rahab hideth.   11 She confesseth the God of Israel.   12 She

---

1:1 ¹ The beginning of this book dependeth on the last chapter of Deut. which was written by Joshua as a preparation to his history.
1:4 ¹ Of Zin, called Kadesh and Paran.
  ² Or, Euphrates.
  ³ Meaning, the whole land of Canaan.
  ⁴ Called Mediterranean.
1:7 ¹ Or, grow stronger and stronger.
  ² He showeth wherein consisteth true prosperity, even to obey the word of God.
1:8 ¹ Showing that it was not possible to govern well, without con-

tinual study of God's word.
  ² Or, govern wisely.
1:11 ¹ Meaning, from the day that this was proclaimed, Josh. 3:2.
1:13 ¹ Which belonged to Sihon the king of the Amorites, and Og king of Bashan.
1:14 ¹ Or, beyond Jordan from Jericho.
1:15 ¹ By your request, but yet by God's secret appointment, Deut. 33:21.
1:17 ¹ They do not only promise to obey him so long as God is with him: but to help to punish all that rebel against him.

requireth a sign for her deliverance.   21 The spies return to Joshua with comfortable tidings.

CHAPTER 2
a Heb. 11:31
James 2:25
b Exod. 14:21,22
c Josh. 4:23
d Num. 21:24

1 Then Joshua the son of Nun sent out of [1]Shittim two men to spy secretly, saying, Go view the land, and *also* Jericho, and they went, and *a*came into an [2]harlot's house, named Rahab, and lodged there.

2 Then report was made to the King of Jericho, saying, Behold, there came men hither tonight, of the children of Israel, to spy out the country.

3 And the king of Jericho sent unto Rahab saying, [1]Bring forth the men that are come to thee, *and* which are entered into thine house: for they be come to search out all the land.

4 (But the woman had taken the two men, and hid them.) Therefore said she thus, There came men unto me, but I wist not whence they were.

5 And when they shut the gate in the dark, the men went out, whither the men went, I wot not: follow ye after them quickly, for ye shall overtake them.

6 (But she had brought them up to the [1]roof of the house, and hid them with the stalks of flax, which she had spread abroad upon the roof.)

7 And certain men pursued after them, the way to Jordan, unto the fords, and as soon as they which pursued after them, were gone out, they shut the gate.

8 ¶ And before they were asleep, she came up unto them upon the roof,

9 And said unto the men, I know that the Lord hath given you the land, and that the [1]fear of you is fallen upon us, and that all the inhabitants of the land faint because of you.

10 For we have heard how the Lord *b*dried up the water of the red Sea *c*before you when ye came out of Egypt, and what you did unto the two kings of the Amorites, that were on the other side Jordan, unto *d*Sihon and to Og, whom ye utterly destroyed:

11 And when we heard it, our hearts [1]did faint, and there remained no more [2]courage in any because of you: for [3]the Lord your God, he is the God in heaven above, and in earth beneath.

12 Now therefore, I pray you, swear unto me by the Lord, that as I have showed you mercy, ye will also show mercy unto my father's house, and give me a true token,

13 And that ye will save alive my father and my mother, and my brethren, and my sisters, and all that they have: and that ye will deliver our [1]souls from death.

14 And the men answered her, [1]Our life for you to die, if ye utter not this our business: and when the Lord hath given us the land, we will deal mercifully and truly with thee.

15 Then she let them down by a cord through the window: for her house *was* upon the town wall, and she dwelt upon the wall.

16 And she said unto them, Go you into the [1]mountain, lest the pursuers meet with you, and hide yourselves there three days, until the pursuers be returned: then afterward may ye go your way.

17 And the men said unto her, [1]We will be blameless of this thine oath which thou hast made us swear.

18 Behold, when we come into the land, thou shalt bind this cord of red thread in the window, whereby thou lettest us down, and thou shalt bring thy father and thy mother, and thy brethren, and all thy father's household home to thee.

19 And whosoever then doth go out at the doors of thine house into the street, [1]his blood shall be upon his head, and we will be guiltless: but whosoever shall be with thee in the house, his blood shall be on our head, if any hand touch him:

20 And if thou utter this our [1]matter, we will be quit of thine oath, which thou hast made us swear.

21 And she answered, According unto your words, so be it: then she sent them away, and they departed, and she bound the [1]red cord in the window.

22 ¶ And they departed, and came into the mountain, and there abode three days, until the pursuers were returned: and the pursuers sought them throughout all the way, but found them not.

23 So the two men returned, and descended from the mountain, and passed [1]over, and came to Joshua the son of Nun, and told him all things that came unto them.

24 Also they said unto Joshua, Surely the Lord hath delivered into our hands all the land: for even all the inhabitants of the country faint because of us.

3 3 *Joshua commandeth them to depart when the Ark removeth.* 7 *The Lord promiseth to exalt Joshua before*

2:1 [1] Which place was in the plain of Moab near unto Jordan.
   [2] Or, taverner's house, or hostess.
2:3 [1] Though the wicked see the hand of God upon them, yet they repent not, but seek how they may by their power and policy resist his working.
2:6 [1] Meaning, upon the house: for then their houses were flat above, so that they might do their business thereupon.
2:9 [1] For so God promised, Deut. 28:7; Josh. 5:1.
2:11 [1] Or, melted.
   [2] Or, spirit.
   [3] Herein appeareth the great mercy of God, that in this common

destruction he would draw a most miserable sinner to repent, and confess his Name.
2:13 [1] Or, lives.
2:14 [1] We warrant you on pain of our lives.
2:16 [1] Which was near unto the city.
2:17 [1] We shall be discharged of our oath if thou dost perform this condition that followeth: for so shalt thou and thine be delivered.
2:19 [1] He shall be guilty of his own death.
2:20 [1] So that others should think to escape by the same means.
2:21 [1] Or, scarlet colored.
2:23 [1] To wit, the river Jordan.

the people.   9 Joshua's exhortation to the people.   16 The waters part asunder while the people pass.

1 Then Joshua rose very early, and they removed from Shittim, and came to [1]Jordan, he, and all the children of Israel, and lodged there before they went over.

2 And after [1]three days, the officers went throughout the host,

3 And commanded the people, saying, When ye see the Ark of the covenant of the Lord your God and the Priests of the Levites bearing it, ye shall depart from your place, and go after it.

4 Yet shall there be a space between you and it, about [1]two thousand cubits by measure: ye shall not come near unto it, that ye may know the way, by the which ye shall go: for ye have not gone this way in times past.

5 (Now Joshua had said unto the people, [a]Sanctify yourselves: for tomorrow the Lord will do wonders among you.)

6 Also Joshua spake unto the Priests, saying, Take up the Ark of the covenant, and go over before the people: so they took up the Ark of the covenant, and went before the people.

7 ¶ Then the Lord said unto Joshua, This day will I begin to magnify thee in the sight of all Israel, which shall know, that [b]as I was with Moses, so will I be with thee.

8 Thou shalt therefore command the Priests that bear the Ark of the covenant, saying, When ye are come to the brink of the waters of Jordan, ye shall stand still [1]in Jordan.

9 ¶ Then Joshua said unto the children of Israel, Come hither, and hear the words of the Lord your God.

10 And Joshua said, [1]Hereby ye shall know that the living God is among you, and that he will certainly cast out before you the Canaanites, and the Hittites, and the Hivites, and the Perizzites, and the Girgashites, and the Amorites, and the Jebusites.

11 Behold, the Ark of the covenant of the Lord of all the world passeth before you into Jordan.

12 Now therefore take from among you [1]twelve men out of the tribes of Israel, out of every tribe a man.

13 And as soon as the soles of the feet of the Priests (that bear the Ark of the Lord God the Lord of all

CHAPTER 3
[a] Lev. 20:7
Num. 11:18
Josh. 7:13
James 16:5
[b] Josh. 1:5
[c] Ps. 114:3
[d] Acts 7:45
[e] 1 Chron. 12:15

CHAPTER 4
[a] Deut. 27:2

the world) shall stay in the waters of Jordan, the waters of Jordan shall be cut off: for the waters that come from above, [c]shall stand still upon an heap.

14 ¶ Then when the people were departed from their tents to go over Jordan, the Priests bearing the [d]Ark of the covenant, *went* before the people.

15 And as they that bare the Ark, came unto Jordan, and the feet of the Priests that bare the Ark were dipped in the brink of the water, ([e]for Jordan useth to fill all his [1]banks all the time of harvest)

16 Then the waters that came down from above, stayed *and* rose upon an heap, and departed far from the city of Adam that was beside Zaretan: but the *waters* that came down toward the Sea of the wilderness, *even* the salt Sea, failed *and* were cut off: so the people went right over against Jericho.

17 But the Priests that bare the Ark of the covenant of the Lord, stood dry within Jordan [1]ready prepared, and all the Israelites went over dry, until all the people were clean gone over through Jordan.

4 *2 God commandeth Joshua to set up twelve stones in Jordan.   18 The waters return to their old course.   20 Other twelve stones are set upon Gilgal.   21 This miracle must be declared to posterity.*

1 And when all the people were wholly gone [a]over Jordan (after the Lord had spoken unto Joshua, saying,

2 Take you twelve men out of the people out of every tribe a man,

3 And command you them, saying, Take you hence out of the midst of Jordan, out of the place where the Priests stood in a [1]readiness, twelve stones, which ye shall take away with you, and leave them in the [2]lodging, where you shall lodge this night)

4 Then Joshua called the twelve men, whom he had prepared of the children of Israel, out of every tribe a man,

5 And Joshua said unto them, Go over before the Ark of the Lord your God, even through the midst of Jordan, and take up every man of you a stone upon his shoulder according unto the number of the tribes of the children of Israel,

6 That this may be a sign among you, that when

3:1 [1] Which according to the Hebrews was in March, and about 40 days after Moses' death.
3:2 [1] Which time was given for to prepare them victuals, Josh. 1:11.
3:4 [1] Or, a mile.
3:8 [1] Even in the channel where the stream had run, as verse 17.
3:10 [1] By this miracle in dividing the water.
3:12 [1] Which should set up twelve stones in remembrance of the

benefit.
3:15 [1] Because the river was accustomed at this time to be full, the miracle is so much the greater.
3:17 [1] Either tarrying till the people were past, or as some read, sure, as though they had been upon the dry land.
4:3 [1] As Josh. 3:17.
       [2] Meaning, the place where they should camp.

your [1]children shall ask their fathers in time to come, saying, What *meant* you by these stones?

7 Then ye may answer them, That the waters of Jordan were cut off before the Ark of the Covenant of the Lord: *for* when it passed through Jordan, the waters of Jordan were cut off: therefore these stones are a memorial unto the children of Israel forever.

8 Then the children of Israel did even so as Joshua had commanded, and took up twelve stones out of the midst of Jordan as the Lord had said unto Joshua, according unto the number of the tribes of the children of Israel, and carried them away with them unto the lodging, and laid them down there.

9 And Joshua set up [1]twelve stones in the midst of Jordan, in the place where the feet of the Priests, which bare the Ark of the Covenant stood, and there have they continued unto this day.

10 ¶ So the Priests, which bare the Ark, stood in the midst of Jordan, until everything was finished that the Lord had commanded Joshua to say unto the people, according to all that Moses charged Joshua: then the people hasted and went over.

11 When all the people were clean passed over, the Ark of the Lord went over also, and the Priests [1]before the people.

12 [b]And the sons of Reuben, and the sons of Gad, and half the tribe of Manasseh went over before the children of Israel armed, as Moses had charged them.

13 Even forty thousand prepared for war, went before the [1]Lord unto battle, into the plain of Jericho.

14 That day the Lord magnified Joshua in the sight of all Israel, and they [1]feared him, as they feared Moses all the days of his life.

15 And the Lord spake unto Joshua, saying,

16 Command the Priests that bear the [1]Ark of the testimony, to come up out of Jordan.

17 Joshua therefore commanded the Priests, saying, Come ye up out of Jordan.

18 And when the Priests that bare the Ark of the Covenant of the Lord, were come up out of the midst of Jordan, and as soon as the soles of the Priests' feet were set on the dry land, the waters of Jordan returned unto their place, and flowed over all the banks thereof, as they did before.

19 ¶ So the people came up out of Jordan the

marginal notes:
[b] Num. 32:27,29
[c] Exod. 14:21,22

CHAPTER 5
[d] Exod. 4:25

tenth *day* of the [1]first month, and pitched in Gilgal, in the East side of Jericho.

20 Also the twelve stones, which they took out of Jordan, did Joshua pitch in Gilgal.

21 And he spake unto the children of Israel, saying, When your children shall ask their fathers in time to come, and say, What *mean* these stones?

22 Then ye shall show your children, and say, Israel came over this Jordan on dry land:

23 For the Lord your God dried up the waters of Jordan before you, until ye were gone over as the Lord your God did the red Sea, [c]which he dried up before us, till we were gone over,

24 That all the people of the [1]world may know that the hand of the Lord is mighty, that ye might fear the Lord your God continually.

5 1 *The Canaanites are afraid of the Israelites.* 2 *Circumcision is commanded the second time.* 10 *The passover is kept.* 12 *Manna ceaseth.* 13 *The Angel appeareth unto Joshua.*

1 Now when all the Kings of the [1]Amorites, which were beyond Jordan Westward, and all the Kings of the Canaanites which were by the Sea, heard that the Lord had dried up the waters of Jordan before the children of Israel until they were gone over, their hearts fainted: and there was no courage in them anymore because of the children of Israel.

2 ¶ That same time the Lord said unto Joshua, [d]Make thee sharp knives, [1]and return, and circumcise the sons of Israel the second time.

3 Then Joshua made him sharp knives, and circumcised the sons of Israel in [1]the hill of the foreskins.

4 And this is the cause why Joshua circumcised all the people, *even* the males that came out of Egypt, because all the men of war were dead in the wilderness by the way after they came out of Egypt.

5 For all the people that came out, were circumcised: but all the people that were born in the wilderness by the way after they came out of Egypt, were [1]not circumcised.

6 For the children of Israel walked forty years in the wilderness, till all the people of the men of war that came out of Egypt, were consumed, because

---

4:6 [1] God commandeth that not only we ourselves profit by this wonderful work, but that our posterity may know the cause thereof and glorify his Name.
4:9 [1] Besides the twelve stones which were carried by the tribes and set up in Gilgal.
4:11 [1] Meaning, in the presence or sight of the people.
4:13 [1] That is, before the Ark.
4:14 [1] Or, reverenced him.
4:16 [1] Because the Ark testified God's presence, and the Tables of the Law contained therein, signified God's will toward his people.

4:19 [1] Called Abib or Nisan, containing part of March and part of April.
4:24 [1] God's benefits serve for a further condemnation to the wicked, and stir up his to reverence him, and obey him.
5:1 [1] The Amorites were on both sides [of] Jordan, whereof two kings were slain already on the side toward Moab.
5:2 [1] For now they had left it off, about 40 years.
5:3 [1] Gilgal was so called, because they were there circumcised.
5:5 [1] For they looked daily to remove at the Lord's commandment, which thing they that were new circumcised, could not do without great danger.

they obeyed not the voice of the Lord: unto whom the Lord sware that he would not show them the land, [b]which the Lord had sworn unto their fathers, that he would give us, *even* a land that floweth with milk and honey.

7 So their sons whom he raised up in their stead, Joshua circumcised: for they were uncircumcised, because they circumcised them not by the way.

8 And when they had made an end of circumcising all the people, they abode in the places in the camp till they [1]were whole.

9 After, the Lord said unto Joshua, This day I have taken away the [1]shame of Egypt from you: wherefore he called the name of that place, Gilgal, unto this day.

10 ¶ So the children of Israel abode in Gilgal, and kept the feast of the Passover the fourteenth day of the month at even, in the plain of Jericho.

11 And they did eat of the corn of the land, on the morrow after the Passover, unleavened bread, and parched corn in the same day.

12 And the Manna ceased on the morrow after they had eaten of the corn of the land, neither had the children of Israel Manna anymore, but did eat of the fruit of the land of Canaan that year.

13 ¶ And when Joshua was by Jericho, he lift up his eyes and looked: and behold, there stood a ʿman against him, having a sword drawn in his hand: and Joshua went unto him, and said unto him, Art thou on our side, or on our adversaries?

14 And he said, Nay, but *as* a captain of the host of the Lord am I now come: then Joshua fell on his face to the earth, and [1]did worship, and said unto him, What saith the Lord unto his servant?

15 And the captain of the Lord's host said unto Joshua, [d]Loose thy shoe of thy foot: for the place whereon thou standest, is holy: and Joshua did so.

6 2 *The Lord instructeth Joshua what he should do as touching Jericho. 6 Joshua commandeth the Priests and warriors what to do. 20 The walls fall. 22 Rahab is saved. 24 All is burnt save gold and metal. 26 The curse of him that buildeth the city.*

1 Now Jericho was [1]shut up, and [2]closed, [3]because of the children of Israel, none might go out nor enter in.

[b] Num. 14:23
[c] Exod. 23:23
[d] Exod. 3:5
Ruth 4:7
Acts 7:33

2 And the Lord said unto Joshua, Behold, I have given into thine hand Jericho and the king thereof, *and* the strong men of war.

3 All ye therefore *that be* men of war, shall compass the city, in going round about the city [1]once: thus shall you do six days:

4 And seven Priests shall bear seven trumpets of [1]rams' horns before the Ark: and the seventh day ye shall compass the city seven times, and the Priests shall blow with the trumpets,

5 And when they make a long *blast* with the ram's horn, and ye hear the sound of the trumpet, all the people shall shout with a great shout: then shall the wall of the city fall down flat, and the people shall ascend up, every man straight before him.

6 ¶ Then Joshua the son of Nun called the Priests and said unto them, Take up the Ark of the Covenant, and let seven Priests bear seven trumpets of rams' horns before the Ark of the Lord.

7 But he said unto the people, [1]Go and compass the city: and let him that is armed go forth before the Ark of the Lord.

8 ¶ And when Joshua had spoken unto the people, the seven priests bare the seven trumpets of rams' horns, and went forth before the Ark of the Lord, and blew with the trumpets, and the ark of the Covenant of the Lord followed them.

9 ¶ And the men of arms went before the priests and blew the trumpets: then the [1]gathering *host* came after the Ark, and they went and blew the trumpets.

10 (Now Joshua had commanded the people, saying, Ye shall not shout, neither make any noise with your voice, neither shall a word proceed out of your mouth, until the day that I say unto you, Shout, then shall ye shout.)

11 So the Ark of the Lord compassed the city, and went about it [1]once: then they returned into the host, and lodged in the camp.

12 And Joshua rose early in the morning, and the Priests bare the Ark of the Lord:

13 Also seven Priests bare seven trumpets of rams' horns, and went before the Ark of the Lord, and going blew with the trumpets: and the men of arms went before them, but the [1]gathering *host* came after the Ark

5:8 [1] For their sore was so grievous, that they were not able to remove.
5:9 [1] By bringing you into this promised land, contrary to the wicked opinion of the Egyptians: or the foreskin whereby you were like to the Egyptians.
5:14 [1] In that that Joshua worshippeth him, he acknowledgeth him to be God: and in that that he calleth himself the Lord's captain, he declareth himself to be Christ.
6:1 [1] That none could go out.
[2] That none could come in.
[3] For fear of the Israelites.
6:3 [1] Every day one.
6:4 [1] That the conquest might not be assigned to man's power, but to the mercy of God, which with most weak things can overcome that which seemeth most strong.
6:7 [1] This is chiefly meant by the Reubenites, Gadites, and half the tribe of Manasseh.
6:9 [1] Meaning, the rearward, wherein was the standard of the tribe of Dan, Num. 10:25.
6:11 [1] For that day.
6:13 [1] The tribe of Dan was so called, because it marched last and gathered up whatsoever was left of others.

of the Lord, as they went and blew the trumpets.

14 And the second day they compassed the city once, and returned into the host: thus they did six days.

15 And when the seventh day came, they rose early, even with the dawning of the day, and compassed the city after the same manner [1]seven times: only that day they compassed the city seven times.

16 And when the Priests had blown the trumpets the seventh time, Joshua said unto the people, Shout: for the Lord hath given you the city.

17 And the city shall be [1]an execrable thing, *both* it, and all that are therein, unto the Lord: only Rahab the harlot shall live, she, and all that are with her in the house: for she hid the messengers that we sent.

18 Notwithstanding, be ye ware of the execrable thing, lest ye make yourselves execrable, and in taking of the execrable thing, make also the host of Israel [b]execrable, and trouble it.

19 But all silver, and gold, and vessels of brass, and iron shall be [1]consecrate unto the Lord, *and* shall come into the Lord's treasury.

20 So the people shouted, when they had blown trumpets: for when the people had heard the sound of the trumpets, they shouted with a great shout: and the wall fell down flat: so the people went up into the city, every man straight before him: and they took the city.

21 And they utterly destroyed all that was in the cities both man and woman, young, and old, and ox, and sheep, and ass with the edge of the sword.

22 But Joshua had said unto the two men that had spied out the country, Go into the harlot's house, and bring out thence the woman, and all that she hath, [d]as ye swore to her.

23 So the young men that were spies, went in and brought out Rahab, and her father, and her mother, and her brethren, and all that she had: also they brought out all her family, and put them [1]without the host of Israel.

24 After, they burnt the city with fire, and all that was therein: only the silver and the gold, and the vessels of brass and iron, they put unto the treasure of the [1]house of the Lord.

25 So Joshua saved Rahab the harlot, and her father's household, and all that she had, and she [1]dwelt in Israel, even unto this day, because she had

CHAPTER 6
[a] Josh. 2:4
[b] Lev. 27:21
Num. 21:2
Deut. 13:15-17
[c] Heb. 11:30
[d] Josh. 2:14
Heb. 11:31

CHAPTER 7
[a] Josh. 22:20
1 Chron. 2:7

hid the messengers, which Joshua sent to spy out Jericho.

26 ¶ And Joshua swore at that time, saying, Cursed be the man before the Lord, that riseth up, and buildeth the city Jericho: [1]he shall lay the foundation thereof in his eldest son, and in his youngest son shall he set up the gates of it.

27 So the Lord was with Joshua, and he was famous through all the world.

7 1 *The Lord is angry with Achan.* 4 *They of Ai put the Israelites to flight.* 6 *Joshua prayeth to the Lord.* 16 *Joshua inquireth out him that sinned, and stoneth him and all his.*

1 But the children of Israel committed a trespass in the [1]excommunicate thing: for [a]Achan the son of Carmi, the son of Zabdi, the son of Zerah of the tribe of Judah, took of the excommunicate thing: wherefore the wrath of the Lord was kindled against the children of Israel.

2 And Joshua sent men from Jericho to [1]Ai, which is beside Beth Aven, on the East side of Bethel, and spake unto them, saying, Go up, and view the country. And the men went up and viewed Ai,

3 And returned to Joshua, and said unto him, Let not all the people go up, *but* let as it were two or three thousand men go up, and smite Ai, and make not all the people to labor thither, for they are few.

4 So there went up thither of the people about three thousand men, and they fled before the men of Ai.

5 And the [1]men of Ai smote of them upon a thirty and six men: for they chased them from before the gate unto Shebarim, and smote them in the going down: wherefore the hearts of the people melted away like water.

6 Then Joshua rent his clothes, and fell to the earth upon his face before the Ark of the Lord, until the eventide, he, and the Elders of Israel, and put dust upon their heads.

7 And Joshua said, Alas, O Lord God, wherefore hast thou brought this people over Jordan, to deliver us into the hand of the Amorites, and to destroy us? would God we had been content to dwell on the [1]other side Jordan.

8 Oh Lord what shall I say, when Israel turn their

6:15 [1] Beside every day once for the space of six days.
6:17 [1] That is appointed wholly to be destroyed.
6:19 [1] And therefore cannot be put to any private use, but must be first molten, and then serve for the Tabernacle.
6:23 [1] For it was not lawful for strangers to dwell among the Israelites, till they were purged.
6:24 [1] Meaning, the Tabernacle.
6:25 [1] For she was married to Salmon prince of the tribe of Judah, Matt. 1:5.

6:26 [1] He shall build it to the destruction of all his stock, which thing was fulfilled in Hiel of Bethel, 1 Kings 16:34.
7:1 [1] In taking that which was commanded to be destroyed.
7:2 [1] This was a city of the Amorites: for there was another so called among the Amorites, Jer. 49:3. The first Ai is called Aiath, Isa. 10:28.
7:5 [1] God would by this overthrow make them more earnest to search out and punish the sin committed.
7:7 [1] This infirmity of his faith showeth how we are inclined of nature to distrust.

backs before their enemies?

9 For the Canaanites, and all the inhabitants of the land shall hear of it, and shall compass us, and destroy our name out of the earth: and what wilt thou do unto thy mighty ¹Name?

10 ¶ And the Lord said unto Joshua, Get thee up: wherefore liest thou thus upon thy face?

11 Israel hath sinned, and they have transgressed my covenant, which I commanded them: for they have even taken of the excommunicate thing, and have also stolen, and dissembled also, and have put it even with their own stuff.

12 Therefore the children of Israel cannot stand before their enemies: *but* have turned their backs before their enemies, because they be execrable: neither will I be with you anymore, except ye ¹destroy the excommunicate from among you.

13 Up *therefore*, sanctify the people, and say, Sanctify yourselves against tomorrow: for thus saith the Lord God of Israel, *There is* an execrable thing among you, O Israel, *therefore* ye cannot stand against your enemies, until ye have put the ¹execrable thing from among you.

14 In the morning therefore ye shall come according to your tribes, and the tribe which the Lord taketh, shall come according to the families: and the family which the Lord shall take, shall come by the households: and the household which the Lord shall take, shall come man by man.

15 And he that is ¹taken with the excommunicate thing, shall be burnt with fire, he, and all that he hath, because he hath transgressed the covenant of the Lord, and because he hath wrought folly in Israel.

16 ¶ So Joshua rose up early in the morning, and brought Israel by their tribes: and the tribe of Judah was taken.

17 And he brought the families of Judah, and took the family of the Zarhites, and he brought the family of the Zarhites, man by man, and Zabdi was taken.

18 And he brought his household, man by man, and Achan the son of Carmi, the son of Zabdi, the son of Zerah of the tribe of Judah was taken.

19 Then Joshua said unto Achan, My son, I beseech thee, give glory to the Lord God of Israel, and ¹make confession unto him, and show me now what thou

CHAPTER 8
ᵃ Deut. 1:29
Deut. 7:18
ᵇ Josh. 6:21
ᶜ Deut. 20:14

hast done: hide it not from me.

20 And Achan answered Joshua, and said, Indeed I have sinned against the Lord God of Israel, and thus, and thus have I done.

21 I saw among the spoil a goodly ¹Babylonish garment, and two hundred shekels of silver, and a wedge of gold of fifty shekels weight, and I coveted them, and took them: and behold, they lie hid in the earth in the midst of my tent, and the silver under it.

22 ¶ Then Joshua sent messengers, which ran unto the tent, and behold, it was hid in his tent, and the silver under it.

23 Therefore they took them out of the tent, and brought them unto Joshua, and unto all the children of Israel, and laid them before the Lord.

24 Then Joshua took Achan the ¹son of Zerah, and the silver, and the garment, and the ²wedge of gold, and his ³sons, and his daughters, and his oxen, and his asses, and his sheep, and his tent, and all that he had: and all Israel with him, brought them unto the valley of Achor.

25 And Joshua said, ¹In as much as thou hast troubled us, the Lord shall trouble thee this day: and all Israel threw stones at him, and burned them with fire, and stoned them with stones.

26 And they cast upon him a great heap of stones unto this day: and *so* the Lord turned from his fierce wrath: therefore he called the name of that place, The valley of Achor, unto this day.

8 *3 The siege, 19 and winning of Ai. 29 The king thereof is hanged. 30 Joshua setteth up an Altar. 32 He writeth the Law upon stones, 35 and readeth it to all the people.*

1 After, the Lord said unto Joshua, ᵃFear not, neither be thou faint hearted: take all the men of war with thee and arise, go up to Ai: behold, I have given into thine hand the king of Ai, and his people, and his city, and his land.

2 And thou shalt do to Ai and to the king thereof, as thou didst unto ᵇJericho and to the king thereof: nevertheless the spoil thereof and ᶜthe cattle thereof shall ye take unto you for a prey: thou shalt lie in wait against the city on the ¹back side thereof.

3 ¶ Then Joshua arose, and all the men of war to go up against Ai: and Joshua chose out thirty thousand strong men, *and* valiant, and sent them

---

7:9 ¹ When thine enemies shall blaspheme thee and say, that thou wast not able to defend us from them.
7:12 ¹ Then to suffer wickedness unpunished, is to refuse God willingly.
7:13 ¹ Meaning, the man that took of the thing forbidden.
7:15 ¹ That is found guilty, either by lots, or by the judgment of Urim, Num. 27:21.
7:19 ¹ By declaring truth: for God is glorified when the truth is confessed.

7:21 ¹ Such a rich garment as the states of Babylon did wear.
7:24 ¹ Or, nephew.
² Some read a plate: others, a rod, and some a tongue.
³ This judgment only appertaineth to God, and to whom he will reveal it, to man he had commanded not to punish the child for the father's fault, Deut. 24:16.
7:25 ¹ He declareth that this is God's judgment because he had offended, and caused others to be slain.
8:2 ¹ Meaning, on the West side, as verse 9.

away by night.

4 And he commanded them, saying, Behold, ye [1]shall lie in wait against the city on the back side of the city: go not very far from the city, but be ye all in a readiness.

5 And I and all the people that are with me, will approach unto the city: and when they shall come out against us, as they did at the first time, then will we flee before them.

6 For they will come out after us, till we have brought them out of the city: for they will say, They flee before us as at the first time: so we will flee before them.

7 Then you shall rise up from lying in wait and [1]destroy the city: for the Lord your God will deliver it into your hand.

8 And when ye have taken the city, ye shall set it on fire: according to the commandment of the Lord shall ye do: behold, I have charged you.

9 ¶ Joshua then sent them forth, and they went to lie in wait, and abode between Bethel and Ai, on the West side of Ai: but Joshua lodged that night [1]among the people.

10 And Joshua rose up early in the morning, and [1]numbered the people: and he and the Elders of Israel went up before the people *against* Ai.

11 Also all the men of war that were with him went up and drew near, and came against the city, and pitched on the North side of Ai: and there was a valley between them and Ai.

12 And he took about five thousand men, [1]and set them to lie in wait between Bethel and Ai on the West side of the city.

13 And the people set all the host that was on the North side against the city, and the liars in wait on the West, against the city: *and* Joshua went the same night into the [1]midst of the valley.

14 ¶ And when the king of Ai saw it, then the men of the city hasted and rose up early, and went out against Israel to battle, he and all his people, at the time appointed, before the plain: for he knew not that *any* lay in wait against him on the back side of the city.

15 Then Joshua and all Israel [1]as beaten before them, fled by the way of the wilderness.

16 And all the people of the city were called together to pursue after them: and they pursued after

margin:
d Deut. 7:2
e Num. 31:22,26
Josh. 8:2

Joshua, and were drawn away out of the city,

17 So that there was not a man left in Ai, nor in Bethel, that went not out after Israel: and they left the city open, and pursued after Israel.

18 Then the Lord said unto Joshua, [1]Stretch out the spear that is in thine hand, toward Ai: for I will give it into thine hand: and Joshua stretched out the spear that he had in his hand, toward the city.

19 And they that lay in wait, arose quickly out of their place, and ran as soon as he had stretched out his hand, and they entered into the city, and took it, and hasted, and set the city on fire.

20 And the men of Ai looked behind them, and saw it: for lo, the smoke of the city ascended up [1]to heaven, and they had no [2]power to flee this way or that way: for the people that fled to the wilderness, turned back upon the pursuers.

21 When Joshua and all Israel saw that they that lay in wait, had taken the city, and that the smoke of the city mounted up, then they turned again and slew the men of Ai.

22 Also the [1]other issued out of the city against them: so were they in the midst of Israel, these *being* on the one side, and the rest on the other side: and they slew them, so that they let none of them [d]remain nor escape.

23 And the King of Ai they took alive, and brought him to Joshua.

24 And when Israel had made an end of slaying all the inhabitants of Ai in the field, *that is*, in the wilderness where they chased them, and when they were all fallen on the edge of the sword, until they were consumed, all the Israelites returned unto Ai, and [1]smote it with the edge of the sword.

25 And all that fell that day, both of men and women, were twelve thousand, even all the men of Ai.

26 For Joshua drew not his hand back again which he had stretched out with the spear, until he had utterly destroyed all the inhabitants of Ai.

27 'Only the cattle and the spoil of this city, Israel took for a prey unto themselves, according unto the word of the Lord, which he commanded Joshua.

28 And Joshua burnt Ai, and made it an heap [1]forever, *and* a wilderness unto this day.

29 And the king of Ai he hanged on a tree, unto the evening. And as soon as the sun was down, Joshua commanded [1]that they should take his carcass down

---

8:4 [1] God would not destroy Ai by miracle, as Jericho, to the intent that other nations might fear the power and policy of his people.
8:7 [1] Or, drive out (the inhabitants) of the city.
8:9 [1] With the rest of the army.
8:10 [1] That is, viewed or mustered them, and set them in array.
8:12 [1] He sent these few, that the others which lay in ambush might not be discovered.
8:13 [1] To the intent that they in the city might the better discover his army.

8:15 [1] As they which feigned to flee for fear.
8:18 [1] Or, lift up the banner, to signify when they shall invade the city.
8:20 [1] Or, toward the heavens.
      [2] Or, place.
8:22 [1] Which came out of the ambush.
8:24 [1] For the fire, which they had before set in the city, was not to consume it, but to signify unto Joshua that they were entered.
8:28 [1] That it could never be built again.
8:29 [1] According as it was commanded, Deut. 21:23.

from the tree, and cast it at the entering of the gate of the city, and /lay thereon a great heap of stones, *that remaineth* unto this day.

30 ¶ Then Joshua built an altar unto the Lord God of Israel, in mount Ebal,

31 As Moses the servant of the Lord had commanded the children of Israel, as it is written in the 8book of the Law of Moses, an altar of whole stone, over which no man had lift an iron: and they offered thereon burnt offerings unto the Lord, and sacrificed peace offerings.

32 Also he wrote there upon the stones, a1rehearsal of the Law of Moses, which he wrote in the presence of the children of Israel.

33 And all Israel (and their Elders, and officers and their Judges stood on this side of the Ark, and on that side, before the Priests of the Levites, which bare the Ark of the covenant of the Lord) as well the stranger, as he that is born in the country: half of them *were* over against mount Gerizim, and half of them over against mount Ebal, *h*as Moses the servant of the Lord had commanded before, that they should bless the children of Israel.

34 Then afterward he read all the words of the Law, the blessings and cursings, according to all that is written in the book of the Law.

35 There was not a word of all that Moses had commanded, which Joshua read not before all the Congregation of Israel, 'as well *before* the 1women and the children, as the stranger that was conversant among them.

9 *1 Divers Kings assemble themselves against Joshua. 3 The craft of the Gibeonites. 15 Joshua maketh a league with them. 23 For their craft they are condemned to perpetual slavery.*

1 And when all the Kings that 1were beyond Jordan, in the mountains and in the valleys, and by all the coasts of the 2great Sea over against Lebanon (*as* the Hittites, and the Amorites, the Canaanites, the Perizzites, the Hivites, and the Jebusites) heard thereof,

2 They gathered themselves together, to fight against Joshua, and against Israel with one 1accord.

3 ¶ *a*But the inhabitants of Gibeon heard what Joshua had done unto Jericho, and to Ai.

4 And therefore they wrought craftily: for they

f Josh. 7:25,26
g Exod. 20:25
Deut. 27:5
h Deut. 11:29
Deut. 27:12,13
i Deut. 31:12,13

CHAPTER 9
a 2 Sam. 21:1

went, and feigned themselves ambassadors, and took old sacks upon their asses, and old bottles for wine, both rent and 1bound up,

5 And old shoes and clouted upon their feet: also the raiment upon them *was* old, and all their provision of bread was dried, and molded.

6 So they came unto Joshua into the host to Gilgal, and said unto him, and unto the men of Israel, We be come from a far country: now therefore make a league with us.

7 Then the men of Israel said unto the 1Hivites, It may be that thou dwellest among us, how then can I make a league with thee?

8 And they said unto Joshua, We are thy servants. Then Joshua said unto them, Who are ye, and whence come ye?

9 And they answered him, From a very far country thy servants are come for 1the Name of the Lord thy God: for we have heard his fame and all that he hath done in Egypt,

10 And all that he hath done to the two kings of the Amorites that were beyond Jordan, to Sihon king of Heshbon, and to Og king of Bashan, which were at Ashtaroth.

11 Wherefore our Elders, and all the inhabitants of our country spake to us, saying, Take vittles 1with you for the journey, and go to meet them, and say unto them, We are your servants: now therefore make ye a league with us.

12 This our 1bread we took it hot with us for victuals out of our houses, the day we departed to come unto you: but now behold, it is dried, and it is molded.

13 Also these bottles of wine which we filled, *were* new, and lo, they be rent, and these our garments and our shoes are old, by reason of the exceeding great journey.

14 ¶ And the 1men accepted *their tale* concerning their victuals, and counseled not with the mouth of the Lord.

15 So Joshua made peace with them, and made a league with them, that he would suffer them to live: also the Princes of the Congregation swore unto them.

16 ¶ But at the end of three days, after they had made a league with them, they heard that they were their neighbors, and that they dwelt among

---

8:32 1 Meaning, the ten commandments, which are the sum of the whole Law.
8:35 1 So neither young nor old, man nor woman, were exempted from hearing the word of the Lord.
9:1 1 In respect of the plain of Moab.
  2 The main sea called Mediterranean.
9:2 1 Hebrew, *one mouth.*
9:4 1 Because they were all worn.

9:7 1 For the Gibeonites and the Hivites were all one people.
9:9 1 Even the idolaters for fear of death will pretend to honor the true God, and receive his religion.
9:11 1 Hebrew, *in your hand.*
9:12 1 The wicked lack no art, nor spare no lies to set forth their policy, when they will deceive the servants of God.
9:14 1 Some think that the Israelites ate of their victuals, and so made a league with them.

them.

17 And the children of Israel took their [1]journey, and came unto their cities the third day, and their cities *were* Gibeon, and Chephirah, and Beeroth and Kirjath Jearim.

18 And the children of Israel slew them not, because the Princes of the Congregation had sworn unto them by the Lord God of Israel: wherefore all the Congregation [1]murmured against the Princes.

19 Then all the Princes said unto all the Congregation, We have sworn unto them by the Lord God of Israel: now therefore we may not touch them.

20 *But* this we will do to them, and let them live, lest the wrath be upon us, because of the [1]oath which we swore unto them.

21 And the Princes said unto them again, Let them live, but they shall hew wood, and draw water unto all the Congregation, as the Princes appoint them.

22 Joshua then called them, and talked with them, and said, Wherefore have ye beguiled us, saying, We are very far from you, when ye dwell among us?

23 Now therefore ye are accursed, and there shall none of you be freed from being bondmen, and hewers of wood, and drawers of water for [1]the house of my God.

24 And they answered Joshua, and said, Because it was told thy servants, that the Lord thy God had [b]commanded his servant Moses to give you all the land, and to destroy all the inhabitants of the land out of your sight, therefore we were exceeding sore afraid for our lives at the presence of you, and have done this thing:

25 And behold now, we are in thine hand: do as it seemeth good and right in thine eyes to do unto us.

26 Even so did he unto them, and delivered them out of the [1]hand of the children of Israel, that they slew them not.

27 And Joshua appointed them that same day *to be* hewers of wood, and drawers of water for the Congregation, and for the [1]altar of the Lord unto this day, in the place which he should choose.

10

1 Five kings make war against Gibeon whom Joshua discomfiteth. 11 The Lord rained hailstones and slew many. 12 The Sun standeth at Joshua's prayer. 26 The five kings are hanged. 29 Many more cities and kings are

Marginal notes (center column):

[b] Deut. 7:1

CHAPTER 10
[a] Josh. 6:16,21
[b] Josh. 8:3,28,29

destroyed.

1 Now when Adoni Zedek king of Jerusalem had heard how Joshua had taken Ai and had destroyed it, (*for* as he had done to Jericho and to the king thereof, so he had done to [b]Ai and to the king thereof) and how the inhabitants of Gibeon had made peace with Israel, and were among them,

2 Then they feared exceedingly: for Gibeon was a great city, as one of the royal cities: for it was greater than Ai, and all the men thereof *were* mighty.

3 Wherefore [1]Adoni Zedek king of Jerusalem sent unto Hoham king of Hebron, and unto Piram king of Jarmuth, and unto Japhia king of Lachish, and unto Debir king of Eglon, saying,

4 Come up unto me, and help me, that we may smite Gibeon: for they have made peace with Joshua and with the children of Israel.

5 Therefore the five kings of the Amorites, the king of Jerusalem, the king of Hebron, the king of Jarmuth, the king of Lachish, *and* the king of Eglon, gathered themselves together, and went up, they with all their hosts, and besieged Gibeon, and made [1]war against it.

6 And the men of Gibeon sent unto Joshua, *even* to the host to Gilgal, saying, Withdraw not thine hand from thy servants: come up to us quickly, and save us, and help us: for all the kings of the Amorites, which dwell in the mountains, are gathered together against us.

7 So Joshua ascended from Gilgal, he, and all the people of war with him, and all the men of might.

8 ¶ And the Lord said unto Joshua, [1]Fear them not: for I have given them into thine hand: none of them shall stand against thee.

9 Joshua therefore came unto them suddenly: *for* he went up from Gilgal all the night.

10 And the Lord discomfited them before Israel, and slew them with a great slaughter at Gibeon, and chased them along the way that goeth up to Beth Horon, and smote them to Azekah, and to Makkedah.

11 And as they fled from before Israel, *and* were in the going down to Beth Horon, the Lord cast down great stones from heaven upon them, until Azekah, and they died: *they were* more that died with the [1]hailstones, than they whom the children

---

9:17 [1] From Gilgal.
9:18 [1] Fearing lest for their fault the plague of God should have light upon them all.
9:20 [1] This doth not establish rash oaths, but showeth God's mercy toward his, which would not punish them for their fault.
9:23 [1] For the uses of the Tabernacle and of the temple when it shall be built.
9:26 [1] Who were minded to put them to death for fear of God's wrath.
9:27 [1] That is, for the service of the Temple, as verse 23.

10:3 [1] That is, Lord of justice: so tyrants take to themselves glorious names, when indeed they be very enemies against God and all justice.
10:5 [1] So envious the wicked are, when any depart from their hand.
10:8 [1] Lest Joshua should have thought that God had sent this great power against him for his unlawful league with the Gibeonites, the Lord here strengtheneth him.
10:11 [1] So we see that all things serve to execute God's vengeance against the wicked.

of Israel slew with the sword.

12 ¶ Then spake Joshua to the Lord, in the day when the Lord gave the Amorites before the children of Israel, and he said in the sight of Israel, 'Sun, stay thou in Gibeon, and thou Moon, in the valley of Aijalon.

13 And the Sun abode, and the moon stood still, until the people avenged themselves upon their enemies: (is not this written in the book of ¹Jasher?) so the Sun abode in the midst of the heaven, and hasted not to go down for a whole day.

14 And there was no day like that before it, nor after it, that the Lord heard the voice of a man: for the Lord ¹fought for Israel.

15 ¶ After, Joshua returned, and all Israel with him unto the camp to Gilgal:

16 But the five kings fled and were hid in a cave at Makkedah.

17 And it was told Joshua, saying, The five kings are found hid in a cave at Makkedah.

18 Then Joshua said, Roll great stones upon the mouth of the cave, and set men by it for to keep them.

19 But stand ye not still: follow after your enemies, and ¹smite all the hindmost, suffer them not to enter into their cities: for the Lord your God hath given them into your hand.

20 And when Joshua and the children of Israel had made an end of slaying them with an exceeding great slaughter till they were consumed, and the rest that remained of them were entered into walled cities,

21 Then all the people returned to the camp, to Joshua at Makkedah in ¹peace: no man moved his tongue against the children of Israel.

22 After, Joshua said, Open the mouth of the cave, and bring out these five kings unto me forth of the cave.

23 And they did so, and brought out those five kings unto him forth of the cave, even the king of Jerusalem, the king of Hebron, the king of Jarmuth, the king of Lachish, and the king of Eglon.

24 And when they had brought out those kings unto Joshua, Joshua called for all the men of Israel, and said unto the chief of the men of war, which went with him, Come near, set your feet upon the ¹necks of these kings, and they came near, and set their feet upon their necks.

25 And Joshua said unto them, Fear not, nor be faint hearted, but be strong and of a good courage: for thus will the Lord do to all your enemies, against

c Isa. 28:21
d Deut. 21:23
Josh. 8:29

whom ye fight.

26 So then Joshua smote them, and slew them, and hanged them on five trees, and they hanged still upon the trees until the evening.

27 And at the going down of the sun, Joshua gave commandment, that they should take ᵈthem down off the trees, and cast them into the cave (wherein they had been hid) and they laid great stones upon the cave's mouth, which remain until this day.

28 ¶ And that same day Joshua took Makkedah and smote it with the edge of the sword, and the king thereof destroyed he with them, and ¹all the souls that were therein, he let none remain: for he did to the king of Makkedah, as he had done unto the king of Jericho.

29 Then Joshua went from Makkedah, and all Israel with him unto Libnah, and fought against Libnah.

30 And the Lord gave it also and the king thereof into the hand of Israel: and he smote it with the edge of the sword, and all the ¹souls that were therein: he let none remain in it: for he did unto the king thereof, as he had done unto the king of Jericho.

31 ¶ And Joshua departed from Libnah, and all Israel with him unto Lachish, and besieged it, and assaulted it.

32 And the Lord gave Lachish into the hand of Israel, which took it the second day, and smote it with the edge of the sword, and all the souls that were therein, according to all as he had done to Libnah.

33 ¶ Then Horam king of Gezer came up to help Lachish: but Joshua smote him and his people, until none of his remained.

34 ¶ And from Lachish Joshua departed unto Eglon, and all Israel with him, and they besieged it, and assaulted it.

35 And they took it the same day, and smote it with the edge of the sword, and all the souls that were therein he utterly destroyed the same day, according to all that he had done to Lachish.

36 Then Joshua went up from Eglon, and all Israel with him unto Hebron, and they fought against it.

37 And when they had taken it, they smote it with the edge of the sword, and the king thereof, and all the cities thereof, and all the souls that were therein: he left none remaining, according to all as he had done to Eglon: for he destroyed it utterly, and all the souls that were therein.

38 ¶ So Joshua returned, and all Israel with him to Debir, and fought against it.

10:13 ¹ Some read the book of the righteous, meaning Moses: the Chaldea text readeth in the book of the Law, but it is like that it was a book thus named, which is now lost.
10:14 ¹ By taking away the enemies' hearts and destroying them with hail stones.
10:19 ¹ Hebrew, cut off all their train or tail.

10:21 ¹ Or in safety, so that none gave them as much as an evil word.
10:24 ¹ Signifying what should become of the rest of God's enemies, seeing that kings themselves were not spared.
10:28 ¹ Or, every person, Josh. 6:21.
10:30 ¹ Or, persons.

39 And when he had taken it, and the king thereof, and all the city thereof, they smote them with the edge of the sword, and utterly destroyed all the souls that were therein, he let none remain: as he did to Hebron, so he did to Debir, and to the king thereof, as he had also done to Libnah, and to the king thereof.

40 ¶ So Joshua smote all the hill countries, and the South countries, and the valleys, and the [1]hillsides, and all their kings, and let none remain, but utterly destroyed every soul, as the Lord God of Israel had commanded.

41 And Joshua smote them from Kadesh Barnea even unto Gaza, and all the country of Goshen, even unto Gibeon.

42 And all these kings, and their land did Joshua take at [1]one time, because the Lord God of Israel fought for Israel.

43 Afterward, Joshua and all Israel with him returned unto the camp in [1]Gilgal.

11 *1 Divers kings and cities, and countries overcome by Joshua. 15 Joshua did all that Moses had commanded him. 20 God hardeneth the enemies' hearts that they might be destroyed.*

1 And when Jabin king of Hazor had heard this, then he [1]sent to Jobab king of Madon, and to the king of Shimron, and to the king of Achshaph,

2 And unto the kings that were by the North in the mountains and plains toward the South side of [1]Chinneroth, and in the valleys, and in the borders of Dor Westward,

3 *And* unto the Canaanites, *both* by East, and by West, and unto the Amorites, and Hittites, and Perizzites, and Jebusites in the mountains, and unto the Hivites, under [1]Hermon in the land of Mizpah.

4 And they came out, and all their hosts with them, many people, as the sand that is on the seashore, for multitude, with horses and chariots exceeding many.

5 So all these kings met together, and came and pitched together at the waters of Merom, for to fight against Israel.

6 ¶ Then the Lord said unto Joshua, Be not afraid for them: for tomorrow about this time will I deliver them all slain before Israel: thou shalt [1]hough their horses, and burn their chariots with fire.

CHAPTER 11
[a] Num. 33:52
  Deut. 7:2
[b] Exod. 34:11
[c] Deut. 7:2
[d] Josh. 9:3

7 Then came Joshua and all the men of war with him, against them, by the waters of Merom suddenly, and fell upon them.

8 And the Lord gave them into the hand of Israel: and they smote them, and chased them unto great Sidon, and unto [1]Misrephoth, and unto the valley of Mizpah Eastward, and smote them until they had none remaining of them.

9 And Joshua did unto them as the Lord bade him: he houghed their horses, and burnt their chariots with fire.

10 ¶ At that time also Joshua turned back, and took Hazor, and smote the King thereof with the sword: for Hazor beforetime was the head of all those kingdoms.

11 Moreover they smote all the [1]persons that were therein with the edge of the sword, utterly destroying *all*, leaving none alive, and he burnt Hazor with fire.

12 So all the cities of those kings, and all the kings of them did Joshua take, and smote them with the edge of the sword, *and* utterly destroyed them, [a]as Moses the servant of the Lord had commanded.

13 But Israel burnt none of the cities that stood still in their [1]strength, save Hazor only, that Joshua burnt.

14 And all the spoil of these cities and the cattle, the children of Israel took for their prey, but they smote every [1]man with the edge of the sword until they had destroyed them, not leaving one alive.

15 ¶ As the Lord [b]had commanded Moses his servant, so did Moses [c]command Joshua, and so did Joshua, he left nothing undone of all that the Lord had commanded Moses.

16 So Joshua took all this land of the mountains, and all the South, and all the land of Goshen, and the low country, and the plain, and the [1]mountain of Israel, and the low country of the same,

17 From the mount [1]Halak, that goeth up to Seir, even unto [2]Baal Gad in the valley of Lebanon, under mount Hermon: and all their kings he took, and smote them, and slew them.

18 Joshua made war [a] long time with all those Kings,

19 Neither was there any city that made peace with the children of Israel, [d]save those Hivites that inhabited Gibeon: all *others* they took by battle.

10:40 [1] Some read, Ashedoth, which signifieth the descents of the hills.
10:42 [1] In one battle.
10:43 [1] Where the ark was, there to give thanks for their victories.
11:1 [1] The more that God's power appeareth, the more the wicked rage against it.
11:2 [1] Which the Evangelists call the lake of Gennesaret, or Tiberias.
11:3 [1] Which was mount Sion, as Deut. 4:48.
11:6 [1] That neither they should serve to the use of war, nor the Isra-

elites should put their trust in them.
11:8 [1] Which signifieth hot waters, or according to some, brine pits.
11:11 [1] Both men, women and children.
11:13 [1] Which were strong by situation and not hurt by war.
11:14 [1] All mankind.
11:16 [1] That is, Samaria.
11:17 [1] So called, because it was bare and without trees.
    [2] Or, the valley of Gad.

20 For it came of the Lord, to [1]harden their hearts that they should come against Israel in battle, to the intent that they should destroy them utterly, *and* show them no mercy, but that they should bring them to nought, as the Lord had commanded Moses.

21 ¶ And that same season came Joshua, and destroyed the Anakims out of the mountains: *as* out of Hebron, out of Debir, out of Anab, and out of all the mountains of Judah, and out of all the mountains of Israel: Joshua destroyed them utterly with their cities.

22 There was no Anakim left in the land of the children of Israel, only in Gaza, [1]in Gath, and in Ashdod were they left.

23 So Joshua took the whole land, according to all that the Lord had said unto Moses: and Joshua gave it for an inheritance unto Israel, [c]according to their portions through their tribes: then the land was at rest without war.

12

1, 7 What kings Joshua and the children of Israel killed on both sides of Jordan. 24 Which were in number thirty and one.

1 And these are the Kings of the land, which the children of Israel smote and possessed their land on the [1]other side Jordan toward the rising of the sun, from the river Arnon, unto mount Hermon, and all the plain Eastward.

2 [a]Sihon king of the Amorites, that dwelt in Heshbon, having dominion from Aroer, which is beside the river of Arnon, and from the middle of the river, and from half Gilead unto the river of Jabbok, in the border of the children of Ammon.

3 And from the plain unto the sea of Chinneroth Eastward, and unto the sea of the [1]plain, even the salt sea Eastward, the way to Beth Jeshimoth, and from the South under the [2]springs of [b]Pisgah.

4 ¶ They *conquered* also the coast of Og king of Bashan of the [c]remnant of the giants, which dwelt at Ashtaroth, and at Edrei,

5 And reigned in mount Hermon, and in Salcah, and in all Bashan, unto the border of the Geshurites, and the Maachathites, and half Gilead: even the border of Sihon king of Heshbon.

6 Moses the servant of the Lord, and the children of Israel smote them: [d]Moses also the servant of the Lord gave *their land* for a possession unto the Reubenites, and unto the Gadites, and to half the tribe of Manasseh.

c Num. 26:53,55

CHAPTER 12
a Num. 21:24
   Deut. 3:6
b Deut. 3:17
   Deut. 4:49
c Deut. 3:11
d Num. 32:29
   Deut. 3:12
   Josh. 13:12
e Josh. 6:2
f Josh. 8:26
g Josh. 10:13
h Josh. 10:33
i Josh. 10:39
j Josh. 10:29,30
k Josh. 10:23
l Josh. 11:19
m Gen. 14:1

7 ¶ These also are the kings of the country, which Joshua and the children of Israel smote on this side Jordan, Westward from Baal Gad in the valley of Lebanon, even unto the mount [1]Halak that goeth up to Seir, and Joshua gave it unto the tribes of Israel for a possession, according to their portions.

8 In the mountains, and in the valleys, and in the plains, and in the [1]hillsides, and in the wilderness, and in the South, *where were* the Hittites, the Amorites, and the Canaanites, the Perizzites, the Hivites, and the Jebusites.

9 ¶ [e]The King of Jericho *was* one: [f]the king of Ai, which is beside Bethel, one:

10 [g]The king of Jerusalem, one: the king of Hebron, one:

11 The king of Jarmuth, one: the king of Lachish, one:

12 The king of Eglon, one: the [h]king of Gezer, one:

13 The [i]king of Debir, one: the king of Geder, one:

14 The king of Hormah, one: the king of Arad, one:

15 The [j]king of Libnah, one: the king of Adullam, one:

16 The [k]king of Makkedah, one: the king of Bethel, one:

17 The king of Tappuah, one: the king of Hepher, one:

18 The king of Aphek, one: the king of Lasharon, one:

19 The king of Madon, one: the [l]king of Hazor, one:

20 The king of Shimron Meron, one: the king of Achshaph, one:

21 The king of Taanach, one: the king of Megiddo, one:

22 The king of Kedesh, one: the king of Jokneam [1]of Carmel, one:

23 The king of Dor, in the country of Dor, one: the king of the [m]nations of Gilgal, one:

24 The king of Tirzah, one. All the kings *were* thirty and one.

13

3 The borders and coasts of the land of Canaan. 8 The possession of the Reubenites, Gadites, and of the half tribe of Manasseh. 14 The Lord is the inheritance of Levi. 22 Balaam was slain.

1 Now when Joshua was old, *and* [1]stricken in

11:20 [1] That is, to give them over to themselves: and therefore they could not but rebel against God and seek their own destruction.
11:22 [1] Out of the which came Goliath, 1 Sam. 17:4.
12:1 [1] From Gilgal where Joshua camped.
12:3 [1] Or, wilderness.
[2] Or, hillsides.
12:7 [1] Read Josh. 11:17.
12:8 [1] Or, in Ashdoth.
12:22 [1] Or, near unto Carmel.
13:1 [1] Being almost an hundred and ten years old.

years, the Lord said unto him, Thou art old and [2]grown in age, and there remaineth exceeding much land to be [3]possessed:

2 This is the land that remaineth, all the [1]regions of the Philistines, and all Geshuri.

3 From [1]Nilus which is [2]in Egypt, even unto the borders of Ekron Northward: this is counted of the Canaanites, even five Lordships of the Philistines, the Gazites, and the Ashdodites, the Ashkelonites, the Gittites, and the Ekronites, and the Avites:

4 From the South, all the land of the Canaanites, and the [1]cave that is beside the Sidonians, unto Aphek, *and* to the borders of the Amorites:

5 And the land of the Gebalites, and all Lebanon toward the Sun rising from [1]Baal Gad under mount Hermon, until one come to Hamath.

6 All the inhabitants of the mountains from Lebanon unto [1]Misrephoth, *and* all the Sidonians, I will cast them out from before the children of Israel: only divide thou it by lot unto the Israelites, to inherit, as I have commanded thee.

7 Now therefore divide this land to inherit, unto the nine tribes, and to the half tribe of Manasseh.

8 *For* with *half* thereof the Reubenites and the Gadites have received their inheritance, [a]which Moses gave them beyond Jordan Eastward, even as Moses the servant of the Lord had given them.

9 From Aroer that is on the brink of the river Arnon, and from the city that is in the midst of the [1]river, and all the plain of Medeba unto Dibon,

10 And all the cities of Sihon king of the Amorites, which reigned in Heshbon, unto the borders of the children of Ammon,

11 And Gilead, and the borders of the Geshurites and of the Maachathites, and all mount Hermon, with all Bashan unto Salcah:

12 All the kingdom of Og in Bashan, which reigned in Ashtaroth and in Edrei: (who remained of [b]the rest of the giants) for these did Moses smite, and cast them out:

13 But the children of Israel [1]expelled not the Geshurites nor the Maachathites: but the Geshurites and the Maachathites dwell among the Israelites even unto this day.

14 Only unto the tribe of Levi he gave none inheritance, *but* the sacrifices of the Lord God of Israel are [1]his inheritance, as he said unto him.

15 ¶ Moses then gave unto the tribe of the children of Reuben *inheritance*, according to their families.

16 And their coast was from Aroer, that is on the brink of the river Arnon, and from the city that is in the midst of the river, and all the plain which is by Medeba:

17 Heshbon with all the cities thereof, that are in the plain: Dibon and [1]Bamoth Baal, and Beth Baal Meon:

18 And Jahaza, and Kedemoth, and Mephaath:

19 Kirjathaim also, and Sibmah, and Zereth Shahar in the mount of [1]Emek:

20 And Beth Peor, and ⸢Ashdoth Pisgah, and Beth Jeshimoth:

21 And all the cities of the plain, and all the kingdom of Sihon king of the Amorites, which reigned in Heshbon, whom Moses [d]smote with the Princes of Midian, Evi and Rekem, and Zur, and Hur, and Reba, the dukes of Sihon, dwelling in the country.

22 And [1]Balaam the son of Beor the soothsayer did the children of Israel slay with the sword, among them that were slain.

23 And the border of the children of Reuben was Jordan with the coasts. This was the inheritance of the children of Reuben according to their families, with the cities and their villages.

24 ¶ Also Moses gave *inheritance* unto the tribe of Gad, *even* unto the children of Gad according to their families.

25 And their coasts were Jazer, and all the cities of Gilead, and half the land of the children of Ammon unto Aroer, which is before Rabbah:

26 And from Heshbon unto Ramath, Mizpah, and Betonim: and from Mahanaim unto the borders of Debir:

27 And in the valley of Beth Haram, and Beth Nimrah, and Succoth, and Zaphon, the rest of the kingdom of Sihon king of Heshbon unto Jordan and the borders even unto the sea coast of Chinnereth, [1]beyond Jordan Eastward.

28 This is the inheritance of the children of Gad, after their families, with the cities and their villages.

29 ¶ Also Moses gave *inheritance* unto the half tribe of Manasseh: and this belonged to the half

CHAPTER 13
[a] Num. 32:33
   Deut. 3:13
   Josh. 22:4
[b] Deut. 3:11
   Josh. 22:4
[c] Deut. 3:17
[d] Num. 31:8

13:1 [2] Hebrew, *commen into years.*
      [3] After that the enemies are overcome.
13:2 [1] Or, borders.
13:3 [1] Hebrew, *Sihor.*
      [2] Hebrew, *upon the face of Egypt.*
13:4 [1] Or, Mearah.
13:5 [1] Or, the plain of Gad.
13:6 [1] Read Josh. 11:8.
13:9 [1] Or, valley.

13:13 [1] Because they destroyed not all as God had commanded, they that remained were snares and pricks to hurt them, Num. 33:35; Josh. 23:13; Judg. 2:3.
13:14 [1] Levi shall live by the sacrifices, Num. 11:23.
13:17 [1] Or, high places of Baal.
13:19 [1] Or, the valley.
13:22 [1] So that both they which obeyed wicked counsel and the wicked counselor perished by the just judgment of God.
13:27 [1] That is, in the land of Moab.

tribe of the children of Manasseh according to their families.

30 And their border was from Mahanaim, *even* all Bashan, *to wit,* all the kingdom of Og king of Bashan, and all the towns of Jair which are in Bashan, threescore cities,

31 And half Gilead, and Ashtaroth, and Edrei, cities of the kingdom of Og in Bashan, *were given* unto the ¹children of Machir the son of Manasseh to half of the children of Machir after their families.

32 These are the heritages, which Moses did distribute in the plain of Moab beyond Jordan *toward* Jericho Eastward.

33 ʲBut unto the tribe of Levi Moses gave none inheritance: *for* the Lord God of Israel is their inheritance, ᵍas he said unto them.

14 1 *The land of Canaan was divided among the nine tribes and the half.* 6 *Caleb requireth the heritage that was promised him.* 13 *Hebron was given him.*

1 These also are the *places* which the children of Israel inherited in the land of Canaan, ᵃwhich Eleazar the Priest, and Joshua the son of Nun and the chief fathers of the tribes of the children of Israel, distributed to them,

2 ᵇBy the lot of their inheritance, as the Lord had commanded by the hand of Moses, to give to the nine tribes, and the half tribe.

3 For Moses had given inheritance unto ¹two tribes and an half tribe, beyond Jordan: but unto the Levites he gave none inheritance among them.

4 For the children of Joseph were ¹two tribes, Manasseh and Ephraim, therefore they gave no part unto the Levites in the land, save cities to dwell in, with the suburbs of the same for their beasts and their substance.

5 ᶜAs the Lord had commanded Moses, so the children of Israel did when they divided the land.

6 ¶ Then the children of Judah came unto Joshua in Gilgal: and Caleb the son of Jephunneh the Kenizzite said unto him, Thou knowest what the Lord said unto Moses the man of God, concerning ¹thee and me in Kadesh Barnea.

7 Forty years old was I, when Moses the servant of the Lord sent me from Kadesh Barnea to espy the land, and I brought him word again, as *I thought* in mine heart.

8 But my ¹brethren that went up with me, dis-

couraged the heart of the people: yet I followed still the Lord my God.

9 Wherefore Moses swore the same day, saying, Certainly the land whereon thy feet have trodden, shall be thine inheritance, and thy children's forever, because thou hast followed constantly the Lord my God.

10 Therefore behold now, the Lord hath kept me alive, as he promised: this is the forty and fifth year since the Lord spake this thing unto Moses, while the children of Israel wandered in the wilderness: and now lo, I am this day four score and five years old:

11 And yet am as strong at this time, as I was when Moses sent me: as strong as I was then, so strong am I now, *either* for war, or ¹for government.

12 Now therefore give me this mountain whereof the Lord spake in that day (for thou heardest in that day, how the ¹Anakim *were* there, and the cities great and walled) ²if so be the Lord will be with me that I may drive them out, as the Lord said.

13 Then Joshua blessed him, and gave unto Caleb the son of Jephunneh, Hebron for an inheritance.

14 ᵈHebron therefore became the inheritance of Caleb the son of Jephunneh the Kenizzite, unto this day: because he followed constantly the Lord God of Israel.

15 And the name of ᵉHebron *was* before time, Kirjath Arba: which *Arba was* a ¹great man among the Anakim: thus the land ceased from war.

15 1 *The lot of the children of Judah, and the names of the cities and villages of the same.* 13 *Caleb's portion.* 18 *The request of Achsah.*

1 This then was the lot of the tribe of the children of Judah by their families: *even* ᵃto the border of Edom and the wilderness of ᵇZin, Southward on the South coast.

2 And their South border was the salt Sea coast, from the ¹point that looketh Southward.

3 And it went out on the South side toward Maaleh Akrabbim, and went along to Zin, and ascended up on the South side unto Kadesh Barnea, and went along to Hezron, and went up to Adar, and set a compass to Karkaa.

4 From thence went it along to Azmon, and reached unto the river of Egypt, and the end of that coast was on the West side: this shall be your South coast.

Marginal notes: ᵉ Num. 32:39 ᶠ Josh. 18:7 ᵍ Num. 18:20 | CHAPTER 14 ᵃ Num. 34:17 ᵇ Num. 26:55 Num. 33:54 ᶜ Num. 35:2 Josh. 21:2,3 ᵈ Josh. 21:11 ᵉ Josh. 15:13 | CHAPTER 15 ᵃ Num. 34:3 ᵇ Num. 33:36

13:31 ¹ Meaning, his nephews and posterity.
14:3 ¹ As Reuben and Gad and half the tribe of Manasseh, Num. 32:33.
14:4 ¹ So though Levi lacked, yet were there still twelve tribes by this means.
14:6 ¹ Which was, that they two only should enter into the land, Num. 14:24.
14:8 ¹ Which were the ten other spies.
14:11 ¹ Hebrew, *to go out and come in.*
14:12 ¹ Or, giants.
  ² This he spake of modesty, and not of doubting.
14:15 ¹ Either for his power or person.
15:2 ¹ The Hebrew word signifieth tongue, whereby is meant either the arm of the Sea that cometh into the land, or a rock, or cape that goeth into the Sea.

5   Also the East border shall be the salt Sea, unto the ¹end of Jordan: and the border on the North quarter from the point of the Sea, *and* from the end of Jordan.

6   And this border goeth up to Beth Hoglah, and goeth along by the North side of Beth Arabah: so the border from thence goeth up to the ¹stone of Bohan the son of Reuben.

7   Again this border goeth up to Debir from the valley of Achor, and Northward, turning toward Gilgal, that lieth before the going unto Adummim, which is on the South side of the river: also this border goeth up to the waters of ¹En Shemesh, and endeth at ʿEn Rogel.

8   Then this border goeth up to the valley of the son of Hinnom; on the South side of the Jebusites: the same is Jerusalem. Also this border goeth up to the top of the mountain that lieth before the valley of Hinnom Westward, which is by the end of the valley of ¹giants Northward.

9   So this border compasseth from the top of the mountain unto the fountain of the water of Nephtoah, and goeth out to the cities of mount Ephron: and this border draweth to Baalah which is ¹Kirjath Jearim.

10   Then this border compasseth from Baalah Westward unto mount Seir, and goeth along unto the side of mount Jearim, which is Chesalon on the North side: it cometh down to Beth Shemesh, and goeth to Timnah.

11   Also this border goeth out unto the side of Ekron Northward: and this border draweth to Shicron, and goeth along to mount Baalah, and stretcheth unto Jabneel: and the ends of this coast are unto the ¹Sea.

12   And the West border *is* to the great sea: so this border shall be the bounds of the children of Judah round about, according to their families.

13   ¶ And unto Caleb the son of Jephunneh did Joshua give a part among the children of Judah, as the Lord commanded him, *even* ᵈKirjath Arba of the father of Anak which is in Hebron.

14   And Caleb ¹drove thence three sons of Anak, Sheshai, and Ahiman, and Talmai, the sons of Anak.

15   And he went up thence to the inhabitants of Debir: and the name of Debir beforetime *was* Kirjath Sepher.

ᶜ 1 Kings 2:9
ᵈ Josh. 14:15

16   Then Caleb said, He that smiteth Kirjath Sepher, and taketh it, even to him will I give Achsah my daughter to wife.

17   And Othniel the son of Kenaz, the ¹brother of Caleb took it: and he gave him Achsah his daughter to wife.

18   And as she went in *to him*, she moved him, to ask of her father a field: ¹and she lighted off her ass, and Caleb said unto her, What wilt thou?

19   Then she answered, ¹Give me a blessing: for thou hast given me the South country; ²give me also springs of water. And he gave her the springs above, and the springs beneath.

20   This shall be the inheritance of the tribe of the children of Judah according to their families.

21   And the utmost cities of the tribe of the children of Judah, toward the coasts of Edom Southward *were* Kabzeel, and Eder, and Jagur,

22   And Kinah, and Dimonah, and Adadah,

23   And Kedesh, and Hazor, and Ithnan,

24   Ziph, and Telem, and Bealoth,

25   And Hazor, Hadattah, and Kerioth, Hezron (which is Hazor.)

26   Amam, and Shema, and Moladah,

27   And Hazar, Gaddah, and Heshmon, and Beth Pelet,

28   And Hazar Shual, and Beersheba, and Bizjothjah,

29   Baalah, and Ijim, and Ezem,

30   And Eltolad, and Chesil, and ¹Hormah,

31   And Ziklag, and Madmannah, and Sansannah,

32   And Lebaoth, and Shilhim, and Ain, and Rimmon: all *these* cities *are* twenty-nine with their villages.

33   ¶ In the low country *were* Eshtaol, and Zorah, and Ashnah,

34   And Zanoah, and En Gannim, Tappuah, and Enam,

35   Jarmuth, and Adullam, Socoh, and Azekah,

36   And Sharaim, and Adithaim, and Gederah, and Gederothaim: fourteen cities with their villages.

37   Zenan, and Hadashah, and Migdal Gad,

38   And Dilean, and Mizpah, and Joktheel,

39   Lachish, and Bozkath, and Eglon,

40   And Cabbon, and Lahmas, and Kithlish,

41   And Gederoth, Beth Dagon, and Naamah, and Makkedah: sixteen cities with their villages.

42   Libnah, and Ether, and Ashan,

15:5 ¹ Meaning the mouth of the river where it runneth into the salt Sea.
15:6 ¹ Which was a mark to part their countries.
15:7 ¹ Or, the fountain of the sun.
15:8 ¹ Hebrew, *Rephaim*.
15:9 ¹ Or, the city of wood.
15:11 ¹ Meaning, toward Syria.
15:14 ¹ This was done after the death of Joshua, Judg. 1:10, 20.
15:17 ¹ Or, cousins.
15:18 ¹ Because her husband tarried too long.
15:19 ¹ Or, grant me this petition.
    ² Because her country was barren, she desired of her father a field that had springs, Judg. 1:14, 15.
15:30 ¹ Which before was called Zephath, Judg. 1:17.

43 And Jiphtah, and Ashnah, and Nezib,

44 And Keilah, and Achzib, and Mareshah: nine cities with their villages.

45 Ekron with her ¹towns and her villages,

46 From Ekron, even unto the Sea, all that lieth about Ashdod with their villages.

47 Ashdod with her towns and her villages: Gaza with her towns and her villages unto the ¹river of Egypt, and the great Sea *was their* coast.

48 ¶ And in the mountains *were* Shamir, and Jattir, and Sochoh,

49 And Dannah, and ¹Kirjath Sannah (which is Debir.)

50 And Anab, and Eshtemoh, and Anim,

51 And Goshen, and Holon, and Giloh: eleven cities with their villages.

52 Arab, and Dumah, and Eshean,

53 And Janum, and Beth Tappuah, and Aphekah,

54 And Humtah, and ʿKirjath Arba, (which is Hebron) and Zior: nine cities with their villages.

55 Maon, Carmel, and Ziph, and Juttah,

56 And Jezreel, and Jokdeam, and Zanoah,

57 Kain, Gibeah, and Timnah: ten cities with their villages.

58 Halhul, Beth Zur, and Gedor,

59 And Maarath, and Beth Anoth, and Eltekon: six cities with their villages.

60 ¶ Kirjath Baal, which is Kirjath Jearim, and Rabbah: two cities with their villages.

61 In the wilderness *were* Beth Arabah, Middin, and Secacah,

62 And Nibshan, and the ¹city of salt, and En Gedi: five cities with their villages.

63 Nevertheless, the Jebusites that were the inhabitants of Jerusalem, could not the children of Judah cast ¹out, but the Jebusites dwell with the children of Judah at Jerusalem unto this day.

16

1 The lot or part of Ephraim. 10 The Canaanites dwelled among them.

1 And the lot fell to the ¹children of Joseph from Jordan by Jericho unto the water of Jericho Eastward, *and* to the wilderness that goeth up from Jericho by the mount Bethel:

2 And goeth out from Bethel to ᵃLuz, and runneth along unto the borders of Archi Ataroth,

3 And goeth down Westward to the coast of Japhlet, unto the coast of Beth Horon the nether:

and to Gezer, and the ends ¹thereof are at the Sea.

4 So the children of Joseph; Manasseh and Ephraim ¹took their inheritance.

5 ¶ Also the borders of the children of Ephraim according to their families, even the borders of their inheritance on the East side were Ataroth Addar, unto Beth Horon the upper.

6 And this border goeth out to the Sea unto Michmethath on the North side, and this border returneth Eastward unto Taanath Shiloh, and passeth it on the East side unto Janohah,

7 And goeth down from Janohah unto Ataroth, and Naarah, and cometh to Jericho, ¹and goeth out at Jordan.

8 And this border goeth from Tappuah Westward unto the river Kanah, and the ends thereof are at the Sea: this is the inheritance of the tribe of the children of Ephraim by their families.

9 And the ¹separate cities for the children of Ephraim *were* among the inheritance of the children of Manasseh: all the cities with their villages.

10 And they cast not out the Canaanite that dwelt in Gezer, but the Canaanite dwelt among the Ephraimites unto this day, and served under tribute.

17

1 The portion of the half tribe of Manasseh. 3 The daughters of Zelophehad. 13 The Canaanites are become tributaries. 14 Manasseh and Ephraim require a greater portion of heritage.

1 This was also the lot of the tribe of Manasseh: for he was the ᵃfirstborn of Joseph, *to wit*, of Machir the firstborn of Manasseh, *and* the father of Gilead: now because he was a man of war, he had Gilead and Bashan.

2 And also ᵇof the ¹rest of the sons of Manasseh by their families, *even* of the sons of Abiezer, and of the sons of Helek, and of the sons of Asriel, and of the sons of Shechem, and of the sons of Hepher, and of the sons of Shemida: these were the males of Manasseh, the son of Joseph according to their families.

3 ¶ But Zelophehad the son of Hepher, the son of Gilead, the son of Machir, the son of Manasseh, had no sons, but daughters: and these are the names of his daughters, Mahlah, and Noah, Hoglah, Milcah and Tirzah:

4 Which came before Eleazar the Priest, and

Margin references: ᶜ Josh. 14:15 / CHAPTER 16 ᵃ Judg. 1:26 / CHAPTER 17 ᵈ Gen. 41:51 Gen. 46:20 Gen. 50:23 Num. 32:39 ᵇ Num. 26:29 ᶜ Num. 26:33 Num. 27:1 Num. 36:2,11

15:45 ¹ Hebrew, *daughters.*
15:47 ¹ Meaning, Nilus, as Josh. 13:3.
15:49 ¹ Which is also called Kirjath Sepher, verse 15.
15:62 ¹ Of this city the salt sea hath his name.
15:63 ¹ That is, utterly, though they slew the most part, and burnt their city, Judg. 1:8.
16:1 ¹ That is, to Ephraim and his children: for Manasseh's portion

followeth.
16:3 ¹ Of their inheritance.
16:4 ¹ Severally, first Ephraim, and then Manasseh.
16:7 ¹ For so far the coasts reach.
16:9 ¹ Because Ephraim's tribe was far greater than Manasseh, therefore he had more cities.
17:2 ¹ For the other half tribe had their portion beyond Jordan.

before Joshua the son of Nun, and before the princes, saying, The Lord commanded Moses to give us an inheritance among our [1]brethren: therefore according to the commandment of the Lord, he gave them an inheritance among the brethren of their father.

5 And there fell ten portions to [1]Manasseh, beside the land of Gilead and Bashan, which is on the other side of Jordan,

6 Because the daughters of Manasseh did inherit among his sons: and Manasseh's other sons had the land of Gilead.

7 ¶ So the borders of Manasseh were from Asher to Michmethath that lieth before Shechem, and this border goeth on the right hand, even to the inhabitants of En Tappuah.

8 The land of Tappuah belonged to Manasseh, but [1]Tappuah beside the border of Manasseh belongeth to the sons of Ephraim.

9 Also this border goeth down unto the [1]river Kanah Southward to the river: these cities of Ephraim are among the cities of Manasseh: and the border of Manasseh is on the North side of the river, and the ends of it are at the [2]Sea,

10 The South pertaineth to Ephraim, and the North to Manasseh, and the sea is his border: and they met together in [1]Asher Northward, and in Issachar Eastward.

11 And Manasseh had in Issachar and in Asher, Beth Shean, and her towns, and Ibleam, and her towns, and the inhabitants of Dor with the towns thereof, and the inhabitants of En Dor with the towns thereof, and the inhabitants of Taanach with her towns, and the inhabitants of Megiddo with the towns of the same, even three countries.

12 Yet the children of Manasseh [1]could not destroy those cities, but the Canaanites dwelled still in that land.

13 Nevertheless, when the children of Israel were strong, they put the Canaanites under tribute, but cast them not out wholly.

14 Then the children of Joseph spake unto Joshua, saying, Why hast thou given me but one lot, and one portion to inherit, seeing I am a great people, forasmuch as the Lord hath [1]blessed me hitherto?

15 Joshua then answered them, If thou be much people, get thee up to the woods, and cut trees for thyself there in the land of the Perizzites, and of the giants, [1]if mount Ephraim be too narrow for thee.

16 Then the children of Joseph said, The mountain will not be enough for us: and all the Canaanites that dwell in the low country have chariots of iron, as well they in Beth Shean, and in the towns of the same, as they in the valley of Jezreel.

17 And Joshua spake unto the house of Joseph, to Ephraim and to Manasseh, saying, Thou art a great people, and hast great power, and shalt not have one lot.

18 Therefore the mountain shall be thine: for it is a wood, and thou shalt cut it down: and the ends of it shall be thine, [1]and thou shalt cast out the Canaanites, though they have iron chariots, and though they be strong.

18 1 The Tabernacle set in Shiloh. 4 Certain are sent to divide the land to the other seven tribes. 11 The lot of the children of Benjamin.

1 And the whole Congregation of the children of Israel came together at Shiloh: for they set up the [1]Tabernacle of the Congregation there, after the land was subject unto them.

2 Now there remained among the children of Israel seven tribes, to whom [1]they had not divided their inheritance.

3 Therefore Joshua said unto the children of Israel, how long are you so slack to enter and possess the land which the Lord God of your fathers hath given you?

4 Give from among you for every tribe three men, that I may send them, and that they may rise and walk through the land, and distribute it according to [1]their inheritance, and return to me.

5 And that they may divide it unto them into seven parts, (Judah shall abide in his coast at the South, and the house of Joseph shall [1]stand in their coasts at the North.)

6 Ye shall describe the land therefore into seven parts, and shall bring them hither to me, and I will cast lots for you here before the [1]Lord our God.

7 But the Levites shall have no part among you: for the [1]Priesthood of the Lord is their inheritance: also Gad and Reuben and half the tribe of Manasseh have

17:4 [1] Among them of our tribe.
17:5 [1] In the land of Canaan: five to the males: and other five to the daughters of Zelophehad.
17:8 [1] Meaning, the city itself.
17:9 [1] Or, the brook of reeds.
[2] That is, toward the main sea.
17:10 [1] In the tribe of Asher, and tribe of Issachar.
17:12 [1] For at the first they lacked courage, and after agreed with them on condition, contrary to God's commandment.
17:14 [1] According to my father Jacob's prophecy, Gen. 48:19.
17:15 [1] If this mount be not large enough, why dost not thou get more by destroying God's enemies, as he hath commanded?
17:18 [1] So that thou shalt enlarge thy portion thereby.
18:1 [1] For they had now removed it from Gilgal, and set it up in Shiloh.
18:2 [1] As Eleazar, Joshua, and the heads of the tribes had done to Judah, Ephraim, and half of Manasseh.
18:4 [1] That is, into seven portions, to every tribe one.
18:5 [1] For these had their inheritance already appointed.
18:6 [1] Before the Ark of the Lord.
18:7 [1] That is, the sacrifices and offerings, Josh. 13:14.

received their inheritance beyond Jordan Eastward, which Moses the servant of the Lord gave them.

8 ¶ Then the men arose, and went their way, and Joshua charged them that went to describe the land, saying, Depart, and go through the land, and [1]describe it, and return to me, that I may here cast lots for you before the Lord in Shiloh.

9 So the men departed, and passed through the land, and described it by cities into seven parts in a book, and returned to Joshua into the camp at Shiloh.

10 ¶ Then Joshua [1]cast lots for them in Shiloh before the Lord, and there Joshua divided the land unto the children of Israel, according to their portions.

11 ¶ And the lot of the tribe of the children of Benjamin came forth according to their families, and the cost of their lot lay [1]between the children of Judah, and the children of Joseph.

12 And their coast on the North side was from Jordan, and the border went up to the side of Jericho on the North part, and went up through the mountains Westward, and the ends thereof are in the wilderness of Beth Aven:

13 And this border goeth along from thence to Luz, even to the South side of Luz (the same is [1]Bethel) and this border descendeth to Ataroth Addar, near the mount that lieth on the South side of Beth Horon the nether.

14 So the border turneth, and compasseth the corner of the Sea Southward, from the mount that lieth before Beth Horon Southward: and the ends thereof are at Kirjath Baal (which is Kirjath Jearim) a city of the children of Judah: this is the West quarter.

15 And the South quarter is from the end of Kirjath Jearim, and this border goeth out [1]Westward, and cometh to the fountain of waters of Nephtoah.

16 And this border descendeth at the end of the mountain, that lieth before the valley of Ben Hinnom, which is in the valley of the [1]giants Northward, and descendeth into the valley of Hinnom by the side of [2]Jebus Southward, and goeth down to En Rogel,

17 And compasseth from the North, and goeth forth to [1]En Shemesh, and stretcheth to Geliloth, which is toward the going up unto Adummim, and goeth down to the [a]stone of Bohan the son of Reuben.

18 So it goeth along to the side over against the

CHAPTER 18
[a] Josh. 15:6

plain Northward, and goeth down into the plain.

19 After, this border goeth along to the side of Beth Hoglah Northward: and the ends thereof, that is, of the border, reach to the point of the salt Sea Northward, and to the [1]end of Jordan Southward: this is the South coast.

20 Also Jordan is the border of it on the East side: this is the inheritance of the children of Benjamin by the coasts thereof round about, according to their families.

21 Now the cities of the tribe of the children of Benjamin, according to their families, are Jericho, and Beth Hoglah, and the valley of Keziz,

22 And Beth Arabah, and Zemaraim, and Bethel,

23 And Avim, and Parah, and Ophrah,

24 And Chephar, Haammoni, and Ophni, and Gaba: twelve cities with their villages:

25 Gibeon, and Ramah, and Beeroth,

26 And Mizpah, and Chephirah, and Mozah,

27 And Rekem, and Irpeel, and Taralah,

28 And Zelah, Eleph, and Jebus, (which is [1]Jerusalem) Gibeath, and Kirjath: fourteen cities with their villages: this is the inheritance of the children of Benjamin, according to their families.

19

1 The portion of Simeon, 10 Of Zebulun, 17 Of Issachar, 24 Of Asher, 32 Of Naphtali, 40 Of Dan. 49 The possession of Joshua.

1 And the second lot came out to Simeon, even for the tribe of the children of Simeon, according to their families: and their inheritance was in the [1]midst of the inheritance of the children of Judah.

2 Now they had in their inheritance Beersheba, and Sheba, and Moladah,

3 And Hazar Shual, and Balah, and Ezem,

4 And Eltolad, and Bethul, and Hormah,

5 And Ziklag, and Beth Marcaboth, and Hazar Susah,

6 And Beth Lebaoth, and Sharuhen: thirteen cities with their villages.

7 Ain, Rimmon, and Ether, and Ashan: four cities with their villages.

8 And all the villages that were round about these cities, unto Baalath Beer, and [1]Ramah, Southward: this is the inheritance of the tribe of the children of Simeon, according to their families.

9 Out of the portion of the children of Judah

18:8 [1] By writing the names of every country and city.
18:10 [1] That everyone should be content with God's appointment.
18:11 [1] Their inheritance bordered upon Judah and Joseph.
18:13 [1] Which was in the tribe of Ephraim: another Bethel was in the tribe of Benjamin.
18:15 [1] Or, to the sea.
18:16 [1] Or, Rephaim.
  [2] Or, Jerusalem.
18:17 [1] Which is in the tribe of Ephraim.
18:19 [1] To the very strait, where the river runneth into the salt sea.
18:28 [1] Which was not wholly in the tribe of Benjamin, but part of it was also in the tribe of Judah.
19:1 [1] According to Jacob's prophecy, that he should be scattered among the other tribes, Gen. 49:7.
19:8 [1] Or, Ramath Negeb.

came the inheritance of the children of Simeon: for the part of the children of Judah was too [1]much for them: therefore the children of Simeon had their inheritance within their inheritance.

10 ¶ Also the third lot arose for the children of Zebulun, according to their families: and the coasts of their inheritance came to Sarid,

11 And their border goeth up [1]Westward, even to Maralah, and reacheth to Dabbasheth, and meeteth with the river that lieth before Jokneam,

12 And turneth from Sarid Eastward toward the Sun rising unto the border of Chisloth Tabor, and goeth out to Daberath, and ascendeth to Japhia,

13 And from thence goeth along Eastward toward the Sun rising to Gath Hepher, to Eth Kazin, and goeth forth to Rimmon, and turneth to Neah.

14 And this border compasseth it on the North side to Hannathon, and the ends thereof are in the valley of Jiphthah El,

15 And Kattath, and Nahallal, and Shimron, and Idalah, and [1]Bethlehem: twelve cities with their villages.

16 This is the inheritance of the children of Zebulun, according to their families, *that is*, these cities and their villages.

17 ¶ The fourth lot came out to Issachar, *even* for the children of Issachar, according to their families.

18 And their coast was Jezreel, and Chesulloth, and Shunem,

19 And Haphraim, and Shion, and Anaharath,

20 And Rabbith, and Kishion, and Abez,

21 And Remeth, and [1]En Gannim, and En Haddah, and Beth Pazzez.

22 And this coast reacheth to Tabor, and Shahazimah, and Beth Shemesh, and the ends of their coast reach to Jordan: sixteen cities with their villages.

23 This is the inheritance of the tribe of the children of Issachar according to their families: *that is*, the cities and their villages.

24 ¶ Also the fifth lot came out for the tribe of the children of Asher according to their families.

25 And their coast was Helkath, and Hali, and Beten, and Achshaph,

26 And Alammelech, and Amad, and Mishal, and came to Carmel Westward, and to Shihor Libnath,

27 And turneth toward the Sun rising to Beth Dagon, and cometh to [1]Zebulun, and to the valley of Jiphtah El, toward the North side of Beth Emek, and Neiel, and goeth out on the left side of Cabul,

28 And to Ebron, and Rehob, and Hammon, and Kanah, unto great Sidon.

29 Then the coast turneth to Ramah and to the strong city of [1]Zor, and this border turneth to Hosah, and the ends thereof are at the Sea from Hebel to Achzib,

30 Ummah also and Aphek, and Rehob: two and twenty cities with their villages.

31 This is the inheritance of the tribe of the children of Asher, according to their families: *that is*, these cities and their villages.

32 ¶ The sixth lot came out to the children of Naphtali, *even* to the children of Naphtali according to their families.

33 And their coast was from [1]Heleph, *and* from Allon in Zaanannim, and Adami Nekeb, and Jabneel, even to Lakkum, and the ends thereof are at Jordan.

34 So this coast turneth Westward to Aznoth Tabor, and goeth out from thence to Hukkok, and reacheth to Zebulun on the South side, and goeth to Asher on the West side, and to Judah [1]by Jordan toward the sun rising.

35 And the strong cities *are* Ziddim, Zer, and Hammath, Rakkath, and [1]Chinnereth,

36 And Adamah, and Ramah, and Hazor,

37 And Kedesh, and Edrei, and En Hazor,

38 And Iron, and Migdal El, Horem, and Beth Anath, and Beth Shemesh: nineteen cities with their villages.

39 This is the inheritance of the tribe of the children of Naphtali according to their families: *that is*, the cities and their villages.

40 ¶ The seventh lot came out for the tribe of the children of Dan, according to their families.

41 And the coast of their inheritance was Zorah, and Eshtaol, and Ir Shemesh,

42 And Shaalabbin, and Aijalon, and Jethlah,

43 And Elon, and Timnah, and Ekron,

44 And Eltekeh, and Gibbethon, and Baalath,

45 And Jehud, and Bene Berak, and Gath Rimmon,

46 And Me Jarkon, and Rakkon, with the border that lieth before [1]Japho.

47 But the coast of the children of Dan fell out *too little* for them: therefore the children of Dan went up to [1]fight against Leshem, and took it, and smote

---

19:9 [1] But this large portion was given them by God's providence to declare their increase in time to come.
19:11 [1] Meaning, toward the great Sea.
19:15 [1] There was another Bethlehem in the tribe of Judah.
19:21 [1] There was another city of this name in the tribe of Judah: for under divers tribes certain cities had all one name, and were distinct by the tribe only.

19:27 [1] Joineth to the tribe of Zebulun, which lay more Eastward.
19:29 [1] Which was Tyre, a strong city in the sea.
19:33 [1] These cities were in the country of Zaanannim.
19:34 [1] Or, even unto Jordan.
19:35 [1] Of the which the lake of Gennesaret had his name.
19:46 [1] Called Joppa.
19:47 [1] According as Jacob had prophesied, Gen. 49:17.

it with the edge of the sword, and possessed it, and dwelt therein, and called Leshem, ^aDan after the name of Dan their father.

48 This is the inheritance of the tribe of the children of Dan according to their families: *that is,* these cities and their villages.

49 ¶ When they had made an end of dividing the land by the coasts thereof, then the children of Israel gave an inheritance unto Joshua the son of Nun among them.

50 According to the word of the Lord they gave him the city which he asked, *even* ^bTimnath Serah in mount Ephraim: and he built the city and dwelt therein.

51 ^cThese are the heritages which Eleazar the Priest, and Joshua the son of Nun, and the chief fathers of the tribes of the children of Israel divided by lot in Shiloh before the Lord at the door of the Tabernacle of the Congregation: so they made an end of dividing the country.

20 *2 The Lord commandeth Joshua to appoint cities of refuge. 3 The use thereof, 7 and their names.*

1 The Lord also spake unto Joshua, saying,

2 Speak to the children of Israel, and say, ^aAppoint you cities of refuge, whereof I spake unto you by the hand of Moses,

3 That the slayer that killeth any person ¹by ignorance, *and* unwittingly, may flee thither, and they shall be your refuge from the avenger of blood.

4 And he that doth flee unto one of those cities, shall stand at the entering of the gate of the city, and shall show his cause ¹to the Elders of the city: and they shall receive him into the city unto them, and give him a place, that he may dwell with them.

5 And if the ¹avenger of blood pursue after him, they shall not deliver the slayer into his hand, because he smote his neighbor ignorantly, neither hated he him beforetime:

6 But he shall dwell in that city until he stand before the Congregation in ¹judgment, ^bor until the death of the high Priest that shall be in those days: then shall the slayer return, and come unto his own city, and unto his own house, *even* unto the city from whence he fled.

7 ¶ Then they appointed Kedesh in ¹Galilee in mount Naphtali, and Shechem in mount Ephraim, and Kirjath Arba, (which is Hebron) in the mountain of Judah.

Cross references

CHAPTER 19
^a Judg. 18:29
^b Josh. 24:30
^c Num. 34:17

CHAPTER 20
^a Exod. 21:13
Num. 35:6,11,14
Deut. 19:2
^b Num. 35:15
^c Deut. 4:43
1 Chron. 6:78

CHAPTER 21
^a Num. 35:2

8 And on the other side Jordan *toward* Jericho Eastward, they appointed ^cBezer in the wilderness upon the plain, out of the tribe of Reuben, and Ramoth in Gilead, out of the tribe of Gad, and Golan in Bashan, out of the ¹tribe of Manasseh.

9 These were the cities appointed for all the children of Israel, and for the stranger that sojourned among them, that whosoever killed any person ignorantly, might flee thither, and not die by the hand of the avenger of blood, until he stood before the ¹Congregation.

21 *3 The cities given to the Levites, 41 in number eight and forty. 44 The Lord according to his promise gave the children of Israel rest.*

1 Then came the ¹principal fathers of the Levites unto Eleazar the Priest, and unto Joshua the son of Nun, and unto the chief fathers of the tribes of the children of Israel,

2 And spake unto them at Shiloh in the land of Canaan, saying, ^aThe Lord commanded ¹by the hand of Moses, to give us cities to dwell in, with the suburbs thereof for our cattle.

3 So the children of Israel gave unto the Levites, out of their inheritance at the commandment of the Lord these cities with their suburbs.

4 And the lot came out for the families of the ¹Kohathites: and the children of Aaron the Priest, *which were* of the Levites, had by lot, out of the tribe of Judah, and out of the tribe of Simeon, and out of the tribe of Benjamin ²thirteen cities.

5 And the rest of the children of Kohath *had* by lot out of the families of the tribe of Ephraim, and out of the tribe of Dan, and out of the half tribe of Manasseh, ten cities.

6 Also the children of Gershon *had* by lot out of the families of the tribe of Issachar, and out of the tribe of Asher, and out of the tribe of Naphtali, and out of the half tribe of Manasseh in Bashan, thirteen cities.

7 The children of Merari according to their families *had* out of the tribe of Reuben, and out of the tribe of Gad, and out of the tribe of Zebulun, twelve cities.

8 So the children of Israel gave by lot unto the Levites these cities with their suburbs, as the Lord had commanded by the hand of Moses.

9 ¶ And they gave out of the tribe of the children of Judah, and out of the tribe of the children of

---

20:3 ¹ At unawares, and bearing him no grudge.
20:4 ¹ Hebrew, *in the ears of the Elders.*
20:5 ¹ That is, the nearest kinsman of him that is slain.
20:6 ¹ Till his cause were proved.
20:7 ¹ Or, Galilee.
20:8 ¹ Out of the half tribe of Manasseh beyond Jordan.

20:9 ¹ Before the Judges.
21:1 ¹ Or, the chief of the fathers.
21:2 ¹ By Moses, by whose ministry God showed his power.
21:4 ¹ He meaneth them that were Priests: for some were but Levites.
   ² Every tribe gave more or fewer cities according as their inheritance was great or little, Num. 35:8.

Simeon, these cities which are here named.

10 And they were the children of ¹Aaron *being* of the families of the Kohathites, *and* of the sons of Levi, (for theirs was the first lot.)

11 So they gave them Kirjath-arba of the father of Anak (which is Hebron) in the mountain of Judah, with the suburbs of the same round about it.

12 (But the land of the city, and the villages thereof, gave they to ᵇCaleb the son of Jephunneh to be his possession.)

13 ¶ Thus they gave to the ¹children of Aaron the Priest, a city of refuge for the slayer, *even* Hebron with her suburbs, and Libnah with her suburbs,

14 And Jattir with her suburbs, and Eshtemoa, and her suburbs,

15 And Holon with her suburbs, and Debir with her suburbs,

16 And Ain with her suburbs, and Juttah with her suburbs, Beth Shemesh with her suburbs: nine cities out of those two tribes.

17 And out of the tribe of Benjamin *they gave* Gibeon with her ¹suburbs, Geba with her suburbs,

18 Anathoth with her suburbs, and Almon with her suburbs: four cities.

19 All the cities of the children of Aaron Priests, *were* thirteen cities with their suburbs.

20 ¶ But to the families of the children of Kohath of the Levites, ¹which were the rest of the children of Kohath (for the cities of their lot were out of the tribe of Ephraim.)

21 They gave them the city of refuge for the slayer, ¹Shechem with her suburbs in mount Ephraim, and Gezer with her suburbs,

22 And Kibzaim with her suburbs, and Beth Horon with her suburbs: four cities.

23 And out of the tribe of Dan, Eltekeh with her suburbs, Gibbethon with her suburbs,

24 Aijalon with her suburbs, Gath Rimmon with her suburbs: four cities.

25 And out of the ¹half tribe of Manasseh, Tanach with her suburbs, and Gath Rimmon with her suburbs: two cities.

26 All the cities for the other families of the children of Kohath *were* ten with their suburbs.

27 ¶ Also unto the children of Gershon of the families of the Levites, *they gave* out of the half tribe

ᵇ Josh. 14:14
1 Chron. 6:56

of Manasseh, the city of refuge for the slayer, ¹Golan in Bashan with her suburbs, and Be Eshterah with her suburbs: two cities.

28 And out of the tribe of Issachar, Kishon with her suburbs, Daberath with her suburbs,

29 Jarmuth with her suburbs, En Gannim with her suburbs: four cities.

30 And out of the tribe of Asher, Mishal with her suburbs, Abdon with her suburbs,

31 Helkath with her suburbs, and Rehob with her suburbs: four cities.

32 And out of the tribe of Naphtali, the city of refuge for the slayer, Kedesh in ¹Galilee with her suburbs, and Hammoth Dor with her suburbs, and Kartan with her suburbs: three cities.

33 All the cities of the Gershonites according to their families, *were* thirteen cities with their suburbs.

34 ¶ Also unto the families of the children of Merari the ¹rest of the Levites, *they gave* out of the tribe of Zebulun, Jokneam with her suburbs, *and* Kartah with her suburbs,

35 Dimnah with her suburbs, Nahalal with her suburbs: four cities.

36 And out of the tribe of Reuben, ¹Bezer with her suburbs, and Jahaz with her suburbs,

37 Kedemoth with her suburbs, and Mephaath with her suburbs: four cities.

38 And out of the tribe of Gad *they gave* for a city of refuge for the slayer, Ramoth in Gilead with her suburbs, and Mahanaim with her suburbs,

39 Heshbon with her suburbs, *and* Jazer with her suburbs: four cities in all.

40 So all the cities of the children of Merari according to their families (which were the rest of the families of the Levites) were by their lot, twelve cities.

41 *And* all the cities of the Levites ¹within the possession of the children of Israel, *were* eight and forty with their suburbs.

42 These cities lay every one *severally* with their suburbs round about them: so were all these cities.

43 ¶ So the Lord gave unto Israel all the land, which he had sworn to give unto their fathers: and they possessed it, and dwelt therein.

44 Also the Lord gave them rest round about according to all that he had sworn unto their fathers:

21:10 ¹ For Aaron came of Kohath, and therefore the Priests' office remained in that family.

21:13 ¹ That is, the Priest of the family of the Kohathites, of whom Aaron was chief.

21:17 ¹ The suburbs were a thousand cubits from the wall of the cities round about, Num. 35:4.

21:20 ¹ That were not Priests.

21:21 ¹ Hebron and Shechem were the two cities of refuge under the Kohathites.

21:25 ¹ Which dwelt in Canaan.

21:27 ¹ Golan and Kadesh were the cities of refuge under the Gershonites.

21:32 ¹ Or, Galilee.

21:34 ¹ They are here called the rest, because they are last numbered, and Merari was the younger brother, Gen. 46:11.

21:36 ¹ Bezer and Ramoth were the cities of refuge under the Merarites and beyond Jordan, Josh. 20:8.

21:41 ¹ Thus according to Jacob's prophecy they were scattered throughout the country, which God used to this end, that his people might be instructed in the true religion by them.

and there stood not a man of all their enemies before them: *for* the Lord delivered all their enemies into their hand.

45 There failed nothing of all the good things, which the Lord had said unto the house of Israel, *but* all came to pass.

22 *1 Reuben, Gad, and the half tribe of Manasseh are sent again to their possessions. 10 They build an altar for a memorial. 15 The Israelites reprove them. 21 Their answer for defense of the same.*

1 Then [1]Joshua called the Reubenites, and the Gadites, and the half tribe of Manasseh,

2 And said unto them, Ye have kept all that Moses the servant of the Lord [1]commanded you, and have obeyed my voice in all that I commanded you:

3 You have not forsaken your brethren this long season unto this day, but have diligently kept the commandment of the Lord your God.

4 And now the Lord hath given rest unto your brethren, as he promised them: therefore now return ye, and go to your tents, to the land of your possession, which Moses the servant of the Lord hath [a]given you beyond Jordan.

5 But take diligent heed, to do the commandment and Law, which Moses the servant of the Lord commanded you: that is, [b]that ye [1]love the Lord your God, and walk in all his ways, and keep his commandments, and cleave unto him, and serve him with all your heart, and with all your soul.

6 So Joshua [1]blessed them, and sent them away, and they went unto their tents.

7 ¶ Now unto *one* half of the tribe of Manasseh Moses had given *a possession* in Bashan: and unto the *other* half thereof gave Joshua among their brethren on this side Jordan Westward: therefore when Joshua sent them away unto their tents, and blessed them,

8 Thus he spake unto them, saying, Return with much riches unto your tents, and with a great multitude of cattle, with silver and with gold, with brass and with iron, and with great abundance of raiment: divide the spoil of your enemies with your [1]brethren.

9 ¶ So the children of Reuben, and the children of Gad, and half the tribe of Manasseh returned, and

c Josh. 23:14,15

CHAPTER 22
a Num. 32:35
Josh. 13:8
b Deut. 10:12
c Num. 25:4

departed from the children of Israel from Shiloh (which is in the land of Canaan) to go unto the country of Gilead to the land of their possession, which they had obtained according to the word of the Lord by the hand of Moses.

10 ¶ And when they came unto the [1]borders of Jordan (which are in the land of Canaan) then the children of Reuben, and the children of Gad, and the half tribe of Manasseh, built [2]there an altar by Jordan, a great altar to see too.

11 ¶ When the children of Israel heard say, Behold, the children of Reuben, and the children of Gad, and the half tribe of Manasseh have built an altar in the forefront of the land of Canaan, upon the borders of Jordan at the passage of the children of Israel:

12 When the children of Israel heard it, then the whole Congregation of the children of Israel gathered them together at Shiloh, to go up [1]to war against them.

13 Then the children of Israel sent unto the children of Reuben, and to the children of Gad, and to the half tribe of Manasseh into the land of Gilead, Phinehas the son of Eleazar the Priest,

14 And with him ten princes, of every chief house a prince, according to all the tribes of Israel: for every one *was* chief of their father's household among the [1]thousands of Israel.

15 ¶ So they went unto the children of Reuben, and to the children of Gad, and to the half tribe of Manasseh, unto the land of Gilead, and spake with them, saying,

16 Thus saith [1]the whole Congregation of the Lord, What transgression is this that ye have transgressed against the God of Israel, to turn away this day from the Lord, in that ye have built you an altar for to rebel this day against the Lord?

17 Have we too little for the wickedness [*]of Peor, whereof we are not [1]cleansed unto this day, though a plague came upon the Congregation of the Lord?

18 Ye also are turned away this day from the Lord: and seeing ye rebel today against the Lord, even tomorrow he will be wroth with all the Congregation of Israel.

19 Notwithstanding, if the land of your possession be [1]unclean, come ye over unto the land of the possession of the Lord, wherein the Lord's Tabernacle dwelleth, and take possession among us: but [2]rebel not against

---

22:1 [1] After that the Israelites enjoyed the land of Canaan.
22:2 [1] Which was to go armed before their brethren, Num. 32:29.
22:5 [1] He showeth wherein consisteth the fulfilling of the Law.
22:6 [1] He commended them to God, and prayed for them.
22:8 [1] Which remained at home and went not to the war, Num. 31:27; 1 Sam. 30:24.
22:10 [1] Hebrew, *Geliloth*, which country also was called Canaan, because the Amorites dwelling there were called Canaanites.
[2] That is, beyond Jordan: for sometimes the whole country on both sides of Jordan is meant by Canaan.

22:12 [1] Such now was their zeal, that they would rather lose their lives, than suffer the true religion to be changed or corrupted.
22:14 [1] Or, multitude.
22:16 [1] Not only of the princes, but also of the common people.
22:17 [1] Meaning, God is not fully pacified, forasmuch as no punishment can be sufficient for such wickedness and idolatry.
22:19 [1] In your judgment.
[2] To use any other service than God hath appointed, is to rebel against God, 1 Sam. 15:23.

the Lord, nor rebel not against us in building you an altar, beside the altar of the Lord our God.

20 Did not Achan the son of Zerah trespass grievously in the execrable thing, and wrath fell on[d]all the Congregation of Israel? and this man alone [1]perished not in his wickedness.

21 ¶ Then the children of Reuben, and the children of Gad, and half the tribe of Manasseh answered, and said unto the heads over the thousands of Israel,

22 The Lord God of gods, the Lord God of gods, he knoweth, and Israel himself shall know: if by rebellion, or by transgression against the Lord *we have done it*, save thou us not this day.

23 If we have built us an altar to return away from the Lord, either to offer thereon burnt offering, or meat offering, or to offer peace offerings thereon, let the Lord [1]himself require it:

24 And if we have not *rather* done it for fear of *this* thing, saying, In time to come your children might say unto our children, What have ye to do with the Lord God of Israel?

25 For the Lord hath made Jordan a border between us and you, ye children of Reuben and of Gad: therefore ye have no part in the Lord: so shall your children make our children [1]cease from fearing the Lord.

26 Therefore we said, We will now go about to make us an altar, not for burnt offering, nor for sacrifice,

27 But it shall be a [e]witness between us and you, and between our generations after us, to execute the service of the Lord before him, in our burnt offerings, and in our sacrifices, and in our peace offerings, and that your children should not say to our children in time to come, Ye have no part in the Lord.

28 Therefore said we, If so be that they should *so* say to us, or to our [1]generations in time to come, then will we answer, Behold the fashion of the altar of the Lord, which our fathers made, not for burnt offering, nor for sacrifice, but it is a witness between us and you.

29 God forbid, that we should rebel against the Lord, and turn this day away from the Lord, to build an altar for burnt offering, *or* for meat offering, or for sacrifice, save the altar of the Lord our God that is before his Tabernacle.

30 ¶ And when Phinehas the Priest, and the princes

[d] Josh. 7:1,5
[e] Gen. 31:48
Josh. 22:34

of the Congregation and heads over the thousands of Israel, which were with him, heard the words that the children of Reuben, and children of Gad, and the children of Manasseh spake, [1]they were well content.

31 And Phinehas the son of Eleazar the Priest said unto the children of Reuben, and to the children of Gad, and to the children of Manasseh, This day we perceive, that the Lord is [1]among us, because ye have not done this trespass against the Lord: now ye have [2]delivered the children of Israel out of the hand of the Lord.

32 ¶ Then Phinehas the son of Eleazar the Priest with the princes, returned from the children of Reuben, and from the children of Gad, out of the land of Gilead, unto the land of Canaan, to the children of Israel, and brought them answer.

33 And the saying pleased the children of Israel: and the children of Israel [1]blessed God, and [2]minded not to go against them in battle for to destroy the land, wherein the children of Reuben and Gad dwelt.

34 Then the children of Reuben, and the children of Gad called the altar [1]*Ed*: for it shall be a witness between us, that the Lord *is* God.

23

2 *Joshua exhorteth the people, that they join not themselves to the Gentiles,* 7 *that they name not their idols.* 14 *The promise if they fear God,* 15 *and threatenings, if they forsake him.*

1 And *a* long season after that the Lord had given rest unto Israel from all their enemies round about, and Joshua was old, and [1]stricken in age,

2 Then Joshua called all Israel, *and* their Elders, and their Heads, and their Judges, and their officers, and said unto them, I am old, *and* stricken in age.

3 Also ye have seen all that the Lord your God hath done unto all these nations [1]before you, how the Lord your God himself hath fought for you.

4 Behold, I have [1]divided unto you by lot these nations that remain, to be an inheritance according to your tribes, from Jordan, with all the nations that I have destroyed, even unto the great Sea [2]Westward.

5 And the Lord your God shall expel [1]them before you, and cast them out of your sight, and ye shall possess their land, as the Lord your God hath said unto you.

22:20 [1] Signifying, that if many suffered for one man's fault, for the fault of many, all should suffer.
22:23 [1] Let him punish us.
22:25 [1] Or, to turn back from the true God.
22:28 [1] They signify a wonderful care that they bare toward their posterity, that they might live in the true service of God.
22:30 [1] Hebrew, *it was good in their eyes.*
22:31 [1] By preserving and governing us.
   [2] Whom if ye had offended; he would have punished with you.

22:33 [1] Or, praised.
   [2] Hebrew, *said.*
22:34 [1] Or, witness, as verse 27.
23:1 [1] Hebrew, *commen into years.*
23:3 [1] Your eyes bearing witness.
23:4 [1] Or, overthrown those nations.
   [2] Hebrew, *at the sunset.*
23:5 [1] Which yet remain and are not overcome, as Josh. 13:2.

6   Be ye therefore of a valiant courage to observe and do all that is written in the book of the Law of Moses, *that ye turn not there from to the right hand nor to the left,

7   Neither company with these nations: *that is,* with them that are [1]left with you, neither *b*make mention of the name of their gods, [2]nor cause to swear *by them,* neither serve them, nor bow unto them:

8   But stick fast unto the Lord your God, as ye have done unto this day.

9   For the Lord hath cast out before you great nations and mighty, and no man hath stood before your face hitherto.

10 *c*One man of you shall chase a thousand: for the Lord your God he fighteth for you, as he hath promised you.

11 Take good heed therefore unto [1]yourselves, that ye love the Lord your God.

12 Else, if ye go back, and cleave unto the rest of these nations: *that is,* of them that remain with you, and shall [1]make marriages with them, and [2]go unto them, and they to you,

13 Know ye for certain, that the Lord your God will cast out no more of these nations from before you: *d*but they shall be a snare and destruction unto you, and a whip on your sides, and thorns in your [1]eyes, until ye perish out of this good land, which the Lord your God hath given you.

14 And behold, this day do I [1]enter into the way of all the world, and ye know in all your [2]hearts and in all your souls, that *e*nothing hath failed of all the good things which the Lord your God promised you, *but* all are come to pass unto you: nothing hath failed thereof.

15 Therefore as all [1]good things are come upon you, which the Lord your God promised you, so shall the Lord bring upon you every [2]evil thing, until he have destroyed you out of this good land, which the Lord your God hath given you.

16 When ye shall [1]transgress the Covenant of the Lord your God, which he commanded you, and shall go and serve other gods, and bow yourselves to them, then shall the wrath of the Lord wax hot against you, and ye shall perish quickly out of the good land which he hath given you.

CHAPTER 23
a Deut. 5:32
Deut. 28:14
b Ps. 16:4
c Lev. 26:8
Deut. 32:30
d Exod. 23:33
Num. 33:55
Deut. 7:16
e Josh. 21:45

CHAPTER 24
a Gen. 11:31
b Gen. 21:2
c Gen. 25:26
d Gen. 36:8
e Gen. 46:6
f Exod. 3:10
g Exod. 12:37
h Exod. 14:9
i Num. 21:29
j Num. 22:5
Deut. 23:4

24

2 Joshua rehearseth God's benefits,   14 and exhorteth the people to fear God.   25 The league renewed between God and the people.   29 Joshua dieth.   32 The bones of Joseph are buried.   33 Eleazar dieth.

1   And Joshua assembled *again* all the [1]tribes of Israel to Shechem, and called the Elders of Israel, and their heads, and their Judges, and their officers, and they presented themselves before [2]God.

2   Then Joshua said unto all the people, Thus saith the Lord God of Israel, *a*Your fathers dwelt beyond the [1]flood in old time, *even* Terah the father of Abraham, and the father of Nachor, and served other gods.

3   And I took your father Abraham from beyond the flood, and brought him through all the land of Canaan, and multiplied his seed, and *b*gave him Isaac.

4   And I gave unto Isaac, *c*Jacob and Esau: and I gave unto *d*Esau mount Seir, to possess it: but Jacob and his children went down into Egypt.

5   *f*I sent Moses also and Aaron, and I plagued Egypt: and when I had *so* done among them, I brought you out.

6   So I *g*brought your fathers out of Egypt, and ye came unto the Sea, and the Egyptians pursued after your fathers with chariots and horsemen unto *h*the red Sea.

7   Then they cried unto the Lord, and he put [1]a darkness between you and the Egyptians, and brought the Sea upon them, and covered them: so your eyes have seen what I have done in Egypt: also ye dwelt in the wilderness a [2]long season.

8   After, I brought you into the land of the Amorites, which dwelt beyond Jordan, *i*and they fought with you: but I gave them into your hand, and ye possessed their country, and I destroyed them out of your sight.

9   *j*Also Balak the son of Zippor king of Moab, arose and warred against Israel, and sent to Balaam the son of Beor for to curse you,

10 But I would not hear Balaam: therefore he blessed you, and I delivered you out of his hand.

11 And ye went over Jordan, and came unto Jericho, and the [1]men of Jericho fought against you, the Amorites, and the Perizzites, and the Canaanites, and the Hittites,

---

23:7 [1] And not yet subdued.
  [2] Let not the Judges admit an oath which any shall swear by their idols.
23:11 [1] Hebrew, *souls.*
23:12 [1] Or, be of their affinity.
  [2] Or, have conversation with them.
23:13 [1] Meaning, they shall be a continual grief unto you, and so the cause of your destruction.
23:14 [1] I die according to the course of nature.
  [2] Most certainly.
23:15 [1] Or, promises.

[2] Or, threatenings, as Josh. 24:20.
23:16 [1] He showeth that no evil can come unto man, except he offend God by disobedience.
24:1 [1] That is, the nine tribes and the half.
  [2] Before the Ark which was brought to Shechem, when they went to bury Joseph's bones.
24:2 [1] Euphrates in Mesopotamia, Gen. 11:26.
24:7 [1] Or, a cloud.
  [2] Even forty years.
24:11 [1] Because it was the chief city, under it he containeth all the country: else they of the city fought not.

and the Girgashites, the Hivites, and the Jebusites, and I delivered them into your hand.

12 And I sent *hornets before you, which cast them out before you, *even the two kings of the Amorites, and not with thy sword, nor with thy bow.

13 And I have given you a land, wherein ye did not labor, and cities which ye built not, and ye dwell in them, and eat of the vineyards and olive trees, which ye planted not.

14 Now therefore ¹fear the Lord, and serve him in uprightness and in truth, and put away the gods, which your fathers served beyond the flood, and in Egypt, and serve ye the Lord.

15 And ¹if it seem evil unto you to serve the Lord, choose you this day whom ye will serve, whether the gods which your fathers served (that were beyond the flood) or the gods of the Amorites, in whose land ye dwell: ²but I and mine house will serve the Lord.

16 Then the people answered and said, God forbid, that we should forsake the Lord, to serve other gods.

17 For the Lord our God, he brought us and our fathers out of the land of Egypt, from the house of bondage, and he did those great miracles in our sight, and preserved us in all the way that we went, and among all the people through whom we came.

18 And the Lord did cast out before us all the people, even the Amorites which dwelt in the land: *therefore* will we also serve the Lord, ¹for he is our God.

19 And Joshua said unto the people, Ye cannot serve the Lord: for he is an holy God: he is a jealous God: he will not pardon your iniquity nor your sins.

20 If ye forsake the Lord and serve strange gods, ¹then he will return and bring evil upon you, and consume you, after that he hath done you good.

21 And the people said unto Joshua, Nay, but we will serve the Lord.

22 And Joshua said unto the people, Ye are witnesses ¹against yourselves, that ye have chosen you the Lord,

k Exod. 23:28
Deut. 7:20
Josh. 11:20
l Josh. 23:15
m Gen. 19:50
Judg. 2:9
n Gen. 50:15
Exod. 13:19
o Gen. 33:19

to serve him: and they said, *We are* witnesses.

23 Then put away now, *said he,* the strange ¹gods which are among you, and bow your hearts unto the Lord God of Israel.

24 And the people said unto Joshua, The Lord our God will we serve, and his voice will we obey.

25 So Joshua ¹made a covenant with the people the same day, and gave them an ordinance and law in Shechem.

26 And Joshua wrote these words in the book of the Law of God, and took a great stone, and pitched it there under an ¹oak that was in the Sanctuary of the Lord.

27 And Joshua said unto all the people, Behold, this stone shall be a witness unto us: for it ¹hath heard all the words of the Lord which he spake with us: it shall be therefore a witness against you, lest you deny your God.

28 Then Joshua let the people depart, every man unto his inheritance.

29 And after these things, Joshua the son of Nun, the servant of the Lord died, being an hundred and ten years old.

30 And they buried him in the border of his inheritance in *m*Timnath Serah, which is in mount Ephraim, on the North side of mount Gaash.

31 And Israel ¹served the Lord all the days of Joshua, and all the days of the Elders that overlived Joshua, and which had known all the works of the Lord that he had done for Israel.

32 And the *n*bones of Joseph, which the children of Israel brought out of Egypt, buried they in Shechem in a parcel of ground, which Jacob bought of *o*the sons of Hamor the father of Shechem, for an hundred pieces of silver, and the children of Joseph had them in their inheritance.

33 Also Eleazar the son of Aaron died, whom they buried in ¹the hill of Phinehas his son, which was given him in mount Ephraim.

24:14 ¹ This is the true use of God's benefits, to learn thereby to fear and serve him with an upright conscience.

24:15 ¹ Hebrew, *if it be evil in your sight.*

² This teacheth us that if all the world would go from God, yet every one of us particularly is bound to cleave unto him.

24:18 ¹ How much more are we bound to serve God in Christ, by whom we have received the redemption of our souls?

24:22 ¹ If you do the contrary, your own mouths shall condemn you.

24:23 ¹ Out of your hearts and otherwise.

24:25 ¹ By joining God and the people together: also he repeated the promises and threatenings out of the Law.

24:26 ¹ Or, elm.

24:27 ¹ Rather than man's dissimulation should not be punished, the dumb creatures shall cry for vengeance.

24:31 ¹ Such are the people commonly as their rulers are.

24:33 ¹ Hebrew, *Gibeath Phinehas.*

THE BOOK OF

JUDGES

1 *After Joshua was dead, Judah was constituted captain.* *6 Adoni-Bezek is taken.* *14 The request of Achsah.* *16 The children of Keni.* *23 The Canaanites are made tributaries, but not destroyed.*

CHAPTER 1
a Judg. 15:14
b Num. 21:3
c Num. 14:24
Josh. 14:13
Josh. 15:14

1 After that Joshua was dead, the children of Israel ¹asked the Lord, saying, ²Who shall go up for us against the Canaanites to fight first against them?

2 And the Lord said, Judah shall go up: behold, I have given the land into his hand.

3 And Judah said unto Simeon his ¹brother, Come up with me into my lot, that we may fight against the Canaanites: and I likewise will go with thee into thy lot: so Simeon went with him.

4 Then Judah went up, and the Lord delivered the Canaanites and the Perizzites into their hands, and they slew of them in Bezek ten thousand men.

5 And they found ¹Adoni-Bezek in Bezek: and they fought against him, and slew the Canaanites, and the Perizzites.

6 But Adoni-Bezek fled, and they pursued after him, and caught him, and ¹cut off the thumbs of his hands and of his feet.

7 And Adoni-Bezek said, Seventy Kings having the thumbs of their hands and of their feet cut off, gathered *bread* under my table: as I have done, so God hath rewarded me, so they brought him to Jerusalem, and there he died.

8 (Now the children of Judah had fought against Jerusalem, and hath taken it and smitten it with the edge of the sword, and had set the ¹city on fire.)

9 ¶ Afterward also the children of Judah went down to fight against the Canaanites, that dwelt in the mountain, and toward the South, and in the low country.

10 And Judah went against the Canaanites that dwelt in Hebron, which Hebron beforetime was called *a*Kirjath Arba: and they slew ¹Sheshai, and Ahiman, and Talmai.

11 And from thence he went to the inhabitants of Debir, and the name of Debir in old time *was* Kirjath Sepher.

12 And Caleb said, He that smiteth Kirjath Sepher, and taketh it, even to him will I give Achsah my daughter to wife.

13 And Othniel the son of Kenaz Caleb's younger brother took it, to whom he gave Achsah his daughter to wife.

14 And when she came *to him*, she moved him to ask of her father a field, ¹and she lighted off her ass, and Caleb said unto her, What wilt thou?

15 And she answered him, Give me a blessing: for thou hast given me a South country, give me also Springs of water: and Caleb gave her the springs above, and the springs beneath.

16 ¶ And the children of ¹Keni Moses' father-in-law went up out of the city of the palm trees with the children of Judah, into the wilderness of Judah, that lieth in the South of Arad, and went and dwelt among the people.

17 But Judah went with Simeon his brother, and they slew the Canaanites that inhabited Zephath, and utterly destroyed it, and called the name of the city *b*Hormah.

18 Also Judah took ¹Gaza with the coasts thereof, and Ashkelon with the coasts thereof, and Ekron with the coasts thereof.

19 And the Lord was with Judah, and he possessed the mountains: for he could not drive out the inhabitants of the valleys, because they had chariots of iron.

20 And they gave Hebron unto Caleb, as *c*Moses had said, and he expelled thence the three sons of Anak.

21 But the children of Benjamin did not cast out the Jebusites, that ¹inhabited Jerusalem: therefore the Jebusites dwell with the children of Benjamin in Jerusalem unto this day.

1:1 ¹ By the judgment of Urim, read Exod. 28:30; Num. 27:21; 1 Sam. 28:6.
  ² Who shall be our captain?
1:3 ¹ For the tribe of Simeon had their inheritance within the tribe of Judah, Josh. 19:1.
1:5 ¹ Or, the lord of Bezek.
1:6 ¹ This was God's just judgment, as the tyrant himself confesseth, that as he had done, so did he receive, Lev. 24:19,20.
1:8 ¹ Which was afterward built again, and possessed by the

Jebusites, 2 Sam. 5:6.
1:10 ¹ These three were giants, and the children of Anak.
1:14 ¹ Read Josh. 15:18.
1:16 ¹ This was one of the names of Moses' father-in-law, read Num. 10:29.
1:18 ¹ These cities and others were afterward possessed of the Philistines, 1 Sam. 6:17.
1:21 ¹ For after that the tribe of Judah had burnt it, they built it again.

22 ¶ They also that were of the house of Joseph, went up to Bethel, and the Lord *was* with them,

23 And the house of Joseph caused to view Bethel (and the name of the city beforetime *was* ^d Luz.)

24 And the spies saw a man come out of the city, and they said unto him, Show us, we pray thee, the way into the city, ^c and we will show thee mercy.

25 And when he had showed them the way into the city, they smote the city with the edge of the sword, but they let the man and all his household depart.

26 Then the man went into the land of the Hittites, and built a city, and called the name thereof Luz, which is the name thereof unto this day.

27 ¶ ^f Neither did Manasseh destroy Beth Shean with her towns, nor Taanach with her towns, nor the inhabitants of Dor with her towns, nor the inhabitants of Ibleam with her towns, neither the inhabitants of Megiddo with her towns: ^1 but the Canaanites dwelled still in that land.

28 Nevertheless when Israel was strong, they put the Canaanites to tribute, and expelled them not wholly.

29 ¶ ^g Likewise Ephraim expelled not the Canaanites that dwelt in Gezer, but the Canaanites dwelt in Gezer among them.

30 ¶ Neither did ^1 Zebulun expel the inhabitants of Kitron, nor the inhabitants of Nahalol, but the Canaanites dwelt among them, and became tributaries.

31 ¶ Neither did Asher cast out the inhabitants of Acco, nor the inhabitants of Sidon, nor of Ahlab, nor of Achzib, nor of Helbah, nor of Aphik, nor of Rehob,

32 But the Asherites dwelt among the Canaanites the inhabitants of the land: for they did not drive them ^1 out.

33 ¶ Neither did Naphtali drive out the inhabitants of Beth Shemesh, nor the inhabitants of Beth Anath, but dwelt among the Canaanites the inhabitants of the land: nevertheless the inhabitants of Beth Shemesh, and of Beth Anath became tributaries unto them.

34 And the Amorites ^1 drove the children of Dan into the mountain: so that they suffered them not to come down to the valley.

35 And the Amorites ^1 dwelt still in mount Heres in Aijalon, and in Shaalbim, and when the ^2 hand of Joseph's family prevailed, they became tributaries:

^d Gen. 28:19
^e Josh. 2:14
^f Josh. 17:11
^g Josh. 16:10

CHAPTER 2
^a Deut. 7:2
^b Deut. 22:3
^c Josh. 23:13

36 And the coast of the Amorites was from Maaleh-Akrabbim, *even* from ^1 Sela and upward.

2 1 *The Angel rebuketh the people, because they had made peace with the Canaanites.* 11 *The Israelites fell to idolatry after Joshua's death.* 14 *They are delivered into the enemies' hands:* 16 *God delivereth them by Judges.* 21 *Why God suffered idolaters to remain among them.*

1 And an ^1 Angel of the Lord came up from Gilgal to Bochim, and said, I made you to go up out of Egypt, and have brought you unto the land which I had sworn unto your fathers, and said, I will never break my covenant with you.

2 ^a Ye also shall make no covenant with the inhabitants of this land, ^b but shall break down their altars: but ye have not obeyed my voice. Why have ye done this?

3 Wherefore, I said also, I will not cast them out before you, but they shall be ^c as thorns unto your sides, and their gods shall be your ^1 destruction.

4 And when the Angel of the Lord spake these words unto all the children of Israel, the people lifted up their voice, and wept.

5 Therefore they called the name of that place, ^1 Bochim, and offered sacrifices there unto the Lord.

6 ¶ Now when Joshua had ^1 sent the people away, the children of Israel went every man into his inheritance, to possess the land.

7 And the people had served the Lord all the days of Joshua, and all the days of the Elders that outlived Joshua, which had seen all the great ^1 works of the Lord that he did for Israel.

8 But Joshua the son of Nun the servant of the Lord died, when he was an hundred and ten years old:

9 And they buried him in the coasts of his inheritance, in ^1 Timnath Heres in mount Ephraim, on the North side of mount Gaash.

10 And so all that generation was gathered unto their fathers, and another generation arose after them, which neither knew the Lord, nor yet the works which he had done for Israel.

11 ¶ Then the children of Israel did wickedly in the sight of the Lord, and served ^1 Baal,

12 And forsook the Lord God of their fathers, which brought them out of the land of Egypt and followed other gods, *even* the gods of the people that were round about them, and bowed unto them, and

---

1:27 ^1 Wherefore God permitted the Canaanites to dwell still in the land, read Judg. 3:5.
1:30 ^1 That is, the tribe of Zebulun as is also to be understood of the rest.
1:32 ^1 But made them pay tribute as the others did.
1:34 ^1 Or, afflicted them.
1:35 ^1 Or, would dwell.
    ^2 Meaning, when he was stronger than they.
1:36 ^1 Which was a city in Arabia, or as some read, from the rock.

2:1 ^1 That is, messenger, or prophet, as some think, Phinehas.
2:3 ^1 Or, snare.
2:5 ^1 Or, weeping.
2:6 ^1 After that he had divided to every man his portion by lot, Josh. 24:28.
2:7 ^1 Meaning, the wonders and miracles.
2:9 ^1 Here, by turning the letters backward is Sereh, as Josh. 24:30.
2:11 ^1 That is, all manner of idols.

provoked the Lord to anger.

13 So they forsook the Lord, and served [d]Baal, and [1]Ashtoreth.

14 And the wrath of the Lord was hot against Israel, and he delivered them into the hands of spoilers, that spoiled them, and he [e]sold them into the hands of their enemies round about them, so that they could no longer stand before their enemies.

15 [1]Whithersoever they went out, the [2]hand of the Lord was sore against them, as the Lord had said, and as the Lord had sworn unto them: so he punished them sore.

16 ¶ Notwithstanding, the Lord raised up [1]Judges, which [2]delivered them out of the hands of their oppressors.

17 But yet they would not obey their Judges for they went a whoring after other gods, and worshipped them, and turned quickly out of the [1]way, wherein their fathers walked, obeying the commandments of the Lord: they did not so.

18 And when the Lord had raised them up Judges, the Lord was with the Judge, and delivered them out of the hand of their enemies all the days of the Judge (for the Lord [1]had compassion of their groanings, [2]because of them that oppressed them and tormented them.)

19 Yet [f]when the Judge was dead, they returned, and [1]did worse than their fathers, in following other gods to serve them and worship them: they ceased not from their own inventions, nor from their rebellious way.

20 Wherefore the wrath of the Lord was kindled against Israel, and he said, Because this people hath transgressed my covenant which I commanded their fathers, and hath not obeyed my voice,

21 Therefore will I no more cast out before them any of the [1]nations, which Joshua left when he died,

22 That through them I may [1]prove Israel, whether they will keep the way of the Lord, to walk therein, as their fathers kept it, or not.

23 So the Lord left those nations, and drove them not out immediately, neither delivered them into the hand of Joshua.

3 1 The Canaanites were left to try Israel. 9 Othniel delivereth Israel. 21 Ehud killeth King Eglon. 31 Shamgar

[d] Judg. 10:6
[e] Ps. 44:12
Isa. 50:1
[f] Judg. 3:12

killeth the Philistines.

1 These now are the nations which the Lord left, that he might prove Israel by them (even as many of Israel as had not known all the [1]wars of Canaan,

2 Only to make the generations of the children of Israel to know, and to teach them war, which doubtless their predecessors knew [1]not.)

3 Five princes of the Philistines, and all the Canaanites, and the Sidonians, and the Hivites that dwelt in mount Lebanon, from mount Baal Hermon until one come to Hamath.

4 And these remained to prove Israel by them, to wit, whether they would obey the commandments of the Lord, which he commanded their fathers by the hand of Moses.

5 And the children of Israel dwelt among the Canaanites, the Hittites, and the Amorites, and the Perizzites, and the Hivites, and the Jebusites,

6 And they took [1]their daughters to be their wives, and gave their daughters to their sons, and served their gods.

7 ¶ So the children of Israel did wickedly in the sight of the Lord, and forgot the Lord their God, and served Baal, and [1]Asherah.

8 Therefore the wrath of the Lord was kindled against Israel, and he sold them into the hand of Cushan-Rishathaim King of [1]Aram-naharaim, and the children of Israel served Cushan-Rishathaim eight years.

9 ¶ And when the children of Israel cried unto the Lord, the Lord stirred up a Savior to the children of Israel, and he saved them, even Othniel the son of Kenaz, Caleb's younger brother.

10 And the [1]Spirit of the Lord came upon him, and he judged Israel, and went out to war: and the Lord delivered Cushan-Rishathaim king of [2]Aram into his hand, and his hand prevailed against Cushan-Rishathaim.

11 So the land had rest [1]forty years, and Othniel the son of Kenaz died.

12 ¶ Then the children of Israel again committed wickedness in the sight of the Lord: and the Lord [1]strengthened Eglon king of Moab against Israel, because they had committed wickedness before the Lord.

13 And he gathered unto him the children of

2:13 [1] These were Idols, which had the form of an ewe or sheep among the Sidonians.
2:15 [1] In all their enterprises.
  [2] The vengeance.
2:16 [1] Or, magistrates.
  [2] Hebrew, saved.
2:17 [1] Meaning, from the true religion.
2:18 [1] Hebrew, repented.
  [2] Seeing their cruelty.
2:19 [1] Hebrew, corrupt themselves.
2:21 [1] As the Hivites, Jebusites, Amorites, etc.
2:22 [1] So that both outward enemies and false prophets are but a

trial to prove our faith, Deut. 13:3 and Judg. 3:1.
3:1 [1] Which were achieved by the hand of God, and not by the power of man.
3:2 [1] For they trusted in God, and he fought for them.
3:6 [1] Contrary to God's commandment, Deut. 3:7.
3:7 [1] Trees or woods erected for idolatry.
3:8 [1] Or, Mesopotamia.
3:10 [1] He was stirred up by the Spirit of the Lord.
  [2] Or, Syria.
3:11 [1] That is, 32 under Joshua, and eight under Othniel.
3:12 [1] So that the enemies of God's people have no power over them, but by God's appointment.

Ammon, and Amalek, and went and smote Israel, and they possessed the city of palm trees.

14 So the children of Israel served Eglon king of Moab eighteen years.

15 But when the children of Israel cried unto the Lord, the Lord stirred them up a savior, Ehud the son of Gera the son of ¹Jemini, a man ²lame of his right hand: and the children of Israel sent a present by him unto Eglon king of Moab.

16 And Ehud ¹made him a dagger with two edges of a cubit length, and he did gird it under his raiment upon his right thigh,

17 And he presented the gift unto Eglon king of Moab (and Eglon was a very fat man.)

18 And when he had now presented the present, he sent away the people that bare the present,

19 But he turned again from the ¹quarries, that were by Gilgal, and said, I have a secret errand unto thee, O King. Who said, Keep ²silence: and all that stood about him went out from him.

20 Then Ehud came unto him, (and he sat alone in a summer parlor, which he had) and Ehud said, I have a message unto thee from God. Then he arose out of his throne.

21 And Ehud put forth his left hand, and took the dagger from his right thigh, and thrust it into his belly,

22 So that the haft went in after the blade, and the fat closed about the blade, so that he could not draw the dagger out of his belly, but the dirt came out.

23 Then Ehud got him out into the ¹porch, and shut the doors of the parlor upon him, and locked them.

24 And when he was gone out, his servants came: who seeing that the doors of the parlor were locked, they said, Surely ¹he doeth his easement in his summer chamber.

25 And they tarried till they were ashamed: and seeing he opened not the doors of the parlor, they took the key, and opened them, and behold, their lord was fallen dead on the earth.

26 So Ehud escaped (while they tarried) and was past the quarries, and escaped unto Seirah,

27 And when he came home, he ¹blew a trumpet in mount Ephraim, and the children of Israel went

CHAPTER 4
ᵃ Ps. 83:9,10

down with him from the mountain, and he went before them.

28 Then said he unto them, Follow me: for the Lord hath delivered your enemies, even Moab into your hand. So they went down after him, and took the passages of Jordan toward Moab, and suffered not a man to pass over.

29 And they slew of the Moabites the same time about ten thousand men, all ¹fed men, and all were warriors, and there escaped not a man.

30 So Moab was ¹subdued that day, under the hand of Israel: and the ²land had rest fourscore years.

31 ¶ And after him was Shamgar the son of Anath, which slew of the Philistines six hundred men with an ox ¹goad, and he also delivered Israel.

4 *1 Israel sin and are given into the hands of Jabin. 4 Deborah judgeth Israel, and exhorteth Barak to deliver the people.   15 Sisera fleeth,.   17 and is killed by Jael.*

1 And the children of Israel ¹began again to do wickedly in the sight of the Lord when Ehud was dead.

2 And the Lord sold them into the hand of ¹Jabin King of Canaan, that reigned in Hazor, whose chief captain was called Sisera, which dwelt in ²Harosheth of the Gentiles.

3 Then the children of Israel cried unto the Lord: (for he had nine hundred chariots of iron, and twenty years he had vexed the children of Israel very sore.)

4 ¶ And at that time Deborah a Prophetess the wife of Lapidoth ¹judged Israel.

5 And this Deborah dwelt under a palm tree, between Ramah and Bethel in mount Ephraim, and the children of Israel came up to her for judgment.

6 Then she sent and called Barak the son of Abinoam out of Kedesh of Naphtali, and said unto him, Hath not the Lord God of Israel ¹commanded, saying, Go, and draw toward mount Tabor, and take with thee ten thousand men of the children of Naphtali, and of the children of Zebulun?

7 And I will draw unto thee to the ᵃ,¹river Kishon, Sisera, the captain of Jabin's army with his chariots, and his multitude, and will deliver him into thine hand.

8 And Barak said unto her, ¹If thou wilt go with me, I will go: but if thou wilt not go with me, I will not go.

3:15 ¹ Or, Benjamin.
     ² Or, left handed.
3:16 ¹ Or, caused a dagger to be made.
3:19 ¹ Or, as some read from the places of idols.
     ² Till all be departed.
3:23 ¹ Or, hall.
3:24 ¹ Hebrew, he covereth his feet.
3:27 ¹ Or, caused the trumpet to be blown, Num. 20:2,3.
3:29 ¹ Or, strong, and big bodied.
3:30 ¹ Hebrew, humbled.
     ² Meaning, the Israelites.
3:31 ¹ So that it is not the number, nor the means that God regard-

eth, when he will get the victory.
4:1 ¹ Hebrew, added, or continued to do evil.
4:2 ¹ There was another Jabin, whom Joshua killed and burnt his city Hazor, Josh. 11:13.
     ² That is in a wood, or strong place.
4:4 ¹ By the spirit of prophecy, resolving of controversies and declaring the will of God.
4:6 ¹ And revealed unto me by the spirit of prophecy.
4:7 ¹ Or, valley.
4:8 ¹ Fearing his own weakness and his enemy's power, he desireth the prophetess to go with him to assure him of God's will from time to time.

9 Then she answered, I will surely go with thee, but this journey that thou takest, shall not be for thine honor: for the Lord shall sell Sisera into the hand of a woman. And Deborah arose and went with Barak to Kedesh.

10 ¶ And Barak called Zebulun and Naphtali to Kedesh, and [1]he went up on his feet with ten thousand men, and Deborah went up with him.

11 (Now Heber the Kenite, which was of the [1]children of [b]Hobab the father-in-law of Moses, was departed from the [2]Kenites, and pitched his tent [3]until the plain of Zaanaim, which is by Kedesh.)

12 Then they showed Sisera, that Barak the son of Abinoam was gone up to mount Tabor.

13 And Sisera called for all his chariots, even nine hundred chariots of iron, and all the people that were with him from Harosheth of the Gentiles, unto the river Kishon.

14 Then Deborah said unto Barak, [1]Up: for this is the day that the Lord hath delivered Sisera into thine hand. Is not the Lord gone out before thee? So Barak went down from mount Tabor, and ten thousand men after him.

15 And the Lord destroyed Sisera and all his chariots, and all his host with the edge of the sword before Barak, so that Sisera lighted down off his chariot, and fled away on his feet.

16 But [c]Barak pursued after the chariots, and after the host unto Harosheth of the Gentiles: and all the host of Sisera fell upon the edge of the sword: there was not a man left.

17 Howbeit Sisera fled away on his feet to the tent of Jael the wife of [1]Heber the Kenite: (for peace was between Jabin the king of Hazor, and between the house of Heber the Kenite.)

18 And Jael went out to meet Sisera, and said unto him, Turn in, my lord, turn into me: fear not. And when he had turned in unto her into her tent, she covered him with a [1]mantel.

19 And he said unto her, Give me, I pray thee, a little water to drink: for I am thirsty. And she opened [d]a bottle of milk, and gave him drink, and covered him.

20 Again he said unto her, Stand in the door of the tent, and when any man doth come and inquire of thee, saying, Is [1]any man there? thou shalt say, Nay.

[b] Num. 10:29
[c] Ps. 38:10
[d] Judg. 5:25

CHAPTER 5
[a] Deut. 4:11
[b] Deut. 2:1
[c] Ps. 97:5
[d] Exod. 19:18
[e] Judg. 3:31
[f] Judg. 4:18

21 Then Jael Heber's wife took a [1]nail of the tent, and took an hammer in her hand, and went softly unto him, and smote the nail into his temples, and fastened it into the ground, (for he was fast asleep and weary) and so he died.

22 And behold, as Barak pursued after Sisera, Jael came out to meet him, and said unto him, Come, and I will show thee the man, whom thou seekest: and when he came into her tent, behold, Sisera lay [1]dead, and the nail in his temples.

23 So God brought down Jabin the king of Canaan that day before the children of Israel.

24 And the hand of the children of Israel [1]prospered, and prevailed against Jabin the king of Canaan, until they had destroyed Jabin king of Canaan.

5   1 The song and thanksgiving of Deborah and Barak, after the victory.

1 Then sang Deborah, and Barak the son of Abinoam the same day, saying,

2 Praise ye the Lord for the avenging of Israel, and for the [1]people that offered themselves willingly.

3 Hear, ye kings, hearken ye princes: I, even I will sing unto the Lord: I will sing praise unto the Lord God of Israel.

4 Lord, [a]when thou wentest out of Seir, when thou departedst out of the field of [b]Edom, the earth trembled, and the heavens rained, the clouds also dropped water.

5 [c]The mountains melted before the Lord, [d]as did that Sinai before the Lord God of Israel.

6 In the days of [e]Shamgar the son of Anath, in the days of [f]Jael, the highways were [1]unoccupied, and the travelers walked through byways.

7 The towns were not inhabited: they decayed, I say, in Israel, until I Deborah came up, which rose up a [1]mother in Israel.

8 They chose new gods: then was war in the gates. Was there a [1]shield or spear seen among forty thousand of Israel?

9 Mine heart is set on the governors of Israel, and on them that are willing among the people: praise ye the Lord.

10 Speak ye that ride on [1]white asses, ye that dwell [2]by Middin, and that walk by the way.

4:10 [1] Or, he led after him 10,000 men.
4:11 [1] Or, posterity.
     [2] Hebrew, from Cain.
     [3] Meaning, that he possessed a great part of that country.
4:14 [1] She still encourageth him to this enterprise by assuring him of God's favor and aid.
4:17 [1] Whose ancestors were strangers, but worshipped the true God, and therefore were joined with Israel.
4:18 [1] Or, blanket.
4:20 [1] To wit, Sisera.
4:21 [1] That is, the pin or stake, whereby it was fastened to the ground.
4:22 [1] So he saw that a woman had the honor, as Deborah prophesied.
4:24 [1] Hebrew, went and was strong.
5:2 [1] To wit, the two tribes of Zebulun and Naphtali.
5:6 [1] For fear of the enemies.
5:7 [1] Miraculously stirred up of God to pity them and deliver them.
5:8 [1] They had no heart to resist their enemies.
5:10 [1] Ye governors.
     [2] As in danger of your enemies.

11 For the noise of the archers *appraised* among the [1]drawers of water: there shall they rehearse the righteousness of the Lord, his righteousness of his towns in Israel: then did the people of the Lord go down to the gates.

12 Up Deborah, up, arise, *and* sing a song: arise Barak, and lead [1]thy captivity captive, thou son of Abinoam.

13 For they that remain, have dominion over the mighty of the people: the Lord hath given me dominion over the strong.

14 Of Ephraim [1]their root *arose* against Amalek: *and* after thee Benjamin *shall fight* against thy people, O *Amalek*, of Machir came rulers, and of Zebulun, they that handle the pen of the [2]writer.

15 And the princes of Issachar were with Deborah, and [1]Issachar, and also Barak: he was set on his feet in the valley: for the divisions of Reuben *were* great [2]thoughts of heart.

16 Why abodest thou among the sheepfolds, to hear the bleatings of the flocks? for the divisions of Reuben *were* great thoughts of heart.

17 [1]Gilead abode beyond Jordan: and why doth Dan remain in ships? Asher sat on the seashore, and tarried in his [2]decayed places.

18 *But* the people of Zebulun and Naphtali have jeopardized their lives unto the death in the high places of the field.

19 The Kings came *and* fought: then fought the Kings of Canaan in Taanach by the waters of Megiddo: they received no gain of [1]money.

20 They fought from heaven, *even* the stars in their courses fought against Sisera.

21 The River Kishon [1]swept them away, that ancient river the river Kishon. O my soul, thou hast marched valiantly.

22 Then were the horse hoofs broken with the oft beating together of their mighty *men*.

23 Curse ye [1]Meroz: (said the Angel of the Lord) curse the inhabitants thereof, because they came not to help the Lord, to help the Lord against the mighty.

24 Jael the wife of Heber the Kenite shall be blessed above *other* women: blessed shall she be above women *dwelling* in tents.

25 He asked water, *and* she gave him milk: she brought forth [1]butter in a lordly dish.

26 She put her hand to the nail, and her right hand to the workman's hammer: with the hammer smote she Sisera: she smote off his head, after she had wounded and pierced his temples.

27 He bowed him down at her feet, he fell down, and lay still: at her feet he bowed him down, and fell: and when he had sunk down, he lay there [1]dead.

28 The mother of Sisera looked out at a window, and cried through the lattice, Why is his chariot so long a coming? why tarry the [1]wheels of his chariots?

29 Her wise ladies answered her, Yea. [1]She answered herself with her own words,

30 Have they not gotten, *and* they divide the spoil? every man hath a maid or two. Sisera hath a prey of diverse colored *garments*, a prey of sundry colors made of needle work: of diverse colors of needle work on both sides, [1]for the chief of the spoil.

31 So let all thine enemies perish, O Lord: but they that love him, shall be as the [1]Sun when he riseth in his might, and the land had rest forty years.

6   *1 Israel is oppressed of the Midianites for their wickedness.*   *14 Gideon is sent to be their deliverer.*   *37 He asketh a sign.*

1 Afterward the children of Israel committed wickedness in the sight of the Lord, and the Lord gave them into the hands of Midian seven years.

2 And the hand of Midian prevailed against Israel, [1]*and* because of the Midianites the children of Israel made them dens in the mountains, and caves, and strongholds.

3 When Israel had sown, then came up the Midianites, the Amalekites, and they of the [1]East, and came upon them,

4 And camped by them, and destroyed the fruit of the earth, even till thou come unto [1]Gaza, and left no food for Israel, neither sheep, nor ox, nor ass.

5 For they went up, and their cattle, and came with their tents as grasshoppers in multitude: so that they and their camels were without number: and they came into the land to destroy it.

5:11 [1] For now you may draw water without fear of your enemies.
5:12 [1] To wit, them that kept thy people in captivity.
5:14 [1] Joshua first fought against Amalek, and Saul destroyed him.
   [2] Even the learned did help to fight.
5:15 [1] Even the whole tribe.
   [2] They marveled, that they came not over Jordan to help them.
5:17 [1] She reproveth all them that came not to help their brethren in their necessity.
   [2] Either by beating of the sea, or by mining.
5:19 [1] They won nothing, but lost all.
5:21 [1] As a besom doeth the filth of the house.

5:23 [1] It was a city near to Tabor, where they fought.
5:25 [1] Some read churned milk in a great cup.
5:27 [1] Hebrew, *destroyed*.
5:28 [1] Or, feet.
5:29 [1] That is, she comforted herself.
5:30 [1] Because he was chief of the army.
5:31 [1] Shall grow daily more and more in God's favor.
6:2 [1] For fear of the Midianites, they fled into the dens of the mountains.
6:3 [1] Or, of Kedem.
6:4 [1] Even almost the whole country.

6 So was Israel exceedingly impoverished by the Midianites: therefore the [1]children of Israel cried unto the Lord.

7 ¶ And when the children of Israel cried unto the Lord because of the Midianites,

8 The Lord sent unto the children of Israel a Prophet, who said unto them, Thus saith the Lord God of Israel, I have brought you up from Egypt, and have brought you out of the house of bondage,

9 And I have delivered you out of the hand of the Egyptians, and out of the hand of all that oppressed you, and have cast them out before you, and given you their land.

10 And I said unto you, I am the Lord your God: [a]fear not the gods of the Amorites in whose land you dwell: but ye have not obeyed my voice.

11 ¶ And the Angel of the Lord came, and sat under the oak which was in Ophrah, that pertained unto Joash the father of the Abiezrites, and his son Gideon threshed wheat by the winepress, [1]to hide it from the Midianites.

12 Then the Angel of the Lord appeared unto him, and said unto him, The Lord is with thee, thou valiant man.

13 To whom Gideon answered, [1]Ah my Lord, if the Lord be with us, why then is all this come upon us? and where be all his miracles which our fathers told us of, and said, Did not the Lord bring us out [of] Egypt? but now the Lord hath forsaken us, and delivered us into the hand of the Midianites.

14 And the [1]Lord looked upon him, and said, Go in this thy [2]might, and thou shalt save Israel out of the hands of the Midianites: have not I sent thee?

15 And he answered him, Ah my Lord, whereby shall I save Israel? behold, my [1]father is poor in Manasseh, and I am the least in my father's house.

16 Then the Lord said unto him, I will therefore be with thee, and thou shalt smite the Midianites, as one man.

17 And he answered him, I pray thee, if I have found favor in thy sight, then show me [1]a sign, that thou talkest with me.

18 Depart not hence, I pray thee, until I come unto thee, and bring mine offering, and lay it before thee. And he said, I will tarry until thou come again.

19 ¶ Then Gideon went in, and made ready a kid,

CHAPTER 6
[a] 2 Kings 17:35,38 Jer. 10:2
[b] Ex. 33:20 Judg. 13:22

and unleavened bread of an [1]Ephah of flour, and put the flesh in a basket, and put the broth in a pot, and brought it out unto him under the oak, and presented it.

20 And the Angel of God said unto him, Take the flesh and the unleavened bread, and lay them upon this stone, and pour out the broth: and he did so.

21 ¶ Then the Angel of the Lord put forth the end of the staff that he held in his hand, and touched the flesh and the unleavened bread: and there arose up fire [1]out of the stone, and consumed the flesh and the unleavened bread, so the Angel of the Lord departed out of his sight.

22 And when Gideon perceived that it was an Angel of the Lord, Gideon then said, Alas, my Lord God: [b]for because I have seen an Angel of the Lord face to face, I shall die.

23 And the Lord said unto him, Peace be unto thee: fear not, thou shalt not die.

24 Then Gideon made an altar there unto the Lord, and called it [1]Jehovah Shalom: unto this day it is in Ophrah, of the father of the Abiezrites.

25 ¶ And the same night the Lord said unto him, Take thy father's young bullock, and another bullock [1]of seven years old, and destroy the altar of Baal that thy father hath, and cut down the grove that is by it,

26 And build an altar unto the Lord thy God upon the top of this rock, in a plain place: and take the second bullock, and offer a burnt offering with the wood of the [1]grove, which thou shalt cut down.

27 Then Gideon took ten men of his servants, and did as the Lord bade him: but because he feared to do it by day for his father's household and the men of the city, he did it by night.

28 ¶ And when the men of the city arose early in the morning, behold, the altar of Baal was broken, and the grove cut down that was by it, and the [1]second bullock offered upon the altar that was made.

29 Therefore they said one to another, Who hath done this thing? and when they inquired and asked, they said, Gideon the son of Joash hath done this thing.

30 Then the men of the city said unto Joash, Bring out thy son, that he may die: for he hath destroyed the altar of Baal, and hath also cut down the grove that was by it.

31 And Joash said unto all that stood by him, Will ye plead Baal's cause? or will ye save him? [1]he that

---

6:6 [1] This is the end of God's punishments, to call his to repentance, that they may seek for help of him.
6:11 [1] Or, to prepare his flight.
6:13 [1] This came not of distrust, but of weakness of faith, which is in the most perfect: for no man in this life can have a perfect faith: yet the children of God have a true faith, whereby they be justified.
6:14 [1] That is, Christ appearing in visible form.
  [2] Which I have given thee.
6:15 [1] Or, family.
6:17 [1] So that we see how the flesh is enemy unto God's vocation,

which cannot be persuaded without signs.
6:19 [1] Of Ephah, read Exod. 16:37.
6:21 [1] By the power of God only, as in the sacrifice of [Elijah], 1 Kings 18:38.
6:24 [1] Or, the Lord of peace.
6:25 [1] That is, as the Chaldea text writeth, fed seven years.
6:26 [1] Which grew about Baal's altar.
6:28 [1] Meaning, the fat bull, which was kept to be offered unto Baal.
6:31 [1] Thus we ought to justify them that are zealous of God's cause, though all the multitude be against us.

will contend for him, let him die or the morning. If he be God, let him plead for himself against him that hath cast down his altar.

32 And in that day was Gideon called Jerubbaal, that is, Let Baal plead for himself because he hath broken down his altar.

33 Then all the Midianites and the Amalekites, and they of the East, were gathered together, and went and pitched in the valley of Jezreel.

34 But the Spirit of the Lord ¹came upon Gideon ᶜand he blew a trumpet, and ²Abiezer was joined with him.

35 And he sent messengers throughout all Manasseh, which was also joined with him, and he sent messengers unto Asher, and to Zebulun and to Naphtali, and they came up to meet them.

36 Then Gideon said unto God, ¹If thou wilt save Israel by mine hand, as thou hast said,

37 Behold, I will put a fleece of wool in the threshing place: if the dew come on the fleece only and it be dry upon all the earth, then shall I be sure, that thou wilt save Israel by mine hand, as thou hast said.

38 And so it was: for he rose up early on the morrow, and thrust the fleece together, and wringed the dew out of the fleece, and filled a bowl of water.

39 Again, Gideon said unto God, Be not angry with me, that ᵈI may speak once more: let me prove once again, I pray thee, with the fleece: let it now be dry only upon the fleece, and let dew be upon all the ground.

40 And God did so the same night: for it was ¹dry upon the fleece only, and there was dew on all the ground.

7 *The Lord commandeth Gideon to send away a great part of his company.   22 The Midianites are discomfitted by a wondrous sort.   25 Oreb and Zeeb are slain.*

1 Then ᵃJerubbaal (who is Gideon) rose up early, and all the people that were with him, and pitched beside ¹the well of Harod, so that the host of the Midianites was on the North side of them, in the valley by the hill of ²Moreh.

2 And the Lord said unto Gideon, The people that are with thee, are too many for me to give the Midianites into their hands, lest Israel make their vaunt ¹against me, and say, Mine hand hath saved me.

Marginal references:
ᶜ Num. 10:3
Judg. 3:27
ᵈ Gen. 18:32

CHAPTER 7
ᵃ Judg. 8:35
ᵇ Deut. 20:8
ᶜ Judg. 6:33

3 Now therefore proclaim in the audience of the people, and say, ᵇWho so is timorous or fearful, let him return, and depart early from mount Gilead. And there returned of the people which were at mount Gilead, two and twenty thousand: so ten thousand remained.

4 And the Lord said unto Gideon, The people are yet too many: bring them down unto the water, and I will ¹try them for thee there: and of whom I say unto thee, This man shall go with thee, the same shall go with thee: and of whomsoever I say unto thee, This man shall not go with thee, the same shall not go.

5 So he brought down the people unto the water. And the Lord said unto Gideon, As many as lap the water with their tongues, as a dog lappeth, them put by themselves, and everyone that shall bow down his knees to drink, ¹put apart.

6 And the number of them that lapped *by putting* their hands to their mouths, *were* three hundred men: but all the remnant of the people kneeled down upon their knees to drink water.

7 ¶ Then the Lord said unto Gideon, By these three hundred men that lapped, will I save you, and deliver the Midianites into thine hand: and let all the *other* ¹people go every man unto his place.

8 ¶ So the people took victuals ¹with them, and their trumpets: and he sent all the rest of Israel, every man unto his tent, and ²retained the three hundred men: and the host of Midian was beneath him in a valley.

9 ¶ And the same night the Lord said unto him, Arise, ¹get thee down unto the host: for I have delivered it into thine hand.

10 But if thou fear to go down, *then* go thou, and Purah thy servant down to the host,

11 And thou shalt hearken what they say, and so shall thine hands be strong to go down unto the host. Then went he down and Purah his servant unto the outside of the soldiers that were in the host.

12 ¶ And the Midianites, and the Amalekites and all ᶜthey of the East, lay in the valley like grasshoppers in multitude, and their camels *were* without number, as the sand which is by the seaside for multitude.

13 And when Gideon was come, behold, a man told a dream unto his neighbor, and said, Behold, I dreamed a dream and lo, a ¹cake of barley bread tumbled from above into the host of Midian, and came into a tent, and smote it that it fell, and overturned it, that the tent fell down.

6:34 ¹ Hebrew, *clad Gideon.*
    ² The family of Abiezer, whereof he was.
6:36 ¹ This request proceeded not of infidelity, but that he might be confirmed in his vocation.
6:40 ¹ Whereby he was assured that it was a miracle of God.
7:1 ¹ Hebrew, *En-harod.*
    ² Hebrew, *Hammoreh.*
7:2 ¹ God will not that any creature deprive him of his glory.
7:4 ¹ I will give thee a proof to know them that shall go with thee.

7:5 ¹ Let them depart as unmeet for this enterprise.
7:7 ¹ That is, the one and thirty thousand, and 700. See verses 3 and 6.
7:8 ¹ Hebrew, *in their hands.*
    ² Or, encouraged.
7:9 ¹ Thus the Lord by divers means doth strengthen him, that he faint not in so great an enterprise.
7:13 ¹ Some read, a trembling noise of barley bread: meaning, that one of no reputation should make their great army to tremble.

14 And his fellow answered, and said, This is nothing else save the sword of Gideon the son of Joash a man of Israel: *for* into his hand hath God delivered Midian and all the host.

15 ¶ When Gideon heard the dream told, and the interpretation of the same, he [1]worshipped, and returned unto the host of Israel, and said, Up: for the Lord hath delivered into your hand the host of Midian.

16 And he divided the three hundred men into three bands, and gave every man a trumpet in his hand with empty pitchers, and [1]lamps [2]within the pitchers.

17 And he said unto them, Look on me, and do likewise, when I come to the side of the host: even as I do, so do you.

18 When I blow with a trumpet and all that are with me, blow ye with trumpets also on every side of the host, and say, [1]For the Lord, and for Gideon.

19 ¶ So Gideon and the hundred men that were with him, came unto the outside of the host, in the beginning of the middle watch, and they raised up the watchmen, and they blew with their trumpets, and brake the pitchers that were in their hands.

20 And the three companies blew with trumpets and brake the pitchers, and held the lamps in their left hands, and the trumpets in their right hands to blow withal: and they cried, The [1]sword of the Lord and of Gideon.

21 And they stood, every man in his place round about the host: and all the host [1]ran, and cried, and fled.

22 And the three hundred blew with trumpets, and [d]the Lord set every man's sword upon his [1]neighbor, and upon all the host: so the host fled to Beth Hashittah in Zererah, *and* to the border of Abel Meholah, unto Tabbath.

23 Then the men of Israel being gathered together out of Naphtali, and out of Asher, and out of all Manasseh, pursued after the Midianites.

24 And Gideon sent messengers unto all mount Ephraim, saying, Come down against the Midianites, and take before them the [1]waters unto Beth Barah and Jordan. Then all the men of Ephraim gathered together and took the waters unto Beth Barah, and

[d] Isa. 9:4
[e] Ps. 83:11
Isa. 10:26

Jordan.

25 And they took two [c]princes of the Midianites, Oreb and Zeeb, and slew Oreb upon the rock Oreb, and slew Zeeb at [1]the winepress of Zeeb, and pursued the Midianites, and brought the heads of Oreb and Zeeb to Gideon beyond Jordan.

8 *1 Ephraim murmureth against Gideon, who appeaseth them. 4 He passeth the Jordan. 16 He revengeth himself on them of Succoth and Penuel. 27 He maketh an Ephod which was the cause of idolatry. 30 Of Gideon's sons and of his death.*

1 Then the men of Ephraim said unto him, [1]Why hast thou served us thus that thou calledst us not, when thou wentest to fight with the Midianites? and they chide with him sharply.

2 To whom he said, What have I now done, in comparison of [1]you? is not the [2]gleaning of grapes of Ephraim better, than the vintage of Abiezer?

3 God hath delivered into your hands the princes of Midian, Oreb and Zeeb: and what was I able to do in comparison of you? and when he had thus spoken, then their spirits abated toward him.

4 ¶ And Gideon came to Jordan to pass over, he, and the three hundred men that were with him, weary, yet pursuing *them.*

5 And he said unto the men of Succoth, Give, I pray you, [1]morsels of bread unto the people [2]that follow me (*for they be weary*) that I may follow after Zebah and Zalmunna Kings of Midian.

6 And the princes of Succoth said, Are the [1]hands of Zebah and Zalmunna now in thine hands, that we should give bread unto thine army?

7 Gideon then said, Therefore when the Lord hath delivered Zebah and Zalmunna into mine hand, I will [1]tear your flesh with thorns of the wilderness and with briers.

8 ¶ And he went up thence to Penuel, and spake unto them likewise, and the men of Penuel answered him, as the men of Succoth answered.

9 And he said also unto the men of Penuel, When I come again [1]in peace, I will break down this tower.

10 ¶ Now Zebah and Zalmunna *were* [1]in Karkor, and their hosts with them, about fifteen thousand, all that were left of all the hosts of them of the East:

7:15 [1] Or, gave God thanks, as it is in the Chaldea text.
7:16 [1] Or, firebrands.
    [2] These weak means God used to signify that the whole victory came of him.
7:18 [1] That is, the victory shall be the Lord's and Gideon's his servant.
7:20 [1] Shall destroy the enemies.
7:21 [1] Or, broke their array.
7:22 [1] The Lord caused the Midianites to kill one another.
7:24 [1] Meaning, the passages or the fords, that they should not escape.
7:25 [1] These places had their names of the acts that were done there.

8:1 [1] They began to cavil, because he had the glory of the victory.
8:2 [1] Which have slain two princes, Oreb and Zeeb.
    [2] This last act of the whole tribe is more famous, than the whole enterprise of one man of one family.
8:5 [1] Or, some small portion.
    [2] Hebrew, *that are at my feet.*
8:6 [1] Because thou hast overcome an handful, thinkest thou to have overcome the whole?
8:7 [1] Hebrew, *beat in pieces.*
8:9 [1] Having gotten the victory.
8:10 [1] A city Eastward beyond Jordan.

for there was slain an hundred and twenty thousand men, that drew swords.

11 ¶ And Gideon went through them that dwelt in [1]Tabernacles on the East side of Nobah and Jogbehah, and smote the host: for the host was careless.

12 And when Zebah and Zalmunna fled, he followed after them, and took the two kings of Midian, Zebah and Zalmunna, and discomfited all the host.

13 ¶ So Gideon the son of Joash returned from battle, [1]the sun being *yet* high,

14 And took a servant of the men of Succoth, and inquired of him: and he [1]wrote to him the princes of Succoth and the Elders thereof, *even* seventy and seven men.

15 And he came unto the men of Succoth, and said, Behold Zebah, and Zalmunna, by whom ye upbraided me, saying, Are the hands of Zebah, and Zalmunna already in thine hands, that we should give bread unto thy weary men?

16 Then he took the Elders of the city, and thorns of the wilderness and briers, and [1]did tear the men of Succoth with them.

17 Also he brake down the tower of [a]Penuel, and slew the men of the city.

18 ¶ Then said he unto Zebah and Zalmunna, What manner of men were they, whom ye slew at Tabor? And they answered, [1]As thou art, so were they, *every* one was like the children of a king.

19 And he said, They were my brethren, even my [1]mother's children: as the Lord liveth, if ye had saved their lives, I would not slay you.

20 Then he said unto Jether his firstborn son, Up, and slay them: but the boy drew not his sword: for he feared, because he was yet young.

21 Then Zebah and Zalmunna said, Rise thou and fall upon us: for [1]as the man is, *so is* his strength. And Gideon arose and slew Zebah and Zalmunna, and took away the [2]ornaments, that were on their camels' necks.

22 ¶ Then the men of Israel said unto Gideon, Reign thou over us, both thou, and thy son and thy [1]son's son: for thou hast delivered us out of the hand of Midian.

CHAPTER 8
[a] 1 Kings 12:25

23 And Gideon said unto them, I will not reign over you, neither shall my child reign over you, *but* the Lord shall reign over you.

24 Again Gideon said unto them, [1]I would desire a request of you, that you would give me every man the earrings of his prey (for they [had] golden earrings because they were Ishmaelites.)

25 And they answered, We will give them. And they spread a garment, and did cast therein every man the earrings of his prey.

26 And the weight of the golden earrings that he required, was a thousand and seven hundred *shekels* of gold, beside collars [1]and jewels, and purple raiment that was on the kings of Midian, and beside the chains that were about the camels' necks.

27 And Gideon made an [1]Ephod thereof, and put it in Ophrah his city: and all Israel went a whoring there after it, which was the destruction of Gideon and his house.

28 Thus was Midian brought low before the children of Israel, so that they lifted up their heads no more: and the country was in quietness forty years in the days of Gideon.

29 ¶ Then Jerubbaal the son of Joash went, and dwelt in his own house.

30 And Gideon had seventy sons [1]begotten of his body: for he had many wives.

31 And his concubine that was in Shechem, bare him a son also, whose name he called Abimelech.

32 So Gideon the son of Joash died in a good age, and was buried in the sepulcher of Joash his father in Ophrah, of the [1]father of the Abiezrites.

33 But when Gideon was dead, the children of Israel turned away, and went a whoring after Baal, and made [1]Baal-Berith their god.

34 And the children of Israel remembered not the Lord their God, which had delivered them out of the hands of all their enemies on every side.

35 Neither [1]showed they mercy on the house of Jerubbaal, *or* Gideon, according to all the goodness which he had showed unto Israel.

9 *1 Abimelech usurpeth the kingdom, and putteth his brethren to death. 7 Jotham proposeth a parable. 23 Hatred between Abimelech and the Shechemites. 26 Gaal conspireth*

8:11 [1] He went by the wilderness where the Arabians dwelt in tents.
8:13 [1] Some read, before the Sun rose up.
8:14 [1] Or, described.
8:16 [1] Hebrew, *break in pieces, as one thresheth corn.*
8:18 [1] Or, they were like unto thee.
8:19 [1] We came all out of one belly: therefore I will be revenged.
8:21 [1] Meaning, that they would be rid out of their pain at once, or else to have a valiant man to put them to death.
　　[2] Or, collars.
8:22 [1] That is, thy posterity.
8:24 [1] His intent was to show himself thankful for this victory by

restoring of religion, which because it was not according as God had commanded, turned to their destruction.
8:26 [1] Or, sweet balls.
8:27 [1] That is, such things as pertained to the use of the Tabernacle. See more of Ephod, Exod. 28:4,6; 1 Sam. 2:18 and 2 Sam. 6:14 and Judg. 17:5.
8:30 [1] Hebrew, *which came out of his thigh.*
8:32 [1] Which city belonged to the family of the Abiezrites.
8:33 [1] That is, Baal, to whom they had bound themselves by covenant.
8:35 [1] They were unmindful of God and unkind toward him, by whom they had received so great a benefit.

against him, and is overcome.   53 *Abimelech is wounded to death by a woman.*

1 Then Abimelech the son of Jerubbaal went to Shechem unto his [1]mother's brethren, and communed with them, and with all the family, *and* house of his mother's father, saying,

2 Say, I pray you, in the audience of all the men of Shechem, Whether is better for you, that all the sons of Jerubbaal, which are seventy persons, reign over you, either that one reign over you? Remember also, that I am your [1]bone, and your flesh.

3 Then his mother's brethren spake of him in the audience of all the men of Shechem, all these words: and their hearts were moved to follow Abimelech: for said they, He is our brother.

4 And they gave him seventy pieces of silver out of the house of Baal-Berith, wherewith Abimelech hired [1]vain and light fellows which followed him.

5 And he went unto his father's house at Ophrah, and [1]slew his brethren, the sons of Jerubbaal, *about* seventy persons upon one stone: yet Jotham the youngest son of Jerubbaal was left: for he hid himself.

6 ¶ And all the men of Shechem gathered together with all the house of [1]Millo, and came and made Abimelech King in the plain, where the stone was erected in Shechem.

7 And when they told it to Jotham, he went and stood in the top of mount Gerizim, and lifted up his voice, and cried, and said unto them, Hearken unto me, you men of Shechem, that God may hearken unto you.

8 [1]The trees went forth to anoint a King over them, and said unto the Olive tree, Reign thou over us.

9 But the Olive tree said unto them, Should I leave my fatness, wherewith by me they honor God and man, and go to advance me above the trees?

10 Then the trees said to the fig tree, Come thou, *and* be king over us.

11 But the fig tree answered them, Should I forsake my sweetness, and my good fruit, and go to advance me above the trees?

12 Then said the trees unto the vine, Come thou, *and* be king over us.

13 But the vine said unto them, Should I leave my wine, whereby I cheer God and man, and go to advance me above the trees?

14 Then said all the trees unto the [1]bramble, Come thou, *and* reign over us.

15 And the bramble said unto the trees, If ye will indeed anoint me king over you, come, and put your trust under my shadow: and if not, the [1]fire shall come out of the bramble, and consume the Cedars of Lebanon.

16 Now therefore, if ye do truly and incorruptly to make Abimelech King, and if ye have dealt well with Jerubbaal and with his house, and have done unto him according to the deserving of his hands,

17 (For my father fought for you, and [1]adventured his life, and delivered you out of the hands of Midian.

18 And ye are risen up against my father's house this day, and have slain his children, *about* seventy persons upon one stone, and have made Abimelech, the son of his maidservant, king over the men of Shechem, because he is your brother.)

19 If ye then have dealt truly and purely with Jerubbaal, and with his house this day, then [1]rejoice ye with Abimelech, and let him rejoice with you.

20 But if not, let a fire come out from Abimelech, and consume the men of Shechem and the house of Millo: also let a fire come forth from the men of Shechem, and from the house of Millo, and consume Abimelech.

21 And Jotham ran away, and fled, and went to Beer, and dwelt there for fear of Abimelech his brother.

22 So Abimelech reigned three years over Israel.

23 But God [1]sent an evil spirit between Abimelech, and the men of Shechem: and the men of Shechem brake their promise to Abimelech,

24 That the cruelty toward the seventy sons of Jerubbaal and their blood might come and be laid upon Abimelech their brother, which had slain them, and upon the men of Shechem, which had aided him to kill his brethren.

25 So the men of Shechem set men in wait for him in the tops of the mountains: who robbed all that passed that way by them: and it was told Abimelech.

26 Then Gaal the son of Ebed came with his brethren, and they went to Shechem: and the men of Shechem put their confidence in him.

27 Therefore they [1]went out into the field, and gathered in their grapes, and trode them, and made merry, and went into the house of their gods, and

---

9:1 [1] To practice with his kinsfolk for the attaining of the kingdom.
9:2 [1] Of your kindred by my mother's side.
9:4 [1] Or, idle fellows and vagabonds.
9:5 [1] Thus tyrants to establish their usurped power, spare not the innocent blood, 2 Kings 10:7; 2 Chron. 21:4.
9:6 [1] Which was as the town house, or common hall, which he calleth the tower of Shechem, verse 49.
9:8 [1] By this parable he declareth that those that are not ambitious, are most worthy of honor, and that the ambitious abuse their honor

both to their own destruction and others.
9:14 [1] Or, thistle, or brier.
9:15 [1] Abimelech shall destroy the nobles of Shechem.
9:17 [1] Hebrew, *he cast his life far from him.*
9:19 [1] That he is your king, and you his subjects.
9:23 [1] Because the people consented with the king in shedding innocent blood, therefore God destroyeth both one and the other.
9:27 [1] Before they were afraid of Abimelech's power, and durst not go out of the city.

did eat and drink, and cursed Abimelech.

28 Then Gaal the son of Ebed said, Who is Abimelech? and who is Shechem, that we should serve him? Is he not the son of Jerubbaal? and Zebul is his officer? Serve rather the men of Hamor the father of Shechem: for why should we serve him?

29 Now would God this people were under mine hand: then would I put away Abimelech. And he said to [1]Abimelech, Increase thine army, and come out.

30 ¶ And when Zebul the ruler of the city heard the words of Gaal the son of Ebed, his wrath was kindled.

31 Therefore he sent messengers unto Abimelech [1]privily, saying, Behold, Gaal the son of Ebed and his brethren be come to Shechem, and behold, they fortify the city against thee.

32 Now therefore arise by night, thou and the people that is with thee, and lie in wait in the field.

33 And rise early in the morning as soon as the sun is up, and assault the city: and when he and the people that is with him, shall come out against thee, do to him [1]what thou canst.

34 ¶ So Abimelech rose up, and all the people that were with him by night: and they lay in wait against Shechem in four bands.

35 Then Gaal the son of Ebed went out, and stood in the entering of the gate of the city: and Abimelech rose up, and the folk that were with him, from lying in wait.

36 And when Gaal saw the people, he said to Zebul, Behold, there come people down from the tops of the mountains: and Zebul said unto him, The [1]shadow of the mountains seem men unto thee.

37 And Gaal spake again, and said, See, there come folk down [1]by the middle of the land, and another band cometh by the way of the plain of [2]Meonenim.

38 Then said Zebul unto him, Where is now thy mouth that said, Who is Abimelech, that we should serve him? Is not this the people that thou hast despised? Go out now, I pray thee and fight with them.

39 And Gaal [1]went out before the men of Shechem, and fought with Abimelech.

40 But Abimelech pursued him, and he fled before him, and many were overthrown and wounded even unto the entering of the gate.

41 And Abimelech dwelt at Arumah: and Zebul thrust out Gaal and his brethren that they should

CHAPTER 9
a 2 Sam. 12:21

not dwell in Shechem.

42 ¶ And on the morrow, the people went out into the field: which was told Abimelech.

43 And he took the [1]people, and divided them into three bands, and laid wait in the fields, and looked, and behold, the people were come out of the city, and he rose up against them, and smote them.

44 And Abimelech, and the bands that were with him, rushed forward, and stood in the entering of the gate of the city: and the two other bands ran upon all the people that were in the field, and slew them.

45 And when Abimelech had fought against the city all that day, he took the city, and slew the people that was therein, and destroyed the city, and sowed [1]salt in it.

46 ¶ And when all the men of the tower of Shechem heard it, they entered into an hold of the house of the god [1]Berith.

47 And it was told Abimelech, that all the men of the tower of Shechem were gathered together.

48 And Abimelech got him up to mount Zalmon, he and all the people that were with him: and Abimelech took axes with him, and cut down boughs of trees, and took them, and bare them on his shoulder, and said unto the folk that were with him, What ye have seen me do, make haste, and do like me.

49 Then all the people also cut down every man his bough, and followed Abimelech, and put them to the hold, and set the hold on fire with them so all the men of the tower of Shechem [1]died also, about a thousand men and women.

50 ¶ Then went Abimelech to Thebez, and besieged Thebez, and took it.

51 But there was a strong tower within the city, and thither fled all the men and women, and all the chiefs of the city, and shut it to them, and went up to the top of the tower.

52 And Abimelech came unto the tower, and fought against it, and went hard unto the door of the tower to set it on fire.

53 But a certain woman [a]cast a piece of a millstone upon Abimelech's head, and brake his brainpan.

54 Then Abimelech called hastily his page that bore his harness, and said unto him, Draw thy sword and slay me, that men say not of me, A woman slew him. And his page [1]thrust him through, and he died.

55 And when the men of Israel saw that Abimelech was dead, they departed every man unto his

---

9:29 [1] Braggingly, as though he had been present, or to his captain Zebul.
9:31 [1] Hebrew, craftily.
9:33 [1] Hebrew, what thine hand can find.
9:36 [1] Thou art afraid of a shadow.
9:37 [1] Hebrew, by the navel.
   [2] Or, charmers.
9:39 [1] As their captain.

9:43 [1] Which were in his company.
9:45 [1] That it should be unfruitful, and never serve to any use.
9:46 [1] That is, of Baal-Berith, as Judg. 8:33.
9:49 [1] Meaning, that all were destroyed as well they in the tower, as the other.
9:54 [1] Thus God by such miserable death taketh vengeance on tyrants even in this life.

own place.

56 Thus God rendered the wickedness of Abimelech, which he did unto his father in slaying his seventy brethren.

57 Also all the wickedness of the men of Shechem did God bring upon their heads. So upon them came the [1]curse of Jotham the son of Jerubbaal.

10

2 *Tola dieth.* 5 *Jair also dieth.* 7 *The Israelites are punished for their sins.* 10 *They cry unto God,* 16 *and he hath pity on them.*

1 After Abimelech, there arose to defend Israel, Tola, the son of Puah, the son of [1]Dodo, a man of Issachar, which dwelt in Shamir in mount Ephraim.

2 And he [1]judged Israel three and twenty years, and died, and was buried in Shamir.

3 ¶ And after him arose Jair a Gileadite, and judged Israel two and twenty years.

4 And he had thirty sons that [1]rode on thirty asscolts, and they had thirty cities, which are called [2]Havoth Jair unto this day, and are in the land of Gilead.

5 And Jair died, and was buried in Camon.

6 ¶ [a]And the children of Israel wrought wickedness again in the sight of the Lord, and served Baal and [b]Ashtoreth, and the gods of [1]Aram, and the gods of Sidon, and the gods of Moab, and the gods of the children of Ammon, and the gods of the Philistines, and forsook the Lord and served not him.

7 Therefore the wrath of the Lord was kindled against Israel, and he [1]sold them into the hands of the Philistines, and into the hands of the children of Ammon:

8 Who from that year vexed and oppressed the children of Israel eighteen years, [1]*even* all the children of Israel that were beyond Jordan, in the land of the Amorites, which is in Gilead.

9 Moreover, the children of Ammon went over Jordan to fight against Judah and against Benjamin, and against the house of Ephraim: so that Israel was sore tormented.

10 Then the children of Israel [1]cried unto the Lord, saying, We have sinned against thee, even because we have forsaken our own God, and have served Baal.

11 And the Lord [1]said unto the children of Israel,

CHAPTER 10
[a] Judg. 2:11
  Judg. 3:7
  Judg. 4:1
  Judg. 6:1
  Judg. 13:1
[b] Judg. 2:13
[c] Deut. 32:15
  Jer. 2:13
[d] Judg. 11:6

Did not I deliver you from the Egyptians and from the Amorites, from the children of Ammon, and from the Philistines?

12 The Sidonians also, and the Amalekites, and the Maonites did oppress you, and ye cried to me, and I saved you out of their hands.

13 Yet ye [c]have forsaken me, and served other gods: Wherefore I will deliver you no more.

14 Go, and cry unto the gods which ye have chosen: let them save you in the time of your tribulation.

15 And the children of Israel said unto the Lord, We have sinned: do thou unto us whatsoever please thee: only we pray thee to deliver us [1]this day.

16 Then they put away the strange gods from among them, and [1]served the Lord: and [2]his soul was grieved for the misery of Israel.

17 Then the children of Ammon gathered themselves together, and pitched in Gilead: and the children of Israel assembled themselves, and pitched in Mizpah.

18 And the people *and* princes of Gilead said one to another, Whosoever will begin the battle against the children of Ammon, the same shall be [d]head over all the inhabitants of Gilead.

11

2 *Jephthah being chased away by his brethren, was after made captain over Israel.* 30 *He maketh a rash vow.* 32 *He vanquisheth the Ammonites,* 39 *and sacrificeth his daughter according to his vow.*

1 Then Gilead begat Jephthah, and Jephthah the Gileadite was [1]a valiant man, but the son of an [2]harlot.

2 And Gilead's wife bare him sons, and when the woman's children were come to age, they thrust out Jephthah, and said unto him, Thou shalt not inherit in our father's house: for thou art the son of a [1]strange woman.

3 Then Jephthah fled from his brethren, and dwelt in the land of [1]Tob: and there gathered idle fellows to Jephthah, and [2]went out with him.

4 ¶ And in process of time, the children of Ammon made war with Israel.

5 And when the children of Ammon fought with Israel, the [1]Elders of Gilead went to fetch Jephthah out of the land of Tob.

9:57 [1] For making a tyrant their king.
10:1 [1] Or, his uncle.
10:2 [1] Or, governed.
10:4 [1] Signifying, they were men of authority.
  [2] Or, the towns of Jair, as Deut. 3:14.
10:6 [1] Or, Syrian.
10:7 [1] Or, delivered.
10:8 [1] As the Reubenites, Gadites, and half the tribe of Manasseh.
10:10 [1] They prayed to the Lord, and confessed their sins.
10:11 [1] By stirring them up some prophets, as Judg. 6:8.

10:15 [1] That is, from this present danger.
10:16 [1] This is true repentance, to put away the evil, and to serve God aright.
  [2] Or, he pitied.
11:1 [1] Hebrew, *a man of mighty force.*
  [2] Or, victualler.
11:2 [1] That is, of an harlot as verse 1.
11:3 [1] Where the governor of the country was called Tob.
  [2] Joined with him, as some think, against his brethren.
11:5 [1] Or, ambassadors, sent for that purpose.

6 And they said unto Jephthah, Come and be our captain, that we may fight ¹with the children of Ammon.

7 Jephthah then answered the Elders of Gilead, Did not ye hate me, and ¹expel me out of my father's house? how then come you unto me now in time of your tribulation?

8 Then the Elders of Gilead said unto Jephthah, Therefore we turn again to thee now, that thou mayest go with us, and fight against the children of Ammon, and be our head over all the inhabitants of Gilead.

9 And Jephthah said unto the Elders of Gilead, If ye bring me home again to fight against the children of Ammon, if the Lord give them before me, shall I be your head?

10 And the Elders of Gilead said unto Jephthah, The Lord ¹be witness between us, if we do not according to thy words.

11 Then Jephthah went with the Elders of Gilead, and the people made him head and captain over them: and Jephthah rehearsed all his words before the Lord in Mizpah.

12 ¶ Then Jephthah sent messengers unto the king of the children of Ammon, saying, What hast thou to do with me, that thou art come against me, to fight in my land?

13 And the king of the children of Ammon answered unto the messengers of Jephthah, ᵃBecause Israel took my land, when they came up from Egypt, from Arnon unto Jabbok, and unto Jordan: now therefore restore those *lands* ¹quietly.

14 Yet Jephthah sent messengers again unto the king of the children of Ammon,

15 And said unto him, Thus saith Jephthah, ᵇIsrael took not the land of Moab, nor the land of the children of Ammon.

16 But when Israel came up from Egypt, and walked through the wilderness unto the red sea, then they came to Kadesh.

17 ᶜAnd Israel sent messengers unto the king of Edom, saying, Let me, I pray thee, go through thy land: but the king of Edom would not consent: and also they sent unto the king of Moab, but he would not: therefore Israel abode in Kadesh.

18 Then they went through the wilderness, and compassed the land of Edom, and the land of Moab, and came by the Eastside of the land of Moab, and

CHAPTER 11
ᵃ Num. 21:13
ᵇ Deut. 2:9
ᶜ Num. 20:14,20
ᵈ Num. 21:13
   Num. 22:14
ᵉ Deut. 2:26
ᶠ Deut. 2:36
ᵍ Num. 22:2
   Deut. 23:4
   Josh. 24:9

pitched on the other side of Arnon, ᵈand came not within the coast of Moab: for Arnon *was* the border of Moab.

19 Also Israel ᵉsent messengers unto Sihon, king of the Amorites, the king of Heshbon, and Israel said unto him, Let us pass, we pray thee, by thy land unto our ¹place.

20 But Sihon ¹consented not to Israel, that he should go through his coast: but Sihon gathered all his people together, and pitched in Jahaz, and fought with Israel.

21 And the Lord God of Israel gave Sihon, and all his folk into the hands of Israel, and they smote them: so Israel possessed all the land of the Amorites, the inhabitants of that country:

22 And they possessed ᶠall the coast of the Amorites, from Arnon unto Jabbok, and from the wilderness even unto Jordan.

23 Now therefore the Lord God of Israel hath cast out the Amorites before his people Israel, and shouldest thou possess it?

24 Wouldest not thou possess that which Chemosh thy god giveth thee to possess? So whomsoever the ¹Lord our God driveth out before us, them will we possess.

25 ᵍAnd art thou now far better than Balak the son of Zippor king of Moab? did he not strive with Israel and fight against them,

26 When Israel dwelt in Heshbon and in her towns, and in Aroer and in her towns, and in all the cities that are by the coasts of Arnon, three hundred years? why did ye not then recover ¹them in that space?

27 Wherefore I have not offended thee: but thou doest me wrong to war against me. The Lord the Judge ¹be judge this day between the children of Israel, and the children of Ammon.

28 Howbeit the king of the children of Ammon hearkened not unto the words of Jephthah, which he had sent him.

29 ¶ Then the ¹Spirit of the Lord came upon Jephthah, and he passed over to Gilead, and to Manasseh, and came to Mizpah in Gilead, and from Mizpah in Gilead he unto the children of Ammon.

30 And Jephthah ¹vowed a vow unto the Lord, and said, If thou shalt deliver the children of Ammon into mine hands,

---

11:6 ¹ Men oft times are constrained to desire help of them, whom before they have refused.

11:7 ¹ Oft times those things which men reject, God chooseth to do great enterprises by.

11:10 ¹ Hebrew, *be the bearer.*

11:13 ¹ Hebrew, *in peace.*

11:19 ¹ Or, country.

11:20 ¹ He trusted them not to go through his country.

11:24 ¹ For we ought more to believe and obey God, than thou thine idols.

11:26 ¹ Meaning, their towns.

11:27 ¹ To punish the offender.

11:29 ¹ That is, the spirit of strength and zeal.

11:30 ¹ As the Apostle commendeth Jephthah for his worthy enterprise in delivering the people, Heb. 11:32, so by his rash vow and wicked performance of the same, his victory was defaced: and here we see that the sins of the godly do not utterly extinguish their faith.

31 Then that thing that cometh out of the doors of mine house to meet me, when I come home in peace from the children of Ammon, shall be the Lord's, and I will offer it for a burnt offering.

32 And so Jephthah went unto the children of Ammon to fight against them, and the Lord delivered them into his hands.

33 And he smote them from Aroer even till thou come to Minnith, twenty cities, and so forth to [1]Abel of the vineyards, with an exceeding great slaughter. Thus the children of Ammon were humbled before the children of Israel.

34 ¶ Now when Jephthah came to Mizpah unto his house, behold, his daughter came out to meet him with [1]timbrels and dances, which was his only child: he had none other son, nor daughter.

35 And when he saw her, he [1]rent his clothes, and said, Alas my daughter, thou hast brought me low, and art of them that trouble me: for I have opened my mouth unto the Lord, and cannot go back.

36 And she said unto him, My father, if thou hast opened thy mouth unto the Lord, do with me as thou hast promised, seeing that the Lord hath avenged thee of thine enemies the children of Ammon.

37 Also she said unto her father, Do thus much for me: suffer me two months, that I may go to the mountains, and [1]bewail my virginity, I and my fellows.

38 And he said, Go: and he sent her away two months: so she went with her companions, and lamented her virginity upon the mountains.

39 And after the end of two months, she turned again unto her father, who did with her according to his vow which he had vowed, and she had known no man. And it was a custom in Israel:

40 The daughters of Israel went year by year to lament the daughter of Jephthah the Gileadite, four days in a year.

12 *6 Jephthah killeth two and forty thousand Ephraimites, 8 After Jephthah succeedeth Ibzan, 11 Elon, 13 and Abdon.*

1 And the men of Ephraim gathered themselves together, and went [1]Northward, and said unto Jephthah, Wherefore wentest thou to fight against the children of Ammon, and didst not call [2]us to go with thee? we will therefore burn thine house upon thee with fire.

2 And Jephthah said unto them, I and my people were at great strife with the children of Ammon, and when I called you, ye delivered me not out of their hands.

3 So when I saw that ye delivered me not, [1]I put my life in mine hands, and went upon the children of Ammon: so the Lord delivered them into mine hands. Wherefore then are ye come upon me now to fight against me?

4 Then Jephthah gathered all the men of Gilead, and fought with Ephraim: and the men of Gilead smote Ephraim, because they said, Ye Gileadites are runagates of Ephraim [1]among the Ephraimites, *and* among the Manassites.

5 Also the Gileadites took the passages of Jordan before the Ephraimites, and when the Ephraimites that were escaped, said, Let me pass, then the men of Gilead said unto him, Art thou an Ephraimite? If he said, Nay,

6 Then said they unto him, Say now [1]Shibboleth: and he said Sibboleth: for he could not so pronounce: then they took him, and slew him at the passages of Jordan: and there fell at that time of the Ephraimites two and forty thousand.

7 And Jephthah judged Israel six years: then died Jephthah the Gileadite, and was buried in *one* of the cities of Gilead.

8 ¶ After him [1]Ibzan of Bethlehem judged Israel,

9 Who had thirty sons and thirty daughters, *which* he sent out, and took in thirty daughters from abroad for his sons: and he judged Israel seven years.

10 Then Ibzan died, and was buried at Bethlehem.

11 ¶ And after him judged Israel Elon, a Zebulunite, and he judged Israel ten years.

12 Then Elon the Zebulunite died, and was buried in Aijalon in the country of Zebulun.

13 ¶ And after him Abdon the son of Hillel the Pirathonite judged Israel.

14 And he had forty sons and thirty [1]nephews that rode on seventy [2]asscolts: and he judged Israel eight years.

15 Then died Abdon the son of Hillel the Pirathonite, and was buried in Pirathon, in the land of Ephraim, in the mount of the Amalekites.

13 *1 Israel for their wickedness is oppressed of the Philistines. 3 The Angel appeareth to Manoah's wife, 16 The Angel commandeth him to sacrifice unto the*

11:33 [1] Or, the plain.

11:34 [1] According to the manner after the victory.

11:35 [1] Being overcome with blind zeal, and not considering whether the vow was lawful or no.

11:37 [1] For it was counted as a shame in Israel, to die without children, and therefore they rejoiced to be married.

12:1 [1] After they had passed Jordan.

[2] Thus ambition envieth God's work in others as they did also against Gideon, Judg. 8:1.

12:3 [1] That is, I ventured my life, and when man's help failed, I put my trust only in God.

12:4 [1] Ye ran from us, and chose Gilead, and now in respect of us, ye are nothing.

12:6 [1] Which signifieth the fall of waters, or an ear of corn.

12:8 [1] Some think that this was Boaz the husband of Ruth.

12:14 [1] Hebrew, *sons' sons.*

[2] Or, horse colts.

Lord.   24 *The birth of Samson.*

1   But the children of Israel continued to commit *a*wickedness in the sight of the Lord, and the Lord delivered them into the hands of the Philistines forty years.

2   ¶ Then there was a man in Zorah of the family of the Danites named Manoah, whose wife was ¹barren, and bare not.

3   And the Angel of the Lord appeared unto the woman, and said unto her, Behold now, thou art barren, and bearest not: but thou shalt conceive, and bear a son.

4   And now therefore beware *b*that thou drink no wine, nor strong drink, neither eat any unclean thing.

5   For lo, thou shalt conceive and bear a son, and no razor shall *c*come on his head: for the child shall be a ¹Nazirite unto God from his birth: and he shall begin to save Israel out of the hands of the Philistines.

6   ¶ Then the wife came and told her husband, saying, A man of God came unto me, and the fashion of him was like the fashion of the Angel of God exceedingly ¹fearful, but I asked him not whence he was, neither told he me his name,

7   But he said unto me, Behold, thou shalt conceive and bear a son, and now thou shalt drink no wine nor strong drink, neither eat any unclean thing, for the child shall be a Nazirite to God from his birth to the day of his death.

8   Then Manoah ¹prayed to the Lord, and said, I pray thee, my Lord, let the man of God, whom thou sentest, come again now unto us, and teach us what we shall do unto the child when he is born.

9   And God heard the voice of Manoah, and the Angel of God came again unto the wife, as she sat in the field, but Manoah her husband was not with her.

10   ¶ And the wife made haste and ran, and showed her husband, and said unto him, Behold, the man hath appeared unto me, that came unto me ¹today.

11   And Manoah arose and went after his wife, and came to the ¹man, and said unto him, Art thou the man that spakest unto the woman? and he said, Yea.

12   Then Manoah said, Now let thy saying come to pass: *but* how shall we order the child and do unto him?

CHAPTER 13
a Judg. 2:11
   Judg. 3:7
   Judg. 4:1
   Judg. 6:1
   Judg. 10:6
b Num. 6:2,3
c 1 Sam. 1:11
d Exod. 33:20
   Judg. 6:22

13   And the Angel of the Lord said unto Manoah, The woman must beware of all that I said unto her.

14   She may eat of nothing that cometh of the vine tree: she shall not drink wine nor strong drink, nor eat any ¹unclean thing: let her observe all that I have commanded her.

15   Manoah then said unto the Angel of the Lord, I pray thee, let us retain thee, until we have made ready a kid for thee.

16   And the Angel of the Lord said unto Manoah, Though thou make me abide, I will not eat of thy bread, and if thou wilt make a burnt offering, offer it unto the ¹Lord: for Manoah knew not that it was an Angel of the Lord.

17   Again Manoah said unto the Angel of the Lord, What is thy name, that when thy saying is come to pass, we may honor thee?

18   And the Angel of the Lord said unto him, Why askest thou thus after my name, which is ¹secret?

19   Then Manoah took a kid with a meat offering, and offered it upon a stone unto the Lord: and *the Angel* did ¹wondrously, while Manoah and his wife looked on.

20   For when the flame came up toward heaven from the altar, the Angel of the Lord ascended up in the flame of the altar, and Manoah and his wife beheld it, and fell on their faces unto the ground.

21   (So the Angel of the Lord did no more appear unto Manoah and his wife.) Then Manoah knew that it was an Angel of the Lord.

22   And Manoah said unto his wife, *d*We shall surely die, because we have seen God.

23   But his wife said unto him, If the Lord would kill us, he would not have received a ¹burnt offering, and a meat offering of our hands, neither would he have showed us all these things, nor would now have told us any such.

24   ¶ And the wife bore a son, and called his name Samson: and the child grew, and the Lord blessed him.

25   And the Spirit of the Lord began to ¹strengthen him in the host of Dan, between Zorah and Eshtaol.

14   2 *Samson desireth to have a wife of the Philistines.*   6 *He killeth a lion.*   12 *He propoundeth*

13:2 ¹ Signifying, that their deliverance came only of God, and not by man's power.

13:5 ¹ Meaning, he should be separate from the world, and dedicated to God.

13:6 ¹ If flesh be not able to abide the sight of an Angel, how much less the presence of God?

13:8 ¹ He showeth himself ready to obey God's will, and therefore desireth to know farther.

13:10 ¹ It seemeth that the Angel appeared unto her twice in one day.

13:11 ¹ He calleth him man, because he so seemed, but he was Christ

the eternal word, which at his time appointed became man.

13:14 ¹ Anything forbidden by the Law.

13:16 ¹ Showing, that he sought not his own honor but God's, whose messenger he was.

13:18 ¹ Or, marvelous.

13:19 ¹ God sent fire from heaven to consume their sacrifice, to confirm their faith in his promise.

13:23 ¹ These graces that we have received of God, and his accepting of our obedience, are sure tokens of his love toward us, so that nothing can hurt us.

13:25 ¹ Or, to come upon him at divers times.

a riddle.   19 He killeth thirty.   20 His wife forsaketh him, and taketh another.

1 Now Samson went down to Timnah, and saw a woman in Timnah of the daughters of the Philistines,

2 And he came up and told his father and his mother and said, I have seen a woman in Timnah of the daughters of the Philistines: now therefore [1]give me her to wife.

3 Then his father and his mother said unto him, Is there [1]never a wife among the daughters of thy brethren, and among all my people, that thou must go to take a wife of the uncircumcised Philistines? And Samson said unto his father, Give me her, for she pleaseth me well.

4 But his father and his mother knew not that it came of the Lord, that he should seek an occasion against the [1]Philistines: for at that time the Philistines reigned over Israel.

5 ¶ Then went Samson, and his father and his mother down to Timnah, and came to the vineyards of Timnah: and behold, a young lion roared upon him.

6 And the Spirit of the Lord [1]came upon him, and he tare him, as one should have rent a kid, and had nothing in his hand, neither told he his father nor his mother what he had done.

7 And he went down, and talked with the woman which was beautiful in the eyes of Samson.

8 ¶ And within a *few* days, when he returned [1]to receive her, he went aside to see the carcass of the lion: and behold, there was a swarm of bees, and honey in the body of the lion.

9 And he took thereof in his hands, and went eating, and came to his father and to his mother, and gave unto them, and they did eat: but he told not them, that he had taken the honey out of the body of the lion.

10 So his father went down unto the woman, and Samson made there a [1]feast: for so used the young men to do.

11 And when [1]they saw him, they brought thirty companions to be with him.

12 Then Samson said unto them, I will now put forth a riddle unto you: and if you can declare it me within seven days of the feast, and find it out, I will give you thirty sheets, and thirty [1]change of garments.

13 But if you cannot declare it me, then shall ye give me thirty sheets and thirty change of garments. And they answered him, Put forth thy riddle, that we may hear it.

14 And he said unto them, Out of the eater came meat, and out of the strong came sweetness: and they could not in three days expound the riddle.

15 And when the seventh day was [1]come, they said unto Samson's wife, Entice thine husband that he may declare us the riddle, lest we burn thee and thy father's house with fire. Have ye called us [2]to possess us? is it not *so*?

16 And Samson's wife wept before him, and said, Surely thou hatest me, and lovest me not: for thou hast put forth a riddle unto the [1]children of my people, and hast not told it me. And he said unto her, Behold, I have not told it my father nor my mother, and shall I tell it thee?

17 Then Samson's wife wept before him [1]seven days, while their feast lasted, and when the seventh day came, he told her, because she was importunate upon him: so she told the riddle to the children of her people.

18 And the men of the city said unto him the seventh day before the sun went down, What is sweeter than honey? and what is stronger than a Lion? Then said he unto them, [1]If ye had not plowed with my heifer, ye had not found out my riddle.

19 And the Spirit of the Lord came upon him, and he went down [1]to Ashkelon, and slew thirty men of them and spoiled them, and gave change of garments unto them, which expounded the riddle: and his wrath was kindled, and he went up to his father's house.

20 Then Samson's wife was *given* to his companion, whom he had used as his friend.

15

4 *Samson tieth firebrands to the foxes' tails.*   6 *The Philistines burnt his father-in-law and his wife.*   15 *With the jawbone of an ass he killeth a thousand men.*   19 *Out of a great tooth in the jaw God gave him water.*

1 But within a while after, in the time of wheat harvest, Samson visited his wife with a kid, saying, I will [1]go in to my wife into the chamber: but her father would not suffer him to go in.

2 And her father said, I thought that thou hadst hated her: therefore gave I her to thy companion. Is not her younger sister fairer than she? take her, I

14:2 [1] Hebrew, *take her for me to wife.*
14:3 [1] Though his parents did justly reprove him, yet it appeareth that this was the secret work of the Lord, verse 4.
14:4 [1] To fight against them for the deliverance of Israel.
14:6 [1] Whereby he had strength and boldness.
14:8 [1] Or, to take her to his wife.
14:10 [1] Meaning, when he was married.
14:11 [1] That is, her parents or friends.

14:12 [1] To wear at feasts, or solemn days.
14:15 [1] Or, drew near: for it was the fourth day.
          [2] Or, to impoverish us.
14:16 [1] Unto them which are of my nation.
14:17 [1] Or, to the seventh day beginning at the fourth.
14:18 [1] If ye had not used the help of my wife.
14:19 [1] Which was one of the five chief cities of the Philistines.
15:1 [1] That is, I will use her as my wife.

pray thee, instead of the other.

3 Then Samson said unto them, Now am I more [1]blameless than the Philistines: therefore will I do them displeasure.

4 ¶ And Samson went out, and took three hundred foxes, and took firebrands, and turned them tail to tail, and put a firebrand in the midst between two tails.

5 And when he had set the brands on fire, he sent them out into the standing corn of the Philistines, and burnt up both the [1]ricks and the standing corn, with the vineyards and olives.

6 Then the Philistines said, Who hath done this? And they answered, Samson the son-in-law of the [1]Timnite, because he had taken his wife, and given her to his companion. Then the Philistines came up and [2]burnt her and her father with fire.

7 And Samson said unto them, Though ye have done this, yet will I be avenged of you, and then I will cease.

8 So he smote them [1]hip and thigh with a mighty plague: then he went and dwelt in the top of the rock Etam.

9 ¶ Then the Philistines came up, and pitched in Judah, and [1]were spread abroad in Lehi.

10 And the men of Judah said, Why are ye come up unto us? And they answered, To [1]bind Samson are we come up, and to do to him as he hath done to us.

11 Then three thousand men of Judah went to the top of the rock Etam, and said to Samson, Knowest thou not that the Philistines are rulers over us? [1]Wherefore then hast thou done thus unto us? And he answered them, As they did unto me, so have I done unto them.

12 Again they said unto him, We are come to bind thee, and to deliver thee into the hand of the Philistines. And Samson said unto them, Swear unto me, that ye will not fall upon me yourselves.

13 And they answered him, saying, No, but we will bind thee and [1]deliver thee unto their hand, but we will not kill thee. And they bound him with two new cords, and brought him from the rock.

14 When he came to Lehi, the Philistines shouted against him, and the Spirit of the Lord came upon him, and the cords that were upon his arms, became as flax that was burnt with fire: for the bands loosed from his hands.

15 And he found a [1]new jawbone of an ass, and put forth his hands, and caught it, and slew a thousand men therewith.

16 Then Samson said, With the jaw of an ass are heaps upon heaps: with the jaw of an ass have I slain a thousand men.

17 And when he had left speaking, he cast away the jawbone out of his hand, and called that place, [1]Ramath Lehi.

18 And he was sore athirst, and [1]called on the Lord, and said, Thou hast given this great deliverance into the hand of thy servant: and now shall I die for thirst, and fall into the hand of the uncircumcised?

19 Then God brake the cheek tooth, that was in the jaw, and water came there out: and when he had drunk, his spirit came again, and he was revived: wherefore the name thereof is called, [1]En Hakkore, which is in Lehi unto this day.

20 And he judged Israel in the days of the Philistines twenty years.

16

3 Samson carrieth away the gates of Gaza. 18 He was deceived by Delilah. 30 He pulleth down the house upon the Philistines, and dieth with them.

1 Then went Samson to [1]Gaza, and saw there [2]an harlot, [3]and went in unto her.

2 And it was told to the Gazites, Samson is come hither. And they went about, and laid wait for him all night in the gate of the city, and were quiet all the night, saying, Abide [1]till the morning early, and we shall kill him.

3 And Samson slept till midnight, and arose at midnight, and took the doors of the gates of the city and the two posts, and lifted them away with the bars, and put them upon his shoulders, and carried them up to the top of the mountain that is before Hebron.

4 And after this he loved a woman by the [1]river of Sorek, whose name was Delilah:

5 Unto whom came the princes of the Philistines, and said unto her, Entice him, and see wherein his great strength lieth, and by what means we may overcome him, that we may bind him, and punish him, and every one of us shall give thee eleven hundred [1]shekels of silver.

15:3 [1] For through his father-in-law's occasion, he was moved again to take vengeance of the Philistines.

15:5 [1] Or, that which was reaped and gathered.

15:6 [1] Or, the citizen of Timnath.

[2] So the wicked punish not vice for love of justice, but for fear of danger, which else might come to them.

15:8 [1] Or, horsemen and footmen.

15:9 [1] Or, camped.

15:10 [1] And so being our prisoner to punish him.

15:11 [1] Such was their gross ignorance, that they judged God's great benefits to be a plague unto them.

15:13 [1] Thus they had rather betray their brother, than use the means that God had given for their deliverance.

15:15 [1] That is, of an ass lately slain.

15:17 [1] Or, the lifting up of the jaw.

15:18 [1] Whereby appeareth that he did these things in faith, and so with a true zeal to glorify God, and deliver his country.

15:19 [1] Or, the fountain of him that prayed.

16:1 [1] One of the five chief cities of the Philistines.

[2] Or, victualler.

[3] That is, he lodged with her.

16:2 [1] Or, to the light of the morning.

16:4 [1] Or, plain.

16:5 [1] Of the value of a shekel, read Gen. 23:15.

6 ¶ And Delilah said to Samson, Tell me, I pray thee, wherein thy great strength *lieth*, and wherewith thou mightest be bound, to do thee hurt.

7 Samson then answered unto her, If they bind me with seven [1]green cords, that were never dried, then shall I be weak, and be as another man.

8 And the princes of the Philistines brought her seven green cords that were not dry, and she bound him therewith.

9 (And she had [1]men lying in wait with her in the chamber) Then she said unto him, The Philistines *be* upon thee, Samson. And he brake the cords, as a thread of tow is broken, when [2]it feeleth fire: so his strength was not known.

10 ¶ After Delilah said unto Samson, See, thou hast mocked me, and told me lies. I pray thee now, [1]tell me wherewith thou mightest be bound.

11 Then he answered her, If they bind me with new ropes that never were occupied, then shall I be weak, and be as another man.

12 Delilah therefore took new ropes, and bound him therewith, and said unto him, The Philistines *be* upon thee, Samson: (and men lay in wait in the chamber) and he brake them from his arms, as a thread.

13 ¶ Afterward Delilah said to Samson, Hitherto thou hast beguiled me, and told me lies: tell me how thou mightest be bound. [1]And he said unto her, If thou plattedst seven locks of mine head with the threads of the woof.

14 And she fastened it with a pin, and said unto him, The Philistines *be* upon thee, Samson. And he awoke out of his sleep, and went away with the [1]pin of the web, and the woof.

15 Again she said unto him, How canst thou say, [1]I love thee, when thine heart is not with me? thou hast mocked me these three times, and hast not told me wherein thy great strength *lieth*.

16 And because she was importunate upon him with her words continually, and vexed him, his soul was pained unto the death.

17 Therefore he told her all his [1]heart, and said unto her, There never came razor upon mine head: for I am a Nazirite unto God from my mother's womb: therefore if I be shaven, my strength will go from me, and I shall be weak, and be like all *other* men.

18 And when Delilah saw that he had told her all his heart, she sent, and called for the Princes of the Philistines, saying, Come up once *again*: for he hath showed me all his heart. Then the Princes of the Philistines came up unto her, and brought the money in their hands.

19 And she made him sleep upon her knees, and she called a man, and made him to shave off the seven locks of his head, and she began to vex him, and his strength was gone [1]from him.

20 Then she said, The Philistines *be* upon thee, Samson. And he awoke out of his sleep, and thought, I will go out now as at other times, and shake myself, but he knew not that the Lord was departed from him.

21 Therefore the Philistines took him, and put out his eyes, and brought him down to Gaza, and bound him with fetters: and he did grind in the prison house.

22 And the hair of his head began to [1]grow again after that it was shaven.

23 Then the Princes of the Philistines gathered them together for to offer a great sacrifice unto Dagon their god, and to rejoice: for they said, Our god hath delivered Samson our enemy into our hands.

24 Also when the people saw him, they praised their god: for they said, Our god hath delivered into our hands our enemy and destroyer of our country, which hath slain many of us.

25 And when their hearts were merry, they said, Call Samson, that he may make us pastime: So they called Samson out of the prison house, and he [1]was a laughing stock unto them, and they set him between the pillars.

26 Then Samson said unto the servant that led him by the hand, Lead me, that I may touch the pillars that the house standeth upon, and that I may lean to them.

27 (Now the house was full of men and women, and there *were* all the princes of the Philistines: also upon the roof *were* about three thousand men and women, that beheld while Samson [1]played)

28 Then Samson called unto the Lord, and said, O Lord God, I pray thee, think upon me: O God, I beseech thee, strengthen me at this time only, that I may be [1]at once [2]avenged of the Philistines for my

---

16:7 [1] Or, new withes.

16:9 [1] Certain Philistines in a secret chamber.

[2] When fire cometh near it.

16:10 [1] Though her falsehood tended to make him lose his life, yet his affection so blinded him, that he could not beware.

16:13 [1] It is impossible if we give place to our wicked affections, but at length we shall be destroyed.

16:14 [1] Or, beam.

16:15 [1] For this Samson used to say, I love thee.

16:17 [1] Thus his immoderate affections toward a wicked woman caused him to lose God's excellent gifts, and become slave unto

them whom he should have ruled.

16:19 [1] Not for the loss of his hair, but for the contempt of the ordinance of God, which was the cause that God departed from him.

16:22 [1] Yet had he not his strength again, till he had called upon God, and reconciled himself.

16:25 [1] Thus by God's just judgments they are made slaves to infidels which neglect their vocation in defending the faithful.

16:27 [1] Or, was mocked.

16:28 [1] Hebrew, *take one vengeance*.

[2] According to my vocation which is to execute God's judgments upon the wicked.

two eyes.

29 And Samson laid hold on the two middle pillars whereupon the house stood, and on which it was borne up: on the one with his right hand, and on the other with his left.

30 Then said Samson, [1]Let me lose my life with the Philistines: and he bowed him with all his might, and the house fell upon the princes, and upon all the people that were therein: so the dead which he slew at his death, were more than they which he had slain in his life.

31 Then his brethren, and all the house of his father came down and took him, and brought him up and buried him between Zorah and Eshtaol, in the sepulcher of Manoah his father: now he had judged Israel twenty years.

17

3 Micah's mother according to her vow, made her son two idols.   5 He made his son a Priest for his idols,   10 and after he hired a Levite.

1 There [1]was a man of mount Ephraim, whose name was Micah,

2 And he said unto his mother, The eleven hundred *shekels* of silver that were taken from thee, for the which thou cursedst, and spakedst it, even in mine hearing, behold, the silver *is* with me, I took it. Then his mother said, Blessed be my son of the Lord.

3 And when he had restored the eleven hundred *shekels* of silver to his mother, his mother said, I had dedicate the silver to the Lord of mine hand for my son, to make [1]a graven and molten image. Now therefore I will give it thee again.

4 And when he had restored the money unto his mother, his mother took two hundred *shekels* of silver, and gave them to the founder, which made thereof a graven and molten image, and it was in the house of Micah.

5 And this man Micah had an house of gods, and made an [a,1]Ephod, and [b,2]Teraphim, and [3]consecrated one of his sons, who was his Priest.

6 [c]In those days there was no [1]King in Israel, *but* every man did that which was good in his own eyes.

7 ¶ There was also a young man out of Bethlehem

CHAPTER 17
[a] Judg. 8:27
[b] Gen. 31:19
Hos. 3:4
[c] Judg. 21:25

Judah, [1]of the family of Judah: who was a Levite, and sojourned there.

8 And the man departed out of the city, *even* out of Bethlehem Judah, to dwell where he could find *a place*: and as he journeyed, he came to mount Ephraim to the house of Micah.

9 And Micah said unto him, Whence comest thou? And the Levite answered him, [1]I *come* from Bethlehem Judah, and go to dwell where I may find *a place*.

10 Then Micah said unto him, Dwell with me, and be unto me a father and a Priest, and I will give thee ten *shekels* of silver by year, and a suit of apparel, and thy meat and drink. So the Levite went in.

11 And the Levite was [1]content to dwell with the man, and the young man was unto him as one of his own sons.

12 And Micah consecrated the Levite, and the young man was his Priest, and was in the house of Micah.

13 Then said Micah, Now I know that the Lord will be [1]good unto me, seeing I have a Levite to my Priest.

18

2 The children of Dan send men to search the land.   11 Then come the six hundred and take the gods, and the Priest of Micah away.   27 They destroy Laish,   28 They build it again.   30 And set up Idolatry.

1 In those days there was no [1]king in Israel, and at the same time the tribe of Dan sought them an inheritance to dwell in: for unto that time *all* their inheritance had not fallen unto them among the tribes of Israel.

2 Therefore the children of Dan sent of their family, five men out of their coasts, *even* men expert in war, out of Zorah and Eshtaol, to view the land and search it out, and said unto them, [1]Go, *and* search out the land. Then they came to mount Ephraim to the house of Micah and lodged there.

3 When they were in the house of Micah, they knew the [1]voice of the young man the Levite: and being turned in thither, they said unto him, Who brought thee hither? or what makest thou in this place? and what hast thou *to do* here?

16:30 [1] He speaketh not this of despair, but humbling himself for neglecting his office and the offence thereby given.

17:1 [1] Some think this history was in the time of Othniel, or as Josephus writeth, immediately after Joshua.

17:3 [1] Contrary to the commandment of God and true religion practiced under Joshua, they forsook the Lord and fell to idolatry.

17:5 [1] He would serve both God and Idols.

  [2] By Teraphim some understand certain idols, having the likeness of a man, but others understand thereby all manner of things and instruments belonging unto those, who sought for any answer at God's hands, as Judg. 18:5,6.

  [3] Hebrew, *filled the hand of one.*

17:6 [1] For where there is no Magistrate fearing God, there can be no

true religion or order.

17:7 [1] Which Bethlehem was in the tribe of Judah.

17:9 [1] For in those days the service of God was corrupt in all estates, and the Levites were not looked unto.

17:11 [1] Not considering that he forsook the true worshipping of God for to maintain his own belly.

17:13 [1] Thus the idolaters persuade themselves of God's favor, when indeed he doth detest them.

18:1 [1] Meaning, no ordinary Magistrate to punish vice according to God's word.

18:2 [1] For the portion which Joshua gave them, was not sufficient for all their tribe.

18:3 [1] They knew him by his speech that he was a stranger there.

4 And he answered them, Thus and thus dealeth Micah with me, and hath hired me, and I am his Priest.

5 Again they said unto him, Ask counsel now of God, that we may know whether the way which we go, shall be prosperous.

6 And the Priest said unto them, ¹Go in peace: for the Lord guideth your way which ye go.

7 Then the five men departed, and came to Laish, and saw the people that were therein, which dwelt careless, after the manner of the Sidonians, quiet and sure, because no man ¹made any trouble in the land, or usurped any dominion: also they were far from the Sidonians, and had no business with *other* men.

8 ¶ So they came again unto their brethren to Zorah and Eshtaol: and their brethren said unto them, What have ye *done?*

9 And they answered, Arise, that we may go up against them: for we have seen the land, and surely it is very good, and ¹do ye sit still? be not slothful to go and enter to possess the land:

10 (If ye will go, ye shall come unto a careless people, and the country *is* large) for God hath given it into your hand. *It is* a place which doth lack nothing that is in the world.

11 ¶ Then there departed thence of the family of the Danites, from Zorah and from Eshtaol, six hundred men appointed with instruments of war.

12 And they went up, and pitched in Kirjath Jearim in Judah: wherefore they called that place ¹Mahaneh Dan unto this day: and it is behind Kirjath Jearim.

13 And they went thence unto mount Ephraim, and came to the house of Micah.

14 Then answered the five men that went to spy out the country of Laish, and said unto their brethren, ¹Know ye not, that there is in these houses an Ephod, and Teraphim, and a graven and a molten image? Now therefore consider what ye have to do.

15 And they turned thitherward and came to the house of the young man the Levite, *even* unto the house of Micah, and saluted him peaceably.

16 And the six hundred men appointed with their weapons of war, which were of the children of Dan, stood by the entering of the gate.

17 Then the five men that went to spy out the land, went in thither, *and* took the ¹graven image and the Ephod, and the Teraphim, and the molten

CHAPTER 18
a Josh. 19:47

image: and the Priest stood in the entering of the gate with the six hundred men that were appointed with weapons of war.

18 And the other went into Micah's house, and fet the graven image, the Ephod and the Teraphim, and the molten image. Then said the Priest unto them, What do ye?

19 And they answered him, Hold thy peace: lay thine hand upon thy mouth, and come with us to be our father and Priest. Whether is it better that thou shouldest be a Priest unto the house of one man, or that thou shouldest be a Priest unto a tribe and to a family in Israel?

20 And the Priest's heart was glad, and he took the Ephod, and the Teraphim, and the graven image, and went among the ¹people.

21 And they turned and departed, and put the children, and the cattle, and the substance ¹before them.

22 ¶ When they were far off from the house of Micah, the men that were in the houses near to Micah's house, gathered together, and pursued after the children of Dan,

23 And cried unto the children of Dan: who turned their faces, and said unto Micah, What aileth thee that thou makest an outcry?

24 And he said, Ye have taken away my ¹gods, which I made, and the Priest, and go your ways: and what have I more? how then say ye unto me, What aileth thee?

25 And the children of Dan said unto him, Let not thy voice be heard among us, lest ¹angry fellows run upon thee, and thou lose thy life with the lives of thine household.

26 So the children of Dan went their ways: and when Micah saw that they were too strong for him, he turned and went back unto his house.

27 And they took the ¹things which Micah had made, and the Priest which he had, and came unto Laish, unto a quiet people, and without mistrust, and smote them with the edge of the sword, and burnt the city with fire:

28 And there was none to ¹help, because ²Laish was far from Sidon, and they had no business with *other* men: also it was in the valley that lieth by Beth Rehob. After, they built the city, and dwelt therein,

29 *a*And called the name of the city Dan, after the name of Dan their father, which was born unto

---

18:6 ¹ Thus God granteth the idolaters sometime their requests to their destruction that delight in errors.

18:7 ¹ Hebrew, *made them ashamed.*

18:9 ¹ Lose ye this good occasion through your slothfulness?

18:12 ¹ Or, the tents of Dan.

18:14 ¹ Because they before had had good success, they would that their brethren should be encouraged by hearing the same tidings.

18:17 ¹ So superstition blinded them that they thought God's power

was in these idols, and that they should have good success by them, though by violence and robbery they did take them away.

18:20 ¹ With the six hundred men.

18:21 ¹ Suspecting them that did pursue them.

18:24 ¹ This declareth what opinion the idolaters have of their idols.

18:25 ¹ Hebrew, *who have their heart bitter.*

18:27 ¹ Meaning, the idols, as verse 18.

18:28 ¹ Or, deliver them.

² Which after was called Cesarea Philippi.

Israel: howbeit the name of the city was Laish at the beginning.

30 Then the children of Dan set them up the ¹graven image: and Jonathan the son of Gershom, the son of Manasseh, and his sons were the Priests in the tribe of the Danites, until the day of the ²captivity of the land.

31 So they set them up the graven image, which Micah had made, all the while the house of God was in Shiloh.

19

1 A Levite's wife being an harlot forsook her husband, and he took her again.   25 At Gibeah she was most villainously abused to the death.   29 The Levite cutteth her in pieces, and sendeth her to the twelve tribes.

1 Also in those days, when there was no king in Israel, a certain Levite dwelt on the side of mount Ephraim, and took to wife a ªconcubine out of Bethlehem Judah,

2 And his concubine played the whore ¹there, and went away from him unto her father's house to Bethlehem Judah, and there continued the space of four months.

3 And her husband arose and went after her, to speak ¹friendly unto her, and to bring her again: *he had* also his servant with him, and a couple of asses: and she brought him unto her father's house, and when the young woman's father saw him, he rejoiced ²of his coming.

4 And his father-in-law, the young woman's father received him: and he abode with him three days: so they did eat and drink, and lodged there.

5 ¶ And when the fourth day came, they arose early in the morning, and ¹he prepared to depart: then the young woman's father said unto his son-in-law, ²Comfort thine heart with a morsel of bread, and then go your way.

6 So they sat down and did eat and drink, both of them together. And the ¹young woman's father said unto the man, Be content, I pray thee, and tarry all night, and let thine heart be merry.

7 And when the man rose up to depart, his father-in-law ¹was earnest: therefore he returned, and lodged there.

8 And he arose up early the fifth day to depart,

CHAPTER 19
ª Judg. 17:6
Judg. 18:1
Gen. 25:6

and the young woman's father said, ¹Comfort thine heart, I pray thee: and they tarried until after midday, and they both did eat.

9 Afterward when the man arose to depart with his concubine and his servant, his father-in-law, the young woman's father said unto him, Behold now, the day ¹draweth toward even: I pray you, tarry all night: behold, the ²sun goeth to rest: lodge here, that thine heart may be merry, and tomorrow get you early upon your way, and go to the ³tent.

10 But the man would not tarry, but arose, and departed, and came over against Jebus, (which is Jerusalem) and his two asses laden, and his concubine *were* with him.

11 When they were near Jebus, the day ¹was sore spent, and the servant said unto his master, Come, I pray thee, and let us turn unto this city of the Jebusites, and lodge all night there.

12 And his master answered him, ¹We will not turn into the city of strangers that are not of the children of Israel, but we will go forth to Gibeah.

13 And he said unto his servant, Come, and let us draw near to one of these places, that we may lodge in Gibeah or in Ramah.

14 So they went forward upon their way, and the Sun went down upon them near to Gibeah, which is in Benjamin.

15 ¶ Then they turned thither to go in and lodge in Gibeah: and when he came, he sat him down in a street of the city: for there was no man that ¹took them into his house to lodging.

16 And behold, there came an old man from his work out of the field at even, and the man was of mount Ephraim, but dwelt in Gibeah: and the men of the place were the children of ¹Jemini.

17 And when he had lifted up his eyes, he saw a ¹wayfaring man in the streets of the city: then this old man said, Whither goest thou, and whence camest thou?

18 And he answered him, We came from Bethlehem Judah, unto the side of mount Ephraim: from thence am I: and I went to Bethlehem Judah, and go *now* to the ¹house of the Lord: and no man receiveth me to house,

19 Although we have straw and provender for

18:30 ¹ Thus instead of giving glory to God, they attributed the victory to their idols, and honored them therefore.

  ² That is, till the Ark was taken, 1 Sam. 5:1.

19:2 ¹ Hebrew, *besides him*, to wit, with others.

19:3 ¹ Hebrew, *to her heart*.

  ² Or, at his meeting.

19:5 ¹ Hebrew, *rose up*.

  ² Or, strengthen.

19:6 ¹ That is, his concubine's father.

19:7 ¹ Or, compelled him.

19:8 ¹ Meaning, that he should refresh himself with meat, as verse 5.

19:9 ¹ Hebrew, *is weak*.

  ² Or, the day lodgeth.

  ³ To wit, to the town or city where he dwelt.

19:11 ¹ Or, went down.

19:12 ¹ Though in these days there were most horrible corruptions, yet very necessity could not compel them, to have to do with them that professed not the true God.

19:15 ¹ Or gathered them.

19:16 ¹ That is, of the tribe of Benjamin.

19:17 ¹ Or, a man walking.

19:18 ¹ To Shiloh of Mizpah where the Ark was.

our asses, and also bread and wine for me and thine handmaid, and for the boy that is with thy servant: we lack nothing.

20 And the old man said, [1]Peace be with thee: as for all that thou lackest, *shalt thou find* with me: only abide not in the street all night.

21 ¶ So he brought him into his house, and gave fodder unto the asses: and they washed their feet, and did eat and drink.

22 And as they were making their hearts merry, behold, the men of the city, [1]wicked men beset the house round about, and [2]smote at the door, and spake to this old man the master of the house, saying, Bring forth the man that came into thine house that we may know him.

23 And [b]this man the master of the house went out unto them, and said unto them, Nay my brethren, do not so wickedly, I pray you, seeing that this man is come into mine house, do not this villainy.

24 Behold, *here is* my daughter, a virgin, and his concubine: them will I bring out now, [1]and humble them, and do with them what seemeth you good: but to this man do not this villainy.

25 But the men would not hearken to him: therefore the man took his concubine, and brought her out unto them: and they knew her and abused her all the night unto the morning and when the day began to spring, they let her go.

26 So the woman came in the dawning of the day, and [1]fell down at the door of the man's house where her lord was, till the light day.

27 And her [1]lord arose in the morning, and opened the doors of the house, and went out to go his way, and behold, the woman his concubine *was* [2]dead at the door of the house, and her hands *lay* upon the threshold.

28 And he said unto her, up, and let us go: but she answered not. Then he took her up upon the ass, and the man rose up, and went unto his [1]place.

29 And when he was come to his house, he took a knife and laid hand on his concubine, and divided her in pieces with her bones into twelve parts, and sent her through all quarters of Israel.

30 And all that saw it, said, There was no [1]such thing done or seen since the time that the children of Israel came up from the land of Egypt unto this day:

[b] Gen. 19:6

CHAPTER 20
[a] Hos. 10:9

consider the matter, consult and give sentence.

20

1 *The Israelites assemble at Mizpah, to whom the Levite declareth his wrong.* 13 *They sent for them that aid the villain.* 45 *The Israelites are twice overcome,* 46 *And at length get the victory.*

1 Then [a]all the children of Israel went out, and the Congregation was gathered together as [1]one man, from Dan to Beersheba, with the land of Gilead, unto the [2]Lord in Mizpah.

2 And the [1]chief of all the people, *and* all the tribes of Israel assembled in the Congregation of the people of God four hundred thousand footmen that [2]drew sword.

3 (Now the children of Benjamin heard that the children of Israel were gone up to Mizpah) Then, the children of Israel [1]said, How is this wickedness committed?

4 And the same Levite, the woman's husband that was slain, answered and said, I came unto Gibeah that is in Benjamin with my concubine to lodge,

5 And the [1]men of Gibeah arose against me, and beset the house round about upon me by night, thinking to have slain me, and have forced my concubine that she is dead.

6 Then I took my concubine, and cut her in pieces, and sent [1]her throughout all the country of the inheritance of Israel: for they have committed abomination and villainy in Israel.

7 Behold, ye are all children of Israel, give your advice, and counsel herein.

8 Then all the people arose as one man, saying, There shall not a man of us go to his tent, neither any turn into his [1]house.

9 But now this is that thing which we will do to Gibeah: *we will go up* by lot against it.

10 And we will take ten men of the hundred throughout all the tribes of Israel, and an hundred of the thousand, and a thousand of ten thousand to bring [1]victual for the people, that they may do (when they come to Gibeah of Benjamin) according to all the villainy, that it hath done in Israel.

11 ¶ So all the men of Israel were gathered against the city, knit together as one man.

12 And the tribes of Israel sent men through all

19:20 [1] Or, be of good comfort.
19:22 [1] Hebrew, *men of Belial*, that is, given to all wickedness.
   [2] To the intent they might break it.
19:24 [1] That is, abuse them, as Gen. 19:8.
19:26 [1] She fell down dead, as verse 27.
19:27 [1] Or, husband.
   [2] Or, fallen.
19:28 [1] Meaning, home unto mount Ephraim.
19:30 [1] For this was like the sin of Sodom for the which God rained down fire and brimstone from heaven.

20:1 [1] That is, all with one consent.
   [2] To ask counsel.
20:2 [1] Hebrew, *corners*.
   [2] Meaning, men able to handle their weapons.
20:3 [1] To the Levite.
20:5 [1] Or, chief, or lord.
20:6 [1] That is, her pieces, to every tribe a piece, Judg. 19:29.
20:8 [1] Before we have revenged this wickedness.
20:10 [1] These only should have the charge to provide for vittles for the rest.

the ¹tribe of Benjamin, saying, What wickedness is this that is committed among you?

13 Now therefore deliver us those wicked men which are in Gibeah, that we may put them to death, and put away evil from Israel: but the children of Benjamin ¹would not obey the voice of their brethren the children of Israel.

14 But the children of Benjamin gathered themselves together out of the cities unto Gibeah, to come out and fight against the children of Israel.

15 ¶ And the children of Benjamin were numbered at that time, out of the cities, six and twenty thousand men that drew sword, beside the inhabitants of Gibeah, which were numbered seven hundred chosen men.

16 Of all this people were seven hundred chosen men, being ᵇleft handed: all these could sling stones at an hair breadth, and not fail.

17 ¶ Also the men of Israel beside Benjamin, were numbered four hundred thousand men that drew sword, even all men of war.

18 And the children of Israel arose, and went up ¹to the house of God, and asked of God, saying, Which of us shall go up first to fight against the children of Benjamin? and the Lord said, Judah shall be first.

19 Then the children of Israel arose up early and camped against Gibeah.

20 And the men of Israel went out to battle against Benjamin, and the men of Israel put themselves in array to fight against them beside Gibeah.

21 And the children of Benjamin came out of Gibeah, and slew down to the ground of the Israelites that day ¹two and twenty thousand men.

22 And the people, the men of Israel plucked up their hearts, and set their battle again in array in the place where they put them in array the first day.

23 (For the children of Israel had gone up and wept before the Lord unto the evening, and had asked of the Lord, saying, Shall I go again to battle against the children of Benjamin my brethren? and the Lord said, Go up against them.)

24 ¶ Then the children of Israel came near against the children of Benjamin the second day.

25 Also the second day Benjamin came forth to meet them out of Gibeah, and slew down to the ground of the children of Israel again eighteen thousand men: ¹all they could handle the sword.

ᵇ Judg. 3:15

26 Then all the children of Israel went up, and all the people came also unto the house of God, and wept, and sat there before the Lord, and fasted that day unto the evening, and offered burnt offerings and peace offerings before the Lord.

27 And the children of Israel asked the Lord (for ¹there was the Ark of the Covenant of God in those days,

28 And Phinehas the son of Eleazar, the son of Aaron ¹stood before it at that time) saying, Shall I yet go anymore to battle against the children of Benjamin my brethren, or shall I cease? And the Lord said, Go up: for tomorrow I will deliver them into your hand.

29 And Israel set men to lie in wait roundabout Gibeah.

30 And the children of Israel went up against the children of Benjamin the third day, and put themselves in array against Gibeah, as at other times.

31 Then the children of Benjamin coming out against the people, were ¹drawn from the city: and they began to smite of the people and kill as at other times, even by the ways in the field (whereof one goeth up to the house of God, and the other to Gibeah) upon a thirty men of Israel.

32 (For the children of Benjamin said, They are fallen before us, as at the first. But the children of Israel said, Let us flee and pluck them away from the city unto the ¹highways.)

33 And all the men of Israel rose up out of their place, and put themselves in array at Baal Tamar: and the men that lay in wait of the Israelites came forth of their place, even out of the meadows of Geba,

34 And they came over against Gibeah, ten thousand chosen men of all Israel, and the battle was sore: for they knew not that the ¹evil was near them.

35 ¶ And the Lord smote Benjamin before Israel, and the children of Israel destroyed of the Benjamites the same day five and twenty thousand and an hundred men: all they could handle the sword.

36 So the children of Benjamin saw that they were stricken down: for the men of Israel ¹gave place to the Benjamites, because they trusted to the men that lay in wait, which they had laid beside Gibeah.

37 And they that lay in wait hasted, and brake forth toward Gibeah, and the ambushment ¹drew themselves along, and smote all the city with the

---

20:12 ¹ That is, every family of the tribe.
20:13 ¹ Because they would not suffer the wicked to be punished, they declared themselves to maintain them in their evil, and therefore were all justly punished.
20:18 ¹ That is, to the Ark, which was in Shiloh some think in Mizpah, as verse 1.
20:21 ¹ This God permitted, because the Israelites partly in their strength, and partly God would by this means punish their sins.
20:25 ¹ All they drawing the sword.

20:27 ¹ To wit, in Shiloh.
20:28 ¹ Or, served in the Priest's office at those days: for the Jews write, that he lived three hundred years.
20:31 ¹ By the policy of the children of Israel.
20:32 ¹ Meaning, crossways or paths to divers places.
20:34 ¹ They knew not that God's judgment was at hand to destroy them.
20:36 ¹ Retired to draw them after.
20:37 ¹ Or, made a long sound with a trumpet.

edge of the sword.

38 Also the men of Israel had appointed a certain time with the ambushments, that they should make a great flame *and* smoke arise up out of the city.

39 And when the men of Israel retired in the battle, Benjamin began to ¹smite and kill of the men of Israel about thirty persons: for they said, Surely they are stricken down before us, as in the first battle.

40 But when the flame began to rise out of the city *as* a pillar of smoke, the Benjamites looked back, and behold, the flame of the city began to ascend up to heaven.

41 Then the men of Israel turned ¹again, and the men of Benjamin were astonished: for they saw that evil was near unto them.

42 Therefore they fled before the men of Israel unto the way of the wilderness, but the battle overtook them: also they which *came out* of the cities, slew them ¹among them.

43 *Thus* they compassed the Benjamites about, *and* ¹chased them at ease, and overran them, even over against Gibeah on the East side.

44 And there were slain of Benjamin eighteen thousand men, which were all men of war.

45 And they turned and fled to the wilderness unto the rock of Rimmon: and the *Israelites* ¹gleaned of them by the way five thousand men, and pursued after them unto Gidom, and slew two thousand men of them,

46 So that all that were slain that day of Benjamin, were ¹five and twenty thousand men that drew sword, which were all men of war.

47 ᶜBut six hundred men turned and fled to the wilderness unto the rock of Rimmon, and abode in the rock of Rimmon four months.

48 Then the men of Israel turned unto the children of Benjamin, and smote them with the edge of the sword, from the men of the city unto the beasts, and all that came to hand: also they set on fire all the ¹cities that they could come by.

21

1 Moreover, the men of Israel ¹sware in Mizpah,

ᶜ Judg. 21:13

CHAPTER 21

ᵈ Num. 31:17

saying, None of us shall give his daughter unto the Benjamites to wife.

2 And the people came unto the house of God and abode there till even before God, and lifted up their voices, and wept with great lamentation,

3 And said, O Lord God of Israel, why is this come to pass in Israel, that this day one tribe of Israel should want?

4 ¶ And on the morrow the people rose up and made there an ¹altar, and offered burnt offerings and peace offerings.

5 Then the children of Israel said, Who is he among all the tribes of Israel, that came not up with the Congregation unto the Lord? for they had made a great oath concerning him that came not up to the Lord to Mizpah, saying, Let him die the death.

6 And the children of Israel ¹were sorry for Benjamin their brother, and said, There is one tribe cut off from Israel this day.

7 How shall we do for wives to them that remain, seeing we have sworn by the Lord, that we will not give them of our daughters to wives?

8 Also they said, is there any of the tribes of Israel that ¹came not up to Mizpah to the Lord? and behold, there came none of Jabesh Gilead unto the host, *and* to the Congregation.

9 For when the people were viewed, behold, none of the inhabitants of Jabesh Gilead were there.

10 Therefore the Congregation sent thither twelve thousand men of the ¹most valiant, and commanded them, saying, Go and smite the inhabitants of Jabesh Gilead with the edge of the sword, both women and children.

11 ᵈAnd this is it that ye shall do: ye shall utterly destroy all the males, and all the women that have lain by men.

12 And they found among the inhabitants of Jabesh Gilead four hundred maids, virgins that had known no man by lying with any male: and they brought them unto the host to Shiloh, which is in the land of Canaan.

13 ¶ Then the whole Congregation ¹sent and spake with the children of Benjamin that were in the rock of Rimmon, and called ²peaceably unto them:

14 And Benjamin came again at that time, and

20:39 ¹ For they were waxen hardy by the two former victories.
20:41 ¹ And withstood their enemies.
20:42 ¹ For they were compassed in on every side.
20:43 ¹ Or, drove them from their rest.
20:45 ¹ They slew them by one and one, as they were scattered abroad.
20:46 ¹ Besides eleven hundred that had been slain in the former battles.
20:48 ¹ If they belonged to the Benjamites.
21:1 ¹ This oath came of rashness, and not of judgment: for after they brake it, in showing secretly the means to marry with certain

of their daughters.
21:4 ¹ According to their custom, when they would consult with the Lord.
21:6 ¹ Or, repented that they had destroyed their brethren, as appeareth verse 15.
21:8 ¹ Condemning them to be favors of vice, which would not put their hand to punish it.
21:10 ¹ Hebrew, *children of strength*.
21:13 ¹ To wit, about four months after the discomfiture, Judg. 20:47.
       ² Or, friendly.

they gave them wives which they had saved alive of the women of Jabesh Gilead: but they had not [1]so enough for them.

15 And the people were sorry for Benjamin, because the Lord had made a breach in the tribes of Israel.

16 Therefore the Elders of the Congregation said, How shall we do for wives to the remnant? for the women of Benjamin are destroyed.

17 And they said, *There must be* [1]an inheritance for them that be escaped of Benjamin, that a tribe be not destroyed out of Israel.

18 Howbeit we may not give them wives of our daughters: for the children of Israel had sworn, saying, Cursed be he that giveth a wife to Benjamin.

19 Therefore they said, Behold, there is a feast of the Lord every year in Shiloh, *in a place*, which is on the [1]North side of Bethel, and on the East side of the way that goeth up from Bethel to Shechem, and on the South of Lebonah.

20 Therefore they commanded the children of Ben-

b Judg. 17:6
Judg. 13:1
Judg. 19:1

jamin, saying, Go, and lie in wait in the vineyards.

21 And when ye see that the daughters of Shiloh come out to dance in dances, then come ye out of the vineyards, and catch you every man a wife of the daughters of Shiloh, and go into the land of Benjamin.

22 And [1]when their fathers or their brethren come unto us to complain, we will say unto them, Have pity on them for our sakes, because we reserved not to each man his wife in the war, and because ye have not given unto them hitherto, ye have sinned.

23 And the children of Benjamin did so, and took wives of them that danced according to their [1]number: which they took, and went away, and returned to their inheritance, and repaired the cities and dwelt in them.

24 So the children of Israel departed thence at that time, every man to his tribe, and to his family, and went out from thence every man to his inheritance.

25 [b]In those days there was no king in Israel, *but* every man did that which was good in his eyes.

21:14 [1] For there lacked two hundred.
21:17 [1] Benjamin must be reserved to have the twelfth portion in the inheritance of Jacob.
21:19 [1] He describeth the place where the maids used yearly to dance as the manner then was, and to sing Psalms and songs of God's works among them.
21:22 [1] Though they thought hereby to persuade men that they kept their oath, yet before God it was broken.
21:23 [1] Meaning, two hundred.

THE BOOK OF

RUTH

1 *1 Elimelech goeth with his wife and children into the land of Moab. 3 He and his sons die. 19 Naomi and Ruth come to Bethlehem.*

1 In the time that the Judges ¹ruled, there was a dearth in the ²land, and a man of Bethlehem ³Judah went for to sojourn in the country of Moab, he, and his wife, and his two sons.

2 And the name of the man *was* Elimelech, and the name of his wife, Naomi, and the names of his two sons, Mahlon, and Chilion, Ephrathites of Bethlehem Judah: and when they came into the land of Moab, they continued there.

3 Then Elimelech the husband of Naomi died, and she remained with her two sons,

4 Which took them wives of the ¹Moabites: the one's name *was* Orpah, and the name of the other Ruth: and they dwelled there about ten years.

5 And Mahlon and Chilion dieth also both twain: so the woman was left, *destitute* of her two sons, and of her husband.

6 ¶ Then she arose with her daughters-in-law, and returned from the country of Moab: for she had heard say in the country of Moab, that the Lord had ¹visited his people, and given them bread.

7 Wherefore she departed out of the place where she was, and her two daughters-in-law with her, and they went on their way to return unto the land of Judah.

8 Then Naomi said unto her two daughters-in-law, Go, return each of you unto her own mother's house: the Lord show favor unto you, as ye have done with the dead, and with me.

9 The Lord grant you, that you may find ¹rest, either of you in the house of her husband. And when she kissed them, they lift up their voice and wept.

10 And they said unto her, Surely we will return with thee unto thy people.

11 But Naomi said, Turn again my daughters: for

what cause will ye go with me? are there any more sons in my womb, that they may be your husbands?

12 Turn again my daughters: go your way: for I am too old to have an husband. If I should say, I have hope, *and* if I had an husband this night: yea, and if I had borne sons,

13 Would ye tarry for them, till they were of age? would ye be deferred for them from taking of husbands? nay my daughters: for it grieveth me ¹much for your sakes that the hand of the Lord is gone out against me.

14 Then they lift up their voice and wept again, and Orpah ¹kissed her mother-in-law, but Ruth abode still with her.

15 And *Naomi* said, Behold, thy sister-in-law is gone back unto her people, and unto her gods: ¹return thou after thy sister-in-law.

16 And Ruth answered, Entreat me not to leave thee, nor to depart from thee: for whither thou goest, I will go: and where thou dwellest, I will dwell: thy people *shall be* my people, and thy God my God.

17 ¶ Where thou diest, will I die, and there will I be buried. The Lord do so to me and more also, if *ought* but death depart thee and me.

18 ¶ When she saw that she was steadfastly minded to go with her, she left speaking unto her.

19 So they went both until they came to Bethlehem: and when they were come to Bethlehem, it was ¹noised of them through all the city, and they said, Is not this Naomi?

20 And she answered them, Call me not ¹Naomi, *but* call me ²Mara: for the Almighty hath given me much bitterness.

21 I went out full, and the Lord hath caused me to return empty: why call ye me Naomi, seeing the Lord hath humbled me, and the Almighty hath brought me unto adversity?

22 So Naomi returned and Ruth the Moabitess

1:1 ¹ Hebrew, *judged.*
² In the land of Canaan.
³ In the tribe of Judah, which was also called Bethlehem Ephrathah, because there was another city so called in the tribe of Zebulun.
1:4 ¹ By this wonderful providence of God Ruth became one of God's household, of whom Christ came.
1:6 ¹ By sending them plenty again.
1:9 ¹ Hereby it appeareth that Naomi by dwelling among idolaters, was waxen cold in the true zeal of God, which rather hath respect to

the ease of the body, than to the comfort of the soul.
1:13 ¹ Or, more than you.
1:14 ¹ When she took leave and departed.
1:15 ¹ No persuasions can prevail to turn them back from God, whom he hath chosen to be his.
1:19 ¹ Whereby appeareth that she was of a great family of good reputation.
1:20 ¹ Or, beautiful.
² Or, bitter.

her daughter-in-law with her, when she came out of the country of Moab: and they came to Bethlehem in the beginning of [1]barley harvest.

2 2 Ruth gathered corn in the fields of Boaz.   8 The gentleness of Boaz toward her.

1 Then Naomi's husband had a kinsman, one of great [1]power of the family of Elimelech, and his name *was* Boaz.

2 And Ruth the Moabitess said unto Naomi, I pray thee, let me go to the field, and [1]gather ears of corn after him, in whose sight I find favor. And she said unto her, Go my daughter.

3 ¶ And she went, and came and gleaned in the field after the reapers, and it came to pass, that she met with the portion of the field of Boaz, who was of the family of Elimelech.

4 And behold, Boaz came from Bethlehem, and said unto the reapers, The Lord *be* with you: and they answered him, The Lord bless thee.

5 Then said Boaz unto his servant that was appointed over the reapers, Whose maid is this?

6 And the servant that was appointed over the reapers, answered, and said, It is the Moabitish maid, that came with Naomi out of the country of Moab:

7 And she said unto us, I pray you, let me glean and gather after the reapers [1]among the sheaves: so she came, and hath continued from that time in the morning unto now, save that she tarried a little in the house.

8 ¶ Then said Boaz unto Ruth, Hearest thou, my daughter? go to none other field to gather, neither go from hence: but abide here by my maidens.

9 [1]Let thine eyes be on the field that they do reap, and go thou after the *maidens*. Have I not charged the servants, that they touch thee not? Moreover when thou art athirst, go unto the vessels, and drink of that which the servants hath drawn.

10 Then she fell on her face, and bowed herself to the ground, and said unto him, How have I found favor in thine eyes, that thou shouldest know me, seeing I am a [1]stranger?

11 And Boaz answered and said unto her, All is told and showed me that thou hast done unto thy mother-in-law, since the death of thine husband, and how thou hast left thy father and thy mother, and

CHAPTER 2
[a] Exod. 16:36

the land where thou wast born, and art come unto a people which thou knewest not in time past.

12 The Lord recompense thy work, and a full reward be given thee of the Lord God of Israel, under whose [1]wings thou art come to trust.

13 Then she said, Let me find favor in thy sight, my lord: for thou hast comforted me, and spoken comfortably unto thy maid, though I be not like to one of thy maids.

14 And Boaz said unto her, At the meal time come thou hither, and eat of the bread, and dip thy morsel in the vinegar. And she sat beside the reapers, and he reached her parched corn: and she did eat, and was sufficed, and [1]left thereof.

15 ¶ And when she arose to glean, Boaz commanded his servants, saying, Let her gather among the sheaves, and do not rebuke her.

16 Also let fall *some* of the sheaves for her, and let it lie, that she may gather it up, and rebuke her not.

17 So she gleaned in the field until evening, and she threshed that she had gathered, and it was about an [a]Ephah of barley.

18 ¶ And she took it up, and went into the city, and her mother-in-law saw what she had gathered: Also she [1]took forth, and gave to her that which she had reserved, when she was sufficed.

19 Then her mother-in-law said unto her, Where hast thou gleaned today? and where wroughtest thou? blessed be he, that knew thee. And she showed her mother-in-law, with whom she had wrought, and said, The man's name with whom I wrought today, is Boaz.

20 And Naomi said unto her daughter-in-law, Blessed be he of the Lord: for he ceaseth not to do good to the living and to the [1]dead. Again Naomi said unto her, The man is near unto us, and of our affinity.

21 And Ruth the Moabitess said, He said also certainly unto me, Thou shalt be with my servants, until they have ended all mine harvest.

22 And Naomi answered unto Ruth her daughter-in-law, It is best, my daughter, that thou go out with his maids, that they [1]meet thee not in another field.

23 Then she kept her by the maids of Boaz, to gather unto the end of barley harvest, and of wheat harvest, and [1]dwelt with her mother-in-law.

1:22 [1] Which was in the month Nisan, that containeth part of March and part of April.
2:1 [1] Both for virtue, authority, and riches.
2:2 [1] This her humility declareth her great affection toward her mother-in-law, forasmuch as she spareth no painful diligence to get both their livings.
2:7 [1] Or, certain handfuls.
2:9 [1] That is, take heed in what field they do reap.

2:10 [1] Even of the Moabites, which are enemies to God's people.
2:12 [1] Signifying, that she shall never want anything, if she put her trust in God, and live under his protection.
2:14 [1] Which she brought home to her mother-in-law.
2:18 [1] To wit, of her bag, as is in the Chaldea text.
2:20 [1] To my husband and children, when they were alive, and now to us.
2:22 [1] Or, fall upon thee.
2:23 [1] Or, returned to her mother-in-law.

3 *1 Naomi giveth Ruth counsel.   8 She sleepeth at Boaz's feet.   12 He acknowledgeth himself to be her kinsman.*

1   Afterward Naomi her mother-in-law said unto her, My daughter, shall not I seek ¹rest for thee, that thou mayest prosper?

2   Now also is not Boaz our kinsman, with whose maids thou wast? Behold, he winnoweth barley tonight in the ¹floor.

3   Wash thyself therefore, and anoint thee, and put thy raiment upon thee, and get thee down to the floor: let not the ¹man know of thee, until he have left eating and drinking.

4   And when he shall sleep, mark the place where he layeth him down, and go, and uncover the place of his feet, and lay thee down, and he shall tell thee what thou shalt do.

5   And she answered her, All that thou biddest me, I will do.

6   ¶ So she went down unto the floor, and did according to all that her mother-in-law bade her.

7   And when Boaz had eaten and drunken, and ¹cheered his heart, he went to lie down at the end of the heap of corn, and she came softly, and uncovered the place of his feet, and lay down.

8   And at midnight the man was afraid ¹and caught hold: and lo, a woman lay at his feet.

9   Then he said, Who art thou? And she answered, I am Ruth thine handmaid: spread therefore the wing of thy garment over thine handmaid: for thou art the kinsman.

10   Then he said, Blessed be thou of the Lord, my daughter: thou hast ¹showed more goodness in the latter end, than at the beginning, inasmuch as thou followedst not young men, were they poor or rich.

11   And now, my daughter, fear not: I will do to thee all that thou requirest: for all the city of my people doth know that thou art a virtuous woman.

12   And now, it is true that I am thy kinsman, howbeit there is a kinsman nearer than I.

13   Tarry tonight, and when morning is come, if he ¹will do the duty of a kinsman unto thee, well, let him do the kinsman's duty: but if he will not do the kinsman's part, then will I do the duty of a kinsman, as the Lord liveth: sleep until the morning.

14   ¶ And she lay at his feet until the morning:

and she arose before one could know another: for he said, Let no man know, that a woman came into the floor.

15   Also he said, Bring the ¹sheet that thou hast upon thee, and hold it. And when she held it, he measured six *measures* of barley, and laid them on her, and she went into the city.

16   And when she came to her mother-in-law, she said, ¹Who art thou, my daughter? And she told her all that the man had done to her,

17   And said, These six *measures* of barley gave he me: for he said to me, Thou shalt not come empty unto thy mother-in-law.

18   Then said she, My daughter, sit still, until thou know how the thing will fall: for the man will not be in rest, until he hath finished the matter this same day.

4 *1 Boaz speaketh to Ruth's next kinsman touching her marriage.   7 The ancient custom in Israel.   10 Boaz marrieth Ruth, of whom he begetteth Obed.   18 The generation of Perez.*

1   Then went Boaz up to the ¹gate, and sat there, and behold, the kinsman, of whom Boaz had spoken, came by: and he said, ²Ho, such one, come, sit down here. And he turned, and sat down.

2   Then he took ten men of the Elders of the city, and said, Sit ye down here. And they sat down.

3   And he said unto the kinsman, Naomi, that is come again out of the country of Moab, will sell a parcel of land, which was our brother Elimelech's.

4   And I thought to advertise thee, saying, Buy it before the ¹assistants, and before the Elders of my people. If thou wilt redeem it, redeem it: but if thou wilt not redeem it, tell me: for I know that there is none ²besides thee to redeem it, and I am after thee. Then he answered, I will redeem it.

5   Then said Boaz, What day thou buyest the field of the hand of Naomi, thou must also buy it of Ruth the Moabitess the wife of the dead, to stir up the name of the dead, upon his ¹inheritance.

6   And the kinsman answered, I cannot redeem it, lest I destroy mine own inheritance: redeem my right to thee, for I can not redeem it.

7   Now this was the manner beforetime in Israel, concerning redeeming and changing for to stablish

3:1 ¹ Meaning, that she would provide her of an husband, with whom she might live quietly.
3:2 ¹ Or, in the barn.
3:3 ¹ Boaz, nor yet any other.
3:7 ¹ That is, had refreshed himself among his servants.
3:8 ¹ Or, turned himself from one side to another.
3:10 ¹ Thou showest thyself from time to time more virtuous.
3:13 ¹ If he will take thee to be his wife by the title of affinity, according to God's law, Deut. 25:5.
3:15 ¹ Or, mantle.
3:16 ¹ Perceiving by her coming home, that he had not taken her to his wife, she was astonied.
4:1 ¹ Which was the place of judgment.
  ² The Hebrews here use two words which have no proper signification, but serve to note a certain person, as we say, Ho sirrah, or ho such one.
4:4 ¹ Or, inhabitants.
  ² For thou art the next of the kin.
4:5 ¹ That his inheritance might bear his name that is dead.

all things: a man did pluck off his shoe, and gave it his neighbor: and this was a sure [1]witness in Israel.

8 Therefore the kinsman said to Boaz, Buy it for thee: and he drew off his shoe.

9 And Boaz said unto the Elders and unto all the people, Ye are witnesses this day, that I have bought all that was Elimelech's, and all that was Chilion's and Mahlon's, of the hand of Naomi.

10 And moreover, Ruth the Moabitess the wife of Mahlon, have I bought to be my wife, to stir up the name of the dead upon his inheritance, and that the name of the dead be not put out from among his brethren, and from the gate of his [1]place: ye are witnesses this day.

11 And all the people that were in the gate, and the Elders said, *We are* witnesses: the Lord make the wife that cometh into thine house, like Rachel and like Leah, which twain did build the house of Israel: and that thou mayest do worthily in [1]Ephrathah, and be famous in Bethlehem.

12 And that thine house be like the house of Perez (*a*whom Tamar bare unto Judah) of the seed which the Lord shall give thee of this young woman.

13 ¶ So Boaz took Ruth, and she was his wife:

CHAPTER 4
a Gen. 38:29
b 1 Chron. 2:4
Matt. 1:3

and when he went in unto her, the Lord gave that she conceived, and bare a son.

14 And the women said unto Naomi, Blessed *be* the Lord, which hath not left thee this day without a kinsman, and [1]his name shall be continued in Israel.

15 And this shall bring thy life again, and cherish thine old age: for thy daughter-in-law which loveth thee, hath borne unto him, and she is better to thee than [1]seven sons.

16 And Naomi took the child, and laid it in her lap, and became nurse unto it.

17 And *the women* her neighbors gave it a name, saying, There is a child born to Naomi, and called the name thereof Obed: the same was the father of Jesse, the father of David.

18 ¶ These now are the generations of [b,1]Perez: Perez begat Hezron,

19 And Hezron begat Ram, and Ram begat Amminadab,

20 And Amminadab begat Nahshon, and Nahshon begat Salmon,

21 And Salmon begat Boaz, and Boaz begat Obed,

22 And Obed begat Jesse, and Jesse begat David.

4:7 [1] That he had resigned his right, Deut. 25:9.
4:10 [1] Or, of the city where he remained.
4:11 [1] Ephrathah and Bethlehem are both one.
4:14 [1] He shall leave continual posterity.

4:15 [1] Meaning, many sons.
4:18 [1] This genealogy is brought in, to prove that David by succession came of the house of Judah.

THE FIRST BOOK

OF

SAMUEL

1 1 *The genealogy of Elkanah father of Samuel.* 2 *His two wives.* 5 *Hannah was barren, and prayed to the Lord.* 15 *Her answer to Eli.* 20 *Samuel is born.* 24 *She doth dedicate him to the Lord.*

CHAPTER 1

a Deut. 16:16

b Num. 6:5
Judg. 13:5

c Ps. 42:5

1 There was a man of one of the two ¹Ramathaim Zophim, of mount Ephraim, whose name *was* Elkanah the son of Jeroham, the son of Elihu, the son of Tohu, the son of Zuph, an Ephraimite.

2 And he had two wives: the name of one *was* Hannah, and the name of the other Peninnah: and Peninnah had children, but Hannah had no children.

3 *a*And this man went up out of his city every year, to worship and to sacrifice unto the Lord of hosts in ¹Shiloh, where were the two sons of Eli, Hophni, and Phinehas, Priests of the Lord.

4 And on a day, when Elkanah sacrificed, he gave to Peninnah his wife and to all her sons and daughters portions,

5 But unto Hannah he gave a worthy ¹portion: for he loved Hannah, and the Lord had made her barren.

6 ¶ And her adversary vexed her sore, forasmuch as she upbraided her, because the Lord had made her barren.

7 (And so did he year by year) *and* as oft as she went up to the house of the Lord, thus she vexed her, that she wept and did not eat.

8 Then said Elkanah her husband to her, Hannah, why weepest thou? and why eatest thou not? and why is thine heart troubled? am not I better to thee than ten ¹sons?

9 So Hannah rose up after that they had eaten and drunk in Shiloh (and Eli the Priest sat upon a stool by one of the posts of the ¹Temple of the Lord)

10 And she was troubled in her mind, and prayed unto the Lord, and wept sore:

11 Also she vowed a vow, and said, O Lord of hosts, if thou wilt look on the trouble of thine handmaid, and remember me, and not forget thine handmaid, but give unto thine handmaid a man-child, then I will give him unto the Lord all the days of his life, *b*and there shall no razor come upon his head.

12 And as she continued praying before the Lord, Eli marked her mouth.

13 For Hannah spake in her heart: her lips did move only, but her voice was not heard: therefore Eli thought she had been drunken.

14 And Eli said unto her, How long wilt thou be drunken? Put away thy ¹drunkenness from thee.

15 Then Hannah answered and said, Nay my lord, *but* I am a woman ¹troubled in spirit: I have drunk neither wine nor strong drink, but have *c*poured out my soul before the Lord.

16 Count not thine handmaid ¹for a wicked woman: for of the abundance of my complaint and my grief have I spoken hitherto.

17 Then Eli answered, and said, Go in peace, and the God of Israel grant thy petition that thou hast asked of him.

18 She said again, Let thine handmaid find ¹grace in thy sight: so the woman went her way, and did eat, and looked no more sad.

19 ¶ Then they rose up early, and worshipped before the Lord, and returned, and came to their house to Ramah. Now Elkanah knew Hannah his wife, and the Lord ¹remembered her.

20 For in process of time Hannah conceived and bare a son, and she called his name Samuel, Because, *said she*, I have asked him of the Lord.

21 ¶ So the man ¹Elkanah and all his house, went up to offer unto the Lord the yearly sacrifice and his vow:

22 But Hannah went not up: for she said unto

1:1 ¹ There were two Ramatus, so that in this city in mount Ephraim were Zophim, that is, the learned men and Prophets.
1:3 ¹ For the Ark was there at that time.
1:5 ¹ Some read, a portion with an hearty cheer.
1:8 ¹ Let this suffice thee, that I love thee no less, than if thou hadst many children.
1:9 ¹ That is of the house where the Ark was.

1:14 ¹ Hebrew, *thy wine*.
1:15 ¹ Hebrew, *of an hard spirit*.
1:16 ¹ Hebrew, *for a daughter of Belial*.
1:18 ¹ That is, pray unto the Lord for me.
1:19 ¹ According to her petition.
1:21 ¹ This Elkanah was a Levite, 1 Chron. 6:27, and as some write once a year they accustomed to appear before the Lord with their families.

her husband, *I will tarry* until the child be weaned, then I will bring him that he may appear before the Lord, and there abide forever.

23 And Elkanah her husband said unto her, Do what seemeth thee best: tarry until thou hast weaned him: only the Lord accomplish his [1]word. So the woman abode, and gave her son suck until she weaned him.

24 ¶ And when she had weaned him, she took him with her with three bullocks and an Ephah of flour and a bottle of wine, and brought him unto the house of the Lord in Shiloh, and the child was [1]young.

25 And they slew a bullock, and brought the child to Eli.

26 And she said, Oh my Lord, as thy [1]soul liveth, my lord, I am the woman that stood with thee here praying unto the Lord.

27 I prayed for this child, and the Lord hath given me my desire which I asked of him.

28 Therefore also I have [1]given him unto the Lord: as long as he liveth he shall be given unto the Lord: and he [2]worshipped the Lord there.

2

1 *The song of Hannah.*   12 *The sons of Eli, wicked.*   13 *The new custom of the Priests.*   18 *Samuel ministereth before the Lord.*   20 *Eli blesseth Elkanah and his wife.*   23 *Eli reproveth his sons.*   27 *God sendeth a Prophet to Eli.*   31 *Eli is menaced for not chastising his children.*

1 And Hannah [1]prayed, and said, Mine heart rejoiceth in the Lord, mine [2]horn is exalted in the Lord: my mouth is [3]enlarged over mine enemies, because I rejoice in thy salvation.

2 There is none holy as the Lord: yea, there is none besides thee, and there is no god like our God.

3 Speak [1]no more presumptuously: let not arrogancy come out of your mouth: for the Lord *is* a God of knowledge, and by him enterprises are established.

4 The bow *and* the mighty men are broken, and the weak have girded themselves with strength.

5 They that were full, are hired forth for [1]bread,

CHAPTER 2
[a] Deut. 32:39
[b] Ps. 113:7
[c] 1 Sam. 7:10

and the hungry are no more *hired*, so that the barren hath borne [2]seven: and she that had many children is feeble.

6 [a]The Lord killeth and maketh alive: bringeth down to the grave and raiseth up.

7 The Lord maketh poor and maketh rich: bringeth low, and exalteth.

8 [b]He raiseth up the poor out of the dust, and lifteth up the beggar from the dunghill, to set *them* among [1]princes, and to make them inherit the seat of glory: for the pillars of the earth are the [2]Lord's, and he hath set the world upon them.

9 He will keep the feet of his Saints, and the wicked shall keep silence in darkness: for in *his own* might shall no man be strong.

10 The Lord's adversaries shall be destroyed, and out of heaven shall he [c]thunder upon them: the Lord shall judge the ends of the world, and shall give power unto his [1]King, and exalt the horn of his Anointed.

11 And Elkanah went to Ramah to his house, and the child did minister unto the [1]Lord before Eli the Priest.

12 ¶ Now the sons of Eli *were* wicked men, *and* [1]knew not the Lord.

13 For the Priest's custom toward the people *was this*: when any man offered sacrifice, the Priest's [1]boy came, while the flesh was seething, and a fleshhook with three teeth in his hand,

14 And thrust it into the kettle, or into the caldron, or into the pan, or into the pot: [1]all that the fleshhook brought up, the Priest took for himself: thus they did unto all the Israelites, that came thither to Shiloh.

15 Yea, before they burnt the [1]fat, the Priest's boy came and said unto the man that offered, Give me flesh to roast for the Priest: for he will not have sodden flesh of thee, but raw.

16 And if any man said unto him, Let them burn the fat according to the [1]custom, then take as much as thine heart [2]desireth: then he would answer, No, but thou shalt give it now: and if thou wilt not, I will take it by force.

17 Therefore the sin of the young men was very great before the Lord: for men [1]abhorred the offering

---

1:23 [1] Because her prayer took effect, therefore it was called the Lord's promise.
1:24 [1] Hebrew, *a child*.
1:26 [1] That is, most certainly.
1:28 [1] Hebrew, *lent*.
　[2] Meaning, Eli gave thanks to God for her.
2:1 [1] After that she had obtained a son by prayer, she gave thanks.
　[2] I have recovered strength and glory by the benefit of the Lord.
　[3] I can answer them that reprove my barrenness.
2:3 [1] In that ye condemn my barrenness, ye show your pride against God.
2:5 [1] They sell their labors for necessary food.
　[2] Or, many.

2:8 [1] He preferreth to honor, and putteth down according to his own will, though man's judgment be contrary.
　[2] Therefore he may dispose all things according to his will.
2:10 [1] She grounded her prayer on Jesus Christ which was to come.
2:11 [1] In all that Eli commanded him.
2:12 [1] That is, they neglected his ordinance.
2:13 [1] Or, son.
2:14 [1] Transgressing the order appointed in the Law, Lev. 7:31, for their belly's sake.
2:15 [1] Which was commanded first to have been offered to God.
2:16 [1] Or, Law.
　[2] Not passing for their own profit, so that God might be served aright.
2:17 [1] Seeing the horrible abuse thereof.

of the Lord.

18 ¶ Now Samuel being a young child ministered before the Lord, girded with a linen ᵈEphod.

19 And his mother made him a little coat, and brought it to him from year to year, when she came up with her husband, to offer the yearly sacrifice.

20 And Eli blessed Elkanah and his wife, and said, The Lord give thee seed of this woman, for ¹the petition that she asked of the Lord: and they departed unto their place.

21 And the Lord visited Hannah, so that she conceived, and bare three sons, and two daughters. And the child Samuel grew before the Lord.

22 ¶ So Eli was very old, and heard all that his sons did unto all Israel, and how they lay with the women that ¹assembled at the door of the Tabernacle of the Congregation.

23 And he said unto them, Why do ye such things? for of all this people I hear evil reports of you.

24 Do no more, my sons: for it is no good report that I hear, which is, that ye make the Lord's people to ¹trespass.

25 If one man sin against another, the Judge shall judge it: but if a man sin against the Lord, who will plead for him? Notwithstanding they obeyed not the voice of their father, because the Lord ¹would slay them.

26 ¶ (Now the child Samuel profited, and grew, and was in favor both with the Lord and also with men.)

27 And there came a man of God unto Eli, and said unto him, Thus saith the Lord, Did not I plainly appear unto the house of thy ¹father, when they were in Egypt in Pharaoh's house?

28 And I chose him out of all the tribes of Israel to be my Priest, to offer upon my altar, and to burn incense, and to wear an Ephod before me, and ᵉI gave unto the house of thy father all the offerings made by fire of the children of Israel.

29 Wherefore have you ¹kicked against my sacrifice and mine offering, which I commanded in my Tabernacle, and honorest thy children above me, to make yourselves fat of the firstfruits of all the offerings of Israel my people?

ᵈ Exod. 28:4
ᵉ Lev. 10:14

30 Wherefore the Lord God of Israel saith, I said, that thine house, and the house of thy father should walk before me forever: but now the Lord saith, ¹It shall not be so: for them that honor me, I will honor, and they that despise me, shall be despised.

31 Behold, the days come, that I will cut off thine ¹arm, and the arm of thy fathers house, that there shall not be an old man in thine house.

32 And thou ¹shalt see thine enemy in the habitation of the Lord in all things wherewith God shall bless Israel, and there shall not be an old man in thine house forever.

33 Nevertheless, I will not destroy every one of thine from mine altar, to make thine eyes to fail, and to make thine heart sorrowful: and all the multitude of thine house shall ¹die when they be men

34 And this shall be a sign unto thee, that shall come upon thy two sons Hophni and Phinehas: in one day they shall die both.

35 And I will stir me up a ¹faithful Priest, that shall do according to mine heart, and according to my mind: and I will build him a sure house, and he shall walk before mine Anointed forever.

36 And all that are left in thine house, shall come and ¹bow down to him for a piece of silver and a morsel of bread, and shall say, Appoint me, I pray thee, to one of the Priest's offices, that I may eat a morsel [of] bread.

3 1 There was no manifest vision in the time of Eli. 4 The Lord calleth Samuel three times, 11 And showeth what shall come upon Eli and his house. 18 The same declareth Samuel to Eli.

1 Now the child Samuel ministered unto the Lord ¹before Eli: and the word of the Lord was ²precious in those days: for there was no manifest vision.

2 And at that time, as Eli lay in his ¹place, his eyes began to wax dim that he could not see.

3 And yer the ¹light of God went out, Samuel slept in the temple of the Lord, where the Ark of God was.

4 Then the Lord ¹called Samuel: and he said, Here I am.

5 And he ran unto Eli, and said, Here am I, for

2:20 ¹ Or, for the thing that she hath lent to the Lord: to wit, Samuel.
2:22 ¹ Which was (as the Hebrews write) after their travail, when they came to be purified, read Exod. 38:8; Lev. 12:6.
2:24 ¹ Because they contemn their duty to God, verse 17.
2:25 ¹ So that to obey good admonitions is God's mercy, and to disobey them is his just judgment for sin.
2:27 ¹ To wit, Aaron.
2:29 ¹ Why have you contemned my sacrifices, and as it were trod them under foot?
2:30 ¹ God's promises are only effectual to such as he giveth constancy unto, to fear and obey him.
2:31 ¹ Thy power and authority.

2:32 ¹ Thy posterity shall see the glory of the chief Priest translated to another, whom they shall envy, 1 Kings 2:27.
2:33 ¹ Or, when they come to man's age.
2:35 ¹ Meaning Zadok, who succeeded Abiathar, and was the figure of Christ.
2:36 ¹ That is, shall be inferior unto him.
3:1 ¹ The Chaldea text readeth, while Eli lived.
   ² Because there were very few Prophets to declare it.
3:2 ¹ In the Court next to the Tabernacle.
3:3 ¹ That is, the lamps which burnt in the night.
3:4 ¹ Josephus writeth that Samuel was 12 years old, when the Lord appeared to him.

thou calledst me. But he said, I called thee not: go again *and* sleep. And he went and slept.

6   And the Lord called once again, Samuel. And Samuel arose, and went to Eli, and said, I am here: for thou didst call me. And he answered, I called thee not my son: go again *and* sleep.

7   Thus *did* Samuel, before he knew ¹the Lord, and before the word of the Lord was revealed unto him.

8   And the Lord called Samuel again the third time: and he arose, and went to Eli, and said, I am here: for thou hast called me. Then Eli ¹perceived that the Lord had called the child.

9   Therefore Eli said unto Samuel, Go *and* sleep: and if he call thee, then say, Speak Lord, for thy servant heareth. So Samuel went, and slept in his place.

10 ¶ And the Lord came, and stood, and called as at other times, Samuel, Samuel. Then Samuel answered, Speak, for thy servant heareth.

11 ¶ Then the Lord said unto Samuel, Behold, I will do a thing in Israel, whereof whosoever shall hear, his two ᵃears shall ¹tingle.

12 In that day I will raise up against Eli all things which I have spoken concerning his house: when I begin, I will also make an end.

13 And I have told him that I will judge his house forever, for the iniquity which he knoweth, because his sons ran into a slander, and he stayed them not.

14 Now therefore I have sworn unto the house of Eli, that the wickedness of Eli's house shall not be purged with sacrifice nor offering ¹forever.

15 Afterward Samuel slept until the morning, and opened the doors of the house of the Lord, and Samuel feared to show Eli the vision.

16 ¶ Then Eli called Samuel, and said, Samuel my son. And he answered, Here I am.

17 Then he said, What is it, that *the Lord* said unto thee? I pray thee hide it not from me. God ¹do so to thee, and more also, if thou hide anything from me, of all that he said unto thee.

18 So Samuel told him every whit, and hid nothing from him. Then he said, It is the Lord: let him do what seemeth him good.

19 ¶ And Samuel grew, and the Lord was with him, and let none of his words ¹fall to the ground.

CHAPTER 3
ᵃ 2 Kings 21:12

20 And all Israel from Dan to Beersheba knew ¹that faithful Samuel *was* the Lord's Prophet.

21 And the Lord appeared again in Shiloh: for the Lord revealed himself to Samuel in Shiloh by ¹his word.

4 *1 Israel is overcome by the Philistines.   4 They do set the Ark, wherefore the Philistines do fear.   10 The Ark of the Lord is taken.   11 Eli and his children die.   19 The death of the wife of Phinehas the son of Eli.*

1   And Samuel spake unto all Israel: ¹and Israel went out against the Philistines to battle, and pitched beside ²Ebenezer: and the Philistines pitched in Aphek.

2   And the Philistines put themselves in array against Israel: and when they joined the battle, Israel was smitten down before the Philistines: who slew of the army in the field about four thousand men.

3   So when the people were come into the camp, the Elders of Israel said, ¹Wherefore hath the Lord smitten us this day before the Philistines? let us bring the Ark of the covenant of the Lord out of Shiloh unto us, that when it cometh among us, it may save us out of the hand of our enemies.

4   Then the people sent to Shiloh, and brought from thence the Ark of the covenant of the Lord of hosts, who ¹dwelleth between the Cherubims: and there *were* the two sons of Eli, Hophni and Phinehas, with the Ark of the covenant of God.

5   And when the Ark of the covenant of the Lord came into the host, all Israel shouted a mighty shout, so that the earth rang again.

6   And when the Philistines heard the noise of the shout, they said, What meaneth the sound of this mighty shout in the host of the Hebrews? and they understood, that the Ark of the Lord was come into the host.

7   And the Philistines were afraid, and said, God is come in the host: therefore said they, ¹Woe unto us: for it hath not been so heretofore.

8   Woe unto us, who shall deliver us out of the hand of these mighty Gods? these are the Gods that smote the Egyptians with all the plagues in the ¹wilderness.

3:7 ¹ By vision.
3:8 ¹ Such was the corruption of those times that the chief Priest was become dull and negligent to understand the Lord's appearing.
3:11 ¹ God declareth what sudden fear shall come upon men, when they shall hear that the Ark is taken, and also see Eli's house destroyed.
3:14 ¹ Meaning that his posterity should never enjoy the chief Priest's office.
3:17 ¹ God punish thee after this and that sort, except thou tell me truth, Ruth 1:17.
3:19 ¹ The Lord accomplished whatsoever he had said.
3:20 ¹ Or, that Samuel was the faithful Prophet of the Lord.

3:21 ¹ Hebrew, *by the word of the Lord.*
4:1 ¹ From the departure of the Israelites out of Egypt, unto the time of Samuel, are about 397 years.
     ² Or, stone of help, 1 Sam. 7:12.
4:3 ¹ For it may seem that this war was undertaken by Samuel's commandment.
4:4 ¹ For he used to appear to the Israelites between the cherubim over the Ark of the covenant, Exod. 25:17.
4:7 ¹ Before we fought against men, and now God is come to fight against us.
4:8 ¹ For in the red sea in the wilderness the Egyptians were destroyed, which was the last of all his plagues.

9   Be strong and play the men, O Philistines, that ye be not servants unto the Hebrews, *as they have served you: be valiant therefore, and fight.

10   And the Philistines fought, and Israel was smitten down, and fled every man into his tent: and there was an exceeding great slaughter, for there fell of Israel [1]thirty thousand footmen.

11   And the Ark of God was taken, and the two sons of Eli, Hophni and Phinehas died.

12   And there ran a man of Benjamin out of the army, and came to Shiloh the same day with his clothes [1]rent, and earth upon his head.

13   And when he came, lo, Eli sat upon a seat by the wayside, waiting: for his heart [1]feared for the Ark of God: and when the man came into the city to tell it, all the city cried out.

14   And when Eli heard the noise of the crying, he said, What meaneth this noise of the tumult? and the man came in hastily, and told Eli.

15   (Now Eli *was* fourscore and eighteen years old, and [b]his eyes were dim that he could not see.)

16   And the man said unto Eli, I came from the army, and I fled this day out of the host: and he said, What thing is done, my son?

17   Then the messenger answered, and said, Israel is fled before the Philistines, and there hath been also a great slaughter among the people: and moreover thy two sons, Hophni and Phinehas [1]are dead, and the Ark of God is taken.

18   ¶ And when he had made mention of the Ark of God, *Eli* fell from his seat backward by the side of the gate, and his neck was broken, and he died: for he was an old man and heavy: and he had [1]judged Israel forty years.

19   And his daughter-in-law, Phinehas' wife, was with child, *near* [1]her travail: and when she heard the report that the Ark of God was taken, and that her father-in-law and her husband were dead, she [2]bowed herself, and travailed: for her pains came upon her.

20   And about the time of her death, the women that stood about her, said unto her, Fear not: for thou hast borne a son: but she answered not, nor regarded it.

21   And she named the child [1]Ichabod, saying, The glory is departed from Israel, because the Ark of God was taken, and because of her father-in-law

CHAPTER 4
a Judg. 13:1
b 1 Sam. 3:2

CHAPTER 5
a Ps. 78:66

and her husband.

22   She said again, [1]The glory is departed from Israel: for the Ark of God is taken.

5 *2 The Philistines bring the Ark into the house of Dagon, which idol fell down before it.   6 The men of Ashdod are plagued.   8 The Ark is carried into Gath, and after to Ekron.*

1   Then the Philistines took the Ark of God and carried it from Ebenezer unto [1]Ashdod,

2   Even the Philistines took the Ark of God, and brought it into the house of Dagon, and set it by [1]Dagon.

3   And when they of Ashdod rose the next day in the morning, behold, Dagon was fallen upon his face on the ground before the Ark of the Lord, and they took up Dagon, and set him in his place again.

4   Also they rose up early in the morning the next day, and behold, Dagon was fallen upon his face on the ground before the Ark of the Lord, and the head of Dagon and the two palms of his hands *were* cut off upon the threshold: only the stump of Dagon was left to him.

5   Therefore the Priests of Dagon, and all that come into Dagon's house, [1]tread not on the threshold of Dagon in Ashdod, unto this day.

6   But the hand of the Lord was heavy upon them of Ashdod, and destroyed them, and smote them with the [a]emerods, *both* Ashdod, and the coasts thereof.

7   And when the men of Ashdod saw this, they said, Let not the Ark of the God of Israel abide with us: for his hand is sore upon us and upon Dagon our god.

8   They sent therefore, and gathered all the princes of the Philistines unto them, and said, [1]What shall we do with the Ark of the God of Israel? And they answered, Let the Ark of the God of Israel be carried about unto Gath: and they carried the Ark of the God of Israel about.

9   And when they had carried it about, the hand of the Lord was against the city with a very great destruction, and he smote the men of the city both small and great, and they had emerods in their secret parts.

10   ¶ Therefore they sent the Ark of God to Ekron: and as soon as the Ark of God came to Ekron, the Ekronites cried out, saying, They have brought the Ark

4:10 [1] David alluding to this place, Ps. 78:63, saith they were con-sumed with fire: meaning they were suddenly destroyed.
4:12 [1] In token of sorrow and mourning.
4:13 [1] Lest it should be taken of the enemies.
4:17 [1] According as God had afore said.
4:18 [1] Or, governed.
4:19 [1] Or, to cry out.
     [2] And settled her body toward her travail.
4:21 [1] Or, No glory, or where is the glory?

4:22 [1] She uttered her great sorrow by repeating her words.
5:1 [1] Which was one of the five principal cities of the Philistines.
5:2 [1] Which was their chief idol, and as some write, from the navel downward was like a fish, and upward like a man.
5:5 [1] Thus instead of acknowledging the true God by this miracle, they fall to a further superstition.
5:8 [1] Though they had felt God's power, and were afraid thereof, yet they would further try him, which thing God turned to their destruction and his glory.

of the God of Israel to us to slay us and our people.

11 Therefore they sent, and gathered together all the princes of the Philistines, and said, Send [1]away the Ark of the God of Israel, and let it return to his own place, that it slay us not and our people: for there was a destruction *and* death throughout all the city, *and* the hand of God was very sore there.

12 And the men that died not, were smitten with the emerods: and the cry of the city went up to heaven.

6 *1 The time that the Ark was with the Philistines, which they sent again with a gift. 12 It cometh to Beth She-mesh. 17 The Philistines offer golden emerods. 19 The men of Beth Shemesh are stricken for looking into the Ark.*

1 So the Ark of the Lord was in the country of the Philistines [1]seven months.

2 And the Philistines called the Priests and the Soothsayers, saying, What shall we do with the Ark of the Lord? tell us wherewith we shall send it home again.

3 And they said, If you send away the Ark of the God of Israel, send it not away empty, but give unto it [1]a sin offering: then shall ye be healed, and it shall be known to you, why his hand departeth not from you.

4 Then said they, What shall be the sin offering, which we shall give unto it? And they answered, Five golden emerods, and five golden mice, according to the number of the princes of the Philistines: for one plague *was* on you all, and on your princes.

5 Wherefore ye shall make the similitudes of your emerods, and the similitudes of your mice that destroy the land: so ye shall give glory unto the God of Israel, that he may take his hand from you, and from your [1]gods, and from your land.

6 Wherefore then should ye harden your hearts, as the Egyptians and Pharaoh hardened their hearts, when he wrought wonderfully among them, *a*did they not let them go, and they departed?

7 Now therefore make a new cart, and take two milch kine, on whom there hath come no yoke: and tie the kine to the cart, and bring the calves home from them.

8 Then take the Ark of the Lord, and set it upon the cart, and put the [1]jewels of gold which ye give it

CHAPTER 6
a Exod. 12:31

for a sin offering in a coffer by the side thereof, and send it away, that it may go.

9 And take heed, if it go up by the way of his own coast to Beth Shemesh, it is [1]he that did us this great evil: but if not, we shall know then, that it is not his hand that smote us, *but* it was a [2]chance that happened us.

10 And the men did so: for they took two kine that gave milk, and tied them to the cart, and shut the calves at home.

11 So they set the Ark of the Lord upon the cart, and the coffer with the mice of gold, and with the similitudes of their emerods.

12 And the kine went the straight way to Beth Shemesh, and kept one path, and lowed as they went, and turned neither to the right hand nor to the left: also the princes of the Philistines went after [1]them unto the borders of Beth Shemesh.

13 Now they of Beth Shemesh were reaping their wheat harvest in the valley, and they lift up their eyes, and spied the Ark, and rejoiced when they saw it.

14 ¶ And the cart came into the field of Joshua a Beth Shemite, and stood still there. There was also a great stone, and [1]they clave the wood of the cart, and offered the kine for a burnt offering unto the Lord.

15 And the Levites took down the Ark of the Lord, and the coffer that was with it, wherein the jewels of gold were, and put them on the great stone, and the men of Beth Shemesh offered burnt offering, and sacrificed sacrifices that same day unto the Lord.

16 And when the five princes of the Philistines had seen it, they returned to Ekron the same day.

17 ¶ So these are the golden emerods, which the Philistines gave for a sin offering to the Lord: for [1]Ashdod one, for Gaza one, for Askelon one, for Gath one, *and* for Ekron one,

18 And golden mice, according to the number of all the cities of the Philistines, *belonging* to the five princes, both of walled towns, and of towns unwalled unto the great *stone* of [1]Abel, whereon they set the Ark of the Lord: *which stone remaineth* unto this day in the field of Joshua the Beth Shemite.

19 And he smote of the men of Beth Shemesh, because they [1]had looked in the Ark of the Lord: he slew even among the people fifty thousand men and threescore and ten men: and the people lamented, because the Lord had slain the people with so great

---

5:11 [1] The wicked when they feel the hand of God, grudge and reject him, where the godly humble themselves, and cry for mercy.
6:1 [1] They thought by continuance of time the plague would have ceased, and so would have kept the Ark still.
6:3 [1] The idolaters confess there is a true God, who justifieth sin justly.
6:5 [1] This is God's judgment upon the idolaters, that knowing the true God, they worship him not aright.
6:8 [1] Meaning, the golden emerods and the golden mice.
6:9 [1] The God of Israel.

[2] The wicked attribute almost all things to fortune and chance, whereas indeed there is nothing done without God's providence and decree.
6:12 [1] For the trial of the matter.
6:14 [1] To wit, the men of Beth Shemesh, which was Israelites.
6:17 [1] These were the five principal cities of the Philistines, which were not all conquered unto the time of David.
6:18 [1] Or, the plaint, or lamentation.
6:19 [1] For it was not lawful to any either to touch or to see it, save only to Aaron and his sons, Num. 4:15, 20.

a slaughter.

20 Wherefore the men of Beth Shemesh said, Who is able to stand before this holy Lord God? and to whom shall he go from us?

21 And they sent messengers to the inhabitants of Kirjath Jearim, saying, The Philistines have brought again the Ark of the Lord: come ye down, *and* take it up to you.

7 1 *The Ark is brought to Kiriath Jearim.* 3 *Samuel exhorteth the people to forsake their sins, and turn to the Lord.* 10 *The Philistines fight against Israel, and are overcome.* 16 *Samuel judgeth Israel.*

1 Then the men of ¹Kirjath Jearim came, and took up the Ark of the Lord, and brought it into the house of Abinadab in the hill: and they sanctified Eleazar his son, to keep the Ark of the Lord.

2 (For while the Ark abode in Kirjath Jearim, the time was long, for it was twenty years) and all the house of Israel lamented ¹after the Lord.

3 ¶ Then Samuel spake unto all the house of Israel, saying, If ye be come again unto the Lord with all your heart, ªput away the strange gods from among you, and ᵇAshtoreth, and direct your hearts unto the Lord, and serve him ᶜonly, and he shall deliver you out of the hand of the Philistines.

4 Then the children of Israel did put away ᵈBaal and Ashtoreth, and served the Lord only.

5 And Samuel said, Gather all Israel to ¹Mizpah, and I will pray for you unto the Lord.

6 And they gathered together to Mizpah, and ¹drew water, and poured it out before the Lord, and fasted the same day, and said there, We have sinned against the Lord. And Samuel judged the children of Israel in Mizpah.

7 When the Philistines heard that the children of Israel were gathered together to Mizpah, the Princes of the Philistines went up against Israel: and when the children of Israel heard that, they were afraid of the Philistines.

8 And the children of Israel said to Samuel, Cease not to ¹cry unto the Lord our God for us, that he may save us out of the hand of the Philistines.

9 Then Samuel took a sucking lamb, and offered it all together for a burnt offering unto the Lord, and Samuel cried unto the Lord for Israel, and the Lord

CHAPTER 7
ª Josh. 24:15,23
ᵇ Judg. 2:13
ᶜ Deut. 6:4
Matt. 4:19
ᵈ Judg. 1:12,13

CHAPTER 8
ª Deut. 16:19
ᵇ Hos. 13:10
Acts 13:21

heard him.

10 And [as] Samuel offered the burnt offering, the Philistines came to fight against Israel: but the Lord ¹thundered with a great thunder that day upon the Philistines, and scattered them: so they were slain before Israel.

11 And the men of Israel went from Mizpah, and pursued the Philistines, and smote them until *they came* under Beth Car.

12 Then Samuel took a stone, and pitched it between Mizpah and ¹Shen, and called the name thereof Ebenezer, and he said, Hitherto hath the Lord helped us.

13 ¶ So the Philistines were brought under, and they came no more again into the coasts of Israel: and the hand of the Lord was against the Philistines all the days of Samuel.

14 Also the cities which the Philistines had taken from Israel, were restored to Israel, from Ekron even to Gath: and Israel delivered the coasts of the same out of the hands of the Philistines: and there was peace between Israel and the ¹Amorites.

15 And Samuel judged Israel all the days of his life,

16 And went about year by year to Bethel, and Gilgal, and Mizpah, and judged Israel in all those places.

17 Afterward he returned to Ramah: for there was his house, and there he judged Israel: also he built an ¹altar there unto the Lord.

8 1 *Samuel maketh his sons Judges over Israel, who follow not his steps.* 5 *The Israelites ask a King.* 11 *Samuel declareth in what state they should be under the King.* 19 *Notwithstanding, they ask one still, and the Lord willeth Samuel to grant unto them.*

1 When Samuel was now become old, he ¹made his sons Judges over Israel,

2 (And the name of his eldest son was ¹Joel, and the name of the second Abijah) *even* Judges in Beersheba.

3 And his sons walked not in his ways, but turned aside after lucre, and ªtook rewards, and perverted the judgment.

4 ¶ Wherefore all the Elders of Israel gathered them together, and came to Samuel unto ¹Ramah,

5 And said unto him, Behold, thou art old, and thy sons walk not in thy ways: ᵇmake us now a King to judge us like all nations.

7:1 ¹ A city in the tribe of Judah, called also Kirjath Baal, Josh. 15:60.
7:2 ¹ Lamented for their sins, and followed the Lord.
7:5 ¹ For Shiloh was now desolate, because the Philistines had taken thence the Ark.
7:6 ¹ The Chaldea text hath, that they drew water out of their heart: that is, wept abundantly for their sins.
7:8 ¹ Signifying, that in the prayers of the godly, there ought to be a vehement zeal.
7:10 ¹ According to the prophecy of Hannah Samuel's mother, 1 Sam. 2:10.
7:12 ¹ Which was a great rock over against Mizpah.
7:14 ¹ Meaning, the Philistines.
7:17 ¹ Which was not contrary to the Law: for as yet a certain place was not appointed.
8:1 ¹ Because he was not able to bear the charge.
8:2 ¹ Who was also called Vasheni, 1 Chron. 6:28.
8:4 ¹ For there his house was, 1 Sam. 7:17.

6 But the thing [1]displeased Samuel, when they said, Give us a King to judge us: and Samuel prayed unto the Lord.

7 And the Lord said unto Samuel, Hear the voice of the people in all that they shall say unto thee: for they have not cast thee away, but they have cast me away, that I should not reign over them.

8 As they have ever done since I brought them out of Egypt even unto this day, (and have forsaken me, and served other gods) even so do they unto thee.

9 Now therefore hearken unto their voice: howbeit, yet [1]testify unto them, and show them the manner of the king that shall reign over them.

10 ¶ So Samuel told all the words of the Lord unto the people that asked a king of him.

11 And he said, This shall be the [1]manner of the king that shall reign over you: he will take your sons, and appoint them to his chariots, and to be his horsemen, and some shall run before his chariot.

12 Also he will make them his captains over thousands, and captains over fifties, and to ear his ground, and to reap his harvest, and to make instruments of war, and the things that serve for his chariots.

13 He will also take your daughters and make them Apothecaries, and Cooks, and Bakers.

14 And he will take your fields, and your vineyards, and your best Olive trees, and give them to his servants.

15 And he will take the tenth of your seed, and of your vineyards, and give it to his [1]Eunuchs, and to his servants.

16 And he will take your menservants, and your maidservants, and the chief of your young men, and your asses, and put them to his work.

17 He will take the tenth of your sheep, and ye shall be his servants.

18 And ye shall cry out at that day, because of your king, whom ye have chosen you, and the Lord will not [1]hear you at that day.

19 But the people would not hear the voice of Samuel, but did say, Nay, but there shall be a king over us.

20 And we also will be like all other nations, and our king shall judge us, and go out before us and fight our battles.

21 Therefore when Samuel heard all the words

CHAPTER 9
ᵃ 1 Sam. 14:15
1 Chron. 8:33

of the people, he rehearsed them in the ears of the Lord.

22 And the Lord said to Samuel, [1]Hearken unto their voice, and make them a king. And Samuel said unto the men of Israel, Go every man unto his city.

9

3 Saul seeking his father's asses, by the counsel of his servant goeth to Samuel.   9 The Prophets called Seers.   15 The Lord revealeth to Samuel Saul's coming, commanding him to anoint him king.   22 Samuel bringeth Saul to the feast.

1 There was now a man of Benjamin, [1]mighty in power, named ᵃKish, the son of Abiel, the son of Zeror, the son of Bechorath, the son of Aphiah, the son of a man of Benjamin.

2 And he had a son called Saul, a [1]goodly young man and a fair: so that among the children of Israel there was none goodlier than he: from the shoulders upward, he was higher than any of the people.

3 And the asses of Kish, Saul's father were lost: therefore Kish said to Saul his son, Take now one of the servants with thee, and arise, go and [1]seek the asses.

4 So he passed through mount Ephraim, and went through the land of Shalisha, but they found them not. Then they went through the land of Shaalim, and there they were not: he went also through the land of Benjamin, but they found them not.

5 When they came to the land of [1]Zuph, Saul said unto his servant that was with him, Come and let us return, lest my father leave the care of asses, and take thought for us.

6 And he said unto him, Behold now, in this city is a man of God, and he is an honorable man: all that he saith cometh to pass: let us now go thither, if so be that he can show us what way we may go.

7 Then said Saul to his servant, Well then, let us go: but what shall we bring unto the man? For the [1]bread is spent in our vessels, and there is no present to bring to the man of God: what have we?

8 And the servant answered Saul again, and said, Behold, I have found about me the fourth part of a [1]shekel of silver: that will I give the man of God, to tell us our way.

9 (Beforetime in Israel when a man went to seek an answer of God, thus he spake, Come, and let us go to the [1]Seer: for he that is called now a Prophet,

---

8:6 [1] Because they were not content with the order that God had appointed, but would be governed as were the Gentiles.
8:9 [1] To prove if they will forsake their wicked purpose.
8:11 [1] Not that kings have this authority by their office, but that such as reign in God's wrath should usurp this over their brethren, contrary to the law, Deut. 17:20.
8:15 [1] Or, chief officers.
8:18 [1] Because ye repent not for your sins, but because ye smart for your afflictions, whereinto ye cast yourselves willingly.
8:22 [1] Or, grant their request.

9:1 [1] That is, both valiant and rich.
9:2 [1] So that it might seem that God approved their request in appointing out such a person.
9:3 [1] All these circumstances were means to serve unto God's providence, whereby Saul (though not approved of God) was made king.
9:5 [1] Where was Ramathaim Zophim, the city of Samuel.
9:7 [1] Or, vittles.
9:8 [1] Which is about five pence, read Gen. 23:15.
9:9 [1] So called because he foresaw things to come.

was in the old time called a Seer)

10 Then said Saul to his servant, Well said, come, let us go: so they went into the city where the man of God was.

11 ¶ And as they were going up the highway to the city, they found maids that came out to draw water, and said unto them, Is there here a Seer?

12 And they answered them, and said, Yea, lo, *he is* before you: make haste now, for he came this day to the city: for there is an ¹offering of the people this day in the high place.

13 When ye shall come into the city, ye shall find him straightway ere he come up to the high place to eat, for the people will not eat until he come, because he will ¹bless the sacrifice; and then eat they that be bidden to the feast: now therefore go up, for even now shall ye find him.

14 Then they went up into the city, and when they were come into the midst of the city, Samuel came out against them, to go up to the high place.

15 ¶ ᵇBut the Lord had revealed to Samuel ¹secretly (a day before Saul came) saying,

16 Tomorrow about this time I will send thee a man out of the land of Benjamin, him shalt thou anoint to be governor over my people Israel, that he may ¹save my people out of the hands of the Philistines; for I have looked upon my people, and their cry is come unto me.

17 When Samuel therefore saw Saul, the Lord answered him, See, this is the man whom I spake to thee of, he shall rule my people.

18 Then went Saul to Samuel in the midst of the gate, and said, Tell me, I pray thee, where the Seer's house is.

19 And Samuel answered Saul, and said, I am the Seer; go up before me unto the high place; for ye shall eat with me today, and tomorrow I will let thee go, and will tell thee all that is in thine ¹heart.

20 And as for thine asses that were lost three days ago, care not for them: for they are found: and ¹on whom *is set* all the desire of Israel? is it not upon thee, and on all thy father's house?

21 ¶ But Saul answered, and said, Am not I the son of Benjamin of the smallest tribe of Israel? and

[margin: ᵇ 1 Sam. 15:1 / Acts 13:21]

[margin: CHAPTER 10 / ᵃ Gen. 35:20]

my family *is* the least of all the families of the tribe of Benjamin. Wherefore then speakest thou so to me?

22 And Samuel took Saul and his servant, and brought them into the ¹chamber, and made them sit in the chiefest place among them that were bidden: which were about thirty persons.

23 And Samuel said unto the cook, Bring forth the portion which I gave thee, *and* whereof I said unto thee, Keep it with thee.

24 And the cook took up the shoulder, and that which was ¹upon it, and set it before Saul. And *Samuel* said, Behold, that which is left, set it before thee, *and* eat: for hitherto hath it been kept for thee, saying, Also I ²have called the people. So Saul did eat with Samuel that day.

25 And when they were come down from the high place into the city, he communed with Saul upon the top of the house.

26 And when they arose early about the spring of the day, Samuel called Saul to the ¹top of the house, saying, Up, that I may send thee away. And Saul arose, and they went out, both he, and Samuel.

27 And when they were come down to the end of the city, Samuel said to Saul, Bid the servant go before us, (and he went) but stand thou still now, that I may show thee ¹the word of God.

10

1 *Saul is anointed King by Samuel.* 9 *God changeth Saul's heart, and he prophesieth.* 17 *Samuel assembleth the people, and showeth them their sins.* 21 *Saul is chosen King by lot.* 25 *Samuel writeth the King's office.*

1 Then Samuel took a vial of ¹oil, and poured it upon his head, and kissed him, and said, Hath not the Lord anointed thee to be governor over his inheritance?

2 When thou shalt depart from me this day, thou shalt find two men by ᵃRachel's sepulcher in the border of Benjamin, even at Zelzah, and they will say unto thee, The ¹asses which thou wentest to seek, are found, and lo, thy father hath left the care of the asses, and sorroweth for you, saying, What shall I do for my son?

3 Then shalt thou go forth from thence, and shalt come to the ¹plain of Tabor, and there shall meet thee three men going up to God to Bethel, one car-

---

9:12 ¹ That is, a feast after the offering, which should be kept in an high place of the city appointed for that use.
9:13 ¹ That is, give thanks and distribute the meat according to their custom.
9:15 ¹ Hebrew, *in his ear.*
9:16 ¹ Notwithstanding their wickedness, yet God was ever mindful of his inheritance.
9:19 ¹ Meaning, all that thou desirest to know.
9:20 ¹ Whom doth Israel desire to be their King, but thee?
9:22 ¹ Where the feast was.
9:24 ¹ That is, the shoulder with the breast, which the Priest had for

his family in all peace offerings, Lev. 10:14.
² That both by the assembling of the people, and by the meat prepared for thee, thou mightest understand that I knew of thy coming.
9:26 ¹ To speak with him secretly: for the houses were flat above.
9:27 ¹ God's commandment as concerning thee.
10:1 ¹ In the Law this anointing signified the gifts of the holy Ghost, which were necessary for them that should rule.
10:2 ¹ Samuel confirmeth him by these signs, that God hath appointed him king.
10:3 ¹ Or, oaks.

rying three kids, and another carrying three loaves of bread, and another carrying a bottle of wine:

4 And they will ask thee ¹if all be well, and will give thee the two *loaves* of bread, which thou shalt receive of their hands.

5 After that shalt thou come to the ¹hill of God, where is the garrisons of the Philistines: and when thou art come thither to the city, thou shalt meet a company of Prophets coming down from the high place with a vial, and a timbrel, and a pipe, and an harp before them, and they shall prophesy.

6 Then the Spirit of the Lord will come upon thee, and thou shalt prophesy with them, and shalt be turned into another man.

7 Therefore when these signs shall come unto thee, do as occasion shall serve: for God *is* with thee.

8 And thou shalt go down before me to Gilgal: and I also will come down unto thee to offer burnt offerings, and to sacrifice sacrifices of peace. ᵇTarry for me seven days, till I come to thee, and show thee what thou shalt do.

9 And when he had turned his ¹back to go from Samuel, God gave him another ²heart; and all those tokens came to pass that same day.

10 ¶ And when they came thither to the hill, behold, the company of Prophets met him, and the Spirit of God came upon him, and he ¹prophesied among them.

11 Therefore all the people that knew him before, when they saw that he prophesied among the Prophets, said each to other, What is come unto the son of Kish? ᶜis Saul also among the Prophets?

12 And one of the same place answered, and said, But who is their ¹father? Therefore it was a proverb, Is Saul also among the ²Prophets?

13 And when he had made an end of Prophesying, he came to the high place.

14 And Saul's uncle said unto him, and to his servant, Whither went ye? And he said, To seek the asses: and when we saw that they were nowhere, we came to Samuel.

15 And Saul's uncle said, Tell me, I pray thee, what Samuel said unto you.

16 Then Saul said to his uncle, He told us plainly that the asses were found: but concerning the kingdom whereof Samuel spake, told he him not.

17 ¶ And Samuel ¹assembled the people unto the Lord in Mizpah,

ᵇ 1 Sam. 13:8
ᶜ 1 Sam. 19:24

18 And he said unto the children of Israel, Thus saith the Lord God of Israel, I have brought Israel out of Egypt, and delivered you out of the hand of the Egyptians, and out of the hands of all kingdoms that troubled you.

19 But ye have this day cast away your God, who only delivereth you out of all your adversities and tribulations: and ye said unto him, *No*, but appoint a king over us. Now therefore stand ye before the Lord according to your tribes, and according to your thousands.

20 And when Samuel had gathered together all the tribes of Israel, the tribe of Benjamin was ¹taken.

21 Afterward he assembled the tribe of Benjamin, according to their families, and the family of Matri was taken. So Saul the son of Kish was taken, and when they sought him, he could not be found.

22 Therefore they asked the Lord again, if that man should yet come thither. And the Lord answered, Behold, he hath ¹hid himself among the stuff.

23 And they ran, and brought him thence: and when he stood among the people, he was higher than any of the people from the shoulders upward.

24 And Samuel said to all the people, See ye not him, whom the Lord hath chosen, that there is none like him among all the people? and all the people shouted and said, ¹God save the King.

25 Then Samuel told the people ¹the duty of the kingdom, and wrote it in a book, and laid it up before the Lord, and Samuel sent all the people away every man to his house.

26 Saul also went home to Gibeah, and there followed him a band of men, whose heart God had touched.

27 But the wicked men said, How shall he save us? So they despised him, and brought him no presents: but he ¹held his tongue.

11

1 Nahash the Ammonite warreth against Jabesh Gilead, who asketh help of the Israelites. 6 Saul promiseth help. 11 The Ammonites are slain. 14 The kingdom is renewed.

1 Then Nahash the Ammonite ¹came up, and besieged Jabesh Gilead: and all the men of Jabesh said unto Nahash, Make a covenant with us, and we will be thy servants.

10:4 ¹ Hebrew, *of peace.*
10:5 ¹ Which was an high place in the city Kirjath Jearim, where the Ark was, 1 Sam. 7:2.
10:9 ¹ Hebrew, *shoulder.*
  ² He gave him such virtues as were meet for a King.
10:10 ¹ Or, *sang praises.*
10:12 ¹ Meaning, that prophecy cometh not by succession, but is given to whom it pleaseth God.
  ² Noting thereby him that from low degree cometh suddenly to honor.

10:17 ¹ Both to declare unto them their fault in asking a King, and also to show God's sentence therein.
10:20 ¹ That is, by casting of lot.
10:22 ¹ As though he were unworthy and unwilling.
10:24 ¹ Hebrew, *let the king live.*
10:25 ¹ As it is written in Deut. 17:15, etc.
10:27 ¹ Both to avoid sedition, and also to win them by patience.
11:1 ¹ After that Saul was chosen king: for fear of whom they asked a king, as 1 Sam. 12:12.

2   And Nahash the Ammonite answered them, On this condition will I make a covenant with you, that I may thrust out all your ¹right eyes, and bring that shame upon all Israel.

3   To whom the Elders of Jabesh said, Give us seven days respite, that we may send messengers unto all the coasts of Israel: and then if no man deliver us, we will come out to thee.

4   ¶ Then came the messengers to Gibeah of Saul, and told these tidings in the ears of the people: and all the people lift up their voices and wept.

5   And behold, Saul came following the cattle out of the field, and Saul said, What aileth this people, that they weep? And they told him the tidings of the men of Jabesh.

6   Then the Spirit of God ¹came upon Saul, when he heard those tidings, and he was exceeding angry,

7   And took a yoke of oxen, and hewed them in pieces, and sent them throughout all the coasts of Israel by the hands of messengers, saying, Whosoever cometh not forth after Saul, and after ¹Samuel, so shall his oxen be served. And the fear of the Lord fell on the people, and they came out ²with one consent.

8   And when he numbered them in Bezek, the children of Israel were three hundred thousand men, and the men of Judah thirty thousand.

9   Then ¹they said unto the messengers that came, So say unto the men of Jabesh Gilead, Tomorrow by then the Sun be hot, ye shall have help. And the messengers came and showed it to the men of Jabesh, which were glad.

10   Therefore the men of Jabesh said, Tomorrow we will come out unto ¹you, and ye shall do with us all that pleaseth you.

11   ¶ And when the morrow was come, Saul put the people in three bands, and they came in upon the host in the morning watch, and slew the Ammonites until the heat of the day: and they that remained, were scattered, so that two of them were not left together.

12   Then the people said unto Samuel, ¹Who is he that said, Shall Saul reign over us? bring those men that we may slay them.

13   But Saul said, There shall no man ¹die this day: for today the Lord hath saved Israel.

14   ¶ Then said Samuel unto the people, Come, that we may go to Gilgal, and renew the kingdom there.

CHAPTER 12
ᵃ Gen. 46:5,6
ᵇ Exod. 4:16
ᶜ Judg. 4:2

15   So all the people went to Gilgal, and made Saul King there before the Lord in Gilgal: and there they offered ¹peace offerings before the Lord: and there Saul and all the men of Israel rejoiced exceedingly.

12   *1 Samuel declaring to the people his integrity, reproveth their ingratitude.   19 God by miracle causeth the people to confess their sin.   20 Samuel exhorteth the people to follow the Lord.*

1   Samuel then said unto all Israel, Behold, I have ¹hearkened unto your voice in all that ye said unto me, and have appointed a King over you.

2   Now therefore behold, *your* King walketh ¹before you, and I am old and gray headed, and behold, my sons *are* with you: and I have walked before you from my childhood unto this day.

3   Behold, here I am: bear record of me before the Lord and before his anointed. ¹Whose ox have I taken? or whose ass have I taken? or whom have I done wrong to? or whom have I hurt? or of whose hand have I received any bribe, to blind mine eyes therewith, and I will restore it you?

4   Then they said, Thou hast done us no wrong, nor hast hurt us, neither hast thou taken ought of any man's hand.

5   And he said unto them, The Lord is witness against you, and his ¹Anointed is witness this day, that ye have found nought in mine hands. And they answered, *He is* witness.

6   Then Samuel said unto the people, It is the Lord that ¹made Moses and Aaron, and that brought your fathers out of the land of Egypt.

7   Now therefore stand still, that I may reason with you before the Lord according to all the ¹righteousness of the Lord, which he showed to you and to your fathers.

8   ᵃAfter that Jacob was come into Egypt, and your fathers cried unto the Lord, then the Lord ᵇsent Moses and Aaron which brought your fathers out of Egypt, and made them dwell in this place.

9   ᶜAnd when they forgot the Lord their God, he sold them into the hand of Sisera ¹captain of the host of Hazor, and into the hand of the Philistines, and into the hand of the king of Moab, and they fought against them.

11:2 ¹ This declareth that the more near the tyrants are to their destruction, the more cruel they are.
11:6 ¹ God gave him the spirit of strength and courage to go against this tyrant.
11:7 ¹ He addeth Samuel because Saul was not yet approved of all.
        ² Hebrew, *as one man.*
11:9 ¹ Meaning, Saul and Samuel.
11:10 ¹ That is, to the Ammonites, dissembling that they had hope of aid.
11:12 ¹ By this victory the Lord won the hearts of the people to Saul.

11:13 ¹ By showing mercy he thought to overcome their malice.
11:15 ¹ In sign of thanksgiving for the victory.
12:1 ¹ I have granted your petition.
12:2 ¹ To govern you in peace and war.
12:3 ¹ God would that this confession should be a pattern for all them that have any charge or office.
12:5 ¹ Your King, who is anointed by the commandment of the Lord.
12:6 ¹ Or, exalted.
12:7 ¹ Or, benefits.
12:9 ¹ Captain of Jabin's host, King of Hazor.

10 And they cried unto the Lord, and said, We have sinned, because we have forsaken the Lord, and have served Baal and Ashtoreth. Now therefore deliver us out of the hands of our enemies, and we will serve thee.

11 Therefore the Lord sent Jerubbaal [1]and Bedan and [d]Jephthah, and [e]Samuel, and delivered you out of the hands of your enemies on every side, and ye dwelled safe.

12 Notwithstanding when you saw, that Nahash the king of the children of Ammon came against you, ye said unto me, [1]No, but a king shall reign over us: when yet the Lord your God was your King.

13 Now therefore behold the King whom ye have chosen, *and* whom ye have desired: lo therefore, the Lord hath set a King over you.

14 If ye will fear the Lord and serve him, and hear his voice, and not disobey the word of the Lord, both ye, and the king that reigneth over you, shall [1]follow the Lord your God.

15 But if ye will not obey the voice of the Lord, but disobey the Lord's mouth, then shall the hand of the Lord be upon you, and on your [1]fathers.

16 Now also stand and see this great thing which the Lord will do before your eyes.

17 Is it not now wheat harvest? I will call unto the Lord, and he shall send thunder and rain, that ye may perceive and see, how that your wickedness is [1]great, which ye have done in the sight of the Lord in asking you a king.

18 Then Samuel called unto the Lord, and the Lord sent thunder and rain the same day: and all the people feared the Lord and Samuel exceedingly.

19 And all the people said unto Samuel, Pray for thy servants unto the Lord thy God, that we die not: for we have sinned in asking us a King, beside [1]all our *other* sins.

20 ¶ And Samuel said unto the people, Fear not, (ye have indeed done all this wickedness, [1]yet depart not from following the Lord, but serve the Lord with all your heart,

21 Neither turn ye back: for that *should be* after vain things which cannot profit you, nor deliver you, for they are but vanity.)

22 For the Lord will not forsake his people for his great Name's sake: because it hath pleased the Lord

[d] Judg. 11:1
[e] 1 Sam. 4:1

to make you [1]his people.

23 Moreover God forbid, that I should sin against the Lord, and cease praying for you, but I will show you the good and right way.

24 Therefore fear you the Lord, and serve him in the truth with all your [1]hearts, and consider how great things he hath done for you.

25 But if ye do wickedly, ye shall perish, both ye and your King.

13

3 *The Philistines are smitten of Saul and Jonathan.* 13 *Saul being disobedient to God's commandment, is showed of Samuel that he shall not reign.* 19 *The great slavery, wherein the Philistines kept the Israelites.*

1 Saul now had been King [1]one year, and he reigned [2]two years over Israel.

2 Then Saul chose him three thousand of Israel: and two thousand were with Saul in Michmash, and in mount Bethel, and a thousand were with Jonathan in Gibeah of Benjamin: and the rest of the people he sent every one to his tent.

3 And Jonathan smote the garrison of the Philistines, that was in the [1]hill: and it came to the Philistines' ears: and Saul blew the [2]trumpet throughout all the land, saying, Hear, O ye Hebrews.

4 And all Israel heard say, Saul hath destroyed a garrison of the Philistines: wherefore Israel was had in abomination with the Philistines: and the people gathered together after Saul to Gilgal.

5 ¶ The Philistines also gathered themselves together to fight with Israel, thirty thousand chariots, and six thousand horsemen: for the people *was* like the sand which is by the seaside in multitude, and came up, and pitched in Michmash Eastward from [1]Beth Aven.

6 And when the men of Israel saw that they were in a strait (*for the people were in distress*) the people hid themselves in caves, and in holds, and in rocks, and in towers, and in pits.

7 And *some* of the Hebrews went over Jordan unto the land of [1]Gad and Gilead: and Saul was yet in Gilgal, and all the people for fear followed him.

8 And he tarried seven days, according unto the time that Samuel had appointed: but Samuel came not to Gilgal, therefore the people were [1]scattered from him.

12:11 [1] That is, Samson, Judg. 13:25.
12:12 [1] Leaving God to seek the help of man, 1 Sam. 8:5.
12:14 [1] Ye shall be preserved as they that follow the Lord's will.
12:15 [1] Meaning, the governors.
12:17 [1] In that ye have forsaken him, who hath all power in his hand, for a mortal man.
12:19 [1] Not only at other times, but now chiefly.
12:20 [1] He showeth that there is no sin so great, but it shall be forgiven, if the sinner turn again to God.
12:22 [1] Of his free mercy, and not of your merits, and therefore he
will not forsake you.
12:24 [1] Unfeignedly, and without hypocrisy.
13:1 [1] While these things were done.
    [2] Before he took upon him the state of a King.
13:3 [1] Of Kirjath Jearim, where the Ark was, 1 Sam. 10:5.
    [2] That everyone should prepare themselves to war.
13:5 [1] Which was also called Bethel, in the tribe of Benjamin.
13:7 [1] Where the two tribes and the half remained.
13:8 [1] Thinking that the absence of the Prophet was a sign, that they should lose the victory.

9 And Saul said, Bring a burnt offering to me and peace offerings: and he offered a burnt offering.

10 And as soon as he had made an end of offering the burnt offering, behold, Samuel came: and Saul went forth to meet him, to [1]salute him.

11 And Samuel said, What hast thou done? Then Saul said, Because I saw that the people was [1]scattered from me, and that thou camest not within the days appointed, and that the Philistines gathered themselves together to Michmash,

12 Therefore said I, the Philistines will come down now upon me to Gilgal, and I have not made supplication unto the Lord. I was bold therefore and offered a burnt offering.

13 And Samuel said to Saul, Thou hast done foolishly: thou hast not kept the commandment of the Lord thy [1]God, which he commanded thee: for the Lord had now stablished thy kingdom upon Israel forever.

14 But now thy kingdom shall not continue: the Lord hath sought him a [1]man after his own heart, and the Lord hath commanded him to be governor over his people, because thou hast not kept that which the Lord had commanded thee.

15 ¶ And Samuel arose, and got him up from Gilgal in [1]Gibeah of Benjamin: and Saul numbered the people that were found with him, about six hundred men.

16 And Saul and Jonathan his son, and the people that were found with them, had their abiding in Gibeah of Benjamin: but the Philistines pitched in Michmash.

17 And there came out of the host of the Philistines [1]three bands to destroy, one band turned unto the way of Ophrah unto the land of Shual,

18 And another band turned toward the way to Beth Horon, and the [1]third band turned toward the way of the coast that looketh toward the valley of Zeboim, toward the wilderness.

19 Then there was no smith found throughout all the land of Israel: for the Philistines said, Lest the Hebrews make them swords or spears.

20 Wherefore, all the Israelites went down to the Philistines, to sharpen every man his share, his mattock, and his axe, and his weeding hook.

21 Yet they had a file for the shares, and for the mattocks, and for the pick forks, and for the axes,

CHAPTER 14
[a] 1 Sam. 4:21
[b] 2 Chron. 14:11

and for to sharpen the goads.

22 So when the day of battle was come, there was neither [1]sword nor spear found in the hands of any of the people that were with Saul and with Jonathan: but *only* with Saul and Jonathan his son was there found.

23 And the garrison of the Philistines came out to the passage of Michmash.

14

14 Jonathan and his armor bearer put the Philistines to flight.   24 Saul bindeth the people by an oath, not to eat till evening.   32 The people eat with the blood.   38 Saul would put Jonathan to death.   45 The people deliver him.

1 Then on a day Jonathan the son of Saul said unto the young man that bare his armor, [1]Come and let us go over toward the Philistines garrison, that *yonder* on the other side, but he told not his father.

2 And Saul tarried in the border of Gibeah under a pomegranate tree, which was in Migron, and the people that were with him, *were* about six hundred men.

3 And Ahijah the son of Ahitub, [a]Ichabod's brother, the son of Phinehas, the son of Eli, *was* the Lord's Priest in Shiloh, and wore an Ephod: and the people knew not that Jonathan was gone.

4 ¶ Now in the way whereby Jonathan sought to go over to the Philistines garrison, there was a [1]sharp rock on the one side, and a sharp rock on the other side: the name of the one *was* called Bozez, and the name of the other Seneh.

5 The one rock stretched from the North toward Michmash, and the other *was* from the South toward Gibeah.

6 And Jonathan said to the young man that bare his armor, Come, and let us go over unto the garrison of these [1]uncircumcised: it may be that the Lord will work with us: for it is [2]not hard to the Lord [b]to save with many, or with few.

7 And he that bare his armor, said unto him, Do all that is in thine heart: go where it pleaseth thee: behold, [1]I am with thee as thine heart desireth.

8 Then said Jonathan, Behold, we go over unto those men, and will show ourselves unto them.

9 [1]If they say on this wise to us, Tarry until we come to you, then we will stand still in our place, and not go up to them.

13:10 [1] Hebrew, *bless him*.
13:11 [1] Though these causes seem sufficient in man's judgment: yet because they had not the word of God, they turned to his destruction.
13:13 [1] Who willed thee to obey him, and rest upon the words spoken by his Prophet.
13:14 [1] That is, David.
13:15 [1] And went to his city Ramah.
13:17 [1] Or, the destroyer: to wit, the captains came out with three bands.
13:18 [1] So that to man's judgment these three armies would have overrun the whole country.

13:22 [1] To declare that the victory only came of God, and not by their force.
14:1 [1] By this example God would declare to Israel that the victory did not consist in multitude or armor, but only came of his grace.
14:4 [1] Or, like a tooth.
14:6 [1] To wit, the Philistines.
       [2] Or, none can let the Lord.
14:7 [1] I will follow thee whithersoever thou goest.
14:9 [1] This he spake by the spirit of prophecy, forasmuch hereby God gave him assurance of the victory.

10 But if they say, Come up unto us, then we will go up: for the Lord hath delivered them into our hand: and this shall be a sign unto us.

11 So they both showed themselves unto the garrison of the Philistines: and the Philistines said, See, the Hebrews come out of the ¹holes wherein they had hid themselves.

12 And the men of the garrison answered Jonathan and his armor bearer, and said, Come up to us: for we will show you a thing. Then Jonathan said unto his armor bearer, Come up after me: for the Lord hath delivered them into the hand of Israel.

13 So Jonathan went up upon ¹his hands and upon his feet, and his armor bearer after him: and *some* fell before Jonathan, and his armor bearer slew *others* after him.

14 So the ¹first slaughter which Jonathan and his armor bearer made, was about twenty men, as it were within half an acre of land which two *oxen plow*.

15 And there was a fear in the host, *and* in the field, and among all the people: the garrison also, and they that went out to spoil, were afraid themselves: and the earth ¹trembled: for it was *stricken* with fear by God.

16 ¶ Then the watchmen of Saul in Gibeah of Benjamin saw: and behold, the multitude was discomfited, and smitten as they went.

17 Therefore said Saul unto the people that were with him, Search now, and see, who is gone from us. And when they had numbered, behold, Jonathan and his armor bearer were not there.

18 And Saul said unto Ahijah, Bring hither the Ark of God (for the Ark of God was at that time with the children of Israel)

19 ¶ And while Saul talked unto the Priest, the noise that was in the host of the Philistines, spread farther abroad, and increased: therefore Saul said unto the Priest, ¹Withdraw thine hand.

20 And Saul was assembled with all the people that were with him, and they came to the battle: and behold, ᶜevery man's sword was against his fellow, *and* there was a very great discomfiture.

21 Moreover, the Hebrews that were with the Philistines beforetime, and were come with them into all parts of the host, even they also turned to be with the ¹Israelites that were with Saul and Jonathan.

ᶜ Judg. 7:21,22
1 Chron. 20:23
ᵈ Lev. 7:26
Lev. 19:26
Deut. 12:16

22 Also all the men of Israel which had hid themselves in mount Ephraim, when they heard that the Philistines were fled, they followed after them in the battle.

23 And so the Lord saved Israel that day: and the battle continued unto Beth Aven.

24 And at that time the men of Israel were pressed *with hunger*: for Saul charged the people with an oath, saying, ¹Cursed be the man that eateth ²food till night, that I may be avenged of mine enemies: so none of the people tasted *any* sustenance.

25 And all they of the land came to a wood, where honey lay upon the ground.

26 And the people came into the wood, and behold, the honey dropped, and no man moved his hand to his mouth: for the people feared the ¹oath.

27 But Jonathan heard not when his father charged the people with the oath: wherefore he put forth the end of the rod that was in his hand, and dipped it in an honey comb, and put his hand to his mouth, and his ¹eyes received sight.

28 Then answered one of the people, and said, Thy father made the people to swear, saying, Cursed be the man that eateth sustenance this day: and the people were ¹faint.

29 Then said Jonathan, My father hath ¹troubled the land: see now how mine eyes are made clear, because I have tasted a little of this honey:

30 How much more, if the people had eaten today of the spoil of their enemies which they found? for had there not been now a greater slaughter among the Philistines?

31 ¶ And they smote the Philistines that day, from Michmash to Aijalon: and the people were exceeding faint.

32 So the people turned to the spoil, and took sheep, and oxen, and calves and slew them on the ground, and the people did eat them ᵈwith the blood.

33 Then men told Saul, saying, Behold, the people sin against the Lord, in that they eat with the blood. And he said, Ye have trespassed: ¹roll a great stone unto me this day.

34 Again Saul said, Go abroad among the people, and bid them bring me every man his ox, and every man his sheep, and slay them here, and eat, and sin not against the Lord in eating with the blood. And

---

14:11 ¹ Thus they spake contemptuously and by derision.
14:13 ¹ That is, he crept up, or went up with all haste.
14:14 ¹ The second was when they slew one another, and the third when the Israelites chased them.
14:15 ¹ In that the insensible creatures tremble for fear of God's judgment, it declareth how terrible his vengeance shall be against his enemies.
14:19 ¹ Let the Ephod alone: for I have no leisure now to ask counsel of God, Num. 27:21.
14:21 ¹ Though before for fear of the Philistines they declared them-

selves as enemies to their brethren.
14:24 ¹ Such was his hypocrisy and arrogancy, that he thought to attribute to his policy that which God had given by the hand of Jonathan.
² Hebrew, *bread*.
14:26 ¹ That is, the punishment, if they break their oath.
14:27 ¹ Which were dim before for weariness and hunger.
14:28 ¹ Or, weary.
14:29 ¹ By making this cruel law.
14:33 ¹ That the blood of the beast that shall be slain, may be pressed out upon it.

the people brought every man his ox in his hand that night, and slew them there.

35 Then Saul made an altar unto the Lord, *and that* [1]*was the first altar that he made unto the Lord.

36 ¶ And Saul said, Let us go down after the Philistines by night, and spoil them until the morning shine, and let us not leave a man of them. And they said, Do whatsoever thou thinkest best. Then said the Priest, Let us [1]draw near hither unto God.

37 So Saul asked of God, *saying*, Shall I go down after the Philistines? wilt thou deliver them into the hands of Israel? But he answered him not at that time.

38 ¶ And Saul said, [c]All [1]ye chief of the people, come ye hither, and know, and see by whom this sin is done this day.

39 For as the Lord liveth, which saveth Israel, though it be *done* by Jonathan my son, he shall die the death. But none of all the people answered him.

40 Then he said unto all Israel, Be ye on one side, and I and Jonathan my son will be on the other side. And the people said unto Saul, Do what thou thinkest best.

41 Then Saul said unto the Lord God of Israel, Give [1]a perfect *lot*. And Jonathan and Saul were taken, but the people escaped.

42 And Saul said, Cast *lot* between me and Jonathan my son. And Jonathan was taken.

43 Then Saul said to Jonathan, Tell me what thou hast done. And Jonathan told him, and said, I tasted a little honey with the end of the rod, that was in mine hand, and lo, I must die.

44 Again Saul answered, God do so and more also, unless thou die the death, Jonathan.

45 And the people said unto Saul, [1]Shall Jonathan die, who hath so mightily delivered Israel? God forbid. As the Lord liveth, there shall not one hair of his head fall to the ground: for he hath wrought with God this day. So the people delivered Jonathan that he died not.

46 Then Saul came up from the Philistines: and the Philistines went to their own place.

47 ¶ So Saul held the kingdom over Israel, and fought against all his enemies on every side, against Moab, and against the children of Ammon, and against Edom, and against the Kings of Zobah, and against the Philistines: and whithersoever he went, he [1]handled them as wicked men.

48 He gathered also an host and smote [1]Amalek, and delivered Israel out of the hands of them that spoiled them.

49 Now the sons of Saul were Jonathan, [1]and Jishui, and Malchishua: and the names of his two daughters, the elder was called Merab, and the younger was named [2]Michal.

50 And the name of Saul's wife was Ahinoam the daughter of Ahimaaz: and the name of his chief captain was [1]Abner the son of Ner, Saul's uncle.

51 And Kish *was* Saul's father: and Ner the father of Abner *was* the son of Abiel.

52 And there was sore war against the Philistines all the days of Saul: *and* [1]whomsoever Saul saw to be a strong man, and meet for the war, he took him unto him.

15

3 Saul is commanded to slay Amalek.   9 He spareth Agag, and the best things.   19 Samuel reproveth him.   28 Saul is rejected of the Lord, and his Kingdom given to another.   33 Samuel heweth Agag in pieces.

1 Afterward Samuel said unto Saul, [a]The Lord sent me to anoint thee King over his people, over Israel: now therefore [1]obey the voice of the words of the Lord.

2 Thus saith the Lord of hosts, I remember what Amalek did to Israel, [b]how they laid *wait* for them in the way, as they came up from Egypt.

3 Now *therefore* go, and smite Amalek, and destroy ye all that pertaineth unto them, and have no compassion on them, but [1]slay both man and woman, both infant and suckling, both ox, and sheep, both camel, and ass.

4 ¶ And Saul assembled the people, and [1]numbered them in Telaim, two hundred thousand footmen, and ten thousand men of Judah.

5 And Saul came to a city of Amalek, and [1]set watch at the river.

6 And Saul said unto the [1]Kenites, Go, depart, *and* get you down from among the Amalekites, lest I destroy you with them: for ye showed [2]mercy to

c Judg. 20:2

CHAPTER 15
a 1 Sam. 9:16
b Exod. 17:14
Num. 24:20

14:35 [1] Or, of that stone began he to build an altar.
14:36 [1] To ask counsel of him.
14:38 [1] Hebrew, *corners*.
14:41 [1] Cause the lot to fall on him that hath broken the oath: but he doth not consider his presumption in commanding the same oath.
14:45 [1] The people thought it their duty to rescue him, who of ignorance had but broken a rash law, and by whom they had received so great a benefit.
14:47 [1] Or, overcame them.
14:48 [1] As the Lord had commanded, Deut. 25:17.
14:49 [1] Called also Abinadab, 1 Sam. 31:2.

[2] Which was the Wife of David, 1 Sam. 18:27.
14:50 [1] Whom Joab the captain of David slew, 2 Sam. 3:27.
14:52 [1] As Samuel had forewarned, 1 Sam. 8:11.
15:1 [1] Because he hath preferred thee to this honor, thou art bound to obey him.
15:3 [1] That this might be an example of God's vengeance against them that deal cruelly with his people.
15:4 [1] Or, knew their number by the lambs which they brought.
15:5 [1] Or, fought in the valley.
15:6 [1] Which were the posterity of Jethro Moses' father-in-law.
[2] For Jethro came to visit them, and gave them good counsel, Exod. 18:19.

all the children of Israel, when they came up from Egypt: and the Kenites departed from among the Amalekites.

7 So Saul smote the Amalekites from Havilah, as thou comest to Shur, that is before Egypt,

8 And took Agag the King of the Amalekites alive, and destroyed all the people with the edge of the sword.

9 But Saul and the people spared Agag, and the better sheep, and the oxen, and the fat beasts, and the lambs, and all that was good, and they would not destroy them; but everything that was vile and nought worth, that they destroyed.

10 ¶ Then came the word of the Lord unto Samuel, saying,

11 It ¹repenteth me that I have made Saul King; for he is turned from me, and hath not performed my commandments. And Samuel was moved, and cried unto the Lord all night.

12 And when Samuel arose early to meet Saul in the morning, one told Samuel, saying, Saul is gone to Carmel; and behold, he hath made him there a place, from whence he returned, and departed, and is gone down to Gilgal.

13 ¶ Then Samuel came to Saul, and Saul said unto him. Blessed be thou of the Lord, I have fulfilled the ¹commandment of the Lord.

14 But Samuel said, What meaneth then the bleating of the sheep in mine ears, and the lowing of the oxen which I hear?

15 And Saul answered, They have brought them from the Amalekites; for the people spared the best of the sheep, and of the oxen, to sacrifice them unto the Lord thy God, and the remnant have we destroyed.

16 Again Samuel said to Saul, Let me tell thee what the Lord hath said to me this night. And he said unto him, Say on.

17 Then Samuel said, When thou wast ¹little in thine own sight, wast thou not made the head of the tribes of Israel? for the Lord anointed thee King over Israel.

18 And the Lord sent thee on a journey, and said, Go, and destroy those sinners the Amalekites, and fight against them, until thou destroy them.

19 Now wherefore hast thou not obeyed the voice

c Hos. 6:6,7
Matt. 9:13
Matt. 12:7
d Exod. 17:11
Num. 14:45

of the Lord, but hast turned to the prey, and hast done wickedly in the sight of the Lord?

20 And Saul said unto Samuel, Yea, ¹I have obeyed the voice of the Lord, and have gone the way which the Lord sent me, and have brought Agag the king of Amalek, and have destroyed the Amalekites.

21 But the people took of the spoil, sheep, and oxen, and the chiefest of the things which should have been destroyed, to offer unto the Lord thy God in Gilgal.

22 And Samuel said, Hath the Lord as great pleasure in burnt offerings and sacrifices, as when the voice of the Lord is obeyed? behold, ᶜto obey is better than sacrifice, and to hearken is better than the fat of rams.

23 For ¹rebellion is as the sin of witchcraft, and transgression is wickedness and idolatry. Because thou hast cast away the word of the Lord, therefore he hath cast away thee from being king.

24 Then Saul said unto Samuel, I have sinned: for I have transgressed the Commandment of the Lord, and thy words, because I feared the people, and obeyed their voice.

25 Now therefore I pray thee, take away my ¹sin, and turn again with me, that I may worship the Lord.

26 But Samuel said unto Saul, I will not return with thee: for thou hast cast away the word of the Lord, and the Lord hath cast away thee, that thou shalt not be King over Israel.

27 And as Samuel turned himself to go away, he caught the lap of his coat, and it rent.

28 Then Samuel said unto him, The Lord hath rent the kingdom of Israel from thee this day, and hath given it to thy ¹neighbor, that is better than thou.

29 For indeed the ¹strength of Israel will not lie nor repent: for he is not a man that he should repent.

30 Then he said, I have sinned: but honor me, I pray thee, before the Elders of my people, and before Israel, and turn again with me, that I may worship the Lord thy God.

31 ¶ So Samuel turned again, and followed Saul: and Saul worshipped the Lord.

32 Then said Samuel, Bring ye hither to me Agag the king of the Amalekites: and Agag came unto him ¹pleasantly, and Agag said, Truly the ²bitterness of death is passed.

15:11 ¹ God in his eternal counsel never changeth nor repenteth, as verse 29, though he seemeth to us to repent when anything goeth contrary to his temporal election.

15:13 ¹ This is the nature of hypocrites to be impudent against the truth, to condemn others, and justify themselves.

15:17 ¹ Meaning, of base condition, as 1 Sam. 9:21.

15:20 ¹ He standeth most impudently in his own defense both against God and his own conscience.

15:23 ¹ God hateth nothing more than the disobedience of

his Commandment, though the intent seems never so good to man.

15:25 ¹ This was not true repentance, but dissimulation, fearing the loss of his kingdom.

15:28 ¹ That is, to David.

15:29 ¹ Meaning, God, who maintaineth and preferreth his.

15:32 ¹ Or, in bonds.

² He suspected nothing less than death, or as some write, he passed not for death.

33 And Samuel said, ^dAs thy sword hath made women childless, so shall thy mother be childless among other women. And Samuel hewed Agag in pieces before the Lord in Gilgal.

34 ¶ So Samuel departed to ¹Ramah, and Saul went up to his house to Gibeah of Saul.

35 And Samuel came no more to ¹see Saul until the day of his death: but Samuel mourned for Saul, and the Lord ²repented that he made Saul King over Israel.

CHAPTER 16
ᵃ 1 Chron. 28:9
Jer. 11:20
Jer. 17:10
Jer. 20:12
Ps. 7:10
ᵇ 2 Sam. 7:8
Ps. 78:71
Ps. 89:21
ᶜ Acts 7:46
Acts 13:22

16 *1 Samuel is reproved of God, and is sent to anoint David. 7 God regardeth the heart. 13 The Spirit of the Lord cometh upon David. 14 The wicked Spirit is sent upon Saul. 19 Saul sendeth for David.*

1 The Lord then said unto Samuel, How long wilt thou mourn for Saul, ¹seeing I have cast him away from reigning over Israel? fill thine horn with oil and come, I will send thee to Jesse the Bethlehemite: for I have provided me a King among his sons.

2 And Samuel said, How can I go? for if Saul shall hear it, he will kill me. Then the Lord answered, Take an heifer ¹with thee, and say, I am come ²to do sacrifice to the Lord.

3 And call Jesse to the sacrifice, and I will show thee what thou shalt do, and thou shalt anoint unto me him whom I name unto thee.

4 So Samuel did that the Lord bade him, and came to Bethlehem, and the elders of the town were ¹astonished at his coming, and said, Comest thou peaceably?

5 And he answered, Yea: I am come to do sacrifice unto the Lord: sanctify yourselves, and come with me to the sacrifice. And he sanctified Jesse and his sons, and called them to the sacrifice.

6 And when they were come, he looked on Eliab, and said, Surely the Lord's ¹Anointed is before him.

7 But the Lord said unto Samuel, Look not on his countenance, nor on the height of his stature, because I have refused him: for *God seeth* not as man seeth: for man looketh on the outward appearance, but the Lord beholdeth the ᵃheart.

8 Then Jesse called Abinadab, and made him come before Samuel. And he said, Neither hath the Lord chosen this.

9 Then Jesse made Shammah come. And he said, Neither yet hath the Lord chosen him.

10 Again Jesse made his seven sons to come before Samuel, and Samuel said unto Jesse, The Lord hath chosen none of these.

11 Finally, Samuel said unto Jesse, ¹Are there no more children *but these*? And he said, There remaineth yet a little one behind, that keepeth the sheep. Then Samuel said unto Jesse, ᵇSend and fet him: for we will not sit down, till he be come hither.

12 And he sent, and brought him in: and he was ruddy, and of a good countenance, and comely visage. And the Lord said, Arise, *and* anoint him: for this is he.

13 Then Samuel took the horn of oil, and anointed him in the midst of his brethren. And the ᶜSpirit of the Lord ¹came upon David, from that day forward: then Samuel rose up, and went to Ramah.

14 ¶ But the Spirit of the Lord departed from Saul, and an ¹evil spirit *sent* of the Lord, vexed him.

15 And Saul's servants said unto him, Behold now, the evil spirit of God vexeth thee.

16 Let our Lord therefore command thy servants *that are* before thee, to seek a man that is a cunning player upon the harp: that when the evil spirit of God cometh upon thee, he may play with his hand, and thou mayest be eased.

17 Saul then said unto his servants, Provide me a man, I pray you, that can play well, and bring him to me.

18 Then answered one of his servants, and said, Behold, I have seen a ¹son of Jesse, a Bethlehemite, that can play, and is strong, valiant, and a man of war, and wise in matters, and a comely person, and the Lord is with him.

19 ¶ Wherefore Saul sent messengers unto Jesse, and said, Send me David thy son, which is with the sheep.

20 And Jesse took an ass *laden* with bread and a flagon of wine and a kid, and sent them by the hand of David his son unto Saul.

21 And David came to Saul, and ¹stood before him: and he loved him very well, and he was his armor bearer.

22 And Saul sent to Jesse, saying, Let David now

15:34 ¹ Where his house was.
15:35 ¹ Though Saul came where Samuel was, 1 Sam. 19:22.
² As verse 11.
16:1 ¹ Signifying, that we ought not to show ourselves more pitiful than God, nor to lament them whom he casteth out.
16:2 ¹ Hebrew, *in thine hand*.
² That is, to make a peace offering, which might be done though the Ark was not there.
16:4 ¹ Fearing, lest some grievous crime had been committed, because the Prophet was not wont to come thither.

16:6 ¹ Thinking that Eliab had been appointed of God to be made King.
16:11 ¹ Hebrew, *are the children ended?*
16:13 ¹ Or, prospered.
16:14 ¹ The wicked spirits are at God's commandment to execute his will against the wicked.
16:18 ¹ Though David was now anointed King by the Prophet, yet God would exercise him in sundry sorts before he had the use of his kingdom.
16:21 ¹ Or, served him.

remain with me: for he hath found favor in my sight.

23 And so when the *evil* spirit of God came upon Saul, David took an harp and played with his hand, and Saul was ¹refreshed and was eased: for the evil spirit departed from him.

17 *1 The Philistines make war against Israel. 10 Goliath defieth Israel. 17 David is sent to his brethren. 34 The strength and boldness of David. 47 The Lord saveth not by sword nor spear. 50 David killeth Goliath, and the Philistines flee.*

1 Now the Philistines gathered their armies to battle, and came together to Sochoh which is in Judah, and pitched between Sochoh and Azekah, ¹in the coast of Dammim.

2 And Saul, and the men of Israel assembled and pitched in the valley ¹of Elah, and put themselves in battle array to meet the Philistines.

3 And the Philistines stood on a mountain on the one side, and Israel stood on a mountain on the other side: so a valley *was* between them.

4 ¶ Then came a man between them ¹both out of the tents of the Philistines, named Goliath of Gath: his height *was* six cubits and an hand breadth,

5 And had an helmet of brass upon his head, and a ¹brigandine upon him: and the weight of his brigandine *was* five thousand ²shekels of brass.

6 And he had ¹boots of brass upon his legs, and a shield of brass upon his shoulders.

7 And the shaft of his spear *was* like a weaver's beam: and his spear head *weighed* six hundred shekels of iron: and one bearing a shield went before him.

8 And he stood, and cried against the host of Israel, and said unto them, Why are ye come to set your battle in array? am not I a Philistine, and you servants to Saul? choose you a man for you, and let him come down to me.

9 If he be able to fight with me, and ¹kill me, then will we be your servants: but if I overcome him, and kill him, then shall ye be our servants, and serve us.

10 Also the Philistine said, I defy the host of Israel this day: give me a man, that we may fight ¹together.

11 When Saul and all Israel heard those words of the Philistine, they were discouraged, and greatly

CHAPTER 17
ᵃ 1 Sam. 16:1
ᵇ Josh. 15:19

afraid.

12 ¶ Now this David *was* the ᵃson of an Ephrathite of Bethlehem Judah, named Jesse, which had eight sons: and ¹this man was taken for an old man in the days of Saul.

13 And the three eldest sons of Jesse went and followed Saul to the battle: and the names of his three sons that went to battle *were* Eliab the eldest, and the next Abinadab, and the third Shammah.

14 So David was the least: and the three eldest went after Saul.

15 David also ¹went, but he returned from Saul to feed his father's sheep in Bethlehem.

16 And the Philistine drew near in the morning, and evening, and continued forty days.

17 And Jesse said unto David his son, ¹Take now for thy brethren an Ephah of this parched corn, and these ten cakes, and run to the host to thy brethren.

18 Also carry these ten fresh cheeses unto the captain, and look how thy brethren fare, and receive their ¹pledge.

19 (Then Saul and they, and all the men of Israel *were* in the valley of Elah, fighting with the Philistines.)

20 ¶ So David rose up early in the morning, and left the sheep with a keeper, and took and went as Jesse had commanded him, and came within the compass of the host: and the host went out in array, and shouted in the battle.

21 For Israel and the Philistines had put themselves in array, army against army.

22 And David left the things which he bare, under the hands of the keeper of the ¹carriage, and ran into the host, and came, and asked his brethren ²how they did.

23 And as he talked with them, behold, the man *that was* between the two *armies*, came up, (whose name *was* Goliath the Philistine of Gath) out of the ¹army of the Philistines, and spake ²such words, and David heard them.

24 And all the men of Israel when they saw the man, ran away from him, and were sore afraid.

25 For every man of Israel said, Saw ye not this man that cometh up? even to revile Israel is he come up: and to him that killeth him, will the King give great riches, and will give him his ᵇdaughter, yea, and

---

16:23 ¹ God would that Saul should receive this benefit as at David's hand: that his condemnation might be the more evident, for his cruel hate toward him.

17:1 ¹ Or, in Ephes Dammim.

17:2 ¹ Or, of the oak.

17:4 ¹ Between the two camps.

17:5 ¹ Or, coat of plate.

     ² That is, 156 pounds 4 ounces after half an ounce the shekel: and 600 shekels weight amounteth to 18 pounds 3 quarters.

17:6 ¹ Or, greaves.

17:9 ¹ Hebrew, *smite me.*

17:10 ¹ Or, hand to hand.

17:12 ¹ Or, he was counted among them that bare office.

17:15 ¹ To serve Saul, as 1 Sam. 16:19.

17:17 ¹ Though Jesse meant one thing, yet God's providence directed David to another end.

17:18 ¹ If they have laid anything to gage for their necessity, redeem it out.

17:22 ¹ Hebrew, *vessels.*

     ² Hebrew, *of peace.*

17:23 ¹ Or, valley.

     ² As are above rehearsed, verses 8 and 9.

make his father's house [1]free in Israel.

26 ¶ Then David spake to the men that stood with him, and said, What shall be done to the man that killeth this Philistine, and taketh away the [1]shame from Israel? for who is this uncircumcised Philistine, that he should revile the host of the living God?

27 And the people answered him after this manner, saying, Thus shall it be done to the man that killeth him.

28 And Eliab his eldest brother heard when he spake unto the men, and Eliab was very angry with David, and said, Why camest thou down hither? and with whom hast thou left those few sheep in the wilderness? I know thy pride and the malice of thine heart, that thou art come down to see the battle.

29 Then David said, What have I now done? Is there not a [1]cause?

30 And he departed from him into the presence of another, and spake of the same manner, and the people answered him according to the former words.

31 ¶ And they that heard the words which David spake, rehearsed them before Saul, which caused him to be brought.

32 So David said to Saul, Let no man's heart fail him, because of him: thy servant will go, and fight with this Philistine.

33 And Saul said to David, Thou art not [1]able to go against this Philistine to fight with him: for thou art a boy, and he is a man of war from his youth.

34 And David answered unto Saul, Thy servant kept his father's sheep, and there came a [1]lion, and likewise a bear, and took a sheep out of the flock,

35 And I went out after him and smote him, and took it out of his mouth: and when he arose against me, I caught him by the beard, and smote him, and slew him.

36 So thy servant slew both the lion, and the bear: therefore this uncircumcised Philistine shall be as one of them, seeing he hath railed on the host of the living God.

37 ¶ Moreover David said, The Lord that delivered me out of the paw of the lion, and out of the paw of the bear, he will deliver me out of the hand of this Philistine. Then Saul said unto David, [1]Go, and the Lord be with thee.

38 And Saul put his raiment upon David, and put an helmet of brass upon his head, and put a brigandine upon him.

39 Then girded David his sword upon his raiment, and [1]began to go: for he never proved it: and David said unto Saul, I can not go with these: for I am not accustomed. Wherefore David put them off him.

40 Then took he his [1]staff in his hand, and chose him five smooth stones out of a brook, and put them in his shepherd's bag or scrip, and his sling *was* in his hand, and he drew near to the Philistine.

41 ¶ And the Philistine came and drew near unto David, and the man that bare the shield *went* before him.

42 Now when the Philistine looked about and saw David, he disdained him: for he was but young, ruddy, and of a comely face.

43 And the Philistine said unto David, Am I a dog, that thou comest to me with staves? And the Philistine [1]cursed David by his gods.

44 And the Philistine said to David, Come to me, and I will give thy flesh unto the fowls of the heaven, and to the beasts of the field.

45 ¶ Then said David to the Philistine, Thou comest to me with a sword, and with a spear, and with a shield, but I come to thee in the Name of the Lord of hosts, the God of the host of Israel, whom thou hast railed upon.

46 This [1]day shall the Lord close thee in mine hand, and I shall smite thee, and take thine head from thee, and I will give the carcasses of the host of the Philistines this day unto the fowls of the heaven, and to the beasts of the earth, that all the world may know that Israel hath a God,

47 And that all this assembly may know, that the Lord saveth not with sword nor with spear, (for the battle is the Lord's) and he will give you into our hands.

48 And when the Philistine arose to come and draw near unto David, David [1]hasted and ran to fight against the Philistine.

49 And David put his hand in his bag, and took out a stone, and slang it, and smote the Philistine in his forehead, that the stone sticked in his forehead, and he fell groveling to the earth.

50 So David overcame the Philistine with a sling and with a stone, and smote the Philistine, and slew

---

17:25 [1] From taxes and payments.
17:26 [1] This dishonor that he doeth to Israel.
17:29 [1] For his father's sending was a just occasion, and also he felt himself inwardly moved by God's Spirit.
17:33 [1] Here Satan proveth David's faith, by the infidelity of Saul.
17:34 [1] David by the experience that he hath had in time past of God's help, nothing doubteth to overcome this danger, seeing he was zealous for God's honor.
17:37 [1] For by these examples he saw that the power of God was

with him.
17:39 [1] Or, assayed.
17:40 [1] To the intent that by these weak means, God might only be known to be the author of this victory.
17:43 [1] He sware by his gods that he would destroy him.
17:46 [1] David being assured both of his cause and of his calling, prophesieth of the destruction of the Philistines.
17:48 [1] Being moved with a fervent zeal to be revenged upon this blasphemer of God's name.

him, when David had no sword in his hand.

51 Then David ran, and stood upon the Philistine, and took his sword and drew it out of his sheath, and slew him, and cut off his head therewith. So when the Philistines saw that their champion was dead, they fled.

52 And the men of Israel and Judah arose, and shouted, and followed after the Philistines, until they came to the ¹valley, and unto the gates of Ekron: and the Philistines fell down wounded by the way of Shaaraim, even to Gath and to Ekron.

53 And the children of Israel returned from pursuing the Philistines, and spoiled their tents.

54 And David took the head of the Philistine, and brought it to Jerusalem, and put his armor in his ¹tent.

55 ¶ When Saul saw David go forth against the Philistine, he said unto Abner the captain of his host, Abner, ¹whose son is this young man? and Abner answered, As thy soul liveth, O king, I cannot tell.

56 Then the King said, Inquire thou whose son this young man is.

57 And when David was returned from the slaughter of the Philistine, then Abner took him and brought him before Saul with the head of the Philistine in his hand.

58 And Saul said to him, Whose son art thou, thou young man? And David answered, I am the son of thy servant Jesse the Bethlehemite.

18

1 The amity of Jonathan and David.   8 Saul envieth David for the praise that the women gave him.   11 Saul would have slain David.   17 He promiseth him Merab to wife, but giveth him Michal.   27 David delivereth to Saul two hundred foreskins of the Philistines.   29 Saul feareth David, seeing that the Lord is with him.

1 And when he had made an end of speaking unto Saul, the ¹soul of Jonathan was knit with the soul of David, and Jonathan loved him, as his own soul.

2 And Saul took him that day, and would not let him return to his father's house.

3 Then Jonathan and David made a covenant: for he loved him as his own soul.

4 And Jonathan put off the robe that was upon him, and gave it David, and his garments, even to his sword, and to his bow, and to his girdle.

5 And David went out whithersoever Saul sent

him, *and* behaved himself ¹wisely: so that Saul set him over the men of war, and he was accepted in the sight of all the people, and also in the sight of Saul's servants.

6 ¶ When they came again, and David returned from the slaughter of the ¹Philistine, the women came out of all cities of Israel singing and dancing to meet king Saul, with timbrels, with *instruments of* joy, and with rebecks.

7 And the women ¹sang by course in their play, and said, ᵃSaul hath slain his thousand, and David his ten thousand.

8 Therefore Saul was exceedingly wroth, and the saying displeased him, and he said, They have ascribed unto David ten thousand, and to me they have ascribed *but* a thousand, *and what can he have* more save the kingdom?

9 Wherefore Saul ¹had an eye on David from that day forward.

10 ¶ And on the morrow, the evil spirit of God came upon Saul, and he ¹prophesied in the midst of the house: and David played with his hand like as at other times, and there *was* a spear in Saul's hand.

11 And Saul took the spear, and said, I will smite David *through* to the wall. But David avoided twice out of his presence.

12 And Saul was afraid of David, because the Lord was with him, and was departed from Saul.

13 Therefore Saul put him from him, and made him a captain over a thousand, and he went ¹out and in before the people.

14 And David behaved himself wisely in all his ways: for the Lord *was* with him.

15 Wherefore when Saul saw that he was very wise, he was afraid of him.

16 For all Israel and Judah loved David, because he went out and in before them.

17 ¶ Then Saul said to David, Behold mine eldest daughter Merab, her I will give thee to wife: only be a valiant son unto me, and ¹fight the Lord's battles: for Saul thought, Mine hand shall not be upon him, but the hand of the Philistines shall be upon him.

18 And David answered Saul, What am I? and what is my life, *or* the family of my father in Israel, that I should be son-in-law to the King?

19 Howbeit when Merab Saul's daughter should have been given to David, ¹she was given unto Adriel

---

17:52 ¹ Or, Gath the city.
17:54 ¹ Or house at Bethlehem.
17:55 ¹ That is, of what family and tribe is he? or else he had forgotten David, albeit he had received so great a benefit by him.
18:1 ¹ His affection was fully bent toward him.
18:5 ¹ That is, he prospered in all his doings.
18:6 ¹ To wit, Goliath.
18:7 ¹ Hebrew, *answered, playing.*

18:9 ¹ Because he bare him envy and hatred.
18:10 ¹ That is, spake as a man beside himself: for so the people abused this word, when they could not understand.
18:13 ¹ Meaning, he was captain over the people.
18:17 ¹ Fight against them that war against God's people.
18:19 ¹ By whom he had five sons which David put to death at the request of the Gibeonites, 2 Sam. 21:8.

a Meholathite to wife.

20 ¶ Then Michal Saul's daughter loved David: and they showed Saul, and the thing pleased him.

21 Therefore Saul said, I will give him her, that she may be a [1]snare to him, and that the hand of the Philistines may be against him. Wherefore Saul said to David, Thou shalt this day be my son-in-law in the *one* of the twain.

22 And Saul commanded his servants, Speak with David secretly, and say, Behold, the king hath a favor to thee, and all his servants love thee: be now therefore the King's son-in-law.

23 And Saul's servants spake these words in the ears of David. And David said, [1]Seemeth it to you a light thing to be a king's son-in-law, seeing that I am a poor man and of small reputation?

24 And then Saul's servants brought him word again, saying, Such words spake David.

25 And Saul said, This wise shall ye say to David, The king desireth no dowry, but an hundred foreskins of the Philistines, to be avenged of the King's enemies: for Saul thought to make David fall into the hands of the Philistines.

26 And when his servants told David these words, it pleased David well, to be the [1]King's son-in-law: and the days were not expired.

27 Afterward David arose with his men, and went and slew of the Philistines two hundred men: and David brought their foreskins, and [1]they gave them wholly to the King that he might be the King's son-in-law: therefore Saul gave him Michal his daughter to wife.

28 Then Saul saw, and understood that the Lord *was* with David, and that Michal the daughter of Saul loved him.

29 Then Saul was more and more afraid [1]of David, and Saul became always David's enemy.

30 And when the Princes of the Philistines went forth, at their going forth [1]David behaved himself more wisely than all the servants of Saul, so that his name was much set by.

19

2 Jonathan declareth to David the wicked purpose of Saul.   11 Michal his wife saveth him.   18 David cometh to Samuel.   23 The Spirit of prophecy cometh on Saul.

1 Then Saul spake to Jonathan his son, and to

CHAPTER 19
a Judg. 12:3
1 Sam. 28:21
Ps. 119:109

all his servants, that they should [1]kill David: but Jonathan Saul's son had a great favor to David.

2 And Jonathan told David, saying, Saul my father goeth about to slay thee: now therefore, I pray thee, take heed unto thyself unto the morning, and abide in a secret *place*, and hide thyself.

3 And I will go out and stand by my father in the field where thou [1]art, and will commune with my father of thee, and I will see what *he saith*, and will tell thee.

4 ¶ And Jonathan spake good of David unto Saul his father, and said unto him, Let not the king sin against his servant, against David: for he hath not sinned against thee, but his works have been to thee very good.

5 For he [1]did [a]put his life in danger, and slew the Philistine, and the Lord wrought a great salvation for all Israel: thou sawest it, and thou rejoicedst: wherefore then wilt thou sin against innocent blood, and slay David without a cause?

6 Then Saul hearkened unto the voice of Jonathan, and Saul [1]swore, As the Lord liveth, he shall not die.

7 So Jonathan called David, and Jonathan showed him all those words, and Jonathan brought David to Saul, and he was in his presence as in times past.

8 ¶ Again the war began, and David went out and fought with the Philistines, and slew them with a great slaughter, and they fled from him.

9 ¶ And the evil spirit of the Lord was upon Saul, as he sat in his house having his spear in his hand, and David [1]played with his hand.

10 And Saul intended to smite David to the wall with the spear: but he turned aside out of Saul's presence, and he smote the spear against the wall: but David fled, and escaped the same night.

11 Saul also sent messengers unto David's house, to watch him, and to slay him in the morning: and Michal David's wife told it him, saying, If thou save not thyself this night, tomorrow thou shalt be slain.

12 So Michal [1]let David down through a window: and he went, and fled, and escaped.

13 Then Michal took an image, and laid it in the bed, and put a pillow stuffed with goat's *hair* under

---

18:21 [1] So his hypocrisy appeareth: for under pretence of favor he sought his destruction.

18:23 [1] Meaning, that he was not able to endow his wife with riches.

18:26 [1] Because he thought himself able to compass the King's request.

18:27 [1] Meaning, David and his soldiers.

18:29 [1] To be deprived of his kingdom.

18:30 [1] That is, David had better success against the Philistines than Saul's men.

19:1 [1] Before Saul sought David's life secretly, but now his hypocrisy bursteth to open cruelty.

19:3 [1] That I may give thee warning what to do.

19:5 [1] Hebrew, *he put his soul in his hand.*

19:6 [1] Whatsoever he pretended outwardly, yet his heart was full of malice.

19:9 [1] He played on his harp to mitigate the rage of the evil spirit, as 1 Sam. 16:23.

19:12 [1] Thus God moved both the son and daughter of this tyrant to favor David against their father.

the head of it, and covered it with a cloth.

14 And when Saul sent messengers to take David, she said, He is sick.

15 And Saul sent the messengers again to see David, saying, Bring him to me in the ¹bed, that I may slay him.

16 And when the messengers were come in, behold, an image *was* in the bed with a pillow of goat's *hair* under the head of it.

17 And Saul said unto Michal, Why hast thou mocked me so, and sent away mine enemy, that he is escaped? And Michal answered Saul, He said unto me, Let me go, or else I will kill thee.

18 ¶ So David fled, and escaped, and came to Samuel to Ramah, and told him all that Saul had done to him: and he and Samuel went and dwelt in ¹Naioth.

19 But one told Saul, saying, Behold, David *is* at Naioth in Ramah.

20 And Saul sent messengers to take David, and when they saw a company of Prophets prophesying, and Samuel standing ¹as appointed over them, the Spirit of God fell upon the messengers of Saul, and they also ²prophesied.

21 And when it was told Saul, he sent other messengers, and they prophesied likewise: again Saul sent the third messengers, and they prophesied also.

22 Then went he himself to Ramah, and came to a great well that is in Sechu, and he asked, and said, Where are Samuel and David? And one said, Behold, *they be* at Naioth in Ramah.

23 And he ¹went thither, *even* to Naioth in Ramah, and the Spirit of God came upon him also, and he went prophesying until he came to Naioth in Ramah.

24 And he stripped off his ¹clothes, and he prophesied also before Samuel, and fell ²down naked all that day and all that night: therefore they say, ᵇIs Saul also among the Prophets?

20

2 Jonathan comforteth David.   3 They renew their league.   33 Saul would have killed Jonathan.   38 Jonathan advertiseth David by three arrows, of his father's fury.

1 And David ¹fled from Naioth in Ramah, and

ᵇ 1 Sam. 10:11

CHAPTER 20

ᵃ 1 Sam. 18:3
1 Sam. 23:18

came and said before Jonathan, What have I done? what *is* mine iniquity? and what sin have I committed before thy father, that he seeketh my life?

2 And he said unto him, God forbid, thou shalt not die: behold, my father will do nothing great nor small, but he will ¹show it me: and why should my father hide this thing from me? he will not do it.

3 And David sware again and said, Thy father knoweth that I have found grace in thine eyes: therefore he thinketh, Jonathan shall not know it, lest he be sorry: but indeed, as the Lord liveth, and as thy soul liveth, there is but a ¹step between me and death.

4 Then said Jonathan unto David, Whatsoever thy soul ¹requireth, that I will do unto thee.

5 And David said unto Jonathan, Behold, tomorrow is the ¹first day of the month, and I should sit with the king at meat: but let me go, that I may hide myself in the fields unto the third *day* at even.

6 If thy father make mention of me, then say, David asked leave of me, that he might go to Bethlehem to his own city: for there is a ¹yearly sacrifice for all that family.

7 And if he say thus, It is well, thy servant shall have peace: but if he be angry, be sure that wickedness is concluded of him.

8 So shalt thou show mercy unto thy servant: ᵃfor thou hast joined thy servant into a covenant of the Lord with thee, and if there be in me iniquity, slay thou me? for why shouldest thou bring me to thy father?

9 ¶ And Jonathan answered, God keep that from thee: for if I knew that wickedness were ¹concluded of my father to come upon thee, would not I tell it thee?

10 Then said David to Jonathan, Who ¹shall tell me? how *shall I know*, if thy father answer thee cruelly?

11 And Jonathan said to David, Come and let us go out into the field: and they twain went out into the field.

12 Then Jonathan said to David, O Lord God of Israel, when I have groped my father's mind tomorrow at this time, *or* within this three days, and if it be well with David, and I then send not unto thee, and show it thee,

13 The Lord ¹do so and much more unto Jonathan:

19:15 ¹ Behold, how the tyrants to accomplish their rage, neither regard oath nor friendship, God nor man.

19:18 ¹ Naioth was a school where the word of God was studieth, near to Ramah.

19:20 ¹ Being their chief instructor.
    ² Changed their minds and praised God.

19:23 ¹ With a mind to persecute them.

19:24 ¹ His kingly apparel.
    ² He humbled himself as others did.

20:1 ¹ For Saul was stayed, and prophesied a day and a night by

God's providence, that David might have time to escape.

20:2 ¹ Hebrew, *reveal it in mine ear.*

20:3 ¹ I am in great danger of death.

20:4 ¹ Hebrew, *saith.*

20:5 ¹ At what time there should be a solemn sacrifice, Num. 28:11, to the which they added peace offerings and feasts.

20:6 ¹ Read 1 Sam. 1:21.

20:9 ¹ That he were fully determined.

20:10 ¹ If thy father do favor me.

20:13 ¹ The Lord punish me most grievously.

but if my father have mind to do thee evil, I will show thee also, and send thee away, that thou mayest go in peace: and the Lord be with thee as he hath been with my father.

14 Likewise *I require* not whiles I live: *for I doubt not* but thou wilt show me the mercy of the Lord, [1]*that I die not.*

15 But *I require* that thou cut not off thy mercy from mine house forever: no, not when the Lord hath destroyed the enemies of David, every one from the earth.

16 So Jonathan made a bond with the house of David, *saying*, Let the Lord require it at the hands of David's enemies.

17 And again Jonathan swore unto David, because he loved him (for he loved him as his own soul,)

18 Then said Jonathan to him, Tomorrow is the first day of the month: and thou shalt be [1]looked for, for thy place shall be empty.

19 Therefore thou shalt hide thyself three days, *then* thou shalt go down quickly and come to the place where thou didst hide thyself, when this matter was in hand, and shalt remain by the stone [1]Ezel.

20 And I will shoot three arrows on the side thereof, as though I shot at a mark.

21 And after I will send a boy, *saying*, Go, seek the arrows. If I say unto the boy, See, the arrows are on this side thee, bring them, and come thou: for it is [1]well with thee, and no hurt, *as* the Lord liveth.

22 But if I say thus unto the boy, Behold, the arrows are beyond thee, go thy way: for the [1]Lord hath sent thee away.

23 As touching the thing which thou and I have spoken of, behold, the Lord *be* between thee and me forever.

24 ¶ So David hid himself in the field: and when the first day of the month came, the king sat to eat meat.

25 And the king sat, as at other times upon his seat, even upon his seat by the wall: and Jonathan arose, and Abner sat by Saul's side, but David's place was empty.

26 And Saul said nothing that day: for he thought, Something hath befallen him, though he were [1]clean, *or else* because he was not purified.

27 But on the morrow which was the second day of the month, David's place was empty again: and Saul said unto Jonathan his son, Wherefore cometh not [1]the son of Jesse to meat, neither yesterday nor today?

28 And Jonathan answered unto Saul, David required of me, *that he might go* to Bethlehem.

29 For he said, Let me go, I pray thee: for our family *offereth* [1]a sacrifice in the city, and my brother hath sent for me: therefore now, if I have found favor in thine eyes, let me go, I pray thee, and see my [2]brethren: this is the cause that he cometh not unto the king's table.

30 Then was Saul angry with Jonathan, and said unto him, Thou [1]son of the wicked rebellious woman, do not I know, that thou hast chosen the son of Jesse to thy confusion, and to the confusion *and* shame of thy mother?

31 For as long as the son of Jesse liveth upon the earth, thou shalt not be established, nor thy kingdom: wherefore now send and fet him unto me, for he [1]shall surely die.

32 And Jonathan answered unto Saul his father, and said unto him, Wherefore shall he [1]die? what hath he done?

33 And Saul cast a spear at him to hit him, whereby Jonathan knew, that it was determined of his father to slay David.

34 ¶ So Jonathan arose from the table in a great anger, and did eat no meat the second day of the month: for he was sorry for David, *and* because his father had reviled him.

35 On the next morning therefore Jonathan went out into the field, [1]at the time appointed with David, and a little boy with him.

36 And he said unto his boy, Run now, seek the arrows which I shoot, and as the boy ran, he shot an arrow beyond him.

37 And when the boy was come to the place where the arrow was that Jonathan had shot, Jonathan cried after the boy, and said, Is not the arrow beyond thee?

38 And Jonathan cried after the boy, [1]Make speed, haste *and* stand not still: and Jonathan's boy gathered up the arrows, and came to his master,

39 But the boy knew nothing: only Jonathan and David knew the matter.

40 Then Jonathan gave his [1]bow and arrows unto the boy that was with him, and said unto him, Go,

---

20:14 [1] I know that if thou werest now preferred to the Kingdom, thou wouldest not destroy me, but show thyself friendly to my posterity.
20:18 [1] Or, mentioned.
20:19 [1] Hebrew, *of the way*, because it served as a sign to show the way to them that passed by.
20:21 [1] Hebrew, *peace*.
20:22 [1] The Lord is the author of thy departure.
20:26 [1] Yet he might have some business to let him.
20:27 [1] Thus he speaketh contemptuously of David.

20:29 [1] That is, a peace offering.
   [2] Meaning, all his kinsfolk.
20:30 [1] Thou art ever contrary unto me as thy mother is.
20:31 [1] Hebrew, *son of death*.
20:32 [1] For it were too great tyranny to put one to death and not to show the cause why.
20:35 [1] For this was the third day, as it was agreed upon, verse 5.
20:38 [1] By these words he admonished David what he ought to do.
20:40 [1] Hebrew, *instruments*.

carry them into the city.

41 ¶ As soon as the boy was gone, David arose out of a place that was toward the [1]South, and fell on his face to the ground, and bowed himself three times: and they kissed one another, and wept both twain, till David exceeded.

42 Therefore Jonathan said to David, Go in peace: that which we have [1]sworn both of us in the name of the Lord, saying, The Lord be between me and thee, and between my seed and between thy seed, *let it* stand forever.

43 And he arose and departed, and Jonathan went into the city.

21

1 David fleeth to Nob to Ahimelech the Priest.   6 He getteth of him the showbread to satisfy his hunger.   7 Doeg Saul's servant was present.   10 David fleeth to King Achish,   13 and there feigneth himself mad.

1 Then came David to [1]Nob, to Ahimelech the Priest, and Ahimelech was astonied at the meeting of David, and said unto him, Why art thou alone, and no man with thee?

2 And David said to Ahimelech the Priest, The [1]King hath commanded me a certain thing, and hath said unto me, Let no man know whereabout I send thee, and what I have commanded thee: and I have appointed my servants to such *and* such places.

3 Now therefore if thou hast ought under thine hand, give me five *cakes* of bread, or what cometh to hand.

4 And the Priest answered David, and said, There is no common bread under mine hand, but here is [a]hallowed bread, if the young men have kept themselves, at least from [1]women.

5 David then answered the Priest, and said unto him, Certainly women have been separate from us these two or three days since I came out: and the [1]vessels of the young men were holy, though the way were profane, and how much more then shall *every one* [2]be sanctified this day in the vessel?

6 So the Priest gave him hallowed *bread*: for there was no bread there, save the showbread that was taken from before the Lord, to put hot bread there, the day that it was taken away.

7 (And there was the same day one of the servants

CHAPTER 21
[a] Exod. 25:30
Lev. 24:5
Matt. 12:3,4
[b] 1 Sam. 17:2
[c] 1 Sam. 17:9
[d] 1 Sam. 18:7
1 Sam. 29:5

of Saul [1]abiding before the Lord, named Doeg the Edomite, the [2]chiefest of Saul's herdmen.)

8 And David said unto Ahimelech, Is there not here under thine hand a spear or a sword? for I have neither brought my sword nor mine harness with me, because the king's business required haste.

9 And the Priest said, The sword of Goliath the Philistine, whom thou slewest in the [b]valley of Elah, behold, it is wrapped in a cloth behind the [1]Ephod: if thou wilt take that to thee, take it: for there is none other save that here: And David said, There is none to that, give it me.

10 And David arose and fled the same day from the [1]presence of Saul, and went to Achish the king of Gath.

11 And the servants of Achish said unto him, Is not this David the [c]King of the land? did they not sing unto him in dances, saying, [d]Saul hath slain his thousand, and David his ten thousand?

12 And David [1]considered these words, and was sore afraid of Achish the king of Gath.

13 And he changed his behavior before them, and feigned himself mad in their hands, and [1]scrabbled on the doors of the gate, and let his spittle fall down upon his beard.

14 Then said Achish unto his servants, Lo, ye see the man is beside himself, wherefore have ye brought him to me?

15 Have I need of mad men, that ye have brought this fellow to play the mad man in my presence? [1]shall he come into mine house?

22

1 David hideth himself in a cave.   2 Many that were in trouble came unto him.   9 Doeg accuseth Ahimelech.   18 Saul causeth the Priests to be slain.   20 Abiathar escapeth.

1 David therefore departed thence, and saved himself in the cave [1]of Adullam: and when his brethren and all his father's house heard it, they went down thither to him.

2 And there gathered unto him all men that were in trouble, and all men that were in debt, and all those that were vexed in mind, and he was their [1]prince, and there were with him about four hundred men.

3 ¶ And David went thence to Mizpah in [1]Moab,

20:41 [1] It seemeth that he had shot on the North side of the stone, lest the boy should have espied David.

20:42 [1] Which oath he calleth in the eighth verse, the covenant of the Lord.

21:1 [1] Where the ark then was to ask counsel of the Lord.

21:2 [1] These infirmities that we see in the Saints of God, teach us that none hath his justice in himself, but receiveth it of God's mercy.

21:4 [1] If they have not accompanied with their wives.

21:5 [1] That is, their bodies.

  [2] Shall be more careful to keep his vessel holy, when he shall have

eaten of this holy food?

21:7 [1] Tarrying to worship before the Ark.

  [2] Or, master of them that kept Saul's castle.

21:9 [1] Behind that place, where the high Priest's garment lay.

21:10 [1] That is, out of Saul's dominion.

21:12 [1] Hebrew, *put these words in his heart.*

21:13 [1] By making marks and toys.

21:15 [1] Is he meet to be in a king's house?

22:1 [1] Which was in the tribe of Judah, and near to Bethlehem.

22:2 [1] Or, captain.

22:3 [1] For there was another so called in Judah.

and said unto the King of Moab, I pray thee, let my father and my mother come *and abide* with you, till I know what God will do for me.

4 And he [1]brought them before the King of Moab, and they dwelt with him all the while that David was in [2]the hold.

5 And the Prophet Gad said unto David, Abide not in the hold, *but* depart and go into the land of Judah. Then David departed and came into the forest of Hereth.

6 ¶ And Saul heard that David was [1]discovered, and the men that were with him, and Saul remained in Gibeah under a tree in Ramah, having his spear in his hand, and all his servants stood about him.

7 And Saul said unto his servants that stood about him, Hear now, the sons [1]of Benjamin, will the son of Jesse give every one of you fields and vineyards: will he make you all captains over thousands, and captains over hundreds:

8 That all ye have conspired against me, and there is none that telleth me that my son hath made a covenant with the son of Jesse? and there is none of you that is sorry for me, or showeth me, that my [1]son hath stirred up my servant to lie in wait against me, as *appeareth* this day?

9 ¶ Then answered Doeg the Edomite, (who was appointed over the servants of Saul) and said, I saw the son of Jesse, when he came to Nob, to Ahimelech the son of Ahitub,

10 Who asked counsel of the Lord for him, and gave him victuals, and he gave him also the sword of Goliath the Philistine.

11 Then the King sent to call Ahimelech the Priest the son of Ahitub, and all his father's house, *to wit*, [1]the Priests that were in Nob: and they came all to the King.

12 And Saul said, Hear now thou son of Ahitub. And he answered, Here I am, my lord.

13 Then Saul said unto him, Why have ye conspired against me, thou and the son of Jesse, in that thou hast given him victual, and a sword, and hast asked counsel of God for him, that he should rise against me, and lie in wait as appeareth this day?

14 And Ahimelech answered the King, and said, Who is so faithful among all thy servants as David, *being* also the king's son-in-law, and goeth at thy

commandment, and is honorable in thine house?

15 [1]Have I this day first begun to ask counsel of God for him? be it far from me, let not the king impute anything unto his servant, nor to all the house of my father: for thy servant knew nothing of all this, less nor more.

16 Then the King said, Thou shalt surely die, Ahimelech, thou, and all thy father's house.

17 And the King said unto the [1]sergeants that stood about him, Turn, and slay the Priests of the Lord, because their hand also is with David, and because they knew when he fled, and showed it not unto me. But the servants of the King [2]would not move their hands to fall upon the Priests of the Lord.

18 Then the King said to Doeg, Turn thou and fall upon the Priests. And Doeg the Edomite turned, and ran upon the Priests, and slew that same day fourscore and five persons, that did wear a linen Ephod.

19 Also Nob the city of the Priests smote he with the edge of the sword, both man and woman, both child and suckling, both ox and ass, and sheep with the edge of the sword.

20 But one of the sons of Ahimelech the son of Ahitub (whose name *was* Abiathar) [1]escaped and fled after David.

21 And Abiathar showed David, that Saul had slain the Lord's Priests.

22 And David said unto Abiathar, I knew it the same day, when Doeg the Edomite *was* there, that he would tell Saul. I am the cause *of the death* of all the persons of thy father's house.

23 Abide thou with me, *and* fear not: for [1]he that seeketh my life, shall seek thy life also: for with me thou shalt be in safeguard.

23 *5 David chaseth the Philistines from Keilah.   13 David departeth from Keilah, and remaineth in the wilderness of Ziph.   16 Jonathan comforteth David.   28 Saul's enterprise is broken in pursuing David.*

1 Then they told David, saying, Behold, the Philistines fight against [1]Keilah, and spoil the barns.

2 Therefore David asked counsel of the Lord, saying, Shall I go and smite these Philistines? And the Lord answered David, Go and smite the Philistines, and save Keilah.

22:4 [1] For he feared the rage of Saul against his house.
    [2] That is, in Mizpah, which was a stronghold.
22:6 [1] That a great brute went on him.
22:7 [1] Ye that are of my tribe and lineage.
22:8 [1] Hereby he would persuade them that this conspiracy was most horrible, where the son conspired against the father, and the servant against his master.
22:11 [1] Which were the remnant of the house of Eli, whose house God threatened to punish.

22:15 [1] Have I not at other times also, when he had great affairs, consulted with the Lord for him?
22:17 [1] Or, footmen.
    [2] For they knew that they ought not to obey the wicked commandment of the king in slaying the innocents.
22:20 [1] This was God's providence, who according to his promise preserved some of the house of Eli, 1 Sam. 2:33.
22:23 [1] Or, he that taketh thy life, shall take mine also.
23:1 [1] Which was a city in the tribe of Judah, Josh. 15:44.

3 And David's men said unto him, See, we be afraid here in [1]Judah, how much more if we come to Keilah against the host of the Philistines?

4 Then David asked counsel of the Lord again. And the Lord answered him, and said, Arise, go down to Keilah: for I will deliver the Philistines into thine hand.

5 ¶ So David and his men went to Keilah, and fought with the Philistines, and brought away their cattle, and smote them with a great slaughter: thus David saved the inhabitants of Keilah.

6 (And when Abiathar the son of Ahimelech [a]fled to David to Keilah, he brought an [1]Ephod [2]with him.)

7 ¶ And it was told Saul that David was come to Keilah, and Saul said, God hath delivered him into mine hand: for he is shut in, seeing he is come into a city that hath gates and bars.

8 Then Saul called all the people together to war for to go down to Keilah, and to besiege David and his men.

9 ¶ And David having knowledge that Saul imagined mischief against him, said to Abiathar the Priest, [1]Bring the Ephod.

10 Then said David, O Lord God of Israel, thy servant hath heard, that Saul is about to come to Keilah to destroy the city for my sake.

11 Will the lords of Keilah deliver me up into his hand? and will Saul come down, as thy servant hath heard? O Lord God of Israel, I beseech thee, tell thy servant. And the Lord said, He will come down.

12 Then said David, Will the [1]lords of Keilah deliver me up, and the men that are with me, into the hand of Saul? And the Lord said, They will deliver thee up.

13 ¶ Then David and his men, which were about six hundred, arose and departed out of Keilah, and went [1]whither they could. And it was told Saul, that David was fled from Keilah, and he left off his journey.

14 And David abode in the wilderness in the [1]holds, and remained in a mountain in the wilderness of Ziph. And Saul sought him every day, but God [2]delivered him not into his hand.

CHAPTER 23
[a] 1 Sam. 22:20

15 And David saw that Saul was come out for to seek his life: and David was in the wilderness of Ziph in the wood.

16 ¶ And Jonathan Saul's son arose and went to David into the wood, and comforted [1]him in God,

17 And said unto him, Fear not: for the hand of Saul my father shall not find thee, and thou shalt be [1]king over Israel, and I shall be next unto thee: and also Saul my father knoweth it.

18 So they twain made a covenant before the Lord: and David did remain in the wood: but Jonathan went to his house.

19 ¶ Then came up the Ziphites to Saul to Gibeah, saying, Doth not David hide himself by us in holds, in the wood in the hill of Hachilah, which is on the right side [1]of Jeshimon?

20 Now therefore, O king, come down according to all that thine heart can desire, and our part shall be to deliver him into the King's hands.

21 Then Saul said, [1]Be ye blessed of the Lord: for ye have had compassion on me.

22 Go, I pray you, and prepare ye yet better: know and see his place where he [1]haunteth, and who hath seen him there: for it is said to me, He is subtle, and crafty.

23 See therefore and know all the secret places where he hideth himself, and come ye again to me with the certainty, and I will go with you: and if he be in the [1]land, I will search him out throughout all the thousands of Judah.

24 Then they arose and went to Ziph before Saul, but David and his men were in the wilderness of Maon, in the plain on the right hand of Jeshimon.

25 Saul also and his men went to seek him, and they told David: wherefore he came down unto a rock, and abode in the wilderness of [1]Maon. And when Saul heard that, he followed after David in the wilderness of Maon.

26 And Saul and his men went on the one side of the mountain: and David and his men on the other side of the mountain: and David made haste to get from the presence of Saul: for Saul and his men compassed David and his men round about, to take them.

27 But there came a [1]messenger to Saul, saying,

23:3 [1] That is, in the midst of Judah, much more when we come to the borders against our enemies.
23:6 [1] By God's providence the Ephod was preserved and kept with David the true king.
    [2] Hebrew, in his hand.
23:9 [1] To consult with the Lord by Urim and Thummim.
23:12 [1] Or, governors.
23:13 [1] Or, to and fro, as having no certain place to go.
23:14 [1] Or, strong places.
    [2] No power nor policy can prevail against God's children, but when he appointeth the time.

23:16 [1] Hebrew, his hand.
23:17 [1] Jonathan assureth David, that God will accomplish his promise, and that his father striveth against his own conscience.
23:19 [1] Or, of the wilderness.
23:21 [1] The Lord recompense this friendship.
23:22 [1] Hebrew, where his foot hath been.
23:23 [1] In your country of Ziph, which is in Judah.
23:25 [1] Which was also in the tribe of Judah, Josh. 15:55.
23:27 [1] Thus the Lord can pull back the bridle of the tyrants and deliver his out of the lion's mouth.

Haste thee, and come: for the Philistines have invaded the land.

28 Wherefore Saul returned from pursuing David, and went against the Philistines. Therefore they called that place, ¹Sela Hammahlekoth.

24

1 David hid in a cave spareth Saul.   10 He showeth to Saul his innocency.   18 Saul acknowledgeth his fault.   22 He causeth David to swear unto him to be favorable to his.

1 And David went thence, and dwelt in ¹holds at En Gedi.

2 When Saul was turned from the Philistines, they told him, saying, Behold, David *is* in the wilderness of ¹En Gedi.

3 Then Saul took three thousand chosen men out of all Israel, and went to seek David and his men upon the rocks *among* the wild goats.

4 And he came to the sheepcotes by the way where there was a cave, and Saul went in ¹to do his easement: and David and his men sat in the ²inward parts of the cave.

5 And the men of David said unto him, See, the day is ¹come, whereof the Lord said unto thee, Behold, I will deliver thine enemy into thine hand, and thou shalt do to him as it shall seem good to thee. Then David arose and cut off the lap of Saul's garment privily.

6 And afterward David ¹was touched in his heart, because he had cut off the lap which was on Saul's *garment.*

7 And he said unto his men, The Lord keep me from doing that thing unto my master the Lord's anointed, to lay mine hand upon him: for he is the Anointed of the Lord.

8 So David overcame his servants with these words, and suffered them not to arise against Saul: for Saul rose up out of the cave and went away.

9 ¶ David also arose afterward, and went out of the cave, and cried after Saul, saying, O my lord the King. And when Saul looked behind him, David inclined his face to the earth, and bowed himself.

10 And David said to Saul, ¹Wherefore givest thou an ear to men's words, that say, Behold, David seeketh evil against thee?

11 Behold, this day thine eyes have seen, that the Lord had delivered thee this day into mine hand in the cave, and some bade me kill thee, but I had compassion on thee, and said, I will not lay mine hand on my master: for he is the Lord's Anointed.

12 Moreover my father, behold: behold, I say, the lap of thy garment in mine hand: for when I cut off the lap of thy garment, I killed thee not. Understand and see, that there is neither evil nor wickedness in me, neither have I sinned against thee, yet thou huntest after my soul, to take it.

13 The Lord be judge between thee and me, and the Lord avenge me of thee, and let not mine hand be upon thee.

14 According as the ¹old proverb saith, Wickedness proceedeth from the wicked, but mine hand be not upon thee.

15 After whom is the king of Israel come out? after whom dost thou pursue? after a dead dog, *and* after a flea?

16 The Lord therefore be judge, and judge between thee and me, and see, and plead my cause, and ¹deliver me out of thine hand.

17 When David had made an end of speaking these words to Saul, Saul said, ¹Is this thy voice, my son David? and Saul lift up his voice, and wept,

18 And said to David, Thou art more righteous than I: for thou hast rendered me good, and I have rendered thee evil.

19 And thou hast showed this day, that thou hast dealt well with me: forasmuch as when the Lord had closed me in thine hands, thou killedst me not.

20 For who shall find his enemy, and let him depart ¹free? wherefore the Lord render thee good for that thou hast done unto me this day.

21 For now behold, I ¹know that thou shalt be king, and that the kingdom of Israel shall be stablished in thine hand.

22 Swear now therefore unto me by the Lord, that thou wilt not destroy my seed after me, and that thou wilt not abolish my name out of my father's house.

23 So David swore unto Saul, and Saul went home: but David and his men went up unto the hold.

25

1 Samuel dieth.   3 Nabal and Abigail.   38 The Lord killeth Nabal.   43 Abigail and Ahinoam

---

23:28 ¹ That is, stone of division, because there they divided themselves one from another.

24:1 ¹ That is, in strong places, which were defensed by nature.

24:2 ¹ A city of Judah, Josh. 15:62.

24:4 ¹ Hebrew, *to cover his feet.*
   ² Hebrew, *in the sides.*

24:5 ¹ Here we see how ready we are to hasten God's promise, if the occasion serve never so little.

24:6 ¹ For seeing it was his own private cause, he repented that he had touched his enemy.

24:10 ¹ Contrary to the false report of them that said, David was Saul's enemy, he proveth himself to be his friend.

24:14 ¹ Or, the proverb of an ancient man.

24:16 ¹ Hebrew, *judge.*

24:17 ¹ Though he was a most cruel enemy to David, yet by his great gentleness his conscience compelled him to yield.

24:20 ¹ Hebrew, *a good way.*

24:21 ¹ Though this tyrant saw and confessed the favor of God toward David, yet he ceaseth not to persecute him against his own conscience.

David's wives.   44 Michal is given to Palti.

CHAPTER 25
ᵈ 1 Sam. 28:3

1 Then ªSamuel died, and all Israel assembled, and mourned for him, and buried him in his ¹own house at Ramah. And David arose and went down to the wilderness of Paran.

2 Now in ¹Maon *was* a man, who had his possession in Carmel, and the man *was* exceeding mighty, and had three thousand sheep, and a thousand goats, and he was shearing his sheep in Carmel.

3 The name also of the man *was* Nabal, and the name of his wife Abigail, and she was a woman of singular wisdom, and beautiful, but the man *was* churlish, and evil conditioned, and was of the family of Caleb.

4 And David heard in the wilderness, that Nabal did shear his sheep.

5 Therefore David sent ten young men, and David said unto the young men, Go up to Carmel, and go to Nabal, and ask him in my name ¹how he doeth.

6 And thus shall ye say ¹,²for salutation, Both thou, and thine house, and all that thou hast, be in peace, wealth and prosperity.

7 Behold, I have heard, that thou hast shearers: now thy shepherds were with us, and we did them no hurt, neither did they miss anything all the while they were in Carmel.

8 Ask thy servants, and they will show thee. Wherefore let these young men find favor in thine eyes: (for we come in a good season) give, I pray thee, whatsoever ¹cometh to thine hand unto thy servants, and to thy son David.

9 ¶ And when David's young men came, they told Nabal all those words in the name of David, and held their peace.

10 Then Nabal answered David's servants, and said, Who is David? and who is the ¹son of Jesse? there be many servants nowadays, that break away every man from his master.

11 Shall I then take my bread, and my water, and my flesh that I have killed for my shearers, and give it unto men, whom I know not whence they be?

12 ¶ So David's servants turned their way, and went again, and came and told him all those things.

13 And David said unto his men, Gird every man his sword *about him.* And they girded every man his sword: David also girded his sword. And about four hundred men went up after David, and two hundred abode by the ¹carriage.

14 Now one of the servants told Abigail Nabal's wife, saying, Behold, David sent messengers out of the wilderness to salute our master, and he ¹railed on them.

15 Notwithstanding, the men were very good ¹unto us, and we had no displeasure, neither missed we anything as long as we were conversant with them, when we were in the fields.

16 They were as a wall unto us both by night and by day, all the while we were with them keeping sheep.

17 Now therefore take heed, and see what thou shalt do: for evil ¹will surely come upon our master, and upon all his family: for he is so wicked, that a man cannot speak to him.

18 ¶ Then Abigail made haste, and took two hundred ¹cakes, and two bottles of wine, and five sheep ready dressed, and five measures of parched corn, and an hundred ²frails of raisins, and two hundred of figs, and laid them on asses.

19 Then she said unto her servants, Go ye before me: behold, I will come after you: yet she told not her ¹husband Nabal.

20 And as she rode on her ass, she came down by a secret place of the mountain, and behold, David and his men came down against her, and she met them.

21 And David said, Indeed I have kept all in vain that this fellow had in the wilderness, so that nothing was missed of all that pertained unto him: for he hath requited me evil for good.

22 So and more also do God unto the enemies of David: *for* surely I will not leave of all that he hath by the dawning of the day, *any* that ¹pisseth against the wall.

23 And when Abigail saw David, she hasted and lighted off her ass, and fell before David on her face, and bowed herself to the ground,

24 And fell at his feet, and said, Oh, my lord, *I have committed* the iniquity, and I pray thee, let thine handmaid speak ¹to thee, and hear thou the words of thine handmaid.

25 Let not my lord, I pray thee, regard this wicked man, Nabal: for as his name is, so is he: ¹Nabal *is* his

---

25:1 ¹ That is, among his own kindred.

25:2 ¹ Maon and Carmel were cities in the tribe of Judah. Carmel the mountain was in Galilee.

25:5 ¹ Hebrew, *of peace.*

25:6 ¹ Some read, so mayest thou live in prosperity the next year, both thou, etc.
   ² Hebrew, *for life.*

25:8 ¹ Whatsoever thou hast ready for us.

25:10 ¹ Thus the covetous wretches instead of relieving the necessity of God's children, used to revile their persons and condemn their cause.

25:13 ¹ Hebrew, *vessel.*

25:14 ¹ Hebrew, *drove them away.*

25:15 ¹ When we kept our sheep in the wilderness of Paran.

25:17 ¹ Hebrew, *is accomplished.*

25:18 ¹ Hebrew, *bread.*
   ² Or, clusters.

25:19 ¹ Because she knew his crooked nature, that he would rather have perished, than consented to her enterprise.

25:22 ¹ Meaning by this proverb, that he would destroy both small and great.

25:24 ¹ Hebrew, *in thine ears.*

25:25 ¹ Or, fool.

name, and folly *is* with him: but I thine handmaid saw not the young men of my lord whom thou sentest.

26 Now therefore my lord, as the Lord liveth, and as thy soul liveth (the Lord, *I say*, that hath withholden thee from coming to *shed* blood, and that thine [1]hand should *not* save thee) so now thine enemies shall be as Nabal, and they that intend to do my lord evil.

27 And now this [1]blessing which thine handmaid hath brought unto my lord, let it be given unto the young men, that [2]follow my lord.

28 I pray thee, forgive the trespass of thine handmaid: for the Lord will make my lord a [1]sure house, because my lord fighteth the battles of the Lord, and none evil hath been found in thee [2]in all thy life.

29 Yet [1]a man hath risen up to persecute thee, and to seek thy soul, but the soul of my lord shall be bound in the [2]bundle of life with the Lord thy God: and the soul of thine enemies shall *God* cast out, as out of the middle of a sling.

30 And when the Lord shall have done to my lord all the good that he hath promised thee, and shall have made thee ruler over Israel,

31 Then shall it be no grief unto thee, nor offence of mind unto my lord, that he hath not shed blood causeless, nor that my lord hath [1]*not* preserved himself: and when the Lord shall have dealt well with my lord, remember thine handmaid.

32 Then David said to Abigail, Blessed be the Lord God of Israel, which sent thee this day to meet me.

33 And blessed be thy counsel, and blessed be thou, which hast kept me this day from coming to *shed* blood, [1]and that mine hand hath *not* saved me.

34 For indeed, as the Lord God of Israel liveth, [1]who hath kept me back from hurting thee, except thou hadst hasted and met me, surely there had not been left unto Nabal by the dawning of the day, *any* that pisseth against the wall.

35 Then David received of her hand that which she had brought him, and said to her, Go up in peace to thine house: behold, I have heard thy voice, and have [1]granted thy petition.

36 ¶ So Abigail came to Nabal, and behold, he made a feast in his house, like the feast of a king, and

b Josh. 15:56

c 2 Sam. 3:14,15

CHAPTER 26
a 1 Sam. 23:19

Nabal's heart was merry within him, for he was very drunken: wherefore she told him [1]nothing, neither less nor more, until the morning arose.

37 Then in the morning, when the wine was gone out of Nabal, his wife told him those words, and his heart died within him, and he was like [1]a stone.

38 And about ten days after, the Lord smote Nabal, that he died.

39 ¶ Now when David heard that Nabal was dead, he said, Blessed be the Lord, that hath [1]judged the cause of my rebuke of the hand of Nabal, and hath kept his servant from evil: for the Lord hath recompensed the wickedness of Nabal upon his own head. Also David sent to commune with Abigail, to [2]take her to his wife.

40 And when the servants of David were come to Abigail to Carmel, they spake unto her, saying, David sent us to thee, to take thee to his wife.

41 And she arose, and bowed herself on her face to the earth, and said, Behold, let thine handmaid be a servant to wash the feet of the servants of my lord.

42 And Abigail hasted, and arose, and rode upon an ass, and her five maids [1]followed her, and she went after the messengers of David, and was his wife.

43 David also took Ahinoam of [b]Jezreel, and they were both his wives.

44 Now Saul had given [c]Michal his daughter, David's wife, to Palti the son of Laish, which was of [1]Gallim.

26 *1 David was discovered unto Saul by the Ziphites. 12 David taketh away Saul's spear, and a pot of water that stood at his head. 21 Saul confesseth his sin.*

1 Again the Ziphites came unto Saul to Gibeah, saying, [a]Doth not David hide himself [1]in the hill of Hachilah before [2]Jeshimon?

2 Then Saul arose, and went down to the wilderness of Ziph, having three thousand [1]chosen men of Israel with him, for to seek David in the wilderness of Ziph.

3 And Saul pitched in the hill of Hachilah, which is before Jeshimon by the wayside. Now David abode in the wilderness, and he saw that Saul came after

---

25:26 [1] That is, that thou shouldest not be revenged of thine enemy.
25:27 [1] Or, present.
    [2] Hebrew, *walk at the feet.*
25:28 [1] Confirm his Kingdom to his posterity.
    [2] Hebrew, *from thy days.*
25:29 [1] To wit, Saul.
    [2] God shall preserve thee long in his service, and destroy thine enemies.
25:31 [1] That he hath not avenged himself, which things would have tormented his conscience.
25:33 [1] Read verse 26.
25:34 [1] He attributeth it to the Lord's mercy, and not to himself that

he was stayed.
25:35 [1] Hebrew, *received thy face.*
25:36 [1] For he had no reason either to consider, or to give thanks for this great benefit of deliverance.
25:37 [1] For fear of the great danger.
25:39 [1] Or, revenged.
    [2] For he had experience of her great godliness, wisdom and humility.
25:42 [1] Hebrew, *went at her feet.*
25:44 [1] Which was a place bordering on the country of the Moabites.
26:1 [1] Or, in Gibeah.
    [2] Or, the wilderness.
26:2 [1] That is, of the most skillful and valiant soldiers.

him into the wilderness.

4 (For David had sent out spies, and understood that Saul was come [1]in very deed.)

5 Then David arose, and came to the place where Saul had pitched, and *when* David beheld the place where Saul lay, and [b]Abner the son of Ner which was his chief captain, (for Saul lay in the fort, and the people pitched round about him.)

6 Then spake David, and said to Ahimelech the [1]Hittite, and to Abishai the son of Zeruiah, brother to [2]Joab, saying, Who will go down with me to Saul to the host? Then Abishai said, I will go down with thee.

7 So David and Abishai came down to the people by night: and behold, Saul lay sleeping within the fort, and his spear did stick in the ground at his [1]head: and Abner and the people lay round about him.

8 ¶ Then said Abishai to David, God hath closed thine enemy into thine hand this day: now therefore, I pray thee, let me smite him once with a spear to the earth, and I will not smite him [1]again.

9 And David said to Abishai, Destroy him not: for who can lay his hand [1]on the Lord's anointed, and be guiltless?

10 Moreover David said, As the Lord liveth, either the Lord shall smite him, or his day shall come to die, or he shall descend into battle, and perish.

11 The Lord keep me from laying mine hand upon the Lord's anointed: but, I pray thee, take now the spear that is at his head, and the pot of water, and let us go hence.

12 So David took the spear and the pot of water from Saul's head, and they got them away, and no man saw it, nor marked it, neither did any awake, but they were all asleep: for [1]the Lord had sent a dead sleep upon them.

13 Then David went unto the other side, and stood on the top of an hill a far off, a great space being between them.

14 And David cried to the people, and to Abner the son of Ner, saying, [1]Hearest thou not, Abner? Then Abner answered, and said, Who art thou that cryest to the King?

15 ¶ And David said to Abner, Art not thou a

[b] 1 Sam. 14:50
1 Sam. 17:55

[1]man? and who is like thee in Israel? wherefore then hast thou not kept thy Lord the King? for there came one of the folk in to destroy the king thy lord.

16 This is not well done of thee: as the Lord liveth, ye are [1]worthy to die, because ye have not kept your master the Lord's anointed: and now see where the King's spear is, and the pot of water that was at his head.

17 And Saul knew David's voice, and said, Is this thy voice, [1]my son David? And David said, It is my voice, my lord, O King.

18 And he said, Wherefore doth my lord thus persecute his servant? for what have I done? or what evil is in mine hand?

19 Now therefore, I beseech thee, let my Lord the King hear the words of his servant. If the Lord have stirred thee up against me, [1]let him smell the savor of a sacrifice: but if the children of men *have done it*, cursed be they before the Lord: for they have cast me out this day from abiding in the inheritance of the Lord, saying, Go, serve [2]other gods.

20 Now therefore, let not my blood fall to the earth before the face of the Lord: for the King of Israel is come out to seek a flea, as one would hunt a partridge in the mountains.

21 Then said Saul, I have sinned: Come again, my son David: for I will do thee no more harm, because my soul was [1]precious in thine eyes this day: behold, I have done foolishly, and have erred exceedingly.

22 Then David answered, and said, Behold the King's spear, let one of the young men come over and fet it.

23 And let the Lord reward every man according to his [1]righteousness and faithfulness: for the Lord had delivered thee into *mine* hands this day, but I would not lay mine hand upon the Lord's anointed.

24 And behold, like as thy life was much set by this day in mine eyes: so let my life be set by in the eyes of the Lord, that he may deliver me out of all tribulation.

25 Then Saul said to David, Blessed art thou, my son David: for thou shalt do great things, and also prevail. So David went his way, and Saul returned to his [1]place.

26:4 [1] Or, to a certain place.

26:6 [1] Who was a stranger, and not an Israelite.
  [2] Who afterward was David's chief captain.

26:7 [1] Or, bolster.

26:8 [1] Meaning, he would make him sure at one stroke.

26:9 [1] To wit, in his own private cause: for Jehu slew two Kings at God's appointment, 2 Kings 9:24.

26:12 [1] Hebrew, *the heavy sleep of the Lord was fallen upon them.*

26:14 [1] Hebrew, *Answerest.*

26:15 [1] Esteemed most valiant and meet to save the King?

26:16 [1] Hebrew, *sons of death.*

26:17 [1] Hereby it appeareth, that the hypocrite persecuted David against his own conscience, and contrary to his promise.

26:19 [1] Let his anger toward us be pacified by a sacrifice.
  [2] As much as lay in them, they compelled him to idolatry because they forced him to flee to the idolaters.

26:21 [1] Because thou savedst my life this day.

26:23 [1] Thus he protesteth his innocency toward Saul, not defending his justice in the sight of God, in whose presence none is righteous, Ps 14:3 and 130:3.

26:25 [1] To Gibeah of Benjamin.

27 2 *David fleeth to Achish King of Gath, who giveth him Ziklag.* 8 *David destroyeth certain of the Philistines.* 10 *Achish is deceived by David.*

1 And David said in his heart, I shall now [1]perish one day by the hand of Saul: is it not better for me that I save myself in the land of the Philistines, and that Saul may have no hope of me to seek me anymore in all the coasts of Israel, and *so* escape out of his hand?

2 David therefore arose, and he, and the six hundred men that were with him, went unto Achish the son of Maoch king of Gath.

3 And David [1]dwelt with Achish at Gath, he, and his men, every man with his household, David with his two wives, Ahinoam the Jezreelite, and Abigail Nabal's wife the Carmelite.

4 And it was told Saul that David was fled to Gath: so he sought no more for him.

5 And David said unto Achish, If I have now found grace in thine eyes, [1]let them give me a place in some *other* city of the country, that I may dwell there: for why should thy servant dwell in the *head* city of the kingdom with thee?

6 Then Achish gave him Ziklag that same day: therefore Ziklag pertaineth unto the kings of Judah unto this day.

7 ¶ And [1]the time that David dwelt in the country of the Philistines, was four months and certain days.

8 Then David and his men went up, and invaded the [1]Geshurites, and the Girzites, and the Amalekites: for they inhabited the land from the beginning, *from the way*, as thou goest to Shur, even unto the land of Egypt.

9 And David smote the land, and left neither man nor woman alive, and took sheep, and oxen, and asses, and camels, and apparel, and returned and came to Achish.

10 And Achish said, [1]Where have ye been a roving this day? And David answered, Against the South of Judah, and against the South of the [2]Jerahmeelites, and against the South of the Kenites.

11 And David saved neither man nor woman alive, to bring them to Gath, saying, Lest they should tell on us, and say, So did David, and so *will be* his manner all the while that he dwelleth in the country of the Philistines.

CHAPTER 28
[a] 1 Sam. 25:1

12 And Achish believed David, saying, [1]He hath made his people of Israel utterly to abhor him: therefore he shall be my servant forever.

28 1 *David hath the chief charge promised about Achish.* 8 *Saul consulteth with a witch, and she causeth him to speak with Samuel,* 18 *Who declareth his ruin.*

1 Now at that time the Philistines assembled their bands and army to fight with Israel: therefore Achish said to David, [1]Be sure, thou shalt go out with me to the battle, thou, and thy men.

2 And David said to Achish, Surely thou shalt know what thy servant can do. And Achish said to David, Surely I will make thee keeper of mine head forever.

3 ([a]Samuel was then dead, and all Israel had lamented him, and buried him in Ramah his own city: and Saul had [1]put away the sorcerers, and the Soothsayers out of the land.)

4 Then the Philistines assembled themselves, and came and pitched in Shunem: and Saul assembled all Israel, and they pitched in Gilboa.

5 And when Saul saw the host of the Philistines, he was afraid, and his heart was sore astonied.

6 Therefore Saul asked counsel of the Lord, and the Lord answered him not, neither by dreams, nor by [1]Urim, nor yet by Prophets.

7 ¶ Then said Saul unto his servants, Seek me a woman that hath a familiar spirit, that I may go to her, and ask of her. And his servants said to him, Behold, there is a woman at En Dor that hath a familiar spirit.

8 Then Saul [1]changed himself, and put on other raiment, and he went, and two men with him, and they came to the woman by night: and he said, I pray thee, conjecture unto me by the familiar spirit, and bring me him up whom I shall name unto thee.

9 And the woman said unto him, Behold, thou knowest what Saul hath done, how he hath destroyed the sorcerers, and the soothsayers out of the land: wherefore then seekest thou to take me in a snare to cause me to die?

10 And Saul swore to her by the Lord, saying, As the Lord liveth, no [1]harm shall come to thee for this thing.

11 Then said the woman, Whom shall I bring up

27:1 [1] David distrusteth God's protection, and therefore fleeth unto the idolaters, who were enemies to God's people.
27:3 [1] Thus God by his providence changeth the enemy's hearts, and maketh them to favor his in their necessity.
27:5 [1] Let thine officers appoint me a place.
27:7 [1] Hebrew, *the number of the days*.
27:8 [1] These were the wicked Canaanites, whom God had appointed to be destroyed.
27:10 [1] Or, against whom.
    [2] Which were a family of the tribe of Judah, 1 Chron. 2:9.
27:12 [1] Or, he doth surely abhor his people.
28:1 [1] Albeit it was a great grief to David to fight against the people of God, yet such was his infirmity, he durst not deny him.
28:3 [1] According to the commandment of God, Exod. 22:18 and Deut. 18:10, 11.
28:6 [1] Meaning, the high Priest, Exod. 28:30.
28:8 [1] He seeketh not to God in his misery, but is let by Satan to unlawful means, which in his conscience he condemneth.
28:10 [1] Or, punishment.

unto thee? And he answered, Bring me up ¹Samuel.

12 And when the woman saw Samuel, she cried with a loud voice, and the woman spake to Saul, saying, Why hast thou deceived me? for thou art Saul.

13 And the king said unto her, Be not afraid: for what sawest thou? And the woman said unto Saul, I saw ¹gods ascending up out of the earth.

14 Then he said unto her, What fashion is he of? And she answered, An old man cometh up lapped in a mantel: and Saul knew that it was ¹Samuel, and he inclined his face to the ground, and bowed himself.

15 ¶ And Samuel said to Saul, Why hast thou disquieted me, to bring me up? Then Saul answered, I am in great distress: for the Philistines make war against me, and God is departed from me, and answereth me no more, neither ¹by Prophets, neither by dreams: therefore I have called thee, that thou mayest tell me, what I shall do.

16 Then said Samuel, Wherefore then dost thou ask of me, seeing, the Lord is gone from thee, and is thine enemy?

17 Even the Lord hath done to ¹him, as he spake ᵇby mine ²hand: for the Lord will rent the kingdom out of thine hand, and give it thy neighbor David.

18 Because thou obeyedst not the voice of the Lord, nor executedst his fierce wrath upon the Amalekites, therefore hath the Lord done this unto thee this day.

19 Moreover the Lord will deliver Israel with thee into the hands of the Philistines: ¹and tomorrow shalt thou and thy sons be with me, and the Lord shall give the host of Israel into the hands of the Philistines.

20 Then Saul fell straightway all along on the earth, and was sore ¹afraid because of the words of Samuel, so that there was no strength in him: for he had eaten no bread all the day nor all the night.

21 Then the woman came unto Saul, and saw that he was sore troubled, and said unto him, See, thine handmaid hath obeyed thy voice, and I ¹have put my soul in mine hand, and have obeyed thy words which thou saidest unto me.

22 Now therefore, I pray thee, hearken thou also unto the voice of thine handmaid, and let me set a

ᵇ 1 Sam. 15:28

CHAPTER 29
ᵃ 1 Chron. 12:19
ᵇ 1 Sam. 18:7
1 Sam. 21:11

morsel of bread before thee, that thou mayest eat and get thee strength, and go on thy journey.

23 But he refused and said, I will not eat: but his servants and the woman together compelled him, and he obeyed their voice: so he arose from the earth, and sat on the bed.

24 Now the woman had a fat calf in the house, and she hasted, and killed it, and took flour, and kneaded it, and baked of it ¹unleavened bread.

25 Then she brought them before Saul, and before his servants: and when they had eaten, they stood up, and went away the same night.

29

4 The princes of the Philistines cause David to be sent back from the battle against Israel, because they distrusted him.

1 So the Philistines were gathered together with all their armies in Aphek: and the Israelites pitched ¹by the fountain, which is in Jezreel.

2 And the ¹princes of the Philistines went forth by ²hundreds and thousands, but David and his men came behind with Achish.

3 Then said the Princes of the Philistines, What do these Hebrews here? And Achish said unto the princes of the Philistines, Is not this David the servant of Saul the King of Israel, who hath been with me these days, ¹or these years, and I have found nothing in him, since he ²dwelt with me unto this day?

4 But the princes of the Philistines were wroth with him, and the princes of the Philistines said unto him, ªSend this fellow back, that he may go again to his place which thou hast appointed him, and let him not go down with us to battle, lest that in the battle he be an adversary to us: for wherewith should he obtain the favor of his master? should it not be with the ¹heads of these men?

5 Is not this David, of whom they sang in dances, saying, ᵇSaul slew his thousand, and David his ten thousand?

6 ¶ Then Achish called David, and said unto him, As the Lord liveth, thou hast been upright and good in my sight, when thou ¹wentest out and in with me in the host, neither have I found evil with thee, since thou camest to me unto this day, but ²the princes do

---

28:11 ¹ He speaketh according to his gross ignorance, not considering the state of the Saints after this life, and how Satan hath no power over them.
28:13 ¹ Or, an excellent person.
28:14 ¹ To his imagination, albeit it was Satan, who to blind his eyes took upon him the form of Samuel, as he can do of an Angel of light.
28:15 ¹ Hebrew, *by the hand of Prophets.*
28:17 ¹ That is, to David.
   ² Or, ministry.
28:19 ¹ Ye shall be dead, 1 Sam. 31:6.
28:20 ¹ The wicked when they hear God's judgments, tremble and

despair, but cannot seek for mercy by repentance.
28:21 ¹ I have ventured my life.
28:24 ¹ Because it required haste.
29:1 ¹ Or, in Ain.
29:2 ¹ Or, captains.
   ² According to their bands, or ensigns.
29:3 ¹ Meaning, a long time, that is, four months and certain days, 1 Sam. 27:7.
   ² Hebrew, *fell,* as Gen. 25:18.
29:4 ¹ Would not Saul receive him to favor, if he would betray us?
29:6 ¹ That is, wast conversant with me.
   ² Hebrew, *thou art not good in the eye of the princes.*

not favor thee.

7 Wherefore now return, and go in peace, that thou displease not the princes of the Philistines.

8 ¶ And David said unto Achish, But what have I done? and what hast thou found in thy servant as long as I have been with thee unto this day, that I may ¹not go and fight against the enemies of my Lord the King?

9 Achish then answered and said to David, I know thou pleasest me as an Angel of God: but the princes of the Philistines have said, Let him not go up with us to battle.

10 Wherefore now rise up early in the morning with thy ¹master's servants that are come with thee: and when ye be up early, as soon as ye have light, depart.

11 So David and his men rose up early to depart in the morning, and to return into the land of the Philistines: and the Philistines went up to Jezreel.

30 1 *The Amalekites burn Ziklag.* 5 *David's two wives are taken prisoners.* 6 *The people would stone him.* 8 *He asketh counsel of the Lord, and pursuing his enemies recovereth the prey.* 24 *He divideth it equally,* 26 *And sendeth part to his friends.*

1 But when David and his men were come to Ziklag ¹the third day, the Amalekites had invaded upon the South, even unto Ziklag, and had ²smitten Ziklag, and burnt it with fire,

2 And had taken the women that were therein, prisoners, both small and great, *and* slew not a man, but carried them away, and went their ways.

3 ¶ So David and his men came to the city, and behold, it was burnt with fire, and their ¹wives and their sons, and their daughters were taken prisoners.

4 Then David and the people that were with him, lift up their voices and wept, until they could weep no more.

5 David's two wives were taken prisoners also, Ahinoam the Jezreelite, and Abigail the wife of Nabal the Carmelite.

6 And David was in great sorrow: for the people ¹intended to stone him, because the hearts of all the people were vexed every man for his sons and for his daughters: but David comforted himself in the Lord his God.

7 ¶ And David said to Abiathar the Priest Ahimelech's son, I pray thee, bring me the Ephod. And Abiathar brought the Ephod to David.

8 Then David asked counsel of the Lord, saying, Shall I follow after this company? shall I overtake them? And he answered him, Follow: for thou shalt surely overtake them, and ¹recover all.

9 ¶ So David and the six hundred men that were with him, went, and came to the river Besor, where a part of them abode:

10 But David and four hundred men followed (for two hundred abode behind, being too weary to go over the river Besor.)

11 And they found an Egyptian in the field, and brought him to David, and gave him ¹bread, and he did eat, and they gave him water to drink.

12 Also they gave him a few figs, and two clusters of raisins: and when he had eaten, his spirit came again to him: for he had eaten no bread, nor drunk any water in three days, and three nights.

13 ¶ And David said unto him, To whom belongest thou? and whence art thou? And he said, I am a young man of Egypt, and servant to an Amalekite: and my master left me three days ago because I fell sick.

14 We roved upon the South of Chereth, and upon the *coast* belonging to Judah, and upon the South of Caleb, and we burnt Ziklag with fire.

15 And David said unto him, Canst thou bring me to this company? And he said, ¹Swear unto me by God, that thou will neither kill me, nor deliver me into the hands of my master, and I will bring thee to this company.

16 ¶ And when he had brought him thither, behold, they lay scattered abroad upon all the earth, ¹eating and drinking, and dancing, because of all the great prey that they had taken out of the land of the Philistines, and out of the land of Judah.

17 And David smote them from the twilight even unto the evening ¹of the next morrow, so that there escaped not a man of them, save four hundred young men, which rode upon camels, and fled.

18 And David recovered all that the Amalekites had taken: also David rescued his two wives.

19 And they lacked nothing, small or great, son or daughter, or of the spoil of all that they had taken

---

29:8 ¹ This dissimulation cannot be excused: for it grieved him to go against the people of God.

29:10 ¹ With them that fled unto thee from Saul.

30:1 ¹ After that he departed from Achish.
  ² That is, destroyed the city.

30:3 ¹ For these only remained in the city, when the men were gone to war.

30:6 ¹ Thus we see that in troubles and adversity we do not consider God's providence, but like raging beasts forget both our own duty, and contemn God's appointment over us.

30:8 ¹ Though God seem to leave us for a time, yet if we trust in him,

we shall be sure to find comfort.

30:11 ¹ God by his providence both provided for the necessity of this poor stranger, and made him a guide to David to accomplish his enterprise.

30:15 ¹ For oaths were in all ages had in most reverence, even among the heathen.

30:16 ¹ The wicked in their pomp and pleasures consider not the judgment of God, which is then at hand to smite them.

30:17 ¹ Some read, and unto the morrow of the two *evenings*: that is, three days.

away: David recovered them all.

20 David also took all the sheep, and the oxen, *and* they drove them before his cattle, and said, This is David's [1]prey.

21 ¶ And David came to the two hundred men that were too weary for to follow David: whom they had made also to abide at the river Besor: and they came to meet David, and to meet the people that were with him: so when David came near to the people, he saluted them.

22 Then answered all the evil and wicked of the men that went with David, and said, Because they went not with us, therefore will we give them none of the prey that we have recovered, save to every man his [1]wife and his children: therefore let them carry them away and depart.

23 Then said David, Ye shall not do so, my brethren, with that which the Lord hath given us, who hath preserved us, and delivered the company that came against us, into our hands.

24 For who will obey you in this matter? but as his part *is* that goeth down to the battle, so *shall* his part *be*, that tarrieth by the stuff: they shall part alike.

25 [1]So from that day forward he made it a statute and a law in Israel, until this day.

26 ¶ When David therefore came to Ziklag, he sent of the prey unto the Elders of Judah and to his friends, saying, See *there is* a blessing for you of the spoil of the enemies of the Lord.

27 He sent to them of Bethel, and to them of South Ramoth, and to them of Jattir,

28 And to them of Aroer, and to them of Siphmoth, and to them of Eshtemoa,

29 And to them of Rachal, and to them of the cities of the Jerahmeelites, and to them of the cities of the Kenites,

30 And to them of Hormah, and to them of Chorashan, and to them of Athach,

31 And to them of Hebron, and [1]to all the places where David and his men had haunted.

31

4 Saul killeth himself. 6 His children are slain in the battle. 12 The men of Jabesh took down his body, which was hanged on the wall.

CHAPTER 31
[a] 1 Chron. 10:1
[b] Jer. 34:5
[c] 2 Sam. 2:4

1 Now [a]the Philistines fought against Israel, and the men of Israel fled away from the Philistines, and they fell down [1]wounded in mount Gilboa.

2 And the Philistines pressed sore upon Saul and his sons, and slew Jonathan, and Abinadab, and Malchishua Saul's sons.

3 And when the battle went sore against Saul, the archers and bowmen [1]hit him, and he was sore [2]wounded of the archers.

4 Then said Saul unto his armor bearer, [1]Draw out thy sword, and thrust me through therewith, lest the uncircumcised come and thrust me through and mock me: but his armor bearer would not, for he was sore afraid. Therefore Saul took a sword and fell upon it.

5 And when his armor bearer saw that Saul was dead, he fell likewise upon his sword, and died with him.

6 So Saul died, and his three sons, and his armor bearer, and all his men that same day together.

7 ¶ And when the men of Israel that were on the other side of the [1]valley, and they of the other side [2]Jordan saw that the men of Israel were put to flight, and that Saul and his sons were dead, then they left the cities, and ran away: and the Philistines came and dwelt in them.

8 ¶ And on the morrow when the Philistines were come to spoil them that were slain, they found Saul and his three sons lying in mount Gilboa,

9 And they cut off his head, and stripped him out of his armor, and sent into the land of the Philistines on every side, that they should [1]publish it in the temple of their idols, and among the people.

10 And they laid up his armor in the house of Ashtoreth, but they hanged up his body on the wall of Beth Shan.

11 ¶ When the inhabitants of [1]Jabesh Gilead heard what the Philistines had done to Saul,

12 Then they arose (as many as were strong men) and went all night, and took the body of Saul, and the bodies of his sons, from the wall of Beth Shan, and came to Jabesh, and [b]burnt them there,

13 And took their bones and buried them under a tree at Jabesh, [c]and [1]fasted seven days.

30:20 [1] Which the Amalekites had taken of others, and David from them, besides the goods of Ziklag.
30:22 [1] Under these are comprehended the cattle and goods, which appertained to every man.
30:25 [1] Some refer these words to David, that he alleged an old custom and law, as if it were written, it is both now, and hath been ever.
30:31 [1] Showing himself mindful of their benefits towards him.
31:1 [1] Or, slain.
31:3 [1] Hebrew, *found him.*

[2] Or, afraid.
31:4 [1] So we see that his cruel life hath a desperate end: as is commonly seen in them that persecute the children of God.
31:7 [1] Near to Gilboa.
[2] The Tribes of Reuben and Gad, and half the tribe of Manasseh.
31:9 [1] In token of victory and triumph.
31:11 [1] Whom he had delivered from their enemies, 1 Sam. 11:11.
31:13 [1] According to the custom of mourners.

THE SECOND BOOK

OF

SAMUEL

1

4 It was told David of Saul's death. 15 He causeth him to be slain that brought the tidings. 19 He lamenteth the death of Saul and Jonathan.

1 After the death of Saul, when David was returned from the ᵃslaughter of the Amalekites, and had been two days in Ziklag,

2 Behold, a man came the third day out of the host from Saul with ¹his clothes rent, and earth upon his head: and when he came to David, he fell to the earth, and did obeisance.

3 Then David said unto him, Whence comest thou? And he said unto him, Out of the host of Israel I am escaped.

4 And David said unto him, What is done? I pray thee, tell me. Then he said, that the people is fled from the battle, and many of the people are overthrown, and dead, and also Saul and Jonathan his son are dead.

5 And David said unto the young man that told it him, How knowest thou that Saul and Jonathan his son be dead?

6 Then the young man that told him, answered, ¹As I came to mount Gilboa, behold, Saul leaned upon his spear, and lo, the chariots and ²horsemen followed hard after him.

7 And when he looked back, he saw me, and called me. And I answered, Here am I.

8 And he said unto me, Who art thou? And I answered him, I am an ¹Amalekite.

9 Then said he unto me, I pray thee,¹come upon me, and slay me: for anguish is come upon me, because my ²life is yet whole in me.

10 So ¹I came upon him, and slew him, and because I was sure that he could not live, after that he had fallen, I took the crown that was upon his head, and the bracelet that was on his arm, and brought them

CHAPTER 1
ᵃ 1 Sam. 30:17
ᵇ 2 Sam. 3:31
2 Sam. 13:31
ᶜ Ps. 105:15
ᵈ Josh. 10:13
ᵉ Mic. 1:10

hither unto my lord.

11 Then David took hold on his clothes, ᵇand rent them, and likewise all the men that were with him.

12 And they mourned and wept, and fasted until even, for Saul and for Jonathan his son, and for the people of the Lord, and for the house of Israel, because they were slain with the sword.

13 ¶ ¹Afterward David said unto the young man that told it him, Whence art thou? And he answered, I am the son of a stranger an Amalekite.

14 And David said unto him, ᶜHow wast thou not afraid, to put forth thine hand to destroy the Anointed of the Lord?

15 Then David called one of his young men, and said, Go near, and fall upon him. And he smote him that he died.

16 Then said David unto him, ¹Thy blood be upon thine own head: for thine own mouth hath testified against thee, saying, I have slain the Lord's Anointed.

17 ¶ Then David mourned with this lamentation over Saul, and over Jonathan his son,

18 (Also he bade them teach the children of Judah to ¹shoot, as it is written in the book of ᵈ,²Jasher.)

19 O noble Israel, ¹he is slain upon thy high places: how are the mighty overthrown!

20 ᵉTell it not in Gath, nor publish it in the streets of Ashkelon, lest the daughters of the Philistines rejoice, lest the daughters of the uncircumcised triumph.

21 Ye mountains of Gilboa, upon you *be* neither dew nor rain, nor ¹*be there* fields of offerings: for there the shield of the mighty is cast down, the shield of Saul, as though he had not been anointed with oil.

22 The bow of Jonathan never turned back, neither did the sword of Saul return empty from the blood

---

1:2 ¹ Seeming to lament the overthrow of the people of Israel.
1:6 ¹ As I fled in the chase.
  ² Or, captains.
1:8 ¹ He was an Amalekite born, but renounced his country, and joined with the Israelites.
1:9 ¹ Hebrew, *stand upon.*
  ² I am sorry, because I am yet alive.
1:10 ¹ Hebrew, *I stood upon him.*

1:13 ¹ After the lamentation, he examined him again.
1:16 ¹ Thou art justly punished for thy fault.
1:18 ¹ That they might be able to match their enemies the Philistines in that art.
  ² Or, righteous.
1:19 ¹ Meaning, Saul.
1:21 ¹ Let their fertile fields be barren, and bring forth no fruit to offer to the Lord.

of the slain, and from the fat of the mighty.

23 Saul and Jonathan were lovely and pleasant in their lives, and in their deaths they were not ¹divided: they were swifter than eagles, they were stronger than lions.

24 Ye daughters of Israel, weep for Saul, which clothed you in scarlet, ¹with pleasures, and hanged ornaments of gold upon your apparel.

25 How were the mighty slain in the midst of the battle! O Jonathan, thou wast slain in thine high places.

26 Woe is me for thee, my brother Jonathan: very kind hast thou been unto me: thy love to me was wonderful, passing the love of ¹women: how are the mighty overthrown, and the weapons of war destroyed!

2

1 David is anointed King in Hebron.   9 Abner maketh Ishbosheth King over Israel.   15 The battle of the servants of David and Ishbosheth.   32 The burial of Asahel.

1 After this, David ¹asked counsel of the Lord, saying, Shall I go up into any of the cities of Judah? And the Lord said unto him, Go up. And David said, Whither shall I go? He then answered, Unto ²Hebron.

2 So David went up thither, and his two wives also, Ahinoam the Jezreelitess, and Abigail Nabal's wife the Carmelite.

3 And David brought up the men that were with ¹him, every man with his household, and they dwelt in the cities of Hebron.

4 ¶ Then the men of Judah came, and there they anointed David King over the house of Judah. And they told David, saying, *ᵃthat the men of Jabesh Gilead buried Saul.

5 And David sent messengers unto the men of Jabesh Gilead, and said unto them, Blessed are ye of the Lord, that ye have showed such kindness unto your lord Saul, that you have buried him.

6 Therefore now the Lord show mercy and ¹truth unto you: and I will recompense you this benefit, because ye have done this thing.

7 Therefore now let your hands be strong, and be you valiant: albeit your master Saul be dead, yet nevertheless the house of Judah hath anointed me ¹King over them.

8 ¶ But Abner the son of Ner that was captain

CHAPTER 2
ᵃ 1 Sam. 31:13

of Saul's host, took Ishbosheth the son of Saul, and brought him to Mahanaim,

9 And made him King over Gilead, and over the Ashurites, and over Jezreel, and over Ephraim, and over Benjamin, and over ¹all Israel.

10 Ishbosheth Saul's son was forty years old when he began to reign over Israel, and reigned two years: but the house of Judah followed David.

11 (And the time which David reigned in Hebron over the house of Judah, *was* seven years and six ¹months.)

12 ¶ And Abner the son of Ner, and the servants of Ishbosheth the son of Saul went out of Mahanaim to Gibeon.

13 And Joab the son of Zeruiah, and the servants of David went out and met one another by the pool of Gibeon: and they sat down, the one on the one side of the pool, and the other on the other side of the pool.

14 Then Abner said to Joab, Let the young men now arise, and ¹play before us. And Joab said, Let them arise.

15 Then there arose and went over twelve of Benjamin by number, which pertained to Ishbosheth the son of Saul, and twelve of the servants of David.

16 And every one caught his ¹fellow by the head, and *thrust* his sword in his fellow's side, so they fell down together: wherefore the place was called ²Helkath Hazzurim, which is in Gibeon.

17 And the battle was exceedingly sore that same day: for Abner and the men of Israel ¹fell before the servants of David.

18 And there were three sons of Zeruiah there, Joab, and Abishai, and Asahel. And Asahel was as light on foot as a wild roe.

19 And Asahel followed after Abner, and in going he turned neither to the right hand nor to the left from Abner.

20 Then Abner looked behind him, and said, Art thou Asahel? And he answered, Yea.

21 Then Abner said, Turn thee either to the right hand or to the left, and take thee one of the young men, and take thee his ¹weapons: and Asahel would not depart from him.

22 And Abner said to Asahel, Depart from me: ¹wherefore should I smite thee to the ground? how

---

1:23 ¹ They died both together in Gilboa.
1:24 ¹ As rich garments and costly jewels.
1:26 ¹ Either toward their husbands, or their children.
2:1 ¹ By the means of the high Priest, as 1 Sam. 23:2 and 2 Sam. 5:19.
    ² Which city was also called Kirjath Arba, Josh. 14:15.
2:3 ¹ In the time of his persecution.
2:6 ¹ According to his promise, which is to recompense them that are merciful.
2:7 ¹ So that you shall not want a Captain and a defender.

2:9 ¹ Over the eleven tribes.
2:11 ¹ After this time was expired, he reigned over all the country 33 years, 2 Sam. 5:5.
2:14 ¹ Let us see how they can handle their Weapons.
2:16 ¹ Meaning, his adversary.
    ² Or, the field of strong men.
2:17 ¹ After that these four and twenty were slain.
2:21 ¹ Or, spoil.
2:22 ¹ Why dost thou provoke me to kill thee?

then should I be able to hold up my face to Joab thy brother?

23 And when he would not depart, Abner with the hinder end of the spear smote him under the [1]fifth *rib*, that the spear came out behind him: and he fell down there, and died in his place. And as many as came to the place where Asahel fell down, and died, stood still.

24 Joab also and Abishai pursued after Abner: and the sun went down when they were come to the hill Ammah, that lieth before Giah by the way of the wilderness of Gibeon.

25 And the children of Benjamin gathered themselves together after Abner, and were on an heap, and stood on the top of an hill.

26 Then Abner called to Joab, and said, Shall the [1]sword devour forever? knowest thou not, that it will be bitterness in the latter end? how long then shall it be, or thou bid the people return from following their brethren?

27 And Joab said, As God liveth, if thou hadst not [1]spoken, surely even in the morning the people had departed every one back from his brother.

28 ¶ So Joab blew a trumpet, and all the people stood still, and pursued after Israel no more, neither fought they anymore.

29 And Abner and his men walked all that night through the [1]plain, and went over Jordan, and past through all Bithron till they came [2]to Mahanaim.

30 Joab also returned back from Abner: and when he had gathered all the people together, there lacked of David's servants nineteen men, and Asahel.

31 But the servants of David had smitten of Benjamin, and of Abner's men, *so that* three [1]hundred and threescore men died.

32 And they took up Asahel, and buried him in the sepulcher of his father, which was in Bethlehem: and Joab and his men went all night, and *when they came* to Hebron, the day arose.

3 1 *Long war between the houses of Saul and David.* 2 *The children of David in Hebron.* 12 *Abner turneth to David.* 27 *Joab killeth him.*

1 There was then [1]long war between the house of Saul and the house of David: but David waxed stronger, and the house of Saul waxed weaker.

CHAPTER 3
[a] 1 Sam. 18:25,27

2 ¶ And unto David were children born in Hebron: and his eldest son was Amnon of Ahinoam the Jezreelitess,

3 And his second, *was* [1]Chileab of Abigail the wife of Nabal the Carmelite: and the third, Absalom the son of Maacah the daughter of Talmai the king of Geshur,

4 And the fourth, Adonijah the son of Haggith: and the fifth, Shephatiah the son of Abital:

5 And the sixth, Ithream by Eglah David's wife: these were born to David in [1]Hebron.

6 ¶ Now while there was war between the house of Saul and the house of David, Abner made all his power for the house of Saul.

7 And Saul had a concubine named Rizpah, the daughter of Aiah. And *Ishbosheth* said to Abner, Wherefore hast thou gone in to my father's concubine?

8 Then was Abner very wroth for the words of Ishbosheth, and said, Am I a [1]dog's head, which against Judah do show mercy this day unto the house of Saul thy father, to his brethren, and to his neighbors, and have not delivered thee into the hand of David, that thou chargest me this day with a fault concerning this woman?

9 [1]So do God to Abner, and more also, except, as the Lord hath sworn to David, even so I do to him,

10 To remove the kingdom from the house of Saul, that the throne of David may be established over Israel, and over Judah, even from Dan to Beersheba.

11 And he durst no more answer to Abner: for he feared him.

12 ¶ Then Abner sent messengers to David [1]on his behalf, saying, Whose is the land? who should *also* say, Make covenant with me, and behold, mine hand *shall be* with thee, to bring all Israel unto thee.

13 Who said, Well, I will make a covenant with thee: but one thing I require of thee, that is, that thou see not my face, except thou bring Michal Saul's daughter when thou comest to see me.

14 ¶ Then David sent messengers to Ishbosheth Saul's son, saying, Deliver me my wife Michal, which I married for [a]an hundred foreskins of the Philistines.

15 And Ishbosheth sent, and took her from her

2:23 [1] Some read, in those parts, whereas the lively parts lie: as the heart, the lungs, the liver, the milt, and the gall.
2:26 [1] Shall we not make an end of murdering?
2:27 [1] If thou hadst not provoked them to battle, as verse 14.
2:29 [1] Or, wilderness.
      [2] Or, to the tents.
2:31 [1] Thus God would confirm David in his kingdom by the destruction of his adversaries.
3:1 [1] That is, without intermission enduring two years, which was

the whole reign of Ishbosheth.
3:3 [1] Who is called also Daniel, 1 Chron. 3:1.
3:5 [1] Within seven years and six months.
3:8 [1] Dost thou esteem me no more than a dog, for all my service done to thy father's house?
3:9 [1] We see how the wicked cannot abide to be admonished of their faults, but seek their displeasure, which go about to bring them from their wickedness.
3:12 [1] Or, secretly.

husband *b*Paltiel the son of Laish.

16 And her husband went with her, and came weeping behind her, unto Bahurim: then said Abner unto him, Go, *and* return. So he returned.

17 ¶ And Abner had ¹communication with the Elders of Israel, saying, Ye fought for David in times past, that he might be your King.

18 Now then do it: for the Lord hath spoken of David, saying, By the hand of my servant David I will save my people Israel out of the hands of the Philistines, and out of the hands of all their enemies.

19 Also Abner spake ¹to Benjamin, and afterward Abner went to speak with David in Hebron, *concerning* all that Israel was content with, and the whole ²house of Benjamin.

20 So Abner came to David to Hebron, having twenty men with him, and David made a feast unto Abner, and to the men that were with him.

21 Then Abner said unto David, I will rise up, and go gather all Israel unto my lord the King, that they may make a covenant with thee, *and* that thou mayest reign over all that thine heart desireth. Then David let Abner depart, who went ¹in peace.

22 ¶ And behold, the servants of David and Joab came ¹from the camp, and brought a great prey with them (but Abner was not with David in Hebron: for he had sent him away, and he departed in peace.)

23 When Joab, and all the host that was with him were come, men told Joab, saying, Abner the son of Ner came to the King, and he hath sent him away, and he is gone in peace.

24 Then Joab came to the King, and said, ¹What hast thou done? behold, Abner came unto thee, why hast thou sent him away, and he is departed?

25 Thou knowest Abner the son of Ner: for he came to deceive thee, and to know thy outgoing and ingoing, and to know all that thou doest.

26 ¶ And when Joab was gone out from David, he sent messengers after Abner, which brought him again from the well of Sirah unknowing to David.

27 And when Abner was come again to Hebron, *c*Joab took him aside in the gate to speak with him ¹peaceably, and smote him under the fifth *rib*, that he died, for the blood of *d*Asahel his brother.

28 ¶ And when afterward it came to David's ear,

b 1 Sam. 25:44
c 1 Kings 2:5
d 2 Sam. 2:23

he said, I and my Kingdom are ¹guiltless before the Lord forever, concerning the blood of Abner the son of Ner.

29 Let the blood fall on the head of Joab, and on all his father's house, that the house of Joab be never without some that have running issues, or leper, or that leaneth on a staff, or that doeth fall on the sword, or that lacketh bread.

30 (So Joab and ¹Abishai his brother slew Abner, because he had slain their brother Asahel at Gibeon in battle.)

31 And David said to Joab, and to all the people that were with him, Rent your clothes, and put on sackcloth, and mourn ¹before Abner: and King David himself followed the bier.

32 And when they had buried Abner in Hebron, the King lift up his voice, and wept beside the sepulcher of Abner, and all the people wept.

33 And the King lamented over Abner, and said, Died Abner ¹as a fool dieth?

34 Thine hands were not bound, nor thy feet tied in fetters of brass: *but* as a man falleth before wicked men, *so* didst thou fall. And all the people wept again for him.

35 Afterward all the people came to cause David eat ¹meat while it was yet day, but David swore, saying, So do God to me and more also, if I taste bread, or ought else till the sun be down.

36 And all the people knew it, and it ¹pleased them: as whatsoever the King did, pleased all the people.

37 For all the people and all Israel understood that day, how that it was not the King's deed that Abner the son of Ner was slain.

38 And the King said unto his servants, Know ye not, that there is a prince and a great man fallen this day in Israel?

39 And I am this day weak and *newly* anointed King: and these men the sons of Zeruiah be too ¹hard for me: the Lord reward the doer of evil according to his wickedness.

4

5 Baanah and Rechab slay Ishbosheth the son of Saul.   12 David commandeth them to be slain.

1 And when Saul's ¹son heard that Abner was

3:17 ¹ Rather for malice that he bare toward Ishbosheth, than for love he bare to David.

3:19 ¹ Hebrew, *in the ears of Benjamin.*
    ² Who challenged the Kingdom, because of their father Saul.

3:21 ¹ Or, without harm.

3:22 ¹ From war against the Philistines.

3:24 ¹ Here appeareth the malicious mind of Joab, who would have had the King to slay Abner for his private grudge.

3:27 ¹ Or, secretly.

3:28 ¹ The Lord knoweth that I did not consent to his death.

3:30 ¹ Abishai is said to slay him with Joab, because he consented

to the murder.

3:31 ¹ Meaning before the corpse.

3:33 ¹ He declareth that Abner died not as a wretch or vile person, but as a valiant man might do, being traitorously deceived by the wicked.

3:35 ¹ According to their custom, which was to banquet at burials.

3:36 ¹ It is expedient sometimes not only to conceive inward sorrow, but also that it may appear to others, to the intent that they may be satisfied.

3:39 ¹ Or, cruel.

4:1 ¹ That is, Ishbosheth.

dead in Hebron, then his hands were [2]feeble, and all Israel was afraid,

2   And Saul's son had two men that were captains of bands: the one called Baanah, and the other called Rechab, the sons of Rimmon a Beerothite of the children of Benjamin: (for [1]Beeroth was reckoned to Benjamin,

3   Because the Beerothites fled to [1]Gittaim, and sojourned there, unto this day.)

4   And Jonathan Saul's son had a son that was lame on his feet: he was five years old when the tidings came of Saul and Jonathan out of Israel: then his nurse took him, and fled away. And as she made haste to flee, the child fell, and began to halt, and his name was Mephibosheth.

5   And the sons of Rimmon the Beerothite, Rechab and Baanah went and came in the heat of the day to the house of Ishbosheth (who slept on a bed at noon.)

6   And behold, Rechab and Baanah his brother came into the midst of the house, as they [1]would have wheat, and they [2]smote him under the fifth rib, and fled.

7   For when they came into the house, he slept on his bed in his bed chamber, and they smote him, and slew him, and beheaded him, and took his head, and got them away through the [1]plain all the night.

8   And they brought the head of Ishbosheth unto David to Hebron, and said to the king, Behold the head of Ishbosheth Saul's son thine enemy, who sought after thy life: and the Lord hath avenged my Lord the King this day of Saul, and of his seed.

9   Then David answered Rechab and Baanah his brother, the sons of Rimmon the Beerothite, and said unto them, As the Lord liveth, who hath delivered my soul out of all adversity,

10   When one [a]told me, and said that Saul was dead, (thinking to have brought good tidings) I took him and slew him in Ziklag, who thought that I would have given him a reward for his tidings:

11   How [1]much more when wicked men have slain a righteous person in his own house, and upon his bed? shall I not now therefore require his blood at your hand, and take you from the earth?

12   Then David commanded his young men, and

CHAPTER 4
[a] 2 Sam. 1:15
[b] 2 Sam. 3:32

CHAPTER 5
[a] 1 Chron. 11:1
[b] Ps. 78:71
[c] 2 Sam. 2:11
[d] 2 Chron. 11:6

they slew them, and cut off their hands and their feet, and hanged them up over the pool in Hebron: but they took the head of Ishbosheth, and buried it in the sepulcher of [b]Abner in Hebron.

5

3 David is made King over all Israel.   7 He taketh the fort of Zion.   19 He asketh counsel of the Lord.   23 And overcometh the Philistines twice.

1   Then [a]came all the tribes of Israel to David unto Hebron, and said thus, Behold, we are thy [1]bones and thy flesh.

2   And in time past when Saul was our King, thou leddest Israel in and out: and the Lord hath said to thee, [b]Thou shalt feed my people Israel, and thou shalt be a captain over Israel.

3   So all the Elders of Israel came to the king to Hebron: and King David made a covenant with them in Hebron [1]before the Lord, and they anointed David King over Israel.

4   ¶ David was thirty years old when he began to reign: and he reigned forty years.

5   In Hebron he reigned over Judah [c]seven years, and six months: and in Jerusalem he reigned thirty and three years over all Israel and Judah.

6   ¶ The King also and his men went to Jerusalem unto the Jebusites, the inhabitants of the land: who spake unto David, saying, Except thou take away the [1]blind and the lame, thou shalt not come in hither: thinking that David could not come thither:

7   But David took the fort of Zion: this is the city of David.

8   Now David had said the same day, Whosoever smiteth the Jebusites, and getteth up to the gutters and smiteth the lame and blind, which David's soul hateth, I will prefer him: [d]therefore they said, The blind and the lame shall not [1]come into that house.

9   So David dwelt in that fort, and called it the city of David, and David built round about it, from [1]Millo, and inward.

10   And David prospered and grew: for the Lord God of hosts was with him.

11   ¶ Hiram also king of [1]Tyre sent messengers to David, and cedar trees, and carpenters, and masons for walls: and they built David an house.

12   Then David knew that the Lord had established

---

[2] Meaning, that he was discouraged.

4:2 [1] This city Beeroth was in the tribe of Benjamin, Josh. 18:25.
4:3 [1] After the death of Saul, for fear of the Philistines.
4:6 [1] They disguised themselves as merchants, which came to buy wheat.
   [2] There is nothing so vile and dangerous, which the wicked will not enterprise in hope of lucre and favor.
4:7 [1] Or, wilderness.
4:11 [1] Forasmuch as neither the example of him that slew Saul, nor duty to their master, nor the innocency of the person, nor reverence of the place, nor time did move them, they deserved most grievous

punishment.

5:1 [1] We are of thy kindred, and most near joined unto thee.
5:3 [1] That is, taking the Lord to witness: for the Ark was as yet in Abinadab's house.
5:6 [1] The children of God called idols blind and lame guides: therefore the Jebusites meant that they should prove that their gods were neither blind nor lame.
5:8 [1] The idols should enter no more into that place.
5:9 [1] He built from the town house round about to his own house, 1 Chron. 11:8.
5:11 [1] Hebrew, Zor.

him King over Israel, and that he had exalted his kingdom for his people Israel's sake.

13 And David took him more [e]concubines and wives out of Jerusalem, after he was come from Hebron, and more sons and daughters were born to David.

14 [f]And these be the names of the sons, that were born unto him in Jerusalem, Shammua, and Shobab, and Nathan, and Solomon,

15 And Ibhar, and Elishua, and Nepheg, and Japhia,

16 And Elishama, and Eliada, and Eliphelet.

17 ¶ [g]But when the Philistines heard that they had anointed David king over Israel, all the Philistines came up to seek David: and when David heard, he went down to a fort.

18 But the Philistines came, and spread themselves in the valley of Rephaim.

19 Then David [1]asked counsel of the Lord, saying, Shall I go up to the Philistines? wilt thou deliver them into mine hands? And the Lord answered David, Go up: for I will doubtless deliver the Philistines into thine hands.

20 ¶ [h]Then David came to Baal Perazim, and smote them there, and said, The Lord hath divided mine enemies asunder before me, as waters be divided asunder: therefore he called the name of that place, [1]Baal Perazim.

21 And there they left their images, and David and his men [i]burnt them.

22 Again the Philistines came up, and spread themselves in the valley of [1]Rephaim.

23 And when David asked counsel of the Lord, he answered, Thou shalt not go up, *but* turn about behind them, and come upon them over against the mulberry trees.

24 And when thou hearest the noise of one going in the tops of the mulberry trees, then remove: for then shall the Lord go out before thee to smite the host of the Philistines.

25 Then David did so as the Lord had commanded him, and smote the Philistines from Geba, until thou come to [1]Gezer.

6

3 The Ark is brought forth of the house of Abinadab. 7 Uzzah is stricken, and dieth. 14 David danceth before it, 16 and is therefore despised of his wife Michal.

1 Again David gathered together all the [1]chosen men of Israel, *even* thirty thousand

2 [a]And David arose, and went with all the people that were with him from [1]Baale of Judah, to bring up from thence the Ark of God, whose Name is called by the Name of the Lord of hosts, that dwelleth upon it between the Cherubims.

3 And they put the Ark of God upon a new cart, and brought it out of the house of Abinadab, that was in [1]Gibeah. And Uzzah and Ahio the sons of Abinadab did drive the new cart.

4 And when they brought the Ark of God out of the house of [b]Abinadab, that was at Gibeah, Ahio went before the Ark.

5 And David and all the house of Israel [1]played before the Lord on all *instruments* made of fir, and on harps, and on Psalteries, and on timbrels, and on cornets, and on cymbals.

6 ¶ [c]And when they came to Nachon's threshing floor, Uzzah put his hand to the Ark of God, and held it: for the oxen did shake it.

7 And the Lord was very wroth with Uzzah, and God [1]smote him in the same place for his fault, and there he died by the Ark of God.

8 And David was displeased because the Lord had [1]smitten Uzzah: and he called the name of the place [2]Perez Uzzah until this day.

9 Therefore David that day feared the Lord, and said, How shall the Ark of the Lord come to me?

10 So David would not bring the Ark of the Lord unto him into the city of David, but David carried it into the house of Obed-Edom [1]a Gittite.

11 And the Ark of the Lord continued in the house of Obed-Edom the Gittite, three months, and the Lord blessed Obed-Edom, and all his household.

12 And one told King David, saying, [d]The Lord hath blessed the house of Obed-Edom, and all that he hath, because of the Ark of God: therefore David went and [1]brought the Ark of God from the house of Obed-Edom, into the city of David with gladness.

13 And when they that bare the Ark of the Lord had gone six paces, he offered an ox, and a fat beast.

14 And David danced before the Lord with all his might, and was girded with a linen [1]Ephod.

15 So David and all the house of Israel brought

[e] 1 Chron. 3:9
[f] 1 Chron. 3:5
[g] 1 Chron. 14:8; 1 Chron. 11:16
[h] Isa. 28:20
[i] 1 Chron. 14:12

CHAPTER 6
[a] 1 Chron. 13:5,6
[b] 1 Sam. 7:1
[c] 1 Chron. 13:10
[d] 1 Chron. 15:25

5:19 [1] By Abiathar the Priest.
5:20 [1] Or, the plain of divisions.
5:22 [1] Meaning, the valley of giants, which David called Baal Perazim, because of his victory.
5:25 [1] Which was in the tribe of Benjamin, but the Philistines did possess it.
6:1 [1] Or, chief.
6:2 [1] This was a city in Judah called also Kirjath Jearim, Josh. 15:9.
6:3 [1] Which was an high place of the city of Baal.
6:5 [1] Praised God, and sang Psalms.
6:7 [1] Here we see what danger it is to follow good intentions, or to do anything in God's service without his express word.
6:8 [1] Hebrew, *made a breach.*
[2] Or, the division of Uzzah.
6:10 [1] Who was a Levite, and had dwelt in Gittaim, 1 Chron. 15:25.
6:12 [1] Meaning, he caused the Levites to bear it, according to the Law.
6:14 [1] With a garment like to the Priest's garment.

the Ark of the Lord with shouting, and sound of trumpet.

16 And as the Ark of the Lord came into the city of David, Michal Saul's daughter looked through a window, and saw King David leap, and dance before the Lord, and she ¹despised him in her heart.

17 And when they had brought in the Ark of the Lord, they set it in his place, in the midst of the Tabernacle that David had pitched for it: then David offered burnt offerings, and peace offerings before the Lord.

18 And as soon as David had made an end of offering burnt offerings and peace offerings, he ᶜblessed the people in the Name of the Lord of hosts,

19 And gave among all the people, *even* among the whole multitude of Israel, as well to the women as men, to every one a cake of bread, and a piece of flesh, and a bottle *of wine*: so all the people departed every one to his house.

20 ¶ Then David returned to ¹bless his house, and Michal the daughter of Saul came out to meet David, and said, O how glorious was the King of Israel this day, which was uncovered today in the eyes of the maidens of his servants, as a ²fool uncovereth himself!

21 Then David said unto Michal, ¹*It was* before the Lord, which chose me rather than thy father, and all his house, and commanded me to be ruler over the people of the Lord, *even* over Israel: and therefore will I play before the Lord,

22 And will yet be more vile than thus, and will be low in mine own sight, and of the very same maidservants, which thou hast spoken of, shall I be had in honor.

23 Therefore Michal the daughter of Saul had ¹no child unto the day of her death.

7 2 David would build God an house, but is forbidden by the Prophet Nathan. 8 God putteth David in mind of his benefits. 12 He promiseth continuance of his kingdom and posterity.

1 Afterward ᵃwhen the King sat in his house, and the Lord had given him rest round about from all his enemies,

2 The King said unto Nathan the Prophet, Behold, now I dwell in an house of cedar trees, and the Ark of God remaineth within the ¹curtains.

Side references:
ᶜ 1 Chron. 16:2
CHAPTER 7
ᵃ 1 Chron. 17:2
ᵇ 1 Sam. 16:12
Ps. 78:70
ᶜ 1 Kings 8:20
ᵈ 1 Kings 5:5
1 Kings 6:12
1 Chron. 22:10
ᵉ Heb. 1:5
ᶠ Ps. 89:31,32

3 Then Nathan said unto the king, Go, and do all that is in thine heart: for the Lord *is* with thee.

4 ¶ And the same night the word of the Lord came unto Nathan, saying,

5 Go and tell my servant David, Thus saith the Lord, ¹Shalt thou build me an house for my dwelling?

6 For I have dwelt in no house since the time that I brought the children of Israel out of Egypt unto this day, but have walked in a tent and Tabernacle.

7 In all the *places* wherein I have walked with all the children of Israel, spake I one ¹word with any of the tribes of Israel when I commanded *the Judges* to feed my people Israel? or said I, Why build ye not me an house of cedar trees?

8 Now therefore so say unto my servant David, Thus saith the Lord of hosts, ᵇI took thee from the sheepcote following the sheep, that thou mightest be ruler over my people, over Israel.

9 And I was with thee wheresoever thou hast walked, and have destroyed all thine enemies out of thy sight, and have made thee a ¹great name, like unto the name of the great men that are in the earth.

10 (Also I will appoint a place for my people Israel, and will plant it, that they may dwell in a place of their own, and move ¹no more, neither shall wicked people trouble them anymore as beforetime,

11 And since the time that I set Judges over my people of Israel) and I will give thee rest from all thine enemies: also the Lord telleth thee, that he will make thee an house.

12 ᶜAnd when thy days be fulfilled, thou shalt sleep with thy fathers, and I will set up thy seed after thee, which shall proceed out of thy body, and will establish his kingdom.

13 ᵈHe shall build an house for my Name, and I will establish the throne of his kingdom forever.

14 ᵉI will be his father, and he shall be my son: and if he ᶠsin, I will chasten him with the ¹rod of men, and with the plagues of the children of men.

15 But my mercy shall not depart away from him, as I took it from Saul whom I have put away before thee.

16 And thine house shall be established and thy kingdom forever before thee, *even* thy throne shall be ¹established forever.

6:16 ¹ The worldlings are not able to comprehend the emotions that move the children of God to praise God by all manner of means.
6:20 ¹ That is, to pray for his house, as he had done for the people. ² Or, vain man.
6:21 ¹ It was for no worldly affection, but only for that zeal that I bare to God's glory.
6:23 ¹ Which was a punishment because she mocked the servant of God.
7:2 ¹ Within the Tabernacle covered with skins, Exod. 26:7.
7:5 ¹ Meaning, he should not: yet Nathan speaking according

to man's judgment and not by the spirit of prophecy, permitted him.
7:7 ¹ As concerning building of an house: meaning, that without God's express word, nothing ought to be attempted.
7:9 ¹ I have made thee famous through all the world.
7:10 ¹ He promiseth them quietness, if they will walk in his fear and obedience.
7:14 ¹ That is, gently, as fathers used to chastise their children.
7:16 ¹ This was begun in Solomon, as a figure, but accomplished in Christ.

17 According to all these words, and according to all this vision, Nathan spake thus unto David.

18 ¶ Then King David went in, and sat before the Lord, and said, Who am I, O Lord God, and what is mine house, that thou hast brought me hitherto?

19 And this was yet a small thing in thy sight, O Lord God, therefore thou hast spoken also of thy servant's house for a great while: but [1]doth this appertain to [2]man, O Lord God?

20 And what can David say more unto thee? for thou, Lord God, knowest thy servant.

21 For thy word's sake, and according to thine own heart hast thou done all these great things, to make them known unto thy servant.

22 Wherefore thou art great, O Lord God: for there is none like thee, neither is there any God besides thee, according to all that we have heard with our ears.

23 [g]And what one people in the earth is like thy people, like Israel? whose God went and redeemed them to himself, that they might be his people, and that he might make him a name, and do for [1]you great things, and terrible for [2]thy land, O Lord, *even* for thy people, whom thou redeemedst to thee out of Egypt, *from* the [3]nations, and their gods?

24 For thou hast [1]ordained to thyself thy people Israel to be thy people forever: and thou Lord art become their God.

25 Now therefore, O Lord God, confirm forever the word that thou hast spoken concerning thy servant and his house, and do as thou hast said.

26 And let thy Name be magnified forever by them that shall say, The Lord of hosts *is* the God over Israel, and let the [1]house of thy servant David be established before thee.

27 For thou, O Lord of hosts, God of Israel, hast revealed unto thy servant, saying, I will build thee an house: therefore hath thy servant [1]been bold to pray this prayer unto thee.

28 Therefore now, O Lord God, (*for thou art* God, and thy words be true, and thou hast told this goodness unto thy servant.)

29 Therefore now let it please thee to bless the house of thy servant, that it may continue forever before thee: for thou, O Lord God, hast [1]spoken it: and let the house of thy servant be blessed forever with thy blessing.

g Deut. 4:7

CHAPTER 8
a 1 Chron. 18:1
Ps. 60:2

8

1 David overcometh the Philistines, and other strange nations, and maketh them tributaries to Israel.

1 After [a]this now, David smote the Philistines and subdued them, and David took [1]the bridle of bondage out of the [2]hand of the Philistines.

2 And he smote Moab, and measured them with a cord, and cast them down to the ground: he measured them with [1]two cords to put them to death, and with one full cord to keep them alive: so became the Moabites David's servants, and brought gifts.

3 ¶ David smote also Hadadezer the son of Rehob king of Zobah, as he went to [1]recover his border at the river [2]Euphrates.

4 And David took of them a thousand and seven hundred horsemen, and twenty thousand footmen, and David [1]destroyed all the chariots, but he reserved an hundred chariots of them.

5 ¶ Then came the [1]Aramites of [2]Dammesek to succor Hadadezer king of Zobah, but David slew of the Aramites two and twenty thousand men.

6 And David put a garrison in [1]Aram of Dammesek: and the Aramites became servants to David, [2]and brought gifts. And the Lord saved David wheresoever he went.

7 And David took the shields of gold that belonged to the servants of Hadadezer, and brought them to [1]Jerusalem.

8 And out of Betah, and Berothai (cities of Hadadezer) king David brought exceedingly much brass.

9 ¶ Then Toi king of [1]Hamath heard how David had smitten all the host of Hadadezer,

10 Therefore Toi sent Joram his son unto king David, [1]to salute him, and to [2,3]rejoice with him, because he had fought against Hadadezer, and beaten him (for Hadadezer had war with Toi) who [4]brought with him vessels of silver, and vessels of

---

7:19 [1] Hebrew, *is this the law of man?*
  [2] Cometh not this rather of thy free mercy, than of any worthiness that can be in man?
7:23 [1] O Israel.
  [2] And inheritance, which is Israel.
  [3] From the Egyptians and their idols.
7:24 [1] He showeth that God's free election is the only cause, why the Israelites were chosen to be his people.
7:26 [1] This prayer is most effectual, when we chiefly seek God's glory, and the accomplishment of his promise.
7:27 [1] Hebrew, *found his heart disposed.*
7:29 [1] Therefore I firmly believe it shall come to pass.
8:1 [1] Or, Metheg Ammah.
  [2] So that they paid no more tribute.

8:2 [1] He slew two parts as it pleased him, and reserved the third.
8:3 [1] Or, enlarge.
  [2] Hebrew, *Perath.*
8:4 [1] Or, bought the horses of the chariots.
8:5 [1] Or, the Syrians.
  [2] Or, of Damascus, that is, which dwelt near Damascus.
8:6 [1] In that part of Syria, where Damascus was.
  [2] They paid yearly tribute.
8:7 [1] For the use of the Temple.
8:9 [1] Or, Antiochia.
8:10 [1] Hebrew, *to ask peace.*
  [2] Hebrew, *bless him.*
  [3] For seeing David victorious, he was glad to entreat of peace.
  [4] Hebrew, *in his hand.*

gold, and vessels of brass.

11 And king David dedicated them unto the Lord with the silver and gold that he had dedicated of all the nations, which he had subdued:

12 Of ¹Aram, and of Moab, and of the children of Ammon, and of the Philistines, and of Amalek, and of the spoil of Hadadezer the son of Rehob king of Zobah.

13 So David got a name after that he returned, and had slain of the Aramites in the ¹valley of salt eighteen thousand men.

14 And he put a garrison in Edom: throughout all Edom put he soldiers, and all they of Edom became David's servants: and the Lord kept David ¹whithersoever he went.

15 Thus David reigned over all Israel, and executed ¹judgment and justice unto all his people.

16 And Joab the son of Zeruiah *was* over the host, and Jehoshaphat the son of Ahilud was ¹Recorder.

17 And Zadok the son of Ahitub, and Ahimelech the son of Abiathar *were* the Priests, and Seraiah the Scribe.

18 And Benaiah the son of Jehoiada ¹and the ²Cherethites and the Pelethites, and David's sons were chief rulers.

9 *9 David restoreth all the lands of Saul's to Mephibosheth the son of Jonathan. 10 He appointeth Ziba to see to the profit of his lands.*

1 And David said, Is there yet any man left of the house of Saul, that I may show him mercy for ¹Jonathan's sake?

2 And there was of the household of Saul a servant whose name was Ziba, and when they had called him unto David, the king said unto him, Art thou Ziba? And he said, I thy servant *am he.*

3 Then the King said, Remaineth there yet none of the house of Saul, on whom I may show the ¹mercy of God? Ziba then answered the King, Jonathan hath yet a son ªlame of his feet.

4 Then the King said unto him, Where is he? And Ziba said unto the king, Behold, he is in the house of Machir the son of Ammiel of Lo Debar.

5 ¶ Then king David sent, and took him out

CHAPTER 9
ª 2 Sam. 4:4

CHAPTER 10
ª 1 Chron. 19:2

of the house of Machir the son of ¹Ammiel of Lo Debar.

6 Now when Mephibosheth the son of Jonathan the son of Saul was come unto David, he fell on his face, and did reverence. And David said, Mephibosheth? And he answered, Behold thy servant.

7 Then David said unto him, Fear not: for I will surely show thee kindness for Jonathan thy father's sake, and will restore thee all the ¹fields of Saul thy father, and thou shalt eat bread at my table continually.

8 And he bowed himself, and said, What is thy servant, that thou shouldest look upon such a ¹dead dog as I am?

9 Then the king called Ziba Saul's servant, and said unto him, I have given unto thy master's ¹son all that pertained to Saul and to all his house.

10 Thou therefore and ¹thy sons and thy servants shall till the land for him, and bring in that thy master's son may have food to eat. And Mephibosheth thy master's son shall eat bread always at my table (now Ziba had fifteen sons, and twenty servants.)

11 Then said Ziba unto the king, According to all that my lord the king hath commanded his servant, so shall thy servant do, ¹that Mephibosheth may eat at my table, as one of the king's sons.

12 Mephibosheth also had a young son named Micha, and all that dwelled in the house of Ziba, *were* servants unto Mephibosheth.

13 And Mephibosheth dwelt in Jerusalem: for he did eat continually at the king's table, and was lame on both his feet.

10 *4 The messengers of David are villainously entreated of the king of Ammon. 7 Joab is sent against the Ammonites.*

1 After this, the ªKing of the children of Ammon died, and Hanun his son reigned in his stead.

2 Then said David, I will show kindness unto Hanun the son of Nahash, as his father ¹showed kindness unto me. And David sent his servants to comfort him for his father. So David's servants came into the land of the children of Ammon.

3 And the princes of the children of Ammon said

8:12 ¹ Or, Syria, or Cœlosyria.
8:13 ¹ Or, in Gemelah.
8:14 ¹ Or, in all his enterprises.
8:15 ¹ He gave judgment in controversies, and was merciful toward the people.
8:16 ¹ Or, writer of Chronicles.
8:18 ¹ Or, was over the Cherethites.
 ² The Cherethites and Pelethites were as the king's guard, and had charge of his person.
9:1 ¹ Because of mine oath and promise made to Jonathan, 1 Sam. 10:15.
9:3 ¹ Such mercy as shall be acceptable to God.
9:5 ¹ Who was also called Eliam the father of Bathsheba David's wife.
9:7 ¹ Or, lands.
9:8 ¹ Meaning, a despised person.
9:9 ¹ Or, nephew.
9:10 ¹ Be ye provident overseers and governors of his lands, that they may be profitable.
9:11 ¹ That Mephibosheth may have all things at commandment, as becometh a king's son.
10:2 ¹ The children of God are not unmindful of a benefit received.

unto Hanun their lord, [1]Thinkest thou that David doth honor thy father, that he hath sent comforters to thee? hath not David *rather* sent his servants unto thee, [2]to search the city, and to spy it out, and to overthrow it?

4 Wherefore Hanun took David's servants, and shaved off the half of their beard, and cut off their garments in the middle, even to their buttocks, and sent them away.

5 ¶ When it was told unto David, he sent to meet them (for the men were exceedingly ashamed) and the king said, Tarry at Jericho, until your beards be grown, then return.

6 ¶ And when the children of Ammon saw that they [1]stank in the sight of David, the children of Ammon sent and hired the [2]Aramites of the house of Rehob, and the Aramites of Zoba, twenty thousand footmen, and of king Maacah a thousand men, and of Ish-Tob twelve thousand men.

7 And when David heard of it, he sent Joab, and all the host of the strong men.

8 And the children of Ammon came out and put their army in array at the entering in of the gate: and the Aramites of [1]Zoba, and of Rehob, and of Ish-Tob, and of Maacah *were* by themselves in the field.

9 When Joab saw that the front of the battle was against him before and behind, he chose of all the choice of Israel, and put them in array against the Aramites.

10 And the rest of the people, he delivered into the hand of Abishai his brother, that he might put them in array against the children of Ammon.

11 And he said, If the Aramites be stronger than I, thou shalt help me, and if the children of Ammon be too strong for thee, I will come and succor thee.

12 Be strong and let us be valiant for [1]our people, and for the cities of our God, and let the Lord do that which is good in his eyes.

13 Then Joab, and the people that was with him, joined in battle with the Aramites, who fled before him.

14 And when the children of Ammon saw that the Aramites fled, they fled also before Abishai, and entered into the city. So Joab returned from the children of Ammon, and came to Jerusalem.

CHAPTER 11
[a] 1 Chron. 20:1
[b] Lev. 15:1,9
Lev. 18:19

15 ¶ And when the Aramites saw that they were smitten before Israel, they gathered them together.

16 And [1]Hadarezer sent, and brought out the Aramites that were beyond the [2]River: and they came to Helam, and Shobach the captain of the host of Hadadezer *went* before them.

17 When it was showed David, then he gathered [1]all Israel together, and passed over Jordan, and came to Helam: and the Aramites set themselves in array against David, and fought with him:

18 And the Aramites fled before Israel: and David destroyed [1]seven hundred chariots of the Aramites, and forty thousand horsemen, and smote Shobach the captain of his host, who died there.

19 And when all the kings, *that were* servants to Hadadezer, saw that they fell before Israel, they made peace with Israel, and served them. and the Aramites feared to help the children of Ammon anymore.

11

1 *The city Rabbah is besieged.* 4 *David committeth adultery.* 17 *Uriah is slain.* 27 *David marrieth Bathsheba.*

1 And when the year was [1]expired in the time when kings go forth *to battle*, David sent [a]Joab, and his servants with him, and all Israel, who destroyed the children of Ammon, and besieged Rabbah: but David remained in Jerusalem.

2 And when it was evening-tide, David arose out of his [1]bed, and walked upon the roof of the king's palace: and from the roof he saw a woman washing herself: and the woman was very beautiful to look upon.

3 And David sent and inquired what woman it was: and *one* said, Is not this Bathsheba the daughter of Eliam, wife to Uriah the [1]Hittite?

4 Then David sent messengers, and took her away: and she came unto him and he lay with her: (now she was [b]purified from her uncleanness) and she returned unto her house.

5 And the woman conceived: therefore she sent and [1]told David, and said, I am with child.

6 ¶ Then David sent to Joab, *saying*, Send me Uriah the Hittite. And Joab sent Uriah to David.

7 And when Uriah came unto him, David demanded

10:3 [1] Hebrew, *in thine eyes doth David.*

[2] Their arrogant malice would not suffer them to see the simplicity of David's heart: therefore their counsel turned to the destruction of their country.

10:6 [1] That they had deserved David's displeasure, for the injury done to his ambassadors.

[2] Or, Syrians.

10:8 [1] These were divers parts of the country of Syria, whereby appeareth that the Syrians served where they might have entertainment, as now the Sweitzers do.

10:12 [1] Here is declared wherefore war ought to be undertaken: of the defense of true religion and God's people.

10:16 [1] Or, Hadarezer.

[2] Or, Euphrates.

10:17 [1] Meaning, the greatest part.

10:18 [1] Which were the chiefest and most principal: for in all he destroyed 7000, as 1 Chron. 19:18, or the soldiers which were in 700 chariots.

11:1 [1] The year following about the spring time.

11:2 [1] Whereupon he used to rest at afternoon, as was read of Ish-bosheth, 2 Sam. 4:7.

11:3 [1] Who was not an Israelite born, but converted to the true religion.

11:5 [1] Fearing lest she should be stoned according to the Law.

him how Joab did, and how the people fared, and how the war prospered.

8   Afterward David said to Uriah, [1]Go down to thine house, and wash thy feet. So Uriah departed out of the king's palace, and the king sent a present after him.

9   But Uriah slept at the door of the king's palace with all the servants of his lord, and went not down to his house.

10   Then they told David, saying, Uriah went not down to his house: and David said unto Uriah, Comest thou not from thy journey? why didst thou not go down to thine house?

11   Then Uriah answered David, [1]The Ark and Israel, and Judah dwell in tents: and my lord Joab and the servants of my lord abide in the open fields: shall I then go into mine house to eat and drink, and lie with my wife? by thy life, and by the life of thy soul, I will not do this thing.

12   Then David said unto Uriah, Tarry yet this day, and tomorrow I will send thee away. So Uriah abode in Jerusalem that day, and the morrow.

13   Then David called him, and he did eat and drink before him, and he made him [1]drunk: and at even he went out to lie on his couch with the servants of his lord, but went not down to his house.

14   And on the morrow David wrote a letter to Joab, and sent it by the hand of Uriah.

15   And he wrote [1]thus in the letter, [2]Put ye Uriah in the forefront of the strength of the battle, and recule ye back from him, that he may be smitten, and die.

16   ¶ So when Joab besieged the city, he assigned Uriah unto a place, where he knew that strong men were.

17   And the men of the city came out, and fought with Joab: and there fell of the people of the servants of David, and Uriah the Hittite also died.

18   Then Joab sent and told David all the things concerning the war.

19   ¶ And he charged the messenger, saying, When thou hast made an end of telling all the matters of the war unto the King,

20   [1]And if the king's anger arise, so that he say unto thee, Wherefore approached ye unto the city

to fight? knew ye not that they would hurl from the wall?

21   Who smote Abimelech son of [1]Jerubbesheth? did not a woman cast a piece of a millstone upon him from the wall, and he died in Thebez? why went you nigh the wall? Then say thou, Thy servant Uriah the Hittite is also dead.

22   So the messenger went, and came and showed David all that Joab had sent him for.

23   And the messenger said unto David, Certainly the men prevailed against us, and came out unto us into the field, but we [1]pursued them unto the entering of the gate.

24   But the shooters shot from the wall against thy servants, and some of the king's servants be dead: and thy servant Uriah the Hittite is also dead.

25   Then David said unto the messenger, [1]Thus shalt thou say unto Joab, Let not this thing trouble thee: for the sword devoureth [2]one as well as another: make thy battle more strong against the city, and destroy it, and encourage thou him.

26   ¶ And when the wife of Uriah heard that her husband Uriah was dead, she mourned for her husband.

27   So when the mourning was past, David sent and took her into his house, and she became his wife, and bare him a son: but the thing that David had done, [1]displeased the Lord.

12   1 David reproved by Nathan, confesseth his sin.   18 The child conceived in adultery, dieth.   24 Solomon is born.   30 Rabbah is taken.   31 The citizens are grievously punished.

1   Then the Lord sent [1]Nathan unto David, who came to him, and said unto him, There were two men in one city, the one rich, and the other poor.

2   The rich man had exceedingly many sheep and oxen:

3   But the poor had none at all, save one little sheep which he had bought and nourished up: and it grew up with him, and with his children also, and did eat of his own morsels, and drank of his own cup, and slept in his bosom, and was unto him as his daughter.

4   Now there came a [1]stranger unto the rich man,

11:8 [1] David thought that if Uriah lay with his wife, his fault might be cloaked.

11:11 [1] Hereby God would touch David's conscience, that seeing the fidelity and religion of his servant, he would declare himself so forgetful of God, and injurious to his servant.

11:13 [1] He made him drink more liberally than he was wont to do, thinking hereby he would have lain by his wife.

11:15 [1] Hebrew, saying.

   [2] Except God continually uphold us with his mighty spirit, the most perfect fall headlong into all vice and abomination.

11:20 [1] Or, thou shalt do this, if.

11:21 [1] Meaning, Gideon, Judg. 9:52, 53.

11:23 [1] Hebrew, were against them.

11:25 [1] He dissembleth with the messenger, to the intent that neither his cruel commandment, nor Joab's wicked obedience might be espied.

   [2] Hebrew, so and so.

11:27 [1] Hebrew, was evil in the eyes of the Lord.

12:1 [1] Because David lay now drowned in sin, the loving mercy of God, which suffereth not his to perish, waketh his conscience by this similitude, and bringeth him to repentance.

12:4 [1] Or, wayfaring man.

who ²refused to take of his own sheep, and of his own oxen to dress for the stranger that was come unto him, but took the poor man's sheep, and dressed it for the man that was come to him.

5   Then ¹David was exceedingly wroth with the man, and said to Nathan, As the Lord liveth, the man that hath done this thing, ²shall surely die,

6   And he shall restore the lamb ᵃfourfold, because he did this thing, and had no pity thereof.

7   Then Nathan said to David, Thou art the man. Thus saith the Lord God of Israel, I ᵇanointed thee King over Israel, and delivered thee out of the hand of Saul.

8   And gave thee thy lord's ¹house, and thy lord's ²wives into thy bosom, and gave thee the house of Israel, and of Judah, and would moreover (if *that had been* too little) have given thee ³such and such things.

9   Wherefore hast thou despised the command-ment of the Lord, to do evil in his sight? thou hast killed Uriah the Hittite with the sword, and hast taken his wife *to be* thy wife, and hast slain him with the sword of the ¹children of Ammon.

10   Now therefore the sword shall never depart from thine house, because thou hast despised me, and taken the wife of Uriah the Hittite to be thy wife.

11   Thus said the Lord, Behold, I will raise up evil against thee out of thine own house, and will ᶜtake thy wives before thine eyes, and give them unto thy neighbor, and he shall lie with thy wives in the sight of his ¹sin.

12   For thou diddest it secretly: but I will do this thing before all Israel, and before the sun.

13   Then David said unto Nathan, I have sinned against the Lord. And Nathan said unto David, The Lord also hath ¹put away thy sin, thou shalt not die.

14   Howbeit, because by this deed thou hast caused the enemies of the Lord to ¹blaspheme, the child that is born unto thee, shall surely die.

15   ¶ So Nathan departed unto his house: and the Lord struck the child that Uriah's wife bare unto David, and it was sick.

CHAPTER 12
ᵃ Exod. 22:1
ᵇ 1 Sam. 16:13
ᶜ Deut. 28:30
2 Sam. 16:22
ᵈ Matt. 1:6
ᵉ 1 Chron. 22:9

16   David therefore besought God for the child, and fasted and ¹went in, and lay all night upon the earth.

17   Then the Elders of his house arose *to come* unto him, and to cause him to rise from the ground: but he would not, neither did he eat ¹meat with them.

18   So on the seventh day the child died: and the servants of David feared to tell him that the child was dead: for they said, Behold, while the child was alive, we spake unto him, and he would not hearken unto our voice: how then shall we say unto him, The child is dead, ¹to vex *him* more?

19   But when David saw that his servants whispered, David perceived that the child was dead: therefore David said unto his servants, Is the child dead? And they said, He is dead.

20   Then David ¹arose from the earth, and washed and anointed himself, and changed his apparel, and came into the house of the Lord, and worshipped, and afterward came to his own house, and bade that they should set bread before him, and he did eat.

21   Then ¹said his servants unto him, What thing is this that thou hast done? thou didst fast and weep for the child while it was alive, but when the child was dead, thou didst rise up, and eat meat,

22   And he said, While the child was yet alive, I fasted, and wept: for I said, Who can tell *whether* God will have mercy on me, that the child may live?

23   But now being dead, wherefore should I now fast? ¹Can I bring him again anymore? I shall go to him, but he shall not return to me.

24   ¶ And David comforted Bathsheba his wife, and went in unto her, and lay with her, ᵈand she bare a son, and ¹he called his name Solomon: also the Lord loved him.

25   For *the Lord* had sent ¹by Nathan the ²Prophet: therefore ³ᵉhe called his name Jedidiah, because the Lord *loved him.*

26   ¶ Then Joab fought against Rabbah of the children of Ammon, and took the ¹city of the Kingdom.

27   Therefore Joab sent messengers to David, say-ing, I have fought against Rabbah, and have taken

---

12:4 ² Or, spared.
12:5 ¹ Hebrew, *the anger of David was kindled.*
    ² Hebrew, *is the child of death.*
12:8 ¹ For David succeeded Saul in his kingdom.
    ² The Jews understand this of Eglah and Michal, or of Rizpah and Michal.
    ³ That is, greater things than these: for God's love and benefits increase toward his, if by their ingratitude they stay him not.
12:9 ¹ Thou hast most cruelly given him into the hands of God's enemies.
12:11 ¹ Meaning, openly, as at noon-days.
12:13 ¹ For the Lord seeketh but that the sinner would turn to him.
12:14 ¹ In saying, that the Lord hath appointed a wicked man to reign over his people.

12:16 ¹ To wit, to his privy chamber.
12:17 ¹ Thinking by his instant prayer that God would have restored his child, but God hath otherwise determined.
12:18 ¹ Hebrew, *and he will do himself evil.*
12:20 ¹ Showing that our lamentations ought not to be excessive, but moderate: and that we must praise God in all his doings.
12:21 ¹ As they which considered not that God granteth many things to the sobs and tears of the faithful.
12:23 ¹ By this consideration he appeased his sorrow.
12:24 ¹ To wit, the Lord, 1 Chron. 22:9.
12:25 ¹ Hebrew, *by the hand of.*
    ² To call him Solomon.
    ³ Meaning, David.
12:26 ¹ Or the chief city.

the city of [1]waters.

28 Now therefore, gather the rest of the people together, and besiege the city, that thou mayest take it, lest [1]the victory be attributed to me.

29 So David gathered all the people together, and went against Rabbah, and besieged it, and took it.

30 [f]And he took their king's crown from his head, (which weighed a [1]talent of gold, with precious stones) and it was *set* on David's head: and he brought away the spoil of the city in exceedingly great abundance.

31 And he carried away the people that was therein, and put them under [1]saws, and under iron harrows, and under axes of iron, and cast them into the tile-kiln: even thus did he with all the cities of the children of Ammon. Then David and all the people returned unto Jerusalem.

13

14 Amnon David's son defileth his sister Tamar. 20 Tamar is comforted by her brother Absalom. 29 Absalom therefore killeth Amnon.

1 Now after this, so it was, that Absalom the son of David having a fair sister, whose name *was* [1]Tamar, Amnon the son of David loved her.

2 And Amnon was so sore vexed, that he fell sick for his sister Tamar: for she was a [1]virgin, and it seemed hard to Amnon to do anything to her.

3 But Amnon had a friend called Jonadab, the son of Shimeah David's brother: and Jonadab was a very subtle man,

4 Who said unto him, Why *art* thou the king's son, so lean from day to day? wilt thou not tell me? Then Amnon answered him, I love Tamar my brother Absalom's sister.

5 And Jonadab said unto him, [1]Lie down on thy bed, and make thyself sick: and when thy father shall come to see thee, say unto him, I pray thee let my sister Tamar come, and give me meat, and let her dress meat in my sight, that I may see it, and eat it of her hand.

6 ¶ So Amnon lay down, and made himself sick: and when the king came to see him, Amnon said unto the king, I pray thee, let Tamar my sister come, and make me a couple of [1]cakes in my sight,

[f] 1 Chron. 20:2

CHAPTER 13
[a] Lev. 18:9

that I may receive meat at her hand.

7 Then David sent home to Tamar, saying, Go now to thy brother Amnon's house, and dress him meat.

8 ¶ So Tamar went to her brother Amnon's house, and he lay down: and she took [1]flour, and knead it, and made cakes in his sight, and did bake the cakes.

9 And she took a pan, and [1]poured them out before him, but he would not eat. Then Amnon said, Cause ye every man to go out from [2]me: so every man went out from him.

10 Then Amnon said unto Tamar, Bring the meat into the chamber, that I may eat of thine hand. And Tamar took the cakes which she had made, and brought them into the chamber to Amnon her brother.

11 And when she had set them before him to eat, he took her, and said unto her, Come, lie with me, my sister.

12 But she answered him, Nay, my brother, do not force me: for no such thing [a]ought to be done in Israel: commit not this folly.

13 And I, [1]whither shall I cause my shame to go? and thou shalt be as one of [2]the fools in Israel: now therefore, I pray thee speak to the king, for he will not deny me unto thee.

14 Howbeit he would not hearken unto her voice, but being stronger than she, forced her, and lay with her.

15 Then Amnon hated her exceedingly, so that the hatred wherewith he hated her, was greater than the love wherewith he had loved her: and Amnon said unto her, Up, get thee hence.

16 And she answered him, [1]There *is* no cause: this evil (to put me away) is greater than the other that thou didst unto me: but he would not hear her,

17 But called his [1]servant that served him, and said, Put this woman now out from me, and lock the door after her.

18 (And she had a garment of [1]diverse colors upon her: for with such garments were the King's daughters that were virgins, apparelled) Then his servant brought her out, and locked the door after her.

19 And Tamar put ashes on her head, and rent the

12:27 [1] That is, the chief city and where all the conduits are, is as good as taken.

12:28 [1] Hebrew, *my name be called upon it.*

12:30 [1] That is: threescore pounds after the weight of the common talent.

12:31 [1] Signifying that as they were malicious enemies of God, so he put them to cruel death.

13:1 [1] Tamar was Absalom's sister both by father and mother, and Amnon's only by father.

13:2 [1] And therefore kept in her father's house, as virgins were accustomed.

13:5 [1] Here we see that there is no enterprise so wicked that can lack

counsel to further it.

13:6 [1] Meaning, some delicate and dainty meat.

13:8 [1] Or, past.

13:9 [1] That is, she served them on a dish.

[2] For the wicked are ashamed to do that before men, which they are not afraid to commit in the sight of God.

13:13 [1] Or, how shall I put away my shame?

[2] As a lewd and wicked person.

13:16 [1] Or, for this cause.

13:17 [1] Or, boy.

13:18 [1] For that which was of divers colors or pieces, in those days was had in great estimation, Gen. 37:3; Judg. 5:30.

garment of diverse colors which was on her, and laid her hand on her head, and went her way crying.

20 And Absalom her brother said unto her, Hath Amnon thy brother been with thee? Now yet be ¹still, my sister: he is thy brother: let not this thing grieve thine heart. So Tamar remained desolate in her brother Absalom's house.

21 ¶ But when King David heard all these things, he was very wroth.

22 And Absalom said unto his brother Amnon neither good nor bad: for Absalom hated Amnon, because he had forced his sister Tamar.

23 ¶ And after the time of two years, Absalom had sheepshearers in ¹Baal Hazor, which is beside Ephraim, and ²Absalom called all the king's sons.

24 And Absalom came to the King, and said, Behold now, thy servant hath sheepshearers: I pray thee, that the king with his servants would go with thy servant.

25 But the King answered Absalom, Nay my son, I pray thee, let us not go all, lest we be chargeable unto thee. Yet Absalom lay sore upon him: howbeit he would not go, but ¹thanked him.

26 Then said Absalom, But, I pray thee, shall not my brother ¹Amnon go with us? And the king answered him, Why should he go with thee?

27 But Absalom was instant upon him, and he sent Amnon with him, and all the king's children.

28 ¶ Now had Absalom commanded his servants, saying, Mark now when Amnon's heart is merry with wine, and when I say unto you, Smite Amnon, kill him, fear not, for have not ¹I commanded you? be bold therefore, and play the men.

29 And the servants of Absalom did unto Amnon, as Absalom had commanded: and all the king's sons arose, and every man got him up upon his mule, and fled.

30 ¶ And while they were in the way, tidings came to David, saying, Absalom hath slain all the King's sons, and there is not one of them left.

31 Then the king arose, and tore his garments, and lay on the ¹ground, and all his servants stood by with their clothes rent.

32 And Jonadab the son of Shimeah David's brother answered and said, Let not my lord suppose

that they have slain all the young men the King's sons: for Amnon only is dead, ¹because Absalom had reported so, since he forced his sister Tamar.

33 Now therefore let not my lord the King ¹take the thing so grievously; to think that all the King's sons are dead: ²for Amnon only is dead.

34 ¶ Then Absalom fled: and the young man that kept the watch, lift up his eyes, and looked, and behold, there came much people by the way of the hill side ¹behind him.

35 And Jonadab said unto the king, Behold, the king's sons come: as thy servant said, ¹so it is.

36 And as soon as he had left speaking, behold, the king's sons came, and lift up their voices, and wept: and the king also and all his servants wept exceedingly sore.

37 But Absalom fled away, and went to ¹Talmai the son of Ammihud king of Geshur: and David mourned for his son every day.

38 So Absalom fled, and went to Geshur, and was there three years.

39 And king David ¹desired to go forth unto Absalom, because he was pacified concerning Amnon, seeing he was dead.

14

2 Absalom is reconciled to his father by the subtlety of Joab. 24 Absalom may not see the King's face. 25 The beauty of Absalom. 30 He causeth Joab's corn to be burnt, and is brought to his father's presence.

1 Then Joab the son of Zeruiah perceived, that the king's ¹heart was toward Absalom,

2 And Joab sent to Tekoa, and brought thence a ¹subtle woman, and said unto her, I pray thee, feign thyself to mourn, and now put on mourning apparel, and ²anoint not thyself with oil: but be as a woman that had now long time mourned for the dead.

3 And come to the king, and speak on this manner unto him, (for Joab ¹taught her what she should say).

4 ¶ Then the woman of Tekoa spake unto the king, and fell down on her face to the ground, and did obeisance, and said, ¹Help, O King.

5 Then the king said unto her, What aileth thee? And she answered, I am indeed a ¹widow, and mine

---

13:20 ¹ For though he conceived sudden vengeance in his heart, yet he dissembled it till occasion served, and comforted his sister.
13:23 ¹ Or, in the plain of Hazor.
² To wit, to a banquet, thinking thereby to fulfill his wicked purpose.
13:25 ¹ Hebrew, blessed.
13:26 ¹ Pretending to the king that Amnon was most dear unto him.
13:28 ¹ Such is the pride of the wicked masters, that in all their wicked commandments they think to be obeyed.
13:31 ¹ Lamenting, as he that felt the wrath of God upon his house, 2 Sam. 12:10.
13:32 ¹ Hebrew, because it was put in Absalom's mouth.
13:33 ¹ Or, take it to heart.

² Or, but.
13:34 ¹ Or, one after another.
13:35 ¹ That only Amnon is dead.
13:37 ¹ For Maacah his mother was the daughter of this Talmai, 2 Sam. 3:3.
13:39 ¹ Or, ceased,
14:1 ¹ That the king favored him.
14:2 ¹ Or, wife.
² In token of mourning: for they used anointing to seem cheerful.
14:3 ¹ Hebrew, put words in her mouth.
14:4 ¹ Hebrew, Save.
14:5 ¹ Hebrew, a widow woman.

husband is dead:

6 And thine handmaid had two ¹sons, and they two strove together in the field, (and there was none to part them) so the one smote the other, and slew him.

7 And behold the whole family is risen against thine handmaid, and they said, Deliver him that smote his brother, that we may kill him for the ¹soul of his brother whom he slew, that we may destroy the heir also: so they shall quench my sparkle which is left, and shall not leave to mine husband neither name nor posterity upon the earth.

8 And the king said unto the woman, Go to thine house, and I will give a charge for thee.

9 Then the woman of Tekoa said unto the King, My lord, O King, this ¹trespass be on me, and on my father's house, and the King and his throne be ²guiltless.

10 And the King said, Bring him to me that speaketh against thee, and he shall touch thee no more.

11 Then said she, I pray thee, let the king ¹remember the Lord thy God, that thou wouldest not suffer many revengers of blood to destroy, lest they slay my son. And he answered, As the Lord liveth, there shall not one hair of thy son fall to the earth.

12 Then the woman said, I pray thee, let thine handmaid speak a word to my lord the King. And he said, Say on.

13 Then the woman said, Wherefore then hast thou ¹thought such a thing against the people of God? or why doth the King, as one which is faulty, speak this thing, that he will not bring again his banished?

14 For we must needs die, and we are as water spilt on the ground, which cannot be gathered up again: neither doth God ¹spare any person, yet doth he appoint ²means, not to cast out from him, him that is expelled.

15 Now therefore, that I am come to speak of this thing unto my lord the King, the cause is that the people ¹have made me afraid: therefore thine handmaid said, Now will I speak unto the King: it may be that the king will perform the request of his handmaid.

16 For the king will hear, to deliver his handmaid out of the hand of the man that would destroy me, and also my son from the inheritance of God.

17 Therefore thine handmaid said, The word of my lord the king shall now be ¹comfortable: for my lord the King is even as an ²Angel of God in hearing of good and bad: therefore the Lord thy God be with thee.

18 Then the king answered, and said unto the woman, Hide not from me, I pray thee, the thing that I shall ask thee. And the woman said, Let my lord the king now speak.

19 And the king said, Is not ¹the hand of Joab with thee in all this? Then the woman answered, and said, As thy soul liveth, my lord the King, I will not turn to the right hand nor to the left, from ought that my lord the king hath spoken: for even thy servant Joab bade me, and he put all these words in the mouth of thine handmaid:

20 For to the intent that I ¹should change the form of speech, thy servant Joab hath done this thing: but ²my lord is wise according to the wisdom of an Angel of God, to understand all things that are in the earth.

21 ¶ And the king said unto Joab, Behold now, I have ¹done this thing: go then, and bring the young man Absalom again.

22 And Joab fell to the ground on his face, and bowed himself and ¹thanked the King. Then Joab said, This day thy servant knoweth, that I have found grace in thy sight, my lord the king, in that the king hath fulfilled the request of his servant.

23 ¶ And Joab arose, and went to Geshur, and brought Absalom to Jerusalem.

24 And the King said, Let him ¹turn to his own house, and not see my face. So Absalom turned to his own house, and saw not the king's face.

25 Now in all Israel there was none to be so much praised for beauty as Absalom: from the sole of his foot even to the top of his head there was no blemish in him.

26 And when he polled his head, (for at every year's end he polled it: because it was too heavy for him, therefore he polled it) he weighed the hair of his head at two hundred ¹shekels by the king's weight.

27 And Absalom had three sons, and one daughter named Tamar, which was a fair woman to look upon.

28 ¶ So Absalom dwelt the space of two years in

14:6 ¹ Under this parable she describeth the death of Amnon by Absalom.
14:7 ¹ Because he hath slain his brother he ought to be slain according to the Law, Gen. 9:6; Exod. 21:12.
14:9 ¹ As touching the breach of the Law which punisheth blood, let me bear the blame.
    ² Or, innocent.
14:11 ¹ Swear that they shall not revenge the blood, which are many in number.
14:13 ¹ Why dost thou give contrary sentence in thy son Absalom?
14:14 ¹ Or, accept.
    ² God hath provided ways (as sanctuaries) to save them oft times,
whom man judgeth worthy death.
14:15 ¹ For I thought they would kill this mine heir.
14:17 ¹ Hebrew, rest.
    ² Is of great wisdom to discern right from wrong.
14:19 ¹ Hast not thou done this by the counsel of Joab.
14:20 ¹ By speaking further in a parable then plainly.
    ² Or, none can hide ought from the King.
14:21 ¹ I have granted thy request.
14:22 ¹ Hebrew, blessed.
14:24 ¹ Covering hereby his affection, and showing some part of justice to please the people.
14:26 ¹ Which weighed 6 pounds 4 ounces after half an ounce the shekel.

Jerusalem, and saw not the king's face.

29 Therefore Absalom sent for Joab to send him to the King, but he would not come to him: and when he sent again, he would not come.

30 Therefore he said unto his servants, Behold, Joab hath a ¹field by my place, and hath barley therein: go, and set it ²on fire: and Absalom's servants set the field on fire.

31 Then Joab arose, and came to Absalom unto his house, and said unto him, Wherefore have thy servants burnt my field with fire?

32 And Absalom answered Joab, Behold, I sent for thee, saying, Come thou hither, and I will send thee to the king for to say, Wherefore am I come from Geshur? It had been better for me to have been there still: now therefore let me see the king's face: and ¹if there be any trespass in me, let him kill me.

33 Then Joab came to the king, and told him: and he called for Absalom, who came to the king, and bowed himself to the ground on his face before the king, and the king kissed Absalom.

15

2 The practices of Absalom to aspire to the kingdom.   14 David and his flee.   31 David's prayer.   34 Hushai is sent to Absalom to discover his counsel.

1 After this, Absalom ¹prepared him chariots, and horses, and fifty men to ²run before him.

2 And Absalom rose up early, and stood hard by the entering in of the gate: and every man that had any ¹matter, and came to the king for judgment, him did Absalom call unto him, and said, Of what city art thou? And he answered, Thy servant *is* of one of the ²tribes of Israel.

3 Then Absalom said unto him, See, thy matters are good and righteous, but there is no man *deputed* of the king to hear thee.

4 Absalom said moreover, ¹Oh that I were made Judge in the land, that every man which hath any matter of controversy, might come to me, that I might do him justice.

5 And when any man came near to him, and did him obeisance, he put forth his hand, and took him, and kissed him.

6 And on this manner did Absalom to all Israel, that came to the King for judgment: so Absalom ¹stole the hearts of the men of Israel.

7 ¶ And after ¹forty years, Absalom said unto the King, I pray thee, let me go to Hebron, and render my vow which I have vowed unto the Lord.

8 For thy servant vowed a vow when I remained at Geshur, in Aram, saying, If the Lord shall bring me again indeed to Jerusalem, I will ¹serve the Lord.

9 And the King said unto him, Go in peace. So he arose, and went to Hebron.

10 ¶ Then Absalom sent spies throughout all the tribes of Israel, saying, When ye hear the sound of the trumpet, ye shall say, Absalom reigneth in Hebron.

11 ¶ And with Absalom went two hundred men out of Jerusalem, that were ¹called: and they went in their simplicity, knowing nothing.

12 Also Absalom sent for Ahithophel the Gilonite David's counselor, from his city Giloh, while he offered sacrifices: and the treason was great: for the people ¹increased still with Absalom.

13 ¶ Then came a messenger to David, saying, The hearts of the men of Israel are turned after Absalom.

14 Then David said unto all his servants that were with him at Jerusalem, Up, and let us flee: for we shall not escape from ¹Absalom: make speed to depart, lest he come suddenly and take us, and bring evil upon us, and smite the city with the edge of the sword.

15 And the king's servants said unto him, Behold, thy servants *are ready to do* according to all that my lord the king shall ¹appoint.

16 So the king departed and all his household ¹after him, and the king left ten concubines to keep the house.

17 And the king went forth and all the people after him, and tarried in a ¹place ²far off.

18 And all his servants went about him, and all the ¹Cherethites and all the Pelethites, and all the Gittites, *even* six hundred men which were come after him from Gath, went before the king.

14:30 ¹ Or, possession.

² The wicked are impatient in their affections, and spare no unlawful means to compass them.

14:32 ¹ If I have offended by revenging my sister's dishonor: thus the wicked justify themselves in their evil.

15:1 ¹ Hebrew, *made him.*

² Which were as a guard to set forth his estate.

15:2 ¹ Or, controversy.

² That is, noting of what city or place he was.

15:4 ¹ Thus by slander, flattery and fair promises the wicked seek preferment.

15:6 ¹ By enticing them from his father to himself.

15:7 ¹ Counting from the time that the Israelites had asked a King of Samuel.

15:8 ¹ By offering a peace offering, which was lawful to do in any place.

15:11 ¹ And bid to his feast in Hebron.

15:12 ¹ Hebrew, *went and increased.*

15:14 ¹ Whose heart he saw that Satan had so possessed, that he would leave no mischief unattempted.

15:15 ¹ Hebrew, *choose.*

15:16 ¹ Hebrew, *at his feet.*

15:17 ¹ Or, *house.*

² To wit, from Jerusalem.

15:18 ¹ These were as the king's guard, or as some write, his counselors.

19 Then said the King to ¹Ittai the Gittite, Wherefore comest thou also with us? Return and abide with the King, for thou art a stranger, depart thou therefore to thy place.

20 Thou camest yesterday, and should I cause thee to wander today and go with us? I will go whither I can: therefore return thou, and carry again thy ¹brethren: mercy and ²truth *be* with thee.

21 And Ittai answered the King, and said, As the Lord liveth, and as my lord the king liveth, in what place my lord the king shall be, whether in death or life, even there surely will thy servant be.

22 Then David said to Ittai, Come, and go forward. And Ittai the Gittite went, and all his men, and all the children that were with him.

23 And all the country wept with a loud voice, and ¹all the people went forward, but the King passed over the brook Kidron: and all the people went over toward the way of the wilderness.

24 ¶ And lo, Zadok also *was there*, and all the Levites with him, ¹bearing the Ark of the covenant of God: and they set down the Ark of God: and Abiathar went ²up until the people were all come out of the city.

25 Then the King said unto Zadok, Carry the Ark of God again into the city: if I shall find favor in the eyes of the Lord, he will bring me again, and show me *both* it, and the ¹Tabernacle thereof.

26 But if he thus say, I have no delight in thee, behold, ¹here am I, let him do to me as seemeth good in his eyes.

27 The King said again unto Zadok the Priest, Art not thou a ᵃSeer? return into the city in peace, and your two sons with you: *to wit*, Ahimaaz thy son, and Jonathan the son of Abiathar.

28 Behold, I will tarry in the fields of the wilderness, until there come some word from you to be told me.

29 Zadok therefore and Abiathar carried the Ark of God again to Jerusalem, and they tarried there.

30 And David went up the mount of olives, and wept as he went up, and had his head ¹covered, and went barefooted: and all the people that was with him, had every man his head covered, and as they went up, they wept.

31 Then one told David, saying, Ahithophel is one of them that have conspired with Absalom: and

CHAPTER 15
ᵃ 1 Sam. 9:9

David said, O Lord, I pray thee, turn the ¹counsel of Ahithophel into foolishness.

32 ¶ Then David came to the top of the mount where he worshipped God: and behold, Hushai the Archite came against him with his coat torn, and having earth upon his head.

33 Unto whom David said, If thou go with me, thou shalt be a burthen unto me.

34 But if thou return to the city, and say unto Absalom, I will be thy ¹servant, O King (as I have been in time past thy father's servant, so will I now be thy servant) then thou mayest bring me the counsel of Ahithophel to nought.

35 And hast thou not there with thee Zadok and Abiathar the Priests? therefore whatsoever thou shalt hear out of the King's house, thou shalt show to Zadok and Abiathar the Priests.

36 Behold, there are with them their two sons: Ahimaaz Zadok's *son*, and Jonathan Abiathar's *son*: by them also shall ye send me everything that ye can hear.

37 So Hushai David's friend went into the city: and Absalom came into Jerusalem.

16

1 *The infidelity of Ziba.* 5 *Shimei curseth David.* 16 *Hushai cometh to Absalom.* 21 *The counsel of Ahithophel for the concubines.*

1 When David was a little past the ¹top *of the hill*, behold, Ziba the servant of Mephibosheth met him with a couple of asses saddled, and upon them two hundred *cakes* of bread, and an hundred bunches of raisins, and an hundred of ²dried figs, and a bottle of wine.

2 And the King said unto Ziba, What meanest thou by these? And Ziba said, They be ¹asses for the king's household to ride on, and bread, and dried figs for the young men to eat, and wine, that the faint may drink in the wilderness.

3 And the King said, But where is thy master's son? Then Ziba answered the King, Behold, he remaineth in Jerusalem: for he said, This day shall the house of Israel restore me the kingdom of my father.

4 Then said the King to Ziba, Behold, thine are all that *pertained* unto Mephibosheth. And Ziba said, ¹I beseech thee, let me find grace in thy sight, my lord, O King.

5 ¶ And when King David came to ¹Bahurim,

15:19 ¹ Who as some write was the king's son of Gath.
15:20 ¹ Meaning, them of his family.
  ² God require thee friendship and fidelity.
15:23 ¹ To wit, the six hundred men.
15:24 ¹ Which was the charge, of the Kohathites, Num. 4:4.
  ² To stand by the Ark.
15:25 ¹ Or, his tabernacle.
15:26 ¹ The faithful in all their afflictions show themselves obedient to God's will.
15:30 ¹ With ashes and dust in sign of sorrow.

15:31 ¹ The counsel of the crafty worldlings doth more harm than the open force of the enemy.
15:34 ¹ Though Hushai dissembled here at the King's request, yet may we not use this example to excuse our dissimulation.
16:1 ¹ Which was the hill of olives, 2 Sam. 15:30.
  ² Or, fig cakes.
16:2 ¹ Commonly there are no viler traitors than they, which under pretence of friendship accuse others.
16:4 ¹ Hebrew, *I worship.*
16:5 ¹ Which was a city in the tribe of Benjamin.

behold, thence came out a man of the family of the house of Saul, named Shimei, the son of Gera: and he came out and cursed.

6 And he cast stones at David, and at all the servants of King David: and all the people, and all the men of war *were* on his ¹right hand, and on his left.

7 And thus said Shimei when he cursed, Come forth, come forth thou ¹murderer, and ²wicked man.

8 The Lord hath brought upon thee all the ¹blood of the house of Saul, in whose stead thou hast reigned: and the Lord hath delivered thy kingdom into the hand of Absalom thy son: and behold, thou art *taken* in thy wickedness, because thou art a murderer.

9 Then said Abishai the son of Zeruiah unto the King, Why doth ªthis dead dog curse my lord the King: let me go, I pray thee, and take away his head.

10 ¶ But the King said, What have I to do with you, ye sons of Zeruiah? for he curseth, even because the Lord hath ¹bidden him curse David: who dare then say, Wherefore hast thou done so?

11 And David said to Abishai, and to all his servants, Behold, my son which came out of mine own bowels, seeketh my life: then how much more now may this son of Benjamin? Suffer him to curse: for the Lord hath bidden him.

12 It may be that the Lord will look on ¹mine affliction, and ²do me good for his cursing this day.

13 And as David and his men went by the way, Shimei went by the side of the mountain over against him, and cursed as he went, and threw stones against him, and cast dust.

14 Then came the King and all the people that were with him weary, and refreshed themselves ¹there.

15 ¶ And Absalom, and all the people the men of Israel, came to Jerusalem, and Ahithophel with him.

16 And when Hushai the Archite, David's friend, was come unto Absalom, Hushai said unto Absalom, ¹God save the King, God save the King.

17 Then Absalom said to Hushai, Is this thy kindness to thy ¹friend? Why wentest thou not with thy friend?

18 Hushai then answered unto Absalom, Nay, but whom the Lord, and this people, and all the men of Israel

CHAPTER 16
ª 1 Sam. 24:14
2 Sam. 3:8

choose, his will I be, and with them will I dwell.

19 And ¹moreover, unto whom shall I do service? not to his son? as I served before thy father, so will I before thee.

20 ¶ Then spake Absalom to Ahithophel, Give counsel what we shall do.

21 And ¹Ahithophel said unto Absalom, Go in to thy father's concubines, which he hath left to keep the house: and when all Israel shall hear that thou art abhorred of thy father, the hands of all that are with thee, shall be strong.

22 So they spread Absalom a tent upon the top of the house, and Absalom went in to his father's concubines in the sight of all Israel.

23 And the counsel of Ahithophel which he counseled in those days, was like as one had asked ¹counsel at the oracle of God: so *was* all the counsel of Ahithophel both with David and with Absalom.

17 *7 Ahithophel's counsel is overthrown by Hushai. 14 The Lord had so ordained. 19 The Priest's sons are hidden in the well. 22 David goeth over Jordan. 23 Ahithophel hangeth himself. 27 They bring victuals to David.*

1 Moreover, Ahithophel said to Absalom, ¹Let me choose out now twelve thousand men, and I will up and follow after David this night,

2 And I will come upon him: for he is weary, and weak handled: so I will fear him, and all the people that are with him shall flee, and I will smite the king only,

3 And I will bring again all the people unto thee, *and* when all shall return, (¹the man whom thou seekest *being slain*) all the people shall be in peace.

4 And the saying ¹pleased Absalom well, and all the Elders of Israel.

5 Then said Absalom, Call now Hushai the Archite also, and let us hear likewise ¹what he saith.

6 So when Hushai came to Absalom, Absalom spake unto him, saying, Ahithophel hath ¹spoken thus: shall we do after his saying, or no? tell thou.

7 Hushai then answered unto Absalom, The counsel that Ahithophel hath given, is not ¹good at this time.

16:6 ¹ That is, round about him.
16:7 ¹ Hebrew, *man of blood*.
  ² Hebrew, *man of Belial*.
16:8 ¹ Reproaching him, as though by his means Ishbosheth and Abner were slain.
16:10 ¹ David felt that this was the judgment of God for his sin, and therefore humbleth himself to his rod.
16:12 ¹ Or, my tears.
  ² Meaning, that the Lord will send comfort to his, when they are oppressed.
16:14 ¹ To wit, at Bahurim.
16:16 ¹ Hebrew, *let the king live*.
16:17 ¹ Meaning, David.

16:19 ¹ Hebrew, *the second time*.
16:21 ¹ Suspecting the change of the Kingdom, and so his own overthrow, he giveth such counsel as might most hinder his father's reconciliation: and also declare to the people that Absalom was in highest authority.
16:23 ¹ It was so esteemed for the success thereof.
17:1 ¹ The wicked are so greedy to execute their malice, that they leave none occasion, that may further the same.
17:3 ¹ Meaning, David.
17:4 ¹ Hebrew, *was right in the eyes of Absalom*.
17:5 ¹ Hebrew, *what is in his mouth*.
17:6 ¹ Or, given such counsel.
17:7 ¹ Hushai showeth himself faithful to David, in that he reproveth this wicked counsel and purpose.

8 For, said Hushai, thou knowest thy father, and his men, that they be strong men, and are chafed in mind as a bear robbed of her whelps in the field: also thy father is a valiant warrior, and will not [1]lodge with the people.

9 Behold, he is hid now in some cave, or in some place: and though some of them be overthrown at the first, yet the *people* shall hear, and say, The people that follow Absalom, [1]be overthrown.

10 Then he also that is valiant, whose heart is as the heart of a lion, shall [1]shrink and faint: for all Israel knoweth that thy father is valiant, and they which be with him, stout men.

11 Therefore my counsel is, that all Israel be gathered unto thee, from Dan even to Beersheba as the sand of the Sea in number, and that thou go to battle in thine own person.

12 So shall we come upon him in some place, where we shall find him, and [1]we will upon him as the dew falleth on the ground: and of all the men that are with him, we will not leave him one.

13 Moreover, if he be gotten into a city, then shall all the men of Israel bring ropes to that city, and we will draw it into the river, until there be not one small stone found there.

14 ¶ Then Absalom and all the men of Israel said, The counsel of Hushai the Archite, is better, than the counsel of Ahithophel: for the Lord had [1]determined to destroy the [2]good counsel of Ahithophel, that the Lord might [3]bring evil upon Absalom.

15 Then said Hushai unto Zadok and to Abiathar the Priests, Of this and that manner did Ahithophel and the Elders of Israel counsel Absalom: and thus and thus have I counseled.

16 Now therefore send quickly, and show David, saying, Tarry not this night in the fields of the wilderness, but rather get thee [1]over, lest the king be devoured, and all the people that are with him.

17 ¶ Now Jonathan and Ahimaaz abode by [1]En Rogel: (for they might not be seen to come into the city) and a maid went, and [2]told them, and they went and showed king David.

18 Nevertheless, a young man saw them, and told it to Absalom. Therefore they both departed quickly,

and came to a man's house in Bahurim, who had a well in his court, into the which they went down.

19 And [1]the wife took and spread a covering over the well's mouth, and spread ground corn thereon, that the thing should not be known.

20 And when Absalom's servants came to the wife into the house, they said, Where is Ahimaaz and Jonathan? And the woman answered them, They be gone over the [1]brook of water. And when they had sought them, and could not find them, they returned to Jerusalem.

21 And as soon as they were departed, the other came out of the well, and went and told king David, and said unto him, Up, and get you quickly over the water: for [1]such counsel hath Ahithophel given against you.

22 Then David arose, and all the people that were with him, and they went over Jordan [1]until the dawning of the day, so that there lacked not one of them, that was not come over Jordan.

23 ¶ Now when Ahithophel saw that his counsel was not followed, he saddled his ass, and arose, and he went home unto his city, and put his household in order, and [1]hanged himself, and died, and was buried in his father's grave.

24 ¶ Then David came to Mahanaim. And Absalom passed over Jordan, he, and all the men of Israel with him.

25 And Absalom made Amasa captain of the host in the stead of Joab: which Amasa was a man's son named Jithra, an Israelite, that went in to Abigail the daughter of [1]Nahash, sister to Zeruiah Joab's mother.

26 So Israel and Absalom pitched in the land of Gilead.

27 ¶ And when David was come to Mahanaim, Shobi the son of Nahash out of Rabbah of the children of Ammon, and Machir the son of Ammiel out of Lo Debar, and Barzillai the Gileadite out of Rogelim,

28 [1]*Brought* beds, and basins, and earthen vessels, and wheat, and barley, and flour, and parched corn, and beans, and lentils, and parched corn.

29 And they brought honey, and butter, and sheep,

17:8 [1] Or, tarry all night.
17:9 [1] Hebrew, *have a breach of ruin.*
17:10 [1] Hebrew, *melt.*
17:12 [1] Or, we will camp against him.
17:14 [1] Or, commanded.
    [2] That counsel which seemed good at the first to Absalom, verse 4.
    [3] For by the counsel of Hushai, he went to the battle, where he was destroyed.
17:16 [1] That is, over Jordan.
17:17 [1] Or, the well of Rogel.
    [2] Meaning, the message from their fathers.

17:19 [1] Thus God sendeth succor to his, in their greatest dangers.
17:20 [1] The Chaldea text readeth: Now they have passed the Jordan.
17:21 [1] To wit, to pursue thee with all haste.
17:22 [1] They traveled all night, and by morning had all their company passed over.
17:23 [1] God's just vengeance even in this life is poured on them which are enemies, traitors, or persecutors of his Church.
17:25 [1] Who was also called Jesse David's Father.
17:28 [1] God showeth himself most liberal to his, when they seem to be utterly destitute.

and cheese of kine for David, and for the people that were with him, to eat: for they said, The people is hungry, and weary, and thirsty in the wilderness.

18 2 David divideth his army into three parts.   9 Absalom is hanged, slain, and cast into a pit.   33 David lamenteth the death of Absalom.

CHAPTER 18
a Gen. 23:15
b Gen. 14:17

1 Then David ¹numbered the people that were with him, and set over them captains of thousands, and captains of hundreds.

2 And David sent forth the third part of the people under the hand of Joab, and the third part under the hand of Abishai Joab's brother, the son of Zeruiah: and the *other* third part under the hand of Ittai the Gittite. And the King said unto the people, I will go with you myself also.

3 But the people answered, Thou shalt not go forth: for if we flee away, they will not regard us, neither will they pass for us, though half of us were slain: but thou art ¹now worth ten thousand of us: therefore now it is better that thou succor us out of the city.

4 Then the king said unto them, What seemeth you best, that I will do. So the king stood by the gate side, and all the people came out by hundreds and by thousands.

5 And the king commanded Joab and Abishai, and Ittai, saying, *Entreat* the young man Absalom gently for my sake. And all the people heard when the King gave all the Captains charge concerning Absalom.

6 So the people went out into the field to meet Israel, and the battle was in the ¹wood of Ephraim:

7 Where the people of Israel were slain before the servants of David: so there was a great slaughter that day, *even* of twenty thousand.

8 ¶ For the battle was scattered over all the country: and the wood devoured much more people that day than did the sword.

9 ¶ Now Absalom met the servants of David, and Absalom rode upon a mule, and the mule came under a great thick oak: and his head caught hold of the oak, and he was taken up ¹between the heaven and the earth: and the mule that was under him

went away.

10 And one that saw it, told Joab, saying, Behold, I saw Absalom hanged in an oak.

11 Then Joab said unto the man that told him, And hast thou indeed seen? why then didst thou not there smite him to the ground, and I would have given thee ten *a*shekels of silver, and a girdle?

12 Then the man said unto Joab, Though I should ¹receive a thousand *shekels* of silver in mine hand, yet would I not lay mine hand upon the King's son: for in our hearing the King charged thee, and Abishai, and Ittai, saying, Beware, lest any *touch* the young man Absalom.

13 If I had done it, *it had been* ¹the danger of my life: for nothing can be hid from the King: yea, thou thyself wouldest have been against me.

14 Then said Joab, I will not thus tarry with thee. And he took three darts in his hand, and thrust them ¹through Absalom, while he was yet alive in the midst of the oak.

15 And ten servants that bare Joab's armor, compassed about and smote Absalom, and slew him.

16 Then Joab ¹blew the trumpet, and the people returned from pursuing after Israel: for Joab held back the people.

17 And they took Absalom, and cast him into a great ¹pit in the wood, and laid a mighty great heap of stones upon him: and all Israel fled every one to his tent.

18 Now Absalom in his life time had taken and reared him up a pillar, which is in the *b*King's dale: for he said, I have no ¹son to keep my name in remembrance: and he called the pillar after his own name, and it is called unto this day, Absalom's place.

19 ¶ Then said Ahimaaz the son of Zadok, I pray thee, let me run and bear the King tidings that the Lord hath ¹delivered him out of the hand of his enemies.

20 And Joab said unto him, Thou ¹shalt not be the messenger today, but thou shalt bear tidings another time, but today thou shalt bear none: for the King's son is dead.

21 Then said Joab to Cushi, Go, tell the King, what thou hast seen. And Cushi bowed himself unto Joab, and ran.

22 Then said Ahimaaz the son of Zadok again

18:1 ¹ For certain of the Reubenites, Gadites, and of the half tribe, could not bear the insolence of the son against the father, and therefore joined with David.

18:3 ¹ Signifying, that a good governor ought to be so dear unto his people, that they will rather lose their lives, than that ought should come unto him.

18:6 ¹ So called, because the Ephraimites (as some say) fed their cattle beyond Jordan in this wood.

18:9 ¹ This is a terrible example of God's vengeance against them that are rebels or disobedient to their parents.

18:12 ¹ Hebrew, *weigh upon mine hand.*

18:13 ¹ Hebrew, *a lie against my soul.*

18:14 ¹ Hebrew, *in the heart of Absalom.*

18:16 ¹ For he had pity of the people, which was seduced by Absalom's flattery.

18:17 ¹ Thus God turned his vain glory to shame.

18:18 ¹ It seemed that God had punished him in taking away his children, 2 Sam. 14:27.

18:19 ¹ Hebrew, *judged.*

18:20 ¹ For Joab bare a good affection to Ahimaaz, and doubted how David would take the report of Absalom's death.

to Joab, What, I pray thee, if I also run after Cushi? And Joab said, Wherefore now wilt thou run my son, seeing that thou hast no tidings to bring?

23 Yet what if I run? Then he said unto him, Run. So Ahimaaz ran by the way of the plain, and overwent Cushi.

24 Now David sat between the two ¹gates. And the watchman went to the top of the gate upon the wall, and lift up his eyes, and saw, and behold, a man came running alone.

25 And the watchman cried, and told the king. And the King said, If he be alone, ¹he bringeth tidings. And he came apace, and drew near.

26 And the watchman saw another man running, and the watchman called unto the potter, and said, Behold, *another* man runneth alone. And the King said, He also bringeth tidings.

27 And the watchman said, ¹Me thinketh the running of the foremost *is* like the running of Ahimaaz the son of Zadok. Then the King said, He is a ²good man, and cometh with good tidings.

28 And Ahimaaz called, and said unto the King, Peace *be with thee*: and he fell down to the earth upon his face before the King, and said, Blessed be the Lord thy God, who hath ¹shut up the men that lift up their hands against my Lord the King.

29 And the King said, Is the young man Absalom safe? And Ahimaaz answered, When Joab sent the King's ¹servant, and *me* thy servant, I saw a great tumult, but I knew not what.

30 And the King said unto him, Turn aside, *and* stand here: so he turned aside and stood still.

31 And behold, Cushi came, and Cushi said, ¹Tidings, my lord the King: for the Lord hath delivered thee this day out of the hand of all that rose against thee.

32 Then the King said unto Cushi, Is the young man Absalom safe? And Cushi answered, The enemies of my lord the King, and all that rise against thee to do thee hurt, be as that young man is.

33 And the King was ¹moved, and went up to the chamber over the gate, and wept: and as he went, thus he said, O my son Absalom, my son, my son Absalom: would God I had died for thee, O Absalom, my son, my son.

19

7 Joab encourageth the king.   8 David is restored.   23 Shimei is pardoned.   24 Mephibosheth meeteth the king.   39 Barzillai departeth.   41 Israel striveth with Judah.

1 And it was told Joab, Behold, the King weepeth and mourneth for Absalom.

2 Therefore the ¹victory of that day was turned into mourning to all the people: for the people heard say that day, The King sorroweth for his son.

3 And the people went that day into the city ¹secretly, as people confounded hide themselves when they flee in battle.

4 So the King ¹hid his face, and the king cried with a loud voice, My son Absalom, Absalom my son, my son.

5 ¶ Then Joab came into the ¹house to the King, and said, Thou hast shamed this day the faces of all thy servants, which this day have saved thy life, and the lives of thy sons, and of thy daughters, and the lives of thy wives, and the lives of thy concubines,

6 In that thou lovest thine enemies, and hatest thy friends: for thou hast declared this day, that thou regardest neither thy ¹princes, nor servants: therefore this day I perceive, that if Absalom had lived, and we all had died this day, that then it would have ²pleased thee well.

7 Now therefore up, come out, and speak ¹comfortably unto thy servants: for I swear by the Lord, except thou come out, there will not tarry one man with thee this night: and that will be worse unto thee, than all the evil that fell on thee from thy youth hitherto.

8 Then the king arose, and sat in the ¹gate: and they told unto all the people, saying, Behold, the king doth sit in the gate: and all the people came before the king: for Israel had fled every man to his tent.

9 ¶ Then all the people were at ¹strife throughout all the tribes of Israel, saying, The King saved us out of the hand of our enemies, and he delivered us out of the hand of the Philistines, and now he is fled out of the land for Absalom.

10 And Absalom, whom we anointed over us, is dead in battle: therefore why are ye so slow to bring the king again?

11 But King David sent to Zadok and to Abiathar the ¹Priests, saying, Speak unto the Elders of Judah,

---

18:24 ¹ He sat in the gate of the city of Mahanaim.
18:25 ¹ Hebrew, *tidings are in his mouth.*
18:27 ¹ Hebrew, *I see the running.*
    ² He had experience of his fidelity, 2 Sam. 17:21.
18:28 ¹ Or, delivered up.
18:29 ¹ To wit, Cushi, who was an Ethiopian.
18:31 ¹ Hebrew, *tidings is brought.*
18:33 ¹ Because he considereth both the judgment of God against his sin, and could not otherwise hide his fatherly affection toward his son.
19:2 ¹ Hebrew, *salvation,* or *deliverance.*

19:3 ¹ Or, by stealth.
19:4 ¹ As they do that mourn.
19:5 ¹ At Mahanaim.
19:6 ¹ Or, captains.
    ² Hebrew, *been right in thine eyes.*
19:7 ¹ Hebrew, *to the heart of thy servant.*
19:8 ¹ Where the most resort of the people haunted.
19:9 ¹ Everyone blamed another and strove who should first bring him home.
19:11 ¹ That they should reprove the negligence of the Elders, seeing the people were so forward.

and say, Why are ye behind to bring the King again to his house (for the saying of all Israel is come unto the King, *even* to his house.)

12 Ye are my brethren: my bones and my flesh are ye: Wherefore then are ye the last that bring the King again?

13 Also say ye to Amasa, Art thou not my bone and my flesh? God do so to me, and more also, if thou be not captain of the host to me forever in the ¹room of Joab.

14 So he bowed the hearts of all the men of Judah, as of one man: therefore they sent to the King, saying, Return thou with all thy servants.

15 ¶ So the king returned, and came to Jordan. And Judah came to Gilgal, for to go to meet the king, *and* to conduct him over Jordan.

16 ¶ And ¹Shimei the son of Gera, the son of Benjamin, which was of Bahurim, hasted and came down with the men of Judah to meet king David,

17 And a thousand men of Benjamin with him, and ᵈZiba the servant of the house of Saul, and his fifteen sons and twenty servants with him: and they went over Jordan before the king.

18 And there went over a boat to carry over the king's household, and to do him pleasure. Then Shimei the son of Gera fell before the king, when he was come over Jordan,

19 And said unto the king, Let not my lord impute ᵇwickedness unto me, nor remember the thing that thy servant did ¹wickedly when my lord the King departed out of Jerusalem, that the king should take it to his heart.

20 For thy servant doth know, that I have done amiss: therefore behold, I am the first this day of all the house of ¹Joseph, that am come to go down to meet my lord the king.

21 But Abishai the son of Zeruiah answered, and said, Shall not Shimei die for this, because he cursed the Lord's anointed?

22 And David said, What have I to do with you, ye sons of Zeruiah, that this day ye should be adversaries unto me? shall there any man die this day in Israel? for do not I know that I am this day king over Israel?

23 Therefore the king said unto Shimei, Thou shalt not ¹die, and the king swore unto him.

CHAPTER 19
ᵃ 2 Sam. 16:2
ᵇ 2 Sam. 16:15
ᶜ 2 Sam. 16:3

24 ¶ And Mephibosheth the son of Saul came down to meet the king, and had neither washed his feet, nor dressed his beard, nor washed his clothes from the time the king departed, until he returned in peace.

25 And when ¹he was come to Jerusalem, and met the king, the king said unto him, Wherefore wentest not thou with me, Mephibosheth?

26 And he answered, My lord the King, my servant deceived me: for thy servant said, I would have mine ass saddled to ride thereon, for to go with the king, because thy servant *is* lame.

27 And he hath ᶜaccused thy servant unto my lord the king: but my lord the king *is* as an ¹angel of God: do therefore thy pleasure.

28 For all my father's house were ¹but dead men before my lord the king, yet didst thou set thy servant among them that did eat at thine own table: what right therefore have I yet to cry anymore unto the king?

29 And the king said unto him, Why speakest thou anymore of thy matters? I have said, Thou, and Ziba, divide the ¹lands.

30 And Mephibosheth said unto the king, Yea, let him take all, seeing my lord the king is come home in peace.

31 ¶ Then Barzillai the Gileadite came down from Rogelim, and went over Jordan with the king, to conduct him over Jordan.

32 Now Barzillai was a very aged man, *even* fourscore years old, and he had provided the king of sustenance, while he lay at Mahanaim: for he was a man of very great substance.

33 And the king said unto Barzillai, Come over with me, and I will feed thee with me in Jerusalem.

34 And Barzillai said unto the king, ¹How long have I to live, that I should go up with the king to Jerusalem?

35 I am this day fourscore years old: and can I discern between good or evil? Hath thy servant any taste in that I eat, or in that I drink? Can I hear anymore the voice of singing men and women? wherefore then should thy servant be anymore a ¹burthen unto my lord the king?

36 Thy servant will go a little way over Jordan with the king, and why will the king recompense it me with such a reward?

19:13 ¹ By this policy David thought that by winning of the captain, he should have the hearts of all the people.
19:16 ¹ Who had before reviled him, 2 Sam. 16:13.
19:19 ¹ For in his adversity he was his most cruel enemy, and now in his prosperity, seeketh by flattery to creep into favor.
19:20 ¹ By Joseph he meaneth Ephraim, Manasseh and Benjamin (whereof he was) because these three were under one standard, Num. 2:18.
19:23 ¹ By my hands, or during my life, as read 1 Kings 2:8, 9.

19:25 ¹ When Mephibosheth being at Jerusalem had met the King.
19:27 ¹ Able for his wisdom to judge in all matters.
19:28 ¹ Worthy to die for Saul's cruelty toward thee.
19:29 ¹ David did evil in taking his lands from him before he knew the cause, but much worse, that knowing the truth, he did not restore them.
19:34 ¹ Hebrew, *how many days are the years of my life?*
19:35 ¹ He thought it not meet to receive benefits of him to whom he was not able to do service again.

37 I pray thee, let thy servant turn back again, that I may die in mine own city, and *be buried* in the grave of my father and of my mother: but behold thy servant [1]Chimham, let him go with my lord the King, and do to him what shall please thee.

38 And the king answered, Chimham shall go with me, and I will do to him that thou shalt be content with: and whatsoever thou shalt [1]require of me, that will I do for thee.

39 So all the people went over Jordan: and the king passed over: and the king kissed Barzillai, and [1]blessed him, and he returned unto his own place.

40 ¶ Then the King went to [1]Gilgal, and Chimham went with him, and all the people of Judah conducted the king, and also half the people of [2]Israel.

41 And behold, all the men of Israel came to the king, and said unto the king, Why have our brethren the men of Judah stolen thee away, and have brought the king and his household, and all David's men with him over [1]Jordan?

42 And all the men of Judah answered the men of Israel, Because the king is near of kin to us: and wherefore now be ye angry for this matter? have we eaten of the king's *cost*, or have we taken any bribes?

43 And the men of Israel answered the men of Judah, and said, We have ten parts in the king, and have also more *right* to David than ye: Why then did ye despise us [1]that our advise should not be first had in restoring our king? And the words of the men of Judah were fiercer than the words of the men of Israel.

20

1 Sheba raiseth Israel against David. 10 Joab killeth Amasa traitorously. 22 The head of Sheba is delivered to Joab. 23 David's chief officers.

1 Then there was come [1]thither a wicked man (named Sheba the son of Bichri, a man of Benjamin) and he blew the trumpet, and said, We have no part in [2]David, neither have we inheritance in the son [3]of Ishai: every man to his tents, O Israel.

2 So every man of Israel went from David and followed Sheba the son of Bichri: but the men of Judah clave fast unto their King, from [1]Jordan even to Jerusalem.

3 When David then came to his house to Jerusalem, the king took the ten women his [a]concubines,

CHAPTER 20
[a] 2 Sam. 16:22
[b] 2 Sam. 8:18

that he had left behind him to keep the house, and put them in ward, and fed them, but lay no more with them: but they were enclosed unto the day of their death, living in widowhood.

4 ¶ Then said the King to [1]Amasa, Assemble me the men of Judah within three days, and be thou here present.

5 So Amasa went to assemble Judah, but he tarried longer than the time which he had appointed him.

6 Then David said to Abishai, Now shall Sheba the son of Bichri do us more harm than *did* Absalom: take thou *therefore* thy [1]lord's servants and follow after him, lest he get him walled cities, and escape us.

7 And there went out after him Joab's men, and the [b]Cherethites and the Pelethites, and all the mighty men: and they departed out of Jerusalem, to follow after Sheba the son of Bichri.

8 When they were at the great stone, which is in Gibeon, Amasa went before them, and Joab's [1]garment, that he had put on, was girded unto him, and upon it was a sword girded, which hanged on his loins in the sheath, and as he went, it used to fall out.

9 And Joab said to Amasa, Art thou in [1]health, my brother? and Joab took Amasa by the beard with the right hand to kiss him.

10 But Amasa took no heed to the sword that was in Joab's hand: for therewith he smote him in the fifth *rib*, and shed out his bowels to the ground, and [1]smote him not the second time: so he died: then Joab and Abishai his brother followed after Sheba the son of Bichri.

11 And one of Joab's men [1]stood by him, and said, He that favoreth Joab, and he that is of David's part, *let him go* after Joab.

12 And Amasa wallowed in blood in the midst of the way: and when the man saw that all the people stood still, he removed Amasa out of the way into the field, and cast a cloth upon him, because he saw that everyone that came by him, stood still.

13 ¶ When he was removed out of the way, every man went after Joab, to follow after Sheba the son of Bichri.

14 And he went through all the tribes of Israel unto Abel, and [1]Beth Maachah and all *places* of Berim: and they gathered together, and went also after him.

15 So they came, and besieged him in Abel, *near*

19:37 [1] My son.
19:38 [1] Or, choose.
19:39 [1] Or, bade him farewell.
19:40 [1] Where the tribe of Judah tarried to receive him.
    [2] Which had taken part with the King.
19:41 [1] Toward Jerusalem.
19:43 [1] Or, have not we first spoken to bring home the King? verse 11.
20:1 [1] Where the ten tribes contended against Judah.
    [2] As they of Judah say.
    [3] He thought by speaking contemptuously of the king, to stir the

people rather to sedition, or else by causing Israel to depart, thought that they of Judah would have less esteemed him.
20:2 [1] From Gilgal, which was near Jordan.
20:4 [1] Who was his chief captain in Joab's room, 2 Sam. 19:13.
20:6 [1] Either them which had been under Joab or David's men.
20:8 [1] Which was his coat, that he used to wear in the wars.
20:9 [1] Hebrew, *peace*.
20:10 [1] Hebrew, *doubled not his stroke*.
20:11 [1] He stood by Amasa at Joab's appointment.
20:14 [1] Unto the city Abel, which was near to Beth Maachah.

to Beth Maachah, and they cast up a mount against the city, and the people thereof stood on the rampart, and all the people that was with Joab, [1]destroyed and cast down the wall.

16 Then cried a wise woman out of the city, Hear, hear, I pray you, say unto Joab, Come thou hither, that I may speak with thee.

17 And when he came near unto her, the woman said, Art thou Joab? And he answered, Yea. And she said to him, Hear the words of thine handmaid. And he answered, I do hear.

18 Then she spake thus, [1]They spake in the old time, saying, They should ask of Abel: and so they have continued.

19 I am [1]one of them that are peaceable, *and* faithful in Israel: and thou goest about to destroy a city, and a mother in Israel: why wilt thou devour the inheritance of the Lord?

20 And Joab answered, and said, God forbid, God forbid it me, that I should devour, or destroy it.

21 The [1]matter is not so, but a man of mount Ephraim (Sheba the son of Bichri by name) hath lift up his hand against the king, *even* against David: deliver us him only, and I will depart from the city. And the woman said unto Joab, Behold, his head shall be thrown to thee over the wall.

22 Then the woman went unto all the people with her wisdom, and they cut off the head of Sheba the son of Bichri, and cast *it* to Joab: then he blew the trumpet, and [1]they retired from the city, every man to his tent: and Joab returned to Jerusalem unto the King.

23 ¶ Then Joab *was* over all the host of Israel, and Benaiah the son of Jehoiada over the Cherethites, and over the Pelethites,

24 And Adoram over the tribute, and Jehoshaphat the son of Ahilud the Recorder,

25 And Sheva *was* Scribe, and Zadok and Abiathar the Priests

26 And also Ira the Jairite *was* [1]chief about David.

c 2 Sam. 8:16

CHAPTER 21
a Josh. 9:3,16,17
b 1 Sam. 18:3
1 Sam. 20:8,42

21 1 *Three dear years.* 9 *The vengeance of the sins of Saul lighteth on his seven sons, which are hanged.* 15 *Four great battles, which David had against the Philistines.*

1 Then there was a famine in the days of David, three years [1]together: and David [2]asked counsel of the Lord, and the Lord answered, It is for Saul, and for his bloody house, because he slew the [3]Gibeonites.

2 Then the King called the Gibeonites, and said unto them, (Now the Gibeonites were not of the children of Israel, but a [a]remnant of the Amorites, unto whom the children of Israel had sworn: but Saul sought to slay them for his zeal toward the children of Israel and Judah)

3 And David said unto the Gibeonites, [1]What shall I do for you, and wherewith shall I make the atonement, that ye may bless the inheritance of the Lord?

4 The Gibeonites then answered him, We will have no silver nor gold of Saul nor of his house, neither for us shalt thou kill [1]any man in Israel. And he said, What ye shall say that will I do for you.

5 Then they answered the king, The man that consumed us, and that imagined evil against us, *so that* we are destroyed from remaining in any coast of Israel,

6 Let seven men of his [1]sons be delivered unto us, and we will hang them up [2]unto the Lord in Gibeah of Saul, the Lord's chosen, And the king said, I will give them.

7 But the king had compassion on Mephibosheth the son of Jonathan the son of Saul, because of the [b]Lord's oath, that was between them, *even* between David and Jonathan the son of Saul.

8 But the king took the two sons of Rizpah the daughter of Aiah, whom she bare unto Saul, *even* Armoni and Mephibosheth, and the five sons of [1]Michal, the daughter of Saul, whom she bare to Adriel the son of Barzillai the Meholathite.

9 And he delivered them unto the hands of the Gibeonites, which hanged them in the mountain before the Lord: so they [1]died *all* seven together: and they were slain in the time of harvest: in the [2]first *days*, and in the beginning of barley harvest.

10 Then Rizpah the daughter of Aiah took [1]sackcloth and hanged it up for her upon the rock, from

---

20:15 [1] That is, he went about to overthrow it.
20:18 [1] She showeth that the old custom was not to destroy a city before peace was offered, Deut. 20:10, 11.
20:19 [1] She speaketh in the name of the city.
20:21 [1] Hearing his fault told him, he gave place to reason, and required only him that was author of the treason.
20:22 [1] Hebrew, *they were scattered.*
20:26 [1] Either in dignity or familiarity.
21:1 [1] Hebrew, *year after year.*
  [2] Hebrew, *sought the face of the Lord.*
  [3] Thinking to gratify the people, because these were not of the seed of Abraham.
21:3 [1] Wherewith may your wrath be appeased, that you may pray

to God to remove this plague from his people.
21:4 [1] Save only of Saul's stock.
21:6 [1] Of Saul's kinsmen.
  [2] To pacify the Lord.
21:8 [1] Here Michal is named for Merab, Adriel's wife, as appeareth, 1 Sam. 18:19, for Michal was the wife of Paltiel, 1 Sam. 25:44, and never had child, 2 Sam. 6:23.
21:9 [1] Hebrew, *fell.*
  [2] Which was in the month Abib or Nisan, which contained part of March and part of April.
21:10 [1] To make her a tent wherein she prayed to God to turn away his wrath.

the beginning of harvest, until ²water dropped upon them from the heaven, and suffered neither the birds of the air to ³light on them by day, nor beasts of the field by night.

11 ¶ And it was told David, what Rizpah the daughter of Aiah the concubine of Saul had done.

12 And David went and took the bones of Saul, and the bones of Jonathan his son from the citizens of Jabesh Gilead, which had stolen them from the street of Beth Shan, where the Philistines had ᶜhanged them, when the Philistines had slain Saul in Gilboa.

13 So he brought thence the bones of Saul, and the bones of Jonathan his son, and they gathered the bones of them that were hanged.

14 And the bones of Saul and of Jonathan his son buried they in the country of Benjamin in Zelah, in the grave of Kish his father: and when they had performed all that the King had commanded, God was then ¹appeased with the land.

15 ¶ Again the Philistines hath war with Israel: and David went down, and his servants with him, and they fought against the Philistines, and David fainted.

16 Then Ishbi-Benob which was of the sons of ¹Haraphah (the head of whose spear weighed three hundred ²shekels of brass) even he being girded with a new sword, thought to have slain David.

17 But Abishai the son of Zeruiah succored him, and smote the Philistine, and killed him. Then David's men swore unto him, saying, Thou shalt go no more out with us to battle, lest thou quench the ¹light of Israel.

18 ¶ And after this also there was a battle with the Philistines at ¹Gob, then Sibbechai the Hushathite slew Saph, which was one of the sons of Haraphah.

19 And there was yet another battle in Gob with the Philistines, where Elhanan the son of Jaare-Oregim, a Bethlehemite slew ¹Goliath the Gittite: the staff of whose spear was like a weaver's beam.

20 Afterward there was also a battle in Gath, where was a man of a great stature, and had on every hand six fingers, and on every foot six toes, four and twenty in number: who was also the son of Haraphah.

21 And when he reviled Israel, Jonathan the son

ᶜ 1 Sam. 31:10
ᵈ 1 Sam. 16:9

CHAPTER 22
ᵃ Ps. 18:2

of ᵈShimea the brother of David slew him.

22 These four were born to Haraphah in Gath, and died by the hand of David, and by the hands of his servants.

22

2 David after his victories praiseth God. 8 The anger of God toward the wicked. 44 He prophesieth of the rejection of the Jews, and vocation of the Gentiles.

1 And David spake the words of this ¹song unto the Lord, what time the Lord had delivered him out of the hands of all his enemies, and out of the hand of Saul.

2 And he said, ᵃThe Lord is my ¹rock and my fortress, and he that delivereth me.

3 God is my ¹strength, in him will I trust: my shield, and the horn of my salvation, my high tower and my refuge: my Savior, thou hast saved me from violence.

4 I will call on the Lord, who is worthy to be praised: so shall I be safe from mine enemies.

5 For the ¹pangs of death have compassed me: the floods of ungodliness have made me afraid.

6 The sorrows of the grave compassed me about: the snares of death overtook me.

7 But in my tribulation did I call upon the Lord, and cry to my God, and he did hear my voice out of his Temple, and my cry did enter into his ears.

8 Then the earth trembled and quaked: the foundations of the heavens moved and shook, because he was angry.

9 ¹Smoke went out at his nostrils, and consuming ²fire out of his mouth: coals were kindled thereat.

10 He ¹bowed the heavens also, and came down, and darkness was under his feet.

11 And he rode upon ¹Cherub and did fly, and he was seen upon the wings of the wind.

12 And he made darkness a Tabernacle round about him, even the gatherings of waters, and the clouds of the air.

13 At the brightness of his presence ¹the coals of fire were kindled.

14 The Lord thundered from heaven, and the most

---

² Because drought was the cause of this famine, God by sending of rain showed that he was pacified.

³ Or, rest.

21:14 ¹ For where the magistrate suffereth faults unpunished, there the plague of God lieth upon the land.

21:16 ¹ That is, of the race of giants.

² Which amount to nine pounds three quarters.

21:17 ¹ For the glory and wealth of the country standeth in the preservation of the godly magistrate.

21:18 ¹ Called Gezer, and Saph is called Sippai, 1 Chron. 20:4.

21:19 ¹ That is, Lahmi the brother of Goliath, whom David slew, 1 Chron. 20:5.

22:1 ¹ In token of the wonderful benefits that he received of God.

22:2 ¹ By the diversity of these comfortable means, he showeth how his faith was strengthened in all tentations.

22:3 ¹ Or, rock.

22:5 ¹ As David (who was the figure of Christ) was by God's power delivered from all dangers: so Christ and his Church shall overcome most grievous dangers, tyranny and death.

22:9 ¹ That is, clouds, and vapors.

² Lightning and thundering.

22:10 ¹ So it seemeth when the air is dark.

22:11 ¹ To fly in a moment through the world.

22:13 ¹ By this description of a tempest he declareth the power of God against his enemies.

High gave his voice.

15 He shot arrows also, and scattered them: *to wit*, lightning, and destroyed them.

16 The [1]channels also of the sea appeared, *even* the foundations of the world were discovered by the rebuking of the Lord, *and* at the blast of the breath of his nostrils.

17 He sent from above, *and* took me: he drew me out of many waters.

18 He delivered me from my strong enemy, *and* from them that hated me: for they were too strong for me.

19 They [1]prevented me in the day of my calamity, but the Lord was my stay,

20 And brought me forth into a large place: he delivered me, because he favored me.

21 The Lord rewarded me according to my [1]righteousness: according to the pureness of mine hands he recompensed me.

22 For I kept the ways of the Lord, and did not [1]wickedly against my God.

23 For all his laws *were* before me, and his statutes: I did not depart therefrom.

24 I was upright also toward him, and have kept me from my wickedness.

25 Therefore the Lord did reward me according to my righteousness, according to my pureness before his eyes.

26 With the godly thou wilt show thyself godly: with the upright man thou wilt show thyself upright.

27 With the pure thou wilt show thyself pure, and with the [1]froward thou wilt show thyself froward.

28 Thus thou wilt save the poor people: but thine eyes *are* upon the haughty, to humble *them*.

29 Surely thou art my light, O Lord: and the Lord will lighten my darkness.

30 For by thee have I broken through an host, and by my God have I leaped over a wall.

31 The way of God is [1]uncorrupt: the word of the Lord is tried *in the fire*: he is a shield to all that trust in him.

32 For who is God besides the Lord? and who is mighty, save our God?

33 God is my strength in battle, and maketh my way upright.

34 He maketh my feet like [1]hinds *feet*, and hath set me upon mine high places.

[b] Rom. 15:9
[c] 2 Sam. 7:13

35 He teacheth mine hands to fight, so that a bowl [1]of brass is broken with mine arms.

36 Thou hast also given me the shield of thy salvation, and thy loving kindness hath caused me to increase.

37 Thou hast enlarged my steps under me, and mine heels have not slid.

38 I have pursued mine enemies, and destroyed them, and have not turned again until I had consumed them.

39 Yea, I have consumed them and thrust them through, and they shall not arise, but shall fall under my feet.

40 For thou hast [1]girded me with power to battle, *and* them that rose against me, hast thou subdued under me.

41 And thou hast given me the necks of mine enemies, that I might destroy them that hate me.

42 They looked about, but there was none to save *them*, *even* unto the [1]Lord, but he answered them not.

43 Then did I beat them as small as the dust of the earth: I did tread them flat as the clay of the street, *and* did spread them abroad.

44 Thou hast also delivered me from the contentions of my [1]people: thou hast preserved me to be the head over nations: the people which I knew not, do serve me.

45 Strangers [1]shall be in subjection to me: as soon as they hear, they shall obey me.

46 Strangers shall shrink away, and fear in their privy chambers.

47 Let the Lord live, [1]and blessed be my strength: and God, *even* the force of my salvation be exalted.

48 *It is* God that giveth me *power* to revenge me, and subdue the people under me,

49 And rescueth me from mine enemies: (thou also hast lift me up from them that rose against me, thou hast delivered me from the cruel man.

50 Therefore I will praise thee, O Lord, among the [b]nations, and will sing unto thy Name.)

51 *He is* the tower of salvation for his King, and showeth mercy to his anointed, *even* to David, and to his seed [c]forever.

23

1 *The last words of David.*   6 *The wicked shall be plucked up as thorns.*   8 *The names and facts of his mighty men.*   15 *He desired water, and would not drink it.*

22:16 [1] He alludeth to the miracle of the red Sea.
22:19 [1] I was so beset, that all means seemed to fail.
22:21 [1] Toward Saul and mine enemies.
22:22 [1] I attempted nothing without his commandment.
22:27 [1] Their wickedness is cause that thou seemest to forget thy wonted mercy.
22:31 [1] The manner that God useth to succor his, never faileth.
22:34 [1] He useth extraordinary means to make me win most strongholds.
22:35 [1] Or, steel.
22:40 [1] He acknowledgeth that God was the author of his victories, who gave him strength.
22:42 [1] The wicked in their necessity are compelled to flee to God, but it is too late.
22:44 [1] Meaning, of the Jews, who conspired against me.
22:45 [1] Not willingly obeying me, but dissemblingly.
22:47 [1] Let him show his power, that he is the governor of all the world.

1 These also be the [1]last words of David, David the son of Jesse saith, even the man who was set up on high, the anointed of the God of Jacob, and the sweet singer of Israel saith,

2 The Spirit of the Lord spake by me, and his word *was* in my [1]tongue.

3 The God of Israel spake to me, the strength of Israel said, *Thou shalt* bear rule over men, being just, *and* ruling in the fear of God.

4 Even as the morning light when the sun riseth, the morning, I say, without clouds, *so shall mine house be, and not* as the [1]grass of the earth *is* by the bright rain.

5 For so shall not mine house *be* with God: for he hath made with me an everlasting covenant, perfect in all points, and sure: therefore all mine health and whole desire *is*, that he will not make it [1]grow *so*.

6 But the wicked *shall be* every one as thorns thrust away, because they cannot be taken with hands.

7 But the man that shall touch them, must be defenced with iron, or with the shaft of a spear: and they shall be burnt with fire in the same place.

8 ¶ These *be* the names of the mighty men whom David hath: He that sat in the seat of [1]wisdom, being chief of the princes, was Adino of Ezni, he slew eight hundred at one time.

9 And after him *was* [a]Eleazar the son of Dodo, the son of Ahohi, one of the three worthies with David, when they [1]defied the Philistines gathered there to battle, when the men of Israel were [2]gone up.

10 He arose and smote the Philistines, until his hand was weary, and his [1]hand clave unto the sword: and the Lord gave great victory the same day, and the people returned after him only to spoil.

11 After him *was* [b]Shammah the son of Agee the Hararite: for the Philistines assembled at a town, where was a piece of a field full of lentils, and the people fled from the Philistines.

12 But he stood in the midst of the field, and defended it, and slew the Philistines: so the Lord gave [1]great victory.

13 ¶ Afterward three of the thirty captains went down, and came to David in the harvest time unto the cave of Adullam, and the host of the Philistines

CHAPTER 23
[a] 1 Chron. 11:12
[b] 1 Chron. 11:27
[c] 1 Chron. 11:20
[d] 2 Sam. 2:18
[e] 1 Chron. 11:27

pitched in the valley of [1]Rephaim.

14 And David *was* then in an hold, and the garrison of the Philistines *was* then in Bethlehem.

15 And David [1]longed, and said, Oh, that one would give me to drink of the water of the well of Bethlehem which is by the gate.

16 Then the three mighty brake into the host of the Philistines, and drew water out of the well of Bethlehem that was by the gate, and took and brought it to David, who would not drink thereof, but [1]poured it *for an offering* unto the Lord,

17 And said, O Lord, be it far from me, that I should do this. *Is* not this the blood of the men that went in jeopardy of their lives? therefore he would not drink it. These things did these three mighty men.

18 ¶ [c]And Abishai the brother of Joab, the son of Zeruiah, was chief among the three, and he lifted up his spear against three hundred, [1]and slew them, and he had the name among the three.

19 For he was most excellent of the three, and was their captain, but he attained not unto *the first* three.

20 And Benaiah the son of Jehoiada the son of [1]a valiant man, which had done many acts, *and was* of Kabzeel, slew two strong men of Moab: he went down also, and slew a lion in the midst of a pit in the time of snow.

21 And he slew an Egyptian a [1]man of great stature, and the Egyptian had a [2]spear in his hand: but he went down to him with a staff, and plucked the spear out of the Egyptian's hand, and slew him with his own spear.

22 These things did Benaiah the son of Jehoiada, and had the name among the three worthies.

23 He was honorable among [1]thirty, but he attained not to the *first* three: and David made him of his counsel.

24 ¶ [d]Asahel the brother of Joab *was* one of the thirty: Elhanan the son of Dodo of Bethlehem:

25 Shammoth the Harorite: Elika the Harodite:

26 Helez the [e,1]Paltite: Ira the son of Ikkesh the Tekoite:

27 Abiezer the Anathothite: [1]Mebunnai the Hushathite:

28 Zalmon an Ahohite: Maharai the Netophathite:

23:1 [1] Which he spake after that he had made the Psalms.
23:2 [1] Meaning, he spake nothing but by the motion of God's Spirit.
23:4 [1] Which groweth quickly, and fadeth soon.
23:5 [1] But that my kingdom may continue forever according to his promise.
23:8 [1] As one of the King's counsel.
23:9 [1] Or, assailed with danger of their lives.
  [2] Meaning, fled from the battle.
23:10 [1] By a cramp which came of weariness and striving.
23:12 [1] Which hath neither respect to many nor few, when he will show his power.
23:13 [1] Or, giants.

23:15 [1] Being overcome with weariness and thirst.
23:16 [1] Bridling his affection, and also desiring God not to be offended for that rash enterprise.
23:18 [1] Hebrew, *slain*.
23:20 [1] Or, Jesse
23:21 [1] Or, a comely man.
  [2] Which was as big as a weaver's beam, 1 Chron. 11:23.
23:23 [1] He was more valiant than the thirty that follow, and not so valiant as the six before.
23:26 [1] Or, Pelonite.
23:27 [1] Divers of these had two names, appeareth 1 Chron. 11, and also many more are there mentioned.

29 Heleb the son of Baanah a Netophathite: Ittai the son of Ribai of Gibeah of the children of Benjamin:

30 Benaiah the Pirathonite: Hiddai of the river of Gaash:

31 Abi-Albon the Arbathite: Azmaveth the Barhumite:

32 Eliahba the Shaalbonite: *of* the sons of Jashen, Jonathan:

33 Shammah the Hararite: Ahiam the son of Sharar the Hararite:

34 Eliphelet the son of Ahasbai, the son of Maachathi: Eliam the son of Ahithophel the Gilonite:

35 Hezrai the Carmelite: Paarai the Arbite:

36 Igal the son of Nathan of Zobah: Bani the Gadite:

37 Zelek the Ammonite: Naharai the Beerothite, the armor-bearer of Joab the son of Zeruiah:

38 Ira the Ithrite: Gareb the Ithrite:

39 Uriah the Hittite, [1]thirty and seven in all.

24

CHAPTER 24
ª 1 Sam. 15:11

1 David causeth the people to be numbered. 10 He repenteth, and chooseth to fall into God's hands. 15 Seventy thousand perish with the pestilence.

1 And the wrath of the Lord was [1]again kindled against Israel, and [2]he moved David against them, in that he said, Go, number Israel and Judah.

2 For the King said to Joab the captain of the host, which was with him, Go speedily now through all the tribes of Israel, from Dan even to Beersheba, and number ye the people, that I may know the [1]number of the people.

3 And Joab said unto the King, The Lord thy God increase the people an hundredfold more than they be, and that the eyes of my lord the King may see it: but why doth my lord the King desire this thing?

4 Notwithstanding the King's word prevailed against Joab and against the captains of the host: therefore Joab and the captains of the host went out from the presence of the King to number the people of Israel.

5 ¶ And they passed over Jordan, and pitched in Aroer at the right side of the city that is in the midst of the [1]valley of Gad, and toward Jazer.

6 Then they came to Gilead, and to [1]Tahtim Hodshi, so they came to Dan Jaan, and so about to Sidon,

7 And came to the fortress of [1]Tyre and to all the cities of the Hivites and of the Canaanites, and went toward the South of Judah, even to Beersheba.

8 ¶ So when they had gone about all the land, they returned to Jerusalem at the end of nine months and twenty days.

9 ¶ And Joab delivered the number *and* sum of the people unto the King: and there were in Israel [1]eight hundred thousand strong men that drew swords, and the men of Judah were [2]five hundred thousand men.

10 Then David's heart smote him, after that he had numbered the people: and David said unto the Lord, I have sinned exceedingly, in that I have done: therefore now, Lord, I beseech thee, take away the trespass of thy servant: for I have done very foolishly.

11 ¶ And when David was up in the morning, the word of the Lord came unto the Prophet Gad David's [1]Seer, saying,

12 Go, and say unto David, Thus saith the Lord, I offer thee three things, choose thee which of them I shall do unto thee.

13 So Gad came to David, and showed him, and said unto him, Wilt thou that [1]seven years famine come upon thee in thy land, or wilt thou flee three months before thine enemies, they following thee, or that there be three days pestilence in my land? now advise thee, and see, what answer I shall give to him that sent me.

14 ¶ And David said unto Gad, I am in a wonderful strait: let us fall now into the hand of the Lord, (for his mercies *are* great) and let me not fall into the hand of man.

15 So the Lord sent a pestilence in Israel from the morning even unto the time appointed: and there died of the people from [1]Dan even to Beersheba seventy thousand men.

16 And when the Angel stretched out his hand upon Jerusalem to destroy it, the Lord ªrepented of the evil, and said to the Angel, that destroyed the people, It is sufficient, [1]hold now thine hand. And the Angel of the Lord was by the threshing place of Araunah the Jebusite.

23:39 [1] These came to David, and helped to restore him to his Kingdom.

24:1 [1] Before they were plagued with famine, 2 Sam. 21:1.
[2] The Lord permitted Satan, as 1 Chron. 21:2.

24:2 [1] Because he did this to try his power, and so to trust therein, it offended God, else it was lawful to number the people, Exod. 30:12; Num. 1:2.

24:5 [1] Or, river.

24:6 [1] Or, to the nether land newly inhabited.

24:7 [1] Or, Zor.

24:9 [1] According to Joab's count: for in all there were eleven hundred thousand, 1 Chron. 21:5.
[2] Concluding under them the Benjamites: for else they had but four hundred and seventy thousand, 1 Chron. 21:5.

24:11 [1] Whom God had appointed for David and his time.

24:13 [1] For three years of famine were past for the Gibeonites' matter: this was the fourth year to the which should have been added other three years more, 1 Chron. 21:12.

24:15 [1] From the one side of the country to the other.

24:16 [1] The Lord spared this place, because he had chosen it to build his Temple there.

17 And David spake unto the Lord (when he saw the Angel that smote the people) and said, Behold, I have sinned, yea, I have done wickedly, but these sheep, what have they [1]done? let thine hand, I pray, thee, be against me and against my father's house.

18 ¶ So Gad came the same day to David, and said unto him, Go up, rear an altar unto the Lord in the threshing floor of Araunah the Jebusite.

19 And David (according to the saying of Gad) went up, as the Lord had commanded.

20 And Araunah looked, and saw the king and his servants coming toward him, and Araunah went out, and bowed himself before the King on his face to the ground.

21 And [1]Araunah said, Wherefore is my lord the king come to his servant? Then David answered, to buy the threshing floor of thee for to build an altar unto the Lord, that the plague may cease from the people.

22 Then Araunah said unto David, Let my lord the King take and offer what seemeth him good in his eyes: behold the oxen for the burnt offering, and chariots, and the instruments of the oxen for wood.

23 (All these things did Araunah [1]as a king give unto the king: and Araunah said unto the king, The Lord thy God be favorable unto thee.)

24 Then the king said unto Araunah, Not so, but I will buy it of thee at a price, and will not offer burnt offering unto the Lord my God of that which doth cost me nothing. So David bought the threshing floor, and the oxen for [1]fifty shekels of silver.

25 And David built there an altar unto the Lord, and offered burnt offerings and peace offerings, and the Lord was appeased toward the land, and the plague ceased from Israel.

24:17 [1] David saw not the just cause why God plagued the people, and therefore he offereth himself to God's corrections as the only cause of this evil.
24:21 [1] Called also Ornan, 1 Chron. 21:20.

24:23 [1] That is, abundantly: for as some write, he was King of Jerusalem before David won the tower.
24:24 [1] Some write that every tribe gave 50 which makes 600, or that afterward he bought as much as came to 550 shekels, 1 Chron. 21:25.

THE FIRST BOOK

OF THE

KINGS

3 *Abishag keepeth David in his extreme age.* 5 *Adonijah usurpeth the kingdom.* 30 *Solomon is anointed king.* 50 *Adonijah fleeth to the altar.*

1 Now when King David was [1]old, and stricken in years, they covered him with clothes, but no [2]heat came unto him.

2 Wherefore his servants said unto him, Let there be sought for my lord the king a young virgin, and let her [1]stand before the king, and cherish him: and let her lie in thy bosom, that my lord the King may get heat.

3 So they sought for a fair young maid throughout all the coasts of Israel, and found one Abishag [1]a Shunammite, and brought her to the king.

4 And the maid was exceedingly fair, and cherished the king, and ministered to him, but the king knew her not.

5 ¶ Then Adonijah the son of Haggith, exalted himself, saying, I will be king. And he got him chariots and horsemen, and [1]fifty men to run before him.

6 And his father would not displease him from his [1]childhood, to say, Why hast thou done so? And he was a very goodly man, and *his mother* bare him next after Absalom.

7 And he [1]took counsel of Joab the son of Zeruiah, and of Abiathar the Priest: and they [2]helped forward Adonijah.

8 But Zadok the Priest, and Benaiah the son of Jehoiada, and Nathan the Prophet, and Shimei, and Rei, and the men of might, which were with David, were not with Adonijah.

9 Then Adonijah sacrificed sheep and oxen, and fat cattle by the stone of Zoheleth, which is by [1]En Rogel, and called all his brethren the king's sons, and all the men of Judah the king's servants.

10 But Nathan the Prophet, and Benaiah, and [1]the mighty men, and Solomon his brother he called not.

11 Wherefore Nathan spake unto Bathsheba the mother of Solomon, saying, Hast thou not heard that Adonijah the son of [a]Haggith doth reign, and David our lord knoweth it not?

12 Now therefore come, *and* I will now give thee counsel, how to save thine own [1]life, and the life of thy son Solomon.

13 Go, and get thee in unto King David, and say unto him, Didst not thou, my lord, O King, swear unto thine handmaid, saying, Assuredly, Solomon thy son shall reign after me, and he shall sit upon my throne? why is then Adonijah King?

14 Behold, while thou yet talkest there with the King, I also will come in after thee, and [1]confirm thy words.

15 ¶ So Bathsheba went in unto the King into the chamber, and the king was very old, and Abishag the Shunammite ministered unto the King.

16 And Bathsheba bowed and made obeisance unto the king. And the King said, What is thy matter?

17 And she answered him, My lord, thou swearest by the Lord thy God unto thine handmaid, *saying,* Assuredly Solomon thy son shall reign after me, and he shall sit upon my throne.

18 And behold, now *is* Adonijah king, and now my lord, O King, thou knowest [1]it not.

19 And he hath offered many oxen, and fat cattle, and sheep, and hath called all the sons of the King, and Abiathar the Priest, and Joab the Captain of the host: but Solomon thy servant hath he not bidden.

20 And thou, my lord, O King, *knowest* that the eyes of all Israel *are* on thee, that thou shouldest tell them, who should sit on the throne of my lord the King after him.

21 For else when my lord the King shall sleep with his fathers, I and my son Solomon shall be [1]reputed [2]vile.

---

[1] He was about 70 years old, 2 Sam. 5:4.
  [2] For his natural heat was worn away with travails.
1:2 [1] Or, serve him.
1:3 [1] Which city was in the tribe of Issachar, as Josh. 19:18.
1:5 [1] Read 2 Sam. 15:1.
1:6 [1] Hebrew, *days.*
1:7 [1] Hebrew, *his words were with Joab.*
  [2] They took his part and followed him.

1:9 [1] Or, the fountains.
1:10 [1] As the Cherethites and Pelethites.
1:12 [1] For Adonijah will destroy thee and thy son, if he reigns.
1:14 [1] By declaring such things, as may further the same.
1:18 [1] The king being worn with age, could not attend to the affairs of the realm, and also Adonijah had many flatterers which kept it from the king.
1:21 [1] And so put to the death as wicked transgressors.
  [2] Hebrew, *sinners.*

22 And lo, while she yet talked with the king, Nathan also the Prophet came in.

23 And they told the King, saying, Behold, Nathan the Prophet. And when he was come in to the King, he made obeisance before the king upon his face [1]to the ground.

24 And Nathan said, My lord, O king, hast thou said, Adonijah shall reign after me, and he shall sit upon my throne?

25 For he is gone down this day, and hath slain many oxen, and fat cattle, and sheep, and hath called all the king's sons, and the captains of the host, and Abiathar the Priest: and behold, they eat and drink before him, and say, [1]God save king Adonijah.

26 But me thy servant, and Zadok the Priest, and Benaiah the son of Jehoiada, and thy servant Solomon hath he not called.

27 Is this thing done by my lord the king, and thou hast not showed it unto thy [1]servant, who should sit on the throne of my lord the king after him?

28 ¶ Then king David answered, and said, Call me Bathsheba. And she came into the king's presence, and stood before the King.

29 And the King sware, saying, As the Lord liveth, who hath redeemed my soul out of all adversity,

30 That as I [1]sware unto thee by the Lord God of Israel, saying, Assuredly Solomon thy son shall reign after me, and he shall sit upon my throne in my place, so will I certainly do this day.

31 Then Bathsheba bowed her face to the earth, and did reverence unto the king, and said, God save my lord king David forever.

32 ¶ And king David said, Call me Zadok the Priest, and Nathan the Prophet, and Benaiah the son of Jehoiada. And they came before the King.

33 Then the king said unto them, Take with you the [1]servants of your lord, and cause Solomon my son to ride upon mine own mule, and carry him down to Gihon.

34 And let Zadok the Priest and Nathan the Prophet anoint him there king over Israel, and blow ye the trumpet, and say, God save King Solomon.

35 Then come up after him, that he may come and sit upon my throne: and he shall be King in my stead: for I have [1]appointed him to be prince over Israel, and over Judah.

36 Then Benaiah the son of Jehoiada answered the king, and said, So be it, *and* the Lord God of my lord the king [1]ratify it.

37 As the Lord hath been with my lord the king, so be he with Solomon, and exalt his throne above the throne of my lord king David.

38 So Zadok the Priest, and Nathan the Prophet, and Benaiah the son of Jehoiada, and the Cherethites, and the Pelethites went down and caused Solomon to ride upon king David's mule, and brought him to Gihon.

39 And Zadok the Priest took an horn of [1]oil out of the Tabernacle, and anointed Solomon: and they blew the trumpet, and all the people said, God save king Solomon.

40 And all the people came up after him, and the people piped with pipes, and rejoiced with great joy, so that the earth [1]rang with the sound of them.

41 ¶ And Adonijah and all the guests that were with him, heard it: (and they had made an end of eating) and when Joab heard the sound of the trumpet, he said, What meaneth this noise and uproar in the city?

42 And as he yet spake, behold, Jonathan the son of Abiathar the Priest came: and Adonijah said, Come in: for thou art a [1]worthy man, and bringest [2]good tidings.

43 And Jonathan answered, and said to Adonijah, Verily our lord king David hath made Solomon king.

44 And the king hath sent with him Zadok the Priest, and Nathan the Prophet, and Benaiah the son of Jehoiada, and the Cherethites, and the Pelethites, and they have caused him to ride upon the king's mule.

45 And Zadok the Priest, and Nathan the Prophet have anointed him king in Gihon: and they are gone up from thence with joy, and the city is moved: this is the noise that ye have heard.

46 And Solomon also sitteth on the throne of the kingdom.

47 And moreover the king's servants came [1]to bless our lord king David, saying, God make the name of Solomon more famous than thy name, and exalt his throne above thy throne: therefore the king worshipped upon the [2]bed.

48 And thus said the king also, Blessed be the

1:23 [1] Acknowledging him to be the true and worthy King appointed of God, as the figure of his Christ.

1:25 [1] Hebrew, *let the king Adonijah live.*

1:27 [1] Meaning, that he ought in such affairs enterprise nothing except he had consulted with the Lord.

1:30 [1] Moved by the Spirit of God so to do, because he foresaw that Solomon should be the figure of Christ.

1:33 [1] Meaning, the king's servants and such as were of his guard.

1:35 [1] Hebrew, *commanded.*

1:36 [1] Hebrew, *say so.*

1:39 [1] Wherewith they accustomed to anoint the Priests and the holy instruments, Exod. 30:23.

1:40 [1] Hebrew, *brake.*

1:42 [1] Hebrew, *a man of power.*

[2] He praised Jonathan, thinking to have heard comfortable news but God wrought things contrary to his expectation, and so did beat down his pride.

1:47 [1] To salute him, and to pray and praise God for him.

[2] He gave God thanks for the good success.

Lord God of Israel, who hath made one to sit on my throne this day, even in my sight.

49 Then all the guests that were with Adonijah, were afraid, and rose up, and went every man his way.

50 ¶ And Adonijah fearing the presence of Solomon, arose and went, and took hold on the horns of the ¹altar.

51 And one told Solomon, saying, Behold, Adonijah doth fear king Solomon: for lo, he hath caught hold on the horns of the altar, saying, Let King Solomon swear unto me this day, that he will not slay his servant with the sword.

52 Then Solomon said, If he will show himself a worthy man, there shall not an hair of him fall to the earth, but if wickedness be found in him, he shall die.

53 Then king Solomon sent, and they brought him from the altar, and he came and did obeisance unto King Solomon. And Solomon said unto him, Go to thine house.

2 1 *David exhorteth Solomon, and giveth charge concerning Joab, Barzillai, and Shimei.* 10 *The death of David.* 17 *Adonijah asketh Abishag to wife.* 25 *He is slain.* 35 *Zadok was placed in Abiathar's room.*

1 Then the days of David drew near that he should die, and he charged Solomon his son, saying,

2 I go the ¹way of all the earth: be strong therefore, and show thyself a man,

3 And take heed to the ¹charge of the Lord thy God, to walk in his ways, and keep his statutes, and his commandments, and his judgments, and his testimonies, as it is written in the Law of Moses, that thou mayest ᵃ,²prosper in all that thou doest, and in everything whereunto thou turnest thee,

4 That the Lord may confirm his word which he spake unto me, saying, If thy sons take heed to their way, that they walk before me in ¹truth, with all their hearts, and with all their souls, ᵇ,²thou shalt not (said he) want one of thy *posterity* upon the throne of Israel.

5 Thou knowest also what Joab the son of Zeruiah did to me, and what he did to the two captains to the hosts of Israel, unto ᶜAbner the son of Ner, and unto ᵈAmasa the son of Jether, whom he slew, and ¹shed blood of battle in peace, and ²put the blood

CHAPTER 2
ᵃ Deut. 29:9
  Josh. 1:7
ᵇ 2 Sam. 7:12
ᶜ 2 Sam. 3:27
ᵈ 2 Sam. 29:10
ᵉ 2 Sam. 19:31
ᶠ 2 Sam. 16:5
ᵍ 2 Sam. 19:23
ʰ Acts 2:29
ⁱ 2 Sam. 5:4
  1 Chron.
  29:26,27
ʲ 1 Chron. 29:25

of war upon his girdle that was about his loins, and in his shoes that were on his feet.

6 Do therefore according to thy wisdom, and let thou not his hoar head go down to the grave in peace.

7 But show kindness unto the sons of ᵉBarzillai the Gileadite, and let them be among them that eat at thy table: ¹for so they came to me when I fled from Absalom thy brother.

8 ¶ And behold, with thee ᶠis Shimei the son of Gera, the son of Benjamin, of Bahurim, which cursed me with an horrible curse in the day when I went to Mahanaim: but he came down to meet me at Jordan, and I sware to him by the Lord, saying, ᵍI will not slay thee with the sword.

9 But thou shalt not count him innocent: for thou art a wise man, and knowest what thou oughtest to do unto him: therefore thou shalt cause his hoar head to go down to the grave with ¹blood.

10 So ʰDavid slept with his fathers, and was buried in the city of David.

11 And the days which David ⁱreigned upon Israel, *were* forty years: seven years reigned he in Hebron, and thirty and three years reigned he in Jerusalem.

12 ¶ʲThen sat Solomon upon the throne of David his father, and his kingdom was established mightily.

13 And Adonijah the son of Haggith came to Bathsheba the mother of Solomon: and she said, ¹Comest thou peaceably? and he said, Yea.

14 He said moreover, I have a suit unto thee. And she said, Say on.

15 Then he said, Thou knowest that the kingdom was mine, and that all Israel set ¹their faces on me, that I should reign: howbeit the kingdom is turned away, and is my brother's: for it came to him by the Lord.

16 Now therefore I ask thee one ¹request, ¹refuse me not. And she said unto him, Say on.

17 And he said, Speak, I pray thee, unto Solomon the King, (for he will not say thee nay) that he give me Abishag the Shunammite to wife.

18 And Bathsheba said, Well, I will speak for thee unto the King.

19 ¶ Bathsheba therefore went unto King Solomon, to speak unto him for Adonijah: and the king rose to meet her, and ¹bowed himself unto her, and sat down on his throne: and he caused a seat to be set for the king's mother, and she sat at his right hand.

20 Then she said, I desire a small request of thee,

1:50 ¹ Which David his father had built in the floor of Araunah, 2 Sam. 24:25.

2:2 ¹ I am ready to die as all men must.

2:3 ¹ He showeth how hard a thing it is to govern, and that none can do it well except he obey God.
   ² Or, do wisely.

2:4 ¹ And without hypocrisy.
   ² Hebrew, *a man shall not be cut off to thee from off the throne.*

2:5 ¹ He shed his blood in time of peace, as if there had been war.

² He put the bloody sword into his sheath.

2:7 ¹ That is, they dealt mercifully with me.

2:9 ¹ Let him be punished with death, see 1 Kings 2:46.

2:13 ¹ For she feared lest he would work treason against the king.

2:15 ¹ In sign of their favor and consent.

2:16 ¹ Hebrew, *cause not my face to turn away.*

2:19 ¹ In token of reverence, and that others by his example might have her in greater honor.

say me not nay. Then the King said unto her, Ask on, my mother: for I will not say thee nay.

21 She said then, Let Abishag the Shunammite be given to Adonijah thy brother to wife.

22 But king Solomon answered and said unto his mother, And why dost thou ask Abishag the Shunammite for Adonijah? ask for him the [1]kingdom also: for he is mine elder brother, and hath for him both Abiathar the Priest, and Joab the son of Zeruiah.

23 Then King Solomon sware by the Lord, saying, God do so to me and more also, if Adonijah hath not spoken this word against his own life.

24 Now therefore as the Lord liveth, who hath established me, and set me on the throne of David my father, who hath also made me an house, as he [k]promised, Adonijah shall surely die this day.

25 And King Solomon sent by the hand of Benaiah the son of Jehoiada, and he [1]smote him that he died.

26 ¶ Then the King said unto Abiathar the Priest, Go to Anathoth unto thine own [1]fields: for thou art [2]worthy of death: but I will not this day kill thee, because thou [3]barest the Ark of the Lord God before David my father, and because thou hast suffered in all, wherein my father hath been afflicted.

27 So Solomon cast out Abiathar from being Priest unto the Lord, that he might [l]fulfill the words of the Lord, which he spake against the house of Eli in Shiloh.

28 ¶ Then tidings came to Joab: (for Joab had [1]turned after Adonijah, but he turned not after Absalom) and Joab fled unto the Tabernacle of the Lord, and caught hold on the horns of the altar.

29 And it was told king Solomon, that Joab was fled unto the Tabernacle of the Lord, and behold, *he is* by the [1]altar. Then Solomon sent Benaiah the son of Jehoiada, saying, Go, fall upon him.

30 And Benaiah came to the Tabernacle of the Lord, and said unto him, Thus saith the King, Come out. And he said, Nay, but I will die here. Then Benaiah brought the king word again, saying, Thus said Joab, and thus he answered me.

31 And the king said unto him, Do as he hath said, and [1]smite him, and bury him, that thou mayest take away the blood, which Joab shed causeless, from me,

and from the house of my father.

32 And the Lord shall bring his blood upon his own head, for he smote two men more righteous and better than he, and slew them with the sword, and my father David knew not: *to wit,* [m]Abner the son of Ner, captain of the host of Israel, and [n]Amasa the son of Jether captain of the host of Judah.

33 Their blood shall therefore return upon the [1]head of Joab, and on the head of his seed forever: but upon David, and upon his seed, and upon his house and upon his throne shall there be peace forever from the Lord.

34 So Benaiah the son of Jehoiada went up, and smote him and slew him, and he was buried in his own house in the wilderness.

35 And the King put Benaiah the son of Jehoiada in his room over the host: and the king set Zadok the [1]Priest in the room of Abiathar.

36 ¶ Afterward the king sent, and called Shimei and said unto him, Build thee an house in Jerusalem, and dwell there, and depart not thence any whither.

37 For that day that thou goest out, and passest over the river of Kidron, know assuredly, that thou shalt die the death: thy blood shall be upon thine own head.

38 And Shimei said unto the king, The thing is good: as my lord the king hath said, so will thy servant do. So Shimei dwelt in Jerusalem many days.

39 And after three years two of the [1]servants of Shimei fled away unto Achish son of Maachah king of Gath: and they told Shimei, saying, Behold, thy servants *be* in Gath.

40 And Shimei arose, and saddled his ass, and went to Gath to Achish, to seek his servants: and [1]Shimei went, and brought his servants from Gath.

41 And it was told Solomon, that Shimei had gone from Jerusalem to Gath, and was come again.

42 And the King sent and called Shimei, and said unto him, Did I not make thee to swear by the Lord, and protested unto thee, saying, That day that thou goest out, and walkest any whither, know assuredly that thou shalt die the death? And thou saidest unto me, The thing is good, *that* I have heard.

43 Why then hast thou not kept the oath of the Lord, and the commandment wherewith I charged thee?

Margin notes:
[k] 2 Sam. 7:12,13
[l] 1 Sam. 2:31,35
[m] 2 Sam. 3:27
[n] 2 Sam. 20:7

2:22 [1] Meaning, that if he should have granted Abishag, which was so dear to his father, he would afterward have aspired to the kingdom.

2:25 [1] Or, fell upon him.

2:26 [1] Or, possessions.
    [2] Hebrew, *man of death.*
    [3] When he fled before Absalom, 2 Sam. 15:24.

2:28 [1] He took Adonijah's part when he would have usurped the kingdom, 1 Kings 1:7.

2:29 [1] Thinking to be saved by the holiness of the place.

2:31 [1] For it was lawful to take the willful murderer from the altar, Exod. 21:14.

2:33 [1] Joab shall be justly punished for the blood that he hath cruelly shed.

2:35 [1] And so took the office of the high Priest from the house of Eli, and restored it to the house of Phinehas.

2:39 [1] Thus God appointeth the ways and means to bring his just judgments upon the wicked.

2:40 [1] His covetous mind moved him rather to venture his life, than to lose his worldly profit, which he had by his servants.

44 The King said also to Shimei, ¹Thou knowest all the wickedness whereunto thine heart is privy, that thou didst to David my father: the Lord therefore shall bring thy wickedness upon thine own head.

45 And let king Solomon be blessed, and the throne of David established before the Lord forever.

46 So the king commanded Benaiah the son of Jehoiada: who went out and smote him that he died. And the ᵉkingdom was ¹established in the hand of Solomon.

3 1 Solomon taketh Pharaoh's daughter to wife.　5 The Lord appeareth to him, and giveth him wisdom.　17 The pleading of the two harlots, and Solomon's sentence therein.

1 Solomon ᵃthen made affinity with Pharaoh king of Egypt, and took Pharaoh's daughter, and brought her into the ¹city of David, until he had made an end of building his own house, and the house of the Lord, and the wall of Jerusalem round about.

2 Only the people sacrificed in the ¹high places, because there was no house built unto the Name of the Lord, until those days.

3 And Solomon loved the Lord, walking in the ordinances of David his ¹father: only he sacrificed and offered incense in the high places.

4 And the King went to ¹Gibeon to sacrifice there, for that was the chief high place: a thousand burnt offerings did Solomon offer upon that altar.

5 In Gibeon the Lord appeared to Solomon in a dream by night: and God said, Ask what I shall give thee.

6 And Solomon said, Thou hast showed unto thy servant David my father great mercy, ¹when he walked before thee in truth, and in righteousness, and in uprightness of heart with thee: and thou hast ²kept for him this great mercy, and hast given him a son, to sit on his throne, as *appeareth* this day.

7 And now, O Lord my God, thou hast made thy servant king instead of David my father: and I am but a young child, and know not how to ¹go out and in.

8 And thy servant *is* in the midst of thy people, which thou hast chosen, even a great people, which cannot be told nor numbered for multitude.

Marginal notes:
ᵒ 2 Chron. 1:1

CHAPTER 3
ᵃ 1 Kings 7:8
ᵇ 2 Chron. 1:10
ᶜ Matt. 6:33
ᵈ 1 Kings 35:5

9 ᵇGive therefore unto thy servant an ¹understanding heart, to judge thy people: that I may discern between good and bad: for who is able to judge this thy ²mighty people?

10 And this pleased the Lord well, that Solomon had desired this thing.

11 And God said unto him, Because thou hast asked this thing, and hast not asked for thyself long life, neither hast asked riches for thyself, nor hast asked the life of thine ¹enemies, but hast asked for thyself understanding to hear judgment,

12 Behold, I have done according to thy words: lo, I have given thee a wise and understanding heart, so that there hath been none like thee before thee, neither after thee shall arise the like unto thee.

13 And I have also ᶜgiven thee that, which thou hast not asked, both riches and honor, so that among the Kings there ¹shall be none like unto thee all thy days.

14 And if thou wilt walk in my ways, to keep mine ordinances and my commandments, ᵈas thy father David did walk, I will prolong thy days.

15 And when Solomon awoke, behold it was ¹a dream, and he came to Jerusalem, and stood before the Ark of the covenant of the Lord, and offered burnt offerings, and made peace offerings, and made a feast to all his servants.

16 ¶ Then came two ¹harlots unto the king, and ²stood before him.

17 And the one woman said, Oh my lord, I and this woman dwell in one house, and I was delivered of a child with her in the house.

18 And the third day after that I was delivered, this woman was delivered also, and we were in the house together: no stranger *was* with us in the house save we twain.

19 And this woman's son died in the night: for she overlay him.

20 And she rose at midnight, and ¹took my son from my side, while thine handmaid slept, and laid him in her bosom, and laid her dead son in my bosom.

21 And when I arose in the morning to give my son suck, behold, he was dead: and when I had well considered him in the morning, behold, it was not my son, whom I had borne.

2:44 ¹ For though thou wouldest deny, yet thine own conscience would accuse thee for reviling and doing wrong to my father, 2 Sam 16:5.
2:46 ¹ Because all his enemies were destroyed.
3:1 ¹ Which was Bethlehem.
3:2 ¹ Where altars were appointed before the temple was built, to offer unto the Lord.
3:3 ¹ For his father had commanded him to obey the Lord and walk in his ways, 1 Kings 2:3.
3:4 ¹ For there the Tabernacle was, 2 Chron. 1:3.
3:6 ¹ Or, as he walked.
² Thou hast performed thy promise.

3:7 ¹ That is, to behave himself in executing this charge of ruling.
3:9 ¹ Or, obedient.
² Which are so many in number.
3:11 ¹ That is, that thine enemy should die.
3:13 ¹ Or, hath been none.
3:15 ¹ He knew that God had appeared unto him in a dream.
3:16 ¹ Or, victuallers.
² By this example it appeareth that God kept his promise with Solomon in granting him wisdom.
3:20 ¹ She stole the quick child away, because she might both avoid the shame and punishment.

22 Then the other woman said, Nay, but my son liveth, and thy son is dead. Again she said, No, but thy son is dead, and mine alive: thus they spake before the king.

23 Then said the king, She saith, This that liveth is my son, and the dead is thy son: and the other saith, Nay, but the dead is thy son, and the living is my son.

24 Then the King said, ¹Bring me a sword: and they brought out a sword before the king.

25 And the king said, Divide ye the living child in twain, and give the one half to the one, and the other half to the other.

26 Then spake the woman, whose the living child was, unto the king, for her compassion was kindled toward her son, and she said, Oh my lord, give her the living child and ¹slay him not: but the other said, Let it be neither mine nor thine, but divide it.

27 Then the king answered, and said, Give her the living child, and slay him not: this is his mother.

28 And all Israel heard the judgment which the king had judged, and they feared the king: for they saw that the wisdom of God was in him to do justice.

4 *2 The princes and rulers under Solomon.   22 The purveyance for his victuals.   26 The number of his horses.   32 His books and writings.*

1 And king Solomon was king over all Israel.

2 And these were ¹his princes, ²Azariah the son of Zadok the Priest,

3 Elihoreph and Ahijah the sons of Shisha, Scribes, Jehoshaphat the son of Ahilud, the Recorder,

4 And Benaiah the son of Jehoiada *was* over the host, and Zadok and ¹Abiathar, Priests,

5 And Azariah the son of Nathan *was* over the officers, and Zabud the son of Nathan, Priest, *was* the king's friend,

6 And Ahishar was over the household, and ᵃAdoniram the son of Abda *was* over the tribute.

7 ¶ And Solomon had twelve officers over all Israel, which provided victuals for the king and his household: each man had a month in the year to provide victuals.

8 And these are their names: the son of Hur in mount Ephraim:

9 The son of Deker in Makaz, and in Shaalbim

CHAPTER 4
ᵃ 1 Kings 5:14
ᵇ 2 Chron. 9:23

and Beth Shemesh, and ¹Elon *and* Beth Hanan:

10 The son of Hesed in Arubboth, to whom pertained Sochoh, and all the land of Hepher:

11 The son of Abinadab in all the region of Dor, which had Taphath the daughter of Solomon to wife:

12 Baana the son of Ahilud in Taanach, and Megiddo, and in all Beth Shean, which is by Zaretan beneath Jezreel, from Beth Shean ¹to Abel Meholah, even till beyond over against Jokneam:

13 The son of Geber in Ramoth Gilead, and his were the towns of ¹Jair, the son of Manasseh, which are in Gilead, and under him was the region of Argob, which is in Bashan: threescore great cities with walls and bars of brass.

14 ¶ Ahinadab the son of Iddo *had* to Mahanaim:

15 Ahimaaz in Naphtali, and he took Basemath the daughter of Solomon to wife:

16 Baanah the son of Hushai in Asher and in Aloth:

17 Jehoshaphat the son of Paruah in ¹Issachar:

18 Shimei the son of Elah in Benjamin:

19 Geber the son of Uri in the country of Gilead, the land of Sihon king of the Amorites, and of Og king of Bashan, and was officer alone in the land.

20 Judah and Israel *were* many, as the sand of the sea in number, ¹eating, drinking, and making merry.

21 And Solomon reigned over all kingdoms, from the ¹River *unto* the land of the Philistines, and unto the border of Egypt, and they brought presents, and served Solomon all the days of his life.

22 And Solomon's victuals for one day were thirty ¹measures of fine flour, and threescore measures of meal:

23 Ten fat oxen, and twenty oxen of the pastures, and an hundred sheep, besides harts, and bucks, and bugles, and fat fowl.

24 For he ruled in all *the region* on the other side of the River, from Tiphsah even unto ¹Gaza, over all the ²kings on the other side the River: and he had peace round about him on every side.

25 And Judah and Israel dwelt without fear every man under his vine, and under his fig tree, from ¹Dan, even to Beersheba, all the days of Solomon.

26 ¶ And Solomon had ᵇforty thousand stalls of horses for his chariots, and twelve thousand horsemen.

3:24 ¹ Except God give Judges understanding, the impudency of the trespasser shall overthrow the just cause of the innocent.
3:26 ¹ Her motherly affection herein appeareth that she had rather endure the rigor of the Law, than see her child cruelly slain.
4:2 ¹ That is, his chief officers.
   ² He was the son of Ahimaaz and Zadok's nephew.
4:4 ¹ Not Abiathar whom Solomon had put from his office, 1 Kings 2:27, but another of that Name.
4:9 ¹ Or, Elon in Beth Aven.
4:12 ¹ Or, to the plain.

4:13 ¹ Which towns bare Jair's name, because he took them of the Canaanites, Num. 32:41.
4:17 ¹ Solomon observed not the division that Joshua made, but divided it as might best serve for his purpose.
4:20 ¹ They lived in all peace and security.
4:21 ¹ Which is Euphrates.
4:22 ¹ Hebrew, *Kors.*
4:24 ¹ Or, Gaza.
   ² For they were all tributaries unto him.
4:25 ¹ Throughout all Israel.

27 And these officers provided victual for king Solomon, and for all that came to king Solomon's table, every man his month, *and* they suffered to lack nothing.

28 Barley also and straw for the horses and mules, brought they unto the place where the officers were, every man according to his charge.

29 ¶ And God gave Solomon wisdom and understanding exceeding much, and [1]a large heart, even as the sand that is on the seashore,

30 And Solomon's wisdom excelled the wisdom of all the children of the [1]East, and all the wisdom of Egypt.

31 For he was wiser than any man: *yea*, than were Ethan the Ezrahite, than Heman, than Chalcol, than Darda the sons of Mahol: and he was famous throughout all nations round about.

32 And Solomon spake three thousand [1]proverbs: and his songs were a thousand and five.

33 And he spake of trees, from the cedar tree that is in Lebanon, even unto the [1]hyssop that springeth out of the wall: he spake also of beasts, and of fowls, and of creeping things, and of fishes.

34 And there came of all people to hear the wisdom of Solomon, from all kings of the earth, which had heard of his wisdom.

5 *1 Hiram sendeth to Solomon, and Solomon to him, purposing to build the house of God.   6 He prepareth the stuff for the building.   13 The number of the workmen.*

1 And Hiram king of [1]Tyre sent his servants unto Solomon, (for he had heard that they had anointed him king in the room of his father) because Hiram had ever loved David.

2 [a]And Solomon sent him to Hiram, saying,

3 Thou knowest that David my father could not build an house unto the name of the Lord his God, for the wars which were about him on every side, until the Lord had put [1]them under the soles of his feet.

4 But now the Lord my God hath given me [1]rest on every side, *so that* there is neither adversary, nor evil to resist.

5 And behold, I purpose to build an house unto the Name of the Lord my God, [b]as the Lord spake unto David my father, saying, Thy son, whom I will

CHAPTER 5
[a] 2 Chron. 2:3
[b] 2 Sam. 7:13
2 Chron. 22:10
[c] 1 Kings 3:12
[d] 1 Kings 4:6

set upon thy throne for thee, he shall build an house unto my Name.

6 Now therefore command, that they hew me cedar trees out of Lebanon, and my servants shall be with thy servants, and unto thee will I give the [1]hire for thy servants, according to all that thou shalt appoint: for thou knowest that there are none among us, that can hew timber like unto the Sidonians.

7 ¶ And when [1]Hiram heard the words of Solomon, he rejoiced greatly, and said, Blessed be the Lord this day, which hath given unto David a wise son over this mighty people.

8 And Hiram sent to Solomon, saying, I have considered the things, for the which thou sentest unto me, and will accomplish all thy desire, concerning the cedar trees and fir trees.

9 My servants shall bring them down from Lebanon to the sea: and I will convey them by sea [1]in rafts unto the place that thou shalt show me, and will cause them to be discharged there, and thou shalt receive them: now thou shalt do me a pleasure to minister food for [2]my family.

10 So Hiram gave Solomon cedar trees and fir trees, *even* his full desire.

11 And Solomon gave Hiram twenty thousand [1]measures of wheat for food to his household, and twenty measures of [2]beaten oil. Thus much gave Solomon to Hiram year by year.

12 ¶ And the Lord gave Solomon wisdom as he [c]promised him. And there was peace between Hiram and Solomon, and they [1]two made a covenant.

13 ¶ And King Solomon raised a sum out of all Israel, and the sum was thirty thousand men:

14 Whom he sent to Lebanon, ten thousand a month by course: they were a month in Lebanon, and two months at home. And [d]Adoniram *was* over the sum.

15 And Solomon had seventy thousand that bare burdens, and fourscore thousand masons in the mountain,

16 Besides the [1]princes, whom Solomon appointed over the work, *even* three thousand and three hundred, which ruled the people that wrought in the work.

17 And the King commanded them, and they brought great stones and costly stones to make the foundations of the house, *even* hewed stones.

4:29 [1] Meaning, great understanding and able to comprehend all things.
4:30 [1] To wit, the Philosophers and Astronomers, which were judged most wise.
4:32 [1] Which for the most part are thought to have perished in the captivity of Babylon.
4:33 [1] From the highest to the lowest.
5:1 [1] Or, Zor.
5:3 [1] Or, his enemies.
5:4 [1] He declareth that he was bound to set forth God's glory, forasmuch as the Lord had sent him rest and peace.

5:6 [1] This was his equity, that he would not receive a benefit without some recompense.
5:7 [1] In Hiram is prefigured the vocation of the Gentiles, who should help to build the Spiritual Temple.
5:9 [1] Or, floats.
     [2] While my servants are occupied about thy business.
5:11 [1] Hebrew, *Kors*.
     [2] Or, pure.
5:12 [1] As touching the furniture of wood and vittles.
5:16 [1] Or, masters of the work.

18 And Solomon's workmen, and the workmen of Hiram, and the [1]masons hewed and prepared timber and stones for the building of the house.

6

1 The building of the Temple and the form thereof. 12 The promise of the Lord to Solomon.

CHAPTER 6
[a] 2 Chron. 3:1
[b] 2 Sam. 7:13

1 And [a]in the four hundred and fourscore year (after the children of Israel were come out of the land of Egypt) and in the fourth year of the reign of Solomon over Israel, in the month [1]Ziv, (which is the second month) he built the [2]house of the Lord.

2 And the house which king Solomon built for the Lord, was threescore cubits long, and twenty broad, and thirty cubits high.

3 And the [1]porch before the Temple of the house *was* twenty cubits long according to the breadth of the house, and ten cubits broad before the house.

4 And in the house he made windows, [1]broad *without*, and narrow *within*.

5 And by the wall of the house he made [1]galleries round about, even by the walls of the house round about the Temple and [2]the oracle, and made chambers round about.

6 And the nethermost gallery *was* five cubits broad, and the middlemost six cubits broad, and the third seven cubits broad: for he made [1]rests round about without the house, that *the beams* should not be fastened in the walls of the house.

7 And when the house was built, it was built of stone perfect, *before* it was brought, so that there was neither hammer, nor axe, nor any tool of iron heard in the house, while it was in building.

8 The door of the middle [1]chamber was in the right side of the house, and men went up with winding stairs into the middlemost, and out of the middlemost into the third.

9 So he built the [1]house and finished it, and ceiled the house, being vaulted with ceiling of cedar trees.

10 And he built the galleries upon all the *wall* of the house of five cubits height, and they were joined to the house with beams of cedar.

11 And the word of the Lord came to Solomon, saying,

12 Concerning this house which thou buildest, if thou wilt walk in mine ordinances, and execute my judgments, and keep all my commandments, to walk in them, then will I perform unto thee my promise, [b]which I promised to David thy father.

13 And I will [1]dwell among the children of Israel, and will not forsake my people Israel.

14 So Solomon built the house and finished it,

15 And built the walls of the house within, with boards of Cedar tree from the pavement of the house unto [1]the walls of the ceiling, and within he covered them with wood, and covered the floor of the house with planks of fir.

16 And he built twenty cubits in the sides of the house with boards of Cedar, from the floor to the walls, and he prepared *a place* within it for the oracle, *even* the most holy place.

17 But the [1]house, that is, the Temple before it, was forty cubits *long*.

18 And the Cedar of the house within was carved with [1]knops, and graven with flowers: all *was* Cedar, *so that* no stone was seen.

19 ¶ Also he prepared the place of the oracle in the midst of the [1]house within, to set the Ark of the covenant of the Lord there.

20 And the place of the oracle within *was* twenty cubits long, and twenty cubits broad, and twenty cubits high: and he covered it with pure gold, and covered the altar with Cedar.

21 So Solomon covered the house within with pure gold, and he [1]shut the place of the oracle with chains of gold, and covered it with gold.

22 And he overlaid all the house with gold, until all the house was made perfect. Also he covered the [1]whole altar, that was before the oracle, with gold.

23 And within the oracle he made two Cherubims of [1]Olive tree, ten cubits high.

24 The wing also of the one Cherub *was* five cubits, and the wing of the other Cherub *was* five cubits: from the uttermost part of *one* of his wings unto the uttermost part of the *other* of his wings, *were* ten cubits.

25 Also the other Cherub was of ten cubits: both the Cherubims were of one measure and one size.

5:18 [1] The Hebrew word is Giblim, which some say were excellent masons.
6:1 [1] Which month containeth part of April and part of May.
[2] Whereby is meant the Temple and the Oracle.
6:3 [1] Or the court where the people prayed, which was before the place where the altar of burnt offerings stood.
6:4 [1] Or, to open and to shut.
6:5 [1] Or, lofts.
[2] Whence God spake between the Cherubims, called also the most holy place.
6:6 [1] Which were certain stones coming out of the wall, as stays for the beams to rest upon.
6:8 [1] Or, Gallery.
6:9 [1] In Exodus it is called the Tabernacle: and the Temple is here called the Sanctuary, and the Oracle the most holy place.
6:13 [1] According as he promised unto Moses, Exod. 25:22.
6:15 [1] Meaning, unto the roof which was also ceiled.
6:17 [1] For when he spake of the house in the first verse, he meant both the Oracle, and the Temple.
6:18 [1] Or, wild cucumbers.
6:19 [1] That is, in the most inward place of the house.
6:21 [1] Hebrew, *he drew through chains of gold before.*
6:22 [1] Meaning, the altar of incense, Exod. 30:1.
6:23 [1] Or, Pine tree

26 *For* the height of the one Cherub *was* ten cubits, and so *was* the other Cherub.

27 And he put the Cherubims within the inner house, ʿand the Cherubims stretched out their wings, so that the wing of the one touched the one wall, and the wing of the other Cherub touched the other wall: and their *other* wings touched one another in the midst of the house.

28 And he ¹overlaid the Cherubims with gold.

29 And he carved all the walls of the house round about with graven figures of Cherubims and of Palm trees, and graven flowers within and without.

30 And the floor of the house he covered with gold within and without.

31 And in the entering of the oracle he made *two* doors of Olive trees: *and* the upper post *and* side posts *were* five square.

32 The two doors also *were* of Olive tree, and he graved them with graving of Cherubims, and Palm trees, and graven flowers, and covered them with gold, and laid ¹thin gold upon the Cherubims and upon the Palm trees.

33 And so made he for the door of the Temple, posts of Olive trees foursquare.

34 But the two doors *were* of fir tree, the two sides of the one door *were* ¹round, and the two sides of the other door *were* round.

35 And he graved Cherubims, and Palm trees, and carved flowers, and covered the carved work with gold finely wrought.

36 ¶ And he built the ¹court within with three rows of hewed stone, and one row of beams of Cedar.

37 In the fourth year was the foundation of the house of the Lord laid in the month of Ziv:

38 And in the eleventh year in the month of ¹Bul, (which is the eighth month) he finished the house with all the furniture thereof, and in every point: so was he seven years in building it.

7 1 *The building of the house of Solomon.* 15 *The excellent workmanship of Hiram in the pieces which he made for the Temple.*

ᶜ Exod. 25:20

CHAPTER 7
ᵃ 1 Kings 9:10
ᵇ 1 Kings 3:1

1 But Solomon was building his own house ᵃthirteen years, and ¹finished all his house.

2 He built also an house ¹*called* the forest of Lebanon, an hundred cubits long, and fifty cubits broad, and thirty cubits high, upon four rows of Cedar pillars: and Cedar beams *were* laid upon the pillars.

3 And it was covered above with cedar upon the beams, that lay on the forty and five pillars, fifteen in a row.

4 And the windows *were* in three rows, and window *was* ¹against window in three ranks.

5 And all the doors, and the side posts *with* the windows were foursquare, and window was over against window in three ranks.

6 And he made a porch of pillars fifty cubits long, and thirty cubits broad, and the porch was before ¹them, *even* before them *were* thirty pillars.

7 ¶ Then he made a porch ¹for the throne, where he judged, even a porch of judgment, and it was ceiled with cedar from pavement to pavement.

8 And in his house where he dwelt *was* another hall more inward than the porch which was of the same work. Also Solomon made an house for Pharaoh's daughter (ᵇwhom he had taken to wife) like unto this porch.

9 All these were ¹of costly stones, hewed by measure, *and* sawed with saws within and without, from the foundation unto ²the *stones* of an ³hand breadth, and on the outside to the great court.

10 And the foundation *was* of costly stones, *and* great stones, *even* of stones of ten cubits, and stones of eight cubits.

11 ¹Above also *were* costly stones squared by rule, and *boards* of cedar.

12 ¶ And the great court round about *was* with three rows of hewed stones, and a row of cedar beams: ¹so *was it* to the inner court of the house of the Lord, and to the porch of the house.

13 ¶ Then King Solomon sent, and fet *one* Hiram out of ¹Tyre.

14 He was a widow's son of the tribe of Naphtali, his father being a man of Tyre, *and* wrought in brass: ¹he was full of wisdom, and understanding, and

6:28 ¹ For the others which Moses made of beaten gold, were taken away with the other jewels by their enemies, whom God permitted divers times to overcome them for their great sins.
6:32 ¹ So that the fashion of the carved work might still appear.
6:34 ¹ Or, folding.
6:36 ¹ Where the Priests were, and was thus called in respect of the great court, which is called in Acts 3:11, the porch of Solomon, where the people used to pray.
6:38 ¹ Which containeth part of October and part of November.
7:1 ¹ After he had built the Temple.
7:2 ¹ For the beauty of the place, and great abundance of cedar trees that went to the building thereof, it was compared to mount Lebanon in Syria: this house he used in summer for pleasure and recreation.

7:4 ¹ There were as many, and like proportion on the one side as the other, and at every end even three in a row one above another.
7:6 ¹ Before the pillars of the house.
7:7 ¹ For his house which was at Jerusalem.
7:9 ¹ Or, precious.
  ² Which were rests and stays for the beams to lie upon.
  ³ Or, span.
7:11 ¹ From the foundation upward.
7:12 ¹ As the Lord's house was built, so was this: only the great court of Solomon's house was uncovered.
7:13 ¹ Or, Zor.
7:14 ¹ Thus when God will have his glory set forth, he raiseth up men, and giveth them excellent gifts for the accomplishment of the same, Exod. 31:2,3.

knowledge to work all manner of work in brass: who came to King Solomon, and wrought all his work.

15 For he cast two pillars of brass: the height of a pillar was eighteen cubits, and a thread of twelve cubits did compass ¹either of the pillars.

16 And he made two ¹chapiters of molten brass to set on the tops of the pillars: the height of one of the chapiters *was* five cubits, and the height of the other chapiter *was* five cubits.

17 He made grates like network and ¹wreathen work like chains for the chapiters that were on the top of the pillars, *even* seven for the one chapiter, and seven for the other chapiter.

18 So he made the pillars and two rows of pomegranates round about in the one grate to cover the chapiters that were upon the top. And thus did he for the other chapiter.

19 And the chapiters that were on the top of the pillars *were* after ¹lily work in the porch, four cubits.

20 And the chapiters upon the two pillars *had* also above, ¹over against the belly ²within the network *pomegranates*: for two hundred pomegranates were in the *two* ranks about upon ³either of the chapiters.

21 And he set up the pillars in the ¹porch of the Temple. And when he had set up the right pillar, he called the name thereof ²Jachin: and when he had set up the left pillar, he called the name thereof ³Boaz.

22 And upon the top of the pillars *was* work of lilies: so was the workmanship of the pillars finished.

23 ¶ And he made a molten ¹sea of ten cubits wide from brim to brim, round in compass, and five cubits high, and a line of thirty cubits did compass it about.

24 And under the brim of it *were* knops like wild cucumbers compassing it round about, ten in one cubit, compassing the sea ʿround about: and the two rows of knops were cast, when it was molten.

25 It stood on twelve bulls, three looking toward the North, and three toward the West, and three toward the South, and three toward the East: and the sea *stood* above upon them, and all their hinder parts were inward.

26 It was ¹an handbreadth thick, and the brim thereof was like the work of the brim of a cup with

ᶜ 2 Chron. 4:3

flowers of lilies: it contained two thousand ²baths.

27 ¶ And he made ten bases of brass, one base *was* four cubits long, and four cubits broad, and three cubits high.

28 ¶ And the work of the bases was on this manner, They had borders, and the borders *were* between the ledges:

29 And on the borders that were between the ledges, were lions, bulls and Cherubims: and upon the ledges there was a base above: and beneath the lions and bulls, were additions made of thin work.

30 And every base had four brazen wheels, and plates of brass: and the four corners had ¹undersetters: under the caldron were undersetters molten at the side of every addition.

31 And the ¹mouth of it was within the chapiter and above *to measure* by the cubit: for the mouth thereof *was* round, made like a base, and it was a cubit and half a cubit: and also upon the mouth thereof *were* graven works, whose borders *were* foursquare, *and* not round.

32 And under the borders *were* four wheels and the axletrees of the wheels *joined* to the base: and the height of a wheel *was* a cubit, and half a cubit.

33 And the fashion of the wheels was like the fashion of a chariot wheel, their axletrees, and their naves and their ¹felloes, and their spokes *were* all molten.

34 And four undersetters *were* upon the four corners of one base: *and* the undersetters thereof were of the base *itself*.

35 And in the top of the base was a round ¹compass of half a cubit high round about: and upon the top of the base the ledges thereof, and the borders thereof *were* of the same.

36 And upon the tables of the ledges thereof, and on the borders thereof he did grave Cherubims, lions and palm trees, on the side of every one, and additions round about.

37 Thus made he the ten bases, *They* had all one casting, one measure, *and* one size.

38 ¶ Then made he ¹ten cauldrons of brass, one cauldron contained forty baths, and every cauldron *was* four cubits, one cauldron *was* upon one base throughout the ten bases.

7:15 ¹ Hebrew, *the second*.
7:16 ¹ Or, pommels.
7:17 ¹ Or, cords like chains.
7:19 ¹ As was seen commonly wrought in costly porches.
7:20 ¹ Or, round about the midst.
  ² Or, bound.
  ³ Hebrew, *the second*.
7:21 ¹ Which was in the inner court between the Temple and the oracle.
  ² That is, he will stablish, to wit, his promise toward this house.
  ³ That is, in strength: meaning the power thereof shall continue.

7:23 ¹ So called for the hugeness of the vessel.
7:26 ¹ Or, a span.
  ² Bath and Ephah seem to be both one measure, Ezek. 45:11, every bath contained about ten pottles.
7:30 ¹ Hebrew, *shoulders*.
7:31 ¹ The mouth of the great base or frame entered into the chapiter, or pillar that bare up the cauldron.
7:33 ¹ Or, rings.
7:35 ¹ Which was called the pillar, chapiter, or small base, wherein the cauldron stood.
7:38 ¹ To keep waters for the use of the sacrifices.

39 And he set the bases, five on the right side of the house, and five on the left side of the house. And he set the sea on the right side of the ¹house Eastward toward the South.

40 ¶ And Hiram made cauldrons, and besoms, and basins, and Hiram finished all the work that he made to King Solomon for the house of the Lord:

41 To wit, two pillars and *two* bowls of the chapiters that were on the top of the two pillars, and two grates to cover the two bowls of the chapiters which were upon the top of the pillars,

42 And four hundred pomegranates for the two grates, even two rows of pomegranates for every grate to cover the two bowls of the chapiters, that were upon the pillars,

43 And the ten bases, and ten cauldrons upon the bases,

44 And the sea, and twelve bulls under that sea,

45 And pots, and besoms, and basins: and all these vessels, which ¹Hiram made to king Solomon for the house of the Lord, were of shining brass.

46 In the plain of Jordan did the King cast them in ¹clay between Succoth and Zaretan.

47 And Solomon left *to weigh* all the vessels, because of the exceeding abundance, neither could the weight of the brass be counted.

48 So Solomon made all the vessels that pertained unto the house of the Lord, the ¹golden altar, and the golden table, whereon the showbread was,

49 And the candlesticks, five at the right side, and five at the left, before the oracle of pure gold, and the flowers, and the lamps, and the snuffers of gold,

50 And the bowls, ¹and the hooks, and the basins, and the spoons, and the ashpans of pure gold, and hinges of gold for the doors of the house within, *even* for the most holy place, *and* for the doors of the house, *to wit*, of the Temple.

51 So was finished all the work that king Solomon made for the house of the Lord, and Solomon brought in the things which ᵈDavid his father had dedicated: the silver and the gold and the vessels, *and* laid them among the treasures of the house of the Lord.

8

4 *The Ark is borne into the Temple.* 10 *A cloud filleth the Temple.* 14 *The king blesseth the people.*

1 Then King Solomon assembled ᵃthe Elders of

ᵈ 2 Chron. 5:1

CHAPTER 8
ᵃ 1 Chron. 5:3
ᵇ Exod. 40:34
ᶜ 2 Chron. 6:1

Israel, even all the heads of the tribes, the chief fathers of the children of Israel unto ¹him in Jerusalem, for to ²bring up the Ark of the covenant of the Lord from the city of David, which is Zion.

2 And all the men of Israel assembled unto King Solomon at the feast in the month of ¹Ethanim, which is the seventh month.

3 And all the Elders of Israel came, and the Priests took the Ark.

4 They bare the Ark of the Lord, and they bare the Tabernacle of the Congregation, and all the holy vessels that were in the Tabernacle: those did the Priests and Levites bring up.

5 And King Solomon and all the Congregation of Israel that were assembled unto him, *were* with him before the Ark, offering sheep and beeves, which could not be told, nor numbered for multitude.

6 So the ¹Priests brought the Ark of the Covenant of the Lord unto his place, into the oracle of the house into the most holy place, even under the wings of the Cherubims.

7 For the Cherubims stretched out their wings over the place of the Ark, and the Cherubims covered the Ark, and the bars thereof above.

8 And they ¹drew out the bars, that the ends of the bars might appear out of the Sanctuary before the oracle, but they were not seen without: and there they are unto this day.

9 Nothing *was* in the Ark ¹save the two tables of stone which Moses had put there at Horeb, where the Lord made a covenant with the children of Israel, when he brought them out of the land of Egypt.

10 And when the Priests were come out of the Sanctuary, the ᵇcloud filled the house of the Lord,

11 So that the Priests could not stand to minister, because of the cloud: for the glory of the Lord had filled the house of the Lord.

12 Then spake Solomon, The Lord ᶜsaid, that he would dwell in the dark cloud.

13 I have built thee an house to dwell in, an habitation for thee to abide in for ¹ever.

14 ¶ And the King turned his face and blessed all the Congregation of Israel: for all the Congregation of Israel stood *there*.

15 And he said, Blessed be the Lord God of Israel, who spake with his mouth unto David my father,

---

7:39 ¹ To wit, of the Temple or Sanctuary.
7:45 ¹ By this name also Hiram the king of Tyre was called.
7:46 ¹ Or, thick earth.
7:48 ¹ This was done according to the form that the Lord prescribed unto Moses in Exodus.
7:50 ¹ Some take this for some instrument of music.
8:1 ¹ Hebrew, *Solomon*.
  ² For David brought it from Obed-edom, and placed it in the Tabernacle which he had made for it, 2 Sam. 6:17.

8:2 ¹ Containing part of September and part of October in the which month they held three solemn feasts, Num. 29:1.
8:6 ¹ That is, the Kohathites, Num. 4:5.
8:8 ¹ They drew them only out so far as they might be seen: for they might not pull them altogether out, Exod. 25:15.
8:9 ¹ For it is like that the enemies when they had the Ark in their hands, took away the rod of Aaron and the pot with Manna.
8:13 ¹ He spake according to the tenor of God's promise which was conditionally that they should serve him aright.

and hath with his hand fulfilled it, saying,

16 Since the day that I brought my people Israel out of Egypt, I chose no city of all the tribes of Israel, to build an house that my Name might be there: but I have chosen ^dDavid to be over my people Israel.

17 And it was in the heart of David my father, to build an house to the Name of the Lord God of Israel.

18 And the Lord said unto David my father, Whereas it was in thine heart to build an house unto my Name, thou didst well, that thou wast so minded:

19 Nevertheless thou shalt not build the house, but thy son that shall come out of thy loins, he shall build the house unto my Name.

20 And the Lord hath ^1made good his word that he spake: and I am risen up in the room of David my father, and sit on the throne of Israel, as the Lord promised, and have built the house for the Name of the Lord God of Israel.

21 And I have prepared therein a place for the Ark, wherein is the ^1covenant of the Lord which he made with our fathers, when he brought them out of the land of Egypt.

22 ¶ Then Solomon stood before ^ethe altar of the Lord in the sight of all the Congregation of Israel, and stretched out his hands toward heaven,

23 And said, O Lord God of Israel, there is no God like thee in heaven above, or in the earth beneath, thou that keepest covenant and mercy with thy servants that walk before thee, with ^1all their heart,

24 Thou that hast kept with thy servant David my father, that thou hast promised him: for thou spakest with thy mouth, and hast fulfilled it with thine hand, as appeareth this day.

25 Therefore, now Lord God of Israel, keep with thy servant David my father that thou hast promised him, saying, ^fThou shalt not want a man in my sight to sit upon the throne of Israel: so that thy children take heed to their way, that they walk before me, as thou hast walked in my sight.

26 And now, O God of Israel, I pray thee, let thy word be verified, which thou spakest unto thy servant David my father.

27 ^1Is it true indeed that God will dwell on the earth? behold, the heavens, and the heavens of heavens are not able to contain thee: how much more *unable* is this house that I have built?

28 But have thou respect unto the prayer of thy servant, and to his supplication, O Lord my God, to

^d 2 Sam. 7:8
^e 2 Chron. 6:13
^f 1 Kings 2:4
^g Deut. 12:11

hear the cry and prayer which thy servant prayeth before thee this day:

29 That thine eyes may be open toward this house, night and day, *even* toward the place whereof thou hast said, ^gMy Name shall be there: that thou mayest hearken unto the prayer which thy servant prayeth in this place.

30 Hear thou therefore the supplication of thy servant, and of thy people Israel which pray in this place, and hear thou ^1in the place of thine habitation, *even* in heaven, and when thou hearest, have mercy.

31 ¶ When a man shall trespass against his neighbor, and ^1he lay upon him an oath to cause him to swear, and ^2the swearer shall come before thine altar into this house,

32 Then hear thou in heaven, and ^1do and judge thy servants, that thou condemn the wicked to bring his way upon his head, and justify the righteous, to give him according to his righteousness.

33 ¶ When thy people Israel shall be overthrown before the enemy, because they have sinned against thee, and turn again to thee, and ^1confess thy Name, and pray and make supplication unto thee in this house,

34 Then hear thou in heaven, and be merciful unto the sin of thy people Israel, and bring them again unto the land, which thou gavest unto their fathers.

35 ¶ When heaven shall be ^1shut up, and there shall be no rain because they have sinned against thee, and shall pray in this place, and confess thy Name, and turn from their sin, when thou dost afflict them,

36 Then hear thou in heaven, and pardon the sin of thy servants and of thy people Israel (when thou hast taught them the good way wherein they may walk) and give rain upon the land that thou hast given thy people to inherit.

37 When there shall be famine in the land, when there shall be pestilence, when there shall be blasting, mildew, grasshopper *or* caterpillar, when their enemies shall besiege them in the ^1cities of their land, *or* any plague, *or* any sickness,

38 *Then* what prayer, *and* supplication soever shall be made of any man *or* of all thy people Israel, when everyone shall know the plague in his own ^1heart, and stretch forth his hands in this house,

39 Hear thou then in heaven, in thy dwelling place, and be merciful, and do, and give every man according to all his ways, as thou knowest his heart,

8:20 ^1 Hebrew, *confirmed*.
8:21 ^1 The two Tables wherein the articles of the covenant were written.
8:23 ^1 Unfainedly and without all hypocrisy.
8:27 ^1 He is ravished with the admiration of God's mercies, who being incomprehensible and Lord over all will become familiar with men.
8:30 ^1 Or, from.

8:31 ^1 To wit, the judge or neighbor.
   ^2 Hebrew, *the oath*.
8:32 ^1 That is, make it known.
8:33 ^1 Acknowledge thy just judgment, and praise thee.
8:35 ^1 So that there be a drought to destroy the fruit of the land.
8:37 ^1 Hebrew, in *the land of their gates*.
8:38 ^1 For such are most meet to receive God's mercies.

(for thou only knowest the hearts of all the children of men)

40 That they may fear thee as long as they live in the land, which thou gavest unto our fathers.

41 Moreover as touching the [1]stranger that is not of thy people Israel, who shall come out of a far country for thy Name's sake,

42 (When they shall hear of thy great Name, and of thy mighty hand, and of thy stretched out arm) and shall come and pray in this house,

43 Hear thou in heaven thy dwelling place, and do according to all that the stranger calleth for unto thee: that all the people of the earth may know thy Name, and fear thee, as do thy people Israel: and that they may know that thy [1]Name is called upon in this house which I have built.

44 ¶ When thy people shall go out to battle against their enemy by the way that thou shalt send them, and shall pray unto the Lord [h]toward the way of the city which thou hast chosen, and toward the house that I have built for thy Name,

45 Hear thou then in heaven their prayer and their supplication, and [1]judge their cause.

46 If they sin against thee, ([i]for there is no man that sinneth not) and thou be angry with them, and deliver them unto the enemies, so that they carry them away prisoners unto the land of the enemies, either far or near,

47 Yet [1]if they turn again unto their heart in the land (to the which they be carried away captives) and return and pray unto thee [2]in the land of them that carried them away captives, saying, We have sinned, we have transgressed, and done wickedly,

48 If they turn again unto thee with all their heart, and with all their soul in the land of their enemies, which led them away captives, and pray unto thee toward [1]the way of their land, which thou gavest unto their fathers, and toward the city which thou hast chosen, and the house which I have built for thy Name,

49 Then hear thou their prayer and their supplication in heaven thy dwelling place, and [1]judge their cause,

50 And be merciful unto thy people that have sinned against thee, and unto all their iniquities (wherein they have transgressed against thee) and cause that they which led them away captives, may [1]have pity and compassion on them.

51 For they be thy people, and thine inheritance, which thou broughtest out of Egypt from the midst of the iron furnace.

52 Let thine eyes be open unto the prayer of thy servant, and unto the prayer of thy people Israel, to hearken unto them, in all that they call for unto thee.

53 For thou didst separate them to thee from among all people of the earth for an inheritance, as thou saidest by the hand of Moses thy servant, when thou broughtest our [j]fathers out of Egypt, O Lord God.

54 And when Solomon had made an end of praying all this [1]prayer and supplication unto the Lord, he rose from before the altar of the Lord, from kneeling on his knees, and stretching of his hands to heaven,

55 And stood and blessed all the Congregation of Israel, with a loud voice, saying,

56 Blessed be the Lord that hath given rest unto his people Israel, according to all that he promised: there hath not failed one word of all his good promise which he promised by the hand of Moses his servant.

57 The Lord our God be with us, as he was with our fathers, that he forsake us not, neither leave us,

58 That he may [1]bow our hearts unto him, that we may walk in all his ways, and keep his commandments, and his statutes, and his laws, which he commanded our fathers.

59 And these my words, which I have prayed before the Lord, be near unto the Lord our God day and night, that he defend the cause of his servant, and the cause of his people Israel [1]always as the matter requireth,

60 That all the people of the earth may know, that the Lord is God, and none other.

61 Let your heart therefore be perfect with the Lord our God, to walk in his statutes, and to keep his commandments, as this day.

62 ¶ [k]Then the king and all Israel with him offered sacrifice before the Lord.

63 And Solomon offered a sacrifice of peace offerings which he offered unto the Lord, to wit, two and twenty thousand beeves, and an hundred and twenty thousand sheep: so the King and all the children of Israel dedicated the [1]house of the Lord.

Marginal references:
[h] Dan. 6:10
[i] 2 Chron. 6:36
Eccl. 7:22
1 John 1:8,10
[j] Exod. 19:6
[k] 2 Chron. 7:4

8:41 [1] He meaneth such as should be turned from their idolatry to serve the true God.
8:43 [1] That this is the true religion wherewith thou wilt be worshipped.
8:45 [1] Or, maintain their right.
8:47 [1] Or, if they repent.
    [2] Though the Temple was the chief place of prayer, yet he secludeth not them, that being let with necessity call upon him in other places.
8:48 [1] As Daniel did, Dan. 6:10.

8:49 [1] Or, avenge their wrong.
8:50 [1] He understood by faith, that God of enemies would make friends unto them that did convert unto him.
8:54 [1] Solomon is a figure of Christ, who continually is the Mediator between God and his Church.
8:58 [1] He concludeth that man of himself is enemy unto God, and that all obedience to his Law proceedeth of his mere mercy.
8:59 [1] Hebrew, the thing of a day in his day.
8:63 [1] Before the oracle where the Ark was.

64 The same day did the King hallow the middle of the court, that was before the house of the Lord: for there he made burnt offerings, and the meat offerings, and the fat of the peace offerings, because the *b*brazen altar that was before the Lord, was too little to receive the burnt offerings, and the meat offerings, and the fat of the peace offerings.

65 And Solomon made at that time a feast and all Israel with him, a very great Congregation, even from the entering in of ¹Hamath unto the river of Egypt, before the Lord our God, ²seven days and seven days, *even* fourteen days.

66 And the eighth day he sent the people away: and they ¹thanked the King, and went unto their tents joyous, and with glad heart, because of all the goodness that the Lord had done for David his servant, and for Israel his people.

9 *2 The Lord appeareth the second time to Solomon. 11 Solomon giveth cities to Hiram. 20 The Canaanites become tributaries. 28 He sendeth forth a navy for gold.*

1 When *a*Solomon had finished the building of the house of the Lord, and the King's palace, and all that Solomon desired and minded to do,

2 Then the Lord appeared unto Solomon the second time, as he *b*appeared unto him at Gibeon.

3 And the Lord said unto him, I have heard thy prayer and thy supplication, that thou hast made before me: I have hallowed this house (which thou hast built) to *c*put my Name there forever, and mine eyes, and my heart shall be there perpetually.

4 And ¹if thou wilt walk before me (as David thy father walked in pureness of heart and in righteousness) to do according to all that I have commanded thee, *and* keep my statutes, and my judgments,

5 Then will I stablish the throne of thy kingdom upon Israel forever, as I promised to David thy father, saying, *d*Thou shalt not want a man upon the throne of Israel.

6 *But* if ye and your children turn away from me, and will ¹not keep my Commandments, *and* my statutes (which I have set before you) but go and serve other gods, and worship them,

7 Then will I cut off Israel from the land, which I have given them, and the house which I have hal-

f 2 Chron. 7:7

CHAPTER 9
a 2 Chron. 7:11
b 1 Kings 3:5
c 1 Kings 8:29
Deut. 12:21
d 2 Sam. 7:12
1 Chron. 22:10
e Jer. 7:14
f Deut. 29:24
Jer. 22:8
g 2 Chron. 8:1

lowed *e*for my Name, will I cast out of my sight, and Israel shall be a ¹proverb, and a common talk among all people.

8 Even this high house shall be *so*: everyone that passeth by it, shall be astonied, and shall hiss, and they shall say, *f*Why hath the Lord done thus unto this land and to this house?

9 And they shall answer, Because they forsook the Lord their God, which brought their fathers out of the land of Egypt, and have taken hold upon other gods, and have worshipped them, and served them, therefore hath the Lord brought upon them all this evil.

10 *g*And at the end of twenty years, when Solomon had built the two houses, the house of the Lord, and the King's palace,

11 (*For the which* Hiram the king of ¹Tyre had brought to Solomon timber of Cedar and fir trees, and gold, and whatsoever he desired) then king Solomon gave to Hiram twenty cities in the land of ²Galilee.

12 And Hiram came out from Tyre to see the cities which Solomon had given him, and they pleased him not.

13 Therefore he said, What cities are these which thou hast given me, my brother? And he called them the land of ¹Cabul unto this day.

14 And Hiram had sent the King ¹sixscore ²talents of gold.

15 ¶ And this is the cause of the tribute, why King Solomon raised tribute, *to wit*, to build the house of the Lord, and his own house, and ¹Millo, and the wall of Jerusalem, and Hazor, and Megiddo, and Gezer.

16 Pharaoh king of Egypt had come up, and taken Gezer, and burnt it with fire, and slew the Canaanites that dwelt in the city, and gave it for a present unto his daughter Solomon's wife.

17 (Therefore Solomon built Gezer and Beth Horon the nether,

18 And Baalath, and Tadmor in the wilderness of the land,

19 And all the cities ¹of store, that Solomon had, even cities for chariots, and cities for horsemen, and *all* that Solomon desired and would build in Jerusalem, and in Lebanon, and in all the land of his dominion)

8:65 ¹ That is, from North to South: meaning all the country.
² Seven days for the dedication, and seven for the feast.
8:66 ¹ Hebrew, *blessed.*
9:4 ¹ If thou walk in my fear, and withdraw thyself from the common manner of men, which follow their sensuality.
9:6 ¹ God declareth that disobedience against him, is the cause of his displeasure, and so of all misery.
9:7 ¹ The world shall make of you a mocking stock for the vile contempt and abusing of God's most liberal benefits.

9:11 ¹ Or, Zor.
² Or, Galilee.
9:13 ¹ Or, dirty, or barren.
9:14 ¹ For his tribute toward the building.
² The common talent was about threescore pounds weight.
9:15 ¹ Millo was as the town house or place of assembly which was open above.
9:19 ¹ Cities for his munitions of war.

20 All the people that were ¹left of the Amorites, Hittites, Perizzites, Hivites, and Jebusites, which were not of the children of Israel

21 *To wit*, their children that were left after them in the land whom the children of Israel were not able to destroy, those did Solomon make tributaries unto this day

22 But of the children of Israel did Solomon ᵇmake no bondmen: but they were men of war and his servants, and his princes, and his captains, and rulers of his chariots and his horsemen.

23 These were the princes of the officers, that were over Solomon's work: *even* ¹five hundred and fifty, and they ruled the people that wrought in the work.

24 ¶ And Pharaoh's daughter came up from the city of David unto the house which *Solomon* had built for her: then did he build Millo.

25 And thrice a year did Solomon offer burnt offerings and peace offerings upon the altar which he built unto the Lord: and he burnt incense upon *the altar* that was before the Lord, when he had finished the house.

26 Also king Solomon made a navy of ships in Ezion Geber, which is beside Elath, and the brink of the red sea, in the land of Edom.

27 And Hiram sent with the navy, his servants, that were mariners, and had knowledge of the sea, with the servants of Solomon.

28 And they came to Ophir, and fet from thence ¹four hundred and twenty talents of gold, and brought it to king Solomon.

10

1 *The Queen of Sheba cometh to hear the wisdom of Solomon.* 18 *His royal throne.* 23 *His power and magnificence.*

1 And the ᵃQueen of ¹Sheba hearing the fame of Solomon (concerning the Name of the Lord) came to prove him with hard questions.

2 And she came to Jerusalem with a very great train, *and* camels that bare sweet odors, and gold exceeding much, and precious stones: and she came to Solomon, and communed with him of all that was in her heart.

3 And Solomon declared unto her all her questions: nothing was hid from the king, which he expounded not unto her.

Margin references:
ᵇ Lev. 25:59

CHAPTER 10
ᵃ 2 Chron. 9:1
   Matt. 12:42
   Luke 11:31
ᵇ 2 Chron. 9:10
ᶜ Exod. 25:39

4 Then the Queen of Sheba saw all Solomon's wisdom, and the house that he had built,

5 And the ¹meat of his table, and the sitting of his servants, and the order of his ministers, and their apparel, and his drinking vessels, and his burnt offerings, that he offered in the house of the Lord, and ²she was greatly astonied.

6 And she said unto the King, It was a true word that I heard in mine own land of thy sayings, and of thy wisdom.

7 Howbeit I believed not this report, till I came, and had seen it with mine eyes: but lo, the one half was not told me: *for* thou hast more wisdom and prosperity, than I have heard by report.

8 Happy are thy men, happy are these thy servants, which stand ever before thee, and hear thy ¹wisdom.

9 Blessed be the Lord thy God, which ¹loved thee, to set thee on the throne of Israel, because the Lord loved Israel forever, and made thee king to do ²equity and righteousness.

10 And she gave the king sixscore talents of gold, and of sweet odors exceeding much, and precious stones. There came no more such abundance of sweet odors, as the queen of Sheba gave to king Solomon.

11 The navy also of Hiram (that carried gold from Ophir) brought likewise great plenty of ᵇAlmuggim trees from Ophir, and precious stones.

12 And the king made of the Almuggim trees pillars for the house of the Lord, and for the king's palace, and made harps and psalteries for singers. There came no more such Almuggim trees, nor were any more seen unto this day.

13 And King Solomon gave unto the Queen of Sheba, whatsoever she would ask, besides that, which Solomon gave her of his ¹kingly liberality: so she returned to her own country, *both* she and her servants.

14 ¶ Also the weight of gold, that came to Solomon in one year, was six hundred threescore and six ᶜtalents of gold,

15 Besides that *he had* of merchant men and of the merchandises of them that sold spices, and of all the kings of Arabia, and of the princes of the ¹country.

16 And King Solomon made two hundred targets of beaten gold, six hundred *shekels* of gold went to a target:

9:20 ¹ These were as bondmen and paid what was required, either labor or money.

9:23 ¹ The overseers of Solomon's works, were divided into three parts: the first contained 3300, the second 300, and the third 250, which were Israelites: so here are contained the two last parts, which make 550, see 2 Chron. 8:10.

9:28 ¹ In 2 Chron. 8:18, is made mention of thirty more, which seem to have been employed for their charges.

10:1 ¹ Josephus saith, that she was Queen of Ethiopia, and that Sheba was the name of the chief city of Meroe, which is an island of Nile.

10:5 ¹ That is, the whole order, and trade of his house.
    ² Hebrew, *there was no more spirit in her.*

10:8 ¹ But much more happy are they, which hear the wisdom of God revealed in his word.

10:9 ¹ It is a chief sign of God's favor, when godly and wise rulers sit in the throne of justice.
    ² This is the cause, why Kings are appointed.

10:13 ¹ Hebrew, *by the hand of the King.*

10:15 ¹ To wit, of Arabia, which for the great abundance of all things was called Happy.

17 And three hundred shields of beaten gold, three pounds of gold went to one shield: and the King put them in the ᵈhouse of the wood of Lebanon.

18 ¶ Then the King made a great throne of ivory, and covered it with the best gold.

19 And the throne had six steps, and the top of the throne *was* round behind, and there were ¹stays on either side on the place of the throne, and two lions standing by the stays.

20 And there stood twelve lions on the six steps on either side: there was not the like made in any kingdom.

21 And all King Solomon's drinking vessels *were* of gold, and all the vessels of the house of the wood of Lebanon *were* of pure gold, none *were* of silver: for it was nothing esteemed in the days of Solomon

22 For the King had on the sea the navy of Tarshish with the navy of Hiram: once in three years came the navy of ¹Tarshish, and brought gold and silver, ivory, and apes and peacocks.

23 So King Solomon exceeded all the kings of the earth both in riches and in wisdom.

24 And all the world sought to see Solomon, to hear his wisdom, which God had put in his heart,

25 And they brought every man his present, vessels of silver, and vessels of gold, and raiment, and armor, and sweet odors, horses and mules, from year to year.

26 Then Solomon gathered together ᶜchariots and horsemen: and he had a thousand and four hundred chariots, and twelve thousand horsemen, whom he placed in the chariot cities, and with the King at Jerusalem.

27 And the King ¹gave silver in Jerusalem as stones, and gave cedars as the wild fig trees that grow abundantly in the plain.

28 Also Solomon had horses brought out of Egypt, and fine linen: ¹the king's merchants received the linen for a price.

29 There came up and went out of Egypt *some* chariot *worth* six hundred *shekels* of silver: that is, one horse, an hundred and fifty. And thus they brought *horses* to all the Kings of the Hittites and to the Kings of Aram by their ¹means.

11 3 Solomon hath a thousand wives and concubines, which bring him to idolatry. 14 His God raiseth up adversaries against him. 43 He dieth.

ᵈ 1 Kings 7:2
ᵉ 2 Chron. 1:14

CHAPTER 11
ᵃ Deut. 17:17
ᵇ Exod. 34:16
ᶜ Judg. 2:15
ᵈ 1 Kings 3:5
  1 Kings 9:2
ᵉ 1 Kings 6:12
ᶠ 1 Kings 2:15

1 But King Solomon loved ᵃmany ¹outlandish women: both the daughter of Pharaoh, *and* the women of Moab, Ammon, Edom, Sidon, and Heth,

2 Of the nations, whereof the Lord had said unto the children of Israel, ᵇGo not ye in to them, nor let them come in to you: *for* surely they will turn your hearts after their gods, to them, *I say*, did Solomon join in love.

3 And he had seven hundred wives, *that were* ¹princesses, and three hundred ²concubines, and his wives turned away his heart.

4 For when Solomon was old, his wives turned his heart after other gods, so that his heart was not ¹perfect with the Lord his God as *was* the heart of David his father.

5 For Solomon followed ᶜAshtoreth the god of the Sidonians, and ¹Milcom the abomination of the Ammonites.

6 So Solomon wrought wickedness in the sight of the Lord, but continued not to follow the Lord, as *did* David his father.

7 Then did Solomon build an high place for Chemosh, the ¹abomination of Moab, in the mountain that is over against Jerusalem, and unto Molech the abomination of the children of Ammon.

8 And so did he for all his outlandish wives, which burnt incense and offered unto their gods.

9 Therefore the Lord was angry with Solomon, because he had turned his heart from the Lord God of Israel, ᵈwhich had appeared unto him twice,

10 And had given him a ᵉcharge concerning this thing, that he should not follow other gods: but he kept not that, which the Lord had commanded him.

11 Wherefore the Lord said unto Solomon, Forasmuch as ¹this is done of thee, and thou hast not kept my Covenant, and my statutes (which I commanded thee) ᶠI will surely rent thy kingdom from thee, and will give it to thy servant.

12 Notwithstanding in thy days I will not do it, because of David thy father, but I will rent it out of the hand of thy son:

13 Howbeit I will not rent all the kingdom, *but* will give one ¹tribe to thy son, because of David my servant, and because of Jerusalem which I have chosen.

14 ¶ Then the Lord stirred up an adversary unto Solomon, *even* Hadad the Edomite, of the king's ¹seed, which was in Edom.

10:19 ¹ As the chair bows, or places to lean upon.
10:22 ¹ By Tarshish is meant Cilicia, which was abundant in variety of precious things.
10:27 ¹ Or, he made silver as plenteous as stones.
10:28 ¹ Or, for the company of the King's merchants did receive a number at a price.
10:29 ¹ Hebrew, *hands*.
11:1 ¹ Which were idolaters.
11:3 ¹ Or, Queens.

² To whom appertained no dowry.
11:4 ¹ He served not God with a pure heart.
11:5 ¹ Who was also called Molech, verse 7, read 2 Kings 23:10.
11:7 ¹ Thus the Scripture termeth whatsoever man doth reverence and serve as God.
11:11 ¹ That thou hast forsaken me and worshipped idols.
11:13 ¹ Because the tribes of Judah and Benjamin had their possessions mixed, they are here taken as one tribe.
11:14 ¹ Of the king of Edom's stock.

15 ᵍFor when David was in Edom, and Joab the captain of the host had smitten all the males in Edom, and was gone up to bury the ¹slain,

16 (For six months did Joab remain there and all Israel, till he had destroyed all the males in Edom.)

17 Then this Hadad ¹fled, and certain other Edomites of his father's servants with him, to go into Egypt, Hadad being yet a little child.

18 And they arose out of Midian, and came to Paran, and took men with them out of Paran, and came to Egypt unto Pharaoh king of Egypt, which gave him an house, and appointed him vittles and gave him land.

19 So Hadad ¹found great favor in the sight of Pharaoh, and he gave him to wife the sister of his own wife, *even* the sister of Tahpenes the Queen.

20 And the sister of Tahpenes bare him Genubath his son, whom Tahpenes weaned in Pharaoh's house: and Genubath was in Pharaoh's house among the sons of Pharaoh.

21 And when Hadad heard in Egypt that David slept with his fathers, and that Joab the captain of the host was dead, Hadad said to Pharaoh, Let me depart, that I may go to mine own country.

22 But Pharaoh said unto him, What hast thou lacked with me, that thou wouldest thus go to thine own country? And he answered, Nothing, but in any wise let me go.

23 ¶ ʰAnd God stirred him up *another* adversary, Rezon the son of Eliadah, which ¹fled from his lord Hadadezer king of Zobah.

24 And he gathered men unto him, and had been captain over the company, when David slew them. And they went to Damascus, and dwelt there, ¹and they made him king in Damascus.

25 Therefore was he an adversary to Israel all the days of Solomon: besides the evil that Hadad *did*, he also abhorred Israel, and reigned over Aram

26 ¶ ⁱAnd Jeroboam the son of Nebat an Ephraimite of Zereda Solomon's servant (whose mother was called Zeruah a widow) lifted up his hand against the king.

27 And this was the cause that he lifted up *his* hand against the king, *When* Solomon built Millo, he repaired the broken places of the city of David his father.

28 And this man Jeroboam was a man of strength

ᵍ 2 Sam. 8:14
ʰ 2 Sam. 8:3
ⁱ 2 Chron. 13:6
ʲ 1 Kings 12:15

and courage, and Solomon seeing that the young man was meet for the work, he made him ¹overseer of all the labor of the house of Joseph.

29 And at that time, when Jeroboam went out of Jerusalem, the Prophet Ahijah the Shilonite found him in the way, having a new garment on him, and they two were alone in the field.

30 Then Ahijah caught the new garment that was on him, and ¹rent it in twelve pieces,

31 And said to Jeroboam, Take unto thee ten pieces: for thus saith the Lord God of Israel, Behold, I will rent the kingdom out of the hands of Solomon, and will give ten tribes to thee.

32 But he shall have one tribe for my servant David's sake, and for Jerusalem the city, which I have chosen out of all the tribes of Israel,

33 Because they have forsaken me, and have worshipped Ashtoreth the god of the Sidonians, and Chemosh the god of the Moabites, and Milcom the god of the Ammonites, and have not walked in my ways (to ¹do right in mine eyes, and my statutes, and my laws) as *did* David his father.

34 But I will not take the whole kingdom out of his hand: for I will make him prince all his life long for David my servant's sake, whom I have chosen, *and* who kept my commandments and my statutes.

35 ʲBut I will take the kingdom out of his son's hand, and will give it unto thee, *even* the ten tribes.

36 And unto his son will I give one tribe, that David my servant may have a ¹light always before me in Jerusalem the city, which I have chosen me to put my Name there.

37 And I will take thee, and thou shalt reign ¹even as thine heart desireth, and shalt be king over Israel.

38 And if thou hearken unto all that I command thee, and wilt walk in my ways, and do right in my sight, to keep my statutes and my commandments as David my servant did, then will I be with thee, and build thee a sure house, as I built unto David, and will give Israel unto thee.

39 And I will ¹for this afflict the seed of David, ²but not forever.

40 ¶ Solomon sought therefore to kill Jeroboam, and Jeroboam arose, and fled into Egypt unto Shishak king of Egypt, and was in Egypt until the death of Solomon.

41 And the rest of the words of Solomon, and all

11:15 ¹ Of the Edomites.
11:17 ¹ Thus God reserved this idolater to be a scourge to punish his people's sins.
11:19 ¹ God brought him to honor, that his power might be more able to compass his enterprises against Solomon's house.
11:23 ¹ When David had discomfited Hadadezer and his army.
11:24 ¹ To wit, the men whom he had gathered unto him.
11:28 ¹ He was overseer of Solomon's works, for the tribe of Ephraim and Manasseh.

11:30 ¹ By these visible signs the Prophets would more deeply print their message into their hearts to whom they were sent.
11:33 ¹ Or, to do that, that pleaseth me.
11:36 ¹ He hath respect unto the Messiah, which should be the bright star that should shine through all the world.
11:37 ¹ Hebrew, *in all that thy soul*.
11:39 ¹ For this idolatry that Solomon hath committed.
² For the whole spiritual kingdom was restored in Messiah.

that he did, and his wisdom, are they not written in the [1]book of the acts of Solomon?

42 The time that Solomon reigned in Jerusalem over all Israel, was [k]forty years.

43 And Solomon slept with his fathers: and was buried in the city of David his father: and Rehoboam his son reigned in his stead.

12

1 Rehoboam succeedeth Solomon. 8 He refuseth the counsel of the Ancient. 20 Jeroboam reigneth over Israel. 21 God commandeth Rehoboam not to fight. 28 Jeroboam maketh golden calves.

1 And [a]Rehoboam went to Shechem: for all Israel were come to Shechem, to make him king.

2 And when Jeroboam the son of Nebat heard of it (who was yet in Egypt, [b]whither Jeroboam had fled from king Solomon, and [1]dwelt in Egypt.)

3 Then they sent and called him: and Jeroboam and all the Congregation of Israel came and spake unto Rehoboam, saying,

4 Thy father made our [c]yoke grievous: now therefore make thou the grievous servitude of thy father, and his sore yoke which he put upon us, [1]lighter, and we will serve thee.

5 And he said unto them, Depart yet for three days, then come again to me. And the people departed.

6 And king Rehoboam took counsel with the old men that [1]had stood before Solomon his father, while he yet lived, and said, What counsel give ye, that I may make an answer to this people?

7 And they spake unto him, saying, If thou be a [1]servant unto this people this day, and serve them, and answer them, and speak kind words to them, they will be thy servants forever.

8 But he forsook the counsel that the old men had given him, and asked counsel of the young men that had been brought up with him, and waited on him.

9 And he said unto them, [1]What counsel give ye, that we may answer this people, which have spoken to me, saying, Make the yoke, which thy father hath put upon us, lighter?

10 Then the young men that were brought up with him, spake unto him, saying, Thus shalt thou say unto this people, that have spoken unto thee, and said, Thy father hath made our yoke heavy, but

[k] 2 Chron. 9:30

CHAPTER 12
[a] 2 Chron. 10:1
[b] 1 Kings 11:40
[c] 1 Kings 4:7
[d] 1 Kings 11:11
[e] 1 Kings 11:13
[f] 2 Chron. 11:2

make thou it lighter unto us: *even* thus shalt thou say unto them, My [1]least part shall be [2]bigger than my father's loins.

11 Now whereas my father did burden you with a grievous yoke, I will yet make your yoke heavier: my father hath chastised you with rods, but I will correct you with [1]scourges.

12 ¶ Then Jeroboam and all the people came to Rehoboam the third day, as the king had [1]appointed, saying, Come to me again the third day.

13 And the king answered the people sharply, and left the old men's counsel that they gave him,

14 And spake to them after the counsel of the young men, saying, My father made your yoke grievous, and I will make your yoke more grievous: my father hath chastised you with rods, but I will correct you with scourges.

15 And the king hearkened not unto the people: for it was the [1]ordinance of the Lord, that he might perform his saying, which the Lord had spoken by [d]Ahijah the Shilonite unto Jeroboam the son of Nebat.

16 So when all Israel saw that the king regarded them not, the people answered the king thus, saying, What portion have we in [1]David? we have none inheritance in the son of Jesse. To your tents, O Israel: now see to thine own house, David. So Israel departed unto their tents.

17 Howbeit over the children of Israel, which dwelt in the cities of Judah, did Rehoboam reign still.

18 ¶ Now the king Rehoboam sent Adoram the receiver of the tribute, and all Israel stoned him to death: then the king Rehoboam [1]made speed to get him up to his chariot, to flee to Jerusalem.

19 And Israel rebelled against the house [1]of David unto this day.

20 ¶ And when all Israel had heard that Jeroboam was come again, they sent and called him to the assembly, and made him king over all Israel: none followed the house of David, but the tribe of Judah [c]only.

21 And when Rehoboam was come to Jerusalem, he [1]gathered all the house of Judah with the tribe of Benjamin, an hundred and fourscore thousand of chosen men (which were good warriors) to fight against the house of Israel, and to bring the kingdom again to Rehoboam the son of Solomon.

22 [f]But the word of God came unto Shemaiah the

11:41 [1] Which book as is thought, was lost in their captivity.
12:2 [1] Or, return from Egypt.
12:4 [1] Oppress us not with so great charges, which we are not able to sustain.
12:6 [1] Or, had been of his ancient counselors.
12:7 [1] They showed him that there was no way to win the people's hearts, but to grant them their just petition.
12:9 [1] There is nothing harder for them that are in authority, than to bridle their affections, and to follow good counsel.
12:10 [1] Or, little finger.

[2] I am much more able to keep you in subjection than my father was.
12:11 [1] Or, scorpions.
12:12 [1] The people declare their obedience in this that they would attempt nothing before the king had given them just occasion.
12:15 [1] Or, the Lord was the cause.
12:16 [1] Though their cause were good, yet it is most hard for the people to bridle their affections, as these vile words declare.
12:18 [1] Hebrew, *strengthened himself*.
12:19 [1] By the just judgment of God for Solomon's sins.
12:21 [1] For as yet he perceived not that the Lord had so appointed it.

¹man of God, saying,

23 Speak unto Rehoboam the son of Solomon king of Judah, and unto all the house of Judah and Benjamin, and the remnant of the people, saying,

24 Thus saith the ¹Lord, Ye shall not go up, nor fight against your brethren the children of Israel: return every man to his house: for this thing is done by me. They obeyed therefore the word of the Lord, and returned, and departed according to the word of the Lord.

25 ¶ Then Jeroboam built Shechem in mount Ephraim, and dwelt therein, and went from thence, and built Penuel.

26 And Jeroboam thought in his heart, Now shall the kingdom return to the house of David.

27 If this people go up and do sacrifice in the house of the Lord ¹at Jerusalem, then shall the hearts of this people turn again unto their lord, *even* to Rehoboam king of Judah: so shall they kill me, and go again to Rehoboam king of Judah.

28 Whereupon the king took counsel, and made two calves of gold, and said unto them, ¹It is too much for you to go up to Jerusalem: Behold, O Israel, thy gods which brought thee up out of the land of Egypt.

29 And he set the one in Bethel, and the other set he in Dan.

30 And this thing turned to sin: for the people went (because of the one) even to Dan.

31 Also he made an ¹house of high places, and made priests of the lowest of the people, which were not of the sons of Levi.

32 And Jeroboam made a feast the ¹fifteenth day of the eighth month, like unto the feast that is in Judah, and offered on the altar. So did he in Bethel and offered unto the calves that he had made: and he placed in Bethel the Priests of the high places, which he had made.

33 And he offered upon the altar, which he had made in Bethel, the fifteenth day of the eighth month, (*even* in the month which he had forged of his own heart) and made a solemn feast unto the children of Israel, and he went up to the altar, to burn incense.

CHAPTER 13
ª 2 Kings 23:17

13

1 Jeroboam is reprehended of the Prophet.   4 His hand drieth up.   13 The Prophet is seduced,   24 and is killed of a lion.   33 The obstinacy of Jeroboam.

1 And behold, there came ¹a man of God out of Judah (by the commandment of the Lord) unto ²Bethel, and Jeroboam stood by the altar to offer incense.

2 And he cried against the altar by the commandment of the Lord, and said, O altar, altar, thus saith the Lord, Behold, a child shall be born unto the house of David, ªJosiah by name, and upon thee shall he sacrifice the priests of the high places that burn incense upon thee, and they shall burn men's bones upon thee.

3 And he gave a sign the same time, saying, This is the ¹sign, that the Lord hath spoken, Behold, the altar shall rent, and the ashes that are upon it, shall ²fall out.

4 And when the king had heard the saying of the man of God, which he had cried against the altar in Bethel, Jeroboam stretched out his hand for the altar, saying, ¹Lay hold on him: but his hand which he put forth against him, dried up, and he could not pull it in again to him.

5 The altar also clave asunder, and the ashes fell out from the altar, according to the sign, which the man of God had given by the ¹commandment of the Lord.

6 Then the king answered and said unto the man of God, ¹I beseech thee, pray unto the Lord thy God, and make intercession for me, that mine hand may be restored unto me. And the man of God besought the Lord, and the King's hand was restored, and became as it was afore.

7 Then the King said unto the man of God, Come home with me, that thou mayest ¹dine, and I will give thee a reward.

8 But the man of God said unto the King, If thou wouldest give me half thine house, I would not go with thee, neither would I eat bread nor drink water in this place.

9 For so ¹was it charged me by the word of the Lord, saying, ²Eat no bread nor drink water, nor turn again by the same way that thou camest.

12:22 ¹ That is, the Prophet.
12:24 ¹ Who of his just judgment will punish the trespasser, and of his mercy spare the innocent people.
12:27 ¹ He feared lest his people should have by this means been enticed to rebel against him.
12:28 ¹ So crafty are carnal persuasions of princes, when they will make a religion to serve to their appetite.
12:31 ¹ That is, a temple, where altars were built for idolatry.
12:32 ¹ Because he would the more bind the people's devotion to his idolatry, he made a new holy day, besides those that the Lord had appointed in the Law.
13:1 ¹ That is, a Prophet.
  ² Not that that was called Luz in Benjamin, but another of that

name.
13:3 ¹ By this sign ye shall know that the Lord hath sent me.
  ² Or, be poured out.
13:4 ¹ The wicked rage against the Prophets of God, when they declare them God's judgments.
13:5 ¹ Hebrew, *mouth*.
13:6 ¹ Though the wicked humble themselves for a time when they feel God's judgment, yet after they return to their old malice, and declare that they are but vile hypocrites.
13:7 ¹ Or, take sustenance.
13:9 ¹ Or, he charged me: to wit, an Angel.
  ² Seeing he had the express word of God, he ought not to have declined therefrom neither for the persuasion of man nor Angel.

10 So he went another way, and returned not by the way that he came to Bethel.

11 ¶ And an old Prophet dwelt in Bethel, and his sons came and told him all the works, that the man of God had done that day in Bethel, and the words which he had spoken unto the king, told they their father.

12 And their father said unto them, What way went he? and his sons ¹showed him what way the man of God went, which came from Judah.

13 And he said unto his sons, Saddle me the ass. Who saddled him the ass, and he rode thereon,

14 And went after the man of God, and found him sitting under an oak: and he said unto him, Art thou the man of God, that camest from Judah? And he said, ¹Yea.

15 Then he said unto him, ¹Come home with me, and eat bread.

16 But he answered, I may not return with thee, nor go in with thee, neither will I eat bread nor drink water with thee in this place.

17 For it was charged me by the word of the Lord, *saying,* Thou shalt eat no bread, nor drink water there, nor turn again to go by the way that thou wentest.

18 And he said unto him, I am a Prophet also as thou art, and an ¹Angel spake unto me by the word of the Lord, saying, Bring him again with thee into thine house, that he may eat bread and drink water: *but* he lied unto him.

19 So he went again with him, and did eat bread in his house, and drank water.

20 And as they sat at the table, the word of the Lord came unto the Prophet, that brought him again.

21 And he cried unto the man of God that came from Judah, saying, Thus saith the Lord, ¹Because thou hast disobeyed the mouth of the Lord, and hast not kept the commandment which the Lord thy God commanded thee,

22 But camest back again, and hast eaten bread and drunk water in the place (whereof he did say unto thee, Thou shalt eat no bread nor drink any water) thy carcass shall not come unto the sepulcher of thy fathers.

23 ¶ And when he had eaten bread and drunk, he saddled him the ass, to wit, to the Prophet whom he had brought again,

24 And when he was gone, ¹a lion met him by the way, and slew him, and his body was cast in the way, and the ass stood thereby: the Lion stood by the corpse also.

25 And behold, men that passed by, saw the carcass cast in the way, and the Lion standing by the corpse: and they came and told it in the town where the old Prophet dwelt.

26 And when the Prophet that brought him back again from the way, heard thereof, he said, It is the man of God, who hath been disobedient unto the Commandment of the Lord: therefore the Lord hath delivered him unto the Lion, which hath rent him and slain him, according to the word of the Lord, which he spake unto him.

27 ¶ And he spake to his sons, saying, Saddle me the ass. And they saddled him.

28 And he went and found his body cast in the way, and the ass and the Lion stood by the corpse: and the lion had ¹not eaten the body, nor torn the ass.

29 And the Prophet took up the body of the man of God, and laid it upon the ass, and brought it again, and the old Prophet came to the city, to lament and bury him.

30 And he laid his body in his ¹own grave, and they lamented over him, *saying,* Alas, my brother.

31 And when he had buried him, he spake to his sons, saying, When I am dead, bury ye me also in the sepulcher, wherein the man of God is buried: lay my bones beside his bones.

32 For that thing which he cried by the word of the Lord against the altar that is in Bethel, and against all the houses of the high places, which are in the cities of Samaria, shall surely come to pass.

33 *Howbeit* after this Jeroboam ¹converted not from his wicked way, but turned again, and made of the lowest of the people priests of the high places. Who would, might ²consecrate himself and be of the priests of the high places.

34 And this thing turned to sin unto the house of Jeroboam, even to root it out, and to destroy it from the face of the earth.

14

2 *Jeroboam sendeth his wife disguised to Ahijah the Prophet, who declareth unto him the destruction of his house.* 25 *Judah is punished by Shishak.*

1 At that time Abijah the son of Jeroboam fell sick.

13:12 ¹ Hebrew, *looked.*
13:14 ¹ Hebrew, *I am.*
13:15 ¹ This he did of a simple mind, thinking it his duty to declare friendship to a Prophet.
13:18 ¹ His fault is here double: first in that he suffereth not the Prophet to obey God's express commandment: and next, that he feigneth to have a revelation to the contrary.
13:21 ¹ God would reprove his folly by him, who was the occasion to bring him into error.

13:24 ¹ By this fearful example, God setteth forth how dangerous a thing it is for men to behave themselves coldly, or deceitfully in their charge whereunto God hath called them.
13:28 ¹ To declare that this was only the judgment of God: for if the Lion had done it for hunger, he would also have devoured the body.
13:30 ¹ Which he had prepared for himself.
13:33 ¹ So the wicked profit not by God's threatenings, but go backward, and become worse and worse, 2 Tim. 3:13.
   ² Hebrew, *fill his hand.*

2 And Jeroboam said unto his wife, Up, I pray thee, [1]and disguise thyself that they know not that thou art the wife of Jeroboam, and go to Shiloh: for there is Ahijah the Prophet, which told me *that I should be king over this people,

3 And take [1]with [2]thee, ten loaves and [3]cracknels, and a bottle of honey, and go to him: he shall tell thee what shall become of the young man.

4 And Jeroboam's wife did so, and arose, and went to Shiloh, and came to the house of Ahijah: but Ahijah could not see, for his [1]sight was decayed for his age.

5 Then the Lord said unto Ahijah, Behold, the wife of Jeroboam cometh to ask a thing of thee for her son, for he is sick: thus and thus shalt thou say unto her: *for when she cometh in, she shall feign herself *to be* [1]another.

6 Therefore when Ahijah heard the sound of her feet as she came in at the door, he said, Come in thou [1]wife of Jeroboam: why feignest thou thus thyself to be another? I am sent to thee *with* heavy tidings.

7 Go tell Jeroboam, Thus saith the Lord God of Israel, Forasmuch as I have exalted [1]thee from among the people, and have made thee prince over my people Israel,

8 And have rent the kingdom away from the house of David, and have given it thee, and thou hast not been as my servant David, which kept my Commandments, and followed me with all his heart, and did only that which was right in mine eyes,

9 But hast done evil above all that were before thee (for thou hast gone and made thee other gods, and [1]molten images, to provoke me, and hast cast me behind thy back.)

10 Therefore behold, I will bring evil upon the house of Jeroboam, and will cut off from Jeroboam him that [b,1]pisseth against the wall, as well him that [2]is shut up, as him that is left in Israel, and will sweep away the remnant of the house of Jeroboam, as a man sweepeth away dung till it be all gone.

11 The dogs shall eat him of Jeroboam's *stock* that dieth in the city, and the fowls of the air shall eat him that dieth in the field: [1]for the Lord hath said it.

CHAPTER 14

[a] 1 Kings 11:31

[b] 1 Kings 21:21
2 Kings 9:8

12 Up therefore and get thee to thine house: for when thy feet enter into the city, the child shall die.

13 And all Israel shall mourn for him, and bury him: for he only of Jeroboam shall come to the grave, because in him there is found [1]some goodness toward the Lord God of Israel in the house of Jeroboam.

14 Moreover, the Lord shall stir him up a King over Israel which shall destroy the house of Jeroboam in that day: [1]what? yea, even now.

15 For the Lord shall smite Israel, as when a reed is shaken in the water, and he shall weed Israel out of this good land, which he gave to their fathers, and shall scatter them beyond the [1]River, because they have made them groves, provoking the Lord to anger.

16 And he shall give Israel up, because of the sins of Jeroboam, who did sin, and [1]made Israel to sin.

17 ¶ And Jeroboam's wife arose, and departed, and came to Tirzah, and when she came to the threshold of the house, the young man died.

18 And they buried him, and all Israel lamented him, according to the word of the Lord which he spake by the hand of his servant Ahijah the Prophet.

19 And the rest of Jeroboam's acts, how he warred, and how he reigned, behold, they are written in the book of the Chronicles of the Kings of Israel.

20 And the days which Jeroboam reigned, were two and twenty years: and he [1]slept with his fathers, and Nadab his son reigned in his stead.

21 ¶ Also Rehoboam the son of Solomon reigned in Judah. Rehoboam was one and forty years old, when he began to reign, and reigned seventeen [1]years in Jerusalem, the city which the Lord did choose out of all the tribes of Israel, to put his name there: and his mother's name was Naamah an Ammonite.

22 And Judah wrought wickedness in the sight of the Lord: and they provoked him more with their sins, which they had committed, [1]than all that which their fathers had done.

23 For they also made them high places, and images, and groves on every high hill, and under every green tree.

24 There were also Sodomites in the [1]land, they did according to all the abominations of the nations,

---

14:2 [1] His own conscience bare him witness, that the Prophet of God would not satisfy his affections, which was a wicked man.

14:3 [1] Hebrew, *in thine hand.*

[2] According to the custom when they went to ask counsel of Prophets, 1 Sam. 9:7.

[3] Or, wafers.

14:4 [1] Hebrew, *eyes stood.*

14:5 [1] Then the wife of Jeroboam.

14:6 [1] For God ofttimes discloseth unto his the craft and subtlety of the wicked.

14:7 [1] Which wast but a servant.

14:9 [1] To wit, two calves.

14:10 [1] Every male even to the dogs, 1 Sam. 25:22.

[2] As well him that is in the stronghold, as him that is abroad.

14:11 [1] They shall lack the honor of burial in token of God's malediction.

14:13 [1] In the midst of the wicked, God hath some on whom he doth bestow his mercies.

14:14 [1] The Lord will begin to destroy it out of hand.

14:15 [1] Meaning, Euphrates.

14:16 [1] The people shall not be excused when they do evil at the commandment of their governors.

14:20 [1] The Lord smote him that he died, 2 Chron. 13:20.

14:21 [1] And died before Jeroboam about four years.

14:22 [1] Or, besides all that their fathers had done by their sins.

14:24 [1] Where idolatry reigneth, all horrible vices are committed, till at length God's just judgment destroy them utterly.

which the Lord hast cast out before the children of Israel.

25 ¶ And in the fifth year of King Rehoboam, Shishak king of Egypt came up against Jerusalem.

26 And took the treasures of the house of the Lord, and the treasures of the King's house, and took away all: so he carried away all the shields of gold 'which Solomon had made.

27 And king Rehoboam made for them brazen shields, and committed them unto the hands of the chief of the guard, which waited at the door of the king's house.

28 And when the King went into the house of the Lord, the guard bare them, and brought them again into the guard chamber.

29 And the rest of the acts of Rehoboam, and all that he did, are they not written in ¹the book of the Chronicles of the kings of Judah?

30 And there was war between Rehoboam and Jeroboam ¹continually.

31 And Rehoboam slept with his fathers, and was buried with his fathers in the city of David: his mother's name was Naamah an ¹Ammonite: and Abijam his son reigned in his stead.

15

1 Abijam reigneth over Judah.   9 Asa succeedeth in his room.   16 The battle between Asa and Baasha.   24 Jehoshaphat succeedeth Asa.   25 Nadab succeedeth Jeroboam.   28 Baasha killeth Nadab.

1 And in the eighteenth year of King ᵃJeroboam the son of Nebat, reigned Abijam over Judah.

2 Three years reigned he in Jerusalem, and his mother's name was Maachah the daughter of ¹Abishalom.

3 And he walked in all the sins of his father, which he had done before him: and his heart was not perfect with the Lord his God, as the heart of David his father.

4 But for David's sake did the Lord his God give him a ¹light in Jerusalem, and set up his son after him, and established Jerusalem,

5 Because David did that which was right in the sight of the Lord, and turned from nothing that he commanded him all the days of his life, ᵇsave only in the matter of Uriah the Hittite.

6 And there was war between Rehoboam and Jeroboam as long as he lived.

ᶜ 1 Kings 10:16

CHAPTER 15
ᵃ 2 Chron. 11:12
ᵇ 2 Sam. 11:4
   2 Sam. 12:9
ᶜ 2 Chron. 13:3
ᵈ 2 Chron. 14:1
ᵉ 2 Chron. 15:16
ᶠ 2 Chron. 16:2

7 The rest also of the acts of Abijam, and all that he did, are they not written in the 'book of the Chronicles of the kings of Judah? there was also war between Abijam and Jeroboam.

8 And Abijam slept with his fathers, and they buried him in the city of David: and Asa his son reigned in his stead.

9 ¶ ᵈAnd in the twenty years of Jeroboam King of Israel, reigned Asa over Judah.

10 He reigned in Jerusalem one and forty years, and his ¹mother's name was Maachah, the daughter of Abishalom.

11 And Asa did right in the eyes of the Lord, as did David his father.

12 And he took away the Sodomites out of the land, and put away all the idols that his fathers had made.

13 And he ¹put down ᵉMaachah his mother also from her estate, because she had made an idol in a grove: and Asa destroyed her idols, and burnt them by the brook Kidron.

14 But they put not down the high places. Nevertheless Asa's heart was ¹upright with the Lord all his days.

15 Also he brought in the holy vessels of his father, and the things that he had dedicated unto the house of the Lord, silver and gold, and vessels.

16 ¶ And there was war between Asa and Baasha king of Israel all their days.

17 Then Baasha King of Israel went up against Judah, and built ¹Ramah, so that he would let none go out or in to Asa king of Judah.

18 Then Asa took all the silver and the gold that was left in the treasures of the house of the Lord, and the treasures of the king's house, and delivered them into the hands of his servants, and king Asa sent them to ᶠBen-Hadad the son of Tabrimmon, the son of Hezion king of ¹Aram that dwelt at Damascus, saying,

19 There is a covenant between me and thee, and between my father and thy father: Behold, I have sent unto thee a present of silver and gold: come, break thy covenant with Baasha King of Israel, that he may ¹depart from me.

20 So Ben-Hadad hearkened unto king Asa, and sent the captains of the hosts, which he had, against the cities of Israel, and smote Ijon, and Dan, and Abel Beth Maachah, and all Chinneroth, with all

---

14:29 ¹ Which books were called the books of Shemaiah and Iddo the Prophets, 2 Chron. 12:15.
14:30 ¹ That is, all the days of Rehoboam's life.
14:31 ¹ Whose idolatry Rehoboam her son followed.
15:2 ¹ Some think that this was Absalom Solomon's son.
15:4 ¹ Meaning, a son to reign over Judah.
15:10 ¹ That is, his grandmother, as David is oft times called father of them, whose grandfather he was.

15:13 ¹ Neither kindred nor authority ought to be regarded, when they blaspheme God, and become idolaters, but must be punished.
15:14 ¹ For in that that he suffered them to worship God in other places, than he had appointed, it came of ignorance, and not of malice.
15:17 ¹ Of the same purpose that Jeroboam did, because the people should not go up to Jerusalem, lest they should follow Asa.
15:18 ¹ Or, Syria.
15:19 ¹ And vex me no longer.

the land of Naphtali.

21 And when Baasha heard thereof, he left building of Ramah, and dwelt in Tirzah.

22 Then king Asa [1]assembled all Judah [2]none excepted, and they took the stones of Ramah, and the timber thereof, wherewith Baasha had built, and king Asa built with them Geba of Benjamin and Mizpah.

23 And the rest of all the acts of Asa, and all his might, and all that he did, and the cities which he built, are they not written in the book of the Chronicles of the Kings of Judah? but in his old age he was diseased in his [1]feet.

24 And Asa slept with his fathers, and was buried with his fathers in the city of David his [1]father. And Jehoshaphat his son reigned in his stead.

25 And Nadab the son of Jeroboam began to reign over Israel the second year of Asa king of Judah, and reigned over Israel two years.

26 And he did evil in the sight of the Lord, walking in the way of his father, and in his sin wherewith he made Israel to sin.

27 And Baasha the son of Ahijah of the house of Issachar conspired against him, and Baasha slew him at Gibbethon, which belonged to the Philistines: for Nadab and all Israel laid siege to Gibbethon.

28 Even in the third year of Asa king of Judah did Baasha slay him, and reigned in his stead.

29 And when he was king, he [1]smote all the house of Jeroboam, he left none alive to Jeroboam, until he had destroyed him, according to the [g]word of the Lord which he spake by his servant Ahijah the Shilonite,

30 Because of the sins of Jeroboam which he committed, and wherewith he made Israel to sin, by his [1]provocation, wherewith he provoked the Lord God of Israel.

31 And the residue of the acts of Nadab, and all that he did, are they not written in the book of the Chronicles of the kings of Israel?

32 And there was war between Asa and Baasha king of Israel, all their days.

33 In the third year of Asa king of Judah, began Baasha the son of Ahijah to reign over all Israel in [1]Tirzah, and reigned four and twenty years.

34 And he did evil in the sight of the Lord, walking in the way of Jeroboam, and in his sin, wherewith he made Israel to sin.

16

1 Of Baasha,   6 Elah,   9 Zimri,   16 Omri.   31 Ahab marrieth Jezebel.   34 Jericho is built again.

1 Then the word of the Lord came to Jehu the son of Hanani against Baasha, saying,

2 [1]Forasmuch as I exalted thee out of the dust, and made thee captain over my people Israel, and thou hast walked in the way of Jeroboam, and hast made my people Israel to sin, to provoke me with their sins,

3 Behold, I will take away the posterity of Baasha, and the posterity of his house, and will make [1]thine house like the [a]house of Jeroboam, the son of Nebat.

4 [b]He that dieth of Baasha's stock in the city, him shall the dogs eat: and that man of him which dieth in the fields, shall the fowls of the air eat.

5 And the rest of the acts of Baasha, and what he did, and his [1]power, are they not written in the book of the [c]Chronicles of the kings of Israel?

6 So Baasha slept with his fathers, and was buried in Tirzah, and Elah his son reigned in his stead.

7 And also [1]by the hand of Jehu the son of Hanani the Prophet, came the word of the Lord to Baasha, and to his house, that he should be like the house of Jeroboam, even for all the wickedness that he did in the sight of the Lord, in provoking him with the work of his hands, and because he killed [2]him.

8 ¶ In the six and twenty years of Asa king of Judah, began Elah the son of Baasha to reign over Israel in Tirzah, and reigned two years.

9 And his servant Zimri, captain of half his chariots, conspired against him, as he was in Tirzah [1]drinking, till he was drunken in the house of Arza steward of his house in Tirzah.

10 And Zimri came and smote him, and killed him in the seven and twenty years of Asa king of Judah, and reigned in his stead.

11 ¶ And when he was king, and sat on his throne, he slew all the house of Baasha, not leaving thereof one to piss against a wall, neither of his kinsfolks, nor of his friends.

12 So did Zimri destroy all the house of Baasha, according to the word of the Lord which he spake against Baasha by the hand of Jehu the [1]Prophet,

13 For all the sins of Baasha, and sins of Elah his son, which they sinned, and made Israel to sin, and

---

g 1 Kings 14:10

CHAPTER 16
a 1 Kings 15:29
b 1 Kings 14:11
c 1 Chron. 16:1

15:22 [1] Or, make a proclamation.
  [2] Hebrew, none innocent.
15:23 [1] He had the gout and put his trust rather in Physicians than in the Lord, 2 Chron. 16:12.
15:24 [1] His great-grandfather.
15:29 [1] So God stirred up one tyrant to punish the wickedness of another.
15:30 [1] By causing the people to commit idolatry with his calves, and so provoking God to anger.

15:33 [1] Which was the place where the kings of Israel remained.
16:2 [1] Thus spake Jehu to Baasha in the Name of the Lord.
16:3 [1] Meaning, the house of Baasha.
16:5 [1] Or, valiantness.
16:7 [1] That is, the Prophet did his message.
  [2] Meaning, Nadab Jeroboam's son.
16:9 [1] The Chaldea text hath thus, Drinking till he was drunken in the Temple of Arza the idol by his house in Tirzah.
16:12 [1] Both Hanani his father and he were Prophets.

provoked the Lord God of Israel with their vanities.

14 And the rest of the acts of Elah, and all that he did, are they not written in the book of the Chronicles of the kings of Israel?

15 ¶ In the seven and twenty years of Asa king of Judah did Zimri reign seven days in Tirzah, and the people was then in camp [1]against Gibbethon, which *belonged* to the Philistines.

16 And the people of the host heard say, Zimri hath conspired, and hath also slain the king. Wherefore all Israel made Omri the captain of the host, king over Israel that same day, *even* in the host.

17 Then Omri went up from Gibbethon, and all Israel with him, and they besieged [1]Tirzah.

18 And when Zimri saw, that the city was taken, he went into the palace of the king's house, and [1]burnt himself, and the king's house with fire, *and* so died,

19 For his sins which he sinned, in doing that which is evil in the sight of the Lord, in walking in the way of Jeroboam, and in his sins which he did, causing Israel to sin.

20 And the rest of the acts of Zimri, and his treason that he wrought, are they not written in the book of the Chronicles of the kings of Israel?

21 Then were the people of Israel divided into two parts: *for* [1]half the people followed Tibni the son of Ginath to make him king, and the other half followed Omri.

22 But the people that followed Omri, prevailed against the people that followed Tibni the son of Ginath: so Tibni died, and Omri reigned.

23 In the one and thirty years of Asa king of Judah began Omri to reign over Israel, *and reigned* twelve years. Six years reigned he in Tirzah.

24 And he bought the mountain [1]Samaria of one Shemer for two talents of silver, and built in the mountain, and called the name of the city, which he built, after the name of Shemer lord of the mountain, Samaria.

25 But Omri did evil in the eyes of the Lord, and did [1]worse than all that were before him.

26 For he walked in all the way of Jeroboam the son of Nebat, and in his sins wherewith he made Israel to sin in provoking the Lord God of Israel with their vanities.

27 And the rest of the acts of Omri, that he did, and

CHAPTER 17
[a] James 5:16,17

his strength that he showed, are they not written in the book of the Chronicles of the Kings of Israel?

28 And Omri slept with his fathers, and was buried in [1]Samaria: and Ahab his son reigned in his stead.

29 Now Ahab the son of Omri began to reign over Israel, in the eight and thirty years of Asa king of Judah, and Ahab the son of Omri reigned over Israel in Samaria two and twenty years.

30 And Ahab the son of Omri did worse in the sight of the Lord than all that were before him.

31 For was it a light thing for him to walk in the sins of Jeroboam the son of Nebat, except he took Jezebel also the daughter of Ethbaal king of the Sidonians [1]to wife, and went and served Baal, and worshipped him?

32 Also he reared up an altar to Baal in the house of Baal, which he had built in Samaria.

33 And Ahab made a grove, and Ahab proceeded, and did provoke the Lord God of Israel more than all the kings of Israel that were before him.

34 In his days did Hiel the Bethelite build [1]Jericho: he laid the foundation thereof in Abiram his eldest son, and set up the gates thereof in his youngest son Segub, according to the word of the Lord which he spake [2]by Joshua the son of Nun.

17 1 *Elijah forewarneth of the famine to come.* 4 *He is fed of Ravens.* 9 *He is sent to Zarephath, where he restoreth his hostess's son to life.*

1 And Elijah the Tishbite one of the inhabitants of Gilead said unto Ahab, [a]As the Lord God of Israel liveth, before whom I [1]stand, there shall be neither dew nor rain these years, but [2]according to my word.

2 ¶ And the word of the Lord came unto him, saying,

3 Go hence, and turn thee Eastward, and hide thyself in the [1]river Cherith, that is over against Jordan,

4 And thou shalt drink of the river: and I have commanded the [1]ravens to feed thee there.

5 So he went and did according unto the word of the Lord: for he went, and remained by the river Cherith that is over against Jordan

6 And the ravens brought him bread and flesh in the morning, and bread and flesh in the evening,

---

16:15 [1] The siege had continued from the time of Nadab Jeroboam's son.

16:17 [1] Where Zimri kept himself in hold.

16:18 [1] Hebrew, *burnt the King's house upon him.*

16:21 [1] That is, the people which were not at the siege of Gibbethon: for there they had chosen Omri.

16:24 [1] Or, Shomeron.

16:25 [1] For such is the nature of idolatry, that the superstition thereof doth daily increase, and the older it is the more abominable it is before God and his Church.

16:28 [1] He was the first king that was buried in Samaria, after that

the kings house was burnt in Tirzah.

16:31 [1] By whose means he fell to all wicked and strange idolatry, and cruel persecution.

16:34 [1] Read Josh. 6:26.

    [2] Hebrew, *by the hand of Joshua.*

17:1 [1] That is, whom I serve.

    [2] But as I shall declare it by God's revelation.

17:3 [1] Or, brook.

17:4 [1] To strengthen his faith against persecution, God promiseth to feed him miraculously.

and he drank of the river.

7   And after a while the river dried up, because there fell no rain upon the earth.

8   ¶ And the ¹word of the Lord came unto him, saying,

9   ᵇUp, *and* get thee to Zarephath, which is in Sidon, and remain there: behold, I have commanded a widow there to sustain thee.

10   So he arose and went to Zarephath: and when he came to the gate of the city, behold, the widow was there ¹gathering sticks: and he called her, and said, Bring me, I pray thee, a little water in a vessel, that I may drink.

11   And as she was going to fetch it, he called to her, and said, Bring me, I pray thee, a morsel of bread in thine hand.

12   And she said, As the Lord thy God liveth, I have not a cake, but even an handful of meal in a barrel, and a little oil in a cruse: and behold, I am gathering ¹a few sticks for to go in, and dress it for me and my son, that we may eat it, and ²die.

13   And Elijah said unto her, Fear not, come do as thou hast said, but make me thereof a little cake first of all, and bring it unto me, and afterward make for thee and thy son.

14   For thus saith the Lord God of Israel, ¹The meal in the barrel shall not be wasted, neither shall the oil in the cruse be diminished, unto the time that the Lord send rain upon the earth.

15   So she went, and did as Elijah said, and she did eat: so did he and her house ¹for a certain time.

16   The barrel of the meal wasted not, nor the oil was spent out of the cruse, according to the word of the Lord, which he spake by the hand of Elijah.

17   ¶ And after these things, the son of the wife of the house fell sick, and his sickness was so sore, ¹that there was no ²breath left in him.

18   And she said unto Elijah, What have I to do with thee, O thou man of God? art thou come unto me to call my sin to remembrance, and to slay my son?

19   And he said unto her, Give me thy son: and he took him out of her bosom, and carried him up into a chamber, where he abode, and laid him upon

ᵇ Luke 4:25,26

his own bed.

20   Then he called unto the Lord, and said, O Lord my God, hast thou ¹punished also this widow, with whom I sojourn, by killing her son?

21   And he stretched himself upon the child three times, and called unto the Lord, and said, O Lord my God, I pray thee, let this child's soul come into him again.

22   Then the Lord heard the voice of Elijah, and the soul of the child came into him again, and he revived.

23   And Elijah took the child, and brought him down out of the chamber into the house, and delivered him unto his mother, and Elijah said, Behold, thy son liveth.

24   And the woman said unto Elijah, Now ¹I know that thou art a man of God, and that the word of the Lord in thy mouth is true.

18

1 Elijah is sent to Ahab.   13 Obadiah hideth an hundred Prophets.   40 Elijah killeth all Baal's prophets.   45 He obtaineth rain.

1   After many days, the word of the Lord came to Elijah, in the ¹third year, saying, Go, show thyself unto Ahab, and I will send rain upon the earth.

2   And Elijah went to show himself unto Ahab, and *there was* a great famine in Samaria.

3   And Ahab called Obadiah the governor of his house: (and Obadiah ¹feared God greatly:

4   For when Jezebel destroyed the Prophets of the Lord, Obadiah took an hundred Prophets, and hid them by fifty in a cave, and he fed them with bread and water.)

5   And Ahab said unto Obadiah, Go into the land, unto all the fountains of water, and unto all the rivers, if so be that we may find grass to save the horses and the mules alive, lest we deprive *the land* of the beasts.

6   And so they divided the land between them to walk through it. Ahab went one way by himself, and Obadiah went another way by himself.

7   ¶ And as Obadiah was in the way, behold, Elijah ¹met him: and he knew him, and fell on his

---

17:8 ¹ As the troubles of the Saints of God are many, so his mercy is ever at hand to deliver them.

17:10 ¹ All this was to strengthen the faith of Elijah, to the intent that he should look upon nothing worldly, but only trust on God's providence.

17:12 ¹ Hebrew, *two.*
    ² For there is no hope of any more sustenance.

17:14 ¹ God receiveth no benefit for the use of his, but he promiseth a most ample recompense for the same.

17:15 ¹ That is, till he had rain and food on the earth.

17:17 ¹ Or, that he died.
    ² God would try whether she had learned by his merciful providence to make her her only stay and comfort.

17:20 ¹ He was afraid lest God's name should have been blasphemed and his ministers contemned, except he should have continued his mercies as he had begun them, specially while he there remained.

17:24 ¹ So hard a thing it is to depend on God, except we be confirmed by miracles.

18:1 ¹ After that he departed from the river Cherith.

18:3 ¹ God had begun to work his fear in his heart, but had not yet brought him to that knowledge, which is also requisite of the godly: that is, to profess his Name openly.

18:7 ¹ God pitieth oft times the wicked for the godly's sake, and causeth Elijah to meet with Obadiah, that the benefit might be known to be granted for God's children's sake.

face, and said, Art not thou my lord Elijah?

8 And he answered him, Yea, go tell thy lord, Behold, Elijah *is here.*

9 And he said, What have I sinned, that thou wouldest deliver thy servant into the hand of Ahab, to slay me?

10 As the Lord thy God liveth, there is no nation or kingdom, whither my lord hath not sent to seek thee: and when they said, He is not here, he took an oath of the kingdom and nation, if they had not found thee.

11 And now thou sayest, Go, tell thy lord, Behold, Elijah *is here.*

12 And when I am gone from thee, the Spirit of the Lord shall carry thee into some place that I do not know: so when I come and tell Ahab, if he cannot find thee, then will he kill me: But I thy servant ¹fear the Lord from my youth.

13 Was it not told my lord, what I did when Jezebel slew the Prophets of the Lord, how I hid an hundred men of the Lord's Prophets by fifties in a cave, and fed them with bread and water?

14 And now thou sayest, Go, tell thy lord, Behold, Elijah *is here,* that he may slay me.

15 And Elijah said, As the Lord of hosts liveth, before whom I stand, I will surely show ¹myself unto him this day.

16 ¶ So Obadiah went to meet Ahab, and told him. And Ahab went to meet Elijah.

17 And when Ahab saw Elijah, Ahab said unto him, Art thou he that troubleth Israel?

18 And he answered, I have not troubled Israel, but ¹thou and thy father's house, in that ye have forsaken the commandments of the Lord, and thou hast followed Baal.

19 Now therefore send, and gather to me all Israel unto mount Carmel, and the prophets of Baal four hundred and fifty, and the prophets of the groves four hundred, which eat at Jezebel's table.

20 ¶ So Ahab sent unto all the children of Israel, and gathered the prophets together unto mount Carmel.

21 And Elijah came unto all the people, and said, How long ¹halt ye between two opinions? If the Lord be God, follow him, but if Baal be he, then go after him. And the people answered him not a word.

22 Then said Elijah unto the people, I only remain

CHAPTER 18
ᵃ Gen. 32:28
2 Kings 17:34

a Prophet of the Lord: but Baal's prophets are four hundred and fifty men.

23 Let them therefore give us two bullocks, and let them choose the one, and cut him in pieces, and lay him on the wood, but put no fire *under,* and I will prepare the other bullock, and lay him on the wood, and will put no fire *under.*

24 Then call ye on the name of your god, and I will call on the Name of the Lord: and then the God that answereth ¹by fire, let him be God. And all the people answered, and said, It is well spoken.

25 And Elijah said unto the prophets of Baal, Choose you a bullock, and prepare him first, (for ye are many) and call on the name of your gods, but put no fire *under.*

26 So they took the one bullock that was given them, and they prepared it, and called on the name of Baal from morning to noon, saying, O Baal, hear us: but there was no voice, nor any to answer: and they ¹leapt upon the altar that was made.

27 And at noon Elijah mocked them, and said, Cry aloud: for he is a ¹god: either he talketh or pursueth *his enemies,* or is in his journey, or it may be that he sleepeth, and must be ²awaked.

28 And they cried loud, and cut themselves as their manner was, with knives and lancers, till the blood gushed out upon them.

29 And when midday was passed, and they had prophesied until the offering of the *evening* sacrifice, there was neither voice, nor one to answer, nor any that regarded.

30 And Elijah said unto all the people, Come to me. And all the people came to him. And he repaired the altar of the Lord that was broken down.

31 And Elijah took twelve stones, according to the number of the tribes of the sons of Jacob, (unto whom the word of the Lord came, saying, ᵃIsrael shall be thy name)

32 And with the stones he built an altar in the Name of the Lord: and he made a ditch round about the altar, as great as would contain two ¹measures of seed.

33 And he put the wood in order, and hewed the bullock in pieces, and laid him in the wood:

34 And said, Fill four barrels with water, and pour it upon the burnt offering and on the wood. Again he said, Do so again. And they did so the second time. And he said, Do it the third time. And they

---

18:12 ¹ I am none of the wicked persecutors that thou shouldest procure unto me such displeasure, but serve God, and favor his children.

18:15 ¹ By my presence I will declare that thou hast told him the truth.

18:18 ¹ The true ministers of God ought not only not to suffer the truth to be unjustly slandered, but to reprove boldly the wicked slanderers without respect of person.

18:21 ¹ Be constant in religion, and make it not as a thing indifferent, whether ye follow God or Baal, or whether ye serve God wholly or in

part, Zeph. 1:5.

18:24 ¹ By sending down fire from heaven to burn the sacrifice.

18:26 ¹ As men ravished with some strange spirit.

18:27 ¹ You esteem him as God.

² He mocketh their beastly madness, which think that by any instance or suit, the dead and vile idols can help their worshippers in their necessity.

18:32 ¹ Hebrew, *seahs,* which some think contain about three pottles and a third part a piece.

did it the third time.

35 And the water ran round about the altar: and he ¹filled the ditch with water also.

36 And when they should offer the *evening* sacrifice, Elijah the Prophet came and said, Lord God of Abraham, Isaac, and of Israel, let it be known this day, that thou art the God of Israel, and that I am thy servant, and that I have done all these things at thy commandment.

37 Hear me, O Lord, hear me, and let this people know that thou art the Lord God, and that thou hast turned their heart again ¹at the last.

38 Then the fire of the Lord fell, and consumed the burnt offering, and the wood, and the stones, and the dust, and licked up the water that was in the ditch.

39 And when all the people saw it, they fell on their faces, and said, The Lord is God, the Lord is God.

40 And Elijah said unto them, Take the prophets of Baal, let not ¹a man of them escape: and they took them, and Elijah brought them to the brook Kishon, and slew them there.

41 ¶ And Elijah said unto Ahab, Get thee up, eat and drink, for *there is* a sound of much rain.

42 So Ahab went up to eat and to drink, and Elijah went up to the top of Carmel: and he crouched unto the earth, and put his face between his knees,

43 And said to his servant, Go up now, and look toward the way of the Sea. And he went up, and looked, and said, There is nothing. Again he said, Go again ¹seven times.

44 And at the seventh time he said, Behold, there ariseth a little cloud out of the Sea like a man's hand. Then he said, Up, and say unto Ahab, Make ready *the chariot*, and get thee down, that the rain stay thee not.

45 And ¹in the meanwhile the heaven was black with clouds and wind, and there was a great rain. Then Ahab went up, and came to Jezreel,

46 And the hand of the Lord was on Elijah, and he girded up his loins, and ran ¹before Ahab till he came to Jezreel.

CHAPTER 19
ᵈ Rom. 11:13

19

5 *Elijah fleeing from Jezebel, is nourished by the Angel of God.* 15 *He is commanded to anoint Hazael, Jehu, and Elisha.*

1 Now Ahab told Jezebel all that Elijah had done, and how he had slain all the ¹prophets with the sword.

2 Then Jezebel sent a messenger unto Elijah, saying, ¹The gods do so to me and more also, if I make not thy life like one of their lives by tomorrow this time.

3 ¶ When he saw that, he arose, and went ¹for his life, and came to Beersheba, which is in Judah, and left his servant there.

4 But he went a day's journey into the wilderness, and came and sat down under a Juniper tree, and desired that he might die, and said, It is now enough: O Lord, ¹take my soul, for I am no better than my fathers.

5 And as he lay and slept under the Juniper tree, behold now, an Angel touched him, and said unto him, Up, *and* eat.

6 And when he looked about, behold, there was a cake baken on the coals, and a pot of water at his head: so he did eat and drink, and returned and slept.

7 And the Angel of the Lord came again the second time, and touched him, and said, Up, *and* eat: for ¹thou hast a great journey.

8 ¶ Then he arose, and did eat and drink, and walked in the strength of that meat forty days and forty nights, unto Horeb the mount of God.

9 And there he entered into a cave, and lodged there: and behold, the Lord spake to him, and said unto him, What doest thou here, Elijah?

10 And he answered, I have ¹been very jealous for the Lord God of hosts: for the children of Israel have forsaken thy covenant, broken down thine altars, and slain thy Prophets with the sword, ᵃand I only am left, and they seek my life to take it away.

11 And he said, Come out, and stand upon the mount before the Lord. And behold, the Lord went by, and a mighty strong wind rent the mountains, and brake the rocks before the Lord: *but* the Lord was ¹not

---

18:35 ¹ Hereby he declared the excellent power of God, who contrary to nature could make the fire burn even in the water, to the intent they should have none occasion to doubt that he is the only God.
18:37 ¹ Though God suffer his to run in blindness and error for a time, yet at the length he calleth them home to him by some notorious sign and work.
18:40 ¹ He commanded them that as they were truly persuaded to confess the only God: so they would serve him with all their power, and destroy the idolaters his enemies.
18:43 ¹ As God's spirit moved him to pray, so was he strengthened by the same, that he did not faint, but continued still till he had obtained.
18:45 ¹ Or, here and there.
18:46 ¹ He was so strengthened with God's spirit, that he ran faster

than the chariot was able to run.
19:1 ¹ To wit, of Baal.
19:2 ¹ Though the wicked rage against God's children, yet he holdeth them back that they cannot execute their malice.
19:3 ¹ Or, whither his mind led him.
19:4 ¹ So hard a thing it is to bridle our impatience in affliction, that the Saints could not overcome the same.
19:7 ¹ He declareth that except God had nourished him miraculously, it had not been possible for him to have gone this journey.
19:10 ¹ He complaineth that the more zealous that he showed himself to maintain God's glory, the more cruelly was he persecuted.
19:11 ¹ For the nature of man is not able to come near unto God, if he should appear in his strength and full majesty, and therefore of his mercy he submitteth himself to our capacity.

in the wind: and after the wind *came* an earthquake: *but* the Lord was not in the earthquake:

12 And after the earthquake *came* fire: *but* the Lord was not in the fire: and after the fire *came* a still and soft voice.

13 And when Elijah heard it, he covered his face with his mantle, and went out, and stood in the entering of the cave: and behold, *there came a* voice unto him, and said, What doest thou here, Elijah?

14 And he answered, I have been very jealous for the Lord God of hosts, ¹because the children of Israel have forsaken thy covenant, cast down thine altars, and slain thy Prophets with the sword, and I only am left, and they seek my life to take it away.

15 And the Lord said unto him, Go, return by the wilderness unto Damascus, and when thou comest *there*, anoint Hazael king over ¹Aram.

16 And Jehu the son of Nimshi shalt thou anoint King over Israel: and Elisha the son of Shaphat of Abel Meholah shalt thou anoint to be Prophet in thy room.

17 And ᵇhim that escapeth from the sword of Hazael, shall Jehu slay: and him that escapeth from the sword of Jehu, shall Elisha slay.

18 Yet will ᶜI leave seven thousand in Israel: *even* ¹all the knees that have not bowed unto Baal, and every mouth that hath not kissed him.

19 ¶ So he departed thence, and found Elisha the son of Shaphat, who was plowing with twelve yoke of oxen before him, and was with the twelfth: and Elijah went towards him, and cast his mantel upon him.

20 And he left the oxen, and ran after Elijah, and said, ¹Let me, I pray thee, kiss my father and my mother, and then I will follow thee. Who answered him, Go, return: for what have I done to thee?

21 And when he went back again from him, he took a couple of oxen, and slew them, and sod their flesh with the ¹instruments of the oxen, and gave unto the people, and they did eat: then he arose and went after Elijah, and ministered unto him.

ᵇ 2 Kings 9:1,3
ᶜ Rom. 11:4

20

1 Samaria is besieged. 13 The Lord promiseth the victory to Ahab by a Prophet. 31 The King of Israel made peace with Ben-Hadad, and is reproved therefore by the Prophet.

1 Then Ben-Hadad the king of ¹Aram assembled all his army, and two and thirty ²kings with him, with horses, and chariots, and went up and besieged ³Samaria, and fought against it.

2 And he sent messengers to Ahab king of Israel, into the city,

3 And said unto him, Thus saith Ben-Hadad, Thy silver and thy gold is mine: also thy women, and thy fair children are mine.

4 And the king of Israel answered, and said, My lord king, according to thy saying, ¹I am thine, and all that I have.

5 And when the messengers came again, they said, Thus commandeth Ben-Hadad, and saith, When I shall send unto thee, and command, thou shalt deliver me thy silver and thy gold, and thy women, and thy children,

6 ¹Or else I will send my servants unto thee by tomorrow this time, and they shall search thine house, and the houses of thy servants: and whatsoever is pleasant in thine eyes, they shall take it in their hands, and bring it away.

7 Then the King of Israel sent for all the Elders of the land, and said, Take heed, I pray you, and see how he seeketh mischief: for he sent unto me for my wives, and for my children, and for my silver, and for my gold, and I denied him not.

8 And all the Elders, and all the people said to him, Hearken ¹not unto him, nor consent.

9 Wherefore he said unto the messengers of Ben-Hadad, Tell my lord the king, All that thou didst send for to thy servant at the first time, that I will do, but this thing I may not do. And the messengers departed, and brought him an answer.

10 And Ben-Hadad sent unto him, and said, The gods do so to me and more also, if the ¹dust of Samaria be enough to all the people that follow me, for every man an handful.

11 And the king of Israel answered, and said, Tell *him*, Let not him that girdeth *his harness*, boast himself, as he that ¹putteth it off.

19:14 ¹ We ought not to depend on the multitude in maintaining God's glory, but because our duty so requireth, we ought to do it.
19:15 ¹ Or, Syria.
19:18 ¹ He declareth that wicked dissemblers and idolaters are not his.
19:20 ¹ Though this natural affection is not to be contemned, yet it ought not to move us when God calleth us to serve him.
19:21 ¹ He would not stay till wood was brought, so great was his desire to follow his vocation.
20:1 ¹ Or, Syria
    ² That is, governors and rulers of provinces.

³ Or, Shomeron.
20:4 ¹ I am content to obey and pay tribute.
20:6 ¹ He would not accept his answer except he did out of hand deliver whatsoever he should ask, for he sought an occasion how to make war against him.
20:8 ¹ They thought it their duties rather to venture their lives, than to grant to that thing which was not lawful, only to satisfy the lust of a tyrant.
20:10 ¹ Much less shall there be found any prey that is worth anything, when they shall be so many.
20:11 ¹ Boast not before the victory be gotten.

12 And when he heard that tidings, as he was with the kings drinking in the pavilions, he said unto the servants, [1]Bring forth *your engines*. And they set them against the city.

13 ¶ And behold, there came a Prophet unto Ahab king of Israel, saying, Thus saith the Lord, Hast thou seen all this great multitude? behold, I will deliver it into thine hand this day, that thou mayest know, [1]that I am the Lord.

14 And Ahab said, By whom? and he said, Thus saith the Lord, By the servants of the princes of the provinces. He said again, Who shall order the battle? and he answered, Thou.

15 ¶ Then he numbered the servants of the princes of the provinces, and they were two hundred, two and thirty: and after them he numbered the whole people of all the children of Israel, *even* seven thousand.

16 And they went out at noon: but Ben-Hadad did drink till he was drunken in the tents, *both* he and the kings: *for* two and thirty kings helped him.

17 So the [1]servants of the princes of the provinces went out first: and Ben-Hadad sent out, and they showed him, saying, There are men come out of Samaria.

18 And he said, Whether they be come out for peace, take them alive; or whether they be come out to fight, take them yet alive.

19 So they came out of the city, *to wit*, the servants of the princes of the provinces, and the host which followed them.

20 And they slew everyone his [1]enemy: and the [2]Aramites fled, and Israel pursued them: but Ben-Hadad the king of Aram escaped on an horse with *his* [3]horsemen.

21 And the king of Israel went out, and smote the horses and chariots, and with a great slaughter slew the Aramites.

22 (For there had come a Prophet to the king of Israel, and had said unto him, Go, be of good courage, and consider, and take heed what thou doest: for when the year is gone about, the king of Aram will come up against thee.)

23 ¶ Then the servants of the king of Aram said unto him, Their [1]gods are gods of the mountains, and therefore they overcame us: but let us fight against them in the plain, and doubtless we shall

overcome them.

24 And this do, Take the kings away, everyone out of his place, and place captains for them.

25 And number thyself an army, like the army that thou hast lost, with such horses, and such chariots, and we will fight against them in the plain, and doubtless we shall overcome them: and he hearkened unto their voice, and did so.

26 And after the year was gone about, Ben-Hadad numbered the Aramites, and went up to Aphek to fight against Israel.

27 And the children of Israel were numbered, and were all [1]assembled, and went against them, and the children of Israel pitched before them like two little flocks of kids: but the Aramites filled the country.

28 And there came a man of God, and spake unto the king of Israel, saying, Thus saith the Lord, Because the Aramites have said, The Lord is the God of the mountains, and not God of the valleys, therefore will I deliver all this great multitude into thine hand, and ye shall know that [1]I am the Lord.

29 And they pitched one over against the other seven days, and in the seventh day the battle was joined: and the children of Israel slew of the Aramites an hundred thousand footmen in one day.

30 But the rest fled to Aphek into the city: and there fell a wall upon seven and twenty thousand men that were left: and Ben-Hadad fled into the city, and came into [1]a secret chamber.

31 ¶ And his servants said unto him, Behold now, we have heard say that the Kings of the house of Israel are merciful Kings: we pray thee, let us put sackcloth about our [1]loins, and ropes about our heads, and go out to the King of Israel: it may be that he will save thy life.

32 Then they girded sackcloth about their loins, and *put* ropes about their heads, and came to the King of Israel, and said, Thy servant Ben-Hadad saith, I pray thee, let me live: and he said, Is he yet alive? he is my brother.

33 Now the men took diligent heed, [1]if they could catch *anything* of him, and made haste, and said, Thy brother [2]Ben-Hadad. And he said, Go, bring him. So Ben-Hadad came out unto him, and he caused him to come up into the chariot.

34 And *Ben-Hadad* said unto him, The cities which

20:12 [1] Or, put yourselves in order.
20:13 [1] Before God went about with signs and miracles to pull Ahab from his impiety, and now again with wonderful victories.
20:17 [1] That is, young men trained in the service of princes.
20:20 [1] Hebrew, *man*.
  [2] Or, Syrians.
  [3] Which them that the wicked blaspheme God in their fury, whom notwithstanding he suffereth not unpunished.
20:23 [1] Thus the wicked blaspheme God in their fury, whom notwithstanding he suffereth not unpunished.

20:27 [1] All they, which were in the battle of the former year, verse 15.
20:28 [1] Who am of like power in the valley, as I am on the hills, and can as well destroy a multitude with few as with many.
20:30 [1] Hebrew, *from chamber, to chamber*.
20:31 [1] In sign of submission, and that we have deserved death, if he will punish us with rigor.
20:33 [1] Or, and caught it of him.
  [2] He is alive.

my father took from thy father, I will restore, and thou shalt make streets for thee in ¹Damascus, as my father did in Samaria. Then *said Ahab,* I will let thee go with this covenant. So he made a covenant with him, and let him go.

35 ¶ Then a certain man of the ¹children of the Prophets said unto his neighbor by the commandment of the Lord, ²Smite me, I pray thee. But the man refused to smite him.

36 Then said he unto him, Because thou hast not obeyed the voice of the Lord, behold, as soon as thou art departed from me, a lion shall ¹slay thee. So when he was departed from him, a lion found him, and slew him.

37 Then he found another man, and said, Smite me, I pray thee. And the man smote him, and in smiting wounded *him.*

38 So the Prophet departed, and waited for the King by the way, and disguised himself with ashes upon his face.

39 And when the King came by, he cried unto the King, and said, ¹Thy servant went into the midst of the battle, and behold, there went away a man, whom *another* man brought unto me, and said, Keep this man: if he be lost, and want, thy life shall go for his life, or else thou shalt pay a talent of silver.

40 And as thy servant had here and there to do, he was gone: And the King of Israel said unto him, So shall thy judgment be: thou hast given sentence.

41 And he hasted, and took the ashes away from his face: and the King of Israel knew him that he was of the Prophets:

42 And he said unto him, Thus saith the Lord, ᵃBecause thou hast let go out of *thine* hands a man whom I appointed to die, thy life shall go for his life, and thy people for his people.

43 And the King of Israel went to his house heavy and in displeasure, and came to ¹Samaria.

21

8 Jezebel commandeth to kill Naboth, for the vineyard that he refused to sell to Ahab. 19 Elijah reproveth Ahab, and he repenteth.

1 After ¹these things, Naboth the Jezreelite had a vineyard in Jezreel, hard by the palace of Ahab king

CHAPTER 20
ᵃ 1 Kings 22:38

of Samaria.

2 And Ahab spake unto Naboth, saying, ¹Give me thy vineyard, that I may make me a garden of herbs thereof, because it is nearby mine house: and I will give thee for it a better vineyard than it is: *or if it* please thee, I will give thee the worth of it in money.

3 And Naboth said to Ahab, The Lord keep me from giving the inheritance of my father unto thee.

4 Then Ahab came into his house heavy and in displeasure, because of the word which Naboth the Jezreelite had spoken unto him. For he had said, I will not give thee the inheritance of my fathers, and he lay ¹upon his bed, and turned his face and would eat no bread.

5 Then Jezebel his wife came unto him, and said unto him, Why is thy spirit so sad that thou eatest no bread?

6 And he said unto her, Because I spake unto Naboth the Jezreelite, and said unto him, Give me thy vineyard for money, or if it please thee, I will give thee *another* vineyard for it: but he answered, I will not give thee my vineyard.

7 Then Jezebel his wife said unto him, ¹Dost thou now govern the kingdom of Israel? Up, eat bread, and ²be of good cheer, I will give thee the vineyard of Naboth the Jezreelite.

8 ¶ So she wrote letters in Ahab's name, and sealed them with his seal, and sent the letters unto the Elders, and to the nobles that were in his city dwelling with Naboth.

9 And she wrote in the letters, saying, Proclaim a ¹fast, and set Naboth among the chief of the people,

10 And set two wicked men before him, and let them witness against him, saying, Thou didst blaspheme God and the king: then carry him out, and stone him that he may die.

11 And the ¹men of the city, *even* the Elders and governors which dwelt in his city, did as Jezebel had sent unto them: as it was written in the letters, which she had sent unto them.

12 They proclaimed a fast, and set Naboth among the chief of the people,

13 And there came two wicked men, and sat before him: and the wicked men witnessed against Naboth

---

20:34 ¹ Thou shalt appoint in my chief city what thou wilt, and I will obey thee.
20:35 ¹ Or, of the disciples.
  ² By this external sign he would more lively touch the king's heart.
20:36 ¹ Because thou hast transgressed the commandment of the Lord.
20:39 ¹ By this parable he maketh Ahab condemn himself, who made a covenant with God's enemy, and let him escape, whom God had appointed to be slain.
20:43 ¹ Or, Shomeron.
21:1 ¹ Or, at this time.
21:2 ¹ Though Ahab's tyranny be condemned by the holy Spirit, yet

he was not so rigorous that he would take from another man his right without full recompense.
21:4 ¹ Thus the wicked consider not what is just and lawful, but fret inwardly, when they cannot have their inordinate appetites satisfied.
21:7 ¹ As though she said, Thou knowest not what it is to reign. Command and entreat not.
  ² Hebrew, *let thine heart be merry.*
21:9 ¹ For then they used to inquire of men's faults: for none could fast truly that were notorious sinners.
21:11 ¹ Thus the worldlings contrary to God's commandment, who willeth not to consent to the shedding of innocent blood, obey rather the wicked commandments of princes than the just laws of God.

in the presence of the people saying, Naboth did [1]blaspheme God and the King. Then they carried him away out of the city, and stoned him with stones, that he died.

14 Then they sent to Jezebel, saying, Naboth is stoned and is dead.

15 ¶ And when Jezebel heard that Naboth was stoned and was dead, Jezebel said to Ahab, [1]Up, *and* take possession of the vineyard of Naboth the Jezreelite, which he refused to give thee for money: for Naboth is not alive, but is dead.

16 And when Ahab heard that Naboth was dead, he rose to go down to the vineyard of Naboth the Jezreelite, to take possession of it.

17 ¶ And the word of the Lord came unto Elijah the Tishbite, saying,

18 Arise, go down to meet Ahab King of Israel, which is in Samaria: lo, *he is* in the vineyard of Naboth, whither he is gone down to take possession of it.

19 Therefore shalt thou say unto him, Thus saith the Lord, [1]Hast thou killed, and also gotten possession? And thou shalt speak unto him, saying, Thus saith the Lord, [2]In the place where dogs licked the blood of Naboth, shall dogs lick even thy blood also.

20 And Ahab said to Elijah, Hast thou found me, O mine enemy? And he answered, I have found *thee*: for thou hast sold thyself to work wickedness in the sight of the Lord.

21 [a]Behold, I will bring evil upon thee, and will take away thy posterity, and will cut off from Ahab him that [b]pisseth against the wall, as well him that is [c]shut up, as him that is left in Israel,

22 And I will make thine house like the house of [d]Jeroboam the son of Nebat, and like the house of [e]Baasha the son of Ahijah, for the provocation wherewith thou hast provoked and made Israel to sin.

23 And also of Jezebel spake the Lord, saying, [f]The dogs shall eat Jezebel, [1]by the wall of Jezreel.

24 The dogs shall eat him of Ahab's *stock*, that dieth in the city: and him that dieth in the fields, shall the fowls of the air eat.

CHAPTER 21

a 1 Kings 14:10
  2 Kings 9:8
b 1 Sam. 15:22
c 1 Kings 14:10
d 1 Kings 15:29
e 1 Kings 16:3
f 2 Kings 9:33,36

CHAPTER 22

a 2 Chron. 18:1,2

25 (But there was none like Ahab, who did [1]sell himself to work wickedness, in the sight of the Lord, whom Jezebel his wife provoked.

26 For he did exceeding abominably in following idols, according to all that the Amorites did, whom the Lord cast out before the children of Israel.)

27 Now when Ahab heard those words, he rent his clothes, and put sackcloth upon [1]him, and fasted, and lay in sackcloth, and went [2]softly.

28 And the word of the Lord came to Elijah the Tishbite, saying,

29 Seest thou how Ahab is humbled before me? because he submitteth himself before me, I will not bring that evil in his days, *but* in his [1]sons' days will I bring evil upon his house.

22

2 Jehoshaphat and Ahab fight against the King of Syria. 15 Micaiah sheweth the king what shall be the success of their enterprise. 24 Zedekiah the false prophet smiteth him. 34 Ahab is slain. 40 Ahaziah his son succeedeth. 41 The reign of Jehoshaphat, 50 and Jehoram his son.

1 And [a]they continued [1]three years without war between Aram and Israel.

2 And in the third year did Jehoshaphat the king of Judah [1]come down to the king of Israel.

3 (Then the king of Israel said unto his servants, Know ye not that [1]Ramoth Gilead was ours? and we stay, and take it not out of the hand of the King of Aram?)

4 And he said unto Jehoshaphat, Wilt thou go with me to battle against Ramoth Gilead? And Jehoshaphat said unto the king of Israel, [1]I am as thou art, my people as thy people, and mine horses as thine horses.

5 Then Jehoshaphat said unto the King of Israel, [1]Ask counsel, I pray thee, of the Lord today.

6 Then the king of Israel gathered the [1]prophets upon a four hundred men, and said unto them, Shall I go against Ramoth Gilead to battle, or shall I let it alone? And they said, Go up, for the Lord shall deliver it into the hands of the King.

21:13 [1] Hebrew, *bless.*
21:15 [1] This example of monstrous cruelty the holy Ghost leaveth to us, to the intent that we should abhor all tyranny, and specially in them whom nature and kind should move to be pitiful and inclined to mercy.
21:19 [1] Dost thou think to have any advantage by murdering of an innocent?
    [2] This was fulfilled in Jehoram his son, as 2 Kings 9:25, 26.
21:23 [1] Or, fortress, or possession.
21:25 [1] By the wicked counsel of his wife he became a vile idolater, and cruel murderer, as one that gave himself wholly to serve sin.
21:27 [1] Hebrew, *his flesh.*
    [2] In token of mourning, or as some read, barefooted.
21:29 [1] Meaning, in Jehoram's time, 2 Kings 9:26.

22:1 [1] Ben-Hadad the king of Syria, and Ahab made a peace which endureth three years.
22:2 [1] To see and visit him.
22:3 [1] The kings of Syria kept Ramoth before this league was made by Ben-Hadad: therefore he thought not himself bound thereby to restore it.
22:4 [1] I am ready to join and go with thee, and all mine is at thy commandment.
22:5 [1] He seemed that he would not go to the war, except God reproved it, yet when Micaiah counseled the contrary, he would not obey.
22:6 [1] Meaning, the false prophets, which were flatterers and served for lucre, whom Jezebel had assembled and kept after the death of those whom Elijah slew.

7 And Jehoshaphat said, Is there here never a Prophet of the ¹Lord more, that we might inquire of him?

8 And the king of Israel said unto Jehoshaphat, There is yet one man (Micaiah the son of Imlah) by whom we may ask counsel of the Lord, but ¹I hate him: for he doth not prophesy good unto me, but evil. And Jehoshaphat said, Let not the king say so.

9 Then the king of Israel called an ¹Eunuch, and said, Call quickly Micaiah the son of Imlah.

10 And the king of Israel and Jehoshaphat the king of Judah sat either *of them* on his throne in their ¹apparel in the void place at the entering in of the gate of Samaria, and all the prophets prophesied before them.

11 And Zedekiah the son of Chenaanah made him ¹horns of iron, and said, Thus saith the Lord, With these shalt thou push the Aramites, until thou hast consumed them.

12 And all the prophets prophesied so, saying, Go up to Ramoth Gilead, and prosper: for the Lord shall deliver it into the king's hand.

13 ¶ And the messenger that was gone to call Micaiah, spake unto him, saying, Behold now, the words of the prophets *declare* good unto the king with ¹,²one accord, let thy word therefore, I pray thee, be like the word of one of them, and speak thou good.

14 And Micaiah said, As the Lord liveth, whatsoever the Lord saith unto me, that will I speak.

15 ¶ So he came to the King, and the king said unto him, Micaiah, shall we go against Ramoth Gilead to battle, or shall we leave off? And he answered him, ¹Go up, and prosper: and the Lord shall deliver it into the hand of the king.

16 And the king said unto him, How oft shall I charge thee that thou tell me nothing but that which is true in the Name of the Lord?

17 Then he said, I saw all Israel scattered upon the mountains, as sheep that had no shepherd. And

b 2 Chron. 18:23

the Lord said, ¹These have no master, let every man return unto his house in peace.

18 (And the king of Israel said unto Jehoshaphat, Did I not tell thee that he would prophesy no good unto me, but evil?)

19 Again he said, Hear thou therefore the word of the Lord. I saw the Lord sit on his throne, and all the ¹host of heaven stood about him on his right hand and on his left hand.

20 And the Lord said, Who shall ¹entice Ahab that he may go and fall at Ramoth Gilead? And one said on this manner, and another said on that manner.

21 Then there came forth a spirit, and ¹stood before the Lord, and said, I will entice him. And the Lord said unto him, Wherewith?

22 And he said, I will go out, and be a ¹false spirit in the mouth of all his prophets. Then he said, Thou shalt entice *him*, and shalt also prevail: go forth, and do so.

23 Now therefore behold, the Lord hath put a lying spirit in the mouth of all these thy prophets, and the Lord hath appointed evil against thee.

24 Then Zedekiah the son of Chenaanah came near, and smote Micaiah on the cheek, and said, *b,*¹When went the spirit of the Lord from me, to speak unto thee?

25 And Micaiah said, Behold, thou shalt see in that day, when thou shalt go from chamber to chamber to hide thee.

26 And the king of Israel said, Take Micaiah and carry him unto Amon the governor of the city, and unto Joash the king's son,

27 And say, Thus saith the King, Put this man in the prison house, and feed him with ¹bread of affliction, and with water of affliction, until I return in peace.

28 And Micaiah said, If thou return in peace, the Lord hath not spoken by me. And he said, ¹Hearken all ye people.

22:7 ¹ Jehoshaphat did not acknowledge the false prophets to be God's ministers, but did contemn them.

22:8 ¹ Whereby we see that the wicked cannot abide to hear the truth, but hate the Prophets of God and molest them.

22:9 ¹ Read Gen. 37:36.

22:10 ¹ In their kingly apparel.

22:11 ¹ The true Prophets of God were accustomed to use signs for the confirmation of their doctrine, Isa. 20:2; Jer. 7:2. Wherein the false Prophets did imitate them, thinking thereby to make their doctrine more commendable.

22:13 ¹ Hebrew, *mouth*.

² This is the common argument of the wicked, who think that none should speak against a thing, if the greater part approve it, be they never so ungodly.

22:15 ¹ He speaketh this in derision, because the king attributed so much to the false prophets, meaning, that by experience he should

try that they were but flatterers.

22:17 ¹ It is better they return home than to be punished and scattered, because they take war in hand without God's counsel and approbation.

22:19 ¹ Meaning, his Angels.

22:20 ¹ Or, persuade and deceive.

22:21 ¹ Here we see that though the devil be ever ready to bring us to destruction, yet he hath no further power than God giveth him.

22:22 ¹ I will cause all his prophets to tell lies.

22:24 ¹ Thus the wicked would seem that none were in the favor of God, but they, and that God hath given his graces to none so much as to them.

22:27 ¹ Let him be pined away with hunger, and be fed with a small portion of bread and water.

22:28 ¹ That when ye shall see these things come to pass, ye may give God the glory, and know that I am his true Prophet.

29 So the king of Israel and Jehoshaphat the king of Judah went up to Ramoth Gilead.

30 And the king of Israel said to Jehoshaphat, I will change mine apparel, and will enter into the battle, but put thou on thine apparel. And the king of Israel changed himself, and went into the battle.

31 And the king of Aram commanded his two and thirty captains over his chariots, saying, Fight neither with small nor great, save only against the king of Israel.

32 And when the captains of the chariots saw Jehoshaphat, they said, Surely it is the king of Israel: and they turned to fight against him: and Jehoshaphat ¹cried.

33 And when the captains of the chariots saw that he was not the king of Israel, they turned back from him.

34 Then a *certain* man drew a bow ¹mightily, and smote the king of Israel between the joints ²of his brigandine. Wherefore he said unto his chariot man, Turn thine hand, and carry me out of the host: for I am ³hurt.

35 And the battle increased that day, and the ¹king stood still in his chariot against the Aramites, and died at even: and the blood ran out of the wound into the midst of the chariot.

36 And there were a proclamation throughout the ¹host about the going down of the Sun, saying, Every man to his city, and every man to his own country.

37 So the king died, and was brought to Samaria, and they buried the king in Samaria.

38 And one washed the chariot in the pool of Samaria, and the dogs licked up his blood (and ¹they washed his armor) according ʿunto the word of the Lord which he spake.

39 Concerning the rest of the acts of Ahab, and all that he did, and the ivory house which he built, and all the cities that he built, are they not written in the book of the Chronicles of the kings of Israel?

40 So Ahab slept with his fathers, and Ahaziah his son reigned in his stead.

marginal references:
ʿ 1 Kings 31:19
ᵈ 2 Chron. 20:31

41 ¶ ᵈAnd Jehoshaphat the son of Asa began to reign upon Judah in the fourth year of Ahab king of Israel.

42 Jehoshaphat was five and thirty years old when he began to reign, and reigned five and twenty years in Jerusalem. And his mother's name was Azubah the daughter of Shilhi.

43 And he walked in all the ways of Asa his father, and declined not there from, but did that which was right in the eyes of the Lord. Nevertheless, ¹the high places were not taken away: *for* the people offered still, and burnt incense in the high places.

44 And Jehoshaphat made peace with the king of Israel.

45 Concerning the rest of the acts of Jehoshaphat, and his worthy deeds that he did, and his battles which he fought, are they not written in the book of the Chronicles of the kings of Judah?

46 And the Sodomites, which remained in the days of his father Asa, he put clean out of the land.

47 There was then no King in Edom: the ¹deputy *was* king.

48 Jehoshaphat made ships of ¹Tarshish to sail to ²Ophir for gold, but they went not, for the ships were broken at Ezion Geber.

49 Then said Ahaziah the son of Ahab unto Jehoshaphat, Let my servants go with thy servants in the ships, But Jehoshaphat would not.

50 And Jehoshaphat did sleep with his fathers, and was buried with his fathers in the city of David his father, and Jehoram his son reigned in his stead.

51 ¶ Ahaziah the son of Ahab began to reign over Israel in Samaria, the seventeenth year of Jehoshaphat king of Judah, and reigned two years over Israel.

52 But he did evil in the sight of the Lord, and walked in the way of his father, and in the way of his mother, and in the way of Jeroboam the son of Nebat, which made Israel to sin.

53 For he served Baal, and worshipped him, and provoked the Lord God of Israel unto wrath, ¹according unto all that his father had done.

22:32 ¹ That is, to the Lord for help.
22:34 ¹ Or, in his simplicity, and ignorantly.
  ² Hebrew, *and between the brigandine.*
  ³ Hebrew, *sick.*
22:35 ¹ To wit, Ahab, king of Israel.
22:36 ¹ Of the Israelites.
22:38 ¹ Or, the harlots washed it.
22:43 ¹ Meaning, that he was led with an error, thinking that they might still sacrifice to the Lord in those places, as well as they did

before the Temple was built.
22:47 ¹ In the time of this king, Idumea was subject to Judah, and was governed by whom they of Judah appointed.
22:48 ¹ By Tarshish the Scripture meaneth Cilicia and all the sea called Mediterranean.
  ² Josephus writeth that Ophir is in India, where the Egyptians and Arabians traffic for gold.
22:53 ¹ Or, in all points as his father did.

THE SECOND BOOK

OF THE

KINGS

---

1 *2 Ahaziah by a fall falleth sick, and consulteth with Baal-Zebub. 3 He is reproved by Elijah. 10 The captains over fifty were sent to Elijah, whereof two were burnt with fire from heaven by his prayer. 17 Ahaziah dieth, and Jehoram his brother succeedeth him.*

1 Then Moab rebelled against Israel after the death of Ahab:

2 And ¹Ahaziah fell through the lattice window in his upper chamber which was in Samaria: so he was sick: then he sent messengers, to whom he said, Go, *and* inquire of ²Baal-Zebub the god of Ekron, if I shall recover of this my disease.

3 Then the Angel of the Lord said to Elijah the Tishbite, Arise, *and* go up to meet the messengers of the king of Samaria, and say unto them, ¹Is it not because there is no God in Israel, that ye go to inquire of Baal-Zebub the god of Ekron?

4 Wherefore thus saith the Lord, Thou shalt not come down from the bed on which thou art gone up, but shalt die the death. So Elijah departed.

5 And the messengers returned unto him, to whom he said, Why are ye now returned?

6 And they answered him, There came a man and met us, and said unto us, Go, *and* return unto the king which sent you, and say unto him, Thus saith the Lord, ¹Is it not because there is no God in Israel, that thou sendest to inquire of Baal-Zebub the God of Ekron? Therefore thou shalt not come down from the bed, on which thou art gone up, but shalt die the death.

7 And he said unto them, What manner of man was he which came and met you, and told you these words?

8 And they said unto him, He was an ¹hairy man,

and girded with a girdle of leather about his loins. Then said he, It is Elijah the Tishbite.

9 Therefore *the King* sent unto him a captain over fifty with his fifty *men*, who went up unto him: for behold, he sat on the top ¹of a mountain, and he said unto him, O man of God, the king hath commanded *that* thou come down.

10 But Elijah answered, and said to the captain over the fifty, If that I be a man of God, let fire come down from the heaven, and devour thee and thy fifty. ¹So fire came down from the heaven and devoured him and his fifty.

11 Again also he sent unto him another captain over fifty with his fifty. Who spake, and said unto him, ¹O man of God, thus saith the King commandeth, Come down quickly.

12 But Elijah answered, and said unto them, ¹If I be a man of God, let fire come down from the heaven and devour thee and thy fifty. So fire came down from the heaven, and devoured him and his fifty.

13 ¶ Yet again he sent the third captain over fifty with his fifty. And the third captain over fifty went up, and came, and fell on his knees before Elijah, and besought him, and said unto him, O man of God, I pray thee, let my ¹life and the life of these thy fifty servants be ²precious in thy sight.

14 Behold, there came fire down from the heaven, and devoured the two former captains over fifty with their fifties: therefore let my life now be precious in thy sight.

15 And the Angel of the Lord said unto Elijah, Go down with him, be ¹not afraid of his presence. So he arose, and went down with him unto the king.

16 And he said unto him, Thus saith the Lord,

1:2 ¹ So that he was punished for his idolatry after two sorts: for the Moabites which were wont to pay him tribute, rebelled, and he fell down at a grate which was upon his house to give light beneath.

² The Philistines which dwelt at Ekron, worshipped this idol, which figureth the god of flies, thinking that he could preserve them from the biting of flies: or else he was so called, because flies were engendered in great abundance of the blood of the sacrifices that were offered to that idol.

1:3 ¹ He showeth that idolaters have not the true God, for else they would seek to none but to him alone.

1:6 ¹ Ignorance is the mother of error and idolatry.

1:8 ¹ Some think that this is meant of his garments, which were rough and made of hair.

1:9 ¹ To wit, Carmel.

1:10 ¹ He declareth what power God's word hath in the mouth of his servants, when they threaten God's judgments against the wicked.

1:11 ¹ He spake this in mockery, and therefore provoked God's wrath so much the more.

1:12 ¹ Meaning, that God would show by effect whether he was a true Prophet or not.

1:13 ¹ Which humble myself before God and his servant.

² That is, spare my life, and let me not die as the other two.

1:15 ¹ Thus the Lord giveth boldness to his, that they fear not the threatenings of tyrants, which otherwise of themselves are afraid to do God's message.

Because thou hast sent messengers to inquire of Baal-Zebub the god of Ekron, (was it not because there was no God in Israel to inquire of his word?) therefore thou shalt not come down off the bed, on which thou art gone up, but shalt die the death.

17 So he died according to the word of the Lord which Elijah had spoken. And Jehoram began to reign in his stead in the second year of [1]Jehoram the son of Jehoshaphat king of Judah, because he had no son.

18 Concerning the rest of the acts of Ahaziah, that he did, are they not written in the book of the Chronicles of the kings of Israel?

2 1 *Elijah divided the waters with his cloak.* 11 *He is taken up into heaven.* 13 *Elisha taketh his cloak and divideth Jordan.* 20 *The bitter and venomous waters are healed.* 23 *The children that mock Elisha, are rent in pieces with bears.*

1 And when the Lord would take up Elijah into heaven by a whirlwind, Elijah went with Elisha from [1]Gilgal.

2 Then Elijah said to Elisha, Tarry here, I pray thee: for the Lord hath sent me to Bethel. But Elisha said, As the Lord liveth, and as thy soul liveth, I will not leave thee. So they came down to Bethel.

3 And the [1]children of the Prophets that were at Bethel, came out to Elisha, and said unto him, Knowest thou that the Lord will take thy master from [2]thine head this day? And he said, Yea, I [3]know it: hold ye your peace.

4 Again Elijah said unto him, Elisha, tarry here, I pray thee: for the Lord hath sent me to Jericho. But he said, As the Lord liveth, and as thy soul liveth, I will not leave thee. So they came to Jericho.

5 And the children of the Prophets that were at [1]Jericho, came to Elisha, and said unto him, Knowest thou, that the Lord will take thy master from thine head this day? And he said, Yea, I know it: hold ye your peace.

6 Moreover Elijah said unto him, Tarry, I pray thee, here: for the Lord hath sent me to Jordan. But he said, As the Lord liveth, and as thy soul liveth, I will not leave thee. So they went both *together*.

7 And fifty men of the sons of the Prophets went and stood on the other side a far off, and they two stood by Jordan.

8 ¶ Then Elijah took his cloak, and wrapped it together, and smote the [1]waters, and they were divided hither and thither, and they twain went over on the dry land.

9 Now when they were passed over, Elijah said unto Elisha, Ask what I shall do for thee before I be taken from thee. And Elisha said, I pray thee, let thy Spirit [1]be double upon me.

10 And he said, Thou hast asked an hard thing: yet if thou see me when I am taken from thee, thou shalt have it so: and if not, it shall not be.

11 And as they went walking and talking, behold, there *appeared* a chariot of fire, and horses of fire, and did separate them twain. So Elijah went up by a whirlwind into [1]heaven.

12 And Elisha saw it, and he cried, My father, my father, the chariot of Israel, and the horsemen thereof: and he saw him no more: and he took his *own* clothes, and rent them in two pieces.

13 ¶ He took up also the cloak of Elijah, that fell from him, and returned, and stood by the bank of Jordan.

14 After, he took the cloak of Elijah, that fell from him, and smote the waters, and said, Where is the Lord God of Elijah? And so he also, after he had stricken the waters, so that they were divided this way and that way, went over, *even* Elisha.

15 And when the children of the Prophets, which were at Jericho, saw him on the other side, they said, [1]The Spirit of Elijah doeth rest on Elisha: and they came to meet him, and fell to the ground before him,

16 And said unto him, Behold now, there be with thy servants fifty strong men: let them go, we pray thee, and seek thy [1]master, if so be the Spirit of the Lord hath taken him up, and cast him upon some mountain, or into some valley. But he said, [2]Ye shall not send.

1:17 [1] Jehoshaphat going to battle against the Syrians, made his son Jehoram king in the 17th year of his reign: and in the 18th year which was the second year of his son, Jehoram the son of Ahab reigned in Israel: and in the fifth year of this Jehoram Jehoshaphat died, and the kingdom of Judah was confirmed to his son.

2:1 [1] Which was that place where the children of Israel were circumcised after they came over Jordan, and had been forty years in the wilderness, as Josh. 5:9.

2:3 [1] So called, because they are begotten as it were anew by the heavenly doctrine.

[2] That is, from being anymore thine head: for to be as the head, is to be the master, as to be at the feet, is to be a scholar.

[3] For the Lord had revealed it unto him.

2:5 [1] Not only at Bethel, but at Jericho and other places were there

Prophets, which had scholars, whom they instructed and brought up in the true fear of God.

2:8 [1] To wit, of Jordan.

2:9 [1] Let thy Spirit have double force in me, because of these dangerous times: or let me have twice so much as the rest of the Prophets: or thy spirit being divided into three parts, let me have two.

2:11 [1] Thus God hath left a testimony in all ages (both before the Law, in the Law, and in the time of the Gospel) of our resurrection.

2:15 [1] The Spirit of prophecy is given to him, as it was to Elijah.

2:16 [1] Meaning, Elijah: for they thought his body had been cast in some mountain.

[2] Because the fact was extraordinary, they doubted where he was become, but Elisha was assured that he was taken up to God.

17 Yet they were instant upon him, till he was ashamed: wherefore he said, Send. So they sent fifty men, which sought three days, but found him not.

18 Therefore they returned to him, (for he tarried at Jericho) and he said unto them, Did not I say unto you, Go not?

19 ¶ And the men of the city said unto Elisha, Behold, we pray thee: the situation of this city is pleasant, as thou, my lord, seest, but the water *is* naught, and the ground [1]barren.

20 Then he said, Bring me a new cruse, and put salt therein. And they brought it to him.

21 And he went unto the spring of the waters, and cast there [1]the salt, and said, Thus saith the Lord, I have healed this water: death shall no more come thereof, neither barrenness *to the ground.*

22 So the waters were healed unto this day, according to the word of Elisha which he had spoken.

23 ¶ And he went up from thence unto Bethel. And as he was going up the way, little children came out of the city, and mocked him, and said unto him, Come up, thou bald head, come up, thou bald head.

24 And he turned back, and looked on them, and [1]cursed them in the name of the Lord. And two bears came out of the forest, and tore in pieces two and forty children of them.

25 So he went from thence to mount Carmel, and from thence he returned to Samaria.

3 1 *The reign of Jehoram.* 6 *He and Jehoshaphat go to war against Moab which rebelled.* 13 *Elisha reproveth him,* 17 *and giveth their hosts water.* 24 *The Moabites are overcome.* 27 *Their King sacrificeth his son.*

1 Now Jehoram the son of Ahab began to reign over Israel in Samaria, the [1]eighteenth year of Jehoshaphat King of Judah, and reigned twelve years.

2 And he wrought evil in the sight of the Lord, but not like his father nor like his mother: for he took away the image of Baal that his father had made.

3 Nevertheless, he cleaved unto the [1]sins of Jeroboam, the son of Nebat, which made Israel to sin, *and* departed not therefrom.

4 ¶ Then [1]Mesha king of Moab had store of sheep, and rendered unto the king of Israel an hundred thousand rams with the wool.

5 But when Ahab was dead, the king of Moab rebelled against the king of Israel.

6 Therefore King Jehoram went out of Samaria the same season, and numbered all Israel,

7 And went, and sent to Jehoshaphat king of Judah, saying, The king of Moab hath rebelled against me: wilt thou go with me to battle against Moab? And he answered, I will go up: *for* [1]I am, as thou art, my people, as thy people, *and* mine horses, as thine horses.

8 Then said he, What way shall we go up? And he answered, The way of the wilderness of Edom.

9 ¶ So went the king of Israel and the king of Judah, and the [1]king of Edom, and when they had compassed the way seven days, they had no water for the host, nor for the cattle that [2]followed them.

10 Therefore the king of Israel said, Alas, that the Lord hath called these three kings, to give them into the hand of Moab.

11 But Jehoshaphat said, Is there not here a Prophet of the Lord, that we may inquire of the Lord by him? And one of the king of Israel's servants answered, and said, Here is Elisha the son of Shaphat, which [1]poured water on the hands of Elijah.

12 Then Jehoshaphat said, [1]The word of the Lord is with him. Therefore the king of Israel, and Jehoshaphat, and the king of Edom went down to him.

13 And Elisha said unto the king of Israel, [1]What have I to do with thee? get thee to the Prophets of thy father, and to the Prophets of thy mother. And the king of Israel said unto him, [2]Nay: for the Lord hath called these three kings, to give them into the hand of Moab.

14 Then Elisha said, As the Lord of hosts liveth, in whose sight I stand, if it were not, that I regard the presence of Jehoshaphat the king of Judah, I would [1]not have looked toward thee, nor seen thee.

15 But now bring me a minstrel. And when the minstrel [1]played, the hand of the Lord came upon him.

16 And he said, Thus saith the Lord, Make this valley full of ditches.

2:19 [1] Or, killeth the inhabitants.

2:21 [1] Thus God gave him power, even contrary to nature, to make that water profitable for man's use, which before was hurtful.

2:24 [1] Perceiving their malicious heart against the Lord and his word, he desireth God to take vengeance of that injury done unto him.

3:1 [1] Read the annotation in the first chapter and seventh verse.

3:3 [1] He sacrificed to the golden calves that Jeroboam had made.

3:4 [1] This was done after that David had made the Moabites tributaries to his successors.

3:7 [1] Read 1 Kings 22:4.

3:9 [1] Meaning, the viceroy, or lieutenant of the king of Judah, read

1 Kings 22:47.

[2] Hebrew, *that were at their feet.*

3:11 [1] That is, who was his servant.

3:12 [1] He is able to instruct us what is God's will in this point.

3:13 [1] He knew that this wicked king would have but used his counsel to serve his turn, and therefore, he disdained to answer him.

[2] The wicked esteem not the servants of God, but when they are driven by every necessity and fear of the present danger.

3:14 [1] God suffereth his word to be declared to the wicked, because of the godly that are among them.

3:15 [1] He sang songs to God's glory, and so stirred up the Prophet's heart to prophesy.

17 For thus saith the Lord, Ye shall neither see wind nor see rain, yet the valley shall be filled with water, that ye may drink, *both* ye and your cattle, and your beasts.

18 But this is a ¹small thing in the sight of the Lord: for he will give Moab into your hand.

19 And ye shall smite every strong town, and every chief city, and shall fell every fair tree, and shall stop all the fountains of water, and ¹mar every good field with stones.

20 And in the morning when the meat offering was offered, behold, there came water by the way of Edom: and the country was filled with water.

21 And when all the Moabites heard that the kings were come up to fight against them, they gathered all that was able ¹to put on harness, and upward, and stood in *their* border.

22 And they rose early in the morning, when the Sun arose upon the water, and the Moabites saw the water over against them, as red as blood.

23 And they said, ¹This is blood: the kings are surely slain, and one hath smitten another: now therefore Moab, to the spoil.

24 And when they came to the host of Israel, the Israelites arose up, and smote the Moabites, so that they fled before them, but they ¹invaded them, and smote Moab.

25 And they destroyed the cities: and on all the good field every man cast his stone, and filled them and they stopped all the fountains of water, and felled all the good trees: only in ¹Kir Haraseth left they the stones thereof: howbeit they went about it with slings, and smote it.

26 And when the King of Moab saw that the battle was too sore for him, he took with him seven hundred men that drew the sword, to break through unto the king of Edom: but they could not.

27 Then he took his eldest son, that should have reigned in his stead, and ¹offered him for a burnt offering upon the wall: so that Israel was sore grieved,

and they departed from him, and returned to their country.

4 4 *God increaseth the oil to the poor widow by Elisha.* 12 *He obtaineth for the Shunammite a son at God's hand.* 18 *Who dying,* 32 *he raiseth him up again.* 40 *He maketh sweet the pottage,* 42 *and multiplied the loaves.*

1 And one of the wives of the sons ¹of the Prophets cried unto Elisha, saying, Thy servant mine husband is dead, and thou knowest, that thy servant did ²fear the Lord: and the creditor is come to take my two sons to be his ³bondmen.

2 Then Elisha said unto her, What shall I do for thee? tell me, what hast thou at home? And she said, Thine handmaid hath nothing at home, save a ¹pitcher of oil.

3 And he said, Go and borrow thee vessels abroad of all thy neighbors, empty vessels, *and* spare not.

4 And when thou art come in, thou shalt shut the door upon thee and upon thy sons, and pour out into ¹all those vessels, and set aside those that are full.

5 So she departed from him, and shut the door upon her, and upon her sons. And they brought to her, and she poured out.

6 And when the vessels were full, she said unto her son, Bring me yet a vessel. And he said unto her, There is no more vessels. And the oil ¹ceased.

7 Then she came and told the man of God. And he said, Go *and* sell the oil, and pay them that thou art in debt unto, and live thou and thy children of the ¹rest.

8 ¶ And on a time Elisha came to Shunem, and there a woman of great *estimation* constrained him to eat bread: and as he passed by, he turned in thither to eat bread.

9 And she said unto her husband, Behold, I know now, that this is an holy man of God that passeth by us continually.

10 Let us make ¹him a little chamber, I pray thee, with walls, and let us set him there a bed, and a table,

---

3:18 ¹ He will not only miraculously give you waters, but your enemies also into your hand.

3:19 ¹ Though God bestow his benefits for a time upon the enemies, yet he hath his seasons, when he will take them away to the intent they might see his vengeance which is prepared against them.

3:21 ¹ Hebrew, *to gird himself with a girdle.*

3:23 ¹ The sudden joy of the wicked is but a preparation to their destruction, which is at hand.

3:24 ¹ Meaning, they followed them into the towns.

3:25 ¹ Which was one of the principle cities of the Moabites, wherein they left nothing but the walls.

3:27 ¹ Some refer it to the king of Edom's son, whom they say he had taken in that skirmish: but rather it seemed to be his own son, whom he offered to his gods to pacify them: which barbarous cruelty moved the Israelites' hearts of pity to depart.

4:1 ¹ Read 2 Kings 2:3.

² And therefore fell not into debt by unthriftiness or prodigality, but by the hand of the Lord.

³ Because I am poor and not able to pay.

4:2 ¹ Thus God suffereth his many times to be brought to extreme necessity, before he succor them, that afterward they may the more praise his mercy.

4:4 ¹ The Prophet declareth hereby unto her, that God never faileth to provide for his servants, their wives and children, if they trust in him.

4:6 ¹ To augment and increase in the vessels.

4:7 ¹ God here did not only provide for his servant, that his debts should be paid and so kept his doctrine and profession without slander, but also for his wife and children.

4:10 ¹ Which should be separate from the rest of the house, that he might more commodiously give himself to study and prayers.

and a stool, and a candlestick, that he may turn in thither when he cometh to us.

11 ¶ And on a day, he came thither and turned into the chamber, and lay therein,

12 And said to Gehazi his servant, Call this Shunammite: and when he called her, she stood before him.

13 Then he said unto him, Say unto her now, Behold, thou hast had all this great care for us, [1]what shall we do for thee? Is there anything to be spoken for thee to the king or to the captain of the host? And she answered, I [2]dwell among mine own people.

14 Again he said, What is then to be done for her? Then Gehazi answered, Indeed she hath [1]no son, and her husband is old.

15 Then said he, Call her. And he called her, and she stood in the door.

16 And he said, [a]At this time appointed, according to the time of life, thou shalt embrace a son. And she said, Oh my Lord, thou man of God, do not lie unto thine handmaid.

17 So the woman conceived, and bore a son at that same season, according to the time of life, that Elisha had said unto her.

18 ¶ And when the child was grown, it fell on a day, that he went out to his father, and to the reapers.

19 And he said to his father, [1]Mine head, mine head. Who said to his servant, Bear him to his mother.

20 And he took him and brought him to his mother, and he sat on her knees till noon, and died.

21 Then she went up, and laid him on the bed of the man of God, and shut the door upon him and went out.

22 ¶ Then she called to her husband, and said, Send with me, I pray thee, one of the young men and one of the asses: for I will haste to the man of God, and come again.

23 And he said, Wherefore wilt thou go to him today? it is neither [1]new moon nor Sabbath day. And she answered, [2]All shall be well.

24 Then she saddled an ass, and said to her servant, Drive, and go forward: stay not for me to get up, except I bid thee.

25 ¶ So she went, and came unto the man of God to mount Carmel. And when the man of God saw

CHAPTER 4
[a] Gen. 18:10

her [1]over against him, he said to Gehazi his servant, Behold, the Shunammite.

26 Run now, I say, to meet her, and say unto her, Art thou in health? is thine husband in health? and is the child in health? And she answered, We are in health.

27 And when she came to the man of God unto the mountain, she [1]caught him by his feet: and Gehazi went to her, to thrust her away: but the man of God said, Let her alone: for her soul is [2]vexed within her, and the Lord hath hid it from me, and hath not told it me.

28 Then she said, Did I desire a son of my lord? did I not say, Deceive me not?

29 Then he said to Gehazi, Gird thy loins, and take my staff in thine hand, and go thy way: [1]if thou meet any, salute him not: and if any salute thee, answer him not: and lay my staff upon the face of the child.

30 And the mother of the child said, As the Lord liveth, and as thy soul liveth, I will not leave thee. Therefore he arose, and followed her.

31 But Gehazi was gone before them, and had laid the staff upon the face of the child, but he neither spake nor heard: wherefore he returned to meet him, and told him, saying, The child is not waken.

32 ¶ Then came Elisha into the house, and behold, the child was dead, and laid upon his bed.

33 He went in therefore, and shut the door upon them twain, and prayed unto the Lord.

34 After he went up, and [1]lay upon the child, and put his mouth on his mouth, and his eyes upon his eyes, and his hands upon his hands, and stretched himself upon him, and the flesh of the child waxed warm.

35 And he went from him, and walked up and down in the house, and went up and spread himself upon him: then the child sneezed [1]seven times, and opened his eyes.

36 Then he called Gehazi, and said, Call this Shunammite. So he called her, which came in unto him. And he said unto her, Take thy son.

37 And she came, and fell at his feet, and bowed herself to the ground, and took up her son, and went out.

38 Afterward Elisha returned to Gilgal, and a famine was in the [1]land, and the children of the Prophets

---

4:13 [1] Thus the servants of God are not unthankful for the benefits they receive.
   [2] I am content with that that God hath sent me, and can want nothing that one can do for another.
4:14 [1] Which then was a reproach, and therefore he would that his master should pray to God for her that she might be fruitful.
4:19 [1] His head ached sore, and therefore he cried thus.
4:23 [1] For at such times the people were wont to resort to the Prophets for doctrine and consolation.
   [2] Hebrew, peace.

4:25 [1] Or, far off.
4:27 [1] In token of humility and joy that she had met with him.
   [2] Hebrew, her soul is in bitterness.
4:29 [1] Make such speed that nothing may let thee in the way, Luke 10:4.
4:34 [1] The like did Elijah to the widow's son at Zarephath, 1 Kings 17:21 and St. Paul, Acts 20:10, signifying the care that ought to be in them, that bear the word of God, and are distributors of the spiritual life.
4:35 [1] Meaning, oftentimes.
4:38 [1] That is, in the land of Israel.

dwelt with him. And he said unto his servant, Set on the great pot, and seethe pottage for the children of the Prophets.

39 And one went out into the field, to gather herbs, and found as it were a wild vine, and gathered thereof [1]wild gourds his garment full, and came and shred them into the pot of pottage: for they knew it not.

40 So they poured out for the men to eat: and when they did eat of the pottage, they cried out, and said, O thou man of God, [1]death *is* in the pot: and they could not eat *thereof*.

41 Then he said, Bring meal. And he cast it into the pot, and said, Pour out for the people, that they may eat: and there was none evil in the pot.

42 ¶ Then came a man from Baal Shalisha, and brought the man of God bread of the firstfruits, *even* twenty loaves of barley, and full ears of corn in the husk. And he said, Give unto the people, that they may eat.

43 And his servant answered, How should I set this before an hundred men? He said again, Give it unto the people, that they may eat: for thus saith the Lord, They [1]shall eat, and there shall remain.

44 So he set it before them, and they did eat, and left over, according to the word of the Lord.

5 1 Naaman the Syrian is healed of his leprosy. 16 Elisha refuseth his gifts. 27 Gehazi is stricken with leprosy, because he took money and raiment of Naaman.

1 Now was there one Naaman captain of the host of the King of Aram, a great man, and honorable in the sight of his lord, because that by him the Lord had [1]delivered the Aramites. He also was a mighty man *and* valiant, *but* a leper.

2 And the Aramites had gone out by bands, and had taken a little maid of the land of Israel, and she [1]served Naaman's wife.

3 And she said unto her mistress, Would God my lord *were* with the [1]Prophet that is in Samaria, he would soon deliver him of his leprosy.

4 And [1]he went in, and told his lord, saying, Thus and thus saith the maid that is of the land of Israel.

5 And the king of Aram said, Go thy way thither,

CHAPTER 5
a Luke 4:27

and I will send a letter unto the King of Israel. And he departed, and [1]took [2]with him ten talents of silver, and six thousand *pieces* of gold, and ten changes of raiments,

6 And brought the letter to the king of Israel to this effect, Now when this letter is come unto thee, understand, that I have sent thee Naaman my servant, that thou mayest heal him of his leprosy.

7 And when the king of Israel had read the letter, he rent his clothes, and said, Am I God to kill and to give life that he doth send to me, that I should heal a man from his leprosy? wherefore consider, I pray you, and see how he seeketh a quarrel against me.

8 But when Elisha the man of God had heard that the King of Israel had rent his clothes, he sent unto the King, saying, [1]Wherefore hast thou rent thy clothes? Let him come now to me, and he shall know that there is a Prophet in Israel.

9 ¶ Then Naaman came with his horses, and with his chariots, and stood at the door of the house of Elisha.

10 And Elisha sent a messenger unto him, saying, Go and wash thee in Jordan seven times, and thy flesh shall come again to thee, and thou shalt be cleansed.

11 But Naaman was [1]wroth and went away, and said, Behold, I thought with myself, He will surely come out, and stand, and call on the Name of the Lord his God, and put his hand on the place, and heal the leprosy.

12 Are not Abanah and Pharpar, rivers of Damascus, better than all the waters of Israel? may I not wash me in them, and be cleansed? so he turned, and departed in displeasure.

13 But his servants came, and spake unto him, and said, [1]Father, *if* the Prophet had commanded thee a great thing, wouldest thou not have done it? how much rather then, when he saith to thee, Wash, and be clean?

14 Then went he down, and *a*washed himself seven times in Jordan, according to the saying of the man of God: and his flesh came again, like unto the flesh of a little child, and he was clean.

15 ¶ And he turned again to the man of God, he,

4:39 [1] Which the Apothecaries call colloquintida, and is most vehement and dangerous in purging.
4:40 [1] They feared that they were poisoned, because of the bitterness.
4:43 [1] It is not the quantity of bread that satisfieth, but the blessing that God giveth.
5:1 [1] Here appeareth that among the infidels God hath his, and also that the infidels have them in estimation which do good to their country.
5:2 [1] Hebrew, *she was before.*
5:3 [1] Meaning, Elisha.
5:4 [1] That is, Naaman told it to the king of Syria.

5:5 [1] To give this as a present to the Prophet.
    [2] Hebrew, *in his hand.*
5:8 [1] The Prophet rebuketh the king because he did not consider that God was true in his promise, and therefore would not leave his Church destitute of a Prophet, whose prayers he would hear, and to whom others should have recourse for comfort.
5:11 [1] Man's reason murmureth, when it considereth only the signs and outward things, and hath not regard to the word of God, which is there contained.
5:13 [1] This declareth that servants ought to reverence and love their masters as children their fathers, and likewise masters toward their servants, must be affectioned as toward their children.

and all his company, and came and stood before him, and said, Behold now, I know that *there is* no God in all the world but in Israel: now therefore, I pray thee, take a ¹reward of thy servant.

16 But he said, As the Lord liveth (before whom I stand) I will not receive it. And he would have constrained him to receive it, ¹but he refused.

17 Moreover Naaman said, Shall there not be given to thy servant two mules' load of this earth? for thy servant will henceforth offer neither burnt sacrifice nor offering unto any other god, save unto the Lord.

18 Herein the Lord be ¹merciful unto thy servant, that when my master goeth into the house of Rimmon, to worship there, and leaneth on mine hand, and I bow myself in the house of Rimmon: when I do bow down, *I say,* in the house of Rimmon, the Lord be merciful unto thy servant in this point.

19 Unto whom he said, ¹Go in peace. So he departed from him about half a day's journey of ground.

20 And Gehazi the servant of Elisha the man of God said, Behold, my master hath spared this Aramite Naaman, receiving not those things at his hand that he brought: As the Lord liveth, I will run after him, and take somewhat of him.

21 So Gehazi followed speedily after Naaman. And when Naaman saw him running after him, ¹he lighted down from the chariot to meet him, and said, Is all well?

22 And he answered, All is well: my master hath set me, saying, Behold, there be come to me, even now from mount Ephraim two young men of the children of the Prophets: give them, I pray thee, a talent of silver, and two changes of garments.

23 And Naaman said, Yea, take two talents: and he compelled him, and bound two talents of silver in two bags, with two changes of garments, and gave them unto two of his servants, that they might bear them before him.

24 And when he came to the ¹tower, he took them out of their hands, and laid them in the house, and sent away the men: and ²they departed.

25 ¶ Then he went in, and stood before his master. And Elisha said unto him, Whence *comest thou,* Ge-

hazi? And he said, Thy servant went no whither.

26 But he said unto him, ¹Went not mine heart *with thee,* when the man turned again from his chariot to meet thee? Is this a time to take money, and to receive garments, ²and olives, and vineyards, and sheep, and oxen, and menservants, and maidservants?

27 The leprosy therefore of Naaman shall cleave unto thee, and to thy ¹seed forever. And he went out from his presence a leper *white* as snow.

6 6 *Elisha maketh iron to swim above the water.* 8 *He discloseth the king of Syria's counsel to the king of Israel,* 13 *who sending certain to take him, were kept fast in Samaria.* 24 *Samaria is besieged, and endureth extreme famine.*

1 And the children of the Prophets said unto Elisha, Behold, we pray thee, the place where we dwell with thee, is too little for us.

2 Let us now go to Jordan, that we may take thence every man a ¹beam, and make us a place to dwell in. And he answered, Go.

3 And one said, Vouchsafe, I pray thee, to go with thy servants. And he answered, I will go.

4 So he went with them, and when they came to Jordan, they cut down wood.

5 And as one was felling of a tree, the ¹iron fell into the water: then he cried, and said, Alas master, it was but borrowed.

6 And the man of God said, Where fell it? And he showed him the place. Then he cut down *a piece* of wood, and cast in thither, and he caused the iron to ¹swim.

7 Then he said, Take it up to thee. And he stretched out his hand, and took it.

8 ¶ Then the king of Aram warred against Israel, and took counsel with his servants, and said, In ¹such and such a place *shall be* my camp.

9 Therefore the man of God sent unto the king of Israel, saying, Beware thou go not over to such a place: for there the Aramites are come down.

10 So the king of Israel sent to the place which the man of God told him, and warned him of, and ¹saved himself from thence, not once, nor twice.

5:15 ¹ Hebrew, *blessing.*

5:16 ¹ So the Lord commandeth that they that receive freely, should give also freely.

5:18 ¹ He feeleth his conscience wounded in being present at idol's service, and therefore desireth God to forgive him, lest others by his example might fall to idolatry: for as for his own part he confesseth that he will never serve any but the true God.

5:19 ¹ The Prophet did not approve his act, but after the common manner of speech he biddeth him farewell.

5:21 ¹ Declaring thereby, what honor and affection he bare to the Prophet his master.

5:24 ¹ Or, fortress, or secret place.
   ² Naaman's servants.

5:26 ¹ Was I not present with thee in spirit?
   ² That is, money to buy possessions with: meaning, that it is detestable in the servants of God to have covetous minds.

5:27 ¹ To be an example to all such, as by whose covetousness God's word might be slandered.

6:2 ¹ Or a piece of wood fit to build with.

6:5 ¹ Or, the axe head.

6:6 ¹ God wrought this miraculously to confirm the authority of Elisha, to whom he had given such abundance of his Spirit.

6:8 ¹ Meaning, that he would lie in ambush, and take the Israelites at unawares.

6:10 ¹ The wicked conspire nothing so craftily, but God can reveal it to his servants, and cause their counsel to be disclosed.

11 And the heart of the king of Aram was troubled for this thing: therefore he called his servants, and said unto them, Will ye not show me, which of us *bewrayeth our counsel* to the king of Israel?

12 Then one of his servants said, None, my lord, O king, but Elisha the Prophet that is in Israel, telleth the king of Israel, *even* the words that thou speakest in thy [1]privy chamber.

13 And he said, Go, and espy where he is, that I may send and fetch him. And one told him, saying, Behold, *he is* in Dothan.

14 ¶ So he sent thither horses, and chariots, and a [1]mighty host: and they came by night, and compassed the city.

15 And when the servant of the man of God arose early to go out, behold, an host compassed the city with horses and chariots. Then his servant said unto him, Alas master, how shall we do?

16 And he answered, [1]Fear not: [a]for they that be with us, are more than they that be with them.

17 Then Elisha prayed, and said, Lord, I beseech thee, open his eyes, [1]that he may see. And the Lord opened the eyes of the servant, and he looked, and behold, the mountain was full of horses and chariots of fire round about Elisha.

18 So [1]they came down to him, but Elisha prayed unto the Lord, and said, Smite this people, I pray thee, with blindness. And he smote them with blindness, according to the word of Elisha.

19 And Elisha said unto them, This is not the way, neither is this the city: follow me, and I will lead you to the man whom ye seek. But he led [1]them to Samaria.

20 And when they were come to Samaria, Elisha said, Lord, open their eyes that they may see. And the Lord opened their eyes, and they saw, and behold, *they were* in the midst of Samaria.

21 And the king of Israel said unto Elisha when he saw them, [1]My father, shall I smite them, shall I smite them?

22 And he answered, Thou shalt not smite them: doest thou not smite them that thou hast taken with

CHAPTER 6
[a] 1 Chron. 32:7
[b] Deut. 28:53-57

thy sword, and with thy bow? *but* set bread and water before them, that they may eat and drink and go to their master.

23 And he made great preparation for them: and when they had eaten and drunken, he sent them away: and they went to their master. So the bands of Aram came [1]no more into the land of Israel.

24 But afterward Ben-Hadad king of Aram gathered all his host, and went up and besieged Samaria.

25 So there was a great famine in Samaria: for lo, they besieged it until an asses head was at four score *pieces* of silver, and the fourth part of a cab of dove's [1]dung at five *pieces* of silver.

26 And as the king of Israel was going upon the wall, there cried a woman unto him, saying, Help, my lord, O King?

27 And he said, *Seeing* the Lord doth not succor thee, how should I help thee with the [1]barn, or with the wine press?

28 Also the king said unto her, What aileth thee? And she answered, This woman said unto me, Give thy son that we may eat him today, and we will eat my son tomorrow,

29 [b]So we sod my son, and did eat him: and I said to her the day after, Give thy son, that we may eat him, but she hath hid her son.

30 And when the king had heard the words of the woman, he rent his clothes, (and as he went upon the wall, the people looked, and behold, he had sackcloth [1]within [2]upon his flesh)

31 And he said, God do so to me and more also, if the head of Elisha the son of Shaphat shall stand on him this day.

32 (Now Elisha sat in his house, and the Elders sat with him.) And *the King* sent a man before him: *but* before the messenger came to him, he said to the Elders, See ye not how this [1]murderer's son hath sent to take away mine head? take heed when the messenger cometh, *and* shut the door, and handle him roughly at the door: is not the sound of his master's feet behind him?

33 While he yet talked with them, behold, the

6:12 [1] There is nothing so secret that thou canst go about, but he knoweth it, and discovereth it unto his King.

6:14 [1] Though it had been nothing in man's judgment to have taken Elisha, yet the wicked ever doubt, and think they are never able to prepare power enough, though it be but against one or a few.

6:16 [1] For he was assured of God's help, and that millions of Angels camped about the godly to deliver them.

6:17 [1] That he may behold how thou hast prepared an army to rescue us.

6:18 [1] Meaning, the Syrians his enemies, which came down, thinking themselves sure of him.

6:19 [1] Thus he did being led by the Spirit of God, and not because he sought his own revengeance, but only to set forth the glory of God.

6:21 [1] The wicked use reverent and grave words toward the servants

of God, when they think to have any commodity by them, though in their heart they cannot abide them.

6:23 [1] For this gentle entreaty and the miracle wrought by the Prophet, did more prevail for common quietness, than if they had been overcome in battle: for they returned no more at that time to fight against Israel, or in that King's days.

6:25 [1] The Hebrews write, that they burned it in the siege for lack of wood.

6:27 [1] Meaning, any kind of vittle, as corn and wine, etc.

6:30 [1] Or, under his clothes.
[2] Thus hypocrites when they feel God's judgments, think to please him with outward ceremonies, whom in prosperity they will not know.

6:32 [1] Meaning, Jehoram Ahab's son, who killed the Prophets, and caused Naboth to be stoned.

messenger came down unto him, and said, Behold, this evil cometh of the Lord: [1]should I attend on the Lord any longer?

7

1 Elisha prophesieth plenty of vittles, and other things to Samaria.   6 The Syrians run away and have no man following them.   17 The prince that would not believe the word of Elisha, is trodden to death.

1 Then Elisha said, Hear ye the word of the Lord: thus saith the Lord, [1]Tomorrow this time a measure of fine flour *shall be* sold for a shekel, and two measures of barley for a shekel in the gate of Samaria.

2 Then a prince, on whose hand the king [1]leaned, answered the man of God, and said, Though the Lord would make [2]windows in the heaven, could this thing come to pass? And he said, Behold, thou shalt see it with thine eyes, but thou shalt not [3]eat thereof.

3 Now there were four leprous men at the [1]entering in of the gate: and they said one to another, Why sit we here until we die?

4 If we say, We will enter into the city, the famine is in the city, and we shall die there: and if we sit here, we die also. Now therefore come, and let us fall into the camp of the Aramites: if they save our lives, we shall live: and if they kill us, we are but dead.

5 So they rose up in the twilight, to go to the camp of the Aramites: and when they were come to the utmost part of the camp of the Aramites, lo, there was no man there.

6 For the Lord had caused the camp of the Aramites to hear a [1]noise of chariots and a noise of horses, *and* a noise of a great army, so that they said one to another, Behold, the King of Israel hath hired against us the kings of the Hittites, and the kings of the Egyptians to come upon us.

7 Wherefore they arose, and fled in the twilight, and left their tents and their horses, and their asses, *even* the camp as it was, and [1]fled for their lives.

8 And when these lepers came to the utmost part of the camp, they entered into one tent, and did eat and drink, and carried thence silver and gold, and raiment, and went and hid it: after, they returned, and entered into another tent, and carried thence *also*, and went and hid it.

9 Then said one to another, We do not well: this day is a day of good tidings, and we hold our peace. If we tarry till daylight, some [1]mischief will come upon us. Now therefore, come, let us go, and tell the king's household.

10 So they came and called unto the porters of the city, and told them, saying, We came to the camp of the Aramites, and lo, there was no man there, neither voice of man, but horses tied and asses tied: and the tents *are* as they were.

11 And the porters cried and declared to the king's house within.

12 Then the King arose in the night, and said unto his servants, [1]I will show you now, what the Aramites have done unto us. They know that we are famished, therefore they are gone out of the camp to hide themselves in the field, saying, When they come out of the city, we shall catch them alive, and get into the city.

13 And one of his servants answered, and said, Let me take now five of the horses that remain, and are left in the *city*, (behold, they are even as all the [1]multitude of Israel that are left therein: behold, *I say*, they are as the multitude of the Israelites that are consumed) and we will send to see.

14 So they took [1]two chariots of horses, and the king sent after the host of the Aramites, saying, Go and see.

15 And they went after them unto Jordan, and lo, all the way was full of clothes and vessels which the Aramites had cast from them in their haste: and the messengers returned, and told the king.

16 Then the people went out and spoiled the camp of the Aramites: so a measure of fine flour was at a shekel, and two measures of barley at a shekel [1]according to the word of the Lord.

17 And the king gave the prince (on whose hand he leaned) the charge of the gate, and the people [1]trode upon him in the gate, and he died, as the man

---

6:33 [1] So the wicked fall into a rage and desperation, if they find not sudden remedy against their afflictions.

7:1 [1] The godly are ever assured of God's help in their necessities, but the times and hours are only revealed by God's Spirit.

7:2 [1] To whom the king gave the charge and oversight of things, as verse 17.

[2] He mocked at the Prophet's words, saying, that if God rained down corn from heaven, yet this could not come to pass.

[3] Thy infidelity shall be punished herein when thou shalt see this miracle, and yet not be partaker thereof.

7:3 [1] For it was commanded in the law that they should dwell apart, and not among their brethren, Lev. 13:46.

7:6 [1] Thus God needeth no great preparation to destroy the wicked, though they be never so many: for he can scatter them with a small noise, or shaking of a leaf.

7:7 [1] The wicked need no greater enemy than their own conscience to pursue them.

7:9 [1] Or, we shall be punished for our faults.

7:12 [1] He mistrusted the Prophet's words, and therefore could believe nothing, as they which are more politic than godly ever cast more perils than needeth.

7:13 [1] There are no more left, but they, or the rest are consumed with the famine, as the rest of the people.

7:14 [1] Or, two horses of the chariot, which were accustomed to draw in the chariot.

7:16 [1] Which he spake by the mouth of Elisha, verse 1.

7:17 [1] As the people preased out of the gate to run to the Syrian's tents, where they had heard was meat, and great spoil left.

of God had said, which spake it, when the king came down to him.

18 And it came to pass, as the man of God had spoken to the King, saying, Two measures of barley at a shekel, and a measure of fine flour shall be at a shekel, tomorrow about this time in the gate of Samaria.

19 But the prince had answered the man of God, and said, Though the Lord would make windows in the heaven, could it come so to pass? And he said, Behold, thou shalt see it with thine eyes, but thou shalt not eat thereof.

20 And so it came unto him: for the people trode upon him in the gate, and he died.

8

1 Elisha prophesieth unto the Shunammite the dearth of seven years.   12 He prophesieth to Hazael, that he shall be king of Syria.   15 He reigneth after Ben-Hadad.   16 Jehoram reigneth over Judah.   20 Edom falleth from Judah.   25 Ahaziah succeedeth Jehoram.

1 Then spake Elisha unto the woman, "whose son he had restored to life, saying, Up, and go, thou, and thine house, and sojourn where thou ¹canst sojourn: for the Lord hath called for a famine, and it cometh also upon the land seven years.

2 And the woman arose, and did after the saying of the man of God, and went both she and her household, and sojourned in the land of the Philistines seven years.

3 ¶ And at the seven year's end, the woman returned out of the land of the Philistines, and went out ¹to call upon the king for her house and for her land.

4 And the King talked with Gehazi the servant of the man of God, saying, Tell me, I pray thee, all the great acts, that Elisha hath done.

5 And as he told ¹the king, how he had restored one dead to life, behold, the woman, whose son he had raised to life, called upon the king for her house and for her land. Then Gehazi said, My lord, O King, this is the woman, and this is her son, whom Elisha restored to life.

6 And when the king asked the woman, she told him: so the King appointed her an Eunuch, saying, Restore thou all that are hers, and all the ¹fruits of

CHAPTER 8
ᵃ 2 Kings 4:35
ᵇ 2 Chron. 21:4

her land since the day she left the land, even until this time.

7 ¶ Then Elisha came to Damascus, and Ben-Hadad the king of Aram was sick: and one told him, saying, The man of God is come hither.

8 And the king said unto Hazael, Take a present in thine hand, and go meet the man of God, that thou mayest inquire of the Lord by him, saying, Shall I recover of this disease?

9 So Hazael went to meet him, and took the present in his hand, and of every ¹good thing of Damascus, *even* the burden of forty camels, and came and stood before him, and said, Thy son Ben-Hadad king of Aram hath sent me to thee, saying, Shall I recover of this disease?

10 And Elisha said to him, Go, *and* say unto him, Thou shalt ¹recover: howbeit the Lord hath showed me, that he shall surely die.

11 And he looked upon him steadfastly, till *Hazael* was ashamed, and the man of God wept.

12 And Hazael said, Why weepeth my lord? And he answered, because I know the evil that thou shalt do unto the children of Israel: *for* their strong cities shalt thou set on fire, and their young men shalt thou slay with the sword, and shalt dash their infants *against the stones*, and rent in pieces their women with child.

13 Then Hazael said, What? is thy servant ¹a dog, that I should do this great thing? And Elisha answered, The Lord hath showed me, that thou shalt be King of Aram.

14 ¶ So he departed from Elisha, and came to his master, who said to him, What said Elisha to thee? And he answered, He told me that thou shouldest recover.

15 And on the morrow he took a thick cloth and dipped in it water, and ¹spread it on his face, and he died: and Hazael reigned in his stead.

16 ¶ ᵇNow in the fifth year of Joram the son of Ahab king of Israel, and of Jehoshaphat King of Judah, ¹Jehoram the son of Jehoshaphat king of Judah began ²to reign.

17 He was two and thirty years old, when he began to reign: and he reigned eight years in Jerusalem.

18 And he walked in the ways of the Kings of Israel, as did the house of Ahab: for the ¹daughter

---

8:1 ¹ Where thou canst find a commodious place to dwell, where as is plenty.

8:3 ¹ That is, to complain on them which had taken her possessions while she was absent.

8:5 ¹ God's wonderful providence appeareth in this, that he caused the King to be desirous to hear of him, whom before he contemned, and also hereby prepared an entrance to the poor widow's suit.

8:6 ¹ The King caused that to be justly restored, which was wrongfully holden from her.

8:9 ¹ Of all the chiefest and precious things of the country.

8:10 ¹ Meaning, that he should recover of this disease: but he knew that this messenger Hazael should slay him to obtain the kingdom.

8:13 ¹ That I should be without all humanity and pity.

8:15 ¹ Under pretence to refresh or ease him, he stifled him with his cloth.

8:16 ¹ Read 2 Kings 1:17.
     ² He was confirmed in his kingdom after his father's death.

8:18 ¹ The holy Ghost showeth hereby what danger it is to join with infidels.

of Ahab was his wife, and he did evil in the sight of the Lord.

19 Yet the Lord would not destroy Judah, for David his servant's sake, ^cas he had promised him to give him a light, *and* to his children forever.

20 ¶ In those days Edom ¹rebelled from under the hand of Judah, and made a King over themselves.

21 Therefore Joram went to Zair, and all his chariots with him, and he arose by night, and smote the Edomites which were about him, with the captains of the chariots, and the people fled into their tents.

22 So Edom rebelled from under the hand of Judah unto this day: then ¹Libnah rebelled at that same time.

23 Concerning the rest of the acts of Joram and all that he did, are they not written in the book of the Chronicles of the kings of Judah?

24 And Joram slept with his fathers, and was buried with his fathers in the city of David. And ^dAhaziah his son reigned in his stead.

25 ¶ In the twelfth year of Joram the son of Ahab King of Israel, did Ahaziah the son of Jehoram king of Judah begin to reign.

26 ¹Two and twenty years old was Ahaziah when he began to reign, and he reigned one year in Jerusalem, and his mother's name *was* Athaliah the daughter of Omri king of Israel.

27 And he walked in the way of the house of Ahab, and did evil in the sight of the Lord, like the house of Ahab: for he was the son in law of the house of Ahab.

28 And he went with Joram the son of Ahab to war against Hazael king of Aram in ¹Ramoth Gilead, and the Aramites smote Joram.

29 And king Joram returned to be healed in ¹Jezreel of the wounds which the Aramites had given him at Ramah, when he fought against Hazael king of Aram. And Ahaziah the son of Jehoram king of Judah went down to see Joram the son of Ahab in Jezreel, because he was sick.

9 6 *Jehu is made king of Israel. 24 And killeth Jehoram the king thereof, 27 And Ahaziah, otherwise called Jehoahaz, the king of Judah. 33 And causeth Jezebel to be cast down out of a window, and the dogs did eat her.*

c 2 Sam. 7:13
d 1 Chron. 22:1

CHAPTER 9
a 1 Kings 19:16,17
b 1 Kings 21:15,25
c 1 Kings 14:10 1 Kings 21:21
d 1 Kings 14:10 1 Kings 21:22
e 1 Kings 16:3-11

1 Then Elisha the Prophet called one of the children of the Prophets, and said unto him, ^{a,1}Gird thy loins, and take this box of oil in thine hand, and get thee to Ramoth Gilead.

2 And when thou comest thither, look where *is* Jehu the son of Jehoshaphat, the son of Nimshi, and go, and make him arise up from among his brethren, and lead him ¹to a secret chamber.

3 Then take the box of oil and pour it on his head, and say, Thus saith the Lord, I have anointed thee for king over Israel: then open the door, and flee without any tarrying.

4 So the servant of the Prophet got him to Ramoth Gilead.

5 And when he came in, behold, the captains of the army were sitting. And he said, I have a message to thee, O captain. And Jehu said, Unto which of all us? And he answered, To thee, O captain.

6 And he arose, and went into the house, and he poured the oil on his head and said unto him, Thus saith the Lord God of Israel, I have ¹anointed thee *for* king over the people of the Lord, *even* over Israel.

7 And thou shalt smite the house of Ahab thy master, that I may avenge the blood of my servants the Prophets, and the blood of all the servants of the Lord ^bof the hand of Jezebel.

8 For the whole house of Ahab shall be destroyed: and ^cI will cut off from Ahab, him that maketh water against the wall, as well him that is shut up, as him that is left in Israel.

9 And I will make the house of Ahab, like the house ^dof Jeroboam the son of Nebat, and like the house ^eof Baasha the son of Ahijah.

10 And the dogs shall eat Jezebel in the field of Jezreel, and there shall be none to bury her. And he opened the door, and fled.

11 ¶ Then Jehu came out to the ¹servants of his lord. And *one* said unto him, Is all well? wherefore came this ²mad fellow to thee? And he said unto them, Ye know the man, and what his talk was.

12 And they said, It is false, tell us it now. Then he said, Thus and thus spake he to me, saying, Thus saith the Lord, I have anointed thee for King over Israel.

8:20 ¹ Which had been subject from David's time, until this time of Jehoram.
8:22 ¹ This was a city in Judah given to the Levites, Josh. 21:13, and after turned from King Jehoram, because of his idolatry.
8:26 ¹ Which is to be understood, that he was made king when his father reigned, but after his father's death he was confirmed king when he was forty-two years old, as 2 Chron. 22:2.
8:28 ¹ Which was a city in the tribe of Gad beyond Jordan.
8:29 ¹ This is a city belonging to the tribe of Issachar.
9:1 ¹ Prepare thyself to go diligently about thy business: for in those countries they used long garments which they tucked up, when they went about earnest business.
9:2 ¹ Hebrew, *from chamber to chamber.*
9:6 ¹ This anointing was for Kings, Priests and Prophets, which were all figures of Messiah, in whom these three offices were accomplished.
9:11 ¹ That is, the rest of the army, whom he called before, his brethren, verse 2.
² In this estimation the world hath the ministers of God: notwithstanding forasmuch as the world hath ever slandered the children of God (yea they called the Son of God a deceiver, and said he had the devil) therefore they ought not to be discouraged.

13 Then they made haste, and took every man his garment, and put it under him on the top of the stairs, and blew the trumpet, saying, Jehu is King.

14 So Jehu the son of Jehoshaphat the son of Nimshi conspired against Joram: (Now Joram kept Ramoth Gilead, he and all Israel, because of Hazael king of Aram.

15 And ʲking Joram returned to be healed in Jezreel of the wounds, which the Aramites had given him, when he fought with Hazael king of Aram) and Jehu said, If it be your minds, let no man depart and escape out of the city, to go and tell in Jezreel.

16 So Jehu got up into a chariot, and went to Jezreel: for Joram lay there, and ¹Ahaziah king of Judah was come down to see Joram.

17 And the watchman that stood in the tower in Jezreel spied the company of Jehu as he came, and said, I see a company. And Jehoram said, Take a horseman and send to meet them, that he may say, Is it peace?

18 So there went one on horseback to meet him, and said, Thus saith the King, Is it peace? And Jehu said, What hast thou to do with peace? ¹turn behind me. And the watchman told, saying, The messenger came to them, but he cometh not again.

19 Then he sent out another on horseback, which came to them, and said, Thus saith the king, Is it peace? And Jehu answered, What hast thou to do with peace? turn behind me.

20 And the watchman told, saying, He came to them also, but cometh not again, and the marching is like the marching of Jehu the son of Nimshi: for he marcheth ¹furiously.

21 ¶ Then Jehoram said, Make ready: and his chariot was made ready. And Jehoram king of Israel, and Ahaziah king of Judah went out either of them in his chariot against Jehu, and met him in the field of Naboth the Jezreelite.

22 And when Jehoram saw Jehu, he said, Is it peace, Jehu? And he answered, What ¹peace? whiles the whoredomes of thy mother Jezebel, and her witchcrafts are yet in great number?

23 Then Jehoram turned his hand, and fled, and

ʲ 2 Kings 8:29
ᵍ 1 Kings 21:29

said to Ahaziah, O Ahaziah, there is treason.

24 But Jehu took a bow in his hand, and smote Jehoram between the shoulders, that the arrow went through his heart: and he fell down in his chariot.

25 Then said Jehu to Bidkar a captain, Take, and cast him in some place of the field of Naboth the Jezreelite: for I remember that when I and thou rode together after Ahab his father, the Lord ¹laid this burden upon him.

26 ᵍSurely I have seen yesterday the blood of Naboth, and the blood of his ¹sons, said the Lord, and I will render it thee in this field, saith the Lord: now therefore take and cast him in the field according to the word of the Lord.

27 But when Ahaziah the king of Judah saw this, he fled by the way of the garden house: And Jehu pursued after him, and said, Smite him also in the chariot: and they smote him in the going up to Gur, which is by Ibleam. And he fled to ¹Megiddo, and there died.

28 And his servants carried him in a chariot to Jerusalem, and buried him in his sepulcher with his fathers in the city of David.

29 ¶ And in the ¹eleventh year of Joram the son of Ahab, began Ahaziah to reign over Judah.

30 And when Jehu was come to Jezreel, Jezebel heard of it, and painted her face, and tired her head, and ¹looked out at a window.

31 And as Jehu entered at the gate, she said, Had ¹Zimri peace, which slew his master?

32 And he lift up his eyes to the window, and said, Who is on my side, who? Then two or three of her ¹Eunuchs looked unto him.

33 And he said, Cast her down: and they cast her down, ¹and he sprinkled of her blood upon the wall, and upon the horses, and he trode her under foot.

34 And when he was come in, he did eat and drink, and said, Visit now yonder cursed woman, and bury her: for she is a ¹King's daughter.

35 And they went to bury her, but they found no more of her, than the skull and the feet, and the palms of her hands.

36 Wherefore they came again and told him.

9:16 ¹ God had thus ordained, as is read, 2 Chron. 22:7, that this wicked and idolatrous King, who was more ready to gratify wicked Joram, than to obey the will of God, should perish with him, by whose means he thought to have been stronger.
9:18 ¹ Or, follow me.
9:20 ¹ As one that went earnestly about his enterprise.
9:22 ¹ Meaning, that forasmuch as God is their enemy because of their sins that he will ever stir up some to revenge his cause.
9:25 ¹ Or, spake this prophecy against him.
9:26 ¹ By this place it is evident, that Jezebel caused both Naboth and his sons to be put to death, that Ahab might enjoy his vineyard more quietly: for else his children might have claimed possession.
9:27 ¹ After that he was wounded in Samaria, he fled to Megiddo,

which was a city of Judah.
9:29 ¹ That is, eleven whole years: for 2 Kings 8:25, before, when he said that he began to reign the twelfth year of Joram, he taketh part of the year for the whole.
9:30 ¹ Being of an harsh and cruel nature she would still retain her princely state and dignity.
9:31 ¹ As though she would say, Can any traitor, or any that riseth against his superior, have good success? read 1 Kings 16:10.
9:32 ¹ Or, chief servants.
9:33 ¹ This he did by the motion of the Spirit of God, that her blood should be shed, that had shed the blood of innocents, to be a spectacle and example of God's judgments to all tyrants.
9:34 ¹ To wit, of the king of Sidon, 1 Kings 16:31.

And he said, This is the word of the Lord, which he spake [1]by his servant Elijah the Tishbite, saying, [b]In the field of Jezreel shall the dogs eat the flesh of Jezebel.

37 And the carcass of Jezebel shall be as dung upon the ground in the field of Jezreel, so that none shall say, [1]This is Jezebel.

10

6 Jehu causeth the seventy sons of Ahab to be slain, 14 And after that forty and two of Ahaziah's brethren. 25 He killeth also all the Priests of Baal. 35 After his death his son reigneth in his stead.

1 Ahab had now seventy [1]sons in Samaria. And Jehu wrote letters, and sent to Samaria unto the rulers of Jezreel, *and* to the Elders, and to the bringers up of Ahab's children, to this effect,

2 Now when this letter cometh to you, (for ye have with you your master's sons, ye have with you both chariots and horses, and a defensed city, and armor)

3 Consider therefore which of your master's sons is best and most meet, and [1]set him on his father's throne, and fight for your master's house.

4 But they were exceedingly afraid, and said, Behold two kings could not stand before him, how shall we then stand?

5 And he that was governor of *Ahab's* house, and he that ruled the city, and the Elders, and the bringers up of the children sent to Jehu, saying, We are thy servants, and will do all that thou shalt bid us: we will make no king: do what seemeth good to thee.

6 ¶ Then he wrote another letter to them, saying, If ye be mine, and will obey my voice, [1]take the heads of the men *that are* your master's sons, and come to me to Jezreel by tomorrow this time. (Now the king's sons, *even* seventy persons *were* with the great men of the city, which brought them up)

7 And when the letter came to them, they took the King's sons, and slew the seventy persons, and laid their heads in baskets, and sent them unto him to Jezreel.

8 ¶ Then there came a messenger and told him, saying, They have brought the heads of the King's sons. And he said, Let them lay them on two heaps

[b] 1 Kings 21:23

CHAPTER 10
[a] 1 Kings 21:29

at the entering in of the gate until the morning.

9 And when it was day he went out, and stood and said to all the people, Ye be [1]righteous: behold, I conspired against my master, and slew him: but who slew all these?

10 Know now that there shall fall unto the earth nothing of the word of the Lord, which the Lord spake concerning the house of Ahab: for the Lord hath brought to pass the things that he spake [1]by his servant [a]Elijah.

11 So Jehu slew all that remained of the house of Ahab in Jezreel, and all that were great with him, and his familiars, and his [1]priests, so that he let none of his remain.

12 ¶ And he arose, and departed, and came to Samaria. *And* as Jehu was in the way by an house where the shepherds did shear,

13 He met with the brethren of Ahaziah king of Judah, and said, Who are ye? And they answered, We are the brethren of Ahaziah, and go down to salute the children of the King and the children of the Queen.

14 And he said, Take them alive. And they took them alive, and slew them at the well beside the house where the sheep are shorn, *even* two and forty men, and he [1]left not one of them.

15 ¶ And when he was departed thence, he met with Jehonadab the son of Rechab coming to meet him, and he [1,2]blessed him, and said to him, Is thine heart upright, as mine heart is toward thine? And Jehonadab answered, Yea, doubtless. *Then* give me thine hand. And when he had given him his hand, he took him up to him into the chariot.

16 And he said, Come with me, and see the zeal that I have for the Lord: so they made him ride in his chariot.

17 And when he came to Samaria, he slew all that remained unto Ahab in Samaria, till he had destroyed him, according to the word of the Lord, which he spake to Elijah.

18 Then Jehu assembled all the people, and said unto them, Ahab served [1]Baal a little, *but* Jehu shall serve him much more.

19 Now therefore call unto me all ye prophets of Baal, all his servants, and all his priests, and let not

---

9:36 [1] Hebrew, *by the hand of.*
9:37 [1] Thus God's judgments appear even in this world against them that suppress his word and persecute his servants.
10:1 [1] The Scripture useth to call them sons, which are either children or nephews.
10:3 [1] He wrote this, to prove them whether they would take his part or no.
10:6 [1] God as a just judge punisheth the wicked children of wicked parents unto the third and fourth generation.
10:9 [1] Ye cannot justly condemn me for the king's death, seeing ye have done the like to his posterity: for the Lord commanded me, and

moved you to execute this his judgment.
10:10 [1] Hebrew, *by the hand of.*
10:11 [1] Meaning, which were the idolatrous priests.
10:14 [1] Thus God's vengeance is upon them that have any part or familiarity with the wicked.
10:15 [1] For he feared God, and lamented the wickedness of those times: therefore Jehu was glad to join with him: of Rechab read Jer. 35:2.
  [2] Or, praised God for him.
10:18 [1] Here Baal is taken for Ashtoreth the idol of the Sidonians, which Jezebel caused to be worshipped, as it is also so used, 1 Kings 16 and 22:53.

a man be lacking: for I have a great sacrifice for Baal: whosoever is lacking, he shall not live. But Jehu did it by a subtlety to destroy the servants of Baal.

20 And Jehu said, [1]Proclaim a solemn assembly for Baal. And they proclaimed it.

21 So Jehu sent unto all Israel, and all the servants of Baal came, and there was not a man left that came not. And they came into the house of Baal, and the house of Baal was full from end to end.

22 Then he said unto him that had the charge of the vestry, Bring forth vestments for all the servants of Baal. And he brought them out vestments.

23 And when Jehu went, and Jehonadab the son of Rechab into the house of Baal, he said unto the servants of Baal, Search diligently, and look, lest there be here with you *any* of the [1]servants of the Lord, but the servants of Baal only.

24 And when they went in to make sacrifice and burnt offering, Jehu appointed four score men without, and said, If any of the men whom I have brought into your hands, escape, [1]his soul *shall be* for his soul.

25 And when he had made an end of the burnt offering, Jehu said to the guard, and to the captains, Go in, slay them, let not a man come out. And they smote them with the edge of the sword. And the guard, and the captains cast them out, and went unto the [1]city, *where was* the temple of Baal.

26 And they brought out the images of the temple of Baal, and burnt them.

27 And they destroyed the image of Baal, and threw down the house of Baal, and made a jakes of it unto this day.

28 So Jehu destroyed Baal out of Israel.

29 But from the sins of Jeroboam the son of Nebat which made Israel to sin, Jehu departed not from them, *neither from* the golden calves that were in Bethel and that were in Dan.

30 ¶ And the Lord said unto Jehu, Because thou hast diligently executed that which was right in mine eyes, *and* hast done unto the house of Ahab according to all things that were in mine heart, *therefore* shall thy [1]sons unto the fourth *generation* sit on the throne of Israel.

31 But Jehu regarded not to walk in the law of

CHAPTER 11
a 2 Chron. 22:10
b 2 Chron. 13:13

the Lord God of Israel with all his heart: *for he* departed not from the sins of Jeroboam, which made Israel to sin.

32 In those days the Lord began to [1]loathe Israel, and Hazael smote them in all the coasts of Israel,

33 From Jordan Eastward, *even* all the land of Gilead, the Gadites, and the Reubenites, and them that were of Manasseh, from Aroer (which is by the river Arnon) and Gilead and Bashan.

34 Concerning the rest of the acts of Jehu, and all that he did, and all his valiant deeds, are they not written in the book of the Chronicles of the kings of Israel?

35 And Jehu slept with his fathers, and they buried him in Samaria, and Jehoahaz his son reigned in his stead.

36 And the time that Jehu reigned over Israel in Samaria is eight and twenty years.

11

1 Athaliah putteth to death all the King's sons, except Joash the son of Ahaziah.   4 Joash is appointed King.   15 Jehoiada causeth Athaliah to be slain.   17 He maketh a covenant between God and the people.   18 Baal and his priests are destroyed.

1 Then *a*Athaliah the mother of Ahaziah when she saw that her son was dead, she arose, and destroyed all the [1]King's seed.

2 But Jehosheba the daughter of king Joram, *and* sister to Ahaziah [1]took Joash the son of Ahaziah, and stole him from among the King's sons that should be slain, *both* him and his nurse, *keeping them* in [2]the bedchamber, and they hid him from Athaliah, so that he was not slain.

3 And he was with her hid in the house of the Lord six years, and Athaliah did reign over the land.

4 ¶ *b*And the seventh year [1]Jehoiada sent and took the captains over hundreds, with *other* captains and them of the guard, and caused them to come unto him into the house of the Lord, and made a covenant with them, and took an oath of them in the house of the Lord, and showed them the King's son.

5 And he commanded them, saying, This is it that ye must do, The third part of [1]you, that cometh on the Sabbath, shall [2]ward toward the King's house:

6 And *another* third part in the gate of [1]Sur: and

10:20 [1] Hebrew, *sanctify.*
10:23 [1] Thus God would have his servants preserved, and idolaters destroyed, as in his law he giveth express commandment, Deut. 13.
10:24 [1] Or, he shall die for him.
10:25 [1] Which city was near to Samaria.
10:30 [1] Thus God approveth and rewardeth his zeal, in executing God's judgment, albeit his wickedness was afterward punished.
10:32 [1] Or, to cut them off.
11:1 [1] Meaning, all the posterity of Jehoshaphat, to whom the kingdom appertained: thus God used the cruelty of this woman to

destroy the whole family of Ahab.
11:2 [1] The Lord promised to maintain the family of David, and not to quench the light thereof, therefore he moved the heart of Jehosheba to preserve him.
  [2] Where the Priests did lie.
11:4 [1] The chief priest, Jehosheba's husband.
11:5 [1] Of the Levites, which had charge of the keeping of the Temple, and kept watch by course.
  [2] That none should come upon them, while they were crowning the king.
11:6 [1] Called the East gate of the Temple, 2 Chron. 23:5.

another third part in the gate behind them of the guard: and ye shall keep watch ²in the house of Massah.

7 And two parts of you, *that is,* all that ¹go out on the Sabbath day, shall keep the watch of the house of the Lord about the king.

8 And ye shall compass the King round about, every man with his weapon in his hand, and whosoever cometh within the ranges, let him be slain: be you with the King, as he goeth out and in.

9 ¶ And the captains of the hundreds did according to all that Jehoiada the Priest commanded, and they took every man of his men that entered *into their charge* on the Sabbath, with them that went out *of it* on the ¹Sabbath, and came to Jehoiada the Priest.

10 And the ¹Priest gave to the captains of hundreds the spears and the shields that were King David's, and were in the house of the Lord.

11 And the guard stood, every man with his weapon in his hand, from the right side of the house to the left side, about the altar and about the house, round about the King.

12 Then he brought out ¹the king's son, and put the crown upon him, and gave him ²the Testimony, and they made him king: also they anointed him, and clapped their hands, and said, God save the King.

13 ¶ And when Athaliah heard the noise of the running of the people, she came into the people in the house of the Lord.

14 And when she looked, behold, the King stood by a ¹pillar, as the manner was, and the princes and the trumpeters by the King, and all the people of the land rejoiced, and blew with trumpets. Then Athaliah rent her clothes, and cried, Treason, treason.

15 But Jehoiada the Priest commanded the captains of the hundreds that had the rule of the host, and said unto them, Have her ¹forth of the ranges, and he that ²followeth her, let him die by the sword: for the Priest had said, Let her not be slain in the house of the Lord.

16 Then they laid hands on her, and she went by the way, by the which the horses go to the house of the King, and there was she slain.

CHAPTER 12
ᵃ 2 Chron. 24:1

17 And Jehoiada made a covenant between the Lord, ¹and the King and the people, that they should be the Lord's people: likewise between the ²King and the people.

18 Then all the people of the land went into the house of Baal, and destroyed it with his altars, and his images brake they down courageously, and slew Mattan the Priest of Baal before the ¹altars: and the ²Priest set a guard over the house of the Lord.

19 Then he took the captains of hundreds, and the *other* captains, and the guard, and all the people of the land: and they brought the King from the house of the Lord, and came by the way of the gate of the guard to the King's house: and he sat him down on the throne of the kings.

20 And all the people of the land rejoiced, and the city was in quiet: ¹for they had slain Athaliah with the sword beside the king's house.

21 Seven years old was Jehoash when he began to reign.

12

6 *Jehoash maketh provision for the repairing of the Temple.* 16 *He slayeth the king of Syria by a present from coming against Jerusalem.* 20 *He is killed by two of his servants.*

1 In ᵃthe seventh year of Jehu Jehoash began to reign, and reigned forty years in Jerusalem, and his mother's name was Zibiah of Beersheba.

2 And Jehoash did that which was good in the sight of the Lord all his time that ¹Jehoiada the Priest taught him.

3 But ¹the high places were not taken away: for the people offered yet and burnt incense in the high places.

4 ¶ And Jehoash said to the Priests, All the silver of dedicated things that be brought to the house of the Lord, *that is,* the money of them that are under the ¹count, the money that every man is set at, *and* all the money that one offereth willingly, and bringeth into the house of the Lord,

5 Let the Priests take it to them, every man of his acquaintance: and they shall repair the ¹broken places

---

² Or, that none break his order.
11:7 ¹ Whose charge is ended.
11:9 ¹ Read verses 5 and 7.
11:10 ¹ To wit, Jehoiada.
11:12 ¹ That is, Joash, which had been kept secret six years.
  ² Meaning, the Law of God, which is his chief charge, and whereby only his throne is established.
11:14 ¹ Where the king's place was in the Temple.
11:15 ¹ Or, out of the Temple.
  ² To take her part.
11:17 ¹ That both the King and the people should maintain the true worship of God and destroy all idolatry.
  ² That he should govern and they obey in the fear of God.
11:18 ¹ Even in the place where he had blasphemed God, and

thought to have been helped by his idol, there God poured his vengeance upon him.
  ² To wit, Jehoiada.
11:20 ¹ Which by her cruelty and persecution had vexed the whole land before.
12:2 ¹ So long as rulers give ear to the true ministers of God, they prosper.
12:3 ¹ So hard a thing it is for them, that are in authority, to be brought to the perfect obedience of God.
12:4 ¹ That is, the money of redemption, Exod. 30:12, also the money which the Priest valued the vows at, Lev. 27:2, and their free liberality.
12:5 ¹ For the Temple which was built an hundred fifty and five years before, had many things decayed in it, both by the negligence of the King's predecessors, and also by the wickedness of the idolaters.

of the house, wheresoever any decay is found.

6 ¶ Yet in the three and twentieth year of King Jehoash the Priests had not mended that which was decayed in the Temple.

7 Then King Jehoash called for Jehoiada the Priest, and the *other* Priests, and said unto them, Why repair ye not the ruins of the Temple? now therefore ¹receive no more money of your acquaintance, except ye deliver it *to repair* the ruins of the Temple.

8 So the Priests consented to receive no more money of the people, neither to repair the decayed places of the Temple.

9 Then Jehoiada the Priest took a chest and bored an hole in the lid of it, and set it beside the altar, on the ¹right side, as every man cometh into the Temple of the Lord. And the Priests that kept the ²door, put therein all the money that was brought into the house of the Lord.

10 And when they saw there was much money in the chest, the king's Secretary came up and the high Priest, and put it up after that they had told the money that was found in the house of the Lord,

11 And they gave the money made ready into the hands of them, ¹that undertook the work, *and* that had the oversight of the house of the Lord: and they paid it out to the carpenters and builders that wrought upon the house of the Lord,

12 And to the masons and hewers of stone, and to buy timber and hewed stone, to repair that was decayed in the house of the Lord, and for all that which was laid out for the reparation of the Temple.

13 Howbeit there was ¹not made for the house of the Lord bowls of silver, instruments of music, basins, trumpets, nor any vessels of gold, or vessels of silver of the money that was brought into the house of the Lord.

14 But they gave it to the workmen, which repaired therewith the house of the Lord.

15 Moreover, they reckoned not with the men, into whose hands they delivered that money to be bestowed on workmen: for they dealt faithfully.

16 The money of the trespass offering, and the money of the sin offerings was not brought into the house of the Lord: *for it was the Priests'.*

17 ¶ Then came up Hazael king of Aram, and fought against Gath, and took it, and Hazael set his face to go up to Jerusalem.

18 And ¹Jehoash king of Judah took all the hallowed things that Jehoshaphat, and Jehoram, and Ahaziah, his fathers, kings of Judah had dedicated, and that he himself had dedicated, and all the gold that was found in the treasures of the house of the Lord, and in the king's house, and sent it to Hazael king of Aram, and he departed from Jerusalem.

19 Concerning the rest of the acts of Joash and all that he did, are they not written in the book of the Chronicles of the kings of Judah?

20 ¶ And his servants arose and wrought treason, and ¹slew Joash in the house of ²Millo, when he came down to Silla.

21 Even ¹Jozachar the son of Shimeath, and Jehozabad the son of Shomer his servants smote him and he died, and they buried him with his fathers in the city of David. And Amaziah his son reigned in his stead.

13 *3 Jehoahaz the son of Jehu is delivered into the hands of the Syrians. 4 He prayeth unto God, and is delivered. 9 Joash his son reigneth in his stead. 20 Elisha dieth. 24 Hazael dieth.*

1 In the three and twentieth year of Joash the son of Ahaziah king of Judah, Jehoahaz the son of Jehu began to reign over Israel in Samaria, *and he reigned* seventeen years.

2 And he did evil in the sight of the Lord, and followed the sins of Jeroboam the son of Nebat, which made Israel to ¹sin, *and* departed not therefrom.

3 And the Lord was angry with Israel, and delivered them into the hand of Hazael king of Aram, and into the hand of Ben-Hadad the son of Hazael, all ¹his days.

4 And Jehoahaz besought the Lord, and the Lord heard him: for he saw the trouble of Israel, wherewith the king of Aram troubled them.

5 (And the Lord gave Israel a ¹deliverer, so that they came out from under the subjection of the Aramites. And the children of Israel ²dwelt in their tents as ³beforetime.

12:7 ¹ He taketh from them the ordering of the money, because of their negligence.
12:9 ¹ That is, on the South side.
    ² Or, vessel.
12:11 ¹ For the King had appointed others which were meet for that purpose, 2 Kings 22:5.
12:13 ¹ For these men had only the charge of the reparation of the Temple, and the rest of the money was brought to the king, who caused these afterward to be made, 2 Chron. 24:14.
12:18 ¹ After the death of Jehoiada, Joash fell to idolatry: therefore God rejected him, and stirreth up his enemy against him, whom he pacified with the treasures of the Temple: for God would not be served with those gifts, seeing the king's heart was wicked.
12:20 ¹ Because he had put Zechariah the son of Jehoiada to death, 2 Chron. 24:25.
    ² Read 2 Sam. 3:9.
12:21 ¹ Or, Jozahar.
13:2 ¹ By worshipping the calves which Jeroboam did erect in Israel.
13:3 ¹ While Jehoahaz lived.
13:5 ¹ To wit, Joash the son of Jehoahaz.
    ² Safely and without danger.
    ³ Hebrew, *as yesterday and before yesterday.*

6 Nevertheless, they departed not from the sins of the house of Jeroboam which made Israel sin, *but* walked in them, even the [1]grove also remained still in Samaria)

7 For he had left of the people to Jehoahaz but fifty horsemen, and ten chariots, and ten thousand footmen, because the king [1]of Aram had destroyed them, and made them like dust beaten to powder.

8 Concerning the rest of the acts of Jehoahaz and all that he did, and his valiant deeds, are they not written in the book of the Chronicles of the kings of Israel?

9 And Jehoahaz slept with his fathers, and they buried him in Samaria, and Joash his son reigned in his stead.

10 ¶ In the seven and thirtieth year of Joash king [1]of Judah began Jehoash the son of Jehoahaz to reign over Israel in Samaria, *and reigned* sixteen years.

11 And did evil in the sight of the Lord: *for* he departed not from all the sins of Jeroboam the son of Nebat that made Israel to sin, but he walked therein.

12 Concerning the rest of the acts of Joash, and all that he did, and his valiant deeds, *and* how he fought against Amaziah king of Judah, are they not written in the book of the Chronicles of the kings of Israel?

13 And Joash slept with his fathers, and Jeroboam sat upon his seat: and Joash was buried in Samaria among the kings of Israel.

14 ¶ When Elisha fell sick of his sickness whereof he died, Joash the king of Israel came down unto him, and wept upon his face, and said, [1]O my father, my father, the chariot of Israel, and the horsemen of the same.

15 Then Elisha said unto him, Take a bow and arrows. And he took unto him bow and arrows.

16 And he said to the king of Israel, Put thine hand upon the bow. And he put his hand upon it. And Elisha put his hands upon the king's hands,

17 And said, Open the window [1]Eastward. And when he had opened it, Elisha said, Shoot. And he

CHAPTER 14
[a] 2 Chron. 25:1

shot. And he said, *Behold*, the arrow of the Lord's deliverance, and the arrow of deliverance against Aram: for thou shalt smite the Aramites in Aphek, till thou hast consumed them.

18 Again he said, Take the arrows. And he took them. And he said unto the king of Israel, Smite the ground. And he smote thrice, and ceased.

19 Then the man of God was [1]angry with him, and said, Thou shouldest have smitten five or six times, so thou shouldest have smitten Aram, till thou hadst consumed it, where now thou shalt smite Aram but thrice.

20 ¶ So Elisha died, and they buried him. And *certain* bands of the Moabites came into the land that year.

21 And as they were burying a man: behold, they saw the soldiers: therefore they cast the man into the sepulcher of Elisha. And when the man was down, and touched the bones of Elisha, he [1]revived and stood upon his feet.

22 ¶ But Hazael king of Aram vexed Israel all the days of Jehoahaz.

23 Therefore the Lord had mercy on them and pitied them, and had respect unto them, because of his covenant with Abraham, Isaac, and Jacob, and would not destroy them, neither cast he them from him as [1]yet.

24 So Hazael the King of Aram died: and Ben-Hadad his son reigned in his stead.

25 Therefore Jehoash the son of Jehoahaz returned, and took out of the hand of Ben-Hadad the son of Hazael the cities which he had taken away by war out of the hand of Jehoahaz his father: *for* three times did Joash beat him, and restored the cities unto Israel.

14 2 Amaziah the king of Judah putteth to death them that slew his father, 7 and after smiteth Edom. 15 Joash dieth, and Jeroboam his son succeedeth him. 29 And after him reigneth Zechariah.

1 The second year of Joash son of Jehoahaz king of Israel, reigned [a]Amaziah the son of Joash king of Judah.

13:6 [1] Wherein they did commit their idolatry, and which the Lord had commanded to be destroyed, Deut. 16:21.

13:7 [1] That is, Hazael and Ben-Hadad his son, as verse 3. Read of Hazael, 2 Kings 8:12.

13:10 [1] His chief purpose is to describe the kingdom of Judah, and how God performed his promise made to the house of David: but by the way he showeth how Israel was afflicted and punished for their great idolatry, who though they had now degenerated, yet God both by sending them sundry Prophets and divers punishments, did call them unto him again.

13:14 [1] Thus they used to call the Prophets and servants of God, by whom God blesseth his people, as 2 Kings 2:12, meaning that by their

prayers they did more prosper their country than by force of arms.

13:17 [1] That is, toward Syria: so that he did not only prophesy with words, but also confirmed him by these signs that he should have the victory.

13:19 [1] Because he seemed content to have victory against the enemies of God for twice or thrice, and had not a zeal to overcome them continually, and to destroy them utterly.

13:21 [1] By this miracle God confirmed the authority of Elisha, whose doctrine in his life they contemned, that at this sight they might return and embrace the same doctrine.

13:23 [1] That is, until their sins were come to a full measure, and there was no more hope of amendment.

2 He was five and twenty years old when he began to reign, and reigned nine and twenty years in Jerusalem, and his mother's name *was* Jehoaddan of Jerusalem.

3 And he did [1]uprightly in the sight of the Lord, yet not like David his father, *but* did according to all that Joash his father had done.

4 Notwithstanding the high places were not taken away: *for* as yet the people did sacrifice, and burnt incense in the high places.

5 ¶ And when the kingdom was confirmed in his hand, he slew his servants which had [b]killed the king his father.

6 But the children of those that did slay *him*, he [1]slew not, according unto that which is written in the book of the Law of Moses, wherein the Lord commanded, saying, 'The fathers shall not be put to death for the children, nor the children put to death for the fathers: but every man shall be put to death for his own sin.

7 He slew *also* of [1]Edom in the valley of salt, ten thousand, and took [2]*the city* of Sela by war, and called the name thereof Joktheel unto this day.

8 ¶ Then Amaziah sent messengers to Jehoash the son of Jehoahaz, son of Jehu king of Israel, saying, Come, [1]let us see one another in the face.

9 Then Jehoash the king of Israel sent to Amaziah king of Judah, saying, The thistle that is in Lebanon, sent to the [1]Cedar that is in Lebanon, saying, Give thy daughter to my son to wife: and the wild beast that was in Lebanon, went and trode down the thistle.

10 *Because* thou hast smitten Edom, thine heart hath made thee proud: [1]brag of glory, and tarry at home. Why doest thou provoke to *thine* hurt, that thou shouldest fall, and Judah with thee?

11 But Amaziah would not hear: therefore Jehoash king of Israel went up: and he and Amaziah king of Judah saw one another in the face at Beth Shemesh which is in Judah.

12 And Judah was put to the worse before Israel, and they fled every man to their tents.

13 But Jehoash king of Israel took Amaziah king

[b] 2 Kings 12:20
[c] Deut. 24:16
    Ezek. 18:20
[d] 2 Chron. 25:27

of Judah, the son of Jehoash the son of Ahaziah at Beth Shemesh, and [1]came to Jerusalem, and brake down the wall of Jerusalem from the gate of Ephraim to the corner gate, four hundred cubits.

14 And he took all the gold and silver, and all the vessels that were found in the house of the Lord, and in the treasures of the king's house, and the children that were in [1]hostage, and returned to Samaria.

15 Concerning the rest of the acts of Jehoash which he did, and his valiant deeds, and how he fought with Amaziah king of Judah, are they not written in the book of the Chronicles of the kings of Israel?

16 And Jehoash slept with his fathers, and was buried at Samaria among the kings of Israel: and Jeroboam his son reigned in his stead.

17 ¶ And Amaziah the son of Joash king of Judah, lived after the death of Jehoash son of Jehoahaz king of Israel, fifteen years.

18 Concerning the rest of the acts of Amaziah, are they not written in the book of the Chronicles of the kings of Judah?

19 But they [d]wrought treason against him in Jerusalem, and he fled to [1]Lachish, but they sent after him to Lachish, and slew him there.

20 And they brought him on horses, and he was buried at Jerusalem with his fathers in the city of David.

21 Then all the people of Judah took [1]Azariah which was sixteen years old, and made him king for his father Amaziah.

22 He built [1]Elath, and restored it to Judah, after that the king slept with his fathers.

23 ¶ In the fifteenth year of Amaziah the son of Joash king of Judah, was Jeroboam the son of Joash made king over Israel in Samaria, *and reigned* one and forty years.

24 And he did evil in the sight of the Lord: *for* he departed not from all the [1]sins of Jeroboam the son of Nebat, which made Israel to sin.

25 He restored the coast of Israel, from the entering of Hamath, unto the sea of the wilderness, according to the word of the Lord God of Israel, which he

---

14:3 [1] In the beginning of his reign he seemed to have an outward show of godliness, but afterward he became an idolater and worshipped the idols of the Idumeans.
14:6 [1] Because they neither consented nor were partakers with their fathers in that act.
14:7 [1] For the Idumeans, whom David had brought to subjection, did rebel in the time of Jehoram son of Jehoshaphat.
   [2] Or, the tower, or rock, 2 Chron. 25:32.
14:8 [1] Let us fight hand to hand, and try it by battle, and not destroy one another's cities.
14:9 [1] By this parable Jehoash compareth himself to a cedar tree, because of his great kingdom over ten tribes, and Amaziah to a thistle, because he ruled but over two tribes, and the wild beasts are

Jehoash's soldiers, that spoiled the cities of Judah.
14:10 [1] Brag of the victory, so that thou tarry at home, and envy me not.
14:13 [1] Or, brought him.
14:14 [1] That is, which the Israelites had given to them of Judah for an assurance of peace.
14:19 [1] Which city Rehoboam built in Judah for a fortress, 2 Chron. 11:9.
14:21 [1] Who is also called Uzziah, 2 Chron. 26:1.
14:22 [1] Which is also called Elanon or Eloth.
14:24 [1] Because this idolatry was so vile and almost incredible, that men should forsake the living God, to worship calves, the work of man's hands, therefore the Scripture doth ofttimes repeat it in the reproach of all idolaters.

spake [1]by his servant Jonah the son of Amittai the Prophet, which was of Gath Hepher.

26 For the Lord saw the exceedingly bitter affliction of Israel, so that there was none [1]shut up, nor any left, neither yet any that could help Israel.

27 Yet the Lord [1]had not decreed to put out the name of Israel from under the heaven: therefore he preserved them by the hand of Jeroboam the son of Joash.

28 Concerning the rest of the acts of Jeroboam, and all that he did, and his valiant deeds, *and* how he fought, and how he restored Damascus, and [1]Hamath to Judah in Israel, are they not written in the book of the Chronicles of the kings of Israel?

29 So Jeroboam slept with his fathers, *even* with the kings of Israel, and Zechariah his son reigned in his stead.

15
1 Azariah the King of Judah becometh a leper. 5 Of Jotham, 10 Shallum, 14 Menahem, 23 Pekahiah, 30 Uzziah, 32 Jotham, 38 and Ahaz.

1 In the [1]seven and twentieth year of Jeroboam king of Israel, began Azariah son of Amaziah king of Judah to reign.

2 Sixteen years old was he, when he was made king, and he reigned two and fifty years in Jerusalem: and his mother's name was Jecholiah of Jerusalem.

3 And he did [1]uprightly in the sight of the Lord, according to all that his father Amaziah did.

4 But the high places were not put away: *for* the people yet offered, and burned incense in the high places.

5 And the Lord [1]smote the king, and he was a leper unto the day of his death, and dwelt in an house apart, and Jotham the king's son governed the house, *and* [2]judged the people of the land.

6 Concerning the rest of the acts of Azariah, and all that he did, are they not written in the book of the Chronicles of the Kings of Judah?

7 So Azariah slept with his fathers, and they buried him with his fathers in the city of David, and Jotham his son reigned in his stead.

8 ¶ In the eight and thirtieth year of Azariah King of Judah, did Zechariah the son of Jeroboam reign over Israel in Samaria six [1]months,

CHAPTER 15
a 2 Kings 10:30

9 And did evil in the sight of the Lord, as did his fathers: *for* he departed not from the sins of Jeroboam the son of Nebat, which made Israel to sin.

10 And Shallum the son of Jabesh conspired against him, and smote him, in the sight of the people, and [1]killed him, and reigned in his stead.

11 Concerning the rest of the acts of Zechariah, behold, they are written in the book of the Chronicles of the Kings of Israel.

12 This was the [a]word of the Lord, which he spake unto Jehu, saying, Thy sons shall sit on the throne of Israel unto the fourth *generation* after thee. And it came so to pass.

13 ¶ Shallum the son of Jabesh began to reign in the nine and thirtieth year of Uzziah King of Judah: and he reigned the space of a month in Samaria.

14 For Menahem the son of Gadi went up from Tirzah, and came to Samaria, and smote Shallum the son of Jabesh in Samaria, and slew him, and reigned in his stead.

15 Concerning the rest of the acts of Shallum, and the treason which he wrought, behold, they are written in the book of the Chronicles of the Kings of Israel.

16 ¶ Then Menahem destroyed [1]Tiphsah, and all that were therein, and the coasts thereof from Tirzah, because they opened not to him, and he smote it, and ripped up all their women with child.

17 The nine and thirtieth year of Azariah King of Judah, began Menahem the son of Gadi to reign over Israel, *and reigned* ten years in Samaria.

18 And he did evil in the sight of the Lord, and departed not all his days from the sin of Jeroboam the son of Nebat, which made Israel to sin.

19 ¶ Then Pul the king of Assyria came against the [1]land: and Menahem gave Pul a thousand [2]talents of silver, that his hand might be with him, and establish the kingdom in his hand.

20 And Menahem exacted the money in Israel that all men of substance should give the king of Assyria fifty shekels of silver a piece: so the king of Assyria returned, and tarried not there in the land.

21 Concerning the rest of the acts of Menahem, and all that he did, are they not written in the book of the Chronicles of the kings of Israel?

14:25 [1] Hebrew, *by the hand of.*
14:26 [1] Read 1 Kings 14:10.
14:27 [1] Hebrew, *had not spoken.*
14:28 [1] Which was also called Antioch of Syria, or Riblah.
15:1 [1] Hebrew, *in the twentieth year and seventh year.*
15:3 [1] So long as he gave ear to Zechariah the Prophet.
15:5 [1] His father and grandfather were slain by their subjects and servants, and he because he would usurp the Priest's office contrary to God's ordinance was smitten immediately by the hand of God with the leprosy, 2 Chron. 26:21.
    [2] As viceroy, or deputy to his father.
15:8 [1] He was the fourth in descent from Jehu, who reigned accord-

ing to God's promise, but in him God began to execute his wrath against the house of Jehu.
15:10 [1] Zechariah was the last in Israel, that had the kingdom by succession, save only Pekahiah the son of Menahem, who reigned but two years.
15:16 [1] Which was a city of Israel that would not receive him to be king.
15:19 [1] That is, of Israel.
    [2] Instead of seeking help of God, he went about by money to purchase the favor of this king being an infidel, and therefore God forsook him, and Pul soon afterward brake promise, destroyed his country, and led his people away captive.

22 And Menahem slept with his fathers, and Pekahiah his son did reign in his stead.

23 ¶ In ye fiftieth year of Azariah king of Judah, began Pekahiah the son of Menahem to reign over Israel in Samaria, *and reigned* two years.

24 And he did evil in the sight of the Lord: *for he* departed not from the sins of Jeroboam the son of Nebat which made Israel to sin.

25 And Pekah the son of Remaliah, his captain conspired against him, and smote him in Samaria in the place of the king's palace with ¹Argob and Arieh, and with him fifty men of the Gileadites: so he killed him, and reigned in his stead.

26 Concerning the rest of the acts of Pekahiah, and all that he did, behold, they are written in the book of the Chronicles of the kings of Israel.

27 ¶ In the two and fiftieth year of Azariah King of Judah, began Pekah the son of Remaliah to reign over Israel in Samaria, *and reigned* twenty years.

28 And he did evil in the sight of the Lord: *for he* departed not from the sins of Jeroboam the son of Nebat that made Israel to sin.

29 In the days of Pekah king of Israel ¹came Tiglath-Pileser king of Assyria, and took Ijon, and Abel Beth Maachah, and Janoah, and Kedesh, and Hazor, and Gilead, and Galilee, *and* all the land of Naphtali, and carried them away to Assyria.

30 And Hoshea the son of Elah wrought treason against Pekah the son of Remaliah, and smote him, and slew him, and reigned in his stead in the twentieth year of Jotham the son of Uzziah.

31 Concerning the rest of the acts of Pekah, and all that he did, behold, they are written in the book of the Chronicles of the kings of Israel.

32 ¶ *b*In the second year of Pekah the son of Remaliah King of Israel, began Jotham son of ¹Uzziah King of Judah to reign.

33 Five and twenty years old was he, when he began to reign, and he reigned sixteen years in Jerusalem: and his mother's name was Jerusha the daughter of Zadok.

34 And he did uprightly in the sight of the Lord: he did according ¹to all that his father Uzziah had done.

35 But the high places were not put away: *for the*

b 2 Chron. 28:6

CHAPTER 16
a Isa. 7:1

people yet offered and burnt incense in the high places: he built the highest gate of the house of the Lord.

36 Concerning the rest of the acts of Jotham, and all that he did, are they not written in the book of the Chronicles of the Kings of Judah?

37 In ¹those days the Lord began to send against Judah, Rezin the king of Aram, and ²Pekah the son of Remaliah.

38 And Jotham slept with his fathers, and was buried with his fathers in the city of David his father, and Ahaz his son reigned in his stead.

16

3 Ahaz King of Judah consecrateth his son in fire. 5 Jerusalem is besieged. 9 Damascus is taken, and Rezin slain. 11 Idolatry. 19 The death of Ahaz. 20 Hezekiah succeedeth him.

1 The seventeenth year of Pekah the son of Remaliah, ¹Ahaz the son of Jotham King of Judah began to reign.

2 Twenty years old was Ahaz, when he began to reign, and he reigned sixteen years in Jerusalem, and did not uprightly in the sight of the Lord his God, like David his father:

3 But walked in the way of the kings of Israel, yea, and made his son to ¹go through the fire, after the abominations of the heathen, whom the Lord had cast out before the children of Israel.

4 Also he offered and burnt incense in the high places, and on the hills, and under every green tree.

5 *a*Then Rezin King of Aram and Pekah son of Remaliah king of Israel came up to Jerusalem, to fight: and they besieged Ahaz, but could not overcome ¹him.

6 At the same time Rezin king of Aram restored ¹Elath to Aram, and drove the Jews from Elath: so the Aramites came to Elath, and dwelt there unto this day.

7 Then Ahaz sent ¹messengers to Tiglath-Pileser king of Assyria, saying, I am thy servant and thy son: come up, and deliver me out of the hand of the king of Aram, and out of the hand of the king of Israel which rise up against me.

8 And Ahaz took the silver and the gold that was found in the ¹house of the Lord, and in the treasures

---

15:25 ¹ Which were of the same conspiracy.
15:29 ¹ For God stirred up Pul and Tiglath-Pileser against Israel for their sins, 1 Chron. 5:26.
15:32 ¹ Or, Azariah.
15:34 ¹ He showeth that his uprightness was not such, but that he had many and great faults.
15:37 ¹ After the death of Jotham.
   ² Which slew of Judah in one day sixscore thousand fighting men, 2 Chron. 28:6, because they had forsaken the true God.
16:1 ¹ This was a wicked son of a godly father, as of him again came godly Hezekiah, and of him wicked Manasseh, save that God in the end showed him mercy. Thus we see how uncertain it is to depend

on the dignity of our fathers.
16:3 ¹ That is, offered him to Molech, or made him to pass between two fires, as the manner of the Gentiles was, Lev. 18:21; Deut. 18:10.
16:5 ¹ For the Lord preserved the city and his people for his promise sake made to David.
16:6 ¹ Which city Azariah had taken from the Aramites and fortified it, 2 Kings 14:22.
16:7 ¹ Contrary to the admonition of the Prophet Isaiah, Isa. 7:4.
16:8 ¹ Thus he spared not to spoil the Temple of God, to have succor of men and would not once lift his heart toward God to desire his help, nor yet hear his Prophet's counsel.

of the king's house, and sent a present unto the king of Assyria.

9 And the king of Assyria consented unto him: and the king of Assyria went up against Damascus. and when he had taken it, he carried the people away to Kir, and slew Rezin.

10 And king Ahaz went unto Damascus to meet Tiglath-Pileser king of Assyria: and when king Ahaz saw the altar that was at Damascus, he sent to Urijah the Priest the pattern of the altar, and the fashion of it, and all the workmanship thereof.

11 And Urijah the Priest made an altar ¹in all points like to that which King Ahaz had sent from Damascus, so did Urijah the Priest against king Ahaz came from Damascus.

12 So when the king was come from Damascus, the king saw the altar: and the king drew near to the altar, and offered ¹thereon.

13 And he burnt his burnt offering, and his meat offering, and poured his drink offering, and sprinkled the blood of his peace offerings besides the altar.

14 And set it by the brazen altar which was before the Lord, and brought it in further before the house between the altar and the house of the Lord, and set it on the ¹North side of the altar.

15 And king Ahaz commanded Urijah the Priest, and said, Upon the great altar set on fire in the morning the burnt offering, and in the even the meat offering, and the king's burnt offering and his meat offering, with the burnt offering of all the people of the land, and their meat offering, and their drink offerings: and pour thereby all the blood of the burnt offering, and all the blood of the sacrifice, and the ¹brazen altar shall be for me to inquire of God.

16 And Urijah the Priest did according to all that King Ahaz had commanded.

17 And King Ahaz brake the borders of the bases, and took the caldrons from off them, and took down the sea from the brazen oxen that were under it, and put it upon a pavement of stones.

18 And the ¹veil for the Sabbath (that they had made in the house) and the king's entry without turned he to the house of the Lord, ²because of the king of Assyria.

CHAPTER 17
ª 2 Kings 18:10

19 Concerning the rest of the acts of Ahaz, which he did, are they not written in the book of the Chronicles of the Kings of Judah?

20 And Ahaz slept with his fathers, and was buried with his fathers in the city of David, and Hezekiah his son reigned in his stead.

17

3 Hoshea King of Israel is taken, 4 And he and all his realm brought to the Assyrians, 18 for their idolatry. 25 Lions destroy the Assyrians that dwelt in Samaria. 29 Every one worshippeth the god of his nation, 35 Contrary to the commandment of God.

1 In the twelfth year of Ahaz king of Judah began Hoshea the son of Elah to reign in Samaria over Israel, and reigned nine years.

2 And he did evil in the sight of the Lord, ¹but not as the kings of Israel, that were before him.

3 And Shalmaneser king of Assyria came up against him, and Hoshea became his servant, and gave him presents.

4 And the king of Assyria found treason in Hoshea: for he had sent messengers to So king of Egypt, and brought no present unto the king of Assyria, ¹as he had done yearly: therefore the king of Assyria shut him up, and put him in prison.

5 Then the king of Assyria came up throughout all the land, and went against Samaria, and besieged it three years.

6 ¶ ªIn the ninth year of Hoshea, the king of Assyria took Samaria, and carried Israel away unto Assyria, and put them in Halah, and in Habor by the river of Gozan, and in the cities of the ¹Medes.

7 For when the children of Israel ¹sinned against the Lord their God, which had brought them out of the land of Egypt, from under the hand of Pharaoh king of Egypt, and feared other gods,

8 And walked according to the fashions of the Heathen, whom the Lord had cast out before the children of Israel, and after the manners of the kings of Israel, which they used,

9 And the children of Israel had done secretly things that were not upright before the Lord their God, and throughout all their cities had built high places, both from the tower ¹of the watch, to the

---

16:11 ¹ We see that there is no prince so wicked, be he shall find flatterers and false ministers to serve his turn.
16:12 ¹ Either offerings for peace or prosperity, or thanksgiving, as Lev. 3:1, or else meaning the morning and evening offering, Exod. 29:38, Num. 28:3, and thus he contemned the means and the altar which God had commanded by Solomon, to serve God after his own fantasy.
16:14 ¹ That is, at the right hand, as men went into the Temple.
16:15 ¹ Here he establisheth by commandment his own wicked proceedings, and doth abolish the commandment and ordinance of God.
16:18 ¹ Or, tent, wherein they lay on the Sabbath, which had served their week in the Temple, and so departed home.

² Either to flatter the King of Assyria, when he should thus see him change the ordinance of God, or else that the Temple might be a refuge for him if the King should suddenly assail his house.
17:2 ¹ Though he invented no new idolatry, or impiety as others did, yet he sought for help at the Egyptians, which God had forbidden.
17:4 ¹ For he had paid tribute for the space of eight years.
17:6 ¹ For at this time the Medes and Persians were subject to the Assyrians.
17:7 ¹ He setteth forth at length the cause of this great plague and perpetual captivity, to admonish all people, and nations to cleave to the Lord God, and only worship him for fear of like judgment.
17:9 ¹ Meaning, throughout all their borders.

defensed city,

10 And had made them images and groves upon every high hill, and under every green tree,

11 And there burnt incense in all the high places, as did the heathen, whom the Lord had taken away before them, and wrought wicked things to anger the Lord,

12 And served idols: whereof the Lord had said unto them, [b]Ye shall do no such thing,

13 Notwithstanding the Lord testified to Israel, and to Judah [1]by all the Prophets, and by all the Seers, saying, [c]Turn from your evil ways, and keep my commandments, *and* my statutes, according to all the Law, which I commanded your fathers, and which I sent to you by my servants the Prophets.

14 Nevertheless they would not obey, [d]but hardened their necks, like to the necks of their [1]fathers, that did not believe in the Lord their God.

15 And they refused his statutes and his covenant, that he made with their fathers, and his testimonies (wherewith he witnessed unto them) and they followed vanity, and became vain, and followed the heathen that were round about them: concerning whom the Lord had charged them, that they should not do like them.

16 Finally they left all the commandments of the Lord their God, and made them molten images, [e]*even* two calves, and made a grove, and worshipped all the [1]host of heaven, and served Baal.

17 And they made their sons and their daughters [1]pass through the fire, and used witchcraft and enchantments, yea, [2]sold themselves to do evil in the sight of the Lord, to anger him.

18 Therefore the Lord was exceedingly wroth with Israel, and put them out of his sight, *and* none was left but the tribe of Judah [1]only.

19 Yet Judah kept not the commandments of the Lord their God, but walked according to the fashion of Israel, which they used.

20 Therefore the Lord cast off all the seed of Israel, and afflicted them, and delivered them into the hands of spoilers, until he had cast them out of his [1]sight.

21 [1]For he cut off Israel from the house of David,

[b] Deut. 4:19
[c] Jer. 18:11
  Jer. 25:5
  Jer. 35:15
[d] Deut. 31:27
[e] Exod. 32:8
  1 Kings 12:28
[f] Jer. 25:9

and they made Jeroboam the son of Nebat King: and Jeroboam drew Israel away from following the Lord, and made them sin a great sin.

22 For the children of Israel walked in all the sins of Jeroboam, which he did, *and* departed not therefrom,

23 Until the Lord put Israel away out of his sight, as he had said [1]by all his servants the [f]Prophets, and carried Israel away out of their land to Assyria unto this day.

24 And the king of Assyria brought folk from Babylon, and from [1]Cuthah, and from Ava, and from Hamath, and from Sepharvaim, and placed them in the cities of Samaria instead of the children of Israel: so they possessed Samaria, and dwelt in the cities thereof.

25 ¶ And at the beginning of their dwelling there, they [1]feared not the Lord: therefore the Lord sent lions among them, which slew them.

26 Wherefore they spake to the king of Assyria, saying, The nations which thou hast removed and placed in the cities of Samaria, know not the manner of the God of the land: therefore he hath sent Lions among them, and behold, they slay them, because they know not the manner of the God of the land.

27 Then the king of Assyria commanded, saying, Carry thither one of the Priests whom ye brought thence, and let him go and dwell there, and teach them the manner of the God [1]of the country.

28 So one of the Priests, which they had carried from Samaria, came and dwelt in Bethel, and taught them how they should fear the Lord.

29 Howbeit, every nation made their gods, and put them in the houses of the high places, which the Samaritans had made, every nation in their cities wherein they dwelt.

30 For the men of Babylon made [1]Succoth Benoth: and the men of Cuth made Nergal, and the men of Hamath made Ashima,

31 And the Avites made Nibhaz, and Tartak: and the Sepharvites burnt their children in the fire to Adrammelech, and Anammelech the gods of Sepharvaim.

32 Thus they feared the Lord, and appointed out

17:13 [1] Hebrew, *by the hand of.*

17:14 [1] So that to allege the authority of our fathers or great antiquity, except we can prove that they were godly, is but to declare that we are the children of the wicked.

17:16 [1] That is, the sun, the moon, and stars, Deut. 4:19.

17:17 [1] Read 2 Kings 16:3.

    [2] Read of this phrase, 1 Kings 21:20, 25.

17:18 [1] No whole tribe was left but Judah, and they of Benjamin and Levi, which remained, were counted with Judah.

17:20 [1] Out of the land where he showed the greatest tokens of his presence and favor.

17:21 [1] That is, God cut off the ten tribes, 1 Kings 12:16, 20.

17:23 [1] Hebrew, *by the hand of.*

17:24 [1] Of these peoples came the Samaritans, whereof mention is so much made in the Gospel, and with whom the Jews would have nothing to do, John 4:9.

17:25 [1] That is, they served him not: therefore, lest they should blaspheme him, as though there were no God, because he chastised the Israelites, he showeth his mighty power among them by this strange punishment.

17:27 [1] That is, how to worship him: thus the wicked rather than to lose their commodities will change to all religions.

17:30 [1] Meaning that every country served that idol, which was most esteemed in that place whence they came.

Priests out of themselves for the high places, who prepared for them *sacrifices* in the houses of the high places.

33 ᵍThey ¹feared the Lord, but served their gods after the manner of the nations whom they carried thence.

34 Unto this day they do after the old manner: they neither fear God, neither do after ¹their ordinances, nor after their customs, nor after the Law, nor after the commandment, which the Lord commanded the children of Jacob ʰwhom he named Israel,

35 And with whom the Lord had made a covenant, and charged them, saying, ¹Fear none other gods, nor bow yourselves to them, nor serve them, nor sacrifice to them:

36 But fear the Lord which brought you out of the land of Egypt with great power, and a stretched out arm: him fear ye, and worship him and sacrifice to him.

37 Also keep ye diligently the statutes and the ordinances and the law, and the commandment, which he wrote for you, that ye do them continually, and fear not other gods.

38 And forget not the covenant that I have made with you, neither fear ye other gods.

39 But fear the Lord your God, and he will deliver you out of the hands of all your enemies.

40 Howbeit they obeyed not, but did after their old custom.

41 So these ¹nations feared the Lord, and served their images *also*: so *did* their children, and their children's children: as did their fathers, *so* do they unto this day.

18

4 Hezekiah king of Judah putteth down the brazen serpent, and destroyeth the idols,   7 and prospereth.   11 Israel is carried away captive.   30 The blasphemy of Sennacherib.

1 Now in the third year of Hoshea, son of Elah king of Israel, ᵃHezekiah the son of Ahaz king of Judah began to reign.

2 He was five and twenty years old when he began to reign, and reigned nine and twenty years in Jerusalem. His mother's name also was Abi the daughter of Zechariah,

3 And he did ¹uprightly in the sight of the Lord,

according to all that David his father had done.

4 He took away the high places, and brake the images, and cut down the groves, and brake in pieces the ᵇbrazen serpent that Moses had made: for unto those days the children of Israel did burn incense to it, and he called it ¹Nehushtan.

5 He trusted in the Lord God of Israel: so that after him was none like him among all the kings of Judah, neither were there any such before him.

6 For he clave to the Lord *and* departed not from him, but kept his commandments, which the Lord had commanded Moses.

7 So the Lord was with him, *and* he prospered in all things which he took in hand, also he rebelled against the king of Assyria, and served him not.

8 He smote the Philistines unto Gaza, and the coasts thereof, ¹from the watchtower unto the defensed city.

9 ¶ ᶜAnd in the fourth year of King Hezekiah, (which was the seventh year of Hoshea son of Elah king of Israel) Shalmaneser king of Assyria came up against Samaria, and besieged it.

10 And after three years they took it, *even* in the sixth year of Hezekiah: that is, ᵈthe ninth year of Hoshea king of Israel was Samaria taken.

11 Then the king of Assyria did carry away Israel unto Assyria, and put them in Halah and in Habor, *by* the river of Gozan, and in the cities of the Medes,

12 Because they would not obey the voice of the Lord their God, but transgressed his covenant: *that is*, all that Moses the servant of the Lord had commanded, and would neither obey nor do them.

13 ¶ ᵉMoreover, in the fourteenth year of king Hezekiah, Sennacherib king of Assyria came up against all the strong cities of Judah, and took them.

14 Then Hezekiah king of Judah sent unto the king of Assyria to Lachish, saying, ¹I have offended: depart from me, *and* what thou layest upon me, I will bear it. And the king of Assyria appointed unto Hezekiah king of Judah three hundred talents of silver, and thirty talents of gold.

15 Therefore Hezekiah gave all the silver that was found in the house of the Lord, and in the treasures of the king's house.

16 At the same season did Hezekiah pull off *the plates* of the doors of the Temple of the Lord,

ᵍ Ezek. 20:39
Zeph. 1:5
ʰ Gen. 32:28
1 Kings 18:34
ⁱ Judg. 6:10
Jer. 10:2

CHAPTER 18
ᵃ 2 Chron. 28:27
2 Chron. 29:1
ᵇ Num. 21:8,9
ᶜ 2 Kings 17:3
ᵈ 2 Kings 17:6
ᵉ 2 Chron. 32:1
Isa. 36:1

17:33 ¹ That is, they had a certain knowledge of God, and feared him because of the punishment, but they continued still idolaters as do the Papist, which worship both God and idols: but this is not to fear God, as appeareth verse 34.

17:34 ¹ He meaneth this by the Israelites to whom God had given his commandments.

17:41 ¹ That is, these strangers which were sent into Samaria by the Assyrians.

18:3 ¹ Although they of Judah were given to idolatry and impiety, as they of Israel were, yet God for his promise sake was merciful unto

the throne of David, and yet by his judgment toward the other, provoked to repentance.

18:4 ¹ That is, a piece of Brass: thus he calleth the serpent by contempt, which notwithstanding was set up by the word of God, and miracles were wrought by it: yet when it was abused to idolatry this good king destroyed it, not thinking it worthy to be called a serpent, but a piece of brass.

18:8 ¹ Read 2 Kings 17:9.

18:14 ¹ As his zeal was before praised, so his weakness is here set forth, that none should glory in himself.

and the pillars (which the said Hezekiah king of Judah had covered over) and gave them to the king of Assyria.

17 ¶ And the king of Assyria sent [1]Tartan, and Rabsaris, and Rabshakeh from Lachish to king Hezekiah with a great host against Jerusalem. And they went up, and came to Jerusalem, and when they were come up, they stood by the conduit of the upper pool, which is by the path of the fuller's field,

18 And called to the king. Then came out to them Eliakim the son of Hilkiah, which was steward of the house, and Shebna the chancellor, and Joah the son of Asaph the [1]recorder.

19 And Rabshakeh said unto them, Tell ye Hezekiah, I pray you, Thus saith the great king, *even* the great king of Assyria, What confidence is this wherein thou trustest?

20 Thou thinkest, Surely I have [1]eloquence, [2]*but* counsel and strength *are* for the war. On whom then doest thou trust, that thou rebellest against me?

21 Lo, thou trustest now in this broken staff of reed, *to wit*, on [1]Egypt, on which if a man lean, it will go into his hand, and pierce it: so *is* Pharaoh king of Egypt unto all that trust on him.

22 But if ye say unto me, We trust in the Lord our God, is not that he whose high places, and whose altars Hezekiah hath [1]taken away, and hath said to Judah and Jerusalem, Ye shall worship before this altar in Jerusalem?

23 Now therefore give [1]hostages to my lord the king of Assyria, and I will give thee two thousand horses, if thou be able to set riders upon them.

24 For how canst thou despise any captain of the least of my master's servants, and put thy trust on Egypt for chariots and horsemen?

25 Am I now come up without the [1]Lord to this place, to destroy it? the Lord said to me, Go up against this land, and destroy it.

26 Then Eliakim the son of Hilkiah, and Shebna, and Joah said unto Rabshakeh, Speak I pray thee, to thy servants in the [1]Aramites' language, for we understand it, and talk not with us in the Jews' tongue, in the audience of the people that are on the wall.

27 But Rabshakeh said unto them, Hath my master sent me to thy master and to thee to speak these words, and not to the men which sit on the wall, that they may eat their own dung, and drink [1]their own piss with you?

28 So Rabshakeh stood, and spake, saying, Hear the words of the great king, of the king of Assyria.

29 Thus saith the king, Let not Hezekiah deceive you: for he shall not be able to deliver you [1]out of mine hand.

30 Neither let Hezekiah make you to trust in the Lord, saying, The Lord will surely deliver us, and this city shall not be given over into the hand of the king of Assyria.

31 Hearken not unto Hezekiah: for thus saith the king of Assyria, Make [1]appointment with me, and come out to me, that every man may eat of his own vine, and every man of his own fig tree, and drink every man of the water of his own well,

32 Till [1]I come, and bring you to a land like your own land, *even* a land of wheat and wine, a land of bread and vineyards, a land of olive's oil, and honey, that ye may live and not die: and obey not Hezekiah, for he deceiveth you, saying, The Lord will deliver us.

33 Hath any of the gods of the nations delivered his land out of the hand of the king of Assyria?

34 Where is the god of Hamath, and of Arpad? where is the god of Sepharvaim, Hena and Ivah? how have they delivered Samaria out of mine hand?

35 Who are they among all the gods of the nations, that have delivered their land out of mine hand, that the [1]Lord should deliver Jerusalem out of mine hand?

36 But the people held their peace, and answered not him a word: for the king's commandment was, saying, Answer ye him not.

37 Then Eliakim the son of Hilkiah which was steward of the house, and Shebna the chancellor, and Joah the son of Asaph the recorder came to Hezekiah with their clothes rent, and told him the words of Rabshakeh.

18:17 [1] After certain years, when Hezekiah ceased to send the tribute appointed by the king of the Assyrians, he sent his captains and army against him.

18:18 [1] Or, writer of Chronicles, or secretary.

18:20 [1] Hebrew, *talk of the lips.*

[2] Thou thinkest that words will serve to persuade thy people, or to move my master.

18:21 [1] Egypt shall not only not be able to succor thee, but shall be an hurt unto thee.

18:22 [1] Thus the idolaters think that God's religion is destroyed, when superstition and idolatry are reformed.

18:23 [1] Meaning, that it was best for him to yield to the king of Assyria, because his power was so small that he had not men to furnish two thousand horses.

18:25 [1] The wicked always in their prosperity flatter themselves, that God doth favor them. Thus he speaketh to fear Hezekiah that by resisting him he should resist God.

18:26 [1] Or, Syrians.

18:27 [1] Hebrew, *the water of their feet.*

18:29 [1] Or, by his hand.

18:31 [1] Hebrew, *blessing:* meaning the conditions of peace.

18:32 [1] He maketh himself so sure, that he will not grant them truce, except they render themselves to him to be led away captives.

18:35 [1] This is an execrable blasphemy against the true God, to make him equal with the idols of other nations: therefore God did most sharply punish it.

19

6 *God promiseth by Isaiah victory to Hezekiah.* 35 *The Angel of the Lord killeth an hundred and fourscore and five thousand men of the Assyrians.* 37 *Sennacherib is killed of his own sons.*

1 And *a*when King Hezekiah heard it, he rent his clothes and put on sackcloth, and came into the house of the Lord,

2 And sent Eliakim which was the steward of the house, and Shebna the chancellor, and the Elders of the Priests clothed in sackcloth ¹to Isaiah, the Prophet the son of Amoz.

3 And they said unto him, Thus saith Hezekiah, This day is a day of tribulation and of rebuke, and blasphemy: for the children are come to ¹the birth, and there is no strength to bring forth.

4 If so be the Lord thy God hath heard all the words of Rabshakeh, whom the king of Assyria his master hath sent to rail on the living God, and to reproach him with words which the Lord thy God hath heard, then lift thou up *thy* prayer for the ¹remnant that are left.

5 ¶ So the servants of king Hezekiah came to Isaiah.

6 And Isaiah said unto them, So shall ye say to your master, Thus saith the Lord, Be not afraid of the words which thou hast heard, wherewith the servants of the king of Assyria have blasphemed me.

7 Behold, I will send a blast ¹upon him, and he shall hear a noise, and return to his own land: and I will cause him to fall by the sword in his own land.

8 ¶ So Rabshakeh returned, and found the king of Assyria fighting against Libnah: for he had heard that he was departed from Lachish.

9 ¹He heard also men say of Tirhakah king of ²Ethiopia, ³Behold, he is come out to fight against thee: he therefore departed and sent *other* messengers unto Hezekiah, saying,

10 Thus shall ye speak to Hezekiah king of Judah, and say, Let not thy ¹God deceive thee in whom thou trustest, saying, Jerusalem shall not be delivered into the hand of the king of Assyria.

11 Behold, thou hast heard what the kings of As-syria have done to all lands, how they have destroyed them: and shalt thou be delivered?

12 Have the gods of the heathen delivered them which my fathers have destroyed? *as* Gozan, and Haran, and Rezeph, and the children of Eden, which were in Telassar?

13 Where is the king of Hamath, and the king of Arpad, and the king of the city of Shepharvaim, Hena and Ivah?

14 ¶ So Hezekiah received the letter of the hand of the messengers, and read it: and Hezekiah went up into the house of the Lord, and Hezekiah spread it before the ¹Lord.

15 And Hezekiah ¹prayed before the Lord, and said, O Lord God of Israel, which dwellest between the Cherubims, thou art very God alone over all the kingdoms of the earth: thou hast made the heaven and the earth.

16 Lord ¹bow down thine ear, and hear: Lord open thine eyes and behold, and hear the words of Sennacherib, who hath sent to blaspheme the ²living God.

17 Truth it is, Lord, that the kings of Assyria have destroyed the nations and their lands,

18 And have set fire on their gods: for they were no gods, but the work of man's hands, *even* wood and stone: therefore they destroyed them.

19 Now therefore, O Lord our God, I beseech thee, save thou us out of his hand, that all the ¹kingdoms of the earth may know, that thou O Lord, art only God.

20 ¶ Then Isaiah the son of Amoz sent to Hezekiah, saying, Thus saith the Lord God of Israel, I have heard that which thou hast prayed me, concerning Sennacherib king of Assyria.

21 This is the word that the Lord hath spoken against him, O ¹Virgin daughter of Zion, he hath despised thee, *and* laughed thee to scorn: O daughter of Jerusalem, he hath shaken his head at thee.

22 Whom hast thou railed on? and whom hast thou blasphemed? and against whom hast thou exalted thy voice, and lifted up thine eyes on high?

19:2 ¹ To hear some new prophecy, and to have comfort of him.
19:3 ¹ The dangers are so great, that we can neither avenge this blasphemy, nor help ourselves no more than a woman in her travail.
19:4 ¹ Meaning, for Jerusalem which only remained of all the cities of Judah.
19:7 ¹ The Lord can with one blast blow away all the strength of man, and turn it into dust.
19:9 ¹ That is, Sennacherib.
² Or, black Moors.
³ For the Kings of Ethiopia and Egypt joined together against the King of Assyria because of his oppression of other countries.

19:10 ¹ The more near that the wicked are to their destruction, the more they blaspheme.
19:14 ¹ Before the Ark of the covenant.
19:15 ¹ He showeth what is the true refuge and succor in all dangers, to wit, to flee to the Lord by earnest prayer.
19:16 ¹ Show by effect that thou wilt not suffer thy Name to be blasphemed.
² By this title he discerneth God from all idols and false gods.
19:19 ¹ He showeth for what end the faithful desire of God to be delivered: to wit, that he may be glorified by their deliverance.
19:21 ¹ Because as yet Jerusalem had not been taken by the enemy, therefore he calleth her virgin.

even ¹against the holy One of Israel.

23 By thy messengers thou hast railed on the Lord, and said, By the multitude of my chariots I am come up to the top of the mountains, by the sides of Lebanon, and will cut down the high cedars thereof, *and* the fair fir trees thereof, and I will go into the ¹lodging of his borders, and into the forest of his ²Carmel.

24 I have dug and drunk the waters of others, and with the plant of my feet have I dried all the ¹floods closed in.

25 Hast thou not heard, how I have of old time made it, and have formed it long ago? ¹and should I now bring it, that it should be destroyed, *and laid* on ruinous heaps, *as* cities defensed?

26 Whose ¹inhabitants have small power, *and* are afraid, and confounded: they are like the grass of the field, and green herb, *or* grass on the house tops, or as corn blasted before it be grown.

27 I know thy dwelling, yea, thy going out and thy coming in, and thy fury against me.

28 And because thou ragest against me, and thy tumult is come up to mine ears, I will put mine ¹hook in thy nostrils, and my bridle in thy lips, and will bring thee back again the same way thou camest.

29 And this shall be a ¹sign unto thee, *O Hezekiah*, Thou shalt eat this year such things as grow of themselves, and the next year such as grow without sowing, and the third year sow ye and reap, and plant vineyards, and eat the fruits thereof.

30 And the remnant that is escaped of the house of Judah, shall again take ¹root downward, and bear fruit upward.

31 For out of Jerusalem shall go a remnant, and some that shall escape out of mount Zion: the ¹zeal of the Lord of hosts shall do this.

32 Wherefore thus saith the Lord, concerning the king of Assyria, He shall not enter into this city, nor shoot an arrow there, nor come before it with shield, nor cast a mount against it:

33 *But* he shall return the way he came, and shall not come into this city, saith the Lord.

b Isa. 37:36

CHAPTER 20
a 2 Chron. 32:24
Isa. 38:1

34 For I will defend this city to save it for mine own sake, and for David my servant's sake.

35 ¶ *b*And the same night the Angel of the Lord went out and smote in the camp of Assyria an hundred four score and five thousand: so when they rose early in the morning, behold, they were all dead corpses.

36 So Sennacherib king of Assyria departed, and went his way, and returned and dwelt in Nineveh.

37 And as he was in the Temple worshipping Nisroch his god, Adrammelech and Sharezer his sons ¹slew him with the sword: and they escaped into the land of Ararat, and Esarhaddon his son reigned in his stead.

20

1 Hezekiah is sick, and receiveth the sign of his health, 12 He receiveth rewards of Berodach, 13 Showeth his treasures, and is reprehended of Isaiah. 21 He dieth, and Manasseh his son reigneth in his stead.

1 About that time *a*was Hezekiah sick unto death: and the Prophet Isaiah the son of Amoz came to him, and said unto him, Thus saith the Lord, Put thine house in an order: for thou shalt die, and not live.

2 Then he turned his face to the ¹wall, and prayed to the Lord, saying,

3 I beseech thee, O lord, remember now, how I have walked before thee in truth and with a ¹perfect heart, and have done that which is good in thy sight: and Hezekiah ²wept sore.

4 ¶ And afore Isaiah was gone out into the middle of the court, the word of the Lord came to him, saying,

5 Turn again, and tell Hezekiah the captain of my people, Thus saith the Lord God of David thy father, I have heard thy ¹prayer, *and* seen thy tears: behold, I have healed thee, *and* the third day thou shalt go up to the ²house of the Lord,

6 And I will add unto thy days fifteen years, and will deliver thee and this city out of the hand of the king of Assyria, and will defend this city for mine own sake, and for David my servant's sake.

19:22 ¹ God counteth that injury done to him, and will revenge it, which is done to any of his Saints.
19:23 ¹ Meaning, Jerusalem, which Isaiah calleth the height of his borders, to wit, of Judah, Isa. 37:24.
    ² Or, pleasant country.
19:24 ¹ Or, the waters of cities besieged.
19:25 ¹ He declareth that forasmuch as he is the author and beginning of his Church, he will never suffer it utterly to be destroyed, as other cities and kingdoms.
19:26 ¹ Thus he describeth the wicked, which for a time flourish, and afterward fade and decay like flowers.
19:28 ¹ I will bridle thy rage, and turn thee to and fro as pleaseth me.
19:29 ¹ God did not only promise him the victory, but giveth him a sign to confirm his faith.

19:30 ¹ The Lord will multiply in great number, that small remnant of Judah that is escaped.
19:31 ¹ The love, that God beareth toward his Church shall overcome the counsels and enterprises of men.
19:37 ¹ This was the just judgment of God for his blasphemy, that he should be slain before that idol, whom he preferred to the living God, and by them, by whom ought by nature to have been defended.
20:2 ¹ That his mind might not be troubled.
20:3 ¹ Meaning, without all hypocrisy.
    ² Not so much for his own death, as for fear that idolatry should be restored, which he had destroyed, and so God's Name be dishonored.
20:5 ¹ Because of his unfained repentance and prayer, God turned away his wrath.
    ² To give thanks for thy deliverance.

7 Then Isaiah said, Take a ¹lump of dry figs. And they took it, and laid it on the boil, and he recovered.

8 ¶ For Hezekiah had said unto Isaiah, What *shall be* the sign that the Lord will heal me, and that I shall go up into the house of the Lord the third day?

9 And Isaiah answered, This sign shalt thou have of the Lord, that the Lord will do that he hath spoken, *Wilt thou* that the shadow go forward ten degrees, or go back ten degrees?

10 And Hezekiah answered, It is a light thing for the shadow to pass forward ten degrees: not so *then*, but let the shadow ¹go back ten degrees.

11 And Isaiah the Prophet called unto the Lord, and he brought again the shadow ten degrees back by the degrees whereby it had gone down in the ¹dial of Ahaz.

12 ᵇThe same season Berodach-Baladan the son of Baladan king of Babylon sent letters and a ¹present to Hezekiah: for he had heard how that Hezekiah was sick.

13 And Hezekiah heard them, and showed them all his treasure house, *to wit*, the silver, and the gold, and the spices, and the precious ointment, and all the house of his armor, and all that was found in his treasures: there was nothing in his house, and in all his ¹realm, that Hezekiah showed them not.

14 Then Isaiah the Prophet came unto King Hezekiah, and said unto him, What said these men? and from whence came they to thee? And Hezekiah said, They be come from a far country, *even* from Babylon.

15 Then said he, What have they seen in thine house? And Hezekiah answered, All that is in mine house have they seen: there is nothing among my treasures, that I have not showed them.

16 And Isaiah said unto Hezekiah, Hear the word of the Lord.

17 Behold, the days come, that all that is in thine house, and whatsoever thy fathers have laid up in store unto this day, ᶜshall be carried into Babylon: Nothing shall be left, saith the Lord.

18 And of thy sons, that shall proceed out of thee, *and* which thou shalt beget, shall they take away, and they shall be eunuchs in the palace of the king of Babylon.

ᵇ Isa. 39:1
ᶜ 2 Kings 24:13
  2 Kings 25:13
  Jer. 27:19

CHAPTER 21
ᵃ 2 Chron. 33:1
ᵇ Deut. 18:9
ᶜ 2 Kings 18:4
ᵈ Jer. 32:34
ᵉ 2 Sam. 7:13
ᶠ 1 Kings 8:19
  1 Kings 9:3
  2 Kings 23:27

19 Then Hezekiah said unto Isaiah, The word of the Lord, which thou hast ¹spoken, is good: for said he, Shall it not *be good* if ²peace and truth be in my days?

20 Concerning the rest of the acts of Hezekiah, and all his valiant deeds, and how he made a pool and a conduit, and brought water into the city, are they not written in the book of the Chronicles of the kings of Judah?

21 And Hezekiah slept with his fathers: and Manasseh his son reigned in his stead.

21

3 King Manasseh restoreth idolatry, 16 And useth great cruelty. 18 He dieth and Amon his son succeedeth, 23 Who is killed of his own servants. 26 After him reigneth Josiah.

1 Manasseh ᵃwas twelve years old when he began to reign, and reigned fifty and five years in Jerusalem: his mother's name also was Hephzibah.

2 And he did evil in the sight of the Lord after the abomination of the heathen, whom the ᵇLord had cast out before the children of Israel.

3 For he went back and built the high places, ᶜwhich Hezekiah his father had destroyed: and he erected up altars for Baal, and made a grove, as did Ahab king of Israel, and worshipped all the host of heaven and served them.

4 Also he ᵈbuilt altars in the house of the Lord, of the which the Lord said, ᵉIn Jerusalem will I put my Name.

5 And he built altars for all the host of the heaven in the two courts of the house of the Lord.

6 And he caused his sons ¹to pass through the fire, and gave himself to witchcraft and sorcery, and he used them that had familiar spirits and were soothsayers, and did much evil in the sight of the Lord to anger him.

7 And he set the image of the grove, that he had made in the house, whereof the Lord had said to David and to Solomon his son, ᶠIn this house and in Jerusalem, which I have chosen out of all the tribes of Israel, will I put my Name forever.

8 Neither will I make the feet of Israel move anymore out of the land, which I gave their fathers: so that they will ¹observe and do all that I have commanded them, *and* according to all the Law that my

---

20:7 ¹ He declareth that albeit God can heal without other medicines, yet he showeth that he will not have these inferior means contemned.

20:10 ¹ Let the sun go so many degrees back, that the hours may be so many the fewer in the king's dial.

20:11 ¹ Which dial was set the top of the stairs that Ahaz had made.

20:12 ¹ Moved with the favor that God showed to Hezekiah, and also because he had declared himself enemy to Sennacherib his enemy which was now destroyed.

20:13 ¹ Being moved with ambition and vain glory, and also because he seemed to rejoice in the friendship of him that was God's enemy

and an infidel.

20:19 ¹ He acknowledgeth Isaiah to be the true Prophet of God, and therefore humbleth himself to his word.

² Seeing that God hath showeth me this favor to grant me quietness during my life: for he was afraid lest the enemies should have had occasion to rejoice, if the Church had decayed in his time, because he had restored religion.

21:6 ¹ Read 2 Kings 16:3.

21:8 ¹ Therefore seeing they obeyed not the commandment of God, they were justly cast forth of that land, which they had but on condition.

servant Moses commanded them.

9   Yet they obeyed not, but Manasseh led them out of the way, to do more wickedly than did the heathen people, whom the Lord destroyed before the children of Israel.

10   Therefore the Lord spake by his servants the Prophets, saying,

11   *Because that Manasseh king of Judah hath done such abominations, and hath wrought more wickedly than all that the Amorites (which were before him) did, and hath made Judah sin also with his idols.

12   Therefore thus saith the Lord God of Israel, Behold, I will bring an evil upon Jerusalem and Judah, that who so heareth of it, both his *ears shall *tingle.

13   And I will stretch over Jerusalem the line *of Samaria, and the plummet of the house of Ahab: and I will wipe Jerusalem, as a man wipeth a dish, which he wipeth, and turneth it upside down.

14   And I will forsake the *remnant of mine inheritance, and deliver them into the hand of their enemies, and they shall be robbed and spoiled of all their adversaries,

15   Because they have done evil in my sight, and have provoked me to anger, since the time their fathers came out of Egypt until this day.

16   Moreover, Manasseh shed *innocent blood exceedingly much, till he replenished Jerusalem from corner to corner, beside his sin wherewith he made Judah to sin, and to do evil in the sight of the Lord.

17   Concerning the rest of the acts of Manasseh, and all that he did, and his sin that he sinned, are they not written in the book of the Chronicles of the kings of Judah?

18   And Manasseh slept with his fathers, and was buried in the garden of his own house, *even* in the garden of Uzza: and Amon his son reigned in his stead.

19   ¶ *Amon was two and twenty years old, when he began to reign, and he reigned two years in Jerusalem: his mother's name also was Meshullemeth the daughter of Haruz of Jotbah.

20   And he did evil in the sight of the Lord, as his father Manasseh did.

21   For he walked in all the way that his father walked in, and served the idols that his father served, and worshipped them.

g Jer. 15:4
h 1 Sam. 3:11
i 2 Chron. 33:20,21

CHAPTER 22
a 2 Chron. 34:1

22   And he forsook the Lord God of his fathers, and walked not in the *way of the Lord.

23   And the servants of Amon conspired against him, and slew the King in his own house.

24   And the people of the land slew all them that had conspired against King Amon, and the people made Josiah his son King in his stead.

25   Concerning the rest of the acts of Amon, which he did, are they not written in the book of the Chronicles of the Kings of Judah?

26   And *they buried him in his sepulcher in the garden of Uzza: and Josiah his son reigned in his stead.

22   *4 Josiah repaireth the Temple.   8 Hilkiah findeth the book of the Law, and causeth it to be presented to Josiah.   12 Who sendeth to Huldah the Prophetess to inquire the Lord's will.*

1   Josiah was *eight years old when he began to reign, and he reigned one and thirty years in Jerusalem. His mother's name also was Jedidah the daughter of Adaiah of Bozkath.

2   And he did uprightly in the sight of the Lord, and *walked in all the ways of David his father, and bowed neither to the right hand, nor to the left.

3   ¶ And in the eighteenth year of King Josiah, the king sent Shaphan the son of Azaliah the son of Meshullam the chancellor, to the house of the Lord, saying,

4   Go up to Hilkiah the high Priest, that he may *sum the silver which is brought into the house of the Lord, which the keepers of the *,*door have gathered of the people.

5   And let *them deliver it into the hand of them that do the work, and have the oversight of the house of the Lord, let them give it to them that work in the house of the Lord, to repair the decayed places of the house:

6   *To wit*, unto the artificers and carpenters, and masons, and to buy timber, and hewed stone to repair the house.

7   Howbeit, let no reckoning be made with them of the money, that is delivered into their hand: for they deal *faithfully.

8   And Hilkiah the high Priest said unto Shaphan

21:12 ¹ Meaning, that whosoever shall hear of this great plague, shall be astonished.
21:13 ¹ As I have destroyed Samaria and the house of Ahab, so will I destroy Judah.
21:14 ¹ Meaning, Judah and Benjamin, which were only left of the rest of the tribes.
21:16 ¹ The Hebrews write that he slew Isaiah the Prophet, who was his father-in-law.
21:22 ¹ That is, according to his commandments.
21:26 ¹ Or, he buried him, to wit, Josiah his son.
22:2 ¹ His zeal was prophesied of, and his name mentioned by Iddo the

Prophet, more than three hundred years before, 1 Kings 13:2, and being but eight years old, he sought the God of his father David, 2 Chron. 34:3.
22:4 ¹ Or, coin, as verse 9.
     ² Or, vessel.
     ³ Certain of the Priests were appointed to this office, as 2 Kings 12:9.
22:5 ¹ From the time of Joash for the space of 244 years, the Temple remained without reparation through the negligence of the priests, this declareth, that they that have a charge and execute it not, ought to have it taken from them.
22:7 ¹ So God provided him of faithful servants, seeing he went about so zealously to set forth the work of God.

the chancellor, I have found the ¹book of the Law in the house of the Lord: and Hilkiah gave the book to Shaphan, and he read it.

9 So Shaphan the chancellor came to the king, and brought him word again, and said, Thy servants have ¹gathered the money that was found in the house, and have delivered it unto the hands of them that do the work, and have the oversight of the house of the Lord.

10 Also Shaphan the chancellor showed the king, saying, Hilkiah the Priest hath delivered me a book. And Shaphan read it before the King.

11 And when the king had heard the words of the book of the Law, he rent his clothes.

12 Therefore the king commanded Hilkiah the Priest, and Ahikam the son of Shaphan, and Achbor the son of Michaiah, and Shaphan the chancellor, and Asahiah the king's servant, saying,

13 Go ye and ¹inquire of the Lord for me and for the people, and for all Judah concerning the words of this book that is found: for great is the wrath of the Lord that is kindled against us, because our fathers have not obeyed the words of this book, to do according unto all that which is written therein for us.

14 ¶ So Hilkiah the Priest, and Ahikam, and Achbor, and Shaphan, and Asahiah went unto Huldah the Prophetess the wife of Shallum, the son of Tikvah, the son of Harhas keeper of the wardrobe: (and she dwelt in Jerusalem in the ¹college) and they communed with her.

15 And she answered them, Thus saith the Lord God of Israel, Tell the man that sent you to me,

16 Thus saith the Lord, Behold, I will bring evil upon this place, and on the inhabitants thereof, even all the words of the book which the king of Judah hath read,

17 Because they have forsaken me, and have burnt incense unto other gods, to anger me with all the ¹works of their hands: my wrath also shall be kindled against this place, and shall not be quenched:

18 But to the king of Judah, who sent you to inquire of the Lord, so shall ye say unto him, Thus

CHAPTER 23
ᵃ 2 Chron. 34:30

saith the Lord God of Israel, The words that thou hast heard, *shall come to pass.*

19 But because thine heart did ¹melt, and thou hast humbled thyself before the Lord when thou heardest what I spake against this place, and against the inhabitants of the same, *to wit,* that it should be destroyed and accursed, and hast rent thy clothes, and wept before me, I have also heard it, saith the Lord.

20 Behold therefore, I will gather thee to thy fathers, and thou shalt be put in thy grave in ¹peace, and thine eyes shall not see all the evil which I will bring upon this place. Thus they brought the king word again.

23 *2 Josiah readeth the Law before the people. 3 He maketh a covenant with the Lord. 4 He putteth down the idols, after he had killed their Priests. 22 He keepeth Passover. 24 He destroyeth the conjurers. 29 He was killed in Megiddo. 30 And his son Jehoahaz reigneth in his stead. 33 After he was taken, his son Jehoiakim was made King.*

1 Then ᵃthe King ¹sent, and there gathered unto him all the Elders of Judah and of Jerusalem.

2 And the king went up into the house of the Lord, with all the men of Judah, and all the inhabitants of Jerusalem with him, and the Priests and Prophets, and all the people both small and great: and he read in their ears all the words of the book of the covenant, which was found in the house of the Lord.

3 And the king stood by ¹the pillar, and made a ²covenant before the Lord, that they should walk after the Lord, and keep his commandments, and his testimonies, and his statutes, with all *their* heart, and with all *their* soul, that they might accomplish the words of this covenant written in this book. And all the people stood to the covenant.

4 Then the king commanded Hilkiah the high ¹Priest, and the Priests of the second order, and the keepers of the door, to bring out of the temple of the Lord all the vessels that were made for Baal, and for the grove, and for all the host of heaven, and he burnt them without Jerusalem in the fields of Kidron, and carried ²the powder of them into Bethel.

22:8 ¹ This was the copy that Moses left them, as appeareth, 2 Chron. 34:14, which either by the negligence of the Priests had been lost, or else by the wickedness of idolatrous kings had been abolished.
22:9 ¹ Hebrew, *melted.*
22:13 ¹ Meaning, to some Prophet whom God revealeth the knowledge of things unto, as Jer. 21:8, though at other times they inquired the Lord by Urim and Thummim.
22:14 ¹ Or the house of doctrine, which was near to the Temple, and where the learned assembled to entreat the Scriptures, and the doctrine of the Prophets.
22:17 ¹ The [works] of man's hand here signify all that man inventeth beside the word of God, which are abominable in God's service.
22:19 ¹ Meaning, that he did repent, as they that do not repent, are

said to harden their heart, Ps. 95:8.
22:20 ¹ Whereupon we may gather that the anger of God is ready against the wicked, when God taketh his servants out of this world.
23:1 ¹ Because he saw the great plagues of God that were threatened, he knew no more speedy way to avoid them, than to turn to God by repentance which cannot come but of faith, and faith by hearing of the word of God.
23:3 ¹ Where the king had his place, 2 Kings 11:14.
   ² As Joshua did, Josh. 24:22, 25.
23:4 ¹ Meaning, them which were next in dignity to the high Priest.
   ² In contempt of that altar, which Jeroboam had there built to sacrifice to his calves.

5 And he put down the ¹Chemarims, whom the kings of Judah had founded to burn incense in the high places, *and* in the cities of Judah and about Jerusalem, and also them that burnt incense unto Baal, to the sun and to the moon, and to the planets, and to all the host of heaven.

6 And he brought out the ¹grove from the Temple of the Lord, without Jerusalem unto the valley of Kidron, and burnt it in the valley Kidron, and stamped it to powder, and cast the dust thereof upon the ²graves of the children of the people.

7 And he brake down the houses of the Sodomites, that were in the house of the Lord, where the women wove hangings for the grove.

8 Also he brought all the priests out of the cities of Judah, and defiled the high places where the Priests had burnt incense, *even* from Geba to Beersheba, and destroyed the high places of the gates, that were in the entering in of the gate of Joshua the governor of the city, which was at the left hand of the gate of the city.

9 Nevertheless the Priests of the high places ¹came not up to the altar of the Lord in Jerusalem, save only they did eat of the unleavened bread among their brethren.

10 He defiled also ¹Topheth, which was in the valley of the children of Hinnom, that no man should make his son or his daughter pass through the fire to Molech.

11 He put down also the ¹horses that the Kings of Judah had given to the sun at the entering in of the house of the Lord, by the chamber of Nethan-Melech the eunuch, which was *ruler* of the suburbs, and burnt the chariots of the sun with fire.

12 And the altars that were on the top of the chamber of Ahaz, which the kings of Judah had made, and the altars which Manasseh had made in the two courts of the house of the Lord did the king break down, and hasted thence, and cast the dust of them in the ¹brook Kidron.

13 Moreover the King defiled the high places that

marginal references:
ᵇ 1 Kings 11:7
ᶜ 2 Chron. 35:1
ᵈ Exod. 12:3
Deut. 16:2

were before Jerusalem, and on the right hand of the ¹mount of corruption (which ᵇSolomon the king of Israel had built for Ashtoreth the idol of the Sidonians, and for Chemosh the idol of the Moabites, and for Milcom the abomination of the children of Ammon)

14 And he brake the images in pieces, and cut down the groves, and filled their places with the bones of men.

15 Furthermore ¹the altar that was at Bethel, *and* the high place made by Jeroboam the son of Nebat, which made Israel to sin, both this altar and also the high place, brake he down, and burnt the high place, *and* stamped it to powder, and burnt the grove.

16 And as Josiah turned himself, he spied the graves that were in the mount, and sent and took the bones out of the graves, and burnt them upon the altar and polluted it, according to the word of the Lord, that the ¹man of God proclaimed, which cried the same words.

17 Then he said, What title is that which I see? And the men of the city said unto him, *It is* the sepulcher of the man of God, which came from Judah, and told these things that thou hast done to the altar of Bethel.

18 Then said he, Let him alone: let none remove his bones. So his bones were saved with the bones of the ¹Prophet that came from Samaria.

19 Josiah also took away all the houses of the high places, which were in the cities of Samaria, which the kings of Israel had made to anger *the Lord*, and did to them according to all the facts that he had done in Bethel.

20 And he sacrificed all the Priests of the high places that were there upon the altars, and burnt men's bones upon them, and returned to Jerusalem.

21 ¶ Then the king commanded all the people, saying, 'Keep the Passover unto the Lord your God, ᵈas it is written in the book of this covenant.

22 And there was no Passover holden ¹like that from the days of the Judges that judged Israel, nor

---

23:5 ¹ Meaning, the priests of Baal, which were called Chemarims, either because they wore black garments, or else were smoked with burning incense to idols.

23:6 ¹ He removed the grove which idolaters for devotion had planted near unto the Temple, contrary to the commandment of the Lord, Deut. 16:21, or as some read, the similitude of a grove which was hung in the Temple.

² Both in contempt of the idols and reproach of them which had worshipped them in their lives.

23:9 ¹ Because that those that had forsaken the Lord to serve idols, were not meet to minister in the service of the Lord for the instruction of others.

23:10 ¹ Which was a valley near to Jerusalem, and signifieth a taboret, because they smote on the taboret while their children were burning, that their cry should not be heard, Lev. 18:21,

where after Josiah commanded carrions to be cast in contempt thereof.

23:11 ¹ The idolatrous kings had dedicated horses and chariots to the sun, either to carry the image thereof about as the heathen did, or else to sacrifice them as a sacrifice most agreeable.

23:12 ¹ Or, valley.

23:13 ¹ That was the mount of olives, so called because it was full of idols.

23:15 ¹ Which Jeroboam had built in Israel, 1 Kings 12:28, 29.

23:16 ¹ According to the prophecy of Iddo, 1 Kings 13:2.

23:18 ¹ Meaning, the Prophet which came after him, and caused him to eat contrary to the commandment of the Lord, which were both two buried in one grave, 1 Kings 13:31.

23:22 ¹ For the multitude and zeal of the people with the great preparation.

in all the days of the kings of Israel, and of the kings of Judah.

23 And in the eighteenth year of King Josiah was this Passover celebrated to the Lord in Jerusalem.

24 Josiah also took away them that had familiar spirits, and the soothsayers, and the images, and the idols, and all the abominations that were espied in the land of Judah and in Jerusalem, to perform the words of the ⁱLaw, which were written in the book that Hilkiah the Priest found in the house of the Lord.

25 Like unto him was there no king before him, that turned to the Lord with all his heart, and with all his soul, and with all his might according to all the Law of Moses, neither after him arose there any like him.

26 Notwithstanding the Lord turned not from the ¹fierceness of his great wrath wherewith he was angry against Judah, because of all the provocations wherewith Manasseh had provoked him.

27 Therefore the Lord said, I will put Judah also out of my sight, as I have put away Israel, and will cast off this city Jerusalem, which I have chosen, and the house whereof I said, ⁱMy name shall be there.

28 Concerning the rest of the acts of Josiah, and all that he did, are they not written in the book of the Chronicles of the kings of Judah?

29 ᵍIn his days Pharaoh Necho king of Egypt ¹went up against the king of Assyria to the river Perath. And king Josiah went against him, whom when *Pharaoh* saw, he slew him at Megiddo.

30 Then his servants carried him dead from Megiddo, and brought him to Jerusalem, and buried him in his own sepulcher. And the people of the land took Jehoahaz the son of Josiah, and anointed him, and made him king in his father's stead.

31 ʰJehoahaz *was* three and twenty years old when he began to reign, and reigned three months in Jerusalem. His mother's name also was Hamutal the daughter of Jeremiah of Libnah.

32 And he did evil in the sight of the Lord, according to all that his ¹fathers had done.

33 And Pharaoh Necho put him in bonds ¹at Riblah in the land of Hamath ²while he reigned in Jerusalem, and put the land to a tribute of an hundred talents of silver, and a talent of gold.

34 ¶ And Pharaoh Necho made Eliakim the son of Josiah king instead of Josiah his father, and

ᵉ Lev. 20:27
Deut. 18:11
ᶠ 1 Kings 8:29
1 Kings 9:3
2 Kings 2:7
ᵍ 2 Chron. 35:20
ʰ 2 Chron. 36:1,2

CHAPTER 24
ᵃ 2 Kings 20:17
2 Kings 23:27

turned his name to Jehoiakim, and took Jehoahaz away, which when he came to Egypt, died there.

35 And Jehoiakim gave the silver and the gold to Pharaoh, and taxed the land to give the money, according to the commandment of Pharaoh: he levied of every man of the people of the land, according to his value, silver and gold to give unto Pharaoh Necho.

36 Jehoiakim was five and twenty years old, when he began to reign, and he reigned eleven years in Jerusalem. His mother's name also was Zebudah the daughter of Pedaiah of Rumah.

37 And he did evil in the sight of the Lord, according to all that his fathers had done.

24

1 *Jehoiakim made subject to Nebuchadnezzar, rebelleth.* 3 *The cause of his ruin and all Judah's.* 6 *Jehoiachin reigneth.* 15 *He, and his people are carried unto Babylon.* 17 *Zedekiah is made king.*

1 In his ¹days came Nebuchadnezzar king of Babylon up, and Jehoiakim became his servant three years: afterward he turned, and rebelled against him.

2 And the Lord sent against him bands of the Chaldeans, and bands of the Aramites, and bands of the Moabites, and bands of the Ammonites, and he sent them against Judah to destroy it, ᵃaccording to the word of the Lord, which he spake by his servants the Prophets.

3 Surely by the ¹commandment of the Lord came this upon Judah, that he might put them out of his sight for the sins of Manasseh, according to all that he did,

4 And for the innocent blood that he shed, (for he filled Jerusalem with innocent blood) therefore the Lord would not pardon it.

5 Concerning the rest of the acts of Jehoiakim, and all that he did, are they not written in the book of the Chronicles of the kings of Judah?

6 So Jehoiakim ¹slept with his fathers, and Jehoiachin his son reigned in his stead.

7 ¶ And the king of Egypt came no more out of his land: for the king of Babylon had taken from the river of Egypt, unto the river ¹Perath, all that pertained to the king of Egypt.

8 ¶ Jehoiachin *was* eighteen years old, when he began to reign, and reigned in Jerusalem three

---

23:26 ¹ Because of the wicked heart of the people, which would not turn unto him by repentance.

23:29 ¹ Because he passed through his country, he feared lest he would have done him harm, and therefore would have stayed him, yet he consulted not with the Lord, and therefore was slain.

23:32 ¹ Meaning, the wicked kings before.

23:33 ¹ Which was Antioch in Syria, called also Hamath.
   ² Or, that he should not reign.

24:1 ¹ In the end of the third year of his reign, and in the beginning of the fourth, Dan. 1:1.

24:3 ¹ Though God used these wicked tyrants to execute his just judgments, yet they are not to be excused, because they proceeded of ambition and malice.

24:6 ¹ Not that he was buried with his fathers, but he died in the way, as they led him prisoner toward Babylon, read Jer. 22:19.

24:7 ¹ Or, Euphrates.

months. His mother's name also *was* Nehushta, the daughter of Elnathan of Jerusalem.

9 And he did evil in the sight of the Lord, according to all that his father had done.

10 [b]In that time came the servants of Nebuchadnezzar king of Babylon up against Jerusalem: so the city was besieged.

11 And Nebuchadnezzar king of Babylon came against the city, and his servants did besiege it.

12 Then Jehoiachin the king of Judah [1]came out against the king of Babylon, he, and his mother and his servants, and his princes, and his eunuchs: and the king of Babylon took him in the eighth year [2]of his reign.

13 [c]And he carried out thence all the treasures of the house of the Lord, and the treasures of the king's house, and brake all the vessels of gold which Solomon king of Israel had made in the Temple of the Lord, as the Lord had said.

14 And he carried away all Jerusalem, and all the princes, and all the strong men of war, *even* ten thousand into captivity, and all the workmen, and cunning men: so none remained saving the poor people of the land.

15 [d]And he carried away Jehoiachin into Babylon, and the king's mother, and the king's wives, and his eunuchs, and the mighty of the land, carried he away into captivity from Jerusalem to Babylon,

16 And all the men of war, *even* seven thousand, and carpenters, and locksmiths a thousand: all that were strong and apt for war, did the king of Babylon bring to Babylon captives.

17 ¶ [e]And the king of Babylon made Mattaniah his uncle king in his stead, and changed his name to Zedekiah.

18 Zedekiah was one and twenty years old, when he began to reign, and he reigned eleven years in Jerusalem. His mother's name also was Hamutal the daughter of Jeremiah of Libnah.

19 And he did evil in the sight of the Lord, according to all that Jehoiakim had done.

20 Therefore certainly the wrath of the Lord was against Jerusalem and Judah, until he cast them out of his [1]sight. And Zedekiah rebelled against the king of Babylon.

Cross references (center column):

[b] Dan. 1:1
[c] 2 Kings 20:17
Isa. 39:6
[d] 2 Chron. 36:10
Esther 2:6
[e] Jer. 37:1
Jer. 52:1

CHAPTER 25
[a] Jer. 39:1
Jer. 52:4
[b] 2 Kings 20:17
Jer. 27:19,20

25

1 *Jerusalem is besieged of Nebuchadnezzar, and taken.* 7 *The sons of Zedekiah are slain before his eyes, and after are his own eyes put out.* 11 *Judah is brought to Babylon.* 25 *Gedaliah is slain.* 27 *Jehoiachin is exalted.*

1 [a]And in the [1]ninth year of his reign, the [2]tenth *month, and* tenth day of the month Nebuchadnezzar king of Babylon came, he, and all his host against Jerusalem, and pitched against it, and they built [3]forts against it round about it.

2 So the city was besieged unto the eleventh year of King Zedekiah.

3 And the ninth *day* of the month the famine was [1]sore in the city, so that there was no bread for the people of the land.

4 Then the city was broken up, and all the men of war *fled* by night, by the way of the [1]gate, *which is* between two walls that was by the king's garden: now the Chaldeans *were* by the city round about: *and the king* went by the way of the wilderness.

5 But the army of the Chaldeans pursued after the king, and took him in the deserts of Jericho, and all his host was scattered from him.

6 Then they took the king, and carried him up to the king of Babylon to Riblah, where they [1]gave judgment upon him.

7 And they slew the sons of Zedekiah before his eyes, and put out the eyes of Zedekiah, and bound him in chains, and carried him to Babylon.

8 And in the fifth month, *and* [1]seventh *day* of the month, which was the nineteenth year of king Nebuchadnezzar king of Babylon, came Nebuzaradan [2]chief steward *and* servant of the king of Babylon, to Jerusalem,

9 And burnt the house of the Lord, and the king's house, and all the houses of Jerusalem, and all the great houses burnt he with fire.

10 And all the army of the Chaldeans that were with the chief steward, brake down the walls of Jerusalem round about.

11 And the rest of the people that were left in the city, and those that were fled and [1]fallen to the king of Babylon, with the remnant of the multitude, did Nebuzaradan chief steward carry away captive.

12 But the chief steward left of the poor of the land to dress the vines, and to till the land.

13 [b]Also the pillars of brass that were in the house of the Lord, and the bases, and the brazen Sea that

---

24:12 [1] That is, yielded himself unto him by the counsel of Jeremiah.
[2] In the reign of the king of Babylon.
24:20 [1] Out of Jerusalem and Judah into Babylon.
25:1 [1] That is, of Zedekiah.
[2] Which the Hebrews call Tebet, and it containeth part of December, and part of January.
[3] Or, a mount.

25:3 [1] Insomuch that the mothers did eat their children, Lam. 4:10.
25:4 [1] Which was a postern door, or some secret gate to issue out at.
25:6 [1] Or, condemned him for his perjury and treason, 2 Chron. 36:13.
25:8 [1] Jeremiah writeth, Jer. 52:12, the tenth day, because the fire continued from the seventh day to the tenth.
[2] Or, captain of the guard.
25:11 [1] While the siege endured.

was in the house of the Lord, did the Chaldeans break, and carried the brass of them to Babylon.

14 The pots [1]also and the besoms, and the instruments of music, and the incense dishes, and all the vessels of brass that they ministered in, took they away.

15 And the ash pans, and the basins, *and all* that was of gold, and that was of silver, took the chief steward away,

16 With the two pillars, one Sea and the bases, which Solomon had made for the house of the Lord: the brass of all these vessels was without weight.

17 ᶜThe height of the one pillar was eighteen cubits, and the chapiter thereon *was* brass, and the height of the chapiter *was* with network three cubits, and pomegranates upon the chapiter round about, all of brass: and likewise *was* the second pillar with the network.

18 And the chief steward took Seraiah the chief Priest, and Zephaniah the [1]second Priest, and the three keepers of the door.

19 And out of the city he took an Eunuch that had the oversight of the men of war, and [1]five men of them that were in the King's presence, which were found in the city, and Sopher captain of the host, who mustered the people of the land, and threescore men of the people of the land, that were found in the city.

20 And Nebuzaradan the chief steward took them, and brought them to the king of Babylon to Riblah.

21 And the king of Babylon smote them, and slew them at Riblah in the land of Hamath. So Judah was carried away captive out of his own land.

22 ᵈHowbeit, there remained people in the land of Judah, whom Nebuchadnezzar king of Babylon

left, and made Gedaliah the son of Ahikam the son of Shaphan ruler over them.

23 Then when all the captains of the host and *their* men heard, that the king of Babylon had made Gedaliah governor, they came to Gedaliah to Mizpah, to wit, Ishmael the son of Nethaniah, and Johanan the son of Careah, and Seraiah the son of Tanhumeth the Netophathite, and Jaazaniah the son of Maachathi, they and their men.

24 And Gedaliah [1]sware to them, and to their men, and said unto them, Fear not to be the servants of the Chaldeans: dwell in the land, and serve the king of Babylon, and ye shall be well.

25 ᵉBut in the seventh month Ishmael the son of Nethaniah the son of Elishama, of the king's seed, came, and ten men with him, and smote Gedaliah, and he died, and so did he the Jews, and the Chaldeans that were with him at Mizpah.

26 Then all the people both small and great, and the captains of the army arose, and came to [1]Egypt: for they were afraid of the Chaldeans.

27 Notwithstanding in the seven and thirtieth year after [1]Jehoiachin King of Judah was carried away, in the twelfth month *and* the seven and twentieth *day* of the month, Evil-Merodach king of Babylon in the year that he began to reign, did lift up the head of Jehoiachin king of Judah out of the prison,

28 And spake kindly to him, and set his throne above the throne of the kings that were with him in Babylon,

29 And changed his prison garments: and he did continually eat bread before him, all the days of his life.

30 And his [1]portion *was* a continual portion given him by the king, every day a certain, all the days of his life.

ᶜ 1 Kings 7:15
Jer. 52:21
1 Chron. 3:15
ᵈ Jer. 40:5,6
ᵉ Jer. 41:1

25:14 [1] Of these read Exod. 27:3.

25:18 [1] That is, one appointed to succeed in the high Priest's room, if he were sick or else otherwise letted.

25:19 [1] Jeremiah maketh mention of seven, but here he speaketh of them that were the chiefest.

25:24 [1] That is, he did exhort them in the Name of the Lord, according to Jeremiah's counsel, to submit themselves to Nebuchadnezzar,

seeing it was the revealed will of the Lord.

25:26 [1] Contrary to Jeremiah's counsel, Jer. 40–43.

25:27 [1] Thus long was he, his wife and his children in Babylon, whom Nebuchadnezzar's son, after his father's death preferred to honor: thus by God's providence the seed of David was preserved even unto Christ.

25:30 [1] Meaning, that he had an ordinary in the court.

THE FIRST BOOK OF THE

¹CHRONICLES,

OR ²PARALIPOMENON

1 1 The genealogy of Adam and Noah until Abra-ham.   27 And from Abraham to Esau.   35 His children.   43 Kings and Dukes came of him.

CHAPTER 1
ᵃ Gen. 10:2
ᵇ Gen. 10:8
ᶜ Gen. 10:22
Gen. 11:10
ᵈ Gen. 11:20
Gen. 17:6
Gen. 21:2
ᵉ Gen. 25:13
ᶠ Gen. 25:4
ᵍ Gen. 21:2
ʰ Gen. 36:9

1 Adam, ¹Seth, Enosh,

2 Cainan, Mahalalel, Jared,

3 Enoch, Methuselah, Lamech,

4 Noah, ¹Shem, Ham, and Japheth.

5 ¶ ᵃThe sons of Japheth were Gomer, and Magog, and Madai, and Javan, and Tubal, and Meshech, and Tiras.

6 And the sons of Gomer, Ashkenaz, and ¹Diphath and Togarmah.

7 Also the sons of Javan, Elishah and Tarshishah, Kittim, and ¹Dodanim.

8 ¶ The sons of Ham were Cush, and Mizraim, Put and Canaan.

9 And the sons of Cush, Seba, and Havilah, and Sabta, and Raama, and Sabtecha. Also the sons of Raama were Sheba and Dedan.

10 And Cush begat ¹ᵇNimrod, who began to be mighty in the earth.

11 And Mizraim begat Ludim and Anamim, Lehabim, and Naphtuhim:

12 Pathrusim also, and Casluhim, of whom came the Philistines, and Caphtorim.

13 Also Canaan begat Sidon his firstborn, and Heth,

14 And the Jebusite, and the Amorite, and the Girgashite,

15 And the Hivite, and the Arkite, and the Sinite,

16 And the Arvadite, and the Zemarite, and the Hamathite.

17 ¶ ᶜThe sons of Shem were Elam and Asshur, and Arphaxad, and Lud, and ¹Aram, and Uz, and Hul, and Gether, and Meshech.

18 Also Arphaxad begat Shelah, and Shelah begat ¹Eber.

19 Unto Eber also were born two sons: the name of the one was Peleg: for in his days was the earth divided, and his brother's name was Joktan.

20 Then Joktan begat Almodad and Sheleph, and Hazarmaveth and Jerah,

21 And Hadoram, and Uzal and Diklah,

22 And Ebal, and Abimael, and Sheba,

23 And Ophir, and Havilah, and Jobab: all these were the sons of Joktan.

24 ¹Shem, ²Arphaxad, Shelah,

25 Eber, Peleg, Reu,

26 Serug, Nahor, Terah,

27 ᵈAbram, which is Abraham.

28 ¶ The sons of Abraham were Isaac, and Ishmael.

29 These are their generations. ᵉThe eldest son of Ishmael was Nebajoth, and Kedar, and Adbeel, and Mibsam,

30 Mishma, and Dumah, Massa, ¹Hadad, and Tema,

31 Jetur, Naphish and Kedemah: these are the sons of Ishmael.

32 ¶ And Keturah Abraham's ¹concubine bare sons, Zimran, and Jokshan, and Medan, and Midian, and Ishbak, and Shuah: and the sons of Jokshan, Sheba, and Dedan.

33 And the sons of Midian were Ephah, and Epher, and Hanoch and Abida, and Eldaah: ᶠAll these are the sons of Keturah.

34 And ᵍAbraham begat Isaac: the sons of Isaac, Esau and Israel.

35 ¶ The sons of Esau were ¹ᵇEliphaz, Reuel, and Jeush, and Jaalam, and Korah.

Title ¹ Hebrew, words of days.
  ² Or, things omitted, to wit, in the books of the kings.
1:1 ¹ Meaning, that Seth was Adam's son, and Enosh Seth's son.
1:4 ¹ It had been sufficient to have named Shem of whom came Abraham and David, but because the world was restored by these three, mention is also made of Ham and Japheth.
1:6 ¹ Or, Riphath.
1:7 ¹ Or, Rodanim.
1:10 ¹ Who did first lift up himself above others.
1:17 ¹ Of whom came the Syrians, and therefore they are called

Aramites throughout all the Scripture.
1:18 ¹ Of him came the Hebrews, which were afterward called Israelites of Israel, which was Jacob: and Jews of Judah because of the excellency of that tribe.
1:24 ¹ He repeateth Shem again because he would come to the stock of Abraham.
  ² Who came of Shem, and of him Shelah.
1:30 ¹ Or, Hadar.
1:32 ¹ Read Gen. 25:4.
1:35 ¹ These were born of three divers mothers, read Gen. 36:4.

36 The sons of Eliphaz, Teman, and Omar, ¹Zephi, and Gatam, Kenaz, and ²Timna, and Amalek.

37 The sons of Reuel, Nahath, Zerah, Shammah and Mizzah.

38 And the sons of ¹Seir, Lotan, and Shobal, and Zibeon, and Anah, and Dishon, and Ezer, and Dishan.

39 And the sons of Lotan, Hori, and Homam, and Timna Lotan's sister.

40 The sons of Shobal were Alian, and Manahath, and Ebal, Shephi, and Onam. And the sons of Zibeon, Ajah and Anah.

41 The son of Anah was Dishon. And the sons of Dishon, Hamran, and Eshban, and Ithran, and Cheran.

42 The sons of Ezer were Bilhan, and Zaavan, and Jaakan. The sons of Dishan were Uz, and Aran.

43 ¶ And these were the ¹Kings that reigned in the land of Edom, before a King reigned over the children of Israel, to wit, Bela the son of Beor, and the name of his city was Dinhabah.

44 Then Bela died, and Jobab the son of Zerah of ¹Bozrah reigned in his stead.

45 And when Jobab was dead, Husham of the land of the Temanites reigned in his stead.

46 And when Husham was dead, Hadad the son of Bedad, which smote Midian in the field of Moab, reigned in his stead, and the name of his city was Avith.

47 So Hadad died, and Samlah of Masrekah reigned in his stead.

48 And Samlah died, and Saul of Rehoboth by the river reigned in his stead.

49 And when Saul was dead, Baal-Hanan the son of Achbor reigned in his stead.

50 And Baal-Hanan died, and Hadad reigned in his stead, and the name of his city was ¹Pai, and his wife's name Mehetabel the daughter of Matred the daughter of Mezahab.

51 Hadad died also, and there were dukes in Edom, duke Timnah, duke ¹Aliah, duke Jetheth,

52 Duke Aholibamah, duke Elah, duke Pinon,

53 Duke Kenaz, duke Teman, duke Mibzar,

54 Duke Magdiel, duke Iram: these were the dukes of Edom.

CHAPTER 2
ᵃ Gen. 29:32
Gen. 30:5
Gen. 35:28
ᵇ Gen. 38:3
Gen. 46:12
1 Chron. 4:1
ᶜ Gen. 38:29
Matt. 1:3
ᵈ Ruth 4:18
ᵉ Josh. 7:1
ᶠ 1 Sam. 16:19
1 Sam. 17:12
ᵍ Exod. 31:2

2

3 The genealogy of Judah unto Jesse the father of David.

1 These are the sons of Israel, ᵃReuben, Simeon, Levi, and Judah, Issachar, and Zebulun,

2 Dan, Joseph, and Benjamin, Naphtali, Gad, and Asher.

3 ᵇThe sons of ¹Judah, Er, and Onan, and Shelah. These three were born to him of the daughter of Shua the Canaanite: but Er the eldest son of Judah was evil in the sight of the Lord, and he slew him.

4 ᶜAnd Tamar his daughter-in-law bare him Perez, and Zerah: so all the sons of Judah were five.

5 ᵈThe sons of Perez, Hezron, and Hamul.

6 The sons also of Zerah were ¹Zimri, and ²Ethan, and Heman, and Calcol, and Dara, which were five in all.

7 And the son of Carmi, ¹ᵉAchar that troubled Israel, transgressing in the thing excommunicate.

8 The son also of Ethan, Azariah.

9 And the sons of Hezron that were born unto him, Jerahmeel, and ¹Ram and Chelubai.

10 And Ram begat Amminadab, and Amminadab begat Nahshon ¹prince of the children of Judah,

11 And Nahshon begat Salma, and Salma begat Boaz,

12 And Boaz begat Obed, and Obed begat ¹Ishai,

13 ᶠAnd Jesse begat his eldest son Eliab, and Abinadab the second, and ¹Shimea the third,

14 Nethanel the fourth, Raddai the fifth,

15 Ozem the sixth, and David the seventh.

16 Whose sisters were Zeruiah and Abigail. And the sons of Zeruiah, Abishai, and Joab, and Asahel.

17 And Abigail bare Amasa: and the father of Amasa was Jether an Ishmaelite.

18 ¶ And ¹Caleb the son of Hezron begat Jerioth of Azubah his wife, and her sons are these, Jesher, and Shobab, and Ardon.

19 And when Azubah was dead, Caleb took unto him Ephrath, which bare him Hur.

20 ᵍAnd Hur begat Uri, and Uri begat Bezalel.

21 And afterward came Hezron to the daughter of Machir the father of ¹Gilead, and took her when he was threescore years old, and she bare him Segub.

22 And Segub begat Jair, which had three and

1:36 ¹ Or, Zepho.
   ² Which was Eliphaz's concubine, read Gen. 36:12.
1:38 ¹ He is also called Seir the Horite, which inhabited mount Seir, Gen. 36:20.
1:43 ¹ He maketh mention of the Kings that came of Esau according to God's promise made to Abraham concerning him, that kings should come of him. These eight kings reigned one after another in Idumea unto the time of David, who conquered their country.
1:44 ¹ Which was the principal city of the Edomites.
1:50 ¹ Or, Pau.
1:51 ¹ Or, Aluah.

2:3 ¹ Though Judah was not Jacob's eldest son, yet he first beginneth at him, because he would come to the genealogy of David, of whom came Christ.
2:6 ¹ Or, Zabdi.
   ² Of these read 1 Kings 4:31.
2:7 ¹ Or, Achan.
2:9 ¹ Whom Saint Matthew calleth Aram, Matt. 1:3.
2:10 ¹ That is, chief of the family.
2:12 ¹ Or, Jesse.
2:13 ¹ Or, Shammah.
2:18 ¹ Who was called Chelubai the son of Hezron, verse 9.
2:21 ¹ Who was prince of mount Gilead, read Num. 32:40.

twenty cities in the land of Gilead.

23 And Geshur with Aram took the towns of Jair ¹from them, *and* Kenath and the towns thereof, *even* threescore cities. All these were the sons of Machir the father of Gilead.

24 And after that Hezron was dead at ¹Caleb Ephrathah, then Abijah Hezron's wife bare him also Ashhur the ²father of Tekoa.

25 And the sons of Jerahmeel the eldest son of Hezron were Ram the eldest, then Bunah, and Oren and Ozem *and* Ahijah.

26 Also Jerahmeel had another wife named Atarah, which was the mother of Onam.

27 And the sons of Ram the eldest son of Jerahmeel were Maaz, and Jamin and Eker.

28 And the sons of Onam were Shammai and Jada. And the sons of Shammai, Nadab and Abishur.

29 And the name of the wife of Abishur *was* called Abihail, and she bare him Ahban and Molid.

30 The sons also of Nadab *were* Seled and Appaim: but Seled died without children.

31 And the son of Appaim *was* Ishi, and the son of Ishi, Sheshan, and the son of Sheshan, ¹Ahlai.

32 And the sons of Jada the brother of Shammai *were* Jether and Jonathan: but Jether died without children.

33 And the sons of Jonathan *were* Peleth and Zaza. These were the sons of Jerahmeel.

34 And Sheshan had no sons, but daughters. And Sheshan had a servant that was an Egyptian named Jarha.

35 And Sheshan gave his daughter to Jarha his servant to wife, and she bare him Attai.

36 And Attai begat Nathan, and Nathan begat Zabad,

37 And Zabad begat Ephlal, and Ephlal begat Obed,

38 And Obed begat Jehu, and Jehu begat Azariah,

39 And Azariah begat Helez, and Helez begat Eleasah,

40 And Eleasah begat Sismai, and Sismai begat Shallum,

41 And Shallum begat Jekamiah, and Jekamiah begat Elishama.

b Josh. 15:17

42 Also the sons of Caleb the brother of Jerahmeel, *were* Mesha his eldest son, which was the ¹father of Ziph: and the sons of Mareshah the father of Hebron.

43 And the sons of Hebron *were* Korah and Tappuah, and Rekem and Shema.

44 And Shema begat Raham the father of Jorkoam: and Rekem begat Shammai.

45 The son also of Shammai *was* Maon: and Maon *was* the father of Beth Zur.

46 And Ephah a ¹concubine of Caleb bare Haran and Moza, and Gazez: Haran also begat Gazez.

47 The sons of Jahdai *were* Regem, and Jotham, and Geshan, and Pelet, and Ephah, and Shaaph.

48 Caleb's concubine Maachah bare Sheber and Tirhanah.

49 She bare also Shaaph the father of Madmannah, *and* Sheva the father of Machbenah, and the father of Gibea. *b*And Achsah was Caleb's daughter.

50 These were the sons of Caleb the son of Hur the eldest son of Ephrathah, Shobal the father of Kirjath Jearim.

51 Salma the father of Bethlehem, *and* Hareph the father of Beth Gader.

52 And Shobal the father of Kirjath Jearim had sons, and he ¹was the overseer of half Manuhoth.

53 And the families of Kirjath Jearim *were* the Ithrites, and the Puthites, and the Shumathites, and the Mishraites: of them came the Zorathites, and the Eshtaolites.

54 The sons of Salma of Bethlehem, and the Netophathites, the ¹crowns of the house of Joab, and ²half the Manahethites *and* the Zorites.

55 And the families of the ¹Scribes dwelling at Jabez, the Tirathites, the Shimeathites, the Suchathites, which are the ²Kenites, that came of Hammath the father of the house of Rechab.

3 1 *The genealogy of David, and his posterity unto the sons of Josiah.*

1 These also were the sons of ¹David, which were born unto him in Hebron: the eldest Amnon of Ahinoam, the Jezreelitess: the second ²Daniel of Abigail the Carmelitess:

2:23 ¹ That is, the Geshurites and Syrians took the towns from Jair's children.

2:24 ¹ Which was a town named of the husband and wife, called also Bethlehem Ephrathah.
　² Meaning, the chief and prince.

2:31 ¹ Who died while his father was alive, and therefore it is said, verse 34, that Sheshan had no sons.

2:42 ¹ That is, the chief governor or prince of the Ziphims, because the prince ought to have a fatherly care and affection toward his people.

2:46 ¹ This difference was between the wife and the concubine, that the wife was taken with certain solemnities of marriage, and her children did inherit: the concubine had no solemnities in marriage,

neither did her children inherit, but had a portion of goods or money given them.

2:52 ¹ Or, he that saw the half, because the prince ought to oversee his subjects.

2:54 ¹ Meaning, the chief and principle.
　² Or, the Zorites, the half of the Manahethites.

2:55 ¹ Which were men learned and expert in the law.
　² Read Num. 10:29; Judg. 1:16.

3:1 ¹ He returneth to the genealogy of David, to show that Christ came of his stock.
　² Which 2 Sam. 3:3, is called Chileab, born of her that was Nabal's wife the Carmelite.

2 The third Absalom the son of Maacah daughter of Talmai King of Geshur: the fourth Adonijah the son of Haggith:

3 The fifth Shephatiah of Abital, the sixth Ithream by Eglah his wife.

4 *These* six were born unto him in Hebron: and there he reigned seven years and six months: and in Jerusalem he reigned three and thirty years.

5 And these four were born unto him in Jerusalem, Shimea, and Shobab, and Nathan, and Solomon of [1]Bathshua the daughter of Ammiel:

6 Ibhar also, and [1]Elishama, and Eliphelet,

7 And Nogah, and Nepheg, and Japhia,

8 And Elishama, and Eliada, and Eliphelet, nine *in number*.

9 *These are* all the sons of David, besides the sons of the concubines, and Tamar their sister.

10 ¶ And Solomon's son *was* Rehoboam, whose son *was* Abijah, *and* Asa his son, *and* Jehoshaphat his son,

11 *And* Joram his son, *and* Ahaziah his son, *and* Joash his son,

12 *And* Amaziah his son, *and* Azariah his son, *and* Jotham his son,

13 *And* Ahaz his son, *and* Hezekiah his son, *and* Manasseh his son,

14 *And* Amon his son, *and* Josiah his son.

15 ¶ And of the sons of Josiah, the [1]eldest *was* [2]Johanan, the second Jehoiakim, the third Zedekiah, *and* the fourth Shallum.

16 And the sons of Jehoiakim *were* Jeconiah his son, *and* Zedekiah his son.

17 And the sons of Jeconiah, Assir *and* Shealtiel his son:

18 Malchiram also and Pedaiah, and Shenazzar, Jecamiah, Hoshama, and Nedabiah.

19 And the sons of Pedaiah *were* [1]Zerubbabel, and Shimei: and the sons of Zerubbabel *were* Meshullam, and Hananiah, and Shelomith their sister,

20 And Hashubah, and Ohel, and Berechiah, and Hasadiah, *and* Jushab-Hesed, five *in number*.

21 And the sons of Hananiah *were* Pelatiah, and Jeshaiah, the sons of Rephaiah, the sons of Arnan, the sons of Obadiah, the sons of Shechaniah.

22 And the son of Shechaniah *was* Shemaiah: and the sons of Shemaiah *were* Hattush and Igal, and

CHAPTER 4
[a] Gen. 38:29
Gen. 46:12
1 Chron. 2:4

Bariah, and Neariah, and Shaphat, [1]six.

23 And the sons of Neariah *were* Elioenai, and Hezekiah, and Azrikam, three.

24 And the sons of Elioenai *were* Hodaviah, and Eliashib, and Pelaiah, and Akkub, and Johanan, and Delaiah, and Anani, seven.

4 *1 The genealogy of the sons of Judah.   5 Of Asher,   9 Of Jabez and his prayer,   11 Of Chelub,   24 And Simeon: their habitations.   38 And conquests.*

1 The [1]sons of Judah *were* [a]Perez, Hezron, and Carmi, and Hur, and Shobal.

2 And Reaiah the son of Shobal begat Jahath, and Jahath begat Ahumai, and Lahad: these are the families of the Zorathites.

3 And these were of the father of Etam, Jezreel, and Ishma and Idbash: and the name of their sister *was* Hazelelponi.

4 And Penuel *was* the father of Gedor, and Ezer the father of Hushah: these are the sons of Hur the [1]eldest son of Ephrathah, the father of Bethlehem.

5 But Ashhur the father of Tekoa had two wives, Helah, and Naarah.

6 And Naarah bare him Ahuzzam, and Hepher, and Temeni and Haahashtari: these were the sons of Naarah.

7 And the sons of Helah *were* Zereth, Zohar and Ethnan.

8 Also Koz begat Anub, and Zobebah, and the families of Aharhel the son of Harum.

9 But Jabez was more honorable than his brethren: and his mother called his name [1]Jabez, saying, Because I bare him in sorrow.

10 And Jabez called on the God of Israel, saying, If thou wilt bless me in deed, and enlarge my coasts, and [1]*if* thine hand be with me, and thou wilt cause me *to be delivered* from evil, that I be not hurt. And God granted the thing that he asked.

11 ¶ And Chelub the brother of Shuhah begat Mehir, which was the father of Eshton.

12 And Eshton begat Beth-Rapha, and Paseah, and Tehinnah the father of the city of Ir-Nahash: these are the men of Rechah.

13 ¶ And the sons of Kenaz *were* Othniel, and Seraiah, and the son of Othniel, Hathath.

3:5 [1] Called also Bathsheba the daughter of Eliam: for they gave them divers names.

3:6 [1] Elishama, or Elishua, 2 Sam. 5:15, and Eliphelet died, and David named those sons, which were next born, by the same names: in the book of Kings his children are mentioned which were alive, and here both they that were alive and dead.

3:15 [1] So called because he was preferred to the dignity royal before his brother Jehoiakim which was the elder.

[2] Or, Jehoahaz, 2 Kings 23:30.

3:19 [1] St. Matthew saith that Zerubbabel was son of Shealtiel, mean-

ing, that he was his nephew according to the Hebrew speech: for he was Pedaiah's son.

3:22 [1] So that Shemaiah was Shechaniah's natural son, and the other five his nephews, and in all were six.

4:1 [1] Meaning, they came of Judah, as nephews and kinsmen: for only Perez was his natural son.

4:4 [1] The firstborn of his mother, and not the eldest son of his father.

4:9 [1] Otherwise called Othniel, Judg. 1:13.

4:10 [1] It is to be understood, that then he would accomplish his vow which he made.

14 And Meonothai begat Ophrah. And Seraiah begat Joab the [1]father of the valley of craftsmen: for they were craftsmen.

15 ¶ And the sons of Caleb the son of [1]Jephunneh were Iru, Elah, and Naam. And the son of Elah was Kenaz.

16 And the sons of Jehallelel were Ziph, and Ziphah, Tiria, and Asarel.

17 And the sons of Ezrah were Jether and Mered, and Epher, and Jalon, and he begat Miriam, and Shammai, and Ishbah the father of Eshtemoa.

18 Also his [1]wife Jehudijah bare Jered the father of Gedor, and Heber the father of Sochoh, and Jekuthiel the father of Zanoah: and these are the sons of Bithiah the daughter of Pharaoh [2]which Mered took.

19 And the sons of the wife of Hodiah, the sister of Naham the father of Keilah were the Garmites, and Eshtemoa the Maachathite.

20 And the sons of Shimon were Amnon and Rinnah, Ben-Hanan and Tilon. And the sons of Ishi were Zoheth, and Ben-Zoheth.

21 ¶ [b]The sons of Shelah, the son of Judah were Er the father of Lecah, and Laadah the father of Mareshah, and the families of the households of them that wrought fine linen in the house of Ashbea.

22 And Jokim, and the men of Chozeba and Joash, and Saraph, which had the dominion in Moab, and [1]Jashubi-Lehem. These also are ancient things.

23 These were porters, and dwelt among plants and hedges: [1]there they dwelt with the king for his work.

24 ¶ [c]The sons of Simeon were Nemuel, and Jamin, Jarib, Zerah, and [1]Shaul.

25 Whose son was Shallum, and his son Mibsam, and his son Mishma.

26 And the sons of Mishma, Hamuel was his son, Zacchur his son, and Shimei his son.

27 And Shimei had sixteen sons, and six daughters, but his brethren had not many children, neither was all their family like to the children of Judah in multitude.

28 And they dwelt at [1]Beersheba, and at Moladah, and at Hazar Shual,

29 And at Bilhah, and at Ezem, and at Tolad,

30 And at Bethuel, and at Hormah, and at Ziklag,

31 And at Beth Marcaboth, and at Hazar Susim, at Beth Biri, and at Shaaraim: these were their cities

Marginal references:
[b] Gen. 38:1,3,8
[c] Gen. 46:10 Exod. 6:15

CHAPTER 5
[a] Gen. 35:22 Gen. 49:4

unto the reign of [1]David.

32 And their towns were Etam, and Ain, Rimmon, and Tochen, and Ashan, five cities.

33 And all their towns that were round about these cities unto Baal, these are their habitations and the declaration of their genealogy,

34 And Meshobab, and Jamlech, and Joshah the son of Amaziah,

35 And Joel and Jehu the son of Joshibiah, the son of Seraiah, the son of Asiel,

36 And Elioenai, and Jaakobah, and Jeshohaiah, and Asaiah, and Adiel, and Jesimiel, and Benaiah,

37 And Ziza the son of Shiphi, the son of Allon, the son of Jedaiah, the son of Shimri, the son of Shemaiah.

38 These were famous Princes in their families, and increased greatly their father's houses.

39 And they [1]went to the entering in of Gedor, even unto the East side of the valley, to seek pasture for their sheep.

40 And they found fat pasture and good, and a wide land both quiet and fruitful: for they of Ham had dwelt there before.

41 And these described by name, came in the days of Hezekiah king of Judah, and smote their tents, and the inhabitants that were found there, and destroyed them utterly unto this day, and dwelt in their room, because there was pasture there for their sheep.

42 And besides these, five hundred men of the sons of Simeon went to mount Seir, and Pelatiah, and Neariah, and Rephaiah, and Uzziel the sons of Ishi were their captains.

43 And they smote the rest of Amalek that had [1]escaped, and they dwelt there unto this day.

5   *1 The birthright taken from Reuben and given to the sons of Joseph. 3 The genealogy of Reuben, 11 and Gad, 23 and of the half tribe of Manasseh.*

1 The sons also of Reuben the eldest son of Israel (for he was the eldest, [a]but had defiled his father's bed, therefore his birthright was given unto the [1]sons of Joseph the son of Israel, so that the genealogy is not reckoned after his birthright.

2 For Judah prevailed above his brethren, and of him came [1]the prince, but the birthright was Joseph's)

4:14 [1] The Lord of that valley where the artificers did work.
4:15 [1] Called also Esron.
4:18 [1] Or, she bare, meaning, the second wife of Ezra.
    [2] Or, of whom he had Mered.
4:22 [1] Or, of the inhabitants of Lehem.
4:23 [1] They were king David's gardeners, and served him in his works.
4:24 [1] His son Ohad is here omitted.
4:28 [1] These cities belonged of Judah, Josh. 19:2, and were given to

the tribe of Simeon.
4:31 [1] Then David restored them to the tribe of Judah.
4:39 [1] For the tribe of Simeon was so great in number, that in the time of Hezekiah they sought new dwellings unto Gedor, which is in the tribe of Dan.
4:43 [1] And were not slain by Saul and David.
5:1 [1] Because they were made two tribes, they had a double portion.
5:2 [1] That is, he was the chiefest of all the tribes according to Jacob's prophecy, Gen. 49:8, and because Christ should come of him.

3 ᵇThe sons of Reuben the eldest son of Israel, *were* Hanoch and Pallu, Hezron and Carmi.

4 The sons of Joel, Shemaiah his son, Gog his son, *and* Shimei his son,

5 Micah his son, Reaiah his son, *and* Baal his son,

6 Beerah his son: whom Tiglath-Pileser king of Assyria ¹carried away, he was a prince of the Reubenites.

7 And when his brethren in their families reckoned the genealogy of their generations, Jeiel and Zechariah *were* the chief,

8 And Bela the son of Azaz, the son of Shema, the son of Joel, which dwelt in ¹Aroer even unto Nebo and Baal Meon.

9 Also Eastward he inhabited unto the entering in of the wilderness from the river ¹Perath: for they had much cattle in the land of Gilead.

10 And in the days of Saul they warred with the ¹Hagrites, which fell by their hands: and they dwelt in their tents in all the East parts of Gilead.

11 ¶ And the children of Gad dwelt over against them in the land of Bashan, unto Salcah.

12 Joel *was* the chiefest, and Shapham the second, but Jaanai and Shaphat *were* in Bashan.

13 And their brethren of the house of their fathers *were* Michael, and Meshullam, and Sheba, and Jorai, and Jachan, and Zia and Eber, seven.

14 These are the children of Abihail, the son of Huri, the son of Jaroah, the son of Gilead, the son of Michael, the son of Jeshishai, the son of Jahdo, the son of Buz.

15 Ahi the son of Abdiel, the son of Guni *was* chief of the household of their fathers.

16 And they dwelt in Gilead in ¹Bashan, and in the towns thereof, and in all the suburbs of Sharon by their borders.

17 All these were reckoned by genealogies in the days of Jotham King of Judah, and in the days of Jeroboam king of Israel.

18 ¶ The sons of Reuben and of Gad, and of half the tribe of Manasseh of those that were valiant men, able to bear shield and sword, and to draw a bow exercised in war, were four and forty thousand, seven hundred and threescore, that went out to the war.

19 And they made war with the Hagrites, with ¹Jetur, and Naphish, and Nodab.

20 And they were ¹helped against them, and the Hagrites were delivered into their hand, and all that were with them: for they cried to God in the battle,

Side references (left column):
ᵇ Gen. 46:9
Exod. 6:14
Num. 26:5
ᶜ 2 Kings 18:11

CHAPTER 6
ᵃ Gen. 46:11
Exod. 6:16
1 Chron. 23:12
ᵇ Lev. 10:1
ᶜ Num. 20:29

and he heard them, because they trusted in him.

21 And they led away their cattle, *even* their camels fifty thousand, and two hundred and fifty thousand sheep, and two thousand asses, and of ¹persons an hundred thousand.

22 For many fell down wounded, because the war *was* of God. And they dwelt in their steads until the ¹captivity.

23 And the children of the half tribe of Manasseh dwelt in the land, from Bashan unto ¹Baal Hermon, and Senir, and unto mount Hermon: *for they* increased.

24 And these were the heads of the households of their fathers, even Epher and Ishi, and Eliel and Azriel, and Jeremiah, and Hodaviah, and Jahdiel, strong men, valiant *and* famous, heads of the households of their fathers.

25 But they transgressed against the God of their fathers, and went a whoring after the gods of the people of the land, whom God had destroyed before them.

26 And the God of Israel ¹stirred up the spirit of Pul king of Assyria, and the spirit of Tiglath-Pileser king of Assyria, and he carried them away: *even* the Reubenites, and the Gadites, and the half tribe of Manasseh, and brought them unto ᶜHalah and Habor, and Hara, and to the river Gozan, unto this day.

6 1 *The genealogy of the sons of Levi.* 31 *Their order in the ministry of the Tabernacle.* 49 *Aaron and his sons Priests.* 54, 57 *Their inhabitations.*

1 The sons of Levi *were* Gershon, Kohath, and Merari.

2 ᵃAnd the sons of Kohath, Amram, Izhar, and Hebron, and Uzziel.

3 And the children of Amram, Aaron, and Moses and Miriam. And the sons of Aaron, ᵇNadab, and Abihu, and ᶜEleazar, and Ithamar.

4 Eleazar begat Phinehas, Phinehas begat Abishua,

5 And Abishua begat Bukki, and Bukki begat Uzzi,

6 And Uzzi begat Zerahiah, and Zerahiah begat Meraioth.

7 Meraioth begat Amariah, and Amariah begat Ahitub,

8 And Ahitub begat ¹Zadok, and Zadok begat Ahimaaz,

5:6 ¹ To wit, in the time of Uzziah King of Israel, 2 Kings 15:23.
5:8 ¹ These places were beyond Jordan toward the East in the land given to the Reubenites.
5:9 ¹ Or, Euphrates.
5:10 ¹ The Ishmaelites that came of Hagar Abraham's concubine.
5:16 ¹ Both the whole country and one peculiar city were called Bashan.
5:19 ¹ These twain were the sons of Ishmael, Gen. 25:15.
5:20 ¹ To wit, by the Lord that gave them the victory.

5:21 ¹ Hebrew, *souls of men*.
5:22 ¹ Meaning, the captivity of the ten tribes under Tiglath Pileser.
5:23 ¹ Otherwise called Baal Gad.
5:26 ¹ Thus God stirred up the wicked, and used them as instruments to execute his just judgment against sinners, although they were led with malice and ambition.
6:8 ¹ Which was high priest after that Abiathar was deposed, according to the prophecy of Eli the Priest, 1 Sam. 2:31, 35.

9 And Ahimaaz begat Azariah, and Azariah begat Johanan,

10 And Johanan begat Azariah (it was he that was ¹Priest in the house that Solomon built in Jerusalem.)

11 And Azariah begat Amariah, and Amariah begat Ahitub,

12 And Ahitub begat Zadok, and Zadok begat Shallum,

13 And Shallum begat Hilkiah, and Hilkiah begat Azariah,

14 And Azariah begat Seraiah, and Seraiah begat Jehozadak,

15 And ¹Jehozadak departed when the Lord carried away into captivity Judah and Jerusalem by the hand of Nebuchadnezzar.

16 ¶ The sons of Levi were Gershon, Kohath and Merari.

17 And these be the names of the sons of Gershon, Libni, and Shimei.

18 And the sons of Kohath were Amram, and Izhar, and Hebron and Uzziel.

19 The sons of Merari, Mahli and Mushi: and these are the families of Levi concerning their fathers.

20 Of Gershon, Libni his son, Jahath his son, Zimmah his son,

21 Joah his son, Iddo his son, Zerah his son, Jeatherai his son.

22 The sons of Kohath, ¹Amminadab his son, ᵈKorah his son, Assir his son,

23 Elkanah his son, and Ebiasaph his son, and Assir his son,

24 Tahath his son, Uriel his son, Uzziah his son, and Shaul his son,

25 And the sons of Elkanah, Amasai, and Ahimoth.

26 Elkanah, the sons of Elkanah, Zophai his son, and Nahath his son,

27 Eliab his son, Jeroham his son, Elkanah his son,

28 And the sons of Samuel, the eldest ¹Vasheni, then Abijah.

29 ¶ The sons of Merari were Mahli, Libni his son, Shimei his son, Uzzah his son,

30 Shimea his son, Haggiah his son, Asaiah his son.

31 And these be they whom David set for to sing in

ᵈ Num. 16:1

the house of the Lord, after that the Ark had ¹rest.

32 And they ministered before the Tabernacle, even the Tabernacle of the Congregation with ¹singing, until Solomon had built the house of the Lord in Jerusalem: then they continued in their office, according to their custom.

33 And these ministered with their children: of the sons of Kohath, Heman a singer, the son of Joel, the son of Samuel,

34 The son of Elkanah, the son of Jeroham, the son of Eliel, the son of Toah,

35 The son of Zuph, the son of Elkanah, the son of Mahath, the son of Amasai,

36 The son of Elkanah, the son of Joel, the son of Azariah, the son of Zephaniah,

37 The son of Tahath, the ¹son of Assir, the son of Ebiasaph, the son of Korah,

38 The son of Izhar, the son of Kohath, the son of Levi, the son of Israel,

39 And his ¹brother ²Asaph stood on his right hand: and Asaph was the son of Berachiah, the son of Shimea,

40 The son of Michael, the son of Baaseiah, the son of Malchijah,

41 The son of Ethni, the son of Zerah, the son of Adaiah,

42 The son of Ethan, the son of Zimmah, the son of Shimei,

43 The son of Jahath, the son of Gershon, the son of Levi.

44 And their brethren the sons of Merari were on the left hand, even Ethan the son of Kishi, the son of Abdi, the son of Malluch,

45 The son of Hashabiah, the son of Amaziah, the son of Hilkiah,

46 The son of Amzi, the son of Bani, the son of Shamer,

47 The son of Mahli, the son of Mushi, the son of Merari, the son of Levi.

48 ¶ And their ¹brethren the Levites were ²appointed unto all the service of the Tabernacle of the house of God,

49 But Aaron and his sons burnt incense upon the altar of burnt offering, and on the altar of incense, for all that was to do in the most holy place, and to make an atonement for Israel according to all that Moses the servant of God had commanded.

6:10 ¹ And did valiantly resist king Uzziah, who would have usurped the Priest's office, 2 Chron. 26:17, 18.

6:15 ¹ That is, he was led into captivity with his father Seraiah the high Priest, 2 Kings 25:18.

6:22 ¹ Who seemeth to be called Izhar, Exod. 6:21.

6:28 ¹ Who is also called Joel, 1 Sam. 8:2 and 1 Chron. 6:33.

6:31 ¹ After it was brought to that place where the Temple should be built and was no more carried to and fro.

6:32 ¹ Read Exod. 27:21.

6:37 ¹ Or, nephews.

6:39 ¹ Or, cousin.

² Meaning, the cousin of Heman, verse 33.

6:48 ¹ The Levites are called the singers brethren because they came of the same stock.

² Read Num. 4:4.

50 These are also the sons of Aaron, Eleazar his son, Phinehas his son, Abishua his son,

51 Bukki his son, Uzzi his son, Zerahiah his son,

52 Meraioth his son, Amariah his son, Ahitub his son,

53 Zadok his son, *and* Ahimaaz his son.

54 ¶ And these are the ¹dwelling places of them throughout their towns and coasts, *even* of the sons of Aaron for the family of the Kohathites, for the ²lot was theirs.

55 So they gave them ¹Hebron in the land of Judah and the suburbs thereof round about it.

56 But the field of the city, and the villages thereof they gave to Caleb the son of Jephunneh.

57 And to the sons of Aaron they gave the cities *of Judah* for ¹refuge, *even* Hebron and Libnah with their suburbs, and Jattir, and Eshtemoa with their suburbs,

58 And ¹Hilen with her suburbs, *and* Debir with her suburbs,

59 And Ashan and her suburbs, and Beth Shemesh and her suburbs:

60 ¶ And of the tribe of Benjamin, Geba and her suburbs, and ¹Alemeth with her suburbs, and Anathoth with her suburbs: all their cities *were* thirteen cities by their families.

61 And unto the sons of ¹Kohath the remnant of the family of the tribe, *even* of the half tribe of the half of Manasseh, by lot ten cities.

62 And to the sons of Gershon according to their families out of the tribe of Issachar, and out of the tribe of Asher, and out of the tribe of Naphtali, and out of the tribe of Manasseh in Bashan, thirteen cities.

63 Unto the sons of Merari according to their families out of the tribe of Reuben, and out of the tribe of Gad, and out of the tribe of Zebulun, by lot twelve cities.

64 Thus the children of Israel gave to the Levites cities with their suburbs.

65 And they gave by lot out of the tribe of the children of Judah, and out of the tribe of the children of Simeon, and out of the tribe of the children of Benjamin, these cities, which they called by *their* names.

66 And they of the families of the sons of Kohath, had cities *and* their coasts out of the tribe of Ephraim.

67 ᵉAnd they gave unto them cities of refuge, Shechem in mount Ephraim, and her suburbs, and Gezer and her suburbs,

68 Jokmeam also and her suburbs, and Beth Horon with her suburbs,

69 And Aijalon and her suburbs, and Gath Rimmon and her suburbs.

70 And out of the half tribe of Manasseh, ¹Aner and her suburbs, and ²Bileam and her suburbs, for the families of the remnant of the sons of Kohath.

71 Unto the sons of ¹Gershon out of the family of the half tribe of Manasseh, Golan in Bashan, and her suburbs, and ²Ashtaroth with her suburbs.

72 And out of the tribe of Issachar, ¹Kedesh and her suburbs, Daberath and her suburbs,

73 ¹Ramoth also and her suburbs, and ²Anem with her suburbs.

74 And out of the tribe of Asher, Mashal and her suburbs, and Abdon and her suburbs,

75 And ¹Hukok and her suburbs, and Rehob and her suburbs.

76 And out of the tribe of Naphtali, Kedesh in Galilee and her suburbs, and ¹Hammon and her suburbs, and ²Kirjathaim and her suburbs.

77 Unto the rest of the children of Merari *were given* out of the tribe of Zebulun ¹Rimmon and her suburbs, ²Tabor and her suburbs,

78 And on the other side Jordan *by* Jericho, *even* on the Eastside of Jordan, out of the tribe of Reuben, ʲBezer in the wilderness with her suburbs, and Jahzah with her suburbs,

79 And Kedemoth with her suburbs, and Mephaath with her suburbs.

80 And out of the tribe of Gad Ramoth in Gilead with her suburbs, and Mahanaim with her suburbs,

81 And Heshbon with her suburbs, and Jazer with her suburbs.

7 1 *The genealogy of Issachar, Benjamin,* 13 *Naphtali,* 14 *Manasseh,* 20 *Ephraim,* 30 *and Asher.*

Marginal: ᵉ Josh 21:21 / ᶠ Josh. 20:8 Josh. 21:36

6:54 ¹ Or, cities which were given to the Levites.
² They were first appointed, and prepared for.
6:55 ¹ Which was also called Kirjath Arba, Gen. 23:2; Josh. 21:11.
6:57 ¹ That he that had killed a man might flee thereunto for succor till his cause were tried, Deut. 19:2.
6:58 ¹ Which Joshua calleth Holon, Josh. 15:51 and 21:15.
6:60 ¹ Or, Almon, Josh. 21:18.
6:61 ¹ That is, they gave a portion to the Kohathites, which were the remnant of the tribe of Levi, out of the half tribe of Manasseh and out of Ephraim, verse 66.
6:70 ¹ Or, Tanach, Josh. 21:25.
² Or, Gath Rimmon.
6:71 ¹ Who in the first verse is called also Gershon.
² Or, Be Eshterah, Josh. 21:27.
6:72 ¹ Or, Kishion, Josh. 21:28.
6:73 ¹ Or, Jarmuth, Josh. 21:29.
² Or, En Gannim, Josh. 21:29.
6:75 ¹ Or, Helkath, Josh. 21:31.
6:76 ¹ Or, Hammoth Dor, Josh. 21:32.
² Or, Kartan, Josh. 21:32.
6:77 ¹ Or, Jokneam.
² Or, Kartah, Josh. 21:34.

1 And the sons of Issachar *were* Tola and [1]Puah, [2]Jashub, and Shimron, four,

2 And the sons of Tola, Uzzi, and Rephaiah and Jeriel, and Jahmai, and Jibsam, and Shemuel, heads in the households of their fathers. Of Tola *were* valiant men of war in their generations, [1]whose number *was* in the days of David two and twenty thousand, and six hundred.

3 And the son of Uzzi *was* Izrahiah, and the sons of Izrahiah, Michael, and Obadiah, and Joel, and Ishiah, [1]five men all princes.

4 And with them in their generations after the household of their fathers *were* bands of men of war for battle six and thirty thousand: for they had many wives and children.

5 And their [1]brethren among all the families of Issachar *were* valiant men of war, reckoned in all by their genealogies fourscore and seven thousand.

6 ¶ The *sons* of Benjamin *were* Bela, and Becher, and [1]Jediael, [2]three.

7 And the sons of Bela, Ezbon, and Uzzi, and Uzziel, and Jerimoth, and Iri five heads of the households of their fathers, valiant men of war, and were reckoned by their genealogies, two and twenty thousand and thirty and four.

8 And the sons of Becher, Zemirah, and Joash, and Eliezer, and Elioenai, and Omri, and Jerimoth, and Abijah, and Anathoth, and Alemeth: all these were the sons of Becher.

9 And they were numbered by their genealogies according to their generations, and the chief of the houses of their fathers, valiant men of war, twenty thousand and two hundred.

10 And the son of Jediael *was* Bilhan, and the sons of Bilhan, Jeush, and Benjamin, and Ehud, and Chenaanah, and Zethan, and Tharshish, and Ahishahar.

11 All these were the sons of Jediael, chief of the fathers, valiant men of war seventeen thousand and two hundred, marching in battle array to the war.

12 And Shuppim, and Huppim were the sons of [1]Ir, *but* Hushim *was* the son [2]of [3]another.

13 ¶ The sons of Naphtali, Jahziel, and Guni, and Jezer, and [1]Shallum [2]of the sons of Bilhah.

CHAPTER 7
a Num. 26:29,31
Josh. 17:1

14 The son of Manasseh *was* Asriel whom she bare unto him, *but* his concubine of Aram bare Machir the *a*father of Gilead.

15 And Machir took to wife *the sister* of Huppim and Shuppim, and the name of their sister was Maachah. And the name of the second *son* was Zelophehad, and Zelophehad had had daughters.

16 And Maachah the wife of Machir bare a son, and called his name [1]Peresh, and the name of his brother was Sheresh: and his sons *were* Ulam and Rakem.

17 And the son of Ulam *was* Bedan. These were the sons of Gilead the son of Machir, the son of Manasseh.

18 And [1]his sister Hammoleketh bare Ishhod, and Abiezer, and Mahlah.

19 And the sons of Shemida *were* Ahian, and Shechem, and Likhi, and Aniam.

20 ¶ The sons also of Ephraim *were* Shuthelah, and Bered his son, and Tahath his son, and his son Eladah, and Tahath his son,

21 And Zabad his son, and Shuthelah his son, and Ezer, and Elead: and the men of [1]Gath that were born in the land, slew them, because they came down to take away their cattle.

22 Therefore Ephraim their father mourned many days, and his [1]brethren came to comfort him.

23 And when he went in to his wife, she conceived, and bare him a son, and he called his name Beriah, because affliction was in his house.

24 And his [1]daughter *was* Sheerah, which built Beth Horon the nether, and the upper, and Uzzen Sheerah.

25 And Rephah *was* his [1]son, and Resheph, and Telah his son, and Tahan his son,

26 Laadan his son, Ammihud his son, Elishama his son,

27 Nun his son, Joshua his son.

28 And their possessions and their habitations *were* Bethel, and the villages thereof, and Eastward Naaran, and Westward Gezer with the villages thereof, Shechem also and the villages thereof, unto [1]Ayyah, and the villages thereof,

29 And by the places of the children of Manasseh,

7:1 [1] Or, Punah.
  [2] Who also is called Job, Gen. 46:13.
7:2 [1] That is, their number was found thus great when David numbered the people, 2 Sam. 24:1.
7:3 [1] Meaning, the four sons, and the father.
7:5 [1] Or, kinsmen.
7:6 [1] Called also Ashbel, Gen. 46:21; Num. 26:38.
  [2] Which were the chief: for else there were seven in all as appeareth, Gen. 46:21.
7:12 [1] Or, Iri.
  [2] Meaning, that he was not the son of Benjamin but of Dan, Gen. 46:23.

[3] Or, of Aher.
7:13 [1] Or Shillem, Gen. 46:24.
  [2] These came of Dan, and Naphtali, which were the sons of Bilhah, Gen. 46:23, 24, 25.
7:16 [1] Or, Jeezer, Num. 26:30.
7:18 [1] Meaning, the sister of Gilead.
7:21 [1] Which was one of the five principal cities of the Philistines, slew the Ephraimites.
7:22 [1] Or, kinsfolk.
7:24 [1] Or, neice.
7:25 [1] To wit, of Ephraim.
7:28 [1] Or, Adaiah.

Beth Shean and her villages, Taanach and her villages, Megiddo and her villages, Dor and her villages. In those dwelt the children of Joseph the son of Israel.

30 ¶ [b]The sons of Asher *were* Imnah, and Ishvah, and Ishvi, and Beriah, and Serah their sister.

31 And the sons of Beriah, Heber, and Malchiel, which is the father of Birzaith.

32 And Heber begat Japhlet, and Shomer, and Hotham, and Shua their sister.

33 And the sons of Japhlet *were* Pasach, and [1]Bimhal, and Ashvath: these were the children of Japhlet.

34 And the sons of Shemer, Ahi, and Rohgah, Jehubbah, and Aram.

35 And the sons of his brother Helem were Zophah and Imna, and Shelesh, and Amal.

36 The sons of Zophah, Suah, and Harnepher, and Shual, and Beri, and Imrah,

37 Bezer and Hod, and Shamma, and Shilshah, and Jithran, and Beera.

38 And the sons of Jether, Jephunneh, and Pispah and Ara.

39 And the sons of Ulla, Arah, and Haniel, and Rizia.

40 All these were the children of Asher, the heads of their father's houses, noble men, valiant men of war *and* chief princes, and they were reckoned by their genealogies for war and for battle to the number of six and twenty thousand men.

8

1 The sons of Benjamin.   33 And race of Saul.

1 Benjamin also [1]begat Bela his eldest son, Ashbel the second, and Aharah the third,

2 Nohah the fourth, and Rapha the fifth.

3 And the sons of Bela were Addar, and Gera, and Abihud,

4 And Abishua, and Naaman, and Ahoah,

5 And Gera, and Shephuphan, and Huram.

6 ¶ And these are the sons of Ehud: these were the chief fathers of those that inhabited Geba: and [1]they were carried away captives to Manahath,

7 And Naaman, and Ahijah, and Gera, he carried them away captives: and [1]he begat Uzza, and Ahihud.

8 And Shaharaim begat *certain* in the country of Moab, after he had sent [1]away Hushim and Baara his wives.

9 He begat, I say, of Hodesh his wife, Jobab and Zibia, and Mesha and Malcam,

b Gen. 45:17

CHAPTER 8
a 1 Chron. 9:35

10 And Jeuz and Sachiah and Mirmah: these were his sons, *and* chief fathers.

11 And of Hushim he begat Abitub and Elpaal.

12 And the sons of Elpaal *were* Eber, and Misham and Shemed (which built Ono and Lod, and the villages thereof.)

13 And Beriah and Shema (which were the chief fathers among the inhabitants of Aijalon: they drave away the inhabitants of Gath.)

14 And Ahio, Shashak, and Jeremoth,

15 And Zebadiah, and Arad, and Eder,

16 And Michael, and Ispah, and Joha, the sons of Beriah,

17 And Zebadiah, and Meshullam, and Hizki, and Heber,

18 And Ishmerai, and Jizliah, and Jobab, the sons of Elpaal,

19 Jakim also, and Zichri, and Zabdi,

20 And Elienai, and Zillethai, and Eliel,

21 And [1]Adaiah, and Beraiah, and Shimrath the sons of Shimei,

22 And Ishpan, and Eber, and Eliel,

23 And Abdon, and Zichri, and Hanan,

24 And Hananiah, and Elam, and Antothijah,

25 Iphdeiah and Penuel the sons of Shashak,

26 And Shamsherai, and Shehariah, and Athaliah,

27 And Jaareshiah, and Elijah, and Zichri, the sons of Jeroham.

28 These were the chief [1]fathers according to their generations, *even* princes, which dwelt in Jerusalem.

29 And at [a]Gibeon dwelt the father of Gibeon, and the name of his wife *was* Maacah.

30 And his eldest son *was* Abdon, then Zur, and Kish, and Baal, and Nadab,

31 And Gedor, and Ahio, and Zecher,

32 And Mikloth begat Shimeah: these also dwelt with their brethren in Jerusalem, *even* by their brethren.

33 And [1]Ner begat Kish, and Kish begat Saul, and Saul begat Jonathan, and Malchishua, and Abinadab, and [2]Esh-Baal.

34 And the son of Jonathan *was* [1]Merib-Baal, and Merib-Baal begat Micah.

35 And the sons of Micah *were* Pithon, and Melech, and Tarea, and Ahaz,

36 And Ahaz begat Jehoaddah, and Jehoaddah begat Alemeth, and Azmaveth, and Zimri, and Zimri begat Moza,

7:33 [1] Or, Kimbal.
8:1 [1] He continueth in the description of the tribe of Benjamin, because his purpose is to set forth the genealogy of Saul.
8:6 [1] Meaning, the inhabitants of the city of Geba.
8:7 [1] To wit, Ehud.
8:8 [1] After he had put away his two wives.

8:21 [1] Or, Araiah.
8:28 [1] The chief of the tribe of Benjamin, that dwelt in Jerusalem.
8:33 [1] Who in 1 Sam. 9:1 is called Abiel.
          [2] He is also named Ishbosheth, 2 Sam. 2:8.
8:34 [1] He is likewise called Mephibosheth, 2 Sam. 9:6.

37 And Moza begat Binea, whose son *was* Raphah, *and* his son Eleasah, *and* his son Azel.

38 And Azel had six sons, whose names are these: Azrikam, Bocheru, and Ishmael, and Sheariah, and Obadiah, and Hanan: all these were the sons of Azel.

39 And the sons of Eshek his brother *were* Ulam his eldest son, Jeush the second, and Eliphelet the third.

40 And the sons of Ulam *were* valiant men of war which shot with the bow, and had many sons and nephews, an hundred and fifty: all these were of the sons of Benjamin.

9

1 All Israel and Judah numbered.   10 Of the Priests and Levites,   11, 18 And of their offices.

1 Thus all Israel were numbered by their genealogies: and behold, they are written in the book of the Kings of Israel and of Judah, *and* they were ¹carried away to Babel for their transgression.

2 ¶ And the chief inhabitants that dwelt in their own possessions, *and* in their own cities, *even* Israel, the Priests, the Levites, and the ¹Nethinim.

3 And in Jerusalem dwelt of the children of Judah, and of the children of Benjamin, and of the children of Ephraim, and Manasseh.

4 Uthai the son of Ammihud the son of Omri, the son of Imri, the son of Bani, of the children of Perez, the son of Judah.

5 And of Shiloni, Asaiah the eldest, and his sons.

6 And the sons of Zerah, Jeuel, and their brethren six hundred and ninety.

7 And of the sons of Benjamin, Sallu, the son of Meshullam, the son of Hodaviah, the son of Hassenuah.

8 And Ibneiah the son of Jeroham, and Elah the son of Uzzi, the son of Michri, and Meshullam the son of Shephatiah, the son of Reuel the son of Ibnijah.

9 And their brethren according to their generations nine hundred, fifty and six: all these men were ¹chief fathers in the households of their fathers.

10 ¶ And of the Priests, Jedaiah, and Jehoiarib, and Jachin,

11 And Azariah the son of Hilkiah, the son of Meshullam, the son of Zadok, the son of Meraioth, the son of Ahitub the ¹chief of the house of God,

12 And Adaiah the son of Jeroham, the son of Pashur, the son of Malchijah, and Maasai the son of Adiel, the son of Jahzerah, the son of Meshullam,

the son of Meshillemith, the son of Immer.

13 And their brethren the chief of the households of their fathers, a thousand seven hundred and threescore valiant men, for the ¹work of the service of the house of God.

14 ¶ And of the Levites, Shemaiah the son of Hasshub, the son of Azrikam, the son of Hashabiah, of the sons of Merari,

15 And Bakbakkar, Heresh and Galal, and Mattaniah the son of Micah, the son of Zichri, the son of Asaph,

16 And Obadiah the son of Shemaiah, the son of Galal, the son of Jeduthun, and Berechiah the son of Asa, the son of Elkanah, that dwelt in the villages of the Netophathites.

17 And the porters were Shallum, and Akkub, and Talmon, and Ahiman, and their brethren: Shallum *was* the chief.

18 For they were porters to this time by companies of the children of Levi unto the ¹King's gate Eastward.

19 And Shallum the son of Kore the son of Ebiasaph the son of Korah, and his brethren the Korahites (of the house of their father) *were* over the work, *and* office to keep the gates of the ¹Tabernacle: so their families *were* over the host of the Lord keeping the entry.

20 And Phinehas the son of Eleazar was their guide, and the Lord *was* with him.

21 Zechariah the son of Meshelemiah *was* the porter of the door of the Tabernacle of the Congregation.

22 All these were chosen for porters of the gates, two hundred and twelve, which were numbered according to their genealogies by their towns. David established these, and Samuel the Seer ¹in their perpetual office.

23 So they and their children had the oversight of the gates of the house of the Lord, even of the house of the Tabernacle by wards.

24 The porters were in four quarters Eastward, Westward, Northward and Southward.

25 And their brethren, *which were* in their towns, came at ¹seven days from time to time with them.

26 For these four chief porters were in perpetual office, and were of the Levites, and had charge of the ¹chambers, and of the treasures in the house of God.

9:1 ¹ Hitherto he hath described their genealogies before they went into captivity, and now he describeth their history after their return.
9:2 ¹ Meaning, the Gibeonites, which served in the Temple, read Josh. 9:13.
9:9 ¹ Or, chief of the families.
9:11 ¹ That is, he was the high Priest.
9:13 ¹ To serve in the Temple, every one according to his office.

9:18 ¹ So called because the king came into the Temple thereby, and not the common people.
9:19 ¹ Their charge was that none should enter into those places, which were only appointed for the Priests to minister in.
9:22 ¹ Or, for their fidelity.
9:25 ¹ They served weekly, as Ezek. 4:10.
9:26 ¹ Or, opening of the doors.

27 And they lay round about the house of God, because the charge *was* theirs, and they caused it to be opened every morning.

28 And certain of them had the rule of the ministering vessels: for they brought them in by tally, and brought them out by tally.

29 Some of them also were appointed over the instruments, and over all the vessels of the Sanctuary, and of the [1]flour, and the wine, and the oil, and the incense, and the sweet odors.

30 And certain of the sons of the Priests made ointments of sweet odors.

31 And Mattithiah one of the Levites which was the eldest son of Shallum the Korahite, had the charge of the things that were made in the frying pan.

32 And other of their brethren the sons of Kohath had the oversight of the [a]showbread to prepare it every Sabbath.

33 And these are the singers, the chief fathers of the Levites, *which dwelt* in the chambers, [1]and had none other charge: for they had to do in that business day and night.

34 These were the chief fathers of the Levites according to their generations, and the principal which dwelt at Jerusalem.

35 [b]And in Gibeon dwelt [1]the father of Gibeon, Jeiel, and the name of his wife *was* Maachah.

36 And his eldest son *was* Abdon, then Zur, and Kish, and Baal, and Ner, and Nadab,

37 And Gedor, and Ahio, and Zechariah, and Mikloth.

38 And Mikloth begat Shimeam: they also dwelt with their brethren at Jerusalem, *even* by their brethren.

39 And [c]Ner begat Kish, and Kish begat Saul, and Saul begat Jonathan, and Malchishua, and Abinadab and Esh-Baal.

40 And the son of Jonathan *was* Merib-Baal, and Merib-Baal begat Micah.

41 And the sons of Micah *were* Pithon, and Melech and Tahrea.

42 And Ahaz begat [1]Jarah, and Jarah begat Alemeth, and Azmaveth, and Zimri, and Zimri begat Moza.

43 And Moza begat Binea, whose son *was* Rephaiah, and his son *was* Eleasah, *and* his son Azel.

44 And Azel had six sons, whose names are these, Azrikam, Bocheru, and Ismael, and Sheariah, and Obadiah, and Hanan: these are the sons of Azel.

CHAPTER 9
[a] Exod. 25:30
[b] 1 Chron. 8:29
[c] 1 Sam. 14:51
1 Chron. 8:33

CHAPTER 10
[a] 1 Sam. 31:1
[b] 1 Sam. 15:23
[c] 1 Sam. 28:8

10

[1] *The battle of Saul against the Philistines,*   4 *In which he dieth,*   6 *And his sons also.*   13 *The cause of Saul's death.*

1 Then [a]the Philistines fought against Israel, and the men of Israel fled before the Philistines, and fell down slain in mount Gilboa.

2 And the Philistines pursued after Saul and after his sons, and the Philistines smote Jonathan, and Abinadab, and Malchishua the sons of Saul.

3 And the battle was sore against Saul, and the archers [1]hit him, and he was wounded of the archers.

4 Then said Saul to his armor-bearer, Draw out thy sword, and thrust me through therewith, lest these uncircumcised come and mock at me: but his armor-bearer would not, for he was sore afraid: therefore Saul took the sword, and fell upon it.

5 And when his armor-bearer saw that Saul was dead, he fell likewise upon the sword, and died.

6 So Saul died, and his three sons, and all his house, they died together.

7 And when all the men of Israel that were in the valley, saw how they fled, and that Saul and his sons were dead, they forsook their cities and fled away, and the Philistines came and dwelt in them.

8 And on the morrow when the Philistines came to spoil them that were slain, they found Saul and his sons [1]lying in mount Gilboa.

9 And when they had stripped him, they took his head and his armor, and sent them into the land of the Philistines round about, to publish it unto their idols, and to the people.

10 And they laid up his armor in the house of their god, and set up his head in the house of [1]Dagon.

11 ¶ When all they of Jabesh Gilead heard all that the Philistines had done to Saul,

12 Then they arose (all the valiant men) and took the body of Saul, and the bodies of his sons, and brought them to Jabesh, and buried the bones of them under an oak in Jabesh, and fasted seven days.

13 So Saul died for his transgression that he committed against the Lord, [b]even against the word of the Lord which he kept not, and in that he sought and asked counsel of a [1,c]familiar spirit,

14 And asked not of the Lord: therefore he slew him, and turned the kingdom unto David the son of Jesse.

11

3 *After the death of Saul, David is anointed in Hebron.*   5 *The Jebusites rebel against David, from whom he taketh the tower of Zion.*   6 *Joab is made*

9:29 [1] Whereof the meat offering was made, Lev. 1:8.
9:33 [1] But were continually occupied in singing praises to God.
9:35 [1] Or, Abi Gibeon.
9:42 [1] Who was also called Jehoaddah, 1 Chron. 8:36.
10:3 [1] Hebrew, *found.*

10:8 [1] Hebrew, *fallen.*
10:10 [1] Which was the idol of the Philistines, and from the belly downward had the form of a fish, and upward of a man.
10:13 [1] Or, witch, and sorceress.

captain.　10 His valiant men.

1　Then ^aall Israel ¹gathered themselves to David unto Hebron, saying, Behold, we are thy bones and thy flesh.

2　And in time past, even when Saul was king, thou leddest Israel out and in: and the Lord thy God said unto thee, Thou shalt feed my people Israel, and thou shalt be captain over my people Israel.

3　So came all the Elders of Israel to the King to Hebron, and David made a covenant with them in Hebron before the Lord. And they anointed David king over Israel, ^baccording to the word of the Lord, by the hand of Samuel.

4　¶ And David and all Israel went to Jerusalem: which is Jebus, where *were* the Jebusites, the inhabitants of the land.

5　And the inhabitants of Jebus said to David, Thou shalt not come in hither. Nevertheless David took the tower of Zion, which is the city of David.

6　And David said, ^cWhosoever smiteth the Jebusites first, shall be the chief and captain. So Joab the son of Zeruiah went first up, and was captain.

7　And David dwelt in the tower: therefore they called it the city of David.

8　^dAnd he built the city on every side, from Millo even round about: and Joab repaired the rest of the city.

9　And David prospered and grew: for the Lord of hosts *was* with him.

10　¶ ^eThese also are the chief of the valiant men that were with David, and joined their force with him in his kingdom with all Israel, to make him king over Israel, according to the word of the Lord.

11　And this is the number of the valiant men whom David had, Jashobeam the son of Hachmoni, the ¹chief among thirty: he lift up his spear against three hundred, *whom* he slew at one time.

12　And after him *was* Eleazar the son of ¹Dodo the Ahohite, which was one of the three valiant men.

13　He was with David at Pasdammim, and there the Philistines were gathered together to battle: and there was a parcel of ground full of barley, and the people fled before the Philistines.

14　And they stood in the midst of the field, ¹and saved it, and slew the Philistines: so the Lord gave a great victory.

15　¶ And three of the ¹thirty captains went to a rock to David, into the cave of Adullam. And

CHAPTER 11
^a 2 Sam. 5:1
^b 2 Sam. 16:13
^c 2 Sam. 5:8
^d 2 Sam. 5:9
^e 2 Sam. 23:8
^f 2 Sam. 23:15
^g 2 Sam. 23:19
^h 2 Sam. 23:23

the army of the Philistines camped in the valley of Rephaim.

16　And when David *was* in the hold, the Philistines garrison *was* at Bethlehem.

17　And David longed, and said, ^fOh, that one would give me to drink of the water of the well of Bethlehem that is at the gate.

18　Then these three brake through the host of the Philistines, and drew water out of the well of Bethlehem that was by the gate, and took it, and brought it to David: but David would not drink of it, but poured it *for an oblation* to the Lord,

19　And said, Let not my God suffer me to do this: should I drink the ¹blood of these men's lives? for they have brought it with the jeopardy of their lives: therefore he would not drink it: these things did these three mighty men.

20　¶ And Abishai the brother of Joab, he was chief of the three, and he lift up his spear against three hundred, *and* slew them, and had the name among the three.

21　Among the three he was more honorable than the two, and he was their captain: ^gbut he attained not unto the *first* three.

22　Benaiah the son of Jehoiada (the son of a valiant man) which had done many acts, *and was* of Kabzeel, he slew two ¹strong men of Moab, he went down also and slew a Lion in the midst of a pit in time of snow.

23　And he slew an Egyptian, a man of great stature, *even* five cubits long, and in the Egyptian's hand *was* a spear like a weaver's beam: and he went down to him with a staff, and plucked the spear out of the Egyptian's hand, and slew him with his own spear.

24　These things did Benaiah the son of Jehoiada, and had the name among the three worthies.

25　Behold, he was honorable among thirty, but he attained not unto the ¹first three. ^hAnd David made him of his counsel.

26　¶ These also *were* valiant men of war, Asahel the brother of Joab, Elhanan the son of Dodo of Bethlehem,

27　¹Shammoth the Harorite, Helez the Pelonite,

28　Ira the son of Ikkesh the Tekoite, Abiezer the Anathothite,

29　¹Sibbechai the Hushathite, Ilai the Ahohite,

30　Maharai the Netophathite, Heled the son of Baanah the Netophathite,

---

11:1 ¹ This was after the death of Ishbosheth Saul's son, when David had reigned over Judah seven years and six months in Hebron, 2 Sam. 5:5.
11:11 ¹ Meaning, the most excellent and best esteemed for his valiantness: some read, the chief of the princes.
11:12 ¹ Or, his uncle.
11:14 ¹ This act is referred to Shammah, 2 Sam. 23:11, which seem-

eth was the chiefest of these.
11:15 ¹ That is, Eleazar and his two companions.
11:19 ¹ That is, this water, for the which they ventured their blood.
11:22 ¹ Or, lions.
11:25 ¹ Meaning, those three which brought the water to David.
11:27 ¹ Called also Shammoth, 2 Sam. 23:25.
11:29 ¹ He is also called Mebunnai, 2 Sam. 23:27.

31 Ithai the son of Ribai of Gibeah of the children of Benjamin, Benaiah the Pirathonite,

32 Hurai of the rivers of Gaash, Abiel the Arbathite,

33 Azmaveth the Baharumite, Eliahba the Shaalbonite,

34 The sons of Hashem the Gizonite, Jonathan the son of Shageh the Harite,

35 Ahiam the son of Sacar the Hararite, Eliphal the son of Ur,

36 Hepher the Mecherathite, Ahijah the Pelonite,

37 Hezro the Carmelite, Naarai the son of Ezbai,

38 Joel the brother of Nathan, Mibhar the son of Hagri,

39 Zelek the Ammonite, Naharai the Berothite, the armor bearer of Joab the son of Zeruiah,

40 Ira the Ithrite, Gareb the Ithrite,

41 Uriah the Hittite, Zabad the son of Ahlai,

42 Adina the son of Shiza the Reubenite, a captain of the Reubenites, and thirty with him.

43 Hanan the son of Maachah, and Joshaphat the Mithnite,

44 Uzzia the Ashterathite, Shama and Jeiel the sons of Hotham the Aroerite,

45 Jediael the son of Shimri, and Joha his brother the Tizite,

46 Eliel the Mahavite, and Jeribai and Joshaviah the sons of Elnaam, and Ithmah the Moabite,

47 Eliel and Obed, and Jaasiel the Mezobaite.

12

3 Who they were that went with David when he fled from Saul.   14 Their valiantness.   23 They that came unto him unto Hebron out of every tribe to make him King.

1 These also are they that came to David to ¹Ziklag, while he was yet kept close, because of Saul the son of Kish: and they were among the valiant and helpers of the battle.

2 They were weaponed with bows, and could use the right and the left hand with stones, and with arrows *and* with bows, *and were* of Saul's ¹brethren, *even* of Benjamin.

3 The chief *were* Ahiezer, and Joash the sons of Shemaah a Gibeathite, and Jeziel, and Pelet the sons of Azmaveth, Berachah and Jehu the Anathothite,

4 And Ishmaiah the Gibeonite, a valiant man among thirty, and above the thirty, and Jeremiah,

CHAPTER 12
ᵃ 1 Sam. 29:4

and Jahaziel, and Johanan, and Jozabad the Gederathite,

5 Eluzai, and Jerimoth, and Bealiah, and Shemariah, and Shephatiah the Haruphite,

6 Elkanah, and Jisshiah, and Azarel, and Joezer, Jashobeam of Korah,

7 And Joelah, and Zebadiah the sons of Jeroham of ¹Gedor,

8 And of the Gadites there separated themselves some unto David into the hold of the wilderness, valiant men of war, *and* men of arms, *and* apt for battle, which could handle ¹spear and shield, and their faces *were like* the faces of ²lions, and *were* like the roes in the mountains in swiftness,

9 Ezer the chief, Obadiah the second, Eliab the third,

10 ¹Mishmannah the fourth, Jeremiah the fifth,

11 Attai the sixth, Eliel the seventh,

12 Johanan the eight, Elzabad the ninth,

13 Jeremiah the tenth, Machbanai the eleventh.

14 These were the sons of Gad, captains of the host: one of the least *could resist* an hundred, and the greatest a thousand.

15 These are they that went over Jordan in the ¹first month, when he had filled over all his banks, and put to flight all them of the valley, toward the East and the West.

16 And there came of the children of Benjamin, and Judah to the hold unto David,

17 And David went out to meet them, and answered and said unto them, If ye be come peaceably unto me to help me, mine heart shall be knit unto you: but if you *come* to betray me to mine adversaries, *seeing* there is no wickedness in mine hands, the God of our fathers behold it, and rebuke it.

18 And the ¹spirit came upon Amasai, which was the chief of thirty, *and he said,* Thine *are* we, David, and with thee, O son of Jesse. Peace, peace be unto thee, and peace be unto thine helpers: for thy God helpeth thee. Then David received them, and made them captains of the garrison.

19 ¶ And of Manasseh, *some* fell to David, when he came with the Philistines against Saul to battle, but they ¹helped them not: for the Princes of the Philistines ᵃby advisement sent him away, saying, He will fall to his master Saul ²for our heads.

20 As he went to Ziklag, there fell to him of Manasseh, Adnah, and Jozabad, and Jediael, and

---

12:1 ¹ To take his part against Saul, who persecuted him.
12:2 ¹ That is, of the tribe of Benjamin, whereof Saul was, and wherein were excellent throwers with slings, Judg. 20:16.
12:7 ¹ Or, Gedua.
12:8 ¹ Or, buckler.
   ² Meaning, fierce and terrible.
12:10 ¹ Or, Mashmannah.

12:15 ¹ Which the Hebrews called Nisan, or Abib, containing half March, and half April, when Jordan was wont to overflow his banks, read Josh. 3:15.
12:18 ¹ The spirit of boldness and courage moved him to speak thus.
12:19 ¹ They came only to help David, and not to succor the Philistines, which were enemies to their country.
   ² Or, on the jeopardy of our heads.

Michael, and Jozabad, and Elihu, and Zillethai, heads of the thousands that were of Manasseh.

21 And they helped David against ¹that band: for they were all valiant men, and were captains in the host.

22 For at that time day by day, there came to David to help him, until it was a great host, like the host of ¹God.

23 And these are the numbers of the captains that were armed to battle, *and* came to David to Hebron to turn the kingdom of Saul to him, according to the word of the Lord.

24 The children of Judah that bare shield and ¹spear, *were* six thousand and eight hundred armed to the war.

25 Of the children of Simeon valiant men of war, seven thousand and an hundred.

26 Of the children of Levi four thousand and six hundred.

27 And Jehoiada *was* the chief of them of ¹Aaron: and with him three thousand and seven hundred.

28 And Zadok a young man very valiant, and of his father's household *came* two and twenty captains.

29 And of the children of Benjamin the brethren of Saul three thousand: for a great part of them unto that time ¹kept the ward of the house of Saul.

30 And of the children of Ephraim twenty thousand, and eight hundred valiant men *and* famous men in the household of their fathers.

31 And of the half tribe of Manasseh eighteen thousand, which were appointed by name to come and make David King.

32 And of the children of Issachar which were men that had understanding of the ¹times, to know what Israel ought to do: the heads of them *were* two hundred, and all their brethren were at their commandment.

33 Of Zebulun that went out to battle, expert in war, *and* in all instruments of war, fifty thousand ¹which could set the battle in array: they were not of a ²double heart.

34 And of Naphtali thousand captains, and with them with shield and spear seven and thirty thousand.

35 And of Dan expert in battle, eight and twenty

CHAPTER 13
a 2 Sam. 6:2

thousand and six hundred.

36 And of Asher that went out to the battle and were trained in the wars, forty thousand.

37 And of the other side of Jordan of the Reubenites, and of the Gadites, and of the half tribe of Manasseh with all instruments of war to fight with, an hundred and twenty thousand.

38 ¹All these men of war ²that could lead an army, came with ³upright heart to Hebron to make David king over all Israel: and all the rest of Israel *was* of one accord to make David King.

39 And there they were with David three days, eating and drinking: for their ¹brethren had prepared for them.

40 Moreover, they that were near them until Issachar, and Zebulun, and Naphtali brought bread upon asses, and on camels, and on mules, and on oxen, *even* meat, flour, figs, and raisins, and wine and oil, and beeves and sheep abundantly: for there was joy in Israel.

13 6 *The Ark is brought again from Kirjath Jearim to Jerusalem.* 10 *Uzza dieth because he toucheth it.*

1 And David counseled with the captains of thousands and of hundreds, *and* with all the governors.

2 And David said to all the Congregation of Israel, If it seem good to you, and that it proceedeth of the Lord our God, we will send to and fro unto our brethren, that are left in all the land of Israel (for with them are the Priests and the Levites in the cities *and* their suburbs) that they may assemble themselves unto us.

3 And we will bring again the ¹Ark of our God to us: for we sought not unto it in the days of Saul.

4 And all the Congregation answered, Let us do so: for the thing seemed good in the eyes of all the people.

5 ¶ ªSo David gathered all Israel together from ¹Shihor in Egypt, even unto the entering of Hamath, to bring the Ark of God from ²Kirjath Jearim.

6 And David went up and all Israel to ¹Baalah in Kirjath Jearim, that was in Judah, to bring up from thence the Ark of God the Lord that dwelleth between the Cherubims, where his Name is called on.

12:21 ¹ To wit, of the Amalekites which had burned the city Ziklag, 1 Sam. 30:1,9.

12:22 ¹ Meaning, mighty or strong: for the Hebrews say a thing is of God, when it is excellent.

12:24 ¹ Or, buckler.

12:27 ¹ Of the Levites which came by descent of Aaron.

12:29 ¹ That is, the greatest number took Saul's part.

12:32 ¹ Men of good experience, which knew at all times what was to be done.

12:33 ¹ Or, set themseves in array.
  ² Hebrew, *heart and heart.*

12:38 ¹ So that his whole host were three hundred twenty and two thousand, two hundred twenty and two.
  ² Or, fight in their array.
  ³ Or, with a good courage.

12:39 ¹ The rest of the Israelites.

13:3 ¹ His first care was to restore religion, which had in Saul's days been corrupted and neglected.

13:5 ¹ Or, Nile.
  ² That is, from Gibea, where the inhabitants of Kirjath Jearim had placed it in the house of Abinadab, 2 Sam. 6:3.

13:6 ¹ Or, Baal, read 2 Sam. 6:2.

7 And they carried the Ark of God in a new cart out of the house of Abinadab: and Uzza and Ahio [1]guided the cart.

8 And David and all Israel played before [1]God with all *their* might, both with songs and with harps, and with viols, and with timbrels, and with cymbals, and with trumpets.

9 ¶ And when they came unto the threshingfloor of [1]Chidon, Uzza put forth his hand to hold the Ark, for the oxen did shake it.

10 But the wrath of the Lord was kindled against Uzza, and he smote him, because he laid his hand upon the Ark: so he died there [1]before God.

11 And David was angry, because the Lord had made a breach in Uzza, and he called the name of that place, Perez Uzza unto this day.

12 And David feared God that day, saying, How shall I bring in to me the Ark of God?

13 Therefore David brought not the Ark to him into the city of David, but caused it to turn into the house of [1]Obed-Edom the Gittite.

14 So the Ark of God remained in the house of Obed-Edom, *even* in his house three months: and the Lord blessed the house of Obed-Edom, and all that he had.

14

1 Hiram sendeth wood and workmen to David.   4 The names of his children.   8, 14 By the counsel of God he goeth against the Philistines, and overcometh them.   15 God fighteth for him.

1 Then [a]sent Hiram the King of [1]Tyre messengers to David, and Cedar trees, with masons and carpenters to build him an house.

2 Therefore David knew that the Lord had confirmed him King over Israel, *and* that his kingdom was lift up on high, because of his [1]people Israel.

3 ¶ Also David took more wives at Jerusalem, and David begat more sons and daughters.

4 And these are the names of the children which he had at Jerusalem, Shammua, and Shobab, Nathan, and Solomon,

5 And Ibhar, and Elishua, and [1]Elpelet,

6 And Nogah, and Nepheg, and Japhia,

7 And Elishama, and [1]Beeliada, and Eliphelet.

8 But when the Philistines heard that David was anointed King over Israel, all the Philistines came

CHAPTER 14
a 2 Sam. 5:11

CHAPTER 15
a Num. 4:2,20

up to seek David. And when David heard, he went out against them.

9 And the Philistines came, and spread themselves in the valley of Rephaim.

10 Then David asked counsel at God, saying, Shall I go up against the Philistines, and wilt thou deliver them into mine hand? And the Lord said unto him, Go up: for I will deliver them into thine hand.

11 So they came up to Baal Perazim, and David smote them there: and David said, God hath divided mine enemies with mine hand, as waters are divided: therefore they called the name of that place, [1]Baal Perazim.

12 And there they had left their gods: and David said, Let them even be burnt with fire.

13 Again the Philistines came and spread themselves in the valley.

14 And when David asked again counsel at God, God said to him, Thou shalt not go up after them, *but* turn away from them, that thou mayest come upon them over against the mulberry trees.

15 And when thou hearest the noise of one going in the tops of the mulberry trees, then go out to battle: for God is gone forth before thee, to smite the host of the Philistines.

16 So David did as God had commanded him: and they smote the host of the Philistines from Gibeon even to Gezer.

17 And the fame of David went out into all lands: and the Lord brought the fear of him upon all nations.

15

1 David prepareth an house for the Ark.   4 The number and order of the Levites.   16 The singers are chosen out among them.   25 They bring again the Ark with joy.   29 David dancing before it is despised of his wife Michal.

1 And *David* made him houses in the [1]city of David, and prepared a place for the Ark of God, and pitched for it a tent.

2 Then David said, [a]None ought to carry the Ark of God, but the Levites: for the Lord hath chosen them to bear the Ark of the Lord, and to minister unto him forever.

3 ¶ And David gathered all Israel together to Jerusalem to bring up the [1]Ark of the Lord unto his

---

13:7 [1] The sons of Abinadab.
13:8 [1] That is, before the Ark, where God showed himself: so that the sign is taken for the thing signified, which is common to all sacraments both in the old and new Testament.
13:9 [1] Called also Nachon, 2 Sam. 6:6.
13:10 [1] Before the Ark for usurping that which did not appertain to his vocation: for this charge was given to the Priests, Num. 4:15, so that here all good intentions are condemned, except they be commanded by the word of God.
13:13 [1] Who was a Levite, and called Gittite, because he had dwelt

at Gath.
14:1 [1] Hebrew, *Zor.*
14:2 [1] Because of God's promise made to the people of Israel.
14:5 [1] Elpelet and Nogah are not mentioned, 2 Sam. 5:14, so there are but eleven, and here thirteen.
14:7 [1] Or, Eliada.
14:11 [1] That is, the valley of divisions, because the enemies were dispersed there like waters.
15:1 [1] That was in the place of the city, called Zion, 2 Sam. 5:7, 9.
15:3 [1] From the house of Obed-Edom, 2 Sam. 6:10, 12.

place, which he had ordained for it.

4 And David assembled the sons of Aaron, and the Levites.

5 Of the sons of Kohath, Uriel the chief, and his [1]brethren six score.

6 Of the sons of Merari, Asaiah the chief, and his brethren two hundred and twenty.

7 Of the sons of Gershom, Joel the chief, and his brethren an hundred and thirty.

8 Of the sons of [1]Elizaphan, Shemaiah the chief, and his brethren two hundred.

9 Of the sons of [1]Hebron, Eliel the chief, and his brethren fourscore.

10 Of the sons of Uzziel, Amminadab the chief, and his brethren an hundred and twelve.

11 ¶ And David called Zadok and Abiathar the Priests, and of the Levites, Uriel, Asaiah and Joel, Shemaiah and Eliel, and Amminadab.

12 And he said unto them, Ye are the chief fathers of the Levites: [1]sanctify yourselves, and your brethren, and bring up the Ark of the Lord God of Israel unto the *place* that I have prepared for it.

13 For [b]because ye were not there at the first, the Lord our God made a breach among us: for we sought him not after *due* [1]order.

14 So the Priests and the Levites sanctified themselves to bring up the Ark of the Lord God of Israel.

15 ¶ And the sons of the Levites bare the Ark of God upon their shoulders with the bars as Moses had commanded, [c]according to the word of the Lord,

16 And David spake to the chief of the Levites, that they should appoint *certain* of their brethren to sing with [1]instruments of music, with viols and harps, and cymbals, that they might make a sound, and lift up their voice with joy.

17 So the Levites appointed Heman the son of Joel, and of his brethren Asaph the son of Berechiah, and of the sons of Merari their brethren, Ethan the son of Kushaiah,

18 And with them their brethren in the [1]second degree, Zechariah, Ben, and Jaaziel, and Shemiramoth, and Jehiel, and Unni, Eliab, and Benaiah, and Maaseiah, and Mattithiah, and Elipheleh, and

Cross references:
[b] 1 Chron. 13:10
[c] Exod. 25:14,15
[d] 2 Sam. 6:12
[e] 2 Sam. 6:16

Mikneiah, and Obed-Edom, and Jeiel the porters.

19 So Heman, Asaph, and Ethan, *were* singers to make a sound with cymbals of brass,

20 And Zechariah, and Aziel, and Shemiramoth, and Jehiel, and Unni, and Eliab, and Maaseiah, and Benaiah with viols on [1]Alamoth,

21 And Mattithiah, and Elipheleh, and Mikneiah, and Obed-Edom, and Jeiel, and Azaziah, with harps upon [1]Sheminith Jenazzeah.

22 But Chenaniah the chief of the Levites had the [1]charge bearing the burden in the charge, for he was able to instruct.

23 And Berechiah and Elkanah were porters for the Ark.

24 And Shebaniah, and Joshaphat and Nethanel and Amasai, and Zechariah, and Benaiah, and Eliezer the Priests did blow with trumpets before the Ark of God, and Obed-Edom and Jehiah *were* porters [1]for the Ark.

25 [d]So David and the Elders of Israel and the captains of thousands went to bring up the Ark of the Covenant of the Lord from the house of Obed-Edom with joy.

26 And because that God [1]helped the Levites that bare the Ark of the covenant of the Lord, they offered [2]seven bullocks and seven rams.

27 And David had on him a linen garment, as all the Levites that bare the Ark, and the singers, and Chenaniah that had the chief charge of the singers: and upon David *was* a linen [1]Ephod.

28 Thus all Israel brought up the Ark of the Lord's covenant with shouting, and sound of cornet, and with trumpets, and with cymbals, making a sound with viols and with harps.

29 And when the Ark of the [1]covenant of the Lord came into the city of David, Michal the daughter of Saul looked out at a window, and saw king David dancing and playing, and [e]she despised him in her heart.

16 *1 The Ark being placed, they offer sacrifices. 4 David ordaineth Asaph and his brethren to minister before the Lord. 8 He appointeth a notable Psalm to be sung in praise of the Lord.*

15:5 [1] Or, kinsmen.
15:8 [1] Who was the son of Uzziel, the fourth son of Kohath, Exod. 6:18, 22; Num. 3:30.
15:9 [1] The third son of Kohath, Exod. 6:18.
15:12 [1] Prepare yourselves and be pure, abstain from all things whereby ye might be polluted, and so not able to come to the Tabernacle.
15:13 [1] According as he hath appointed in the law.
15:16 [1] These instruments and other ceremonies, which they observed, were instructions of their infancy, which continued to the coming of Christ.
15:18 [1] Which were inferior in dignity.

15:20 [1] This was an instrument of music, or a certain tune, whereunto they accustomed to sing Psalms.
15:21 [1] Which was the eighth tune, over the which he that was most excellent had charge.
15:22 [1] To wit, to appoint Psalms, and songs to them that sung.
15:24 [1] With Berechiah and Elkanah, verse 23.
15:26 [1] That is, gave them strength to execute their office.
   [2] Besides the bullock and the fat beast which David offered at every sixth pace, 2 Sam. 6:13.
15:27 [1] Read 2 Sam. 6:14.
15:29 [1] It was so called because it put the Israelites in remembrance of the Lord's covenant made with them.

1 So *they brought in the Ark of God, and set it in the midst of the Tabernacle that David had pitched for it, and they offered burnt offerings and peace offerings before God.

2 And when David had made an end of offering the burnt offering and the peace offerings, he ¹blessed the people in the Name of the Lord.

3 And he dealt to every one of Israel both man and woman, to every one a cake of bread, and a piece of flesh, and a bottle of *wine*.

4 And he appointed certain of the Levites to minister before the Ark of the Lord, and to ¹rehearse and to thank and praise the Lord God of Israel:

5 Asaph the chief, and next to him Zechariah, Jeiel, and Shemiramoth, and Jehiel, and Mattithiah, and Eliab, and Benaiah, and Obed-Edom, even Jeiel with instruments, viols, and harps, and Asaph to make a sound with cymbals,

6 *And* Benaiah and Jahaziel Priests, with trumpets continually before the Ark of the covenant of God.

7 Then at that time David did ¹appoint at the beginning to give thanks to the Lord by the hand of Asaph and his brethren.

8 ᵇPraise the Lord *and* call upon his Name: declare his ¹works among the people.

9 Sing unto him, sing praise unto him, *and* talk of all his ¹wonderful works.

10 Rejoice in his holy Name: let the hearts of them that seek the Lord, rejoice.

11 Seek the Lord and his strength: seek his face continually.

12 Remember his marvelous works that he hath done, his wonders, and the ¹judgments of his mouth,

13 O seed of Israel his servant, O the children of Jacob his ¹chosen.

14 He is the Lord our God: his judgments *are* throughout all the earth.

15 Remember his Covenant forever, *and* the word, which he commanded to a thousand generations:

16 ᶜWhich he made with Abraham, and his oath

CHAPTER 16
ᵃ 2 Sam. 6:17
ᵇ Ps. 105:1
Isa. 12:4
ᶜ Gen. 22:16,
17,28
Luke 1:73
Heb. 6:17
ᵈ Ps. 95:1

to Isaac:

17 And hath confirmed it to Jacob for a Law, *and* to Israel for an everlasting Covenant,

18 Saying, To thee will I give the land of Canaan, the ¹lot of your inheritance.

19 When ye were ¹few in number, yea, a very few, and strangers therein,

20 And walked about from nation to nation, and from *one* kingdom to another people,

21 He suffered no man to do them wrong, but rebuked ¹Kings for their sakes, saying,

22 Touch not mine ¹anointed, and do my ²Prophets no harm.

23 ᵈSing unto the Lord all the earth: declare his salvation from day to day.

24 Declare his glory among the nations, and his wonderful works among all people.

25 For the Lord *is* great and much to be praised, and he is to be feared above all gods.

26 For all the gods of the people *are* ¹idols, but the Lord made the heavens.

27 Praise and glory *are* before him: power and beauty *are* in his place.

28 Give unto the Lord, ye families of the people: give unto the Lord glory and power.

29 Give unto the Lord the glory of his Name: bring an offering and come before him, *and* worship the Lord in the glorious Sanctuary.

30 ¹Tremble ye before him all the earth, surely the world shall be, *and* not move.

31 Let the ¹heavens rejoice, and let the earth be glad, and let them say among the nations, The Lord reigneth.

32 Let the sea roar, and all that therein is: let the field be joyful and all that is in it.

33 Let the trees of the wood then rejoice at the presence of the Lord: for he cometh to ¹judge the earth.

34 Praise the Lord, for he is good, for his mercy *endureth* forever.

35 And say ye, Save us, O God, our salvation, and gather us, and deliver us from the heathen, that we may praise thine holy Name, and ¹glory in thy praise.

16:2 ¹ He called upon the Name of God, desiring him to prosper the people, and give good success to their beginnings.

16:4 ¹ To wit, God's benefits toward his people.

16:7 ¹ David gave them this Psalm to praise the Lord, signifying, that in all our enterprises the Name of God ought to be praised and called upon.

16:8 ¹ Whereof this is the chiefest, that he hath chosen himself a Church to call upon his Name.

16:9 ¹ Who of his wonderful providence hath chosen a few of the stock of Abraham to be his children.

16:12 ¹ In overcoming Pharaoh, which judgments were declared by God's mouth to Moses.

16:13 ¹ Meaning hereby that the promise of adoption only appertaineth to the Church.

16:18 ¹ Hebrew, *cord*, whereby parcels of land were measured.

16:19 ¹ Meaning, from the time that Abraham entered, unto the time that Jacob went into Egypt for famine.

16:21 ¹ As Pharaoh and Abimelech.

16:22 ¹ Mine elect people and them whom I have sanctified.
² To whom God declared his word, and they declared it to their posterity.

16:26 ¹ His strong faith appeareth herein, though all the world would follow idols, yet he would cleave to the living God.

16:30 ¹ Humble yourselves under the mighty hand of God.

16:31 ¹ He exhorteth the dumb creatures to rejoice with him in considering the greatness of the grace of God.

16:33 ¹ To restore all things to their estate.

16:35 ¹ He esteemeth this to be the chiefest felicity of man.

36 Blessed *be* the Lord God of Israel forever and ever: and let all people say, [1]So be it, and praise the Lord.

37 ¶ Then he left there before the Ark of the Lord's Covenant Asaph and his brethren to minister continually before the Ark, that which was to be done every day:

38 And Obed-Edom and his brethren, threescore and eight: and Obed-Edom the son of Jeduthun, and Hosah *were* porters.

39 And Zadok the Priest and his brethren the Priests *were* before the Tabernacle of the Lord, in the high place that was at Gibeon,

40 To offer burnt offerings unto the Lord, upon the burnt offering altar continually, in the morning and in the evening, even according unto all that is written in the Law of the Lord, which he commanded Israel.

41 And with [1]them were Heman, and Jeduthun, and the rest that were chosen (which were appointed by names) to praise the Lord, because his mercy *endureth* forever.

42 Even with them *were* Heman and Jeduthun, to make a sound with the cornets and with the cymbals, with excellent instruments of music: and the sons of Jeduthun were at the gate.

43 And all the people departed, every man to his house: and David returned to [1]bless his house.

17

3 *David is forbidden to build an house unto the Lord.* 12 *Christ is promised under the figure of Solomon.* 18 *David giveth thanks,* 23 *and prayeth unto God.*

1 Now [a]afterward when David dwelt in his house, he said to Nathan the Prophet, Behold, I dwell in an house of [1]cedar trees, but the Ark of the Lord's Covenant remaineth under [2]curtains.

2 Then Nathan said to David, Do [1]all that is in thine heart: for God is with thee.

3 And the same [1]night even the word of God came to Nathan, saying,

4 Go, and tell David my servant, Thus saith the

CHAPTER 17
[a] 2 Sam. 7:2

Lord, Thou shalt not build me an house to dwell in:

5 For I have dwelt in no house since the day that I brought out the children of Israel unto this day, but I have been from tent to [1]tent, and from habitation *to habitation.*

6 Wherefore I have [1]walked with all Israel, spake I one word to any of the Judges of Israel (whom I commanded to feed my people) saying, Why have ye not built me an house of cedar trees?

7 Now therefore thus shalt thou say unto my servant David, Thus saith the Lord of hosts, I took thee from the sheepcote [1]and from following the sheep, that thou shouldest be a prince over my people Israel.

8 And I have been with thee whithersoever thou hast walked, and have destroyed all thine enemies out of thy sight, and have [1]made thee a name, like the name of the great men that are in the earth.

9 (Also I will appoint a place for my people Israel, and will [1]plant it, that they may dwell in their place, and move no more: neither shall the [2]wicked people [3]vex them anymore, as at the beginning,

10 And since the time that I commanded judges over my people Israel) And I will subdue all thine enemies: therefore I say unto thee, that the Lord will [1]build thee an house.

11 And when thy days shall be fulfilled to go with thy fathers, then will I raise up thy seed after thee, which shall be of thy sons, and will establish his kingdom.

12 He shall build me an house, and I will establish his throne [1]forever.

13 I will be his father, and he shall be my son, and I will not take my mercy away from him, as I took it from him that was before [1]thee.

14 But I will establish him in mine house, and in my kingdom forever, and his throne shall be established forever,

15 According to all these words, and according to all this vision. So Nathan spake to David.

16 ¶ And David the king [1]went in and [2]sat before the Lord, and said, Who am I, O Lord God, and what is mine house, that thou hast brought me [3]hitherto?

16:36 [1] He willeth all the people both in heart and mouth to consent to these praises.
16:41 [1] With Zadok and the rest of the Priests.
16:43 [1] Declaring that after our duty to God we are chiefly bound to our own house, for the which as for all other things we ought to pray unto God, and instruct our families to praise his Name.
17:1 [1] Well built and fair.
  [2] That is, in tents covered with skin.
17:2 [1] As yet God had not revealed to the Prophet what he purposed concerning David: therefore seeing God favored David, he spake what he thought.
17:3 [1] After that Nathan had spoken to David.
17:5 [1] That is, in a tent which removed to and fro.
17:6 [1] Meaning, wheresoever his Ark went, which was a sign of his presence.

17:7 [1] Of a shepherd of sheep I made thee a shepherd of men: so that thou camest not to this dignity through thine own merits, but by my pure grace.
17:8 [1] Or, gotten thee fame.
17:9 [1] Make them sure that they shall not remove.
  [2] Hebrew, *sons of iniquity.*
  [3] Or, consume.
17:10 [1] Will give thee great posterity.
17:12 [1] That is, unto the coming of Christ: for then these figures should cease.
17:13 [1] Which was Saul.
17:16 [1] He went into the tent where the Ark was, showing what we ought to do when we receive any benefits of the Lord.
  [2] Or, remained.
  [3] Meaning to this kingly estate.

17 Yet thou esteeming this a small thing, O God, hast also spoken concerning the house of thy servant for a great while, and hast regarded me according to the estate of a man of ¹high degree, O Lord God.

18 What can David *desire* more of thee for the honor of thy servant? for thou knowest thy servant.

19 O Lord, for thy servant's sake, even according to thine ¹heart hast thou done all this great thing to declare all magnificence.

20 Lord, there is none like thee, neither *is there* any God besides thee according to all that we have heard with our ears.

21 Moreover what one nation in the earth *is* like thy people Israel, whose God went to redeem them *to be* his people, and to make thyself a Name, *and to do* great and terrible things by casting out Nations from before thy people, whom thou hast delivered out of Egypt?

22 For thou hast ordained thy people Israel to be thine own people forever, and thou Lord art become their God.

23 Therefore now Lord, let the thing that thou hast spoken concerning thy servant, and concerning his house, be confirmed forever, and do as thou hast said,

24 And let thy Name be stable and magnified forever, that it may be said, The Lord of hosts, God of Israel, *is* the God of ¹Israel, and let the house of David thy servant be established before thee.

25 For thou, O my God, hast ¹revealed unto the ear of thy servant, that thou wilt build him an house: therefore thy servant hath ²been bold to pray before thee.

26 Therefore now Lord (*for* thou art ¹God, and hast spoken this goodness unto thy servant.)

27 Now therefore it hath pleased thee to bless the house of thy servant, that it may be before thee forever: for thou, O Lord, hast blessed it, and it shall be blessed forever.

18

1 *The battle of David against the Philistines,* 2 *And against Moab,* 3 *Zobah,* 5 *Aram,* 12 *And Edom.*

1 And after this, David smote the Philistines,

CHAPTER 18
ᵃ 2 Sam. 8:4
ᵇ 1 Kings 7:23
Jer. 52:20

and subdued them, and took ¹Gath, and the villages thereof out of the hand of the Philistines.

2 And he smote Moab, and the Moabites became David's servants, and ¹brought gifts.

3 ¶ And David smote ¹Hadadezer King of Zobah unto Hamath, as he went to establish his border by the river ²Perath.

4 And David took from him a thousand chariots, and seven thousand horsemen, and twenty thousand footmen, and ᵃdestroyed all the chariots, but he reserved of them an hundred chariots.

5 ¶ Then came the Aramites of Damascus to succor Hadadezer king of Zobah, but David slew of the Aramites two and twenty thousand.

6 And David put *a garrison* in Aram of ¹Damascus, and the Aramites became David's servants, and brought gifts: and the Lord ²preserved David wheresoever he went.

7 And David took the shields of gold that were of the servants of Hadadezer, and brought them to Jerusalem.

8 And from ¹Tibhath, and from Chun (cities of Hadadezer) brought David exceeding much brass, wherewith Solomon made the brazen ᵇSea, and the pillars and the vessels of brass.

9 ¶ Then Tou King of Hamath heard how David had smitten all the host of Hadadezer king of Zobah:

10 Therefore he sent ¹Hadoram his son to king David, to salute him, and to rejoice with him, because he had fought against Hadadezer, and beaten him (for Tou had war with Hadadezer) *who brought* all vessels of gold and silver and brass.

11 And king David did dedicate them unto the Lord, with the silver and gold that he brought from all the nations, from ¹Edom, and from Moab, and from the children of Ammon, and from the Philistines, and from Amalek.

12 ¶ And Abishai the son of Zeruiah smote of Edom in the salt valley ¹eighteen thousand,

13 And he put a garrison in Edom, and all the Edomites became David's servants: and the Lord preserved David wheresoever he went.

14 So David reigned over all Israel, and executed

17:17 ¹ Thou hast promised a kingdom that shall continue to me and my posterity, and that Christ shall proceed of me.
17:19 ¹ Freely and according to the purpose of thy will, without any deserving.
17:24 ¹ That is, he showeth himself in deed to be their God, by delivering them from dangers, and preserving them.
17:25 ¹ Thou hast declared unto me by Nathan the Prophet.
  ² Hebrew, *hath found.*
17:26 ¹ And canst not break promise.
18:1 ¹ Which in 2 Sam. 8:1, is called the bridle of bondage, because it was a strong town, and kept the country round about in subjection.

18:2 ¹ Or, paid tribute.
18:3 ¹ Or, Hadadezer.
  ² Or, Euphrates.
18:6 ¹ Or, Darmesek.
  ² That is, in all things that he enterprised.
18:8 ¹ Which in 2 Sam. 8:8, are called Betah and Berothai.
18:10 ¹ Called also Joram, 2 Sam. 8:10.
18:11 ¹ Because the Edomites and the Syrians joined their power together, it is said, 2 Sam. 8:12, that the Aramites were spoiled.
18:12 ¹ Which is understood that Joab slew twelve thousand, as is in the title of the threescore Psalm and Abishai the rest.

judgment and justice to all his people.

15 And Joab the son of Zeruiah was over the host, and Jehoshaphat the son of Ahilud Recorder,

16 And Zadok the son of Ahitub, and Abimelech the son of Abiathar *were* the Priests, and ¹Shavsha the Scribe,

17 ʿAnd Benaiah the son of Jehoiada was over the ¹Cherethites and the Pelethites: and the sons of David *were* chief about the King.

19

4 Hanun King of the children of Ammon doeth great injuries to the servants of David.   6 He prepareth an army against David,   15 and is overcome.

1 After this also ªNahash the king of the children of Ammon died, and his son reigned in his stead.

2 And David said, I will show kindness unto Hanun the son of Nahash, because his ¹father showed kindness unto me. And David sent messengers to comfort him for his father. So the servants of David came into the land of the children of Ammon to Hanun, to comfort him.

3 And the princes of the children of Ammon said to Hanun, Thinkest thou that David doth honor thy father, that he hath sent comforters unto thee? Are not his servants come to thee to ¹search, to seek and to spy out the land?

4 Wherefore Hanun took David's servants, and ¹shaved them, and cut off their ²garments by the half unto the buttocks, and sent them away.

5 And there went *certain* and told David concerning the men: and he sent to meet them (for the men were exceedingly ashamed) and the King said, Tarry at Jericho, until your beards be grown: then return.

6 ¶ When the children of Ammon saw that they ¹stank in the sight of David, then sent Hanun and the children of Ammon a thousand talents of silver, to hire them chariots and horsemen out ᵇof Aram Naharaim, and out of Aram Maachah, and out of ²Zobah.

7 And they hired them two and thirty thousand chariots, and the king of Maachah and his people, which came and pitched before ¹Medeba: and the children of Ammon gathered themselves together from their cities, and came to the battle.

8 ¶ And when David heard it, he sent Joab and

ᶜ 2 Sam. 8:17,18

CHAPTER 19
ª 2 Sam. 10:1
ᵇ 2 Sam. 10:6,8

all the host of the valiant men.

9 And the children of Ammon came out, and set their battle in array at the gate of the city. And the kings that were come, were by themselves in the field.

10 When Joab saw that the front of the battle was against him before and behind, then he chose out of all the choice of Israel, and set himself in array to meet the Aramites.

11 And the rest of the people he delivered unto the hand of Abishai his brother, and they put themselves in array against the children of Ammon.

12 And he said, If Aram be too strong for me, then thou shalt succor me: and if the children of Ammon prevail against thee, then I will succor thee.

13 Be strong, and let us show ourselves valiant for our ¹people, and for the cities of our God, and let the Lord do that which is good in his own sight.

14 So Joab and the people that was with him, came near before the Aramites unto the battle, and they fled before him.

15 And when the children of Ammon saw that the Aramites fled, they fled also before Abishai his brother, and entered into the city: so Joab came to Jerusalem.

16 ¶ And when the Aramites saw that they were discomfited before Israel, they sent messengers, and caused the Aramites to come forth that were beyond the ¹river: and Shophach the captain of the host of Hadadezer *went* before them.

17 And when it was showed David, he gathered all Israel, and went over Jordan, and came unto them, and put himself in array against them: And when David had put himself in battle array to meet the Aramites, they fought with him.

18 But the Aramites fled before Israel, and David destroyed of the Aramites ¹seven thousand chariots, and forty thousand footmen, and killed Shophach the captain of the host.

19 And when the servants of Hadadezer saw that they fell before Israel, they made peace with David, and served him. And the Aramites would no more succor the children of Ammon.

20

1 Rabbah destroyed.   3 The Ammonites tormented.   4 The Philistines are thrice overcome with their giants.

18:16 ¹ Or, Seraiah.
18:17 ¹ Read 2 Sam. 8:18.
19:2 ¹ Because Nahash received David and his company, when Saul persecuted him he would now show pleasure to his son for the same.
19:3 ¹ Thus the malicious ever interpret the purpose of the godly in the worst sense.
19:4 ¹ They shaved off the half of their beards, 2 Sam. 10:4.
     ² To put them to shame and villainy, whereas the ambassadors ought to have been honored: and because the Jews used to wear

side garments and beards, they thus disfigured them, to make them odious to others.
19:6 ¹ Or, had made themselves to be abhorred of David.
     ² Which were five in all.
19:7 ¹ Which was a city of the tribe of Reuben beyond Jordan.
19:13 ¹ He declareth that where the cause is evil, the courage cannot be valiant, and that in good causes men ought to be courageous, and commit the success to God.
19:16 ¹ That is, Euphrates.
19:18 ¹ For this place, read 2 Sam. 10:18.

1 And [a]when the year was expired, in the time that kings go out *a warfare*, Joab carried out the strength of the army, and destroyed the country of the children of Ammon, and came and besieged [1]Rabbah (but David tarried at Jerusalem) and Joab smote Rabbah, and destroyed it.

2 [b]Then David took the crown of their king from off his head, and found it the weight of a [1]talent of gold with precious stones in it: and it was *set* on David's head, and he brought away the spoil of the city exceeding much.

3 And he carried away the people that were in it, and cut them with saws, and with harrows of iron, and with axes: even thus did David with all the cities of the children of Ammon. Then David and all the people came again to Jerusalem.

4 ¶[c]And after this also there arose war at [1]Gezer with the Philistines: then Sibbechai the Hushathite slew [2]Sippai of the children of [3]Haraphah, and they were subdued.

5 And there was yet *another* battle with the Philistines: and Elhanan the son of Jair slew [1]Lahmi the brother of Goliath the Gittite, whose spear staff *was* like a weaver's beam.

6 And yet again there was a battle at Gath, where was a man of a *great* stature, and his fingers *were* by [1]sixes, *even* four and twenty, and was also the son of Haraphah.

7 And when he reviled Israel, Jonathan the son of Shimea David's brother did slay him.

8 These were born unto Haraphah at Gath, and fell by the hand of David, and by the hands of his servants.

21 *1 David causeth the people to be numbered,   14 and there dieth seventy thousand men of the pestilence.*

1 And [1]Satan stood up against Israel, and provoked David to number Israel.

2 Therefore David said to Joab, and to the rulers of the people, Go, *and* number Israel from [1]Beersheba even to Dan, and bring it to me, that I may know the number of them.

3 And Joab answered, The Lord increased his people an hundred times so many as they be, O my

CHAPTER 20
[a] 2 Sam. 11:1
[b] 2 Sam. 12:29,30
[c] 2 Sam. 21:18

lord the king: are they not all my lord's servants? wherefore doeth my lord require this thing? why should he be a cause of [1]trespass to Israel?

4 Nevertheless, the king's word prevailed against Joab. And Joab departed and went through all Israel, and returned to Jerusalem.

5 And Joab gave the number *and* sum of the people unto David: and all Israel were [1]eleven hundred thousand men that drew sword: and Judah was [2]four hundred and seventy thousand men that drew sword.

6 But the Levites and Benjamin counted he not among them: for the King's word was abominable to Joab.

7 ¶ And God was displeased with this thing: therefore he smote Israel.

8 Then David said unto God, I have sinned greatly, because I have done this thing: but now, I beseech thee, remove the iniquity of thy servant: for I have done very foolishly.

9 And the Lord spake unto Gad David's [1]Seer, saying,

10 Go and tell David, saying, Thus saith the Lord, I offer thee three things: choose thee one of them, that I may do it unto thee.

11 So Gad came to David, and said unto him, Thus saith the Lord, Take to thee,

12 Either three years famine, or three months to be destroyed before thine adversaries, and the sword of thine enemies [1]to take *thee*, or else the sword of the Lord and pestilence in the land three days, that the Angel of the Lord may destroy throughout all the coasts of Israel: now therefore advise thee, what word I shall bring again to him that sent me.

13 And David said unto Gad, I am in a wonderful strait, let me now fall into the hand of the Lord: for his mercies *are* exceedingly great, and let me not fall into the hand of man.

14 So the Lord sent a pestilence in Israel, and there fell of Israel seventy thousand men.

15 ¶ And God sent the Angel into Jerusalem to destroy it. And [1]as he was destroying, the Lord beheld, and [2]repented of the evil, and said to the Angel that destroyed, It is now enough, let thine hand cease. Then the Angel of the Lord stood by the threshing

---

20:1 [1] Which was the chief city of the Ammonites.
20:2 [1] Which mounteth about the value of seven thousand and seventy crowns, which is about threescore pound weight.
20:4 [1] Or, Gob, 2 Sam. 21:18.
   [2] Or, Saph.
   [3] Or, Raphaim, or the giants.
20:5 [1] Read 2 Sam. 21:19.
20:6 [1] Meaning, that he had six apiece on hands and feet.
21:1 [1] He tempted David, in setting before his eyes his excellency and glory, his power and victories, read 2 Sam. 24:1.
21:2 [1] That is, from South to North.
21:3 [1] It was a thing indifferent and usual to number the people, but

because he did it of an ambitious mind, as though his strength stood in his people, God punished him.
21:5 [1] Joab partly for grief, and partly through negligence, gathered not the whole sum as it is here declared.
   [2] In Samuel is mention of thirty thousand more, which was either by joining to them some of the Benjamites which were mixed with Judah, or as the Hebrews write, here the chief and princes are left out.
21:9 [1] Or, Prophet.
21:12 [1] Or, smite thee.
21:15 [1] Read 2 Sam. 24:16.
   [2] When God draweth back his plagues, he seemeth to repent, read Gen. 6:6.

floor of ³Ornan the Jebusite.

16 And David lifted up his eyes, and saw the Angel of the Lord stand between the earth and the heaven, with his sword drawn in his hand *and* stretched out toward Jerusalem. Then David and the Elders of Israel which were clothed in sack, fell upon their faces.

17 And David said unto God, Is it not I that commanded to number the people? It is even I that have sinned and have committed evil, but these sheep, what have they done? O Lord my God, I beseech thee, let thine hand be on me and on my father's house, and not on ¹thy people for *their* destruction.

18 ¶ Then the Angel of the Lord commanded Gad to say to David, that David should go up, and set up an altar unto the Lord in the threshing floor of Ornan the Jebusite.

19 So David went up according to the saying of Gad, which he had spoken in the Name of the Lord.

20 And Ornan turned about and saw the Angel, and his four sons *that were* with him, ¹hid themselves, and Ornan threshed wheat.

21 And as David came to Ornan, Ornan looked and saw David, and went out of the threshing floor, and bowed himself to David with his face to the ground.

22 And David said to Ornan, Give me the place of *thy* threshing floor, that I may build an ¹altar therein unto the Lord: give it me for sufficient money, that the plague may be stayed from the people.

23 Then Ornan said unto David, Take it to thee, and let my lord the king do that which seemeth him good: lo, I give thee bullocks for burnt offerings, and threshing instruments for wood, and wheat for meat offering, I give it all.

24 And King David said to Ornan, Not so: but I will buy it for sufficient ¹money: for I will not take that which is thine for the Lord, nor offer burnt offerings without cost.

25 So David gave to Ornan for that place ¹six hundred shekels of gold by weight.

26 And David built there an altar unto the Lord, and offered burnt offerings, and peace offerings, and

CHAPTER 22
a 2 Sam. 7:13

called upon the Lord, and he ¹answered him by fire from heaven upon the altar of burnt offering.

27 And when the Lord had spoken to the Angel, he put up his sword again into his sheath.

28 At that time when David saw that the Lord had heard him in the threshing floor of Ornan the Jebusite, then he sacrificed there.

29 (But the Tabernacle of the Lord which Moses had made in the wilderness, and the altar of burnt offering *were* at that season in the high place at Gibeon.

30 And David could not go before it to ask counsel at God: for he was afraid of the sword of the Angel of the Lord.)

22

2 *David prepareth things necessary for the building of the Temple.* 6 *He commandeth his son Solomon to build the Temple of the Lord, which thing he himself was forbidden to do.* 9 *Under the figure of Solomon Christ is promised.*

1 And David said, This is the ¹house of the Lord God, and this is the altar for the burnt offering of Israel.

2 And David commanded to gather together the ¹strangers that were in the land of Israel, and he set masons to hew and polish stones to build the house of God.

3 David also prepared ¹much iron for the nails of the doors *and* of the gates, and for the joinings, and abundance of brass passing weight,

4 And cedar trees without number: for the Sidonians and they of Tyre brought much cedar wood to David.

5 And David said, Solomon my son is young and tender, and we must build an house for the Lord, magnifical, excellent and of great fame and dignity throughout all countries: I will *therefore* now prepare for him. So David prepared very much before his death.

6 Then he called Solomon his son, and charged him to build an house for the Lord God of Israel.

7 And David said to Solomon, *a*My son, I purposed with myself to build an house to the Name of the Lord my God,

8 But the word of the Lord came to me, saying,

21:15 ³ Or, Araunah.

21:17 ¹ Thus he both showeth a true repentance and a fatherly care toward his people, which desireth God to spare them, and to punish him and his.

21:20 ¹ If man hide himself at the sight of an Angel which is a creature, how much as a sinner able to appear before the face of God?

21:22 ¹ Thus he did by the commandment of God, as verse 18, for else it had been abominable, except he had either God's word, or revelation.

21:24 ¹ That is, as much as it is worth: for having enough of his own, and yet to have taken of another man's goods to offer unto the Lord,

it had been theft and not acceptable to God.

21:25 ¹ Read 2 Sam. 24:24.

21:26 ¹ God declared that he heard his request, in that he sent down fire from heaven, for else they might use no fire in sacrifice, but of that which was reserved still upon the altar, Lev. 6:13, and came down from heaven, Lev. 9:24, as appeared by the punishment of Nadab and Abihu, Lev. 10:1.

22:1 ¹ That is, the place wherein he will be worshipped.

22:2 ¹ Meaning, cunning men of other nations which dwelt among the Jews.

22:3 ¹ To wit, which weighed fifty shekels of gold, 2 Chron. 3:9.

b,1Thou hast shed much blood, and hast made great battles: thou shalt not build an house unto my name: for thou hast shed much blood upon the earth in my sight.

9 Behold, a son is born to thee, which shall be a man of rest, for I will give him rest from all his enemies round about: therefore his name is Solomon: and I will send peace and quietness upon Israel in his days.

10 ᶜHe shall build an house for my Name, and he shall be my son, and I will be his father, and I will establish the throne of his kingdom upon Israel forever.

11 Now *therefore* my son, the Lord shall be with thee, and thou shalt ¹prosper, and thou shalt build an house to the Lord thy God, as he hath spoken of thee.

12 Only the Lord give thee ¹wisdom and understanding, and give thee charge over Israel, even to keep the Law of the Lord thy God.

13 Then thou shalt prosper, if thou take heed to observe the statutes and the judgments which the Lord commanded Moses for Israel: be strong and of good courage: fear not, neither be afraid.

14 For behold, according to my ¹poverty have I prepared for the house of the Lord an hundred thousand talents of gold, and a thousand thousand talents of silver, and of brass and of iron passing weight: for there was abundance. I have also prepared timber and stone, and thou mayest provide more thereto.

15 Moreover thou hast workmen with thee enough, ¹hewers of stone, and workmen of timber, and all men expert in every work.

16 Of gold, of silver, *and* of brass, and of iron there is no number: ¹Up *therefore*, and be doing, and the Lord will be with thee.

17 David also commanded all the princes of Israel to help Solomon his son, *saying,*

18 Is not the Lord your God with you, and hath given you rest on every side? for he hath given the ¹inhabitants of the land into mine hand, and the land is subdued before the Lord, and before his people.

19 Now set ¹your hearts and your souls to seek the Lord your God, and arise, and build the Sanctuary of the Lord God, to bring the Ark of the covenant of the Lord, and the holy vessels of God into the

Marginal references:
b 1 Chron. 28:3
c 2 Sam. 7:13
  1 Kings 5:5

CHAPTER 23
a 1 Kings 1:30
b 1 Chron. 6:1
c Exod. 6:17
d Exod. 2:2
  Exod. 6:20
  Heb. 5:4,5
e Exod. 2:22
  Exod. 18:3

house built for the Name of the Lord.

23

1 David being old, ordaineth Solomon King. 3 He causeth the Levites to be numbered, 4 and assigneth them to their offices. 13 Aaron and his sons are for the high Priest. 14 The sons of Moses.

1 So when David was old and full of days, ᵃhe made Solomon his son King over Israel.

2 And he gathered together all the princes of Israel with the Priests and the Levites.

3 And the Levites were numbered from the age of thirty years and above, and their number according to their sum was eight and thirty thousand men.

4 Of these four and twenty thousand *were set* to ¹advance the work of the house of the Lord, and six thousand were overseers and judges.

5 And four thousand *were* porters, and four thousand praised the Lord with instruments which ¹he made to praise *the Lord.*

6 ᵇSo David divided offices unto them, *to wit,* to the sons of Levi, to ᶜGershon, Kohath, and Merari.

7 Of the Gershonites *were* ¹Laadan and Shimei.

8 The sons of Laadan, the chief *was* Jehiel, and Zetham and Joel, three.

9 The Sons of Shimei, Shelomith, and Haziel, and Haran, three: these were the chief fathers of Laadan.

10 Also the sons of Shimei *were* Jahath, Zina, Jeush, and Beriah: these four were the sons of Shimei.

11 And Jahath was the chief, and ¹Zizah the second, but Jeush and Beriah had not many sons: therefore they were in the families of *their* father, counted but as one.

12 ¶ The sons of Kohath *were* Amram, Izhar, Hebron and Uzziel, four.

13 ᵈThe sons of Amram, Aaron and Moses: and Aaron was separated to ¹sanctify the most holy place, he and his sons forever to burn incense before the Lord, to minister to him, and to bless in his Name forever.

14 ¶ Moses also the man of God *and* his children were named with the ¹tribe of Levi.

15 The sons of Moses *were* Gershon, and Eliezer.

16 Of the sons of ᵉGershon *was* Shebuel the chief.

22:8 ¹ This declareth how greatly God detesteth the shedding of blood, seeing David for this cause is stayed to build the Temple of the Lord, albeit he enterprised no war, but by God's commandment and against his enemies.
22:11 ¹ He showeth that there can be no prosperity, but when the Lord is with us.
22:12 ¹ These are only the means whereby Kings govern their subjects aright, and whereby the Realms do prosper and flourish.
22:14 ¹ For David was poor in respect of Solomon.
22:15 ¹ Or, masons and carpenters.
22:16 ¹ That is, go about it quickly.
22:18 ¹ The nations round about.

22:19 ¹ For else he knew that God would plague them, and not prosper their labor, except they sought with all their hearts to set forth his glory.
23:4 ¹ Or, to have care over.
23:5 ¹ Hebrew, *I made,* meaning David.
23:7 ¹ Or, Libni, 1 Chron. 6:17.
23:11 ¹ Or, Zina.
23:13 ¹ That is, to serve in the most holy place, and to consecrate the holy things.
23:14 ¹ They were but of the order of the Levites, and not of the Priests as Aaron's sons.

17 And the son of Eliezer *was* Rehabiah the ¹chief: for Eliezer had none other sons: but the sons of Rehabiah were very many.

18 The son of Izhar *was* Shelomith the chief.

19 The sons of Hebron *were* Jeriah the first, Amariah the second, Jahaziel the third, and Jekameam the fourth.

20 The sons of Uzziel *were* Michah the first, and Jesshiah the second.

21 ¶ The sons of Merari *were* Mahli and Mushi. The sons of Mahli, Eleazar and Kish.

22 And Eleazar died, and had no sons, but daughters, and their ¹brethren the sons of Kish took them.

23 The sons of Mushi *were* Mahli, and Eder, and Jeremoth, three.

24 These were the sons of Levi according to the house of their fathers, *even* the chief fathers according to their offices, according to the number of names, *and* their sum that did the work for the service of the house of the Lord from the age of ¹twenty years and above.

25 For David said, The Lord God of Israel hath given rest unto his people, that they may dwell in Jerusalem forever.

26 And also the Levites shall no more bear the Tabernacle and all the vessels for the service thereof.

27 Therefore according to the last words of David, the Levites were numbered from twenty years and above,

28 And their office *was* under the hand of the sons of Aaron, for the service of the house of the Lord in the courts, and chambers, and in the ¹purifying of all holy things, and in the work of the service of the house of God,

29 Both for the showbread, and for the fine flour, for the meat offering, and for the unleavened cakes, and for the fried things, and for that which was roasted, and for all measures and size,

30 And for to stand every morning, to give thanks and praise to the Lord, and likewise at even,

31 And to offer all burnt offerings unto the Lord in the Sabbaths, in the months, *and* at the appointed times, according to the number and according to their custom, continually before the Lord,

32 And that they should keep the charge of the Tabernacle of the Congregation, and the charge of the holy place, and the charge of the sons of Aaron their brethren in the service of the house of the Lord.

CHAPTER 24
ᵃ Lev. 10:4,6
Num. 3:4
Num. 26:60

24

3 David assigneth offices to the sons of Aaron.

1 These are also the ᵃdivisions of the sons of Aaron: The sons of Aaron *were* Nadab, and Abihu, Eleazar, and Ithamar.

2 But Nadab and Abihu died ¹before their father, and had no children: therefore Eleazar and Ithamar executed the Priest's office.

3 And David distributed them, even Zadok of the ¹sons of Eleazar, and Ahimelech of the sons of Ithamar according to their offices in their ministration.

4 And there were found more of the sons of Eleazar by the ¹number of men, than of the sons of Ithamar, and they divided them, *to wit*, among the sons of Eleazar, sixteen heads, according to the household of their fathers, and among the sons of Ithamar, according to the household of their fathers, eight.

5 Thus they distributed them by lot the one from the other, and so the rulers of the Sanctuary and the rulers *of the house* of God *were* of the sons of Eleazar, and of the sons of Ithamar.

6 And Shemaiah the son of Nethanel the Scribe of the Levites, wrote them before the king and the princes, and Zadok the Priest, and Ahimelech the son of Abiathar, and *before* the chief fathers of the Priests and of the Levites, one family being reserved for Eleazar, and another reserved for Ithamar.

7 And the first ¹lot fell to Jehoiarib, and the second to Jedaiah,

8 The third to Harim, the fourth to Seorim,

9 The fifth to Malchijah, the sixth to Mijamin,

10 The seventh to Hakkoz, the eight to ¹Abijah,

11 The ninth to Jeshua, the tenth to Shecaniah,

12 The eleventh to Eliashib, the twelfth to Jakim,

13 The thirteenth to Huppah, the fourteenth to Jeshebeab,

14 The fifteenth to Bilgah, the sixteenth to Immer,

15 The seventeenth to Hezir, the eighteenth to Happizzez,

16 The nineteenth to Pethahiah, the twentieth to Jehezekel,

17 The one and twenty to Jachin, the two and twenty to Gamul,

18 The three and twenty to Delaiah, the four and twenty to Maaziah.

19 These were their orders according to their offices, when they entered into the house of the Lord according to their custom under ¹the hand of

---

23:17 ¹ The Scripture useth to call chief or the firstborn, although he be alone and there be none born after, Matt. 1:25.

23:22 ¹ Meaning, their cousins.

23:24 ¹ David did choose the Levites twice, first at the age of thirty, as verse 3 and again afterward at 20, as the necessity of the office did require: at the beginning they had no charge in the Temple, before they were five and twenty years old, and had none after fifty, Num. 4:3.

23:28 ¹ In washing and cleansing all the holy vessels.

24:2 ¹ While their father yet lived.

24:3 ¹ Or, cousins.

24:4 ¹ Hebrew, *heads.*

24:7 ¹ This lot was ordained to take away all occasion of envy or grudging of one against another.

24:10 ¹ Zacharias the father of John the Baptist was of this course or lot of Abija, Luke 1:5.

24:19 ¹ By the dignity that God gave to Aaron.

Aaron their father, as the Lord God of Israel had commanded him.

20 ¶ And of the sons of Levi that remained of the sons of Amram, *was* Shubael, of the sons of Shubael, Jehdeiah,

21 Of Rehabiah, *even* of the sons of Rehabiah, the first Isshiah,

22 Of Izhari, Shelomoth, of the sons of Shelomoth, Jahath,

23 And *his* sons, Jeriah *the first*, Amariah the second, Jahaziel the third, *and* Jekameam the fourth,

24 The son of Uzziel *was* Michah, the son of Michah *was* Shamir,

25 The brother of Michah *was* Isshiah, the son of Isshiah, Zechariah,

26 The sons of Merari, *were* Mahli and Mushi, the son of Jaaziah *was* Beno,

27 The sons of Merari, of Jaaziah *were* Beno, and Shoham, and Zaccur and Ibri.

28 Of Mahli *came* Eleazar, which had no sons.

29 Of Kish: the son of Kish *was* Jerahmeel,

30 And the sons of [1]Mushi *were* Mahli, and Eder, and Jerimoth: these were sons of the Levites after the household of their fathers.

31 And these also cast [1]lots with their brethren the sons of Aaron before King David, and Zadok and Ahimelech and the chief fathers of the Priests, and of the Levites, *even* the chief of the families against their younger brethren.

25

The singers are appointed with their places and lots.

1 So David and the captains of the army [1]separated for the ministry the sons of Asaph, and Heman, and Jeduthun, who should *sing* prophesies with harps, with viols, and with cymbals, and their number was *even* of the men for the office of their ministry, *to wit*,

2 Of the sons of Asaph, Zaccur, and Joseph, and Nethaniah, and Asharelah the sons of Asaph *were* under the hand of Asaph, *which sang* prophecies by the [1]commission of the King.

3 Of Jeduthun, the sons of Jeduthun, Gedaliah, and Zeri, and Jeshaiah, Hashabiah and Mattithiah, [1]six, under the hands of their father: Jeduthun *sang* [2]prophecies with an harp, for to give thanks and to praise the Lord.

4 Of Heman, the sons of Heman, Bukkiah, Mattaniah, Uzziel, Shebuel, and Jerimoth, Hananiah, Hanani, Eliathah, Giddalti, and Romamti-Ezer, Joshbekashah, Mallothi, Hothir, *and* Mahazioth.

5 All these were the sons of Heman, the King's [1]Seer in the words of God to lift up the [2]horn: and God gave to Heman fourteen sons and three daughters.

6 All these were under the [1]hand of their father singing in the house of the Lord with cymbals, viols and harps, for the service of the house of God, and Asaph, and Jeduthun, and Heman *were* at the King's [2]commandment.

7 So was their number with their brethren that were instructed in the songs of the Lord, *even* of all that were cunning, two hundred fourscore and eight.

8 And they cast lots, [1]charge against *charge*, as well [2]small as great, the cunning man as the scholar.

9 And the first lot fell to [1]Joseph, *which was* of Asaph, the second, to Gedaliah, who with his brethren and his sons were twelve.

10 The third, to Zaccur, *he*, his sons and his brethren *were* twelve.

11 The fourth, to [1]Jizri, *he*, his sons and his brethren twelve.

12 The fifth, to Nethaniah, *he*, his sons and his brethren twelve.

13 The sixth, to Bukkiah, *he*, his sons and his brethren twelve.

14 The seventh, to Jesharelah, *he*, his sons and his brethren twelve.

15 The eighth to Jeshaiah, *he*, his sons and his brethren twelve.

16 The ninth to Mattaniah, *he*, his sons and his brethren twelve.

17 The tenth to Shimei, *he*, his sons and his brethren twelve.

18 The eleventh to Azarel, *he*, his sons and his brethren twelve.

19 The twelfth to Hashabiah, *he*, his sons and his brethren twelve.

20 The thirteenth to Shubael, *he*, his sons and his brethren twelve.

21 The fourteenth to Mattithiah, *he*, his sons and his brethren twelve.

22 The fifteenth to Jeremoth, *he*, his sons and his brethren twelve.

23 The sixteenth to Hananiah, *he*, his sons and

24:30 [1] Which was the second son of Merari.
24:31 [1] That is, every one had that dignity, which fell unto him by lot.
25:1 [1] The singers were divided into 24 courses, so that every course or order contained twelve, and in all there were 288, as verse 7.
25:2 [1] Hebrew, *hands*.
25:3 [1] Whereof one is not here numbered.
　　 [2] Meaning, Psalms and songs to praise God.
25:5 [1] Or, Prophet.

[2] Or, power, meaning of the king.
25:6 [1] Or, government.
　　 [2] Hebrew, *hand*.
25:8 [1] Who should be in every company and course.
　　 [2] Without respect to age or cunning.
25:9 [1] So that he served in the first turn, and the rest everyone as his turn followed orderly.
25:11 [1] Or, the Zerites.

his brethren twelve.

24 The seventeenth to Joshbekashah, *he*, his sons and his brethren twelve.

25 The eighteenth to Hanani, *he*, his sons and his brethren twelve.

26 The nineteenth to Mallothi, *he*, his sons and his brethren twelve.

27 The twentieth to Eliathah, *he*, his sons and his brethren twelve.

28 The one and twentieth to Hothir, *he*, his sons and his brethren twelve.

29 The two and twentieth to Giddalti, *he*, his sons and his brethren twelve.

30 The three and twentieth to Mahazioth, *he*, his sons and his brethren twelve.

31 The four and twentieth to Romamti-Ezer, *he*, his sons and his brethren twelve.

26 ¹ *The porters of the Temple are ordained, every man to the gate, which he should keep,* 20 *and over the treasure.*

1 Concerning the ¹divisions of the porters, of the Korahites, Meshelemiah the son of Kore of the sons of ²Asaph.

2 And the sons of Meshelemiah, Zechariah the eldest, Jediael the second, Zebadiah the third, Jathniel the fourth,

3 Elam the fifth, Jehohanan the sixth, *and* Eliehoe-nai the seventh.

4 And the sons of Obed-Edom, Shemaiah the eldest, Jehozabad the second, Joah the third, and Sacar the fourth, and Nethanel the fifth,

5 Ammiel the sixth, Issachar the seventh, Peulthai the eight: for God had ¹blessed him.

6 And to Shemaiah his son were sons born that ¹ruled in the house of their father, for they were men of might.

7 The sons of Shemaiah *were* Othni, and Rephael, and Obed, Elzabad, *and* his brethren, strong men: Elihu also, and Semachiah.

8 All these were of the ¹sons of Obed-Edom, they and their sons and their brethren mighty and ²strong to serve, *even* threescore and two of Obed-Edom.

9 And of Meshelemiah sons and brethren, eighteen mighty men.

10 And of Hosah of the sons of Merari, the sons *were* Shimri the chief, and (though he was not the eldest, yet his father made him the chief)

11 Hilkiah the second, Tebaliah the third, *and* Zechariah the fourth: all the ¹sons and the brethren of Hosah *were* thirteen.

12 Of these *were* the ¹divisions of the porters, of the chief men, *having* the charge ²against their brethren, to serve in the house of the Lord.

13 And they cast lots both small and great, for the house of their fathers, for every gate.

14 And the lot on the East side fell to ¹Shelemiah: then they cast lots for Zechariah his son a ²wise counselor, and his lot came out Northward:

15 To Obed-Edom Southward, and to his sons the house of ¹Asuppim:

16 To Shuppim and to Hosah Westward with the gate ¹of Shallecheth by the paved street that goeth upward, ward over against ward.

17 Eastward *were* six Levites, *and* Northward four a day, *and* Southward four a day, and toward Asuppim ¹two *and* two.

18 In ¹Parbar toward the West *were* four by the paved street, and two in Parbar.

19 These are the divisions of the porters of the sons of Korah, and of the sons of Merari.

20 ¶ And of the Levites. Ahijah *was* over the treasures of the house of God, and over the treasures of the dedicate things.

21 Of the sons of Laadan the sons of the Gershonites *descending* of Laadan, the chief fathers of Laadan *were* Gershon *and* Jehieli.

22 The sons of Jehieli *were* Zetham and Joel his brother, *appointed* over the treasures of the house of the Lord.

23 Of the ¹Amramites, of the Izharites, of the Hebronites, *and* of the Uzzielites.

24 And Shebuel the son of Gershom, the son of Moses, a ruler over the treasures.

25 And of his ¹brethren *which came* of Eliezer, was Rehabiah his son, and Jeshaiah his son, and Joram his son, and Zichri his son, and Shelomith his son.

26 Which Shelomith and his brethren *were* over all the treasures of the dedicate things, which David the king, and the chief fathers, the captains over

26:1 ¹ Or, courses, or turns.
² This Asaph was not the notable musician, but another of that name called also Ebiasaph, 1 Chron. 6:23, 37 and 9:19 and also Jasaph.
26:5 ¹ In giving him many children.
26:6 ¹ Or, like their father's house, meaning, worthy men, and valiant.
26:8 ¹ Or, nephews.
² And meet to serve the office of the portership.
26:11 ¹ Or, cousins.
26:12 ¹ Or, courses.
² According to their turns as well the one as the other.

26:14 ¹ Or, Meshelemiah.
² One expert and meet to keep that gate.
26:15 ¹ This was an house, where they used to resort to consult of things concerning the Temple, as a convocation house.
26:16 ¹ Whereat they used to cast out the filth of the city.
26:17 ¹ Meaning two one day, and two another.
26:18 ¹ Which was an house wherein they kept the instruments of the Temple.
26:23 ¹ These also had charge over the treasures.
26:25 ¹ Or, cousins.

thousands, and hundreds, and the captains of the army had [1]dedicated.

27 (*For* of the battles and of the spoils they did dedicate to maintain the house of the Lord.)

28 And all that Samuel the Seer had dedicated, and Saul the son of Kish, and Abner the son of Ner, and Joab the son of Zeruiah, *and* whosoever had dedicated *anything, it was* under the hand of Shelomith, and his brethren.

29 Of the Izharites *was* Chenaniah and his sons, for the business [1]without over Israel, for officers and for Judges.

30 Of the Hebronites, Hashabiah and his brethren, men of activity, a thousand and seven hundred were officers for Israel beyond Jordan Westward in all the business of the Lord, and for the service of [1]the King.

31 Among the Hebronites *was* Jerijah the chiefest, even the Hebronites by his generations according to the families. And in the fortieth year of the reign of David they were sought for: and there were found among them men of activity at Jazer in Gilead.

32 And his [1]brethren men of activity, two thousand and seven hundred chief fathers, whom King David made rulers over the Reubenites, and the Gadites, and the half tribe of Manasseh, for every matter *pertaining* to [2]God, and for the king's business.

27 Of the princes and rulers that ministered unto the King.

1 The children of Israel also after their number, *even* the chief fathers and captains of thousands and of hundreds, and their officers that served the king by divers [1]courses, [2]which came in and went out, month by month throughout all the months of the year: in every course *were* four and twenty thousand.

2 Over the first course for the first month *was* Jashobeam the son of Zabdiel: and in his course *were* four and twenty thousand.

3 Of the sons of Perez *was* the chief over all the princes of the armies for the first month.

4 And over the course of the second month was Dodai an Ahohite, and *this was* his course, and Mikloth *was* [1]a captain, and in his course *were* four and twenty thousand.

5 The captain of the third host for the third month *was* Benaiah the son of Jehoiada the chief Priest: and in his course *were* four and twenty thousand.

CHAPTER 27
[a] 2 Sam. 23:20
2 Sam. 22:23

6 This Benaiah was mighty among [a]thirty and above the thirty, and in his course *was* Ammizabad his son.

7 The fourth for the fourth month *was* Asahel the brother of Joab, and Zebadiah his son after him: and in his course *were* four and twenty thousand.

8 The fifth for the fifth month *was* prince Shamhuth the Izrahite: and in his course four and twenty thousand.

9 The sixth for the sixth month *was* Ira the son of Ikkesh the Tekoite: and in his course four and twenty thousand.

10 The seventh for the seventh month *was* Helez the Pelonite, of the sons of Ephraim: and in his course four and twenty thousand.

11 The eight for the eight month *was* Sibbechai the Hushathite of the Zarhites: and in his course four and twenty thousand.

12 The ninth for the ninth month *was* Abiezer the Anathothite of the sons of [1]Jemini: and in his course four and twenty thousand.

13 The tenth for the tenth month *was* Maharai the Netophathite of the Zarhites: and in his course four and twenty thousand.

14 The eleventh for the eleventh month *was* Benaiah the Pirathonite of the sons of Ephraim: and in his course four and twenty thousand.

15 The twelfth for the twelfth month *was* Heldai the Netophathite, of Othniel: and in his course four and twenty thousand.

16 ¶ Moreover [1]*the rulers* over the tribes of Israel *were these*: over the Reubenites *was* ruler, Eliezer the son of Zichri: over the Simeonites, Shephatiah the son of Maachah:

17 Over the Levites, Hashabiah the son of Kemuel: over *them* of Aaron, *and* Zadok:

18 Over Judah, Elihu of the brethren of David: over Issachar, Omri the son of Michael:

19 Over Zebulun, Ishmaiah the son of Obadiah: over Naphtali, Jerimoth the son of Azriel:

20 Over the sons of Ephraim, Hoshea the son of Azaziah: over the half tribe of Manasseh, Joel the son of Pedaiah:

21 Over the [1]*other* half of Manasseh in Gilead, Iddo the son of Zechariah: over Benjamin, Jaasiel the son of Abner:

22 Over Dan, Azarel the son of Jeroham. These are the princes of the tribes of Israel.

26:26 [1] According as the Lord commanded, Num. 31:28.
26:29 [1] Meaning, of things that were out of the city.
26:30 [1] That is, for the king's house.
26:32 [1] To wit, the cousins of Jerijah.
    [2] Both in spiritual and temporal things.
27:1 [1] Hebrew, *divisions*, or *bands*.
    [2] Which executed their charge and office, which is meant by com-

ing in, and going out.
27:4 [1] That is, Dodai's lieutenant.
27:12 [1] Or, Benjamin.
27:16 [1] Meaning, besides these twelve captains.
27:21 [1] Which is beyond Jordan, in respect of Judah: also one captain was over the Reubenites and the Gadites.

23 But David took not the number of them from twenty years old and under, because the Lord had said that he would increase Israel like unto the stars of the heavens.

24 And [b]Joab the son of Zeruiah began to number: but he finished it not, [1]because there came wrath for it against Israel: neither was the number put into the [2]Chronicles of king David.

25 And over the king's treasures *was* Azmaveth the son of Adiel: and over the treasures in the fields, in the cities and in the villages, and in the towers *was* Jehonathan the son of Uzziah:

26 And over the workmen in the field that tilleth the ground, *was* Ezri the son of Chelub:

27 And over them that dressed the vines, *was* Shimei the Ramathite: and over that which appertained to the vines, and over the store of the wine *was* Zabdi the Shiphmite:

28 And over the olive trees and mulberry trees that were in the valleys, *was* Baal-Hanan the Gederite: and over the store of the oil *was* Joash:

29 And over the oxen that fed in Sharon, *was* Shitrai the Sharonite: and over the oxen in the valleys *was* Shaphat the son of Adlai:

30 And over the camels *was* Obil the Ishmaelite: and over the asses *was* Jehdeiah the Meronothite:

31 And over the sheep *was* Jaziz the Hagrite: all these were the rulers of the substance that was king David's.

32 And Jehonathan David's uncle a man of counsel and understanding (for he was a [1]scribe) and Jehiel the son of Hachmoni *were* with the King's [2]sons.

33 And Ahithophel *was* the king's counselor, and Hushai the Archite the king's friend.

34 And [1]after Ahithophel *was* Jehoiada the son of Benaiah and Abiathar: and captain of the King's army *was* Joab.

28

3 *Because David was forbidden to build the Temple, he willeth Solomon and the people to perform it.* 8 *Exhorting him to fear the Lord.*

1 Now David assembled all the princes of Israel: the princes of the tribes, and the captains of the bands that served the King, and the captains of thousands, and the captains of hundreds, and the rulers of all

b 1 Chron. 21:7

CHAPTER 28
a Ps. 96:5
b 2 Sam. 7:5,13
1 Chron. 22:8
c 1 Sam. 16:7
Ps. 7:9
Jer. 11:20
Jer. 17:10
Jer. 20:12

the substance and possession of the king, and of his sons, with the [1]eunuchs, and the mighty, and all the men of power, unto Jerusalem.

2 And King David stood up upon his feet, and said, Hear ye me, my brethren and my people: I purposed to have built an house of [1]rest for the Ark of the covenant of the Lord, and for a [a]footstool of our God, and have made ready for the building,

3 But God said unto me, [b]Thou shalt not build an house for my Name, because thou hast been a man of war, and hast shed blood.

4 Yet *as* the Lord God of Israel chose me before all the house of my father, to be King over Israel forever (for in Judah would he choose a prince, and of the house of [1]Judah is the house of my father, and among the sons of my father he delighted in me to make me king over all Israel)

5 So of all my sons (for the Lord hath given me many sons) he hath even chosen Solomon my son to sit upon the throne of the kingdom of the Lord over Israel.

6 And he said unto me, Solomon thy son, he shall build mine house and my courts: for I have chosen him to be my son, and I will be his father.

7 I will establish therefore his kingdom forever, if he endeavor himself to do my commandments, and my judgments, as [1]this day.

8 Now therefore in the sight of all Israel the congregation of the Lord, and in the audience of our God, keep and seek for all the commandments of the Lord your God, that ye may possess this [1]good land, and leave it for an inheritance for your children after you [2]forever.

9 And thou, Solomon my son, know thou the God of thy father, and serve him with a perfect heart, and with a willing mind: [c]For the Lord searcheth all hearts, and understandeth all the imaginations of thoughts: if thou seek him, he will be found of thee, but if thou forsake him, he will cast thee off forever.

10 Take heed now, for the Lord hath chosen thee to build [1]the house of the Sanctuary: be strong *therefore* and [2]do it.

11 ¶ Then David gave to Solomon his son the pattern of the porch and of the houses thereof, and of the closets thereof, and of the galleries thereof, and of the chambers thereof that are within, and of

---

27:24 [1] And the commandment of the King was abominable to Joab, 1 Chron. 21:6.
  [2] The Hebrews make both these books of Chronicles but one, and at this verse make the midst of the book as touching the number of verses.
27:32 [1] That is, a man learned in the word of God.
  [2] To be their schoolmasters and teachers.
27:34 [1] After that Ahithophel had hanged himself, 2 Sam. 17:23, Jehoiada was made counselor.
28:1 [1] Or, chief servants, Gen. 37:36.

28:2 [1] Where the Ark should remain, and remove no more to and fro.
28:4 [1] According to the prophecy of Jacob, Gen. 49:8.
28:7 [1] If he continue to keep my law and depart not therefrom, as he doeth hitherto.
28:8 [1] To wit, of Canaan.
  [2] He declareth that nothing can separate them from the commodity of this land, both for themselves and their posterity, but their sins and iniquity.
28:10 [1] Meaning, for his Ark.
  [2] Put it in execution.

the house of the mercy seat,

12 And the pattern of all that [1]he had in his mind for the courts of the house of the Lord, and for all the chambers round about, for the treasures of the house of God, and for the treasures of the dedicate things,

13 And for the courses of the Priests, and of the Levites, and for all the work for the service of the house of the Lord, and for all the vessels of the ministry of the house of the Lord.

14 *He gave* of gold by weight, for *the vessels* of gold, for all the vessels of all manner of service, *and* all the vessels of silver by weight, for all manner vessels of all manner of service.

15 The weight also of gold for the [1]candlesticks, and gold for their lamps, with the weight for every candlestick, and for the lamps thereof, and for the candlesticks of silver by the weight of the candlestick, and the lamps thereof according to the use of every candlestick,

16 And the weight of the gold for the tables of showbread, for every table, and silver for the tables of silver,

17 And pure gold for the fleshhooks, and the bowls, and [1]plates, and for basins, gold in weight for every basin, and for silver basins, by weight for every basin,

18 And for the altar of incense, pure gold by weight, and gold for the pattern of [1]the chariot of the Cherubs that spread themselves, and covered the Ark of the covenant of the Lord:

19 All, *said* he, by writing sent to me [1]by the hand of the Lord, *which* made me understand all the workmanship of the pattern.

20 And David said to Solomon his son, Be strong and of a valiant courage, and do it: fear not, nor be afraid: for the Lord God, *even* my God *is* with thee: he will not leave thee, nor forsake thee, till thou hast finished all the work for the service of the house of the Lord.

21 Behold also, the companies of the Priests and the Levites for all the service of the house of God, even *they shall be* with thee for the whole work, [1]with every free heart that is skillful in any manner of service. The princes also and all the people *will be* [2]wholly at thy commandment.

CHAPTER 29
[a] Ps. 122:1

29

2 *The offering of David and of the princes for the building of the Temple.* 10 *David giveth thanks to the Lord.* 20 *He exhorteth the people to do the same.* 22 *Solomon is created king.* 28 *David dieth, and Solomon his son reigneth in his stead.*

1 Moreover, David the King said unto all the Congregation, God hath chosen Solomon mine only son, young and tender, and the work *is* great: for this house *is* not for man, but for the [1]Lord God.

2 Now I have prepared with all my power for the house of my God, gold for *vessels* of gold, and silver for *them* of silver, and brass for *things* of brass, iron for *things* of iron, and wood for *things* of wood, and onyx stones, and stones to be set, and carbuncle stones, and of divers colors, and all precious stones, and marble stones in abundance.

3 Moreover, because I have [1]delight in the house of my God, I have of mine own gold and silver, which I have given to the house of my God, beside all that I have prepared for the house of the Sanctuary,

4 Even [1]three thousand talents of gold of the gold of Ophir, and seven thousand talents of fined silver to overlay the walls of the houses.

5 The gold for the *things* of gold, and the silver for *things* of silver, and for all the work by the hands of artificers: and who is [1]willing [2]to fill his hand today unto the Lord?

6 So the princes of the families, and the princes of the tribes of Israel, and the captains of thousands and of hundreds, with the rulers of the king's work, offered willingly,

7 And they gave for the service of the house of God, five thousand talents of gold, and ten thousand pieces, and ten thousand talents of silver, and eighteen thousand talents of brass, and one hundred thousand talents of iron.

8 And they with whom *precious* stones were [1]found, gave them to the treasure of the house of the Lord, by the hand of Jehiel the Gershonite.

9 And the people rejoiced when they offered willingly: for they offered willingly unto the Lord, with a [1]perfect heart. And David the king also [a]rejoiced with great joy.

10 Therefore David blessed the Lord before all the Congregation, and David said, Blessed *be* thou, O Lord God of [1]Israel our father, forever and ever.

28:12 [1] Hebrew, *that were in his spirit with him.*
28:15 [1] That is, the ten candlesticks, 1 Kings 7:49.
28:17 [1] Or, coverings.
28:18 [1] Meaning, of the mercy seat which covered the Ark, which was called the chariot, because the Lord declared himself there.
28:19 [1] For all this was left in writing in the book of the Law, Exod. 25:40, which book the king was bound to put in execution, Deut. 17:19.
28:21 [1] That is, everyone will be ready to help thee with those gifts that God hath given him.
      [2] Hebrew, *at all thy words.*

29:1 [1] And therefore is taught to be excellent in all points.
29:3 [1] His great zeal toward the furtherance of the Temple made him to spare no expenses, but to bestow his own peculiar treasure.
29:4 [1] He showeth what he had of his own store for the Lord's house.
29:5 [1] He was not only liberal himself, but provoked others to set forth the works of God.
      [2] Or, to offer.
29:8 [1] Meaning, them that had any.
29:9 [1] That is, with a good courage and without hypocrisy.
29:10 [1] Which didst reveal thyself to our father Jacob.

11 Thine, O Lord, is greatness and power, and glory and victory, and praise: for all that is in heaven and in earth *is thine*: thine is the kingdom, O Lord, and thou excellest as head over all.

12 Both riches and honor *come* of thee, and thou reignest over all, and in thine hand is power and strength, and in thine hand it is to make great, and to give strength unto all.

13 Now therefore, our God, we thank thee, and praise thy glorious Name.

14 But who am I, and what is my people, that we should be able to offer willingly after this sort? for all things ¹come of thee: and of thine own hand we have given thee.

15 For we are ¹strangers before thee, and sojourners like all our fathers: our days *are* like the shadow upon the earth, and there is none ²abiding.

16 O Lord our God, all this abundance that we have prepared to build thee an house for thine holy Name, is of thine hand, and all *is* thine.

17 I know also my God, that thou ᵇtriest the heart, and hast pleasure in righteousness: I have offered willingly in the uprightness of mine heart all these things: now also have I seen thy people which are found here, to offer unto thee willingly with joy.

18 O Lord God of Abraham, Isaac, and Israel our fathers, keep this forever in the ¹purpose, *and* the thoughts of the heart of thy people, and prepare their hearts unto thee.

19 And give unto Solomon my son a perfect heart to keep thy commandments, thy testimonies, and thy statutes, and to do all things, and to build the house which I have prepared.

20 ¶ And David said to all the congregation, Now bless the Lord your God. And all the Congregation

ᵇ 1 Sam. 16:7
1 Chron. 28:9
ᶜ 1 Kings 2:11

blessed the Lord God of their fathers, and bowed down their heads, and worshipped the Lord and the ¹king.

21 And they offered sacrifices unto the Lord, and on the morrow after that day, they offered burnt offerings unto the Lord, *even* a thousand young bullocks, a thousand rams, *and* a thousand sheep, with their ¹drink offerings, and sacrifices in abundance for all Israel.

22 And they did eat and drink before the Lord the same day with great joy, and they made Solomon the son of David king the second time, and anointed him prince before the Lord, and Zadok for the high Priest.

23 So Solomon sat on the ¹throne of the Lord, as king instead of David his father, and prospered: and all Israel obeyed him.

24 And all the princes and men of power, and all the sons of king David ¹submitted themselves under king Solomon.

25 And the Lord magnified Solomon in dignity, in the sight of all Israel, and gave him so glorious a kingdom, as no king had before him in Israel.

26 ¶ Thus David the son of Jesse reigned over all Israel.

27 And the space that he reigned over Israel, *was* forty years: seven years reigned he in Hebron, and three and thirty years reigned he in Jerusalem:

28 And he died in a good age, full of days, riches and honor, and Solomon his son reigned in his stead.

29 Concerning the acts of David the king, first and last, behold they are written in the book of Samuel the Seer, and in the book of ¹Nathan the Prophet, and in the book of Gad the Seer,

30 With all his reign and his power, and ¹times that went over him, and over Israel, and over all the kingdoms of the earth.

29:14 ¹ We gave thee nothing of our own, but that which we have received of thee: for whether the gifts be corporal or spiritual, we receive them all of God, and therefore must give him the glory.

29:15 ¹ And therefore have this land but lent to us for a time.
² Hebrew, *waiting for them to return.*

29:18 ¹ Continue them in his good mind, that they may serve thee willingly.

29:20 ¹ That is, did reverence the king.

29:21 ¹ Meaning, all kind of liquor which they mingled with their sacrifices, as wine, oil, etc.

29:23 ¹ This declareth that the Kings of Judah were figures of Christ, who was the true anointed, and to whom God gave the chief government of all things.

29:24 ¹ Hebrew, *gave the hand.*

29:29 ¹ The books of Nathan and Gad are thought to have been lost in the captivity.

29:30 ¹ Meaning, the troubles and griefs.

THE SECOND BOOK

OF THE

CHRONICLES

1 6 *The offering of Solomon at Gibeon.* 8 *He prayeth unto God to give him wisdom:* 11 *Which he giveth him, and more.* 14 *The number of his chariots and horsemen,* 15 *and of his riches.*

1 Then Solomon the son of David was ¹confirmed in his kingdom: and the Lord his God *was* with him, and magnified him highly.

2 And Solomon ¹spake unto all Israel, to the captains of thousands, and of hundreds, and to the judges, and to all the governors in all Israel, *even* the chief fathers.

3 So Solomon and all the Congregation with him went to the high place that was at ¹Gibeon: for there was the Tabernacle ²of the Congregation of God which Moses the servant of the Lord had made in the wilderness.

4 But the Ark of God had David brought up from Kirjath Jearim, when David had made preparation for it: for he had pitched a tent for it in Jerusalem.

5 Moreover, the ¹brazen altar ªthat Bezalel the son of Uri, the son of Hur had made, did he set before the Tabernacle of the Lord: and Solomon and the Congregation sought it.

6 And Solomon offered there before the Lord upon the brazen altar that was in the Tabernacle of the Congregation: ᵇeven a thousand burnt offerings offered he upon it.

7 ¶ The same night did God appear unto Solomon, and said unto him, Ask what I shall give thee.

8 And Solomon said unto God, Thou hast showed great mercy unto David my father, and hast made me to reign in his stead.

9 Now *therefore,* O Lord God, let thy promise unto David my father be ¹true: for thou hast made me King over a great people, like to the dust of the earth.

10 Give me now wisdom and knowledge, that I may ¹go out and go in before this people: for who

ª Exod. 38:1,2
ᵇ 2 Kings 3:4
ᶜ 1 Kings 10:26
ᵈ Isa. 19:9
Ezek. 27:7

can judge this thy great people?

11 And God said to Solomon, Because this was in thine heart, and thou hast not asked riches, treasures nor honor, nor the ¹lives of thine enemies, neither yet hast asked long life, but hast asked for thee wisdom and knowledge, that thou mightest judge my people, over whom I have made thee King,

12 Wisdom and knowledge is granted unto thee, and I will give thee riches and treasures and honor, so that there hath not been the like among the kings which were before thee, neither after thee shall there be the like.

13 Then Solomon came from the high place that was at Gibeon, to Jerusalem from before the Tabernacle of the Congregation, and reigned over Israel.

14 ᶜAnd Solomon gathered the chariots and horsemen: and he had a thousand and four hundred chariots, and twelve thousand horsemen, whom he placed in the ¹chariot cities, and with the King at Jerusalem.

15 And the king gave gold and silver at Jerusalem as ¹stone, and gave cedar trees as the wild fig trees, that are abundantly in the plain.

16 Also Solomon had horses brought out of Egypt, and ᵈfine linen: ¹the King's merchants received the fine linen for a price.

17 They came up also and brought out of Egypt *some* chariot, *worth* six hundred *shekels* of silver, that is an horse for an hundred and fifty: and thus they brought *horses* to all the kings of the Hittites, and to the kings of Aram by their ¹means.

2 2 *The number of Solomon's workmen to build the Temple.* 3 *Solomon sendeth to Huram the King of Tyre for wood and workmen.*

1 Then Solomon determined to build an house for the Name of the Lord, and an ¹house for his kingdom.

1:1 ¹ Or, stablished, and strong, read 1 Kings 2:46.
1:2 ¹ That is, he proclaimed a solemn sacrifice, and commanded that all should be at the same.
1:3 ¹ Read 1 Kings 3:4.
  ² So called, because that God thereby showed certain signs to the congregation of his presence.
1:5 ¹ Which was for the burnt offerings, Exod. 27:1.
1:9 ¹ Perform thy promise made to my father concerning me.

1:10 ¹ That I may govern this people, read 1 Chron. 27:1 and 1 Kings 3:7.
1:11 ¹ That is, to be revenged on thine enemies.
1:14 ¹ Which were cities appointed to keep and maintain the chariots.
1:15 ¹ He caused so great plenty, that it was no more esteemed than stones.
1:16 ¹ Read 1 Kings. 10:28.
1:17 ¹ Hebrew, *hands.*
2:1 ¹ Or, Palace.

2 And Solomon told out seventy thousand that bare burdens, and fourscore thousand men to hew *stones* in the mountain, and three thousand and [1]six hundred to oversee them.

3 And Solomon sent to [1]Huram the king of Tyre, saying, As thou hast done to David my father, and didst [a]send him cedar trees to build him an house to dwell in *so do to me.*

4 Behold, I build an house unto the Name of the Lord my God, to sanctify it unto him, and to burn sweet incense before him, and for the continual showbread, and for the burnt offerings of the morning and evening, on the Sabbath days, and in the new months, and in the solemn feasts of the Lord our God: this is a perpetual thing for Israel.

5 And the house which I build, *is* great: for great *is* our God above all gods.

6 Who is he then that can be able to build him an house, when the heaven and the heaven of heavens can not contain him? who am I then that I should build him an house? but *I do it* to burn [1]incense before him.

7 Send me now therefore a cunning man that can work in gold, in silver, and in brass, and in iron, and in purple, and in [1]crimson and blue silk, and that can grave in graven work with the cunning men that are with me in Judah and in Jerusalem, whom David my father hath prepared.

8 Send me also cedar trees, fir trees and [1,2]Algummim trees from Lebanon: for I know that thy servants can skill to hew timber in Lebanon: and behold, my servants *shall be* with thine,

9 That they may prepare me timber in abundance: for the house which I do build, *is* great and wonderful.

10 And behold, I will give to thy servants the cutters and the hewers of timber twenty thousand [1]measures of beaten wheat, and twenty thousand measures of barley, and twenty thousand baths of wine, and twenty [2]thousand baths of oil.

11 Then Huram king of Tyre answered in writing which he sent to Solomon, Because the Lord hath loved his people, he hath made thee King over them.

CHAPTER 2
[a] 2 Sam. 5:11

CHAPTER 3
[a] 1 Kings 6:1
[b] 2 Sam. 24:16,21

12 Huram said moreover, Blessed *be* the Lord God of Israel, which made the heaven and the earth, and that hath given unto David the King a [1]wise son, that hath discretion, prudence and understanding to build an house for the Lord, and a palace for his kingdom.

13 Now therefore I have sent a wise man, *and* of understanding of my father Huram's,

14 The son of a woman, of the [1]daughters of Dan: and his father was a man of Tyre, and he can skill to work in gold, in silver, in brass, in iron, in stone, and in timber, in purple, in blue silk, and in fine linen, and in crimson, and can grave in all graven works, and broider in all broidered work that shall be given him, with thy cunning men, and with the cunning men of my lord David thy father.

15 Now therefore the wheat and the barley, the oil and the wine, which my lord hath spoken of, let him send unto his servants.

16 And we will cut wood in Lebanon as much as thou shalt need, and will bring it to thee in [1]rafts by the sea to [2]Japho, so thou mayest carry them to Jerusalem.

17 ¶ And Solomon numbered all the strangers that were in the land of Israel, after the numbering that his father David had numbered them: and they were found an hundred and three and fifty thousand, and six hundred.

18 And he set seventy thousand of them to the burden, and fourscore thousand to hew *stones* in the mountain, and three thousand and six hundred overseers to cause the people to work.

3

1 *The Temple of the Lord, and the porch are built, with other things thereto belonging.*

1 So [a]Solomon began to build the house of the Lord in Jerusalem, in mount [1]Moriah which had been declared unto David his father, in the place that David prepared in the threshing floor of [b]Ornan the Jebusite.

2 And he began to build in the second month *and* the second day, in the fourth year of his reign.

3 And these are the *measures whereon* Solomon grounded to build the house of God: the length of cubits after the first [1]measure *was* threescore cubits,

---

2:2 [1] Which is to be understood of all sorts of officers and overseers: for else the chief officers were but 3300, as in 1 Kings 5:16.
2:3 [1] Or, Hiram.
2:6 [1] That is, to do the service which he hath commanded, signifying that none is able to honor and serve God in that perfection as his majesty deserveth.
2:7 [1] Or, scarlet.
2:8 [1] Some take it for Brasil, or the wood called Ebenum, others for coral.
  [2] Or, Almuggim.
2:10 [1] Hebrew, *Corins.*
  [2] Of Bath read 1 Kings 7:26, it is called also Ephah, but Ephah is to measure dry things, as Bath is a measure for liquors.

2:12 [1] The very heavens confessed that it was a singular gift of God, when he gave to any nation a King that was wise and of understanding, albeit it appeareth that this Hiram had the true knowledge of God.
2:14 [1] It is also written that she was of the tribe of Naphtali, 1 Kings 7:14, which may be understood that by reason of the confusion of tribes, which then began to be, they married in divers tribes, so that by her father she might be of Dan, and by her mother of Naphtali.
2:16 [1] Or, ships.
  [2] Or, Joppa.
3:1 [1] Which is the mountain where Abraham thought to have sacrificed his son, Gen. 22:2.
3:3 [1] According to the whole length of the Temple, comprehending the most holy place with the rest.

and the breadth twenty cubits:

4   And the porch that was before the length in the front ¹of the breadth *was* twenty cubits, and the height *was* an ²hundred and twenty, and he overlaid it within with pure gold.

5   And the greater house he ceiled with fir tree which he overlaid with good gold, and graved thereon palm trees and chains.

6   And he overlaid the house with precious stones for beauty: and the gold *was* gold of ¹Parvaim.

7   The house, I say, the beams, posts, and walls thereof and the doors thereof overlaid he with gold, and graved Cherubims upon the walls.

8   ¶ He made also the house of the most holy place: the length thereof *was* in the front of the breadth of the house, twenty cubits, and the breadth thereof twenty cubits: and he overlaid it with the best gold, of six hundred talents.

9   And the weight of the nails *was* fifty shekels of gold, and he overlaid the chambers with gold.

10   ¶ And in the house of the most holy place he made two Cherubims wrought like children, and overlaid them with gold.

11   ᶜAnd the wings of the Cherubims *were* twenty cubits long: the one wing *was* five cubits, reaching to the wall of the house, and the other wing five cubits, reaching to the wing of the other Cherub.

12   Likewise the wing of the other Cherub was five cubits, reaching to the wall of the house, and the other wing five cubits, joining to the wing of the other Cherub.

13   The wings of these Cherubims were spread abroad twenty cubits, they stood on their feet, and their faces *were* toward the house.

14   ¶ He made also the ¹veil of blue silk and purple, and crimson, and fine linen, and wrought Cherubims thereon.

15   ¶ And he made before the house two pillars ¹of five and thirty cubits high: and the chapiter that was upon the top of *each* of them, *was* five cubits.

16   He made also chains for the Oracle, and put them on the heads of the pillars, and made an ¹hundred pomegranates, and put them among the chains.

17   And he set up the pillars before the Temple, one on the right hand, and the other on the left, and

ᶜ 1 Kings 6:14

called that on the right hand Jachin, and that on the left hand Boaz.

4   *1 The altar of brass. 2 The molten sea. 6 The caldrons. 7 The candlesticks, etc.*

1   And he made an altar of brass twenty cubits long, and twenty cubits broad, and ten cubits high.

2   And he made a molten ¹Sea of ten cubits from brim to brim, round in compass, and five cubits high: and a line of thirty cubits did compass it about.

3   And under ¹it was the fashion of oxen, which did compass it round about, ²ten in a cubit compassing the Sea about: two rows of oxen were cast when it was molten.

4   It stood upon twelve oxen: three looked toward the North, and three looked toward the West, and three looked toward the South, and three looked toward the East, and the Sea *stood* above upon them, and all their hinder parts were inward.

5   And the thickness thereof *was* an hand breadth, and the brim thereof *was* like the work of the brim of a cup, with flowers of ¹lilies: it contained ²three thousand baths.

6   ¶ He made also ten caldrons, and put five on the right hand, and five on the left, to wash in them, *and* to cleanse in them that which appertained to the burnt offerings: but the Sea *was* for the Priests to wash in.

7   ¶ And he made ten candlesticks of gold (according to ¹their form) and put them in the Temple, five on the right hand, and five on the left.

8   ¶ And he made ten tables, and put them in the Temple, five on the right hand, and five on the left: and he made an hundred basins of gold.

9   And he made the ¹court of the Priests, and the great court and doors for the court, and overlaid the doors thereof with brass.

10   And he set the Sea on the right side Eastward toward the South.

11   And Huram made ¹pots and besoms and basins, and Huram finished the work that he should make for King Solomon for the house of God,

12   *To wit,* two pillars, and the bowls and the chapiters on the top of the two pillars, and two grates to cover the two bowls of the chapiters which were

---

3:4 ¹ It contained as much as did the breadth of the Temple, 1 Kings 6:3.
    ² From the foundation to the top: for in the book of the kings mention is made from the foundation to the first stage.
3:6 ¹ Some think it is that place which is called Peru.
3:14 ¹ Which separated the Temple from the most holy place.
3:15 ¹ Every one was eighteen cubits long, but the half cubit could not be seen, for it was hid in the roundness of the chapiter, and therefore he giveth to every one but 17 and an half.
3:16 ¹ For every pillar an hundred, read 1 Kings 7:20.
4:2 ¹ A great vessel of brass, so called, because of the great quantity of water, which it contained, 1 Kings 7:24.

4:3 ¹ Meaning, under the brim of the vessel, as 1 Kings 7:24.
    ² In the length of every cubit were ten heads or knops which in all are 300.
4:5 ¹ Or, flower delices.
    ² In 1 Kings 7:26, mention is only made of two thousand, but the less number was taken there, and here according as the measures proved afterward, is declared.
4:7 ¹ Even as they should be made.
4:9 ¹ Called also the porch of Solomon, Act 3:11. It is also taken for the Temple where Christ preached, Matt. 21:23.
4:11 ¹ Or, cauldrons.

upon the top of the pillars:

13 And four hundred pomegranates for the two grates, two rows of pomegranates for every grate to cover the two bowls of the chapiters, that were upon the pillars.

14 He made also bases, and made caldrons upon the bases:

15 *And* a Sea, and twelve bulls under it:

16 Pots also and besoms, and flesh hooks, and all these vessels made Huram [1]his father to King Solomon for the house of the Lord of shining brass.

17 In the plain of Jordan did the King cast them in clay between Succoth and Zeredathah.

18 And Solomon made all these vessels in great abundance: for the weight of brass could not be reckoned.

19 And Solomon made all the vessels that were for the house of God: the golden altar also and the tables, whereon the [1]showbread stood.

20 Moreover, the candlesticks with their lamps, to burn them after the manner before the Oracle, of pure gold.

21 And the flowers and the lamps, and the snuffers of gold, which was fine gold.

22 And the [1]hooks, and the basins, and the spoons, and the ash pans of pure gold: the entry also of the house *and* doors thereof within, *even* of the most holy place: and the doors of the house, *to wit*, of the Temple were [2]of gold.

5 1 *The things dedicated by David are put in the Temple.* 2 *The Ark is brought into the Tmple.* 10 *What was within it.* 12 *They sing praise to the Lord.*

1 So [a]was all the work finished that Solomon made for the house of the Lord, and Solomon brought in the things that David his father had dedicated, with the silver and the gold, and all the vessels, *and* put them among the treasures of the house of God.

2 Then Solomon assembled the Elders of Israel, and all the heads of the tribes, the chief fathers of the children of Israel unto Jerusalem, to bring up the Ark of the covenant of the Lord from the [1]city of David, which is Zion.

3 And all the men of Israel assembled unto the king at the [1]feast: it was in the seventh [2]month.

CHAPTER 5
[a] 1 Kings 7:51
1 Kings 8:1

4 And all the Elders of Israel came, and the Levites took up the Ark.

5 And they carried up the Ark, and the Tabernacle of the Congregation: and all the holy vessels that were in the Tabernacle, those did the Priests *and* Levites bring up.

6 And king Solomon and all the Congregation of Israel that were assembled unto him, *were* before the Ark, offering sheep and bullocks, which could not be told nor numbered for multitude.

7 So the Priests brought the Ark of the covenant of the Lord unto his place, into the Oracle of the house, into the most Holy place, *even* under the wings of the Cherubims.

8 For the Cherubims stretched out *their* wings over the place of the Ark, and the Cherubims covered the Ark and the bars thereof above.

9 And they drew out the bars, that the ends of the bars might be seen out of the Ark before the Oracle, but they were not seen [1]without: and there they are unto this day.

10 Nothing *was* in the Ark, save [1]the two Tables, which Moses gave at Horeb, where the Lord made a covenant with the children of Israel when they came out of Egypt.

11 And when the Priests were come out of the Sanctuary (for all the Priests that were present, were [1]sanctified *and* did not wait by course.

12 And the Levites the singers of all sorts, *as* of Asaph, of Heman, of Jeduthun, and of their sons and of their brethren, being clad in fine linen, stood with cymbals, and with viols, and harps at the East end of the Altar, and with them an hundred and twenty Priests blowing with trumpets.

13 And they were [1]as one, blowing trumpets, and singing, and made one sound to be heard in praising and thanking the Lord, and when they lifted up *their* voice with trumpets, and with cymbals, and with instruments of music, and when they praised the Lord, *singing*, [2]For he is good, because his mercy *lasteth* forever) then the house, *even* the house of the Lord was filled with a cloud,

14 So that the Priests could not stand to minister, because of the cloud: for the glory of the Lord had filled the house of God.

4:16 [1] Whom Solomon reverenced for the gifts that God had given him, as a father: he had the same name also that Huram the king of Tyre had, his mother was a Jewess, and his father a Tyrian. Some read for his father, the author of this work.

4:19 [1] In Hebrew, *the bread of the faces*, because they were set before the Ark, where the Lord showed his presence.

4:22 [1] Or, instruments of music.
[2] That is, covered with plates of gold.

5:2 [1] Read 2 Sam. 6:12.

5:3 [1] When the things were dedicated and brought into the Temple.
[2] Called in Hebrew *Ethanim*, containing part of September and

part of October, 1 Kings 8:2, which moveth the Jews called the first month, because they say, that the world was created in that month, and after they came from Egypt, they began at March: but because this opinion is uncertain, we make March ever the first, as best writers do.

5:9 [1] Or, without the Oracle.

5:10 [1] For Aaron's rod and Manna were taken thence before it was brought to this place.

5:11 [1] Were prepared to serve the Lord.

5:13 [1] They agreed all in one tune.
[2] This was the effect of their songs, Ps. 118:1 and 136:1.

6 *3 Solomon blesseth the people. 4 He praiseth the Lord. 14 He prayeth unto God for those that shall pray in the Temple.*

CHAPTER 6
a 1 Kings 8:12
b 2 Sam. 7:5
c 1 Kings 8:27
d 1 Kings 8:31

1 Then *a*Solomon [1]said, The Lord hath said that he would dwell in the dark cloud:

2 And I have built thee an house to dwell in, an habitation for thee to dwell in forever.

3 And the King turned his face, and blessed all the Congregation of Israel (for all the Congregation of Israel stood *there*.)

4 And he said, Blessed *be* the Lord God of Israel, who spake with his mouth unto David my father, and hath with his [1]hand fulfilled it, saying,

5 Since the day that I brought my people out of the land of Egypt, I chose no city of all the tribes of Israel to build an [1]house, that my Name might be there, neither chose I any man to be a ruler over my people Israel:

6 But I have chosen Jerusalem, that my Name might be there, and have chosen David to be over my people Israel.

7 *b*And it was in the heart of David my father to build an house unto the Name of the Lord God of Israel.

8 But the Lord said to David my father, Whereas it was in thine heart to build an house unto my Name, thou diddest well, that [1]thou wast so minded.

9 Notwithstanding, thou shalt not build the house, but thy son, which shall come out of thy loins, he shall build an house unto my Name.

10 And the Lord hath performed his word that he spake: and I am risen up in the room of David my father, and am set on the throne of Israel as the Lord promised, and have built an house to the Name of the Lord God of Israel.

11 And I have set the Ark there, wherein is the [1]covenant of the Lord, that he made with the children of Israel.

12 And the [1]king stood before the altar of the Lord, in the presence of all the Congregation of Israel, and stretched out his hands,

13 (For Solomon had made a brazen scaffold, and set it in the midst of the court, of five cubits long, and five cubits broad, and three cubits of height, and upon it he stood, and kneeled down upon his knees before all the Congregation of Israel, and [1]stretched out his hands toward heaven.)

14 And said, O Lord God of Israel, there *is* no God like thee in heaven nor in earth, which keepest covenant and mercy unto thy servants, that walk before thee with all their heart.

15 Thou that hast kept with thy servant David my father, that thou hast promised him: for thou spakest with thy mouth, and hast fulfilled it with thine [1]hand, as *appeareth* this day.

16 Therefore now, Lord God of Israel, keep with thy servant David my father, that thou hast promised him, saying, Thou [1]shalt not want a man in my sight, that shall sit upon the throne of Israel, so that thy sons take heed to their ways to walk in my Law, as thou hast walked before me.

17 And now, O Lord God of Israel, let thy word be verified, which thou spakest unto thy servant David.

18 (Is it true indeed that God will dwell with man on earth? behold, the *c*heavens, and the heavens of heavens are not able to contain thee: how much more *unable* is this house which I have built?)

19 But have thou respect to the prayer of thy servant, and to his supplication, O Lord my God, to hear the cry and prayer which thy servant prayeth before thee,

20 That thine [1]eyes may be open toward this house day and night, *even* toward the place, whereof thou hast said, that thou wouldest put thy Name there, that thou mayest hearken unto the prayer, which thy servant prayeth in this place.

21 Hear thou therefore the supplication of thy servant, and of thy people Israel, which they pray in this place: and hear thou in the place of thine habitation, *even* in heaven, and when thou hearest, be merciful.

22 ¶ *d*When a man shall sin against his [1]neighbor, and he lay upon him an oath to cause him to swear, and the [2]swearer shall come before thine altar in this house,

23 Then hear thou in heaven, and do, and judge thy servants, in recompensing the wicked to bring his way [1]upon his head, and in justifying the righteous, to give him according to his righteousness.

24 ¶ And when thy people Israel shall be overthrown before the enemy, because they have sinned against thee, and turn again, and [1]confess thy Name,

---

6:1 [1] After that he had served the glory of the Lord in the cloud.
6:4 [1] Or, power.
6:5 [1] Or, Temple.
6:8 [1] Hebrew, *that it was in thine heart.*
6:11 [1] Meaning, the two Tables, wherein is contained the effect of the covenant that God made with our fathers.
6:12 [1] On a scaffold that was made for that purpose, that he praying for the whole people might be heard of all, as 1 Kings 8:22.
6:13 [1] Both to give thanks for the great benefits of God bestowed upon him, and also to pray for the perseverance and prosperity of his people.
6:15 [1] Or, in effect, or by thy power.
6:16 [1] Hebrew, *a man shall not be cut off.*
6:20 [1] That thou mayest declare in effect that thou hast a continual care over this place.
6:22 [1] By retaining anything from him, or by denying that which he hath left him to keep, or do him any wrong.
      [2] Hebrew, *oath.*
6:23 [1] Meaning, to give him that which he hath deserved.
6:24 [1] Or, praise.

and pray, and make supplication before thee in this house,

25 Then hear thou in heaven, and be merciful unto the sin of thy people Israel, and bring them again unto the land which thou gavest to them and to their fathers.

26 When heaven shall be shut up, and there shall be no rain, because they have sinned against thee, and shall pray in this place and confess thy Name, and ¹turn from their sin, when thou dost afflict them,

27 Then hear thou in heaven, and pardon the sin of thy servants, and of thy people Israel (when thou hast taught them the good way wherein they may walk) and give rain upon thy land, which thou hast given unto thy people for an inheritance.

28 ¶ ᵉWhen there shall be famine in the land, when there shall be pestilence, blasting, or mildew, when there shall be grasshopper, or caterpillar, when their enemy shall besiege them ¹in the cities of their land, *or* any plague or any sickness,

29 *Then* what prayer *and* supplication soever shall be made of any man, or of all thy people Israel, when every one shall know his own plague, and his own disease, and shall stretch forth his hands toward this house,

30 Hear thou then in heaven, thy dwelling place, and be merciful, and give every man according unto all his ways, as thou dost know his ¹heart (for thou only knowest the hearts of the children of men)

31 That they may fear thee, and walk in thy ways, as long as they live in the land which thou gavest unto our fathers.

32 ¶ Moreover, as touching the stranger which is not of thy people Israel, who shall come out of a far country for thy great Name's sake, and thy mighty hand, and thy stretched out arm: when they shall come and ¹pray in this house,

33 Hear thou in heaven, thy dwelling place, and do according to all that the stranger calleth for unto thee, that all the people of the earth may know thy Name, and fear thee like thy people Israel, and that they may know that thy Name is called upon in this house which I have built.

34 ¶ When thy people shall go out to battle against their enemies, by the way that ¹thou shalt send them, and they pray to thee, ²in the way toward this city, which thou hast chosen, even toward the house

ᵉ 2 Chron. 20:9
ᶠ 1 Kings 8:46
  1 John 1:8
ᵍ Ps. 132:8

which I have built to thy Name,

35 Then hear thou in heaven their prayer and their supplication, and judge their cause.

36 If they sin against thee (ᶠfor there is no man that sinneth not) and thou be angry with them, and deliver them unto the enemies, and they take them and carry them away captive unto a land far or near,

37 If they ¹turn again to their heart in the land whither they be carried in captives, and turn and pray unto thee in the land of their captivity, saying, We have sinned, we have transgressed and have done wickedly,

38 If they turn again to thee with all their heart, and with all their soul in the land of their captivity, whither they have carried them captives, and pray toward their land, which thou gavest unto their fathers, and *toward* the city which thou hast chosen, and toward the house which I have built for thy Name,

39 Then hear thou in heaven, in the place of thine habitation, their prayer and their supplication, and ¹judge their cause, and be merciful unto thy people, which have sinned against thee.

40 Now my God, I beseech thee, let thine eyes be open, and thine ears attent unto the prayer *that is made* in this place.

41 ᵍNow therefore arise, O Lord God, *to come* into thy ¹rest, thou, and the Ark of thy strength: O Lord God, let thy Priests be clothed with ²salvation, and let thy Saints rejoice in goodness.

42 O Lord God, refuse not the face of ¹thine anointed: remember the mercies *promised* to David thy servant.

7 1 *The fire consumeth the sacrifice.* 2 *The glory of the Lord filleth the Temple.* 12 *He heareth his prayer,* 17 *and promised to exalt him and his throne.*

1 And when Solomon had made an end of praying, ¹fire came down from heaven, and consumed the burnt offering and the sacrifices: and the glory of the Lord filled the house,

2 So that the Priests could not enter into the house of the Lord, because the glory of the Lord had filled the Lord's house.

3 And when all the children of Israel saw the fire, and the glory of the Lord come down upon the

---

6:26 ¹ Or, toward this place.
6:28 ¹ Hebrew, *in the land of their gates.*
6:30 ¹ He declareth that the prayers of hypocrites cannot be heard, nor of any but of them which pray unto God with an unfeigned faith and in true repentance.
6:32 ¹ He showeth that before God there is no deception of person, but all people that feareth him and worketh righteousness, are accepted, Acts 10:35.
6:34 ¹ Meaning, that none ought to enterprise any war, but at the

Lord's commandment, that is, which is lawful by his word.
  ² Or, according to the manner of this city.
6:37 ¹ Or, repent.
6:39 ¹ Or, maintain their right.
6:41 ¹ That is, into the Temple.
  ² Let them be preserved by thy power, and made virtuous and holy.
6:42 ¹ Hear my prayer which am thine anointed king.
7:1 ¹ Hereby God declared that he was pleased with Solomon's prayer.

house, they bowed themselves with *their* faces to the earth upon the pavement, and worshipped and praised the Lord, *saying*, For he is good, because his mercy *lasteth* forever.

4 [a]Then the King and all the people offered sacrifices before the Lord.

5 And king Solomon offered a sacrifice of two and twenty thousand bullocks, and an hundred and twenty thousand sheep. So the king and all the people dedicated the house of God.

6 And the Priests waited on their offices, and the Levites with the instruments of music of the Lord, which king David had made to praise the Lord, because his mercy *lasteth* forever: when David praised God [1]by them, the Priests also blew trumpets over against them: and all they of Israel stood by.

7 Moreover, Solomon hallowed the middle of the court that was before the house of the Lord: for there he had prepared burnt offerings, and the fat of the peace offerings, because the brazen altar which Solomon had made, was not able to receive the burnt offering, and the meat offering, and the fat.

8 And Solomon made [1]a feast at that time of seven days, and all Israel with him, a very great Congregation, from the entering in of Hamath, unto the river of Egypt.

9 And in the eight day they [1]made a solemn assembly: for they had made the dedication of the altar seven days, and the feast seven days.

10 And the [1]three and twentieth day of the seventh month, he sent the people away into their tents, joyous and with glad heart, because of the goodness that the Lord had done for David and for Solomon, and for Israel his people.

11 [b]So Solomon finished the house of the Lord, and the king's house, and all that came into Solomon's heart to make in the house of the Lord: and he prospered in his house.

12 ¶ And the Lord [c]appeared to Solomon by night, and said to him, I have heard thy prayer, and have chosen this place for myself to be an house of sacrifice.

13 If I shut the heaven that there be no rain, or if I command the grasshopper to devour the land, or if I send pestilence among my people,

14 If my people, among whom my Name is called upon, do humble themselves, and pray and seek my

CHAPTER 7
[a] 1 Kings 8:62,63
[b] 1 Kings 9:1
[c] Num. 12:6
[d] 2 Chron. 6:16

CHAPTER 8
[a] 1 Kings 9:10

presence, and turn from their wicked ways, then will I hear in heaven and be merciful to their sin, and will [1]heal their land:

15 Then mine eyes shall be open and mine ears attent unto the prayer *made* in this place.

16 For I have now chosen and sanctified this house, that my Name may be there forever: and mine eyes and mine heart shall be there perpetually.

17 And if thou wilt walk before me, as David thy father walked, to do according unto all that I have commanded thee, and shalt observe my statutes and my judgments,

18 Then will I establish the throne of thy kingdom, according as I made the covenant with David thy father, saying, [d]Thou shalt not want a man to be ruler in Israel.

19 But if ye turn away, and forsake my statutes and my commandments which I have set before you, and shall go and serve other gods, and worship them,

20 Then will I pluck them up out of my land, which I have given them, and this house which I have [1]sanctified for my Name, will I cast out of my sight, and will make it to be a proverb and a common talk among all people.

21 And this house which is most high, shall be an astonishment to everyone that passeth by it, so that he shall say, Why hath the Lord done thus to this land, and to this house?

22 And they shall answer, Because they forsook the Lord God of their fathers, which brought them out of the land of Egypt, and have taken hold on other gods, and have worshipped them, and served them, therefore hath he brought all this evil upon them.

8 *2 The cities that Solomon built.   7 People that were made tribute unto him.   12 His sacrifices.   17 He sendeth to Ophir.*

1 And [a]after [1]twenty years when Solomon had built the house of the Lord, and his own house,

2 Then Solomon built the cities that Huram [1]gave to Solomon, and caused the children of Israel to dwell there.

3 And Solomon went to Hamath Zobah, and overcame it.

4 And he built Tadmor in the wilderness, and repaired all [1]the cities of store which he built in Hamath.

7:6 [1] Hebrew, *by their hands.*
7:8 [1] The feast of the Tabernacles which was kept in the seventh month.
7:9 [1] They assembled to hear the word of God, after that they had remained seven days in the booths or Tabernacles.
7:10 [1] They had leave to depart the two and twentieth day, 1 Kings 8:66, but they went not away till the next day.
7:14 [1] I will cause the pestilence to cease and destroy the beasts that hurt the fruits of the earth, and send rain in due season.

7:20 [1] Which thing declareth that God had more respect to their salvation, than to the advancement of his own glory: and whereas men abuse those things which God hath appointed to set forth his praise, he doth withdraw his graces thence.
8:1 [1] Signifying that he was twenty years in building them.
8:2 [1] That is, which Hiram gave again to Solomon because they pleased him not: and therefore called them Cabul, that is, dirt or filth, 1 Kings 9:13.
8:4 [1] Meaning, of Munitions and treasures for the war.

5 And he built [1]Beth Horon the upper, and Beth Horon the nether, cities defensed with walls, gates and bars:

6 Also Baalath, and all the cities of store that Solomon had, and all the chariot cities, and the cities of the horsemen, and every pleasant place that Solomon had a mind to build in Jerusalem, and in [1]Lebanon, and throughout all the land of his dominion.

7 *And* all the people that were left to the Hittites, and the Amorites, and Perizzites, and the Hivites, and the Jebusites, which were not of Israel,

8 *But* of their children which were left after them in the land, whom the children of Israel had not consumed, even them did Solomon make [1]tributaries until this day.

9 But of the children of Israel did Solomon make no servants for his work: for they were men of war, and his chief princes, and the captains of his chariots and of his horsemen.

10 So these were the chief, of the officers which Solomon had, *even* [1]two hundred and fifty that bare rule over the people.

11 ¶ Then Solomon brought up the daughter of Pharaoh out of the city of David, into the house that he had built for her: for he said, My wife shall not dwell in the house of David king of Israel: for it is holy, because that the Ark of the Lord came unto it.

12 ¶ Then Solomon offered burnt offerings unto the Lord, on the [b]altar of the Lord, which he had built before the porch,

13 To [c]offer according to the commandment of Moses [1]every day, in the Sabbaths, and in the new moons, and in the solemn feasts, [2]three times in the year, *that is*, in the feast of the Unleavened bread, and in the feast of the Weeks, and in the feast of the Tabernacles.

14 And he set the courses of the Priests to their offices according to the order of David his father, and the Levites in their watches, for to praise and minister before the Priests every day, and the porters by their [d]courses, at every gate: for so *was* the commandment of David the man of God.

15 And they declined not from the commandment of the king, concerning the Priests and the Levites, touching all things, and touching the treasures.

[b 2 Chron. 4:1
c Exod. 29:39
d 1 Chron. 24:1

CHAPTER 9
a 1 Kings 10:1
Matt. 12:42
Luke 11:3

16 ¶ Now Solomon had made provision for all the [1]work from the day of the foundation of the house of the Lord, until it was finished: *so* the house of the Lord was perfect.

17 Then went Solomon to Ezion Geber, and to Eloth by the [1]Sea side in the land of Edom.

18 And Huram sent him by the hands of his servants, ships and servants that had knowledge of the sea: and they went with the servants of Solomon to Ophir, and brought thence [1]four hundred and fifty talents of gold, and brought them to King Solomon.

9 *1, 9 The Queen of Sheba cometh to see Solomon, and bringeth gifts. 13 His yearly revenues. 30 The time of his reign. 31 His death.*

1 And [a]when the Queen of Sheba heard of the fame of Solomon, she came to [1]prove Solomon with hard questions at Jerusalem, with a very great train, and camels that bare sweet odors and much gold, and precious stones: and when she came to Solomon, she communed with him of all that was in her heart.

2 And Solomon declared her all her questions, and there was [1]nothing hid from Solomon, which he declared not unto her.

3 Then the Queen of Sheba saw the wisdom of Solomon, and the house that he had built,

4 And the meat of his table, and the sitting of his servants, and the order of his waiters, and their apparel, and his butlers, and their apparel, and his [1]burnt offerings which he offered in the house of the Lord, and she was greatly [2]astonied.

5 And she said to the King, *It was* a true word which I heard in mine own land of thy [1]sayings, and of thy wisdom:

6 Howbeit, I believed not their report, until I came, and mine eyes had seen it: and behold, the one half of thy great wisdom was not told me: *for* thou exceedest the fame that I heard.

7 Happy are thy men, and happy are these thy servants, which stand before thee always, and hear thy wisdom.

8 Blessed be the Lord thy God, which loved thee, to set thee on his [1]throne as king, in the stead

---

8:5 [1] That is, he repaired and fortified them: for they were built long before by Sheerah a noble woman of the tribe of Ephraim, 1 Chron. 6:68 and 7:24.
8:6 [1] Read 1 Kings 7:2
8:8 [1] Hebrew, *to come up to tribute.*
8:10 [1] For in all there were 3300 but here he meaneth of them that had the principal charge, read 1 Kings 9:23.
8:13 [1] Or, after the manner of every day.
    [2] Read Lev. 23.
8:16 [1] Both for the matter and also for the workmanship.
8:17 [1] Meaning, the red Sea.

8:18 [1] Which sum is thought to mount to three million and six hundred thousand crowns, for here is mention made of thirty more than are spoken of, 1 Kings 9:28.
9:1 [1] To know whether his wisdom were so great as the report was.
9:2 [1] There was no question so hard that he did not resolve.
9:4 [1] Or, galleries whereby he went up.
    [2] Hebrew, *there was no spirit in her.*
9:5 [1] Or, acts.
9:8 [1] Meaning, that the Israelites were God's peculiar people, and that Kings are the lieutenants of God, which ought to grant unto him the superiority, and minister justice to all.

of the Lord thy God: because thy God loveth Israel, to establish it forever, therefore hath he made thee king over them, to execute judgments and justice.

9 Then she gave the King sixscore talents of gold, and of sweet odors exceedingly much, and precious stones: neither was there such sweet odors *since*, as the Queen of Sheba gave unto King Solomon.

10 And the servants also of Huram, and the servants of Solomon which brought gold from Ophir, brought [1]Algummim wood and precious stones.

11 And the King made of the Algummim wood [1]stairs in the house of the Lord, and in the king's house, and harps and viols for singers: and there was no such seen before in the land of Judah.

12 And King Solomon gave to the Queen of Sheba every pleasant thing that she asked, [1]besides for that which she had brought unto the king: so she returned and went to her own country, *both* she, and her servants.

13 ¶ Also the weight of gold that came to Solomon in one year, was six hundred threescore and six talents of gold,

14 Besides that which chapmen and merchants brought: and all the Kings of Arabia, and the princes of the country brought gold and silver to Solomon.

15 And King Solomon made two hundred targets of beaten gold, *and* [1]six hundred *shekels* of beaten gold went to one target.

16 And three hundred shields of beaten gold: three hundred [1]*shekels* of gold went to one shield, and the king put them in the house of the wood of Lebanon.

17 And the king made a great throne of ivory, and overlaid it with pure gold.

18 And the throne had six steps, with a footstool of gold [1]fastened to the throne, and stays on either side on the place of the seats, and two lions standing by the [2]stays.

19 And twelve lions stood there on the six steps on either side: there was not the like made in any kingdom.

20 And all King Solomon's drinking vessels *were* of gold, and all the vessels of the house of the wood of Lebanon *were* of pure gold: *for* silver was nothing esteemed in the days of Solomon.

21 For the king's ships went to Tarshish with the servants of Huram, every three years once came the ships of [1]Tarshish, and brought gold, and silver, ivory, and apes, and peacocks.

22 So king Solomon excelled all the kings of the earth in riches and wisdom.

23 And all the Kings of the earth sought the presence of Solomon, to hear his wisdom that God had put in his heart.

24 And they brought every man his present, vessels of silver, and vessels of gold, and raiment, armor, and sweet odors, horses, and mules, from year to year.

25 And Solomon had [1]four thousand stalls of horses, and chariots, and twelve thousand horsemen, whom he bestowed in the chariot cities, and with the king at Jerusalem.

26 And he reigned over all the kings from the [1]River even unto the land of the Philistines, and to the border of Egypt.

27 And the king gave silver in Jerusalem, [1]as stones, and gave cedar trees as the wild fig trees, that are abundant in the plain.

28 And they brought unto Solomon horses out of Egypt, and out of all lands.

29 Concerning the rest of the acts of Solomon first and last, are they not written in the book of Nathan the Prophet, and in the prophecy of Ahijah the Shilonite, and in the visions of [1]Iddo the Seer [2]against Jeroboam the son of Nebat?

30 And Solomon reigned in Jerusalem over all Israel forty years.

31 And Solomon [b]slept with his fathers, and they buried him in the city of David his father: and Rehoboam his son reigned in his stead.

10

4, 14 The rigor of Rehoboam.   13 He followeth lewd counsel.   16 The people rebel.

1 Then [a]Rehoboam [1]went to Shechem: for to Shechem came all Israel to make him king.

2 And when Jeroboam the son of Nebat heard it (which was in Egypt, whither he had fled from the presence of Solomon the king) he returned out of Egypt.

3 And they sent and called him: so came Jeroboam

Marginal notes:
[b] 1 Kings 11:41,42
CHAPTER 10
[a] 1 Kings 12:1

9:10 [1] Read 2 Chron. 2:8 and 1 Kings 10:11.
9:11 [1] Or pillars: meaning, the garnishing, and trimming of the stairs or pillars.
9:12 [1] That is, which the King gave her for recompense of the treasure which she brought.
9:15 [1] Which sum mounteth to 2400 crowns of the sun, Budeus De Asse.
9:16 [1] Or, pounds called mina, whereof every one seemed to make an hundred shekels.
9:18 [1] That is, the steps and the footstool were fastened to the throne.
     [2] Upon the pommels or knops.

9:21 [1] Which country of the best writers is thought to be Cilicia, read 1 Kings 10:22.
9:25 [1] That is, ten horses in every stable, which in all amounts to forty thousand , as 1 Kings 4:26.
9:26 [1] Or, Euphrates.
9:27 [1] The abundance of these temporal treasures in Solomon's kingdom is a figure of the Spiritual treasures, which the elect shall enjoy in the heavens under the true Solomon, Christ.
9:29 [1] Or, Iddo.
     [2] That is, which prophesied against him.
10:1 [1] After the death of Solomon.

and all Israel, and communed with Rehoboam, saying,

4 Thy father [1]made our yoke grievous: now therefore make thou the grievous servitude of thy father, and his sore yoke that he put upon us, lighter, and we will serve thee.

5 And he said to them, *Depart* yet three days, then come again unto me. And the people departed.

6 And King Rehoboam took counsel with the old men that had stood before Solomon his father, while he yet lived, saying, What counsel give ye that I may answer this people?

7 And they spake unto him, saying, If thou be kind to this people, and please them, and speak loving words to them, they will be thy servants forever.

8 But he left the counsel of the ancient men that they had given him, and took counsel of the young men that were brought up with him, and [1]waited on him.

9 And he said unto them, What counsel give ye, that we may answer this people, which have spoken to me, saying, Make the yoke which thy father did put upon us, lighter?

10 And the young men that were brought up with him, spake unto him, saying, Thus shalt thou answer the people that spake to thee, saying, Thy father made our yoke heavy, but make thou it lighter for us: thus shalt thou say unto them, My [1]least part shall be bigger than my father's loins.

11 Now whereas my father did burden you with a grievous yoke, I will yet increase your yoke: my father hath chastised you with rods, but I *will correct you* with [1]scourges.

12 ¶ Then Jeroboam and all the people came to Rehoboam the third day, as the king had appointed, saying, Come again to me the third day.

13 And the king answered them sharply: and king Rehoboam left the counsel of the ancient men,

14 And spake to them after the counsel of the young men, saying, My father made your yoke grievous, but I will increase it: my father chastised you with rods, but I *will correct you* with scourges.

15 So the king hearkened not unto the people: for it was the [1]ordinance of God, that the Lord might perform his saying, which he had spoken [2]by Ahijah

b 1 Kings 12:16

CHAPTER 11

a 1 Kings 12:20,21

the Shilonite to Jeroboam the son of Nebat.

16 So when all Israel saw that the king would not hear them, the people answered the king, saying, [b]What portion have we in David? for we have none inheritance in the son of Jesse. O Israel, every man to your tents: now see to thine own house, David. So all Israel departed to their tents.

17 Howbeit Rehoboam reigned over the children of Israel, that dwelt in the cities of Judah.

18 Then King Rehoboam sent Hadoram that was [1]over the tribute, and the children of Israel stoned him with stones, that he died: then King Rehoboam [2]made speed to get him up to his chariot, to flee to Jerusalem.

19 And Israel rebelled against the house of David unto this day.

11

4 *Rehoboam is forbidden to fight against Jeroboam.* 5 *Cities which he built.* 21 *He hath eighteen wives, and threescore concubines, and by them eight and twenty sons, and threescore daughters.*

1 And [a]when Rehoboam was come to Jerusalem, he gathered of the house of Judah and [1]Benjamin ninescore thousand chosen men of war to fight against [2]Israel, and to bring the kingdom again to Rehoboam.

2 But the word of the Lord came to Shemaiah the man of God, saying,

3 Speak unto Rehoboam the son of Solomon King of Judah, and to all Israel that are in Judah and Benjamin, saying,

4 Thus saith the Lord, Ye shall not go up, nor fight against your brethren: return every man to his house: for this thing is done of me. They obeyed therefore the word of the Lord, and returned from going against Jeroboam.

5 And Rehoboam dwelt in Jerusalem, and [1]built strong cities in Judah.

6 He built also Bethlehem, and Etam, and Tekoa,

7 And Beth Zur, and Sochoh, and Adullam,

8 And Gath, Mareshah, and Ziph,

9 And Adoraim, and Lachish, and Azekah,

10 And Zorah, and Aijalon, and Hebron, which were in Judah and Benjamin strong cities.

11 And he [1]repaired the strongholds and put captains in them, and store of vittles, and oil and wine.

10:4 [1] That is, handled us rudely, it seemeth that God hardened their hearts, so that they thus murmured without cause: which declareth also the inconstancy of the people.

10:8 [1] Or, that stood by him, that is, which were of his counsel and secrets.

10:10 [1] Or, little finger, meaning that he was of far greater power, than was his father.

10:11 [1] Or, scorpions.

10:15 [1] God's will imposeth such a necessity to the second causes, that nothing can be done but according to the same, and yet man's will worketh as of itself, so that it cannot be excused in doing that it

is God's ordinance.

[2] Hebrew, *by the hand of.*

10:18 [1] Or, receiver.

[2] Hebrew, *strengthened himself.*

11:1 [1] That is, the half tribe of Benjamin: for the other half was gone after Jeroboam.

[2] Meaning the ten tribes which rebelled.

11:5 [1] Or, repaired them and made them strong to be more able to resist Jeroboam.

11:11 [1] Or, strengthened.

12 And in all cities he put shields and spears and made them exceedingly strong: so Judah and Benjamin were his.

13 ¶ And the Priests and the Levites that were in all Israel, [1]resorted unto him out of all their coasts.

14 For the Levites left their suburbs and their possessions, and came to Judah and to Jerusalem: [b]for Jeroboam and his sons had cast them out from ministering in the Priests' office unto the Lord.

15 [c]And he ordained him Priests for the high places, and for the [1]devils and for the calves which he had made.

16 And after the Levites there came to Jerusalem of all the tribes of Israel, such as set their [1]hearts to seek the Lord God of Israel, to offer unto the Lord God of their fathers.

17 So they strengthened the kingdom of Judah, and made Rehoboam the son of Solomon mighty, three years long: for three years they [1]walked in the way of David and Solomon.

18 ¶ And Rehoboam took him Mahalath the daughter of Jerimoth the son of David to wife, *and* Abihail the daughter of Eliah the son of Jesse,

19 Which bare him sons Jeush, and Shamariah, and Zaham.

20 And after her he took Maachah the daughter of Absalom which bare him Abijah, and Attai, and Ziza, and Shelomith.

21 And Rehoboam loved Maachah the daughter of Absalom above all his wives and his concubines: for he took eighteen wives and threescore concubines, and begat eight and twenty sons, and threescore daughters.

22 And Rehoboam made [1]Abijah the son of Maachah the chief ruler among his brethren: *for* he thought to make him King.

23 And he taught him: and dispersed all his sons throughout all the countries of Judah and Benjamin unto every strong city: and he gave them abundance of vittles, and [1]desired many wives.

12

1 *Rehoboam forsaketh the Lord, and is punished by Shishak.* 5 *Shemaiah reproveth him.* 6 *He humbleth himself.* 7 *God sendeth him succor.* 9 *Shishak taketh his treasures.* 13 *His reign and death.* 16 *Abijah*

[b] 2 Chron. 13:5
[c] 1 Kings 12:31
CHAPTER 12
[a] 2 Chron. 9:15,16

his son succeedeth him.

1 And when [1]Rehoboam had established the kingdom and made it strong, he forsook the Law of the Lord, and [2]all Israel with him.

2 Therefore in the fifth year of king Rehoboam, Shishak the king of Egypt came up against Jerusalem (because they had transgressed against the Lord)

3 With twelve hundred chariots, and threescore thousand horsemen, and the people were without number, that came with him from Egypt, *even* the Lubim, [1]Sukkiim, and the [2]Ethiopians.

4 And he took the strong cities which were of Judah, and came unto Jerusalem.

5 ¶ Then came Shemaiah the Prophet to Rehoboam, and to the princes of Judah that were gathered together in Jerusalem, because of Shishak, and said unto them, Thus saith the Lord, Ye have forsaken me, [1]therefore have I also left you in the hands of Shishak.

6 Then the princes of Israel, and the King humbled themselves, and said, The Lord *is* [1]just.

7 And when the Lord saw that they humbled themselves, the word of the Lord came to Shemaiah, saying, They have humbled themselves, *therefore* I will not destroy them, but I will send them deliverance shortly, and my wrath shall not [1]be poured out upon Jerusalem by the hand of Shishak.

8 Nevertheless they shall be his servants: so shall they know my [1]service, and the service of the kingdoms of the earth.

9 ¶ Then Shishak king of Egypt came up against Jerusalem, and took the treasures of the house of the Lord, and the treasures of the King's house: he took *even* all, and he carried away the shields of gold, [a]which Solomon had made.

10 In stead whereof King Rehoboam made shields of brass, and committed them to the hands of the chief of the guard, that waited at the door of the king's house.

11 And when the king entered into the house of the Lord, the guard came and bare them and brought them again unto the guard chamber.

12 And because he [1]humbled himself, the wrath of the Lord turned from him, that he would not

---

11:13 [1] Hebrew, *stood.*
11:15 [1] Meaning, idols, read Isa. 44:15.
11:16 [1] Which were zealous of true religion, and feared God.
11:17 [1] So long as they feared God, and set forth his word, they prospered.
11:22 [1] Called also Abijam, who reigned three years, 1 Kings 15:2.
11:23 [1] He gave himself to have many wives.
12:1 [1] Or, when the Lord had established Rehoboam's kingdom.
[2] For such is the inconstancy of the people, that for the most part they follow the vices of their governors.
12:3 [1] Which were a people of Africa called the Troglodytes because they dwelled in holes.
[2] Or, black Moores.
12:5 [1] Signifying, that no calamity can come unto us except we forsake God, and that he never leaveth us till we have cast him off.
12:6 [1] And therefore doth justly punish you for your sins.
12:7 [1] Hebrew, *drop down.*
12:8 [1] He showeth that God's punishments are not to destroy his utterly, but to chastise them, to bring them to the knowledge of themselves, and to know how much better it is to serve God than tyrants.
12:12 [1] Which declareth that God seeketh not the death of a sinner, but his conversion, Ezek. 18:32 and 23:11.

destroy all together. And also in Judah the things prospered.

13 [b]So King Rehoboam was strong in Jerusalem and reigned: for Rehoboam was one and forty years old, when he began to reign, and reigned [1]seventeen years in Jerusalem, the city which the Lord had chosen out of all the tribes of Israel to put his Name there. And his mother's name was Naamah an Ammonitess.

14 And he did evil: for he prepared not his heart to seek the Lord.

15 The acts also of Rehoboam, first and last, are they not written in the [1]book of Shemaiah the Prophet, and Iddo the Seer, in rehearsing the genealogy? and there *was* war always between Rehoboam and Jeroboam.

16 And Rehoboam slept with his fathers, and was buried in the city of David, and [1]Abijah his son reigned in his stead.

13

1 *Abijah maketh war against Jeroboam.* 4 *He showeth the occasion.* 12 *He trusteth in the Lord and overcometh Jeroboam.* 21 *Of his wives and children.*

1 In the eighteenth year of King Jeroboam, began Abijah to reign over [1]Judah.

2 He reigned three years in Jerusalem: (his mother's name also was [1]Michaiah the daughter of [2]Uriel of Gibeah) and there was war between Abijah and Jeroboam.

3 And Abijah set the battle in array with the army of valiant men of war, *even* four hundred thousand chosen men. Jeroboam also set the battle in array against him with eight hundred thousand chosen men which were strong *and* valiant.

4 And Abijah stood up upon mount [1]Zemaraim, which is in mount Ephraim, and said, O Jeroboam, and all Israel, hear you me,

5 Ought you not to know that the Lord God of Israel hath given the kingdom over Israel to [1]David forever, *even* to him and to his sons by a covenant [2]of salt?

6 And Jeroboam the son of Nebat the servant

[b] 1 Kings 14:21

CHAPTER 13
[a] 1 Kings 11:26
[b] Lev. 26:36
[c] 1 Kings 12:31
2 Chron. 11:14

of Solomon the son of David is risen up, and hath [a]rebelled against his lord:

7 And there are gathered to him [1]vain men *and* [2]wicked, and made themselves strong against Rehoboam the son of Solomon: for Rehoboam was [3]*but* a child and [4,b]tender hearted, and could not resist them.

8 Now therefore ye think that ye be able to resist against the kingdom of the Lord, *which is* in the hands of the sons of David, and ye be a great multitude, and the golden calves *are* with you which Jeroboam made you for gods.

9 [c]Have ye not driven away the Priests of the Lord the sons of Aaron and the Levites, and have made you Priests like the people of *other* countries? whosoever cometh to [1]consecrate with a [2]young bullock and seven rams, the same may be a Priest of them that are no gods.

10 But we belong unto the Lord our God, and have not forsaken him, and the Priests the sons of Aaron minister unto the Lord, and the Levites in *their* office.

11 And they burn unto the Lord every [1]morning and every evening burnt offerings and sweet incense, and the bread is set in order upon the pure table, and the candlestick of gold with the lamps thereof, to burn every evening: for we keep the watch of the Lord our God: but ye have forsaken him.

12 And behold, this God *is* [1]with us as a captain, and his Priests with the sounding trumpets to cry an alarm against you. O ye children of Israel, fight not against the Lord God of your fathers: for ye shall not prosper.

13 ¶ But Jeroboam caused an ambushment [1]to compass, *and* come behind them, when they were before Judah, and the ambushment behind them.

14 Then Judah looked, and behold, the battle *was* before and behind them, and they cried unto the Lord, and the Priests blew with the trumpets,

15 And the men of Judah gave a shout: and even

12:13 [1] That is, twelve years after that he had been overcome by Shishak, verse 2.

12:15 [1] Hebrew, *sayings.*

12:16 [1] Or, Abijam.

13:1 [1] He meaneth Judah and Benjamin.

13:2 [1] Or, Maachah, 1 Kings 15:2.

[2] Called also Abishalom, for Abishalom was her grandfather, 1 Kings 15:2.

13:4 [1] Which was one of the tops of mount Ephraim.

13:5 [1] And therefore whosoever doth usurp it or take it from that stock, transgresseth the ordinance of the Lord. Thus like an hypocrite he allegeth the word of God for his advantage.

[2] That is, perpetual because that thing which is salted, is preserved from corruption: he meaneth also that it was made solemnly, and confirmed by offering of sacrifices, where as they used salt according

as was ordained, Num. 18:19.

13:7 [1] This word in the Chaldean tongue is Raca, which our Savior useth, Matt. 5:22.

[2] Hebrew, *children of Belial.*

[3] Meaning, in heart and courage.

[4] Or, faint hearted.

13:9 [1] Hebrew, *fill his hand.*

[2] He showeth the nature of idolaters which take no trial of the vocation, life and doctrine of their ministers, but think the most vilest and greatest beasts sufficient to serve their turn.

13:11 [1] As it was appointed in the Law, Exod. 29:39.

13:12 [1] Because their cause was good and approved by the Lord, they doubted not of the success and victory.

13:13 [1] Contemning the good counsel which came of the Spirit of God, he thought to have overcome by deceit.

as the men of Judah shouted, God [1]smote Jeroboam and also Israel before Abijah and Judah.

16 And the children of Israel fled before Judah, and God delivered them into their hand.

17 And Abijah and his people slew a great slaughter of them, so that there fell down wounded of Israel five hundred thousand chosen men.

18 So the children of Israel were brought under at that time: and the children of Judah prevailed, [1]because they stayed upon the Lord God of their fathers.

19 And Abijah pursued after Jeroboam, and took cities from him, *even* Bethel and the [1]villages thereof, and Jeshanah with her villages, and Ephron with her villages.

20 And Jeroboam recovered no strength again in the days of Abijah, but the Lord plagued him, and he died.

21 So Abijah waxed mighty, and married fourteen wives, and begat two and twenty sons, and sixteen daughters.

22 The rest of the acts of Abijah, and his manners and his sayings, are written in the story of the Prophet Iddo.

CHAPTER 14
[a] 1 Kings 15:8
[b] 1 Sam. 14:6

14

3 Asa destroyeth idolatry, and commandeth his people to serve the true God.   11 He prayed unto God when he should go to fight.   12 He obtaineth the victory.

1 So [a]Abijah slept with his fathers, and they buried him in the city of David, and Asa his son reigned in his stead: in whose days the land was quiet ten years.

2 And Asa did that was good and right in the eyes of the Lord his God.

3 For he took away the altars of the strange *gods*, and the high places, and brake down the images, and cut down the [1]groves,

4 And commanded Judah to seek the Lord God of their fathers, and to do *according* to the Law and the Commandment.

5 And he took away out of all the cities of Judah the high places, and the images: therefore the Kingdom was [1]quiet before him.

6 He built also strong cities in Judah, because the land was in rest, and he had no war in those years: for the Lord had given him rest.

7 Therefore he said to Judah, Let us build these cities, and make walls about, and towers, gates, and bars, while the land is [1]before us: because we have sought the Lord our God, we have sought him, and he hath given us rest on every side: so they built and prospered.

8 And Asa had an army of Judah, that bare shields and spears, three hundred thousand, and of Benjamin that bare shields and drew bows, two hundred and fourscore thousand: all these were valiant men.

9 ¶ And there came out against him Zerah [1]of Ethiopia with an host of ten hundred thousand, and three hundred chariots, and came unto [2]Mareshah.

10 Then Asa went out before him, and they set the battle in array in the valley of Zephathah, beside Mareshah.

11 And Asa cried unto the Lord his God, and said, Lord, [b]it is nothing with thee to help [1]with many, *or* with no power: help us, O Lord our God: for we rest on thee, and in thy Name are we come against this multitude: O Lord, thou art our God: [2]let not man prevail against thee.

12 ¶ So the Lord smote the Ethiopians before Asa and before Judah, and the Ethiopians fled.

13 And Asa and the people that was with him, pursued them unto Gerar. And the Ethiopians' host was overthrown, *so that* there was no life in them: for they were destroyed before the Lord and before his host: and they carried away a mighty great spoil.

14 And they smote all the cities round about Gerar: for the [1]fear of the Lord came upon them, and they spoiled all the cities, for there was exceeding much spoil in them.

15 Yea, and they smote the tents of cattle, and carried away plenty of sheep and camels, and returned to Jerusalem.

15

2 The exhortation of Azariah.   8 Asa purgeth his country of idolatry.   11 He sacrificeth with the people.   14 They swear together to serve the Lord.   16 He deposeth his mother for her idolatry.

1 Then the Spirit of God came upon [1]Azariah the son of Obed.

2 And he went out to meet Asa, and said unto him, O Asa, and all Judah and Benjamin, hear ye me, The Lord *is* with you, while ye be with him: and if ye

---

13:15 [1] Or, gave him the overthrow.
13:18 [1] He showeth that the stay of all kingdoms, and assurance of victories depend upon our trust and confidence in the Lord.
13:19 [1] Hebrew, *daughters.*
14:3 [1] Which were planted contrary to the Law, Deut. 16:21.
14:5 [1] He showeth that the rest and quietness of kingdoms standeth in abolishing idolatry, and advancing true religion.
14:7 [1] While we have the full government thereof.
14:9 [1] The king of Ethiopia, or Egypt.
     [2] Which was a city in Judah, Josh. 15:44, where Michaiah the Prophet

was born.
14:11 [1] Or, against many, without power.
     [2] Thus the children of God neither trust in their own power or policy, neither fear the strength and subtlety of their enemies, but consider the cause and see whether their enterprises tend to God's glory, and thereupon assure themselves of the victory by him, which is only Almighty, and can turn all flesh into dust with the breath of his mouth.
14:14 [1] The Lord had stricken them with fear.
15:1 [1] Who was called Obed, as his father was, verse 8.

seek him, he will be found of you, but if ye forsake him, he will forsake you.

3 Now for a long season Israel *hath been* without the ¹true God, and without Priest to teach, and without Law.

4 But *whosoever* returned in his affliction to the Lord God of Israel, and sought him, he ¹was found of him.

5 And in that time there *was* no peace to him, that did go out and go in: but great troubles *were* to all the inhabitants of the earth.

6 For nation was destroyed of nation, and city of city: for God troubled them with all adversity.

7 Be ye strong therefore, and let not your hands be weak: for your ¹work shall have a reward.

8 ¶ And when Asa heard these words, and the prophecy of Obed the Prophet, he was encouraged, and took away the abominations out of all the land of Judah and Benjamin, and out of the cities which he had taken of mount Ephraim, and he renewed the altar of the Lord, that was before the porch of the Lord.

9 And he gathered all Judah and Benjamin, and the strangers with them out of Ephraim, and Manasseh, and out of Simeon: for there fell many to him out of Israel, when they saw that the Lord his God *was* with him.

10 So they assembled to Jerusalem in the ¹third month, in the fifteenth year of the reign of Asa.

11 And they offered unto the Lord the same time of the ¹spoil *which* they had brought, *even* seven hundred bullocks, and seven thousand sheep.

12 And they made a covenant to seek the Lord God of their fathers, with all their heart, and with all their soul.

13 And ¹whosoever will not seek the Lord God of Israel, shall be slain, whether he were small or great, man or woman.

14 And they sware unto the Lord with a loud voice, and with shouting, and with trumpets, and with cornets.

CHAPTER 15
ª 1 Kings 15:13

CHAPTER 16
ª 1 Kings 15:17

15 And all Judah rejoiced at the oath: for they had sworn unto the Lord with all their heart, and sought him with a whole desire, and he was ¹found of them. And the Lord gave them rest round about.

16 ¶ And King Asa deposed ªMaachah *his* ¹mother from her regency, because she had made an idol in a grove: and Asa brake down her idol, and stamped it, and burnt it at the brook Kidron.

17 But the high places were not ¹taken away out of ²Israel: yet the heart of Asa was ³perfect all his days.

18 Also he brought into the house of God the things that his father had dedicated, and that he had dedicated, silver, and gold, and vessels.

19 And there was no war unto the five and thirtieth year of the reign of Asa.

16 *2 Asa for fear of Baasha king of Israel, maketh a covenant with Ben-Hadad king of Aram. 7 He is reproved by the Prophet. 10 Whom he putteth in prison. 12 He putteth his trust in the Physicians. 13 His death.*

1 In the six and thirtieth year of the reign of Asa came ¹ªBaasha king of Israel up against Judah, and built ²Ramah, to let none pass out or go in to Asa king of Judah.

2 Then Asa brought out silver and gold out of the treasures of the house of the Lord, and of the king's house, and sent to Ben-Hadad king of Aram that dwelt at ¹Damascus, saying,

3 There *is* a covenant between me and thee, and between my father and thy father: behold, I have sent thee silver and gold: come, ¹break thy league with Baasha king of Israel, that he may depart from me.

4 And Ben-Hadad hearkened unto King Asa, and sent the captains of the army which he had, against the cities of Israel. And they smote Ijon, and Dan, and Abel Maim, and all the store cities of Naphtali.

5 And when Baasha heard it, he left building of Ramah, and let his work cease.

6 Then Asa the king took all Judah, and carried away the stones of Ramah and the timber thereof,

---

15:3 ¹ For the space of twelve years under Rehoboam, and three years under Abijah, religion was neglected, and idolatry planted.
15:4 ¹ He showeth, that notwithstanding the wickedness of tyrants and their rage, yet God hath his, whom he heareth in their tribulation, as he delivered him from Zerah king of the Ethiopians, 2 Chron. 14:9, 12, and out of all other dangers, when they called upon the Lord.
15:7 ¹ Your confidence and trust in God shall not be frustrated.
15:10 ¹ Called Sivan, containing part of May, and part of June.
15:11 ¹ Which they had taken of the Ethiopians.
15:13 ¹ These were the words of their covenant, which commanded all idolaters to be put to death, according to the Law of God, Deut. 13:5, 9, 15.
15:15 ¹ So long as they served him aright, so long did he preserve and prosper them.
15:16 ¹ Or grandmother: and herein he showed that he lacked zeal, for she ought to have died both by the covenant, as verse 13, and

by the Law of God: but he gave place to foolish pity and would also seem after a sort to satisfy the Law.
15:17 ¹ Which partly came through lack of zeal in him, partly through the negligence of his officers, and partly by the superstition of the people, that all were not taken away.
² Because that God was called the God of Israel, by reason of his promise to Jacob: therefore Israel is sometimes taken for Judah, because Judah was his chief people.
³ In respect of his predecessors.
16:1 ¹ Who reigned after Nadab the son of Jeroboam.
² He fortified it with walls and ditches: it was a city in Benjamin near to Gibeon.
16:2 ¹ Or, Darmesek.
16:3 ¹ He thought to repulse his adversary by an unlawful means, that is, by seeking help of infidels, as they that seek the Turks' amity, thinking thereby to make themselves more strong.

wherewith Baasha did build, and he built therewith Geba and Mizpah.

7 ¶ And at that same time Hanani the [1]Seer came to Asa king of Judah, and said unto him, Because thou hast rested upon the king of Aram, and not rested in the Lord thy God, therefore is the host of the king of Aram escaped out of thine hand.

8 [b]The Ethiopians and the Lubim, were they not a great host with chariots and horsemen, exceedingly many? yet because thou didst rest upon the Lord, he delivered them into thine hand.

9 For the eyes of the Lord behold all the earth, to show himself strong with them that are of perfect heart toward him: thou hast then done foolishly in this: therefore from henceforth thou shalt have wars.

10 Then Asa was wroth with the Seer, and put him into a [1]prison: for he was [2]displeased with him, because of this thing. And Asa oppressed *certain* of the people at the same time.

11 And behold, the acts of Asa first and last, lo, they are written in the book of the Kings of Judah and Israel.

12 ¶ And Asa in the nine and thirtieth year of his reign was [1,c]diseased in his feet, *and* his disease was [2,3]extreme: yet he sought not the Lord in his disease, but to the [4]Physicians.

13 So Asa slept with his fathers, and died in the one and fortieth year of his reign.

14 And they buried him in *one* of his sepulchers, which he had made for himself in the city of David, and laid him in the bed, which they had filled with sweet odors and divers kinds *of* spices made by the art of the Apothecary: and they burnt *odors* for him with an exceeding great fire.

[b] 2 Chron. 14:9
[c] 1 Kings 15:23

17

5 Jehoshaphat trusting in the Lord, prospereth in riches and honor.   6 He abolisheth idolatry.   7 and causeth the people to be taught.   11 He receiveth tribute of strangers.   13 His munitions, and men of war.

1 And Jehoshaphat his son reigned in his stead, and prevailed against Israel.

2 And he put garrisons in all the strong cities of Judah, and set bands in the land of Judah and in the cities of Ephraim, which Asa his father had taken.

3 And the Lord was with Jehoshaphat, because he walked in the [1]first ways of his father David, and sought not [2]Baalim,

4 But sought the Lord God of his father, and walked in his commandment, and not after the [1]trade of Israel.

5 Therefore the Lord established the kingdom in his hand, and all Judah brought presents to Jehoshaphat, so that he had of riches and honor in abundance.

6 And he [1]lifted up his heart unto the ways of the Lord, and he took away moreover the high places and the groves out of Judah.

7 ¶ And in the third year of his reign he sent his princes, Ben-Hail, and Obadiah, and Zechariah, and Nethanel, and Michaiah, that they should [1]teach in the cities of Judah,

8 And with them Levites, Shemaiah, and Nethaniah, and Zebadiah, and Asahel, and Shemiramoth, and Jehonathan, and Adonijah, and Tobijah, and Tobadonijah, Levites, and with them Elishama and Jehoram, Priests.

9 And they taught in Judah, and had the book of the Law of the Lord with them, and went about throughout all the cities of Judah, and taught the people.

10 And the fear of the Lord fell upon all the kingdoms of the lands that were round about Judah, and they [1]fought not against Jehoshaphat.

11 Also *some* of the Philistines brought Jehoshaphat gifts and tribute silver, and the Arabians brought him flocks, seven thousand and seven hundred rams, and seven thousand and seven hundred he goats.

12 So Jehoshaphat prospered and grew up on high, and he built in Judah palaces and cities of store.

13 And he had great works in the cities of Judah, and men of war, *and* valiant men in Jerusalem.

14 And these are the numbers of them after the house of their fathers, In Judah *were* captains of thousands, Adnah the captain, and [1]with him valiant men three hundred thousand.

15 And [1]at his hand Jehohanan a captain, and with him two hundred and fourscore thousand.

16:7 [1] Or, Prophet.
16:10 [1] Hebrew, *prison house.*
[2] Thus instead of turning to God by repentance, he disdained the admonition of the Prophet, and punished him, as the wicked do when they be told of their faults.
16:12 [1] Or, gouty, or swollen.
[2] Or, to the top of his head.
[3] God plagued his rebellion, and hereby declareth that it is nothing to begin well, except we so continue to the end, that is, zealous of God's glory, and put our whole trust in him.
[4] He showeth that it is in vain to seek to the Physicians, except we first seek to God to purge our sins, which are the chief cause of all our diseases, and after use the help of the Physician, as a means by whom God worketh.

17:3 [1] That is, his virtues: meaning before he had committed with Bathsheba, and against Uriah.
[2] Sought not help at strange Gods.
17:4 [1] Hebrew, *work.*
17:6 [1] He gave himself wholly to serve the Lord.
17:7 [1] He knew it was in vain to profess religion, except such were appointed which could instruct the people in the same, and had authority to put away all idolatry.
17:10 [1] Thus God prospereth all such that with a pure heart seek his glory, and keepeth their enemies in fear, that they cannot be able to execute their rage against them.
17:14 [1] Hebrew, *in his hand.*
17:15 [1] Or, next to him.

16 And at his hand Amasiah the son of Zichri, ¹which willingly offered himself unto the Lord, and with him two hundred thousand valiant men.

17 And of Benjamin, Eliada a valiant man, and with him armed men with bow and shield, two hundred thousand.

18 And at his hand Jehozabad, and with him an hundred and fourscore thousand armed to the war.

19 These ¹waited on the king, besides those which the king put in the strong cities throughout all Judah.

18

1 Jehoshaphat maketh affinity with Ahab. 10 Four hundred Prophets counsel Ahab to go to war. 16 Michaiah is against them. 23 Zedekiah smiteth him. 25 The king putteth him in prison. 29 The effect of his prophecy.

1 And ᵈJehoshaphat had riches and honor in abundance, but he was joined in ¹affinity with Ahab.

2 And after certain ¹years he went down to Ahab to Samaria: and Ahab slew sheep and oxen for him in great number, and for the people that he had with him, and enticed him to go up unto ²Ramoth Gilead.

3 And Ahab king of Israel said unto Jehoshaphat king of Judah, Wilt thou go with me to Ramoth Gilead? And he answered him, I am as thou art, and my people as thy people, and we *will join* with thee in the war.

4 And Jehoshaphat said unto the king of Israel, Ask counsel, I pray thee, at the ¹word of the Lord this day.

5 Therefore the King of Israel gathered of ¹Prophets four hundred men, and said unto them, Shall we go to Ramoth Gilead to battle, or shall I cease? And they said, Go up: for God shall deliver it into the king's hand.

6 But Jehoshaphat said, Is there here never a Prophet more of the Lord that we might inquire of him?

7 And the king of Israel said unto Jehoshaphat, There is yet one man by whom we may ask counsel of the Lord: but I ¹hate him: for he doth not prophesy good unto me, but always evil: it is Michaiah the son of Imla. Then Jehoshaphat said, Let not the king say ²so.

8 And the king of Israel called an eunuch, and

CHAPTER 18
ᵈ 1 Kings 22:3

said, Call quickly Michaiah the son of Imla.

9 ¶ And the king of Israel, and Jehoshaphat King of Judah sat either of them on his throne clothed in their ¹apparel: they sat even in the threshing floor at the entering in of the gate of Samaria: and all the Prophets prophesied before them.

10 And Zedekiah the son of Chenaanah made him ¹horns of iron, and said, Thus saith the Lord, With these shalt thou push the Aramites until thou hast consumed them.

11 And all the Prophets prophesied so, saying, Go up in Ramoth Gilead, and prosper: for the Lord shall deliver it unto the hand of the king.

12 ¶ And the messenger that went to call Michaiah, spake to him, saying, Behold, the words of the Prophets *declare* good to the king with one ¹accord: let thy word therefore, I pray thee, be like one of theirs, and speak thou good.

13 And Michaiah said, As the Lord liveth, whatsoever my God saith, that will I speak.

14 ¶ So he came to the king, and the King said unto him, Michaiah, shall we go to Ramoth Gilead to battle, or shall I leave off? And he said, ¹Go ye up, and prosper, and they shall be delivered into your hand.

15 And the King said to him, How oft shall I charge thee, that thou tell me nothing but the truth in the Name of the Lord?

16 Then he said, I saw all Israel scattered in the mountains, as sheep that have no shepherd: and the Lord said, ¹These have no master: let them return every man to his house in peace.

17 And the King of Israel said to Jehoshaphat, Did I not tell thee, that he would not prophesy good unto me, but evil?

18 Again he said, Therefore hear ye the word of the Lord: I saw the Lord sit upon his throne, and all the ¹host of heaven standing at his right hand, and at his left.

19 And the Lord said, Who shall ¹persuade Ahab King of Israel, that he may go up, and fall at Ramoth Gilead? And one spake and said thus, and another said that.

20 Then there came forth a spirit and stood before the Lord, and said, I will persuade him. And the

---

17:16 ¹ Meaning, which was a Nazirite, Num. 6.

17:19 ¹ That is, they were as his ordinary guard.

18:1 ¹ For Joram Jehoshaphat's son married Ahab's daughter.

18:2 ¹ That is, the third year, 1 Kings 22:2.
  ² To recover it out of the hands of the Syrians.

18:4 ¹ Hear the advice of some Prophet, to know whether it be God's will.

18:5 ¹ Which were the prophets of Baal, signifying that the wicked esteem none but flatterers, and such as will bear with their inordinate affections.

18:7 ¹ Yet the true ministers of God ought not to cease to do their duty, though the wicked magistrates cannot abide them to speak the truth.

² Meaning, that he ought not to refuse to hear any that was of God.

18:9 ¹ That is, in their majesty and royal apparel.

18:10 ¹ Read 1 Kings 22:11.

18:12 ¹ Thinking, that whereas four hundred prophets had agreed in one thing, that he being but one man and in least estimation, durst not gainsay it.

18:14 ¹ He spake this by derision of the false prophets, as the King well perceived.

18:16 ¹ He prophesieth of how the people should be dispersed and Ahab slain.

18:18 ¹ Meaning, his Angels.

18:19 ¹ Or, deceive.

Lord said unto him, Wherein?

21 And he said, I will go out, and be a false spirit in the mouth of all his Prophets. And [1]he said, Thou shalt persuade, and shalt also prevail: go forth and do so.

22 Now therefore behold, the Lord hath put a [1]false spirit in the mouth of these thy Prophets, and the Lord hath determined evil against thee.

23 Then Zedekiah the son of Chenaanah came near, and smote Michaiah upon the [1]cheek, and said, By what way went the Spirit of the Lord from me, to speak with thee?

24 And Michaiah said, Behold, thou shalt see that day when thou shalt go from chamber to chamber to hide thee.

25 And the King of Israel said, Take ye Michaiah, and carry him to Amon the governor of the city, and to Joash the king's son,

26 And say, Thus saith the king, Put this man in the prison house, and feed him with bread of [1]affliction and with water of affliction, until I return in peace.

27 And Michaiah said, If thou return in peace, the Lord hath not spoken by me. And [1]he said, Hear, all ye people.

28 So the King of Israel and Jehoshaphat the King of Judah went up to Ramoth Gilead.

29 And the King of Israel said unto Jehoshaphat, I will [1]change myself, and enter into the battle: but put thou on thine apparel. So the king of Israel changed himself, and they went into the battle.

30 And the king of Aram had commanded the captains of the chariots that were with him, saying, Fight you not with small nor great, but against the king of Israel only.

31 And when the captains of the chariots saw Jehoshaphat, they said, It is the king of Israel: and they compassed about him to fight. But Jehoshaphat [1]cried, and the Lord helped him and moved them *to depart* from him.

32 For when the captains of the chariots saw that he was not the King of Israel, they turned

CHAPTER 19
a Deut. 10:17
Job 34:19
Acts 10:34
Rom. 2:11
Gal. 2:6
Eph. 6:9
Col. 3:25
1 Pet. 1:17

back from him.

33 Then *a certain* man drew a bow [1]mightily, and smote the King of Israel between the joints [2]of his brigandine: Therefore he said to his chariotman, Turn thine hand, and carry me out of the host: for I am hurt.

34 And the battle increased that day: and the king of Israel [1]stood still in his chariot against the Aramites until even, and died at the time of the sun going down.

19 *4 After Jehoshaphat was rebuked by the Prophet, he called again the people to the honoring of the Lord. 5 He appointed Judges and minsters, 9 and exhorteth them to fear God.*

1 And Jehoshaphat the king of Judah returned [1]safe to his house in Jerusalem.

2 And Jehu the son of Hanani the Seer went out to meet him, and said to King Jehoshaphat, [1]Wouldest thou help the wicked, and love them that hate the Lord? therefore for this thing the wrath [2]of the Lord is upon thee.

3 Nevertheless good things are found in thee, because thou hast taken away the groves out of the land, and hast prepared thine heart to seek God.

4 ¶ So Jehoshaphat dwelt at Jerusalem, and returned and went [1]through the people from Beersheba to mount Ephraim, and brought them again unto the Lord God of their fathers.

5 And he set judges in the land throughout all the strong cities of Judah, city by city,

6 And said to the judges, Take heed what ye do: for ye execute not the judgments of man, but of the Lord, and *he will be* [1]with you in the cause *and* judgment.

7 Wherefore now let the fear of the Lord be upon you: take heed, and do it: for there is no [1]iniquity with the Lord our God, neither *a*respect of persons, nor receiving of reward.

8 Moreover in Jerusalem did Jehoshaphat set of the Levites, and of the Priests and of the chief of the families of Israel, for the judgment and cause of the

---

18:21 [1] That is, the Lord.

18:22 [1] To them that will not believe the truth, God sendeth strong delusion that they should believe lies, 2 Thess. 2:10.

18:23 [1] By this cruelty, his ambition and hypocrisy was discovered: thus the hypocrites boast of the Spirit which they have not, and declare their malice against them in whom the true Spirit is.

18:26 [1] Keep him straitly in prison, and let him feel hunger and thirst.

18:27 [1] Or, Micaiah.

18:29 [1] Thus the wicked think by their own subtlety to escape God's judgments which he threateneth by his word.

18:31 [1] He cried to the Lord by acknowledging his fault in going with this wicked king to war against the word of the Lord by his Prophet, and also by desiring mercy for the same.

18:33 [1] Hebrew, *in his simplicity,* or *ignorantly.*

[2] Or, between the habergeon.

18:34 [1] He dissembled his hurt that his soldiers might fight more courageously.

19:1 [1] Hebrew, *in peace.*

19:2 [1] He declareth that the wrath and judgment of God is over all such that support the wicked, and rather show not in deed that they are enemies to all such as hate the Lord.

[2] Hebrew, *wrath from the Lord.*

19:4 [1] He visited all his country, and brought his people from idolatry to the knowledge of the true God.

19:6 [1] Both to preserve you, if you do justly, or to punish you, if you do the contrary.

19:7 [1] He will declare by the sharpness of the punishment, that he hateth all iniquity.

Lord: and they ¹returned to Jerusalem.

9   And he charged them, saying, Thus shall ye do in the fear of the Lord faithfully and with a perfect heart.

10   And in every cause that shall come to you of your brethren that dwell in your cities, between ¹blood and blood, between law and precept, statutes and judgments, *ye shall judge them* and admonish them that they trespass not against the Lord, that ²wrath come not upon you and upon your brethren. This shall ye do and trespass not.

11   And behold, Amariah the Priest *shall be* the chief over you in all matters of the Lord, and Zebadiah the son of Ishmael, a ruler of the house of Judah, *shall be* for all the ¹King's affairs, and the Levites *shall be* officers ²before you. Be of courage, and do it, and the Lord shall be with the ³good.

20 ³ *Jehoshaphat and the people pray unto the Lord. 22 The marvelous victory that the Lord gave him against his enemies. 30 His reign and acts.*

1   After this also came the children of Moab and the children of Ammon, and with them of the ¹Ammonites against Jehoshaphat to battle.

2   Then there came that told Jehoshaphat, saying, There cometh a great multitude against thee from beyond the ¹Sea, out of Aram: and behold, they be in Hazazon Tamar, which is En Gedi.

3   And Jehoshaphat feared, and set himself ¹to seek the Lord, and proclaimed a fast throughout all Judah.

4   And Judah gathered themselves together to ask counsel of the Lord: they came even out of all the cities of Judah to inquire of the Lord.

5   And Jehoshaphat stood in the Congregation of Judah and Jerusalem in the house of the Lord before the new court,

6   And said, O Lord God of our fathers, art not thou God in heaven? and reignest not thou on all the kingdoms of the heathen? and in thine hand is power and might, and none is able to withstand thee.

CHAPTER 20
ᵃ 1 Kings 8:37
2 Chron. 6:28
ᵇ Deut. 2:9
Neh. 13:1
ᶜ Exod. 14:13,14

7   Didst not thou our God cast out the inhabitants of this land before thy people Israel, and ¹gavest it to the seed of Abraham thy friend forever?

8   And they dwelt therein, and have built thee a Sanctuary therein for thy Name, saying,

9   ᵃIf evil come upon us, as the ¹sword of judgment, or pestilence, or famine, we will stand before this house and in thy presence (for thy name ²is in this house) and will cry unto thee in our tribulation, and thou wilt hear and help.

10   And now, behold, the children of ᵇAmmon and Moab, and mount Seir, by whom thou wouldest not let Israel go, when they came out of the land of Egypt: but they turned aside from them, and destroyed them not:

11   Behold, I say, they reward us, in coming to cast us out of thine inheritance, which thou hast caused us to inherit.

12   O our God, wilt thou not judge them? for there is no strength in us *to stand* before this great multitude that cometh against us, neither do we know what to do: but our eyes ¹are toward thee.

13   And all Judah stood ¹before the Lord with their young ones, their wives, and their children.

14   And Jahaziel the son of Zechariah, the son of Benaiah, the son of Jeiel, the son of Mattaniah, a Levite of the sons of Asaph, *was there*, upon whom came ¹the Spirit of the Lord, in the midst of the Congregation.

15   And he said, Hearken ye all Judah, and ye inhabitants of Jerusalem, and thou, King Jehoshaphat: thus saith the Lord unto you, Fear you not, neither be afraid for this great multitude: for the ¹battle *is* not yours, but God's.

16   Tomorrow go ye down against them: behold, they come up by the cleft of Ziz, and ye shall find them at the end of the brook before the wilderness of Jeruel.

17   Ye shall not need to fight in this *battle*: 'stand still, move not, and behold the ¹salvation of the Lord

---

19:8 ¹ The Priests and Levites, which should judge matters according to the word of the Lord.

19:10 ¹ That is, to try whether the murder was done at unawares, or else on set purpose, Num. 35:11; Deut. 4:41.

² Meaning, that God would punish them most sharply, if they would not execute justice aright.

19:11 ¹ Shall be chief overseer of the public's affairs of the Realm.

² They shall have the handling of inferior causes.

³ God will assist them that do justice.

20:1 ¹ That is, which counterfeited the Ammonites in language and apparel. The Hebrews think that they were the Amalekites, but as may appear by the tenth verse they were the Idumeans of mount Seir.

20:2 ¹ Called the dead Sea, where God destroyed the five cities for sin.

20:3 ¹ This declareth what the fear of the godly is, which is as the prick to stir them to prayer, and to depend on the Lord, whereas it

moveth the wicked either to seek after worldly means and policies, or else to fall into despair.

20:7 ¹ He groundeth his prayer upon God's power, whereby he is able to help, and also on his mercy, which he will continue toward his, forasmuch as he hath once chosen them and began to show his graces toward them.

20:9 ¹ Meaning war which cometh by God's just judgments for our sins.

² That is, it is here called upon, and thou declarest thy presence and favor.

20:12 ¹ We only put our trust in thee, and wait for our deliverance from heaven.

20:13 ¹ That is, before the Ark of the Covenant.

20:14 ¹ Which was moved by the Spirit of God to prophesy.

20:15 ¹ They fight against God and not against you, therefore he will fight for you.

20:17 ¹ Or, deliverance.

towards you: O Judah, and Jerusalem, fear ye not, neither be afraid: tomorrow go out against them, and the Lord *will be* with you.

18 ¶ Then Jehoshaphat ¹bowed down with his face to the earth, and all Judah and the inhabitants of Jerusalem fell down before the Lord, worshipping the Lord.

19 ¶ And the Levites of the children of the Kohathites, and of the children of the Korahites stood up to praise the Lord God of Israel with a loud voice on high.

20 And when they arose early in the morning, they went forth to the wilderness of Tekoa: and as they departed, Jehoshaphat stood and said, Hear ye me, O Judah, and ye inhabitants of Jerusalem: put your trust in the Lord your God, and ye shall be assured: believe his ¹Prophets, and ye shall prosper.

21 And when he had consulted with the people, and appointed singers unto the Lord, and them that should praise *him that is* in the beautiful Sanctuary, in going forth before the men of arms, and saying, ¹Praise ye the Lord, for his mercy *lasteth* forever.

22 And when they began to shout, and to praise, the Lord laid ambushments against the children of Ammon, Moab, and ¹mount Seir, which were come against Judah, and they slew one another.

23 For the children of Ammon and Moab rose against the inhabitants of mount Seir, to slay and to destroy *them*: and when they had made an end of the inhabitants of Seir, every one helped to ¹destroy another.

24 And when Judah came toward Mizpah in the wilderness, they looked unto the multitude: and behold, the carcasses were fallen to the earth, and none escaped.

25 And when Jehoshaphat and his people came to take away the spoil of them, they found among them in abundance both of substance and also of bodies *laden* with precious jewels, which they took for themselves, till they could carry no more: they were three days in gathering of the spoil: for it was much.

26 And in the fourth day they ¹assembled themselves in the valley of Berachah: for there they blessed the

d 1 Kings 22:42
e 1 Kings 16:1
f 1 Kings 2:48,49

Lord: therefore they called the name of that place, The valley of Berachah unto this day.

27 Then every man of Judah and Jerusalem returned with Jehoshaphat their head to go again to Jerusalem with joy: for the Lord had made them to rejoice over their enemies.

28 And they came to Jerusalem with viols, and with harps, and with trumpets, *even* unto the house of the Lord.

29 And the ¹fear of God was upon all the kingdoms of the earth, when they had heard that the Lord had fought against the enemies of Israel.

30 So the kingdom of Jehoshaphat was quiet, and his God gave him rest on every side.

31 ¶ And *d*Jehoshaphat reigned over Judah, and *was* five and thirty years old, when he began to reign: and reigned five and twenty years in Jerusalem, and his mother's name was Azubah the daughter of Shilhi.

32 And he walked in the way of ¹Asa his father, and departed not there from, doing that which was right in the sight of the Lord.

33 Howbeit the high places were ¹not taken away: for the people had not yet prepared their hearts unto the God of their fathers.

34 Concerning the rest of the acts of Jehoshaphat first and last, behold, they are written in the book of Jehu the son of Hanani, which *e*is mentioned in the book of the kings of Israel.

35 ¶ Yet after this did Jehoshaphat king of Judah join himself with Ahaziah king of Israel, who was given to do evil.

36 And he joined with him, to *f*make ships to go to Tarshish: and they made the ships in Ezion Geber.

37 Then Eliezer the son of Dodavah of Mareshah prophesied against Jehoshaphat, saying, Because thou hast ¹joined thyself with Ahaziah, the Lord hath broken thy works: and the ships were broken, that they were not able to go to Tarshish.

21 *1 Jehoshaphat died. 3 Jehoram succeedeth him, 4 which killeth his brethren. 6 He was brought to idolatry, 11 and succeedeth the people. 16 He is oppressed of the Philistines. 18 His miserable end.*

20:18 ¹ Declaring his faith and obedience to the word of the Lord, and giving thanks for the deliverance promised.
20:20 ¹ Give credit to their words and doctrine.
20:21 ¹ This was a Psalm of thanksgiving which they used commonly to sing when they praised the Lord for his benefits, and was made by David, Ps. 136.
20:22 ¹ Meaning, the Idumeans which dwelt in mount Seir.
20:23 ¹ Thus the Lord according to Jehoshaphat's prayer declared his power, when he delivered his by causing their enemies to kill one another.
20:26 ¹ To give thanks to the Lord for the victory: and therefore the valley was called Berachah, that is, blessing or thanksgiving, which was also called the Valley of Jehoshaphat, Joel 3:2,12, because the

Lord judged the enemies according to Jehoshaphat's prayer.
20:29 ¹ He declareth hereby, that the works of God bring ever comfort or deliverance to his, and fear or destruction to his enemies.
20:32 ¹ Meaning, in his virtues, and those ways wherein he followed God.
20:33 ¹ If the great care and diligence of this good king was not able utterly to abolish all superstition of this people, but that they would still retain theirs, how much less are they able to reform evil, which either have little zeal, or not such as he had: though here he was not to be excused?
20:37 ¹ Thus God would not have his to join in society with idolaters and wicked men.

1 Jehoshaphat then slept with his fathers, and was buried with his fathers in the city of David: and Jehoram his son reigned in his stead.

2 And he had brethren the sons of Jehoshaphat, Azariah, and Jehiel, and Zechariah, and Azariah, and Michael, and Shephatiah. All these were the sons of Jehoshaphat king of ¹Israel.

3 And their father gave them great gifts of silver and of gold, and of precious things, with strong cities in Judah, but the kingdom gave he to Jehoram: for he was the eldest.

4 ªAnd Jehoram rose up upon the kingdom of his father, and made himself strong, and ¹slew all his brethren with the sword, and also of the princes of ²Israel.

5 Jehoram was two and thirty years old, when he began to reign, and he reigned eight years in Jerusalem.

6 And he walked in the way of the kings of Israel, as the house of Ahab had done: for he had the daughter of Ahab to ¹wife, and he wrought evil in the eyes of the Lord.

7 Howbeit the Lord would not destroy the house of David, because of the ᵇcovenant that he had made with David, and because he had promised to give a light to him, and to his sons forever.

8 ¶ In his days Edom rebelled from under the hand of Judah, and made a king over them.

9 And Jehoram went forth with his princes, and all his chariots with him: and he rose up by night, and smote Edom, which had compassed him in, and the captains of the chariots.

10 But Edom rebelled from under the hand of Judah unto this day. Then did ¹Libnah rebel at the same time from under his hand, because he had forsaken the Lord God of his fathers.

11 ¶ Moreover he made high places in the mountains of Judah, and caused the inhabitants of Jerusalem to commit ¹fornication, and compelled Judah thereto.

12 And there came a writing to him from ¹Elijah the Prophet, saying, Thus saith the Lord God of David thy father, Because thou hast not walked in the ways of Jehoshaphat thy father, nor in the ways

CHAPTER 21
ª 2 Kings 8:16
ᵇ 2 Sam. 7:12,16
1 Kings 2:4
1 Kings 9:5
2 Kings 8:19
2 Chron. 6:16

CHAPTER 22
ª 2 Kings 8:24

of Asa king of Judah,

13 But hast walked in the way of the kings of Israel, and hast made Judah and the inhabitants of Jerusalem to go a whoring, as the house of Ahab went a whoring, and hast also slain thy brethren of thy father's house, which were better than thou.

14 Behold, with a great plague will the Lord smite thy people, and thy children, and thy wives, and all thy substance,

15 And thou shalt be in great diseases in the disease of thy bowels, until ¹thy bowels fall out for the disease, day by day.

16 ¶ So the Lord stirred up against Jehoram the spirit of the Philistines, and the Arabians that were beside the ¹Ethiopians.

17 And they came up into Judah, and brake into it, and carried away all the substance that was found in the king's house, and his sons also, and his wives, so that there was not a son left him, save ¹Jehoahaz the youngest of his sons.

18 And after all this, the Lord smote him in his bowels with an incurable disease.

19 And in process of time, even after the end of two years, his guts fell out with his disease: so he died of sore diseases: and his people made no burning for him like the burning of his fathers.

20 When he began to reign, he was two and thirty years old, and reigned in Jerusalem eight years, ¹and lived without being desired: yet they buried him in the city of David, but not among the sepulchers of the Kings.

22 Ahaziah reigneth after Jehoram.   9 Jehu king of Israel killeth Ahaziah.   10 Athaliah putteth to death all the King's lineage.   11 Joash escapeth.

1 And ªthe inhabitants of Jerusalem made Ahaziah his youngest son King in his stead: for the army that came with ¹the Arabians to the camp, had slain all the eldest: therefore Ahaziah the son of Jehoram king of Judah reigned.

2 Two and ¹forty years old was Ahaziah when he began to reign, and he reigned ²one year in Jerusalem. And his mother's name was Athaliah

---

21:2 ¹ Read 2 Chron. 15:17, how by Israel he meant Judah.

21:4 ¹ Because the wicked live ever in fear, and also are ambitious, they become cruel, and spare not to murder them, whom by nature they ought most to cherish and defend.
  ² Meaning, of Judah and Benjamin.

21:6 ¹ So that we see how it cannot be that we should join with the wicked, and serve God.

21:10 ¹ Read 2 Kings 8:22.

21:11 ¹ Meaning, idolatry because that the idolater breaketh promise with God, as doth the adulteress to her husband.

21:12 ¹ Some think that this was Elisha, so called because he had the Spirit in abundance, as had Elijah.

21:15 ¹ We see this example daily practiced upon them that fall away from God, and become idolaters and murderers of their brethren.

21:16 ¹ There were other Arabians in Africa Southward toward Egypt.

21:17 ¹ Called also Ahaziah, as 2 Chron. 22:1, or Azariah, verse 6 following.

21:20 ¹ That is, as some write, he was not regarded, but deposed for his wickedness, and idolatry: so that his son reigned 22 years (his father yet living) without honor, and after his father's death he was confirmed to reign still, as 2 Chron. 22:2.

22:1 ¹ Meaning, the Philistines.

22:2 ¹ Read 2 Chron. 21:20.
  ² That is, after the death of his father.

the daughter ³of Omri.

3 He walked also in the ways of the house of Ahab: for his mother counseled him to do wickedly.

4 Wherefore he did evil in the sight of the Lord, like the house of Ahab: for they were his ¹counselors after the death of his father, to his destruction.

5 And he walked after their counsel, and went with Jehoram the son of Ahab king of Israel to fight against Hazael king of Aram at Ramoth Gilead: and the Aramites smote Joram.

6 ¶ And he returned to be healed in Jezreel, because of the wounds wherewith they had wounded him at Ramah, when he fought with Hazael king of Aram. Now Azariah the son of Jehoram king of Judah went down to see Jehoram the son of Ahab at Jezreel, because he was diseased.

7 And the destruction of Ahaziah ¹came of God, in that he went to Joram: for when he was come, he went forth with Jehoram against Jehu the son of Nimshi, ᵇwhom the Lord had anointed to destroy the house of Ahab.

8 Therefore when Jehu ¹executed judgment upon the house of Ahab, and found the princes of Judah and the sons of the brethren of Ahaziah that waited on Ahaziah, he slew them also.

9 And he sought Ahaziah, and they caught him where he was hid in Samaria, and brought him to Jehu, and slew him and buried him, because said they, he is the son of ¹Jehoshaphat, which sought the Lord with all his heart. So the house of Ahaziah was not able to retain the kingdom.

10 ¶ ᶜTherefore when Athaliah the mother of Ahaziah saw that her son was dead, she arose and ¹destroyed all the king's seed of the house of Judah.

11 But Jehoshabeath the daughter of the king, took Joash the son of Ahaziah, and stole him from among the king's sons, that should be slain, and put him and his nurse in the bed chamber: so Jehoshabeath the daughter of king Jehoram the wife of Jehoiada the Priest (for she was the sister of Ahaziah) hid him from Athaliah: so she slew him not.

12 And he was with them hid in the ¹house of God six years, while Athaliah reigned over the ²land.

ᵇ 2 Kings 9:7
ᶜ 2 Kings 11:1

CHAPTER 23
ᵃ 2 Kings 11:4
ᵇ 2 Sam. 7:12,16
1 Kings 2:4
2 Chron. 21:7
ᶜ 2 Kings 11:6

23

Joash the son of Ahaziah is made king.   15 *Athaliah is put to death.*   17 *The temple of Baal is destroyed.*   16 *Jehoiada appointeth ministers in the Temple.*

1 And ᵃʼ¹in the seventh year Jehoiada waxed bold, and took the captains of hundreds, *to wit,* Azariah the son of Jeroham, and Ishmael the son of Jehohanan, and Azariah the son of Obed, and Maaseiah the son of Adaiah, and Elishaphat the son of Zichri in covenant with him.

2 And they went about in Judah, and gathered the Levites out of all the cities of Judah, and the ¹chief fathers of Israel: and they came to Jerusalem.

3 And all the congregation made a covenant with the King in the house of God: and he said unto them, Behold, the King's son must reign, ᵇas the Lord hath said of the sons of David.

4 This is it that ye shall do, The third part of you that come on the Sabbath of the Priests, and the Levites, *shall be* porters of the doors.

5 And *another* third part toward the King's house, and *another* third part at the ᶜgate of the ¹foundation, and all the people *shall be* in the courts of the house of the Lord.

6 But let none come into the house of the Lord, save the Priests, and the Levites that minister, they shall go in, for they are holy: but all the people shall keep the watch of the Lord.

7 And the Levites shall compass the King round about, and every man with his weapon in his hand, and he that entereth ¹into the house, shall be slain, and be you with the king, when he cometh in, and when he goeth out.

8 ¶ So the Levites and all Judah did according to all things that Jehoiada the Priest had commanded, and took every man his men that came on the Sabbath, with them that ¹went out on the Sabbath: for Jehoiada the Priest did not discharge the courses.

9 And Jehoiada the Priest delivered to the captains of hundreds spears, and shields, and bucklers which had been King David's, and were in the house of God.

10 And he caused all the people to stand (every man with his weapon in his hand) from the right side of the house, to the left side of the house by the altar and by the ¹house round about the king.

---

³ She was Ahab's daughter, who was the son of Omri.

22:4 ¹ He showeth that it must needs follow that the rulers are such as their counselors be, and that there cannot be a good King, that suffereth wicked counselors.

22:7 ¹ Hereby we see how nothing can come to any but by God's providence and as he hath appointed, and therefore he causeth all means to serve to his will.

22:8 ¹ Or, took vengeance.

22:9 ¹ This was the just plague of God, because he joined himself with God's enemies: yet God to declare the worthiness of Jehoshaphat his grandfather, moved them to give him the honor of burial.

22:10 ¹ To the intent that there should be none to make title to the

crown, and so she might usurp the government.

22:12 ¹ Meaning, in the chamber, where the Priests and Levites slept, which kept their courses weekly in the Temple.

² To wit, of Judah.

23:1 ¹ Of the reign of Athaliah, or after the death of Ahaziah.

23:2 ¹ Meaning of Judah and Benjamin: read why they are called Israel, 2 Chron. 15:17.

23:5 ¹ Which was the chief gate of the Temple toward the East.

23:7 ¹ Meaning, to make any tumult, or to hinder their enterprise.

23:8 ¹ Which had finished their course on the Sabbath, and so the other part entered to keep their turn.

23:10 ¹ Meaning, the most holy place where the Ark stood.

11 Then they brought out the king's son, and put upon him the crown and *gave him* the [1]testimony, and made him King. And Jehoiada and his sons anointed him, and said, God save the king.

12 ¶ But when Athaliah heard the noise of the people running and praising the King, she came to the people into the house of the Lord.

13 And when she [1]looked, behold, the king stood by his pillar at the entering in, and the princes and the trumpets by the King, and all the people of the land rejoiced, and blew the trumpets, and the singers *were* with instruments of music, and they that could sing praise: then Athaliah rent her clothes, and said, [2]Treason, treason.

14 Then Jehoiada the Priest brought out the captains of hundreds that were governors of the host, and said unto them, Have her forth of the ranges, and he that [1]followeth her, let him die by the sword: for the Priest had said, Slay her not in the house of the Lord.

15 So they laid hands on her: and when she was come to the entering of the horse gate by the king's house, they slew her there.

16 ¶ And Jehoiada made a [1]covenant between him and all the people, and the king, that they would be the Lord's people.

17 And all the people went to the house of Baal, and [1]destroyed, and brake his altars and his images, and slew [2]Mattan the priest of Baal before the altars.

18 And Jehoiada appointed officers for the house of the Lord, under the [1]hands of the Priests and Levites, whom David had distributed for the house of the Lord, to offer burnt offerings unto the Lord, [d]as it is written in the Law of Moses, with rejoicing and singing by the appointment of David.

19 And he set porters by the gates of the house of the Lord, that none that was unclean in anything, should enter in.

20 And he took the captains of hundreds, and the noble men, and the governors of the people, and all the people of the land, and he caused the king to come down out of the house of the Lord, and they went through the [1]high gate of the king's house, and set the king upon the throne of the kingdom.

[d] Num. 28:3

CHAPTER 24
[a] 2 Kings 12:1
[b] Exod. 30:13
[c] 2 Kings 12:9
[d] Exod. 30:13

21 Then all the people of the land rejoiced, and the city was quiet [1]after that they had slain Athaliah with the sword.

24

Joash repaireth the house of the Lord.   17 After the death of Jehoiada he falleth to idolatry.   21 He stoneth to death Zechariah the Prophet.   25 Joash is killed of his own servants.   27 After him reigneth Amaziah.

1 Joash [a]*was* seven years old when he began to reign, and he reigned forty years in Jerusalem: and his mother's name was Zibiah of Beersheba.

2 And Joash did uprightly in the sight of the Lord all the days of [1]Jehoiada the Priest.

3 And Jehoiada [1]took him two wives, and he begat sons and daughters.

4 ¶ And afterward it came into Joash's mind to renew the house of the Lord.

5 And he assembled the Priests and the Levites, and said to them, Go out unto the cities of Judah, and gather of all [1]Israel money to repair the house of your God, from year to year, and haste the thing, but the Levites hasted not.

6 Therefore the king called Jehoiada the [1]chief, and said unto him, Why hast thou not required of the Levites to bring in out of Judah and Jerusalem [b]the tax of Moses the servant of the Lord, and of the Congregation of Israel, for the Tabernacle of the testimony?

7 For [1]wicked Athaliah, and her children brake up the house of God: and all the things that were dedicated for the house of the Lord, did they bestow upon Baal.

8 Therefore the king commanded, [c]and they made a chest, and set it at the gate of the house of the Lord without.

9 And they made proclamation through Judah and Jerusalem, to bring unto the Lord [d]the tax of Moses the servant of God, *laid* upon Israel in the wilderness.

10 And all the princes and all the people rejoiced, and brought in, and cast into the chest, until they had finished.

11 And when it was time, [1]they brought the chest

23:11 [1] That is, the book of the Law, or as some read, they put upon him his royal apparel.

23:13 [1] Or, saw the king standing.
[2] Declaring her vile impudence, which having unjustly and by murder usurped the crown, would still have defeated the true possessor, and therefore called true obedience treason.

23:14 [1] To join with her party, and to maintain her authority.

23:16 [1] That they would only serve him and renounce all idolatry.

23:17 [1] According to their covenant made to the Lord.
[2] As the Lord commanded in his Law both for the person and also the city, Deut. 13:9 and 15.

23:18 [1] Or, charge.

23:20 [1] Which was the principal gate, that the King might be seen

of all the people.

23:21 [1] For where a tyrant and an idolater reigneth, there can be no quietness for the plagues of God are ever among such people.

24:2 [1] Who was a faithful counselor, and governed him by the word of God.

24:3 [1] Or, gave him two wives.

24:5 [1] He meaneth not the ten tribes, but only the two tribes of Judah and Benjamin.

24:6 [1] For he was the high Priest.

24:7 [1] The Scriptures doth term her thus, because she was a cruel murderer, and a blasphemous idolatress.

24:11 [1] Such as were faithful men, whom the king had appointed for that matter.

unto the King's officer by the hand of the Levites: and when they saw that there was much silver, then the King's Scribe (and one appointed by the high Priest) came and emptied the chest, and took it, and carried it to his place again: thus they did day by day, and gathered silver in abundance.

12 And the King and ¹Jehoiada gave it to such as did the labor *and* work in the house of the Lord, and hired masons and carpenters to repair the house of the Lord: *they gave it* also to workers of iron and brass, to repair the house of the Lord.

13 So the workmen wrought, and the work ¹amended through their hands: and they restored the house of God to his state, and strengthened it.

14 And when they had finished it, they brought the rest of the silver before the king and Jehoiada, and he made thereof ¹vessels for the house of the Lord, *even* vessels to minister, both mortars and *incense* cups, and vessels of gold, and of silver: and they offered burnt offerings in the house of the Lord continually all the days of Jehoiada.

15 ¶ But Jehoiada waxed old and was full of days, and died. An hundred and thirty years old *was* he when he died.

16 And they buried him in the city of David with the ¹kings, because he had done good in Israel, and toward God and his house.

17 ¶ And after the death of Jehoiada, came the ¹princes of Judah, and did reverence to the king, and the king hearkened unto them.

18 And they left the house of the Lord God of their fathers, and served groves and idols: and wrath came upon Judah and Jerusalem, because of this their trespass.

19 And *God* sent Prophets among them, to bring them again unto the Lord: and they ¹made protestation among them, but they would not hear.

20 And the Spirit of God came upon Zechariah the son of Jehoiada the Priest, which stood ¹above the people, and said unto them, Thus saith God,

Why transgress ye the commandments of the Lord? surely ye shall not prosper: because ye have forsaken the Lord, he also hath forsaken you.

21 Then they conspired against him, and stoned him with stones at the ¹commandment of the king, in the court of the house of the Lord.

22 Thus Joash the king remembered not the kindness which Jehoiada his father had done to him, but slew his son. And when he died, he said, The Lord ¹look upon it and require it.

23 ¶ And when the year was out, the host of Aram came up against him, and they came against Judah and Jerusalem, and destroyed all the princes of the people from among the people, and sent all the spoil of them unto the king of Damascus.

24 Though the army of Aram came with a small company of men, yet the Lord delivered a very great army into their hand, because they had forsaken the Lord God of their fathers: and they ¹gave sentence against Joash.

25 And when they were departed from him, (for they left him in great diseases) his own servants conspired against him for the blood of the ¹children of Jehoiada the Priest, and slew him on his bed, and he died, and they buried him in the city of David: but they buried him not in the sepulchers of the kings.

26 And these are they that conspired against him, Zabad the son of Shimrath an Ammonitess, and Jehozabad the son of Shimrith a Moabitess.

27 But ¹his sons, and the sum of the tax *gathered* by him, and the ²foundation of the house of God, behold, they are written in the story of the book of the Kings. And Amaziah his son reigned in his stead.

25 *Amaziah putteth him to death which slew his father. 10 He sendeth back them of Israel. 11 He overcometh the Edomites. 14 He falleth to idolatry. 17 And Joash king of Israel overcometh Amaziah. 27 He is slain by a conspiracy.*

1 Amaziah was five and twenty years old when he

24:12 ¹ Signifying that this thing was done by advice and counsel, and not by any one man's affection.
24:13 ¹ Hebrew, *a medicine was upon the work,* meaning it was repaired.
24:14 ¹ For the wicked kings his predecessors, and Athaliah had destroyed the vessels of the Temple, or turned them to the use of their idols.
24:16 ¹ Signifying that they could not honor him too much, who had so excellently served in the work of the Lord, and in the affairs of the commonwealth.
24:17 ¹ Which were flatterers, and knew now that the king was destitute of him who did watch over him as a father, and therefore brought him to most vile idolatry.
24:19 ¹ They took heaven and earth and all creatures to witness, that except they returned to the Lord, he would most grievously punish their infidelity and rebellion, Neh. 9:26.
24:20 ¹ In a place above the people, to the intent that he might be heard.
24:21 ¹ There is no rage so cruel and beastly as of them whose hearts God hath hardened, and which delight more in superstition and idolatry than in the true service of God and pure simplicity of his word.
24:22 ¹ Revenge my death and require my blood at your hands: or he speaketh this by prophecy, because he knew that God would do it. This Zechariah is also called the son of Berechiah, Matt. 23:35, because his progenitors were Iddo, Berechiah, Jehoiada, etc.
24:24 ¹ That is, reproved and checked him, and handled him rigorously.
24:25 ¹ Meaning, Zechariah, which was one of Jehoiada's sons, and a Prophet of the Lord.
24:27 ¹ That is, concerning his sons, etc.
² That is, the reparation.

began to reign, and he reigned nine and twenty years in ªJerusalem, and his mother's name *was* Jehoaddan of Jerusalem.

2 And he did ¹uprightly in the eyes of the Lord, but not with a perfect heart.

3 And when the kingdom was established unto him, he slew his servants, that had slain the king his father.

4 But he slew not their children, but *did* as it is written in the Law, *and* in the book of Moses, where the Lord commanded, saying, ᵇThe fathers shall not die for the ¹children, neither shall the children die for the fathers, but every man shall die for his own sin.

5 ¶ And Amaziah assembled Judah, and made them captains over thousands, and captains over hundreds, according to the houses of their fathers, throughout all Judah and Benjamin: and he numbered them from ¹twenty years old and above, and found among them three hundred thousand chosen men, to go forth to the war, and to handle spear and shield.

6 He hired also an hundred thousand valiant men ¹out of Israel for an hundred talents of silver.

7 But a man of God came to him, saying, O king, let not the army of Israel go with thee: for the Lord is not ¹with Israel, *neither* with all the house of Ephraim.

8 If ¹not, go thou on, do it, make thyself strong to the battle, *but* God shall make thee fall before the enemy: for God hath power to help, and to cast down.

9 And Amaziah said to the man of GOD, What shall we do then for the hundred talents, which I have given to the host of Israel? Then the man of God answered, The Lord is able to ¹give thee more than this.

10 So Amaziah separated them, *to wit*, the army that was come to him out of Ephraim, to return to their place: wherefore their wrath was kindled greatly against Judah, and they returned to their places with great anger.

CHAPTER 25
ª 2 Kings 14:2
ᵇ Deut. 24:16
2 Kings 14:6
Jer. 31:30
Ezek. 18:10
ᶜ 2 Kings 14:9

11 Then Amaziah was encouraged, and led forth his people, and went to the salt valley, and smote the children of ¹Seir, ten thousand.

12 And *other* ten thousand did the children of Judah take alive, and carried them to the top of a ¹rock, and cast them down from the top of the rock, and they all burst to pieces.

13 But the men of the ¹army, which Amaziah sent away, that they should not go with his people to battle, fell upon the cities of Judah from Samaria unto Beth Horon, and smote three thousand of them, and took much spoil.

14 Now after that Amaziah was come from the slaughter of the Edomites, he brought the gods of the children of Seir, and set them up to be his gods, and ¹worshipped them, and burned incense unto them.

15 Wherefore the Lord was wroth with Amaziah, and sent unto him a Prophet, which said unto him, Why hast thou sought the gods of the people, which were not able to ¹deliver their own people out of thine hand?

16 And as he talked with him, ¹he said unto him, Have they made thee the King's counselor? cease thou: why should they ²smite thee? And the Prophet ceased, but said, I know that God hath determined to destroy thee, because thou hast done this, and hast not obeyed my counsel.

17 ¶ Then Amaziah King of Judah took counsel, and sent to Joash the son of Jehoahaz, the son of Jehu king of Israel, saying, Come, ¹let us see one another in the face.

18 But Joash king of Israel sent to Amaziah king of Judah, saying, The thistle that is in Lebanon, sent to the cedar that is in Lebanon, saying, ᶜGive thy daughter to my son to wife: and the wild beast that was in Lebanon went and trode down the thistle.

19 Thou thinkest: lo, thou hast smitten Edom, and thine heart lifteth thee up to brag: abide now at home: why dost thou provoke to thine hurt, that thou shouldest fall, and Judah with thee?

25:2 ¹ Meaning, in respect of his predecessors albeit he had his imperfections.
25:4 ¹ That is, for that fault wherefore the child is punished, except he be culpable of the same.
25:5 ¹ So many as were able men to bear weapons and go to the war.
25:6 ¹ That is, out of the ten tribes, which had separated themselves before, both from God and their true king.
25:7 ¹ And therefore to think to have help of them, whom the Lord favoreth not, is to cast off the help of the Lord.
25:8 ¹ If thou wilt not give credit to my words.
25:9 ¹ He showeth that if we depend only upon God, we shall not need to be troubled with these worldly respects, for he will give at all times that which shall be necessary, if we obey his word.
25:11 ¹ For the Idumeans whom David had brought to subjection, rebelled under Jehoram Jehoshaphat's son.

25:12 ¹ In 2 Kings 14:7, this rock is called the city Sela.
25:13 ¹ That is, the hundred thousand of Israel.
25:14 ¹ Thus where he should have given the praise to God for his benefits and great victory, he fell from God, and did most vilely dishonor him.
25:15 ¹ He proveth that whatsoever cannot save himself nor his worshippers, is no God but an idol.
25:16 ¹ Meaning, the King.
² So hard it is, for the carnal man to be admonished of his fault, that he contemneth, mocketh, and threateneth him that warneth him: yea, imprisoneth him and putteth him to death, 2 Chron. 16:10 and 18:26 and 24:21.
25:17 ¹ That is, let us try the matter hand to hand: for he was offended, that the army of the Israelites, whom he had in wages, and dismissed by the counsel of the Prophet, had destroyed certain of the cities of Judah.

20 But Amaziah would not hear: for ¹it was of God, that he might deliver them into his hand, because they had sought the gods of Edom.

21 So Joash the king of Israel went up: and he and Amaziah king of Judah saw one another in the face at Bethshemesh, which is in Judah.

22 And Judah was put to the worse before Israel, and they fled every man to his tents.

23 But Joash the king of Israel took Amaziah king of Judah, the son of Joash, the son of Jehoahaz, in Bethshemesh, and brought him to Jerusalem, and brake down the wall of Jerusalem, from the gate of Ephraim unto the corner gate, four hundred cubits.

24 And *he took* all the gold and the silver, and all the vessels that were found in the house of God with ¹Obed Edom, and in the treasures of the king's house, and the children that were in hostage, and returned to Samaria.

25 ¶ And Amaziah the son of Joash king of Judah lived after the death of Joash son of Jehoahaz king of Israel, fifteen years.

26 Concerning the rest of the acts of Amaziah first and last, are they not written in the book of the kings of Judah and Israel?

27 Now after the time that Amaziah did turn away from the Lord, ᵈthey wrought treason against him in Jerusalem: and when he was fled to Lachish, they sent to Lachish after him, and slew him there.

28 And they brought him upon horses, and buried him with his fathers in the city of Judah.

26

1, 5 Uzziah obeying the Lord, prospereth in his enterprises.   16 He waxeth proud and usurpeth the Priests' office.   19 The Lord plagueth him.   20 The Priests drive him out of the Temple, and exclude him out of the Lord's house.   23 His burial, and his successor.

1 Then all the ᵃpeople of Judah took ¹Uzziah which was sixteen years old, and made him king in the stead of his father Amaziah.

2 He built ¹Eloth, and restored it to Judah, after that the king slept with his fathers.

3 ᵇSixteen years old *was* Uzziah, when he began to reign, and he reigned two and fifty years in Jerusalem,

ᵈ 2 Kings 14:19

CHAPTER 26
ᵈ 2 Kings 14:21
ᵇ 1 Kings 15:2
ᶜ Neh. 3:19,24

and his mother's name *was* Jecholiah of Jerusalem.

4 And he did uprightly in the sight of the Lord, according to all that his father Amaziah did.

5 And he sought God in the days of ¹Zechariah (which understood the visions of God) and when as ²he sought the Lord, God made him to prosper.

6 For he went forth and fought against the Philistines and brake down the wall of Gath, and the wall of Jabneh, and the wall of Ashdod, and built cities in Ashdod, and among the Philistines.

7 And God helped him against the Philistines, and against the Arabians that dwelt in Gur Baal and Hammeunim.

8 And the Ammonites gave ¹gifts to Uzziah, and his name spread to the entering in of Egypt: for he did most valiantly.

9 Moreover Uzziah built towers in Jerusalem at the corner gate, and at the valley gate, and at the ᶜ,¹turning, and made them strong.

10 And he built towers in the wilderness, and dug many ¹cisterns: for he had much cattle both in the valleys and plains, plowmen, and dressers of vines in the mountains, and in ²Carmel: for he loved husbandry.

11 Uzziah also had an host of fighting men that went out to war by bands, according to the count of their number under the hand of Jeiel the Scribe, and Maaseiah the ruler, *and* under the hand of Hananiah, one of the King's captains.

12 The whole ¹number of the chief of the families of the valiant men *were* two thousand and six hundred.

13 And under their hand *was* the army for war, three hundred and seven thousand, and five hundred that fought valiantly to help the King against the enemy.

14 And Uzziah prepared them throughout all the host, shields, and spears, and helmets, and brigandines, and bows, and stones to sling.

15 He made also very ¹artificial engines in Jerusalem, to be upon the towers and upon the corners, to shoot arrows and great stones: and his name spread far abroad, because God did help him marvelously till he was mighty.

25:20 ¹ Thus God oft times plagueth by those means wherein men most trust, to teach them to have their recourse only to him, and to show his judgments, moveth their hearts to follow that which shall be their destruction.

25:24 ¹ Meaning, the successors of Obed Edom: for the house bare the name of the chief father.

26:1 ¹ Called also Azariah.

26:2 ¹ He fortified it and made it strong: this city was also called Elath and Elanon near to the red Sea.

26:5 ¹ This was not that Zechariah that was the son of Jehoiada, but some other Prophet of that name.

² For God never forsakes any that seeketh unto him, and therefore man is the cause of his own destruction.

26:8 ¹ That is, they paid tribute in sign of subjection.

26:9 ¹ Whereas the wall or tower turneth.

26:10 ¹ Or, pits.

² That is, in mount Carmel, or as the word signifieth in the fruitful field: it is also taken for a green ear of corn, when it is full, as Lev. 2:14.

26:12 ¹ Of the chief officers of the king's house, or of the captains and sergeants for war.

26:15 ¹ Hebrew, *engines by the invention of an inventive man.*

16 ¶ But when he was strong, his heart ¹was lifted up to *his* destruction: for he transgressed against the Lord his God, and went into the Temple of the Lord to burn incense upon the altar of incense.

17 And Azariah the Priest went in after him, and with him fourscore Priests of the Lord, valiant men.

18 And they withstood Uzziah the King, and said unto him, ᵈIt pertaineth not to thee, Uzziah, to burn incense unto the Lord, but to the Priests the sons of Aaron, that are consecrated for to offer incense: ¹go forth of the Sanctuary: for thou hast transgressed, and thou shalt have none honor of the Lord God.

19 Then Uzziah was wroth, and had incense in his hand to burn it: and while he was wroth with the Priests, the leprosy rose up in his forehead before the Priests in the house of the Lord beside the incense altar.

20 And when Azariah the chief Priest with all the Priests looked upon him, behold, he was leprous in his forehead, and they caused him hastily to depart thence: and he was even compelled to go out, because the Lord had smitten him.

21 ‘And Uzziah the King was a leper unto the day of his death, and dwelt as a leper in an ¹house apart, because he was cut off from the house of the Lord: and Jotham his son *ruled* over the King's house, and judged the people of the land.

22 Concerning the rest of the acts of Uzziah, first and last, did Isaiah the Prophet the son of Amoz write.

23 So Uzziah slept with his fathers, and they buried him with his fathers in the field of the burial, which pertained to the Kings: for they said, He ¹is a leper. And Jotham his son reigned in his stead.

27

1 Jotham reigned, and overcometh the Ammon-ites.   8 His reign and death.   9 Ahaz his son reigneth in his stead.

1 Jotham ᵃ*was* five and twenty years old when he began to reign, and reigned sixteen years in Jerusalem, and his mother's name *was* Jerushah the daughter of Zadok.

2 And he did uprightly in the sight of the Lord, according to all that his father Uzziah did, save that

ᵈ Num. 18:7

ᵉ 2 Kings 15:5

CHAPTER 27
ᵃ 2 Kings 15:33

CHAPTER 28
ᵃ 2 Kings 16:2

he entered not into the ¹Temple of the Lord, and the people did yet ²corrupt *their ways.*

3 He built the high ¹gate of the house of the Lord, and he built very much on the wall of the castle.

4 Moreover he built cities in the mountains of Judah, and in the forests he built palaces and towers.

5 And he fought with the kings of the children of Ammon, and prevailed against them. And the children of Ammon gave him the same year an hundred talents of silver, and ten thousand ¹measures of wheat, and ten thousand of barley: this did the children of Ammon give him ²both in the second year and the third.

6 So Jotham became mighty, ¹because he directed his way before the Lord his God.

7 Concerning the rest of the acts of Jotham and all his wars and his ways, lo, they are written in the book of the Kings of Israel, and Judah.

8 He was five and twenty years old, when he began to reign, and reigned sixteen years in Jerusalem.

9 And Jotham slept with his fathers, and they buried him in the city of David: and Ahaz his son reigned in his stead.

28

1 Ahaz an idolater is given into the hands of the Syrians and the king of Israel.   9 The Prophet reproveth the Israelites' cruelty.   18 Judah is molested with enemies.   23 Ahaz increaseth his idolatry.   26 His death and successor.

1 Ahaz ᵃ*was* twenty years old when he began to reign, and reigned sixteen years in Jerusalem, and did not uprightly in the sight of the Lord, like David his ¹father.

2 But ¹he walked in the ways of the kings of Israel, and made even molten images for ²Baalim.

3 Moreover he burnt incense in the valley of Ben-hinnom, and ¹burnt his sons with fire, after the abominations of the heathen whom the Lord had cast out before the children of Israel.

4 He sacrificed also and burnt incense in the high places, and on hills, and under every green tree.

5 Wherefore the Lord his God delivered him into the hand of the king of the Aramites, and they smote

26:16 ¹ Thus prosperity causeth men to trust in themselves, and by forgetting him which is the author thereof, procure their own perdition.
26:18 ¹ Though his zeal seemed to be good and also his intention, yet because they were not governed by the word of God, he did wickedly, and was therefore both justly resisted and also punished.
26:21 ¹ According to the commandment of the Lord, Lev. 13:46.
26:23 ¹ And therefore was buried apart in the same field, but not in the same sepulchers with his predecessors.
27:2 ¹ To wit, to offer incense against the word of God, which thing is spoken in the commendation of Jotham.
   ² They were not clean purged from idolatry.

27:3 ¹ Which was sixscore cubits high, and was for the height called Ophel: it was at the East gate, and mention is made of it, 2 Chron. 3:4.
27:5 ¹ Hebrew, *Corim.*
   ² Or, yearly.
27:6 ¹ He showeth that all prosperity cometh of God, who never faileth when we put our trust in him.
28:1 ¹ Or, predecessor.
28:2 ¹ He was an idolater like them.
   ² As the idolaters have certain chief idols, who are as patrons (as were these Baalim) so have they others which are inferior and do represent the great idols.
28:3 ¹ Or, made them pass through the fire, as 2 Chron. 33:6; Lev. 13:21.

him, and took of his [1]many prisoners, and brought them to Damascus: and he was also delivered into the hand of the king of Israel, which smote him with a great slaughter.

6 For [1]Pekah the son of Remaliah slew in Judah sixscore thousand in one day, all [2]valiant men, because they had forsaken the Lord God of their fathers.

7 And Zichri a [1]mighty man of Ephraim slew Maaseiah the king's son, and Azrikam the governor of the house, and Elkanah the second after the king.

8 And the children of Israel took prisoners of their brethren, [1]two hundred thousand of women, sons and daughters, and carried away much spoil of them, and brought the spoil to Samaria.

9 ¶ But there was a Prophet of the Lord, (whose name *was* Oded) and he went out before the host that came to Samaria, and said unto them, Behold, [1]because the Lord God of your fathers is wroth with Judah, he hath delivered them into your hand, and ye have slain them in a rage, that reacheth up to heaven.

10 And now ye purpose to keep under the children of Judah and Jerusalem, as servants and handmaids unto you, but are not you *such that* [1]sins *are* with you before the Lord your God?

11 Now therefore hear me, and deliver the captives again, which ye have taken prisoners of your brethren: for the fierce wrath of the Lord *is* toward you.

12 Wherefore certain of the chiefs of the children of [1]Ephraim, Azariah the son of Johanan, Berechiah the son of Meshillemoth, and Jehizkiah the son of Shallum, and Amasa the son of Hadlai, stood up against them that came from the war,

13 And said unto them, Bring not in the captives hither: for *this shall be* [1]a sin upon us *against* the Lord: ye intended to add more to our sins and to our trespass, though our trespass be great, and the fierce wrath *of God is* against Israel.

14 So the army left the captives and the spoil before the princes and all the Congregation.

15 And the men that were [1]named by name, rose up and took the prisoners, and with the spoil clothed all that were naked among them, and arrayed them,

[b] 2 Kings 16:8

and shod them, and gave them meat, and gave them drink, and [2]anointed them, and carried all that were feeble of them upon asses, and brought them to Jericho the city of Palm trees to their [3]brethren: so they returned to Samaria.

16 ¶ At that time did King Ahaz send unto the [1]kings of Assyria to help him.

17 (For the Edomites came moreover, and slew of Judah, and carried away captives.

18 The Philistines also invaded the cities in the low country, and toward the South of Judah, and took Beth Shemesh, and Aijalon, and Gederoth and Sochoh, with the villages thereof, and Timnah, with her villages, and Gimzo, with her villages, and they dwelt there.

19 For the Lord had humbled Judah, because of Ahaz king of [1]Israel: for he had brought vengeance upon Judah, and had grievously transgressed against the Lord.)

20 And Tilgath-Pilneser king of Assyria came unto him, who troubled him and did not strengthen him.

21 For Ahaz [1]took a portion [b]out of the house of the Lord and out of the king's house and of the princes', and gave unto the king of Assyria: yet it helped him not.

22 And in the time of his tribulation did he yet trespass more against the Lord, (this is king Ahaz)

23 For he sacrificed unto the gods of Damascus, which [1]plagued him, and he said, Because the gods of the kings of Aram helped them, I will sacrifice unto them, and they will [2]help me: yet they were his ruin, and of all [3]Israel.

24 And Ahaz gathered the vessels of the house of God, and brake the vessels of the house of God, and shut up the doors of the house of the Lord, and made him altars in every corner of Jerusalem.

25 And in every city of Judah he made high places, to burn incense unto other gods, and provoked to anger the Lord God of his fathers.

26 Concerning the rest of his acts, and all his ways first and last, behold, they are written in the book of the Kings of Judah, and Israel.

28:5 [1] Hebrew, *a great captivity.*
28:6 [1] Who was king of Israel.
   [2] Hebrew, *sons of strength.*
28:7 [1] Or, tyrant.
28:8 [1] Thus by the just judgment of God, Israel destroyed Judah.
28:9 [1] For they thought they had overcome them by their own valiantness, and did not consider that God had delivered them into their hands, because Judah had offended him.
28:10 [1] May not God as well punish you for your sins as he hath done these men for theirs, seeing yours are greater?
28:12 [1] Which tribe was now greatest, and had most authority.
28:13 [1] God will not suffer this sin, which we commit against him, to be unpunished.
28:15 [1] Whose name were rehearsed before, verse 12.

[2] Either for their wounds or weariness.
[3] To them of the tribe of Judah.
28:16 [1] To Tiglath-Pileser and those kings that were under his dominion, 2 Kings 16:7.
28:19 [1] He meaneth Judah, because Ahaz forsook the Lord and sought help of the infidels. Read of Israel taken for Judah, 2 Chron. 15:17.
28:21 [1] Hebrew, *divided.*
28:23 [1] As he falsely supposed.
[2] Thus the wicked measure God's favor by prosperity and adversity: for if idolaters prosper, they make their idols gods, not considering that God punisheth them oft times whom he loveth, and giveth his enemies good success for a time, whom afterward he will destroy.
[3] Or, Judah and Benjamin.

27 And Ahaz slept with his fathers, and they buried him in the city ¹of Jerusalem, but brought him not unto the ²sepulchers of the Kings of Israel: and Hezekiah his son reigned in his stead.

29 3, 5 *Hezekiah repaireth the Temple, and advertiseth the Levites of the corruption of religion.* 12 *The levites prepare the Temple.* 20 *The king and his princes sacrifice in the Temple.* 25 *The Levites sing praises.* 31 *The oblation of the people.*

1 Hezekiah ᵃbegan to reign, when he was five and twenty years old, and reigned nine and twenty years in Jerusalem: and his mother's name *was* ¹Abijah the daughter of Zechariah.

2 And he did uprightly in the sight of the Lord, according to all that David his father had done.

3 He opened the ¹doors of the house of the Lord in the ²first year, and in the first month of his reign, and repaired them.

4 And he brought in the Priests and the Levites, and gathered them into the East street,

5 And said unto them, Hear me, ye Levites: sanctify now yourselves, and sanctify the house of the Lord God of your fathers, and carry forth ¹the filthiness out of the Sanctuary.

6 For our fathers have trespassed and done evil in the eyes of the Lord our God, and have forsaken him, and turned away their faces from the Tabernacle of the Lord, and turned their backs.

7 They have also shut the doors of the porch, and quenched the lamps, and have neither burnt incense, nor offered burnt offerings in the Sanctuary unto the God of Israel.

8 ¹Wherefore the wrath of the Lord hath been on Judah and Jerusalem, and he hath made them a ²scattering, a desolation, and an hissing, as ye see with your eyes.

9 For lo, our fathers are fallen by the sword, and our sons, and our daughters, and our wives *are* in captivity for the same cause.

10 Now ¹I purpose to make a covenant with the Lord God of Israel, that he may ²turn away his fierce wrath from us.

11 Now my sons, be not deceived: for the Lord hath ᵇchosen you to stand before him, to serve him, and to be his ministers, and to burn incense.

12 ¶ Then the Levites arose, Mahath the son of Amasai, and Joel the son of Azariah of the sons of the Kohathites: and of the sons of Merari, Kish the son of Abdi, and Azariah the son of Jehallelel: and of the Gershonites, Joah the son of Zimmah, and Eden the son of Joah:

13 And of the sons of Elizaphan, Shimri, and Jeiel: and of the sons of Asaph, Zechariah, and Mattaniah:

14 And of the sons of Heman, Jehiel, and Shimei: and of the sons of Jeduthun, Shemaiah and Uzziel.

15 And they gathered their brethren, and sanctified themselves and came according to the commandment of the king, *and* ¹by the words of the Lord, for to cleanse the house of the Lord.

16 And the Priests went into the inner parts of the house of the Lord, to ¹cleanse it and brought out all the uncleanness that they found in the Temple of the Lord, into the court of the house of the Lord: and the Levites took it, to carry it out unto the brook Kidron.

17 They began the first *day* of the ¹first month to sanctify it, and the eight day of the month came they to the porch of the Lord: so they sanctified the house of the Lord in eight days, and in the sixteenth day of the first month, they made an end.

18 ¶ Then they went in to Hezekiah the king and said, We have cleansed all the house of the Lord, and the altar of burnt offering, with all the vessels thereof, and the ¹showbread table, with all the vessels thereof:

19 And all the vessels which King Ahaz had cast aside when he reigned, *and* transgressed, have we prepared and sanctified: and behold, they are before the altar of the Lord.

20 ¶ And Hezekiah the king ¹rose early, and gathered the princes of the city, and went up to the house of the Lord.

21 And they brought seven bullocks, and seven rams, and seven lambs, and seven he goats for a ᶜsin offering for the kingdom, and for the sanctuary, and for Judah. And he commanded the Priests the sons of Aaron, to offer *them* on the altar of the Lord.

22 So they slew the bullocks, and the Priests

28:27 ¹ Or, in Jerusalem.
² They buried him not in the city of David, where were the sepulchers of the kings.
29:1 ¹ Or, Abi.
29:3 ¹ Which Ahaz had shut up, 2 Chron. 28:24.
² This is a notable example for all princes, first to establish the pure religion of God, and to procure that the Lord may be honored and served aright.
29:5 ¹ Meaning, all the idols, altars, groves and whatsoever was occupied in their service, and wherewith the Temple was polluted.
29:8 ¹ He showeth that the contempt of religion is the cause of all God's plagues.
² Or, a nodding of the head and mockery.
29:10 ¹ Hebrew, *it is in mine heart.*
² He proveth by the judgments of God upon those that have contemned his word, that there is no way to avoid his plagues, but by conforming themselves to his will.
29:15 ¹ Or, concerning the things of the Lord.
29:16 ¹ From the pollutions and filth that Ahaz had brought in.
29:17 ¹ Which contained part of March and part of April.
29:18 ¹ Or, table where the bread was set in order.
29:20 ¹ By this manner of speech the Hebrews mean a certain diligence and speed to do a thing: and when there is no delay.

received the blood, and [1]sprinkled it upon the altar: they slew also the rams, and sprinkled the blood upon the altar, and they slew the lambs, and they sprinkled the blood upon the altar.

d 1 Chron. 16:4
e Lev. 3:2,3

23 Then they brought the he goats for the sin offering before the king and the Congregation, [1]and they laid their hands upon them.

24 And the Priests slew them, and with the blood of them they cleansed the altar to reconcile all Israel: for the king had commanded for all Israel the burnt offering, and the sin offering.

25 He appointed also the Levites in the house of the Lord with cymbals, with viols, and with harps, [d]according to the commandment of David, and Gad the King's Seer, and Nathan the Prophet: for the [1]commandment *was* by the hand of the Lord, *and* by the hand of his Prophets.

26 And the Levites stood with the instruments of David, and the priests with the trumpets.

27 And Hezekiah commanded to offer the burnt offering upon the altar: and when the burnt offering began, the song of the [1]Lord began with the trumpets, and the instruments [2]of David king of Israel.

28 And all the congregation worshipped, singing a song, and they blew the trumpets: all this *continued* until the burnt offering was finished.

29 And when they had made an end of offering, the king and all that were present with him, bowed themselves, and worshipped.

30 ¶ Then Hezekiah the king and the princes commanded the Levites to praise the Lord with the [1]words of David, and of Asaph the Seer. So they praised with joy, and they bowed themselves, and worshipped.

31 And Hezekiah spake, and said, Now ye have [1]consecrated yourselves to the Lord: come near and bring the sacrifices and *offerings* of praise into the house of the Lord. And the Congregation brought sacrifices and *offerings* of praises, and every man that was willing in heart *offered* burnt offerings.

32 And the number of the burnt offerings, which the Congregation brought, was seventy bullocks, an hundred rams, *and* two hundred lambs: all these were for a burnt offering to the Lord:

33 And for [1]sanctification six hundred bullocks, and three thousand sheep.

34 But the Priests were too few, and were not able to flay all the burnt offerings: therefore their brethren the Levites did help them, till they had ended the work, and until *other* Priests were sanctified: for the Levites were [1]more upright in heart to sanctify themselves than the Priests.

35 And also the burnt offerings were many, with the [e]fat of the peace offerings and the drink offerings for the burnt offering: so the service of the house of the Lord was set in order.

36 Then Hezekiah rejoiced, and all the people, that God had made the people so [1]ready: for the thing was done suddenly.

30

1, 13 The keeping of the Passover by the king's commandment.   6 He exhorteth Israel to turn to the Lord.   18 He prayeth for the people.   24 His oblation and the princes'.   27 The Levites bless the people.

1 And Hezekiah sent to all Israel and Judah, and also wrote letters to [1]Ephraim and Manasseh, that they should come to the house of the Lord at Jerusalem, to keep the Passover unto the Lord God of Israel.

2 And the king and his princes and all the Congregation had taken counsel in Jerusalem to keep the Passover in the [1]second month.

3 For they could not keep it at this time, because there were not Priests enough sanctified, neither was the people gathered to Jerusalem.

4 And the thing pleased the king, and all the Congregation.

5 And they decreed to make proclamation throughout all Israel from [1]Beersheba even to Dan, that they should come to keep the Passover unto the Lord God of Israel at Jerusalem: for they had not done it of a great *time*, [2]as it was written.

6 ¶ So the posts went with letters by the commission of the King, and his princes, throughout all Israel and Judah, and with the commandment of the King, saying, Ye children of Israel, turn again unto the Lord God of Abraham, Isaac, and Israel, and [1]he will return to the remnant that are

---

29:22 [1] For without sprinkling of blood nothing could be sanctified, Heb. 9:21; Exod. 24:8.

29:23 [1] That is, the King and the Elders, as Lev. 4:15, for they that offered a sin offering, must lay their hands upon it, to signify that they had deserved that death, and also that they did consecrate it to God to be thereby sanctified, Exod. 29:10.

29:25 [1] This thing was not appointed of man, but it was the commandment of God.

29:27 [1] The Psalm which David had appointed to be sung for thanksgiving.
   [2] Which David had appointed to praise the Lord with.

29:30 [1] With that Psalm whereof mention is made, 1 Chron. 16:7.

29:31 [1] Hebrew, *filled your hands.*

29:33 [1] That is, for the holy offerings.

29:34 [1] Meaning, were more zealous to set forward the religion.

29:36 [1] He showeth that religion cannot proceed except God touch the heart of the people.

30:1 [1] Meaning, all Israel, whom Tiglath-Pileser had not taken away into the captivity, 2 Kings 15:29.

30:2 [1] Though they ought to have done it in the first month, as Exod. 12:18; Num. 9:3, yet if any were not clean, or else had a long journey, they might defer it unto the second month, as Num. 9:10, 11.

30:5 [1] From one end of the land to the other, North and South.
   [2] In such sort and perfection as God had appointed.

30:6 [1] He will have compassion on them, and preserve them.

escaped of you, out of the hands of the kings of Assyria.

7   And be not ye like your fathers, and like your brethren, which trespassed against the Lord God of their fathers: *and* therefore he made them desolate, as ye see.

8   Be not ye now stiff-necked like your fathers, *but* ¹give the hand to the Lord, and come into his Sanctuary, which he hath sanctified forever, and serve the Lord your God, and the fierceness of his wrath shall turn away from you.

9   For if ye return unto the Lord, your brethren and your children *shall find* mercy before them that led them captives, and they shall ¹return unto this land: for the Lord your God is gracious and merciful, and will not turn away his face from you, if ye convert unto him.

10   ¶ So the posts went from city to city through the land of Ephraim and Manasseh, even unto Zebulun: but they ¹laughed them to scorn and mocked them.

11   Nevertheless, divers of Asher, and Manasseh, and of Zebulun, submitted themselves, and came to Jerusalem.

12   And the hand of God was in Judah, so that he gave them one ¹heart to do the commandment of the king, and of the rulers, according to the word of the Lord.

13   And there assembled to Jerusalem much people, to keep the feast of the unleavened bread in the second month, a very great assembly.

14   ¶ And they arose, and took away the ¹altars that were in Jerusalem, and all those for incense took they away, and cast them into the brook Kidron.

15   Afterward they slew the Passover the fourteenth *day* of the second month: and the Priests and Levites were ¹ashamed, and sanctified themselves, and brought the burnt offerings into the house of the Lord.

16   And they stood in their place after their manner, according to the Law of Moses the man of God: *and* the Priests sprinkled the ¹blood *returned* of the hands of the Levites.

17   Because there were many in the Congregation that were not sanctified, therefore the Levites had the charge of the killing of the Passover for all that were not clean, to sanctify it to the Lord.

18   For a multitude of the people, *even* a multitude of Ephraim, and Manasseh, Issachar and Zebulun had not cleansed themselves, yet did eat the Passover, *but* not as it was written: wherefore Hezekiah prayed for them, saying, The ¹good Lord be merciful toward *him*,

19   That prepareth his whole heart to seek the Lord God, the God of his fathers, though he be not *cleansed*, according to the purification of the Sanctuary.

20   And the Lord heard Hezekiah, and ¹healed the people.

21   And the children of Israel that were present at Jerusalem, kept the feast of the unleavened bread seven days with great joy, and the Levites, and the priests praised the Lord day by day, singing with loud instruments unto the Lord.

22   And Hezekiah ¹spake comfortably unto all the Levites that had good knowledge *to sing* unto the Lord: and they did eat in that feast seven days, and offered peace offerings, and praised the Lord God of their fathers.

23   And the whole assembly took counsel to keep it another seven days. So they kept it seven days with joy.

24   For Hezekiah king of Judah had given to the Congregation a ¹thousand bullocks, and seven thousand sheep. And the princes had given to the Congregation a thousand bullocks, and ten thousand sheep: and many Priests were sanctified.

25   And all the Congregation of Judah rejoiced with the Priests and the Levites, and all the Congregation that came out of Israel, and the strangers that came out of the land of Israel, and that dwelt in Judah.

26   So there was great joy in Jerusalem: for since the time of Solomon the son of David king of Israel there *was* not the like thing in Jerusalem.

27   Then the Priests and the Levites arose, and ¹blessed the people, and their voice was heard, and

---

30:8 ¹ Submit yourselves to the Lord, and rebel no more.

30:9 ¹ God will not only preserve you, but through your repentance restore your brethren, which for their sins he gave into the hands of the enemies.

30:10 ¹ Though the wicked mock at the servants of God, by whom he calleth them to repentance, as Gen. 19:14, yet the word ceaseth not to fructify in the hearts of God's elect.

30:12 ¹ He showeth the cause why some obey and some mock at God's calling, to wit, because his Spirit is with the one sort, and moveth their heart, and the others are left to themselves.

30:14 ¹ Which declareth that we must put away those things wherewith God is offended, before we can serve him aright.

30:15 ¹ Seeing their own negligence (who should have been most

prompt) and the readiness of the people, 2 Chron. 29:36.

30:16 ¹ To wit, of the lamb of the Passover.

30:18 ¹ He knew that faith and sincerity of heart was more agreeable to God, than the observation of the ceremonies, and therefore he prayed unto God to pardon this fault unto the people which did not offend of malice but of ignorance.

30:20 ¹ That is, did accept them as purified.

30:22 ¹ Hebrew, *spake to the heart*.

30:24 ¹ This great liberality declareth how kings, princes, and all they to whom God hath given wherewith, ought to be most ready to bestow it in setting forth of God's glory.

30:27 ¹ According to that which is written, Num. 6:23, when they should dismiss the people.

their prayer came up unto heaven, to his holy habitation.

31 *1 The people destroy idolatry. 2 Hezekiah appointeth Priests and Levites, 4 And provideth for their livings. 13 He ordaineth overseers to distribute to every one his portion.*

1 And when all these things were finished, all Israel, that were found in the cities of Judah, went out and ¹brake the images, and cut down the groves, and brake down the high places, and the altars throughout all Judah and Benjamin, in Ephraim also and Manasseh, until they had made an end: afterward all the ²children of Israel returned every man to his possession, into their own cities.

2 And Hezekiah appointed the courses of the Priests and Levites by their turns, every man according to his office, *both* Priests and Levites for the burnt offering and peace offerings, to minister and to give thanks, and to praise in the gates of the ¹tents of the Lord.

3 (And the king's portion *was* of his own substance for the burnt offerings, *even* for the burnt offerings of the morning and of the evening, and the burnt offerings for the Sabbaths, and for the new moons and for the solemn feasts, *a*as it is written in the Law of the Lord)

4 He commanded also the people that dwelt in Jerusalem, to give a ¹part to the Priests, and Levites, that they might be ²encouraged in the law of the Lord.

5 ¶ And when the commandment was ¹spread, the children of Israel brought abundance of firstfruits, of corn, wine, and oil, and honey, and of all the increase of the field, and the tithes of all things brought they abundantly.

6 And the children of Israel and Judah that dwelt in the cities of Judah, they also brought the tithes of bullocks and sheep, and the holy tithes ¹which were consecrated unto the Lord their God, and laid them on ²many heaps.

7 In the third month they began to lay the foundation of the heaps, and finished them in the seventh month.

8 ¶ And when Hezekiah and the princes came, and saw the heaps, they ¹blessed the Lord and his people Israel.

9 And Hezekiah questioned with the Priests and the Levites concerning the heaps.

10 And Azariah the chief Priest of the house of Zadok answered him, and said, Since the people began to bring the offerings into the house of the Lord, we have ¹eaten, and have been satisfied, and there is left in abundance: for the Lord hath blessed his people, and this abundance that is left.

11 ¶ And Hezekiah commanded to prepare chambers in the house of the Lord: and they prepared them,

12 And carried in the firstfruits, and the tithes, and the dedicated things faithfully: and over them *was* Conaniah the Levite the chief, and Shimei his brother the second.

13 And Jehiel, and Azaziah and Nahath, and Asahel, and Jerimoth, and Jozabad, and Eliel, and Ismachiah, and Mahath, and Benaiah *were* overseers ¹by the appointment of Conaniah, and Shimei his brother, *and* by the commandment of Hezekiah the King, and of Azariah the chief of the house of God.

14 And Kore the son of Imnah the Levite, porter toward the East, *was* over the things that were willingly offered unto God, to distribute the oblations of the Lord, and the holy things that were consecrated.

15 And at his hand *were* Eden, and Miniamin, and Jeshua, and Shemaiah, Amariah, and Shechaniah, in the cities of the Priests, to distribute with fidelity to their brethren by courses, both to the great and small,

16 Their daily portion: beside their generation, being males ¹from three years old and above, *even* to all that entered into the house of the Lord to their office in their charge, according to their courses:

17 Both to the generation of the Priests after the house of their fathers, and to the Levites from twenty years old and above, according to their charge in their courses:

18 And to the generation of all their children, their wives, and their sons, and their daughters throughout all the Congregation: for by their ¹fidelity are they partakers of the holy things.

19 Also to the sons of Aaron, the Priests, *which were* in the fields *and* suburbs of their cities, in every city the men that were appointed by names, should give portions to all the males of the Priests, and to

---

31:1 ¹ According to the commandment of the Lord, Deut. 7:25; Josh. 7:1.
  ² That is, all they which came to the Passover.
31:2 ¹ That is, in the Temple, where they assembled as in a tent.
31:4 ¹ The tithes and first fruits for the maintenance of the Priests and Levites.
  ² That their minds might not be entangled with provision of worldly things, but that they might wholly and cheerfully serve the Lord.
31:5 ¹ Or, published.
31:6 ¹ Which they had dedicated to the Lord by a vow.
  ² For the relief of the Priests, Levites, widows, pupils, fatherless, strangers, and such as were in necessity.

31:8 ¹ They praised the Lord and prayed for all prosperity to his people.
31:10 ¹ He showeth that this plenteous liberality is expedient for the maintenance of the ministers, and that God therefore prospereth his people, and increaseth by his blessing that which is given.
31:13 ¹ Hebrew, *by the hand.*
31:16 ¹ Who had also a portion and allowance in this distribution.
31:18 ¹ Meaning, that either by the faithful distributions of the officers, everyone had their part in the things that were offered, or else that their wives and children were relieved, because the Levites were faithful in their office, and so depended on them.

all the generation of the Levites.

20 And thus did Hezekiah throughout all Judah, and did well, and uprightly, and truly before the Lord his God.

21 And in all the works that he began for the service of the house of God, both in the Law and in the commandments, to seek his God, he did it with all his heart, and prospered.

32 1 *Sennacherib invadeth Judah.* 3 *Hezekiah prepareth for the war.* 7 *He exhorteth the people to put their trust in the Lord.* 9 *Sennacherib blasphemeth God.* 20 *Hezekiah prayeth.* 21 *The Angel destroyeth the Assyrians and the king is slain.* 25 *Hezekiah is not thankful toward the Lord.* 33 *His death.*

1 After these things faithfully *described,* ᵃSennacherib king of Assyria came and entered into Judah, and besieged the strong cities, and thought to ¹win them for himself.

2 When Hezekiah saw that Sennacherib was come, and that his ¹purpose *was* to fight against Jerusalem,

3 Then he took counsel with his princes and his nobles, to stop the water of the fountains without the city: and they did help him.

4 So many of the people assembled themselves, and stopped all the fountains, and the river that ran through the midst of the country, saying, Why should the kings of Assyria come, and find much water?

5 And ¹he took courage, and built all the broken wall, and made up the towers, and another wall without, and repaired ²Millo in the ³city of David, and made many ⁴darts and shields.

6 And he set captains of war over the people, and assembled them to him in the broad place of the gate of the city, and ¹spake comfortably unto them, saying,

7 Be strong and courageous: fear not, neither be afraid for the king of Assyria, neither for all the multitude that is with him: ᵇfor there *be* more with us, then *is* with him.

8 With him *is* an ¹arm of flesh, but with us *is* the ²Lord our God for to help us, and to fight our battles. Then the people were confirmed by the words

ᵃ 2 Kings 18:13
Isa. 30:1
ᵇ 2 Kings 6:16
ᶜ 2 Kings 18:17

of Hezekiah king of Judah.

9 ᶜAfter this, did Sennacherib king of Assyria send his servants to Jerusalem (while he was ¹against Lachish, and all his dominion with him) unto Hezekiah king of Judah, and unto all Judah that were at Jerusalem, saying,

10 Thus saith Sennacherib the king of Assyria, Wherein do ye trust, that ye will remain in Jerusalem, *during* the siege?

11 Doth not Hezekiah entice you to give over yourselves unto death by famine and by thirst, saying, The Lord our God shall deliver us out of the hand of the king of Assyria?

12 Hath not the same Hezekiah taken away his high places, and his ¹altars, and commanded Judah, and Jerusalem, saying, Ye shall worship before one altar, and burn incense upon it?

13 Know ye not what I and my fathers have done unto all the people of *other* countries? were the gods of the nations of *other* lands able to deliver their land out of mine hand?

14 Who is he of all the ¹gods of those nations (that my fathers have destroyed) that could deliver his people out of mine hand, that your God should be able to deliver you out of mine hand?

15 Now therefore let not Hezekiah deceive you, nor seduce you after this sort, neither believe ye him: for none of all the gods of any nation or kingdom was able to deliver his people out of ¹mine hand, and out of the hand of my fathers: how much less shall your gods deliver you out of mine hand?

16 And his servants spake yet more against the Lord God, and against his ¹servant Hezekiah.

17 He wrote also letters, blaspheming the Lord God of Israel, and speaking against him, saying, As the gods of the nations of *other* countries could not deliver their people out of mine hand, so shall not the God of Hezekiah deliver his people out of mine hand.

18 Then they ¹cried with a loud voice in the Jews speech unto the people of Jerusalem that were on the wall, to fear them and to astonish them, that they might take the city.

19 Thus they spake against the God of Jerusalem,

32:1 ¹ Hebrew, *break them up.*
32:2 ¹ Hebrew, *face.*
32:5 ¹ Hebrew, *he was strengthened.*
   ² He made a double wall.
   ³ Read 2 Sam. 5:9.
   ⁴ Some read, swords or daggers.
32:6 ¹ Hebrew, *he spake to their heart.*
32:8 ¹ That is, the power of man.
   ² This declareth that Hezekiah did ever put his trust in God, and yet made himself strong and used lawful means, lest he should seem to tempt God.
32:9 ¹ While he besieged Lachish.

32:12 ¹ Thus the wicked put no difference between true religion and false, God and idols: for Hezekiah only destroyed idolatry, and placed true religion. Thus the Papists slander the servants of God: for when they destroy idolatry, they say that they abolish religion.
32:14 ¹ This is his blasphemy, that he will compare the living God to vile idols.
32:15 ¹ When man hath prosperity, he swelleth in pride, and thinketh himself able to resist and overcome even God himself.
32:16 ¹ Herein we see that when the wicked speak evil of the servants of God, they care not to blaspheme God himself: for if they feared God, they would love his servants.
32:18 ¹ Their words are written, 2 Kings 18:19.

as against the gods of the people of the earth, *even* the ¹works of man's hands,

20 But Hezekiah the King, and the Prophet Isaiah the son of Amoz ¹prayed against this and cried to heaven.

21 And the Lord sent an Angel, which destroyed all the valiant men, and the princes and ¹captains of the host of the king of Assyria: so he returned ²with shame to his own land. And when he was come into the house of his god, they that came forth of his ³own bowels, slew him there with the sword.

22 So the Lord saved Hezekiah and the inhabitants of Jerusalem from the hand of Sennacherib king of Assyria, and from the hand of all *others*, and ¹maintained them on every side.

23 And many brought offerings unto the Lord to Jerusalem, and presents to Hezekiah king of Judah, so that he was ¹magnified in the sight of all nations from thenceforth.

24 ᵈIn those days Hezekiah was sick unto the death, and prayed unto the Lord, who spake unto him, and gave him ¹a sign.

25 But Hezekiah did not render according to the reward *bestowed* upon him: for his heart ¹was lifted up, and wrath came upon him, and upon Judah and Jerusalem.

26 Notwithstanding Hezekiah humbled himself (after that his heart was lifted up) he and the inhabitants of Jerusalem, and the wrath of the Lord came not upon them in the days of Hezekiah.

27 Hezekiah also had exceeding much riches and honor, and he got him treasures of silver, and of gold, and of precious stones, and of sweet odors, and of shields, and of all pleasant vessels:

28 And of store houses for the increase of wheat and wine and oil, and stalls for all beasts, and ¹rows for the ²stables.

29 And he made him cities, and *had* possession of sheep and oxen in abundance: for God had given him substance exceeding much.

30 This same Hezekiah also stopped the upper water springs of ¹Gihon, and led them straight underneath toward the city of David Westward: so Hezekiah prospered in all his works.

Cross references:
ᵈ 2 Kings 20:1
Isa. 38:1

CHAPTER 33
ᵃ 2 Kings 21:5
ᵇ Deut. 18:9
ᶜ 2 Kings 18:4
ᵈ Jer. 32:34
2 Kings 17:10
ᵉ 2 Kings 11:4
ᶠ 1 Kings 8:39
1 Kings 9:3
1 Kings 21:7
1 Kings 23:17

31 But because of the ambassadors of the princes of Babel, which sent unto him to inquire of the wonder that was done in the land, God left him to ¹try him, *and* to know all that was in his heart.

32 Concerning the rest of the acts of Hezekiah, and his goodness, behold, they are written in the vision of Isaiah the Prophet the son of Amoz, in the book of the kings of Judah and Israel.

33 So Hezekiah slept with his fathers, and they buried him in the highest sepulcher of the sons of David: and all Judah and the inhabitants of Jerusalem did him honor at his death, and Manasseh his son reigned in his stead.

33

Manasseh an idolater.   9 He causeth Judah to err.   11 He is led away prisoner into Babylon.   12 He prayeth to the Lord, and is delivered.   14 He abolisheth idolatry,   16 and setteth up true religion.   20 He dieth, and Amon his son succeedeth.   24 Whom his own servants slay.

1 Manasseh *was* twelve years old, ᵃwhen he began to reign, and he reigned five and fifty years in Jerusalem:

2 And he did evil in the sight of the Lord, like the abominations of the heathen, ᵇwhom the Lord had cast out before the children of Israel.

3 For he went back and built the high places, ᶜwhich Hezekiah his father had broken down: ᵈand he set up altars for Baal, and made groves and worshipped all the host of the heaven, and served them.

4 Also he built altars in the house of the Lord, whereof the Lord had said, ᵉIn Jerusalem shall my Name be forever.

5 And he built altars for all the host of the heaven in the two courts of the house of the Lord.

6 And he caused his sons to ¹pass through the fire in the valley of Ben-hinnom: he gave himself to witchcraft and to charming, and to sorcery, and he used them that had familiar spirits, and soothsayers: he did very much evil in the sight of the Lord to anger him.

7 He put also the carved image, which he had made, in the house of God: whereof God had said to David and to Solomon his son, ᶠIn this house and in Jerusalem, which I have chosen before all the tribes

---

32:19 ¹ Which were invented, made and authorized by man.

32:20 ¹ This showeth what is the best refuge in all troubles and dangers.

32:21 ¹ To the number of an hundred fourscore and five thousand, as 2 Kings 19:35, 36.
   ² Hebrew, *with shame of face.*
   ³ Meaning, Adrammelech and Sharezer his sons.

32:22 ¹ Or, governed.

32:23 ¹ Thus after trouble God sendeth comfort to all them that patiently wait on him, and constantly put their trust in his mercies.

32:24 ¹ To confirm his faith in God's promise, who declared to him

by his Prophet that his life should be prolonged fifteen years.

32:25 ¹ He was lifted up with the pride of his victory and treasures, and showeth them for an ostentation to the ambassadors of Babylon.

32:28 ¹ Or, ranges and partitions.
   ² Or, racks.

32:30 ¹ Which also was called Shiloah [Siloam], whereof mention is made, Isa. 8:6; John 9:7.

32:31 ¹ Here we see the cause, why the faithful are tempted, which is to try whether they have faith or no, and that they may feel the presence of God, who suffereth them not to be overcome by tentations, but in their weakness ministereth strength.

33:6 ¹ Read 2 Kings 16:3.

of Israel, will I put my Name forever.

8   Neither will I [g]make the foot of Israel to remove anymore out of the land which I have appointed for your fathers, so that they take heed, and do all that I have commanded them, according to the Law and statutes and judgments by the [1]hand of Moses.

9   So Manasseh made Judah and the inhabitants of Jerusalem to err, *and* to do worse than the heathen, whom the Lord had destroyed before the children of Israel.

10   ¶ And the Lord spake to [1]Manasseh and to his people, but they would not regard.

11   Wherefore the Lord brought upon them the captains of the host of the king of Assyria, which took Manasseh *and put him* in fetters, and bound him in chains, and carried him to Babel.

12   And when he was in tribulation, he prayed to the Lord his God, and humbled himself greatly before the God of his fathers,

13   And prayed unto him: and God was [1]entreated of him, and heard his prayer, and brought him again to Jerusalem into his kingdom: then Manasseh knew that the Lord was God.

14   Now after this he built a wall without the city of David, on the West side of [1]Gihon in the valley, even at the entry of the fish gate, and compassed about [2]Ophel, and raised it very high, and put captains of war in all the strong cities of Judah.

15   And he took away the strange gods and the image out of the house of the Lord, and all the altars that he had built in the mount of the house of the Lord, and in Jerusalem, and cast them out of the city.

16   Also he prepared the [1]altar of the Lord, and sacrificed thereon peace offerings, and of thanks, and commanded Judah to serve the Lord God of Israel.

17   Nevertheless the people did sacrifice still in the high places, but unto the [1]Lord their God.

18   ¶ Concerning the rest of the acts of Manasseh, and his [1]prayer unto his God, and the words of the Seers, that spake to him in the Name of the Lord God of Israel, behold, they are *written* in the book of the Kings of Israel.

19   And his prayer and how God was entreated of

him, and all his sin, and his trespass, and the places wherein he built high places, and set groves and images (before he was humbled) behold, they are written in the book of the [1]Seers.

20   So Manasseh slept with his fathers, and they buried him in his own [1]house: and Amon his son reigned in his stead.

21   ¶ Amon *was* two and twenty years old, when he began to reign, and reigned two years in Jerusalem.

22   But he did evil in the sight of the Lord, as did Manasseh his father: for Amon sacrificed to all the images, which Manasseh his father had made, and served them.

23   And he humbled not himself before the Lord, as Manasseh his father had humbled himself: but this Amon trespassed more and more.

24   And his servants [b]conspired against him, and slew him in his own house.

25   But the people of the land slew all them that had conspired against King Amon: and the people of the land made Josiah his son King in his stead.

34

1 *Josiah destroyeth the idols.*   8 *And restoreth the Temple.*   14 *The book of the Law is found.*   21 *He sendeth to Huldah the Prophetess for counsel.*   27 *God heareth his prayer.*   31 *He maketh a covenant with God.*

1   Josiah [a]was eight years old when he began to reign, and he reigned in Jerusalem one and thirty years.

2   And he did uprightly in the sight of the Lord, and walked in the ways of [1]David his father, and bowed neither to the right hand nor to the left.

3   And in the eighth year of his reign (when he was yet a [1]child) he began to seek after the God of David his father: and in the twelfth year he began to purge Judah, and Jerusalem from the high places, and the groves, and the carved images, and molten images.

4   And they brake down [1]in his sight the altars of Baal, and he caused to cut down the images that were on high upon them: he brake also the groves, and the carved images and the molten images, and stamped them to powder, and strowed it upon the graves of them that had sacrificed unto them.

5   Also he burnt the [1]bones of the Priests upon

[g] 2 Sam. 7:10
[b] 2 Kings 21:23

CHAPTER 34
[a] 2 Kings 22:1

33:8 [1] By the charge given to Moses.

33:10 [1] Meaning by his Prophets, but their hearts were not touched to believe and repent, without the which the preaching of the word taketh no place.

33:13 [1] This affliction giveth understanding: for he that hated God in his prosperity, now in his misery he seeketh unto him.

33:14 [1] Read 2 Chron. 32:30.
  [2] Read 2 Chron. 27:3.

33:16 [1] Which Solomon had caused to be made.

33:17 [1] Thus by ignorance they were deceived, thinking it nothing to keep the altars, so that they worshipped God: but it is idolatry to worship God any otherwise than he hath appointed.

33:18 [1] Which albeit that it is not contained in the Hebrew, yet

because it is here mentioned and is written in the Greek, we have placed it in the end of this book.

33:19 [1] Or, Hozai.

33:20 [1] Because he had so horribly offended against the Lord, they did not bury him in the sepulchers of the Kings, but in the garden of the King's house.

34:2 [1] He followed David in all points that he followed the Lord.

34:3 [1] When he was but sixteen years old he showed himself zealous of God's glory, and at twenty years old he abolished idolatry, and restored the true religion.

34:4 [1] Which showeth that he would see the reformation with his own eyes.

34:5 [1] Read 2 Kings 23:16.

their altars, and purged Judah and Jerusalem.

6 And in the cities of Manasseh, and Ephraim, and Simeon, even unto Naphtali, with their mauls *they brake all* round about.

7 And when he had ¹destroyed the altars, and the groves, and had broken and stamped to powder the images, and had cut down all the idols throughout all the land of Israel, he returned to Jerusalem.

8 ¶ ᵇThen in the eighteenth year of his reign, when he had purged the land and the temple, he sent Shaphan the son of Azaliah and Maaseiah the governor of the city, and Joah the son of Joahaz the Recorder to repair the house of the Lord his God.

9 And when they came to Hilkiah the high Priest, they delivered the money that was brought into the house of God, which the Levites that kept the door, had gathered at the hand of Manasseh, and Ephraim, and of all the residue of Israel, and of all Judah and Benjamin, and ¹of the inhabitants of Jerusalem.

10 And they put it in the hands of ¹them that should do the work, *and* had the oversight in the house of the Lord: and they gave it to the workmen that wrought in the house of the Lord to repair and amend the house.

11 Even to the workmen and to the builders gave they it to buy hewed stone and timber for couples, and for beams of the ¹houses, which the kings of Judah had destroyed.

12 And the men did the work ¹faithfully, and the overseers of them *were* Jahath and Obadiah the Levites, of the children of Merari, and Zechariah, and Meshullam, of the children of the Kohathites to set it forward: and of the Levites all that could skill of instruments of music.

13 And *they were* over the bearers of burdens, and them that set forward all the workmen in every work: and of the Levites *were* scribes, and officers and porters.

14 ¶ And when they brought out the money that was brought into the house of the Lord, Hilkiah the Priest found the ¹book of the Law of the Lord *given* by the hand of Moses.

15 Therefore Hilkiah answered and said to Shaphan

ᵇ 2 Kings 33:5

the chancellor, I have found the book of the Law in the house of the Lord: and Hilkiah gave the book to Shaphan.

16 And Shaphan carried the book to ¹the King, and brought the King word again, saying, All that is committed to the hand of thy servants, that do they.

17 For they have gathered the money that was found in the house of the Lord, and have delivered it into the hands of the overseers, and to the hands of the workmen.

18 Also Shaphan the chancellor declared to the King, saying, Hilkiah the Priest hath given me a book, and Shaphan read it before the King.

19 And when the King had heard the words of the Law, he ¹tare his clothes,

20 And the King commanded Hilkiah and Ahikam the son of Shaphan, and Abdon the son of Micah, and Shaphan the chancellor, and Asaiah the king's servant, saying,

21 Go *and* inquire of the Lord for me, and for the rest in Israel and Judah, concerning the words of this book that is found: for great *is* the wrath of the Lord that is fallen upon us, because our ¹fathers have not kept the word of the Lord, to do after all that is written in this book.

22 Then Hilkiah and they that the king *had appointed* went to Huldah the prophetess the wife of Shallum, the son of ¹Tokhath, the son of ²Hasrah keeper of the ³wardrobe (and she dwelt in Jerusalem within the ⁴college) and they communed hereof with her.

23 And she answered them, Thus saith the Lord God of Israel, Tell ye ¹the man that sent you to me,

24 Thus saith the Lord, Behold, I will bring evil upon this place, and upon the inhabitants thereof, *even* all the curses, that are written in the book which they have read before the King of Judah:

25 Because they have forsaken me, and burnt incense unto other gods, to anger me with all the works of their ¹hands, therefore shall my wrath fall upon this place, and shall not be quenched.

26 But to the king of Judah, who sent you to inquire of the Lord, so shall ye say unto him, Thus saith the Lord God of Israel, The words which thou

---

34:7 ¹ This great zeal of this godly King the holy Ghost setteth forth as an example and pattern to other kings and rulers, to teach them what God requireth of them.
34:9 ¹ Or, they returned to Jerusalem.
34:10 ¹ Meaning Shaphan, etc.
34:11 ¹ For there were many portions and pieces annexed to the Temple.
34:12 ¹ Meaning, that they were in such credit for their fidelity, that they made none accounts of that which they received, 2 Kings 22:7, 9.
34:14 ¹ Read 2 Kings 22:8.
34:16 ¹ For the king was commanded to have continually a copy of this book, and to read therein day and night, Deut. 17:18.

34:19 ¹ For sorrow that the word of God had been so long suppressed and the people kept in ignorance, considering also the curses contained therein against the transgressors.
34:21 ¹ Thus the godly do not only lament their own sins, but also that their fathers and predecessors have offended God.
34:22 ¹ Or, Tiknah.
² Or, Harhas.
³ Meaning, either of the Priest's apparel, or of the King's.
⁴ Read hereof, 2 Kings 22:15.
34:23 ¹ That is, to the King.
34:25 ¹ This she speaketh in contempt of the idolaters, who contrary to reason and nature make that a god, which they have made and framed with their own hands.

hast heard, *shall come to pass.*

27 *But* because thine heart did [1]melt, and thou didst humble thyself before God, when thou heardest his words against this place, and against the inhabitants thereof, and humbledst thyself before me, and tearest thy clothes, and weptest before me, I have also heard it, saith the Lord.

28 Behold, I will gather thee to thy fathers, and thou shalt be put in thy grave in peace, and thine eyes shall not see all the evil, which I will bring upon this [1]place and upon the inhabitants of the same. Thus they brought the King word again.

29 ¶ Then the King sent and gathered all the Elders of Judah and Jerusalem.

30 And the King went up into the house of the Lord, and all the men of Judah, and the inhabitants of Jerusalem, and the Priests and the Levites, and all the people from the greatest to the [1]smallest, and he read in their ears all the words of the book of the Covenant that was found in the house of the Lord.

31 And the King stood by his pillar, and made a covenant before the Lord, to walk after the Lord, and to keep his commandments, and his testimonies, and his statutes with all his heart, and with all his soul, *and* that he would accomplish the words of the Covenant written in the same book.

32 And he caused all that were found in Jerusalem, and Benjamin to stand to it: and the inhabitants of Jerusalem did according to the Covenant of God, *even* the God of their fathers.

33 So Josiah took away all the abominations out of all the countries that pertained to the children of Israel, and compelled all [1]that were found in Israel, to serve the Lord their God: so all his days they turned not back from the Lord God of their fathers.

35

1 Josiah keepeth the Passover. 2 He setteth forth God's service. 20 He fighteth against the king of Egypt, and dieth. 24 The people bewail him.

1 Moreover, [a]Josiah kept a Passover unto the Lord in Jerusalem, and they slew the [1]Passover in

CHAPTER 35
[a] 2 Kings 23:21
[b] 1 Chron. 13:24-26

the fourteenth day of the first month.

2 And he appointed the Priests to their charges, and encouraged them to the service of the house of the Lord,

3 And he said unto the Levites that [1]taught all Israel and were sanctified unto the Lord, Put the holy Ark in the house which Solomon the son of David King of Israel did build: it *shall be* no more a [2]burden upon your shoulders: serve now the Lord your God, and his people Israel,

4 And prepare yourselves by the houses of your fathers according to your courses, as [b]David the king of Israel hath written, and according to the writing of Solomon his son,

5 And stand in the Sanctuary according to the division of the families of your brethren [1]the children of the people, and *after* the division of the family of the Levites:

6 So kill the Passover, and sanctify yourselves, and [1]prepare your brethren that they may do according to the word of the Lord by the hand of Moses.

7 Josiah also gave to the [1]people sheep, lambs and kids, all for the Passover, *even* to all that were present, to the number of thirty thousand, and three thousand bullocks: these were of the king's substance.

8 And his princes offered willingly unto the people, to the Priests and to the Levites: Hilkiah, and Zechariah, and Jehiel, rulers of the house of God gave unto the Priests for the Passover, *even* two thousand and six hundred *sheep*, and three hundred bullocks.

9 [1]Conaniah also and Shemaiah and Nethanel his brethren, *and* Hashabiah and Jeiel, and Jozabad, chief of the Levites gave unto the Levites for the Passover, five thousand *sheep*, and five hundred bullocks.

10 Thus the service was prepared, and the Priests stood in their places, also the Levites in their orders, according to the king's commandment:

11 And they slew the Passover, and the Priests [1]sprinkled *the blood* with their hands, and the Levites flayed *them*.

34:27 [1] This declareth what is the end of God's threatenings, to call his to repentance, and to assure the unrepentant of their destruction.

34:28 [1] It may appear that very few were touched with true repentance, seeing that God spared them for a time only for the king's sake.

34:30 [1] Forasmuch as neither young nor old could be exempted from the curses contained therein, if they did transgress, he knew it pertained to all, and was his duty to see it read to all sorts, that everyone might learn to avoid those punishments by serving God aright.

34:33 [1] Because he had charge over all, and must answer for everyone that perished: he thought it his duty to see that all should make profession to receive the word of God.

35:1 [1] The Scripture useth in sundry places to call the lamb the Passover, which was but the sign of the Passover, because in all sacra-

ments the signs have the names of the things which are signified.

35:3 [1] So that the Levite's charge was not only to minister in the Temple, but also to instruct the people in the word of God.

[2] As it was before the Temple was built: therefore your office only is now to teach the people, and to praise God.

35:5 [1] Or, the people.

35:6 [1] Exhort everyone to examine themselves, that they be not unmeet to eat of the Passover.

35:7 [1] Hebrew, *sons of the people.*

35:9 [1] So that everyone and of all sorts gave of that they had, a liberal portion to the service of God.

35:11 [1] Meaning, of the Lamb, which was called the Passover: for only the Priests might sprinkle, and in necessity the Levites might kill the sacrifice.

12 And they took away *from* the ¹burnt offering to give it according to the divisions of the families of the children of the people, to offer unto the Lord, as it is written in the book of Moses, and so of the bullocks.

13 And ʿthey roasted the Passover with fire, according to the custom, but the sanctified things they sod in pots, pans, and cauldrons, and distributed them quickly to all the people.

14 Afterward also they prepared for themselves and for the Priests: for the Priests the sons of Aaron *were occupied* in offering of burnt offerings, and the fat until night: therefore the Levites prepared for themselves, and for the Priests the sons of Aaron.

15 And the singers the sons of Asaph *stood* in their standing ᵈaccording to the commandment of David, and Asaph, and Heman, and Jeduthun the king's ¹Seer: and the porters at every gate, who might not depart from their service: therefore their brethren the Levites prepared for them.

16 So all the service of the Lord was prepared the same day to keep the Passover, and to offer burnt offerings upon the altar of the Lord, according to the commandment of King Josiah.

17 And the children of Israel that were present, kept the Passover the same time, and the feast of the unleavened bread seven days.

18 And there was no Passover kept like that in Israel, from the days of Samuel the Prophet: neither did all the kings of Israel keep such a Passover as Josiah kept, and the Priests and the Levites, and all Judah, and Israel that were ¹present, and the inhabitants of Jerusalem.

19 This Passover was kept in ¹the eighteenth year of the reign of Josiah.

20 ¶ ʿAfter all this, when Josiah had prepared the Temple Necho king of Egypt came up to fight against ¹Carchemish by ²Perath and Josiah went out against him.

21 But he sent messengers to him, saying, What have I to do with thee, thou king of Judah? *I come* not against thee this day, but against the house ¹of mine enemy, and God commanded me to make haste: leave off *to come* against God, which is with me, lest he destroy thee.

ᶜ Exod. 12:8
ᵈ 1 Chron. 25:1
ᵉ 2 Kings 23:29

CHAPTER 36

ᵃ 2 Kings 23:30

22 But Josiah would not turn his face from him, but ¹changed his apparel to fight with him, and hearkened not unto the words of Necho, which were of the mouth of God, but came to fight in the valley of Megiddo.

23 And the shooters shot at king Josiah: then the king said to his servants, Carry me away, for I am very sick.

24 So his servants took him out of that chariot, and put him in the second chariot which he had, and when they had brought him to Jerusalem, he died, and was buried in the sepulchers of his fathers: and all Judah and Jerusalem ¹mourned for Josiah.

25 And Jeremiah lamented Josiah, and all singing men and singing women mourned for Josiah in their lamentations to this day, and made the same for an ordinance unto Israel: and behold, they be written in the ¹Lamentations.

26 Concerning the rest of the acts of Josiah, and his goodness, *doing* as it was written in the Law of the Lord,

27 And his deeds first and last, behold, they are written in the book of the Kings of Israel, and Judah.

36

After Josiah reigneth Jehoahaz. 4 After Jehoahaz, Jehoiakim. 8 After him Jehoiachin. 11 After him Zedekiah. 14, 17 In whose time all the people were carried away to Babel for contemning the Admonition of the Prophets, 22 and were restored again the seventieth year after by king Cyrus.

1 Then ᵃthe people of the land took Jehoahaz the son of Josiah, and made him King in his father's stead in Jerusalem.

2 Jehoahaz *was* three and twenty years old when he began to reign, and he reigned three ¹months in Jerusalem.

3 And the king of Egypt took him away at Jerusalem, and condemned the land in an ¹hundred talents of silver, and a talent of gold.

4 ¶ And the king of Egypt made Eliakim his brother king over Judah and Jerusalem, and turned his name to Jehoiakim: and Necho took Jehoahaz his brother, and carried him to Egypt.

5 Jehoiakim *was* five and twenty years old when

35:12 ¹ They reserved for the people that which was not expedient to be offered, that every man might offer peace offerings, and so have his portion.
35:15 ¹ Meaning hereby his Prophet, because he appointed the Psalms and prophecies which were to be sung.
35:18 ¹ Hebrew, *found.*
35:19 ¹ Which was in his six and twentieth year of his age.
35:20 ¹ Which was a city of the Assyrians, and Josiah fearing lest he passing through Judah, would have taken his kingdom, made war against him, and consulted not with the Lord.
   ² Or, Euphrates.
35:21 ¹ Hebrew, *of my battle.*

35:22 ¹ That is, armed himself, or disguised himself, because he might not be known.
35:24 ¹ The people so much lamented the loss of this good king, that after when there was any great lamentation this was spoken of as a proverb, read Zech. 12:11.
35:25 ¹ Which some think Jeremiah made, wherein he lamenteth the state of the Church after this king's death.
36:2 ¹ For three months after the death of Josiah, came Necho to Jerusalem, and so the plagues began, which Huldah and the Prophetess forewarned should come upon Jerusalem.
36:3 ¹ To pay this as a yearly tribute.

he began to reign, and he reigned eleven years in Jerusalem, and did [1]evil in the sight of the Lord his God.

6 Against him came up Nebuchadnezzar king of Babel, and bound him with chains to carry him to Babel.

7 Nebuchadnezzar also [b]carried of the vessels of the house of the Lord to Babel, and put them in his temple at Babel.

8 Concerning the rest of the acts of Jehoiakim, and his abominations which he did, and [1]that which was found upon him, behold, they are written in the book of the kings of Israel and Judah, and Jehoiachin his son reigned in his stead.

9 ¶ Jehoiachin *was* [1]eight years old when he began to reign, and he reigned three months and ten days in Jerusalem, and did evil in the sight of the Lord.

10 And when the year was out, king Nebuchadnezzar sent and brought him to Babel, with the precious vessels of the house of the Lord, and he made Zedekiah his [1]brother king over Judah and Jerusalem.

11 Zedekiah *was* one and twenty years old when he began to reign, and reigned eleven years in Jerusalem.

12 'And he did evil in the sight of the Lord his God, and humbled not himself before Jeremiah the Prophet at the commandment of the Lord.

13 But he rebelled moreover against Nebuchadnezzar, which had caused him to swear by God: and he hardened his neck and made his heart obstinate, that he might not return to the Lord God of Israel.

14 All the chief of the Priests also and of the people trespassed wonderfully, according to all the abominations of the heathen, and polluted the houses of the Lord which he had sanctified in Jerusalem.

15 Therefore the Lord God of their fathers sent to them [1]by his messengers, [2]rising early and sending:

(margin: [b] 2 Kings 24:13 / [c] 1 Kings 24:17,19 Jer. 52:2 / [d] Jer. 25:13 Jer. 29:10)

for he had compassion on his people, and on his habitation.

16 But they mocked the messengers of God, and despised his words, and misused his Prophets, until the wrath of the Lord arose against his people, and till there was no [1]remedy.

17 For he brought upon them the king of the Chaldeans, who slew their young men with the sword [1]in the house of their Sanctuary, and spared neither young man nor virgin, ancient, nor aged. *God* [2]gave all into his hand,

18 And all the vessels of the house of God great and small, and the treasures of the house of the Lord, and the treasures of the king, and of his princes: all these carried he to Babel.

19 And they burnt the house of God, and brake down the wall of Jerusalem, and burnt all the palaces thereof with fire, and all the precious vessels thereof, to destroy *all*.

20 And they that were left by the sword, carried he away to Babel, and they were servants to him, and to his sons, until the kingdom of the [1]Persians had rule,

21 To fulfill the word of the Lord by the [1]mouth of Jeremiah, until the land had her fill of her Sabbaths: *for* all the days that she lay desolate, she kept Sabbath, to fulfill seventy years.

22 ¶ [d]But in the [1]first year of Cyrus king of Persia (when the word of the Lord, *spoken* by the mouth of Jeremiah, was finished) the Lord stirred up the spirit of Cyrus king of Persia, and he made a proclamation through all his kingdom, and also by writing, saying,

23 Thus saith Cyrus king of Persia, All the kingdoms of the earth hath the Lord God of heaven given me, and hath [1]commanded me to build him an house in Jerusalem, that is in Judah. Who is among you of all his people, with whom the Lord his God *is*? let him go up.

36:5 [1] Because he and the people turned not to God by his first plague, he brought a new upon him, and at length rooted them out.

36:8 [1] He meaneth superstitious marks which were found upon his body, when he was dead, which thing declared how deeply idolatry was rooted in his heart, seeing he bare the marks in his flesh.

36:9 [1] That is, he began his reign at eight years old, and reigned ten years when his father was alive, and after his father's death, which was the eighteenth year of his age, he reigned alone three months and ten days.

36:10 [1] Or, uncle.

36:15 [1] Hebrew, *by the hand of his.*

[2] By this phrase the Scripture meaneth, oftentimes, and diligently, as Jer. 11:7 and 25:3 and 26:5 and 32:33.

36:16 [1] Till God could no longer suffer their sins, but must needs punish them.

36:17 [1] Whither they fled, thinking to have been saved for the holi-

ness thereof.

[2] Which is not because God approveth him, which yet is the minister of his justice, but because God would by his just judgment punish this people: for this king was led with ambition and vain glory, whereunto were joined fury and cruelty: therefore his work was condemnable, notwithstanding it was just and holy on God's part, who used this wicked instrument to declare his justice.

36:20 [1] When Cyrus King of Persia had made the Babylonians subject.

36:21 [1] Who threatened the vengeance of God and seventy years captivity, which he calleth the Sabbaths or rest of the land, Jer. 25:11.

36:22 [1] In the first year that he reigned over the Chaldeans, Ezra 1:1.

36:23 [1] God had so forewarned by his Prophet above an hundred years before Cyrus was born, Isa. 44:28, that Jerusalem and the Temple should be built again by Cyrus his anointed: so called, because God used his service for a time to deliver his Church.

EZRA

1

1 Cyrus sendeth again the people that was in captivity, 8 and restoreth them their holy vessels.

1 Now [a]in [1]the first year of Cyrus King of Persia (that the word of the LORD, *spoken* by the [2]mouth of Jeremiah, might be accomplished) the Lord stirred up the [3]spirit of Cyrus King of Persia, and he made a proclamation through all his kingdom, and also by writing, saying,

2 Thus saith Cyrus King of Persia, The Lord God of heaven hath given me [1]all the kingdoms of the earth, and he hath commanded me to build him an house in Jerusalem, which is in Judah.

3 Who is he among you of all his people with whom his God is? let him go up to Jerusalem which is in Judah, and build the house of the Lord God of Israel: he is the God, which is in Jerusalem.

4 And everyone that remaineth in any place (where he sojourneth) [1]let the men of his place relieve him with silver and with gold, and with substance, and with cattle, [2]*and* with a willing offering, for the house of God that is in Jerusalem.

5 Then the chief fathers of Judah and Benjamin, and the Priests and the Levites rose up, with all them whose spirit God had raised to go up, to build the house of the Lord which is in Jerusalem.

6 And all [1]they that were about them, strengthened their hands with vessels of silver, with gold, with substance and with cattle, and with precious things, besides all that was willingly offered.

7 Also the king Cyrus brought forth the vessels of the house of the Lord, [b]which Nebuchadnezzar had taken out of Jerusalem, and had put them in the house of his god.

8 Even them did Cyrus king of Persia bring forth by the hand of Mithredath the treasurer, and counted

CHAPTER 1
[a] 2 Chron. 3:22
Jer. 25:12
Jer. 29:10
[b] 2 Kings 25:13
2 Chron. 36:7
Jer. 27:19,20
Dan. 1:2

CHAPTER 2
[a] Neh. 7:6

them unto [1]Sheshbazzar the Prince of Judah.

9 And this is the number of them, thirty basins of gold, a thousand basins of silver, nine and twenty [1]knives,

10 Thirty bowls of gold, *and* of silver bowls of the second sort, four hundred and ten, *and* of other vessels, a thousand.

11 All the vessels of gold and silver *were* five thousand and four hundred. Sheshbazzar brought up all [1]with them of the captivity that came up from Babel to Jerusalem.

2

The number of them that returned from the captivity.

1 These [a]also are the sons [1]of the province that went up out of the captivity (whom Nebuchadnezzar king of Babel had carried away unto Babel) and returned to Jerusalem, and to Judah, everyone unto his city,

2 Which came up with [1]Zerubbabel, *to wit*, Jeshua, Nehemiah, Seraiah, Reelaiah, [2]Mordecai, Bilshan, Mispar, Bigvai, Rehum, Baanah. The number of the men [3]of the people of Israel *was*,

3 The sons of Parosh, two thousand, an hundred seventy and two:

4 The sons of Shephatiah, three hundred, seventy and two:

5 The sons of Arah, seven hundred, and seventy and five:

6 The sons of [1]Pahath-Moab, of the sons of Jeshua, and Joab, two thousand, eight hundred and twelve:

7 The sons of Elam, a thousand, two hundred and four and fifty:

8 The sons of Zattu, nine hundred and five and forty:

1:1 [1] After that he and Darius had won Babylon.
[2] Who promised them deliverance after that seventy years were past, Jer. 25:12.
[3] That is, moved him, and gave him heart.
1:2 [1] For he was chief Monarch, and had many nations under his dominion, which this heathen king confesseth to have received of the living God.
1:4 [1] If any through poverty were not able to return, the king's commission was that he should be furnished with necessaries.
[2] Which they themselves should send toward the reparation of the Temple.
1:6 [1] The Babylonians and Chaldeans gave them these presents: thus rather than the children of God should want for their necessities,

he would stir up the heart of the very infidels to help them.
1:8 [1] So the Chaldeans called Zerubbabel who was the chief governor, so that the preeminence still remained in the house of David.
1:9 [1] Which served to kill the beasts that were offered in sacrifice.
1:11 [1] With the Jews that had been kept captives in Babylon.
2:1 [1] Meaning, Judea, which was a province, that is, a country which was in subjection.
2:2 [1] Zerubbabel was chief captain, and Jeshua the high Priest: but Nehemiah a man of great authority went not now, but came after 64 years.
[2] This was not that Mordecai which was Esther's kinsman.
[3] Meaning, of the common people.
2:6 [1] Or, of the Duke of Moab.

9 The sons of Zaccai, seven hundred and three-score:

10 The sons of Bani, six hundred and two and forty:

11 The sons of Bebai, six hundred, and three and twenty:

12 The sons of Azgad, a thousand, two hundred and two and twenty:

13 The sons of Adonikam, six hundred, three score and six:

14 The sons of Bigvai, two thousand, and six and fifty:

15 The sons of Adin, four hundred and four and fifty:

16 The sons of Ater of [1]Hezekiah, ninety and eight:

17 The sons of Bezai, three hundred and three and twenty:

18 The sons of Jorah, an hundred and twelve:

19 The sons of Hashum, two hundred and three and twenty:

20 The sons of Gibbar, ninety and five:

21 [1]The sons of Bethlehem, an hundred and three and twenty:

22 The men of Netophah, six and fifty:

23 The men of Anothoth, an hundred and eight and twenty:

24 The sons of Azmaveth, two and forty:

25 The sons of Kirjath Arim, of Chephirah, and Beeroth, seven hundred and three and forty:

26 The sons of Ramah and Geba, six hundred and one and twenty:

27 The men of Michmas, an hundred and two and twenty:

28 The sons of Bethel, and Ai, two hundred and three and twenty:

29 The sons of Nebo, two and fifty:

30 The sons of Magbish, an hundred and six and fifty:

31 The sons of the other Elam, a thousand, and two hundred and four and fifty:

32 The sons of Harim, three hundred and twenty:

33 The sons of Lod, Hadid, and Ono, seven hundred and five and twenty:

34 The sons of Jericho, three hundred and five and forty:

35 The sons of Senaah, three thousand six hundred and thirty:

36 The [1]Priests: of the sons of Jedaiah of the house of Jeshua, nine hundred seventy and three:

37 The sons of Immer, a thousand and two and fifty:

38 The sons of Pashur, a thousand, two hundred and seven and forty:

39 The sons of Harim, a thousand and seventeen.

40 ¶ The Levites: the sons of Jeshua, and Kadmiel of the sons of Hodaviah, seventy and four.

41 ¶ The Singers: the sons of Asaph, an hundred and eight and twenty.

42 ¶ The sons of the porters: the sons of Shallum, the sons of Ater, the sons of Talmon, the sons of Akkub, the sons of Hatita, the sons of Shobai: all *were* an hundred and nine and thirty.

43 ¶ The [1]Nethinim: the sons of Ziha, the sons of Hasupha, the sons of Tabbaoth,

44 The sons of Keros, the sons of Siaha, the sons of Padon,

45 The sons of Lebanah, the sons of Hagabah, the sons of Akkub,

46 The sons of Hagab, the sons of Shamlai, the sons of Hanan,

47 The sons of Giddel, the sons of Gahar, the sons of Reaiah,

48 The sons of Rezin, the sons of Nekoda, the sons of Gazzam,

49 The sons of Uzza, the sons of Paseah, the sons of Besai,

50 The sons of Asnah, the sons of Meunim, the sons of Nephusim,

51 The sons of Bakbuk, the sons of Hakupha, the sons of Harhur,

52 The sons of Bazluth, the sons of Mehida, the sons of Harsha,

53 The sons of Barkos, the sons of Sisera, the sons of Thamah,

54 The sons of Neziah, the sons of Hatipha,

55 The sons of Solomon's [1]servants: the sons of Sotai, the sons of Sophereth, the sons of Peruda,

56 The sons of Jaala, the sons of Darkon, the sons of Giddel,

57 The sons of Shephatiah, the sons of Hattil, the sons of Pochereth Hazzebaim, the sons of Ami.

58 All the Nethinim, and the sons of Solomon's servants *were* three hundred ninety and two.

59 ¶ And these went up from Tel Melah, and from Tel Harsha, Cherub, Addan, *and* Immer, but they could not discern their father's house and their seed, whether they were of Israel.

60 The sons of Delaiah, the sons of Tobiah, the

2:16 [1] Which were of the posterity of Hezekiah.
2:21 [1] That is, inhabitants, for so this word (some) signifieth when it is joined with the names of places.
2:36 [1] Before he hath declared the two tribes of Judah and Benjamin, and now cometh to the tribe of Levi, and beginneth at the Priests.

2:43 [1] So called, because they were given to the Temple, to cut wood and bear water for the use of the sacrifices, and came of the Gibeonites, which were appointed to this use by Joshua, Josh. 9:23.
2:55 [1] Which came of them that Solomon had appointed for the work of the Temple.

sons of Nekoda, six hundred and two and fifty.

61 And of the sons of the Priests, the sons of Habaiah, the sons of Koz, the sons of ¹Barzillai: which took of the daughters of Barzillai the Gileadite to wife, and was called after their name.

62 These sought their writing of the genealogies, but they were not found: therefore were they put from the Priesthood.

63 And ¹Tirshatha said unto them, that they should not eat of the most holy thing, till there rose up a Priest with ²Urim and Thummim.

64 The whole Congregation together *was* two and forty thousand, three hundred and threescore,

65 Beside their servants and their maids: of whom *were* seven thousand, three hundred and seven and thirty: and among them *were* two hundred singing men and singing women.

66 Their horses *were* seven hundred, and six and thirty: their mules, two hundred, and five and forty:

67 Their camels four hundred, and five and thirty: their asses, six thousand, seven hundred and twenty.

68 And certain of the chief fathers, when they came to the house of the Lord, which was in Jerusalem, they offered willingly for the house of God, to set it up upon his foundation.

69 They gave after their ability unto the treasure of the work, *even* one and threescore thousand ¹drams of gold, and five thousand ²pieces of silver, and an hundred Priests' garments.

70 So the Priests and the Levites, and a *certain* of the people, and the singers, and the porters, and the Nethinim dwelt in their cities, and all Israel in their cities.

3 2 *They build the Altar of God.* 6 *They offer to the Lord.* 7 *They prepare for the Temple,* 11 *And sing unto the Lord.*

1 And when the ¹seventh month was come, and the children of Israel *were* in their cities, the people assembled themselves as one man unto Jerusalem.

2 Then stood up Jeshua the son of Jozadak, and his brethren the Priests, and Zerubbabel the ¹son of Shealtiel, and his brethren, and built the Altar of

CHAPTER 3
ᵃ Exod. 23:16
ᵇ 1 Chron. 16:7,8

the God of Israel to offer burnt offerings thereon, as it is written in the Law of Moses the man of God,

3 And they set the Altar upon ¹his bases (for fear was among them, because of the people of those countries) therefore they offered burnt offerings thereon unto the Lord, *even* burnt offerings in the morning, and at even.

4 They kept also the feast of the Tabernacles, as it is written, and they burnt offering ᵃdaily, by number according to the custom day by day,

5 And afterward ¹the continual burnt offering, both in the new months and in all the feast days that were consecrated unto the Lord, and in all the oblations willingly offered unto the Lord.

6 From the first day of the seventh month began they to offer burnt offerings unto the Lord: but the foundation of the Temple of the Lord was not laid.

7 They gave money also unto the masons, and to the workmen, and meat and drink, and oil unto them of Zidon and of Tyre, to bring them cedar wood from Lebanon to the sea unto ¹Japho, according to the grant that they had of Cyrus king of Persia.

8 ¶ And in the second year of their coming unto the house of God in Jerusalem, in the ¹second month began Zerubbabel the son of Shealtiel, and Jeshua the son of Jozadak, and the remnant of their brethren the Priests, and the Levites, and all they that were come out of the captivity unto Jerusalem, and appointed the Levites from twenty years old and above, to set forward the work of the house of the Lord.

9 And Jeshua ¹stood with his sons, and his brethren, *and* Kadmiel with his sons, *and* the sons of Judah together, to set forward the workmen in the house of God, and the sons of Henadad with their sons, and their brethren the Levites.

10 And when the builders laid the foundation of the Temple of the Lord, they appointed the Priests in their apparel with trumpets, and the Levites the sons of Asaph with cymbals, to praise the Lord, ᵇafter the ordinance of David king of Israel.

11 Thus they sang when they gave praise, and when they gave thanks unto the Lord, For he is good, for his mercy *endureth* forever toward Israel.

2:61 ¹ Of him is made mention, 2 Sam. 17:27 and 19:31, and because the Priest's office was had in contempt, these would have changed their estate by their name, and so by God's just judgment lost both the estimation of the world and the dignity of their office.

2:63 ¹ This is a Chaldean name, and signifieth him that hath authority over others.

² Read Exod. 28:30.

2:69 ¹ Which mount to of our money, 24,826 pounds, 13 shillings and 4 pence, esteeming the French crown at 6 shillings and 4 pence for the dram is the eighth part of an ounce, and the ounce the eighth part of a mark.

² Which are called, *mina*, and contain a piece two marks: so 50,000 *minas* make 55,000 franks, which mount to of our money 69,666

pounds, 13 shillings 4 pence so that the whole sum was 94,493 pounds, 6 shillings, 8 pence.

3:1 ¹ Called Tishri which answereth to part of September and part of October.

3:2 ¹ Meaning, nephew: for he was the son of Pedaiah, read 1 Chron. 3:19.

3:3 ¹ In the place where Solomon had placed it.

3:5 ¹ That is, after the feast of Tabernacles.

3:7 ¹ Or, Joppa.

3:8 ¹ Which month contained part of April and part of May: for in the mean season they had provided for things necessary for the work.

3:9 ¹ They gave them exhortations, and encouraged every man forward in the work.

And all the people shouted with a great shout, when they praised the Lord, because the foundation of the house of the Lord was laid.

12 Many also of the Priests and the Levites and the chief of the fathers, ancient men which had seen the first house, (when the foundation of this house was laid before their eyes) [1]wept with a loud voice, and many shouted aloud for joy,

13 So that the people could not discern the sound of the shout for joy, from the noise of the weeping of the people: for the people shouted with a loud cry, and the noise was heard far off.

4 *2 The building of the Temple is hindered, and how, 11 Letters to Artaxerxes, and the answer.*

1 But [1]the adversaries of Judah and Benjamin heard, that the children of the captivity built the Temple unto the Lord God of Israel.

2 And they came to Zerubbabel, and to the chief fathers, and said unto them, We will build with you: for we seek the Lord your God as ye *do*, and we have sacrificed unto him since the time of Esarhaddon king of Assyria, which brought us up hither.

3 Then Zerubbabel, and Jeshua, and the rest of the chief fathers of Israel said unto them, It is not for you, but for us to build the house unto our God: [1]for we ourselves together will build it unto the Lord God of Israel, as king Cyrus the king of Persia hath commanded us.

4 Wherefore the people of the land [1]discouraged the people of Judah, and troubled them in building.

5 And they [1]hired counselors against them, to hinder their devise all the days of Cyrus king of Persia, even until the reign of Darius king of Persia.

6 And in the reign of [1]Ahasuerus (in the beginning of his reign) wrote they an accusation against the inhabitants of Judah and Jerusalem.

7 And in the days of [1]Artachshashta, Mithredath, Tabeel, and the rest of their companions wrote when it was peace, unto Artaxerxes king of Persia, and the writing of the letter was the Aramites writing, and the thing declared *was* in the language of the Aramites.

8 Rehum the [1]chancellor, and Shimshai the scribe wrote a letter against Jerusalem to Artaxerxes the king, in this sort.

9 Then *wrote* Rehum the chancellor, and Shimshai the scribe, and their companions [1]Dinai, and Apharsathcai, Tarpelai, Persia, Archevai, Bablai, Shushanchai, Dehave, Elamai,

10 And the rest of the people whom the great and noble [1]Osnapper brought over, and set in the cities of Samaria, and other that are beyond the [2]River and [3]Cheeneth.

11 ¶ This is the copy of the letter that they sent unto King Artaxerxes, THY SERVANTS the men beyond the River and Cheeneth, *salute thee.*

12 Be it known unto the King that the Jews, which came up from thee to us, are come unto Jerusalem (a city rebellious and wicked) and build, and lay the foundations of the walls, and have joined the foundations.

13 Be it known now unto the king, that if this city be built, and the foundations of the walls laid, they will not give toll, tribute, nor [1]custom: so shalt thou hinder the king's tribute.

14 Now therefore because [1]we have been brought up in the *King's* palace, it was not meet for us to see the King's dishonor: for this cause have we sent and certified the King,

15 That one may search in the book of the Chronicles of thy fathers, and thou shalt find in the book of the Chronicles, and perceive that this city is rebellious and noisome unto kings and provinces, and that they have moved sedition of old time, for the which cause this city was destroyed.

16 We certify the king *therefore*, that if this city be built, and the foundation of the walls laid, by this means the portion beyond the River shall not be thine.

17 ¶ The King sent an answer unto Rehum the chancellor, and Shimshai the scribe, and to the rest of their companions that dwelt in Samaria, and unto the other beyond the River, [1]Shelam and [2]Cheeth.

3:12 [1] Because they saw that it was nothing so glorious as that Temple, which Solomon had built, notwithstanding Aggeus comforteth them, and prophesieth that it shall be more beautiful than the first: meaning the spiritual Temple, which are the members of Christ's body.

4:1 [1] Meaning, the inhabitants of Samaria, whom the king of Assyria had placed in the stead of the ten tribes, 2 Kings 17:24 and 19:37. These professed God, but worshipped idols also, and therefore were the greatest enemies to the true servants of God.

4:3 [1] For they perceived what their pretence was, to wit, to erect idolatry instead of true religion.

4:4 [1] Hebrew, *made their hands weak.*

4:5 [1] They bribed the governors under the king to hinder their work: Thus they that halt, cannot abide that God should be purely served.

4:6 [1] He was also called Artaxerxes, which is a Persian name, some think it was Cambises Cyrus' son, or Darius, as verse 5.

4:7 [1] Called Artaxerxes, which signifieth in the Persian tongue, an excellent warrior.

4:8 [1] Or, counselor.

4:9 [1] These were certain people which the Assyrians placed in Samaria instead of the ten tribes.

4:10 [1] Some think it was Sennacherib, but rather Shalmaneser.
  [2] To wit, Euphrates: and he meaneth in respect of Babel that they dwelt beyond it.
  [3] Which were a certain people that envied the Jews.

4:13 [1] Meaning, the gifts that are wont to be given to kings when they pass by any country.

4:14 [1] Hebrew, in the Chaldea, *we have eaten the salt of the palace.*

4:17 [1] Some read for Shalom, salutation or greeting.
  [2] Called also Cheeneth, as verse 11.

18 ¶ The letter which ye sent unto us, hath been openly read before me,

19 And I have commanded and they have searched, and found, that this city of old time hath made insurrection against kings, and hath rebelled, and rebellion hath been committed therein.

20 There have been mighty kings also over Jerusalem, which have ruled over all beyond the River, and toll, tribute and custom was given unto them.

21 Make ye now a decree that those men may cease, and that the city be not built, till I have given *another* commandment.

22 Take heed now that ye fail not to do this: why should damage grow to hurt the king?

23 When the copy of king Artaxerxes's letter was read before Rehum and Shimshai the scribe, and their companions, they went up in all the haste to Jerusalem unto the Jews, and caused them to cease by force and power.

24 Then ¹ceased the work of the house of God, which was in Jerusalem, and did stay unto the second year of Darius king of Persia.

5 *1 Haggai and Zechariah do prophesy.   3 The work of the Temple goeth forward contrary to the mind of Tattenai.   6 His letters to Darius.*

1 Then ¹ᵃHaggai a Prophet, and Zechariah the son of Iddo a Prophet prophesied unto the Jews that were in Judah, and Jerusalem, in the Name of the God of Israel, *even* unto them.

2 Then Zerubbabel the son of Shealtiel, and Jeshua the son of Jozadak arose, and began to build the house of God at Jerusalem, and with them *were* the Prophets of God, which ¹helped them.

3 ¶ At the same time came to them Tattenai which was captain beyond the River, and Shethar-Boznai, and their companions, and said thus unto them, Who hath given you commandment to build this house, and to lay the foundations of these walls?

4 ¹Then said we unto them after this manner, What are the names of the men that build this building?

5 But the ¹eye of their God was upon the Elders of the Jews, that they could not cause them to cease, till the matter came to Darius: and then they answered by letters thereunto.

6 The copy of the letter, that Tattenai captain beyond the River, and Shethar-Boznai and his companions, Persians, (which were beyond the river)

CHAPTER 5
ᵃ Hag. 1:1
ᵇ 1 Kings 6:2
2 Chron. 3:2
ᶜ 2 Kings 24:12
2 Kings 25:9

sent unto King Darius.

7 They sent a letter unto him, wherein it was written thus, UNTO DARIUS the king, all peace.

8 Be it known unto the king, that we went into the province of Judea, to the house of the great God, which is built with ¹great stones, and beams are laid in the walls, and this work is wrought speedily, and prospereth in their hands.

9 Then asked we those Elders, and said unto them thus, Who hath given you commandment to build this house, and to lay the foundation of these walls?

10 We asked their names also that we might certify thee, *and* that we might write the names of the men that were their rulers.

11 But they answered us thus, and said, We are the servants of the God of heaven and earth, and build the house that was built of old *and* many years ago, which a ¹great king of Israel ᵇbuilt, and founded it.

12 But after that our fathers had provoked the God of heaven unto wrath, ᶜhe gave them over into the hand of Nebuchadnezzar king of Babel the Chaldean, and he destroyed this house, and carried the people away captive unto Babel.

13 But in the ¹first year of Cyrus king of Babel, King Cyrus made a decree to build this house of God.

14 And the vessels of gold and silver of the house of God, which Nebuchadnezzar took out of the Temple, that was in Jerusalem, and brought them into the Temple of Babel, those did Cyrus the king take out of the Temple of Babel, and they gave them unto *one* ¹Sheshbazzar by his name, whom he had made captain.

15 And he said unto him, Take these vessels and go thy way, and put them in the Temple that is in Jerusalem, and let the house of God be built in his place.

16 Then came the same Sheshbazzar and laid the foundation of the house of God, which is in Jerusalem, and since that time even until now, hath it been in building, yet is it not finished.

17 Now therefore if it please the king, let there be search made in the house of the king's ¹treasures, which is there in Babel, whether a decree hath been made by king Cyrus, to build this house of God in Jerusalem, and let the King send *his* mind concerning this.

6 *At the commandment of Darius king of Persia, after the Temple was built and dedicated, the children of Israel keep the feast of unleavened bread.*

4:24 ¹ Not altogether for the Prophets exhorted them to continue, but they used less diligence because of the troubles.
5:1 ¹ Or, Haggeni.
5:2 ¹ Which encouraged them to go forward, and accused them that they were more careful to build their own houses, than zealous to build the Temple of God.
5:4 ¹ That is, the enemies asked this, as verse 10.

5:5 ¹ His favor and the spirit of strength.
5:8 ¹ Or, masonry.
5:11 ¹ To wit, Solomon.
5:13 ¹ Read Ezra 1:1, 2.
5:14 ¹ Read Ezra 1:8.
5:17 ¹ Meaning, in the library, or places where lay the register or records of times.

1 Then king Darius gave commandment, and they made search in the ¹library of the treasures, which were there laid up in Babel.

2 And there was found in a ¹coffer (in the palace that was in the province of the Medes) a volume, and therein was it thus written, *as* a memorial,

3 IN THE FIRST year of King Cyrus, King Cyrus made a decree for the house of God in Jerusalem, Let the house be built, *even* the place where they offered sacrifices, and let the walls thereof be joined together: let the height thereof *be* threescore cubits, *and* the breadth thereof threescore cubits,

4 Three ¹orders of ²great stones, and one order of timber, and let the expenses be given of the king's house.

5 And also let them render the vessels of the house of God (of gold and silver, which Nebuchadnezzar took out of the Temple, which was in Jerusalem, and brought unto Babel) and let ¹him go unto the Temple that is in Jerusalem to his place, and put them in the house of God.

6 Therefore Tattenai captain beyond the river, and Shethar-Boznai, (and their companions Apharsecai, which are beyond the River) be ye far ¹from thence.

7 Suffer ye the work of this house of God, that the captain of the Jews and the Elders of the Jews may build this house of God in his place.

8 For I have given a commandment what ye shall do to the Elders of these Jews, for the building of this house of God, that of the revenues of the King, which is of the tribute beyond the River, there be incontinently expenses given unto these men that they ¹cease not.

9 And that which they shall have need of, let it be given unto them day by day, whether it be young bullocks, or rams, or lambs for the burnt offerings of the God of heaven, wheat, salt, wine, and oil, according to the appointment of the Priests that are in Jerusalem, that there be no fault,

10 That they may have to offer sweet odors unto the God of heaven, and pray for the king's life, and for his sons.

11 And I have made a decree, that whosoever shall alter this sentence, the wood shall be pulled down from his house, and shall be set up, *and* he shall

CHAPTER 6
ᵃ Num. 3:6
Num. 8:9

be hanged thereon, and his house shall be made a dunghill for this.

12 And the God that hath caused his Name ¹to dwell there, destroy all kings and people that put to their hand to alter *and* to destroy this house of God, which is in Jerusalem. I Darius have made a decree, let it be done with speed.

13 ¶ Then Tattenai the Captain beyond the River, *and* Shethar-Boznai and their companions, according to that which Darius had sent, so they did speedily.

14 So the elders of the Jews built, and they prospered by the prophesying of ¹Haggai the Prophet, and Zechariah the son of Iddo, and they built and finished it, by the appointment of the God of Israel, and by the commandment of Cyrus and Darius, and Artaxerxes king of Persia.

15 And this house was finished the third day of the month ¹Adar, which was ²the sixth year of the reign of King Darius.

16 ¶ And the children of Israel, the Priests, and the Levites, and the residue of the children of the captivity kept the dedication of this house of God with joy,

17 And offered at the dedication of this house of God an hundred bullocks, two hundred rams, four hundred lambs, and twelve goats, for the sin of all Israel, according to the number of the tribes of Israel.

18 And they set the Priests in their order, and the Levites in their courses over the service of God in Jerusalem, as it is written in the ᵃbook of Moses.

19 And the children of the captivity kept the Passover on the fourteenth *day* of the first month.

20 (For the Priests and the Levites were purified altogether) and they killed the Passover for all the children of the captivity, and for their brethren the Priests, and for themselves.

21 So the children of Israel which were come again out of captivity, and all such as had ¹separated themselves unto them, from the filthiness of the Heathen of the land to seek the Lord God of Israel, did eat,

22 And they kept the feast of unleavened bread seven days with joy: for the Lord had made them glad, and turned the heart of the king of ¹Assyria

---

6:1 ¹ Hebrew, *house of books.*
6:2 ¹ Wherein were the acts of the kings of the Medes and Persians.
6:4 ¹ Or, rows, or courses.
   ² Or, Marble.
6:5 ¹ Meaning, Zerubbabel to whom he giveth charge.
6:6 ¹ Meddle not with them neither hinder them.
6:8 ¹ For lack of money.
6:12 ¹ Who hath appointed that place to have his Name called upon there.

6:14 ¹ Whom God stirs up to assure them that he would give their work good success.
6:15 ¹ This is the twelfth month and containeth part of February and part of March.
   ² And the two and fortieth year after their first return.
6:21 ¹ Which were of the heathen, and forsaked their idolatry to worship the true God.
6:22 ¹ Meaning, Darius who was king of the Medes, Persians, and Assyrians.

unto them, to [2]encourage them in the work of the house of God, *even* the God of Israel.

7 *13 By the commandment of the king, Ezra and his companions come to Jerusalem. 27 He giveth thanks to God.*

1 Now after these things, in the reign of [1]Artaxerxes king of Persia, *was* Ezra the son of Seraiah, the son of Azariah, the son of Hilkiah,

2 The son of Shallum, the son of Zadok, the son of Ahitub,

3 The son of Amariah, the son of Azariah, the son of Meraioth,

4 The son of Zerahiah, the son of Uzzi, the son of Bukki,

5 The son of Abishua, the son of Phinehas, the son of Eleazar, the son of [1]Aaron, the chief Priest.

6 This Ezra came up from Babel, and was a [1]Scribe, prompt in the Law of Moses, which the Lord God of Israel had given, and the king gave him all his request according to the hand of the Lord his God, *which was* upon him.

7 And there went up *certain* of the children of Israel, and of the Priests, and the Levites, and the singers, and the porters, and the Nethinim unto Jerusalem, in the seventh year of king Artaxerxes.

8 And he came to Jerusalem in the [1]fifth month, which was in the seventh year [2]of the king.

9 For upon the first *day* of the first month began he to go up from Babel, and on the first *day* of the fifth month came he to Jerusalem according to the good hand of his God *that was* upon him.

10 For Ezra had prepared his heart to seek the Law of the Lord, and to do it, and to teach the precepts and judgments in Israel.

11 ¶ And this is the copy of the letter that king Artaxerxes gave unto Ezra the Priest *and* Scribe, *even* a writer of the words of the commandments of the Lord, and of his statutes over Israel.

12 ARTAXERXES king of kings, to Ezra the Priest and perfect Scribe of the Law of the God of heaven, and to [1]Cheeneth.

13 I have given commandment, that everyone that is willing in my kingdom of the people of Israel, and of the Priests, and Levites, [1]to go to Jerusalem with thee, shall go.

14 Therefore art thou sent of the king and his seven counselors, to [1]enquire in Judah and Jerusalem, according to the Law of thy God, which is in [2]thine hand,

15 And to carry the silver and the gold, which the king and his counselors willingly offer unto the God of Israel (whose habitation is in Jerusalem)

16 And all the silver and gold that thou canst find in all the province of Babel, with the free offering of the people, and that which the Priests offer willingly to the house of their God which is in Jerusalem,

17 That thou mayest buy speedily with this silver, bullocks, rams, lambs, with their meat offerings, and their drink offerings: and thou shalt offer them upon the Altar of the house of your God, which is in Jerusalem.

18 And whatsoever it pleaseth thee and thy brethren to do with the rest of the silver and gold, do ye it according to the will of your [1]God.

19 And the vessels that are given thee for the service of the house of thy God, those deliver thou before God in Jerusalem.

20 And the residue that shall be needful for the house of thy God, which shall be meet for thee to bestow, thou shalt bestow it out of the King's treasure house,

21 And I king Artaxerxes have given commandment to all the treasurers which are beyond [1]the River, that whatsoever Ezra the Priest and Scribe of the Law of the God of heaven shall require of you, that it be done incontinently,

22 Unto an hundred talents of silver, unto an hundred [1]measures of wheat, and unto an hundred [2]baths of wine, and unto an hundred baths of oil, and salt without writing.

23 Whatsoever *is* by the commandment of the God of heaven, let it be done speedily for the house of the God of heaven: for why should he be wroth [1]against the realm of the King and his children?

24 And we certify you, that upon any of the Priests, Levites, singers, porters, Nethinim, or Ministers in

---

[2] Hebrew, *to strengthen their hands.*

7:1 [1] The Hebrews write, that divers of the kings of Persia were called by this name, as Pharaoh was a common name to the kings of Egypt, and Caesar to the Emperors Roman.

7:5 [1] Ezra deduceth his kindred, till he cometh to Aaron, to prove that he came of him.

7:6 [1] He showeth here what a Scribe is, who had charge to write the Law and to expound it, whom Mark calleth a Scribe, Mark 12:28, Matthew and Luke called him a Lawyer or doctor of the Law, Matt. 22:35; Luke 10:25.

7:8 [1] That contained part of July, and part of August.

[2] Of king Darius.

7:12 [1] Some take this for the name of a people, some for time or continuance, meaning that the king wished him long life.

7:13 [1] Which remained as yet in Babylon and had not returned with Zerubbabel.

7:14 [1] To examine who lived according to the Law.

[2] Whereof thou art expert.

7:18 [1] As ye know best may serve to God's glory.

7:21 [1] Which was the river Euphrates, and they were beyond it in respect of Babylon.

7:22 [1] Hebrew, *Corim.*

[2] Read 1 Kings 7:26; 2 Chron. 2:10.

7:23 [1] This declareth that the fear of God's judgments causeth him to use this liberality, and not the love that he bare to God's glory: or affection to his people.

this house of God, there shall no governor lay upon them toll, tribute nor custom.

25 And thou Ezra (after the wisdom of thy God, that is in thine hand) [1]set judges and arbiters, which may judge all the people that is beyond the River, *even* all that know the law of thy God, and teach ye *them* that know it not.

26 And whosoever will not do the Law of thy God, and the king's law, let him have judgment without delay, whether it be unto death, or to banishment, or to confiscation of goods, or to imprisonment.

27 [1]Blessed *be* the Lord God of our fathers, which so hath put in the king's heart, to beautify the house of the Lord that is in Jerusalem,

28 And hath inclined mercy toward me, before the king and his counselors, and before all the king's mighty Princes: and I was comforted by the hand of the Lord my God *which was* upon me, and I gathered the chief of Israel to go up with me.

8

1 *The number of them that returned to Jerusalem with Ezra.* 21 *He causeth them to fast.* 24 *He admonisheth the Priests of their duty.* 31 *What they did when they came to Jerusalem.*

1 These are now the chief fathers of them, and the genealogy of them that came up with me from Babel, in the reign of king [1]Artaxerxes.

2 Of the sons of Phinehas, Gershom: of the sons of Ithamar, Daniel: of the sons of David, Hattush:

3 Of the sons of Shechaniah, of the sons of Pharosh, Zechariah, and with him the count of the males, an hundred and fifty.

4 Of the sons of [1]Pahath-Moab, Elihoenai, the son of Zerahiah, and with him two hundred males.

5 Of the sons of Shechaniah, the son of Jahaziel, and with him three hundred males.

6 And of the sons of Adin, Ebed the son of Jonathan, and with him fifty males.

7 And of the sons of Elam, Jeshaiah the son of Athaliah, and with him seventy males.

8 And of the sons of Shephatiah, Zebadiah the son of Michael, and with him fourscore males.

9 Of the sons of Joab, Obadiah the son of Jehiel, and with him two hundred and eighteen males.

10 And of the sons of Shelomith the son of Josiphiah, and with him an hundred and threescore males.

11 And of the sons of Bebai, Zechariah the son of Bebai, and with him eight and twenty males.

12 And of the sons of Azgad, Johanan the son of Hakkatan, and with him an hundred and ten males.

13 And of the sons of Adonikam, *that were* the [1]last, whose names are these: Eliphelet, Jehiel and Shemaiah, and with them threescore males.

14 And of the sons of Bigvai, Uthai, and Zabbud, and with them seventy males.

15 And I gathered them to the [1]river that goeth toward Ahava, and there abode we three days: then I viewed the people, and the Priests, and found there none of the sons of Levi.

16 Therefore sent I to Eliezer, to Ariel, to Shemeiah, and to Elnathan, and to Jarib, and to Elnathan, and to Nathan, and to Zechariah, and to Meshullam the chief, and to Joiarib, and to Elnathan men of understanding,

17 And I gave them commandment, to Iddo the [1]chiefest at the place of Casiphia, and I [2]told them the words that they should speak to Iddo, *and* to his brethren the Nethinim at the place of Casiphia, that they should cause the ministers of the house of our God to come unto us.

18 So by the good hand of our God, *which was* upon us, they brought us a man of understanding of the sons of Mahli the son of Levi the son of Israel, and Sherebiah with his sons and his brethren, *even* eighteen.

19 Also Hashabiah, and with him Jeshaiah of the sons of Merari, with his brethren, and their sons twenty.

20 And of the [1]Nethinim, whom David had set, and the Princes for the service of the Levites, two hundred and twenty of the Nethinim, which all were named by name.

21 And there at the river, by Ahava, I proclaimed a fast, that we might humble [1]ourselves before our God, and seek of him a right way for us, and for our children, and for all our substance.

22 For I was [1]ashamed to require of the king an army and horsemen, to help us against the enemy in the way, because we had spoken to the king, saying, The hand of our God *is* upon all them that seek him in goodness, but his power and his wrath *is* against

---

7:25 [1] He gave Ezra full authority to restore all things according to the word of God, and to punish them that resisted, and would not obey.
7:27 [1] Thus Ezra gave God thanks for that he gave him so good success in his affairs by reason of the king.
8:1 [1] Read Ezra 7.
8:4 [1] Or, captains of Moab.
8:13 [1] That came to go with Ezra.
8:15 [1] To that place of Euphrates, where Ahava the river entereth into it.
8:17 [1] He was the chiefest that taught there the Law of God unto

the Levites.
[2] Hebrew, *put words in their mouth.*
8:20 [1] Read Ezra 2:43.
8:21 [1] He showeth that the end of fasting, is to humble the body to the spirit, which must proceed of the heart lively touched, or else it is but hypocrisy.
8:22 [1] He thought it better to commit himself to the protection of God, than by seeking these ordinary means to give occasion to others to think that he did doubt of God's power.

all them that forsake him.

23 So we fasted, and besought our God for this: and he was entreated of us.

24 Then I separated twelve of the chief of the Priests, Sherebiah, *and* Hashabiah, and ten of their brethren with them,

25 And weighed them the silver and the gold and the vessels, *even* the offering of the house of our God, *which* the king and his counselors and his Princes, and all Israel that were present had offered.

26 And I weighed unto their hand six hundred and fifty ¹talents of silver, and in silver vessel an hundred talents, *and* in gold, an hundred talents,

27 And twenty basins of gold, of a thousand ¹drams, and two vessels of shining brass very good, and precious as gold.

28 ¶ And I said unto them, Ye are consecrated unto the Lord, and the vessels *are* consecrated, and the gold and the silver *are* freely offered unto the Lord God of your fathers.

29 Watch ye, and keep *them* until ye weigh them before the chief Priests and the Levites, and the chief fathers of Israel in Jerusalem in the chambers of the house of the Lord.

30 So the Priests and the Levites received the weight of the silver, and of the gold, and of the vessels to bring *them* to Jerusalem, unto the house of our God.

31 ¶ Then we departed from the river of Ahavah on the twelfth *day* of the first month, to go unto Jerusalem, and the hand of our God was upon us, and delivered us from the hand of the enemy, and of such as laid ¹wait by the way.

32 And we came to Jerusalem, and abode there three days.

33 And on the fourth day was the silver weighed, and the gold, and the vessel, in the house of our God, by the hand of Meremoth the son of Uriah the Priest, and with him *was* Eleazar the son of Phinehas, and with them *was* Jozabad the son of Jeshua, and Noadiah the son of Binnui the ¹Levites,

34 By number and by weight of every one, and all the weight was written at the same time.

35 Also the children of the captivity, which were come out of captivity, offered burnt offerings unto the God of Israel, twelve bullocks for all Israel, ninety and six rams, seventy and seven lambs, *and* twelve he goats for sin: all *was* a burnt offering of the Lord.

36 And they delivered the King's commission unto the King's officers, and to the captains beyond the river: and they promoted the people, and the house of God.

9 *1 Ezra complaineth on the people that had turned themselves from God, and married with the Gentiles. 5 He prayeth unto God.*

1 When as these things were done, the rulers came to me, saying, The people of Israel, and the Priests, and the Levites are not ¹separated from the people of the lands (as touching their abominations) *to wit*, of the Canaanites, the Hittites, the Perizzites, the Jebusites, the Ammonites, the Moabites, the Egyptians, and the Amorites.

2 For they have taken their daughters to themselves, and to their sons, and they have mixed the holy seed with the people of the lands, and the hand of the ¹Princes and rulers have been chief in this trespass.

3 But when I heard this saying, I rent my clothes and my garment, and plucked off the hair of mine head, and of my beard, and sat down ¹astonied.

4 And there assembled unto me all that feared the words of the God of Israel, because of the transgression of them of the captivity. And I sat down astonied until the ᵃevening sacrifice.

5 And at the evening sacrifice I rose up from mine heaviness, and when I had rent my clothes and my garment, I fell upon my knees, and spread out mine hands unto the Lord my God,

6 And said, O my God, I am confounded and ashamed to lift up mine eyes unto thee my God: for our iniquities are increased over ¹our head, and our trespass is grown up unto the ²heaven.

7 From the days of our fathers have we been in a great trespass unto this day, and for our iniquities have we, our kings, *and* our Priests been delivered into the hand of the kings of the lands, unto the sword, into captivity, into a spoil, and into confusion of face, as *appeareth* this day.

8 And now for a little space grace hath been showed from the Lord our God, in causing a remnant to escape, and in giving us a ¹nail in his holy place, that our God may light our eyes, and give us a little reviving in our servitude.

9 For *though* we were bondmen, yet our God hath

8:26 ¹ Read 1 Kings 9:14.
8:27 ¹ Read Ezra 2:29.
8:31 ¹ This declared that their journey was full of danger, and yet God delivered them according to their prayer.
8:33 ¹ This was a token of a good conscience and of his integrity, that he would have witnesses of his fidelity.
9:1 ¹ From the time they came home under Zerubbabel until the coming of Ezra, they had degenerated contrary to the Law of God,

and married where it was not lawful, Deut. 7:3.
9:2 ¹ That is, the governors are the chief beginners hereof.
9:3 ¹ As one doubting whether God would continue his benefits towards us, or else destroy this which he had begun.
9:6 ¹ That is, we are drowned in sin.
² They so exceed that they cannot grow greater.
9:8 ¹ In giving us a resting place. It is a similitude taken of them that remain still in a place, which smite nails to hang things upon, Isa. 22:23.

not forsaken us in our bondage, but hath inclined mercy unto us in the sight of the kings of Persia, to give us life, *and* to erect the house of our God, and to redress the desolate places thereof, and to give us a wall in Judah and in Jerusalem.

10 And now, our God, what shall we say after this? for we have forsaken thy commandments,

11 Which thou hast commanded by thy servants the Prophets, saying, [b]The land whereunto ye go to possess it, is an unclean land, because of the filthiness of the people of the lands, which by their abominations, *and* by their uncleanness have filled it from corner to corner.

12 Now therefore shall ye not give your daughters unto their sons, neither shall ye take their daughters unto your sons, nor seek their 'peace nor wealth forever, that ye may be strong and eat the goodness of the land, and leave it for an inheritance to your sons forever.

13 And after all that is come upon us for our evil deeds, and for our great trespasses, (seeing that thou our God hast stayed *us from being* beneath [1]for our iniquities, and hast given us such deliverance.)

14 Should we return to break thy commandments, and join in affinity with the people of such abominations? wouldest not thou be angry toward us till thou hadst consumed *us*, so that there *should be* no remnant nor any escaping?

15 O Lord God of Israel, thou art just, for we have been [1]reserved to escape, as *appeareth* this day: behold, we are before thee in our trespass: therefore we cannot stand before thee because of it.

10

1 The people repent and turn, and put away their strange wives.

1 While Ezra prayed thus, and [1]confessed himself weeping, and falling down before the house of God, there assembled unto him of Israel a very great Congregation of men and women and children: for the people wept with a great lamentation.

2 Then Shechaniah the son of Jehiel one of the sons of Elam answered, and said to Ezra, We have trespassed against our God, and have taken strange wives of the people of the land, yet now there is [1]hope in Israel concerning this.

3 Now therefore let us make a covenant with our

[b] Exod. 23:32
Exod. 34:12, 15-16
Deut. 7:13
[c] Deut. 23:6

God, to put away [1]all the wives (and such as are born of them) according to the counsel of the Lord, and of those that fear the commandments of our God, and let it be done according to the Law.

4 Arise: for the matter [1]belongeth unto thee: we also will be with thee: be of comfort and do it.

5 ¶ Then arose Ezra, and caused the chief Priests, the Levites, and all Israel, to swear that they would do according to this word. So they sware.

6 And Ezra rose up from before the house of God, and went into the chamber of Johanan the son of Eliashib: he went even thither, *but* he did eat neither bread nor drunk water: for he mourned, because of the transgression of them of the captivity.

7 And they caused a proclamation to go throughout Judah and Jerusalem, unto [1]all them of the captivity, that they should assemble themselves unto Jerusalem.

8 And whosoever would not come within three days according to the counsel of the Princes and Elders, all his substance should be [1]forfeit, and he should be separate from the Congregation of them of the captivity.

9 ¶ Then all the men of Judah and Benjamin assembled themselves unto Jerusalem within three days, which was the twentieth *day* of the [1]ninth month, and all the people sat in the street of the house of God, trembling for this matter, and for the [2]rain.

10 And Ezra the Priest stood up, and said unto them, Ye have transgressed, and have taken strange wives, to [1]increase the trespass of Israel.

11 Now therefore [1]give praise unto the Lord God of your fathers, and do his will, and separate yourselves from the people of the land, and from the strange wives.

12 And all the Congregation answered, and said with a loud voice, So will we do according to thy words unto us.

13 But the people are many, and it is a rainy weather, and we are not able to stand without, neither *is it* the work of one day or two: for we are many that have offended in this thing.

14 Let our rulers stand therefore [1]before all the Congregation, and let all them which have taken strange wives in our cities, come at the time appointed, and with [them] the Elders of every city and the judges thereof, till the fierce wrath of our God for this matter turn away from us.

9:13 [1] Hast not utterly cast us down and destroyed us for our sins, Deut. 28:13.

9:15 [1] He showeth that God is just in punishing his people, and yet merciful in reserving a residue in whom he showeth favor.

10:1 [1] He confessed his sins, and the sins of the people.

10:2 [1] Meaning, that God would receive them to mercy.

10:3 [1] Which are strangers and married contrary to the Law of God.

10:4 [1] Because God hath given thee authority and learning to persuade the people herein, and to command them.

10:7 [1] Hebrew, *the sons of the captivity.*

10:8 [1] Or, condemned.

10:9 [1] Which contained part of November and part of December.

[2] For the season was given to rain and so the weather was more sharp and cold, and also their conscience touched them.

10:10 [1] Ye have laid one sin upon another.

10:11 [1] Read Josh. 7:19.

10:14 [1] Let them be appointed to examine this matter.

15 Then were appointed Jonathan the son of Asahel, and Jahaziah the son of Tikvah over this matter, and Meshullam and Shabbethai the Levites helped them.

16 And they of the captivity did so, and [1]departed, *even* Ezra the Priest, *and* the men *that were* chief fathers to the family of their fathers by name, and sat down in the first day of the tenth month to examine the matter.

17 And until the first day of the first month they were finishing the business with all the men that had taken strange wives.

18 And of the sons of the Priests there were men found, that had taken strange wives, *to wit*, of the sons of Jeshua, the son of Jozadak, and of his brethren, Maaseiah, Eliezer, and Jarib, and Gedaliah.

19 And they gave [1]their hands, that they would put away their wives, and they that had trespassed *gave* a ram for their trespass.

20 And of the sons of Immer, Honani, and Zebadiah.

21 And of the sons of Harim, Maaseiah, and Elijah, and Shemaiah, and Jehiel, and Uzziah.

22 And of the sons of Pashur, Elioenai, Maaseiah, Ishmael, Nethanel, Jozabad, and Elasah.

23 And of the Levites, Jozabad and Shimei, and Kelaiah, (which is Kelita) Pethahiah, Judah and Eliezer.

24 And of the singers, Eliashib. And of the porters, Shallum, and Telem, and Uri.

25 And of [1]Israel: of the sons of Parosh, Ramiah, and Jeziah, and Malchiah, and Mijamin, and Eleazar, and Malchijah, and Benaiah.

26 And of the sons of Elam, Mattaniah, Zechariah, and Jehiel, and Abdi, and Jeremoth, and Eliah.

27 And of the sons of Zattu, Elioenai, Eliashib, Mattaniah, and Jerimoth, and Zabad, and Aziza.

28 And of the sons of Bebai, Jehohanan, Hananiah, Zabbai, Athlai.

29 And of the sons of Bani, Meshullam, Malluch, and Adaiah, Jashub, and Sheal, Jeremoth.

30 And of the sons of [1]Pahath-Moab, Adna, and Chelal, Benaiah, Maaseiah, Mattaniah, Bezaleel, and Binnui, and Manasseh.

31 And of the sons of Harim, Eliezer, Ishijah, Malchiah, Shemaiah, Shimeon,

32 Benjamin, Malluch, Shamariah.

33 Of the sons of Hashum, Mattenai, Mattattah, Zabad, Eliphelet, Jeremai, Manasseh, Shimei.

34 Of the sons of Bani, Maadai, Amram, and Uel,

35 Banaiah, Bedeiah, Chelluh,

36 Vaniah, Meremoth, Eliashib,

37 Mattaniah, Mattenai, and Jaasai,

38 And Bani, and Binnui, Shimei,

39 And Shelemiah, and Nathan, and Adaiah,

40 Machnadebai, Shashai, Sharai,

41 Azarel, and Shelemiah, Shemariah,

42 Shallum, Amariah, Joseph.

43 Of the sons of Nebo, Jeiel, Mattithiah, Zabad, Zebina, Jadai, and Joel, Benaiah.

44 All these had taken strange wives: and among them were women that had [1]children.

10:16 [1] They went to the chief cities to sit on this matter which was three months in finishing.
10:19 [1] As a token that they would keep promise and do it.
10:25 [1] Meaning, of the common people: for before he spake of the Priests and Levites.
10:30 [1] Or, the captain of Moab.
10:44 [1] Which also were made illegitimate because the marriage was unlawful.

NEHEMIAH

1

4 Nehemiah bewaileth the calamity of Jerusalem. 5 He confesseth the sins of the people, and praiseth God for them.

CHAPTER 1
a Dan. 9:4
b Deut. 29:21,28
c Deut. 30:4

1 The words of Nehemiah the son of Hachaliah. In the month ¹Chislev, in the twentieth year, as I was in the palace of Shushan,

2 Came Hanani, one of my ¹brethren, he and the men of Judah, and I asked them concerning the Jews that were delivered, which were of the residue of the captivity, and concerning Jerusalem.

3 And they said unto me, The residue that are left of the captivity there in the ¹province, *are* in great affliction and in reproach, and the wall of Jerusalem *is* broken down, and the gates thereof are burnt with fire.

4 And when I heard these words, I sat down and wept, and mourned *certain* days, and I fasted and prayed before the God of heaven,

5 And said, ªO Lord God of heaven, the great and terrible God, that keepeth covenant and mercy for them that love him, and observe his commandments,

6 I pray thee let thine ears be attent, and thine eyes open, to hear the prayer of thy servant, which I pray before thee daily, day and night for the children of Israel thy servants, and confess the sins of the children of Israel, which we have sinned against thee, both I and my father's house have sinned:

7 We have ¹grievously sinned against thee, and have not kept the commandments, nor the statutes, nor the judgments, which thou commandedst thy servant Moses.

8 I beseech thee, remember the word that thou commandedst thy servant Moses, saying, Ye will transgress, and ᵇI will scatter you abroad among the people.

9 But if ye return unto me, and keep my commandments, and do them, ᶜthough your scattering were to the uttermost part of the heaven, *yet* will I gather you from thence, and will bring you unto the place that I have chosen to place my Name there.

10 Now these are thy servants and thy people whom thou hast redeemed by thy great power, and by thy mighty hand.

11 O Lord, I beseech thee, let thine ear now hearken to the prayer of thy servant, and to the prayer of thy servants, who desire to ¹fear thy Name, and I pray thee, cause thy servant to prosper this day, and give him favor in the presence of ²this man: for I was the king's butler.

2

1 After Nehemiah had obtained letters of Artaxerxes, 11 he came to Jerusalem, 17 and built the walls.

1 Now in the month ¹Nisan in the twentieth year of king ²Artaxerxes, the wine *stood* before him, and I took up the wine, and gave it unto the king. Now I was not *before time* sad in his presence.

2 And the king said unto me, Why is thy countenance sad, seeing thou art not sick? this is nothing, but sorrow of heart. Then was I sore afraid,

3 And I said to the King, God save the king forever: why should not my countenance be sad, when the city *and* house of the sepulchers of my fathers lieth waste, and the gates thereof are devoured with fire?

4 And the king said unto me, For what thing doest thou require? Then I prayed ¹to the God of heaven,

5 And said unto the king, If it please the king, and if thy servant have found favor in thy sight, *I desire* that thou wouldest send me to Judah unto the city of the sepulchers of my fathers, that I may build it.

6 And the King said unto me, (the Queen also sitting by him:) How long shall thy journey be? and when wilt thou come again? So it pleased the king, and he sent me, and I set him a time.

7 After I said unto the King, If it please the King, let them give me letters to the captains beyond the ¹River, that they may convey me over, till I come into Judah,

8 And letters unto Asaph the keeper of the king's ¹park, that he may give me timber to build the gates of the palace (which appertained to the house) and for the walls of the city, and for the house that I shall enter into. And the king gave me according to ²the

---

1:1 ¹ Which containeth part of November and part of December, and was their ninth month.
1:2 ¹ A Jew as I was.
1:3 ¹ Meaning, in Judea.
1:7 ¹ Hebrew, *corrupted.*
1:11 ¹ That is, to worship thee.
    ² To wit, the king Artaxerxes.

2:1 ¹ Which was the first month of the year, and containeth part of March and part of April.
    ² Who is also called Darius, read Ezra 7:1, and was the son of Hystaspis.
2:4 ¹ I desired God in mine heart to prosper mine enterprise.
2:7 ¹ Or, Euphrates.
2:8 ¹ Or, Paradise.
    ² As God moved me to ask, and as he gave me good success therein.

good hand of my God upon me.

9 ¶ Then came I to the captains beyond the River, and gave them the king's letters. And the king had sent captains of the army and horsemen with me.

10 But [1]Sanballat the Horonite, and Tobiah a servant an Ammonite heard it, and it grieved them sore, that there was come a man which sought the wealth of the children of Israel.

11 So I came to Jerusalem, and was there three days.

12 And I rose in the night, I, and a few men with me: for I told no man, what God had put in mine heart to do at Jerusalem, and there was not a beast with me, save the beast whereon I rode.

13 And I went out by night by the gate of the valley, and came before the dragon well, and to the dung port, and viewed the walls of Jerusalem, how they were broken down, and the ports thereof devoured with the fire.

14 Then I went forth unto the gate of the [1]fountain, and to the king's fish pool, and there was no room for the beast that was under me to pass.

15 Then went I up in the night by the brook, and viewed the wall, and turned back, and coming back, I entered by the gate of the valley, and returned.

16 And the rulers knew not whither I was gone, nor what I did, neither did I as yet tell it unto the Jews, nor to the Priests, nor to the noble men, nor to the rulers, nor to the rest that labored in the work.

17 Afterward I said unto them, Ye see the misery that we are in, how Jerusalem lieth waste, and the gates thereof are burnt with fire: come, and let us build the wall of Jerusalem, that we be no more [1]a reproach.

18 Then I told them of the hand of my God, (which was good over me) and also of the king's words that he had spoken unto me. And they said, Let us rise, and build. So they [1]strengthened their hand to good.

19 But when Sanballat the Horonite, and Tobiah the servant an Ammonite, and [1]Geshem the Arabian heard it, they mocked us, and despised us, and said, What a thing is this that ye do? Will ye [2]rebel against

CHAPTER 3
[a] Isa. 22:11

the king?

20 Then answered I them, and said to them, The God of heaven, he will prosper us, and we his servants will rise up and build: but as for you, ye have no portion nor right, nor [1]memorial in Jerusalem.

3

The number of them that built the walls.

1 Then arose Eliashib the high Priest with his brethren the Priests, and they built the sheep gate: they [1]repaired it, and set up the doors thereof: even unto the tower of Meah repaired they it, *and* unto the tower of Hananel.

2 And next unto him built the men of Jericho, and beside him Zaccur the son of Imri.

3 But the fish port did the sons of Senaah build, which also laid the beams thereof, and set on the doors thereof, the locks thereof, and the bars thereof.

4 And next unto them fortified Meremoth, the son of Urijah, the son of Koz: and next unto them fortified Meshullam, the son of Berechiah, the son of Meshezabel: and next unto them fortified Zadok, the son of Baana:

5 And next unto them fortified the Tekoites: but the great men of them [1]put not their necks to the works of their lords.

6 And the gate of the [a]old *fish pool* fortified Jehoiada the son of Paseah, and Meshullam the son of Besodeiah: they laid the beams thereof, and set on the doors thereof, and the locks thereof, and the bars thereof.

7 Next unto them also fortified Melatiah the Gibeonite, and Jadon the Meronothite, men of Gibeon, and of Mizpah, unto the [1]throne of the Duke, *which was* beyond the River.

8 Next unto him fortified Uzziel the son of Harhaiah [1]of the goldsmiths: next unto him also fortified Hananiah the son [2]of Harakkahim, and they repaired Jerusalem unto the broad wall.

9 Also next unto them fortified Rephaiah, the son of Hur, the ruler of the half part of Jerusalem.

10 And next unto him fortified Jedaiah the son of Harumaph, even over against his house: and next unto him fortified Hattush the son of Hashabniah.

2:10 [1] These were great enemies to the Jews, and labored always both by force and subtlety to overcome them, and Tobiah, because his wife was a Jewess, had advertisement ever of their affairs, and so wrought them great trouble.
2:14 [1] Or, conduit.
2:17 [1] That is, contemned of other nations, as though God had forsaken us.
2:18 [1] They were encouraged, and gave themselves to do well, and to travel in this worthy enterprise.
2:19 [1] These were three chief governors under the king of Persia beyond Euphrates.
[2] Thus the wicked when they will burden the children of God, ever lay treason unto their charge, both because it maketh them most

odious to the world, and also stirreth the hatred of princes most against them.
2:20 [1] Neither are ye of the number of the children of God (to whom he hath appointed this city only) neither did any of your predecessors ever fear God.
3:1 [1] In Hebrew, they sanctified it, that is, they finished it, and so dedicated it to the Lord by prayer, in desiring him to maintain it.
3:5 [1] The rich and mighty would not obey them which were appointed officers in this work, neither would they help thereunto.
3:7 [1] Unto the place where the Duke was wont to sit in judgment, who governed the country in their absence.
3:8 [1] Or, Zorephim.
[2] Or, of the Apothecaries.

11 Malchijah the son of Harim, and Hashub the son of Pahath-Moab fortified the second [1]portion, and the tower of the furnaces.

12 Next unto him also fortified Shallum the son of Hallohesh, the ruler of the half part of Jerusalem, he and his daughters.

13 The valley gate fortified Hanun, and the inhabitants of Zanoah: they built it, and set on the doors thereof, the locks thereof, and the bars thereof, even a thousand cubits on the wall unto the dung port.

14 But the dung port fortified Malchijah the son of Rechab, the ruler of the fourth part of Beth Haccarem: he built it, and set on the doors thereof, the locks thereof, and the bars thereof.

15 But the gate of the fountain fortified Shallun the son of Col-Hozeh, the ruler of the fourth part of Mizpah: he built it, and covered it, and set on the doors thereof, the locks thereof, and the bars thereof, and the wall unto the fish pool of [1]Shelah by the king's garden, and unto the steps that go down from the city of David.

16 After him fortified Nehemiah the son of Azbuk, the ruler of the half part of Beth Zur until the other side over against the sepulchers of David and to the fish pool that was repaired, and unto the house of the mighty.

17 After him fortified the Levites, Rehum the son of Bani, and the next unto him fortified Hashabiah the ruler of the half part of Keilah in his quarter.

18 After him fortified their brethren: Bavai, the son of Henadad the ruler of the half part of Keilah:

19 And next unto him fortified Ezer, the son of Jeshua the ruler of Mizpah, the other portion over against the going up to the [1]corner of the armor.

20 After him was earnest Baruch the son of Zabbai, *and* fortified another portion from the corner unto the door of the house of Eliashib the high Priest.

21 After him fortified Meremoth the son of Urijah, the son of Koz, another portion from the door of the house of Eliashib, even as long as the house of Eliashib extended.

22 After him also fortified the Priests, the men of [1]the plain.

23 After them fortified Benjamin, and Hasshub over against their house: after him fortified Azariah the son of Maaseiah, the son of Ananiah, by his house.

24 After him fortified Binnui, the son of Henadad

another portion, from the house of Azariah unto the turning and unto the corner.

25 Palal, the son of Uzai, from over against the corner, and the high tower, that lieth out from the King's house, which is beside the court of the prison. After him Pedaiah the son of Parosh.

26 And the [1]Nethinim they dwelt in the fortress unto the *place* over against the water gate Eastward, and to the tower that lieth out.

27 After him fortified the Tekoites another portion over against the great tower that lieth out even unto the wall of the fortress.

28 From above the horse gate forth fortified the Priests, every one over against his house.

29 After them fortified Zadok the son of Immer over against his house: and after him fortified Shemaiah the son of Shechaniah the keeper of the East gate.

30 After him fortified Hananiah the son of Shelemiah, and Hanun the son of Zalaph, the [1]sixth, another portion: after him fortified Meshullam, the son of Berechiah, over against his chamber.

31 After him fortified Malchijah the goldsmith's son, until the house of the Nethinim, and of the Merchants over against the gate [1]Miphkad, and to the chamber in the corner.

32 And between the chamber of the corner unto the sheep gate fortified the goldsmiths and the merchants.

4

7 The building of Jerusalem is hindered, 15 but God breaketh their enterprise. 17 The Jews build with one hand, and hold their weapons in the other.

1 But when Sanballat heard that we built the wall, then was he wroth and sore grieved, and mocked the Jews,

2 And said before his [1]brethren and the army of Samaria, thus he said, What do these [2]weak Jews? will they fortify themselves? will they sacrifice? will they finish it in a day? will they make the stones whole again out of the heaps of dust, seeing they are burnt?

3 And Tobiah the Ammonite *was* beside him, and said, Although they build, *yet* if a fox go up, he shall even break down their stony wall.

4 [1]Hear, O our God (for we are despised) and turn their shame upon their own head, and give them unto a prey [2]in the land of their captivity,

---

3:11 [1] Or, measure.

3:15 [1] Or, Shoa.

3:19 [1] Where the weapons and armor of the city lay.

3:22 [1] Which dwelt in the plain country by Jordan and Jericho.

3:26 [1] Read Ezra 2:43.

3:30 [1] Meaning the sixth of his sons.

3:31 [1] Which was the place of judgment or execution.

4:2 [1] Of his companions that dwelt in Samaria.

[2] Thus the wicked that consider not that God's power is ever in a readiness for the defense of his, mock them as though they were weak and feeble.

4:4 [1] This is the remedy that the children of God have against the derision and threatenings of their enemies, to flee to God by prayer.

[2] Let them be spoiled and led away captive.

5 And cover not their ¹iniquity, neither let their sin be put out in thy presence: for they have provoked *us* before the builders.

6 So we built the wall, and all the wall was joined unto the ¹half thereof, and the heart of the people was to work.

7 ¶ But when Sanballat, and Tobiah, and the Arabians, and the Ammonites, and the Ashdodims heard that the walls of Jerusalem were repaired, (for the breaches began to be stopped) then they were very wroth,

8 And conspired all together to come and to fight against Jerusalem, and to ¹hinder them.

9 Then we prayed unto our God, and set watchmen by them, day and night, because of them.

10 And Judah said, The strength of the bearers is weakened, and there *is* much earth, so that we are not able to build the wall.

11 Also our adversaries had said, They shall not know, neither see, till we come into the midst of them, and slay them, and cause the work to cease.

12 But when the Jews (which dwelt beside them) came, they told us ¹ten times, ²From all places, whence ye shall return, *they will be* upon us.

13 Therefore set I in the lower places behind the wall upon the tops of the stones, and placed the people by their families, with their swords, their spears, and their bows.

14 Then I beheld, and rose up, and said unto the princes, and to the rulers, and to the rest of the people, Be not afraid of them: ¹remember the great Lord, and fearful, and fight for your brethren, your sons, and your daughters, your wives, and your houses.

15 And when our enemies heard that it was known unto us, then God brought their counsel to nought, and we turned all again to the wall, every one unto his work.

16 And from that day half of the young men did the labor, and the other half part of them held the spears, and shields, and bows, and habergeons: and the Rulers *stood* ¹behind all the house of Judah.

17 They that built on the wall, and they that bare burdens, *and* they that laded, did the work with one hand, and with the other held the sword.

18 For every one of the builders *had* his sword girded on his loins, and *so* built: and he that blew the trumpet, *was* beside me.

19 Then said I unto the Princes, and to the rulers, and to the rest of the people, The work is great and large, and we are separated upon the wall, one far from another.

20 In what place *therefore* ye hear the sound of the trumpet, ¹resort ye thither unto us: our God shall fight for us.

21 So we labored in the work, and half of them held the spears, from the appearing of the morning, till the stars came forth.

22 And at the same time said I unto the people, Let everyone with his servant lodge within Jerusalem, that they may be a watch for us in the night, and labor in the day.

23 So neither I, nor my brethren, nor my servants, nor the men of the ward (which followed me) none of us did put off our clothes, *save* everyone put them off ¹for washing.

5 *1 The people are oppressed and in necessity.   6 Nehemiah remedieth it.   14 He took not the portion of others that had ruled before, lest he should grieve the people.*

1 Now there was a great cry of the people, and of their wives ¹against their brethren the Jews.

2 For there were that said, We, our sons and our daughters are many, therefore we take up ¹corn, that we may eat and live.

3 And there were that said, We must gage our lands, and our vineyards, and our houses, and take up corn for the famine.

4 There were also that said, We have borrowed money for the king's ¹tribute *upon* our lands and our vineyards.

5 And now our flesh *is* as ¹the flesh of our brethren, *and* our sons as their sons: and lo, we bring into subjection our sons and our daughters, as servants, and there be of our daughters *now* in subjection, and there *is* no power ²in our hands: for other men *have* our lands and our vineyards.

6 Then was I very angry when I heard their cry and these words.

4:5 ¹ Let the plagues declare to the world that they set themselves against thee and against thy Church: that he prayeth only having respect to God's glory and not for any private affection, or grudge.
4:6 ¹ Or, half height.
4:8 ¹ Hebrew, *make to stay*, meaning the people.
4:12 ¹ That is, oftentimes.
² They which brought the tidings, said thus, When you leave your work, and go either to eat or to rest, your enemies will assail you.
4:14 ¹ Who is ever at hand to deliver his out of danger: and therefore seeing they should fight for the maintenance of God's glory, and for the preservation of their own lives and of theirs, he encourageth them to play the valiant men.

4:16 ¹ To oversee them and to encourage them to their work.
4:20 ¹ Meaning, to resist their enemies, if need required.
4:23 ¹ That is, when they purified themselves, or else when they washed their clothes.
5:1 ¹ Against the rich which oppressed them.
5:2 ¹ This is the complaint of the people, showing to what extremity they were brought unto.
5:4 ¹ To pay our tribute to the king of the Persians, which was exacted yearly of us.
5:5 ¹ By nature the rich is no better than the poor.
² We are not able to redeem them, but for poverty are constrained to hire them to others.

7 And I thought in my mind, and I rebuked the princes, and the rulers, and said unto them, You lay [1]burdens every one upon his brethren: and I set a great [2]assembly against them,

8 And I said unto them, We (according to our ability) have redeemed our brethren the Jews, which were sold unto the heathen: and will you sell your brethren again, or shall they be [1]sold unto us? Then held they their peace, and could not answer.

9 [1]I said also, That which ye do, is not good. Ought ye not to walk in the fear of our God, for the [2]reproach of the heathen our enemies?

10 For even I, my brethren, and my servants do lend them money and corn: I pray you, let us leave off this [1]burden.

11 Restore, I pray you, unto them this day their lands, their vineyards, their olives, and their houses, and remit the hundredth part of the silver and of the corn, of the wine, and of the oil [1]that ye exact of them.

12 Then said they, We will restore it, and will not require it of them: we will do as thou hast said. Then I called the Priests and caused them to swear, that they should do according to this promise.

13 So I shook my lap, and said, So let God shake out every man that will not perform this promise, from his house, and from his labor: even thus let him be shaken out and emptied. And all the Congregation said, Amen, and praised the Lord: and the people did according to this promise.

14 And from the time that the King gave me charge to be governor in the land of Judah, from the twentieth year, even unto the two and thirtieth year of King Artaxerxes, that is, twelve years, I, and my brethren have not eaten the [1]bread of the governor.

15 For the former governors that were before me, had been chargeable unto the people, and had taken of them bread and wine, besides forty shekels of silver: yea, and their servants bare rule over the people: but so did not I, because of the fear of God.

16 But rather I fortified a portion in the work of this wall, and we bought no land, and all my servants came thither together unto the work.

17 Moreover there were at my table an hundred and fifty of the Jews, and rulers, which came unto us from among the heathen that are about us.

18 And there was prepared daily an ox, and six chosen sheep, and birds were prepared for me, and [1]within ten days wine for all [2]in abundance. Yet for all this I required not the bread of the governor: for the bondage was grievous unto this people.

19 Remember me, O my God, in goodness, according to all that I have done for this people.

6 *8 Nehemiah answereth with great wisdom and zeal to his adversary. 11 He is not discouraged by the false Prophets.*

1 And when Sanballat, and Tobiah, and Geshem the Arabian, and the rest of our enemies heard that I had built the wall, and that there were no more [1]breaches therein (though at that time I had not set up the doors upon the gates)

2 Then sent Sanballat and Geshem unto me, saying, come thou that we may meet together in the villages in the plain of Ono: and they thought to do me evil.

3 Therefore I sent messengers unto them, saying, I have a great work to do, and I cannot come down: [1]why should the work cease, while I leave it and come down to you?

4 Yet they sent unto me four times after this sort. And I answered them after the same manner.

5 Then sent Sanballat his servant after this sort unto me the fifth time, with an open letter in his hand,

6 Wherein was written, It is reported among the heathen, and [1]Gashmu hath said it, that thou and the Jews think to rebel, for the which cause thou buildest the wall, and thou wilt be their king according to these [2]words.

7 Thou hast also ordained [1]the Prophets to preach of thee at Jerusalem, saying, There is a King in Judah: and now according to these words it shall come to the King's ears: come now therefore, and let us take

---

5:7 [1] You press them with usury, and seek how to bring all things into your hands.

[2] Both because they should be moved with pity, seeing how many were by them oppressed, and also hear the judgment of others, which should be as it were witnesses of their dealings toward their brethren.

5:8 [1] Seeing God hath once delivered them from the bondage of the heathen, shall we make them our slaves?

5:9 [1] Meaning, Nehemiah.

[2] Who by this occasion will blaspheme the Name of God, seeing that our acts are no better than theirs.

5:10 [1] Or, usury.

5:11 [1] Which ye take of them for the loan.

5:14 [1] I received not that portion and diet, which the governors that were before me exacted, wherein he declareth that he rather sought the wealth of the people than his own commodity.

5:18 [1] Or, once in ten days.

[2] Whereas at other times they had by measure, at this time they had most liberally.

6:1 [1] That is, that they were joined together, as Neh. 4:6.

6:3 [1] Meaning, that if he should obey their request, the work which God had appointed, should cease: showing hereby that we should not commit ourselves to the hands of the wicked.

6:6 [1] Or, Geshem.

[2] As the same goeth.

6:7 [1] Thou hast bribed and set up false prophets, to make thyself king, and so to defraud the king of Persia of that subjection which you owe unto him.

counsel together.

8 Then I sent unto him, saying, It is not done according to these words that thou sayest: for thou feignest them of thine own heart.

9 For all they afraid us, saying, Their hands shall be weakened from the work, and it shall not be done: now therefore [1]encourage thou me.

10 ¶ And I came to the house of Shemaiah the son of Delaiah the son of Mehetabel, and he was [1]shut up, and he said, Let us come together into the house of God in the midst of the Temple, and shut the doors of the Temple: for they will come to slay thee: yea, in the night will they come to kill thee.

11 Then I said, [1]Should such a man as I, flee? Who is he, being as I am, that would go into the Temple to live? I will not go in.

12 And lo, I perceived that God had not sent him, but that he pronounced this prophecy against me: for Tobiah and Sanballat had hired him.

13 Therefore was he hired, that I might be afraid, and do thus, and sin, and that they might have an evil report, that they might reproach me.

14 My God, remember thou Tobiah, and Sanballat according unto these their works, and Noadiah the [1]Prophetess also, and the rest of the prophets that would have put me in fear.

15 ¶ Notwithstanding the wall was finished on the five and twentieth *day* of [1]Elul, in two and [2]fifty days.

16 And when all our enemies heard thereof, *even* all the heathen that were about us, they were afraid, and their courage failed them: for they knew that this work was wrought by our God.

17 And in these days *were* there many of the princes of Judah, whose [1]letters went unto Tobiah, and those of Tobiah came unto them.

18 For there *were* many in Judah, that were sworn unto him: for he was the son in law of Shechaniah, the son of Arah: and his son Jehohanan had the daughter of Meshullam, the son of Berechiah.

19 Yea, they spake in his praise before me, and told him my words, *and* Tobiah sent letters to put me in fear.

CHAPTER 7
[a] Ezra 2:2

7

[1] After the wall once built, is the watch appointed.   6 They that returned from the captivity are numbered.

1 Now when the wall was built, and I had set up the doors, and the porters, and the singers and the Levites were appointed,

2 Then I commanded my brother Hanani and Hananiah, the prince of the palace in Jerusalem (for he was doubtless a faithful man, and feared God above many)

3 And I said unto them, Let not the gates of Jerusalem be opened, until the heat of the sun: and while [1]they stand by, let them shut the doors, and [2]make them fast: and I appointed wards of the inhabitants of Jerusalem, everyone in his ward, and everyone over against his house.

4 Now the city *was* large and great, but the people *were* few therein, and the houses were not built.

5 And my God put into mine heart, and I gathered the princes, and the rulers, and the people, to count their genealogies: and I found a book of the genealogy of them, [a]which came up at the first, and found written therein,

6 These are the [1]sons of the province that came up from the captivity that was carried away (whom Nebuchadnezzar king of Babel had carried away) and they returned to Jerusalem and to Judah, every one unto his city.

7 They which came with Zerubbabel, Jeshua, Nehemiah, [1]Azariah, Raamiah, Nahamani, Mordecai, Bilshan, Mispereth, Bigvai, Nehum, Baanah. This is the number of the men of the people of Israel.

8 The sons of Parosh, two thousand an hundred seventy and two.

9 The sons of Shephatiah, three hundred seventy and two.

10 The sons of Arah, six hundred fifty and two.

11 The sons of [1]Pahath-Moab of the sons of Jeshua and Joab, two thousand eight hundred and eighteen.

12 The sons of Elam, a thousand two hundred fifty and four.

13 The sons of Zattu, eight hundred and five and forty.

14 The sons of Zaccai, seven hundred and three-

6:9 [1] Hebrew, *strengthen thou mine hand.*

6:10 [1] As though he would be secret, to the intent that he might pray unto God with greater liberty, and receive some revelation, which in him was but hypocrisy.

6:11 [1] He doubted not but God was able to preserve him, and knew that if he had obeyed this counsel he should have discouraged all the people: thus God giveth power to his to resist false prophecies, though they seem to have never so great probability.

6:14 [1] Very grief caused him to pray against such, which under the pretence of being the ministers of God, were adversaries to his glory, and went about to overthrow his Church, declaring also hereby that where there is one true minister of God, the devil hath a great sort

of hirelings.

6:15 [1] Which was the sixth month and contained part of August, and part of September.

  [2] After that I had sent Sanballat his answer.

6:17 [1] Thus the Church of God hath evermore enemies within itself, which are more dangerous than the outward and professed enemy.

7:3 [1] To wit, they that are mentioned, verse 2.

  [2] Hebrew, *hold them*, meaning, till the bars were put in.

7:6 [1] That is, the inhabitants of Judah.

7:7 [1] Azariah in Ezra is called Seraiah, and Raamiah, Reelaiah, Ezra 2:2.

7:11 [1] Or, the captain of Moab.

score.

15 The sons of Binnui, six hundred and eight and forty.

16 The sons of Bebai, six hundred and eight and twenty.

17 The sons of Azgad, two thousand three hundred and two and twenty.

18 The sons of Adonikam, six hundred threescore and seven.

19 The sons of Bigvai, two thousand threescore and seven.

20 The sons of Adin, six hundred and five and fifty.

21 The sons of Ater of Hezekiah, ninety and eight.

22 The sons of Hashum, three hundred and eight and twenty.

23 The sons of Bezai, three hundred and four and twenty.

24 The sons of Hariph, an hundred and twelve.

25 The ¹sons of Gibeon, ninety and five.

26 The men of Bethlehem and Netophah, an hundred fourscore and eight.

27 The men of Anathoth, an hundred and eight and twenty.

28 The men of Beth Azmaveth, two and forty.

29 The men of Kirjath Jearim, Chephirah, and Beeroth, seven hundred and three and forty.

30 The men of Ramah and Geba, six hundred and one and twenty.

31 The men of Michmas, an hundred and two and twenty.

32 The men of Bethel and Ai, an hundred and three and twenty.

33 The men ¹of the other Nebo, two and fifty.

34 The sons of the other Elam, a thousand two hundred and four and fifty.

35 The sons of Harim, three hundred and twenty.

36 The sons of Jericho, three hundred and five and forty.

37 The sons of Lod, Hadid and Ono, seven hundred and one and twenty.

38 The sons of Senaah, three thousand nine hundred and thirty.

39 The Priests: the sons of Jedaiah of the house of Jeshua, nine hundred seventy and three.

40 The sons of Immer, a thousand and two and fifty.

41 The sons of Pashur, a thousand two hundred and seven and forty.

42 The sons of Harim, a thousand and seven-

teen.

43 ¶ The Levites: the sons of Jeshua of Kadmiel, and of the sons of ¹Hodevah, seventy and four.

44 ¶ The singers: the children of Asaph, an hundred and eight and forty.

45 The porters: the sons of Shallum, the sons of Ater, the sons of Talmon, the sons of Akkub, the sons of Hatita, the sons of Shobai, an hundred and eight and thirty.

46 ¶ The ¹Nethinim: the sons of Ziha, the sons of Hasupha, the sons of Tabbaoth,

47 The sons of Keros, the sons of Sia, the sons of Padon,

48 The sons of Lebana, the sons of Hagaba, the sons of Shalmai,

49 The sons of Hanan, the sons of Giddel, the sons of Gahar,

50 The sons of Reaiah, the sons of Rezin, the sons of Nekoda,

51 The sons of Gazzam, the sons of Uzza, the sons of Paseah,

52 The sons of Besai, the sons of Meunim, the sons of Nephishesim,

53 The sons of Bakbuk, the sons of Hakupha, the sons of Harhur,

54 The sons of Bazlith, the sons of Mehida, the sons of Harsha,

55 The sons of Barkos, the sons of Sisera, the sons of Tamah,

56 The sons of Neziah, the sons of Hatipha,

57 The sons of Solomon's servants, the sons of Sotai, the sons of Sophereth, the sons of Perida,

58 The sons of Jaala, the sons of Darkon, the sons of Giddel,

59 The sons of Shephatiah, the sons of Hattil, the sons of Pochereth of Zebaim, the sons of Amon.

60 All the Nethinim, and the sons of Solomon's servants *were* three hundred, ninety and two.

61 ¶ And these came up from Tel Melah, Tel Harsha, Cherub, Addon, and Immer: but they could not show their father's house, nor their seed, *or* if they were of Israel.

62 The sons of Delaiah: the sons of Tobiah, the sons of Nekoda, six hundred and two and forty.

63 And of the Priests: the sons of Habaiah, the sons of Koz, the sons of Barzillai, which took one of the daughters of Barzillai the Gileadite to wife, and was named after their name.

64 These sought their writing of the genealogies, but it was not found: therefore they were put from the Priesthood.

65 And ¹the Tirshatha said unto them, that they

7:25 ¹ That is, the inhabitants of Gibeon.
7:33 ¹ For there were two cities of this name.
7:43 ¹ Or, Hodaiah.
7:46 ¹ Read Ezra 2:43.
7:65 ¹ Meaning, Nehemiah: for Tirshatha in the Chaldean tongue signifieth a butler.

should not eat of the most holy, till there rose up a Priest with [b]Urim and Thummim.

66 All the Congregation together *was* two and forty thousand, three hundred and threescore,

67 Besides their servants and their maids, which were seven thousand, three hundred and seven and thirty: and they had two hundred and five and forty singing men and singing women.

68 Their horses *were* seven hundred and six and thirty, *and* their mules two hundred and five and forty.

69 The camels four hundred and five and thirty, *and* six thousand seven hundred and twenty asses.

70 And certain of the chief fathers gave unto the work. The Tirshatha gave to the treasure, a thousand [1]drams of gold, fifty basins, five hundred and thirty Priest's garments.

71 And *some* of the chief fathers gave unto the treasure of the work, twenty thousand drams of gold, and two thousand and two hundred [1]pieces of silver.

72 And the rest of the people gave twenty thousand drams of gold, and two thousand pieces of silver, and threescore and seven Priest's garments.

73 And the Priests, and the Levites, and the porters and the singers, and the rest of the people and the Nethinim, and all Israel dwelt in their cities: and when the [1]seventh month came, the children of Israel were in their cities.

8 *2 Ezra gathereth together the people, and readeth to them the Law. 12 They rejoice in Israel for the knowledge of the word of God. 15 They keep the feast of Tabernacles or booths.*

1 And all the people assembled themselves [1]together, in the street that was before the water gate, and they spake unto Ezra the [2]Scribe, that he would bring the book of the Law of Moses, which the Lord had commanded to Israel.

2 And Ezra the Priest brought the Law before the Congregation both of men and women, and of all [1]that could hear and understand it, in the first day of the seventh month,

3 And he read therein in the street that was before the water gate (from the morning until [1]the midday) before men and women, and them that understood it, and the ears of all the people *hearkened* unto the book of the Law.

4 And Ezra the Scribe stood upon a pulpit of

[b] Exod. 28:30

CHAPTER 8
[a] Lev. 23:24

wood which he had made for the preaching, and beside him stood Mattithiah, and Shema, and Anaiah, and Urijah, and Hilkiah, and Maaseiah on his right hand, and on his left hand Pedaiah, and Mishael, and Malchijah, and Hashum, and Hashbadana, Zechariah, *and* Meshullam.

5 And Ezra opened the book before all the people: for he was [1]above all the people: and when he opened it, all the people stood up.

6 And Ezra praised the Lord the great God, and all the people answered, Amen, Amen, with lifting up their hands: and they bowed themselves, and worshipped the Lord with their faces toward the ground.

7 Also Jeshua, and Bani, and Sherebiah, Jamin, Akkub, Shabbethai, Hodijah, Maaseiah, Kelita, Azariah, Jozabad, Hanan, Pelaiah, and the Levites caused the people to understand the Law, and the people *stood* in their place.

8 And they read in the book of the Law of God distinctly, and gave the sense, and caused them to understand the reading.

9 Then Nehemiah (which is Tirshatha) and Ezra the Priest and Scribe, and the Levites that instructed the people, said unto all the people, This day is holy unto the Lord your God: mourn not, neither weep: for all the people [1]wept, when they heard the words of the Law.

10 He said also unto them, Go *and* eat of the fat, and drink the sweet, and send part unto them, for whom none is [1]prepared: for this day is holy unto our Lord: be ye not sorry therefore: for the [2]joy of the Lord is your strength.

11 And the Levites made silence throughout all the people, saying, Hold your peace: for the day is holy, be not sad therefore.

12 Then all the people went to eat and to drink, and to send away part, and to make great joy, because they had understood the words that they had taught them.

13 And on the second day the chief fathers of all the people, the Priests and the Levites were gathered unto Ezra the Scribe, that he also might instruct them in the words of the Law.

14 And they found written in the Law, (that the Lord had commanded Moses) that the children of Israel should dwell in [a]booths in the feast of the seventh month,

---

7:70 [1] Read Ezra 2:69.
7:71 [1] Or, minas.
7:73 [1] Which containeth part of September and part of October.
8:1 [1] Hebrew, *as one man.*
      [2] Read Ezra 7:6.
8:2 [1] Which had age and discretion to understand.
8:3 [1] This declareth the great zeal, that the people had to hear the

word of God.
8:5 [1] To the intent that his voice might be the better heard.
8:9 [1] In considering their offences against the Law. Therefore the Levites do not reprove them for mourning, but assure them of God's mercies forasmuch as they are repentant.
8:10 [1] That is, remember the poor.
       [2] Rejoice in the Lord, and he will give you strength.

15 And that they should cause it to be declared and proclaimed in all their cities, and in Jerusalem, saying, Go forth unto the mount, and bring olive branches, and pine branches, and branches of ¹myrtle, and palm branches, and branches of thick trees, to make booths, as it is written.

16 So the people went forth and brought *them*, and made them booths, every one upon the ¹roof of his house, and in their courts, and in the courts of the house of God, and in the street by the water gate, and in the street of the gate of Ephraim.

17 And all the Congregation of them that were come again out of the captivity, made booths, and sat under the booths: for since the ¹time of Jeshua the son of Nun unto this day, had not the children of Israel done so, and there was very great joy.

18 And he read in the book of the Law of God every day, from the first day unto the last day. And they kept the feast seven days, and on the eighth day a solemn assembly, according unto the manner.

9 *The people repent, and forsake their strange wives.* 5 *The Levites exhort them to praise God,* 6 *Declaring his wonders,* 26 *And their ingratitude,* 30 *And God's great mercies toward them.*

1 In the four and twentieth day of this ¹month the children of Israel were assembled with fasting, and with sackcloth, and earth upon them.

2 (And they that were of the seed of Israel were separated from all the ¹strangers) and they stood and confessed their sins and the iniquities of their fathers.

3 And they stood up in their place and read in the book of the Law of the Lord their God four times on the day, and they ¹confessed and worshipped the Lord their God four times.

4 Then stood up upon the stairs of the Levites, Jeshua, and Bani, Kadmiel, Shebaniah, Bunni, Sherebiah, Bani, *and* Chenani, and cried with a loud voice unto the Lord their God.

5 And the Levites said, *even* Jeshua and Kadmiel, Bani, Hashabniah, Sherebiah, Hodijah, Shebaniah *and* Pethahiah, Stand up *and* praise the Lord your God forever and ever, and let them praise thy glorious Name, O God, which excelleth above all thanksgiving and praise.

6 Thou art Lord alone: thou hast made heaven, and the heaven of all heavens, with all their host, the earth, and all things that are therein, the seas, and all that are in them and thou preservest them all and the host of the heaven worshippeth thee.

7 Thou art, O Lord, the God, that hast chosen

CHAPTER 9
a Gen. 11:31
b Gen. 17:5
c Gen. 15:18
d Exod. 2:76
Exod. 14:16
e Exod. 14:10
f Exod. 13:10
g Exod. 19:18,20
Exod. 20:1
h Exod. 16:18
i Exod. 17:6
j Deut. 1:8
k Exod. 13:22
Num. 14:14
1 Cor. 10:1

Abram, and broughtest him out of *a*Ur in Chaldeans, and *b*madest his name Abraham,

8 And foundest his heart faithful before thee, *c*and madest a Covenant with him, to give unto his seed the land of the Canaanites, Hittites, Amorites, and Perizzites, and Jebusites, and Girgashites, and hast performed thy words, because thou art just.

9 *d*Thou hast also considered the affliction of our fathers in Egypt, and heard their cry by the red Sea,

10 And showed tokens and wonders upon Pharaoh, and on all his servants, and on all the people of his land: for thou knewest that they dealt proudly against them: therefore thou madest thee a Name, as *appeareth* this day.

11 *e*For thou didst break up the Sea before them, and they went through the midst of the sea on dry land: and those that pursued them, hast thou cast into the bottoms as a stone, in the mighty waters:

12 And *f*leddest them in the day with a pillar of a cloud, and in the night with a pillar of fire to give them light in the way that they went.

13 *g*Thou camest down also upon mount Sinai, and spakest unto them from heaven, and gavest them right judgments, and true laws, ordinances and good Commandments,

14 And declaredst unto them thine holy Sabbath, and commandedst them precepts, and ordinances, and laws, by the hand of Moses thy servant:

15 *h*And gavest them bread from heaven for their hunger, *i*and broughtest forth water for them out of the rock for their thirst: and *j*promisedst them that they should go in, and take possession of the land: for the which thou hadst lifted up thine hand for to give them.

16 But they and our fathers behaved themselves proudly and hardened their neck, so that they hearkened not unto thy Commandments,

17 But refused to obey, and would not remember thy marvelous works that thou hadst done for them, but hardened their necks, and had in their heads to return to their bondage by their rebellion: but thou, O God of mercies, gracious and full of compassion, of long-suffering, and of great mercy, yet forsookest them not.

18 Moreover, when they made them a molten calf (and said, This is thy God that brought thee up out of the land of Egypt) and committed great blasphemies,

19 Yet thou for thy great mercies forsookest them not in the wilderness: *k*the pillar of the cloud departed not from them by day to lead them the way, neither

---

8:15 ¹ Or, goodly branches, as Lev. 3:40.
8:16 ¹ For their houses were made flat above, read Deut. 22:8.
8:17 ¹ Which was almost a thousand years.

9:1 ¹ Meaning, the seventh.
9:2 ¹ Hebrew, *strange children*.
9:3 ¹ They made confession of their sins, and used prayers.

the pillar of fire by night, to show them light, and the way whereby they should go.

20 Thou gavest also thy good Spirit to instruct them, and withheldest not thy Manna from their mouth, and gavest them water for their thirst.

21 Thou didst also feed them forty years in the wilderness: they lacked nothing: [1]their clothes waxed not old, and their feet [1]swelled not.

22 And thou gavest them kingdoms and people, and [1]scatteredst them into corners: so they possessed [m]the land of Sihon, and the land of the king of Heshbon, and the land of Og king of Bashan.

23 And thou didst multiply their children like the stars of the heaven, and broughtest them into the land, whereof thou hadst spoken unto their fathers, that they should go, and possess it.

24 So the children went in, and possessed the land, and thou subduedst before them the inhabitants of the land, even the Canaanites, and gavest them into their hands, with their kings and the people of the land, that they might do with them what they would.

25 And they took their strong cities and the fat land, and possessed houses full of all goods, cisterns dug out, vineyards and olives, and trees for food in abundance, and they did eat, and were filled, and became fat, and lived in pleasure through thy great goodness.

26 Yet they were disobedient, and rebelled against thee, and cast thy Law behind their backs, and slew thy Prophets (which [1]protested among them to turn them unto thee) and committed great blasphemies.

27 Therefore thou deliveredst them into the hand of their enemies that vexed them: yet in the time of their affliction, when they cried unto thee, thou heardest them from the heaven, and through thy great mercies thou gavest them saviors, who saved them out of the hand of their adversaries.

28 But when they had [1]rest, they returned to do evil before thee: therefore leftest thou them in the hand of their enemies, so that they had the dominion over them, yet when they converted and cried unto thee, thou heardest them from heaven, and deliveredst them according to thy great mercies many times,

29 And protestedst among them, that thou mightest bring them again unto thy Law: but they behaved themselves proudly, and hearkened not unto thy commandments, but sinned against thy judgments

[l] Deut. 8:4
[m] Num. 21:26
[n] Lev. 18:5
Ezek. 20:11
Rom. 10:5
Gal. 3:12
[o] Exod. 34:6,7
[p] Ps. 143:1,2

("which a man should do and live in them) and [1]pulled away the shoulder, and were stiff-necked, and would not [2]hear.

30 Yet thou [1]didst forbear them many years, and protestedst among them by thy Spirit, even by the hand of thy Prophets, but they would not hear: therefore gavest thou them into the hand of the people of the lands.

31 Yet for thy great mercies thou hast not consumed them, neither forsaken them: for thou art a gracious and merciful God.

32 Now therefore our God, [o]thou great God, mighty and terrible, that keepest covenant and [p]mercy, let not all the affliction that hath come unto us, seem a little before thee, that is, to our Kings, to our Princes, and to our Priests, and to our Prophets, and to our fathers, and to all thy people since the time of the [1]kings of Assyria unto this day.

33 Surely thou art just in all that is come upon us: for thou hast [1]dealt truly, but we have done wickedly.

34 And our kings and our princes, our priests and our fathers have not done thy Law, nor regarded thy commandments, nor thy protestations, wherewith thou hast [1]protested among them.

35 And they have not served thee in their kingdom, and in thy great goodness that thou showedst unto them, and in the large and fat land which thou didst set before them, and have not converted from their evil works.

36 Behold, we are servants this day, and the land that thou gavest unto our fathers, to eat the [1]fruit thereof, and the goodness thereof, behold, we are servants therein.

37 And it yieldeth much fruit unto the kings whom thou hast set over us, because of our sins: and they have dominion over our bodies, and over our cattle at their pleasure, and we are in great affliction.

38 Now because of all this we make [1]a sure covenant, and write it, and our princes, our Levites, and our Priests seal unto it.

10

1 The names of them that sealed the covenant between God and the people.

1 Now they that sealed, were Nehemiah the [1]Tirshatha the son of Hachaliah, and Zidkijah,

---

9:21 [1] Though the way was tedious and long.
9:22 [1] Meaning, the heathen whom he drove out.
9:26 [1] Taking heaven and earth to witness, that God would destroy them, except they returned, as 2 Chron. 24:19.
9:28 [1] He declareth how God's mercies ever contended with the wickedness of the people, who ever in their prosperity forgat God.
9:29 [1] Which is a similitude taken of oxen that shrink at the yoke or burden, as Zech. 7:11.
    [2] When thou didst admonish them by thy Prophets.
9:30 [1] Hebrew, thou didst prolong upon them many years.

9:32 [1] By whom we were led away into captivity, and have been appointed to be slain, as Esther 3:13.
9:33 [1] He confesseth that all these things came to them justly for their sins, but he appealeth from God's justice to his mercies.
9:34 [1] That thou wouldest destroy them, except they would return to thee, as verse 26.
9:36 [1] That is, to be the Lord's therof.
9:38 [1] Thus by affliction they promise to keep God's commandments, whereunto they could not be brought by God's great benefits.
10:1 [1] Or, butler.

2 Seraiah, Azariah, Jeremiah,

3 Pashur, Amariah, Malchijah,

4 Hattush, Shebaniah, Malluch,

5 Harim, Meremoth, Obadiah,

6 Daniel, Ginnethon, Baruch,

7 Meshullam, Abijah, Mijamin,

8 Maaziah, Bilgai, Shemaiah: these are ¹the Priests.

9 ¶ And the Levites: Jeshua the son of Azaniah, Binnui, of the sons of Henadad, Kadmiel.

10 And their brethren, Shebaniah, Hodijah, Kelita, Pelaiah, Hanun,

11 Micha, Rehob, Hashabiah,

12 Zaccur, Sherebiah, Shebaniah,

13 Hodijah, Bani, Beninu.

14 ¶ The chief of the people were Parosh, ¹Pahath-Moab, Elam, Zattu, Bani,

15 Bunni, Azgad, Bebai,

16 Adonijah, Bigvai, Adin,

17 Ater, Hezekiah, Azzur,

18 Hodijah, Hashum, Bezai,

19 Hariph, Anathoth, Nebai,

20 Magpiash, Meshullam, Hezir,

21 Meshezabeel, Zadok, Jaddua,

22 Pelatiah, Hanan, Anaiah,

23 Hoshea, Hananiah, Hashub,

24 Hallohesh, Pileha, Shobek,

25 Rehum, Hashabnah, Maaseiah,

26 And Ahijah, Hanan, Anan,

27 Malluch, Harim, Baanah.

28 And the rest of the people, the Priests, the Levites, the porters, the singers, the ¹Nethinim, and all that were ²separated from the people of the lands unto the Law of God, their wives, their sons and their daughters, all that could understand.

29 The chief of them ¹received it for their brethren, and they came to the ²curse and to the oath to walk in God's Law, which was given by Moses the servant of God, to observe and do all the commandments of the Lord our God, and his judgments and his statutes:

30 And that we would not give our daughters to the people of the land, neither take their daughters for our sons.

31 And if the people of the land brought ware on

CHAPTER 10
ᵃ Lev. 25:4
Deut. 15:1
ᵇ Num. 18:26

the Sabbath, or any vittles to sell, ¹that we would not take it of them on the Sabbath, and on the holy days: ᵃand that we would let the seventh year be free, and the debts of every ²person.

32 And we made statutes for ourselves to give by the year, the third part of a shekel for the service of the house of our God,

33 For the ¹showbread, and for the daily offering, and for the daily burnt offering, the Sabbaths, the new moons, for the solemn feasts, and for the things that were sanctified, and for the sin offerings, to make an atonement for Israel, and for all the work of the house of our God.

34 We cast also lots for the offering of the wood, even the Priests, the Levites, and the people, to bring it into the house of our God, ¹by the house of our fathers, yearly at the times appointed, to burn it upon the Altar of the Lord our God, as it is written in the Law,

35 And to bring the firstfruits of our land, and the first of all the fruits of all trees, year by year, into the house of the Lord,

36 And the firstborn of our sons, and of our cattle, as it is ¹written in the Law, and the firstborn of our bullocks, and of our sheep, to bring it into the house of our God, unto the Priests that minister in the house of our God,

37 And that we should bring the firstfruit of our dough, and our offerings, and the fruit of every tree, of wine and of oil, unto the Priests, to the chambers of the house of our God: and the tithes of our land unto the Levites, that the Levites might have the tithes in all the cities of our ¹travail.

38 And the Priest, the son of Aaron shall be with the Levites, when the Levites take tithes, and the Levites shall ᵇbring up the tenth part of the tithes unto the house of our God, unto the chambers of the treasure house.

39 For the children of Israel, and the children of Levi shall bring up the offering of the corn, of the wine, and of the oil, unto the chambers: and there shall be the vessels of the Sanctuary, and the Priests that minister, and the porters, and the singers, and ¹we will not forsake the house of our God.

10:8 ¹ Which subscribed to keep the promise.

10:14 ¹ Or, captain of Moab.

10:28 ¹ Read Ezra 2:43.

    ² Which being idolaters forsook their wickedness, and gave themselves to serve God.

10:29 ¹ They made the oath in the name of the whole multitude.

    ² Whereunto they gave themselves if they brake the Law, as Deut. 28:15.

10:31 ¹ Which notwithstanding they brake soon after, as Neh. 13:15.

    ² Hebrew, hand.

10:33 ¹ This declareth wherefore they gave this third part of the

shekel, which was besides the half shekel that they were bound to pay, Exod. 30:13.

10:34 ¹ Or, into the house of.

10:36 ¹ By this rehearsal is meant that there was no part nor ceremony in the Law, whereunto they did not bind themselves by covenant.

10:37 ¹ Wheresoever we labored, or travailed, there the tithes were due unto the Lord both by the Law, and according to the oath and covenant that we made.

10:39 ¹ We will not leave it destitute of that that shall be necessary for it.

11

1 Who dwelled in Jerusalem after it was built,   20 and who in the cities of Judah.

1 And the rulers of the people dwelt in Jerusalem: the other people also cast lots, [1]to bring one out of ten to dwell in Jerusalem the holy city, and nine parts *to be* in the cities.

2 And the people thanked all the men that were willing to dwell in Jerusalem.

3 These now are the chief of the province, that dwelt in Jerusalem, but in the cities of Judah, everyone dwelt in his own possession in their cities of Israel, the Priests and the Levites, and the Nethinim, and the sons of Solomon's servants.

4 And in Jerusalem dwelt *certain* of the children of Judah, and of the children of Benjamin: Of the sons of Judah, Athaiah, the son of Uziah, the son of Zechariah, the son of Amariah, the son of Shephatiah, the son of Mahalalel, of the sons of [1]Perez,

5 And Maaseiah the son of Baruch, the son of Col-Hozeh, the son of Hazaiah, the son of Adaiah, the son of Joiarib, the son of Zechariah, the son of [1]Shiloni.

6 All the sons of Perez that dwelt at Jerusalem, *were* four hundred threescore and eight valiant men.

7 These also are the sons of Benjamin, Sallu, the son of Meshullam, the son of Joed, the son of Pedaiah, the son of Kolaiah, the son of Maaseiah, the son of Ithiel, the son of Jeshaiah.

8 And after him Gabbai, Sallai, nine hundred and twenty and eight.

9 And Joel the son of Zichri *was* governor over them: and Judah the son of Senuah *was* the second over the city:

10 Of the Priests, Jedaiah, the son of Joiarib, Jachin.

11 Seraiah, the son of Hilkiah, the son of Meshullam, the son of Zadok, the son of Meraioth, the son of Ahitub, [1]*was* chief of the house of God.

12 And their brethren [1]that did the work in the Temple, *were* eight hundred, twenty and two: and Adaiah, the son of Jeroham, the son of Pelaliah, the son of Amzi, the son of Zechariah, the son of Pashur, the son of Malchijah:

13 And his brethren, chief of the fathers, two hundred and two and forty: and Amashsai the son of Azarel, the son of Ahazai, the son of Meshilemoth, the son of Immer:

14 And their brethren valiant men, an hundred and eight and twenty: and their overseer *was* Zabdiel the son [1]of Haggedolim.

15 And of the Levites, Shemaiah, the son of Hashub, the son of Azrikam, the son of Hashabiah, the son of Bunni.

16 And Shabbethai, and Jozabad of the chief of the Levites *were* over the works of the house of God without.

17 And Mattaniah, the son of Micha, the son of Zabdi, the son of Asaph *was* the chief to [1]begin the thanksgiving *and* prayer: and Bakbukiah the second of his brethren, and Abda, the son of Shammua, the son of Galal, the son of Jeduthun.

18 All the Levites in the holy city *were* two hundred fourscore and four.

19 And the porters Akkub, Talmon, and their brethren that kept the [1]gates, *were* an hundred twenty and two.

20 And the [1]residue of Israel, of the Priests, *and* of the Levites *dwelt* in all the cities of Judah, everyone in his inheritance.

21 And the Nethinim dwelt in the [1]fortress, and Ziha, and Gispa *was* over the Nethinim.

22 And the overseer of the Levites in Jerusalem *was* Uzzi the son of Bani, the son of Hashabiah, the son of Mattaniah, the son of Micha: of the sons of Asaph singers *were* over the work of the house of God.

23 For it *was* the king's commandment concerning them, that faithful *provision should be* for the singers every day.

24 And Pethahiah the son of Meshezabel, of the sons of Zerah, the son of Judah [1]*was* at the king's hand in all matters concerning the people.

25 And in the villages in their lands, *some* of the children of Judah dwelt in Kirjath Arba, and in the villages thereof, and in Dibon, and in the villages thereof, and in Jekabzeel, and in the villages thereof,

26 And in Jeshua, and in Moladah, and in Beth Pelet,

27 And in Hazar Shual, and in Beersheba, and in the villages thereof,

28 And in Ziklag, and in Mekonah, and in the villages thereof,

29 And in En Rimmon, and in Zorah, and in Jarmuth,

30 Zanoah, Adullam, and in their villages, in Lachish, and in the fields thereof, at Azekah, and in the villages thereof: and they dwelt from Beersheba,

---

11:1 [1] Because their enemies dwelt round about them, they provided that it might be replenished with men, and used this policy, because there were few that offered themselves willingly.

11:4 [1] Which came of Perez the son of Judah.

11:5 [1] Or, of a Shilonite.

11:11 [1] That is, was the high Priest.

11:12 [1] That served and ministered in the Temple.

11:14 [1] Or, of one of the great men.

11:17 [1] That is, he began the Psalm, and was the chanter.

11:19 [1] Meaning, of the Temple.

11:20 [1] Of them, which dwelt not in Jerusalem.

11:21 [1] Or, Ophel.

11:24 [1] Was chief about the king for all his affairs.

unto the valley of Hinnom.

31 And the sons of Benjamin from Geba, in Michmash, and Aija, and Bethel, and in the villages thereof,

32 And Anathoth, Nob, Ananiah,

33 Hazor, Ramah, Gittaim,

34 Hadid, Zeboim, Neballat,

35 Lod and Ono, in the carpenters valley.

36 And of the Levites *were* divisions in Judah and in Benjamin.

12

1 *The Priests and Levites which came with Zerubbabel unto Jerusalem, are numbered,* 27 *and the wall is dedicated.*

1 These also are the Priests and the Levites that [1]went up with Zerubbabel, the son of Shealtiel, and Jeshua: *to wit,* Seraiah, Jeremiah, Ezra,

2 Amariah, Malluch, Hattush,

3 Shecaniah, Rehum, Meremoth,

4 Iddo, Ginnethoi, Abijah,

5 Mijamin, Maadiah, Bilgah,

6 Shemaiah, and Joiarib, Jedaiah,

7 Sallu, Amok, Hilkiah, Jedaiah: these were the [1]chief of the Priests, and of their brethren in the days of Jeshua.

8 And the Levites, Jeshua, Binnui, Kadmiel, Sherebiah, Judah, Mattaniah [1]*were* over the thanksgivings, he, and his brethren.

9 And Bakbukiah and Unni, *and* their brethren *were* about them in the [1]watches.

10 And Jeshua begat Joiakim: Joiakim also begat Eliashib, and Eliashib begat Joiada.

11 And Joiada begat Jonathan, and Jonathan begat Jaddua.

12 And in the days of Joiakim were *these* the chief fathers of the Priests: under [1]Seraiah *was* Meraiah, under Jeremiah, Hananiah,

13 Under Ezra, Meshullam, under Amariah, Jehohanan,

14 Under Melichu, Jonathan, under Shebaniah, Joseph,

15 Under Harim, Adna, under Maraioth, Helkai,

16 Under Iddo, Zechariah, under Ginnethon, Meshullam,

17 Under [1]Abijah, Zichri, under Minjamin, *and* under Moadiah, Piltai,

18 Under Bilgah, Shammua, under Shemaiah, Jehonathan,

19 Under Joiarib, Mattenai, under Jedaiah, Uzzi,

20 Under Sallai, Kallai, under Amok, Eber,

21 Under Hilkiah, Hashabiah, under Jedaiah, Nethanel.

22 In the days of Eliashib, Joiada, and Johanan and Jaddua *were* the chief fathers of the Levites written, and the Priests in the reign of Darius the Persian.

23 The sons of Levi, the chief fathers *were* written in the book of the Chronicles even unto the days of Johanan the son of Eliashib.

24 And the chief of the Levites *were* Hashabiah, Sherebiah, and Jeshua the son of Kadmiel, and their brethren about them to give praise and thanks, according to the ordinances of David the man of God, ward over [1]against ward.

25 Mattaniah and Bakbukiah, Obadiah, Meshullam, Talmon *and* Akkub *were* porters keeping the ward at the thresholds of the gates.

26 These were in the days of Joiakim the son of Jeshua, the son of Jozadak, and in the days of Nehemiah the captain, and of Ezra the Priest and Scribe.

27 And in the dedication of the wall at Jerusalem, they sought the Levites out of all their places to bring them to Jerusalem to keep the dedication and gladness, both with thanksgivings and with songs, cymbals, viols, and with harps.

28 Then the [1]singers gathered themselves together both from the plain country about Jerusalem, and from the villages of [2]Netophathi,

29 And from the house of Gilgal, and out of the countries of Geba, and Azmaveth: for the singers had built them villages round about Jerusalem.

30 And the Priests and Levites were purified, and cleansed the people, and the gates, and the wall.

31 And [1]I brought up the princes of Judah upon the wall, and appointed two great companies to give thanks, and the *one* went on the right hand of the wall toward the dung gate.

32 And after them went Hoshaiah, and half of the princes of Judah,

33 And Azariah, Ezra and Meshullam,

34 Judah, Benjamin, and Shemaiah, and Jeremiah,

35 And of the Priest's sons with trumpets, Zechariah, the son of Jonathan, the son of Shemaiah, the

---

12:1 [1] From Babylon to Jerusalem.
12:7 [1] Next in dignity to the high Priests, and which were of the stock of Aaron.
12:8 [1] Had charge of them that sang the Psalms.
12:9 [1] They kept the wards and watches according to their turns, as 2 Chron. 23:6.
12:12 [1] That is, next to Seraiah, or rather of the order, which was

called after the name of Seraiah.
12:17 [1] Whereof was Zacharias, John Baptist's father.
12:24 [1] That is, one after another, and every one in his course.
12:28 [1] Hebrew, *the sons of the singers.*
[2] Which were a certain family, and had their possessions in the fields, 1 Chron. 2:54.
12:31 [1] Meaning, Nehemiah.

son of Mattaniah, the son of Michaiah, the son of Zaccur, the son of Asaph.

36 And [1]his brethren, Shemaiah, and Azarel, Milalai, Gilalai, Maai, Nethanel, and Judah, Hanani, with the musical instruments of David the man of God: and Ezra the Scribe *went* before them.

37 And to the gate of the fountain, even over against them went they up by the [1]stairs of the city of David, at the going up of the wall beyond the house of David, even unto the water gate Eastward.

38 And the second company of them that gave thanks, went on the other side, and I after them, and the half of the people *was* upon the wall, *and* upon the tower of the furnaces even unto the broad wall.

39 And upon the gate of Ephraim, and upon the old gate, and upon the fish gate, and the tower of Hananel, and the tower of Meah, even unto the sheep gate: and they stood in the gate of the ward.

40 So stood the two companies (of them that gave thanks) in the house of God, and I and the half of the rulers with me.

41 The Priests also, Eliakim, Maaseiah, Minjamin, Michaiah, Elioenai, Zechariah, Hananiah, with trumpets,

42 And Maaseiah, and Shemaiah, and Eleazar, and Uzzi, and Jehohanan, and Malchijah, and Elam, and Ezer: and the singers [1]sang loud, having Jezrahiah which *was* the overseer.

43 And the same day they offered great sacrifices and rejoiced: for God had given them great joy, so that both the women, and the children were joyful: and the joy of Jerusalem was heard far off.

44 Also at the same time were men appointed [1]over the chambers of the store for the offerings, (for the firstfruits, and for the tithes) to gather into them out of the fields of the cities, the portions of the Law for the Priests, and the Levites, for Judah rejoiced for the Priests and for the Levites, that served.

45 And both the singers and the Levites kept the ward of their God, and the ward of the purification according to the commandment of David, *and* Solomon his son.

46 [a]For in the days of David and Asaph, of old *were* chief singers, and songs of praise and thanksgiving unto God.

47 And in the days of Zerubbabel, and in the days

CHAPTER 12
[a] 1 Chron. 15:16

CHAPTER 13
[a] Deut. 23:3
[b] Num. 22:5,6

of Nehemiah did all Israel give portions unto the singers and porters, every day his portion, and they gave the holy things unto the Levites, and the Levites [1]gave the holy things unto the sons of Aaron.

13

1 The Law is read.   3 They separate from them all strangers.   15 Nehemiah reproveth them that break the Sabbath.   30 An ordinance to serve God.

1 And on that day they did read in the book of Moses, in the audience of the people, and it was found written therein, that the Ammonite, and the Moabite [a]should not enter into the Congregation of God,

2 Because they met not the children of Israel with bread and with water, [b]but hired Balaam against them, that he should curse them: and our God turned the curse into a blessing.

3 Now when they had heard the Law, they separated from Israel [1]all those that were mixed.

4 ¶ And before [1]this had the Priest Eliashib the oversight of the chamber of the house of our God, being [2]kinsman to Tobiah:

5 And he had made him a great chamber, and there had they aforetime laid the offerings, the incense, and the vessels, and the tithes of corn, of wine, and of oil (appointed for the Levites, and the singers, and the porters) and the offerings of the Priests.

6 But in all this *time* was not I in Jerusalem: for in the two and thirtieth year of [1]Artachshashta King of Babel, came I unto the King, and [2]after certain days I obtained of the King.

7 And when I was come to Jerusalem, I understood [1]the evil that Eliashib had done for Tobiah, in that he had made him a chamber in the court of the house of God,

8 And it grieved me sore: therefore I cast forth all the vessels of the house of Tobiah out of the chamber.

9 And I commanded them to cleanse the chambers: and thither brought I again the vessels of the house of God with the meat offering and the incense.

10 And I perceived that the portions of the Levites had not been given, and that everyone was fled to his land, *even* the Levites and singers that executed the work.

11 Then reproved I the rulers and said, Why is the house of God forsaken? And I assembled them, and set them in their place.

12:36 [1] That is, the brethren of Zaccur.
12:37 [1] Which was the going up to the mount Zion, which is called the city of David.
12:42 [1] Hebrew, *caused to hear.*
12:44 [1] Which were chambers appointed by Hezekiah to put in the tithes, and such things, 2 Chron. 31:11 and now were repaired again for the same use.
12:47 [1] That is, the tenth part of the tithes.
13:3 [1] That is, all such which had joined in unlawful marriage, and also those with whom God had forbidden them to have

society.
13:4 [1] That the separation was made.
    [2] He was joined in affinity with Tobiah the Ammonite and enemy of the Jews.
13:6 [1] Called also Darius, Ezra 7:1.
    [2] Or, at the year's end.
13:7 [1] Thus we see to what inconveniences the people fall into, when they are destitute of one that hath the fear of God, seeing that their chief governor was but a while absent, and yet they fell into such great absurdities: as appeareth also, Exod. 32:1.

12 Then brought all Judah the tithes of corn and of wine, and of oil unto the treasures.

13 And I made treasurers over the treasures, Shelemiah the Priest, and Zadok the scribe, and of the Levites, Pedaiah, and under their hand Hanan the son of Zaccur the son of Mattaniah: for they were counted faithful, and their office was to distribute unto their brethren.

14 Remember me, O my God, herein, and wipe not out my [1]kindness that I have showed on the house of my God, and on the offices thereof.

15 In those days saw I in Judah them, that trod wine presses on the Sabbath, and that brought in sheaves, and which laded asses also with wine, grapes, and figs, and all burdens, and brought them into Jerusalem upon the Sabbath day: and [1]I protested to them in the day that they sold vittles.

16 There dwelt men of Tyre also therein, which brought fish and all wares, and sold on the Sabbath unto the children of Judah even in Jerusalem.

17 Then reproved I the rulers of Judah, and said unto them, What evil thing is this that ye do, and break the Sabbath day?

18 Did not your fathers [1]thus, and our God brought all this plague upon us, and upon this city? yet ye increase the wrath upon Israel, in breaking the Sabbath.

19 And when the gates of Jerusalem began to be [1]dark before the Sabbath, I commanded to shut the gates, and charged, that they should not be opened till after the Sabbath, and *some* of my servants set I at the gates, that there should no burden be brought in on the Sabbath day.

20 So the chapmen and merchants of all merchandise remained once or twice all night without Jerusalem.

21 And I protested among them, and said unto them, Why tarry ye all night about the wall? If ye

c 2 Kings 3:7,12
d 2 Sam. 12:24,25
e 1 Kings 11:1,4

do it once again, I will lay hands upon you. From that time came they no more on the Sabbath.

22 ¶ And I said unto the Levites, that they should cleanse themselves, and that they should come and [1]keep the gates, to sanctify the Sabbath day. Remember me, O my God, concerning this, and pardon me according to thy great mercy.

23 In those days also I saw Jews that married wives of [1]Ashdod, of Ammon, and of Moab.

24 And their children spake half in the speech of Ashdod, and could not speak in the Jews' language, and according to the language of the *one* people, and of the *other* people.

25 Then I reproved them, and [1]cursed them, and smote certain of them, and pulled off their hair, and took an oath of them by God, Ye shall not give your daughters unto their sons, neither shall ye take of their daughters unto your sons nor for yourselves.

26 ⸠Did not Solomon the king of Israel sin by these things? yet among many nations was there no King like him: for he was ᵈbeloved of his God, and God had made him King over Israel: ᵉyet strange women caused him to sin.

27 Shall we then obey unto you, to do all this great evil, and to transgress against our God, *even* to marry strange wives?

28 And *one* of the sons of Joiada the son of Eliashib the high Priest was the son-in-law of Sanballat the Horonite: but I chased him from me.

29 Remember them, O my God, that [1]defile the Priesthood, and the covenant of the Priesthood, and of the Levites.

30 Then cleansed I them from all strangers, and appointed the wards of the Priests and of the Levites, every one in his office,

31 And for the offering of the wood at times appointed, and for the firstfruits. Remember me, O my God, [1]in goodness.

13:14 [1] He protesteth that he did his duty with a good conscience, yet he doth not justify himself in therein, but desireth God to favor him and to be merciful unto him for his own goodness sake, as verse 22 and 31.

13:15 [1] I declared unto them, that God would not suffer such transgressors of his Law to be unpunished.

13:18 [1] Was not this a great cause, why God plagued us in times past: meaning, that if they transgressed now in the same again, their plague should be greater.

13:19 [1] About the time that the Sun went down: for the Sabbath lasted

from the Sun going down of the one day, to the Sun setting of the other.

13:22 [1] Meaning, of the Temple, that none that was unclean, should enter.

13:23 [1] Which was a city of the Philistines, and they had married wives thereof, and so had corrupted their speech and Religion.

13:25 [1] That is, I did excommunicate them, and drive them out of the congregation.

13:29 [1] Punish them according to their fault and evil example, which they have given to the rest of thy people contrary to their vocation.

13:31 [1] That is, to show mercy unto me.

ESTHER

1

CHAPTER 1
ᵃ Neh. 1:1

1 In the days of ¹Ahasuerus (this is Ahasuerus that reigned from India even unto Ethiopia, over an ²hundred, and seven and twenty provinces.)

2 In those days when the king Ahasuerus ¹sat on his throne, which was in the palace of ᵃShushan,

3 In the third year of his reign, he made a feast unto all his princes and his servants, even the power of Persia and Media, and to the captains and governors of the provinces which were before him,

4 That he might show the riches and glory of his kingdom, and the honor of his great majesty many days, even an hundred and fourscore days.

5 And when these days were expired, the king made a feast to all the people that were found in the palace of Shushan, both unto great and small, seven days, in the court of the garden of the king's palace,

6 Under an hanging of white, green, and blue cloths, fastened with cords of fine linen and purple, in silver rings, and pillars of marble: the ¹beds were of gold and of silver upon a pavement of porphyry, and marble and alabaster, and blue color.

7 And they gave them drink in vessels of gold, and changed vessel after vessel, and royal wine in abundance, according to the ¹power of the king.

8 And the drinking was by an order, none might ¹compel: for so the king had appointed unto all the officers of his house, that they should do according to every man's pleasure.

9 ¶ The Queen Vashti made a feast also for the women in the royal house of King Ahasuerus.

10 Upon the ¹seventh day when the King was merry with wine, he commanded Mehuman, Biztha, Harbona, Bigtha, and Abagtha, Zethar, and Carcas, the seven eunuchs, (that served in the presence of king Ahasuerus)

11 To bring Queen Vashti before the king with the crown royal, that he might show the people and the princes her beauty: for she was fair to look upon.

12 But the Queen Vashti refused to come at the king's word, ¹which he had given in charge to the eunuchs: therefore the King was very angry, and his wrath kindled in him.

13 Then the King said to the wise men, ¹that knew the times (for so was the King's manner towards all that knew the law and the judgment:

14 And the next unto him was Carshena, Shethar, Admatha, Tarshish, Meres, Marsena, and Memucan the seven Princes of Persia, and Media, which saw the ¹King's face, and sat the first in the kingdom.)

15 What shall we do unto the Queen Vashti according to the law, because she did not according to the word of the King Ahasuerus by the commission of the eunuchs?

16 Then Memucan answered before the king and the Princes, The Queen Vashti hath not only done ¹evil against the King, but against all the Princes, and against all the people that are in all the provinces of King Ahasuerus.

17 For the ¹act of the Queen shall come abroad unto all women, so that they shall despise their husbands in their own eyes, and shall say, The King Ahasuerus commanded Vashti the Queen to be brought in before him, but she came not.

18 So shall the ¹Princesses of Persia and Media this day say unto all the King's Princes, when they hear of the act of the Queen: thus shall there be much despitefulness and wrath.

19 If it please the King, let a royal decree proceed

1:1 ¹ Called also Darius, who was now the sovereign Monarch and had the government of the Medes, Persians, and Chaldeans, some think he was Darius Hystaspis' son called also Artaxerxes.

  ² Dan. 6:1, maketh mention but of sixscore, leaving out the number that is unprecise as the Scripture in divers places useth.

1:2 ¹ That is, had rest and quietness.

1:6 ¹ Which they used in those countries instead of tables.

1:7 ¹ As was beseeming for so magnificent a king.

1:8 ¹ None might be compelled to drink more than it pleased him.

1:10 ¹ Which was the last day of the feast that the king made for the people, as verse 5.

1:12 ¹ Hebrew, which was in the hand of the eunuchs.

1:13 ¹ That had experience of things as they had learned by diligent marking in continuance of time.

1:14 ¹ Which were his chief counselors, that might have always access to him.

1:16 ¹ By her disobedience she hath given an example to all women to do the like to their husbands.

1:17 ¹ That is, her disobedience.

1:18 ¹ Meaning, that they would take first occasion thereof to do the like, and that the rest of women would by continuance do the same.

from him, and let it be written among the statutes of Persia and Media, (and let it not be transgressed) that Vashti come [1]no more before king Ahasuerus: and let the king give her royal estate unto her companion that is better than she.

20 And when the decree of the King which shall be made, shall be published throughout all his kingdom (though it be [1]great) all the women shall give their husbands honor, both great and small.

21 And this saying pleased the King and the Princes, and the King did according to the word of Memucan.

22 For he sent letters into all the provinces of the King, into every province according to the writing thereof, and to every people after their language, that every man should [1]bear rule in his own house, and that he should publish it in the language of that same people.

2

2 After the Queen is put away, certain young maids are brought to the king. 17 Esther pleaseth the King, and is made Queen. 22 Mordecai discloseth unto the king those that would betray him.

1 After these things, when the wrath of King Ahasuerus was appeased, he [1]remembered Vashti, and what she had done, and what was decreed [2]against her.

2 And the King's servants that ministered unto him, said, Let them seek for the King beautiful young virgins,

3 And let the King appoint officers through all the provinces of his Kingdom, and let them gather all the beautiful young virgins unto the palace of Shushan, into the house of the women, under the hand of Hegai the King's eunuch, [1]keeper of the women, to give them their things [2]for purification.

4 And the maid that shall please the King, let her reign in the stead of Vashti. And this pleased the king, and he did so.

5 ¶ In the city of Shushan there was a certain Jew, whose name was Mordecai, the son of Jair, the son of Shimei, the son of Kish a man of Benjamin,

6 Which had been carried away from Jerusalem [a]with the captivity that was carried away with Jeconiah King of Judah (whom Nebuchadnezzar king of Babel had carried away.)

CHAPTER 2
[a] 2 Kings 14:15

7 And he nourished Hadassah, that is, Esther, his uncle's daughter: for she had neither father nor mother, and the maid was fair and beautiful to look on: and after the death of her father, and her mother, Mordecai took her for his own daughter.

8 And when the king's commandment, and his decree was published, and many maids were brought together to the palace of Shushan, under the hand of Hegai, Esther was brought also unto the King's house under the hand of Hegai the keeper of the women.

9 And the maid pleased him, and she found favor in his sight, therefore he caused her things for purification to be given her speedily, and her [1]state, and seven comely maids to be given her out of the King's house, and he gave change to her and to her maids of the best in the house of the women.

10 But Esther showed not her people and her kindred: for Mordecai had charged her that she should not tell it.

11 And Mordecai walked [1]every day before the court of the women's house, to know if Esther did well, and what should be done with her.

12 And when the course of every maid came, to go in to King Ahasuerus, after that she had been twelve months according to the manner of the women (for so were the days of their purifications accomplished, six months with oil of myrrh, and six months with sweet odors and in the purifying of the women:

13 And thus went the maids unto the King) whatsoever she required, was [1]given her to go with her out of the women's house unto the king's house.

14 In the evening she went, and on the morrow she returned into the second house of the women under the hand of Shaashgaz the King's eunuch, which kept the concubines: she came in to the King no more, except she pleased the King, and that she were called by name.

15 Now when the course of Esther the daughter of Abihail the uncle of Mordecai (which had taken her as his own daughter) came, that she should go in to the king, she desired nothing, but what [1]Hege the king's eunuch the keeper of the women [2]said: and Esther found favor in the sight of all them that looked upon her.

1:19 [1] Let her be divorced, and another made Queen.
1:20 [1] For he had under him an hundred twenty and seven countries.
1:22 [1] That is, that the wife should be subject to the husband and at his commandment.
2:1 [1] That is, he called the matter again into communication.
  [2] By the seven wise men of his counsel.
2:3 [1] The abuse of these countries was so great, that they invented many means to serve the lusts of Princes, and therefore as they ordained wicked laws, that the king might have whose daughters he would, so they had divers houses appointed, as one for them while they were virgins, another when they were concubines and for the

Queens another.
  [2] Read what this purification was, verse 12.
2:9 [1] Hebrew, portions.
2:11 [1] For though she was taken away by a cruel law, yet he ceased not to have a fatherly care over her, and therefore did resort ofttimes to hear of her.
2:13 [1] What apparel she asked of the eunuch, that was he bound to give her.
2:15 [1] Or, Hegai.
  [2] Wherein her modesty appeared, because she sought not apparel to commend her beauty, but stood to the Eunuch's appointment.

16 ¶ So Esther was taken unto king Ahasuerus into his house royal in the tenth month, which is the [1]month Tebeth, in the seventh year of his reign.

17 And the King loved Esther above all the women, and she found grace and favor in his sight more than all the virgins: so that he set the crown of the kingdom upon her head, and made her Queen instead of Vashti.

18 Then the king made a great feast unto all his princes, and his servants, *which was* [1]the feast of Esther, and gave rest [2]unto the provinces, and gifts, according to the [3]power of a king.

19 And when the virgins were gathered the [1]second time, then Mordecai sat in the king's gate.

20 Esther had not yet showed her kindred nor her people, as Mordecai had charged her: for Esther did after the word of Mordecai, as when she was nourished with him.

21 ¶ In those days when Mordecai sat in the king's gate, two of the king's eunuchs, Bigthan and Teresh, which kept the door, were wroth, and sought to lay [1]hand on the King Ahasuerus.

22 And the thing was known to Mordecai, and he told it unto Queen Esther, and Esther certified the king thereof in Mordecai's name: and when inquisition was made, it was found so: therefore they were both hanged on a tree: and it was written in the book of the [1]Chronicles before the king.

3 *1 Haman, after he was exalted, obtained of the King, that all the Jews should be put to death, because Mordecai had not done him worship as others had.*

1 After these things did king Ahasuerus promote Haman the son of Hammedatha the Agagite, and exalted him, and set his seat above all the princes that were with him.

2 And all the king's servants that were at the king's gate, bowed their knees, and reverenced Haman: for the king had so commanded concerning him: but Mordecai [1]bowed not the knee, neither did reverence.

3 Then the king's servants which were at the king's gate, said unto Mordecai, Why transgressest thou the king's commandment?

4 And albeit they spake daily unto him, yet he would not hear them: therefore they [1]told Haman, that they might see how Mordecai's matters would stand: for he had told them, that he was a Jew.

5 And when Haman saw that Mordecai bowed not the knee unto him, nor did reverence unto him, then Haman was full of wrath.

6 Now he [1]thought it too little to lay hands only on Mordecai: and because they had showed him the people of Mordecai, Haman sought to destroy all the Jews that were throughout the whole kingdom of Ahasuerus, *even* the people of Mordecai.

7 In the first month (that is the month [1]Nisan) in the twelfth year of king Ahasuerus, they cast Pur (that is a lot) [2]before Haman, from day to day, and from month to month *unto* the twelfth month, that is the month [3]Adar.

8 Then Haman said unto king Ahasuerus, There is a people scattered, and dispersed among the people in all the provinces of thy kingdom, and their laws *are* divers from all people, and they do not observe the [1]King's laws: therefore it is not the king's profit to suffer them.

9 If it please the king, let it be written that they may be destroyed, and I will [1]pay ten thousand talents of silver by the hands of them that have the charge of this business to bring it into the king's treasury.

10 Then the king took his ring from his hand, and gave it unto Haman the son of Hammedatha the Agagite the Jews' adversary.

11 And the king said unto Haman, Let the silver be thine, and the people to do with them as it pleaseth thee.

12 Then were the king's [1]Scribes called on the thirteenth day of the first month, and there was written (according to all that Haman commanded) unto the king's officers, and to the captains that were over every province, and to the rulers of every people, *and* to every province, according to the writing thereof, and to every people according to their language: in the name of king Ahasuerus was it written, and sealed with the king's ring.

13 And the letters were sent [1]by posts into all the

2:16 [1] Which contained part of December and part of January.
2:18 [1] That is, made for her sake.
   [2] He released their tribute.
   [3] That is, great and magnificent.
2:19 [1] That is, at the marriage of Esther, which was the second marriage of the king.
2:21 [1] Meaning, to kill him.
2:22 [1] In the Chronicles of the Medes and Persians, as Esther 10:2.
3:2 [1] The Persians' manner was to kneel down and reverence their kings, and such as he appointed in chief authority, which Mordecai would not do to this ambitious and proud man.
3:4 [1] Thus we see that there is none so wicked, but they have their flatterers to accuse the godly.

3:6 [1] Hebrew, *despised in his eyes.*
3:7 [1] Which answereth to part of March and part of April.
   [2] To know what month and day should be good to enterprise this thing, that it might have good success: but God disappointed their lots, and expectation.
   [3] Containing part of February and part of March.
3:8 [1] These be the two arguments which commonly the worldlings and the wicked use toward princes against the godly, that is, the contempt of their laws, and diminishing of their profit: without respect how God is either pleased or displeased.
3:9 [1] Hebrew, *weigh.*
3:12 [1] Or, secretaries.
3:13 [1] Hebrew, *the hands of posts.*

king's provinces, to root out, to kill and to destroy all the Jews, both young and old, children and women, in one day upon the thirteenth day of the twelfth month (which is the month Adar) and to spoil them as a prey.

14 The contents of the writing was, that there should be given a commandment in all provinces, and published unto all people, that they should be ready against the same day.

15 And the posts compelled by the King's commandment went forth, and the commandment was given in the palace at Shushan: and the king and Haman sat drinking, but the [1]city of Shushan was in perplexity.

4 5 *Mordecai giveth the Queen knowledge of the cruel decree of the king against the Jews.* 16 *She willeth that they pray for her.*

1 Now when Mordecai perceived all that was done, Mordecai rent his clothes, and put on sackcloth, and ashes, and went out into the midst of the city, and cried with a great cry, and a bitter.

2 And he came even before the King's [1]gate, but he might not enter within the king's gate, being clothed with sackcloth.

3 And in every province *and* place, whither the king's charge and his commission came, there was great sorrow among the Jews, and fasting, and weeping, and mourning, and [1]many lay in sackcloth and in ashes.

4 ¶ Then Esther's maids and her Eunuchs came and told it her: therefore the queen was very heavy, and she sent raiment to clothe Mordecai, and to take away his sackcloth from him, but he received it not.

5 Then called Esther Hathach *one* of the King's eunuchs, whom he [1]had appointed to serve her, and gave him a commandment unto Mordecai, to know what it was, and why it was.

6 So Hathach went forth to Mordecai unto the street of the city, which was before the king's gate.

7 And Mordecai told him of all that which had come unto him, and of the [1]sum of the silver that Haman had promised to pay unto the King's treasures, because of the Jews, for to destroy them.

8 Also he gave him the [1]copy of the writing *and* commission that was given at Shushan, to destroy them, that he might show it unto Esther and declare it unto her, and to charge her that she should go in to the king, and make petition and supplication before him for her people.

9 ¶ So when Hathach came, he told Esther the words of Mordecai.

10 Then Esther said unto Hathach, and commanded him *to say* unto Mordecai,

11 All the king's servants and the people of the King's provinces do know, That whosoever, man or woman, that cometh to the king into the inner court, which is not called, there *is* a law of his, that he shall die, except him to whom the king holdeth out the golden rod, that he may live. Now I have not been called to come unto the king these thirty days.

12 And they certified Mordecai of Esther's words.

13 And Mordecai said, that they should answer Esther *thus*, Think not with thyself that thou shalt escape in the king's house, more than all the Jews.

14 For if thou holdest thy peace at this time, [1]comfort and deliverance [2]shall appear to the Jews out of another place, but thou and thy father's house shall perish: and who knoweth whether thou art come to the kingdom for [3]such a time?

15 Then Esther commanded to answer Mordecai,

16 Go, *and* assemble all the Jews that are found in Shushan, and fast ye for me, and eat not, nor drink in three days, day nor night. I also and my maids will fast likewise, and so will I go in to the King, which is not according to the law: and if I perish, [1]I perish.

17 So Mordecai went his way, and did according to all that Esther had commanded him.

5 1 *Esther entereth to the King, and biddeth him and Haman to a feast.* 14 *Haman prepareth a gallows for Mordecai.*

1 And on the third [1]day Esther put on her royal apparel, and stood in the court of the King's palace within, over against the King's house: and the King sat upon his royal throne in the king's palace over against the gate of the house.

2 And when the King saw Esther the Queen standing in the court, she found favor in his sight: and the King [1]held out the golden scepter that was in his hand: so Esther drew near, and touched the top of the scepter.

3:15 [1] To wit, the Jews that were in Shushan.
4:2 [1] Because he would advertise Esther of this cruel proclamation.
4:3 [1] Hebrew, *sackcloth and ashes were spread for many.*
4:5 [1] Hebrew, *had caused to stand before her.*
4:7 [1] Hebrew, *declaration.*
4:8 [1] Or, contents.
4:14 [1] Hebrew, *breathing.*
[2] Thus Mordecai spake in the confidence of that faith which all God's children ought to have: which is, that God will deliver them, though all worldly means fail.
[3] For to deliver God's Church out of these present dangers.
4:16 [1] I will put my life in danger and refer the success to God, seeing it is for his glory and the deliverance of his Church.
5:1 [1] To wit, after that the Jews had begun to fast.
5:2 [1] Which was a sign that her coming was agreeable unto him, as Esther 4:11.

3 Then said the King unto her, What wilt thou, Queen Esther? and what is thy request? it shall be even ¹given thee to the half of the kingdom.

4 Then said Esther, If it please the king, let the King and Haman come this day unto the banquet, that I have prepared for him.

5 And the king said, Cause Haman to make haste, that he may do as Esther hath said. So the king and Haman came to the banquet that Esther had prepared.

6 And the king said unto Esther at the banquet of ¹wine, What is thy petition, that it may be given thee? and what is thy request? it shall even be performed unto the half of the kingdom.

7 Then answered Esther, and said, My petition, and my request *is*,

8 If I have found favor in the sight of the king, and if it please the king to give me my petition, and to perform my request, let the king and Haman come to the banquet that I shall prepare for them, and I will do tomorrow according to the king's ¹saying.

9 ¶ Then went Haman forth the same day joyful, and with a glad heart. But when Haman saw Mordecai in the king's gate, that he stood not up, nor moved for him, then was Haman full of indignation at Mordecai.

10 Nevertheless, Haman refrained himself: and when he came home, he sent, and called for his friends, and Zeresh his wife.

11 And Haman told them of the glory of his riches, and the multitude of his children, and all the things wherein the king had ¹promoted him, and how that he had set him above the princes and servants of the king.

12 Haman said moreover, Yea, Esther the queen did let no man come in with the king to the banquet that she had prepared, save me: and tomorrow am I bidden unto her also with the king.

13 But all this doth nothing avail me, as long as I see Mordecai the Jew sitting at the king's gate.

14 Then said Zeresh his wife and all his friends unto him, Let them make a tree of fifty ¹cubits high, and tomorrow speak thou unto the king, that Mordecai may be hanged thereon: then shalt thou go joyfully with the king unto the banquet. And the thing pleased Haman, and he caused to make the tree.

CHAPTER 6
ª Esther 2:22

6

2 The king turneth over the Chronicles, and findeth the fidelity of Mordecai, 10 and commandeth Haman to cause Mordecai to be had in honor.

1 The same night ¹the king slept not, and he commanded to bring the book of the Records, *and* the Chronicles: and they were read before the king.

2 Then it was found written that Mordecai ªhad told of Bigthana and Teresh, two of the king's eunuchs keepers of the door, who sought to lay hands on King Ahasuerus.

3 Then the king said, What honor and dignity hath been given to Mordecai ¹for this? And the king's servants that ministered unto him, said, There is nothing done for him.

4 And the king said, Who is in the court? (Now Haman was come into the inner court of the king's house, that he might speak unto the king to ¹hang Mordecai on the tree that he had prepared for him.)

5 And the king's servants said unto him, Behold, Haman standeth in the court. And the king said, Let him come in.

6 And when Haman came in, the king said unto him, What shall be done unto the man whom the king will honor? Then Haman thought in his heart, To whom would the king do honor more than to me?

7 And Haman answered the king, The man whom the king would honor,

8 Let them bring *for him* royal apparel, which the king *useth* to wear, and the ¹horse that the king rideth upon, and that the crown royal may be set upon his head.

9 And let the raiment and the horse be delivered by the hand of one of the king's most noble princes, and let them apparel the man (whom the king will honor) and cause him to ride upon the horse through the street of the city, and proclaim before him, Thus shall it be done unto the man whom the king will honor.

10 Then the king said to Haman, Make haste, take the raiment and the horse, as thou hast said, and do so unto Mordecai the Jew, that sitteth at the king's gate: let nothing fail of all that thou hast spoken.

11 So Haman took the raiment and the horse, and arrayed Mordecai, and brought him on horseback through the street of the city, and proclaimed before him, Thus shall it be done to the man whom the king

---

5:3 ¹ Meaning hereby, that whatsoever she asked should be granted, as Mark 6:23.
5:6 ¹ Because they used to drink excessively in their banquets, they called the banquet by the name of that which was most in use or esteemed.
5:8 ¹ I will declare what thing I demand.
5:11 ¹ Thus the wicked when they are promoted, instead of acknowledging their charge and humbling themselves, wax ambitious, disdainful, and cruel.

5:14 ¹ Meaning, the highest that could be found.
6:1 ¹ Hebrew, *the king's sleep departed*.
6:3 ¹ For he thought it unworthy his estate to receive a benefit, and not reward it.
6:4 ¹ Thus while the wicked imagine the destruction of others, they themselves fall into the same pit.
6:8 ¹ Meaning hereby that the king should make him next unto himself, as Joseph hereby was known to be next to Pharaoh, Gen. 41:41.

will honor.

12 And Mordecai came again to the king's gate, but Haman hasted home mourning and his head covered.

13 And Haman told Zeresh his wife, and all his friends, all that had befallen him. Then said his wise men, and Zeresh his wife unto him, If Mordecai be of the seed of the Jews, before whom thou hast begun to fall, thou shalt not prevail against him, [1]but shalt surely fall before him.

14 And while they were yet talking with him, came the king's eunuchs and hasted to bring Haman unto the banquet that Esther had prepared.

7 *3 The queen biddeth the king and Haman again, and prayeth for herself and her people. 6 She accuseth Haman, and he is hanged on the gallows which he had prepared for Mordecai.*

1 So the king and Haman came to banquet with the queen Esther.

2 And the king said again unto Esther on the second day at the banquet of [1]wine, What is thy petition, Queen Esther, that it may be given thee? and what is thy request? It shall be even performed unto the half of the kingdom.

3 And Esther the queen answered, and said, If I have found favor in thy sight, O king, and if it please the king, let my life be given me at my petition, and my people at my request.

4 For we are sold, I, and my people, to be destroyed, to be slain, and to perish: but if we were sold for servants, and for handmaids, I would have held my tongue, although the adversary could not [1]recompense the king's loss.

5 Then king Ahasuerus answered, and said unto the queen Esther, Who is he? and where is he that [1]presumeth to do thus?

6 And Esther said, The adversary and enemy is this wicked Haman. Then Haman was afraid before the king and the queen.

7 And the king arose from the banquet of wine in his wrath, *and went* into the palace garden: but Haman stood up to make request for his life to the queen Esther: for he saw that there was a [1]mischief prepared for him of the king.

8 And when the king came again out of the palace garden, into the house where they drank wine, Haman was [1]fallen upon the bed whereon Esther *sat*: therefore the King said, Will he force the Queen also before me in the house? As the word went out of the King's mouth, they [2]covered Haman's face.

9 And Harbonah one of the eunuchs, said in the presence of the King, Behold, there standeth yet the tree in Haman's house fifty cubits high, which Haman had prepared for Mordecai, that spake [1]good for the king. Then the King said, Hang him thereon.

10 So they hanged Haman on the tree, that he had prepared for Mordecai: then was the King's wrath pacified.

8 *1 After the death of Haman was Mordecai exalted. 14 Comfortable letters are sent unto the Jews.*

1 The same day did King Ahasuerus give the house of Haman the adversary of the Jews, unto the Queen Esther. And Mordecai [1]came before the King: for Esther told what he was [2]unto her.

2 And the King took off his ring, which he had taken from Haman, and gave it unto Mordecai: and Esther set Mordecai over the house of Haman.

3 And Esther spake yet more before the King, and fell down at his feet weeping, and besought him that he would put away the [1]wickedness of Haman the Agagite, and his device that he had imagined against the Jews.

4 And the King held out the golden [1]scepter toward Esther. Then arose Esther, and stood before the King,

5 And said, If it please the King, and if I have found favor in his sight, and the thing be acceptable before the King, and I please him, let it be written, that the letters of the device of Haman the son of Hammedatha the Agagite may be called again, which he wrote to destroy the Jews, that are in all the King's provinces.

6 For how can I suffer and see the evil, that shall come unto my people? Or how can I suffer and see the destruction of my kindred?

7 And the king Ahasuerus said unto the Queen Esther, and to Mordecai the Jew, Behold, I have given Esther the house of Haman, whom they have hanged upon the tree, because he [1]laid hand upon

---

6:13 [1] Thus God sometimes putteth in the mouth of the very wicked, to speak that thing which he hath decreed shall come to pass.
7:2 [1] Read Esther 5:6.
7:4 [1] Haman could not so much profit the king by this his malice, as he should hinder him by the loss of the Jews, and the tribute which he hath of them.
7:5 [1] Hebrew, *filleth his heart.*
7:7 [1] His conscience did accuse him that as he had conspired the death of innocents, so the vengeance of God might fall upon him for the same.
7:8 [1] He fell down at the bed's feet or couch, whereupon she sat, and

made request for his life.
[2] This was the manner of the Persians, when one was out of the King's favor.
7:9 [1] Which discovered the conspiracy against the king, Esther 2:21, 22.
8:1 [1] That is, was received into the king's favor and presence.
[2] That he was her uncle, and had brought her up.
8:3 [1] Meaning, that he should abolish the wicked decrees, which had made for the destruction of the Jews.
8:4 [1] Read Esther 5:2.
8:7 [1] Or, went about to slay the Jews.

the Jews.

8 Write ye also for the Jews, as it liketh you in the King's name, and seal it with the King's ring, (for the writings written in the King's name, and sealed with the king's ring, may ¹no man revoke.)

9 Then were the King's Scribes called at the same time, even in the third month, that is the month ¹Sivan, on the three and twentieth *day* thereof: and it was written, according to all as Mordecai commanded, unto the Jews and to the princes, and captains and rulers of the provinces, which were from India even unto Ethiopia, an hundred and seven and twenty provinces, unto every province according to the ²writing thereof, and to every people after their speech, and to the Jews, according to their writing, and according to their language.

10 And he wrote in the King Ahasuerus's name, and sealed it with the King's ring, and he sent letters by posts on horseback *and* that rode on *beasts* of price, *as* dromedaries, *and* ¹colts of mares.

11 Wherein the King granted the Jews (in what cities soever they were) to gather themselves together, and to stand for ¹their life, *and* to root out, to slay and to destroy all the power of the people and of the province that vexed them, *both* children and women, and to spoil their goods:

12 Upon one day in all the provinces of King Ahasuerus, *even* in the thirteenth *day* of the twelfth month, which is the month ¹Adar.

13 The copy of the writing *was*, how there should be a commandment given in all and every province, published among all the people, and that the Jews should be ready against that day, to ¹avenge themselves on their enemies.

14 *So* the posts rode upon *beasts* of price, *and* dromedaries, *and* went forth with speed, to execute the King's commandment, and the decree was given at Shushan the palace.

15 And Mordecai went out from the King in royal apparel of blue, and white, and with a great crown of gold, and with a garment of fine linen and purple, and the city of Shushan rejoiced and was glad.

16 *And* unto the Jews was come light and ¹joy and gladness, and honor.

17 Also in all and every province, and in all and every city and place, where the King's commandment and his decree came, *there was* joy and gladness to the Jews, a feast and good day, and many of the people of the land ¹became Jews: for the fear of the Jews fell upon them.

9 1 *At the commandment of the King, the Jews put their adversaries to death.* 14 *The ten sons of Haman are hanged.* 17 *The Jews keep a feast in remembrance of their deliverance.*

1 So in the twelfth month, which is the month Adar, upon the thirteenth day of the same, when the King's commandment and his decree drew near to be put in execution, in the day that the enemies of the Jews hoped to have power over them (but it ¹turned contrary: for the Jews had rule over them that hated them.)

2 The Jews gathered themselves together into their cities throughout all the provinces of the King Ahasuerus, to lay hand on such as sought their hurt, and no man could withstand them: for the fear of them fell upon all people.

3 And all the rulers of the provinces, and the princes and the captains, and the officers of the King ¹exalted the Jews: for the fear of Mordecai fell upon them.

4 For Mordecai was great in the King's house, and the report of him went through all the provinces: for this man Mordecai waxed greater and greater.

5 Thus the Jews smote all their ¹enemies with strokes of the sword and slaughter, and destruction, and did what they would unto those that hated them.

6 And at Shushan the palace slew the Jews and destroyed ¹five hundred men,

7 And Parshandatha, and Dalphon, and Aspatha,

8 And Poratha, and Adalia, and Aridatha,

9 And Parmashta, and Arisai, and Aridai, and Vajezatha,

10 The ten sons of Haman, the son of Hammedatha, the adversary of the Jews slew they: but they laid not their hands ¹on the spoil.

11 On the same day came the number of those that were slain, unto the palace of Shushan before the King.

8:8 ¹ This was the law of the Medes and Persians, as Dan. 6:15, notwithstanding the king revoked the former decree granted to Haman, for Esther's sake.
8:9 ¹ Which containeth part of May and part of June.
  ² That is, in such letters and language, as was usual in every province.
8:10 ¹ Or, mules.
8:11 ¹ That is, to defend themselves against all that would assail them.
8:12 ¹ Which hath part of February and part of March.
8:13 ¹ The king gave them liberty to kill all that did oppress them.
8:16 ¹ He showeth by these words that follow, what this light was.
8:17 ¹ Conformed themselves to the Jew's religion.
9:1 ¹ This was by God's great providence, who turneth the joy of the wicked into sorrow, and the tears of the godly into gladness.
9:3 ¹ Did them honor, and showed them friendship.
9:5 ¹ Which had conspired their death by the permission of the wicked Haman.
9:6 ¹ Besides those three hundred, that they slew the second day, as verse 15.
9:10 ¹ Whereby they declared that this was God's just judgment upon the enemies of his Church, forasmuch as they sought not their own gain, but to execute his vengeance.

12 And the King said unto the Queen Esther, The Jews have slain in Shushan the palace, and destroyed five hundred men, and the ten sons of Haman: what have they done in the rest of the King's provinces? and what is thy petition, that it may be given thee? or what is thy request moreover, that it may be performed?

13 Then said Esther, If it please the King, let it be granted also tomorrow to the Jews that are in Shushan, to do according ¹unto this day's decree, that they may hang upon the tree Haman's ten sons.

14 And the King charged to do so, and the decree was given at Shushan, and they hanged Haman's ten sons.

15 ¶ So the Jews that were in Shushan, assembled themselves upon the fourteenth day of the month Adar, and slew three hundred men in Shushan, but on the spoil they laid not their hand.

16 And the rest of the Jews that were in the King's provinces assembled themselves, and stood for ¹their lives, and had rest from their enemies, and slew of them that ²hated them, seventy and five thousand: but they laid not their hand on the spoil.

17 *This they did* on the ¹thirteenth day of the month Adar, and rested the fourteenth day thereof, and kept it a day of feasting and joy.

18 But the Jews that were in Shushan assembled themselves on the thirteenth *day*, and on the fourteenth thereof, and they rested on the fifteenth of the same, and kept it a day of feasting and joy.

19 Therefore the Jews of the villages that dwelt in the unwalled towns, ¹kept the fourteenth day of the month Adar with joy and feasting, *even* a joyful day, and everyone sent presents unto his neighbor.

20 ¶ And Mordecai wrote ¹these words, and sent letters unto all the Jews that were through all the provinces of the King Ahasuerus, *both* near and far,

21 Enjoining them that they should keep the fourteenth day of the month Adar, and the fifteenth day of the same, every year.

22 According to the days wherein the Jews rested from their enemies, and the month which was turned unto them from sorrow to joy, and from mourning into a joyful day, to keep them the days of feasting and joy, and to ¹send presents every man to his neighbor, and gifts to the poor.

23 And the Jews promised to do as they had begun, and as Mordecai had written unto them,

24 Because Haman the son of Hammedatha the Agagite all the Jews' adversary had imagined against the Jews to destroy them, and had ¹cast Pur (that is a lot) to consume and destroy them.

25 And when ¹she came before the king, he commanded by letters, Let this wicked ²device (which he imagined against the Jews) turn upon his own head, and let them hang him and his sons on the tree.

26 Therefore they called these days Purim, by the name of Pur, *and* because of all the words of this letter, and of that which they had seen besides this, and of that which had come unto them.

27 The Jews *also* ordained, and promised for them and for their seed, and for all that joined unto them, that they would not ¹fail to observe those two ²days every year, according to their writing, and according unto their season,

28 And that these days should be remembered, and kept throughout every generation and every family, and every province, and every city: even these days of Purim should not fail among the Jews, and the memorial of them should not perish from their seed.

29 And the Queen Esther the daughter of Abihail and Mordecai the Jew wrote with all ¹authority (to confirm this letter of Purim the second time.)

30 And he sent letters unto all the Jews to the hundred and seven and twenty provinces of the kingdom of Ahasuerus, with ¹words of peace and truth,

31 To confirm these days of Purim according to their seasons, as Mordecai the Jew and Esther the Queen had appointed them, and as they had promised for ¹themselves and for their seed with ²fasting and prayer.

32 And the decree of Esther confirmed these words of Purim, and was written in the book.

10

1 *The estimation and authority of Mordecai.*

9:13 ¹ This she requireth not for desire of vengeance, but with zeal to see God's judgments executed against his enemies.

9:16 ¹ Read Esther 8:11.
    ² Meaning, that they laid hands on none that were not this enemies of God.

9:17 ¹ Meaning, in all places saving in Shushan.

9:19 ¹ As the Jews do even to this day, calling it in the Persian language Purim, that is, the day of lots.

9:20 ¹ The Jews gather hereof that Mordecai wrote this story: but it seemeth that he wrote but only these letters and decrees that follow.

9:22 ¹ He setteth before our eyes the use of this feast, which was for the remembrance of God's deliverance, the maintenance of mutual friendship and relief of the poor.

9:24 ¹ Read Esther 3.

9:25 ¹ That is, Esther.
    ² These are the words of the king's commandment to disannul Haman's wicked enterprise.

9:27 ¹ Or, transgress.
    ² Meaning, the fourteenth and fifteenth day of the month of Adar.

9:29 ¹ Or, strength, or efficacy.

9:30 ¹ Which were letters declaring unto them quietness, and assurance and putting them out of doubt and fear.

9:31 ¹ Hebrew, *souls.*
    ² That they would observe this feast with fasting and earnest prayer, which in Hebrew is signified by this word (they cry).

1   And the King Ahasuerus laid a tribute upon the land, and upon the isles of the sea.

2   And all the acts of his power, and of his might, and the declaration of the dignity of Mordecai, wherewith the King magnified him, are they not written in the book of the Chronicles of the Kings of Media and Persia?

3   For Mordecai the Jew was the second unto king Ahasuerus, and great among the Jews, and [1]accepted among the multitude of his brethren, who procured the wealth of his people, and spake peaceably to all his seed.

10:3 [1] These three points are here set forth as commendable and necessary for him that is in authority, to have the favor of the people, to procure their wealth, and to be gentle and loving toward them.

JOB

1 1 The holiness, riches, and care of Job for his children. 10 Satan hath permission to tempt him. 13 He
tempteth him by taking away his substance, and his children. 20 His faith and patience.

1 There was a man in the land of [1]Uz called Job,
and this man [2]was an upright and just man, [3]one that
feared God, and eschewed evil.

2 And he had seven sons, and three daughters.

3 His [1]substance also was seven thousand sheep,
and three thousand camels, and five hundred yoke
of oxen, and five hundred she asses, and his family
was very great, so that this man was the greatest of
all the [2]men of [3]the East.

4 And his sons went and banqueted in their
houses, every one his day, and sent, and called their
three sisters to eat and to drink with them.

5 And when the days of their banqueting were
gone about, Job sent, and [1]sanctified them, and rose
up early in the morning, and [2]offered burnt offerings
according to the number of them all. For Job thought,
It may be that my sons have sinned, and [3]blasphemed
God in their hearts, thus did Job [4]every day.

6 ¶ Now on a day when the [1]children of God
came and stood [2]before the Lord, Satan [3]came also
among them.

7 Then the Lord said unto Satan, Whence [1]comest
thou? And Satan answered the Lord, saying, [2]From
compassing the earth to and fro, and from walking
in it.

8 And the Lord said unto Satan, Hast thou not
considered my servant Job, how none *is* like him in
the earth? an upright and just man, one that feareth
God, and escheweth evil?

9 Then Satan answered the Lord, and said, Doth
Job fear God for [1]nought?

10 Hast thou not made [1]an hedge about him and
about his house, and about all that he hath on every
side? thou hast blessed the work of his hands, and
his substance is increased in the land.

11 But stretch out now thine hand and [1]touch all
that he hath, *to see* if he will not blaspheme thee [2]to
thy face.

12 Then the Lord said unto Satan, Lo, all that he
hath *is* in [1]thine hand: only upon himself shalt thou
not stretch out thine hand. So Satan departed from
the [2]presence of the Lord.

13 ¶ And on a day, when his sons and his daughters were eating and drinking wine in their eldest
brother's house,

14 There came a messenger unto Job, and said,
The oxen were plowing, and the asses feeding in
their places,

1:1 [1] That is, of the country of Idumea, as Lam. 4:21, or bordering
thereupon: for the land was called by the name of Uz, the son of
Dishan the son of Seir, Gen. 36:28.

[2] Forasmuch as he was a Gentile, and not a Jew, and yet is pronounced upright, and without hypocrisy, it declareth that among the
heathen God hath his.

[3] Hereby is declared, what is meant by an upright and just man.
1:3 [1] His children and riches are declared, to commend his virtue in
his prosperity and his patience, and constancy, when God had taken
them from him.

[2] Hebrew, *children*.

[3] Meaning, the Arabians, Chaldeans, Idumeans, etc.
1:5 [1] That is, commanded them to be sanctified: meaning, that they
should consider the faults that they had committed, and reconcile
themselves for the same.

[2] That is, he offered for every one of his children an offering of reconciliation, which declared his religion toward God, and the care that
he had toward his children.

[3] In Hebrew it is, *and blessed God*, which is sometimes taken for
blaspheming and cursing, as here and 1 Kings 21:10, 13, etc.

[4] While the feast lasted.
1:6 [1] Meaning, the Angels, which are called the sons of God, because
they are willing to execute his will.

[2] Because our infirmity cannot comprehend God in his majesty,
he is set forth unto us as a King, that our capacity may be able to
understand that which is spoken of him.

[3] This declareth, that although Satan be adversary to God, yet he
is compelled to obey him, and do him all homage, without whose
permission and appointment he can do nothing.
1:7 [1] This question is asked for our infirmity: for God knew whence
he came.

[2] Herein is described the nature of Satan, which is ever ranging for
his prey, 1 Pet. 5:8.
1:9 [1] He feareth thee not for thine own sake, but for the commodity
that he received by thee.
1:10 [1] Meaning, the grace of God, which served Job as a rampart
against all tentations.
1:11 [1] This signifieth, that Satan is not able to touch us, but it is God
that must do it.

[2] Satan noteth the vice whereunto men are commonly subject,
that is, to hide their rebellion, and to be content with God in the time
of prosperity, which view is disclosed in the time of their adversity.
1:12 [1] God giveth not Satan power over man to gratify him, but to declare
that he hath no power over man, but that which God giveth him.

[2] That is, went to execute that which God had permitted him to
do: for else he can never go out of God's presence.

15 And the [1]Sabeans came violently, and took them: yea, they have slain the servants with the edge of the sword: but I only am escaped alone to tell thee.

16 And while he was yet speaking, another came, and said, The [1]fire of God is fallen from the heaven, and hath burnt up the sheep and the servants, and devoured them: but I only am escaped alone to tell thee.

17 And while he was yet speaking, there came another, and said, The Chaldeans set on three bands, and fell upon the camels, and have taken them, and have slain the servants with the edge of the sword: but I only am escaped alone to tell thee.

18 And while he was yet speaking, came another, and said, Thy [1]sons, and thy daughters were eating, and drinking wine in their eldest brother's house,

19 And behold, there came a great wind from beyond the wilderness, and smote the four corners of the house, which fell upon the children, and they are dead, and I only am escaped alone to tell thee.

20 Then Job arose, and [1]rent his garment, and shaved his head, and fell down upon the ground, and worshipped,

21 And said, [a]Naked came I out of my mother's womb, and naked shall I return [1]thither: the Lord hath given, and the Lord hath taken it: [2]blessed be the Name of the Lord.

22 In all this did not Job sin, nor charge God [1]foolishly.

2 6 Satan hath permission to afflict Job.   9 His wife tempteth him to forsake God.   11 His three friends visit him.

CHAPTER 1
a Eccl. 5:14
1 Tim. 6:7

CHAPTER 2
a Ezek. 14:14
Job 1:1

1 And on a day the [1]children of God came and stood before the Lord, and [2]Satan came also among them, and stood before the Lord.

2 Then the Lord said unto Satan, Whence comest thou? And Satan answered the Lord, and said, From compassing the earth to and fro, and from walking in it.

3 And the Lord said unto Satan, Hast thou not considered my servant Job, how none is like him in the earth? [a]an upright and just man, one that feareth God, and escheweth evil? for yet he continueth in his uprightness, [1]although thou movedst me against him, to destroy [2]him without cause.

4 And Satan answered the Lord, and said, [1]Skin for skin, and all that ever a man hath, will he give for his life.

5 But stretch now out thine hand, and touch his [1]bones and his flesh, to see if he will not blaspheme thee to thy face.

6 Then the Lord said unto Satan, Lo, he is in thine hand, but save [1]his life.

7 ¶ So Satan departed from the presence of the Lord, and smote Job with sore [1]boils, from the sole of his foot unto his crown.

8 And he took a [1]potsherd to scrape him, and he sat down among the ashes.

9 Then said his [1]wife unto him, Dost thou [2]continue yet in thine uprightness? [3]Blaspheme God, and die.

10 But he said unto her, Thou speakest like a foolish woman: what? shall we receive good at the hand of God, and not [1]receive evil? In all this did not Job sin with his [2]lips.

1:15 [1] That is, the Arabians.
1:16 [1] Which thing was also done by the craft of Satan, to tempt Job the more grievously, forasmuch as he might see, that not only men were his enemies, but that God made war against him.
1:18 [1] This last plague declareth, that when one plague is past which seemeth hard to be borne, God can send us another far more grievous, to try his, and teach them obedience.
1:20 [1] Which came not of impatience, but declareth that the children of God are not insensible like blocks, but that in their patience they feel affliction and grief of mind: yet they keep a mean herein, and rebel not against God, as the wicked do.
1:21 [1] That is, into the belly of the earth, which is the mother of all.
[2] Hereby he confesseth that God is just, and good, although his hand be sore upon him.
1:22 [1] But declared that God did all things according to justice and equity.
2:1 [1] That is, the Angels, as Job 1:6.
[2] Read Job 1:6.
2:3 [1] He proveth Job's integrity by this that he ceased not to fear God when his plagues were grievously upon him.
[2] That is, when thou hadst nought against him, or when thou wast not able to bring thy purpose to pass.
2:4 [1] Hereby he meant, that a man's own skin is dearer unto him than another man's.

2:5 [1] Meaning, his own person.
2:6 [1] Thus Satan can go no further in punishing, than God hath limited him.
2:7 [1] This sore was most vehement, wherewith also God plagued the Egyptians, Exod. 9:9, and threateneth to punish the rebellious people, Deut. 28:27, so that this tentation was most grievous: for if Job had measured God's favor by the vehemency of his disease, he might have thought that God had cast him off.
2:8 [1] As destitute of all other help and means, and wonderfully afflicted with the sorrow of his disease.
2:9 [1] Satan useth the same instrument against Job, as he did against Adam.
[2] Meaning, what gainest thou to serve God, seeing he thus plagueth thee, as though he were thine enemy? This is the most grievous temptation of the faithful, when their faith is assailed, and when Satan goeth about to persuade them that they trust in God in vain.
[3] For death was appointed to the blasphemer, and so she meant that he should soon be rid out of his pain.
2:10 [1] That is, to be patient in adversity, as we rejoice when he sendeth prosperity, and so to acknowledge him to be both merciful and just.
[2] He so bridled his affections, that his tongue through impatience did not murmur against God.

11 Now when Job's three ¹friends heard of all this evil that was come upon him, they came every one from his own place, *to wit*, Eliphaz the Temanite, and Bildad the Shuhite, and Zophar the Naamathite: for they were agreed together to come to lament with him, and to comfort him.

12 So when they lifted up their eyes afar off, they knew him not: therefore they lifted up their voices and wept, and every one of them rent his garment and sprinkled ¹dust upon their heads toward the heaven.

13 So they sat by him upon the ground seven days, and seven nights, and none spake a word unto him: for they saw that the grief *was* very ¹great.

3

1 Job complaineth, and curseth the day of his birth. 11 He desireth to die, as though death were the end of all man's misery.

1 Afterward ¹Job opened his mouth, and ²cursed his day.

2 And Job cried out, and said,

3 Let the day ¹perish wherein I was born, and the night when it was said, There is a man child conceived.

4 Let that day be darkness, let not God ¹regard it from above, neither let the light shine upon it,

5 *But* let darkness and the ¹shadow of death stain it: let the cloud remain upon it, and let them make it fearful as a bitter day.

6 Let darkness possess that night, let it not be joined unto the days of the year, nor let it come into the count of the months.

7 Yea, desolate be that night, and let no joy be in it.

8 Let them that curse the day, (being ¹ready to renew their mourning) curse it.

9 Let the stars of that twilight be dim through darkness of it: let it look for light, but have none: neither let it ¹see ²the dawning of the day,

10 Because it shut not up the doors of my *mother's* womb, nor hid sorrow from mine eyes.

11 ¹Why died I not in the birth? or why died I not, when I came out of the womb?

12 Why did the knees prevent me? and why did I suck the breasts?

13 For *so* should I now have ¹lain and been quiet, I should have slept then, *and* been at rest,

14 With the kings and counselors of the earth, which have built themselves ¹desolate places:

15 Or with the princes that had gold, *and* have filled their houses with silver.

16 Or *why* was I not hid, as an untimely birth, *either* as infants, *which* have not seen the light?

17 The wicked ¹have there ceased from *their* tyranny, and there they that labored valiantly, are at rest.

18 The ¹prisoners rest together, *and* hear not the voice of the oppressor.

19 There are small and great, and the servant *is* free from his master.

20 Wherefore is the light given to him that is in misery? and ¹life unto them that have heavy hearts?

21 Which long for death, and if it come not, they would even search it more than treasures:

22 Which joy for gladness, *and* rejoice, when they can find the grave.

23 *Why is the light given* to the man whose way is ¹hid, and whom God hath hedged in?

24 For my sighing cometh before I eat, and my roarings are poured out like the water.

25 For the thing I ¹feared, is come upon me, and the thing that I was afraid of, is come unto me.

2:11 ¹ Which were men of authority, wise and learned, and as the Septuagint writes, Kings, and came to comfort him, but when they saw how he was visited, they conceived an evil opinion of him, as though he had been but an hypocrite, and so justly plagued of God for his sins.

2:12 ¹ This was also a ceremony, which they used in those countries, as the renting of their clothes in sign of sorrow, etc.

2:13 ¹ And therefore thought that he would not have hearkened unto their counsel.

3:1 ¹ The seven days ended, Job 2:13.

² Here Job beginneth to feel his great imperfection in this battle between the spirit and the flesh, Rom. 7:18, and after a manner yieldeth, yet in the end he getteth victory, though he was in the mean time greatly wounded.

3:3 ¹ Men ought not to be weary of their life, and curse it, because of the infirmities that it is subject unto, but because they are given to sin and rebellion against God.

3:4 ¹ Let it be put out of the number of days, and let it not have the light of the Sun to separate it from the night.

3:5 ¹ That is, most obscure darkness, which maketh them afraid of death that are in it.

3:8 ¹ Which curse the day of their birth, let them lay that curse upon this night.

3:9 ¹ Let it be always night, and never see day.

² Hebrew, *The eyelids of the morning.*

3:11 ¹ This, and that which followeth, declareth, that when man giveth place to his passions, he is not able to stay nor keep measure, but runneth headlong into all evil, except God call him back.

3:13 ¹ The vehemency of his afflictions made him to utter these words, as though death were the end of all miseries, and as if there were no life after this, which he speaketh not as though it were so, but the infirmities of his flesh caused him to burst out in this error of the wicked.

3:14 ¹ He noteth the ambition of them, which for their pleasure as it were change the order of nature, and build in most barren places, because they would hereby make their names immortal.

3:17 ¹ That is, by death the cruelty of the tyrants hath ceased.

3:18 ¹ All they that sustain any kind of calamity and misery in this world: which he speaketh after the judgment of the flesh.

3:20 ¹ He showeth that the benefits of God are not comfortable, expect the heart be joyful, and the conscience quieted.

3:23 ¹ That seeth not how to come out of his miseries, because he dependeth not on God's providence.

3:25 ¹ In my prosperity I looked ever for a fall, as is come now to pass.

26 I had no peace, neither had I quietness, neither had I rest, [1]yet trouble is come.

4

5 *Job is reprehended of impatience,* 7 *and of injustice,* 17 *and of the presumption of his own righteousness.*

1 Then Eliphaz the Temanite, answered and said,

2 If we assay to commune with thee, wilt thou be grieved? but [1]who can withhold himself from speaking?

3 Behold, thou hast taught many, and [1]hast strengthened the weary hands.

4 Thy words have confirmed him that was falling, and thou hast strengthened the weak knees.

5 But now it is come upon thee, and thou art grieved: it toucheth thee, and thou art troubled.

6 Is not this thy [1]fear, thy confidence, thy patience, and uprightness of thy ways?

7 Remember, I pray thee: who *ever* perished, being an [1]innocent? or where were the upright destroyed?

8 As I have seen, they that [1]plow iniquity, and sow wickedness, reap the same.

9 With the [1]blast of God they perish, and with the breath of his nostrils are they consumed.

10 The roaring of the [1]Lion, and the voice of the Lioness, and the teeth of the Lion's whelps are broken.

11 The Lion perisheth for lack of prey, and the Lion's whelps are scattered abroad.

12 But a thing was brought to me [1]secretly, and mine ear hath received a little thereof.

13 In the thoughts of the visions of the night, when sleep falleth on men,

14 Fear came upon me, and dread which made all my bones [1]to tremble.

15 And the wind passed before me, and made the hairs of my flesh to stand up.

16 *Then* stood *one*, and I knew not his face: an image *was* before mine eyes, *and in* [1]silence heard I a voice, *saying*,

17 Shall man be more [1]just than God? or shall a man be more pure than his Maker?

18 Behold, he found no steadfastness in his servants, and laid folly upon his [1]Angels.

19 How much more in them that dwell in houses of [1]clay, whose foundation is in the dust, which shall be destroyed before the moth?

20 They be destroyed from the [1]morning unto the evening: they perish forever, [2]without regard.

21 Doth not their dignity go away with them? do they not die, and that without [1]wisdom?

5

1, 2 *Eliphaz showeth the difference between the children of God and the wicked.* 3 *The fall of the wicked.* 9 *God's power who destroyeth the wicked, and delivereth his.*

1 Call now, if any will [1]answer thee, and to which of the Saints wilt thou turn?

2 Doubtless [1]anger killeth the foolish, and envy slayeth the idiot.

3 I have seen the [1]foolish well rooted, and suddenly I [2]cursed his habitation, *saying*,

4 His [1]children shall be far from salvation, and they shall be destroyed in the [2]gate, and none shall deliver them.

3:26 [1] The fear of troubles that should ensue, caused my prosperity to seem to me as nothing, and yet I am not exempted from trouble.

4:2 [1] Seeing this thine impatience.

4:3 [1] Thou hast comforted others in their afflictions, and canst not now comfort thyself.

4:6 [1] This he concludeth that Job was but an hypocrite, and had no true fear nor trust in God.

4:7 [1] He concludeth that Job was reproved, seeing that God handled him so extremely, which is the argument that the carnal men make against the children of God.

4:8 [1] They that do evil, cannot but receive evil.

4:9 [1] He showeth that God needeth no great preparation to destroy his enemies: for he can do it with the blast of his mouth.

4:10 [1] Though men according to their office do not punish tyrants (whom for their cruelty he compareth to lions, and their children to their whelps) yet God both is able, and his justice will punish them.

4:12 [1] A thing that I knew not before, was declared unto me by vision, that is, that whosoever thinketh himself just, shall be found a sinner, when he cometh before God.

4:14 [1] In these visions which God showeth to his creatures, there is ever a certain fear joined, that the authority thereof might be had in greater reverence.

4:16 [1] When all things were quiet, or when the fear was somewhat assuaged, as God appeared to Elijah, 1 Kings 19:12.

4:17 [1] He proveth that if God did punish the innocent, the creature should be more just than the Creator, which were a blasphemy.

4:18 [1] If God find imperfection in his Angels, when they are not maintained by his power, how much more shall he lay folly to man's charge when he would justify himself against God?

4:19 [1] That is, in this mortal body, subject to corruption, as 2 Cor. 5:1.

4:20 [1] They see death continually before their eyes, and daily approaching toward them.

[2] No man for all this doth consider it.

4:21 [1] That is, before that any of them were so wise, as to think on death.

5:1 [1] He willeth Job to consider the example of all them that have lived or do live godly, whether any of them be like unto him in raging against God as he doth.

5:2 [1] Murmuring against God in afflictions increaseth the pain, and uttered man's folly.

5:3 [1] That is, the sinner that hath not the fear of God.

[2] I was not moved with his prosperity, but knew that God had cursed him and his.

5:4 [1] Though God sometimes suffer the fathers to pass in this world, yet his judgments will light upon their wicked children.

[2] By public judgment they shall be condemned, and none shall pity them.

5 The hungry shall eat up his harvest: yea, they shall take it from among the ¹thorns, and the thirsty shall drink up their substance.

6 For misery cometh not forth of the dust, ¹neither doeth affliction spring out of the earth.

7 But man is born unto ¹travail, as the sparks fly upward.

8 But I would inquire at ¹God, and turn my talk unto God:

9 Which ¹doeth great things, and unsearchable, and marvelous things without number.

10 He ¹giveth rain upon the earth, and poureth water upon the streets,

11 And setteth up on high them that be low, that the sorrowful may be exalted to salvation.

12 He scattereth the devices of the crafty: so that their hands cannot accomplish that which they do enterprise.

13 ᵃHe taketh the wise in their craftiness, and the counsel of the wicked is made foolish.

14 They meet with ¹darkness in the daytime, and ²grope at noonday, as in the night.

15 But he saveth the ¹poor from the sword, from their ²mouth, and from the hand of the violent man,

16 So that the poor hath his hope, but iniquity shall ¹stop her mouth.

17 Behold, blessed is the man whom God correcteth: therefore refuse not thou the chastising of the Almighty.

18 For he maketh the wound, and bindeth it up: he smiteth, and his hands make whole.

19 He shall deliver thee in ¹six troubles, and in the seventh the evil shall not touch thee.

20 In famine he shall deliver thee from death: and

CHAPTER 5
ᵃ 1 Cor. 3:19

in battle from the power of the sword.

21 Thou shalt be hid from the scourge of the tongue, and thou shalt not be afraid of destruction when it cometh.

22 But thou shalt ¹laugh at destruction and dearth, and shalt not be afraid of the beast of the earth.

23 For the stones of the field ¹shall be in league with thee, and the beasts of the field shall be at peace with thee.

24 And thou shalt know, that peace shall be in thy tabernacle, and thou shalt visit thine habitation, and shalt not ¹sin.

25 Thou shalt perceive also that thy seed shall be great, and thy posterity as the grass of the earth.

26 Thou shalt go to thy grave in ¹a full age, as a rick of corn cometh in due season into the barn.

27 Lo, ¹thus have we inquired of it, and so it is: hear this and know it for thyself.

6 1 Job answereth, that his pain is more grievous than his fault. 8 He wisheth death. 14 He complaineth of his friends.

1 But Job answered and said,

2 Oh that my grief were well weighed, and my miseries were laid together in the ¹balance!

3 For it would be now heavier than the sand of the sea: therefore my words are ¹swallowed up.

4 For the arrows of the Almighty are in me, the venom whereof doth drink up my spirit, and the terrors of God ¹fight against me.

5 Doth the ¹wild ass bray when he hath grass? or loweth the ox when he hath fodder?

6 That which is ¹unsavory, shall it be eaten without salt? or is there any taste in the white of an egg?

7 Such things as my soul refused to touch, as

5:5 ¹ Though there be but two or three ears left in the hedges, yet these shall be taken from him.

5:6 ¹ That is, the earth is not the cause of barrenness and man's misery, but his own sin.

5:7 ¹ Which declareth that sin is ever in our corrupt nature: for before sin it was not subject to pain and affliction.

5:8 ¹ If I suffered as thou doest, I would seek unto God.

5:9 ¹ He counselleth Job to humble himself unto God to whom all creatures are subject and whose works declare that man is inexcusable except he glorify God in all his works.

5:10 ¹ He showeth by particular examples, what the works of God are.

5:14 ¹ In things plain and evident they show themselves fools instead of wise men.

² This declareth that God punisheth the worldly wise, as he threatened, Deut. 28:29.

5:15 ¹ That is, he that humbleth himself before God.

² He compareth the slander of the wicked to sharp swords.

5:16 ¹ If the wicked be compelled at God's works to stop their mouths, much more they that profess God.

5:19 ¹ He will send trouble after trouble that his children may not for one time, but continually trust in him: but they shall have a comfortable issue, even in the greatest and the last, which is here called the

seventh.

5:22 ¹ Whereas the wicked lament in their troubles, thou shalt have occasion to rejoice.

5:23 ¹ When we are in God's favor, all creatures shall serve us.

5:24 ¹ God shall so bless thee, that thou shalt have occasion to rejoice in all things, and not to be offended.

5:26 ¹ Though the children of God have not always this promise performed, yet God doth recompense it otherwise to their advantage.

5:27 ¹ We have learned these points by experience, that God punisheth not the innocent, that man cannot compare in justice with him, that the hypocrites shall not long prosper, and that the affliction which man sustaineth, cometh for his own sin.

6:2 ¹ To know whether I complain without just cause.

6:3 ¹ My grief is so great that I lack words to express it.

6:4 ¹ Which declareth that he was not only afflicted in body, but wounded in conscience, which is the greatest battle that the faithful can have.

6:5 ¹ Think you that I cry without cause, seeing the brute beasts do not complain when they have what they would.

6:6 ¹ Can a man's taste delight in that, that hath no savor? meaning, that none take pleasure in affliction, seeing they cannot [do] away with things that are unsavory to the mouth.

were sorrows, are my meat.

8 Oh that I might have my ¹desire, and that God would grant me the thing that I long for!

9 That is, that God would destroy me: that he would let his hand go, and cut me off.

10 Then should I yet have comfort, (though I burn with sorrow, let him not spare) ¹because I have not denied the words of the Holy one.

11 What power have I that I should endure? or what is mine ¹end, if I should prolong my life?

12 Is my strength the strength of stones? *or* is my flesh of brass?

13 Is it not so, that there is in me no ¹help? and that ²strength is taken from me?

14 He that is in misery, ought to be comforted of his neighbor: but men have forsaken the fear of the Almighty.

15 My brethren have deceived me as a ¹brook, *and* as the rising of the rivers they pass away.

16 Which are blackish with ice, *and* wherein the snow is hid.

17 But in time they are dried up with heat *and* are consumed: and when it is hot they fail out of their places,

18 *Or* they depart from their way and course, *yea,* they vanish and perish.

19 They that go to Tema, ¹considered them, *and* they that go to Sheba, waited for them.

20 *But* they were confounded: when they hoped, they came thither, and were ashamed.

21 Surely now are ye *like* ¹unto it: ye have seen *my* fearful plague, and are afraid.

22 Was it because I said, Bring unto me? or give a reward to me of your ¹substance?

23 And deliver me from the enemy's hand, or ransom me out of the hand of tyrants?

24 Teach me, and I will ¹hold my tongue: and

cause me to understand, wherein I have erred.

25 How ¹steadfast are the words of righteousness? and what can any of you justly reprove?

26 Do ye imagine to reprove ¹words, that the talk of the afflicted should be as the wind?

27 Ye make your wrath to fall upon the fatherless, and dig a pit for your friend.

28 Now therefore be content to ¹look upon me: for I will not lie before your face.

29 Turn, I pray you, let there be none iniquity: return, I say, *and ye shall see* yet my righteousness in that behalf. Is there iniquity in my tongue? doth not my mouth feel sorrows?

7 *1 Job showeth the shortness and misery of man's life.*

1 Is there not an appointed time to man upon earth? and *are not* his days as the days of an ¹hireling?

2 As a servant longeth for the shadow, and as an hireling looketh for *the end* of his work,

3 So have I had as an inheritance the ¹months of vanity, and painful nights have been appointed unto me.

4 If I laid me down, I said, When shall I arise? and measuring the evening, I am even full with tossing to and fro unto the dawning of the day.

5 My flesh is ¹clothed with worms and filthiness of the dust: my skin is rent, and become horrible.

6 My days are swifter than ¹a weaver's shuttle, and they are spent without hope.

7 Remember that my life is but a wind, *and that* mine eye shall not return to see pleasure.

8 The eye that hath seen me, shall see me no more: thine eyes *are* upon me, and I shall be no longer.

9 ¹*As* the cloud vanisheth and goeth away, so he that goeth down to the grave, shall ²come up no more.

6:8 ¹ Herein he sinneth double, both in wishing through impatience to die, and also in desiring of God a thing which was not agreeable to his will.

6:10 ¹ That is, let me die at once, before I come to distrust in God's promise through my impatience.

6:11 ¹ He fearest lest he should be brought to inconveniences, if his sorrows should continue.

6:13 ¹ Have I not sought to help myself as much as was possible?
  ² Or, wisdom, or law.

6:15 ¹ He compareth those friends which comfort us not in misery, to a brook, which in summer, when we need water, is dry, in winter is hard frozen, and in the time of rain, when we have no need, overfloweth with water.

6:19 ¹ They that pass thereby to go into the hot countries of Arabia, think to find water there to quench their thirst, but they are deceived.

6:21 ¹ That is, like to this brook which deceiveth them that think to have water there in their need, as I looked for consolation at your hands.

6:22 ¹ He toucheth the worldlings, which for necessity will give part of their goods, and much more these men, which would not give

him comfortable words.

6:24 ¹ Show me wherein I have erred, and I will confess my fault.

6:25 ¹ He that hath a good conscience doth not shrink at the sharp words or reasonings of others, except they be able to persuade him by reason.

6:26 ¹ Do you cavil at my words because I should be thought to speak foolishly, which am now in misery?

6:28 ¹ Consider whether I speak as one that is driven to this impatience through very sorrow, or as an hypocrite as you condemn me.

7:1 ¹ Hath not an hired servant some rest and ease? then in this my continual torment I am worse than an hireling.

7:3 ¹ My sorrow hath continued from month to month, and I have looked for hope in vain.

7:5 ¹ This signifieth that his disease was rare and most horrible.

7:6 ¹ Thus he speaketh in respect of the brevity of man's life, which passeth without hope of returning: in consideration whereof he desireth God to have compassion on him.

7:9 ¹ If thou behold me in thine anger, I shall not be able to stand in thy presence.
  ² Shall no more enjoy this mortal life.

10 He shall return no more to his house, neither shall his place know him anymore.

11 Therefore I will not ¹spare my mouth, *but* will speak in the trouble of my spirit, *and* muse in the bitterness of my mind.

12 Am I a sea ¹or a whalefish, that thou keepest me in ward?

13 When I say, My couch shall relieve me, *and* my bed shall bring *comfort* in my meditation,

14 Then fearest thou me ¹with dreams, and astonishest me with visions.

15 Therefore my soul ¹chooseth rather to be strangled *and* to die, than *to be in* my bones.

16 I abhor it: I shall not live always: ¹spare me then, for my days *are* but vanity.

17 What is man, that thou ¹dost magnify him, and that thou settest thine heart upon him?

18 And dost visit him every morning, and triest him every moment?

19 How long will it be *ere* thou depart from me? thou wilt not let me alone while I may swallow my spittle.

20 I have ¹sinned, what shall I do unto thee? O thou preserver of men, why hast thou set me *as a mark* against thee, so that I am a burden unto myself?

21 And why dost thou not pardon my trespass? and take away mine iniquity? for now shall I sleep in the dust, and if thou seek me in the morning, I shall ¹not be *found*.

8

1 Bildad showeth that Job is a sinner, because that God punisheth the wicked, and preserveth the good.

1 Then answered Bildad the Shuhite, and said,

2 How long wilt thou talk of these things? and how long shall the words of thy mouth ¹*be as* a mighty wind?

3 Doth God pervert judgment? or doth the Almighty subvert justice?

4 If thy sons have sinned against him, and he hath sent them into the place of their ¹iniquity,

5 *Yet* if thou ¹wilt early seek unto God, and pray to the Almighty,

6 If thou be pure and upright, then surely he will awake up unto thee, and he will make the habitation of thy righteousness prosperous.

7 And though thy beginning ¹be small, yet thy latter end shall greatly increase.

8 ¹Inquire therefore, I pray thee, of the former age, and prepare thyself to search of their fathers.

9 (For we are but ¹of yesterday, and are ignorant: for our days upon earth *are* but a shadow)

10 Shall not they teach thee *and* tell thee, and utter the words of their heart?

11 Can a rush ¹grow without mire? or can the grass grow without water?

12 Though it were in green *and* not cut down, yet shall it wither before any other herb.

13 So *are* the paths of all that forget God, and the hypocrite's hope shall perish.

14 His confidence also shall be cut off, and his trust *shall be as* the house of a ¹spider.

15 He shall lean upon his house, but it shall not stand: he shall hold him fast by it, yet shall it not endure.

16 The ¹*tree* is green before the Sun, and the branches spread over the garden thereof.

17 The roots thereof are wrapped about the fountain, *and* are folded *about* the house of stones.

18 If *any* pluck it from his place, and it ¹deny, *saying*, I have not seen thee,

---

7:11 ¹ Seeing I can by none other means comfort myself, I will declare my grief by words, and thus he speaketh as one overcome with grief of mind.

7:12 ¹ Am not I a poor wretch? what needest thou then to lay so much pain on me?

7:14 ¹ So that I can have no rest, night nor day.

7:15 ¹ He speaketh as one overcome with sorrow, and not of judgment, or of the examination of his faith.

7:16 ¹ Seeing my term of life is so short, let me have some rest and ease.

7:17 ¹ Seeing that man of himself is so vile, why dost thou give him that honor to contend against him? Job useth all kinds of persuasion with God, that he might stay his hand.

7:20 ¹ After all tentations faith bursteth forth and leadeth Job to repentance: yet it was not in such perfection, that he could bridle himself from reasoning with God, because that he still tried his faith.

7:21 ¹ That is, I shall be dead.

8:2 ¹ He declareth that their words which would diminish anything from the justice of God, is but as a puff of wind that vanisheth away.

8:4 ¹ That is, hath rewarded them according to their iniquity: meaning, that Job ought to be warned by the example of his children, that he offend not God.

8:5 ¹ That is, if thou turn betime while God calleth thee to repentance.

8:7 ¹ Though the beginnings be not so pleasant as thou wouldest desire, yet in the end thou shalt have sufficient occasion to content thyself.

8:8 ¹ He willeth Job to examine all antiquity, and he shall find it true which he here saith.

8:9 ¹ Meaning, that it is not enough to have the experience of ourselves, but to be confirmed by the examples of them that went before us.

8:11 ¹ As a rush cannot grow without moistness, so cannot the hypocrite, because he hath not faith, which is moistened with God's Spirit.

8:14 ¹ Which is today, and tomorrow swept away.

8:16 ¹ He compareth the just to a tree, which although it be removed out of one place unto another, yet flourisheth: so the affliction of the godly turneth to their profit.

8:18 ¹ That is, so that there remain nothing there to prove whether the tree had grown there or no.

19 Behold, it will rejoice [1]by this means, that it may grow in another mold.

20 Behold, God will not cast away an upright man, neither will he take the wicked by the hand,

21 Till he have filled thy mouth with [1]laughter, and thy lips with joy.

22 They that hate thee, shall be clothed with shame, and the dwelling of the wicked shall not *remain*.

9 *2 Job declareth the mighty power of God, and that man's righteousness is nothing.*

1 Then Job answered, and said,

2 I know verily that it is so: for how should man *compared* unto God, be [1]justified?

3 If he would dispute with him, he could not answer him one thing of [1]thousand.

4 He is wise in heart, and mighty in strength: who hath been fierce against him, and hath prospered?

5 He removeth the mountains, and they feel not when he overthroweth them in his wrath.

6 He [1]removeth the earth out of her place, that the pillars thereof do shake.

7 He commandeth the Sun, and it riseth not: he closeth up the stars, as under a signet.

8 He himself alone spreadeth out the heavens, and walketh upon the height of the Sea.

9 He maketh *the stars* [1]Arcturus, Orion, and Pleiades, and the climates of the South.

10 He doeth great things, and unsearchable: yea, marvelous things without number.

11 Lo, when he goeth [1]by me, I see him not: and when he passeth by, I perceive him not:

12 Behold, when he taketh a prey, [1]who can make him to restore it? who shall say unto him, What doest thou?

13 God [1]will not withdraw his anger, *and* the most mighty helpers [2]do stoop under him.

14 How much less shall I answer him? or how should I find out [1]my words with him?

15 For though I were just, yet could I [1]not answer, *but* I would make supplication to my Judge.

16 If I [1]cry, and he answer me, *yet* would I not believe, that he heard my voice.

17 For he destroyeth me with a tempest, and woundeth me [1]without cause.

18 He will not suffer me to take my breath, but filleth me with bitterness.

19 If *we speak* of strength, behold, he is [1]strong: if *we speak* of judgment, who shall bring me in to plead?

20 If I should justify myself, mine own mouth shall condemn me: [1]if I would be perfect, he shall judge me wicked.

21 *Though* I were perfect, *yet* I know not my soul: *therefore* abhor I my life.

22 This is one point: therefore I said, He destroyeth the [1]perfect and the wicked.

23 If the scourge should suddenly [1]slay, should God [2]laugh at the punishment of the innocent?

24 The earth is given into the hand of the wicked: [1]he covereth the faces of the judges thereof: if not, where [2]is he? or who is he?

25 My days have been more swift than a post: they have fled, and have seen no good thing.

26 They are passed *as* with the most swift ships, and as the Eagle that flieth to the prey.

27 If [1]I say, I will forget my complaint, I will cease from my wrath, and comfort me,

28 *Then* I am afraid of all my sorrows, knowing that thou wilt not judge me innocent.

8:19 [1] To be planted in another place, where it may grow at pleasure.

8:21 [1] If thou be godly, he will give thee occasion to rejoice, and if not, thine affliction shall increase.

9:2 [1] Job here answereth to that point of Eliphaz and Bildad's oration, touching the justice of God, and his innocency, confessing God to be infinite in justice, and man to be nothing in respect.

9:3 [1] Of a thousand things, which God could lay to his charge, man cannot answer him one.

9:6 [1] He declareth what is the infirmity of man, by the mighty and incomprehensible power that is in God, showing what he could do if he would set forth his power.

9:9 [1] These are the names of certain stars whereby he meaneth that all stars both known and unknown are at his appointment.

9:11 [1] I am not able to comprehend his works, which are common and daily before my eyes, much less in those things, which are hid and secret.

9:12 [1] He showeth that when God doth execute his power, he doeth it justly, forasmuch as none can control him.

9:13 [1] God will not be appeased for ought that man can say for himself for his justification.

[2] That is, all the reasons that men can lay to approve their cause.

9:14 [1] How should I be able to answer him by eloquence? whereby he noteth his friends, that albeit they were eloquent in talk, yet they felt not in heart, that which they spake.

9:15 [1] Meaning, in his own opinion, signifying, that man will sometimes flatter himself to be righteous, which before God is abomination.

9:16 [1] While I am in my pangs, I cannot but burst forth into many inconveniences, although I know still that God is just.

9:17 [1] I am not able to feel my sins so great, as I feel the weight of his plagues; and this he speaketh to condemn his dullness, and to justify God.

9:19 [1] After he hath accused his own weakness, he continueth to justify God and his power.

9:20 [1] If I would stand in mine own defense, yet God hath just cause to condemn me, if he examine mine heart and conscience.

9:22 [1] If God punish according to his justice, he will destroy as well them, that are counted perfect as them that are wicked.

9:23 [1] To wit, the wicked.

[2] This is spoken according to our apprehension, as though he would say, If God destroy but the wicked, as Job 5:3, why should he suffer the innocent to be so long tormented by them?

9:24 [1] That they cannot see to do justice.

[2] That can show the contrary?

9:27 [1] I think not to fall into these afflictions, but my sorrows bring me to these manifold infirmities, and my conscience condemneth me.

29 *If* I be wicked, why ¹labor I thus in vain?

30 If I wash ¹myself with snow water, and purge mine hands most clean,

31 Yet shalt thou plunge me in the pit, and mine own ¹clothes shall make me filthy.

32 For he is not a man as I am, that I should answer him, *if* we come together to judgment.

33 Neither is there any umpire ¹that might lay his hand upon us both.

34 Let him take his rod away from me, and let not his fear astonish me:

35 *Then* will I speak, and fear him not: ¹*but* because I am not so, I hold me still.

10

1 *Job is weary of his life, and setteth out his fragility before God.* 20 *He desireth him to stay his hand.* 22 *A description of death.*

1 My soul is cut off ¹though I live: I will leave my ²complaint upon myself, *and* will speak in the bitterness of my soul.

2 I will say unto God, ¹Condemn me not: show me, wherefore thou contendest with me.

3 Thinkest thou it ¹good to oppress me, *and* to cast off the ²labor of thine hands, and to favor the ³counsel of the wicked?

4 Hast thou ¹carnal eyes? or dost thou see as man seeth?

5 Are thy days as man's ¹days? or thy years as the time of man,

6 That thou inquirest of mine iniquity, and searchest out my sin?

7 Thou knowest that I cannot do ¹wickedly: for none can deliver me out of thine hand.

8 Thine ¹hands have made me, and fashioned me wholly round about, and wilt thou destroy me?

9 Remember, I pray thee, that thou hast made me as ¹the clay, and wilt thou bring me into dust again?

10 Hast thou not poured me out as milk? and turned me to curds like cheese?

11 Thou hast clothed me with skin and flesh, and joined me together with bones and sinews.

12 Thou hast given me life, and ¹grace: and the ²visitation hath preserved my spirit.

13 Though thou hast hid these things in thine heart, *yet* I know ¹that it is so with thee.

14 If I have sinned, then thou wilt straightly look unto me, and wilt not hold me guiltless of mine iniquity.

15 If I have done wickedly, woe unto me: if I have done righteously, I will not ¹lift up mine head, being full of confusion, because I see mine affliction.

16 But let it increase: hunt thou me as a lion: return and show thyself ¹marvelous upon me.

17 Thou renewest thy plagues against me, and thou increasest thy wrath against me: ¹changes and armies *of sorrows* are against me.

18 Wherefore then hast thou brought me out of the womb? Oh that I had perished, and that none eye had seen me!

19 *And* that I were as I had not been, *but* brought from the womb to the grave!

20 Are not my days few? let him ¹cease, *and* leave off from me, that I may take a little comfort,

21 Before I go and shall not ¹return, *even* to the land of darkness and shadow of death:

22 Into a land, I *say*, dark as darkness itself, *and*

9:29 ¹ Why doth not God destroy me at once? thus he speaketh according to the infirmity of the flesh.

9:30 ¹ Though I seem never so pure in mine own eyes, yet all is but corruption before God.

9:31 ¹ Whatsoever I would use to cover my filthiness with, shall disclose me so much more.

9:33 ¹ Which might make an accord between God and me, speaking of impatience, and yet confessing God to be just in punishing him.

9:35 ¹ Signifying that God's judgments keep him in awe.

10:1 ¹ I am more like to a dead man, than to one that liveth.

² I will make an ample declaration of my torments, accusing myself and not God.

10:2 ¹ He would not that God should proceed against him by his secret justice, but by the ordinary means that he punisheth others.

10:3 ¹ Is it agreeable to thy justice to do me wrong?

² Wilt thou be without compassion?

³ Wilt thou gratify the wicked and condemn me?

10:4 ¹ Doest thou this of ignorance?

10:5 ¹ Art thou inconstant and changeable, as the times, today a friend, tomorrow an enemy?

10:7 ¹ By affliction thou keepest me as in a prison, and restrainest me from doing evil, neither can any set me at liberty.

10:8 ¹ In these eight verses following he describeth the mercy of God, in the wonderful creation of man: and thereon groundeth that God should not show himself rigorous against him.

10:9 ¹ As brittle as a pot of clay.

10:12 ¹ That is, reason and understanding, and many other gifts, whereby man excelleth all earthly creatures.

² That is, thy fatherly care and providence whereby thou preservest me, and without the which I should perish straightway.

10:13 ¹ Though I be not fully able to comprehend these things, yet I must needs confess that it is so.

10:15 ¹ I will always walk in fear and humility, knowing that none is just before thee.

10:16 ¹ Job being sore assaulted in this battle between the flesh and the spirit, bursteth out into these affections, wishing rather short days than long pain.

10:17 ¹ That is, diversity of diseases and in great abundance: showing that God hath infinite means to punish man.

10:20 ¹ He wisheth that God would leave off his affliction, considering his great misery and the brevity of his life.

10:21 ¹ He speaketh thus in the person of a sinner, that is overcome with passions and with the feeling of God's judgments, and therefore cannot apprehend in that state the mercies of God, and comfort of the resurrection.

into the shadow of death, where is none ¹order, but the light *is there* as darkness.

CHAPTER 11
ᵃ Lev. 26:5,6

11

1 Job is unjustly reprehended of Zophar. 7 God is incomprehensible. 14 He is merciful to the repentant. 18 Their assurance that live godly.

1 Then answered Zophar the Naamathite, and said,

2 Should not the multitude of words be answered? or should a great ¹talker be justified?

3 Should men hold their peace at thy lies? and when thou mockest *others*, shall none make thee ashamed?

4 For thou hast said, ¹My doctrine is pure, and I am clean in thine eyes.

5 But, oh that God would speak and open his lips against thee!

6 That he might show thee the ¹secrets of wisdom how thou hast *deserved* double, according to right: know therefore that God hath forgotten thee for thine iniquity.

7 Canst thou by searching find out God? canst thou find out the Almighty to *his* perfection?

8 The heavens are high, what canst thou do? ¹it is deeper than the hell, how canst thou know it?

9 The measure thereof is longer than the earth, and it is broader than the Sea.

10 If he cut off and ¹shut up, or gather together, who can turn him back?

11 For he knoweth vain men, and seeth iniquity, and him that understandeth nothing.

12 Yet vain man would be wise, though man *new*born is like a wild ¹ass colt.

13 If thou ¹prepare thine heart, and stretch out thine hands toward him:

14 If iniquity be in thine ¹hand, put it far away,

CHAPTER 12
ᵃ Prov. 14:2

and let no wickedness dwell in thy Tabernacle.

15 Then truly shalt thou lift up thy ¹face without spot, and shalt be stable, and shalt not fear.

16 But thou shalt forget *thy* misery, and remember it as waters that are past.

17 Thine age also shall appear more *clear* than the noon day: thou shalt shine *and* be as the morning.

18 And thou shalt be bold, because there is hope: and thou shalt dig pits, *and* shalt lie down safely.

19 ᵃFor when thou takest thy rest, none shall make thee afraid: yea, many shall make suit unto thee.

20 But the eyes ¹of the wicked shall fail, and their refuge shall perish, and their hope *shall be* sorrow of mind.

12

2 Job accuseth his friends of ignorance. 7 He declareth the might, and power of God. 17 And how he changeth the course of things.

1 Then Job answered, and said,

2 Indeed because that ye are the people *only*, ¹wisdom must die with you.

3 But I have understanding as well as you, and am not inferior unto you: yea, who knoweth not such things?

4 ᵃI am ¹as one mocked of his neighbor, who calleth upon God, and he ²heareth him: the just *and* the upright is laughed to scorn.

5 ¹He that is ready to fall, *is as* a lamp despised in the opinion of the rich.

6 The tabernacles of robbers do prosper, and they are in safety, that provoke God, ¹whom God hath enriched with his hand.

7 Ask now the beasts, ¹and they shall teach thee, and the fowls of the heaven, and they shall tell thee:

8 Or speak to the earth, and it shall show thee: or the fishes of the sea, and they shall declare unto thee.

10:22 ¹ No distinction between light and darkness, but where all is very darkness itself.

11:2 ¹ Should he persuade by his great talk, that he is just?

11:4 ¹ He chargeth Job with this, that he should say, that the thing which he spake was true, and that he was without sin in the sight of God.

11:6 ¹ Which is not to stand in justifying of thyself: he signifieth that man will never be overcome, while he reasoneth with another, and therefore God must break off the controversy, and stop man's mouth.

11:8 ¹ That is, this perfection of God, and if man be not able to comprehend the height of the heaven, the depth of hell, the length of the earth, the breadth of the Sea, which are but creatures: how can he attain to the perfection of the Creator?

11:10 ¹ If God should turn the state of things, and establish a new order in nature, who could control him?

11:12 ¹ That is, without understanding: so that whatsoever gifts he hath afterward, come of God, and not of nature.

11:13 ¹ If thou repent, pray unto him.

11:14 ¹ Renounce thine own evil works, and see that they offend not God, over whom thou hast charge.

11:15 ¹ He declareth what quietness of conscience and success in all things such shall have, which turn to God by true repentance.

11:20 ¹ He showeth that contrary things shall come unto them that do not repent.

12:2 ¹ Because you feel not that which you speak, you think the whole standeth in words, and so flatter yourselves as though none knew anything, or could know but you.

12:4 ¹ He reproveth these his friends of two faults: the one that they thought they had better knowledge than indeed they had: and the other, that instead of true consolation, they did deride and despise their friend in his adversity.

² The which neighbor being a mocker and a wicked man, thinketh that no man is in God's favor but he, because he hath all things that he desireth.

12:5 ¹ As the rich esteem not a light, or torch that goeth out, so is he despised that falleth from prosperity to adversity.

12:6 ¹ Hebrew, *to whom God hath brought in with his hand*.

12:7 ¹ He declareth to them that did dispute against him, that their wisdom is common to all, and such as the very brute beasts do daily teach.

9 Who is ignorant of all these, but that the hand of the Lord hath made these?

10 In whose hand is the soul of every living thing, and the breath of all [1]mankind.

11 Doth not the ears [1]discern the words, and the mouth taste meat for itself?

12 Among the [1]ancient *is* wisdom, and in the length of days *is* understanding.

13 With him *is* wisdom and strength: he hath counsel and understanding.

14 Behold, he will break down, and it cannot be built: he shutteth a man up, and he cannot be loosed.

15 Behold, he withholdeth the waters, and they dry up: but when he sendeth them out, they destroy the earth.

16 With him *is* strength and wisdom: he that is deceived, and that [1]deceiveth, are his.

17 He causeth the counselors to go *as* spoiled, and maketh the judges fools.

18 [1]He looseth [2]the collar of kings, and girdeth their loins with a girdle.

19 He leadeth away the princes *as* a prey, and overthroweth the mighty.

20 He taketh away the speech from the [1]faithful *counselors*, and taketh away the judgment of the ancient.

21 He poureth contempt upon princes, and maketh the strength of the mighty weak.

22 He discovereth the deep places from *their* darkness, and bringeth forth the shadow of death to light.

23 He [1]increaseth the people, and destroyeth them: he enlargeth the nations, and bringeth them in again.

24 He taketh away the hearts of them that are the chief over the people of the earth, and maketh them to wander in the wilderness out of the way.

25 They grope in the dark without light: and he maketh them to stagger like a drunken man.

13

3 Job compareth his knowledge with the experience of his friends. 16 The penitent shall be saved, and the hypocrite condemned, 20 He prayeth unto God, that he would not handle him rigorously.

1 Lo, mine eye hath seen all *this*: mine ear hath heard, and understood it.

2 I know also as much as you know: I am not inferior unto you.

3 But I will speak to the Almighty, and I desire [1]to dispute with God.

4 For indeed ye forge lies, and all you are [1]physicians of no value.

5 Oh, that you would hold your tongue, that it might be imputed to you for wisdom!

6 Now hear my disputation, and give ear to the arguments of my lips.

7 Will ye speak [1]wickedly for God's *defense*, and talk deceitfully for his cause?

8 Will ye accept his person? or will ye contend for God?

9 Is it well that he should seek of you? will you make a lie for him, as one lieth for a man?

10 He will surely reprove you, if ye do secretly accept any person.

11 Shall not his excellency make you afraid? and his fear fall upon you?

12 Your [1]memories may be compared unto ashes, *and* your bodies unto bodies of clay.

13 Hold your tongues in my presence, that I may speak, and let come upon what will.

14 Wherefore do I [1]take my flesh in my teeth, and put my soul in my hand?

15 Lo, though he slay me, *yet* will I trust in him, and I will reprove my ways in his sight.

16 He shall be my salvation also: for the [1]hypocrite shall not come before him.

17 Hear diligently my words, and mark my talk.

12:10 [1] Or, flesh.

12:11 [1] He exhorteth them to be wise in judging, and as well to know the right use why God hath given them ears, as he hath done a mouth.

12:12 [1] Though men by age, and continuance of time attain to wisdom, yet it is not comparable to God's wisdom, nor able to comprehend his judgments, wherein he answereth to that which was alleged, Job 8:8.

12:16 [1] He showeth that there is nothing done in this world without God's will and ordinance, for else he should not be Almighty.

12:18 [1] He taketh wisdom from them.

[2] He abateth the honor of princes, and bringeth them into the subjection of others.

12:20 [1] He causeth that their words have no credit, which is when he will punish sin.

12:23 [1] In this discourse of God's wonderful works, Job showeth that whatsoever is done in this world both in the order and change of things, is by God's will and appointment: wherein he declareth that

he thinketh well of God, and is as able to set forth his power in words as they that reasoned against, were.

13:3 [1] For although he knew that God had a justice, which was manifest in his ordinary working and another in his secret counsel, yet he would utter his affection to God, because he was not able to understand the cause why he did thus punish him.

13:4 [1] You do not well apply your medicine to the disease.

13:7 [1] He condemneth their zeal, which had not knowledge, neither regarded they to comfort him, but always grated on God's justice, as though it was not evidently seen in Job, except they had undertaken the probation thereof.

13:12 [1] Your fame shall come to nothing.

13:14 [1] Is not this a manifest sign of mine affliction, and that I do not complain without cause, seeing that I am thus tormented as though I should tear mine own flesh, and put my life in danger?

13:16 [1] Whereby he declareth that he is not an hypocrite as they charged him.

18 Behold now: *if* I prepare me to judgment, I know that I shall be ¹justified.

19 Who is he that will plead ¹with me? for *if* I now hold my tongue, I ²die.

20 But do not these two things unto me: then will I not hide myself from thee.

21 ¹Withdraw thine hand from me, and let not thy fear make me afraid.

22 Then call thou, and I will answer: or let me speak, and answer thou me.

23 How many are ¹mine iniquities and sins, show me my rebellion and my sin.

24 Wherefore hidest thou thy face, and takest me for thine enemy?

25 Wilt thou break a leaf driven to and fro? and wilt thou pursue the dry stubble?

26 For thou writest bitter things against me, and makest me to possess the ¹iniquities of my youth.

27 Thou puttest my feet also in the ¹stocks, and lookest narrowly unto all my paths, and makest the print *thereof* in the ²heels of my feet.

28 Such a one consumeth like a rotten thing, *and* as a garment that is moth-eaten.

14

1 Job describeth the shortness and misery of the life of man. 14 Hope sustaineth the godly. 21 The condition of man's life.

1 Man ¹that is born of woman, is of short continuance and full of trouble.

2 He shooteth forth as a flower, and is cut down: he vanisheth also as a ªshadow, and continueth not.

3 *And* yet thou openest thine eyes upon such ¹one, and causest me to enter into judgment with thee.

4 ᵇWho can bring a clean thing out of filthiness? there is not one.

5 Are not his days determined? the number of his months *are* with thee: thou hast appointed his

CHAPTER 14
ª Job 8:9
  Ps. 144:4
ᵇ Ps. 51:5,7
ᶜ Prov. 5:21

bound, which he cannot pass.

6 Turn from him that he may cease until his desired day, ¹as an hireling.

7 For there is hope of a tree, if it be cut down, that it will yet sprout, and the branches thereof will not cease.

8 Though the root of it wax old in the earth, and the stock thereof be dead in the ground,

9 *Yet* by the scent of water it will bud, and bring forth boughs like a plant.

10 ¹But man is sick, and dieth, and man perisheth, and where is he?

11 *As* the waters pass from the sea, and as the flood decayeth and drieth up,

12 So man sleepeth and riseth not: *for* he shall not wake again, nor be raised from his sleep till the heaven be no more.

13 Oh that thou wouldest hide me in the grave, and keep me secret, until thy ¹wrath were past, *and* wouldest give me term, and ²remember me!

14 If a man die, shall he live again? All the days of mine appointed time will I wait, till ¹my changing shall come.

15 Thou shalt call me, and I will ¹answer thee: thou lovest the work of thine own hands.

16 But now thou ᶜnumberest my steps, *and* doest not delay my sins.

17 Mine iniquity is sealed up, *as* in a ¹bag, and thou addest unto my wickedness.

18 And surely *as* the mountain that falleth, cometh to nought, and the ¹rock that is removed from his place:

19 *As* the water breaketh the stones, *when* thou overflowest the things which grow in the dust of the earth: so thou destroyest the hope of man.

20 Thou prevailest always against him, so that he passeth away: he changeth his face when thou castest him away.

13:18 ¹ That is, cleared and not cast off for my sins, as you reason.
13:19 ¹ To prove that God doth thus punish me for my sins.
  ² If I defend not my cause, every man will condemn me.
13:21 ¹ He showeth what these two things are.
13:23 ¹ His pangs thus move him to reason with God, not denying but that he had sinned: but he desired to understand what were his great sins that had deserved such rigor, wherein he offended that he would know a cause of God why he did punish him.
13:26 ¹ Thou punishest me now for the faults that I committed in my youth.
13:27 ¹ Thou makest me thy prisoner, and dost so press me that I cannot stir hand nor foot.
  ² Hebrew, *roots.*
14:1 ¹ Taking occasion of his adversary's words, he describeth the state of man's life from his birth to his death.
14:3 ¹ His meaning is, that seeing that man is so frail a creature, God should not handle him so extremely, wherein Job showeth the wickedness of the flesh, when it is not subject to the Spirit.

14:6 ¹ Until the time that thou hast appointed for him to die, which he desireth as the hireling waiteth for the end of his labor to receive his wages.
14:10 ¹ He speaketh not here as though he had not hope of the immortality, but as a man in extreme pain, when reason is overcome by affections and torments.
14:13 ¹ Hereby he declareth that the fear of God's judgment was the cause why he desired to die.
  ² That is, release my pains and take me to mercy.
14:14 ¹ Meaning, unto the day of the resurrection when he should be changed, and renewed.
14:15 ¹ Though I be afflicted in this life, yet in the resurrection I shall feel thy mercies and answer when thou callest me.
14:17 ¹ Thou layest them all together, and sufferest none of my sins unpunished.
14:18 ¹ He murmureth through the impatience of the flesh against God, as though he used as great severity against him as against the hard rocks, or waters that overflow, so that hereby all the occasion of his hope is taken away.

21 And he knoweth not if his sons shall be honorable, neither shall he understand concerning them, whether they shall be of low degree,

22 But *while* his [1]flesh *is* upon him, he shall be sorrowful, and *while* his soul *is* in him, it shall mourn.

15

1 *Eliphaz reprehendeth Job, because he ascribeth wisdom and pureness to himself.* 16 *He describeth the curse that falleth on the wicked, reckoning Job to be one of the number.*

1 Then answered Eliphaz the Temanite, and said,

2 Shall a wise man speak words of the [1]wind? and fill his belly [2]with the East wind?

3 Shall he dispute with words not comely? or with talk that is not profitable?

4 Surely thou hast cast off [1]fear, and restrainest prayer before God:

5 For thy mouth declareth thine iniquity, seeing thou hast chosen the [1]tongue of the crafty.

6 Thine own mouth condemneth thee, and not I, and thy lips testify against thee.

7 Art thou the [1]first man that was born? and wast thou made before the hills?

8 Hast thou heard the secret counsel of God, and dost thou restrain wisdom [1]to thee?

9 What knowest thou that we know not? *and* understandest that is not in us?

10 With us are both ancient and very aged men, far older than thy father.

11 *Seem* the consolations of God [1]small unto thee? is this thing strange unto thee?

12 Why doth thine heart [1]take thee away, and what do thine eyes mean,

13 That thou answerest to God [1]at thy pleasure, and bringest *such* words out of thy mouth?

14 What is man, that he should be clean? and he that is born of woman, that he should [1]be just?

15 Behold, he found no steadfastness in his Saints: yea, the heavens are not clean in his sight.

16 How much more *is* man abominable, and filthy, which [1]drinketh iniquity like water?

17 I will tell thee: hear me, and I will declare that which I have seen:

18 Which wise men have told, *as they have heard* of their fathers, and have not kept it secret:

19 To whom alone the land was [1]given, and no stranger passed through them.

20 The wicked man is continually as one that travaileth of child, and the number [1]of years is hid from the tyrant.

21 A sound of fear *is* in his ears, *and* in his prosperity the destroyer shall come upon him.

22 He believeth not to return out of [1]darkness: for he seeth the sword before him.

23 He wandereth [1]to and fro for bread where *he may*: he knoweth that the day of darkness is prepared at hand.

24 Affliction and [1]anguish shall make him afraid: they shall prevail against him as a king ready to the battle.

25 For he hath stretched out his hand against God, and made himself strong against the Almighty.

26 *Therefore God* shall run upon him, *even* upon his neck, and against the most thick part of his shield.

27 Because he hath covered his face with [1]his fatness, and hath collops in *his* flank.

28 Though he dwell [1]in desolate cities, *and* in houses which no man inhabiteth, but are become heaps,

29 He shall not be rich, neither shall his substance continue, neither shall he prolong the [1]perfection thereof in the earth.

30 He shall never depart out of darkness: the flame shall dry up his branches, and he shall go away with the breath of his mouth.

14:22 [1] Yet while he shall be in pain, and misery.
15:2 [1] That is, vain words, and without consolation?
[2] Meaning, with matters that are of none importance, which are forgotten as soon as they are uttered, as the East wind drieth up the moisture as soon as it falleth.
15:4 [1] He chargeth Job as though his talk caused men to cast off the fear of God, and prayer.
15:5 [1] Thou speakest as do the mockers and contemners of God.
15:7 [1] That is, the most ancient, and so by reason the most wise?
15:8 [1] Art thou only wise?
15:11 [1] He accuseth Job's pride and ingratitude, that will not be comforted by God, nor by their counsel.
15:12 [1] Why dost thou stand in thine own conceit?
15:13 [1] Hebrew, *in thy spirit.*
15:14 [1] His purpose is to prove that Job as an unjust man, and an hypocrite is punished for his sins, like as he did before, Job 4:8.
15:16 [1] Which hath a desire to sin, as he that is thirsty to drink.
15:19 [1] Who by their wisdom so governed, that no stranger invaded them, and so the land seemed to be given to them alone.
15:20 [1] The cruel man is ever in danger of death, and is never quiet in conscience.
15:22 [1] Out of that misery whereunto he once falleth.
15:23 [1] God doth not only impoverish the wicked oft times, but even in their prosperity he punisheth them with a greediness evermore to gather: which is as a beggary.
15:24 [1] He showeth what weapons God useth against the wicked, which lift up themselves against him, to wit, terror of conscience, and outward afflictions.
15:27 [1] That is, he was so puffed up with great prosperity and abundance of all things, that he forgat God: noting, that Job in his felicity had not the true fear of God.
15:28 [1] Though he build and repair ruinous places to get him fame, yet God shall bring all to naught, and turn his great prosperity into extreme misery.
15:29 [1] Meaning, that his sumptuous buildings should never come to perfection.

31 He [1]believeth not that he erreth in vanity: therefore vanity shall be his change.

32 His branch shall not be green, but shall be cut off before his day.

33 *God* shall destroy him as the vine her sour [1]grape, and shall cast him off, as the olive *doth* her flower.

34 For the congregation of the hypocrite shall be desolate, and fire shall devour the houses of [1]bribes.

35 *For* they [1]conceive mischief and bring forth vanity, and their belly hath prepared deceit.

16

1 Job moved by the importunacy of his friends,   7 Counteth in what extremity he is.   19 And taketh God to witness of his innocence.

1 But Job answered and said,

2 I have oftentimes heard such things: miserable comforters are ye all.

3 Shall there be none end of words of [1]wind? or what maketh thee bold so to [2]answer?

4 I could also speak as ye do: (but would God your [1]soul were in my soul's stead) I could keep you company in speaking, and could [2]shake mine head at you,

5 But I would strengthen you [1]with my mouth, and the comfort of my lips should assuage *your sorrow.*

6 Though I speak, my sorrow [1]cannot be assuaged: though I cease, what release have I?

7 But now [1]he maketh me weary: O *God*, thou hast made all my [2]congregation desolate,

8 And hast made me full of [1]wrinkles which is a witness thereof, and my leanness riseth up in me, testifying *the same* in my face.

9 [1]His wrath hath torn *me*, and he hateth me, *and* gnasheth upon me with his teeth: mine enemy hath sharpened his eyes against me.

10 They have opened their mouths upon me, and smitten me on the [1]cheek in reproach: they gathered themselves together against me.

11 God hath delivered me to the unjust, and hath made me to turn out of the way by the [1]hands of the wicked.

12 I was in wealth, but he hath brought me to nought: he hath taken me by the neck and beaten me, and set me as a mark for himself.

13 His [1]archers compass me round about: he cutteth my reins, and doth not spare, and poureth my gall [2]upon the ground.

14 He hath broken me with one breaking upon another, and runneth upon me like a giant.

15 I have sowed a sackcloth upon my skin, and have abased mine [1]horn unto the dust.

16 My face is withered with weeping, and the shadow of death *is* upon mine eyes,

17 Though *there be* no wickedness in [1]mine hands, and my prayer [2]*be* pure.

18 O earth, cover not thou my [1]blood, and let my crying find no place.

19 For lo, now my [1]witness *is* in the heaven, and my record *is* on high.

20 My friends [1]speak eloquently against me: *but* mine eye poureth out *tears* unto God.

21 Oh that a man might [1]plead with God, as man with his neighbor!

22 For the years accounted come, and I shall go the way, whence I shall not return.

17

1 Job sayeth that he consumeth away, and yet doth patiently abide it.   10 He exhorteth his friends to repentance,   13 showing that he looketh out for death.

1 My breath is corrupt: my days are cut off, and the grave *is ready* for me.

2 There are none but [1]mockers with me, and

15:31 [1] He standeth so in his own conceit, that he will give no place to good counsel, therefore his own pride shall bring him to destruction.

15:33 [1] As one that gathereth grapes before they be ripe.

15:34 [1] Which were built or maintained by powling and bribery.

15:35 [1] And therefore all their vain devises shall turn to their own destruction.

16:3 [1] Which serve for vain ostentation and for no true comfort.

[2] For Eliphaz did reply against Job's answer.

16:4 [1] I would you felt that which I do.

[2] That is, mock at your misery, as you do at mine.

16:5 [1] If this were in my power, yet would I comfort you, and not do as ye do to me.

16:6 [1] If they would say, Why dost thou not then comfort thyself? he answereth, that the judgments of God are more heavy than he is able to assuage either by words or silence.

16:7 [1] Meaning, God.

[2] That is, destroyed most of my family.

16:8 [1] In token of sorrow and grief.

16:9 [1] That is, God by his wrath: and in this diversity of words

and high style, he expresseth how grievous the hand of God was upon him.

16:10 [1] That is, hath handled me most contemptuously: for so smiting on the cheek signified, 1 Kings 22:24; Mark 14:65.

16:11 [1] They have led me whither they would.

16:13 [1] His manifold afflictions.

[2] I am wounded to the heart.

16:15 [1] Meaning, his glory was brought low.

16:17 [1] Signifying, that he is not able to comprehend the cause of this his grievous punishment.

[2] That is, unfeigned, and without hypocrisy.

16:18 [1] Let my sin be known if I be such a sinner as mine adversaries accuse me, and let me find no favor.

16:19 [1] Though man condemn me, yet God is witness of my cause.

16:20 [1] Use painted words instead of true consolation.

16:21 [1] Thus by his great torments he is carried away, and breaketh out into passions, and speaketh unadvisedly, as though God should entreat man more gently, seeing he hath but a short time here to live.

17:2 [1] Instead of comfort, being now at death's door, he had but them that mocked at him, and discouraged him.

mine eye continueth in [2]their bitterness.

3 [1]Lay down now, *and* put me in surety for thee: who is he, that [2]will touch mine hand?

4 For thou hast hid their heart from [1]understanding: therefore shalt thou not set *them* up on high.

5 [1]For the eyes of his children shall fail, that speaketh flattery to *his* friends.

6 He hath also made me a [1]byword of the people, and I am as a tabret [2]before them.

7 Mine eye therefore is dim for grief, and all my strength *is* like a shadow.

8 The righteous shall be astonied at [1]this, and the innocent shall be moved against the hypocrite.

9 But the righteous will hold his [1]way, and he whose hands are pure, shall increase *his* strength.

10 All [1]you therefore turn you, and come now, and I shall not find one wise among you.

11 My days are past, mine enterprises are broken, *and* the thoughts of mine heart

12 Have changed the [1]night for the day, and the light that approached, for darkness.

13 Though I hope, [1]*yet* the grave shall be mine house, *and* I shall make my bed in the dark.

14 I shall say to corruption, Thou art my [1]father, *and* to the worm, Thou art my mother and my sister.

15 Where is then now mine hope? or who shall consider the thing that I hoped for?

16 [1]They shall go down into the bottom of the pit: surely it shall lie together in the dust.

18

1 Bildad rehearseth the pains of the unfaithful and wicked.

1 Then answered Bildad the Shuhite, and said,

2 When will [1]ye make an end of *your* words? [2]cause us to understand, and then we will speak.

3 Wherefore are we counted as beasts, *and* are vile in your sight?

4 Thou art [1]*as one* that teareth his soul in his anger. Shall the [2]earth be forsaken for thy sake? or the rock removed out of his place?

5 Yea, the light of the wicked shall be [1]quenched, and the spark of his fire shall not shine.

6 The light shall be dark in his dwelling, and his candle shall be put out with him.

7 The steps of his strength shall be restrained, and his own counsel shall cast him down.

8 For he is taken in the net by his feet, and he [1]walketh upon the snares.

9 The grenne shall take him by the heel, and the chief shall come upon him.

10 A snare is laid for him in the ground, and a trap for him in the way.

11 Fearfulness shall make him afraid on every side, and shall drive him to his feet.

12 His strength shall be [1]famine: and destruction shall be ready at his side.

13 It shall devour the inner parts of his skin, *and* the [1]firstborn of death shall devour his strength.

14 His hope shall be rooted out of his dwelling, and shall cause him to go to the [1]king of fear.

15 *Fear* shall dwell in his house (because it is not [1]his) [2]and brimstone shall be scattered upon his habitation.

16 His roots shall be dried up beneath, and above shall his branch be cut down.

17 His remembrance shall perish from the earth, and he shall have no name in the street.

18 They shall drive him out of the [1]light unto darkness, and chase him out of the world.

19 He shall neither have son nor nephew among

17:2 [2] I see still that they seek but to vex me.

17:3 [1] He reasoneth with God as a man beside himself, to the intent that his cause might be brought to light.

[2] And answers for thee?

17:4 [1] That these mine afflictions are thy just judgments, though man know not the cause.

17:5 [1] He that flattereth a man, and only judgeth him happy in his prosperity, shall not himself only but in his posterity be punished.

17:6 [1] God hath made all the world to speak of me, because of mine afflictions.

[2] That is, as a continual sound in their ears.

17:8 [1] To wit, when they see the godly punished: but in the end they shalt come to understanding, and know what shall be the reward of the hypocrite.

17:9 [1] That is, will not be discouraged, considering that the godly are punished as well as the wicked.

17:10 [1] Job speaketh to them three that came to comfort him.

17:12 [1] That is, have brought me sorrow instead of comfort.

17:13 [1] Though I should hope to come from adversity to prosperity, as your discourse pretendeth.

17:14 [1] I have no more hope in father, mother, sister, or any worldly

thing: for the dust and worms shall be to me instead of them.

17:16 [1] All worldly hope and prosperity fail which you say, are only signs of God's favor: but seeing that these things perish, I set mine hope in God and in the life everlasting.

18:2 [1] Which count yourselves just, as Job 12:4.

[2] Whom you take to be but beasts, as Job 12:7.

18:4 [1] That is, like a madman.

[2] Shall God change the order of nature for thy sake, by dealing with thee otherwise than he doth with all men?

18:5 [1] When the wicked is in his prosperity, then God changeth his state: and this is his ordinary working for their sins.

18:8 [1] Meaning, that the wicked are in continual danger.

18:12 [1] That which should nourish him shall be consumed by famine.

18:13 [1] That is, some strong and violent death shall consume his strength: or as the Hebrew word signifieth, his members or parts.

18:14 [1] That is, with most great fear.

18:15 [1] Meaning, not truly come by.

[2] Though all the world would favor him, yet God would destroy him and his.

18:18 [1] He shall fall from prosperity to adversity.

his people, nor any posterity in his dwellings.

20 The posterity shall be astonied at his [1]day, and fear shall come upon the ancient.

21 Surely such are the habitations of the wicked, and this is the place of him that knoweth not God.

19

2 Job reproveth his friends,   8 and reciteth his miseries and grievous pains.   25 He assureth himself of the general resurrection.

1 But Job answered, and said,

2 How long will ye vex my soul, and torment me with words?

3 Ye have now [1]ten times reproached me, and are not ashamed: ye are impudent toward me.

4 And though I had indeed erred, mine error [1]remaineth with me.

5 But indeed if ye will advance yourselves against me, and rebuke me for my reproach,

6 Know now, that God hath [1]overthrown me, and hath compassed me with his net.

7 Behold, I cry out of violence, but I have none answer: I cry, but there *is* no judgment.

8 He hath hedged up my way that I cannot [1]pass, and he hath set darkness in my paths.

9 He hath spoiled me of mine honor, and taken the [1]crown away from mine head.

10 He hath destroyed me on every side, and I am gone: and he hath removed mine hope like [1]a tree.

11 And he hath kindled his wrath against me, and counteth me as one of his enemies.

12 His [1]armies came together, and made their way upon me, and camped about my tabernacle.

13 He hath removed my brethren far from me, and also mine acquaintance were strangers unto me.

14 My neighbors have forsaken me, and my familiars have forgotten me.

15 [1]They that dwell in mine house, and my maids took me for a stranger: for I was a stranger in their sight.

16 I called my servant, but he would not answer, *though* I prayed him with my mouth.

17 My breath was strange unto my wife, though I prayed her for the children's sake of mine [1]own body.

18 The wicked also despised me, *and* when I rose, they spake against me.

19 All my secret friends abhorred me, and they whom I loved, are turned against me.

20 My bone [1]cleaveth to my skin and to my flesh, and I have escaped with the [2]skin of my teeth.

21 Have pity upon me: have [1]pity upon me, (O ye my friends) for the hand of God hath touched me.

22 Why do ye persecute me, as [1]God? and are not satisfied with my [2]flesh?

23 Oh that my words were now written! oh that they were written even in a book,

24 *And* graven with [1]an iron pen in lead, or in stone forever!

25 For I am sure that my [1]Redeemer liveth, and he shall stand the last on the earth.

26 And though after my skin *worms* destroy this *body,* yet shall I see God [1]in my flesh.

27 Whom I myself shall see, and mine eyes shall behold, and none other *for me, though* my reins are consumed within me.

28 But ye said, Why is he persecuted? And there was a [1]deep matter in me.

29 Be ye afraid of the sword: for the sword will be [1]avenged of wickedness, that ye may know that there is a judgment.

20

1 Zophar showeth, that the wicked and the covetous shall have a short end,   22 though for a time they flourish.

1 Then answered Zophar the Naamathite, and said,

2 Doubtless my thoughts cause me to answer, and therefore I make haste.

18:20 [1] When they shall see what came unto him.
19:3 [1] That is, many times, as Neh. 4:12.
19:4 [1] That is, I myself shall be punished for it, or you have not yet confuted it.
19:6 [1] He bursteth out again into his passions, and declareth still that his affliction cometh of God, though he be not able to feel the cause in himself.
19:8 [1] Meaning, out of his afflictions.
19:9 [1] Meaning, his children, and whatsoever was dear unto him in this world.
19:10 [1] Which is plucked up, and hath no more hope to grow.
19:12 [1] His manifold afflictions.
19:15 [1] Mine household servants: by all these losses Job showeth that touching the flesh he had great occasion to be moved.
19:17 [1] Which were hers and mine.
19:20 [1] Besides these great losses and most cruel unkindness, he was touched in his own person, as followeth.
    [2] All my flesh was consumed.

19:21 [1] Seeing I have these just causes to complain, condemn me not as an hypocrite, specially ye which should comfort me.
19:22 [1] Is it not enough that God doth punish me, except you by reproaches increase my sorrow?
    [2] To see my body punished, except ye trouble my mind?
19:24 [1] He protesteth that notwithstanding his sore passions his religion is perfect: and that he is not a blasphemer as they judged him.
19:25 [1] I do not so justify myself before the world, but I know that I shall come before the great Judge, who shall be my deliverer and Savior.
19:26 [1] Herein Job declareth plainly that he had a full hope, that both the soul and body should enjoy the presence of God in the last resurrection.
19:28 [1] Though his friends thought that he was but persecuted of God for his sins, yet he declareth that there was a deeper consideration, to wit, the trial of his faith and patience, and so to be an example for others.
19:29 [1] God will be revenged of this hasty judgment, whereby you condemned me.

3 I have heard [1]the correction of my reproach: therefore the spirit of mine understanding causeth me to answer.

4 Knowest thou not this of old? *and* since *God* placed man upon the earth,

5 That the rejoicing of the wicked *is* short, and that the joy of the hypocrites is but a moment?

6 Though [1]his excellency mount up to the heaven, and his head reach unto the clouds,

7 *Yet* shall he perish forever like his dung, *and* they which have seen him, shall say, Where is he?

8 He shall flee away as a dream, and they shall not find him, and shall pass away as a vision of the night.

9 So that the eye which had seen him, shall do so no more, and his place shall see him no more.

10 His children shall [1]flatter the poor, and his hands shall [2]restore his substance.

11 His bones are full *of the sin* of his youth, and [1]it shall lie down with him in the dust.

12 When wickedness was [1]sweet in his mouth, *and* he hid it under his tongue,

13 *And* favored it, and would not forsake it, but kept it close in his mouth,

14 *Then* his meat in his bowels was turned: the gall of Asps *was* in the midst of him.

15 He hath devoured substance, and he shall vomit it: *for* God shall draw it out of his belly.

16 He shall suck the [1]gall of Asps, *and* the viper's tongue shall slay him.

17 He shall not see the [1]rivers, *nor* the floods *and* streams of honey and butter.

18 He shall restore the labor, and shall devour no more: *even* according to the substance *shall be* his exchange, [1]and he shall enjoy it no more.

19 For he hath undone *many*: he hath forsaken the poor, *and* hath spoiled houses which he built not.

20 Surely he shall feel no quietness in his body, *neither* shall he reserve of that which he desired.

21 There shall none of his [1]meat be left: therefore none shall hope for his goods.

22 When he shall be filled with his abundance, he shall be in pain, *and* the hand [1]of all the wicked shall assail him.

23 He shall be about to fill his belly, *but God* shall send upon him his fierce wrath, [1]and shall cause to rain upon him, *even* upon his meat.

24 He shall flee from the iron weapons, *and* the bow of steel shall strike him through.

25 *The arrow* is drawn out, and cometh forth of the [1]body, and shineth of his gall, *so* fear cometh upon him.

26 [1]All darkness shall be hid in his secret places: the fire that is not [2]blown shall devour him, *and* that which remaineth in his tabernacle shall be destroyed.

27 The heaven shall declare his wickedness, and the earth shall rise up against him.

28 The [1]increase of his house shall go away: it shall flow away in the day of his wrath.

29 This is the portion of the wicked man from [1]God, and the heritage *that he shall have* of God, for his [2]words.

21

7 Job declareth how the prosperity of the wicked maketh them proud.   15 Insomuch that they blaspheme God.   16 Their destruction is at hand.   23 None ought to be judged wicked for affliction, neither good for prosperity.

1 But Job answered, and said,

2 Hear diligently my words, and this [1]shall be instead of your consolations.

3 Suffer me that I may speak, and when I have spoken, mock on.

4 Do I *direct* my talk to man? If it [1]were so, how

20:3 [1] He declareth that two things moved him to speak: to wit, because Job seemed to touch him, and because he thought he had knowledge sufficient to confute him.

20:6 [1] His purpose is to prove Job to be a wicked man, and an hypocrite, because God punished him, and changed his prosperity into adversity.

20:10 [1] Whereas the father through ambition and tyranny oppressed the poor, the children through poverty and misery, shall seek favor at the poor.

[2] So that the thing which he hath taken away by violence shall be restored again by force.

20:11 [1] Meaning, that he shall carry nothing away with him but his sin.

20:12 [1] As poison that is sweet in the mouth, bringeth destruction when it cometh into the body: so all vice at the first is pleasant, but afterward God turneth it to destruction.

20:16 [1] He compareth evil gotten goods to the venom of Asps, which serpent is most dangerous: noting that Job's great riches were not truly come by and therefore God did plague him justly for the same.

20:17 [1] Though God give to all other abundance of his blessings, yet he shall have no part thereof.

20:18 [1] That is, these raveners and spoilers of the poor shall enjoy their theft but for a time: for after, God will take it from them, and cause them to make restitution, so that it is but an exchange.

20:21 [1] He shall leave nothing to his posterity.

20:22 [1] The wicked shall never be in rest: for one wicked man shall seek to destroy another.

20:23 [1] Some read, upon his flesh, alluding to Job, whose flesh was smitten with a scab.

20:25 [1] Some read, of the quiver.

20:26 [1] All fear and sorrow shall light upon him, when he thinketh to escape.

[2] That is, fire from heaven, or the fire of God's wrath.

20:28 [1] Meaning, the children of the wicked shall flow away like rivers, and be dispersed in divers places.

20:29 [1] Thus God will plague the wicked.

[2] Against God, thinking to excuse himself, and to escape God's hand.

21:2 [1] Your diligent marking of my words shall be to me a great consolation.

21:4 [1] As though he would say, I do not talk with man but with God, who will not answer me, and therefore my mind must needs be troubled.

should not my spirit be troubled?

5 Mark me, and be abashed, and lay your hand upon *your* [1]mouth.

6 Even when I remember, I am afraid, and fear taketh hold on my flesh.

7 Wherefore do the wicked [1]live, *and* wax old, and grow in wealth?

8 Their seed is established in their sight with them, and their generation before their eyes.

9 Their houses are peaceable without fear, and the rod of God is not upon them.

10 Their bullock gendereth, and faileth not: their cow calveth, and casteth not her calf.

11 They send forth their children [1]like sheep, and their sons dance.

12 They take the tambourine and harp, and rejoice in the sound of the organs.

13 They spend their days in wealth, and suddenly [1]they go down to the grave.

14 They say also unto God, Depart from us: for we desire not the [1]knowledge of thy ways.

15 Who is the Almighty, that we should serve him? and what profit should we have, if we should pray unto him?

16 Lo, their wealth is not in their [1]hand: *therefore* let the counsel of the wicked [2]be far from me.

17 How oft shall the candle of the wicked be put out and their destruction come upon them? he will divide *their* lives in his wrath.

18 They shall be as stubble before the wind, and as chaff that the storm carrieth away.

19 God will lay up the sorrow *of the father* for his children: when he rewardeth him, he shall know it.

20 [1]His eyes shall see his destruction, and he shall drink of the wrath of the Almighty.

21 For what pleasure hath he in his house after him, when the number of his months is cut off?

22 Shall any teach [1]God knowledge, who judgeth

CHAPTER 22
a Job 35:7

the highest things?

23 One [1]dieth in his full strength, being in all ease and prosperity.

24 His breasts are full of milk, and his bones run full of marrow.

25 And another [1]dieth in the bitterness of his soul, and never eateth with pleasure.

26 They shall sleep both in [1]the dust, and the worms shall cover them.

27 Behold, I know your thoughts, and the enterprises *wherewith* ye do me wrong.

28 For ye say, Where is the prince's [1]house? and where is the tabernacle of the wicked's dwelling?

29 May ye [1]not ask them that go by the way? and ye cannot deny their signs.

30 But the wicked is kept unto the day of [1]destruction, *and* they shall be brought forth to the day of wrath.

31 Who shall declare his way [1]to his face? and who shall reward him for that he hath done?

32 Yet shall he be brought to the grave, and remain in the heap.

33 The [1]slimy valley shall be sweet unto him, and every man shall draw after him, as before him there were innumerable.

34 How then comfort [1]ye me in vain, seeing in your answer there remain but lies?

22 2 *Eliphaz affirmeth that Job is punished for his sins.* 6 *He accuseth him of unmercifulness.* 13 *And that he denied God's providence.* 21 *He exhorteth to repentance.*

1 Then Eliphaz the Temanite answered, and said,

2 May a man be [1]profitable unto God, as he that is wise may be profitable to himself?

3 [a]Is it anything unto the Almighty, that thou art

21:5 [1] He chargeth them as though they were not able to comprehend this his feeling of God's judgment, and exhorteth them therefore to silence.

21:7 [1] Job proveth against his adversaries that God punisheth not straightways the wicked, but oft times giveth them long life, and prosperity: so that we must not judge God just or unjust by the things that appear to our eyes.

21:11 [1] They have store of children, lusty and healthful, and in these points he answereth to that which Zophar alleged before.

21:13 [1] Not being tormented with long sickness.

21:14 [1] They desire nothing more than to be exempt from all subjection that they should bear to God: thus Job showeth his adversaries, that if they reason only by that which is seen by common experience, the wicked that hate God, are better dealt withal, than they that love him.

21:16 [1] It is not their own, but God only lendeth it unto them.
  [2] God keep me from their prosperity.

21:20 [1] When God recompenseth his wickedness, he shall know that his prosperity was but vanity.

21:22 [1] Who sendeth to the wicked prosperity, and punisheth the godly.

21:23 [1] Meaning, the wicked.

21:25 [1] To wit, the godly.

21:26 [1] As concerning their bodies: and this he speaketh according to the common judgment.

21:28 [1] Thus they called Job's house in derision, concluding that it was destroyed because he was wicked.

21:29 [1] Which through long travailing have experience and tokens thereof, to wit, that the wicked do prosper, and the godly live in affliction.

21:30 [1] Though the wicked flourish here, yet God will punish him in the last day.

21:31 [1] Though men do flatter him, and none dare reprove him in this world, yet death is a token that he will bring him to an account.

21:33 [1] He shall be glad to lie in a slimy pit, which before could not be content with a royal palace.

21:34 [1] Saying, that the just in this world have prosperity, and the wicked adversity.

22:2 [1] Though man were just, yet God could have no profit of this his justice: and therefore when he punished him, he hath no regard to his justice, but to his sin.

righteous? or is it profitable *to him*, that thou makest thy ways upright?

4 Is it for fear ¹of thee that he will accuse thee? *or* go with thee into judgment?

5 Is not thy wickedness great, and thine iniquities innumerable?

6 For thou hast taken the ¹pledge from thy brother for nought, and spoiled the clothes of the naked.

7 To such as were weary, thou hast not given water to drink, and hast withdrawn bread from the hungry.

8 But the mighty man ¹had the earth, and he that was in authority, dwelt in it.

9 Thou hast cast out widows empty, and the arms of the ¹fatherless were broken.

10 Therefore snares *are* round about thee, and fear shall suddenly trouble thee.

11 Or darkness that thou shouldest not see, and ¹abundance of waters shall cover thee.

12 Is not God on ¹high in the heaven? and behold the height of the ²stars how high they are.

13 But thou sayest, How should God ¹know? can he judge through the dark cloud?

14 The clouds hide him that he cannot see, and he walketh in the circle of heaven.

15 Hast thou marked the way of the world, ¹wherein wicked men have walked?

16 Which were ¹cut down before the time, whose foundation *was as* a river that overflowed:

17 Which said unto God, Depart from us, and *asked* what the Almighty could do for them.

18 Yet he ¹filled their houses with good things: but let the counsel of the wicked *be* far from me.

19 The righteous shall see them, and shall rejoice, ¹and the innocent shall laugh them to scorn.

20 Surely ¹our substance is hid: but the fire hath devoured the remnant of ²them.

21 Therefore acquaint thyself, I pray thee, ¹with him, and make peace: thereby thou shalt have prosperity.

22 Receive, I pray thee, the law of his mouth, and lay up his words in thine heart.

23 If thou return to the Almighty, thou shalt ¹be built up, *and* thou shalt put iniquity far from thy tabernacle.

24 Thou shalt lay up gold for ¹dust, and the gold of Ophir, as the flints of the rivers.

25 Yea, the Almighty shall be thy defense, and thou shalt have plenty of silver.

26 And thou shalt then delight in the Almighty, and lift up thy face unto God.

27 Thou shalt make thy prayer unto him, and he shall hear thee, and thou shalt render thy vows.

28 Thou shalt also decree a thing, and he shall establish it unto thee, and the ¹light shall shine upon thy ways.

29 ¹When *others* are cast down, then shalt thou say, I am lifted up: and *God* shall save the humble person.

30 The innocent shall deliver the ¹island, and it shall be preserved by the pureness of thine hands.

23 *Job affirmeth that he both knoweth and feareth the power and sentence of the Judge,* 10 *And that he is not punished only for his sins.*

1 But Job answered, and said,

2 Though my talk be this day in ¹bitterness, *and* my plague greater than my groaning,

3 Would God *yet* I knew how to find him, I would enter unto his place.

4 I would plead the cause before him, and fill my mouth with arguments.

22:4 ¹ Lest thou shouldest reprove or hurt him?
22:6 ¹ Thou hast been cruel and without charity, and wouldest do nothing for the poor, but for thine own advantage.
22:8 ¹ When thou wast in power and authority, thou didst not justice but wrong.
22:9 ¹ Thou hast not only not showed pity, but oppressed them.
22:11 ¹ That is, manifold afflictions.
22:12 ¹ He accuseth Job of impiety and contempt of God, as though he would say, If thou pass not for men, yet consider the height of God's majesty.
² That so much the more by that excellent work thou mayest fear God, and reverence him.
22:13 ¹ He reproveth Job, as though he denied God's providence and that he could not see the things that were done in this world.
22:15 ¹ How God hath punished them from the beginning?
22:16 ¹ He proveth God's providence by the punishment of the wicked, whom he taketh away before they can bring their wicked purposes to pass.
22:18 ¹ He answereth to that which Job had said, Job 21:7, that the wicked have prosperity in this world: desiring that he might not be partaker of the like.
22:19 ¹ The just rejoice at the destruction of the wicked for two causes: first, because God showeth himself judge of the world and by this means continueth his honor and glory: secondly, because God showeth that he hath care over his in that he punished their enemies.
22:20 ¹ That is, the state and preservation of the godly, is hid under God's wings.
² Meaning, of the wicked.
22:21 ¹ He exhorteth Job to repentance, and to return to God.
22:23 ¹ God will restore unto thee all thy substance.
22:24 ¹ Which shall be in abundance like dust.
22:28 ¹ That is, the favor of God.
22:29 ¹ God will deliver his when the wicked are destroyed round about them, as in the flood and in Sodom.
22:30 ¹ God will deliver a whole country from peril, even for the just man's sake.
23:2 ¹ He showeth the just cause of his complaining, and as touching that Eliphaz had exhorteth him to return to God, Job 22:21, he declareth that he desireth nothing more, but it seemed that God would not be found of him.

5 I would know the words, *that* he would answer me, and would understand what he would say unto me.

6 Would he ¹plead against me with his great power? No, but he would ²put *strength* in me.

7 ¹There the righteous might reason with him, so I should be delivered forever from my Judge.

8 ¹Behold, *if* I go to the East, he is not there: if to the West, yet I cannot perceive him:

9 *If* to the North where he worketh, yet I cannot see him: he will hide himself in the South, and I cannot behold him.

10 But he knoweth my ¹way, *and* trieth me, *and* I shall come forth like gold.

11 My foot hath followed his steps: his way have I kept, and have not declined:

12 Neither have I departed from the commandment of his lips, *and* I have ¹esteemed the words of his mouth more than mine appointed food.

13 Yet he is in one *mind*, and who can ¹turn him? yea, he doeth what his mind desireth.

14 For he will perform that which is decreed of me, and ¹many such things *are* with him.

15 Therefore I am troubled at his presence, and in considering it, I am afraid of him.

16 For ¹God hath softened mine heart, and the Almighty hath troubled me.

17 For I am not cut off in ¹darkness, but he hath hid the darkness from my face.

24 2 *Job describeth the wickedness of men, and showeth what curse belongeth to the wicked.   12 How all things are governed by God's providence.   17 And the destruction of the wicked.*

1 How should not the times ¹be hid from the Almighty, seeing that they which know him, see not his ²days?

2 *Some* remove the landmarks, that rob the flocks and feed *thereof.*

3 They lead away the ass of the fatherless, *and* take the widow's ox to pledge.

4 They make the poor to turn out of the way, so that the poor of the earth hide themselves ¹together.

5 Behold, *others as* wild asses in the wilderness, go forth to their business, and ¹rise early for a prey: the wilderness ²*giveth* him *and* his children food.

6 They reap ¹his provision in the field, but they gather the late ²vintage of the wicked.

7 They cause the naked to lodge without garment, and without covering in the cold.

8 They are wet with the showers of the mountains, ¹and they embrace the rock for want of a covering.

9 They pluck the fatherless ¹from the breast, and take the pledge of ²the poor.

10 They cause him to go naked without clothing, and take the gleaning from the hungry.

11 They that make oil ¹between their walls, and tread their winepresses, suffer thirst.

12 Men ¹cry out of the city, and the souls of the slain ²cry out: yet God ³doth not charge them with folly.

13 These are they that abhor the ¹light: they know not the ways thereof, nor continue in the paths thereof.

14 The murderer riseth early, *and* killeth the poor and the needy: and in the night he is as a thief.

15 The eye also of the ¹adulterer waiteth for the twilight, and saith, None eye shall see me, and disguiseth his face.

23:6 ¹ Using his absolute power, and saying, because I am God, I may do what I will.

² Of his mercy he would give me power to answer him.

23:7 ¹ When he of his mercy hath given strength to maintain their cause.

23:8 ¹ Meaning, that if he consider God's justice, he is not able to comprehend his judgments on what side or what part soever he turneth himself.

23:10 ¹ God hath this preeminence about me, that he knoweth my way: to wit, that I am innocent, and I am not able to judge of his works: he showeth also his confidence, that God doth use him for his profit.

23:12 ¹ His word is more precious unto me, than the meat wherewith the body is sustained.

23:13 ¹ Job confesseth that at this present he felt not God's favor, and yet was assured that he had appointed him to a good end.

23:14 ¹ In many points man is not able to attain to God's judgments.

23:16 ¹ That I should not be without fear.

23:17 ¹ He showeth the cause of his fear, which is, that he being in trouble seeth none end, neither yet knoweth the cause.

24:1 ¹ Thus Job speaketh in his passions, and after the judgment of the flesh: that is, that he seeth not the things that are done at times, neither yet hath a peculiar care over all, because he punisheth not the wicked, nor revengeth the godly.

² When he punisheth the wicked, and rewardeth the good.

24:4 ¹ And for cruelty and oppression dare not show their faces.

24:5 ¹ That is, spareth diligence.

² He and his live by robbing and murdering.

24:6 ¹ Meaning, the poor man's.

² Signifying, that one wicked man will not spoil another, but for necessity.

24:8 ¹ The poor are driven by the wicked into the rocks and holes where they cannot lie dry for the rain.

24:9 ¹ That is, they so powle and pill the poor widow, that she cannot have to sustain herself that she may be able to give her child suck.

² That is, his garment, wherewith he should be covered or clad.

24:11 ¹ In such places which are appointed for that purpose: meaning, that those that labor for the wicked, are pined for hunger.

24:12 ¹ For the great oppression and extortion.

² Cry out and call for vengeance.

³ God doth not condemn the wicked, but seemeth to pass over it by his long silence.

24:13 ¹ That is, God's word, because they are reproved thereby.

24:15 ¹ By these particular vices and the licence thereunto, he would prove that God punished not the wicked, and rewardeth the just.

16 They dig through houses in the dark, *which* they marked for themselves in the day: they know not the light.

17 But the morning *is* even to them as the shadow of death: if one know them, *they are* in the terrors of the shadow of death.

18 He is swift upon the ¹waters: their ²portion shall be cursed in the earth: he will not behold the way of the vineyards.

19 *As* the dry ground and heat consume the snow waters, *so shall* the grave ¹the sinners.

20 ¹The pitiful man shall forget him: the worm *shall feel* his sweetness: he shall be no more remembered, and the wicked shall be broken like a tree.

21 He ¹doth evil entreat the barren that doth not bear, neither doeth he good to the widow.

22 He draweth also the ¹mighty by his power, *and* when he riseth up, none is sure of life.

23 Though men give him assurance to be in safety, yet his eyes *are* upon their ways.

24 They are exalted for a little, but they are gone, and are brought low as all *others*: they are destroyed, and cut off as the top of an ear of corn.

25 But if it be not ¹so, where is he? *or* who will prove me a liar, and make my words of no value?

25

Bildad proveth that no man is clean nor without sin before God.

1 Then answered Bildad the Shuhite, and said,

2 ¹Power and fear *is* with him, that maketh peace in his places.

3 Is there any number in his armies? ¹and upon whom shall not ²his light arise?

4 And how may a man ¹be justified with God? or how can he be clean that is born of woman?

5 Behold, he will give no light to the Moon, ¹and the Stars are unclean in his sight.

6 How much more man, a worm, even the son of man, *which is but* a worm?

26

Job showeth that man cannot help God, and proveth it by his miracles.

1 But Job answered, and said,

2 ¹Whom helpest thou? him that hath no power? savest thou the arm that hath no strength?

3 Whom counselest thou? him that hath no wisdom? ¹thou showest right well as the thing is.

4 To whom dost thou declare *these* words? or whose spirit ¹cometh out of thee?

5 The ¹dead things are formed under the waters, and near unto them.

6 The grave is ¹naked before him, and there is no covering for ²destruction.

7 He stretcheth out the ¹North over the empty place, and hangeth the earth upon nothing.

8 He bindeth the waters in his clouds, and the cloud is not broken under them.

9 He holdeth back the face of his throne, and spreadeth his cloud upon it.

10 He hath set bounds ¹about the waters, until the ²day and night come to an end.

11 The ¹pillars of heaven tremble and quake at his reproof.

12 The sea is calm by his power, and by his understanding he smiteth the pride *thereof*.

13 His Spirit hath garnished the heavens, *and* his hand hath formed the crooked ¹serpent.

14 Lo, these are part of his ways: but ¹how little a portion hear we of him? and who can understand his fearful power?

24:18 ¹ He fleeth to the waters for his succor.
   ² They think that all the world is bent against them, and dare not go by the high way.
24:19 ¹ As the dry ground is never full with waters, so will they never cease sinning till they come to the grave.
24:20 ¹ Though God suffer the wicked for a time, yet their end shall be most vile destruction, and in this point Job committeth to himself, and showeth his confidence.
24:21 ¹ He showeth why the wicked shall not be lamented, because he did not pity others.
24:22 ¹ He declareth that after that the wicked have destroyed the weakest, they will do like to the stranger, and therefore are justly punished by God's judgments.
24:25 ¹ That is, that contrary to your reasoning no man can give perfect reasons of God's judgments, let me be reproved.
25:2 ¹ His purpose is to prove that albeit God try and afflict the just, yet soon after he sendeth prosperity, and because he did not so to Job he concludeth that he is wicked.
25:3 ¹ Who can hide him from his presence?
25:4 ¹ That is, be just in respect of God?
25:5 ¹ If God show his power, the Moon and Stars cannot have that light which is given them, much less can man have any excellency,

but of God.
26:2 ¹ Thou concludest nothing: for neither thou helpest me, which am destitute of all help, neither yet speakest sufficiently on God's behalf, who hath no need of thy defense.
26:3 ¹ But thou dost not apply it to the purpose.
26:4 ¹ That is, moveth thee to speak this?
26:5 ¹ Job beginneth to declare the force of God's power and providence in the mines and metals in the deep places of the earth.
26:6 ¹ There is nothing hid in the bottom of the earth but he seeth it.
   ² Meaning, the grave wherein things putrify.
26:7 ¹ He causeth the whole heaven to turn about the North pole.
26:10 ¹ That is, he hid the heavens which are called his throne.
   ² So long as this world endureth.
26:11 ¹ Not that heaven hath pillars to uphold it, but he speaketh by a similitude, as though he would say, The heaven itself is not able to abide his reproach.
26:13 ¹ Which is a figure of stars fashioned like a serpent, because of the crookedness.
26:14 ¹ If these few things, which we see daily with our eyes, declare his great power and providence, how much more would they appear, if we were to comprehend all his works?

27

3 The constancy and perfectness of Job.   13 The reward of the wicked and of the tyrants.

1 Moreover Job proceeded and continued his parable, saying,

2 The living God hath taken away my [1]judgment: for the Almighty hath put my soul in bitterness.

3 Yet so long as my breath is in me, and the Spirit of God in my nostrils,

4 [1]My lips surely shall speak no wickedness, and my tongue shall utter no deceit.

5 God forbid, that I should [1]justify you: until I die, I will never take away mine [2]innocency from myself.

6 I will keep my righteousness, and will not forsake it: mine heart shall not reprove me of my [1]days.

7 Mine enemy shall be as the wicked, and he that riseth against me, as the unrighteous.

8 For what [1]hope hath the hypocrite when he hath heaped up riches, if God take away his soul?

9 Will God hear his cry, when trouble cometh upon him?

10 Will he set his delight on the Almighty? will he call upon God at all times?

11 I will teach you *what is* in the hand of [1]God, *and* I will not conceal that which is with the Almighty.

12 Behold, all ye yourselves [1]have seen it: why then do you thus vanish [2]vanity?

13 This is the [1]portion of a wicked man with God, and the heritage of tyrants, *which* they shall receive of the Almighty.

14 If his children be in great number, the sword *shall destroy* them, and his posterity shall not be satisfied with bread.

15 His remnant shall be buried in death, and his widows [1]shall not weep.

16 Though he should heap up silver as the dust, and prepare raiment as the clay,

17 He may prepare it, but the just shall put it on, and the innocent shall divide the silver.

18 He buildeth his house as the [1]moth, and as a lodge that the watchman maketh.

19 When the rich man sleepeth, [1]he shall not be gathered *to his fathers*: they opened their eyes, and he was gone.

20 Terrors shall take him as waters, *and* a tempest shall carry him away by night.

21 The East wind shall take him away, and he shall depart: and it shall hurl him out of his place.

22 And *God* shall cast upon him and not spare, *though* he would fain flee out of his hand.

23 *Every man* shall clap their hands at him, and hiss at him out of their place.

28

Job showeth that the wisdom of God is unsearchable.

1 The silver surely hath his vein, [1]and the gold his palace, *where* they take it.

2 Iron is taken out of the dust, and brass is molten out of the stone.

3 *God* putteth an end to darkness, [1]and he trieth the perfection of all things: he setteth a bond of darkness, and of the shadow of death.

4 The flood breaketh out against the [1]inhabitant, *and the waters* [2]forgotten of the foot, being higher than man, are gone away.

5 Out of the same earth cometh [1]bread, and under it, as it were fire is turned up.

6 The stones thereof *are* a place [1]of Sapphires, and the dust of it *is* gold.

7 There is a path which no fowl hath known, neither hath the kite's eye seen it.

8 The Lion's whelps have not walked it, nor the Lion passed thereby.

9 He putteth his hand upon the [1]rocks, and overthroweth the mountains by the roots.

27:2 [1] He hath so sore afflicted me, that men cannot judge of mine uprightness: for they judge only by outward signs.

27:4 [1] However men judge of me, yet will I not speak contrary to that which I have said, and so do wickedly in betraying the truth.

27:5 [1] Which condemns me as a wicked man, because the hand of God is upon me.

   [2] I will not confess that God doth thus punish me for my sins.

27:6 [1] Of my life past.

27:8 [1] What advantage hath the dissembler to gain never so much, seeing he shall lose his own soul?

27:11 [1] That is, what God reserveth to himself, and whereof he giveth not the knowledge to all.

27:12 [1] That is, these secret judgments of God, and yet do not understand them.

   [2] Why maintain you then this error?

27:13 [1] Thus will God order the wicked, and punish him even unto his posterity.

27:15 [1] None shall lament him.

27:18 [1] Which breedeth in another man's possession or garment, but is soon shaken out.

27:19 [1] He meaneth, that the wicked tyrants shall not have a quiet death, nor be buried honorably.

28:1 [1] His purpose is to declare that man may attain in this world to divers secrets of nature, but man is never able to comprehend the wisdom of God.

28:3 [1] There is nothing but it is compassed within certain limits, and hath an end, but God's wisdom.

28:4 [1] Meaning, him that dwelleth thereby.

   [2] Which a man cannot wade through.

28:5 [1] That is, come, and underneath is brimstone or coal, which easily conceiveth fire.

28:6 [1] He alludeth to the mines and secrets of nature, which are under the earth, whereinto neither fowls nor beasts can enter.

28:9 [1] After that he hath declared the wisdom of God in the secrets of nature he describeth his power.

10 He breaketh rivers in the roots, and his eye seeth every precious thing.

11 He bindeth the floods, that they do not overflow, and the thing that is hid, bringeth he to light.

12 But where is wisdom found? [1]and where is the place of understanding?

13 Man knoweth not [1]the price thereof: for it is not found in the land of the living.

14 The depth saith, It is not in me: the Sea also saith, It is not with me.

15 [1]Gold shall not be given for it, neither shall silver be weighed for the price thereof.

16 It shall not be valued with the wedge of gold of Ophir, *nor* with the precious onyx, nor the sapphire.

17 The gold nor the crystal shall be equal unto it, nor the exchange *shall be* for plate of fine gold.

18 No mention shall be made of coral, nor of the [1]gabish: for wisdom is more precious than pearls.

19 The Topaz of Ethiopia shall not be equal unto it, neither shall it be valued with the wedge of pure gold.

20 Whence then cometh wisdom? and where is the place of understanding,

21 Seeing it is hid from the eyes of all the living, and is hid from the [1]fowls of the heaven?

22 Destruction and death say, We have heard the fame thereof with our ears.

23 *But* God understandeth the [1]way thereof, and he knoweth the place thereof.

24 For he beholdeth the ends of the world, *and* seeth all that is under heaven,

25 To make the weight of the winds and to weigh the waters by measure.

26 When he made a decree for the rain, and a way for the lightning of the thunders,

27 Then did he see it, and counted it: he prepared it, and also considered it.

28 And unto man he said, Behold, [a]the [1]fear of the Lord is wisdom, and to depart from evil *is* understanding.

CHAPTER 28
[a] Prov. 1:7

29

1 Job complaineth of the prosperity of the time past. 7, 21 His authority.   22 Justice and equity.

1 So Job proceeded, and continued his parable, saying,

2 Oh that I were as [1]in times past, when God preserved me!

3 When his [1]light shined upon mine head: *and when* by his light I walked through the [2]darkness,

4 As I was in the days of my youth: when [1]God's providence *was* upon my tabernacle;

5 When the Almighty was yet with me, *and* my children round about me;

6 when I washed my paths [1]with butter, and when the rock poured me out rivers of oil;

7 When I went out to the gate, *even* to the judgment seat, *and when* I caused them to prepare my seat in the street.

8 The young men saw me, and [1]hid themselves, and the aged arose, *and* stood up.

9 The princes stayed talk, and laid their hand on their [1]mouth.

10 The voice of princes was hid, and their tongue cleaved to the roof of their mouth.

11 And when the [1]ear heard me, it blessed me, and when the eye saw *me*, it gave witness to [2]me.

12 For I delivered the [1]poor that cried, and the fatherless, and him that had none to help him.

13 [1]The blessing of him that was ready to perish, came upon me, and I caused the widow's heart to rejoice.

14 I put [1]on justice, and it covered me: my judgment *was* as a robe, and a crown.

15 I was the eyes to the blind, and I was the feet to the lame.

16 I was a father unto the poor, and *when* I knew not the cause, I sought it out diligently.

17 I brake also the jaws of the unrighteous man, and plucked the prey out of his teeth.

18 Then I said, I shall die in my [1]nest, and I shall multiply *my* days as the sand.

19 *For* my root is [1]spread out by the water, and the dew shall lie upon my branch.

28:12 [1] Though God's power and wisdom may be understood in earthly things, yet his heavenly wisdom cannot be attained unto.
28:13 [1] It is too high a thing for man to attain unto in this world.
28:15 [1] It can neither be bought for gold nor precious stones, but is only the gift of God.
28:18 [1] Which is thought to be a kind of precious stone.
28:21 [1] Meaning, that there is no natural means whereby man might attain to the heavenly wisdom: which he meaneth by the souls that fly high.
28:23 [1] He maketh God only the author of this wisdom, and the giver thereof.
28:28 [1] He declareth that man hath so much of this heavenly wisdom, as he showeth by fearing God, and departing from evil.
29:2 [1] Hebrew, *month before.*
29:3 [1] When I felt his favor.

[2] I was free from affliction.
29:4 [1] That is, seemed by evident tokens to be more present with me.
29:6 [1] By these similitudes he declareth the great prosperity that he was in, so that he had none occasion to be such a sinner as they accused him.
29:8 [1] Being ashamed of their lightness and afraid of my gravity.
29:9 [1] Acknowledging my wisdom.
29:11 [1] All that heard me, praised me.
[2] Testifying, that I did good justice.
29:12 [1] Because his adversaries did so much charge him with wickedness, he is compelled to render account of his life.
29:13 [1] That is, I did succor him that was in distress, and so he had cause to praise me.
29:14 [1] I delighted to do justice, as others did to wear costly apparel.
29:18 [1] That is, at home in my bed without all trouble and unquietness.
29:19 [1] My felicity doth increase.

20 My glory shall renew toward me, and my bow shall be restored in mine hand.

21 Unto me men gave ear, and waited, and held their tongue at my counsel.

22 After my words they replied not, and my talk ¹dropped upon them.

23 And they waited for me, as for the rain, and they opened their mouth ¹as for the latter rain.

24 *If* I ¹laughed on them, they believed it not: neither did they cause the light of my countenance ²to fall.

25 I appointed out ¹their way, and did sit as chief, and dwelt as a King in the army, *and* like him that comforteth the mourners.

30

1 *Job complaineth that he is contemned of the most contemptible,* 11, 21 *because of his adversity and affliction.* 23 *Death is the house of all flesh.*

1 But now they that are younger than I, ¹mock me: *yea,* they whose fathers I have refused to set with the ²dogs of my flocks.

2 For whereto should the strength of their hands have served me, *seeing* age ¹perished in them?

3 For poverty and famine *they were* solitary, fleeing into the wilderness, *which is* dark, desolate and waste.

4 They cut up ¹nettles by the bushes, and the juniper roots *was* their meat.

5 They were ¹chased forth from among *men:* they shouted at them, as at a thief.

6 Therefore they dwelt in the clefts of rivers, in the holes of the earth and rocks.

7 They roared among the bushes, and under the thistles they gathered themselves.

8 *They were* the children of fools, and the children of villains, which were more vile than the earth.

9 And now am I their ¹song, and I am their talk.

10 They abhor me, *and* flee far from me, and spare not to spit in my face.

11 Because that *God* hath loosed my ¹cord and humbled me, ²they have loosed the bridle before me.

12 The youth rise up at my right hand: they have pushed my feet, and have trode on me *as on the* ¹paths of their destruction.

13 They have destroyed my paths: they took pleasure at my calamity, they had no ¹help.

14 They came as a great breach *of waters, and* ¹under this calamity they come on heaps.

15 Fear is turned upon me: *and* they pursue my soul as the wind, and mine health passeth away as a cloud.

16 Therefore my soul is now ¹poured out upon me, and the days of affliction have taken hold on me.

17 ¹It pierceth my bones in the night, and my sinews take no rest.

18 For the great vehemency is my garments changed, *which* compasseth me about, as the collar of my coat.

19 ¹He hath cast me into the mire, and I am become like ashes and dust.

20 When I cry unto thee, thou dost not hear me, neither regardest me, *when* I stand up.

21 Thou turnest thyself ¹cruelly against me, and art enemy unto me with the strength of thine hand.

22 Thou takest me up *and* causest me to ride upon the ¹wind, and makest my ²strength to fail.

23 Surely I know that thou wilt bring me to death, and to the house appointed for all the living.

24 Doubtless none can stretch his hand ¹unto the grave, though they cry in his destruction.

25 Did not I weep with him that was in trouble? was not my soul in heaviness for the poor?

26 Yet when I looked for good, ¹evil came unto me: and when I waited for light, there came darkness.

27 My bowels did boil without rest: *for* the days of affliction are come upon me.

28 I went mourning ¹without sun: I stood up in

29:22 ¹ That is, was pleasant unto them.

29:23 ¹ As the dry ground thirsteth for the rain.

29:24 ¹ That is, they thought it not to be a rest, or they thought not that I would condescend unto them.

  ² They were afraid to offend me and cause me to be angry.

29:25 ¹ I had them at commandment.

30:1 ¹ That is, mine estate is changed, and whereas before the ancient men were glad to do me reverence, the young men now contemn me.

  ² Meaning to be my shepherds, or to keep my dogs.

30:2 ¹ That is, their fathers died for famine before they came to age.

30:4 ¹ Or, mallows.

30:5 ¹ Job showeth that these that mocked him in his affliction, were like to their fathers, wicked and lewd fellows, such as he here describeth.

30:9 ¹ They make songs of me, and mock at my misery.

30:11 ¹ God hath taken from me the force, credit, and authority wherewith I kept them in subjection.

  ² He said that the young men when they saw him, hid themselves, as Job 29:8, and now in his misery they were impudent and licentious.

30:12 ¹ That is, they sought by all means how they might destroy me.

30:13 ¹ They need none to help them.

30:14 ¹ By my calamity they took an occasion against me.

30:16 ¹ My life faileth me, and I am as half dead.

30:17 ¹ Meaning, sorrow.

30:19 ¹ That is, God hath brought me into contempt.

30:21 ¹ He speaketh not thus to accuse God, but to declare the vehemency of his affliction, whereby he was carried beside himself.

30:22 ¹ He compareth his afflictions to a tempest or whirlwind.

  ² Or, wisdom, or law.

30:24 ¹ None can deliver me thence, though they lament at my death.

30:26 ¹ Instead of comforting they mocked at me.

30:28 ¹ Not delighting in any worldly thing, no not so much as in the use of the Sun.

the Congregation ²*and* cried.

29 I am a brother to the ¹Dragons, and a companion to the Ostriches.

30 My skin is black upon me, and my bones are burnt with ¹heat.

31 Therefore mine harp is turned to mourning, and mine organs into the voice of them that weep.

31

1 Job reciteth the innocence of his living and number of his virtues, which declareth what ought to be the life of the faithful.

1 I made a covenant with mine ¹eyes: why then should I think on ²a maid?

2 For what portion *should I have* of God from above? and *what* inheritance of the almighty from on high?

3 Is not destruction to the wicked, and strange *punishment* to ¹the workers of iniquity?

4 Doth not he behold my ways, and tell all my steps?

5 If I have walked in vanity, or if my foot hath made haste to deceit?

6 Let God weigh me in the just balance, and he shall know my ¹uprightness.

7 If my step hath turned out of the way, or mine heart hath ¹walked after mine eye, or if any blot hath cleaved to mine hands,

8 Let me sow, and let another ¹eat: yea, let my plants be rooted out.

9 If mine heart hath been deceived by a woman, or if I have laid wait at the door of my neighbor,

10 Let my wife ¹grind unto another man, and let other men bow down upon her.

11 For this is a wickedness, and iniquity to be condemned.

12 Yea, this is a fire that shall devour ¹to destruction, and which shall root out all my increase.

13 If I did contemn the judgment of my servant, and of my maid, when they ¹did contend with me,

14 What then shall I do when ¹God standeth up? and when he shall visit *me*, what shall I answer?

15 He that hath made me in the womb, hath he not made ¹him? hath not he alone fashioned us in the womb?

16 If I restrained the poor of *their* desire, or have caused the eyes of the widow ¹to fail,

17 Or have eaten my morsels alone, and the fatherless hath not eaten thereof,

18 (For from my youth hath he grown up with me ¹as *with* a father, and from my mother's womb have I been a guide unto her.)

19 If I have seen any perish for want of clothing, or any poor without covering,

20 If his loins have not blessed me, because he was warmed with the fleece of my sheep,

21 If I have lifted ¹up mine hand against the fatherless, when I saw that I might help him in the gate,

22 Let mine ¹arm fall from my shoulder, and mine arm be broken from the bone.

23 For God's punishment was ¹fearful unto me, and I could not *be delivered* from his Highness.

24 If I made gold mine hope, or have said to the wedge of gold, *Thou* art my confidence,

25 If I rejoiced because my substance was great, or because mine hand had gotten much,

26 If I did behold the ¹sun, when it shined, or the moon walking in *her* brightness,

27 If mine heart did flatter me in secret, or if my mouth did kiss mine ¹hand,

28 (This also had been an iniquity to be condemned: for I had denied the God ¹above.)

29 If I rejoiced at his destruction that hated me, or was moved *to joy* when evil came upon him,

30 Neither have I suffered my mouth to sin, by wishing a curse unto his soul.

31 Did not the men of my ¹Tabernacle say, Who shall give us of his flesh? we cannot be satisfied.

32 The stranger did not lodge in the street, *but I*

30:28 ² Lamenting them that were in affliction, and moving others to pity them.

30:29 ¹ I am like the wild beasts that desire most solitary places.

30:30 ¹ With the heat of affliction.

31:1 ¹ I kept my eyes from all wanton looks.

² Would not God then have punished me?

31:3 ¹ Job declareth that the fear of God was a bridle to stay him from all wickedness.

31:6 ¹ He showeth wherein his uprightness standeth, that is, inasmuch as he was blameless before men, and sinned not against the second Table.

31:7 ¹ That is, hath accomplished the lust of mine eyes.

31:8 ¹ According to the curse of the law, Deut. 28:33.

31:10 ¹ Let her be made a slave.

31:12 ¹ He showeth that albeit man neglect the punishment of adultery, yet the wrath of God will never cease till such be destroyed.

31:13 ¹ When they thought themselves evil entreated by me.

31:14 ¹ If I had oppressed others, how should I have escaped God's judgment.

31:15 ¹ He was moved to show pity unto servants, because they were God's creatures as he was.

31:16 ¹ By long waiting for her request.

31:18 ¹ He nourished the fatherless, and maintained the widow's cause.

31:21 ¹ To oppress him and to do him injury.

31:22 ¹ Let me rot in pieces.

31:23 ¹ I refrained not from sinning for fear of men, but because I feared God.

31:26 ¹ If I was proud of my worldly prosperity and felicity, which is meant by the shining of the sun, and brightness of the moon.

31:27 ¹ If mine own doings delighted me.

31:28 ¹ By putting confidence in anything but in him alone.

31:31 ¹ My servants moved me to be revenged of mine enemy, yet did I never wish him hurt.

opened my doors unto him, that went by the way.

33 If I have hid ¹my sins, as Adam, concealing mine iniquity in my bosom,

34 Though I could have made afraid a great multitude, yet the most contemptible of the families did ¹fear me: so I kept ²silence, and went not out of the door.

35 Oh that I had some to hear me! behold my ¹sign that the Almighty will witness for me: though mine adversary should write a book *against me*,

36 Would not I take it upon my shoulder, *and* bind it as a ¹crown unto me?

37 I will tell him the number of my goings, and go unto him as to a ¹prince.

38 If my land ¹cry against me, or the furrows thereof complain together,

39 If I have eaten the fruits thereof without silver: or *if* I have grieved ¹the souls of the masters thereof,

40 Let thistles grow instead of wheat, and cockle in the stead of barley.

THE ¹WORDS OF JOB ARE ENDED.

32

2 Elihu reproveth them of folly.   8 Age maketh not a man wise, but the spirit of God.

1 So these three men ceased to answer Job, because he ¹esteemed himself just.

2 Then the wrath of Elihu the son of Barachel the ¹Buzite, of the family of ²Ram, was kindled: his wrath, *I say*, was kindled against Job, because he justified himself ³more than God.

3 Also his anger was kindled against his three friends, because they could not find an answer, *and* yet condemned Job.

4 (Now Elihu had waited till Job had spoken: for ¹they were more ancient in years than he.)

5 So when Elihu saw, that there was none answer in the mouth of the three men, his wrath was kindled.

6 Therefore Elihu the son of Barachel, the Buzite answered and said, I am young in years, and ye are ancient: therefore I doubted, and was afraid to show you mine opinion.

7 *For* I said, The days ¹shall speak, and the multitude of years shall teach wisdom.

8 Surely there is a spirit in man, ¹but the inspiration of the Almighty giveth understanding.

9 Great men are not *always* wise, neither do the aged *always* understand judgment.

10 Therefore I say, Hear me *and* I will show also mine opinion.

11 Behold, I did wait upon your words, *and* hearkened unto your knowledge, while you sought out ¹reasons.

12 Yea, when I had considered you, lo, there was none of you that reproved Job, nor answered his words:

13 Lest ye should say, We have ¹found wisdom: *for* God hath cast him down, *and* no man.

14 Yet hath ¹he not directed *his* words to me, neither will I answer ²him by your words.

15 Then they fearing, answered no more, *but* left off their talk.

16 When I had waited (for they spake not, but stood still *and* answered no more)

17 Then answered I in my turn, and I showed mine opinion.

18 For I am full of ¹matter, *and* the spirit within me compelleth me.

19 Behold, my belly *is* as the wine, which hath no vent, *and* like the new bottles that burst.

20 *Therefore* will I speak, that I may take breath: I will open my lips, and will answer.

21 I will not now accept the person of man, ¹neither will I give titles to man.

22 For I may not give ¹titles, *lest* my Maker should take me away suddenly.

33

5 Elihu accuseth Job of ignorance.   14 He showeth that God hath divers means to instruct man and to draw him from sin.   19, 29 He afflicteth man and suddenly delivereth

---

31:33 ¹ And not confessed it freely: whereby it is evident that he justified himself before men, and not before God.
31:34 ¹ That is, I reverenced the most weak and contemned, and was afraid to offend them.
    ² I suffered them to speak evil of me, and went not out of my house to revenge it. .
31:35 ¹ This is a sufficient token of my righteousness, that God is my witness and will justify my cause.
31:36 ¹ Should not this book of his accusations be a praise and commendation to me?
31:37 ¹ I will make him account of all my life, without fear.
31:38 ¹ As though I had withheld their wages that labored in it.
31:39 ¹ Meaning, that he was no briber nor extortioner.
31:40 ¹ That is, the talk which he had with his three friends.
32:1 ¹ Hebrew, *was just in his own eyes.*
32:2 ¹ Which came of Buz, the son of Nahor, Abraham's brother.

² Or, as the Chaldean paraphrase readeth, Abram.
³ By making himself innocent, and by charging God of rigor.
32:4 ¹ That is, the three mentioned before.
32:7 ¹ Meaning, the ancient, which have experience.
32:8 ¹ It is a special gift of God that man hath understanding, and cometh neither of nature nor by age.
32:11 ¹ To prove that Job's affliction came for his sins.
32:13 ¹ And flatter yourselves, as though you had overcome him.
32:14 ¹ To wit, Job.
    ² He useth almost the like arguments, but without taunting and reproaches.
32:18 ¹ I have conceived in my mind great store of reasons.
32:21 ¹ I will neither have regard to riches, credit, nor authority, but will speak the very truth.
32:22 ¹ The Hebrew word signifieth, to change the name, as to call a fool a wise man: meaning, that he would not cloak the truth to flatter men.

him.   26 Man being delivered giveth thanks to God.

1 Wherefore, Job, I pray thee, hear my talk, and hearken unto all my words.

2 Behold now, I have opened my mouth: my tongue hath spoken in my mouth.

3 My words *are* in the uprightness of mine heart, and my lips shall speak pure knowledge.

4 The ¹Spirit of God hath made me, and the breath of the Almighty hath given me life.

5 If thou canst give me answer, prepare thyself *and* stand before me.

6 Behold, I am according to thy wish in ¹God's stead: I am also formed of the clay.

7 Behold, my terror shall not fear thee, neither shall mine hand ¹be heavy upon thee.

8 Doubtless thou hast spoken in mine ears, and I have heard the voice of *thy* words.

9 I am ¹clean, without sin: I am innocent and there is none iniquity in me.

10 Lo, he hath found occasions against me, and counted me for his enemy.

11 He hath put my feet in the stocks, and looketh narrowly unto all my paths.

12 Behold, in this hast thou not done right: I will answer thee, that God is greater than man.

13 Why dost thou strive against him? for he doth not ¹give account of all his matters.

14 For God speaketh ¹once or twice, and one seeth it not.

15 In dreams *and* ¹visions of the night, when sleep falleth upon men, and they sleep upon *their* beds,

16 Then he openeth the ears of men, even by their corrections, *which* he ¹had sealed,

17 That he might cause man to turn away from *his* enterprise, and that he might hide the ¹pride of man,

18 And keep back his soul from the pit, and that his life should not pass by the sword.

19 He is also stricken with sorrow upon his bed, and the grief of his bones *is* sore,

20 So that his ¹life causeth him to abhor bread, and his soul dainty meat.

21 His flesh faileth that it cannot be seen, and his bones *which* were not seen, clatter.

22 So his soul draweth to the grave, and his life ¹to the buriers.

23 If there be a ¹messenger with him, *or* an interpreter, one of a thousand ²to declare unto man his righteousness,

24 Then will he have ¹mercy upon him, and will say, ²Deliver him, that he go not down into the pit: for I have received a reconciliation.

25 *Then* shall his flesh be ¹as fresh as a child's, *and* shall return as in the days of his youth.

26 He shall pray unto God, and he will be favorable unto him, and he shall see his face with joy: for he will render unto man his ¹righteousness.

27 He looketh upon men, and if one say, I have sinned, and ¹perverted righteousness, and it did not profit ²me,

28 ¹He will deliver his soul from going into the pit, and his life shall see the light.

29 Lo, all these things will God work ¹twice or thrice with a man,

30 That he may turn back his soul from the pit, to be illuminated in the light of the living.

31 Mark well, O Job, *and* hear me: keep silence and I will speak.

32 If there be ¹matter, answer me, *and* speak: for I desire to ²justify thee.

33 If thou hast not, hear me: hold thy tongue, and I will teach thee wisdom.

34

5 Elihu chargeth Job, that he called himself righteous.   12 He showeth that God is just in his

---

33:4 ¹ I confess the power of God, and am one of his, therefore thou oughtest to hear me.

33:6 ¹ Because Job had wished to dispute his cause with God, Job 16:21, so that he might do it without fear, Elihu saith, he will reason in God's stead, whom he needeth not to fear, because he is a man made of the same matter that he is.

33:7 ¹ I will not handle thee so roughly as these others have done.

33:9 ¹ He repeateth Job's words, whereby he protested his innocence in divers places, but specially in Job 13, 16 and 30.

33:13 ¹ The cause of his judgments is not always declared to man.

33:14 ¹ Though God by sundry examples of his judgments speak unto man, yet the reason thereof is not known: yea and though God should speak, yet is he not understood.

33:15 ¹ God saith he, speaketh commonly, either by visions to teach us the cause of his judgments, or else by afflictions, or by his messenger.

33:16 ¹ That is, determined to send upon them.

33:17 ¹ He showeth for what end God sendeth afflictions: to beat down man's pride, and to turn from evil.

33:20 ¹ That is, his painful and miserable life.

33:22 ¹ To them that shall bury him.

33:23 ¹ A man sent of God to declare his will.

² A singular man, and as one chosen out of a thousand, which is able to declare the great mercies of God unto sinners: and wherein man's righteousness standeth, which is through the justice of Jesus Christ and faith therein.

33:24 ¹ He showeth that it is a sure token of God's mercy toward sinners, when he causeth his word to be preached unto them.

² That is, the minister shall by the preaching of the word pronounce unto him the forgiveness of his sins.

33:25 ¹ He shall feel God's favor and rejoice: declaring hereby wherein standeth the true joy of the faithful, and that God will restore him to health of body, which is a token of his blessing.

33:26 ¹ God will forgive his sins, and accept him as just.

33:27 ¹ That is, done wickedly.

² But my sins hath been the cause of God's wrath toward me.

33:28 ¹ God will forgive the penitent sinner.

33:29 ¹ Meaning, oftentimes, even as oft as a sinner doth repent.

33:32 ¹ If thou doubt of anything, or see occasion to speak against it.

² That is, to show thee, wherein man's justification consisteth.

judgments.   24 God destroyeth the mighty.   30 By him the hypocrite reigneth.

CHAPTER 34
a Job 26:23

1 Moreover Elihu answered and said,

2 Hear my words, ye [1]wise men, and hearken unto me ye that have knowledge.

3 For the ear trieth the words, as the mouth tasteth meat.

4 Let us seek [1]judgment among us, and let us know among ourselves what is good.

5 For Job hath said, I am righteous, and God hath taken [1]away my judgment.

6 Should I lie in my [1]right? my *wound* of the arrow is [2]grievous without *my* sin.

7 What man is like Job, that drinketh [1]scornfulness like water?

8 Which goeth in the [1]company of them that work iniquity, and walketh with wicked men?

9 For he hath said, It [1]profiteth a man nothing that he should [2]walk with God.

10 Therefore hearken unto me, ye men of wisdom, God forbid that wickedness *should be* in God, and iniquity in the Almighty.

11 For he will render unto man *according* to his work, and cause everyone to find according to his way.

12 And certainly God will not do wickedly, neither will the Almighty pervert judgment.

13 Whom [a]hath he appointed over the earth besides himself? or who hath placed the whole world?

14 If [1]he set his heart upon *man*, and gather unto himself his spirit [2]and his breath,

15 All flesh shall perish together, and man shall return unto dust.

16 And if thou hast understanding, hear this, *and* hearken to the voice of my words.

17 Shall he that hateth judgment, [1]govern? and wilt thou judge him wicked that is most just?

18 Wilt thou say unto a king, *Thou art* [1]wicked? or to princes, *Ye are* ungodly?

19 *How much less* to him that accepteth not the persons of princes, and regardeth not the rich, more than the poor? for they be all the work of his hands.

20 They shall die suddenly, [1]and the people shall be troubled at midnight, [2]and they shall pass forth and take away the mighty without hand.

21 For his eyes *are* upon the ways of man, and he seeth all his goings.

22 There is no darkness nor shadow of death, that the workers of iniquity might be hid therein.

23 For he will not lay on man so much, that he should [1]enter into judgment with God.

24 He shall break the mighty without [1]seeking, and shall set up others in their stead.

25 Therefore shall he declare their [1]works: he shall turn the [2]night, and they shall be destroyed.

26 He striketh them as wicked men in the places of the [1]seers,

27 Because they have turned back from him, and would not consider all his ways:

28 So that they have caused the voice of the poor to [1]come unto him, and he hath heard the cry of the afflicted.

29 And when he giveth quietness, who can make trouble? and when he hideth his face, who can behold him, whether *it be* upon nations, or upon a man only?

30 Because the [1]hypocrite doth reign, *and* because the people are snared.

31 Surely *it appertaineth* unto God [1]to say, I have pardoned, I will not destroy.

32 [1]But if I see not, teach thou me: if I have done wickedly, I will do no more.

33 Will he perform the thing through [1]thee? for thou hast reproved [2]it, because that thou hast chosen, and not I: now speak what thou knowest.

34:2 [1] Which are esteemed wise of the world.

34:4 [1] Let us examine the matter uprightly.

34:5 [1] That is, hath afflicted me without measure.

34:6 [1] Should I say, I am wicked, being an innocent?
  [2] I am sorer punished, than my sin deserveth.

34:7 [1] Which is compelled to receive thy reproach and scorns of many for his foolish words.

34:8 [1] Meaning, that Job was like to the wicked, because he seemed not to glorify God and submit himself to his judgments.

34:9 [1] He wresteth Job's words who said that God's children are ofttimes punished in this world, and the wicked go free.
  [2] That is, live godly, as Gen. 5:22.

34:14 [1] To destroy him.
  [2] The breath of life which he gave man.

34:17 [1] If God were not just, how could he govern the world?

34:18 [1] If man of nature fear to speak evil of such as have power, then much more ought they to be afraid to speak evil of God.

34:20 [1] When they look not for it.
  [2] The messengers of visitation that God shall send.

34:23 [1] God doth not afflict man above measure, so that he should have occasion to contend with him.

34:24 [1] For all his creatures are at hand to serve him, so that he needeth not to seek for any other army.

34:25 [1] Make them manifest that they are wicked.
  [2] Declare the things that were hid.

34:26 [1] Meaning, openly in the sight of all men.

34:28 [1] By their cruelty and extortion.

34:30 [1] When tyrants sit in the throne of justice which under pretence of executing justice are but hypocrites and oppress the people, it is a sign that God hath drawn back his countenance of favor from that place.

34:31 [1] Only it belongeth to God to moderate his corrections, and not unto man.

34:32 [1] Thus Elihu speaketh in the person of God, as it were mocking Job, because he would be wiser than God.

34:33 [1] Will God use thy counsel in doing his works?
  [2] Thus he speaketh in the person of God, as though Job should choose and refuse affliction at his pleasure.

34 Let men of understanding tell me, and let a wise man hearken unto me.

35 Job hath not spoken of knowledge, neither were his words according to wisdom.

36 I desire that Job may be ¹tried, unto the end, touching the answers for wicked men.

37 For he ¹addeth rebellion unto his sin, he clappeth his hands among us, and multiplieth his words against God.

35

6 Neither doth godliness profit, or ungodliness hurt God, but man. 13 The wicked cry unto God and are not heard.

1 Elihu spake moreover, and said,

2 Thinkest thou this right, that thou hast said, I am ¹more righteous than God?

3 For thou hast said, What profiteth it thee, and what availeth it me, to purge me from my sin?

4 Therefore will I answer thee, and thy ¹companions with thee.

5 Look unto the heaven, and see and behold the ¹clouds which are higher than thou.

6 If thou sinnest, what doest thou ¹against him, yea, when thy sins be many, what doest thou unto him?

7 If thou be righteous, what givest thou unto him? or what receiveth he at thine hand?

8 Thy wickedness may hurt a man as thou art: and thy righteousness may profit the son of man.

9 They cause many that are oppressed, ¹to cry, which cry out for the violence of the mighty.

10 But none saith, Where is God that made me, which giveth songs in the night?

11 Which teacheth us more than the beasts of the earth, and giveth us more wisdom than the fowls of the heaven.

12 Then they cry because of the violence of the wicked, ¹but he answereth not.

13 Surely God will not hear vanity, neither will

the Almighty regard it.

14 Although thou sayest to God, Thou wilt not regard it, ¹yet judgment is before him: trust thou in him.

15 But now because his anger hath not visited, nor called to count the evil with great extremity,

16 Therefore Job ¹openeth his mouth in vain, and multiplieth words without knowledge.

36

1 Elihu showeth the power of God. 6 And his justice. 9 And wherefore he punisheth. 13 The property of the wicked.

1 Elihu also proceeded and said,

2 Suffer me a little and I will instruct thee: for I have yet to speak on God's behalf.

3 I will fetch ¹my knowledge afar off, and will attribute righteousness unto my maker.

4 For truly my words shall not be false, and he that is ¹perfect in knowledge, speaketh with thee.

5 Behold, the mighty God casteth away none that is ¹mighty and valiant of courage.

6 He ¹maintaineth not the wicked, but he giveth judgment to the afflicted.

7 He withdraweth not his eyes from the righteous, but they are with ¹kings in the throne, where he placeth them forever: thus they are exalted.

8 And if they be bound in fetters and tied with the cords of affliction,

9 Then will he show them their ¹work and their sins, because they have been proud.

10 He openeth also their ear to discipline, and commandeth them that they return from iniquity.

11 ᵃIf they obey and serve him, they shall end their days in prosperity, and their years in pleasures:

12 But if they will not obey, they shall pass by the sword and perish ¹without knowledge.

13 But the hypocrites ¹of heart increase the wrath:

34:36 ¹ That he may speak as much as he can, that we may answer him and all the wicked that shall use such arguments.

34:37 ¹ He standeth stubbornly in the maintenance of his cause.

35:2 ¹ Job never spake these words: but because he maintained his innocence, it seemed as though he would say, that God tormented him without just cause.

35:4 ¹ Such as are in the like error.

35:5 ¹ If thou canst not control the clouds, wilt thou presume to instruct God?

35:6 ¹ Neither doth thy sin hurt God, nor thy justice profit for: for he will be glorified without thee.

35:9 ¹ The wicked may hurt man and cause him to cry, who if he sought to God which sendeth comfort should be delivered.

35:12 ¹ Because they pray not in faith, as feeling God's mercies.

35:14 ¹ God is just, howsoever thou judgest of him.

35:16 ¹ For if he did punish thee as thou deservest, thou shouldest

not be able to open thy mouth.

36:3 ¹ He showeth that when we speak of God, we must lift up our spirits more high, than our natural sense is able to reach.

36:4 ¹ Thou shalt perceive that I am a faithful instructor, and that I speak to thee in the name of God.

36:5 ¹ Strong and constant, and of understanding: for these are the gifts of God, and he loveth them in man: but forasmuch as God punished now Job, it is a sign that these are not in him.

36:6 ¹ Therefore he will not preserve the wicked: but to the humble and afflicted heart he will show grace.

36:7 ¹ He preferreth the godly to honor.

36:9 ¹ He will move their hearts to feel their sins that they may come to him by repentance as he did Manasseh.

36:12 ¹ That is, in their folly or obstination, and so shall be cause of their own destruction.

36:13 ¹ Which are maliciously bent against God, and flatter themselves in their vices.

for they [2]call not when he bindeth them.

14 Their soul dieth in [1]youth, and their life among the whoremongers.

15 He delivereth the poor in his afflictions, and openeth their ear in trouble.

16 Even so would he have taken thee out of the straight place *into* a broad place, and not shut up beneath: and [1]that which resteth upon thy table had been full of fat.

17 But thou art full of the [1]judgment of the wicked, *though* judgment and equity maintain *all things*.

18 [1]For *God's* wrath is, lest he should take thee away in *thine* abundance: for no multitude of gifts can deliver thee.

19 Will he regard thy riches? *he regardeth* not gold, nor all them that excel in strength.

20 [1]Be not careful in the night, how he destroyeth the people out of their place.

21 Take thou heed: look not to [1]iniquity: for thou hast chosen it rather than affliction.

22 Behold, God exalteth by his power: what teacher is like him?

23 Who hath appointed to him his way? or who can say, Thou hast done wickedly?

24 Remember that thou magnify his work, which men behold.

25 All men see it, and men behold it [1]afar off.

26 Behold, God *is* excellent, [1]and we know him not, neither can the number of his years be searched out.

27 When he restraineth the drops of water, the rain [1]poureth down by the vapor thereof,

28 Which rain the clouds do drop *and* let fall abundantly upon man.

29 Who can know the divisions of the clouds, *and* the thunders of his [1]Tabernacle?

30 Behold, he spreadeth his light upon [1]it, and covereth the [2]bottom of the sea.

31 For thereby he judgeth [1]the people, and giveth meat abundantly.

32 He covereth the light with the clouds, and commanded them to go [1]against it.

33 [1]His companion showeth him therefore, and there is anger in rising up.

37

1 *Elihu proveth that the unsearchable wisdom of God is manifest by his works.* 4 *As by the thunders.* 6 *The snow.* 9 *The whirlwind.* 11 *And the rain.*

1 At this also mine heart is [1]astonied, and is moved out of his place.

2 Hear the [1]sound of his voice, and the noise that goeth out of his mouth.

3 He directeth it under the whole heaven, and his light unto the ends of the world.

4 After it a noise soundeth: he thundereth with the voice of his majesty, and he will not stay [1]them when his voice is heard.

5 God thundereth marvelously with his voice: he worketh great things, which we know not.

6 For he saith to the snow, Be thou upon the earth [1]likewise to the small rain and to the great rain of his power.

7 With the force *thereof* he [1]shutteth up every man, that all men may know his work.

8 Then the beasts go into the den, and remain in their places.

9 The whirlwind cometh out of the South, and the cold from the [1]North wind.

10 At the breath of God the frost is given, and the breadth of the waters [1]*is* made narrow.

11 He maketh also the clouds to [1]labor, to water *the earth, and* scattereth the cloud of [2]his light.

---

[2] When they are in affliction, they seek not to God for succor, as Asa in 2 Chron. 16:12; Rev.16:11.

36:14 [1] They die of some vile death, and that before they come to age.

36:16 [1] If thou hadst been obedient to God, he would have brought thee to liberty and wealth.

36:17 [1] Thou art altogether after the manner of the wicked: for thou dost murmur against the justice of God.

36:18 [1] God doth punish thee, lest thou shouldest forget God in thy wealth and so perish.

36:20 [1] Be not thou curious in seeking the cause of God's judgments, when he destroyeth any.

36:21 [1] And so murmur against God through impatience.

36:25 [1] The works of God are so manifest, that a man may see them afar off, and know God by the same.

36:26 [1] Our infirmity hindereth us so, that we cannot attain to the perfect knowledge of God.

36:27 [1] That is, the rain cometh of those drops of water, which he keepeth in the clouds.

36:29 [1] Meaning, of the clouds, which he calleth the Tabernacle of God.

36:30 [1] Upon the cloud.

[2] That men cannot come to the knowledge of the springs thereof.

36:31 [1] He showeth that the rain hath double use: the one that it declareth God's judgments, when it doth overflow any places, and the other that it maketh the land fruitful.

36:32 [1] That is, one cloud to dash against another.

36:33 [1] The cold vapor showeth him: that is, the cloud of the hot exhalation, which being taken in the cold cloud mounteth up toward the place where the fire is, and so anger is engendered: that is, noise, and thunderclaps.

37:1 [1] At the marvelling of the thunder and lightnings: whereby he declareth that the faithful are lively touched with the majesty of God, when they behold his works.

37:2 [1] That is, the thunder, whereby he speaketh to men to waken their dullness, and to bring them to the consideration of his works.

37:4 [1] Meaning, the rains and thunders.

37:6 [1] So that neither small rain, nor great, snow nor anything else cometh without God's appointment.

37:7 [1] By rains and thunders God causeth men to keep themselves within their houses.

37:9 [1] In Hebrew it is called the scattering wind, because it driveth away the clouds and purgeth the air.

37:10 [1] That is, is frozen up and dried.

37:11 [1] Gather the vapors and move to and fro to water the earth.

[2] That is, the cloud that hath lightning in it.

12 And it is turned about by his government, that they may do whatsoever he commandeth them upon the whole world:

13 Whether it be for ¹punishment, or for his land, or of mercy, he causeth it to come.

14 Hearken unto this, O Job: stand and consider the wondrous works of God.

15 Didst thou know when God disposed them? and caused the ¹light of his cloud to shine?

16 Hast thou known the ¹variety of the cloud, *and* the wondrous works of him that is perfect in knowledge?

17 *Or* how thy clothes are ¹warm, when he maketh the earth quiet through the South wind?

18 Hast thou stretched out the heavens, which are strong, *and* as a molten ¹glass?

19 Tell us what we shall say unto him: *for* we cannot dispose *our matter* because of ¹darkness.

20 Shall it be ¹told him when I speak? or shall man speak when he shall be ²destroyed?

21 And now men see not the light, ¹which shineth in the clouds, but the wind passeth and cleanseth them.

22 The ¹brightness cometh out of the North: the praise *thereof is* to God, which is terrible.

23 *It is* the Almighty: we cannot find him out: *he is* excellent in power and judgment, and abundant in justice: he ¹afflicteth not.

24 Let men therefore fear him: *for* he will not regard any that are wise in their own conceit.

38

1 *God speaketh to Job, and declareth the weakness of man in the consideration of his creatures, by whose excellency the power, justice, and providence of the Creator is known.*

1 Then answered the Lord unto Job out of the ¹whirlwind, and said,

2 Who is this that ¹darkeneth the counsel by words without knowledge?

3 Gird up now thy loins like a man: I ¹will demand of thee, and declare thou unto me.

4 Where wast thou when I ¹laid the foundations of the earth? declare, if thou hast understanding.

5 Who hath laid the measures thereof, if thou knowest, or who hath stretched the line over it:

6 Whereupon are the foundations thereof set? or who laid the cornerstone thereof:

7 When the stars of the morning ¹praised *me* together, and all the ²children of God rejoiced:

8 Or *who* hath shut up the Sea with doors, when it issued and came forth *as* out of the womb:

9 When I made the clouds *as* a covering thereof, and darkness *as* the ¹swaddling bands thereof:

10 When I establisheth my commandment upon it, and set bars and doors,

11 And said, hitherto shalt thou come, but no further, and here shall it ¹stay thy proud waves.

12 Hast thou commanded the ¹morning since thy days? hast thou caused the morning to know his place?

13 That it might take hold of the corners of the earth, and that the wicked might be ¹shaken out of it?

14 It is turned as clay to fashion, ¹and all stand up as a garment.

15 And from the wicked their light shall be taken away, and the high arm shall be broken.

16 Hast thou entered into the bottoms of the sea? or hast thou walked to seek out the ¹depth?

17 Have the gates of death been opened unto thee? or hast thou seen the gates of the shadow of death?

18 Hast thou perceived the breadth of the earth?

37:13 ¹ Rain, cold, heat, tempests and such like are sent of God, either to punish man, or to profit the earth, or to declare his favor toward man, as Job 36:31.

37:15 ¹ That is, the lightning to break forth in the clouds?

37:16 ¹ Which is sometimes changed into rain, or snow, hail, or such like.

37:17 ¹ Why thy clothes should keep thee warm when the South wind bloweth, rather than when any other wind bloweth?

37:18 ¹ For their clearness.

37:19 ¹ That is, our ignorance: signifying that Job was so presumptuous, that he would control the works of God.

37:20 ¹ Hath God need that any should tell him when man murmureth against him?

² If God would destroy a man, should he repine?

37:21 ¹ The cloud stoppeth the shining of the sun, that man cannot see it till the wind have chased away the cloud: and if man be not able to attain to the knowledge of these things, how much less of God's judgments?

37:22 ¹ In Hebrew, *gold*, meaning, fair weather and clear as gold.

37:23 ¹ Meaning, without cause.

38:1 ¹ That his words might have greater majesty, and that Job might know with whom he had to do.

38:2 ¹ Which by seeking out the secret counsel of God by man's reason, maketh it more obscure, and showeth his own folly.

38:3 ¹ Because he had wished to dispute with God, Job 23:3, God reasoneth with him, to declare his rashness.

38:4 ¹ Seeing he could not judge of those things which were done so long before he was born, he was not able to comprehend all God's works: much less the secret causes of his judgments.

38:7 ¹ The stars and dumb creatures are said to praise God, because his power, wisdom and goodness is manifest and known therein.

² Meaning, the Angels.

38:9 ¹ As though the great sea were but as a little babe in the hands of God to turn to and fro.

38:11 ¹ That is, God's decree and commandment, as verse 10.

38:12 ¹ To wit, to rise, since thou wast born?

38:13 ¹ Who having in the night been given to wickedness, cannot abide the light, but hide themselves.

38:14 ¹ The earth which seemed in the night to have no form, by the rising of the sun, is as it were created anew, and all things therein clad with new beauty.

38:16 ¹ If thou art not able to seek out the depth of the sea, how much less art thou able to comprehend the counsel of God?

tell if thou knowest all this.

19 Where is the way *where* light dwelleth? and where is the place of darkness,

20 That thou [1]shouldest receive it in the bounds thereof, and that thou shouldest know the paths to the house thereof?

21 Knewest thou it, because thou wast then born? and *because* the number of thy days *is* great?

22 Hast thou entered into the treasures of the snow? or hast thou seen the treasures of the hail,

23 Which I have hid [1]against the time of trouble, against the day of war and battle?

24 By what way is the light parted, *which* scattereth the East wind upon the earth?

25 Who hath divided the spouts for the rain? or the way for the lightning of the thunders,

26 To cause it to rain on the earth where no man is, *and* in the wilderness where there is no man?

27 To fulfill the wild and waste place, and to cause the bud of the herb to spring forth?

28 Who is the father of the rain? or who hath begotten the drops of the dew?

29 Out of whose womb came the ice? who hath engendered the frost of the heaven?

30 The waters are hid [1]as *with* a stone: and the face of the depth is frozen.

31 Canst thou restrain the sweet *influences* of [1]the Pleiades, or loose the bands of [2]Orion?

32 Canst thou bring forth [1]Mazzaroth in their time? canst thou also guide [2]Arcturus with his sons?

33 Knowest thou the course of heaven, or canst thou set the [1]rule thereof in the earth?

34 Canst thou lift up thy voice to the clouds, that the abundance of water may cover thee?

35 Canst thou send the lightnings that they may walk, and say unto thee, Lo, here we are?

36 Who hath put wisdom in the [1]reins? or who hath given the heart understanding?

37 Who can number clouds by wisdom? or who can cause to cease the [1]bottles of heaven,

38 When the earth groweth into hardness, [1]and the clots are fast together?

39

The bounty and providence of God, which extendeth even to the young ravens, giveth man full occasion to put his confidence in God. 37 Job confesseth and humbleth himself.

1 Wilt [1]thou hunt the prey for the lion? or fill the appetite of the lion's whelps,

2 When they crouch in their places, *and* remain in the covert to lie in wait?

3 Who prepareth for the raven his meat, when his birds [1]cry unto God, wandering for lack of meat?

4 Knowest thou the time when the wild goats bring forth young? *or* dost thou mark when the [1]hinds do calve?

5 Canst thou number the months that they [1]fulfill? or knowest thou the time when they bring forth?

6 They bow themselves: they [1]bruise their young and cast out their sorrows.

7 *Yet* their young wax fat, and grow up with corn: they go forth and return not unto them.

8 Who hath set the wild ass at liberty? or who hath loosed the bonds of the wild ass?

9 *It is* I which have made the wilderness his house, and the [1]salt places his dwellings.

10 He derideth the multitude of the city: he heareth not the cry of the driver.

11 He seeketh out the mountain for his pasture, and searcheth after every green thing.

12 Will the unicorn [1]serve thee? or will he tarry by thy crib?

13 Canst thou bind the unicorn with his band *to labor* in the furrow? or will he plow the valleys after thee?

14 Wilt thou trust in him, because his strength is great, and cast off thy labor unto him?

15 Wilt thou believe him, that he will bring home thy seed, and gather it unto thy barn?

16 *Hast thou given* the pleasant wings unto the peacocks? or wings and feathers unto the ostrich?

17 Which leaveth his eggs in the earth, and maketh them [1]hot in the dust,

18 And forgetteth that the foot might scatter them,

38:20 [1] That thou mightest appoint it highway and limits.
38:23 [1] To punish mine enemies with them, Exod. 9:18; Josh. 10:11.
38:30 [1] The ice covereth it, as though it were paved with stone.
38:31 [1] Which stars arise when the sun is in Taurus, which is the springtime, and bring flowers.
[2] Which star bringeth in winter.
38:32 [1] Certain stars so called: some think they were the twelve signs.
[2] The North star with those that are about him.
38:33 [1] Canst thou cause the heavenly bodies to have any power over the earthly bodies?
38:36 [1] In the secret parts of man.
38:37 [1] That is, the clouds wherein the water is contained as in bottles.
38:38 [1] For when God doth not open these bottles, the earth cometh to this inconvenience.

39:1 [1] After he had declared God's works in the heavens, he showeth his marvelous providence in earth, even toward the brute beasts.
39:3 [1] Read Ps. 147:9.
39:4 [1] He chiefly maketh mention of wild goats and hinds, because they bring forth their young with most difficulty.
39:5 [1] That is, how long they go with young?
39:6 [1] They bring forth with great difficulty.
39:9 [1] That is, the barren ground where no good fruits grow.
39:12 [1] Is it possible to make the unicorn tame? signifying that if man cannot rule a creature, that it is much more impossible that he should appoint the wisdom of God, whereby he governeth all the world.
39:17 [1] They write that the ostrich covereth her eggs in the sand, and because the country is hot and the sun still keepeth them warm, they are hatched.

or that the wild beast might break them.

19 He showeth himself cruel unto his young ones, *as they were not his, and* is without fear, as if he travailed ¹in vain.

20 For God had deprived him of ¹wisdom, and hath given him no part of understanding.

21 When ¹time *is*, he mounteth on high: he mocketh the horse and his rider.

22 Hast thou given the horse strength, *or* covered his neck with ¹neighing?

23 Hast thou made him afraid as the grasshopper? his strong neighing is fearful.

24 He ¹diggeth in the valley, and rejoiceth in *his* strength: he goeth forth to meet the harnessed *man*.

25 He mocketh at fear, and is not afraid, and turneth not back from the sword,

26 *Though* the quiver rattle against him, the glittering spear and the shield.

27 He ¹swalloweth the ground for fierceness and rage, and he believeth not that it is the noise of the trumpet.

28 He saith among the trumpets, Ha, ha: he smelleth the battle afar off, and the noise of the captains, and the shouting.

29 Shall the hawk fly by thy wisdom, *stretching out* his wings even toward the ¹South?

30 Doth the eagle mount up at thy commandment, or make his nest on high?

31 She abideth and remaineth in the rock, *even* upon the top of the rock, and the tower,

32 From thence she spieth for meat, *and* her eyes behold afar off.

33 His young ones also suck up blood: and where the slain *are*, there is she.

34 Moreover the Lord spake unto Job, and said,

35 Is this ¹to learn, to strive with the Almighty? he that reproveth God, let him answer to it.

36 ¶ Then Job answered the Lord, saying,

37 Behold, I am ¹vile: what shall I answer thee? I will lay mine hand upon my mouth.

38 Once have I spoken, but I will answer no more, yea twice, but I will proceed no further.

40

2 How weak man's power is, being compared to the work of God: 10 Whose power appeareth in the creation, and governing of the great beasts.

1 Again the Lord answered Job out of ᵃthe whirlwind, and said,

2 Gird up now thy loins like a man: I will demand of thee, and declare thou unto me.

3 Wilt thou disannul ¹my judgment? *or* wilt thou condemn me, that thou mayest be justified?

4 Or hast thou an arm like God? or dost thou thunder with a voice like him?

5 Deck thyself now with ¹majesty and excellency, and array thyself with beauty and glory.

6 Cast abroad the indignation of thy wrath, and behold everyone that is proud, and abase him.

7 Look on everyone that is arrogant, *and* bring him low: and destroy the wicked in their place.

8 Hide them in the dust together, *and* bind ¹their faces in a secret place.

9 Then will I confess unto thee also, that thy right hand can ¹save thee.

10 ¶ Behold now ¹Behemoth (whom I made ²with thee) which eateth ³grass as an ox.

11 Behold now, his strength *is* in his loins, and his force *is* in the navel of his belly.

12 *When* he taketh pleasure, his tail is like a cedar: the sinews of his stones are wrapped together.

13 His bones *are like* staves of brass, *and* his small bones like staves of iron.

14 ¹He is the chief of the ways of God: ²he that made him, will make his sword to approach unto him.

15 Surely the mountains bring him forth grass, where all the beasts of the field play.

16 Lieth he under the trees in the covert of the reed and fens?

17 Can the trees cover him with their shadow? or can the willows of the river compass him about?

18 Behold, he spoileth the river, ¹and hasteth not: he trusteth that he can draw up Jordan into his mouth.

19 He taketh it with his eyes, and thrusteth *his* nose through whatsoever meeteth him.

39:19 ¹ If he should take care of them.
39:20 ¹ That is, to have a care and natural affection toward his young.
39:21 ¹ When the young ostrich is grown up, he outrunneth the horse.
39:22 ¹ That is, given him courage? which is meant by neighing and shaking his mane: for with his breath he covereth his neck.
39:24 ¹ He beateth with his hoof.
39:27 ¹ He so rideth the ground that it seemeth nothing under him.
39:29 ¹ That is, when cold cometh, to fly into the warm countries.
39:35 ¹ Is this the way for a man that will learn, to strive with God? which thing he reproveth in Job.
39:37 ¹ Whereby he showeth that he repented, and desired pardon for his faults.
40:3 ¹ Signifying that they that justify themselves, condemn God as unjust.

40:5 ¹ Meaning, that these were proper unto God, and belonged to no man.
40:8 ¹ Cause them to die if thou canst.
40:9 ¹ Proving hereby that whosoever attributeth to himself power and ability to save himself, maketh himself God.
40:10 ¹ This beast is thought to be the elephant, or some other, which is unknown.
    ² Whom I made as well as thee.
    ³ This commendeth the providence of God toward man: for if he were given to devour as a lion, nothing were able to resist him, or content him.
40:14 ¹ He is one of the chiefest works of God among the beasts.
    ² Though man dare not come near him, yet God can kill him.
40:18 ¹ He drinketh at leisure, and feareth nobody.

20 ¶ Canst thou draw out [1]Leviathan with an hook, and with a line which thou shalt cast down unto his tongue?

21 Canst thou cast an hook into his nose? canst thou [1]pierce his jaws with an angle?

22 Will he make many prayers unto thee? *and* speak thee fair?

23 Will he make a covenant with thee? *and* wilt thou take [1]him as a servant forever?

24 Wilt thou play with him as with a bird? or wilt thou bind him for thy maids?

25 Shall the companions banquet with him? shall they divide him among the merchants?

26 Canst thou fill the basket with his skin? or the fishpanier with his head?

27 Lay thine hand upon him: remember [1]the battle, *and* do no more so.

28 Behold, [1]his hope is in vain: *for* shall not one perish even at the sight of him?

41 *1 By the greatness of this monster Leviathan, God showeth his greatness and his power, which nothing can resist.*

1 None *is* so fierce that dare stir him up. Who is he then that can [1]stand before me?

2 Who hath prevented me that I should [1]make an end? All under heaven is mine.

3 I will not keep silence *concerning* [1]his parts, nor *his* power, nor his comely proportion.

4 Who can discover the face [1]of his garment? *or* who shall come to him with a double [2]bridle?

5 Who shall [1]open the doors of his face? his teeth are fearful round about.

6 The majesty *of his* scales is like strong shields, *and* are sure sealed.

7 One is set to another, that no wind can come between them.

8 One is joined to another: they stick together, that they cannot be sundered.

9 His sneezings [1]make the light to shine, and his eyes *are* like the eyelids of the morning.

10 Out of his mouth go lamps, *and* sparks of fire leap out.

11 Out of his nostrils cometh out smoke, as out of a boiling pot or caldron.

12 His breath maketh the coals burn: for a flame goeth out of his mouth.

13 In his neck remaineth strength, and [1]labor is rejected before his face.

14 The members of his body are joined: they are strong in themselves, *and* cannot be moved.

15 His heart is as strong as a stone, and as hard as the nether millstone.

16 The mighty are afraid of his majesty, *and* for fear they faint in themselves.

17 When the sword doth touch him, he will not rise up, *nor for* the spear, dart nor habergeon.

18 He esteemeth iron as straw, and brass as rotten wood.

19 The archer cannot make him flee: the stones of the sling are turneth into stubble unto him.

20 The darts are counted as straw: and he laugheth at the shaking of the spear.

21 Sharp stones [1]are under him, and he spreadeth sharp things upon the mire.

22 He maketh the depth to [1]boil like a pot, and maketh the Sea like *a pot* of ointment.

23 He maketh a path to [1]shine after him, one would think the depth as an hoar head.

24 In the earth there is none like him: he is made without fear.

25 He beholdeth [1]all high things: he is a King over all the children of pride.

42 *6 The repentance of Job. 9 He prayeth for his friends. 12 His goods are restored double unto him. 13 His children, age and death.*

1 Then Job answered the Lord, and said,

2 I know that thou canst do all things, and that there is no [1]thought hid from thee.

3 Who is he that hideth counsel without [1]knowledge? therefore have I spoken that I understood not, *even* things too wonderful for me, [2]and *which* I knew not.

40:20 [1] Meaning, the whale.
40:21 [1] Because he feareth lest thou shouldest take him.
40:23 [1] To do thy business, and be at thy commandment?
40:27 [1] If thou once consider the danger, thou wilt not meddle with him.
40:28 [1] To wit, that trusteth to take him.
41:1 [1] If none dare stand against a whale, which is but a creature, who is able to compare with God the Creator?
41:2 [1] Who hath taught me to accomplish my work?
41:3 [1] The parts and members of the whale?
41:4 [1] That is, who dare pull off his skin?
    [2] Who dare put a bridle in his mouth?
41:5 [1] Who dare look in his mouth?
41:9 [1] That is, casteth out flames of fire.
41:13 [1] Nothing is painful or hard unto him.
41:21 [1] His skin is so hard that he lieth with a great ease on the stones as in the mire.
41:22 [1] Either he maketh the sea to seem as it boiled by his wallowing, or else he spouteth water in such abundance as it would seem that the sea boiled.
41:23 [1] That is, a white froth and shining stream before him.
41:25 [1] He despiseth all other beasts and monsters, and is the proudest of all others.
42:2 [1] No thought so secret, but thou dost see it, nor anything that thou thinkest, but thou canst bring it to pass.
42:3 [1] Is there any but I? for this God laid to his charge, Job 38:2.
    [2] I confess herein mine ignorance, and that I spake I wist not what.

4 Hear, I beseech thee, and I will speak: I will demand of thee, [1]and declare thou unto me.

5 I have [1]heard of thee by the hearing of the ear, but now mine eye seeth thee.

6 Therefore I abhor *myself*, and repent in dust and ashes.

7 Now after that the Lord had spoken these words unto Job, the Lord also said unto Eliphaz the Temanite, My wrath is kindled against thee and against thy two friends: for ye have not spoken of me the thing that is [1]right, like my servant [2]Job.

8 Therefore take unto you now seven bullocks, and seven rams, and go to my servant Job, and offer up for yourselves a burnt offering, and my servant Job shall [1]pray for you: for I will accept him, lest I should put you to shame, because ye have not spoken of me the thing which is right, like my servant Job.

9 So Eliphaz the Temanite, and Bildad the Shuhite, *and* Zophar the Naamathite, went, and did according as the Lord had said unto them, and the Lord accepted Job.

10 ¶ Then the Lord turned the [1]captivity of Job, when he prayed for his friends: also the Lord gave Job twice so much as he had before.

11 Then came unto him all his [1]brethren, and all his sisters, and all they that had been of his acquaintance before, and did eat bread with him in his house, and had compassion on him, and comforted him for all the evil that the Lord had brought upon him, and every man gave him a [2]piece of money, and everyone an earring of gold.

12 So the Lord blessed the last days of Job more than the first: for he had [1]fourteen thousand sheep, and six thousand camels, and a thousand yoke of oxen, and a thousand she asses.

13 He had also seven sons, and three daughters.

14 And he called the name of one [1]Jemimah, and the name of the second [2]Keziah, and the name of the third [3]Keren-Happuch.

15 In all the land were no women found so fair as the daughters of Job, and their father gave them inheritance among their brethren.

16 And after this lived Job an hundred and forty years, and saw his sons, and his son's sons, *even* four generations.

17 So Job died, being old, and full of days.

42:4 [1] He showeth that he will be God's scholar to learn of him.

42:5 [1] I knew thee only before by hearsay: but now thou hast caused me to feel what thou art to me, that I may resign myself over unto thee.

42:7 [1] You took in hand an evil cause, in that you condemned him by his outward afflictions, and not comforted him with my mercies.

[2] Who had a good cause, but handled it evil.

42:8 [1] When you have reconciled yourselves to him for the faults that you have committed against him, he shall pray for you, and I will hear him.

42:10 [1] He delivered him out of the affliction wherein he was.

42:11 [1] That is, all his kindred, read Job 19:13.

[2] Or, lamb, or money so marked.

42:12 [1] God made him twice so rich in cattle as he was afore, and gave him as many children as he had taken from him.

42:14 [1] That is, of long life, or beautiful as the day.

[2] As pleasant as cassia or sweet spice.

[3] That is, the horn of beauty.

THE
¹PSALMS
OF DAVID

1 *Whether it was Esdras, or any other that gathered the Psalms into a book, it seemeth he did set this Psalm first in manner of a preface, to exhort all godly men to study and meditate the heavenly wisdom.   For the effect hereof is,   1 That they be blessed which give themselves wholly all their life to the holy Scriptures;   4 and that the wicked contemners of God, though they seem for a while happy, yet at length shall come to miserable destruction.*

1 Blessed *is* the man that doth not walk in the ¹counsel of the wicked, nor stand in the way of sinners, nor sit in the seat of the scornful.

2 But his delight *is* in the *ª*law of the Lord, and in his ¹law doth he meditate day and night.

3 For he shall be like a *ᵇ*tree planted by the rivers of waters, that will bring forth her fruits in due season: whose leaf shall not fade: so ¹whatsoever he shall do, shall prosper.

4 ¹The wicked *are* not so, but as the chaff, which the wind driveth away.

5 Therefore the wicked shall not stand in the ¹judgment, nor sinners in the assembly of the righteous.

6 For the Lord ¹knoweth the way of the righteous, and the way of the wicked shall perish.

2 *The Prophet David rejoiceth, that notwithstanding his enemies' rage, yet God will continue his kingdom forever, and advance it even to the end of the world,   10 and therefore exhorteth kings and rulers, that they would humbly submit*

CHAPTER 1
ª Deut. 6:6
Josh. 1:8
Prov. 6:10
ᵇ Jer. 17:8

CHAPTER 2
ª Acts 4:25
ᵇ Prov. 1:26
ᶜ Acts 13:23,33
Heb. 1:5
ᵈ Rev. 2:27

themselves under God's yoke, because it is in vain to resist God. Herein is figured Christ's kingdom.

1 Why do the ¹heathen *ª*rage, and the people murmur in vain.

2 The kings of the earth band themselves, and the Princes are assembled together against the Lord, and against his ¹Christ.

3 ¹Let us break their bands, and cast their cords from us.

4 *ᵇBut* he that dwelleth in the heaven shall laugh: the Lord shall have them in derision.

5 ¹Then shall he speak unto them in his wrath, and vex them in his sore displeasure, *saying,*

6 *Even* I have set my King upon Zion mine holy mountain.

7 I will declare the ¹decree: *that is,* the Lord hath said unto me, ᶜThou art my son; this ²day have I begotten thee.

8 Ask of me, and I shall give thee the heathen for thine inheritance, and the ¹ends of the earth for thy possession.

9 *ᵈ*Thou shalt crush them with a scepter of iron, *and* break them in pieces like a potter's vessel.

10 ¹Be wise now therefore, ye kings: be learned ye judges of the earth.

11 Serve the Lord in fear, and rejoice in trembling.

12 ¹Kiss the Son, lest he be angry, and ye ²perish in the way, when his wrath shall suddenly burn. Blessed *are* all that trust in him.

Title ¹ Or, praises, according to the Hebrews: and were chiefly instituted to praise and give thanks to God for his benefits. They are called the Psalms or Songs of David, because the most part were made by him.

1:1 ¹ When a man hath given once place to evil counsel, or to his own concupiscence, he beginneth to forget himself in his sin, and so falleth into contempt of God, which contempt is called the seat of the scorners.

1:2 ¹ In the holy Scriptures.

1:3 ¹ God's children are so moistened ever with his grace, that whatsoever cometh unto them, tendeth unto their salvation.

1:4 ¹ Though the wicked seem to bear the swinge in this world, yet the Lord driveth them down that they shall not rise nor stand in the company of the righteous.

1:5 ¹ But tremble when they feel God's wrath.

1:6 ¹ Doth approve and prosper, like as not to know, is to reprove and reject.

2:1 ¹ The conspiracy of the Gentiles, the murmuring of the Jews, and power of kings cannot prevail against Christ.

2:2 ¹ Or, anointed.

2:3 ¹ Thus the wicked say, that they will cast off the yoke of God, and of his Christ.

2:5 ¹ God's plagues will declare that in resisting his Christ, they fought against him.

2:7 ¹ To show that my vocation to the kingdom, is of God.

² That is to say, as touching man's knowledge, because it was the first time that David appeared to be elected of God. So is it applied to Christ in his first coming and manifestation to the world.

2:8 ¹ Not only the Jews, but the Gentiles also.

2:10 ¹ He exhorteth all rulers to repent in time.

2:12 ¹ In sign of homage.

² When the wicked shall say, Peace and rest, seeming yet to be but in the mind way of their purposes, then shall destruction suddenly come, 1 Thess. 5:3.

3 David driven forth of his kingdom, was greatly tormented in mind for his sins against God: 4 And therefore calleth upon God, and waxeth bold through his promises, against the great railings and terrors of his enemies, yea against death itself, which he saw present before his eyes. 7 Finally, he rejoiceth for the good success that God gave him and all the Church.

**A Psalm of David,
when he fled from his son Absalom.**

1 Lord, how are mine adversaries [1]increased? how many rise against me?

2 Many say to my soul, *There is* no help for him in God. [1]Selah.

3 But thou Lord art a buckler for me, my glory, and the lifter up of mine head.

4 I did call unto the Lord with my voice, and he heard me out of his holy mountain. Selah.

5 I laid me down and slept, *and* rose up again: for the Lord sustained me.

6 I will not be afraid for [1]ten thousand of the people, that should beset me round about.

7 O Lord, arise: help me, my God: for thou hast smitten all mine enemies upon the cheekbone: thou hast broken the teeth of the wicked.

8 [1]Salvation *belongeth* unto the Lord, *and* thy blessing *is* upon thy people. Selah.

4 When Saul persecuted him, he called upon God, trusting most assuredly in his promise, and therefore boldly reproveth his enemies, who willfully resisted his dominion, 7 and finally preferreth the favor of God before all worldly treasures.

**[1]To him that excelleth on Neginoth.
A Psalm of David.**

1 Hear me when I call, [1]O God of my righteousness: thou hast set me at liberty, *when I was* in [2]distress: have mercy upon me, and hearken unto my prayer.

2 O ye [1]sons of men, how long *will ye turn* my glory into shame, [2]*loving vanity, and* seeking lies? Selah.

3 For be ye sure that the Lord hath chosen to himself [1]a godly man, the Lord will hear when I call

unto him.

4 [1]Tremble and sin not: examine your own heart upon your bed, and be [2]still. Selah.

5 [1]Offer the sacrifices of righteousness, and trust in the Lord.

6 Many say, Who will show us *any* [1]good? *but* Lord, lift up the light of thy countenance upon us.

7 Thou hast given me more joy of heart, than *they have had*, when their wheat and their wine did abound.

8 I will lay me down, and also sleep in peace: for thou, [1]Lord, only makest me dwell in safety.

5 David oppressed with the cruelty of his enemies, and fearing greater dangers, calleth to God for succor, showing how requisite it is that God should punish the malice of his adversaries. 7 After, being assured of prosperous success, he conceiveth comfort, 12 concluding, that when God shall deliver him, others also shall be partakers of the same mercies.

**To him that excelleth upon [1]Nehiloth.
A Psalm of David.**

1 Hear my words, O Lord: understand my [1]meditation.

2 Hearken unto the voice of my cry, my king and my God: for unto thee do I pray.

3 Hear my voice in the morning, O Lord: *for in the* morning will I direct *me* unto thee, and I will [1]wait.

4 For thou art not a God that loveth [1]wickedness, neither shall evil dwell with thee.

5 [1]The foolish shall not stand in thy sight: *for* thou hatest all them that work iniquity.

6 Thou shalt destroy them that speak lies: the Lord will abhor the bloody man and deceitful.

7 But I [1]will come into thine house in the multitude of thy mercy: *and* in thy fear will I worship toward thine holy Temple.

8 Lead me, O Lord, in thy righteousness, [1]because of *mine* enemies: make thy way plain before my face.

9 For no constancy *is* in their mouth: within

3:1 [1] This was a token of his stable faith, that for all his troubles he had his recourse to God.
3:2 [1] Selah here signifieth a lifting up of the voice, to cause us to consider the sentence, as a thing of great importance.
3:6 [1] When he considered the truth of God's promise, and tried the same, his faith increased marvelously.
3:8 [1] Be the dangers never so great or many, yet God hath ever means to deliver his.
4:Title [1] Among them that were appointed to sing the Psalms, and to play on the instruments, one was appointed chief to set the tune, and to begin: who had the charge, because he was most excellent, and he began this Psalm on the instrument calleth Neginoth, or in a tune so called.
4:1 [1] Thou that art the defender of my just cause.
  [2] Both of mind and body.
4:2 [1] Ye that think yourselves noble in this world.
  [2] Though your enterprises please your never so much, yet God will bring them to nought.
4:3 [1] A king that walketh in his vocation.

4:4 [1] For fear of God's judgment.
  [2] Cease your rage.
4:5 [1] Serve God purely, and not with outward ceremonies.
4:6 [1] The multitude seek worldly wealth, but David setteth his felicity in God's favor.
4:8 [1] This word in Hebrew may be referred to God, as it is here translated, or to David, signifying that he should dwell as joyful alone, as if he had many about him, because the Lord is with him.
5:Title [1] Or, a musical instrument or tune.
5:1 [1] That is, my vehement prayer, and secret complaint and sighings.
5:3 [1] With patience and trust till I be heard.
5:4 [1] Seeing that God of nature hateth wickedness, he must needs punish the wicked, and save the godly.
5:5 [1] Which run most ragingly after their carnal affections.
5:7 [1] In the deepest of his tentations he putteth his full confidence in God.
5:8 [1] Because thou art just, therefore lead me out of the dangers of mine enemies.

they are very corruption: their *throat *is* an open sepulcher, *and* they flatter with their tongue.

10 Destroy them, O God, [1]let them [2]fall from their counsels: cast them out for the multitude of their iniquities, because they have rebelled against thee.

11 And [1]let all them that trust in thee, rejoice *and* triumph forever, and cover thou them: and let them that love thy name, rejoice in thee.

12 For thou Lord, wilt [1]bless the righteous, *and* with favor [2]wilt compass him, as with a shield.

6 *When David by his sins had provoked God's wrath, and now felt not only his hand against him, but also conceived the horrors of death everlasting, he desireth forgiveness. 6 Bewailing that if God took him away in his indignation, he should lack occasion to praise him as he was wont to do while he was among men. 9 Then suddenly feeling God's mercy, he sharply rebuketh his enemies which rejoiced in his affliction.*

**To him that excelleth on Neginoth, upon the eight *tune*.
A Psalm of David.**

1 O Lord, *,[1]rebuke me not in thine anger, neither chastise me in thy wrath.

2 Have mercy upon me, O Lord, for I am weak: O Lord heal me, for my [1]bones are vexed.

3 [1]My soul is also sore troubled: but Lord, how long wilt thou delay?

4 Return, O Lord: deliver my soul: save me for thy mercy's sake.

5 For in [1]death *there is* no remembrance of thee: in the grave who shall praise thee?

6 I fainted in my mourning: I cause my bed every night to swim, *and* water my couch with my tears.

7 [1]Mine eye is dimmed for despite, and sunk in because of all mine enemies.

8 [1]Away from me all ye workers of iniquity: for the Lord hath heard the voice of my weeping.

9 The Lord hath heard my petition: the Lord will receive my prayer.

10 All mine enemies shall be confounded and sore vexed: they shall be turned back, *and* put to shame [1]suddenly.

CHAPTER 5
a Rom. 3:13

CHAPTER 6
a Jer. 10:24

CHAPTER 7
a 2 Sam. 16:7

7 *Being falsely accused by Cush one of Saul's kinsmen, he calleth to God to be his defender, 3 to whom he commendeth his innocence, 9 first showing that his conscience did not accuse him of any evil toward Saul. 10 Next that it touched God's glory to award sentence against the wicked. 12 And so entering into the consideration of God's mercies and promise, he waxeth bold, and derideth the vain enterprises of his enemies, 15 threatening that that shall fall on their own neck which they have purposed for others.*

[1]Shiggaion of David, which he sang unto the Lord, concerning the [2]words of *Cush the son of Benjamin.

1 O Lord my God, in thee I put my trust: save me from all that persecute me, and deliver me,

2 Lest [1]he devour my soul like a lion, and tear it in pieces, while there is none to help.

3 O Lord my God, if I have done [1]this thing, if there be *any* wickedness in mine hands,

4 [1]If I have rewarded evil unto him that had peace with me, (yea I have delivered him that vexed me without cause.)

5 *Then* let the enemies persecute my soul, and take it: yea, let him tread my life down upon the earth, and lay mine [1]honor in the dust. Selah.

6 Arise, O Lord, in thy wrath, and lift up thyself against the rage of mine enemies, and awake for me *according* to the [1]judgment *that* thou hast appointed.

7 So shall the congregation of the people compass thee about: for their sakes therefore [1]return on high.

8 The Lord shall judge the people: judge thou me, O Lord, according to my [1]righteousness, and according to mine innocency *that is* in me.

9 Oh let the malice of the wicked come to an end: but guide thou the just: for the righteous God trieth the [1]hearts and reins.

10 My defense *is* in God, who preserveth the upright in heart.

11 God judgeth the righteous, and him that contemneth God, [1]every day.

12 Except [1]he turn, he hath whet his sword: he hath bent his bow, and made it ready.

13 He hath also prepared him deadly weapons: he

5:10 [1] Or, cause them to err.
  [2] Let their devices come to nought.
5:11 [1] Thy favor toward me shall confirm the faith of all others.
5:12 [1] Or, give good success.
  [2] So that he shall be safe from all dangers.
6:1 [1] Though I deserve destruction, yet let thy mercy pity my frailty.
6:2 [1] For my whole strength is abated.
6:3 [1] His conscience is also touched with the fear of God's judgment.
6:5 [1] He lamenteth that occasion should be taken from him to praise God in the congregation.
6:7 [1] Or, mine eye is eaten as it were with worms.
6:8 [1] God sendeth comfort and boldness, in affliction, that we may triumph over our enemies.
6:10 [1] When the wicked think that the godly shall perish, God delivereth them suddenly, and destroyeth their enemies.
7:Title [1] Or, kind of tune.

[2] Or, accusation.
7:2 [1] He desireth God to deliver him from the rage of cruel Saul.
7:3 [1] Wherewith Cush chargeth me.
7:4 [1] If I reverenced not Saul for affinities sake and preserved his life, 1 Sam. 26:8,9.
7:5 [1] Let me not only die, but be dishonored forever.
7:6 [1] In promising me the kingdom.
7:7 [1] Not only for mine, but for thy Church's sake, declare thy power.
7:8 [1] As touching my behavior toward Saul and mine enemies.
7:9 [1] Though they pretend a just cause against me: yet God shall judge their hypocrisy.
7:11 [1] He doth continually call the wicked to repentance by some signs of his judgments.
7:12 [1] Except Saul turn his mind, I die: for he hath both men and weapons to destroy me. Thus considering his great danger, he magnifieth God's grace.

will ordain his arrows for them that persecute *me*.

14 ᵇBehold, he shall travail with wickedness: for he hath conceived mischief, but he shall bring forth a lie.

15 He hath made a pit, and dug it, and is fallen into the pit *that* he made.

16 His mischief shall return upon his own head, and his cruelty shall fall upon his own pate.

17 I will praise the Lord according to his ¹righteousness, and will sing praise to the Name of the Lord most high.

8 1 *The Prophet considering the excellent liberality and Fatherly providence of God toward man, whom he made as it were a god over all his works, doth not only give great thanks, but is astonished with the admiration of the same, as one nothing able to compass such great mercies.*

To him that excelleth on ¹Gittith.
A Psalm of David.

1 O Lord our Lord, how ¹excellent is thy Name in all the world! which hast set thy glory above the heavens.

2 Out of the mouth ¹of babes and sucklings hast thou ²ordained strength, because of thine enemies, that thou mightest ³still the enemy and the avenger.

3 When I behold thine heavens, *even* the works of thy fingers, the moon and the stars, which thou hast ordained,

4 What is ¹man, *say I*, that thou art mindful of him? and the son of man that thou visitest him?

5 For thou hast made him a little lower than ¹God, and crowned him with glory and worship.

6 Thou hast made him to have dominion in the works of thine hands, thou hast put all things under his feet:

7 All ¹sheep and oxen: yea, and the beasts of the field:

8 The fowls of the air, and the fish of the sea, *and* that which passeth through the paths of the seas.

9 O Lord our Lord, how excellent is thy Name in all the world!

9 1 *After he had given thanks to God for the sundry victories that he had sent him against his enemies, and also proved*

ᵇ Isa. 59:4
Job 15:35

by manifold experience, how ready God was at hand in all his troubles. 14 He being now likewise in danger of new enemies, desireth God to help him according to his wont, 17 and to destroy the malicious arrogance of his adversaries.

To him that excelleth upon ¹Muth Labben.
A Psalm of David.

1 I will praise the Lord with my ¹whole heart: I will speak of all thy marvelous works.

2 I will be glad, and rejoice in thee: I will sing praise to thy Name, O most High.

3 For that mine enemies are turned back: they shall fall and perish at thy presence.

4 For ¹thou hast maintained my right and my cause: thou art set in the throne, *and* judgest right.

5 Thou hast rebuked the heathen: thou hast destroyed the wicked: thou hast put out their name forever and ever.

6 ¹O enemy, destructions are come to a perpetual end, and thou hast destroyed the cities: their memorial is perished with them.

7 But the Lord ¹shall sit forever: he hath prepared his throne for judgment.

8 For he shall judge the world in righteousness, *and* shall judge the people with equity.

9 The Lord also will be a refuge for the ¹poor, a refuge in *due* time, *even* in affliction.

10 And they that know thy Name, will trust in thee: for thou, Lord, hast not failed them that seek thee.

11 Sing praises to the Lord, which dwelleth in Zion: show the people his works.

12 For ¹when he maketh inquisition for blood, he remembereth it, *and* forgetteth not the complaint of the poor.

13 Have mercy upon me, O Lord: consider my trouble *which I suffer* of them that hate me, thou that liftest me up from the gates of death,

14 That I may show all thy praises within the ¹gates of the daughter of Zion, *and* rejoice in thy salvation.

15 The heathen are ¹sunken down in the pit *that* they made: in the net that they hid, is their foot taken.

16 ¹The Lord is known by executing judgment: the wicked is snared in the work of his own hands,

7:17 ¹ In keeping faithfully his promise with me.
8:Title ¹ Or, kind of instrument, or tune.
8:1 ¹ Or, noble, or marvelous.
8:2 ¹ Though the wicked would hide God's praises, yet the very babes are sufficient witnesses of the same.
² Or, established.
³ Or, confound.
8:4 ¹ It had been sufficient, for him to have set forth his glory by the heavens, though he had not come so low as to man, which is but dust.
8:5 ¹ Touching his first creation.
8:7 ¹ By the temporal gifts of man's creation, he is led to consider the benefits which he hath by his regeneration through Christ.
9:Title ¹ Or, kind of instrument, or tune, or for the death of Labben or Goliath.

9:1 ¹ God is not praised, except the whole glory be given to him alone.
9:4 ¹ Howsoever the enemy seems for a time to prevail, yet God preserveth the just.
9:6 ¹ A derision of the enemy, that mindeth nothing but destruction: but the Lord will deliver his, and bring him into judgment.
9:7 ¹ Or, reign as Judge.
9:9 ¹ Our miseries are means to cause us to feel God's present care over us.
9:12 ¹ Though God revengeth not suddenly the wrong done to his, yet he suffereth not the wicked unpunished.
9:14 ¹ In the open assembly of the Church.
9:15 ¹ For God overthroweth the wicked in their enterprises.
9:16 ¹ The mercy of God toward his Saints must be declared, and the fall of the wicked must always be considered.

²Higgaion. Selah.

17 The wicked shall turn into hell, *and* all nations that forget God.

18 For the poor shall not be always forgotten: the hope ¹of the afflicted shall not perish forever.

19 Up Lord: let not man prevail: let the heathen be judged in thy sight.

20 Put them in fear, O Lord, that the heathen may know that they are but ¹men. Selah.

10 *1 He complaineth of the fraud, rapine, tyranny, and all kinds of wrong, which worldly men use, assigning the cause thereof, that wicked men, being as it were drunken with worldly prosperity, and therefore setting apart all fear and reverence towards God, think they may do all things without controlling. 15 Therefore he calleth upon God to send some remedy against these desperate evils, 16 and at length comforteth himself with hope of deliverance.*

1 Why standest thou far off, O Lord, *and* hidest thee in ¹*due* time, *even* in affliction?

2 The wicked with pride doth persecute the poor; let them be taken in the crafts that they have imagined.

3 For the wicked hath ¹made boast of his own heart's desire, and the covetous blesseth *himself*, he contemneth the Lord.

4 The wicked is so proud, that he seeketh not *for God*: he thinketh always, There is no God.

5 His ways always prosper: thy judgments are high above his sight; therefore ¹defieth he all his enemies.

6 He saith in his heart, I shall ¹never be moved, ²nor be in danger.

7 His mouth is full of cursing, and deceit, and fraud; under his tongue is mischief and iniquity.

8 ¹He lieth in wait in the villages; in the secret places doth he murder the innocent; his eyes are bent against the poor.

9 He lieth in wait secretly, *even* as a lion in his den; he lieth in wait to spoil the poor; he doth spoil the poor, when he draweth him into his net.

10 He croucheth *and* boweth; therefore heaps of the ¹poor do fall by his might.

11 He hath said in his heart, God hath forgotten, he hideth away his face, *and* will never see.

12 ¹Arise, O Lord God, lift up thine hand; forget not the poor.

13 Wherefore doth the wicked contemn God? he saith in his heart, Thou wilt not ¹regard.

14 *Yet* thou hast seen it; for thou beholdest mischief and wrong; that thou mayest ¹take it into thine hands; the poor committeth himself unto thee; *for* thou art the helper of the fatherless.

15 Break thou the arm of the wicked and malicious; search his wickedness, *and* thou shalt find ¹none.

16 The Lord *is* King forever and ever; the ¹heathen are destroyed forth of his land.

17 Lord, thou hast heard the desire of the poor; thou preparest their heart; thou bendest thine ear *to them*,

18 ¹To judge the fatherless and poor, that earthly man ²cause to fear no more.

11 *1 This Psalm containeth two parts. In the first David showeth how hard assaults of temptations he sustained, and in how great anguish of mind he was, when Saul did persecute him. 4 Then next he rejoiceth that God sent him succor in his necessity, declaring his justice as well in governing the good, and the wicked men, as the whole world.*

To him that excelleth. A *Psalm* of David.

1 In the Lord put I my trust; how say ye then to my soul, ¹Flee to your mountain *as* a bird?

2 For lo, the wicked bend their bow, *and* make ready their arrows upon the string, that they may secretly shoot at them which are upright in heart.

3 For the ¹foundations are cast down, what hath the ²righteous done?

4 The Lord *is* in his holy palace; the Lord's throne *is* in the heaven; his eyes ¹will consider; his eyelids will try the children of men.

5 The Lord will try the righteous; but the wicked,

---

² Or, this is worthy to be noted.

9:18 ¹ God promiseth not to help us before we have felt the cross.

9:20 ¹ Which they cannot learn without the fear of thy judgment.

10:1 ¹ So soon as we enter into affliction, we think God should help us, but that is not always his due time.

10:3 ¹ The wicked man rejoiceth in his own lust, he boasteth when he hath that he would: he braggeth of his wit and wealth, and blesseth himself, and thus blasphemeth the Lord.

10:5 ¹ Or, snuffeth at.

10:6 ¹ Or, not be moved, because he was never in evil.

² The evil shall not touch me, Isa. 28:15, or else he speaketh thus because he never felt evil.

10:8 ¹ He showeth that the wicked have many means to hide their cruelty, and therefore ought to be feared.

10:10 ¹ By the hypocrisy of them that have authority, the poor are

devoured.

10:12 ¹ He calleth to God for help, because wickedness is so far overgrown, that God must now help or never.

10:13 ¹ Therefore thou must needs punish this their blasphemy.

10:14 ¹ To judge between the right and the wrong.

10:15 ¹ For thou hast utterly destroyed him.

10:16 ¹ The hypocrites or such as live not after God's Law, shall be destroyed.

10:18 ¹ God helpeth when man's help ceaseth.

² Or, destroy no more man upon the earth.

11:1 ¹ This is the wicked counsel of his enemies to him and his companions to drive him from the hope of God's promise.

11:3 ¹ All hope of succor is taken away.

² Yet am I innocent and my cause good.

11:4 ¹ Though all things in earth be out of order, yet God will execute judgment from heaven.

and him that loveth iniquity, doth his soul hate.

6 Upon the wicked he shall rain snares, [1]fire, and brimstone, and stormy tempest; *this is* the [2]portion of their cup.

7 For the righteous Lord loveth righteousness: his countenance doth behold the just.

12 *1 The Prophet lamenting the miserable estate of the people, and the decay of all good order, desireth God speedily to send succor to his children. 7 Then comforting himself, and others with the assurance of God's help, he commendeth the constant verity that God observeth in keeping his promises.*

To him that excelleth upon the eight *tune*. A Psalm of David.

1 Help Lord, for there is not [1]a godly man left: for the faithful are failed from among the children of men.

2 They speak deceitfully every one with his neighbor, [1]flattering with their lips, *and* speak with a double heart.

3 The Lord cut off all flattering lips, *and* the tongue that speaketh proud things:

4 Which have said, [1]With our tongue will we prevail; our lips are our own; who is Lord over us?

5 [1]Now for the oppression of the needy, *and* for the sighs of the poor, I will up, saith the Lord, *and* will [2]set at liberty him, *whom the wicked hath* [snared].

6 The words of the Lord *are* pure words, *as* the silver, tried in a furnace of earth, fined sevenfold.

7 Thou wilt keep [1]them, O Lord; thou wilt preserve him from this generation forever.

8 The wicked walk on every side; when they are exalted, [1]*it is* a shame for the sons of men.

13 *1 David as it were overcome with sundry and new afflictions, fleeth to God as his only refuge, 3 and so at the length being encouraged through God's promises, he conceiveth most sure confidence against the extreme horrors of death.*

CHAPTER 14
[a] Ps. 53

To him that excelleth. A Psalm of David.

1 How long wilt thou forget me, O Lord, [1]forever? how long wilt thou hide thy face from me?

2 How long shall I take [1]counsel within myself *having* weariness daily in mine heart? how long shall mine enemy be exalted above me?

3 Behold, *and* hear me, O Lord my God: lighten mine eyes, that I sleep not in death.

4 Lest mine enemy say, I have [1]prevailed against him: *and* they that afflict me, rejoice, when I slide.

5 But I trust in thy [1]mercy: mine heart shall rejoice in thy salvation; I will sing to the Lord, because he hath [2]dealt lovingly with me.

14 *1 He describeth the perverse nature of men, which were so grown to licentiousness, that God was brought to utter contempt. 7 For the which thing, although he was greatly grieved, yet being persuaded that God would send some present remedy, he comforteth himself and others.*

To him that excelleth. *A Psalm of David.*

1 The [a]fool hath said in his heart, [1]There *is* no God: they have [2]corrupted, and done an abominable work: *there is* none that doeth good.

2 The Lord looked down from heaven upon the children of men, to see if there were any that would understand, and seek God.

3 [1]All are gone out of the way: they are all corrupt: there is none that doeth good, no not one.

4 Do not all the workers of iniquity know that they eat up my people, *as* they eat bread? they call not upon the Lord.

5 [1]There they shall be taken with fear, because God *is* in the generation of the just.

6 You have made [1]a mock at the counsel of the poor, because the Lord *is* his trust.

7 Oh give salvation unto [1]Israel out of Zion: when the Lord turneth the captivity of his people, *then* Jacob shall rejoice, and Israel shall be glad.

Note that of Psalm 14:5-7, which are put into the common translation, and may seem unto some to be left out in this, are not in the same Psalm in the Hebrew text, but rather are put in more fully to express the manners

---

11:6 [1] As in the destruction of Sodom and Gomorrah.
 [2] Which they shall drink even to the dregs, Ezek. 23:34.
12:1 [1] Which dare defend the truth and show mercy to the oppressed.
12:2 [1] He meaneth the flatterers of the court which hurt him more with their tongues, than with their weapons.
12:4 [1] They think themselves able to persuade whatsoever they take in hand.
12:5 [1] The Lord is moved with the complaints of his, and delivereth in the end from all dangers.
 [2] Because the Lord's word and promise is true and unchangeable, he will perform it and preserve the poor from this wicked generation.
12:7 [1] That is, thine though he were but one man.
12:8 [1] For they suppress the godly and maintain the wicked.
13:1 [1] He declareth that his afflictions lasted a long time, and that

his faith fainted not.
13:2 [1] Changing my purposes as the sick man doth his place.
13:4 [1] Which might turn to God's dishonor: if he did not defend his.
13:5 [1] The mercy of God is the cause of our salvation.
 [2] Both by the benefits past, and by others to come.
14:1 [1] He showeth that the cause of all wickedness is to forget God.
 [2] There is nothing but disorder and wickedness among them.
14:3 [1] David here maketh comparison between the faithful and the reprobate, but S. Paul speaketh the same of all men naturally, Rom. 3:10.
14:5 [1] Where they think themselves most sure.
14:6 [1] You mock them that put their trust in God.
14:7 [1] He prayeth for the whole Church whom he is assured God will deliver: for none but he only can do it.

of the wicked, and are gathered out of Psalms 5, 10, 36, 140; Isa. 59, and are alleged by S. Paul, and placed together in Romans 3.

CHAPTER 16
a Exod. 23:13

15 *1 This Psalm teacheth on what condition God did choose the Jews for his peculiar people; and wherefore* he placed his Temple among them, which was to the intent that they by living uprightly and godly, might witness that they were his special and holy people.

A Psalm of David.

1   Lord, who shall dwell in thy Tabernacle? who shall rest in thine holy Mountain?

2   He that [1]walketh uprightly and worketh righteousness, and speaketh the truth in his heart.

3   He that slandereth not with his tongue, nor doeth evil to his neighbor, nor receiveth a false report against his neighbor.

4   [1]In whose eyes a vile person is contemned, but he *honoreth* them that fear the Lord: he that sweareth to his *own* hindrance and changeth not.

5   He that [1]giveth not his money unto usury, nor taketh reward against the innocent: he that doeth these things, [2]shall never be moved.

16 *1 David prayeth to God for succor not for his works, but for his faith's sake.   4 Protesting that he hateth all* idolatry, taking God only for his comfort and felicity.   8 Who suffereth his to lack nothing.

[1]Michtam of David.

1   Preserve me, O GOD: for in thee do I [1]trust.

2   *O my soul,* thou hast said unto the Lord, Thou art my Lord: my [1]well doing *extendeth* not to thee,

3   *But* to the Saints that are in the earth, and to the excellent: all my delight is in them.

4   The [1]sorrows of them, that offer to another *god,* shall be multiplied: [2]their offerings of blood will I not offer, neither make *a*mention of their names with my lips.

5   The Lord *is* the portion of mine inheritance and of my cup: thou shalt maintain my lot.

6   The [1]lines are fallen unto me in pleasant places:

yea, I have a fair heritage.

7   I will praise the Lord, who hath given me counsel: my [1]reins also teach me in the nights.

8   I have set the Lord always before me: for he is at my right hand: *therefore* I [1]shall not slide.

9   Wherefore [1]mine heart is glad, and my tongue rejoiceth: my flesh also doth rest in hope.

10   For thou [1]wilt not leave my soul in the grave: neither wilt thou suffer thine holy One to see corruption.

11   Thou wilt show me the path of life: in thy [1]presence *is* the fullness of joy: *and* at thy right hand there *are* pleasures forevermore.

17 *1 Here he complaineth to God of the cruel pride and arrogance of Saul, and the rest of his enemies, who* thus raged without any cause given on his part.   6 Therefore he desireth God to revenge his innocence and deliver him.

The prayer of David.

1   Hear [1]the right, O Lord, consider my cry: hearken unto my prayer of lips unfeigned.

2   Let my [1]sentence come forth from thy presence, *and* let thine eyes behold equity.

3   Thou hast [1]proved and visited mine heart in the night: thou hast tried me, *and* foundest nothing: *for* I was purposed that my [2]mouth should not offend.

4   Concerning the works of men, by the [1]words of thy lips I kept me from the paths of the cruel man.

5   Stay my steps in thy paths, that my feet do not slide.

6   I have called upon thee: [1]surely thou wilt hear me, O God: incline thine ear to me, *and* hearken unto my words.

7   Show thy marvelous mercies: *thou* that art the Savior of them that trust *in thee,* from such as [1]resist thy right hand.

8   Keep me as the apple of the eye: hide me under the shadow of thy wings,

9   From the wicked that oppress me, *from mine* enemies, which compass me round about for [1]*my* soul.

10   They are enclosed in their own [1]fat, *and* they

15:2 [1] First God requireth uprightness of life, next doing well to others, and thirdly, truth and simplicity in our words.

15:4 [1] He that flattereth not the ungodly in their wickedness.

15:5 [1] To the hindrance of his neighbor.

[2] That is, shall not be cast forth of the Church as hypocrites.

16:Title [1] Or, a certain tune.

16:1 [1] He showeth that we cannot call upon God except we trust in him.

16:2 [1] Though we can not enrich God, yet we must bestow God's gifts to the use of his children.

16:4 [1] As grief of conscience and miserable destruction.

[2] He would neither by outward profession nor in heart, nor in mouth consent to their idolatries.

16:6 [1] Wherewith my portion is measured.

16:7 [1] God teacheth me continually by secret inspiration.

16:8 [1] The faithful are sure to persevere to the end.

16:9 [1] That is, I rejoice both in body and in soul.

16:10 [1] This is chiefly meant of Christ, by whose resurrection all his members have immortality.

16:11 [1] Where God favoreth, there is perfect felicity.

17:1 [1] My righteous cause.

17:2 [1] The vengeance that thou shalt show against mine enemies.

17:3 [1] When thy Spirit examined my conscience.

[2] I was innocent toward mine enemy both in deed and thought.

17:4 [1] Though the wicked provoked me to do evil for evil, yet thy word kept me back.

17:6 [1] He was assured that God would not refuse his request.

17:7 [1] For all rebel against thee, which trouble thy Church.

17:9 [1] For their cruelty cannot be satisfied but with my death.

17:10 [1] They are puffed up with pride, as the stomach that is choked with fat.

have spoken proudly with their mouth.

11 They have compassed us now in our steps: they have set their eyes to bring down to the ground:

12 Like as a lion that is greedy of prey, and as it were a Lion's whelp lurking in secret places.

13 Up Lord, [1]disappoint him: cast him down: deliver my soul from the wicked [2]with thy sword,

14 From men by thine [1]hand, O Lord, from men [2]of the world, who have their [3]portion in this life, whose bellies thou fillest with thine hid treasure: their children have enough, and leave the rest of their substance for their children.

15 *But* I will behold thy face [1]in righteousness, *and* when I [2]wake, I shall be satisfied with thine image.

18

1 This Psalm is the first beginning of his gratulation, and thanksgiving in the entering into his kingdom, wherein he extolleth and praiseth most highly the marvelous mercies and grace of God, who hath thus preserved and defended him. 32 Also he setteth forth the image of Christ's kingdom, that the faithful may be assured that Christ shall always conquer and overcome by the unspeakable power of his Father, though all the whole world should strive there against.

To him that excelleth. A Psalm of David the servant of the Lord, which spake unto the Lord the words of this song (in the day that the Lord delivered him from the hand of all his enemies, and from the hand of Saul) and said,

1 I will love thee dearly, O Lord my strength.

2 [a,1]The Lord *is* my rock, and my fortress, and he that delivereth me, my God *and* my strength: in him will I trust, my shield, the horn also of my salvation, *and* my refuge.

3 I will call upon the Lord, which is worthy to be [1]praised: so shall I be safe from mine enemies.

4 [1]The sorrows of death compassed me, and the floods of wickedness made me afraid.

5 The [1]sorrows of the grave have compassed me about: the snares of death overtook me.

6 *But* in my trouble did I call upon the Lord,

CHAPTER 18
[a] 2 Sam. 22:2

and cried unto my God: he heard my voice out of his Temple, and my cry did come before him, *even* into his ears.

7 [1]Then the earth trembled and quaked: the foundations also of the mountains moved and shook, because he was angry.

8 Smoke went out at his nostrils, and a [1]consuming fire out of his mouth: coals were kindled thereat.

9 He bowed the heavens also and came down, and [1]darkness *was* under his feet.

10 And he rode upon [1]Cherub, and did fly, and he came flying upon the wings of the wind.

11 He made darkness his [1]secret place, *and* his pavilion round about him, *even* darkness of waters, *and* clouds of the air.

12 At the brightness of his presence his clouds passed, hailstones and coals of fire.

13 The Lord also thundered in the heaven, and the Highest gave [1]his voice, hailstones and coals of fire.

14 Then he sent out [1]his arrows and scattered them, and he increased lightnings and destroyed them.

15 And the channels of waters were seen, and the [1]foundations of the world were discovered at thy rebuking, O Lord, at the blasting of the breath of thy nostrils.

16 He hath sent down from above *and* taken me: he hath drawn me out of many [1]waters.

17 He hath delivered me from my [1]strong enemy, and from them which hate me: for they were [2]too strong for me.

18 They prevented me in the day of my calamity: but the Lord was my stay.

19 He brought me forth also into a large place: [1]he delivered me because he favored me.

20 The Lord rewarded me according to my [1]righteousness: according to the pureness of mine hand he recompensed me:

21 Because I kept the ways of the Lord, and did not wickedly against my God.

17:13 [1] Stop his rage.
 [2] Or, which is thy sword.
17:14 [1] By thine heavenly power.
 [2] Or, whose tyranny hath too long endured.
 [3] And feel not the smart that God's children oft times do.
17:15 [1] This is the full felicity, comforting against all assaults, to have the face of God and favorable countenance opened unto us.
 [2] And am delivered out of my great troubles.
18:2 [1] He useth this diversity of names, to show that as the wicked have many means to hurt, so God hath many ways to help.
18:3 [1] For none can obtain their requests of God, that join not his glory with their petition.
18:4 [1] He speaketh of the dangers and malice of his enemies from the which God had delivered him.
18:5 [1] Or, cords, or, cables
18:7 [1] A description of the wrath of God against his enemies, after he had heard his prayers.

18:8 [1] He showeth how horrible God's judgments shall be to the wicked.
18:9 [1] Darkness signifieth the wrath of God as the clear light signifieth God's favor.
18:10 [1] This is described at large, Ps. 104.
18:11 [1] As a king angry with the people, will not show himself unto them.
18:13 [1] Thundered, lightninged and hailed.
18:14 [1] His lightnings.
18:15 [1] That is, the deep bottoms were seen when the red sea was divided.
18:16 [1] Out of sundry and great dangers.
18:17 [1] To wit, Saul.
 [2] Therefore God sent me succor.
18:19 [1] The cause of God's deliverance is his only favor and love to us.
18:20 [1] David was sure of his righteous cause, and good behavior toward Saul and his enemies, and therefore was assured of God's favor and deliverance.

22 For all his laws *were* before me, and I did not cast away his [1]commandments from me.

23 I was upright also with him, and have kept me from my [1]wickedness.

24 Therefore the Lord rewarded me according to my righteousness, *and* according to the pureness of mine hands in his sight.

25 With the [1]godly thou wilt show thyself godly: with the upright man thou wilt show thyself upright.

26 With the pure thou wilt show thyself pure, and with the froward thou wilt show thyself froward.

27 Thus thou wilt save the poor people, and wilt [1]cast down to proud looks.

28 Surely thou wilt light my candle: the Lord my God will lighten my darkness.

29 For by thee I have [1]broken through an host, and by my God I have leaped over a wall.

30 The way of God is uncorrupt: the [1]word of the Lord is tried *in the fire*: he is a shield to all that trust in him.

31 For who is God besides the Lord? and who is mighty save our God?

32 God girdeth me with strength, and maketh my [1]way upright.

33 He maketh my feet like hind's *feet*, and setteth me upon mine [1]high places.

34 He teacheth mine hands to fight: so that a bow of [1]brass is broken with mine arms.

35 Thou hast also given me the [1]shield of thy salvation, and thy right hand hath stayed me, and thy [2]lovingkindness hath caused me to increase.

36 Thou hast enlarged my steps under me, and my heels have not slid.

37 [1]I have pursued mine enemies, and taken them, and have not turned again till I had consumed them.

38 I have wounded them, that they were not able to rise, they are fallen under my feet.

39 For thou hast girded me with strength to battle: them that rose against me, thou hast subdued under me.

40 And thou hast [1]given me the necks of mine enemies, that I might destroy them that hate me.

41 They [1]cried, but there was none to save *them*, *even* unto the Lord, but he answered them not.

42 Then I did beat them small as the dust before the wind: I did tread them flat as the clay in the streets.

43 Thou hast delivered me from the contentions of the people: thou hast made me the head of the [1]heathen, a people, *whom* I have not [2]known, shall serve me.

44 As soon as they hear they shall obey me: the strangers shall [1]be in subjection to me.

45 Strangers shall [1]shrink away, and fear in their pure chambers.

46 Let the Lord live, and blessed be my strength, and the God of my salvation be exalted.

47 *It is* God that giveth me *power* to avenge me, and subdued the people under me.

48 O my deliverer from mine enemies, even thou hast set me up from those that rose against me; thou hast delivered me from the [1]cruel man.

49 Therefore [1]I will praise thee, O Lord, among the nations, and will sing unto thy Name.

50 Great deliverances giveth he unto his king, and showeth mercy to his anointed, *even* to David, and to his [1]seed forever.

19 1 *To the intent he might move the faithful to deeper consideration of God's glory, he setteth before their eyes the most exquisite workmanship of the heavens, with their proportion, and ornaments.* 8 *And afterward calleth them to the Law, wherein God hath revealed himself more familiarly to his chosen people. The which peculiar grace by commending the Law, he setteth forth more at large.*

18:22 [1] For all his dangers he exercised himself in the Law of God.
18:23 [1] I neither gave place to their wicked tentations, nor to mine own affections.
18:25 [1] Here he speaketh of God according to our capacity, who showeth mercy to his and punisheth the wicked, as is said also, Lev. 26:21, 24.
18:27 [1] When their sin is come to the full measure.
18:29 [1] He attributeth it to God that he both got the victory in the field, and also destroyed the cities of his enemies.
18:30 [1] Be the dangers never so many or great, yet God's promise must take effect.
18:32 [1] He giveth good success to all mine enterprises.
18:33 [1] As towers and forts, which he took out of the hands of God's enemies.
18:34 [1] Or, steel.
18:35 [1] To defend me from dangers.
   [2] He attributed the beginning, continuance and increase in well doing only to God's favor.

18:37 [1] David declareth that he did nothing besides his vocation, but was stirred up by God's Spirit to execute his judgments.
18:40 [1] Thou hast given them into mine hands to be slain.
18:41 [1] They that reject the cry of the afflicted, God will also reject them, when they cry for help: for either pain or fear cause those hypocrites to cry.
18:43 [1] Which dwell round about me.
   [2] The kingdom of Christ is in David's kingdom prefigured, who by the preaching of his word bringeth all to his subjection.
18:44 [1] Or, lie: signifying a subjection constrained and not voluntary.
18:45 [1] Fear shall cause them to be afraid and come forth of their secret holes and holds to seek pardon.
18:48 [1] That is, Saul, who of malice persecuted him.
18:49 [1] This prophecy appertaineth to the kingdom of Christ and vocation of the Gentiles, as Rom. 15:9.
18:50 [1] This did not properly appertain to Solomon, but to Jesus Christ.

To him that excelleth. A Psalm of David.

1 The ^{a,1}heavens declare the glory of God, and the firmament showeth the work of his hands.

2 ¹Day unto day uttereth the same, and night unto night teacheth knowledge.

3 There is no speech nor ¹language, where their voice is not heard.

4 Their ¹line is gone forth through all the earth, and their words into the ends of the world: in them hath he set a tabernacle for the Sun.

5 Which cometh forth as a bridegroom out of his ¹chamber, and rejoiceth like a mighty man to run his race.

6 His going out is from the end of the heaven, and his compass is unto the ends of the same, and none is hid from the heat thereof.

7 The ¹Law of the Lord is perfect, converting the soul: the testimony of the Lord is sure, and giveth wisdom unto the simple.

8 The statutes of the Lord are right, and rejoice the heart, the commandment of the Lord is pure, and giveth light unto the eyes.

9 The fear of the Lord is clean, and endureth forever: the judgments of the Lord are ¹truth: they are righteous ²altogether,

10 And more to be ¹desired than gold, yea, than much fine gold: sweeter also than honey, and the honeycomb.

11 Moreover by them is thy servant made circumspect, and in keeping of them there is great ¹reward.

12 Who can understand his ¹faults? cleanse me from secret faults.

13 Keep thy servant also from ¹presumptuous sins: let them not reign over me: ²so shall I be upright, and made clean from much wickedness.

14 Let the words of my mouth, and the ¹meditation of mine heart be acceptable in thy sight, O Lord my strength, and my redeemer.

CHAPTER 19
^a Rom. 1:20

20 *A prayer of the people unto God, that it would please him to hear their king and receive his sacrifice, which he offered before he went to battle against the Ammonites.*

To him that excelleth. A Psalm of David.

1 The ¹Lord hear thee in the day of trouble: the ²Name of the God of Jacob defend thee:

2 Send thee help from the Sanctuary, and strengthen thee out of Zion.

3 Let him remember all thine offerings, and ¹turn thy burnt offerings into ashes. Selah.

4 And grant thee according to thine heart, and fulfill all thy purpose:

5 That we may rejoice in thy ¹salvation, and set up the banner in the Name of our God, when the Lord shall perform all thy petitions.

6 Now ¹know I that the Lord will help his anointed, and will hear him from his ²Sanctuary, by the mighty help of his right hand.

7 Some trust in chariots, and some in horses: but we will remember the Name of the Lord our God.

8 ¹They are brought down and fallen, but we are risen, and stand upright.

9 Save Lord: ¹Let the King hear us in the day that we call.

21 *1 David in the person of the people praiseth God for the victory, attributing it to God, and not to the strength of man.   Wherein the holy Ghost directeth the faithful to Christ, who is the perfection of this kingdom.*

To him that excelleth. A Psalm of David.

1 The King shall ¹rejoice in thy strength, O Lord: yea how greatly shall he rejoice in thy salvation?

2 Thou hast given him his heart's desire, and hast not denied him the request of his lips. Selah.

3 For thou ¹didst prevent him with liberal blessings, and didst set a crown of pure gold upon his head.

4 ¹He asked life of thee, and thou gavest him a

19:1 ¹ He reproacheth unto man his ingratitude, seeing the heavens, which are dumb creatures, set forth God's glory.

19:2 ¹ The continual success of the day and the night is sufficient to declare God's power and goodness.

19:3 ¹ The heavens are a Schoolmaster to all nations, be they never so barbarous.

19:4 ¹ The heavens are as a line of great capital letters to show unto us God's glory.

19:5 ¹ Or, veil. The manner was that the bride and bridegroom should stand under a veil together, and after come forth with great solemnity, and rejoicing of the assembly.

19:7 ¹ Though the creatures cannot serve, yet this ought to be sufficient to lead us unto him.

19:9 ¹ So that all man's inventions and intentions are lies.

² Everyone without exception.

19:10 ¹ Except God's word be esteemed above all worldly things, it is contemned.

19:11 ¹ For God accepteth our endeavor, though it be far imperfect.

19:12 ¹ Then there is no reward of duty, but of grace: for where sin is,

there death is the reward.

19:13 ¹ Which are done purposely and of malice.

² If thou suppress my wicked affections by thine holy spirit.

19:14 ¹ That I may obey thee in thought, word and deed.

20:1 ¹ Hereby kings are also admonished to call to God in their affairs.

² The virtue, power and grace of God.

20:3 ¹ In token that they are acceptable unto him.

20:5 ¹ Granted to the King in whose wealth our felicity standeth.

20:6 ¹ The Church feeleth that God has heard their petition.

² As by the visible Sanctuary God's familiarity appeared toward his people, so by the heavenly is meant his power and majesty.

20:8 ¹ The worldlings that put not their only trust in God.

20:9 ¹ Let the king be able to deliver us by thy strength, when we seek unto him for succor.

21:1 ¹ When he shall overcome his enemies, and so be assured of his vocation.

21:3 ¹ Thou declarest thy liberal favor toward him before he prayed.

21:4 ¹ David did not only obtain life, but also assurance that his posterity should reign forever.

long life forever and ever.

5 His glory *is* great in thy salvation: dignity and honor hast thou laid upon him.

6 For thou hast set him *as* [1]blessings forever: thou hast made him glad with the joy of thy countenance.

7 Because the king trusteth in the Lord, and in the mercy of the most high, he shall not slide.

8 [1]Thine hand shall find out all thine enemies, *and* thy right hand shall find out them that hate thee.

9 Thou shalt make them like a fiery oven in time of thine anger: the Lord shall destroy them in his [1]wrath, and the fire shall devour them.

10 Their fruit shalt thou destroy from the earth, and their seed from the children of men.

11 For they [1]intended evil against thee, *and* imagined mischief, *but* they shall not prevail.

12 Therefore shalt thou put them [1]apart, *and* the strings of thy bow shalt thou make ready against their faces.

13 [1]Be thou exalted, O Lord, in thy strength: *so* will we sing and praise thy power.

22

1 David complained because he was brought into such extremities that he was past all hope, but after he had rehearsed the sorrows and griefs, wherewith he was vexed. 10 He recovereth himself from the bottomless pit of tentations, and groweth in hope. And here under his own person he setteth forth the figure of Christ, whom he did foresee by the spirit of prophecy, that he should marvelously, and strangely be rejected, and abased, before his Father should raise and exalt him again.

**To him that excelleth upon [1]Aijeleth Hashahar.
A Psalm of David.**

1 My [1]God, my God, why hast thou forsaken me, *and* art so far from mine health, *and from* the words of my [2]roaring?

2 O my God, I cry by day, but thou hearest not: and by night, but [1]have no audience.

CHAPTER 22
a Matt. 27:43

3 But thou art holy, and dost inhabit the [1]praises of Israel.

4 Our fathers trusted in thee: they trusted, and thou didst deliver them.

5 They called upon thee, and were delivered: they trusted in thee, and were not confounded.

6 But I am a [1]worm, and not a man: a shame of men, and the contempt of the people.

7 All they that see me, have me in derision: they make a mow *and* nod the head, *saying,*

8 [1,a]He trusted in the Lord, let him deliver him: let him save him, seeing he loveth him.

9 But thou didst draw me out of the [1]womb: thou gavest me hope, *even* at my mother's breasts.

10 I was cast upon thee, *even* from the [1]womb: thou art my God from my mother's belly.

11 Be not far from me, because trouble is near: for *there is* none to help *me.*

12 Many young bulls have compassed me: mighty [1]bulls of Bashan have closed me about.

13 They gape upon me with their mouths, *as* a ramping and roaring lion.

14 I am like [1]water poured out, and all my bones are out of joint: mine heart is like wax: it is molten in the midst of my bowels.

15 My strength is dried up like a potsherd, and my tongue cleaveth to my jaws, and thou [1]hast brought me into the dust of death.

16 For dogs have compassed me, *and* the assembly of the wicked have enclosed me: they [1]pierced mine hands and my feet.

17 I may tell all my bones, *yet* they behold, *and* look upon me.

18 They part my garments among them, and cast lots upon my vesture.

19 But be not thou far off, O Lord, my strength: hasten to help me.

20 Deliver my soul from the sword: my [1]desolate

21:6 [1] Thou hast made him thy blessings to others, and a perpetual example of thy favor forever.

21:8 [1] Here he describeth the power of Christ's kingdom against the enemies thereof.

21:9 [1] This teacheth us patiently to endure the cross till God destroy the adversary.

21:11 [1] They laid as it were their nets to make God's power to give place to their wicked enterprises.

21:12 [1] As a mark to shoot at.

21:13 [1] Maintain thy Church against thine adversaries, that we may have ample occasion to praise thy Name.

22:Title [1] Or, the hind of the morning: and this was the name of some common song.

22:1 [1] Here appeareth that horrible conflict, which he sustained between faith and desperation.

[2] Being tormented with extreme anguish.

22:2 [1] Or, I cease not.

22:3 [1] He meaneth the place of praising, even the Tabernacle: or else it is so called, because he gave the people continually occasion to

praise him.

22:6 [1] And seeming most miserable of all creatures, which was meant of Christ. And herein appeareth the unspeakable love of God toward man, that he would thus abase his Son for our sakes.

22:8 [1] Hebrew, *rolled upon God.*

22:9 [1] Even from my birth thou hast given me occasion to trust in thee.

22:10 [1] For except God's providence preserve the infants, they should perish a thousand times in the mother's womb.

22:12 [1] He meaneth, that his enemies were so fat, proud, and cruel, that they were rather beasts than men.

22:14 [1] Before he spake of the cruelty of his enemies, and now he declareth the inward griefs of the mind, so that Christ was tormented both in soul and body.

22:15 [1] Thou had suffered me to be without all hope of life.

22:16 [1] Thus David complaineth as though he were nailed by his enemies both hands and feet: but this was accomplished in Christ.

22:20 [1] My life that is solitary, left alone and forsaken of all, Ps. 35:17 and 25:16.

soul from the power of the dog.

21 ¹Save me from the lion's mouth, and answer me *in saving me* from the horns of the unicorns.

22 ᵇI will declare thy Name unto my brethren: in the midst of the Congregation will I praise thee, *saying,*

23 ¹Praise the Lord, ye that fear him: magnify ye him, all the seed of Jacob, and fear ye him all the seed of Israel.

24 For he hath not despised nor abhorred the affliction of the ¹poor: neither hath he hid his face from him, but when he called unto him, he heard.

25 My praise *shall be* of thee in the great Congregation: my ¹vows will I perform before them that fear him.

26 ¹The poor shall eat and be satisfied: they that seek after the Lord, shall praise him: your heart shall live forever.

27 All the ends of the world shall remember *themselves* and turn to the Lord, and all the kindreds of the nations shall worship before thee.

28 For the kingdom *is* the Lord's, and he ruleth among the nations.

29 All they that be fat ¹in the earth shall eat and worship: all they that go down into the dust, shall bow before him, ²even he that cannot quicken his own soul.

30 ¹*Their* seed shall serve him: it shall be counted unto the Lord for a generation.

31 They shall come and shall declare his righteousness unto a people that shall be born, because he hath ¹done it.

23 *1 Because the Prophet had proved the great mercies of God at divers times, and in sundry manners, he gathereth a certain assurance, fully persuading himself that God will continue the very same goodness towards him forever.*

A Psalm of David.

1 The Lord *is* my ªshepherd, ¹I shall not want.

Marginal references (center column):
ᵇ Heb. 2:12

CHAPTER 23
ª Isa. 40:11
Jer. 23:5
Ezek. 34:23
John 10:11
1 Pet. 2:25

CHAPTER 24
ª Deut. 10:14
Job 18:14
1 Cor. 10:26

2 He maketh me to rest in green pasture, *and* leadeth me by the still waters.

3 He ¹restoreth my soul, *and* leadeth me in the ²paths of righteousness for his Name's sake.

4 Yea, though I should walk through the valley of the ¹shadow of death, I will fear no evil; for thou art with me: thy rod and thy staff, they comfort me.

5 Thou dost prepare a ¹table before me in the sight of mine adversaries: thou dost ²anoint mine head with oil, *and* my cup runneth over.

6 Doubtless kindness and mercy shall follow me all the days of my life, and I shall remain a long season in the ¹house of the Lord.

24 *1 Albeit the Lord God hath made, and governeth all the world, yet toward his chosen people, his gracious goodness doth most abundantly appear, in that among them he will have his dwelling place.   Which thought it was appointed among the children of Abraham, yet only they do enter aright into this Sanctuary, which are the true worshippers of God, purged from the sinful filth of this world.   7 Finally he magnifieth God's grace for the building of the Temple, to the end he might stir up all the faithful to the true service of God.*

A Psalm of David.

1 The earth ª*is* the Lord's, and all that therein is; the world and they that dwell therein.

2 For he hath founded it upon the ¹seas; and established it upon the floods.

3 Who shall ascend into the mountain of the Lord? and who shall stand in his holy place?

4 *Even he that hath* innocent hands, and a pure heart; which hath not lifted up his mind unto vanity, nor sworn deceitfully.

5 He shall receive a blessing from the Lord, and righteousness from the God of his salvation.

6 This is the ¹generation of them that seek him, of them that seek thy face, *this is* Jacob. Selah.

7 ¹Lift up your heads ye gates, and be ye lifted up ye

22:21 ¹ Christ is delivered with a more mighty deliverance by overcoming death, than if he had not tasted death at all.
22:23 ¹ He promiseth to exhort the Church that they by his example might praise the Lord.
22:24 ¹ The poor afflicted are comforted by this example of David, or Christ.
22:25 ¹ Which were sacrifices of thanksgiving, which they offered by God's commandment, when they were delivered out of any great danger.
22:26 ¹ He doth allude still to the sacrifice.
22:29 ¹ Though the poor be first named, as verse 26, yet the wealthy are not separated from the grace of Christ's kingdom.
² In whom there is no hope that he shall recover life: so neither poor nor rich, quick nor dead shall be rejected from his kingdom.
22:30 ¹ Meaning, the prosperity, which the Lord keepeth as a seed to the Church to continue his praise among men.
22:31 ¹ That is, God hath fulfilled his promise.
23:1 ¹ He hath care over me and ministereth unto me all things.
23:3 ¹ He comforteth or refresheth me.

² Plain, or straight ways.
23:4 ¹ Though he were in danger of death, as the sheep that wandereth in the dark valley without his shepherd.
23:5 ¹ Albeit his enemies sought to destroy him, yet God delivereth him, and dealeth most liberally with him in despite of them.
² As was the manner of great feasts.
23:6 ¹ He setteth not his felicity in the pleasures of this world, but in the fear and service of God.
24:2 ¹ He noteth two things: the one, that the earth to man's judgment seemeth above the waters: and next, that God miraculously preserveth the earth, that it is not drowned with the waters, which naturally are above it.
24:6 ¹ Though circumcision separate the carnal seed of Jacob, from the Gentiles, yet he that seeketh God, is the true Jacob and the very Israelite.
24:7 ¹ David desireth the building up of the Temple, wherein the glory of God should appear, and under the figure of this Temple, he also prayeth for the spiritual Temple, which is eternal, because of the promise which was made to the Temple, as it is written, Ps. 132:14.

everlasting doors, and the King of glory shall come in.

8 Who is this King of glory? the Lord, strong and mighty, *even* the Lord mighty in battle.

9 Lift up your heads, ye gates, and lift up *yourselves* ye everlasting doors, and the King of glory shall come in.

10 Who is this King of glory? the Lord of hosts, he is the King of glory. Selah.

CHAPTER 25
a Isa. 28:26
Rom. 10:11

25 *1 The Prophet touched with the consideration of his sins, and also grieved with the cruel malice of his enemies,   6 Prayeth to God most fervently to have his sins forgiven.   7 Especially such as he had committed in his youth.   He beginneth every verse according to the Hebrew letters, two or three except.*

A Psalm of David.

1 Unto thee, [1]O Lord, lift I up my soul.

2 My God, I [1]trust in thee; let me not be confounded: let not mine enemies rejoice over me.

3 *a*So all that hope in thee, shall not be ashamed; *but* let them be confounded, that transgress without cause.

4 [1]Show me thy ways, O Lord, *and* teach me thy paths.

5 Lead me forth in thy truth, and teach me: for thou art the God of my salvation: in thee do I trust [1]all the day.

6 Remember, O Lord, thy tender mercies, and thy lovingkindness: for they have been forever.

7 Remember not the [1]sins of my youth, nor my rebellions, *but* according to thy kindness remember thou me, *even* for thy goodness sake, O Lord.

8 Gracious and righteous *is* the Lord: therefore will he [1]teach sinners in the way.

9 Them that be meek, will he [1]guide in judgment, and teach the humble his way.

10 All the paths of the Lord *are* mercy and truth unto such as keep his covenant and his testimonies:

11 For thy [1]Name's sake, O Lord, be merciful unto mine iniquity, for it is great.

12 What [1]man is he that feareth the Lord? him will he teach the way *that* he shall [2]choose.

13 His soul shall dwell at [1]ease, and his seed shall inherit the land.

14 The [1]secret of the Lord *is revealed* to them that fear him: and his Covenant to give them understanding.

15 Mine eyes *are* ever toward the Lord: for he will bring my feet out of the net.

16 Turn thy face unto me, and have mercy upon me: for I am desolate and poor.

17 The sorrows of mine heart [1]are enlarged: draw me out of my troubles.

18 Look upon mine affliction and my travail, and forgive all my sins.

19 Behold mine [1]enemies, for they are many, and they hate me with cruel hatred.

20 Keep my soul and deliver me: let me not be confounded: for I trust in thee.

21 Let [1]*mine* uprightness and equity preserve me; for mine hope is in thee.

22 Deliver Israel, O God, out of all his troubles.

26 *1 David oppressed with many injuries, finding no help in the world, calleth for aid from God: and assured of his integrity towards Saul, desireth God to be his judge, and to defend his innocence.   6 Finally he maketh mention of his sacrifice, which he will offer for his deliverance, and desireth to be in the company of the faithful in the Congregation of God, whence he was banished by Saul, promising integrity of life, and open praises and thanksgiving.*

A Psalm of David.

1 Judge me, [1]O Lord, for I have walked in mine innocency: my trust hath been also in the Lord: *therefore* shall I not slide.

2 Prove me, O Lord, and try me: examine my [1]reins, and mine heart.

3 For thy [1]lovingkindness *is* before mine eyes: therefore have I walked in thy truth.

4 I have not [1]haunted with vain persons, neither kept company with the dissemblers.

5 I have hated the assembly of the evil, and have not companied with the wicked.

6 I will [1]wash mine hands in innocency, O Lord,

25:1 [1] I put not my trust in any worldly thing.

25:2 [1] That thou wilt take away mine enemies, which are thy rods.

25:4 [1] Retain me in the faith of thy promise, that I swerve not on any side.

25:5 [1] Constantly, and against all tentations.

25:7 [1] He confesseth that his manifold sins were the cause that his enemies did thus persecute him, desiring that the cause of the evil may be taken away, to the intent that the effect may cease.

25:8 [1] That is, call them to repentance.

25:9 [1] He will govern and comfort them that are truly humbled for their sins.

25:11 [1] And for none other respect.

25:12 [1] Meaning, the number is very small.

  [2] He will direct such with his spirit to follow the right way.

25:13 [1] He shall prosper both in spiritual and corporal things.

25:14 [1] His counsel contained in his word, whereby he declareth

that he is the protector of the faithful.

25:17 [1] My grief is increased because of mine enemies' cruelty.

25:19 [1] The greater that his afflictions were and the more that his enemies increased, the more near felt he God's help.

25:21 [1] Forasmuch as I have behaved myself uprightly toward mine enemies, let them know that thou art the defender of my just cause.

26:1 [1] He fleeth to God to be the Judge of his just cause; seeing there is no equity among men.

26:2 [1] My very affections and inward motions of the heart.

26:3 [1] He showeth what stayed him, that he did not recompense evil for evil.

26:4 [1] He declareth that they cannot walk in simplicity before God, that delight in the company of the ungodly.

26:6 [1] I will serve thee with a pure affection, and with the godly that sacrifice unto thee.

and compass thine altar,

7 That I may declare with the voice of thanksgiving, and set forth all thy wondrous works.

8 O Lord, I have loved the habitation of thine house, and the place where thine honor dwelleth.

9 ¹Gather not my soul with the sinners, nor my life with the bloody men:

10 In whose hand *is* ¹wickedness, and their right hand is full of bribes.

11 But I will walk in mine innocency: redeem me *therefore*, and be merciful unto me.

12 My foot standeth in ¹uprightness: I will praise thee, O Lord, in the Congregations.

27 *1 David maketh this Psalm being delivered from great perils, as appeareth by the praises and thanksgiving annexed: 6 Wherein we may see the constant faith of David against the assaults of all his enemies.   7 And also the end wherefore he desireth to live and to be delivered, only to worship God in his Congregation.*

A Psalm of David.

1 The Lord *is* my ¹light and my salvation, whom shall I fear? the Lord *is* the strength of my life, of whom shall I be afraid?

2 When the wicked, *even* mine enemies and my foes came upon me to eat up my flesh, they stumbled and fell.

3 Though an host pitched against me, mine heart should not be afraid: though war be raised against me, I will trust in ¹this.

4 ¹One thing have I desired of the Lord, that I will require, *even* that I may dwell in the house of the Lord all the days of my life, to behold the beauty of the Lord, and to visit his Temple.

5 For in the time of trouble he shall hide me in his Tabernacle: in the secret *place* of his pavilion shall he hide me, *and* set me up upon a rock.

6 ¹And now shall he lift up mine head above mine enemies round about me: therefore will I offer in his Tabernacle sacrifices of joy: I will sing

and praise the Lord.

7 Hearken unto my voice, O Lord, *when* I cry: have mercy also upon me and hear me.

8 *When thou saidest*, ¹Seek ye my face, mine heart answered unto thee, O Lord, I will seek thy face.

9 Hide not *therefore* thy face from me, nor cast thy servant away in displeasure: thou hast been my succor, leave me not, neither forsake me, O God of my salvation.

10 ¹Though my father and my mother should forsake me, yet the Lord will gather me up.

11 Teach me thy way, O Lord, and lead me in a right path, because of mine enemies.

12 Give me not unto the ¹lust of mine adversaries: for there are false witnesses risen up against me, and such as speak cruelly.

13 *I should have fainted*, except I had believed to see the goodness of the Lord ¹in the land of the living.

14 ¹Hope in the Lord: be strong, and he shall comfort thine heart, and trust in the Lord.

28 *1 Being in great fear and heaviness of heart to see God dishonored by the wicked, he desireth to be rid of them.   4 And crieth for vengeance against them: and at length assureth himself, that God hath heard his prayer,   9 Unto whose tuition he commendeth all the faithful.*

A Psalm of David.

1 Unto thee, O Lord, do I cry: O my strength, be not deaf toward me, lest if thou answer me not, I be like ¹them that go down into the pit.

2 Hear the voice of my petitions, when I cry unto thee, when I hold up my hands toward thine ¹holy Oracle.

3 ¹Draw me not away with the wicked, and with the workers of iniquity: which speak friendly to their neighbors, when malice *is* in their hearts.

4 ¹Reward them according to their deeds, and according to the wickedness of their inventions: recompense them after the work of their hands: render them their reward.

26:9 ¹ Destroy me not in the overthrow of the wicked.

26:10 ¹ Whose cruel hands do execute the malicious devices of their hearts.

26:12 ¹ I am preserved from mine enemies by the power of God, and therefore will praise him openly.

27:1 ¹ Because he was assured of good success in all his dangers, and that his salvation was surely laid up in God, he feared not the tyranny of his enemies.

27:3 ¹ That God will deliver me and give my faith the victory.

27:4 ¹ The loss of country, wife, and all worldly commodities grieve me not in respect of this one thing, that I may not praise thy Name in the midst of the congregation.

27:6 ¹ David assured himself by the Spirit of prophecy that he should overcome his enemies, and serve God in his Tabernacle.

27:8 ¹ He groundeth upon God's promise, and showeth that he is

most willing to obey his commandment.

27:10 ¹ He magnifieth God's love toward his, which far passeth the most tender love of parents towards their children.

27:12 ¹ But either pacify their wrath, or bridle their rage.

27:13 ¹ In this present life before I die, as Isa. 38:11.

27:14 ¹ He exhorteth himself to depend on the Lord, seeing he never failed in his promises.

28:1 ¹ He counteth himself as a dead man, till God show his favor toward him, and grant him his petition.

28:2 ¹ He used this outward means to help the weakness of his faith: for in that place was the Ark, and there God promised to show the tokens of his favor.

28:3 ¹ Destroy not the good with the bad.

28:4 ¹ He thus prayeth in respect to God's glory and not for his own cause, being assured that God would punish the persecutors of his Church.

5 For they reward not the works of the Lord, nor the operation of his hands: *therefore* [1]break them down, and build them not up.

6 [1]Praised *be* the Lord, for he hath heard the voice of my petitions.

7 The Lord *is* my strength and my shield: mine heart trusted in him, and I was helped: therefore mine heart shall rejoice, and with my song will I praise him.

8 The Lord *is* [1]their strength, and he is the strength of the deliverances of his anointed.

9 Save thy people, and bless thine inheritance: feed them also, and exalt them forever.

CHAPTER 30
[a] 1 Sam. 7:2
[b] Deut. 20:5
[c] Ps. 145:8
Isa. 54:8
2 Cor. 4:17

29

1 The Prophet exhorteth the princes and rulers of the world (which for the most part think there is no God.) 3 At the least to fear him for the thunders and tempests, for fear whereof all creatures tremble. 11 And though thereby God threateneth sinners, yet he is always merciful to his, and moveth them thereby to praise his Name.

A Psalm of David.

1 Give unto the Lord, ye [1]sons of the mighty, give unto the Lord glory and strength.

2 Give unto the Lord glory *due* unto his Name: worship the Lord in the glorious Sanctuary.

3 The [1]voice of the Lord *is* upon the waters: the God of glory maketh it to thunder: the Lord *is* upon the great waters.

4 The voice of the Lord *is* mighty: the voice of the Lord *is* glorious.

5 The [1]voice of the Lord breaketh the cedars: yea, the Lord breaketh the cedars of Lebanon.

6 He maketh them also to leap like a calf: Lebanon *also* and [1]Shirion like a young unicorn.

7 The voice of the Lord divideth the [1]flames of fire.

8 The voice of the Lord maketh the wilderness to tremble: the Lord maketh the wilderness of [1]Kadesh

to tremble.

9 The voice of the Lord maketh the hinds to [1]calve, and [2]discovereth the forests: *therefore* in his [3]Temple doth every man speak of *his* glory.

10 The Lord sitteth upon the [1]floods, and the Lord doth remain King forever.

11 The Lord shall give strength unto his people: the Lord shall bless his people with peace.

30

1 When David was delivered, from great danger, he rendered thanks to God, exhorting others to do the like, and to learn by his example, that God is rather merciful than severe and rigorous towards his children. 7 And also that the fall from prosperity to adversity is sudden. 8 This done, he returneth to prayer, promising to praise God forever.

[a]A Psalm or song of the [b]dedication of the [1]house of David.

1 I will magnify thee, O Lord: [1]thou hast exalted me, and hast not made my foes to rejoice over me.

2 O Lord my God, I cried unto thee, and thou hast [1]restored me.

3 O Lord, thou hast brought up my [1]soul out of the grave: thou hast revived me from them that go down into the pit.

4 Sing praises unto the Lord, ye [1]his Saints, and give thanks [2]before the remembrance of his Holiness.

5 'For *he endureth but* a while in his anger: *but* in his favor *is* life: weeping may abide at evening, but joy *cometh* in the morning.

6 And in my [1]prosperity I said, I shall never be moved.

7 *For* thou Lord of thy goodness hadst made my [1]mountain to stand strong: *but* thou didst hide thy face, *and* I [2]was troubled.

8 *Then* cried I unto thee, O Lord, and prayed to my Lord.

9 What profit *is there* in my blood, when I go down to the pit! shall the [1]dust give thanks unto

28:5 [1] Let them be utterly destroyed, as Mal. 1:4.
28:6 [1] Because he felt the assurance of God's help in his heart, his mouth was opened to sing his praises.
28:8 [1] Meaning, his soldiers, who were as means, by whom God declared his power.
29:1 [1] He exhorteth the proud tyrants to humble themselves under God's hand, and not to be inferior to brute beasts and dumb creatures.
29:3 [1] The thunder claps that are heard out of the clouds, ought to make the wicked to tremble for fear of God's anger.
29:5 [1] That is, the thunderbolt breaketh the most strong trees, and shall men think their power to be able to resist God?
29:6 [1] Called also Hermon.
29:7 [1] It causeth the lightnings to shoot and glide.
29:8 [1] In places most desolate, whereas seemeth there is no presence of God.
29:9 [1] For fear maketh them to cast their calves.
[2] Maketh the trees bare, or pierceth the most secret places.
[3] Though the wicked are nothing moved with these lights, yet the

faithful praise God.
29:10 [1] To moderate the rage of the tempest and waters, that they destroy not all.
30:Title [1] After that Absalom had polluted it with most filthy fornication.
30:1 [1] He condemneth them of great ingratitude, which do not praise God for his benefits.
30:2 [1] Restored from the rebellion of Absalom.
30:3 [1] Meaning, that he escaped death most narrowly.
30:4 [1] The word signifieth them that have received mercy, and show mercy liberally unto others.
[2] Before his Tabernacle.
30:6 [1] I put too much confidence in my quiet state, as Jer. 31:18; 2 Chron. 32:24, 25.
30:7 [1] I thought thou hadst established me in Zion most surely.
[2] After that thou hast withdrawn thine help, I felt my misery.
30:9 [1] David meaneth that the dead are not profitable to the Congregation of the Lord here in the earth: therefore he would live to praise his Name, which is the end of man's creation.

thee? or shall it declare thy truth?

10 Hear, O Lord, and have mercy upon me: Lord, be thou mine helper.

11 Thou hast turned my mourning into joy: thou hast loosed my sack, and girded me with gladness.

12 Therefore shall *my* [1]tongue praise thee and not cease: O Lord my God, I will give thanks unto thee forever.

31

1 David delivered from some great danger, first rehearseth what meditation he had by the power of faith, when death was before his eyes, his enemy being ready to take him.   15 Then he affirmeth that the favor of God is always ready to those that fear him.   20 Finally he exhorteth all the faithful to trust in God and to love him, because he preserveth and strengtheneth them, as they may see by his example.

To him that excelleth. A Psalm of David.

1 In [a]thee, O Lord, have I put my trust: let me never be confounded: deliver me in thy [1]righteousness.

2 Bow down thine ear to me: make haste to deliver me: be unto me a strong rock, *and* an house of defense to save me.

3 For thou art my rock and my fortress: therefore for thy Name's sake direct me and guide me.

4 Draw me out of the [1]net, that they have laid privily for me: for thou art my strength.

5 Into thine [1]hand I commend my spirit: *for* thou hast redeemed me, O Lord God of truth.

6 I have hated them that give themselves to deceitful vanities: for I [1]trust in the Lord.

7 I will be glad and rejoice in thy mercy: for thou hast seen my trouble: thou hast known my soul in adversities,

8 And thou hast not shut me up in the hand of the enemy, *but* hast set my feet at [1]large.

9 Have mercy upon me, O Lord: for I am in trouble: mine [1]eye, my soul and my belly are consumed with grief.

CHAPTER 31
[a] Ps. 71:1

10 For my life is wasted with heaviness, and my years with mourning: my strength faileth for my pain, and my bones are consumed.

11 I was a [1]reproach among all mine enemies, but specially among my neighbors: and a fear to mine acquaintance, [2]who seeing me in the street, fled from me.

12 I am forgotten as a dead man out of mind: I am like a broken vessel.

13 For I have heard the railing of [1]great men: fear *was* on every side, while they conspired together against me, *and* consulted to take my life.

14 But I trusted in thee, O Lord: I said, [1]Thou art my God.

15 My [1]times are in thine hand: deliver me from the hand of mine enemies, and from them that persecute me.

16 Make thy face to shine upon thy servant: *and* save me through thy mercy.

17 Let me not be confounded, O Lord: for I have called upon thee: let the wicked be put to confusion, *and* to [1]silence in the grave.

18 Let the lying lips be made dumb, which cruelly, proudly, and spitefully speak against the righteous.

19 How great is thy goodness, which thou [1]hast laid up for them that fear thee! *and* done to them that trust in thee, *even* before the sons of men!

20 Thou dost hide them [1,2]privily in thy presence from the pride of men: thou keepest them secretly in thy Tabernacle from the strife of tongues.

21 Blessed *be* the Lord: for he hath showed his marvelous kindness toward me in a [1]strong city.

22 Though I said in mine [1]haste, I am cast out of thy sight, yet thou heardest the voice of my prayer, when I cried unto thee.

23 Love ye the Lord all his [1]Saints: *for* the Lord preserveth the faithful, and rewardeth abundantly the proud doer.

30:12 [1] Because thou hast preserved me that my tongue should praise thee, I will not be unmindful of my duty.

31:1 [1] For then God declareth himself just, when he preserveth his according as he hath promised.

31:4 [1] Preserve me from the crafty counsels and subtle practice of mine enemies.

31:5 [1] He desireth God not only to take care for him in this life, but that his soul may be saved after this life.

31:6 [1] This affection ought to be in all God's children, to hate whatsoever thing is not grounded upon a sure trust in God, as deceitful and vain.

31:8 [1] Largeness signifieth comfort, as straightness, sorrow and peril.

31:9 [1] Meaning, that his sorrow and torment had continued a great while.

31:11 [1] Mine enemies had drawn all men to their part against me, even my chief friends.

[2] They were afraid to show me any token of friendship.

31:13 [1] They that were in authority, condemned me as a wicked doer.

31:14 [1] I had this testimony of conscience, that thou wouldest defend mine innocence.

31:15 [1] Whatsoever changes come, thou governest them by thy providence.

31:17 [1] Let death destroy them to the intent that they may hurt no more.

31:19 [1] The treasures of God's mercy are always laid up in store for his children, albeit at all times they do not enjoy them.

31:20 [1] Hebrew, *in the secret of thy face.*

[2] That is, in a place where they shall have thy comfort, and be hid safely from the enemies' pride.

31:21 [1] Meaning, there was no city so strong to preserve him, as the defense of God's favor.

31:22 [1] And so by my rashness and infidelity deserved to have been forsaken.

31:23 [1] Or, ye that feel his mercies.

24 All ye that trust in the Lord, be [1]strong, and he shall establish your heart.

32 1 David punished with grievous sickness for his sins, counteth them blessed to whom God doth not impute their transgressions. 5 And after that he had confessed his sins, and obtained pardon, 6 he exhorteth the wicked men to live godly, 11 and the good to rejoice.

A Psalm of David to give [1]instruction.

1 Blessed *is* he whose wickedness is [1]forgiven, *and* whose sin is covered.

2 Blessed *is* the man, unto whom the Lord imputeth not iniquity, and in whose spirit *there is* no guile.

3 When I held my [1]tongue, my bones consumed, *or* when I [2]roared all the day,

4 (For thine hand is heavy upon me day and night: *and* my moisture is turned into the drought of Summer. Selah.)

5 Then I [1]acknowledged my sin unto thee, neither hid I mine iniquity: *for* I thought, I will confess against myself my wickedness unto the Lord, and thou forgavest the punishment of my sin. Selah.

6 Therefore shall everyone that is godly, make his prayer unto thee in a [1]time, when thou mayest be found: surely in the flood of great waters [2]they shall not come near him.

7 Thou art my secret place: thou preservest me from trouble: thou compassest me about with joyful deliverance. Selah.

8 I will [1]instruct thee, and teach thee in the way that thou shalt go, *and* I will guide thee with mine eye.

9 Be ye not like an horse, *or* like a mule *which* understand not: whose [1]mouths thou dost bind with bit and bridle, lest they come near thee.

10 Many sorrows *shall come* to the wicked: but he that trusteth in the Lord, mercy shall compass him.

11 Be glad ye righteous, and [1]rejoice in the Lord,

and be joyful all ye, that are upright in heart.

33 1 He exhorteth good men to praise God, for that he hath not only created all things, and by his providence governeth the same, but also is faithful in his promises, 10 he understandeth man's heart, and scattereth the counsel of the wicked, 16 so that no man can be preserved by any creature or man's strength: by they, that put their confidence in his mercy, shall be preserved from all adversities.

1 Rejoice in the Lord, O ye righteous: *for* it [1]becometh upright men to be thankful.

2 Praise the Lord with harp: sing unto him with viol *and* [1]instrument of ten strings.

3 Sing unto him a new song: sing cheerfully with a loud voice.

4 For the [1]word of the Lord *is* righteous, and all his [2]works *are* faithful.

5 He [1]loveth righteousness and judgment: the earth is full of the goodness of the Lord.

6 By the word of the Lord were the heavens made, and all the host of them by the breath of his mouth.

7 He [1]gathereth the waters of the sea together as upon an heap, and layeth up the depths in *his* treasures.

8 Let all the earth fear the Lord: let all them that dwell in the world, fear him.

9 For he spake, and it was done: he commanded, and it [1]stood.

10 The Lord breaketh the [1]counsel of the heathen, *and* bringeth to nought the devices of the people.

11 The counsel of the Lord shall stand forever, *and* the thoughts of his heart throughout all ages.

12 Blessed *is* that nation, whose [1]God is the Lord: *even* the people *that* he hath chosen for his inheritance.

13 The Lord [1]looketh down from heaven, *and*

31:24 [1] Be constant in your vocation, and God will confirm you with heavenly strength.

32:Title [1] Concerning the free remission of sins, which is the chiefest point of our faith.

32:1 [1] To be justified by faith, is to have our sins freely remitted, and to be reputed just, Rom. 4:6.

32:3 [1] Between hope and despair.

   [2] Neither by silence nor crying found I ease, signifying that before the sinner be reconciled to God, he feeleth a perpetual torment.

32:5 [1] He showeth that as God's mercy is the only cause of forgiveness of sins, so the means thereof are repentance and confession which proceed of faith.

32:6 [1] When necessity causeth him to seek to thee for help, Isa. 55:6.

   [2] To wit, the waters and great dangers.

32:8 [1] David promiseth to make the rest of God's children partakers of the benefits which he felt, and that he will diligently look and take care to direct them in the way of salvation.

32:9 [1] If men can rule brute beasts, think they that God will not bridle and tame their rage?

32:11 [1] He showeth that peace and joy of conscience in the holy

Ghost, is the fruit of faith.

33:1 [1] It is the duty of the godly to set forth the praises of God for his mercy and power showed toward them.

33:2 [1] To sing on instruments, was a part of the ceremonial service of the Temple, which doth no more appertain unto us, than the sacrifices, censings, and lights.

33:4 [1] That is, counsel or commandment in governing the world.

   [2] That is, the effect and execution.

33:5 [1] Howsoever the world judgeth of God's works, yet he doeth all things according to justice and mercy.

33:7 [1] By the creation of the heavens and beautiful ornament with the gathering also of the waters, he setteth forth the power of God, that all creatures might fear him.

33:9 [1] Or, was created.

33:10 [1] No counsel can prevail against God, but he defeateth it, and it shall have evil success.

33:12 [1] He showeth that all our felicity standeth in this, that the Lord is our God.

33:13 [1] He proveth, that all things are governed by God's providence and not by fortune.

beholdeth all the children of men.

14 From the habitation of his dwelling, he beholdeth all them that dwell in the earth.

15 He [1]fashioneth their hearts every one, *and* understandeth all their works.

16 The [1]King is not saved by the multitude of an host, *neither* is the mighty man delivered by great strength.

17 A horse is a vain help, and shall not deliver *any* by his great strength.

18 Behold, [1]the eye of the Lord *is* upon them that fear him, *and* upon them that trust in his mercy,

19 To deliver their souls from death, and to preserve them in famine.

20 [1]Our soul waiteth for the Lord: *for* he is our help and our shield.

21 Surely our heart shall rejoice in him, because we trusted in his holy Name.

22 Let thy mercy, O Lord, be upon us, as we trusted in thee.

34 *1 After David had escaped Achish, according as it is written in 1 Sam. 2:11, whom in this title he calleth Abimelech (which was a general name to all the Kings of the Philistines) he praiseth God for his deliverance, 3 provoking all others by his example to trust in God, to fear and serve him, 7 who defendeth the godly with his Angels, 16 and utterly destroyeth the wicked in their sins.*

A *Psalm* of David, when he changeth his behavior before Abimelech, who drave him away, and he departed.

1 I will [1]always give thanks unto the Lord: his praise *shall be* in my mouth continually.

2 My soul shall glory in the Lord: the [1]humble shall hear it and be glad.

3 Praise ye the Lord with me, and let us magnify his Name together.

4 I sought the Lord, and he heard me: yea, he delivered me out of all my [1]fear.

5 They [1]shall look unto him, and run *to him*: and their faces shall not be ashamed, *saying,*

6 This poor man cried, and the Lord heard *him,*

and saved him out of all his troubles.

7 The [1]Angel of the Lord pitched round about them, that fear him, and delivereth them.

8 Taste ye and see, how gracious the Lord is: blessed *is* the man that trusteth in him.

9 Fear the Lord ye his Saints: for nothing wanteth to them that fear him.

10 The [1]lions do lack and suffer hunger, but they which seek the Lord, shall [2]want nothing that is good.

11 Come children, hearken unto me: I will teach you the [1]fear of the Lord.

12 [a]What man is he that desireth life, and loveth *long* days for to [1]see good?

13 Keep thy tongue from evil, and thy lips, that they speak no guile.

14 Eschew evil and do good: seek peace and follow after it.

15 The eyes of the Lord *are* upon the righteous, and his ears *are open* unto their cry.

16 But the [1]face of the Lord *is* against them that do evil, to cut off their remembrance from the earth.

17 The *righteous* cry, and the Lord heareth *them,* and delivereth them out of all their troubles.

18 The Lord is near unto them that are of a [1]contrite heart, and will save such as be afflicted in spirit.

19 Great *are* the troubles of the righteous: but the Lord delivereth him out of them all.

20 [1]He keepeth all his bones: not one of them is broken.

21 *But* malice shall slay the [1]wicked: and they that hate the righteous, shall perish.

22 The Lord [1]redeemeth the souls of his servants: and none that trust in him, shall perish.

35 *1 So long as Saul was enemy to David, all that had any authority under him, to flatter their king (as is the course of the world) did also most cruelly persecute David: against whom he prayeth God to plead and to avenge his cause, 8 that they may be taken in their nets and snares, which they laid for him, that his innocency may be declared, 27 and that the in-*

33:15 [1] Therefore he knoweth their wicked enterprises.

33:16 [1] If kings and the mighty of the world cannot be saved by worldly means, but only by God's providence, what have others to trust in, that have not like means?

33:18 [1] God showeth that toward his of his mercy, which man by no means is able to compass.

33:20 [1] Thus he speaketh in the name of the whole Church, which only depend on God's providence.

34:1 [1] He promised never to become unmindful of God's great benefit for his deliverance.

34:2 [1] They that are beaten down with the experience of their own evils.

34:4 [1] Which I conceived for the danger wherein I was.

34:5 [1] They shall be bold to flee to thee for succor, when they shall see thy mercies toward me.

34:7 [1] Though God's power be sufficient to govern us, yet for man's

infirmity he appointeth his Angels to watch over us.

34:10 [1] The godly by their patient obedience profit more than they which ravine and spoil.

    [2] If they abide the last trial.

34:11 [1] That is, the true religion and worship of God.

34:12 [1] Seeing all men naturally desire felicity, he wondereth why they cast themselves willingly into misery.

34:16 [1] The anger of God doth not only destroy the wicked, but also abolisheth their name forever.

34:18 [1] When they seem to be swallowed up with afflictions, then God is at hand to deliver them.

34:20 [1] And as Christ saith, all the hairs of his head.

34:21 [1] Their wicked enterprises shall turn to their own destruction.

34:22 [1] For when they seem to be overcome with great dangers and death itself, then God showeth himself their redeemer.

nocent, which taketh part with him, may rejoice and praise the Name of the Lord, that thus delivereth his servant. 28 And so he promiseth to speak forth the justice of the Lord, and to magnify his Name all the days of his life.

A Psalm of David.

1 Plead thou my [1]cause, O Lord, with them that strive with me: fight thou against them that fight against me.

2 [1]Lay hand upon the shield and buckler, and stand up for my help.

3 Bring out also the spear, and stop *the way* against them that persecute me, say unto my [1]soul, I am thy salvation.

4 Let them be confounded and put to shame, that seek after my soul: let them be turned back, and brought to confusion, that imagine mine hurt.

5 Let them be as chaff before the wind, and let the Angel of the Lord [1]scatter *them.*

6 Let their way be dark and slippery: and let the Angel of the Lord persecute them.

7 For [1]without cause they have hid the pit *and* their net for me: without cause have they dug *a pit* for my soul.

8 Let destruction come upon [1]him at unawares, and let his net, that he hath laid privily, take him: let him fall into [2]the same destruction.

9 Then my soul shall be joyful in the Lord: it shall rejoice in his salvation.

10 All my [1]bones shall say, Lord, who is like unto thee, which deliverest the poor from him, that is too strong for him! yea, the poor and him that is in misery, from him that spoileth him!

11 [1]Cruel witnesses did rise up: they asked of me things that I knew not.

12 They rewarded me evil for good, to [1]have spoiled my soul.

13 Yet I, when they were sick, I was clothed with a sack: I humbled my soul with fasting: and [1]my prayer was turned upon my bosom.

14 I behaved myself as to *my* friend, *or* as to my brother: I humbled myself, mourning as one that bewaileth his mother.

15 But in mine [1]adversity they rejoiced, and gathered themselves together: the abjects assembled themselves against me, and I knew not: they tare [2]me, and ceased not,

16 With the false scoffers at [1]banquets, gnashing their teeth against me.

17 Lord, how long wilt thou behold *this?* deliver my soul from their tumult, *even* my desolate *soul* from the lions.

18 *So* will I give thee thanks in a great Congregation: I will praise thee among much people.

19 Let not them that are mine enemies unjustly rejoice over me, neither let them [1]wink with the eye, that hate me without a cause.

20 For they speak not as friends: but they imagine deceitful words against the [1]quiet of the land.

21 And they gaped on me with their mouths, saying, Aha, aha, [1]our eye hath seen.

22 Thou hast seen it, O Lord: keep not silence: be not far from me, O Lord.

23 Arise and wake to my judgment, *even* to my cause, my God, and my Lord.

24 Judge me, O Lord my God, according to thy [1]righteousness, and let them not rejoice over me.

25 Let them not say in their hearts, [1]O our soul rejoice: neither let them say, We have devoured him.

26 Let them be confounded, and put to shame [1]together, that rejoice at mine hurt: let them be clothed [2]with confusion and shame, that lift up themselves against me.

27 *But* let them be joyful and glad, [1]that love my righteousness: yea, let them say always, Let the Lord be magnified, which loveth the [2]prosperity of his servant.

35:1 [1] He desireth God to undertake his cause against them that did persecute him and slander him.

35:2 [1] Albeit God can with his breath destroy all his enemies, yet the holy Ghost attributeth unto him these outward weapons to assure us of his present power.

35:3 [1] Assure me against these tentations, that thou art the author of my salvation.

35:5 [1] Smite them with the spirit of giddiness that their enterprises may be foolish, and they received just reward.

35:7 [1] Showing that we may not call God to be a revenger, but only for his glory, and when our cause is just.

35:8 [1] When he promiseth to himself peace.

[2] Which he prepared against the children of God.

35:10 [1] He attributeth his deliverance only to God, praising him therefore both in soul and body.

35:11 [1] That would not suffer me to purge myself.

35:12 [1] To have taken from me all comfort and brought me into despair.

35:13 [1] I prayed for them with inward affection, as I would have done for myself: or, I declared mine affection with bowing down mine head.

35:15 [1] When they saw me ready to slip, and as one that halted for infirmity.

[2] With their railing words.

35:16 [1] The word signifieth cakes: meaning that the proud courtiers at their dainty feasts scoff, rail, and conspire his death.

35:19 [1] In token of contempt and mocking.

35:20 [1] Or, clefts of the earth: meaning, himself and others in their misery.

35:21 [1] They rejoiced as though they had now seen David overthrown.

35:24 [1] It is the justice of God to give to the oppressors affliction and torment, and to the oppressed aid and relief, 2 Thess. 1:6.

35:25 [1] Because we have that which we sought for, seeing he is destroyed.

35:26 [1] That is, at once, were they never so many or mighty.

[2] This prayer shall always be verified against them that persecute the faithful.

35:27 [1] That at least favor my right, though they be not able to help me.

[2] He exhorteth the Church to praise God for the deliverance of his servants, and for the destruction of his adversaries.

28 And my tongue shall utter thy righteousness, *and* thy praise every day.

36

1 The Prophet grievously vexed by the wicked, doth complain of their malicious wickedness.   6 Then he turneth to consider the unspeakable goodness of God toward all creatures.   9 But specially towards his children, that by the faith thereof he may be comforted and assured of his deliverance by this ordinary course of God's work.   12 Who in the end destroyeth the wicked, and saveth the just.

To him that excelleth.
A Psalm of David, the servant of the Lord.

1 Wickedness saith to the wicked man, ¹even in mine heart, *that there is* no fear of God before his eyes.

2 For he ¹flattereth himself in his own eyes, while his iniquity is found *worthy* to be hated.

3 The words of his mouth *are* iniquity and ¹deceit: he hath left off to understand *and* to do good.

4 He ¹imagineth mischief upon his bed: he setteth himself upon a way, *that is* not good, *and* doth not abhor evil.

5 Thy ¹mercy, O Lord, *reacheth* unto the heavens, *and* thy faithfulness unto the clouds.

6 Thy righteousness *is* like the ¹mighty mountains: thy judgments *are like* a great ²deep: thou Lord, dost save man and beast.

7 How excellent is thy mercy, O God! therefore the children of men trust under the shadow of thy wings.

8 They shall be ¹satisfied with the fatness of thine house, and thou shalt give them drink out of the river of thy pleasures.

9 For with thee *is* the well of life, and in thy light shall we see light.

10 Extend thy loving-kindness unto them that ¹know thee, and thy righteousness unto them that are upright in heart.

11 Let not the ¹foot of pride come against me, and let not the hand of the wicked men move me.

12 ¹There they are fallen that work iniquity: they are cast down, and shall not be able to rise.

37

1 This Psalm containeth exhortation and consolation for the weak, that are grieved at the prosperity of the wicked, and the affliction of the godly.   7 For how prosperously soever the wicked do live for the time, he doth affirm their felicity to be vain and transitory, because they are not in the favor of God, but in the end they are destroyed as his enemies.   11 And how miserably that the righteous seemeth to live in the world, yet his end is peace, and he is in the favor of God, he is delivered from the wicked, and preserved.

A Psalm of David.

1 Fret not ¹thyself because of the wicked men, neither be envious for the evildoers.

2 For they shall soon be ¹cut down like grass, and shall wither as the green herb.

3 ¹Trust thou in the Lord and do good: dwell in the land, and thou shalt be fed assuredly:

4 And delight thyself in the Lord, and he shall give thee thine heart's desire.

5 ¹Commit thy way unto the Lord, and trust in him, and he shall bring it to pass.

6 And he shall bring forth thy righteousness as the light, and thy ¹judgment as the noon day.

7 Wait patiently upon the Lord, and hope in him: fret not thyself for him ¹which prospereth in his way, *nor* for the man that bringeth *his* enterprises to pass.

8 Cease from anger, and leave off wrath: fret not thyself ¹also to do evil.

9 For evildoers shall be cut off, and they that wait upon the Lord, they shall inherit the land.

10 ¹Therefore yet a little while and the wicked shall not *appear*, and thou shalt look after his place, and he shall not *be found.*

36:1 ¹ I see evidently by his deeds, that sin pusheth forward the reprobate from wickedness to wickedness, albeit he go about to cover his impiety.

36:2 ¹ Though all others detest his vile sin, yet he himself seeth it not.

36:3 ¹ The reprobate mock at wholesome doctrine, and put not difference between good and evil.

36:4 ¹ By describing at large the nature of the reprobate, he admonisheth the godly to beware of these vices.

36:5 ¹ Though wickedness seemeth to overflow all the world, yet by thine heavenly providence thou governest heaven and earth.

36:6 ¹ Hebrew, *the mountains of God*: for whatsoever is excellent, is thus called.

    ² The depth of thy providence governeth all things, and disposeth them, albeit the wicked seem to overwhelm the world.

36:8 ¹ Only God's children have enough of all things both concerning this life and the life to come.

36:10 ¹ He showeth who are God's children, to wit, they that know him, and lead their lives uprightly.

36:11 ¹ Let not the proud advance himself against me, neither the power of the wicked drive me away.

36:12 ¹ That is, in their pride wherein they flatter themselves.

37:1 ¹ He admonisheth us neither to vex ourselves for the prosperous estate of the wicked, neither to desire to be like them to make our state the better.

37:2 ¹ For God's judgment cutteth down their state in a moment.

37:3 ¹ To trust in God, and do according to his will, are sure tokens that his providence will never fail us.

37:5 ¹ Be not led by thine own wisdom, but obey God, and he will finish his work in thee.

37:6 ¹ As the hope of the daylight causeth us not to be offended with the darkness of the night: so ought we patiently to trust that God will clear our cause and restore us to our right.

37:7 ¹ When God suffereth the wicked to prosper, it seemeth to the flesh that he favoreth their doings, Job 21:7 etc.

37:8 ¹ Meaning, except he moderate his affections, he shall be led to do as they do.

37:10 ¹ He correcteth the impatience of our nature, which cannot abide till the fullness of God's time be come.

11 But "meek men shall possess the earth, and shall have their delight in the multitude of peace.

12 ¹The wicked practiceth against the just, and gnasheth his teeth against him.

13 But the Lord shall laugh him to scorn: for he seeth that his day is coming.

14 The wicked have drawn their sword and have bent their bow, to cast down the poor and needy, and to slay such as be of upright conversation.

15 But their sword shall enter into their own heart, and their bows shall be broken.

16 ¹A small thing unto the just man is better than great riches to the wicked and mighty.

17 For the arms of the wicked shall be broken: but the Lord upholdeth the just men.

18 The Lord ¹knoweth the days of upright men, and their inheritance shall be perpetual.

19 They shall not be confounded in the perilous time, and in the days of famine they shall have ¹enough.

20 But the wicked shall perish, and the enemies of the Lord shall be consumed as the ¹fat of lambs: even with the smoke shall they consume away.

21 The wicked borroweth and payeth not again: but the righteous is merciful and ¹giveth.

22 For such as be blessed of God shall inherit the land, and they that be cursed of him, shall be cut off.

23 ¹The paths of man are directed by the Lord: for he loveth his way.

24 Though he ¹fall, he shall not be cast off, for the Lord putteth under his hand.

25 I have been young, and am old: yet I saw never the righteous forsaken, nor his ¹seed begging bread.

26 But he is ever merciful and lendeth, and his seed enjoyeth the blessing.

27 Flee from evil and do good, and dwell forever.

28 For the Lord loveth judgment, and forsaketh not his Saints: they shall be preserved forevermore: but the seed of the wicked shall be cut off.

29 The righteous men shall inherit the land, and

CHAPTER 37
a Matt. 5:5

dwell therein ¹forever.

30 The ¹mouth of the righteous will speak of wisdom, and his tongue will talk of judgment.

31 For the Law of his God is in his heart, and his steps shall not slide.

32 The wicked watched the righteous, and seeketh to slay him.

33 But the Lord will not leave him in his hand, nor condemn him, when he is ¹judged.

34 Wait thou on the Lord, and keep his way, and he shall exalt thee, that thou shalt inherit the land: when the wicked men shall perish, thou shalt see.

35 I have seen the wicked strong, and spreading himself like a green bay tree.

36 Yet he ¹passed away, and lo, he was gone, and I sought him, but he could not be found.

37 ¹Mark the upright man, and behold the just: for the end of that man is peace.

38 But their transgressors shall be destroyed together, and the end of the wicked shall be cut off.

39 But the ¹salvation of the righteous men shall be of the Lord: he shall be their strength in the time of trouble.

40 For the Lord shall help them, and deliver them: he shall deliver them from the wicked, and shall save them, because they trust in him.

38 1 David lying sick of some grievous disease, acknowledgeth himself to be chastised of the Lord for his sins, and therefore prayeth God to turn away his wrath. 5 He uttereth the greatness of his grief by many words and circumstances, as wounded with the arrows of God's ire, forsaken of his friends, evil intreated of his enemies. 22 But in the end with firm confidence he commendeth his cause to God, and hopeth for speedy help at his hand.

A Psalm of David for ¹remembrance.

1 O Lord, rebuke me not in thine ¹anger, neither chastise me in thy wrath.

37:12 ¹ The godly are assured that the power and craft of the wicked shall not prevail against them, but fall on their own necks, and therefore ought patiently to abide God's time, and in the meanwhile bewail their sins, and offer up their tears, is a sacrifice of their obedience.

37:16 ¹ For they are daily fed as with Manna from heaven, and have sufficient, when the wicked have never enough, but ever hunger.

37:18 ¹ God knoweth what dangers hang over his, and by what means to deliver them.

37:19 ¹ For God will give them contented minds: and that which shall be necessary.

37:20 ¹ They shall vanish away suddenly, for they are fed for the day of slaughter.

37:21 ¹ God so furnisheth him with his blessings, that he is able to help others.

37:23 ¹ God prospereth the faithful, because they walk in his ways with an upright conscience.

37:24 ¹ When God doth exercise his faith with divers tentations.

37:25 ¹ Though the just man die, yet God's blessings are extended to his posterity, and though God suffer some just man to lack temporal benefits, yet he recompenseth him with spiritual treasures.

37:29 ¹ They shall continually be preserved under God's wings, and have at least inward rest.

37:30 ¹ These three points are required of the faithful, that their talk be godly, that God's law be in their heart, and that their life be upright.

37:33 ¹ For though it be sometime so expedient both for God's glory and their salvation, yet he will approve their cause, and revenge their wrong.

37:36 ¹ So that the prosperity of the wicked is but as a cloud, which vanisheth away in a moment.

37:37 ¹ He exhorteth the faithful to mark diligently the examples both of God's mercies, and also of his judgments.

37:39 ¹ He showeth that the patient hope of the godly is never in vain, but in the end hath good success, though for a time God prove them by sundry tentations.

38:Title ¹ To put himself and others in mind of God's chastisement for sin.

38:1 ¹ He desireth not to be exempted from God's rod, but that he would so moderate his hand, that he might be able to bear it.

2 For thine [1]arrows have light upon me, and thine hand lieth upon me.

3 There *is* nothing sound in my flesh, because of thine anger: neither *is* there rest in my bones, because of my [1]sin.

4 For mine [1]iniquities are gone over mine head, *and* as a weighty burden they are too heavy for me.

5 My wounds are putrefied, and corrupt because of [1]my foolishness.

6 I am bowed, *and* crooked very sore: I go [1]mourning all the day.

7 For my reins are full of burning, and there *is* nothing sound in my flesh.

8 I am weakened and sore broken: I [1]roar for the very grief of mine heart.

9 Lord, *I* pour my whole desire before thee, and my sighing is not hid from thee.

10 Mine heart [1]panteth: my strength faileth me, and the light of mine eyes, even [2]they are not mine own.

11 My lovers and my friends stand aside from my plague, and my [1]kinsmen stand afar off.

12 They also that seek after my life, lay snares, and they that go about to do me evil, talk wicked things and imagine deceit continually.

13 But I as a [1]deaf man heard not, and *am* as a dumb man, *which* openeth not his mouth.

14 Thus am I as a man, that heareth not, and in whose mouth *are* no reproofs.

15 For on thee, O Lord, do I wait: thou wilt hear *me*, my Lord, my God.

16 For I said, *Hear me*, lest they rejoice over me: for [1]when my foot slippeth, they extol themselves against me.

17 Surely I am ready to [1]halt, and my sorrow *is* ever before me.

18 When I declare my pain, *and* am sorry for my sin,

19 Then mine [1]enemies are alive, *and* are mighty, and they that hate me wrongfully are many.

20 They also, that reward evil for good, are mine adversaries, because I follow [1]goodness.

21 Forsake me not, O Lord, be not thou far from me, my God.

22 Haste thee, to help me, O my Lord, my [1]salvation.

39

1 *David uttereth with what great grief and bitterness of mind he was driven to these outrageous complaints of his infirmities.* 2 *For he confesseth that when he had determined silence, that he brast forth yet into words, that he would not, through the greatness of his grief.* 4 *Then he rehearseth certain requests which taste of the infirmity of man.* 8 *And mixeth with them many prayers: but all do show a mind wonderfully trembled, that it may plainly appear how he did strive mightily against death and desperation.*

To the excellent *Musician* [1]Jeduthun. A Psalm of David.

1 I thought, [1]I will take heed to my ways, that I sin not with my tongue: I will keep my mouth bridled, while the wicked is in my sight.

2 I was dumb and spake nothing: I kept silence *even* from good, [1]and my sorrow was more stirred.

3 Mine heart was hot within me, *and* while I was musing, the fire kindled, *and* I [1]spake with my tongue, *saying,*

4 Lord, let me know mine end, and the measure of my days, what it is: let me know how long I have to live.

5 Behold, thou hast made my days as an hand breadth, and mine age as nothing in respect of thee: surely every man *in his best* state is altogether [1]vanity. Selah.

6 Doubtless man walketh in a shadow, and disquieteth himself in vain: he heapeth up *riches*, and cannot tell who shall gather them.

7 And now Lord, what wait I for? mine hope is even in thee.

38:2 [1] Thy sickness, wherewith thou hast visited me.

38:3 [1] David acknowledgeth God to be just in his punishments, because his sins had deserved much more.

38:4 [1] He confesseth his sins, God's justice, and maketh prayer his refuge.

38:5 [1] That rather gave place to mine own lusts, than to the will of God.

38:6 [1] Or, black as one that is disfigured and consumed with sickness.

38:8 [1] This example warneth us never to despair, be the torment never so great: but always to cry unto God with sure trust for deliverance.

38:10 [1] Hebrew, *runneth about*, or, *is tossed to and fro*, meaning, that he was destitute of all help and counsel.

[2] My sight faileth me for very sorrow.

38:11 [1] Partly for fear and partly for pride, they denied all duty and friendship.

38:13 [1] For I can have no audience before men, and therefore patiently wait for the help of God.

38:16 [1] That is, if they see that thou succor me not in time, they will mock and triumph, as though thou hadst forsaken me.

38:17 [1] I am without hope to recover my strength.

38:19 [1] In my greatest misery they most rejoice.

38:20 [1] He had rather have the hatred of all the world, than to fail in any part of his duty to Godward.

38:22 [1] Which are the author of my salvation: and this declareth that he prayed with sure hope of deliverance.

39:Title [1] This was one of the chief singers, 1 Chron. 16:41.

39:1 [1] Albeit he had appointed with himself patiently to have tarried God's leisure, yet the vehemency of his pain caused him to break his purpose.

39:2 [1] Though when the wicked ruled, he thought to have kept silence, yet his zeal caused him to change his mind.

39:3 [1] He confesseth that he grudged against God, considering the greatness of his sorrows, and the shortness of his life.

39:5 [1] Yet David offended in that that he reasoned with God as though that he were too severe toward his weak creature.

8 Deliver me from all my transgressions, and make me not a rebuke unto the [1]foolish.

9 I should have been dumb, and not have opened my mouth, because [1]thou didst it.

10 Take thy plague away from me: for I am consumed by the stroke of thine hand.

11 When thou with rebukes dost chastise man for iniquity, thou as a moth [1]makest his [2]beauty to consume: surely every man is vanity. Selah.

12 Hear my prayer, O Lord, and hearken unto my cry: keep not silence at my tears, for I am a stranger with thee, and a sojourner as all my fathers.

13 Stay thine anger from me, that I may recover my strength, [1]before I go hence and be not.

40

1 David delivered from great danger doth magnify and praise the grace of God for his deliverance, and commendeth his providence toward all mankind. 5 Then doth he promise to give himself wholly to God's service, and so declareth how God is truly worshipped. 14 Afterwards he giveth thanks and praiseth God, and having complained of his enemies, with good courage he calleth for aid and succor.

To him that excelleth. A Psalm of David.

1 I waited [1]patiently for the Lord, and he inclined unto me, and heard my cry.

2 He brought me also out of the [1]horrible pit, out of the miry clay, and set my feet upon the rock, and ordered my goings.

3 And he hath put in my mouth [1]a new song of praise unto our God: many shall see it and fear, and shall trust in the Lord.

4 Blessed is the man that maketh the Lord his trust, and regardeth [1]not the proud, nor such as turn aside to lies.

5 [1]O Lord my God, thou hast made thy wonderful works so many, that none can count in order to thee

thy thoughts toward us: I would declare and speak of them, but they are more than I am able to express.

6 Sacrifice and offering thou didst not desire: (for [1]mine ears hast thou prepared) burnt offering and sin offering hast thou not required.

7 [1]Then said I, Lo, I come: for in the roll of the book it is written of me.

8 I desired to do thy good will, O my God: yea, thy Law is within mine heart.

9 I have declared thy righteousness in the [1]great congregation: lo, I will not refrain my lips: O Lord, thou knowest.

10 I have not hid thy righteousness within mine heart, but I have declared thy [1]truth and thy salvation: I have not concealed thy mercy, and thy truth from the great Congregation.

11 Withdraw not thou thy tender mercy from me, O Lord, let thy mercy and thy truth always preserve me.

12 For innumerable troubles have compassed me: my sins have taken such hold upon me, that I am not able to look up: yea, they are more in number than the hairs of mine head: therefore mine heart hath [1]failed me.

13 Let it please thee, O Lord, to deliver me: make haste, O Lord, to help me.

14 Let them be [1]confounded and put to shame together, that seek my soul to destroy it: let them be driven backward and put to rebuke that desire mine hurt.

15 Let them be [1]destroyed for a reward of their shame, which say unto me, Aha, aha.

16 Let all them that seek thee, rejoice and be glad in thee, and let them that love thy salvation, say always, [1]The Lord be praised.

17 Though I be poor and needy, the Lord thinketh on me: thou art mine helper and my deliverer: my God, make no tarrying.

39:8 [1] Make me not a mocking stock to the wicked, or wrap me not up with the wicked, when they are put to shame.

39:9 [1] Seeing my troubles came of thy providence, I ought to have endured them patiently.

39:11 [1] Though thine open plagues light not evermore upon them, yet thy secret curse continually fretteth them.

[2] The word signifieth all that he desireth, as health, force, strength, beauty, and in whatsoever he hath delight, so that the rod of God taketh away all that is desired in this world.

39:13 [1] For his sorrow caused him to think that God would destroy him utterly: whereby we see how hard it is for the very Saints to keep a measure in their words, when death and despair assail them.

40:1 [1] Though God deferred his help, yet he patiently abode till he was heard.

40:2 [1] He hath delivered me from most great dangers.

40:3 [1] That is, a special occasion to praise him: for God's benefits are so many occasions for us to praise his Name.

40:4 [1] To follow their example, which he must needs do that trusteth not only in the Lord.

40:5 [1] David goeth from one kind of God's favor to the contemplation of his providence over all, and confesseth that his counsels

towards us are far above our capacities: we cannot so much as tell them in order.

40:6 [1] Thou hast opened mine ears to understand the spiritual meaning of the sacrifices: and here David esteemeth the ceremonies of the law nothing in respect of the spiritual service.

40:7 [1] When thou hadst opened mine ears and heart, I was ready to obey thee, being assured that I was written in the book of thine elect for this end.

40:9 [1] In the Church assembled in the Sanctuary.

40:10 [1] David here numbereth 3 degrees of our salvation: God's mercy, whereby he pitieth us: his righteousness, which signifieth his continual protection: and his truth, whereby appeareth his constant favor, so that hereof proceedeth our salvation.

40:12 [1] As touching the judgment of the flesh, I was utterly destitute of all counsel, yet faith inwardly moved mine heart to pray.

40:14 [1] He desireth that God's mercy may contend for him against the rage of his enemies.

40:15 [1] Let the same shame and confusion light upon them, which they intended to have brought upon me.

40:16 [1] As the faithful always praise God for his benefits, so the wicked mocked God's children in their afflictions.

41

1 *David being grievously afflicted, blesseth them that pity his case,* 9 *and complaineth of the treason of his own friends and familiars, as came to pass in Judas, John 13:18. After he feeling the great mercies of God gently chastising him, and not suffering his enemies to triumph against him,* 13 *giveth most hearty thanks to God.*

To him that excelleth. A Psalm of David.

1 Blessed *is* he that [1]judgeth wisely of the poor: the Lord shall deliver him in the time of trouble.

2 The Lord will keep him and preserve him alive, he shall be blessed upon the earth: and thou wilt not deliver him unto the will of his enemies.

3 The Lord will strengthen him upon the [1]bed of sorrow: thou hast turned all his [2]bed in his sickness.

4 *Therefore* I said, Lord have mercy upon me: heal my soul, for I have sinned against thee.

5 Mine enemies [1]speak evil of me, *saying,* When shall he die, and his name perish?

6 And if he come to see me, he speaketh [1]lies, *but* his heart heapeth iniquity within him, *and when* he cometh forth, he telleth it.

7 All they that hate me whisper together against me: *even* against me do they imagine mine hurt.

8 [1]A mischief is light upon him, and he that lieth, shall no more rise.

9 Yea, my [1]familiar friend, whom I trusted, which did eat of my bread, [2]hath lifted up the heel against me.

10 Therefore, O Lord, have mercy upon me, and raise me up: so shall I reward them.

11 By this I know that thou favorest me, because mine enemy doth not triumph against me.

12 And as for me thou upholdest me [1]in mine integrity, and dost set me before thy [2]face forever.

13 Blessed *be* the Lord God of Israel world without end. [1]So be it, even so be it.

42

1 *The Prophet grievously complaineth, that being letted by his persecutors, he could not be present in the congregation of God's people, protesting that although he was separated in body from them, yet his heart was thitherward affectioned.* 7 *And least of all he showed that he was not so far overcome with these sorrows and thoughts,* 8 *but that he continually put his confidence in the Lord.*

To him that excelleth. A Psalm to give instruction, [1]committed to the sons of Korah.

1 As the Hart brayeth for the rivers of water, so [1]panted my soul after thee, O God.

2 My soul thirsteth for God, *even* for the living God: when shall I come and appear *before* the presence of God?

3 [1]Mine tears have been my meat day and night, while they daily say unto me, Where is thy God?

4 When I remembered [1]these things, I poured out my very heart, because I had gone with the multitude, *and* led them into the house of God with the voice of singing, *and* praise, *as* a multitude that keepeth a feast.

5 Why art thou cast down, my soul, and unquiet within me? [1]wait on God: for I will yet give him thanks for the help of his presence.

6 My God, my soul is cast down within me, [1]because I remembered thee, from the land of Jordan, and Hermon, *and* from the mount Mizar.

7 One [1]deep calleth *another* deep by the noise of thy waterspouts: all thy waves and thy floods are gone over me.

8 The Lord [1]will grant his loving-kindness in the day, and in the night shall I sing of him, *even* a prayer unto the God of my life.

9 I will say unto God, *which is* my rock, Why hast thou forgotten me? why go I mourning, when the enemy oppresseth *me*?

10 My [1]bones are cut asunder, while mine enemies reproach me, saying daily unto me, Where is thy God?

41:1 [1] Not condemning him as accursed whom God doth visit, knowing that there are divers causes why God layeth his hand upon us, yea and afterward he restoreth us.

41:3 [1] When for sorrow and grief of mind he calleth himself upon his bed.

[2] Thou hast restored him in his sick bed and sent him comfort.

41:5 [1] That is, curse me and cannot have their cruel hate quenched, but with my shameful death.

41:6 [1] For pretending to comfort me, he conspireth my death in his heart, and braggeth thereof.

41:8 [1] The enemies thought by his sharp punishments that God was become his mortal enemy.

41:9 [1] Hebrew, *the man of my peace.*

[2] As David felt this falsehood, and as it was chiefly accomplished in Christ, John 13:18, so shall his members continually prove the same.

41:12 [1] Meaning, either in prosperity of life, or in the true fear of God against all tentations.

[2] Showing me evident signs of thy fatherly providence.

41:13 [1] By this repetition he stirreth up the faithful to praise God.

42:Title [1] As a treasure to be kept of them, which were of the number of the Levites.

42:1 [1] By these similitudes of thirst and panting, he showeth his fervent desire to serve God in his Temple.

42:3 [1] As others take pleasure in eating and drinking, so he was altogether given to weeping.

42:4 [1] That is, how I led the people to serve thee in thy Tabernacle; and now seeing my contrary estate, I die for sorrow.

42:5 [1] Though he sustained grievous assaults of the flesh to cast him into despair, yet his faith grounded on God's accustomed mercies getteth the victory.

42:6 [1] That is, when I remember thee in this land of my banishment among the mountains.

42:7 [1] Afflictions came so thick upon me, that I felt my self as overwhelmed: whereby he showeth there is no end of our misery till God be pacified and send remedy.

42:8 [1] He assureth himself of God's help in time to come.

42:10 [1] That is, I am most grievously tormented.

11 ¹Why art thou cast down, my soul? and why art thou disquieted within me? wait on God: for I will yet give him thanks: *he is* my present help and my God.

43

1 He prayeth to be delivered from them that conspire against him, that he might joyfully praise God in his holy congregation.

1 Judge ¹me, O God, and defend my cause against the unmerciful ²people: deliver me from the deceitful and wicked man.

2 For thou art the God of my strength: why hast thou put me away? why go I so mourning, when the enemy oppressed *me?*

3 Send thy ¹light and thy truth: let them lead me: let them bring me unto thine holy Mountain, and to thy Tabernacles.

4 Then ¹will I go unto the altar of God, *even* unto the God of my joy *and* gladness: and upon the harp will I give thanks unto thee, O God my God.

5 Why art thou cast down, my soul? and why art thou disquieted within me: ¹wait on God: for I will yet give him thanks, *he is* my present help and my God.

44

1 The faithful remember the great mercy of God toward his people. 9 After they complain, because they feel it no more. 17 Also they allege the covenant made with Abraham, for the keeping whereof they show what grievous things they suffered. 23 Finally, they pray unto God not to contemn their affliction, seeing the same redoundeth to the contempt of his honor.

To him that excelleth. *A Psalm to give instruction, committed* to the sons of Korah.

1 We have heard with our ¹ears, O God: our fathers have told us the works *that* thou hast done in their days, in the old time:

CHAPTER 44
ᵃ Rom. 8:36

2 *How* thou hast driven out the ¹heathen with thine hand, and planted ²them: *how* thou hast destroyed the ³people, and caused ⁴them to grow.

3 For they inherited not the land by their own sword, neither did their own arm save them: but thy right hand, and thine arm, and the light of thy countenance, because thou didst ¹favor them.

4 Thou art my king, O God: send help unto ¹Jacob.

5 ¹Through thee have we thrust back our adversaries: by thy Name have we trodden down them that rose up against us.

6 For I do not trust in my bow, neither can my sword save me.

7 But thou hast saved us from our adversaries, and hast put them to confusion that hate us.

8 *Therefore* will we praise God continually, and will confess thy Name forever. Selah.

9 But *now* thou art far off, and puttest us to ¹confusion, and goest not forth with our armies.

10 Thou makest us to turn back from the adversary, and they which hate us, spoil ¹for themselves.

11 ᵃThou givest us ¹as sheep to be eaten, and dost scatter us among the nations.

12 Thou sellest thy people ¹without gain, and dost not increase their price.

13 Thou makest us a reproach to our neighbors, a jest and laughing stock to them that are round about us.

14 Thou makest us a proverb among the nations, and a nodding of the head among the people.

15 My ¹confusion *is* daily before me, and the shame of my face hath covered me,

16 For the voice of the slanderer and rebuker, for the enemy and ¹avenger.

17 All this is come upon us, yet do we not ¹forget thee, neither deal we falsely concerning thy covenant.

42:11 ¹ This repetition doth declare that David did not overcome at once, to teach us to be constant, forasmuch as God will certainly deliver his.

43:1 ¹ He desireth God to undertake his cause against the enemies but chiefly that he would restore him to the Tabernacle.
² That is, the cruel company of mine enemies.

43:3 ¹ To wit, thy favor, which appeareth by the performance of thy promises.

43:4 ¹ He promiseth to offer a solemn sacrifice of thanksgiving in token of his great deliverance.

43:5 ¹ Whereby he admonisheth the faithful not to relent, but constantly to wait on the Lord, though their troubles be long and great.

44:1 ¹ This psalm seemeth to have been made by some excellent Prophet for the use of the people, when the Church was in extreme misery, either at their return from Babylon, or under Antiochus, or in such like affliction.

44:2 ¹ That is, the Canaanites.
² To wit, our fathers.
³ Of Canaan.
⁴ That is, our fathers.

44:3 ¹ God's free mercy and love is the only fountain and beginning of the Church, Deut. 4:37.

44:4 ¹ Because thou art our king, therefore deliver thy people from their misery.

44:5 ¹ Because they and their forefathers made both one Church, they apply that to themselves which before they did attribute to their fathers.

44:9 ¹ As they confessed before that their strength came of God, so now they acknowledge that this affliction came by his just judgment.

44:10 ¹ Or, at their pleasure.

44:11 ¹ Knowing God to be author of this calamity, they murmur not, but seek remedy at his hands, who wounded them.

44:12 ¹ As slaves which are sold for a low price, neither lookest thou for him that offereth most, but takest the first chapman.

44:15 ¹ I dare not lift up my head for shame.

44:16 ¹ Meaning, the proud and cruel tyrant.

44:17 ¹ They boast not of their virtues, but declare that they rest upon God in the midst of their afflictions: who punished not now their sins, but by hard afflictions called them to the consideration of the heavenly joys.

18 Our heart is not turned back: neither our steps gone out of thy paths,

19 Albeit thou hast smitten us down into the place of [1]dragons, and covered us with the shadow of death.

20 If we have forgotten the Name of our God, and held up our hands to a [1]strange god,

21 Shall not God [1]search this out? for he knoweth the secrets of the heart.

22 Surely for thy sake [1]are we slain continually, and are counted as sheep for the slaughter.

23 Up, why sleepest thou, O Lord? awake, be not far off forever.

24 Wherefore hidest thou thy face? and forgettest our misery and our affliction?

25 For our soul is [1]beaten down unto the dust: our belly cleaveth to the ground.

26 Rise up for our succor, and redeem us for thy [1]mercy's sake.

45

1 *The majesty of Solomon, his honor, strength, beauty, riches, and power are praised, and also his marriage with the Egyptian being an heathen woman, is blessed.* 10 *If that she can renounce her people and the love of her country, and gave herself wholly to her husband. Under the which figure, the wonderful majesty and increase of the kingdom of Christ and his Church his spouse, now taken of the Gentiles, is described.*

To him that excelleth on [1]Shoshannim, a song of [2]love to give instruction, *committed* to the sons of Korah.

1 Mine heart will utter forth a good matter: I will entreat *in* my works of the king: my tongue *is as* the pen of a swift writer.

2 Thou art [1]fairer than the children of men: grace is poured in thy lips, because God hath blessed thee forever.

3 Gird thy sword upon *thy* thigh, O most mighty,

to wit, thy worship and thy glory:

4 And prosper with thy glory: [1]ride upon the word of truth and of meekness *and* of righteousness: so thy right hand shall teach thee terrible things.

5 Thine arrows *are* sharp *to pierce* the heart of the King's enemies: *therefore* the people shall fall under thee.

6 Thy [1]throne, O God, *is* forever and ever: the scepter of thy kingdom, *is* a scepter of righteousness.

7 Thou lovest righteousness, and hatest wickedness, because God, *even* thy God, hath [1]anointed thee with the oil of gladness above thy fellows.

8 All thy garments *smell* of myrrh and aloes, *and* cassia, *when thou comest* out of the ivory palaces [1]where they have made thee glad.

9 King's daughters *were* among thine honorable *wives*: upon thy right hand did stand the [1]Queen in a vesture of gold of Ophir.

10 [1]Hearken, O daughter, and consider, and incline thine ear: forget also thine own people and thy father's house.

11 So shall the King have pleasure in thy beauty: for he is thy Lord, and reverence thou him.

12 And the [1]daughter of [2]Tyre *with* the rich of the people, shall do homage before thy face with presents.

13 The King's daughter is all glorious [1]within: her clothing is of broidered gold.

14 She shall be brought unto the King in raiment of needlework: the virgins *that follow* after her, *and* her companions shall be brought unto thee.

15 With joy and gladness shall they be brought, *and* shall enter into the king's palace.

16 Instead of thy fathers shall thy [1]children be: thou shalt make them princes [2]through all the earth.

17 I will make thy [1]Name to be remembered through all generations: therefore shall the people

---

44:19 [1] Or, whales: meaning, the bottomless seas of tentations: here we see the power of faith, which can be overcome by no perils.

44:20 [1] They show that they honored God aright, because they trusted in him alone.

44:21 [1] They take God to witness that they were upright to himward.

44:22 [1] The faithful make this their comfort, that the wicked punish them not for their sins, but for God's cause, Matt. 5:10; 1 Pet. 4:14.

44:25 [1] There is no hope of recovery, except thou put to thine hand and raise us up.

44:26 [1] Which is the only sufficient ransom to deliver both body and soul from all kinds of slavery and misery.

45:Title [1] This was a certain tune or an instrument.
[2] Of that perfect love that ought to be between the husband and the wife.

45:2 [1] Solomon's beauty and eloquence to win favor with his people, and his power to overcome his enemies, is here described.

45:4 [1] He alludeth to them that ride in chariots in their triumphs, showing that the quiet state of a kingdom standeth in truth, meekness and justice, not in worldly pomp and vanity.

45:6 [1] Under this figure of this kingdom of justice is set forth the

everlasting kingdom of Christ.

45:7 [1] Hath established thy kingdom as the figure of Christ, which is the peace and joy of the Church.

45:8 [1] In the which palace the people made thee joyful to see them give thanks and rejoice for thee.

45:9 [1] Though he had many Kings' daughters among his wives, yet he loved Pharaoh's daughter best.

45:10 [1] Under the figure of Pharaoh's daughter, he showeth that the Church must cast off all carnal affections to obey Christ only.

45:12 [1] He signifieth that divers of them that be rich shall be benefactors to the Church, albeit they give not perfect obedience to the Gospel.
[2] Or, Zor.

45:13 [1] There is nothing feigned, nor hypocritical, but she is glorious both within and without: and howbeit the Church hath not at all times this outward glory, the fault is to be imputed only to their own ingratitude.

45:16 [1] They shall have greater graces than their fathers.
[2] He signifieth the great compass of Christ's kingdom, which shall be sufficient to enrich all his members.

45:17 [1] This only must be referred to Christ and not to Solomon.

give thanks unto thee, world without end.

46

1 A song of triumph or thanksgiving for the deliverance of Jerusalem, after Sennacherib with his army was driven away, or some other like sudden and marvelous deliverance by the mighty hand of God. 8 Whereby the Prophet commending this great benefit, doth exhort the faithful to give themselves wholly into the hand of God, doubting nothing but that under his protection they shall be safe against all the assaults of their enemies, because this is his delight to assuage the rage of the wicked, when they are most busy against the just.

To him that excelleth upon ¹Alamoth,
a song *committed* to the sons of Korah.

1 God *is* our ¹hope and strength, *and* help in ²troubles, ready to be found.

2 Therefore will not we ¹fear, though the earth be moved, and though the mountains fall into the midst of the sea,

3 *Though* the waters thereof ¹rage *and* be troubled, *and* the mountains shake at the surges of the same. Selah.

4 Yet there *is* a ¹River, whose stream shall make glad the City of God: *even* the Sanctuary of the Tabernacles of the most High.

5 God *is* in the midst of it: *therefore* shall it not be moved: God shall help it ¹very early.

6 *When* the nations raged, *and* the kingdoms were moved, God ¹thundered, *and* the earth melted.

7 The Lord of hosts *is* ¹with us; the God of Jacob *is* our refuge. Selah.

8 Come *and* behold the works of the Lord, ¹what desolations he hath made in the earth.

9 He maketh wars to cease unto the ends of the world, he breaketh the bow, and cutteth the spear, *and* burneth the chariots with fire.

10 Be ¹still and know that I am God, I will be exalted among the heathen, *and* I will be exalted in the earth.

11 The Lord of hosts *is* with us; the God of Jacob *is* our refuge. Selah.

47

1 The Prophet exhorteth all people to the worship of the true and everlasting God, commending the mercy of God toward the posterity of Jacob. 9 And after prophesieth of the kingdom of Christ in the time of the Gospel.

To him that excelleth.
A Psalm *committed* to the sons of Korah.

1 All people ¹clap your hands; sing loud unto God with a joyful voice.

2 For the Lord *is* high, *and* terrible; a great King over all the earth.

3 He hath ¹subdued the people under us, and the nations under our feet.

4 He hath chosen ¹our inheritance for us: *even* the glory of Jacob whom he loved. Selah.

5 God is gone up with triumph, *even* the Lord with the ¹sound of the trumpet.

6 Sing praises to God, sing praises: sing praises unto our King, sing praises.

7 For God *is* the king of all the earth: sing praises *everyone* that hath ¹understanding.

8 God reigneth over the heathen: God sitteth upon his holy Throne.

9 The princes of the people are gathered unto the people of the God of Abraham: for the shields of the world *belong* to God: he ¹is greatly to be exalted.

48

1 A notable deliverance of Jerusalem from the hands of many kings is mentioned, for the which thanks are given to God, and the state of that city is praised, that hath God so presently at all times ready to defend them.   This Psalm seemeth to be made in the time of Ahaz, Jehoshaphat, Asa, or Hezekiah: for in their times chiefly was the city by foreign princes assaulted.

46:Title ¹ Which was either a musical instrument or a solemn tune, unto the which this Psalm was sung.

46:1 ¹ Or, protection.
² In all manner of troubles God showeth his speedy mercy and power in defending his.

46:2 ¹ That is, we will not be overcome with fear.

46:3 ¹ Though the afflictions rage never so much, yet the rivers of God's mercies bring sufficient comfort to his.

46:4 ¹ The river of Shiloah, which passed through Jerusalem: meaning, though the defense seem never so small, yet if God have appointed it, it is sufficient.

46:5 ¹ Always when need requireth.

46:6 ¹ Hebrew, *gave his voice.*

46:7 ¹ They are assured that God can and will defend his Church from all dangers and enemies.

46:8 ¹ To wit, how oft he hath destroyed his enemies, and delivered his people.

46:10 ¹ He warneth them that persecute the Church, to cease their

cruelty: for else they shall feel that God is too strong for them against whom they fight.

47:1 ¹ Here is figured Christ, unto whom all his should give willing obedience, and who would show himself terrible to the wicked.

47:3 ¹ He hath made the Jews, who were the keepers of the Law and Prophets, schoolmasters to the Gentiles, that they should with gladness obey them.

47:4 ¹ God hath chosen us above all other nations, to enjoy a most glorious inheritance.

47:5 ¹ He doth allude unto the trumpets, that were blown at solemn feasts: but he doth further signify the triumph of Christ and his glorious ascension into the heavens.

47:7 ¹ He requireth that understanding be joined with singing, lest the Name of God be profaned with vain crying.

47:9 ¹ He praiseth God's highness, for that he joineth the great princes of the world (whom he calleth shields) to the fellowship of his Church.

¹A song or Psalm committed to the sons of Korah.

1 Great *is* the Lord, and greatly to be praised in the ¹City of our God, *even* upon his holy Mountain.

2 Mount Zion, *lying* Northward, *is* fair in situation: it *is* the ¹joy of the whole earth, *and* the City of the great king.

3 In the palaces thereof God is known for a ¹refuge.

4 For lo, the kings were ¹gathered, *and* went together.

5 When they saw ¹it, they marveled: they were astonied, *and* suddenly driven back.

6 Fear came there upon them, *and* sorrow, as upon a woman in travail.

7 *As* with an East wind thou breakest the ships ¹of Tarshish, *so were they destroyed.*

8 As we have ¹heard, so have we seen in the City of the Lord of hosts, in the city of our God: God will establish it forever. Selah.

9 We wait for thy loving-kindness, O God, in the midst of thy Temple.

10 O God, according to thy Name, so is thy praise unto the ¹world's end: thy right hand is full of righteousness.

11 Let ¹mount Zion rejoice, *and* the daughters of Judah be glad, because of thy judgments.

12 ¹Compass about Zion, and go round about it, *and* tell the towers thereof.

13 Mark well the wall thereof: behold her towers, that ye may tell your posterity.

14 For this God *is* our God forever and ever, he shall be our guide unto the death.

49 *1 The holy Ghost calleth all men to the consideration of man's life, 7 showing them not to be most blessed that are most wealthy, and therefore not to be feared:*

but contrariwise he lifteth up our minds to consider how all things are ruled by God's providence: *14 Who as he judgeth these worldly misers to everlasting torments, 15 so doth he preserve his, and will reward them in the day of the resurrection, 1 Thess. 1:6.*

To him that excelleth.
A Psalm *committed* to the sons of Korah.

1 Hear ¹this all *ye* people: give ear, all ye that dwell in the world,

2 As well low as high, both rich and poor.

3 My mouth shall speak of wisdom, and the meditation of mine heart *is* of knowledge.

4 I will incline mine ear to a parable, *and* utter my grave matter upon the harp.

5 Wherefore should I ¹fear in the evil days, *when* iniquity shall compass me about, *as at* mine heels?

6 They trust in their ¹goods, and boast themselves in the multitude of their riches.

7 Yet a man can by no means redeem *his* brother: he cannot give his ransom to God,

8 (So ¹precious is the redemption of their souls, ²and the continuance forever)

9 That he may live still forever, *and* not see the grave.

10 For he seeth that wise men ¹die: *and* also that the ignorant and foolish perish, and leave their riches for ²others.

11 *Yet* they think their houses *and* their habitations *shall continue* forever, *even* from generation to generation, and ¹call *their* lands by their names.

12 But man shall not continue in honor; he is like the ¹beasts *that* die.

13 This their way *uttereth* their foolishness; *yet* their posterity ¹delight in their talk. Selah.

14 ¹Like sheep they lie in grave; ²death devoureth them; and the righteous shall have domination over

---

48:Title ¹ Some put this difference between a song and Psalm, saying that it is called a song, when there is no instrument, but the voice: and the Psalm, the contrary. The song of the Psalm is when the instruments begin, and the voice followeth. The Psalm of the song the contrary.

48:1 ¹ Albeit God shows his wonders through all the world, yet he will be chiefly praised in his Church.

48:2 ¹ Because the word of salvation came thence to all them that should believe.

48:3 ¹ Except God were the defense thereof, neither situation nor munition could prevail.

48:4 ¹ They conspired and went against God's people.

48:5 ¹ The enemies were afraid at the sight of the City.

48:7 ¹ That is, of Cilicia, or of the sea called Mediterranean.

48:8 ¹ To wit, of our fathers: so have we proved: or God hath performed his promise.

48:10 ¹ In all places where thy Name shall be heard of, men shall praise thee, when they hear of thy marvelous works.

48:11 ¹ Let Jerusalem and the cities of Judea rejoice, for thy just judgments against thine enemies.

48:12 ¹ For in this outward defense and strength God's blessings did

also appear: but the chief is to be referred to God's favor and secret defense, who never leaveth his.

49:1 ¹ He will entreat how God governeth the world by his providence, which cannot be perceived by the judgment of the flesh.

49:5 ¹ Though wickedness reign, and enemies rage, seeing God will execute his judgments against the wicked in time convenient.

49:6 ¹ To trust in riches is mere madness, seeing they can neither restore life, nor prolong it.

49:8 ¹ That is, so rare or not to be found, as prophecy was precious in the days of Eli, 1 Sam. 3:1.

² Meaning, it is impossible to live forever: also that life and death are only in God's hands.

49:10 ¹ In that that death maketh no difference between the persons.

² That is, not to their children, but to strangers. Yet the wicked profit not by these examples, but still dream an immortality in earth.

49:11 ¹ Or, labor that their name may be famous in earth.

49:12 ¹ As touching the death of the body.

49:13 ¹ They speak and do the same thing that their fathers did.

49:14 ¹ As sheep are gathered into the fold, so shall they be brought to the grave.

² Because they have no part of life everlasting.

them in the [3]morning; for their beauty shall consume, *when they shall go* from their house to grave.

15 But God shall deliver my soul from the power of the grave; [1]for he will receive me. Selah.

16 Be not thou afraid when one is made rich, *and* when the glory of his house is increased.

17 [a]For he shall take nothing away, when he dieth, neither shall his pomp descend after him.

18 For while he lived, [1]he rejoiced himself; and [2]men will praise thee, when thou makest much of thyself.

19 [1,2]He shall enter into the generation of his fathers, [3]*and* they shall not live forever.

20 Man *is* in honor; and [1]understandeth not; he is like to beasts *that* perish.

CHAPTER 49
[a] Job 27:19
1 Tim. 6:7

50

1 Because the Church is always full of hypocrites, 8 which do imagine that God will be worshipped with outward ceremonies only without the heart: and especially the Jews were of this opinion, because of their figures and ceremonies of the Law, thinking that their sacrifices were sufficient. 21 Therefore the Prophet doth reprove this gross error, and pronounceth the Name of God to be blasphemed where holiness is set in ceremonies. 23 For he declareth the worship of God to be spiritual, whereof are two principal parts, invocation and thanksgiving.

A Psalm of [1]Asaph.

1 The God of gods, *even* the Lord hath spoken and called the [1]earth from the rising up of the Sun, unto the going down thereof.

2 Out of Zion, *which is* the [1]perfection of beauty, hath God shined.

3 Our God shall come, and shall not keep silence: [1]a fire shall devour before him, and a mighty tempest shall be moved round about him.

4 He shall call the heaven above, and [1]the earth to judge his people.

5 Gather my [1]Saints together unto me, those that make a covenant with me with [2]sacrifice.

6 And the heavens shall declare his righteousness: for God is Judge himself. Selah.

7 Hear, O my people and I will speak: *hear*, O Israel, and I will testify unto thee: *for* I am God, *even* thy God.

8 I will not [1]reprove thee for thy sacrifices, or thy burnt offerings, *that have not been* continually before me.

9 I will take no bullock out of thine house, *nor* goats out of thy folds.

10 [1]For all the beasts of the forest are mine, *and* the beasts on a thousand mountains.

11 I know all the fowls on the mountains, and the wild beasts of the field are mine.

12 If I be hungry, I will not tell thee: for the world is mine and all that therein is.

13 [1]Will I eat the flesh of bulls? or drink the blood of goats?

14 Offer unto God praise, and [1]pay thy vows unto the most High,

15 And call upon me in the day of trouble: *so* will I deliver thee, and thou shalt glorify me.

16 But unto the wicked said God, [1]What hast thou to do to declare mine ordinances, that thou shouldest take my covenant in thy mouth,

17 Seeing thou hatest [1]to be reformed, and hast cast my words behind thee?

18 For when thou seest a thief, [1]thou runnest with him, and thou art partaker with the adulterers.

19 Thou givest thy mouth to evil, and with thy tongue thou forgest deceit.

20 Thou [1]sittest, *and* speakest against thy brother, *and* slanderest thy mother's son.

---

[3] Christ's coming is as the morning, when the elect shall reign with Christ their head over the wicked.
49:15 [1] Or, because he hath received me.
49:18 [1] Hebrew, *he blessed his soul.*
[2] The flatterers praise them that live in delight and pleasures.
49:19 [1] Or, his soul.
[2] And not pass the term appointed for life.
[3] Both they and their fathers shall live here but a while, and at length die forever.
49:20 [1] He condemneth man's ingratitude, who having received excellent gifts of God, abuseth them like a beast to his own condemnation.
50:Title [1] Who was either the author, or a chief singer, to whom it was committed.
50:1 [1] To plead against his dissembling people before heaven and earth.
50:2 [1] Because God had chosen it to have his Name there called upon, and also his image shined there, in the doctrine of the Law.
50:3 [1] As when God gave his Law in mount Sinai, he appeared terrible with thunder and tempest, so will he appear terrible to take account for the keeping thereof.
50:4 [1] As witnesses against the hypocrites.
50:5 [1] God in respect of his elect calleth the whole body holy, Saints, and his people.
[2] Which should know that Sacrifices are sealed of the covenant between God and his people, and not set religion therein.
50:8 [1] For I pass not for sacrifices, except the true use be there, which is to confirm your faith in my promises.
50:10 [1] Though he did delight in sacrifice, yet had he no need of man's help thereunto.
50:13 [1] Though man's life for the infirmity thereof hath need of food, yet God whose life quickeneth all the world, hath no need of such means.
50:14 [1] Show thyself mindful of God's benefits by thanksgiving.
50:16 [1] Why dost thou feign to be of my people, and talkest of my covenant, seeing thou art but an hypocrite?
50:17 [1] And to live according to my word.
50:18 [1] He showeth what are the fruits of them that contemn God's word.
50:20 [1] He noteth the cruelty of hypocrites, which spare not in their talk or judgment their own mother's sons.

21 These things hast thou done, and I held my tongue: *therefore* thou thoughtest that I was like thee: *but* I will reprove thee, and ¹set *them* in order before thee.

22 Oh consider this ye that forget God, lest I tear you in pieces, and there be none that can deliver *you*.

23 He that offereth ¹praise, shall glorify me: and to him that ²disposeth his way *aright*, will I ³show the salvation of God.

51

When David was rebuked by the Prophet Nathan for his great offenses, he did not only acknowledge the same to God, with protestation of his natural corruption and iniquity, but also left a memorial thereof to his posterity. 7 Therefore first he desireth God to forgive his sins, 10 And to renew in him his holy Spirit. 13 With promise that he will not be unmindful of those great graces. 18 Finally, fearing lest God would punish the whole Church for his fault, he requireth that he would rather increase his graces toward the same.

To him that excelleth. A Psalm of David, when the Prophet Nathan ¹came unto him, after he had gone in to Bathsheba.

1 Have mercy upon me, O God, ¹according to thy loving-kindness: according to the multitude of thy compassions put away mine iniquities.

2 Wash me ¹thoroughly from mine iniquity, and cleanse me from mine sin.

3 For I ¹know mine iniquities, and my sin *is* ever before me.

4 Against thee, against thee only have I sinned, and done evil in thy sight, that thou mayest be just when thou ¹speakest, *and* pure when thou judgest.

5 Behold, I was born in iniquity, and in sin hath my mother conceived me.

6 Behold, thou ¹lovest truth in the inward affections: therefore hast thou taught me wisdom in the secret *of* mine heart.

7 Purge me with ᵃhyssop, and I shall be clean:

wash me, and I shall be whiter than snow.

8 Make me to hear ¹joy and gladness, *that* the ²bones, *which* thou hast broken, may rejoice.

9 Hide thy face from my sins, and put away all mine iniquities.

10 ¹Create in me a clean heart, O God, and renew a right spirit within me.

11 Cast me not away from thy presence, and take not thine holy Spirit from me.

12 Restore to me the joy of thy salvation, and establish me with *thy* ¹free Spirit.

13 Then shall I teach thy ¹ways unto the wicked, and sinners shall be converted unto thee.

14 Deliver me from ¹blood, O God, *which art* the God of my salvation, *and* my tongue shall sing joyfully of thy righteousness.

15 ¹Open thou my lips, O Lord, and my mouth shall show forth thy praise.

16 For thou desirest no sacrifice, though I would give it: thou delightest not in burnt offering.

17 The sacrifices of God *are* a ¹contrite spirit: a contrite and a broken heart, O God, thou wilt not despise.

18 Be favorable unto ¹Zion for thy good pleasure: build the walls of Jerusalem.

19 Then shalt thou accept the sacrifices of ¹righteousness, *even* the burnt offering and oblation: then shall they offer calves upon thine altar.

52

1 David describeth the arrogant tyranny of his adversary Doeg: who by false surmises cause Ahimelech with the rest of the Priests to be slain. 5 David prophesieth his destruction, 6 and encourageth the faithful to put their confidence in God, whose judgments are most sharp against his adversaries. 9 And finally, he rendereth thanks to God for his deliverance. In this Psalm is timely set forth the kingdom of Antichrist.

50:21 ¹ I will write all thy wicked deeds in a roll, and make thee to read and acknowledge them, whither thou wilt or no.

50:23 ¹ Under the which is contained faith and invocation.

² As God hath appointed.

³ That is, declare myself to be his Savior.

51:Title ¹ To reprove him because he had committed so horrible sins, and lain in the same without repentance more than a whole year.

51:1 ¹ As his sins were manifold and great, so he requireth that God would give him the feeling of his excellent and abundant mercies.

51:2 ¹ My sins strike so fast in me, that I have need of some singular kind of washing.

51:3 ¹ My conscience accuseth me so, that I can have no rest till I be reconciled.

51:4 ¹ When thou givest sentence against sinners, they must needs confess thee to be just, and themselves sinners.

51:6 ¹ He confesseth that God who loveth pureness of heart, may justly destroy man, who of nature is a sinner much more him, whom he had instructed in his heavenly wisdom.

51:8 ¹ He meaneth God's comfortable mercies toward repentant sinners.

² By the bones he understandeth all strength of soul and body, which by cares and mourning are consumed.

51:10 ¹ He confesseth that when God's Spirit is cold in us, to have it again revived, is as a new creation.

51:12 ¹ Which may assure me that I am drawn out of the slavery of sin.

51:13 ¹ He promiseth to endeavor that others by his example may turn to God.

51:14 ¹ From the murder of Uriah, and the others that were slain with him, 2 Sam. 11:17.

51:15 ¹ By giving me occasion to praise thee, when thou shalt forgive my sins.

51:17 ¹ Which is a wounding of the heart, proceeding of faith, which seeketh unto God for mercy.

51:18 ¹ He prayeth for the whole Church, because through his sin it was in danger of God's judgment.

51:19 ¹ That is, just and lawful, applied to the right end, which is the exercise of faith and repentance.

To him that excelleth. *A Psalm* of David to give instruction. When Doeg the Edomite came and showed Saul, and said to him, David is come to the house of Ahimelech.

1 Why boastest thou thyself in *thy* wickedness, O [1]man of power? the loving-kindness of God *endureth* daily.

2 Thy tongue imagineth [1]mischief, *and is* like a sharp razor, that cutteth deceitfully.

3 Thou dost love evil more than good, *and* lies more than to speak the [1]truth. Selah.

4 Thou lovest all words that may destroy: O deceitful tongue!

5 So shall God [1]destroy thee forever: he shall take thee and pluck thee out of *thy* tabernacle, and [2]root thee out of the land of the living. Selah.

6 The [1]righteous also shall see it, [2]*and* fear, and shall laugh at him, *saying*,

7 Behold the man that took not God for his strength, but trusteth unto the multitude of his riches, *and* put his strength [1]in his malice.

8 But I shall be like a [1]green olive tree in the house of God: *for* I trusted in the mercy of God forever and ever.

9 I will always praise thee, for that thou hast done [1]*this*, and I will [2]hope in thy name, because it is good before thy Saints.

53 *1 He describeth the crooked nature.   4 The cruelty,   5 And punishment of the wicked, when they look not for it,   6 And desireth the deliverance of the godly, that they may rejoice together.*

To him that excelleth on [1]Mahalath.
A Psalm of David to give instruction.

1 The fool hath said in his heart, *There is* [1]no God, they have corrupted and done abominable wickedness, *there is* none that doeth good.

2 God looked down from heaven upon the children of men, to see if there were any that would

CHAPTER 53
a Rom. 3:10

CHAPTER 54
a 1 Sam. 13:19

understand and [1]seek God.

3 [a]Everyone is gone back: they are altogether corrupt: there is none that doeth good, no not one.

4 Do not the [1]workers of iniquity know that they eat up my people *as* they eat bread? they call not upon God.

5 There they were afraid for fear, *where* no [1]fear was: for God hath scattered the [2]bones of him that besieged thee: thou hast put them to confusion, because God hath cast them off.

6 Oh give salvation unto Israel out of Zion: when God turneth the captivity of his people, *then* Jacob shall rejoice, and Israel shall be glad.

54 *1 David brought into great danger by reason of the Ziphites,   5 Calleth upon the Name of God to destroy his enemies,   6 Promising sacrifices and free offerings for so great deliverance.*

To him that excelleth on Neginoth.
A Psalm of David, to give instruction. When the Ziphims came and said unto Saul, [a]'Is not David hid among us?'

1 Save me, O God, [1]by thy Name, and by thy power judge me.

2 O God, hear my prayer: hearken unto the words of my mouth.

3 For [1]strangers are risen up against me, and [2]tyrants seek my soul: they have not set God before them. Selah.

4 Behold, God *is* mine helper: the Lord *is* with [1]them that uphold my soul.

5 He shall reward evil unto mine enemies: Oh cut them off in thy [1]truth!

6 [1]*Then* I will sacrifice [1]freely unto thee: I will praise thy Name, O Lord, because it is good.

7 For he hath delivered me out of all trouble, and mine eye hath [1]seen *my desire* upon mine enemies.

52:1 [1] O Doeg, which hast credit with the tyrant Saul, and hast power to murder the Saints of God.

52:2 [1] Thy malice moveth thee by crafty flatteries and lies to accuse and destroy the innocents.

52:3 [1] Hebrew, *righteousness*.

52:5 [1] Though God forbear for a time, yet at length he will recompense thy falsehood.

[2] Albeit thou seem to be never so sure settled.

52:6 [1] For the eyes of the reprobate are shut up at God's judgments.

[2] With joyful reverence, seeing that he taketh their part against the wicked.

52:7 [1] Or, in his substance.

52:8 [1] He rejoiceth to have a place among the servants of God, that he may grow in the knowledge of godliness.

52:9 [1] Executed his vengeance.

[2] Or, wait upon thy grace and promise.

53:Title [1] Which was an instrument or kind of note.

53:1 [1] Whereas no regard is had of honesty or dishonesty, of virtue nor of vice, there the Prophet pronounceth that the people have no God.

53:2 [1] Whereby he condemneth all knowledge and understanding, that tendeth not to seek God.

53:4 [1] David pronounceth God's vengeance against cruel governors, who having charge to defend and preserve God's people, do most cruelly devour them.

53:5 [1] When they thought there was none occasion to fear, the sudden vengeance of God lighted upon them.

[2] Be the enemy's power never so great, nor the danger so fearful, yet God delivereth his in due time.

54:1 [1] He declareth that when all means do fail, God will deliver even as it were by miracle, them that call unto him with an upright conscience.

54:3 [1] To wit, the Ziphims.

[2] Saul and his army, which were like cruel beasts, and could not be satisfied but by his death.

54:4 [1] Be they never so few, as he was with Jonathan.

54:5 [1] According to thy faithful promise for my defense.

54:6 [1] For hypocrites serve God for fear or upon conditions.

54:7 [1] We may lawfully rejoice for God's judgments against the wicked, if our affections be pure.

55

1 David being in great heaviness and distress, complaineth of the cruelty of Saul,   13 and of the falsehood of his familiar acquaintance,   17 Uttering the most ardent affections to move the Lord to pity him.   22 After, being assured of deliverance, he setteth forth the grace of God, as though he had already obtained his request.

To him that excelleth on Neginoth.
A Psalm of David to give instruction.

1 Hear ¹my prayer, O God, and hide not thyself from my supplication.

2 Hearken unto me, and answer me: I mourn in my prayer, and make a noise,

3 For the ¹voice of the enemy, *and* for the vexation of the wicked, because ²they have brought iniquity upon me, and furiously hate me.

4 Mine heart trembleth within me, and the terrors of death are fallen upon me.

5 Fear and trembling are come upon me, and an horrible fear hath ¹covered me.

6 And I said, Oh that I had wings like a dove: then would I ¹fly away and rest.

7 Behold I would take my flight far off, *and* lodge in the wilderness. Selah.

8 He would make haste for my deliverance ¹from the stormy wind and tempest.

9 Destroy, O Lord, *and* ¹divide their tongues: for I have seen cruelty and strife in the city.

10 Day and night they go about it upon the walls thereof, both ¹iniquity and mischief *are* in the midst of it.

11 Wickedness *is* in the midst thereof: deceit and guile depart not from her streets.

12 Surely mine ¹enemy did not defame me, for I could have borne it: neither did mine adversary exalt himself against me: for I would have hid me from him.

13 But *it was* thou, O man, even my ¹companion, my guide, and my familiar:

14 Which delighted in consulting together, *and* went into the house of God as companions.

15 Let death seize upon them: let them ¹go down quick into the grave: for wickedness *is* in their dwellings *even* in the midst of them.

16 *But* I will call unto God, and the Lord will save me.

17 Evening and morning, and at noon will I pray ¹and make a noise, and he will hear my voice.

18 He hath delivered my soul in peace from the battle *that was* against me: for ¹many were with me.

19 God shall hear and afflict them, even he that reigneth of old, Selah: because they ¹have no changes, therefore they fear not God.

20 He ¹laid his hand upon such as be at peace with him, *and* he brake his covenant.

21 *The* words of his mouth were softer than butter, yet war *was* in his heart, his words were more gentle than oil, yet they were swords.

22 Cast thy ¹burden upon the Lord, and he shall nourish thee: he will not suffer the righteous to fall ²forever.

23 And thou, O God, shalt bring them down into the pit of corruption: the bloody, and deceitful men shall not live ¹half their days: but I will trust in thee.

56

1 David being brought to Achish the king of Gath, 1 Sam. 21:12, complaineth of his enemies, demandeth succor,   3 Putteth his trust in God and in his promises,   12 And promiseth to perform his vows which he had taken upon him, whereof this was the effect, to praise God in his Church.

To him that excelleth. A Psalm of David on Michtam,
concerning the ¹dumb dove in a far country, when the
Philistines took him in Gath.

1 Be merciful unto me, O God, for ¹man would swallow me up: he fighteth continually *and* vexeth me.

55:1 ¹ The earnestness of his prayer declareth the vehemency of his grief insomuch as he is compelled to burst out into cries.
55:3 ¹ For the threatnings of Saul and his adherents.
² They have defamed me as a wicked person, or they have imagined my destruction.
55:5 ¹ There was no part of him, that was not astonished with extreme fear.
55:6 ¹ Fear had driven him to so great distress, that he wished to be hid in some wilderness, and to be banished from that kingdom which God had promised that he should enjoy.
55:8 ¹ From the cruel rage and tyranny of Saul.
55:9 ¹ As in the confusion of Babylon when the wicked conspired against God.
55:10 ¹ All laws and good orders are broken, and only vice and dissolation reigneth under Saul.
55:12 ¹ If mine open enemy had sought mine hurt, I could the better have avoided him.
55:13 ¹ Which was not only joined to me in friendship and counsel

in worldly matters, but also in religion.
55:15 ¹ As Korah, Dathan and Abiram.
55:17 ¹ Which signifieth a fervent mind and sure trust to obtain his portion, which thing made him earnest at all times in prayer.
55:18 ¹ Even the Angels of God fought on my side against mine enemies, 2 Kings 6:16.
55:19 ¹ But their prosperous estate still continueth.
55:20 ¹ I did not provoke him, but was as at peace with him, yet he made war against me.
55:22 ¹ Or, gift, to wit, which thou wouldest that God should give thee.
² Though for their bettering and trial, he suffer them to slip for a time.
55:23 ¹ Though they sometimes live longer, yet their life is cursed of God, unquiet, and worse than any death.
56:Title ¹ Being chased by the fury of his enemies into a strange country, he was a dumb dove not seeking revengeance.
56:1 ¹ He showeth that it is either now time or never, that God help him, for all the world is against him and ready to devour him.

2 Mine enemies would daily swallow me up: for many fight against me, O thou most High.

3 When I was afraid, I trusted in thee.

4 I will rejoice in God, *because* of his ¹word, I trust in God, *and* will not fear what flesh can do unto me.

5 Mine own ¹words grieve *me* daily: all their thoughts *are* against me to do me hurt.

6 ¹They gather together, and keep themselves close: they mark my steps, because they wait for my soul.

7 ¹They *think* they shall escape by iniquity: O God, cast *these* people down in *thine* anger.

8 Thou hast counted my wanderings; put my ¹tears into thy bottle; are they not in thy register?

9 When I cry, then mine enemies shall turn back; this I know, for God is with me.

10 I will rejoice in God *because of his* word; in the Lord will I rejoice *because of his* word.

11 In God do I trust; I will not be afraid what man can do unto me.

12 ¹Thy vows *are* upon me, O God, I will render praises unto thee.

13 For thou hast delivered my soul from death, and also my feet from falling, that I may ¹walk before God in the ²light of the living.

57 1 *David being in the desert of Ziph, where the inhabitants did betray him, and at length in the same cave with Saul,* 2 *Calleth most earnestly unto God, with full confidence that he will perform his promise, and take his cause in hand.* 5 *Also that he will show his glory in the heavens and the earth against his cruel enemies.* 9 *Therefore doth he render laud and praise.*

To him that excelleth. ¹Destroy not. *A Psalm* of David on
Michtam. ᵃWhen he fled from Saul in the cave.

1 Have mercy upon me, O God, have mercy upon me; for my soul trusteth in thee, and in the shadow of thy wings will I ¹trust, till *these* ²afflictions overpass.

CHAPTER 57
ᵃ 1 Sam. 24:4

2 I will call unto the most high God, *even* the God, that ¹performeth *his promise* toward me.

3 He will send from ¹heaven, and save me from the reproof of him that would swallow me. Selah. God will send his mercy, and his truth.

4 My soul *is* among lions; I lie *among* the children of men, that are set on fire; whose teeth *are* ¹spears and arrows, and their tongue a sharp sword.

5 ¹Exalt thyself, O God, above the heaven, *and* let thy glory *be* upon all the earth.

6 They have laid a net for my steps; ¹my soul is pressed down, they have dug a pit before me, *and* are fallen into the midst of it. Selah.

7 Mine heart is ¹prepared, O God, mine heart is prepared; I will sing and give praise.

8 ¹Awake my tongue, awake viol and harp: I will awake early.

9 I will praise thee, O Lord, among the people, *and* I will sing unto thee among the nations.

10 For thy mercy is great unto the heavens, *and* thy truth unto the ¹clouds.

11 Exalt thyself, O God, above the heavens, *and* let thy glory *be* upon all the earth.

58 1 *He describeth the malice of his enemies, the flatterers of Saul, who both secretly and openly sought his destruction, from whom he appealeth to God's judgment,* 10 *Showing that the just shall rejoice, when they see the punishment of the wicked to the glory of God.*

To him that excelleth. Destroy not.
A Psalm of David on Michtam.

1 Is it true? O ¹congregation, speak ye justly? O sons of men judge ye uprightly?

2 Yea, rather ye imagine mischief in *your* heart: ¹your hands execute cruelty upon the earth.

3 The wicked ¹are strangers from the womb: *even* from the belly have they erred, and speak lies.

56:4 ¹ He stayeth his conscience upon God's promise, though he see not present help.
56:5 ¹ All my counsels have evil success, and turn to mine own sorrow.
56:6 ¹ As all the world against one man, and cannot be satiate, except they have my life.
56:7 ¹ They think not only to escape punishment, but the more wicked they are, the more impudent they wax.
56:8 ¹ If God keep the tears of his Saints in store, much more will he remember their blood, to avenge it: and though tyrants burn the bones, yet can they not blot the tears and blood out of God's register.
56:12 ¹ Having received that which I required, I am bound to pay my vows of thanksgiving, as I promised.
56:13 ¹ As mindful of his great mercies, and giving him thanks for the same.
² That is, in this life and light of the sun.
57:Title ¹ This was either the beginning of a certain song, or the words which David uttered when he stayed his affection.
57:1 ¹ Or, dwell most safely.

² He compareth the afflictions which God layeth upon his children, to a storm that cometh and goeth.
57:2 ¹ Who leaveth not his works begun imperfect.
57:3 ¹ He would rather deliver me by a miracle, than that I should be overcome.
57:4 ¹ He meaneth their calumnies and false reports.
57:5 ¹ Suffer me not to be destroyed to the contempt of thy Name.
57:6 ¹ For very fear seeing the great dangers on all sides.
57:7 ¹ That is, wholly bent to give thee praise for my deliverance.
57:8 ¹ He showeth that both his heart shall praise God, and his tongue shall confess him, and also he will use other means to provoke himself forward to the same.
57:10 ¹ Thy mercies do not only appertain to the Jews, but also to the Gentiles.
58:1 ¹ Ye counselors of Saul, who under pretence of consulting for the common wealth, conspire my death being an innocent.
58:2 ¹ Ye are not ashamed to execute that cruelty publicly, which ye have imagined in your hearts.
58:3 ¹ That is, enemies to the people of God even from their birth.

4   Their poison is even like the poison of a serpent; like the deaf [1]adder *that* stoppeth his ear.

5   Which heareth not the voice of the enchanter, though he be most expert in charming.

6   Break their [1]teeth, O God, in their mouths: break the jaws of the young lions, O Lord.

7   Let them [1]melt like the waters, let them pass away; when he shooteth his arrows, *let them be* as broken.

8   Let them consume like a snail that melteth, *and like* the untimely fruit of a woman, *that* hath not seen the sun.

9   [1]As raw flesh before your pots feel *the fire* of thorns: *so* let them carry them away as with a whirlwind in *his* wrath.

10   The righteous shall [1]rejoice when he seeth the vengeance; he shall wash his feet in the [2]blood of the wicked.

11   And men shall say, [1]Verily there is fruit for the righteous; doubtless there is a God that judgeth in the earth.

59 *1 David being in great danger of Saul, who sent to slay him in his bed, prayeth unto God,   3 Declaring his innocency, and their fury,   5 Desiring God to destroy all those that sin of malicious wickedness.   11 Whom though he keep alive for a time to exercise his people, yet in the end he will consume them in his wrath,   13 That he may be known to be the God of Jacob to the end of the world.   16 For this he singeth praises to God assured of his mercies.*

To him that excelleth. Destroy not.
A Psalm of David, on [1]Michtam. [a]*When Saul sent and they did watch the house to kill him.*

1   O my God, [1]deliver me from mine enemies; defend me from them that rise up against me.

2   Deliver me from the wicked doers, and save me from the bloody men.

3   For lo, they have laid wait for my soul; the

mighty men are gathered against me, not for mine [1]offense, nor for my sin, O Lord.

4   They run and prepare themselves without a fault *on my part*: arise *therefore* to assist me, and behold.

5   Even thou, O Lord God of hosts, O God of Israel, awake to visit all the heathen, *and* be not [1]merciful unto all that transgress maliciously. Selah.

6   They go to and fro in the evening: they bark like [1]dogs, and go about the city.

7   Behold, they [1]brag in their talk, *and* swords *are* in their lips: for who, *say they*, doth hear?

8   But thou, O Lord, shalt have them in derision, *and* thou shalt laugh at all the heathen.

9   [1]He is strong: *but* I will wait upon thee: for God *is* my defense.

10   My merciful God will [1]prevent me: God will let me see *my desire* upon mine enemies.

11   Slay them [1]not, lest my people forget it: *but* scatter them abroad by thy power, and put them down, O Lord, our shield,

12   *For* the sin of their mouth, *and* the words of their lips: and let them be [1]taken in their pride, even for their perjury and lies, *that* they speak.

13   [1]Consume *them* in *thy* wrath: consume *them* that they be no more: and let them know that God ruleth in Jacob, *even* unto the ends of the world. Selah.

14   And in the evening they [1]shall go to and fro, *and* bark like dogs, and go about the city.

15   They shall run here and there for meat, *and* surely they shall not be satisfied, though they tarry all night.

16   But I will sing of thy [1]power, and will praise thy mercy in the morning: for thou hast been my defense and refuge in the day of my trouble.

17   Unto thee, O my [1]Strength will I sing: for God is my defense, *and* my merciful God.

58:4 [1] They pass in malice and subtlety the crafty serpent which could preserve himself by stopping his ear from the enchanter.
58:6 [1] Take away all occasions and means whereby they hurt.
58:7 [1] Considering God's divine power, he showeth that God in a moment can destroy their force whereof they brag.
58:9 [1] As flesh is taken raw out of the pot before the water seethe: so he desireth God to destroy their enterprises before they bring them to pass.
58:10 [1] With a pure affection.
   [2] Their punishment and slaughter shall be so great.
58:11 [1] Seeing God governeth all by his providence, he must needs put difference between the godly and the wicked.
59:Title [1] Read Ps. 16.
59:1 [1] Though his enemies were even at hand to destroy him, yet he assureth himself that God had ways now in hand to deliver him.
59:3 [1] For I am innocent to themwards, and have not offended them.
59:5 [1] Seeing it appertaineth to God's judgments to punish the wicked, he desireth God to execute his vengeance on the reprobate, who maliciously persecute his Church.

59:6 [1] He compareth their cruelty to hungry dogs, showing that they are never weary in doing evil.
59:7 [1] They boast openly in their wicked devices, and every word is as a sword: for they neither fear God nor are ashamed of men.
59:9 [1] Though Saul have never so great power, yet I know that thou dost bridle him: therefore will I patiently hope on thee.
59:10 [1] He will not fail to succor me when need requireth.
59:11 [1] Altogether, but by little and little, that the people seeing oftentimes thy judgments, may be mindful of thee.
59:12 [1] That in their misery and shame they may be as glasses and examples of God's vengeance.
59:13 [1] When thy time shall come, and when they have sufficiently served for an example of thy vengeance unto others.
59:14 [1] He mocketh at their vain enterprises, being assured that they shall not bring their purpose to pass.
59:16 [1] Which didst use the policy of a weak woman to confound the enemy's strength, as 1 Sam. 19:12.
59:17 [1] Confessing himself to be void of all virtue and strength, he attributeth the whole to God.

60

1 *David being now king over Judah, and having had many victories, showeth by evident signs that God elected him King, assuring the people that God will prosper them, if they approve the same.* 14 *After, he prayeth unto God to finish that that he hath begun.*

CHAPTER 60
ª 2 Sam. 8:1
2 Sam. 10:1
1 Chron. 18:13

CHAPTER 62
ª 1 Chron. 16:41

To him that excelleth upon ¹Shushan Eduth, *or* Michtam. *A Psalm* of David to teach. ªWhen he fought against ²Aram Naharaim, and against Aram ³Zobah, when Joab returned and slew twelve thousand Edomites in the salt valley.

1   O God, thou hast cast us out, thou hast ¹scattered us, thou hast been angry, turn again unto us.

2   Thou hast made the land to tremble, and hast made it to ¹gape: heal the breaches thereof, for it is shaken.

3   Thou hast ¹showed thy people heavy things: thou hast made us to drink the wine of giddiness.

4   *But now* thou hast given ¹a banner to them that fear thee, that it may be displayed because of *thy* truth. Selah.

5   That thy beloved may be delivered, help with thy right hand and hear me.

6   God hath spoken in his ¹holiness: *therefore* I will rejoice: I shall divide Shechem, and measure the valley of Succoth.

7   Gilead *shall be* mine, and Manasseh *shall be* mine: Ephraim also *shall be* the ¹strength of mine head: ²Judah *is* my lawgiver.

8   Moab *shall be* my ¹washpot: over Edom will I cast out my shoe: ²Philistia show thyself joyful for me.

9   Who will lead me into the ¹strong city? who will bring me unto Edom?

10   Wilt not thou, O God, *which* hadst cast us off, and didst not go forth, O God, with our armies?

11   Give us help against trouble: for vain is the help of man.

12   Through God we shall do valiantly; for he shall tread down our enemies.

61

1 *Whether that he were in danger of the Ammonites, or being pursued of Absalom, here he crieth to be heard and delivered,* 7 *And confirmed in his kingdom.* 8 *He promiseth perpetual praises.*

To him that excelleth on Neginoth. A Psalm of David.

1   Hear my cry, O God: give ear unto my prayer.

2   From ¹the ends of the earth will I cry unto thee: when mine heart is oppressed, bring me upon the rock that is ²higher than I.

3   For thou hast been my hope, *and* a strong tower against the enemy.

4   I will dwell in thy Tabernacle forever, *and* my trust shall be under the covering of thy wings. Selah.

5   For thou, O God, ¹hast heard my desires; thou hast given an heritage unto those that fear thy Name.

6   Thou shalt give the King a ¹long life; his years *shall be* as many ages.

7   He shall dwell before God forever; prepare ¹mercy and faithfulness, *that* they may preserve him.

8   So will I always sing praise unto thy Name, in performing daily my vows.

62

This Psalm partly containeth meditation, whereby David encourageth himself to trust in God against the assaults of temptations.   And because our minds are easily drawn from God by the allurements of the world, he sharply reproveth this vanity, to the intent he might cleave fast to the Lord.

To the excellent *Musician* ªJeduthun. A Psalm of David.

1   Yet ¹my soul keepeth silence unto God; of him *cometh* my salvation.

2   ¹Yet he is my strength and my salvation, *and* my defense; *therefore* I shall not much be moved.

3   How long will ye imagine mischief against a ¹man? ye shall be all slain; *ye shall be* as a bowed wall, *or* as a ²wall shaken.

4   Yet they consult to cast him down from his

60:Title ¹ These were certain songs after the note whereof this Psalm was sung.

   ² Or, Syria, called Mesopotamia.

   ³ Called also Sophene, which standeth by Euphrates.

60:1 ¹ For when Saul was not able to resist the enemy, the people fled hither and thither: for they could not be safe in their own houses.

60:2 ¹ As cleft with an earthquake.

60:3 ¹ Thou hast handled thy people sharply, in taking from them sense and judgment, in that they aided Saul the wicked King, and pursued him to whom God had given the just title of the realm.

60:4 ¹ In making me king, thou hast performed thy promise, which seemed to have lost the force.

60:6 ¹ It is so certain as if it were spoken by an oracle, that I shall possess those places which Saul hath left to his children.

60:7 ¹ For it was strong and well peopled.

   ² David meaneth, that in this tribe his kingdom shall be established, Gen. 49:10.

60:8 ¹ In most vile subjection.

   ² For thou wilt dissemble, and feign as though thou werest glad.

60:9 ¹ He was assured that God would give him the strong cities of his enemies, wherein they thought themselves sure.

61:2 ¹ From the place where I was banished, being driven out of the city and Temple by my son Absalom.

   ² Unto the which without thy help I cannot attain.

61:5 ¹ There is nothing that doth more strengthen our faith, than the remembrance of God's succor in times past.

61:6 ¹ This chiefly is referred to Christ, who liveth eternally not only in himself, but also in his members.

61:7 ¹ For the stability of my kingdom standeth in thy mercy and truth.

62:1 ¹ Though Satan tempted him to murmur against God, yet he bridled his affections, and resting upon God's promise.

62:2 ¹ It appeareth by the oft repetition of this word, that the Prophet abode manifold tentations, but by resting on God, and by patience he overcame them all.

62:3 ¹ He meaneth himself, being the man whom God had appointed to the kingdom.

   ² Though, ye seem to be in honor, yet God will suddenly destroy you.

dignity; their delight is in lies: they bless with their mouths, but curse with their hearts. Selah.

5 [1]Yet my soul, keep thou silence unto God: for mine hope *is* in him.

6 Yet is he my strength and my salvation, *and* my defense: *therefore* I shall not be moved.

7 In God *is* my salvation and my [1]glory, the rock of my strength; in God is my trust.

8 Trust in him always, ye people; [1]pour out your hearts before him, *for God is* our hope. Selah.

9 Yet the children of men *are* vanity, the chief men *are* liars: to lay them upon a balance they are altogether lighter than vanity.

10 Trust not in oppression nor in robbery: [1]be not vain: if riches increase, set not your heart thereon.

11 God spake [1]once or twice, I have heard it, that power *belongeth* unto God,

12 And to thee, O Lord, mercy: for thou [1]rewardest everyone according to his work.

63 [1] *David after he had been in great danger by Saul in the desert of Ziph, made this Psalm.   3 Wherein he giveth thanks to God for his wonderful deliverance, in whose mercies he trusted, even in the midst of his miseries.   9 Prophesying the destruction of God's enemies: 11 And contrariwise happiness to all them that trust in the Lord.*

A Psalm of David, when he was in the [1]wilderness of Judah.

1 O God, thou art my God, early will I seek thee: my soul [1]thirsteth for thee: my flesh longeth greatly after thee in a barren and dry land without water:

2 Thus [1]I behold thee *as* in the Sanctuary, when I behold thy power and thy glory.

3 For thy loving-kindness *is* better than life: *therefore* my lips shall praise thee.

4 Thus will I magnify thee *all* my life, *and* lift up mine hands in thy Name.

5 My soul shall be satisfied, as with [1]marrow and fat-

ness, and my mouth shall praise *thee* with joyful lips,

6 When I remember thee on my bed, *and when* I think upon thee in the *night* watches.

7 Because thou hast been mine helper, therefore under the shadow of thy wings will I rejoice.

8 My soul [1]cleaveth unto thee: *for* thy right hand upholdeth me.

9 Therefore they that seek my soul to destroy it, they shall go into the lowest parts of the earth.

10 [1]They shall cast him down with the edge of the sword, *and* they shall be a portion for foxes.

11 But the king shall rejoice in God, *and* all that [1]swear by him shall rejoice *in him*: for the mouth of them that speak lies, shall be stopped.

64 [1] *David prayeth against the fury and false reports of his enemies.   7 He declareth their punishment and destruction.   10 To the comfort of the just and the glory of God.*

To him that excelleth. A Psalm of David.

1 Hear my [1]voice, O God, in my prayer: preserve my life from fear of the enemy.

2 Hide me from the [1]conspiracy of the wicked, *and* from the [2]rage of the works of iniquity.

3 Which have whet their tongue like a sword, and shot *for* their arrows [1]bitter words:

4 To shoot at the upright in secret: they shoot at him suddenly and [1]fear not.

5 They [1]encourage themselves *in* a wicked purpose: they commune together to lay snares privily, *and* say, Who shall see them?

6 They have sought out iniquities, *and* have accomplished that which they sought out, even everyone [1]*his* secret *thoughts*, and the depth of his heart.

7 But God will shoot an arrow at them suddenly: their strokes shall be *at once.*

8 They shall cause their own tongue to fall upon

62:5 [1] David was greatly moved with these troubles, therefore he stirreth up himself to trust in God.

62:7 [1] These vehement and often repetitions were necessary to strengthen his faith against the horrible assault of Satan.

62:8 [1] He admonisheth us of our wicked nature, which rather hide our sorrow and bite on the bridle, than utter our grief to God to obtain remedy.

62:10 [1] Give yourselves wholly to God by putting away all things that are contrary to his Law.

62:11 [1] He hath plainly borne witness of his power, so that none needeth to doubt thereof.

62:12 [1] So that the wicked shall feel thy power, and the godly thy mercy.

63:Title [1] To wit, of Ziph, 1 Sam. 23:14.

63:1 [1] Though he was both hungry and in great distress, yet he made God his sufficiency and above all meat and drink.

63:2 [1] In this misery I exercise myself in the contemplation of thy power and glory, as if I were in the Sanctuary.

63:5 [1] The remembrance of thy favor is more sweet unto me than all

the pleasures and dainties of the world.

63:8 [1] He assureth himself by the Spirit of God to have the gift of constancy.

63:10 [1] He prophecieth of the destruction of Saul and them that take his part, whose bodies shall not be buried, but be devoured with wild beasts.

63:11 [1] All that swear by God aright or profess him, shall rejoice in this worthy king.

64:1 [1] In that he calleth to God with his voice, it is a sign that his prayer was vehement, and that his life was in a danger.

64:2 [1] That is, from their secret malice.
[2] To wit, their outward violence.

64:3 [1] False reports and slanders.

64:4 [1] To be without fear of God, and reverence of man, is a sign of reprobation.

64:5 [1] The more that the wicked see God's children in misery, the more bold and impudent are they in oppressing them.

64:6 [1] There is no way so secret and subtle to do hurt, which they invented not for his destruction.

them: *and* whosoever shall see them, shall [1]flee away.

9 And all men shall see it, and declare the work of God, and they shall understand, what he hath wrought.

10 *But* the righteous [1]shall be glad in the Lord, and trust in him: and all that are upright of heart, shall rejoice.

65 1 *A praise and thanksgiving unto God by the faithful, who are signified by Zion,*   4 *For the choosing, preservation, and governance of them,*   9 *And for the plentiful blessings poured forth upon all the earth, but especially toward his Church.*

To him that excelleth. A Psalm *or* song of David.

1 O God, [1]praise waiteth for thee in Zion, and unto thee shall the vow be performed.

2 *Because thou* hearest the prayer, unto thee shall all [1]flesh come.

3 Wicked deeds [1]have prevailed against me: *but* thou wilt be merciful unto our transgressions.

4 Blessed *is he, whom* thou choosest and causest to come *to thee*: he shall dwell in thy courts, *and* we shall be satisfied with the pleasures of thine House, *even* of thine holy Temple.

5 O God of our salvation, thou wilt [1]answer us with fearful *signs* in *thy* righteousness, O *thou* the hope of all the ends of the earth, and of them that are far off in the [2]Sea.

6 He establisheth the mountains by his power: *and* is girded about with strength.

7 He appeaseth the [1]noise of the seas, *and* the noise of the waves thereof, and the tumults of the people.

8 They also that dwell in the uttermost parts *of the earth,* shall be afraid of thy signs; thou shalt make [1]the East and the West to rejoice.

9 Thou [1]visitest the earth, and waterest it; thou makest it very rich: the [2]river of God is full of water,

thou preparest them corn; for so thou appointest [3]it.

10 Thou [1]waterest abundantly the furrows thereof; thou causest *the rain* to descend into the valleys thereof; thou makest it soft with showers, *and* blessest the bud thereof.

11 Thou crownest the year with thy goodness, and thy steps drop fatness.

12 They drop *upon* the pastures of the wilderness: and the hills shall be compassed with gladness.

13 The pastures are clad with sheep; the valleys also shall be covered with corn; *therefore* they shout for joy, [1]and sing.

66 1 *He provoketh all men to praise the Lord and to consider his works.*   6 *He setteth forth the power of God to affray the rebels.*   10 *And showeth how God hath delivered Israel from great bondage and afflictions.*   13 *He promiseth to give sacrifice,*   16 *And provoketh all men to hear what God hath done for him, and to praise his Name.*

To him that excelleth. A song *or* Psalm.

1 Rejoice in God, [1]all ye *inhabitants* of the earth.

2 Sing forth the glory of his Name: make his praise glorious.

3 Say unto God, How terrible art thou *in* thy works! through the greatness of thy power shall thine enemies be [1]in subjection unto thee.

4 All the world shall worship thee, and sing unto thee, *even* sing of thy Name. Selah.

5 [1]Come and behold the works of God: he is terrible in *his* doings toward [2]the sons of men.

6 He hath turned the sea into dry land: they passed through the river on foot: there did we rejoice in him.

7 He ruleth the world with his power: his eyes behold the nations: the rebellious shall not [1]exalt themselves. Selah.

8 Praise our God, ye people, and make the voice of his praise to be heard.

64:8 [1] To see God's heavy judgments against them, and how he hath caught them in their own snares.

64:10 [1] When they shall consider that he will be favorable to them as he was to his servant David.

65:1 [1] Thou givest daily new occasion to thy Church to praise thee.

65:2 [1] Not only the Jews but also the Gentiles in the kingdom of Christ.

65:3 [1] He imputeth it to his sins and to the sins of the people, that God who was accustomed to assist them withdraweth his succor from them.

65:5 [1] Thou wilt declare thyself to be the preserver of thy Church in destroying thine enemies, as thou didst in the red Sea.

[2] As of all barbarous nations and far off.

65:7 [1] He showeth that there is no part nor creature in the world which is not governed by God's power and providence.

65:8 [1] Hebrew, *the going forth of the morning and of the evening.*

65:9 [1] To wit, with rain.

[2] That is, Shiloh or the rain.

[3] Thou hast appointed the earth to bring forth food to man's use.

65:10 [1] By this description he showeth that all the order of nature is a testimony of God's love toward us, who causeth all creatures to serve our necessity.

65:13 [1] That is, the dumb creatures shall not only rejoice for a time for God's benefits, but shall continually sing.

66:1 [1] He prophecieth that all nations shall come to the knowledge of God, who then was only known in Judea.

66:3 [1] As the faithful shall obey God willingly, so the infidels for fear shall dissemble themselves to be subject.

66:5 [1] He toucheth the slothful dullness of man, who is cold in the consideration of God's works.

[2] His providence is wonderful in maintaining their estate.

66:7 [1] He proveth that God will extend his grace also to the Gentiles, because he punisheth among them such as will not obey his calling.

9 Which [1]holdeth our souls in life, and suffereth not our feet to slip.

10 For thou, O God, hast proved us, thou hast tried us as silver is tried.

11 Thou hast brought us unto the [1]snare, *and* laid a strait *chain* upon our loins.

12 Thou hast caused men to ride over our heads: we went into fire and into water, but thou broughtest us out into a wealthy *place*.

13 I will go into thine [1]House with burnt offerings, *and* will pay thee my vows,

14 Which my lips have promised, and my mouth hath spoken in mine affliction.

15 I will offer unto thee the burnt offerings of fat rams with incense: I will prepare bullocks and goats. Selah.

16 [1]Come *and* hearken, all ye that fear God, and I will tell you what he hath done to my soul.

17 I called unto him with my mouth, and he was exalted with my tongue.

18 [1]If I regard wickedness in mine heart, the Lord will not hear me.

19 But God hath heard *me, and* considered the voice of my prayer.

20 Praised *be* God, which hath not put back my prayer, nor his mercy from me.

67

1 *A prayer of the Church to obtain the favor of God and to be lightened with his countenance.* 2 *To the end that his way and judgment may be known throughout the earth.* 7 *And finally is declared the kingdom of God, which should be universally erected at the coming of Christ.*

To him that excelleth on Neginoth.
A Psalm *or* song.

1 God be merciful unto us, and bless us, *and* [1]cause his face to shine among us. (Selah.)

2 That [1]they may know thy way upon earth, *and* thy saving health among all nations.

3 Let the people praise thee, O God: let all the people praise thee.

4 [1]Let the people be glad and rejoice: for thou shalt judge the people righteously, and govern the nations upon the earth. Selah.

5 Let the people praise thee, O God: let all the people praise thee.

6 *Then* shall [1]the earth bring forth her increase, *and* God, *even* our God shall bless us.

7 God shall bless us, and all the ends of the earth [1]shall fear him.

68

1 *In this Psalm David setteth forth as in a glass the wonderful mercies of God toward his people:* 5 *Who by all means and most strange sorts declared himself to them.* 15 *And therefore God's Church by reason of his promises, graces, and victories, doth excel without comparison all worldly things.* 34 *He exhorteth therefore all men to praise God forever.*

To him that excelleth. A Psalm *or* song of David.

1 God [1]will arise, *and* his enemies shall be scattered: they also that hate him, shall flee before him.

2 As the smoke vanisheth, *so* shalt thou drive them away: *and* as wax melteth before the fire, *so* shall the wicked perish at the presence of God.

3 [1]But the righteous shall be glad, *and* rejoice before God: yea, they shall leap for joy.

4 Sing unto God, *and* sing praises unto his name: exalt him that rideth upon the heavens, in his Name [1]Jah, and rejoice before him.

5 *He is* a Father of the fatherless, and a Judge of the widows, *even* God in his holy habitation.

6 God [1]maketh the solitary to dwell in families, *and* delivereth them that were prisoners in stocks: but the rebellious shall dwell in a [2]dry land.

7 [1]O God, when thou wentest forth before thy

66:9 [1] He signifieth some special benefit, that God had showed to his Church of the Jews, in delivering them from some great danger: whereof or of the like he promiseth that the Gentiles shall be partakers.

66:11 [1] The condition of the Church is here described, which is to be led by God's providence into troubles to be subject under tyrants, and to enter into manifold dangers.

66:13 [1] The duty of the faithful is here described, which are never unmindful to render God praise for his benefits.

66:16 [1] It is not enough to have received God's benefits and to be mindful thereof, but also we are bound to make others to profit thereby and praise God.

66:18 [1] If I delight in wickedness, God will not hear me, but if I confess it, he will receive me.

67:1 [1] That is, move our hearts with his holy Spirit, that we may feel his favor towards us.

67:2 [1] That both Jews and Gentiles may know God's covenant made with them.

67:4 [1] By these oft repetitions he showeth that the people can never rejoice sufficiently and give thanks for the great benefits that they

shall receive under the kingdom of Christ.

67:6 [1] He showeth that where God favoreth, there shall be abundance of all other things.

67:7 [1] When they feel his great benefits both spiritual and corporal toward them.

68:1 [1] The Prophet showeth that albeit God suffereth the wicked tyrants to oppress his Church for a time, yet at length he will be revenged of them.

68:3 [1] He showeth that when God declareth his power against the wicked, that it is for the commodity and salvation of his Church, which praise him therefore.

68:4 [1] Yah and Jehovah are the names of God, which do signify his essence and majesty incomprehensible, so that hereby is declared that all idols are but vanity, and that the God of Israel is the only true God.

68:6 [1] He giveth children to them that be childless, and increaseth their families.

[2] Which is barren of God's blessings, which before they had abused.

68:7 [1] He teacheth that God's favor peculiarly belongeth to his Church, as appeareth by their wonderful deliverance out of Egypt.

people: when thou wentest through the wilderness, (Selah.)

8 The earth shook, and the heavens dropped at the presence of this God: *even* Sinai *was moved* at the presence of God, *even* the God of Israel.

9 Thou, O God, sentest a gracious rain *upon* thine inheritance, and thou didst refresh it when it was weary.

10 Thy Congregation dwelled therein: *for* thou, O God, hast of thy ¹goodness prepared it for the poor.

11 The Lord gave matter to the ¹women to tell of the great army.

12 Kings of the armies did flee: they did flee, and ¹she that remained in the house, divided the spoil.

13 Though ye have lain among ¹pots, *yet shall ye be as* the wings of a dove that is covered with silver, and whose feathers *are like* yellow gold.

14 When the Almighty scattered kings ¹in it, it was white as the snow in Zalmon.

15 ¹The mountain of God *is like* the mountain of Bashan: *it is* an high mountain, *as* mount Bashan.

16 ¹Why leap ye, ye high mountains? as for this Mountain, God delighteth to dwell in it: yea, the Lord will dwell in it forever.

17 The chariots of God *are* twenty thousand thousand Angels, *and* the Lord is among them, *as* in the Sanctuary of Sinai.

18 Thou art gone up on high: thou hast ¹led captivity captive, *and* received gifts for men: yea, even the rebellious hast thou led, that the Lord God might dwell there.

19 Praised *be* the Lord, *even* the God of our salvation, which ladeth us daily *with benefits.* Selah.

20 This *is* our God, *even* the God that saveth *us*: and to the Lord God *belong* the ¹issues of death.

21 Surely God will wound the head of his enemies, *and* the hairy pate of him that walketh in his sins.

22 The Lord hath said, I will bring *my people* again from ¹Bashan: I will bring them again from the depths of the Sea:

23 That thy foot may be dipped in blood, *and* the tongue of thy dogs *in the blood* of the enemies, *even* in ¹it.

24 They have seen, O God, thy ¹goings, the goings of my God, *and* my king, *which* art in the Sanctuary.

25 The ¹singers went before, the players of instruments after: in the midst *were* the maids playing with timbrels.

26 Praise ye God in the assemblies, *and* the Lord, *ye that are* of the fountain ¹of Israel.

27 There *was* ¹little Benjamin *with* their ²ruler, *and* the Princes of Judah *with* their assembly, the princes of Zebulun, *and* the princes of Naphtali.

28 Thy GOD hath appointed thy strength: establish, O God, that *which* thou first wrought in us,

29 ¹Out of thy Temple upon Jerusalem, *and* kings shall bring presents unto thee.

30 Destroy the company of the spearmen, *and* multitude of the mighty bulls with the calves of the people, that ¹tread under feet pieces of silver: scatter the people that delight in war.

31 Then shall the princes come out ¹of Egypt: Ethiopia shall haste to stretch her hands unto God.

32 Sing unto God, O ye kingdoms of the earth: sing praise unto the Lord, (Selah)

33 To him that rideth upon the most high heavens, *which were from* the beginning: behold, he will send out by his ¹voice a mighty sound.

34 Ascribe the power to God: *for* his majesty *is* upon Israel, and his strength *is* in the clouds.

68:10 ¹ God blessed the land of Canaan, because he had chosen that place for his Church.

68:11 ¹ The fashion then was that women sang songs after the victory, as Miriam, Deborah, Judith, and others.

68:12 ¹ The prey was so great, that not only the soldiers, but women also had part thereof.

68:13 ¹ Though God suffer his Church for a time to lie in black darkness, yet he will restore it, and make it most shining and white.

68:14 ¹ In the land of Canaan, where his Church was.

68:15 ¹ Zion the Church of God, doth excel all worldly things, not in pomp and outward show, but by the inward grace of God, which there remaineth, because of his dwelling there.

68:16 ¹ Why boast ye of your strength and beauty against this Mountain of God?

68:18 ¹ As God overcame the enemies of his Church, took them prisoners, and made them tributaries: so Christ, which is God manifested in the flesh, subdued Satan and sin under us, and gave unto his Church most liberal gifts of his Spirit, Eph. 4:8.

68:20 ¹ In most extreme dangers God hath infinite ways to deliver his.

68:22 ¹ As he delivered his Church once from Og of Bashan, and

other tyrants, and from the danger of the red Sea, so will he still do as oft as necessity requireth.

68:23 ¹ That is, in the blood of that great slaughter, where dogs shall lap blood.

68:24 ¹ That is, how thou which art chief King goest out with thy people to war, and givest them the victory.

68:25 ¹ He describeth the order of the people, when they went to the Temple to give thanks for the victory.

68:26 ¹ Which come of the Patriarch Jacob.

68:27 ¹ Benjamin is called little, because he was the youngest son of Jacob.

   ² Who was some chief ruler of the tribe.

68:29 ¹ Declare out of thine holy palace thy power for the defense of thy Church Jerusalem.

68:30 ¹ He desireth that the pride of the mighty may be destroyed, which accustomed to garnish their shoes with silver, and therefore for their glittering pomp thought themselves above all men.

68:31 ¹ He prophecieth that the Gentiles shall come to the true knowledge and worship of God.

68:33 ¹ By his terrible thunders he will make himself to be known the God of all the world.

35 O God, thou art ¹terrible out of thine holy ²places: the God of Israel is he that giveth strength and power unto the people: praised *be* God.

69

1 The complaints, prayers, fervent zeal and great anguish of David is set forth as a figure of Christ and all his members. 21 The malicious cruelty of the enemies. 22 And their punishment also. 26 Where Judas and such traitors are accursed. 30 He gathereth courage in his affliction, and offereth praises unto God, 32 Which are more acceptable than all sacrifices: whereof all the afflicted may take comfort. 35 Finally, he doth provoke all creatures to praises, prophesying of the kingdom of Christ, and the preservation of the Church, where all the faithful, 27 And their seed shall dwell forever.

To him that excelleth upon ¹Shoshannim.
A Psalm of David.

1 Save me, O God: for the ¹waters are entered even to *my* soul.

2 I stick fast in the deep mire, where no ¹stay *is*: I am come into deep waters, and the streams run over me.

3 I am weary of crying: my throat is dry: mine ¹eyes fail, while I wait for my God.

4 They that hate me without a cause, are more than the hairs of mine head: they that would destroy me, *and* are mine enemies ¹falsely, are mighty, so that I restored that which I ²took not.

5 O God, thou knowest my ¹foolishness, and my faults are not hid from thee.

6 Let not them that trust in thee, O Lord God of hosts, be ashamed for ¹me: let not those that seek thee, be confounded through me, O God of Israel.

7 For thy sake have I suffered reproof: shame hath covered my face.

8 I am become a stranger unto my brethren, even an alien unto my mother's sons.

9 ¹For the zeal of thine house hath eaten me, and the rebukes of them that rebuked thee, are fallen upon me.

10 I ¹wept and my soul fasted, but that was to my reproof.

11 I put on a sack also: and I became a proverb unto them.

12 They that ¹sat in the gate, spake of me, and the drunkards sang *of me.*

13 But Lord, *I make* my prayer unto thee in an ¹acceptable time, *even* in the multitude of thy mercy: O God, hear me in the truth of thy salvation.

14 Deliver me out of the mire, that I sink not: let me be delivered from them that hate me, and out of the ¹deep waters.

15 Let not the water flood drown me, neither let the deep swallow me up: and let not the pit shut her mouth upon me.

16 Hear me, O Lord, for thy loving-kindness is good: turn unto me according to the multitude of thy tender mercies.

17 And ¹hide not thy face from thy servant, for I am in trouble; make haste *and* hear me.

18 Draw near unto my soul *and* redeem it: deliver me because of mine enemies.

19 Thou hast known my reproof and my shame, and my dishonor: all mine ¹adversaries *are* before thee.

20 Rebuke hath broken mine heart, and I am full of heaviness, and ¹I looked *for some* to have pity *on me*, but there was none: and for comforters, but I found none.

21 For they gave me gall in my meat, and in my thirst they gave me vinegar to drink.

22 Let their ¹table be a snare before them, and their prosperity *their* ruin.

23 Let their eyes be blinded that they see not: and make their ¹loins always to tremble.

24 Pour out thine anger upon them, and let thy wrathful displeasure take them.

68:35 ¹ In showing fearful judgments against thine enemies for the salvation of thy people.

  ² He alludeth to the Tabernacle which was divided in three parts.

69:Title ¹ Of Shoshannim, read Ps. 45.

69:1 ¹ David signifieth by the waters, in what great dangers he was, out of the which God did deliver him.

69:2 ¹ No firmity of stableness to settle my feet.

69:3 ¹ Though his senses failed him, yet his faith was constant and encouraged him still to pray.

69:4 ¹ Condemning me guiltless.

  ² They judged me poor innocent as a thief, and gave my goods to others, as though I had stolen them.

69:5 ¹ Though I be guilty to theeward, yet am I innocent toward them.

69:6 ¹ Let not mine evil entreaty of the enemies be an occasion, that the faithful fall from thee.

69:9 ¹ When I saw thine enemies pretend thy Name only in mouth, and in their life deny the same, thine holy Spirit, thrust me forward, to reprove them and defend thy glory.

69:10 ¹ My zeal moved me to lament and pray for my salvation.

69:12 ¹ The more he sought to win them to God, the more they were against him both poor and rich.

69:13 ¹ Knowing that albeit I suffer now trouble, yet thou hast a time wherein thou hast appointed my deliverance.

69:14 ¹ He showeth a lively faith, in that that he assureth himself, that God is favorable to him, when he seemeth to be angry: and at hand when he seemeth to be far off.

69:17 ¹ Not that he feared that God would not hear him, but that care made him to think that God deferred long.

69:19 ¹ Thou seest that I am beset as a sheep among many wolves.

69:20 ¹ He showeth that it is in vain to put our trust in men in our great necessities, but that our comfort only dependeth of God: for man rather increaseth our sorrows, than diminisheth them, John 19:29.

69:22 ¹ He desireth God to execute his judgments against the reprobate, which cannot by any means be turned, Rom. 11:9.

69:23 ¹ Take both judgment and power from them, Acts 1:20.

25 Let their [1]habitation be void, *and* let none dwell in their tents.

26 For they persecute him, whom thou hast smitten: and they add unto the sorrow of them, whom thou hast wounded.

27 Lay [1]iniquity upon their iniquity, and let them not come into thy righteousness.

28 Let them be put out of the [1]book of life, neither let them be written with the righteous.

29 When I am poor and in heaviness, thine help, O God, shall exalt me.

30 I will praise the Name of God with a song, and magnify him with thanksgiving.

31 This also shall please the Lord better than a [1]young bullock that hath horns and hoofs.

32 The humble shall see this, *and* they that seek God shall be glad, and your heart shall live.

33 For the Lord heareth the poor, and despiseth not his [1]prisoners.

34 Let heaven and earth praise him: the seas and all that moveth in them.

35 For God will save Zion, and build the cities of Judah, that men may dwell there and have it in possession.

36 The [1]seed also of his servants shall inherit it: and they that love his name shall dwell therein.

70

1 He prayeth to be right speedily delivered.   2 He desireth the shame of his enemies,   4 And the joyful comfort of all those that seek the Lord.

To him that excelleth.
A Psalm of David, to put [1]in remembrance.

1 O [a]God, [1]haste *thee* to deliver me: make haste to help me, O Lord.

2 Let them be [1]confounded and put to shame, that seek my soul: let them be turned backward and put to rebuke, that desire mine hurt.

CHAPTER 70
[a] Ps. 40:13

CHAPTER 71
[a] Ps. 31:1

3 Let them be turned back for a reward of their [1]shame, which say, Aha, aha.

4 *But* let all those that seek thee, be joyful and glad in thee, and let all that love thy salvation, say always, God be praised.

5 Now I am [1]poor and needy: O God, make haste to me: thou art my helper, and my deliverer: O Lord, make no tarrying.

71

He prayeth in faith, established by the word of promise,   5 And confirmed by the work of God from his youth.   10 He complaineth of the cruelty of his enemies,   17 And desireth God to continue his graces toward him,   22 Promising to be mindful and thankful for the same.

1 In [a,1]thee, O Lord, I trust: let me never be ashamed.

2 Rescue me and deliver me in thy [1]righteousness: incline thine ear unto me and save me.

3 Be thou my strong rock, whereunto I may always resort: thou [1]hast given commandment to save me: for thou art my rock, and my fortress.

4 Deliver me, O my God, out of the hand [1]of the wicked: out of the hand of the evil and cruel man.

5 For thou art mine hope, O Lord God, *even* my [1]trust from my youth.

6 Upon thee have I been stayed from the womb: thou art he that took me out of my mother's bowels: my praise shall be always of thee.

7 I am become as it were a [1]monster unto many: but thou art my sure trust.

8 Let my mouth be filled with thy praise, *and* with thy glory every day.

9 Cast me not off in the time of [1]age: forsake me not when my strength faileth.

10 For mine enemies speak of me, and they that lay wait for my soul, take their counsel together,

11 Saying, [1]God hath forsaken him: pursue and

69:25 [1] Punish not only them, but their posterity, which shall be like unto them.

69:27 [1] By their continuance and increasing in their sins, let it be known that they be of the reprobate.

69:28 [1] They which seemed by their profession to have been written in thy book, yet by their fruits prove the contrary, let them be known as reprobate.

69:31 [1] There is no sacrifice, which God more esteemeth, than thanksgiving for his benefits.

69:33 [1] For as he delivered his servant David, so will he do all that are in distress, and call upon him.

69:36 [1] Under the temporal promise of the land of Canaan, he comprehendeth the promise of life everlasting to the faithful and their posterity.

70:Title [1] Which might put him in remembrance of his deliverance.

70:1 [1] He teacheth us to be earnest in prayer, though God seem to stay: for at his time he will hear us.

70:2 [1] He was assured that the more they raged, the nearer they were to destruction, and he the nearer to his deliverance.

70:3 [1] Hereby we are taught not to mock at others in their misery,

lest the same fall on our own necks.

70:5 [1] Because he had felt God's help before, he groundeth on experience, and boldly seeketh unto him for succor.

71:1 [1] He prayeth to God with full assurance of faith, that he will deliver him from his adversaries.

71:2 [1] By declaring thyself true of promise.

71:3 [1] Thou hast infinite means, and all creatures are at thy commandment: therefore show some sign, whereby I shall be delivered.

71:4 [1] That is, from Absalom, Ahithophel and that conspiracy.

71:5 [1] He strengtheneth his faith by the experience of God's benefits, who did not only preserve him in his mother's belly, but took him thence, and ever since hath preserved him.

71:7 [1] All the world wondereth at me because of my miseries: as well they in authority as the common people, yet being assured of thy favor, I remained steadfast.

71:9 [1] Thou that didst help me in my youth, when I had more strength, help me now so much the more in mine old age and weakness.

71:11 [1] Thus the wicked both blaspheme God, and triumph against his Saints, as though he had forsaken them, if he suffer them to fall into their hands.

take him, for there is none to deliver *him*.

12　Go not far from me, O God: [1]my God haste thee to help me.

13　Let them be confounded *and* consumed that are against my soul: let them be covered with reproof and confusion, that seek mine hurt.

14　But I will wait continually, and will praise thee more and more.

15　My mouth shall daily rehearse thy righteousness, *and* thy salvation: [1]for I know not the number.

16　I will [1]go forward in the strength of the Lord God, *and* will make mention of thy righteousness, *even* of thine only.

17　O God, thou hast taught me from my youth even until now: *therefore* will I tell of thy wondrous works,

18　[1]Yea even unto *mine* old age and gray head, O God: forsake me not, until I have declared thine arm unto *this* generation, *and* thy power to all them that shall come.

19　And thy [1]righteousness, O God, *I will exalt* on high: for thou hast done great things: [2]O God, who is like unto thee!

20　Which hast showed me great troubles and [1]adversities, *but* thou wilt return *and* revive me, and wilt come again, *and* take me up from the depth of the earth.

21　Thou wilt increase mine honor, and return *and* comfort me.

22　Therefore will I praise thee *for* thy [1]faithfulness, O God, upon instrument *and* viol: unto thee will I sing upon the harp, O Holy one of Israel.

23　My lips will rejoice when I sing unto thee, and my [1]soul which thou hast delivered.

24　My tongue also shall talk of thy righteousness daily: for they are confounded and brought unto shame, that seek mine hurt.

72

1 He prayeth for the prosperous estate of the kingdom of Solomon, who was the figure of Christ,　4 under whom shall be righteousness, peace, and felicity.　10 Unto whom all Kings and nations shall do homage,　17 Whose name and power shall endure forever, and in whom all nations shall be blessed.

A Psalm [1]of Solomon.

1　Give thy [1]judgments to the King, O God, and thy righteousness to the King's [2]son.

2　Then shall he judge thy people in righteousness, and thy poor with equity.

3　The [1]mountains, and the hills shall bring peace to the people by justice.

4　He shall [1]judge the poor of the people: he shall save the children of the needy, and shall subdue the oppressor.

5　They shall [1]fear thee as long as the sun and moon endureth, from generation to generation.

6　He shall come [1]down like the rain upon the mown grass, *and* as the showers that water the earth.

7　In his days shall the righteous flourish, and abundance of peace *shall be* so long as the moon endureth.

8　His dominion shall be also from [1]sea to sea, and from the river unto the ends of the land.

9　They that dwell in the wilderness, shall kneel before him, and his enemies shall lick the dust.

10　The kings of [1]Tarshish and of the isles shall bring presents: the kings [2]of Sheba and Seba shall bring gifts.

11　Yea, all kings shall worship him: all nations shall serve him.

12　For he shall deliver the poor when he crieth: the needy also, and him that hath no helper.

13　He shall be merciful to the poor and needy, and shall preserve the souls of the poor.

14　He shall redeem their souls from deceit and violence, and [1]dear shall their blood be in his sight.

71:12 [1] In calling him his God, he putteth back the false reports of the adversaries, that said, God had forsaken him.

71:15 [1] Because thy benefits toward me are innumerable, I cannot but continually meditate and rehearse them.

71:16 [1] I will remain steadfast, being upholden with the power of God.

71:18 [1] He desireth that as he hath begun, he would so continue his benefits, that his liberality may have perfect praise.

71:19 [1] Thy just performance of thy promise.

[2] His faith breaketh through all tentations, and by this exclamation he praiseth the power of God.

71:20 [1] As he confesseth that God is the only author of his deliverance: so he acknowledgeth that these evils were sent unto him by God's providence.

71:22 [1] He confesseth that his long tarriance was well recompensed, when God performed his promise.

71:23 [1] For there is no true praising of God, except it come from the heart: and therefore he promiseth to delight in nothing, but wherein God be glorified.

72:Title [1] Composed by David as touching the reign of his son Solomon.

72:1 [1] Endue the king with the Spirit of wisdom and justice, that he reign not as do the worldly tyrants.

[2] To wit, to his posterity.

72:3 [1] When justice reigneth, even the places most barren shall be enriched with thy blessings.

72:4 [1] He showeth wherefore the sword is committed to Kings: to wit, to defend the innocent, and suppress the wicked.

72:5 [1] The people shall embrace thy true religion, when thou givest a King that ruleth according to thy word.

72:6 [1] As this is true in all godly kings, so it is chiefly verified in Christ, who with his heavenly dew, maketh his Church ever to flourish.

72:8 [1] That is, from the red sea to the sea called Syriacum, and from Euphrates forward, meaning, that Christ's Kingdom should be large and universal.

72:10 [1] Of Cilicia, and of all other countries, beyond the sea, which he meaneth by the isles.

[2] That is, of Arabia that rich country, whereof Sheba was a part bordering upon Ethiopia.

72:14 [1] Though tyrants pass not to shed blood, yet this godly king shall preserve his subjects from all kind of wrong.

15 Yea, he shall live, and unto him shall they give of the [1]gold of Sheba: they shall also pray for him continually, *and* daily bless him.

16 An handful of corn shall be *sown* in the earth, *even* in the top of the mountains, and the [1]fruit thereof shalt shake like *the trees* of Lebanon: and the *children* shall flourish out of the city like the grass of the earth.

17 His name shall be forever: his name shall endure as long as the Sun: all nations shall bless [1]him, and be blessed in him.

18 Blessed *be* the Lord God, *even* the God of Israel which only doeth [1]wondrous things.

19 And blessed *be* his glorious Name forever: and let all the earth be filled with his glory. So be it, even so be it.

[20] Here end the [1]prayers of David the son of Jesse.

73

1 *The Prophet teacheth by his example that neither* the worldly prosperity of the ungodly, 14 nor yet *the affliction of the good ought to discourage God's children: but rather ought to move us to consider our Father's providence, and to cause us to reverence God's judgments, 19 forasmuch as the wicked vanish away, 24 and the godly enter into life everlasting, 28 in hope whereof he resigneth himself into God's hands.*

A Psalm *committed* to Asaph.

1 Yet [1]God is good to Israel: *even* to the pure in heart.

2 As for me, my feet were almost gone: my steps had well near slipped.

3 For I fretted at the foolish, *when* I saw the prosperity of the wicked.

4 For there are [1]no bands in their death, but they are lusty *and* strong.

5 They are not in trouble *as other* men, neither are they plagued with *other* men.

6 [1]Therefore pride *is* as a chain unto them, *and* cruelty covereth them *as* a garment.

7 Their eyes stand out for fatness: [1]they have more than heart can wish.

8 They are licentious, and speak wickedly of *their* oppression: they talk presumptuously.

9 They [1]set their mouth against heaven, and their tongue walketh through the earth.

10 Therefore his [1]people turn hither: for waters of a full *cup* are wrung out to them.

11 And they [1]say, How doth God know it? or is there knowledge in the most High?

12 Lo these are the wicked, yet prosper they always, *and* increase in riches.

13 Certainly I have cleansed mine heart in vain, and washed mine hands in innocency.

14 For daily have I been punished, and chastened *every* morning.

15 If I say, [1]I will judge thus, behold the generation of thy children, I have trespassed.

16 Then thought I to know this, *but* it was too painful for me,

17 Until I went into the [1]Sanctuary of God: *then* understood I their end.

18 Surely thou hast set them in slippery places, *and* castest them down into desolation.

19 How suddenly are they destroyed, perished *and* [1]horribly consumed,

20 As a dream when one awaketh! O Lord, when [1]thou raisest us up, thou shalt make their image despised.

21 Certainly mine heart was vexed, and I was pricked in my reins.

22 So foolish was I and ignorant: I was a [1]beast before thee.

23 Yet I was always [1]with thee: thou hast holden *me* by my right hand.

72:15 [1] God will both prosper his life, and also make the people most willing to obey him.

72:16 [1] Under such a king shall be most great plenty, both of fruit and also of the increase of mankind.

72:17 [1] They shall pray to God for his continuance, and know that God doth prosper them for his sake.

72:18 [1] He confesseth that except God miraculously preserve his people, that neither the king nor the kingdom can continue.

72:20 [1] Concerning his son Solomon.

73:1 [1] As it were between hope and despair he bursteth forth into this affection, being assured that God would continue his favor toward such as were godly indeed, and not hypocrites.

73:4 [1] The wicked in this life live at pleasure and are not drawn to death like prisoners: that is, by sickness which is death's messenger.

73:6 [1] They glory in their pride as some do in their chains, and in cruelty, as some do in apparel.

73:7 [1] Hebrew, *they pass the desires of the heart.*

73:9 [1] They blaspheme God, and fear not his power and rail upon men, because they esteem themselves above all others.

73:10 [1] Not only the reprobate, but also the people of God oftentimes fall back, seeing the prosperous estate of the wicked, and are overwhelmed with sorrows, thinking that God considereth not aright the estate of the godly.

73:11 [1] Thus the flesh moveth even the godly to dispute with God touching their poor estate, and the prosperity of the wicked.

73:15 [1] If I give place to this wicked thought, I offend against thy providence, seeing thou disposeth all things most wisely and preservest thy children in their greatest dangers.

73:17 [1] Until I entered into thy school and learned by thy word and holy Spirit, that thou orderest all things most wisely and justly.

73:19 [1] By thy fearful judgment.

73:20 [1] When thou openest our eyes to consider thy heavenly felicity, we contemn all their vain pomp.

73:22 [1] For the more that man goeth about by his own reason to seek out God's judgments, the more doth he declare himself a beast.

73:23 [1] By faith I was assured that thy providence did watch always over me, to preserve me.

24 Thou wilt guide me by thy counsel, and afterward receive me to glory.

25 Whom have I in [1]heaven *but thee?* and I have desired none in the earth with thee.

26 My flesh faileth and mine heart *also: but God is* the strength of mine heart, and my [1]portion forever.

27 For lo, that they withdraw themselves from thee, shall perish: thou destroyest all them that [1]go a whoring from thee.

28 As for me, it is good for me [1]to draw near to God: *therefore* I have put my trust in the Lord God, that I may declare all thy works.

74

1 *The faithful complain of the destruction of the Church and true religion,* 2 *Under the Name of Zion, and the Temple destroyed:* 11 *and trusting in the might and free mercies of God,* 20 *by his covenant,* 21 *they require help and succor for the glory of God's holy Name, for the salvation of his poor afflicted servants,* 23 *and the confusion of his proud enemies.*

A *Psalm* to give instruction, *committed* to Asaph.

1 O God, [1]why hast thou put us away forever? *why* is thy wrath kindled against the sheep of thy pasture?

2 Think upon the congregation, *which* thou hast possessed of old, and on the [1]rod of thine inheritance, *which* thou hast redeemed, *and* on this mount Zion, wherein thou hast dwelt.

3 Lift up thy [1]strokes, that thou mayest forever destroy every enemy that doeth evil to the Sanctuary.

4 Thine adversaries roar in the midst of thy congregation, *and* [1]set up their banners for signs.

5 He that [1]lifted the axes upon the thick trees, was renowned as one that brought a thing to perfection:

6 But now they break down the carved work thereof with axes and hammers.

7 They have cast thy Sanctuary into the fire, *and* razed *it* to the ground, *and* have defiled the dwelling place of thy Name.

8 They said in their [1]hearts, Let us destroy them altogether: they have burnt all the Synagogues of God in the land.

9 We see not our signs: there is not one Prophet more, nor any with us that knoweth [1]how long.

10 O God, how long shall the adversary reproach *thee?* shall the enemy blaspheme thy Name forever?

11 Why withdrawest thou thine hand, even thy right hand? *draw it* out of thy bosom, *and* [1]consume them.

12 Even God *is* my king of old, working salvation [1]in the midst of the earth.

13 Thou didst divide the sea by thy power: thou brakest the heads of the [1]dragons in the waters.

14 Thou brakest the head of [1]Leviathan in pieces, *and* gavest him to be [2]meat for the people in wilderness.

15 Thou brakest up the fountain and river: thou driest up mighty rivers.

16 The [1]day is thine, and the night is thine: thou hast prepared the light and the sun.

17 Thou hast set all the borders of the earth: thou hast made Summer and Winter.

18 Remember this, *that* the enemy hath reproached the Lord, and the foolish people hath blasphemed thy Name.

19 Give not the soul of thy [1]turtle dove unto the beast, *and* forget not the Congregation of thy poor forever.

20 Consider *thy* covenant: for [1]the dark places of the earth are full of the habitations of the cruel.

21 O let not the oppressed return ashamed, *but* let the poor and needy praise thy Name.

22 Arise, O God: maintain thy [1]own cause: remember thy daily reproach by the foolish man.

23 Forget not the voice of thine enemies: *for* the tumult of them that rise against thee, [1]ascendeth continually.

73:25 [1] He sought neither help nor comfort of any save of God only.

73:26 [1] He teacheth us to deny ourselves, to have God our whole sufficiency, and only contentment.

73:27 [1] That is, forsake thee to seek others.

73:28 [1] Though all the world shrink from God, yet he promiseth to trust in him and to magnify his works.

74:1 [1] The Church of God being oppressed by the tyranny, either of the Babylonians or of Antiochus, prayeth to God by whose hand this yoke was laid upon them for their sins.

74:2 [1] Which inheritance thou hast measured out for thyself as with a line or rod.

74:3 [1] Or, feet.

74:4 [1] They have destroyed thy true religion, and spread their banners in sign of defiance.

74:5 [1] He commendeth the temple for the costly matter, the excellent workmanship, and beauty thereof, which notwithstanding the enemies did destroy.

74:8 [1] They encouraged one another to cruelty, that not only God's people might be destroyed, but also his religion utterly in all places suppressed.

74:9 [1] They lament that they have no Prophet among them to show them how long their misery should endure.

74:11 [1] They join their deliverance with God's glory and power, knowing that the punishment of the enemy should be their deliverance.

74:12 [1] Meaning, in the sight of all the world.

74:13 [1] To wit, Pharaoh's army.

74:14 [1] Which was a great monster of the sea, or whale, meaning, Pharaoh.

[2] His destruction did rejoice them as meat refresheth the body.

74:16 [1] Seeing that God by his providence governeth and disposeth all things, he gathereth that he will take care chiefly for his children.

74:19 [1] He meaneth the Church of God, which is exposed as a prey to the wicked.

74:20 [1] That is, all places where thy word shineth not, there reigneth tyranny and ambition.

74:22 [1] He showeth that God cannot suffer his Church to be oppressed, except he loose his own right.

74:23 [1] Or, increaseth more and more.

75

1 The faithful do praise the Name of the Lord,   2 Which shall come to judge at the time appointed: 8 When the wicked shall be put to confusion, and drink of the cup of his wrath.   10 Their pride shall be abated, and the righteous shall be exalted to honor.

To him that excelleth. ¹Destroy not.
A Psalm, *or song* committed to Asaph.

1   We will praise thee, O God, we will praise *thee*, for thy Name *is* near: *therefore* ¹they will declare thy wondrous works.

2   ¹When I shall take a convenient time, I will judge righteously.

3   The earth and all the inhabitants thereof are dissolved: *but* I will establish the pillars ¹of it. Selah.

4   I said unto the foolish, Be not so foolish, and to the wicked, Lift not up the horn.

5   Lift not up your ¹horn on high, neither speak with a stiff neck.

6   For to come to preferment *is* neither from the East, nor from the West, nor from the South,

7   But God *is* the judge: he maketh low, and he maketh high.

8   For in the hand of the Lord *is* a ¹cup, and the wine is red: it is full mixed, and he poureth out of the same: surely all the wicked of the earth shall wring out *and* drink the dregs thereof.

9   But I will declare forever, and sing praises unto the God of Jacob.

10   All the horns of the wicked also will I break: *but* the horns of the ¹righteous shall be exalted.

76

1 This Psalm setteth forth the power of God, and care for the defense of his people in Jerusalem, in the destruction of the army of Sennacherib: 11 and exhorteth the faithful to be thankful for the same.

CHAPTER 77
ª Ps. 39
Ps. 62
1 Chron. 16:41

To him that excelleth on Neginoth.
A Psalm, *or song* committed to Asaph.

1   God is ¹known in Judah: his Name *is* great in Israel.

2   For in ¹Salem is his Tabernacle, and his dwelling in Zion.

3   There brake he the arrows of the bow, the shield, and the sword, and the battle. Selah.

4   Thou art more bright and puissant, than ¹the mountains of prey.

5   The stouthearted are spoiled: they have slept their sleep, and all the men of strength have not ¹found their hands.

6   At thy rebuke, O God of Jacob, both the chariot and horse are cast asleep.

7   Thou, *even* thou art to be feared; and who shall stand in thy ¹sight, when thou art angry!

8   Thou didst cause *thy* judgment to be heard from heaven; *therefore* the earth feared, and was still,

9   When thou, O God, arose to judgment, to ¹help all the meek of the earth. Selah.

10   Surely the ¹rage of man shall turn to thy praise; the remnant of the rage shalt thou restrain.

11   Vow and perform unto the Lord your God, all *ye* that be ¹round about him; let them bring presents unto him that ought to be feared.

12   He shall ¹cut off the spirit of princes; he is terrible to the kings of the earth.

77

1 The Prophet in the Name of the Church rehearseth the greatness of his affliction, and his grievous temptations,   6 Whereby he was driven to this end to consider his former conversation,   11 and the continual course of God's works in the preservation of his servants, and so he confirmeth his faith against these temptations.

For the excellent *Musician* ªJeduthun.
A Psalm committed to Asaph.

1   My ¹voice *came* to God, when I cried: my voice *came* to God; and he heard me.

75:Title ¹ Read Ps. 57:1.
75:1 ¹ He declareth how the faithful shall ever have just occasion to praise God, forasmuch as in their need they shall feel his power at hand to help them.
75:2 ¹ When I see my time (saith God) to help your miseries, I will come and set all things in good order.
75:3 ¹ Though all things be brought to ruin, yet I can restore and preserve them.
75:5 ¹ The Prophet warneth the wicked that they would not set themselves against God's people, seeing that God at his time destroyeth them that rule wickedly.
75:8 ¹ God's wrath is compared to a cup of strong and delicate wine, wherewith the wicked are made so drunk, that by drinking till they come to the very dregs they are utterly destroyed.
75:10 ¹ The godly shall better prosper by their innocent simplicity, than the wicked shall by all their craft and subtlety.
76:1 ¹ He declareth that God's power is evidently seen in preserving his people and destroying his enemies.

76:2 ¹ Which afterward was called Jerusalem.
76:4 ¹ He compareth the kingdoms full of extortion and rapine to the mountains that are full of ravening beasts.
76:5 ¹ God hath taken their spirits and strength from them as though their hands were cut off.
76:7 ¹ God with a look is able to destroy all the power and activity of the enemies, were they never so many, or mighty.
76:9 ¹ To revenge the wrongs done to thy Church.
76:10 ¹ For the end shall show that the enemy was able to bring nothing to pass: also thou shalt bridle their rage that they shall not compass their purpose.
76:11 ¹ To wit, the Levites, that dwell about the Tabernacle, or the people among whom he doth dwell.
76:12 ¹ The Hebrew word signifieth to vintage, or gather grapes: meaning, that he shall make the counsels and enterprises of wicked tyrants foolish and vain.
77:1 ¹ The Prophet teacheth us by his example to flee unto God for help in our necessities.

2 In the day of my trouble I sought the Lord: [1]my sore ran and ceased not in the night: my soul refused comfort.

3 I did think upon God, and was [1]troubled: I prayed, and my spirit was full of anguish. Selah.

4 Thou keepest mine eyes [1]waking: I was astonied, and could not speak.

5 Then I considered the days of old: *and* the years of ancient time.

6 I called to remembrance my [1]song in the night: I communed with mine own heart, and my spirit searched [2]diligently.

7 Will the Lord absent himself forever? and will he show no more favor?

8 Is his [1]mercy clean gone forever? doth his promise fail forevermore?

9 Hath God forgotten to be merciful? hath he shut up his tender mercies in displeasure? Selah.

10 And I said, This is my [1]death: *yet I remembered* the years of the right hand of the most High.

11 I remembered the works of the Lord: certainly I remembered thy wonders of old.

12 I did also meditate all thy works, and did devise of thine acts, *saying,*

13 Thy way, O God, *is* [1]in the Sanctuary: who is so great a [2]God, as *our* God!

14 Thou art the God that doest wonders; thou hast declared thy power among the people.

15 Thou hast redeemed thy people with *thine* arm, *even* the sons of Jacob and Joseph. Selah.

16 The [1]waters saw thee, O God: the waters saw thee, *and* were afraid: yea, the depths trembled.

17 The clouds poured out water: the heavens gave a [1]sound: yea, thine arrows went abroad.

18 The voice of thy thunder was round about; the lightnings lightened the world: the earth trembled and shook.

19 Thy way *is* in the sea, and thy paths in the great waters, and thy footsteps are not [1]known.

20 Thou didst lead thy people like sheep by the hand of Moses and Aaron.

78

1 He showeth how God of his mercy chose his Church of the posterity of Abraham, 8 Reproaching the stubborn rebellion of their fathers, that the children might not only understand. 11 That God of his free mercy made his Covenant with their ancestors, 17 But also seeing them so malicious and perverse, might be ashamed, and so turn wholly to God. In this Psalm the holy Ghost hath comprehended, as it were, the sum of all God's benefits, to the intent the ignorant and gross people might see in few words the effect of the whole histories of the Bible.

A Psalm to give [1]instruction, *committed* to Asaph.

1 Hear my [1]doctrine, O my people: incline your ears unto the words of my mouth.

2 I will open my mouth in a parable: I will declare high sentences of old.

3 Which we have heard and known, and our [1]fathers have told us.

4 We will not hide them from their children, *but* to the generation to come we will show the praise of the Lord, his power also, and his wonderful works that he hath done:

5 How he established a [1]testimony in Jacob, and ordained a Law in Israel, which he commanded our fathers, that they should teach their children:

6 That the [1]posterity might know it, *and* the children, which should be born, should stand up, and declare it to their children:

7 That they might [1]set their hope on God, and not forget the works of God, but keep his commandments:

8 And not to be as their [1]fathers, a disobedient and rebellious generation: a generation that set not

---

77:2 [1] Or, mine hand was stretched out.

77:3 [1] He showeth that we must patiently abide, although God deliver us not out of our troubles at the first cry.

77:4 [1] Meaning, that his sorrows were as watchmen that kept his eyes from sleeping.

77:6 [1] Of thanksgiving, which I was accustomed to sing in my prosperity.

[2] Both the causes why I was chastened, and when my sorrows should have an end.

77:8 [1] As if he should say, It is impossible: whereby he exhorteth himself to patience.

77:10 [1] Though I first doubted of my life, yet considering that God had his years, that is, change of times, and was accustomed also to lift up them, whom he hath beaten, I took heart again.

77:13 [1] That is in heaven, whereunto we must ascend by faith, if we will know the ways of God.

[2] He condemneth all that worship anything save the only true God, whose glory appeareth through the world.

77:16 [1] He declareth wherein the power of God was declared when

he delivered the Israelites through the red sea.

77:17 [1] That is, thundered and lightninged.

77:19 [1] For when thou hadst brought over thy people, the water returned to her course, and the enemies that thought to have followed them, could not pass through, Exod. 14:28, 29.

78:Title [1] Read Ps. 32.

78:1 [1] The Prophet under the name of a teacher calleth the people his, and the doctrine his, as Paul calleth the Gospel his, whereof he was but the preacher, as Rom. 2:16 and 16:25.

78:3 [1] Which were the people of God.

78:5 [1] By the testimony, and law, he meaneth the law written, which they were commanded to teach their children, Deut. 6:7.

78:6 [1] He showeth wherein the children should be like their fathers: that is, in maintaining God's pure Religion.

78:7 [1] He showeth wherein the use of this doctrine standeth: in faith, in the meditation of God's benefits, and in obedience.

78:8 [1] Though these fathers were the seed of Abraham and the chosen people, yet he showeth by their rebellion, provocation, falsehood, and hypocrisy, that the children ought not to follow their examples.

their heart aright, and whose spirit was not faithful unto God.

9 The children of ¹Ephraim being armed and shooting with the bow, turned back in the day of battle.

10 They kept not the Covenant of God, but refused to walk in his Law,

11 And forgate his acts, and his wonderful works that he had showed them.

12 He did marvelous things in the sight of their ¹fathers in the land of Egypt; *even* in the field of Zoan.

13 ⁿHe divided the Sea, and led them through: he made also the waters to stand as an heap.

14 ᵇIn the daytime also he led them with a cloud, and all the night with a light of fire.

15 ᶜHe clave the rocks in the wilderness, and gave them drink as of the great depths.

16 ᵈHe brought floods also out of the stony rock, so that he made the waters to descend like the rivers.

17 Yet they ¹sinned still against him, and provoked the Highest in the wilderness,

18 And tempted God in their hearts in ¹requiring meat for their lust.

19 ᵉThey spake against God also, saying, Can God ¹prepare a table in the wilderness?

20 ᶠBehold, he smote the rock, that the water gushed out, and the streams overflowed: can he give bread also? or prepare flesh for his people?

21 Therefore the Lord heard, and was angry, and the ᵍfire was kindled in Jacob, and also wrath came upon Israel,

22 Because they believed not in God, and ¹trusted not in his help.

23 Yet he had commanded the ¹clouds above, and had opened the doors of heaven,

24 And had rained down Manna upon them for to eat, and had given them of the wheat of heaven.

25 ʰMan did eat the bread of Angels: he sent them

CHAPTER 78
ᵃ Exod. 14:21
ᵇ Exod. 14:24
ᶜ Exod. 17:6
Num. 20:12
Ps. 105:41
ᵈ 1 Cor. 10:4
ᵉ Num. 11:1
ᶠ Exod. 17:6
Num. 20:11
Ps. 105:41
1 Cor. 10:4
ᵍ Num. 11:1
ʰ John 6:31
1 Cor. 10:3

meat enough.

26 He caused the ¹East wind to pass in the heaven: and through his power he brought in the South wind.

27 He rained flesh also upon them as dust, and feathered fowl as the sand of the sea.

28 And he made it fall in the midst of their camp, *even* round about their habitations.

29 So they did eat, and were well filled: for he gave them their desire.

30 They were not turned from their ¹lusts, *but* the meat *was* yet in their mouths,

31 When the wrath of God came even upon them, and slew ¹the strongest of them, and smote down the chosen men of Israel.

32 For all this they ¹sinned still, and believed not his wondrous works.

33 Therefore their days did he consume in vanity, and their years hastily.

34 And when he ¹slew them, they sought him, and they returned, and sought God early.

35 And they remembered that God *was* their strength, and the most high God their redeemer.

36 But they flattered him with their mouth, and dissembled with him with their tongue.

37 For their ¹heart was not upright with him: neither were they faithful in his covenant.

38 Yet he being merciful, ¹forgave *their* iniquity, and destroyed *them* not, but oft times called back his anger, and did not stir up all his wrath.

39 For he remembered that they were flesh: *yea,* a wind that passeth and cometh not again.

40 How oft did they provoke him in the wilderness? *and* grieve him in the desert?

41 Yea, they ¹returned and tempted God, and ²limited the Holy one of Israel.

42 They ¹remembered not his hand, *nor* the day when he delivered them from the enemy,

43 *Nor* him that set his signs in Egypt, and his

78:9 ¹ By Ephraim he meaneth also the rest of the tribes, because they were most in number: whose punishment declareth that they were unfaithful to God, and by their multitude and authority had corrupt all others.

78:12 ¹ He proveth that not only the posterity but also their forefathers were wicked and rebellious to God.

78:17 ¹ Their wicked malice could be overcome by no benefits, which were great and many.

78:18 ¹ Then to require more than is necessary, and to separate God's power from his will, is to tempt God.

78:19 ¹ Thus when we give place to sin, we are moved to doubt of God's power, except he will always be ready to serve our lust.

78:22 ¹ That is, in his fatherly providence, whereby he careth for his, and provideth sufficiently.

78:23 ¹ So that they had that, which was necessary and sufficient: but their lust made them to covet that which they knew God had denied them.

78:26 ¹ God used the means of the wind to teach them that all ele-

ments were at his commandment, and that no distance or place could let his working.

78:30 ¹ Such is the nature of concupiscence, that the more it hath, the more it lusteth.

78:31 ¹ Though others were not spared, yet chiefly they suffered, which trusted in their strength against God.

78:32 ¹ Thus sin by continuance maketh man insensible, so that by no plagues they can be amended.

78:34 ¹ Such was their hypocrisy, that they sought unto God for fear of punishment, though in their heart they loved him not.

78:37 ¹ Whatsoever cometh not from the pure fountain of the heart, is hypocrisy.

78:38 ¹ Because he would ever have some remnant of a Church to praise his Name in earth, he suffered not their sins to overcome his mercy.

78:41 ¹ That is, they tempted him oft times.
² As they all do that measure the power of God by their capacity.

78:42 ¹ The forgetfulness of God's benefits is the root of rebellion and all vice.

wonders in the field of Zoan,

44 And turned their rivers into blood, and their floods, that they could not drink.

45 He sent ¹a swarm of flies among them, which devoured them, and frogs, which destroyed them.

46 He ¹gave also their fruits unto the caterpillar, and their labor unto the grasshopper.

47 He destroyed their vines with hail, and their wild fig trees with the hailstone.

48 He gave their cattle also to the hail, and their flocks to the thunderbolts.

49 He cast upon them the fierceness of his anger, indignation and wrath, and vexation by the sending out of ¹evil angels.

50 He made a way to his anger: he spared not their soul from death, *but* gave their life to the pestilence,

51 And smote all the firstborn in Egypt, *even* the ¹beginning of *their* strength in the tabernacles of ²Ham.

52 But he made his people to go out like sheep, and led them in the wilderness like a flock.

53 Yea, he carried them out safely, and they ¹feared not, and the Sea covered their enemies.

54 And he brought them unto the borders of his ¹Sanctuary: *even* to this Mountain *which* his right hand purchased.

55 ¹He cast out the heathen also before them, and caused them to fall to the lot of *his* inheritance, and made the tribes of Israel to dwell in their tabernacles.

56 Yet they tempted, and provoked the most high God, and kept not his testimonies,

57 But turned back, and dealt ¹falsely like their fathers: they turned like a deceitful bow.

58 And they ¹provoked him to anger with their high places, and moved him to wrath with their graven images.

i Josh. 11:6
Josh. 13:6

59 God heard *this* and was wroth, and greatly abhorred Israel,

60 So that he ¹forsook the habitation of Shiloh, *even* the Tabernacle where he dwelt among men,

61 And delivered his ¹power into captivity, and his beauty into the enemy's hand.

62 And he gave up his people to the sword, and was angry with his inheritance.

63 The fire ¹devoured their chosen men, and their maids were not ²praised.

64 Their Priests fell by the sword, and their ¹widows lamented not.

65 But the Lord awaked as one out of sleep, *and* as a strong man that after *his* ¹wine crieth out,

66 And smote his enemies in the hinder *parts*, *and* put them to a perpetual shame.

67 Yet he refused the tabernacle of ¹Joseph, and chose not the tribe of Ephraim:

68 But chose the tribe of Judah, *and* mount Zion which he loved.

69 And he ¹built his Sanctuary as an high *palace*, like the earth, which he established forever.

70 He chose David also his servant, and took him from the sheepfolds.

71 Even from behind the ewes with young, brought he him to feed his people in Jacob, and his inheritance in Israel.

72 So ¹he fed them according to the simplicity of his heart, and guided them by the discretion of his hands.

79

1 *The Israelites complain to God for the great calamity and oppression that they suffered by God's enemies,* 8 *and confessing their sins, flee to God's mercies with full hope of deliverance,* 10 *Because their calamities were joined with the contempt of his Name,* 13 *for the which they promise to be thankful.*

78:45 ¹ This word signifieth a confused mixture of flies and venomous worms. Some take it for all sorts of serpents: some for all wild beasts.

78:46 ¹ He repeateth not here all the miracles that God did in Egypt, but certain which might be sufficient to convince the people of malice and ingratitude.

78:49 ¹ So called either of the effect, that is, of punishing the wicked: or else because they were wicked spirits, whom God permitted to vex men.

78:51 ¹ The firstborn are so called, as Gen. 49:3.

² That is, Egypt: for it was called Mizraim, or Egypt of Mizraim that was the son of Ham.

78:53 ¹ That is, they had none occasion to fear, forasmuch as God destroyed their enemies, and delivered them safely.

78:54 ¹ Meaning, Canaan, which God had consecrated to himself, and appointed to his people.

78:57 ¹ Nothing more displeaseth God in the children, than when they continue in that wickedness, which their fathers had begun.

78:58 ¹ By serving God otherwise than he had appointed.

78:60 ¹ For their ingratitude he suffered the Philistines to take the Ark, which was the sign of his presence, from among them.

78:61 ¹ The Ark is called his power and beauty, because thereby he defended his people, and beautifully appeared unto them.

78:63 ¹ They were suddenly destroyed, 1 Sam. 4:10.

² They had no marriage songs: that is, they were not married.

78:64 ¹ Either they were slain before, or taken prisoners of their enemies, and so were forbidden.

78:65 ¹ Because they were drunken in their sins, they judged God's patience to be a slumbering, as though he were drunken, therefore he answering their beastly judgment, saith, he will awake and take sudden vengeance.

78:67 ¹ Showing that he spared not altogether the Israelites, though he punished their enemies.

78:69 ¹ By building the Temple, and established the kingdom, he declareth that the signs of his favor were among them.

78:72 ¹ He showeth wherein a king's charge standeth: to wit, to provide faithfully for his people, to guide them by counsel, and defend them by power.

A Psalm *committed* to Asaph.

1 O God, ¹the heathen are come into thine inheritance: thine holy Temple have they defiled, and made Jerusalem heaps *of stones.*

2 The ¹dead bodies of thy servants have they given to be meat unto fowls of the heaven, *and* the flesh of thy saints unto the beasts of the earth.

3 Their blood have they shed like waters, round about Jerusalem, and there was none to ¹bury them.

4 We are a reproach to our ¹neighbors, *even* a scorn and derision unto them that are round about us.

5 Lord, how long wilt thou be angry, forever? shall thy jealousy ¹burn like fire?

6 ªPour out thy wrath upon the heathen that have not known thee, and upon the kingdoms that have not called upon thy Name.

7 For they have devoured Jacob, and made his dwelling place desolate.

8 Remember not against us the ¹former iniquities, *but* ²make haste, *and* let thy tender mercies prevent us: for we are in great misery.

9 Help us, O God of our ¹salvation, for the glory of thy Name, and deliver us, and be merciful unto our sins for thy Name's sake.

10 Wherefore should the heathen say, Where is their God? let them be known among the heathen in our sight by the vengeance of the blood of thy servants that is shed.

11 Let the sighing of the ¹prisoners come before thee: according to thy mighty arm preserve ²the children of death,

12 And render to our neighbors sevenfold into their bosom their reproach, wherewith they have reproached thee, O Lord.

13 So we thy people, and sheep of thy pasture shall praise thee forever: and from generation to

CHAPTER 79
ª Jer. 10:25

generation ¹we will set forth thy praise.

80

1 A lamentable prayer to God to help the miseries of his Church, 8 Desiring him to consider their first estate, when his favor shined toward them, to the intent that he might finish that work which he had begun.

To him that excelleth on Shoshannim Eduth,
A Psalm *committed* to Asaph.

1 Hear, ¹O thou shepherd of Israel, thou that leadest Joseph like sheep: show *thy* brightness, thou that sittest between the ²Cherubims.

2 Before Ephraim and Benjamin and Manasseh stir up thy strength, and come to help us.

3 ¹Turn us again, O God, and cause thy face to shine that we may be saved.

4 O Lord God of hosts, how long wilt thou be ¹angry against the prayer of thy people?

5 Thou hast fed them with the bread of tears, and given them tears to drink with great measure.

6 Thou hast made us a ¹strife unto our neighbors, and our enemies laugh *at us* among themselves.

7 ¹Turn us again, O God of hosts: cause thy face to shine, and we shall be saved.

8 Thou hast brought a ¹vine out of Egypt: thou hast cast out the heathen, and planted it.

9 Thou madest room for it, and didst cause it to take root, and it filled the land.

10 The mountains were covered with the shadow of it, and the boughs thereof *were like* the ¹goodly cedars.

11 She stretched out her branches unto the Sea, and her boughs unto the ¹river.

12 Why hast thou *then* broken down her hedges, so that all they, which pass by the way, have plucked her?

13 The wild ¹boar out of the wood hath destroyed it, and the wild beasts of the field have eaten it up.

79:1 ¹ The people cry unto God against the barbarous tyranny of the Babylonians, who spoiled God's inheritance, polluted his Temple, destroyed his religion, and murdered his people.
79:2 ¹ The Prophet showeth to what extremities God suffereth sometime his Church to fall, to exercise their faith, before he set his hand to deliver them.
79:3 ¹ Their friends and kinsfolks durst not bury them for fear of the enemies.
79:4 ¹ Whereof some came of Abraham but were degenerate: and others were open enemies to thy religion, but they both laughed at our miseries.
79:5 ¹ Wilt thou utterly consume us for our sins, before thou takest us to mercy?
79:8 ¹ Which we and our fathers have committed.
² And stay not till we have recompensed for our sins.
79:9 ¹ Seeing we have none other Savior, neither can we help ourselves, and also by our salvation thy Name shall be praised: therefore, O Lord, help us.
79:11 ¹ Who though in respect of God they were justly punished for their sins: yet in consideration of their cause were unjustly murdered.
² Which were captives among their enemies, and could look for

nothing but death.
79:13 ¹ We ought to desire no benefit of God, but on this condition to praise his name, Isa. 43:21.
80:1 ¹ This Psalm was made as a prayer for to desire God to be merciful to the ten tribes.
² Move their hearts, that they may return to worship God aright: that is, in the place where thou hast appointed.
80:3 ¹ Join thy whole people, and all thy tribes together again.
80:4 ¹ The faithful fear God's anger, when they perceive that their prayers are not forthwith heard.
80:6 ¹ Our neighbors have continual strife and war against us.
80:7 ¹ Because that repentance only cometh of God, they most instantly and ofttimes call to God for it as a means whereby they shall be saved.
80:8 ¹ Seeing that of thy mercy thou hast made us a most dear possession to thee, and we through our sins are made open for wild beasts to devour us, declare again thy love, and finish the work that thou hast begun.
80:10 ¹ Hebrew, *cedars of God.*
80:11 ¹ To wit, Euphrates.
80:13 ¹ That is, as well they that hate our religion, as they that hate our persons.

14 Return, we beseech thee, O God of hosts: look down ¹from heaven and behold, and visit this vine,

15 And the vineyard, that thy right hand hath planted, and the young vine, *which* thou madest ¹strong for thyself.

16 It is burnt with fire, *and* cut down: *and* they perish at the ¹rebuke of thy countenance.

17 Let thine hand be upon the ¹man of thy right hand, *and* upon the son of man, *whom* thou madest strong for thine own self.

18 So will not we go back from thee, ¹revive thou us, and we shall call upon thy Name.

19 Turn us again, O Lord God of hosts: cause thy face to shine, and we shall be saved.

81 *1 An exhortation to praise God both in heart and voice for his benefits, 8 and to worship him only. 11 God condemneth their ingratitude, 12 and showeth what great benefit they have lost through their own malice.*

To him that excelleth upon ¹Gittith.
A Psalm committeth to Asaph.

1 Sing ¹joyfully unto God our strength: sing loud unto the God of Jacob.

2 Take the song and bring forth the timbrel, the pleasant harp with the viol.

3 Blow the trumpet in the ¹new moon, *even in* the time appointed at our feast day.

4 For this is a statute for Israel, *and* a Law of the God of Jacob.

5 He set this in ¹Joseph for a testimony, when he came out of the land of Egypt, *where* I heard a language, that ²I understood not.

6 I have withdrawn his shoulder from the burden, *and* his hands have left the ¹pots.

7 Thou calledst in affliction, and I delivered thee, *and* ¹answered thee in the secret of the thunder: I proved thee at the waters of ²Meribah. Selah.

8 ¹Hear, O my people, and I will protest unto thee: O Israel, if thou wilt hearken unto me,

9 And wilt have no strange god in thee, neither worship any strange god,

10 (*For* I am the Lord thy God, which brought thee out of the land of Egypt:) ¹open thy mouth wide, and I will fill it.

11 But my people would not hear my voice, and Israel would none of me,

12 So I gave them up unto the hardness of their heart, *and* they have walked in their own counsels.

13 ¹Oh that my people had hearkened unto me, *and* Israel had walked in my ways!

14 I would soon have humbled their enemies, and turned mine hand ¹against their adversaries.

15 The haters of the Lord should have been subject unto him, and their time ¹should have endured forever.

16 And *God* would have fed them with the ¹fat of wheat, and with honey out of the rock would I have sufficed thee.

82 *1 The Prophet declaring God to be present among the Judges and Magistrates, 2 Reproveth their partiality. 3 And exhorteth them to do justice. 5 But seeing none amendment, 8 He desireth God to undertake the matter and execute justice himself.*

A Psalm committeth to Aspah.

1 God standeth in the assembly of ¹gods: he judgeth among gods.

2 How long will ye judge unjustly, and accept the persons of the ¹wicked? Selah.

3 Do right to the poor and fatherless: do justice to the poor and needy.

4 Deliver the poor and ¹needy: save *them* from

80:14 ¹ They gave not place to tentation, knowing that albeit there were no help in earth, yet God was able to succor them from heaven.
80:15 ¹ So that no power can prevail against it, and which as a young bud thou raisest up again as out of the burnt ashes.
80:16 ¹ Only when thou art angry and not of the sword of the enemy.
80:17 ¹ That is, upon this vine or people, whom thou hast planted with thy right hand, that they should be as one man or one body
80:18 ¹ For none can call upon God but such as are raised up as it were from death to life, and regenerate by the holy Spirit.
81:Title ¹ An instrument of music brought from Geth.
81:1 ¹ It seemeth that this Psalm was appointed for solemn feasts and assemblies of the people to whom for a time these ceremonies were ordained, but now under the Gospel are abolished.
81:3 ¹ Under this feast he comprehendeth all other solemn days.
81:5 ¹ That is, in Israel: for Joseph's family was counted the chief before that Judah was preferred.
² God speaketh in the person of the people because he was their leader.
81:6 ¹ If they were never able to give sufficient thanks to God for this deliverance from corporal bondage, how much more are we indebted to him for our spiritual deliverance from the tyranny of Satan and sin?
81:7 ¹ By a strange and wonderful fashion.
² Or, contention, Exod. 17:7.
81:8 ¹ He condemneth all assemblies, where the people are not attentive to hear God's voice, and to give obedience to the same.
81:10 ¹ God accuseth their incredulity, because they opened not their mouths to receive God's benefits in such abundance as he poureth them out.
81:13 ¹ God by his word calleth all, but his secret election appointeth who shall hear with fruit.
81:14 ¹ If their sins had not letted.
81:15 ¹ If the Israelites had not broken covenant with God, he would have given them victory against their enemies.
81:16 ¹ That is, with most fine wheat and abundance of honey.
82:1 ¹ The Prophet showeth that if princes and judges do not their duty, God whose authority is above them, will take vengeance on them.
82:2 ¹ For thieves and murderers find favor in judgment, when the cause of the godly cannot be heard.
82:4 ¹ Not only when they cry for help, but when their cause requireth aid and support.

the hand of the wicked.

5   They know not and understand nothing: they walk in darkness, *albeit* all the [1]foundations of the earth be moved.

6   I have said, Ye are gods, and ye all are children of the most High.

7   [1]But ye shall die as a man, and ye princes shall fall like others.

8   O God, arise, *therefore* judge thou the earth: for thou shalt inherit [1]all nations.

83

1 The people of Israel pray unto the Lord to deliver them from their enemies both at home and far off, which imagined nothing but their destruction.   9 And they desire that all such wicked people may according as God was accustomed, be stricken with the stormy tempest of God's wrath,   18 That they may know that the Lord is most high upon the earth.

A song *or* Psalm *committed* to Asaph.

1   Keep [1]not thou silence, O God: be not still, and cease not, O God.

2   For lo, thine [1]enemies make a tumult, and they that hate thee, have lifted up the head.

3   They have taken crafty counsel against thy people, and have consulted against thy [1]secret ones.

4   They have said, Come and let us [1]cut them off from being a nation: and let the name of Israel be no more in remembrance.

5   For they have consulted together in [1]heart, *and* have made a league [2]against thee:

6   The tabernacles of Edom, and the Ishmaelites, Moab and the Hagarites:

7   Gebal and Ammon, and Amalek, the Philistines, with the inhabitants of [1]Tyre.

8   Assyria also is joined with them: they have been an arm to the children [1]of Lot. Selah.

9   Do thou to them as unto the [1]Midianites: as

CHAPTER 83
[a] Judg. 7:25
Judg. 8:21

to Sisera *and* as to Jabin at the river of Kishon.

10   They perished at En Dor, *and* were [1]dung for the earth.

11   Make them, *even* their princes, like [a]Oreb and like Zeeb: yea, all their princes like Zebah and like Zalmunna,

12   Which have said, Let us take for our possession the [1]habitations of God.

13   O my God, make them like unto a [1]wheel, *and* as the stubble before the wind.

14   As the fire burneth the forest, and as the flame setteth the mountains on fire:

15   So persecute them with thy tempest, and make them afraid with thy storm.

16   Fill their faces with shame, that they may [1]seek thy Name, O Lord.

17   Let them be confounded and troubled forever: yea, let them be put to shame, and perish,

18   That they may [1]know that thou, which art calleth Jehovah, art alone, *even* the most High over all the earth.

84

1 David driven forth of his country,   2 Desireth most ardently to come again to the tabernacle of the Lord and the assembly of the Saints to praise God,   4 pronouncing them blessed that may so do.   6 Then he praiseth the courage of the people, that pass through the wilderness to assemble themselves in Zion.   10 Finally, with praise of this matter and confidence of God's goodness, he endeth the Psalm.

To him that excelleth upon Gittith.
A Psalm *committed* to the sons of Korah.

1   O [1]Lord of hosts, how amiable *are* thy Tabernacles?

2   My soul longeth, yea, and fainted for the [1]courts of the Lord: *for* my heart and my flesh rejoice in the living God.

3   Yea, the sparrow hath found *her* an house, and

82:5 [1] That is, all things are out of order either by their tyranny or careless negligence.

82:7 [1] No title of honor shall excuse you, but you shall be subject to God's judgment, and render account as well as other men.

82:8 [1] Therefore no tyrant shall pluck thy right and authority from thee.

83:1 [1] This Psalm seemeth to have been composed as a form of prayer against the dangers that the Church was in, in the days of Jehoshaphat.

83:2 [1] He calleth them God's enemies, which are enemies to his Church.

83:3 [1] The elect of God are his secret ones: for he hideth them in the secret of his tabernacle, and preserveth them from all dangers.

83:4 [1] They were not content to take the Church as prisoner: but sought utterly to destroy it.

83:5 [1] By all secret means.
[2] They thought to have subverted thy counsel wherein the perpetuity of the Church was established.

83:7 [1] Or, Zor.

83:8 [1] The wickedness of the Ammonites and Moabites is described in that they provoked these other nations to fight against the Israelites their brethren.

83:9 [1] By these examples they were confirmed, that God would not suffer his people to be utterly destroyed, Judg. 7:21 and 4:15.

83:10 [1] Trodden under feet as mire.

83:12 [1] That is, Judea: for where his Church is, there dwelleth he among them.

83:13 [1] Because the reprobate could by no means be amended, he prayeth that they may utterly be destroyed, be unstable, and led with all winds.

83:16 [1] That is, be compelled by thy plagues to confess thy power.

83:18 [1] Though they believe not, yet they may prove by experience, that it is in vain to resist against thy counsel in establishing thy Church.

84:1 [1] David complaineth that he cannot have access to the Church of God to make profession of his faith, and to profit in religion.

84:2 [1] For none but the Priests could enter into the Sanctuary, and the rest of the people into the courts.

the swallow a nest for her, where she may lay her young: *even* by thine ¹altars, O Lord of hosts, my king *and* my God.

4 Blessed *are* they that dwell in thine house, they will ever praise thee. Selah.

5 Blessed *is* the man whose ¹strength *is* in thee, *and* in whose heart *are* thy ways.

6 They going through the valley of ¹Baca, make wells therein: the rain also covereth the pools.

7 They go from ¹strength to strength, *till every* one appear before God in Zion.

8 O Lord God of hosts, hear my prayer, hearken, O God of Jacob. Selah.

9 Behold, O God, our shield, and look upon the face of thine ¹Anointed.

10 For ¹a day in thy courts is better than a thousand *other where*: I had rather be a doorkeeper in the house of my God, than to dwell in the tabernacles of wickedness.

11 For the Lord God is the sun and shield *unto us*: the Lord will give grace and glory, and no ¹good thing will he withhold from them that walk uprightly.

12 O Lord of hosts, blessed *is* the man that trusteth in thee.

85 1 *Because God withdrew not his rods from his Church after their return from Babylon, first they put him in mind of their deliverance, to the intent that he should not leave the work of his grace imperfect.* 5 *Next they complain of their long affliction.* 8 *And thirdly, they rejoice in hope of felicity promised.* 9 *For their deliverance was a figure of Christ's kingdom, under the which should be perfect felicity.*

To him that excelleth.
A Psalm *committed* to the sons of Korah.

1 Lord, thou hast been ¹favorable unto thy land: thou hast brought again the captivity of Jacob.

2 Thou hast forgiven the iniquity of thy people, *and* ¹covered all their sins. Selah.

3 Thou hast withdrawn all thine anger, and hast turned back from the ¹fierceness of thy wrath.

4 Turn us, O God of our salvation, and release thine anger toward us.

5 Wilt thou be angry with us ¹forever? *and* wilt thou prolong thy wrath from one generation to another?

6 Wilt thou not turn again *and* quicken us, that thy people may rejoice in thee?

7 Show us thy mercy, O Lord, and grant us thy ¹salvation.

8 I will hearken what the Lord God will say: for he will speak ¹peace unto his people, and to his Saints, that they turn not again to folly.

9 Surely his salvation is near to them that fear him, that glory may dwell in our land.

10 Mercy and truth shall meet, righteousness and peace shall kiss *one another*.

11 ¹Truth shall bud out of the earth, and righteousness shall look down from heaven.

12 Yea, the Lord shall give good things, and our land shall give her increase.

13 ¹Righteousness shall go before him, and shall set her steps in the way.

86 1 *David sore afflicted and forsaken of all, prayeth fervently for deliverance: sometimes rehearsing his miseries,* 5 *Sometimes the mercies received.* 11 *Desiring also to be instructed of the Lord, that he may fear him, and glorify his Name.* 14 *He complaineth also of his adversaries, and requireth to be delivered from them.*

A prayer of David.

1 Incline ¹thine ear, O Lord, *and* hear me: for I am poor and needy.

2 Preserve thou my soul, for I am ¹merciful: my God, save thou thy servant, that trusteth in thee.

3 Be merciful unto me, O Lord: for I ¹cry upon thee continually.

4 Rejoice the soul of thy servant: for unto thee,

84:3 ¹ So that the poor birds have more liberty than I.
84:5 ¹ Who trusteth nothing in himself, but in thee only, and learneth of thee to rule his life.
84:6 ¹ That is of mulberry trees, which was a barren place: so that they which passed through, must dig pits for water: signifying, that no lets can hinder them that are fully bent to come to Christ's Church, neither yet that God will ever fail them.
84:7 ¹ They are never weary but increase in strength and courage till they come to God's house.
84:9 ¹ That is, for Christ's sake, whose figure I represent.
84:10 ¹ He would wish to live but one day rather in God's Church, than a thousand among the worldlings.
84:11 ¹ But will from time to time increase his blessings toward his more and more.
85:1 ¹ They confess that God's free mercy was the cause of their deliverance, because he loved the land which he had chosen.
85:2 ¹ Thou hast buried them that they shall not come into judgment.
85:3 ¹ Not only in withdrawing thy rod, but in forgiving of sins, and

in touching our hearts to confess them.
85:5 ¹ As in times past they had felt God's mercies, so now being oppressed by the long continuance of evils, they pray unto God that according to his nature he would be merciful unto them.
85:7 ¹ He confesseth that our salvation cometh only of God's mercy.
85:8 ¹ He will send all prosperity to his Church, when he hath sufficiently corrected them, also by his punishments the faithful shall learn to beware that they return not like offences.
85:11 ¹ Though for a time God thus exerciseth them with his rods, yet under the kingdom of Christ they should have peace and joy.
85:13 ¹ Justice shall then flourish, and have free course and passage in every place.
86:1 ¹ David persecuted of Saul, thus prayed, leaving the same to the Church as a monument, how to seek redress against their miseries.
86:2 ¹ I am not enemy to them, but pity them though they be cruel toward me.
86:3 ¹ Which was a sure token that he believed that God would deliver him.

O Lord, do I lift up my soul.

5 For thou, Lord, art good and [1]merciful, and of great kindness unto all them that call upon thee.

6 Give ear, Lord, unto my prayer, and [1]hearken to the voice of my supplication.

7 In the day of my trouble I will call upon thee: for thou hearest me.

8 Among the gods there is none like thee, O Lord, and there is none [1]that can do like thy works.

9 All nations whom thou hast made, shall come and [1]worship before thee, O Lord, and shall glorify thy Name.

10 For thou art great and doest wondrous things: thou art God alone.

11 [1]Teach me thy way, O Lord, and I will walk in thy truth: knit mine heart unto thee, that I may fear thy Name.

12 I will praise thee, O Lord my God, with all mine heart: yea, I will glorify thy Name forever.

13 For great is thy mercy toward me, and thou hast delivered my soul from [1]the lowest grave.

14 O God, the proud are risen against me, and the assemblies of violent men have [1]sought my soul, and have not set thee before them.

15 But thou, O Lord, art a pitiful God and merciful, slow to anger, and great in kindness and truth.

16 Turn unto me, and have mercy upon me: give thy strength unto thy servant, and save the [1]son of thine handmaid.

17 Show a token of thy goodness toward me, that they which hate me, may see it, and be ashamed, because thou, O Lord, hast helped me and comforted me.

87
1 The holy Ghost promiseth, that the condition of the Church which was in misery after the captivity of Babylon, should be restored to great excellency. 4 So that

there should be nothing more comfortable, than to be numbered among the members thereof.

A Psalm or song committed to the sons of Korah.

1 God laid his [1]foundations among the holy mountains.

2 The Lord loveth the gates of Zion above all the habitations of Jacob.

3 [1]Glorious things are spoken of thee, O city of God. Selah.

4 I will make mention of [1]Rahab and Babel among them that know me: behold Palestine and Tyre with Ethiopia, [2]There is he born.

5 And of Zion it shall be said, [1]Many are born in her: and he, even the most High shall stablish her.

6 The Lord shall count, when he [1]writeth the people, He was born there. Selah.

7 As well the singers as the players on instruments shall praise thee: all my [1]springs are in thee.

88
1 A grievous complaint of the faithful, sore afflicted by sickness, persecutions and adversity, 7 Being as it were left of God without any consolation. 13 Yet he calleth on God by faith, and striveth against desperation. 18 Complaining himself to be forsaken of all earthly help.

A song or Psalm of [a]Heman the Ezrahite to give instruction, committed to the sons of Korah for him that excelleth upon Mahalath [1]Leannoth.

1 O Lord God of my salvation, I cry day and night [1]before thee.

2 Let my prayer enter into thy presence: incline thine ear unto my cry.

3 For my soul is filled with evils, and my life draweth near to the grave.

4 I am counted among them that go down unto the pit, and am as a man without strength,

5 [1]Free among the dead, like the slain laying in

86:5 [1] He doth confess that God is good to all, but only merciful to poor sinners.

86:6 [1] By crying and calling continually, he showeth how we may not be weary, though God grant not forthwith our request, but that we must earnestly and often call upon him.

86:8 [1] He condemneth all idols, forasmuch as they can do no works to declare that they are gods.

86:9 [1] This proveth that David prayed in the Name of Christ the Messiah, of whose kingdom he doth here prophesy.

86:11 [1] He confesseth himself ignorant till God hath taught him, and his heart variable and separate from God, till God join it to him, and confirm it in his obedience.

86:13 [1] That is, from most great danger of death: out of the which none but only the almighty hand of God could deliver him.

86:14 [1] He showeth that there can be no moderation nor equity, where proud tyrants reign, and that the lack of God's fear is as a privilege to all vice and cruelty.

86:16 [1] He boasteth not of his own virtues, but confesseth that God of his free goodness hath ever been merciful unto him, and given him power against his enemies, as to one of his own household.

87:1 [1] God did choose that place among the hills, to establish Jeru-

salem and his Temple.

87:3 [1] Though thy glorious estate does not yet appear, yet wait with patience, and God will accomplish his promise.

87:4 [1] That is, Egypt and these other countries shall come to the knowledge of God.

[2] It shall be said of him that is regenerate and come to the Church, that he is as one that was born in the Church.

87:5 [1] Out of all quarters they shall come to the Church, and be counted as citizens.

87:6 [1] When he calleth by his word them into the Church, whom he had elected and written in the book.

87:7 [1] The Prophet setteth his whole affections and comfort in the Church.

88:Title [1] That is, to humble. It was the beginning of a song, by the tune whereof this Psalm was sung.

88:1 [1] Though many cry in their sorrows, yet they cry not earnestly to God for remedy, as he did whom he confessed to be the author of his salvation.

88:5 [1] For he that is dead, is free from all cares and business of this life: and thus he saith, because he was unprofitable for all matters concerning man's life, and as it were cut off from this world.

the grave, when thou rememberest no more, and they are cut off from thy [2]hand.

6 Thou hast laid me in the lowest pit, in darkness, *and* in the deep.

7 Thine indignation lieth upon me, and thou hast vexed me with all thy [1]waves. Selah.

8 Thou hast put away mine [1]acquaintance far from me, *and* made me to be abhorred of them: [2]I am shut up, and cannot get forth.

9 [1]Mine eye is sorrowful through mine affliction: Lord, I call daily upon thee: I stretch out mine hands unto thee.

10 Wilt thou show [1]a miracle to the dead? or shall the dead rise *and* praise thee? Selah.

11 Shall thy loving kindness be declared in the grave? *or* thy faithfulness in destruction?

12 Shall thy wondrous works be known in the dark? and thy righteousness in the land [1]of oblivion?

13 But unto thee, have I cried, O Lord, and early shall my prayer come before thee.

14 Lord, why dost thou reject my soul, *and* hidest thy face from me?

15 I am afflicted and at the point of death: [1]from *my* youth I suffer thy terrors, doubting *of my life.*

16 Thine indignations go over me, and thy fear hath cut me off.

17 They came round about me daily like water, *and* compassed me together.

18 My lovers and friends hast thou put away from me, *and* mine acquaintance [1]hid themselves.

89

1 *With many words doth the Prophet praise the good-ness of God,* 23 *For his testament and covenant, that he had made between him and his elect by Jesus Christ the son of David.* 38 *Then doth he complain of the great ruin, and desolation of the kingdom of David, so that to the outward appearance the promise was broken.* 46 *Finally, he prayeth to* be delivered from his afflictions, making mention of the shortness of man's life, and confirming himself by God's promise.

A *Psalm* **to give instruction, of Ethan the Ezrahite.**

1 I will [1]sing the mercies of the Lord forever: with my mouth will I declare thy truth from generation to generation.

2 For I [1]said, Mercy shall be set up forever: thy truth shalt thou [2]stablish in the very heavens.

3 [1]I have made a covenant with my chosen: I have sworn to David my servant,

4 Thy seed will I stablish forever, and set up thy throne from generation to generation. Selah.

5 O Lord, even the [1]heavens shall praise thy wondrous work: yea, thy truth in the [2]Congregation of the Saints.

6 For who is equal to the Lord in the heaven? *and* who is like the Lord among the [1]sons of the gods?

7 God is very terrible in the assembly of the [1]Saints, and to be reverenced above all *that are* about him.

8 O Lord God of hosts, who is like unto thee, *which art* a mighty Lord, and thy truth *is* about thee?

9 [1]Thou rulest the raging of the Sea: when the waves thereof arise, thou stillest them.

10 Thou hast beaten down Rahab as a man slain: thou hast scattered thine enemies with thy mighty arm.

11 The heavens are thine, the earth also is thine: thou hast laid the foundation of the world, and all that therein is.

12 Thou hast created the North and the South: [1]Tabor and Hermon shall rejoice in thy Name.

13 Thou hast a mighty arm: strong is thy hand, *and* high is thy right hand.

14 [1]Righteousness and equity *are* the stablishment of thy throne: mercy and truth go before thy face.

15 Blessed *is* the people that can [1]rejoice *in thee*: they

---

88:5 [2] That is, from thy providence and care, which is meant according to the judgment of the flesh.

88:7 [1] The storms of thy wrath have overwhelmed me.

88:8 [1] He attributeth the loss and displeasure of his friends to God's providence, whereby he partly punisheth and partly trieth his.

[2] I see none end of my sorrows.

88:9 [1] Mine eyes and face declare my sorrows.

88:10 [1] He showeth that the time is more convenient for God to help, when men call unto him in their dangers, than to tarry till they be dead, and then raise them up again.

88:12 [1] That is, in the grave, where only the body lieth without all sense and remembrance.

88:15 [1] I am ever in great dangers and sorrows, as though my life should utterly be cut off every moment.

88:18 [1] Hebrew, *were in darkness.*

89:1 [1] Though the horrible confusion of things might cause them to despair of God's favor, yet the manifold examples of his mercies cause them to trust in God, though to man's judgment they saw none occasion.

89:2 [1] As he that surely believed in heart.

[2] As thine invisible heaven is not subject to any alteration and change: so shall the truth of thy promise be unchangeable.

89:3 [1] The Prophet showeth what was the promise of God, whereon he grounded his faith.

89:5 [1] The Angels shall praise thy power and faithfulness in delivering thy Church.

[2] That is, in the heavens.

89:6 [1] Meaning, the Angels.

89:7 [1] If the Angels tremble before God's majesty and infinite justice, what earthly creature by oppressing the Church, dare set himself against God?

89:9 [1] For as he delivered the Church by the red Sea, and by destroying Rahab, that is, the Egyptians: so will he eftsoons deliver it, when the dangers be great.

89:12 [1] Tabor is a mountain Westward from Jerusalem, and Hermon Eastward: so the Prophet signifieth that all parts and places of the world shall obey God's power for the deliverance of his Church.

89:14 [1] For hereby he judgeth the world, and showeth himself a merciful Father, and faithful protector unto his.

89:15 [1] Feeling in their conscience that God is their Father.

shall walk in the light of thy ²countenance, O Lord.

16 They shall rejoice continually in thy Name, and in thy righteousness shall they exalt themselves.

17 For thou art the ¹glory of their strength, and by thy favor our horns shall be exalted.

18 For our ¹shield *appertaineth* to the Lord, and our King to the Holy one of Israel.

19 Thou spakest then in a vision unto ¹thine Holy one, and saidest, I have laid help upon one that is ²mighty: I have exalted one chosen out of the people.

20 I have found David my servant: with mine holy oil have I anointed him.

21 Therefore mine hand shall be established with him, and mine arm shall strengthen him.

22 The enemy shall not oppress him, neither shall the wicked hurt him.

23 But I will ¹destroy his foes before his face, and plague them that hate him.

24 My truth also and my ¹mercy *shall be* with him, and in my Name shall his ²horn be exalted.

25 I will set his hand also in the sea, and his right hand in the ¹floods.

26 He shall cry unto me, Thou art my ¹Father, my God, and the rock of my salvation.

27 Also I will make him my firstborn, higher than the kings of the earth.

28 My mercy will I keep for him for evermore, and my Covenant shall stand fast with him.

29 His seed also will I make to endure ¹forever, and his throne as the days of heaven.

30 *But* if his children forsake my Law, and walk not in my judgments:

31 ªIf they break my statutes, and keep not my commandments:

32 Then will I visit their transgression with the

CHAPTER 89
ª 2 Sam. 7:14

rod, and their iniquity with strokes.

33 ¹Yet my loving kindness will I not take from him, neither will I falsify my truth.

34 My Covenant will I not break, nor ¹alter the thing that is gone out of my lips.

35 I have sworn once by mine holiness, ¹that I will not fail David, *saying,*

36 His seed shall endure forever, and his throne *shall be* as the sun before me.

37 He shall be established for evermore as the moon, and *as* a faithful ¹witness in the heaven. Selah.

38 But thou hast rejected and abhorred, thou hast been angry with thine anointed.

39 Thou hast ¹broken the Covenant of thy servant, *and* profaned his ²crown, *casting it* on the ground.

40 Thou hast broken down all his walls: thou hast laid his fortresses in ruin.

41 All that go by the way, spoil him: he is a rebuke unto his neighbors.

42 Thou hast set up the right hand of his enemies, *and* made all his adversaries to rejoice.

43 Thou hast also turned the edge of his sword, and hast not made him to stand in the battle.

44 Thou hast caused his dignity to decay, and cast his throne to the ground.

45 The days of his ¹youth hast thou shortened, *and* covered him with shame. Selah.

46 ¹Lord, how long wilt thou hide thyself, forever? shall thy wrath burn like fire?

47 Remember ¹of what time I am: wherefore shouldest thou create in vain all the children of men?

48 What man liveth, and shall not see death? shall he deliver his soul from the hand of the grave? Selah.

49 Lord, where are thy former mercies, *which* thou swarest unto David in thy truth?

---

² They shall be preserved by thy Fatherly providence.

89:17 ¹ In that they are preserved and continue, they ought to give the praise and glory only to thee.

89:18 ¹ In that that our King hath power to defend us, it is the gift of God.

89:19 ¹ To Samuel and to others, to assure that David was thy chosen one.

² Whom I have both chosen and given him strength to execute his office, as verse 21.

89:23 ¹ Though there shall be evermore enemies against God's kingdom, yet he promiseth to overcome them.

89:24 ¹ I will mercifully perform my promises to him, notwithstanding his infirmities and offences.

² His power, glory and estate.

89:25 ¹ He shall enjoy the land round about.

89:26 ¹ His excellent dignity shall appear herein, that he shall be named the son of God, and the firstborn wherein he is a figure of Christ.

89:29 ¹ Though for the sins of the people the state of this kingdom decayed: yet God reserved still a root, till he had accomplished this promise in Christ.

89:33 ¹ Though the faithful answer not in all points to their profes-

sion, yet God will not break his Covenant with them.

89:34 ¹ For God in promising hath respect to his mercy, and not to man's power in performing.

89:35 ¹ Hebrew, *If I lie unto David,* which is a manner of oath.

89:37 ¹ As long as the Sun and Moon endure, they shall be witnesses to me of this promise.

89:39 ¹ Because of the horrible confusion of things, the Prophet complaineth to God, as though he saw not the performance of his promise. And thus discharging his cares on God, he resisteth doubt and impatience.

² By this he meaneth the horrible dissipation and renting of the kingdom, which was under Jeroboam: or else by the Spirit of prophecy Ethan speaketh of those great miseries, which came soon afterward to pass at the captivity of Babylon.

89:45 ¹ He showeth that the kingdom fell before it came to perfection, or was ripe.

89:46 ¹ The Prophet in joining prayer with his complaint, showeth that his faith never failed.

89:47 ¹ Seeing man's life is short, and thou hast created man to bestow thy benefits upon him, except thou haste to help, death will prevent thee.

50 Remember, O Lord, the rebuke of thy servants, which I bear in my [1]bosom of all the mighty people.

51 For [1]thine enemies have reproached *thee*, O Lord, because they have reproached the [2]footsteps of thine Anointed.

52 Praised *be* the Lord for evermore. So be it, even so be it.

90

1 Moses in his prayer setteth before us the eternal favor of God toward his, 3 who are neither admonished by the brevity of their life, 7 nor by his plagues to be thankful, 12 therefore Moses prayeth God to turn their hearts, and continue his mercies toward them and their posterity forever.

A prayer of Moses, [1]the man of God.

1 Lord, thou hast been our [1]habitation from generation to generation.

2 Before the [1]mountains were made, and *before* thou hadst formed the earth, and the world, even from everlasting to everlasting thou art *our* God.

3 Thou [1]turnest man to destruction: again thou sayest, Return ye sons of Adam.

4 [1]For a thousand years in thy sight *are* as yesterday when it is past, and *as* a watch in the night.

5 Thou hast [1]overflowed them, they are *as* a sleep, in the morning he groweth like the grass:

6 In the morning it flourisheth and groweth, *but* in the evening it is cut down and withereth.

7 For we are [1]consumed by thine anger, and by thy wrath are we troubled.

8 Thou hast set our iniquities before thee, *and* our secret sins in the light of thy countenance.

9 For all our days are past in thine anger: we have [1]spent our years as a thought.

10 The time of our life *is* threescore years and ten, and if they be of strength, [1]fourscore years: yet their strength *is* but labor and sorrow: for it is cut off quickly, and we flee away.

11 [1]Who knoweth the power of thy wrath? for according to thy fear *is* thine anger.

12 Teach us so to number our days, that we may apply *our* hearts unto [1]wisdom.

13 Return (O Lord, [1]how long?) and be [2]pacified toward thy servants.

14 Fill us with thy mercy in the morning: so shall we rejoice and be glad all our days?

15 Comfort us according to the days that thou hast afflicted us, *and according* to the years that we have seen evil.

16 [1]Let thy work be seen toward thy servants, and thy glory upon their [2]children.

17 And let the [1]beauty of the Lord our God be upon us, and [2]direct thou the work of our hands upon us, even direct the work of our hands.

91

1 Here is described in what assurance he liveth, that putteth his whole trust in God, and committeth himself wholly to his protection in all temptations. 14 A promise of God to those that love him, know him, and trust in him to deliver them, and give them immortal glory.

1 Who so dwelleth in the [1]secret of the most High, shall abide in the shadow of the Almighty.

2 [1]I will say unto the Lord, O my hope, and my fortress: *he is* my God, in him will I trust.

3 Surely I will deliver thee from the [1]snare of the hunter, *and* from the noisome pestilence.

4 He will cover thee under his wings, and thou shalt be sure under his feathers: his [1]truth shall be thy shield and buckler.

5 [1]Thou shalt not be afraid of the fear of the

89:50 [1] He meaneth that God's enemies did not only slander him behind his back: but also mocked him to his face, and as it were cast their injuries in his bosom.

89:51 [1] So he calleth them that persecute the Church.

[2] They laugh at us which patiently wait for the coming of thy Christ.

90:Title [1] Thus the Scripture useth to call the Prophets.

90:1 [1] Thou hast been as an house and defense unto us in all our troubles and travels now this four hundred years.

90:2 [1] Thou hast chosen us to be thy people before the foundations of the world were laid.

90:3 [1] Moses by lamenting the frailty and shortness of man's life moveth God to pity.

90:4 [1] Though man thinks his life long, which is indeed most short, yea though it were a thousand years: yet in God's sight it is as nothing, and as the watch that lasteth but three hours.

90:5 [1] Thou takest them away suddenly as with a flood.

90:7 [1] Thou callest us by thy rods to consider the shortness of our life, and for our sins thou abridgest our days.

90:9 [1] Our days are not only short, but miserable, forasmuch as our sins daily provoke thy wrath.

90:10 [1] Meaning, according to the common state of life.

90:11 [1] If man's life for the brevity be miserable, much more if thy wrath lie upon it, as they which fear thee, only know.

90:12 [1] Which is, by considering the shortness of our life, and by meditating the heavenly joys.

90:13 [1] Meaning, wilt thou be angry?

[2] Or, take comfort in thy servants.

90:16 [1] Even thy mercy, which is the chiefest work.

[2] As God's promises appertained as well to their posterity, as to them, so Moses prayeth for the posterity.

90:17 [1] Meaning, that is was obscured, when he ceaseth to do good to his Church.

[2] For except thou guide us with thine holy Spirit, our enterprises can have no good success.

91:1 [1] He that maketh God his defense and trust, shall perceive his protection to be a most sure safeguard.

91:2 [1] Being assured of this protection, he prayeth unto the Lord.

91:3 [1] That is, God's help is most ready for us, whether Satan assail us secretly, which he calleth a snare: or openly, which is here meant by the pestilence.

91:4 [1] That is, his faithful keeping of promise to help thee in thy necessity.

91:5 [1] The care that God hath over his, is most sufficient to defend them from all dangers.

night: *nor* of the arrow that flieth by day:

6 *Nor* of the pestilence that walketh in the darkness: *nor* of the plague that destroyeth at noon day.

7 A thousand shall fall at thy side, and ten thousand at thy right hand, *but* it shall not come near thee.

8 Doubtless with thine ¹eyes shalt thou behold and see the reward of the wicked.

9 For thou *hast said*, The Lord *is* mine hope: thou hast set the most High for thy refuge.

10 There shall none evil come unto thee, neither shall any plague come near thy tabernacle.

11 ¹For he shall give his Angels charge over thee to keep thee in all thy ways.

12 They shall bear thee in their hands, that thou hurt not thy foot against a stone.

13 Thou shalt walk upon the lion and asp: the ¹young lion, and the dragon shalt thou tread under feet.

14 ¹Because he hath loved me, therefore will I deliver him: I will exalt him because he hath known my Name.

15 He shall call upon me, and I will hear him: I will be with him in trouble: I will deliver him, and glorify him.

16 With ¹long life will I satisfy him, and show him my salvation.

92 *1 This Psalm was made to be sung on the Sabbath, to stir up the people to acknowledge God, and to praise him in his works: the Prophet rejoiceth therein. 6 But the wicked is not able to consider, that the ungodly, when he is most flourishing, shall most speedily perish. 12 In the end is described the felicity of the just, planted in the house of God to praise the Lord.*

A Psalm *or* song for the ¹Sabbath day.

1 It is a good thing to praise the Lord, and to sing unto thy Name, O most High,

2 To declare thy loving kindness in the ¹morning, and thy truth in the night,

3 Upon an ¹instrument of ten strings, and upon the viol, with the song upon the harp.

4 For thou Lord, hast made me glad by thy ¹works, *and* I will rejoice in the works of thine hands.

5 O Lord, how glorious are thy works! *and* thy thoughts are very deep.

6 An ¹unwise man knoweth it not, and a fool doth not understand this,

7 (When the wicked grow as the grass, and all the workers of wickedness do flourish) that they shall be destroyed forever.

8 But thou, O Lord, art ¹most High forevermore.

9 For lo, thine enemies, O Lord: for lo, thine enemies shall perish: all the workers of iniquity shall be destroyed.

10 ¹But thou shalt exalt mine horn, like the unicorns, *and* I shall be anointed with fresh oil.

11 Mine eye also shall see *my desire* against mine enemies: and mine ears shall hear *my wish* against the wicked, that rise up against me.

12 The righteous shall ¹flourish like a palm tree, *and* shall grow like a cedar in Lebanon.

13 Such as be planted in the house of the Lord, shall flourish in the courts of our God.

14 They shall still bring forth fruit in *their* ¹age: they shall be fat and flourishing,

15 To declare that the Lord my rock is righteous, and that none iniquity *is* in him.

93 *1 He praiseth the power of God in the creation of the world, and beateth down all people which lift them up against his majesty, 5 and provoked to consider his promises.*

1 The Lord ¹reigneth, *and* is clothed with majesty: the Lord is clothed, *and* girded with power, the world also shall be established, that it cannot be moved.

2 Thy ¹throne is established of old: thou art from everlasting.

3 ¹The floods have lifted up, O Lord: the floods have

91:8 ¹ The godly shall have some experience of God's judgments against the wicked even in this life, but fully they shall see it at that day when all things shall be revealed.

91:11 ¹ God hath not appointed every man one Angel, but many to be ministers of his providence to keep his, and defend them in their vocation, which is the way to walk in without tempting God.

91:13 ¹ Thou shalt not only be preserved from all evil, but overcome it whether it be secret or open.

91:14 ¹ To assure the faithful of God's protection, he bringeth in God to confirm the same.

91:16 ¹ For he is contented with that life that God giveth: for by death the shortness of this life is recompensed with immortality.

92:Title ¹ Which teacheth that the use of the Sabbath standeth in praising God, and not only in ceasing from work.

92:2 ¹ For God's mercy and fidelity in his promises toward his, bind them to praise him continually both day and night.

92:3 ¹ These instruments were then permitted, but at Christ's coming abolished.

92:4 ¹ He showeth what is the use of the Sabbath: to wit, to meditate God's works.

92:6 ¹ That is, the wicked consider not God's works, nor his judgments against them, and therefore most justly perish.

92:8 ¹ Thy judgments are most constant against the wicked and pass our reach.

92:10 ¹ Thou wilt strengthen them with all power, and bless them with all felicity.

92:12 ¹ Though the faithful seem to wither and be cut down by the wicked, yet they shall grow again and flourish in the Church of God as the cedars do in mount Lebanon.

92:14 ¹ The children of God shall have a power above nature, and their age shall bring forth most fresh fruits.

93:1 ¹ As God by his power and wisdom hath made and governeth the world: so must the same be our defense against all enemies and dangers.

93:2 ¹ Wherein thou sittest and governest the world.

93:3 ¹ God's power appeareth in ruling the furious waters.

lifted up their voice: the floods lift up their waves.

4 The waves of the sea *are* marvelous through the noise of many waters, *yet* the Lord on high is more mighty.

5 Thy [1]testimonies are very sure: holiness becometh thine House, O Lord, forever.

94

1 He prayeth unto God against the violence and arrogance of tyrants,   10 warning them of God's judgments.   12 Then doth he comfort the afflicted by the good issue of their afflictions, as he felt in himself, and did set in others, and by the ruin of the wicked,   23 whom the Lord will destroy.

1 O Lord God [1]the avenger, O God the avenger, show thyself [2]clearly.

2 Exalt thyself, O Judge of the world, *and* render a reward to the proud.

3 Lord, how long shall the wicked, how long shall the wicked [1]triumph?

4 They prate *and* speak fiercely: all the workers of iniquity vaunt themselves.

5 They [1]smite down thy people, O Lord, and trouble thine heritage.

6 They slay the widow and the stranger, and murder the fatherless.

7 [1]Yet they say, The Lord shall not see: neither will the God of Jacob regard it.

8 Understand, ye unwise among the people: and ye fools, when will ye be wise?

9 He that [1]planted the ear, shall he not hear? or he that formed the eye, shall he not see?

10 Or he that chastiseth the [1]nations, shall he not correct? he that teacheth man knowledge, *shall he not know?*

11 The Lord knoweth the thoughts of man, that they are vanity.

12 Blessed *is* the man whom thou [1]chastisest, O Lord, and teachest him in thy Law,

13 That thou mayest give him rest from the days of evil, while the pit is dug for the wicked.

14 Surely the Lord will not fail his people, neither will he forsake his inheritance.

15 For [1]judgment shall return to justice, and all the upright in heart *shall follow* after it.

16 Who will rise up with me against the wicked? or who will take my part against the workers of iniquity?

17 If the Lord had not [1]helped me, my soul had almost dwelt in silence.

18 When I said, [1]My foot slideth, thy mercy, O Lord, stayed me.

19 In the multitude of my [1]thoughts in mine heart, thy comforts have rejoiced my soul.

20 Hath the throne of iniquity [1]fellowship with thee, which forgeth wrong for a Law?

21 They gather them together against the soul of the righteous, and condemn the innocent blood.

22 But the Lord is my refuge, and my God *is* the rock of mine hope.

23 And he will recompense them their wickedness, and [1]destroy them in their own malice, *yea,* the Lord our God shall destroy them.

95

1 An earnest exhortation to praise God,   4 for the government of the world and the election of the Church.   8 An admonition not to follow the rebellion of the old fathers, that tempted God in the wilderness.   11 For the which they might not enter into the land of promise.

1 Come, let us rejoice unto the Lord: let us sing [1]aloud unto the rock of our salvation.

2 Let us come before his face with praise: let us sing loud unto him with Psalms.

3 For the Lord *is* a great God, and a great King above all [1]gods,

4 In whose hand *are* the deep places of the earth, and the [1]heights of the mountains *are* his,

---

93:5 [1] Besides God's power and wisdom in creating and governing, his great mercy also appeareth in that he hath given his people his word and covenant.

94:1 [1] Whose office it is to take vengeance on the wicked.
[2] Show by effect that thou art Judge of the world to punish the wicked.

94:3 [1] That is, brag of their cruelty and oppression: or esteem themselves above all others.

94:5 [1] Seeing the Church was then so sore oppressed, it ought not to seem strange to us, if we see it so now, and therefore we must call to God, to take our cause in hand.

94:7 [1] He showeth that they are desperate in malice, forasmuch as they feared not God, but gave themselves wholly to do wickedly.

94:9 [1] He showeth that it is impossible, but God should hear, see, and understand their wickedness.

94:10 [1] If God punish whole nations for their sins, it is mere folly for any one man, or else a few to think that God will spare them.

94:12 [1] God hath care over his, and chastised them for their wealth,

that they should not perish forever with the wicked.

94:15 [1] God will restore the state and government of things to their right use, and then the Godly shall follow him cheerfully.

94:17 [1] He complaineth of them which would not help him to resist the enemies: yet was assured that God's help would not fail.

94:18 [1] When I thought there was no way but death.

94:19 [1] In my trouble and distress I ever found thy present help.

94:20 [1] Though the wicked judges pretend justice in oppressing the Church, yet they have not that authority of God.

94:23 [1] It is a great token of God's judgment when the purpose of the wicked is broken, but most, when they are destroyed in their own malice.

95:1 [1] He showeth that God's service standeth not in dead ceremonies, but chiefly in the sacrifice of praise and thanksgiving.

95:3 [1] Even the Angels (who in respect of men are thought as gods) are nothing in his sight, much less the idols, which man's brain inventeth.

95:4 [1] All things are governed by his providence.

5   To whom the Sea *belongeth*, for he made it, and his hands formed the dry land.

6   Come, let us [1]worship and fall down, and kneel before the Lord our maker.

7   For he is our God, and we are the people of his pasture, and the sheep of his [1]hand: today, if ye will hear his voice,

8   [1]Harden not your heart, as in [2]Meribah, *and* as in the day of [3]Massah in the wilderness,

9   When your fathers [a]tempted me, proved me, though they had seen my work.

10   Forty years have I contended with *this* generation, and said, They are a people that [1]err in heart, for they have not known my ways.

11   Wherefore I sware in my wrath, *saying*, Surely they shall not enter into [1]my rest.

96

1 An exhortation both to the Jews and Gentiles to praise God for his mercy. And this specially ought to be referred to the kingdom of Christ.

1   Sing [1]unto the Lord a new song: sing unto the Lord all the earth.

2   Sing unto the Lord, *and* praise his Name: declare his salvation from day to day.

3   Declare his glory among all nations, *and* his wonders among all people.

4   For the Lord *is* [1]great and much to be praised: he is to be feared above all gods.

5   For all the gods of the people *are* [1]idols: but the Lord [2]made the heavens.

6   [1]Strength and glory *are* before him: power and beauty *are* in his Sanctuary.

7   Give unto the Lord, ye families of the people: give unto the Lord glory and [1]power.

8   Give unto the Lord the glory of his Name: bring [1]an offering, and enter into his courts.

CHAPTER 95
[a] Exod. 17:1

9   Worship the Lord in the glorious Sanctuary: tremble before him all the earth.

10   Say among the [1]Nations, The Lord reigneth: Surely the world shall be stable, *and* not move, *and* he shall judge the people [2]in righteousness.

11   Let the heavens rejoice, and let the earth be glad: let the sea roar, and all that therein is.

12   Let the field be joyful, and all that is in it: let all the [1]trees of the wood then rejoice,

13   Before the Lord: for he cometh, for he cometh to judge the earth: he will judge the world with righteousness, and the people in his truth.

97

1 The Prophet exhorteth all to rejoice for the coming of the kingdom of Christ, 7 dreadful to the rebels and idolaters, 8 and joyful to the just, whom he exhorteth to innocency, 12 to rejoicing and thanksgiving.

1   The [1]Lord reigneth: let the earth rejoice: let the [2]multitude of the Isles be glad.

2   [1]Clouds and darkness *are* round about him: righteousness and judgment *are* the foundation of his throne.

3   There shall go a fire before him, and burn up his enemies round about.

4   His lightnings gave light unto the world: the earth saw it and was [1]afraid.

5   The mountains melted like wax at the presence of the Lord, at the presence of the Lord of the whole earth.

6   The heavens declare his righteousness, and all the people see his glory.

7   [1]Confounded be all they that serve graven images, *and* that glory in idols: worship him [2]all ye gods.

8   Zion heard of it, and was glad: and the [1]daughters of Judah rejoiced, because of thy judgments, O Lord.

95:6 [1] By these three words he signifieth one thing: meaning that they must wholly give themselves to serve God.
95:7 [1] That is, the flock, whom he governeth with his own hand. He showeth wherein they are God's flock, that is, if they hear his voice.
95:8 [1] By the contemning of God's word.
[2] Or, in strife: whereof the place was so called.
[3] Or, tentation, read Exod. 17:7.
95:10 [1] They were without judgment and reason.
95:11 [1] That is, into the land of Canaan, where he promised them rest.
96:1 [1] The Prophet showeth that the time shall come, that all nations shall have occasion to praise the Lord for the revealing of his Gospel.
96:4 [1] Seeing he will reveal himself to all nations contrary to their own expectation, they ought all to worship him contrary to their own imaginations, and only as he hath appointed.
96:5 [1] Or, vanities.
[2] Then the idols, or whatsoever made not the heavens, are not God.
96:6 [1] God cannot be known, but by his strength and glory, the signs whereof appear in his Sanctuary.
96:7 [1] As by experience ye see that it is only due unto him.
96:8 [1] By offering up yourselves wholly unto God, declare that you worship him only.
96:10 [1] He prophecieth that the Gentiles shall be partakers with the Jews of God's promise.
[2] He shall regenerate them anew with his Spirit, and restore them to the image of God.
96:12 [1] If the insensible creatures shall have cause to rejoice, when God appeareth, much more we, from whom he hath taken malediction and sin.
97:1 [1] He showeth that where God reigneth, there is all felicity, and spiritual joy.
[2] For the Gospel shall not be only preached in Judea, but through all isles and countries.
97:2 [1] He is thus described to keep his enemies in fear, which commonly contemn God's power.
97:4 [1] This fear bringeth not the wicked to true obedience, but maketh them to run away from God.
97:7 [1] He signifieth that God's judgments are in a readiness to destroy the idolaters.
[2] Let all that which is esteemed in the world fall down before him.
97:8 [1] The Jews shall have occasion to rejoice, that the Gentiles are made partakers with them of God's favor.

9 For thou, Lord, art most High above all the earth: thou art much exalted above all gods.

10 Ye that ¹love the Lord, hate evil: he preserveth the souls of his Saints: he will deliver them from the hand of the wicked.

11 ¹Light is sown for the righteous, and joy for the upright in heart.

12 Rejoice ye righteous in the Lord, and give thanks for his holy ¹remembrance.

98

1 An earnest exhortation to all creatures to praise the Lord for his power, mercy and fidelity in his promise by Christ, 10 by whom he hath communicated his salvation to all nations.

A Psalm.

1 Sing ¹unto the Lord a new song: for he hath done marvelous things: ªhis right hand, and his holy ²arm have gotten him the victory.

2 The Lord declared his ¹salvation: his righteousness hath he revealed in the sight of the nations.

3 He hath ¹remembered his mercy and his truth toward the house of Israel: all the ends of the earth have seen the salvation of our God.

4 All the earth, sing ye loud unto the Lord: cry out and rejoice, and sing praises.

5 Sing praise to the Lord upon the harp, *even* upon the harp with a singing voice.

6 With ¹shalms and sound of trumpets sing loud before the Lord the king.

7 Let the sea roar, and all that therein is, the world, and they that dwell therein.

8 Let the floods clap their hands, *and* let the mountains rejoice together,

9 Before the Lord: for he is come to judge the earth: with righteousness shall he judge the world: and the people with equity.

99

1 He commendeth the power, equity, and excellency of the kingdom of God by Christ over the Jews and Gentiles, 5 And provoketh them to magnify the same, and

CHAPTER 98
ª Isa. 59:16

CHAPTER 99
ª Exod. 25:22

to serve the Lord, 6 following the example of the ancient fathers, Moses, Aaron, Samuel, who calling upon God, were heard in their prayers.

1 The Lord reigneth, let the ¹people tremble: he sitteth *between* the ªCherubims, let the earth be moved.

2 The Lord *is* great in Zion, and he is high above all the people.

3 They shall ¹praise thy great and fearful Name (*for it is holy.*)

4 And the King's power, that loveth judgment: *for* thou hast prepared equity: thou hast executed judgment and justice in Jacob.

5 Exalt the Lord our God, and fall down before his ¹footstool: *for* he is holy.

6 Moses and Aaron *were* among his Priests, ¹and Samuel among such as call upon his Name: these called upon the Lord, and he heard them.

7 He spake unto them in the cloudy pillar: they kept his testimonies, *and* the Law *that* he gave them.

8 Thou heardest them, O Lord our God: thou wast a favorable God unto them, though thou didst take vengeance for ¹their inventions.

9 Exalt the Lord our God and fall down before his holy Mountain: for the Lord our God is holy.

100

1 He exhorteth all to serve the Lord, 3 who hath chosen us, and preserved us, 4 and to enter into his assemblies to praise his Name.

A Psalm of praise.

1 Sing ¹ye loud unto the Lord, all the earth.

2 Serve the Lord with gladness; come before him with joyfulness.

3 Know ye that even the Lord is God; he hath ¹made us, and not we ourselves: *we are* his people, and the sheep of his pasture.

4 ¹Enter into his gates with praise, *and* into his courts with rejoicing: praise him *and* bless his Name.

97:10 ¹ He requireth two things of his children: the one that they detest vice, the other, that they put their trust in God for their deliverance.

97:11 ¹ Though God's deliverance appear not suddenly, yet it is sown and laid up in store for them.

97:12 ¹ Be mindful of his benefits and only trust in his defense.

98:1 ¹ That is, some song newly made in token of their wonderful deliverance by Christ.

² He preserveth his Church miraculously.

98:2 ¹ For the deliverance of his Church.

98:3 ¹ God was moved by none other means to gather his Church of the Jews and Gentiles, but because he would perform his promise.

98:6 ¹ By this repetition and earnest exhortation to give praises with instruments, and also of the dumb creatures, he signifieth that the world is never able to praise God sufficiently for their deliverance.

99:1 ¹ When God delivereth his Church, all the enemies shall have cause to tremble.

99:3 ¹ Though the wicked rage against God, but the godly shall praise his Name and mighty power.

99:5 ¹ That is, before his Temple or Ark, where he promised to hear when they worshipped him, as now he promiseth his spiritual presence, wheresoever his Church is assembled.

99:6 ¹ Under these three he comprehendeth the whole people of Israel, with whom God made his promise.

99:8 ¹ For the more liberally that God dealeth with his people, the more doth he punish them that abuse his benefits.

100:1 ¹ He prophecieth that God's benefit in calling the Gentiles shall be so great, that they shall have wonderful occasion to praise his mercy and rejoice.

100:3 ¹ He chiefly meaneth, touching the spiritual regeneration, whereby we are his sheep and people.

100:4 ¹ He showeth that God will not be worshipped, but by that means which he hath appointed.

5 For the Lord is good: his mercy is [1]everlasting, and his truth *is* from generation to generation.

101

1 David describeth what government he will observe in his house and kingdom. 5 He will punish and correct, by rooting forth the wicked, 6 and cherishing the godly persons.

A Psalm of David.

1 I will [1]sing mercy and judgment: unto thee, O Lord, will I sing.

2 I will do wisely in the perfect way, [1]till thou comest to me, I will walk in the uprightness of mine heart in the midst of my house.

3 I will set no wicked thing before mine eyes: I hate [1]the work of them that fall away: it shall not cleave unto me.

4 A froward heart shall depart from me; I will know none evil.

5 Him that privily [1]slandereth his neighbor, will I destroy: him that hath a proud look and high heart, I cannot *suffer*.

6 Mine eyes *shall be* unto the [1]faithful of the land, that they may dwell with me: he that walketh in a perfect way, he shall serve me.

7 There shall no deceitful person dwell within my house: he that telleth lies, shall not remain in my sight.

8 [1]Betimes will I destroy all the wicked of the land that I may cut off all the workers of iniquity from the City of the Lord.

102

1 It seemeth that this prayer was appointeth to the faithful to pray in the captivity of Babylon. 16 A consolation for the building of the Church: 18 whereof followeth the praise of God to be published unto all posterity. 22 The conversion of the Gentiles, 28 and the stability of the Church.

A prayer [1]of the afflicted, when he shall be in distress, and pour forth his meditation before the Lord.

1 O Lord hear my prayer, and let my [1]cry come unto thee.

2 Hide not thy face from me in the time of my trouble: incline thine ears unto me, when I call, make haste to hear me.

3 For my days are [1]consumed like smoke, and my bones are burnt like an hearth.

4 Mine heart is smitten, and withered like grass, because I forgat [1]to eat my bread.

5 For the voice of my groaning, my bones do cleave to my skin.

6 I am like a [1]pelican of the wilderness: I am like an owl of the deserts.

7 I watch, and am as a sparrow alone upon the house top.

8 Mine enemies revile me daily, *and* they that rage against me, have [1]sworn against me.

9 Surely I have [1]eaten ashes as bread, and mingled my drink with weeping,

10 Because of thine [1]indignation and thy wrath: for thou hast heaved me up, and cast me down.

11 My days *are* like a shadow that fadeth, and I am withered like grass.

12 But thou, O Lord, dost [1]remain forever, and thy remembrance from generation to generation.

13 Thou wilt arise *and* have mercy upon Zion: for the time to have mercy thereon, for the [1]appointed time is come.

14 For thy servants delight in the [1]stones thereof, and have pity on the dust thereof.

15 Then the heathen shall fear the Name of the Lord, and all the kings of the earth thy glory,

16 When the Lord shall build up Zion, *and* shall appear [1]in his glory,

17 *And* shall turn unto the prayer of the desolate,

100:5 [1] He declareth that we ought never to be weary in praising him, seeing his mercies towards us last forever.

101:1 [1] David considereth what manner of King he would be, when God should place him in the throne, promising openly, that he would be merciful and just.

101:2 [1] Though as yet thou deferrest to place me in the Kingly dignity, yet will I give myself to wisdom and uprightness being a private man.

101:3 [1] He showeth that Magistrates do not their duties, except they be enemies to all vice.

101:5 [1] In promising to punish these vices, which are most pernicious in them that are about Kings, he declareth that he will punish all.

101:6 [1] He showeth what is the true use of the sword: to punish the wicked, and to maintain the good.

101:8 [1] Magistrates must immediately punish vice, lest it grow to further inconvenience: and if heathen magistrates are bound to do this, how much more they that have the charge of the Church of God?

102:Title [1] Whereby is signified, that albeit we be in never so great miseries, yet there is ever place left for prayer.

102:1 [1] He declareth that in our prayer we must lively feel that, which we desire, and steadfastly believe to obtain.

102:3 [1] These excessive kinds of speech show how much the affliction of the Church ought to wound the hearts of the godly.

102:4 [1] My sorrows were so great, that I passed not for mine ordinary food.

102:6 [1] Ever mourning and solitary, casting out fearful cries.

102:8 [1] Have conspired my death.

102:9 [1] I have not risen out of my mourning to take my refection.

102:10 [1] He showeth that the afflictions did not only thus move him, but chiefly the feeling of God's displeasure.

102:12 [1] Howsoever we be frail, yet thy promise is sure, and the remembrance thereof shall confirm us forever.

102:13 [1] That is, the seventy years for which by the Prophet Jeremiah thou didst appoint, Jer. 29:12.

102:14 [1] The more that the Church is in misery and desolation, the more ought the faithful to love and pity it.

102:16 [1] That is, when he shall have drawn his church out of the darkness of death.

and not despise their prayer.

18 This shall be written for the generation to come: and the people which shall be ¹created, shall praise the Lord.

19 For he hath looked down from the height of his Sanctuary: out of the heaven did the Lord behold the earth,

20 That he might hear the mourning of the prisoner, and deliver the ¹children of death.

21 That they may declare the Name of the Lord in Zion, and his praise in Jerusalem,

22 When the people shall be gathered ¹together, and the kingdoms to serve the Lord.

23 He ¹abated my strength in the way, *and* shortened my days.

24 *And* I said, O my God, take me not away in the midst of my days: thy years *endure* from generation to generation.

25 Thou hast aforetime laid the foundation of the earth, and the heavens *are* the work of thine hands.

26 ¹They shall perish, but thou shalt endure: even they all shall wax old as doth a garment: as a vesture shalt thou change them, and they shall be changed.

27 But thou art the same, and thy years shall not fail.

28 The children of thy servants shall continue, and their seed shall stand ¹fast in thy sight.

103

1 He provoketh all to praise the Lord, which hath pardoned his sins, delivered him from destruction and given him sufficient of all good things. 10 Then he addeth the tender mercies of God, which he showeth like a most tender Father toward his children. 14 The frailty of man's life. 20 An exhortation to man and Angels to praise the Lord.

A Psalm of David.

1 My soul, ¹praise thou the Lord, and all that is within me, *praise* his holy Name.

2 My soul, praise thou the Lord, and forget not all his benefits.

3 Which ¹forgiveth all thine iniquity, and healeth all thine infirmities.

4 Which redeemeth thy life from the ¹grave; and crowneth thee with mercy and compassions.

5 Which satisfieth thy mouth with good things: and thy ¹youth is renewed like the eagle's.

6 The Lord executeth righteousness and judgment to all that are oppressed.

7 He made his ways known unto ¹Moses, *and* his works unto the children of Israel.

8 The Lord is full of compassion and mercy, slow to anger and of great kindness.

9 He will not always ¹chide, neither keep *his* anger forever.

10 He hath not ¹dealt with us after our sins, nor rewarded us according to our iniquities.

11 For as high as the heaven is above the earth, so great is his mercy toward them that fear him.

12 As far as ¹the East is from the West: so far hath he removed our sins from us.

13 As a father hath compassion on his children, so hath the Lord compassion on them that fear him.

14 For he knoweth whereof we be made: he remembereth that we are but dust.

15 The days of ¹man are as grass: as a flower of the field, so flourisheth he.

16 For the wind goeth over it, and it is gone, and the place thereof shall know it no more.

17 But the loving kindness of the Lord *endureth* forever and ever upon them that fear him, and his ¹righteousness upon children's children,

18 Unto them that keep his ¹covenant, and think

102:18 ¹ The deliverance of the Church is a most excellent benefit, and therefore he compareth it to a new creation: for in their banishment the body of the Church seemed to have been dead, which by deliverance was as it were created anew.

102:20 ¹ Who now in their banishment could look for nothing but death.

102:22 ¹ He showeth that God's Name is never more praised, than when religion flourisheth and the church increaseth: which thing is chiefly accomplished under the kingdom of Christ.

102:23 ¹ The Church laments that they see not the time of Christ, which was promised, but have but few years and short days.

102:26 ¹ If heaven and earth perish, much more man shall perish: but the Church by reason of God's promise endureth forever.

102:28 ¹ Seeing thou hast chosen thy Church out of the world, and joined it to thee, it cannot but continue forever: for thou art everlasting.

103:1 ¹ He wakeneth his dullness to praise God, showing that both understanding and affections, mind and heart are too little to set forth his praise.

103:3 ¹ That is, the beginning and chiefest of all benefits, remission of sin.

103:4 ¹ For before that we have remission of our sins, we are as dead men in the grave.

103:5 ¹ As the eagle, when her beak overgroweth, sucketh blood, and so is renewed in strength, even so God miraculously giveth strength to his Church above all man's expectation.

103:7 ¹ As to his chief minister, and next to his people.

103:9 ¹ He showeth first his severe judgment, but so soon as the sinner is humbled, he received him to mercy.

103:10 ¹ Who have proved by continual experience, that his mercy hath ever prevailed against our offences.

103:12 ¹ As great as the world is, so full is it of signs of God's mercies toward his faithful, when he hath removed their sins.

103:15 ¹ He declareth that man hath nothing in himself to move God to mercy, but only the confession of his infirmity and misery.

103:17 ¹ His just and faithful keeping of his promise.

103:18 ¹ To whom he giveth grace to fear him, and to obey his word.

upon his commandments to do them.

19 The Lord hath prepared his throne in heaven, and his kingdom ruleth over all.

20 Praise the Lord, ye [1]his Angels, that excel in strength, that do his commandment in obeying the voice of his word.

21 Praise the Lord all ye his hosts, ye his servants that do his pleasure.

22 Praise the Lord all ye his works, in all places of his dominion: my soul, praise thou the Lord.

104
1 An excellent Psalm to praise God for the creation of the world, and the governance of the same by his marvelous providence. 35 Wherein the Prophet prayeth against the wicked, who are occasions that God diminisheth his blessings.

1 My soul, praise thou the Lord: O Lord my God, thou art exceeding great, thou art [1]clothed with glory and honor.

2 Which covereth himself with light, as with a garment, and spreadeth the heavens like a curtain.

3 Which layeth the beams of his chambers in the waters, and maketh the clouds his chariot, and walketh upon the wings of the wind.

4 Which [1]maketh the spirits his messengers, and a flaming fire his ministers.

5 He set the earth upon her foundations, so that it shall never move.

6 Thou coverest it with the [1]deep as with a garment: the [2]waters would stand above the mountains.

7 But at thy rebuke they flee: at the voice of thy thunder they haste away.

8 And the mountains ascend, and the valleys descend to the place which thou hast established for them.

9 But thou hast set them a bound which they shall not pass: they shall not return to cover the earth.

10 He sendeth the springs into the valleys, which run between the mountains.

11 They shall give drink to all the [1]beasts of the field, and the wild asses shall quench their thirst.

12 By these [1]springs shall the fowls of the heaven dwell, and sing among the branches.

13 He watereth the mountains from his [1]chambers, and the earth is filled with the fruit of thy works.

14 He causeth grass to grow for the cattle, and herb for the use of [1]man, that he may bring forth bread out of the earth,

15 And wine that maketh glad the heart of man, and oil to make his face to shine, and bread that strengtheneth man's heart.

16 The high trees are satisfied, even the cedars of Lebanon, which he hath planted,

17 That the birds may make their nests there: the stork dwelleth in the fir trees.

18 The high mountains are for the [1]goats: the rocks are a refuge for the conies.

19 He appointed [1]the moon for certain seasons: [2]the sun knoweth his going down.

20 Thou makest darkness, and it is night, wherein all the beasts of the forest creep forth.

21 The lions roar after their prey, and seek their meat [1]at God.

22 When the sun riseth, they retire, and couch in their dens.

23 [1]Then goeth man forth to his work, and to his labor until the evening.

24 O Lord, how [1]manifold are thy works! in wisdom hast thou made them all: the earth is full of thy riches.

25 So is the sea great and wide: for therein are things creeping innumerable, both small beasts and great.

26 There go the ships, yea that [1]Leviathan, whom thou hast made to play therein.

27 [1]All these wait upon thee, that thou mayest

103:20 [1] In that that we, which naturally are slow to praise God, exhort the Angels, who willingly do it, we stir up ourselves to consider our duty, and awake out of our sluggishness.

104:1 [1] The Prophet showeth that we need not to enter into the heavens to seek God, forasmuch as all the order of nature, with the propriety, and placing of the elements, are most lively mirrors to see his majesty in.

104:4 [1] As the Prophet here showeth that all visible powers are ready to serve God: so the Apostle to the Hebrews 1:7, beholdeth in this glass how the very Angels also, are obedient to his commandment.

104:6 [1] Thou makest the sea to be an ornament unto the earth.

[2] If by thy power thou didst not bridle the rage of the waters, it were not possible, but the whole world should be destroyed.

104:11 [1] If God provide for the very beasts, much more will he extend his provident care to man.

104:12 [1] There is no part of the world so barren, where most evident signs of God's blessings appear not.

104:13 [1] From the clouds.

104:14 [1] He describeth God's provident care over man, who doth not only provide necessary things for him, as herbs and other meat: but also things to rejoice and comfort him as wine and oil, or ointments.

104:18 [1] Or, does, roes, and such like.

104:19 [1] As to separate the night from the day, and to note days, months and years.

[2] That is, by his course, either far or near, it noteth summer, winter and other seasons.

104:21 [1] That is, they only find meat according to God's providence, who careth even for the brute beasts.

104:23 [1] To wit, when the day springeth: for the light is as it were a shield to defend man against the tyranny and fierceness of beasts.

104:24 [1] He confesseth that no tongue is able to express God's works, nor mind to comprehend them.

104:26 [1] Or, whale.

104:27 [1] God is a most nourishing Father, who provideth for all creatures their daily foods.

give them food in due season.

28 Thou givest it to them, *and* they gather it, thou openest thy hand, *and* they are filled with good things.

29 *But if* thou ¹hide thy face, they are troubled: *if* thou take away their breath, they die and return to their dust:

30 *Again if* thou ¹send forth thy spirit, they are created, and thou renewest the face of the earth.

31 Glory be to the Lord forever: let the Lord rejoice in his works.

32 He looketh on the earth and it trembleth: he toucheth the mountains, and they ¹smoke.

33 I will sing unto the Lord *all* my life: I will praise my God, while I live.

34 Let my words be acceptable unto him: I will rejoice in the Lord.

35 Let the sinners be ¹consumed out of the earth, and the wicked till there be no more: O my soul, praise thou the Lord. Praise ye the Lord.

105

1 He praiseth the singular grace of God, who hath of all the people of the world chosen a peculiar people to himself, and having chosen them, never ceaseth to do them good, even for his promise's sake.

1 Praise the Lord, *and* call upon his Name: ¹declare his works among the people.

2 Sing unto him, sing praise unto him, *and* talk of all his wondrous works.

3 Rejoice in his holy Name, let the heart of them that seek the Lord, rejoice.

4 Seek the Lord and his ¹strength: seek his face continually.

5 Remember his ¹marvelous works that he hath done, his wonders, and the ²judgments of his mouth,

6 Ye seed of Abraham his servant, ye children of Jacob, which are his elect.

7 He is the Lord our God: his judgments *are*

through all the earth.

8 He hath always remembered his covenant, *and* promise, that he made to a thousand generations,

9 *Even* that which he ¹made with Abraham, and his oath unto Isaac:

10 And *since* hath confirmed it to Jacob for a law, *and* to Israel for an everlasting covenant,

11 Saying, ¹Unto thee will I give the land of Canaan, the lot of your inheritance.

12 Albeit they were few in number, *yea* very few, and strangers in the land,

13 And walked about from nation to nation, from *one* kingdom to another people,

14 *Yet* suffered he no man to do them wrong, but reproved ¹Kings for their sakes, *saying*,

15 Touch not mine ¹anointed, and do my ²Prophets no harm.

16 Moreover, he called a famine upon the land, *and* utterly brake the ¹staff of bread.

17 *But* he sent a man before them: Joseph was sold for a slave.

18 They held his feet in the stocks, *and* he was laid in irons,

19 Until ¹his appointed time came, *and* the counsel of the Lord had tried him.

20 The King sent and loosed him: *even* the Ruler of the people delivered him.

21 He made him lord of his house, and ruler of all his substance,

22 That he should bind his ¹princes unto his will, and teach his Ancients wisdom.

23 Then Israel came to Egypt, and Jacob was a stranger in the land of Ham.

24 And he increased his people exceedingly, and made them stronger than their oppressors.

25 ¹He turned their heart to hate his people, and to deal craftily with his servants.

26 *Then* sent he Moses his servant, *and* Aaron

104:29 ¹ As by thy presence all things have life: so if thou withdraw thy blessings, they all perish.

104:30 ¹ As the death of creatures showeth that we are nothing of ourselves: so their generation declareth that we receive all things of our Creator.

104:32 ¹ God's merciful face giveth strength unto the earth, but his severe countenance burneth the mountains.

104:35 ¹ Who infect the world, and so cause God that he cannot rejoice in his works.

105:1 ¹ Forasmuch as the Israelites were exempted from the common condemnation of the world, and were elected to be God's people, the Prophet willeth them to show themselves mindful by thanksgiving.

105:4 ¹ By the strength and face he meaneth the Ark where God declared his power and his presence.

105:5 ¹ Which he hath wrought in the deliverance of his people.
² Because his power was thereby as lively declared, as if he should have declared it by mouth.

105:9 ¹ The promise which God made to Abraham to be his God, and the God of his seed after him, he renewed and repeated it again to his seed after him.

105:11 ¹ He showeth that they should not enjoy the land of Canaan by any other means, but by reason of his covenant made with their fathers.

105:14 ¹ That is, the king of Egypt and the king of Gerar, Gen. 12:17 and 20:3.

105:15 ¹ Those whom I have sanctified to be my people.
² Meaning, the old fathers, to whom God showed himself plainly, and who were setters forth of his word.

105:16 ¹ Either by sending scarcity, or by taking away the strength and nourishment thereof.

105:19 ¹ So long he suffered adversity as God had appointed, and till he had tried sufficiently his patience.

105:22 ¹ That the very princes of the countries should be at Joseph's commandment, and learn wisdom at him.

105:25 ¹ So it is in God, either to move the hearts of the wicked to love or to hate God's children.

whom he had chosen.

27 They showed among them the message of his signs, and wonders in the land of Ham.

28 He sent darkness, and made it dark: and they were not [1]disobedient unto his commission.

29 [a]He turned their waters into blood, and slew their fish.

30 [b]Their land brought forth frogs, *even* in their King's chambers.

31 He [1]spake, and there came swarms of flies *and* lice in all their quarters.

32 He gave them [1]hail for rain, *and* flames of fire in their land.

33 He smote their vines also and their fig trees, and brake down the trees in their coasts.

34 [1]He spake and the grasshoppers came, and caterpillars innumerable,

35 And did eat up all the grass in their land, and devoured the fruit of their ground.

36 [c]He smote also all the firstborn in their land, *even* the beginning of all their strength.

37 He brought them forth also with silver and gold, and there was [1]none feeble among their tribes.

38 Egypt was [1]glad at their departing: for the fear of them had fallen upon them.

39 He spread a cloud to be a covering, and fire to give light in the night.

40 They [1]asked, and he brought quails, and he filled them with the bread of heaven.

41 He opened the rock, and the water flowed out, *and* ran in the dry places *like* a river.

42 For he remembered his holy [1]promise to Abraham his servant,

43 And he brought forth his people with [1]joy, *and* his chosen with gladness,

44 And gave them the lands of the heathen, and they took the labors of the people in possession,

45 That they might [1]keep his statutes, and observe his Laws. Praise ye the Lord.

CHAPTER 105
[a] Exod. 7:20
[b] Exod. 8:6
[c] Exod. 12:29

CHAPTER 106
[a] Exod. 14:27

106

1 *The people dispersed under Antiochus, do magnify the goodness of God among the just and repentant:* 4 *Desiring to be brought again into the land by God's merciful visitation.* 8 *And after the manifold marvels of God wrought in their deliverance forth of Egypt, And the great ingratitude of the people rehearsed.* 47 *They do pray and desire to be gathered from among the heathen, to the intent that they may praise the Name of the God of Israel.*

Praise ye the Lord.

1 Praise [1]ye the Lord because he is good, for his mercy *endureth* forever.

2 Who can express the noble acts of the Lord, *or* show forth all his praise?

3 Blessed *are* they that [1]keep judgment, and do righteousness at all times.

4 Remember me, O Lord, with the [1]favor of thy people: visit me with thy salvation,

5 That I may see the felicity of thy chosen, and rejoice in the joy of thy people, and glory with thine inheritance.

6 We have [1]sinned with our fathers: we have committed iniquity, *and* done wickedly.

7 Our fathers understood not thy wonders in Egypt, neither remembered they the multitude of thy mercies, but rebelled at the Sea, *even* at the red sea.

8 Nevertheless he [1]saved them for his Name's sake, that he might make his power to be known.

9 And he rebuked the red sea, and it was dried up, and he led them in the deep, as in the wilderness.

10 And he saved them from the adversary's hand, and delivered them from the hand of the enemy.

11 [a]And the waters covered their oppressors: not one of them was left.

12 Then [1]believed they his words, *and* sang praise unto him.

13 But incontinently they forgat his works, they waited not for his [1]counsel,

105:28 [1] Meaning, Moses and Aaron.
105:31 [1] So that this vermin came not by fortune, but as God had appointed, and his prophet Moses spake.
105:32 [1] It was strange to see rain in Egypt, much more it was fearful to see hail.
105:34 [1] He showeth that all creatures are armed against man when God is his enemy, as at his commandment the grasshoppers destroyed the land.
105:37 [1] When their enemies felt God's plagues his children by his providence were exempted.
105:38 [1] For God's plagues caused them rather to depart with the Israelites, than with their lives.
105:40 [1] Not for necessity, but for satisfying of their lust.
105:42 [1] Which he confirmeth to the posterity, in whom after a sort the dead live and enjoy the promises.
105:43 [1] When the Egyptians lamented and were destroyed.
105:45 [1] This is the end, why God preserveth his Church, because they should worship, and call upon him in this world.

106:1 [1] The Prophet exhorteth the people to praise God for his benefits past, that thereby their minds may be strengthened against all present troubles and despair.
106:3 [1] He showeth that it is not enough to praise God with the mouth, except the whole heart agree thereunto, and all our life be thereunto framed.
106:4 [1] Let the good will that thou bearest to thy people, extend unto me, that thereby I may be received into the number of thine.
106:6 [1] By earnest confession as well of their own, as of their fathers' sins, they show that they had hope that God according to his promise would pity them.
106:8 [1] The inestimable goodness of God appeareth in this, that he would change the order of nature, rather than his people should not be delivered, although they were wicked.
106:12 [1] The wonderful works of God caused them to believe for a time, and to praise him.
106:13 [1] They would prevent his wisdom and providence.

14　But lusted with concupiscence in the wilderness, and tempted God in the desert.

15　Then he gave them their desire: but he sent [1]leanness into their soul.

16　They envied Moses also in the tents, *and* Aaron the holy one of the Lord.

17　*Therefore* the earth opened and [1]swallowed up Dathan, and covered the company of Abiram.

18　And the fire was kindled in their assembly: the flame burnt up the wicked.

19　They made a calf in Horeb, and worshipped the molten image.

20　Thus they turned their [1]glory into the similitude of a bullock, that eateth grass.

21　They forgat God their Savior, which had done great things in Egypt,

22　Wondrous works in the land of Ham, and fearful things by the red sea.

23　Therefore he minded to destroy them, had [1]not Moses his chosen stood in the breach before him to turn away his wrath, lest he should destroy *them*.

24　Also they contemned [1]that pleasant land, *and* believed not his word,

25　But murmured in their tents, *and* hearkened not unto the voice of the Lord.

26　Therefore [1]he lifted up his hand against them, to destroy them in the wilderness,

27　And to destroy their seed among the nations, and to scatter them throughout the countries.

28　They joined themselves also unto [1]Baal of Peor, and did eat the offerings of the [2]dead.

29　Thus they [1]provoked *him* unto anger with their own inventions, and the plague brake in upon them.

30　But [1]Phinehas stood up, and executed judgment, and the plague was stayed.

31　[b]And it was [1]imputed unto him for righteousness from generation to generation forever.

b Num. 25:12
c Num. 20:13
Ps. 95:8

32　They angered him also at the waters of [c]Meribah, so that [1]Moses was punished for their sakes,

33　Because they vexed his Spirit, so that he spake unadvisedly with his lips.

34　Neither destroyed they the people, as the Lord had commanded them,

35　But were mingled among the heathen, and learned their works,

36　And served their idols, which were their ruin.

37　Yea, they offered their [1]sons, and their daughters unto devils,

38　And shed innocent blood, *even* the blood of their sons, and of their daughters whom they offered unto the idols of Canaan, and the land was defiled with blood.

39　Thus were they stained with their own works, and went [1]a whoring with their own inventions.

40　Therefore was the wrath of the Lord kindled against his people, and he abhorred his own inheritance.

41　And he gave them into the hand of the heathen: and they that hated them were lords over them.

42　Their enemies also oppressed them, and they were humbled under their hand.

43　Many [1]a time did he deliver them, but they provoked him by their counsels: therefore they were brought down by their iniquity.

44　Yet he saw when they were in affliction, and he heard their cry.

45　And he remembered his covenant toward them, and [1]repented according to the multitude of his mercies,

46　And gave them favor in the sight of all them that led them captives.

47　Save us, O Lord our God, and [1]gather us from among the heathen, that we may praise thine holy Name, and glory in thy praise.

48　Blessed *be* the Lord God of Israel forever and ever, and let all the people say, So be it. Praise ye the Lord.

106:15 [1] The abundance that God gave them, profited not, but made them pine away, because God cursed it.

106:17 [1] By the greatness of the punishment the heinous offence may be considered: for they that rise against God's ministers, rebel against him.

106:20 [1] He showeth that all idolaters renounce God to be their glory, when instead of him they worship any creature, much more wood, stone, metal, or calves.

106:23 [1] If Moses by his intercession had not obtained God's favor against their rebellions.

106:24 [1] That is, Canaan, which was as it were an earnest penny of the heavenly inheritance.

106:26 [1] That is, he sware. Sometimes also it meaneth, to punish.

106:28 [1] Which was the idol of the Moabites.

[2] Sacrifices offered to the dead idols.

106:29 [1] Signifying that whatsoever man inventeth of himself to serve God by, is detestable, and provoketh his anger.

106:30 [1] When all others neglected God's glory, he in his zeal killed the adulterers and prevented God's wrath.

106:31 [1] This act declared his lively faith, and for his faith's sake was accepted.

106:32 [1] If so notable a Prophet of God escape not punishment, though others provoked him to sin, how much more shall they be subject to God's judgment, which cause God's children to sin?

106:37 [1] He showeth how monstrous a thing idolatry is, which can win us to things abhorring to nature, whereas God's word cannot obtain most small things.

106:39 [1] Then true chastity is to cleave wholly and only unto God.

106:43 [1] The prophet showeth that neither by menaces, nor promises we can come to God, except we be altogether newly reformed, and that his mercy overcover and hide our malice.

106:45 [1] Not that God is changeable in himself, but that then he seemeth to us to repent when he altereth his punishment, and forgiveth us.

106:47 [1] Gather thy Church, which is dispersed, and give us constancy under the cross, that with one consent we may all praise thee.

107

1 The Prophet exhorteth all those that are redeemed by the Lord and gathered unto him, to give thanks, 9 for this merciful providence of God governing all things at his good pleasures, 20 sending good and evil, prosperity and adversity to bring men unto him. 42 Therefore as the righteous thereat rejoice, so shall the wicked have their mouth stopped.

1 Praise ¹the Lord, because he is good: for his mercy *endureth* forever.

2 Let them, ¹which have been redeemed of the Lord, show how he hath delivered them from the hand of the oppressor,

3 And gathered them out of the lands, from the East and from the West, from the North and from the ¹South.

4 *When* they wandered in the desert *and* wilderness out of the way, *and* found no city to dwell in,

5 ¹Both hungry *and* thirsty, their soul fainted in them.

6 Then they cried unto the Lord in their trouble, *and* he delivered them from their distress,

7 And led them forth by the right way, that they might go to a city of habitation.

8 Let them *therefore* confess before the Lord his loving kindness, and his wonderful works before the sons of men.

9 For he satisfied the thirsty soul, and filled the hungry soul with goodness.

10 They that dwell in darkness and in the shadow of death, being bound in misery and iron,

11 Because they ¹rebelled against the words of the Lord, and despised the counsel of the most High,

12 When he humbled their heart with heaviness, *then* they fell down, and there was no helper.

13 Then they ¹cried unto the Lord in their trouble, *and* he delivered them from their distress.

14 He brought them out of darkness, and *out of* the shadow of death, and brake their bands asunder.

15 Let them *therefore* confess before the Lord his loving-kindness, and his wonderful works before the sons of men.

16 For he hath broken the ¹gates of brass, and burst the bars of iron asunder,

17 ¹Fools by reason of their transgression, and because of their iniquities are afflicted.

18 Their soul abhorreth all meat, and they are brought to death's door.

19 Then they cry unto the Lord in their trouble, *and* he delivereth them from their distress.

20 ¹He sendeth his word and healeth them, and delivereth them from their ²graves.

21 Let them *therefore* confess before the Lord his loving kindness, and his wonderful works before the sons of men,

22 And let them offer sacrifices of ¹praise, and declare his works with rejoicing.

23 They that go down to the ¹sea in ships, *and* occupy by the great waters,

24 They see the works of the Lord, and his wonders in the deep.

25 For he commandeth and raiseth the stormy wind, and it lifteth up the waves thereof.

26 They mount up to the heaven, *and* descend to the deep, so that their soul ¹melteth for trouble.

27 They are tossed to and fro, and stagger like a drunken man, and all their ¹cunning is gone.

28 Then they cry unto the Lord in their trouble, *and* he bringeth them out of their distress.

29 He turneth the storm to calm, so that the waves thereof are still.

30 When they are ¹quieted, they are glad, and he bringeth them unto the haven, where they would be.

31 Let them *therefore* confess before the Lord his loving kindness, and his wonderful works before the sons of men.

32 And let them exalt him in the ¹congregation of the people, and praise him in the assembly of the Elders.

33 He turneth the floods to a wilderness, and the

107:1 ¹ This notable sentence was in the beginning used as the foot or tenor of the song, which was oftentimes repeated.

107:2 ¹ As this was true in the Jews, so there is none of God's elect, that feel not his help in their necessity.

107:3 ¹ Or, from the sea: meaning the red sea, which is on the South part of the land.

107:5 ¹ He showeth that there is none affliction so grievous, out of the which God will not deliver his, and also exhorteth them that are delivered to be mindful of so great a benefit.

107:11 ¹ Then the true way to obey God, is to follow his express commandment: also hereby all are exhorted to descend into themselves, forasmuch as none are punished but for their sins.

107:13 ¹ He showeth that the cause why God doth punish us extremely, is because we can be brought unto him by none other means.

107:16 ¹ When there seemeth to man's judgment no recovery, but all things are brought to despair, then God chiefly showeth his mighty power.

107:17 ¹ They that have no fear of God, by his sharp rods are brought to call upon him, and so find mercy.

107:20 ¹ By healing them he declareth his good will toward them.
² Meaning, their diseases, which had almost brought them to the grave and corruption.

107:22 ¹ Praise and confession of God's benefits are the true sacrifices of the godly.

107:23 ¹ He showeth by the sea what care God hath over man, for in that that he delivereth them from the great danger of the sea, he delivereth them, as it were from a thousand deaths.

107:26 ¹ Their fear and danger is so great.

107:27 ¹ When their art and means fail them, they are compelled to confess that only God's providence doth preserve them.

107:30 ¹ Though before every drop seemed to fight one against another, yet at his commandment they are as still, as though they were frozen.

107:32 ¹ This great benefit ought not only to be considered particularly, but magnified in all places and assemblies.

springs of waters into dryness,

34 *And* a fruitful land into [1]barrenness, for the wickedness of them that dwell therein.

35 *Again* he [1]turneth the wilderness into pools of water, and the dry land into water springs.

36 And there he placeth the hungry, and they build a city to dwell in,

37 And sow the fields, and plant vineyards, which bring forth fruitful [1]increase.

38 For he blesseth them, and they multiply exceedingly, and he diminisheth not their cattle.

39 [1]*Again men* are diminished, and brought low by oppression, evil and sorrow.

40 He poureth [1]contempt upon princes, and causeth them to err in desert places out of the way.

41 Yet he raiseth up the poor out of misery, and maketh him families like a flock of sheep.

42 The [1]righteous shall see it, and rejoice, and all iniquity shall stop her mouth.

43 Who is wise that he may observe these things? for they shall understand the loving kindness of the Lord.

108 *This Psalm is composed of two other Psalms before the seven and fiftieth and the sixtieth. The matter here contained is,   1 That David giveth himself with heart and voice to praise the Lord,   7 and assureth himself of the promise of God concerning his kingdom over Israel, and his power against other nations: 11 Who though he seem to forsake us for a time, yet he alone will in the end cast down our enemies.*

A song or Psalm of David.

1 O God, mine heart *is* [1]prepared, so *is* [2]my tongue: I will sing and give praise.

2 Awake viol and harp, I will awake early.

3 I will praise thee, O Lord, among the [1]people, and I will sing unto thee among the nations.

4 For thy mercy is great above the heavens, and thy truth unto the clouds.

5 [1]Exalt thyself, O God, above the heavens, and

let thy glory *be* upon all the earth,

6 That thy beloved may be delivered: [1]help with thy right hand and hear me.

7 God hath spoken in his [1]holiness: *therefore* I will rejoice, I shall divide Shechem and measure the valley of Succoth.

8 Gilead *shall be* mine, *and* Manasseh *shall be* mine: Ephraim also *shall be* the strength of mine head: Judah *is* my lawgiver.

9 *a*Moab *shall be* my washpot: over Edom will I cast out my shoe: upon Palestine will I triumph.

10 Who will lead me into the strong city? who will bring me unto Edom?

11 [1]Wilt not thou, O God, *which* hadst forsaken us, and didst not go forth, O God, with our armies?

12 Give us help against trouble: for vain is the help of man.

13 Through God we shall do valiantly: for he shall tread down our enemies.

109 *1 David being falsely accused by flatterers unto Saul, prayeth God to help him, and to destroy his enemies.   8 And under them he speaketh of Judas the traitor unto Jesus Christ, and of all the like enemies of the children of God: 27 And desireth so to be delivered, that his enemies may know the work to be of God.   30 Then doth he promise to give praise unto God.*

To him that excelleth. A Psalm of David.

1 Hold not thy tongue, O God of my [1]praise.

2 For the mouth of the wicked, and the mouth *full* of deceit are opened upon me: they have spoken to me with a lying tongue.

3 They compassed me about also with words of hatred, and fought against me without a cause.

4 For my friendship they were my adversaries, [1]but I gave myself to prayer.

5 And they have rewarded me evil for good, and hatred for my friendship.

6 [1]Set thou the wicked over him, and let the adversary stand at his right hand.

107:34 [1] Or, saltness.

107:35 [1] For the love that he beareth to his Church, he changeth the order of nature for their commodity.

107:37 [1] Continual increase and yearly.

107:39 [1] As God by his providence doth exalt men, so doth he also humble them by afflictions to know themselves.

107:40 [1] For their wickedness and tyranny he causeth the people and subjects to contemn them.

107:42 [1] They, whose faith is lightened by God's spirit, shall rejoice to see God's judgments against the wicked and ungodly.

108:1 [1] This earnest affection declareth that he is free from hypocrisy, and that sluggishness stayeth him not.

[2] Or, my glory, because it chiefly setteth forth the glory of God.

108:3 [1] He prophecieth of the calling of the Gentiles: for except they were called, they could not hear the goodness of God.

108:5 [1] Let all the world see thy judgments in that that thou art God

over all, and so confess that thou art glorious.

108:6 [1] When God by his benefits maketh us partakers of his mercies, he admonisheth us to be earnest in prayer, to desire him to continue and finish his graces.

108:7 [1] As he hath spoken to Samuel concerning me, so will he show himself constant, and holy in his promise, so that these nations following shall be subject unto me.

108:11 [1] From the sixth verse of this Psalm unto the last, read the exposition of Ps. 60:5.

109:1 [1] Though all the world condemn me, yet thou wilt approve mine innocence, and that is a sufficient praise to me.

109:4 [1] To declare that I had no other refuge, but thee, in whom my conscience was at rest.

109:6 [1] Whether it were Doeg, or Saul, or some familiar friend that had betrayed him, he prayeth not of private affection, but moved by God's Spirit, that God would take vengeance upon him.

7　When he shall be judged, let him be condemned, and let his [1]prayer be turned into sin.

8　Let his days be few, and let another take his [1]charge.

9　Let his children be fatherless, and his wife a widow.

10　Let his children be vagabonds, and beg and seek *bread, coming out* of their places destroyed.

11　Let [1]the extortioner catch all that he hath, and let the strangers spoil his labor.

12　Let there be none to extend mercy unto him: neither let there be any to show mercy upon his fatherless children.

13　Let his posterity be destroyed, *and* in the generation following, let their name be put out.

14　[1]Let the iniquity of his fathers be had in remembrance with the Lord: and let not the sin of his mother be done away.

15　*But* let them always be before the Lord, that he may cut off their memorial from the earth.

16　Because [1]he remembered not to show mercy, but persecuted the afflicted and poor man, and the sorrowful hearted to slay him.

17　As he loved cursing, [1]so shall it come unto him, *and* as he loved not blessing, so shall it be far from him.

18　As he clothed himself with cursing like a raiment, so shall it come into his bowels like water, and like oil into his bones.

19　Let it be unto him as a garment to cover him, and for a girdle, wherewith he shall be always girded.

20　Let this be the reward of mine adversary [1]from the Lord, and of them that speak evil against my soul.

21　But thou, O Lord my God, deal with me according unto thy [1]Name: deliver me, (for thy mercy is good)

22　Because I am poor and needy, and mine heart is wounded within me.

23　I depart like the shadow that declineth, and am shaken off as the [1]grasshopper.

24　My knees are weak through fasting, and my flesh [1]hath lost *all* fatness.

25　I became also a rebuke unto them: they that looked upon me, shaked their heads.

26　Help me, O Lord my God: [1]save me according to thy mercy.

27　And they shall know that this is thine hand, *and that* thou, Lord, hast done it.

28　*Though* [1]they curse, yet thou wilt bless: they shall arise and be confounded, but thy servant shall rejoice.

29　Let mine adversaries be clothed with shame, and let them cover themselves with their confusion as with a cloak.

30　I will give thanks unto the Lord greatly with my [1]mouth, and praise him among the multitude.

31　For he will stand at the right hand of the poor, to save him from them that would [1]condemn his soul.

110

1 David prophesieth of the power and everlasting kingdom given to Christ, 4 and of his Priesthood, which should put an end to the Priesthood of Levi.

A Psalm of David.

1　The [1]Lord said unto my Lord, Sit thou at my right hand, until I make thine enemies thy footstool.

2　The Lord shall send the rod of thy power out of [1]Zion: be thou ruler in the midst of thine enemies.

3　Thy people *shall come* willingly at the time *of assembling* [1]thine army in holy beauty: the youth of thy womb *shall be* as the morning dew.

4　The Lord sware, and will not repent, Thou art a Priest forever, after the order of [1]Melchizedek.

5　The Lord *that is* at thy right hand, shall wound kings in the day of his wrath.

109:7 [1] As to the elect all things turn to their profit: so to the reprobate, even those things that are good, turn to their damnation.

109:8 [1] This was chiefly accomplished in Judas, Acts 1:20.

109:11 [1] He declareth that the curse of God lieth upon the extortioners, who thinking to enrich their children by their unlawfull gotten goods, are by God's just judgment deprived of all.

109:14 [1] Thus punisheth the Lord to the third and fourth generation the wickedness of the parents in their wicked children.

109:16 [1] He showeth that God accustometh to plague them after a strange sort that show themselves cruel toward others.

109:17 [1] Thus giveth the Lord to every man the thing wherein he delighteth, that the reprobate cannot accuse God of wrong, when they are given up to their lusts and reprobate minds.

109:20 [1] For being destitute of man's help, he fully trusted in the Lord, that he would deliver him.

109:21 [1] As thou art named merciful, gracious and long suffering, so show thyself in effect.

109:23 [1] Meaning, that he hath no stay nor assurance in this world.

109:24 [1] For hunger, that came of sorrow, he was lean, and his natural moisture failed him.

109:26 [1] The more grievously Satan assailed him, the more earnest and instant was he in prayer.

109:28 [1] They shall gain nothing by cursing me.

109:30 [1] Not only in confessing it secretly in myself, but also in declaring it before all the congregation.

109:31 [1] Hereby he showeth that he had not to do with them that were of little power, but with the judges and princes of the world.

110:1 [1] Jesus Christ in Matt. 22:44, giveth the interpretation hereof, and showeth that this cannot properly be applied unto David but to himself.

110:2 [1] And thence it shalt stretch through all the world: and this power chiefly standeth in the preaching of his word.

110:3 [1] By the word thy people shall be assembled into thy Church whose increase shall be so abundant and wonderous as the drops of the water.

110:4 [1] As Melchizedek the figure of Christ was both a King and Priest, so this effect cannot be accomplished on any king save only Christ, Heb. 7:26.

6 He shall be judge among the heathen: he shall fill *all* with dead bodies, *and* smite the [1]head over great countries.

7 He shall [1]drink of the brook in the way: therefore shall he lift up *his* head.

111

1 He giveth thanks to the Lord for his merciful works toward his Church,   10 and declareth wherein true wisdom and right knowledge consisteth.

Praise ye the Lord.

1 I will [1]praise the Lord with my whole heart in the assembly and the congregation of the just.

2 The works of the Lord *are* [1]great, and ought to be sought out of all them that love them.

3 His work *is* beautiful and glorious, and his righteousness endureth forever.

4 He hath made his wonderful works to be had in remembrance: the Lord *is* merciful and full of compassion.

5 He hath given [1]a [2]portion unto them that fear him: he will ever be mindful of his covenant.

6 He hath showed to his people the power of his works, in giving unto them the heritage of the heathen.

7 The [1]works of his hands *are* truth and judgment: all his statutes are true.

8 They are established forever and ever, and are done in truth and equity.

9 He sent redemption unto his people: he hath commanded his covenant forever: holy and fearful *is* his Name.

10 [1]The beginning of wisdom *is* the fear of the Lord: all they that observe [2]them, have good understanding: his praise endureth forever.

112

1 He praiseth the felicity of them that fear God,   10 and condemneth the cursed state of the contemners of God.

Praise ye the Lord.

1 Blessed *is* the man that [1]feareth the Lord, *and* delighteth greatly in his commandments.

2 His seed shall be mighty upon earth: the generation of the righteous shall be blessed.

3 [1]Riches and treasures *shall be* in his house, and his righteousness endureth forever.

4 Unto the [1]righteous ariseth light in darkness: *he is* merciful and full of compassion and righteous.

5 A good man *is* merciful, and [1]lendeth, *and* will measure his affairs by judgment.

6 Surely he shall never be moved: *but* the righteous shall be had in everlasting remembrance.

7 He will not be afraid of evil tidings: *for* his heart is fixed, *and* believeth in the Lord.

8 His heart is established: *therefore* he will not fear, until he see *his desire* upon his enemies.

9 He hath [1]distributed *and* given to the poor: his righteousness remaineth forever: his [2]horn shall be exalted with glory.

10 The wicked shall see it, and be angry: he shall gnash with his teeth, and [1]consume away: the desire of the wicked shall perish.

113

1 An exhortation to praise the Lord for his providence   7 in that that contrary to the course of nature he worketh in his Church.

Praise ye the Lord.

1 Praise, O ye servants of the Lord, [1]praise the Name of the Lord.

2 Blessed be the Name of the Lord from henceforth and forever.

3 The Lord's Name is praised from the rising of the sun, unto the going down of the same.

4 The Lord is high above all [1]nations, *and* his

110:6 [1] No power shall be able to resist him.
110:7 [1] Under this similitude of a captain that is so greedy to destroy his enemies, that he will not scarce drink by the way, he showeth how God will destroy his enemies.
111:1 [1] The Prophet declareth that he will praise God both privately and openly, and that from the heart, as he that consecrateth himself wholly and only unto God.
111:2 [1] He showeth that God's works are a sufficient cause wherefore we should praise him, but chiefly his benefits toward his Church.
111:5 [1] God hath given to his people all that was necessary for them, and will do still even for his covenant's sake, and in this sense the Hebrew word is taken, Prov. 30:8 and 31:15.
   [2] Or, prey, and food.
111:7 [1] As God promised to take the care of his Church: so in effect doth he declare himself just and true in the government of the same.
111:10 [1] They only are wise, that fear God, and none have understanding, but they that obey the word.
   [2] To wit, his commandments, as verse 7.
112:1 [1] He meaneth that reverent fear, which is in the children of

God, which causeth them to delight only in the word of God.
112:3 [1] The godly shall have abundance, and contentment, because their heart is satisfied in God only.
112:4 [1] The faithful in all their adversities, know that all shall go well with them, for God will be merciful and just.
112:5 [1] He showeth what is the fruit of mercy to lend freely; and not for gain; and so to measure his doings that he may be able to help where need requireth, and not to bestow all on himself.
112:9 [1] The godly pinch not niggardly, but distribute liberally, as the necessity of the poor requireth, and as his power is able.
   [2] His power and prosperous estate.
112:10 [1] The blessings of God upon his children shall cause the wicked to die for envy.
113:1 [1] By this oft repetition he stirreth up our cold dullness to praise God, seeing his works are so wonderful, and that we are created for the same cause.
113:4 [1] If God's glory shine through all the world, and therefore of all ought to be praised, what great condemnation were it to his people, among whom chiefly it shineth, if they should not earnestly extol his Name?

glory above the heavens.

5 Who is like unto the Lord our God, that hath his dwelling on high.

6 Who abaseth himself to behold *things* in the heavens and in the earth!

7 He raiseth the needy out of the dust, *and* lifteth up the ¹poor out of the dung,

8 That he may set him with the princes, *even* with the princes of his people.

9 He maketh the barren woman to dwell with a family, *and* a joyful mother of children. Praise ye the Lord.

114

1 How the Israelites were delivered forth of Egypt, and of the wonderful miracles that God wrought at that time.   Which put us in remembrance of God's great mercy toward his Church, who when the course of nature faileth, preserveth his miraculously.

1 When ªIsrael went out of Egypt, *and* the house of Jacob from the ¹barbarous people,

2 Judah was his ¹sanctification, *and* Israel his dominion.

3 The sea saw it, and fled: Jordan was turned back.

4 The ¹mountains leaped like rams, *and* the hills as lambs!

5 What ailed thee, O sea, that thou fleddest? O Jordan, *why* wast thou turned back?

6 Ye mountains *why* leaped ye like rams, *and* ye hills as lambs?

7 The ¹earth trembled at the presence of the Lord, at the presence of the God of Jacob,

8 Which ¹turneth the rock into waterpools, *and* the flint into a fountain of water.

115

1 A prayer of the faithful oppressed by idolatrous tyrants, against whom they desire that God would succor them,   9 trusting most constantly that God will preserve them in this their need, seeing, that he hath adopted and received them into his favor.   13 Promising finally that they will not be unmindful of so great a benefit if

CHAPTER 114
ª Exod. 13:5

it would please God to hear their prayer, and deliver them by his omnipotent power.

1 Not ¹unto us, O Lord, not unto us, but unto thy Name give the glory for thy loving mercy, *and* for thy truth's sake.

2 Wherefore shall the heathen say, ¹Where is now their God?

3 But our God *is* in heaven: he doeth whatsoever he ¹will.

4 Their idols *are* ¹silver and gold, *even* the work of men's hands.

5 They have a mouth, and speak not: they have eyes, and see not.

6 They have ears, and hear not: they have noses and smell not.

7 They have ¹hands, and touch not: they have feet, and walk not: neither make they a sound with their throat.

8 They that make them are ¹like unto them: *so are* all that trust in them.

9 O Israel, trust thou in the Lord: *for* he is their help, and their shield.

10 ¹O house of Aaron trust ye in the Lord, *for* he is their help, and their shield.

11 Ye that fear the Lord, trust in the Lord: *for* he is their helper, and their shield.

12 The Lord hath been mindful of us, he will bless, he ¹will bless the house of Israel, he will bless the house of Aaron.

13 He will bless them that fear the Lord, both small and great.

14 The Lord will increase *his graces* toward you, *even* toward you, and toward your children.

15 Ye are blessed of the Lord, which ¹made the heaven and the earth.

16 The ¹heavens, *even* the heavens *are* the Lord's: but he hath given the earth to the sons of men.

17 The dead praise not the Lord, neither any that ¹go down into the *place of* silence.

113:7 ¹ By preferring the poor to high honor and giving the barren children, he showeth that God worketh not only in his Church by ordinary means, but also by miracles.

114:1 ¹ That is, from them that were of a strange language.

114:2 ¹ The whole people were witnesses of his holy majesty, in adopting them, and of his mighty power in delivering them.

114:4 ¹ Seeing that these dead creatures felt God's power, and after a sort saw it, much more his people ought to consider it, and glorify him for the same.

114:7 ¹ Ought then his people to be insensible when they see his power and majesty?

114:8 ¹ That is, caused miraculously water to come out of the rock in most abundance, Exod. 17:6.

115:1 ¹ Because God promised to deliver them, not for their sakes, but for his Name, Isa. 48:11, therefore they ground their prayer upon this promise.

115:2 ¹ When the wicked see that God accomplisheth not his prom-

ise as they imagine, they think there is no God.

115:3 ¹ No impediments can let his work, but he useth even the impediments to serve his will.

115:4 ¹ Seeing that neither the matter nor the form can commend their idols, it followeth that there is nothing why they should be esteemed.

115:7 ¹ He showeth what great vanity it is to ask help of them, which not only have no help in them, but lack sense and reason.

115:8 ¹ As much without sense, as blocks and stones.

115:10 ¹ For they were appointed by God as instructors and teachers of faith and religion for others to follow.

115:12 ¹ That is, he will continue his graces toward his people.

115:15 ¹ And therefore doth still govern and continue all things therein.

115:16 ¹ And they declare enough his sufficiency, so that the world serveth him nothing, but to show his fatherly care toward men.

115:17 ¹ Though the dead set forth God's glory, yet he meaneth here, that they praise him not in his Church and Congregation.

18 But we will praise the Lord from henceforth and forever. Praise ye the Lord.

CHAPTER 117
ᵈ Rom. 15:11

116

1 David being in great danger of Saul in the desert of M[...], perceiving the great and inestimable love of God toward him, magnifieth such great mercies, 13 and protesteth that he will be thankful for the same.

1 I ¹love the Lord, because he hath heard my voice *and* my prayers.

2 For he hath inclined his ear unto me, when I did call *upon him* ¹in my days.

3 *When* the snares of death compassed me, and the griefs of the grave caught me: *When* I found trouble and sorrow.

4 Then I called upon the Name of the Lord, *saying,* I beseech thee, O Lord, deliver my soul.

5 The Lord *is* ¹merciful and righteous, and our God *is* full of compassion.

6 The Lord preserveth the simple: I was in misery, and he saved me.

7 Return unto thy rest, O ¹my soul: for the Lord hath been beneficial unto thee,

8 Because thou hast delivered my soul from death, mine eyes from tears, *and* my feet from falling.

9 I shall ¹walk before the Lord in the land of the living.

10 ¹I believed, therefore did I speak: *for* I was sore troubled.

11 I said in my ¹fear, All men are liars.

12 What shall I render unto the Lord for all his benefits toward me?

13 I will ¹take the cup of salvation, and call upon the Name of the Lord.

14 I will pay my vows unto the Lord, *even* now in the presence of all his people.

15 Precious in the sight of the Lord *is* the ¹death of his Saints.

16 Behold, Lord: for I am thy servant, I am thy servant, *and* the son of thine handmaid: thou hast

broken my bonds.

17 I will offer to thee a sacrifice of praise, and will call upon the Name of the Lord.

18 I will pay my ¹vows unto the Lord, *even* now in the presence of all his people,

19 In the courts of the Lord's house, *even* in the midst of thee, O Jerusalem. Praise ye the Lord.

117

1 He exhorteth the Gentiles to praise God, because he hath accomplished as well to them as to the Jews, the promise of life everlasting by Jesus Christ.

1 All ᵃnations, praise ye the Lord: all ye people, praise him.

2 For his loving kindness is great toward us, and the ¹truth of the Lord *endureth* forever. Praise ye the Lord.

118

1 David rejected of Saul and of the people at the time appointed obtained the kingdom. 4 For the which he biddeth all them, that fear the Lord, to be thankful. And under his person in all this was Christ lively set forth, who should be of his people rejected.

1 Praise ¹ye the Lord, because he is good: for his mercy *endureth* forever.

2 Let Israel now say, That his mercy *endureth* forever.

3 Let the house of Aaron now say, That his mercy *endureth* forever.

4 Let them that fear the Lord, now say, That his mercy *endureth* forever.

5 I called upon the Lord in ¹trouble, *and* the Lord heard me, *and* set *me* at large.

6 The Lord *is* with me: *therefore* I will not fear what ¹man can do unto me.

7 The Lord *is* with me among them that help me: therefore shall I see *my* desire upon mine enemies.

8 It is better to trust in the Lord, than to have confidence ¹in man.

9 It is better to trust in the Lord, than to have

116:1 ¹ He granteth that no pleasure is so great as to feel God's help in our necessity, neither that anything more stirreth up our love toward him.
116:2 ¹ That is in convenient time to seek help, which was when he was in distress.
116:5 ¹ He showeth forth the fruit of his love in calling upon him, confessing him to be just and merciful, and to help them that are destitute of aid and counsel.
116:7 ¹ Which was unquieted before, now rest upon the Lord, for he hath been beneficial towards thee.
116:9 ¹ The Lord will preserve me, and save my life.
116:10 ¹ I felt all these things, and therefore was moved by faith to confess them, 2 Cor. 4:13.
116:11 ¹ In my great distress I thought God would not regard man, which is but lies and vanity, yet I overcame this tentation, and felt the contrary.
116:13 ¹ In the Law they used to make a banquet when they gave solemn thanks to God, and to take the cup and drink in sign of thanksgiving.

116:15 ¹ I perceive that God hath a care over his, so that he both disposeth their death, and taketh an account.
116:18 ¹ I will thank him for his benefits, for that is a just payment, to confess that we owe all to God.
117:2 ¹ That is, the most certain and continual testimonies of his Fatherly graces.
118:1 ¹ Because God by creating David King, showed his mercy toward his afflicted Church, the Prophet doth not only himself thank God, but exhorteth all the people to do the same.
118:5 ¹ We are here taught that the more that troubles oppress us, the more ought we to be instant in prayer.
118:6 ¹ Being exalted to this estate, he assured himself to have man ever to be his enemy. Yet he doubted not, but God would maintain him, because he had placed him.
118:8 ¹ He showeth that he had trusted in vain if he had put his confidence in man, to have been preferred to the kingdom and therefore he put his trust in God and obtained.

confidence in princes.

10 All nations have compassed me: but in the Name of the Lord shall I destroy them.

11 They have compassed me, yea, they have compassed me: but in the Name of the Lord I shall destroy them.

12 They came about me like bees, *but* they were quenched as a fire of thorns: for in the Name of the Lord I shall destroy them.

13 [1]Thou hast thrust sore at me, that I might fall: but the Lord hath helped me.

14 The Lord *is* my strength and [1]song: for he hath been my deliverance.

15 The [1]voice of joy and deliverance *shall be* in the tabernacles of the righteous, *saying*, The right hand of the Lord hath done valiantly.

16 [1]The right hand of the Lord is exalted: the right hand of the Lord hath done valiantly.

17 I shall not die, but live, and declare the works of the Lord.

18 The Lord had chastened me sore, but he hath not delivered me to death.

19 Open ye unto me the [1]gates of righteousness, *that* I may go into them, *and* praise the Lord.

20 This is the gate of the Lord: the righteous shall enter into it.

21 I will praise thee: for thou hast heard me, and hast been my deliverance.

22 [a]The stone, *which* the builders [1]refused, is the head of the corner.

23 This was the Lord's doing, *and* it is marvelous in our eyes,

24 This is the [1]day, *which* the Lord hath made: let us rejoice and be glad in it.

25 [1]O Lord, I pray thee, save now: O Lord, I pray thee now give prosperity.

26 Blessed *be he*, that cometh in the Name of the Lord: [1]we have blessed you out of the house of the Lord.

CHAPTER 118
[a] Isa. 28:16
Matt. 21:42
Acts 4:11
Rom. 9:33
1 Pet. 2:6,7

27 The Lord *is* mighty, and hath given us [1]light: bind the sacrifice with cords unto the horns of the altar.

28 Thou art my God, and I will praise thee, *even* my God: therefore I will exalt thee.

29 Praise ye the Lord, because he is good: for his mercy *endureth* forever.

119

1 The Prophet exhorteth the children of God to frame their lives according to his holy word. 123 Also he showeth wherein the true service of God standeth, that is, when we serve him according to his word, and not after our own fantasies.

ALEPH

1 Blessed *are* [1]those that are upright in *their* way, *and* walk in the Law of the Lord.

2 Blessed *are* they that keep his testimonies, *and* seek him with their whole heart.

3 Surely they work [1]none iniquity, *but* walk in his ways.

4 Thou hast commanded to keep thy precepts diligently.

5 [1]Oh that my ways were directed to keep thy statutes!

6 Then should I not be confounded, when I have respect unto all thy commandments.

7 I will praise thee with an upright [1]heart, when I shall learn the [2]judgments of thy righteousness.

8 I will keep thy statutes: forsake me not [1]overlong.

BETH

9 Wherewith shall a [1]young man redress his way? in taking heed *thereto* according to thy word.

10 With my whole heart have I sought thee: let me not wander from thy commandments.

11 I have [1]hid thy promise in mine heart, that I might not sin against thee.

12 Blessed art thou, O Lord: teach me thy statutes.

13 With my lips have I declared all the judgments

118:13 [1] He noteth Saul his chief enemy.

118:14 [1] In that he was delivered, it came not of himself, nor of the power of man, but only of God's favor, therefore he will praise him.

118:15 [1] He promiseth both to render graces himself, and to cause others to do the same, because that in his person the Church was restored.

118:16 [1] So that all, that are both far and near, may see his mighty power.

118:19 [1] He willeth the doors of the Tabernacle to be opened, that he may declare his thankful mind.

118:22 [1] Though Saul and the chief powers refused me to be King, yet God hath preferred me above them all.

118:24 [1] Wherein God hath showeth chiefly his mercy, by appointing me king and delivering his Church.

118:25 [1] The people pray for the prosperity of David's kingdom, who was the figure of Christ.

118:26 [1] Which are the Priests, and have the charge thereof, as Num. 6:23.

118:27 [1] Because he hath restored us from darkness to light, we will offer sacrifices and praises unto him.

119:1 [1] Here they are not called blessed, which think themselves wise in their own judgment, nor which imagine to themselves a certain holiness, but they whose conversation is without hypocrisy.

119:3 [1] For they are ruled by God's Spirit and embrace no doctrine but his.

119:5 [1] David acknowledgeth his imperfection, desiring God to reform it, that his life may be conformable to God's word.

119:7 [1] For true religion standeth in serving God without hypocrisy.
[2] That is, thy precepts, which contain perfect righteousness.

119:8 [1] He refuseth not to be tried by tentations, but he feareth to faint, if God succor not his infirmity in time.

119:9 [1] Because youth is most given to licentiousness, he chiefly warneth them to frame their lives betimes to God's word.

119:11 [1] If God's word be graven in our hearts, we shall be more able to resist the assaults of Satan: and therefore the Prophet desireth God to instruct him daily more and more therein.

of thy mouth.

14 I have had as great [1]delight in the way of thy testimonies, as in all riches.

15 I will meditate in thy precepts, and consider thy ways.

16 I will delight in thy statutes, *and* I will not forget thy word.

GIMEL

17 Be beneficial unto thy servant, *that* I may [1]live and keep thy word.

18 Open mine eyes, that I may see the wonders of thy Law.

19 I am a [1]stranger upon earth: hide not thy commandments from me.

20 Mine heart breaketh for the desire to thy judgments always.

21 Thou [1]hast destroyed the proud: cursed are they that do err from thy commandments.

22 Remove from me shame and contempt: for I have kept thy testimonies.

23 [1]Princes also did sit, *and* speak against me: *but* thy servant did meditate in thy statutes.

24 Also thy testimonies *are* my delight, *and* my counselors.

DALETH

25 My soul cleaveth to the [1]dust: quicken me according to thy word.

26 I have [1]declared my ways, and thou heardest me: teach me thy statutes.

27 Make me to understand the way of thy precepts, and I will meditate in thy wondrous works.

28 My soul melteth for heaviness: raise me up according to thy [1]word.

29 Take from me the [1]way of lying, and grant me graciously thy Law.

30 I have chosen the way of truth, *and* thy judg-

ments have I laid *before me*.

31 I have cleaved to thy testimonies, O Lord: confound me not.

32 I will run the way of thy commandments, when thou [1]shalt enlarge mine heart.

HE

33 Teach [1]me, O Lord, the way of thy statutes, and I will keep it unto the end.

34 Give me understanding and I will keep thy Law, yea, I will keep it with *my* whole [1]heart.

35 Direct me in the path of thy commandments: for therein is my delight.

36 Incline mine heart unto thy testimonies: and not to [1]covetousness.

37 Turn away mine [1]eyes from regarding vanity, *and* quicken me in thy way.

38 Stablish thy promise to thy servant, because he feareth thee.

39 Take away [1]my rebuke that I fear: for thy judgments are good.

40 Behold, I desire thy commandments: [1]quicken me in thy righteousness.

VAU

41 And let thy loving [1]kindness come unto me, O Lord, *and* thy salvation according to thy promise.

42 So shall I [1]make answer unto my blasphemers: for I trust in thy word.

43 And take not the word of truth utterly out of my mouth: for I wait for thy judgments.

44 So shall I always keep thy Law forever and ever.

45 And I will [1]walk at liberty: for I seek thy precepts.

46 I will speak also of thy testimonies before [1]Kings, and will not be ashamed.

47 And my delight shall be in thy Commandments, which I have loved.

119:14 [1] The Prophet not boast of his virtues, but setteth forth an example for others to follow God's word, and leave worldly vanities.

119:17 [1] He showeth that we ought not to desire to live but to serve God, and that we cannot serve him aright except he open our eyes and minds.

119:19 [1] Seeing man's life in this world is but a passage, what should become of him, if thy word were not his guide?

119:21 [1] In all ages thou hast plagued all such which maliciously and contemptuously depart from thy truth.

119:23 [1] When the powers of the world gave false sentence against me, thy word was a guide and counselor to teach me what to do, and to comfort me.

119:25 [1] That is, it is almost brought to the grave, and without thy word I cannot live.

119:26 [1] I have confessed mine offences, and now depend wholly on thee.

119:28 [1] If God did not maintain us by his word, our life would drop away like water.

119:29 [1] Instruct me in thy word, whereby my mind may be purged from vanity, and taught to obey thy will.

119:32 [1] By this he showeth that we can neither choose good,

cleave to God's word, nor turn forward in his way, except he make our hearts large to receive grace, and willing to obey.

119:33 [1] He showeth that he cannot follow on to the end, except God teach him ofttimes, and lead him forward.

119:34 [1] Not only in outward conversation, but also with inward affection.

119:36 [1] Hereby meaning all other vices, because that covetousness is the root of all evil.

119:37 [1] Meaning, all his senses.

119:39 [1] Let me not fall to thy dishonor, but let mine heart still delight in thy gracious word.

119:40 [1] Give me strength to continue in thy word even to the end.

119:41 [1] He showeth that God's mercy and love is the first cause of our salvation.

119:42 [1] By trusting in God's word he assureth himself to be able to confute the slanders of his adversaries.

119:45 [1] They that simply walk after God's word, have no lets to entangle them, whereas they that do contrary, are ever in nets and snares.

119:46 [1] He showeth that the children of God ought not to suffer their father's glory to be obscured by the vain pomp of princes.

48 Mine hands also will I lift up unto thy Commandments, which I have loved, and I will meditate in thy statutes.

ZAIN

49 Remember [1]the promise *made* to thy servant, wherein thou hast caused me to trust.

50 It is my comfort in my trouble; for thy promise hath quickened me.

51 The [1]proud have had me exceedingly in derision: *yet* have I not declined from thy Law.

52 I remembered thy [1]judgments of old, O Lord, and have been comforted.

53 [1]Fear is come upon me for the wicked, that forsake thy Law.

54 Thy statutes have been my songs in the house of my [1]pilgrimage.

55 I have remembered thy Name, O Lord, in the [1]night, and have kept thy Law.

56 [1]This I had because I kept thy precepts.

CHETH

57 O Lord, *that art* my [1]portion, I have determined to keep thy words.

58 I made my supplication in thy presence with *my* whole heart: be merciful unto me according to thy promise.

59 I have considered my [1]ways, and turned my feet into thy testimonies.

60 I made haste and delayed not to keep thy commandments.

61 The bands of the wicked have [1]robbed me: *but* I have not forgotten thy Law.

62 At midnight will I rise to give thanks unto thee, because of thy righteous judgments.

63 I am [1]companion of all them that fear thee, and keep thy precepts.

64 The earth, O Lord, is full of thy mercy: [1]teach me thy statutes.

TETH

65 O Lord, thou hast dealt [1]graciously with thy servant, according unto thy word.

66 Teach me good judgment and knowledge: for I have believed thy commandments.

67 Before I was [1]afflicted, I went astray: but now I keep thy word.

68 Thou art good and gracious: teach me thy statutes.

69 The proud have imagined a lie against me: *but* I will keep thy precepts with *my* whole heart.

70 [1]Their heart is fat as grease, *but* my delight is in thy Law.

71 It is [1]good for me that I have been afflicted, that I may learn thy statutes.

72 The Law of thy mouth is better unto me, than thousands of gold and silver.

JOD

73 Thine hands have [1]made me and fashioned me: give me understanding *therefore*, that I may learn thy commandments.

74 So they that [1]fear thee, seeing me, shall rejoice, because I have trusted in thy word.

75 I know, O Lord, that thy judgments *are* right, and that thou hast afflicted me [1]justly.

76 I pray thee that thy mercy may comfort me, according to thy promise unto thy servant.

77 Let thy tender mercies come unto me, that I may [1]live: for thy Law *is* my delight.

78 Let the proud be ashamed: for they have dealt wickedly *and* falsely with me: *but* I meditate in thy precepts.

79 Let such as fear thee [1]turn unto me, and they that [2]know thy testimonies.

80 Let mine heart be upright in thy statutes, that I be not ashamed.

119:49 [1] Though he feel God's hand still to lie upon him, yet he resteth on his promise, and comforteth himself therein.

119:51 [1] Meaning, the wicked, which contemn God's word, and tread his Religion under foot.

119:52 [1] That is, the examples, whereby thou declarest thyself to be judge of the world.

119:53 [1] That is, a vehement zeal to thy glory and indignation against the wicked.

119:54 [1] In the course of this life and sorrowful exit.

119:55 [1] Even when others sleep.

119:56 [1] That is, all these benefits.

119:57 [1] I am persuaded that to keep thy Law is an heritage and great gain for me.

119:59 [1] He showeth that none can embrace the word of God, except he consider his own imperfections and ways.

119:61 [1] They have gone about to draw me into their company.

119:63 [1] Not only in mutual consent, but also with aid and succor.

119:64 [1] For the knowledge of God's word is a singular token of his favor.

119:65 [1] Having proved by experience that God was true in his promise, he desireth that he would increase in him knowledge and judgment.

119:67 [1] So Jeremiah saith, that before the Lord touched him, he was like a calf untamed: so that the use of God's rod is to call us home to God.

119:70 [1] Their heart is indurated and hardened, puffed up with prosperity and vain estimation of themselves.

119:71 [1] He confesseth that before that he was chastened, he was rebellious, as man by nature is.

119:73 [1] Because God leaveth not his work that he hath begun, he desireth a new grace: that is, that he would continue his mercies.

119:74 [1] When God showeth his grace toward any, he testifieth to others, that he faileth not them that trust in him.

119:75 [1] Hebrew, *in truth*.

119:77 [1] He declareth, that when he felt not God's mercies, he was as dead.

119:79 [1] That is, be comforted by mine example.

[2] He showeth that there can be no true fear of God without the knowledge of his word.

CAPH

81 My soul ¹fainted for thy salvation: *yet* I wait for thy word.

82 Mine eyes fail for thy promise, saying, When wilt thou comfort me?

83 For I am like a ¹bottle in the smoke; *yet* do I not forget thy statutes.

84 How many are the ¹days of thy servant? When wilt thou execute judgment on them that persecute me?

85 The proud have ¹dug pits for me, which is not after thy Law.

86 All thy commandments *are* true: they persecute me falsely: ¹help me.

87 They had almost consumed ¹me upon the earth: but I forsook not thy precepts.

88 Quicken me according to thy loving kindness: so shall I keep the testimony of thy mouth.

LAMED

89 O Lord, thy word endureth forever in ¹heaven.

90 Thy truth *is* from generation to generation: thou hast laid the foundation of the earth, and it abideth.

91 They ¹continue *even* to this day by thine ordinances: for all *are* thy servants.

92 Except thy law had been my delight, I should now have perished in mine affliction.

93 I will never forget thy precepts: for by them thou hast quickened me.

94 I am ¹thine, save me: for I have sought thy precepts.

95 The wicked have waited for me to destroy me: *but* I will consider thy testimonies.

96 I ¹have seen an end of all perfection: *but* thy commandment *is* exceeding large.

MEM

97 Oh how love I thy law! it is my meditation ¹continually.

98 By thy commandments thou hast made me wiser than mine enemies: for they are ever with me.

99 I have had more ¹understanding than all my teachers: for thy testimonies are my meditation.

100 I understood more than the ancient, because I kept thy precepts.

101 I have refrained my feet from every evil way, that I might keep thy word.

102 I have not declined from thy judgments: for ¹thou didst teach me.

103 How sweet are thy promises unto my mouth! *yea*, more than honey unto my mouth.

104 By thy precepts I have gotten understanding: therefore I hate all the ways of falsehood.

NUN

105 Thy word *is* a ¹lantern unto my feet, and a light unto my paths.

106 I have ¹sworn and will perform it, that I will keep thy righteous judgments.

107 I am very sore afflicted: O Lord, quicken me according to thy word.

108 O Lord, I beseech thee, accept the ¹free offering of my mouth, and teach me thy judgments.

109 My ¹soul is continually in mine hand: yet do I not forget thy law.

110 The wicked have laid a snare for me: but I swerved not from thy precepts.

111 Thy testimonies have I taken *as* an ¹heritage forever: for they are the joy of mine heart.

112 I have applied mine heart to fulfill thy statutes always, *even* unto the end.

SAMECH

113 I hate ¹vain inventions: but thy Law do I love.

119:81 ¹ Though my strength fail me, yet my soul groaneth and sigheth, resting still in thy word.

119:83 ¹ Like a skin bottle or bladder that is parched in the smoke.

119:84 ¹ How long wilt thou afflict thy servant.

119:85 ¹ They have not only oppressed me violently, but also craftily conspired against me.

119:86 ¹ He assureth himself, that God will deliver his, and destroy such as unjustly persecute them.

119:87 ¹ Finding no help in earth, he lifteth up his eyes to heaven.

119:89 ¹ Because none should esteem God's word according to the changes of things in this world, he showeth that it abideth in heaven, and therefore is immutable.

119:91 ¹ Seeing the earth and all creatures remain in that estate wherein thou hast created them, much more thy truth remaineth constant and unchangeable.

119:94 ¹ He proveth by effect that he is God's child, because he seeketh to understand his word.

119:96 ¹ There is nothing so perfect in earth, but it hath an end, only God's word lasteth forever.

119:97 ¹ He showeth that we cannot love God's word, except we exercise ourselves therein and practice it.

119:99 ¹ Whosoever doth submit himself only to God's word, shall not only be safe against the practices of his enemies, but also learn more wisdom than they that profess it, and are men of experience.

119:102 ¹ So then of ourselves we can do nothing: but when God doth inwardly instruct us with his spirit, we feel his graces sweeter than honey.

119:105 ¹ Of ourselves we are but darkness and cannot see except we be lightened with God's Word.

119:106 ¹ So all the faithful ought to bind themselves to God by a solemn oath and promises, to stir up their zeal to embrace God's word.

119:108 ¹ That is, my prayers and thanksgiving which sacrifice Hosea calleth the calves of the lips, Hos. 14:3.

119:109 ¹ That is, I am in continual danger of my life.

119:111 ¹ I esteemed no worldly things, but made thy word mine inheritance.

119:113 ¹ Whosoever will embrace God's word aright, must abhor all fantasies and imaginations both of himself and others.

114 Thou art my refuge and shield, *and* I trust in thy word.

115 [1]Away from me, ye wicked: for I will keep the commandments of my God.

116 Stablish me according to thy promise, that I may live, and disappoint me not of mine hope.

117 [1]Stay thou me, and I shall be safe, and I will delight continually in thy statutes.

118 Thou hast trodden down all them that depart from thy statutes: for their [1]deceit *is* vain.

119 Thou hast taken away all the wicked of the earth *like* [1]dross: therefore I love thy testimonies.

120 My flesh [1]trembleth for fear of thee, and I am afraid of thy judgments.

AIN

121 I have executed judgment and justice: leave me not to mine oppressor.

122 [1]Answer for thy servant in that which is good, *and* let not the proud oppress me.

123 Mine eyes have failed *in waiting* for thy salvation, and for thy just promise.

124 Deal with thy [1]servant according to thy mercy, and teach me thy statutes.

125 I am thy servant: grant me *therefore* understanding, that I may know thy testimonies.

126 It is [1]time for thee, Lord, to work: *for* they have destroyed thy Law.

127 Therefore love I thy commandments above gold, yea, above most fine gold.

128 Therefore I esteem all thy precepts most just, and hate all false [1]ways.

PE

129 Thy testimonies *are* [1]wonderful: therefore doth my soul keep them.

130 The entrance into thy [1]words showeth light, *and* giveth understanding to the simple.

131 I opened my mouth, and [1]panted, because I

CHAPTER 119
a Ps. 69:9
John 2:17

loved thy commandments.

132 Look upon me and be merciful unto me, as thou usest to do unto those that love thy Name.

133 Direct my steps in thy word, and let none iniquity have dominion over me.

134 Deliver me from the oppression of men, and I will keep thy precepts.

135 Show the light of thy countenance upon thy servant, and teach me thy statute.

136 Mine eyes gush [1]out with rivers of water, because they keep not thy Law.

TZADDI

137 Righteous art thou, O Lord, and just *are* thy judgments.

138 Thou hast commanded [1]justice by thy testimonies and truth especially.

139 [a]My zeal hath even consumed me: because mine enemies have forgotten thy words.

140 Thy word is proved [1]most pure, and thy servant loveth it.

141 I am [1]small and despised: *yet* do I not forget thy precepts.

142 Thy righteousness *is* an everlasting righteousness, and thy Law *is* truth.

143 Trouble and anguish are come upon me: *yet are* the commandments my delight.

144 The righteousness of thy testimonies *is* everlasting: grant me understanding, and I shall [1]live.

KOPH

145 I have [1]cried with *my* whole heart: hear me, O Lord, *and* I will keep thy statutes.

146 I called upon thee: save me, and I will keep thy testimonies.

147 I prevented the morning light, and cried: *for* I waited on thy word.

148 Mine eyes [1]prevent the *night* watches, to meditate in thy word.

119:115 [1] And hinder me not to keep the Law of the Lord.

119:117 [1] He desireth God's continual assistance, lest he should faint in this race, which he had begun.

119:118 [1] The crafty practices of them that contemn thy Law, shall be brought to naught.

119:119 [1] Which infected thy people, as dross doth the metal.

119:120 [1] Thy judgments do not only teach me obedience, but cause me to fear, considering mine own weakness, which fear causeth repentance.

119:122 [1] Put thyself between mine enemies and me, as if thou were my pledge.

119:124 [1] He boasteth not that he is God's servant, but hereby putteth God in mind that as he made him his by his grace, so he would continue his favor toward him.

119:126 [1] The Prophet showeth that when the wicked have brought all things to confusion, and God's word to utter contempt, then it is God's time to help and send remedy.

119:128 [1] That is, whatsoever dissenteth from the purity of thy word.

119:129 [1] Containing high and secret mysteries, so that I am moved with admiration and reverence.

119:130 [1] The simple idiots that submit themselves to God, have their eyes opened and their minds illuminated, so soon as they begin to read God's word.

119:131 [1] My zeal toward thy word was so great.

119:136 [1] He showeth what ought to be the zeal of God's children, when they see his word contemned.

119:138 [1] We cannot confess God to be righteous, except we live uprightly and truly, as he hath commanded.

119:140 [1] Gold hath need to be fined, but thy word is perfection itself.

119:141 [1] This is the true trial, to praise God in adversity.

119:144 [1] So that the life of man without the knowledge of God, is death.

119:145 [1] He showeth that all his affections and whole heart were bent to Godward for to have help in his dangers.

119:148 [1] He was more earnest in the study of God's word, than they that kept the watch were in their charge.

149 Hear my voice according to thy loving kindness: O Lord, quicken me according to thy ¹judgment.

150 They draw near that follow after ¹malice, *and* are far from thy Law.

151 Thou art near, O Lord: for all thy commandments are true.

152 I have known long since ¹by thy testimonies, that thou hast established them forever.

RESH

153 Behold mine affliction, and deliver me: for I have not forgotten thy law.

154 Plead my cause, and deliver me: quicken me according unto thy ¹word.

155 Salvation *is* far from the wicked, because they seek not thy statutes.

156 Great art thy tender mercies, O Lord: quicken me according to thy ¹judgments.

157 My persecutors and mine oppressors *are* many: *yet* do I not swerve from thy testimonies.

158 I saw the transgressors and was ¹grieved, because they kept not thy word.

159 Consider, O Lord, how I ¹love thy precepts: quicken me according to thy loving kindness.

160 The ¹beginning of thy word is truth, and all the judgments of thy righteousness *endure* forever.

SCHIN

161 Princes have ¹persecuted me without cause: but mine heart stood in awe of thy words.

162 I rejoice at thy word, as one that findeth a great spoil.

163 I hate falsehood and abhor it, *but* thy Law do I love.

164 ¹Seven times a day do I praise thee, because of thy righteous judgments.

165 They that ¹love thy law, shall have great prosperity, and they shall have none hurt.

166 Lord, I have ¹trusted in thy salvation, and have done thy commandments.

167 My soul hath kept thy testimonies: for I love them exceedingly.

168 I have kept thy precepts and thy testimonies: ¹for all my ways are before thee.

TAU

169 Let my complaint come before thee, O Lord, *and* give me understanding ¹according unto thy word.

170 Let my supplication come before thee, *and* deliver me according to thy promise.

171 My lips shall ¹speak praise, when thou hast ²taught me thy statutes.

172 My tongue shall entreat of thy word: for all thy commandments *are* righteous.

173 Let thine hand help me: for I have chosen thy precepts.

174 I have longed for thy salvation, O Lord, and thy Law *is* my delight.

175 Let my soul live, and it shall praise thee, and thy ¹judgments shall help me.

176 I have ¹gone astray like a lost sheep: seek thy servant, for I do not forget thy commandments.

120 *1 The prayer of David being vexed by the false reports of Saul's flatterers. 5 And therefore he lamenteth his long abode among those infidels, 7 Who were given to all kinds of wickedness and contention.*

A song of ¹degrees.

1 I called unto the Lord in my ¹trouble, and he heard me.

2 Deliver my soul, O Lord, from lying lips, *and* from a deceitful tongue.

3 What doth *thy* ¹deceitful tongue bring unto thee? or what doth it avail thee?

4 *It is as* the ¹sharp arrows of a mighty man, and *as* the coals of Juniper.

119:149 ¹ Or, custom.
119:150 ¹ He showeth the nature of the wicked to be to persecute against their conscience.
119:152 ¹ His faith is grounded upon God's word, that he would ever be at hand when his children be oppressed.
119:154 ¹ For without God's promise there is no hope of deliverance.
119:156 ¹ According to thy promise made in the law, which because the wicked lack, they can have no hope of salvation.
119:158 ¹ My zeal consumed me when I saw their malice and contempt of thy glory.
119:159 ¹ It is a sure sign of our adoption, when we love the Law of God.
119:160 ¹ Since thou first promised it, even to the end all thy sayings are true.
119:161 ¹ The threatenings and persecutions of princes could not cause me to shrink to confess thee whom I more fear than men.
119:164 ¹ That is, often and sundry times.
119:165 ¹ For their conscience assureth them that they please thee, whereas they that love not thee, have the contrary.
119:166 ¹ He showeth that we must first have faith before we can work and please God.
119:168 ¹ I had no respect of men, but set thee always before mine eyes, as the judge of my doings.
119:169 ¹ As thou hast promised to be the schoolmaster unto all them that depend upon thee.
119:171 ¹ The word signifieth to pour forth continually.
² All his prayer and desire is to profit in the word of God.
119:175 ¹ That is, thy provident care over me, and wherewith thou wilt judge mine enemies.
119:176 ¹ Being chased to and fro by mine enemies, and having no place to rest in.
120:Title ¹ That is, of lifting up the tune and rising in singing.
120:1 ¹ Albeit the children of God ought to rejoice when they suffer for righteous sake, yet it is a great grief to the flesh to hear evil for well doing.
120:3 ¹ He assured himself that God would turn their craft to their own destruction.
120:4 ¹ He showeth that there is nothing so sharp to pierce, nor so hot to set on fire, as a slanderous tongue.

5   Woe is to me that I remain in [1]Meshech, *and* dwell in the tents of [2]Kedar.

6   My soul hath too long dwelt with him that hateth peace.

7   I *seek* [1]peace, and when I speak *thereof*, they are *bent* to war.

121

1 This Psalm teacheth that the faithful ought only to look for help at God,   7 who only doth maintain, preserve and prosper his Church.

A song of degrees.

1   I will lift up mine eyes [1]unto the mountains, from whence my help shall come.

2   Mine help *cometh* from the Lord, which hath made the [1]heaven and the earth.

3   He will not suffer thy foot to slip: *for* he that keepeth thee, will not [1]slumber.

4   Behold, he that keepeth Israel, will neither slumber nor sleep.

5   The Lord *is* thy keeper: the Lord *is* thy shadow at thy right hand.

6   The sun shall not [1]smite thee by day, nor the moon by night.

7   The Lord shall preserve thee from all evil: he shall keep thy soul.

8   The Lord shall preserve thy [1]going out, and thy coming in from henceforth and forever.

122

1 David rejoiceth in the name of the faithful, that God hath accomplished his promise and placed his Ark in Zion.   5 For the which he giveth thanks,   8 And prayeth for the prosperity of the Church.

A song of degrees, or *Psalm* of David.

1   I [a,1]rejoiced when they said to me, We will go into the house of the Lord.

2   Our [1]feet shall stand in thy gates, O Jerusalem.

3   Jerusalem *is* built as a city, that is [1]compact together in itself:

CHAPTER 122
[a] 1 Chron. 29:9

4   Whereunto [1]the Tribes, *even* the Tribes of the Lord go up *according* to the testimony to Israel, to praise the Name of the Lord.

5   For there are thrones set for judgment, *even* the thrones of the house of [1]David.

6   Pray for the peace of Jerusalem: let them prosper that love thee.

7   Peace be within thy [1]walls, *and* prosperity within thy palaces.

8   For my [1]brethren and neighbors' sakes, I will wish thee now prosperity.

9   Because of the House of the Lord our God, I will procure thy wealth.

123

A prayer of the faithful, which were afflicted either in Babylon or under Antiochus, by the wicked worldlings and contemners of God.

A song of degrees.

1   I lift up mine eyes to thee, that dwellest in the heavens.

2   Behold, as the eyes of [1]servants *look* unto the hand of their masters, *and* as the eyes of a maiden unto the hand of her mistress: so our eyes *wait* upon the Lord our God, until he have mercy upon us.

3   Have mercy unto us, O Lord, have mercy upon us: for we have [1]suffered too much contempt.

4   Our soul is filled too full of the mocking of the wealthy, *and* of the despitefulness of the proud.

124

The people of God, escaping a great peril, do acknowledge themselves to be delivered, not by their own force, but by the power of God.   4 They declare the greatness of the peril.   6 And praise the Name of God.

A song of degrees, or *Psalm* of David.

1   If the Lord had not been [1]on our side, (may Israel now say)

2   If the Lord had [not] been on our side, when men rose up against us,

---

120:5 [1] These were people of Arabia, which came of Japheth, Gen. 10:2.   [2] That is, of the Ishmaelites.

120:7 [1] He declareth what he meaneth by Meshech, and Kedar, to wit, the Israelites which had degenerate from their godly fathers, and hated and contended against the faithful.

121:1 [1] Or, about the mountains: meaning, that there is nothing so high in this world, wherein he can trust, but only in God.

121:2 [1] He accuseth man's ingratitude, which cannot depend on God's power.

121:3 [1] He showeth that God's providence not only watcheth over his Church in general: but also over every member thereof.

121:6 [1] Neither heat nor cold, nor any incommodity shall be able to destroy God's Church, albeit for a time they may molest it.

121:8 [1] Whatsoever thou dost enterprise, shall have good success.

122:1 [1] He rejoiceth that God had appointed a place, where the Ark should still remain.

122:2 [1] Which were wont to wander to and fro, as the Ark removed.

122:3 [1] By the artificial joining and beauty of the houses, he meaneth the concord and love that was between the citizens.

122:4 [1] All the tribes according to God's covenant shall come and pray there.

122:5 [1] In whose house God placed the throne of justice, and made it a figure of Christ's kingdom.

122:7 [1] The favor of God prosper thee both within and without.

122:8 [1] Not only for mine own sake, but for all the faithful.

123:2 [1] He compareth the condition of the godly, to servants that are destitute of all help, assuring that when all other helps fail, God is ever at hand and like himself.

123:3 [1] He declareth that when the faithful are so full, that they can no more endure the oppressions and scornings of the wicked, there is always help above, if with hungry desires they call for it.

124:1 [1] He showeth that God was ready to help at need, and that there was none other way to be saved, but by his only means.

3 They had then swallowed us up ¹quick, when their wrath was kindled against us.

4 Then the ¹waters had drowned us, *and* the stream had gone over our soul:

5 Then had the swelling waters gone over our soul.

6 Praised *be* the Lord, which hath not given us *as* a prey unto their teeth.

7 Our soul is escaped, even as a bird out of the ¹snare of the fowlers: the snare is broken, and we are delivered.

8 Our help *is* in the Name of the Lord, which hath made heaven and earth.

125 *1 He describeth the assurance of the faithful in their afflictions. 4 And desireth their wealth, 5 And the destruction of the wicked.*

A song of degrees.

1 They that trust in the Lord, *shall be* as mount Zion, *which* cannot ¹be removed, *but* remaineth forever.

2 *As* the mountains *are* about Jerusalem: so *is* the Lord about his people from henceforth and forever.

3 For the ¹rod of the wicked shall not rest on the lot of the righteous, lest the righteous put forth their hand unto wickedness.

4 Do well, O Lord, unto those that be good and true in their hearts.

5 ¹But these that turn aside by their crooked *ways*, them shall the Lord lead with the workers of iniquity: *but* peace *shall be* upon Israel.

126 *1 This Psalm was made after the return of the people from Babylon, and showeth that the means of their deliverance was wonderful after the seventy years of captivity forspoken by Jeremiah, in Jer. 25:12 and 29:10.*

A song of degrees, or *Psalm* of David.

1 When the Lord brought again the captivity of Zion, we were like them that ¹dream.

2 Then was our mouth ¹filled with laughter, and our tongue with joy: then said they among the ²heathen, The Lord hath done great things for them.

3 The Lord hath done great things for us, *whereof* we rejoice.

4 O Lord, bring again our captivity, as the ¹rivers in the South.

5 They that sow in tears, shall reap in joy.

6 They went weeping, and carried ¹precious seed: *but* they shall return with joy, and bring their sheaves.

127 *1 He showeth that the whole estate of the world, both domestical and political, standeth by God's mere providence and blessing. 3 And that to have children well nurtured, is an especial grace and gift of God.*

A song of degrees, or Psalm of Solomon.

1 Except the Lord ¹build the house, they labor in vain that build it: except the Lord keep the ²city, the keeper watcheth in vain.

2 It is in vain for ¹you to rise early, *and* to lie down late, *and* eat the bread ²of sorrow: but he will surely give ³rest to his beloved.

3 Behold, children are the inheritance of the Lord, *and* the fruit of the womb *his* reward.

4 As *are* the arrows in the hand of the strong man; so *are* the ¹children of youth.

5 Blessed *is* the man that hath his quiver full of them: *for* they ¹shall not be ashamed, when they speak with *their* enemies in the gate.

128 *He showeth that blessedness appertaineth not to all universally, but to them only that fear the Lord, and walk in his ways.*

A song of degrees.

1 Blessed *is* everyone that feareth the Lord, and walketh in his ¹ways.

124:3 ¹ So unable were we to resist.

124:4 ¹ He useth most proper similitudes to express the great danger that the Church was in, and out of the which God miraculously delivered them.

124:7 ¹ For the wicked did not only furiously rage against the faithful, but craftily imagined to destroy them.

125:1 ¹ Though the world be subject to mutations, yet the people of God shall stand sure, and be defended by God's providence.

125:3 ¹ Though God suffer his to be under the cross, lest they should embrace wickedness, yet this cross shall not so rest upon them, that it should drive them from hope.

125:5 ¹ He desireth God to purge his Church from hypocrites, and such as have no zeal of the truth.

126:1 ¹ Their deliverance was as a thing incredible, and therefore took away all excuse of ingratitude.

126:2 ¹ He showeth how the godly ought to rejoice when God gathereth his Church or delivereth it.

² If the infidels confess God's wonderful work, the faithful can never show themselves sufficiently thankful.

126:4 ¹ It is no more impossible to God to deliver his people, than to cause the rivers to run in the wilderness and barren places.

126:6 ¹ That is, seed which was scarce and dear: meaning, that they which trusted in God's promise to return, had their desire.

127:1 ¹ That is, govern and dispose all things pertaining to the family.

² The public estate of the commonwealth.

127:2 ¹ Which watch and ward, and are also magistrates, and rulers of the city.

² Either that which is gotten by hard labor, or eaten with grief of mind.

³ Not exempting them from labor, but making their labors comfortable, and as it were a rest.

127:4 ¹ That is, endued with strength and virtues from God: for these are signs of God's blessings, and not the number.

127:5 ¹ Such children shall be able to stop their adversaries' mouths, when their godly life is maliciously accused before Judges.

128:1 ¹ God approveth not our life, except it be reformed according to his word.

2 When thou eatest the labors of thine ¹hands, thou shalt be blessed, and it shall be well with thee.

3 Thy wife *shall be* as the fruitful vine on the sides of thine house, *and* thy ¹children like the olive plants round about thy table.

4 Lo, surely thus shall the man be blessed, that feareth the Lord.

5 The Lord out of Zion shall ¹bless thee, and thou shalt see the wealth of ²Jerusalem all the days of thy life.

6 Yea, thou shalt see thy children's children, *and* peace upon Israel.

129

1 He admonisheth the Church to rejoice though it be afflicted.   4 For by the righteous Lord it shall be delivered.   6 And the enemies for all their glorious show, shall suddenly be destroyed.

A song of degrees.

1 They have oftentimes afflicted me from my youth (may ¹Israel now say)

2 They have oftentimes afflicted me from my youth: but they could not prevail against me.

3 The plowers plowed upon my back, *and* made long furrows.

4 *But* the ¹righteous Lord hath cut the cords of the wicked.

5 They that hate Zion, shall be all ashamed and turned backward.

6 ¹They *shall be* as the grass on the house tops, which withereth afore it cometh forth.

7 Whereof the mower filleth not his hand, neither the gleaner his lap:

8 ¹Neither they which go by, say, The blessing of the Lord *be* upon you, *or*, We bless you in the Name of the Lord.

130

The people of God from their bottomless miseries do cry unto God, and are heard.   3 They confess their sins, and flee unto God's mercies.

A song of degrees.

1 Out of the ¹deep places have I called unto thee, O Lord.

2 Lord, hear my voice: let thine ears attend to the voice of my prayers.

3 If thou, O Lord, straightly markest iniquities, O Lord, ¹who shall stand?

4 But mercy *is* with thee, that thou ¹mayest be feared.

5 I have waited on the Lord: my soul hath waited, and I have trusted in his word.

6 My soul *waiteth* on the Lord more than the morning watch watcheth for the morning.

7 Let Israel wait on the Lord: for with the Lord *is* ¹mercy, and with him *is* great redemption.

8 And he shall redeem Israel from all his iniquities.

131

1 David charged with ambition and greedy desire to reign, protesteth his humility and modesty before God, and teacheth all men what they should do.

A song of degrees, or Psalm of David.

1 Lord, ¹mine heart is not haughty, neither are mine eyes lofty, neither have I walked in great ²matters and hid from me.

2 Surely I have behaved myself, like one weaned from his mother, and kept silence: I am in myself as one that is ¹weaned.

3 Let Israel wait on the Lord from henceforth and forever.

132

1 The faithful grounding on God's promise made unto David, desire that he would establish the same, both as touching his posterity, and the building of the Temple, to pray there as was forspoken, Deut. 12:5.

A song of degrees.

1 Lord, remember David with all his ¹affliction,

2 Who sware unto the Lord, *and* vowed unto the mighty God, of Jacob, *saying*,

---

128:2 ¹ The world esteemeth them happy, which live in wealth and idleness: but the holy Ghost approveth them best that live of the mean profit of their labors.

128:3 ¹ Because God's favor appeareth in none outward thing, more than in increase of children, he promiseth to enrich the faithful with this gift.

128:5 ¹ Because of the spiritual blessing which God hath made to his Church, these temporal things shall be granted.

² For except God blessed his Church publicly, this private blessing were nothing.

129:1 ¹ The Church now afflicted ought to remember how her condition hath ever been such from the beginning to be molested most grievously by the wicked: yet in time it hath ever been delivered.

129:4 ¹ Because God is righteous, he cannot but plague his adversary, and deliver his, as oxen out of the plough.

129:6 ¹ The enemies that lift themselves most high, and as it were

approach near to the Sun, are consumed with the heat of God's wrath, because they are not grounded in godly humility.

129:8 ¹ That is, the wicked shall perish, and none shall pass for them.

130:1 ¹ Being in great distress and sorrow.

130:3 ¹ He declareth that we cannot be just before God but by forgiveness of sins.

130:4 ¹ Because of nature thou art merciful: therefore the faithful reverence thee.

130:7 ¹ He showeth to whom the mercy of God doth appertain: to Israel, that is, to the Church and not to the reprobate.

131:1 ¹ He setteth forth his great humility, as an example to all rulers and governors.

² Which pass the measure and limits of his vocation.

131:2 ¹ He was void of ambition and wicked desires.

132:1 ¹ That is, with how great difficulty he came to the kingdom, and with how great zeal and care he went about to build thy Temple.

3 I [1]will not enter into the Tabernacle of mine house, nor come upon my pallet *or* bed,

4 Nor suffer mine eyes to sleep, nor mine eyelids to slumber,

5 Until I find out a place for the [1]Lord, an habitation for the mighty *God* of Jacob.

6 Lo, we heard of it in [1]Ephrathah, *and* found it in the fields of the forest.

7 We will enter into his Tabernacles, *and* worship before his footstool.

8 Arise, O Lord, *to come* into thy [1]rest, thou, and the Ark of thy strength.

9 Let thy Priests be clothed with [1]righteousness, and let thy Saints rejoice.

10 For thy [1]servant David's sake refuse not the face of thine Anointed.

11 The Lord hath sworn in truth unto David, and he will not shrink from it, *saying,* Of the fruit of thy body will I set upon thy throne.

12 If thy sons keep my Covenant, and my testimonies, that I shall teach them, their sons also shall sit upon thy throne [1]forever.

13 For the Lord hath chosen Zion, *and* loved to dwell in it, *saying,*

14 This is my rest forever: here will I dwell, for I have a [1]delight therein.

15 I will surely bless her vittles, *and* will satisfy her poor with bread,

16 And will clothe her Priests with [1]salvation, and her Saints shall shout for joy.

17 There will I make the [1]horn of David to bud: *for* I have ordained a light for mine Anointed.

18 His enemies will I clothe with shame, but on him his crown shall flourish.

133

[1] This Psalm containeth the commendation of brotherly amity among the servants of God.

A song of degrees, *or* Psalm of David.

1 Behold, how good and how comely a thing it is, brethren to dwell even [1]together.

2 *It is* like to the precious [1]ointment upon the head, that runneth down upon the beard, *even* unto Aaron's beard, which went down on the border of his garments,

3 *And* as the dew of [1]Hermon which falleth upon the mountains of Zion: for [2]there the Lord appointed the blessing *and* life forever.

134

[1] He exhorteth the Levites watching in the Temple, to praise the Lord.

A song of degrees.

1 Behold, praise ye the Lord, all ye [1]servants of the Lord, ye that by night stand in the house of the Lord.

2 Lift up your [1]hands to the Sanctuary, and praise the Lord.

3 The Lord that [1]hath made heaven and earth, bless thee out of Zion.

135

[1] He exhorteth all the faithful, of what estate soever they be, to praise God for his marvelous works. 12 And specially for his graces toward his people, wherein he hath declared his Majesty, 15 To the confusion of all idolaters and their idols.

Praise ye the Lord.

1 Praise, the Name of the Lord; ye servants of the Lord, praise *him.*

2 Ye that [1]stand in the House of the Lord, *and* in the [2]courts of the House of our God,

3 Praise ye the Lord: for the Lord is good: sing praises unto his Name: for it is a comely thing.

132:3 [1] Because the chief charge of the king was to set forth God's glory, he showeth that he could take no rest, neither would go about any worldly thing, were it never so necessary, before he had executed his office.

132:5 [1] That is, the Ark, which was a sign of God's presence.

132:6 [1] The common bruit was that the Ark should remain in Ephrathah, that is, in Bethlehem a plentiful place: but after we perceived that thou wouldest place it in Jerusalem, which was barren as a forest, and compassed about only with hills.

132:8 [1] That is, Jerusalem, because that afterward his Ark should remove to none other place.

132:9 [1] Let the effect of thy grace both appear in the Priests and in the people.

132:10 [1] As thou first madest promise to David, so continue it to his posterity, that whatsoever they shall ask for their people, it may be granted.

132:12 [1] Because this cannot be accomplished but in Christ, it followeth, that the promise was spiritual.

132:14 [1] Meaning, for his own sake, and not for the plentifulness of the place: for he promiseth to bless it, declaring before that it was barren.

132:16 [1] That is, with my protection, whereby they shall be safe.

132:17 [1] Though his force for a time seemed to be broken, yet he promiseth to restore it.

133:1 [1] Because the greatest part were against David, though some favored him, yet when he was established king at length, they joined all together like brethren: and therefore he showeth by these similitudes the commodity of brotherly love.

133:2 [1] The ointment was a figure of the graces which come from Christ the head upon his Church.

133:3 [1] By Hermon and Zion he meaneth the plentiful country about Jerusalem.

[2] Where there is such concord.

134:1 [1] Ye that are Levites and chiefly appointed to this office.

134:2 [1] For their charge was not only to keep the Temple, but to pray there, and to give God thanks.

134:3 [1] And therefore hath all power, bless thee with his Fatherly love declared in Zion. Thus the Levites used to praise the Lord, and bless the people.

135:2 [1] Ye Levites that are in his Sanctuary.

[2] Meaning, the people: for the people and Levites had their courts, which were places of the Temple separate.

4 For the Lord hath ¹chosen Jacob to himself, *and* Israel for his chief treasure.

5 For I know that the Lord *is* great, and that our Lord *is* above all gods.

6 Whatsoever pleased the Lord, that ¹did he in heaven and in earth, in the sea, and in all the depths.

7 He bringeth up the clouds from the ends of the earth, and maketh the ªlightnings with the rain: he draweth forth the wind out of his treasures.

8 ᵇHe smote the firstborn of Egypt both of man and beast.

9 He hath sent tokens and wonders into the midst of thee, O Egypt, upon Pharaoh, and upon all his servants.

10 ᶜHe smote many nations, and slew mighty Kings:

11 *As* Sihon King of the Amorites, and Og king of Bashan, and all the kingdoms of Canaan:

12 And ¹gave their land for an inheritance, *even* an inheritance unto Israel his people.

13 Thy Name, O Lord, *endureth* forever: O Lord, thy remembrance *is* from generation to generation.

14 For the Lord will ¹judge his people, and be pacified toward his servants.

15 The ¹idols of the heathen *are* silver and gold, *even* the work of men's hands.

16 They have a mouth, and speak not: they have eyes and see not.

17 They have ears and hear not, neither is there any breath in their mouth.

18 They that make them, are like unto them: *so are* all that trust in them.

19 Praise the Lord, ye house of Israel: praise the Lord, ye house of Aaron.

20 Praise the Lord, ye house of Levi; ye that fear the Lord, praise the Lord.

21 Praised *be* the Lord out of Zion, which dwelleth in Jerusalem. Praise ye the Lord.

136

1 *A most earnest exhortation to give thanks unto God for the creation and governance of*

CHAPTER 135
ª Jer. 10:13
ᵇ Exod. 12:29
ᶜ Num. 21:24,34

all things, which standeth in confessing that he giveth us all of his mere liberality.

1 Praise ye the Lord, because he is good: for his ¹mercy *endureth* forever.

2 Praise ye the God of gods: for his mercy *endureth* forever:

3 Praise ye the Lord of lords: for his mercy *endureth* forever:

4 Which only doeth great wonders; for his mercy *endureth* forever:

5 Which by *his* wisdom made the heavens: for his mercy *endureth* forever:

6 Which hath stretched out the earth upon the waters: for his ¹mercy *endureth* forever:

7 Which made great lights: for his mercy *endureth* forever:

8 *As* the Sun to rule the day; for his mercy *endureth* forever:

9 The Moon and the stars to govern the night: for his mercy *endureth* forever:

10 Which smote Egypt with their firstborn, (for his mercy *endureth* forever)

11 And ¹brought out Israel from among them; for his mercy *endureth* forever:

12 With a mighty hand and ¹stretched out arm; for his mercy *endureth* forever:

13 Which divideth the Sea into two parts; for his mercy *endureth* forever:

14 And made Israel to pass through the midst of it; for his mercy *endureth* forever:

15 And overthrew Pharaoh and his host in the red Sea; for his mercy *endureth* forever:

16 Which led his people through the ¹wilderness; for his mercy *endureth* forever:

17 Which smote great Kings: for his mercy *endureth* forever:

18 And slew ¹mighty Kings: for his mercy *endureth* forever:

19 *As* Sihon King of the Amorites: for his mercy *endureth* forever:

20 And Og the king of Bashan: for his mercy *endureth* forever:

135:4 ¹ That is, hath freely loved the posterity of Abraham.

135:6 ¹ He joined God's power with his will, to the intent that we should not separate them, and hereby he willeth God's people to depend on his power which he confirmeth by examples.

135:12 ¹ He showeth what fruit the godly conceive of God's power, whereby they see how he destroyeth his enemies, and delivereth his people.

135:14 ¹ That is, govern and defend his people.

135:15 ¹ By showing what punishment God appointeth for the heathen idolaters, he warneth his people to beware the like offenses, seeing that idols have neither power nor life, and that their deliverance came not by idols, but by the mighty power of God, read Ps. 115:4.

136:1 ¹ By this repetition he showeth that the least of God's benefits bind us to thanksgiving: but chiefly his mercy, which is principally

declared towards his Church.

136:6 ¹ This was a common kind of thanksgiving, which the whole people used, when they had received any benefit of God, as 2 Chron. 7:6 and 20:21, meaning, that God was not only merciful to their fathers, but also continued the same to their posterity.

136:11 ¹ God's merciful providence toward man appeareth in all his creatures, but chiefly in that that he delivered his Church from the thraldom of their enemies.

136:12 ¹ In doing such a work as was never done before, nor that any other could do.

136:16 ¹ Where for the space of forty years he showed infinite and most strange wonders.

136:18 ¹ Declaring thereby that no power nor authority was so dear unto him, as the love of his Church.

21 And gave their land for an heritage; for his mercy *endureth* forever:

22 *Even* an heritage unto Israel his servant; for his mercy *endureth* forever:

23 Which remembered us in our [1]base estate; for his mercy *endureth* forever:

24 And hath rescued us from our oppressors; for his mercy *endureth* forever:

25 Which giveth food to all [1]flesh; for his mercy *endureth* forever:

26 [1]Praise ye the God of heaven; for his mercy *endureth* forever.

137

1 The people of God in their banishment seeing God's true Religion decay, lived in great anguish and sorrow of heart: the which grief the Chaldeans did so little pity, 3 That they rather increased the same daily with taunts, reproaches and blasphemies against God. 7 Wherefore the Israelites desire God, first to punish the Edomites, who provoked the Babylonians against them, 8 And moved by the Spirit of God, prophesy the destruction of Babylon, where they were handled so tyrannously.

1 By the rivers of Babel we [1]sat, and there we wept, when we remembered Zion.

2 We hanged our harps upon the willows in the midst [1]thereof.

3 Then they that led us captive, [1]required of us songs and mirth, when we had hanged up *our harps*, *saying,* Sing us *one* of the songs of Zion.

4 How shall we sing, *said we,* a song of the Lord in a strange land?

5 [1]If I forget thee, O Jerusalem, let my right hand forget *to play.*

6 If I do not remember thee, let my tongue cleave to the roof of my mouth: *yea,* if I prefer not Jerusalem to my [1]chief joy.

7 Remember the children of [1]Edom, O Lord, in the [2]day of Jerusalem, which said, Raze it, raze it to

the foundation thereof.

8 O daughter of Babel, worthy to be destroyed, blessed *shall he be* that rewardeth thee, as thou hast served us.

9 [1]Blessed *shall he be* that taketh and dasheth thy children against the stones.

138

1 David with great courage praiseth the goodness of God toward him, the which is so great, 4 That it is known to foreign princes, who shall praise the Lord together with him. 6 And he is assured to have the like comfort of God in the time following, as he had heretofore.

A Psalm of David.

1 I will praise thee with my whole heart: *even* before the [1]gods will I praise thee.

2 I will worship toward thine holy [1]Temple and praise thy Name, because of thy loving-kindness and for thy truth: for thou hast magnified thy Name above all things by thy word.

3 When I called, then thou heardest me, *and* hast [1]increased strength in my soul.

4 All the [1]kings of the earth shall praise thee, O Lord: for they have heard the words of thy mouth.

5 And they shall sing of the ways of the Lord, because the glory of the Lord *is* great.

6 For the Lord is high, yet he beholdeth the lowly, but the proud he knoweth [1]afar off.

7 Though I walk in the midst of trouble, *yet* wilt thou revive me: thou wilt stretch forth thine hand upon the wrath of mine enemies, and thy right hand shall save me.

8 The Lord will [1]perform *his work* toward me: O Lord, thy mercy *endureth* forever: forsake not the works of thine hands.

139

1 David cleanseth his heart from all hypocrisy, showeth that there is nothing so hid, which God seeth not. 13 Which he confirmeth by the creation of

---

136:23 [1] In our greatest affliction and slavery, when we looked for nothing less than to have had any succor.

136:25 [1] Seeing that God provideth even for the beasts, much more hath he care over his.

136:26 [1] Seeing that all ages have had most plain testimonies of God's benefits.

137:1 [1] That is, we abode a long time, and albeit that the country was pleasant, yet could not stay our tears, nor turn us from the true service of our God.

137:2 [1] To wit, of that country.

137:3 [1] The Babylonians speak thus in mocking us, as though by our silence we should signify that we hoped no more in God.

137:5 [1] Albeit the faithful are touched with their particular griefs, yet the common sorrow of the Church is most grievous unto them, and is such as they cannot but remember and lament.

137:6 [1] The decay of God's religion in their country was so grievous, that no joy could make them glad, except it were restored.

137:7 [1] According as Ezekiel 25:13 and Jer. 49:7, prophesied: and Obadiah, verse 10, showeth that the Edomites which came of Esau,

conspired with the Babylonians against their brethren and kinsfolk.

[2] When thou didst visit Jerusalem.

137:9 [1] He alludeth to Isaiah's prophecy, Isa. 13:16, promising good success to Cyrus and Darius, whom ambition moved to fight against Babylon, but God used them as his rods to punish his enemies.

138:1 [1] Even in the presence of Angels and of them that have authority among men.

138:2 [1] Both the Temple and ceremonial service at Christ's coming were abolished: so that now God will be worshipped only in spirit and truth, John 4:23.

138:3 [1] Thou hast strengthened me against mine outward and inward enemies.

138:4 [1] All the world shall confess that thou hast wonderfully preserved me, and performed thy promise.

138:6 [1] Distance of place cannot hinder God to show mercy to his, and to judge the wicked though they think that he is far off.

138:8 [1] Though mine enemies rage never so much, yet the Lord, which hath begun his work in me, will continue his grace to the end.

man. 14 *After declaring his zeal and fear of God, he professeth to be enemy to all them that contemn God.*

To him that excelleth. A Psalm of David.

1 O Lord, thou hast tried me, and known *me.*

2 Thou knowest my ¹sitting and my rising: thou understandest my thought afar off.

3 Thou ¹compassest my paths, and my lying down, and art accustomed to all my ways.

4 For there is not a word in my ¹tongue, *but* lo, thou knowest it wholly, O Lord.

5 Thou holdest me strait behind and before, and layest thine ¹hand upon me.

6 *Thy* knowledge is too wonderful for me: it is so high that I cannot *attain* unto it.

7 Whither shall I go from thy ¹Spirit? or whither shall I flee from thy presence?

8 If I ascend into heaven, thou art there: if I lie down in hell, thou art there.

9 Let me take the wings of the morning, *and* dwell in the uttermost parts of the sea:

10 Yet thither shall thine hand ¹lead me, and thy right hand hold me.

11 If I say, Yet the darkness shall hide me, even the night *shall be* ¹light about me.

12 Yea, the darkness hideth not from thee: but the night shineth as the day: the darkness and light are both alike.

13 For thou hast ¹possessed my reins: thou hast covered me in my mother's womb.

14 I will praise thee, for I am ¹fearfully and wondrously made: marvelous *are* thy works, and my soul knoweth it well.

15 My bones are not hid from thee, though I was made in a secret *place, and* fashioned ¹beneath in the earth.

16 Thine eyes did see me, when I was without form: ¹for in thy book were all things written, *which*

in continuance were fashioned, when there was none of them *before.*

17 How ¹dear therefore are thy thoughts unto me, O God! how great is the sum of them!

18 If I should count them, they are more than the sand: when I awake, ¹I am still with thee.

19 Oh that thou wouldest [slay], O God, the wicked and bloody men, *to whom I say,* Depart ye from me:

20 Which speak wickedly of thee, *and* being thine enemies are lifted up in vain.

21 Do not I ¹hate them, O Lord, that hate thee? and do not I earnestly contend with those that rise up against thee?

22 I hate them with an unfeigned hatred, as they were mine *utter* enemies.

23 Try me, O God, and know mine heart: prove me and know my thoughts,

24 And consider if there be any ¹way of wickedness in me, and lead me in the ²way forever.

140 1 *David complaineth of the cruelty, falsehood and injuries of his enemies.* 8 *Against the which he prayeth unto the Lord, and assureth himself of his help and succor.* 12 *Wherefore he provoketh the just to praise the Lord, and to assure themselves of his tuition.*

To him that excelleth. A Psalm of David.

1 Deliver me, O Lord, from the evil man: preserve me from the ¹cruel man:

2 Which imagine evil things in *their* ¹heart, *and* make war continually.

3 They have sharpened their tongues like a serpent: ¹adders' poison *is* under their lips. Selah.

4 Keep ¹me, O Lord, from the hands of the wicked; preserve me from the cruel man, which purposeth to cause my steps to slide.

5 The proud have laid a snare for me, and spread

139:2 ¹ He confesseth that neither our actions, thoughts, or any part of our life can be hid from God, though he seem to be far off.
139:3 ¹ So that they are evidently known to thee.
139:4 ¹ Thou knowest my meaning before I speak.
139:5 ¹ Thou so guidest me with thine hand, that I can turn no way, but where thou appointest me.
139:7 ¹ From thy power and knowledge?
139:10 ¹ Thy power doth so fast hold me, that I can escape by no means from thee.
139:11 ¹ Though darkness be an hindrance to man's sight, yet it serveth thine eyes as well as the light.
139:13 ¹ Thou hast made me in all parts, and therefore must needs know me.
139:14 ¹ Considering thy wonderful work in forming me, I cannot but praise thee and fear thy mighty power.
139:15 ¹ That is, in my mother's womb: which he compareth to the inward parts of the earth.
139:16 ¹ Seeing that thou didst know me before I was composed of either flesh or bone, much more now must thou know me when

thou hast fashioned me.
139:17 ¹ How ought we to esteem the excellent declaration of thy wisdom in the creation of man?
139:18 ¹ I continually see new occasions to meditate in thy wisdom, and to praise thee.
139:21 ¹ He teacheth us boldly to contemn all the hatred of the wicked, and friendship of the world, when they would let us to serve God sincerely.
139:24 ¹ Or any heinous way or rebellious: meaning, that though he were subject to sin, yet he was not given to wickedness, and to provoke God by rebellion.
² That is, continue thy favor towards me to the end.
140:1 ¹ Which persecuteth me of malice and without cause.
140:2 ¹ That is, by their false cavillations and lies they kindle the hatred of the wicked against me.
140:3 ¹ He showeth what weapons the wicked use, when power and force fail them.
140:4 ¹ He declareth what is the remedy of the godly, when they are oppressed by the worldlings.

a net with cords in my pathway, *and* set gins for me. Selah.

6   *Therefore* I said unto the Lord, Thou art my God: hear, O Lord, the voice of my prayers.

7   O Lord God the strength of my salvation, thou [1]hast covered my head in the day of battle.

8   Let not the wicked have his desire, O Lord; [1]perform not his wicked thought, *lest* they be proud. Selah.

9   *As for* [1]the chief of them that compass me about, let the mischief of their own lips come upon them.

10   Let coals fall upon them: let [1]him cast them into the fire, *and* into the deep pits that they rise not.

11   *For* the backbiter shall not be established upon the earth, evil shall [1]hunt the cruel man to destruction.

12   I know that the Lord will avenge the afflicted, *and* judge the poor.

13   Surely the righteous shall praise thy Name, *and* the just shall [1]dwell in thy presence.

141

1 David being grievously persecuted under Saul, only fleeth unto God to have succor.   *3 Desiring him to bridle his affections, that he may patiently abide till God take vengeance of his enemies.*

A Psalm of David.

1   O Lord, I [1]call upon thee: haste thee unto me: hear my voice, when I cry unto thee.

2   Let my prayer be directed in thy sight *as* incense, *and* the [1]lifting up of mine hands *as* an evening sacrifice.

3   Set a watch, O Lord, before my mouth, *and* keep the [1]door of my lips.

4   Incline not mine heart to evil, that I should commit wicked works with them that work iniquity: and let me not eat of their [1]delicates.

5   Let the righteous smite me: *for that is* a benefit:

and let [1]him reprove me, *and it shall be* a precious oil that shall not break mine head: for within a while I shall even [2]pray in their miseries.

6   When their judges shall be cast down in stony places, they shall [1]hear my words, for they are sweet.

7   Our bones lie scattered at the [1]grave's mouth, as he that heweth *wood* or diggeth in the earth.

8   But mine eyes *look* unto thee, O Lord God: in thee is my trust: leave not my soul destitute.

9   Keep me from the snare, *which* they have laid for me, and from the gins of the workers of iniquity.

10   Let the wicked fall into [1]his nets [2]together, while I escape.

142

The Prophet neither astonied with fear, nor carried away with anger, nor forced by desperation, would kill Saul: but with a quiet mind directed his earnest prayer to God, who did preserve him.

A Psalm of David, to give instruction,
and a prayer when he was in the cave.

1   I cried unto the Lord with my voice: with my voice I [1]prayed unto the Lord.

2   I poured out my meditation before him, *and* declared mine affection in his presence.

3   Though my spirit [1]was in perplexity in me, yet thou knewest my path: in the way wherein I walked, have they privily laid a snare for me.

4   I looked upon my right hand, and beheld, but there was none that would know me: all refuge failed me, *and* [1]none cared for my soul.

5   *Then* cried I unto thee, O Lord, *and* said, Thou art mine [1]hope, *and* my portion in the land of the living.

6   Hearken unto my cry, for I am brought very low: deliver me from my persecutors, for they are too strong for me.

7   Bring my soul out of [1]prison, that I may praise

140:7 [1] He calleth to God with lively faith, being assured of his mercies, because he had before time proved, that God helped him ever in his dangers.

140:8 [1] For it is in God's hand to overthrow the counsels and enterprises of the wicked.

140:9 [1] It seemeth that he alludeth to Saul.

140:10 [1] To wit, God: for David saw that they were reprobate, and that there was no hope of repentance in them.

140:11 [1] God's plagues shall light upon him in such sort, that he shall not escape.

140:13 [1] That is, shall be defended and preserved by thy fatherly providence and care.

141:1 [1] He showeth that there is none other refuge in our necessities, but only to flee unto God for comfort of soul.

141:2 [1] He meaneth his earnest zeal and gesture, which he used in prayer: alluding of the sacrifices which were by God's commandment offered in the old Law.

141:3 [1] He desireth God to keep his thoughts and ways either from thinking or executing vengeance.

141:4 [1] Let not their prosperity allure me to be wicked as they are.

141:5 [1] He could abide all corrections, that came of a loving heart.

[2] By patience I shall see the wicked so sharply handled, that I shall for pity pray for them.

141:6 [1] The people which followeth their wicked rulers in persecuting the Prophet, shall repent and turn to God, when they see their wicked rulers punished.

141:7 [1] Here appeareth that David was miraculously delivered out of many deaths, as 2 Cor. 1:9, 10.

141:10 [1] Into God's nets, whereby he catcheth the wicked in their own malice.

[2] So that none of them escape.

142:1 [1] David's patience and instant prayer to God condemneth their wicked rage, which in their troubles either despair and murmur against God, or else seek to others than to God, to have redress in their miseries.

142:3 [1] Hebrew, *was folden or wrapped in me*: meaning, as a thing that could have no issue.

142:4 [1] Or, sought for myself.

142:5 [1] Though all means failed him, yet he knew that God would never forsake him.

142:7 [1] For he was on all sides beset with his enemies, as though he had been in a most straight prison.

thy Name: *then* shall the righteous ²come about me, when thou art beneficial unto me.

143

1 An earnest prayer for remission of sins, acknowledging that the enemies did thus cruelly persecute him by God's just judgment.   8 He desireth to be restored to grace,   10 To be governeth by his holy Spirit, that he may spend the remnant of his life in the true fear and service of God.

A Psalm of David.

1 Hear my prayer, O Lord, *and* hearken unto my supplication: answer me in thy ¹truth, *and* in thy ²righteousness.

2 (And enter not into judgment with thy servant: for in thy ¹sight shall none that liveth, be justified.)

3 For the enemy hath persecuted my soul: he hath smitten my life down to the earth: he hath laid me in the darkness, as they that have been dead ¹long ago:

4 And my spirit was in perplexity in me, *and* mine ¹heart within me was amazed.

5 *Yet* do I remember the time ¹past: I meditate in all thy works, *yea*, I do meditate in the works of thine hands.

6 I stretch forth mine hands unto thee: my soul desireth after thee, as the thirsty land. Selah.

7 Hear me speedily, O Lord, *for* my spirit faileth: hide not thy face from me, else I shall be like unto them that go down into the pit.

8 Let me hear thy loving-kindness in the ¹morning, for in thee is my trust; ²show me the way, that I should walk in, for I lift up my soul unto thee.

9 Deliver me, O Lord, from mine enemies: *for* ¹I hid me with thee.

10 ¹Teach me to ²do thy will, for thou art my God: let thy good Spirit lead me unto the land of righteousness.

11 Quicken me, O Lord, for thy Name's sake, *and* for thy righteousness bring my soul out of trouble.

12 And for thy mercy ¹slay mine enemies, and destroy all them that oppress my soul: for I am thy ²servant.

144

He praiseth the Lord with great affection and humility for his kingdom restored, and for his victories obtained.   5 Demanding help, and the destruction of the wicked,   9 Promising to acknowledge the same with songs of praises,   15 And declareth wherein the felicity of any people consisteth.

A Psalm of David.

1 Blessed *be* the Lord my strength, which ¹teacheth mine hands to fight, *and* my fingers to battle.

2 *He is* my goodness and my fortress, my tower and ¹my deliverer, my shield and in him I trust, ²which subdueth my people under me.

3 Lord, what is man that thou ¹regardest him! *or* the son of man that thou thinkest upon him?

4 Man is like to vanity; his days *are* like a shadow that vanisheth.

5 ¹Bow thine heavens, O Lord, and come down; touch the mountains, and they shall smoke.

6 ¹Cast forth the lightning and scatter them; shoot out thine arrows and consume them.

7 Send thine hand from above: deliver me, and take me out of the great ¹waters, *and* from the hand of strangers,

8 Whose mouth talketh vanity, and their right hand *is* a right hand ¹of falsehood.

---

² Either to rejoice at my wonderful deliverance, or to set a crown upon mine head.

143:1 ¹ That is, as thou hast promised to be faithful in thy promise to all that trust in thee.

² That is, according to thy free goodness, whereby thou defendest thine.

143:2 ¹ He know that his afflictions were God's messengers to call him to repentance for his sins, though toward his enemies he was innocent, and that in God's sight all men are sinners.

143:3 ¹ He acknowledgeth that God is the only and true physician and heal him: and that he is able to raise him to life, though he were dead long ago, and turned to ashes.

143:4 ¹ So that only by faith and by the grace of God's Spirit was he upheld.

143:5 ¹ To wit, thy great benefits of old, and the manifold examples of thy favor towards thine.

143:8 ¹ That is, speedily and in due season.

² Let thine holy Spirit counsel me how to come forth of these great cares and troubles.

143:9 ¹ I hid myself under the shadow of thy wings that I might be defended by thy power.

143:10 ¹ He confesseth that both the knowledge and obedience of God's will cometh by the Spirit of God, who teacheth us by his word, giveth understanding by his Spirit, and frameth our hearts by his grace to obey him.

² That is, justly and aright: for so soon as we decline from God's will, we fall into error.

143:12 ¹ Which shall be a sign of thy Fatherly kindness toward me.

² Resigning myself wholly unto thee, and trusting in thy protection.

144:1 ¹ Who of a poor shepherd hath made me a valiant warrior and mighty conqueror.

144:2 ¹ Hebrew, *my deliverer unto me*: for the Prophet cannot satisfy himself with any words.

² He confesseth that neither by his own authority, power or policy his kingdom was quiet, but by the secret grace of God.

144:3 ¹ To give unto God just praise, is to confess ourselves to be unworthy of so excellent benefits, and that he bestoweth them upon us of his free mercy.

144:5 ¹ He desireth God to continue his graces, and to send help for the present necessity.

144:6 ¹ By these manner of speeches he showeth that all the lets in the world cannot hinder God's power, which he apprehended by faith.

144:7 ¹ That is, deliver me from the tumults of them that should be my people, but are corrupt in their judgment and enterprises, as though they were strangers.

144:8 ¹ For though they shake hands, yet they keep not promise.

9 I will sing a ¹new song unto thee, O God, *and* sing unto thee upon a viol, *and* an instrument of ten strings.

10 *It is he* that giveth deliverance unto kings, *and* rescueth David his ¹servant from the hurtful sword.

11 Rescue me, and deliver me from the hand of strangers, whose mouth talketh vanity, and their right hand *is* a right hand of falsehood:

12 ¹That our sons *may be* as the plants growing up in their youth, *and* our daughters as the corner *stones*, graven after the similitude of a palace:

13 That our ¹corners *may be* full *and* abounding with divers sorts, *and* that our sheep may bring forth thousands and ten thousand in our streets.

14 That our ¹oxen may be strong to labor; that there be none invasion, nor going out, nor no crying in our streets.

15 Blessed *are* the people, that be ¹so, *yea* blessed *are* the people whose God is the Lord.

145

This Psalm was composed when the kingdom of David flourished. 1 Wherein he describeth the wonderful providence of God, as well in governing man, as in preserving all the rest of his creatures. 17 He praiseth God for his justice and mercy. 18 But specially for his loving-kindness toward those that call upon him, that fear him, and love him: 21 For the which he promiseth to praise him forever.

A Psalm of David of praise.

1 O my God *and* King, ¹I will extol thee, and will bless thy Name forever and ever.

2 I will bless thee daily, and praise thy Name forever and ever.

3 ¹Great *is* the Lord, and most worthy to be

CHAPTER 145
ᵃ Exod. 34:6
ᵇ Luke 1:33
Dan. 7:14

praised, and his greatness *is* incomprehensible.

4 Generation shall praise thy works unto ¹generation, and declare thy power.

5 I will meditate of the beauty of thy glorious majesty, and thy wonderful works.

6 And they shall speak of the power of thy ¹dreadful acts, and I will declare thy greatness.

7 They shall break out into the mention of thy great goodness, and shall sing aloud of thy righteousness.

8 ᵃThe Lord is gracious, and ¹merciful, slow to anger, and of great mercy.

9 The Lord is good to all, and his mercies *are* over all his works.

10 All thy works praise thee, O Lord, and thy Saints bless thee.

11 ¹They show the glory of thy kingdom, and speak of thy power,

12 To cause his ¹power to be known to the sons of men, and the glorious renown of his kingdom.

13 Thy ᵇkingdom *is* an everlasting kingdom, and thy dominion *endureth* throughout all ages.

14 The Lord upholdeth all that ¹fall, and lifteth up all that are ready to fall.

15 The eyes of ¹all wait upon thee, and thou givest them their meat in due season.

16 Thou openest thine hand, and fillest all things living of *thy* good pleasure.

17 The Lord *is* ¹righteous in all his ways, and holy in all his works.

18 The Lord *is* near unto all that call upon him, *yea*, to all that call upon him in ¹truth.

19 He will fulfill the ¹desire of them that fear him;

144:9 ¹ That is, a rare and excellent song, as thy great benefits deserve.

144:10 ¹ Though wicked kings be called God's servants, as Cyrus, Isa. 45:1, forasmuch as he useth them to execute his judgments: yet David because of God's promise, and they that rule godly, are properly so called, because they serve not their own affections, but set forth God's glory.

144:12 ¹ He desireth God to continue his benefits toward his people, counting the procreation of children and their good education among the chiefest of God's benefits.

144:13 ¹ That the very corners of our houses may be full of store for the great abundance of thy blessings.

144:14 ¹ He attributeth not only the great commodities, but even the least also to God's favor.

144:15 ¹ And if God give not to all his children all these blessings, yet he recompenseth them with better things.

145:1 ¹ He showeth what sacrifices are pleasant and acceptable unto God, even praise and thanksgiving, and seeing that God still continueth his benefits towards us, we ought never to be weary in praising him for the same.

145:3 ¹ Hereby he declareth that all power is subject unto God, and that no worldly promotion ought to obscure God's glory.

145:4 ¹ Forasmuch as the end man's creation, and of his preservation in this life is to praise God, therefore he requireth not only that we ourselves do this, but cause all others to do the same.

145:6 ¹ Of thy terrible judgments against the wicked.

145:8 ¹ He describeth after what sort God showeth himself to all his creatures, though our sins have provoked his vengeance against all: to wit, merciful, not only in pardoning the sins of his elect, but in doing good even to the reprobate, albeit they cannot feel the sweet comfort of the same.

145:11 ¹ The Praise of thy glory appeareth in all thy creatures: and though the wicked would obscure the same by their silence, yet the faithful are ever mindful of the same.

145:12 ¹ He showeth that all things are out of order; but only where God reigneth.

145:14 ¹ Who being in misery and affliction would faint and fall away, if God did not uphold them, and therefore they ought to reverence him that reigneth in heaven, and suffer themselves to be governed by him.

145:15 ¹ To wit, as well of man, as of beast.

145:17 ¹ He praiseth God, not only because he is beneficial to all his creatures, but also in that he justly punisheth the wicked, and mercifully examineth his by the cross, giving them strength and delivering them.

145:18 ¹ Which only appertaineth to the faithful: and this virtue is contrary to infidelity, doubting, impatience and murmuring.

145:19 ¹ For they will ask or wish for nothing, but according to his will, 1 John 5:14.

he will also hear their cry, and will save them.

20 The Lord preserveth all them that love him; but he will destroy the wicked.

21 My mouth shall speak the praise of the Lord, and all [1]flesh shall bless his holy Name forever and ever.

146

1 David declareth his great zeal that he hath to praise God. 3 And teacheth, not to trust in man, but only in God Almighty, 7 Which delivereth the afflicted, 9 Defendeth the strangers, comforteth the fatherless, and the widows, 10 And reigneth forever.

Praise ye the Lord.

1 Praise thou the Lord, O my [1]soul.

2 I will praise the Lord during my life; as long as I have any being, I will sing unto my God.

3 Put not your trust in [1]Princes, nor in the son of man, for there is no help in him.

4 His breath departeth, and he returneth to his earth; then his [1]thoughts perish.

5 Blessed is he that hath the God of Jacob for his help, whose hope is in the Lord his God,

6 Which made [1]heaven and earth, the sea, and all that therein is; which keepeth his fidelity forever,

7 Which executeth justice [1]for the oppressed, which giveth bread to the hungry; the Lord looseth the prisoners.

8 The Lord giveth sight to the blind: the Lord raiseth up the crooked: the Lord [1]loveth the righteous.

9 The Lord keepeth the [1]strangers: he relieveth the fatherless and widow: but he overthroweth the way of the wicked.

10 The Lord shall [1]reign forever: O Zion, thy God endureth from generation to generation. Praise

ye the Lord.

147

1 The Prophet praiseth the bounty, wisdom, power, justice, and providence of God upon all his creatures. 2 But specially upon his Church, which he gathereth together after their dispersion, 19 Declaring his word and judgment so unto them, as he hath done to none other people.

1 Praise ye the Lord, for it is good to sing unto our God: for it is a [1]pleasant thing, and praise is comely.

2 The Lord doth build up [1]Jerusalem, and gather together the dispersed of Israel.

3 He healeth those that are [1]broken in heart, and bindeth up their sores.

4 He [1]counteth the number of the stars, and calleth them all by their names.

5 Great is our Lord, and great is his power: his wisdom is infinite.

6 The Lord relieveth the meek, and abaseth the wicked to the [1]ground.

7 Sing unto the Lord with praise: sing upon the harp unto our God,

8 Which [1]covereth the heaven with clouds, and prepareth rain for the earth, and maketh the grass to grow upon the mountains:

9 Which giveth to beasts their food, and to the young ravens that [1]cry.

10 He hath no pleasure in the [1]strength of an horse, neither delighteth he in the legs of man.

11 But the Lord delighteth in them that fear him, and attend upon his mercy.

12 Praise the Lord, O Jerusalem: praise thy God, O Zion.

13 For he hath made the bars of the gates [1]strong,

145:21 [1] That is, all men shall be bound to praise him.

146:1 [1] He stirreth up himself and all his affections to praise God.

146:3 [1] That God may have the whole praise: wherein he forbiddeth all vain confidence, showing that of nature we are more inclined to put our trust in creatures, than in God the Creator.

146:4 [1] As their vain opinions, whereby they flattered themselves and so imagined wicked enterprises.

146:6 [1] He encourageth the godly to trust only in the Lord, both for that his power is able to deliver them from all danger, and from his promise sake, his will is most ready to do it.

146:7 [1] Whose faith and patience for a while he trieth, but at length he punisheth the adversaries, that he may be known to be judge of the world.

146:8 [1] Though he visit them by affliction, hunger, imprisonment and such like, yet his fatherly love and pity never faileth them, yea, rather to his these are signs of his love.

146:9 [1] Meaning, all them that are destitute of worldly means and succor.

146:10 [1] He assureth the Church that God reigneth forever for the preservation of the same.

147:1 [1] He showeth wherein we ought to exercise ourselves continually, and to take our pastime: to wit, in praising God.

147:2 [1] Because the Lord is the founder of the Church, it cannot be destroyed, though the members thereof be dispersed, and seem as it were for a time to be cut off.

147:3 [1] With affliction, or sorrow for sin.

147:4 [1] Though it seem to man incredible, that God should assemble his Church, being so dispersed, yet nothing can be too hard to him that can number and name all the stars.

147:6 [1] For the more high that the wicked climb the greater is their fall in the end.

147:8 [1] He showeth by the examples of God's mighty power, goodness, and wisdom, that he can never want most just occasion to praise God.

147:9 [1] For their crying is as it were a confession of their need, which cannot be relieved, but by God only, then if God show himself mindful of the most contemptible souls, can he suffer them to die with famine, whom he hath assured of life everlasting?

147:10 [1] Though to use lawful means is both profitable and pleaseth God, yet to put our trust in them, is to defraud God of his honor.

147:13 [1] He doth not only furnish his Church with all things necessary, but preserveth also the same, and maketh it strong against all outward force.

and hath blessed thy children within thee.

14 He setteth peace in thy borders, *and* satisfieth thee with the [1]flour of wheat.

15 He sendeth forth his [1]commandment upon earth, *and* his word runneth very [2]swiftly.

16 He giveth snow like wool, *and* scattereth the hoary frost like ashes.

17 He casteth forth his ice like morsels: who can abide the cold thereof?

18 He sendeth his word and melteth them: he causeth his wind to blow, *and* the waters flow.

19 He showeth his [1]word unto Jacob, his statutes and his judgments unto Israel.

20 He hath not dealt so with every nation, neither have they [1]known *his* judgments. Praise ye the Lord.

148

1 He provoketh all creatures to praise the Lord in heaven and earth, and all places. 14 Specially his Church, for the power that he hath given to the same, after that he had chosen them and joined them unto him.

Praise ye the Lord.

1 Praise ye the Lord from the heaven: praise ye him in the high places.

2 Praise ye him, all ye [1]his Angels: praise him, all his army.

3 Praise ye him, [1]sun and moon: praise ye him all bright stars.

4 Praise ye him [1]heavens of heavens, and [2]waters, that be above the heavens.

5 Let them praise the Name of the Lord: for he commanded, and they were created.

6 And he hath established them forever and ever: he hath made an ordinance, which shall not pass.

7 Praise ye the Lord from the earth, *ye* [1]dragons and all depths:

8 [1]Fire and hail, snow and vapors, stormy wind, which execute his word.

9 Mountains and all hills, fruitful trees, and all cedars:

10 Beasts and all cattle, creeping things and feathered fowls:

11 [1]Kings of the earth and all people, princes and all judges of the world:

12 Young men and maidens, also old men and children:

13 Let them praise the Name of the Lord: for his Name only is to be exalted, *and* his praise above the earth and the heavens.

14 For he hath exalted the [1]horn of his people, *which is* a praise for all his Saints, *even* for the [2]children of Israel, a people *that is* near unto him. Praise ye the Lord.

149

1 An exhortation to the Church to praise the Lord for his victory and conquest, that he giveth his Saints against all man's power.

Praise ye the Lord.

1 Sing ye unto the Lord [1]a new song: let his praise *be heard* in the Congregation of Saints.

2 Let Israel rejoice in him that [1]made him, and let the children of Zion rejoice in their [2]King.

3 Let them praise his Name with the flute: let them sing praises unto him with the timbrel and harp.

4 For the Lord hath pleasure in his people: he will make the meek glorious by deliverance.

5 Let the Saints be joyful with glory: let them sing loud upon their [1]beds.

6 Let the high Acts of God be in their mouth, and a two edged sword in their hands,

7 [1]To execute vengeance upon the heathen, *and* corrections among the people:

147:14 [1] Hebrew, *fat.*

147:15 [1] His secret working in all creatures is as a commandment to keep them in order, and to give them moving and force.

[2] For immediately and without resisting all things obey him.

147:19 [1] As before he called God's secret working in all his creatures his word: so he meaneth here by his word the doctrine of life everlasting, which he hath left to his Church as a most precious treasure.

147:20 [1] The cause of this difference is God's free mercy, which hath elected his in his Son Christ Jesus to salvation: and his just judgment, whereby he hath appointed the reprobate to eternal damnation.

148:2 [1] Because they are members of the same body, he setteth them before our eyes, which are most willing hereunto, and by their prompt obedience teach us to do our duty.

148:3 [1] In that God's glory shineth in these insensible creatures, this their beauty is as a continual praising of God.

148:4 [1] Not that there are divers heavens, but because of the spheres and of the situation of the fixed stars and planets, he comprehendeth by this word the whole heaven.

[2] That is, the rain which is in the middle region of the air, which he here comprehendeth under the name of the heavens.

148:7 [1] Meaning, the great and monstrous fishes, as whales and such like.

148:8 [1] Which come not by chance or fortune, but by God's appointed ordinance.

148:11 [1] For the greater gifts that any hath received, and the more high that one is preferred, the more bound is he to praise God for the same: but neither high nor low condition or degree can be exempted from this duty.

148:14 [1] That is, the dignity, power and glory of his Church.

[2] By reason of his covenant made with Abraham.

149:1 [1] For his rare and manifold benefits bestowed on his Church.

149:2 [1] In that they were preferred before all other nations, it was as a new creation, and therefore, Ps. 95:7, they were called the sheep of God's hands.

[2] For God as he is the creator of the soul and body, so wills he that both … serve him and that his people be continually subject to him, as to their most lawful king.

149:5 [1] He alludeth to that continual rest and quietness which they should have if they would suffer God to rule them.

149:7 [1] This is chiefly accomplished in the kingdom of Christ when God's people for just causes execute God's judgments against his enemies: and it giveth no liberty to any to revenge their private injuries.

8   To bind [1]their kings in chains, and their nobles with fetters of iron,

9   That they may execute upon them the judgment that is [1]written: this honor shall be to all his Saints. Praise ye the Lord.

150

1 An exhortation to praise the Lord without cease by all manner of ways for all his mighty and wonderful works.

Praise ye the Lord.

1   Praise ye God in his [1]Sanctuary: praise ye him in the [2]firmament of his power.

2   Praise ye him in his mighty Acts: praise ye him according to his excellent greatness.

3   Praise ye him in the sound of the [1]trumpet: praise ye him upon the viol and the harp.

4   Praise ye him with timbrel and flute: praise ye him with virginals and organs.

5   Praise ye him with sounding cymbals: praise ye him with high sounding cymbals.

6   Let everything that hath [1]breath praise the Lord. Praise ye the Lord.

149:8 [1] Not only the people, but the kings that were their enemies should be destroyed.

149:9 [1] Hereby God bindeth the hands and minds of all his to enterprise no farther than he appointeth.

150:1 [1] That is, in the heaven.

[2] For his wonderful power appeareth in the firmament, which in Hebrew is called a stretching out, or spreading abroad, wherein the mighty work of God shineth.

150:3 [1] Exhorting the people only to rejoice in praising God, he maketh mention of those instruments which by God's commandment were appointed in the old Law, but under Christ the use thereof is abolished in the Church.

150:6 [1] He showeth that all the order of nature is bound to this duty, and much more God's children, who ought never to cease to praise him, till they be gathered into that kingdom, which he hath prepared for his, where they shall sing everlasting praise.

THE
¹PROVERBS
OF SOLOMON

1 *2 The power and use of the word of God. 7 Of the fear of God and knowledge of his word. 10 We may not consent to the enticings of sinners. 20 Wisdom complaineth that she is contemned. 24 The punishment of them that contemn her.*

CHAPTER 1
a Ps. 111:10
Eccl. 1:16

1 The Parables of Solomon the son of David king of Israel,

2 To know wisdom, ¹and instruction, to understand the words ²of knowledge,

3 To receive ¹instruction to do wisely, *by* ²justice and judgment and equity,

4 To give unto the ¹simple sharpness of wit, *and* to the child knowledge and discretion.

5 And wise man shall hear and increase in learning, and a man of ¹understanding shall attain unto wise counsels,

6 To understand a parable, and the interpretation, the words of the wise, and their dark sayings.

7 ¶ *a*The fear of the Lord *is* the beginning of knowledge: *but* fools despise wisdom and instruction.

8 My son, hear thy ¹father's instruction, and forsake not thy ²mother's teaching.

9 For they shall be ¹a comely ornament unto thine head, and *as* chains for thy neck.

10 ¶ My son, ¹if sinners do entice thee, consent thou not.

11 If they say, Come with us, we will lay wait for ¹blood, *and* lie privily for the innocent without a cause:

12 We will swallow them up alive like a ¹grave, even whole, as those that go down into the pit:

13 We shall find all precious riches, *and* fill our houses with spoil:

14 Cast in thy lot among us, we will all have one ¹purse:

15 My son, walk not thou in the way with them: refrain thy foot from their ¹path.

16 For their feet run to evil, and make haste to shed blood.

17 Certainly *as* without cause the net is spread before the eyes of all that hath wing:

18 So they lay wait for blood, *and* lie privily for ¹their lives.

19 Such *are* the ways of everyone that is greedy of gain: he would take away ¹the life of the owners thereof.

20 ¶ ¹Wisdom crieth without: she uttereth her voice in the ²streets.

21 She calleth in the high *street, among* the prease in the enterings of the gates, *and* uttereth her words in the city, *saying,*

22 O ye ¹foolish, how long will ye love foolishness? and the scornful take their pleasure in scorning? and the fools hate knowledge?

Title ¹ This word Proverb, or Parable, signifieth a grave and notable sentence, worthy to be kept in memory: and is sometimes taken in the evil part for a mock or scoff.

1:2 ¹ That is, what we ought to know and follow, and what we ought to refuse.

² Meaning, the word of God wherein is the only true knowledge.

1:3 ¹ To learn to submit ourselves to the correction of those that are wise.

² By living justly and rendering to every man that which appertaineth unto him.

1:4 ¹ To such as have no discretion to rule themselves.

1:5 ¹ As he showeth that these parables containing the effect of religion as touching manners and doctrine, do appertain to the simple people: so doth he declare that the same is also necessary for them that are wise and learned.

1:8 ¹ He speaketh this in the Name of God, which is the universal Father of all creatures, or in the name of the pastor of the Church, who is as a father.

² That is, of the Church, wherein the faithful are begotten by the incorruptible seed of God's word.

1:9 ¹ Hebrew, *increase of grace.*

1:10 ¹ To wit, the wicked which have not the fear of God.

1:11 ¹ He speaketh not only of the shedding of blood with hand, but of all crafty practices which tend to the detriment of our neighbor.

1:12 ¹ As the grave is never satiated, so the avarice of the wicked and their cruelty hath none end.

1:14 ¹ He showeth whereby the wicked are allured to join together, because they have every one part of the spoil of the innocent.

1:15 ¹ That is, have nothing at all to do with them.

1:18 ¹ He showeth that there is no cause to move these wicked to spoil the innocent, but their avarice and cruelty.

1:19 ¹ Whereby he concludeth, that the covetous man is a murderer.

1:20 ¹ This wisdom is the eternal word of God.

² So that none can pretend ignorance.

1:22 ¹ Wisdom reproveth three kinds of men: the foolish or simple which err of ignorance, and the mockers that cannot suffer to be taught, and the fools which are drowned in worldly lusts and hate the knowledge of godliness.

23 (Turn you at my correction: lo, I will pour out my mind unto you, *and* make you understand my words.)

24 Because I have called, and ye refused: I have stretched out mine hand, and none would regard.

25 But ye have despised all my counsel, and would none of my correction,

26 I will also [1]laugh at your destruction, *and* mock when your fear cometh.

27 When [1]your fear cometh like *sudden* desolation, and your destruction shall come like a whirlwind: when affliction and anguish shall come upon you,

28 Then shall they call upon me, but I will not answer: they shall seek me early, but they shall not [1]find me,

29 Because they hated knowledge, and did not choose the fear of the Lord.

30 They would none of my counsel, *but* [1]despised all my correction.

31 Therefore shall they eat of the [1]fruit of their own way, and be filled with their own devices.

32 For [1]ease slayeth the foolish, and the prosperity of fools destroyeth them.

33 But he that obeyeth me, shall dwell safely, and be quiet from fear of evil.

2 1 *Wisdom exhorteth to obey her.* 5 *She teacheth the fear of God.* 6 *She is given of God.* 10 *She preserveth from wickedness.*

1 My son, if thou wilt receive my words, and [1]hide my commandments within thee,

2 And cause thine ears to hearken unto wisdom, *and* incline [1]thine heart to understanding,

3 (For if thou callest after knowledge, [1]*and* cryest for understanding:

4 If thou seekest her as silver, and searchest for her as for [1]treasures,

5 Then shalt thou understand the fear of the Lord, and find the [1]knowledge of God.

6 For the Lord giveth wisdom, out of his mouth cometh knowledge and understanding.

7 He [1]preserveth the state of the righteous, *he is* a shield to them that walk uprightly,

8 That they may keep the ways of judgment: and he preserveth the way of his Saints).

9 Then shalt thou understand righteousness and judgment, and equity, *and* every good path.

10 ¶ When wisdom entereth into thine heart, and knowledge delighteth thy soul,

11 Then shall [1]counsel preserve thee, *and* understanding shall keep thee,

12 And deliver thee from the evil way, and from the man that speaketh froward things,

13 *And from* them that leave the [1]ways of righteousness to walk in the ways of darkness:

14 Which rejoice in doing evil, *and* delight [1]in the frowardness of the wicked,

15 Whose ways are crooked, and they are lewd in their paths.

16 And it shall deliver thee from the strange [1]woman, *even* from the stranger which flattereth with her words.

17 Which forsaketh the [1]guide of her youth, and forgetteth the [2]covenant of her God.

18 Surely her [1]house tendeth to death, and her paths unto [2]the dead.

19 All they that go unto her, return not again, neither take they hold of the ways of life.

20 Therefore walk thou in the way of good men, and keep the ways of the righteous.

21 For the just shall dwell in the [1]land, and the upright men shall remain in it.

22 But the wicked shall be cut off from the earth, and the transgressor shall be rooted out of it.

3 1 *The words of God giveth life.* 5 *Trust in God.* 7 *Fear him.* 9 *Honor him.* 11 *Suffer his correction:* 21 *To them that follow the word of God, all things shall succeed well.*

1 My son, forget not thou my Law, but let thine

1:26 [1] This is spoken according to our capacity, signifying that the wicked, which mock and jest at God's word, shall have the just reward of their mocking.
1:27 [1] That is, your destruction, which thing you feared.
1:28 [1] Because they sought not with an affection to God, but for ease of their own grief.
1:30 [1] Showing that without faith and obedience, we can not call upon God aright.
1:31 [1] They shall feel what commodity their wicked life shall give them.
1:32 [1] That is, the prosperity and sensuality wherein they delight.
2:1 [1] That is, keep them in thine heart.
2:2 [1] If thou give thyself to the true knowledge of God without hypocrisy.
2:3 [1] Meaning, that we must seek the knowledge of God with care and diligence.
2:4 [1] Showing that no labor must be spared.
2:5 [1] This (saith he) is the true wisdom, to know and fear God.
2:7 [1] Or, hideth the salvation.
2:11 [1] The word of God shall teach thee, and counsel thee how to govern thyself.
2:13 [1] That is, the word of God, which is the only light, to follow their own fantasies which are darkness.
2:14 [1] When they see any given to evil as they are.
2:16 [1] Meaning, that wisdom which is the word of God, shall preserve us from all vices: naming this vice of whoredom whereunto man is most prone.
2:17 [1] That is, her husband, which is her head and guide to govern her, from whom she ought not to depart, but remain in his subjection.
[2] Which is the promise made in marriage.
2:18 [1] Her acquaintance with her familiars, and them that haunt her.
[2] To them that are dead in body and soul.
2:21 [1] They shall enjoy the temporal and spiritual promises of God, as the wicked shall be void of them.

heart *keep my commandments.

2 For they shall increase the length of thy [1]days and the years of life, and *thy* prosperity.

3 Let not [1]mercy and truth forsake thee: bind them on thy [2]neck, *and* write them upon the table of thine [3]heart.

4 So shalt thou find favor and good understanding in the sight of God and man.

5 ¶ Trust in the Lord with all thine heart, and lean not unto thine own wisdom.

6 In all thy ways acknowledge him, and he shall direct thy ways.

7 ¶ Be not wise in thine own eyes: *but* fear the Lord, and depart from evil.

8 *So* health shall be unto thy [1]navel, and marrow unto thy bones.

9 [1]Honor the Lord with thy riches, and with the first *fruits* of all thine increase.

10 So shall thy barns be filled with abundance, and thy presses shall [1]burst with new wine.

11 ¶ My son, refuse not the chastening of the Lord, neither be grieved with his correction.

12 [b]For the Lord correcteth him, whom he loveth, even as the father *doth* the child, in *whom* he delighteth.

13 Blessed *is* the man that findeth wisdom, and the man that getteth understanding.

14 For the merchandise thereof is better than the merchandise of silver, and the gain thereof *is better* than gold.

15 It is more precious than pearls: and all things that thou canst desire, are not to be compared unto her.

16 Length of days *is* in her right hand, [1]*and* in her right hand riches and glory.

17 Her ways *are* ways of pleasure, and all her paths prosperity.

18 She is a tree [1]of life to them that lay hold on her, and blessed is he that retaineth her.

CHAPTER 3
a Deut. 8:1
Deut. 30:16
b Heb. 12:5
Rev. 3:19

19 The Lord by wisdom hath laid the [1]foundation of the earth, and hath stablished the heavens through understanding.

20 By his knowledge the depths are broken up, and the clouds drop down the dew.

21 My son, let not *these things* depart from thine eyes, *but* observe wisdom and counsel.

22 So they shall be life to thy soul, and grace unto thy [1]neck.

23 Then shalt thou walk safely by the way: and thy foot shall not stumble.

24 If thou sleepest, thou shalt not be afraid: and when thou sleepest, thy sleep shall be sweet.

25 [1]Thou shalt not fear for *any* sudden fear, neither for destruction of the wicked, when it cometh.

26 For the Lord shall be for thine assurance, and shall preserve thy foot from taking.

27 ¶ Withhold not the good from [1]the owners thereof, though there be power in [thine] hand to do it.

28 Say not unto thy neighbor, Go and come again, and tomorrow will I give *thee*, if thou *now* have it.

29 ¶ Intend none hurt against thy neighbor, seeing he doth dwell [1]without fear by thee.

30 ¶ Strive not with a man causeless, when he hath done thee no harm.

31 ¶ Be not [1]envious for the wicked man, neither choose any of his ways,

32 For the froward *is* abomination unto the Lord: but his [1]secret *is* with the righteous.

33 The curse of the Lord is in the house of the wicked: but he blesseth the habitation of the righteous.

34 With the scornful [1]he scorneth, but he giveth grace unto the humble.

35 The wise shall inherit glory: but fools dishonor, *though* they be exalted.

4 *1 Wisdom and her fruits ought to be searched. 14 The way of the wicked must be refused. 20 By the word of*

3:2 [1] Long life is the blessing of God which he giveth to his, so far forth as it is expedient for them.

3:3 [1] By mercy and truth he meaneth the commandments of the first and second table: or else the mercy and faithfulness that we ought to use toward our neighbors.

[2] Keep them as a most precious jewel.

[3] Have them ever in remembrance.

3:8 [1] By this part he comprehendeth the whole body, as by health he meaneth all the benefits promised in the Law both corporal and spiritual.

3:9 [1] As was commanded in the Law, Exod. 23:19; Deut. 26:2, and by this they acknowledged that God was the giver of all things, and that they were ready to bestow all at his commandment.

3:10 [1] For the faithful distributor God giveth in greater abundance.

3:16 [1] Meaning, that he that seeketh wisdom, that is, suffereth himself to be governeth by the Word of God, shall have all prosperity both corporal and spiritual.

3:18 [1] Which bringeth forth such fruit that they that eat thereof have life: and he alludeth to the tree of life in paradise.

3:19 [1] Hereby he sheweth that this wisdom, whereof he speaketh, is everlasting, because it was before all creatures, and that all things even the whole world were made by it.

3:22 [1] Or, throat, read Prov. 1:9.

3:25 [1] For when God destroyeth the wicked, he will save his as he did Lot in Sodom.

3:27 [1] Not only from them to whom the possession belongeth, but also thou shalt not keep it from them which have need of the use thereof.

3:29 [1] That is, putteth his trust in thee.

3:31 [1] Desire not to be like unto him.

3:32 [1] That is, his covenant and fatherly affection which is hid and secret from the world.

3:34 [1] He will show by his plagues, that their scorns shall turn to their own destruction, as Prov. 1:26.

God the heart, eyes, and course of life must be guided.

1 Hear, O ye children, the instruction of a ¹father, and give ear to learn understanding.

2 For I do give you a good doctrine: *therefore* forsake ye not my law.

3 For I was my father's son, tender and dear in the sight of my mother,

4 When he ¹taught me, and said unto me, Let thine heart hold fast my words: keep my commandments, and thou shalt live.

5 Get wisdom: get understanding: forget not, neither decline from the words of my mouth.

6 Forsake her not, and she shall keep thee: love her and she shall preserve thee.

7 ¹Wisdom *is* the beginning: get wisdom *therefore:* and above all thy possession get understanding.

8 Exalt her, and she shall exalt thee: she shall bring thee to honor, if thou embrace her.

9 She shall give a comely ornament unto thine head, *yea,* she shall give thee a crown of glory.

10 ¶ Hear, my son: and receive my words, and the years of thy life shall be many.

11 I have ¹taught thee in the way of wisdom, *and* led thee in the paths of righteousness.

12 When thou goest, thy gait shall not be ¹strait, and when thou runnest, thou shalt not fall.

13 Take hold of instruction, *and* leave not: keep her, for she is thy life.

14 ¶ Enter not into the way of the wicked, and walk not in the way of evil men.

15 Avoid it, *and* go not by it: turn from it, and pass by.

16 For they cannot ¹sleep, except they have done evil, and their sleep departeth except they cause *some* to fall.

17 For they eat the bread of ¹wickedness, and drink the wine of violence.

18 But the way of the righteous shineth as the light, that ¹shineth more and more unto the perfect day.

19 The way of the wicked *is* as the darkness: they know not wherein they shall fall.

20 ¶ My son, hearken unto my words, incline thine ear unto my sayings.

21 Let them not depart from thine eyes, *but* keep them in the midst of thine heart.

22 For they are life unto those that find them: and health unto all their ¹flesh.

23 Keep thine heart with all diligence: for thereout cometh ¹life.

24 Put away from thee a froward mouth, and put wicked lips far from thee.

25 Let thine eyes behold the right, and let thine eyelids direct thy way before thee.

26 ¹Ponder the path of thy feet, and let all thy ways be ordered aright.

27 Turn not to the right hand, nor to the left, *but* remove thy foot from evil.

5

3 Whoredom is forbidden,   9 And prodigality.   15 He willeth a man to live on his labors and to help others,   18 To love his wife.   22 The wicked taken in their own wickedness.

1 My son, hearken unto my wisdom, *and* incline thine ear unto my ¹knowledge,

2 That thou mayest regard counsel, and thy lips observe knowledge.

3 For the lips ¹of a strange woman drop *as* an honeycomb, and her mouth is more soft than ²oil.

4 But the end of her is bitter as wormwood, *and* sharp as a two-edged sword.

5 Her ¹feet go down to death, and her steps take hold on hell.

6 She weigheth not the way of life: ¹her paths are moveable: thou canst not know *them.*

7 Hear ye me now therefore, O children, and depart not from the words of my mouth.

8 Keep thy way far from her, and come not near the door of her house,

9 Lest thou give thine ¹honor unto others, and thy years to the cruel:

10 Lest the stranger should be filled with thy strength, and thy ¹labors be in the house of a stranger,

---

4:1 ¹ He speaketh this in the person of a Preacher and Minister, which is as a father unto the people, read Prov. 2:8.
4:4 ¹ Meaning, David his father.
4:7 ¹ He showeth that we must first begin at God's word, if so be we will that other things prosper with us, contrary to the judgment of the world, which make it their last study, or else care not for it at all.
4:11 ¹ Solomon declareth what care his father had to bring him up in the true fear of God: for this was David's protestation.
4:12 ¹ Thou shalt walk at liberty without offence.
4:16 ¹ Meaning, that to do evil is more proper and natural to the wicked than to sleep, eat or drink.
4:17 ¹ Gotten by wicked means and cruel oppression.
4:18 ¹ Signifying, that the godly increase daily in knowledge and perfection, till they come to full perfection, which is when they shall

be joined to their head in the heavens.
4:22 ¹ That is, they shall have health of body: under the which all other blessings promised in the law are contained.
4:23 ¹ For as the heart is either pure or corrupt, so is the whole course of man's life.
4:26 ¹ Keep a measure in all thy doings.
5:1 ¹ Or, understanding.
5:3 ¹ That is, an harlot which giveth herself to another than to her husband.
    ² By oil and honey he meaneth flattering and crafty enticements.
5:5 ¹ All her doings lead to destruction.
5:6 ¹ She hath ever new means to allure to wickedness.
5:9 ¹ That is, thy strength and goods to her that will have no pity upon thee: as is read of Samson, and the prodigal son.
5:10 ¹ The goods gotten by thy travel.

11 And thou mourn at thine end, (when thou hast consumed thy flesh and thy body)

12 And say, How have I hated instruction, and mine heart despised correction!

13 And have not obeyed the voice of them that taught me, nor inclined mine ear to them that instructed me!

14 I was almost *brought* into all evil in the midst of the Congregation and [1]assembly.

15 ¶ Drink the water of [1]thy cistern, and of the rivers out of the midst of thine own well.

16 Let thy fountains flow forth, and the rivers of waters in the streets.

17 But let them be thine, *even* [1]thine only, and not the strangers with thee.

18 Let thy [1]fountain be blessed, and rejoice with the wife of thy [2]youth.

19 *Let her be as* the loving hind and pleasant roe: let her breasts satisfy thee at all times, *and* delight in her love continually.

20 For why shouldest thou [1]delight, my son, in a strange woman, or embrace the bosom of a stranger?

21 For the ways of man *are* before the [1]eyes of the Lord, and he pondereth all his paths.

22 His own iniquities shall take the wicked himself, and he shall be holden with the cords of his own sin.

23 He shall [1]die for fault of instruction, and shall go astray through his great folly.

6

1 Instruction for sureties.   6 The slothful and sluggish is stirred to work.   12 He describeth the nature of the wicked.   16 The things that God hateth.   20 To observe the word of God.   24 To flee adultery.

1 My son, if thou be surety for thy neighbor, *and* hast stricken hands with the stranger,

2 Thou art [1]snared with the words of thy mouth: thou art *even* taken with the words of thine own mouth.

3 Do this now, my Son, and deliver thyself: seeing thou art come into the hand of thy neighbor, go, and humble thyself, and solicit thy friends.

4 Give no sleep to thine eyes, nor slumber to thine eyelids.

5 Deliver thyself as a Doe from the hand *of the hunter*, and as a bird from the hand of the fowler.

6 ¶ Go to [1]the pismire, O sluggard: behold her ways, and be wise.

7 For she having no guide, governor, nor ruler,

8 Prepareth her meat in the summer, *and* gathereth her food in harvest.

9 How long wilt thou sleep, O sluggard? when wilt thou arise out of the sleep?

10 *aYet* a little sleep, a little slumber, [1]a little folding of the hands to sleep.

11 Therefore thy poverty cometh as one that [1]traveleth by the way, and thy necessity like [2]an armed man.

12 The unthrifty man [1]*and* the wicked man walketh with a froward mouth.

13 He maketh a sign with his eyes: he [1]signifieth with his feet: he [2]instructeth with his fingers.

14 Lewd things *are* in his heart: he imagineth evil at all times, *and* raiseth up contentions.

15 Therefore shall his destruction come speedily: he shall be destroyed suddenly without recovery.

16 ¶ These six things doth the Lord hate: yea, his soul abhorreth seven:

17 The haughty eyes, a lying tongue, and the hands that shed innocent blood,

18 An heart that imagineth wicked enterprises, [1]feet that be swift in running to mischief,

19 A false witness that speaketh lies, and him that raiseth up contentions among [1]brethren.

20 ¶ My son, keep thy father's commandment, and forsake not thy mother's instruction.

21 Bind them always upon thine [1]heart, *and* tie them about thy neck.

5:14 [1] Although I was faithfully instructed in the truth, yet had I almost fallen to utter shame and destruction notwithstanding my good bringing up in the assembly of the godly.

5:15 [1] He teacheth us sobriety, exhorting us to live of our own labors and to be beneficial to the godly that want.

5:17 [1] Distribute them not to the wicked and infidels, but reserve them for thyself, thy family and them that are of the household of faith.

5:18 [1] Thy children which shall come of thee in great abundance, showing that God blesseth marriage, and curseth whoredom.

[2] Which thou didst marry in thy youth.

5:20 [1] Or, go astray with a stranger?

5:21 [1] He declareth that except man do join to his wife both in heart and in outward conversation, that he shall not escape the judgments of God.

5:23 [1] Because he will not give ear to God's word and be admonished.

6:2 [1] He forbiddeth us not to become surety for one another, according to the rule of charity, but that we consider for whom and

after what sort, so that the creditor may not be defrauded.

6:6 [1] If the word of God cannot instruct thee, yet learn at the little pismire to labor for thyself and not to burden others.

6:10 [1] He expresseth lively the nature of the sluggards, which though they sleep never so long, yet have never enough, but ever seek occasions thereunto.

6:11 [1] That is, suddenly, and when thou lookest not for it.

[2] It shall come in such sort, as thou are not able to resist it.

6:12 [1] He showeth to what inconvenience the idle persons and sluggards come, by calling them unthrifty, or the men of Belial, and slanderous.

6:13 [1] Hebrew, *speaketh*.

[2] Thus all his gesture tendeth to wickedness.

6:18 [1] Meaning, the raging affections, which carry a man away in such sort that he cannot tell what he doeth.

6:19 [1] Or, neighbors.

6:21 [1] Read Prov. 3:3.

22 It shall lead thee when thou walkest: it shall watch for thee when thou sleepest, *and* when thou wakest, it shall talk with thee.

23 For the [1]commandment *is* a lantern, and instruction a light: and [2]corrections for instruction *are* the way of life,

24 To keep thee from the wicked woman, *and* from the flattery of the tongue of a strange woman.

25 Desire not her beauty in thine heart, neither let her take thee with her [1]eye lids.

26 For because of the whorish woman, *a man is brought* to a morsel of bread, and a woman will hunt for the precious life of a man.

27 [1]Can a man take fire in his bosom, and his clothes not be burnt?

28 Or can a man go upon coals, and his feet not be burnt?

29 So he that goeth into his neighbor's wife, shall not be innocent, whosoever toucheth her.

30 Men do not [1]despise a thief, when he stealeth to satisfy his [2]soul, because he is hungry.

31 But if he be found, he shall restore sevenfold, *or* he shall give all the substance of his house.

32 But he that commiteth adultery with a woman, he [1]is destitute of understanding: he that doeth it, destroyeth his own soul.

33 He shall find [1]a wound and dishonor, and his reproach shall never be put away.

34 For jealousy *is* the rage of a man: therefore he will not [1]spare in the day of vengeance.

35 He cannot bear the sight of any ransom: neither will he consent, though thou augment the gifts.

7 1 *An exhortation to wisdom and to the word of God.* 5 *Which will preserve us from the harlot,* 6 *Whose manners are described.*

1 My son keep my words, and hide my commandments with thee.

2 Keep my commandments, and thou shalt live, and mine instruction, as the [1]apple of thine eyes.

3 Bind them upon thy fingers, *and* write them upon the table of thine heart.

4 Say unto wisdom, Thou art my sister, and call understanding *thy* kinswoman,

5 That they may keep thee from the strange woman, *even* from the strange that is smooth in her words.

6 ¶ [1]As *I was* in the window of mine house, I looked through my window,

7 And I saw among the fools, *and* considered among the children a young man destitute of understanding,

8 Who passed through the street by her corner, and went toward her house,

9 In the twilight in the evening, when the night began to be [1]black and dark.

10 And behold, there met him a woman with an harlot's [1]behavior, and [2]subtle in heart.

11 (She [1]is babbling and loud, whose feet cannot abide in her house.

12 Now *she is* without, now in the streets, and lieth in wait at every corner)

13 So she caught him and kissed him, and [1]with an impudent face said unto him,

14 I have [1]peace offerings: this [2]day have I paid my vows.

15 Therefore came I forth to meet thee, that I might seek thy face: and I have found thee.

16 I have decked my bed with ornaments, [1]carpets and laces of Egypt.

17 I have perfumed my bed with myrrh, aloes, and cinnamon.

18 Come, let us take our fill of love until the morning: let us take our pleasure in dalliance.

6:23 [1] By the commandment, he meaneth the word of God: and by the instruction, the preaching and declaration of the same, which is committed to the Church.

[2] And reprehensions when the word is preached bring us to life.

6:25 [1] With her wanton looks and gesture.

6:27 [1] Meaning, that she will never cease till she have brought thee to beggary, and then seek thy destruction.

6:30 [1] He reproveth not theft, but showeth that it is not so abominable as whoredom, forasmuch as theft might be redeemed: but adultery was a perpetual infamy, and death by the law of God.

[2] Meaning, for very necessity.

6:32 [1] Hebrew, *faileth in heart.*

6:33 [1] That is, death appointed by the Law.

6:34 [1] He showeth that man by nature seeketh his death, that hath abused his wife, and so concludeth, that neither God's Law nor the law of nature admitteth any ransom for the adultery.

7:2 [1] By this diversity of words, he meaneth that nothing ought to be so dear unto us as the word of God, nor that we look on anything more nor mind anything so much.

7:6 [1] Solomon useth this parable to declare their folly, that suffer themselves to be abused by harlots.

7:9 [1] He showeth that there was almost none so impudent, but they were afraid to be seen, and also their own consciences did accuse them which caused them to seek the night to cover their filthiness.

7:10 [1] Or, garment.

[2] Or, hid.

7:11 [1] He describeth certain conditions, which are peculiar to harlots.

7:13 [1] Hebrew, *she strengthened her face.*

7:14 [1] Because that in peace offerings a portion returned to them that offered, she showeth him that she hath meat at home to make good cheer with: or else she would use some cloak of holiness till she had gotten him in her snares.

[2] Which declareth that harlots outwardly will seem holy and religious: both because they may the better deceive others, and also thinking by observing of ceremonies and offerings to make satisfaction for their sins.

7:16 [1] Or, carved work.

19 For *mine* husband is not at home: he is gone a journey far off.

20 He hath taken [1]with him a bag of silver, *and* will come home at the day appointed.

21 Thus with her great craft she caused him to yield, and with her flattering lips she enticed him.

22 And he followed her straightway, as an [1]ox that goeth to the slaughter, and [2]as a fool to the stocks for correction,

23 Till a dart strike through his liver, as a bird hasteth to the snare, not knowing that [1]he is in danger.

24 ¶ Hear me now therefore, O children, and hearken to the words of my mouth.

25 Let not thine heart decline to her ways: wander thou not in her paths.

26 For she hath caused many to fall down wounded, *and* the [1]strong men *are* all slain by her.

27 Her house is the way [a]unto the grave, which goeth down to the chambers of death.

8 *1 Wisdom declareth her excellency, 11 riches, 15 power, 22 eternity. 32 She exhorteth all to love and follow her.*

1 Doth [a]not [1]wisdom cry? and understanding utter her voice?

2 She standeth in the top of the high places, by the way in the place of the paths.

3 She crieth besides [1]the gates before the city at the entry of the doors,

4 O men, I call unto you, and *utter* my voice to the children of men.

5 O *ye* foolish men, understand wisdom, and ye, O fools, be wise in heart.

6 Give ear, for I will speak of excellent things, and the opening of my lips *shall teach* things that be right.

7 For my mouth shall speak the truth, and my lips abhor wickedness.

8 All the words of my mouth *are* righteous: there

CHAPTER 7
a Prov. 2:18

CHAPTER 8
a Prov. 1:20

is no lewdness, nor frowardness in them.

9 They are all [1]plain to them that will understand, and straight to them that would find knowledge.

10 Receive mine instruction, and not silver, and knowledge rather than fine gold.

11 For wisdom is better than precious stones: and all pleasures are not to be compared unto her.

12 I wisdom dwell with [1]prudence, and I find forth knowledge *and* counsels.

13 The fear of the Lord *is* to hate [1]evil, *as* pride, and arrogancy, and the evil way: and a mouth *that speaketh* lewd things I do hate.

14 I have counsel and wisdom: I am understanding, *and* I have strength.

15 By me [1]kings reign, and princes decree justice.

16 By me princes rule, and the nobles, *and* all the judges of the earth.

17 I love them that love me: and they that seek me [1]early shall find me.

18 Riches and honor *are* with me: [1]*even* durable riches and righteousness.

19 My fruit is better than gold, *even* than fine gold, and my revenues *better* than fine silver.

20 I cause to walk in the way of righteousness, *and* in the midst of the paths of [1]judgment,

21 That I may cause them that love me, to inherit substance, and I will fill their treasures.

22 The Lord hath possessed me in the beginning of his way: *I was* [1]before his works of old.

23 [1]I was set up from everlasting, from the beginning, *and* before the earth.

24 When there were no depths, was I begotten, when there were no fountains abounding with water.

25 Before the mountains were settled: *and* before the hills, was I begotten.

26 He had not yet made the earth, nor the open places, nor the height of the dust in the world.

27 When he prepared the heavens, I was there,

7:20 [1] Hebrew, *in his hand.*
7:22 [1] Which thinking he goeth to the pasture, goeth willingly to his own destruction.
[2] Which goeth cheerfully, not knowing that he shall be chastised.
7:23 [1] Hebrew, *It is for his life.*
7:26 [1] Neither wit nor strength can deliver them that fall into the hands of the harlot.
8:1 [1] Solomon declareth that man is cause of his own perdition, and that he can pretend no ignorance, forasmuch as God calleth to all men by his word, and by his works to follow virtue, and to flee from vice.
8:3 [1] Where the people did most resort, and which was the place of justice.
8:9 [1] Meaning, that the word of God is easy unto all that have a desire unto it, and which are not blinded by the prince of this world.
8:12 [1] That is, except a man have wisdom, which is the true knowledge of God, he can neither be prudent nor good counselor.

8:13 [1] So that he that doth not hate evil, feareth not God.
8:15 [1] Whereby he declareth that honors, dignity or riches come not of man's wisdom or industry, but by the providence of God.
8:17 [1] That is, study the word of God diligently, and with a desire to profit.
8:18 [1] Signifying that he chiefly meaneth the spiritual treasures and heavenly riches.
8:20 [1] For there can be no true justice or judgment, which is not rejected by this wisdom.
8:22 [1] He declareth hereby the divinity and eternity of this wisdom, which he magnifieth and praiseth through this book: meaning thereby the eternal son of God Jesus Christ our Savior, whom Saint John calleth that word that was in the beginning, John 1:1.
8:23 [1] He declareth the eternity of the Son of God, which is meant by this word, wisdom, who was before all time, and ever present with the father.

when he set the compass upon the deep:

28 When he established the clouds above: when he confirmed the fountains of the deep:

29 When he gave his decree to the sea, that the waters should not pass his commandment, when he appointed the foundations of the earth.

30 Then was I with him ¹*as* a nourisher, and I was daily *his* delight, rejoicing always before him,

31 And took my ¹solace in the compass of ²his earth: and my delight *is* with the children of men.

32 Therefore now hearken, O children, unto me: for blessed *are they that* keep my ways.

33 Hear instruction, and be ye wise, and refuse it not: blessed *is* the man that heareth me, watching daily at my gates, *and* giving attendance at the posts of my doors.

34 For he that findeth me, findeth life, and shall obtain favor of the Lord.

35 But he that sinneth against me, hurteth his own soul: *and* all that hate me, love death.

9

2 Wisdom calleth all to her feast.　7 The scorner will not be corrected.　10 The fear of God.　13 The conditions of the harlot.

1 Wisdom hath built her ¹house, *and* hewn out her ²seven pillars.

2 She hath killed her victuals, drawn her wine, and ¹prepared her table.

3 She hath sent forth her ¹maidens, *and* crieth upon the highest places of the city, *saying,*

4 Who so is ¹simple, let him come hither, *and* to him that is destitute of wisdom, she saith,

5 Come, *and* eat of my ¹meat, and drink of the wine *that* I have drawn.

6 Forsake *your way,* ye foolish, and ye shall live: and walk in the way of understanding.

7 He that reproveth a scorner, purchaseth to himself shame: and he that rebuketh the wicked,

getteth himself a ¹blot.

8 Rebuke not a ¹scorner, lest he hate thee: *but* rebuke a wise man, and he will love thee.

9 Give *admonition* to the wise, and he will be the wiser: teach a righteous man, and he will increase in learning.

10 The beginning of wisdom *is* the fear of the Lord, and the knowledge of holy things, *is* ¹understanding.

11 For thy days shall be multiplied by me, and the years of thy life shall be augmented.

12 If thou be wise, thou shalt be wise for ¹thyself, *and if* thou be a scorner, thou alone shalt suffer.

13 ¶ A ¹foolish woman *is* troublesome; she *is* ignorant and knoweth nothing.

14 But she sitteth at the door of her house on a seat in the high places of the city,

15 To call them that pass by the way, that go right on their way, *saying,*

16 Who so is simple let him come hither, and to him that is destitute of wisdom, she saith also,

17 Stolen waters are sweet, and hid bread is pleasant.

18 But he knoweth not, that the dead *are* there, *and that* her guests *are* in the depth of hell.

10

In this Chapter, and all that follow, unto the thirtieth, the wise man exhorteth by divers sentences, which he calleth Parables, to follow virtue, and flee vice: and also showeth what profit cometh of wisdom, and what hindrance proceedeth of foolishness.

THE PARABLE OF SOLOMON.

1 A wise ᵃson maketh a glad father: but a foolish son *is* an heaviness to his mother.

2 The treasures of ¹wickedness profit nothing: but righteousness delivereth from death.

3 The Lord will ¹not famish the soul of the righteous: but he casteth away the substance of the wicked.

8:30 ¹ Some read, a chief worker: signifying that this wisdom, even Christ Jesus, was equal with God his father, and created, preserveth and still worketh with him, as John 5:17.

8:31 ¹ Whereby is declared that the work of the creation was no pain, but a solace unto the wisdom of God.

² By earth he meaneth man, which is the work of God in whom wisdom took pleasure: insomuch as for man's sake the divine wisdom took man's nature, and dwelt among us, and filled us with unspeakable treasures: and this is that solace and pastime whereof is here spoken.

9:1 ¹ Christ hath prepared him a Church.

² That is, many chief stays and principal parts of his Church, as were the Patriarchs, Prophets, Apostles, Pastors, and Doctors.

9:2 ¹ He compareth wisdom with great princes that keep open house for all that come.

9:3 ¹ Meaning, true preachers, which are not infected with man's wisdom.

9:4 ¹ He that knoweth his own ignorance, and is void of malice.

9:5 ¹ By the meat and drink, is meant the word of God, and the min-

istration of the Sacraments, whereby God nourisheth his servants in his house, which is the Church.

9:7 ¹ For the wicked will contemn him and labor to defame him.

9:8 ¹ Meaning them that are incorrigible, which Christ calleth dogs and swine: or he speaketh not in this comparison, not that the wicked should not be rebuked, but he showeth their malice, and the small hope of profit.

9:10 ¹ He showeth what true understanding is, to know the will of God in his word which is meant by holy things.

9:12 ¹ Thou shalt have the chief profit and commodity thereof.

9:13 ¹ By the foolish woman, some understand the wicked preachers, who counterfeit the word of God: as appeareth verse 16, which were the words of the true preachers, as verse 4, but their doctrine is but as stolen waters: meaning, that they are but men's traditions, which are more pleasant to the flesh than the word of God, and therefore they themselves boast thereof.

10:2 ¹ That is, wickedly gotten.

10:3 ¹ Though he suffer the just to want for a time, yet he will send him comfort in due season.

4 A ¹slothful hand maketh poor: but the hand of the diligent maketh rich.

5 He that gathereth in summer, *is* the son of wisdom: *but* he that sleepeth in harvest, *is* the son of confusion.

6 Blessings *are* upon the head of the righteous: but iniquity shall cover the mouth of ¹the wicked.

7 The memorial of the just *shall be* blessed: but the name of the wicked shall ¹rot.

8 The wise in heart will receive commandments: but the foolish in ¹talk shall be beaten.

9 He that walketh uprightly, walketh ¹boldly: but he that perverteth his ways, shall be known.

10 He that ¹winketh with the eye, worketh sorrow, and he that is ²foolish in talk, shall be beaten.

11 The mouth of a righteous man is a wellspring of life: but iniquity covereth the mouth of the wicked.

12 Hatred stirreth up contentions: ᵇbut love covereth all trespasses.

13 In the lips of him that hath understanding, wisdom is found, and ¹a rod shall be for the back of him that is destitute of wisdom.

14 Wise men lay up knowledge: but the mouth of the fool *is* a present destruction.

15 The rich man's goods are his ¹strong city: *but* the fear of the needy *is* their poverty.

16 The labor of the righteous *tendeth* to life: *but* the revenues of the wicked to sin.

17 He that regardeth instruction *is in* the way of life: but he that refuseth correction, goeth out of the way.

18 He that dissembleth hatred with lying lips, and he that inventeth slander, is a fool.

19 In many words there cannot want iniquity: but he that refraineth his lips, is wise:

20 The tongue of the just man *is as* fined silver: *but* the heart of the wicked *is* little worth.

21 The lips of the righteous do ¹feed many: but fools shall die for want of wisdom.

22 The blessing of the Lord, it maketh rich, and he doth add ¹no sorrows with it.

23 *It is* a pastime to a fool to do wickedly: but

ᵇ 1 Cor. 13:4
1 Pet. 4:8

CHAPTER 11
ᵃ Ezek. 7:19

wisdom *is* understanding to a man.

24 That which the wicked feareth, shall come upon him: but *God* will grant the desire of the righteous.

25 As the whirlwind passeth, so *is* the wicked no more: but the righteous *is as* an everlasting foundation.

26 As vinegar *is* to the teeth, and as smoke to the eyes, so *is* the slothful to them that ¹send him.

27 The fear of the Lord increaseth the days: but the years of the wicked ¹shall be diminished.

28 The patient abiding of the righteous *shall be* gladness: but the hope of the wicked shall perish.

29 The way of the Lord *is* strength to the upright man: but fear shall be for the workers of iniquity.

30 The righteous shall ¹never be removed: but the wicked shall not dwell in the land.

31 The mouth of the just shall be fruitful in wisdom: but the tongue of the froward shall be cut out.

32 The lips of the righteous know what is acceptable: but the mouth of the wicked *speaketh* froward things.

11

1 False ¹balances *are* an abomination unto the Lord: but a perfect ²weight pleaseth him.

2 When pride cometh, then cometh ¹shame: but with the lowly *is* wisdom.

3 The uprightness of the just shall guide them: but the frowardness of the transgressors shall destroy them.

4 ᵃRiches avail not in the day of wrath: but righteousness delivereth from death.

5 The righteousness of the upright shall direct his way: but the wicked shall fall in his own wickedness.

6 The righteousness of the just shall deliver them: but the transgressors shall be taken in *their* own wickedness.

7 When a wicked man dieth, *his* hope perisheth, and the hope of the unjust shall perish.

8 The righteous escapeth out of trouble, and the wicked shall come in his ¹stead.

10:4 ¹ Or, deceitful.
10:6 ¹ When their wickedness shall be discovered, they shall be as dumb, and not know what to say.
10:7 ¹ Shall be vile and abhorred both of God and man, contrary to their own expectation, which think to make their name immortal.
10:8 ¹ Hebrew, *lips.*
10:9 ¹ Or, surely.
10:10 ¹ That beareth a fair countenance, and imagineth mischief in his heart, as Prov. 6:13.
   ² For the corruption of his heart is known by his talk.
10:13 ¹ That is, God will find him out to punish him.
10:15 ¹ And so maketh him bold to do evil, whereas poverty bridleth the poor from many evil things.

10:21 ¹ For they speak truth, and edify many by exhortations, admonition, and counsel.
10:22 ¹ Meaning, that all worldly things bring care, and sorrow, whereas they that feel the blessings of God, have none.
10:26 ¹ He is but a trouble and grief to him about any business.
10:27 ¹ The time of their prosperity shall be short because of their great fall, though they seem to live long.
10:30 ¹ They enjoy in this life by faith and hope, their everlasting life.
11:1 ¹ Under this word he condemneth all false weights, measures and deceit.
   ² Hebrew, *stone.*
11:2 ¹ When man so getteth himself, and thinketh to be exalted above his vocation, then God bringeth him to confusion.
11:8 ¹ That is, shall enter into trouble.

9 An [1]hypocrite with *his* mouth hurteth his neighbor: but the righteous shall be delivered by knowledge.

10 In the prosperity of the righteous the city [1]rejoiceth: and when the wicked perish, *there is* joy.

11 By the [1]blessing of the righteous the city is exalted: but it is subverted by the mouth of the wicked.

12 He that despiseth his neighbor, is destitute of wisdom: but a man of understanding will [1]keep silence.

13 He that goeth about *as* a slanderer, discovereth a secret: but he that is of a faithful heart, concealeth a matter.

14 Where no counsel is, the people fall: but where many [1]counselors are, *there is* health.

15 He shall be sore vexed, that is surety for a [1]stranger, and he that hateth suretiship, is sure.

16 A [1]gracious woman attaineth honor, and the strong men attain riches.

17 He that is merciful, [1]rewardeth his own soul: but he that troubleth his own [2]flesh, *is* cruel.

18 The wicked worketh a deceitful work: but he that soweth righteousness, *shall receive* a sure reward.

19 As righteousness *leadeth* to life: so he that followeth evil, *seeketh* his own death.

20 They that are of a froward heart, *are* abomination to the Lord: but they that are upright in *their* way, *are* his delight.

21 [1]*Though* hand *join* in hand, the wicked shall not be unpunished: but the seed of the righteous shall escape.

22 *As a* jewel of gold in a swine's snout: *so is* a fair woman which [1]lacketh discretion.

23 The desire of the righteous is only good: *but* the hope of the wicked [1]*is* indignation.

24 There is that scattereth, [1]and is more increased: but he that spareth more [2]than is right, surely *cometh* to poverty.

25 The [1]liberal person shall have plenty: and he

that watereth, shall also have rain.

26 He that withdraweth the corn, the people will curse him: but blessing *shall be* upon the head of him that [1]selleth corn.

27 He that seeketh good things getteth favor: but he that seeketh evil, it shall come to him.

28 He that trusteth in his riches, shall fall: but the righteous shall flourish as a leaf.

29 He that troubleth his own [1]house, shall inherit the wind, and the fool *shall be* [2]servant to the wise in heart.

30 The fruit of the righteous *is as* a tree of life, and he that [1]winneth souls *is* wise.

31 Behold, the righteous shall be [1]recompensed in the earth: how much more the wicked and the sinner?

12 1 He that loveth instruction, loveth knowledge: but he that hateth correction, *is* a fool.

2 A good man getteth favor of the Lord: but the man of wicked imaginations will he condemn.

3 A man cannot be established by wickedness: but the [1]root of the righteous shall not be moved.

4 A [1]virtuous woman *is* the crown of her husband: but she that maketh *him* ashamed, *is* as corruption in his bones.

5 The thoughts of the just *are* right: but the counsels of the wicked are deceitful.

6 The talking of the wicked *is* to lie in wait for blood: but the mouth of the righteous will [1]deliver them.

7 God overthroweth the wicked, and they are not: but the house of the righteous shall stand.

8 A man shall be commended for his wisdom: but the froward of heart shall be despised.

9 He that is despised, [1]and *is* his own servant, is better than he that boasteth himself, and lacketh bread.

10 A righteous man [1]regardeth the life of his beast:

11:9 [1] A dissembler that pretendeth friendship, but is a privy enemy.

11:10 [1] The country is blessed, where there are godly men, and they ought to rejoice when the wicked are taken away.

11:11 [1] Or, prosperity.

11:12 [1] Will not make light report of others.

11:14 [1] Where God giveth store of men of wisdom and counsel: whose conversation he knoweth not.

11:15 [1] He that doeth not without judgment and consideration of the circumstances, puts himself in danger, as Prov. 6:1.

11:16 [1] Or, modest.

11:17 [1] Is both good to himself and to others.

[2] Or, neighbor.

11:21 [1] Though they make never so many friends, or think themselves never so sure, yet they shall not escape.

11:22 [1] Or, of uncomely behavior.

11:23 [1] They can look for nothing but God's vengeance.

11:24 [1] Meaning them that give liberally, whom God blesseth.

[2] That is, the niggard.

11:25 [1] Or, generous.

11:26 [1] That provideth for the use of them that are in necessity.

11:29 [1] The covetous men that spare their riches to the hindrance of their families, shall be deprived thereof miserably.

[2] For though the wicked be rich, yet are they but slaves to the godly, which are the true possessors of the gifts of God.

11:30 [1] That is, bringeth them to the knowledge of God.

11:31 [1] Shall be punished as he deserveth, 1 Pet. 4:18.

12:3 [1] They are so grounded in the favor of God, that their root shall prosper continually.

12:4 [1] Hebrew, *strong*, or *painful*.

12:6 [1] As their conscience is upright, so shall they be able to speak for themselves against their accusers.

12:9 [1] The poor man that is contemned and yet liveth of his own travail.

12:10 [1] Is merciful, even to the very beast that doeth him service.

but the mercies of the wicked *are* cruel.

11 [a]He that tilleth his land, shall be satisfied with bread: but he that followeth the idle, *is* destitute of [1]understanding.

12 The wicked desireth the [1]net of evils: but the [2]root of the righteous giveth *fruit.*

13 The evil man is snared by the wickedness of *his* lips, but the just shall come out of adversity.

14 A man shall be satiate with good things by the fruit of *his* mouth, and the recompense of a man's hands shall God give unto him.

15 The way of a fool *is* [1]right in his own eyes: but he that heareth in counsel, *is* wise.

16 A fool in a day shall be known by his anger: but he [1]that covereth shame, *is* wise.

17 He that speaketh truth, will show righteousness: but a false witness *useth* deceit.

18 [b]There is that speaketh *words* like the prickings of [1]a sword: but the tongue of wise men *is* health.

19 The lip of truth shall be stable forever: but a lying tongue *varieth* incontinently.

20 Deceit *is* in the heart of them that imagine evil: but to the counselors of peace *shall be* joy.

21 There shall none iniquity come to the just: but the wicked are full of evil.

22 The lying lips *are* an abomination to the Lord: but they that deal truly *are* his delight.

23 A wise man concealeth knowledge: but the heart of the fools publisheth foolishness.

24 [c]The hand of the diligent shall bear rule: but the idle *shall be* under tribute.

25 Heaviness in the heart of man doth bring it down: but a [1]good word rejoice it.

26 The righteous [1]*is* more excellent than his neighbor: but the way of the wicked will deceive them.

27 The deceitful man roasteth not that he [1]took in hunting: but the riches of the diligent man *are* precious.

28 Life *is* in the way of righteousness, and *in that* pathway *there is* no death.

13

1 A wise son *will obey* the instruction of his father: but a scorner will hear no

CHAPTER 12
[a] Prov. 28:19
[b] Prov. 14:5
[c] Prov. 10:4

CHAPTER 13
[d] Prov. 25:13

rebuke.

2 A man shall eat good things by the fruit [1]of his mouth: but the soul of the trespasser *shall suffer* violence.

3 He that keepeth his mouth, keepeth his life: *but* he that openeth his lips, destruction *shall be* to him.

4 The sluggard [1]lusteth, but his soul hath nought: but the soul of the diligent shall have plenty.

5 A righteous man hateth lying words: but the wicked causeth slander and shame.

6 Righteousness preserveth the upright of [1]life: but wickedness overthroweth the sinner.

7 There is that maketh himself rich, and hath nothing, *and* that maketh himself poor, having great riches.

8 A man *will give* his riches for the ransom of *his* life: but the poor [1]cannot hear the reproach.

9 The light of the righteous rejoiceth: but the candle of the wicked shall be put out.

10 Only by pride [1]doth *man* make contention: but with the well-advised *is* wisdom.

11 The [1]riches of vanity shall diminish: but he that gathereth with [2]the hand, shall increase *them.*

12 The hope that *is* deferred, *is* the fainting of the heart, but when the desire cometh, *it is as* a tree of life.

13 He that despiseth [1]the word, he shall be destroyed, but he that feareth the commandment, he shall be rewarded.

14 The instruction of a wise man *is as* the wellspring of life, to turn away from the snares of death.

15 Good understanding maketh acceptable: but the way of the disobedient *is* hated.

16 Every wise man will work by knowledge: but a fool will spread abroad folly.

17 [d]A wicked messenger falleth [1]into evil: but a faithful ambassador *is* preservation.

18 Poverty and shame *is* to him that refuseth instruction: but he that regardeth correction, shall be honored.

19 A desire accomplished, delighteth the soul: but *it is* an abomination to fools to depart from evil.

12:11 [1] Or, defense.
12:12 [1] Continually imagineth means how to do harm to others.
  [2] Meaning, their heart within, which is upright, and doeth good to all.
12:15 [1] He standeth in his own conceit, and condemneth all others in respect of himself.
12:16 [1] Which bridleth his affections.
12:18 [1] Which seek nothing more than to provoke others to anger.
12:25 [1] That is, words of comfort, or, a cheerful mind which is declared by his words, rejoiceth a man, as a covetous mind killeth him.
12:26 [1] That is, more liberal in giving.
12:27 [1] Although he get much by unlawful means, yet will he not spend it upon himself.

13:2 [1] If he use his tongue to God's glory, and the profit of his neighbor, God shall bless him.
13:4 [1] He ever desireth, but taketh no pains to get anything.
13:6 [1] Hebrew, *way.*
13:8 [1] For his poverty, he is not able to escape the threatenings, which the cruel oppressors use against him.
13:10 [1] When as every man contendeth to have the preeminence, and will not give place to another.
13:11 [1] That is, goods evil gotten.
  [2] That is, with his own labor.
13:13 [1] Meaning, the word of God, whereby he is admonished of his duty.
13:17 [1] Bringeth many inconveniences both to himself and to others.

20 He that walketh with the wise shall be wise: but a companion of fools shall be ¹afflicted.

21 Affliction followeth sinners: but unto the righteous, *God* will recompense good.

22 The good man shall give inheritance unto *his* children's children: and the ¹riches of the sinner is laid up for the just.

23 Much food *is* in the field of the ¹poor, but *the field* is destroyed without discretion.

24 ᵇHe that spareth his rod, hateth his son: but he that loveth him chasteneth him betime.

25 The righteous eateth to the contentation of his mind: but the belly of the wicked shall want.

14

1 A wise woman ¹buildeth her house: but the foolish destroyeth it with her own hands.

2 ᵃHe that walketh in his ¹righteousness, feareth the Lord: but he that is lewd in his ways, despiseth him.

3 In the mouth of the foolish *is* the ¹rod of pride: but the lips of the wise preserve them.

4 Where none ¹oxen *are*, there the crib *is* empty: but much increase *cometh* by the strength of the ox.

5 A faithful witness will not lie: but a false record will speak lies.

6 ¹A scorner seeketh wisdom, and *findeth* it not: but knowledge *is* easy to him that will understand.

7 Depart from the foolish man, when thou perceivest not *in him* the lips of knowledge.

8 The wisdom of the prudent *is* to understand his way: but the foolishness of the fools *is* deceit.

9 The fool maketh a mock of ¹sin: but among the righteous *there is* favor.

10 The heart knoweth the ¹bitterness of his soul, and the stranger shall not meddle with his joy.

11 The house of the wicked shall be destroyed: but the tabernacle of the righteous shall flourish.

12 ᵇThere is a way that seemeth right to a man: but the issues thereof *are* the ways of death.

13 Even in laughing the heart is sorrowful, ¹and the end of that mirth *is* heaviness.

ᵇ Prov. 23:13

CHAPTER 14
ᵃ Job 12:4
ᵇ Prov. 16:25
ᶜ Prov. 17:5

14 The heart that declineth, ¹shall be satiated with his own ways: but a good man *shall depart* from him.

15 The foolish will believe everything: but the prudent will consider his steps.

16 A wise man feareth, and departeth from evil, but a fool rageth, and is careless.

17 He that is hasty to anger, commiteth folly, and a ¹busybody is hated.

18 The foolish do inherit folly: but the prudent are crowned with knowledge.

19 The evil shall bow before the good, and the wicked ¹at the gates of the righteous.

20 The poor is hated even of his own neighbor: but the friends of the rich *are* many.

21 The sinner despiseth his neighbor: but he that hath mercy on the poor, *is* blessed.

22 Do not they err that imagine evil? but to them that think on good things, *shall be* mercy and truth.

23 In all labor there is abundance: but the talk of the lips *bringeth* only want.

24 The crown of the wise *is* their riches, *and* the folly of fools *is* foolishness.

25 A faithful witness delivereth souls: but a deceiver speaketh lies.

26 In the fear of the Lord *is* an assured strength, and his children shall have hope.

27 The fear of the Lord *is as* a wellspring of life, to avoid the snares of death.

28 In the multitude of the ¹people is the honor of a King, and for the want of people *cometh* the destruction of the Prince.

29 He that is slow to wrath, *is* of great wisdom: but he that is of an hasty mind, exalteth folly.

30 A sound heart *is* the life of the ¹flesh: but envy *is* the rotting of the bones.

31 ᶜHe that oppresseth the poor, reproveth him that made him: but he honoreth him, that hath mercy on the poor.

32 The wicked shall be cast away for his malice: but the righteous hath hope in his death.

33 Wisdom resteth in the heart of him that hath understanding, and is known ¹in the midst of fools.

13:20 ¹ As he is partaker of their wickedness, and beareth with their vices, so shall he be punished alike as they are.
13:22 ¹ Read Job 27:16, 17.
13:23 ¹ God blesseth the labor of the poor, and consumeth their goods which are negligent, because they think they have enough.
14:1 ¹ That is, taketh pain to profit her family, and to do that which concerneth her duty in her house.
14:2 ¹ That is, in uprightness of heart, and without hypocrisy.
14:3 ¹ His proud tongue shall cause him to be punished.
14:4 ¹ By the ox is meant labor, and by the crib the barn: meaning, without labor there is no profit.
14:6 ¹ For the maintenance of his own ambition, and not for God's glory, as Simon Magus.
14:9 ¹ Doth not know the grievousness thereof, nor God's judg-

ments against the same.
14:10 ¹ As a man's conscience is witness of his own grief, so another cannot feel the joy and comfort which a man feeleth in himself.
14:13 ¹ He showeth the allurement unto sin, seemeth sweet, but the end thereof is destruction.
14:14 ¹ He that forsaketh God shall be punished, and made weary of his sins, wherein he delighted.
14:17 ¹ Hebrew, *the man of imaginations*.
14:19 ¹ If this come not daily to pass, we must consider that it is because of our sins, which let God's working.
14:28 ¹ That is, the strength of a king standeth in many people.
14:30 ¹ Or, body.
14:33 ¹ Forasmuch as they are convicted thereby and put to silence.

34 Justice exalteth a nation, [1]but sin is a shame to the people.

35 The pleasure of a King *is* in a wise servant: but his wrath shall be toward him that is lewd.

15

1 [*a*]A soft answer putteth away wrath: but grievous words stir up anger.

2 The tongue of the wise useth knowledge aright: but the mouth of fools [*b*]babbleth out foolishness.

3 The eyes of the Lord in every place behold the evil and the good.

4 A wholesome tongue *is as* a tree of life: but the frowardness thereof *is* the breaking of the mind.

5 A fool despiseth his father's instruction, but he that regardeth correction, is prudent.

6 The house of the righteous *hath* much treasure: but in the revenues of the wicked is [1]trouble.

7 The lips of the wise do spread abroad knowledge: but the heart of the foolish *doth* not so.

8 The [1]sacrifice of the wicked *is* abomination unto the Lord: but the prayer of the righteous is acceptable unto him.

9 The way of the wicked is an abomination unto the Lord: but he loveth him that followeth righteousness.

10 Instruction is evil to him that [1]forsaketh the way, *and* he that hateth correction, shall die.

11 [1]Hell and destruction *are* before the Lord, how much more the hearts of the sons of men?

12 A scorner loveth not him that rebuketh him, neither will he go unto the wise.

13 [*c*]A joyful heart maketh a cheerful countenance: but by the sorrow of the heart the mind is heavy.

14 The heart of him that hath understanding, seeketh knowledge: but the mouth of the fool is fed with foolishness.

15 All the days of the afflicted *are* evil; but a good [1]conscience is a continual feast.

16 [*d*]Better *is* a little with the fear of the Lord, than great treasure and trouble therewith.

17 Better *is* a dinner of green herbs where love *is*, than a stalled ox and hatred therewith.

18 [*e*]An angry man stirreth up strife: but he that

CHAPTER 15
a Prov. 25:15
b Prov. 15:18
c Prov. 17:22
d Ps. 37:16
e Prov. 29:22
f Prov. 10:1

is slow to wrath, appeaseth strife.

19 The way of a slothful man *is* as an hedge of [1]thorns: but the way of the righteous is plain.

20 [*f*]A wise son rejoiceth the father: but a foolish man despiseth his mother.

21 Foolishness *is* joy to him that is destitute of understanding: but a man of understanding walketh uprightly.

22 Without counsel, thoughts come to nought: but [1]in the multitude of counselors there is steadfastness.

23 A joy *cometh* to a man by the answer of his mouth: and how good *is* a word [1]in due season?

24 The way of life *is* on high to the prudent, to avoid from hell beneath.

25 The Lord will destroy the house of the proud men: but he will stablish the borders of the widow.

26 The thoughts of the wicked are abomination to the Lord: but the pure *have* [1]pleasant words.

27 He that is greedy of gain, troubleth his own house: but he that beareth gifts, shall live.

28 The heart of the righteous studieth to answer: but the wicked man's mouth babbleth evil things.

29 The Lord is far off from the wicked: but he heareth the prayer of the righteous.

30 The light of the eyes rejoiceth the heart, and a good name maketh the bones fat.

31 The ear that hearkeneth to the [1]correction of life, shall lodge among the wise.

32 He that refuseth instruction, despiseth his own soul: but he that obeyeth correction, getteth understanding.

33 The fear of the Lord *is* the instruction of wisdom: and before honor *goeth* [1]humility.

16

1 The [1]preparations of the heart *are* in man: but the answer of the tongue *is* of the Lord.

2 All the ways of a man *are* [1]clean in his own eyes: but the Lord pondereth the spirits.

3 [1]Commit thy works unto the Lord, and thy thoughts shall be directed.

4 The Lord hath made all things for his own sake: yea, even the wicked for the day of [1]evil.

14:34 [1] Or, and the mercy of the people is a sacrifice for sin.
15:6 [1] For though they have much, yet it is full of trouble and care.
15:8 [1] That thing is abominable before God, which the wicked think to be most excellent, and whereby they think most to be accepted.
15:10 [1] He that swerveth from the word of God, cannot abide to be admonished.
15:11 [1] There is nothing so deep or secret that can be hid from the eyes of God, much less man's thoughts.
15:15 [1] Hebrew, *heart.*
15:19 [1] That is, he ever findeth some let or stay, and dare not go forward.
15:22 [1] Read Prov. 11:14.
15:23 [1] If we will that our talk be comfortable, we must wait for time and season.

15:26 [1] That is, wholesome and profitable to the hearers.
15:31 [1] That suffereth himself to be admonished by God's word, which bringeth life: and so amendeth.
15:33 [1] Meaning, that God exalteth none but them that are truly humbled.
16:1 [1] He derideth the presumption of man, who dare attribute to himself any thing, as to prepare his heart or such like, seeing that he is not able to speak a word, except God give it him.
16:2 [1] He showeth hereby that man flattereth himself in his doings, calling that virtue, which God termeth vice.
16:3 [1] Hebrew, *role.*
16:4 [1] So that the justice of God shall appear to his glory, even in the destruction of the wicked.

5 All that are proud in heart, *are* an abomination to the Lord: *though* ªhand *join* in hand, he shall not be unpunished.

6 By [1]mercy and truth iniquity shall be forgiven, and by the fear of the Lord they depart from evil.

7 When the ways of a man please the Lord, he will make also his enemies at peace with him.

8 [b]Better is a little with righteousness, than great revenues without equity.

9 The heart of [1]man purposeth his way: but the Lord doth direct his steps.

10 A divine sentence *shall be* in the lips of the king: his mouth shall not transgress in judgment.

11 ᶜA true weight and balance are of the Lord: and the weights of the bag *are* his [1]work.

12 It is an abomination to kings to commit wickedness: for the throne is stablished [1]by justice.

13 Righteous lips are the delight of kings, and the king loveth him that speaketh right things.

14 The wrath of a king *is as* [1]messengers of death: but a wise man will pacify it.

15 In the light of the king's countenance *is* life: and his favor *is* [1]as a cloud of the latter rain.

16 ᵈHow much better is it to get wisdom than gold? and to get understanding, is more to be desired than silver.

17 The path of the righteous is to decline from evil, and he keepeth his soul that keepeth his way.

18 Pride *goeth* before destruction, and an high mind before the fall.

19 Better it is to be of humble mind with the lowly, than to divide the spoils with the proud.

20 He that is wise in *his* business, shall find good: and ᶜhe that trusteth in the Lord, he is blessed.

21 The wise in heart shall be called prudent and [1]the sweetness of the lips shall increase doctrine.

22 Understanding *is* a wellspring of life unto them that have it: and the [1]instruction of fools *is* folly.

23 The heart of the wise guideth his mouth wisely, and addeth doctrine to his lips.

24 Fair words *are as* an honey comb, sweetness to

CHAPTER 16
ª Prov. 11:21
ᵇ Prov. 15:16
  Ps. 37:16
ᶜ Prov. 11:1
ᵈ Prov. 8:10
ᵉ Ps. 125:1
ᶠ Prov. 14:12

CHAPTER 17
ª Prov. 14:31

the soul, and health to the bones.

25 ᶠThere is a way that seemeth right unto man, but the issue thereof *are* the ways of death.

26 The person that travaileth, travaileth for himself: for his mouth [1]craveth it of him.

27 A wicked man diggeth up evil, and in his lips *is* like [1]burning fire.

28 A froward person soweth strife: and a taleteller maketh division among princes.

29 A wicked man deceiveth his neighbor, and leadeth him into the way that is not good.

30 [1]He shutteth his eyes to devise wickedness: he moveth his lips, *and* bringeth evil to pass.

31 Age is a crown of glory, *when* it is found in the way of [1]righteousness.

32 He that is slow unto anger, is better than the mighty man: and he that ruleth his own mind, *is better* than he that winneth a city.

33 The lot is cast into the lap: but the whole disposition thereof *is* [1]of the Lord.

17

1 Better is a dry morsel, if peace *be* with it, than an house full of [1]sacrifices *with* strife.

2 A discrete servant shall have rule over a lewd son, and he shall divide the [1]heritage among the brethren.

3 *As is* the fining pot for silver, and the furnace for gold, so the Lord trieth the hearts.

4 The wicked giveth heed to false lips, *and* a liar hearkeneth to the naughty tongue.

5 ªHe that mocketh the poor, reproacheth him that made him: and he that rejoiceth at destruction, shall not be unpunished.

6 Children's children are the crown of the elders: and the glory of the children *are* their fathers.

7 [1]High talk becometh not a fool, much less a lying talk a prince.

8 A reward *is as* a stone pleasant in the eyes of them that have it: it prospereth, whithersoever it [1]turneth.

16:6 [1] Their upright and repenting life shall be a token that their sins are forgiven.

16:9 [1] He showeth the folly of man, which thinketh that his ways are in his own hand, and yet it is able to remove one foot except God give force.

16:11 [1] If they be true and just, they are God's work, and he delighteth therein, but otherwise if they be false, they are the work of the devil, and to their condemnation that use them.

16:12 [1] They are appointed by God to rule according to equity and justice.

16:14 [1] That is, he findeth out many means to execute his wrath.

16:15 [1] Which is most comfortable to the dry ground, Deut. 11:14.

16:21 [1] The sweet words of consolation, which come forth of a godly heart.

16:22 [1] Either that which the wicked teach others, or else it is folly to

teach them that are malicious.

16:26 [1] Hebrew, *boweth upon him.*

16:27 [1] For he consumeth himself and others.

16:30 [1] With his whole endeavor he laboreth to bring his wickedness to pass.

16:31 [1] That is, when it is joined with virtue: or else the elder that the wicked are, the more they are to be abhorred.

16:33 [1] So that there is nothing that ought to be attributed to fortune: for all things are determined in the counsel of God which shall come to pass.

17:1 [1] For whereas were many sacrifices, there were many portions given to the people, wherewith they feasted.

17:2 [1] That is, shall be made governor over the children.

17:7 [1] Hebrew, *the lip of excellency.*

17:8 [1] The reward hath great force to gain the hearts of men.

9　He that covereth a transgression, seeketh love: but he that repeateth a matter, separateth the [1]prince.

10　A reproof entereth more into him that hath understanding, than an hundred stripes into a fool.

11　A seditious person seeketh only evil, and a cruel [1]messenger shall be sent against him.

12　*It is better* for a man to meet a bear robbed of her whelps, than [1]a fool in his folly.

13　[b]He that rewardeth evil for good, evil shall not depart from his house.

14　The beginning of strife *is as* one that openeth the waters: therefore, or the contention be meddled with, leave off.

15　[c]He that justifieth the wicked, and he that condemneth the just, even they both are abomination to the Lord.

16　Wherefore is there a [1]price in the hand of the fool to get wisdom, and *he hath* none heart?

17　A friend loveth at all times; and a [1]brother is born for adversity.

18　A man destitute of understanding, [1]toucheth the hand, and becometh surety for his neighbor.

19　He loveth transgression that loveth strife: *and* he that exalteth his [1]gate, seeketh destruction.

20　The froward heart findeth no good: and he that hath a naughty tongue, shall fall into evil.

21　He that begetteth a fool, *getteth* himself sorrow, and the father of a fool can have no joy.

22　[d]A joyful heart causeth good health: but a sorrowful mind drieth the bones.

23　A wicked man taketh a gift out of the [1]bosom to wrest the ways of judgment.

24　[e]Wisdom *is* in the face of him that hath understanding: but the eyes of a fool *are* in the [1]corners of the world.

25　A foolish son is a grief unto his father, and a [f]heaviness to her that bare him.

26　Surely it is not good to condemn the just, nor that the princes should smite *such* [1]for equity.

27　He that hath knowledge, spareth his words, and a man of understanding *is* of an excellent spirit.

28　Even a fool, (when he holdeth his peace) is counted wise, and he that stoppeth his lips, prudent.

18

1　For the desire *thereof* he will [1]separate himself to seek it, *and* occupy himself in all wisdom.

2　A fool hath no delight in understanding: but that his heart may be [1]discovered.

3　When the wicked cometh, then cometh [1]contempt, and with the vile man reproach.

4　The words of a man's mouth *are like* deep [1]waters, *and* the wellspring of wisdom *is like* a flowing river.

5　It is not good to [1]accept the person of the wicked, to cause the righteous to fall in judgment.

6　A fool's lips come with strife, and his mouth calleth for stripes.

7　A fool's mouth *is* his own destruction, and his lips *are* a snare for his soul.

8　The words of a talebearer *are* as flatterings, and they go down into the [1]bowels of the belly.

9　He also that is slothful in his work, is even the brother of him that is a great waster.

10　The name of the Lord *is* a strong tower: the righteous runneth [1]unto it, and is exalted.

11　[a]The rich man's riches *are* his strong city: and as an high wall in his imagination.

12　[b]Before destruction the heart of a man is haughty, and before glory *goeth* lowliness.

13　He that answereth a matter before he hear it, it is folly and shame unto him.

14　The spirit of a man will sustain his infirmity: but [1]a wounded spirit, who can bear it?

15　A wise heart getteth knowledge, and the ear of the wise seeketh learning.

16　A man's gift [1]enlargeth him, and leadeth him before great men.

17　[1]*He that is* first in his own cause, *is* just: then cometh his neighbor and maketh inquiry of him.

18　The lot [1]causeth contentions to cease, and

Cross-references (center column):

[b] Rom. 12:17
1 Thess. 5:15
1 Pet. 3:9

[c] Isa. 5:23
Prov. 24:24

[d] Prov. 15:13

[e] Eccl. 2:14
Eccl. 8:1

[f] Prov. 10:1

CHAPTER 18
[a] Prov. 10:15
[b] Prov. 16:18

17:9 [1] He that admonisheth the prince of his fault, maketh him his enemy.

17:11 [1] By the messenger is meant such means as God useth to punish the rebels.

17:12 [1] Whereby he meaneth the wicked in his rage, who hath no fear of God.

17:16 [1] What availeth it the wicked to be rich, seeing he setteth not his mind to wisdom?

17:17 [1] So that he is more than a friend, even a brother that helpeth in time of adversity.

17:18 [1] Read Prov. 6:1.

17:19 [1] Lifteth up himself above his degree.

17:23 [1] That is, secretly and out of the bosom of the rich.

17:24 [1] That is, wander to and fro, and seek not after wisdom.

17:26 [1] For their well doing.

18:1 [1] He that loveth wisdom, will separate himself from all impediments, and give himself wholly to seek it.

18:2 [1] That is, that he may talk licentiously of whatsoever cometh to mind.

18:3 [1] Meaning, such one as contemneth all others.

18:4 [1] Which can never be drawn empty, but bring ever profit.

18:5 [1] That is, to favor him and support him.

18:8 [1] They are soon believed, and enter most deeply.

18:10 [1] He showeth what is the refuge of the godly against all trouble.

18:14 [1] The mind can well bear the infirmity of the body, but when the spirit is wounded, it is a thing most hard to sustain.

18:16 [1] Getteth him liberty to speak, and favor of them that are most in estimation.

18:17 [1] He that speaketh first, is best heard of the wicked judge, but when his adversary inquireth out the matter, it turneth to his shame.

18:18 [1] If a controversy cannot otherwise be decided, it is best to cast lots to know whose the thing shall be.

²maketh a partition among the mighty.

19 A brother offended *is harder to win* than a strong city, and *their* contentions *are* like the ¹bar of a palace.

20 With the fruit of a man's mouth shall his belly be satisfied, *and* with the increase of his lips shall he be filled.

21 Death and life *are* in the power of the tongue, and they that ¹love it, shall eat the fruit thereof.

22 He that findeth a ¹wife, findeth a good thing, and receiveth favor of the Lord.

23 The poor speaketh *with* prayers: but the rich answereth roughly.

24 A man *that hath* friends, *ought* to show himself friendly: for a friend is nearer ¹than a brother.

19

1 Better ᵃis the poor that walketh in his uprightness, than he that abuseth his lips, and is a fool.

2 For without knowledge the mind is not good, and he that hasteth with his feet, sinneth.

3 The foolishness of a man perverteth his way, and his heart fretteth against the Lord.

4 Riches gather many friends: but the poor is separated from his neighbor.

5 ᵇA false witness shall not be unpunished: and he that speaketh lies, shall not escape.

6 Many reverence the face of the prince, and every man *is* friend to him that giveth gifts.

7 All the brethren of the poor do hate him: how much more will his friends depart far from him? though he be instant ¹with words, *yet* they will not.

8 He that possesseth understanding, ¹loveth his own soul, and keepeth wisdom to find goodness.

9 A false witness shall not be unpunished: and he that speaketh lies, shall perish.

10 ¹Pleasure is not comely for a fool, much less for a servant to have rule over princes.

11 The discretion of man deferreth his anger: and his glory *is* ¹to pass by an offence.

12 ᶜThe king's wrath *is* like the roaring of a lion: but his favor *is* like the dew upon the grass.

CHAPTER 19
ᵃ Prov. 28:6
ᵇ Deut. 19:19
Dan. 13:62
ᶜ Prov. 20:2
ᵈ Prov. 17:21
ᵉ Prov. 21:9
ᶠ Prov. 18:22
ᵍ Prov. 26:15
ʰ Prov. 21:11

13 ᵈA foolish son *is* the calamity of his father, ᵉand the contentions of a wife *are like* a continual ¹dropping.

14 House and riches *are* the inheritance of the fathers: but a ᶠprudent wife *cometh* of the Lord.

15 Slothfulness causeth to fall asleep, and a deceitful person shall be affamished.

16 He that keepeth the commandment, keepeth his own soul: *but* he that despiseth his ways, shall die.

17 He that hath mercy upon the poor, lendeth unto the Lord: and the Lord will recompense him that which he hath given.

18 Chasten thy son while there is hope, and let not thy soul spare for his murmuring.

19 *A man* of much anger shall suffer punishment, and though thou ¹deliver *him*, yet will *his anger* come again.

20 Hear counsel and receive instruction, that thou mayest be wise in thy latter end.

21 Many devices *are* in a ¹man's heart: but the counsel of the Lord shall stand.

22 That that is to be desired of a man, *is* his ¹goodness, and a poor man is better than a liar.

23 The fear of the Lord *leadeth* to life: and he that is filled *therewith*, shall continue, *and* shall not be visited with evil.

24 ᵍThe slothful hideth his hand in *his* bosom, and will not put it to his mouth again.

25 ʰSmite a scorner, and the ¹foolish will beware: and reprove the prudent, and he will understand knowledge.

26 He that destroyeth *his* father, *or* chaseth away *his* mother, *is* a lewd and shameful child.

27 My son, hear no more the instruction, that causeth to err from the words of knowledge.

28 A wicked witness mocketh at judgment, and the mouth of the wicked ¹swalloweth up iniquity.

29 *But* judgments are prepared for the scorners, and stripes for the back of the fools.

20

1 Wine ¹*is* a mocker, *and* strong drink is raging: and whosoever is deceived thereby,

---

² Appeaseth their controversy, which are so stout that cannot otherwise be pacified.

18:19 ¹ Which for the strength thereof will not bow nor yield.

18:21 ¹ By the using of the tongue well or evil, cometh the fruit thereof either good or bad.

18:22 ¹ He that is joined with a virtuous woman in marriage, is blessed of the Lord, as Prov. 19:14.

18:24 ¹ That is, ofttimes such are found which are more ready to do pleasure, than he that is more bound by duty.

19:7 ¹ To have comfort of them.

19:8 ¹ He that is upright in judgment findeth favor of God.

19:10 ¹ The free use of things are not to be permitted to him that cannot use them aright.

19:11 ¹ That is, to cover it by charity, and to do therein as may most

serve to God's glory.

19:13 ¹ As rain that droppeth and rotteth the house.

19:19 ¹ Though for a time he give place to counsel, yet soon after will he give place to his raging affections.

19:21 ¹ Man's device shall not have success, except God govern it, whose purpose is unchangeable.

19:22 ¹ That is, that he be honest: for the poor man that is honest, is to be esteemed above the rich which is not virtuous.

19:25 ¹ That is, the simple and ignorant men learn, when they see the wicked punished.

19:28 ¹ Taketh a pleasure and delight therein, as gluttons and drunkards in delicate meats and drinks.

20:1 ¹ By wine here is meant him that is given to wine, and so by strong drink.

is not wise.

2 "The fear of the King *is* like the roaring of a lion: he that provoketh him unto anger [1]sinneth against his own soul.

3 *It is* a man's honor to cease from strife: but every fool will be meddling.

4 The slothful will not plow, because of winter: *therefore* shall he beg in summer, but have nothing.

5 The counsel in the heart of [1]man *is like* deep waters: but a man that hath understanding, will draw it out.

6 Many men will boast every one of his own goodness: but who can find a faithful man?

7 He that walketh in his integrity, *is* just, *and* blessed *shall* his children *be* after him.

8 A king that sitteth in the throne of judgment, [1]chaseth away all evil with his eyes.

9 "Who can say, I have made mine heart clean, I am clean from my sin?

10 Divers [1]weights, and divers measures, both [2]these are even abomination unto the Lord.

11 A child also is known by his doings, whether his word be pure and right.

12 The Lord hath made both these, even the ear to hear, and the eye to see.

13 Love not sleep, lest thou come unto poverty: open thine eyes, *and* thou shalt be satisfied with bread.

14 It is naught, it is naught, saith the buyer: but when he is gone apart, he boasteth.

15 There is gold, and a multitude of precious stones: but the lips of knowledge *are* a precious jewel.

16 'Take his [1]garment, that is surety for a stranger, and a pledge of him for the stranger.

17 The bread of deceit *is* sweet to a man: but afterward his mouth shall be filled with gravel.

18 Establish thy thoughts by counsel; and by counsel make war.

19 He that goeth about *as* a slanderer, discovereth [d]secrets: therefore meddle not with him that flattereth with his lips.

20 'He that curseth his father or his mother, his

CHAPTER 20
a Prov. 19:12
b 1 Kings 8:46
2 Chron. 6:36
Eccl. 7:22
1 John 1:8
c Prov. 27:13
d Prov. 11:13
e Exod. 21:17
Lev. 20:9
Matt. 15:4
f Deut. 32:35
Prov. 17:13
Prov. 24:29
Rom. 12:17
1 Thess. 5:15
1 Pet. 3:9
g Prov. 11:1
Prov. 20:10
h Jer. 10:13
i Prov. 19:14

CHAPTER 21
a Prov. 16:2
b Mic. 6:8
c Prov. 13:11
d Prov. 19:13
Prov. 25:24

light shall be put out in obscure darkness.

21 An heritage *is* hastily gotten at the beginning, but the end thereof shall not be blessed.

22 Say not thou, [f]I will recompense evil, *but* wait upon the Lord, and he shall save thee.

23 [g]Diverse weights *are* an abomination unto the Lord, and deceitful balances *are* not good.

24 [h]The steps of man *are ruled* by the Lord: how can a man then understand his own way?

25 It is a destruction for a man to [1]devour that which is sanctified, and after the vows to inquire.

26 A wise King scattereth the wicked, and causeth the [1]wheel to turn over them.

27 The [1]light of the Lord *is* the breath of man, and searcheth all the bowels of the belly.

28 [i]Mercy and truth preserve the king: for his throne shall be established with mercy.

29 The beauty of young men *is* their strength, and the glory of the aged *is* the gray head.

30 [1]The blueness of the wound serveth to purge the evil, and the stripes within the bowels of the belly.

21 1 The [1]King's heart *is* in the hand of the Lord, *as* the rivers of waters: he turneth it whithersoever it pleaseth him.

2 Every "way of a man *is* right in his own eyes: but the Lord pondereth the hearts.

3 [b]To do justice and judgment is more acceptable to the Lord than sacrifice.

4 A haughty look, and a proud heart *which is* the [1,2]light of the wicked, *is* sin.

5 The thoughts of the diligent *do* surely *bring* abundance; but [1]whosoever is hasty, *cometh* surely to poverty.

6 'The gathering of treasures by a deceitful tongue, *is* vanity tossed to and fro of them that seek death.

7 The [1]robbery of the wicked shall destroy them; for they have refused to execute judgment.

8 The way of some *is* perverted and strange, but of the pure man, his work *is* right.

9 [d]It is better to dwell in a corner of the house top, than with a contentious woman in a [1]wide house.

20:2 [1] Putteth his life in danger.
20:5 [1] It is hard to find out: for it is as deep waters, whose bottom cannot be found: yet the wise man will know a man either by his words or manners.
20:8 [1] Where righteous judgment is executed, there sin ceaseth, and vice dare not appear.
20:10 [1] Hebrew, *stone and stone, ephah and ephah.*
    [2] Read Prov. 16:11.
20:16 [1] Teach him wit, that he cast not himself rashly into danger.
20:25 [1] That is, to apply it, or take it to his own use, which was appointed to God's, and then inquire how they may be exempted from the fault.
20:26 [1] Which was a kind of punishment then used.
20:27 [1] The word of God giveth life unto man, and causeth us to see

and try the secret of our dark hearts, Heb. 4:12.
20:30 [1] Sharp punishment that pierceth even the inward parts, is profitable for the wicked, to bring them to amendment.
21:1 [1] Though Kings seem to have all things at commandment, yet are they not able to bring their own purposes to pass any otherwise than God hath appointed: much less are the inferiors able.
21:4 [1] Or, plowing.
    [2] That is, the thing whereby he is guided or which he bringeth forth as the fruit of his work.
21:5 [1] He that goeth rashly about his business, and without counsel.
21:7 [1] He meaneth this chiefly of Judges, and Princes which leave that vocation, whereunto God hath called them, and powle their subjects to maintain their lusts.
21:9 [1] Or, in a great family.

10 The soul of the wicked wisheth evil, *and* his neighbor hath no favor in his eyes.

11 [1]When the scorner is punished, the foolish is wise, and when one instructeth the wise, he will receive knowledge.

12 The righteous [1]teacheth the house of the wicked; *but God* overthroweth the wicked for *their* evil.

13 He that stoppeth his ear at the crying of the poor, he shall also cry and not be heard.

14 A [1]gift in secret pacifieth anger, and a gift in the bosom, great wrath.

15 It is joy to the just to do judgment; but destruction *shall be* to the workers of iniquity.

16 A man that wandereth out of the way of wisdom, shall remain in the congregation of the dead.

17 He that loveth pastime, *shall be* a poor man; *and* he that loveth wine and oil, shall not be rich.

18 The [1]wicked *shall be* a ransom for the just, and the transgressor for the righteous.

19 It is better to dwell in the wilderness, than with a contentious and angry woman.

20 In the house of the wise is a pleasant treasure and [1]oil; but a foolish man devoureth it.

21 He that followeth after righteousness and mercy, shall find life, righteousness and glory.

22 A [1]wise man goeth up into the city of the mighty, and casteth down the strength of the confidence thereof.

23 He that keepeth his mouth and his tongue, keepeth his soul from afflictions.

24 Proud, haughty, *and* scornful *is* his name that worketh in *his* arrogancy wrath.

25 The desire of the slothful [1]slayeth him; for his hands refuse to work.

26 He coveteth evermore greedily: but the righteous giveth and spareth not.

27 The ᶜsacrifice of the wicked *is* an abomination: how much more when he bringeth it with a wicked mind?

28 ᶠA false witness shall perish: but he that heareth, [1]speaketh continually.

29 A wicked man hardeneth his face: but the just,

e Prov. 15:8 Isa. 1:13
f Prov. 19:5

CHAPTER 22
a Eccl. 7:1
b Prov. 29:13
c Prov. 27:12

he will direct his way.

30 There is no wisdom, neither understanding, nor counsel against the Lord.

31 The horse is prepared against the day of battle: but salvation *is* of the Lord.

22

1 ᵃA good name is to be chosen above great riches, and [1]loving favor is above silver and above gold.

2 ᵇThe rich and poor [1]meet together, the Lord *is* the maker of them all.

3 ᶜA prudent man [1]seeth the plague, and hideth himself: but the foolish go on still, and are punished.

4 The reward of humility, *and* the fear of God *is* riches, and glory, and life.

5 Thorns *and* snares *are* in the way of the froward: *but* he that regardeth his soul, will depart far from them.

6 Teach a child [1]in the trade of his way, and when he *is* old he shall not depart from it.

7 The rich ruleth the poor, and the borrower *is* servant to the man that lendeth.

8 He that soweth iniquity, shall reap affliction, and the [1]rod of his anger shall fail.

9 He that hath a good [1]eye, he shall be blessed: for he giveth of his bread unto the poor.

10 Cast out the scorner, and strife shall go out: so contention and reproach shall cease.

11 He that loveth pureness of heart *for the grace* of his lips, the [1]king *shall be* his friend.

12 The eyes of the Lord preserve [1]knowledge: but he overthroweth the words of the transgressor.

13 The slothful man saith, [1]A lion *is* without, I shall be slain in the street.

14 The mouth of strange women *is as* a deep pit: he with whom the Lord is angry, [1]shall fall therein.

15 Foolishness *is* bound [1]in the heart of a child: but the rod of correction shall drive it away from him.

16 He that oppresseth the poor to increase himself, *and* giveth unto the rich, *shall* surely *come* to poverty.

21:11 [1] Read Prov. 19:25.
21:12 [1] Though the godly admonish them both by words and example of life, yet the wicked will not amend, till God destroy them.
21:14 [1] To do a pleasure to the angry man pacifieth him.
21:18 [1] God shall cause that to fall on their own heads, which they intended against the just by delivering the just, and putting the wicked in their places.
21:20 [1] Meaning, abundance of all things.
21:22 [1] Wisdom overcometh strength and confidence in worldly things.
21:25 [1] He thinketh to live by wishing and desiring all things, but will take no pain to get ought.
21:28 [1] He may boldly testify the truth that he hath heard.
22:1 [1] Which cometh by well doing.
22:2 [1] Live together, and have need the one of the other.

22:3 [1] That is, the punishment, which is prepared for the wicked, and fleeth [not to] God for succor.
22:6 [1] Bring him up virtuously, and he shall so continue.
22:8 [1] His authority, whereby he did oppress others, shall be taken from him.
22:9 [1] He that is merciful and liberal.
22:11 [1] He showeth that princes should use their familiarity, whose conscience is good, and their talk wise and godly.
22:12 [1] Favor them that love knowledge.
22:13 [1] He derideth them that invent vain excuses, because they would not do their duty.
22:14 [1] So God punisheth one sin by another, when he suffereth the wicked to fall into the acquaintance of an harlot.
22:15 [1] He is naturally given unto it.

17 ¶ Incline thine ear, and hear the words of the wise, and apply thine heart unto my knowledge.

18 For *it shall be* pleasant, if thou keep them in thy belly, *and if* they be directed together in thy lips.

19 That thy confidence may be in [1]the Lord, I have showed thee this day: thou therefore *take heed.*

20 Have not I written unto thee [1]three times in counsels and knowledge,

21 That I might show thee the assurance of the words of truth, to answer the words of truth to them that send to thee?

22 Rob not the poor, because he is poor, neither oppress the afflicted [1]in judgment.

23 For the Lord [d]will defend their cause, and spoil the soul of those that spoil them.

24 Make [1]no friendship with an angry man, neither go with the furious man,

25 Lest thou learn his ways, and receive destruction to thy soul.

26 Be not thou of them that [1]tough the hand, *nor* among them that are surety for debts.

27 If thou hast nothing to pay, why *causest thou* that he should take thy bed from under thee?

28 Thou shalt not [e]remove the ancient bounds which thy fathers have made.

29 Thou seest that a diligent man in his business standeth before Kings, *and* standeth not before the base sort.

23

1 When thou sittest to eat with a ruler, [1]consider diligently what is before thee,

2 [1]And put thy knife to thy throat, if thou be a man given to the appetite.

3 Be not desirous of his dainty meats: [1]for it is a deceivable meat.

4 Travail not too much to be rich: *but* cease from thy [1]wisdom.

5 Wilt thou cast thine eyes upon it, which is nothing? for *riches* taketh her to her wings, as an Eagle, and flieth into the heaven.

6 Eat thou not the bread of him that hath an [1]evil eye, neither desire his dainty meats.

7 For as though he thought it in his heart: so will he say unto thee, Eat and drink: but his heart is not with thee.

8 Thou shalt vomit thy [1]morsel that thou hast eaten, and thou shalt lose thy sweet words.

9 Speak not in the ears of a fool: for he will despise the wisdom of thy words.

10 [a]Remove not the ancient bounds, and enter not into the fields of the fatherless.

11 For he that redeemeth them, is mighty: he will [b]defend their cause against thee.

12 Apply thine heart to instruction, and thine ears to the words of knowledge.

13 [c]Withhold not correction from the child: if thou smite him with the rod, he shall not die.

14 Thou shalt smite him with the rod, and shalt deliver his soul from [1]hell.

15 My son, if thine heart be wise, mine heart shall rejoice, and I also,

16 And my reins shall rejoice, when thy lips speak righteous things.

17 [d]Let not thine heart be envious against sinners: but *let it be* in the fear of the Lord continually.

18 For surely there is an end, [1]and thy hope shall not be cut off.

19 O thou my son, hear, and be wise, and guide thine heart in the [1]way.

20 Keep not company with [1]drunkards, *nor* with [2]gluttons.

21 For the drunkard and the glutton shall be poor, and the sleeper shall be clothed with rags.

22 Obey thy father that hath begotten thee, and despise not thy mother when she is old.

23 Buy [1]the truth, but sell it not: *likewise* wisdom, instruction, and understanding.

24 The father of the righteous shall greatly rejoice, and he that begetteth a wise child, shall have joy of him.

25 Thy father and thy mother shall be glad, and she that bare thee shall rejoice.

26 My son, give me [1]thine heart, and let thine eyes delight in my ways.

27 [e]For a whore *is as* a deep ditch, and a strange woman *is as* a narrow pit.

---

d Prov. 23:11
e Deut. 17:17
  Prov. 23:10

CHAPTER 23
a Deut. 27:17
  Prov. 22:28
b Prov. 12:13
c Prov. 13:24
  Prov. 19:18
d Ps. 37:1
  Prov. 24:1
e Prov. 22:14

22:19 [1] He showeth what the end of wisdom is: to wit, to direct us to the Lord.

22:20 [1] That is, sundry times.

22:22 [1] Hebrew, *in the gates.*

22:24 [1] Have not to do with him that is not able to rule his affections: for he would hurt thee by his evil conversation.

22:26 [1] Which rashly put themselves in danger for others, as Prov. 6:2.

23:1 [1] Eat with sobriety.

23:2 [1] Bridle thine appetite, as it were by force and violence.

23:3 [1] For ofttimes the rich when they bid their inferiors to their tables, it is not for the love they bear them, but for their own secret purposes.

23:4 [1] Bestow not the gifts that God hath given thee, to get worldly riches.

23:6 [1] That is, covetous, as contrary a good eye is taken for liberal, as Prov. 22:9.

23:8 [1] He will not cease till he hath done thee some harm, and his flattering words shall come to no use.

23:14 [1] That is, from destruction.

23:18 [1] The prosperity of the wicked shall not continue.

23:19 [1] In the observation of God's commandments.

23:20 [1] Hebrew, *wine-bibbers.*
    [2] Hebrew, *devourers of flesh.*

23:23 [1] Spare no cost for truth's sake, neither depart from it for any gain.

23:26 [1] Give thyself wholly to wisdom.

28 ʃAlso she lieth in wait as for a prey, ¹and she increaseth the transgressors among men.

29 To whom is woe? to whom is sorrow? to whom is strife? to whom is murmuring? to whom are wounds without cause? *and* to whom is the redness of the eyes?

30 *Even* to them that tarry long at the wine, to them that go, ¹and seek mixed wine.

31 Look not thou upon the wine, when it is red, *and* when it showeth his color in the cup, *or* goeth down pleasantly.

32 In the end thereof it will bite like a serpent, and hurt like a cockatrice.

33 Thine ¹eyes shall look upon strange women, and thine heart shall speak lewd things.

34 And thou shalt be as one that sleepeth in the midst of the ¹sea, and as he that sleepeth in the top of the mast.

35 They have stricken me, *shalt thou say, but* I was not sick: they have beaten me, *but* I knew not, when I awoke: *therefore* will I ¹seek it yet still.

24

1 ᵃBe not thou envious against evil men, neither desire to be with them.

2 For their heart imagineth destruction, and their lips speak mischief.

3 Through wisdom is an house built, and with understanding it is established.

4 And by knowledge shall the chambers be filled with all precious and pleasant riches.

5 A wise man *is* strong: for a man of understanding increaseth *his* strength.

6 ᵇFor with counsel thou shalt enterprise thy war, and in the multitude of them that can give counsel, *is* health.

7 Wisdom is high to a fool: *therefore* he cannot open his mouth in the ¹gate.

8 He that imagineth to do evil, men shall call him an author of wickedness.

9 The wicked thought of a fool *is* sin, and the scorner *is* an abomination unto men.

10 *If* thou be ¹faint in the day of adversity, thy strength *is* small.

11 Deliver them that are drawn ¹to death, and wilt thou not preserve them that are led to be slain?

12 If thou say, Behold, we knew not of it: he that pondereth the hearts, doth not he understand it? and he that keepeth thy soul, knoweth he it not? will he not also recompense every man according to his works?

13 My son, eat ¹honey, for it is good, and the honey comb, *for it is* sweet unto thy mouth.

14 So shall the knowledge of wisdom be unto thy soul if thou find it, and there shall be an ¹end, and thine hope shall not be cut off.

15 Lay no wait, O wicked man, against the house of the righteous, and spoil not his resting place.

16 For a just man ¹falleth seven times, and riseth again: but the wicked fall into mischief.

17 Be thou not glad when thine enemy falleth, and let not thine heart rejoice when he stumbleth,

18 Lest the Lord see it, and it displease him, and he turn his wrath ¹from him.

19 ᶜFret not thyself because of the malicious, neither be envious at the wicked.

20 For there shall be none end *of plagues* to the evil man, ᵈthe light of the wicked shall be put out.

21 My son, fear the Lord, and the King *and* meddle not with them that are seditious.

22 For their destruction shall rise suddenly, and who knoweth the ruin of them ¹both?

23 Also these things pertain to the wise, It is not good ¹to have respect of any person in judgment.

24 He that saith to the wicked, ᵉThou art righteous, him shall the people curse, and the multitude shall abhor him.

25 But to them that rebuke *him*, shall be pleasure, and upon them shall come the blessing of goodness.

26 They shall kiss the lips of him that answereth upright words.

27 Prepare thy work without, and make ready thy things in the field, ¹and after, build thine house.

28 Be not a witness against thy neighbor without cause: for wilt thou deceive with thy lips?

29 ʃSay not, I will do to him as he hath done to me, I ¹will recompense every man according to his work.

30 I passed by the field of the slothful, and by the

ʃProv. 7:12

CHAPTER 24
ᵃPs. 37:1
Prov. 23:17
ᵇProv. 20:18
ᶜPs. 37:1
Prov. 33:17
ᵈProv. 13:9
ᵉProv. 17:25
Isa. 5:23
ʃProv. 20:22

23:28 ¹ She seduceth many and causeth them to offend God.
23:30 ¹ Which by art make wine stronger and more pleasant.
23:33 ¹ That is, drunkenness shall bring thee to whoredom.
23:34 ¹ In such great danger shalt thou be.
23:35 ¹ Though drunkenness make them more insensible than beasts, yet can they not refrain.
24:7 ¹ In the place where wisdom should be showed.
24:10 ¹ Man hath no trial of his strength till he be in troubles.
24:11 ¹ None can be excused, if he help not the innocent when he is in danger.
24:13 ¹ As honey is sweet and pleasant to the taste, so wisdom is

to the soul.
24:14 ¹ Or, reward.
24:16 ¹ He is subject to many perils, but God delivereth him.
24:18 ¹ To be avenged on thee.
24:22 ¹ Meaning, either of the wicked and seditious, as verse 19 and 21, or, of them that fear not God, nor obey their King.
24:23 ¹ Hebrew, *to know the face.*
24:27 ¹ Be sure of the means how to compass it, before thou take any enterprise in hand.
24:29 ¹ He showeth what is the nature of the wicked, to revenge wrong for wrong.

vineyard of the man destitute of understanding.

31 And lo, it was all grown over with thorns, *and* nettles had covered the face thereof, and the stone wall thereof was broken down.

32 Then I beheld, *and* I considered it well: I looked upon it, *and* received [1]instruction.

33 Yet a little sleep, [1]a little slumber, a little folding of the hands to sleep.

34 So thy poverty cometh *as* one that traveleth by the way, and thy necessity like an armed man.

CHAPTER 25
[a] Luke 14:10
[b] Rom. 12:20
[c] Prov. 21:9

25

1 These are also parables of Solomon, which the [1]men of Hezekiah King of Judah [2]copied out.

2 The glory of God *is* to [1]conceal a thing secret: but the [2]King's honor *is* to search out a thing.

3 The heaves in height, and the earth in deepness: and the [1]king's heart can no man search out.

4 Take the [1]dross from the silver, and there shall proceed a vessel for the finer.

5 Take [1]away the wicked from the King, and his throne shall be established in righteousness.

6 Boast not thyself before the King, and stand not in the place of great men.

7 [a]For it is better, that it be said unto thee, Come up hither, than thou to be put lower in the presence of the Prince whom thine eyes have seen.

8 Go not forth hastily to strife, lest thou know not what to do in the end thereof, when thy neighbor hath put thee to shame.

9 Debate thy matter with thy neighbor, and discover not the secret to another,

10 Lest he that heareth it, put thee to shame, and thine infamy do not [1]cease.

11 A word spoken in his place, *is like* apples of gold with pictures of silver.

12 He that reproveth the wise *and* the obedient ear, *is as* a golden earring, and an ornament of fine gold.

13 As the cold of the snow [1]in the time of harvest, *so is* a faithful messenger to them that send him: for he refresheth the soul of his masters.

14 A man that boasteth of false liberality, *is like* [1]clouds and wind without rain.

15 A Prince is pacified by staying of [1]anger, and a soft tongue breaketh the [2]bones.

16 *If* thou have found honey, eat that is [1]sufficient for thee, lest thou be overfull, and vomit it.

17 Withdraw thy foot from thy neighbor's house, lest he be weary of thee, and hate thee.

18 A man that beareth false witness against his neighbor, *is like* an hammer and a sword, and a sharp arrow.

19 Confidence in an unfaithful man in time of trouble, *is like* a broken tooth and a sliding foot.

20 He that taketh away the garment in the cold season, *is like* vinegar *poured* upon [1,2]nitre, or *like* him that singeth songs to an heavy heart.

21 [b]If he that hateth thee be hungry, give him bread to eat, and if he be thirsty, give him water to drink:

22 For thou shalt lay [1]coals upon his head, and the Lord shall recompense thee.

23 *As* the Northwind driveth away the rain, so doth an angry countenance the slandering tongue.

24 [c]It is better to dwell in a corner of the house top, than with a contentious woman in a wide house.

25 *As are* the cold waters to a weary soul, so *is* good news from a far country.

26 A righteous man falling down before the wicked, *is like* a troubled well and a corrupt spring.

27 It is not good to eat much honey: so to search their own glory, *is not* glory.

28 A man that refraineth not his appetite, *is like* a city which is [1]broken down *and* without walls.

26

1 As the snow in the Summer, and as the rain in the Harvest *are not meet*, so is honor unseemly for a fool.

2 As the sparrow by flying, and the swallow by flying *escape*, so the curse *that is* causeless, shall not come.

3 Unto the horse *belongeth* a whip, to the ass a bridle, and a rod to the fool's back.

24:32 [1] That I might learn by another man's fault.

24:33 [1] Read Prov. 6:10.

25:1 [1] Whom Hezekiah appointed for this purpose.
  [2] That is, gathered out of divers books of Solomon.

25:2 [1] God doth not reveal the cause of his judgments to man.
  [2] Because the king ruleth by the revealed word of God, the cause of his doings must appear, and therefore he must use diligence in trying out of causes.

25:3 [1] He showeth that it is too hard for man to attain to the reason of all the secret doings of the King, even when he is upright, and doeth his duty.

25:4 [1] When vice is removed from a king, he is a meet vessel for the Lord's use.

25:5 [1] It is not enough that he be pure himself: but that he put away others that be corrupted.

25:10 [1] Lest whereas thou thinkest by this means to have an end of the matter, it put thee to further trouble.

25:13 [1] In the time of great heat, when men desire cold.

25:14 [1] Which have an outward appearance, and are nothing within.

25:15 [1] By not ministering occasion to provoke him further.
  [2] That is, the heart that is bent to anger, as Prov. 15:1.

25:16 [1] Use moderately the pleasures of this world.

25:20 [1] Which melteth it, and consumeth it.
  [2] Or, alum.

25:22 [1] Thou shalt, as it were by force, overcome him, insomuch that his own conscience shall move him to acknowledge the benefits, and his heart shall be inflamed.

25:28 [1] And so is in extreme danger.

4 Answer not a fool ¹according to his foolishness, lest thou also be like him.

5 Answer a fool ¹according to his foolishness, lest he be wise in his own ²conceit.

6 He that sendeth a message by the hand of a fool, *is as* he that cutteth off ¹the feet, ²and drinketh iniquity.

7 *As* they that lift up the legs of the lame, so *is* a parable in a fool's mouth.

8 As the closing up of a *precious* stone in an heap of stones, so *is* he that giveth glory to a fool.

9 *As* a thorn standing ¹up in the hand of a drunkard, so *is* a parable in the mouth of fools.

10 ¹The Excellent that formed all things, both rewardeth the fool, and rewardeth the transgressors.

11 ᵈAs a dog turneth again to his own vomit, *so* a fool turneth to his foolishness.

12 Seest thou a man wise in his own conceit? ¹more hope *is* of a fool than of him.

13 The slothful man saith, ¹A lion *is* in the way: a lion *is* in the streets.

14 *As* the door turneth upon his hinges, so *doth* the slothful man upon his bed.

15 ᵇThe slothful hideth his hand in *his* bosom, *and* it grieveth him to put it again to his mouth.

16 The sluggard is wiser in his own conceit, than seven *men* that can render a reason.

17 He that passeth by and medleth with the strife *that belongeth* not unto him, *is as* one that taketh a dog by the ears.

18 As he that feigneth himself mad, casteth firebrands, arrows, and mortal things,

19 So *dealeth* the deceitful man with ¹his friend, and saith, Am not I in sport?

20 Without wood the fire is quenched, and without a talebearer strife ceaseth.

21 *As* the coal *maketh* burning coals, and wood a fire, so the contentious man *is* apt to kindle strife.

22 ᶜThe words of a talebearer *are* as flatterings, and they go down into the bowels of the belly.

23 *As* silver dross overlaid upon a potsherd, *so are* burning lips, and ¹an evil heart.

24 He that hateth, will counterfeit with his lips, but in his heart he layeth up deceit.

25 Though he speak favorably, believe him not: for *there are* ¹seven abominations in his heart.

26 Hatred may be covered by deceit: *but* the malice thereof shall be discovered in the ¹congregation.

27 ᵈHe that diggeth a pit shall fall therein, and he that rolleth a stone, it shall return unto him.

28 A false tongue hateth the afflicted, and a flattering mouth causeth ruin.

27 1 Boast not thyself of ¹tomorrow, for thou knowest not what a day may bring forth.

2 Let another man praise thee, and not thine own mouth: a stranger, and not thine own lips.

3 A stone *is* heavy, and the sand weighty: but a fool's wrath *is* heavier than them both.

4 Anger is cruel, and wrath *is* raging: but who can stand before ¹envy?

5 Open rebuke *is* better than secret love.

6 The wounds of a lover *are* faithful, and the kisses of an enemy *are* ¹pleasant.

7 ᵃThe person that is full, despiseth an honeycomb: but unto the hungry soul every bitter thing is sweet.

8 As a bird that wandereth from her nest, so is a man that wandereth from his own place.

9 *As* ointment and perfume rejoice the heart, so *doth* the sweetness of a man's friend by hearty counsel.

10 Thine own friend and thy father's friend forsake thou not: neither enter into thy brother's ¹house in the day of thy calamity: *for* better is a neighbor *that is* near, than a brother far off.

11 My son, be wise, and rejoice mine heart, that I may answer him that reproacheth me.

12 ¹A prudent man seeth the plague, and hideth himself: *but* the foolish go on still, *and* are punished.

13 ᵇTake his garment that is surety for a stranger, and a pledge of him for the stranger.

14 He that ¹praiseth his friend with a loud voice, rising ²early in the morning, it shall be counted to him as a curse.

15 A ᶜcontinual dropping in the day of rain, and a contentious woman are alike.

16 He that hideth her, hideth the wind, and *she is as* the oil in his right hand that uttereth itself.

17 Iron sharpeneth iron, so doth [1]man sharpen the face of his friend.

18 He that keepeth the fig tree, shall eat the fruit thereof: so he that waiteth upon his master, shall come to honor.

19 As in water face *answereth* to face, [1]so the heart of man to man.

20 The grave and destruction can never be full, so the eyes of man can never be satisfied.

21 [d]*As is* the fining pot for silver, and the furnace for gold, so *is* every man according to his [1]dignity.

22 Though thou shouldest bray a fool in a mortar among wheat brayed with a pestle, *yet* will not his foolishness depart from him.

23 Be diligent to know the state of thy flock, and take heed to the herds.

24 For riches *remain* not always, nor the crown from generation to generation.

25 The hay discovereth itself, and the grass appeareth, and the herbs of the mountains are gathered.

26 The [1]lambs *are* for thy clothing, and the goats *are* the price of the field.

27 And let the milk of the goats *be* sufficient for thy food, for the food of thy family, and for the sustenance of thy maids.

28

1 The wicked [1]flee when none pursueth: but the righteous are bold as a lion.

2 For the transgression of the land [1]*there are* many princes thereof: but by a man of understanding and knowledge *a realm* likewise endureth long.

3 A poor man, if he oppress the poor, is like a raging rain that *leaveth* no food.

4 They that forsake the Law, praise the wicked: but they that keep the Law, set themselves against them.

5 Wicked men understand not judgment: but they that seek the Lord, understand all things.

6 [a]Better is the poor that walketh in his uprightness, than he that perverteth *his* ways, though he be rich.

7 He that keepeth the Law, is a child of understanding: but he that feedeth the gluttons, shameth his father.

[d] Prov. 17:3

CHAPTER 28
[a] Prov. 19:1
[b] Prov. 29:2
[c] Prov. 12:11
[d] Prov. 13:11
Prov. 20:21

8 He that increaseth his riches by usury and interest, gathereth [1]them for him that will be merciful unto the poor.

9 He that turneth away his ear from hearing the Law, even his prayer shall be [1]abominable.

10 He that causeth the righteous to go astray by an evil way, shall fall into his own pit, and the upright shall inherit good things.

11 The rich man is wise in his own conceit: but the poor that hath understanding, can try [1]him.

12 [b]When righteous men rejoice, *there is* great glory: but when the wicked come up, the man [1]is tried.

13 He that hideth his sins, shall not prosper: but he that confesseth, and forsaketh *them*, shall have mercy.

14 Blessed *is* the man that [1]feareth always: but he that hardeneth his heart, shall fall into evil.

15 As a roaring lion, and an hungry bear, *so is* [1]a wicked ruler over the poor people.

16 A prince destitute of understanding is also a great oppressor: but he that hateth covetousness, shall prolong *his* days.

17 A man that doeth violence against the blood of a person, shall flee unto the grave, *and* they shall not [1]stay him.

18 He that walketh uprightly shall be saved: but he that is froward in *his* ways, shall once fall.

19 [c]He that tilleth his land, shall be satisfied with bread, but he that followeth the idle, shall be filled with poverty.

20 A faithful man shall abound in blessings, and [d]he that maketh haste to be rich, shall not be innocent.

21 To have respect of persons is not good: for *that* man will transgress for a piece of [1]bread.

22 A man with a wicked [1]eye hasteth to riches, and knoweth not that poverty shall come upon him.

23 He that rebuketh a man, shall find more favor at the length, than he that flattereth with *his* tongue.

24 He that robbeth his father and mother, and saith, It is no transgression, is the companion of a man that destroyeth.

25 He that is of a proud heart, stirreth up strife: but he that trusteth in the Lord, shall be [1]fat.

27:17 [1] One hasty man provoketh another to anger.
27:19 [1] There is no difference between man and man by nature, but only the grace of God maketh the difference.
27:21 [1] That is, he is either known to be ambitious, and glorious, or humble and modest.
27:26 [1] This declareth the great goodness of God towards man, and the diligence that he requireth of him for the preservation of his gifts.
28:1 [1] Because their own conscience accuseth them.
28:2 [1] The state of the commonweal is oftentimes changed.
28:8 [1] For God will take away the wicked usurer, and give his goods

to him that shall bestow them well.
28:9 [1] Because it is not of faith which is grounded of God's word or Law, which the wicked contemn.
28:11 [1] And judge that he is not wise.
28:12 [1] He is known by his doings to be wicked.
28:14 [1] Which standeth in awe of God, and is afraid to offend him.
28:15 [1] For he can never be satisfied, but ever oppresseth and spoileth.
28:17 [1] None shall be able to deliver him.
28:21 [1] He will be abused for nothing.
28:22 [1] Meaning, him that is covetous.
28:25 [1] Shall have all things in abundance.

26 He that trusteth in his own heart, is a fool: but he that walketh in wisdom, shall be delivered.

27 He that giveth unto the poor, shall not lack: but he that hideth his eyes, *shall have* many curses.

28 *When the wicked rise up, men hide themselves: but when they perish, the righteous increase.

29

1 A man that hardeneth his neck when he is rebuked, shall suddenly be destroyed, and cannot be cured.

2 *When the righteous [1]are in authority, the people rejoice: but when the wicked beareth rule, the people sigh.

3 A man that loveth wisdom rejoiceth his father: but [b]he that feedeth harlots wasteth *his* substance.

4 A king by judgment maintaineth the country: but a man *receiving* gifts, destroyeth it.

5 A man that flattereth his neighbor, [1]spreadeth a net for his steps.

6 In the transgression of an evil man *is* his [1]snare: but the righteous doth sing and rejoice.

7 The righteous knoweth the cause of the poor: *but* the wicked regardeth not knowledge.

8 Scornful men bring a city into a snare: but wise men turn away wrath.

9 *If* a wise man contend with [1]a foolish man, whether he be angry or laugh, there *is* no rest.

10 Bloody men hate him that is upright: but the just have care of his soul.

11 A fool poureth out all his mind: but a wise man keepeth it in till afterward.

12 Of a prince that hearkeneth to lies, all his servants *are* wicked.

13 *The poor and the usurer meet together, *and* the Lord lighteneth both their eyes.

14 A [d]King that judgeth the poor in truth, his throne shall be established forever.

15 The rod and correction give wisdom, but a child set at liberty, maketh his mother ashamed.

16 When the wicked are increased, transgression increaseth: but the righteous shall see their fall.

17 Correct thy son, and he will give thee rest, and will give pleasures to thy soul.

18 [1]Where there *is* no vision, the people decay: but he that keepeth the law *is* blessed.

19 A [1]servant will not be chastised with words: though he understand, yet he will not [2]answer.

20 Seest thou a man hasty in his matters? *there is* more hope of a fool, than of him.

21 He that delicately bringeth up his servant from youth, at length he will be even *as* his son.

22 *An angry man stirreth up strife, and a furious man aboundeth in transgression.

23 [f]The pride of a man shall bring him low: but the humble in spirit shall enjoy glory.

24 He that is partner with a thief, hateth his own soul: he heareth cursing and declareth it not.

25 The fear of man bringeth a [1]snare: but he that trusteth in the Lord shall be exalted.

26 Many do seek the face of the ruler: but every man's [1]judgment *cometh* from the Lord.

27 A wicked man *is* abomination to the just, and he that is upright in *his* way, *is* abomination to the wicked.

30

2 To humble ourselves in consideration of God's works. 5 The word of God is perfect. 11 Of the wicked and hypocrites. 15 Of things that are never satiate. 18 Of others that are wonderful.

THE WORDS OF [1]AGUR THE SON OF JAKEH.

1 The prophecy *which* the man spake unto Ithiel, *even* to [1]Ithiel, and Ucal.

2 Surely I am more [1]foolish than any man, and have not the understanding of a man in me.

3 For I have not learned wisdom, nor attained to the knowledge of holy things.

4 Who hath ascended up to [1]heaven, and descended? Who hath gathered the wind in his fist? Who hath bound the waters in a garment? Who hath established all the ends of the world? What is his name, and what is his son's name, if thou canst tell?

5 [a]Every word of God is pure: he is a shield to those that trust in him.

6 [b]Put nothing unto his words, lest he reprove thee, and thou be found a liar.

7 Two [1]things have I required of thee: deny me them not before I die.

8 Remove far from me vanity and lies: give me not poverty, nor riches: feed me with food convenient for me,

c Prov. 29:2

CHAPTER 29
a Prov. 28:12,28
b Luke 15:13
c Prov. 22:2
d Prov. 20:28
e Prov. 15:28
f Job 22:29

CHAPTER 30
a Ps. 19:8
b Deut. 4:2
Deut. 12:32

29:2 [1] Or, are increased.
29:5 [1] He that giveth ear to the flatterer, is in danger as the bird is before the fowler.
29:6 [1] He is ever ready to fall into the snare that he layeth for others.
29:9 [1] He can hear no admonition in what sort soever it is spoken.
29:18 [1] Where there are not faithful ministers of the word of God.
29:19 [1] He that is of a servile and rebellious nature.
    [2] Or, regard.
29:25 [1] He that feareth man more than God, falleth into a snare and is destroyed.

29:26 [1] He needeth not to flatter the ruler: for what God hath appointed, that shall come to him.
30:Title [1] Who was an excellent man in virtue and knowledge in the time of Solomon.
30:1 [1] Which were Agur's scholars or friends.
30:2 [1] Herein he declareth his great humility, who would not attribute any wisdom to himself, but all unto God.
30:4 [1] Meaning, to know the secrets of God, as though he would say, None.
30:7 [1] He maketh this request to God.

9 Lest I be full, and deny *thee*, and say, [1]Who is the Lord? or lest I be poor and steal, and take the Name of my God *in vain*.

10 Accuse not a servant unto his master, lest he curse thee, [1]when thou hast offended.

11 *There is* a generation that curseth their father, and doth not bless their mother.

12 *There is* a generation that are pure in their own conceit, and *yet* are not washed from their filthiness.

13 *There is* a generation whose eyes are haughty, and their eye lids are lifted up.

14 *There is* a generation, whose teeth *are as* swords, and their chaws *as* knives to eat up the afflicted out of the earth, and the poor from among men.

15 The horseleech hath two [1]daughters *which cry*, Give, give. There be three things that will not be satisfied: *yea*, four that say not, It is enough.

16 The grave, and the barren womb, the earth, that cannot be satisfied with water, and the fire that saith not, It is enough.

17 The eye that mocketh *his* father and despiseth the instruction of *his* mother, let the ravens [1]of the valley pick it out, and the young eagles eat it.

18 There be three things hid from me: yea, four that I know not:

19 The way of an eagle in the air, the way of a serpent upon a stone, the way of a ship in the midst of the sea, and the way of a man with a maid.

20 Such is the way also of an adulterous woman: she eateth and [1]wipeth her mouth, and saith, I have not committed iniquity.

21 For three things the earth is moved: yea, for four it cannot sustain itself:

22 For [1]a servant when he reigneth, and a fool when he is filled with meat;

23 For the hateful woman, when she is married, and for a handmaid that is [1]heir to her mistress.

24 These be four small things in the earth, yet they are [1]wise, and full of wisdom.

25 The pismires a people not strong, yet prepare they their meat in summer:

26 The conies a people not mighty, yet make they their houses in the rock:

27 The grasshopper hath no king, yet go they forth all by bands:

28 The spider taketh hold [1]with *her* hands, and is in king's palaces.

29 There be three things that order well *their* going: yea, four are comely in going:

30 A lion which is strong among beasts, and turneth not at the sight of any:

31 A lusty greyhound, and a goat, and a king against whom there is no rising up.

32 If thou hast been foolish in lifting thyself up, and if thou hast thought wickedly, *lay* thine hand [1]upon *thy* mouth.

33 When one churneth milk, he bringeth forth butter: and he that wringeth his nose, causeth blood to come out, so he that forceth wrath, bringeth forth strife.

31

2 He exhorteth to chastity and justice,   10 and showeth the conditions of a wise and worthy woman.

1 THE WORDS OF KING [1]LEMUEL: The [2]prophecy which his mother taught him.

2 What my son! and what the son of [1]my womb! and what, O son of my desires!

3 Give not thy strength unto women, [1]nor thy ways *which is* to destroy kings.

4 It is not for kings, O Lemuel, it is not for kings to drink wine, nor for princes [1]strong drink,

5 Lest he drink and forget the decree, and change the judgment of all the children of affliction.

6 Give ye strong drink unto him that is ready to perish, and wine unto them that have grief of heart.

7 Let him drink, that he may forget [1]his poverty, and remember his misery no more.

8 Open thy mouth for the [1]dumb in the cause of all the children of destruction.

9 Open thy mouth, judge righteously, and judge the afflicted, and the poor.

10 ¶ Who shall find a virtuous woman? for her price *is* far above the pearls.

11 The heart of her husband trusteth in her, and he shall have no need of [1]spoil.

30:9 [1] Meaning, that they that put their trust in their riches, forget God, and that by too much wealth men have an occasion to the same.

30:10 [1] In accusing him without cause.

30:15 [1] The leech hath two forks in her tongue, which here he calleth her two daughters, whereby she sucketh the blood, and is never satiated: even so are the covetous extortioners insatiable.

30:17 [1] Which haunt in the valley for carrions.

30:20 [1] She hath her desires, and after counterfeiteth as though she were an honest woman.

30:22 [1] These commonly abuse the state whereunto they are called.

30:23 [1] Which is married to her master after the death of her mistress.

30:24 [1] They contain great doctrine and wisdom.

30:28 [1] If man be not able to compass these common things by his wisdom, we cannot attribute wisdom to man, but folly.

30:32 [1] Make a stay, and continue not in doing evil.

31:1 [1] That is, of Solomon, who was called Lemuel, that is, of God, because God had ordained him to be king over Israel.

[2] The doctrine which his mother Bathsheba taught him.

31:2 [1] By this often repetition of one thing, she declareth her motherly affection.

31:3 [1] Meaning, that women are the destruction of kings, if they haunt them.

31:4 [1] That is, the King must not give himself to wantonness, and neglect of his office, which is to execute judgment.

31:7 [1] For wine doth comfort the heart, as Ps. 104:15.

31:8 [1] Defend their cause that are not able to help themselves.

31:11 [1] He shall not need to use any unlawful means to gain his living.

12 She will do him good, and not evil all the days of her life.

13 She seeketh wool and flax, and laboreth cheerfully with her hands.

14 She is like the ships of merchants: she bringeth her food from afar.

15 And she ariseth, while it is yet night: and giveth ¹the portion to her household, and the ²ordinary to her maids.

16 She considereth a field, and ¹getteth it: *and* with the fruit of her hands she planteth a vineyard.

17 She girdeth her loins with strength, and strengtheneth her arms.

18 She feeleth that her merchandise is good: her candle is not put out by night.

19 She putteth her hands to the wheel, and her hands handle the spindle.

20 She stretcheth out her hand to the poor, and putteth forth her hands to the needy.

21 She feareth not the snow for her family: for all her family is clothed with ¹scarlet.

22 She maketh herself carpets: fine linen and purple *is* her garment.

23 Her husband is known in the ¹gates, when he sitteth with the Elders of the land.

24 She maketh ¹sheets, and selleth them, and giveth girdles unto the merchant.

25 ¹Strength and honor *is* her clothing, and in the latter day she shall rejoice.

26 She openeth her mouth with wisdom, and the ¹law of grace *is* in her tongue.

27 She overseeth the ways of her household, and eateth not the bread of idleness.

28 Her children rise up, and ¹call her blessed: her husband also shall praise her, *saying,*

29 Many daughters have done virtuously: but thou surmountest them all.

30 Favor *is* deceitful, and beauty *is* vanity: *but* a woman that feareth the Lord she shall be praised.

31 Give ¹her of the fruit of her hands, and let her own works praise her in the ²gates.

31:15 ¹ Or, meat, as Ps. 111:5
  ² She prepareth their meat betime.
31:16 ¹ She purchaseth it with the gains of her travail.
31:21 ¹ Or, with double.
31:23 ¹ In the assemblies and places of judgment.
31:24 ¹ Or, linen cloth.
31:25 ¹ After that he had spoken of the apparel of the body, he now declareth the apparel of the spirit.
31:26 ¹ Her tongue is as a book whereby one might learn many good things: for she delighteth to talk of the word of God.
31:28 ¹ That is, do her reverence.
31:31 ¹ Confess her diligent labors, and commend her therefore.
  ² Forasmuch as the most honorable are clad in the apparel that she made.

ECCLESIASTES,

OR

THE PREACHER

---

1 *2 All things in this world are full of vanity, and of none endurance. 13 All man's wisdom is but folly and grief.*

1 The words of the ¹Preacher, the son of David king in Jerusalem.

2 ¹Vanity of vanities, saith the Preacher: vanity of vanities, all *is* vanity.

3 What remaineth unto man in all his ¹travail, which he suffereth under the sun?

4 *One* generation passeth, and *another* generation succeedeth: but the earth remaineth ¹forever.

5 The sun riseth, and the sun goeth down, and draweth to his place where he riseth.

6 The ¹wind goeth toward the South, and compasseth toward the North: the wind goeth round about, and returneth by his circuits.

7 All the rivers go into the sea, yet the sea is not full: *for* the rivers go unto the place ¹whence they return, and go.

8 All things are full of labor: man cannot utter it: the eye is not satisfied with seeing, nor the ear filled with hearing.

9 ¹What is it that hath been? that that shall be: and what is it that hath been done? that which shall be done: and there *is* no new thing under the sun.

10 Is there anything, whereof one may say, Behold this, it is new? it hath been already in the old time that was before us.

11 There is no memory of the former, neither shalt

there be a remembrance of the latter that shall be, with them that shall come after.

12 ¶ ¹I the Preacher have been king over Israel in Jerusalem:

13 And I have given mine heart to search and find out wisdom by all things that are done under the heaven: (this sore travail hath God given to the sons of men, ¹to humble them thereby.)

14 I have considered all the works that are done under the sun, and behold, all *is* vanity, and vexation of the spirit.

15 That which is ¹crooked, can none make straight: and that which faileth, cannot be numbered.

16 I thought in mine heart, and said, Behold, I am become great, and excel in wisdom all them that have been before me in Jerusalem: and mine heart hath seen much wisdom and knowledge.

17 And I gave mine heart to know wisdom and knowledge, ¹madness and foolishness: I knew also that this is a vexation of the spirit.

18 For in the multitude of wisdom *is* much ¹grief: and he that increaseth knowledge, increaseth sorrow.

2 *Pleasures, sumptuous buildings, riches and possessions are but vanity. 14 The wise and the fool have both one end touching the bodily death.*

1 I said in mine heart, Go to now, I will prove ¹thee with joy: therefore take thou pleasure in pleas-

---

1:1 ¹ Solomon is here called a preacher, or one that assembleth the people, because he teacheth the true knowledge of God, and how men ought to pass their life in this transitory world.

1:2 ¹ He condemneth the opinions of all men that set felicity in any thing, but in God alone, seeing that in this world all things are as vanity and nothing.

1:3 ¹ Solomon doth not condemn man's labor or diligence, but showeth that there is no full contentation in any thing under the heaven, forasmuch as all things are transitory.

1:4 ¹ One man dieth after another, and the earth remaineth longest, even to the last day, which yet is subject to corruption.

1:6 ¹ By the sun, wind and rivers, he showeth that the greatest labor and longest hath an end, and therefore there can be no felicity in this world.

1:7 ¹ The sea which compasseth all the earth, filleth the veins thereof, the which pour out springs and rivers into the sea again.

1:9 ¹ He speaketh of times and seasons, and things done in them,

which as they have been in times past, so come they to pass again.

1:12 ¹ He proveth that if any could have attained to felicity in this world by labor, and study, he chiefly should have obtained it, because he had gifts and aids of God thereunto above all others.

1:13 ¹ Man of nature hath a desire to know, and yet is not able to come to the perfection of knowledge, which is the punishment of sin, to humble man, and to teach him to depend only upon God.

1:15 ¹ Man is not able by all his diligence to cause things to go otherwise than they do: neither can he number the faults that are committed, much less remedy them.

1:17 ¹ That is, vain things, which served unto pleasure, wherein was no commodity, but grief and trouble of conscience.

1:18 ¹ Wisdom and knowledge cannot be come by without great pain of body and mind: for when a man hath attained to the highest, yet is his mind never fully content: therefore in this world is no true felicity.

2:1 ¹ Solomon maketh this discourse with himself, as though he would try whether there were contentation in ease and pleasures.

ant things: and behold, this also is vanity.

2 I said of laughter, Thou art mad: and of joy, What is this that thou doest?

3 I sought in mine heart [1]to give myself to wine, and to lead mine heart in [2]wisdom, and to take hold of folly, till I might see where is that goodness of the children of men, which they [3]enjoy under the Sun, the *whole* number of the days of their life.

4 I have made my great works: I have built me houses: I have planted me vineyards.

5 I have made me gardens and [1]orchards, and planted in them trees of all fruit.

6 I have made me cisterns of water, to water therewith the woods that grow with trees.

7 I have gotten servants and maids, and had children *born* in the [1]house: also I had great Possession of beeves and sheep above all that were before me in Jerusalem.

8 I have gathered unto me also silver and gold, and the chief treasures of Kings and provinces: I have provided me men singers, and women singers, and the [1]delights of the sons of men, *as* a woman [2]taken captive, and women taken captives.

9 And I was great, and increased above all that were before me in Jerusalem: also my wisdom [1]remained with me.

10 And whatsoever mine eyes desired, I withheld it not from them: I withdrew not mine heart from any joy: for mine heart rejoiced in all my labor: and this was my [1]portion of all my travail.

11 Then I looked on all my works that mine hands had wrought, and on the travail that I had labored to do: and behold, *all* is vanity and vexation of the spirit: and there *is* no profit under the Sun.

12 ¶ And I turned to behold [1]wisdom, and madness, and folly: (for who is the man that [2]will come after the King in things, which men now have done?)

13 Then I saw that there is profit in wisdom more than in folly: as the light is more excellent than darkness.

CHAPTER 2
[d] Prov. 17:24

14 [d]For the wise man's [1]eyes *are* in his head, but the fool walketh in darkness: yet I know also that the same [2]condition falleth to them all.

15 Then I thought in mine heart, It befalleth unto me, as it befalleth to the fool. Why therefore do I then labor to be more wise? And I said in mine heart, that this also is vanity.

16 For there shall be no remembrance of the wise, nor of the fool [1]forever: for that that now is, in the days to come, shall all be forgotten. And [2]how dieth the wise man, as doth the fool?

17 Therefore I hated life: for the work that is wrought under the Sun is grievous unto me: for all *is* vanity, and vexation of the spirit.

18 I hated also all my labor, wherein I had travailed under the Sun, which I shall leave to the man that shall be after me.

19 And who knoweth whether he shall be wise or foolish? yet shall he have rule over all my labor, wherein I have travailed, and wherein I have showed myself wise under the Sun. This is also vanity.

20 Therefore I went about to make mine heart [1]abhor all the labor, wherein I had travailed under the Sun.

21 For there is a man whose travail is in wisdom, and in knowledge, and in equity: yet to a man that hath not travailed herein, shall he [1]give his portion: this also is vanity, and a great grief.

22 For what hath man of all his travail and grief of his heart, wherein he hath travailed under the Sun?

23 For all his days are sorrows, and his travail grief: his heart also taketh not rest in the night: which also is vanity.

24 There *is* no profit to man, but that he eat and drink, and [1]delight his soul with the profit of his labor: I saw also this, that it was of the hand of God.

25 For who could eat, and who could haste to [1]outward things more than I?

26 Surely to a man that is good in his sight, *God* giveth wisdom, and knowledge, and joy: but to the

---

2:3 [1] Hebrew, *draw my flesh to wine.*
 [2] Albeit I gave myself to pleasures, yet I thought to keep wisdom and the fear of God in mine heart, and govern mine affairs by the same.
 [3] Hebrew, *do.*
2:5 [1] Hebrew, *paradises.*
2:7 [1] Meaning, of the servants or slaves, which he had bought: so the children born in their servitude, were the master's.
2:8 [1] That is, whatsoever men take pleasure in.
 [2] Which were the most beautiful of them that were taken in war, as Judg. 5:30. Some understand by these words, no women, but instruments of music.
2:9 [1] For all this God did not take his gift of wisdom from me.
2:10 [1] This was the fruit of all my labor, a certain pleasure mixed with care, which he calleth vanity in the next verse.
2:12 [1] I bethought with myself whether it were better to follow wisdom, or mine own affections and pleasures, which he calleth

madness.
 [2] Or, compare with the King.
2:14 [1] He forseeth things, which the fool cannot for lack of wisdom.
 [2] For both die and are forgotten as verse 16, or they both alike have prosperity or adversity.
2:16 [1] Meaning, in this world.
 [2] He wondereth that men forget a wise man, being dead, as soon as they do a fool.
2:20 [1] That I might seek the true felicity which is in God.
2:21 [1] Among other griefs that was not the least, to leave that which he had gotten by great travail, to one that had taken no pain therefore, and whom he knew not whether he were a wise man or a fool.
2:24 [1] When man hath all labored, he can get no more than food and refreshing, yet he confesseth also that this cometh of God's blessing, as Eccl. 3:13.
2:25 [1] Meaning, to pleasures.

sinner he giveth pain to gather, and to heap to give to him that is good before God: this also is vanity, and vexation of the spirit.

3 *1 All things have their time. 14 The works of God are perfect, and cause us to fear him. 17 God shall judge both the just and unjust.*

1 To all things *there is* an [1]appointed time, and a time to every purpose under the heaven.

2 A time to be born, and a time to die: a time to plant, and a time to pluck up that which is planted.

3 A time to slay, and a time to heal: a time to break down, and a time to build.

4 A time to weep, and a time to laugh: a time to mourn, and a time to dance.

5 A time to cast away stones, and a time to gather stones: a time to embrace, and a time to be far from embracing.

6 A time to seek, and a time to lose: a time to keep, and a time to cast away.

7 A time to rent, and a time to sow: a time to keep silence, and a time to speak.

8 A time to love, and a time to hate: a time of war, and a time of peace.

9 What profit *hath* he that worketh of the thing wherein he travaileth?

10 I have seen the travail that God hath given to the sons of men, [1]to humble them thereby.

11 He hath made everything beautiful in his time: also he hath set the [1]world in their heart, yet cannot man find out the work that God hath wrought from the beginning even to the end.

12 I know that there is nothing good in them, but to rejoice, and to do good in his life.

13 And also that every man eateth and drinketh, and seeth the commodity of all his labor. This is the [1]gift of God.

14 I know that whatsoever God shall do, it shall be [1]forever: to it can no man add, and from it can none diminish: for God hath done it, that they should fear before him.

15 What is that that hath been? that is now: and that that shall be, hath now been: for God [1]requireth that which is past.

16 And moreover, I have seen under the Sun the place of judgment, where *was* wickedness, and the place of justice, where *was* iniquity.

17 I thought in mine heart, God will judge the just and the wicked: for time is [1]there for every purpose and for every work.

18 I considered in mine heart the state of the children of men, that God had [1]purged them: yet to see too, they are in themselves *as* beasts.

19 For the condition of the children of men, and the condition of beasts *are* even *as* one [1]condition unto them. As the one dieth, so dieth the other: for they have all one breath, and there is no excellency of man above the beast: for all *is* vanity.

20 All go to one place, and all was of the dust, and all shall return to the dust.

21 Who [1]knoweth whether the spirit of man ascend upward, and the spirit of the beast descend downward to the earth?

22 Therefore I see that there is nothing better than that a man should [1]rejoice in his affairs, because that is his portion. For who shall bring him to see what shall be after him?

4 *2 The innocents are oppressed. 4 Man's labors are full of abuse and vanity. 9 Man's society is necessary. 13 A young man poor and wise, is to be preferred to an old King that is a fool.*

1 So [1]I turned and considered all the oppressions that are wrought under the sun, and behold, the tears of the oppressed, and none comforteth them, and *lo*, the strength *is* of the hand of them that oppress them, and none comforteth them.

2 Wherefore I praised the [1]dead which now are dead, above the living, which are yet alive.

3 And *I count* him [1]better than them both, which

3:1 [1] He speaketh of this diversity of time for two causes: first to declare that there is nothing in this world perpetual: next to teach us not to be grieved, if we have not all things at once according to our desires, neither enjoy them so long as we would wish.

3:10 [1] Read Eccl. 1:13.

3:11 [1] God hath given man a desire, and affection to seek out the things of this world, and to labor therein.

3:13 [1] Read Eccl. 2:24, and these places declare that we should do all things with sobriety and in the fear of God, forasmuch as he giveth not his gifts to the intent that they should be abused.

3:14 [1] That is, man shall never be able to let God's work, but as he hath determined, so it shall come to pass.

3:15 [1] God only causeth that, which is past, to return.

3:17 [1] Meaning, with God, howsoever man neglect his duty.

3:18 [1] And made them pure in their first creation.

3:19 [1] Man is not able by his reason and judgment to put differ-

ence between man and beast, as touching those things whereunto both are subject: for the eye cannot judge any otherwise of a man being dead, than of a beast, which is dead: yet by the word of God and faith we easily know the diversity, as verse 21.

3:21 [1] Meaning, that reason cannot comprehend that which faith believeth herein.

3:22 [1] By the often repetition of this sentence, as Eccl. 2:24; 3:12, 22; 5:17 and 8:15, he declareth that man by reason can comprehend nothing better in this life, than to use the gifts of God soberly and comfortably: for to know further, is a special gift of God revealed by his Spirit.

4:1 [1] He maketh here another discourse with himself concerning the tyranny of them that oppressed the poor.

4:2 [1] Because they are no more subject to these oppressions.

4:3 [1] He speaketh according to the judgment of the flesh, which cannot abide to feel or see troubles.

hath not yet been: for he hath not seen the evil works which are wrought under the sun.

4 Also I beheld all travail, and all [1]perfection of works, that this is the envy of a man against his neighbor: this also *is* vanity and vexation of spirit.

5 The fool foldeth his hands, and [1]eateth up his own flesh.

6 Better is an handful with quietness, than two handfuls with labor and vexation of spirit.

7 Again I returned, and saw vanity under the sun.

8 There is one *alone*, and there *is* not a second, which hath neither son nor brother, yet *is* there none end of all his travail, neither can his eye be satisfied with riches: neither *doth he think*, For whom do I travail and defraud my soul of pleasures? this also is vanity, this is an evil travail.

9 [1]Two *are* better wages for their labor.

10 For if they fall, the one will lift up his fellow: but woe unto him *that is* alone: for he falleth, and there *is* not a second to lift him up.

11 Also if two sleep *together*, then shall they have heat: but to one how should there be heat?

12 And if one overcome him, two shall stand against him: and a threefold [1]cord is not easily broken.

13 Better is a poor and wise child, than an old and foolish King, which will no more be admonished.

14 For out of the [1]prison he cometh forth to reign: when as he that is [2]born in his kingdom, is made poor.

15 I beheld all the living, which walk under the Sun [1]with the second child, which shall stand up in his place.

16 There is none [1]end of all the people, *nor* of all that were before them, and they that come after, shall not rejoice in him: surely this is also vanity and vexation of spirit.

17 Take heed to thine [1]foot when thou enterest into the house of God, and be more near to hear than to give the sacrifice of [2]fools: for they know

CHAPTER 5
ᵃ Deut. 23:21

not that they do evil.

5

1 Not to speak lightly, chiefly in God's matters. 9 The covetous can never have enough. 11 The laborer's sleep is sweet. 14 Man when he dieth, taketh nothing with him. 18 To live joyfully, and with a contented mind, is the gift of God.

1 Be not [1]rash with thy mouth, nor let thine heart be hasty to utter a thing before God: for God *is* in the heavens, and thou art on the earth: therefore let thy words be [2]few.

2 For *as* a dream cometh by the multitude of business: so the voice of a fool *is* in the multitude of words.

3 ᵃWhen thou hast vowed a vow to God, defer not to pay it: for he delighteth not in fools: pay *therefore* that thou hast [1]vowed.

4 It is better that thou shouldest not vow, than that thou shouldest vow and not pay it.

5 Suffer not thy mouth to make thy [1]flesh to sin: neither say before the [2]Angel, that this is ignorance: wherefore shall God be angry by thy voice, and destroy the work of thine hands?

6 For in the multitude of dreams, and vanities *are* also many words: but fear thou God.

7 If in a country thou seest the oppression of the poor, and the defrauding of judgment and justice, be not astonied at the matter: for he that is [1]higher than the highest, regardeth, and *there be* higher than they.

8 And the [1]abundance of the earth is over all: the king [2]*also consisteth* by the field that is tilled.

9 He that loveth silver, shall not be satisfied with silver, and he that loveth riches, *shall be* without the fruit *thereof*: this is also vanity.

10 When goods increase, they are increased that eat them: and what good cometh to the owners thereof, but the beholding *thereof* with their eyes?

4:4 [1] The more perfect that the work is, the more it is envied of the wicked.

4:5 [1] For idleness he is compelled to destroy himself.

4:9 [1] Forasmuch as when man is alone, he can neither help himself nor others, he showeth that men ought to live in mutual society to the intent they may be profitable one to another, and that their things may increase.

4:12 [1] By this proverb he declareth how necessary it is, that men should live in society.

4:14 [1] That is, from a poor and base estate, or out of trouble and prison, as Joseph did, Gen. 41:14.

[2] Meaning, that is born a King.

4:15 [1] Which follow and flatter the King's son, or him that shall succeed, to enter into credit with them in hope of gain.

4:16 [1] They never cease by all means to creep into favor, but when they obtain not, their greedy desires, they think themselves abused, as others have been in time past, and so care no more for him.

4:17 [1] That is, with what affection thou comest to hear the word of God.

[2] Meaning, of the wicked, which think to please God with common uses, and have neither faith nor repentance.

5:1 [1] Either in vowing or in praying: meaning, that we should use all reverence to Godward.

[2] He heareth thee not for thy many words' sake, or often repetitions, but considereth thy faith and servant mind.

5:3 [1] He speaketh of vows, which are approved by God's word, and serve to his glory.

5:5 [1] Cause not thyself to sin by vowing rashly: as they do which make a vow to live unmarried, and such like.

[2] That is, before God's messenger, when he shall examine thy doing, as though thy ignorance should be a just excuse.

5:7 [1] Meaning, that God will redress these things, and therefore we must depend upon him.

5:8 [1] The earth is to be preferred above all things which appertain to this life.

[2] Kings and Princes cannot maintain their estate without tillage, which thing commendeth the excellency of tillage.

11 The sleep of him that travaileth, *is* sweet, whether he eat little or much: but the [1]satiety of the rich will not suffer him to sleep.

12 There is an evil sickness *that* I have seen under the sun: *to wit*, riches [1]reserved to the owners thereof for their evil.

13 And these riches perish by evil travail, and he begetteth a son, and in his [1]hand *is* nothing.

14 [b]As he came forth of his mother's belly, he shall return naked to go as he came, and shall bear away nothing of his labor, which he hath caused to pass by his hand.

15 And this also is an evil sickness, *that* in all points as he came, so shall he go, and what profit hath he that he hath travailed for the [1]wind?

16 Also all his days he eateth in [1]darkness with much grief, and *in* his sorrow and anger.

17 Behold then, what I have seen good, that it is comely to [1]eat, and to drink, and to take pleasure in all his labor, wherein he travaileth under the sun, the *whole* number of the days of his life, which God giveth him: for this is his portion.

18 Also to every man to whom God hath given riches and treasures, and giveth him power to eat thereof, and to take his part, and to enjoy his labor: this is the gifts of God.

19 Surely he will not much remember the days of his [1]life, because God answereth to the joy of his heart.

6 *The miserable estate of him to whom God hath given riches, and not the grace to use them.*

1 There is an evil, which I saw under the sun, and it is much among men:

2 A man to whom God hath given riches and treasures and honor, and he wanteth nothing for his soul of all that he desireth: but [1]God giveth him not power to eat thereof, but a strange man shall eat it up: this is vanity, and this is an evil sickness.

3 If a man beget an hundred *children* and live many years, and the days of his years be multiplied: and his

b Job 1:21
1 Tim. 6:7

CHAPTER 7
a Job 14:2
Ps. 144:4
b Prov. 22:1

soul be not [1]satisfied with good things, and he be not [2]buried, I say that an untimely fruit is better than he.

4 For [1]he cometh into vanity, and goeth into darkness: and his name shall be covered with darkness.

5 Also he hath not seen the sun, nor known it: *therefore* this hath more rest than the other.

6 And if he had lived a thousand years twice told, and had seen no good, shall not all go to one place?

7 All the labor of man *is* for his mouth: yet the [1]soul is not filled.

8 For what hath the wise man more than the fool? what hath the poor that [1]knoweth how to walk before the living?

9 The [1]sight of the eye is better than to walk in the lusts: this also is vanity, and vexation of spirit.

10 What is that that hath been? the name thereof is now named: and it is known that it is man: and he cannot strive with him that is [1]stronger than he.

7 *Divers precepts to follow that which is good, and to avoid the contrary.*

1 Surely there be many things that increase vanity, *and* what availeth it a man?

2 For who knoweth what is [1]good for man in the life, *and* in the number of the days of the life of his vanity, seeing he maketh them as a [a]shadow? for who can show unto man what shall be after him under the sun?

3 [b]A good name *is better* than a good ointment, and the day of [1]death, than the day that one is born.

4 It is better to go to the house of [1]mourning, than to go to the house of feasting, because this is the end of all men: and the living shall lay it to his heart.

5 Anger is better than laughter: for by a sad look the heart is made better.

6 The heart of the wise *is* in the house of mourning: but the heart of fools *is* in the house of mirth.

7 Better it is to hear the rebuke of a wise man, than that a man should hear the song of fools.

8 For like the noise of the [1]thorns under the pot, so *is* the laughter of the fool: this also is vanity.

5:11 [1] That is, his great abundance of riches, or the surfeiting, which cometh by his great feeding.

5:12 [1] When covetous men heap up riches, which turn to their destruction.

5:13 [1] He doth not enjoy his father's riches.

5:15 [1] Meaning, in vain, and without profit.

5:16 [1] In affliction and grief of mind.

5:17 [1] Read Eccl. 3:22.

5:19 [1] He will take no great thought for the pains that he hath endured in time past.

6:2 [1] He showeth that it is the plague of God when the rich man hath not a liberal heart to use his riches.

6:3 [1] If he can never have enough.

[2] As we see oftentimes that the covetous man either falleth into crimes that deserve death, or is murdered or drowned or hangeth

himself, or such like, and so lacketh the honor of burial, which is the last office of humanity.

6:4 [1] Meaning, the untimely fruit whose life did neither profit or hurt any.

6:7 [1] His desire and affection.

6:8 [1] That knoweth to use his goods well in the judgment of men.

6:9 [1] To be content with that which God hath given, is better than to follow the desires that never can be satisfied.

6:10 [1] Meaning, God who will make him to feel that he is mortal.

7:2 [1] There is no state wherein man can live to have perfect quietness in this life.

7:3 [1] He speaketh thus after the judgment of the flesh, which thinketh death to be the end of all evils, or else, because that this corporal death is the entering into life everlasting.

7:4 [1] Where we may see the hand of God, and learn to examine our lives.

7:8 [1] Which crackle for a while and profit nothing.

9 Surely oppression maketh a wise man [1]mad: and the reward destroyeth the heart.

10 The [1]end of a thing is better than the beginning thereof, *and* the patient in spirit is better than the proud in spirit.

11 Be not thou of an hasty spirit to be angry: for anger resteth in the bosom of fools.

12 Say not thou, Why is it that the former days were better than these? for thou dost not inquire [1]wisely of this thing.

13 Wisdom is good with an [1]inheritance, and excellent to them that see the sun.

14 For *man shall rest* in the shadow of wisdom, and in the shadow of silver: but the excellency of the knowledge of wisdom giveth life to the possessors thereof.

15 Behold the work of God; for who can make 'straight that which he hath made crooked?

16 In the day of wealth be of good comfort, and in the day of affliction [1]consider: God also hath made this contrary to that, to the intent that man should find [2]nothing after him.

17 I have seen all things in the days of my vanity: there is a just man that perisheth in his [1]justice, and there is a wicked man that continueth long in his malice.

18 Be not thou just [1]overmuch, neither make thyself overwise: wherefore shouldest thou be desolate?

19 Be not thou wicked [1]overmuch, neither be thou foolish: wherefore shouldest thou perish not in thy time?

20 It is good that thou lay hold on [1]this: but yet withdraw not thine hand from [2]that: for he that feareth God shall come forth of them all.

21 Wisdom shall strengthen the wise men more than ten mighty princes that are in the city.

22 [d]Surely there is no man just in the earth that doeth good and sinneth not.

23 Give not thine [1]heart also to all the words that men speak, lest thou do hear thy servant cursing thee.

c Eccl. 1:15
d 1 Kings 8:36
2 Chron. 6:36
Prov. 20:9
1 John 1:8

24 For oftentimes also thine heart knoweth that thou likewise hast [1]cursed others.

25 All this have I proved by wisdom: I thought, I will be wise, but it went far from me.

26 It is far off, what may [1]it be? and it is a profound deepness, who can find it?

27 I have compassed about, *both* I and mine heart to know and to inquire and to search wisdom, and reason, and to know the wickedness of folly, and the foolishness of madness,

28 And I find more bitter than death the woman whose heart is *as* nets and snares, *and* her hands *as* bands: he that is good before God, shall be delivered from her, but the sinner shall be taken by her.

29 Behold, saith the Preacher, this have I found, *seeking* one by one to [1]find the count:

30 And yet my soul seeketh, but I find it not. I have found one man of a thousand: but a woman among them all have I not found.

31 Only lo, this have I found, that God hath made man righteous: but they have sought many [1]inventions.

8

2 *To obey Princes and Magistrates.*   17 *The works of God pass man's knowledge.*

1 Who is as the wise man? and who knoweth the interpretation of a thing? the wisdom of a man doth make his face [1]to shine: and [2]the strength of his face shall be changed.

2 *I advertise thee* to take heed to the [1]mouth of the king, and to the word of the oath of God.

3 [1]Haste not to go forth of his sight: stand not in an evil thing: for he will do whatsoever pleaseth him.

4 Where the word of the King is, *there is* power, and who shall say unto him, What doest thou?

5 He that keepeth the commandment, shall know none evil thing, and the heart of the wise shall know the [1]time, and judgment.

6 For to every purpose there is a time and judgment, because the [1]misery of man is great upon him.

7:9 [1] A man that is esteemed wise, when he falleth to oppression, becometh like a beast.

7:10 [1] He noteth their lightness which enterprise a thing and suddenly leave it off again.

7:12 [1] Murmur not against God when he sendeth adversities for man's sins.

7:13 [1] He answereth to them that esteem not wisdom except riches be joined therewith, showing that both are the gifts of God, but that wisdom is far more excellent, and may be without riches.

7:16 [1] Consider wherefore God doth send it and what may comfort thee.

[2] That man should be able to control nothing in his works.

7:17 [1] Meaning, that cruel tyrants put the godly to death and let the wicked go free.

7:18 [1] Boast not too much of thine own justice and wisdom.

7:19 [1] Tarry not long when thou art admonished to come out of the way of wickedness.

7:20 [1] To wit, on these admonitions that go before.

[2] Consider what desolation and destruction shall come, if thou do not obey them.

7:23 [1] Credit them not, neither care for them.

7:24 [1] Or, spoken evil of others.

7:26 [1] Meaning, wisdom.

7:29 [1] That is, to come to a conclusion.

7:31 [1] And so are cause of their own destruction.

8:1 [1] That is, doth get him favor and prosperity.

[2] Whereas before he was proud and arrogant, he shall become humble and meek.

8:2 [1] That is, that thou obey the king and keep the oath that thou hast made for the same cause.

8:3 [1] Withdraw not thyself lightly from the obedience of thy prince.

8:5 [1] That is, when time is to obey, and how far he should obey.

8:6 [1] Man of himself is miserable, and therefore ought to do nothing to increase the same, but to work all things by wisdom and counsel.

7 For he knoweth not that which shall be: for who can tell him when it shall be?

8 Man is not Lord [1]over the spirit to retain the spirit: neither hath he power in the day of death, nor deliverance in the battle, neither shall wickedness deliver the possessors thereof.

9 All this have I seen, and have given mine heart to every work which is wrought under the sun, *and I saw* a time that man ruleth over man to his own [1]hurt.

10 And likewise I saw the wicked buried, and [1]they returned, and they that came from the holy [2]place, were yet forgotten in the city, where they had done right: this also is vanity.

11 Because sentence against an evil work is not [1]executed speedily, therefore the heart of the children of men is fully set in them to do evil.

12 Though a sinner do evil an hundred times, and *God* prolongeth *his days*, yet I know that it shall be well with them that fear the Lord, and do reverence before him.

13 But it shall not be well to the wicked, neither shall he prolong *his* days: *he shall be* like a shadow, because he feareth not before God.

14 There is a vanity, which is done upon the earth, that there be righteous men to whom it cometh according to the [1]work of the wicked: and there be wicked men to whom it cometh according to the work of the just: I thought also that this is vanity.

15 And I praised joy, for there is no goodness to man under the sun, save [1]to eat and to drink and to rejoice: for this is adjoined to his labor the days of his life that God hath given him under the sun.

16 When I applied mine heart to know wisdom, and to behold the business that is done on earth, that neither day nor night the eyes of man take sleep,

17 Then I beheld the whole work of God, that man cannot find out the work that is wrought under the sun: for the which man laboreth to seek it, and cannot find it: yea, and though the wise man think to know it, he cannot find it.

9 1 By no outward thing can man know whom God loveth or hateth.   12 No man knoweth his end.   16 Wisdom

CHAPTER 9
[a] Eccl. 5:18

excelleth strength.

1 I have surely given mine heart to all this, and to declare all this, that the just, and the wise, and their works *are* in the hand of God: and no man knoweth either love or [1]hatred of all *that is* before them.

2 All things *come* alike to all: and the same condition *is* to the just and to the wicked, to the good and to the pure, and to the polluted, and to him that sacrificeth, and to him that sacrificeth not: as *is* the good, so *is* the sinner, he that sweareth, as he that feareth an oath.

3 This is evil among all that is done under the sun, that there is one [1]condition to all, and also the heart of the sons of men is full of evil, and madness *is* in their hearts while they live, and after that, *they go* to the dead.

4 Surely whosoever is joined to all the living, there is hope: for it is better to a [1]living dog, than to a dead lion.

5 For the living know that they shall die, but the dead know nothing at all: neither have they anymore a reward: for their remembrance is forgotten.

6 Also their love and their hatred, and their envy is now perished, and they have no more portion forever, in all that is done under the sun.

7 Go, eat thy bread with joy, and drink thy wine with a cheerful heart: for God now [1]accepteth thy works.

8 At all times let thy garments be [1]white, and let not oil be lacking upon thine head.

9 [1,a]Rejoice with the wife whom thou hast loved all the days of the life of thy vanity, which *God* hath given thee under the sun all the days of thy vanity: for this is thy portion in the life, and in thy travail wherein thou laborest under the sun.

10 All that thine hand shall find to do, do it with *all* thy power: for there is neither work nor invention, nor knowledge, nor wisdom in the grave whither thou goest.

11 I returned, and I saw under the sun that the race is not to the swift, nor the battle to the strong, nor yet bread to the wise, nor also riches to men of understanding, neither yet favor to men of knowledge:

8:8 [1] Man hath no power to save his own life, and therefore must not rashly cast himself into danger.

8:9 [1] As cometh ofttimes to tyrants and wicked rulers.

8:10 [1] That is, others as wicked as they.

[2] They that feared God and worshipped him according as he had appointed.

8:11 [1] Where justice is delayed, there sin reigneth.

8:14 [1] Which are punished as though they were wicked, as Eccl. 7:17.

8:15 [1] Read Eccl. 3:22.

9:1 [1] Meaning, what things he ought to choose or refuse: or man knoweth not by these outward things, that is, by prosperity or adversity, whom God doth favor or hate, for he sendeth them as well to the wicked as to the godly.

9:3 [1] In outward things, as riches and poverty, sickness and health, there is no difference between the godly and the wicked: but the difference is that the godly are assured by faith of God's favor and assistance.

9:4 [1] He noteth the Epicureans and carnal men, which made their belly their god, and had no pleasure, but in this life, wishing rather to be an abased and vile person in this life, than a man of authority, and so to die, which is meant by the dog and lion.

9:7 [1] They flatter themselves to be in God's favor, because they have all things in abundance.

9:8 [1] Rejoice, be merry, and spare for no cost, thus speak the wicked belly-gods.

9:9 [1] Hebrew, *regard the life*.

but time and [1]chance cometh to them all.

12 For neither doth man know his [1]time, *but* as the fishes which are taken in an evil net, and as the birds that are caught in the snare: so are the children of men snared in the evil time, when it falleth upon them suddenly.

13 I have also seen this wisdom under the sun, and it is great unto me.

14 A little city and few men in it, and a great King came against it, and compassed it about, and built forts against it.

15 And there was found therein a poor and wise man, and he delivered the city by his wisdom, but none remembered this poor man.

16 Then said I, Better is wisdom than strength: yet the wisdom of the poor is despised, and his words are not heard.

17 The words of the wise are more heard in quietness, than the cry of him that ruleth among fools.

18 Better is wisdom than weapons of war: but one sinner destroyeth much good.

10

1 The difference of foolishness and wisdom. 11 A slanderer is like a serpent that cannot be charmed. 16 Of foolish kings and drunken princes, 17 And of good Kings and Princes.

1 Dead flies cause to stink, and putrefy the ointment of the apothecary: *so doth* a little folly him that is in estimation for wisdom, *and* for glory.

2 The heart of a [1]wise man *is* at his right hand: but the heart of a fool *is* at his left hand.

3 And also when the fool goeth by the way, his heart faileth, and he [1]telleth unto all that he is a fool.

4 If the [1]spirit of him that ruleth, rise up against thee, leave not thy place: for gentleness pacifieth great sins.

5 There is an evil *that* I have seen under the sun, as an [1]error that proceedeth from the face of him that ruleth.

6 Folly is set in great excellency, and the [1]rich sit in the low place.

7 I have seen servants on horses, and princes walking as servants on the ground.

8 [a]He that diggeth a pit, shall fall into it, and he

CHAPTER 10
[a] Ps. 7:15
Prov. 26:27

that breaketh the hedge, a serpent shall bite him.

9 He that removeth stones, shall hurt himself thereby, *and* he that cutteth wood, shall be in danger thereby.

10 If the iron be blunt, and one hath not whet the edge, he must then put to more [1]strength: but the excellency to direct a thing *is* wisdom.

11 If the serpent bite, when he is not charmed: no better is a babbler.

12 The words of the mouth of a wise man *have* grace: but the lips of a fool devour himself.

13 The beginning of the words of his mouth *is* foolishness, and the latter end of his mouth *is* wicked madness.

14 For the fool multiplieth words, *saying*, Man knoweth not what shall be: and who can tell him what shall be after him?

15 The labor of the foolish doth weary him: for he knoweth not to go into the [1]city.

16 Woe to thee, O land, when thy king *is* a [1]child, and thy princes [2]eat in the morning.

17 Blessed art thou, O land, when thy King *is* the son [1]of nobles, and thy princes eat in time, for strength and not for drunkenness.

18 By slothfulness the roof of the house goeth to decay, and by the idleness of the hands the house droppeth through.

19 They prepare bread for laughter, and wine comforteth the living, but silver answereth to all.

20 Curse not the king, no not in thy thought, neither curse the rich in thy bed chamber: for the [1]fowl of the heaven shall carry the voice, and that which hath wings, shall declare the matter.

11

1 To be liberal to the poor. 4 Not to doubt of God's providence. 8 All worldly prosperity is but vanity. 9 God will judge all.

1 Cast thy bread upon the [1]waters: for after many days thou shalt find it.

2 Give a portion to seven, and also to eight: for thou knowest not what evil shall be upon the earth.

3 If the [1]clouds be full, they will pour forth rain upon the earth: and if the [2]tree do fall toward the

---

9:11 [1] Thus the worldlings say to prove that all things are lawful for them, and attribute that to chance and fortune, which is done by the providence of God.

9:12 [1] That is, he doth not foresee what shall come.

10:2 [1] So that he doeth all things well and justly, where as the fool doeth the contrary.

10:3 [1] By his doings he betrayeth himself.

10:4 [1] If thy superior be angry with thee, be thou discrete, and not moved.

10:5 [1] Meaning, that it is an evil thing when they that are in authority, fail and do not their duty.

10:6 [1] They that are rich in wisdom and virtue.

10:10 [1] Without wisdom whatsoever a man taketh in hand, turneth

to his own hurt.

10:15 [1] The ignorance and beastliness of the wicked is such that they know not common things, and yet will they discuss high matters.

10:16 [1] That is, without wisdom and counsel.
[2] Are given to their lusts, and pleasures.

10:17 [1] Meaning, when he is noble for virtue and wisdom, and with the gifts of God.

10:20 [1] Thou canst not work evil so secretly, but it shall be known.

11:1 [1] That is, be liberal to the poor, and though it seem to be as a thing ventured on the sea, yet it shall bring thee profit.

11:3 [1] As the clouds that are full, pour out rain, so the rich that have abundance, must distribute it liberally.
[2] He exhorteth to be liberal while we live: for after, there is no power.

South, or toward the North, in the place that the tree falleth, there it shall be.

4   He that observeth the [1]wind shall not sow, and he that regardeth the clouds, shall not reap.

5   As thou knowest not which is the way of the spirit, *nor* how the bones *do grow* in the womb of her that is with child: so thou knowest not the work of God that worketh all.

6   In the morning sow thy seed, and in the evening let not thine hand [1]rest: for thou knowest not whether shall prosper, this or [2]that, or whether both shall be a like good.

7   Surely the light is a pleasant thing: and it is a good thing to the eyes to see the sun.

8   Though a man live many years, *and* in them all he rejoice, yet he shall remember the days of [1]darkness, because they are many, all that cometh *is* vanity.

9   [1]Rejoice, O young man, in thy youth, and let thine heart cheer thee in the days of thy youth: and walk in the ways of thine heart, and in the sight of thine eyes: but know that for all these things, God will bring thee to judgment.

10   Therefore take away [1]grief out of thine heart, and cause evil [2]to depart from thy flesh: for childhood and youth *are* vanity.

12   *1 To think on God in youth, and not to defer till age.   7 The soul returneth to God.   11 Wisdom is the gift of God, and consisteth in fearing him and keeping his commandments.*

1   Remember now thy Creator in the days of thy youth, while the evil days come not, nor the years approach, wherein thou shalt say, I have no pleasure in them:

2   While the sun is not dark, nor the light, nor the moon, nor the stars, nor the [1]clouds return after the rain.

3   When the [1]keepers of the house shall tremble, and the [2]strong men shall bow themselves, and the [3]grinders shall cease, because they are few, and they wax dark that [4]look out by the windows:

4   And the [1]doors shall be shut without by the base sound of the [2]grinding, and he shall rise up at the voice of the [3]bird: and all the [4]daughters of singing shall be abased:

5   Also they shall be afraid of the [1]high thing, and fear *shall be* in the [2]way, and the almond tree shall [3]flourish, and the [4]grasshopper shall be a burden, and concupiscence shall be driven away: for man goeth to the house of his age, and the mourners go about in the street.

6   While the [1]silver cord is not lengthened, nor the golden [2]ewer broken, nor the [3]pitcher broken at the [4]well, nor the [5]wheel broken at the [6]cistern,

7   And dust return to the earth as it was, and the [1]spirit return to God that gave it.

8   Vanity of vanities, saith the Preacher, all *is* vanity.

9   And the more wise the Preacher was, the more he taught the people knowledge, and caused them to hear, and searched forth, and prepared many parables.

10   The Preacher sought to find out pleasant words, and an upright writing, *even* the words of truth.

11   The words of the wise are like goads, and like nails [1]fastened by the masters of the assemblies, *which* are given by one [2]pastor.

12   And of other things beside these, my son, take thou heed: for there is none end in making many [1]books, and much reading is a weariness of the flesh.

13   Let us hear the end of all: fear God and keep his commandments: for this is the whole *duty* of man.

14   For God will bring every work unto judgment, with every secret thing, whether it be good or evil.

11:4 [1] He that feareth inconveniences, when necessity requireth, shall never do his duty.

11:6 [1] Be not weary of well doing.

[2] That is, which of thy works are most agreeable to God.

11:8 [1] That is, of affliction and trouble.

11:9 [1] He derideth them that set their delight in worldly pleasures, as though God would not call count.

11:10 [1] To wit, anger, and envy.

[2] Meaning, carnal lusts, whereunto youth is given.

12:2 [1] Before thou come to a continual misery: for when the clouds remain after the rain, man's grief is increased.

12:3 [1] The hands, which keep the body.

[2] The legs.

[3] The teeth.

[4] The eyes.

12:4 [1] The lips, or mouth.

[2] When the jaws, shall scarce open, and not be able to chew anymore.

[3] He shall not be able to sleep.

[4] That is, the wind pipes, or the ears shall be deaf and not able to hear singing.

12:5 [1] To climb high because of their weakness, or they stoop down, as though they were afraid, lest anything should hit them.

[2] They shall tremble as they go, as though they were afraid.

[3] Their head shall be as white as the blossoms of an almond tree.

[4] They shall be able to bear nothing.

12:6 [1] Meaning, the marrow of the backbone and the sinews.

[2] The little skin that covereth the brain, which is in color like gold.

[3] That is, the veins.

[4] Meaning, the liver.

[5] Which is the head.

[6] That is, the heart, out of which the head draweth the powers of life.

12:7 [1] The soul incontinently goeth either to joy or torment, and sleepeth not as the wicked imagine.

12:11 [1] Which are well applied by the ministers, whom he calleth masters.

[2] That is, by God.

12:12 [1] These things cannot be comprehended in books or learned by study, but God must instruct thine heart that thou mayest only know that wisdom is the true felicity, and the way thereunto is to fear God.

AN [1]EXCELLENT

SONG

WHICH WAS SOLOMON'S

---

1 1 *The familiar talk and mystical communication of the spiritual love between Jesus Christ and his Church.* 5 *The domestical enemies that persecute the Church.*

1 Let [1]him kiss me with the kisses of his mouth: for thy love is better than wine.

2 Because of the [1]savor of thy good ointments, thy name *is as* an ointment poured out: therefore the [2]virgins love thee.

3 [1]Draw me: we will run after thee: the King hath brought me into his [2]chambers: we will rejoice and be glad in thee: we will remember thy love more than wine: the righteous do love thee.

4 I am [1]black, O daughters of Jerusalem, but comely, as the tents of [2]Kedar, *and* as the [3]curtains of Solomon.

5 Regard ye me not because I am [1]black: for the [2]sun hath looked upon me. The [3]sons of my mother were angry against me: they made me the keeper of the vines: but I [4]kept not mine own vine.

6 Show me, [1]O *thou* whom my soul loveth, where thou feedest, where thou liest at noon: for why should I be as she that turneth aside to the stocks of [2]thy companions?

7 [1]If thou know not, O thou the fairest among women, get thee forth by the steps of the flock, and feed thy kids by the tents of the shepherds.

8 I have compared thee, O my love, to the troupe of horses in the [1]chariots of Pharaoh.

9 Thy cheeks are comely with rows of stones, and thy neck with chains.

10 We will make thee borders of gold with floods of silver.

11 [1]While the King was at his repast, my spikenard gave the smell thereof.

12 My well-beloved *is as* a bundle of myrrh unto me: he shall lie between my [1]breasts.

13 My well-beloved *is as* a cluster of camphire unto me in the vines of En Gedi.

14 My love, behold, thou art [1]fair: behold, thou art fair: thine eyes *are like* the doves.

15 My well-beloved, behold, thou art fair, and pleasant: also our [1]bed is green.

16 The beams of our house *are* cedars, our rafters *are* of fir.

2 3 *The Church desireth to rest under the shadow of Christ.* 8 *She heareth his voice.* 14 *She is compared to the dove.* 15 *And the enemies to the foxes.*

1 I am the rose of the field, *and* the lily of the valleys.

2 Like a lily among the thorns, so *is* my [1]love among the daughters.

3 [1]Like the apple tree among the trees of the forest, so *is* my well-beloved among the sons *of men*: under his shadow had I delight, and sat down: and his fruit *was* sweet unto my mouth.

Title [1] Hebrew, *a song of songs*: so called because it is the chiefest of those 1005, which Solomon made, as is mentioned, I Kings 4:32.

1:1 [1] This is spoken in the person of the Church, or of the faithful soul inflamed with the desire of Christ, whom she loveth.

1:2 [1] The feeling of thy great benefits.

[2] They that are pure in heart and conversation.

1:3 [1] The faithful confess that they cannot come to Christ, except they be drawn.

[2] Meaning, the secret joy that is not known to the world.

1:4 [1] The Church confesseth her spots and sin, but hath confidence in the favor of Christ.

[2] Kedar was Ishmael's son, of whom came the Arabians that dwelt in tents.

[3] Which within were all set with precious stones and Jewels.

1:5 [1] Consider not the Church by the outward appearance.

[2] The corruption of nature through sin and afflictions.

[3] Mine own brethren, which should have most favored me.

[4] She confesseth her own negligence.

1:6 [1] The spouse feeling her fault fleeth to her husband only for succor.

[2] Whom thou hast called to the dignity of pastors, and they set forth their own dreams instead of thy doctrine.

1:7 [1] Christ speaketh to his Church, bidding them that are ignorant, to go to the pastors to learn.

1:8 [1] For thy spiritual beauty and excellency there was no worldly treasure to be compared unto thee.

1:11 [1] The Church rejoiceth that she is admitted to the company of Christ.

1:12 [1] He shall be most dear unto me.

1:14 [1] Christ accepteth his Church, and commendeth her beauty.

1:15 [1] That is, the heart of the faithful, wherein Christ dwelleth by his Spirit.

2:2 [1] Thus Christ preferreth his Church above all other things.

2:3 [1] The spouse testifieth her great desire toward her husband, but her strength faileth her, and therefore she desireth to be comforted, and felt it.

4   He brought me into the wine cellar, and love *was* his banner over me.

5   Stay me with flagons, and comfort me with apples: for I am sick of love.

6   His left hand *is* under mine head, and his right hand doth embrace me.

7   [1]I charge you, O daughters of Jerusalem, by the roes and by the hinds of the field, that ye stir not up, nor waken *my* love, until she please.

8   [1]*It is* the voice of my well-beloved: behold, he cometh leaping by the mountains, and skipping by the hills.

9   My well-beloved is like a roe, or a young hart: lo, he [1]standeth behind our wall, looking forth of the windows, showing himself through the [2]grates.

10   My well-beloved spake and said unto me, Arise, my love, my fair one, and come thy way.

11   For behold, [1]winter is past: the rain is changed, and is gone away.

12   The flowers appear in the earth: the time of the singing of birds is come, and the voice of the turtle is heard in our land.

13   The fig tree hath brought forth her young figs: and the vines with *their* small grapes have cast a savor: arise my love, my fair one, and come away.

14   My dove, that art in the [1]holes of the rock, in the secret places of the stairs, show me thy sight, let me hear thy voice: for thy voice is sweet, and thy sight comely.

15   Take us the foxes, the [1]little foxes, which destroy the vines: for our vines *have* small grapes.

16   My well-beloved *is* mine, and I am his: he feedeth among the lilies,

17   Until the daybreak, and the shadows flee away: return, my well-beloved, *and* be like a [1]roe, or a young hart upon the mountains of Bether.

3   1 *The Church desireth to be joined inseparably to Christ her husband.   6 Her deliverance out of the wilderness.*

1   In my bed by [1]night I sought him that my soul loved: I sought him, but I found him not.

2   I will rise *therefore* now, and go about in the city, by the streets, and by the open places, *and* will [1]seek him that my soul loveth: I sought him, but I found him not.

3   The [1]watchmen that went about the city, found me: *to whom I said*, Have you seen him whom my soul loveth?

4   When I had passed a little from them, then I found him whom my soul loved: I took hold on him, and left him not, till I had brought him unto my mother's house, into the chamber of her that conceived me.

5   [1]I charge you, O daughters of Jerusalem, by the roes and by the hinds of the field, that ye stir not up, nor waken *my* love until she please.

6   Who is she that cometh up out of the [1]wilderness like pillars of smoke perfumed with myrrh and incense, *and* with all the [2]spices of the merchant?

7   Behold his [1]bed, which is Solomon's: threescore strong men *are* round about it, of the valiant men of Israel.

8   They all handle the sword, *and are* expert in war, everyone *hath* his sword upon his thigh for the fear [1]by night.

9   King Solomon made himself a [1]palace of the trees of Lebanon.

10   He made the pillars thereof of silver, *and* the pavement thereof of gold, the hangings thereof of purple, whose midst *was* paved with the love of the daughters of Jerusalem.

11   Come forth, ye [1]daughters of Zion, and behold the King Solomon with the [2]crown, wherewith his mother crowned him in the day of his marriage, and in the day of the gladness of his heart.

4   1 *The praises of the Church.   7 She is without blemish in his sight.   9 The love of Christ towards her.*

1   Behold, thou art [1]fair, my love: behold, thou art fair: thine eyes *are like* the doves: among thy locks

---

2:7 [1] Christ chargeth them which have to do in the Church as it were by a solemn oath, that they trouble not the quietness thereof.

2:8 [1] This is spoken of Christ, who took upon his our nature to come to help his Church.

2:9 [1] Forasmuch as his divinity was hid under the cloak of our flesh.

[2] So that we cannot have full knowledge of him in this life.

2:11 [1] That is, sin and error is driven back by the coming of Christ, which is here described by the spring time, when all things flourish.

2:14 [1] Thou that art ashamed of thy sins, come and show thyself unto me.

2:15 [1] Suppress the heretics while they are young, that is, when they begin to show their malice, and destroy the vine of the Lord.

2:17 [1] The Church desireth Christ to be most ready to help her in all dangers.

3:1 [1] The Church by night, that is, in troubles, seeketh to Christ, but is not incontinently heard.

3:2 [1] Showing that although we be not heard at the first, yet we must still continue in prayer, till we feel comfort.

3:3 [1] Which declareth that we must seek unto all of whom we hope to have any succor.

3:5 [1] Read Song 2:7.

3:6 [1] This is referred to the Church of Israel, which was led by the wilderness forty years.

[2] Hebrew, *powder*.

3:7 [1] By the bed is meant the Temple which Solomon made.

3:8 [1] He alludeth to the watch which kept the Temple.

3:9 [1] Or, chariot.

3:11 [1] All ye that are of the number of the faithful.

[2] Christ become man was crowned by the love of God with the glorious crown of his divinity.

4:1 [1] Because Christ delighteth in his Church, he commendeth all that is in her.

ᵃthine hair is like the ²flock of goats, which look down from the mountain of Gilead.

2 Thy teeth *are* like a flock of *sheep* in good order, which go up from the washing: which every one brings out twins, and none is barren among them.

3 Thy lips are like a thread of scarlet, and thy talk is comely: thy temples *are* within thy locks as a piece of a pomegranate.

4 Thy neck is as the tower of David built for defense: a thousand shields hang therein, *and* all the targets of the strong men.

5 Thy two ¹breasts *are* as two young roes that are twins, feeding among the lilies.

6 Until the day break, and the shadows fly away, I will go into the mountain of myrrh, and to the mountain of incense.

7 Thou art all fair my love, and there is no spot in thee.

8 ¹Come with me from Lebanon, *my* spouse, *even* with me from Lebanon, *and* look from the top of Amana, from the top of Senir, and Hermon, from the dens of the lions, *and* from the mountains of the leopards.

9 My ¹sister, *my* spouse, thou hast wounded mine heart: thou hast wounded mine heart with one of thine ²eyes, *and* with a chain of thy neck.

10 My sister, *my* Spouse, how fair is thy love? how much better is thy love than wine? and the savor of thine ointments than all spices?

11 Thy ¹lips, *my* Spouse, drop *as* honeycombs: honey and milk are under thy tongue, and the savor of thy garment *is* as the savor of Lebanon.

12 My sister, my spouse *is as* a garden enclosed, as a spring shut up, *and* a fountain sealed up.

13 Thy plants *are as* an orchard of pomegranates with sweet fruits, *as* camphire, spikenard,

14 *Even* spikenard, and saffron: calamus, and cinnamon, with all the trees of incense, myrrh and aloes, with all the chief spices.

15 ¹O fountain of the gardens, O well of living waters, and the springs of Lebanon.

CHAPTER 4
ᵃ Song 6:4

16 Arise, O ¹North, and come, O South, *and* blow on my garden, that the spices thereof may flow out: let my well-beloved come to his garden, and eat his pleasant fruit.

5 *1 Christ calleth his Church to the participation of all his treasures. 2 She heareth his voice. 3 She confesseth her nakedness. 10 She praiseth Christ her husband.*

1 I am come into my ¹garden, my sister, my spouse, I gathered my myrrh with my spice: I ate mine honeycomb with mine honey, I drank my wine with my milk: eat, O friends, drink, and make you merry, O well-beloved.

2 ¹I sleep, but mine heart waketh, *it is* the voice of my well-beloved that knocketh, *saying,* Open unto me, my sister, my love, my dove, my undefiled: for mine head is full of dew, and my locks with the drops of the ²night.

3 I have put off my ¹coat, how shall I defile [put] it on? I have washed my feet, how shall I defile them?

4 My well-beloved put in his hand by the hole *of the door,* and ¹mine heart was affectioned toward him.

5 I rose up to open to my well-beloved, and mine hands did drop down myrrh, and my ¹fingers pure myrrh upon the handles of the bar.

6 I opened to my well-beloved: but my well-beloved was gone and past: mine heart was gone when he did speak: I sought him, but I could not find him: I called him, but he answered me not.

7 The ¹watchmen that were about the city, found me: they smote me, *and* wounded me: the watchmen of the walls took away my veil from me.

8 I charge you, ¹O daughters of Jerusalem, if you find my well-beloved, that you tell him that I am sick of love.

9 ¹O the fairest among women, what is thy well-beloved more than *other* well-beloved? what is thy well-beloved more than *another* lover, that thou dost

---

² He hath respect to the multitude of the faithful, which are many in number.

4:5 ¹ Wherein are knowledge and zeal two precious jewels.

4:8 ¹ Christ promiseth his Church to call his faithful from all the corners of the world.

4:9 ¹ Christ calleth his Church sister, in respect that he had taken the flesh of man.

² In that he made his Church beautiful and rich, he loved his gifts in her.

4:11 ¹ Because of thy confession and thanksgiving.

4:15 ¹ The Church confesseth that all her glory and beauty cometh of Christ, who is the true fountain of all grace.

4:16 ¹ She desireth Christ to comfort her and to pour the graces of his Spirit upon her, which Spirit is meant by the North and South wind.

5:1 ¹ The garden signifieth the kingdom of Christ, where he prepar-

eth the banquet for his elect.

5:2 ¹ The spouse saith that she is troubled with the cares of worldly things, which is meant by sleeping.

² Declaring the long patience of the Lord toward sinners.

5:3 ¹ The spouse confesseth her nakedness, and that of herself she hath nothing, or seeing that she is once made clean, she promiseth not to defile herself again.

5:4 ¹ Hebrew, *my bowels were moved towards him.*

5:5 ¹ The spouse which should be anointed of Christ, shall not find him if she think to anoint him with her good works.

5:7 ¹ These are the false teachers, which wound the conscience with their traditions.

5:8 ¹ She asketh of them which are godly (forasmuch as the law and salvation should come out of Zion and Jerusalem) that they would direct her to Christ.

5:9 ¹ Thus say they of Jerusalem.

so charge us?

10 My well-beloved is white and ruddy, the chiefest of ten thousand.

11 His [1]head is as fine gold, his locks curled, and black as a raven.

12 His eyes are like doves upon the rivers of waters, which are washed with milk, and remain by the full vessels.

13 His cheeks are as a bed of spices, and as sweet flowers, and his lips like lilies dropping down pure myrrh.

14 His hands as rings of gold set with the [1]chrysolite, his belly like white ivory covered with sapphires.

15 His legs are as pillars of marble set upon sockets of fine gold: his countenance as Lebanon, excellent as the cedars.

16 His mouth is as sweet things, and he is wholly delectable: this is my well-beloved, and this is my lover, O daughters of Jerusalem.

17 [1]O the fairest among women, whither is thy well-beloved gone? whither is thy well-beloved turned aside, that we may seek him with thee?

6

1 The Church assureth herself of the love of Christ. 3 The praises of the Church. 8 She is but one and undefiled.

1 My well-beloved is gone down into his [1]garden to the beds of spices, to feed in the gardens, and to gather lilies.

2 I am my well-beloved's, and my well-beloved is mine, who feedeth among the lilies.

3 Thou art beautiful, my love, as [1]Tirzah, comely as Jerusalem, terrible as an army with banners.

4 [1]Turn away thine eyes from me: for they overcome me: [a]thine hair is like a flock of goats, which look down from Gilead.

5 Thy teeth are like a flock of sheep, which go up from the washing, which every one bring out twins, and none is barren among them.

6 Thy temples are within thy locks as a piece of a pomegranate.

7 There are [1]threescore Queens, and fourscore concubines, and of the damsels without number.

8 But my dove is alone, and my undefiled, she

CHAPTER 6
[a] Song 4:1

is the only daughter of her mother, and she is dear to her that bare her: the daughters have seen her, and counted her blessed: even the Queens and the concubines, and they have praised her.

9 [1]Who is she that looketh forth as the morning, fair as the moon, pure as the sun, terrible as an army with banners!

10 I went down to the [1]garden of nuts, to see the fruits of the valley, to see if the vine budded, and if the pomegranates flourished.

11 [1]I knew nothing, my soul set me [2]as the chariots of my noble people.

12 Return, return, O [1]Shulamite, return: return that we may behold thee. What shall you see in the Shulamite, but as the company of an army?

7

1 The beauty of the Church in all her members. 10 She is assured of Christ's love towards her.

1 How beautiful are thy [1]goings with shoes, O prince's daughter! the joints of thy thighs are like jewels: the work of the hand of a cunning workman.

2 Thy navel is as a round cup that wanteth not liquor: thy belly is as an heap of wheat compassed about with lilies.

3 [1]Thy two breasts are as two young roes that are twins.

4 Thy neck is like a tower of ivory; thine eyes are like the fish pools in Heshbon by the gate of Bath Rabbim: thy nose is as the tower of Lebanon that looketh toward Damascus.

5 Thine head upon thee is as scarlet, and the bush of thine head like purple: the king is tied [1]in the [2]rafters.

6 How fair art thou, and how pleasant art thou, O my love, in pleasures!

7 This thy stature is like a palm tree, and thy breasts like clusters.

8 I said, I will go up into the palm tree, I will take hold of her boughs: thy breasts shall now be like the clusters of the vine: and the savor of thy nose like apples,

9 And the roof of thy mouth like good wine, which goeth straight to my well-beloved, and causeth

---

5:11 [1] She describeth Christ to be of perfect beauty and comeliness.
5:14 [1] Hebrew, Tarshish.
5:17 [1] Hearing of the excellency of Christ, the faithful desire to know how to find him.
6:1 [1] That is, is conversant here in earth among men.
6:3 [1] Which was a fair and strong city, 1 Kings 14:17.
6:4 [1] This declareth the exceeding love of Christ toward his Church.
6:7 [1] Meaning, that the gifts are infinite which Christ giveth to his Church: or that his faithful are many in number
6:9 [1] He showeth that the beginning of the Church was small, but that it grew up to a great multitude.

6:10 [1] He went down into the Synagogue to see what fruits came of the Law, and the Prophets.
6:11 [1] I found nothing but rebellion.
    [2] Or, set me on the chariots of my willing people.
6:12 [1] O ye people of Jerusalem: for Jerusalem was called Salem which signifieth peace.
7:1 [1] He describeth the comely beauty of the Church in every part, which is to be understood spiritually.
7:3 [1] Read Song 4:5.
7:5 [1] He delighteth to come near thee, and to be in thy company.
    [2] Or, galleries.

the lips of the ancient to speak.

10 [1]I am my well-beloved's, and his desire is toward me.

11 Come my well-beloved, let us go forth into the field: let us remain in the villages.

12 Let us get up early to the vines, let us see if the [1]vine flourish, *whither* it hath budded the small grape, *or whither* the pomegranates flourish: there will I give thee my love.

13 The mandrakes have given a smell, and in our gates are all sweet things, new and old: my well-beloved, I have kept *them* for thee.

8

2 The Church will be taught by Christ.   3 She is upheld by him.   6 The vehement love wherewith Christ loveth her.   11 She is the vine that bringeth forth fruit to the spiritual Solomon, which is Jesus Christ.

1 Oh [1]that thou werest as my brother that sucked the breasts of my mother: I would find thee without, I would kiss thee, then they should not despise [2]thee.

2 I will lead thee *and* bring thee into my mother's house: *there* thou shalt teach me: *and* I will cause thee to drink spiced wine, *and* new wine of the pomegranate.

3 [1]His left hand *shall be* under mine head, and his right hand shall embrace me.

4 [1]I charge you, O daughters of Jerusalem, that you stir not up, nor waken *my* love until she please.

5 (Who is this that cometh up out of the wilderness, leaning upon her well-beloved?) I raised thee up under an apple tree: there the mother conceived thee: there she conceived that bare thee.

6 [1]Set me as a seal on thine heart, *and* as a signet upon thine arm: for love *is* strong as death: jealousy is cruel as the grave: the coals thereof *are* fiery coals, *and* a vehement flame.

7 Much water cannot quench love, neither can the floods drown it: if a man should give all the substance of his house for love, they would greatly contemn it.

8 [1]We have a little sister, and she hath no breasts: what shall we do for our sister when she shall be spoken for?

9 [1]If she be a wall, we will build upon her a silver palace: and if she be a door, we will keep her in with boards of cedar.

10 [1]I am a wall, and my breasts *are* as towers: then was I in his eyes as one that findeth peace.

11 [1]Solomon had a vine in Baal Hamon: he gave the vineyard unto keepers: everyone bringeth for the fruit thereof a thousand *pieces* of silver.

12 *But* my vineyard which is mine, *is* before me: to thee, O Solomon, *appertaineth* a thousand *pieces of silver*, and two hundred to them that keep the fruit thereof.

13 O thou that dwellest in the [1]gardens, the companions hearken unto thy voice: cause me to hear it.

14 O my well-beloved, [1]flee away and be like unto the roe, or to the young hart upon the mountains of spices.

7:10 [1] This the spouse speaketh.
7:12 [1] If the people that are called to Christ, bring forth any fruit.
8:1 [1] The Church called of the Gentiles, speaketh thus to the Church of Jerusalem.
    [2] Or, me.
8:3 [1] Read Song 2:6.
8:4 [1] Read Song 3:5.
8:6 [1] The spouse desireth Christ to be joined in perpetual love with him.
8:8 [1] The Jewish Church speaketh this of the Church of the Gentiles.
8:9 [1] If she be sure and fast, she is meet for the husband to dwell in.
8:10 [1] The Church promiseth fidelity and constancy.
8:11 [1] This is the vineyard of the Lord hired out, Matt. 21:33.
8:13 [1] Christ dwelleth in his Church, whose voice the faithful hear.
8:14 [1] The Church desireth Christ that if he depart from them, yet that he would haste to help them in their troubles.

ISAIAH

1 *2 Isaiah reproveth the Jews of their ingratitude and stubbornness, that neither for benefits nor punishments would amend. 11 He showed why their sacrifices are rejected, and wherein God's true service standeth. 24 He prophesieth of the destruction of Jerusalem, 25 and of the restitution thereof.*

1 A ¹vision of Isaiah, the son of Amoz, which he saw ²concerning Judah and Jerusalem, in the days of ³Uzziah, Jotham, Ahaz, *and* Hezekiah Kings of Judah.

2 Hear, O ¹heavens, and hearken, O earth: for the Lord hath said, I have nourished and brought up ²children, but they have rebelled against me.

3 The ¹ox knoweth his owner, and the ass his master's crib: *but* Israel hath not known: my people hath not understood.

4 Ah, sinful nation, a people laden with iniquity: a ¹seed of the wicked, corrupt children: they have forsaken the Lord: they have provoked the ²Holy one of Israel to anger: they are gone backward.

5 Wherefore should ye be ¹smitten anymore? for ye fall away more and more: the whole ²head is sick, and the whole heart is heavy.

6 From the ¹sole of the foot unto the head, there *is* nothing whole therein, *but* wounds and swelling, and sores full of corruption: they have not been wrapped, ²nor bound up nor mollified with oil.

7 Your land is waste: your cities *are* burnt with fire: strangers devour your land in your presence, and *it is* desolate like the overthrow of ¹strangers.

8 And the daughter of ¹Zion shall remain like a cottage in a vineyard, like a lodge in a garden of cucumbers, *and* like a besieged city.

9 Except the Lord of hosts ¹had reserved unto us even a small remnant, we should have been ²as Sodom, *and* should have been like unto Gomorrah.

10 Hear the word of the Lord, O ¹princes of Sodom: hearken unto the Law of our God, O people of Gomorrah.

11 What have I to do with the multitude of your sacrifices, saith the Lord? I am full of the burnt offerings of rams, and of the fat of fed beasts: and I ¹desire not the blood of bullocks, nor of lambs, nor of goats.

12 When ye come to appear before me, who required this of your hands to tread in my courts?

13 Bring no more oblations, ¹in vain: incense is an abomination unto me: I cannot suffer *your* new moons, nor Sabbath, *nor* solemn days (*it is* iniquity) nor solemn assemblies.

14 My soul hateth your ¹new moons and your appointed feasts: they are a burden unto me: I am weary to bear *them*.

15 And when you shall stretch out your hands, I will hide mine eyes from you: and though ye make many prayers, I will not hear: *for* your hands are full ¹of blood.

1:1 ¹ That is, a revelation or prophecy, which was one of the two means whereby God declared himself to his servants in old time, as Num. 12:6, and therefore the Prophets were called Seers, 1 Sam. 9:9.

² Isaiah was chiefly sent to Judah and Jerusalem, but not only: for in this book are prophecies concerning other nations also.

³ Called also Azariah, 2 Kings 15:1, of these Kings, read 2 Kings 14–21, and 2 Chron. 25–33.

1:2 ¹ Because men were obstinate and insensible, he calleth to the dumb creatures, which were more prompt to obey God's word, as Deut. 32:1.

² He declareth his great mercy toward the Jews forasmuch as he chose them above all other nations to be his people and children, as Deut. 10:15.

1:3 ¹ The most dull and brute beasts do more acknowledge their duty toward their masters, than my people do toward me, of whom they have received benefits without comparison.

1:4 ¹ They were not only wicked as were their fathers, but utterly corrupt, and by their evil example infected others.

² That is, him that sanctifieth Israel.

1:5 ¹ What availeth it to seek to amend you by punishment, seeing the more I correct you, the more ye rebel?

² By naming the chief parts of the body, he signifieth that there was no part of the whole body of the Jews free from his rods.

1:6 ¹ Every part of the body as well the least as the chiefest, was plagued.

² Their plagues were so grievous, that they were incurable, and yet they would not repent.

1:7 ¹ Meaning, of them that dwell far off, which because they look for no advantage of that which remaineth destroy all before them.

1:8 ¹ That is, Jerusalem.

1:9 ¹ Because that he will ever have a Church to call upon his Name.

² That is, all destroyed.

1:10 ¹ Ye that for your vices deserved all to be destroyed, as they of Sodom, save that God of his mercy reserved a little number, Lam. 3:22.

1:11 ¹ Although God commanded these sacrifices for a time, as aids and exercises of their faith: yet because the people had not faith nor repentance, God detesteth them, Ps. 50:13; Jer. 6:20; Amos 5:22; Mic. 6:7.

1:13 ¹ Without faith and repentance.

1:14 ¹ Your sacrifices offered in the new moons and feasts: he condemneth hereby hypocrites, which think to please God with ceremonies, and they themselves are void of faith and mercy.

1:15 ¹ He showeth that where men be given to avarice, deceit, cruelty and extortion, which is meant by blood, there God will show his anger, and not accept them, though they seem never so holy, as Isa. 59:3.

16 ¹Wash you, make you clean, take away the evil of your works from before mine eyes: cease to do evil.

17 Learn to ¹do well: seek judgment, relieve the oppressed: judge the fatherless, *and* defend the widow.

18 Come now, ¹and let us reason together, saith the Lord: though your sins were as crimson, they shall be made ²white as snow: though they were red like scarlet, they shall be as wool,

19 If ye ¹consent and obey, ye shall eat the good *things* of the land.

20 But if ye refuse and be rebellious, ye shall be devoured with the sword: for the mouth of the Lord hath spoken it.

21 How is the ¹faithful city become an harlot? it was full of judgment, *and* justice lodged therein, but now ²*they are* murderers.

22 Thy ¹silver is become dross: thy wine is mixed with water.

23 Thy princes *are* rebellious, and companions of ¹thieves: every one loveth gifts, and followeth after rewards: they judge not the fatherless, neither doth the widow's cause come before them.

24 Therefore saith the Lord God of hosts, the ¹Mighty one of Israel, Ah, I will ²ease me of mine adversaries, and avenge me of mine enemies.

25 Then I will turn mine hand upon thee, and burn out thy dross, till it ¹be pure, and take away all thy tin.

26 ¹And I will restore thy Judges as at the first, and thy counselors as at the beginning: afterward shalt

CHAPTER 2
a Mic. 4:1
b Mic. 4:2

thou be called a city of righteousness, *and* a faithful city.

27 Zion shall be redeemed in judgment, and they that return in her, in ¹justice.

28 And the ¹destruction of the transgressors and of the sinners shall be together: and they that forsake the Lord, shall be consumed.

29 For they shall be confounded for the ¹oaks, which ye have desired, and ye shall be ashamed of the gardens that ye have chosen,

30 For ye shall be as an oak, whose leaf fadeth: and as a garden that hath no water.

31 And the strong shall be as ¹tow, and the maker thereof as a spark: and they shall both burn together, and none shall quench *them*.

2

2 *The Church shall be restored by Christ, and the Gentiles called.* 6 *The punishment of the rebellious and obstinate.*

1 The word that Isaiah the son of Amoz saw upon Judah and Jerusalem,

2 ᵃIt ¹shall be in the last days, that the mountain of the House of the Lord shall be prepared in the top of the mountains, and ²shall be exalted above the hills, and all nations shall ³flow unto it.

3 And many people shall go, and say, Come, and let us go up to ¹the mountain of the Lord, to the house of the God of Jacob; and he will teach us his ways, and we will walk in his paths, ᵇfor the ²Law shall go forth of Zion, and the word of the Lord from ³Jerusalem.

4 And ¹he shall judge among the nations, and

1:16 ¹ By this outward washing, he meaneth the spiritual: exhorting the Jews to repent and amend their lives.

1:17 ¹ This kind of reasoning by the second Table, the Scriptures use in many places against the hypocrites, who pretend most holiness and religion in word, but when the charity and love toward their brethren should appear, they declare that they have neither faith nor religion.

1:18 ¹ To know if I do accuse you without cause.
² Lest sinners should pretend any rigor on God's part, he only willeth them to be pure in heart, and he will forgive all their sins, were they never so many or great.

1:19 ¹ He showeth that whatsoever adversity man endureth, it ought to be attributed to his own incredulity and disobedience.

1:21 ¹ That is, Jerusalem, which had promised fidelity unto me, as a wife to her husband.
² Given to covetousness and extortion, which he signified before by blood, verse 15.

1:22 ¹ Whatsoever was pure in thee before, is now corrupt, though thou have an outward show.

1:23 ¹ That is, they maintain the wicked and the extortioners: and not only do not punish them, but are themselves such.

1:24 ¹ When God will show himself merciful to his Church, he calleth himself, The Holy one of Israel, but when he hath to do with his enemies, he is called Mighty, as against whom no power is able to resist.
² I will take vengeance of mine adversaries the Jews, and so satisfy my desire by punishing them. Which thing yet he doeth with a grief, because of his Covenant.

1:25 ¹ Lest the faithful among them should be overcome with his threatening, he addeth this consolation.

1:26 ¹ It is only the work of God to purify the heart of man, which thing he doeth because of his promise, made concerning the salvation of his Church.

1:27 ¹ By justice is meant God's faithful promise, which is the cause of the deliverance of his Church.

1:28 ¹ The wicked shall not be partakers of God's promise, Ps. 92:9.

1:29 ¹ That is, the trees and pleasant places, where ye commit idolatry, which was forbidden, Deut. 16:22.

1:31 ¹ The false god, wherein ye put your confidence, shall be consumed as easily as a piece of tow.

2:2 ¹ The decree and ordinance of God, touching the restoration of the Church, which is chiefly meant of the time of Christ.
² In an evident place to be seen and discerned.
³ When the kingdom of Christ shall be enlarged by the preaching of the doctrine. Here also is declared the zeal of the children of God, when they are called.

2:3 ¹ Alluding to mount Zion, where the visible Church then was.
² Meaning, the whole doctrine of salvation.
³ This was accomplished, when the Gospel was first preached in Jerusalem, and from thence went through all the world.

2:4 ¹ The Lord, which is Christ, shall have all power given him.

²rebuke many people: they shall ³break their swords also into mattocks, and their spears into scythes: nation shall not lift up a sword against nation, neither shall they learn ⁴to fight anymore.

5 O house of Jacob, come ye, and let us ¹walk in the Law of the Lord.

6 Surely thou ¹hast forsaken thy people, the house of Jacob, because they are ²full of the East *manners*, and *are* sorcerers as the Philistines, ³and abound with strange children.

7 Their land also was full of ¹silver and gold, and there *was* none end of their treasures: and their land was full of horses, and their chariots *were* infinite.

8 Their land was also full of idols; they worshipped the work of their own hands, which their own fingers have made.

9 And a man bowed himself, and a man ¹humbled himself: therefore ²spare them not.

10 Enter into the rock, and hide thee in the dust from before the fear of the Lord, and from the glory of his Majesty.

11 The high look of man shall be humbled, and the loftiness of men shall be abased, and the Lord only shall be exalted in ¹that day.

12 For the day of the Lord of hosts *is* upon all the proud and haughty, and upon all that is exalted: and it shall be made low.

13 Even upon all the cedars of Lebanon, that are high and exalted, and upon all the oaks of Bashan,

14 And upon all the high ¹mountains, and upon all the hills that are lifted up,

15 And upon every high tower, and upon every strong wall,

16 And upon ¹all the ships of Tarshish, and upon all pleasant pictures.

17 And the haughtiness of men shall be brought

ᶜ Hos. 10:8
Luke 23:30
Rev. 6:16
Rev. 9:6

low, and the loftiness of men shall be abased, and the Lord shall only be exalted in that day.

18 And the idols will he utterly destroy.

19 Then shall they go ᶜinto the holes of the rocks, and into the caves of the earth from before the fear of the Lord, and from the glory of his majesty, when he shall arise to destroy the earth.

20 At that day shall man cast away his silver idols and his golden idols (which they had made themselves to worship them) ¹to the moles, and to the backs,

21 To go into the holes of the rocks, and into the tops of the ragged rocks from before the fear of the Lord, and from the glory of his majesty, when he shall rise to destroy the earth.

22 Cease you from the man, whose ¹breath is in his nostrils: for wherein is he to be esteemed?

3 *1 For the sin of the people, God will take away the wise men, and give them foolish princes. 14 The covetousness of the governors. 26 The pride of the women.*

1 For lo, the Lord God of hosts will take away from Jerusalem and from Judah the stay ¹and the strength: *even* all the stay of bread, and all the stay of water,

2 The strong man, and the man of war, ¹the judge, and the Prophet, the prudent and the aged,

3 The captain of fifty, and the honorable, and the counselor, and the cunning artificer, and ¹eloquent man.

4 And I will appoint ¹children *to be* their princes, and babes shall rule over them.

5 The people shall be ¹oppressed one of another, and every one by his neighbor: the children shall presume against the ancient, and the vile against the honorable.

2:4 ² That they may acknowledge their sins, and turn to him.
³ He showeth the fruit of the peace, which the Gospel should bring: to wit, that men should do good one to another, whereas before they were enemies.
⁴ He speaketh not against the use of weapons and lawful war, but showeth how the hearts of the godly shall be affected one toward another: Which peace and love doth begin and grow in this life, but shall be perfected when we are joined with our Head Christ Jesus.
2:5 ¹ Seeing the Gentiles will be so ready, make you haste, and show them the way to worship God.
2:6 ¹ The Prophet seeing the small hope that the Jews would convert, complaineth to God, as though he had utterly forsaken them for their sins.
² Full of the corruptions that reigned chiefly in the East parts.
³ They altogether gave themselves to the fashions of other nations.
2:7 ¹ The Prophet first condemned their superstition and idolatry: next their covetousness, and thirdly their vain trust in worldly means.
2:9 ¹ He noteth the nature of the idolaters, which are never satisfied in their superstitions.
² Thus the Prophet spake, being inflamed with the zeal of God's

glory, and that he might fear them with God's judgment.
2:11 ¹ Meaning, as soon as God shall begin to execute his judgments.
2:14 ¹ By high trees and mountains are meant them that are proud and lofty, and think themselves most strong in this world.
2:16 ¹ He condemneth their vain confidence, which they had in strongholds, and in their rich merchandise, which brought in vain pleasures, wherewith men's minds became effeminate.
2:20 ¹ They shall cast them into most vile and filthy places, when they perceive that they are not able to help them.
2:22 ¹ Cast off your vain confidence of man, whose life is so frail, that if his nose be stopped, he is dead, and consider that you have to do with God.
3:1 ¹ Because they trusted in their abundance and prosperity, he showeth that they should be taken from them.
3:2 ¹ The temporal governor and the minister.
3:3 ¹ By these he meaneth that God would take away everything that was in any estimation, and wherein they had any occasion to vaunt themselves.
3:4 ¹ Not only in age: but in wit, manners, knowledge and strength.
3:5 ¹ For lack of good regiment and order.

6 When everyone shall [1]take hold of his brother of the house of his father, *and say*, Thou hast clothing, thou shalt be our prince, and let this fall be under thine hand:

7 In that day he shall [1]swear, saying, I cannot be an helper: for there is no bread in mine house, nor clothing: *therefore* make me no prince of the people.

8 Doubtless Jerusalem is fallen, and Judah is fallen down, because their tongue and works *are* against the Lord, to provoke the eyes of his glory.

9 The [1]trial of their countenance testifieth against them, yea, they declare their sins, as Sodom, they hide them not. Woe be unto their souls: for they have rewarded evil unto themselves.

10 [1]Say ye, Surely it shall be well with the just: for they shall eat the fruit of their works.

11 Woe be to the wicked, it shall be evil *with him*: for the reward of his hands shall be given him.

12 [1]Children *are* extortioners of my people, and women have rule over them: O my people, they that lead thee, cause thee to err, and destroy the way of thy paths.

13 The Lord standeth up to plead, yea, he standeth to judge the people.

14 The Lord shall enter into judgment with the [1]Ancients of his people and the princes thereof: for ye have eaten up the vineyard: the spoil of the poor *is* in your houses.

15 What have ye to do that ye beat my people to pieces, [1]and grind the faces of the poor, saith the Lord, *even* the Lord of hosts?

16 The Lord also saith, [1]Because the daughters of Zion are haughty, and walk with [2]stretched out necks, and with [3]wandering eyes, walking and [4]mincing as they go, and making a [5]tinkling with their feet,

17 Therefore shall the Lord make the heads of the daughters of Zion bald, and the Lord shall discover their secret parts.

18 In that day shall the Lord take away the ornament of the slippers, and the cauls, and the round tyres,

19 The sweet balls, and the bracelets, and the bonnets,

20 The tyres of the head, and the slops, and the headbands, and the tablets, and the earrings,

21 The rings and the mufflers,

22 The costly apparel and the veils, and the wimples, and the crisping pins,

23 And the glasses and the fine linen, and the hoods and the [1]lawns.

24 And instead of sweet savor, there shall be stink, and instead of girdle, a rent, and instead of dressing of the hair, baldness, and instead of a stomacher, a girding of sackcloth, *and* burning instead of beauty.

25 Thy men shall fall by the [1]sword, and thy strength in the battle.

26 Then shall her gates mourn and lament, and she being desolate, shall sit upon the ground.

4 1 *The small remnant of men after the destruction of Jerusalem.* 2 *The graces of God upon them that remain.*

1 And in that day shall [1]seven women take hold of one man, saying, We will eat our own bread, and we will wear our own garments: only [2]let us be called by thy name, *and* take away our [3]reproach.

2 In that day shall the [1]bud of the Lord be beautiful and glorious, and the fruit of the earth shall be excellent and pleasant for them that are escaped of Israel.

3 Then he that shall be left in Zion, and he that shall remain in Jerusalem, shall be called holy,

---

3:6 [1] He showeth that this plague shall be so horrible, that contrary to the common manner of men, which by nature are ambitious, none shall be found able or willing to be their governor.

3:7 [1] Fear shall rather cause him to forswear himself, than to take such a dangerous charge upon him.

3:9 [1] When God shall examine their deeds whereupon they now set an impudent face, he shall find the mark of their impiety in their forehead.

3:10 [1] Be ye that are godly, assured that God will defend you in the midst of these troubles.

3:12 [1] Because the wicked people were more addicted to their princes, than to the commandments of God, he showeth that he would give them such princes, by whom they should have no help, but that should be manifest tokens of his wrath, because they should be fools and effeminate.

3:14 [1] Meaning, that the rulers and governors had destroyed his Church, and not preserved it, according to their duty.

3:15 [1] That is, ye show all cruelty against them.

3:16 [1] He meaneth the people because of the arrogancy and pride of their women, which gave themselves to all wantonness and dissolution.

[2] Which declared their pride.

[3] As a sign, that they were not chaste.

[4] Which showed their wantonness.

[5] They delighted then in slippers that did creak, or had little plates sewed upon them, which tinkled as they went.

3:23 [1] In rehearsing all these things particularly, he showeth the lightness and vanity of such as cannot be content with comely apparel according to their degree.

3:25 [1] Meaning, that God will not only punish the women, but their husbands which have suffered this dissoluteness, and also the commonweal, which hath not remedied it.

4:1 [1] When God shall execute this vengeance, there shall not be one man found to be the head to many women, and they contrary to womanly shamefacedness, shall seek unto men, and offer themselves to any condition.

[2] Be thou our husband, and let us be called thy wives.

[3] For so they thought it to be without an head and husband.

4:2 [1] He comforteth the Church in this desolation, which shall spring up like a bud, signifying that God's graces should be as plentiful toward the faithful, as though they sprang out of the earth, as Isa. 45:8. Some by the bud of the Lord mean Christ.

and every one shall be [1]written among the living in Jerusalem,

4 When the Lord shall wash the filthiness of the daughters of Zion, and purge the [1]blood of Jerusalem out of the midst thereof by the spirit of [2]judgment, and by the spirit of burning.

5 And the Lord shall create upon every place of mount Zion, and upon the assemblies thereof, [1]a cloud and smoke by day, and the shining of a flaming fire by night: for upon all the [2]glory *shall be* a defense.

6 And a covering shall be for a shadow in the day for the heat, and a place of refuge and a covert for the storm [1]and for the rain.

5

1 *Under the similitude of the vine, he describeth the state of the people.* 8 *Of their avarice.* 11 *Their drunkenness.* 13 *Of their captivity.*

1 Now will [1]I sing to my [2]beloved a song of my beloved to his vineyard, [a]My beloved had a [3]vineyard in a very fruitful hill.

2 And he hedged it, and gathered out the stones of it, and he planted it with the best plants, [1]and he built a tower in the midst thereof, and made a winepress therein, then he looked that it should bring forth grapes: but it brought forth [2]wild grapes.

3 Now therefore, O inhabitants of Jerusalem and men of Judah, judge, I pray you, [1]between me and my vineyard.

4 What could I have done anymore to my vineyard that I have not done unto it? why have I looked that it should bring forth grapes, and it bringeth forth wild grapes?

5 And now I will tell you what I will do to my vineyard: I [1]will take away the hedge thereof, and it

CHAPTER 5
[a] Jer. 2:21
Matt. 21:33

shall be eaten up: I will break the wall thereof, and it shall be trodden down:

6 And I will lay it waste: it shall not be cut, nor dug, but briers and thorns shall grow up: I will also command the clouds that they rain no rain upon it.

7 ¶ Surely the vineyard of the Lord of hosts *is* the house of Israel, and the men of Judah *are* his pleasant plant, and he looked for [1]judgment, but behold oppression: for righteousness, but behold [2]a crying.

8 Woe unto them that join house to house, *and* lay field to field, till there be no [1]place, that ye may be placed by yourselves in the midst of the earth.

9 *This is* in mine [1]ears, *saith* the Lord of hosts. Surely many houses shall be desolate, *even* great and fair without inhabitant.

10 For ten acres of vines shall yield one [1]bath, and the seed of an [2]homer shall yield an [3]ephah.

11 ¶ Woe unto them, that [1]rise up early to follow drunkenness, and to them that continue until [2]night, *till* the wine do inflame them,

12 And the harp and viol, timbrel and pipe, and wine *are* in their feasts: but they regard not the [1]work of the Lord, neither consider the work of his hands.

13 Therefore my people [1]is gone into captivity, because they had [2]no knowledge, and the glory thereof *are* men famished, and the multitude thereof is dried up with thirst.

14 Therefore [1]hell hath enlarged itself, and hath opened his mouth without measure, and their glory, and their multitude, and their pomp, and he that rejoiceth among them, shall descend *into it.*

15 And man shall be brought down, and man

4:3 [1] He alludeth to the book of life, whereof read Exod. 32:32, meaning, God's secret counsel, wherein his elect are predestinate to life everlasting.

4:4 [1] That is, the cruelty, extortion, avarice, and all wickedness.
  [2] When things shall be redressed that were amiss.

4:5 [1] He alludeth to the pillar of the cloud, Exod. 13:21, meaning, that God's favor and protection should appear in every place.
  [2] The faithful are called the glory of God, because his image and tokens of his grace shine in them.

4:6 [1] God promiseth to be the defense of his Church against all troubles and dangers.

5:1 [1] The Prophet by this song doth set before the people's eyes their ingratitude, and God's mercy.
  [2] That is, to God.
  [3] Meaning, that he had planted his Church in a place most plentiful and abundant.

5:2 [1] He spared no diligence nor cost.
  [2] In the seventh verse he declareth what they were.

5:3 [1] He maketh them judges in their own cause, forasmuch as it was evident that they were the cause of their own ruin.

5:5 [1] I will take no more care for it: meaning, that he would take from them his word and ministers, and all other comforts, and send them

contrary plagues.

5:7 [1] Judgment and righteousness are true fruits of the fear of God, and therefore in the cruel oppression there is no religion.
  [2] Of them that are oppressed.

5:8 [1] To wit, for the poor to dwell in.

5:9 [1] I have heard the complaint and cry of the poor.

5:10 [1] Which containeth about ten pottels: so that every acre should but yield one pottel.
  [2] Which containeth an hundred pottels.
  [3] An Ephah containeth ten pottels and is in dry things as much as Bath is in liquors.

5:11 [1] That spare no pain nor diligence to follow their lusts.
  [2] Which are never weary of their rioting and excessive pleasures, but use all means to provoke to the same.

5:12 [1] They regard not the provident care of God over them, nor for what end he hath created them.

5:13 [1] That is, shall certainly go: for so the Prophets use to speak, as though the thing which shall come to pass, were done already.
  [2] Because they would not obey the word of God.

5:14 [1] Meaning, the grave shall swallow up them that shall die for hunger and thirst, and yet for all this great destruction it shall ever be satiate.

shall be humbled, even the eyes of the proud shall be humbled.

16 And the Lord of hosts shall be exalted in judgment, and the holy God shall be sanctified in justice.

17 Then shall [1]the lambs feed after their manner, and the strangers shall eat the desolate places of the fat.

18 ¶ Woe unto them that draw iniquity with [1]cords of vanity, and sin, as with cart ropes:

19 Which say, [1]Let him make speed: let him hasten his work, that we may see it: and let the counsel of the Holy One of Israel draw near and come, that we may know it.

20 Woe unto them that speak good of evil, [1]and evil of good, which put darkness for light, and light for darkness, that put bitter for sweet, and sweet for sour.

21 Woe unto them that are [1]wise in their own eyes, and prudent in their own sight.

22 Woe unto them that are [1]mighty to drink wine, and unto them that are strong to pour in strong drink:

23 Which justify the wicked for a reward, and take away the righteousness of the righteous from him.

24 Therefore as the flame of fire devoureth the stubble, and as the chaff is consumed of the flame: so their [1]root shall be a rottenness, and their bud shall rise up like dust, because they have cast off the Law of the Lord of hosts, and contemned the word of the Holy one of Israel.

25 Therefore is the wrath of the Lord kindled against his people, and he hath stretched out his [1]hand upon them, and hath smitten them that the mountains did tremble: and their carcasses were torn in the midst of the streets, *and* for all this his wrath was not turned away, but his hand was stretched out still.

26 And he will lift up a sign [1]unto the nations afar, and will hiss unto them from the end of the earth: and behold, they shall come hastily with speed.

27 None shall [1]faint nor fall among them: none shall slumber nor sleep, neither shall the girdle of his loins be loosed, nor [2]the latchet of his shoes be broken.

28 Whose arrows shall be sharp, and all his bows bent: his horse hoofs shall be thought like flint, and his wheels like whirlwind.

29 His roaring *shall be* like a lion, and he shall roar like lion's whelps: they shall [1]roar, and lay hold of the prey: they shall take it away, and none shall deliver it.

30 And in that day they shall roar upon them, as the roaring of the sea: and if [1]they look unto the earth, behold darkness *and* sorrow, and the light shall be darkened in their [2]sky.

6 *1 Isaiah showeth his vocation by the vision of the divine majesty. 9 He showeth the obstinacy of the people. 11 The destruction of the land. 13 The remnant reserved.*

1 In the year of the death of king Uzziah, [1]I saw also the Lord sitting upon an [2]high throne, and lifted up, and the lower [3]parts thereof filled the Temple.

2 The [1]Seraphims stood upon it, every one had six wings: with twain he covered his [2]face, and with twain he covered his [3]feet, and with twain he did [4]fly.

3 And one cried to another, and said, [1]Holy, holy, holy *is* the Lord of hosts: the whole [2]world is full of his glory.

5:17 [1] God comforteth the poor lambs of his Church, which had been strangers in other countries, promising that they should dwell in these places again, whereof they had been deprived by the fat and cruel tyrants.

5:18 [1] Which use all allurements, occasions, and excuses to harden their conscience in sin.

5:19 [1] He showeth what are the words of the wicked, when they are menaced with God's judgments, 2 Pet. 3:4.

5:20 [1] Which are not ashamed of sin, nor care for honesty, but are grown to a desperate impiety.

5:21 [1] Which are contemners of all doctrine and admonition.

5:22 [1] Which are never weary, but show their strength, and brag in gluttony and drunkenness.

5:24 [1] Both they and their posterity, so that nothing shall be left.

5:25 [1] He showeth that God had so sore punished this people, that the dumb creatures, if they had been so plagued, would have been more sensible, and therefore his plagues must continue, till they begin to feel them.

5:26 [1] He will make the Babylonians to come against them at his beck, and to fight under his standard.

5:27 [1] They shall be prompt and lusty to execute God's vengeance.

 [2] The enemy shall have none impediment.

5:29 [1] Whereby is declared the cruelty of the enemy.

5:30 [1] The Jews shall find no succor.

 [2] In the land of Judah.

6:1 [1] God showeth not himself to man in his majesty, but according as man's capacity is able to comprehend him, that is, by visible signs, as John Baptist saw the holy Ghost in the form of a dove.

 [2] As a Judge ready to give sentence.

 [3] Of his garment, or of his throne.

6:2 [1] They were Angels, so called, because they were of a fiery color, to signify that they burnt in the love of God, or were light as fire to execute his will.

 [2] Signifying, that they were not able to endure the brightness of God's glory.

 [3] Whereby was declared that man was not able to see the brightness of God in them.

 [4] Which thing declareth the prompt obedience of the Angels to execute God's commandment.

6:3 [1] This oft repetition signifieth that the Holy Angels cannot satisfy themselves in praising God, to teach us that in all our lives we should give ourselves to the continual praise of God.

 [2] His glory doth not only appear in the heavens, but through all the world, and therefore all creatures are bound, to praise him.

4 And the lintels of the door cheeks [1]moved at the voice of him that cried, and the house was filled with smoke.

5 Then I said, [1]Woe is me: for I am undone, because I am a man of polluted lips, and I dwell in the midst of a people of polluted lips: for mine eyes have seen the King, *and* Lord of hosts.

6 Then flew one of the Seraphims unto me with an hot coal in his hand, *which* he had taken from the [1]altar with the tongs:

7 And he touched my mouth, and said, Lo, this hath touched thy lips, and thine iniquity shall be taken away, and thy [1]sin shall be purged.

8 Also I heard the voice of the Lord, saying, Whom shall I send? and who shall go for us? Then I said, Here am I, send me.

9 And he said, Go, and say unto this people, [1]Ye shall hear indeed, but ye shall not understand: ye shall plainly see, and not perceive.

10 Make the heart of this people fat, make their ears heavy, and shut their eyes, lest they see with their eyes, and hear with their ears, and understand with their heart, and convert, and he heal them.

11 Then said I, Lord, [1]how long? And he answered, Until the cities be wasted without inhabitant, and the houses without man, and the land be utterly desolate,

12 And the Lord have removed men far away, and *there be* a great desolation in the midst of the land.

13 But yet in it *shall be* [1]a tenth, and shall return, and shall be eaten up as an elm [2]or an oak, which have a substance in them, when they cast *their leaves: so* the holy seed shall be the substance thereof.

7

1 *Jerusalem is besieged.*   4 *Isaiah comforteth the king.*   14 *Christ is promised.*

1 And in the days of [a]Ahaz, the son of Jotham, the son of Uzziah king of Judah, Rezin the king of [1]Aram [2]came up, and Pekah the son of Remaliah king of Israel, to Jerusalem to fight against it, but he could not overcome it.

2 And it was told the house of [1]David, saying, Aram is joined with [2]Ephraim: therefore his heart was [3]moved, and the heart of his people, as the trees of the forest are moved by the wind.

3 ¶ Then said the Lord unto Isaiah, Go forth now to meet Ahaz (thou and [1]Shear-Jashub thy son) at the end of the conduit of the upper pool, in the path of the fuller's field,

4 And say unto him, Take heed, and be still: fear not, neither be fainthearted for the two tails of these smoking [1]firebrands, for the furious wrath of Rezin and of Aram, and of Remaliah's son,

5 Because Aram hath taken wicked counsel against thee, *and* Ephraim and Remaliah's son, saying,

6 Let us go up against Judah, and let us waken them up, and make a breach therein for us, and set a king in the midst thereof, *even* the son of [1]Tabel.

7 Thus saith the Lord God, It shall not stand, neither shall it be.

8 For the head of Aram *is* Damascus, and the head of Damascus *is* Rezin: and within five and [1]threescore years, Ephraim shall be destroyed from being a people.

9 And the head of Ephraim *is* Samaria, and the head of Samaria *is* Remaliah's son. If ye believe not, surely ye shall not be established.

10 ¶ And the Lord spake again unto Ahaz, saying,

11 Ask [1]a sign for thee of the Lord thy God: ask it

6:4 [1] Which things were to confirm the Prophet, that it was not the voice of man: and by the smoke was signified the blindness that should come upon the Jews.

6:5 [1] He speaketh this for two causes: the one because he that was a mortal creature, and therefore had more need to glorify God than the Angels, did it not: and the other because the more near that man approacheth to God, the more doth he know his own sin and corruption.

6:6 [1] Of the burnt offerings, where the fire never went out.

6:7 [1] This declareth that man cannot render due obedience to God, till he have purged us.

6:9 [1] Whereby is declared that for the malice of man God will not immediately take away his word, but he will cause it to be preached to their condemnation, when as they will not learn thereby to obey his will, and be saved: hereby he exhorteth the ministers to do their duty, and answereth to the wicked murmurers, that through their own malice their heart is hardened, Matt. 13:14; Acts 28:26; Rom. 11:8.

6:11 [1] As he was moved with the zeal of God's glory, so was he touched with a charitable affection toward the people.

6:13 [1] Meaning, the tenth part: or as some write, it was revealed to Isaiah for the confirmation of his prophecy, that ten Kings should come before their captivity, as were from Uzziah to Zedekiah.

[2] For the fewness they shall seem to be eaten up: yet they shall after flourish as a tree, which in winter loseth leaves, and seemeth to be dead, yet in Summer is fresh and green.

7:1 [1] Or, Syria.

[2] To wit, the second time: for in the first battle Ahaz was overcome.

7:2 [1] Meaning, the King's house.

[2] That is, Israel, because that tribe was the greatest, Gen. 48:19.

[3] For fear.

7:3 [1] That is to say, the rest shall return, which name Isaiah gave his son, to signify that the rest of the people should return out of their captivity.

7:4 [1] Which have but a little smoke and shall quickly be quenched.

7:6 [1] Which was an Israelite, and as seemeth, enemy to the house of David.

7:8 [1] Counting from the five and twentieth year of the reign of Uzziah, at what time Amos prophesied this thing, and now Isaiah confirmeth that the Israelites should be led into perpetual captivity, which thing came to pass within 20 years after that Isaiah did this message.

7:11 [1] For the confirmation of this thing that thine enemies shall be destroyed and thou preserved.

either in the depth beneath, or in the height above.

12 But Ahaz said, I will not ask, neither will I ¹tempt the Lord.

13 Then he said, Hear you now, O house of David, is it a small thing for you to grieve ¹men, that ye will also grieve my God?

14 Therefore the Lord ¹himself will give you a sign. Behold, the virgin shall conceive and bear a son, and she shall call his name ²Immanuel.

15 ¹Butter and honey shall he eat, till he have knowledge to refuse the evil, and to choose the good.

16 For afore the ¹child shall have knowledge to eschew the evil, and to choose the good, the land that thou abhorrest, shall be forsaken of both her kings.

17 The Lord shall bring upon thee, and upon thy people, and upon thy Father's house (the days that are not come from the day that ¹Ephraim departed from Judah) *even* the King of ²Assyria.

18 And in that day shall the Lord hiss for the ¹fly that is at the uttermost parts of the floods of Egypt, and for the Bee which is in the land of Assyria,

19 And they shall come and shall light all in the desolate valleys, and in the holes of the rocks, and upon all thorny places, and upon all bushy ¹places.

20 In that day shall the Lord shave with a razor that is hired, *even* by them beyond the River, by the King of Assyria, the head and the hair of the ¹feet, and it shall consume the beard.

21 And in the same day shall a man ¹nourish a young cow, and two sheep.

22 And for the ¹abundance of milk, that they shall give, he shall eat butter: for butter and honey shall everyone eat, which is left within the land.

23 And at the same day every place, wherein shall be a thousand vines, shall be at a thousand *pieces* of silver: *so* it shall be for the briers and for the thorns.

24 With arrows and with ¹bow shall one come thither: because all the land shall be briers and thorns.

25 But on ¹all the mountains, which shall be dug with the mattock, there shall not come thither the fear of briers and thorns: but they shall be for the sending out of bullocks, and for the treading of sheep.

8 1 *The captivity of Israel and Judah by the Assyrians.* 6 *The infidelity of the Jews.* 9 *The destruction of the Assyrians.* 14 *Christ the stone of stumbling to the wicked.* 19 *The word of God must be inquired at.*

1 Moreover the Lord said unto me, Take thee a ¹great roll, and write it ²with a man's pen, Make speed to the spoil: haste to the prey.

2 Then I took unto me ¹faithful witnesses to record, Uriah the Priest, and Zechariah the son of Jeberechiah.

3 After, I came unto the ¹Prophetess, which conceived, and bare a son. Then said the Lord to me, Call his name, ²Maher-Shalal-Hash-Baz.

4 For before the ¹child shall have knowledge to cry, My father, and my mother, he shall take away the riches of Damascus, and the spoil of Samaria, before the ²King of Assyria.

5 ¶ And the Lord spake yet again unto me, saying,

6 Because this people hath refused the waters of ¹Shiloah that run softly, and rejoice with Rezin, and the son of Remaliah,

7:12 ¹ Not to believe God's word without a sign, is to tempt God, but to refuse a sign when God offereth it for the aid and help of our infirmity, is to rebel against him.
7:13 ¹ You think you have to do with men, when ye contemn God's messengers: but it is God against whom you bend yourselves.
7:14 ¹ Forasmuch as thou art unworthy, the Lord for his own promise sake will give a sign, which shall be that Christ the Savior of his Church, and the effect of all signs and miracles shall be revealed.
² Or, God with us, which name can agree to none, but to him that is both God and man.
7:15 ¹ Meaning, that Christ is not only God, but man also, because he shall be nourished as other men until the age of discretion.
7:16 ¹ Not meaning Christ, but any child: for before a child can come to the years of discretion, the kings of Samaria and Syria shall be destroyed.
7:17 ¹ Since the time that the twelve Tribes rebelled under Rehoboam.
² In whom thou hast put thy trust.
7:18 ¹ Meaning, the Egyptians: for by reason the country is hot and moist, it is full of flies, as Assyria is full of bees.
7:19 ¹ Signifying, that no place shall be free from them.
7:20 ¹ That is, that which is from the belly downward: meaning, that he would destroy both great and small.
7:21 ¹ He that before had a great number of cattle, shall be content with one cow and two sheep.
7:22 ¹ The number of men shall be so small, that a few beasts shall be able to nourish all abundantly.
7:24 ¹ As they that go to seek wild beasts among the bushes.
7:25 ¹ The mountains contrary to their wont, shall be tilled by such as shall flee to them for succor.
8:1 ¹ That thou mayest write in great letters, to the intent it may be more easily read.
² Meaning, after the common fashion, because all men might read it.
8:2 ¹ Because the thing was of great importance, he took these two witnesses, which were of credit with the people, when he set this up upon the door of the Temple, albeit Uriah was a flattering hypocrite, 2 Kings 16:11.
8:3 ¹ Meaning, to his wife, and this was done in a vision.
² Or, make speed to the spoil: haste to the prey.
8:4 ¹ Before any child be able to speak.
² That is, the army of Assyria.
8:6 ¹ Which was a fountain at the foot of mount Zion, out of the which ran a small river through the city: meaning, that they of Judah, distrusting their own power, which was small, desired such power and riches as they saw in Syria and Israel.

7 Now therefore, behold, the Lord bringeth up upon them the waters of [1]the River mighty and great, *even* the King of Assyria with all his glory, and he shall come up upon all their rivers, and go over all their banks,

8 And shall break into Judah, *and* shall overflow, and pass through, *and* shall come up to the [1]neck, and the stretching out of his wings shall fill the breadth of thy land, O [2]Immanuel.

9 Gather together on heaps, O ye [1]people, and ye shall be broken in pieces, and hearken all ye of far countries: gird yourselves, and you shall be broken in pieces: gird yourselves, and you shall be broken in pieces.

10 Take counsel together, yet, it shall be brought to naught: pronounce a decree, yet shall it not stand: for God is with us.

11 For the Lord spake thus to me, in taking [1]of *mine* hand, and taught me, that I should not walk in the way of this people, saying,

12 Say ye not, A [1]confederacy, to all them to whom this people saith a confederacy, neither fear you [2]their fear, nor be afraid of them.

13 [1]Sanctify the Lord of hosts, and let him be your fear, and let him be your dread,

14 And he shall be as a [1]Sanctuary: *but* as a stumbling stone, and as a rock to fall upon, to both the houses of Israel, *and* as a snare and as a net to the inhabitants of Jerusalem.

15 And many among them shall stumble, and shall fall, and shall be broken, and shall be snared, and shall be taken,

16 [1]Bind up the testimony: seal up the Law among my disciples.

17 Therefore I will wait upon the Lord that hath hid his face from the house of Jacob, and I will look for him.

18 Behold, I and the [1]children whom the Lord hath given me, *are* as signs and as wonders in Israel, [2]by the Lord of hosts, which dwelleth in Mount Zion.

19 And when they shall say unto you, Inquire at them that have a spirit of divination, and at the soothsayers which whisper and murmur, [1]Should not a people inquire at their God? from the [2]living to the dead?

20 To the [1]Law, and to the testimony, if they speak not according to this word: *it is* because there *is* no [2]light in them.

21 Then he that is afflicted and famished, shall go to and fro in [1]it: and when he shall be hungry, he shall even fret himself, [2]and curse his king and his gods, and shall look upward.

22 And when he shall look to the earth, behold trouble, and [1]darkness, vexation, *and* anguish, and he *is* driven to darkness.

9

1 The vocation of the Gentiles. 6 A prophecy of Christ. 14 The destruction of the ten tribes for their pride and contempt of God.

1 Yet [1]the darkness shall not *be* according to the affliction, [2]that it had when at the first he touched lightly the land of Zebulun and the land of Naphtali, nor afterward *when* he was more grievous by the way of the sea beyond Jordan in Galilee of [3]the Gentiles.

2 The people that [1]walked in darkness, have seen a great [2]light: they that dwelled in the land

---

8:7 [1] That is, the Assyrians which dwell beyond Euphrates.

8:8 [1] It shall be ready to drown them.

[2] He speaketh this to Messiah, or Christ, in whom the faithful were comforted, and who would not suffer his Church to be destroyed utterly.

8:9 [1] To wit, ye that are enemies to the Church, as the Assyrians, Egyptians, Syrians, etc.

8:11 [1] To encourage me that I should not shrink for the infidelity of this people, and so neglect mine office.

8:12 [1] Consent not ye that are godly, to the league and friendship that this people seek with strangers and idolaters.

[2] Meaning, that they should not fear the thing that they feared, which have no hope in God.

8:13 [1] In putting your trust only in him, in calling upon him in adversity, patiently looking for his help, and fearing to do anything contrary to his will.

8:14 [1] He will defend you which are his elect, and reject all the rest, which is meant of Christ, against whom the Jews should stumble and fall, Luke 2:34; Rom. 9:33; 1 Pet. 2:7, 8.

8:16 [1] Though all forsake me, yet ye that are mine, keep my word sure sealed in your hearts.

8:18 [1] Meaning, them that were willing to hear and obey the word of God, whom the world hated, as though they were monsters and not worthy to live.

[2] This was a consolation in their troubles, knowing that nothing could come unto them, but by the will of the Lord.

8:19 [1] Answer the wicked thus, Should not God's people seek succor only at him?

[2] This is, will they refuse to be taught of the Prophet, who is the mouth of God, and seek help at the dead, which is the illusion of Satan?

8:20 [1] Seek remedy in the word of God, where his will is declared.

[2] They have no knowledge, but are blind leaders of the blind.

8:21 [1] That is, in Judah, where they should have had rest, if they had not thus grievously offended God.

[2] In whom afore they put their trust.

8:22 [1] They shall think that heaven and earth and all creatures are bent against them to trouble them.

9:1 [1] He comforteth the Church again after these great threatenings, promising to restore them to great glory in Messiah.

[2] Wherewith Israel was punished, first by Tiglath-pilesar, which was a light scourge in respect of that which they suffered afterward by Shalmaneser, who carried the Israelites away captives.

[3] Whereas the Jews and Gentiles dwelt together by reason of those twenty cites, which Solomon gave to Hiram.

9:2 [1] Which were captivity in Babylon: and the Prophet speaketh of that thing which should come to pass threescore years after, as though it were now done.

[2] Meaning, the comfort of their deliverance.

of the shadow of death, upon them hath the [3]light shined.

3 Thou hast [1]multiplied the nation, *and* not increased *their* joy: they have rejoiced before thee according to the joy in harvest, *and* as men rejoice when they divide a spoil.

4 For the [1]yoke of their burden, and the staff of their shoulder, *and* the rod of their oppressor hast thou broken, as in the day of Midian.

5 Surely every battle of the warrior *is* with noise, and with tumbling of garments in blood: but *this* shall be [1]with burning, *and* devouring of fire.

6 For unto us a child is born, *and* unto us a Son is given: and the government is upon his shoulder, and he shall call his name, Wonderful, Counselor, The mighty God, The everlasting [1]Father, The prince of peace.

7 The increase of *his* government and peace shall have none end: he shall sit upon the throne of David, and upon his kingdom, to order it, and to stablish it with judgment, and with justice, from henceforth, *even* forever: [1]the zeal of the Lord of hosts will perform this.

8 ¶ The Lord hath sent a word into Jacob, and it lighted upon [1]Israel.

9 And all the people shall know, *even* Ephraim, and the inhabitant of Samaria, that say in the pride and presumption of their heart,

10 The [1]bricks are fallen, but we will build it with hewn stones: the wild fig trees are cut down, but we will change them into cedars.

11 Nevertheless, the Lord will raise up the adversaries of [1]Rezin against him, and join his enemies together.

12 Aram before and the Philistines behind, and they shall devour Israel with open mouth: *yet* for all this his wrath is not turned away, but his hand *is* stretched out still.

13 For the people turneth not unto him that smiteth them, neither do they seek the Lord of hosts.

14 Therefore will the Lord cut off from Israel head and tail, branch and rush in one day.

15 The ancient and the honorable man, he is the head: and the prophet that teacheth lies, he is the tail.

16 For the leaders of the people cause them to err: and they that are led by them are devoured.

17 Therefore shall the Lord have no pleasure in their young men, neither will he have compassion of their fatherless and of their widows: for everyone is an hypocrite and wicked, and every mouth speaketh folly: *yet* for all this his wrath is not turned away, but his hand *is* stretched out still.

18 For wickedness [1]burneth as a fire: it devoureth the briers and the thorns, and will kindle in the thick places of the forest: and they shall mount up *like* the lifting up of smoke.

19 By the wrath of the Lord of hosts shall the land be darkened, and the people shall be as the meat of the fire: no man shall [1]spare his brother.

20 And he shall snatch at the right hand, and be hungry: and he shall eat on the left hand, and shall not be satisfied: everyone shall eat the [1]flesh of his own arm.

21 Manasseh Ephraim: and Ephraim Manasseh, *and* they both shall be against Judah: *yet* for all this his wrath is not turned away, but his hand *is* stretched out still.

10 1 *Of wicked lawmakers.* 5 *God will punish his people by the Assyrians and after destroy them.* 21 *The remnant of Israel shall be saved.*

1 Woe unto them that decree wicked decrees, and [1]write grievous things,

2 To keep back the poor from judgment, and to take away the judgment of the poor of my people, that widows may be their prey, and that they may spoil the fatherless.

3 What will ye do now in the day of visitation, and of destruction, which shall come from [1]far? to

---

[3] This captivity and deliverance were figures of our captivity by sin, and of our deliverance by Christ through the preaching of the Gospel, Matt. 4:15, 16.

9:3 [1] Their number was greater when they went into captivity, than when they returned, but their joy was greater at their return, Hag. 2:9.

9:4 [1] Thou gavest them perfect joy by delivering them, and by destroying the tyrants, that had kept them in cruel bondage, as thou didst deliver them by Gideon from the Midianites, Judg. 7:21.

9:5 [1] He speaketh of the deliverance of his Church, which he hath delivered miraculously from his enemies, but especially by the coming of Christ, of whom he prophesieth in the next verse.

9:6 [1] The author of eternity, and by whom the Church and every member thereof shall be preserved forever, and have immortal life.

9:7 [1] His singular love and care for his elect.

9:8 [1] This is another prophecy against them of Samaria, which were mockers and contemners of God's promises and menaces.

9:10 [1] We were but weak, when the enemy overcame us, but we will make ourselves so strong, that we will neither care for our enemies, nor fear God's threatenings.

9:11 [1] Rezin king of Syria, who was in league with Israel, was slain by the Assyrians, after whose death Aram, that is, the Syrians were against Israel, which on the other side were assailed by the Philistines.

9:18 [1] Wickedness as a bellows kindleth the fire of God's wrath, which consumeth all his obstinate enemies.

9:19 [1] Though there were no foreign enemy, yet they shall destroy one another.

9:20 [1] Their greediness shall be insatiable, so that one brother shall eat up another, as though he should eat his own flesh.

10:1 [1] Which write and pronounce a wicked sentence to oppress the poor: meaning, that the wicked magistrates, which were the chief cause of mischief, should be first punished.

10:3 [1] To wit, from Assyria.

whom will ye flee for help and where will ye leave your ²glory?

4 ¹Without me *everyone* shall fall among them that are bound, and they shall fall down among the slain: *yet* for all this his wrath is not turned away, but his hand *is* stretched out still.

5 ¶ O ¹Assyria, the rod of my wrath: and the staff in their hands is mine indignation.

6 I will send ¹him to a dissembling nation, and I will give him a charge against the people of my wrath to take the spoil and to take the prey, and to tread them under feet like the mire in the street.

7 But he thinketh not so, neither doth his heart esteem it so: but he imagineth to destroy and to cut off not a few nations.

8 For he saith, Are not my princes altogether Kings?

9 Is not Calno as ¹Carchemish? Is not Hamath like Arpad? Is not Samaria as Damascus?

10 Like as mine hand hath found the kingdoms of the idols, seeing their idols *were* above Jerusalem, and above Samaria:

11 Shall not I, as I have done to Samaria, and to the idols thereof, so do to Jerusalem, and to the idols thereof?

12 ¶ But when the Lord hath accomplished ¹all his work upon mount Zion and Jerusalem, I will visit the fruit of the proud heart ²of the king of Assyria, and his glorious and proud looks,

13 Because he said, By the power of mine own hand have I done it, and by my wisdom, because I am wise: therefore I have removed the borders of the people, and have spoiled their treasures, and have pulled down the inhabitants like a valiant man.

14 And mine hand hath found as a nest the riches of the people, and as one that gathereth eggs that are left, *so* have I gathered all the earth: and there was none to move the wing or to open the mouth, or to whisper.

15 Shall the ¹axe boast itself against him that heweth therewith? or shall the saw exalt itself against him that moveth it? as if the rod should lift up itself against him that taketh it up, *or* the staff should exalt itself *as it were* no wood.

16 Therefore shall the Lord God of hosts send among his fat men leanness, and under his glory he shall kindle a burning, like the burning of fire.

17 And the light of Israel shall be as a ¹fire, and the Holy one thereof as a flame, and it shall burn, and devour ²his thorns and his briers in one day:

18 And shall consume the glory of his forest, and of his fruitful fields both soul ¹and flesh: and he shall be as the ²fainting of a standard bearer.

19 And the rest of the trees of his forest shall be few, that a child may tell them.

20 ¶ And at that day shall the remnant of Israel and such as are escaped of the house of Jacob, stay no more upon him that smote them, but shall ¹stay upon the Lord, the Holy one of Israel in truth.

21 The remnant shall return, *even* the remnant of Jacob unto the mighty God.

22 For though thy people, O Israel, be as the sand of the sea, *yet* shall the remnant of them return. The consumption ¹decreed shall overflow with righteousness.

23 For the Lord God of hosts shall make the consumption even ¹determined, in the midst of all the land.

24 Therefore thus saith the Lord God of hosts, O my people, that dwellest in Zion, be not afraid of Assyria: he shall smite thee with a rod, and shall lift up his staff against thee after the manner of ¹Egypt.

25 But yet a very little time, and the wrath shall be consumed, and mine anger in their destruction.

26 And the Lord of hosts shall raise up a scourge for him, according to the plague of ¹Midian in the rock Oreb: and *as* his staff *was* upon the ²Sea, so he

---

10:3 ² Your riches and authority, that they may be safe, and that ye may receive them again.

10:4 ¹ Because they have forsaken me, some shall go into captivity, and the rest shall be slain.

10:5 ¹ God calleth for the Assyrians to be the executioners of his vengeance.

10:6 ¹ That is, the Assyrians against the Jews, which are but hypocrites: and in the sixth and seventh verse is declared the difference of the work of God, and of the wicked in one very thing and act: for God's intention is to chastise them for their amendment, and the Assyrians' purpose is to destroy them to enrich themselves: thus in respect of God's justice, it is God's work, but in respect of their own malice, it is the work of the devil.

10:9 ¹ Seeing that I have overcome as well one city as another, so that none could resist, shall Jerusalem be able to escape mine hands?

10:12 ¹ When he hath sufficiently chastised his people (for he beginneth at his own house) then will he burn the rods.

² Meaning of Sennacherib.

10:15 ¹ Here we see that no creature is able to do anything, but as God appointeth him, and that they are all but his instruments to do his work, though the intentions be divers, as verse 6.

10:17 ¹ Meaning, that God is a light to comfort his people, and a fire to burn his enemies.

² That is, the Assyrians.

10:18 ¹ To wit, body and soul utterly.

² When the battle is lost and the standard taken.

10:20 ¹ This is the end of God's plagues toward his, to bring them to him, and to forsake all trust in others.

10:22 ¹ This small number which seemed to be consumed, and yet according to God's decree is saved, shall be sufficient to fill all the world with righteousness.

10:23 ¹ God will destroy this land as he hath determined, and after save a small portion.

10:24 ¹ As the Egyptians did punish thee.

10:26 ¹ Read Isa. 9:4.

² When the Israelites passed through by the lifting up of Moses' rod, and the enemies were drowned, Exod. 14:28.

will lift it up after the manner of Egypt.

27 And at that day shall his burden be taken away from off thy shoulder, and his yoke from off thy neck: and the yoke shall be destroyed because of [1]the anointing.

28 He is come to [1]Aiath: he is passed into Migron: at Michmash shall he lay up his armor.

29 They have gone over the ford: they lodged in the lodging at Geba: Ramah is afraid: Gibeah of Saul is fled away.

30 Lift up thy voice, O daughter Gallim, cause Laish to hear, O poor Anathoth.

31 Madmenah is removed: the inhabitants of Gebim have gathered themselves together.

32 Yet there is a time that he will stay at Nob: he shall lift up his hand toward the mount of the daughter Zion, the hill of Jerusalem.

33 Behold, the Lord God of hosts shall cut off the [1]bough with fear, and they of high stature shall be cut off, and the high shall be humbled.

34 And he shall cut away the thick places of the forest with iron, and Lebanon shall have a mighty fall.

11

1 Christ born of the root of Jesse.   2 His virtues and kingdom.   6 The fruits of the Gospel.   10 The calling of the Gentiles.

1 But there shall come a [1]rod forth of the stock of Jesse, and a grass shall grow out of his roots.

2 And the Spirit of the Lord shall rest upon him: the Spirit of wisdom and understanding, the Spirit of counsel and strength, the Spirit of knowledge, and of the fear of the Lord,

3 And shall make him prudent in the fear of the Lord: for he shall not judge after the sight of his eyes, neither reprove by the hearing of his ears.

4 But with righteousness shall he judge the poor, and with equity shall he reprove for the meek of the earth: and he shall [1]smite the earth with the rod of his mouth, and with the breath of his lips shall he slay the wicked.

5 And justice shall be the girdle of his loins, and faithfulness the girdle of his reins.

6 The [1]wolf also shall dwell with the lamb, and the leopard shall lie with the kid, and the calf, and the lion, and the fat beast together, and a little child shall lead them.

7 And the cow and the bear shall feed: their young ones shall lie together: and the lion shall eat straw like the bullock.

8 And the sucking child shall play upon the hole of the asp, and the weaned child shall put his hand upon the cockatrice hole.

9 Then shall none hurt nor destroy in all the mountain of mine holiness: for the earth shall be full of the knowledge of the Lord, as [1]the waters that cover the sea.

10 And in that day the root of Jesse, which shall stand up for a sign unto the [1]people, the nations shall seek unto it, and his [2]rest shall be glorious.

11 And in the same day shall the Lord *stretch out* his hand [1]again the second time, to possess the remnant of his people, (which shall be left) of Assyria, and of Egypt, and of Pathros, and of Ethiopia, and of Elam, and of Shinar, and of Hamath, and of the isles of the sea.

12 And he shall set up a sign to the nations, and assemble the dispersed of Israel, and gather the scattered of Judah from the four corners of the world.

13 The hatred also of Ephraim shall depart, and the adversaries of Judah shall be cut off: Ephraim shall not envy [1]Judah, neither shall Judah vex Ephraim:

14 But they shall flee upon the shoulders of the Philistines toward the West: they shall spoil them of the East together: Edom and Moab shall be the stretching out of their hands, and the children of Ammon *in* their obedience.

15 The Lord also shall utterly destroy the [1]tongue of the Egyptian's sea, and with his mighty wind shall

---

10:27 [1] Because of the promise made to that kingdom, whereby Christ's kingdom was prefigured.

10:28 [1] He describeth by what way the Assyrians should come against Jerusalem, to confirm the faithful, when it should come to pass, that as their plague was come, so should they be delivered.

10:33 [1] Fear and destruction shall come upon Judah for the princes and the people shall be all led away captives.

11:1 [1] Because the captivity of Babylon was a figure of the spiritual captivity under sin, he showeth that our true deliverance must come by Christ: for as David came out of Jesse a man without dignity, so Christ should come of a poor carpenter's house as out of a dead stock, Isa. 53:2.

11:4 [1] All these properties can agree to none, but only unto Christ: for it is he that toucheth the hearts of the faithful, and mortifieth their concupiscences: and to the wicked he is the savor of death, and to them that shall perish: so that all the world shall be smitten with his rod, which is his word.

11:6 [1] Men because of their wicked affections are named by the names of beasts, wherein the like affections reign: but Christ by his Spirit shall reform them, and work in them such mutual charity, that they shall be like lambs, favoring and loving one another, and cast off all their cruel affections, Isa. 65:25.

11:9 [1] It shall be in as great abundance as the waters in the sea.

11:10 [1] He prophesieth of the calling of the Gentiles.
   [2] That is, the Church, which he also calleth his rest, Ps. 132:14.

11:11 [1] For God first delivered his people out of Egypt, and now promiseth to deliver them out of their enemies' hands as from the Parthians, Persians, Chaldeans, and them of Antiochia, among whom they were dispersed: and this is chiefly meant of Christ, who calleth his people being dispersed through all the world.

11:13 [1] Here he describeth the consent that shall be in his Church, and their victory against their enemies.

11:15 [1] Meaning, a corner of the sea, that entereth into the land, and hath the form of a tongue.

lift up his hand [2]over the river, and shall smite him in *his* seven streams, and cause men to walk *therein* with shoes.

16 And there shall be a path to the remnant of his people which are left of Assyria, like as it was unto Israel in the day that he came up out of the land of Egypt.

12

A thanksgiving of the faithful for the mercies of God.

1 And thou [1]shalt say in that day, O Lord, I will praise thee: though thou wast angry with me, thy wrath is turned away, and thou comfortest me.

2 Behold, God *is* my [1]salvation: I will trust, and will not fear: for the Lord God *is* [a]my strength and song: he is also become my salvation.

3 Therefore with joy shall ye [1]draw waters out of the wells of salvation.

4 And ye shall say in that day, [b]Praise the Lord: call upon his Name: declare his works among the people: make mention of them, for his Name is exalted.

5 Sing unto the Lord, for he hath done excellent things: this is known in all the world.

6 Cry out, and shout, [1]O inhabitant of Zion: for great *is* the Holy one of Israel in the midst of thee.

13

The Medes and Persians shall destroy Babylon.

1 The [1]burden of Babel, which Isaiah the son of Amoz did see.

2 Lift up a standard upon the high mountain: lift up the voice unto them: wag the [1]hand, that they may go into the gates of the nobles.

3 I have commanded them, that I have [1]sanctified: and I have called the mighty to my wrath, *and* them that rejoice in my [2]glory.

4 The noise of a multitude *is* in the mountains like a great people: a tumultuous voice of the kingdoms

CHAPTER 12
[a] Exod. 15:2
Ps. 118:14
[b] 1 Chron. 16:8

CHAPTER 13
[a] Ps. 137:9

of the nations gathered together: the Lord of hosts numbereth the host of the battle.

5 They come from a far country, from the end of the heaven: *even* the Lord with the [1]weapons of his wrath to destroy the whole land.

6 Howl [1]you, for the day of the Lord is at hand: it shall come as a destroyer from the Almighty.

7 Therefore shall all hands be weakened, and all men's hearts shall melt.

8 And they shall be afraid: anguish and sorrow shall take *them*, and they shall have pain, as a woman that travaileth: everyone shall be amazed at his neighbor, and their faces *shall be like* [1]flames of fire.

9 Behold, the day of the Lord cometh, cruel, with wrath and fierce anger to lay the land waste: and he shall destroy the sinners out of it.

10 For the [1]stars of heaven and the planets thereof shall not give their light: the sun shall be darkened in his going forth, and the moon shall not cause her light to shine.

11 And I will visit the wickedness upon the [1]world, and their iniquity upon the wicked, and I will cause the arrogancy of the [2]proud to cease, and will cast down the pride of tyrants.

12 I will make a [1]man more precious than fine gold, even a man above the wedge of gold of Ophir.

13 Therefore I will shake the heaven, and the earth shall remove out of her place in the wrath of the Lord of hosts, and in the day of his fierce anger.

14 And [1]it shall be as a chased Doe, and as a sheep that no man taketh up; every man shall turn to his own people, and flee each one to his own land.

15 Everyone that is found, shall be stricken through: and whosoever joineth himself, shall fall by the sword.

16 [a]Their [1]children also shall be broken in pieces before their eyes: their houses shall be spoiled; and their wives ravished.

11:15 [2] To wit, Nile, the great river of Egypt, which entereth into the sea with seven streams.

12:1 [1] He showeth how the Church shall praise God, when they are delivered from their captivity.

12:2 [1] Our salvation standeth only in God, who giveth us an assured confidence, constancy, and occasion, to praise him for the same.

12:3 [1] The graces of God shall be so abundant, that ye may receive them in as great plenty, as waters out of a fountain that is full.

12:6 [1] Ye that are of the Church.

13:1 [1] That is, the great calamity, which was prophesied to come on Babel, as a most grievous burden, which they were not able to bear. In these twelve chapters following, he speaketh of the plagues wherewith God would smite the strange nations (whom they knew) to declare that God chastised the Israelites as his children, and these others as his enemies: and also if that God spare not these that are ignorant, that they must not think strange, if he punish them which have knowledge of his Law, and keep it not.

13:2 [1] To wit, the Medes and Persians.

13:3 [1] That is, prepared and appointed to execute my judgments.

[2] Which willingly go about to the work whereunto I appoint them, but how the wicked do this, read Isa. 10:6.

13:5 [1] The army of the Medes and the Persians against Babylon.

13:6 [1] Ye Babylonians.

13:8 [1] The Babylonians' anger and grief shall be so much, that their faces shall burn as fire.

13:10 [1] They that are overcome shall think that all the powers of heaven and earth are against them, Ezek. 32:7; Joel 3:15; Matt. 24:29.

13:11 [1] He compareth Babylon to the whole world, because they so esteemed themselves by reason of their great empire.

[2] He noteth the principal vice, whereunto they are most given, as are all that abound in wealth.

13:12 [1] He noteth the great slaughter that shall be, seeing the enemy shall neither for gold, or silver spare a man's life, as verse 17.

13:14 [1] Meaning, the power of Babylon with their hired soldiers.

13:16 [1] This was not accomplished when Cyrus took Babylon, but after the death of Alexander the great.

17 Behold, I will stir up the Medes against them, which shall not regard silver, nor be desirous of gold.

18 With bows also shall they destroy the children, and shall have no compassion upon the fruit of the womb, and their eyes shall not spare the children.

19 And Babel the glory of kingdoms, the beauty and pride of the Chaldeans, shall be as the destruction of God [b]in Sodom and Gomorrah.

20 It shall not be inhabited forever, neither shall it be dwelled in from generation to generation: neither shall the [1]Arabian pitch his tents there, neither shall their shepherds make their folds there.

21 But [1]Zijm shall lodge there, and their houses shall be full of Ohim: Ostriches shall dwell there, and the Satyrs shall dance there.

22 And Iim shall cry in their palaces, and dragons in their pleasant palaces: and the time thereof is ready to come, and the days thereof shall not be prolonged.

[b] Gen. 19:24
Jer. 50:40

14

1 *The return of the people from captivity.* 4 *The derision of the King of Babylon.* 11 *The death of the king.* 29 *The destruction of the Philistines.*

1 For [1]the Lord will have compassion of Jacob, and will yet choose Israel, and cause them to rest in their own land: and the stranger [2]shall join himself unto them, and they shall cleave to the house of Jacob.

2 And the people shall receive them and bring them to their own place, and the house of Israel shall possess them in the land of the Lord, for [1]servants and handmaids: and they shall take them prisoners, whose captives they were, and have rule over their oppressors.

3 ¶ And in that day when the Lord shall give thee rest from thy sorrow, and from thy fear, and from the sore bondage, wherein thou didst serve,

4 Then shalt thou take up this proverb against the King of Babel, and say, How hath the oppressor ceased? and the gold thirsty *Babel* rested?

5 The Lord hath broken the rod of the wicked, *and* the scepter of the rulers:

6 Which smote the people in anger with a continual plague, *and* ruled the nations in wrath: if any were persecuted, he did [1]not let.

7 The whole world is at [1]rest *and* is quiet: they sing for joy.

8 Also the fir trees rejoiced of thee, *and* the cedars of Lebanon, *saying,* Since thou art laid down, no hewer came up against us.

9 Hell beneath is moved for thee to [1]meet thee at thy coming, raising up the dead for thee, *even* all the princes of the earth, and hath raised from their thrones all the Kings of the nations.

10 All they shall cry and say unto thee, Art thou become weak also as we? art thou become like unto us?

11 Thy pomp is brought down to the grave, *and* the sound of the viols: the worm [1]is spread under thee, and the worms cover thee.

12 How art thou fallen from heaven, O [1]Lucifer, son of the morning? *and* cut down to the ground, which didst cast lots upon the nations?

13 Yet thou saidest in thine heart, I will ascend into heaven, and exalt my throne above beside the stars of God: I will sit also upon the mount of the congregation in the sides of the [1]North.

14 I will ascend above the height of the clouds, *and* I will be like the most high.

15 But thou shalt be brought down to the grave, to the side of the pit.

16 They that see thee, shall [1]look upon thee *and* consider thee, *saying,* Is this the man that made the earth to tremble, *and* that did shake the kingdoms?

17 He made the world as a wilderness, and destroyed the cities thereof, *and* opened not [1]the house of his prisoners.

18 All the kings of the nations, *even* they all sleep in glory, everyone in his own house.

19 But thou art [1]cast out of thy grave like an abominable branch: *like* the raiment of those that are slain, *and* thrust through with a sword, which go

---

13:20 [1] Who useth to go from country to country to find pasture for their beasts, but there shall they find none.

13:21 [1] Which were either wild beasts, or fowls, or wicked spirits, whereby Satan deluded man, as by the fairies, goblins, and such like fantasies.

14:1 [1] He showeth why God will haste to destroy his enemies, to wit, because he will deliver his Church.

[2] Meaning, that the Gentiles shalt be joined with the Church, and worship God.

14:2 [1] Signifying, that the Jews should be superiors to the Gentiles, and that they should be brought under the service of Christ by the preaching of the Apostles, whereby all are brought to the subjection of Christ, 2 Cor. 10:5.

14:6 [1] That is, he suffered all violence and injuries to be done.

14:7 [1] Meaning, that when tyrants reign, there can be no rest nor quietness, and also how detestable a thing tyranny is, seeing the insensible creatures have occasion to rejoice at their destruction.

14:9 [1] As though they feared, lest thou shouldest trouble the dead, as thou didst the living: and here he derideth the proud tyranny of the wicked, which know not that all creatures wish their destruction, that they may rejoice.

14:11 [1] Instead of thy costly carpets and coverings.

14:12 [1] Thou that thoughtest thyself most glorious, and as it were placed in the heaven: for the morning star that goeth before the sun, is called Lucifer, to whom Nebuchadnezzar is compared.

14:13 [1] Meaning, Jerusalem, whereof the Temple was of the North side, Ps. 48:2, whereby he meaneth that tyrants fight against God, when they persecute his Church, and would set themselves in his place.

14:16 [1] In marveling at thee.

14:17 [1] To set them at liberty: noting his cruelty.

14:19 [1] Thou wast not buried in the sepulchre of thy fathers, thy tyranny was so abhorred.

down to the stones of the pit, as a carcass trodden under feet.

20 Thou shalt not be joined with them in the grave, because thou hast destroyed thine own land, *and* slain thy people: the seed of the wicked shall not be renowned forever.

21 [1]Prepare a slaughter for his children, for the iniquity of their fathers: let them not rise up nor possess the land, nor fill the face of the world with enemies.

22 ¶ For I will rise up against them (saith the Lord of hosts) and will cut off from Babel the name and the remnant, and the son, and the nephew, saith the Lord:

23 And I will make it a possession to the [1]hedge-hog, and pools of water, and I will sweep it with the besom of destruction, saith the Lord of hosts.

24 The Lord of hosts hath sworn, saying, Surely like as I have purposed, so shall it come to pass, and as I have consulted, it shall stand:

25 [1]That I will break to pieces Assyria in my land, and upon my mountains will I tread him under foot, so that his yoke shall depart from [2]them, and his burden shall be taken from off their shoulder.

26 This is the counsel that is consulted upon the whole world, and this is the hand stretched out over all the nations,

27 Because the Lord of hosts hath determined, and who shall disannul it? and his hand is stretched out, and who shall turn it away?

28 ¶ In the year that king Ahaz died, was this [1]burden.

29 Rejoice not, (thou whole [1]Philistia) because the rod of him that did beat thee is broken: for out of the serpent's root shall come forth a cockatrice, and the fruit thereof *shall be* a fiery flying serpent.

30 For the [1]first born of the poor shall be fed, and the needy shall lie down in safety: and I will kill thy root with famine, and [2]it shall slay thy remnant.

31 Howl, O gate, cry, O city: thou whole land of Philistia art dissolved, for there shall come from the [1]North a smoke, and none *shall be* [2]alone, at his time appointed.

32 What shall then one answer the [1]messengers of the Gentiles? that the Lord hath stablished [2]Zion, and the poor of his people shall trust in it.

15   *A prophecy against Moab.*

1 The [1]burden of Moab. Surely [2]Ar of Moab was destroyed, *and* brought to silence in a night: surely Kir of Moab was destroyed, *and* brought to silence in a night.

2 [1]He shall go up to the Temple, and to Dibon to the high places to weep: for [2]Nebo and for Medeba shall Moab howl: upon all [3]their heads *shall be* bald-ness, and every beard shaven.

3 In their streets shall they be girded with sackcloth: on the tops of their houses, and in their streets everyone shall howl, *and* come down with weeping.

4 And Heshbon shall cry, and Elealeh: their voice shall be heard unto Jahaz: therefore the warriors of Moab shall shout: the soul of everyone shall lament in himself.

5 Mine [1]heart shall cry for Moab: his fugitives *shall flee* unto Zoar, [2]an heifer of three years old: for they shall go up with weeping by the mounting up of Luhith: and by the way of Horonaim they [3]shall raise up a cry of destruction.

6 For the waters of Nimrim shall be dried up: therefore the grass is withered, the herbs consumed, *and* there was no green herb.

7 Therefore what *every man* hath left, and their sub-stance shall they bear to the [1]brook of the willows.

8 For the cry went round about the borders of Moab, *and* the howling thereof unto Eglaim, and the skriking thereof unto Beer Elim,

9 Because the waters of Dimon shall be full [1]of blood: for I will bring more upon Dimon, even

---

14:21 [1] He called to the Medes and Persians, and all those that should execute God's vengeance.

14:23 [1] Or, tortoise.

14:25 [1] As I have begun to destroy the Assyrians in Sennacherib: so will I continue, and destroy them wholly, when I shall deliver you from Babylon. [2] From the Jews.

14:28 [1] Read Isa. 13:1.

14:29 [1] He willeth the Philistines not to rejoice because the Jews are diminished in their power, for their strength shall be greater than ever it was.

14:30 [1] The Israelites, which were brought to most extreme misery. [2] To wit, my people.

14:31 [1] That is, from the Jews or Assyrians: for they were brought to most extreme misery. [2] But they shall be all ready, and join together.

14:32 [1] Which shall come to inquire of the state of the Church. [2] They shall answer that the Lord doth defend his Church, and them that join themselves thereunto.

15:1 [1] Read Isa. 13:1. [2] The chief city, whereby the whole country was meant.

15:2 [1] The Moabites shall flee to their idols for succor, but it shall be too late. [2] Which were cites of Moab. [3] For as in the west parts the people used to let their hair grow long, when they mourned, so in the East part they cut it off.

15:5 [1] The Prophet speaketh this in the person of the Moabites: or as one that felt the great judgment of God that God should come upon them. [2] Meaning, that it was a city that ever lived in pleasure, and never felt sorrow. [3] He describeth the miserable dissipation and flight of the Moabites.

15:7 [1] To hide themselves, and their goods there.

15:9 [1] Of them that are slain.

lions ²upon him that escapeth of Moab, and to the remnant of the land.

16
The causes wherefore the Moabites are destroyed.

1   Send ¹ye a lamb to the ruler of the world from the rock of the wilderness, unto the mountain of the daughter Zion.

2   For it shall be as a bird that ¹flieth, and a nest forsaken: the daughters of Moab shall be at the fords of Arnon.

3   Gather a counsel, execute judgment, ¹make thy shadow as the night in the midday: hide them that are chased out: bewray not him that is fled.

4   Let my banished dwell with thee: Moab, be thou their covert from the face of the destroyer: for the extortioner ¹shall end: the destroyer shall be consumed, *and* the oppressor shall cease out of the land.

5   And in mercy shall the throne be prepared, ¹and he shall sit upon it in steadfastness, in the tabernacle of David, judging, and seeking judgment, and hasting justice.

6   We have heard of the pride of Moab (he is very proud) *even* his pride, and his arrogancy, and his indignation, *but* his ¹lies *shall* not *be* so.

7   Therefore shall Moab howl unto Moab, everyone shall howl: for the foundations of Kir Hareseth shall ye mourn, yet they shall be ¹stricken.

8   For the vineyards of Heshbon are cut down, *and* the vine of Sibmah: ¹the lords of the heathen have broken the principal vines thereof: they are come unto ²Jazer: they wandered in the wilderness: her goodly branches stretched out themselves, *and* went over the sea.

9   Therefore will ¹I weep with the weeping of Jazer, and of the vine of Sibmah, O Heshbon: and Elealeh,

I will make thee drunk with my tears, because upon thy summer fruits, and upon thy harvest ²a shouting is fallen.

10   And gladness is taken away, and joy out of the plentiful field: and in the vineyards shall be no singing nor shouting for joy: the treader shall not tread wine in the wine presses: I have caused the rejoicing to cease.

11   Wherefore, my ¹bowels shall sound like an harp for Moab, and mine inward parts for Kir Heres.

12   And when it shall appear that Moab shall be weary of his high places, then shall he come to his ¹temple to pray, but he shall not prevail.

13   This is the word that the Lord hath spoken against Moab since that time.

14   And now the Lord hath spoken, saying, ¹In three years as the years of an ²hireling, and the glory of Moab shall be contemned in all the great multitude, and the remnant shall be very small *and* feeble.

17
1 *A prophecy of the destruction of Damascus and Ephraim,* 7 *calamity moveth to repentance.*

1   The ¹burden of ²Damascus. Behold, Damascus is taken away from being a city, for it shall be a ruinous heap.

2   The cities of ¹Aroer *shall be* forsaken: they shall be for the flocks: for they shall lie *there*, and none shall make them afraid.

3   The munition also shall cease from ¹Ephraim, and the kingdom from Damascus, and the remnant of Aram shall be as the ²glory of the children of Israel, saith the Lord of hosts.

4   And in that day the glory of ¹Jacob shall be made clean.

5   And it shall be as when the harvest man gathereth ¹the corn, and reapeth the ears with his arm,

---

² So that by no means they should escape the hand of God: thus will God punish the enemies of his Church.

16:1 ¹ That is, offer a sacrifice, whereby he derideth their long delay, which would not repent when the Lord called them, showing them that it is now too late, seeing the vengeance of God is upon them.

16:2 ¹ There is no remedy, but you must flee.

16:3 ¹ He showeth what Moab should have done, when Israel their neighbor was in affliction, to whom because they would give no shadow nor comfort, they are now left comfortless.

16:4 ¹ The Assyrians shall oppress the Israelites, but for a while.

16:5 ¹ Meaning, Christ.

16:6 ¹ Their vain confidence, and proud brags shall deceive them, Jer. 48:2.

16:7 ¹ For all your mourning, yet the city shall be destroyed, even unto the foundation.

16:8 ¹ That is, the Assyrians and other enemies.

² Meaning, that the country of Moab was now destroyed, and all the precious things thereof were carried into the borders, yea into other countries, and over the sea.

16:9 ¹ He showeth that their plague was so great, that it would have moved any man to lament with them, as Ps. 141:5.

² The enemies are come upon thee, and shout for joy, when they carry thy commodities from thee, as Jer. 48:33.

16:11 ¹ For very sorrow and compassion.

16:12 ¹ They shall use all means to seek help of their idols, and all in vain: for Chemosh their great god shall not be able to help them.

16:14 ¹ He appointed a certain time to punish the enemies in.

² Who will observe justly the time for the which he is hired, and serve no longer, but will ever long for it.

17:1 ¹ Read Isa. 13:1.

² The chief city of Syria.

17:2 ¹ It was a country of Syria by the river Arnon.

17:3 ¹ It seemeth that the Prophet would comfort the Church in declaring the destruction of these two kings of Syria and Israel, when as they had conspired the overthrow of Judah.

² The ten tribes gloried in their multitude and alliance with other nations: therefore he saith that they shall be brought down, and the Syrians also.

17:4 ¹ Meaning, of the ten tribes, which boasted themselves of their nobility, prosperity, strength and multitude.

17:5 ¹ As the abundance of corn doth not fear the harvest men that should cut it down: no more shall the multitude of Israel make the enemies to shrink, whom God shall appoint to destroy them.

and he shall be as he that gathereth the ears in the valley of ²Rephaim.

6 Yet a gathering of grapes shall ¹be left in it: as the shaking of an olive tree, two or three berries are in the top of the upmost boughs, and four or five in the high branches of the fruit thereof, saith the Lord God of Israel.

7 At that day shall a man look to his ¹maker, and his eyes shall look to the holy one of Israel.

8 And he shall not look to the altars, the works of his own hands, neither shall he look to those things which his own fingers have made, as groves and images.

9 In that day shall the cities of their strength be as the forsaking of boughs and branches, which ¹they did forsake, because of the children of Israel, and there shall be desolation.

10 Because thou hast forgotten the God of thy salvation, and hast not remembered the God of thy strength, therefore shalt thou set pleasant plants, and shalt graft strange ¹vine branches.

11 In the day shalt thou make thy plant to grow, and in the morning shalt thou make thy seed to flourish: but the harvest shall be gone in the day ¹of possession, and there shall be desperate sorrow.

12 ¹Ah, the multitude of many people, they shall make a sound like the noise of the sea: for the noise of the people shall make a sound like the noise of mighty waters.

13 The people shall make a sound like the noise of many waters: but God shall ¹rebuke them, and they shall flee far off, and shall be chased as the chaff of the mountains before the wind, and as a rolling thing before the whirlwind.

14 And lo, in the evening there is ¹trouble: but afore the morning it is gone. This is the portion of them that spoil us, and the lot of them that rob us.

18

1 Of the enemies of the Church. 7 And of the vocation of the Gentiles.

1 Oh, the ¹land shadowing with wings, which is beyond the rivers of Ethiopia,

2 Sending ambassadors by the sea, even in vessels of ¹reeds upon the waters, saying, ²Go, ye swift messengers, to a nation that is scattered abroad, and spoiled, unto a terrible ³people from their beginning even hitherto: a nation by little and little even trodden under foot: whose land the ⁴floods have spoiled.

3 All ye the inhabitants of the world, and dwellers in the earth, shall see when ¹he setteth up a sign in the mountains, and when he bloweth the trumpet, ye shall hear.

4 For so the Lord said unto me, I will ¹rest and behold in my tabernacle, as ²the heat drying up the rain, and as a cloud of dew in the heat of harvest.

5 For afore the harvest, when the flower is finished, and the fruit is ripening in the flower, then he shall cut down the branches with hooks, and shall take away, and cut off the boughs:

6 They shall be left together unto the fowls of the mountains, and to the ¹beasts of the earth: for the fowl shall summer upon it, and every beast of the earth shall winter upon it.

7 At that time shall a ¹present be brought unto the Lord of hosts (a people that is scattered abroad, and spoiled, and of a terrible people from their beginning hitherto, a nation by little and little even trodden under foot, whose land the rivers have spoiled) to the place of the name of the Lord of hosts, even the mount Zion.

19

1 The destruction of the Egyptians by the Assyrians. 18 Of their conversion to the Lord.

1 The ¹burden of Egypt. Behold, the Lord

17:5 ² Which valley was plentiful and fertile.

17:6 ¹ Because God would have his covenant stable, he promiseth to reserve some of this people, and to bring them to repentance.

17:7 ¹ He showeth that God's corrections ever bring forth some fruit, and cause his to turn from their sins, and to humble themselves to him.

17:9 ¹ As the Canaanites left their cities when God did place the Israelites there, so the cities of Israel shall no more be able to defend their inhabitants than bushes, when God shall send the enemy to plague them.

17:10 ¹ Which are excellent, and brought out of other countries.

17:11 ¹ As the Lord threateneth the wicked in his Law, Lev. 26:16.

17:12 ¹ The Prophet lamenteth, considering the horrible plague that was prepared against Israel by the Assyrians, which were infinite in number, and gathered of many nations.

17:13 ¹ He addeth this for the consolation of the faithful which were in Israel.

17:14 ¹ He compareth the enemies the Assyrians to a tempest, which riseth overnight, and in the morning is gone.

18:1 ¹ He meaneth that part of Ethiopia, which lieth toward the sea, which was so full of ships that the sails (which he compareth to

wings) seemed to shadow the sea.

18:2 ¹ Which in those countries were great, insomuch as they made ships of them for swiftness.

² This may be taken, that they sent others to comfort the Jews, and to promise them help against their enemies, and so the Lord did threaten to take away their strength, that the Jews should not trust therein: or that they did solicit the Egyptians, and promised them aid to go against Judah.

³ To wit, the Jews, who because of God's plague, made all other nations afraid of the like, as God threatened, Deut. 28:37.

⁴ Meaning, the Assyrians, as Isa. 8:7.

18:3 ¹ When the Lord prepared to fight against the Ethiopians.

18:4 ¹ I will stay a while from punishing the wicked.

² Which two seasons are most profitable for the ripening of fruits, whereby he meaneth, that he will seem to favor them, and give them abundance for a time, but he will suddenly cut them off.

18:6 ¹ Not only men shall contemn them, but the brute beasts.

18:7 ¹ Meaning, that God will pity his Church, and receive that little remnant as an offering unto himself.

19:1 ¹ Read Isa. 13:7.

²rideth upon a swift cloud, and shall come into Egypt, and the idols of Egypt shall be moved at his presence, and the heart of Egypt shall melt in the midst of her.

2   And I will set the Egyptians against the Egyptians: so everyone shall ¹fight against his brother, and everyone against his neighbor, city against city, *and* kingdom against kingdom.

3   And the ¹spirit of Egypt shall fail in the midst of her, and I will destroy their counsel, and they shall seek at the idols, and at the sorcerers, and at them that have spirits of divination, and at the soothsayers.

4   And I will deliver the Egyptians into the hand of the cruel lords, and a mighty king shall rule over them, saith the Lord God of hosts.

5   Then the waters of the sea shall ¹fail, and the river shall be dried up, and wasted.

6   And the ¹rivers shall go far away: the rivers of defense shall be emptied and dried up: the reeds and flags shall be cut down.

7   The grass in the river, *and* at the ¹head of the rivers, and all that groweth by the river shall wither, *and* be driven away, and be no more.

8   The fishers also shall ¹mourn, and all they that cast angle into the river, shall lament, and they that spread their net upon the waters, shall be weakened.

9   Moreover, they that work in flax of divers sorts, shall be confounded, and they that weave nets.

10   For their nets shall be broken, and all they that make ponds *shall be* heavy in heart.

11   Surely the princes of ¹Zoan *are* fools: the counsel of the wise counselors of Pharaoh, is become foolish: how say ye unto Pharaoh, I ²am the son of the wise? I am the son of the ancient kings?

12   Where are now the wise men, that they may tell thee, or may know what the Lord of hosts hath determined against Egypt?

13   The princes of Zoan are become fools: the princes of ¹Noph are deceived, they have deceived Egypt, *even* the ²corners of the tribes thereof.

14   The Lord hath mingled among them the spirits ¹of errors: and they have caused Egypt to err in every work thereof, as a drunken man erreth in his vomit.

15   Neither shall there be any work in Egypt, which the head may ¹do, nor the tail, the branch nor the rush.

16   In that day shall Egypt be like unto women: for it shall be afraid and fear because of the moving of the hand of the Lord of hosts, which he shaketh over it.

17   And the land of Judah shall be a fear ¹unto Egypt: everyone that maketh mention of it, shall be afraid thereat, because of the counsel of the Lord of hosts, which he hath determined upon it.

18   In that day shall five cities in the land of Egypt ¹speak the language of Canaan, and shall ²swear by the Lord of hosts: one shall be called the city of ³destruction.

19   In that day shall the altar of the Lord be in the midst of the land of Egypt, and ¹a pillar by the border thereof unto the Lord.

20   And it shall be for a sign and for a witness unto the Lord of hosts in the land of Egypt: for they shall cry unto the Lord, because of the oppressors, and he shall send them ¹a Savior, and a great man, and shall deliver them.

21   And the Lord shall be known of the Egyptians, and the Egyptians shall know the Lord in that day, and do ¹sacrifice and oblation, and shall vow vows unto the Lord, and perform *them*.

---

² Because the Egyptians trusted in the defense of their country, in the multitude of their idols, and in the valiantness of their men, the Lord showeth that he will come over all their munitions in a swift cloud, and that their idols shall tremble at his coming and that men's hearts shall faint.

19:2 ¹ As he caused the Ammonites, Moabites and Idumeans to kill one another, when they came to destroy the Church of God, 2 Chron. 20:22; Isa. 49:26.

19:3 ¹ Meaning, their policy and wisdom.

19:5 ¹ He showeth that the sea and Nile their great river, whereby they thought themselves most sure, should not be able to defend them from his anger, but that he would send the Assyrians among them, that should keep them under as slaves.

19:6 ¹ For the Nile ran into the sea by seven streams, as though they were so many rivers.

19:7 ¹ The Hebrew word is mouth, whereby they mean the spring out of the which the water gusheth as out of a mouth.

19:8 ¹ The Scriptures used to describe the destruction of a country by taking away of the commodities thereof, as by vines, flesh, fish, and such other things, whereby countries are enriched.

19:11 ¹ Called also Tanis, a famous city upon the Nile.

² He noteth the flatterers of Pharaoh: who persuaded the king that he was wise and noble, and that his house was most ancient, and so he flattered himself, saying, I am wise.

19:13 ¹ Or, Memphis, others Alexandria, and now called the great Cairo.

² The principal upholders thereof are the chiefest cause of their destruction.

19:14 ¹ For the spirit of wisdom he hath made them drunken and giddy with the spirit of error.

19:15 ¹ Neither the great nor the small, the strong nor the weak.

19:17 ¹ Considering that through their occasion the Jews made not God their defense: but put their trust in them, and were therefore now punished, they shall fear lest the like light upon them.

19:18 ¹ Shall make one confession of faith with the people of God: by the speech of Canaan, meaning the language wherein God was then served.

² Shall renounce their superstitions and protest to serve God aright.

³ Meaning, of six cities, five should serve God, and the sixth remain in their wickedness: and so of the sixth part there should be but one lost.

19:19 ¹ There shall be evident signs and tokens, that God's religion is there: which manner of speech is taken of the Patriarchs and ancient times, when God had not as yet appointed the place, and full manner how he would be worshipped.

19:20 ¹ This declareth that this prophecy should be accomplished in the time of Christ.

19:21 ¹ By these ceremonies he comprehendeth the spiritual service under Christ.

22 So the Lord shall smite Egypt, he shall smite and heal it: for he shall return unto the Lord, and he shall be entreated of them and shall heal them.

23 In that day shall there be a path from ¹Egypt to Assyria, and Assyria shall come into Egypt, and Egypt into Assyria: so the Egyptians shall worship with Assyria.

24 In that day shall Israel be the third with Egypt and Assyria: *even* a blessing in the midst of the land.

25 For the Lord of hosts shall bless it, saying, Blessed *be* my people Egypt and Assyria, the work of mine hands, and Israel mine inheritance.

20

2 The three years captivity of Egypt and Ethiopia described by the three years going naked of Isaiah.

1 In the year that ¹Tartan came to ²Ashdod, (when ³Sargon king of Assyria sent him) and had fought against Ashdod, and taken it,

2 At the same time spake the Lord by the hand of Isaiah the son of Amoz, saying, Go, and loose the ¹sackcloth from thy loins, and put off thy shoe from thy foot. And he did so, walking naked and barefoot.

3 And the Lord said, Like as my servant Isaiah hath walked naked and barefoot three years *as* a sign and wonder upon Egypt, and Ethiopia;

4 So shall the king of Assyria take away the captivity of Egypt, and the captivity of Ethiopia, *both* young men and old men, naked and barefoot, with their buttocks uncovered, to the shame of Egypt.

5 And they shall fear, and be ashamed of ¹Ethiopia their expectation, and of Egypt their ²glory.

6 Then shall the inhabitants of this ¹isle say in that day, Behold, such is our expectation, whither we fled for help to be delivered from the king of Assyria, and how shall we be delivered?

CHAPTER 21
ᵃ Jer. 51:8
Rev. 14:8

21

1 Of the destruction of Babylon by the Persians and Medes.   11 The ruin of Idumea,   13 and of Arabia.

1 The burden of the ¹desert sea. As the whirlwinds in the South used to pass from the wilderness, *so* shall it ²come from the horrible land.

2 A grievous vision was showed unto me, The ¹Transgressor *against* a transgressor, and the destroyer *against* a destroyer. Go up ²Elam, besiege Media: I have caused all the mourning ³thereof to cease.

3 Therefore are my ¹loins filled with sorrow: sorrows have taken me as the sorrows of a woman that travaileth: I was bowed down when I heard it, *and* I was amazed when I saw it.

4 Mine heart failed: fearfulness troubled me: the night ¹of my pleasures hath he turned into fear unto me.

5 Prepare thou the table: watch in the watch tower: eat, drink: ¹arise, ye princes, anoint the shield:

6 For thus hath the ¹Lord said unto me, Go, set a watchman, to tell what he seeth.

7 And he saw a chariot with two horsemen: ¹a chariot of an ass, *and* a chariot of a camel: and he hearkened *and* took diligent heed.

8 And he cried, A ¹lion: my Lord, I stand continually upon the watch tower in the daytime, and I am set in my watch every night:

9 And behold, this man's chariot cometh with two horsemen. And ¹he answered and said, ᵃBabel is fallen: it is fallen, and all the images of her gods hath he broken unto the ground.

10 O ¹my threshing, and the ²corn of my floor. That which I have heard of the Lord of hosts the God of Israel, have I showed unto you.

11 ¶ The burden of ¹Dumah, he calleth unto me out of ²Seir, Watchman, what was in the night? Watchman, what was in the night?

19:23 ¹ By these two nations, which were then chief enemies of the Church, he showeth that the Gentiles and the Jews should be joined together in one faith and religion, and should be all one fold under Christ their shepherd.

20:1 ¹ Who was captain of Sennacherib, 2 Kings 18:17.

² A city of the Philistines.

³ The Hebrews write that Sennacherib was so called.

20:2 ¹ Which signifieth that the Prophet did lament the misery that he saw prepared, before the three years that he went naked and barefooted.

20:5 ¹ In whose aid they trusted.

² Of whom they boasted and gloried.

20:6 ¹ Meaning, Judea, which was compassed about with their enemies, as an isle with waters.

21:1 ¹ On the seaside between Judea and Chaldea was a wilderness, whereby he meaneth Chaldea.

² That is, the ruin of Babylon by the Medes and Persians.

21:2 ¹ The Assyrians and Chaldeans, which had destroyed other nations, shall be overcome of the Medes and Persians: and this he prophesied an hundred years before it came to pass.

² By Elam he meaneth the Persians.

³ Because they shall find no succor, they shall mourn no more, or, I have caused them to cease mourning, whom Babylon had afflicted.

21:3 ¹ This the Prophet speaketh in the person of the Babylonians.

21:4 ¹ He prophesieth the death of Belshazzar, as Dan. 5:30, who in the midst of his pleasures was destroyed.

21:5 ¹ While they are eating and drinking, they shall be commanded to run to their weapons.

21:6 ¹ To wit, in a vision by the spirit of prophecy.

21:7 ¹ Meaning, chariots of men of war, and others that carried the baggage.

21:8 ¹ Meaning, Darius, which overcame Babylon.

21:9 ¹ The watchman whom Isaiah set up, told him who came toward Babylon, and the Angel declared that it should be destroyed: all this was done in a vision.

21:10 ¹ Meaning, Babylon.

² Hebrew, *son.*

21:11 ¹ Which was a city of the Ishmaelites, and was so named of Dumah, Gen. 25:14.

² A mountain of the Idumeans.

12 The watchman said, The ¹morning cometh, and also the night. If ye will as he, inquire: return *and* come.

13 ¶ The burden against Arabia. In ¹the forest of Arabia shall ye tarry all night, *even* in the ways of Dedanites.

14 O inhabitants of the land of Tema, bring forth ¹water to meet the thirsty, *and* prevent him that fleeth with his bread.

15 For they flee from the drawn swords, *even* from the drawn sword, and from the bent bow, and from the grievousness of war.

16 For thus hath the Lord said unto me, Yet a year ¹according to the years of an ²hireling, and all the glory of Kedar shall fail.

17 And the residue of the number of the strong archers of the sons of ¹Kedar shall be few: for the Lord God of Israel hath spoken it.

22 1 *He prophesieth of the destruction of Jerusalem by Nebuchadnezzar.* 15 *A threatening against Shebna.* 20 *To whose office Eliakim is preferred.*

1 The burden of the ¹valley of vision. What ²aileth thee now that thou art wholly gone up unto the house tops?

2 Thou that art full of ¹noise, a city full of brute, a joyous city, thy slain men shall not *be* slain ²with sword, nor die in battle.

3 All thy princes shall flee together from the bow: they shall be ¹bound: all that shall be found in thee, shall be bound together, which have fled from ²far.

4 Therefore said I, Turn away from me, I will weep ¹bitterly: labor not to comfort me for the destruction of the daughter of my people.

5 For *it is* a day of trouble, and of ruin, and of perplexity by the Lord God of hosts in the valley of vision, breaking down the city: and a ¹crying unto the mountains.

6 ¶ And Elam ¹bare the quiver in a man's chariot with horsemen, and Kir uncovered the shield.

7 And thy chief valleys were full of chariots, and the horsemen set themselves in array against the gate.

8 And he discovered the ¹covering of Judah: and thou didst look in that day to the armor of the house of the forest.

9 And ye have seen ¹the breaches of the city of David: for they were many, and ye gathered the waters of the lower pool.

10 And ye numbered the houses ¹of Jerusalem, and the houses have ye broken down to fortify the wall,

11 And have also made a ditch between the two walls, for the ¹waters of the old pool, and have not looked unto the maker ²thereof, neither had respect unto him that formed it of old.

12 And in that day did the Lord God of hosts call unto weeping and mourning, and to baldness and girding with sackcloth.

13 And behold, joy and gladness, slaying oxen and killing sheep, eating flesh, and drinking wine, ¹eating and drinking, for tomorrow we shall die.

14 And it was declared in the ears of the Lord of hosts. Surely this iniquity shall not be purged from you, till ye die, saith the Lord God of hosts.

15 Thus saith the Lord God of hosts, Go, get thee to that ¹treasurer, to Shebna, the steward of the house, *and say,*

21:12 ¹ He describeth the unquietness of the people of Dumah, who were night and day in fear of their enemies, and ever ran to and fro to inquire news.

21:13 ¹ For fear, the Arabians shall flee into the woods, and he appointeth what way they shall take.

21:14 ¹ Signifying, that for fear they shall not tarry to eat nor drink.

21:16 ¹ He appointeth them respite for one year only, and then they should be destroyed.

² Read Isa. 16:14.

21:17 ¹ Which was the name of a people of Arabia: and by the horrible destruction of all these nations, he teacheth the Jews that there is no place for refuge or to escape God's wrath, but only to remain in his Church, and to live in his fear.

22:1 ¹ Meaning, Judea, which was compassed about with mountains, and was called the valley of visions, because of the Prophets, which were always there, whom they named Seers.

² He speaketh to Jerusalem, whose inhabitants were fled up to the housetops for fear of their enemies.

22:2 ¹ Which was wont to be full of people and joy.

² But for hunger.

22:3 ¹ And led into captivity.

² Which have fled from other places to Jerusalem for succor.

22:4 ¹ He showeth what is the duty of the godly, when God's plagues hang over the Church, and especially of the ministers, Jer. 9:1.

22:5 ¹ That is, the shout of the enemies whom God had appointed to destroy the city.

22:6 ¹ He putteth them in mind how God delivered them once from Sennacherib, who brought the Persians and Cyrenians with him, that they might by returning to God avoid that great plague which they should else suffer by Nebuchadnezzar.

22:8 ¹ The secret place where the armor was: to wit, in the house of the forest, 1 Kings 7:2.

22:9 ¹ Ye forfeited the ruinous places which were neglected in times of peace: meaning, the whole City, and the City of David, which was within the compass of the other.

22:10 ¹ Either to pull down such as might hurt, or else to know what men they were able to make.

22:11 ¹ To provide if need should be of water.

² To God that made Jerusalem: that is, they trusted more in these worldly means, than in God.

22:13 ¹ Instead of repentance ye were joyful and made great cheer, contemning the admonitions of the Prophets, saying, Let us eat and drink for our Prophets say, that we shall die tomorrow.

22:15 ¹ Because the Hebrew word doth also signify one that doth nourish and cherish, there are of the learned that think that this wicked man did nourish secret friendship with the Assyrians and Egyptians to betray the Church, and to provide for himself against all dangers: in the mean season he packed craftily, and got of the best offices into his hand under Hezekiah, ever aspiring to the highest.

16 What hast thou to do here? and whom hast thou ¹here? that thou shouldest here hew thee out a sepulcher, as he that heweth out his sepulcher in a high place, or that graveth an habitation ²for himself in a rock?

17 Behold, the Lord will carry thee away with a great captivity, and will surely cover thee.

18 He will surely roll and turn thee like a ball in a large country: there shalt thou die, and there the chariots of thy glory shall be the ¹shame of thy lord's house.

19 And I will drive thee from thy station, and out of thy dwelling will he destroy thee.

20 And in that day will I ¹call my servant Eliakim the son of Hilkiah,

21 And with thy garments will I clothe him, and with thy girdle will I strengthen him: thy power also will I commit into his hand, and he shall be a father of the inhabitants of Jerusalem, and of the house of Judah.

22 And the ¹key of the house of David will I lay upon his shoulder: so he shall open, and no man shall shut: and he shall shut, and no man shall open.

23 And I will fasten him as a ¹nail in a sure place, and he shall be for the throne of glory to his father's house.

24 And they shall hang upon him all the glory of his father's house, even of the nephews and posterity ¹all small vessels, from the vessels of the cups, even to all the instruments of music.

25 In that day saith the Lord of hosts, shall the ¹nail that is fastened in the sure place, depart and shall be broken and fall, and the burden that was upon it, shall be cut off: for the Lord hath spoken it.

23

1 A Prophecy against Tyre.   17 A promise that it shall be restored.

1 The ¹burden of Tyre. Howl ye ships of ²Tarshish: for ³it is destroyed, so that there is none house: none

shall come from the land of ⁴Kittim: it is ⁵revealed unto them.

2 Be still, ye that dwell in the isles: the merchants of Sidon, and such as pass over the sea, have ¹replenished thee.

3 The ¹seed of Nile growing by the abundance of waters, and the harvest of the river was her revenues, and she was a mart of the nations.

4 Be ashamed, thou Sidon: for the ¹sea hath spoken, even the strength of the sea, saying, I have not ²travailed, nor brought forth children, neither nourished young men, nor brought up virgins.

5 When the fame cometh to the Egyptians, they shall be ¹sorry, concerning the rumor of Tyre.

6 Go you over to ¹Tarshish: howl, ye that dwell in the isles.

7 Is not this that your glorious city? her antiquity is of ancient days: her own feet shall lead her afar off to be a sojourner.

8 Who hath decreed this against Tyre (that ¹crowneth men) whose merchants are princes? whose chapmen are the nobles of the world?

9 The Lord of hosts hath decreed this, to stain the pride of all glory, and to bring to contempt all them that be glorious in the earth.

10 Pass through thy land like a flood to the ¹daughter of Tarshish: there is no more strength.

11 He stretched out his hand upon the sea: he shook the kingdoms: the Lord hath given a commandment concerning the place of merchandise, to destroy the power thereof.

12 And he said, Thou shalt no more rejoice when thou art oppressed: ¹O virgin ²daughter of Sidon: rise up, go out unto Kittim: yet there thou shalt have no rest.

13 Behold the land of the Chaldeans: this was no people: ¹Assyria founded it by the inhabitants of the wilderness: they set up the towers thereof:

22:16 ¹ Meaning, that he was a stranger, and came up of nothing.
   ² Whereas he thought to make his name immortal by his famous sepulcher, he died most miserably among the Assyrians.
22:18 ¹ Signifying that whatsoever dignity the wicked attain unto, at length it will turn to the shame of those princes, by whom they are preferred.
22:20 ¹ To be steward again, out of the which office he had been put, by the craft of Shebna.
22:22 ¹ I will commit unto him the full charge and government of the king's house.
22:23 ¹ I will establish him, and confirm him in his office: of this phrase, read Ezra 9:9.
22:24 ¹ Meaning that both small and great that shall come of Eliakim, shall have praise and glory by his faithful officer.
22:25 ¹ He meaneth Shebna, who in man's judgment should never have fallen.
23:1 ¹ Read Isa. 13:1.
   ² Ye of Cilicia that come thither for merchandise.
   ³ Tyre is destroyed by Nebuchadnezzar.

⁴ By Kittim they meant all the isles and countries Westward from Palestine.
   ⁵ All men know of this destruction.
23:2 ¹ Have haunteth thee, and enriched thee.
23:3 ¹ Meaning, the corn of Egypt, which was fed by the overflowing of the Nile.
23:4 ¹ That is, Tyre, which was the chief part of the sea.
   ² I have no people left in me, and am as a barren woman that never had children.
23:5 ¹ Because these two countries were joined in league together.
23:6 ¹ Tyre willeth other merchants to go to Cilicia, and to come no more there.
23:8 ¹ Who maketh her merchants like princes.
23:10 ¹ Thy strength will no more serve thee: therefore flee to other countries for succor.
23:12 ¹ For Tyre was never touched nor afflicted before.
   ² Because Tyre was built by them of Sidon.
23:13 ¹ The Chaldeans which dwelt in tents in the wilderness, were gathered by the Assyrians into cities.

they raised the palaces thereof, *and* he [2]brought it to ruin.

14 Howl ye ships of Tarshish, for your [1]strength is destroyed.

15 And in that day shall Tyre be forgotten seventy years (according to the years of one King) at the end of [1]seventy years shall Tyre [2]sing as an harlot.

16 Take an harp *and* go about the city (thou harlot that hast been forgotten) [1]make sweet melody, sing more songs that thou mayest be remembered.

17 And at the end of seventy years shall the Lord visit Tyre, and she shall return to her [1]wages, and shall commit fornication with all the kingdoms of the earth, *that are* in the world.

18 Yet her occupying and her wages shall be [1]holy unto the Lord: it shall not be laid up nor kept in store, but her merchandise shall be for them that dwell before the Lord, to eat sufficiently, and to have durable clothing.

24

1 *A prophecy of the curse of God for the sins of the people.* 13 *A remnant reserved shall praise the Lord.*

1 Behold, the Lord maketh the [1]earth empty, and he maketh it waste: he turneth it upside down, and scattereth abroad the inhabitants thereof.

2 And there shall be like people, like [1]Priest, and like servant, like master, like maid, like mistress, like buyer, like seller, like lender, like borrower, like giver, like taker to usury.

3 The earth shall be clean emptied, and utterly spoiled: for the Lord hath spoken this word.

4 The earth lamenteth and fadeth away, the world is feebled and decayed: the proud people of the earth are weakened.

5 The earth [1]also deceiveth, because of the inhabitants thereof: for they transgressed the laws: they changed the ordinances, *and* brake the everlasting Covenant.

6 Therefore hath the [1]curse devoured the earth, and the inhabitants thereof are desolate. Wherefore the inhabitants of the land are [2]burned up, and few men are left.

7 The wine faileth, the vine hath no might: all that were of merry heart, do mourn.

8 The mirth of tabrets ceaseth: the noise of them that rejoice, endeth: the joy of the harp ceaseth.

9 They shall not drink wine with mirth: strong drink shall be bitter to them that drink it.

10 The city of [1]vanity is broken down: every house is shut up, that no man may come in.

11 There is a crying for wine in the streets: all joy is darkened: the [1]mirth of the world is gone away.

12 In the cities is left desolation, and the gate is smitten with destruction.

13 ¶ Surely thus shall it be in the midst of the earth, among the people, [1]as the shaking of an olive tree, *and* as the grapes when the vintage is ended.

14 They shall lift up their voice: they shall shout for the magnificence of the Lord: they shall rejoice from [1]the sea.

15 Wherefore praise ye the Lord in the valleys, *even* the Name of the Lord God of Israel, in the isles of the sea.

16 From the uttermost part of the earth we have heard praises, *even* glory to the [1]just, and I said, [2]My

---

[2] The people of the Chaldeans destroyed the Assyrians: whereby the Prophet meaneth, that seeing the Chaldeans were able to overcome the Assyrians which were so great a nation, much more shall these two nations of Chaldea and Assyria be able to overthrow Tyre.

23:14 [1] That is, Tyre by whom ye are enriched.

23:15 [1] Tyre shall lie destroyed seventy years which he calleth the reign of one King, or a man's age.

[2] Shall use all craft and subtlety to entice men again unto her.

23:16 [1] She shall labor by all means to recover her first credit: as an harlot when she is long forgotten, seeketh by all means to entertain her lovers.

23:17 [1] Though she have been chastised of the Lord, yet she shall return to her old wicked practices, and for gain shall give herself to all men's lusts like an harlot.

23:18 [1] He showeth that God yet by the preaching of the Gospel will call Tyre to repentance, and turn her heart from avarice and filthy gain, unto the true worshipping of God, and liberality toward his Saints.

24:1 [1] This prophecy is as a conclusion of that which hath been threatened to the Jews, and other nations from chap. 13, and therefore by the earth he meaneth those lands which were before named.

24:2 [1] Because this was a name of dignity, it was also applied to them, which were not of Aaron's family, and so signifieth also a man of dignity, as 2 Sam. 8:18 and 20:25; 1 Chron. 18:17, and by these words the Prophet signifieth an horrible confusion, where there shall be neither religion, order, nor policy, Hos. 4:9.

24:5 [1] That is, rendereth not her fruit for the sin of the people, whom the earth deceived of their nourishment, because they deceived God of his honor.

24:6 [1] Written in the Law, as Lev. 26:14; Deut. 28:16, thus the Prophets used to apply particularly the menaces and promises, which are general in the Law.

[2] With heat and drought, or else that they were consumed with the fire of God's wrath.

24:10 [1] Which as it was without order, so now should it be brought to desolation and confusion: and this was not only meant of Jerusalem, but of all the other wicked cities.

24:11 [1] Because they did not use God's benefits aright, their pleasures should fail, and they fall to mourning.

24:13 [1] He comforteth the faithful, declaring that in this great desolation the Lord will assemble his Church which shall praise his Name, as Isa. 10:22.

24:14 [1] From the utmost coasts of the world, where the Gospel shall be preached, as verse 16.

24:16 [1] Meaning, to God, who will publish his Gospel through all the world.

[2] I am consumed with care, considering the affliction of the Church, both by foreign enemies and domestic. Some read, my secret, my secret: that is, it was revealed to the Prophet, that the good should be preserved, and the wicked destroyed.

leanness, my leanness, woe is me: the transgressors have offended: yea, the transgressors have grievously offended.

17 Fear, and the pit, and the snare *are* upon thee, O inhabitant of the earth.

18 And he that fleeth from the noise of the fear, shall fall into the pit: and he that cometh up out of the pit, shall be taken in the snare: for the [1]windows from on high are open, and the foundations of the earth do shake.

19 The earth is utterly broken down: the earth is clean dissolved: the earth is moved exceedingly.

20 The earth shall reel to and fro like a drunken man, and shall be removed like a tent, and the iniquity thereof shall be heavy upon it: so that it shall fall, and rise no more.

21 ¶ And in that day shall the Lord [1]visit the host above that is on high, even the kings of the world that are upon the earth.

22 And they shall be gathered together as the prisoners in the pit: and they shall be shut up in the prison, and after many days shall they be [1]visited.

23 [1]Then the moon shall be abashed, and the sun ashamed, when the Lord of hosts shall reign in mount Zion and in Jerusalem: and glory shall be before his ancient men.

25

A thanksgiving to God in that that he showeth himself judge of the world, by punishing the wicked, and maintaining the godly.

1 O Lord, thou [1]art my God: I will exalt thee, I will praise thy Name: for thou hast done wonderful things, *according* to the counsels of old, with a stable truth.

2 For thou hast made of a [1]city an heap, of a strong city, a ruin: *even* the place [2]of strangers of a city, it shall never be built.

3 Therefore shall the [1]mighty people give glory unto thee: the city of the strong nations shall fear thee.

4 For thou hast been a strength unto the poor, *even* a strength to the needy in his trouble, a refuge against the tempest, a shadow against the heat: for the blast [1]of the mighty is like a storm *against* the wall.

5 Thou shalt bring down the noise of the strangers, [1]as the heat in a dry place; he will bring down the song of the mighty, *as* [2]the heat in the shadow of a cloud.

6 And in this [1]mountain shall the Lord of hosts make unto all people a feast of fat things, *even* a feast of fined *wines, and* of fat things full of marrow, of *wines* fined *and* purified.

7 And he will destroy in this mountain [1]the covering that covereth all people, and the veil that is spread upon all nations.

8 He will destroy death forever: and the Lord God will [1]wipe away the tears from all faces, and the rebuke of his people will he take away out of all the earth: for the Lord hath spoken it.

9 And in that day shall men say, Lo, this is our God: we have waited for him, and he will save us. This is the Lord, we have waited for him, we will rejoice and be joyful in salvation.

10 For in this mountain shall the hand of the Lord rest, and [1]Moab shall be threshed under him even as straw is threshed in [2]Madmenah.

11 And he shall stretch out his hand in the midst of them (as he that swimmeth stretcheth *them* out to swim) and with the strength of his hands shall he bring down their pride.

12 The defense also of the height of thy walls shall he bring down and lay low, *and* cast them to the ground, *even* unto the dust.

26

A song of the faithful, wherein is declared, in what consisteth the salvation of the Church, and wherein they ought to trust.

24:18 [1] Meaning, that God's wrath and vengeance should be over and under them: so that they should not escape no more than they did at Noah's flood.

24:21 [1] There is no power so high or mighty, but God will visit him with his rods.

24:22 [1] Not with his rods, as verse 21, but shall be comforted.

24:23 [1] When God shall restore his Church, the glory thereof shall so shine, and his ministers (which are called his ancient men) that the sun and the moon shall be dark in comparison thereof.

25:1 [1] Thus the Prophet giveth thanks to God because he will bring under subjection these nations by his corrections, and make them of his Church, which before were his enemies.

25:2 [1] Not only of Jerusalem, but also of these other cities which have been thine enemies.

[2] That is, a place whereas all vagabonds may live without danger, and as it were at ease, as in a palace.

25:3 [1] The arrogant and proud, which before would not know thee, shall by thy corrections fear and glorify thee.

25:4 [1] The rage of the wicked is furious, till God break the force thereof.

25:5 [1] Meaning, that as the heat is abated by the rain, so shall God bring down the rage of the wicked.

[2] As a cloud shadoweth from the heat of the sun, so shall God assuage the rejoicing of the wicked against the godly.

25:6 [1] To wit, in Zion, whereby he meaneth his Church, which should under Christ be assembled of the Jews and the Gentiles, and is here described under the figure of a costly banquet, as Matt. 22:2.

25:7 [1] Meaning, that ignorance and blindness, whereby we are kept back from Christ.

25:8 [1] He will take away all occasions of sorrow and fill his with perfect joy, Rev. 7:17 and 21:4.

25:10 [1] By Moab are meant all the enemies of his Church.

[2] There were two cities of this name: one in Judah, 1 Chron. 2:49, and another in the land of Moab, Jer. 48:2, which seemeth to have been a plentiful place of corn, Isa. 10:31.

1 In that day shall ¹this song be sung in the land of Judah, We have a strong city: ²salvation shall *God* set for walls and bulwarks.

2 ¹Open ye the gates that the righteous nation, which keepeth the truth, may enter in.

3 By an assured ¹purpose wilt thou preserve perfect peace, because they trusted in thee.

4 Trust in the Lord forever: for in the Lord God *is* strength forevermore.

5 For he will bring down them that dwell on high: ¹the high city he will abase: *even* unto the ground will he cast it down, and bring it unto dust.

6 The foot shall tread it down, *even* the feet of the ¹poor, *and* the steps of the needy.

7 The way of the just *is* righteousness: thou wilt make equal the righteous path of the just.

8 Also we, O Lord, have waited for thee in the way of thy ¹judgments: the desire of *our* soul *is* to thy Name, and to the remembrance of thee.

9 With my soul have I desired thee in the night, and with my spirit within me will I seek thee in the morning: for seeing thy judgments *are* in the earth, the inhabitants of the world shall learn ¹righteousness.

10 Let mercy ¹be showed to the wicked, *yet* he will not learn righteousness: in the land of uprightness will he do wickedly, and will not behold the majesty of the Lord.

11 O Lord, they will not behold thine high hand: *but* they shall see it, and be confounded with ¹the zeal of the people, and the fire of thine ²enemies shall devour them.

12 Lord unto us thou wilt ordain peace: for thou also hast wrought all our works for us.

13 O Lord our God, *other* ¹lords beside thee, have ruled us, *but* we will remember thee only, *and* thy Name.

14 The ¹dead shall not live, *neither* shall the dead arise, because thou hast visited and scattered them, and destroyed all their memory.

15 Thou hast increased ¹the nation, O Lord: thou hast increased the nation: thou art made glorious, thou hast enlarged all the coasts of the earth.

16 Lord, in trouble have they ¹visited thee: they poured out a prayer when thy chastening *was* upon them.

17 Like as a woman with child, that draweth near to the travail, is in sorrow, *and* crieth in her pains, so have we been in thy ¹sight, O Lord.

18 We have conceived, we have born in pain, as though we should have brought forth ¹wind: there was no help in the earth, neither did the inhabitants of ²the world fall.

19 ¶ ¹Thy dead men shall live: *even* with my body shall they rise. Awake and sing, ye that dwell in dust: for thy ²dew *is* as the dew of herbs, and the earth shall cast out the dead.

20 Come, my people: ¹enter thou into thy chambers, and shut thy doors after thee: hide thyself for a very little while, until the indignation pass over.

21 For lo, the Lord cometh out of his place, to visit the iniquity of the inhabitants of the earth upon them: and the earth shall disclose her ¹blood, and shall no more hide her slain.

27

A prophecy against the kingdom of Satan.   2 And of the joy of the Church for their deliverance.

1 In that ¹day the Lord with his sore and great and mighty ²sword shall visit Leviathan, that piercing serpent, even Leviathan, that crooked serpent, and

---

26:1 ¹ This song was made to comfort the faithful when their captivity should come, assuring them also of their deliverance, for the which they should sing this song.
² God's protection and defense shall be sufficient for us.

26:2 ¹ He assureth the godly to return after the captivity to Jerusalem.

26:3 ¹ Thou hast decreed so, and thy purpose cannot be changed.

26:5 ¹ There is no power so high that can let God, when he will deliver his.

26:6 ¹ God will set the poor afflicted over the power of the wicked.

26:8 ¹ We have constantly aboade in the adversities wherewith thou had afflicted us.

26:9 ¹ Meaning, that by afflictions men shall learn to fear God.

26:10 ¹ The wicked though God show them evident signs of his grace, shall be never the better.

26:11 ¹ Through envy and indignation against thy people.
² The fire and vengeance, wherewith thou dost destroy thine enemies.

26:13 ¹ The Babylonians, which have not governed according to thy word.

26:14 ¹ Meaning, that the reprobate, even in this life shall have the beginning of everlasting death.

26:15 ¹ To wit, the company of the faithful by the calling of the Gentiles.

26:16 ¹ That is, the faithful by the rods were moved to pray unto thee for deliverance.

26:17 ¹ To wit, in extreme sorrow.

26:18 ¹ Our sorrows had none end, neither did we enjoy the comfort that we looked for.
² The wicked and men without religion were not destroyed.

26:19 ¹ He comforteth the faithful in their afflictions, showing them that even in death they shall have life: and that they should most certainly rise to glory, the contrary should come to the wicked, as verse 14.
² As herbs dead in winter flourisheth again by the rain in the springtime: so they that lie in the dust, shall rise up to joy, when they feel the dew of God's grace.

26:20 ¹ He exhorteth the faithful to be patient in their afflictions, and to wait upon God's work.

26:21 ¹ The earth shall vomit and cast out the innocent blood, which it hath drunk, that it may cry for vengeance against the wicked.

27:1 ¹ At the time appointed.
² That is, by his mighty power, and by his word. He prophesieth here of the destruction of Satan and his kingdom under the name of Leviathan, Assyria, and Egypt.

he shall slay the dragon that is in the sea.

2 In that day sing of the vineyard ¹of red wine.

3 I the Lord do keep it: I will water it every moment: lest any assail it, I will keep it night and day.

4 Anger ¹is not in me: who would set the briers and the thorns *against* me in battle? I would go through them, I would burn them together.

5 Or will he ¹feel my strength, that he may make peace with me, *and* be at one with me?

6 ¹Hereafter Jacob shall take root: Israel shall flourish and grow: and the world shall be filled with fruit.

7 Hath he smitten ¹him, as he smote those that smote him? or is he slain according to the slaughter of them that were slain by him?

8 In ¹measure in the branches thereof wilt thou contend with it, *when* he bloweth with his rough wind in the day of the East wind.

9 By this therefore shall the iniquity of Jacob be purged, and this is all the ¹fruit, the taking away of his sin: when he shall make all the stones of the altars, as chalk stones broken in pieces, *that* the groves and images may not stand up.

10 Yet the ¹defensed city *shall be* desolate, *and* the habitation *shall be* forsaken, and left like a wilderness. There shall the calf feed, and there shall he lie and consume the branches thereof.

11 When the boughs of it are dry, they shall be broken: the ¹women come and set them on fire: for it is a people of none understanding: therefore he that made them shall not have compassion of them, and he that formed them, shall have no mercy on them.

12 And in that day shall the Lord thresh from the channel of the ¹river unto the river of Egypt, and ye shall be gathered, one by one, O children of Israel.

13 In that day also shall the great trumpet be ¹blown, and they shall come, which perished in the land of Assyria, and they that were chased into the land of Egypt, and they shall worship the Lord in the holy Mount at Jerusalem.

28

Against the pride and drunkenness of Israel. 9 *The untowardness of them that should learn the word of God.* 24 *God doeth all things in time and place.*

1 Woe to the ¹crown of pride, the drunkards of Ephraim: for his glorious beauty *shall be* a fading flower, which is upon the head of the ²valley of them that be fat, *and* are overcome with wine.

2 Behold, the Lord hath a mighty and ¹strong *host* like a tempest of hail, *and* a whirlwind that overthroweth, like a tempest of mighty waters that overflow, which throw to the ground mightily.

3 They shall be trodden under foot, *even* the crown *and* the pride of the drunkards of Ephraim.

4 For his glorious beauty shall be a fading flower, which is upon the head of the valley of them that be fat, *and* as ¹the hasty fruit afore Summer, which when he hath looketh upon it, seeth it, while it is in his hand, he eateth it.

5 In that day shall the Lord of hosts be for a crown of glory, and for a diadem of beauty unto the ¹residue of his people:

6 And for a spirit of judgment to him that sitteth in judgment, and for ¹strength unto them that turn away the battle to the gate.

7 But ¹they have erred because of wine, and are out of the way by strong drink: the Priest and the prophet have erred by strong drink: they are swallowed up with wine: they have gone astray through strong drink: they fail in vision: they stumble in judgment.

27:2 ¹ Meaning, of the best wine, which this vineyard, that is, the Church should bring forth, as most agreeable to the Lord.

27:4 ¹ Therefore he will destroy the kingdom of Satan, because he loveth his Church for his own mercy's sake, and cannot be angry with it, but wisheth that he may pour his anger upon the wicked infidels, whom he meaneth by briers and thorns.

27:5 ¹ He marveleth that Israel will not come by gentleness, except God make them to feel his rods, and so bring them unto him.

27:6 ¹ Though I afflict and diminish my people for a time, yet shall the root spring again and bring forth in great abundance.

27:7 ¹ He showeth that God punisheth his in mercy, and his enemies in justice.

27:8 ¹ That is, thou wilt not destroy the root of thy Church, though the branches thereof seem to perish by the sharp wind of affliction.

27:9 ¹ He showeth that there is no true repentance, nor full reconciliation to God, till the heart be purged from all idolatry, and the monuments thereof be destroyed.

27:10 ¹ Notwithstanding his favor that he will show them after, yet Jerusalem shall be destroyed, and grass for cattle shall grow in it.

27:11 ¹ God shall not have need of mighty enemies: for the very women shall do it to their great shame.

27:12 ¹ He shall destroy all from Euphrates to the Nile: for some fled toward Egypt, thinking to have escaped.

27:13 ¹ In the time of Cyrus, by whom they should be delivered: but this was chiefly accomplished under Christ.

28:1 ¹ Meaning, the proud kingdom of the Israelites, which were drunken with worldly prosperity.

² Because the Israelites for the most part dwelt in plentiful valleys, he meaneth hereby the valley of them that had abundance of worldly prosperity, and were as it were crowned therewith as with garlands.

28:2 ¹ He seemeth to mean the Assyrians, by whom the ten tribes were carried away.

28:4 ¹ Which is not of long continuance, but is soon ripe and first eaten.

28:5 ¹ Signifying, that the faithful, which put not their trust in any worldly prosperity, but made God their glory, shall be preserved.

28:6 ¹ He will give counsel to the governor, and strength to the captain, to drive the enemies in at their own gates.

28:7 ¹ Meaning, the hypocrites which were among them, and were altogether corrupt in life and doctrine, which is here meant by drunkenness and vomiting.

8 For all *their* tables are full of filthy vomiting: no place *is clean*.

9 ¹Whom shall he teach knowledge? and whom shall he make to understand the things that he heareth? them that are weaned from the milk, *and* drawn from the breasts.

10 For ¹precept *must be* upon precept, precept upon precept, line unto line, line unto line, there a little, *and* there a little.

11 For with a stammering ¹tongue, and with a strange language shall he speak unto this people.

12 Unto whom ¹he said, ²This is the rest: ³give rest unto him that is weary, and this is the refreshing: but they would not hear.

13 Therefore shall the word of the ¹Lord be unto them precept upon precept, precept upon precept, line unto line, line unto line, there a little *and* there a little: that they may go and fall backward, and be broken, and be snared, and be taken.

14 Wherefore hear the word of the Lord, ye scornful men, that rule this people, which is at Jerusalem.

15 Because ye have said, We have made a ¹covenant with death, and with hell are we at agreement: though a scourge run over, and pass through, it shall not come at us: for we have made ²falsehood our refuge, and under vanity are we hid,

16 Therefore thus saith the Lord God, Behold, I will lay in Zion a stone, a ¹tried stone, a precious cornerstone, a sure foundation. He that believeth, ²shall not make haste.

17 Judgment also will I lay to the rule, and ¹righteousness to the balance, and the ²hail shall sweep away the vain confidence, and the waters shall overflow ³the secret place.

18 And your covenant with death shall be disannulled, and your agreement with hell shall not stand: when a scourge shall run over and pass through, then shall ye be trodden down by it.

19 When it passeth over, it shall take you away: for it shall pass through every morning in the day and in the night, and there shall be only ¹fear, to make *you* to understand the hearing.

20 For the bed is ¹strait, that it cannot suffice, and the covering narrow, that one cannot wrap himself.

21 For the Lord shall stand as in mount ¹Perazim: he shall be wroth as in the valley ²of Gibeon, that he may do his work, his strange work, and bring to pass his act, his strange act.

22 Now therefore be no mockers, lest your bonds increase: for I have heard of the Lord of hosts a consumption, even determined upon the whole earth.

23 Hearken ye, and hear my voice: hearken ye, and hear my speech.

24 Doth the plowman plow all the day, to sow? doth he open, and break the clots of his ground?

25 When he hath made it ¹plain, will he not then sow the fitches, and sow cumin, and cast in wheat by measure, and the appointed barley and rye in their place?

26 For his God doth instruct him to have discretion, *and* doth teach him.

27 For fitches shall not be threshed with a threshing instrument, neither shall a cartwheel be turned about upon the cumin: but the fitches are beaten out with a staff, and cumin with a rod.

28 Bread *corn* when it is threshed, he doth not always thresh it, neither doth the wheel of his cart *still* make a noise, neither will he break it with the teeth thereof.

29 This also cometh from the Lord of hosts, which is wonderful in counsel, *and* excellent in works.

29 *1 A prophecy against Jerusalem.   13 The vengeance of God on them that follow the traditions of men.*

28:9 ¹ For there was none that was able to understand any good doctrine: but were foolish and as unmeet as young babes.

28:10 ¹ They must have one thing ofttimes told.

28:11 ¹ Let one teach what he can, yet they shall no more understand him, than if he spake in a strange language.

28:12 ¹ That is, the Prophet, whom God should send.

² This is the doctrine, whereupon ye ought to stay and rest.

³ Show to them that are weary and have need of rest, what is the true rest.

28:13 ¹ Because they will not receive the word of God, when it is offered, it cometh of their own malice, if after their hearts be so hardened, that they care not for it, as before, Isa. 6:9.

28:15 ¹ They thought they had shifts to avoid God's judgments, and that they could escape though all others perished.

² Though the prophets condemned their idols and vain trust of falsehood and vanity, yet the wicked thought in themselves that they would trust in these things.

28:16 ¹ That is, Christ, by whom all the building must be tried and upheld, Ps. 118:22; Matt. 21:42; Acts 4:11; Rom. 9:33; 1 Pet. 2:6.

² He shall be quiet, and seek none other remedies, but be content with Christ.

28:17 ¹ In the restitution of his Church, judgment and justice shall reign.

² God's corrections and afflictions.

³ Affliction shall discover their vain confidence, which they kept secret to themselves.

28:19 ¹ Terror and destruction shall make you to learn that, which exhortations and gentleness could not bring you unto.

28:20 ¹ Your affliction shall be so sore, that you are not able to endure it.

28:21 ¹ When David overcame the Philistines, 2 Sam. 5:20; 1 Chron. 14:11.

² Where Joshua discomfited five kings of the Amorites, Josh. 10:12.

28:25 ¹ As the plowman hath his appointed time, and divers instruments for his labor, so hath the Lord for his vengeance: for he punisheth some at one time, and some at another, some after one sort, and some after another, so that his chosen seed is beaten and tried, but not broken, as are the wicked.

1 Ah [1]altar, altar of the city that David dwelt in: add year unto year: [2]let them kill lambs.

2 But I will bring the altar into distress, and there shall be heaviness and sorrow, and it shall be unto me like [1]an altar.

3 And I will besiege thee as a circle, and fight against thee on a mount, and will cast up ramparts against thee.

4 So shalt thou be humbled, and shalt speak out of the [1]ground, and thy speech shall be as out of the dust: thy voice also shall be out of the ground like him that hath a spirit of divination, and thy talking shall whisper out of the dust.

5 Moreover, multitude of thy [1]strangers shall be like small dust, and the multitude of strong men shall be as chaff that passeth away: and it shall be in a moment, even suddenly.

6 Thou shalt be visited of the Lord of hosts with thunder, and shaking, and a great noise, a whirlwind, and a tempest, and a flame of a devouring fire.

7 And the [1]multitude of all the nations that fight against the altar, shall be as a dream or vision by night: even all they that make the war against it, and strongholds against it, and lay siege unto it.

8 And it shall be like as an hungry man dreameth, and behold, [1]he eateth: and when he awaketh, his soul is empty: or like as a thirsty man dreameth, and lo, he is drinking, and when he awaketh, behold, he is faint, and his soul longeth: so shall the multitude of all nations be that fight against mount Zion.

9 [1]Stay yourselves and wonder: they are blind, and make you blind: they are drunken, but not with wine: they stagger, but not by strong drink.

10 For the Lord hath covered you with a spirit of slumber, and hath shut up your eyes: the Prophet, and your chief Seers hath he covered.

11 And the vision of them all is become unto you, as the words of a book that is sealed up, which they deliver to one that can read, saying, Read this, I pray thee. Then shall he say, I [1]cannot; for it is sealed.

12 And the book is given unto him that cannot read, saying, Read this, I pray thee. And he shall say, I cannot read.

13 Therefore the Lord said, Because this people [1]come near unto me with their mouth, and honor me with their lips, but have removed their heart far from me, and their [2]fear toward me was taught by the precept of men,

14 Therefore behold, I will again do a marvelous work in this people, even a marvelous work, and a wonder: for the wisdom of their wise men shall [1]perish, and the understanding of their prudent men shall be hid.

15 Woe unto them that [1]seek deep to hide their counsel from the Lord: for their works are in darkness, and they say, Who seeth us? and who knoweth us?

16 Your turning of devices shall it not be esteemed [1]as the potter's clay? for shall the work say of him that made it, He made me not? or the thing formed, say of him that fashioned it, He had none understanding?

17 Is it not yet but a little while, and Lebanon shall be [1]turned into Carmel? and Carmel shall be counted as a forest?

18 And in that day shall the deaf hear the words of the book, and the eyes of the blind shall see out of obscurity, and out of darkness.

19 The meek in the Lord shall receive joy again, and the poor men shall rejoice in the Holy one of Israel.

20 For the cruel man shall cease, and the scornful shall be consumed: and all that hasted to iniquity, shall be cut off:

21 Which made a man to sin in the [1]word, and took him in a snare: which reproved them in the gate,

---

29:1 [1] The Hebrew word Ariel signifieth the Lion of God, and signifieth the Altar, because the altar seemed to devour the sacrifice that was offered to God, as Ezek. 43:16.

[2] Your vain confidence in your sacrifices shall not last long.

29:2 [1] Your city shall be full of blood, as an altar whereon they sacrifice.

29:4 [1] Thy speech shall be no more so lofty, but abased and low as the very charmers, which are in low places, and whisper, so that their voice can scarce be heard.

29:5 [1] Thine hired soldiers in whom thou trustest, shall be destroyed as dust or chaff in a whirlwind.

29:7 [1] The enemies that I will bring to destroy thee, and that which thou makest thy vain trust, shall come at unawares, even as a dream in the night. Some read, as if this were a comfort to the Church for the destruction of their enemies.

29:8 [1] That is, he thinketh that he eateth.

29:9 [1] Muse hereon as long as ye list, yet shall ye find nothing but occasion to be astonied: for your Prophets are blind, and therefore cannot direct you.

29:11 [1] Meaning, that it is all alike, either to read, or not to read,

except God open the heart to understand.

29:13 [1] Because they are hypocrites and not sincere in heart, as Matt. 15:8.

[2] That is, their religion was learned by man's doctrine, and not by my word.

29:14 [1] Meaning, that where as God is not worshipped according to his word, both magistrates and ministers are but fools and without understanding.

29:15 [1] This is spoken of them which in heart despised God's word, and mocked at the admonitions, but outwardly bare a good face.

29:16 [1] For all your craft saith the Lord, you cannot be able to escape mine hands no more than the clay, that is in the potter's hands, hath power to deliver itself.

29:17 [1] Shall there not be a change of all things? And Carmel that is a plentiful place in respect of that it shall be then, may be taken as a forest, as Isa. 32:15, and thus he speaketh to comfort the faithful.

29:21 [1] They that went about to find fault with the Prophet's words, and would not abide admonitions, but would entangle them and bring them into danger.

and made the just to fall without cause.

22 Therefore thus saith the Lord unto the house of Jacob, *even* he that redeemed Abraham: Jacob shall not now be confounded, neither now shall his face be pale.

23 But when he seeth his children, the work of mine hands, in the midst of him, they shall sanctify my Name, and sanctify the Holy one of Jacob, and shall fear the God of Israel.

24 Then they that erred in spirit, [1]shall have understanding, and they that murmured, shall learn doctrine.

30 *1 He reproveth the Jews, which in their adversity used their own counsels, 2 and sought help of the Egyptians, 10 despising the Prophets. 16 Therefore he showeth what destruction shall come upon them, 18 but offereth mercy to the repentant.*

1 Woe to the [1]rebellious children, saith the Lord, that take counsel, but not of me, and [2]cover with a covering, but not by my spirit, that they may lay sin upon sin:

2 Which walk forth to go down into Egypt (and have not asked at my mouth) to strengthen themselves with the strength of Pharaoh, and trust in the shadow of Egypt.

3 But the strength of Pharaoh shall be your shame, and the trust in the shadow of Egypt your confusion.

4 For his [1]princes were at Zoan, and his ambassadors came unto Hanes.

5 They shall be all ashamed of the people that cannot profit them, nor help, nor do them good, but *shall be* a shame and also a reproach.

6 ¶ The [1]burden of the beasts of the South, in a land of trouble and anguish, from whence shall come the young and old lion, the viper and fiery flying serpent *against them* that shall bear their riches upon the shoulders of the colts, and their treasures upon the bunches of the camels, to a people that cannot

profit.

7 For the Egyptians are vanity, and they shall help in vain. Therefore have I cried unto [1]her, Their strength [2]*is* to sit still.

8 Now go, *and* write [1]it before them in a table, and note it in a book, that it may be for the [2]last day forever and ever:

9 That it is a rebellious people, lying children, *and* children that would not [1]hear the Law of the Lord.

10 Which say unto the Seers, See not: and to the Prophets, Prophesy not unto us right things: *but* speak flattering things unto us: prophesy [1]errors.

11 Depart out of the way: go aside out of the path: cause the Holy one of Israel to cease from us.

12 Therefore thus saith the Holy one of Israel, Because you have cast off this word, and trust in [1]violence, and wickedness, and stay thereupon,

13 Therefore this iniquity shall be unto you as a breach that falleth, *or* a swelling in an high wall, whose breaking cometh suddenly in a moment.

14 And the breaking thereof is like the breaking of a potter's pot, which is broken without pity, and in the breaking thereof is not found [1]a shard to take fire out of the hearth, or to take water out of the pit.

15 For thus said the [1]Lord God, the Holy one of Israel, In rest and quietness shall ye be saved: in quietness and in confidence shall be your strength, but ye would not.

16 For ye have said, No, but we will flee away upon [1]horses. Therefore shall ye flee. We will ride upon the swiftest. Therefore shall your persecutors be swifter.

17 A thousand *as* one *shall flee* at the rebuke of one: at the rebuke of five shall ye flee, till ye be left as a ship mast upon the [1]top of a mountain, and as a beacon upon an hill.

18 Yet therefore will the Lord wait, that he may have [1]mercy upon you, and therefore will he be exalted, that he may have compassion upon you:

29:24 [1] Signifying, that except God give understanding, and knowledge, man cannot but still err and murmur against him.

30:1 [1] Who contrary to their promise take not me for their protector, and contrary to my commandment seek help at strangers.

[2] They seek shifts to cloak their doings, and not godly means.

30:4 [1] The chief of Israel went into Egypt in embassy to seek help, and abode at these cities.

30:6 [1] That is, a heavy sentence or prophecy against the beasts that carried their treasures into Egypt, by the wilderness, which was south from Judah, signifying that if the beasts should not be spared, the men should be punished much more grievously.

30:7 [1] To wit, to Jerusalem.

[2] And not to come to and fro to seek help.

30:8 [1] That is, this prophecy.

[2] That it may be a witness against them for all posterity.

30:9 [1] He showeth what was the cause of their destruction, and

bringeth also all misery to man: to wit, because they would not hear the word of God, but delighted to be flattered, and led in error.

30:10 [1] Threaten us not by the word of God, neither be so rigorous, nor talk unto us in the Name of the Lord, as Jer. 11:21.

30:12 [1] Meaning, in their stubbornness against God and the admonitions of his Prophets.

30:14 [1] Signifying, that the destruction of the wicked shall be without recovery.

30:15 [1] Ofttimes by his Prophets he put you in remembrance of this, that you should only depend on him.

30:16 [1] We will trust to escape by our horses.

30:17 [1] Whereas all the trees are cut down save two or three to make masts.

30:18 [1] He commendeth the great mercies of God, who with patience waiteth to call sinners to repentance.

for the Lord *is* the God of [2]judgment. Blessed *are* all they that wait for him.

19 Surely a people shall dwell in Zion, *and* in Jerusalem: thou shalt weep no more: he will certainly have mercy upon thee at the voice of thy cry: when he heareth thee, he will answer thee.

20 And when the Lord hath given you the bread of adversity, and the water of affliction, thy rain shall be no more kept back, but thine eyes shall see thy [1]rain.

21 And thine ears shall hear a word behind thee, saying, This is the way, [1]walk ye in it, when thou turnest to the right hand, and when thou turnest to the left.

22 And ye shall [1]pollute the covering of the images of silver, and the rich ornament of thine images of gold, *and* cast them away as a menstruous cloth, and thou shalt say unto it, [2]Get thee hence.

23 Then shall he give rain unto thy seed, when thou shalt sow the ground, and bread of the increase of the earth, and it shall be fat and as oil: in that day shall thy cattle be fed in large pastures.

24 The oxen also and the young asses, that till the ground, shall eat clean provender, which is winnowed with the shovel and with the fan.

25 And upon every high [1]mountain, and upon every high hill shall there be rivers, *and* streams of waters, in the day of the great slaughter, when the towers shall fall.

26 Moreover, the light of the Moon shall be as the light of the [1]Sun, and the light of the Sun shall be sevenfold, and like the light of seven days in the day that the Lord shall bind up the breach of his people, and heal the stroke of their wound.

27 Behold, [1]the Name of the Lord cometh from far, his face is burning, and the burden thereof *is* heavy: his lips are full of indignation, and his tongue *is* as a devouring fire.

28 And his spirit *is* as a river that overfloweth up to the neck: it divideth asunder, to fan the nations with the fan of [1]vanity, and there *shall be* a bridle to cause them to err in the jaws of the people.

29 *But* there shall be a song unto you as in the [1]night, when a solemn feast is kept; and gladness of heart, as he that cometh with a pipe to go unto the mount of the Lord, to the Mighty one of Israel.

30 And the Lord shall cause his glorious voice to be heard, and shall declare the lighting down of his arm with the anger of *his* countenance, and flame of a devouring fire, with scattering and tempest, and hailstones.

31 For with the voice of the Lord shall Assyria be destroyed, which smote with the [1]rod.

32 And in every place that the staff shall pass, it shall [1]cleave fast, which the Lord shall lay upon him with [2]tabrets and beards and with battles, *and* lifting up *of hands* shall he fight [3]against it.

33 For [1]Tophet is prepared of old; it is even prepared for the [2]King; he hath made it [3]deep and large: the burning thereof *is* fire and much wood; the breath of the Lord, like a river of brimstone, doth kindle it.

31

[1] He curseth them that forsake God, and seek for the help of men.

1 Woe unto them that [1]go down into Egypt for help, and stay upon horses, and trust in chariots, because they are many, and in horsemen, because they be very strong; but they look not unto the Holy one of Israel, nor [2]seek unto the Lord.

2 But he yet is [1]wisest; therefore he will bring evil, and not turn back his word, but he will arise against the house of the wicked, and against the help of them that work vanity.

30:18 [2] Not only in punishing, but in using moderation in the same, as Jer. 10:24 and 30:11.

30:20 [1] Or, instructor.

30:21 [1] God shall direct all thy ways, and appoint thee how to go either hither or thither.

30:22 [1] Ye shall cast away your idols, which you have made of gold, and silver, with all that belongeth unto them, as a most filthy thing, and polluted.

[2] Showing, that there can be no true repentance, except both in heart and deed we show ourselves enemies to idolatry.

30:25 [1] By these divers manners of speech he showeth that the felicity of the Church shall be so great, that none is able sufficiently to express it.

30:26 [1] When the Church shall be restored, the glory thereof shall pass seven times the brightness of the Sun: for by the Sun and Moon, which are two excellent creatures, he showeth what shall be the glory of the children of God in the kingdom of Christ.

30:27 [1] This threatening is against the Assyrians the chief enemies of the people of God.

30:28 [1] To drive thee to nothing: and thus God consumeth the wicked by that means, whereby he cleanseth his.

30:29 [1] Ye shall rejoice at the destruction of your enemies, as they that sung for joy of the solemn feast, which began in the evening.

30:31 [1] God's plague.

30:32 [1] It shall destroy.

[2] With joy and assurance of the victory.

[3] Against Babel: meaning the Assyrians and Babylonians.

30:33 [1] Here it is taken for hell, where the wicked are tormented, read 2 Kings 23:10.

[2] So that their estate or degree cannot exempt the wicked.

[3] By these figurative speeches he declareth the condition of the wicked after this life.

31:1 [1] There were two special causes, why the Israelites should not join amity with the Egyptians: first, because the Lord had commanded them never to return thither, Deut. 17:16 and 28:68, lest they should forget the benefit of their redemption: and secondly, lest they should be corrupted with the superstition and idolatry of the Egyptians, and so forsake God, Jer. 2:18.

[2] Meaning, that they forsake the Lord, that put their trust in worldly things: for they cannot trust in both.

31:2 [1] And knoweth their crafty enterprises, and will bring all to naught.

3 Now the Egyptians *are* men and not God, and their horses flesh, and not spirit; and when the Lord shall stretch out his hand, the [1]helper shall fall, and he that is helped shall fall, and they shall altogether fail.

4 For this hath the Lord spoken unto me, As the lion or lion's whelp roareth upon his prey, against whom *if* a multitude of shepherds be called, he will not be afraid at their voice, neither will humble himself at their noise: so shall the Lord of hosts come [1]down to fight for mount Zion, and for the hill thereof.

5 As birds that fly, so shall the Lord of hosts defend Jerusalem by defending and delivering, by passing through and preserving it.

6 O ye children of Israel, turn again, in as much as ye are [1]sunken deep in rebellion.

7 For in that day every man shall [1]cast out his idols of silver, and his idols of gold, which your hands have made you, *even* a sin.

8 [1]Then shall Assyria fall by the sword, not of man, neither shall the sword of man devour him, and he shall flee from the sword, and his young men shall faint.

9 And he shall go for fear to his [1]tower, and his princes shall be afraid of the standard, saith the Lord, whose [2]fire is in Zion, and his furnace in Jerusalem.

32 *The conditions of good rulers and officers describeth by the government of Hezekiah, who was the figure of Christ.*

1 Behold, [1]a King shall reign in justice, and the princes shall [2]rule in judgment.

2 And *that* man shall be as an hiding place from the wind, and as a refuge for the tempest, as rivers of water in a dry place, *and* as the shadow of a great rock in [1]a weary land.

3 The eyes of [1]the seeing shall not be shut, and the ears of them that hear, shall hearken.

4 And the heart of the foolish shall understand knowledge, and the tongue of the stutters shall be ready to speak distinctly.

5 A [1]niggard shall no more be called liberal, nor the churl rich.

6 But the niggard will speak of niggardness, and his heart will work iniquity, and do wickedly, and speak falsely against the Lord, to make empty the hungry soul, and to cause the drink of the thirsty to fail.

7 For the weapons of the churl *are* wicked: he deviseth wicked counsels to undo the poor with lying words, and to speak *against* the poor in judgment.

8 But the liberal man will devise of liberal things, and he will continue *his* liberality.

9 ¶ Rise up ye women that are at ease: hear my voice, ye [1]careless daughters, hearken to my words.

10 Ye women that are careless, shall be in fear [1]above a year in days, [2]for the vintage shall fail, *and* the gatherings shall come no more.

11 Ye women that are at ease, be astonied; fear, O ye careless women: put off the clothes; make bare, and gird *sackcloth* upon the loins.

12 Men shall lament for the [1]teats, *even* for the pleasant fields, *and* for the fruitful vine.

13 Upon the land of my people shall grow thorns *and* briers: yea, upon all the houses of joy in the city of rejoicing,

14 Because the palace shall be forsaken, *and* the [1]noise of the city shall be left: the tower and fortress shall be dens forever, *and* the delight of wild asses, *and* a pasture for flocks,

15 Until the [1]Spirit be poured upon us from above, and the wilderness become a fruitful field, and the

---

31:3 [1] Meaning, both the Egyptians and the Israelites.
31:4 [1] He showeth the Jews, that if they would put their trust in him, he is so able, that none can resist his power: and so careful over them, as a bird over her young, which ever flieth about them for their defense: which similitude the scripture useth in divers places, as Deut. 32:11; Matt. 23:37.
31:6 [1] He toucheth their conscience, that they might earnestly feel their grievous sins, and so truly repent, forasmuch as now they are almost drowned and past recovery.
31:7 [1] By these fruits your repentance shall be known, as Isa. 2:20.
31:8 [1] When your repentance appeareth.
31:9 [1] This was accomplished soon after when Sennacherib's army was discomfited, and he fled to his castle in Nineveh for succor.
[2] To destroy his enemies.
32:1 [1] This prophecy is of Hezekiah, who was a figure of Christ, and therefore it ought chiefly to be referred to him.
[2] By judgment and justice is meant an upright government, both in policy, and religion.
32:2 [1] Where men are weary with traveling for lack of water.

32:3 [1] He promiseth to give the true light, which is the pure doctrine of God's word, and understanding, and zeal of the same, are contrary to the threatenings against the wicked, Isa. 6:9 and 29:10.
32:5 [1] Vice shall no more be called virtue, nor virtue esteemed by power and riches.
32:9 [1] He prophesieth of such calamity to come, that they will not spare the women and children, and therefore willeth them to take heed and provide.
32:10 [1] Meaning, that the affliction should continue long, and when one year were past, yet they should look for new plagues.
[2] God will take from you the means and occasions, which made you to contemn him: to wit, abundance of worldly goods.
32:12 [1] By the teats he meaneth the plentiful fields, whereby men are nourished as children with the teat: or, the mothers for sorrow and heaviness shall lack milk.
32:14 [1] Or, multitude.
32:15 [1] That is, when the Church shall be restored: thus the Prophets, after they have denounced God's judgments against the wicked, used to comfort the godly, lest they should faint.

²plenteous field be counted as a forest.

16 And judgment shall dwell in the desert, and justice shall remain in the fruitful field.

17 And the work of justice shall be peace, even the work of justice and quietness, and assurance forever.

18 And my people shall dwell in the tabernacle of peace, and in sure dwellings, and in safe resting places.

19 When it haileth, it shall fall on the forest, and the ¹city shall be in the low place.

20 Blessed are ye ¹that sow upon all waters, and ²drive *thither* the feet of the ox and the ass.

33

1 *The destruction of them by whom God hath punished his Church.*

1 Woe to thee that ¹spoilest, and wast not spoiled: and doest wickedly, and they did not wickedly against thee: when thou shalt ²cease to spoil, thou shalt be spoiled: when thou shalt make an end of doing wickedly, ³they shall do wickedly against thee.

2 ¹O Lord, have mercy upon us, we have waited for thee: be thou, *which wast* ²their arm in the morning, our help also in time of trouble.

3 At the noise of the tumult, the ¹people fled: at thine ²exalting the nations were scattered.

4 And your spoil shall be gathered *like* the gathering of ¹caterpillars: and ²he shall go against him like the leaping of grasshoppers.

5 The Lord is exalted: for he dwelleth on high: he hath filled Zion with judgment and justice.

6 And there shall be stability of ¹the times, strength, salvation, wisdom, and knowledge: *for the* fear of the Lord shall be his treasure.

7 Behold, ¹their messengers shall cry without, and the ²ambassadors of peace shall weep bitterly.

8 The ¹paths are waste: the wayfaring man ceaseth: he hath broken the covenant: he hath contemned the cities: he regardeth no man.

9 The earth mourneth and fainteth: Lebanon is ashamed, and hewn down: ¹Sharon is like a wilderness, and Bashan is shaken and Carmel.

10 Now will I ¹arise, saith the Lord: now will I be exalted, now will I lift up myself.

11 ¹Ye shall conceive chaff, *and* bring forth stubble: the fire of your breath shall devour you.

12 And the people shall be *as* the burning of lime: *and as* the thorns cut up, shall they be burnt in the fire.

13 Hear, ye that are ¹far off, what I have done, and ye that are near, know my power.

14 The ¹sinners in Zion are afraid: a fear is come upon the hypocrites: who among us shall dwell with the devouring fire? who among us shall dwell with the everlasting burnings?

15 He that walketh in justice, and speaketh righteous things, refusing gain of oppression, shaking his hands from taking of gifts, stopping his ears from hearing of blood, and shutting his eyes from seeing evil,

16 He shall dwell on ¹high: his defense *shall be* the munitions of rocks: bread shall be given him, *and*

32:15 ² The field which is now fruitful, shall be but as a barren forest in comparison of that it shall be then, as Isa. 29:17, which shall be fulfilled in Christ's time, for then they that were before as the barren wilderness, being regenerate shall be fruitful, and they that had some beginning of godliness, shall bring forth fruits in such abundance, that their former life shall seem but as a wilderness where no fruits were.

32:19 ¹ They shall not need to build it in high places for fear of the enemy: for God will defend it, and turn away the storms from hurting of their commodities.

32:20 ¹ That is, upon fat ground and well watered, which bringeth forth in abundance, or in places which before were covered with waters, and now made dry for your uses.

² The fields shall be so rank, that they shall send out their cattle to eat up the first crop, which abundance shall be signs of God's love and favor toward them.

33:1 ¹ Meaning, the enemies of the Church, as were the Chaldeans and Assyrians, but chiefly of Sennacherib, but not only.

² When thine appointed time shall come that God shall take away thy power: and that which thou hast wrongfully gotten, shall be given to others, as Amos 5:11.

³ The Chaldeans shall do like to the Assyrians, as the Assyrians did to Israel, and the Medes and Persians shall do the same to the Chaldeans.

33:2 ¹ He declareth hereby what is the chief refuge of the faithful, when troubles come, to pray, and seek help of God.

² Which helped our fathers so soon as they called upon thee.

33:3 ¹ That is, the Assyrians fled before the army of the Chaldeans, or the Chaldeans for fear of the Medes and Persians.

² When thou, O Lord, didst lift up thine arm to punish thine enemies.

33:4 ¹ Ye that as caterpillars destroyed with your number the whole world, shall have no strength to resist your enemies the Chaldeans: but shall be gathered on an heap and destroyed.

² Meaning, the Medes and Persians against the Chaldeans.

33:6 ¹ That is, in the days of Hezekiah.

33:7 ¹ Sent from Sennacherib.

² Whom they of Jerusalem sent to entreat of peace.

33:8 ¹ These are the words of the ambassadors, when they returned from Sennacherib.

33:9 ¹ Which was a plentiful country, meaning, that Sennacherib would destroy all.

33:10 ¹ To help and deliver my Church.

33:11 ¹ This is spoken against the enemies, who thought all was their own: but he showeth that their enterprise shall be in vain, and that the fire which they had kindled for others, should consume them.

33:13 ¹ His vengeance shall be so great, that all the world shall talk thereof.

33:14 ¹ Which do not believe the words of the Prophet, and the assurance of their deliverance.

33:16 ¹ Meaning, that God will be a sure defense to all them that live according to his word.

his waters shall be sure.

17 Thine eyes shall [1]see the King in his glory: they shall behold the [2]land far off.

18 Thine heart [1]shall meditate fear, Where is the scribe? where is the receiver? where is he that counted the towers?

19 Thou shalt not see a fierce people, a people of a dark speech, that thou canst not perceive, and of a stammering tongue that thou canst not understand.

20 Look upon Zion the city of our solemn feasts: thine eyes shall see Jerusalem a quiet habitation, a tabernacle that cannot be removed: and the stakes thereof can never be taken away, neither shall any of the cords thereof be broken.

21 For surely there the mighty Lord will be unto us, as a place [1]of floods, and broad rivers, whereby shall pass no ship with oars, neither shall great ship pass thereby.

22 For the Lord is our Judge, the Lord is our lawgiver: the Lord is our King, he will save us.

23 Thy [1]cords are loosed: they could not well strengthen their mast, neither could they spread the sail: then shall the [2]prey be divided for a great spoil: yea, the lame shall take away the prey.

24 And none inhabitant shall say, I am sick: the people that dwell therein, shall have their iniquity forgiven.

34

1 He showeth that God punisheth the wicked for the love that he beareth toward his Church.

1 Come near, ye [1]nations and hear, and hearken, ye people: let the earth hear and all that is therein, the world and all that proceedeth thereof.

2 For the indignation of the Lord is upon all nations, and his wrath upon all their armies: he hath [1]destroyed them and delivered them to the slaughter.

3 And their slain shall be cast out, and their stink shall come up out of their bodies, and the mountains shall be melted with their blood.

4 And all the host of heaven [1]shall be dissolved, and the heavens shall be folded like a book: and all their hosts shall fall as the leaf falleth from the vine, and as it falleth from the fig tree.

5 For my sword shall be [1]drunken in the heaven: behold, it shall come down upon Edom, even upon the people of [2]my curse to judgment.

6 The sword of the Lord is filled with blood: it is made fat with the fat and with the blood of the [1]lambs and the goats, with the fat of the kidneys of the rams: for the Lord hath a sacrifice in [2]Bozrah, and a great slaughter in the land of Edom.

7 And the [1]unicorn shall come down with them, and the heifers with the bulls, and their land shall be drunken with blood, and their dust made fat with fatness.

8 For it is the day of the Lord's vengeance, and the year of recompense for the judgment of Zion.

9 And the rivers thereof shall be turned into pitch, and the dust thereof into [1]brimstone, and the land thereof shall be burning pitch.

10 It shall not be quenched night nor day: the smoke thereof shall go up evermore: it shall be desolate from generation to generation; none shall pass through it forever.

11 But the pelican [1]and the hedgehog shall possess it, and the great owl, and the raven shall dwell in it, and he shall stretch out upon it the line of [2]vanity, and the stones of emptiness.

12 [1]The nobles thereof shall call to the kingdom, and there shall be none, and all the princes thereof shall be as nothing.

13 And it shall bring forth thorns in the palaces thereof, nettles, and thistles in the strongholds thereof, and it shall be an habitation for dragons, and a court for ostriches.

14 There shall [1]meet also Ziim and Iim, and the Satyr shall cry to his fellow, and the screech owl

---

33:17 [1] They shall see Hezekiah delivered from his enemies, and restored to honor and glory.

[2] They shall be no more shut in as they were of Sennacherib, but go where it pleaseth them.

33:18 [1] Before that this liberty cometh thou shalt think that thou art in great danger: for the enemy shall so sharply assail you, that one shall cry, where is the clerk that writeth the names of them that are taxed? another, Where is the receiver? another shall cry for him that valueth the rich houses, but God will deliver you from this fear.

33:21 [1] Let us be content with this small river of Shiloah and not desire the great streams and rivers, whereby the enemies may bring in ships and destroy us.

33:23 [1] He derideth the Assyrians and enemies of the Church, declaring their destruction as they that perish by shipwreck.

[2] He comforteth the Church, and showeth that they shall be enriched with all benefits both of body and soul.

34:1 [1] He prophesieth of the destruction of the Edomites and other nations which were enemies to the Church.

34:2 [1] God hath determined in his counsel, and hath given sentence

for their destruction.

34:4 [1] He speaketh this in respect of man's judgment, who in great fear and horrible troubles, thinketh that heaven and earth perisheth.

34:5 [1] I have determined in my secret counsel, and in the heavens to destroy them till my sword be weary with shedding of blood.

[2] They had an opinion of holiness, because they came of the Patriarch Isaac, but in effect were accursed of God, and enemies unto his Church, as the Papists are.

34:6 [1] That is, both of young and old, poor and rich of his enemies.

[2] That famous city shall be consumed as a sacrifice burnt to ashes.

34:7 [1] The mighty and rich shall be as well destroyed as the inferiors.

34:9 [1] He alludeth to the destruction of Sodom and Gomorrah, Gen. 19:24.

34:11 [1] Read Isa. 13:21 and Zeph. 2:14.

[2] In vain shall any man go about to build it again.

34:12 [1] Meaning, here shall be neither order nor policy, nor state of commonweal.

34:14 [1] Read Isa. 13:21.

shall rest there, and shall find for herself a quiet dwelling.

15 There [1]shall the owl make her nest, and lay and hatch, and gather them under her shadow: there shall the vultures also be gathered, every one with her make.

16 Seek in the [1]book of the Lord, and read: none of [2]these shall fail, none shall want her make: for [3]his mouth hath commanded, and his very spirit hath gathered them.

17 And he hath cast the [1]lot for them, and his hand hath divided unto them by line: they shall possess it forever: from generation to generation shall they dwell in it.

35

1 The great joy of them that believe in Christ. 3 Their office which preach the Gospel. 8 The fruits that follow thereof.

1 The [1]desert and the wilderness shall rejoice, and the waste ground shall be glad and flourish as the rose.

2 It shall flourish abundantly, and shall greatly rejoice also and joy: the glory of Lebanon shall be given unto it: the beauty of [1]Carmel, and of Sharon, they shall [2]see the glory of the Lord, *and* the excellency of our God.

3 [1]Strengthen the weak hands, and comfort the feeble knees.

4 Say unto them that are fearful, Be you strong, fear not: behold, your God cometh with [1]vengeance: *even* God with a recompense, he will come and save you.

5 Then shall the eyes of the [1]blind be lightened, and the ears of the deaf be opened.

6 Then shall the lame man leap as an hart, and the dumb man's tongue shall sing: for in the [1]wilderness

shall waters break out, and rivers in the desert.

7 And the dry ground shall be as a pool, and the thirsty as springs of water: in the habitation of dragons, where they lay, *shall be* a place for reeds and rushes.

8 And there shall be a path and a way, and the way shall be called [1]holy: the polluted shall not pass by it: for [2]he shall be with them, and walk in the way, and the fools shall not err.

9 There shall be [1]no lion, nor noisome beasts shall ascend by it, neither shall they be found there, that the redeemed may walk.

10 Therefore the [1]redeemed of the Lord shall return and come to Zion with praise: and everlasting joy shall be upon their heads: they shall obtain joy and gladness, and sorrow and mourning shall flee away.

36

1 Sennacherib sendeth Rabshakeh to besiege Jerusalem. 15 His blasphemies against God.

1 Now [1]in the [2]fourteenth year of King Hezekiah, Sennacherib King of Assyria came up against all the strong cities of Judah, and took them.

2 And the King of Assyria sent Rabshakeh from Lachish toward Jerusalem unto king Hezekiah, with a great host, and he stood by the conduit of the upper pool in the path of the fuller's field.

3 Then came forth unto him Eliakim the son of Hilkiah the [1]steward of the house, and Shebna [2]the chancellor, and Joah the son of Asaph the recorder.

4 And [1]Rabshakeh said unto them, Tell you Hezekiah, I pray you, Thus saith the great king, the King of Assyria, What confidence is this, wherein thou trustest?

5 I say, [1]Surely *I have* eloquence, *but* counsel and strength *are* for the war: on whom then dost thou

---

34:15 [1] Signifying, that Edom should be an horrible desolation and barren wilderness.

34:16 [1] That is, in the Law where such curses are threatened against the wicked.

[2] To wit, beasts and souls.

[3] That is, the mouth of the Lord.

34:17 [1] He hath given the beasts and fowls Edom for an inheritance.

35:1 [1] He prophesieth of the full restoration of the Church both of the Jews and Gentiles under Christ, which shall be fully accomplished at the last day: albeit as yet it is compared to a desert and wilderness.

35:2 [1] The Church which was before compared to a barren wilderness shall by Christ be made most plenteous and beautiful.

[2] He showeth that the presence of God is the cause that the Church doth bring forth fruit and flourish.

35:3 [1] He willeth all to encourage one another, and specially the ministers to exhort and strengthen the weak, that they may patiently abide the coming of God, which is at hand.

35:4 [1] To destroy your enemies.

35:5 [1] When the knowledge of Christ is revealed.

35:6 [1] They that were barren and destitute of the graces of God, shall have them given by Christ.

35:8 [1] It shall be for the Saints of God and not for the wicked.

[2] God shall lead and guide them, alluding to the bringing forth of Egypt.

35:9 [1] As he threateneth to the wicked to be destroyed hereby, Isa. 30:6.

35:10 [1] Whom the Lord shall deliver from the captivity of Babylon.

36:1 [1] This history is rehearsed because it is as a seal and confirmation of the doctrine afore, both for the threatenings and promises: to wit, that God would suffer his Church to be afflicted, but at length would send deliverance.

[2] When he had abolished superstition, and idolatry, and restored religion, yet God would exercise his Church to try their faith and patience.

36:3 [1] For he was now restored to his office, as Isaiah had prophesied, Isa. 22:20.

[2] This declareth that there were few godly to be found in the king's house, when he was driven to send this wicked man in such a weighty matter.

36:4 [1] Sennacherib's chief captain.

36:5 [1] He speaketh this in the person of Hezekiah, falsely charging him that he put his trust in his wit and eloquence, whereas his only confidence was in the Lord.

trust, that thou rebellest against me?

6 Lo, thou trustest in this broken staff of reed, on Egypt, whereupon if a man lean, it will go into his hand, and pierce it: so *is* ¹Pharaoh King of Egypt unto all that trust in him.

7 But if thou say unto me, We trust in the Lord our God, is not that he, whose high places and whose altars Hezekiah took down, and said to Judah and to Jerusalem, Ye shall worship before this altar?

8 Now therefore give hostages to my Lord the king of Assyria, and I will give thee two thousand horses, if thou be able on thy part to set riders upon them.

9 For how canst thou ¹despise any captain of the ²least of my lord's servants? and put thy trust on Egypt for chariots and for horsemen?

10 And am I now come up without the Lord to this land to destroy it? The Lord said unto me, ¹Go up against this land and destroy it.

11 ¶ Then said Eliakim, and Shebna and Joah unto Rabshakeh, ¹Speak, I pray thee, to thy servants in the Aramite's language (for we understand it) and talk not with us in the Jews' tongue, in the audience of the people that are on the wall.

12 Then said Rabshakeh, Hath my master sent me to thy master, and to thee, to speak these words, and not to the men that sit on the wall? that they may eat their own thing, and drink their own ¹piss with you?

13 So Rabshakeh stood, and cried with a loud voice in the Jews' language, and said, Hear the words of the great King, of the King of Assyria.

14 Thus saith the king, Let not Hezekiah deceive you: for he shall not be able to deliver you.

15 Neither let Hezekiah make you to trust in the Lord, saying, The Lord will surely deliver us: this city shall not be given over into the hand of the king of Assyria.

16 Hearken not to Hezekiah: for thus saith the king of Assyria, Make ¹appointment with me, and

CHAPTER 37
ᵈ 2 Kings 19:1

come out to me, that every man may eat of his own vine, and every man of his own fig tree, and drink every man the water of his own well,

17 Till I come and bring you to a land like your own land, *even* a land of wheat and wine, a land of bread and vineyards,

18 Lest Hezekiah deceive you, saying, The Lord will deliver us. Hath any of the gods of the nations delivered his land out of the hand of the king of Assyria?

19 Where is the god of ¹Hamath, and of Arpad? where is the god of Sepharvaim? or how have they delivered Samaria out of my hand?

20 Who is he among all the gods of these lands, that hath delivered their country out of mine hand, that the Lord should deliver Jerusalem out of mine hand?

21 Then they ¹kept silence, and answered him not a word: for the king's commandment was, saying, Answer him not.

22 Then came Eliakim the son of Hilkiah the steward of the house, and Shebna the chancellor, and Joah the son of Asaph the recorder, unto Hezekiah with rent clothes, and told him the words of Rabshakeh.

37

2 Hezekiah asketh counsel of Isaiah, who promiseth him the victory.   10 The blasphemy of Sennacherib.   16 Hezekiah's prayer.   36 The army of Sennacherib is slain of the Angel.   38 And he himself of his own sons.

1 And ᵈwhen the King Hezekiah heard it, he ¹rent his clothes, and put on sackcloth and came into the house of the Lord.

2 And he sent Eliakim the steward of the house, and Shebna the chancellor, with the Elders of the Priests, clothed in sackcloth unto ¹Isaiah the Prophet the son of Amoz.

3 And he said unto him, Thus saith Hezekiah, This day is a day of tribulation and of rebuke and blasphemy: for the children are come to the ¹birth, and there is no strength to bring forth.

36:6 ¹ Satan labored to pull the godly King from one vain confidence to another: to wit, from trust in the Egyptians, whose power was weak and would deceive them, to yield himself to the Assyrians, and so not to hope for any help of God.
36:9 ¹ Or, turn back.
    ² He reproacheth to Hezekiah his small power, which is not able to resist one of Sennacherib's least captains.
36:10 ¹ Thus the wicked to deceive us, will pretend the Name of the Lord: but we must try the spirits, whether they be of God or no.
36:11 ¹ They were afraid, lest by his words, he should have stirred up the people against the King, and also pretended to grow to some appointment with him.
36:12 ¹ Hebrew, *the water of their feet.*
36:16 ¹ The Hebrew word signifieth blessing, whereby this wicked captain would have persuaded the people, that their condition should be better under Sennacherib than under Hezekiah.

36:19 ¹ That is, of Antioch in Syria, of the which these two other cities also were: whereby we see how every town had his peculiar idol, and how the wicked make God an idol because they do not understand that God maketh them his scourge, and punisheth cities for sin.
36:21 ¹ Not that they did not show by evident signs that they did detest his blasphemy: for they had now rent their clothes, but they knew it was in vain to use long reasoning with this infidel, whose rage they should have so much more provoked.
37:1 ¹ In sign of grief and repentance.
37:2 ¹ To have comfort of him by the word of God, that his faith might be confirmed and so his prayer be more earnest: teaching hereby that in all dangers these two are the only remedies, to seek unto God and his ministers.
37:3 ¹ We are in as great sorrow as a woman that travaileth of child, and cannot be delivered.

4 If so be the Lord thy God hath [1]heard the words of Rabshakeh, whom the King of Assyria his master hath sent to rail on the living God, and to reproach him with words, which the Lord thy God hath heard, then [2]lift thou up *thy* prayer for the remnant that are left.

5 So the servants of the King Hezekiah came to Isaiah.

6 And Isaiah said unto them, Thus say unto your master, Thus saith the Lord, Be not afraid of the words that thou hast heard, wherewith the servants of the King of Assyria have blasphemed me.

7 Behold, I will send a blast upon him, and he shall hear a [1]noise, and return to his own land, and I will cause him to fall by the sword in his own land.

8 ¶ So Rabshakeh returned, and found the King of Assyria fighting against [1]Libnah: for he had heard that he was departed from Lachish.

9 He heard also men say of Tirhakah, King of Ethiopia, *Behold*, he is come out to fight against thee: and when he heard it, he sent *other* messengers to Hezekiah, saying,

10 Thus shall ye speak to Hezekiah King of Judah, saying, Let not thy God [1]deceive thee, in whom thou trustest, saying, Jerusalem shall not be given into the hand of the King of Assyria.

11 Behold, thou hast heard what the Kings of Assyria have done to all lands in destroying them, and shalt thou be delivered?

12 Have the gods of the nations delivered them, which my fathers have destroyed? *as* [1]Gozan, and [2]Haran, and Rezeph, and the children of Eden, which were at Telassar?

13 Where is the king of Hamath, and the King of Arpad, and the King of the city of Sepharvaim, Hena, and Ivah?

14 ¶ So Hezekiah received the letter of the hand of the messengers, and read it, and he went up into the house of the Lord, and Hezekiah spread it before the Lord.

15 And Hezekiah prayed unto the Lord, saying,

16 O Lord of hosts, God of Israel, which [1]dwellest between the Cherubims, thou art very God alone over all the kingdoms of the earth: thou hast made the heaven and the earth.

17 Incline thine ear, O Lord, and hear: open thine eyes, O Lord, and see, and hear all the words of Sennacherib, who hath sent to blaspheme the living God.

18 Truth it is, O Lord, that the Kings of Assyria have destroyed all lands and [1]their country,

19 And have cast their gods in the fire: for they were no gods, but the work of men's hands, *even* wood or stone: therefore they destroyed them.

20 Now therefore, O Lord our God, save thou us out of his hand, that [1]all the kingdoms of the earth may know, that thou only art the Lord.

21 ¶ Then Isaiah the son of Amoz sent unto Hezekiah, saying, Thus saith the Lord God of Israel, Because thou hast prayed unto me, concerning Sennacherib king of Assyria,

22 This is the word that the Lord hath spoken against him, The [1]virgin, the daughter of Zion, hath despised thee, *and* laughed thee to scorn: the daughter of Jerusalem hath shaken her head at thee.

23 Whom hast thou railed on and blasphemed? and against whom hast thou exalted *thy* voice, and lifted up thine eyes on high? *even* against the [1]holy One of Israel.

24 By thy servants hast thou railed on the Lord, and said, By the multitude of my chariots I am come up to the top of the mountains to the sides of Lebanon, and will cut down the high cedars thereof, *and* the fair fir trees thereof, and I will go up to the heights of his top, *and* to the forest of his fruitful places.

25 I have dug, [1]and drunk the waters, and with the plant of my feet have I dried all the rivers closed in.

26 Hast thou not heard how I have of old time made it, [1]and have formed it long ago? and should

---

37:4 [1] That is, will declare by effect that he hath heard it: for when God deferreth to punish, it seemeth to the flesh, that he knoweth not the sin, or heareth not the cause.

[2] Declaring that the minister's office doth not only stand in comforting by the word, but also in praying for the people.

37:7 [1] Of the Egyptians and Ethiopians, that shall come and fight against him.

37:8 [1] Which was a city toward Egypt, thinking thereby to have stayed the force of his enemies.

37:10 [1] Thus God would have him to utter a most horrible blasphemy before his destruction: as to call the author of all truth, a deceiver: some gather hereby that Shebna had disclosed unto Sennacherib the answer that Isaiah sent to the king.

37:12 [1] Which was a city of the Medes.

[2] Called also Charre a city in Mesopotamia, whence Abraham came after his father's death.

37:16 [1] He groundeth his prayer on God's promise, who promised to hear them from between the Cherubims.

37:18 [1] Meaning, the ten tribes.

37:20 [1] He declareth for what cause he prayed, that they might be delivered: to wit, that God might be glorified thereby through all the world.

37:22 [1] Whom God had chosen to himself as a chaste virgin, and over whom he had care to preserve her from the lusts of the tyrant, as a father would have over his daughter.

37:23 [1] Declaring hereby that they that are enemies to God's Church, fight against him whose quarrel his Church only maintaineth.

37:25 [1] He boasteth of his policy, in that that he can find means to nourish his army: and of his power in that that his army is so great, that it is able to dry up whole rivers, and to destroy the waters which the Jews had closed in.

37:26 [1] Signifying, that God made not his Church to destroy it, but to preserve it: and therefore he saith that he formed it of old, even in his eternal counsel which cannot be changed.

I now bring it, that it should be destroyed, *and laid* on ruinous heaps, *as* cities defensed?

27 Whose inhabitants have [1]small power, *and are* afraid and confounded: they are like the grass of the field and green herb, *or* grass on the house tops, or corn blasted [2]afore it be grown.

28 But I know thy dwelling, and thy [1]going out, and thy coming in, and thy fury against me.

29 Because thou ragest against me, and thy tumult is come unto mine ears, therefore will I put mine [1]hook in thy nostrils, and my bridle in thy lips, and will bring thee back again the same way thou [2]camest.

30 And this shall be a [1]sign unto thee, *O Hezekiah*, Thou shalt eat this year such as groweth of itself: and the [2]second year such things as grow without sowing: and in the third year, sow ye and reap, and plant vineyards, and eat the fruit thereof.

31 And [1]the remnant that is escaped of the house of Judah, shall again take root downward and bear fruit upward.

32 For out of Jerusalem shall go a remnant, and they that escape out of mount Zion: the zeal of the Lord of hosts shall do this.

33 Therefore thus saith the Lord concerning the King of Assyria, He shall not enter into this city, nor shoot an arrow there, nor come before it with shield, nor cast a mount against it.

34 By the same way that he came, he shall return, and not come into this city, saith the Lord.

35 For I will defend this city to save it, for mine own sake, and for my servant [1]David's sake.

36 ¶ [b]Then the Angel of the Lord went out, and smote in the camp of Assyria, an hundred fourscore, and five thousand: so when they arose early in the morning, behold, they were all dead corpses.

b 2 Kings 19:35
2 Chron. 32:21

CHAPTER 38
a 2 Kings 20:1
2 Chron. 32:4

37 So Sennacherib king of Assyria departed, and went away and returned and dwelt at [1]Nineveh.

38 And as he was in the Temple worshipping of Nisroch his god, Adrammelech and Sharezer his sons slew him with the sword, and they escaped into the land of [1]Ararat: and [2]Esarhaddon his son reigned in his stead.

38 *1 Hezekiah is sick.   5 He is restored to health by the Lord, and liveth fifteen years after.   10 He giveth thanks for his benefit.*

1 About [a]that [1]time was Hezekiah sick unto the death, and the Prophet Isaiah son of Amoz came unto him, and said unto him, Thus saith the Lord, Put thine house in an order, for thou shalt die, and not live.

2 Then Hezekiah [1]turned his face to the wall, and prayed to the Lord,

3 And said, I beseech thee, Lord, remember now how I have walked before thee in truth, and with a perfect heart, and have done that which is good in thy sight: and Hezekiah wept sore.

4 ¶ Then came the word of the Lord to Isaiah, saying,

5 Go, and say unto Hezekiah, Thus saith the Lord God of David thy father, I have heard thy prayer, *and* seen thy tears: behold, I will add unto thy days fifteen years.

6 And I will deliver thee [1]out of the hand of the king of Assyria, and this city: for I will defend this city.

7 And [1]this sign shalt thou have of the Lord, that the Lord will do this thing that he hath spoken,

8 Behold, I will bring again the shadow of the degrees (whereby it is gone down in the dial of Ahaz by the [1]sun) ten degrees backward: so the sun

---

37:27 [1] Hebrew, *are short in hand.*
    [2] He showeth that the state and power of most flourishing cities endureth but a moment in respect of the Church, which shall remain forever, because God is the maintainer thereof.
37:28 [1] Meaning, his counsels and enterprises.
37:29 [1] Because Sennacherib showed himself, as a devouring fish and furious beast, he useth these similitudes, to teach how he will take him and guide him.
    [2] Thou shalt lose thy labor.
37:30 [1] God giveth signs after two sorts: some go before the thing, as the signs that Moses wrought in Egypt, which were for the confirmation of their faith, and some go after the thing, as the sacrifice, which they were commanded to make three days after their departure: and these latter are to keep the benefits of God in our remembrance: of the which sort here is.
    [2] He promiseth that for two years the ground of itself should feed them.
37:31 [1] They whom God hath delivered out of the hands of the Assyrians, shall prosper: and this properly belongeth to the Church.
37:35 [1] For my promise sake made to David.
37:37 [1] Which was the chiefest city of the Assyrians.

37:38 [1] Or, Armenia.
    [2] Who was also called Sardanapalus, in whose days ten years after Sennacherib's death the Chaldeans overcame the Assyrians by Merodach their king.
38:1 [1] Soon after that the Assyrians were slain: so that God will have the exercise of his children continually, that they may learn only to depend upon God and aspire to the heavens.
38:2 [1] For his heart was touched with fear of God's judgment, seeing he had appointed him to die so quickly after his deliverance from so great calamity, as one unworthy to remain in that estate, and also foreseeing the great change that should come in the Church, forasmuch as he left no son to reign after him: for as yet Manasseh was not born, and when he reigned, we see what a tyrant he was.
38:6 [1] He doth not only promise to prolong his life, but to give him rest and quietness from the Assyrians, who might have renewed their army to revenge their former discomfiture.
38:7 [1] For Hezekiah had asked for the confirmation of his faith, a sign, as verse 22, and 2 Kings 20:8, whereunto he was moved by the singular motion of God's spirit.
38:8 [1] Read 2 Kings 20:10.

returned by ten degrees, by the which degrees it was gone down.

9 ¹The writing of Hezekiah king of Judah, when he had been sick, and was recovered of his sickness.

10 I said in the ¹cutting off of my days, I shall go to the gates of the grave: I am deprived of the residue of my years.

11 I said, ¹I shall not see the Lord, *even* the Lord in the land of the living: I shall see man no more among the inhabitants of the world.

12 Mine habitation is departed, and is removed from me, like a shepherd's tent: I ¹have cut off like a weaver my life: he will cut me off from the height: from day ²to night, thou wilt make an end of me.

13 I reckoned ¹to the morning: but he brake all my bones like a lion, from day to night wilt thou make an end of me.

14 Like a crane *or* a swallow, so did I ¹chatter: I did mourn as a dove: mine eyes were lifted up on high: O Lord, ²it hath oppressed me, comfort me.

15 What shall I say, ¹for he hath said it to me, and he hath done it: I shall walk ²weakly all my years in the bitterness of my soul.

16 O Lord, ¹*to them* that overlive them, and to all *that are* in them, the life of my spirit *shall be known*, that thou causest me to ²sleep and hast given life to me.

17 Behold, for ¹felicity I had bitter grief, but it was thy pleasure *to deliver* my soul from the pit of corruption: for thou hast cast all my ²sins behind thy back.

18 For ¹the grave cannot confess thee: death cannot praise thee: they that go down into the pit, cannot

CHAPTER 39
ᵈ 2 Kings 20:12

hope for thy truth.

19 *But* the living, the living, he shall confess thee, as I *do* this day: the father to the ¹children shall declare thy truth.

20 The Lord *was ready* to save me: therefore we will sing my song, all the days of ¹our life in the house of the Lord.

21 Then said Isaiah, Take a lump of dry figs and ¹lay it upon the boil, and he shall recover.

22 Also Hezekiah ¹had said, What is the sign, that I shall go up into the house of the Lord?

39

Hezekiah is reproved because he showed his treasures unto the ambassadors of Babylon.

1 At ᵃthe same time, ¹Merodach Baladan, the son of Baladan, King of Babel, sent ²letters, and a present to Hezekiah: for he had heard that he had been sick, and was recovered.

2 And Hezekiah was ¹glad of them, and showed them the house of the treasures, the silver, and the gold, and the spices, and the precious ointment, and all the house of his armor, and all that was found in his treasures; there was nothing in his house, nor in all his kingdom that Hezekiah showed them not.

3 Then came Isaiah the Prophet unto King Hezekiah, and said unto him, What said these men? and from whence came they to thee? And Hezekiah said, They are come from a far country unto me, from Babel.

4 Then said he, What have ¹they seen in thine house? And Hezekiah answered, All that is in mine house have they seen; there is nothing among my treasures, that I have not showed them.

38:9 ¹ He left this song of his lamentation and thanksgiving to all posterity, as a monument of his own infirmity and thankful heart for God's benefits, as David did, Ps. 51.
38:10 ¹ At what time it was told me, that I should die.
38:11 ¹ I shall no more praise the Lord here in this Temple among the faithful: thus God suffereth his dearest children to want his consolation for a time, that his grace afterward may the more appear when they feel their own weakness.
38:12 ¹ By my sin I have provoked God to take my life from me.
² That is, in one day, or shortly.
38:13 ¹ Over night I thought that I should live till morning, but my pangs in the night persuaded me the contrary: he showeth the horror that the faithful have when they apprehend God's judgment against their sin.
38:14 ¹ I was so oppressed with sorrow, that I was not able to utter my words, but only to groan and sigh.
² To wit, sorrow and grief both of the body and mind.
38:15 ¹ God hath declared by his Prophet that I shall die and therefore I will yield unto him.
² I shall have no release, but continual sorrows while I live.
38:16 ¹ They that shall overlive the men that are now alive, and all they that are in these years shall acknowledge this benefit.
² That after that thou hadst condemned me to death thou restoredst me to life.
38:17 ¹ Whereas I thought to have lived in rest and ease being deliv-

ered from mine enemy, I had grief upon grief.
² He esteemeth more the remission of his sins, and God's favor than a thousand lives.
38:18 ¹ Forasmuch as God hath placed man in this world to glorify him, the godly take it as a sign of his wrath, when their days were shortened, either because that they seemed unworthy for their sins to live longer in his service, or for their zeal to God's glory, seeing that there are so few in earth that do regard it, as Ps. 6:5; 115:17.
38:19 ¹ All posterity shall acknowledge, and the fathers according to their duty toward their children shall instruct them in thy graces, and mercies toward me.
38:20 ¹ He showeth what is the use of the Congregation and Church, to wit, to give the Lord thanks for his benefits.
38:21 ¹ Read 2 Kings 20:7.
38:22 ¹ As verse 7.
39:1 ¹ This was the first king of Babylon, which overcame the Assyrians in the tenth year of his reign.
² Partly moved with the greatness of the miracle, partly because he showed himself enemy to his enemies, but chiefly because he would join with them whom God favored, and have their help, if occasion served.
39:2 ¹ Read 2 Kings 20:13 and 2 Chron. 32:25, 31.
39:4 ¹ He asketh him of the particulars, to make him understand the craft of the wicked, which he before being overcome with their flattery and blinded with ambition, could not see.

5 And Isaiah said to Hezekiah, Hear the word of the Lord of hosts,

6 Behold, the days come, that all that is in thine house, and which thy fathers have laid up in store until this day, shall be ¹carried to Babel: nothing shall be left, saith the Lord.

7 And of thy sons, that shall proceed out of thee, *and* which thou shalt beget, shall they take away, and they shall be ¹eunuchs in the palace of the King of Babel.

8 ¹Then said Hezekiah to Isaiah, The word of the Lord is good, which thou hast spoken: and he said, Yet let there be peace, and truth in my days.

40

2 *Remission of sins by Christ.* 3 *The coming of John Baptist.* 18 *The Prophet reproveth the Idolaters, and them that trust not in the Lord.*

1 Comfort ¹ye, comfort ye my people, will your God say.

2 Speak comfortably to Jerusalem, and cry unto her, that her ¹warfare is accomplished, that her iniquity is pardoned; for she hath received of the Lord's hand ²double for all her sins.

3 A ¹voice crieth in the ²wilderness, ³Prepare ye the way of the Lord: make straight in the desert a path for our God.

4 Every valley shall be exalted, and every ¹mountain and hill shall be made low; and the crooked shall be straight, and the rough places plain.

5 And the glory of the Lord shall be revealed, and all ¹flesh shall see it together: for the mouth of the Lord hath spoken it.

6 A ¹voice said, Cry. And he said, What shall I cry? All flesh *is* grass, and all the ²grace thereof *is* as the flowers of the field.

7 The grass withereth, the flower fadeth, because the ¹Spirit of the Lord bloweth upon it: surely the people *is* grass.

8 The grass withereth, the flower fadeth: but the ¹word of our God shall stand forever.

9 ¶ O Zion, that bringest good tidings, get thee up into the high ¹mountain: O Jerusalem, that bringest tidings, lift up thy voice with strength: lift it up, be not afraid: say unto the cities of Judah, Behold ²your God.

10 Behold, the Lord God will come with power, and ¹his arm shall rule for him: behold, his reward *is* with him, and his work before him.

11 He shall feed his flock like a shepherd: he shall gather the lambs with his arm, and carry them in his bosom, *and* shall guide them with ¹young.

12 Who hath measured the waters in his ¹fist? and counted heaven with the span, and comprehended the dust of the earth in a measure? and weighed the mountains in a weight, and the hills in a balance?

13 Who hath instructed the spirit of the Lord? or *was* ¹his counselor, *or* taught him?

14 Of whom took the counsel, and *who* instructed him and taught him in the way of judgment? or taught him knowledge, and showed unto him the way of understanding?

15 Behold, the nations *are* as a drop of a bucket, and are counted as the dust of the balance: behold, he taketh away the isles as a little dust.

16 And Lebanon *is* not sufficient for fire, nor the beasts thereof sufficient for a burnt offering.

17 All nations before him *are* as ¹nothing, and they are counted to him, less than nothing, and vanity.

18 To whom then ¹will ye liken God? or what

39:6 ¹ By the grievousness of the punishment is declared how greatly God detested ambition and vain glory.

39:7 ¹ That is, officers and servants.

39:8 ¹ Read 2 Kings 20:19.

40:1 ¹ This is a consolation for the Church, assuring them, that they shall be never destitute of Prophets whereby he exhorteth the true ministers of God that then were, and those also that should come after him, to comfort the poor afflicted, and to assure them of their deliverance both of body and soul.

40:2 ¹ The time of her affliction.
² Meaning, sufficient, as Isa. 61:7, and full correction, or double grace, whereas she deserved double punishment.

40:3 ¹ To wit, of the Prophets.
² That is, in Babylon and other places, where they were kept in captivity, and misery.
³ Meaning Cyrus and Darius which should deliver God's people out of captivity, and make them a ready way to Jerusalem: and this was fully accomplished, when John the Baptist brought tidings of Jesus Christ's coming, who was the true deliverer of his Church from sin and Satan, Matt. 3:3.

40:4 ¹ Whatsoever may let or hinder this deliverance, shall be removed.

40:5 ¹ This miracle shall be so great, that it shall be known through all the world.

40:6 ¹ The voice of God which spake to the Prophet Isaiah.
² Meaning, all man's wisdom and natural powers, James 1:10; 1 Pet. 1:24.

40:7 ¹ The spirit of God shall discover the vanity in all that seem to have any excellency of themselves.

40:8 ¹ Though considering the frailty of man's nature many of the Jews should perish, and so not be partakers of this deliverance, yet God's promise should be fulfilled, and they that remained, should feel the fruit thereof.

40:9 ¹ To publish this benefit through all the world.
² He showeth at one word the perfection of all man's felicity, which is to have God's presence.

40:10 ¹ His power shall be sufficient without help of any other, and shall have all means in himself to bring his will to pass.

40:11 ¹ He shall show his care and favor over them that are weak and tender.

40:12 ¹ Declaring that as God only hath all power, so doth he use the same for the defense and maintenance of his Church.

40:13 ¹ He showeth God's infinite wisdom for the same.

40:17 ¹ He speaketh all this to the intent that they should neither fear man nor put their trust in any, save only in God.

40:18 ¹ Hereby he armeth them against the idolatry, wherewith they should be tempted in Babylon.

similitude will ye set up unto him?

19 The workman melteth an image, or the goldsmith beateth it out in gold, or the goldsmith *maketh* silver plates.

20 Doth not ¹the poor choose out a tree that will not rot, for an oblation? he seeketh also unto him a cunning workman, to prepare an image that shall not be moved.

21 Know ye nothing? have ye not heard ¹it? hath it not been told you from the beginning? have ye not understood it by the ²foundation of the earth?

22 He sitteth upon the circle of the earth, and the inhabitants thereof *are* as grasshoppers, he stretcheth out the heavens as a curtain, and spreadeth them out, as a tent to dwell in.

23 He bringeth the princes to nothing, *and* maketh the judges of the earth, as vanity,

24 As though they were not planted, as though they were not sown, as though their stock took no root in the earth: for he did even ¹blow upon them, and they withered, and the whirlwind will take them away as stubble.

25 To whom now will ye liken me, that I should be like *him*, saith the Holy one?

26 Lift up your eyes on high, and behold who hath created these things, and bringeth ¹out their armies by number, and calleth them all by names: by the greatness of *his* power and mighty strength nothing faileth.

27 Why sayest thou, O Jacob, and speakest O Israel, ¹My way is hid from the Lord, and my judgment is passed over of my God?

28 Knowest thou not? *or* hast thou not heard, that the everlasting God, the Lord hath created the ¹ends of the earth? he neither fainteth, nor is weary: there *is* no searching of his ²understanding.

29 *But* he giveth strength unto him that fainteth, and unto him that hath no strength, he increaseth power.

30 ¹Even the young men shall faint, and be weary, and the young men shall stumble and fall.

31 But they that wait upon the Lord, shall renew *their* strength: they shall lift up the wings, as the eagles: they shall run, and not be weary, and they shall walk and not faint.

41

2 *God's mercy in choosing his people.*　6 *Their idolatry.*　27 *Deliverance promised to Zion.*

1 Keep ¹silence before me, O islands, and let the people ²renew *their* strength: let them come near, and let them speak: let us come together into judgment.

2 Who raised up ¹justice from the East, *and* called him to his foot? *and* gave the nations before him, and subdued the kings? he gave them as dust to his sword, *and* as scattered stubble unto his bow.

3 He pursued them, and passed safely by the way that he had not gone with his feet.

4 Who hath wrought and done it? he that calleth the ¹generations from the beginning. I the Lord *am* the ²first, and with the last I am the same.

5 The isles saw it, and did ¹fear, *and* the ends of the earth were abashed, drew near, and ²came.

6 Every man helped his neighbor, and said to his brother, ¹Be strong.

7 So the workman comforted the founder, *and* he that smote with the hammer, him that smote by course, saying, It is ready for the soldering, and he fastened it with nails that it should not be moved.

8 ¶ But thou, Israel, *art* my ¹servant, *and* thou Jacob, whom I have chosen, the seed of Abraham my friend.

9 For I have taken thee from the ends of the earth, and called thee before the chief thereof, and said unto thee, Thou *art* my servant: I have chosen thee, and not cast thee away.

10 Fear thou not, for I *am* with thee: be not afraid, for I *am* thy God: I will strengthen thee, and help thee, and will sustain thee with the ¹right hand of

---

40:20 ¹ He showeth the rage of the idolaters, seeing that the poor that have not to suffice their own necessities, will defraud themselves to serve their idols.

40:21 ¹ Have ye not the word of God, which plainly condemneth idolatry?

² Can you not learn by the visible creatures whom God hath made to observe your use, that you should not serve them nor worship them?

40:24 ¹ So that his power appeareth in every place wheresoever we turn our eyes.

40:26 ¹ Who hath set in order the infinite number of the stars.

40:27 ¹ He rebuketh the Jews, because they did not rest on the providence of God, but thought that he had forsaken them in their troubles.

40:28 ¹ And therefore all power is in his hand to deliver when his time cometh.

² Showing that men must patiently abide, and not curiously seek out the cause of God's delay in our afflictions.

40:30 ¹ They that trust in their own virtue, and do not acknowledge that all cometh of God.

41:1 ¹ God as though he pleaded his cause with all nations, requireth silence, that he may be heard in his right.

² That is, gather all their power and supports.

41:2 ¹ Who called Abraham (who was the pattern of God's justice in delivering his Church) from the idolatry of the Chaldeans to go to and fro at his commandment, and placed him in the land of Canaan.

41:4 ¹ Who hath created man and maintained his succession.

² Though the world set up never so many gods, yet they diminish nothing of my glory: for I am all one, unchangeable, which have ever been, and shall be forever.

41:5 ¹ Considering mine excellent works among my people.

² They assembled themselves and conspired against me to maintain their idolatry.

41:6 ¹ He noteth the obstinacy of the idolaters to maintain their superstitions.

41:8 ¹ And therefore oughtest not to pollute thyself with the superstition of the Gentiles.

41:10 ¹ That is, by the force of promise, in the performance whereof I will show myself faithful and just.

my justice.

11 Behold, all they that provoke thee, shall be ashamed, and confounded: they shall be as nothing, and they that strive with thee shall perish.

12 Thou shalt seek them and shalt not ¹find them: *to wit*, the men of thy strife, *for* they shall be as nothing, and the men that war against thee, as a thing of nought.

13 For I the Lord thy God will hold thy right hand, saying unto thee, Fear not, I will help thee.

14 Fear not thou ¹worm, Jacob, *and* ye men of Israel: I will help thee, saith the Lord, and thy redeemer the holy One of Israel.

15 Behold, I will make thee a roller, and a new threshing instrument having teeth: thou shalt thresh the ¹mountains, and bring them to powder, and shalt make the hills as chaff.

16 Thou shalt fan them, and the wind shall carry them away, and the whirlwind shall scatter them: and thou shalt rejoice in the Lord, *and* shalt glory in the holy One of Israel.

17 When ¹the poor and the needy seek water, and there *is* none (their tongue faileth for thirst: I the Lord will hear them: I the God of Israel will not forsake them:)

18 I will open rivers in the tops of the hills, and fountains in the midst of the valleys: I will make the wilderness as a pool of water, and the waste ¹land as springs of water.

19 I will set in the wilderness the cedar, the Shittah, and the myrrhe tree, and the pine tree, *and* I will set in the wilderness the fir tree, the elm and the box tree together.

20 Therefore let them see and know, and let them consider and understand together that the hand of the Lord hath done this, and the holy One of Israel

¹hath created it.

21 ¹Stand to your cause, saith the Lord: bring forth your strong reasons saith the King of Jacob.

22 Let them bring them forth, and let them tell us what shall come, let them show the former things what they be, that we may consider them, and know the latter end of them: either declare us things for to come.

23 Show the things that are to come hereafter, that we may know that ye are gods: yea, do good or do evil, that we may declare it, and behold it together.

24 Behold, ye are of no value, and your making is of naught: *man* hath ¹chosen an abomination by them.

25 ¶ I have raised up from the ¹North, and he shall come: from the East sun shall he ²call upon my name, and shall come upon ³princes as upon clay, and as the potter treadeth mire under the foot.

26 Who hath declared from the beginning, that we may know? or before time, that we may say, He is righteous? Surely there is none that showeth: surely there is none that declareth: surely there is none that heareth ¹your words.

27 I *am* the first, *that saith* to Zion, Behold, behold ¹them: and I will give to Jerusalem ²one that shall bring good tidings.

28 But when ¹I beheld, there was none: and when I inquired of them, there *was* no counselor, and when I demanded of them, they answered not a word.

29 Behold, they are all vanity: their work is of nothing, their images are wind and confusion.

42

1 *The obedience and humility of Christ.* 6 *Why he was sent into the world.* 11 *The vocation of the Gentiles.*

1 Behold, ¹my servant: ²I will stay upon him: mine elect, *in whom* my soul ³delighteth: I have put

---

41:12 ¹ Because they shall be destroyed.

41:14 ¹ Thus he calleth them because they were contemned of all the world, and that they considering their own poor estate, should seek unto him for help.

41:15 ¹ I will make thee able to destroy all thine enemies, be they never so mighty: and this chiefly is referred to the kingdom of Christ.

41:17 ¹ That is, they that shall be afflicted in the captivity of Babylon.

41:18 ¹ God will rather change the order of nature than they should want anything, that cry to him by true faith in their miseries: declaring to them hereby that they shall lack nothing by the way, when they return from Babylon.

41:20 ¹ That is, hath appointed and determined that it shall come so to pass.

41:21 ¹ He biddeth the idolaters to prove their religion, and to bring forth their idols, that they may be tried whether they know all things, and can do all things: which if they cannot do, he concludeth that they are no gods, but vile idols.

41:24 ¹ So that a man cannot make an idol, but he must do that which God detesteth and abhoreth: for he chooseth his own devices and forsaketh the Lord's.

41:25 ¹ Meaning, the Chaldeans.

² That is, Cyrus, who shall do all things in my name and by my direction: whereby he meaneth that both their captivity and deliverance shall be ordered by God's providence and appointment.

³ Both of the Chaldeans and others.

41:26 ¹ Meaning, that none of the Gentile gods can work any of these things.

41:27 ¹ That is, the Israelites which return from the captivity.

² To wit, a continual succession of Prophets and ministers.

41:28 ¹ When I looked whether the idols could do these things, I found that they had neither wisdom nor power to do anything: therefore he concludeth that all are wicked, that trust in such vanities.

42:1 ¹ That is, Christ, who in respect of his manhood is called here servant. The Prophets used to make mention of Christ after that they have declared any great promise, because he is the foundation whereupon all the promises are made and ratified.

² For I have committed all my power to him, as to a most faithful steward: Some read, I will establish him: to wit, in his office by giving him the fullness of my Spirit.

³ He only is acceptable to me, and they that come unto me by him: for there is no other means of reconciliation, Matt. 12:18; Eph. 4:1.

my Spirit upon him: he shall bring forth ⁴judgment to the Gentiles.

2 He shall not ¹cry, nor lift up, nor cause his voice to be heard in the street.

3 A ¹bruised reed shall he not break, and the smoking ²flax shall he not quench: he shall bring forth judgment in ³truth.

4 He shall not fail nor be discouraged till he have ¹set judgment in the earth: and the ²isles shall wait for his Law.

5 Thus saith God the Lord (he that created the heavens and spread them abroad: he that stretched forth the earth, and the buds thereof: he that giveth breath unto the people upon it, and spirit to them that walk therein)

6 I the Lord have called thee in ¹righteousness, and will hold ²thine hand, and I will keep thee, and give thee for a ³covenant of the people, *and* for a light of the Gentiles,

7 That thou mayest open the eyes of the blind, *and* bring out the prisoners from the prison: and them that sit in darkness, out of the prison house.

8 I am the Lord, this is my Name, and my ¹glory will I not give to another, neither my praise to graven images.

9 Behold, the former things are ¹come to pass, and new things do I declare: before they come forth, I tell you of them.

10 Sing unto the Lord a new song, *and* his praise from the end of the earth: ye that go down to the sea, and all that is therein, the isles and the inhabitants thereof.

11 Let the wilderness and the cities thereof lift up *their voice*, the towns that ¹Kedar doth inhabit: let the inhabitants of the rocks sing: let them shout from the top of the mountains.

12 Let them give glory unto the Lord, and declare his praise in the islands.

13 The Lord shall go forth as a ¹giant; he shall stir up *his* courage like a man of war: he shall shout and cry, *and* shall prevail against his enemies.

14 I have a long time held my peace: I have been still *and* refrained myself; now will I cry like a ¹travailing woman: I will destroy and devour at once.

15 I will make waste mountains, and hills, and dry up all their herbs, and I will make the floods islands, and I will dry up the pools.

16 ¶ And I will bring the ¹blind by a way, that they knew not, *and* lead them by paths that they have not known: I will make darkness light before them, and crooked things straight. These things will I do unto them, and not forsake them.

17 They shall be turned back: they shall be greatly ashamed, that trust in graven images, and say to the molten images, Ye are our gods.

18 ¶ Hear, ye deaf: and ye blind, regard, that ye may see.

19 Who is blind but my ¹servant? or deaf as my ²messenger, that I sent? who is blind as the ³perfect, and blind as the Lord's servant?

20 Seeing many things, but thou keepest them not? opening the ears, but he heareth not?

21 The Lord is willing for his righteousness sake, *that* he may magnify the Law and exalt it.

22 But this people is ¹robbed and spoiled, and shall be all snared in dungeons, and they shall be hid in prison houses; they shall be for prey, and none shall deliver: a spoil, and none shall say, ²Restore.

23 Who among you shall hearken to this, *and* take heed, and hear for ¹afterwards?

24 Who gave Jacob for a spoil, and Israel to the robbers? Did not the Lord, because we have sinned against him? for they would not walk in his ways, neither be obedient unto his Law.

42:1 ⁴ He shall declare himself governor over the Gentiles, and call them by his word, and rule them by his Spirit.

42:2 ¹ His coming shall not be with pomp and noise, as earthly princes.

42:3 ¹ He will not hurt the weak and feeble, but support and comfort them.

² Meaning, the wick of a lamp, or candle which is almost out, but he will cherish it and snuff it, that it may shine brighter.

³ Although he favor the weak, yet will he not spare the wicked, but will judge them according to truth and equity.

42:4 ¹ Till he have set all things in good order.

² The Gentiles shall be desirous to receive his doctrine.

42:6 ¹ Meaning, unto a lawful and just vocation.

² To assist and guide thee.

³ As him, by whom the promise made to all nations in Abraham shall be fulfilled.

42:8 ¹ I will not suffer my glory to be diminished: which I should do if I were not faithful in performing the same, and the idolaters thereby would extol their idols above me.

42:9 ¹ As in time past I have been true in my promises, so will I be in time to come.

42:11 ¹ Meaning, the Arabians, under whom he comprehendeth all the people of the East.

42:13 ¹ He showeth the zeal of the Lord, and his power in the conservation of his Church.

42:14 ¹ I will haste to execute my vengeance, which I have so long deferred as a woman that desireth to be delivered, when she is in travail.

42:16 ¹ That is, my poor people, which are in perplexity and care.

42:19 ¹ To wit, Israel, which should have most light because of my Law.

² The Priest to whom my word is committed, which should not only hear it himself, but cause others to hear it.

³ As the Priests and Prophets that should be lights to others?

42:22 ¹ Because they will not acknowledge this benefit of the Lord, who is ready to deliver them, he suffereth them to be spoiled of their enemies through their own fault and incredulity.

² There shall be none to succor them, or to will the enemy to restore that which he hath spoiled.

42:23 ¹ Meaning, God's wrath.

25 Therefore he hath poured upon him his fierce wrath, and the strength of battle; and it set him on fire round about, and he knew not, and it burned him up, yet he considered not.

43

1 *The Lord comforteth his people.* *He promiseth deliverance to the Jews.* *11 There is no God but one alone.*

1 But now thus saith the Lord, [1]that created thee, O Jacob: and he that formed thee, O Israel, [2]Fear not: for I have redeemed thee: I have called thee by thy name, thou art mine.

2 When thou passest through the [1]waters, I will be with thee, and through the floods, that they do not overflow thee. When thou walkest through the very fire, thou shalt not be burnt, neither shall the flame kindle upon thee.

3 For I am the Lord thy God, the holy one of Israel, thy Savior: I gave [1]Egypt for thy ransom, Ethiopia, and Seba for thee.

4 Because thou wast precious in my sight, *and* thou wast honorable, and I loved thee, therefore will I give [1]man for thee, and people for thy sake.

5 Fear not, for I am with thee: I will bring thy seed from the [1]East, and gather thee from the West.

6 I will say to the North, Give: and to the South, Keep not back: bring my sons from far, and my daughters from the ends of the earth.

7 Everyone shall be called by my [1]Name: for I created him for my glory, formed him and made him.

8 I will bring forth the blind people, and they shall have eyes, and the deaf, and they shall have ears.

9 Let all the nations be gathered [1]together, and let the people be assembled: who among them can declare this, and show us former things? let them bring forth their [2]witnesses, that they may be justi-

fied: but let them [3]hear, and say, It *is* truth.

10 You [1]are my witnesses, saith the Lord, and my [2]servant, whom I have chosen: therefore ye shall know and believe me, and ye shall understand that I am: before me there was no God formed, neither shall there be after me.

11 I, *even* I am the Lord, and beside me there is no Savior.

12 I have declared, and I have saved, and I have showed, when there was no strange *god* among you: therefore you are my witnesses, saith the Lord, that I am God.

13 Yea, before the day *was*, I am, and there is none that can deliver out of mine hand: I will do it, and who shall let it?

14 Thus saith the Lord your redeemer, the holy one of Israel, For your sake I have sent to Babel, and [1]brought it down: they are all fugitives, and the Chaldeans cry in [2]the ships.

15 I am the Lord your holy one, the creator of Israel, your King.

16 Thus saith the Lord which maketh a way in [1]the Sea, and a path in the mighty [2]waters.

17 When he [1]bringeth out the [2]chariot and horse, the army and the power lie together, *and* shall not rise, they are extinct, and quenched as tow.

18 Remember ye not the former things, neither regard the things of old.

19 Behold, I do a new thing: now shall it come forth: shall you not know it? I will even make a way in the [1]desert, *and* floods in the wilderness.

20 The wild [1]beasts shall honor me, the dragons and the ostriches, because I gave water in the desert, *and* floods in the wilderness to give drink to my people, even to mine elect.

21 This people have I formed for myself: they shall show forth my praise.

22 And thou hast not [1]called upon me, O Jacob,

43:1 [1] After these threatenings he promiseth deliverance to his Church, because he hath regenerated them, adopted them, and called them.

[2] When thou seest dangers and conspiracies on all sides, remember this benefit and the love of thy God, and it shall encourage thee.

43:2 [1] By water and fire he meaneth all kind of troubles and perils.

43:3 [1] I turned Sennacherib's power against these countries, and made them to suffer that affliction which thou shouldest have done, and so were as the payment of thy ransom, Isa. 37:9.

43:4 [1] I will not spare any man, rather than thou shouldest perish, for God more esteemeth one of his faithful than all the wicked in the world.

43:5 [1] He prophesieth of their deliverance from the captivity of Babylon, and so of the calling of the universal Church, alluding to that which is written, Deut. 30:3.

43:7 [1] Meaning, that he could not be unmindful of them, except he would neglect his own Name and glory.

43:9 [1] Signifying, that no power can resist him in doing this miraculous work, nor all their idols are able to do the like, as Isa. 41:22.

[2] To prove that the things which are spoken of them, are true.

[3] Showing, that the malice of the wicked hindereth them in the

knowledge of the truth, because they will not hear when God speaketh by his word.

43:10 [1] The Prophets and people to whom I have given my Law.

[2] Meaning specially Christ, and by him all the faithful.

43:14 [1] By Darius and Cyrus.

[2] They shall cry when they would escape by my water, seeing that the course of Euphrates is turned another way by the enemy.

43:16 [1] When he delivered Israel from Pharaoh, Exod. 14:22.

[2] When the Israelites passed through Jordan, Josh. 3:17.

43:17 [1] When he delivered his people out of Egypt.

[2] Pharaoh and his mighty army.

43:19 [1] Meaning, that their deliverance out of Babylon should be more famous than that from Egypt was, Jer. 23:7; Hag. 2:10; 2 Cor. 5:17; Rev. 21:5, 7.

43:20 [1] They shall have such abundance of all things as they return home, even in the dry and barren places, that the very beasts shall feel my benefits, and shall acknowledge them: much more men ought to be thankful for the same.

43:22 [1] Thou hast not worshipped me as thou oughtest to have done.

but thou hast ²wearied me, O Israel.

23 Thou ¹hast not brought me the sheep of thy burnt offerings, neither hast thou honored me with thy sacrifices. I have not caused thee to serve with an offering, nor wearied thee with incense.

24 Thou broughtest me no sweet ¹savor with money, neither hast thou made me drunk with the fat of thy sacrifices, but thou hast made me to ²serve with thy sins, *and* wearied me with thine iniquities.

25 I, *even* I am he that putteth away thine iniquities for mine own sake, and will not remember thy sins.

26 Put me in ¹remembrance: let us be judged together: count thou that thou mayest be justified.

27 Thy ¹first father hath sinned, and thy ²teachers have transgressed against me.

28 Therefore I have ¹profaned the rulers of the Sanctuary, and have made Jacob a curse, and Israel a reproach.

44

1 *The Lord promiseth comfort, and that he will assemble his Church of divers nations.* 9 *The vanity of Idols.* 17 *The beastliness of idolaters.*

1 Yet now hear, O Jacob my servant, and Israel whom I have chosen.

2 Thus saith the Lord, that made thee, and formed ¹thee from the womb: he will help thee. Fear not, O Jacob, my servant, and thou righteous ²whom I have chosen.

3 For I will pour water upon the ¹thirsty, and floods upon the dry ground: I will pour my spirit upon thy seed, and my blessing upon thy buds.

4 And they ¹shall grow as among the grass, *and* as the willows by the rivers of waters.

5 One shall say, I am the Lord's: another ¹shall be called by the name of Jacob: and another shall subscribe with his hand unto the Lord, and name himself by the name of Israel.

6 Thus saith the Lord the King of Israel and his redeemer, the Lord of hosts, ¹I am the first, and I am the last, and without me *is* there no God.

7 And who is like me, that shall ¹call and shall declare it, and set ²it in order before me, since I appointed the ³ancient people? and what is at hand, and what things are to come? let ⁴them show unto them.

8 Fear ye not, neither be afraid: have not I told thee of old, and have declared it? ¹you are even my witnesses, whether there be a God beside me, and that there is no God that I know not.

9 All they that make an image, are vanity, and ¹their delectable things shall nothing profit: and they are their own witnesses, ²that they see not nor know: therefore they shall be confounded.

10 Who hath made a ¹god, or molten an image, that is ²profitable for nothing?

11 Behold, all that are of the ¹fellowship thereof, shall be confounded: for the workmen themselves are men: let them all be gathered together, and ²stand up, *yet* they shall fear, and be confounded together.

12 The smith *taketh* an instrument, and worketh in the coals, and fashioneth it with hammers, and worketh it with the strength of his arms, yea, he is ¹an hungered, and his strength faileth, he drinketh no water, and is faint.

---

² Because thou hast not willingly received that which I did command thee, thou didst grieve me. Whereby he showeth that his mercies were the only cause of their deliverance, forasmuch as they had deserved the contrary.

43:23 ¹ Meaning, in true faith and obedience.

43:24 ¹ Either for the composition of the sweet ointment, Exod. 30:34, or for the sweet incense, Exod. 30:7.

² Thou hast made me to bear an heavy burden by thy sins.

43:26 ¹ If I forget anything that may make for thy justification, put me in remembrance and speak for thyself.

43:27 ¹ Thine ancestors.

² Thy Priests and thy Prophets.

43:28 ¹ That is, rejected, abhorred, and destroyed them in the wilderness and at other times.

44:2 ¹ He treated and chose thee from the beginning of his own mercy, and before thou couldest merit anything.

² Whom God accepteth as righteous: or which haddest occasion thereunto because of the Law, and of thine holy vocation.

44:3 ¹ Because man of himself is as the dry and barren land, he promiseth to moisten him with the waters of his holy Spirit, Joel 2:28; John 7:38; Acts 2:17.

44:4 ¹ That is, thy children and posterity shall increase wonderfully after their deliverance from Babylon.

44:5 ¹ By this diversity of speech he meaneth one thing, that is, that the people shall be holy, and receive the true religion of God, as Ps. 87:5.

44:6 ¹ I am always like myself, that is, merciful toward my Church, and most able to maintain it, as Isa. 41:4 and 48:12; Rev. 1:17 and 22:13.

44:7 ¹ And appoint them that shall deliver the Church.

² That is, declare unto me how I ought to proceed herein.

³ God calleth the Israelites ancient, because he preferred them to all others in his eternal election.

⁴ Meaning, their idols.

44:8 ¹ Read Isa. 43:10.

44:9 ¹ Whatsoever they bestow upon their idols, to make them to seem glorious.

² That is, the idolaters seeing their idols blind, most needs be witnesses of their own blindness, and feeling that they are not able to help them, must confess that they have no power.

44:10 ¹ Meaning, that whatsoever is made by the hand of man, if he be esteemed as God, is most detestable.

² Whereby appeareth their blasphemy, which call images the books of the laity, seeing that they are not only here called unprofitable, but Isa 41:24 abominable, and Jeremiah calleth them the work of errors, Jer. 10:15; Habakkuk, a lying teacher, Hab. 2:18.

44:11 ¹ That is, which by any way consent either to the making or worshipping.

² Signifying, that the multitude shall not then save the idolaters, when God will take vengeance, although they excuse themselves thereby among men.

44:12 ¹ He describeth the raging affection of the idolaters, which forget their own necessities to set forth their devotion toward their idols.

13 The carpenter stretcheth forth a line, he fashioneth it with a red thread, he planeth it, and he portrayeth it with the compass, and maketh it after the figure of a man, *and* according to the beauty of a man, that it may remain in [1]an house.

14 He will hew him down cedars, and take the pine tree and the oak, and taketh courage among the trees of the forest; he planteth a fir tree, and the rain doth nourish it.

15 And man burneth thereof; for he will take thereof, and [1]warm himself: he also kindleth it, and baketh bread, yet he maketh a god, and worshippeth it; he maketh it an idol, and boweth unto it.

16 He burneth the half thereof even in the fire, *and* upon the half thereof he [1]eateth flesh; he roasteth the roast, and is satisfied; also he warmeth himself and saith, Aha, I am warm, I have been at the fire.

17 And the residue thereof he maketh a god, *even* his idol; he boweth unto it, and worshippeth and prayeth unto it, and saith, Deliver me; for thou art my god.

18 They have not known, nor understood: [1]for *God* hath shut their eyes that they cannot see, *and* their heart, that they cannot understand.

19 And none [1]considereth in his heart, neither *is* there knowledge nor understanding to say, I have burnt half of it, even in the fire, and have baked bread also upon the coals thereof: I have roasted flesh, and eaten it, and shall I make the residue thereof an abomination? shall I bow to the stock of a tree?

20 He feedeth [1]of ashes: a seduced heart hath deceived him, that he cannot deliver his soul, nor say, Is there not a lie in my right hand?

21 [1]Remember these (O Jacob and Israel) for thou art my servant: I have formed thee; thou art my servant: O Israel forget me not.

22 I have put away thy transgressions like a cloud, and thy sins as a mist; turn unto me, for I have redeemed thee.

23 [1]Rejoice ye heavens; for the Lord hath done it; shout, ye lower parts of the earth; burst forth into praises, ye mountains, O forest and every tree therein: for the Lord hath redeemed Jacob, and will be glorified in Israel.

24 Thus saith the Lord thy redeemer, and he that formed thee from the womb, I am the Lord that made all things, that spread out the heavens alone, and stretched out the earth by myself.

25 I destroy the [1]tokens of the soothsayers, and make them that conjecture, fools, and turn the wise men backward, and make their knowledge foolishness.

26 ¶ He confirmeth the word of his [1]servant, and performeth the counsel of his messengers, saying to Jerusalem, Thou shalt be inhabited: and to the cities of Judah, Ye shall be built up, and I will repair the decayed places thereof.

27 He saith to the [1]deep, Be dry, and I will dry up thy floods.

28 He saith to [1]Cyrus, *Thou art* my shepherd, and he shall perform all my desire: saying also to Jerusalem, Thou shalt be built, and to the Temple, Thy foundation shall be surely laid.

45 1 *The deliverance of the people by Cyrus.*   9 *God is just in all his works.*   20 *The calling of the Gentiles.*

1 Thus saith the Lord unto [1]Cyrus his [2]anointed, whose right hand I have holden to [3]subdue nations before him: therefore will I weaken the loins of kings, and open the doors before him, and the gates shall not be shut.

2 I will go before thee, and make the [1]crooked straight: I will break the brazen doors, and burst the iron bars.

3 And I will give thee the treasures of darkness, and the things hid in secret places, that thou mayest [1]know that I am the Lord which call thee by thy name, even the God of Israel.

44:13 [1] To place it in some Temple.

44:15 [1] He setteth forth the obstinacy and malice of the idolaters, which though they see by daily experience that their idols are no better than the rest of the matter whereof they are made, yet they refuse the one part, and make a god of the other, as the Papists make their cake god, and the rest of their idols.

44:16 [1] That is, he either maketh a table or trenchers.

44:18 [1] The Prophet giveth here an answer to all them that wonder how it is possible that any should be so blind to commit such abomination, saying, that God hath blinded their eyes, and hardened their hearts.

44:19 [1] Hebrew, *turneth*.

44:20 [1] He is abused as one that would eat ashes, thinking to satisfy his hunger.

44:21 [1] Showing that man's heart is most inclined to idolatry, and therefore he warneth his people by these examples, that they should not cleave to any but to the living God, when they should be among the idolaters.

44:23 [1] He showeth that the work of the Lord toward his people shall be so great, that the insensible creatures shall be moved therewith.

44:25 [1] He armeth them against the soothsayers of Babylon, which would have borne them in hand, that they knew by the stars, that God would not deliver them, and that Babylon should stand.

44:26 [1] Of Isaiah and the rest of his Prophets, which did assure the Church of God's favor and deliverance.

44:27 [1] He showeth that God's work should be no less notable in this their deliverance, than when he brought them out of Egypt, through the sea.

44:28 [1] To assure them of their deliverance, he nameth the person by whom it should be, more than an hundred years before he was born.

45:1 [1] To assure the Jews of their deliverance against the great tentations that they should abide, he nameth the person and the means.

[2] Because Cyrus should execute the office of a deliverer, God called him his anointed for a time, but after another sort than he called David.

[3] To guide him in the deliverance of my people.

45:2 [1] I will take away all impediments and lets.

45:3 [1] Not that Cyrus did know God to worship him aright, but he had a certain particular knowledge as profane men may have of his power, and so was compelled to deliver God's people.

4 For Jacob my servant's [1]sake, and Israel mine elect, I will even call *thee* by thy name, *and* name thee, though thou hast not known me.

5 I am the Lord, and there is none other; there is no God besides me: I [1]girded thee, though thou hast not known me.

6 That they may know from the rising of the sun, and from the West, that there is none besides me. I am the Lord, and there is none other.

7 I form the [1]light, and create darkness: I make peace, and create evil: I the Lord do all these things.

8 Ye heavens send the dew from above, and let the clouds drop down [1]righteousness: let the earth open, and let salvation and justice grow forth: let it bring them forth together: I the Lord have [2]created him.

9 [1]Woe be unto him that striveth with his maker, the potsherd with the potsherds of the earth: shall the clay say to him that fashioneth it, What makest thou? or thy work, [2]It hath none hands?

10 Woe unto him that saith to *his* father, What hast thou begotten? or to *his* mother, What hast thou brought forth?

11 Thus saith the Lord, the only one of Israel, and his maker, Ask me [1]of things to come concerning my sons, and concerning the works of mine hands: commend you me.

12 I have made the earth, and created man upon it: I, whose hands have spread out the heavens, I have even commanded all their [1]army.

13 I have raised [1]him up in righteousness, and I will direct all his ways: he shall build my city, and he shall let go my captives, not for [2]price nor reward, saith the Lord of hosts.

14 Thus saith the Lord, The labor [1]of Egypt, and the merchandise of Ethiopia, and of the Sabeans, men of stature shall come unto thee, and they shall be [2]thine: they shall follow thee, *and* shall go in chains: they shall fall down before thee, and make supplication unto thee, *saying,* Surely God is in thee, and there *is* none other God besides.

15 Verily, thou O God [1]hidest thyself, O God, the Savior of Israel.

16 All they shall be ashamed and also confounded: they shall go to confusion together, that are the makers of images.

17 *But* Israel shall be saved in the Lord, with an everlasting salvation: ye shall not be ashamed nor confounded world without end.

18 For this saith the Lord (that created heaven, God himself that formed the earth, and made it: he that prepared it, he created it not in vain: he formed it to be [1]inhabited) I am the Lord, and there *is* none other.

19 I have not spoken in secret, *neither* [1]in a place of darkness in the earth: I said not in vain unto the seed of Jacob, Seek you me: I the Lord do speak righteousness, and declare righteous things.

20 Assemble yourselves, and come: draw near together, [1]ye abject of the Gentiles: they have no knowledge, that set up the wood of their idol, and pray unto a god, that cannot save them.

21 Tell ye and bring them, and let them take counsel together, who hath declared this from the beginning, *or* hath told it of old? Have not I the Lord? and there *is* none other God beside me, a just God, and a Savior: there *is* none beside me.

22 Look unto me, and ye shall be saved: all [1]the ends of the earth shall be saved: for I am God, and there *is* none other.

23 I have sworn by myself: the word is gone out of my mouth in [1]righteousness, and shall not return, That every [2]knee shall bow unto me, *and* every tongue shall swear *by me.*

45:4 [1] Not for any thing that is in thee, or for thy worthiness.

45:5 [1] I have given thee strength, power and authority.

45:7 [1] I send peace and war, prosperity and adversity, as Amos 3:6.

45:8 [1] He comforteth the Jews, as if he would say, Though when ye look to the heavens and earth for succor, ye see nothing now but signs of God's wrath, yet will cause them to bring forth most certain tokens of your deliverance, and of the performance of my promise: which is meant by righteousness.

[2] I have appointed Cyrus to this use and purpose.

45:9 [1] Hereby he bridleth their impatience, which in adversity and trouble murmur against God, and will not tarry his pleasure: willing that man should match with his like, and not contend against God.

[2] That is, it is not perfectly made.

45:11 [1] Instead of murmuring, humble yourselves, and ask what ye will for the consolation of my children, and you shall be sure of it, as ye are of these things which are at your commandment. Some read it with an interrogation, and make the application of the similitude.

45:12 [1] That is, the stars.

45:13 [1] To wit, Cyrus, that I may show by him the faithfulness of my promise in delivering my people.

[2] Meaning, freely and without ransom, or any grievous condition.

45:14 [1] These people were tributaries to the Persians, and so king Arta-xerxes gave this money toward the building of the Temple, Ezra 7:27.

[2] Whereas to fore they were thine enemies, they shall now honor thee, and thou shalt rule them: which was accomplished in the time of Christ.

45:15 [1] Hereby he exhorteth the Jews to patience, though their deliverance be deferred for a time: showing that they should not repent their long patience, but the wicked and idolaters shall be destroyed.

45:18 [1] To wit, of men, but chiefly of his Church.

45:19 [1] As do the false gods, which give uncertain answers.

45:20 [1] All ye idolaters which though you seem to have never so much worldly dignity, yet in God's sight you are vile and abject.

45:22 [1] He calleth the idolaters to repentance, willing them to look unto him with the eye of faith.

45:23 [1] That is, that the thing which I have promised shall be faithfully performed.

[2] The knowledge of God and the true worshipping shall be through all the world, Rom. 14:11; Phil. 2:10, whereby he signifieth that we must not only serve God in heart, but declare the same also by outward profession.

24 Surely [1]he shall say, In the Lord have I righteousness and strength: he shall come unto him, and all that [2]provoke him shall be ashamed.

25 The whole seed of Israel shall be justified, and glory in the Lord.

46

1 *The destruction of Babylon and of their idols.* 3 *He calleth the Jews to the consideration of his works.*

1 Bel is bowed down: [1]Nebo is fallen: their idols were upon their [2]beasts, and upon the cattle: they which did bear you, *were* laden with a weary burden.

2 [1]They are bowed down, *and* fallen together, for they could not rid them of the burden, and their [2]soul is gone into captivity.

3 Hear ye me, O house of Jacob, and all that remain of the house of Israel, which are [1]born of me *from the* womb, and brought up of me *from the* birth.

4 Therefore unto [1]old age, I the same, even I will bear *you* until the hoary hairs: I have made *you*: I will also bear *you*, and I will carry *you*, and I will deliver *you*.

5 ¶ To whom will ye make me like, or make me equal, or [1]compare me that I should be like him?

6 They draw gold out of the bag, and weigh silver in the balance, *and* hire a goldsmith to make a god of it, *and* they bow down and worship it.

7 They bear it upon the shoulders: they carry him and set him in his place: so doth he stand, *and* cannot remove from his place. Though one cry unto him, yet can he not answer, nor deliver him out of his tribulation.

8 Remember this, and be ashamed: bring it again to [1]mind, O you transgressors.

9 Remember the former things of old: for I am God, and there *is* none other God, and there *is* nothing like me,

10 Which declare the last thing from the beginning, and from of old: the things that were not done, saying, My counsel shall stand, and I will do whatsoever I will.

11 I call a [1]bird from the East, *and* the man of my [2]counsel from far: as I have spoken, so will I bring it to pass: I have purposed it, and I will do it.

12 Hear me ye stubborn hearted, that are far from [1]justice.

13 I bring [1]near my justice: it shall not be far off, and my salvation shall not tarry: for I will give salvation in Zion, *and* my glory unto Israel.

47

The destruction of Babylon, and the causes wherefore.

1 Come down and sit in the dust: O [1]virgin, daughter Babel, sit on the ground: there is no [2]throne, O daughter of the Chaldeans; for thou shalt no more be called, Tender and delicate.

2 Take the millstones, and [1]grind meal; loose thy locks: [2]make bare the feet: uncover the leg, *and* pass through the floods.

3 Thy filthiness shall be discovered, and thy shame shall be seen: I will take vengeance, and I will not meet *thee as* a [1]man.

4 [1]Our redeemer, the Lord of hosts *is* his Name, the holy One of Israel.

5 [1]Sit still, and get thee into darkness, O daughter of the Chaldeans; for thou shalt no more be called, The lady of kingdoms.

6 I was wroth with my people: I have polluted mine inheritance, and given them into thine hand, thou didst show them no [1]mercy, but thou didst lay thy very heavy yoke upon the ancient.

7 And thou saidest, I shall be a lady forever, so that thou didst not set thy mind to these things, neither

---

45:24 [1] Meaning, the faithful shall feel and confess this.

[2] All the contemners of God.

46:1 [1] These were the chief idols of Babylon.

[2] Because they were of gold and silver, the Medes and Persians carried them away.

46:2 [1] The beasts that carried the idols, fell down under their burden.

[2] He derideth the idols, which had neither soul nor sense.

46:3 [1] He showeth the difference between the idols and the true God: for they must be carried of others, but God himself carrieth his, as Deut. 32:11.

46:4 [1] Seeing I have begotten you, I will nourish and preserve you forever.

46:5 [1] The people of God, setting their own calamity, and the flourishing estate of the Babylonians, should be tempted to think that their God was not so mighty as the idols of their enemies: therefore he describeth the original of all the idols to make them to be abhorred of all men: showing that the most that can be spoken in their commendation, is but to prove them vile.

46:8 [1] Become wise, meaning, that all idolaters are without wit or sense, like mad men.

46:11 [1] That is, Cyrus, which shall come as swift as a bride, and fight

against Babylon.

[2] Him by whom I have appointed to execute that which I have determined.

46:12 [1] Which by your incredulity would let the performance of my promise.

46:13 [1] He showeth that man's incredulity cannot abolish the promise of God, Rom. 3:3.

47:1 [1] Which hast lived in wealth and wantonness, and hast not yet been overcome by any enemy.

[2] Thy government shall be taken from thee.

47:2 [1] Thou shalt be brought to most vile servitude: for to turn the mill was the office of slaves.

[2] The things wherein she setteth her greatest pride, shall be made vile, even from the head to the foot.

47:3 [1] I will use no humanity nor pity toward thee.

47:4 [1] The Israelites shall confess that the Lord doeth this for his Church's sake.

47:5 [1] For very shame, and hide thyself.

47:6 [1] They abused God's judgments, thinking that he punished the Israelites, because he would utterly cast them off, and therefore instead of pitying their misery, thou didst increase it.

didst thou remember the latter end thereof.

8 Therefore now hear, thou that art given to pleasures, and dwellest careless, She saith in her heart, I am and none else: I shall not sit *as* a widow, neither shall know the loss of children.

9 But these two things shall come to thee suddenly on one day, the loss of children and widowhood; they shall come upon thee in their [1]perfection, for the multitude of thy divinations, and for the great abundance of thine enchanters.

10 For thou hast trusted in thy wickedness; thou hast said, None seeth me. Thy [1]wisdom and thy knowledge, they have caused thee to rebel, and thou hast said in thine heart, I am, and none else.

11 Therefore shall evil come upon thee, and thou shalt not know the morning thereof; destruction shall fall upon thee, which thou shalt not be able to put away: destruction shall come upon thee suddenly, or thou beware.

12 Stand now among thine enchanters, and in the multitude of thy soothsayers (with whom thou hast [1]wearied thyself from thy youth) if so be thou mayest have profit, *or* if so be thou mayest have strength.

13 Thou art wearied in the multitude of thy counsels: let now the astrologers, the stargazers, and prognosticators stand up, and save thee from these things that shall come upon thee.

14 Behold, they shall be as stubble: the fire shall burn them; they shall not deliver their own lives from the power of the flame: there *shall be* no coals [1]to warm at, *nor* light to sit by.

15 Thus shall they serve thee, with whom thou hast wearied thee, *even* thy merchants from thy youth; every one shall wander to his own [1]quarters: none shall save thee.

48 1 *The hypocrisy of the Jews is reproved.* 12 *The Lord alone will be worshipped.* 20 *Of their deliver-*

---

ance out of Babylon.

1 Hear ye this, O house of Jacob, which are [1]called by the name of Israel, and are come out of [2]the waters of Judah: which swear by the name of the Lord, and make mention of the God of Israel, *but* not in truth nor in righteousness.

2 For they are called of the holy city, and stay themselves [1]upon the God of Israel, whose Name *is* the Lord of hosts.

3 I have declared the former things of old, and they went out of my mouth, and I showed [1]them: I did them suddenly and they came to pass.

4 Because I knew that [1]thou art obstinate, and thy neck *is* an iron sinew, and thy brow brass,

5 Therefore I have declared it to thee of old: before it came to pass, I showed [1]it thee, lest thou shouldest say, Mine idol hath done them, and my carved image, and my molten image hath commanded them.

6 Thou hast heard, behold all this, and will not ye [1]declare it? I have showed thee new things, even now, and hid things, which thou knewest not.

7 They are created now, and not of old, and even before this thou heardest them not, lest thou shouldest say, Behold, I [1]knew them.

8 Yet thou heardest them not, neither didst know them, neither yet was thine ear opened of old; for I knew that thou wouldest grievously transgress: therefore have I called thee a transgressor from the [1]womb.

9 For my Name's sake will I defer my wrath, and for my praise, will I refrain it from thee, [1]that I cut thee not off.

10 Behold, I have fined thee, but [1]not as silver: I have [2]chosen thee in the furnace of affliction.

11 For mine own sake, for mine own sake will I do it; for how should *my Name* [1]be polluted? [2]surely I will not give my glory unto another.

12 Hear me, O Jacob and Israel, my called, [1]I am,

47:9 [1] So that thy punishment shall be so great, as is possible to be imagined.

47:10 [1] Thou didst think that thine own wisdom and policy would have saved thee.

47:12 [1] He derideth their vain confidence, that put their trust in anything but in God, condemning also such vain sciences, which serve to no use, but to delude the people, and to bring them from depending only on God.

47:14 [1] They shall utterly perish, and no part of them remain.

47:15 [1] They shall flee everyone to that place, which he thought by his speculations to be most sure: but that shall deceive them.

48:1 [1] He detecteth their hypocrisy which vaunteth themselves to be Israelites, and were not so indeed.

  [2] Meaning, the fountain and stock.

48:2 [1] They make a show, as though they would have none other God.

48:3 [1] He showeth that they could not accuse him in anything, forasmuch as he had performed whatsoever he had promised.

48:4 [1] I have done for thee more than I promised, that thy stubbornness and impudence might have been overcome.

48:5 [1] How thou shouldest be delivered out of Babylon.

48:6 [1] Will ye not acknowledge this my benefit, and declare it unto others?

48:7 [1] Showing that man's arrogance is the cause why God doth not declare all things at once, lest they should attribute this knowledge to their own wisdom.

48:8 [1] From the time that I brought thee out of Egypt: for that deliverance was as the birth of the Church.

48:9 [1] As it was my free mercy that I did choose thee: so it is my free mercy that must save thee.

48:10 [1] For I had respect to thy weakness and infirmity: for in silver there is some pureness, but in us there is nothing but dross.

  [2] I took thee out of the furnace where thou shouldest have been consumed.

48:11 [1] God joineth the salvation of his with his own honor: so that they cannot perish, but his glory should be diminished, as Deut. 32:27.

  [2] Read Isa. 42:8.

48:12 [1] Read Isa. 41:4.

I am the first, and I am the last.

13 Surely mine hand hath laid the foundation of the earth, and my right hand hath spanned the heavens: when I call them, [1]they stand up together.

14 All you, assemble yourselves, and hear: which among them hath declared these things? The Lord hath loved [1]him, he will do his will in Babel, and his arm *shall be* against the Chaldeans.

15 I, *even* I have spoken it, and I have called him, I have brought him, and his way shall prosper.

16 Come near unto me: hear ye this: I have not spoken it in secret from the [1]beginning: from the time that the thing was, I was there, and now the Lord God and his Spirit hath [2]sent me.

17 Thus saith the Lord thy redeemer, the Holy one of Israel, I am the Lord thy God, which teach thee [1]to profit, and lead thee by the way that thou shouldest go.

18 Oh, that thou hadst hearkened to my commandments! then had thy prosperity been as the flood, and thy righteousness as the waves of the sea.

19 Thy seed also had been as the sand, and the fruit of thy body like the gravel thereof: his [1]name should not have been cut off nor destroyed before me.

20 [1]Go ye out of Babel: flee ye from the Chaldeans with a voice of joy: tell and declare this: show it forth to the end of the earth: say ye, The Lord hath redeemed his servant Jacob.

21 And they [1]were not thirsty: he led them through the wilderness: he caused the waters to flow out of the rock for them: for he clave the rock and the water gushed out.

22 There is no [1]peace, saith the Lord, unto the wicked.

49

1 The Lord God exhorteth all nations to believe his promises. 6 Christ is the salvation of all that believe,

and will deliver them from the tyranny of their enemies.

1 Hear ye me, O isles, and hearken, ye people from far. The Lord hath called [1]me from [2]the womb, and made mention of my name from my mother's belly.

2 And he hath made my mouth like a sharp [1]sword: under the shadow of his hand hath he [2]hid me, and made me a chosen shaft, *and* hid me in his quiver,

3 And said unto me, Thou art my servant [1]Israel, for I will be glorious in thee.

4 And I said, I have [1]labored in vain: I have spent my strength in vain and for nothing; but my judgment *is* with the Lord, and my work with my God.

5 And now saith the Lord that formed me from the womb to be his servant, that I may bring Jacob again to him (though Israel be not gathered, [1]yet shall I be glorious in the eyes of the Lord; and my God shall be my strength.)

6 And he said, It is a small thing that thou shouldest be my servant to raise up the tribes of Jacob, and to restore the desolations of Israel: I will also give [1]thee for a light of the Gentiles, that thou mayest be my salvation unto the end of the world.

7 Thus saith the Lord the redeemer of Israel, *and* his holy One, to him that is despised in soul, to a nation that is abhorred, to a [1]servant of rulers, Kings shall see, and [2]arise, and princes shall worship, because of the Lord, that is faithful: and the holy One of Israel, which hath chosen thee.

8 Thus saith the Lord, [1]In an acceptable time have I heard thee, and in a day of salvation have I helped thee: and I will preserve thee, and will give [2]thee for a covenant of the people, that thou mayest raise up the [3]earth, and obtain the inheritance of the desolate heritages:

48:13 [1] To obey me, and to do whatsoever I command them.

48:14 [1] Meaning, Cyrus, whom he had chosen to destroy Babylon.

48:16 [1] Since the time that I declared myself to your fathers.

[2] Thus the Prophet speaketh for himself, and to assure them of these things.

48:17 [1] What things shall do thee good.

48:19 [1] That is, the prosperous estate of Israel.

48:20 [1] After that he had forewarned them of their captivity, and of the cause thereof, he showeth them the great joy that shall come of their deliverance.

48:21 [1] He showeth that it shall be as easy to deliver them, as he did their fathers out of Egypt.

48:22 [1] Thus he speaketh that the wicked hypocrites should not abuse God's promise, in whom was neither faith nor repentance, as Isa. 57:21.

49:1 [1] This is spoken in the person of Christ, to assure the faithful that these promises should come to pass: for they were all made in him, and in him should be performed.

[2] This is meant of the time that Christ should be manifested to the world, as Ps. 2:7.

49:2 [1] By the sword and shaft, he signifieth the virtue and efficacy

of Christ's doctrine.

[2] God hath taken me to his protection and defense: this chiefly is meant of Christ, and may also be applied to the ministers of his word.

49:3 [1] By Israel is meant Christ, and all the body of the faithful, as the members, and their head.

49:4 [1] Thus Christ in his members complaineth, that his labor and preaching take none effect, yet he is contented that his doings are approved of God.

49:5 [1] Though the Jews refuse my doctrine, yet God will approve my ministry.

49:6 [1] To declare my Gospel, to the Gentiles, Isa. 42:6; Acts 13:47; Luke 2:32.

49:7 [1] Meaning, the Jews, whom tyrants kept in bondage.

[2] The benefit of their deliverance shall be so great, that great and small shall acknowledge it, and reverence God for it.

49:8 [1] Thus he speaketh of his Church when he would show his mercy toward it, 2 Cor. 6:2.

[2] Meaning, Christ alone.

[3] Signifying, that before Christ renew the earth by his word, there is nothing but confusion and disorder.

9 That thou mayest say to the ¹prisoners, Go forth; and to them that are in darkness, Show yourselves; they shall feed in the ways, and their ²pastures shall be in all the tops of the hills.

10 They shall not be hungry, neither shall they be thirsty, neither shall the heat smite them, nor the sun, for he that hath compassion ¹on them, shall lead them; even to the springs of water shall he drive them.

11 And I will make all my mountains, as a way, and my paths shall be exalted.

12 Behold, these shall come from far: and lo, these from the North and from the West, and these from the land of ¹Sinim.

13 Rejoice, O ¹heavens; and be joyful, O earth; burst forth into praise, O mountains; for God hath comforted his people, and will have mercy upon his afflicted.

14 But Zion said, The Lord hath ¹forsaken me, and my Lord hath forgotten me.

15 Can a woman forget her child, and not have compassion on the son of her womb? though they should forget, yet will I not forget thee.

16 Behold, I have graven thee upon the palm of mine ¹hands: thy ²walls are ever in my sight.

17 Thy builders make ¹haste: thy destroyers and they that made thee waste, are departed from thee.

18 Lift up thine eyes round about and behold: all these gather themselves together and come to thee: as I live, saith the Lord, thou shalt surely ¹put them all upon thee as a garment, and gird thyself with them like a bride.

19 For thy desolations, and thy waste places, and thy land destroyed, shall surely be now narrow for them that shall dwell in it, and they that dwell devour thee, shall be far away.

20 The children of thy barrenness shall say again in thine ears, The place is strait for me: give place to me that I may dwell.

21 Then shalt thou say in thine heart, Who hath begotten me these, seeing I am barren and desolate, a captive and a wanderer to and fro? and who hath nourished them? behold, I was left alone: whence are these?

22 Thus saith the Lord God, Behold, I will lift up mine hand to the ¹Gentiles, and set up my standard to the people, and they shall bring thy sons in their arms: and thy daughters shall be carried upon their shoulders.

23 And Kings ¹shall be thy nursing fathers, and Queens shall be thy nurses: they shall worship thee with their faces toward the earth, and lick up the ²dust of thy feet: and thou shalt know that I am the Lord: for they shall not be ashamed that wait for me.

24 Shall the prey be ¹taken from the mighty? or the just captivity delivered?

25 But thus saith the Lord, ¹Even the captivity of the mighty shall be taken away: and the prey of the tyrant shall be delivered: for I will contend with him that contendeth with thee, and I will save thy children,

26 And will feed them that spoil thee, with ¹their own flesh, and they shall be drunken with their own blood, as with sweet wine; and all flesh shall know that I the Lord am thy Savior and thy Redeemer, the mighty one of Jacob.

50

1 The Jews forsaken for a time.　2 Yet the power of God is not diminished.　5 Christ's obedience and victory.

1 Thus saith the Lord, Where is that ¹bill of your mother's divorcement, ²whom I have cast off? or who is the creditor ³to whom I sold you? Behold, for your iniquities are ye sold, and because of your transgressions is your mother forsaken.

49:9 ¹ To them that are in the prison of sin and death.
² Being in Christ's protection, they shall be safe against all dangers, and free from the fear of the enemies.
49:10 ¹ Meaning, that there should be nothing in their way from Babylon that should hinder or hurt them: but this is accomplished spiritually.
49:12 ¹ Meaning, the South country, so that Christ shall deliver his from all the parts of the world.
49:13 ¹ Read Isa. 44:23.
49:14 ¹ He objecteth what the faithful might say in their long affliction, and answereth thereunto to comfort them, with a most proper similitude, and full of consolation.
49:16 ¹ Because I would not forget thee.
² Meaning, the good order of policy, and discipline.
49:17 ¹ I have continual care to build thee up again, and to destroy thine enemies.
49:18 ¹ He showeth what are the ornaments of the Church: to have many children, which are assembled by the word of God, and governed by his Spirit.

49:22 ¹ He showeth that Christ will not only gather this great number of the Jews, but also of the Gentiles.
49:23 ¹ Meaning, that Kings shall be converted to the Gospel, and bestow their power and authority for the preservation of the Church.
² Being joined with the Church, they shall humble themselves to Christ their head, and give him all honor.
49:24 ¹ He maketh this as an objection, as though the Chaldeans were strong, and had them in just possession.
49:25 ¹ This is the answer to their objection, that none is stronger than the Lord, neither hath a more just title unto them.
49:26 ¹ I will cause them to destroy one another, as Judg. 7:22; 2 Chron. 20:22; Isa. 19:2.
50:1 ¹ Meaning, that he hath not forsaken her, but through her own occasion, as Hos. 2:2.
² Which should declare that I have cut her off: meaning, that they could show none.
³ Signifying, that he sold them not for any debt or poverty, but that they sold themselves to sins to buy their own lusts and pleasures.

2 [1]Wherefore came I, and there was no man? I called, and none answered: is mine hand so [2]shortened, that it cannot help? or have I no power to deliver? Behold, at my rebuke I dry up the sea: I make the floods desert; their fish rotteth for want of water, and dieth for thirst.

3 I clothe the heavens with darkness, and make a [1]sack their covering.

4 The Lord God hath given [1]me a tongue of the learned, that I should know to minister a word in time to him that is [2]weary; he will raise me up in the morning, in the morning he will waken mine ear to hear, [3]as the learned.

5 The Lord God hath opened mine ear, and I was not rebellious, neither turned I back.

6 I gave my back unto the [1]smiters, and my cheeks to the nippers: I hid not my face from shame and spitting.

7 For the Lord God will help me, therefore shall I not be confounded: therefore have I set my face like a flint, and I know that I shall not be ashamed.

8 He is near that justifieth me: who will contend with me? Let us stand together? who is mine adversary? let him come near to me.

9 Behold, the Lord God will help me: who is he that can condemn me? lo, they shall wax old as a garment: the moth shall eat them up.

10 [1]Who is among you that feareth the Lord? let him hear the voice of his servant: he that walketh in darkness and hath no light, let him trust in the Name of the Lord, and stay upon his God.

11 Behold, all you kindle [1]a fire, and are compassed about with sparks: walk in the light of your fire, and in the sparks that ye have kindled. This shall ye have of mine hand: ye shall lie down in sorrow.

51

1 To trust in God alone by Abraham's example.   7 Not to fear men.   17 The great affliction of Jerusalem,   22 and her deliverance.

1 Hear me [1]ye that follow after righteousness, and ye that seek the Lord: look unto the [2]rock, whence you are hewn, and to the hole of the pit, whence ye are dug.

2 Consider Abraham your father, and Sarah that bare you: for I called him alone, and blessed him and increased him.

3 Surely the Lord shall comfort Zion: he shall comfort all her desolations, and he shall make her desert [1]like Eden, and her wilderness like the garden of the Lord: joy and gladness shall be found therein: praise, and the voice of singing.

4 Hearken ye unto me my people, and give ear unto me, O my people: for a [1]Law shall proceed from me, and I will bring forth my judgment for the light of the people.

5 My [1]righteousness is near: my salvation goeth forth, and mine [2]arm shall judge the people: the isles shall wait for me, and shall trust unto mine arm.

6 Lift up your eyes to the heavens, and look upon the earth beneath: for the [1]heavens shall vanish away like smoke, and the earth shall wax old like a garment, and they that dwell therein, shall perish in like manner: but my salvation shall be forever, and my righteousness shall not be abolished.

7 Hearken unto me ye that know righteousness, the people in whose heart is my Law. Fear ye not the reproach of men, neither be ye afraid of their rebukes.

8 For the moth shall eat them up like a garment, and the worm shall eat them like wood: but my righteousness shall be forever, and my salvation from generation to generation.

9 Rise up, Rise up, and put on strength, O arm of the Lord: rise up as [1]in the old time in the generations of the world. Art not thou the same, that hath cut [2]Rahab, and wounded the [3]dragon?

10 Art not thou the same, which hath dried the Sea, even the waters of the great deep, making the

---

50:2 [1] He came by his Prophets and ministers, but they would not believe their doctrine and convert.

[2] Am I not able to help you, as I have helped your fathers of old, when I dried up the red Sea, and killed the fish in the rivers, and also afterward in Jordan?

50:3 [1] As I did in Egypt in token of my displeasure, Exod. 10:21.

50:4 [1] The Prophet doth represent here the person and charge of them that are justly called to the ministry of God's word.

[2] To him that is oppressed by affliction and misery.

[3] As they that are taught, and made meet by him.

50:6 [1] I did not shrink from God for any persecution or calamity. Whereby he showeth that the true ministers of God can look for none other recompense of the wicked, but after this sort, and also what is their comfort.

50:10 [1] Showing that it is a rare thing that any should obey aright God's true ministers, though they labor to bring them from hell to heaven.

50:11 [1] You have sought consolation by your own devices, and have

refused the light, and consolation which God hath offered: therefore ye shall remain in sorrow, and not be comforted.

51:1 [1] He comforteth the Church, that they should not be discouraged for their small number.

[2] That is, to Abraham, of whom ye were begotten, and to Sarah, of whom we were born.

51:3 [1] As plentiful as Paradise, Gen. 2:8.

51:4 [1] I will rule and govern my Church by my word and doctrine.

51:5 [1] The time that I will accomplish my promise.

[2] My power and strength.

51:6 [1] He forewarneth them of the horrible changes and mutations of all things, and how he will preserve his church in the midst of all these dangers.

51:9 [1] He putteth them in remembrance of his great benefit for their deliverance out of Egypt, that thereby they might learn to trust in him constantly.

[2] Meaning, Egypt, Ps. 87:4.

[3] To wit, Pharaoh, Ezek. 29:3.

depth of the sea a way for the redeemed to pass over?

11 Therefore the redeemed of the Lord shall [1]return, and come with joy unto Zion, and everlasting joy shall be upon their head: they shall obtain joy and gladness: *and* sorrow and mourning shall flee away.

12 I, *even* I am he that comfort you. Who art thou that thou shouldest fear a mortal man, and the son of man, which shall be made as grass?

13 And forgettest the Lord thy maker, that hath spread out the heavens, and laid the foundations of the earth? and hast feared continually all the day, because of the rage of the oppressor, which is ready to destroy? Where is now the rage of the oppressor?

14 The captive [1]hasteneth to be loosed, and that he should not die in the pit, nor that his bread should fail.

15 And I am the Lord thy God that divided the sea, when his waves roared: the Lord of hosts *is* his Name.

16 And I have put my words in thy [1]mouth, and have defended thee in the shadow of mine hand, that I may plant the [2]heavens, and lay the foundation of the earth, and say unto Zion, Thou art my people.

17 Awake, awake, and stand up, O Jerusalem, which hast drunk at the hand of the Lord the [1]cup of his wrath: thou hast drunken the dregs of the cup of trembling, and wrung them out.

18 There is none to guide her among all her sons, whom she hath brought forth: there *is* none that taketh her by the hand of all the sons that she hath brought up.

19 These two [1]things are come unto thee: who will lament thee? desolation and destruction and famine, and the sword: by whom shall I comfort thee?

20 Thy sons have fainted, and lie at the head of all the streets as a wild bull in a net, and are full of the wrath of the Lord, *and* rebuke of thy God.

21 Therefore hear now this, thou miserable and drunken, but [1]not with wine.

22 Thus saith thy Lord God, even God that pleadeth the cause of his people, Behold, I have taken out of thine hand the cup of trembling, *even* the dregs of the cup of my wrath: thou shalt drink it no more.

23 But I will put it into their hand that spoil thee, which have said to thy soul, Bow down that we may go over, and thou hast laid thy body as the ground, and as the streets to them that went over.

52

1 A consolation to the people of God.   7 Of the messengers thereof.

1 Arise, arise: put on thy strength, O Zion: put on the garments of thy beauty, O Jerusalem, the holy City: for henceforth there shall no [1]more come into thee the uncircumcised and the unclean.

2 Shake thyself from the [1]dust, arise, and sit down, O Jerusalem: loose the bands of thy neck, O thou captive daughter Zion.

3 For thus saith the Lord, Ye were sold for [1]naught; therefore shall ye be redeemed without money.

4 For thus saith the Lord God, My people went [1]down afore time into Egypt to sojourn there, and Assyria [2]oppressed them without cause.

5 Now therefore what have I here, saith the Lord, that my people is taken away for naught, and they that rule over them, make them to howl, saith the Lord? and my Name all the day continually is [1]blasphemed?

6 Therefore my people shall know my name: therefore *they shall know* in that day, that I am he that do speak: behold, it is I.

7 How [1]beautiful upon the mountains are the feet of him, that declareth *and* publisheth peace! that declareth good tidings, *and* publisheth salvation, saying unto Zion, Thy God reigneth!

8 [1]The voice of thy watchmen *shall be heard*: they shall lift up their voice, and shout together: for they

---

51:11 [1] From Babylon.
51:14 [1] He comforteth them by the short time of their banishment: for in seventy years they were restored, and the greatest empire of the world destroyed.
51:16 [1] Meaning, of Isaiah, and of all true ministers, who are defended by his protection.
[2] That all things may be restored in heaven and earth, Eph. 1:10.
51:17 [1] Thou hast been justly punished and sufficiently as Isa. 40:2, and this punishment in the elect is by measure, and according as God giveth grace to bear it: but in the reprobate it is the just vengeance of God to drive them to an insensibleness and madness, as Jer. 25:15, 16.
51:19 [1] Whereof the one is outward, as of the things that come to the body, as war, and famine, and the other is inward, and appertaineth to the mind: that is, to be without comfort: therefore he saith, How shalt thou be comforted?
51:21 [1] But with trouble and fear.
52:1 [1] No wicked tyrant, which shall subvert God's true religion, and

oppress the conscience.
52:2 [1] Put off the garments of sorrow and heaviness, and put on the apparel of joy and gladness.
52:3 [1] The Babylonians paid nothing to me for you: therefore I will take you again without ransom.
52:4 [1] When Jacob went thither in time of famine.
[2] The Egyptians might pretend some cause to oppress my people because they went thither, and remained among them, but the Assyrians have no title to excuse their tyranny by, and therefore will I punish them more than I did the Egyptians.
52:5 [1] To wit, by the wicked, which think that I have no power to deliver them.
52:7 [1] Signifying, that the joy and good tidings of their deliverance should make their affliction in the mean time more easy: but this is chiefly meant of the spiritual joy, as Nah. 1:15; Rom. 10:15.
52:8 [1] The Prophets which are thy watchmen shall publish this thy deliverance: this was begun under Zerubbabel, Ezra, and Nehemiah, but was accomplished under Christ.

shall see eye to eye, when the Lord shall bring again Zion.

9 O ye desolate places of Jerusalem, be glad and rejoice together, for the Lord hath comforted his people: he hath redeemed Jerusalem.

10 The Lord hath made ¹bare his holy arm in the sight of all the Gentiles, and all the ends of the earth shall see the salvation of our God.

11 ¹Depart, depart ye: go ye out from thence, and touch no unclean thing, go out of the midst of her, be ye clean, that ²bear the vessels of the Lord.

12 For ye shall not go out ¹with haste, nor depart by fleeing away: but the Lord will go before you, and the God of Israel will gather you together.

13 Behold, my ¹servant shall prosper: he shall be exalted and extolled, and be very high.

14 As many were astonied at thee (his visage was so ¹deformed of men, and his form of the sons of men) so ²shall he sprinkle many nations: the Kings shall shut their ³mouths at him: for that which had not been told them, shall they see, and that which they had not heard shall they ⁴understand.

53

1 Of Christ and his kingdom, whose word few will believe. 6 All men are sinners. 11 Christ is our righteousness, 12 and is dead for our sins.

1 Who ¹will believe our report? and to whom is the ²arm of the Lord revealed?

2 But he shall grow up before him as a branch, and as a ¹root out of a dry ²ground; he hath neither form nor beauty: when we shall see him, there shall be no form that we should desire him.

3 He is despised and rejected of men: he is a man full of sorrows, and hath experience of ¹infirmities: we hid as it were our faces from him: he was despised, and we esteemed him not.

4 Surely, he hath born our infirmities, and carried ¹our sorrows, yet we did judge him as ²plagued and smitten of God, and humbled.

5 But he was wounded for our transgressions: he was broken for our iniquities: the ¹chastisement of our peace was upon him, and with his stripes are we healed.

6 All we like sheep have gone astray: we have turned every one to his own way, and the Lord hath laid upon him the ¹iniquity of us all.

7 He was oppressed, and he was afflicted, yet did he not ¹open his mouth: he is brought as a sheep to the slaughter, and as a sheep before her shearer is dumb, so he opened not his mouth.

8 He was taken out from ¹prison, and from judgment: ²and who shall declare his age? for he was cut out of the land of the living: for the transgression of my people was he plagued.

9 ¹And he made his grave with the wicked, and with the rich in his death, though he had done no wickedness, neither was any deceit in his mouth.

10 Yet the Lord would break him and make him subject to infirmities: when ¹he shall make his soul an offering for sin, he shall see his seed and shall prolong his days, and the will of the Lord shall prosper in his hand.

11 He shall see of the ¹travail of his soul, and shall be satisfied; by his knowledge shall my ²righteous servant justify many: for he shall bear their iniquities.

12 Therefore will I give him a portion with the great, and he shall divide the spoil with the strong, because ¹he hath poured out his soul unto death; and

---

52:10 ¹ As ready to smite his enemies, and to deliver his people.
52:11 ¹ He warneth the faithful not to pollute themselves with the superstitions of the Babylonians, as Isa. 48:20; 2 Cor. 6:17.
  ² For the time is at hand that the Priests and Levites chiefly (and so by them all the people, which shall be as the Levites in this office) shall carry home vessels of the Temple which Nebuchadnezzar had taken away.
52:12 ¹ As your fathers did out of Egypt.
52:13 ¹ Meaning, Christ, by whom our spiritual deliverance should be wrought, whereof this was a figure.
52:14 ¹ In the corrupt judgment of man, Christ in his person was not esteemed.
  ² He shall spread his word through many nations.
  ³ In sign of reverence, and as being astonished at his excellency.
  ⁴ By the preaching of the Gospel.
53:1 ¹ The Prophet showeth that very few shall receive this their preaching of Christ, and of their deliverance by him, John 12:38; Rom. 10:16.
  ² Meaning, that none can believe, but whose hearts God toucheth with the virtue of his holy Spirit.
53:2 ¹ The beginning of Christ's kingdom shall be small and contemptible in the sight of man, but it shall grow wonderfully, and flourish before God.
  ² Read Isa. 11:1.

53:3 ¹ Which was by God's singular providence for the comfort of sinners, Heb. 4:15.
53:4 ¹ That is, the punishment due to our sins: for the which he hath both suffered and made satisfaction, Matt. 8:17; 1 Pet. 2:24.
  ² We judgeth evil, thinking that he was punished for his own sins, and not for ours.
53:5 ¹ He was chastised for our reconciliation, 1 Cor. 15:3.
53:6 ¹ Meaning, the punishment of our iniquity, and not the fault itself.
53:7 ¹ But willingly and patiently obeyed his father's appointment, Matt. 26:63; Acts 8:32.
53:8 ¹ From the cross and grave, after that he was condemned.
  ² Though he died for sin, yet after his resurrection he shall live forever and this his death is to restore life to his members, Rom. 6:9.
53:9 ¹ God the Father delivered him into the hands of the wicked, and to the powers of the world to do with him what they would.
53:10 ¹ Christ by offering up himself shall give life to his Church, and so cause them to live with him forever.
53:11 ¹ That is, the fruit and effect of his labor, which is the salvation of his Church.
  ² Christ shall justify by faith through his word, whereas Moses could not justify by the law.
53:12 ¹ Because he humbled himself, therefore he shall be extolled to glory, Phil. 2:7-12.

he was counted with the transgressors, and he bare the sin ²of many, and prayed for the trespassers.

54

1 More of the Gentiles shall believe the Gospel than of the Jews. 7 God leaveth his for a time, to whom afterward he showeth mercy.

1 Rejoice, O ¹barren that didst not bear: break forth into joy and rejoice, thou that didst not travail with child; for the ²desolate hath more children than the married wife, saith the Lord.

2 ¹Enlarge the place of thy tents, and let them spread out the curtains of thine habitations: spare not: stretch out thy cords, and make fast thy stakes.

3 For thou shalt increase on the right hand and on the left, and thy seed shall possess the Gentiles, and dwell in the desolate cities.

4 Fear not: for thou shalt not be ashamed, neither shalt thou be confounded: for thou shalt not be put to shame: yea, thou shalt forget the shame of thy ¹youth, and shalt not remember the reproach of thy ²widowhood anymore.

5 For he that ¹made thee, *is* thine husband, (whose name *is* the Lord of hosts) and thy redeemer the holy One of Israel, shall be called the God of the whole ²world.

6 For the Lord hath called thee, being as a woman forsaken, and afflicted in spirit, and *as* a ¹young wife when thou wast refused, saith thy God.

7 For a little while have I forsaken thee, but with great compassion will I gather thee.

8 For a moment in *mine* anger, I hid my face from thee for a little season, but with everlasting mercy have I had compassion on thee, saith the Lord thy redeemer.

9 For this is unto me *as* the ¹waters of Noah; for as I have sworn that the waters of Noah should no more go over the earth, so have I sworn that I would not be angry with thee, nor rebuke thee.

10 For the mountains shall remove, and the hills shall fall down; but my mercy shall not depart from thee, neither shall the covenant of my peace fall away, saith the Lord, that hath compassion on thee.

11 O thou afflicted and tossed with tempest, that hast no comfort, behold, I will lay thy stones with the ¹carbuncle, and lay thy foundation with sapphires,

12 And I will make thy windows of ¹emeralds, and thy gates shining stones, and all thy borders of pleasant stones.

13 And all thy children *shall be* ¹taught of the Lord, and much peace shall be to thy children.

14 In ¹righteousness shalt thou be established, *and* be far from oppression; for thou shalt not fear it: and from fear; for it shall not come near thee.

15 Behold, *the enemies* shall gather himself, but without ¹me: whosoever shall gather himself in thee, ²against thee, shall fall.

16 Behold, I have created the ¹smith that bloweth the coals in the fire, and him that bringeth forth an instrument for his work, and I have created the destroyer to destroy.

17 But all the weapons that are made against thee, shall not prosper: and every tongue that shall rise against thee in judgment, thou shalt condemn. This is the heritage of the Lord's servants, and their righteousness *is* of me, saith the Lord.

55

1 An exhortation to come to Christ. 8 God's counsels are not as man's. 12 The joy of the faithful.

1 Ho, everyone that ¹thirsteth, come ye to the waters, and ye that have ²no silver, come, buy and eat: come, I say, buy ³wine and milk without silver and without money.

2 Wherefore do ye lay out silver, *and* not for bread? ¹and your labor without being satisfied? hearken diligently unto me, and eat that which is

---

53:12 ² That is, of all that believe in him.
54:1 ¹ After that he hath declared the death of Christ, he speaketh to the Church, because it should feel the fruit of the same, and calleth her barren, because that in the captivity she was a widow without hope to have any children.
   ² The Church in this her affliction and captivity shall bring forth more children, than when she was at liberty: or this may be spoken by admiration, considering the great number that should come of her. Her deliverance under Cyrus was as her childhood, and therefore this was accomplished, when she came to her age, which was under the Gospel.
54:2 ¹ Signifying, that for the great number of children that God should give her, she should seem to lack room to lodge them.
54:4 ¹ The afflictions which thou suffered at the beginning.
   ² When as thou wast refused for thy sins, Isa. 50:1.
54:5 ¹ That did regenerate thee by his holy Spirit.
   ² His glory shall shine through the whole World, which seemed before to be shut up in Judea.
54:6 ¹ As a wife which wast forsaken in thy youth.
54:9 ¹ As sure as the promise that I made to Noah, that the waters should no more overflow the earth.

54:11 ¹ Hereby he declareth the excellent estate of the Church under Christ.
54:12 ¹ Or, jasper, or pearl.
54:13 ¹ By the hearing of his word and inward moving of his Spirit.
54:14 ¹ In stability and sureness, so that it shall stand forever.
54:15 ¹ And therefore shall not prevail.
   ² Meaning, the domestical enemies of the Church, as are the hypocrites.
54:16 ¹ Signifying hereby, that man can do nothing, but so far as God giveth power: for seeing that all are his creatures, he must needs govern and guide them.
55:1 ¹ Christ by proposing his graces and gifts to his Church, exempteth the hypocrites which are full with their imagined works, and the Epicureans, which are full with their worldly lusts, and so thirst not after these waters.
   ² Signifying, that God's benefits cannot be bought for money.
   ³ By waters, wine, milk and bread, he meaneth all things necessary to the spiritual life, as these are necessary to this corporal life.
55:2 ¹ He reproveth their ingratitude, which refuse those things that God offereth willingly, and in the meantime spare neither cost nor labor to obtain those which are nothing profitable.

3 Incline your ears, and come unto me: hear, and your soul shall live, and I will make an everlasting covenant with you, *even* the 1sure mercies of David.

4 Behold, I gave 1him for a witness to the people, for a prince and a master unto the people.

5 Behold, thou shalt call a nation that thou knowest not, 1and a nation that knew not thee, shall run unto thee because of the Lord thy God, and the Holy one of Israel: for he hath glorified thee.

6 Seek ye the Lord while he may be 1found: call ye upon him while he is near.

7 Let the wicked 1forsake his ways, and the unrighteous his own imaginations, and return unto the Lord, and he will have mercy upon him; and to our God, for he is very ready to forgive.

8 For my 1thoughts *are* not your thoughts, neither *are* your ways my ways, saith the Lord.

9 For as the heavens are higher than the earth, so are my ways higher than your ways, and my thoughts above your thoughts.

10 Surely as the rain cometh down, and the snow from heaven, and returneth not thither but watereth the earth, and maketh it to bring forth and bud, that it may give seed to the sower, and bread unto him that eateth,

11 So shall my 1word be, that goeth out of my mouth: it shall not return unto me void, but it shall accomplish that which I will, and it shall prosper in the thing whereto I sent it.

12 Therefore ye shall go out with joy, and be led forth with peace; the 1mountains and the hills shall break forth before you into joy, and all the trees of the field shall clap *their* hands.

13 For thorns there shall grow fir trees; for nettles shall grow the myrrh tree, and it shall be to the Lord 1for a name, *and* for an everlasting 2sign that shall

not be taken away.

56 *1 An exhortation to judgment and justice.   10 Against shepherds that devour their flock.*

1 Thus saith the Lord, 1Keep judgment and do justice, for my salvation is at hand to come, and my 2righteousness to be revealed.

2 Blessed *is* the man that doeth this, and the son of man which layeth hold on it; he that keepeth the 1Sabbath, and polluteth it not, and keepeth his hand from doing any evil.

3 And let not the son of the strangers, which 1is joined to the Lord, speak and say, The Lord hath surely separated me from his people; neither let the Eunuch say, Behold, I am a dry tree.

4 For thus saith the Lord unto the Eunuchs that keep my Sabbaths, and choose the thing that pleaseth me, and take hold of my covenant,

5 Even unto them will I give in mine 1House and within my walls, a place, and a 2name better than of the sons and of the daughters; I will give them an everlasting name, that shall not be put out.

6 Also the strangers that cleave unto the Lord, to serve him, and to love the Name of the Lord, and to be his servants; everyone that keepeth the Sabbath, and polluteth it not, and embraceth my covenant,

7 Them will I bring also to mine holy mountain, and make them joyful in mine House of prayer; their burnt 1offerings and their sacrifices *shall be* accepted upon mine altar: for mine house shall be called an house of prayer for 2all people.

8 The Lord God saith, which gathereth the scattered of Israel, Yet will I gather to them those that are to be gathered to them.

9 All ye 1beasts of the field, come to devour, *even* all ye beasts of the forest.

---

2 You shall be fed abundantly.
55:3 1 The same covenant which through my mercy I ratified and confirmed to David, that it should be eternal, 2 Sam. 7:13; Acts 13:34.
55:4 1 Meaning Christ, of whom David was a figure.
55:5 1 To wit, the Gentiles, which before thou didst not receive to be thy people.
55:6 1 When he offereth himself by the preaching of his word.
55:7 1 Hereby he showeth that repentance must be joined with faith, and how we cannot call upon God aright, except the fruits of our faith appear.
55:8 1 Although you are not soon reconciled one to another and judge me by yourselves, yet I am most easy to be reconciled, yea, I offer my mercies to you.
55:11 1 If these small things have their effect, as daily experience showeth, much more shall my promise which I have made and confirmed, bring to pass the things which I have spoken for your deliverance.
55:12 1 Read Isa. 44:23 and 49:13.
55:13 1 To set forth his glory.
2 Of God's deliverance, and that he will never forsake his Church.
56:1 1 God showeth what he requireth of them after that he hath

delivered them: to wit, the works of charity whereby true faith is declared.
2 Which I will declare toward you, and pour into your hearts by my Spirit.
56:2 1 Under the Sabbath he comprehendeth the whole service of God and true religion.
56:3 1 Let none think himself unmeet to receive the graces of the Lord: for the Lord will take away all impediments, and will forsake none which will keep his true religion, and believe in him.
56:5 1 Meaning, in his Church.
2 They shall be called after my people, and be of the same religion: yea, under Christ the dignity of the faithful shall be greater than the Jews were at that time.
56:7 1 Hereby he meaneth the spiritual service of God, to whom the faithful offer continual thanksgiving, yea themselves and all that they have, as a lively and acceptable sacrifice.
2 Not only for the Jews, but for all others, Matt. 21:13.
56:9 1 Meaning, the enemies of the Church, as the Babylonians, Assyrians, etc., thus he speaketh to fear the hypocrites and to assure the faithful that when this cometh, they may know it was told them before.

10 Their [1]watchmen are all blind: they have no knowledge: they are all dumb dogs: they cannot bark: they lie and sleep, and delight in sleeping.

11 And these greedy dogs can never have enough: and these shepherds cannot understand: *for* they all look to their own way, everyone for his advantage, *and* for his own purpose.

12 Come, I will bring wine, and we will fill ourselves with strong drink, and [1]tomorrow shall be as this day, *and* much more abundant.

57

1 *God taketh away the good, that he should not see the horrible plagues to come.* 3 *Of the wicked idolaters,* 9 *and their vain confidence.*

1 The righteous perisheth, and no man considereth it in heart, and merciful men are taken away, and no man understandeth that the righteous is taken away [1]from the evil *to* come.

2 [1]Peace shall come: they shall rest in their beds, *everyone* that walketh before him.

3 But you [1]witches' children, come hither, the seed of the adulterer and of the whore.

4 On whom have ye jested? upon whom have ye gaped and thrust out your tongue? are not ye rebellious children, *and* a false seed?

5 Inflamed with idols under every green tree? and sacrificing the [1]children in the valleys under the tops of the rocks?

6 Thy portion *is* in the smooth stones [1]of the river: they, they are thy lot: even to them hast thou poured a drink offering: thou hast offered a sacrifice. Should I delight in [2]these?

7 Thou hast made thy [1]bed upon a very high mountain: thou wentest up thither, even thither wentest thou to offer sacrifice.

8 Behind the [1]doors also and posts hast thou set up thy remembrance: for thou hast discovered thyself *to another*, than me, and wentest up, *and* didst [2]enlarge thy bed, and make a covenant between thee and them, and lovedst their bed in *every* place where thou sawest it.

9 Thou wentest [1]to the kings with oil, and didst increase thine ointments, *and* send thy messengers far off, and didst humble thyself unto hell.

10 Thou weariedst thyself in thy manifold journeys, *yet* saidest thou not, [1]There is no hope: thou [2]hast found life by thine hand, therefore thou wast not grieved.

11 And whom didst thou reverence or fear, seeing thou hast [1]lied unto me, and hast not remembered me, neither set thy mind thereon? is it not *because* I hold my peace, and that of long [2]time? therefore thou fearest not me.

12 I will declare thy righteousness [1]and thy works, and they shall not profit thee.

13 When thou cryest, let them that thou hast gathered together, deliver thee: but the wind [1]shall take them all away: vanity shall pull them away: but he that trusteth in me shall inherit the land, and shall possess mine holy Mountain.

14 [1]And he shall say, Cast up, cast up: prepare the way: take up the stumbling blocks out of the way of my people.

15 For thus saith he that is high and excellent, he that inhabiteth the eternity, whose Name is the Holy one, I dwell in the high and holy place: with him also that is of a contrite and humble spirit to revive the spirit of the humble, and to give life to them that are of a contrite heart.

16 For I will not contend forever: neither will I be

56:10 [1] He showeth that this affliction shall come through the fault of the governors, prophets, and pastors, whose ignorance, negligence, avarice and obstinacy provoked God's wrath against them.

56:12 [1] We are well yet, and tomorrow shall be better: therefore let us not fear the plagues before they come: thus the wicked contemned the admonitions and exhortations which were made them in the Name of God.

57:1 [1] From the plague that is at hand, and also because God will punish the wicked.

57:2 [1] The soul of the righteous shall be in joy, and their body shall rest in the grave unto the time of the resurrection, because they walked before the Lord.

57:3 [1] He threateneth the wicked hypocrites, who under the pretence of the name of God's people, derided God's word and his promises: boasting openly that they were the children of Abraham, but because they were not faithful and obedient as Abraham was, he calleth them bastards, and the children of sorcerers, which forsook God, and fled to wicked means for succor.

57:5 [1] Read Lev. 18:21; 2 Kings 23:10.

57:6 [1] Meaning, every place was polluted with their idolatry: or every fair stone that they found, they made an idol of it.

[2] In the sacrifices which you offering before these idols, thought

you did serve God.

57:7 [1] To wit, thine altars in an open place, like an impudent harlot, that careth not for the sight of her husband.

57:8 [1] Instead of setting up the word of God in the open places on the posts and doors to have it in remembrance, Deut. 6:9 and 27:1, thou hast set up signs and marks of thine idolatry in every place.

[2] That is, didst increase thine idolatry more and more.

57:9 [1] Thou didst seek the favor of the Assyrians by gifts and presents to help thee against the Egyptians: and when they failed thou soughtest to the Babylonians, and more and more didst torment thyself.

57:10 [1] Although thou sawest all thy labors to be in vain, yet wouldest thou never acknowledge thy fault, and leave off.

[2] He derideth their unprofitable diligence, which thought to have made all sure, and yet were deceived.

57:11 [1] Broken promise with me.

[2] Meaning, that the wicked abuse God's lenity, and grow to further wickedness.

57:12 [1] That is, thy naughtiness, idolatries, and impieties which the wicked call God's service: thus he derideth their obstinacy.

57:13 [1] Meaning, the Assyrians and others, whose help they looked for.

57:14 [1] God shall say to Darius and Cyrus.

always wroth, ¹for the spirit should fail before me: and I have made the breath.

17 For his ¹wicked covetousness I am angry with him, and have smitten him: I hid me, and was angry, yet he went away, and turned after the way of his own heart.

18 I have seen his ways, and will ¹heal him: I will lead him also, and restore comfort unto him, and to those that lament him.

19 I create the ¹fruit of the lips, *to be* peace: peace unto them that are ²far off, and to them that are near, saith the Lord: for I will heal him.

20 But the wicked *are* like the raging sea, that ¹cannot rest, whose waters cast up mire and dirt.

21 There is no peace, saith my God, to the wicked.

58 *1 The office of God's ministers.   2 The works of the hypocrites.   6 The fast of the faithful.   13 Of the true Sabbath.*

1 Cry ¹aloud, spare not: lift up thy voice like a trumpet, and show my people their transgression, and to the house of Jacob their sins.

2 Yet they ¹seek me daily, and will know my ways, even as a nation that did righteously, and had not forsaken the statutes of their God: they ask of me the ordinances of justice: they will draw near unto God, *saying,*

3 ¹Wherefore have we fasted, and thou seest it not? we have punished ourselves, and thou regardest it not. Behold, in the day of your fast you will seek ²*your* will, and require all your debts.

4 Behold, ye fast to strife and debate, and to smite with the fist of wickedness: ye shall not fast as *ye do* today, to make your voice to be ¹heard above.

5 Is it such a fast that I have chosen, that a man should afflict his soul for a day, and to bow down his head, as a bull rush, and to lie down in sackcloth and ashes? wilt thou call this a fasting, or an acceptable day to the Lord?

6 Is not this the fasting that I have chosen? to loose the bands of wickedness, to take off the heavy burdens, and to let the oppressed go free, and that ye break every ¹yoke?

7 Is it not to deal thy bread to the hungry, and that thou bring the poor that wander, unto thine house? when thou seest the naked, that thou cover him, and hide not thyself from ¹thine own flesh?

8 Then shall thy ¹light break forth as the morning, and thine health shall grow speedily: thy ²righteousness shall go before thee, *and* the glory of the Lord shall embrace thee.

9 Then shalt thou call, and the Lord shall answer: thou shalt cry, and he shall say, Here I am: if thou take away from the midst of thee the yoke, the putting forth of the ¹finger, and wicked speaking:

10 If thou ¹pour out thy soul to the hungry, and refresh the troubled soul: then shall thy light spring out in the ²darkness, and thy darkness *shall be* as the noon day.

11 And the Lord shall guide thee continually, and satisfy thy soul in drought, and make fat thy bones, and thou shalt be like a watered garden, and like a spring of water, whose waters fail not.

12 And they shall be of thee, that shall build the old ¹waste places: thou shalt raise up the foundations for many generations, and thou shalt be called the repairer of the breach, *and* the restorer of the paths to dwell in.

13 If thou ¹turn away thy foot from the Sabbath, from doing thy will on mine Holy day, and call the Sabbath a delight to consecrate it, *as* glorious to the Lord, and shalt honor him, not doing thine own ways, nor seeking thine own will, nor speaking a vain word,

14 Then shalt thou delight in the Lord, and I will cause thee to mount upon the high places of the earth, and feed thee with the heritage of Jacob thy father: for the mouth of the Lord hath spoken it.

57:16 ¹ I will not use my power against frail man, whose life is but a blast.

57:17 ¹ That is, for the vices and faults of the people, which is meant here by covetousness.

57:18 ¹ Though they were obstinate, yet I did not withdraw my mercy from them.

57:19 ¹ That is, I frame the speech and words of my messengers which shall bring peace.

² As well to him that is in captivity as to him that remaineth at home.

57:20 ¹ Their evil conscience doth ever torment them, and therefore they can never have rest, read Isa. 48:22.

58:1 ¹ The Lord thus speaketh to the Prophet, willing him to use all diligence and severity to rebuke the hypocrites.

58:2 ¹ They will seem to worship me and have outward holiness.

58:3 ¹ He setteth forth the malice and disdain of the hypocrites, which grudge against God, if their works be not accepted.

² Thus he convinceth the hypocrites by the second table, and by their duty toward their neighbor, that they have neither faith nor religion.

58:4 ¹ So long as you use contention and oppression, your fasting and prayers shall not be heard.

58:6 ¹ That you leave off all your extortions.

58:7 ¹ For in him thou seest thyself as in a glass.

58:8 ¹ That is, the prosperous estate wherewith God will bless thee.

² The Testimony of thy goodness shall appear before God and man.

58:9 ¹ Whereby is meant all manner of injury.

58:10 ¹ That is, have compassion on their miseries.

² Thine adversity shall be turned into prosperity.

58:12 ¹ Signifying, that of the Jews should come such as should build again the ruins of Jerusalem and Judea: but chiefly this is meant of the spiritual Jerusalem, whose builders were the Apostles.

58:13 ¹ If thou refrain thyself from thy wicked works.

59 1 *The wicked perish through their own iniqui-*
ties. 12 *The confession of sins.* 16 *God alone*
will preserve his Church though all men fail.

CHAPTER 59
a Num. 11:23
Isa. 50:2
b Jer. 5:25

1 Behold, *a*the Lord's hand is not shortened, that
it cannot save: neither is his ear heavy, that it cannot
hear.

2 But *b*your iniquities have separated between
you and your God, and your sins have hid *his* face
from you, that he will not hear.

3 For your hands are defiled with [1]blood, and
your fingers with iniquity: your lips have spoken
lies, *and* your tongue hath murmured iniquity.

4 No man calleth for justice: no man [1]contendeth
for truth: they trust in vanity, and speak vain things:
they conceive mischief, and [2]bring forth iniquity.

5 They hatch cockatrice [1]eggs, and weave the
spider's [2]web: he that eateth of their eggs, died,
and that which is trode upon, breaketh out into a
serpent.

6 Their webs shall be no garment, neither shall
they cover themselves with their labors: *for* their
works *are* works of iniquities, and the work of cruelty
is in their hands.

7 Their feet turn to evil, and they make haste
to shed innocent blood: their thoughts are wicked
thoughts: desolation and destruction *is* in their
paths.

8 The way of peace they know not, and there *is*
none equity in their goings: they have made them
crooked paths: whosoever goeth therein, shall not
know peace.

9 Therefore is [1]judgment far from us, neither
doth [2]justice come near unto us: we wait for light,
but lo, it *is* darkness: for brightness, *but* we walk in
darkness.

10 We grope for the wall like the [1]blind, and we
grope as one without eyes: we stumble at the noon
day as in the twilight: *we are* in solitary places, as
dead men.

11 We roar all like [1]bears, and mourn like doves:
we look for equity, but there *is* none: for health, *but*
it is far from us.

12 For our trespasses are many before thee, and
our [1]sins testify against us: for our trespasses *are*
with us, and we know our iniquities

13 In trespassing and lying against the Lord, and we
have departed away from our God, *and* have spoken
of cruelty and rebellion, conceiving and uttering out
of the heart [1]false matters.

14 Therefore [1]judgment is turned backward, and
justice standeth far off: for truth is fallen in the street,
and equity cannot enter.

15 Yea, truth faileth, and he that refraineth from
evil, maketh himself [1]a prey: and when the Lord saw
it, it displeased him, that there *was* no judgment.

16 And when he saw that there *was* no man, he
wondered that none would offer himself. [1]Therefore
his arm did [2]save it, and his righteousness itself did
sustain it.

17 For he put on righteousness, as an habergeon,
and an [1]helmet of salvation upon his head, and he
put on the garments of vengeance for clothing, and
was clad with zeal as a cloak.

18 As *to make* recompense, as to requite the fury
of the adversaries *with* a recompense to his enemies:
he will fully repair the [1]islands.

19 So shall they fear the Name of the Lord from
the West, and his glory from the rising of the Sun;
for the enemy shall [1]come like a flood; *but* the Spirit
of the Lord shall chase him away.

20 And the Redeemer shall come unto Zion, and
unto [1]them that turn from iniquity in Jacob, saith
the Lord.

21 And I will make this my Covenant with them,
saith the Lord, My Spirit that is upon thee, and my
words, which I have put in thy mouth, [1]shall not
depart out of thy mouth, nor out of the mouth of
thy seed, nor out of the mouth of the seed of thy
seed, saith the Lord, from henceforth even forever.

59:3 [1] Read Isa. 1:15.
59:4 [1] All men wink at the injuries and oppressions, and none go
about to remedy them.
[2] According to their wicked devices, they hurt their neighbors.
59:5 [1] Whatsoever cometh from them is poison, and bringeth
death.
[2] They are profitable to no purpose.
59:9 [1] That is, God's vengeance to punish our enemies.
[2] God's protection to defend us.
59:10 [1] We are altogether destitute of counsel, and can find no end
of our miseries.
59:11 [1] We express our sorrows by outward signs, some more, some
less.
59:12 [1] This confession is general to the Church to obtain remission
of sins, and the Prophets did not exempt themselves from the same.
59:13 [1] To wit, against our neighbors.
59:14 [1] There is neither justice nor uprightness among men.

59:15 [1] The wicked will destroy him.
59:16 [1] Meaning, to do justice, and to remedy the things that were
so far out of order.
[2] That is, his Church or his arm did help itself, and did not seek aid
of any other.
59:17 [1] Signifying, that God hath all means at hand to deliver his
Church and to punish their enemies.
59:18 [1] To wit, your enemies, which dwell in divers places, and
beyond the sea.
59:19 [1] He showeth that there shall be great affliction in the Church,
but God will ever deliver his.
59:20 [1] Whereby he declareth that the true deliverance from sin
and Satan belongeth to none, but to the children of God, whom he
justifieth.
59:21 [1] Because the doctrine is made profitable by the virtue of the
Spirit, he joineth the one with the other, and promiseth to give them
both to his Church forever.

60 *3 The Gentiles shall come to the knowledge of the Gospel. 8 They shall come to the Church in abundance. 16 They shall have abundance though they suffer for a time.*

1 Arise, O *Jerusalem*; be bright, for thy [1]light is come, and the glory of the Lord is risen upon thee.

2 For behold, darkness shall cover the [1]earth, and gross darkness the people; but the Lord shall arise upon thee, and his glory shall be seen upon thee.

3 And the Gentiles shall walk in [1]thy light, and Kings at the brightness of thy rising up.

4 Lift up thine eyes round about, and behold: all [1]these are gathered, *and* come to thee: thy sons shall come from far, and thy daughters shall be nourished at *thy* side.

5 Then thou shalt see and shine: thine heart shall be astonied [1]and enlarged, because the multitude of the sea shall be converted unto thee, and the riches of the Gentiles shall come unto thee.

6 The [1]multitude of camels shall cover thee: and the dromedaries of Midian and of Ephah: all they of Sheba shall come: they shall bring gold and incense, and show forth the praises of the Lord.

7 All the sheep of [1]Kedar shall be gathered unto thee: the rams of Nebajoth shall serve thee: they shall come up to be accepted upon mine [2]altar: and I will beautify the house of my glory.

8 Who are these [1]that fly like a cloud, and as the doves to their windows?

9 Surely the isles shall wait for me, and the ships [1]of Tarshish, as at the beginning, that they may bring thy sons from far, *and* their silver and their gold with them unto the Name of the Lord thy God, and to the Holy one of Israel, because he hath glorified thee.

10 And the sons of strangers shall build up thy walls, and their [1]Kings shall minister unto thee: for in my wrath I smote thee, but in my mercy I had compassion on thee.

11 Therefore thy gates shall be open continually: neither day nor night shall they be shut, that men may bring unto thee the riches of the Gentiles, and that their kings may be brought.

12 For the nation and the [1]kingdom, that will not serve thee, shall perish: and those nations shall be utterly destroyed.

13 The [1]glory of Lebanon shall come unto thee, the fir tree, the elm and the box tree together to beautify the place of my Sanctuary: for I will glorify the place of my [2]feet.

14 The sons also of them that afflicted thee, shall come and bow unto thee: and all they that despised thee, shall fall [1]down at the soles of thy feet: and they shall call thee; The city of the Lord, Zion of the Holy one of Israel.

15 Whereas thou hast been forsaken and hated, so that no man went *by thee*, I will make thee an eternal glory, and a joy from generation to generation.

16 Thou shalt also suck the milk of the Gentiles, and shalt suck the [1]breasts of Kings: and thou shalt know, that I the Lord am thy Savior, and thy Redeemer, the mighty one of Jacob.

17 For brass will I bring gold, and for iron will I bring silver, and for wood brass, and for stones iron. I will also make thy government [1]peace, and thine exactors righteousness.

18 Violence shall no more be heard of in thy land, neither desolation, nor destruction within thy borders: but thou shalt [1]call salvation, thy walls, and praise, thy gates.

19 Thou shalt have no more Sun to shine by day, neither shall the brightness of the [1]Moon shine unto thee: for the Lord shall be thine everlasting light, and thy God, thy glory.

20 Thy Sun shall never go down, neither shall thy Moon be hid: for the Lord shall be thine everlasting light, and the days of thy sorrow shall be ended.

60:1 [1] The time of thy prosperity and felicity: whereas speaking of Babylon, he commanded her to go down, Isa. 47:1.

60:2 [1] Signifying, that all men are in darkness till God give them the light of his Spirit, and that this light shineth to none, but to those that are in his Church.

60:3 [1] Meaning, that Judea should be as the morning star, and that the Gentiles should receive light of her.

60:4 [1] An infinite number from all countries, as Isa. 49:18.

60:5 [1] For joy, as the heart is drawn in for sorrow.

60:6 [1] Meaning, that everyone shall honor the Lord with what wherewith he is able: signifying, that it is no true serving of God, except we offer ourselves to serve his glory, and all that we have.

60:7 [1] That is, the Arabians, that have great abundance of cattle.

[2] Because the Altar was a figure of Christ, Heb. 13:10, he showeth that nothing can be acceptable to him, which is not offered to him by this Altar, who was both the offering and the altar itself.

60:8 [1] Showing what great number shall come to the Church, and with what great diligence and zeal.

60:9 [1] The Gentiles that are now enemies, shall become friends and setters forth of the Church.

60:10 [1] Meaning, Cyrus and his successors, but chiefly this is accomplished in them that serve Christ, being converted by his Gospel.

60:12 [1] He showeth that God hath given all power and authority here in earth for the use of his Church, and that they which will not serve and profit the same, shall be destroyed.

60:13 [1] There is nothing so excellent which shall not serve the necessity of the Church.

[2] Signifying, that God's Majesty is not included in the Temple, which is but the place for his feet, that we may learn to rise us to the heavens.

60:14 [1] To worship their head Christ, by obeying his doctrine.

60:16 [1] Both high and low shall be ready to help and succor thee.

60:17 [1] Thy governors shall love thee, and seek thy wealth and prosperity.

60:18 [1] Meaning, not a temporal felicity, but a spiritual, which is fulfilled in Christ's kingdom.

60:19 [1] Signifying, that all worldly means shall cease, and that Christ shall be all in all, as Rev. 21:23 and 22:5.

21 Thy people also shall be all righteous: they shall possess the land forever, the [1]grass of my planting shall be the work of mine hands, that I may be glorified.

22 A little one shall become as a [1]thousand, and a small one as a strong nation: I the Lord will hasten it in due time.

61

1 He prophesieth that Christ shall be anointed, and sent to preach.   10 The joy of the faithful.

1 The "Spirit of the Lord God *is* [1]upon me, therefore hath the Lord anointed me: he hath sent me to preach good tidings unto the poor, to bind up the [2]broken hearted, to preach liberty to the [3]captives, and to them that are bound, the opening of the prison,

2 To preach the [1]acceptable year of the Lord, and the day of [2]vengeance of our God, to comfort all that mourn,

3 To appoint unto them that mourn in Zion, *and* to give unto them beauty for [1]ashes, the oil of joy for mourning, the garment of gladness for the spirit of heaviness, that they might be called [2]trees of righteousness, the planting of the Lord, that he might be glorified.

4 And they shall build the old waste places, *and* raise up the former desolations, and they shall repair the cities that were desolate and waste through many [1]generations.

5 And the strangers shall [1]stand and feed your sheep, and the sons of the strangers shall be your plowmen, and dressers of your vines.

6 But ye shall be named the [1]Priests of the Lord, and men shall say unto you, The ministers of our God: Ye shall eat the [2]riches of the Gentiles, and shall be exalted with their glory.

7 For your shame *you shall receive* [1]double, and for confusion, [2]they shall rejoice in [3]their portion: for in

their land they shall possess the [4]double: everlasting joy shall be unto them.

8 For I the Lord love judgment, *and* hate [1]robbery for burnt offering, and I will direct their work in truth, and I will make an everlasting covenant with them.

9 And [1]their seed shall be known among the Gentiles, and their buds among the people. All that see them, shall know them, that they are the seed which the Lord hath blessed.

10 [1]I will greatly rejoice in the Lord, *and* my soul shall be joyful in my God: for he hath clothed me with the garments of salvation, and covered me with the robe of righteousness: he hath decked me like a bridegroom, and as a bride attireth herself with her jewels.

11 For as the earth bringeth forth her bud, and as the garden causeth to grow that which is sown in it: so the Lord God will cause righteousness to grow, and praise before all the heathen.

62

1 The great desire that the Prophets have had for Christ's coming.   6 The diligence of the Pastors to preach.

1 For Zion's sake I will not [1]hold my tongue, and for Jerusalem's sake I will not rest, until the righteousness thereof break forth as the [2]light, and salvation thereof as a burning lamp.

2 And the Gentiles shall see thy righteousness, and all Kings thy glory: and thou shalt be called by [1]a new name, which the mouth of the Lord shall name.

3 Thou shalt also be a [1]crown of glory in the hand of the Lord, and a royal diadem in the hand of thy God.

4 It shall no more be said unto thee, [1]Forsaken, neither shall it be said anymore to thy land, Desolate, but thou shalt be called [2]Hephzibah, and thy land [3]Beulah: for the Lord delighteth in thee, and thy

---

60:21 [1] The children of the Church.
60:22 [1] Meaning, that the Church should be miraculously multiplied.
61:1 [1] Thus appertaineth to all the Prophets and ministers of God, but chiefly to Christ, of whose abundant graces everyone receiveth according as it pleaseth him to distribute.
   [2] To them that are lively touched with the feeling of their sins.
   [3] Which are in the bondage of sin.
61:2 [1] The time when it pleased God to show his good favor to man, which S. Paul calleth the fullness of time, Gal. 4:4.
   [2] For when God delivereth his Church, he punisheth his enemies.
61:3 [1] Which was the sign of mourning.
   [2] Trees that bring forth good fruits, as Matt. 3:8.
61:4 [1] That is, for a long time.
61:5 [1] They shall be ready to serve you in all your necessities.
61:6 [1] This is accomplished in the time of Christ, by whom all the faithful are made Priests and Kings, 1 Pet. 2:9; Rev. 1:6 and 5:10.
   [2] Read Isa. 6:11, 16.
61:7 [1] Abundant recompense, as this word is used, Isa. 40:2.
   [2] That is, the Jews.
   [3] To wit, of the Gentiles.

[4] Whereas the Gentiles had dominion over the Jews in times past, now they shall have double authority over them and possess twice so much.
61:8 [1] I will not receive their offerings which are extortioners, deceivers, hypocrites, or that deprive me of my glory.
61:9 [1] That is, of the Church.
61:10 [1] He showeth what shall be the affection, when they feel this their deliverance.
62:1 [1] The Prophet saith that he will never cease to declare unto the people the good tidings of their deliverance.
   [2] Till they have full deliverance: and this the Prophet speaketh to encourage all other ministers to the setting forth of God's mercies toward his Church.
62:2 [1] Thou shalt have a more excellent fame than thou hast had hitherto.
62:3 [1] He shall esteem thee as dear and precious as a king doth his crown.
62:4 [1] Thou shalt no more be contemned as a woman forsaken of her husband.
   [2] Or, my delight in her.
   [3] Or, married.

land shalt have an [4]husband.

5   For *as* a young man marrieth a virgin, *so* shall thy sons [1]marry thee: and *as* a bridegroom is glad of the bride, *so* shall thy God rejoice over thee.

6   I have set [1]watchmen upon thy walls, O Jerusalem, which all the day and all the night continual shall not cease: [2]ye that are mindful of the Lord, keep not silence,

7   And give him no rest, till he repair, and until he set up Jerusalem the [1]praise of the world.

8   The Lord hath sworn by his right hand and by his strong arm, Surely I will no more give thy corn to be meat for thine enemies, and surely the sons of the strangers shall not drink thy wine, for the which thou hast labored.

9   But they that have gathered it, shall eat it, and praise the Lord, and the gatherers thereof shall drink it in the courts of my Sanctuary.

10   [1]Go through, go through the gates: prepare you the way for the people: cast up, cast up the way, and gather out the stones, *and* set up a standard for the people.

11   Behold, the Lord hath proclaimed unto the ends of the world, [1]tell the daughter Zion, Behold, thy Savior cometh: Behold, his wages *is* with him, and [2]his work *is* before him.

12   And they shall call them, The holy people, the redeemed of the Lord, and thou shalt be named, A [1]city sought out *and* not forsaken.

63

1 God shall destroy his enemies for his Church's sake. 7 God's benefits toward his Church.

1   Who is this that cometh [1]from Edom, with red garments from Bozrah? he is glorious in his apparel, and walketh in his great strength. [2]I speak in righteousness, *and* am mighty to save.

2   [1]Wherefore is thine apparel red, and thy garments like him that treadeth in the winepress?

3   I have trodden the winepress alone, and of all people there *was* none with me: for I will tread them in mine anger, and tread them under foot in my wrath, and their blood shall be sprinkled upon my garments, and I will stain all my raiment.

4   For the day of vengeance *is* in mine heart, and the [1]year of my redeemed is come.

5   And I looked, and there was none to help, and I wondered that there was none to uphold: therefore mine own [1]arm helped me, and my wrath itself sustained me.

6   Therefore I will tread down the people in my wrath, and make them [1]drunken in mine indignation, and will bring down their strength to the earth.

7   I will [1]remember the mercy of the Lord, *and* the praises of the Lord, according unto all that the Lord hath given us, and for the great goodness toward the house of Israel, which he hath given them according to his tender love, and according to his great mercies.

8   For he said, Surely they are my [1]people, children that will not lie: so he was their Savior.

9   In all their troubles he was [1]troubled, and the Angel [2]of his presence saved them: in his love and in his mercy he redeemed them, and he bare them and carried them always continually.

10   But they rebelled and vexed his holy Spirit: therefore was he turned to be their enemy, *and* he fought against them.

11   Then he [1]remembered the old time of Moses and

---

[4] That it may be replenished with children.

62:5 [1] Forasmuch as they confess one faith and religion with thee, they are in the same bond of marriage with thee, and they are called the children of the Church, inasmuch as Christ maketh her plentiful to bring forth children unto him.

62:6 [1] Prophets, Pastors, and Ministers.

[2] He exhorteth the ministers never to cease to call upon God by prayer for the deliverance of his Church, and to teach others to do the same.

62:7 [1] For the restoration whereof all the world shall praise him.

62:10 [1] Signifying the great number that should come to the Church, and what means he would prepare for the restitution of the same, as Isa. 57:14.

62:11 [1] Ye Prophets and Ministers show the people of this their deliverance: which was chiefly meant of our salvation by Christ, Zech. 9:9; Matt. 21:5.

[2] He shall have all power to bring his purpose to pass, as Isa. 40:10.

62:12 [1] That is, one over whom God hath had a singular care to recover her when she was lost.

63:1 [1] This prophecy is against the Idumeans and enemies which persecuted the Church, on whom God will take vengeance, and is here set forth all bloody after he hath destroyed them in Bozrah, the chief city of the Idumeans: for these were their greatest enemies, and under the title of circumcision and the kindred of Abraham, claimed to them-

selves the chief religion, and hated the true worshippers, Ps. 137:7.

[2] God answereth them that asked this question, Who is this? etc. and saith, Ye see now performed in deed the vengeance which my Prophets threatened.

63:2 [1] Another question, to the which the Lord answereth.

63:4 [1] Showing that when God punisheth his enemies, it is for the profit and deliverance of his Church.

63:5 [1] God showeth that he hath no need of man's help for the deliverance of his, and though men refuse to do their duty through negligence and ingratitude, yet he himself will deliver his Church, and punish the enemies, read Isa. 59:16.

63:6 [1] I will so astonish them and make them so giddy, that they shall not know which way to go.

63:7 [1] The Prophet speaketh this to move the people to remember God's benefits in times past, that they may be confirmed in their troubles.

63:8 [1] For I did choose them to be mine, that they should be holy, and not deceive mine expectation.

63:9 [1] He bare their afflictions and griefs as though they had been his own.

[2] Which was a witness of God's presence, and this may be referred to Christ, to whom belongeth the office of Salvation.

63:11 [1] That is, the people of Israel, being afflicted, called to remembrance God's benefits, which he had bestowed upon their fathers in times past.

his people, saying, Where is he that brought them up out of the sea with the ²shepherd of his sheep? Where is he that put his holy Spirit within ³him?

12 He led *them* by the right hand of Moses with his own glorious arm, dividing the water before them, to make himself an everlasting Name.

13 He led them through the deep, as an ¹horse in the wilderness, that they should not stumble.

14 As the beast goeth down into the valley, the Spirit of the Lord gave them rest: so didst thou lead thy people, to make thyself a glorious Name.

15 ¹Look down from heaven, and behold from the dwelling place of thine holiness, and of thy glory. Where is thy ²zeal and thy strength, the multitude of thy mercies, and of thy compassion? they are restrained from ³me.

16 Doubtless thou art our Father: though ¹Abraham be ignorant of us, and Israel know us not, *yet* thou, O Lord, art our Father, *and* our redeemer: thy Name *is* forever.

17 O Lord, why hast ¹thou made us to err from thy ways? *and* hardened our heart from thy fear? Return for thy ²servant's sake, *and* for the tribes of thine inheritance.

18 The people of thine holiness have possessed it, but a little ¹while: for our adversaries have trodden down thy Sanctuary.

19 We have been *as they*, over whom thou never barest rule, and upon whom thy name was not called.

64

1 *The Prophet prayeth for the sins of the people.*   6 *Man's righteousness is like a filthy cloth.*

1 Oh, that thou wouldest ¹break the heavens, *and* come down, *and* that the mountains might melt at

thy presence!

2 As the melting fire burned, *as* the fire caused ¹the waters to boil, (that thou mightest declare thy Name to thine adversaries) the people did tremble at thy presence.

3 When thou didst terrible things, which we looked not for, thou camest down, *and* the mountains melted at thy presence.

4 For since the beginning of the world, they have not ¹heard nor understood with the ear, neither hath the eye seen *another* God beside thee, which doeth *so* to him that waiteth for him.

5 Thou didst meet him, ¹that rejoiced *in thee*, and did justly: they remembered thee in thy ²ways: behold, thou art angry, for we have sinned: *yet* in ³them *is* continuance, and we ⁴shall be saved.

6 But we have all been as an unclean thing, and all our ¹righteousness *is* as filthy cloths, and we all do fade like a leaf, and our iniquities like the wind have taken us away.

7 And there *is* none that calleth upon thy Name, neither that stirreth up himself to take hold of thee: for thou hast hid thy face from us, and hast consumed us because of our iniquities.

8 But now, O Lord, thou art our Father: we are the ¹clay, and thou art our potter, and we all are the work of thine hands.

9 Be not angry, O Lord, ¹above measure, neither remember iniquity forever: Lo, we beseech thee, behold, we are all thy people.

10 ¹Thine holy cities lie waste: Zion is a wilderness, *and* Jerusalem a desert.

11 The house of our Sanctuary, and of our glory, ¹where our fathers praised thee, is burnt up with fire, and all our pleasant things are wasted.

63:11 ² Meaning, Moses.

³ That is, in Moses that he might well govern the people: some refer this giving of the spirit to the people.

63:13 ¹ Peaceably and gentle, as an horse is led to his pasture.

63:15 ¹ Having declared God's benefits showed to their forefathers, he turned himself to God by prayer, desiring him to continue the same graces toward them.

² Thy great affection, which thou barest towards us.

³ Meaning, from the whole body of the Church.

63:16 ¹ Though Abraham would refuse us to be his children, yet thou wilt not refuse to be our father.

63:17 ¹ By taking away the holy Spirit from us, by whom we were governed, and so for our ingratitude didst deliver us up to our own concupiscence, and didst punish sin by sin according to thy just judgment.

² Meaning, for the Covenant's sake made to Abraham, Isaac, and Jacob his servants.

63:18 ¹ That is, in respect of the promise, which is perpetual: albeit they had now possessed the land of Canaan, a thousand and four hundred years: and thus they lament, to move God rather to remember his Covenant, than to punish their sins.

64:1 ¹ The Prophet continueth his prayer, desiring God to declare his love toward his Church by miracles, and mighty power, as he did

in mount Sinai.

64:2 ¹ Meaning, the rain, hail, fire, thunder, and lightnings.

64:4 ¹ S. Paul useth the same kind of admiration, 1 Cor. 2:9, marveling at God's great benefit showed to his Church, by the preaching of the Gospel.

64:5 ¹ Thou showedst favor toward our fathers, when they trusted in thee, and walked after thy Commandments.

² They considered thy great mercies.

³ That is, in thy mercies, which he calleth the ways of the Lord.

⁴ Thou wilt have pity upon us.

64:6 ¹ We are justly punished and brought into captivity, because we have provoked thee to anger, and though we would excuse ourselves, yet our righteousness, and best virtues are before thee as vile cloths, or (as some read) like the menstruous clothes of a woman.

64:8 ¹ Albeit, O Lord, by thy just judgment thou mayest utterly destroy us as the potter may his pot, yet we appeal to thy mercies, whereby it hath pleased thee to adopt us to be thy children.

64:9 ¹ For so the flesh judgeth when God doth not immediately send succor.

64:10 ¹ Which were dedicated to thy service, and to call upon thy Name.

64:11 ¹ Wherein we rejoiced and worshipped thee.

12 Wilt thou hold thyself still ¹at these things, O Lord? wilt thou hold thy peace and afflict us above measure?

65

1 The vocation of the Gentiles, and the rejection of the Jews. 13 The joy of the elect, and the punishment of the wicked.

1 I have been sought of them that ¹asked not: I was found of them that sought me not: I said, Behold me, behold me, unto a nation that called not upon my Name.

2 I have ¹spread out mine hands all the day unto a rebellious people, which walked in a way that was not good, *even* after their own ²imaginations.

3 A people that provoked me ever unto my face: that sacrificeth in ¹gardens, and burneth incense upon ²bricks.

4 Which remain among the ¹graves, and lodge in the deserts, which eat ²swine's flesh, and the broth of things polluted *are* in their vessels.

5 Which say, ¹Stand apart, come not near to me; for I am holier than thou; these are a smoke in my wrath, *and* a fire that ²burneth all the day.

6 Behold, it is ¹written before me; I will not keep silence, but will render it and recompense it into their bosom.

7 Your iniquities, and the iniquities of your fathers, *shall be* ¹together (saith the Lord) which have burnt incense upon the mountains, and blasphemed me upon the hills; therefore will I measure their old work into their bosom.

8 Thus saith the Lord, As the wine is found in the cluster, and one saith, Destroy it not, for a ¹blessing *is* in it, so will I do for my servants' sakes, that I may not destroy them whole.

9 But I will bring a seed out of Jacob, and out of Judah that shall inherit my mountain; and mine elect shall inherit it, and my servants shall dwell there.

10 And ¹Sharon shall be a sheepfold, and the valley of Achor shall be a resting place for the cattle of my people, that have sought me.

11 But ye are they that have forsaken the Lord, and forgotten mine holy Mountain, and have prepared a table for the ¹multitude, and furnish the drink offerings unto the number.

12 Therefore will I ¹number you to the sword, and all you shall bow down to the slaughter, because I called, and ye did not answer; I ²spake, and ye heard not, but did evil in my sight, and did choose that thing which I would not.

13 Therefore thus saith the Lord God, Behold, my servants shall ¹eat, and ye shall be hungry; behold, my servants shall drink, and ye shall be thirsty; behold, my servants shall rejoice, and ye shall be ashamed.

14 Behold, my servants shall sing for joy of heart, and ye shall cry for sorrow of heart, and shall howl for vexation of mind.

15 And ye shall leave your name as a curse unto my ¹chosen; for the Lord God shall slay you, and call his servants by ²another name.

16 He that shall bless in the ¹earth, shall bless himself in the true God; and he that sweareth in the earth, shall swear by the true God; for the former ²troubles are forgotten, and shall surely hide themselves from mine eyes.

17 For lo, I will create ¹new heavens and a new earth; and the former shall not be remembered nor come into mind.

18 But be you glad and rejoice forever in the things

64:12 ¹ That is, at the contempt of thine own glory? though our sins have deserved this, yet thou wilt not suffer thy glory thus to be diminished.

65:1 ¹ Meaning, the Gentiles which knew not God, should seek after him, when he had moved their heart with his holy Spirit, Rom. 10:20.

65:2 ¹ He showeth the cause of the rejection of the Jews, because they would not obey him for any admonition of his Prophets, by whom he called them continually and stretched out his hand to draw them.

² He showeth that to delight in our own fantasies, is the declining from God and the beginning of all superstition and Idolatry.

65:3 ¹ Which were dedicated to idols.

² Meaning, their altars, which he thus named by contempt.

65:4 ¹ To consult with spirits, and to conjure devils, which was forbidden, Deut.18:11.

² Which was contrary to God's Commandment, Lev. 11:7; Deut. 14:8.

65:5 ¹ He showeth that hypocrisy is ever joined with pride and contempt of others.

² Their punishment shall never have end.

65:6 ¹ So that the remembrance thereof cannot be forgotten.

65:7 ¹ Shall be both punished together: and this declareth how the children are punished for their fathers' faults, to wit, when the same faults or like are found in them.

65:8 ¹ That is, it is profitable: meaning, that God will not destroy the faithful branches of his vineyard, when he destroyeth the rotten stocks, that is, the hypocrites.

65:10 ¹ Which was a plentiful place in Judea to feed sheep, as Achor was for cattle.

65:11 ¹ By the multitude and number he meaneth their innumerable idols of whom they thought they could never have enough.

65:12 ¹ Seeing you cannot number your gods, I will number you with the sword.

² By my Prophets, whom ye would not obey.

65:13 ¹ By these words, Eat and drink, he meaneth, the blessed life of the faithful, which have always consolation and full contentment of all things in their God, though sometimes they lack these corporal things.

65:15 ¹ Meaning, that he would call the Gentiles, who should abhor even the very name of the Jews for their infidelities' sake.

² Than by the name of the Jews.

65:16 ¹ By blessing, and by swearing is meant the praising of God for his benefits, and the true worshipping of him, which shall not be only in Judea, but through all the world.

² I will no more suffer my Church to be desolate as in times past.

65:17 ¹ I will so alter and change the state of my church, that it shall seem to dwell in a new world.

that I shall create; for behold, I will create Jerusalem, *as* a rejoicing, and her people *as* a joy.

19 And I will rejoice in Jerusalem, and joy in my people, and the voice of weeping shall be no more heard in her, nor the voice of crying.

20 There shall be no more there a child of years, nor an old man that hath [1]not filled his days: for he that shall be an hundred years old, shall die *as a* young man: but the sinner being [2]an hundred years old shall be accursed.

21 And they shall [1]build houses, and inhabit them, and they shall plant vineyards, and eat the fruit of them.

22 They shall not build, and another inhabit: they shall not plant, and another eat: for as the days of the tree are the days of my people, and mine elect shall enjoy in old age the work of their hands.

23 They shall not labor in vain, nor bring forth in fear: for they are the seed of the blessed of the Lord, and their buds with them.

24 Yea, before they call, I will answer, and whiles they speak, I will hear.

25 The [1]wolf and the lamb shall feed together, and the lion shall eat straw like the bullock: and to the serpent dust *shall be* his meat. They shall no more hurt nor destroy in all mine holy Mountain, saith the Lord.

66

1 *God dwelleth not in Temples made with hands.* 3 *He despiseth sacrifices done without mercy and faith.* 5 *God comforteth them that are troubled for his sake.* 19 *The vocation of the Gentiles.* 23 *The perpetual Sabbath.* 24 *The punishment of the wicked is everlasting.*

1 Thus saith the Lord, "The [1]heaven *is* my throne, and the earth *is* my footstool: where is that house that ye will build unto me? and where is that place of my rest?

CHAPTER 66
a Acts 7:48,49

2 For all these things hath mine hand mad[e] [1]and all these things have been, saith the Lord: an[d] to him will I look, even to him that is poor, and [of] [2]a contrite spirit, and trembleth at my words.

3 He that killeth a bullock, *is as* if he [1]slew a ma[n;] he that sacrificeth a sheep, *as if* he cut off a dog's nec[k:] he that offereth an oblation, *as if* he offered swine['s] blood: he that remembereth incense, *as if* he blesse[d] an idol: yea, they have chosen their own ways, an[d] their soul delighteth in their abominations.

4 Therefore will I [1]choose out their delusions, an[d] I will bring their fear upon them, because I calle[d,] and none would answer: I speak, and they wou[ld] not hear: but they did evil in my sight, and chos[e] the things which I would not.

5 Hear the word of the Lord, all ye that tremb[le] at his [1]word, Your brethren that hated you, and cas[t] you out for my Name's sake, said, Let the Lord b[e] glorified: but he shall appear to your joy, and the[y] shall be ashamed.

6 [1]A voice soundeth from the city, *even* a voic[e] from the Temple, the voice of the Lord, that recom[-] penseth his enemies fully.

7 Before [1]she travailed, she brought forth: and befor[e] her pain came, she was delivered of a man child.

8 Who hath heard such a thing? who hath see[n] such things? shall the earth be brought forth in on[e] [1]day? or shall a nation be born at once? for as soo[n] as Zion travailed, she brought forth her children.

9 Shall I [1]cause to travail, and not bring forth[?] shall I cause to bring forth, and shall be barren, sait[h] thy God?

10 Rejoice ye with Jerusalem, and be glad wit[h] her, all ye that love her: rejoice for joy with her, a[ll] ye that mourn for her,

11 That ye may suck, [1]and be satisfied with th[e]

65:20 [1] Meaning, in this wonderful restoration of the Church there should be no weakness of youth, nor infirmities of age, but all should be fresh and flourishing: and this is accomplished in the heavenly Jerusalem, when all sin shall cease, and the tears shall be wiped away.

[2] Whereby he showeth that the infidels and unrepentant sinners have no part of this benediction.

65:21 [1] He proposeth to the faithful the blessings which are contained in the Law, and so under temporal things comprehendeth the spiritual promises.

65:25 [1] Read Isa. 11:6.

66:1 [1] My majesty is so great, that it filleth both heaven and earth, and therefore cannot be included in a temple like an idol: condemning hereby their vain confidence, which trusted in the Temple and sacrifices.

66:2 [1] Seeing that both the Temple and the things therein, with the sacrifices, were made and done by his appointment, he showeth that he hath no need thereof, and that he can be without them, Ps. 50:10.

[2] To him that is humble and pure in heart, which receiveth my doctrine with reverence and fear.

66:3 [1] Because the Jews thought themselves holy by offering of their sacrifices, and in the mean season had neither faith nor repentance, God showeth that he doth no less detest these ceremonies than he

doth the sacrifices of the heathen, who offered men, dogs, and swine to their idols, which things were expressly forbidden in the Law.

66:4 [1] I will discover their wickedness and hypocrisy, wherewith the[y] think to blind mine eyes, to all the world.

66:5 [1] He encourageth the faithful by promising to destroy the[ir] enemies, which pretended to be as brethren, but were hypocrites and hated them that feared God.

66:6 [1] The enemies shall shortly hear a more terrible voice, even fir[e] and slaughter, seeing they would not hear the gentle voice of the Prophets, which called them to repentance.

66:7 [1] Meaning, that the restoration of the Church should be so sud[-] den and contrary to all men's opinions, as when a woman is delivere[d] before she looked for it, and that without pain in travail.

66:8 [1] This shall pass the capacity of man to see such a multitud[e] that shall come up at once, meaning, under the preaching of the Gospel, whereof they that came up out of Babylon were a sign.

66:9 [1] Declaring hereby, that as in his power and providence wome[n] travailed and delivered, so he giveth the power to bring forth the Church at his time appointed.

66:11 [1] That is, may rejoice for all the benefits that God bestoweth upon his Church.

breasts of her consolation: that ye may milk out, and be delighted with the brightness of her glory.

12 For thus saith the Lord, behold, I will extend ¹peace over her like a flood, and the glory of the ²Gentiles like a flowing stream: then shall ye suck, ye shall be ³born upon *her* sides, and be joyful upon *her* knees.

13 As one whom his mother comforteth, so will I comfort you, and ye shall be comforted in Jerusalem.

14 And when ye see this, your hearts shall rejoice, and your ¹bones shall flourish like an herb: and the hand of the Lord shall be known among his servants, and *his* indignation against his enemies.

15 For behold, the Lord will come with fire, and his chariots like a whirlwind, that he may ¹recompense his anger with wrath, and his indignation with the flame of fire.

16 For the Lord will judge with fire, and with his sword all flesh, and the flame of the Lord shall be many.

17 They that sanctify ¹themselves, and purify themselves in the gardens behind one *tree* in the midst eating ²swine's flesh, and such abomination, even the mouse, shall be consumed together, saith the Lord.

18 For I *will visit* their works, and their imaginations,

for it shall come that I will gather all nations, and tongues, and they shall come, and see my ¹glory.

19 And I will set a ¹sign among them, and will send those that ²escape of them unto the nations of ³Tarshish, ⁴Pul, and ⁵Lud, *and* to them that draw the ⁶bow, to ⁷Tubal and ⁸Javan, isles afar off, that have not heard my fame, neither have seen my glory, and ⁹they shall declare my glory among the Gentiles.

20 And they shall bring all your ¹brethren for an offering unto the Lord out of all nations, upon ²horses, and in chariots, and in horse litters, and upon mules, and swift beasts, to Jerusalem mine holy Mountain, saith the Lord, as the children of Israel offer in a clean vessel in the House of the Lord.

21 And I will take of them for ¹Priests, *and* for Levites, saith the Lord.

22 For as the new ¹heavens, and the new earth, which I will make, shall remain before me, saith the Lord, so shall your seed and your name continue.

23 And from month to month, and from Sabbath to Sabbath shall all flesh come to worship before me, saith the Lord.

24 And they shall go forth, and look upon the ¹carcasses of the men that have transgressed against me: for their ²worm shall not die, neither shall their fire be quenched, and they shall be an abhorring ³unto all flesh.

66:12 ¹ I will give her felicity and prosperity in great abundance.
  ² Read Isa. 60:16.
  ³ Ye shall be cherished as her dearly beloved children.
66:14 ¹ Ye shall have new strength and new beauty.
66:15 ¹ This vengeance God began to execute at the destruction of Babylon, and hath ever continued it against the enemies of his Church, and will do till the last day, which shall be the accomplishment thereof.
66:17 ¹ Meaning, the hypocrites.
  ² Whereby are meant them that did maliciously transgress the Law, by eating beasts forbidden, even to the mouse, which nature abhoreth.
66:18 ¹ The Gentiles shall be partakers of that glory, which before I showed to the Jews.
66:19 ¹ I will make these that I chose, that they perish not with the rest of the infidels: whereby he alludeth to the marking of the posts of his people, whom he preserved, Exod. 12:7.
  ² I will scatter the rest of the Jews, which escaped destruction, into divers nations.
  ³ That is, Cilicia.
  ⁴ Meaning Africa.
  ⁵ To wit, Lydia, or Asia minor.
  ⁶ Signifying the Parthians.

  ⁷ Italy.
  ⁸ Greece.
  ⁹ Meaning, the Apostles, Disciples, and others, which he did first choose of the Jews to preach unto the Gentiles.
66:20 ¹ That is, the Gentiles, which by faith shall be made the children of Abraham as you are.
  ² Whereby he meaneth that no necessary means shall want, when God shall call the Gentiles to the knowledge of the Gospel.
66:21 ¹ To wit, of the Gentiles, as he did Luke, Timothy, and Titus first, and others after to preach his word.
66:22 ¹ Hereby he signifieth the kingdom of Christ wherein his Church shall be renewed, and whereas before there were appointed seasons to sacrifice, in this there shall be one continual Sabbath, so that all times and seasons shall be meet.
66:24 ¹ As he that declared the felicity that shall be within the Church for the comfort of the godly, so doth he show what horrible calamity shall come to the wicked, that are out of the Church.
  ² Meaning, a continual torment of conscience, which shall ever gnaw them, and never suffer them to be at rest, Mark 9:44.
  ³ This is the just recompense for the wicked, which contemning God and his word, shall be by God's just judgment abhorred of all his creatures.

JEREMIAH

1 *1 In what time Jeremiah prophesied. 6 He acknowledgeth his imperfection, and is strengthened of the Lord. 11 The Lord showeth him the destruction of Jerusalem. 17 He commandeth him to preach his word without fear.*

1 The ¹words of Jeremiah the son of ²Hilkiah *one* of the Priests that were at ³Anathoth in the land of Benjamin.

2 To whom the ¹word of the Lord came in the days of Josiah the son of Amon King of Judah in the thirteenth year of his reign:

3 And also in the days of Jehoiakim the ¹son of Josiah king of Judah unto the end of the eleventh year of Zedekiah, the son of Josiah king of Judah, *even* unto the carrying away of Jerusalem captive in the fifth ²month.

4 Then the word of the Lord came unto me, saying,

5 Before I ¹formed thee in the womb, I knew thee, and before thou camest out of the womb, I sanctified thee, *and* ordained thee to be a Prophet unto the ²nations.

6 Then said I, ¹Oh, Lord God, behold, I cannot speak, for I am a child.

7 But the Lord said unto me, Say not, I am a child: for thou shalt go to all that I shall send thee, and whatsoever I command thee, shalt thou speak.

8 Be not afraid of their faces: for I am with thee to deliver thee, saith the Lord.

9 Then the Lord stretched out his hand, and ¹touched my mouth, and the Lord said unto m[e], Behold, I have put my words in thy mouth.

10 Behold, this day have I set thee over the ¹nation[s] and over the kingdoms, to pluck up, and to root out, an[d] to destroy, and throw down, to build, and to plant.

11 After this the word of the Lord came unto m[e], saying, Jeremiah, what seest thou? And I said, I se[e] a ¹rod of almond tree.

12 Then said the Lord unto me, Thou hast see[n] aright: for I will hasten my word to perform it.

13 Again the word of the Lord came unto me th[e] second time, saying, What seest thou? And I said, [I] see a seething ¹pot looking out of the North.

14 Then said the Lord unto me, Out of the ¹Nort[h] shall a plague be spread upon all the inhabitants o[f] the land.

15 For lo, I will call all the families of the kingdom[s] of the North, saith the Lord, and they shall com[e] and everyone shall set his throne in the entering o[f] the gates of Jerusalem, and on all the walls thereo[f] round about, and in all the cities of Judah.

16 And I will declare unto them my ¹judgment[s] touching all the wickedness of them that have for[-] saken me, and have burnt incense unto other god[s,] and worshipped the works of their own hands.

17 Thou therefore truss up thy loins, and aris[e] and speak unto them all that I command thee: b[e] not afraid of their faces, lest I ¹destroy thee befor[e] them.

1:1 ¹ That is, the sermons and prophecies.
² Which is thought to be he that found the book of the Law under king Josiah, 2 Kings 22:8.
³ This was a city about three miles distant from Jerusalem, and belonged to the Priests, the sons of Aaron, Josh. 21:18.
1:2 ¹ This is spoken to confirm his vocation and office, forasmuch as he did not presume of himself to preach and prophesy, but was called thereunto by God.
1:3 ¹ Meaning, the nephew of Josiah: for Jehoahaz was his father, who reigned but three months, and therefore is not mentioned, no more is Jehoiakim that reigned no longer.
² Of the eleventh year of Zedekiah, who was also called Mattaniah, and at this time the Jews were carried away into Babylon by Nebuchadnezzar.
1:5 ¹ The scripture useth this manner of speech, to declare that God hath appointed his minsters to their offices before they were born, as Isa. 49:1; Gal. 1:15.
² For Jeremiah did not only prophesy against the Jews, but also against the Egyptians, Babylonians, Moabites, and other nations.
1:6 ¹ Considering the great judgments of God, which according to his threatening should come upon the world, he was moved with a certain compassion on the one side to pity them that should thus perish, and on the other side by the infirmity of man's nature, know-ing how hard a thing it was to enterprise such a charge, as Isa. 6:1[?] Exod. 3:21 and 4:1.
1:9 ¹ Which declareth that God maketh them meet, and assuret[h] them, whom he calleth to set forth his glory: giving them all mean[s] necessary for the same, Exod. 4:12; Isa. 6:7.
1:10 ¹ He showeth what is the authority of God's true ministe[r] which by his word have power to bear down whatsoever lifteth itse[lf] up against God: and to plant and assure the humble, and such as giv[e] themselves to the obedience of God's word, 2 Cor. 10:4, 5; Heb. 4:12, an[d] these are the keys which Christ hath left to loose, and bind, Matt. 18:1[8.]
1:11 ¹ He joineth the sign with the word, for a more ample confirma[-] tion: signifying by the rod of the Almond tree, which first budet[h] the hasty coming of the Babylonians against the Jews.
1:13 ¹ Signifying, that the Chaldeans and Assyrians should be as [a] pot to seethe the Jews which boiled in their pleasures and lust.
1:14 ¹ Syria and Assyria were Northward in respect of Jerusale[m] which were the Chaldeans' dominion.
1:16 ¹ I will give them charge and power to execute my vengeanc[e] against the Idolaters which have forsaken me for their idols.
1:17 ¹ Which declareth that God's vengeance is prepared agains[t] them, which dare not execute their duty faithfully, either for fear o[f] man, or for any other cause, 1 Cor. 9:16.

18 For I, behold, I this day have made thee a defenced city, and an ¹iron pillar and walls of brass against the whole land, against the Kings of Judah, *and* against the Princes thereof, against the Priests thereof, and against the people of the land.

19 For they shall fight against thee, but they shall not prevail against thee: for I am with thee to deliver thee, saith the Lord.

2 *2 God rehearseth his benefits done unto the Jews.   8 Against the priests and false prophets.   12 The Jews are destroyed because they forsake God.*

1 Moreover, the word of the Lord came unto me, saying,

2 Go and cry in the ears of Jerusalem, saying, Thus saith the Lord, I remember thee, with the ¹kindness of thy youth *and* the love of thy marriage, when thou wentest after me in the wilderness ²in a land that was not sown.

3 Israel *was as* a thing ¹hallowed unto the Lord, *and* his firstfruits: all they ²that eat it, shall offend: evil shall come upon them, saith the Lord.

4 Hear ye the word of the Lord, O house of Jacob, and all the families of the house of Israel.

5 Thus saith the Lord, What iniquity have your fathers found in me, that they are gone ¹far from me, and have walked after vanity, and are become ²vain?

6 For they said not, Where is the Lord that brought us up out of the land of Egypt, that led us through the wilderness, through a desert, and waste land, through a dry land, and by ¹the shadow of death, by a land that no man passed through, and where no man dwelt?

7 And I brought you into a plentiful country, to eat the fruit thereof, and the commodities of the same: but when ye entered, ye defiled ¹my land, and made mine heritage an abomination.

8 The priests said not, ¹Where is the Lord? and they that should minister the ²Law, knew me not: the ³pastors also offended against me, and the prophets prophesied in ⁴Baal, and went after *things* that did not profit.

9 Wherefore I will yet ¹plead with you, saith the Lord, and I will plead with your children's children.

10 For go ye to the isles of ¹Chittim, and behold, and send unto ²Kedar, and take diligent heed, and see whether there be such things.

11 Hath *any* nation changed their gods, which yet are no gods? but my people have changed their ¹glory, for that which doth not ²profit.

12 O ye ¹heavens, be astonied at this: be afraid and utterly confounded, saith the Lord.

13 For my people have committed two evils: they have forsaken me ¹the fountain of living waters, to dig them pits, *even* broken pits that can hold no water.

14 Is Israel a ¹servant, or is he born in the house? why *then* is he spoiled?

15 The ¹Lions roared upon him *and* yelled, and they have made his land waste: his cities are burnt without ²an inhabitant.

16 Also the children of ¹Noph and Tahapanes have ²broken thine head.

17 Hast not thou procured this unto thyself,

1:18 ¹ Signifying, on the one part, that the more that Satan and the world rage against God's Ministers, the more present will he be to help them, Josh. 1:5; Heb. 13:5, and on the other part, that they are utterly unmeet to serve God in his Church, which are afraid, and do not resist wickedness, whatsoever danger depend thereon, Isa. 50:7; Ezek. 3:8.

2:2 ¹ According to that grace and favor which I showed thee from the beginning, when I did first choose thee to be my people, and married thee to myself, Ezek. 16:8.

² When I had delivered thee out of Egypt.

2:3 ¹ Chosen above all others to serve the Lord only, and the first offered to the Lord of all other nations.

² Whosoever did challenge this people, or else did annoy them, was punished.

2:5 ¹ That is, fallen to most vile idolatry.

² Altogether given to vanity, and are become blind and insensible as the idols that they serve.

2:6 ¹ Where for lack of all things necessary for life, ye could look for nothing every hour but present death.

2:7 ¹ By your idolatry and wicked manners, Ps. 78:58 and 106:38.

2:8 ¹ They taught not the people to seek after God.

² As the Scribes, which should have expounded the Law to the people.

³ Meaning, the Princes and Ministers: signifying, that all estates were corrupt.

⁴ That is, spake vain things, and brought the people from the true worship of God to serve idols: for by Baal, which was the chief idol of the Moabites, are meant all idols.

2:9 ¹ Signifying that he would not as he might, straightway condemn them, but showeth them by evident examples their great ingratitude that they might be ashamed and repent.

2:10 ¹ Meaning, the Grecians and Italians.

² Unto Arabia.

2:11 ¹ That is, God which is their glory, and who maketh them glorious above all other people, reproving the Jews that they were less diligent to serve the true God, than were the idolaters to honor their vanities.

² Meaning, the idols which were their destruction, Ps. 106:36.

2:12 ¹ He showeth that the insensible creatures abhor this vile ingratitude, and as it were tremble for fear of God's great judgments against the same.

2:13 ¹ Signifying, that when men forsake God's word, which is the fountain of life, they reject God himself, and so fall to their own inventions, and vain confidence, and procure to themselves destruction, Jonah 2:8; Zech. 10:2.

2:14 ¹ Have I ordered them like servants and not like dearly beloved children? Exod. 4:22, therefore it is their fault only, if the enemy spoil them.

2:15 ¹ The Babylonians, Chaldeans, and Assyrians.

² Not one shall be left to dwell there.

2:16 ¹ That is, the Egyptians: for these were two great cities in Egypt.

² Have grievously vexed thee at sundry times.

because thou hast forsaken the Lord thy God, when he [1]led thee by the way?

18 And what hast thou now to do in the way of [1]Egypt? to drink the water of Nilus? or what makest thou in the way of Assyria? to drink the water of the [2]River?

19 Thine own wickedness shall [1]correct thee, and thy turnings back shall reprove thee: know therefore and behold, that it is an evil thing, and bitter, that thou hast forsaken the Lord thy God, and that my fear is not in thee, saith the Lord God of hosts.

20 For of old time I have broken thy yoke, and burst thy bonds, and thou saidest, [1]I will no more transgress, but like an harlot thou runnest about upon all high hills, and under all green trees.

21 Yet I had planted thee a noble vine, whose [1]plants were all natural: how then art thou turned unto me into the plants of a strange vine?

22 Though thou wash thee with [1]nitre, and take thee much soap, yet thine iniquity is marked before me, saith the Lord God.

23 How canst thou say, I am not polluted, neither have I [1]followed Baal? behold thy ways in the valley, and know what thou hast done: thou art like a swift [2]dromedary, that runneth by his ways.

24 And as a wild [1]ass used to the wilderness that snuffeth up the wind by occasion at her pleasure: who can turn her back? all they that seek her, will not weary themselves, but will find her in her [2]month.

25 Keep thou thy feet from [1]bareness, and thy throat from thirst: but thou saidest desperately, No, for I have loved strangers, and them will I follow.

26 As the [1]thief is ashamed when he is found, so is the house of Israel ashamed, they, their kings, their princes and their priests, and their prophets,

27 Saying to a tree, Thou art my [1]father, and to a stone, Thou hast begotten me: for they have turned their back unto me, and not their face: but in the time of their trouble they will say, Arise, and help us.

28 But where are thy gods, that thou hast made thee? let them arise, if they can help thee in the time of thy trouble: for according [1]to the number of thy cities, are thy gods, O Judah.

29 Wherefore will [1]ye plead with me? ye all have rebelled against me, saith the Lord.

30 I have smitten your children in vain, they received no correction: your own [1]sword hath devoured your Prophets like a destroying lion.

31 O generation, take heed to the word of the Lord: have I been as a [1]wilderness unto Israel? or a land of darkness? Wherefore saith my people then, We are lords, [2]we will come no more unto thee?

32 Can a maid forget her ornament, or a bride her attire? yet my people have forgotten me, days without number.

33 Why dost thou prepare thy way, to [1]seek amity? even therefore will I teach thee, that thy ways are wickedness.

34 Also in thy [1]wings is found the blood of the souls of the poor innocents: I have not found it in holes, but upon all these places.

35 Yet thou sayest, Because I am guiltless, surely his wrath shall turn from me: behold, I will enter with thee into judgment, because thou sayest, I have

---

2:17 [1] Showing that God would have still led them aright, if they would have followed him.

2:18 [1] To seek help of man, as though God were not able enough to defend thee, which is to drink of the puddles, and to leave the fountain, read Isa. 31:1.
   [2] To wit, Euphrates.

2:19 [1] Meaning, that the wicked are insensible, till the punishment for their sin waken them as verse 26; Isa. 3:9.

2:20 [1] When I delivered thee out of Egypt, Exod. 19:8; Deut. 5:27; Josh. 24:16; Ezra 10:12; Heb. 8:6.

2:21 [1] Hebrew, seed was all true.

2:22 [1] Though thou use all the purifications and ceremonies of the law, thou canst not escape punishment, except thou turn to me by faith and repentance.

2:23 [1] Meaning, that hypocrites deny that they worship the idols, but that they honor God in them, and therefore they call their doings, God's service.
   [2] He compareth the idolaters to these beasts, because they never cease running to and fro: for both valleys and hills are full of their idolatry.

2:24 [1] He compareth the idolaters to a wild ass: for she can never be tamed nor yet wearied: for as she runneth she can take her wind at every occasion.
   [2] That is, when she is with foal, and therefore the hunters wait their time: so though thou canst not be turned back now from thine idolatry, yet when thine iniquity shall be at the full, God will meet with thee.

2:25 [1] Hereby he warneth them that they should not go into strange countries to seek help: for they should but spend their labor, and hurt themselves, which is here meant by the bare foot and thirst, Isa. 57:10.

2:26 [1] As a thief will not acknowledge his fault, till he be taken with the deed, and ready to be punished, so they will not confess their idolatry, till the plagues due to the same light upon them.

2:27 [1] Meaning, that idolaters spoil God of his honor: and whereas he hath taught to call him the father of all flesh, they attribute this title to their idols.

2:28 [1] Thou thoughtest that thy gods of blocks and stones could have helped thee, because they were many in number and present in every place: but now let us see whether either the multitude, or their presence can deliver thee from my plague, Jer. 11:13.

2:29 [1] As though I did you injury in punishing you, seeing that your faults are so evident.

2:30 [1] That is, you have killed your Prophets, that exhorted you to repentance, as Zechariah, Isaiah, etc.

2:31 [1] Have I not given them abundance of all things?
   [2] But will trust in our own power and policy.

2:33 [1] With strangers.

2:34 [1] The Prophets and the faithful are slain in every corner of your country.

not sinned.

36 Why runnest thou about so much to change thy ways? for thou shalt be confounded of Egypt, ¹as thou art confounded of Assyria.

37 For thou shalt go forth from thence, and thine hands upon ¹thine head, because the Lord hath rejected thy confidence, and thou shalt not prosper thereby.

3 God calleth his people unto repentance. 14 He promiseth the restitution of his Church. 20 He reproveth Judah and Israel, comparing them to a woman disobedient to her husband.

1 They ¹say, If a man put away his wife, and she go from him, and become another man's, shall he return again unto her? shall not this land ²be polluted? but thou hast played the harlot with many ³lovers: yet ⁴turn again to me, saith the Lord.

2 Lift up thine eyes unto the high places, and behold, where thou hast not played the harlot: thou hast sat *waiting* for them in the ways, as the ¹Arabian in the wilderness: and thou hast polluted the land with thy whoredoms, and with thy malice.

3 Therefore the showers have been restrained, and the ¹latter rain came not, and thou haddest a ²whore's forehead: thou wouldest not be ashamed.

4 Didst thou not still cry ¹unto me, Thou art my father, *and* the guide of my youth?

5 Will he keep *his anger* forever? will he reserve it to the end? thus hast thou spoken, but thou doest evil, even more and more.

6 The Lord said also unto me, in the days of Josiah the King, Hast thou seen what this rebel ¹Israel hath done? *for* she hath gone up upon every high mountain, and under every green tree, and there played the harlot.

7 And I said, when she had done all this, Turn thou unto me: but she returned not, as her rebellious sister Judah saw.

8 When I saw, how that by all occasions rebellious Israel had played the harlot, I cast ¹her away, and gave her a bill of divorcement: yet her rebellious sister Judah was not afraid, but she went also and played the harlot.

9 So that for the ¹lightness of her whoredom she hath even defiled the land: for she hath committed fornication with stones and stocks.

10 Nevertheless for all this, her rebellious sister Judah hath not returned unto me with ¹her whole heart, but feignedly, saith the Lord.

11 And the Lord said unto me, The rebellious Israel hath ¹justified herself more than the rebellious Judah.

12 Go and cry these words toward ¹the North, and say, Thou disobedient Israel, return, saith the Lord, *and* I will not let my wrath fall upon you: for I am merciful, saith the Lord, and I will not always keep *mine anger.*

13 But know thine iniquity: for thou hast rebelled against the Lord thy God, and hast ¹scattered thy ways to the strange *gods* under every green tree, but ye would not obey my voice, saith the Lord.

14 O ye disobedient children, turn again, saith the Lord, for I am your Lord, and I will take you one of a city, and two of a tribe, and will bring you to Zion,

15 And I will give you pastors according to mine heart, which shall feed you with knowledge and understanding.

16 Moreover, when ye be increased and multiplied in the land, in those days, saith the Lord, they shall say no more, The ¹Ark of the covenant of the Lord: for it shall come no more to mind, neither shall they remember it, neither shall they visit it, for that shall be no more done.

17 At that time they shall call Jerusalem, ¹The

2:36 ¹ For the Assyrians had taken away the ten tribes out of Israel, and destroyed Judah even unto Jerusalem: and the Egyptians slew Josiah, and vexed the Jews in sundry sorts.
2:37 ¹ In sign of lamentation, as 2 Sam. 13:19.
3:1 ¹ According as it is written, Deut. 24:4.
² If he take such one to wife again.
³ That is, with idols, and with them whom thou hast put thy confidence in.
⁴ And I will not cast thee off, but receive thee, according to my mercy.
3:2 ¹ Which dwelleth in tents and waiteth for them that pass by to spoil them.
3:3 ¹ As God threatened by his Law, Deut. 28:24.
² Thou wouldest never be ashamed of thine acts and repent: and this impudency is common to idolaters, which will not give off, though they be never so manifestly convicted.
3:4 ¹ He showeth that the wicked in their miseries will cry unto God and use outward prayer as the godly do, but because they turn not

from their evil, they are not heard, Isa. 58:3, 4.
3:6 ¹ Meaning, the ten tribes.
3:8 ¹ And gave her into the hands of the Assyrians.
3:9 ¹ The Hebrew word may either signify lightness, and wantonness, or noise and brute.
3:10 ¹ Judah feigned for a time that she did return, as under Josiah and other good kings, but she was never truly touched, or wholly reformed, as appeared when occasion was offered by any wicked prince.
3:11 ¹ Israel hath not declared herself so wicked as Judah, which yet hath had more admonitions and examples to call her to repentance.
3:12 ¹ Whereas the Israelites were now kept in captivity by the Assyrians, to whom he promiseth mercy, if they will repent.
3:13 ¹ There was no way, which thou didst not haunt to seek after the idols, and to trot a pilgrimage.
3:16 ¹ This is to be understood of the coming of Christ: for then they shall not seek the Lord by ceremonies, and all figures shall cease.
3:17 ¹ Meaning, the Church, where the Lord will be present to the world's end, Matt. 28:20.

throne of the Lord, and all the nations shall be gathered unto it, *even* to the Name of the Lord in Jerusalem: and thence forth they shall follow no more the hardness of their wicked heart.

18 In those days the house of Judah shall walk with the house of Israel, and they shall come together out of the land of the ¹North, into the land that I have given for an inheritance unto your fathers.

19 But I said, How did I take thee for children, and give thee a pleasant land, *even* the glorious heritage of the armies of the heathen, and say, Thou shalt call me, *saying*, My father, and shall not turn from me?

20 But *as* a woman rebelleth against her ¹husband: so have ye rebelled against me, O house of Israel, saith the Lord.

21 ¹A voice was heard upon the high places, weeping, and supplications of the children of Israel: for they have perverted their way, *and* forgotten the Lord their God.

22 O ye disobedient children, return *and* I will heal your rebellions. ¹Behold, we come unto thee, for thou art the Lord our God.

23 Truly *the hope* of the hills *is* but vain, *nor* the multitude of mountains: but in the Lord our God is the health of Israel.

24 For confusion hath devoured our ¹father's labor, from our youth, their sheep and their bullocks, their sons and their daughters.

25 We lie down in our confusion, and our shame covereth us: ¹for we have sinned against the Lord our God, we and our fathers from our youth, even unto this day, and have not obeyed the voice of the Lord our God.

4 1 True repentance.   4 He exhorteth to the circumcision *of the heart.*   5 The destruction of Judah is prophesied for the malice of their hearts.   19 The Prophet lamenteth it.

1 O Israel, if thou return, ¹return unto me, saith the Lord: and if thou put away thine abominations out of my sight, then shalt thou not remove.

2 And thou shalt ¹swear, The Lord liveth in truth, in judgment and in righteousness, and the nations shall be blessed in him, and shall glory in him.

3 For thus saith the Lord to the men of Judah, and to Jerusalem,

4 Break up ¹your fallow ground, and sow not among the thorns: be circumcised to the Lord, and take away the foreskins of your hearts, ye men of Judah, and inhabitants of Jerusalem, lest my wrath come forth like fire, and burn, that none can quench it, because of the wickedness of your inventions.

5 ¹Declare in Judah, and show forth in Jerusalem, and say, Blow the trumpet in the land: cry, and gather together, and say, Assemble yourselves, and let us go into strong cities.

6 Set up the standard in Zion: ¹prepare to flee, *and* stay not: for I will bring a plague from the North, and a great destruction.

7 The ¹lion is come up from his den, and the destroyer of the Gentiles is departed, *and* gone forth of his place to lay thy land waste, *and* thy cities shall be destroyed without an inhabitant.

8 Wherefore gird you with sackcloth: lament, and howl, for the fierce wrath of the Lord is not turned back from us.

9 And in that day, saith the Lord, the heart of the king shall perish, and the heart of the princes and the Priests shall be astonished, and the ¹Prophets shall wonder.

10 Then said I, Ah, Lord God, surely thou hast ¹deceived this people, and Jerusalem, saying, Ye shall have peace, and the sword pierceth unto the heart.

11 At that time shall it be said to this people and to Jerusalem, A dry ¹wind in the high places of the wilderness *cometh* toward the daughter of my people, *but* neither ²to fan nor to cleanse.

3:18 ¹ Where they are now in captivity.

3:20 ¹ The Hebrew word signifieth a friend or companion, and here may be taken for a husband, as it is used also, Hos. 3:1.

3:21 ¹ Signifying, that God, whom they had forsaken, would bring their enemies unto them, who should lead them captive, and make them to cry and lament.

3:22 ¹ This is spoken in the person of Israel to the shame of Judah, which stayed so long to turn unto God.

3:24 ¹ For their idolatry God's vengeance hath light upon them and theirs.

3:25 ¹ They justify not themselves, or say that they would follow their fathers, but condemn their wicked doings and desire forgiveness of the same, as Ezra 9:7; Ps. 106:6; Isa. 64:6.

4:1 ¹ That is, wholly, and without hypocrisy, Joel 2:12, not dissembling to turn and serve God as they do which serve him by halves, as Hos. 7:16.

4:2 ¹ Thou shalt detest the name of idols, Ps. 16:4, and shalt with reverence swear by the living God, when thine oath may advance God's glory, and profit others: and here, by swearing he meaneth the true religion of God.

4:4 ¹ He willeth them to pluck up the impiety and wicked affection and worldly respects out of their heart, that the true seed of God's word may be sown therein, Hos. 10:12, and this is the true circumcision of the heart, Deut. 10:16; Rom. 2:29; Col. 2:11.

4:5 ¹ He warneth them of the great dangers that shall come upon them by the Chaldeans, except, they repent and turn to the Lord.

4:6 ¹ He speaketh this to admonish them of the great danger when every man shall prepare to save himself, but it shall be too late, 2 Kings 25:4.

4:7 ¹ Meaning, Nebuchadnezzar King of Babylon, 2 Kings 24:1.

4:9 ¹ That is, the false prophets, which still prophesied peace and security.

4:10 ¹ By the false prophets which promised peace and tranquility: and thus thou hast punished their rebellious stubbornness by causing them to hearken unto lies which would not believe thy truth, 1 Kings 22:23; Ezek. 14:9; 2 Thess. 2:11.

4:11 ¹ The North wind whereby he meaneth Nebuchadnezzar.
   ² But to carry away both corn, and chaff.

12 A mighty wind shall come unto me from those *places*, and now will I also give sentence upon them.

13 Behold, he shall come up as the [1]clouds, and his chariots *shall be* as a tempest: his horses are lighter than eagles. [2]Woe unto us, for we are destroyed.

14 O Jerusalem, wash thine heart from wickedness, that thou mayest be saved: how long shall thy wicked thoughts remain within thee?

15 For a voice declareth from [1]Dan, and publisheth affliction from mount [2]Ephraim.

16 Make ye mention of the heathen, *and* publish in Jerusalem, Behold, the scouts come from a far country, and cry out against the cities of Judah.

17 They have compassed her about as the watchmen of the [1]field, because it hath provoked me unto wrath, saith the Lord.

18 Thy ways and thine inventions have procured thee these things, such is thy wickedness: therefore it shall be bitter, therefore it shall pierce unto thine heart.

19 My belly, my [1]belly, I am pained, even at the very heart: mine heart is troubled within me: I cannot be still: for my soul hath heard the sound of the trumpet, *and* the alarm of the battle.

20 Destruction upon destruction is cried, for the whole land is wasted: suddenly are my [1]tents destroyed, *and* my curtains in a moment.

21 How long shall I see the standard, *and* hear the sound of the trumpet?

22 For my people is foolish, they have not known me: they are foolish children, and have none understanding: [1]they are wise to do evil, but to do well they have no knowledge.

23 I have looked upon the earth, and lo, it was without form and [1]void: and to the heavens, and they had no light.

24 I beheld the mountains: and lo, they trembled, and all the hills shook.

25 I beheld, and lo, there was no man, and all the birds of the heaven were departed.

26 I beheld, and lo, the fruitful place *was* a wilderness, and all the cities thereof were broken down at the presence of the Lord, and by his fierce wrath.

27 For thus hath the Lord said, The whole land shall be desolate: yet will I [1]not make a full end.

28 Therefore shall the earth mourn, and the heavens above shall be darkened, because I have pronounced it: I have thought it, and will not repent, neither will I turn back from it.

29 The whole city shall flee, for the noise of the horsemen and bowmen: they shall go into thickets, and climb up upon the rocks: every city shall be forsaken, and not a man dwell therein.

30 And when thou shalt be destroyed, what wilt thou do? Though thou [1]clothest thyself with scarlet, though thou deckest thee with ornaments of gold, though thou paintest thy face with colors, yet shalt thou trim thyself in vain: *for* thy lovers will abhor thee *and* seek thy life.

31 For I have heard a noise as of a woman travailing, or as one laboring of her first child, *even* the voice of the daughter Zion that sigheth and stretcheth out her hands: [1]woe is me now: for my soul fainteth because of the murderers.

5 1 *In Judah no righteous man is found, neither among the people nor the rulers.* 15 *Wherefore Judah is destroyed of the Chaldeans.*

1 Run to and fro by the streets of Jerusalem, and behold now, and know, and inquire in the open places thereof, if ye can find a man, *or* if there be any that executeth judgment, and seeketh the truth, and I will spare [1]it.

2 For though they say, The [1]Lord liveth, yet do they swear falsely.

3 O Lord, are not thine eyes upon the [1]truth? thou hast [2]stricken them, but they have not sorrowed: thou hast consumed them, *but* they have refused to receive correction: they have made their faces harder than a stone, *and* have refused to return.

4:13 [1] Meaning, that Nebuchadnezzar should come as suddenly, as a cloud that is carried with the wind.

[2] This is spoken in the person of all the people, who in their affliction should cry thus.

4:15 [1] Which was a city in the utmost border of Israel Northward toward Babylon.

[2] Which was in the mid-way between Dan and Jerusalem.

4:17 [1] Which keep the fruits so straightly, that nothing can come in nor out: so should the Babylonians compass Judah.

4:19 [1] He showeth that the true ministers are lively touched with the calamities of the Church, so that all the parts of their body feel the grief of their heart, albeit with zeal to God's glory they pronounce his judgments against the people.

4:20 [1] Meaning, the cities, which were as easily cast down as a tent.

4:22 [1] Their wisdom and policy tend to their own destruction and pulleth them from God.

4:23 [1] By these manner of speeches he showeth the horrible destruction that should come upon the land, and also condemneth the obstinacy of the people, who repent not at the fear of these terrible tidings, seeing that the insensible creatures are moved therewith, as if the order of nature should be changed, Isa. 13:10 and 24:23; Ezek. 32:7; Joel 2:31 and 3:15.

4:27 [1] But for his mercy's sake, he will reserve himself a residue to be his Church, and to praise him in earth, Isa. 1:9.

4:30 [1] Neither thy ceremonies nor rich gifts shall deliver thee.

4:31 [1] As the Prophets were moved to pity the destruction of their people, so they declared it to the people to move them to repentance, Isa. 22:4; Jer. 9:1.

5:1 [1] That is, the city.

5:2 [1] Though they pretend religion and holiness, yet all is but hypocrisy: for under this kind of swearing is contained the true religion.

5:3 [1] Dost not thou love uprightness and faithful dealing?

[2] Thou hast ofttimes punished them, but all is in vain, Isa. 9:13.

4 Therefore I said, Surely they are poor, they are foolish, for they know not the way of the Lord, *nor* the judgment of their God.

5 I will get me unto the ¹great men, and will speak unto them: for they have known the way of the Lord, *and* the judgment of their God: but these have altogether broken the yoke, and burst the bonds.

6 Wherefore a ¹lion out of the forest shall slay them, and a wolf of the wilderness shall destroy them: a leopard shall watch over their cities: everyone that goeth out thence, shall be torn in pieces, because their trespasses are many, *and* their rebellions are increased.

7 How should I spare thee for this? thy children have forsaken me, and ¹sworn by them that are no gods: though I fed them to the full, yet they committed adultery, and assembled themselves by companies in the harlot's houses.

8 They rose up in the morning *like* fed horses: *for* every man ªneighed after his neighbor's wife.

9 Shall I not visit for these things, saith the Lord? shall not my soul be avenged on such a nation as this?

10 ¹Climb up upon their walls, and destroy them, but make not a full end: ²take away their battlements, for they are not the Lord's.

11 For the house of Israel, and the house of Judah have grievously trespassed against me, saith the Lord.

12 They have ¹denied the Lord, and said, It is not he, neither shall the plague come upon us, neither shall we see sword nor famine.

13 And the Prophets shall be *as* ¹wind, and the word is ²not in them: thus shall it come unto them.

14 Wherefore thus saith the Lord God of hosts, Because ye speak such words, behold, I will put my words into ¹thy mouth, like a fire, and this people shall be *as* wood, and it shall devour them.

15 Lo, I will bring a nation upon you ¹from far, O house of Israel, saith the Lord, which is a mighty nation, and an ancient nation, a nation whose language thou knowest not, neither understandest what they say.

16 Whose quiver is as an ¹open sepulcher: they

CHAPTER 5
ª Ezek. 22:11
b Jer. 16:10
c Isa. 6:9
Matt. 13:14
Acts 28:27
Rom. 11:8
d Job 26:10
e Isa. 1:23
Ezek. 7:9

are all very strong.

17 And they shall eat thine harvest and thy bread: they shall devour thy sons and thy daughters: they shall eat up thy sheep and thy bullocks: they shall eat thy vines and thy fig trees: they shall destroy with the sword thy fenced cities, wherein thou didst trust.

18 Nevertheless, at those days, saith the Lord, I will not make a full end of ¹you.

19 And when ᵇye shall say, Wherefore doth the Lord our God do these things unto us? then shalt ¹thou answer them, Like as ye have forsaken me and served strange gods in your land, so shall ye serve strangers in a land that is not yours.

20 Declare this in the house of Jacob, and publish it in Judah, saying,

21 Hear now this, O foolish people, and ¹without understanding, which have ᶜeyes and see not, which have ears and hear not.

22 Fear ye not me, saith the Lord? or will ye not be afraid at my presence, which have placed the sand for the ᵈbounds of the sea by the perpetual decree that it cannot pass it, and though the waves thereof rage, yet can they not prevail, though they roar, *yet* can they not pass over it?

23 But this people hath an unfaithful and rebellious heart: they are departed and gone.

24 For they say not in their heart, Let us now fear the Lord our God, that giveth rain both early and late in due season: he reserveth unto us the appointed weeks of the harvest.

25 *Yet* your ¹iniquities have turned away these things, and your sins have hindered good things from you.

26 For among my people are found wicked persons, that lay wait as he that setteth snares: they have made a pit, to catch men.

27 As a cage is full of birds, so are their houses full of deceit: thereby they are become great and waxen rich.

28 They are waxen fat *and* shining: they do overpass the deeds of the wicked: ᶜthey execute no judgment, no not the judgment of the fatherless: yet they ¹prosper, though they execute no judgment for the poor.

5:5 ¹ He speaketh this to the reproach of them which should govern and teach others, and yet are farther out of the way than the simple people.
5:6 ¹ Meaning, Nebuchadnezzar and his army.
5:7 ¹ He showeth that to swear by anything than by God, is to forsake him.
5:10 ¹ He commandeth the Babylonians and enemies to destroy them.
  ² Read Jer. 4:27.
5:12 ¹ Because they gave no credit to the words of his Prophets, as Isa. 28:15.
5:13 ¹ Their words shall be of none effect, but vain.
² They are not sent of the Lord, and therefore that which they threaten to us shall come upon them.
5:14 ¹ Meaning, Jeremiah.
5:15 ¹ To wit, the Babylonians and Chaldeans.
5:16 ¹ Who shall kill many with their arrows.
5:18 ¹ Here the Lord declareth his unspeakable favor toward his Church, as Jer. 4:27.
5:19 ¹ Meaning, the Prophet Jeremiah.
5:21 ¹ Hebrew, *without heart.*
5:25 ¹ If there be any stay, that we receive not God's blessings in abundance, we must consider that it is for our own iniquities, Isa. 59:1, 2.
5:28 ¹ They feel not the plague of God for it.

29 Shall I not visit for these things, saith the Lord? or shall not my soul be avenged on such a nation as this?

30 An horrible and filthy thing is committed in the land.

31 The ¹prophets prophesy lies, and the priests ²receive *gifts* in their hands, and my people delight therein. What will ye then do in the end thereof?

6

1 The coming of the Assyrians and Chaldeans.   16 He exhorteth the Jews to repentance.

1 O ye children of ¹Benjamin, prepare to flee out of the midst of Jerusalem, and blow the trumpet in ²Tekoa: set up a standard upon ³Beth-Haccerem: for a plague appeareth out of the North and great destruction.

2 I have compared the daughter of Zion to ¹a beautiful and dainty woman.

3 The Pastors with their flocks ¹shall come unto her: they shall pitch *their* tents round about by her, *and* everyone shall feed in his place.

4 ¹Prepare war against her: arise, and let us go up toward the South: woe unto us: for the day declineth, and the shadows of the evening are stretched out.

5 Arise, and let us go up by night, and destroy her palaces.

6 For thus hath the Lord of hosts said, Hew down wood, and cast a mount against Jerusalem: this city must be visited; all oppression is in the midst of it.

7 As the fountain casteth out her waters, so she casteth out her malice; ¹cruelty and spoil is continually heard in her before me, *with* sorrow and strokes.

8 Be thou instructed, O ¹Jerusalem, lest my soul depart from thee, lest I make thee desolate *as* a land that none inhabiteth.

9 Thus saith the Lord of hosts, They shall gather as a vine, the residue of Israel: turn ¹back thine hand as the grape gatherer into the baskets.

10 Unto whom shall I speak, and admonish that they may hear? behold, their ears *are* ¹uncircumcised, and they cannot hearken: behold, the word of the Lord is unto them as a reproach: they have no delight in it.

11 Therefore I am full of the wrath of the Lord: I am weary with holding it: ¹I will pour it out upon the ²children in the street, and likewise upon the assembly of the young men: for the husband shall even be taken with the wife, *and* the aged with him that is full of days.

12 And their houses *with* their lands, and wives also shall be turned unto strangers: for I will stretch out mine hand upon the inhabitants of the land, saith the Lord.

13 For from the least of them, even unto the greatest of them, everyone is given unto covetousness, and from the Prophet even unto the Priest, they all deal falsely.

14 They have healed also the hurt of the daughter of my people with sweet words, saying, ¹Peace, peace, when there is no peace.

15 Were they ashamed when they had committed abomination? nay, they were not ashamed, no neither could they have any shame: therefore they shall fall among the ¹slain: when I shall visit them, they shall be cast down, saith the Lord.

16 Thus saith the Lord, Stand in the ways and behold, and ask for the ¹old way, which is the good way, and walk therein, and ye shall find rest for your souls: but they said, We will not walk *therein*.

17 Also I set ¹watchmen over you, *which said*, Take heed to the sound of the trumpet: but they said, We will not take heed.

18 Hear therefore, ye ¹Gentiles, and thou Congregation know, what is among them.

19 Hear, O earth, behold, I will cause a plague to come upon this people, *even* the fruit of their own imaginations: because they have not taken heed unto

---

5:31 ¹ Meaning that there could be nothing but disorder, where the ministers were wicked persons and corrupt.
 ² Or, [bearest].
6:1 ¹ He speaketh to them chiefly because they should take heed by the example of their brethren, the other half of their tribe, which were now carried away prisoners.
 ² Which was a city in Judah, six miles from Bethlehem, 2 Chron. 11:6.
 ³ Read Neh. 3:14.
6:2 ¹ I have entreated her gently, and given her abundance of all things.
6:3 ¹ She shall be so destroyed; that the sheep may be fed in her.
6:4 ¹ He speaketh this in the person of the Babylonians, which complain that the time faileth them before they have brought their enterprises to pass.
6:7 ¹ He showeth the cause why it should be destroyed, and how it cometh of themselves.
6:8 ¹ He warneth them to amend by his correction, and turn to him by repentance.
6:9 ¹ He exhorteth the Babylonians to be diligent to search out all

and to leave none.
6:10 ¹ They delight to hear vain things, and to shut up their ears to true doctrine.
6:11 ¹ As the Lord had given him his word to be as a fire of his indignation to burn the wicked, Jer. 5:14, so he kindleth it now when he seeth that all remedies are past.
 ² None shall be spared.
6:14 ¹ When the people began to fear God's judgments, the false prophets comforted them by flatterings, showing that God would send peace and not war.
6:15 ¹ Hebrew, *them that fall*.
6:16 ¹ Wherein the Patriarchs and Prophets walked, directed by the word of God: signifying that there is no true way, but that which God prescribeth.
6:17 ¹ Prophets which should warn you of the dangers that were at hand.
6:18 ¹ God taketh all the world to witness, and the insensible creatures, of the ingratitude of the Jews.

my words, nor to my Law, but cast it off.

20 To what purpose bringest thou me ¹incense from Sheba, and sweet calamus from a far country? Your burnt offerings are not pleasant, nor your sacrifices sweet unto me.

21 Therefore thus saith the Lord, Behold, I will lay stumbling blocks before this people, and the fathers and the sons together shall fall upon them: the neighbor and his friend shall perish.

22 Thus saith the Lord, Behold, a people cometh from the ¹North country, and a great nation shall arise from the sides of the earth.

23 With bow and shield shall they be weaponed: they are cruel and will have no compassion: their voice roareth like the sea, and they ride upon horses well appointed, like men of war against thee, O daughter Zion.

24 We have heard their fame, *and* our hands wax ¹feeble: sorrow is come upon us, as the sorrow of a woman in travail.

25 Go not forth into the field, nor walk by the way: for the sword of the enemy *and* fear *is* on every side.

26 O daughter of my people, gird thee with sackcloth, and wallow thyself in the ashes: make lamentation, and bitter mourning *as* for thine only son: for the destroyer shall suddenly come upon us.

27 I have set ¹thee for a defense *and* fortress among my people, that thou mayest know and try their ways.

28 They are all rebellious traitors, walking craftily; *they are* brass and iron, they all are destroyers,

29 The ¹bellows are burnt; the lead is consumed in the fire; the founder melteth in vain; for the wicked are not taken away.

30 They shall call them reprobate silver, because the Lord hath rejected them.

7

2 Jeremiah is commanded to show unto the people the words of God, which trusteth in the outward service of the Temple. 13 The evils that shall come to the Jews, for the despising of their Prophets. 21 Sacrifices doth not the Lord chiefly require of the Jews, but that they should obey his word.

CHAPTER 7
ᵃ Jer. 26:13

1 The words that came to Jeremiah from the Lord, saying,

2 Stand in the gate of the Lord's house, and cry this word there, and say, Hear the word of the Lord, all ye of Judah that enter in at these gates to worship the Lord.

3 Thus saith the Lord of hosts, the God of Israel, ᵃAmend your ways and your works, and I will let you dwell in this place.

4 Trust not in ¹lying words, saying, The Temple of the Lord, the Temple of the Lord; this is the Temple of the Lord.

5 For if you amend *and* redress your ways and your works; if you execute judgment between a man and neighbor,

6 *And* oppress not the stranger, the fatherless, and the widow, and shed no innocent blood in this place, neither walk after other gods to your destruction,

7 Then ¹will I let you dwell in this place in the land that I gave unto your fathers forever and ever.

8 Behold, you trust in lying words, that cannot profit.

9 Will you steal, murder, and commit adultery, and swear falsely, and burn incense unto Baal, and walk after other gods whom ye know not?

10 And come and stand before me in this House, whereupon my Name is called, and say, We are delivered, though we have done all these abominations?

11 Is this House become ¹a den of thieves, whereupon my Name is called before your eyes? Behold, even I see it, saith the Lord.

12 But go ye now unto my place which was in Shiloh, ¹where I set my Name at the beginning, and behold, what I did to it for the wickedness, of my people Israel.

13 Therefore now because ye have done all these works, saith the Lord, (and I ¹rose up early and spake unto you: but when I spake, ye would not hear me, neither when I called, would ²ye answer.)

14 Therefore will I do unto this house, whereupon my Name is called, wherein also ye trust, even unto

---

6:20 ¹ Read Isa. 1:11 and Amos 5:21.
6:22 ¹ From Babylon by Dan, which was North from Jerusalem.
6:24 ¹ For fear of the enemy: he speaketh this in the person of the Jews.
6:27 ¹ Meaning, Jeremiah, whom God had appointed to try out the godly from the wicked, as a founder doth the pure metal from the dross.
6:29 ¹ All the pain and labor that hath been taken with them, is lost.
7:4 ¹ Believe not the false prophets, which say that for the Temple's sake, and the sacrifices there, the Lord will preserve you, and so nourish you in your sin, and vain confidence.
7:7 ¹ God showeth on what condition he made his promise to this Temple: that they should be an holy people unto him, as he would

be a faithful God to them.
7:11 ¹ As thieves hid in holes and dens think themselves safe, so when you are in my Temple, you think to be covered with the holiness thereof, and that I cannot see your wickedness, Matt. 21:13.
7:12 ¹ Because they depended so much on the Temple, which was for his promise, that he would be present and defend them where the Ark was, he sendeth them to God's judgments against Shiloh, where the Ark had remained about 300 years, and after was taken, the Priests slain, and the people miserably discomfited, 1 Sam. 4:11; Jer. 26:6.
7:13 ¹ That is, I never ceased to warn you, as Isa. 65:2; Prov. 1:23.
² He showeth what is the only remedy to redress our faults: to suffer God to lead us into the way, and to obey his calling, Isa. 66:4.

the place that I gave to you, and to your fathers, as I have done unto Shiloh.

15 And I will cast ¹you out of my sight, as I have cast out all your brethren, *even* the whole seed of Ephraim.

16 Therefore thou shalt not ¹pray for this people, neither lift up cry or prayer for them, neither entreat me, for I will not hear thee.

17 Seest thou not what they do in the cities of Judah, and in the streets of Jerusalem?

18 The children gather wood, and the fathers kindle the fire, and the women kneed the dough to make cakes to ¹the Queen of heaven, and to pour out drink offerings unto other gods, that they may provoke me unto anger.

19 Do they provoke me to anger, saith the Lord, and not themselves to the confusion of their own faces?

20 Therefore thus saith the Lord God, Behold, mine anger and my wrath shall be poured upon this place; upon man and upon beast, and upon the tree of the field, and upon the fruit of the ground, and it shall burn and not be quenched.

21 Thus saith the Lord of hosts, the God of Israel, Put your burnt offerings unto your sacrifices, and eat the flesh.

22 For ¹I spake not unto your fathers, nor commanded them, when I brought them out of the land of Egypt, concerning burnt offerings and sacrifices.

23 But this thing commanded I them, saying, Obey my voice, and I will be your God, and ye shall be my people: and walk ye in all the ways which I have commanded you, that it may be well unto you.

24 But they would not obey, nor incline their ear, but went after the counsels, *and* the stubbornness of their wicked heart, and went backward and not forward.

25 Since the day that your fathers came up out of the land of Egypt, unto ¹this day, I have even sent unto you all my servants the Prophets, ²rising up early every day, and sending them.

26 Yet would they not hear me, nor incline their ear, but hardened their neck, *and* did worse than their fathers.

b Ezek. 26:13

27 Therefore shalt thou speak all these words unto them, but they ¹will not hear thee: thou shalt also cry unto them, but they will not answer thee.

28 But thou shalt say unto them, This is a nation that heareth not the voice of the Lord their God, nor receiveth discipline: truth is perished, and is clean gone out of their mouth.

29 Cut off thine ¹hair, O Jerusalem, and cast it away, and take up a complaint on the high places: for the Lord hath rejected and forsaken the generation of his ²wrath.

30 For the children of Judah have done evil in my sight, saith the Lord: they have set their abominations in the house, whereupon my Name is called to pollute it.

31 And they have built the high place of ¹Tophet, which is in the valley of Ben-Hinnom to burn their sons and their daughters in the fire, which I ²commanded them not, neither came it in mine heart.

32 Therefore behold, the days come, saith the Lord, that it shall no more be called Tophet, nor the valley of Ben-Hinnom, but the valley of slaughter: for they shall bury in Tophet till there be no place.

33 And the carcasses of this people shall be meat for the fowls of the heaven, and for the beasts of the earth, and none shall fray them away.

34 *b*Then I will cause to cease from the cities of Judah, and from the streets of Jerusalem the voice of mirth, and the voice of gladness, the voice of the bridegroom, and the voice of the bride: for the land shall be desolate.

8

1 The destruction of the Jews. 4 The Lord moveth the people to amendment. 10 He reprehendeth the lying doctrine and the covetousness of the Prophets and Priests.

1 At that time, saith the Lord, they shall bring out the bones of the kings of Judah, and the bones of their Princes, and the bones of the Priests, and the bones of the Prophets, and the bones of the inhabitants of Jerusalem out of their ¹graves.

2 And they shall spread them before the sun, and the moon, and all the host of heaven, whom they

---

7:15 ¹ I will send you into captivity as I have done Ephraim, that is, the ten tribes.

7:16 ¹ To assure them that God had determined with himself to punish their wickedness, he showeth that the prayer of the godly can nothing avail them, whiles they remain in their obstinacy against God, and will not use the means that he useth to call them to repentance, Jer. 11:14 and 14:11.

7:18 ¹ That is, they sacrifice to the Sun, Moon and Stars, which they called the queen of heaven, Jer. 44:17; 2 Kings 23:5.

7:22 ¹ Showing that it was not his chief purpose and intent, that they should offer sacrifices: but that they should regard, wherefore they were ordained: to wit, to be joined to the word as seals and confirmations of remissions of sins in Christ: for without the word

they were vain and unprofitable.

7:25 ¹ Which was about fourteen hundred years.
² Read verse 13.

7:27 ¹ Whereby he showeth that the pastors ought not to leave their flocks in their obstinacy, for the Lord will use the means of his servants to make the wicked more faulty and to prove his.

7:29 ¹ In sign of mourning, as Job 1:20.
² Against whom he had just occasion to pour out his wrath, Mic. 1:6.

7:31 ¹ Of Tophet, read 2 Kings 23:10.
² But commanded the contrary, as Lev. 18:21 and 20:3; Deut. 18:10.

8:1 ¹ The enemy for greediness of gain shall rifle your graves, and lay you before those idols, which in your life you worshipped, to see if they can help you.

have loved, and whom they have served, and whom they have followed, and whom they have sought, and whom they have worshipped: they shall not be gathered nor be buried, *but* shall be as dung upon the earth.

3　And death shall be desired [1]rather than life of all the residue that remaineth of this wicked family, which remain in all the places where I have scattered them, saith the Lord of hosts.

4　Thou shalt say unto them also, Thus saith the Lord, Shall they [1]fall, and not arise? shall he turn away and not turn again?

5　Wherefore is this people of Jerusalem turned back by a perpetual rebellion? they gave themselves to deceit, *and* would not return.

6　I hearkened and heard, *but* none spake aright: no man repented him of his wickedness, saying, What have I done? [1]everyone turned to their race, as the horse rusheth into the battle.

7　Even the stork in the air knoweth her appointed times, and the turtle, and the crane and the swallow observe the time of their coming, but my people knoweth not the [1]judgment of the Lord.

8　How do ye say, We are wise, and the Law of the Lord *is* with us? Lo, [1]certainly in vain made he it, the pen of the scribes is in vain.

9　The [1]wise men are ashamed: they are afraid and taken: lo, they have rejected the word of the Lord, and what wisdom is in them?

10　Therefore will I give their wives unto others, *and* their fields to them that shall possess them: "for everyone from the least even unto the greatest is given to covetousness, *and* from the Prophet even unto the Priest, everyone dealeth falsely.

11　For they have healed the hurt of the daughter of my people with sweet words, saying, [1]Peace, peace, when there is no peace.

12　Were they ashamed when they had committed abomination? nay, they were not ashamed, neither could they have any shame: therefore shall they fall

CHAPTER 8
[a] Isa. 56:11
Jer. 5:31
Jer. 6:13
[b] Jer. 14:19

among the slain: when I shall visit them, they shall be cast down, saith the Lord.

13　I will surely consume them, saith the Lord: there shall be no grapes on the vine, nor figs on the fig tree, and the leaf shall fade, and the things that I have given them shall depart from them.

14　Why do we stay? [1]assemble yourselves, and let us enter into the strong cities, and let us be quiet there: for the Lord our God hath put us to silence, and given us water with [2]gall to drink, because we have sinned against the Lord.

15　[b]We looked for peace, but no good *came, and* for a time of health, and behold troubles.

16　The neighing of his horses was heard from [1]Dan, the whole land trembled at the noise of the neighing of his strong *horses*: for they are come, and have devoured the land with all that is in it, the city and those that dwell therein.

17　For behold, I will [1]send serpents, *and* cockatrices among you, which will not be charmed, and they shall sting you, saith the Lord.

18　I would have [1]comforted myself against sorrow, but *mine* heart is heavy in me.

19　Behold, the voice of the cry of the daughter of my people *for fear of them* of a far country, Is not the Lord in Zion? is not her king in her? Why [1]have they provoked me to anger with their graven images, and with the vanities of a strange *god*?

20　The [1]harvest is past, the Summer is ended, and we are not holpen.

21　I am [1]sore vexed for the hurt of the daughter of my people, I am heavy, *and* astonishment hath taken me.

22　Is there no balm [1]at Gilead? is there no Physician there? Why then is not the health of the daughter of my people recovered?

9 *1 The complaint of the Prophet for the malice of the people. 24 In the knowledge of God ought we only to rejoice. 26 The uncircumcision of the heart.*

8:3 [1] Because of the afflictions that they shall feel through God's judgments.
8:4 [1] Is there no hope that they will return?
8:6 [1] They are full of hypocrisy, and everyone followeth his own fantasy without any consideration.
8:7 [1] He accuseth them in that that they are more ignorant of God's judgments, than these birds are of their appointed seasons to discern the cold and heat, as Isa. 1:3.
8:8 [1] The Law doth not profit you, neither need it to have been written for ought that you have learned by it.
8:9 [1] They that seem wise, may be ashamed of their ignorance, for all wisdom consisteth in God's word.
8:11 [1] Read Jer. 6:14.
8:14 [1] He speaketh in the person of the people, who when the enemy cometh, will turn about to hide themselves, and acknowledge that it is God's hand.

[2] That is, hath brought us into extreme affliction, and thus they shall not attribute this plague to fortune, but to God's just judgment, Jer. 9:15 and 23:15.
8:16 [1] Read Jer. 4:15.
8:17 [1] God threateneth to send the Babylonians among them, who shall utterly destroy them in such sort, as by no means they shall escape.
8:18 [1] Read Jer. 4:19.
8:19 [1] Thus the Lord speaketh.
8:20 [1] The people wonder that they have so long time looked for succor in vain.
8:21 [1] The Prophet speaketh this.
8:22 [1] Meaning, that no man's help or means could save them: for in Gilead was precious balm, Jer. 46:11, or else deriding the vain confidence of the people, who looked for help at their Priests, who should have been the Physicians of their souls, and dwelt at Gilead, Hos. 6:8.

1 Oh, that mine head were *full* of [1]water, and mine eyes a fountain of tears, that I might weep day and night for the slain of the daughter of my people.

2 Oh, that I had in the wilderness a [1]cottage of wayfaring men, that I might leave my people, and go from them: for they be all [2]adulterers, and an assembly of rebels.

3 And they bend their tongues *like* their bows for [1]lies: but they have no courage for the truth upon the earth, for they proceed from evil to worse, and they have not known me, saith the Lord.

4 Let everyone take heed of his neighbor, and trust you not in any [1]brother: for every brother will use deceit, and every friend will deal deceitfully.

5 And everyone will deceive his friend, and will not speak the truth: *for* they [1]have taught their tongue to speak lies, and take great pains to do wickedly.

6 Thine habitation is in the midst of deceivers: [1]because of *their* deceit they refuse to know me, saith the Lord.

7 Therefore thus saith the Lord of hosts, Behold, I will [1]melt them, and try them: for what should I *else* do for the daughter of my people?

8 Their tongue [a]*is* as an arrow shot out, *and* speaketh deceit: one speaketh peaceably to his neighbor with his mouth, but in his heart he layeth wait for him.

9 Shall I not visit them for these things, saith the Lord? or shall not my soul be avenged on such a nation as this?

10 Upon the [1]mountains will I take up a weeping and a lamentation, and upon the fair places of the wilderness a mourning, because they are burnt up, so that none can pass through them, neither can men hear the voice of the flock: both the fowl of the air, and the beast are fled away *and* gone.

11 And I will make Jerusalem an heap, *and* a den of dragons, and I will make the cities of Judah waste without an inhabitant.

12 Who is [1]wise to understand this? and to whom

CHAPTER 9
[a] Ps. 28:3
Ps. 120:4

the mouth of the Lord hath spoken, even he shall declare it. Why doth the land perish, *and* is burnt up like a wilderness, that none passeth through?

13 And the Lord saith, because they have forsaken my Law, which I set before them, and have not obeyed my voice, neither walked thereafter,

14 But have walked after the stubbornness of their own heart, and after Baal, which [1]their fathers taught them.

15 Therefore thus saith the Lord of hosts, the God of Israel, Behold, I will feed this people with wormwood, and give them waters of gall [1]to drink:

16 I will scatter them also among the heathen, whom neither they nor their fathers have known, and I will send a sword after them, till I have consumed them.

17 Thus saith the Lord of hosts, Take heed, and call for [1]the mourning women, that they may come, and send for skillful women, that they may come,

18 And let them make haste, and let them take up a lamentation for us, that our eyes may cast out tears, and our eyelids gush out of water.

19 For a lamentable noise is heard out of Zion, How are we destroyed, *and* utterly confounded, for we have forsaken the land, and our dwellings [1]have cast us out.

20 Therefore hear the word of the Lord, O ye women, and let your ears regard the words of his mouth, and [1]teach your daughters to mourn, and everyone her neighbor to lament.

21 For death is come up into our [1]windows, *and* is entered into our palaces, to destroy the children without, and the young men in the streets.

22 Speak, Thus saith the Lord, The carcasses of men shall lie, even as the dung upon the field, and as the handful after the mower, and none shall gather *them.*

23 Thus saith the Lord, Let not the [1]wise man glory in his wisdom, nor the strong man glory in his strength, neither the rich man glory in his riches.

9:1 [1] The Prophet showeth the great compassion that he had toward this people, seeing that he could never sufficiently lament the destruction that he saw to hang over them, which is a special note to discern the true pastors from the hirelings, read Jer. 4:19.
9:2 [1] He showeth that this were more quietness and greater safety for him to dwell among the wild beasts than among this wicked people, save that God hath enjoined him this charge.
    [2] Utterly turned from God.
9:3 [1] To belie and slander their neighbors.
9:4 [1] Meaning, that all were corrupt, and none could find an honest man.
9:5 [1] They have so practiced deceit, that they cannot forsake it.
9:6 [1] They had rather forsake God, than leave their wicked trade.
9:7 [1] With the fire of affliction.
9:10 [1] Signifying, that all the places about Jerusalem should be destroyed.
9:12 [1] Meaning, that they are all without sense and understanding, and that God hath taken his spirit from them.

9:14 [1] He showeth that the children cannot excuse themselves by their fathers: for both father and child if they be wicked shall perish.
9:15 [1] Read Jer. 8:14.
9:17 [1] Seeing you cannot lament your own sins, call for those foolish women, whom of a superstition you have to lament for the dead, that they by their feigned tears may provoke you to some sorrow.
9:19 [1] As though they were weary of us, because of our iniquities, Lev. 18:28 and 20:22.
9:20 [1] He derideth the superstition of the women which made an art of mourning, and taught to weep with feigned tears.
9:21 [1] Signifying, that there is no means to deliver the wicked from God's judgments: but when they think to be most sure, and most far off, then they are soonest taken.
9:23 [1] Forasmuch as none can save himself by his own labor, or any worldly means, he showeth that it is vain to put our trust therein, but that we trust in the Lord, and rejoice in him, who only can deliver us, 1 Cor. 1:31; 2 Cor. 10:17.

24 But let him that glorieth, glory in this, that he understandeth and knoweth me: for I am the Lord, which ¹show mercy, judgment, and righteousness in the earth: for in these things I delight, saith the Lord.

25 Behold, the days come saith the Lord, that I will visit all them which are ¹circumcised with the uncircumcised:

26 Egypt and Judah, and Edom, and the children of Ammon, and Moab, and all the utmost corners of them that dwell in the wilderness: for all *these* nations *are* uncircumcised, and all the house of Israel *are* uncircumcised in the heart.

10 *The constellations of the stars are not to be feared. 5 The weakness of idols. 6 Of the power of God. 21 Their Pastors are become brute beasts.*

1 Hear ye the word of the Lord that he speaketh unto you, O house of Israel.

2 Thus saith the Lord, Learn not the way of the heathen, and be not afraid for the ¹signs of heaven, though the heathen be afraid of such.

3 For the ¹customs of the people are vain: for one cutteth a tree out of the forest (which is the work of the hands of the carpenter) with the axe,

4 And *another* decketh it ¹with silver, and with gold: they fasten it with nails and hammers that it fall not.

5 The *idols* stand up as the palm tree, but speak not: they are borne because they cannot go: fear them not, for they cannot do evil, neither can they do good.

6 There is none like unto thee, O Lord: ¹thou art great, and thy Name *is* great in power.

7 Who would not fear thee, O king of nations? for to thee appertaineth *the dominion*: for among all the wise men of the Gentiles, and in all their kingdoms there is none like thee.

8 But altogether they dote, and are foolish: *for* the stock is a ¹doctrine of vanity.

9 Silver plates are brought from Tarshish, and gold ¹from Uphaz, *for* the work of the workman, and the hands of the founder: the blue silk, and the purple *is* their clothing: all these things are made by cunning men.

10 But the Lord *is* the God of truth: he is the living God, and an everlasting King: at his anger the earth shall tremble, and the nations cannot abide his wrath.

11 (Thus shall you say unto them, The gods ¹that have not made the heavens and the earth, shall perish from the earth, and from under these heavens.)

12 He hath made the earth by his power, and established the world by his wisdom, and hath stretched out the heaven by his discretion.

13 He giveth by *his* voice the multitude of waters in the heaven, and he causeth the clouds to ascend from the ends of the earth: he turneth lightnings to rain, and bringeth forth the wind out of his treasures.

14 Every man is a ¹beast by *his own* knowledge: every founder is confounded by the graven image: for his melting is but falsehood, and there is no breath therein.

15 They are vanity, *and* the work of errors: in the time of their visitation they shall perish.

16 The ¹portion of Jacob *is* not like them: for he is the maker of all things, and Israel *is* the rod of his inheritance: the Lord of hosts *is* his Name.

9:24 ¹ These three points are necessary to know aright: his mercy, wherein consisteth our salvation; his judgment, which he executeth continually against the wicked, and his justice, whereby he defendeth and maintaineth the faithful.

9:25 ¹ Meaning, both Jews and Gentiles, as in this next verse he showeth the cause, read Jer. 4:4.

10:2 ¹ God forbiddeth his people to give credit or fear the constellations and conjunctions of stars and planets which have no power of themselves, but are governed by him, and their secret motions and influences are not known to man and therefore there can be no certain judgment thereof, Deut. 18:9.

10:3 ¹ Meaning, not only in the observation of the stars, but their laws and ceremonies whereby they confirm their idolatry, which is forbidden, Deut. 12:30.

10:4 ¹ The Prophets use thus plainly and simply to set forth the vile absurdity of the idolaters, that men might learn to be ashamed of that whereunto their corrupt nature is most subject, read Isa. 44:12.

10:6 ¹ He teacheth the people to lift up their eyes to God, who hath all power and therefore ought only to be feared: and herein he showeth them not only the evil that they ought to eschew: but the good which they ought to follow, Rev. 15:4.

10:8 ¹ Because the people thought that to have images, was a means to serve God, and to bring them to the knowledge of him, he showeth that nothing more displeaseth God, nor bringeth man into greater errors and ignorance of God: and therefore he calleth them the doctrine of vanity, the work of errors, verse 15, and Hab. 2:18 calleth them the teachers of lies: contrary to that wicked opinion, that they are the books of the lay people.

10:9 ¹ Whereas they found the best gold: showing that they thought nothing too dear for their idols, some read Ophir, as 1 Kings 9:28.

10:11 ¹ This declareth that all that hath been in this chapter spoken of idols, was to arm the Jews when they should be in Chaldea among the idolaters, and now with one sentence he instructeth them both how to protect their own religion against the idolaters, and how to answer them to their shame which should exhort them to idolatry, and therefore he writeth this sentence in the Chaldean's tongue for a memorial, whereas all the rest of his writing is Hebrew.

10:14 ¹ The more that man thinketh to do anything well by his own wisdom, and not as God instructeth him, the more doth he prove himself to be a vile beast.

10:16 ¹ By these words Portion and Rod, he signifieth their inheritance, meaning, that God should be all sufficient for them: and that their felicity consisted in him alone, and therefore they ought to renounce all other helps and succors as of idols, etc. Deut. 32:9; Ps. 16:5.

17 ¶ [1]Gather up thy wares out of the land, O thou that dwellest in the strong place.

18 For thus saith the Lord, Behold, at this time I will throw as with a sling the inhabitants of the land, and will trouble them, and they shall find it *so*.

19 Woe is me for my destruction, *and* my grievous plague: but I thought, Yet it [1]is my sorrow, and I will bear it.

20 [1]My Tabernacle is destroyed, and all my cords are broken: my children are gone from me, and are not: there is none to spread out my tent anymore, and to set up my curtains.

21 For the Pastors [1]are become beasts, and have not sought the Lord: therefore have they none understanding: and all the *flocks* of their pastures are scattered.

22 Behold, the noise of the bruit is come, and a great commotion out of the [1]North country, to make the cities of Judah desolate, *and* a den of dragons.

23 O Lord, I know that [1]the way of man is not in himself, neither *is it* in man to walk and to direct his steps.

24 O Lord, correct me, but with [1]judgment, not in thine anger, lest thou bring me to nothing.

25 Pour out [1]thy wrath upon the heathen that know thee not, and upon the families that call not on thy Name: for they have eaten up Jacob, and devoured him, and consumed him, and have made his habitation desolate.

11

3 *A curse of them that obey not the word of God's covenant.* 10 *The people of Judah following the steps of their fathers, worship strange gods.* 15 *The Lord forbiddeth Jeremiah to pray for them.*

1 The word that came to Jeremiah from the Lord, saying,

2 Hear ye the words of this covenant, and speak unto the men of Judah, and to the inhabitants of Jerusalem,

3 And say thou unto them, Thus saith the Lord God of Israel, [1]Cursed be the man that obeyeth not the words of this covenant,

4 Which I commanded unto your fathers, when I brought them out of the land of Egypt, from the iron furnace, saying, Obey my voice, and do according to all these things which I command you: so shall ye be my people, and I will be your God,

5 That I may confirm the oath, that I have sworn unto your fathers, to give them a land, which floweth with milk and honey, as *appeareth* this day. Then answered [1]I, and said, So be it, O Lord.

6 Then the Lord said unto me, Cry all these words in the cities of Judah, and in the streets of Jerusalem, saying, Hear ye the words of this covenant, and do them.

7 For I have protested unto your fathers, when I brought them up out of the land of Egypt unto this day, [1]rising early and protesting, saying, Obey my voice.

8 Nevertheless they would not obey, nor incline their ear: but everyone walked in the stubbornness of his [1]wicked heart: therefore I will bring upon them all the [2]words of this covenant which I commanded them to do, but they did it not.

9 And the Lord said unto me, A [1]conspiracy is found among the men of Judah, and among the inhabitants of Jerusalem.

10 They are turned back to the iniquities of their forefathers, which refused to hear my words: and they went after other gods to serve them: *thus* the house of Israel and the house of Judah have broken my covenant, which I made with their fathers.

11 Therefore thus saith the Lord, Behold, I will bring a plague upon them, which they shall not be able to escape, and though they cry unto me, [1]I will

---

10:17 [1] The Prophet willeth the Jews to prepare themselves to this captivity, showing that it was now at hand that they should feel the things whereof he had told them.

10:19 [1] It is my just plague, and therefore I will take it patiently: whereby he teacheth the people how to behave themselves toward God.

10:20 [1] He showeth how Jerusalem shall lament.

10:21 [1] The governors and ministers.

10:22 [1] Read Jer. 4:15.

10:23 [1] He speaketh this because that Nebuchadnezzar purposed to have made war against the Moabites and Ammonites, but hearing of Zedekiah's rebellion, he turned his power to go against Jerusalem, Ezek. 21:21, therefore the Prophet saith, that this was the Lord's direction.

10:24 [1] Considering that God had revealed unto him the certitude of their captivity, Jer. 7:16, he only prayeth, that he would punish them with mercy, which Isaiah calleth in measure, Isa. 27:8, measuring his rods by their infirmity, 1 Cor. 10:13, for here by judgment is meant not only the punishment, but also the merciful moderation of the same, as Jer. 30:11.

10:25 [1] Forasmuch as God cannot only be known and glorified by his mercy, that he useth toward his Church, but also by his justice in punishing his enemies, he prayeth that this glory may fully appear both in the one and the other, Ps. 79:6.

11:3 [1] He calleth the Jews to the consideration of God's mercy, who freely chose them, made a covenant of eternal felicity with them, and how he ever performed it on his behalf, and how they ever showed themselves rebellious and ingrate toward him, and brake it on their part, and so are subject to the curse of the Law, Deut. 27:26.

11:5 [1] Thus he speaketh in the person of the people, which agreed to the covenant.

11:7 [1] Read Jer. 7:13.

11:8 [1] According to his own fantasy, and not as my word appointed him.

[2] Meaning, the menaces and curses contained in the Law, Lev. 26:14; Deut. 28:16.

11:9 [1] That is, a general consent to rebel against me.

11:11 [1] Because they will not pray with true faith and repentance, but for the smart and grief which they feel, Prov. 1:28.

not hear them.

12 Then shall the cities of Judah, and the inhabitants of Jerusalem go, and cry unto the gods unto whom they offer incense, but they shall not be able to help them in time of their trouble.

13 [1]For according to the number of thy cities were thy gods, O Judah, and *according* to the number of the streets of Jerusalem have ye set up altars of confusion, *even* altars to burn incense unto Baal.

14 Therefore thou shalt not [1]pray for this people, neither lift up a cry or prayer for them: for when they cry unto me in their trouble, I will not hear them.

15 What should my [1]beloved *tarry* in mine house, seeing they have committed abomination with many, and the holy flesh [2]goeth away from thee: yet when thou doest evil, thou rejoicest.

16 The Lord called thy name, A green olive tree, fair, *and* of goodly fruit: *but* with [1]noise and great tumult he hath set fire upon it, and the branches of it are broken.

17 For the Lord of hosts that planted thee, hath pronounced a plague against thee, for the wickedness of the house of Israel, and of the house of Judah, which they have done against themselves to provoke me to anger in offering incense unto Baal,

18 And the Lord hath taught me, and I know it, *even* then thou showedst me [1]their practices.

19 But I was like a lamb, *or* a bullock, that is brought to the slaughter, and I knew not that they had devised thus against me, *saying*, Let us [1]destroy the tree with the fruit thereof, and cut him out of the land of the living, that his name may be no more in memory,

20 But O Lord of hosts, that judgest righteously, and triest the reins and the heart, let me see thy [1]vengeance on them: for unto thee have I opened my cause.

21 The Lord therefore speaketh thus of the men of [1]Anathoth, (that seek thy life, and say, [2]Prophesy not in the name of the Lord, that thou die not by our hands.)

22 Thus therefore saith the Lord of hosts, Behold, I will visit them: the young men shall die by the sword: their sons and their daughters shall die by famine,

23 And none of them shall remain: for I will bring a plague upon the men of Anathoth, *even* the year of their visitation.

12 1 *The Prophet marvelleth at the prosperity of the wicked, although he confess God to be righteous.* 7 *The Jews are forsaken of the Lord.* 10 *He speaketh against pastors and preachers, that seduce the people.* 14 *The Lord threateneth destruction unto the nations that troubled Judah.*

1 O Lord, if I dispute with thee, thou art [1]righteous: yet let me talk with thee of *thy* judgments: wherefore doth the way of the wicked [2]prosper? why are all they in wealth that rebelliously transgress?

2 Thou hast planted them, and they have taken root: they grow, and bring forth fruit, thou art near in their mouth, and far from their [1]reins.

3 But thou, Lord, knowest me: thou hast seen me, and tried mine heart toward thee: pull them out like sheep for the slaughter, and [1]prepare them for the day of slaughter.

4 How long shall the land mourn, and the herbs of every field wither, for the wickedness of them that dwell therein? the beasts are consumed, and the birds, because they said, [1]He will not see our last end.

5 If thou hast run with the [1]footmen, and they have wearied thee, then how canst thou match thyself with horses? and if thou thoughtest thyself safe in

---

11:13 [1] Read Jer. 2:28.

11:14 [1] Read Jer. 7:16 and 14:11.

11:15 [1] My people of Israel, whom I have hitherto so greatly loved.
[2] Meaning, that they offer not in the Temple to God, but on the altars of Baal and the idols, and so rejoiced in their wickedness.

11:16 [1] Of the Babylonians and Chaldeans.

11:18 [1] Which went about privily to conspire my death.

11:19 [1] Let us destroy the Prophet and his doctrine. Some read, Let us corrupt his meat with wood, meaning, poison.

11:20 [1] Thus he spake, not for hatred, but being moved with the Spirit of God, he desireth the advancement of God's glory, and the verifying of his word, which is by the destruction of his enemies.

11:21 [1] To wit, both the Priests and the rest of the people: for this town was the Priests, and they dwelt in it, read Jer. 1:1.
[2] Not that they could not abide to hear God named: (for herein they would show themselves most holy) but because they could not abide to be sharply reproved, and therefore desired to be flattered, Isa. 30:10, and to be maintained in their pleasures, Mic. 2:11, and not to hear vice condemned, Amos 7:12.

12:1 [1] The Prophet confesseth God to be just in all his doings, although man be not able to give a reason of all his acts.

[2] This question hath been always a great tentation to the godly, to see the wicked enemies of God in prosperity, and his dear children in adversity, as Job 21:7; Ps. 37:1 and 73:3; Hab. 1:3.

12:2 [1] They profess God in mouth, but deny him in heart, which is here meant by the reins, Isa. 29:13; Matt. 15:8.

12:3 [1] The Hebrew word is, Sanctify them, meaning, that God would be sanctified in the destruction of the wicked, to whom God for a while giveth prosperity, that afterward they should the more feel his heavy judgment when they lack their riches which were a sign of his mercy.

12:4 [1] Abusing God's lenity and his promises, they flattered themselves as though God would ever be merciful, and not utterly destroy them: therefore they hardened themselves in sin, till at length the beasts and insensible creatures felt the punishment of their stubborn rebellion against God.

12:5 [1] Some think that God reproveth Jeremiah, in that that he would reason with him, saying, that if he were not able to march with men, that he were far unable to dispute with God. Others, by the footmen, mean them of Anathoth: and by the horsemen, them of Jerusalem, which should trouble the Prophet worse than his own countrymen did.

a peaceable land, what wilt thou do in the swelling of Jordan?

6 For even thy brethren and the house of thy father, even they have dealt unfaithfully with thee, and they have cried out altogether upon thee: *but* believe them not, though they speak fair to thee.

7 I have forsaken ¹mine house: I have left mine heritage: I have given the dearly beloved of my soul into the hands of her enemies.

8 Mine heritage is unto me, as a ¹lion in the forest: it crieth out against me, therefore have I hated it.

9 Shall mine heritage be unto me, as a bird ¹of divers colors? are not the birds about her, *saying*, Come, assemble all the beasts of the field, come to eat her?

10 Many pastors have destroyed my ¹vineyard, and trodden my portion under foot: of my pleasant portion they have made a desolate wilderness.

11 They have laid it waste, and it, being waste mourneth unto me, *and* the whole land lieth waste, because no man setteth *his* mind on ¹it.

12 The destroyers are come upon all the high places in the wilderness: for the sword of the Lord shall devour from the one end of the land, even to the *other* end of the land: no flesh shall have peace.

13 ¹They have sown wheat, and reaped thorns: they were ²sick, *and* had no profit: and they were ashamed of ³your fruits, because of the fierce wrath of the Lord.

14 Thus saith the Lord against all mine evil ¹neighbors, that touch the inheritance, which I have caused my people Israel to inherit, Behold, I will pluck them out of their land, and pluck out the house of Judah from among them.

15 And after that I have plucked them out, I ¹will return, and have compassion on them, and will bring again every man to his heritage, and every man to his land.

16 And if they will learn the ¹ways of my people, to swear by my Name, (The ²Lord liveth, as they taught my people to swear by Baal) then shall they be built ³in the midst of my people.

17 But if they will not obey, then will I utterly pluck up, and destroy that nation, saith the Lord.

13 *The destruction of the Jews is prefigured.* 11 Why *Israel was received to be the people of God, and why they were forsaken.* 15 He exhorteth them to repentance.

1 Thus saith the Lord unto me, Go, and buy thee a linen girdle, and put it upon thy loins, and put it not in water.

2 So I bought the girdle according to the commandment of the Lord, and put it upon my loins.

3 And the word of the Lord came unto me the second time, saying,

4 Take the girdle that thou hast bought, which is upon thy loins, and arise, go toward ¹Perath, and hide it there in the cleft of the rock.

5 So I went, and hid it by Perath, as the Lord had commanded me.

6 And after many days the Lord said unto me, Arise, go toward Perath, and take the girdle from thence, which I commanded thee to hide there.

7 Then went I to Perath, and dug, and took the girdle from the place where I had hid it, and behold, the girdle was corrupt, *and* was profitable for nothing.

8 Then the word of the Lord came unto me, saying,

9 Thus saith the Lord, After this manner will I destroy the pride of Judah, and the great pride of Jerusalem.

10 This wicked people have refused to hear my word, and walk after the stubbornness of their own heart, and walk after other gods to serve them, and to worship them: therefore they shall be as this girdle, which is profitable to nothing.

11 For as the girdle cleaveth to the loins of a man, so have I tied to me the whole house of Israel, and the whole house of Judah, saith the Lord, that they might be my people: that they might have a name, and praise, and glory, but they would not hear.

12:7 ¹ God willeth the Prophet to denounce his judgments against Jerusalem, notwithstanding that they shall both by threatenings and flatteries, labor to put him to silence.
12:8 ¹ Ever ramping and raging against me and my Prophets.
12:9 ¹ Instead of bearing my livery, and wearing only my colors, they have change and diversity of colors of their idols and superstitions, therefore their enemies as thick as the fowls of the air shall come about them to destroy them.
12:10 ¹ He prophecieth of the destruction of Jerusalem, by the captains of Nebuchadnezzar, whom he calleth pastors.
12:11 ¹ Because no man regardeth my word, or the plagues that I have sent upon the land.
12:13 ¹ To wit, the Prophets.
² They lamented the sins of the people.
³ For instead of amendment, you grew worse and worse, as God's plagues testified.
12:14 ¹ Meaning, the wicked enemies of his Church, which blasphemed his Name, and whom he would punish after that he hath delivered his people.
12:15 ¹ After that I have punished the Gentiles, I will have mercy upon them.
12:16 ¹ The true doctrine and manner to serve God.
² Read Jer. 4:2.
³ They shall be of the number of the faithful, and have a place in my Church.
13:4 ¹ Because this river Perath or Euphrates was far from Jerusalem, it is evident that this was a vision, whereby was signified that the Jews should pass over Euphrates to be captives in Babylon, and there for length of time should seem to be rotten, although they were joined to the Lord before as a girdle about a man.

12 Therefore thou shalt say unto them this word, Thus saith the Lord God of Israel, Every ¹bottle shall be filled with wine, and they shall say unto thee, do we not know that every bottle shall be filled with wine?

13 Then shalt thou say unto them, Thus saith the Lord, Behold, I will fill all the inhabitants of this land, even the kings that sit upon the throne of David, and the Priests and the Prophets, and all the inhabitants of Jerusalem with drunkenness.

14 And I will ¹dash them one against another, even the fathers and the sons together, saith the Lord: I will not spare, I will not pity, nor have compassion, but destroy them.

15 Hear and give ear, be not proud: for the Lord hath spoken it.

16 Give glory to the Lord your God before he bring ¹darkness, and or ever your feet stumble in the dark mountains, and while you look for ²light, he turn it into the shadow of death *and* make it as darkness.

17 But if ye will not hear this, my soul shall ¹weep in secret for *your* pride, and mine eye shall weep and drop down tears, because the Lord's flock is carried away captive.

18 Say unto the ¹King and to the Queen: Humble yourselves, sit down, for the crown of your glory shall come down from your heads.

19 The cities of ¹the South shall be shut up, and no man shall open them: all Judah shall be carried away captive: it shall be wholly carried away captive:

20 Lift up your eyes, and behold them that come from the North: where is the ¹flock that was given thee, *even* thy beautiful flock?

21 What wilt thou say when he shall visit thee? (for thou hast ¹taught them to be captains *and* as chief over thee) shall not sorrow take thee as a woman in travail?

22 And if thou say in thine heart, Wherefore come these things upon me? For the multitude of thine iniquities are thy skirts ¹discovered *and* thy heels made bare.

23 Can the black Moor change his skin? or the leopard his spots, *then* may ye also do good, that are accustomed to do evil?

24 Therefore will I scatter them, as the stubble that is taken away with the South wind.

25 This is thy portion, *and* the part of thy measures from me, saith the Lord, because thou hast forgotten me, and trusted in lies.

26 Therefore I have also discovered thy skirts upon thy face, ¹that thy shame may appear.

27 I have seen thine adulteries, and thy ¹neighings, the filthiness of thy whoredom on the hills in ²the fields, *and* thine abominations. [Woe] unto thee, O Jerusalem: wilt thou not be made clean? when shall it once be?

14 1 Of the death that should come. 7 The prayer of the people asking mercy of the Lord. 10 The unfaithful people are not heard. 12 Of prayer, fasting, and of false prophets that seduce the people.

1 The word of the Lord that came unto Jeremiah, concerning the ¹,²dearth.

2 Judah hath mourned, and the gates thereof are desolate, they have been ¹brought to heaviness unto the ground, and the cry of Jerusalem goeth up.

3 And their nobles have sent their inferiors to the water, who came to the wells, *and* found no water: they returned with their vessels empty: they were ashamed and confounded: and ¹covered their heads.

4 For the ground was destroyed, because there was no rain in the earth: the plowmen were ashamed, *and* covered their heads.

5 Yea, the hind also calved in the field, and forsook ¹it, because there was no grass.

6 And the wild asses did stand in the high places, and drew in their wind like ¹dragons: their eyes did fail, because there was no grass.

7 ¹O Lord, though our iniquities testify against us, deal *with us* according to thy Name: for our

13:12 ¹ Every one of you shall be filled with spiritual drunkenness, and be without all knowledge to seek how to help yourselves.

13:14 ¹ It shall be as easy for me to destroy the greatest and the strongest, as it is for a man to break earthen bottles.

13:16 ¹ That is, affliction and misery by the Babylonians, Isa. 8:22.
² Meaning, for help and support of the Egyptians.

13:17 ¹ You shall surely be led away captive, and I, according to mine affection towards you, shall weep and lament for your stubbornness.

13:18 ¹ For Jehoiachin and his mother rendered themselves by Jeremiah's counsel to the king of Babylon, 2 Kings 24:12.

13:19 ¹ That is, of Judah, which lieth Southward from Babylon.

13:20 ¹ He asketh the king, where his people be become.

13:21 ¹ By seeking to strangers for help, thou hast made them skillful to fight against thee.

13:22 ¹ The cloak of hypocrisy shall be pulled off, and thy shame seen.

13:26 ¹ As thine iniquities have been manifest to all the world, so shall thy shame and punishment.

13:27 ¹ He compareth idolaters to horses inflamed after mares.
² There is no place so high nor low, whereas the marks and signs of thine idolatry appear not.

14:1 ¹ Which came for lack of rain, as verse 4.
² Or, restraint.

14:2 ¹ The word signifieth to be made black, and so is here taken for extreme sorrow.

14:3 ¹ To wit, with ashes in token of sorrow.

14:5 ¹ Meaning, that the brute beasts for drought were compelled to forsake their young, contrary to nature, and to go seek water which they could not find.

14:6 ¹ Which are so hot of nature, that they cannot be cooled with drinking of water, but still gape for the air to resisteth them.

14:7 ¹ He showeth the only way to remedy to God's plagues, which is by unfeigned confession of our sins, and returning to him by repentance.

rebellions are many, we sinned against thee.

8 O thou hope of Israel, the savior thereof in the time of trouble, why art thou as a ¹stranger in the land, as one that passeth by, to tarry for a night?

9 Why art thou as a man astonied, and as ¹a strong man that cannot help? yet thou, O Lord, art in the midst of us, and thy name is called upon us: forsake us not.

10 Thus saith the Lord unto this people, Thus have they delighted to wander: they have not refrained their feet, therefore the Lord hath no delight in them: *but* he will now remember their iniquity, and visit their sins.

11 Then said the Lord unto me, ¹Thou shalt not pray to do this people good.

12 When they fast, I will not hear their cry, and when they offer burnt offering, and an oblation, I will not accept them: but I will consume them by the sword, and by the famine, and by the pestilence.

13 Then answered I, Ah Lord God, behold, the ¹prophets say unto them, Ye shall not see the sword, neither shall famine come upon you, but I will give you assured peace in this place.

14 Then the Lord said unto me, The prophets prophesy lies in my name: ªI have not sent them, neither did I command them, neither spake I unto them, *but* they prophesy unto you a false vision, and divination, and vanity, and deceitfulness of their own heart.

15 Therefore thus saith the Lord, Concerning the prophets that prophesy in my Name, whom I have not sent, yet they say, Sword and famine shall not be in this land, by sword and famine shall those prophets be consumed.

16 And the people to whom these prophets do prophesy shall be cast out in the streets of Jerusalem, because of the famine, and the sword, and there shall be none to bury them: *both* they and their wives, and their sons, and their daughters: for I will pour their wickedness upon them.

17 Therefore thou shalt say this word unto them, Let mine eyes drop down ¹tears night and day with-

CHAPTER 14
ª Jer. 23:21
Jer. 27:10,15
Jer. 29:9

CHAPTER 15
ª Zech. 11:9

out ceasing: for the virgin daughter of my people is destroyed with a great destruction, *and* with a sore grievous plague.

18 For if I go into the field, behold the slain with the sword: and if I enter into the city, behold them that are sick for hunger also: moreover, the Prophet also and the Priest go a wandering ¹into a land that they know not.

19 Hast thou utterly rejected ¹Judah, or hath thy soul abhorred Zion? why hast thou smitten us, that we cannot be healed? We looked for peace, and there is no good, and for the time of health, and behold trouble.

20 We ¹acknowledge, O Lord, our wickedness, *and* the iniquity of our fathers: for we have sinned against thee.

21 Do not abhor *us*: for thy Name's sake cast not down the throne of thy glory: remember *and* break not thy covenant with us.

22 Are there any among the ¹vanities of the Gentiles, that can give rain? or can the heavens give showers? Is it not thou, O Lord our God? therefore we will wait upon thee: for thou hast made all these things.

15

1 *The Lord would hear no prayer for the Jews,* 3 *but threateneth to destroy them with four plagues.*

1 Then said the Lord unto me, ¹Though Moses and Samuel stood before me, *yet* mine affection could not be toward this people: cast *them* out of my sight, and let them depart.

2 And if they say unto thee, Whither shall we depart? then tell them, Thus saith the Lord, ªSuch as are *appointed* to death, unto death: and such as are for the sword, to the sword: and such as are for the famine, to the famine: and such as are for the captivity, to the captivity.

3 And I will appoint over them four kinds, saith the Lord, the sword to slay, and the ¹dogs to tear in pieces, and the fowls of the heaven, and the beasts of the earth to devour, and to destroy.

4 I will ¹scatter them also in all kingdoms of the

14:8 ¹ That taketh no care for us.
14:9 ¹ As one that hath strength to help, and yet is afraid to put to his hand.
14:11 ¹ Read Jer. 7:16 and 11:14.
14:13 ¹ He pitieth the people, and accuseth the false prophets, which deceived them: but the Lord answered, that both the prophets, which deceived, and the people, which suffered themselves to be seduced, shall perish, Jer. 23:15 and 27:8, 9 and 29:8.
14:17 ¹ The false prophets promised peace and assurance, but Jeremiah calleth to tears, and repentance for their affliction, which is at hand, as Jer. 9:1; Lam. 1:16 and 2:18.
14:18 ¹ Both high and low shall be led captives into Babylon.
14:19 ¹ Though the Prophet knew that God had cast off the multitude, which were hypocrites, and bastard children, yet he was

assured that for his promise sake he would have still a Church, for the which he prayeth.
14:20 ¹ He teacheth the Church a form of prayer to humble themselves to God by true repentance, which is the only means to avoid this famine, which was the beginning of God's plagues.
14:22 ¹ Meaning, their idols, read Jer. 10:15.
15:1 ¹ Meaning, that if there were any man living moved with so great zeal toward the people as were these two, yet that he would not grant this request, forasmuch as he had determined the contrary, Ezek. 14:14.
15:3 ¹ The dogs, birds, and beasts should devour them that were slain.
15:4 ¹ The word signifieth to run to and fro for fear, and unquietness of conscience, as did Cain.

earth, ²because of Manasseh the son of Hezekiah King of Judah for that which he did in Jerusalem.

5 Who shall then have pity upon thee, O Jerusalem? or who shall be sorry for thee? or who shall go to pray for thy peace?

6 Thou hast forsaken me, saith the Lord, *and* gone backward: therefore will I stretch out mine hand against thee, and destroy thee: *for* I ¹am weary with repenting.

7 And I will scatter them with the fan ¹in the gates of the earth: I have wasted, *and* destroyed my people, *yet* they would not return from their ways.

8 Their widows ¹are increased by me above the sand of the sea: I have brought upon them, *and* against the ²assembly of the young men, a destroyer at noon day: I have caused *him* to fall upon them, *and* the city, suddenly and ³speedily.

9 She that hath borne ¹seven, hath been made weak: her heart hath failed: the sun hath failed ²her, while it was day, she hath been confounded, and ashamed, and the residue of them will I deliver unto the sword before their enemies, saith the Lord.

10 ¶ ¹Woe is me, my mother, that thou hast borne me, a contentious man, and a man that striveth with the whole earth: I have neither ²lent on usury, nor men have lent unto me on usury: *yet* everyone doth curse me.

11 The Lord said, ¹Surely thy remnant shall have wealth: surely I will cause thine enemy to entreat thee in the time of trouble, and in the time of affliction.

12 Shall the ¹iron break the iron, and the brass *that cometh* from the North?

13 Thy substance and thy treasures will I give to be spoiled without ¹gain, and that for all thy sins even in all thy borders.

14 And I will make thee to go with thine enemies into a land that thou knowest not, for a fire is kindled in mine anger, *which* shall burn you.

15 O Lord, thou knowest, remember me, and visit me, and revenge me of my ¹persecutors: take me not away in the continuance of thine anger: know that for thy sake I have suffered rebuke.

16 Thy words were found *by me*, and I did ¹eat them, and thy word was unto me the joy and rejoicing of mine heart: for thy Name is called upon me, O Lord God of hosts.

17 I sat not in the assembly of the mockers, neither did I rejoice, but sat alone ¹because of thy plague: for thou hast filled me with indignation.

18 Why is mine heaviness continual? and my plague desperate *and* cannot be healed, *why* art thou unto me ¹as a liar, *and as* waters that fail?

19 Therefore thus saith the Lord, If thou ¹return, then will I bring thee again, *and* thou shalt stand before me: and if thou take away the ²precious from the vile, thou shalt be ³according to my word: let them return ⁴unto thee, but return not thou unto them.

20 And I will make thee unto this people a strong brazen wall, and they shall fight against thee, but they shall not ¹prevail against thee: for I am with thee to save thee, and to deliver thee, saith the Lord.

21 And I will deliver thee out of the hand of the wicked, and I will redeem thee out of the hand of the tyrants.

16 *2 The Lord forbidding Jeremiah to marry, showeth him what should be the afflictions upon Judah. 13 The captivity of Babylon. 15 Their deliverance. 19 The calling of the Gentiles.*

15:4 ² Not that the people was punished for the king's sin only, but for their own sins also, because they consented to his wickedness, 2 Kings 21:9.

15:6 ¹ That is, I will not call back my plagues or spare thee any more.

15:7 ¹ Meaning, the cities.

15:8 ¹ Because I had slain their husbands.

² Or, mother.

³ Or, fearfully.

15:9 ¹ She that had many, lost all her children.

² She was destroyed in the midst of her prosperity.

15:10 ¹ By these are the Prophet's words, complaining of the obstinacy of the people and that he was reserved to so wicked a time: wherein also he showeth what is the condition of God's ministers, to wit, to have all the world against them, though they give none occasion.

² Which is an occasion of contention and hatred.

15:11 ¹ In this perplexity the Lord comforted me, and said that my last days should be quiet: and by the enemy he meaneth here, Nebuzaradan the captain of Nebuchadnezzar, who gave Jeremiah the choice either to remain in his country, or to go whither he would: or by the enemy he meaneth the Jews, which should afterward know Jeremiah's fidelity, and therefore favor him.

15:12 ¹ As for the people, though they seemed strong as iron, yet should they not be able to resist the hard iron of Babylon, but should be led captives.

15:13 ¹ Or, ransom.

15:15 ¹ He speaketh not this for desire of revengeance, but wishing that God would deliver his Church of them whom he knew to be hardened and incorrigible.

15:16 ¹ I received them with a great joy, as he that is famished, eateth meat.

15:17 ¹ I had nothing a do with the wicked contemners of thy word, but lamented bitterly for thy plagues: showing what the faithful should do when they see tokens of God's anger.

15:18 ¹ And hast not assisted me according to the promise? wherein appeareth that in the Saints of God is imperfection of faith, which through impatience is ofttimes assailed, as Jer. 20:7.

15:19 ¹ If thou forget these carnal considerations, and faithfully execute thy charge.

² That is, seek to win the good from the bad.

³ To wit, as my mouth hath pronounced, Jer. 1:18, and as here followeth, verse 20.

⁴ Conform not thyself to their wickedness, but let them follow thy godly example.

15:20 ¹ I will learn thee with an invincible strength and constancy, so that all the powers of the world shall not overcome thee.

1 The word of the Lord came also unto me, saying,

2 Thou shalt not take ¹thee a wife, nor have sons nor daughters in this place.

3 For thus saith the Lord concerning the sons, and concerning the daughters, that are born in this place, and concerning their mothers that bear them, and concerning their fathers that beget them in this land,

4 They shall die of deaths *and* diseases: they shall not be lamented, neither shall they be buried, *but* they shall be as dung upon the earth, and they shall be consumed by the sword, and by famine, and their carcasses shall be meat for the fowls of the heaven, and for the beasts of the earth.

5 For thus saith the Lord, ¹Enter not into the house of mourning, neither go to lament, nor be moved for them: for I have taken my peace from this people, saith the Lord, *even* mercy and compassion.

6 Both the great, and the small shall die in this land: they shall not be buried, neither shall men lament for them, ¹nor cut themselves, nor make themselves bald for them.

7 They shall not stretch out *the hands* for them in the mourning to comfort them for the dead, neither shall they give them the ¹cup of consolation to drink for their father or for their mother.

8 Thou shalt not also go into the house of feasting, to sit with them to eat and to drink.

9 For thus saith the Lord of hosts, the God of Israel, Behold, I will cause to cease out of this place in your eyes, even in your days, the voice of mirth, and the voice of gladness, the voice of the bridegroom, and the voice of the bride.

10 And when thou shalt show this people all these words, and they shall say unto thee, ªWherefore hath the Lord pronounced all this great plague against us? or what is ¹our iniquity? and what is our sin that we have committed against the Lord our God?

11 Then shalt thou say unto them, Because your fathers have forsaken me, saith the Lord, and have walked after other gods, and have served them, and worshipped them, and have forsaken me, and have not kept my Law,

12 (ᵇAnd ye have done worse than your fathers:

CHAPTER 16
ª Jer. 5:19
ᵇ Jer. 7:26
ᶜ Jer. 23:7

for behold, you walk everyone after the stubbornness of his wicked heart, and will not hear me.)

13 Therefore will I drive you out of this land into a land that ye know not, *neither* you nor your fathers, and there ye shall serve other gods day and night: for I will show you no grace.

14 ᶜBehold therefore saith the Lord, the days come that it shall no more be said, The Lord liveth, which brought up the children of Israel out of the land of Egypt,

15 But, The Lord liveth, that brought up the children of Israel ¹from the land of the North, and from all the lands where he had scattered them, and I will bring them again into their land that I gave unto their fathers.

16 Behold, saith the Lord, I will send out many ¹fishers, and they shall fish them, and after will I send out many hunters, and they shall hunt them from every mountain, and from every hill, and out of the caves of the rocks.

17 For mine eyes *are* upon all their ways: they are not hid from my face, neither is their iniquity hid from mine eyes.

18 And first I will recompense their iniquity and their sin double, because they have defiled my land, *and* have filled mine inheritance with their filthy ¹carrions and their abominations.

19 O Lord, *thou art* my ¹fortress, and my strength and my refuge in the day of affliction: the Gentiles shall come unto thee from the ends of the world, and shall say, Surely our fathers have inherited ²lies, *and* vanity, wherein there was no profit.

20 Shall a man make gods unto himself, and they are no gods?

21 Behold, therefore I will this once ¹teach them: I will show them mine hand and my power, and they shall know that my Name is the Lord.

17 1 *The frowardness of the Jews.* 5 *Cursed be those that put their confidence in man.* 9 *Man's heart is wicked.* 10 *God is the searcher of the heart.* 13 *The living waters are forsaken.* 21 *The right keeping of the Sabbath commanded.*

16:2 ¹ Meaning, that the affliction should be so horrible in Jerusalem, that wife and children should but increase his sorrow.

16:5 ¹ Signifying, that the affliction should be so great, that one should not have leisure to comfort another.

16:6 ¹ That is, should not rent their clothes in sign of mourning.

16:7 ¹ For in these great extremities all consolation and comfort shall be in vain.

16:10 ¹ Because the wicked are always rebellious, and dissemble their own sins, and murmur against God's judgments, as though he had no just cause to punish them, he showeth him what to answer.

16:15 ¹ Signifying, the benefit of their deliverance out of Babylon should be so great, that it should abolish the remembrance of their deliverance from Egypt: but he hath here chiefly respect to the spiri-

tual deliverance under Christ.

16:16 ¹ By the fishers and hunters are meant the Babylonians and Chaldeans, who should destroy them in such sort, that if they escaped the one, the other should take them.

16:18 ¹ That is, their sons and daughters, which they offered to Molech.

16:19 ¹ He wondereth at the great mercy of God in this deliverance, which shall not only extend to the Jews, but also to the Gentiles.

² Our fathers were most vile idolaters, therefore it cometh only of God's mercy, that he performeth his promise, and hath not utterly cast us off.

16:21 ¹ They shall once again feel my power and mercy for their deliverance, that they may learn to worship me.

1 The sin of Judah is [1]written with a pen of iron, *and* with the point of a diamond, *and* graven upon the [2]table of their heart, and upon the horns of your [3]altars.

2 [1]They remember their altars as their children, with their groves by the green trees upon the high hills.

3 [1]O my mountain in the field, I will give thy substance, *and* all thy treasures to be spoiled, for the sin of thy high places throughout all thy borders.

4 And thou shalt rest, [1]and in thee *shall be a rest* from thine heritage that I gave thee, and I will cause thee to serve thine enemies in the land, which thou knowest not: for ye have kindled a fire in mine anger, *which* shall burn forever.

5 ¶ Thus saith the Lord, [1]Cursed *be* the man that trusteth in man, and maketh flesh his arm, and withdraweth his heart from the Lord.

6 For he shall be like the heath in the wilderness, and shall not see when *any* good cometh, but shall inhabit the parched places in the wilderness, in a salt land, and not inhabited.

7 Blessed *be* the man that trusteth in the Lord, and whose hope the Lord is.

8 [1]For he shall be as a tree that is planted by the water, which spreadeth out her roots by the river, and shall not feel when the heat cometh, but her leaf shall be green, and shall not care for the year of drought, neither shall cease from yielding fruit.

9 [1]The heart is deceitful and wicked above all things, who can know it?

10 I the Lord search the heart, *and* try the reins, even to give every man according to his ways, *and* according to the fruit of his works.

11 [1]*As* the partridge gathereth *the young*, which she hath not brought forth: *so* he that getteth riches, and not by right, shall leave them in the midst of his days, and at his end shall be a fool.

12 *As* a glorious throne [1]exalted from the beginning, *so is* the place of our Sanctuary.

13 O Lord, the hope of Israel, that forsake thee, shall be confounded: they that depart from thee, shall be written [1]in the earth, because they have forsaken the Lord, the fountain of living waters.

14 Heal me, O Lord, and I shall be whole: [1]save me, and I shall be saved: for thou art my praise.

15 Behold, [1]they say unto me, Where is the word of the Lord? let it come now.

16 But [1]I have not thrust in myself for a pastor after thee, neither have I desired the day of misery, thou knowest that which came out of my lips was *right* before thee.

17 Be not [1]terrible unto me: thou art mine hope in the day of adversity.

18 Let them be confounded, that persecute me, but let not me be confounded: let them be afraid, but let not me be afraid: bring upon them the day of adversity, [1]and, destroy them with double destruction.

19 Thus hath the Lord said unto me, Go and stand in the [1]gate of the children of the people, whereby the Kings of Judah come in, and by the which they go out, and in all the gates of Jerusalem,

20 And say unto them, Hear the word of the Lord, ye kings of Judah, and all Judah, and all the inhabitants of Jerusalem, that enter in by these gates.

21 Thus saith the Lord, Take heed to your souls, and bear no burden in the [1]Sabbath day, nor bring it in by the gates of Jerusalem.

17:1 [1] The remembrance of their contempt of God cannot pass, albeit for a time he defer the punishment, for it shall be manifest to men and Angels.

[2] Instead of the Law of God, they have written idolatry and all abominations in their heart.

[3] Your sins appear in all the altars that you have erected to idols.

17:2 [1] Some read, So that their children remember their altars, that is, follow their fathers' wickedness.

17:3 [1] Zion that was my mountain, shall now be left as a waste field.

17:4 [1] Because thou wouldest not give the land rest, at such times, days, and years as I appointed, thou shalt hereafter be carried away, and it shall rest for lack of laborers.

17:5 [1] The Jews were given to worldly policies, and thought to make themselves strong by the friendship of the Egyptians, Isa. 31:3, and strangers, and in the mean season did not depend on God, and therefore he denounceth God's plagues against them, showing that they prefer corruptible man to God, which is immortal, Isa. 2:22; Jer. 48:6, 7.

17:8 [1] Read Ps. 1:3.

17:9 [1] Because the wicked have ever some excuse to defend their doings, he showeth that their own lewd imaginations deceive them, and bring them to these inconveniences: but God will examine their deeds by the malice of their hearts, 1 Sam. 16:7; 1 Chron. 28:9; Ps. 7:10; Jer. 11:20 and 20:12; Rev. 2:13.

17:11 [1] As the Partridge by calling gathered others which forsake her, when they see that she is not their dam: so the covetous man is forsaken of his riches, because he cometh by them falsely.

17:12 [1] Showing that the godly ought to glory in nothing, but in God, who doth exalt his, and hath left a sign of his favor in his Temple.

17:13 [1] Their names shall not be registered in the book of life.

17:14 [1] He desireth God to preserve him that he fall not into tentation, considering the great contempt of God's word, and the multitude that fall from God.

17:15 [1] The wicked say that my prophecy shall not come to pass, because thou deferrest the time of thy vengeance.

17:16 [1] I am assured of my vocation, and therefore know that the thing which thou speakest by me, shall come to pass, and that I speak not of any worldly affection.

17:17 [1] Howsoever the wicked deal rigorously with me, yet let me find comfort in thee.

17:18 [1] Read Jer. 11:20.

17:19 [1] Whereas thy doctrine may be best understood both of high and low.

17:21 [1] By naming the Sabbath day, he comprehendeth the thing that is thereby signified: for if they transgressed in the ceremony, they must needs be culpable of the rest, read Exod. 20:8, and by the breaking of this one commandment, he maketh them transgressors of the whole law, forasmuch as the first and second table are contained herein.

22 Neither carry forth burdens out of your houses in the Sabbath day: neither do ye any work, but sanctify the Sabbath, as I commanded your fathers.

23 But they obeyed not, neither inclined their ears, but made their necks stiff, and would not hear, nor receive correction.

24 Nevertheless, if ye will hear me, saith the Lord, and bear no burden through the gates of the city in the Sabbath day, but sanctify the Sabbath day, so that ye do no work therein,

25 Then shall the Kings and the Princes enter in at the gates of this city, and shall sit ᵃupon the throne of David, and shall ride upon chariots and upon horses, *both* they and their princes, the men of Judah, and the inhabitants of Jerusalem: and this city shall remain forever.

26 And they shall come from the cities of Judah, and from about Jerusalem, and from the land of Benjamin, and from the plain, and from the mountains, and from the South, which shall bring burnt offerings, and sacrifices, and meat offerings, and incense, *and* shall bring sacrifice of praise into the house of the Lord.

27 But if ye will not hear me to sanctify the Sabbath day, and not to bear a burden, nor to go through the gates of Jerusalem in the Sabbath day, then will I kindle a fire in the gates thereof, and it shall devour the palaces of Jerusalem, and it shall not be quenched.

18

2 God showeth by the example of a potter, that it is in his power to destroy the despisers of his word. 18 The conspiracy of the Jews against Jeremiah. 19 His prayer against his adversaries.

1 The word which came to Jeremiah from the Lord, saying,

2 Arise, and go down into the potter's house, and there shall I show thee my words.

3 Then I went down to the potter's house, and behold, he wrought a work on the wheels.

4 And the vessel that he made ¹of clay, was broken in the hand of the potter, so he returned, and made it another vessel, as seemed good to the potter to make it.

CHAPTER 17
ᵃ Jer. 22:4

5 Then the word of the Lord came unto me, saying,

6 O house of Israel, cannot I do with you as this potter, saith the Lord? behold, as the clay *is* in the potter's hand, so are you in mine hand, O house of Israel.

7 I will speak suddenly against a nation, or against a kingdom to pluck it up, and to root it out, and to destroy it.

8 But if this nation against whom I have pronounced turn from their wickedness, I will ¹repent of the plague that I thought to bring upon them.

9 And I will speak suddenly concerning a nation, and concerning a kingdom to build it and to plant it.

10 But if it do evil in my sight, and hear not my voice, I will repent of the good that I thought to do for them.

11 Speak thou now therefore unto the men of Judah, and to the inhabitants of Jerusalem, saying, Thus saith the Lord, Behold, I prepare a plague for you, and purpose a thing against you: return you therefore every one from his evil way, and make your ways and your works good.

12 But they said ¹desperately, Surely we will walk after our own imaginations, and do every man *after* the stubbornness of his wicked heart.

13 Therefore thus saith the Lord, Ask now among the heathen, who hath heard such things? the virgin of Israel hath done very filthily.

14 Will a man forsake the snow of Lebanon, *which cometh* from the rock of the field? ¹or shall the cold flowing waters, that come from another place, be forsaken?

15 Because my people hath forgotten me, *and* have burnt incense to vanity, and *their prophets* have caused them to stumble in their ways *from* the ¹ancient ways, to walk in the paths *and* way that is not trodden,

16 To make their land desolate, *and* a perpetual derision, *so that* everyone that passeth thereby, shall be astonished and wag his head,

17 I will scatter them with an East wind before the enemy: I will show them the back, and ¹not the face in the day of their destruction.

18 Then said they, Come, and let us imagine some device against Jeremiah: for the Law ¹shall not perish

---

18:4 ¹ As the potter hath power over the clay to make what pot he will, or to break them, when he hath made them: so have I power over you to do with you as seemeth good to me, Isa. 45:9; Rom. 9:20, 21.

18:8 ¹ When the Scripture attributeth repentance unto God, it is not that he doeth contrary to that which he hath ordained in his secret counsel: but when he threateneth, it is a calling to repentance, and when he giveth man grace to repent, the threatening (which ever containeth a condition in it) taketh no place: and this the scripture calleth repentance in God, because it so appeareth to man's judgment.

18:12 ¹ As men that had no remorse, but were altogether bent to rebellion and to their own self-will.

18:14 ¹ As no man that hath thirst refuseth fresh conduit waters which he hath at home, to go and seek waters abroad to quench his thirst: so they ought not to seek for help and succor at strangers, and leave God which was present with them.

18:15 ¹ That is, the way of truth which God had taught by his law, read Jer. 6:16.

18:17 ¹ I will show mine anger and not my favor toward them.

18:18 ¹ This argument the wicked have ever used against the servants of God. The Church cannot err: we are the Church, and therefore whosoever speaketh against us, they ought to die, 1 Kings 22:24; Jer. 7:4 and 20:2; Mal. 2:4, and thus the false Church persecuteth the true Church, which standeth not in outward pomp, and in multitude, but is known by the graces of the holy Ghost.

from the Priest, nor counsel from the wise, nor the word from the Prophet: come, and let us smite him with the ²tongue, and let us not give heed to any of his words.

19 Hearken unto me, O Lord, and hear the voice of them that contend with me.

20 Shall evil be recompensed for good? for they have dug a pit for my soul: remember that I stood before thee, to speak good for them, *and* to turn away thy wrath from them.

21 Therefore, ¹deliver up their children to famine, and let them drop away by the force of the sword, let their wives be robbed of their children, and be widows: and let their husbands be put to death, *and* let their young men be slain by the sword in the battle.

22 Let the cry be heard from their houses, when thou shalt bring an host suddenly upon them: for they have dug a pit to take me, and hid snares for my feet.

23 Yet Lord thou knowest all their counsel against me *tendeth* to death: forgive not their iniquity, neither put out their sin from thy sight, but let them be overthrown before thee: deal *thus* with them in the time of thine anger.

CHAPTER 19
a Jer. 18:16
Jer. 49:13
Jer. 50:13
b Deut. 28:53
Lam. 4:10

19

He prophesieth the destruction of Jerusalem for the contempt and despising of the word of God.

1 Thus saith the Lord, Go, and buy an earthen bottle of a potter, and *take* of the ancients for the people, and of the ancients of the Priests,

2 And go forth unto the valley of Ben-Hinnom, which is by the entry of the ¹East gate: and thou shalt preach there the words, that I shall tell thee,

3 And shalt say, Hear ye the word of the Lord, O ¹Kings of Judah, and inhabitants of Jerusalem, Thus saith the Lord of hosts, the God of Israel, Behold, I will bring a plague upon this place, the which whosoever heareth, his ears shall ²tingle.

4 Because they have forsaken me, and profaned this place, and have burnt incense in it unto other gods, whom *neither* they, nor their fathers have known, nor the Kings of Judah (they have filled this place also with the blood of innocents,

5 And they have built the high places of Baal, to burn their sons with fire for burnt offerings unto

Baal, which I ¹commanded not, nor spake it, neither came it into my mind)

6 Therefore behold, the days come, saith the Lord, that this place shall no more be called ¹Topheth, nor the valley of Ben-Hinnom, but the valley of slaughter.

7 And I will bring the counsel of Judah and Jerusalem to nought in this place, and I will cause them to fall by the sword before their enemies, and by the hand of them that seek their lives: and their carcasses will I give to be meat for the fowls of the heaven, and to the beasts of the field.

8 ªAnd I will make this city desolate, and an hissing, *so that* everyone that passeth thereby, shall be astonished and hiss because of all the plagues thereof.

9 ᵇAnd I will feed them with the flesh of their sons, and with the flesh of their daughters, and everyone shall eat the flesh of his friend in the siege and straitness, wherewith their enemies that seek their lives, shall hold them strait.

10 Then shalt thou break the bottle in the sight of the men that go with thee,

11 And shalt say unto them, Thus saith the Lord of hosts, Even so will I break this people and this city, as one breaketh a ¹potter's vessel, that cannot be made whole again, and they shall bury *them* in Topheth till there be no place to bury.

12 Thus will I do unto this place, saith the Lord, and to the inhabitants thereof, and I will make this city like Topheth.

13 For the houses of Jerusalem, and the houses of the Kings of Judah shall be defiled as the place of Topheth, because of all the ¹houses upon whose ²roofs they have burnt incense unto all the host of heaven, and have poured out drink offerings unto other gods.

14 Then came Jeremiah from Topheth, where the Lord had sent him to prophesy, and he stood in the court of the Lord's house, and said to all the people,

15 Thus saith the Lord of hosts, the God of Israel, Behold, I will bring upon this city, and upon all her towns, all the plagues that I have pronounced against it, because they have hardened their necks, and would not hear my words.

18:18 ² Let us slander him, and accuse him: for we shall be believed.
18:21 ¹ Seeing the obstinate malice of the adversaries, which grew daily more and more, the Prophet being moved with God's Spirit, without any carnal affection prayeth for their destruction, because he knew that it should tend to God's glory, and profit of his Church.
19:2 ¹ Or, gate of the sun.
19:3 ¹ By Kings here and in other places are meant counselors and governors of the people: which he calleth the ancients, verse 1.
    ² Read of this phrase, 1 Sam. 3:11.

19:5 ¹ Whereby is declared, that whatsoever is not commanded by God's word touching his service, is against his word.
19:6 ¹ Read Jer. 7:31 and 2 Kings 23:10; Isa. 30:33.
19:11 ¹ This visible sign was to confirm them touching the assurance of this plague, which the Lord threatened by his prophet.
19:13 ¹ He noteth the great rage of the idolaters, which left no place free from their abominations, insomuch as they polluted their own houses therewith, as we see yet among the Papists.
    ² Read Deut. 22:8.

20

Jeremiah is smitten and cast into prison for preaching of the word of God. 3 *He prophesieth the captivity of Babylon.* 7 *He complaineth that he is a mocking stock for the word of God.* 9 *He is compelled by the spirit to preach the word.*

CHAPTER 20
ª 1 Sam. 16:7
1 Chron. 28:9
Ps. 7:9
Jer. 11:20
Jer. 17:10

1 When Pashhur, the son of Immer, the priest, which was appointed governor in the house of the Lord, heard that Jeremiah prophesied these things,

2 Then Pashhur smote Jeremiah the Prophet, and put him in the ¹stocks that were in the high gate of Benjamin, which was by the house of the Lord.

3 And on the morning, Pashhur brought Jeremiah out of the stocks. Then said Jeremiah unto him, The Lord hath not called thy name Pashhur, but ¹Magor-Missabib.

4 For thus saith the Lord, behold, I will make thee to be a terror to thyself, and to all thy friends, and they shall fall by the sword of their enemies, and thine eyes shall behold it, and I will give all Judah into the hand of the king of Babel, and he shall carry them captive into Babel, and shall slay them with the sword.

5 Moreover, I will deliver all the substance of this city, and all the labors thereof, and all the precious things thereof, and all the treasures of the Kings of Judah will I give into the hand of their enemies, which shall spoil them, and take them away and carry them to Babel.

6 And thou Pashhur, and all that dwell in thine house, shall go into captivity, and thou shalt come to Babel, and there thou shalt die, and shalt be buried there, thou and all thy ¹friends, to whom thou hast prophesied lies.

7 O Lord, thou hast deceived me, and I am ¹deceived: thou art stronger than I, and hast ²prevailed: I am in derision daily: everyone mocketh me.

8 For since I spake, I cried out of wrong, and proclaimed ¹desolation: therefore the word of the Lord was made a reproach unto me, and in derision daily.

9 Then I said, I will not make mention of him, nor speak anymore in his Name. But *his word* was in mine heart as a burning fire shut up in my bones,

and I was weary with forbearing, and I could not *stay.*

10 For I had heard the railing of many, *and* fear on every side. ¹Declare, *said they,* and we will declare it: all my familiars watched for mine halting, *saying,* It may be that he is deceived: so we shall prevail against him, and we shall execute our vengeance upon him.

11 ¹But the Lord is with me like a mighty giant: therefore my persecutors shall be overthrown, and shall not prevail, *and* shall be greatly confounded: for they have done unwisely, *and their* everlasting shame shall never be forgotten.

12 ªBut, O Lord of hosts, that triest the righteous, and seest the reins and the heart, let me see thy vengeance on them: for unto thee have I opened my cause.

13 Sing unto the Lord, praise ye the Lord: for he hath delivered the soul of the poor from the hand of the wicked.

14 ¶ ¹Cursed *be* the day wherein I was born: and let not the day wherein my mother bare me, be blessed.

15 Cursed *be* the man that showed my father, saying, A man child is born unto thee, and comforted him.

16 And let that man be as the ¹cities, which the Lord hath overturned and repented not: and let him hear the cry in the morning, and the shouting at noon tide,

17 Because he hath not slain me, *even* from the womb, or that my mother might have been my grave, or her womb a perpetual ¹conception.

18 How is it, *that* I came forth of the womb, to see labor and sorrow, that my days should be consumed with shame?

21

He prophesieth that Zedekiah shall be taken, and the city burned.

1 The word which came unto Jeremiah from the Lord, when king Zedekiah sent unto him Pashhur, the son of Melchiah, and Zephaniah, the son of Maaseiah the Priest, saying,

---

20:2 ¹ Thus we see that the thing which neither the King, nor the princes, nor the people durst enterprise against the Prophet of God, this Priest as a chief instrument of Satan first attempted, read Jer. 18:18.

20:3 ¹ Or, fear round about.

20:6 ¹ Which have suffered themselves to be abused by thy false prophecies.

20:7 ¹ Herein appeareth the impatience, which oftentimes overcometh the servants of God, when they see not their labors to profit, and also feel their own weakness, read Jer. 15:18.

² Thou didst thrust me forth to this work against my will.

20:8 ¹ He showeth that he did his office in that he reproved the people of their vices, and threatened them with God's judgments:

but because he was derided and persecuted for this, he was discouraged, and thought to have ceased to preach, save that God's Spirit did force him thereunto.

20:10 ¹ Thus the enemies conferred together to know what they had heard him say, that they might accuse him thereof, read Isa. 29:21.

20:11 ¹ Here he showeth how his faith did strive against tentation, and sought to the Lord for strength.

20:14 ¹ How the children of God are overcome in this battle of the flesh and the Spirit, and into what inconveniences they fall till God raise them up again: read Job 3:1 and Jer. 15:10.

20:16 ¹ Alluding to the destruction of Sodom and Gomorrah, Gen. 19:25.

20:17 ¹ Meaning, that the fruit thereof might never come to profit.

2 ¹Inquire, I pray thee, of the Lord for us, (for Nebuchadnezzar king of Babel maketh war against us) if so be that the Lord will deal with us according to all his wondrous works, that he may return up from us.

3 Then said Jeremiah, Thus shall you say to Zedekiah,

4 Thus saith the Lord God of Israel, Behold, I will ¹turn back the weapons of war that are in your hands, wherewith ye fight against the king of Babel, and against the Chaldeans, which besiege you without the walls, and I will assemble them into the midst of this city.

5 And I myself will fight against you with an outstretched hand, and with a mighty arm, even in anger and in wrath, and in great indignation.

6 And I will smite the inhabitants of this city, both man and beast: they shall die of a great pestilence.

7 And after this, saith the Lord, I will deliver Zedekiah the King of Judah, and his servants, and the people, and such as are left in this city, from the pestilence, from the sword, and from the famine, into the hand of Nebuchadnezzar king of Babel, and into the hand of their enemies, and into the hand of those that seek their lives, and he shall smite them with the edge of the sword: he shall not spare them, neither have pity nor compassion.

8 And unto this people thou shalt say, Thus saith the Lord, Behold, I set before you the ¹way of life, and the way of ²death.

9 ᵃHe that abideth in this city, shall die by the sword, and by the famine, and by the pestilence: but he that goeth out, and falleth to the Chaldeans, that besiege you, he shall live, and his life shall be unto him for a ¹prey.

10 For I have set my face against this city, for evil and not for good, saith the Lord: it shall be given into the hand of the king of Babel, and he shall burn it with fire.

11 ¶ And say unto the house of the King of Judah, Hear ye the word of the Lord.

12 O house of David, Thus saith the Lord, ᵇExecute judgment ¹in the morning, and deliver the oppressed

CHAPTER 21
ᵃ Jer. 38:2
ᵇ Jer. 22:3

CHAPTER 22
ᵃ Jer. 21:12
ᵇ Jer. 17:25

out of the hand of the oppressor, lest my wrath go out like fire, and burn that none can quench it, because of the wickedness of your works.

13 Behold, I *come* against thee, ¹O inhabitant of the valley, *and* rock of the plain, saith the Lord, which say, Who shall come down against us? or who shall enter into our habitations?

14 But I will visit you according to the fruit of your works, saith the Lord, and I will kindle a fire ¹in the forest thereof, and it shall devour round about it.

22 *1 He exhorteth the King to judgment and righteousness. 9 Why Jerusalem is brought into captivity. 11 The death of Shallum the son of Josiah is prophesied.*

1 Thus said the Lord, Go down to the house of the King of Judah, and speak there this thing,

2 And say, Hear the word of the Lord, O King of Judah, that sittest upon the throne of David, thou and thy servants, and thy people that enter in by these gates.

3 Thus saith the Lord, ᵃExecute ye judgment and ¹righteousness, and deliver the oppressed from the hand of the oppressor, and vex not the stranger, the fatherless, nor the widow: do no violence, nor shed innocent blood in this place.

4 For if ye do this thing, then shall the kings sitting upon the throne of David enter in by the gates of this House, ᵇand ride upon chariots and upon horses, *both* he and his servants and his people.

5 But if ye will not hear these words, I ¹swear by myself, saith the Lord, that this House shall be waste.

6 For thus hath the Lord spoken upon the king's house of Judah, Thou art ¹Gilead unto me, *and* the head of Lebanon, *yet* surely I will make thee a wilderness, *and as* cities not inhabited.

7 And I will ¹prepare destroyers against thee, everyone with his weapons, and they shall cut down thy chief ²cedar trees, and cast them in the fire.

8 ¹And many nations shall pass by this city, and they shall say every man to his neighbor, Wherefore hath the Lord done thus unto this great city?

9 Then shall they answer, Because they have

21:2 ¹ Not that the King was touched with repentance of his sins, and so sought to God, as did Hezekiah, when he sent to Isaiah, 2 Kings 19:1; Isa. 37:2, but because the Prophet might pray unto God to take this present plague away, as Pharaoh sought unto Moses, Exod. 9:28.
21:4 ¹ To wit, from your enemies to destroy yourselves.
21:8 ¹ By yielding yourselves to Nebuchadnezzar.
   ² By resisting him.
21:9 ¹ As a thing recovered from extreme danger, Jer. 37:2, 39:18 and 45:5.
21:12 ¹ Be diligent to do justice.
21:13 ¹ Meaning, Jerusalem which was built part on the hill, and part in the valley, and was compassed about with mountains.
21:14 ¹ That is, in the houses thereof, which stood as thick as trees

in the forest.
22:3 ¹ This was his ordinary manner of preaching before the Kings, from Josiah unto Zedekiah, which was about forty years.
22:5 ¹ Showing that there is none greater than he is, Heb. 6:13, and that he will most certainly perform his oath.
22:6 ¹ He compareth Jerusalem to Gilead, which was beyond Jordan, and the beauty of Judea to Lebanon.
22:7 ¹ The Hebrew word signifieth to sanctify, because the Lord doth dedicate to his use and purpose such as he prepareth to execute his work, Isa. 13:3; Jer. 6:4 and 12:3.
   ² Thy buildings made of Cedar trees.
22:8 ¹ As they that wonder at a thing which they thought would never have come so to pass, Deut. 29:24; 1 Kings 9:8.

forsaken the covenant of the Lord their God, and worshipped other gods, and served them.

10 ¶ Weep not for the dead, and be not moved for them, *but* weep for him [1]that goeth out: for he shall return no more, nor see his native country.

11 For thus saith the Lord, As touching [1]Shallum the son of Josiah King of Judah, which reigned for Josiah his father, which went out of this place, he shall not return thither,

12 But he shall die in the place, whither they have led him captive, and shall see this land no more.

13 ¶ Woe unto him that buildeth his house by [1]unrighteousness, and his chambers without equity: he useth his neighbor without wages, and giveth him not for his work.

14 He saith, I will build me a wide house and large chambers: so he will make himself large windows, and ceiling with cedar, and paint them with vermilion.

15 Shalt thou reign, because thou closest thyself in cedar? did not thy [1]father eat and drink and prosper, when he executed judgment and justice?

16 When he judged the cause of the afflicted and the poor, he prospered: was not this because he knew me, saith the Lord?

17 But thine eyes and thine heart are but only for thy covetousness, and for to shed innocent blood, and for oppression, and for destruction, *even* to do this.

18 Therefore thus saith the Lord against Jehoiakim, the son of Josiah king of Judah, They shall not [1]lament him, *saying*, Ah, my brother, or ah sister: neither shall they mourn for him, *saying*, Ah, lord, or ah, his glory.

19 He shall be buried, as an ass [1]is buried, *even* drawn and cast forth without the gates of Jerusalem.

20 ¶ Go up to [1]Lebanon, and cry: shout in [2]Bashan, and cry by the passages: for all thy lovers are destroyed.

21 I spake unto thee when thou wast in prosper-

ity: *but* thou saidest, I will not hear, this hath been thy manner from thy youth, that thou wouldest not obey my voice.

22 The wind shall feed all thy pastors, [1]and thy lovers shall go into captivity: and then shalt thou be ashamed and confounded of all thy wickedness.

23 Thou that dwellest in Lebanon, *and* makest thy nest in the [1]cedars, how beautiful shalt thou be when sorrows come upon thee, as the sorrow of a woman in travail?

24 As I live, saith the Lord, though [1]Coniah the son of Jehoiakim king of Judah, were the signet of my right hand, yet would I pluck thee thence.

25 And I will give thee into the hand of them that seek thy life, and into the hand of them, whose face thou fearest, even into the hand of Nebuchadnezzar king of Babel, and into the hand of the Chaldeans.

26 And I will cause them to carry thee away, and thy mother that bare thee into another country, where ye were not born, and there shall ye die.

27 But to the land, whereunto they desire to return, they shall not return thither.

28 Is not this man Coniah *as* a despised *and* broken idol? or *as* a vessel, wherein is no pleasure? wherefore are they carried away, he and his seed, and cast out into a land that they know not?

29 O [1]earth, earth, earth, hear the word of the Lord.

30 Thus saith the Lord, Write this [1]man destitute of *children*, a man that shall not prosper in his days: for there shall be no man of his seed that shall prosper and sit upon the throne of David, or bear rule anymore in Judah.

23

1 Against false pastors.　5 A prophecy of the great Pastor Jesus Christ.

1 Woe *be* unto [1]the pastors that destroy and scatter the [2]sheep of my pasture, saith the Lord.

22:10 [1] Signifying, that they should lose their king: for Jehoiachin went forth to meet Nebuchadnezzar and yielded himself, and was carried into Babylon, 2 Kings 24:12.

22:11 [1] Whom some think to be Jehoiachin, and that Josiah was his grandfather: but as seemeth, this was Jehoiakim, as verse 18.

22:13 [1] By bribes, and extortion.

22:15 [1] Meaning, Josiah, who was not given to ambition and superfluity, but was content with mediocrity, and did only delight in setting forth God's glory, and to do justice to all.

22:18 [1] For everyone shall have enough to lament for himself.

22:19 [1] Not honorably among his fathers, but as carrions are cast in a hole, because their stink should not infect, read 2 Kings 24:9. Josephus Antiquities 10:8, writeth that the enemy slew him in the city and commanded him to be cast before the walls unburied, see Jer. 36:30.

22:20 [1] To call to the Assyrians for help.

　[2] For this was the way out of India to Assyria, whereby is meant that all help should fail: for the Chaldeans have subdued both them and the Egyptians.

22:22 [1] Both thy governors and they that should help thee, shall vanish away as wind.

22:23 [1] Thou that art built of the fair Cedar trees of Lebanon.

22:24 [1] Who was called Jehoiachin, or Jeconiah, whom he calleth here Coniah in contempt, who thought his kingdom could never depart from him, because he came of the stock of David, and therefore for the promise sake could not be taken from his house: but he abused God's promise, and therefore was justly deprived of the kingdom.

22:29 [1] He showeth that all posterities shall be witnesses of his just plague, as though it were registered for perpetual memory.

22:30 [1] Not that he had no children (for after that he begat Shealtiel in the captivity, Matt. 1:12) but that none should reign after him as King.

23:1 [1] Meaning, the princes, governors and false prophets, as Ezek. 34:2.

　[2] For the which I have especial care, and have prepared good pastures for them.

2 Therefore thus saith the Lord God of Israel unto the pastors that [1]feed my people, Ye have scattered my flock, and thrust them out, and have not visited them: behold, I will visit you for the wickedness of your works, saith the Lord.

3 And I will gather the [1]remnant of my sheep out of all countries, whither I had driven them, and will bring them again to their folds, and they shall grow and increase:

4 And I will set up shepherds over them, which shall feed them: and they shall dread no more nor be afraid, neither shall any of them be lacking, saith the Lord.

5 Behold, the days come, saith the Lord, that I will raise unto David a righteous [1]branch, and a King shall reign and prosper, and shall execute judgment and justice in the earth.

6 In his days Judah shall be saved, and [a]Israel shall dwell safely, and this is the Name whereby they shall call him, [b]The Lord our righteousness.

7 Therefore behold, the days come, saith the Lord, that they shall no more say, The [1]Lord liveth, which brought up the children of Israel out of the land of Egypt.

8 But the Lord liveth, which brought up and led the seed of the house of Israel out of the North country, and from all countries where I had scattered them, and they shall dwell in their own land.

9 Mine heart breaketh within me, because of the [1]prophets, all my bones shake: I am like a drunken man (and like a man whom wine hath [2]overcome) for the presence of the Lord and for his holy words.

10 For the land is full of adulterers, *and* because of oaths the land mourneth, the pleasant places of the wilderness are dried up, and their [1]course is evil, and their force is not right.

11 For both the Prophet and the Priest [1]do wickedly: and their wickedness have I found in mine [2]House, saith the Lord.

12 Wherefore their way shall be unto them as slippery *ways* in the darkness: they shall be driven forth

CHAPTER 23
[a] Deut. 33:28
[b] Jer. 33:16
[c] Jer. 14:13,14
Jer. 27:15
Jer. 29:8,9

and fall therein: for I will bring a plague upon them, *even* the year of their visitation, saith the Lord.

13 And I have seen foolishness in the prophets of Samaria that prophesied in Baal, and caused my people Israel to err.

14 I have seen also in the prophets of Jerusalem [1]filthiness: they commit adultery and walk in lies: they strengthen also the hands of the wicked, that none can return from his wickedness: they are all [2]unto me as Sodom, and the inhabitants thereof as Gomorrah.

15 Therefore thus saith the Lord of hosts concerning the prophets, Behold, I will feed them with [1]wormwood, and make them drink the water of gall: for from the prophets of Jerusalem is [2]wickedness gone forth into all the land.

16 Thus saith the Lord of hosts, Hear not the words of the prophets that prophesy unto you, and teach you vanity: they speak the vision of their own [1]heart, *and* not out of the mouth of the Lord.

17 They say still unto them that despise me, The Lord hath said, Ye [1]shall have peace: and they say unto everyone that walketh after the stubbornness of his own heart, No evil shall come upon you.

18 For [1]who hath stood in the counsel of the Lord that he hath perceived, and heard his word? Who hath marked his word and heard it?

19 Behold, the tempest of the Lord goeth forth in *his* wrath, and a violent whirlwind shall fall down upon the head of the wicked.

20 The anger of the Lord shall not return until he have executed, and till he have performed the thoughts of his heart: in the latter days ye [1]shall understand it plainly.

21 [1]I have not sent these prophets, saith the Lord, yet they ran; I have not spoken to them, and yet they prophesied.

22 But if they had stood in my counsel, and [1]had declared my words to my people, then they should have turned them from their evil way, and from the wickedness of their inventions.

23:2 [1] Whose charge is to feed the flock, but they eat the fruit thereof, Ezek. 34:3.

23:3 [1] Thus the Prophets ever used to mix the promises with the threatenings, lest the godly should be too much beaten down, and therefore he showeth how God will gather his Church after this dispersion.

23:5 [1] This prophecy is of the restitution of the Church in the time of Jesus Christ, who is the true branch, read Isa. 11:1 and 45:8; Jer. 35:15; Dan. 9:24.

23:7 [1] Read Jer. 16:14.

23:9 [1] Meaning, the false prophets which deceive the people: wherein appeareth his great love toward his nation, read Jer. 14:13.

[2] Hebrew, *passed over* or *troubled.*

23:10 [1] They run headlong to wickedness, and seek vain help.

23:11 [1] Or, are hypocrites.

[2] My Temple is full of their idolatry and superstitions.

23:14 [1] They which should have profited by my rods against Samaria, are become worse than they.

[2] Though to the world they seem holy fathers, yet I detest them as I did these abominable cities.

23:15 [1] Read Jer. 8:14.

[2] Or, hypocrisy.

23:16 [1] Which they have invented of their own brain.

23:17 [1] Read Jer. 6:14 and 8:11.

23:18 [1] Thus they did deride Jeremiah, as though the word of God were not revealed unto him: so also spake Zedekiah to Micaiah, 1 Kings 22:24.

23:20 [1] Both that God hath sent me, and that my words shall be true.

23:22 [1] He showeth the difference between the true Prophets and the false, between the hireling and the true minister.

23 Am I a God at *hand*, saith the Lord, and not a God ¹far off?

24 Can any hide himself in secret places, that I shall not see him, saith the Lord? Do not I fill heaven and earth, saith the Lord?

25 I have heard what the prophets said, that prophesied lies in my Name, saying, I ¹have dreamed, I have dreamed.

26 How long? ¹Do the prophets delight to prophesy lies, even prophesying the deceit of their own heart?

27 Think they to cause ¹my people to forget my Name by their dreams, which they tell every man to his neighbor, as their forefathers have forgotten my Name for Baal?

28 The prophet that hath a dream, let him ¹tell a dream, and he that hath my word, let him speak my word faithfully: ²what is the chaff to the wheat, saith the Lord?

29 Is not my word even like a fire, saith the Lord? and like an hammer, that breaketh the stone?

30 Therefore behold, I *will come* against the prophets, saith the Lord, that ¹steal my word every one from his neighbor.

31 Behold, I *will come* against the prophets, saith the Lord, which have sweet tongues, and say, ¹He saith.

32 Behold, I *will come* against them that prophesy false dreams, saith the Lord, and do tell them, and cause my people to err by their lies, and by their flatteries, and I sent them not, nor commanded them: therefore they bring no profit unto this people, saith the Lord.

33 And when this people, or the prophet, or a Priest shall ask thee, saying, What is the ¹burden of the Lord? thou shalt then say unto them, What burden? I will even forsake you, saith the Lord.

34 And the prophet, or the priest, or the people that shall say, The ¹burden of the Lord, I will even visit every such one, and his house.

35 Thus shall ye say every one to his neighbor,

d Jer. 20:11

and every one to his brother, What hath the Lord answered? and what hath the Lord spoken?

36 And the burden of the Lord shall ye mention no more: for every man's ¹word shall be his burden: for ye have perverted the words of the living God, the Lord of hosts our God.

37 Thus shalt thou say to the Prophet, What hath the Lord answered thee? and what hath the Lord spoken?

38 And if you say, The burden of the Lord, Then thus saith the Lord, Because ye say this word, The burden of the Lord, and I have sent unto you, saying, Ye shall not say, The burden of the Lord.

39 Therefore behold, I, even I will utterly ¹forget you, and I will forsake you, and the city that I gave you and your fathers, *and cast you* out of my presence,

40 And will bring ᵈan everlasting reproach upon you, and a perpetual shame which shall never be forgotten.

24

The vision of the baskets of figs, 5 *Signifieth that part of the people should be brought again out of captivity.* 8 *And that Zedekiah and the rest of the people should be carried away.*

1 The Lord showed me, and behold, two ¹baskets of figs were set before the Temple of the Lord, after that Nebuchadnezzar king of Babel had carried away captive Jeconiah the son of Jehoiakim king of Judah, and the princes of Judah with the workmen, and cunning men of Jerusalem, and had brought them to Babel.

2 One basket *had* very good figs, *even* like the figs that are first *ripe*, and the other basket *had* very naughty figs, which could not be eaten, they were so evil.

3 Then said the Lord unto me, What seest thou, Jeremiah? And I said, Figs: the good figs very good, and the naughty very naughty, which cannot be eaten, they are so evil.

4 Again the word of the Lord came unto me,

23:23 ¹ Do I not see your falsehood, however you cloak it, and wheresoever you commit it?
23:25 ¹ I have a prophecy revealed unto me, as Num. 12:6.
23:26 ¹ Hebrew, *Is it in the heart of the Prophets?*
23:27 ¹ He showeth that Satan raiseth up false prophets to bring the people from God.
23:28 ¹ Let the false prophet declare that it is his own fantasy, and not slander my word as though it were a cloak to cover his lies.
² Meaning, that it is not sufficient for God's ministers to abstain from lies, and to speak the word of God: but that there be judgment in alleging it, and that it may appear to be applied to the same purpose that it was spoken, Ezek. 3:27; 1 Cor. 2:13 and 4:2; 2 Tim. 2:25; 2 Pet. 4:10, 11.
23:30 ¹ Which set forth in my Name that which I have not commanded.

23:31 ¹ To wit, the Lord.
23:33 ¹ The Prophets called their threatenings God's burden, which the sinners were not able to sustain, therefore the wicked in deriding the word, would ask of the Prophets, what was the burden, as though they would say, You seek nothing else, but to lay burdens on our shoulders: and thus they rejected the word of God, as a grievous burden.
23:34 ¹ Because this word was brought to contempt and derision, he will teach them another manner of speech, and will cause this word burden to cease, and teach them to ask with reverence, What saith the Lord?
23:36 ¹ The thing which they mock and contemn, shall come upon them.
23:39 ¹ Or, take you away.
24:1 ¹ The good figs signified them that were gone into captivity, and so saved their life, as Jer. 21:8, and the naughty figs them that remained, which were yet subject to the sword, famine and pestilence.

saying,

5　Thus saith the Lord the God of Israel, Like these good figs, so will I know them that are carried away captive of Judah to be good, whom I have sent out of this ¹place, into the land of the Chaldeans.

6　For I will set mine eyes upon them for good, and I will bring them again to this land, and I will build them and not destroy them, and I will plant them, and not root them out.

7　And I will give them ¹an heart to know me, that I am the Lord, and they shall be ªmy people, and I will be their God: for they shall return unto me with their whole heart.

8　ᵇAnd as the naughty figs which cannot be eaten, they are so evil (surely thus saith the Lord) so will I give Zedekiah the King of Judah, and his princes, and the residue of Jerusalem, that remain in this land, and them that dwell ¹in the land of Egypt:

9　I will even give them for a terrible plague to all the kingdoms of the earth, *and* for a reproach and for a proverb, for a common talk, and for a curse, in all places where I shall cast them.

10　And I will send the sword, the famine, and the pestilence among them, till they be consumed out of the land, that I gave unto them, and to their fathers.

25

1 *He prophesieth that they shall be in captivity seventy years.* 12 *And that after the seventy years the Babylonians should be destroyed.* 15 *The destruction of all nations is prophesied.*

1　The word that came to Jeremiah, concerning all the people of Judah, in the ¹fourth year of Jehoiakim the son of Josiah king of Judah, that was in the first year of Nebuchadnezzar king of Babel:

2　The which Jeremiah the Prophet spake unto all the people of Judah, and to all the inhabitants of Jerusalem, saying,

3　From the thirteenth year of Josiah the son of Amon king of Judah, even unto ¹this day (that is the three and twentieth year) the word of the Lord hath

CHAPTER 24
ª Jer. 31:33
Heb. 8:10
ᵇ Jer. 29:17

CHAPTER 25
ª Jer. 16:9

come unto me, and I have spoken unto you ²rising early and speaking, but ye would not hear.

4　And the Lord hath sent unto you all his servants the Prophets, rising early, and sending *them*, but ye would not hear, nor incline your ears, to obey.

5　They ¹said, Turn again now everyone from his evil way, and from the wickedness of your inventions, and ye shall dwell in the land that the Lord hath given unto you, and to your fathers forever and ever.

6　And go not after other gods to serve them and to worship them, and provoke me not to anger with the works of your hands, and I will not punish you.

7　Nevertheless, ye would not hear me, saith the Lord, but have provoked me to anger with the works of your hands to your own hurt.

8　Therefore thus saith the Lord of hosts, Because ye have not heard my words,

9　Behold, I will send and take *to me* all the ¹families of the North, saith the Lord, and Nebuchadnezzar the king of Babel my ²servant, and will bring them against this land, and against the inhabitants thereof, and against all these nations ³round about, and will destroy them, and make them an astonishment and an hissing, and a continual desolation.

10　ªMoreover I will ¹take from them the voice of mirth and the voice of gladness, the voice of the bridegroom and the voice of the bride, the noise of the ²millstones, and the light of the candle.

11　And this whole land shall be desolate, and an astonishment, *and* these nations shall serve the king of Babel seventy years.

12　And when the ¹seventy years are accomplished, I will visit ²the king of Babel and that nation, saith the Lord, for their iniquities, even the land of the Chaldeans, and will make it a perpetual desolation.

13　And I will bring upon that land all my words which I have pronounced against it, *even* all that is written in this book, which Jeremiah hath prophesied against all nations.

14　For many nations, and great kings shall even

24:5 ¹ Whereby he approveth the yielding of Jeconiah and his company, because they obeyed the Prophet, who exhorted them thereunto.

24:7 ¹ Which declareth that man of himself can know nothing, till God give the heart and understanding.

24:8 ¹ Which fled thither for succor.

25:1 ¹ That is, in the third year accomplished and in the beginning of the fourth: for though Nebuchadnezzar began to reign in the end of the third year of Jehoiakim's reign, yet that year is not here counted, because it was almost expired, Dan. 1:1.

25:3 ¹ Which was the fifth year and the ninth month of Jehoiakim's reign.

² That is, I have spared no diligence or labor, Jer. 7:13.

25:5 ¹ He showeth that the Prophets, wholly with one consent did labor to pull the people from those vices, which then reigned, to wit,

from idolatry, and the vain confidence of men: for under these two all others were contained, 2 Kings 17:13; Jer. 18:11 and 35:15; Jonah 3:8.

25:9 ¹ The Chaldeans and all their power.

² So the wicked and Satan himself are God's servants, because he maketh them to serve him by constraint, and turneth that which they do of malice, to his honor and glory.

³ As the Philistines, Ammonites, Egyptians and others.

25:10 ¹ Or, destroy.

² Meaning, that bread and all things that should serve unto their feasts, should be taken away.

25:12 ¹ This revelation was for the confirmation of his prophecy, because he told them of the time that they should enter and remain in captivity, 2 Chron. 36:22; Ezra 1:1; Jer. 29:10; Dan. 9:2.

² For seeing the judgment began at his own house, the enemies must needs be punished most grievously, Ezek. 9:6, 1 Pet. 4:17.

[1]serve themselves of them: thus will I recompense them according to their deeds, and according to the works of their own hands.

15 For thus hath the Lord God of Israel spoken unto me, [1]Take the cup of wine of this *mine* indignation at mine hand, and cause all the nations, to whom I send thee, to drink it.

16 And they shall drink, and be moved, and be mad, because of the sword that I will send among them.

17 Then took I the cup at the Lord's hand, and made all people to drink, unto whom the Lord had sent me:

18 *Even* Jerusalem, and the cities of Judah, and the kings thereof, and the princes thereof, to make them desolate, an astonishment, an hissing, and a curse, [1]as *appeareth* this day:

19 Pharaoh *also*, King of Egypt, and his servants, and his princes, and all his people:

20 And all sorts of people, and all the Kings of the land [1]of Uz: and all the kings of the land of the Philistines, and [2]Ashkelon, and Gaza, and Ekron, and the remnant of Ashdod:

21 [1]Edom, and Moab, and the Ammonites,

22 And all the Kings of Tyre, and all the kings of Sidon, and the kings of the [1]Isles, that are beyond the sea,

23 And [1]Dedan, and Tema, and Buz, and all that dwell in the uttermost corners,

24 And all the kings of Arabia, and all the kings of Arabia that dwell in the [1]desert,

25 And all the kings of Zimri, and all the kings of [1]Elam, and all the kings of the Medes,

26 And all the kings of the North, far and near one to another, and all the kingdoms of the world, which are upon the earth, and the king of [1]Sheshach shall drink after them.

27 Therefore say thou unto them, Thus saith the Lord of hosts, the God of Israel, Drink and be drunken, and spew and fall, and rise no more, because of the sword, which I will send among you.

28 ¶ But if they refuse to take the cup at thine hand to drink, then tell them, Thus saith the Lord of hosts, Ye shall certainly drink.

b Joel 3:16
Amos 1:2
c Jer. 30:23

29 For lo, [1]I begin to plague the city, where my Name is called upon, and should you go free? Ye shall not go acquited: for I will call for a sword upon all the inhabitants of the earth, saith the Lord of hosts.

30 Therefore prophesy thou against them all these words, and say unto them, [b]The Lord shall roar from above, and thrust out his voice from his holy habitation: he shall roar upon his habitation, and cry aloud, as they that press the grapes, against all the inhabitants of the earth.

31 The sounds shall come to the ends of the earth: for the Lord hath a controversy with the nations, and will enter into judgment with all flesh, *and* he will give them that are wicked, to the sword, saith the Lord.

32 ¶ Thus saith the Lord of hosts, Behold, a plague shall go forth from nation to nation, and a [c]great whirlwind shall be raised up from the coasts of the earth.

33 And [1]the slain of the Lord shall be at that day, from *one* end of the earth, even unto the *other* end of the earth: they shall not be mourned, neither gathered nor buried, *but* shall be as the dung upon the ground.

34 Howl, [1]ye shepherds, and cry, and wallow yourselves in the ashes, ye principal of the flock: for your days of slaughter are accomplished, and of your dispersion, and ye shall fall like [2]precious vessels.

35 And the [1]flight shall fail from the shepherds, and the escaping from the principal of the flock.

36 A voice of the cry of the shepherds, and an howling of the principal of the flock, *shall be heard*: for the Lord hath destroyed their pasture.

37 And the [1]best pastures are destroyed because of the wrath and indignation of the Lord.

38 He hath forsaken his covert, as the lion: for their land is waste, because of the wrath of the oppressor, and because of the wrath of his indignation.

26 2 *Jeremiah moveth the people to repentance.* 7 *He is taken of the false prophets and priests, and brought to judgment.* 23 *Urijah the Prophet is killed of Jehoiakim contrary to the will of God.*

25:14 [1] That is, of the Babylonians, as Jer. 27:7.
25:15 [1] Signifying, the extreme affliction, that God had appointed for everyone, as Ps. 75:8; Isa. 51:17, and this cup, which the wicked drink, is more bitter than that which he giveth to his children, for he measureth the one by mercy, and the other by justice.
25:18 [1] For now it beginneth and shall so continue till it be accomplished.
25:20 [1] Read Job 1:1.
   [2] Which were cities of the Philistines.
25:21 [1] Edom is here taken for the whole country, and Uz for a part thereof.
25:22 [1] As Greece, Italy and the rest of those countries.

25:23 [1] These were people of Arabia which came of Dedan the son of Abraham and Keturah.
25:24 [1] For there were two countries so named, the one called plentiful, and the other barren, or desert.
25:25 [1] Or, Persia.
25:26 [1] That is, of Babylon, as Jer. 51:41.
25:29 [1] That is, Jerusalem, read verse 12.
25:33 [1] They which are slain at the Lord's appointment.
25:34 [1] Ye that are chief rulers, and governors.
   [2] Which are most easily broken.
25:35 [1] It shall not help them to seek to flee.
25:37 [1] Hebrew, *peaceable*.

1 In the beginning of the reign of Jehoiakim the son of Josiah King of Judah, came this word from the Lord, saying,

2 Thus saith the Lord, Stand in the ¹court of the Lord's House, and speak unto all the cities of Judah, which come to worship in the Lord's House, all the words that I command thee to speak unto them: keep not ²a word back,

3 If so be they will hearken, and turn every man from his evil way, that I may ¹repent me of the plague, which I have determined to bring upon them because of the wickedness of their works.

4 And thou shalt say unto them, Thus saith the Lord, If ye will not hear me to walk in my Laws, which I have set before you,

5 And to hear the words of my servants the Prophets, whom I sent unto you, both rising up early, and sending *them*, and will not obey *them*,

6 Then will I make this House like ¹Shiloh, and will make this city ²a curse to all nations of the earth.

7 So the Priests, and the Prophets, and all the people heard Jeremiah speaking these words in the House of the Lord.

8 Now when Jeremiah had made an end of speaking all that the Lord had commanded *him* to speak unto all the people, then the Priests, and the Prophets, and all the people took him, and said, Thou shalt die the death.

9 Why hast thou prophesied in the name of the Lord, saying, ¹This House shall be like Shiloh, and this city shall be desolate without an inhabitant? and all the people were gathered against Jeremiah in the house of the Lord.

10 And when the Princes of Judah heard of these things, they came up from the king's house into the House of the Lord, and sat down in the entry of the ¹new gate of the Lord's *House*.

11 Then spake the Priests, and the Prophets unto the Princes, and to all the people, saying, ¹This man is worthy to die: for he hath prophesied against this city, as ye have heard with your ears.

12 Then spake Jeremiah unto all the Princes and

CHAPTER 26
ᵃ Mic. 1:1
Mic. 3:12

to all the people, saying, The Lord hath ¹sent me to prophesy against this House and against this city all the things that ye have heard.

13 Therefore now amend your ways, and your works, and hear the voice of the Lord your God, that the Lord may repent him of the plague, that he hath pronounced against you.

14 As for me, behold, I am in your hands: do with me as ye think good and right:

15 But know ye for certain, that if ye put me to death, ye shall surely bring innocent blood upon yourselves, and upon this city, and upon the inhabitants thereof: for of a truth the Lord hath sent me unto you, to speak all these words in your ears.

16 Then said the Princes and all the people unto the Priests, and to the Prophets, This man is not worthy to die: for he hath spoken unto us in the Name of the Lord our God.

17 ¶ Then rose up certain of the Elders of the land, and spake to all the assembly of the people, saying,

18 Micah the Morashite ᵃprophesied in the days of Hezekiah king of Judah, and spake to all the people of Judah, saying, Thus saith the Lord of hosts, Zion shall be plowed *like* a field, and Jerusalem shall be an heap, and the mountain of the ¹house *shall be* as the high places of the forest.

19 Did Hezekiah King of Judah, and all Judah put him to death? did he not fear the Lord, and prayed before the Lord, and the Lord repented him of the ¹plague, that he had pronounced against them? Thus might we procure great evil against our souls.

20 And there was also a man that prophesied in the Name of the Lord, *one* Urijah the son of Shemaiah, of Kirjath Jearim, who prophesied against this city, and against this land, according to all the words of Jeremiah.

21 Now when Jehoiakim the king with all his men of power, and all the princes heard his words, the King sought to slay him. But when Urijah heard it, he was afraid and fled, and went into Egypt.

22 Then Jehoiakim the king ¹sent men into Egypt, *even* Elnathan the son of Achbor, and certain with him into Egypt.

26:2 ¹ That is, in that place of the Temple whereunto the people resort out of all Judah to sacrifice.
² To the intent that they should pretend no ignorance, as Acts 20:27.
26:3 ¹ Read Jer. 18:8
26:6 ¹ Read Jer. 7:12.
² So that when they would curse any, they shall say, God do to thee as to Jerusalem.
26:9 ¹ Because of God's promises to the Temple, Ps. 132:14, that he would forever remain there, the hypocrites thought this Temple could never perish, and therefore thought it blasphemy to speak against it, Matt. 26:61; Acts 6:13, not considering that this was meant of the Church, where God will remain forever.
26:10 ¹ So called, because it was repaired by Jotham, 2 Kings 15:35.

26:11 ¹ Hebrew, *judgments of death belongeth to this man.*
26:12 ¹ He both showeth the cause of his doings plainly, and also threateneth them that they should nothing avail, though they should put him to death, but heap greater vengeance upon their heads.
26:18 ¹ That is, of the House of the Lord, to wit, Zion, and these examples the godly alleged to deliver Jeremiah out of the Priests' hands, whose rage else would not have been satisfied but by his death.
26:19 ¹ So that the city was not destroyed, but by miracle was delivered out of the hands of Sennacherib.
26:22 ¹ Here is declared the fury of tyrants, who cannot abide to hear God's word declared, but persecute the ministers thereof, and yet in the end they prevail nothing but provoke God's judgments so much the more.

23 And they fetched Urijah out of Egypt, and brought him unto Jehoiakim the king, who slew him with the sword, and ¹cast his dead body into the graves of the children of the people.

24 But the hand of Ahikam ¹the son of Shaphan was with Jeremiah that they should not give him into the hand of the people to put him to death.

27 ¹ *Jeremiah at the commandment of the Lord sendeth bonds to the King of Judah and to the other Kings that were near, whereby they are monished to be subjects unto Nebuchadnezzar. 9 He warneth the people, and the Kings and rulers that they believe not false Prophets.*

1 In the beginning of the reign of ¹Jehoiakim the son of Josiah King of Judah came this word unto Jeremiah from the Lord, saying,

2 Thus saith the Lord to me, Make thee ¹bonds, and yokes, and put them upon thy neck,

3 And send them to the king of Edom, and to the king of Moab, and to the king of the Ammonites, and to the king of Tyre, and to the king of Sidon, by the hand of the messengers which come to Jerusalem unto Zedekiah the king of Judah,

4 And command them to say unto their masters, Thus saith the Lord of hosts the God of Israel, Thus shall ye say unto your masters,

5 I have made the earth, the man, and the beast that are upon the ground, by my great power, and by my outstretched arm, and have given it unto whom it pleased me.

6 But now I have given all these lands into the hand of Nebuchadnezzar the king of Babel my ¹servant, and the beasts of the field have I also given him to serve him.

7 And all nations shall serve him, and his ¹son, and his son's son until the very time of his land come also: then many nations and great kings shall ²serve themselves of him.

8 And the nation and kingdom which will not serve the same Nebuchadnezzar king of Babel, and that will not put their neck under the yoke of the king of Babel, the same nation will I visit saith the Lord, with the sword, and with the famine, and with the pestilence, until I have wholly *given* them into

CHAPTER 27
ᵃ Jer. 14:14
Jer. 23:11
Jer. 29:9
ᵇ Jer. 28:3
ᶜ 2 Kings 25:13

his hands.

9 Therefore hear not your prophets nor your soothsayers, nor your dreamers, nor your enchanters, nor your sorcerers which say unto you thus, Ye shall not serve the king of Babel.

10 For they prophesy a lie unto you to cause you to go far from your land, and that I should cast you out, and you should perish.

11 But the nation that put their necks under the yoke of the king of Babel, and serve him, those will I let remain still in their own land, saith the Lord, and they shall occupy it, and dwell therein.

12 ¶ I spake also to Zedekiah king of Judah according to all these words, saying, Put your necks under the yoke of the king of Babel, and serve him and his people, that ye may live.

13 Why will ye die, thou, and thy people by the sword, by the famine, and by the pestilence, as the Lord hath spoken against the nation, that will not serve the king of Babel?

14 Therefore hear not the words of the prophets that speak unto you, saying, Ye shall not serve the king of Babel: for they prophesy a lie unto you.

15 For I have not ᵃsent them, saith the Lord, yet they prophesy a lie in my Name, that I might cast you out, and that ye might perish, *both* you, and the Prophets that prophesy unto you.

16 Also I spake to the Priests, and to all this people, saying, Thus saith the Lord, Hear not the words of your prophets that prophesy unto you, saying, Behold, ᵇthe vessels of the house of the Lord shall now shortly be ¹brought again from Babel: for they prophesy a lie unto you.

17 Hear them not, *but* serve the king of Babel, that ye may live: wherefore should this city be desolate?

18 But if they be Prophets, and if the word of the Lord be with them, let them ¹entreat the Lord of hosts, that the vessels, which are left in the House of the Lord, and in the house of the king of Judah, and at Jerusalem, go not to Babel.

19 For thus saith the Lord of hosts, concerning the ᶜpillars, and concerning the sea, and concerning the bases, and concerning the residue of the vessels that remain in this city,

---

26:23 ¹ As in the first Hezekiah's example is to be followed, so in this other Jehoiakim's act is to be abhorred: for God's plague did light on him, and his household.
26:24 ¹ Which declareth that nothing could have appeased their fury, if God had not moved this noble man to stand valiantly in his defense.
27:1 ¹ As touching the disposition of these prophecies, they that gathered them into a book, did not altogether observe the order of times, but did set some afore, which should be after, and contrary wise, which if the reader mark well it shall avoid many doubts, and make the reading much more easy.
27:2 ¹ By such signs the Prophets used sometimes to confirm their

prophecies which notwithstanding they could not do of themselves, but in as much as they had a revelation for the same, Isa. 20:2, and therefore the false Prophets to get more credit, did use also such visible signs, but they had no revelation, 1 Kings 22:12.
27:6 ¹ Read Jer. 25:9.
27:7 ¹ Meaning, Evil-Merodach, and his son Belshazzar.
² They shall bring him and his kingdom in subjection, as Jer. 25:14.
27:16 ¹ Which were taken when Jeconiah was led captive into Babel.
27:18 ¹ For it was not only the Prophet's office to show the word of God, but also to pray for the sins of the people, Gen. 20:7, which these could not do because they had no express word: for God had pronounced the contrary.

20 Which Nebuchadnezzar King of Babel took not, when he carried ^daway captive Jeconiah the son of Jehoiakim king of Judah from Jerusalem to Babel, with all the nobles of Judah, and Jerusalem.

21 For thus saith the Lord of hosts the God of Israel, concerning the vessels that remain in the house of the Lord, and in the house of the king of Judah, and at Jerusalem,

22 They shall be brought to Babel, and there they shall be until the day that I visit ¹them, saith the Lord: then will I bring them up, and restore them unto this place.

28 ¹ *The false prophecy of Hananiah. 12 Jeremiah reproveth Hananiah, and prophesieth.*

1 And that same year in the beginning of the ¹reign of Zedekiah King of Judah, in the ²fourth year, *and* in the fifth month, Hananiah the son of Azur the prophet, which was of ³Gibeon, spake to me in the house of the Lord in the presence of the Priests, and of all the people, and said,

2 Thus speaketh the Lord of hosts, the God of Israel, saying, I have broken the yoke of the King of Babel.

3 ¹Within two years space I will bring into this place all the vessels of the Lord's House, that Nebuchadnezzar king of Babel took away from this place, and carried them into Babel.

4 And I will bring again to this place Jeconiah the son of Jehoiakim King of Judah, with all them that were carried away captive of Judah, and went into Babel, saith the Lord: for I will break the yoke of the king of Babel.

5 Then the Prophet Jeremiah said unto the ¹Prophet Hananiah in the presence of the Priests, and in the presence of all the people that stood in the House of the Lord.

6 Even the Prophet Jeremiah said, So be it: the ¹Lord so do, the Lord confirm thy words which thou hast prophesied, to restore the vessels of the Lord's house, and all that is carried captive from Babel, into this place.

7 But hear thou now this word that I will speak in thine ears, and in the ears of all the people.

^d 2 Kings 24:12,15

8 The Prophets that have been before me, and before thee in time past, ¹prophesied against many countries, and against great kingdoms, of war, and of plagues, and of pestilence.

9 *And* the Prophet which prophesieth of peace, when the word of the Prophet shall come to pass, *then* shall the Prophet be known that the Lord hath truly sent him.

10 Then Hananiah the Prophet took the yoke from the Prophet Jeremiah's neck, and ¹brake it.

11 And Hananiah spake in the presence of all the people, saying, Thus saith the Lord, Even so will I break the yoke of Nebuchadnezzar king of Babel, from the neck of all nations within the space of two years: and the Prophet Jeremiah went his way.

12 ¶ Then the word of the Lord came unto Jeremiah the Prophet, (after that Hananiah the Prophet had broken the yoke from the neck of the Prophet Jeremiah) saying,

13 Go and tell Hananiah, saying, Thus saith the Lord, Thou hast broken the yokes of wood, but thou shalt make for them yokes of iron.

14 For thus saith the Lord of hosts the God of Israel, I have put a ¹yoke of iron upon the neck of all these nations, that they may serve Nebuchadnezzar King of Babel: for they shall serve him, and I have given him the ²beasts of the field also.

15 Then said the Prophet Jeremiah, unto the Prophet Hananiah, Hear now Hananiah, the Lord hath not sent thee, but thou makest this people to trust in a lie.

16 Therefore thus saith the Lord, Behold, I will cast thee from of the earth: this year thou shalt die, because thou hast spoken rebelliously against the Lord.

17 So Hananiah the Prophet ¹died the same year in the seventh month.

29 ¹ *Jeremiah writeth unto them that were in captivity in Babylon. 10 He prophesieth their return after seventy years. 16 He prophesieth the destruction of the King and of the people that remain in Jerusalem. 21 He threateneth the prophets that seduce the people. 25 The death of Shemaiah is prophesied.*

1 Now these are the words of the ¹book that

27:22 ¹ That is, for the space of seventy years till I have caused the Medes and Persians to overcome the Chaldeans.

28:1 ¹ When Jeremiah began to bear these bonds and yokes.

   ² After that the land hast rested, as Lev. 25:2.

   ³ This was a city in Benjamin belonging to the sons of Aaron, Josh. 21:17.

28:3 ¹ Hebrew, *two years of days.*

28:5 ¹ He was so esteemed though he was a false prophet.

28:6 ¹ That is, I would wish the same for God's honor, and wealth of my people, but he hath appointed the contrary.

28:8 ¹ Meaning, that the Prophets that did either denounce war or peace, were tried either true or false by the success of their prophecies, albeit God maketh to come to pass sometimes that which the

false prophet speaketh to try the faith of his, Deut. 13:3.

28:10 ¹ This declareth the impudence of the wicked hirelings, which have no zeal to the truth, but are led with ambition to get the favor of men, and therefore cannot abide any that might discredit them but burst forth into rages and contrary to their own conscience, pass not what lies they report or how wickedly they do, so that they may maintain their estimation.

28:14 ¹ That is, a hard and cruel servitude.

   ² Signifying, that all should be his, as Dan. 2:38.

28:17 ¹ Seeing this thing was evident in the eyes of the people, and yet they returned not to the Lord, it is manifest, that miracles cannot move us, neither the word itself, except God touch the heart.

29:1 ¹ Or, letter.

Jeremiah the Prophet sent from Jerusalem unto [2]the residue of the Elders, which were carried away captives, and to the Priests, and to the Prophets, and to all the people, whom Nebuchadnezzar had carried away captive from Jerusalem to Babel:

2 (After that Jeconiah the King, and the [1]Queen, and the eunuchs, the [a]princes of Judah, and of Jerusalem, and the workmen, and cunning men were departed from Jerusalem)

3 By the hand of Elasah the son of Shaphan and Gemariah the son of Hilkiah, (whom Zedekiah king of Judah [1]sent unto Babel to Nebuchadnezzar king of Babel) saying,

4 Thus hath the Lord of hosts the God of Israel spoken unto all that are carried away captives, whom I have [1]caused to be carried away captives from Jerusalem unto Babel:

5 Build you houses to dwell in, and plant you gardens, and eat the fruits of them.

6 Take you wives, and beget sons and daughters, and take wives for your sons, and give your daughters husbands, that they may bear sons and daughters, that ye may be increased there, and not diminished.

7 And seek the prosperity of the city, whither I have caused you to be carried away captives, and [1]pray unto the Lord for it: for in the peace thereof shall you have peace.

8 ¶ For thus saith the Lord of hosts the God of Israel, Let not your prophets, and your soothsayers that be among you, deceive you, neither give ear to your dreams, which you dream.

9 For they prophesy you a lie in my Name: I have not sent them, saith the Lord.

10 But thus saith the Lord, that after seventy years be accomplished at Babel, I will visit you, and perform my good promise toward you, and cause you to return to this place.

11 For I know the thoughts, that I have thought towards you, saith the Lord, *even* the thoughts of peace, and not of trouble, to give you an end, and *your* hope.

12 Then shall you cry unto me, and ye shall go and pray unto me, and I will hear you,

13 And ye shall seek me, and find *me*, because ye shall seek me with all [1]your heart.

CHAPTER 29
[a] Jer. 24:1

14 And I will be found of you, saith the Lord, and I will turn away your captivity, and I will gather you from all the nations, and from all the places, whither I have cast you, saith the Lord, and will bring you again unto the place, whence I caused you to be carried away captive.

15 Because ye have said, The Lord hath raised us up [1]Prophets in Babel.

16 Therefore thus saith the Lord of the King, that sitteth upon the throne of David, and of all the people that dwell in this city, your brethren that are not gone forth with you into captivity:

17 *Even* thus saith the Lord of hosts, Behold, I will send upon them the [1]sword, the famine, and the pestilence, and will make them like vile [2]figs, that cannot be eaten, they are so naughty.

18 And I will persecute them with the sword, with the famine, and with the pestilence: and I will make them a terror to all kingdoms of the earth, *and* [1]a curse, and astonishment, and an hissing and a reproach among all the nations whither I have cast them,

19 Because they have not heard my words saith the Lord, which I sent unto them by my servants the Prophets, [1]rising up early, and sending *them*, but ye would not hear, saith the Lord.

20 ¶ Hear ye therefore the word of the Lord, all ye of the captivity, whom I have sent from Jerusalem to Babel.

21 Thus saith the Lord of hosts, the God of Israel, of Ahab the son of Kolaiah, and of Zedekiah the son of Maaseiah, which prophesy lies unto you in my Name, Behold, I will deliver them into the hand of Nebuchadnezzar King of Babel, and he shall slay them before your eyes.

22 And all they of the captivity of Judah, that are in Babel, shall take up this curse against them, and say, The Lord make thee like Zedekiah, and like Ahab, whom the King of Babel burnt [1]in the fire,

23 Because they have committed [1]villainy in Israel, and have committed adultery with their neighbor's wives, and have spoken lying words in my Name, which I have not commanded them, even I know it, and testify it, saith the Lord.

24 ¶ Thou shalt also speak to Shemaiah the

---

[2] For some died in the way.
29:2 [1] Meaning, Jeconiah's mother.
29:3 [1] To entreat of some equal conditions.
29:4 [1] To wit, the Lord, whose work this was.
29:7 [1] The Prophet speaketh not this for the affection that he bare to the tyrant, but that they should pray for the common rest and quietness, that their troubles might not be increased, and that they might with more patience and less grief wait for the time of their deliverance, which God had appointed most certain: for else not only the Israelites, but all the world, yea, and the insensible creatures should rejoice when these tyrants should be destroyed, as Isa. 14:4.

29:13 [1] When your oppression shall be great, and your afflictions cause you to repent your disobedience, and also when the seventy years of your captivity shall be expired, 2 Chron. 36:22; Ezra 1:1; Jer. 25:12; Dan. 9:2.
29:15 [1] As Ahab, Zedekiah and Shemaiah.
29:17 [1] Whereby he assureth them, that there shall be no hope of returning before the time appointed.
[2] According to the comparison, Jer. 24:1, 2.
29:18 [1] Read Jer. 26:6.
29:19 [1] Read Jer. 7:13, 25:3 and 26:5.
29:22 [1] Because they gave the people hope of speedy returning.
29:23 [1] Which was adultery, and falsifying the word of God.

¹Nehelamite, saying,

25 Thus speaketh the Lord of hosts, the God of Israel, saying, Because thou hast sent letters in thy name unto all the people, that are at Jerusalem, and to Zephaniah the son of Maaseiah the Priest, and to all the Priests, saying,

26 The Lord hath made thee Priest, for ¹Jehoiada the Priest, that ye should be officers in the House of the Lord, for every man that raveth and maketh himself a Prophet, to put him in prison and in the stocks.

27 Now therefore why hast not thou reproved Jeremiah of Anathoth, which prophesieth unto you?

28 For, for this cause he sent unto us in Babel, saying, This *captivity* is long: build houses to dwell in, and plant gardens, and eat the fruits of them.

29 And Zephaniah the Priest read this letter in the ears of Jeremiah the Prophet.

30 Then came the word of the Lord unto Jeremiah, saying,

31 Send to all them of the captivity, saying, Thus saith the Lord of Shemaiah the Nehelamite, Because that Shemaiah hath prophesied unto you, and I sent him not, and he caused you to trust in a lie,

32 Therefore thus saith the Lord, Behold, I will visit Shemaiah the Nehelamite, and his seed: he shall not have a man ¹to dwell among this people, neither shall he behold the good, that I will do for my people, saith the Lord, because he hath spoken rebelliously against the Lord.

30

1 *The return of the people from Babylon.*   16 *He menaceth the enemies,*   18 *and comforteth the Church.*

1 The word, that came to Jeremiah from the Lord, saying,

2 Thus speaketh the Lord God of Israel, saying, Write thee all the words that I have spoken unto thee, in ¹a book.

3 For lo, the days come, saith the Lord, that I will bring again the captivity of my people Israel and Judah, saith the Lord: for I will restore them unto the land, that I gave to their fathers, and they shall possess it.

4 Again, these are the words that the Lord spake concerning Israel, and concerning Judah.

5 For thus saith the Lord, We have heard a ¹terrible voice, of fear and not of peace.

6 Demand now and behold, if man travail with child: wherefore do I behold every man with his hands on his loins as a woman in travail, and all faces are turned into a paleness?

7 Alas, for this ¹day is great: none *hath been* like it: it is even the time of Jacob's trouble, yet shall he be delivered from it.

8 ¹For in that day, saith the Lord of hosts, I will break ²his yoke from off thy neck, and break thy bonds, and strangers shall no more serve themselves ³of him.

9 But they shall serve the Lord their God, and ¹David their King, whom I will raise up unto them.

10 Therefore fear not, O my servant Jacob, saith the Lord, neither be afraid, O Israel: for lo, I will deliver thee from a far *country*, and thy seed from the land of their captivity, and Jacob shall turn again, and shall be in rest and prosperity, and none shall make him afraid.

11 For I am with thee saith the Lord, to save thee: though I utterly destroy all the nations where I have scattered thee, yet will I not utterly destroy thee, but I will correct thee by judgment, and not utterly cut thee off.

12 For thus saith the Lord, Thy bruising is incurable, *and* thy wound is dolorous.

13 There is none to judge thy cause, *or to lay* a plaster: there are no medicines, nor help for thee.

14 All thy lovers have forgotten thee: they seek thee not: for I have stricken thee with the wound of an enemy, *and* with a sharp chastisement for the multitude of thine iniquities, *because* thy sins were increased.

15 Why cryest thou for thine affliction? thy sorrow is incurable, for the multitude of thine iniquities: *because* thy sins were increased, I have done these things unto thee.

16 ¹Therefore all they that devour thee, shall be devoured, and all thine enemies everyone shall go into

---

29:24 ¹ Or, dreamer.

29:26 ¹ Shemaiah the false prophet flattereth Zephaniah the chief Priest, as though God had given him the spirit and zeal of Jehoiada to punish whosoever trespassed against the word of God, of the which he would have made Jeremiah one, calling him a raver and a false prophet.

29:32 ¹ He and his seeds shall be destroyed, so that none of them should see the benefit of this deliverance.

30:2 ¹ Because they should be assured and their posterity confirmed in the hope of this deliverance promised.

30:5 ¹ He showeth that before that this deliverance shall come, the Chaldeans should be extremely afflicted by their enemies, and that they should be in such perplexity and sorrow as a woman in her tra-

vail, as Isa. 13:8.

30:7 ¹ Meaning, that the time of their captivity should be grievous.

30:8 ¹ When I shall visit Babylon.

² Of the King of Babylon.

³ To wit, of Jacob.

30:9 ¹ That is, Messiah which should come of the stock of David, according to the flesh and should be the true pastor, as Ezek. 34:23, who is set forth and his kingdom that should be everlasting in the person of David, Hos. 3:5.

30:16 ¹ Herein is commended God's great mercy toward his, who doth not destroy them for their sins, but correct and chastise them till he have purged and pardoned them, and so burneth the rods by the which he did punish them, Isa. 33:1.

captivity, and they that spoil thee, shall be spoiled, and all they that rob thee, will I give to be robbed.

17 For I will restore health unto thee, and I will heal thee of thy wounds, saith the Lord, because they called thee, The castaway, *saying*, This is Zion whom no man seeketh after.

18 Thus saith the Lord, Behold, I will bring again the captivity of Jacob's tents, and have compassion on his dwelling places, and the city shall be built upon her own heap, [1]and the palace shall remain after the manner thereof.

19 And out of them shall proceed [1]thanksgiving, and the voice of them that are joyous, and I will multiply them, and they shall not be few: I will also glorify them, and they shall not be diminished.

20 Their children also shall be as afore time, and their congregation shall be established before me: and I will visit all that vex them.

21 And their [1]noble *ruler* shall be of themselves, and their governor shall proceed from the midst of them, and I will cause him to draw near and approach unto me: for who is this that directeth his [2]heart to come unto me, saith the Lord?

22 And ye shall be my people, and I will be your God.

23 Behold, [1]the tempest of the Lord goeth forth with wrath: the whirlwind that hangeth over, shall light upon the head of the wicked.

24 The fierce wrath of the Lord shall not return, until he have done, and until he have performed the intents of his heart: in the [1]latter days ye shall understand it.

31
1 *He rehearseth God's benefits after their return from Babylon.* 13 *And the spiritual joy of the faithful in the Church.*

1 At the [1]same time, saith the Lord, will I be the God of all the families of Israel, and they shall be my people.

2 Thus saith the Lord, The people which [1]escaped the sword, found grace in the wilderness: [2]he walketh *before* Israel to cause him to rest.

3 The Lord hath appeared unto me [1]of old, *say they*: [2]Yea, I have loved thee with an everlasting love, therefore with mercy I have drawn thee.

4 Again I will build thee, and thou shalt be built, O virgin Israel: thou shalt still [1]be adorned with thy timbrels, and shalt go forth in the dance of them that be joyful.

5 Thou shalt yet plant vines upon the mountains of [1]Samaria, and the planters that plant them, [2]shall make them common.

6 For the days shall come, that the [1]watchmen upon the mount of Ephraim shall cry, Arise, and let us go up unto [2]Zion to the Lord our God.

7 For thus saith the Lord, Rejoice with gladness for Jacob, and shout for joy among the chief of the Gentiles: publish praise and say, O Lord, save thy people, the remnant of Israel.

8 [1]Behold, I will bring them from the North country, and gather them from the coasts of the world, *with* the blind and the lame among them, *with* the woman with child, and her that is delivered also: a great company shall return hither.

9 They shall come [1]weeping, and with mercy will I bring them again: I will lead them by the rivers of [2]water in a straight way, wherein they shall not stumble: for I am a father to Israel, and Ephraim is [3]my firstborn.

10 ¶ Hear the word of the Lord, O ye Gentiles, and declare in the isles afar off, and say, He that scattered Israel, will gather him, and will keep him, as a shepherd *doth* his flock.

11 For the Lord hath redeemed Jacob, and ransomed him from the hand [1]of him, that was stronger than he.

12 Therefore they shall come, and rejoice in the

30:18 [1] Meaning, that the city and the Temple should be restored to their former estate.

30:19 [1] He showeth how the people shall with praise and thanksgiving acknowledge these benefits.

30:21 [1] Meaning, Zerubbabel, who was the figure of Christ, in whom this was accomplished.

[2] Signifying, that Christ doth willingly submit himself to the obedience of God his father.

30:23 [1] Lest the wicked hypocrites should flatter themselves with these promises, the Prophets showeth what shall be their portion.

30:24 [1] When this Messiah and deliverer is sent.

31:1 [1] When this noble governor shall come, meaning, Christ, not only Judah, and Israel, but the rest of the world shall be called.

31:2 [1] Which were delivered from the cruelty of Pharaoh.

[2] To wit, God.

31:3 [1] The people thus reason as though he were not so beneficial to them now, as he had been of old.

[2] Thus the Lord answereth that his love is not changeable.

31:4 [1] Thou shalt have still occasion to rejoice: which is meant by timbrels, and dancing, as their custom was after notable victories, Exod. 15:20; Judg. 5:2 and Jer. 18:34.

31:5 [1] Because the Israelites, which were the ten tribes never returned to Samaria, therefore this must be spiritually understood under the kingdom of Christ, which was the restoration of the true Israel.

[2] That is, shall eat the fruit thereof, as Lev. 19:23-25; Deut. 20:6.

31:6 [1] The Ministers of the word.

[2] They shall exhort all to the embracing of the Gospel, as Isa. 2:3.

31:8 [1] He showeth what shall be the concord and love of all under the Gospel, when none shall be refused for their infirmities: and everyone shall exhort one another to embrace it.

31:9 [1] That is, lamenting their sins, which had not given ear to the Prophets, and therefore it followeth that God received them to mercy, Jer. 50:4. Some take it that they should weep for joy.

[2] Where they found no impediments, but abundance of all things.

[3] That is, my dearly beloved, as the first child is to the father.

31:11 [1] That is, from the Babylonians, and other enemies.

height of Zion, and shall run to the bountifulness of the Lord, *even* for the ¹wheat and for the wine, and for the oil, and for the increase of sheep and bullocks: and their soul shall be as a watered garden, and they shall have no more sorrow.

13 Then shall the virgin rejoice in the ¹dance, and the young men and the old men together: for I will turn their mourning into joy, and will comfort them, and give them joy for their sorrows.

14 And I will replenish the soul of the Priests with ¹fatness, and my people shall be satisfied with my goodness, saith the Lord.

15 Thus saith the Lord, A voice was heard on high, a mourning, *and* bitter weeping. ¹Rachel weeping for her children, refused to be comforted for her children, because they were not.

16 Thus saith the Lord, Refrain the voice from weeping, and thine eyes from tears: for thy work shall be rewarded, saith the Lord, and they shall come again from the land of the enemy:

17 And there is hope in thine end, saith the Lord, that *thy* children shall come again to their own borders.

18 I have heard ¹Ephraim lamenting *thus*, Thou hast corrected me, and I was chastised as an ²untamed calf: ³convert thou me, and I shall be converted: for thou art the Lord my God.

19 Surely after that I was converted, I repented, and after that I was instructed, I smote upon *my* ¹thigh: I was ashamed, yea, even confounded, because I did bear the reproach of my youth.

20 Is Ephraim ¹my dear son or pleasant child? yet since I spake unto him, I still ²remembered him: therefore my bowels are troubled for him. I will surely have compassion upon him, saith the Lord.

21 Set thee up ¹signs: make thee heaps: set thine heart toward the path and way, that thou hast walked: turn again, O virgin of Israel: turn again to these thy cities.

22 How long wilt thou go astray, O thou rebellious daughter? for the Lord hath created ¹a new thing in the earth: A WOMAN shall compass a man.

23 Thus saith the Lord of hosts the God of Israel, Yet shall they say this thing in the land of Judah, and in the cities thereof, when I shall bring again their captivity, The Lord bless thee, O habitation of justice *and* holy mountain.

24 And Judah shall dwell in it, and all the cities thereof together, the husbandmen and they that go forth with the flock.

25 For I have satiated the weary soul, and I have replenished every sorrowful soul.

26 Therefore I awaked and beheld, and my sleep ¹was sweet unto me.

27 Behold, the days come, saith the Lord, that I will sow the house of Israel, and the house of Judah ¹with the seed of man, and with the seed of beast.

28 And like as I have watched upon them, to pluck up and to root out, and to throw down, and to destroy, and to plague *them*, so will I watch over them, to build and to plant *them*, saith the Lord.

29 In those days shall they say no more, The fathers have ¹eaten a sour grape, and the children's teeth are set on edge.

30 But everyone shall die for his own iniquity, every man that eateth the sour grape, his teeth shall be set on edge.

31 ¶ Behold, the days come, saith the Lord, that I will make a ¹new covenant with the house of Israel, and with the house of Judah,

32 Not according to the covenant that I made with their fathers, when I took them by the hand to bring them out of the land of Egypt, the which my covenant they ¹brake, although I was ²an husband

---

31:12 ¹ By these temporal benefits he meaneth the spiritual graces, which are in the Church, and whereof there should be ever plenty, Isa. 58:11, 12.

31:13 ¹ In the company of the faithful, which ever praise God for his benefits.

31:14 ¹ Meaning, the spirit of wisdom, knowledge, and zeal.

31:15 ¹ To declare the greatness of God's mercy in delivering the Jews, he showeth them that they were like to the Benjamites of Israelites, that is, utterly destroyed and carried away, insomuch, that if Rachel the mother of Benjamin could have risen again to seek for her children, she should have found none remaining.

31:18 ¹ That is, the people that were led captive.
   ² Which was wanton and could not be subject to the yoke.
   ³ He showeth how the faithful used to pray: that is, desire God to turn them forasmuch as they cannot turn of themselves.

31:19 ¹ In sign of repentance and detestation of my sin.

31:20 ¹ As though he would say: No, for by his iniquity he did what lay in him to cast me off.
   ² To wit, in pity him for my promise's sake.

31:21 ¹ Mark by what way thou didst go into captivity, and thou shalt turn again by the same.

31:22 ¹ Because their deliverance from Babylon, was a figure of their deliverance from sin, he showeth how this should be procured, to wit, by Jesus Christ, whom a woman should conceive and bear in her womb. Which is a strange thing in earth, because he should be born of a virgin without man, or he meaneth that Jerusalem, which was like a barren woman in her captivity, should be fruitful as she, that is joined in marriage, and whom God blesseth with children.

31:26 ¹ Having understood this vision of the Messiah to come, in whom the two houses of Israel and Judah should be joined, I rejoiced.

31:27 ¹ I will multiply and enrich them with people and cattle.

31:29 ¹ The wicked used this proverb, when they did murmur against God's judgments pronounced by the Prophets, saying, That their fathers had committed the fault and that the children were punished, Ezek. 18:3.

31:31 ¹ Though the covenant of redemption made to the fathers, and this which was given after, seem divers, yet they are all one, and grounded on Jesus Christ, save that this is called new, because of the manifestation of Christ, and the abundant graces of the holy Ghost given to his Church under the Gospel.

31:32 ¹ And so were the occasion of their own divorcement through their infidelity, Isa. 50:1.
   ² Or, master.

unto them, saith the Lord.

33 But this shall be the covenant that I will make with the house of Israel, After ¹those days, saith the Lord, I will put my law in their inward parts, and write it in their hearts, and will be their God, and they shall be my people.

34 And they shall ¹teach no more every man his neighbor, and every man his brother, saying, Know the Lord: for they shall all know me from the least of them unto the greatest of them, saith the Lord: for I will forgive their iniquity, and will remember their sins no more.

35 Thus saith the Lord, which giveth ¹the sun for a light to the day, *and* the courses of the moon and of the stars for a light to the night, which breaketh the sea, when the waves thereof roar: his Name *is* the Lord of hosts.

36 If these ordinances depart out of my sight, saith the Lord, then shall the seed of Israel cease from being a nation before me, forever.

37 Thus saith the Lord, If the heavens can be measured, ¹or the foundations of the earth be searched out beneath, then will I cast off all the seed of Israel, for all that they have done, saith the Lord.

38 Behold, the days come, saith the Lord, that the ¹city shall be built to the Lord from the tower of Hananel, unto the gate of the corner.

39 And the line of the measure shall go forth [in] his presence upon the hill Gareb, and shall compass about to Goath.

40 And the whole valley of the dead bodies, and of the ashes, and all the fields unto the brook of Kidron, *and* unto the corner of the horsegate toward the East, *shall be* holy unto the Lord, neither shall it be plucked up nor destroyed anymore forever.

32 *Jeremiah is cast into prison because he prophesied that the city should be taken of the king of Babylon. 7 He showeth that the people should come again to*

CHAPTER 32
ᵃ Jer. 29:16,17
Jer. 34:2

their own possession. 38 *The people of God are his servants, and he is their Lord.*

1 The word that came unto Jeremiah from the Lord, in the ¹tenth year of Zedekiah king of Judah, which was the eighteenth year of Nebuchadnezzar.

2 For then the king of Babel's host besieged Jerusalem: and Jeremiah the Prophet was shut up in the court of the prison, which was in the King of Judah's house.

3 For Zedekiah king of Judah had shut him up, saying, Wherefore dost thou prophesy, and say, Thus saith the Lord, ᵃBehold, I will give this city into the hands of the King of Babel, and he shall take it?

4 And Zedekiah the king of Judah shall not escape out of the hand of the Chaldeans, but shall surely be delivered into the hands of the king of Babel, and shall speak with him mouth to mouth, and his eyes shall behold his face,

5 And he shall lead Zedekiah to Babel, and there shall he be, until ¹I visit him, saith the Lord: though ye fight with the Chaldeans, ye shall not prosper.

6 ¶ And Jeremiah said, The word of the Lord came unto me, saying,

7 Behold, Hanamel, the son of Shallum thine uncle, shall come unto thee and say, ¹Buy unto thee my field, that is in Anathoth: for the ²title by kindred *appertaineth* unto thee ³to buy it.

8 So Hanamel mine uncle's son came to me in the court of the prison, according to the word of the Lord, and said unto me, Buy my ¹field, I pray thee, that is in Anathoth, which is in the country of Benjamin: for the right of the possession *is* thine, and the purchase *belongeth* unto thee: buy it for thee. Then I knew that this was the word of the Lord.

9 And I bought the field of Hanamel, mine uncle's son, that was in Anathoth, and weighed him the silver, *even* seven ¹shekels, and ten *pieces* of silver.

10 And I wrote it in the book and signed it, and took witnesses, and weighed him the silver in the balances.

31:33 ¹ In the time of Christ, my law shall instead of tables of stone be written in their hearts by mine holy Spirit, Heb. 8:10.

31:34 ¹ Under the kingdom of Christ there shall be none blinded with ignorance, but I will give them faith, and knowledge of God for remission of their sins and daily increase the same: so that it shall not seem to come so much by the preaching of my ministers, as by the instruction of my holy Spirit, Isa. 54:13, but the full accomplishing hereof is referred to the kingdom of Christ, when we shall be joined with our head.

31:35 ¹ If the sun, moon and stars cannot but give light according to mine ordinance, so long as this world lasteth, so shall my Church never fail, neither shall anything hinder it: and as sure as I will have a people, so certain is it, that I will leave them my word forever to govern them with.

31:37 ¹ The one and the other is impossible.

31:38 ¹ As it was performed, Neh. 3:1. By this description he showeth that the city should be as ample, and beautiful as ever it was: but he

alludeth to the spiritual Jerusalem, whose beauty should be incomparable.

32:1 ¹ So that Jeremiah had now prophesied from the thirteenth year of Josiah unto the last year save one of Zedekiah's reign, which was almost forty years.

32:5 ¹ Till I take Zedekiah away by death: for he shall not die by the sword, as Jer. 34:4.

32:7 ¹ Whereby was meant that the people should return again out of captivity and enjoy their possessions and vineyards, as verses 15 and 44.

² Or, right to redeem it.

³ Because he was next of the kindred, as Ruth 4:4.

32:8 ¹ Of the possession of the Levites, read Lev. 25:32.

32:9 ¹ Which mounteth to of our money about ten shillings six pence, if this shekel were the common shekel, read Gen. 23:15, for the shekel of the Temple was of double value, and ten pieces of silver were half a shekel: for twenty made the shekel.

11 So I took the book of the possession, being sealed ¹*according* to the Law, and custom, with the book that was open,

12 And I gave the book of the possession unto Baruch the son of Neriah, the son of Mahseiah, in the sight of Hanamel mine uncle's *son*, and in the presence of the witnesses, written in the book of the possession, before all the Jews that sat in the court of the prison.

13 And I charged Baruch before them, saying,

14 Thus saith the Lord of hosts the God of Israel, Take the writings, *even* this book of the possession, both that is sealed, and this book that is open, and put them in an earthen ¹vessel, that they may continue a long time.

15 For the Lord of hosts, the God of Israel saith thus, Houses and fields, and vineyards shall be possessed again in this land.

16 ¶ Now when I had delivered the book of the possession unto Baruch the son of Neriah, I prayed unto the Lord, saying,

17 Ah Lord God, behold, thou hast made the heaven and the earth by thy great power, and by thy stretched out arm, and there is nothing ¹hard unto thee.

18 ᵇThou showest mercy unto thousands, and recompensest the iniquity of the fathers into the bosom of their ¹children after them: O God the great and mighty, whose name *is* the Lord of hosts,

19 Great in counsel, and mighty in work, (for thine eyes are open upon all the ways of the sons of men, to give to everyone according to his ways, and according to the fruit of his works)

20 Which hast set signs and wonders in the land of Egypt unto this day, and in Israel and among *all* men, and hast made thee a Name, ¹*as appeareth* this day,

21 And hast brought thy people Israel out of the land of Egypt with signs, and with wonders, and with a strong hand, and a stretched out arm, and with great terror,

22 And hast given them this land, which thou didst swear to their fathers to give them, *even* a land that floweth with milk and honey,

23 And they came in, and possessed it, but they

ᵇ Exod. 34:7
Deut. 5:9

obeyed not thy voice, neither walked in thy Law: all that thou commandedst them to do, they have not done: therefore thou hast caused this whole plague to come upon them.

24 Behold, the ¹mounts, they are come into the city to take it, and the city is given into the hand of the Chaldeans, that fight against it by means of the sword, and of the famine, and of the pestilence, and what thou hast spoken, is come to pass, and behold, thou seest it.

25 And thou hast said unto me, O Lord God, Buy unto thee the field for silver, and take witnesses: for the city shall be given into the hand of the Chaldeans.

26 ¶ Then came the word of the Lord unto Jeremiah, saying,

27 Behold, I am the LORD GOD of all ¹flesh: is there anything too hard for me?

28 Therefore thus saith the Lord, Behold, I will give this city into the hand of the Chaldeans, and into the hand of Nebuchadnezzar, king of Babel, and he shall take it.

29 And the Chaldeans shall come and fight against this city, and set fire on this city, and burn it with the houses, upon whose roofs they have offered incense unto Baal, and poured drink offerings unto other gods, to provoke me unto anger.

30 For the children of Israel, and the children of Judah have surely done evil before me, from their ¹youth: for the children of Israel have surely provoked me to anger with the works of their hands, saith the Lord.

31 Therefore this city hath been unto me *as a provocation* of mine anger, and of my wrath, from the day that they built it, even unto this day, that I should remove it out of my sight,

32 Because of all the evil of the children of Israel, and of the children of Judah, which they have done to provoke me to anger, *even* they, their Kings, their Princes, their Priests, and their Prophets, and the men of Judah, and the inhabitants of Jerusalem.

33 And they have turned unto me the back and not the face: though I taught them, ¹rising up early, and instructing them, yet they were not obedient to receive doctrine,

34 But they set their abominations in the house

32:11 ¹ According to the custom the instrument or evidence was sealed up with the common seal, and a copy thereof remained, which contained the same in effect, but was not so authentical as the other, but was left open to be seen if anything should be called into doubt.

32:14 ¹ And so to hide them in the ground, that they might be preserved as a token of their deliverance.

32:17 ¹ Or, hid.

32:18 ¹ Because the wicked are subject to the curse of God, he showeth that their posterity which by nature are under this malediction, shall be punisheth both for their own wickedness, and that the iniquity of their fathers, which is likewise in them, shall be also revenged on their head.

32:20 ¹ Meaning, that his miracles in delivering his people, should never be forgotten.

32:24 ¹ The word signifieth anything that is cast up, as a mount or rampart, and is also used for engines of war, which were laid on an high place to shoot into a city before that guns were in use.

32:27 ¹ That is, of every creature: who as they are his work, so doth he govern and guide them as pleaseth him, whereby he showeth that as he is the author of this their captivity for their sins, so will he for his mercies be their redeemer to restore them again to liberty.

32:30 ¹ From the time that I brought them out of Egypt, and made them my people, and called them my firstborn.

32:33 ¹ Read Prov. 1:24; Isa. 65:2; Jer. 7:13 and 13:3 and 26:5 and 29:19; and 2 Chron. 36:15; Jer. 35:14 and 44:4.

(whereupon my Name was called) to defile it.

35 And they built the high ¹places of Baal, which are in the valley of ²Ben-Hinnom, to cause their sons and their daughters to ³pass through *the fire* unto Molech, which I commanded them not, neither came it into my mind, that they should do such abomination, to cause Judah to sin.

36 And now ¹therefore, thus hath the Lord God of Israel spoken concerning this city, whereof ye say, It shall be delivered into the hand of the king of Babel by the sword, and by the famine, and by the pestilence.

37 ᶜBehold, I will gather them out of all countries, wherein I have scattered them in mine anger, and in my wrath, and in great indignation, and I will bring them again unto this place, and I will cause them to dwell safely.

38 And they shall be ᵈmy people, and I will be their God.

39 And I will give them ¹one heart and one way, that they may fear me forever for the wealth of them, and of their children after them.

40 And I will make an everlasting ¹covenant with them, that I will never turn away from them to do them good, but I will put my fear in their hearts, that they shall not depart from me.

41 Yea, I will delight in them to do them good, and I will plant them in this land assuredly with my whole heart, and with all my soul.

42 For thus saith the Lord, Like as I have brought all this great plague upon this people, so will I bring upon them all the good that I have promised them.

43 And the fields shall be possessed in this land, whereof ye say, it is desolate without man or beast, and shall be given into the hand of the Chaldeans.

44 Men shall buy ¹fields for silver, and make writings and seal them, and take witnesses in the land of Benjamin, and round about Jerusalem, and in the cities of Judah, and in the cities of the mountains, and in the cities of the plain, and in the cities of the South: for I will cause their captivity to return, saith the Lord.

ᶜ Deut. 30:3
ᵈ Jer. 30:22

33 *1 The Prophet is monished of the Lord to pray for the deliverance of the people which the Lord promised. 8 God forgiveth sins for his own glory. 15 Of the birth of Christ. 20 The kingdom of Christ in the Church shall never be ended.*

1 Moreover the word of the Lord came unto Jeremiah the second time (while he was yet shut up in the ¹court of prison) saying,

2 Thus saith the Lord, the ¹maker thereof, the Lord that formed it, and established it, the Lord is his Name.

3 Call unto me, and I will answer thee, and show thee great and mighty things, which thou knowest not.

4 For thus saith the Lord God of Israel, concerning the houses of this city, and concerning the houses of the Kings of Judah, which are destroyed by the ¹mounts, and by the sword,

5 They come to ¹fight with the Chaldeans, but it *is* to fill themselves with the dead bodies of men, whom I have slain in mine anger and in my wrath: for I have hid my ²face from this city, because of all their wickedness.

6 ¶ Behold, I ¹will give it health and amendment: for I will cure them, and will reveal unto them the abundance of peace, and truth.

7 And I will cause the captivity of Judah and the captivity of Israel to return, and will build them as at the first.

8 And I will ¹cleanse them from all their iniquity, whereby they have sinned against me: yea, I will pardon all their iniquities, whereby they have sinned against me, and whereby they have rebelled against me.

9 And it shall be to me a name, a ¹joy, a praise, and an honor before all the nations of the earth, which shall hear all the good that I do unto them: and they shall fear and tremble for all the goodness, and for all the wealth, that I show unto this *city*.

10 Thus saith the Lord, Again there shall be heard in this place (which ye say shall be desolate, without man, and without beast, *even* in the cities of Judah, and in the streets of Jerusalem, that are desolate without man, and without inhabitant, and without beast)

11 The voice of joy and the voice of gladness, the

32:35 ¹ That is, the altars which were made to offer sacrifices upon to their idols.
  ² Read Jer. 7:31; 2 Kings 21:4, 6.
  ³ Read 2 Kings 16:3.
32:36 ¹ Read Jer. 30:16.
32:39 ¹ One consent and one religion, as Ezek. 11:19 and 36:27.
32:40 ¹ Read Jer. 31, 32, 33.
32:44 ¹ This is the declaration of that which was spoken verse 8.
33:1 ¹ Which was in the king's house at Jerusalem, as Jer. 32:1, 2.
33:2 ¹ To wit, of Jerusalem, who as he made it, so will he preserve it, read Isa. 37:26.
33:4 ¹ Read Jer. 32:24.

33:5 ¹ The Jews think to overcome the Chaldeans, but they seek their own destruction.
  ² He showeth that God's favor is cause of all prosperity, as his anger is of all adversity.
33:6 ¹ In the midst of his threatenings God remembereth his, and comforteth them.
33:8 ¹ Declaring that there is no deliverance nor joy, but whereas we feel remission of sins.
33:9 ¹ Whereby he showeth that the Church wherein is remission of sins, is God's honor and glory, so that whosoever is enemy to it, laboreth to dishonor God.

voice of the bridegroom, and the voice of the bride, the voice of them that shall say, ¹Praise the Lord of hosts, because the Lord is good: for his mercy *endureth* forever, *and* of them that offer *the sacrifice* of praise in the house of the Lord, for I will cause to return the captivity of the land, as at the first, saith the Lord.

12 Thus saith the Lord of hosts, Again in this place, which is desolate, without man, and without beast, and in all the cities thereof there shall be dwelling for shepherds to rest their flocks.

13 In the cities of the ¹mountains, in the cities in the plain, and in the cities of the South, and in the land of Benjamin and about Jerusalem, and in the cities of Judah shall the sheep pass again, under the hand of him that telleth them, saith the Lord.

14 Behold, the days come, saith the Lord, that I will perform that good thing, which I have promised unto the house of Israel, and to the house of Judah.

15 In those days, and at that time will I cause ¹the Branch of righteousness to grow up unto David, and he shall execute judgment and righteousness in the land.

16 In those days shall Judah be saved, and Jerusalem shall dwell safely, and he that shall call ¹her, is the Lord our ²righteousness.

17 For thus saith the Lord, David shall never want a man to sit upon the throne of the house of Israel.

18 Neither shall the Priests and Levites want a man before me to offer ¹burnt offerings, and to offer meat offerings, and to do sacrifice continually.

19 ¶ And the word of the Lord came unto Jeremiah, saying,

20 Thus saith the Lord, If you can break my covenant of the ¹day, and my covenant of the night, that there should not be day and night in their season,

21 Then may my covenant be broken with David my servant, that he should not have a son to reign upon his throne, and with the Levites, *and* Priests my ministers.

22 As the army of heaven cannot be numbered, neither the sand of the sea measured: so will I multiply the seed of David my servant, and the Levites, that minister unto me.

23 ¶ Moreover, the word of the Lord came to Jeremiah, saying,

CHAPTER 34
ª 2 Chron. 36:19
Jer. 29:16,17
Jer. 32:3

24 Considerest thou not what ¹this people have spoken, saying, The two families, which the Lord hath chosen, he hath even cast them off? thus they have despised my people, that they should be no more a nation before them.

25 Thus saith the Lord, If my covenant be not with day and night, *and if* I have not appointed the order of heaven and earth,

26 Then will I cast away the seed of Jacob and David my servant, and not take of his seed to be rulers over the seed of Abraham, Isaac, and Jacob: for I will cause their captivity to return, and have compassion on them.

34 1 *He threateneth that the city, and the King Zedekiah shall be given into the hands of the king of Babylon.* 11 *He rebuketh their cruelty toward their servants.*

1 The word which came unto Jeremiah from the Lord (when ¹Nebuchadnezzar king of Babel, and all his host, and all the kingdoms of the earth, *that were* under the power of his hand, and all people fought against Jerusalem, and against all the cites thereof) saying,

2 Thus saith the Lord God of Israel, Go, and speak to Zedekiah king of Judah, and tell him, Thus saith the Lord, behold, ªI will give this city into the hand of the king of Babel, and he shall burn it with fire,

3 And thou shall not escape out of his hand, but shalt surely be taken, and delivered into his hand, and thine eyes shall behold the face of the king of Babel, and he shall speak with thee mouth to mouth, and thou shalt go to Babel.

4 Yet hear the word of the Lord, O Zedekiah king of Judah, thus saith the Lord of thee, Thou shalt not die by the sword,

5 *But* thou shalt die in ¹peace: and according to the burning for thy fathers the former kings which were before thee, so shall they burn *odors* for thee, and they shall lament thee, *saying*, Oh ²Lord: for I have pronounced the word, saith the Lord.

6 Then Jeremiah the Prophet spake all these words unto Zedekiah king of Judah in Jerusalem,

7 (When the King of Babel's host fought against Jerusalem, and against all the cities of Judah, that were left, *even* against Lachish, and against Azekah: for

33:11 ¹ Which was a song appointed for the Levites to praise God by, 1 Chron. 16:8; Ps. 105:1; Isa. 12:4; Ps. 106:1; 107:1; 118:1; 136:1.
33:13 ¹ Meaning, that all the country of Judah shall be inhabited again.
33:15 ¹ That is, I will send the Messiah, which shall come of the house of David, of whom this prophecy is meant, as testify all the Jews, and that which is written, Jer. 23:5.
33:16 ¹ To wit, Christ that shall call his Church.
² That is, Christ is our Lord God, our righteousness, sanctification, and redemption, 1 Cor. 1:30.
33:18 ¹ That is chiefly meant of the spiritual sacrifice of thanksgiving,

which is left to the Church in the time of Christ, who was the everlasting Priest, and the everlasting sacrifice figured by the sacrifices of the Law.
33:20 ¹ Read Jer. 31:35.
33:24 ¹ Meaning, the Chaldeans and other infidels which thought God had utterly cast off Judah and Israel or Benjamin, because he did correct them for a time for their amendment.
34:1 ¹ Who commonly of Jeremiah was called Nebuchadrezzar, and of others Nebuchadnezzar.
34:5 ¹ Not of any violent death.
² The Jews shall lament for thee their lord and king.

these strong cities remained of the cities of Judah)

8 This *is* the word that came unto Jeremiah from the Lord, after that the king Zedekiah had made a covenant with all the people, which were at Jerusalem, [1]to proclaim liberty unto them,

9 That every man should let his [1]servant go free, and every man his handmaid, which was an Hebrew or an Hebrewess, and that none should serve himself of them, *to wit*, of a Jew his brother.

10 Now when all the princes, and all the people which was agreed to the covenant, heard that everyone should let his servant go free, and everyone his handmaid, and that none should serve themselves of them anymore, they obeyed and let them go.

11 But afterward they [1]repented and caused the servants and the handmaids, whom they had let go free, to return, and held them in subjection as servants and handmaids.

12 Therefore the word of the Lord came unto Jeremiah from the Lord, saying,

13 Thus saith the Lord God of Israel, I made a covenant with your fathers, when I brought them out of the land of Egypt, out of the house of [1]servants, saying,

14 [b]At the term of seven years, let ye go every man his brother an Hebrew which hath been sold unto thee: and when he hath served thee six years, thou shalt let him go free from thee: but your fathers obeyed me not, neither inclined their ears.

15 And ye were now turned, and had done right in my sight in proclaiming liberty, every man to his neighbor, and ye had made a covenant before me in [1]the house, whereupon my Name is called.

16 But ye repented, and polluted my Name: for ye have caused every man his servant, and every man his handmaid, whom ye had set at liberty at their pleasure, to return, and hold them in subjection to be unto you as servants and as handmaids.

17 Therefore thus saith the Lord, Ye have not obeyed me, in proclaiming freedom every man to his brother, and every man to his neighbor: behold, I proclaim a liberty for you, saith the Lord, to [1]the sword, to the pestilence, and to the famine, and I will make you a terror to all the kingdoms of the earth.

18 And I will give those men that have broken

[b] Deut. 15:1,12

my Covenant, and have not kept the words of the Covenant, which they had made before me, when they [1]cut the calf in twain, and passed between the parts thereof,

19 The princes of Judah, and the princes of Jerusalem, the Eunuchs, and the Priests, and all the people of the land, which passed between the parts of the calf,

20 I will even give them into the hand of their enemies, and into the hands of them that seek their life: and their dead bodies shall be for meat unto the fowls of the heaven, and to the beasts of the earth.

21 And Zedekiah king of Judah, and his princes will I give into the hand of their enemies, and into the hand of them that seek their life, and into the hand of the king of Babel's host, which [1]are gone up from you.

22 Behold, I will command, saith the Lord, and cause them to return to this city, and they shall fight against it, and take it and burn it with fire: and I will make the cities of Judah desolate without an inhabitant.

35

He purposeth the obedience of the Rechabites, and thereby confoundeth the pride of the Jews.

1 The word which came unto Jeremiah from the Lord, in the days [1]of Jehoiakim the son of Josiah king of Judah, saying,

2 Go unto the house of the [1]Rechabites, and speak unto them, and bring them into the house of the Lord into one of the chambers, and give them wine to drink.

3 Then took I Jaazaniah, the son of Jeremiah the son of Habazziniah, and his brethren, and all his sons, and the whole house of the Rechabites,

4 And I brought them into the house of the Lord, into the chamber of the sons of Hanan the son of Igdaliah a man [1]of God, which was by the chamber of the princes, which was above the chamber of Maaseiah the son of Shallum, the keeper of the [2]treasure.

5 And I set before the sons of the house of the Rechabites pots full of wine, and cups, and [1]said unto them, Drink wine.

34:8 [1] When the enemy was at hand, and they saw themselves in danger, they would seem holy, and so began some kind of reformation: but soon after they uttered their hypocrisy.

34:9 [1] According to the Law, Exod. 21:2; Deut. 15:12.

34:11 [1] Hebrew, *returneth*.

34:13 [1] Or, bondage.

34:15 [1] Meaning, in the Temple, to declare that it was a most solemn and straight covenant, made in the Name of the Lord.

34:17 [1] That is, I give the sword liberty to destroy you.

34:18 [1] As touching this manner of solemn covenant which the ancients used by passing between the two parts of a beast, to signify

that the transgressor of the same covenant should be so divided in pieces, read Gen. 15:10.

34:21 [1] To fight against the Egyptians, as Jer. 37:11.

35:1 [1] For the disposition and order of these prophecies, read Jer. 27:1.

35:2 [1] They came of Hobab Moses' father-in-law, who was no Israelite, but after joined with them in the service of God.

35:4 [1] That is, a Prophet.

[2] Or, door.

35:5 [1] The Prophet saith not, The Lord saith thus, for then they ought to have obeyed, but he tendeth to another end: that is, to declare their obedience to man, seeing the Jews would not obey God himself.

6 But they said, We will drink no wine: for ¹Jonadab the son of Rechab our father commanded us, saying, ²Ye shall drink no wine, *neither* you nor your sons forever.

7 Neither shall ye build house, nor sow seed, nor plant vineyard, nor have any, but all your days ye shall dwell in tents, that ye may live a long time in the land where ye be strangers.

8 Thus have we obeyed the voice of Jonadab the son of Rechab our father, in all that he hath charged us, and we drink no wine all our days, *neither* we, our wives, our sons, nor our daughters.

9 Neither build we houses for us to dwell in, neither have we vineyard, nor field, nor seed,

10 But we have remained in tents, and have obeyed, and done according to ¹all that Jonadab our father commanded us.

11 But when Nebuchadnezzar king of Babel came up into the land, we said, Come, and let us go to Jerusalem, from the host of the Chaldeans, and from the host of Aram: so we ¹dwell at Jerusalem.

12 Then came the word of the Lord unto Jeremiah, saying,

13 Thus saith the Lord of hosts, the God of Israel, Go, and tell the men of Judah, and the inhabitants of Jerusalem, Will ¹ye not receive doctrine to obey my words, saith the Lord?

14 The commandment of Jonadab the son of Rechab that he commanded his sons, that they should drink no wine, is surely kept: for unto this day they drink none, but obey their father's commandment: notwithstanding I have spoken unto you, ¹rising early, and speaking, but ye would not obey me.

15 I have sent also unto you all my servants the Prophets: rising up early, and sending *them*, saying, ªReturn now every man from his evil way, and amend your works, and go not after other gods to serve them, and ye shall dwell in the land which I have given unto you, and to your fathers, but ye would not incline your ear, nor obey me.

16 Surely the sons of Jonadab the son of Rechab, have kept the commandment of their father, which he gave them, but this people hath not obeyed me.

17 ªTherefore thus saith the Lord of hosts, the

CHAPTER 35
ª Jer. 18:11
Jer. 25:5

God of Israel, Behold, I will bring upon Judah, and upon all the inhabitants of Jerusalem, all the evil that I have pronounced against them, because I have ¹spoken unto them, but they would not hear, and I have called unto them, but they would not answer.

18 And Jeremiah said to the house of the Rechabites, Thus saith the Lord of hosts, the God of Israel, Because ye have obeyed the commandment of Jonadab your father, and kept all his precepts, and done according unto all that he hath commanded you,

19 Therefore thus saith the Lord of hosts, the God of Israel, Jonadab the son of Rechab shall ¹not want a man, to stand before me forever.

36 *Baruch writeth as Jeremiah inditeth, the book of the curses against Judah and Israel. 9 He is sent with the book unto the people, and readeth it before them all. 14 He is called before the rulers, and readeth it before them also. 23 The king casteth it in the fire. 28 There is another written at the commandment of the Lord.*

1 And in the fourth ¹year of Jehoiakim the son of Josiah king of Judah came this word unto Jeremiah from the Lord, saying,

2 Take thee a roll *or* book, and write therein all the words that I have spoken to thee against Israel, and against Judah, and against all the nations, from the day that I spake unto thee, *even* ¹from the days of Josiah unto this day.

3 It may be that the house of Judah will hear of all the evil, which I determined to do unto them, that they may return every man from his evil way, that I may forgive their iniquity and their sins.

4 Then Jeremiah called Baruch the son of Neriah, and Baruch wrote ¹at the mouth of Jeremiah all the words of the Lord, which he had spoken unto him, upon a roll *or* book.

5 And Jeremiah commanded Baruch, saying, I am ¹shut up, *and* cannot go into the House of the Lord.

6 Therefore go thou, and read the roll wherein thou hast written at my mouth the words of the Lord, in the audience of the people in the Lord's house upon the ¹fasting day: also thou shalt read them in the hearing of all Judah, that come out of their cities.

35:6 ¹ Whom Jehu the King of Israel favored for his zeal, 2 Kings 10:15.
² Teaching them hereby to flee all occasion of intemperancy, ambition and avarice, and that they might know that they were strangers in the earth, and be ready to depart at all occasions.
35:10 ¹ Which was now for the space of three hundred years from Jehu to Jehoiakim.
35:11 ¹ Which declareth that they were not so bound to their vow, that it could not be broken for any necessity: for where they were commanded to dwell in tents, they dwell now at Jerusalem for fear of the wars.
35:13 ¹ Whom I have chosen to be my children, seeing these which were the children of an heathen man, obeyed the commandment of their father.
35:14 ¹ I have most diligently exhorted and warned you both by

myself and my Prophet.
35:17 ¹ That is, by his Prophets and ministers, which showeth that it is as much, as though he should speak to us himself, when he sendeth his ministers to speak in his Name.
35:19 ¹ His posterity shall continue and be in my favor forever.
36:1 ¹ Read Jer. 25:1.
36:2 ¹ Which were twenty and three years, as Jer. 25:3, counting from the thirteenth year of Josiah's reign.
36:4 ¹ As he did indite.
36:5 ¹ Meaning, in prison, through the malice of the Priests.
36:6 ¹ Which was proclaimed for fear of the Babylonians, as their custom was when they feared war, or any great plague of God.

7 It may be that they will ¹pray before the Lord, and everyone return from his evil way, for great is the anger and the wrath that the Lord hath declared against this people.

8 So Baruch the son of Neriah did according unto all, that Jeremiah the Prophet commanded him, reading in the book the words of the Lord in the Lord's house.

9 ¶ And in the fifth ¹year of Jehoiakim the son of Josiah King of Judah, in the ninth month, they proclaimed a fast before the Lord to all the people in Jerusalem, and to all the people that came from the cities of Judah unto Jerusalem.

10 Then read Baruch in the book the words of Jeremiah in the house of the Lord, in the chamber of Gemariah the son of Shaphan the Secretary, in the higher court at the entry of the ¹new gate of the Lord's house in the hearing of all the people.

11 When Michaiah the son of Gemariah, the son of Shaphan had heard out of the book all the words of the Lord,

12 Then he went down to the King's house into the Chancellor's chamber, and lo, all the princes sat there, even Elishama the Chancellor, and Delaiah the son of Shemaiah, and Elnathan the son of Achbor, and Gemariah the son of Shaphan, and Zedekiah the son of Hananiah, and all the princes.

13 Then Michaiah declared unto them all the words that he had heard when Baruch read in the book in the audience of the people.

14 Therefore all the princes sent Jehudi the son of Nethaniah, the son of Shelemiah, the son of Cushi, unto Baruch, saying, Take in thine hand the roll, wherein thou hast read in the audience of the people, and come. So Baruch the son of Neriah took the roll in his hand, and came unto them.

15 And they said unto him, Sit down now, and read it, that we may hear. So Baruch read it in their audience.

16 Now when they had heard all the words, they were ¹afraid both one and other, and said unto Baruch, We will certify the King of all these words.

17 And they examined Baruch, saying, Tell us now, how didst thou write all these words at his mouth?

18 Then Baruch answered them, He pronounced all these words unto me with his mouth, and I wrote them with ink in the book.

19 Then said the princes unto Baruch, Go, ¹hide thee, thou and Jeremiah, and let no man know where ye be.

20 ¶ And they went in to the king to the court, but they laid up the roll in the chamber of Elishama the Chancellor, and told the King all the words, that he might hear.

21 So the King sent Jehudi to fetch the roll, and he took it out of Elishama the Chancellor's chamber, and Jehudi read it in the audience of the King, and in the audience of all the princes, which stood beside the King.

22 Now the King sat in the winter house, in the ¹ninth month, and there was a fire burning before him.

23 And when Jehudi had read three or four sides, he cut it with the penknife, and cast it into the fire that was on the hearth, until all the roll was consumed in the fire, that was on the hearth.

24 Yet they were not afraid, nor rent ¹their garments, neither the King, nor any of his servants that heard all these words.

25 Nevertheless, Elnathan, and Delaiah, and Gemariah had besought the King, that he would not burn the roll: but he would not hear them.

26 But the King commanded Jerahmeel the son of Hammelech, and Seraiah the son of Azriel, and Shelemiah the son of Abdeel, to take Baruch the Scribe, and Jeremiah the Prophet, but the Lord ¹hid them.

27 ¶ Then the word of the Lord came to Jeremiah (after that the King had burnt the roll and the words that Baruch wrote at the mouth of Jeremiah) saying,

28 Take thee again ¹another roll, and write in it all the former words that were in the first roll which Jehoiakim the King of Judah hath burnt,

29 And thou shalt say to Jehoiakim King of Judah, Thus saith the Lord, thou hast burnt this roll, saying, ¹Why hast thou written therein, saying, That the King of Babel shall certainly come and destroy this land, and shall take thence both man and beast?

36:7 ¹ He showeth that fasting without prayer and repentance, availeth nothing, but is mere hypocrisy.

36:9 ¹ The fast was then proclaimed, and Baruch read this rule, which was a little before that Jerusalem was first taken, and then Jehoiakim, and Daniel and his companions were led away captives.

36:10 ¹ Which is the East gate of the Temple.

36:16 ¹ The godly were afraid, seeing God so offended, and the wicked were astonied for the horror of the punishment.

36:19 ¹ They that were godly among the princes gave this counsel, by whose means it is like that Jeremiah was delivered: for they knew the rage of the king and of the wicked to be such, that they could not escape without danger of their lives.

36:22 ¹ Which contained part of November, and part of December.

36:24 ¹ Showing that the wicked instead of repenting when they hear God's judgments, grow into further malice against him and his word.

36:26 ¹ Thus we see the continual care, that God hath ever over his to preserve them from the rage of the wicked.

36:28 ¹ Though the wicked think to have abolished the word of God, when they have burnt the book thereof: yet this declareth that God will not only raise it up again, but also increase it in greater abundance to their condemnation, as verse 32.

36:29 ¹ These are Jehoiakim's words.

30 Therefore thus saith the Lord of Jehoiakim King of Judah, He shall have [1]none to sit upon the throne of David, and his [2]dead body shall be cast out in the day to the heat, and in the night to the frost.

31 And I will visit him and his seed, and his servants for their iniquity, and I will bring upon them, and upon the inhabitants of Jerusalem, and upon the men of Judah all the evil that I have pronounced against them: but they would not hear.

32 Then took Jeremiah another roll, and gave it to Baruch the Scribe the son of Neriah, which wrote therein at the mouth of Jeremiah all the words of the book which Jehoiakim King of Judah had burnt in the fire, and there were added besides them many like words.

37

1 Zedekiah succeedeth Jeconiah. 3 He sendeth unto Jeremiah to pray for him. 12 Jeremiah going into the land of Benjamin is taken. 15 He is beaten and put in prison.

1 And [a]King Zedekiah the son of Josiah reigned for [1]Coniah the son of Jehoiakim, whom Nebuchadnezzar king of Babel [2]made king in the land of Judah.

2 But neither he, nor his servants, nor the people of the land would obey the words of the Lord which he spake by the [1]ministry of the Prophet Jeremiah.

3 And Zedekiah the king [1]sent Jehucal the son of Shelemiah, and Zephaniah the son of Maaseiah the Priest to the Prophet Jeremiah, saying, Pray now unto the Lord our God for us.

4 (Now Jeremiah went [1]in and out among the people: for they had not put him into the prison.

5 Then Pharaoh's host was [1]come out of Egypt: and when the Chaldeans that besieged Jerusalem, heard tidings of them, they [2]departed from Jerusalem.)

6 Then came the word of the Lord unto the Prophet Jeremiah, saying,

7 Thus saith the Lord God of Israel, Thus shall ye say to the King of Judah, that sent you unto me to inquire of me, Behold, Pharaoh's host, which is come forth to help you, shall return to Egypt into their own land.

8 And the Chaldeans shall come again, and fight against this city, and take it and burn it with fire.

9 Thus saith the Lord, [1]Deceive not yourselves, saying, The Chaldeans shall surely depart from us:

CHAPTER 37
a 2 Kings 24:17
2 Chron. 36:10
Jer. 52:1
b Jer. 28:4

for they shall not depart.

10 For though ye had smitten the whole host of the Chaldeans that fight against you, and there remained, *but* wounded men among them, *yet* should every man rise up in his tent, and burn this city with fire.

11 ¶ When the host of the Chaldeans was broken up from Jerusalem, because of Pharaoh's army,

12 Then Jeremiah went out of Jerusalem to go into the [1]land of Benjamin, separating himself thence from among the people.

13 And when he was in the [1]gate of Benjamin, there was a chief officer, whose name was Irijah, the son of Shelemiah, the son of Hananiah, and he took Jeremiah the Prophet, saying, Thou [2]fleest to the Chaldeans.

14 Then said Jeremiah, That is false, I flee not to the Chaldeans: but he would not hear him: so Irijah took Jeremiah, and brought him to the princes.

15 Wherefore the princes were angry with Jeremiah, and smote him, and laid him in prison in the house of Jehonathan the Scribe: for they had made that the [1]prison.

16 When Jeremiah was entered into the dungeon, and into the prisons, and had remained there a long time,

17 Then Zedekiah the king sent, and took him out, and the king asked him secretly, in his house, and said, Is there any word from the Lord? And Jeremiah said, Yea: for, said he, thou shalt be delivered into the hand of the king of Babel.

18 Moreover, Jeremiah said unto king Zedekiah, What have I offended against thee, or against thy servants, or against this people, that ye have put me in prison?

19 [b]Where are now your prophets, which prophesied unto you, saying, The king of Babel shall not come against you, nor against this land?

20 Therefore hear now, I pray thee, O my lord the King: let my prayer be [1]acceptable before thee, that thou cause me not to return to the house of Jehonathan the scribe, lest I die there.

21 Then Zedekiah the King commanded, that they should put Jeremiah in the court of the prison, and that they should give him daily a piece of bread out of the baker's street until all the [1]bread in the city were eaten up. Thus Jeremiah remained in the court of the prison.

36:30 [1] Though Jehoiachin his son succeeded him, yet because he reigned but three months, it was esteemed as no reign.
[2] Read Jer. 22:19.
37:1 [1] Who was called Jehoiachin, or Jeconiah.
[2] And called him Zedekiah, whereas before his name was Mattaniah, 2 Kings 24:17.
37:2 [1] Hebrew, *hand.*
37:3 [1] Because he was afraid of the Chaldeans that came against him.
37:4 [1] That is, was out of prison, and at liberty.
37:5 [1] To help the Jews.

[2] Hebrew, *went up.*
37:9 [1] Or, lift not up your minds.
37:12 [1] As some think, to go to Anathoth his own town.
37:13 [1] By the which men went into the country of Benjamin.
[2] Hebrew, *fallest.*
37:15 [1] Because it was a vile and straight prison.
37:20 [1] Hebrew, *fall.*
37:21 [1] That is, so long as there was any bread in the city: thus God provideth for his, that he will cause their enemies to preserve them to that end whereunto he hath appointed them.

38

1 By the motion of the rulers Jeremiah is put into a dungeon. 14 At the request of Ebed-Melech the King commandeth Jeremiah to be brought forth of the dungeon. 17 Jeremiah showeth the King how he might escape death.

1 Then Shephatiah the son of Mattan, and Gedaliah the son of Pashhur, and Jucal the son of Shelemiah, and Pashhur the son of ¹Malchiah, heard the words that Jeremiah had spoken unto all the people, saying,

2 Thus saith the Lord, He that remaineth in this city, shall die by the sword, by the famine and by the pestilence: but he that goeth forth to the Chaldeans, shall live: for he shall have his life for ¹a prey, and shall live.

3 Thus saith the Lord, This city shall surely be given into the hand of the king of Babel's army, which shall take it.

4 Therefore the Princes said unto the king, We beseech you, let this man be put to death: for thus he ¹weakeneth the hands of the men of war ²that remain in this city, and the hands of all the people, in speaking such words unto them: for this man seeketh not the wealth of this people, but the hurt.

5 Then Zedekiah the king said, Behold, he is in your hands, for the king can *deny* ¹you nothing.

6 Then took they Jeremiah, and cast him into the dungeon of Malchiah the son of Hammelech, that was in the court of the prison: and they let down Jeremiah with cords: and in the dungeon there was no water but mire: so Jeremiah stuck fast in the mire.

7 Now when Ebed-Melech ye ¹black Moor, one of the Eunuchs which was in the king's house, heard that they had put Jeremiah in the dungeon, (then the king sat in the ²gate of Benjamin)

8 And Ebed-Melech went out of the king's house, and spake to the king, saying,

9 My lord the king, ¹these men have done evil in all that they have done to Jeremiah the Prophet, whom they have cast into the dungeon, and he dieth for hunger in the place where he is: for there is no more bread in the city.

10 Then the king commanded Ebed-Melech the black Moor, saying, Take from hence thirty men

¹with thee, and take Jeremiah the Prophet out of the dungeon before he die.

11 So Ebed-Melech took the men with him, and went to the house of the king under the treasury, and took there old rotten *rags*, and old worn *clouts*, and let them down by cords into the dungeon to Jeremiah.

12 And Ebed-Melech the black Moor said unto Jeremiah, Put now these old rotten *rags* and worn, under thine arm holes, between the cords. And Jeremiah did so.

13 So they drew up Jeremiah with cords, and took him up out of the dungeon, and Jeremiah remained in the ¹court of the prison.

14 ¶ Then Zedekiah the king sent, and took Jeremiah the Prophet unto him, into the third entry that is in the House of the Lord, and the king said unto Jeremiah, I will ask thee a thing: hide nothing from me.

15 Then Jeremiah said to Zedekiah, If I declare it unto thee, wilt thou not slay me? and if I give thee counsel, thou wilt not hear me.

16 So the King sware secretly unto Jeremiah, saying, As the Lord liveth, that made us these souls, I will not slay thee, nor give thee into the hands of those men that seek thy life.

17 Then said Jeremiah unto Zedekiah, Thus saith the Lord God of hosts the God of Israel, If thou wilt go forth unto the king of Babel's ¹princes, then thy soul shall live, and this city shall not be burnt up with fire, and thou shalt live, and thine house.

18 But if thou wilt not go forth to the king of Babel's princes, then shall this city be given into the hand of the Chaldeans, and they shall burn it with fire, and thou shalt not escape out of their hands.

19 And Zedekiah the king said unto Jeremiah, I am careful for the Jews that are fled unto the Chaldeans, lest they deliver me into their hands, and they ¹mock me.

20 But Jeremiah said, They shall not deliver *thee*: hearken unto the voice of the Lord, I beseech thee, which I speak unto thee: so shall it be well unto thee, and thy soul shall live.

21 But if thou wilt refuse to go forth, this is the word that the Lord hath showed me.

38:1 ¹ For Zedekiah had sent these to Jeremiah, to inquire at the Lord for the state of the country now when Nebuchadnezzar came, as Jer. 21:1.

38:2 ¹ Read Jer. 21:9 and 45:5.

38:4 ¹ Or, discourageth.

² Thus we see how the wicked when they cannot abide to hear the truth of God's word, seek to put the ministers to death, as transgressors of policies.

38:5 ¹ Wherein he grievously offended in that that not only he would not hear the truth spoken by the Prophet, but also gave him to the lusts of the wicked to be cruelly entreated.

38:7 ¹ Hebrew, *Cushite,* or *Ethiopian.*

² To hear matters and give sentence.

38:9 ¹ Hereby is declared that the Prophet found more favor at this stranger's hands, than he did by all them of his country, which was to their great condemnation.

38:10 ¹ Hebrew, *under thine hand.*

38:13 ¹ Where the king had set him before to be at more liberty, as Jer. 37:21.

38:17 ¹ And yield thyself unto them.

38:19 ¹ Which declareth that he more feared the reproach of men, than the threatenings of God.

22 And behold, all the women that are ¹left in the king of Judah's house, shall be brought forth to the king of Babel's princes, and those *women* shall say, Thy friends have persuaded thee, and have prevailed against thee: thy feet are fastened in the mire, *and* they are turned back.

23 So they shall bring out all thy wives, and thy children to the Chaldeans, and thou shalt not escape out of their hands, but shalt be taken by the hand of the king of Babel: and this city shalt thou cause to be burnt with fire.

24 Then said Zedekiah unto Jeremiah, Let no man know of these words, and thou shalt not die.

25 But if the princes understand that I have talked with thee, and they come unto thee, and say unto thee, Declare unto us now, what thou hast said unto the king, hide it not from us, and we will not slay thee: also what the King said unto thee,

26 Then shalt thou say unto them, I humbly ¹besought the king that he would not cause me to return to Jonathan's house, to die there.

27 Then came all the princes unto Jeremiah and asked him, And he told them according to all these words that the king had commanded: so they left off speaking with him, for the matter was not perceived.

28 So Jeremiah abode still in the court of the prison until the day that Jerusalem was taken: and he was *there* when Jerusalem was taken.

39

2 Nebuchadnezzar beseigeth Jerusalem.   4 Zedekiah fleeing, is taken of the Chaldeans.   6 His sons are slain.   7 His eyes are thrust out.   11 Jeremiah is provided for.   26 Ebed-Melech is delivered from captivity.

1 In ᵃthe ninth year of Zedekiah King of Judah in the tenth month, came Nebuchadnezzar King of Babel and all his host against Jerusalem, and they besieged it.

2 *And* in the eleventh year of Zedekiah in the fourth month, the ninth *day* of the month, the city was broken ¹up.

3 And all the princes of the King of Babel came in, and sat in the middle gate, *even* Nergal-Sharezer, Samgar-Nebo, Sarsechim, Rabsaris, Nergal-Sharezer, Rabmag, with all the residue of the princes of the king of Babel.

CHAPTER 39
ᵃ 2 Kings 25:15
Jer. 52:4

4 And when Zedekiah the king of Judah saw them, and all the men of war, then they fled, and went out of the city by night, through the king's garden, *and* by the ¹gate between the two walls, and he went toward the wilderness.

5 But the Chaldean's host pursued after them, and overtook Zedekiah in the desert of Jericho: and when they had taken him, they brought him to Nebuchadnezzar king of Babel unto ¹Riblah in the land of Hamath, where he gave judgment upon him.

6 Then the king of Babel slew the sons of Zedekiah in Riblah before his eyes: also the king of Babel slew all the nobles of Judah.

7 Moreover he put out Zedekiah's eyes, and bound him in chains to carry him to Babel.

8 And the Chaldeans burnt the king's house, and the houses of the people with fire, and brake down the walls of Jerusalem.

9 Then Nebuzaradan the ¹chief steward carried away captive into Babel the remnant of the people that remained in the city, and those that were fled and fallen unto him, with the rest of the people that remained.

10 But Nebuzaradan the chief steward left the ¹poor that had nothing in the land of Judah, and gave them vineyards and fields at the same time.

11 Now Nebuchadnezzar king of Babel gave charge concerning Jeremiah ¹unto Nebuzaradan the chief steward, saying,

12 Take him, and ¹look well to him, and do him no harm, but do unto him ²even as he shall say unto thee.

13 So Nebuzaradan the chief steward sent, and Nebushasban, Rabsaris, and Nergal-Sharezar, Rabmag, and all the King of Babel's princes:

14 Even they sent, and took Jeremiah out of the court of the prison, and committed him unto ¹Gedaliah the son of Ahikam the son of Shaphan, that he should carry him home: so he dwelt among the people.

15 Now the word of the Lord came unto Jeremiah, while he was shut up in the court of the prison, saying,

16 Go and speak to Ebed-Melech the black Moor, saying, Thus saith the Lord of hosts the God of Israel,

---

38:22 ¹ When Jeconiah and his mother, with others, were carried away, these women of the king's house were left: which shall be taken, saith the Prophet, and tell the king of Babel how Zedekiah hath been seduced by his familiar friends and false prophets, which have left him in the mire.

38:26 ¹ Herein appeareth the infirmity of the Prophet, who did dissemble to save his life albeit it was not to the denial of his doctrine, or to the hurt of any.

39:2 ¹ The gates and walls were broken down.

39:4 ¹ Which was a postern door, read 2 Kings 25:4.

39:5 ¹ Which is called Antioch in Syria.

39:9 ¹ Or, captain of the guard.

39:10 ¹ For the rich and the mighty which put their trust in their shifts and means, were by God's just judgments most rigorously handled.

39:11 ¹ Hebrew, *by the hand of.*

39:12 ¹ Hebrew, *set thine eyes upon them.*

² Thus God preserved his prophet by his means, whom he made the scourge to punish the king, and them that were his enemies.

39:14 ¹ Whom the King of Babel had now appointed governor over the rest of the Jews that he left behind.

Behold, I will bring my words upon this city for evil, and not for good, and they shall be *accomplished* in that day before thee.

17 But I will deliver thee in that day, saith the Lord, and thou shalt not be given into the hand of the men whom thou fearest.

18 For I will surely deliver thee, and thou shalt not fall by the sword, but thy life shall be for a prey unto thee, because thou [1]hast put thy trust in me, saith the Lord.

40

Jeremiah hath license to go whither he will. 6 He dwelleth with the people that remain with Gedaliah.

1 The word which came to Jeremiah from the Lord after that Nebuzaradan the chief steward had let him go from Ramah, when he had taken him being bound in chains among all that were carried away captive of Jerusalem and Judah, which were carried away captive unto Babel.

2 [1]And the chief steward took Jeremiah and said unto him, The Lord thy God hath pronounced this plague upon this place.

3 Now the Lord hath brought it, and done according as he hath said: because ye have [1]sinned against the Lord, and have not obeyed his voice, therefore this thing is come upon you.

4 And now behold, I loose thee this day from the chains which were on thine hands: if it please thee to come with me into Babel, come, and I will look well unto thee: but if it please thee not to come with me into Babel, [1]tarry still: behold, all the land *is* [2]before thee: whither it seemeth good, and convenient for thee to go, thither go.

5 For yet he was not returned: therefore *he said,* Return to Gedaliah the son of Ahikam, the son of Shaphan, whom the king of Babel hath made governor over all the cities of Judah, and dwell with him among the people, or go wheresoever it pleaseth thee to go. So the chief steward gave him vittles and a reward, and let him go.

6 Then went Jeremiah unto Gedaliah the son of Ahikam, to [1]Mizpah, and dwelt there with him among the people that were left in the land.

7 Now when all the captains of the host, [1]which were in the fields, *even* they and their men heard,

CHAPTER 40
a 2 Kings 25:24

that the king of Babel had made Gedaliah the son of Ahikam governor in the land, and that he had committed unto him men, and women, and children, and of the poor of the land, that were not carried away captive to Babel,

8 Then they came to Gedaliah to Mizpah, even [1]Ishmael the son of Nethaniah, and Johanan, and Jonathan the sons of Kareah, and Seraiah the son of Tanhumeth, and the sons of Ephai, the Netophathite, and Jezaniah the son of Maachathi, they and their men.

9 And Gedaliah the son of Ahikam, the son of Shaphan [a]sware unto them, and to their men, saying, Fear not to serve the Chaldeans: dwell in the land, and serve the king of Babel, and it shall be well with you:

10 As for me, Behold, I will dwell at Mizpah to [1]serve the Chaldeans, which will come unto us: but you, gather you wine, and summer fruits, and oil, and put them in your vessels, and dwell in your cities, that ye have [2]taken.

11 Likewise when all the Jews that were in [1]Moab, and among the Ammonites, and in Edom, and that were in all the countries, heard that the king of Babel had left a remnant of Judah, and that he had set over them Gedaliah the son of Ahikam the son of Shaphan,

12 Even all the Jews returned out of all places where they were driven, and came to the land of Judah to Gedaliah unto Mizpah, and gathered wine and summer fruits, very much.

13 Moreover Johanan the son of Kareah, and all the captains of the host, that were in the fields, came to Gedaliah to Mizpah,

14 And said unto him, Knowest thou not that [1]Baalis the King of the Ammonites hath sent Ishmael the son of Nethaniah to slay thee? But Gedaliah the son of Ahikam believed them not.

15 Then Johanan the son of Kareah spake to Gedaliah in Mizpah secretly, saying, Let me go, I pray thee, and I will slay Ishmael the son of Nethaniah, and no man shall know it. Wherefore should he kill thee, that all the Jews, which are gathered unto thee, should be scattered, and the remnant in Judah perish?

16 But Gedaliah the son of Ahikam said unto Johanan the son of Kareah, Thou shalt [1]not do this thing: for thou speakest falsely of Ishmael.

39:18 [1] Thus God recompensed his zeal and favor, which he showed to his Prophet in his troubles.

40:2 [1] From this second verse unto Jer. 42:7, it seemeth to be as a parenthesis, and separated matter: and there this story beginneth again, and this vision is declared what it was.

40:3 [1] God moved this infidel to speak this to declare the great blindness and obstinacy of the Jews, which could not feel that which this heathen man confessed.

40:4 [1] Hebrew, *cease.*
[2] Or, at thy commandment.

40:6 [1] Which was a city of Judah.

40:7 [1] Which were scattered abroad for fear of the Chaldeans.

40:8 [1] Who was of the king's blood and after slew him, Jer. 41:2.

40:10 [1] Or, to receive them, or to entreat them for you.
[2] Or, chosen to dwell in.

40:11 [1] Which were fled also for fear of the Chaldeans.

40:14 [1] For under the color of entertaining of Ishmael, he sought only to make them destroy one another.

40:16 [1] Thus the godly, which think no harm to others, are soonest deceived, and never lack such as conspire their destruction.

41

2 Ishmael killeth Gedaliah guilefully, and many others with him.   11 Johanan followeth after Ishmael.

1 But in the ¹seventh month came Ishmael the son of Nethaniah, the son of Elishama of the seed royal, and the princes of the ²king, and ten men with him, unto Gedaliah the son of Ahikam to Mizpah, and there they did ³eat bread together in Mizpah.

2 Then arose Ishmael the son of Nethaniah with these ten men that were with him, and smote Gedaliah the son of Ahikam the son of Shaphan with the sword, and slew him whom the king of Babel had made governor over the land.

3 Ishmael also slew all the Jews that were with Gedaliah at Mizpah, and all the Chaldeans that were found there, *and* the men of war.

4 Now the second day that he had slain Gedaliah, and no man knew it,

5 There came men from Shechem, from Shiloh, and from Samaria, *even* fourscore men having their beards shaven, and their clothes rent and cut, with ¹offerings and incense in their hands to offer in the house of the Lord.

6 And Ishmael the son of Nethaniah went forth from Mizpah to meet them, weeping, as he went: and when he met them, he said unto them, Come ¹to Gedaliah the son of Ahikam.

7 And when they came into the midst of the city, Ishmael the son of Nethaniah slew them, *and cast them* into the midst of the pit, he and the men that were with him.

8 But ten men were found among them, that said unto Ishmael, Slay us not: for we have treasures in the field, of wheat, and of barley, and of oil, and of honey: so he stayed, and slew them not among their brethren.

9 Now the [pit] wherein Ishmael had cast the dead bodies of the men (whom he had slain because of Gedaliah) is it, which Asa the king had ¹made because of Baasha king of Israel, *and* Ishmael the son of Nethaniah filled it with them that were slain.

10 Then Ishmael carried away captive all the residue of the people that were in Mizpah, *even* the King's daughters, and all the people that remained in Mizpah, whom Nebuzaradan the chief steward had committed to Gedaliah the son of Ahikam, and Ishmael the son of Nethaniah carried them away cap-

tive, and departed to go over to the Ammonites.

11 But when Johanan the son of Kareah, and all the ¹captains of the host that were with him, heard of all the evil that Ishmael the son of Nethaniah had done,

12 Then they all took *their* men, and went to fight with Ishmael the son of Nethaniah, and found him by the great waters that are in Gibeon.

13 Now when all the people whom Ishmael carried away captive, saw Johanan the son of Kareah, and all the captains of the host, that were with him, they were glad.

14 So all the people that Ishmael had carried away captive from Mizpah, returned and came again, and went unto Johanan the son of Kareah.

15 But Ishmael the son of Nethaniah, escaped from Johanan with eight men, and went to the ¹Ammonites.

16 Then took Johanan the son of Kareah, and all the captains of the host that were with him, all the remnant of the people, whom Ishmael the son of Nethaniah had carried away captive from Mizpah, (after that he had slain Gedaliah the son of Ahikam) *even* the strong men of war, and the women, and the children, and the eunuchs, whom he had brought again from Gibeon.

17 And they departed and dwelt in Geruth ¹Chimham, which is by Bethlehem, to go *and* to enter into Egypt,

18 Because of the Chaldeans: for they feared them, because Ishmael the son of Nethaniah had slain Gedaliah the son of Ahikam, whom the king of Babel made governor in the land.

42

1 The captains ask counsel of Jeremiah what they ought to do.   7 He admonisheth the remnant of the people not to go into Egypt.

1 Then all the captains of the host, and Johanan the son of Kareah, and Jezaniah the son of Hoshaiah, and all the people from the least unto the most, came,

2 And said unto Jeremiah the Prophet, ¹Hear our prayer, we beseech thee, and pray for us unto the Lord thy God, even for all this remnant (for we are left, *but* a few of many, as thine eyes do behold)

3 That the Lord thy God may show us the way

41:1 ¹ The city was destroyed in the fourth month: and in the seventh month, which contained part of September, and part of October, was the governor Gedaliah slain.

² Meaning, Zedekiah.

³ They did eat together as familiar friends.

41:5 ¹ For they thought that the Temple had not been destroyed and therefore came up to the feast of Tabernacles: but hearing of the burning thereof in the way, they showed these signs of sorrow.

41:6 ¹ For his death was kept secret, and he feigned that he lament

for the destruction of Jerusalem, and the Temple: but after slew them when they seemed to favor Gedaliah.

41:9 ¹ Asa fortified Mizpah for fear of the enemy, and cast ditches and trenches, 1 Kings 15:22.

41:11 ¹ Which had been captains under Zedekiah.

41:15 ¹ For Baalis the king of the Ammonites was the cause of this murder.

41:17 ¹ Which place David of old had given to Chimham the son of Barzillai the Gileadite, 2 Sam. 19:38.

42:2 ¹ Hebrew, *Let our prayer fall before thee*, as Jer. 36:7

wherein we may walk, and the thing that we may ¹do.

4 Then Jeremiah the Prophet said unto them, I have heard *you*: behold, I will pray unto the Lord your God according to your words, and whatsoever thing the Lord shall answer you, I will declare it unto you: I will keep nothing back from you.

5 Then they said to Jeremiah, ¹The Lord be a witness of truth, and faith between us, if we do not even according to all things for the which the Lord thy God shall send thee to us.

6 Whether it be good or evil, we will obey the voice of the Lord God, to whom we send thee, that it may be well with us, when we obey the voice of the Lord our God.

7 ¶ ¹And so after ten days came the word of the Lord unto Jeremiah.

8 Then called he Johanan the son of Kareah, and all the captains of the host, which were with him, and all the people from the least to the most,

9 And said unto them, Thus saith the Lord God of Israel, unto whom ye sent me to present your prayers before him,

10 If ye will dwell in this land, then I will build you, and not destroy *you*, and I will plant you, and not root *you* out: for I ¹repent me of the evil that I have done unto you.

11 Fear not for the king of Babel, of whom ye are afraid: be not afraid of him, saith the Lord: for I am with you, to save you, and to deliver you ¹from his hand,

12 And I will grant you mercy that he may have compassion upon you, and he shall cause you to ¹dwell in your own land.

13 But if ye say, We will not dwell in this land, neither hear the voice of the Lord your God,

14 Saying, Nay, but we will go into the land of Egypt, where we shall see no war, nor hear the sound of the trumpet, nor have hunger of bread, and there will we dwell,

15 (And now therefore hear the word of the Lord, ye remnant of Judah: thus saith the Lord of hosts, the God of Israel, If ye set your faces to enter into Egypt, and go to dwell there,)

16 Then the sword that ye feared, ¹shall take you there in the land of Egypt, and the famine, for the which ye care, shall there hang upon you in Egypt, and there shall ye die.

17 And all the men that set their faces to enter into Egypt to dwell there, shall die by the sword, by the famine, and by the pestilence, and none of them shall remain, nor escape from the plague, that I will bring upon them.

18 For thus saith the Lord of hosts, the God of Israel, As mine anger and my wrath hath been poured forth upon the inhabitants of Jerusalem: so shall my wrath be poured forth upon you, when ye shall enter into Egypt, and ye shall be a detestation, and an astonishment, and a ¹curse, and a reproach, and ye shall see this place no more.

19 O ye remnant of Judah, the Lord hath said concerning you, Go not into Egypt: know certainly that I have admonished you this day.

20 Surely ye ¹dissembled in your hearts when ye sent me unto the Lord your God, saying, Pray for us unto the Lord our God, and declare unto us even according unto all that the Lord our God shall say, and we will do it.

21 Therefore I have this day declared it you, but you have not obeyed the voice of the Lord your God, nor anything for the which he hath sent me unto you.

22 Now therefore, know certainly that ye shall die by the sword, by the famine, and by the pestilence ¹in the place whither ye desire to go and dwell.

43 *Johanan carrieth the remnant of the people into Egypt, contrary to the mind of Jeremiah.* *8 Jeremiah prophesieth the destruction of Egypt.*

1 Now when Jeremiah had made an end of speaking unto the whole people all the words of the Lord their God, for the which the Lord their God had sent him to them, *even* all these words,

2 Then spake ¹Azariah the son of Hoshaiah, and Johanan the son of Kareah, and all the ²proud men, saying unto Jeremiah, ³Thou speakest falsely:

42:3 ¹ This declareth the nature of hypocrites, which would know of God's word what they should do, but will not follow it, but inasmuch as it agreeth with that thing, which they have purposed to do.
42:5 ¹ There are none more ready to abuse the Name of God and take it in vain, than the hypocrites, which to color their falsehood use it without all reverence, and make it a means for them to deceive the simple and the godly.
42:7 ¹ Here is declared the vision and the occasion thereof, whereof mention was made, Jer. 40:1.
42:10 ¹ Read Jer. 18:8.
42:11 ¹ Because all kings' hearts and ways are in his hands, he can turn them and dispose them as it pleaseth him, and therefore they need not to fear man, but only obey God, Prov. 21:1.
42:12 ¹ Or, return.

42:16 ¹ Thus God turneth the policy of the wicked to their own destruction: for they thought themselves sure in Egypt, and there Nebuchadnezzar destroyed them and the Egyptians, Jer. 46:25.
42:18 ¹ Read Jer. 26:6 and 24:12, showing that this should come upon them for their infidelity and stubbornness.
42:20 ¹ For ye were fully minded to go into Egypt, whatsoever God spake to the contrary.
42:22 ¹ To wit, in Egypt.
43:2 ¹ Who was also called Jezaniah, Jer. 42:1.
² This declareth that pride is the cause of rebellion: and contempt of God's ministers.
³ When the hypocrisy of the wicked is discovered, they burst forth into open rage: for they can abide nothing but flattery, read Isa. 30:10.

the Lord our God hath [4]not sent thee to say, Go not into Egypt to dwell there,

3 But Baruch the son of Neriah [1]provoketh thee against us, for to deliver us into the hand of the Chaldeans, that they might slay us, and carry us away captives into Babel.

4 So Johanan the son of Kareah, and all the captains of the host, and all the people obeyed not the voice of the Lord, to dwell in the land of Judah.

5 But Johanan the son of Kareah, and all the captains of the host took all the remnant of Judah that were returned from all [1]nations, whither they had been driven, to dwell in the land of Judah:

6 *Even* men and women, and children, and the king's daughters, and every person that Nebuzaradan the chief steward had left with Gedaliah the son of Ahikam, the son of Shaphan, and Jeremiah the [1]Prophet, and Baruch the son of Neriah.

7 So they came into the land of Egypt: for they obeyed not the voice of the Lord: thus came they to [1]Tahpanhes.

8 ¶ Then came the word of the Lord unto Jeremiah in Tahpanhes, saying,

9 Take great stones in thine hand, and [1]hide them in the clay in the brick kiln, which is at the entry of Pharaoh's house in Tahpanhes in the sight of the men of Judah,

10 And say unto them, Thus saith the Lord of hosts the God of Israel, Behold, I will send and bring Nebuchadnezzar the king of Babel [1]my servant, and will set his throne upon these stones that I have hid, and he shall spread his pavilion over them.

11 And when he shall come, he shall smite the land of Egypt: [1]such as are *appointed* for death, to death, and such as are for captivity, to captivity, and such as are for the sword, to the sword.

12 And I will kindle a fire in the houses of the gods of Egypt, and he shall burn them and carry them away captives, and he shall array himself with the land of Egypt, as a [1]shepherd putteth on his garment, and shall depart from thence in peace.

13 He shall break also the images of [1]Beth Shemesh,

that is in the land of Egypt, and the houses of the gods of the Egyptians shall he burn with fire.

44 *He reproveth the people for their idolatry.* 15 They *that set light by the threatening of the Lord, are* chastened. 26 *The destruction of Egypt, and of the Jews therein, is prophesied.*

1 The word that came to Jeremiah concerning all the Jews, which dwell in the land of Egypt, and remained at Migdol and at [1]Tahpanhes, and at Noph, and in the country of Pathros, saying,

2 Thus saith the Lord of hosts the God of Israel, Ye have seen all the evil that I have brought upon Jerusalem, and upon all the cities of Judah: and behold, this day they are desolate and no man dwelleth therein,

3 Because of their wickedness which they have committed, to provoke me to anger in that they went to burn incense, *and* to serve other gods whom they knew not, *neither* they *nor* you, nor your fathers.

4 Howbeit I sent unto you all my servants the Prophets [1]rising early, and sending *them*, saying, Oh do not this abominable thing that I hate.

5 But they would not hear nor incline their ear to turn from their wickedness, and to burn no more incense unto other gods.

6 Wherefore [1]my wrath, and mine anger was poured forth, and was kindled in the cities of Judah, and in the streets of Jerusalem, and they are desolate, *and* wasted, as *appeareth* this day.

7 Therefore now thus saith the Lord of hosts the God of Israel, wherefore commit ye *this* great evil against your souls, to cut off from you man and woman, child and suckling out of Judah, and leave you none to remain?

8 In that ye provoke me unto wrath with the works of your hands, burning incense unto other gods in the land of Egypt, whither ye be gone to dwell: that ye might bring destruction unto yourselves, and that ye might be a curse and a reproach among all nations of the earth.

9 Have ye forgotten the wickedness of your fathers,

43:2 [4] He showeth what is the nature of the hypocrites: to wit, to feign that they would obey God and embrace his word, if they were assured that his messenger spake the truth: though indeed they be most far from all obedience.

43:3 [1] Thus the wicked do not only contemn and hurt the messengers of God, but slander, and speak wickedly of all them that support or favor the godly.

43:5 [1] As from the Moabites, Ammonites, and Edomites, Jer. 40:11.

43:6 [1] Whom these wicked lead away by force.

43:7 [1] A city in Egypt near to Nilus.

43:9 [1] Which signified that Nebuchadnezzar should come even to the gates of Pharaoh, where were his brick kilns for his buildings.

43:10 [1] Read Jer. 25:9.

43:11 [1] Everyone shall be slain by that means that God hath appointed, Jer. 15:2.

43:12 [1] Meaning, most easily and suddenly shall he carry the Egyptians away.

43:13 [1] Or, the house of the Sun.

44:1 [1] These were all famous and strange cities in Egypt, where the Jews that were fled, dwelt for their safety: but the Prophet declareth that there is no hold so strong that can preserve them from God's vengeance.

44:4 [1] Read Jer. 7:25; 25:3; 36:5; 29:19 and 32:33.

44:6 [1] He setteth before their eyes God's judgments against Judah and Jerusalem for their idolatry, that they might beware by their example, and not with the like wickedness provoke the Lord: for then they should be double punished.

and the wickedness of the [1]kings of Judah, and the wickedness of their wives, and your own wickedness, and the wickedness of your wives, which they have committed in the land of Judah, and in the streets of Jerusalem?

10 They are not [1]humbled unto this day, neither have they feared nor walked in my law nor in my statutes, that I set before you and before your fathers.

11 Therefore thus saith the Lord of hosts, the God of Israel, Behold, I will set my face against you [a]to evil, and to destroy all Judah,

12 And I will take the remnant of Judah that [1]have set their faces to go into the land of Egypt there to dwell, and they shall all be consumed and fall in the land of Egypt: they shall even be consumed by the sword and by the famine: they shall die from the least unto the most, by the sword, and by the famine and they shall be a detestation and an astonishment, and a [2]curse and a reproach.

13 For I will visit them that dwell in the land of Egypt, as I have visited Jerusalem, by the sword, by the famine, and by the pestilence,

14 So that none of the remnant of Judah, which are gone into the land of Egypt to dwell there shall escape or remain, that they should return into the land of Judah to the which they [1]have a desire to return to dwell there: for none shall return but [2]such as shall escape.

15 Then all the men which knew that their wives had burnt incense unto other gods, and all the women that stood by, a great multitude, even all the people that dwelt in the land of Egypt in Pathros, answered Jeremiah, saying,

16 The word that thou hast spoken unto us in the Name of the Lord, we will [1]not hear it of thee,

17 But we will do whatsoever thing goeth out of our own mouth, as to burn incense unto [1]the Queen of heaven, and to pour out drink offerings unto her, as we have done, both we and our fathers, our

CHAPTER 44
[a] Amos 9:4

kings and our princes in the cities of Judah, and in the streets of Jerusalem: for then [2]had we [3]plenty of vittles and were well and [4]felt none evil.

18 But since we left off to burn incense to the Queen of heaven, and to pour out drink offerings unto her, we have had [1]scarceness of all things, and have been consumed by the sword and by the famine.

19 And when we burnt incense unto the Queen of heaven, and poured out drink offerings unto her, did we make her cakes [1]to make her glad, and pour out drink offerings unto her without [2]our husbands?

20 Then said Jeremiah unto all the people, to the men, and to the women, and to all the people which had given him that answer, saying,

21 Did not the Lord remember the incense, that ye burnt in the cities of Judah, and in the streets of Jerusalem, both you and your fathers, your kings, and your Princes, and the people of the land, and [1]hath he not considered it?

22 So that the Lord could no longer forbear, because of the wickedness of your inventions, and because of the abominations, which ye have committed: therefore is your land desolate, and an astonishment, and a curse, and without inhabitant, as appeareth this day.

23 Because you have burnt incense, and because ye have sinned against the Lord, and have not obeyed the voice of the Lord, nor walked in his law, nor in his statutes, nor in his testimonies, therefore this plague is come upon you, as appeareth this day.

24 Moreover Jeremiah said unto all the people and to all the women, Hear the word of the Lord, all Judah, that are in the land of Egypt.

25 ¶ Thus speaketh the Lord of hosts, the God of Israel, saying, Ye and your wives have both spoken with your mouths, and fulfilled with your [1]hand, saying, We will perform our vows that we have vowed to burn incense to the Queen of heaven, and to pour out drink offerings to her: ye will perform

---

44:9 [1] He showeth that we ought to keep in memory God's plagues from the beginning, that considering them, we might live in his fear, and know if he have not spared our fathers, yea, kings, princes, and rulers, and also whole countries, and nations for their sins, that we vile worms, cannot look to escape punishment for ours.
44:10 [1] Or, beaten down.
44:12 [1] Which have fully set their minds, and are gone thither on purpose. Whereby he excepteth the innocents, as Jeremiah and Baruch that were forced: therefore the Lord showeth that he will set his face against them: that is, purposely destroy them.
[2] Read Jer. 26:6 and 41:18.
44:14 [1] Hebrew, lift up their souls.
[2] Meaning, but a few.
44:16 [1] This declareth how dangerous a thing it is to decline once from God, and to follow our own fantasies: for Satan ever soliciteth such, and doth not leave them till he have brought them to extreme impudency and madness, even to justify their wickedness against God and his Prophets.
44:17 [1] Read Jer. 7:18, it seemeth that the Papists gathered of this

place Salve Regina, and Regina caeli latare, calling the virgin Mary Queen of heaven, and so of the blessed virgin and mother of our Savior Christ, made an idol: for here the Prophet condemneth their idolatry.
[2] Hebrew, we were satiated with bread.
[3] This is still the argument of idolaters, which esteem religion by the belly, and instead of acknowledging God's works, who sendeth both plenty and dearth, health and sickness, they attribute it to their idols, and so dishonor God.
[4] Or, saw.
44:18 [1] Or, want.
44:19 [1] Or, to appease her.
[2] This teacheth us how great danger it is for the husbands to permit their wives anything whereof they be not assured by God's word: for thereby they take an occasion to justify their doings, and their husbands shall give an account thereof before God, read Isa. 3:25.
44:21 [1] Hebrew, is it not come up into his heart?
44:25 [1] You have committed double evil in making wicked vows, and in performing the same.

your vows, and do the things that ye have vowed.

26 Therefore hear the word of the Lord, all Judah that dwell in the land of Egypt, Behold, I have sworn by my great Name, saith the Lord, that my Name [1]shall no more be called upon by the mouth of any man of Judah, in all the land of Egypt, saying, The Lord God liveth.

27 Behold, I will watch over them for evil, and not for good, and all men of Judah that are in the land of Egypt, shall be consumed by the sword, and by the famine, until they be utterly destroyed.

28 Yet a small number that escape the sword, [1]shall return out of the land of Egypt into the land of Judah: and all the remnant of Judah that are gone into the land of Egypt to dwell there, shall know whose words shall stand, mine or theirs.

29 And this shall be a sign unto you, saith the Lord, when I visit you in this place, that ye may know that my words shall surely stand against you for evil.

30 Thus saith the Lord, Behold, I will [1]give Pharaoh Hophra King of Egypt into the hand of his enemies, and into the hand of them that seek his life: as I gave Zedekiah king of Judah into the hand of Nebuchadnezzar king of Babel his enemy, who also sought his life.

45

2 Jeremiah comforteth Baruch, assuring him that he should not perish in the destruction of Jerusalem.

1 The word that Jeremiah the Prophet spake unto [1]Baruch the son of Neriah, when he had written these [2]words in a book at the mouth of Jeremiah, in the fourth year of Jehoiakim, the son of Josiah king of Judah, saying,

2 Thus saith the Lord God of Israel unto thee, O Baruch,

3 Thou didst say, Woe is me now: for the Lord hath laid sorrow unto my sorrow: I [1]fainted in my mourning, and I can find no rest.

4 Thus shalt thou say unto him, The Lord saith thus, Behold, that which I have built, will I [1]destroy, and that which I have planted, will I pluck up, even this whole land.

5 And seekest [1]thou great things for thyself? seek them not: for behold, I will bring a plague upon all flesh, saith the Lord: but thy life will I give thee for [2]a prey in all places, whither thou goest.

46

He prophesieth the destruction of Egypt. 27 Deliverance is promised to Israel.

1 The words of the Lord, which came to Jeremiah the Prophet against the [1]Gentiles,

2 As against Egypt, against the army of [1]Pharaoh Necho king of Egypt, which was by the river Perath in Carchemish, which Nebuchadnezzar king of Babel smote in the fourth year of Jehoiakim the son of Josiah king of Judah.

3 [1]Make ready buckler and shield, and go forth to battle.

4 Make ready the horses, and let the horsemen get up, and stand up with *your* sallets, furbish the spears, and put on the brigandines.

5 [1]Wherefore have I seen them afraid, *and* driven back? for their mighty men are smitten, and are fled away, and look not back: *for* fear *was* round about, saith the Lord.

6 The swift shall not flee away, nor the strong man escape: they shall stumble, and [1]fall toward the North by the river Perath.

7 Who is this that cometh up as [1]a flood, whose waters are moved like the rivers?

8 Egypt riseth up like the flood, and *his* waters are moved like the rivers, and he saith, I will go up, *and* will cover the earth: I will destroy the city with them that dwell therein.

9 Come up ye horses, and rage ye chariots, and let the valiant men come forth, [1]the black Moors, and the Libyans that bear the shield, and the Lydians that handle *and* bend the bow.

44:26 [1] This declareth an horrible plague toward idolaters, seeing that God will not vouchsafe to have his Name mentioned by such as have polluted it.

44:28 [1] We see therefore that God hath a perpetual care over his, wheresoever they are scattered: for though they be but two or three, yet he will deliver them when he destroyeth his enemies.

44:30 [1] He showeth the means whereby they should be destroyed to assure them of the certainty of the plague, and yet they remain still in their obstinacy till they perish: for Josephus, lib. 10, de Antiq., cap. 11, writeth that five years after the taking of Jerusalem, Nebuchadnezzar the younger having overcome the Moabites and the Ammonites, went against Egypt, and slew the king, and so brought these Jews and others into Babylon.

45:1 [1] Which was Jeremiah's disciple, and wrote his prophecies under him.
    [2] Whereof read Jer. 36:9, 10.

45:3 [1] Baruch moved with an inconsiderate zeal of Jeremiah's imprisonment, but chiefly for the destruction of the people, and the Temple, maketh this lamentation, as Ps. 6:6.

45:4 [1] Meaning, that God might destroy this people, because he had planted them.

45:5 [1] Thinkest thou to have honor and credit? wherein he showeth his infirmity.
    [2] Read Jer. 21:9.

46:1 [1] That is, nine nations, which are round about the land of Egypt.

46:2 [1] Read 2 Kings 23:29 and 24:7; 2 Chron. 35:20.

46:3 [1] He warneth the Egyptians to prepare themselves to war.

46:5 [1] The Prophet had this vision of the Egyptians, which should be put to flight by the Babylonians at Carchemish.

46:6 [1] The Babylonians shall discomfit them at the river Euphrates.

46:7 [1] He derideth the boastings of the Egyptians, who thought by their riches and power to have overcome all the world, alluding to the river Nilus, which at certain times overfloweth the country of Egypt.

46:9 [1] For these nations took part with the Egyptians.

10 ¶ For this is the day of the Lord God of hosts, *and* a day of vengeance, that he may avenge him of his enemies: for the sword shall devour, and it shall be satiate, and made drunk with their blood: for the Lord God of hosts hath [1]a sacrifice in the North country [2]by the river Perath.

11 Go up unto Gilead, [1]and take balm, [2]O virgin, the daughter of Egypt: in vain shalt thou use many [3]medicines: *for* thou shalt have no health.

12 The nations have heard of thy shame, and thy cry hath filled the land: for the strong hath stumbled against the strong, *and* they are fallen both together.

13 ¶ The word that the Lord spake to Jeremiah the Prophet, how Nebuchadnezzar king of Babel should come and smite the land of Egypt.

14 Publish in Egypt and declare in Migdol, and proclaim in Noph, and in Tahpanhes, *and* say, Stand still and prepare thee, for the sword shall devour round about thee.

15 Why are thy valiant men put back? they could not stand, because the Lord did drive them.

16 He made many to fall, and one fell upon another: and they said, Arise, let us go again to our [1]own people, and to the land of our nativity from the sword of the violent.

17 They did cry there, Pharaoh king of Egypt, *and* of a great multitude, [1]hath passed the time appointed.

18 As I live, saith the King, whose Name is the Lord of hosts, surely as Tabor *is* in the mountains, and as Carmel *is* in the sea: so shall [1]it come.

19 O thou daughter dwelling in Egypt, make thee gear to go into captivity: for Noph shall be waste and desolate, without an inhabitant.

20 Egypt *is like* a [1]fair calf, *but* destruction cometh: out of the North it cometh.

21 Also her hired men [1]*are* in the midst of her like fat calves: they are also turned back and fled away together: they could not stand, because the day of their destruction was come upon them, *and* the time of their visitation.

22 The voice thereof shall go forth like a [1]serpent: for they shall march with an army, and come against [2]her with axes, as hewers of wood.

23 They shall cut down [1]her forest, saith the Lord: for they cannot be counted, because they are more than the [2]grasshoppers, and are innumerable.

24 The daughter of Egypt shall be confounded: she shall be delivered into the hands of the people of the North.

25 ¶ Thus saith the Lord of hosts, the God of Israel, Behold, I will visit thy [1]common people of No and Pharaoh, and Egypt, with their gods and their kings, even Pharaoh, and all them that trust in him,

26 And I will deliver them into the hands of those that seek their lives, and into the hand of Nebuchadnezzar king of Babel, and into the hands of his servants, and afterward she shall dwell as [1]in the old time, saith the Lord.

27 ¶ [1]But fear not thou, O my servant Jacob, and be not thou afraid, O Israel: for behold, I will deliver thee from a far *country*, and thy seed from the land of their captivity, and Jacob shall return and be in rest, and prosperity, and none shall make him afraid.

28 Fear thou not, O Jacob my servant, saith the Lord, for I am with thee, and I will utterly destroy all the nations, whither I have driven thee: but I will not utterly destroy thee, but correct [1]thee by judgment, and not utterly cut thee off.

47

The word of the Lord against the Philistines.

1 The words of the Lord that came to Jeremiah the Prophet, against the Philistines, before that Pharaoh smote [1]Gaza.

2 Thus saith the Lord, Behold, waters rise up out of the [1]North, and shall be as a swelling flood, and shall overflow the land, and all that is therein, and the cities with them that dwell therein: then the men shall cry, and all the inhabitants of the land shall howl,

---

46:10 [1] He calleth the slaughter of God's enemies a sacrifice, because it is a thing that doth please him, Isa. 34:6.

[2] That is, at Carchemish.

46:11 [1] For at Gilead did grow most sovereign balm for wounds.

[2] So called, because Egypt had not yet been overcome by the enemy.

[3] He showeth that no salve or medicine can prevail whereas God giveth the wound.

46:16 [1] As they that should repent that they helped the Egyptians.

46:17 [1] He derideth them which shall impute their overthrow to lack of counsel and policy, or to fortune, and not observing of time: not considering that it is God's just judgment.

46:18 [1] To wit, that the Egyptians shall be destroyed.

46:20 [1] They have abundance of all things, and therefore are disobedient and proud.

46:21 [1] As verse 9.

46:22 [1] They shall be scarce able to speak for fear of the Chaldeans.

[2] Meaning, Egypt.

46:23 [1] That is, they shall slay the great and mighty men of power.

[2] To wit, Nebuchadnezzar's army.

46:25 [1] Some take the Hebrew word Amon for the King's name of No, that is, of Alexandria.

46:26 [1] Meaning, that after the space of forty years Egypt should be restored, Isa. 19:23; Ezek. 29:13.

46:27 [1] God comforteth all his that were in captivity, but specially the small Church of the Jews, whereof were Jeremiah and Baruch, which remained among the Egyptians: for the Lord never forsaketh his, Isa. 44:2; Jer. 30:10.

46:28 [1] Read Jer. 10:14.

47:1 [1] Which was also called Gaza, a city of the Philistines.

47:2 [1] He meaneth the army of the Chaldeans, Isa. 8:7, 8.

3 At the noise *and* stamping of the hoofs of his strong *horses*, at the noise of his chariots, and at the rumbling of his wheels: [1]the fathers shall not look back to *their* children, for feebleness of [2]hands,

4 Because of the day that cometh to destroy all the Philistines, and to destroy Tyre, and Sidon, *and* all the rest that take their part: for the Lord will destroy the Philistines, the remnant of the isle of [1]Caphtor.

5 [1]Baldness is come upon Gaza: Ashkelon is cut up *with* the rest of their valleys. How long wilt [2]thou cut thyself?

6 O thou sword of the Lord, how long will it be or thou cease! turn again into thy scabbard, rest and be still.

7 How can it [1]cease, seeing the Lord hath given it a charge against Ashkelon, and against the sea bank? even there hath he appointed it.

48

The word of the Lord against the Moabites.   *26 Because of their pride and cruelty.*

1 Concerning Moab, thus saith the Lord of hosts, the God of Israel, Woe unto [1]Nebo: for it is wasted: Kirjathaim is confounded *and* taken: Misgab is confounded and afraid.

2 Moab shall boast no more of Heshbon: *for* they have devised evil against it. [1]Come, and let us destroy it, that it be no more a nation: also thou shalt be destroyed, [2]O Madmen, *and* the sword shall pursue thee.

3 A voice of crying *shall be* from Horonaim *with* desolation and great destruction.

4 Moab is destroyed: her little ones have caused their cry to be heard.

5 For at the going up of [1]Luhith, the mourner shall go up with weeping: for in the going down of Horonaim, the enemies have heard a cry of destruction.

6 Flee and save your lives, and be like unto the [1]heath in the wilderness.

7 For because thou hast trusted in thy [1]works and in thy treasures, thou shalt also be taken, and [2]Chemosh shall go forth into captivity with his Priests and his Princes together.

8 And the destroyer shall come upon all cities, and no city shall escape: the valley also shall perish and the plain shall be destroyed as the Lord hath spoken.

9 Give wings unto Moab, that it may flee and get away: for the cities thereof shall be desolate, without any to dwell therein.

10 [1]Cursed *be he* that doeth the work of the Lord [2]negligently, and cursed *be he* that keepeth back his sword from blood.

11 Moab hath been at rest from his youth, and he hath settled on his lees, and hath not been [1]poured from vessel to vessel, neither hath he gone into captivity: therefore his taste remained in him, and his scent is not changed.

12 ¶ Therefore behold, the days come, saith the Lord, that I will send unto him such as shall carry him away, and shall empty his vessels, and break their bottles.

13 And Moab shall be ashamed of Chemosh, as the house of Israel was ashamed of [1]Bethel their confidence.

14 How think you *thus*, We are mighty and strong men of war?

15 Moab is destroyed, and his cities [1]burnt up, and his chosen young men are gone down to slaughter, saith the King, whose name *is*, The Lord of hosts.

16 The destruction of Moab is ready to come, and his plague hasteth fast.

17 All ye that are about him, mourn for him, and all ye that know his name, say, [1]How is the strong staff broken, *and* the beautiful rod!

18 Thou daughter that dost inhabit Dibon, come

47:3 [1] The great fear shall take away their natural affection.
  [2] Their heart shall so fail them.
47:4 [1] For the Caphtorims, which are also called Cappadocians, had destroyed in old time the Philistines, and dwelt in their land even to Gaza, Deut. 2:23.
47:5 [1] They that pilled off their hair for sorrow and heaviness.
  [2] As the heathen used in their mourning, which the Lord forbade his people to do, Deut. 14:1.
47:7 [1] Meaning, that it is not possible that the wicked should by any means escape or stay the Lord, when he will take vengeance.
48:1 [1] These were cities of the Moabites, which Nebuchadnezzar took before he went to fight against Necho king of Egypt.
48:2 [1] Thus shall the Babylonians encourage one another.
  [2] Read Isa. 25:10.
48:5 [1] Horonaim and Luhith were two places whereby the Moabites should flee, Isa. 15:5.
48:6 [1] Hide yourselves in barren places, where the enemy will not pursue after you, Jer. 17:6.

48:7 [1] That is, the idols which are the works of thine hands. Some read, in thy possessions, for so the word may signify, as 1 Sam. 25:2.
  [2] Both thy great idol and his maintainers shall be led away captives, so that they shall then know that it is in vain to look for help at idols, Isa. 15:2.
48:10 [1] He showeth that God would punish the Chaldeans, if they did not destroy the Egyptians, and that with a courage, and calleth this executing of his vengeance against his enemies, his work: though the Chaldeans sought another end, Isa. 10:11.
  [2] Or, deceitfully.
48:11 [1] Hath not been removed as the Jews have, but have lived at ease, and as a wine that feedeth itself on his lees.
48:13 [1] As the calf of Bethel was not able to deliver the Israelites: no more shall Chemosh deliver the Moabites.
48:15 [1] Hebrew, *gone up*, or *destroyed*.
48:17 [1] How are they destroyed that put their trust in their strength and riches?

down from *thy* glory, and sit in thirst: for the destroyer of Moab shall come upon thee, *and* he shall destroy thy strongholds.

19 Thou that dwellest in Aroer, stand by the way, and behold ask him that fleeth and that escapeth, *and* say, What is done?

20 ¹Moab is confounded: for it is destroyed, howl and cry, tell ye it in Arnon, that Moab is made waste,

21 And judgment is come upon the plain country, upon Holon and upon Jahzah, and upon Mephaath,

22 And upon Dibon, and upon Nebo, and upon the house of Diblathaim,

23 And upon Kirjathaim, and upon Beth Gamul, and upon Beth Meon,

24 And upon Kerioth, and upon Bozrah, and upon all the cities of the land of Moab far or near.

25 The ¹horn of Moab is cut off, and his arm is broken, saith the Lord.

26 Make ye him ¹drunken: for he magnified himself against the Lord: Moab shall ²wallow in his vomit, and he also shall be in derision.

27 For didst not thou deride Israel, as though he had been found among thieves? for when thou speakest of him, thou art ¹moved.

28 O ye that dwell in Moab, leave the cities, and dwell in the rocks, and be like the dove that maketh her nest in the sides of the hole's mouth.

29 ᵃWe have heard the pride of Moab (*he is* exceeding proud) his stoutness, and his arrogancy, and his pride, and the haughtiness of his heart.

30 I know his wrath, saith the Lord, ¹but *it shall* not *be* so: *and* his dissimulations, *for* they do not right.

31 ¹Therefore will I howl for Moab, and I will cry out for all Moab: *mine heart* shall mourn for the men of Kir Heres.

32 O vine of Sibmah, I will weep for thee, as I wept for Jazer: thy plants are gone over the sea, they are come to the sea ¹of Jazer: the destroyer is fallen upon thy summer fruits, and upon thy vintage,

33 And joy, and gladness is taken from the plentiful field, and from the land of Moab: and I have caused wine to fail from the winepress: none shall tread with

CHAPTER 48
ᵃ Isa. 16:6
ᵇ Isa. 15:2,3
Ezek. 7:18

shouting: *their* shouting *shall be* no shouting.

34 From the cry of Heshbon unto Elealeh *and* unto Jahaz have they made their noise: from Zoar unto Horonaim, the ¹heifer of three years old *shall go lowing*: for the waters also of Nimrim shall be wasted.

35 Moreover, I will cause to cease in Moab, saith the Lord, him that offereth in the high places, and him that burneth incense to his gods.

36 Therefore mine heart shall sound for Moab like a ¹shawm, and mine heart shall sound like a shawm for the men of Kir Heres, because the riches that he hath gotten is perished.

37 ᵇFor every head *shall be* ¹bald, and every beard plucked: upon all the hands *shall be* cuttings, and upon the loins sackcloth.

38 *And* mourning shall be upon all the house tops of Moab, and in all the streets thereof: for I have broken Moab like a vessel wherein is no pleasure, saith the Lord.

39 They shall howl, *saying*, How is he destroyed? how hath Moab turned the back with shame? so shall Moab be a derision, and a fear to all them about him.

40 For thus saith the Lord, Behold, ¹he shall flee as an eagle, and shall spread his wings over Moab.

41 The cities are taken, and the strongholds are won, and the mighty men's hearts in Moab at that day shall be as the heart of a woman in travail.

42 And Moab shall be destroyed from being a people, because he hath set up himself against the Lord:

43 ¹Fear, and pit, and snare *shall be* upon thee, O inhabitant of Moab, saith the Lord.

44 He that escapeth from the fear, shall fall in the pit, and he that getteth up out of the pit, shall be taken [in] the snare: for I will bring upon it, *even* upon Moab the year of their visitation, saith the Lord.

45 They that fled, stood under the shadow ¹of Heshbon, because of the force: for ²the fire came out of Heshbon, and a flame from Sihon, and devoured the corner of Moab, and the top of the seditious children.

46 Woe *be* unto thee, O Moab: the people of

48:20 ¹ Thus they that flee, shall answer.
48:25 ¹ That is, his power and strength.
48:26 ¹ He willed the Chaldeans to lay afflictions enough upon them, till they be like drunken men that fall down to their shame and are derided of all.
² Or, shall be full, or clap his hands.
48:27 ¹ Thou rejoicest to hear of his misery.
48:30 ¹ He shall not execute his malice against his neighbors.
48:31 ¹ Read Isa. 16:7.
48:32 ¹ Which city was in the utmost border of Moab: and hereby he signifieth that the whole land should be destroyed, and the people

carried away.
48:34 ¹ Read Isa. 15:5.
48:36 ¹ Their custom was to play on flutes or instruments, heavy and grave tunes at burials and in the time of mourning, as Matt. 9:23.
48:37 ¹ Or, shaven.
48:40 ¹ That is, Nebuchadnezzar, as Jer. 49:22.
48:43 ¹ He that escapeth one danger shall be taken of another, Isa. 24:17.
48:45 ¹ They fled thither, thinking to have succor of the Amorites.
² The Amorites had destroyed the Moabites in times past, and now because of their power, the Moabites shall seek to them for help.

[1]Chemosh perisheth: for thy sons are taken captives, and thy daughters *led* into captivity.

47 Yet will I bring again the captivity of Moab in the [1]latter days, saith the Lord. Thus far of the judgment of Moab.

49

[1] *The word of the Lord against the Ammonites,* 7 *Edom,* 23 *Damascus,* 28 *Kedar,* 34 *and Elam.*

1 Unto the children of [1]Ammon thus saith the Lord, Hath Israel no sons? or hath he none heir? Why *then* hath their king [2]possessed Gad? and his people dwelt in [3]his cities?

2 Therefore behold, the days come, saith the Lord, that I will cause a noise of war to be heard in [1]Rabbah of the Ammonites, and it shall be a desolate heap, and her daughters shall be burnt with fire: then shall Israel possess those that possessed him, saith the Lord.

3 Howl, O Heshbon, for Ai is wasted: cry ye daughters of Rabbah: gird you with sackcloth: mourn and run to and fro by the hedges: for their king shall go into captivity; *and* his Priests, and his Princes likewise.

4 Wherefore gloriest thou in the [1]valleys? thy valley floweth away, O rebellious daughter: she trusted in her treasures, *saying*, Who shall come unto me?

5 Behold, I will bring [1]a fear upon thee, saith the Lord God of hosts, of all those that be about thee, and ye shall be scattered every man [2]right forth, and none shall gather him that fleeth.

6 And [1]afterward I will bring again the captivity of the children of Ammon.

7 ¶ To Edom thus saith the Lord of hosts, Is wisdom no more in [1]Teman? is counsel perished from *their* children? is their wisdom vanished?

8 Flee, ye inhabitants of Dedan ([1]they are turned back, and have consulted to dwell) for I have brought the destruction of Esau upon him, *and* the time of his visitation.

9 If the [1]grape gatherers come to thee, would they not leave *some* grapes? if thieves come by night, they will destroy till they have enough.

10 For I have discovered Esau: I have uncovered his secrets, and he shall not be able to hide himself: his seed is wasted, and his brethren and his neighbors, and there shall be none *to say*,

11 Leave thy [1]fatherless children, *and* I will preserve them alive, and let thy widows trust in me.

12 For thus saith the Lord, [1]Behold, they whose judgment was not to drink of the cup, have assuredly drunken, and art thou he that shall escape free? thou shalt not go free, but thou shalt surely drink of it.

13 For I have sworn by myself, saith the Lord, that [1]Bozrah shall be waste, and for a reproach, and a desolation, and a curse, and all the cities thereof shall be perpetual desolations.

14 I have heard a rumor from the Lord, and an ambassador is sent unto the heathen, *saying*, Gather you together, and come against [1]her, and rise up to the battle.

15 For lo, I will make thee but small among the heathen, and despised among men.

16 Thy [1]fear, *and* the pride of thine heart hath deceived thee, thou that dwellest in the clefts of the rock, and keepest the height of the hill: though thou shouldest make thy nest as high as the eagle, I will bring thee down from thence, saith the Lord.

17 Also Edom shall be desolate: everyone that goeth by it, shall be astonished, and shall hiss at all the plagues thereof,

18 As in the overthrow of Sodom and of Gomorrah, and the places thereof near about, saith the Lord: no man shall dwell there, neither shall the sons of men remain in it.

19 Behold, [1]he shall come up like a lion from the swelling of Jordan unto the strong dwelling place: for I will make *Israel* to rest, *even* I will make [2]him to haste away from her, and who is a chosen man

---

48:46 [1] Which vaunted themselves of their idol, as though he could have defended them.

48:47 [1] That is, they shall be restored by the Messiah.

49:1 [1] They were separated from the Moabites by the river Arnon, and after that the ten tribes were carried away into captivity, they invaded the country of Gad.

[2] To wit, of the Ammonites.

[3] Meaning, of the Israelites.

49:2 [1] Which was one of the chief cities of the Ammonites, as were Heshbon and Ai: there was also a city called Heshbon among the Moabites.

49:4 [1] In thy plentiful country.

49:5 [1] Signifying, that power and riches cannot prevail, when as God will execute his judgments.

[2] That is, without looking back, and as everyone can find a way to escape.

49:6 [1] In the time of Christ, when the Gentiles shall be called.

49:7 [1] Which was a city of Edom, called by the name of Teman Eliphaz' son, who came of Esau.

49:8 [1] The enemies that shall dissemble as though they fled away, shall turn back and invade your land, and possess it.

49:9 [1] Meaning, that God would utterly destroy them, and not spare one, though the grape gatherers leave some grapes, and thieves seek but till they have enough, Obad. 1:5.

49:11 [1] The destruction shall be so great, that there shall be none left to take care over the widows and the fatherless.

49:12 [1] I have not spared mine own people, and how should I pity thee?

49:13 [1] Which was a chief city of Edom.

49:14 [1] That is, Bozrah.

49:16 [1] Or, idol.

49:19 [1] To wit, Nebuchadnezzar after he hath overcome Judah, which is meant by the swelling of Jordan, shall come against mount Seir and Edom.

[2] That is, the Israelites, whom the Edomites kept as prisoners, to haste away from thence.

that I may appoint against her? for who is like me? and who will appoint me the time? and who is the [3]shepherd that will stand before me?

20 Therefore hear the counsel of the Lord that he hath devised against Edom, and his purpose that he hath conceived, against the inhabitants of Teman: surely the least [1]of the flock shall draw them out: surely [2]he shall make their habitations desolate with them.

21 The earth is moved at the noise of their fall: the cry of their voice is heard in the red sea.

22 Behold, he shall come up, and fly as the eagle, [1]and spread his wings over Bozrah, and at that day shall the heart of the strong men of Edom be as the heart of a woman in travail.

23 ¶ Unto [1]Damascus he saith, Hamath is confounded and Arpad, for they have heard evil tidings, and they are faint hearted as one on the fearful sea that can not rest:

24 Damascus is discouraged, and turneth herself to flight, [1]and fear hath seized her: anguish and sorrows have taken her as a woman in travail.

25 How is the glorious [1]city not reserved, the city of my joy?

26 Therefore her young men shall fall in her streets, and all her men of war shall be cut off in that day, saith the Lord of hosts.

27 And I will kindle a fire in the wall of Damascus, which shall consume the palaces of [1]Ben-Hadad.

28 Unto [1]Kedar, and to the kingdoms of Hazor, which Nebuchadnezzar king of Babel shall smite, thus saith the Lord, Arise, and go up unto Kedar, and destroy the men of the East.

29 Their tents and their flocks shall they take away: yea, they shall take to themselves their [1]curtains and all their vessels, and their camels, and they shall cry unto them, Fear is on every side.

30 Flee, get you far off ([1]they have consulted to dwell) O ye inhabitants of Hazor, saith the Lord: for Nebuchadnezzar king of Babel hath taken counsel against you, and hath devised a purpose against you.

31 [1]Arise, and get you up unto the wealthy nation that dwelleth without care, saith the Lord, which have neither gates nor bars, but dwell alone.

32 And their camels shall be a bootie, and the multitude of their cattle a spoil, and I will scatter them into all winds, and to the utmost corners, and I will bring their destruction from all the sides thereof, saith the Lord.

33 And Hazor shall be a dwelling for dragons, and desolation forever: there shall no man dwell there, nor the sons of men remain in it.

34 ¶ The words of the Lord that came to Jeremiah the Prophet, concerning [1]Elam, in the beginning of the reign of Zedekiah king of Judah, saying,

35 Thus saith the Lord of hosts, Behold, I will break the [1]bow of Elam, even the chief of their strength.

36 And upon Elam I will bring the four winds from the four quarters of heaven, and will scatter them towards all these winds, and there shall be no nation, whither the fugitives of Elam shall not come.

37 For I will cause Elam to be afraid before their enemies, and before them that seek their lives, and will bring upon them a plague, even the indignation of my wrath, saith the Lord, and I will send the sword after them, till I have consumed them.

38 And I will set my [1]throne in Elam, and I will destroy both the king and the princes from thence, saith the Lord: but [2]in the latter days I will bring again the captivity of Elam, saith the Lord.

50

He prophesieth the destruction of Babylon, and the deliverance of Israel which was in captivity.

1 The word that the Lord spake concerning Babel, and concerning the land of the Chaldeans by the [1]ministry of Jeremiah the Prophet.

2 Declare among the nations, and publish it, and set up a standard, proclaim it and conceal it not: say, [1]Babel is taken, Bel is confounded, [2]Merodach is broken down: her idols are confounded, and their images are burst in pieces.

---

[3] The captain and governor of the army, meaning, Nebuchadnezzar.

49:20 [1] They shall not be able to resist his petty captains.

[2] To visit, the enemy.

49:22 [1] As Jer. 48:40, was said of Moab.

49:23 [1] Which was the chief city of Syria, whereby he meaneth the whole country.

49:24 [1] When she heard the sudden coming of the enemy.

49:25 [1] He speaketh this in the person of the king and of them of the country, who shall wonder to see Damascus the chief city destroyed.

49:27 [1] Who was king of Syria, 1 Kings 20:26, and had built these palaces, which were still called the palaces of Ben-Hadad.

49:28 [1] Meaning, the Arabians, and their borderers.

49:29 [1] Because they used to dwell in tents, he nameth the things that pertain thereunto.

49:30 [1] The enemies will dwell in your places.

49:31 [1] He showeth that they of Hazor will flee to the Arabians for succor, but that shall not avail him.

49:34 [1] That is, Persia, so called of Elam the son of Shem.

49:35 [1] Because the Persians were good archers, he showeth that the thing wherein they put their trust, should not profit them.

49:38 [1] I will place Nebuchadnezzar there, and in these prophecies Jeremiah speaketh of those countries, which should be subdued under the first of those four monarchies whereof Daniel maketh mention.

[2] This may be referred to the Empire of Persians and Medes after the Chaldeans, or unto the time of Christ, as Jer. 48:47.

50:1 [1] Hebrew, *hands.*

50:2 [1] After that God had used the Babylonians' service to punish other nations, he showeth that their turn shall come to be punished.

[2] These were two of their chief idols.

3 For out of the North ¹there cometh up a nation against her, which shall make her land waste, and none shall dwell therein: they shall flee, *and* depart, both man and beast.

4 In those days, and at that time, saith the Lord, the children of Israel shall ¹come, they, and the children of Judah together, going, and ²weeping shall they go, and seek the Lord their God.

5 They shall ask the way to Zion, with their faces thitherward, *saying*, Come, and let us cleave to the Lord in a perpetual covenant that shall not be forgotten.

6 ¶ My people hath been *as* lost sheep: their ¹shepherds have caused them to go astray, and have turned them away to the mountains: they have gone from ²mountain to hill, *and* forgotten their resting place.

7 All that found them have devoured them, and their enemies said, We offend not, because they have sinned against the Lord, ¹the habitation of justice, even the Lord the hope of their fathers.

8 ¹Flee from the midst of Babel, and depart out of the land of the Chaldeans, and be ye as the he goats ²before the flock.

9 For lo, I will raise and cause to come up against Babel a multitude of mighty nations from the North country, and they shall set themselves in array against her, whereby she shall be taken: their arrows *shall be* as of a strong man, which is expert, *for* none shall return in vain.

10 And Chaldea shall be a spoil: all that spoil her, ¹shall be satisfied, saith the Lord.

11 Because you were glad and rejoiced in destroying mine heritage, *and* because ye are grown fat, as the calves in the grass, ¹and neighed like strong *horses*,

12 *Therefore* your mother shall be sore confounded, and she that bare you shall be ashamed, behold, the uttermost of the nations *shall be* a desert, a dry land, and a wilderness.

13 Because of the wrath of the Lord it shall not be inhabited, but shall be wholly desolate: everyone that goeth by Babel, shall be astonished, ¹and hiss at all her plagues.

CHAPTER 50
ᵃ Ezek. 23:13

14 ¹Put yourselves in array against Babel round about: all ye that bend the bow, shoot at her, spare no arrows: for she hath ²sinned against the Lord.

15 Cry against her round about: she hath ¹given her hand: her foundations are fallen, *and* her walls are destroyed: for it is the vengeance of the Lord: take vengeance upon her: as she hath done, do unto her.

16 Destroy the ¹sower from Babel, and him that handleth the scythe in the time of harvest: because of the sword of the oppressor they shall turn everyone to his people, and they shall flee everyone to his own land.

17 Israel *is like* scattered sheep: the lions have dispersed them: first the king of ¹Assyria hath devoured him, and last this Nebuchadnezzar king of Babel hath broken his ²bones.

18 Therefore thus saith the Lord of hosts the God of Israel, Behold, I will visit the king of Babel, and his land, as I have visited the King of Assyria.

19 And I will bring Israel again to his habitation: he shall feed on Carmel and Bashan, and his soul shall be satisfied upon the mount Ephraim and Gilead.

20 In those days, and at that time, saith the Lord, the iniquity of Israel shall be sought for, and there shall be none: and the sins of Judah, and they shall not be found: for I will be merciful unto them whom I reserve.

21 Go up against the land of the ¹rebels, *even* against it and against the inhabitants ᵃof ²Pekod: destroy, and lay it waste after them, saith the Lord, and do according to all that I have commanded thee.

22 A cry of battle is in the land, and of great destruction.

23 How is the ¹hammer of the whole world destroyed, and broken! how is Babel become desolate among the nations!

24 I have snared thee, and thou art taken, O Babel, and thou wast not aware: thou art found, and also caught, because thou hast striven against the Lord.

25 The Lord hath opened his treasure, and hath brought forth the weapons of his wrath: for this is the work of the Lord God of hosts in the land of the Chaldeans.

50:3 ¹ To wit, the Medes and the Persians.
50:4 ¹ When Cyrus shall take Babel.
　² Read Jer. 31:9.
50:6 ¹ Their governors and ministers by their examples have provoked them to idolatry.
　² They have committed idolatry in every place.
50:7 ¹ For the Lord dwelt among them in his Temple, and would have maintained them by his justice against their enemies.
50:8 ¹ When God shall deliver you by Cyrus.
　² That is, most forward and without fear.
50:10 ¹ Shall be made rich thereby.
50:11 ¹ For joy of the victory, that ye had against my people.
50:13 ¹ In sign of contempt and disdain.

50:14 ¹ He speaketh to the enemies the Medes and Persians.
　² Though the Lord called the Babylonians his servants, and their work his work in punishing his people, yet because they did it not to glorify God, but for their own malice, and to profit themselves, it is here called sin.
50:15 ¹ Or, yielded, or made peace.
50:16 ¹ Destroy her so that none be left to labor the ground, or to take the fruit thereof.
50:17 ¹ Meaning, Tiglath-Pilesar, who carried away the ten tribes.
　² He carried away the rest, to wit, Judah, and Benjamin.
50:21 ¹ That is, Babylon: thus the Lord raised up Cyrus.
　² Or, of them that should be visited.
50:23 ¹ Nebuchadnezzar, who had smitten down all the princes and people of the world.

26 Come against her ¹from the utmost border: open her storehouses, tread on her as on sheaves, and destroy her utterly: let nothing of her be left.

27 Destroy all her ¹bullocks: let them go down to the slaughter. Woe unto them, for their day is come, *and* the time of their visitation.

28 The voice of them that ¹flee, and escape out of the land of Babel to declare in Zion, the vengeance of the Lord our God, *and* the vengeance of his Temple.

29 Call up the archers against Babel: all ye that bend the bow, besiege it round about: let none thereof escape: ᵇrecompense her according to her work, *and* according to all that she hath done, do unto her: for she hath been proud against the Lord, *even* against the holy One of Israel.

30 Therefore shall her young men fall in the streets, and all her men of war shall be destroyed in that day, saith the Lord.

31 Behold, I *come* unto thee, O proud *man*, saith the Lord God of hosts: for thy day is come, *even* the time that I will visit thee.

32 And the proud shall stumble and fall, and none shall raise him up: and I will kindle a fire in his cities, and it shall devour all round about him.

33 Thus saith the Lord of hosts, The children of Israel, and the children of Judah were oppressed together: and all that took them captives, held them, *and* would not let them go.

34 *But* their strong redeemer, whose Name *is* the Lord of hosts, he shall maintain their cause, that he may give rest to the land, ¹and disquiet the inhabitants of Babel.

35 A sword *is* upon the Chaldeans, saith the Lord, and upon the inhabitants of Babel, and upon her princes, and upon her wise men.

36 A sword *is* upon the ¹soothsayers, and they shall dote: a sword *is* upon her strong men, and they shall be afraid.

37 A sword *is* upon their horses, and upon their chariots, and upon all the multitude that are in the midst of her, and they shall be like women: a sword is upon her treasures, and they shall be spoiled.

38 A ¹drought *is* upon her waters, and they shall be dried up: for it is the land of graven images, and they dote upon their idols.

39 Therefore the ¹Ziims with the Iims shall dwell

ᵇ Rev. 18:6
ᶜ Gen. 19:24
Isa. 13:19
ᵈ Jer. 49:19

there, and ²the ostriches shall dwell therein: for it shall be no more inhabited, neither shall it be inhabited from generation unto generation.

40 As God destroyed ᶜSodom and Gomorrah with the places thereof near about, saith the Lord: so shall no man dwell there, neither shall the son of man remain therein.

41 ¶ Behold, a people shall come from the North, and a great nation, and many kings shall be raised up from ¹the coasts of the earth.

42 They shall hold the bow and the buckler: they are cruel and unmerciful: their voice shall roar like the sea, and they shall ride upon horses, *and* be put in array like men to the battle against thee, O daughter of Babel.

43 The king of Babel hath heard the report of them, and his hands ¹waxed feeble: sorrow came upon him, *even* sorrow as of a woman in travail.

44 Behold, he ᵈshall come up like a lion from the swelling of Jordan unto the strong habitation: for I will make *Israel* to rest, and I will make them to haste away from her: and who is a chosen man that I may appoint against her? for who is like me, and who will appoint me the time? and who is the ¹shepherd that will stand before me?

45 Therefore hear the counsel of the Lord, that he hath devised against Babel, and his purpose that he hath conceived against the land of the Chaldeans: surely the least of the flock shall draw them out: surely he shall make *their* habitation desolate with them.

46 At the noise of the winning of Babel the earth is moved, and the cry is heard among the nations.

51

6 *Why Babylon is destroyed.* 41 *The vain confidence of the Babylonians.* 43 *The vanity of idolaters.* 59 *Jeremiah giveth his book to Seraiah.*

1 Thus saith the Lord, Behold, I will raise up against Babel, and against the inhabitants ¹that lift up *their* heart against me, a destroying ²wind,

2 And will send unto Babel fanners that shall fan her, and shall empty her land, for in the day of trouble they shall be against her on every side.

3 Also to the bender that bendeth his bow, and to him that lifteth himself up in his brigandine, *will I say*, Spare not her young men, but destroy all her host.

50:26 ¹ Hebrew, *from the end.*
50:27 ¹ Her princes and mighty men.
50:28 ¹ Of the Jews which should be delivered by Cyrus.
50:34 ¹ He showeth that when God executeth his judgments against his enemies, that his Church shall then have rest.
50:36 ¹ Hebrew, *liars.*
50:38 ¹ For Cyrus did cut the river Euphrates, and divided the course thereof into many streams, so that it might be passed over as though there had been no water: which thing he did by the counsel of two of Belshazzar's captains, who conspired against their king, because he

had gelded the one of them in despite, and slain the son of the other.
50:39 ¹ Read Isa. 13:21.
   ² Hebrew, *sons of the ostriches,* or *young.*
50:41 ¹ Meaning, that the Persians should gather their army of many nations.
50:43 ¹ Which is meant of Belshazzar, Dan. 5:6.
50:44 ¹ Read Jer. 49:19.
51:1 ¹ Or, *of the land that riseth up.*
   ² The Medes and Persians that shall destroy them as the wind doth the chaff.

4 Thus the slain shall fall in the land of the Chaldeans, and they that are thrust through in her streets.

5 For Israel hath been no [1]widow, nor Judah from his God, from the Lord of hosts, though their land was filled with sin against the holy one of Israel.

6 ¶ [1]Flee out of the midst of Babel, and deliver every man his soul: be not destroyed in her iniquity: for this is the time of the Lord's vengeance: he will render unto her a recompense.

7 Babel *hath been as* a golden cup in the [1]Lord's hand, that made all the earth drunken, the nations have drunken of her wine, therefore do the nations [2]rage.

8 [a]Babel is suddenly fallen, and destroyed: howl for her, bring balm for her sore, if she may be healed.

9 We would have cured Babel, but she could not be healed: forsake her, and let [1]us go everyone into his own country: for her judgment is come up into heaven, and is lifted up to the clouds.

10 The Lord hath brought forth our [1]righteousness: come and let us declare in Zion the work of the Lord our God.

11 Make bright the arrows: [1]gather the shields: the Lord hath raised up the spirit of the King of the Medes: for his purpose is against Babel to destroy it, because it is the [2]vengeance of the Lord, *and* the vengeance of his Temple.

12 Set up the standard upon the walls of Babel, make the watch strong: set up the watchmen: prepare the scouts: for the Lord hath both devised, and done that which he spake against the inhabitants of Babel.

13 O thou that dwellest upon many [1]waters, abundant in treasures, thine end is come, *even* the [2]end of thy covetousness.

14 The Lord of hosts hath sworn by [1,b]himself, *saying,* Surely I will fill thee with men, as with caterpillars, and they shall cry and shout against thee.

15 [c]He hath made the earth by his power, and established the world by his wisdom, and hath stretched out the heaven by his discretion.

CHAPTER 51
[a] Isa. 21:9
Rev. 14:8
[b] Amos 6:8
[c] Jer. 10:12

16 He giveth by *his* voice the multitude of waters in the heaven, and he causeth the clouds to ascend from the ends of the earth, he turneth lightnings to rain, and bringeth forth the wind out of his treasures.

17 Every man is a beast by *his own* [1]knowledge: every founder is confounded by the graven image: for his melting is but falsehood, and there is no breath therein.

18 They are vanity, *and* the work of errors: in the time of their [1]visitation they shall perish.

19 The [1]portion of Jacob *is* not like them: for he is the maker of all things, and *Israel is* the rod of his inheritance: the Lord of hosts *is* his Name.

20 Thou art mine [1]hammer, *and* weapons of war: for with thee will I break the nations, and with thee will I destroy kingdoms,

21 And by thee will I break horse and horseman, and by thee will I break the chariot and him that rideth therein.

22 By thee also will I break man and woman, and by thee will I break old and young, and by thee will I break the young man and the maid.

23 I will also break by thee the shepherd and his flock, and by thee will I break the husbandman and his yoke of oxen, and by thee will I break the dukes and princes.

24 And I will render unto Babel, and to all the inhabitants of the Chaldeans all their evil, that they have done in Zion, *even* in your sight, saith the Lord.

25 Behold, I *come* unto thee, O destroying [1]mountain, saith the Lord, which destroyest all the earth: and I will stretch out mine hand upon thee, and roll thee down from the [2]rocks, and will make thee a burnt mountain.

26 They shall not take of thee a stone for a corner, nor a stone for foundations: but thou shalt be destroyed forever, saith the Lord.

27 Set up a standard in the land: blow the trumpets among the nations: prepare the nations against her: call up the kingdoms of [1]Ararat, Minni, and Ashkenaz against her, appoint the prince against her, cause

---

51:5 [1] Though they were forsaken for a time, yet they were not utterly cast off as though their husbands were dead.
51:6 [1] He showeth that there remaineth nothing for them that abide in Babylon, but destruction, Jer. 17:6 and 48:6.
51:7 [1] By whom the Lord poured out the drink of his vengeance, to whom it pleased him.
    [2] For the great afflictions that they have felt by the Babylonians.
51:9 [1] Thus the people of God exhort one another to go to Zion and praise God.
51:10 [1] In approving our cause and punishing our enemies.
51:11 [1] Or, fill, or multiply.
    [2] For the wrong done to his people and to his Temple, Jer. 50:28.
51:13 [1] For the land of Chaldea was full of rivers, which ran into Euphrates.

[2] Or, measures.
51:14 [1] Hebrew, *his soul.*
51:17 [1] Read Jer. 10:14.
51:18 [1] When God shall execute his vengeance.
51:19 [1] That is, the true God of Israel is not like to these idols: for he can help when all things are desperate.
51:20 [1] He meaneth the Medes and Persians, as he did before call the Babylonians his hammer, Jer. 50:23.
51:25 [1] Not that Babylon stood on a mountain, but because it was strong and seemed invincible.
    [2] From thy strongholds and fortresses.
51:27 [1] By these three nations he meaneth Armenia the higher, Armenia the lower, and Scythia: for Cyrus had gathered an army of divers nations.

horses to come up as the rough caterpillars.

28 Prepare against her the nations with the kings of the Medes, the dukes thereof, and the princes thereof, and all the land of his dominion.

29 And the land shall tremble and sorrow: for the device of the Lord shall be performed against Babel, to make the land of Babel waste without an inhabitant.

30 The strong men of Babel have ceased to fight: they have remained in their holds: their strength hath failed, *and* they were like women: they have burnt her dwelling places, *and* her bars are broken.

31 A post shall run to meet the post, and a messenger to meet the messenger, to show the King of Babel, that his city is taken on a ¹side thereof,

32 And that the passages are stopped, and the reeds burnt with fire, and the men of war troubled.

33 For thus saith the Lord of hosts the God of Israel, The daughter of Babel *is* like a threshingfloor: the time of her threshing *is come*: yet a little while, and the time of her harvest ¹shall come.

34 Nebuchadnezzar the King of Babel hath ¹devoured me, and destroyed me: he hath made me an empty vessel: he swallowed me up like a dragon: and filled his belly with my delicates, *and* hath cast me out.

35 The spoil of me, and that which was left of me, *is brought* unto Babel, shall the inhabitant of Zion say: and my blood unto the inhabitants of Chaldea, shall Jerusalem say.

36 Therefore thus saith the Lord, Behold, I will maintain thy ¹cause, and take vengeance for thee, and I will dry up the sea, and dry up her springs.

37 And Babel shall be *as* heaps, a dwelling place for dragons, an astonishment, and an hissing, without an inhabitant.

38 They shall roar together like lions, and yell as the lion's whelps.

39 In their ¹heat I will make them feasts, and I will make them drunken that they may rejoice, and sleep a perpetual sleep, and not wake, saith the Lord.

40 I will bring them down like lambs to the slaughter, *and* like rams and goats.

41 How is ¹Sheshach taken! and how is the glory of the whole earth taken! how is Babel become an astonishment among the nations!

42 The ¹sea is come up upon Babel: she is covered with the multitude of the waves thereof.

43 Her cities are desolate: the land is dry and a wilderness, a land wherein no man dwelleth, neither doth the son of man pass thereby.

44 I will also visit Bel in Babel, and I will bring out of his mouth, that which ¹he hath swallowed up, and the nations shall run no more unto him, and the wall of Babel shall fall.

45 My people, go out of the midst of her, and deliver ye every man his soul from the fierce wrath of the Lord,

46 Lest your heart even faint, and ye fear the rumor that shall be heard in the land: the rumor shall come *this* year, and after that in the *other* ¹year *shall come* a rumor, and cruelty in the land, and ruler against ruler.

47 Therefore behold, the days come, that I will visit the images of Babel, and the whole land shall be confounded, and all her slain shall fall in the midst of her.

48 Then the heaven and ¹the earth, and all that is therein, shall rejoice for Babel: for the destroyers shall come unto her from the North, saith the Lord.

49 As Babel caused the ¹slain of Israel to fall, so by Babel the slain of all the earth did fall.

50 Ye that ¹have escaped the sword, go away, stand not still: remember the Lord afar off, and let Jerusalem come into your mind.

51 We are ¹confounded because we have heard reproach: shame hath covered our faces, for strangers are come into the Sanctuaries of the Lord's house.

52 Wherefore behold, the days come, saith the Lord, that I will visit her graven images, and through all her land the wounded shall groan.

53 Though Babel should mount up to ¹heaven, and

51:31 ¹ By turning the course of the river one side was made open and the reeds that did grow in the water were destroyed, which Cyrus did by the counsel of Gobria and Gabatha Belshazzar's captains.

51:33 ¹ When she shall be cut up and threshed.

51:34 ¹ This is spoken in the person of the Jews bewailing their state and the cruelty of the Babylonians.

51:36 ¹ Thus the Lord esteemed the injury done to his Church, as done to himself, because their cause is his.

51:39 ¹ When they are inflamed with surfeiting and drinking, I will feast with them, alluding to Belshazzar's banquet, Dan. 5:2.

51:41 ¹ Meaning, Babel, as Jer. 25:26.

51:42 ¹ The great army of the Medes and Persians.

51:44 ¹ That is, his gifts and presents which he had received as part of the spoil of other nations, and which the idolaters brought unto him from all countries.

51:46 ¹ Meaning, that Babylon should not be destroyed all at once, but little by little should be brought to nothing: for the first year came the tidings, the next year the siege, and in the third year it was taken: yet this is not that horrible destruction which the prophets threatened in many places: for that was after this when they rebelled and Darius overcame them by the policy of Zopyrus, and hanged three thousand gentlemen besides the common people.

51:48 ¹ All creatures in heaven and earth shall rejoice, and praise God for the destruction of Babylon the great enemy of his Church.

51:49 ¹ Babylon did not only destroy Israel, but many other nations.

51:50 ¹ Ye that are now captives in Babylon.

51:51 ¹ He showeth how they should remember Jerusalem by lamenting the miserable affliction thereof.

51:53 ¹ For the walls were two hundred foot high.

though she should defend her strength on high, *yet* from me shall her destroyers come, saith the Lord.

54 A sound of a cry *cometh* from Babel, and great destruction from the land of the Chaldeans,

55 Because the Lord hath laid Babel waste, and destroyed from her the great voice, and her waves shall roar like great waters, *and* a sound was made by their noise:

56 Because the destroyer is come upon her, *even* upon Babel, and her strong men are taken, their bows are broken: for the Lord God that recompenseth, shall surely recompense.

57 And I will ¹make drunk her princes, and her wise men, her dukes, and her nobles, and her strong men: and they shall sleep a perpetual sleep, and not wake, saith the King, whose Name *is* the Lord of hosts.

58 Thus saith the Lord of hosts, The ¹thick wall of Babel shall be broken, and her high gates shall be burnt with fire, and the people shall labor in vain, and the folk in the fire, for they shall be weary.

59 The word which Jeremiah the Prophet commanded Seraiah the son of Neriah, the son of Mahseiah, when he went with Zedekiah the king of Judah into Babel, in the ¹fourth year of his reign, and this Seraiah was a peaceable Prince.

60 So Jeremiah wrote in a book all the evil that should come upon Babel, *even* all these things that are written against Babel.

61 And Jeremiah said to Seraiah, When thou comest unto Babel, and shalt see and shalt read all these words,

62 Then shalt thou say, O Lord, thou hast spoken against this place, to destroy it, that none should remain in it, neither man nor beast, but that it should be desolate forever.

63 And when thou hast made an end of reading this book, thou shalt bind a ¹stone to it, and cast it in the midst of Euphrates,

64 And shalt say, Thus shall Babel be drowned and shall not rise from the evil, that I will bring upon her: and they shall ¹be weary. Thus far *are* the words of Jeremiah.

52

4 *Jerusalem is taken.* 10 *Zedekiah's sons are killed before his face, and his eyes put out.* 13 *The city is burned.* 31 *Jehoiachin is brought forth of prison, and fed*

CHAPTER 52
a 2 Kings 24:18
2 Chron. 39:11
b 2 Kings 25:1
Jer. 39:1

like a king.

1 Zedekiah *ᵃwas* one and twenty years old when he began to reign, and he reigned eleven years in Jerusalem, and his mother's name *was* Hamutal, the daughter of Jeremiah of Libnah.

2 And he did evil in the eyes of the Lord, according to all that Jehoiakim had done.

3 ¹Doubtless because the wrath of the Lord was against Jerusalem and Judah, till he had cast them out from his presence, therefore Zedekiah rebelled against the king of Babel.

4 *ᵇBut* in the ninth year of his reign, in the tenth month the tenth *day* of the month came Nebuchadnezzar King of Babel, he and all his host against Jerusalem, and pitched against it, and built forts against it round about.

5 So the city was besieged unto the eleventh year of the king Zedekiah.

6 Now in the fourth month, the ninth *day* of the month, the famine was sore in the city, so that there was no more bread for the people of the land.

7 Then the city was broken up, and all the men of war fled, and went out of the city by night, by the ¹way of the gate between the two walls, which was by the King's garden: (now the Chaldeans *were* by the city round about) and they went by the way of the wilderness.

8 But the army of the Chaldeans pursued after the king, and took Zedekiah in the desert of Jericho, and all the host was scattered from him.

9 Then they took the King and carried him up unto the king of Babel to Riblah in the land of Hamath, ¹where he gave judgment upon him.

10 And the king of Babel slew the sons of Zedekiah before his eyes: he slew also all the princes of Judah in Riblah.

11 Then he put out the eyes of Zedekiah, and the king of Babel bound him in chains, and carried him to Babel, and put him in prison till the day of his death.

12 Now in the fifth month in the ¹tenth *day* of the month (which was the nineteenth year of the king Nebuchadnezzar King of Babel) came Nebuzaradan chief steward *which* ²stood before the king of Babel in Jerusalem,

13 And burnt the House of the Lord, and the

51:57 ¹ I will so astonish them by afflictions that they shall not know which way to turn them.

51:58 ¹ The thickness of the wall was fifty foot thick.

51:59 ¹ This was not in the time of his captivity, but seven years before, when he went either to gratulate Nebuchadnezzar, or to entreat of some matters.

51:63 ¹ St. John in his Revelation alludeth to this place, when he saith that the Angel took a millstone and cast it into the sea: signifying thereby the destruction of Babylon, Rev. 18:21.

51:64 ¹ They shall not be able to resist, but shall labor in vain.

52:3 ¹ So the Lord punished sin by sin, and gave him up to his rebellious heart, till he had brought the enemy upon him to lead him away and his people.

52:7 ¹ Read Jer. 39:4.

52:9 ¹ Read 2 Kings 25:6; Jer. 39:5.

52:12 ¹ In 2 Kings 25:8, it is called the seventh day, because the fire began then, and so continued to the tenth.

² That is, which was his servant, as 2 Kings 25:8.

King's house, and all the houses of Jerusalem, and all the great houses burnt he with fire.

14 And all the army of the Chaldeans that were with the chief steward, brake down all the walls of Jerusalem round about.

15 Then Nebuzaradan the chief steward carried away captive *certain* of the poor of the people, and the residue of the people that remained in the city, and those that were fled, and fallen to the King of Babel, with the rest of the multitude.

16 But Nebuzaradan the chief steward left *certain* of the poor of the land, to dress the vines, and to till the land.

17 Also the [1]pillars of brass that were in the House of the Lord, and the bases, and the brazen Sea, that was in the House of the Lord, the Chaldeans brake, and carried all the brass of them to Babel.

18 The pots also and the [1]besoms, and the instruments of music, and the basins, and the incense dishes, and all the vessels of brass wherewith they ministered, took they away.

19 And the bowls, and the ashpans, and the basins, and the pots, and the candlesticks, and the incense dishes, and the cups, *and all* that was of gold, and that was of silver, took the chief steward away,

20 With the two pillars, one Sea, and twelve brazen bulls, that were under the bases, which King Solomon had made in the House of the Lord: the brass of all these vessels was without [1]weight.

21 And concerning the pillars, the height of one pillar *was* eighteen cubits, and a thread of twelve cubits did compass it, and the thickness thereof *was* four fingers: *it was* hollow.

22 And a chapiter of brass *was* upon it, and the height of one chapiter was five cubits with network, and pomegranates upon the chapiters round about, all of brass: the second pillar also, and the pomegranates *were* like unto these.

23 And there were ninety and six pomegranates on a side: *and* all the pomegranates upon the network *were* an [1]hundred round about.

24 And the chief steward took Seraiah the chief Priest, and Zephaniah [1]the second Priest, and the three keepers of the door.

25 He took also out of the city an Eunuch, which had the oversight of the men of war, and [1]seven men that were in the King's presence, which were found in the city, and Sopher captain of the host, who mustered the people of the land, and threescore men of the people of the land, that were found in the midst of the city.

26 Nebuzaradan the chief steward took them, and brought them to the King of Babel to Riblah.

27 And the king of Babel smote them, and slew them in Riblah, in the land of Hamath: thus Judah was carried away captive out of his own land.

28 ¶ This is the people, whom Nebuchadnezzar carried away captive, in the [1]seventh year, *even* three thousand Jews, and three and twenty.

29 In the [1]eighteenth year of Nebuchadnezzar, he carried away captive from Jerusalem eight hundred thirty and two [2]persons.

30 In the three and twentieth year of Nebuchadnezzar, Nebuzaradan the chief steward carried away captive of the Jews seven hundred forty and five persons: all the persons *were* four thousand and six hundred.

31 And in the seven and thirtieth year of the captivity of Jehoiachin King of Judah, in the twelfth month, in the five and twentieth *day* of the month, Evil-Merodach king of Babel, in the *first* year of his reign, [1]lifted up the head of Jehoiachin king of Judah, and brought him out of prison,

32 And spake kindly unto him, and set his throne above the throne of the Kings, that were with him in Babel,

33 And changed his prison [1]garments, and he did continually eat bread before him all the days of his life.

34 His portion *was* a [1]continual portion given him of the king of Babel, every day a certain, all the days of his life until he died.

52:17 [1] Of these pillars, read 1 Kings 7:15.

52:18 [1] Which were also made of brass, as 1 Kings 7:45.

52:20 [1] It was so much in quantity.

52:23 [1] But because of the roundness, no more could be seen but ninety and six.

52:24 [1] Which served in the high Priest's stead, if he had any necessary impediment.

52:25 [1] In 2 Kings 25:19, is read but of five: those were the most excellent, and the other two, which were not so noble, are not there mentioned with them.

52:28 [1] Which was the latter end of the seventh year of his reign, and the beginning of the eighth.

52:29 [1] In the latter end also of that year, and the beginning of the nineteenth.
       [2] Hebrew, *souls*.

52:31 [1] That is, restored him to liberty and honor.

52:33 [1] And gave him princely apparel.

52:34 [1] That is he had allowance in the court, and thus at length he had rest and quietness because he obeyed Jeremiah the Prophet, whereas the others were cruelly ordered, that would not obey him.

LAMENTATIONS

1 *The Prophet bewaileth the miserable estate of Jerusalem. 5 And showeth that they are plagued because of their sins. The first and second Chapter begin every verse according to the letters of the Hebrew Alphabet. The third hath three verses for every letter, and the fourth is as the first.*

CHAPTER 1
a Jer. 14:17
Lam. 2:18

1 How doth ¹the city remain solitary that was full of people? she is as a widow: she that was great among the nations, ²*and* princess among the provinces, is made tributary.

2 She weepeth continually in the ¹night, and her tears *run down* by her cheeks: among all her ²lovers, she hath none to comfort her: all her friends have dealt unfaithfully with her, *and* are her enemies.

3 Judah is carried away captive, because ¹of affliction, and because of great servitude, she dwelleth among the heathen, *and* findeth no rest: all her persecutors took her in the straits.

4 The ways of Zion lament, because no man cometh¹to the solemn feasts, all her gates are desolate: her Priests sigh: her virgins are discomfited, and she is in ²heaviness.

5 Her adversaries ¹are the chief, *and* her enemies prosper: for the Lord hath afflicted her, for the multitude of her transgressions, *and* her children are gone into captivity before the enemy.

6 And from the daughter of Zion all her beauty is departed: her princes are become ¹like harts that find no pasture, and they are gone without strength before the pursuer.

7 Jerusalem remembered the days of her affliction, and of her rebellion, *and* all her pleasant things that she had in times past, when her people ¹fell into the hand of the enemy, and none did help her: the adversary saw her, *and* did mock at her ²Sabbaths.

8 Jerusalem hath grievously sinned, therefore she is ¹in derision: all that honored her, despise her, because they have seen her filthiness: yea, she sigheth, and turneth backward.

9 ¹Her filthiness is in her skirts: she remembered not her last end, therefore she came down wonderfully: she had no comforter: O Lord, behold mine affliction: for the enemy ²is proud.

10 The enemy hath stretched out his hand upon all her pleasant things: for she hath seen the heathen enter into her Sanctuary, whom ¹thou didst command, that they should not enter into thy Church.

11 All her people sigh and seek *their* bread: they have given their pleasant things for meat to refresh the soul: see, O Lord, and consider: for I am become vile.

12 Have ye no regard, all ye that pass by *this* way? behold and see, if there be any ¹sorrow like unto my sorrow, which is done unto me wherewith the Lord hath afflicted *me* in the day of his fierce wrath.

13 From above hath ¹he sent fire into my bones, which prevail against them: he hath spread a net for my feet, *and* turned me back: he hath made me desolate, *and* daily in heaviness.

14 The ¹yoke of my transgressions is bound upon his hand: they are wrapped, and come up upon my neck: he hath made my strength to fall: the Lord hath delivered me into *their* hands, neither am I able to rise up.

15 The Lord hath trodden under foot all my valiant men in the midst of me: he hath called an assembly against me to destroy my young men: the Lord hath trodden ¹the winepress upon the virgin the daughter of Judah.

16 ᵃFor these things I weep: mine eye, *even* mine eye casteth out water, because the comforter that

---

1:1 ¹ The Prophet wondereth at the great judgment of God, seeing Jerusalem, which was so strong and so full of people, to be now destroyed and desolate.

² Which had chief rule over many provinces and countries.

1:2 ¹ So that she taketh no rest.

² Meaning, the Egyptians and Assyrians, which promised help.

1:3 ¹ For her cruelty toward the poor and oppression of servants, Jer. 34:11.

1:4 ¹ As they used to come up with mirth and joy, Ps. 42:4.

² Hebrew, *bitterness.*

1:5 ¹ That is, have rule over her, Deut. 28:41.

1:6 ¹ As men pined away with sorrow and that have no courage.

1:7 ¹ In her misery she considered the great benefits and commodities that she had lost.

² At her religion and serving of God, which was the greatest grief

to the godly.

1:8 ¹ Or, driven away.

1:9 ¹ She is not ashamed of her sin, although it be manifest.

² Hebrew, *hath magnified himself.*

1:10 ¹ God forbiddeth that the Ammonites and Moabites should enter into the Congregation of the Lord, and under them he comprehendeth all enemies, Deut. 23:3.

1:12 ¹ Thus Jerusalem lamenteth moving others to pity her and to learn by her example.

1:13 ¹ This declareth that we should acknowledge God to be the author of all our afflictions to the intent that we might seek unto him for remedy.

1:14 ¹ Mine heavy sins are continually before his eyes, as he that tieth a thing to his hand for a remembrance.

1:15 ¹ He hath trodden them underfoot as they tread grapes in the winepress.

should refresh my soul, is far from me: my children are desolate, because the enemy prevailed.

17 Zion stretcheth out her hands, and there *is* none to comfort her: the Lord hath appointed the enemies of Jacob round about him: Jerusalem is [1]as a menstruous woman in the midst of them.

18 The Lord is righteous: for I have rebelled against his [1]commandment: hear, I pray you, all people, and behold my sorrow: my virgins and my young men are gone into captivity.

19 I called for my lovers, *but* they deceived me: my Priests and mine Elders perished in the city, while they [1]sought their meat to refresh their souls.

20 Behold, O Lord, how I am troubled: my bowels swell: mine heart is turned within me, for I am full of heaviness: the sword spoileth abroad, as death *doeth* at home.

21 They have heard that I mourn, *but* there is none to comfort me: all mine enemies have heard of my trouble, *and* are glad, that thou hast done it: thou wilt bring the day, that thou hast pronounced, and they shall be like unto me.

22 [1]Let all their wickedness come before thee: [2]do unto them, as thou hast done unto me, for all my transgressions: for my sighs are many, and mine heart is heavy.

2

1 How hath the Lord [1]darkened the daughter of Zion in his wrath! and hath cast down from [2]heaven unto the earth the beauty of Israel, and remembered not his [3]footstool in the day of his wrath!

2 The Lord hath destroyed all the habitations of Jacob, and not spared: he hath thrown down in his wrath the strongholds of the daughter of Judah: he hath cast them down to the ground: he hath polluted the kingdom and the princes thereof.

3 He hath cut off in his fierce wrath all the [1]horn of Israel: he hath drawn back his [2]right hand from before the enemy, and there was kindled in Jacob like a flame of fire, which devoured round about.

4 He [1]hath bent his bow like an enemy: his right hand was stretched up as an adversary, and slew all that was pleasant to the eye in the Tabernacle of the daughter of Zion: he poured out his wrath like fire.

5 The Lord was as an enemy: he hath devoured Israel *and* consumed all his palaces: he hath destroyed his strongholds, and hath increased in the daughter of Judah lamentation and mourning.

6 For he hath destroyed his Tabernacle, as a garden he hath destroyed his Congregation: the Lord hath caused the feasts and Sabbaths to be forgotten in Zion, and hath despised in the indignation of his wrath, the King and the Priest.

7 The Lord hath forsaken his altar: he hath abhorred his Sanctuary: he hath given into the hand of the enemy the walls of her palaces: they have made a [1]noise in the House of the Lord, as in the day of solemnity.

8 The Lord hath determined to destroy the wall of the daughter of Zion: he stretched out a line: he hath not withdrawn his hand from destroying: therefore he made the rampart, [1]and the wall to lament: they were destroyed together.

9 Her gates are sunk to the ground: he hath destroyed and broken her bars: her King and her Princes *are* among the Gentiles: the Law *is* no more, neither can her Prophets [1]receive *any* vision from the Lord.

10 The Elders of the daughter of Zion sit upon the ground, and keep silence: they have cast up dust upon their heads: they have girded themselves with sackcloth: the virgins of Jerusalem hang down their heads to the ground.

11 Mine eyes do fail with tears: my bowels swell: my liver is poured upon the earth, for the destruction of the daughter of my people, because the children and sucklings [1]swoon in the streets of the city.

12 They have said to their mothers, Where is [1]bread and drink? when they swooned as the wounded in the streets of the city, *and* when they [2]gave up the ghost in their mother's bosom.

13 [1]What thing shall I take to witness for thee? What thing shall I compare to thee, O daughter Jerusalem? what shall I liken to thee, that I may

---

1:17 [1] Which because of her pollution was separate from her husband, Lev. 15:19, and was abhorred for the time.

1:18 [1] Hebrew, *mouth*.

1:19 [1] That is, they died for hunger.

1:22 [1] Of desiring vengeance against the enemy, read Jer. 11:20 and 18:21.
[2] Or, gather them like grapes.

2:1 [1] That is, brought her from prosperity to adversity.
[2] Hath given her a most sore fall.
[3] Alluding to the Temple, or to the Ark of the covenant, which was called the footstool of the Lord, because they should not set their minds so low, but lift up their hearts toward the heavens.

2:3 [1] Meaning, the glory and strength, as 1 Sam. 2:1.
[2] That is, his succor which he was wont to send us, when our enemies oppressed us.

2:4 [1] Showing that there is no remedy but destruction, where God is the enemy.

2:7 [1] As the people were accustomed to praise God to the solemn feasts with a loud voice, so now the enemies blaspheme him with shouting and cry.

2:8 [1] This is a figurative speech, as that was, when he said, the ways did lament, Lam. 1:4, meaning, that this sorrow was so great, that the insensible things had their part thereof.

2:9 [1] Or, find.

2:11 [1] Or, faint.

2:12 [1] Hebrew, *wheat and wine*.
[2] Hebrew, *poured out the soul*.

2:13 [1] Meaning, that her calamity was so evident, that it needed no witnesses.

comfort thee, O virgin daughter Zion? for thy breach *is* great like the sea: who can heal thee?

14 Thy Prophets have[1]looked out vain and foolish things for thee, and they have not discovered thine iniquity, to turn away thy captivity, but have looked out for thee false [2]prophecies, and causes of banishment.

15 All that pass by the way, clap their hands at thee: they hiss and wag their head upon the daughter Jerusalem, *saying*, Is this the city that men call, The perfection of beauty, *and* the joy of the whole earth?

16 All thine enemies have opened their mouth against thee: they hiss and gnash the teeth, saying, Let us devour it: certainly this is the day that we looked for: we have found *and* seen it.

17 *a*The Lord hath done that which he had purposed: he hath fulfilled his word that he had determined of old time: he hath thrown down, and not spared: he hath caused thine enemy to rejoice over thee, and set up the horn of thine adversaries.

18 Their heart *b*cried unto the Lord, O wall of the daughter Zion, let tears run down like a river, day and night: take thee no rest, neither let the apple of thine eye cease.

19 Arise, cry in the night: in the beginning of the watches, pour out thine heart like water before the face of the Lord: lift up thine hands toward him for the life of thy young children, that faint for hunger in the corners of all the streets.

20 Behold, O Lord, and consider to whom thou hast done thus: shall the women eat their fruit, *and* children of a [1]span long? shall the Priest and the Prophet be slain in the Sanctuary of the Lord?

21 The young and the old lie on the ground in the streets: my virgins and my young men are fallen by the sword: thou hast slain *them* in the day of thy wrath: thou hast killed, and not spared.

22 Thou hast called as in a solemn day my [1]terrors round about, so that in the day of the Lord's wrath none escaped nor remained: those that I have nourished and brought up, hath mine enemy consumed.

CHAPTER 2
a Lev. 26:15,25
Deut. 28:15,25
b Jer. 14:17
Lam. 1:16

3

1 I am the man that hath seen [1]affliction in the rod of his indignation.

2 He hath led me, and brought me into darkness, but not to light.

3 Surely he is turned against me: he turneth his hand *against me* all the day.

4 My flesh and my skin hath he caused to wax old, *and* he hath broken my bones.

5 He hath [1]built against me, and compassed *me* with gall and labor.

6 He hath set me in dark places, as they that be dead forever.

7 He hath hedged about me, that I cannot get out: he hath made my chains heavy.

8 Also when I cry and shout, he shutteth out my [1]prayer.

9 He hath [1]stopped up my ways with hewn stone, *and* turned away my paths.

10 [1]He was unto me *as* a bear lying in wait, *and* as a lion in secret places.

11 He hath stopped my ways, and pulled me in pieces: he hath made me desolate.

12 He hath bent his bow, and made me a mark for the arrow.

13 He caused [1]the arrows of his quiver to enter into my reins.

14 I was a derision to all my people, *and* their song all the day.

15 He hath filled me with bitterness, *and* made me drunken with [1]wormwood.

16 He hath also broken my teeth with stones, *and* hath covered me with ashes.

17 Thus my soul was far off from peace: I forgot prosperity,

18 And I said, My strength and my [1]hope is perished from the Lord,

19 Remembering mine affliction, and my mourning, the wormwood and the gall.

20 My soul hath them in remembrance, and is humbled [1]in me.

21 I consider this in mine heart: therefore have I hope.

2:14 [1] Because the false prophets called themselves Seers, as the others were called, therefore he showeth that they saw amiss, because they did not reprove the people's faults, but flattered them in their sins, which was the cause of their destruction.

[2] Or, burdens.

2:20 [1] Or, brought up in their own hands.

2:22 [1] Or, enemies, whom I feared.

3:1 [1] The Prophet complaineth of the punishments and afflictions that he endured by the false prophets and hypocrites, when he declared the destruction of Jerusalem, as Jer. 20:1, 2.

3:5 [1] He speaketh this, as one that felt God's heavy judgment, which he greatly feared, and therefore setteth them out with this diversity of words.

3:8 [1] This is a great tentation to the godly when they see not the fruit

of their prayers, and causeth them to think that they are not heard, which thing God useth to do, that they might pray more earnestly and the oftener.

3:9 [1] And keepeth me in hold as a prisoner.

3:10 [1] He hath no pity on me.

3:13 [1] Hebrew, *sons*.

3:15 [1] With great anguish and sorrow he hath made me to lose my sense.

3:18 [1] Thus with pain he was driven to and fro between hope and despair, as the godly ofttimes are, yet in the end the spirit getteth the victory.

3:20 [1] He showeth that God thus useth to exercise his, to the intent that hereby they may know themselves, and feel his mercies.

22 It is the Lord's [1]mercies that we are not consumed, because his compassions fail not.

23 They are renewed [1]every morning: great is thy faithfulness.

24 The Lord is my [1]portion, saith my soul: therefore will I hope in him.

25 The Lord is good unto them that trust in him, and to the soul that seeketh him.

26 It is good both to trust, and to wait for the salvation of the Lord.

27 It is good for a man that he bear the yoke in his [1]youth.

28 He sitteth alone, [1]and keepeth silence, because he hath borne it upon him.

29 He putteth his [1]mouth in the dust, if there may be hope.

30 He giveth his cheek to him that smiteth him: he is filled full with reproaches.

31 For the Lord will not forsake forever.

32 But though he send affliction, yet will he have compassion according to the multitude of his mercies.

33 For he doth not [1]punish [2]willingly, nor afflict the children of men,

34 In stamping under his feet all the prisoners of the earth,

35 In overthrowing the right of a man before the face of the most High,

36 In subverting a man in his cause: the Lord [1]seeth it not.

37 Who is he then that saith, and it cometh to pass, and the Lord [1]commandeth it not?

38 Out of the mouth of the most High proceedeth not [1]evil and good?

39 Wherefore then is the living [1]man sorrowful? man suffereth for his sin.

40 Let us search and try our ways, and turn again to the Lord.

41 Let us lift up [1]our hearts with our hands unto God in the heavens.

42 We have sinned, and have rebelled, therefore thou hast not spared.

43 Thou hast covered us with wrath, and persecuted

CHAPTER 3
[a] 1 Cor. 4:13
[b] Ps. 28:4

us: thou hast slain, and not spared.

44 Thou hast covered thyself with a cloud, that our prayer should not pass through.

45 Thou hast made us as the [a]offscouring and refuse in the midst of the people.

46 All our enemies have opened their mouth against us.

47 Fear, and a snare is come upon us with desolation and destruction.

48 Mine eye casteth out rivers of water, for the destruction of the daughter of my people.

49 Mine eye droppeth without stay, and ceaseth not,

50 Till the Lord look down, and behold from heaven.

51 Mine eye [1]breaketh mine heart because of all the daughters of my city.

52 Mine enemies chased me sore, like a bird, without cause.

53 They have shut up my life [1]in the dungeon, and cast a stone upon me.

54 Waters flowed over mine head, then thought I, I am destroyed.

55 I called upon thy Name, O Lord, out of the low dungeon.

56 Thou hast heard my voice: stop not thine ear from my sigh, and from my cry.

57 Thou drewest near in the day that I called upon thee: thou saidest, Fear not.

58 O Lord, thou hast maintained the cause of my [1]soul, and hast redeemed my life.

59 O Lord, thou hast seen my wrong, judge thou my cause.

60 Thou hast seen all their vengeance, and all their devises against me:

61 Thou hast heard their reproach, O Lord, and all their imaginations against me.

62 The lips also of those that rose against me, and their whispering against me continually.

63 Behold, their sitting down, and their rising up, how I am their song.

64 [b]Give them a recompense, O Lord, according to the work of their hands.

3:22 [1] Considering the wickedness of man, it is [a] marvel that any remaineth alive: but only that God for his own mercy's sake and for his promise, will ever have his Church to remain, though they be never so few in number, Isa. 1:9.

3:23 [1] We feel thy benefits daily.

3:24 [1] The godly put their whole confidence in God, and therefore look for none other inheritance, as Ps. 16:5.

3:27 [1] He showeth that we can never begin too timely to be exercised under the cross, that when the afflictions grow greater, our patience also by experience may be stronger.

3:28 [1] He murmureth not against God, but is patient.

3:29 [1] He humbleth himself as they that fall down with their face to the ground, and so with patience waiteth for succor.

3:33 [1] He taketh no pleasure in it, but doeth it of necessity for our amendment, when he suffereth the wicked to oppress the poor.

   [2] Hebrew, with his heart.

3:36 [1] He doth not delight therein.

3:37 [1] He showeth that nothing is done without God's providence.

3:38 [1] That is, adversity and prosperity, Amos 3:6.

3:39 [1] When God afflicteth him.

3:41 [1] That is, both hearts and hands: for else to lift up the hands, is but hypocrisy.

3:51 [1] I am overcome with sore weeping for all my people.

3:53 [1] Read Jer. 37:16, how he was in the miry dungeon.

3:58 [1] Meaning, the cause wherefore his life was in danger.

65 Give them [1]sorrow of heart *even* thy curse to them.

66 Persecute with wrath and destroy them from under the heaven, O Lord.

CHAPTER 4
[a] Gen. 19:25
[b] Num. 6:2

4 1 How is the [1]gold become so [2]dim? the most fine gold is changed, and the stones of the Sanctuary are scattered in the corner of every street.

2 The noble [1]men of Zion comparable to fine gold, how are they esteemed as earthen [2]pitchers, *even* the work of the hands of the potter!

3 Even the dragons [1]draw out the breasts, and give suck to their young: *but* the daughter of my people *is become* cruel like the [2]ostriches in the wilderness.

4 The tongue of the sucking child cleaveth to the roof of his mouth for thirst: the young children ask bread, *but* no man breaketh it unto them.

5 They that did feed delicately, perish in the streets: they that were brought up in scarlet, embrace the dung.

6 For the iniquity of the daughter of my people is become greater than the sin of Sodom, that was [a]destroyed as in a moment, and [1]none pitched camps against her.

7 Her [b]Nazirites were purer than the snow, *and* whiter than the milk: they were more ruddy in body, than the red precious stones: they were *like* polished sapphire.

8 *Now* their [1]visage is blacker than a coal: they cannot know them in the streets: their skin cleaveth to their bones: it is withered like a stock.

9 They that be slain with the sword, are better than they that are killed with hunger: for they fade away *as* they were stricken through for the [1]fruits of the field.

10 The hands of the pitiful women have sodden their own children, *which* were their meat in the destruction of the daughter of my people.

11 The Lord hath accomplished his indigna-

tion: he hath poured out his fierce wrath, he hath kindled a fire in Zion, which hath devoured the foundations thereof.

12 The kings of the earth, and all the inhabitants of the world would not have believed that the adversary and the enemy should have entered into the gates of Jerusalem:

13 For the sins of her prophets, *and* the iniquities of her priests, that have shed the blood of the just in the midst of [1]her.

14 They have wandered *as* blind men[1]in the streets, and they were polluted with blood, so that[2]they would not touch their garments.

15 *But* they cried unto them, Depart ye polluted, depart, depart, touch not: therefore they fled away, and wandered: they have said among the heathen, They shall no more dwell there.

16 The [1]anger of the Lord hath scattered them, he will no more regard them: [2]they reverenced not the face of the Priest, nor had compassion on the Elders.

17 While we waited for our vain help, our eyes failed: for in our waiting we looked for [1]a nation that could not save us.

18 They hunt our steps, that we cannot go in our streets: our end is near, our days are fulfilled, for our end is come.

19 Our persecutors are swifter than the eagles of the heaven: they pursued us upon the mountains, and laid wait for us in the wilderness.

20 The [1]breath of our nostrils, the Anointed of the Lord was taken in their nets, of whom we said, Under his shadow we shall be preserved alive among the heathen.

21 Rejoice and be glad, [1]O daughter Edom: that dwellest in the land of Uz, the cup also shall pass through unto thee: thou shalt be drunken [2]and vomit.

22 Thy punishment is accomplished, O daughter Zion: he [1]will no more carry thee away into captivity, *but* he will visit thine iniquity, O daughter Edom, he will discover thy sins.

3:65 [1] Or, an obstinate heart.

4:1 [1] By the gold, he meaneth the princes, as by the stones he understandeth the Priests.

[2] Or, hid.

4:2 [1] Or, sons.

[2] Which are of small estimation, and have none honor.

4:3 [1] Though the dragons be cruel, yet they pity their young, and nourish them, which things Jerusalem doth not.

[2] The women forsake their children, as the ostrich doth her eggs, Job 39:17.

4:6 [1] Or, no strength was against her.

4:8 [1] They that were before most in God's favor, are now in greatest abomination unto him.

4:9 [1] For lack of food they pine away and consume.

4:13 [1] He meaneth that these things are come to pass therefore, contrary to all men's expectation.

4:14 [1] Some refer this to the blind men, which as they went, stumbled on the blood, whereof the city was full.

[2] Meaning, the heathen which came to destroy them, could not abide them.

4:16 [1] Or, face. [2] That is, the enemies.

4:17 [1] He showeth two principal causes of their destruction: their cruelty and their vain confidence in man: for they trusted in the help of the Egyptians.

4:20 [1] Our king Josiah, in whom stood our hope of God's favor, and on whom depended our state and life, was slain, whom he calleth Anointed, because he was a figure of Christ.

4:21 [1] This is spoken by derision.

[2] Or, show thy nakedness.

4:22 [1] He comforteth the Church, by that after seventy years their sorrows shall have an end, whereas the wicked should be tormented forever.

5

The prayer of Jeremiah.

1 Remember, O Lord, what is come upon us: [1]consider, and behold our reproach.

2 Our inheritance is turned to the strangers, our houses to the aliens.

3 We are fatherless, even without father, *and* our mothers are as widows.

4 We have drunk our [1]water for money, *and* our wood is sold *unto us.*

5 Our necks are under persecution: we are weary, and have no rest.

6 We have given our [1]hands to the Egyptians, *and* to Assyria, to be satisfied with bread.

7 Our fathers have sinned, and are not, and we have borne [1]their iniquities.

8 Servants have ruled over us, none would deliver us out of their hands.

9 We got our bread with the *peril* of our lives, because of the sword [1]of the wilderness.

10 Our skin was black like as an oven because of the terrible famine.

11 They defiled the women in Zion, *and* the maids in the cities of Judah.

12 The princes are hanged up by [1]their hand: the faces of the Elders were not had in honor.

13 They took the young men to grind, and the children fell under [1]the wood.

14 The Elders have ceased from the [1]gate *and* the young men from their songs.

15 The joy of our heart is gone, our dance is turned into mourning.

16 The crown of our head is fallen: woe now unto us, that we have sinned.

17 Therefore our heart is heavy for these things, our [1]eyes are dim,

18 Because of the mountain of Zion, which is desolate: the foxes run upon it.

19 *But* thou, O Lord, remainest [1]forever: thy throne is from generation to generation.

20 Wherefore dost thou forget us forever, *and* forsake us so long time?

21 [1]Turn thou us unto thee, O Lord, and we shall be turned: renew our days as of old.

22 But thou hast utterly rejected us: thou art exceedingly angry against us.

5:1 [1] This prayer as is thought, was made when some of the people were carried away captive, others, as the poorest remained, and some went into Egypt, and other places for succor: albeit it seemeth that the Prophet foreseeing their miseries to come, thus prayed.

5:4 [1] Meaning, their extreme servitude and bondage.

5:6 [1] We are joined in league and amity with them, or have submitted ourselves unto them.

5:7 [1] As our fathers have been punished for their sins: so we that are culpable of the same sins, are punished.

5:9 [1] Because of the enemy that came from the wilderness, and would not suffer us to go and seek our necessary food.

5:12 [1] That is, by the enemy's hand.

5:13 [1] Their slavery was so great, that they were not able to abide it.

5:14 [1] There were no more laws nor form of commonwealth.

5:17 [1] With weeping.

5:19 [1] And therefore thy covenant and mercies can never fail.

5:21 [1] Whereby is declared that it is not in man's power to turn to God, but is only his work to convert us, and thus God worketh in us before we can turn to him, Jer. 31:18.

EZEKIEL

1

1 It came to pass in the ¹thirtieth year in the fourth *month, and* in the fifth *day* of the month (as I was among the captives by the river ²Chebar) that the heavens were opened, and I saw visions of ³GOD.

2 In the fifth *day* of the month (which was the fifth year of king Jehoiachin's captivity)

3 The word of the Lord came unto Ezekiel the Priest, the son of Buzi, in the land of the Chaldeans, by the river Chebar, where the ¹hand of the Lord was upon him.

4 And I looked, and behold, a ¹whirlwind came out of the North, a great cloud and a fire wrapped about it, and a brightness *was* about it, and in the midst thereof, *to wit,* in the midst of the fire *came out* as the likeness of ²amber.

5 Also out of the midst thereof *came* the likeness of ¹four beasts, and this was their form: they had the appearance of a man,

6 And every one had four faces, and every one had four wings.

7 And their feet *were* straight feet, and the sole of their feet *was* like the soles of a calf's foot, and they sparkled like the appearance of bright brass.

8 And the hands of a man *came out* from under their wings in the four parts of them, and they four had their faces, and their wings.

9 They where ¹joined by their wings one to another, *and* when they went forth, they returned not, *but* every one went straight forward.

10 And the similitude of their faces *was as* ¹the face of a man: and they four had the face of a lion on the right side, and they four had the face of a bullock on the left side: they four also had the face of an Eagle.

11 Thus were their faces: but their wings *were* spread out above: two *wings* of every one were joined one to another, and two covered their bodies.

12 And every one went straight forward: they went whither their ¹spirit led them, *and* they returned not when they went forth.

13 The similitude also of the beasts, *and* their appearance *was* like burning coals of fire, and like the appearance of lamps: *for the fire* ran among the beasts, and the fire gave a glister, and out of the fire there went lightning.

14 And the beasts ran, and ¹returned like unto lightning.

15 Now as I beheld the beasts, behold, a wheel *appeared* upon the earth by the beasts, having four faces.

16 The fashion of the wheels and their work *was* like unto a ¹Chrysolite: and they four had one form, and their fashion and their work *was* as one wheel in *another* wheel.

17 When they went, they went upon their four sides, *and* they returned not when they went.

18 They had also ¹rings, and height, and were *fearful* to behold, and their rings were full of eyes, round about them four.

19 And when the beasts went, the wheels went with them: and when the beasts were lifted up from the earth, the wheels were lifted up.

20 Whither their spirit led them, they went, *and* thither did the spirit of the wheels lead them, and the wheels were lifted up besides them: for the spirit of the beasts *was* in the wheels.

21 When the *beasts* went, they went, and when they stood, they stood, and when they were lifted up from the earth, the wheels were lifted up besides them: for the spirit of the beasts *was* in the wheels.

22 And the similitude of the firmament upon the heads of the beasts *was* wonderful, like unto crystal spread over their heads above.

23 And under the firmament *were* their wings

1:1 ¹ After that the book of the Law was found, which was the eighteenth year of the reign of Josiah, so that five and twenty years after this book was found, Jeconiah was led away captive with Ezekiel and many of the people, who the first year after saw these visions.

² Which was a part of Euphrates so called.

³ That is notable and excellent visions, so that it might be known, it was no natural dream, but came of God.

1:3 ¹ That is, the spirit of prophecy, as Ezek. 3:22 and 37:1.

1:4 ¹ By this diversity of words he signifieth the fearful judgment of God and the great afflictions that should come upon Jerusalem.

² Or, pale fellow.

1:5 ¹ Which were the four Cherubims that represented the glory of God, as Ezek. 3:23.

1:9 ¹ The wing of the one touched the wing of the other.

1:10 ¹ Every Cherubim had four faces, the face of a man, and of a lion on the right side, and the face of a bullock and of an Eagle on the left side.

1:12 ¹ Hebrew, *whither their spirit or w[ings] was to go.*

1:14 ¹ That is, when they had executed God's will: for afore they returned not till God had changed the state of things.

1:16 ¹ The Hebrew word is tarshish meaning that the color was like the Cilician Sea, or a precious stone so called.

1:18 ¹ Or, the trent.

straight, the one toward the other: every one had two which covered them, and every one had two which covered their bodies.

24 And when they went forth, I heard the noise of their [1]wings, like the noise of great waters, *and* as the voice of the Almighty, *even* the voice of speech, as the noise of an host: *even* when they stood, they [2]let down their wings.

25 And there was a voice from the firmament that was over their heads, when they stood, *and* had let down their wings.

26 And above the firmament that was over their heads, *was* the fashion of a throne like unto a Sapphire stone, and upon the similitude of the throne *was* by appearance, as the similitude of a man above upon it.

27 And I saw as the appearance of amber, *and* as the similitude of fire [1]round about within it to look too, even from his loins upward: and to look too, even from his loins downward, I saw as a likeness of fire, and brightness round about it.

28 As the likeness of the bow, that is in the cloud in the day of rain, so *was* the appearance of the light round about.

29 This was the appearance of the similitude of the glory of the Lord: and when I saw it, I fell [1]upon my face, and I heard a voice of one that spake.

2

The Prophet is sent to call the people from their error.

1 And [1]he said unto me, [2]Son of man, stand up upon thy feet, and I will speak unto thee.

2 [1]And the Spirit entered into me, when he had spoken unto me, and set me upon my feet, so that I heard him that spake unto me.

3 And he said unto me, Son of Man, I send thee to the children of Israel, to a rebellious nation that hath rebelled against me: *for* they and their fathers have rebelled against me, even unto this very day.

4 For *they are* [1]impudent children, and stiff-hearted: I do send thee unto them, and thou shalt say unto them, Thus saith the Lord God.

5 But surely they will not hear, neither indeed

will they cease: for they are a rebellious house: yet shall they know that [1]there hath been a Prophet among them.

6 And thou son of man, [1]fear them not, neither be afraid of their words, although rebels and thorns *be* with thee, and thou remainest with scorpions: fear not their words, nor be afraid at their looks, for they are a rebellious house.

7 Therefore thou shalt speak my words unto them: *but* surely they will not hear, neither will they indeed cease: for they are rebellious.

8 But thou son of man, hear what I say unto thee: be not thou rebellious, like *this* rebellious house: open thy mouth, and [1]eat that I give thee.

9 And when I looked up, behold, an hand was sent unto me, and lo, a roll of a book *was* therein.

10 And he spread it before me, and it was written within and without, and there was written therein, [1]Lamentations and mourning, and woe.

3

1 *The Prophet being fed with the word of God and with the constant boldness of the spirit, is sent unto the people that were in captivity.* 17 *The office of true ministers.*

1 Moreover he said unto me, Son of man, eat that thou findest: [1]eat this roll, and go, *and* speak unto the house of Israel.

2 So I opened my mouth, and he gave me this roll to eat.

3 And he said unto me, Son of man, cause thy belly to eat, and fill thy bowels with this roll that I give thee. Then did I eat, and it was in my mouth as sweet as honey.

4 And he said unto me, Son of man, go *and* enter into the house of Israel, and declare them my words.

5 For thou art not sent to a people of an [1]unknown tongue, or of an hard language, *but* to the house of Israel,

6 Not to many people of an unknown tongue, or of an hard language, whose words thou canst not understand: yet if I should send thee to them, they would obey thee.

1:24 [1] Which declared the swiftness and the fearfulness of God's judgments.
[2] Which signified that they had no power of themselves, but only waited to execute God's commandment.
1:27 [1] Whereby was signified a terrible judgment toward the earth.
1:29 [1] Considering the majesty of God, and the weakness of flesh.
2:1 [1] That is, the Lord.
[2] Meaning, man which is but earth and ashes, which was to humble him, and cause him to consider his own state, and God's grace.
2:2 [1] So that he could not abide God's presence, till God's Spirit did enter into him.
2:4 [1] Hebrew, *hard of face.*
2:5 [1] This declareth on the one part God's great affection toward his people, that notwithstanding their rebellion, yet he will send his

Prophets among them, and admonisheth his ministers on the other part that they cease not to do their duty, though the people be never so obstinate: for the word of God shall be either to their salvation or greater condemnation.
2:6 [1] Read Jer. 1:17, he showeth that for none afflictions they should cease to do their duties.
2:8 [1] He doth not only exhort him to his duty, but also giveth him the means wherewith he may be able to execute it.
2:10 [1] He showeth what were the contents of this book: to wit, God's judgments against the wicked.
3:1 [1] Whereby is meant that none is meet to be God's messenger before he have received the word of God in his heart, as verse 10, and have a zeal thereunto, and delight therein, as Jer. 15:16; Rev. 10:10.
3:5 [1] Hebrew, *deep lips.*

7 But the house of Israel will not obey thee: for they will not obey me: yea, all the house of Israel are impudent and stiff-hearted.

8 Behold, I have made thy ¹face strong against their faces, and thy forehead hard against their foreheads.

9 I have made thy forehead as the adamant, *and* harder than the flint: fear them not therefore, neither be afraid at their looks: for they are a rebellious house.

10 He said moreover unto me, Son of man, ¹receive in thine heart all my words that I speak unto thee, and hear *them* with thine ears,

11 And go *and* enter to them that are led away captives unto the children of thy people, and speak unto them, and tell them, Thus saith the Lord God: *but* surely they will not hear, neither will they indeed cease.

12 Then the spirit took me up, and I heard behind me a noise of a great rushing, *saying,* ¹Blessed *be* the glory of the Lord out of his place.

13 I *heard* also the noise of the wings of the beasts, that touched one another, and the rattling of the wheels that were by them, even a noise of a great rushing.

14 So the spirit lifted me up, and took me away, and I ¹went in bitterness *and* indignation of my spirit, but the hand of the Lord was strong upon me.

15 Then I came to them that were led away captives to ¹Tel Abib, that dwelt by the river Chebar, and I sat where they sat, and remained there astonished among them ²seven days.

16 And at the end of seven days, the word of the Lord came again unto me, saying,

17 Son of man, I have made thee a ¹watchman unto the house of Israel: therefore hear the word at my mouth, and give them warning from me

18 When I shall say unto the wicked, Thou shalt surely die, and thou givest not him warning, nor speakest to admonish the wicked of his wicked way, that he may live, the same wicked man shall die in his iniquity: but his blood will I require at thine hand.

19 Yet, if thou warn the wicked, and he turn not from his wickedness, nor from his wicked way, he shall die in his iniquity, but thou hast delivered thy soul.

20 Likewise if a ¹righteous man turn from his righteousness, and commit iniquity, I will lay a ²stumbling block before him and he shall die, because thou hast not given him warning, he shall die in his sin, and his ³righteous deeds, which he hath done, shall not be remembered: but his blood will I require at thine hand.

21 Nevertheless, if thou admonish that righteous man, that the righteous sin not, and that he doth not sin, he shall live because he is admonished: also thou hast delivered thy soul.

22 And the ¹hand of the Lord was there upon me, and he said unto me, Arise, *and* go into the ²field, and I will there talk with thee.

23 So when I had risen up, and gone forth into the field, behold, the glory of the Lord stood there, as the ¹glory which I saw by the river Chebar, and I fell down upon my face.

24 Then the Spirit entered into me, which ¹set me up upon my feet, and spake unto me, and said to me, Come, *and* ²shut thyself within thine house.

25 But thou, O son of man, behold, they shall put bands upon thee, and shall bind thee with them, and thou shalt not go out among them.

26 And I will make thy tongue ¹cleave to the roof of thy mouth, that thou shalt be dumb, and shalt not be to them as a man that rebuketh: for they are a rebellious house.

27 But when I shall have spoken unto thee, I will open thy mouth, and thou shalt say unto them, Thus saith the Lord God, He that heareth, let him hear, and he that leaveth off, ᵃlet him leave: for they are a rebellious house.

4

1 The besieging of the city of Jerusalem is signified. 9 The long continuance of the captivity of Israel. 16 An hunger is prophesied to come.

1 Thou also son of man, take thee a brick, and

3:8 ¹ God promiseth his assistance to his ministers, and that he will give them boldness and constancy in their vocation, Isa. 50:7; Jer. 1:18; Mic. 3:8.
3:10 ¹ He showeth what is meant by the eating of the book, which is that the ministers of God may speak nothing as of themselves, but that only, which they have received of the Lord.
3:12 ¹ Whereby he signifieth, that God's glory should not be diminished, although he departed out of his Temple, for this declared that the city and Temple should be destroyed.
3:14 ¹ This showeth that there is ever an infirmity of the flesh which can never be ready to render full obedience to God, and also God's grace who ever assisteth his, and overcometh their rebellious affections.
3:15 ¹ Which was a place by Euphrates, where the Jews were prisoners.
² Declaring hereby that God's ministers must with advisement and

deliberation utter his judgments.
3:17 ¹ Of this read Ezek. 33:2.
3:20 ¹ If he that hath been instructed in the right way turn back.
² I will give him up to a reprobate mind, Rom. 1:28.
³ Which seemed to have been done in faith, and were not.
3:22 ¹ That is, the Spirit of prophecy.
² Or, valley.
3:23 ¹ Meaning, the vision of the Cherubims, and the wheels.
3:24 ¹ Read Ezek. 2:2.
² Signifying, that not only he should not profit, but they should grievously trouble and afflict him.
3:26 ¹ Which declareth the terrible plague of the Lord, when God stoppeth the mouths of his ministers, and that all such are the rods of his vengeance that do it.

lay it before thee, and portray upon it the city, *even* Jerusalem,

2   And lay siege against it, and build a fort against it, and cast a mount against it, set the camp also against it, and lay engines of war against it round about.

3   Moreover, take an [1]iron pan, and set it for a wall of iron between thee and the city, and direct thy face toward it, and it shall be besieged, and thou shalt lay siege against it: this shall be a sign unto the house of Israel.

4   Sleep thou also upon thy left side, and lay the iniquity of the [1]house of Israel upon it: *according* to the number of the days, that thou shalt sleep upon it, thou shalt bear their iniquity.

5   For I have laid upon thee the years of their iniquity according to the number of the days, *even* three hundred and ninety days: so shalt thou bear the iniquity of the house of Israel.

6   And when thou hast accomplished them, sleep again upon thy [1]right side, and thou shalt bear the iniquity of the house of Judah forty days: I have appointed thee a day for a year, *even* a day for a year.

7   Therefore thou shalt direct thy face toward the siege of Jerusalem, and thine [1]arm *shall be* uncovered, and thou shalt prophesy against it.

8   And behold, I will lay [1]bands upon thee, and thou shalt not turn thee from one side to another, till thou hast ended the days of thy siege.

9   Thou shalt take also unto thee wheat, and barley, and beans, and lentils, and millet, [1]and fitches, and put them in one vessel, and make thee bread thereof *according* to the number of the days, that thou shalt sleep upon thy side: *even* [2]three hundred and ninety days shalt thou eat thereof.

10   And the meat, whereof thou shalt eat *shall be* by weight, *even* [1]twenty shekels a day: *and* from time to time shalt thou eat thereof.

11   Thou shalt drink also water by measure, *even* the sixth part of [1]an Hin: from time to time shalt thou drink.

12   And thou shalt eat it *as* barley cakes, and thou shalt bake it [1]in the dung that cometh out of man in their sight.

13   And the Lord said, So shall the children of Israel eat their defiled bread among the Gentiles, whither I will cast them.

14   Then said I, Ah, Lord God, behold, my soul hath not been polluted: for from my youth up, even unto this hour, I have not eaten of a thing dead or torn in pieces, neither came there any [1]unclean flesh in my mouth.

15   Then he said unto me, Lo, I have given thee bullocks [1]dung for man's dung, and thou shalt prepare thy bread therewith.

16   Moreover, he said unto me, Son of man, behold, I will break [1]the staff of bread in Jerusalem, and they shall eat bread by weight, and with care, and they shall drink water by measure, and with astonishment.

17   Because that bread and water shall fail, they shall be astonied one with another, and shall consume away for their iniquity.

5   The sign of the hairs, whereby is signified the destruction of the people.

1   And thou son of man, take thee a sharp knife, *or* take thee a barber's razor, and cause it [1]to pass upon thine head, and upon thy beard: then take thee balances to weigh, and divide the *hair*.

2   Thou shalt burn with fire the third part in the midst of the [1]city, when the days of the siege are fulfilled, and thou shalt take the *other* third part, and smite about it with a knife, and the *last* third part thou shalt scatter in the wind, and I will draw out a sword after them.

3   Thou shalt also take thereof a few in number, and bind them in thy [1]lap.

4   Then take of them again and cast them into the midst of the fire, and burn them in the fire: [1]for thereof shall a fire come forth into all the house of Israel.

5   Thus saith the Lord God, This is Jerusalem, I

4:3 [1] Which signified the stubbornness and hardness of their heart.
4:4 [1] Hereby he represented the idolatry and sin of the ten tribes (for Samaria was on his left hand from Babylon) and how they had remained therein three hundred and ninety years.
4:6 [1] Which declared Judah, who had now from the time of Josiah slept in their sins forty years.
4:7 [1] In token of a speedy vengeance.
4:8 [1] The people should so straightly be besieged, that they should not be able, to turn them.
4:9 [1] Meaning, that the famine should be so great, that they should be glad to eat whatsoever they could get.
    [2] Which were fourteen months that the city was besieged, and this was as many days as Israel sinned years.
4:10 [1] Which make a pound.
4:11 [1] Read Exod. 29:40.
4:12 [1] Signifying hereby the great scarcity of fuel and matter to burn.

4:14 [1] Much less such vile corruption.
4:15 [1] To be as fire to bake thy bread with.
4:16 [1] That is, the force and strength wherewith it should nourish, Isa. 3:1; Ezek. 5:17 and 14:13.
5:1 [1] To shave thine head and thy beard.
5:2 [1] To wit, of that city which he had portrayed upon the brick, Ezek. 4:1. By the fire and pestilence he meaneth the famine, wherewith one part perished during the siege of Nebuchadnezzar. By the sword, those that were slain whom Zedekiah fled, and those that were carried away captive. And by the scattering into the wind, those that fled into Egypt, and into other parts after the city was taken.
5:3 [1] Meaning, that a very few should be left, which the Lord should preserve among all these storms, but not without troubles and trial.
5:4 [1] Out of that fire which thou kindlest shall a fire come, which shall signify the destruction of Israel.

have set it in the midst of the nations and countries, *that* are round about her.

6   And she hath changed my [1]judgments into wickedness more than the nations, and my statutes more than the countries, that are round about her: for they have refused my judgments, and my statutes, *and* they have not walked in them.

7   Therefore thus saith the Lord God, Because your [1]multitude is greater than the nations that are round about you, and ye have not walked in my statutes, neither have ye kept my judgments: no, ye have not done according to the judgments of the nations, that are round about you.

8   Therefore thus saith the Lord God, Behold, I, even I *come* against thee, and will execute judgment in the midst of thee, *even* in the sight of the nations.

9   And I will do in thee that I never did *before*, neither will do anymore the like, because of all thine abominations.

10   For in the midst of thee, the fathers *a*shall eat their sons, and the sons shall eat their fathers, and I will execute judgment in thee, and the whole remnant of thee will I scatter into all the winds.

11   Wherefore as I live, saith the Lord God, Surely, because thou hast defiled my Sanctuary with all thy filthiness, and with all thine abominations, therefore will I also destroy thee, neither shall mine eye spare *thee*, neither will I have any pity.

12   The third part of thee shall die with the pestilence, and with famine shall they be consumed in the midst of thee: and *another* third part shall fall by the sword round about thee: and I will scatter the *last* third part into all winds, and I will draw out a sword after them.

13   Thus shall mine anger be accomplished, and I will cause my wrath to cease in them, and I will be [1]comforted: and they shall know, that I the Lord have spoken it in my zeal, when I have accomplished my wrath in them.

14   Moreover, I will make thee waste, and abhorred among the nations that are round about thee, *and* in the sight of all that pass by.

15   So thou shalt be a reproach and shame, a chastisement and an astonishment unto the nations, that are round about thee, when I shall execute judgments in thee in anger and in wrath, and in sharp rebukes:

CHAPTER 5
a Lev. 26:29
Deut. 28:53
2 Kings 6:29
Lam. 4:10
b Ezek. 14:13

CHAPTER 6
a Ezek. 36:1
b 2 Kings 23:20

I the Lord have spoken it.

16   When I shall send upon them the [1]evil [2]arrows of famine, which shall be for *their* destruction, *and* which I will send to destroy you: and I will increase the famine upon you, and will break your staff of bread.

17   [b]So I will send upon you famine, and evil beasts, and they shall spoil thee: and pestilence and blood shall pass through thee: and I will bring the sword upon thee: I the Lord have spoken it.

6 *He showeth that Jerusalem shall be destroyed for their idolatry.   8 He prophesieth the repentance of the remnant of the people, and their deliverance.*

1   Again the word of the Lord came unto me, saying,

2   Son of man, Set thy face towards the *a*mountains of Israel, and prophesy against them,

3   And say, Ye mountains of Israel, hear the word of the Lord God: thus saith the Lord God to the [1]mountains and to the hills, to the rivers and to the valleys, Behold, I, *even* I will bring a sword upon you, and I will destroy your high places:

4   And your altars shall be desolate, and your images of the [1]Sun shall be broken: and I will cast down your slain men before your idols.

5   And I will lay the dead carcasses of the children of Israel before their [1]idols, and I will [b]scatter your bones round about your altars.

6   In all your dwelling places the cities shall be desolate, and the high places shall be laid waste, so that your altars shall be made waste and desolate, and your idols shall be broken and cease, and your images of the Sun shall be cut in pieces, and your works shall be abolished.

7   And the slain shall fall in the midst of you, and ye shall know that I am the Lord.

8   Yet will I leave a remnant, [1]that you may have *some* that shall escape the sword among the nations, when you shall be scattered through the countries.

9   And they that escape of you, shall remember me among the nations, where they shall be in captivity, because I am grieved for their whorish hearts, which have departed from me, and for their eyes, which have gone a whoring after their idols, and they [1]shall be displeased in themselves for the evils which they have committed in all their abominations.

5:6 [1] My word and law into idolatry and superstitions.
5:7 [1] Because your idols are in greater number, and your superstitions more than among the professed idolaters, read Isa. 65:11, or he condemneth their ingratitude in respect of his benefits.
5:13 [1] That is, I will not be pacified, till I be revenged, Isa. 1:24.
5:16 [1] Or, dangerous.
  [2] Which were the grasshoppers, mildew, and whatsoever occasions of famine.

6:3 [1] He speaketh to all the places where the Israelites accustomed to commit their idolatries, threatening them destruction.
6:4 [1] Read 2 Kings 23:11.
6:5 [1] In contempt of their power and force, which shall neither be able to deliver you nor themselves.
6:8 [1] He showeth that in all dangers God will preserve a few, which shall be as the seed of his Church and call upon his Name.
6:9 [1] They shall be ashamed to see that their hope in idols was but vain, and so shall repent.

10 And they shall know that I am the Lord, *and* that I have not said in vain, that I would do this evil unto them.

11 Thus saith the Lord God, ¹Smite with thine hand, and stretch forth with thy foot, and say, Alas, for all the wicked abominations of the house of Israel: for they shall fall by the sword, by the famine, and by the pestilence.

12 He that is far off, shall die of the pestilence, and he that is near, shall fall by the sword, and he that remaineth and is besieged, shall die by the famine: thus will I accomplish my wrath upon them.

13 Then ¹ye shall know, that I am the Lord, when their slain men shall be among their idols round about their altars, upon every high hill in all the tops of the mountains, and under every green tree, and under every thick oak, *which is* the place where they did offer sweet savor to all their idols.

14 So will I ᶜstretch mine hand upon them, and make the land waste and desolate ¹from the wilderness unto Diblath in all their habitations, and they shall know that I am the Lord.

7

The end of all the land of Israel shall suddenly come.

1 Moreover the word of the Lord came unto me, saying,

2 Also thou son of man, thus saith the Lord God, An end *is* come unto the land of Israel: the end is come upon the four corners of the land.

3 Now *is* the end *come* upon thee, and I will send my wrath upon thee, and will judge thee according to thy ways, and will lay upon thee all ¹thine abominations.

4 Neither shall mine eye spare thee, neither will I have pity: but I will lay thy ways upon thee: and thine abomination shall be in the midst of thee, and ye shall know that I am the Lord.

5 Thus saith the Lord God, ¹Behold, one evil, *even one* evil is come.

6 An end is come, the end is come, it ¹watched

Marginal references:
ᶜ Ezek. 5:14

CHAPTER 7
ᵃ Isa. 13:7
Jer. 6:24

for thee: behold, it is come.

7 The ¹morning is come unto thee, that dwellest in the land: the time is come, the day of trouble is near, and not the ²sounding again of the mountains.

8 Now I will shortly pour out my wrath upon thee, and fulfill mine anger upon thee: I will judge thee according to thy ways, and will lay upon thee all thine abominations.

9 Neither shall mine eye spare *thee*, neither will I have pity, *but* I will lay upon thee according to thy ways, and thine abominations shall be in the midst of thee, and ye shall know that I am the Lord that smiteth.

10 Behold, the day, behold, it is come: the morning is gone forth, the ¹rod flourisheth: ²pride hath budded.

11 ¹Cruelty is risen up into a rod of wickedness: none of them *shall remain*, nor of their riches, nor of any of theirs, neither shall there be ²lamentation for them.

12 The time is come, the day draweth near: let not the buyer ¹rejoice, nor let him that selleth ²mourn: for the wrath is upon all the multitude thereof.

13 For he that selleth, shall not ¹return to that which is sold, although they were yet alive: for the ²vision was unto all the multitude thereof, *and* they returned not, ³neither doth any encourage himself in the punishment of his life.

14 ¹They have blown the trumpet, and prepared all, but none goeth to the battle: for my wrath is upon all the multitude thereof.

15 The sword *is* without, and the pestilence, and the famine within: he that is in the field, shall die with the sword, and he that is in the city, famine and pestilence shall devour him.

16 But they that flee away from them, shall escape, and shall be in the mountains, like the doves of the valleys: all they shall mourn, every one for his iniquity.

17 ᵃAll hands shall be weak, and all knees shall fall away *as* water.

6:11 ¹ By these signs he would that the Prophet should signify the great destruction to come.

6:13 ¹ That is, all nations when you shall see my judgments.

6:14 ¹ Some read, more desolate than the wilderness of Diblath, which was in Syria, and bordered upon Israel, or from the wilderness, which was South unto Diblath, which was North: meaning, the whole country.

7:3 ¹ I will punish thee as thou hast deserved for thine idolatry.

7:5 ¹ Or, behold, evil cometh after evil.

7:6 ¹ He showeth that the judgments of God ever watch to destroy the sinners, which notwithstanding he delayeth till there be no more hope of repentance.

7:7 ¹ The beginning of his punishments is already come.
² Which was a voice of joy and mirth.

7:10 ¹ The scourge is in a readiness.
² That is, the proud tyrant Nebuchadnezzar, hath gathered his

force and is ready.

7:11 ¹ This cruel enemy shall be a sharp scourge for their wickedness.
² Their own affliction shall be so great, that they shall have no regard to lament for others.

7:12 ¹ For the present profit.
² For he shall lose nothing.

7:13 ¹ In the year of the Jubilee, meaning that none should enjoy the privilege of the law, Lev. 25:13, for they should all be carried away captives.
² This vision signified, that all should be carried away, and none should return for the Jubilee.
³ No man for all this endeavoreth himself, or taketh heart to repent for his evil life. Some read, for none shall be strengthened in his iniquity of his life: meaning, that they should gain nothing by flattering themselves in evil.

7:14 ¹ The Israelites made a brag, but their hearts failed them.

18 [b]They shall also gird themselves with sackcloth, and fear shall cover them, and shame *shall be* upon all faces, and baldness upon their heads.

19 They shall cast their silver in the streets, and their gold shall be *cast* far off: their [c]silver and their gold cannot deliver them in the day of the wrath of the Lord: they shall not satisfy their souls, neither fill their bowels: for *this* ruin is for their iniquity.

20 He had also set the beauty of his [1]ornament in majesty: but they made images of their abominations, *and* of their idols therein: therefore have I set it far from them.

21 And I will give it into the hands of the [1]strangers to be spoiled, and to the wicked of the earth to be robbed, and they shall pollute it.

22 My face will I turn also from them, and they shall pollute my [1]secret place: for the destroyers shall enter into it, and defile it.

23 ¶ Make a [1]chain: for the land is full of the [2]judgment of blood, and the city is full of cruelty.

24 Wherefore I will bring the most wicked of the heathen, and they shall possess their houses: I will also make the pomp of the mighty to cease, and their [1]holy places shall be defiled.

25 When destruction cometh, they shall seek peace, and shall not *have* it.

26 Calamity shall come upon calamity, and rumor shall be upon rumor: then shall they seek a vision of the Prophet: but the Law shall perish from the Priest, and counsel from the Ancient.

27 The king shall mourn, and the prince shall be clothed with desolation, and the hands of the people in the land shall be troubled: I will do unto them according to their ways, and according to their judgments will I judge them, and they shall know that I am the Lord.

8

1 *An appearance of the similitude of God.* 3 *Ezekiel is brought to Jerusalem in the spirit.* 6 *The Lord showeth the Prophet the idolatries of the house of Israel.*

1 And in the [1]sixth year, in the [2]sixth *month, and* in the fifth *day* of the month, as I sat in mine house,

[b] Is. 15:3
Jer. 48:37
[c] Prov. 11:4
Zeph. 1:18
Eccl. 5:8

and the Elders of Judah sat before me, the hand of the Lord God fell there upon me.

2 Then I beheld, and lo, *there was* a likeness, as the appearance of [1]fire, to look to, from his loins downward, and from his loins upward, as the appearance of brightness, and like unto amber.

3 And he stretched out the likeness of an hand, and took me by an hairy lock of mine head, and the Spirit lifted me up between the earth and the heaven, and brought me [1]by a Divine [2]vision to Jerusalem, into the entry of the inner [3]gate that lieth toward the North, where remained the idol of [4]indignation, which provoked indignation.

4 And behold, the glory of the God of Israel *was* there according to the vision, that I saw [1]in the field.

5 Then said he unto me, Son of man, lift up thine eyes now toward the North. So I lifted up mine eyes toward the North, and behold, Northward, at the gate of the [1]altar, this idol of indignation *was* in the entry.

6 He said furthermore unto me, Son of man, seest thou not what they do? *even* the great abominations that the house of Israel committeth here to cause *me* to depart from [1]my Sanctuary? but yet turn thee *and* thou shalt see greater abominations.

7 And he caused me to enter at the gate of the court: and when I looked, behold, an hole *was* in the wall.

8 Then said he unto me, Son of man, dig now in the wall. And when I had dug in the wall, behold, *there was* a door.

9 And he said unto me, Go in, and behold the wicked abominations that they do here.

10 So I went in, and saw, and behold, *there was* every similitude of creeping things, and [1]abominable beasts, and all the idols of the house of Israel painted upon the wall round about.

11 And there stood before them seventy [1]men of the Ancients of the house of Israel, and in the midst of them stood Jaazaniah, the son of Shaphan, with every man his censor in his hand, and the vapor of the incense went up *like* [2]a cloud.

12 Then said he unto me, Son of man, hast thou seen what the Ancients of the house of Israel [1]do in

---

7:20 [1] Meaning, the Sanctuary.
7:21 [1] That is, of the Babylonians.
7:22 [1] Which signifieth the most holy place, whereinto none might enter but the high Priest.
7:23 [1] Signifying, that they should be bound and led away captives.
[2] That is, of sins that deserve death.
7:24 [1] Which was the Temple that was divided into three parts, Ps. 63:35.
8:1 [1] Of the captivity of Jeconiah.
[2] Which contained part of August, and part of September.
8:2 [1] As Ezek. 1:27.
8:3 [1] Hebrew, *in the visions of God.*
[2] Meaning, that he was thus carried in spirit, and not in body.

[3] Which was the porch or the court where the people assembled.
[4] So called, because it provoked God's indignation, which was the idol of Baal.
8:4 [1] Read Ezek. 3:22.
8:5 [1] That is, in the court where the people had made an altar to Baal.
8:6 [1] For God will not be where idols are.
8:10 [1] Which were forbidden in the Law, Lev. 11:4.
8:11 [1] Thus they that should have kept all the rest in the fear, and true service of God, were the ringleaders of all abomination, and by their example pulled others from God.
[2] It was in such abundance.
8:12 [1] For besides their common idolatry they had particular service, which they had in secret chambers.

the dark, everyone in the chamber of his imagery? for they say, The Lord seeth us not, the Lord hath forsaken the earth.

13 Again he said also unto me, Turn thee again, *and* thou shalt see greater abominations that they do.

14 And he caused me to enter into the entry of the gate of the Lord's house, which was toward the North: and behold, there sat women mourning for [1]Tammuz.

15 Then said he unto me, Hast thou seen *this*, O son of man? Turn thee again, *and* thou shalt see greater abominations than these.

16 And he caused me to enter into the inner court of the Lord's house, and behold, at the door of the Temple of the Lord, between the porch and the altar *were* about five and twenty men with their backs toward the Temple of the Lord, and their faces toward the East, and they worshipped the sun, toward the East.

17 Then he said unto me, Hast thou seen *this*, O son of man? Is it a small thing to the house of Judah to commit these abominations which they do here? for they have filled the land with cruelty, and have returned to provoke me: and lo, they have cast out [1]stink before their noses.

18 Therefore will I also execute *my* wrath: mine eye shall not spare *them*, neither will I have pity, and [a]though they cry in mine ears with a loud voice, *yet* will I not hear them.

9

1 The destruction of the city. 4 They that shall be saved, are marked. 8 A complaint of the Prophet for the destruction of the people.

1 He cried also with a loud voice in mine ears, saying, The visitations of [1]the city draw near, and every man hath a weapon in his hand to destroy it.

2 And behold, six [1]men came by the way of the high gate, which lieth toward the [2]North, and every man a weapon in his hand to destroy it: and one man among them was clothed with linen, with a writer's [3]inkhorn by his side, and they went in and stood beside the brazen altar.

CHAPTER 8
a Prov. 1:28
Isa. 46:7
Jer. 11:11
Mic. 3:4

CHAPTER 10
a Ezek. 1:22

3 And the glory of the God of Israel was [1]gone up from the Cherub, whereupon he was, *and* stood on the [2]door of the house, and he called to the man clothed with linen, which had the writer's inkhorn by his side.

4 And the Lord said unto him, Go through the midst of the city, *even* through the midst of Jerusalem, and [1]set a mark upon the foreheads of them that [2]mourn, and cry for all the abominations that be done in the midst thereof.

5 And to the other he said, that I might hear, Go ye after him through the city, and smite: let your eye spare none, neither have pity.

6 Destroy utterly the old, *and* the young, and the maids, and the children, and the women, but touch no man, upon whom *is* the [1]mark, and begin at my Sanctuary. Then they began at the [2]ancient men, which were before the house.

7 And he said unto them, Defile the house, and fill the courts with the slain, *then* go forth: and they went out and slew *them* in the city.

8 Now when they had slain them, and I had escaped, I fell down upon my face, and cried, saying, [1]Ah Lord God, wilt thou destroy all the residue of Israel, in pouring out thy wrath upon Jerusalem?

9 Then said he unto me, The iniquity of the house of Israel, and Judah *is* exceeding great, so that the land is full of [1]blood, and the city full of corrupt judgment: for they say, The Lord hath forsaken the earth, and the Lord seeth *us* not.

10 As touching me also, mine eye shall not spare *them*, neither will I have pity, *but* will recompense their ways upon their heads.

11 And behold, the man clothed with linen which had the inkhorn by his side, made report, and said, *Lord*, I have done as thou hast commanded me.

10

1 Of the man that took hot burning coals out of the middle of the wheels of the Cherubims. 8 A rehearsal of the vision of the wheels, of the beasts, and of the Cherubims.

1 And as I looked, behold in the [a]firmament that was above the head of the [1]Cherubims there

---

8:14 [1] The Jews write, that this was a Prophet of the idols, who after his death was once a year mourned for in the night.
8:17 [1] Declaring that the censings and service of the idolaters, are but infection and villainy before God.
9:1 [1] The time to take vengeance.
9:2 [1] Which were Angels in the similitude of men.
  [2] Signifying, that the Babylonians should come from the North to destroy the city and the Temple.
  [3] To mark them that should be saved.
9:3 [1] Which declared that he was not bound thereunto, neither would remain any longer, than there was hope that they would return from their wickedness and worship him aright.
  [2] Or, Threshold.

9:4 [1] Or, mark with [x].
  [2] He showeth what is the manner of God's children, whom he marketh to salvation: to wit, to mourn and cry out against the wickedness, which they see committed against God's glory.
9:6 [1] Thus in all his plagues the Lord preserveth his small number, which he marketh, as Exod. 12:12; Rev. 7:3, but the chief mark is the Spirit of adoption, wherewith the heart is sealed up to life everlasting.
  [2] Which were the chief occasion of all these evils, as Ezek. 8:11.
9:8 [1] This declareth that the servants of God have a compassion, when they see his judgments executed.
9:9 [1] That is, with all kinds of wickedness, read Isa. 1:15.
10:1 [1] Which in Ezek. 1:5, he called the four beasts.

appeared upon them like unto the similitude of a throne, as *it were* a sapphire stone.

2 And he spake unto the man clothed with linen, and said, Go in between the wheels, *even* under the Cherub, and fill thine hands with coals of fire from between the Cherubims, and scatter them over ¹the city. And he went in my sight.

3 Now the Cherubims stood upon the right side of the house, when the man went in, and the cloud filled the inner court.

4 Then the glory of the Lord ¹went up from the Cherub, *and stood* over the door of the house, and the house was filled with the cloud, and the court was filled with the brightness of the Lord's glory.

5 And the ¹sound of the Cherubims' wings was heard into the utter court, as the voice of the Almighty God, when he speaketh.

6 And when he had commanded the man clothed with linen, saying, Take fire from between the wheels, *and* from between the Cherubims, then he went in and stood beside the wheel.

7 And one Cherub stretched forth his hand from between the Cherubims unto the fire that was between the Cherubims, and took *thereof*, and put it into the hands of him that was clothed with linen: who took it and went out.

8 And there appeared in the Cherubims, the likeness of a man's hand under their wings.

9 And when I looked up, behold, four wheels *were* beside the Cherubims, one wheel by one Cherub, and another wheel by another Cherub, and the appearance of the wheels *was* as the color of a ¹Chrysolite stone.

10 And their appearance (*for they were all* four of one fashion) was as if one wheel had been in *another* wheel.

11 When they went forth, they went upon their four sides, and they returned not as they went: but to the place whither the first went, they went after it, *and* they ¹turned not as they went.

12 And their whole body, and their ¹rings, and their hands, and their wings, and the wheels were full of eyes round about, *even* in the same four wheels.

13 And the *Cherub* cried to these wheels in mine hearing, *saying*, O wheel.

14 And every *beast* had four faces: the first face *was* the face of a Cherub, and the second face *was* the face of a man, and the third the face of a lion,

ᵇ Ezek. 1:5
ᶜ Ezek. 1:15

and the fourth the face of an Eagle.

15 And the Cherubims were lifted up: ᵇthis is the beast that I saw at the river Chebar.

16 And when the Cherubims went, the wheels went by them: and when the Cherubims lifted up their wings to mount up from the earth, the same wheels also turned not from beside them.

17 When the *Cherubims* stood, they stood: and when they were lifted up, they lifted themselves up *also*: for the ¹spirit of the beast *was* in them.

18 ¹Then the glory of the Lord departed from above the door of the house, and stood upon the Cherubims.

19 And the Cherubims lifted up their wings and mounted up from the earth in my sight: when they went out, the wheels also *were* beside them: and *everyone* stood at the entry of the gate of the Lord's House at the East side, and the glory of the God of Israel *was* upon them on high.

20 'This is the ¹beast that I saw under the God of Israel by the river Chebar, and I knew that they were the Cherubims.

21 Every one had four faces, and every one four wings, and the likeness of man's hands *was* under their wings.

22 And the likeness of their faces *was* the selfsame faces, which I saw by the river Chebar, *and* the appearance of the *Cherubims was* the selfsame, *and* they went every one straight forward.

11 1 *Who they were that seduced the people of Israel.* 5 *Against these he prophesieth, showing them how they shall be dispersed abroad.* 19 *The renewing of the heart cometh of God.* 21 *He threateneth them that lean unto their own counsels.*

1 Moreover, the Spirit lifted me up, and brought me unto the East gate of the Lord's house, which lieth Eastward, and behold, at the entry of the gate *were* five and twenty men: among whom I saw Jaazaniah the son of Azzur, and Pelatiah the son of Benaiah, the princes of the people.

2 Then said he unto me, Son of man, these are the men that imagine mischief, and devise wicked counsel in this city.

3 *For* they say, ¹It is not near, let us build houses: this *city* is the ²caldron, and we be the flesh.

4 Therefore prophesy against them, son of man,

10:2 ¹ This signified, that the city should be burnt.
10:4 ¹ Meaning, that the glory of God should depart from the Temple.
10:5 ¹ Read Ezek. 1:24.
10:9 ¹ Read Ezek. 1:16.
10:11 ¹ Until they had executed God's judgments.
10:12 ¹ Or, trents.
10:17 ¹ There was one consent between the Cherubims and the wheels.
10:18 ¹ Read Ezek. 9:3.
10:20 ¹ That is, the whole body of the four beasts or Cherubims.
11:3 ¹ Thus the wicked derided the Prophets, as though they preached but errors, and therefore gave themselves still to their pleasures.
² We shall not be pulled out of Jerusalem, till the hour of our death come, as the flesh is not taken out of the caldron till it be sod.

prophesy.

5 And the Spirit of the Lord fell upon me, and said unto me, Speak, Thus saith the Lord, O ye house of Israel, this have ye said, and I know that which riseth up of your minds.

6 Many have ye murdered in this city, and ye have filled the streets thereof with the slain.

7 Therefore thus saith the Lord God, They that ye have slain, and have laid in the midst of it, they are [1]the flesh, and this *city* is the caldron, but I will bring you forth of the midst of it.

8 Ye have feared the sword, and I will bring a sword upon you, saith the Lord God.

9 And I will bring you out of the midst thereof, and deliver you into [1]the hands of strangers, and will execute judgments among you.

10 Ye shall fall by the sword, *and* I will judge you in the border of [1]Israel, and ye shall know that I am the Lord.

11 This *city* shall not be your caldron, neither shall ye be the flesh in the midst thereof, *but* I will judge you in the border of Israel.

12 And ye shall know that I am the Lord: for ye have not walked in my statutes, neither executed my judgments, but have done after the manners of the heathen that are round about you.

13 ¶ And when I prophesied, Pelatiah the son of [1]Benaiah died: then fell I down upon my face, and cried with a loud voice, and said, Ah Lord God, wilt thou then utterly destroy all the remnant of Israel?

14 Again the word of the Lord came unto me, saying,

15 Son of man, thy [1]brethren, *even* thy brethren, the men of thy kindred, and all the house of Israel, wholly *are they* unto whom the inhabitants of Jerusalem have said, Depart ye far from the Lord: *for* the land is given us in possession.

16 Therefore say, Thus saith the Lord God, Although I have cast them far off among the heathen, and although I have scattered them among the countries, yet will I be to them as a little [1]Sanctuary in the countries where they shall come.

17 Therefore say, Thus saith the Lord God, I will gather you again from the people, and assemble you out of the countries where ye have been scattered, and I will give you the land of Israel.

18 And they shall come thither, and they shall take away all the idols thereof, and all the abominations thereof from thence.

19 [a]And I will give them one heart, and I will put a new spirit within their bowels: and I will take the [1]stony heart out of their bodies, and will give them an heart of flesh,

20 That they may walk in my statutes, and keep my judgments, and execute them: and they shall be my people, and I will be their God.

21 But upon them, whose heart is toward their idols, and whose affection goeth after their abominations, I will lay their way upon their own heads saith the Lord God.

22 ¶ Then did the Cherubims lift up their wings, and the wheels beside them, and the glory of the God of Israel *was* upon them on high.

23 And the glory of the Lord went up from the midst of the city, and stood upon the mountain which is toward the East side of the city.

24 Afterward the Spirit took me up, and brought me in a vision by the Spirit of God into Chaldea to them that were led away captives: so the vision that I had seen, went up from me.

25 Then I declared unto them that were [1]led away captives, all the things that the Lord had showed me.

12

1 *The parable of the captivity.*   18 *Another parable whereby the distress of hunger and thirst is signified.*

1 The word of the Lord also came unto me, saying,

2 Son of man, thou dwellest in the midst of a rebellious house, which have eyes to see, and see [1]not: they have ears to hear, and hear not: for they are a rebellious house.

3 Therefore thou son of man, [1]prepare thy stuff to go into captivity, and go forth by day in their sight: and thou shalt pass from thy place to another place in their sight, if it be possible that they may consider it: for they are a rebellious house.

4 Then shalt thou bring forth thy stuff by day in their sight, as the stuff of him that goeth into captivity: and thou shalt go forth at even in their sight, as they that go forth into captivity.

11:7 [1] Contrary to their vain confidence he showeth in what sense the city is the caldron: that is, because of the dead bodies that have been murdered therein, and so lie as flesh in the caldron.

11:9 [1] That is, of the Chaldeans.

11:10 [1] That is, in Riblah, read 2 Kings 25:6.

11:13 [1] It seemeth that this noble man died of some terrible death, and therefore the Prophet feared some strange judgment of God toward the rest of the people.

11:15 [1] They that remained still at Jerusalem thus reproached them that were gone into captivity, as though they were cast off and for-

saken of God.

11:16 [1] They shall be yet a little Church: showing that the Lord will ever have some to call upon his Name, whom he will preserve and restore, though they be for a time afflicted.

11:19 [1] Meaning, the heart whereunto nothing can enter, and regenerate them anew, so that their heart may be soft, and ready to receive my graces.

11:25 [1] When Jeconiah was led away captive.

12:2 [1] That is, they receive not the fruit of that which they see and hear.

12:3 [1] Hebrew, *make thee vessels to go into captivity.*

5 Dig thou through the wall in their sight, and carry out thereby.

6 In their sight shalt thou bear it upon *thy* shoulders *and* carry it forth in the dark: thou shalt cover thy face that thou see not the earth: for I have set thee *as* a [1]sign unto the house of Israel.

7 And as I was commanded, so I brought forth my stuff by day, as the stuff of one that goeth into captivity: and by night I dug through the wall with mine hand, and brought it forth in the dark, *and* I bore it upon *my* shoulder in their sight.

8 And in the morning came the word of the Lord unto me, saying,

9 Son of man, hath not the house of Israel, the rebellious house, said unto thee, What [1]doest thou?

10 *But* say thou unto them, Thus saith the Lord God, This [1]burden *concerneth* the chief in Jerusalem, and all the house of Israel that are among them.

11 Say, I am your sign: like as I have done, so shall it be done unto them: they shall go into bondage *and* captivity.

12 And the chiefest that is among them, shall bear upon his shoulder in the dark, and shall go forth: they shall dig through the wall, to carry out thereby: he shall cover his face, that he see not the ground with *his* eyes.

13 My net also will I spread upon [1]him, and he shall be taken in my net, and I will bring him to Babel to the land of the Chaldeans, yet shall he not see it, though he shall die there.

14 And I will scatter toward every wind all that are about him to help him, and all his garrisons, and I will draw out the sword after them.

15 And they shall know that I am the Lord, when I shall scatter them among the nations, and disperse them in the countries.

16 But I will leave a [1]little number of them from the sword, from the famine, and from the pestilence, that they may declare all these abominations among the heathen, where they come, and they shall know, that I am the Lord.

17 ¶ Moreover, the word of the Lord came unto me, saying,

18 Son of man, eat thy bread with trembling, and drink thy water with trouble, and with carefulness,

19 And say unto the people of the land, Thus saith the Lord God of the inhabitants of Jerusa-

CHAPTER 13
[a] Ezek. 14:9

lem, *and* of the land of Israel, They shall eat their bread with carefulness, and drink their water with desolation: for the land shall be desolate from her abundance, because of the cruelty of them that dwell therein.

20 And the cities that are inhabited, shall be left void, and the land shall be desolate, and ye shall know that I am the Lord.

21 ¶ And the word of the Lord came unto me, saying,

22 Son of man, what is that proverb that you have in the land of Israel, saying, The days [1]are prolonged, and all visions [2]fail?

23 Tell them therefore, Thus saith the Lord God, I will make this proverb to cease, and they shall no more use it as a proverb in Israel: but say unto them, The days are at hand, and the effect of every vision.

24 For no vision shall be anymore in vain, neither *shall there be* any flattering divination within the house of Israel.

25 For I am the Lord: I will speak, *and* that thing that I shall speak, shall come to pass: it shall be no more prolonged: for in your days, O rebellious house, will I say the thing, and will perform it, saith the Lord God.

26 Again the word of the Lord came unto me, saying,

27 Son of man, behold, they of the house of Israel say, The vision that he seeth, is for [1]many days *to come*, and he prophesieth of the times that are far off.

28 Therefore say unto them, Thus saith the Lord God, All my words shall no longer be delayed, but that thing which I have spoken, shall be done, saith the Lord God.

13

2 *The word of the Lord against false prophets, which teach the people the counsels of their own hearts.*

1 And the word of the Lord came unto me, saying,

2 Son of man, prophesy against the prophets of [a]Israel, that prophesy, and say thou unto them, that prophesy out of their [1]own hearts, Hear the word of the Lord.

3 Thus saith the Lord God, Woe unto the foolish Prophets that follow their own spirit, and have seen nothing.

4 O Israel, thy Prophets are like the foxes [1]in the

12:6 [1] That as thou doest, so shall they do, and therefore in thee they shall see their own plague and punishment.

12:9 [1] Do not they deride thy doings?

12:10 [1] Or, prophecy.

12:13 [1] When the king shall think to escape by fleeing, I will take him in my net, as Ezek. 17:20 and 32:3.

12:16 [1] Which should bear his Name, and should be his Church, read Ezek. 11:16.

12:22 [1] Because they did not immediately see the prophecies

accomplished, they contemned them as though they should never be fulfilled.

    [2] Or, take none effect.

12:27 [1] That is, it shall not come to pass in our days, and therefore we care not for it: thus the wicked ever abuse God's patience and benignity.

13:2 [1] After their own fantasy, and not as having the revelation of the Lord, Jer. 23:16.

13:4 [1] Watching to destroy the vineyard.

waste places.

5 [1]Ye have not risen up in the gaps, neither made up the hedge for the house of Israel, to stand in the battle in the day of the Lord.

6 They have seen vanity, and lying divination, saying, The Lord saith it, and the Lord hath not sent them: and they have made *others* to hope that they would confirm the word *of their prophecy.*

7 Have ye not seen a vain vision? and have ye not spoken a lying divination? [1]ye say, The Lord saith it, albeit I have not spoken.

8 Therefore thus saith the Lord God, Because ye have spoken vanity and have seen lies, therefore behold, I am against you, saith the Lord God,

9 And mine hand shall be upon the Prophets that see vanity, and divine lies: they shall not be in the assembly of my people, neither shall they be written in the [1]writing of the house of Israel, neither shall they enter into the land of Israel: and ye shall know that I am the Lord God.

10 And therefore, because they have deceived my people, saying, [1]Peace, and there was no peace: and one built up a [2]wall, and behold, the others daubed it with untempered *mortar,*

11 Say unto them which daub it with untempered *mortar,* that it shall fall: *for* there shall come a great shower, and I will send hailstones, *which* shall cause it to fall, and a stormy wind shall break it.

12 Lo, when the wall is fallen, shall it not be said unto you, Where is the daubing wherewith ye have daubed it?

13 Therefore thus saith the Lord God, I will cause a stormy wind to break forth in my wrath, and a great shower shall be in mine anger, and hailstones in *mine* indignation to consume it.

14 So I will destroy the wall that ye have daubed with untempered *mortar,* and bring it down to the ground, so that the foundation thereof shall be discovered, and it shall fall, and ye shall be consumed in the midst thereof, and ye shall know, that I am the Lord.

15 Thus will I accomplish my wrath upon the wall, and upon them that have daubed it with [1]untempered

mortar, and will say unto you, The wall is no more, neither the daubers thereof,

16 *To wit,* the Prophets of Israel, which prophesy upon Jerusalem, and see visions of peace for it, and there is no peace, saith the Lord God.

17 Likewise thou son of man, set thy face against the daughters of thy people, which prophesy out of their own heart: and prophesy thou against them, and say,

18 Thus saith the Lord God, Woe unto the *women* that sow [1]pillows under all armholes, and make veils upon the head of everyone that standeth up, to hunt souls: will ye hunt the souls of my people, and will ye give life to the souls that come unto you?

19 And will ye pollute me among my people for handfuls of [1]barley, and for pieces of bread to slay the souls of them that should not die, and [2]to give life to the souls that should not live, in lying to my people, that hear *your* lies?

20 Wherefore thus saith the Lord God, Behold, I will *have to do* with your pillows, wherewith ye hunt the [1]souls to make them to flee, and I will tear them from your arms, and will let the souls go, *even* the souls that ye hunt to make them to flee.

21 Your veils also will I tear, and deliver my people out of your hand, and they shall be no more in your hands to be hunted, and ye shall know that I am the Lord.

22 Because with *your* lies ye have made the heart of the [1]righteous sad, whom I have not made sad, and strengthened the hands of the wicked, that he should not return from his wicked way, by promising him life,

23 Therefore ye shall see no more vanity, nor divine divinations: for I will deliver my people out of your hand, and ye shall know that I am the Lord.

14

4 *The Lord sendeth false Prophets for the ingratitude of the people.* 22 *He reserveth a small portion for his Church.*

1 Then came certain of the Elders of Israel unto

13:5 [1] He speaketh to the governors, and true ministers that should have resisted them.

13:7 [1] Ye promised peace to this people, and now ye see their destruction, so that it is manifest, that ye are false prophets.

13:9 [1] That is, in the book of life, wherein the true Israelites are written.

13:10 [1] Read Jer. 6:14.
    [2] Whereas the true Prophets prophesied the destruction of the city to bring the people to repentance, the false prophets spake the contrary, and flattered them in their vanities, so that what one false prophet said (which is here called the building of the wall) another false prophet would affirm, though he had neither occasion nor good ground to bear him.

13:15 [1] Whereby is meant whatsoever man of himself setteth forth

under the authority of God's word.

13:18 [1] These superstitious women for lucre would prophesy and tell every man his fortune, giving them pillows to lean upon, and kerchiefs to cover their heads, to the intent they might the more allure them and bewitch them.

13:19 [1] Will ye make my word to serve your bellies?
    [2] These sorcerers made the people believe that they could preserve life or destroy it, and that it should come to everyone according as they prophesied.

13:20 [1] That is, to cause them to perish, and that they should depart from the body.

13:22 [1] By threatening them that were godly, and upholding the wicked.

me, and [1]sat before me.

2 And the word of the Lord came unto me, saying,

3 Son of man, these men have set up their idols in their [1]heart, and put the stumbling block of their iniquity before their face: should I, being required, answer them?

4 Therefore speak unto them, and say unto them, Thus saith the Lord God, Every man of the house of Israel that setteth up his idols in his heart, and putteth the stumbling block of his iniquity before his face, and cometh to the [1]Prophet, I the Lord will answer him that cometh, according to the multitude [2]of his idols:

5 That [1]I may take the house of Israel in their own heart, because they are all departed from me through their idols.

6 Therefore say unto the house of Israel, Thus saith the Lord God, Return, and withdraw yourselves, and turn your faces from your idols, and turn your faces from all your abominations.

7 For everyone of the house of Israel, or of the stranger that sojourneth in Israel, which departeth from me, and setteth up his idols in his heart, and putteth the stumbling block of his iniquity before his face, and cometh to a Prophet, for to inquire of him for me, I the Lord will answer him [1]for myself,

8 And I will set my face against that man, and will make him an example and proverb, and I will cut him off from the midst of my people, and ye shall know that I am the Lord.

9 And if the Prophet be [1]deceived, when he hath spoken a thing, I the Lord have deceived that Prophet, and I will stretch out mine hand upon him, and will destroy him from the midst of my people of Israel.

10 And they shall bear their punishment: the punishment of the Prophet shall be even as the punishment of him that asketh,

11 That the house of [1]Israel may go no more astray from me, neither be polluted anymore with all their

CHAPTER 14
[a] Ezek. 5:17

transgressions, but that they may be my people, and I may be their God, saith the Lord God.

12 ¶ The word of the Lord came again unto me, saying,

13 Son of man, when the land sinneth against me by committing a trespass, then will I stretch out mine hand upon it, [1]and will break the staff of the bread thereof, and will send famine upon it, and I will destroy man and beast forth of it.

14 Though these three men [1]Noah, Daniel, and Job were among them, they should deliver but their own souls by their [2]righteousness, saith the Lord God.

15 If I bring noisome beasts into the land and they spoil it, so that it be desolate, that no man may pass through, because of beasts,

16 Though these three men were in the midst thereof, As I live, saith the Lord God, they shall save neither sons nor daughters: they only shall be delivered, but the land shall be waste.

17 Or if I bring a sword upon this land, and say, Sword, go through the land, so that I destroy man and beast out of it,

18 Though these three men were in the midst thereof, As I live, saith the Lord God, they shall deliver neither sons nor daughters, but they only shall be delivered themselves.

19 Or if I send a pestilence into this land, and pour out my wrath upon it in blood, to destroy out of it man and beast,

20 And though Noah, Daniel and Job were in the midst of it, As I live, saith the Lord God, they shall deliver neither son nor daughter: they shall but deliver their own souls by their righteousness.

21 For thus saith the Lord God, How much more when I send my [a]four sore judgments upon Jerusalem, even the sword, and famine, and the noisome beast, and pestilence, to destroy man and beast out of it?

22 Yet behold, therein shall be left a [1]remnant of them that shall be carried away both sons and

---

14:1 [1] He showeth the hypocrisy of the idolaters, who will dissemble to hear the Prophets of God, though in their heart they follow nothing less than their admonitions, and also how by one means or other God doth discover them.

14:3 [1] They are not only idolaters in heart, but also worship their filthy idols openly, which lead them in blindness, and cause them to stumble, and cast them out of God's favor, so that he will not hear them when they call unto him, read Jer. 10:15.

14:4 [1] To inquire of things which the Lord hath appointed to come to pass.

[2] As his abomination hath deserved: that is, he shall be led with lies according as he delighted therein, 2 Thess. 2:10.

14:5 [1] That is, convince them by their own conscience.

14:7 [1] Or, by myself.

14:9 [1] The Prophet declareth that God for man's ingratitude raiseth up false prophets to seduce them that delight in lies

rather than in the truth of God, and thus he punisheth sin by sin, 1 Kings 22:20, 22, and destroyeth as well those Prophets as that people.

14:11 [1] Thus God's judgments against the wicked, are admonitions to the godly, to cleave unto the Lord, and not to defile themselves with like abominations.

14:13 [1] Read Ezek. 4:16 and 5:17; Isa. 3:1.

14:14 [1] Though Noah and Job were now alive, which in their time were most godly men (for at this time Daniel was in captivity with Ezekiel) and so these three together should pray for this wicked people, yet would I not hear them, read Jer. 15:1.

[2] Meaning, that a very few (which he calleth the remnant, verse 22) should escape these plagues, whom God hath sanctified and made righteous, so that this righteousness is a sign that they are the Church of God, whom he would preserve for his own sake.

14:22 [1] Read Ezek. 5:3.

daughters: behold, they shall come forth unto you, and ye shall see their way, and their enterprises: and ye shall be comforted, concerning the evil that I have brought upon Jerusalem, *even* concerning all that I have brought upon it.

23 And they shall comfort you, when ye see their way and their enterprises: and ye shall know, that I have not done without cause all that I have done in it, saith the Lord God.

15
2 As the unprofitable wood of the vine tree is cast into the fire, so Jerusalem shall be burnt.

1 And the word of the Lord came unto me, saying,

2 Son of man, what cometh of the vine tree above all *other* trees? and of the vine branch, which is among the ¹trees of the forest?

3 Shall wood be taken thereof to do any work? or will men take a pin of it to hang any vessel thereon?

4 Behold, it is cast in the fire to be consumed: the fire consumeth both the ends of it, and the midst of it is burnt. Is it meet for *any* work?

5 Behold, when it was whole, it was meet for no work: how much less shall it be meet for any work, when the fire hath consumed it, and it is burnt?

6 Therefore thus saith the Lord God, as the vine tree, *that is* among the trees of the forest, which I have given to the fire to be consumed, so will I give the inhabitants of Jerusalem.

7 And I will set my face against them: they shall go out from *one* ¹fire, and *another* fire shall consume them: and ye shall know, that I am the Lord, when I set my face against them,

8 And *when* I make the land waste, because they have greatly offended, saith the Lord God.

16
The Prophet declared the benefits of God toward Jerusalem. 15 Their unkindness. 46 He justifieth the wickedness of other people in comparison of the sins of Jerusalem. 49 The cause of the abominations, into which the Sodomites fell. 60 Mercy is promised to the repentant.

1 Again, the word of the Lord came unto me, saying,

2 Son of man, cause Jerusalem to know her abominations,

3 And say, Thus saith the Lord God unto Jerusalem, Thine habitation and thy kindred is of the land ¹of Canaan: thy father was an Amorite, and thy mother an Hittite.

4 And in thy nativity when thou wast ¹born, thy navel was not cut: thou wast not washed in water to soften *thee*: thou wast not salted with salt, nor swaddled in clouts.

5 None eye pitied thee to do any of these unto thee, for to have compassion upon thee, but thou wast cast out in the open field to the contempt of thy person in the day that thou wast born.

6 And when I passed by thee, I saw thee polluted in thine ¹own blood, and I said unto thee, when thou wast in thy blood, Thou shalt live: even when thou wast in thy blood, I said unto thee, Thou shalt live.

7 I have caused thee to multiply as the bud of the field, and thou hast increased and waxen great, and thou hast gotten excellent ornaments: *thy* breasts are fashioned, thine hair is grown, whereas thou wast naked and bare.

8 Now when I passed by thee, and looked upon thee, behold, thy time *was as* the time of love, and I spread my skirts over thee, and covered ¹thy filthiness: yea, I swear unto thee, and entered into a covenant with ²thee, saith the Lord God, and thou becamest mine.

9 Then washed I thee with ¹water: yea, I washed away thy blood from thee, and I ²anointed thee with oil.

10 I clothed thee also with broidered work, and shod thee with badgers' skin, and I girded thee about with fine linen, and I covered thee with silk.

11 I decked thee also with ornaments, and I put bracelets upon thine hands, and a chain on thy neck.

12 And I put a frontlet upon thy face, and earrings in thine ears, and a beautiful ¹crown upon thine head.

13 Thus wast thou decked with gold and silver, and thy raiment was of fine linen, and silk, and broidered work: thou didst eat fine flour, and honey and oil, and thou wast very beautiful, and

---

15:2 ¹ Which brings forth no fruit, no more than the other trees of the forest do: meaning that if Jerusalem, which bore the name of his Church, did not bring forth fruit it would be utterly destroyed.
15:7 ¹ Though they escape one danger, yet another will take them.
16:3 ¹ Thou boastest to be of the seed of Abraham, but thou art degenerate and followest the abominations of the wicked Canaanites, as children do the manners of their fathers, Isa. 1:4 and 57:3.
16:4 ¹ When I first brought thee out of Egypt, and planted thee in this land to be my Church.
16:6 ¹ Being thus in thy filthiness and forsaken of all men, I took thee and gave thee life: whereby is meant that before God wash his

Church, and give life, there is nothing but filthiness and death.
16:8 ¹ These words, as blood, pollution, nakedness, and filthiness, are oftentimes repeated to beat down their pride, and to cause them to consider what they were before God received them to mercy, favored them and covered their shame.
² That thou shouldest be a chaste wife unto me, and that I should maintain thee and endue thee with all graces.
16:9 ¹ I washed away thy sins.
² I sanctified thee with mine holy Spirit.
16:12 ¹ Hereby he showeth how he saved his Church, enriched it, and gave it power and dominion to reign.

thou didst grow up into a kingdom.

14 And thy name was spread among the heathen for thy beauty: for it was perfect through my [1]beauty which I had set upon thee, saith the Lord God.

15 Now thou didst [1]trust in thine own beauty, and playedst the harlot, because of thy renown, and hast poured out [2]thy fornications on everyone that passed by, *thy desire* was to him.

16 And thou didst take thy garments, and deckedst thine high places with divers colors, [1]and playedst the harlot thereupon: the like things shall not come, neither hath any done so.

17 Thou hast also taken thy fair jewels *made of* my gold and of my silver, which I had given thee, and [1]madest to thyself images of men, and didst commit whoredom with them,

18 And tookest thy broidered garments, and coveredst them: and thou hast set mine oil and my perfume before them.

19 My meat also, which I gave thee, *as* fine flour, oil and honey, *wherewith* I fed thee, thou hast even set it before them for a sweet savor: thus it was, saith the Lord God.

20 Moreover thou hast taken thy sons and thy daughters, whom thou hast borne unto me, and these hast thou sacrificed unto them, to [1]be devoured: is *this* thy whoredom a small matter?

21 That thou hast slain my children, and delivered them to cause them to pass *through fire* for them?

22 And in all thine abominations and whoredoms thou hast not remembered the days of thy youth, when thou wast naked and bare, *and* wast polluted in thy blood.

23 And beside all thy wickedness (woe, woe unto thee, saith the Lord God)

24 Thou hast also built unto thee an high place, and hast made thee an high place in every street.

25 Thou hast built thine high place at every [1]corner of the way, and hast made thy beauty to be abhorred: thou hast opened thy feet to everyone that passed by, and multiplied thy whoredom.

26 Thou hast also committed fornication with the [1]Egyptians thy neighbors, which have great members, and hast increased thy whoredom, to provoke me.

27 Behold, therefore I did stretch out mine hand over thee, and will diminish thine ordinary, and deliver thee unto the will of them that hate thee, *even* to the [1]daughters of the Philistines, which are ashamed of thy wicked way.

28 Thou hast played the whore also with the Assyrians, because thou wast insatiable: yea, thou hast played the harlot with them, and yet couldest not be satisfied.

29 Thou hast moreover multiplied thy fornication from the land of Canaan unto Chaldea, and yet thou wast not satisfied herewith.

30 How weak is thine heart, saith the Lord God, seeing thou doest all these things, *even* the work of a [1]presumptuous whorish woman?

31 In that thou buildest thine high place in the corner of every way, and makest thine high place in every street, and hast not been as an harlot [1]that despiseth a reward,

32 But *as* a wife that playeth the harlot, *and* taketh others for her husband:

33 They give gifts to all *other* whores, but thou givest gifts unto all thy lovers, and rewardest them that they may come unto thee on every side for thy fornication.

34 And the contrary is in thee from *other* women in thy fornications, neither *the like* fornication *shall be* after thee: for in that thou givest a reward and no reward is given unto thee, therefore thou art contrary.

35 Wherefore, O harlot, hear the word of the Lord.

36 Thus saith the Lord God, Because thy [1]shame was poured out, and thy filthiness discovered through thy fornications with thy lovers, and with all the idols of thine abominations, and by the blood of thy children, which thou didst offer unto them,

37 Behold, therefore I will gather all [1]thy lovers, with whom thou hast taken pleasure, and all them that thou hast loved, with all them that thou hast hated: I will even gather them round about against thee, and will discover thy filthiness unto them, that they may see all thy filthiness.

38 And I will judge thee *after* the manner of them

16:14 [1] He declareth wherein the dignity of Jerusalem stood: to wit, in that that the Lord gave them of his beauty and excellency.

16:15 [1] In abusing my gifts, and in putting thy confidence in thine own wisdom and dignity, which were the occasions of thine idolatry.

[2] There was none idolatry so vile wherewith thou didst not pollute thyself.

16:16 [1] This declareth how the idolaters put their chief delight in those things, which please the eyes and outward senses.

16:17 [1] Thou hast converted my vessels and instruments, which I gave thee to serve me with, to the use of thine idols.

16:20 [1] Meaning, by fire: read Lev. 18:21; 2 Kings 23:10.

16:25 [1] Or, head.

16:26 [1] He noteth the great impiety of this people, who first falling from God to seek help at strange nations, did also at length embrace their idolatry, thinking thereby to make their amity more strong.

16:27 [1] Or, cities.

16:30 [1] Or, that will bear rule.

16:31 [1] Meaning, that some harlots contemn small rewards, but no lovers gave a reward to Israel, but they gave to all others: signifying that the idolaters bestow all their substance, which they receive of God for his glory, to serve their vile abominations.

16:36 [1] Or, … parts.

16:37 [1] Egyptians, Assyrians and Chaldeans, whom thou tookest to be thy lovers, shall come and destroy thee, Ezek. 23:9.

that are [1]harlots, and of them that shed blood, and I will give thee the blood of wrath, and jealousy.

39 I will also give thee into their hands, and they shall destroy thine high place, and shall break down thine high places: they shall strip thee also out of thy clothes, and shall take thy fair jewels, and leave thee naked and bare.

40 They shall also bring up a company against thee, and they shall stone thee with stones, and thrust thee through with their swords.

41 And they [a]shall burn up thine houses with fire, and execute judgments upon thee in the sight of many women: and I will cause thee to cease from playing the harlot, and thou shalt give no reward anymore.

42 So will I make my wrath toward thee to rest, and my [1]jealousy shall depart from thee, and I will cease, and be no more angry.

43 Because thou hast not remembered the days of thy youth, but hast provoked me with all these things, behold, therefore I also have [1]brought thy way upon thine head, saith the Lord God: yet hast not thou had consideration of all thine abominations.

44 Behold, all that use proverbs, shall use this proverb against thee, saying, As is the mother, [1]so is her daughter.

45 Thou art thy mother's daughter, that hath cast off her husband and her children, and thou art the sister of thy [1]sisters, which forsook their husbands and their children: your mother is an Hittite, and your father an Amorite.

46 And thine elder sister is Samaria, and her [1]daughters, that dwell at thy left hand, and [2]thy younger sister, that dwelleth at thy right hand, is Sodom, and her daughters.

47 Yet hast thou [1]not walked after their ways, nor done after their abominations: but as it had been a very little thing, thou wast corrupted more than they in all thy ways.

48 As I live, saith the Lord God, Sodom thy sister hath not done, neither she nor her daughters, as thou

CHAPTER 16
[a] 2 Kings 25:9

hast done and thy daughters.

49 Behold, this was the iniquity of thy sister Sodom, [1]pride, fullness of bread and abundance of idleness was in her, and in her daughters: neither did she strengthen the hand of the poor and needy.

50 But they were haughty, and committed abomination before me: therefore I took them away as pleased me.

51 Neither [1]hath Samaria committed half of thy sins, but thou hast exceeded them in thine abominations, and hast [2]justified thy sisters in all thine abominations which thou hast done.

52 Therefore thou which hast justified thy sisters, bear thine own shame for thy sins, that thou hast committed more abominable than they which are more righteous than thou art: be thou therefore confounded also, and bear thy shame, seeing that thou hast justified thy sisters.

53 Therefore I will bring again [1]their captivity, with the captivity of Sodom, and her daughters, and with the captivity of Samaria, and her daughters: even the captivity of thy captives in the midst of them,

54 That thou mayest bear thine own shame, and mayest be confounded in all that thou hast done, in that thou hast [1]comforted them.

55 And thy sister Sodom and her daughters shall return to their former state: Samaria also and her daughters shall return to their former state: [1]when thou and thy daughters shall return to your former state.

56 For thy sister Sodom [1]was not heard of [2]by thy report in the day of thy pride,

57 Before thy wickedness was [1]discovered, as in that same time of the reproach of the daughters of Aram, and of all the daughters of the Philistines round about [2]her, which despise thee on all sides.

58 Thou hast borne therefore thy wickedness and thine abomination, saith the Lord.

59 For thus saith the Lord God, I might even deal with thee, as thou hast done: when thou didst despise the [1]oath, in breaking the covenant.

16:38 [1] I will judge thee to death, as the adulterers and murderers.
16:42 [1] I will utterly destroy thee, and so my jealousy shall cease.
16:43 [1] I have punished thy faults, but thou wouldest not repent.
16:44 [1] As were the Canaanites, and the Hittites and others your predecessors, so are you their successors.
16:45 [1] That is, of Samaria and Sodom.
16:46 [1] That is, her cities.
    [2] Hebrew, thy sister younger than thou.
16:47 [1] But done far worse.
16:49 [1] He allegeth these four vices, pride, excess, idleness and contempt of the poor, as four principal causes of such abomination, wherefore they were so horribly punished, Gen. 19:24.
16:51 [1] Which worshipped the calves in Bethel and Dan.
    [2] Thou art so wicked, that in respect of thee Sodom and Samaria

were just.
16:53 [1] This he speaketh in comparison, seeing that he would restore Jerusalem when Sodom should be restored, that is, never: and this is meant of the greatest part of the Jews.
16:54 [1] In that thou hast showed thyself worse than they and yet thoughtest to escape punishment.
16:55 [1] Meaning, that it should never come to pass.
16:56 [1] Hebrew, was not a rumor in thy mouth.
    [2] Thou wouldest not call her punishment to mind when thou wast aloft, to learn by her example to fear my judgments.
16:57 [1] That is, till thou wast brought under by the Syrians and Philistines, 2 Chron. 28:19.
    [2] Which joined with the Syrians, or compassed about Jerusalem.
16:59 [1] When thou brakest the covenant which was made between thee and me, as verse 8.

60 Nevertheless, I will [1]remember my covenant *made* with thee in the days of thy youth, and I will confirm unto thee an everlasting Covenant.

61 Then thou shalt remember thy ways, and be ashamed, when thou shalt receive [1]thy sisters, *both* thy elder and thy younger, and I will give them unto thee for daughters, but not [2]by thy covenant.

62 And I will establish my covenant with thee, and thou shalt know that I am the Lord,

63 That thou mayest remember, and be [1]ashamed, and never open thy mouth anymore: because of thy shame when I am pacified toward thee, for all that thou hast done, saith the Lord God.

17 The parable of the two Eagles.

1 And the word of the Lord came unto me, saying,

2 Son of man, put forth a parable and speak a proverb unto the house of Israel,

3 And say, Thus saith the Lord God, The great [1]eagle with great wings *and* long wings, *and* full of feathers, which had diverse colors, came unto Lebanon, and took the highest branch of the cedar,

4 And brake off the top of his twig, *and* carried it into the land of [1]merchants, *and* set it in a city of merchants.

5 He took also of the [1]seed of the land, and planted it in a fruitful ground: he placed it by great waters, and set it *as* a willow tree.

6 And it budded up, and was like [1]a spreading vine of [2]low stature, whose branches turned toward it, and the roots thereof were under it: so it became a vine, and it brought forth branches, and shot forth buds.

7 There was also [1]another great Eagle with great wings and many feathers, and behold, this vine did turn her roots toward it, and spread forth her branches toward it, that she might water it by the trenches of her plantation.

8 It was planted in a good soil by great [1]waters, that it should bring forth branches, and bear fruit, and be an excellent vine.

9 Say thou, Thus saith the Lord God, Shall it prosper? shall [1]he not pull up the roots thereof, and destroy the fruit thereof, and cause them to dry? all the leaves of her bud shall wither without great power, or many people, to pluck it up by the roots thereof.

10 Behold, it was planted: but shall it prosper? shall it not be dried up, and wither? [1]when the East wind shall touch it, it shall wither in the trenches, where it grew.

11 Moreover, the word of the Lord came unto me, saying,

12 Say now to this rebellious house, Know ye not what these things *mean*? tell them, behold, the king of Babel is come to Jerusalem, and hath taken [1]the king thereof and the princes thereof, and led them with him to Babel,

13 And hath taken *one* of the King's seed, and made a covenant with him, and hath taken [1]an oath of him: he hath also taken the princes of the land,

14 That the kingdom might be in subjection, and not lift itself up, *but* keep their covenant, and stand to it.

15 But he rebelled against him, and sent his ambassadors into Egypt, that they might give him horses, and much people: shall he prosper? shall he escape that doeth such things? or shall he break the covenant, and be delivered?

16 As I live, saith the Lord God, he shall die in the midst of Babel, in the place of the king that had made him king, whose oath he despised, and whose covenant *made* with him, he brake.

17 Neither shall Pharaoh with *his* mighty host, and great multitude of people, maintain him in the war, when they have cast up mounts, and built ramparts to destroy many persons.

18 For he hath despised the oath, and broken the covenant (yet lo, he had given [1]his hand) because he hath done all these things, he shall not escape.

19 Therefore, thus saith the Lord God, As I live, I will surely bring mine oath that he hath despised, and my covenant that he hath broken, upon his own

---

16:60 [1] That is, of mercy and love I will pity thee, and so stand to my covenant though thou hast deserved the contrary.

16:61 [1] Whereby he showeth that among the most wicked, he had ever some seed of his Church, which he would cause to fructify in due time: and here he declareth how he will call the Gentiles.

[2] But of my free mercy.

16:63 [1] This declareth what fruits God's mercies work in his, to wit, sorrow and repentance for their former life.

17:3 [1] That is, Nebuchadnezzar, who hath great power, riches, and many countries under him, shall come to Jerusalem, and take away Jeconiah the King, as verse 12.

17:4 [1] Meaning, to Babylon.

17:5 [1] That is, Zedekiah, who was of the King's blood and was left at Jerusalem, and made King instead of Jeconiah, 2 Kings 24:17; Jer. 37:1.

17:6 [1] This was Zedekiah's kingdom.

[2] That is, might not have power to rebel against Babylon, as verse 14.

17:7 [1] Meaning, the king of Egypt, of whom Zedekiah sought succor against Nebuchadnezzar.

17:8 [1] They thought to be moistened by the waters of Nilus.

17:9 [1] Shall not Nebuchadnezzar destroy it?

17:10 [1] By this dry wind he meaneth the Babylonians.

17:12 [1] That is, Jeconiah, 2 Kings 24:15.

17:13 [1] For his subjection and obedience.

17:18 [1] Because he took the Name of God in vain, and brake his oath which he had confirmed by giving his hand: therefore the Prophet declareth that God would not suffer such perjury and infidelity to escape punishment.

head.

20 ªAnd I will spread my net upon him, and he shall be taken in my net, and I will bring him to Babel, and will enter into judgment with him there for his trespass that he hath committed against me.

21 And all that flee from him with all his host, shall fall by the sword, and they that remain shall be scattered toward all the winds: and ye shall know that I the Lord have spoken it.

22 Thus saith the Lord God, I will also take off the top¹of this high cedar, and will set it, and cut off the ²top of the tender plant thereof, and I will plant it upon an high mountain and great.

23 *Even* in the high mountain of Israel will I plant it: and it shall bring forth boughs, and bear fruit, and be an excellent cedar, and under it shall remain all birds, and every ¹fowl shall dwell in the shadow of the branches thereof.

24 And all the ¹trees of the field shall know that I the Lord have brought down the high tree, and exalted the low tree: that I have dried up the green tree, and made the dry tree to flourish: I the Lord have spoken it, and have done it.

18

2 He sheweth that every man shall bear his own sin.   21 To him that amendeth, salvation is promised.   24 Death is prophesied to the righteous, which turneth back from the right way.

1 The word of the Lord came unto me again, saying,

2 What mean ye that ye speak this proverb concerning the land of Israel, saying, ¹The fathers have eaten sour grapes, and the children's teeth are set on edge?

3 As I live, saith the Lord God, ye shall use this proverb no more in Israel.

4 Behold, all souls are mine, both the soul of the father, and also the soul of the son are mine: the soul that sinneth, it shall die.

5 But if a man be just, and do that which is lawful and right,

6 *And* hath not eaten ¹upon the mountains, neither hath lift up his eyes to the idols of the house of Israel, neither hath ªdefiled his neighbor's wife, neither hath ²lain with a ᵇmenstruous woman,

7 Neither hath oppressed any, *but* hath restored the pledge to his debtor: he that hath spoiled none

CHAPTER 17
ᵈ Ezek. 12:13
Ezek. 32:3

CHAPTER 18
ᵃ Lev. 18:20
ᵇ Lev. 20:18
ᶜ Isa. 58:7
Matt. 25:35
ᵈ Exod. 22:25
Lev. 25:37
Deut. 23:19
Ps. 15:5
ᵉ Deut. 24:16
2 Kings 4:6
2 Chron. 25:4

by violence, ᶜ*but* hath given his bread to the hungry, and hath covered the naked with a garment,

8 And hath not given forth upon ᵈusury, neither hath taken any increase, *but* hath withdrawn his hand from iniquity, and hath executed true judgment between man and man,

9 And hath walked in my statutes, and hath kept my judgments to deal truly, he is just, he shall surely live, saith the Lord God.

10 ¶ If he beget a son, that is a ¹thief, *or* a shedder of blood, if he do anyone of these things,

11 Though he do not all these things, but either hath eaten upon the mountains, or defiled his neighbor's wife,

12 Or hath oppressed the poor and needy, *or* hath spoiled by violence, *or* hath not restored the pledge, or hath lifted up his eyes unto the idols, *or* hath committed abomination,

13 Or hath given forth upon usury, or hath taken increase, shall he live? he shall not live: seeing he hath done all these abominations, ¹he shall die the death, *and* his blood shall be upon him.

14 ¶ But if he beget a son, that seeth all his father's sins, which he hath done, and feareth, neither doeth such like,

15 That hath not eaten upon the mountains, neither hath lifted up his eyes to the idols of the house of Israel, nor hath defiled his neighbor's wife,

16 Neither hath oppressed any, nor hath withheld the pledge, neither hath spoiled by violence, *but* hath given his bread to the hungry, and hath covered the naked with a garment,

17 *Neither* hath withdrawn his hand from the afflicted, nor received usury nor increase, *but* hath executed my judgments, *and* hath walked in my statutes, he shall not die in the iniquity of his father, *but* he shall surely live.

18 His father, because he cruelly oppressed and spoiled his brother by violence, and hath not done good among his people, lo, even he dieth in his iniquity.

19 Yet say ye, Wherefore shall not the son bear the iniquity of the father? because the son hath executed judgment and justice, *and* hath kept all my statutes, and done them, he shall surely live.

20 ᶜThe same soul that sinneth, shall die: the son shall not bear the iniquity of the father, neither

---

17:22 ¹ This promise is made to the Church which shall be as a small remnant, and as the top of a tree.

² I will trim it, and dress it.

17:23 ¹ Both the Jews and Gentiles shall be gathered into it.

17:24 ¹ All the world shall know that I have plucked down the proud enemies, and set up my Church which was low and contemned.

18:2 ¹ The people murmured at the chastisings of the Lord, and therefore used this proverb, meaning, that their fathers had sinned, and their

children were punished for their transgressions, read Jer. 31:29.

18:6 ¹ If he hath not eaten of the flesh that hath been offered up to idols, to honor them thereby.

² Hebrew, *come near.*

18:10 ¹ Or, a cruel man.

18:13 ¹ He sheweth how the son is punished for his father's fault: that is, if he be wicked as his father was, and doth not repent, he shall be punished as his father was, or else not.

shall the father bear the iniquity of the son, *but the righteousness* of the righteous shall be upon him, and the wickedness of the wicked shall be upon himself.

21 But if the wicked will return from all his sins that he hath committed, and keep all my ¹statutes, and do that which is lawful and right, he shall surely live, *and* shall not die.

22 All his transgressions that he hath committed, they shall not be ¹mentioned unto him, *but* in his ²righteousness that he hath done, he shall live.

23 ¹Have I any desire that the wicked should die, saith the Lord God? ²or shall he not live, if he return from his ways?

24 But if the righteous turn away from his righteousness, and commit iniquity, *and* do according to all the abominations that the wicked man doeth, shall he live? all his ¹righteousness that he hath done, shall not be mentioned: *but* in his transgression that he hath committed, and in his sin that he hath sinned, in them shall he die.

25 Yet ye say, The way of the Lord is not ¹equal: hear now, O house of Israel. Is not my way equal? *or* are not your ways unequal?

26 *For* when a righteous man turneth away from his righteousness, and committeth iniquity, he shall even die for the same, he shall *even* die for his iniquity that he hath done.

27 Again, when the wicked turneth away from his wickedness that he hath committed, and doeth that which is lawful and right, he shall save his soul alive.

28 Because he considereth, and turneth away from all his transgressions that he hath committed, he shall surely live, *and* shall not die.

29 Yet saith the house of Israel, The way of the Lord is not equal. O house of Israel, are not my ways equal? *or* are not your ways unequal?

30 Therefore I will judge you, O house of Israel, everyone according to his ways, saith the Lord God: return *therefore*, and cause *others* to turn away from all your transgressions: so iniquity shall not be your

destruction.

31 Cast away from you all your transgressions, whereby ye have transgressed and make ¹you a new heart and a new spirit: for why will ye die, O house of Israel?

32 For I desire not the death of him that dieth, saith the Lord God: cause therefore *one another* to return, and live ye.

19

1 *The captivity of the kings of Judah signified by the lion's whelps and by the lion.* 10 *The prosperity of the city of Jerusalem that is past, and the misery thereof that is present.*

1 Thou also take up a lamentation for the ¹princes of Israel,

2 And say, Wherefore lay thy ¹mother *as* a lioness among the lions? she nourished her young ones among the lion's whelps,

3 And she brought up one of her whelps, *and* it became a lion, and it learned to catch the prey, *and* it devoured men.

4 The ¹nations also heard of him, *and* he was taken in their nets, and they brought him in chains unto the land of Egypt.

5 Now when she saw that she had waited, and her hope was lost, she took another of her ¹whelps, and made him a lion.

6 Which went among the lions, *and* became a lion, and learned to catch the prey, *and* he devoured ¹men.

7 And he knew their widows, and he destroyed their cities, and the land was wasted, and all that was therein by the noise of his roaring.

8 Then the ¹nations set against him on every side of the countries, and laid their nets for him: so he was taken in their pit.

9 And they put him in prison *and* in chains, and brought him to the king of Babel, *and* they put him in holds, that his voice should no more be heard upon the mountains of Israel.

10 Thy ¹mother *is* like a vine in thy blood, planted

18:21 ¹ He joineth the observation of the commandments with repentance: for none can repent in deed, except he labor to keep the Law.
18:22 ¹ Or, not laid to his charge.
² That is, in the fruits of his faith which declare that God doth accept him.
18:23 ¹ He speaketh this to commend God's mercy to poor sinners, who rather is ready to pardon than to punish, as his long suffering declareth, Ezek. 33:11. Albeit God in his eternal counsel appointed the death and damnation of the reprobate, yet the end of his counsel was not their death only, but chiefly his own glory. Also because he doth not approve sin, therefore it is here said that he would have them to turn away from it, that they might live.
² Or, rather that he may return from his ways, and live.
18:24 ¹ That is, the false opinion that the hypocrites have of their righteousness.

18:25 ¹ In punishing the father with the children.
18:31 ¹ He showeth that man cannot forsake his wickedness, till his heart be changed, which is only the work of God.
19:1 ¹ That is, Jehoahaz and Jehoiakim Josiah's sons, who for their pride and cruelty are compared unto lions.
19:2 ¹ To wit, Jehoahaz's mother, or Jerusalem.
19:4 ¹ By Pharaoh Necho king of Egypt, 2 Kings 23:33.
19:5 ¹ Which was Jehoiakim.
19:6 ¹ He slew of the prophets, and them that feared God, and ravished their wives.
19:8 ¹ Nebuchadnezzar with his great army which was gathered of divers nations.
19:10 ¹ He speaketh this in the reproach of this wicked king, in whose blood, that is, in the race of his predecessors, Jerusalem should have been blessed, according to God's promise, and flourished as a fruitful vine.

by the waters: she brought forth fruit and branches by the abundant waters,

11 And she had strong rods for the scepters of them that bear rule, and her stature was exalted among the branches, and she appeared in her height with the multitude of her branches.

12 But she was plucked up in wrath: she was cast down to the ground, and the ¹East wind dried up her fruit: *her branches* were broken and withered: *as for* the rod of her strength, the fire consumed it.

13 And now she is planted in the wilderness in a dry and thirsty ground.

14 And fire is gone out ¹of a rod of her branches, which hath devoured her fruit, so that she hath no strong rod *to be* a scepter to rule: this is a lamentation, and shall be for a lamentation.

20

3 The Lord denieth that he will answer them when they pray, because of their wickedness.   33 He promiseth that his people shall return from captivity.   46 By the forest that should be burnt, is signified the burning of Jerusalem.

1 And in the ¹seventh year, in the fifth *month*, the tenth *day* of the month, came certain of the Elders of Israel to inquire of the Lord, and sat before me.

2 Then came the word of the Lord unto me, saying,

3 Son of man, speak unto the Elders of Israel, and say unto them, Thus saith the Lord God, Are ye come to inquire of me? as I live, saith the Lord God, when I am asked, I will not answer you.

4 Wilt thou judge them, son of man? wilt thou judge *them*? cause ¹them to understand the abominations of their fathers,

5 And say unto them, Thus saith the Lord God, In the day when I chose Israel, and ¹lifted up mine hand unto the seed of the house of Jacob, and made myself known unto them in the land of Egypt, when I lift up mine hand unto them, and said, I am the Lord your God,

6 In the day that I lifted up mine hand unto them, to bring them forth of the land of Egypt, into a land that I had provided for them, flowing with milk and honey, which is pleasant among all lands,

CHAPTER 20
ᵃ Lev. 18:5
Rom. 10:5
Gal. 3:12
ᵇ Exod. 20:8
Exod. 31:13
Deut. 5:12
ᶜ Num. 14:28,29
Num. 26:65

7 Then said I unto them, Let every man cast away the abominations of his eyes, ¹and defile not yourselves with the idols of Egypt: *for* I am the Lord your God.

8 But they rebelled against me, and would not hear me: *for* none cast away the abominations of ¹their eyes, neither did they forsake the idols of Egypt: then I thought to pour out mine indignation upon them, *and* to accomplish my wrath against them in the midst of the land of Egypt.

9 But I had respect to my ¹Name, that it should not be polluted before the heathen, among whom they were, and in whose sight I made myself known unto them in bringing them forth of the land of Egypt.

10 Now I carried them out of the land of Egypt, and brought them into the wilderness.

11 And I gave them my statutes, and declared my judgments unto them, ᵃwhich if a man do, he shall live in them.

12 Moreover I gave them also my ᵇSabbaths to be a sign between me and them, that they might know that I am the Lord, that sanctify them.

13 But the house of Israel rebelled against me in the wilderness: they walked not in my statutes, and they cast away my judgments, which if a man do, he shall live in them, and my Sabbaths have they greatly polluted: then I thought to pour out mine indignation upon them ᶜin the wilderness to consume them,

14 But I had respect to my name, that it should not be polluted before the ¹heathen in whose sight I brought them out.

15 Yet nevertheless, I lifted up mine hand unto them in the wilderness, that I would not bring them into the land, which I had given them, flowing with milk and honey, which was pleasant above all lands,

16 Because they cast away my judgments, and walked not in my statutes, but have polluted my ¹Sabbaths: for their heart went after their idols.

17 Nevertheless, mine eye spared them, that I would not destroy them, neither would I consume them in the wilderness.

18 But I said unto their children in the wilder-

19:12 ¹ Meaning, that the Chaldeans should destroy them as the East wind doth the fruit of the vine.

19:14 ¹ Destruction is come by Zedekiah, who was the occasion of this rebellion.

20:1 ¹ Of the captivity of Jeconiah.

20:4 ¹ This declareth the great lenity and patience of God, which calleth sinners to repentance before he condemns them.

20:5 ¹ I sware that I would be their God, which manner of oath was observed from all antiquity, where they used to lift up their hands toward the heaven, acknowledging God to be the author of truth, and the defender thereof, and also the Judge of the heart, wishing that he should take vengeance, if they concealed anything which they knew to be truth.

20:7 ¹ God had forbidden them to make mention of the idols, Exod. 23:13; Ps. 16:4.

20:8 ¹ Which thing declareth the wickedness of man's heart, which judge God's service by their eyes and outward senses.

20:9 ¹ God had ever this respect to his glory, that he would not have his Name evil spoken of among the Gentiles for the punishment that his people deserved, in confidence whereof the godly ever prayed, as Exod. 32:12; Num. 14:13.

20:14 ¹ Who might thereby take an occasion to blaspheme my Name and to accuse me of lack of ability, or else that I had sought a means to destroy them more commodiously.

20:16 ¹ That is, my true religion, which I had commanded them, and gave themselves to serve me according to their own fantasies.

ness, Walk ye not in the ordinances of your [1]fathers, neither observe their manners, nor defile yourselves with their idols.

19 I am the Lord your God: walk in my statutes, and keep my judgments and do them,

20 And sanctify my Sabbaths, and they shall be a sign between me and you, that ye may know that I am the Lord your God.

21 Notwithstanding the children rebelled against me: they walked not in my statutes, nor kept my judgments to do them, which if a man do, he shall live in them, *but* they polluted my Sabbaths: then I thought to pour out mine indignation upon them, *and* to accomplish my wrath against them in the wilderness.

22 Nevertheless, I withdrew mine hand and had respect to my Name, that it should not be polluted before the heathen, in whose sight I brought them forth.

23 Yet I lifted up mine hand unto them in the wilderness, that I would scatter them among the heathen, and disperse them through the countries,

24 Because they had not executed my judgments, but had cast away my statutes, and had polluted my Sabbaths, and their eyes were after [1]their fathers' idols.

25 Wherefore I gave [1]them also statutes that were not good, and judgments, wherein they should not live.

26 And I polluted them in their own [1]gifts in that they caused to pass *by the fire* all that *first* openeth the womb, that I might destroy them, to the end that they might know that I am the Lord.

27 Therefore, son of man, speak unto the house of Israel and say unto them, Thus saith the Lord God, Yet in this your fathers have blasphemed me, though they had *before* grievously transgressed against me.

28 [1]For when I had brought them into the land, for the which I lifted up mine hand to give it to them, then they saw every high hill, and all the thick trees, and they offered there their sacrifices, and there they presented their offering of provocation: there also they made their sweet savor, and poured out there their drink offerings.

29 Then I said unto them, What is the high place whereunto ye go? And the name thereof was called [1]Bamah unto this day.

30 Wherefore, say unto the house of Israel, Thus saith the Lord God, Are ye not polluted [1]after the manner of your fathers? and commit ye not whoredom after their abominations?

31 For when you offer your gifts, and make your sons to pass through the fire, you pollute yourselves with all your idols unto this day: shall I answer you when I am asked, O house of Israel? As I live, saith the Lord God, [1]I will not answer you when I am asked.

32 Neither shall that be done that cometh into your mind: for ye say, we will be as the heathen, and as the families of the countries, and serve wood, and [1]stone.

33 As I live, saith the Lord God, I will surely rule you with a mighty hand, and with a stretched out arm, and in *my* wrath poured out,

34 And will bring you from the people, and will gather you out of the countries, wherein ye are scattered, with a mighty hand, and with a stretched out arm, and in *my* wrath poured out,

35 And I will bring you into the [1]wilderness of the people, and there will I plead with you face to face.

36 Like as I pleaded with your fathers in the wilderness of the land of Egypt, so will I plead with you, saith the Lord God.

37 And I will cause you to pass under the rod, and will bring you into the bond of the covenant.

38 And I will [1]choose out from among you the rebels, and them that transgress against me: I will bring them out of the land where they dwell, and they shall not enter into the land of Israel, and ye shall know that I am the Lord.

20:18 [1] Whereby the holy Ghost confuteth them that say that they will follow the religion and example of their fathers, and not measure their doings by God's word whether they be approvable thereby or no.

20:24 [1] Meaning, that they set their delight upon them.

20:25 [1] Because they would not obey my laws, I gave them up to themselves, that they should obey their own fantasies, as verse 39; Rom. 1:21, 24.

20:26 [1] I condemned those things, and counted them as abominable, which they thought had been excellent, and to have declared most zeal, Luke 16:15, for that which God required, as most excellent, that they gave to their idols.

20:28 [1] Not only in the wilderness, when I brought them out of Egypt, but since I placed them in this land: which declareth how prompt man's heart is to idolatry, seeing that by no admonitions he can be drawn back.

20:29 [1] Which signifieth an high place, declaring that they vaunted themselves of their idolatry, and were not ashamed thereof, though God had commanded them expressly that they should have no altar lifted upon high by stairs, Exod. 20:26.

20:30 [1] Hebrew, *in the way.*

20:31 [1] He showeth that the ingratitude of the people deserveth that God should cut them off, and that they should not have the comfort of his word.

20:32 [1] He declareth that man of nature is wholly enemy unto God, and to his own salvation, and therefore God calleth him to the right way, partly by chastising, but chiefly by his mercy in forgiving his rebellion, and wickedness.

20:35 [1] I will bring you among strange nations as into a wilderness, and there will visit you, and so call you to repentance, and then bring the godly home again, Isa. 65:9.

20:38 [1] Signifying, that he will not burn the corn with the chaff, but choose out the wicked to punish them when he will spare his.

39 As for you, O house of Israel, thus saith the Lord God, ¹Go you, and serve everyone his idol, seeing that ye will not obey me, and pollute mine holy Name no more with your gifts, and with your idols.

40 For in mine holy mountain, *even* in the high mountain of Israel, saith the Lord God, there shall all the house of Israel, and all in the land serve me: there will I accept them, and there will I require your offerings, and the firstfruits of your oblations, with all your holy things.

41 I will accept your sweet savor, when I bring you from the people, and gather you out of the countries, wherein ye have been scattered, that I may be sanctified in you before the heathen.

42 And ye shall know that I am the Lord, when I shall bring you into the land of Israel, into the land for the which I lifted up mine hand to give it to your fathers.

43 And there shall ye remember your ways, and all your works, wherein ye have been defiled, and ye ¹shall judge yourselves worthy to be cut off, for all your evils, that ye have committed.

44 And ye shall know that I am the Lord, when I have respect unto you for my Name's sake, *and* not after your wicked ways, nor according to your corrupt works, O ye house of Israel, saith the Lord God.

45 ¶ Moreover, the word of the Lord came unto me, saying,

46 Son of man, Set thy face toward the way of Teman, and drop *thy word* toward ¹the South, and prophesy toward the forest of the field of the South,

47 And say to the forest of the South, Hear the word of the Lord: thus saith the Lord God, Behold, I will kindle a fire in thee, and it shall devour all the ¹green wood in thee, and all the dry wood: the continual flame shall not be quenched, and every face from the South to the North shall be burnt therein.

48 And all flesh shall see, that I the Lord have kindled it, *and* it shall not be quenched. Then said I, Ah Lord God, they say of me, Doth not he speak ¹parables?

21 ³ *He threateneth the sword and destruction to Jerusalem.* 25 *He showeth the fall of king Zed-*

ekiah.   29 *He is commanded to prophesy the destruction of the children of Ammon.*   30 *The Lord threateneth to destroy Nebuchadnezzar.*

1 The word of the Lord came to me again, saying,

2 Son of man, set thy face toward Jerusalem, ¹and drop *thy word* toward the holy places, and prophesy against the land of Israel,

3 And say to the land of Israel, Thus saith the Lord, Behold, I *come* against thee, and will draw my sword out of his sheath, and cut off from thee *both* the ¹righteous and the wicked.

4 Seeing then that I will cut off from thee *both* the righteous and wicked, therefore shall my sword go out of his sheath against all flesh from the South to the ¹North,

5 That all flesh may know that I the Lord have drawn my sword out of his sheath, *and* it shall not return anymore.

6 Mourn therefore thou son of man, *as* in the pain of *thy* ¹reins, and mourn bitterly before them.

7 And if they say unto thee, Wherefore mournest thou? Then answer, Because ¹of the bruit: for it cometh, and every heart shall melt, and all hands shall be weak, and all minds shall faint, and all knees shall fall away *as* water: behold, it cometh, and shall be done, saith the Lord God.

8 ¶ Again, the word of the Lord came unto me, saying,

9 Son of man, prophesy, and say, Thus saith the Lord God, say, A sword, a sword both sharp and furbished.

10 It is sharpened to make a sore slaughter, *and* it is furbished that it may ¹glitter: how shall we rejoice? *for* it contemneth the ²rod of my son, *as* ³all *other* trees.

11 And he hath given it to be furbished, that he may handle it: this sword is sharp, and is furbished that he may give it into the hand of the ¹slayer.

12 Cry and howl, son of man: for this shall come to my people, *and* it shall come unto all the princes of Israel: the terrors of the sword shall be upon my people, ¹smite therefore upon thy thigh.

13 For *it is* a trial, ¹and what shall this be, if *the sword* contemn even the rod? It shall be *no more*,

20:39 ¹ This is spoken to the hypocrites.
20:43 ¹ Your own consciences shall convict you after, that you have felt my mercies.
20:46 ¹ For Judah stood South from Babylon.
20:47 ¹ Both strong and weak in Jerusalem.
20:48 ¹ The people said that the Prophet spake darkly: therefore he desireth the Lord to give them a plain declaration thereof.
21:2 ¹ Speak sensibly, that all may understand.
21:3 ¹ That is such which seem to have an outward show of righteousness, by observation of the ceremonies of the law.
21:4 ¹ Meaning, through all the land.
21:6 ¹ As though thou were in extreme anguish.

21:7 ¹ Because of the great noise of the army of the Chaldeans.
21:10 ¹ And so cause a fear.
² Meaning, the scepter: showing that it will not spare the King, who should be as the son of God, and in his place.
³ That is, the rest of the people.
21:11 ¹ To wit, unto the army of the Chaldeans.
21:12 ¹ Read Jer. 31:19.
21:13 ¹ Ezekiel moved with compassion, thus complaineth, fearing the destruction of the kingdom which God had confirmed to David and his posterity by promise, which promise God performed, although here it seemed to man's eye that it should utterly perish.

saith the Lord God.

14 Thou therefore, son of man, prophesy and smite [1]hand to hand, and let the sword be doubled: let the sword that hath killed, *return* the third time: it is the sword of the great slaughter entering into their privy chambers.

15 I have brought the fear of the sword into all their gates to make *their* heart to faint, and to multiply *their* ruins. Ah, it is made bright, *and* it is dressed for the slaughter.

16 Get thee [1]alone: go to the right hand, *or* get thyself to the left hand, whithersoever thy face turneth.

17 I will also smite mine hands together, and will cause my wrath to cease. I the Lord have said it.

18 ¶ The word of the Lord came unto me again, saying,

19 Also thou son of man, appoint thee [1]two ways, that the sword of the King of Babel may come: both twain shall come out of one land, and choose a place, and choose it in the corner of the way of the city.

20 Appoint a way, that the sword may come to Rabbah of the Ammonites, and [1]to Judah in Jerusalem the strong *city*.

21 And the King of Babel stood at the [1]parting of the way, at the head of the two ways, consulting by divination, *and* made his arrows bright: he consulted with idols, *and* looked in [2]the liver.

22 At his right hand was the divination for Jerusalem to appoint captains to open *their* mouth in the slaughter, and to lift up their voice with shouting, to lay engines of war against the gates, to cast a mount, *and* to build a fortress.

23 And it shall be unto them [1]as a false divination in their sight for the oaths made unto them: [2]but he will call to remembrance *their* iniquity, to the intent they should be taken.

24 Therefore thus saith the Lord God, Because ye have made your iniquity to be remembered in discovering your rebellion, that in all your works your

sins might appear: because, *I say*, that ye are come to remembrance, ye shall be taken with the hand.

25 And thou [1]Prince of Israel polluted, *and* wicked, whose day is come, when iniquity *shall have* an end,

26 Thus saith the Lord God, I will take away the [1]diadem, and take off the crown: this shall be no more the same: I will exalt the humble, and will abase him that is high.

27 I will overturn, overturn, overturn it, and it shall be no more until he [1]come, whose right it is, and I will give it him.

28 ¶ And thou, son of man, prophesy, and say, Thus saith the Lord God to the children of Ammon, and to their blasphemy: say thou, I say, The sword, the sword is drawn forth *and* furbished to the slaughter, to consume, because of the glittering,

29 While they see [1]vanity unto thee, and prophesied a lie unto thee to bring thee upon the necks of the wicked that are slain, whose day is come, when their iniquity *shall have* an end.

30 Shall I cause it to return into his sheath? I will judge thee in the place where thou wast created, *even* in the land of thine habitation.

31 And I will pour out mine indignation upon thee, and will blow against thee in the fire of my wrath, and deliver thee into the hand of beastly men, *and* skillful to destroy.

32 Thou shalt be in the fire to be devoured: thy blood shall be in the midst of the land, *and* thou shalt be no more remembered: for I the Lord have spoken it.

22

1 Jerusalem is reproved for cruelty.   25 Of the wicked doctrine of the false prophets and priests, and of their unsatiable covetousness.   26 The tyranny of rulers.   29 The wickedness of the people.

1 Moreover, the word of the Lord came unto me, saying,

2 Now thou son of man, wilt thou [1]judge, wilt

21:14 [1] That is, encourage the sword.

21:16 [1] Provide for thyself: for thou shalt see God's plague of all parts on this country.

21:19 [1] This was spoken, because that when Nebuchadnezzar came against Judah, his purpose was also to go against the Ammonites: but doubting in the way, which enterprise to undertake first he consulted with his soothsayers, and so went against Judah.

21:20 [1] That is, to the tribe of Judah that kept themselves in Jerusalem.

21:21 [1] To know whether he should go against the Ammonites or them of Jerusalem.

[2] He used conjuring and sorcery.

21:23 [1] Because there was a league between the Jews, and the Babylonians, they of Jerusalem shall think nothing less than that this thing should come to pass.

[2] That is, Nebuchadnezzar will remember the rebellion of Zedekiah,

and so come upon them.

21:25 [1] Meaning, Zedekiah, who practiced with the Egyptians to make himself high and able to resist the Babylonians.

21:26 [1] Some refer this to the Priest's attire: for Jehozadak the Priest went into captivity with the king.

21:27 [1] That is, unto the coming of Messiah: for though the Jews had some sign of government afterward under the Persians, Greeks and Romans, yet this restitution was not till Christ's coming, and at length should be accomplished, as was promised, Gen. 49:10.

21:29 [1] Though the Jews and Ammonites would not believe that thou, to wit, the sword, shouldest come upon them, and said, that the Prophets, which threatened, spake lies, yet thou shalt as surely come, as though thou werest already upon their necks.

22:2 [1] Art thou ready to execute thy charge, which I commit unto thee against Jerusalem, that murdereth the Prophets and them that are godly?

thou judge this bloody city? wilt thou show her all her abominations?

3 Then say, Thus saith the Lord God, The city sheddeth blood in the midst of it, that her ¹time may come, and maketh idols against ²herself, to pollute herself.

4 Thou hast offended in thy blood, that thou hast shed, and hast polluted thyself in thine idols, which thou hast made, and thou hast caused thy days to draw near, and art come unto thy term: therefore have I made thee a reproach to the heathen, and a mocking to all countries.

5 Those that be near, and those that be far from thee, shall mock thee, *which art* vile in ¹name *and* sore in affliction.

6 Behold, the princes of Israel everyone in thee was *ready* to his power, to shed blood.

7 In thee have they despised father and mother: in the midst of thee ¹have they oppressed the stranger: in thee have they vexed the fatherless and the widow.

8 Thou hast despised mine holy things, and hast polluted my Sabbaths.

9 In thee are men that carry tales to shed blood: in thee *are they* that eat upon the mountains: in the midst of thee they commit abomination.

10 ᵃIn thee have they discovered their fathers' shame: in thee have they vexed her that was polluted in *her* flowers.

11 And everyone ᵇhath committed abomination with his neighbor's wife, and everyone hath wickedly defiled his daughter-in-law, and in thee hath every man forced his own sister, *even* his father's daughter.

12 In thee have they taken gifts to shed blood: thou hast taken usury and the increase, and thou hast defrauded thy neighbors by extortion, and hast forgotten me, saith the Lord God.

13 Behold, therefore I have ¹smitten mine hands upon thy covetousness, that thou hast used, and upon the blood, which hath been in the midst of thee.

14 Can thine heart endure, or can thine hands ¹be strong, in the days that I shall have to do with thee? I the Lord have spoken it, and will do it.

15 And I will scatter thee among the heathen, and disperse thee in the countries, and will cause

CHAPTER 22
ᵃ Lev. 20:11,18
ᵇ Jer. 5:8
ᶜ Mic. 3:11
  Zeph. 3:3

thy ¹filthiness to cease from thee.

16 And thou shalt take thine ¹inheritance in thyself in the sight of the heathen, and thou shalt know that I am the Lord.

17 ¶ And the word of the Lord came unto me, saying,

18 Son of man, the house of Israel is unto me as ¹dross: all they are brass, and tin, and iron, and lead, in the midst of the furnace: they are *even* the dross of silver.

19 Therefore thus saith the Lord God, Because ye are all as dross, behold, therefore I will gather you in the midst of Jerusalem.

20 As they gather silver and brass, and iron, and lead, and tin into the midst of the furnace, to blow the fire upon it to melt it, so will I gather you in mine anger and in my wrath, and will put you *there* ¹and melt you.

21 I will gather you, I say, and blow the fire of my wrath upon you, and you shall be melted in the midst thereof.

22 As silver is melted in the midst of the furnace, so shall ye be melted in the midst thereof, and ye shall know that I the Lord have poured out my wrath upon you.

23 And the word of the Lord came unto me, saying,

24 Son of man, say unto her, Thou art the land, that is unclean, ¹*and* not rained upon in the day of wrath.

25 *There is* a conspiracy ¹of her prophets in the midst thereof like a roaring lion, ravening the prey: they have devoured souls: they have taken the riches and precious things: they have made her many widows in the midst thereof.

26 Her Priests have broken my Law, and have defiled mine holy things: they have put no difference between the holy and profane, neither discerned between the unclean and the clean, and have hid their ¹eyes from my Sabbaths, and I am profaned among them.

27 Her princes in 'the midst thereof *are* like wolves, ravening the prey to shed blood, *and* to destroy souls for their own covetous lucre.

28 And her ¹prophets have daubed them with untempered *mortar*, seeing vanities, and divining

22:3 ¹ That is, the time of her destruction.
      ² To her own undoing.
22:5 ¹ Whose very name all men hate.
22:7 ¹ He meaneth hereby that there was no kind of wickedness which was not committed in Jerusalem, and therefore the plagues of God should speedily come upon her.
22:13 ¹ In token of my wrath and vengeance.
22:14 ¹ That is, able to defend thyself.
22:15 ¹ I will thus take away the occasion of thy wickedness.
22:16 ¹ Thou shalt be no more the inheritance of the Lord, but forsaken.

22:18 ¹ Which before was most precious.
22:20 ¹ Meaning, hereby that the godly should be tried, and the wicked destroyed.
22:24 ¹ Thou art like a barren land which the Lord plagueth with drought.
22:25 ¹ The false prophets have conspired together to make their doctrine more probable.
22:26 ¹ They have neglected my service.
22:28 ¹ They which should have reproved them, flattered them in their vices, and covered their doings with lies, Ezek. 13:10.

lies unto them, saying, Thus saith the Lord God, when the Lord had not spoken.

29 The people of the land have violently oppressed by spoiling and robbing, and have vexed the poor and the needy: yea, they have oppressed the stranger against right.

30 And I sought for a man among them, that should ¹make up the hedge, and stand in the gap before me for the land, that I should not destroy it, but I found none.

31 Therefore have I poured out mine indignation upon them, and consumed them with the fire of my wrath: their own ways have I rendered upon their heads, saith the Lord God.

23

Of the Idolatry of Samaria and Jerusalem, under the names of Oholah and Oholibah.

1 The word of the Lord came again unto me, saying,

2 Son of man, there were two women, the daughters of one ¹mother.

3 And they committed fornication in ¹Egypt, they committed fornication in their youth: there were their breasts pressed, and there they bruised the teats of their virginity.

4 And the names of ¹them *were* Oholah the elder, and Oholibah her sister: and they were mine, and they bare sons and daughters: thus *were* their names: Samaria *is* Oholah, and Jerusalem Oholibah.

5 And Oholah played the harlot ¹when ²she was mine, and she was set on fire with her lovers, *to wit*, with the Assyrians *her* neighbors,

6 Which were clothed with blue silk, *both* captains and princes they were all pleasant young men, *and* horsemen riding upon horses.

7 Thus she committed her whoredom with them, *even* with all them that were the chosen men of Assyria, and with all on whom she doted, *and* defiled herself with all their idols.

8 Neither left she her fornications, *learned* of the Egyptians: for in her youth they ¹lay with her, and they bruised the breasts of her virginity, and poured their whoredom upon her.

9 Wherefore I delivered her into the hands of her lovers, *even* into the hands of the Assyrians, upon whom she doted.

10 These discovered her shame: they took away her sons and her daughters, and slew her with the sword, and she had an *evil* name among women: for ¹they had executed judgment upon her.

11 And when her sister Oholibah saw this, she marred herself with inordinate love more than she, and with her fornications more than her sister with *her* fornications.

12 She doted upon the Assyrians *her* neighbors, *both* captains and princes clothed with divers suits, horsemen riding upon horses: they were all pleasant young men.

13 Then I saw that she was defiled, *and* that they were both after one sort,

14 And that she increased her fornications: for when she saw men ¹painted upon the wall, the images of the Chaldeans painted with vermilion,

15 And girded with girdles upon their loins, and with dyed attire upon their heads (looking all like princes after the manner of the Babylonians in Chaldea, the land of their nativity)

16 As soon, I say, as she saw them, she doted upon them, and sent messengers unto them, into Chaldea.

17 Now when the Babylonians came to her into the bed of love, they defiled her with their fornication, and she was polluted with them, and her lust departed from them.

18 So she discovered her fornication, and disclosed her shame: then mine heart forsook her, like as mine heart had forsaken her sister.

19 Yet she increased her whoredom more, and called to remembrance the days of her youth wherein she had played the harlot in the land of Egypt.

20 For she doted upon their servants whose members are *as* the members of asses, and whose issue is *like* the issue of horses.

21 Thou calledst to remembrance the wickedness of thy youth, when thy teats were bruised by the Egyptians: therefore the paps of thy youth *are thus.*

22 Therefore, O Oholibah, thus saith the Lord God, Behold, I will raise up thy lovers against thee, from whom thine heart is departed, and I will bring them against thee on every side,

---

22:30 ¹ Which would show himself zealous in my cause by resisting vice, Isa. 59:16 and 63:5, and also pray unto me to withhold my plagues, Ps. 106:23.
23:2 ¹ Meaning, Israel and Judah, which came both out of one family.
23:3 ¹ They became idolaters after the manner of the Egyptians.
23:4 ¹ Oholah signifieth a mansion or dwelling in herself, meaning Samaria, which was the royal city of Israel and Oholibah signifieth my mansion in her, whereby is meant Jerusalem, where God's Temple was.
23:5 ¹ Hebrew, *under me.*

² When the Israelites were named the people of God, they became idolaters, and forsook God, and put their trust in the Assyrians.
23:8 ¹ The holy Ghost useth these terms which seem strange to chaste ears, to cause this wicked vice of idolatry so to be abhorred, that [...] any should abide to hear the name thereof.
23:10 ¹ Meaning, the Assyrians.
23:14 ¹ This declareth that no words are able sufficiently to express the rage of idolaters, and therefore the holy Ghost here compareth them to those which in their raging love and filthy lusts dote upon the images and paintings of them after whom they lust.

23 *To wit*, the Babylonians, and all the Chaldeans, [1]Pekod, and Shoa, and Koa, *and* all the Assyrians with them: they were all pleasant young men, captains and princes: all they were valiant and renowned, riding upon horses.

24 Even these shall come against thee with chariots, wagons, and wheels, and with a multitude of people, *which* shall set against thee buckler and shield, and helmet round about, and [1]I will leave the punishment unto them, and they shall judge thee according to their [2]judgments.

25 And I will lay mine indignation upon thee, and they shall deal cruelly with thee: they shall cut off thy [1]nose and thine ears, and thy remnant shall fall by the sword: they shall carry away thy sons and thy daughters, and thy residue shall be devoured by the fire.

26 They shall also strip thee out of thy clothes, and take away thy fair jewels.

27 Thus will I make thy wickedness to cease from thee, and thy fornication out of the land of Egypt: so that thou shalt not lift up thine eyes unto them, nor remember Egypt anymore.

28 For thus saith the Lord God, Behold, I will deliver thee into the hand of them, whom thou hatest, *even* into the hands of them from whom thine heart is departed.

29 And they shall handle thee despitefully, and shall take away all thy [1]labor, and shall leave thee naked and bare, and the shame of thy fornications [2]shall be discovered, both thy wickedness, and thy whoredom.

30 I will do these things unto thee, because thou hast gone a whoring after the heathen, *and* because thou art polluted with their idols.

31 Thou hast walked in the way of thy sister: therefore will I give her [1]cup into thine hand.

32 Thus saith the Lord God, Thou shalt drink of thy sister's cup, deep and large: thou shalt be laughed to scorn and had in derision, because it containeth much.

33 Thou shalt be filled with [1]drunkenness and sorrow, *even* with the cup of destruction, and desolation, with the cup of thy sister Samaria.

34 Thou shalt even drink it, and wring it out *to the dregs*, and thou shalt break the shards thereof, and tear thine own breasts: for I have spoken it, saith

the Lord God.

35 Therefore thus saith the Lord God, Because thou hast forgotten me, and cast me behind thy back, therefore thou shalt also bear thy wickedness and thy whoredom.

36 ¶ The Lord said moreover unto me, Son of man, wilt thou judge Oholah and Oholibah? and wilt thou declare to them their abominations?

37 For they have played the whores, and blood *is* in their hands, and with their idols have they committed adultery, and have also caused their sons, whom they bore unto me, to pass *by the fire* to be their [1]meat.

38 Moreover, thus have they done unto me: they have defiled my Sanctuary in the same day, and have profaned my Sabbaths.

39 For when they had slain their children to their idols, they came the same day into my Sanctuary to defile it: and lo, thus have they done in the midst of mine house.

40 And how much more *is it* that they sent for men to come from [1]far, unto whom a messenger was sent, and lo, they came? for whom thou didst wash thyself, and paintedst thine eyes, and deckedst thee with ornaments,

41 And satest [1]upon a costly bed, and a table prepared before it, whereupon thou hast set mine incense and mine oil.

42 And a voice of a multitude being at ease, *was* with her: and with the men to make the company great, were brought men of [1]Saba from the wilderness, which put bracelets upon their hands, and beautiful crowns upon their heads.

43 Then I said unto her that was old in adulteries, Now shall she and her fornications come to an end.

44 And they went in unto her as they go to a common harlot: so went they to Oholah and Oholibah the wicked women.

45 And the righteous men they shall judge them after the manner of [1]harlots, and after the manner of murderers: for they are harlots, and blood *is* in their hands.

46 Wherefore thus saith the Lord God, I will bring a multitude upon them, and will give them unto the tumult and to the spoil,

47 And the multitude shall stone them with stones,

23:23 [1] These were the names of certain princes and captains under Nebuchadnezzar.

23:24 [1] Hebrew, *I will give judgment before them.*
    [2] Or, laws.

23:25 [1] They shall destroy thy princes and priests with the rest of thy people.

23:29 [1] All thy treasures and riches which thou hast gotten by labor.
    [2] All the world shall see thy shameful forsaking of God to serve idols.

23:31 [1] I will execute the same judgments and vengeance against

thee, and that with greater severity.

23:33 [1] Meaning, that its afflictions should be so great that they should cause them to lose their senses, and reason.

23:37 [1] That is, to be sacrifices to their idols, read Ezek. 16:20.

23:40 [1] They sent into other countries to have such as should teach the service of their idols.

23:41 [1] He meaneth the altar that was prepared for the idols.

23:42 [1] Which should teach the manner of worshipping their gods.

23:45 [1] That is, worthy of death, read Ezek. 16:38.

and cut them with their swords: they shall slay their sons, and their daughters, and burn up their houses with fire.

48 Thus will I cause wickedness to cease out of the land, that all [1]women may be taught not to do after your wickedness.

49 And they shall lay your wickedness upon you, and ye shall bear the sins of your idols, and ye shall know that I am the Lord God.

24

He showeth the destruction of Jerusalem by a parable of a seething pot. 16 *The parable of Ezekiel's wife being dead.*

CHAPTER 24
[a] Nah. 3:1
Hab. 2:12

1 Again in the [1]ninth year, in the tenth month, in the tenth *day* of the [2]month, came the word of the Lord unto me, saying,

2 Son of man, write thee the name of the day, *even* of this same day: *for* the King of Babel set himself against Jerusalem this same day.

3 Therefore speak a parable unto the rebellious house, and say unto them, Thus saith the Lord God, Prepare a [1]pot, prepare it, and also pour water into it.

4 Gather the [1]pieces thereof into it, *even* every good piece, *as* the thigh and the shoulder, *and* fill it with the chief bones.

5 Take one of the best sheep, and [1]burn also the [2]bones under it, *and* make it boil well, and seethe the bones of it therein,

6 Because the Lord God saith thus, Woe to the bloody city, *even* to the pot, [1]whose scum is therein, and whose scum is not gone out of it: bring it out [2]piece by piece: let no [3]lot fall upon it.

7 For her blood is in the midst of her: she set it upon an high [1]rock, *and* poured it not upon the ground to cover it with dust,

8 That it might cause wrath to arise, and take vengeance: *even* I have set her blood upon an high rock that it should not be covered.

9 Therefore thus saith the Lord God, [a]Woe to the bloody city, for I will make [1]the burning great.

10 Heap on much wood: [1]kindle the fire, consume the flesh, and cast in spice, and let the bones be burnt.

11 Then set it empty upon the coals thereof, that [1]the brass of it may be hot, and may burn, and that the filthiness of it may be molten in it, *and* that the scum of it may be consumed.

12 [1]She hath wearied herself with lies, and her great scum went not out of her: *therefore* her scum *shall be consumed* with fire.

13 *Thou remainest* in thy filthiness *and* wickedness: because I would [1]have purged thee, and thou wast not purged, thou shalt not be purged from thy filthiness, till I have caused my wrath to light upon thee.

14 I the Lord have spoken it: it shall come to pass, and I will do it: I will not go back, neither will I spare, neither will I repent: according to thy ways, and according to thy works shall [1]they judge thee, saith the Lord God.

15 ¶ Also the word of the Lord came unto me, saying,

16 Son of man, behold, I take away from thee the [1]pleasure of thine eyes with a plague: yet shalt thou neither mourn nor weep, neither shall thy tears run down.

17 Cease from sighing: make no mourning for the dead, *and* bind the tire of thine head upon thee, [1]and put on thy shoes upon thy feet, *and* cover not thy lips, and eat [2]not the bread of men.

18 So I spake unto the people in the morning, and at even my wife died: and I did in [1]the morning, as I was commanded.

19 And the people said unto me, Wilt thou not tell us what these things mean toward us that thou doest so?

20 Then I answered them, The word of the Lord came unto me, saying,

21 Speak unto the house of Israel, Thus saith the Lord God, behold, I will [1]pollute my Sanctuary, *even* the [2]pride of your power, the pleasure of your eyes, and

---

23:48 [1] Meaning, all other cities and countries.
24:1 [1] Of Jeconiah's captivity, and of the reign of Zedekiah, 2 Kings 25:1.
  [2] Called Tebeth, which containeth part of December and part of January: in the which month and day Nebuchadnezzar besieged Jerusalem.
24:3 [1] Whereby was meant Jerusalem.
24:4 [1] That is the citizens, and the chief men thereof.
24:5 [1] Or, heap.
  [2] Meaning, of the innocents, whom they had slain, who were the cause of the kindling of God's wrath against them.
24:6 [1] Whose iniquities and wicked citizens there yet remain.
  [2] Signifying that they should not be destroyed all at once, but by little and little.
  [3] Spare none estate or condition.
24:7 [1] The city showed her cruelty to all the world, and was not ashamed thereof, neither yet hid it.
24:9 [1] Or, an heap of wood.
24:10 [1] Meaning, that the city should be utterly destroyed, and that he would give the enemies an appetite thereunto.
24:11 [1] Or, bottom.
24:12 [1] The city hath flattered herself in vain.
24:13 [1] I labored by sending my Prophets to call thee to repentance, but thou wouldest not.
24:14 [1] That is, the Babylonians.
24:16 [1] Meaning, his wife, in whom he delighted, as verse 18.
24:17 [1] For in mourning they went bareheaded and barefooted, and also covered their lips.
  [2] That is, which the neighbors sent to them that mourned.
24:18 [1] Meaning, the morning following.
24:21 [1] By sending the Chaldeans to destroy it, as Ezek. 7:22.
  [2] Wherein you boast and delight.

your heart's desire, and your sons, and your daughters whom ye have left, shall fall by the sword.

22 And ye shall do as I have done: ye shall not cover your lips, neither shall ye eat the bread of men.

23 And your tire *shall be* upon your heads, and your shoes upon your feet: ye shall not mourn nor weep, but ye shall pine away for your iniquities, and mourn one toward another.

24 Thus Ezekiel is unto you a sign: according to all that he hath done, ye shall do: and when this cometh, ye shall know that I am the Lord God.

25 Also, thou son of man, shall it not be in the day when I take from them their power, the joy of their honor, the pleasure of their eyes, and the ¹desire of their heart, their sons and their daughters,

26 That he that escapeth in that day, shall come unto thee *to tell thee* that which he hath heard with *his* ears?

27 In that day shall thy mouth be opened to him which is escaped, and thou shalt speak, and be no more dumb, and thou shalt be a sign unto them, and they shall know that I am the Lord.

25

1 The word of the Lord came again unto me, saying,

2 Son of man, set thy face against the Ammonites, and prophesy against them,

3 And say unto the Ammonites, Hear the word of the Lord God, Thus saith the Lord God, Because thou saidest, ¹Ha, ha, against my Sanctuary, when it was polluted, and against the land of Israel, when it was desolate, and against the house of Judah, when they went into captivity,

4 Behold, therefore I will deliver thee to the ¹men of the East for a possession, and they shall set their ²palaces in thee, and make their dwellings in thee: they shall eat thy fruit, and they shall drink thy milk:

5 And I will make ¹Rabbah a dwelling place for camels, and the Ammonites a sheepcote, and ye shall know that I am the Lord.

6 For thus saith the Lord God, Because thou hast clapped the hands, and stamped with the feet, and rejoiced in heart with all thy despite against the land of Israel,

7 Behold, therefore I will stretch out mine hand

upon thee, and will deliver thee to be spoiled of the heathen, and I will root thee out from the people, and I will cause thee to be destroyed out of the countries, *and* I will destroy thee, and thou shalt know that I am the Lord.

8 Thus saith the Lord God, Because that Moab and Seir do say, Behold, the house of Judah is like unto all the heathen,

9 Therefore, behold, I will open the side of Moab, *even* of the cities ¹of his cities, *I say,* in his frontiers with the pleasant country, Beth Jeshimoth, Baal Meon, and Kirjathaim.

10 *I will call* the men of the East against the Ammonites, and will give them in possession, so that the Ammonites shall no more be remembered among the nations.

11 And I will execute judgments upon Moab, and they shall know that I am the Lord.

12 ¶ Thus saith the Lord God, because that Edom hath done *evil* by taking vengeance upon the house of Judah, and hath committed great offence, and revenged himself upon them,

13 Therefore thus saith the Lord God, I will also stretch out mine hand upon Edom, and destroy man and beast out of it, and I will make it desolate from Teman, and they of Dedan shall fall by the sword.

14 And I will execute my vengeance upon Edom by the hand of my people Israel, and they shall do in Edom according to mine anger, and according to mine indignation, and they shall know my vengeance, saith the Lord God.

15 Thus saith the Lord God, Because the Philistines have executed vengeance, and revenged themselves with a despiteful heart, to destroy it for the old hatred,

16 Therefore thus saith the Lord God, behold, I will stretch out mine hand upon the Philistines, and I will cut off the ¹Cherethims, and destroy the remnant of the seacoast.

17 And I will execute great vengeance upon them with rebukes of mine indignation, and they shall know that I am the Lord, when I shall lay my vengeance upon them.

26

1 And in the ¹eleventh year in the first day of

24:25 ¹ Hebrew, *lifting up of their souls.*
25:3 ¹ Because ye rejoiced when the enemy destroyed my city and Temple.
25:4 ¹ That is, to the Babylonians.
² They shall chase thee away, and take thy gorgeous houses to dwell in.
25:5 ¹ Called also Philadelphin, which was the chief city of the Ammonites, and full of conduits, 2 Sam. 12:27.

25:9 ¹ So that no power or strength should be able to resist the Babylonians.
25:16 ¹ Which were certain garrisons of Philistines, whereby they ofttimes molested the Jews, of the Cherethims David also had a guard, 2 Sam. 8:18.
26:1 ¹ Either of the captivity of Jeconiah, or of the reign of Zedekiah.

the month, the word of the Lord came unto me, saying,

2 Son of man, because that Tyre hath said against Jerusalem, Aha, the ¹gate of the people is broken: it is turned unto me: *for* seeing she is desolate, I shall be ²replenished,

3 Therefore thus saith the Lord God, Behold, I come against thee, O Tyre, and I will bring up many nations against thee, as the sea mounteth up with his waves.

4 And they shall destroy the walls of Tyre and break down her towers: I will also scrape her dust from her, and make her like the top of a rock.

5 Thou shalt be for the spreading of nets in the midst of the sea: for I have spoken it, saith the Lord God, and it shall be a spoil to the nations.

6 And her ¹daughters which are in the field, shall be slain by the sword, and they shall know that I am the Lord.

7 For thus saith the Lord God, Behold, I will bring upon Tyre Nebuchadnezzar king of Babel, a King of kings from the North, with horses and with chariots, and with horsemen, with a multitude and much people.

8 He shall slay with the sword thy daughters in the field, and he shall make a fort against thee, and cast a mount against thee, and lift up the buckler against thee.

9 He shall set engines of war before him against thy walls, and with his weapons break down thy towers.

10 The dust of his horses shall cover thee, for their multitude: thy walls shall shake at the noise of the horsemen, and of the wheels, and of the chariots, when he shall enter into thy gates as into the entry of a city that is broken down.

11 With the hooves of his horses shall he tread down all thy streets: he shall slay the people by the sword, and the ¹pillars of thy strength shall fall down to the ground.

12 And they shall rob thy riches, and spoil thy merchandise, and they shall break down thy walls, and destroy thy pleasant houses, and they shall cast thy stones and thy timber and thy dust into the midst of the water.

13 ᵃThus will I cause the sound of thy songs to

CHAPTER 26
ᵃ Jer. 7:34

cease, and the sound of thine harps shall be no more heard.

14 I will lay thee like the top of a rock: ¹thou shalt be for a spreading of nets: thou shalt be built no more: for I the Lord have spoken it, saith the Lord God.

15 Thus saith the Lord God to Tyre, Shall not the isles tremble at the sound of thy fall? and at the cry of the wounded, when they shall be slain and murdered in the midst of thee?

16 Then all the princes of the ¹sea shall come down from their thrones: they shall lay away their robes, and put off their broidered garments, and shall clothe themselves with astonishment: they shall sit upon the ground and be astonished at *every* moment, and be amazed at thee.

17 And they shall take up a lamentation for thee, and say to thee, How art thou destroyed, that wast inhabited ¹of the Sea *men*, the renowned city which was strong in the sea, *both* she and her inhabitants, which cause their fear to be on all that haunt therein!

18 Now shall the isles be astonished in the day of thy fall: yea, the isles that are in the sea, shall be troubled at thy departure.

19 For thus saith the Lord God, when I shall make thee a desolate city, like the cities that are not inhabited, and when I shall bring the deep upon thee, and great waters shall cover thee,

20 When I shall cast thee down with them that descend into the pit, with the people ¹of old time, and shall set thee in the low parts of the earth, like the old ruins, with them, *I say*, which go down to the pit, so that thou shalt not be inhabited, and I shall show my glory in the land of the ²living.

21 I will ¹bring thee to nothing, and thou shalt be no *more*: though thou be sought for, yet shalt thou never be found again, saith the Lord God.

27
The Prophet bewaileth the desolation of Tyre, showing what were the riches, power and authority thereof in times past.

1 The word of the Lord came again unto me, saying,

2 Son of man, take up a lamentation for Tyre,

3 And say unto Tyre that is situated at the entry

26:2 ¹ That is, the famous city Jerusalem, whereunto all people resorted.
² My riches and fame shall increase: thus the wicked rejoice at their fall by whom they may have any profit or advantage.
26:6 ¹ The towns that belonged unto her.
26:11 ¹ For Tyre was much built by art and by labor of men was won out of the Sea. Some refer this unto the images of the noble men which they had erected up for their glory and renown.
26:14 ¹ I will make thee so bare that thou shalt have nothing to

cover thee.
26:16 ¹ The governors and rulers of other countries that dwell by the sea: whereby he signifieth that her destruction should be so horrible, that all the world should hear thereof and be afraid.
26:17 ¹ Meaning, merchants which by their traffic did enrich her wonderfully and increase her power.
26:20 ¹ Which were dead long ago.
² Meaning, in Judea, when it shall be restored.
26:21 ¹ Or, make thee a terror.

of the sea, which is the mart [1]of the people for many isles, Thus saith the Lord God, O Tyre, thou hast said, I am of perfect beauty.

4   Thy borders are in the [1]midst of the sea, *and* thy builders have made thee of perfect beauty.

5   They have made all thy *ship* boards of fir trees of [1]Senir: they have brought cedars from Lebanon, to make masts for thee.

6   Of the oaks of Bashan have they made thine ores: the company of the Assyrians have made thy banks of ivory, *brought* out of the isles of [1]Kittim.

7   Fine linen with broidered work, *brought* from Egypt, was spread over thee to be thy sail, blue silk and purple, *brought* from the isles of Elishah was thy covering.

8   The inhabitants of Sidon, and Arvad were thy mariners, O Tyre: thy wise men that were in thee, they were thy [1]pilots.

9   The ancients of Gebal, and the wise men thereof were in thee thy [1]caulkers, all the ships of the sea with their mariners were in thee to occupy thy merchandise.

10   They of Persia, and of Lud and of Put were in thine army: thy men of war they hanged the shield and helmet in thee: they set forth thy beauty.

11   The men of Arvad with thine army *were* upon thy walls round about, and the [1]Gammadims were in thy towers: they hanged their shields upon thy walls round about: they have made thy beauty perfect.

12   They of Tarshish *were* thy merchants for the multitude of all riches, for silver, iron, tin, and lead, *which* they brought to thy fairs.

13   They of [1]Javan, Tubal and Meshech were thy merchants, [2]concerning the lives of men, and they brought vessels of brass for thy merchandise.

14   They of the house of [1]Togarmah brought to thy fairs, horses and horsemen, and mules.

15   The men of Dedan *were* thy merchants: and the merchandise of many isles *were* in thine hands: they brought thee for a present, [1]horns, teeth, and peacocks.

16   They of Aram *were* thy merchants for the multitude of thy [1]wares: they occupied in thy fairs, with [2]emeralds, purple, and broidered work, and [3]fine linen, and coral, and pearl.

17   They of Judah and of the land of Israel were thy merchants: they brought for thy merchandise wheat of [1]Minnith, and Pannag, and honey, and oil, and [2]balm.

18   They of Damascus *were* thy merchants in the multitude of thy wares, for the multitude of all riches, *as* in the wine of Helbon and white wool.

19   They of Dan also and of Javan, going to and fro, occupied in thy fairs: iron work, cassia and calamus were among thy merchandise.

20   They of Dedan *were* thy merchants in precious clothes for the chariots.

21   They of Arabia, and all the princes of Kedar [1]occupied with thee, in lambs, and rams and goats: in these were thy merchants.

22   The merchants of Sheba, and Raamah were thy merchants: they occupied in thy fairs with the chief of all spices, and with all precious stones and gold.

23   They of Haram and Canneh and Eden, the merchants of Sheba, Assyria *and* Chilmad *were* thy merchants.

24   These were thy merchants in all sorts *of things*, in raiment of blue silk, and of broidered work, and in coffers for the rich apparel, which were bound with cords: chains also *were* among thy merchandise.

25   The ships of Tarshish [1]were thy chief in thy merchandise, and thou wast replenished and made very glorious in the midst of the sea.

26   Thy [1]robbers have brought thee into great waters: the [2]East wind hath broken thee in the midst of the sea.

27   Thy riches and thy fairs, thy merchandise, thy mariners and pilots, thy caulkers, and the occupiers of thy merchandise, and all thy men of war that are in thee, and all thy multitude which is in the midst of thee, shall fall in the midst of the sea in the day of thy ruin.

28   The [1]suburbs shall shake at the sound of the cry of thy pilots.

27:3 [1] Which servest all the world with thy merchandise.
27:4 [1] Hebrew, *heart*.
27:5 [1] This mountain was called Hermon, but the Amorites called it Senir, Deut. 3:9.
27:6 [1] Which is taken for Greece and Italy.
27:8 [1] Or, shipmasters.
27:9 [1] Meaning, that they built the walls of the city, which is here meant by the ship: and of these were the builders of Solomon's Temple, 1 Kings 5:18.
27:11 [1] That is, they of Cappadocia, or Pygmies and dwarfs, which were so called, because that out of the high towers they seemed little.
27:13 [1] Of Greece, Italy and Cappadocia.
  [2] By selling slaves.
27:14 [1] Which are taken for a people of Asia minor.
27:15 [1] Meaning, Unicorn's horns, and Elephant's teeth.
27:16 [1] Or, works.
  [2] Or, carbuncle.
  [3] Or, silk.
27:17 [1] Where the best wheat grew.
  [2] Or, turpentine, or, treacle.
27:21 [1] Or, were merchants whose merchandise passed through thine hands.
27:25 [1] Or, came in company toward thee.
27:26 [1] Or, rowers.
  [2] That is, Nebuchadnezzar.
27:28 [1] That is, the cities near about thee, as was Zidon, Arvad, and others.

29 And all that handle the oar, the mariners *and* all the pilots of the sea shall come down from their ships, *and* shall stand upon the land,

30 And shall cause their voice to be heard against thee, and shall cry bitterly, and shall cast dust upon their heads, and wallow themselves in the ashes.

31 They shall pluck off their hair for thee, and gird them with a sackcloth, and they shall weep for thee with sorrow of heart *and* bitter mourning.

32 And in their mourning, they shall take up a lamentation for thee, *saying*, What *city* is like Tyre so destroyed in the midst of the sea!

33 When thy wares went forth of the seas, thou filledst many people, *and* thou didst enrich the Kings of the earth with the multitude of thy riches and of thy merchandise.

34 When thou shalt be broken by the seas in the depths of the waters, thy merchandise and all thy multitude which was in the midst of thee, shall fall.

35 All the inhabitants of the isles shall be astonished at thee, and all their Kings shall be sore afraid *and* troubled in their countenance.

36 The merchants among the people shall hiss at thee: thou shalt be a terror, and never shalt be [1]anymore.

28

2 The word of God against the king of Tyre for his pride.   21 The word of the Lord against Sidon.   25 The Lord promises that he will gather together the children of Israel.

1 The word of the Lord came again unto me, saying,

2 Son of man, say unto the prince of Tyre, Thus saith the Lord God, because thine heart is exalted, and thou hast said, [1]I am a god, I sit in the seat of God in the midst of the sea, yet thou art but a man and not God, and [2]though thou didst think in thine heart, that thou wast equal with God,

3 Behold, thou art wiser than [1]Daniel: there is no secret that they can hide from thee.

4 With thy wisdom and thine understanding thou hast gotten thee riches, and hast gotten gold and silver into thy treasures.

5 By thy great wisdom *and* by thine occupying hast thou increased thy riches, and thine heart is lifted up because of thy riches.

6 Therefore thus saith the Lord God, Because thou didst think in thine heart, that thou wast equal with God,

7 Behold, therefore I will bring strangers upon thee, *even* the terrible nations: and they shall draw their swords against the beauty of thy wisdom, and they shall defile thy brightness.

8 They shall cast thee down to the pit, and thou shalt die the death of them, that are slain in the midst of the sea.

9 Wilt thou say *then* before him that slayeth thee, I am a god? but thou shalt be a man, and no god, in the hands of him that slayeth thee.

10 Thou shalt die the death of the [1]uncircumcised by the hands of strangers: for I have spoken it, saith the Lord God.

11 ¶ Moreover, the word of the Lord came unto me, saying,

12 Son of man, take up a lamentation upon the King of Tyre, and say unto him, Thus saith the Lord God, Thou sealest up the sum, *and* art full of [1]wisdom, and perfect in beauty.

13 Thou hast been in Eden the garden of God: every precious stone *was* in thy garment, the ruby, the topaz, and the [1]diamond, the chrysolite, the onyx, and the jasper, the sapphire, [2]emerald, and the carbuncle and gold: the workmanship of thy timbrels, and of thy pipes was prepared in thee in the day that thou wast created.

14 Thou art [1]the anointed Cherub, that covereth, and I have set thee [2]in honor: thou wast upon the holy mountain of God: thou hast walked in the midst of the [3]stones of fire.

15 Thou wast perfect in thy ways from the day that thou wast [1]created, till iniquity was found in thee.

16 By the multitude of thy merchandise, they have filled the midst of thee with cruelty, and thou hast sinned: therefore I will cast thee as profane out of the [1]mountain of God: and I will destroy thee, O covering Cherub, from the midst of the stones of fire.

17 Thine heart was lifted up because of thy beauty,

27:36 [1] Whereby is meant a long time: for it was prophesied to be destroyed but seventy years, Isa. 23:15.

28:2 [1] I am safe that none can come to hurt me, as God is in the heaven.

   [2] Hebrew, *though thou set thine heart as the heart of God.*

28:3 [1] Thus he speaketh by derision: for Daniel had declared notable signs of his wisdom in Babylon, when Ezekiel wrote this.

28:10 [1] Like the rest of the heathen and infidels, which are God's enemies.

28:12 [1] He derideth the vain opinion and confidence that the Tyrians had in their riches, strength and pleasures.

28:13 [1] Or, jasper.
   [2] Or, carbuncle.

28:14 [1] He meaneth the royal state of Tyre, which for the excellency and glory thereof he compareth to the Cherubims which covered the Ark: and by this word *anointed* he signifieth the same.
   [2] I did thee this honor to make thee one of the builders of my Temple, which was when Hiram sent unto Solomon things necessary for the work.
   [3] To wit, among my people Israel, which shined as precious stones.

28:15 [1] Which was when I first called thee to this dignity.

28:16 [1] Thou shalt have no part among my people.

and thou hast corrupted thy wisdom by reason of thy brightness: I will cast thee to the ground. I will lay thee before kings that they may behold thee.

18 Thou hast defiled thy [1]sanctification by the multitude of thine iniquities, *and* by the iniquity of thy merchandise: therefore will I bring forth a fire from the midst of thee, which shall devour thee: and I will bring thee to ashes upon the earth, in the sight of all them that behold thee.

19 All they that know thee among the people, shall be astonished at thee: thou shalt be [1]a terror, and never shalt thou be anymore.

20 ¶ Again the word of the Lord came unto me, saying,

21 Son of man, set thy face against Sidon, and prophesy against it,

22 And say, Thus saith the Lord God, Behold, I *come* against thee, O Sidon, and I will be [1]glorified in the midst of thee: and they shall know that I am the Lord, when I shall have executed judgments in her, and shall be sanctified in her.

23 For I will send into her pestilence, and blood into her streets, and the slain shall fall in the midst of her: [1]*the enemy shall come* against her with the sword on every side, and they shall know that I am the Lord.

24 And they shall be no more a pricking thorn unto the house of Israel, nor *any* grievous thorn of all that are round about them, and despised them, and they shall know that I am the Lord God.

25 Thus saith the Lord God, When I shall have gathered the house of Israel from the people where they are scattered, and shall be [1]sanctified in them in the sight of the heathen, then shall they dwell in the land, that I have given to my servant Jacob.

26 And they shall dwell safely therein, and shall build houses, and plant vineyards: yea, they shall dwell safely, when I have executed judgments upon all round about them that despise them, and they shall know that I am the Lord their God.

29

He prophesieth against Pharaoh and Egypt.   13 The Lord promiseth that he will restore Egypt after forty years.   18 Egypt is the reward of King Nebuchadnezzar for the labor which he took against Tyre.

1 In the [1]tenth year *and* in the tenth month, in the twelfth *day* of the month, the word of the Lord came unto me, saying,

2 Son of man, set thy face against Pharaoh the king of Egypt, and prophesy against him, and against all Egypt.

3 Speak, and say, Thus saith the Lord God, Behold, I *come* against thee, Pharaoh king of Egypt, the great [1]dragon, that lieth in the midst of his rivers, which hath said, The river is mine, and I have made it for myself.

4 But I will put [1]hooks in thy jaws, and I will cause the fish of thy rivers to stick unto thy scales, and I will draw thee out of the midst of thy rivers, and all the fish of thy rivers shall stick unto thy scales.

5 And I will leave thee in the wilderness, *both* thee and all the fish of thy rivers: thou shalt fall upon the open field: thou shalt not be brought together, nor gathered: *for* I have given thee for meat to the beasts of the field, and to the fowls of heaven.

6 And all the inhabitants of Egypt shall know that I am the Lord, because they have been a staff of [1]reed to the house of Israel.

7 When they took hold of thee with their hand, thou didst break and rent all their shoulder: and when they leaned upon thee, thou brakest and madest all their loins to [1]stand [2]upright.

8 Therefore thus saith the Lord God, Behold, I will bring a sword upon thee, and destroy man and beast out of thee.

9 And the land of Egypt shall be desolate, and waste, and they shall know that I am the Lord: because he hath said, [1]The river is mine, and I have made it.

10 Behold, therefore I *come* upon thee, and upon thy rivers, and I will make the land of Egypt utterly waste and desolate from the tower of Syene, even unto the borders of the [1]black Moors.

11 No foot of man shall pass by it, nor foot of beast shall pass by it, neither shall it be inhabited forty years.

12 And I will make the land of Egypt desolate in the midst of the countries that are desolate, and her cities shall be desolate among the cities that are desolate for forty years: and I will scatter the Egyptians among the nations, and will disperse them through the countries.

28:18 [1] That is, the honor, whereunto I called them.
28:19 [1] Or, brought to nothing.
28:22 [1] By executing my judgments against thy wickedness.
28:23 [1] That is, Nebuchadnezzar.
28:25 [1] He showeth for what cause God will assemble his Church, and preserve it still, though he destroy his enemies: to wit, that they should praise him, and give thanks for his great mercies.
29:1 [1] To wit, of the captivity of Jeconiah, or of the reign of Zedekiah. Of the order of these prophecies, and how the former sometimes standeth after the latter, read Jer. 27:1.

29:3 [1] He compareth Pharaoh to a dragon which hideth himself in the river Nile, as Isa. 51:9.
29:4 [1] I will send enemies against thee, which shall pluck thee, and thy people which trust in thee, out of thy sure places.
29:6 [1] Read 2 Kings 18:21; Isa. 36:6.
29:7 [1] Or, shake.
[2] When they felt their hurt, they would stay no more upon thee, but stood upon their feet, and put their trust in others.
29:9 [1] Thus God cannot suffer that man should arrogate anything to himself, or put his trust in anything save in him alone.
29:10 [1] Hebrew, *Cush*, or *Ethiopia*.

13 Yet thus saith the Lord God, ^aAt the end of forty years will I gather the Egyptians from the people, where they were scattered,

14 And I will bring again the captivity of Egypt, and will cause them to return into the land of Pathros, into the land of their habitation, and they shall be there a ¹small kingdom.

15 It shall be the smallest of the kingdoms, neither shall it exalt itself anymore above the nations: for I will diminish them, that they shall no more rule the nations.

16 And it shall be no more the confidence of the house of Israel, to bring their ¹iniquity to remembrance by looking after them, so shall they know that I am the Lord God.

17 ¶ In the ¹seven and twentieth year also in the first month, and in the first day of the month, came the word of the Lord unto me, saying,

18 Son of man, Nebuchadnezzar king of Babel caused his army to serve a great ¹service against Tyre: every head was made bald, and every shoulder was made bare: yet he had no wages, ²nor his army for Tyre, for the service that he served against it.

19 Therefore thus saith the Lord God, Behold, I will give the land of Egypt unto Nebuchadnezzar the king of Babel, and he shall take her multitude, and spoil her spoil, and take her prey, and it shall be the wages for his army.

20 I have given him the land of Egypt for his labor, that he served ¹against it, because they wrought ²for me, saith the Lord God.

21 In that day will I cause the horn of the house of Israel to grow, and I will give thee an open mouth in the midst of them, and they shall know that I am the Lord.

30

The destruction of Egypt and the cities thereof.

1 The word of the Lord came again unto me, saying,

2 Son of man, prophesy, and say, Thus saith the Lord God, Howl and cry, Woe be unto this day.

3 For the day is near, and the day of the Lord is at hand, a cloudy day, and it shall be the time of the heathen.

4 And the sword shall come upon Egypt, and

CHAPTER 29
^a Jer. 46:26

fear shall be in Ethiopia, when the slain shall fall in Egypt, when they shall take away her multitude, and when her foundations shall be broken down.

5 ¹Ethiopia and Put, and Lud, and all the common people, and Chub, and the men of the land, that is in league, shall fall with them by the sword.

6 Thus saith the Lord, They also that maintain Egypt, shall fall, and the pride of her power shall come down: from the tower of ¹Syene shall they fall by the sword, saith the Lord God.

7 And they shall be desolate in the midst of the countries that are desolate, and her cities shall be in the midst of the cities that are wasted.

8 And they shall know that I am the Lord, when I have set a fire in Egypt, and when all her helpers shall be destroyed.

9 In that day shall there messengers go forth from me in ships, to make the careless Moors afraid, and fear shall come upon them, as in the day of Egypt: for lo, it cometh.

10 Thus saith the Lord God, I will also make the multitude of Egypt to cease by the hand of Nebuchadnezzar king of Babel.

11 For he and his people with him, even the terrible nations shall be brought to destroy the land: and they shall draw their swords against Egypt, and fill the land with the slain.

12 And I will make the rivers dry, and sell the land into the hands of the wicked, and I will make the land waste, and all that therein is by the hands of strangers: I the Lord have spoken it.

13 Thus saith the Lord God, I will also destroy the idols, and I will cause their idols to cease out of ¹Noph, and there shall be no more a prince of the land of Egypt, and I will send a fear in the land of Egypt.

14 And I will make Pathros desolate, and will set fire in ¹Zoan, and I will execute judgment in No.

15 And I will pour my wrath upon ¹Sin, which is the strength of Egypt: and I will destroy the multitude of ²No.

16 And I will set fire in Egypt: Sin shall have great sorrow, and No shall be destroyed, and Noph shall have sorrows daily.

17 The young men of ¹Aven, and of ²Pi Beseth

29:14 ¹ Meaning, that they should not have full dominion, but be under the Persians, Greeks and Romans, and the cause is that the Israelites should no more put their trust in them, but learn to depend on God.
29:16 ¹ Lest I should by this means punish their sins.
29:17 ¹ Counting from the captivity of Jeconiah.
29:18 ¹ He took great pains at the siege of Tyre, and his army was sore handled.
    ² Signifying that Nebuchadnezzar had more pains than profit, by the taking of Tyre.

29:20 ¹ Or, in it.
    ² Or, evil against me.
30:5 ¹ By Put and Lud are meant Africa and Libya.
30:6 ¹ Which was a strong city of Egypt, Ezek. 29:10.
30:13 ¹ Or, Memphis, or Cairo.
30:14 ¹ Or, Tanis.
30:15 ¹ Or, Pelusium.
    ² Or, Alexandria.
30:17 ¹ Or, Heliopolis.
    ² Or, Pubastum.

shall fall by the sword: and these *cities* shall go into captivity.

18 At Tehaphnehes the day [1]shall restrain *his light*, when I shall break there the [2]bars of Egypt: and when the pomp of her power shall cease in her, the cloud shall cover her, and her daughters shall go into captivity.

19 Thus will I execute judgments in Egypt, and they shall know that I am the Lord.

20 ¶ And in the [1]eleventh year, in the first *month*, *and* in the seventh *day* of the month, the word of the Lord came unto me, saying,

21 Son of man, [1]I have broken the arm of Pharaoh king of Egypt: and lo, it shall not be bound up to be healed, neither shall they put a roll to bind it, and *so* make it strong to hold the sword.

22 Therefore thus saith the Lord God, Behold, I *come* against Pharaoh King of Egypt, and will break [1]his arm that was strong, but is broken, and I will cause the sword to fall out of his hand.

23 And I will scatter the Egyptians among the nations, and will disperse them through the countries.

24 And I will strengthen the arm of the king of Babel, and put my sword in his hand, but I will break Pharaoh's arms, and he shall cast out sighings, as the sighings of him that is wounded before him.

25 But I will strengthen the arms of the king of Babel, and the arms of Pharaoh shall fall down, and they shall know, that I am the Lord, [1]when I shall put my sword into the hand of the king of Babel, and he shall stretch it out upon the land of Egypt.

26 And I will scatter the Egyptians among the nations, and disperse them among the countries, and they shall know, that I am the Lord.

31

2 A comparison of the prosperity of Pharaoh with the prosperity of the Assyrians. 10 He prophesieth a like destruction to them both.

1 And in the [1]eleventh year, in the third *month*, *and* in the first *day* of the month the word of the Lord came unto me, saying,

2 Son of man, speak unto Pharaoh king of Egypt, and to his multitude, Whom art thou [1]like in thy greatness?

3 Behold, Assyria *was like* a cedar in Lebanon with fair branches, and with thick shadowing boughs, and shot up very high, and his top was among the thick boughs.

4 The waters nourished him, and the deep exalted him on high with her rivers running round about his plants, and sent out her [1]little rivers unto all the trees of the [2]field.

5 Therefore his height was exalted above all the trees of the field, and his boughs were multiplied, and his branches were long, because of the multitude of the waters, which *the deep* sent out.

6 All the fowls of the heavens made their nests in his boughs, and under his branches did all the beasts of the field bring forth their young, and under his shadow dwelt all mighty nations.

7 Thus was he fair in his greatness, *and* in the length of his branches: for his root was near great waters.

8 The cedars in the garden [1]of God could not hide him: no fir tree was like his branches: and the chestnut trees were not like his boughs: all the trees in the garden of God were not like unto him in his beauty.

9 I made him fair by the multitude of his branches: so that all the trees of Eden, that were in the garden of God, envied him.

10 Therefore thus saith the Lord God, Because [1]he is lifted up on high, and hath shot up his top among the thick boughs, and his heart is lifted up in his height,

11 I have therefore delivered him into the hands of the [1]mightiest among the heathen: he shall handle him, *for* I have cast him away for his wickedness.

12 And the strangers have destroyed him, *even* the terrible nations, and they have left him upon the mountains, and in all the valleys his branches are fallen, and his boughs are [1]broken by all the rivers of the land: and all the people of the earth are departed from his shadow, and have forsaken him.

13 Upon his ruin shall all the fowls of the heaven remain, and all the beasts of the field shall be upon his branches,

14 So that none of all the trees by the waters shall be exalted by their height, neither shall shoot up their top among the thick boughs, neither shall

---

30:18 [1] Meaning, that there shall be great sorrow and affliction.
[2] That is, the strength and force.
30:20 [1] Of the captivity of Jeconiah, or of Zedekiah's reign.
30:21 [1] For Nebuchadnezzar destroyed Pharaoh Necho at Carchemish, Jer. 46:26.
30:22 [1] His force and power.
30:25 [1] Whereby we see that tyrants have no power of themselves, neither can do anymore harm than God appointeth, and when he will they must cease.
31:1 [1] Of Zedekiah's reign, or of Jeconiah's captivity.
31:2 [1] Meaning, that he was not like in strength to the King of the Assyrians, whom the Babylonians overcame.
31:4 [1] Many other nations were under their dominion.
[2] Or, country.
31:8 [1] Signifying, that there was no greater power in the world than his was.
31:10 [1] Or, thou wast lifted up.
31:11 [1] That is, of Nebuchadnezzar, who afterward was the monarch and only ruler of the world.
31:12 [1] Hereby is signified the destruction of the power of the Assyrians by the Babylonians.

their leaves stand up in their height, which drink so much water: for they are all delivered unto death in the nether parts of the earth in the midst of the children of men among them that go down to the pit.

15 Thus saith the Lord God, In the day when he went down to hell, I caused them to mourn, *and* I [1]covered the deep for him, and I did restrain the floods thereof, and the great waters were stayed: I caused Lebanon to mourn for him, and all the trees of the field fainted.

16 I made the nations to shake at the sound of his fall, when I cast him down to hell, with them that descend into the pit, and all the excellent trees of Eden, and the best of Lebanon: *even* all that are nourished with waters, shall [1]be comforted in the nether parts of the earth.

17 They also went down to hell with him unto them that were slain with the sword, and his arm, *and* they that dwelt under his shadow in the midst of the heathen.

18 To whom [1]art thou thus like in glory and in greatness among the trees of Eden? yet thou shalt be cast down with the trees of Eden unto the nether parts of the earth: thou shalt sleep in the midst of the [2]uncircumcised, with them that be slain by the sword: this is Pharaoh and all his multitude, saith the Lord God.

32

2 *The Prophet is commanded to bewail Pharaoh King of Egypt.* 12 *He prophesieth that destruction shall come unto Egypt through the King of Babylon.*

1 And in the [1]twelfth year in the twelfth month, *and* in the first *day* of the month, the word of the Lord came unto me, saying,

2 Son of man, take up a lamentation for Pharaoh king of Egypt, and say unto him, Thou art like a [1]lion of the nations, and art as a [2]dragon in the sea: thou castedst out thy rivers [3]and troubledst the waters with thy feet, and stampedst in their rivers.

3 Thus saith the Lord God, [d]I will therefore spread my net over thee a great multitude of people, and they shall make thee come up into my net,

4 Then will I leave thee upon the land, *and* I will

CHAPTER 32
[d] Ezek. 12:13
Ezek. 17:20
[b] Isa. 13:10
Joel 2:31
Joel 3:15
Matt. 24:29

cast thee upon the open field, and I will cause all the fowls of the heaven to remain upon thee, and I will fill all the beasts of the field with thee.

5 And I will lay thy flesh upon the mountains, and fill the valleys [1]with thine height.

6 I will also water with thy blood the land wherein thou [1]swimmest, *even* to the mountains, and the rivers shall be full of thee.

7 And when I shall [1]put thee out, I will cover the heaven, and make the stars thereof dark: [b]I will cover the sun with a cloud, and the moon shall not give her light.

8 All the lights of heaven will I make dark for thee, and bring [1]darkness upon thy land, saith the Lord God.

9 I will also trouble the hearts of many people, when I shall bring thy destruction among the nations, *and* upon the countries which thou hast not known.

10 Yea, I will make many people amazed at thee, and their kings shall be astonished with fear for thee, when I shall make my sword to glitter against their faces, and they shall be afraid at every moment: every man for his own life in the day of thy fall.

11 For thus saith the Lord God, The sword of the king of Babel shall come upon thee.

12 By the swords of the mighty will I cause thy multitude to fall: they all shall be terrible nations, and they shall destroy the [1]pomp of Egypt, and all the multitude thereof shall be consumed.

13 I will destroy also all the beasts thereof from the great watersides, neither shall the foot of man trouble them anymore, nor the hooves of beasts trouble them.

14 Then will I make [1]their waters deep, and cause their rivers to run like oil, saith the Lord God.

15 When I shall make the land of Egypt desolate, and the country with all that is therein, shall be laid waste: when I shall smite all them which dwell therein, then shall they know that I am the Lord.

16 This is the mourning wherewith they shall lament her: the daughters of the nations shall lament her: they shall lament for Egypt, and for all her multitude, saith the Lord God.

31:15 [1] The deep waters that caused him to mount so high (meaning his great abundance and pomp) shall now lament as though they were covered with sackcloth.
31:16 [1] To cause this destruction of the king of Assyria to seem more horrible, he setteth forth other kings and princes which are dead, as though they rejoiced at the fall of such a tyrant.
31:18 [1] Meaning, that Pharaoh's power was nothing so great as his was.
[2] Read Ezek. 28:10.
32:1 [1] Which was the first year of the general captivity under Zedekiah.
32:2 [1] Thus the scriptures compare tyrants to cruel and huge beasts which devour all that are weaker than they, and such as they may

overcome.
[2] Or, whale.
[3] Thou preparest great armies.
32:5 [1] With heaps of the carcasses of thine army.
32:6 [1] As Nile overfloweth Egypt, so will I make the blood of thine host to overflow it.
32:7 [1] The word signifieth to be put out as a candle is put out.
32:8 [1] By this manner of speech is meant the great sorrow that shall be for the slaughter of the king and his people.
32:12 [1] This came to pass in less than four years after this prophecy.
32:14 [1] To wit, of the Chaldeans thine enemies, which shall quietly enjoy all thy commodities.

17 ¶ In the twelfth year also in the fifteenth *day* of the month, came the word of the Lord unto me, saying,

18 Son of man, lament for the multitude of Egypt, and [1]cast them down, *even* them and the daughters of the mighty nations under the nether parts of the earth, with them that go down into the pit.

19 Whom dost thou pass [1]in beauty? go down and sleep with the uncircumcised.

20 They shall fall in the midst of them that are slain by the sword: [1]she is delivered to the sword: draw her down, and all her multitude.

21 The most mighty *and* strong shall speak to [1]him out of the midst of hell with them that help her: they are gone down, *and* sleep with the uncircumcised that be slain by the sword.

22 Assyria is there and all his company: their graves are about him: all they are slain *and* fallen by the sword.

23 Whose graves are made in the side of the pit, and his multitude are round about his grave: all they are slain *and* fallen by the sword, which caused fear *to be* in the land of the living.

24 There *is* [1]Elam and all his multitude round about his grave: all they are slain *and* fallen by the sword, which are gone down with the uncircumcised into the nether parts of the earth, which caused themselves to be feared in the land of the [2]living, yet have they borne their shame with them that are gone down to the pit.

25 They have made his bed in the midst of the slain with all his multitude: their graves *are* round about him: all these uncircumcised are slain by the sword: though they have caused their fear in the land of the living, yet have they borne their shame with them that go down to the pit: they are laid in the midst of them that be slain.

26 There *is* [1]Meshech, Tubal, and all their multitude: their graves *are* round about them: all these uncircumcised were slain by the sword, though they caused their fear *to be* in the land of the living.

27 And they shall not lie with the valiant [1]of the uncircumcised, that are fallen, which are gone down to the grave with their weapons of war, and have laid their swords under their heads, but their iniquity shall be upon their bones: because *they were* the fear of the mighty in the land of the living.

28 Yea, thou shalt be broken in the midst of the uncircumcised, and lie with them that are slain by the sword.

29 There *is* Edom, his kings, and all his princes, which with their strength are laid by them that were slain by the sword: they shall sleep with the uncircumcised, and with them that go down to the pit.

30 There *be* all the princes of the [1]North, with all the Sidonians, which are gone down with the slain, with their fear; they are ashamed of their strength, and the uncircumcised sleep with them that be slain by the sword, and bear their shame with them that go down to the pit.

31 Pharaoh shall see them, and he shall be [1]comforted over all his multitude: Pharaoh, and all his army *shall be* slain by the sword, saith the Lord God.

32 For I have caused my [1]fear *to be* in the land of the living: and he shall be laid in the midst of the uncircumcised with them, that are slain by the sword, *even* Pharaoh and all his multitude, saith the Lord God.

33

2 *The office of the governors and ministers.* 14 *He strengtheneth them that despair, and boldeneth them with the promise of mercy.* 30 *The word of the Lord against the mockers of the Prophet.*

1 Again, the word of the Lord came unto me, saying,

2 Son of man, speak to the children of thy people, and say unto them, When I bring the sword upon a land, if the people of the land take a man [1]from among them, and make him their [2]watchman,

3 If when he seeth the sword come upon the land, he blow the trumpet, and warn the people,

4 Then he that heareth the sound of the trumpet, and will not be warned, if the sword come, and take him away, his blood shall be upon his own head.

5 For he heard the sound of the trumpet, and would not be admonished: *therefore* his blood shall be upon him: but he that receiveth warning, shall save his life.

32:18 [1] That is, prophesy, that they shall be cast down: thus the Lord giveth his Prophets power both to plant and to destroy by his word, read Jer. 1:10.

32:19 [1] Have not other kingdoms, more beautiful than thou, perished?

32:20 [1] That is, Egypt.

32:21 [1] To make the matter more sensible, he bringeth in Pharaoh whom the dead shall meet and marvel at him, read Isa. 14:9.

32:24 [1] Meaning, the Persians.
[2] Whom in his life all the world feared.

32:26 [1] That is, the Cappadocians and Italians, or Spaniards, as Josephus writeth.

32:27 [1] Which died not by cruel death, but by the course of nature, and are honorably buried with their coat armor, and signs of honor.

32:30 [1] The Kings of Babylon.

32:31 [1] As the wicked rejoice when they see others partakers of their miseries.

32:32 [1] I will make the Egyptians afraid of me, as they caused others to fear them.

33:2 [1] Or, of their coasts.
[2] He showeth that the people ought to have continually governors and teachers which may have a care over them, and to warn them ever of the dangers which are at hand.

6 But if the watchman see the sword come, and blow not the trumpet, and the people be not warned: if the sword come, and take any person from among them, he is taken away for his [1]iniquity, but his blood will I require at the watchman's hand.

7 [a]So thou, O son of man, I have made thee a watchman unto the house of Israel: therefore thou shalt hear the word at my [1]mouth, and admonish them from me.

8 When I shall say unto the wicked, O wicked man, thou shalt die the death, if thou dost not speak and admonish the wicked of his way, that wicked man shall die for his iniquity, but his blood will I [1]require at thine hand.

9 Nevertheless, if thou warn the wicked of his way to turn from it, if he do not turn from his way, he shall die for his iniquity, but thou hast delivered thy soul.

10 Therefore, O thou son of man, speak unto the house of Israel, Thus ye speak and say, If our transgressions and our sins be upon us, and we are consumed because of them, [1]how should we then live?

11 Say unto them, As I live, saith the Lord God, [1]I desire not the death of the wicked, but that the wicked turn from his way and live: turn you, turn you from your evil ways, for why will ye die, O ye house of Israel?

12 Therefore thou son of man, say unto the children of thy people, The [1]righteousness of the righteous shall not deliver him in the day of his transgression, nor the wickedness of the wicked shall cause him to fall therein, in the day that he returneth from his wickedness, neither shall the righteous live for his righteousness in the day that he sinneth.

13 When I shall say unto the righteous, that he shall surely live, if he trust to his own righteousness, and commit iniquity, all his righteousness shall be no more remembered, but for his iniquity that he hath committed, he shall die for the same.

14 Again when I shall say unto the wicked, Thou shalt die the death, if he turn from his sin, and do that which is lawful and [1]right,

CHAPTER 33
[a] Ezek. 3:17
[b] Ezek. 18:25

15 To wit, if the wicked restore the pledge, and give again that he had robbed, and walk in the statutes of life, without committing iniquity, he shall surely live, and not die.

16 None of his sins that he hath committed, shall be mentioned unto him: because he hath done that, which is lawful and right, he shall surely live.

17 Yet the children of thy people say, [b]The way of the Lord is not equal: but their own way is unequal.

18 When the righteous turneth from his righteousness, and committeth iniquity, he shall even die thereby.

19 But if the wicked return from his wickedness, and do that which is lawful and right, he shall live thereby.

20 Yet ye say, The way of the Lord is not equal, O ye house of Israel, I will judge you every one after his ways.

21 Also in the twelfth year of our [1]captivity, in the tenth month, and in the fifth day of the month, one that had escaped out of Jerusalem, came unto me, and said, The city is smitten.

22 Now the [1]hand of the Lord had been upon me in the evening afore he that had escaped, came, and had opened my mouth until he came to me in the morning: and when he had opened my [2]mouth, I was no more dumb.

23 Again the word of the Lord came unto me, and said,

24 Son of man, these that dwell in the desolate places of the land of Israel, talk and say, [1]Abraham was but one, and he possessed the land: but we are many, therefore the land shall be given us in possession.

25 Wherefore say unto them, Thus saith the Lord God, Ye eat with the [1]blood, and lifted up your eyes toward your idols, and shed blood: should ye then possess the land?

26 Ye lean upon your [1]swords, ye work abomination, and ye defile every one his neighbor's wife: should ye then possess the land?

27 Say thus unto them, Thus saith the Lord God, As I live, so surely they that are in the desolate places,

---

33:6 [1] Signifying, that the wicked shall not escape punishment though the watchman be negligent: but if the watchman blow the trumpet, and then he will not obey, he shall deserve double punishment.

33:7 [1] Which teacheth that he that receiveth not his charge at the Lord's mouth, is a spy, and not a true watchman.

33:8 [1] The watchman must answer for the blood of all that perish through his negligence.

33:10 [1] Thus the wicked when they hear God's judgments for their sins, despair of his mercies, and murmur.

33:11 [1] Read Ezek. 18:23.

33:12 [1] Read of this righteousness, Ezek. 18:21, 24.

33:14 [1] Hereby he condemneth all them of hypocrisy, which pretend

to forsake wickedness, and yet declare not themselves such by their fruits, that is, in obeying God's commandments, and by godly life.

33:21 [1] When the Prophet was led away captive with Jeconiah.

33:22 [1] I was endued with the Spirit of prophecy, Ezek. 8:1.

[2] Whereby is signified that the ministers of God cannot speak till God give them courage, and open their mouths, Ezek. 24:27 and 29:21; Eph. 6:19.

33:24 [1] Thus the wicked think themselves more worthy to enjoy God's promises than the Saints of God, to whom they were made: and would bind God to be subject to them, though they would not be bound to him.

33:25 [1] Contrary to the Law, Lev. 17:14.

33:26 [1] As they that are ready still to shed blood.

shall fall by the sword: and him that is in the open field, will I give unto the beasts to be devoured: and they that be in the forts and in the caves, shall die of the pestilence.

28 For I will lay the land desolate and waste, and the ᶜpomp of her strength shall cease: and the mountains of Israel shall be desolate, and none shall pass through.

29 Then shall they know that I am the Lord, when I have laid the land desolate and waste, because of all their abominations, that they have committed.

30 Also thou son of man, the children of thy people that ¹talk of thee by the walls and in the doors of houses, and speak one to another, everyone to his brother, saying, Come, I pray you, and hear what is the word that cometh from the Lord.

31 For they come unto thee, as the people *useth* to come: and my people sit before thee, and hear thy words, but they will not do them: for with their mouths they make ¹jests, *and* their heart goeth after their covetousness.

32 And lo, thou art unto them, as a ¹jesting song of one that hath a pleasant voice, and can sing well: for they hear thy words, but they do them not.

33 And when this cometh to pass (*for* lo, it will come) then shall they know, that a Prophet hath been among them.

34 *2 Against the shepherds that despised the flock of Christ, and seek their own reign. 7 The Lord saith that he will visit his dispersed flock, and gather them together. 23 He promiseth the true shepherd Christ, and with him peace.*

1 And the word of the Lord came unto me, saying,

2 Son of man, prophesy against the shepherds of Israel, prophesy and say unto them, Thus saith the Lord God unto the shepherds, ᵃWoe *be* unto the ¹shepherds of Israel, that feed themselves: should not the shepherds feed the flocks?

3 Ye eat the ¹fat, and ye clothe you with the wool: ye kill them that are fed, but ye feed not the sheep.

4 The ¹weak have ye not strengthened: the sick have ye not healed, neither have ye bound up that broken, nor brought again that which was driven away, neither have ye sought that which was lost, but

ᶜ Ezek. 7:24
Ezek. 24:21
Ezek. 30:6,7

CHAPTER 34
ᵃ Jer. 13:1

with cruelty, and with rigor have ye ruled them.

5 And they were scattered without a shepherd: and when they were dispersed, they were ¹devoured of all the beasts of the field.

6 My sheep wandered through all the mountains, and upon every high hill: yea, my flock was scattered through all the earth, and none did seek or search *after them*.

7 Therefore ye shepherds, hear the word of the Lord.

8 As I live, saith the Lord God, surely because my flock was spoiled, and my sheep were devoured of all the beasts of the field, having no shepherd, neither did my shepherds seek my sheep, but the shepherds fed themselves, and fed not my sheep,

9 Therefore, hear ye the word of the Lord, O ye shepherds.

10 Thus saith the Lord God, Behold, I *come* against the shepherds, and will require my sheep at their hands, and cause them to cease from feeding the sheep: neither shall the shepherds feed themselves anymore: for I will deliver thy sheep from ¹their mouths, and they shall no more devour them.

11 For thus saith the Lord God, Behold, I will search my sheep, and seek them out.

12 As a shepherd searcheth out his flock, when he hath been among his sheep that are scattered, so will I seek out my sheep and will deliver them out of all places, where they have been scattered in ¹the cloudy and dark day,

13 And I will bring them out from the people, and gather them from the countries, and will bring them to their own land, and feed them upon the mountains of Israel, by the rivers, and in all the inhabited places of the country.

14 I will feed them in a good pasture, and upon the high mountains of Israel shall their fold be: there shall they lie in a good fold, and in fat pasture shall they feed upon the mountains of Israel.

15 I will feed my sheep, and bring them to their rest, saith the Lord God.

16 I will seek that which was lost, and bring again that which was driven away, and will bind up that which was broken, and will strengthen the weak, but I will destroy the fat and the ¹strong, *and* I will

---

33:30 ¹ In derision.
33:31 ¹ This declareth that we ought to hear God's word with such zeal and affection, that we should in all points obey it, else we abuse the word to our own condemnation, and make of his ministers, as though they were jests to serve men's foolish fantasies.
33:32 ¹ Or, pleasant, and love song.
34:2 ¹ By the shepherds he meaneth the king, the Magistrates, Priests, and Prophets.
34:3 ¹ Ye seek to enrich yourselves by their commodities, and to spoil their riches and substance.
34:4 ¹ He describeth the office and duty of a good pastor, who

ought to love and succor his flock, and not to be cruel toward them.
34:5 ¹ For lack of good government and doctrine they perished.
34:10 ¹ By destroying the covetous hirelings, and restoring true shepherds, whereof we have a sign so oft as God sendeth true preachers, who both by doctrine and life labor to feed his sheep in the pleasant pastures of his word.
34:12 ¹ In the day of their affliction and misery: and this promise is to comfort the Church in all dangers.
34:16 ¹ Meaning, such as lift up themselves above their brethren, and think they have no need to be governed by me.

feed them with ²judgment.

17 Also you my sheep, thus saith the Lord God, Behold, I judge between sheep and sheep, *between* the rams and the goats.

18 Seemeth it a small thing unto you to have eaten up the good ¹pasture, but ye must tread down with your feet, the residue of your pasture? and to have drunk of the deep waters, but ye must trouble the residue with your feet.

19 And my sheep eat that which ye have trodden with your feet, and drink that which ye have troubled with your feet.

20 Therefore thus saith the Lord God unto them, Behold, I, *even* I will judge between the fat sheep and the lean sheep.

21 Because ye have thrust with side and with shoulder, and pushed all the weak with your horns, till ye have scattered them abroad,

22 Therefore will I help my sheep, and they shall no more be spoiled, and I will judge between sheep and sheep.

23 And I will set up a shepherd over them, and he shall feed them, *even* my servant ¹David, he shall feed them, and he shall be their shepherd.

24 And I the Lord will be their God, and my servant David *shall be* the Prince among them, I the Lord have spoken it.

25 And I will make with them a covenant of peace, and will cause the evil beasts to cease out of the land, and they shall ¹dwell safely in the wilderness, and sleep in the woods.

26 And I will set them, *as* a blessing, even round about my mountains, and I will cause rain to come down in due season: and there shall be rain of blessing.

27 And the ¹tree of the field shall yield her fruit, and the earth shall give her fruit, and they shall be safe in their land, and shall know that I am the Lord, when I have broken the cords of their yoke, and delivered them out of the hands of those that served themselves of them.

28 And they shall no more be spoiled of the heathen, neither shall the beasts of the land devour them, but they shall dwell safely, and none shall make them afraid.

29 And I will raise up for them a ¹plant of renown, and they shall be no more consumed with hunger in the land, neither bear the reproach of the heathen anymore.

30 Thus shall they understand, that I the Lord their God am with them, and that they, *even* the house of Israel are my people, saith the Lord God.

31 And ye my sheep, the sheep of my pasture are men, *and* I am your God, saith the Lord God.

35

2 *The destruction that shall come on mount Seir, because they troubled the people of Israel.*

1 Moreover, the word of the Lord came unto me, saying,

2 Son of man, Set thy face against mount ¹Seir, and prophesy against it,

3 And say unto it, Thus saith the Lord God, Behold, O mount Seir, I *come* against thee, and I will stretch out mine hand against thee, and I will make thee desolate and waste.

4 I will lay thy cities waste, and thou shalt be desolate, and thou shalt know that I am the Lord.

5 Because thou hast had a perpetual hatred, and hast put the children of Israel to flight by the force of the sword in the time of their calamity, when *their* ¹iniquity had an end,

6 Therefore as I live, saith the Lord God, I will prepare thee unto blood, and blood shall pursue thee: except thou ¹hate blood, even blood shall pursue thee.

7 Thus will I make mount Seir desolate and waste, and cut off from it him that passeth out and him that returneth.

8 And I will fill his mountains with his slain men: in thine hills, and in thy valleys, and in all thy rivers shall they fall, that are slain with the sword.

9 I will make thee perpetual desolations, and thy cities shall not ¹return, and ye shall know that I am the Lord.

10 Because thou hast said, ¹These two nations and these two countries shall be mine, and we will possess them (seeing the Lord was ²there)

11 Therefore as I live, saith the Lord God, I will even do according to thy ¹wrath, and according to thine indignation, which thou hast used in thine

---

34:16 ² That is, by putting difference between the good and the bad, and so give to either as they deserve.
34:18 ¹ By good pasture and deep waters is meant the pure word of God and the administration of justice, which they did not distribute to the poor till they had corrupted it.
34:23 ¹ Meaning Christ, of whom David was a figure, Jer. 30:9; Hos. 3:5.
34:25 ¹ This declareth that under Christ the flock should be truly delivered from sin, and hell, and so be safely preserved in the Church, where they should never perish.
34:27 ¹ The fruits of God's grace shall appear in great abundance in

his Church.
34:29 ¹ That is, the rod that shall come out of the root of Jesse, Isa. 11:1.
35:2 ¹ Where the Edomites dwelt.
35:5 ¹ When by their punishment I called them from their iniquity.
35:6 ¹ Except thou repent thy former cruelty.
35:9 ¹ To wit, to their former estate.
35:10 ¹ Meaning, Israel and Judah.
     ² And so by fighting against God's people, they should go about to put him out of his own possession.
35:11 ¹ As thou hast done cruelly, so shalt thou be cruelly handled.

hatred against them: and I will make myself known among [2]them, when I have judged thee.

12 And thou shalt know, that I the Lord have heard all the blasphemies which thou hast spoken against the mountains of Israel, saying, They lie waste, they are given us to be devoured.

13 Thus with your mouths ye have boasted against me, and I have multiplied your words against me: I have heard *them.*

14 Thus saith the Lord God, So shall all the world rejoice, *when* I shall make thee desolate.

15 As thou didst rejoice at the inheritance of the house of Israel, because it was desolate, so will I do unto thee: thou shalt be desolate, O mount Seir, and all Idumea wholly, and they shall know that I am the Lord.

36

1 *He promiseth to deliver Israel from the Gentiles.* 22 *The benefits done unto the Jews, are to be ascribed to the mercy of God, and not unto their deservings.* 26 *God reneweth our hearts that we may walk in his commandments.*

1 Also thou son of man, prophesy unto the [a]mountains of Israel, and say, Ye mountains of Israel, hear the word of the Lord.

2 Thus saith the Lord God, Because the [1]enemy hath said against you, Aha, even the [2]high places of the world are ours in possession,

3 Therefore prophesy and say, Thus saith the Lord God, Because that they have made you desolate, and swallowed you up on every side that ye might be a possession unto the residue of the heathen, and ye are come unto the lips and [1]tongues *of men*, and unto the reproach of the people,

4 Therefore ye mountains of Israel, hear the word of the Lord God, Thus saith the Lord God to the mountains, and to the hills, to the rivers and to the valleys, and to the waste *and* desolate places, and to the cities that are forsaken, which are spoiled and had in derision of the residue of the heathen that are round about.

5 Therefore thus saith the Lord God, Surely in the fire of mine indignation have I spoken against the residue of the heathen, and against all Idumea, which have [1]taken my land for their possession, with

CHAPTER 36
[a] Ezek. 6:2

the joy of all *their* heart, *and* with despiteful minds to cast it out for a prey.

6 Prophesy therefore upon the land of Israel, and say unto the mountains and to the hills, to the rivers, and to the valleys, Thus saith the Lord God, Behold, I have spoken in mine indignation and in my wrath, because ye have suffered the [1]shame of the heathen.

7 Therefore thus saith the Lord God, I have [1]lifted up mine hand, surely the heathen that are about you, shall bear their shame.

8 But you, O mountains of Israel, ye shall [1]shoot forth your branches, and bring forth your fruit to my people of Israel: for they are ready to come.

9 For behold, I *come* unto you, and I will turn unto you, and ye shall be tilled and sown.

10 And I will multiply the men upon you, *even* all the house of Israel wholly, and the cities shall be inhabited, and the desolate places shall be built.

11 And I will multiply upon you man and beast, and they shall increase, and bring fruit, and I will cause you to dwell after your old estate, and I will bestow benefits upon you more than [1]at the first, and ye shall know that I am the Lord.

12 Yea, I will cause men to walk upon [1]you, *even* my people Israel, and they shall possess [2]you, and ye shall be their inheritance, and ye shall no more henceforth deprive them *of men*.

13 Thus saith the Lord, Because they say unto you, Thou [1]*land* devourest up men, and hast been a waster of thy people,

14 Therefore thou shalt devour men no more, neither waste thy people henceforth, saith the Lord God,

15 Neither will I cause men to hear in thee the shame of the heathen anymore, neither shalt thou bear the reproach of the people anymore, neither shalt cause thy folk to fall anymore, saith the Lord God.

16 ¶ Moreover, the word of the Lord came unto me, saying,

17 Son of man, when the house of Israel dwelt in their own land, they defiled it by their own ways, and by their deeds: their way was before me as the filthiness of the menstruous.

18 Wherefore I poured my wrath upon them, for

---

[2] Showing that when God punisheth the enemies, the godly ought to consider that he hath a care over them, and so praise his Name: and also that the wicked rage as though there were no God, till they feel his hand to their destruction.

36:2 [1] That is, the Edomite.
  [2] That is, Jerusalem, which for God's promises was the chiefest of all the world.
36:3 [1] Ye are made a matter of talk and derision to all the world.
36:5 [1] They appointed with themselves to have it, and therefore came with Nebuchadnezzar against Jerusalem for this purpose.

36:6 [1] Because you have been a laughingstock unto them.
36:7 [1] By making a solemn oath, read Ezek. 20:5.
36:8 [1] God declareth his mercies and goodness toward his Church, who still preserveth his, even when he destroyeth his enemies.
36:11 [1] Which was accomplished under Christ, to whom all these temporal deliverances did direct them.
36:12 [1] That is, upon the mountains of Jerusalem.
  [2] Or, thee.
36:13 [1] This the enemies imputed as the reproach of the land, which God did for the sins of the people according to his just judgments.

the blood that they had shed in the land, and for their idols, *wherewith* they had polluted it.

19 And I scattered them among the heathen, and they were dispersed through the countries: *for according* to their ways, and according to their deeds, I judged them.

20 [b]And when they entered unto the heathen, whither they went, they polluted mine holy Name, when they said of them, These are the people of the Lord, and are gone out of his land.

21 But I favored mine holy [1]Name, which the house of Israel had polluted among the heathen, whither they went.

22 Therefore say unto the house of Israel, Thus saith the Lord God, I do not this for your sakes, O house of Israel, but for mine [1]holy Name's sake, which ye polluted among the heathen, whither ye went.

23 And I will sanctify my great Name, which was polluted among the heathen, among whom you have polluted it, and the heathen shall know that I am the Lord, saith the Lord God, when I shall be sanctified in you before [1]their eyes.

24 For I will take you from among the heathen, and gather you out of all countries, and will bring you into your own land.

25 Then will I pour clean [1]water upon you, and ye shall be clean: *yea*, from all your filthiness, and from all your idols will I cleanse you.

26 [c]A new heart also will I give you, and a new spirit will I put within you, and I will take away the stony heart out of your body, and I will give you an heart of flesh.

27 And I will put my spirit within you, and cause you to walk in my statutes, and ye shall keep my judgments and do them.

28 And ye shall dwell in the land that I gave to your fathers, and ye shall be my people, and I will be your God.

29 I will also deliver you from all your filthiness, and I will call for [1]corn, and will increase it, and lay no famine upon you.

30 For I will multiply the fruit of the trees, and the increase of the field, that ye shall bear no more the reproach of famine among the heathen.

31 Then shall ye remember your own wicked ways,

and your deeds that were not good, and shall judge yourselves worthy to have been [1]destroyed for your iniquities, and for your abominations.

32 Be it known unto you that I do not this for your sakes, saith the Lord God: *therefore*, O ye house of Israel, be ashamed and confounded for your own ways.

33 Thus saith the Lord God, What time as I shall have cleansed you from all your iniquities, I will cause *you* to dwell in the cities, and the desolate places shall be built.

34 And the desolate land shall be tilled, whereas it lay waste in the sight of all that passed by.

35 For they said, This waste land was like the garden of Eden, and these waste, and desolate, and ruinous cities were strong, *and* were inhabited.

36 Then the residue of the heathen, that are left round about you, shall [1]know that I the Lord build the ruinous places, *and* plant the desolate places: I the Lord have spoken it, and will do it.

37 Thus saith the Lord God, I will yet for this be sought of the house of Israel, to perform it unto them: I will increase them with men like a flock.

38 As the holy flock, as the flock of Jerusalem in their solemn feasts, so shall the desolate cities be filled with flocks of men, and they shall know that I am the Lord.

37
He prophesieth the bringing again of the people, being in captivity. 16 He showeth the union of the ten tribes with the two.

1 The hand of the Lord was upon me, and carried me out in the Spirit of the Lord, and set me down in the midst of the [1]field, which was full of [2]bones:

2 And he led me round about by them, and behold, they *were* very many in the open field, and lo, *they were* very dry.

3 And he said unto me, Son of man, can these bones live? And I answered, O Lord God, thou knowest.

4 Again he said unto me, Prophesy upon these bones, and say unto them, O ye dry bones, hear the word of the Lord.

5 Thus saith the Lord God unto these bones, Behold, I will cause breath to enter into you, and

---

b Isa. 52:5
Rom. 2:24
c Jer. 32:39
Ezek. 11:19

36:21 [1] And therefore would not suffer my Name to be had in contempt, as the heathen would have reproached me, if I had suffered my Church to perish.

36:22 [1] This excludeth from man all dignity, and means to deserve anything by, seeing that God referreth the whole to himself, and that only for the glory of his holy Name.

36:23 [1] Or, your.

36:25 [1] That is, his spirit, whereby he reformeth the heart, and regenerateth his, Isa. 44:3.

36:29 [1] Under the abundance of temporal benefits he concludeth the spiritual graces.

36:31 [1] Ye shall come to true repentance, and think yourselves unworthy to be of the number of God's creatures, for your ingratitude against him.

36:36 [1] He declareth that it ought not to be referred to the soil or plentifulness of the earth that any country is rich and abundant, but only to God's mercies, as his plagues and curses declare, when he maketh it barren.

37:1 [1] Or, valley.

[2] He showeth by a great miracle that God hath power, and also will deliver his people from their captivity, inasmuch as he is able to give life to the dead bones, and bodies, and raise them up again.

ye shall live.

6 And I will lay sinews upon you, and make flesh grow upon you, and cover you with skin, and put breath in you, that ye may live, and ye shall know that I am the Lord.

7 So I prophesied as I was commanded: and as I prophesied, there was a noise, and behold, *there was* a shaking, and the bones came together, bone to his bone.

8 And when I beheld, lo, the sinews, and the flesh grew upon them, and above the skin covered them, but there was no breath in them.

9 Then said he unto me, Prophesy unto the wind: prophesy, son of man, and say to the wind, Thus saith the Lord God, Come from the four ¹winds, O breath, and breathe upon these slain, that they may live.

10 So I prophesied as he had commanded me: and the breath came into them, and they lived, and stood up upon their feet, an exceeding great army.

11 Then he said unto me, Son of man, these bones are the whole house of Israel. Behold, they say, Our bones are dried, and our hope is gone, *and* we are clean cut off.

12 Therefore prophesy, and say unto them, Thus saith the Lord God, Behold, my people, I will open your graves, and cause you to come up out of your sepulchers, and bring you into the land of Israel,

13 And ye shall know that I am the Lord, ¹when I have opened your graves, O my people, and brought you up out of your sepulchers,

14 And shall put my Spirit in you, and ye shall live, and I shall place you in your own land: then ye shall know that I the Lord have spoken it, and performed it, saith the Lord.

15 ¶ The word of the Lord came again unto me, saying,

16 Moreover, thou son of man, take thee a *piece* of wood, and write upon it, Unto Judah, and to the children of Israel his companions: then take ¹another *piece* of wood, and write upon it, Unto Joseph the tree of Ephraim, and to all the house of Israel his companions,

17 And thou shalt join them one to another into one tree, and they shall be as one in thine hand.

18 And when the children of thy people shall speak unto thee, saying, Wilt thou not show us what thou meanest by these?

19 Thou shalt answer them, Thus saith the Lord God, Behold, I will take the tree ¹of Joseph, which

CHAPTER 37
ᵃ John 10:16
ᵇ Isa. 40:11
Jer. 23:5
Ezek. 34:23
Dan. 9:24
ᶜ Ps. 109:4
Ps. 116:2

is in the hand of Ephraim, and the tribes of Israel his fellows, and will put them with him *even* with the tree of Judah, and make them one tree, and they shall be one in mine hand.

20 And the *pieces* of wood whereon thou writest, shall be in thine hand, in their sight.

21 And say unto them, Thus saith the Lord God, Behold, I will take the children of Israel from among the heathen whither they be gone, and will gather them on every side, and bring them into their own land.

22 And I will make them one people in the land, upon the mountains of Israel, ᵃand one king shall be king to them all: and they shall be no more two peoples, neither be divided anymore henceforth into two kingdoms.

23 Neither shall they be polluted anymore with their idols, nor with their abominations, nor with any of their transgressions: but I will save them out of all their dwelling places, wherein they have sinned, and will cleanse them: so shall they be my people, and I will be their God.

24 And David my ᵇservant *shall be* king over them, and they shall all have one shepherd: they shall also walk in my judgments, and observe my statutes, and do them.

25 And they shall dwell in the ¹land, that I have given unto Jacob my servant, where your fathers have dwelt, and they shall dwell therein, *even* they, and their sons, and their sons' sons forever, and my servant David *shall be* their prince forever.

26 Moreover, I will make a ᶜcovenant of peace with them: it shall be an everlasting covenant with them, and I will place them, and multiply them, and will set my sanctuary among them forevermore.

27 My tabernacle also shall be with them: yea, I will be their God, and they shall be my people.

28 Thus the heathen shall know, that I the Lord do sanctify Israel, when my Sanctuary shall be among them forevermore.

38

2 He prophesieth that Gog and Magog shall fight with great power against the people of God. 21 Their destruction.

1 And the word of the Lord came unto me, saying,

2 Son of men, set thy face against ¹Gog, *and against* the land of Magog, the chief prince of Meshech and

---

37:9 ¹ Signifying, all parts whereas the Israelites were scattered: that is, the faithful shall be brought to the same unity of spirit and doctrine, wheresoever they are scattered through the world.
37:13 ¹ That is, when I have brought you out of those places, and towns where you are captives.
37:16 ¹ Which signifieth the joining together of the two houses, of Israel, and Judah.
37:19 ¹ That is, the house of Israel.
37:25 ¹ Meaning, that the elect by Christ shall dwell in the heaven by Jerusalem, which is meant by the land of Canaan.
38:2 ¹ Which was a people that came of Magog the son of Japheth, Gen. 10:2. Magog also here signifieth a certain country so that by these two countries which had the government of Greece and Italy, he meaneth the principal enemies of the Church, Rev. 20:8.

Tubal, and prophesy against him,

3   And say, Thus saith the Lord God, Behold, I come against thee, O Gog, the chief prince of Meshech and Tubal.

4   And I will destroy thee, and put hooks in thy jaws, and I will bring thee forth and all thine host, both horses and horsemen, all clothed with all sorts of armor, even a great multitude with bucklers and shields, all [1]handling swords.

5   They of [1]Paras, of Cush, and Put with them, even all they that bear shield and helmet.

6   [1]Gomer and all his bands, and the house of Togarmah of the North quarters, and all his bands, and much people with thee.

7   Prepare thyself, and make thee [1]ready, both thou, and all thy multitude that are assembled unto thee, and be thou their safeguard.

8   After many days thou shalt be visited: for in the latter years thou shalt come into the land that hath been destroyed with the sword, and is gathered out of many people upon the mountains of Israel, which have long lain waste: yet [1]they have been brought out of the people, and they shall dwell all safe.

9   Thou shalt ascend and come up like a tempest, and shalt be like a cloud to cover the land, both thou, and all thy bands, and many people with thee.

10   Thus saith the Lord God, Even at the same time shall many things come into thy mind, and thou shalt think [1]evil thoughts.

11   And thou shalt say, I will go up to the land that hath no walled towers: [1]I will go to them that are at rest and dwell in safety, which dwell all without walls, and have neither bars nor gates,

12   Thinking to spoil the prey, and to take a booty, to turn thine hand upon the desolate places that are now inhabited, and upon the people that are gathered out of the nations which have gotten cattle, and goods, and dwell in the midst of the land.

13   Sheba and Dedan, and the merchants of Tarshish with all the lions thereof shall say unto thee, [1]Art thou come to spoil the prey? hast thou gathered

CHAPTER 38
ᵃ Ezek. 36:23
Ezek. 37:28

thy multitude to take a booty? to carry away silver and gold, to take away cattle and goods, and to spoil a great prey?

14   Therefore, son of man, prophesy, and say unto Gog, Thus saith the Lord God, In that day, when my people of Israel [1]dwelleth safe shalt thou not know it,

15   And come from thy place out of the North parts, thou and much people with thee? all shall ride upon horses, even a great multitude and a mighty army.

16   And thou shalt come up against my people of Israel, as a cloud to cover the land, thou shalt be in the [1]latter days, and I will bring thee upon my land, that the heathen may know me, when I [2]shall be sanctified in thee, O Gog, before their eyes.

17   Thus saith the Lord God, Art not thou he, of whom I have spoken in old time, [1]by the hand of my servants the Prophets of Israel which prophesied in those days and years, that I would bring thee upon them?

18   At the same time also when Gog shall come against the land of Israel, saith the Lord God, my wrath shall arise in mine anger.

19   For in mine indignation, and in the fire of my wrath have I spoken it: surely at that time there shall be a great shaking in the land of Israel,

20   So that the fishes of the Sea, and the fowls of the heaven, and the beasts of the field, and all that move and creep upon the earth, and all the men that are upon the earth, shall tremble at my presence, and the mountains shall be overthrown, and the [1]stairs shall fall, and every wall shall fall to the ground.

21   For I will call for a sword against him [1]throughout all my mountains, saith the Lord God: every man's sword shall be against his brother.

22   And I will plead against him with pestilence, and with blood, and I will cause to rain upon him and upon his bands, and upon the great people that are with him, a sore rain, and hailstones, fire, and brimstone.

23   Thus will I be ᵃmagnified, and sanctified, and

38:4 [1] He showeth that the enemies should bend themselves against the Church, but it should be to their own destruction.

38:5 [1] The Persians, Ethiopians and men of Africa.

38:6 [1] Gomer was Japheth's son, and Togarmah the son of Gomer, and are thought to be they that inhabit Asia Minor.

38:7 [1] Signifying, that all the people of the world should assemble themselves against the Church and Christ their head.

38:8 [1] Or, it: meaning, the land of Israel.

38:10 [1] That is, to molest and destroy the Church.

38:11 [1] Meaning, Israel, which had now been destroyed, and was not yet built again: declaring hereby the simplicity of the godly, who seek not so much to fortify themselves by outward force, as to depend on the providence and goodness of God.

38:13 [1] One enemy shall envy another because everyone shall think

to have the spoil of the Church.

38:14 [1] Shalt not thou spy thine occasions to come against my Church when they suspect nothing?

38:16 [1] Meaning, in the last age, and from the coming of Christ unto the end of the world.

   [2] Signifying, that God will be sanctified by maintaining his Church, and destroying his enemies, as Ezek. 36:23 and 37:28.

38:17 [1] Hereby he declareth that none affliction can come to the Church, whereof they have not been advertised aforetime, to teach them to endure all things with more patience, when they know that God hath so ordained.

38:20 [1] All means whereby man should think to save himself, shall fail, the affliction in those days shall be so great, and the enemies' destruction shall be so terrible.

38:21 [1] Against the people of Gog and Magog.

known in the eyes of many nations, and they shall know, that I am the Lord.

39

1 He showeth the destruction of Gog, and Ma-gog.   11 The graves of Gog and his host.   17 They shall be devoured of birds and beasts.   23 Wherefore the house of Israel is captive.   24 Their bringing again from captivity is promised.

1   Therefore thou son of man, prophesy against Gog, and say, Thus saith the Lord God, Behold, I *come* against thee, O Gog, the chief prince of Meshech and Tubal.

2   And I will destroy thee ¹and leave but the sixth part of thee, and will cause thee to come up from the North parts, and will bring thee upon the mountains of Israel:

3   And I will smite thy bow out of thy left hand, and I will cause thine arrows to fall out of thy right hand.

4   Thou ¹shalt fall upon the mountains of Israel, and all thy bands and the people, that is with thee: *for* I will give thee unto the birds, *and* to every feathered fowl and beast of the field to be devoured.

5   Thou shalt fall upon the open field: for I have spoken it, saith the Lord God.

6   And I will send a fire on Magog, and among them that dwell safely in the ¹isles, and they shall know that I am the Lord.

7   So will I make mine holy Name known in the midst of my people Israel, and I will not suffer them to pollute mine holy Name anymore, and the heathen shall know that I am the Lord, the Holy one of Israel.

8   Behold, ¹it is come, and it is done, saith the Lord God: and this is the day whereof I have spoken.

9   And they that dwell in the cities of Israel shall ¹go forth, and shall burn and set fire upon the weapons, and on the shields, and bucklers, upon the bows, and upon the arrows, and upon the staves *in their* hands, and upon the spears, and they shall burn them with fire seven years.

10   So that they shall bring no wood out of the field, neither cut down *any* out of the forests: for they shall burn the weapons with fire, and they shall rob those that robbed them, and spoil those that spoiled them, saith the Lord God.

11   And at the same time will I give unto Gog ¹a place there for burial in Israel, *even* the valley, whereby men go toward the East part of the sea: and it shall cause them that pass by, to stop their ²noses, and there shall they bury Gog with all his multitude: and they shall call it the valley of ³Hamon Gog.

12   ¹And seven months long shall the house of Israel be burying of them, that they may cleanse the land.

13   Yea, all the people of the land shall bury them, and they shall have a name, when I shall be glorified, saith the Lord God.

14   And they shall choose out men to go continually through the ¹land with them that travail, to bury those that remain upon the ground, to cleanse it: they shall search to the end of seven months.

15   And the travelers that pass through the land, if *any* see a man's bone, then shall he set up a sign by it, till the buriers have buried it in the valley of Hamon Gog.

16   And also the name of the city *shall be* ¹Hamonah: thus shall they cleanse the land.

17   And thou son of man, thus saith the Lord God, Speak unto every feathered fowl, and to all the beasts of the field, Assemble yourselves, and come: ¹gather yourselves on every side to my sacrifice: for I do sacrifice a great sacrifice for you upon the mountains of Israel, that ye may eat flesh, and drink blood.

18   Ye shall eat the flesh of the valiant, and drink the blood of the princes of the earth, of the weathers, of the lambs, and of the goats, *and* of bullocks, *even* of all fat beasts of Bashan.

19   And ye shall eat fat till ye be full, and drink blood till ye be drunken of my sacrifice, which I have sacrificed for you.

20   Thus you shall be filled at my table with horses and chariots, with valiant men, and with all men of war, saith the Lord God.

21   And I will set my glory among the heathen, and all the heathen shall see my judgment, that I have executed, and mine hand, which I have laid upon them.

22   So the house of Israel shall know, that I am the Lord their God from that day and so forth.

39:2 ¹ Or, destroy thee with six plagues, as Ezek. 38:22.
39:4 ¹ Meaning, that by the virtue of God's word the enemy shall be destroyed wheresoever he assaileth his Church.
39:6 ¹ That is, among all nations where the enemies of my people dwell, seem they never so far separated.
39:8 ¹ That is, this plague is fully determined, in my counsel, and cannot be changed.
39:9 ¹ After this destruction the Church shall have great peace and tranquility, and burn all their weapons, because they shall no more fear the enemies, and this is chiefly meant of the accomplishment of Christ's kingdom when by their head Christ, all enemies shall be overcome.
39:11 ¹ Which declareth that the enemies shall have an horrible fall.
² For the stink of the carcasses.
³ Or, the multitude of Gog.
39:12 ¹ Meaning, a long time.
39:14 ¹ Partly that the holy land should not be polluted, and partly for the compassion that the children of God have, even on their enemies.
39:16 ¹ Or, multitude.
39:17 ¹ Whereby he signifieth the horrible destruction that should come upon the enemies of his Church.

23 And the heathen shall know that the house of Israel went into captivity for [1]their iniquity, because they trespassed against me: therefore hid I my face from them, and gave them into the hand of their enemies: so fell they all by the sword.

24 According to their uncleanness, and according to their transgressions have I done unto them, and hid my face from them.

25 Therefore thus saith the Lord God, Now will I bring again the captivity of Jacob, and have compassion upon the whole house of Israel, and will be jealous for mine holy Name,

26 After that they have borne their shame, and all their transgression, whereby they have transgressed against me, when they dwelt safely in their land, and without fear of any.

27 When I have brought them again from the people, and gathered them out of their enemies' lands, and am [a]sanctified in them in the sight of many nations,

28 Then shall they know, that I am the Lord their God, which caused them to be led into captivity among the heathen: but I have gathered them unto their own land, and have left none of them anymore there,

29 Neither will I hide my face anymore from them: for I have poured out my Spirit upon the house of Israel, saith the Lord God.

40

The restoring of the city and the Temple.

1 In the five and twentieth year of our being in captivity, in the [1]beginning of the year, in the tenth *day* of the month, in the fourteenth year after that the city was smitten, in the selfsame day, the hand of the Lord was upon me, and brought me thither.

2 Into the land of Israel brought he me by [1]a divine vision, and set me upon a very high mountain, whereupon *was* as the building of a city, toward the South.

3 And he brought me thither, and behold, there *was* a [1]man, whose similitude *was* to look to, like brass, with a linen thread in his hand, and a reed to measure with: and he stood at the gate.

4 And the man said unto me, Son of man, behold with thine eyes, and hear with thine ears, and set thine heart upon all that I shall show thee: for to the intent that they might be showed thee, art thou brought hither: declare all that thou seest unto the house of Israel.

CHAPTER 39
[a] Ezek. 36:23

5 And behold, *I saw* a wall on the outside of the house round about: and in the man's hand *was* a reed to measure with, of six cubits long, by the cubit, and an hand breadth: so he measured the breadth of the building with one reed, and the height with one reed.

6 Then came he unto the gate which looketh toward the East, and went up the stairs thereof, and measured the [1]post of the gate, *which was* one reed broad, and [2]the other post of the gate, *which was* one reed broad.

7 And *every* chamber was one reed long, and one reed broad, and between the chambers *were* five cubits: and the post of the gate by the porch of the gate within *was* one reed.

8 He measured also the porch of the gate within with one reed.

9 Then measured he the porch of the gate of eight cubits and the [1]posts thereof, of two cubits, and the porch of the gate *was* inward.

10 And the Chambers of the gate Eastward, *were* three on this side, and three on that side: they three *were* of one measure, and the posts had one measure on this side, and one on that side.

11 And he measured the breadth of the entry of the gate ten cubits, *and* the height of the gate thirteen cubits.

12 The space also before the chambers *was* one cubit *on this side* and the space *was* one cubit on that side, and the chambers *were* six cubits on this side, and six cubits on that side.

13 He measured then the gate from the roof of a chamber to the top of the *gate*: the breadth *was* five and twenty cubits, door against door.

14 He made also posts of threescore cubits, and the posts of the court, *and* of the gate, *had one measure* round about.

15 And upon the forefront of the entry of the gate unto the forefront of the porch of the gate within *were* fifty cubits.

16 And *there were* narrow windows in the chambers, and in their posts within the gate round about, and likewise to the arches: and the windows *went* round about within: and upon the posts *were* palm trees.

17 ¶ Then brought he me into the outward court, and lo, *there were* chambers, and a pavement made for the court round about, *and* thirty chambers *were* upon the pavement.

18 And the pavement *was* by the side of the gates

39:23 [1] The heathen shall know that they overcame not my people by their strength, neither yet by the weakness of mine arm, but that this was for my people's sins.
40:1 [1] The Jews counted the beginning of the year after two sorts: for their feasts, they began to count in March, and for their other affairs in September: so that this is to be understood of September.

40:2 [1] Or, visions of God.
40:3 [1] Which was an Angel in form of a man, that came to measure out this building.
40:6 [1] Or, threshold.
    [2] Or, upper posts.
40:9 [1] Or, pentises.

over against the length of the gates, *and* the pavement *was* beneath.

19 Then he measured the breadth from the fore-front of the lower gate without, unto the forefront of the court within, an hundred cubits Eastward and Northward.

20 And the gate of the outward court, that looked toward the North, measured he after the length and breadth thereof.

21 And the chambers thereof *were* three on this side, and three on that side, and the posts thereof and the arches thereof were after the measure of the first gate: the length thereof *was* fifty cubits, and the breadth five and twenty cubits.

22 And their windows, and their arches with their palm trees, *were* after the measure of the gate that looketh toward the East, and the going up unto it *had* seven steps, and the arches thereof *were* before them.

23 And the gate of the inner court *stood* over against the gate toward the North, and toward the East, and he measured from gate to gate an hundred cubits.

24 After that, he brought me toward the South, and lo, *there was* a gate toward the South, and he measured the posts thereof, and the arches thereof according to these measures.

25 And *there were* windows in it, and in the arches thereof round about, like those windows: the height *was* fifty cubits, and the breadth five and twenty cubits.

26 And there were seven steps to go up to it, and the arches thereof *were* before them, and it had palm trees, one on this side, and another on that side upon the post thereof.

27 ¶ And *there was* a gate in the inner court toward the South, and he measured from gate to gate toward the South an hundred cubits.

28 And he brought me into the inner court by the South gate, and he measured the South gate, according to these measures,

29 And the chambers thereof, and the posts thereof, and the arches thereof according to these measures, and *there were* windows in it, and in the arches thereof round about, *it was* fifty cubits long, and five and twenty cubits broad.

30 And the arches round about *were* five and twenty cubits long, and five cubits broad.

31 And the arches thereof *were* toward the utter Court, and palm trees *were* upon the posts thereof, and the going up to it *had* eight steps.

32 ¶ Again he brought me into the inner court toward the East, and he measured the gate according to these measures.

33 And the chambers thereof, and the posts thereof, and the arches thereof were according to these measures, and *there were* windows therein, and in the arches thereof round about: *it was* fifty cubits long, and five and twenty cubits broad.

34 And the arches thereof *were* toward the utter court, and palm trees *were* upon the posts thereof, on this side and on that side, and the going up to it *had* eight steps.

35 ¶ After he brought me to the North gate, and measured it, according to these measures,

36 The chambers thereof, the posts thereof, and the arches thereof, and *there were* windows therein round about: the height *was* fifty cubits, and the breadth five and twenty cubits.

37 And the posts thereof *were* toward the utter court, and palm trees *were* upon the posts thereof on this side, and on that side, and the going up to it *had* eight steps.

38 And *every* chamber, and the entry thereof *was* under the posts of the gates: there they washed the burnt offering.

39 And in the porch of the gate *stood* two tables on this side, and two tables on that side, upon the which they slew the burnt offering, and the sin of-fering, and the trespass offering.

40 And at the side beyond the steps, at the entry of the North gate *stood* two tables, and on the other side, which was at the porch of the gate *were* two tables.

41 Four tables *were* on this side, and four tables on that side by the side of the gate *even* eight tables whereupon they slew *their sacrifice.*

42 And the four tables *were* of hewn stone for the burnt offering, of a cubit and an half long, and a cubit and an half broad, and one cubit high: whereupon also they laid the instruments wherewith they slew the burnt offering and the sacrifice.

43 And within *were* borders an hand broad, fastened round about, and upon the tables *lay* the flesh of the offering.

44 And without the inner gate *were* the chambers of the singers in the inner court, which was at the side of the North gate: and their prospect *was* toward the South, and one *was* at the side of the East gate, having the prospect toward the North.

45 And he said unto me, This chamber whose prospect is toward the South *is* for the Priests, that have charge to keep the house.

46 And the chamber whose prospect is toward the North, *is* for the Priests that have the charge to keep the Altar: these are the sons of Zadok among the sons of Levi, which may come near to the Lord to minister unto him.

47 So he measured the court an hundred cubits long, and an hundred cubits broad, *even* four square: likewise the Altar *that was* before the house.

48 And he brought me to the porch of the house, and measured the posts of the porch, five cubits on this side, and five cubits on that side: and the breadth of the gate *was* three cubits on this side, and three

cubits on that side.

49 The length of the porch *was* twenty cubits, and the breadth eleven cubits, and *he brought me* by the steps whereby they went up to it, and *there were* pillars by the posts, one on this side and another on that side.

41   *1 The disposition and order of the building of the Temple, and the other things thereunto belonging.*

1 Afterward, he brought me to the Temple and measured the posts, six cubits broad on the one side, and six cubits broad on the other side, *which was the* breadth of the Tabernacle.

2 And the breadth of the entry *was* ten cubits, and the sides of the entry *were* five cubits, on the one side, and five cubits on the other side, and he measured the length thereof forty cubits, and the breadth twenty cubits.

3 Then went he in, and measured the posts of the entry two cubits, and the entry six cubits, and the breadth of the entry seven cubits.

4 So he measured the length thereof twenty cubits, and the breadth twenty cubits before the Temple, and he said unto me, This is the most holy place.

5 After, he measured the wall of the house, six cubits, and the breadth of *every* chamber four cubits round about the house, on every side.

6 And the chambers *were* chamber upon chamber, three and thirty foot *high*, and they entered into the wall made for the chambers which was round about the house, that *the posts* might be fastened *therein*, and not be fastened in the wall of the house.

7 And it was large, and went round mounting upward to the chambers: for the stairs of the house *was* mounting upward, round about the house: therefore the house was larger upward: so they went up from the lowest *chamber* to the highest by the midst.

8 I saw also the house high round about: the foundations of the chambers *were* a full reed of six great cubits.

9 The thickness of the wall which was for the chamber without, *was* five cubits, and that which remained, *was* the place of the chambers that were within.

10 And between the chambers was the wideness of twenty cubits round about the House on every side.

11 And the doors of the chambers *were* toward the place that remained, one door toward the North, and another door toward the South, and the breadth of the place that remained, *was* five cubits round about.

12 Now the building that was before the separate place toward the West corner, *was* seventy cubits

broad, and the wall of the building was five cubits thick round about, and the length ninety cubits.

13 So he measured the house an hundred cubits long, and the separate place and the building with the walls thereof *were* an hundred cubits long.

14 Also the breadth of the forefront of the house and of the separate place toward the East, *was* an hundred cubits.

15 And he measured the length of the building over against the separate place, which was behind it, and the chambers on the one side and on the other side an hundred cubits with the Temple within, and the arches of the court.

16 The posts and the narrow windows, and the chambers round about, on three sides over against the posts, ceiled with *cedar* wood round about, and from the ground up to the windows, and the windows were ceiled.

17 And from above the door unto the inner house and without, and by all the wall round about within and without it was *ceiled according* to the measure.

18 And it was made with Cherubims and palm trees, so that a palm tree *was* between a Cherub and a Cherub: and *every* Cherub had two faces.

19 So that the face of a man *was* toward the palm tree on the one side, and the face of a lion toward the palm tree on the other side: *thus* was it made through all the house round about.

20 From the ground unto above the door *were* Cherubims, and palm trees made as in the wall of the Temple.

21 The posts of the Temple were squared, *and* thus to look unto *was* the similitude *and* form of the Sanctuary.

22 The altar of wood *was* three cubits high, and the length thereof two cubits, and the corners thereof and the length thereof and the sides thereof *were* of wood. And he said unto me, This is the Table that shall be before the Lord.

23 And the Temple and the Sanctuary had two doors.

24 And the doors had two wickets, *even* two turning wickets, two wickets for one door, and two wickets for another door.

25 And upon the doors of the Temple there were made Cherubims and palm trees, like as was made upon the walls, and *there were* thick planks upon the forefront of the porch without.

26 And *there were* narrow windows and palm trees on the one side, and on the other side, by the sides of the porch, and *upon* the sides of the house, and thick planks.

42   *Of the chambers of the Temple for the Priests, and the holy things.*

1 Then brought he me into the utter court by the way toward the North, and he brought me into the chamber that was over against the separate place, and which was before the building toward the North.

2 Before the length of an hundred cubits, *was* the North door, and *it was* fifty cubits broad.

3 Over against the twenty *cubits* which were for the inner court, and over against the pavement, which was for the utter court, was chamber against chamber in three rows.

4 And before the chambers *was* a gallery of ten cubits wide, *and* within *was* a way of one cubit, and their doors toward the North.

5 Now the chambers above were narrower: for those chambers *seemed* to eat up these, *to wit,* the lower, and those that were in the midst of the building.

6 For they were in three rows, but had not pillars as the pillars of the court: therefore there was a difference from them beneath and from the middlemost, *even* from the ground.

7 And the wall that was without over against the chambers, toward the utter court on the forefront of the chambers, *was* fifty cubits long.

8 For the length of the chambers that were in the utter court, *was* fifty cubits: and lo, before the Temple *were* an hundred cubits.

9 And under these chambers *was* the entry, on the East side, as one goeth into them from the outward court.

10 The chambers *were* in the thickness of the wall of the court toward the East, over against the separate place, and over against the building.

11 And the way before them *was* after the manner of the chambers, which were toward the North, as long as they, *and* as broad as they: and all their entries were like, both according to their fashions, and according to their doors.

12 And according to the doors of the chambers, that were toward the South, *was* a door in the corner of the way, *even* the way directly before the wall toward the East, as one entereth.

13 Then said he unto me, The North chambers *and* the South chambers which are before the separate place, they be holy chambers wherein the Priests that approach unto the Lord, shall eat the most holy things: there shall they lay the most holy things, and the meat offering, and the sin offering, and the trespass offering: for the place *is* holy.

14 When the Priests enter therein, they shall not go out of the holy place into the utter court, but there they shall lay their garments wherein they minister: for they

CHAPTER 43
a Ezek. 9:3

are holy, *and* shall put on other garments, and so shall approach to those things, which are for the people.

15 Now when he had made an end of measuring the inner house, he brought me forth toward the gate whose prospect is toward the East, and measured it round about.

16 He measured the East side with the measuring rod, five hundred reeds *even* with the measuring reed round about.

17 He measured *also* the North side, five hundred reeds, *even* with the measuring reed round about.

18 And he measured the South [1]side five hundred reeds with the measuring reed.

19 He turned about *also* to the West side, *and* measured five hundred reeds with the measuring reed.

20 He measured it by the four sides: it had a wall round about, five hundred *reeds* long, and five hundred broad to make a separation between the Sanctuary, and the profane place.

43

2 He seeth the glory of God going into the Temple, from whence it had before departed. 7 He mentioneth the idolatry of the children of Israel, for the which they were consumed and brought to naught. 9 He is commanded to call them again to repentance.

1 Afterward he brought me to the gate *even* the gate that turneth toward the East.

2 And behold, the glory of the God of Israel, came from out of the East, whose voice was like a noise of great waters, and the earth was made light with his glory.

3 And the vision which I saw *was* *a*like the vision, *even* as the vision that I saw [1]when I came to destroy the city: and the visions *were* like the vision that I saw by the river Chebar, *and* I fell upon my face.

4 And the [1]glory of the Lord came into the house by the way of the gate, whose prospect is toward the East.

5 So the Spirit took me up and brought me into the inner court, and behold, the glory of the Lord filled the house.

6 And I heard one speaking unto me out of the house: and there stood a man by me,

7 Which said unto me, Son of man *this* place is my throne, and the place of the soles of my feet, whereas I will dwell among the children of Israel forever, and the house of Israel shall no more [1]defile mine holy Name, neither they, nor their kings by their fornication, nor by the carcasses of [2]their kings *in* their high places.

8 Albeit they set their thresholds by my thresh-

42:18 [1] Or, wind.
43:3 [1] When I prophesied the destruction of the city of the Chaldeans.
43:4 [1] Which was departed afore, Ezek. 10:4 and 12:22.

43:7 [1] By their idolatries.
[2] He alludeth to Amnon and Manasseh, who were buried in their gardens near the Temple, and there had erected up monuments to their idols.

olds, and their posts by my posts (for there *was but* a wall between me and them) yet have they defiled mine holy Name with their abominations, that they have committed: wherefore I have consumed them in my wrath.

9 Now *therefore* let them put away their fornication, and the carcasses of their kings far from me, and I will dwell among them forever.

10 ¶ Thou son of man, show this House to the house of Israel, that they may be ashamed of their wickedness, and let them measure the pattern.

11 And if they be ashamed of all that they have done, show them the form of the house, and the pattern thereof, and the going out thereof, and the coming in thereof, and the whole fashion thereof, and all the ordinances thereof, and all the figures thereof, and all the laws thereof: and write it in their sight, that they may keep the whole fashion thereof, and all the ordinances thereof, and do them.

12 This is the [1]description of the house, *It shall be* upon the top of the mount: all the limits thereof round about shall be most holy. Behold, this is the description of the house.

13 And these are the measures of the Altar, after the cubits, the cubit *is* a cubit, and an hand breadth, even the bottom *shall be* a cubit, and the breadth a cubit, and the border thereof by the edge thereof round about *shall be* a span: and this *shall be* the height of the Altar.

14 And from the bottom *which toucheth* the ground to the lower piece *shall be* two cubits and the breadth one cubit, and from the little piece to the great piece *shall be* four cubits, and the breadth one cubit.

15 So the altar *shall be* four cubits, and from the altar upward *shall be* four horns.

16 And the altar *shall be* twelve *cubits* long and twelve broad, *and* foursquare in the four corners thereof.

17 And the frame *shall be* fourteen *cubits* long, and fourteen broad in the foursquare corners thereof, and the border about it *shall be* half a cubit, and the bottom thereof *shall be* a cubit about, and the steps thereof *shall be* turned toward the East.

18 ¶ And he said unto me, Son of man, thus saith the Lord God, These are the ordinances of the altar in the day when they shall make it to offer the burnt offering thereon, and to sprinkle blood thereon.

19 And thou shalt give to the Priests, *and* to the Levites that be of the seed of Zadok, which approach unto me, to minister unto me, saith the Lord God, a young bullock for a sin offering.

20 And thou shalt take of the blood thereof, and put it on the four horns of it, and on the four corners of the frame, and upon the border round about: thus shalt thou cleanse it, and reconcile it.

21 Thou shalt take the bullock also of the sin offering, and burn it in the appointed place of the house without the Sanctuary.

22 But the second day thou shalt offer an he goat without blemish for a sin offering, and they shall cleanse the altar, as they did cleanse it with the bullock.

23 When thou hast made an end of cleansing it, thou shalt offer a young bullock without blemish, and a ram out of the flock without blemish.

24 And thou shalt offer them before the Lord, and the Priests shall cast salt upon them, and they shall offer them for a burnt offering unto the Lord.

25 Seven days shalt thou prepare every day an he goat for a sin offering: they shall also prepare a young bullock and a ram out of the flock without blemish.

26 Thus shall they seven days purify the altar, and cleanse it, and [1]consecrate it.

27 And when these days are expired upon the eighth day and so forth, the Priests shall make your burnt offerings upon the altar, and your peace offerings, and I will accept you, saith the Lord God.

44 *He reproveth the people for their offense.* 7 *The uncircumcised in heart, and in the flesh.* 9 *Who are to be admitted to the service of the Temple, and who to be refused.*

1 Then he brought me toward the gate of the outward Sanctuary, which turneth toward the East, and it was shut.

2 Then said the Lord unto me, This gate shall be [1]shut, *and* shall not be opened, and no man shall enter by it, because the Lord God of Israel hath entered by it, and it shall be shut.

3 *It appertaineth* to the Prince: the Prince himself shall sit in it to eat bread before the Lord: he shall enter by the way of the porch of that gate, and shall go out by the way of the same.

4 ¶ Then brought he me toward the North gate before the house: and when I looked, behold, the glory of the Lord, filled the house of the Lord, and I fell upon my face.

5 And the Lord said unto me, Son of man, [1]mark well and behold with thine eyes, and hear with thine ears, all that I say unto thee, concerning all the ordinances of the house of the Lord, and all the laws thereof, and mark well the entering in of the house with every going forth of the Sanctuary.

43:12 [1] Hebrew, *law.*
43:26 [1] Hebrew, *fill his hand.*
44:2 [1] Meaning, from the common people, but not from the Priests, nor the Prince, read Ezek. 46:8,9.
44:5 [1] Hebrew, *set thine hearts.*

6 And thou shalt say to the rebellious, *even* to the house of Israel, Thus saith the Lord God, O house of Israel, ye have enough of all your abominations,

7 Seeing that ye have brought into my Sanctuary [1]strangers uncircumcised in heart, and uncircumcised in flesh, to be in my Sanctuary, to pollute mine house, when ye offer my bread, *even* fat, and blood: and they have broken my covenant, because of all your abominations.

8 For ye have not kept the [1]ordinances of mine holy things: but you yourselves have set *others* to take the charge of my Sanctuary.

9 Thus saith the Lord God, No stranger uncircumcised in heart, nor uncircumcised in flesh, shall enter into my Sanctuary, of any stranger that is among the children of Israel,

10 Neither yet the [1]Levites that are gone back from me, when Israel went astray, which went astray from me after their idols, but they shall bear their iniquity.

11 And they shall serve in my Sanctuary, and keep the gates of the House, and minister in the House: they shall slay the burnt offering and the sacrifice for the people: and they shall stand before them to serve them.

12 Because they served before their idols, and caused the house of Israel to fall into iniquity, therefore have I lifted up mine hand against them, saith the Lord God, and they shall bear their iniquity,

13 And they shall not come near unto me to do the office of the Priest unto me, neither shall they come near unto any of mine holy things in the most holy place, but they shall bear their shame, and their abominations, which they have committed.

14 And I will make them keepers of the watch of the House, for all the service thereof, and for all that shall be done therein.

15 But the Priests of the Levites, the sons of Zadok, that [1]kept the charge of my Sanctuary, when the children of Israel went astray from me, they shall come near to me to serve me, and they shall stand before me to offer me the fat and the blood, saith the Lord God.

16 They shall enter into my Sanctuary, and shall come near to my table, to serve me, and they shall keep my charge.

17 And when they shall enter in at the gates of the inner court, they shall be clothed with linen garments, and no wool shall come upon them while they serve in the gates of the inner court, and within.

CHAPTER 44
a Lev. 10:9
b Lev. 21:13,14
c Lev. 21:1,2,11
d Deut. 18:1
Num. 18:20
e Exod. 18:2
Exod. 22:29
Exod. 34:15
Num. 3:13
f Exod. 22:31
Lev. 22:8

18 They shall have linen bonnets upon their heads, and shall have linen breeches upon their loins: they shall not gird themselves in the sweating *places*.

19 But when they go forth into the utter court, *even* to the utter court to the people, they shall put off their garments, wherein they ministered, and lay them in the holy chambers, and they shall put on other garments: for they shall not sanctify the people with their garments.

20 They shall not also [1]shave their heads, nor suffer their locks to grow long, *but* round their heads.

21 [a]Neither shall any Priests drink wine when they enter into the inner court.

22 Neither shall they take for their [b]wives a widow, or her that is divorced: but they shall take maidens of the seed of the house of Israel, or a widow that hath been the widow of a Priest.

23 And they shall teach my people *the difference* between the holy and profane, and cause them to discern between the unclean and the clean.

24 And in controversy they shall stand to judge, and they shall judge it according to my judgments: and they shall keep my laws and my statutes in all mine assemblies, and they shall sanctify my Sabbaths.

25 [c]And they shall come at no dead person to defile themselves, except at *their* father or mother, or son or daughter, brother or sister, that hath had yet none husband: in *these* may they [1]be defiled.

26 And when he is cleansed, they shall reckon unto him seven days.

27 And when he goeth into the Sanctuary, unto the inner court, to minister in the Sanctuary, he shall offer his sin offering, saith the Lord God.

28 [d]And the *Priesthood* shall be their inheritance, *yea*, I am their inheritance: therefore shall ye give them no possession in Israel, *for* I am their possession.

29 They shall eat the meat offering, and the sin offering, and the trespass offering, and every dedicated thing in Israel shall be theirs.

30 [e]And all the first of all the firstborn, and every oblation, *even* all of every sort of your oblations shall be the Priest's. Ye shall also give unto the Priest the first of your dough, that he may cause the blessing to rest in thine house.

31 The Priests shall not eat of anything that is [f]dead, or torn, whether it be fowl or beast.

45 *1 Out of the land of promise are there separate four portions, of which the first is given to the Priests*

44:7 [1] For they had brought idolaters which were of other countries, to teach them their idolatry, Ezek. 23:40.
44:8 [1] Ye have not offered unto me according to my Law.
44:10 [1] The Levites which had committed idolatry, were put from their dignity and could not be received into the Priests' office,

although they had been of the house of Aaron, but must serve in the inferior offices, as to watch and to keep the doors, read 2 Kings 23:9.
44:15 [1] Which observed the Law of God, and fell not to idolatry.
44:20 [1] As did the infidels and heathen.
44:25 [1] They may be at their burial, which was a defiling.

and to the Temple, the second to the Levites, the third to the city, the fourth to the prince. 9 An exhortation unto the heads of Israel. 10 Of just weights and measures. 14 Of the firstfruits, etc.

1 Moreover, when ye shall divide the land for inheritance, ye shall offer an oblation unto the Lord an ¹holy portion of the land, five and twenty thousand reeds long, and ten thousand broad: this shall be holy in all the borders thereof round about.

2 Of this there shall be for the Sanctuary five hundred *in length*, with five hundred *in breadth*, all square round about, and fifty cubits round about for the suburbs thereof.

3 And of this measure shalt thou measure the length of five and twenty thousand, and the breadth of ten thousand: and in it shall be the Sanctuary, *and* the most holy place.

4 The holy portion of the land shall be the Priests, which minister in the Sanctuary, which came near to serve the Lord: and it shall be a place for their houses, and an holy place for the Sanctuary.

5 And *in* the five and twenty thousand of length, and the ten thousand of breadth shall the Levites that minister in the house, have their possession for twenty chambers.

6 Also ye shall appoint the possession of the city, five thousand broad, and five and twenty thousand long over against the oblation of the holy portion: it shall be for the whole house of Israel.

7 And *a portion shall be* for the prince on the one side, and on that side of the oblation of the holy portion, and of the possession of the city, *even* before the oblation of the holy portion, and before the possession of the city from the West corner Westward, and from the East corner Eastward, and the length *shall be* by one of the portions from the West border unto the East border.

8 In this land shall be his possession in Israel: and my princes shall no more oppress my people, and *the* rest of the land shall they give to the house of Israel, according to their tribes.

9 Thus saith the Lord God, Let it ¹suffice you, O princes of Israel: leave off cruelty and oppression, and execute judgment and justice: take away your exactions from my people, saith the Lord God.

10 Ye shall have just balances, and a true ¹Ephah, and a true Bath.

11 The Ephah and the Bath shall be equal: a Bath shall contain the tenth part of an Homer, and an

CHAPTER 45
ᵃ Exod. 30:13
Lev. 27:25
Num. 3:47
ᵇ Exod. 22
Lev. 23:5

Ephah the tenth part of an Homer: the equality thereof shall be after the Homer.

12 ᵃAnd the shekel *shall be* twenty Gerahs, *and* twenty shekels, and ¹five and twenty shekels and fifteen shekels shall be your Mina.

13 ¶ This is the oblation that ye shall offer, the sixth part of an Ephah of an Homer of wheat, and ye shall give the sixth part of an Ephah of an Homer of Barley.

14 Concerning the ordinance of the oil, *even of the* Bath of oil, *ye shall offer* the tenth part of a Bath out of the Cor (ten Baths *are* an Homer: for ten Baths *fill* an Homer)

15 And one Lamb of two hundred sheep out of the fat pastures of Israel for a meat offering, and for a burnt offering and for peace offerings, to make reconciliation for them, saith the Lord God.

16 All the people of the land shall *give* this oblation for the prince in Israel.

17 And it shall be the prince's part to give burnt offerings, and meat offerings, and drink offerings in the solemn feasts and in the new moons, and in the Sabbaths, *and* in all the high feasts of the house of Israel: he shall prepare the sin offering, and the meat offering, and the burnt offering, and the peace offerings to make reconciliation for the house of Israel.

18 ¶ Thus saith the Lord God, In the first *month*, in the first *day* of the ¹month, thou shalt take a young bullock without blemish and cleanse the Sanctuary.

19 And the Priest shall take of the blood of the sin offering, and put it upon the posts of the house, and upon the four ¹corners of the frame of the altar, and upon the posts of the gate of the inner court.

20 And so shalt thou do the seventh *day* of the month, for everyone that hath erred, and for him that is deceived: so shall you reconcile the house.

21 ᵇIn the first *month* in the fourteenth day of the month, ye shall have the Passover, a feast of seven days, *and* ye shall eat unleavened bread.

22 And upon that day, shall the prince prepare for himself and for all the people of the land, a bullock for a sin offering.

23 And in the seven days of the feast he shall make a burnt offering to the Lord, *even* of seven bullocks, and seven rams without blemish daily for seven days, and an he goat daily for a sin offering.

24 And he shall prepare a meat offering of an Ephah for a bullock, an Ephah for a ram, and an

---

45:1 ¹ Of all the land of Israel the Lord only requireth this portion for the Temple and for the Priests, for the city and for the Prince.
45:9 ¹ The Prophet showeth that the heads must be first reformed afore any good order can be established among the people.
45:10 ¹ Ephah and Bath were both of one quantity, save that Ephah contained in dry things that which Bath did in liquor, Lev. 5:11;

1 Kings 5:11.
45:12 ¹ That is, three-score shekels make a weight called Mina, for he joineth these three parts to a Mina.
45:18 ¹ Which was Nisan, containing part of March and part of April.
45:19 ¹ Or, court.

¹Hin of oil for an Ephah.

25 In the seventh *month*, in the fifteenth day of the month, shall he do the like in the feast for seven days, according to the sin offering, according to the burnt offering, and according to the meat offering, and according to the oil.

46 1 *The sacrifices of the Sabbath and of the new moon.* 8 *Through which doors they must go in, or come out of the Temple, etc.*

1 Thus saith the Lord God, The gate of the inner court, that turneth toward the East, shall be shut the six working days: but on the Sabbath it shall be opened, and in the day of the new moon it shall be opened.

2 And the prince shall enter by the way of the porch of that gate without, and shall stand by the post of the gate, and the Priests shall make his burnt offering, and his peace offerings, and he shall worship at the threshold of the gate: after he shall go forth, but the gate shall not be shut till the evening.

3 Likewise the people of the land shall worship at the entry of this gate before the Lord on the Sabbaths, and in the new moons.

4 And the burnt offering that the prince shall offer unto the Lord on the Sabbath day, *shall be* six lambs without blemish, and a ram without blemish.

5 And the meat offering *shall be* an Ephah for a ram: and the meat offering for the lambs ¹a gift of his hand, and an Hin of oil to an Ephah.

6 And in the day of the new moon *it shall be* a young bullock without blemish, and six lambs and a ram: they shall be without blemish.

7 And he shall prepare a meat offering, *even* an Ephah for a bullock, and an Ephah for a ram, and for the lambs ¹according as his hand shall bring, and an Hin of oil to an Ephah.

8 And when the prince shall enter, he shall go in by the way of the porch of that gate, and he shall go forth by the way thereof.

9 But when the people of the land shall come before the Lord in the solemn feasts, he that entereth in by the way of the North gate to worship, shall go out by the way of the South gate: and he that entereth by the way of the South gate, shall go forth by the way of the North gate: he shall not return by the way of the gate whereby he came in, but they shall go forth over against it.

10 And the prince shall be in the midst of them: he shall go in when they go in, and when they go forth, they shall go forth *together*.

11 And in the feasts, and in the solemnities the meat offering shall be an Ephah to a bullock, and an Ephah to a ram, and to the lambs, the gift of his hand, and an Hin of oil to an Ephah.

12 Now when the prince shall make a free burnt offering, or peace offerings freely unto the Lord, one shall then open him the gate that turneth toward the East, and he shall make his burnt offering and his peace offerings, as he did on the Sabbath day: after he shall go forth, and when he is gone forth, one shall shut the gate.

13 Thou shalt daily make a burnt offering unto the Lord of a lamb of one year, without blemish: thou shalt do it every morning.

14 And thou shalt prepare a meat offering for it every morning, the sixth part of an Ephah, and the third part of an Hin of oil, to mingle with the fine flour: *this* meat offering shall be continually by a perpetual ordinance unto the Lord.

15 Thus shall they prepare the lamb, and the meat offering, and the oil every morning, for a continual burnt offering.

16 ¶ Thus saith the Lord God, If the prince give a gift of his inheritance unto any of his sons, it shall be his sons, *and* it shall be their possession by inheritance.

17 But if he give a gift of his inheritance to one of his servants, then it shall be his to the ¹year of liberty: after, it shall return to the Prince, but his inheritance shall remain to his sons for them.

18 Moreover the prince shall not ¹take of the people's inheritance, nor thrust them out of their possession: *but* he shall cause his sons to inherit of his own possession, that my people be not scattered every man from his possession.

19 ¶ After he brought me through the entry, which was at the side of the gate, into the holy chambers of the Priests, which stood toward the North: and behold, there was a place at the West side of them.

20 Then said he unto me, This is the place where the Priests shall seethe the trespass offering and the sin offering, where they shall bake the meat offering, that they should not bear them into the utter court, ¹to sanctify the people.

21 Then he brought me forth into the utter court, and caused me to go by the four corners of the court: and behold, in every corner of the court there *was* a court.

22 In the four corners of the court there were courts joined of forty *cubits* long, and thirty broad:

45:24 ¹ Read Exod. 29:40.
46:5 ¹ That is, as much as he will.
46:7 ¹ Meaning, as he shall think good.
46:17 ¹ Which was at the Jubilee, Lev. 25:9.
46:18 ¹ But be content with that portion that God hath assigned him, as Ezek. 45:8.
46:20 ¹ That the people should not have to do with those things which appertain to the Lord, and think it lawful for them to eat them.

these four corners were of one measure.

23 And there *went* a wall about them, *even* about those four, and kitchens were made under the walls round about.

24 Then said he unto me, This is the kitchen where the ministers of the house shall seethe the sacrifice of the people.

47

1 The vision of the waters that came out of the Temple. 13 The coasts of the land of promise, and the division thereof by tribes.

1 Afterward he brought me unto the door of the house: and behold, ¹waters issued out from under the threshold of the house Eastward: for the forefront of the house *stood* toward the East, and the waters ran down from under the right side of the house, at the South side of the altar.

2 Then brought he me out toward the North gate, and led me about by the way without unto the utter gate by the way that turneth Eastward: and behold, there came forth waters on the right side

3 And when the man that had the line in his hand, went forth Eastward, he measured a thousand cubits, and he brought me through the waters: the waters *were* to the ankles.

4 Again he measured a thousand and brought me through the waters: the waters *were* to the knees: again he measured a thousand, and brought me through: the waters *were* to the loins.

5 Afterward he measured a thousand, *and it was* a ¹river, that I could not pass over: for the waters were risen, *and* the waters did flow, *as* a river that could not be passed over.

6 And he said unto me, Son of man, hast thou seen this? Then he brought me, and caused me to return to the brink of the river:

7 Now when I turned, behold, at the brink of the river *were* very many ¹trees on the one side and on the other.

8 Then said he unto me, These waters issue out toward the East country, and run down into the plain, and shall go into one ¹sea: they shall run into *another* sea, and the waters shall be wholesome.

9 And everything that liveth, which moveth,

CHAPTER 47
ᵃ Gen. 48:22
ᵇ Gen. 12:7
Gen. 13:15
Gen. 15:18
Gen. 26:4
Deut. 34:4

wheresoever the rivers shall come, shall live, and there shall be a very great multitude of fish, because these waters shall come thither: ¹for they shall be wholesome, and everything shall live whither the river cometh.

10 And then the ¹fishers shall stand upon it, *and* from En Gedi even unto ²En Eglaim, they shall spread out their nets: *for* their fish shall be according to their kinds, as the fish of ³the main sea, exceeding many.

11 But ¹the miry places thereof, and the marshes thereof shall not be wholesome: they shall be made salt pits.

12 And by this river upon the brink thereof, on this side, and on that side shall grow all ¹fruitful trees, whose leaf shall not fade, neither shall the fruit thereof fail: it shall bring forth new fruit according to his months, because their waters run out of the Sanctuary: and the fruit thereof shall be meat, and the leaf thereof shall be for ²medicine.

13 ¶ Thus saith the Lord God, This shall be the border, whereby ye shall inherit the land according to the twelve tribes ᵃof Israel: Joseph shall have *two* portions.

14 And ye shall inherit it, one as well as another: ᵇconcerning the which I lifted up mine hand to give it unto your fathers, and this land shall fall unto you for inheritance.

15 And this shall be the border ¹of the land toward the North side, from the main sea toward Hethlon, as men go to Zedad:

16 Hamath, Berothah, Sibraim, which is between the border of Damascus, and the border of Hamath, *and* Hazar, Hatticon, which is by the coast of Hauran.

17 And the border from the sea shall be Hazar, Enan, *and* the border of Damascus, and the residue of the North Northward, and the border of Hamath: so *shall be* the North part.

18 But the East side shall ye measure from Hauran, and from Damascus, and from Gilead, and from the land of Israel by Jordan, *and* from the border unto the East sea: and so *shall be* the East part.

19 And the South side *shall be* toward Teman, from Tamar to the waters of ¹Meriboth *in* Kadesh, *and* the river to the main sea: so *shall be* the South

---

47:1 ¹ Whereby are meant the spiritual graces that should be given to the Church under the kingdom of Christ.

47:5 ¹ Signifying that the graces of God should never decrease, but ever abound in his Church.

47:7 ¹ Meaning, the multitude of them that should be refreshed by the spiritual waters.

47:8 ¹ Showing that the abundance of these graces should be so great, that all the world should be full thereof, which is here meant by the Persian sea, or Genezareth, and the sea called Mediterranean, Zech. 14:8.

47:9 ¹ The waters which of nature are salt, and unwholesome shall be made sweet and comfortable.

47:10 ¹ Signifying, that when God bestoweth his mercies in such abundance, the ministers shall by their preaching win many.

² Which were cities at the corners of the salt or dead sea.

³ They shall be here of all sorts, and in as great abundance as in the great Ocean where they are bred.

47:11 ¹ That is, the wicked and reprobate.

47:12 ¹ Or, tree for meat.

² Or, for bruises and sores.

47:15 ¹ By the land of promise he signifieth the spiritual land whereof this was a figure.

47:19 ¹ Or, strife.

part toward Teman.

20 The West part also *shall be* the great sea from the border, till a man come over against Hamath: this shall be the west part.

21 So shall ye divide this land unto you, according to the tribes of Israel.

22 And you shall divide it by lot for an inheritance unto you, and to the strangers that dwell among you, which shall beget children among you, and they shall be unto you, as born in the country among the children of Israel, [1]they shall part inheritance with you in the midst of the tribes of Israel.

23 And in what tribe the stranger dwelleth, there shall ye give him his inheritance, saith the Lord God.

48

The lots of the tribes. 9 The parts of the possession of the Priests, of the Temple, of the Levites, of the city, and of the Prince are rehearsed.

1 Now these are the names of the [1]tribes. From the North side, to the coast toward Hethlon as one goeth to Hamath, Hazar, Enan, *and* the border of Damascus Northward the coast of Hamath, even *from* the East side to the West shall be *a portion* for Dan.

2 And by the border of Dan from the East side unto the West side, *a portion* for Asher.

3 And by the border of Asher from the East part even unto the West part, *a portion* for Naphtali.

4 And by the border of Naphtali from the East quarter unto the West side, *a portion* for Manasseh.

5 And by the border of Manasseh, from the East side unto the West side, *a portion* for Ephraim.

6 And by the border of Ephraim, from the East part even unto the West part, *a portion* for Reuben.

7 And by the border of Reuben, from the East quarter unto the West quarter, *a portion* for Judah.

8 And by the border of Judah from the East part unto the West part [1]shall be the offering which they shall offer of five and twenty thousand *reeds* broad, and of length as one of the *other* parts, from the East side unto the West side, and the Sanctuary shall be in the midst of it.

9 The oblation that ye shall offer unto the Lord, *shall be* of five and twenty thousand long, and of ten thousand the breadth.

10 And for them, *even* for the Priests shall be this holy oblation, toward the North five and twenty thousand *long*, and toward the West, ten thousand

CHAPTER 48
a Ezek. 44:5

broad, and toward the East ten thousand broad, and toward the South five and twenty thousand long, and the Sanctuary of the Lord shall be in the midst thereof.

11 *It shall be* for the Priests that are sanctified of the sons of *a*Zadok, which have kept my charge, which went not astray, when the children of Israel went astray, as the Levites went astray.

12 Therefore *this* oblation of the land that is offered shall be theirs, *as* a thing most holy by the border of the Levites.

13 And over against the border of the Priests the Levites *shall have* five and twenty thousand long, and [ten] thousand broad: all the length *shall be* five and twenty thousand, and the breadth ten thousand.

14 And they shall not sell of it, neither change it, nor alienate the firstfruits of the land: for it is holy unto the Lord.

15 And the five thousand that are left in the breadth over against the five and twenty thousand, shall be a profane place for the city, for housing, and for suburbs, and the city shall be in the midst thereof.

16 And these shall be the measures thereof, the North part five hundred and four thousand, and the South part [1]five hundred and four thousand, and the East part five hundred and four thousand, and the West part five hundred and four thousand.

17 And the suburbs of the city shall be toward the North two hundred and fifty, and toward the South two hundred and fifty, and toward the East two hundred and fifty, and toward the West two hundred and fifty.

18 And the residue in length over against the oblation of the holy portion *shall be* ten thousand Eastward, and ten thousand Westward: and it shall be over against the oblation of the holy portion, and the increase thereof shall be for food unto them that serve in the city.

19 And they that serve in the city, *shall be* of all the tribes of Israel that shall serve therein.

20 All the oblation *shall be* five and twenty thousand with [1]five and twenty thousand: you shall offer this oblation foursquare for the Sanctuary, and for the possession of the city.

21 And the residue *shall be* for the prince on the one side and on the other of the oblation of the Sanctuary, and of the possession of the city, over against the five and twenty thousand of the oblation toward the East border, and Westward over against the five and twenty thousand toward the West border,

---

47:22 [1] Meaning, that in this spiritual kingdom there should be no difference between Jew nor Gentile, but that all should be partakers of this inheritance in their head Christ.
48:1 [1] The tribes after that they entered into the land under Joshua, divided the land somewhat otherwise than is here set forth by this vision.

48:8 [1] That is, the portion of the ground which they shall separate and appoint to the Lord, which shall be divided into three parts, for the Priests, for the Prince, and for the city.
48:16 [1] Meaning, that it should be square.
48:20 [1] Every way it shall be five and twenty thousand.

over against *shall be* for the portion of the prince: this shall be the holy oblation, and the house of the Sanctuary *shall be* in the midst thereof.

22 Moreover, from the possession of the Levites, and from the possession of the city, that which is in the midst shall be the prince's: between the border [1]of Judah, and between the border of Benjamin shall be the Princes.

23 And the rest of the tribes *shall be thus*: from the East part unto the West part, Benjamin *shall be a portion*.

24 And by the border of Benjamin, from the East side unto the West side, Simeon *a portion*.

25 And by the border of Simeon from the East part unto the West part, Issachar *a portion*.

26 And by the border of Issachar, from the East side unto the West, Zebulun *a portion*.

27 And by the border of Zebulun, from the East part unto the West part, Gad *a portion*.

28 And by the border of Gad at the South side, toward [1]Temath, the border shall be even from [2]Tamar, *unto* the waters of Meribah *in* Kadesh, *and* to the [3]river, *that runneth* into the main sea.

29 This is the land, which ye shall distribute unto the tribes of Israel for inheritance, and these are their portions, saith the Lord God.

30 And these are the bounds of the city, on the North side five hundred, and four thousand measures.

31 And the gates of the city *shall be* after the names of the tribes of Israel, the gates Northward, one gate of Reuben, one gate of Judah, *and* one gate of Levi.

32 And at the East side five hundred and four thousand, and three gates, and one gate of Joseph, one gate of Benjamin, *and* one gate of Dan.

33 And at the South side, five hundred and four thousand measures, and three ports, one gate of Simeon, one gate of Issachar, *and* one gate of Zebulun.

34 At the West side, five hundred and four thousand, *with* their three gates, one gate of Gad, one gate of Asher, *and* one gate of Naphtali.

35 *It was* round about eighteen thousand *measures*, and the name of the city from that day *shall be*, [1]The Lord is there.

48:22 [1] So that Judah was on the North side of the Prince's and Levites' portions, and Benjamin on the South side.
48:28 [1] Which is here taken for Edom.

[2] Which was Jericho the city of palm trees.
[3] Meaning, Nile that runneth into the Sea, called Mediterranean.
48:35 [1] Hebrew, *Jehovah Shammah*.

DANIEL

1 *1 The captivity of Jehoiakim king of Judah. 4 The king chooseth certain young men of the Jews to learn his law. 5 They have the king's ordinary appointed, 8 but they abstain from it.*

1 In the ¹third year of the reign of Jehoiakim king of Judah, came Nebuchadnezzar King of Babel unto Jerusalem and besieged it.

2 And the Lord gave Jehoiakim king of Judah into his hand with part of the vessels of the house of God, which he carried into the land of ¹Shinar, to the house of his god, and he brought the vessels into his god's treasury.

3 And the King spake unto ¹Ashpenaz the master of his ²Eunuchs, that he should bring *certain* of the children of Israel, of the ³King's seed, and of the princes:

4 Children in whom was no blemish, but well ¹favored, and instruct in all wisdom, and well seen in knowledge, and able to utter knowledge, and such as were able to stand in the king's palace, and whom they might ²teach the learning, and the tongue of the Chaldeans.

5 And the king appointed them provision every day of a ¹portion of the king's meat, and of the wine, which he drank, so nourishing them ²three years, that at the end thereof, they might stand ³before the king.

6 Now among these were *certain* of the children of Judah, Daniel, Hananiah, Mishael and Azariah.

7 Unto whom the chief of the Eunuchs ¹gave *other* names: for he called Daniel, Belteshazzar, and Hananiah, Shadrach, and Mishael, Meshach, and Azariah, Abednego.

8 ¶ But Daniel had determined in his heart, that he would not ¹defile himself with the portion of the King's meat, nor with the wine which he drank: therefore he required the chief of the Eunuchs that he might not defile himself.

9 (Now God had brought Daniel into favor, and tender love with the chief of the Eunuchs.)

10 And the chief of the Eunuchs said unto Daniel, ¹I fear my lord the King, who hath appointed your meat and your drink: therefore if he see your faces worse liking than the *other* children which are of your sort, then shall you make me lose mine head unto the King.

11 Then said Daniel to Melzar, whom the chief of the Eunuchs had set over Daniel, Hananiah, Mishael, and Azariah,

12 Prove thy servants, I beseech thee, ¹ten days, and let them give us ²pulse to eat, and water to drink.

13 Then let our countenances be looked upon

1:1 ¹ Read 2 Kings 24:1 and Jer. 25:1.
1:2 ¹ Which was a plain by Babylon, where was the Temple of their great god, and is here taken for Babylon.
1:3 ¹ Who was as master of the wards.
² He calleth them Eunuchs whom the King nourished and brought up to be rulers of other countries afterward.
³ His purpose was to keep them as hostages, and that he might show himself victorious, and also by their good entreaty and learning of his religion, they might favor rather than the Jews, and so to be able to serve him as governors in their land: moreover by this means the Jews might be better kept in subjection, fearing otherwise to procure hurt to these noble men.
1:4 ¹ The King required three things, that they should be of noble birth, that they should be witty and learned, and that they should be of a strong and comely nature, that they might do him better service: this he did for his own commodity, therefore it is not to praise his liberality: yet in this he is worthy praise, that he esteemed learning, and knew that it was a necessary means to govern by.
² That they might forget their own religion, and country fashions to serve him the better to his purpose: yet it is not to be thought that Daniel did learn any knowledge that was not godly: in all points he refused the abuse of things and superstition, insomuch that he would not eat the meat which the King appointed him, but was content to learn the knowledge of natural things.
1:5 ¹ That by their good entertainment they might learn to forget the mediocrity of their own people.
² To the intent that in this time they might both learn the manners of the Chaldeans, and also their tongue.
³ As well to serve at the table, as in other offices.
1:7 ¹ That they might altogether forget their religion: for the Jews gave their children names, which might ever put them in remembrance of some point of religion: therefore this was a great tentation and a sign of servitude, which they were not able to resist.
1:8 ¹ Not that he thought any religion to be in the meat or drink, (for afterward he did eat) but because the king should not entice him by this sweet poison to forget his religion and accustomed sobriety, and that in his meat and drink he might daily remember of what people he was: and Daniel bringeth this in to show how God from the beginning assisted him with his Spirit, and at length called him to be a Prophet.
1:10 ¹ He supposed they did this for their religion, which was contrary to the Babylonians, and therefore herein he representeth them, which are of no religion: for neither he would condemn theirs, nor maintain his own.
1:12 ¹ Meaning, that within this space he might have the trial, and that no man should be able to discern it: and thus he spake, being moved by the Spirit of God.
² Not that it was a thing abominable to eat dainty meats, and to drink wine, as both before and after they did, but if they should have hereby been won to the King, and have refused their own religion, that meat and drink had been accursed.

before thee, and the countenances of the children that eat of the portion of the King's meat: and as thou seest, deal with thy servants.

14 So he consented to them in this matter, and proved them ten days.

15 And at the end of ten days, their [1]countenances appeared fairer, and in [2]better liking than all the children's, which did eat the portion of the King's meat.

16 Thus Melzar took away the portion of their meat, and the wine that they should drink, and gave them pulse.

17 As for these four children, God gave them knowledge, and understanding in all learning [1]and wisdom: also he gave Daniel understanding of all [2]visions and dreams.

18 Now when the time [1]was expired, that the King had appointed to bring them in, the chief of the Eunuchs brought them before Nebuchadnezzar.

19 And the King communed with them: and among them all was found none like Daniel, Hananiah, Mishael, and Azariah: therefore stood they before the king.

20 And in all matters of wisdom, and understanding that the King enquired of them, he found them ten times better than all the enchanters and astrologians that were in all his realm.

21 And Daniel was unto [1]the first year of king Cyrus.

2 1 The dreams of Nebuchadnezzar. 13 The king commandeth all the wise men of Babylon to be slain, because they could not interpret his dream. 16 Daniel requireth time to solute the question. 24 Daniel is brought unto the king, and showeth him his dream, and the interpretation thereof. 44 Of the everlasting kingdom of Christ.

1 And in the [1]second year of the reign of Nebuchadnezzar, Nebuchadnezzar dreamed [2]dreams wherewith his spirit was [3]troubled, and his [4]sleep was upon him.

2 Then the king commanded to call the enchanters, and the astrologians, and the sorcerers, and the [1]Chaldeans for to show the king his dreams: so they came and stood before the King.

3 And the king said unto them, I have dreamed a dream, and my spirit was troubled to know the dream.

4 Then spake the Chaldeans to the king in the [1]Aramite's language, O king, live forever: show thy servants thy dream, and we shall show the interpretation.

5 And the King answered and said to the Chaldeans, The thing is gone from me. If ye will not make me understand the dream with the interpretation thereof, ye [1]shall be drawn in pieces, and your houses shall be made a jakes.

6 But if ye declare the dream and the interpretation thereof, ye shall receive of me gifts and rewards, and great honor: therefore show me the dream and the interpretation of it.

7 They answered again, and said, Let the king show [1]his servants the dream, and we will declare the interpretation thereof.

8 Then the king answered, and said, I know certainly that ye [1]would gain the time, because ye see the thing is gone from me.

9 But if ye will not declare me the dream, there is but one judgment for you: for ye have prepared lying and corrupt words, to speak before me till the time be changed: therefore tell me the dream, that I may know, if ye can declare me the interpretation thereof.

10 Then the Chaldeans answered before the king, and said, There is no man upon earth that can declare the king's matter: yea, there is neither King nor Prince nor lord that asked such things at an enchanter, or

---

1:15 [1] This bare feeding and that also of Moses, when he fled from the court of Egypt, declareth that we must live in such sobriety as God doth call us unto, seeing he will make it more profitable unto us than all dainties: for his blessing only sufficeth.

[2] Hebrew, fatter in flesh.

1:17 [1] Meaning, in the liberal sciences, and natural knowledge, and not in the magical arts which are forbidden, Deut. 18:11.

[2] So that he only was a Prophet and none of the others: for by dreams and visions God appeared to his Prophets, Num. 12:6

1:18 [1] Of the three years above mentioned, verse 5.

1:21 [1] That is, he was esteemed in Babylon as a Prophet so long as that commonwealth stood.

2:1 [1] The father and the son were both called by this name, so that this is meant of the son, when he reigned alone: for he reigned also after a sort with his father.

[2] Not that he had many dreams, but because many matters were contained in this dream.

[3] Because it was so rare and strange a dream: that he had not had the like.

[4] He was so heavy with sleep, that he began to sleep again. Some read, and his sleep was broken from him.

2:2 [1] For all these Astrologers and sorcerers called themselves by this name of honor, as though all the wisdom and knowledge of the country depended upon them, and that all other countries were void of the same.

2:4 [1] That is, in the Syrian tongue which differed not much from the Chaldeans, save it seemed to be more eloquent, and therefore the learned used to speak it, as the Jewish writers do to this day.

2:5 [1] This is a just reward of their arrogance (which vaunted of themselves that they had the knowledge of all things) that they should be proved fools, and that to their perpetual shame and confusion.

2:7 [1] Herein appeared their ignorance, that notwithstanding their brags, yet were they not able to tell the dream, except he entered them into the matter, and therefore they would pretend knowledge where was but mere ignorance, and so as deluders of the people, they were worthy to die.

2:8 [1] Hebrew, redeem the time.

astrologian, or Chaldean.

11 For it is a rare thing that the king requireth, and there is none other that can declare it before the king, except the gods whose dwelling is not with flesh.

12 For this cause the king was angry and in great fury, and commanded to destroy all the wise men of Babel.

13 ¶ And when sentence was given, the wise men were slain: and they ¹sought Daniel and his fellows to be put to death.

14 Then Daniel answered with counsel and wisdom to Arioch the king's ¹chief steward, which was gone forth to put to death the wise men of Babel.

15 *Yea*, he answered and said unto Arioch the king's captain, Why is the sentence so hasty from the king? Then Arioch declared the thing to Daniel.

16 So Daniel went and desired the king that he would give him leisure, and that he would show the king the interpretation thereof.

17 ¶ Then Daniel went to his house, and showed the matter to Hananiah, Mishael, and Azariah his companions,

18 That they should beseech the God of heaven for grace in this secret, that Daniel and his fellows should not perish with the rest of the wise men of Babel.

19 Then was the secret revealed unto Daniel in a vision by night: therefore Daniel praised the God of heaven.

20 And Daniel answered and said, ᵃThe Name of God be praised forever and ever: for wisdom and strength are his.

21 And he changeth the times and seasons: he taketh away kings: he setteth up kings: he giveth wisdom unto the wise, and understanding to those that understand.

22 He discovereth the deep and secret things: he knoweth what is in darkness, and the ¹light dwelleth with him.

23 I thank thee and praise thee, O thou God of my ¹fathers, that thou hast given me wisdom and

CHAPTER 2
ᵃ Ps. 113:2
Ps. 115:18

²strength, and hast showed me now the thing that we desired of thee: for thou hast declared unto us the king's matter.

24 ¶ Therefore Daniel went unto Arioch, whom the King had ordained to destroy the wise men of Babel: he went and said thus unto him, Destroy not ¹the wise men of Babel, *but* bring me before the king, and I will declare unto the king the interpretation.

25 Then Arioch brought Daniel before the king in all haste, and said thus unto him, I have found a man of the children of Judah that were brought captives, that will declare unto the king the interpretation.

26 Then answered the king, and said unto Daniel, whose name was Belteshazzar, Art thou able to show me the dream which I have seen, and the interpretation thereof?

27 Daniel answered in the presence of the king, and said, The secret which the king hath demanded, can neither the wise, the astrologians, the enchanters, *nor* the soothsayers declare unto the king.

28 But there is a God in ¹heaven that revealeth secrets, and showeth the king Nebuchadnezzar what shall be in the latter days. Thy dream, and the things which thou hast seen in thine head upon thy bed, is this:

29 O king, when thou wast in thy bed, thoughts came into thy *mind*, what should come to pass hereafter, and he that revealeth secrets, telleth thee what shall come.

30 As ¹for me, this secret is not showed me for any wisdom that I have more than any other living, but only to show the king the interpretation, and that thou mightest know the thoughts of thine heart.

31 O king, thou sawest, and behold, there *was* a great image: this great image whose glory was so excellent, stood before thee, and the form therefore *was* terrible.

32 This image's head was of fine ¹gold, his breast, and his arms of silver, his belly and his thighs of brass,

33 His legs of iron, *and* his feet *were* part of iron,

2:13 ¹ Which declareth that God would not have his servant joined in the company of these sorcerers and Astrologers, whose arts were wicked, and therefore justly ought to die, though the king did it upon a rage and no zeal.

2:14 ¹ Or, the captain of the guards.

2:22 ¹ He showeth that man hath neither wisdom nor knowledge, but very dark blindness and ignorance of himself: for it cometh only of God, that man understandeth anything.

2:23 ¹ To whom thou madest thy promise, and who lived in thy fear: whereby he excludeth all other gods.

² Meaning, power to interpret it.

2:24 ¹ Whereby appeareth that many were slain, as verse 13, and the rest at Daniel's offer were preserved on condition: not that Daniel favored their wicked profession, but that he had respect to equity, because the King proceeded according to his wicked affection, and not considering if their science were lawful or no.

2:28 ¹ He affirmeth that man by reason and art is not able to attain

to the cause of God's secrets, but the understanding only thereof must come of God: whereby he smiteth the king with a certain fear and reverence of God, that he might be the more apt to receive the high mysteries, that should be revealed.

2:30 ¹ Because he had said that God only must reveal the signification of this dream, the King might have asked, why Daniel did enterprise to interpret it, and therefore he showeth that he was but God's minister and had no gifts, but such as God had given him to set forth his glory.

2:32 ¹ By gold, silver, brass and iron, are meant the Chaldean, Persian, Macedonian and Roman kingdoms, which should successively rule all the world till Christ (which is here called the stone) come himself, and destroy the last: and this was to assure the Jews, that their affliction should not end with the empire of the Chaldeans, but that they should patiently abide the coming of Messiah, which should be at the end of this fourth monarchy.

and part of clay.

34 Thou beheldest it till a stone was cut without hands, which smote the image upon his feet, that were of iron and clay, and brake them to pieces.

35 Then was the iron, the clay, the brass, the silver and the gold broken all together, and became like the chaff of the summer flowers, and the wind carried them away, that no place was found for them: and the stone that smote the image, became a great mountain, and filled the whole earth.

36 This is the dream, and we will declare before the king the interpretation thereof.

37 ¶ O king, thou art a king of kings: for the God of heaven hath given thee a kingdom, power, and strength, and glory.

38 And in all *places* where the children of men dwell, the beasts of the field, and the fowls of the heaven hath he given into thine hand, and hath made thee ruler over them all: thou art ¹this head of gold.

39 And after thee shall rise another kingdom, ¹inferior to thee, *of silver*, and another ²third kingdom *shall be* of brass, which shall bear rule over all the earth.

40 And the fourth kingdom shall be strong as iron: for as iron breaketh in pieces, and subdueth all things, and as iron bruiseth all these things, *so* shall it break in ¹pieces, and bruise *all*.

41 Whereas thou sawest the feet and toes, part of potter's clay, and part of iron: the kingdom shall be ¹divided, but there shall be in it of the strength of the iron, as thou sawest the iron mixed with the clay, *and* earth.

42 And *as* the toes of the feet *were* part of iron, and part of clay, *so* shall the kingdom be partly strong, and partly broken.

43 And whereas thou sawest iron mixed with clay *and* earth, they shall mingle themselves with ¹the seed of men: but they shall not join one with another, as iron cannot be mixed with clay.

44 And in the days of these kings, shall the God of heaven set up a kingdom, which ¹shall never be destroyed: and this kingdom shall not be given to another people, but it shall break, and destroy all these kingdoms, and it shall stand forever.

45 Whereas thou sawest, that the ¹stone was cut of the mountain without hands, and that it brake in pieces the iron, the brass, the clay, the silver, and the gold: *so* the great God hath showed the king, what shall come to pass hereafter, and the dream *is* true, and the interpretation thereof *is* sure.

46 ¶ Then the king Nebuchadnezzar fell upon his face, and ¹bowed himself unto Daniel, and commanded that they should offer meat offerings, and sweet odors unto him.

47 *Also* the King answered unto Daniel, and said, I *know* of a truth that your ¹God is a God of gods, and the Lord of kings, and the revealer of secrets, seeing thou couldest open this secret.

48 So the king made Daniel a great man, and gave him many and great ¹gifts. He made him governor over the whole province of Babel, and chief of the rulers, *and* above all the wise men of Babel.

49 Then Daniel ¹made request to the King, and he set Shadrach, Meshach, and Abednego over the charge of the province of Babel: but Daniel *sat* in the ²gate of the king.

3

1 *The king setteth up a golden image.* 8 *Certain are accused because they despised the king's commandment,*

2:38 ¹ Daniel leaveth out the kingdom of the Assyrians, which was before the Babylonian, both because it was not a Monarchy and general empire, and also because he would declare the things that were to come, to the coming of Christ, for the comfort of the elect among these wonderful alterations, and he calleth the Babylonian kingdom the golden head, because in respect of the other three, it was the best, and yet it was of itself wicked and cruel.

2:39 ¹ Meaning, the Persians which were not inferior in dignity, power, and riches, but were worse touching ambition, cruelty, and all kind of vice, showing that the world should grow worse and worse, till it was restored by Christ.

² That is, of the Macedonians shall be of brass, not alluding to the hardness thereof, but to the vileness in respect of silver.

2:40 ¹ That is, the Roman empire shall subdue all these other aforenamed, which after Alexander were divided into the Macedonians, Grecians, Syrians and Egyptians.

2:41 ¹ They shall have civil wars, and continual discords among themselves.

2:43 ¹ They shall by marriages and affinities think to make themselves strong: yet shall they never be joined in hearts.

2:44 ¹ His purpose is to show, that all the kingdoms of the world are transitory, and that the kingdom of Christ shall only remain forever.

2:45 ¹ Meaning Christ, who was sent of God, and not set up by

man, whose kingdom at the beginning should be small and without beauty to man's judgment, but should at length grow and fill the whole earth, which he calleth a great mountain, as verse 35. And this kingdom which is not only referred to the person of Christ, but also to the whole body of his Church, and to every member thereof, shall be eternal: for the Spirit that is in them is life eternal, Rom. 8:10.

2:46 ¹ Though this humbling of the king seemed to deserve commendation, yet because he joined God's honor with the Prophet's, it is to be reproved, and Daniel herein erred, if he suffered it: but it is credible that Daniel admonished him of his fault, and did not suffer it.

2:47 ¹ This confession was but a sudden motion, as it was also in Pharaoh, Exod. 9:28, but his heart was not touched, as appeared soon afterward.

2:48 ¹ Not that the Prophet was desirous of gifts or honor, but because by this means he might relieve his poor brethren, which were grievously oppressed in this their captivity, and also he received them, lest he should offend this cruel king, which willingly gave them.

2:49 ¹ He did not this for their private profit: but that the whole Church, which was then there in affliction, might have some release and ease by this benefit.

² Meaning, that either he was a judge, or that he had the whole authority, so than none could be admitted to the king's presence, but by him.

and are put into a burning oven.   15 By belief in God they are delivered from the fire.   25 Nebuchadnezzar confesseth the power of God after the sight of the miracle.

1 Nebuchadnezzar the king made [1]an image of gold, whose height *was* threescore cubits, *and* the breadth thereof six cubits: he set it up in the plain of Dura, in the province of Babel.

2 Then Nebuchadnezzar the king sent forth to gather together the nobles, the princes and the dukes, the judges, the receivers, the counselors, the officers, and all the governors of the provinces, that they should come to the [1]dedication of the image, which Nebuchadnezzar the [2]King had set up.

3 So the nobles, princes, and dukes, the judges, the receivers, the counselors, the officers, and all the governors of the provinces were assembled unto the dedicating of the image that Nebuchadnezzar the King had set up and they stood before the image which Nebuchadnezzar had set up.

4 Then an herald cried aloud, Be it known to you, O people, [1]nations, and languages,

5 That when ye hear the sound of the cornet, trumpet, harp, sackbut, psaltery, dulcimer, and all instruments of music, ye fall down, and worship the golden image, that Nebuchadnezzar the king hath set up.

6 And whosoever falleth not down, and worshippeth, shall the same hour be cast into the midst of an hot fiery furnace.

7 Therefore as soon as all the people heard the sound of the cornet, trumpet, harp, sackbut, psaltery, and all instruments of music, all the people, nations, and languages fell down, and worshipped the golden image, that Nebuchadnezzar the king had set up.

8 ¶ By reason whereof at that same time came men of the Chaldeans, and grievously accused the Jews.

9 *For* they spake and said to the king Nebuchad-nezzar, O King, live forever.

10 Thou, O King, hast made a decree, that every man that shall hear the sound of the cornet, trumpet, harp, sackbut, psaltery, and dulcimer, and all instruments of music, shall fall down, and worship the golden image.

11 And whosoever falleth not down, and worshippeth, that he should be cast into the midst of an hot fiery furnace.

12 There are certain Jews whom thou hast set over the charge of the province of Babel, [1]Shadrach, Meshach, and Abednego: these men, O King, have not regarded thy commandment, neither will they serve thy gods, nor worship the golden image that thou hast set up.

13 ¶ Then Nebuchadnezzar in *his* anger and wrath commanded that they should bring Shadrach, Meshach, and Abednego, so these men were brought before the king.

14 *And* Nebuchadnezzar spake, and said unto them, What disorder? will not you, Shadrach, Meshach, and Abednego, serve my god, nor worship the golden image that I have set up?

15 [1]Now therefore are ye ready when ye hear the sound of the cornet, trumpet, harp, sackbut, psaltery, and dulcimer, and all instruments of music, to fall down, and worship the image which I have made? for if ye worship it not, ye shall be cast immediately into the midst of an hot fiery furnace: for who is that God, that can deliver you out of mine hands?

16 Shadrach, Meshach, and Abednego answered and said to the King, O Nebuchadnezzar, we [1]are not careful to answer thee in this matter.

17 Behold, our God whom we serve, is [1]able to deliver us from the hot fiery furnace, and he will deliver us out of thine hand, O king.

18 But if not, be it known to thee, O king, that

3:1 [1] Under pretence of religion, and holiness in making an image to his idol Bel, he sought his own ambition and vain glory: and this declareth that he was not toucheth with the true fear of God before but that he confessed him on a sudden motion as the wicked when they are overcome with the greatness of his works. The Greek interpreters write, that this was done eighteen years after the dream, and as may appear, the King feared lest the Jews by their religion, should have altered the state of his commonwealth, and therefore he meant to bring all to one kind of religion, and so rather sought his own quietness than God's glory.

3:2 [1] Showing that the idol is not known for an idol so long as he is with workmen: but when the ceremonies and customs are recited and used, and the consent of the people is there, then of a block they think they have made a god.

[2] This was sufficient with the wicked at all times to approve their religion, if the king's authority were alleged for the establishment thereof, not considering in the mean season what God's word did permit.

3:4 [1] These are the two dangerous weapons, wherewith Satan used to fight against the children of God, the consent of the multitude, and the cruelty of the punishment: for though some feared God, yet the multitude, which consented to the wickedness, astonied them: and here the King required, not an inward consent, but an outward gesture, that the Jews might by little and little learn to forget their true religion.

3:12 [1] It seemeth that they named not Daniel, because he was greatly in the king's favor, thinking if these three had been destroyed, they might have had better occasion to accuse Daniel: and this declareth that this policy of erecting this image was invented by the malicious flatterers which sought nothing but the destruction of the Jews, whom they accused of rebellion and ingratitude.

3:15 [1] Signifying that he would receive them to grace if they should now at the length obey his decree.

3:16 [1] For they should have done injury to God, if they should have doubted in this holy cause, and therefore they say, that they are resolved to die for God's cause.

3:17 [1] They ground on two points, first on the power and providence of God over them, and secondly on their cause, which was God's glory, and the testifying of his true religion with their blood, and so make open confession, that they will not so much as outwardly consent to idolatry.

we will not serve thy gods, nor worship the golden image which thou hast set up.

19 ¶ Then was Nebuchadnezzar full of rage, and the form of his visage was changed against Shadrach, Meshach, and Abednego: *therefore* he charged and commanded that they should heat the furnace at once seven [1]times more than it was wont to be heated.

20 And he charged the most valiant men of war that were in his army, to bind Shadrach, Meshach, and Abednego, *and* to cast them into the hot fiery furnace.

21 So these men were bound in their coats, their hosen, and their cloaks, with their *other* garments, and cast into the midst of the hot fiery furnace.

22 Therefore, because the king's commandment was strait, that the furnace should be exceeding hot, the flame of the fire slew those men that brought forth Shadrach, Meshach and Abednego.

23 And these three men, Shadrach, Meshach and Abednego fell down bound into the midst of the hot fiery furnace.

24 ¶ Then Nebuchadnezzar the king was astonied, and rose up in haste, *and* spake, and said unto his counselors, Did not we cast three men bound into the midst of the fire? Who answered, and said unto him, It is true, O king.

25 *And* he answered, and said, Lo, I see four men loose, walking in the midst of the fire, and they have no hurt, and the form of the fourth is like the [1]son of God.

26 Then the King Nebuchadnezzar came near to the mouth of the hot fiery furnace, *and* spake and said, Shadrach, Meshach and Abednego, the servants of the high God, go forth and come *hither*: so Shadrach, Meshach and Abednego [1]came forth of the midst of the fire.

27 Then the nobles, princes, and dukes, and the king's counselors came together to see these men, because the fire had no power over their bodies: for not an hair of their head was burnt, neither were their coats

changed, nor any smell of fire came upon them.

28 *Wherefore* Nebuchadnezzar spake and said, [1]Blessed *be* the God of Shadrach, Meshach and Abednego, who hath sent his Angel, and delivered his servants, that put their trust in him, and have changed the king's commandment, and yielded their bodies rather than they would serve or worship any god save their own God.

29 Therefore I make a decree that every people, nation, and language, which speak any [1]blasphemy against the God of Shadrach, Meshach, and Abednego, shall be drawn in pieces, and their houses shall be made a jakes, because there is no god that can deliver after this sort.

30 Then the King promoted Shadrach, Meshach and Abednego in the province of Babel.

31 Nebuchadnezzar king unto all people, nations and languages, that dwell in all the [1]world, Peace be multiplied unto you:

32 I thought it good to declare the signs and wonders, that the high God hath wrought toward me.

33 How great are his signs, and how mighty are his wonders! [1]his kingdom *is* an everlasting kingdom, and his dominion *is* from generation to generation.

4 *2 Another dream of Nebuchadnezzar, which Daniel declareth.   29 The Prophet declareth how of a proud king, he should become as a beast.   31 After he confesseth the power of God, and is restored to his former dignity.*

1 I Nebuchadnezzar being at [1]rest in mine house, and flourishing in my palace,

2 Saw a [1]dream, which made me afraid, and the thoughts upon my bed, and the visions of mine head troubled me.

3 Therefore made I a decree, that they should bring all the wise men of Babel before me, that they might declare unto me the interpretation of the dream.

4 So came the enchanters, the astrologians, the Chaldeans and the soothsayers, to whom I told the dream, but [1]they could not show me the interpreta-

---

3:19 [1] This declareth that the more that tyrants rage, and the more witty they show themselves inventing strange and cruel punishments, the more is God glorified by his servants to whom he giveth patience and constancy to abide the cruelty of their punishment: for either by delivereth them from death, or else for this life giveth them a better.

3:25 [1] For the Angels were called the sons of God, because of their excellency: therefore the king called this Angel whom God sent to comfort his in these great torments, the son of God.

3:26 [1] This commendeth their obedience unto God, that they would not for any fear depart out of this furnace, till the time appointed, as Noah remained in the ark, till the Lord called him forth.

3:28 [1] He was moved by the greatness of the miracle to praise God, but his heart was not touched. And here we see that miracles are not sufficient to convert men to God, but that doctrine most chiefly be adjoined, without the which there can be no faith.

3:29 [1] If this heathen king moved by God's Spirit would not see blas-

phemy unpunished, but made a law and set a punishment to such transgressors, much more ought all they that profess religion, take order that such impiety reign not, lest according as their knowledge and charge is greater, so they suffer double punishment.

3:31 [1] Meaning, so far as his dominion extended.

3:33 [1] Read Dan. 2:44.

4:1 [1] There was no trouble that might cause me to dream, and therefore it came only of God.

4:2 [1] This was another dream besides that which he saw of the four Empires, for Daniel both declared what that dream was, and what it meant, and here he only expoundeth the dream.

4:4 [1] In that that he sent abroad to others, whose ignorance in times past he had experimented, and left Daniel which was ever ready at hand, it declareth the nature of the ungodly, which never seek to the servants of God, but for very necessity, and then they spare no flatterings.

tion thereof,

5 Till at the last Daniel came before me, (whose name *was* [1]Belteshazzar, according to the name of my god, which hath the spirit of the holy gods in him) and before him I told the dream, *saying,*

6 O Belteshazzar, [1]chief of the enchanters, because I know, that the spirit of the holy gods is in thee, and no secret troubleth thee, tell me the visions of my dream, that I have seen, and the interpretation thereof.

7 Thus *were* the visions of my head in my bed, and behold, I saw a [1]tree in the midst of the earth, and the height thereof *was* great:

8 A great tree and strong, and the height thereof reached unto heaven, and the sight thereof to the ends of all the earth.

9 The boughs thereof *were* fair and the fruit thereof much, and in it was meat for all: it made a shadow under it for the beasts of the field, and the fowls of the heaven dwelt in the boughs thereof, and all flesh fed of it.

10 I saw in the visions of mine head upon my bed, and behold, a [1]watchman and an holy one came down from heaven,

11 And cried aloud, and said thus, Hew down the tree, and break off his branches: shake off his leaves, and scatter his fruit, that the beasts may flee from under it, and the fowls from his branches.

12 Nevertheless, leave the stump of his roots in the earth, and with a band of iron and brass *bind it* among the grass of the field, and let it be wet with the dew of heaven, and let his portion *be* with the beasts among the grass of the field.

13 [1]Let his heart be changed from man's *nature,* and let a beast's heart be given unto him, and let seven times be passed over him.

14 [1]The sentence *is* according to the decree of the watchmen, and according to the word of the holy ones: the demand *was answered,* to the intent that living men may know, that the most High hath power over the kingdom of men, and giveth it to whomsoever he will,

and appointeth over it the most abject among men.

15 This is the dream, *that* I King Nebuchadnezzar have seen: therefore thou, O Belteshazzar, declare the interpretation thereof: for all the wise men of my kingdom are not able to show me the interpretation: but thou art able, for the spirit of the holy gods *is* in thee.

16 ¶ Then Daniel (whose name *was* Belteshazzar) held his [1]peace by the space of one hour, and his thoughts troubled him, *and* the King spake and said, Belteshazzar, let neither the dream, nor the interpretation thereof trouble thee. Belteshazzar answered and said, My lord, the dream *be* to them that hate thee, and the interpretation thereof to thine enemies.

17 The tree that thou sawest, which was great and mighty, whose height reached unto the heaven, and the sight thereof through all the world,

18 Whose leaves *were* fair, and the fruit thereof much, and in it was meat for all, under the which the beasts of the field dwelt, and upon whose branches the fowls of the heaven did sit,

19 It is thou, O king, that art great and mighty: for thy greatness is grown, and reacheth unto heaven, and thy dominion to the ends of the earth.

20 Whereas the King saw a watchman, and an holy one that came down from heaven, and said, Hew down the tree, and destroy it, yet leave the stump of the roots thereof in the earth, and with a band of iron and brass *bind it* among the grass of the field, and let it be wet with the dew of heaven, and let his portion be with the beasts of the field, [1]till seven times pass over him.

21 This *is* the interpretation, O king, and it is the decree of the most High, which is come upon my lord the king,

22 That they shall drive thee from men, and thy dwelling shall be with the beasts of the field: they shall make thee to eat grass as the [1]oxen, and they shall wet thee with the dew of heaven: and seven times shall pass over thee, till thou know, that [2]the

---

4:5 [1] This no doubt was a great grief to Daniel not only to have his name changed, but to be called by the name of a vile idol, which thing Nebuchadnezzar did to make him forget the true religion of God.
4:6 [1] Which also was a great grief to the Prophet to be numbered among the sorcerers and men whose practices were wicked and contrary to God's word.
4:7 [1] By the tree is signified the dignity of a king whom God ordaineth to be a defense for all kind of men, and whose state is profitable for mankind.
4:10 [1] Meaning the Angel of God, which neither eateth nor sleepeth, but is ever ready to do God's will, and is not infected with man's corruption, but is ever holy: and in that that he commandeth to cut down this tree, he knew that it should not be cut down by man, but by God.
4:13 [1] Hereby he meaneth that Nebuchadnezzar should not only for a time lose his kingdom, but be like a beast.
4:14 [1] God hath decreed this judgment and the whole army of heaven

have as it were subscribed unto it, like as also they desire the execution of his decree against all them that lift up themselves against God.
4:16 [1] He was troubled for the great judgment of God, which he saw ordained against the king, and so the Prophets used on the one part to denounce God's judgments for the zeal they bare to his glory, and on the other part to have compassion upon man, and also to consider that they should be subject to God's judgments, if he did not regard them with pity.
4:20 [1] Whereby he meaneth a long space, as seven years. Some interpret seven months, and others seven weeks, but it seemeth he means of years.
4:22 [1] Not that his shape or form was changed into a beast, but that he was either stricken mad, and so avoided man's company, or was cast out for his tyranny, and so wandered among the beasts, and ate herbs and grass.
[2] Daniel showeth the cause why God thus punished him.

most High beareth rule over the kingdom of men, and giveth it to whomsoever he will.

23 Whereas they said, that one should leave the stump of the tree roots, thy kingdom shall remain unto thee: after that, thou shalt know, that the heavens have the rule.

24 Wherefore, O king, let my counsel be acceptable unto thee, and [1]break off thy sins by righteousness, and thine iniquities by mercy towards the poor: lo, let there be a [2]healing of thine error.

25 All these things shall come upon the king Nebuchadnezzar.

26 ¶ At the end of twelve [1]months, he walked in the royal palace of Babel.

27 And the king spake and said, Is not this great Babel that I have built for the house of the kingdom by the might of my power, and for the honor of my majesty?

28 While the word was in the king's mouth, a voice came down from heaven, saying, O king Nebuchadnezzar, to thee be it spoken, Thy kingdom is departed from thee,

29 And they shall drive thee from men, and thy dwelling shall be with the beasts of the field: they shall make thee to eat grass, as the oxen, and seven times shall pass over thee, until thou knowest, that the most High beareth rule over the kingdom of men, and giveth it unto whomsoever he will.

30 The very same hour was this thing fulfilled upon Nebuchadnezzar, and he was driven from men, and did eat grass as the oxen, and his body was wet with the dew of heaven, till his hairs were grown as eagles feathers, and his nails like birds claws.

31 And at the end of these [1]days, I Nebuchadnezzar lifted up mine eyes unto heaven, and mine understanding was restored unto me, and I gave thanks unto the most High, and I praised and honored him, that liveth forever, [a]whose power is an everlasting power, and his kingdom is from generation to generation.

CHAPTER 4
[a] Dan. 7:14
Mic. 4:17
Luke 1:33

32 And all the inhabitants of the earth are reputed as nothing: and according to his [1]will he worketh in the army of heaven, and in the inhabitants of the earth: and none can stay his hand, nor say unto him, What doest thou?

33 At the same time was mine understanding restored unto me, and I returned to the honor of my kingdom: my glory and my beauty was restored unto me, and my counselors and [1]my princes sought unto me, and I was established in my kingdom, and my glory was augmented toward me.

34 Now therefore I Nebuchadnezzar [1]praise, and extol and magnify the king of heaven, whose works are all truth, and his ways judgment: and those that walk in pride, he is able to abase.

5 5 Belshazzar king of Babylon seeth an handwriting on the wall. 8 The soothsayers called of the king, cannot expound the writing. 25 Daniel readeth it, and interpreteth it also. 30 The king is slain. 31 Darius enjoyeth the kingdom.

1 King [1]Belshazzar made a great feast to a thousand of his princes, and drank wine [2]before the thousand.

2 And Belshazzar [1]while he tasted the wine, commanded to bring him the golden and silver vessels, which his [2]father Nebuchadnezzar had brought from the Temple in Jerusalem, that the king and his princes, his wives, and his concubines might drink therein.

3 Then were brought the golden vessels, that were taken out of the Temple of the Lord's house at Jerusalem, and the king and his princes, his wives and his concubines drank in them.

4 They drank wine, and praised the [1]gods of gold, and of silver, of brass, of iron, of wood, and of stone.

5 At the same hour appeared fingers of a man's hand, which wrote over [1]against the candlestick upon the plaster of the wall of the king's palace, and the

---

4:24 [1] Cease from provoking God to anger any longer by thy sins, that he may mitigate his punishment, if thou show by thine upright life that thou hast true faith and repentance.
  [2] Suffer the errors of thy former life to be redressed.
4:26 [1] After that Daniel had declared this vision: and this his pride declareth that it is not in man to convert to God, except his Spirit move him: seeing that these terrible threatenings could not move him to repent.
4:31 [1] When the term of these seven years was accomplished.
4:32 [1] He confesseth God's will to be the rule of all justice, and a most perfect law, whereby he governeth both man and Angels and devils, so that none ought to murmur or ask a reason of his doings, but only to stand content therewith and give him the glory.
4:33 [1] By whom it seemeth that he had been put from his kingdom before.
4:34 [1] He doth not only praise God for his deliverance, but also confesseth his fault that God may only have the glory, and man the shame, and that he may be exalted and man cast down.

5:1 [1] Daniel reciteth this history of king Belshazzar, Evil-merodach's son, to show God's judgments against the wicked for the deliverance of his Church: and how the prophecy of Jeremiah was true, that they should be delivered after seventy years.
  [2] The kings of the East parts then used to sit alone commonly, and disdained that any should sit in their company: and now to show his power, and how little he set by his enemy, which then besieged Babylon, he made a solemn banquet, and used excess in their company, which is meant here by drinking wine: thus the wicked are most dissolute and negligent, when their destruction is at hand.
5:2 [1] Or, overcome with wine.
  [2] Meaning, his grandfather.
5:4 [1] In contempt of the true God, they praise their idols, not that they thought that the gold or silver were gods, but that there was a certain virtue and power in them to do them good, which is also the opinion of all idolaters.
5:5 [1] That it might the better be seen.

king saw the palm of the hand that wrote.

6 Then the king's countenance was changed, and his thoughts troubled him, so that the joints of his loins were loosed, and his [1]knees smote one against the other.

7 *Wherefore* the king cried loud, that they should bring [1]the astrologians, the Chaldeans and the soothsayers. And the king spake, and said to the wise men of Babel, Whosoever can read this writing, and declare me the interpretation thereof, shall be clothed with purple, and *shall have* a chain of gold about his neck, and shall be the third ruler in the kingdom.

8 Then came all the king's wise men, but they could neither read the writing, nor show the king the interpretation.

9 Then was king Belshazzar greatly troubled, and his countenance was changed in him, and his princes were astonied.

10 *Now* the [1]Queen by reason of the talk of the King and his princes, came into the banquet house, *and* the Queen spake, and said, O king, live forever: let not thy thoughts trouble thee, nor let thy countenance be changed.

11 There is a man in thy kingdom, in whom is the spirit of the holy gods, and in the days of thy father, light and understanding and wisdom like the wisdom of the gods, was found in him: whom the king Nebuchadnezzar thy father, the king, *I say*, thy father, made chief of the [1]enchanters, astrologians, Chaldeans, *and* soothsayers,

12 Because a more excellent spirit, and knowledge, and understanding (*for* he did expound dreams, and declare hard sentences, and dissolved doubts) were found in him, *even* in Daniel, whom the king named Belteshazzar: now let Daniel be called, and he will declare the interpretation.

13 ¶ Then was Daniel brought before the king, *and* the king spake and said unto Daniel, Art thou that Daniel, which art of the children of the captivity of Judah, whom my father the king brought out of Jewry?

14 Now I have heard of thee, that [1]the spirit of the holy gods *is* in thee, and that light and understanding, and excellent wisdom is found in thee.

15 Now therefore wise men *and* Astrologians have

been brought before me, that they should read this writing, and show me the interpretation thereof: but they could not declare the interpretation of the thing.

16 Then heard I of thee, that thou couldest show interpretations, and dissolve doubts: now if thou canst read the writing, and show me the interpretation thereof, thou shalt be clothed with purple, and *shall have* a chain of gold about thy neck, and shalt be the third ruler in the kingdom.

17 Then Daniel answered, and said before the king, Keep thy rewards to thyself, and give thy gifts to another: yet I will read the writing unto the king, and show him the interpretation.

18 O king, *hear* thou, The most high God gave unto [1]Nebuchadnezzar thy father a kingdom, and majesty, and honor, and glory.

19 And for the majesty that he gave him, all people, nations, and languages trembled, and feared before him: he put to death whom he would: he smote whom he would: whom he would he set up, and whom he would he put down.

20 But when his heart was puffed up, and his mind hardened in pride, he was deposed from his kingly throne, and they took his honor from him.

21 And he was driven from the sons of men, and his heart was made like the beasts, and his dwelling was with the wild asses: they fed him with grass like oxen, and his body was wet with the dew of the heaven, till he knew that the most high God bare rule over the kingdom of men, and that he appointeth over it, whomsoever he pleaseth.

22 And thou his son, O Belshazzar, hast not humbled thine heart, though thou knewest all these things,

23 But hast lifted thyself up against the Lord of heaven, and they have brought the vessels of his House before thee, and thou and thy princes, thy wives and thy concubines have drunk wine in them, and thou hast praised the gods of silver and gold, of brass, iron, wood and stone, which neither see, neither hear, nor understand: and the God in whose hand thy breath is and all thy ways, him hast thou not glorified.

24 [1]Then was the palm of the hand sent from him, and hath written this writing.

5:6 [1] So he that before contemned God, was moved by this sight to tremble for fear of God's judgments.
5:7 [1] Thus the wicked in their troubles seek many means, who draw them from God, because they seek not to him who is the only comfort in all afflictions.
5:10 [1] To wit, his grandmother Nebuchadnezzar's wife, which for her age was not before at the feast, but came thither when she heard of these strange news.
5:11 [1] Read Dan. 4:6, and this declareth that both this name was odious unto him, and also he did not use these vile practices, because

he was not among them when all were called.
5:14 [1] For the idolaters thought that the Angels had power as God, and therefore had them in like estimation, as they had God, thinking that the spirit of prophecy and understanding came of them.
5:18 [1] Before he read the writing, he declareth to the king his great ingratitude toward God, who could not be moved to give him the glory, considering his wonderful work toward his grandfather, and so showeth that he doth not sin of ignorance but of malice.
5:24 [1] After that God had so long time deferred his anger, and patiently waited for thine amendment.

25 And this is the writing that he hath written, ¹MENE, MENE, TEKEL UPHARSIN.

26 This is the interpretation of the thing, MENE, God hath numbered thy kingdom, and hath finished it.

27 TEKEL, thou art weighed in the balance, and art found ¹too light.

28 PERES, thy kingdom is divided and given to the Medes and Persians.

29 Then at the commandment of Belshazzar they clothed Daniel with purple, and put a chain of gold about his neck, and made a proclamation concerning him that he should be the third ruler in the kingdom.

30 The same night was Belshazzar the King of the Chaldeans slain.

31 And Darius ¹of the Medes took the kingdom, being threescore and two years old.

6 1 Daniel is made ruler over the governors. 5 An act against Daniel. 16 He is put into a den of lions by the commandment of the king. 23 He is delivered by faith in God. 24 Daniel's accusers are put unto the lions. 25 Darius by a decree magnifieth the God of Daniel.

1 It pleased Darius to set over the kingdom ¹an hundred and twenty governors, which should be over the whole kingdom,

2 And over these three rulers, (of whom Daniel was one) that the governors might give accompts unto them, and the king ¹should have no damage.

3 Now this Daniel ¹was preferred above the rulers, and governors, because the spirit was excellent in him, and the king thought to set him over the whole realm.

4 ¶ Wherefore the rulers and governors ¹sought an occasion against Daniel concerning the kingdom: but they could find none occasion nor fault: for he was so faithful that there was no blame nor fault found in him.

5 Then said these men, We shall not find an occasion against this Daniel, except we find it against him concerning the Law of his God.

6 Therefore the rulers and these governors went together to the king, and said thus unto him, King Darius, live forever.

7 All the rulers of thy kingdom, the officers and governors, the counselors and dukes have consulted together to make a decree for the king, and to establish a statute, that whosoever shall ask a petition of any god or man for thirty days save of thee, O king, he shall be cast into the den of lions.

8 Now, O king, confirm the decree, and seal the writing, that it be not changed, according to the law of the Medes and Persians, which altereth not.

9 Wherefore king Darius ¹sealed the writing and the decree.

10 ¶ Now when Daniel understood that he had sealed the writing, he went into his house, and his ¹window being open in his chamber toward Jerusalem, he kneeled upon his knees three times a day, and prayed and praised his God, as he did aforetime.

11 Then these men assembled, and found Daniel praying, and making supplication unto his God.

12 So they came and spake unto the king concerning the king's decree, Hast thou not sealed the decree, that every man that shall make a request to any god or man within thirty days, save to thee, O King, shall be cast into the den of lions? The King answered, and said, The thing is true, according to the law of the Medes and Persians, which altereth not.

13 Then answered they, and said unto the King, This Daniel which is of the children of the captivity of Judah, regardeth not thee, O king, nor the decree that thou hast sealed, but maketh his petition three times a day.

14 When the King heard these words, he was sore displeased with himself, and set his heart on Daniel, to deliver him: and he labored till the sun went down, to deliver him.

15 Then these men assembled unto the king, and said unto the King, Understand, O King, that the law of the Medes and Persians is, that no decree nor statute which the king confirmeth, may be ¹altered.

5:25 ¹ This word is twice written for the certainty of the thing: showing that God had most surely counted: signifying also that God hath appointed a term for all kingdoms, and that a miserable end shall come on all that raise themselves against him.

5:27 ¹ Or, wanting.

5:31 ¹ Cyrus his son-in-law gave him this title of honor, although Cyrus in effect had the dominion.

6:1 ¹ Read Esther 1:1.

6:2 ¹ Or, not be troubled.

6:3 ¹ This heathen king preferred Daniel a stranger to all his nobles and familiars, because the graces of God were more excellent in him than in others.

6:4 ¹ Thus the wicked cannot abide the graces of God in others, but seek by all occasions to deface them, therefore against such assaults there is no better remedy than to walk upright in the fear of God, and to have a good conscience.

6:9 ¹ Herein is condemned the wickedness of the king, who would be set up as a god, and passed not what wicked laws he approved for the maintenance of the same.

6:10 ¹ Because he would not by his silence show that he consented to this wicked decree, he set open his windows toward Jerusalem, when he prayed: both to stir up himself with the remembrance of God's promises to his people, when they should pray toward that Temple, and also that others might see, that he would neither consent in heart nor deed for these few days to anything that was contrary to God's glory.

6:15 ¹ Thus the wicked maintain evil laws by constancy and authority, which is ofttimes either lightness, or stubbornness, when as the innocents thereby perish, and therefore governors neither ought to fear, nor be ashamed to break such.

16 ¶ Then the King commanded, and they brought Daniel, and cast him into the den of lions: now the king spake, and said unto Daniel, Thy God, whom thou always servest, *even* he will deliver thee.

17 And a stone was brought, and laid upon the mouth of the den, and the King sealed it with his own signet, and with the signet of his princes, that the purpose might not be changed, concerning Daniel.

18 Then the king went unto his palace, and remained fasting, neither were the instruments of music brought before him, and his sleep went from him.

19 ¶ Then the king arose early in the morning, and went in all haste unto the den of lions.

20 And when he came to the den, he cried with a lamentable voice unto Daniel: and the king spake, and said to Daniel, O Daniel the servant of the living God, is not thy God (whom thou always servest) [1]able to deliver thee from the lions?

21 Then said Daniel unto the King, O king, live forever.

22 My God hath sent his Angel and hath shut the lion's mouths, and they have not hurt me: for [1]my justice was found out before him: and unto thee, O king, I have done [2]no hurt.

23 Then was the King exceeding glad for him, and commanded that they should take Daniel out of the den: so Daniel was brought out of the den, and no manner of hurt was found upon him, because he [1]believed in his God.

24 And by the commandment of the King these men which had accused Daniel, were brought, and were [1]cast into the den of lions, *even* they, their children, and their wives: and the lions had the mastery of them, and brake all their bones a pieces, or ever they came at the ground of the den.

25 ¶ Afterward King Darius wrote, Unto all people, nations and languages, that dwell in all the world: Peace be multiplied unto you.

26 I make a decree, that in all the dominion of my kingdom, men tremble and fear [1]before the God of Daniel: for he is the [2]living God, and remaineth forever: and his kingdom shall not perish, and his dominion *shall be* everlasting.

27 He rescueth and delivereth, and he worketh signs and wonders in heaven and in earth: who hath delivered Daniel from the power of the lions.

28 So this Daniel prospered in the reign of Darius and in the reign of Cyrus of Persia.

7 *3 A vision of four beasts is showed unto Daniel. 8 The ten horns of the fourth beast. 27 Of the everlasting kingdom of Christ.*

1 In the first year of Belshazzar King of Babel, Daniel saw a dream, and there *were* visions in his head, upon his bed: [1]then he wrote the dream, and declared the sum of the matter.

2 Daniel spake and said, I saw in my vision by night, and behold, the four winds of the heaven strove upon [1]the great sea:

3 And four great beasts came up from the sea one divers from another.

4 The first *was* as a [1]lion, and had eagle's wings: I beheld till the wings thereof were plucked off, and it was lifted up from the earth, and set upon *his* feet as a man, and a man's heart was given him.

5 And behold, another beast *which was* the second, was like a [1]bear, and stood upon the [2]one side: and he had three ribs in his [3]mouth between his teeth, [4]and they said thus unto him, Arise, *and* devour much flesh.

6:20 [1] This declareth that Darius was not touched with the true knowledge of God, because he doubted of his power.

6:22 [1] My just cause and uprightness in this thing wherein I was charged, is approved of God.

[2] For he did disobey the king's wicked commandment to obey God, and so did no injury to the king, who ought to command nothing whereby God should be dishonored.

6:23 [1] Because he committed himself wholly unto God whose cause he did defend, he was assured that nothing but good could come unto him: wherein we see the power of faith, as Heb. 11:33.

6:24 [1] This is a terrible example against all the wicked which do against their conscience make cruel laws to destroy the children of God, and also admonisheth Princes how to punish such when their wickedness is come to light: though not in every point, or with like circumstances, yet to execute true justice upon them.

6:26 [1] This proveth not that Darius did worship God aright, or else was converted: for then he would have destroyed all superstition and idolatry: and not only given God the chief place, but also have set him up, and caused him to be honored according to his word: but this was a certain confession of God's power, whereunto he was compelled by this wonderful miracle.

[2] Which hath not only life in himself, but is the only fountain of life, and quickeneth all things, so that without him there is no life.

7:1 [1] Whereas the people of Israel looked for a continual quietness, after their seventy years, as Jeremiah had declared, he sheweth that this rest shall not be a deliverance from all troubles, but a beginning, and therefore encourageth them to look for a continual affliction, till the Messiah be uttered and revealed, by whom they should have a spiritual deliverance, and all the promises be fulfilled: whereof they should have a certain token in the destruction of the Babylonian kingdom.

7:2 [1] Which signified that there should be horrible troubles and afflictions in the world in all corners of the world, and at sundry times.

7:4 [1] Meaning, the Assyrian and Chaldean empire, which was most strong and fierce in power, and most soon come to their authority, as though they had wings to fly: yet their wings were pulled by the Persians, and they went on their feet, and were made like other men, which is here meant by man's heart.

7:5 [1] Meaning, the Persians which were barbarous and cruel.

[2] They were small in the beginning and were shut up in the mountains and had no bruit.

[3] That is, destroyed many kingdoms, and was insatiable.

[4] To wit, the Angels by God's commandment, who by this means punished the ingratitude of the world.

6 After this, I beheld, and lo, there *was* another like a ¹leopard, which had upon his back ²four wings of a fowl: the beast had also four heads, and ³dominion was given him.

7 After this, I saw in the visions by night, and behold, the ¹fourth beast *was* fearful and terrible and very strong. It had great ²iron teeth: it devoured and brake in pieces, and stamped ³the residue under his feet: and it was unlike to the beasts that were before it: for it had ⁴ten horns.

8 As I considered the horns, behold, there came up among them another little ¹horn, before whom there were ²three of the first horns plucked away: and behold, in this horn *were* ³eyes like the eyes of man, and a mouth speaking presumptuous things.

9 I beheld till the ¹thrones were set up, and the ²Ancient of days did sit, whose garment was white as snow, and the hair of his head like the pure wool: his throne *was like* the fiery flame, *and* his wheels, *as* burning fire.

10 A fiery stream issued, and came forth from before him: thousand thousands ministered unto him, and ten thousand ¹thousands stood before him: the judgment was set, and the ²books opened.

11 Then I beheld, ¹because of the voice of the presumptuous words which the horn spake: I beheld, even till the beast was slain, and his body destroyed, and given to the burning fire.

12 As ¹concerning the other beasts, they had taken away their dominion: yet their lives were prolonged for a certain time and season.

13 ¶ As I beheld in visions by night, behold, ¹one like the son of man came in the clouds of heaven, and ²approached unto the Ancient of days, and they brought him before him.

14 And he gave him ¹dominion, and honor, and a kingdom, that all people, nations and languages should serve him: his dominion *is* an everlasting dominion, which shall never be taken away: and his dominion shall never be destroyed.

15 ¶ I Daniel was ¹troubled in my spirit, in the midst of my body, and the visions of mine head made me afraid.

16 Therefore I came unto ¹one of them that stood by, and asked him the truth of all this: so he told me, and showed me the interpretation of these things.

17 These great beasts which are four, *are* four kings, which shall arise out of the earth,

7:6 ¹ Meaning, Alexander the king of Macedonia.
² That is, his four chief captains, which had the empire among them after his death. Seleucus had Asia the great, Antigonus the less, Cassander and after him Antipater was king of Macedonia, and Ptolemy had Egypt.
³ It was not of himself nor of his own power that he got all these countries: for his army contained but thirty thousand men, and he overcame in one battle Darius, which had ten hundred thousand, when he was so heavy with sleep, that his eyes were scarce open, as the stories report: therefore this power was given him of God.
7:7 ¹ That is, the Roman Empire which was a monster, and could not be compared to any beasts, because the nature of none was able to express it.
² Signifying, the tyranny and greediness of the Romans.
³ That which the Romans could not quietly enjoy in other countries, they would give it to other Kings and rulers, that at all times when they would, they might take it again: which liberality is here called the stamping of the rest under the feet.
⁴ That is, sundry and divers provinces which were governed by the deputies and proconsuls, whereof everyone might be compared to a King.
7:8 ¹ Which is meant of Julius Caesar, Augustus, Tiberius, Caligula, Claudius, and Nero, etc., who were as kings in effect, but because they could not rule, but by the consent of the Senate, their power is compared to a little horn. For Muhammad came not of the Roman Empire, and the Pope hath no vocation of government: therefore this cannot be applied unto them, and also in this prophecy the Prophet's purpose is chiefly to comfort the Jews unto the revelation of Christ. Some take it for the whole body of Antichrist.
² Meaning, a certain portion of the ten horns: that is, a part from the whole estate was taken away. For Augustus took from the Senate the liberty of choosing the deputies to send into the provinces, and took the government of certain countries to himself.
³ These Roman Emperors at the first used a certain humanity and gentleness, and were content that others, as the Consuls, and Sen-

ate, should bear the names of dignity, so that they might have the profit, and therefore in election and counsels would behave themselves according as did other Senators: yet against their enemies and those that would resist them, they were fierce and cruel, which is here meant by the proud mouth.
7:9 ¹ Meaning, the places where God and his Angels should come to judge these Monarchies, which judgment should begin at the first coming of Christ.
² That is, God which was before all times, and is here described as man's nature is able to comprehend some portion of his glory.
7:10 ¹ That is, an infinite number of Angels, which were ready to execute his commandment.
² This is meant of the first coming of Christ, when as the will of God was plainly revealed by his Gospel.
7:11 ¹ Meaning, that he was astonied when he saw these Emperors in such dignity and pride, and so suddenly destroyed at the coming of Christ, when this fourth Monarchy was subject to men of other nations.
7:12 ¹ As the three former Monarchies had an end at the time that God appointed, although they flourished for a time, so shall this fourth have, and they that patiently abide God's appointment, shall enjoy the promises.
7:13 ¹ Which is meant of Christ, who had not yet taken upon him man's nature, neither was the son of David according to the flesh, as he was afterward: but appeared then in a figure, and that in the clouds: that is, being separate from the common sort of men by manifest signs of his divinity.
² To wit, when he ascend into the heavens, and his divine majesty appeared, and all power was given unto him, in respect of that that he was our Mediator.
7:14 ¹ This is meant of the beginning of Christ's kingdom, when God the Father gave unto him all dominion, as to the Mediator, to the intent that he should govern here his Church in earth continually, till the time that he brought them to eternal life.
7:15 ¹ Through the strangeness of the vision.
7:16 ¹ Meaning, of the Angels, as verse 10.

18 And they shall take the ¹kingdom of the Saints of the ²most High, and shall possess the kingdom forever, even forever and ever.

19 ¶ After this, I would *know* the truth of the fourth beast, which was ¹so unlike to all the others, very fearful, whose teeth were of iron, and his nails of brass: *which* devoured brake in pieces, and stamped the ²residue under his feet.

20 Also *to know* of the ten horns that were in his head, and of the others which came up, before whom three fell, and of the horn that had eyes, and of the mouth that spake presumptuous things, whose ¹look was more stout than his fellows.

21 I beheld, and the same ¹horn made battle against the Saints, yea, and prevailed against them,

22 Until ¹the Ancient of days came, and judgment was given to the Saints of the most High: and the time approached, that the Saints possessed the kingdom.

23 Then he said, The fourth beast shall be the fourth kingdom in the earth, which was be unlike to all the kingdoms, and shall devour the whole earth, and shall tread it down and break it in pieces.

24 And the ten horns out of this kingdom *are* ten Kings that shall rise: and another shall rise after them, and he shall be unlike to the first, and he shall subdue ¹three Kings,

25 And shall speak words against ¹the most High, and shall consume the Saints of the most High, and think that he may ²change times and laws, and they

shall be given into his hand until a ³time, and times, and the dividing of time.

26 But the ¹judgment shall sit, and they shall take away his dominion to consume and destroy it unto the end.

27 And the ¹kingdom, and dominion, and the greatness of the kingdom under the whole heaven shall be given to the holy people of the most High, whose kingdom *is* an everlasting kingdom, and all ²powers shall serve and obey him.

28 Even this is the end of the matter, I Daniel had many ¹cogitations *which* troubled me, and my countenance changed in me: but I kept the matter in mine heart.

8 *A vision of a battle between a ram and a goat:* 20 *The understanding of the vision.*

1 In the third year of the reign of king Belshazzar, a vision appeared unto me, *even* unto me Daniel, ¹after that *which* appeared unto me at the first.

2 And I saw in a vision, and when I saw it, I was in the palace of Shushan, which is in the province ¹of Elam, and in a vision me thought I was by the river of Ulai.

3 Then I looked up and saw, and behold, there stood before the river a ¹ram which had two horns, and these two horns *were* high: but one was ²higher than another, and the highest came up last.

4 I saw the ram pushing against the West, and

7:18 ¹ Because Abraham was appointed heir of all the world, Rom. 4:13, and in him all the faithful, therefore the kingdom thereof is theirs by right, which these four beasts or tyrants should invade, and usurp until the world were restored by Christ: and this was to confirm them that were in troubles, that their afflictions should have an end at length.

² That is, of the most high things, because God hath chosen them out of this world, that they should look up to the heavens, whereon all their hope dependeth.

7:19 ¹ For the other three Monarchies were governed by a King, and the Roman Empire by Consuls: the Romans changed their governors yearly, and the other Monarchies retained them for term of life: also the Romans were the strongest of all the others, and were never quiet among themselves.

² Read verse 7.

7:20 ¹ This is meant of the fourth beast, which was more terrible than the others.

7:21 ¹ Meaning the Roman Emperors, who were most cruel against the Church of God both of the Jews and of the Gentiles.

7:22 ¹ Till God showed his power in the person of Christ, and by the preaching of the Gospel gave unto his some rest, and so obtained a famous Name in the world, and were called the Church of God, or the kingdom of God.

7:24 ¹ Read the exposition hereof, verse 8.

7:25 ¹ That is, shall make wicked decrees and proclamations against God's word, and send throughout all their dominion, to destroy all that did profess it.

² These Emperors shall not consider that they have their power of God, but think it is in their own power to change God's laws and

man's, and as it were the order of nature, as appeareth by Octavius, Tiberius, Caligula, Nero, Domitian, etc.

³ God shall suffer them thus to rage against his Saints for a long time, which is meant by the time and times, but at length he will assuage these troubles, and shorten the time for his elect's sake, Matt. 24:22, which is here meant by the dividing of time.

7:26 ¹ God by his power shall restore things that were out of order, and so destroy this little horn, that it shall never rise up again.

7:27 ¹ He showeth wherefore the beast should be destroyed, to wit, that his Church might have rest and quietness, which though they do not fully enjoy here, yet they have it in hope, and by the preaching of the Gospel enjoy the beginning thereof, which is meant by these words: Under the heaven: and therefore he here speaketh of the beginning of Christ's kingdom in this world, which kingdom the faithful have by the participation that they have with Christ their head.

² That is, some of every sort that bear rule.

7:28 ¹ Though he had many motions in his heart which moved him to and fro to seek out this matter curiously, yet he was content with that which God revealed, and kept it in memory, and wrote it for the use of the Church.

8:1 ¹ After the general vision, he cometh to certain particular visions as touching the destruction of the Monarchy of the Persians, and Macedonians: for the ruin of the Babylonians was at hand, and also he had sufficiently spoken thereof.

8:2 ¹ That is, of Persia.

8:3 ¹ Which represented the kingdom of the Persians and Medes, which were joined together.

² Meaning, Cyrus, which after grew greater in power than Darius his uncle and father-in-law.

against the North, and against the South: so that no ¹beasts might stand before him, nor could deliver out of his hand, but he did what he listed, and became great.

5 And as I considered, behold, ¹a goat came from the West over the whole earth, and touched not the ground: and this goat had an ²horn that appeared between his eyes.

6 And he came unto the ram that had the two horns, whom I had seen standing by the river, and ran unto him in his fierce rage.

7 And I saw him come unto the ram, and being moved against him, he ¹smote the ram, and brake his two horns: and there was no power in the ram to stand against him, but he cast him down to the ground, and stamped upon him, and there was none that could deliver the ram out of his power.

8 Therefore the goat waxed exceeding great, and when he was at the strongest, his great ¹horn was broken: and for it came up four that ²appeared toward the four winds of the heaven.

9 And out of one of them came forth a ¹little horn, which waxed very great toward the ²South, and toward the ³East, and toward the ⁴pleasant land.

10 Yea, it grew up unto the ¹host of heaven, and it cast down some of the host, and of the stars to the ground, and trode upon them,

11 And extolled himself against the ¹prince of the host, from whom the ²daily sacrifice was taken away, and the place of his Sanctuary was cast down.

12 And ¹a time shall be given him over the daily sacrifice for the iniquity: and it shall ²cast down the truth to the ground, and thus shall it do, and prosper.

13 Then I heard one of the ¹Saints speaking, and one of the Saints spake unto a certain one, saying, How long shall endure the vision of the daily sacrifice, and the iniquity of the ²desolation to tread both the Sanctuary and the ³army underfoot?

14 And ¹he answered me, Unto the ²evening and the morning, two thousand and three hundred: then shall the Sanctuary be cleansed.

15 ¶ Now when I Daniel had seen the vision, and sought for the meaning, behold, there stood before me ¹like the similitude of a man.

16 And I heard a man's voice between the banks of Ulai, which called, and said, Gabriel, ¹make this man to understand the vision.

17 So he came where I stood: and when he came, I was afraid, and fell upon my face: but he said unto me, Understand, O son of man: for ¹in the last time shall be the vision.

18 Now as he was speaking unto me, I being asleep fell on my face to the ground: but he touched me, and set me up in my place.

19 And he said, Behold, I will show thee what shall be in the last ¹wrath: for in the end of the time appointed it shall come.

20 The ram which thou sawest having two horns, are the Kings of the Medes and Persians.

21 And the goat is the King of Greece, and the great horn that is between his eyes, is the first king.

8:4 ¹ That is, no kings or nations.
8:5 ¹ Meaning, Alexander that came from Greece with great speed and expedition.

² Though he came in the name of all Greece, yet he bore the title and dignity of the general captain, so that the strength was attributed to him, which is meant by this horn.
8:7 ¹ Alexander overcame Darius in two sundry battles, and so had the two kingdoms of the Medes and Persians.
8:8 ¹ Alexander's great power was broken: for when he had overcome all the East, he thought to return toward Greece to subdue them that had rebelled, and so died by the way.

² That is, which were famous; for almost in the space of fifteen years there were fifteen divers successors before this monarchy was divided to these four, whereof Cassander had Macedonia, Seleucus Syria, Antigonus Asia the less, and Ptolemy Egypt.
8:9 ¹ Which was Antiochus Epiphanes, who was of a servile and flattering nature, and also there were others between him and the kingdom, and therefore is here called the little horn, because neither princely conditions, nor any other thing was in him, why he should obtain this kingdom.

² That is, toward Egypt.
³ Whereby he meaneth Ptolemeus.
⁴ That is, Judea.
8:10 ¹ Antiochus raged against the elect of God, and trode his precious stars under feet, which are so called, because they are separated from the world.

8:11 ¹ That is, God, who governeth and maintaineth his Church.
² He labored to abolish all religion, and therefore cast God's service out of his Temple, which God had chosen as a little corner from all the rest of the world to have his Name there truly called upon.
8:12 ¹ He showeth that their sins are the cause of these horrible afflictions: and yet comforteth them, in that he appointeth this tyrant a time, whom he would not suffer utterly to abolish his religion.

² This horn shall abolish for a time the true doctrine, and so corrupt God's service.
8:13 ¹ Meaning, that he heard one of the Angels asking this question of Christ, whom he called a certain one, or a secret one, or a marvelous one.

² That is, the Jews' sins, which were cause of his destruction.
³ That is, which suppresseth God's religion, and his people.
8:14 ¹ Christ answered me for the comfort of the Church.

² That is, until so many natural days be past, which make 6 years, 3 months and an half: for so long under Antiochus was the Temple profaned.
8:15 ¹ Which was Christ who in this manner declared himself to the old fathers, how he would be God manifest in flesh.
8:16 ¹ This power to command the Angel, declared that he was God.
8:17 ¹ The effect of this vision shall not yet appear, but a long time after.
8:19 ¹ Meaning, that great rage which Antiochus should show against the Church.

22 And that that is broken, and four stood up for it, *are* four kingdoms, which shall stand up [1]of that nation, but not [2]in his strength.

23 And in the end of their kingdom, when the rebellious shall be consumed, a King of [1]fierce countenance, and understanding dark sentences, shall stand up.

24 And his power shall be mighty, but not [1]in his strength: and he shall destroy wonderfully, and shall prosper, and practice, and shall destroy the [2]mighty, and the holy people.

25 And through his [1]policy also he shall cause craft to prosper in his hand, and he shall extol himself in his heart, and by [2]peace shall destroy many: he shall also stand up against the [3]prince of princes, but he shall be broken down [4]without hand.

26 And the vision of the [1]evening and the morning, which is declared, is true: therefore seal thou up the vision, for it *shall be* after many days.

27 And I Daniel was stricken and sick [1]*certain* days: but when I rose up, I did the king's business, and I was astonished at the vision, but none understood it.

9 *3 Daniel desireth to have that performed of God, which he had promised concerning the return of the people from their banishment in Babylon. 5 A true confession. 20 Daniel's prayer is heard. 21 Gabriel the Angel expoundeth unto him the vision of the seventy weeks. 24 The anointing of Christ. 25 The building again of Jerusalem. 26 The death of Christ.*

1 In the first year of Darius the son of [1]Ahasuerus, of the seed of the Medes, which was made king over the [2]realm of the Chaldeans,

2 *Even* in the first year of his reign, I Daniel understood by [1]books the number of the years, whereof the Lord had spoken unto Jeremiah the Prophet, that he would accomplish seventy years

in the desolation of Jerusalem.

3 And I turned my face unto the Lord God, and [1]sought by prayer and supplications with fasting and sackcloth and ashes.

4 And I prayed unto the Lord my God, and made my confession, saying, Oh Lord God *which art* [1]great and fearful, and keepest covenant and mercy toward them which love [2]thee, and toward them that keep thy commandments,

5 We have sinned and have committed iniquity, and have done wickedly, yea, we have rebelled, and have departed from thy precepts, and from thy judgments.

6 For we would not obey thy servants the Prophets, which spake in thy name to our kings, to our princes, and to our fathers, and to all the people of the land.

7 O Lord, [1]righteousness *belongeth* unto thee, and unto us [2]open shame, as *appeareth* this day unto every man of Judah, and to the inhabitants of Jerusalem, yea, unto all Israel, *both* near and far off, through all the country, whither thou hast driven them, because of their offences, that they have committed against thee.

8 O Lord, unto us *appertaineth* open shame, to our [1]Kings, to our princes, and to our fathers, because we have sinned against thee.

9 *Yet* compassion and forgiveness *is* in the Lord our God, albeit we have rebelled against him.

10 For we have not obeyed the [1]voice of the Lord our God, to walk in his laws, which he hath laid before us by the ministry of his servants the Prophets.

11 Yea, all Israel have transgressed thy Law, and are turned back, and have not heard thy voice: therefore the [1]curse is poured upon us, and the oath that is written in the Law of Moses the servant of God, because we have sinned against him.

12 And he hath confirmed his words, which he

8:22 [1] That is, out of Greece.
[2] They shall not have like power as had Alexander.
8:23 [1] Noting that this Antiochus was impudent and cruel, and also crafty that he could not be deceived.
8:24 [1] That is, not like Alexander's strength.
[2] Both the Gentiles that dwelt about him, and also the Jews.
8:25 [1] Whatsoever he goeth about by his craft, he shall bring it to pass.
[2] That is, under pretence of peace, or as it were in sport.
[3] Meaning, against God.
[4] For God would destroy him with a notable plague, and so comfort his Church.
8:26 [1] Read verse 14.
8:27 [1] For fear and astonishment.
9:1 [1] Who was also called Astyages.
[2] For Cyrus led with ambition, went about wars in other countries, and therefore Darius had the title of the kingdom, though Cyrus was king in effect.
9:2 [1] For though he was an excellent Prophet, yet he daily increased in knowledge by reading of the Scriptures.

9:3 [1] He speaketh not of that ordinary prayer, which he used in his house thrice a day, but of a rare and vehement prayer, least their sins should cause God to delay the time of their deliverance prophesied by Jeremiah.
9:4 [1] That is, hast all power in thyself to execute thy terrible judgments against obstinate sinners, as thou art rich in mercy to comfort them which obey thy word and love thee.
[2] Hebrew, *him.*
9:7 [1] He showeth that whensoever God punisheth, he doeth it for just cause: and thus the godly never accuse him of rigor as the wicked do, but acknowledge that in themselves there is just cause why he should so entreat them.
[2] Hebrew, *confusion of face.*
9:8 [1] He doth not excuse the kings because of their authority, but prayeth chiefly for them as the chief occasions of these great plagues.
9:10 [1] He showeth that they rebel against God, which serve him not according to his commandment and word.
9:11 [1] As Deut. 27:15, or the curse confirmed by an oath.

spake against us, and against our judges that ¹judged us, by bringing upon us a great plague: for under the whole heaven hath not been the like, as hath been brought upon Jerusalem.

13 All this plague is come upon us, as it is written in the Law of Moses: yet made we not our prayer before the Lord our God, that we might turn from our iniquities and understand thy truth.

14 Therefore hath the Lord ¹made ready the plague, and brought it upon us: for the Lord our God is righteous in all his works which he doeth: for we would not hear his voice.

15 ᵃAnd now, O Lord our God, that hast brought thy people out of the land of Egypt with a mighty hand, and hast gotten thee renown, as *appeareth* this day, we have sinned, we have done wickedly.

16 O Lord, according to all thy ¹righteousness, I beseech thee, let thine anger and thy wrath be turned away from thy city Jerusalem thine holy Mountain: because of our sins, and for the iniquities of our fathers, Jerusalem and thy people *are* a reproach to all *that are* about us.

17 Now therefore, O our God, hear the prayer of thy servant, and his supplications, and cause thy face to ¹shine upon thy Sanctuary, that lieth waste for the ²Lord's sake.

18 O my God, incline thine ear and hear: open thine eyes, and behold our desolations, and the city whereupon thy Name is called: for we do not present our supplications before thee for our own ¹righteousness, but for thy great tender mercies.

19 O Lord hear, O Lord forgive, O Lord ¹consider, and do it: defer not, for thine own sake, O my God: for thy Name is called upon thy city, and thy people.

20 ¶ And while I was speaking and praying, and

CHAPTER 9
ᵃ Exod. 14:28
ᵇ Dan. 8:16

confessing my sin, and the sin of my people Israel, and did present my supplication before the Lord my God, for the holy Mountain of my God,

21 Yea, while I was speaking in prayer, even the man ᵇGabriel, whom I had seen before in the vision, came flying, and touched me about the time of the evening oblation.

22 And he informed *me*, and talked with me, and said, O Daniel, I am now come forth to give thee knowledge *and* understanding.

23 At the beginning of thy supplications the commandment came forth, and I am come to show *thee*, for thou art greatly beloved: therefore understand the matter and consider the vision.

24 Seventy ¹weeks are determined upon ²thy people and upon thine holy city, to finish the wickedness, and to seal up ³the sins, and to reconcile the iniquity, and to bring in everlasting righteousness, and to seal up the vision and prophecy, and to anoint the most Holy.

25 Know therefore and understand that from ¹the going forth of the commandment to bring again *the people*, and to build Jerusalem, unto Messiah the Prince, *shall be* seven ²weeks and ³threescore and two weeks, *and* the street shall be built again, and the wall even in a ⁴troublous time.

26 And after threescore and two ¹weeks, shall Messiah be slain, and shall ²have nothing, and the people of the ³prince that shall come, shall destroy the city and the Sanctuary, and the end thereof *shall be* with a flood: and unto the end of the battle it shall be destroyed by desolations.

27 And he ¹shall confirm the covenant with many for one week: and in the midst of the week he shall cause the sacrifice and the oblation to ²cease, ³and for the overspreading of the abominations, he shall

9:12 ¹ Or, governed us.
9:14 ¹ Hebrew, *watched upon the evil.*
9:16 ¹ That is, according to all thy merciful promises and the performance thereof.
9:17 ¹ Show thyself favorable.
² That is, for thy Christ's sake in whom thou wilt accept all our prayers.
9:18 ¹ Declaring, that the godly flee only unto God's mercies, and renounce their own works, when they seek for remission of their sins.
9:19 ¹ Thus he could not content himself with any vehemence of words: for he was so led with a fervent zeal considering God's promise made to the city in respect of his Church, and for the advancement of God's glory.
9:24 ¹ He alludeth to Jeremiah's prophecy: who prophesied that their captivity should be seventy years: but now God's mercy should sevenfold exceed his judgment, which should be four hundred and ninety years, even to the coming of Christ, and so then it should continue forever.
² Meaning, Daniel's nation, over whom he was careful.
³ To show mercy and to put sin out of remembrance.
9:25 ¹ That is, from the time that Cyrus gave them leave to depart.

² These weeks make forty-nine years, whereof 46 are referred to the time of the building of the Temple, and three to the laying of the foundation.
³ Counting from the sixth year of Darius, who gave the second commandment for the building of the Temple are 62 weeks, which make 434 years, which comprehend the time from the building of the Temple unto the baptism of Christ.
⁴ Hebrew, *in straits of time.*
9:26 ¹ In this least week of the seventy, shall Christ come and preach and suffer death.
² He shall seem to have no beauty, nor to be of any estimation, as Isa. 53:2.
³ Meaning Titus, Vespasian's son, who should come and destroy both the Temple and the people without all hope of recovery.
9:27 ¹ By the preaching of the Gospel he confirmed his promise, first to the Jews, and after to the Gentiles.
² Christ accomplished this by his death and resurrection.
³ Meaning, that Jerusalem and the Sanctuary should be utterly destroyed for their rebellion against God, and their idolatry: or as some read, that the plague shall be so great, that they shall be all astonied at them.

make it desolate, even until the consummation determined shall be poured upon the desolate.

CHAPTER 10
a Jer. 10:9

10

1 There appeareth unto Daniel a man clothed in linen, 11 which showeth him wherefore he is sent.

1 In the ¹third year of Cyrus King of Persia, a thing was revealed unto Daniel (whose name was called Belteshazzar) and the word *was* true, but the time appointed *was* ²long, and he understood the thing, and had understanding of the vision.

2 At the same time I Daniel was in heaviness for three weeks of days.

3 I ate no pleasant bread, neither came flesh nor wine in my mouth, neither did I anoint myself at all, till three weeks of days were fulfilled.

4 And in the four and twentieth day of the ¹first month, as I ²was by the side of that great river, even Hiddekel,

5 And I lifted mine eyes, and looked, and behold, there *was* a man ¹clothed in linen, whose loins were girded with fine gold of ᵃUphaz.

6 His body also *was* like the Chrysolite, and his face (to look upon) like the lightning, and his eyes as lamps of fire, and his arms and his feet *were* like in color to polished brass, and the voice of his words *was* like the voice of a multitude.

7 And I Daniel alone saw the vision: for the men that were with me, saw not the vision: but a great fear fell upon them, so that they fled away and hid themselves.

8 Therefore I was left alone, and saw this great vision, and there remained no strength in me: for ¹my strength was turned in me into corruption, and I retained no power.

9 Yet heard I the voice of his words: and when I heard the voice of his words, I slept on my face, and my face *was* toward the ground.

10 And behold, an ¹hand touched me, which set me up upon my knees, and upon the palms of mine hands,

11 And he said unto me, O Daniel, a man greatly beloved, understand the words that I speak unto thee, and stand in thy place: for unto thee am I now sent. And when he had said this word unto me, I stood trembling.

12 Then said he unto me, Fear not, Daniel: for from the first day that thou didst set thine heart to understand, and to humble thyself before thy God, thy words were heard, and I am come for thy words.

13 But the ¹prince of the kingdom of Persia withstood me one and twenty days: but lo, ²Michael one of the chief princes, came to help me, and I remained there by the Kings of Persia.

14 Now I am come to show thee what shall come to thy people in the latter days: for yet the ¹vision *is* for *many* days.

15 And when he spake these words unto me, I set my face toward the ground, and held my tongue.

16 And behold, ¹one like the similitude of the sons of man touched my lips: then I opened my mouth, and spake, and said unto him that stood before me, O my Lord, ²by the vision my sorrows are returned upon me, and I have retained no strength.

17 For how can the servant of this my Lord talk with my Lord *being* such one? for as for me, straightway there remained no strength in me, neither is there breath left in me.

18 Then there came again, and touched me, one like the appearance of a man, and he strengthened me,

19 And said, O man, greatly beloved, fear not: ¹peace *be* unto thee: be strong and of good courage. And when he had spoken unto me, I ²was strengthened, and said, Let my Lord speak: for thou hast strengthened me.

20 Then said he, Knowest thou wherefore I am come unto thee? but now will I return to fight with the Prince of Persia: and when I am gone forth, lo,

---

10:1 ¹ He noteth this third year, because at this time the building of the Temple began to be hindered by Cambyses Cyrus' son, when the father made war in Asia minor against the Scythians, which was a discouraging to the godly, and a great fear to Daniel.

² Which is to declare that the godly should not hasten too much, but patiently to abide the issue of God's promise.

10:4 ¹ Called Abib, which containeth part of March, and part of April.

² Being carried by the Spirit of prophecy to have the sight of this river Tigris.

10:5 ¹ This was the Angel of God, which was sent to assure Daniel in this prophecy that followeth.

10:8 ¹ The word also signifieth comeliness, or beauty, so that for fear he was like a dead man for deformity.

10:10 ¹ Which declareth that when we are struck down with the majesty of God, we cannot rise, except he also lift us up with his hand, which is his power.

10:13 ¹ Meaning, Cambyses who reigned in his father's absence,

and did not only for this space hinder the building of the Temple, but would have further raged, if God had not sent me to resist him, and therefore have I stayed for the profit of the Church.

² Though God could by one Angel destroy all the world, yet to assure his children of his love, he sendeth forth double power, even Michael, that is, Christ Jesus the head of Angels.

10:14 ¹ For though the Prophet Daniel should end and cease, yet his doctrine should continue till the coming of Christ, for the comfort of his Church.

10:16 ¹ This was the same Angel that spake with him before in the similitude of a man.

² I was overcome with fear and sorrow, when I saw the vision.

10:19 ¹ He declareth hereby that God would be merciful to the people of Israel.

² Which declareth that when God smiteth down his children, he doth not immediately lift them up at once (for now the Angel had touched him twice) but by little and little.

the [1]Prince of Greece shall come.

21 But I will show thee that which is decreed in the Scripture of truth: [1]and there is none that holdeth with me in these things, but Michael your prince.

11

A prophecy of the kingdoms, which should be enemies to the Church of God, as of Persia, 3 Of Greece, 5 of Egypt, 28 of Syria, 36 and of the Romans.

1 Also I, in the first year of Darius of the Medes, even I [1]stood to encourage and to strengthen him.

2 And now will I show thee the truth. Behold, there shall stand up yet [1]three kings in Persia, and the fourth shall be far richer than they all: and by his strength, and by his riches he shall stir up [2]all against the realm of Greece.

3 But a [1]mighty King shall stand up, that shall rule with great dominion, and do according to his pleasure.

4 And when he shall stand up, [1]his kingdom shall be broken, [2]and shall be divided toward the [3]four winds of heaven: and not to his [4]posterity, nor according to [5]his dominion, which he ruled: for his kingdom shall be plucked up even to be for others besides [6]those.

5 And the [1]King of the South shall be mighty, and one of [2]his princes, and shall prevail against him, and bear rule: his dominion shall be a great dominion.

6 And in the end of years they shall be joined together: for the King's [1]daughter of the South shall come to the King of the North to make an agreement, but she shall not retain the power of the [2]arm, neither shall [3]he continue, nor his [4]arm: but she shall be delivered to death, and they that brought her, and he [5]that begat her, and he that comforted her, in these times.

7 But out of the bud of her [1]roots shall one stand up in his stead, [2]which shall come with an army, and shall enter into the fortress of the King of the North, and do with them as he list, and shall prevail,

8 And shall also carry captives into Egypt their gods: with their molten images, and with their precious vessels of silver and of gold, and he shall continue [1]more years than the king of the North.

9 So the king of the South shall come into his kingdom, and shall return into his own land.

10 Wherefore his [1]sons shall be stirred up, and shall assemble a mighty great army: and one [2]shall come, and overflow, and pass through: then shall he [3]return, and be stirred up at his fortress.

11 And the King of the South shall be angry, and shall come forth, and fight with him, even with the king of the North: for he shall set forth a great [1]multitude, and the multitude shall be given into his hand.

12 Then the multitude shall be proud, and their heart shall be lifted up: for he shall cast down thou-

---

10:20 [1] Meaning, that he would not only himself bridle the rage of Cambyses, but also the other Kings of Persia by Alexander the King of Macedonia.

10:21 [1] For this Angel was appointed for the defense of the Church under Christ, who is the head thereof.

11:1 [1] The Angel assureth Daniel that God hath given him power to perform these things, seeing he appointed him to assist Darius when he overcame the Chaldeans.

11:2 [1] Whereof Cambyses that now reigned, was the first, the second Smerdis, the third Darius the son of Hystaspis, and the fourth Xerxes, which all were enemies to the people of God, and stood against them.

[2] For he raised up all the East countries to fight against the Greeks, and albeit he had in his army nine hundred thousand men, yet in four battles he was discomfited and fled away with shame.

11:3 [1] That is, Alexander the great.

11:4 [1] For when his estate was most flourishing, he overcame himself with drink, and so fell into a disease: or as some write, was poisoned by Cassander.

[2] For his twelve chief Princes first divided his kingdom among themselves.

[3] After this his Monarchy was divided into four: for Seleucus had Syria, Antigonus Asia minor, Cassander the kingdom of Macedonia, and Ptolemy Egypt.

[4] Thus God revenged Alexander's ambition and cruelty in causing his posterity to be murdered, partly of the father's chief friends, and partly one of another.

[5] None of these four shall be able to be compared to the power of Alexander.

[6] That is, his posterity having no part thereof.

11:5 [1] To wit, Ptolemy king of Egypt.

[2] That is, Antiochus the son of Seleucus, and one of Alexander's princes shall be more mighty: for he should have both Asia and Syria.

11:6 [1] That is, Berenice the daughter of Ptolemy Philadelphus shall be given in marriage to Antiochus Theos, thinking by this affinity that Syria and Egypt should have a continual peace together.

[2] That force and strength shall not continue: for soon after Berenice and her young son after her husband's death, was slain of her stepson Seleucus Callinicus the son of Laodice, the lawful wife of Antiochus, but put away for this woman's sake.

[3] Neither Ptolemy nor Antiochus.

[4] Some read, seed, meaning, the child begotten of Berenice.

[5] Some read, she that begate her, and thereby understand her nurse, which brought her up: so that all they that were occasion of this marriage, were destroyed.

11:7 [1] Meaning, that Ptolemeus Euergetes after the death of his father Philadelphus should succeed in the kingdom being of the same stock that Berenice was.

[2] To revenge the sister's death against Antiochus Callinicus king of Syria.

11:8 [1] For this Ptolemy reigned six and forty years.

11:10 [1] Meaning, Seleucus and Antiochus the great, the sons of Callinicus, shall make war against Ptolemy Philopater the son of Philadelphus.

[2] For his elder brother Seleucus died, or was slain while the wars were preparing.

[3] That is, Philopater when he shall see Antiochus to take great dominions from him in Syria, and also ready to invade Egypt.

11:11 [1] For Antiochus had six thousand horsemen, and threescore thousand footmen.

sands: but he shall not *still* prevail,

13 For the King of the North [1]shall return, and shall set forth a greater multitude than afore, and shall come forth (after certain years) with a mighty army, and great riches.

14 And at the same time there shall [1]many stand up against the king of the South: also the rebellious children of thy [2]people shall exalt themselves to establish the vision, but they shall fall.

15 So the King of the North shall come, and cast up a mount, and take the strong city: and the arms of the South shall [1]not resist, neither his chosen people, neither *shall* there *be* any strength to withstand.

16 But he that shall come, shall do unto him as he list, and none shall stand against him: and he shall stand in the [1]pleasant land, which by his hand shall be consumed.

17 Again he shall [1]set his face to enter with the power of his whole kingdom, and his confederates with him: thus shall he do, and he shall give him the [2]daughter of women to destroy [3]her: but [4]she shall not stand *on his side*, neither be for him.

18 After this shall he turn his face unto the [1]isles, and shall take many, but a prince [2]shall cause his shame to light upon him, besides that he shall cause his own shame to turn upon [3]himself.

19 For he shall turn his face toward the forts of [1]his own land: but he shall be overthrown and fall, and be no more [2]found.

20 [1]Then shall stand up in his place in the glory of the kingdom, one that shall raise taxes: but after few days he shall be destroyed, neither in [2]wrath, nor in battle.

21 And in his place shall stand up a [1]vile person, to whom they shall not give the honor of the kingdom: but he shall come in peaceably and obtain the kingdom by flatteries.

22 And the [1]arms shall be overthrown with a flood before him, and shall be broken: and also the prince of the [2]covenant.

23 And after [1]the league *made* with him, he shall work deceitfully: for he shall come up, and overcome with a [2]small people.

24 He shall enter into the quiet and plentiful province, and he shall do that which his fathers [1]have not done, nor his fathers' fathers: he shall divide among them the prey and the spoil, and the substance, yea, and he shall forecast his devices against the strongholds, even for a [2]time.

25 Also he shall stir up his power, and his courage against the King of the South with a great army, and the King of the South shall be stirred up to battle with a very great and mighty army: but he shall not [1]stand: for they shall forecast and practice against him.

26 Yea, they that feed of the portion of [1]his meat, shall destroy him: and his army [2]shall overflow: and many shall fall, and be slain.

27 And both these Kings' hearts *shall be* to do [1]mischief, and they shall talk of deceit at one table:

11:13 [1] After the death of Ptolemy Philopater, who left Ptolemeus Epiphanes his heir.

11:14 [1] For not only Antiochus came against him but also Philip King of Macedonia, and these two brought great power with them.

[2] For under Onias which falsely alleged that place of Isa. 19:19, certain of the Jews retired with him into Egypt to fulfill this prophecy: also the Angel showeth that all these troubles which are in the Church, are by the providence and counsel of God.

11:15 [1] The Egyptians were not able to resist Scopas Antiochus' captain.

11:16 [1] He showeth that he shall not only afflict the Egyptians, but also the Jews, and shall enter into their country, whereof he admonisheth them before, that they may know that all these things came by God's providence.

11:17 [1] This was the second battle that Antiochus fought against Ptolemy Epiphanes.

[2] To wit, a beautiful woman which was Cleopatra Antiochus' daughter.

[3] For he regarded not the life of his daughter in respect of the kingdom of Egypt.

[4] She shall not agree to his wicked counsel, but shall love her husband, as her duty requireth, and not seek his destruction.

11:18 [1] That is, toward Asia, Greece, and those isles which are in the sea called Mediterranean: for the Jews called all countries isles which were divided from them by sea.

[2] For whereas Antiochus was wont to contemn the Romans, and put their ambassadors to shame in all places, Atilius the Consul, or Lucius Scipio put him to flight, and caused his shame to turn on his own head.

[3] By his wicked life, and obeying of foolish counsel.

11:19 [1] For fear of the Romans he shall flee to his holds.

[2] For when as under the pretence of poverty he would have robbed the Temple of Jupiter Dodomeus, the countrymen slew him.

11:20 [1] That is, Seleucus shall succeed his father Antiochus.

[2] Not by foreign enemies, or battle, but by treason.

11:21 [1] Which was Antiochus Epiphanes, who as is thought was the occasion of Seleucus his brother's death, and was of a vile, cruel and flattering nature, and defrauded his brother's son of the kingdom, and usurped the kingdom without the consent of the people.

11:22 [1] He showeth that great foreign powers shall come to help the young son of Seleucus against his uncle Antiochus: and yet shall be overthrown.

[2] Meaning, Ptolemais Philopater's son who was this child's cousin germane, and is here called the prince of the covenant, because he was the chief, and all others followed his conduct.

11:23 [1] For after the battle Philometor and his uncle Antiochus made a league.

[2] For he came upon him at unawares, and when he suspected his uncle Antiochus nothing.

11:24 [1] Meaning, in Egypt.

[2] He will content himself with the small holds for a time, but ever labor by craft to attain to the chiefest.

11:25 [1] He shall be overcome with treason.

11:26 [1] Signifying his princes and the chief about him.

[2] Declaring that his soldiers shall brast out and venture their life to slay and to be slain for the safeguard of their prince.

11:27 [1] The uncle and the nephew shall take truce, and banquet together, yet in their hearts they shall imagine mischief one against the other.

but it shall not avail: for [2]yet the end *shall be* at the time appointed.

28 Then shall he return into his land with great [1]substance: for his heart shall be against the holy covenant: so shall he do and return to his own land.

29 At the time appointed he shall return, and come toward the South: but the last shall not be as the first.

30 For the ships [1]of Chittim shall come against him: therefore he shall be sorry and return and fret against the holy covenant: so shall he do, he shall even return [2]and have intelligence with them that forsake the holy covenant.

31 And arms [1]shall stand on his part, and they shall pollute the Sanctuary [2]of strength, and shall take away the daily *sacrifice*, and they shall set up the abominable desolation.

32 And such as wickedly [1]break the covenant, shall he cause to sin by flattery: but the people that do know their God, shall prevail and prosper.

33 And they that understand among the [1]people, shall instruct many: [2]yet they shall fall by sword, and by flame, by captivity and by spoil many days.

34 Now when they shall fall, they shall be holpen with a [1]little help: but many shall cleave unto them [2]feignedly.

35 And some of them [1]of understanding shall fall to try them, and to purge, and to make them white, till the time be out: for there *is* a time appointed.

36 And the [1]king shall do what him list: he shall exalt himself, and magnify himself against all, *that is* God, and shall speak marvelous things against the God of gods, and shall prosper, till the wrath [2]be accomplished: for the determination is made.

37 Neither shall he regard the [1]God of his fathers, nor the desires [2]of women, nor care for any God: for he shall magnify himself above all.

38 But in his place shall he honor the [1]god Mauzzim, and the god whom his fathers knew not, shall he honor with [2]gold and with silver, and with precious stones, and pleasant things.

39 Thus shall he do in [1]the holds of Mauzzim with a strange god whom he shall acknowledge: he shall increase *his* glory, and shall cause them to rule over many, and shall divide the land for gain.

40 And at the end of time shall the king of the [1]South push at him, and the king of the North shall come against him like a whirlwind with chariots, and with horsemen, and with many ships, and he shall enter into the countries, and shall overflow and pass through.

41 He shall enter also into the [1]pleasant land, and many *countries* shall be overthrown: but these shall

---

11:27 [2] Signifying, that it standeth not in the counsel of men to bring things to pass, but in the providence of God, who ruleth the Kings by a secret bridle, that they cannot do what they list themselves.
11:28 [1] Which he shall take of the Jews in spoiling Jerusalem and the Temple, and this is told them before to move them to patience, knowing that all things are done by God's providence.
11:30 [1] That is, the Roman power shall come against him: for P. Popilius the Ambassador appointed him to depart in the Romans' name, to which thing he obeyed, although with grief, and to revenge his rage he came against the people of God the second time.
[2] With the Jews which shall forsake the covenant of the Lord: for first he was called against the Jews by Jason the high Priest, and this second time by Menelaus.
11:31 [1] A great faction of the wicked Jews shall hold with Antiochus.
[2] So called because the power of God was nothing diminished, although this tyrant set up in the Temple the image of Jupiter Olympius, and so began to corrupt the pure service of God.
11:32 [1] Meaning, such as bare the name of Jews, but indeed were nothing less, for they sold their souls, and betrayed their brethren for gain.
11:33 [1] They that remain constant among the people shall teach others by their example, and edify many in the true religion.
[2] Whereby he exhorteth the godly to constancy, although they should perish a thousand times, and though their miseries endure never so long.
11:34 [1] As God will not leave his Church destitute, yet will he not deliver it all at once, but so help, as they may still seem to fight under the cross, as he did in the time of the Maccabees, whereof he here prophesieth.
[2] That is, there shall be even of this small number many hypocrites.
11:35 [1] To wit, of them that fear God and will lose their life for the defense of true religion. Signifying also that the Church must con-

tinually be tried and purged, and ought to look for one persecution after another: for God hath appointed the time: therefore we must obey.
11:36 [1] Because the Angel's purpose is to show the whole course of the persecutions of the Jews unto the coming of Christ, he now speaketh of the Monarchy of the Romans which he noteth by the name of a King, who were without religion and condemned the true God.
[2] So long the tyrants shall prevail as God hath appointed to punish his people: but he showeth that it is but for a time.
11:37 [1] The Romans shall observe no certain form of religion as other nations, but shall change their gods at their pleasures, yea, contemn them and prefer themselves to their gods.
[2] Signifying that they should be without all humanity: for the love of women is taken for singular or great love, as 2 Sam. 1:26.
11:38 [1] That is, the god of power and riches: they shall esteem their own power above all their gods and worship it.
[2] Under pretence of worshipping the gods, they shall enrich their city with the most precious jewels of all the world, because that hereby all men should have them in admiration for their power and riches.
11:39 [1] Although in their hearts they had no religion, yet they did acknowledge the gods, and worshipped them in their temples, lest they should have been despised as Atheists: but this was to increase their fame and riches: and when they got any country, they so made others the rulers thereof, that the profit ever came to the Romans.
11:40 [1] That is, both the Egyptians and the Syrians shall at length fight against the Romans, but they shall be overcome.
11:41 [1] The Angel forewarneth the Jews that when they should see the Romans invade them, and that the wicked should escape their hands, that then they should not think but that all this was done by God's providence, forasmuch as he warned them of it so long afore, and therefore he would still preserve them.

escape out of his hand, *even* Edom and Moab, and the chief of the children of Ammon.

42 He shall stretch forth his hands also upon the countries, and the land of Egypt shall not escape.

43 But he shall have power over the treasures of gold and of silver, and over all the precious things of Egypt, and of the Libyans, and of the black Mores where he shall pass.

44 But the tidings out of the East and the North shall ¹trouble him: therefore he shall go forth ²with great wrath to destroy and root out many.

45 And he shall plant the tabernacles ¹of his palace between the seas in the glorious *and* holy mountain, yet he shall come to his end, and none shall help him.

12
1 *Of the deliverance of the Church by Christ.*

1 And at that ¹time shall Michael stand up, the great prince, which standeth for the children of thy people, and there shall be a time of trouble, such as never was since there began to be a nation unto that same time: and at that time thy people shall be delivered, everyone that shall be found written in the book.

2 And many ¹of them that sleep in the dust of the earth, shall awake, some to everlasting life, and some to shame and perpetual contempt.

3 And they that be ¹wise, shall shine, as the brightness of the firmament: and they that ²turn many to righteousness, *shall shine* as the stars, forever and ever.

4 But thou, O Daniel, ¹shut up the words, and seal the book ²till the end of the time: many shall

run to and fro, and knowledge shall be increased.

5 ¶ Then I Daniel looked, and behold, there stood other two, the one on this side of the brink of the ¹river, and the other on that side of the brink of the river.

6 And *one* said unto the man clothed in linen, which was upon the waters of the river, When *shall be* the end of these wonders?

7 And I heard the man clothed in linen which was upon the waters of the river, when he held up his ¹right hand, and his left hand unto heaven, and sware by him that liveth forever, that *it shall tarry* for a ²time two times and an half: and when he shall have accomplished ³to scatter the power of the holy people, all these things shall be finished.

8 Then I heard it, but I understood it not: then said I, O my Lord, what shall be the end of these things?

9 And he said, Go thy way, Daniel: for the words are closed up, and sealed, till the end of the time.

10 Many shall be purified, made white, and tried: but the wicked shall do wickedly, and none of the wicked shall have understanding: but the wise shall understand.

11 And from the time that the ¹daily *sacrifice* shall be taken away, and the abominable desolation set up, there ²*shall be* a thousand, two hundred and ninety days.

12 Blessed *is* he that waiteth and cometh to the thousand, three hundred and ¹five and thirty days.

13 But go ¹thou thy way till the end *be*: for thou shalt rest and stand up in thy lot, at the end of the days.

11:44 ¹ Hearing that Crassus was slain, and Antonius discomfited.

² For Augustus overcame the Parthians, and recovered that which Antonius had lost.

11:45 ¹ The Romans after this reigned quietly throughout all countries, and from sea to sea, and in Judea: but at length for their cruelty God shall destroy them.

12:1 ¹ The Angel here noteth two things: first that the Church shall be in great affliction and trouble at Christ's coming, and next that God will send his Angel to deliver it, whom here he calleth Michael, meaning Christ, which is published by the preaching of the Gospel.

12:2 ¹ Meaning, all shall rise at the general resurrection, which thing he here nameth because the faithful should have ever respect to that: for in the earth there shall be no sure comfort.

12:3 ¹ Who have kept the true fear of God and his religion.

² He chiefly meaneth the ministers of God's word, and next all the faithful which instruct the ignorant, and bring them to the true knowledge of God.

12:4 ¹ Though the most part despise this prophecy, yet keep thou it sure and esteem it as a treasure.

² Till the time that God hath appointed for the full revelation of these things: and then many shall run to and fro to search the knowl-

edge of these mysteries which things they obtain now by the light of the Gospel.

12:5 ¹ Which was Tigris.

12:7 ¹ Which was as were a double oath, and did the more confirm the thing.

² Meaning, a long time, a longer time, and at length a short time: signifying that their troubles should have an end.

³ When the Church shall be scattered and diminished in such sort as it shall seem to have no power.

12:11 ¹ From the time that Christ by his sacrifice shall take away the sacrifice and ceremonies of the Law.

² Signifying that the time shall be long of Christ's second coming, and yet the children of God ought not to be discouraged, though it be deferred.

12:12 ¹ In this number he addeth a month and a half to the former number, signifying that it is not in man to appoint the time of Christ's coming, but that they are blessed that patiently abide his appearing.

12:13 ¹ The Angel warneth the Prophet patiently to abide; till the time appointed come, signifying that he should depart this life, and rise again with the elect, when God had sufficiently humbled and purged his Church.

HOSEA

1 *1 The time wherein Hosea prophesied.   2 The idolatry of the people.   10 The calling of the Gentiles.   11 Christ is the head of all people.*

1   The word of the Lord that came unto Hosea the son of Beeri, in the days [1]of Uzziah, Jotham, Ahaz, *and* Hezekiah, [2]kings of Judah, and in the days of Jeroboam the son of Joash king of Israel.

2   At the beginning the Lord spake by Hosea, and the Lord said unto Hosea, Go, take unto thee a wife [1]of fornications, and children of fornications: for the land hath committed great whoredom, *departing* from the Lord.

3   So he went, and took [1]Gomer, the daughter of Diblaim, which conceived and bare him a son.

4   And the Lord said unto him, Call his name [1]Jezreel: for yet a little, and I will visit the blood of Jezreel upon the house of [2]Jehu, and will cause to cease the kingdom of the house of Israel.

5   And at that [1]day will I also break the bow of Israel in the valley of Jezreel.

6   She conceived yet again, and bare a daughter, and *God* said unto him, Call her name [1]Lo-Ruhamah: for I will no more have pity upon the house of Israel: but I will utterly [2]take them away.

7   Yet I will have mercy upon the house of Judah, and will [1]save them by the Lord their God, and will not save them by bow, nor by sword, nor by battle, by horses, nor by horsemen.

8   Now when she had weaned Lo-Ruhamah, she conceived, and bare a son.

9   Then said *God*, Call his name [1]Lo-Ammi: for ye are not my people: therefore will I not be yours.

10   Yet the number of the [1]children of Israel shall be as the sand of the sea, which cannot be measured nor told: and in the place where it was said unto them, Ye are not my people, it shall be said unto them, *Ye are* the sons of the living God.

11   Then shall the children of Judah, and the children of Israel be [1]gathered together, and appoint themselves one head, and they shall come up out of the land: for great *is* the [2]day of Jezreel.

2 *1 The people is called to repentance.   5 He showeth their idolatry and threateneth them except they repent.*

1   Say unto your [1]brethren, Ammi, and to your sisters, Ruhamah,

2   Plead with your [1]mother: plead *with her*: for she is not my wife, neither am I her husband: but let her take away her fornications out of her sight, and her adulteries [2]from between her breasts.

3   Lest I strip her naked, and [1]set her as in the day that she was [2]born, and make her as a wilderness, and

1:1 [1] Called also Azariah, who being a leper was disposed from his kingdom.

[2] So that it may be gathered by the reign of these four kings, that he preached above threescore years.

1:2 [1] That is, one that of long time hath accustomed to play the harlot: not that the Prophet did this thing in effect, but he saw this in a vision, or else was commanded by God to set forth under this parable or figure the idolatry of the Synagogue, and of the people her children.

1:3 [1] Gomer signifieth a consumption or corruption, and Diblaim clusters of figs, declaring that they were all corrupt like rotten figs.

1:4 [1] Meaning, that they should be no more called Israelites of the which name they boasted because Israel, did prevail with God: but that they were as bastard, and therefore should be called Jezreelites, that is scattered people, alluding to Jezreel, which was the chief city of the ten tribes under Ahab where Jehu shed so much blood, 2 Kings 10:8.

[2] I will be revenged upon Jehu for the blood that he shed in Jezreel: for albeit God stirred him up to execute his judgments, yet he did them for his own ambition, and not for the glory of God as the end declared: for he built up that idolatry which he had destroyed.

1:5 [1] When the measure of their iniquity is full, and I shall take vengeance and destroy all their policy and force.

1:6 [1] That is, not obtaining mercy: whereby he signifieth, that God's favor was departed from them.

[2] For the Israelites never returned after that they were taken captives by the Assyrians.

1:7 [1] For after their captivity he restored him miraculously by the means of Cyrus, Ezra 1:1.

1:9 [1] That is, not my people.

1:10 [1] Because they thought that God could not have been true in his promise except he had preserved them, he declareth though they were destroyed, yet the true Israelites, which are the sons of the promise, should be without number, which stand both of the Jews and the Gentiles, Rom. 9:26.

1:11 [1] To wit, after the captivity of Babylon when the Jews were restored, but chiefly this is referred to the time of Christ, who should be the head both of the Jews and Gentiles.

[2] The calamity and destruction of Israel shall be so great, that to restore them shall be as a miracle.

2:1 [1] Seeing that I have promised you deliverance, it remaineth that you encourage one another to embrace the same, considering that ye are my people on whom I will have mercy.

2:2 [1] God showeth that the fault was not in him, but in their Synagogue, and their idolatries, that he forsook them, Isa. 50:1.

[2] Meaning, that their idolatry was so great, that they were not ashamed, but boasted of it, Ezek. 16:25.

2:3 [1] For though this people were as an harlot for their idolatries, yet he had left them with their apparel and dowry and certain signs of his favor, but if they continued still, he would utterly destroy them.

[2] When I brought her out of Egypt, Ezek. 16:4.

leave her like a dry land, and slay her for thirst.

4   And I will have no pity upon her children: for they be the [1]children of fornication.

5   For their mother hath played the harlot: she that conceived them, hath done shamefully: for she said, I will go after thy [1]lovers that give me my bread and my water, my wool, and my flax, mine oil and my drink.

6   Therefore behold, I will stoop [1]thy way with thorns, and make an hedge, that she shall not find her paths.

7   Though she follow after her lovers, yet shall she not come at them: though she seek them, yet shall she not find *them*: then shall she say, [1]I will go and return to my first husband: for at that time was I better than now.

8   Now she did not know that I [1]gave her corn, and wine, and oil, and multiplied her silver and gold, *which* they bestowed upon Baal.

9   Therefore will I return, and take away [1]my corn in the time thereof, and my wine in the season thereof, and will recover my wool and my flax *lent*, to cover her shame.

10   And now will I discover her [1]lewdness in the sight of her lovers, and no man shall deliver her out of mine hand.

11   I will also cause all her mirth to cease, her feast days, her new moons, and her Sabbaths, and all her solemn feasts.

12   And I will destroy her vines and her fig trees, whereof she hath said, These are my rewards that my lovers have given me: and I will make them as a forest, and the wild beasts shall eat them.

13   And I will visit upon her the days of [1]Baal, wherein she burnt incense to them: and she decked herself with her [2]earrings and her jewels, and she followed her lovers, and forgot me, saith the Lord.

14   Therefore behold, I will [1]allure her, and bring

CHAPTER 2
a Rom. 9:25
1 Pet. 2:10

her into the wilderness, and speak friendly unto her.

15   And I will give her her vineyards from thence, and the valley [1]of Achor for the door of hope, and she shall [2]sing there as in the days of her youth, and as in the day when she came up out of the land of Egypt.

16   And at that day, saith the Lord, thou shalt call me [1]Ishi, and shalt call me no more [2]Baali.

17   For I will take away the names of Baal out of her mouth, and they shall be no more remembered by their [1]names.

18   And in that day will I make a covenant for them with the [1]wild beasts, and with the fowls of the heaven, and with that that creepeth upon the earth: and I will break the bow, and the sword and the battle out of the earth: and will make them to sleep safely.

19   And I will marry thee unto me forever: yea, I will marry thee unto me in righteousness, and in judgment, and in mercy, and in compassion.

20   I will even marry thee unto me in [1]faithfulness, and thou shalt know the Lord.

21   And in that day I will hear, saith the Lord, I will *even* hear [1]the heavens, and they shall hear the earth,

22   And the earth shall hear the corn, and the wine, and the oil, and they shall hear Jezreel.

23   And I will sow her unto me in the earth, and I will have mercy upon her, that was not pitied, [a]and I will say to them which were not my people, Thou art my people. And they shall say, *Thou art* my God.

3   *1 The Jews shall be cast off for their idolatry.   5 Afterward they shall return to the Lord.*

1   Then said the Lord to me, [1]Go yet, *and* love a woman (beloved of *her* husband, and was an harlot)

2:4 [1] That is, bastards and begotten in adultery.

2:5 [1] Meaning, the idol which they served, and by whom they thought they had wealth and abundance.

2:6 [1] I will punish thee that then thou mayest try whether thine idols can help thee, and bring thee into such straightness that thou shalt have no lust to play the wanton.

2:7 [1] This he speaketh of the faithful, which are truly converted, and also showeth the use and profit of God's rods.

2:8 [1] This declareth that idolaters defraud God of his honor, when they attribute his benefits to their idols.

2:9 [1] Signifying, that God will take away his benefits when man by his ingratitude doth abuse them.

2:10 [1] That is, all her service, ceremonies and inventions whereby she worshipped her idols.

2:13 [1] I will punish her for her idolatry.

[2] By showing how harlots trim themselves to please others, he declareth how that superstitious idolaters set a great part of their religion, in decking themselves on their holy days.

2:14 [1] By my benefits in offering her grace and mercy, even in that

place where she shall think herself destitute of all help and comfort.

2:15 [1] Which was a plentiful valley, and wherein they had great comfort when they came out of the wilderness, as Josh. 7:26, and is called the door of hope, because it was a departing from death and an entry into life.

[2] She shall then praise God as she did when she was delivered out of Egypt.

2:16 [1] That is, mine husband, knowing that I am joined to thee by an inviolable covenant.

[2] That is, my master: which name was applied to their idols.

2:17 [1] No idolatry shall once come into their mouth, but they shall serve me purely according to my word.

2:18 [1] Meaning, that he will so bless them that all creatures shall favor them.

2:20 [1] With a covenant that never shall be broken.

2:21 [1] Then shall the heaven desire rain for the earth which shall bring forth for the use of man.

3:1 [1] Herein the Prophet representeth the person of God, which loved his Church before he called her, and did not withdraw the same when she gave herself to idols.

according to the love of the Lord toward the children of Israel: yet they looked to other gods, and [2]loved the wine bottles.

2 So [1]I bought her to me for fifteen *pieces* of silver, and for an homer of barley, and an half *homer* of barley.

3 And I said unto her, Thou shalt abide with [1]me many days: thou shalt not play the harlot, and thou shalt be to none *other* man, and I will be so unto thee.

4 For the children of Israel shall [1]remain many days without a king and without a [2]prince, and without an offering, and without an image, and without an Ephod, and without Teraphim.

5 Afterward shall the children of Israel convert and seek the Lord their God, and [1]David their king, and shall fear the Lord and his goodness in the latter days.

4

A complaint against the people and the priests of Israel.

1 Hear the word of the Lord, ye children of Israel: for the Lord [1]hath a controversy with the inhabitants of the land, because there is no truth, nor mercy, nor knowledge of God in the land.

2 By swearing, and lying, and killing, and stealing, and whoring, they break out, and [1]blood toucheth blood.

3 Therefore shall the land mourn, and everyone that dwelleth therein shall be cut off, with the beasts of the field, and with the fowls of the heaven, and also the fishes of the sea shall be taken away.

4 Yet [1]let none rebuke, nor reprove another: for thy people *are* as they that rebuke the Priest.

5 Therefore shalt thou fall in the [1]day, and the Prophet shall fall with thee in the night, and I will destroy thy [2]mother.

6 My people are destroyed for lack of knowledge: because [1]thou hast refused knowledge, I will also refuse thee that thou shalt be no Priest to me: and seeing [2]thou hast forgotten the Law of thy God, I will also forget thy children.

7 As they were [1]increased, so they sinned against me: *therefore* will I change their glory into shame.

8 [1]They eat up the sins of my people, and lift up their minds in their iniquity.

9 And there shall be like people like [1]priest: for I will visit their ways upon them, and reward them their deeds.

10 For they shall eat, and not have enough, they shall [1]commit adultery, and shall not increase, because they have left off to take heed to the Lord.

11 [1]Whoredom, and wine, and new wine take away *their* heart.

12 My [1]people ask counsel at their stocks, and their staff teacheth them: for the [2]spirit of fornications hath caused *them* to err, and they have gone a whoring from under their God.

13 They sacrifice upon the tops of the mountains, and burn incense upon the hills under the oaks, and the poplar tree, and the elm, because the shadow thereof is good: therefore your daughters shall be [1]harlots, and your spouses shall be whores.

14 I will not [1]visit your daughters when they are harlots: nor your spouses, when they are whores: for they themselves are separated with harlots, and sacrifice with whores: therefore the people that doth not understand, shall fall.

3:1 [2] That is, gave themselves wholly to pleasure, and could not take up, as they that are given to drunkenness.

3:2 [1] Yet I loved her and paid a small portion for her, lest she perceiving the greatness of my love, should have abused me, and not been under duty: for fifteen pieces of silver were but half the price of a slave, Exod. 21:32.

3:3 [1] I will try thee a long time as in thy widowhood whether thou wilt be mine or no.

3:4 [1] Meaning, not only all the time of their captivity, but also unto Christ.
[2] That is, they should neither have policy nor religion, and their idols also wherein they put their confidence, should be destroyed.

3:5 [1] This is meant of Christ's kingdom, which was promised unto David to be eternal, Ps. 72:17.

4:1 [1] Because the people would not obey the admonitions of the Prophet, he citeth them before the judgment seat of God, against whom they chiefly offended, Isa. 7:13; Zech. 12:10; Mic. 6:1, 2.

4:2 [1] In every place appeareth a liberty to most heinous vices, so that one followeth in the neck of another.

4:4 [1] As though he would say that it were in vain to rebuke them: for no man can abide it: yea, they will speak against the prophets and priests whose office it is chiefly to rebuke them.

4:5 [1] Ye shall perish all together the one because he would not obey, and the other, because he would not admonish.

[2] That is, the Synagogue wherein thou boastest.

4:6 [1] That is, the Priests shall be cast off, because that for lack of knowledge, they are not able to execute their charge, and instruct others, Deut. 33:3; Mal. 2:7.
[2] Meaning, the whole body of the people, which were weary with hearing the word of God.

4:7 [1] The more I was beneficial unto them.

4:8 [1] To wit, the Priests seek to eat the people's offerings, and flatter them in their sins.

4:9 [1] Signifying, that as they have sinned together, so shall they be punished together.

4:10 [1] Showing that their wickedness shall be punished on all sorts: for though they think by the multitude of wives to have many children, yet they shall be deceived of their hope.

4:11 [1] In giving themselves to pleasures, they become like brute beasts.

4:12 [1] Thus he speaketh by derision in calling them his people, which now for their sins they were not: for they sought help of stocks and sticks.
[2] They are carried away with a rage.

4:13 [1] Because they take away God's honor, and give it to idols: therefore he will give them up to their lusts, that they shall dishonor their own bodies, Rom. 1:28.

4:14 [1] I will not correct your shame to bring you to amendment, but let you run headlong to your own damnation.

15 Though thou Israel, play the harlot, *yet* [1]let not Judah sin: come not ye unto [2]Gilgal, neither go ye up to [3]Beth Aven, nor swear, The Lord liveth.

16 For Israel is rebellious as an unruly heifer. Now the Lord will feed them as a [1]lamb in a large place.

17 Ephraim *is* joined to idols: let him alone.

18 Their drunkenness stinketh: they have committed whoredom: their rulers love *to say* with shame, [1]Bring ye.

19 The wind hath [1]bound them up in her wings, and they shall be ashamed of their sacrifices.

5

1 Against the Priests and rulers of Israel.   13 The help of man is in vain.

1 O ye Priests, hear this, and hearken ye, O house of Israel, and give ye ear, O house of the King: for judgment is toward you, because you have been a [1]snare on Mizpah, and a net spread upon Tabor.

2 Yet they were profound to decline to [1]slaughter, though I have been a [2]rebuker of them all.

3 I know [1]Ephraim, and Israel is not hid from me: for now, O Ephraim, thou art become an harlot, *and* Israel is defiled.

4 They will not give their minds to turn unto their God: for the spirit of fornication is in the midst of them, and they have not known the Lord.

5 And the [1]pride of Israel doth testify to his face: therefore shall Israel and Ephraim fall in their iniquity: Judah also shall fall with them.

6 They shall go with their sheep, and with their bullocks, to seek the Lord: but they shall not find him: *for* he hath withdrawn himself from them.

7 They have transgressed against the Lord: for they have begotten [1]strange children: now shall [2]a month devour them with their portions.

8 Blow ye the trumpet in Gibeah, *and* the shame in Ramah: cry out at Beth Aven, after thee, O [1]Ben-jamin.

9 Ephraim shall be desolate in the day of rebuke: among the tribes of Israel have I caused to [1]know the truth.

10 The princes of Judah were like them that [1]remove the bound: *therefore* will I pour out my wrath upon them like water.

11 Ephraim is oppressed *and* broken in judgment, because he willingly walked after the [1]commandment.

12 Therefore will I be unto Ephraim as a moth, and to the house of Judah as a rottenness.

13 When Ephraim saw his sickness, and Judah his wound, then went Ephraim unto [1]Assyria, and sent unto King [2]Jareb: yet could he not heal you, nor cure you of your wound.

14 For I will be unto Ephraim as a lion, and as a lion's whelp, to the house of Judah: I, *even* I will spoil and go away: I will take away, and none shall rescue it.

15 I will go, *and* return to my place, till they acknowledge their fault, and seek me: in their affliction, they will seek me diligently.

6

1 Affliction causeth a man to turn to God.   9 The wickedness of the Priests.

1 Come, and let [1]us return to the Lord: for he hath spoiled, and he will heal us: he hath wounded us, and he will bind us up.

2 After two days will [1]he revive us, *and* in the third day he will raise us up, and we shall live in his sight.

3 Then shall we have knowledge, and endeavor ourselves to know the Lord: his going forth is prepared as the morning, and he shall come unto us as the rain, *and* as the latter rain unto the earth.

4 O Ephraim, what shall I do unto thee? O Judah, how shall I entreat thee? for [1]your goodness *is* as a morn-

---

4:15 [1] God complaineth that Judah is infected, and willeth them to learn to return in time.

[2] For albeit the Lord had honored this place in time past by his presence, yet because it was abused by their idolatry, he would not that his people should resort thither.

[3] He calleth Bethel, that is, the house of God, Beth Aven, that is, the house of iniquity, because of their abominations set up there, signifying that no place is holy, where God is not purely worshipped.

4:16 [1] God will so disperse them, that they shall not remain in any certain place.

4:18 [1] They are so impudent in receiving bribes, that they will command men to bring them unto them.

4:19 [1] To carry them suddenly away.

5:1 [1] The Priests and Princes caught the poor people in their snares, as the fowlers did the birds, in these two high mountains.

5:2 [1] Notwithstanding they seemed to be given altogether to holiness, and to sacrifices which here he calleth slaughter in contempt.

[2] Though I had admonished them continually by my Prophets.

5:3 [1] They boasted themselves not only to be Israelites, but also Ephraimites, because their king Jeroboam came of that tribe.

5:5 [1] Meaning, their contemning of all admonitions.

5:7 [1] That is, their children are degenerate, so that there is no hope in them.

[2] Their destruction is not far off.

5:8 [1] That is, all Israel comprehended under this part, signifying that the Lord's plagues should pursue them from place to place till they were destroyed.

5:9 [1] By the success they shall know that I have surely determined this.

5:10 [1] They have turned upside down all political order and all manner of religion.

5:11 [1] To wit, after king Jeroboam's commandment, and did not rather follow God.

5:13 [1] Instead of seeking for remedy at God's hand.

[2] Who was king of the Assyrians.

6:1 [1] He showeth the people how they ought to turn to the Lord, that he might call back his plagues.

6:2 [1] Though he correct us from time to time, yet his help will not be far off, if we return to him.

6:4 [1] You seem to have a certain holiness and repentance, but it is upon the sudden, and as a morning cloud.

ing cloud, and as the morning dew it goeth away.

5 Therefore have I [1]cut down by the Prophets: I have slain them by the words of my mouth, and thy [2]judgments *were as* the light that goeth forth.

6 For I desired [1]mercy, and not sacrifice, and the knowledge of God more than burnt offerings.

7 But they [1]like men have transgressed the covenant: there have they trespassed against me.

8 [1]Gilead *is* a city of them that work iniquity, *and is* polluted with blood.

9 And as the thieves wait for a man, *so* the company of Priests murder in the way by consent: for they work mischief.

10 I have seen villainy in the house of Israel: there *is* the whoredom of Ephraim: Israel is defiled.

11 Yea, Judah hath set a [1]plant for thee, while I would return the captivity of my people.

7

1 Of the vices and wantonness of the people.   12 Of their punishment.

1 When I would have healed Israel, then the iniquity of Ephraim was discovered, and the wickedness of Samaria: for they have dealt falsely: and [1]the thief cometh in, and the robber spoileth without.

2 And they consider not in their hearts, *that* I remember all their wickedness: now their own inventions have beset them about: they are in my sight.

3 They make the [1]king glad with their wickedness, and the princes with their lies.

4 They are all adulterers, *and* as a very [1]oven heated by the baker, which ceaseth from raising up, *and* from kneading the dough until it be leavened.

5 *This is* the [1]day of our king: the princes have made him sick with flagons of wine: he stretcheth out his hand to scorners.

6 For they have made ready their heart like an oven while they lie in wait: their baker sleepeth all the

night: in the morning it burneth as a flame of fire.

7 They are all hot as an oven, and have [1]devoured their judges: all their kings are fallen: there is none among them that calleth unto me.

8 Ephraim hath [1]mixed himself among the people. Ephraim is as a cake on the hearth not turned.

9 Strangers have devoured his strength, and he knoweth it not: yea, [1]gray hairs are here, and there upon him, yet he knoweth not.

10 And the pride of Israel testifieth to his face, and they do not return to the Lord their God, nor seek him for all this.

11 Ephraim also is like a dove deceived without [1]heart: they call to Egypt: they go to Assyria.

12 *But* when they shall go, I will spread my net upon them, *and* draw them down as the fowls of the heaven: I will chastise them as their [1]Congregation hath heard.

13 Woe unto them: for they have fled away from me: destruction *shall be* unto them, because they have transgressed against me: though I have [1]redeemed them, yet they have spoken lies against me.

14 And they have not cried unto me with their hearts, [1]when they howled upon their beds: [2]they assembled themselves for corn, and wine, *and* they rebel against me.

15 Though I have bound *and* strengthened their arm, yet do they imagine mischief against me.

16 They return, *but* not to the most high: they are like a deceitful bow: their princes shall fall by the sword, for the rage [1]of their tongues: this shall be their derision in the land of Egypt.

8

1 The destruction of Judah and Israel, because of their idolatry.

1 Set the trumpet to thy [1]mouth: *he shall come* as an eagle against the House of the Lord, because

---

6:5 [1] I have still labored by my prophets, and as it were framed you to bring you to amendment, but all was in vain: for my word was not food to feed them, but a sword to slay them.

    [2] My doctrine which I taught thee, was most evident.

6:6 [1] He showeth to what scope his doctrine tended, that they should join the obedience of God, and the love of their neighbor with outward sacrifices.

6:7 [1] That is, like light and weak persons.

6:8 [1] Which was the place where the Priests dwelt, and which should have been best instructed in my word.

6:11 [1] That is, doth imitate thine idolatry, and hath taken grafts of thy trees.

7:1 [1] Meaning, that there was no one kind of vice among them, but that they were subject to all wickedness, both secret and open.

7:3 [1] They esteem their wicked king Jeroboam above God, and seek but how to flatter and please him.

7:4 [1] He compareth the rage of the people to a burning oven which the baker heateth, still till his dough be leavened and raised.

7:5 [1] They used all riot and excess in their feasts, and solemnities whereby their king was overcome with surfeit, and brought into dis-

eases, and delighted in flatteries.

7:7 [1] By their occasion God hath deprived them of all good rulers.

7:8 [1] That is, he counterfeited the religion of the Gentiles, yet is but as a cake baked on the one side, and raw on the other, that is, neither thoroughly hot, nor thoroughly cold, but partly a Jew, and partly a Gentile.

7:9 [1] Which are a token of his manifold afflictions.

7:11 [1] That is, without all judgment, as they that cannot tell whether it is better to cleave only to God, or to seek the help of man.

7:12 [1] According to my curses made to the whole Congregation of Israel.

7:13 [1] That is, divers times redeemed them, and delivered them from death.

7:14 [1] When they were in affliction, and cried out for pain, they sought not unto me for help.

    [2] They only seek their own commodity and wealth, and pass not for me their God.

7:16 [1] Because they boast of their own strength, and pass not what they speak against me and my servants, Ps. 73:9.

8:1 [1] God encourageth the Prophet to signify the speedy coming of the enemy against Israel, which was once the people of God.

they have transgressed my covenant, and trespassed against my Law.

2 Israel shall [1]cry unto me, My God, we know thee.

3 Israel hath cast off the thing that is good: the enemy shall pursue him.

4 They have set up a [1]king, but not by me: they have made princes, and I knew it not: of their silver and their gold have they made them idols: therefore shall they be destroyed.

5 Thy calf, O Samaria, hath cast thee off: mine anger is kindled against them: how long will they be without [1]innocency!

6 [1]For it came even from Israel: the workman made it, therefore it is not God: but the calf of Samaria shall be *broken* in pieces.

7 For they have [1]sown the wind, and they shall reap the whirlwind: it hath no stalk: the bud shall bring forth no meal: if so be it brought forth, the strangers shall devour it.

8 Israel is devoured, now shall they be among the Gentiles as a vessel wherein *is* no pleasure.

9 For they are gone up to Assyria: *they are as* a [1]wild ass alone by himself: Ephraim hath hired lovers.

10 Yet though they have hired among the nations, now will I gather them and they shall sorrow a little for the [1]burden of the king *and* the princes.

11 Because Ephraim hath made many altars to sin, his altars *shall be* to sin.

12 I have written to them the great things of my Law: but they were counted as a [1]strange thing.

13 They sacrifice flesh for the sacrifices of mine offerings, and eat it: *but* the [1]Lord accepteth them not: now will he remember their iniquity, and visit their sins: they shall return to Egypt.

14 For Israel hath forgotten his maker, and buildeth

Temples, and Judah hath increased strong cities: but I will send a fire upon his cities, and it shall devour the palaces thereof.

9 *Of the hunger and captivity of Israel.*

1 Rejoice not, O Israel for joy [1]as *other* people: for thou hast gone a whoring from thy God: thou hast loved [2]a reward upon every corn floor.

2 [1]The floor, and the winepress shall not feed them, and the new wine shall fail in her.

3 They will not dwell in the Lord's land, but Ephraim will return to Egypt, and they will eat unclean things in Assyria.

4 They shall not offer [1]wine to the Lord, neither shall their sacrifices be pleasant unto him: *but they shall be* unto them as the bread of mourners: all that eat thereof, shall be polluted: for their bread [2]for their souls shall not come into the house of the Lord.

5 What will ye do [1]then in the solemn day, and in the day of the feast of the Lord?

6 For lo, they are gone from [1]destruction: *but* Egypt shall gather them up, and Memphis shall bury them: the nettle shall possess the pleasant *places* of their silver, *and* the thorn *shall be* in their tabernacles.

7 The days of visitation are come: the days of recompense are come: Israel shall know it: [1]the Prophet *is* a fool: the spiritual man *is* mad, for the multitude of thine iniquity: therefore the hatred is great.

8 The watchman of Ephraim [1]*should be* with my God: *but* the Prophet *is* the snare of a fowler in all his ways, *and* hatred in the house of his God.

9 They [1]are deeply set: they are corrupt as in the days of Gibeah: *therefore* he will remember their iniquity, he will visit their sins.

10 I found Israel like [1]grapes in the wilderness: I saw your fathers as the first ripe in the fig tree at her first time: *but* they went to Baal Peor, and separated

---

8:2 [1] They shall cry like hypocrites, but not from the heart, as their deeds declare.

8:4 [1] That is, Jeroboam by whom they sought their own liberty, and not to obey my will.

8:5 [1] That is, upright judgment and godly life.

8:6 [1] Meaning, the calf was invented by themselves, and of their fathers in the wilderness.

8:7 [1] Showing that their religion hath but a show, and in itself is but vanity.

8:9 [1] They never cease, but run to and fro to seek help.

8:10 [1] That is, for the king and the princes shall lay upon them: which means the Lord useth to bring them to repentance.

8:12 [1] Thus the idolaters count the word of God as strange in respect of their own inventions.

8:13 [1] Saying that they offer it to the Lord, but he accepteth no service, which he himself hath not appointed.

9:1 [1] For though all other people should escape, yet thou shalt be punished.

[2] Thou hast committed idolatry in hope of reward, and to have thy

barns filled, Jer. 44:17, as an harlot that had rather live by playing the whore, than to be entertained of her own husband.

9:2 [1] These outward things that thou seekest, shall be taken from thee.

9:4 [1] All their doings both touching policy and religion, shall be rejected as things polluted.

[2] The meat offering which they offered for themselves.

9:5 [1] When the Lord shall take away all the occasions of serving him, which shall be the most grievous point of your captivity, when ye shall see yourselves cut off from God.

9:6 [1] Though they think to escape by fleeing the destruction that is at hand, yet shall they be destroyed in the place whither they flee for succor.

9:7 [1] Then they shall know that they were deluded by them, who challenged to themselves to be their prophets and spiritual men.

9:8 [1] The Prophet's duty is to bring men to God, and not to be a snare to pull them from God.

9:9 [1] This people is so rooted in their wickedness, that Gibeah which was like to Sodom, was never more corrupt, Judg. 19:22.

9:10 [1] Meaning, that he so esteemed them and delighted in them.

themselves unto that shame, and *their* abominations were according to ²their lovers.

11 Ephraim their glory shall flee away like a bird: from the birth ¹and from the womb, and from the conception.

12 Though they bring up their children, yet I will deprive them from being men: yea, woe to them, when I depart from them.

13 Ephraim, as I saw, *is as a tree* ¹in Tyre planted in a cottage: but Ephraim shall bring forth his children to the murderer.

14 O Lord, give them: what wilt thou give them? give them a ¹barren womb and dry breasts.

15 All their wickedness *is* in ¹Gilgal: for there do I hate them: for the wickedness of their inventions, I will cast them out of mine House: I will love them no more: all their princes are rebels.

16 Ephraim is smitten, their root is dried up: they can bring no fruit: yea, though they bring forth, yet will I slay even the dearest of their body.

17 My God will cast them away, because they did not obey him: and they shall wander among the nations.

10
¹ *Against Israel and his idols.* 14 *His destruction for the same.*

1 Israel *is* a ¹empty vine, *yet* hath it brought forth fruit unto itself, *and* according to the multitude of the fruit thereof he hath increased the altars: according to the ²goodness of their land they have made fair images.

2 Their heart is ¹divided: now shall they be found faulty: he shall break down their altars; he shall destroy their images.

3 For now they shall say, We have no ¹King because we feared not the Lord: and what should a

CHAPTER 10
ᵃ Isa. 2:19
Luke 23:30
Rev. 6:16
Rev. 9:6

King do to us?

4 They have spoken words, swearing falsely in making ¹a covenant: thus ²judgment groweth as wormwood in the furrows of the field.

5 The inhabitants of Samaria shall ¹fear because of the calf of Beth Aven: for the people thereof shall mourn over it, and the ²Chemarims thereof, that rejoiced on it for the glory thereof, because it is departed from it.

6 It shall be also brought to Assyria, for a present unto king Jareb: Ephraim shall receive shame, and Israel shall be ashamed of his own counsel.

7 Of Samaria, the king thereof is destroyed, as the foam upon the water.

8 The high places also of ¹Aven shall be destroyed, *even* the sin of Israel: the thorn and the thistle shall grow upon their altars, and they shall say to the mountains, ᵃCover us, and to the hills, Fall upon us.

9 O Israel, thou hast ¹sinned from the days of Gibeah: there they ²stood: the battle in Gibeah against the children of iniquity did not ³touch them.

10 It is my desire ¹that I should chastise them, and the people shall be gathered against them, when they shall gather themselves in their two ²furrows.

11 And Ephraim *is as* a heifer used to delight in ¹threshing: but I will pass by her ²fair neck: I will make Ephraim to ride: Judah shall plow, *and* Jacob shall break his clods.

12 Sow to yourselves in righteousness: reap after the measure of mercy: ¹break up your fallow ground: for *it is* time to seek the Lord, till he come and rain righteousness upon you.

13 *But* you have plowed wickedness: ye have reaped iniquity: you have eaten the fruit of lies: because thou didst trust in thine own ways, *and* in the multitude of thy strong men,

---

9:10 ² They were as abominable unto me, as their lovers the idols.
9:11 ¹ Signifying, that God would destroy their children by these sundry means, and so consume them by little and little.
9:13 ¹ As they kept tender plants in their houses in Tyre to preserve them from the cold air of the sea, so was Ephraim at the first unto me, but now I will give him to the slaughter.
9:14 ¹ The Prophet seeing the great plagues of God toward Ephraim, prayeth to God to make them barren, rather than that this great slaughter should come upon their children.
9:15 ¹ The chief cause of their destruction is that they commit idolatry, and corrupt my Religion in Gilgal.
10:1 ¹ Whereof though the grapes were gathered, yet ever as it gathered new strength, it increased new wickedness, so that the correction which should have brought them to obedience, did but utter their stubbornness.
² As they were rich and had abundance.
10:2 ¹ To wit, from God.
10:3 ¹ The day shall come that God shall take away their king, and then they shall feel the fruit of their sins, and how they trusted in him in vain, 2 Kings 17:6, 7.

10:4 ¹ In promising to be faithful toward God.
² Thus their integrity and fidelity, which they pretended, was nothing but bitterness and grief.
10:5 ¹ When the calf shall be carried away.
² Chemarims were certain idolatrous priests, which did wear black apparel in their sacrifices, and cried with a loud voice: which superstition Elijah derided, 1 Kings 18:27, read 2 Kings 23:5.
10:8 ¹ This he speaketh in contempt of Bethel, read Hos. 4:15.
10:9 ¹ In those days wast thou as wicked as the Gibeonites, as God there partly declared: for thy zeal could not be good in executing God's judgments, seeing thine own deeds were as wicked as theirs.
² To wit, to fight, or the Israelites remained in that stubbornness from that time.
³ The Israelites were not moved by their example to cease from their sins.
10:10 ¹ Because they are so desperate, I will delight to destroy them.
² That is, when they have gathered all their strength together.
10:11 ¹ Wherein is pleasure, as in plowing is labor and pain.
² I will lay my yoke upon her fat neck.
10:12 ¹ Read Jer. 4:4.

14 Therefore shall a tumult arise among thy people, and all thy munitions shall be destroyed, as [1]Shalman destroyed Beth Arbel in the day of battle: the mother with the children was dashed in pieces.

15 So shall Bethel do unto you, because of your malicious wickedness: in a morning shall the king of Israel be destroyed.

11
1 The benefits of the Lord toward Israel.   5 Their ingratitude against him.

1 When Israel [1]*was* a child, then I loved him, and called my son out of Egypt.

2 They called them, *but* they [1]went thus from them: they sacrificed unto Baal, and burnt incense to images.

3 I led Ephraim also, *as one* should bear them in his arms: but they knew not that I healed them.

4 I led them with cords [1]of a man, *even* with bands of love, and I was to them, as he was taketh off the yoke from their jaws, and I laid the meat unto them.

5 He shall no more return into the land of Egypt: but Assyria shall be his [1]King, because they refused to convert.

6 And the sword shall fall on his cities, and shall consume his bars, and devour them, because of their own counsels.

7 And my people are bent to rebellion against me: though [1]they called them to the most high, *yet* none at all would exalt *him.*

8 [1]How shall I give thee up, Ephraim? *how* shall I deliver thee, Israel? how shall I make thee, as [2]Admah? *how* shall I set thee, as Zeboim? mine heart is turned within me: [3]my repentings are rouled together.

9 I will not execute the fierceness of my wrath: I will not return to destroy Ephraim: for I am God, and not man, the holy one in the midst of thee, and

I will not [1]enter into the city.

10 They shall walk after the Lord: he shall roar like a lion: when he shall roar, then the children of the West shall fear.

11 [1]They shall fear as a sparrow out of Egypt, and as a dove out of the land of Assyria, and I will place them in their houses, saith the Lord.

12 Ephraim compasseth me about with lies, and the house of Israel with deceit: but Judah yet ruleth with [1]God, and is faithful with the Saints.

12
He admonisheth by Jacob's example to trust in God, and not in riches.

1 Ephraim is fed [1]with the wind, and followeth after the East wind: he increaseth daily lies and destruction, and they do make a covenant with Assyria, and [2]oil is carried into Egypt.

2 The Lord hath also a controversy with [1]Judah, and will visit Jacob, according to his ways: according to his works, will he recompense him.

3 He took his brother by the heel in the womb, and by his strength he had [1]power with God,

4 And had [1]power over the Angel, and prevailed: he wept and prayed unto him: [2]he found him in Bethel, and there he spake with us.

5 Yea, the Lord God of hosts, the Lord *is* himself his memorial.

6 Therefore turn thou to thy God: keep mercy and judgment, and hope still in thy God.

7 *He is* [1]Canaan: the balances of decree *are* in his hand: he loveth to oppress.

8 And Ephraim said, Notwithstanding I am rich, I have found me out riches in all my labors: they shall find none iniquity in me, [1]that were wickedness.

9 Though I am the Lord thy God, from the land of Egypt, yet will I make thee to dwell in the

---

10:14 [1] That is, Shalmaneser in the destruction of that city spared neither kind nor age.

11:1 [1] While the Israelites were in Egypt, and did not provoke my wrath by their malice and ingratitude.

11:2 [1] They rebelled and went a contrary way when the Prophets called them to repentance.

11:4 [1] That is, friendly: and not as beasts or slaves.

11:5 [1] Seeing they contemn all this kindness, they shall be led captive into Assyria.

11:7 [1] To wit, the Prophets.

11:8 [1] God considereth with himself, and that with a certain grief, how to punish them.

[2] Which were two of the cities that were destroyed with Sodom, Deut. 29:23.

[3] Meaning, that his love wherewith he first loved them, made him between doubt and assurance what to do: and herein appeareth his Fatherly affection: that his mercy toward his shall overcome his judgments, as he declareth in the next verse.

11:9 [1] To consume thee, but will cause thee to yield, and so receive

thee to mercy: and this is meant of the final number who shall walk after the Lord.

11:11 [1] The Egyptians, and the Assyrians shall be afraid when the Lord maintaineth his people.

11:12 [1] Governeth their state according to God's word, and doth not degenerate.

12:1 [1] That is, flattereth himself with vain confidence.

[2] Meaning, presents to get friendship.

12:2 [1] Which in those points was like to Ephraim, but not in idolatries.

12:3 [1] Seeing that God did thus prefer Jacob their father, Judah's ingratitude was the more to be abhorred.

12:4 [1] Read Gen. 32:24-32.

[2] God found Jacob as he lay sleeping in Bethel, Gen. 28:12, and so spake with him there, that the fruit of that speech appertained to the whole body of the people, whereof we are.

12:7 [1] As for Ephraim he is more like the wicked Canaanites, than godly Abraham or Jacob.

12:8 [1] Thus the wicked measure God's favor by outward prosperity and like hypocrites cannot abide that any should reprove their doings.

tabernacles, as in [1]the days of the solemn feast.

10 I have also spoken by the Prophets, and I have multiplied visions, and used similitudes by the ministry of the Prophets.

11 Is there [1]iniquity in Gilead? surely they are vanity: they sacrifice bullocks in Gilgal, and their altars *are* as heaps in the furrows of the field.

12 [1]And Jacob fled into the country of Aram, and Israel served for a wife, and for a wife he kept *sheep,*

13 And by a [1]Prophet the Lord brought Israel out of Egypt, and by a Prophet was he reserved.

14 *But* Ephraim provoked him with high places: therefore shall his blood be poured upon him, and his reproach shall his Lord reward him.

13

1 *The abomination of Israel,* 9 *and cause of their destruction.*

1 When Ephraim spake, there *was* [1]trembling: he [2]exalted himself in Israel, but he hath sinned in Baal, [3]and is dead.

2 And now they sin more and more, and have made them molten images of their silver, *and* idols according to their own understanding: they were all the work of the craftsmen: they say one to another while they sacrifice a [1]man, Let them kiss the calves.

3 Therefore they shall be as the morning cloud, and as the morning dew that passeth away, as the chaff that is driven with a whirlwind out of the floor, and as the smoke that goeth out of the chimney.

4 Yet I am the Lord thy God [1]from the land of Egypt, and thou shalt know no God but me: for there is no Savior beside me.

5 I did know thee in the wilderness, in the land of drought.

6 As in their pastures, so were they filled: they were filled, and their heart was exalted: therefore have they forgotten me.

7 And I will be unto them as a very lion, *and* as a leopard in the way of Assyria.

8 I will meet them, as a bear that is robbed of her whelps, and I will break the caul of their heart, and there will I devour them like a lion: the wild beasts shall tear them.

9 O Israel, one [1]hath destroyed thee, but in me *is* thine help.

10 [1]I am: where is thy king that should help thee in all thy cities? and thy judges, of whom thou saidest, Give me a king and princes?

11 I gave thee a king in mine anger, and I took him away in my wrath.

12 The iniquity of Ephraim is [1]bound up: his sin *is* hid.

13 The sorrows of a travailing woman shall come upon him: he is an unwise son, else would he not stand still at the time, *even* at the [1]breaking forth of the children.

14 I will redeem them from the power of the grave: I will deliver them from death: O [1]death, I will be thy death: O grave, I will be thy destruction: [2]repentance is hid from mine eyes.

15 Though he grew up among *his* brethren, an East wind shall come, *even* the wind of the Lord shall come up from the wilderness, and dry up his vein, and his fountain shall be dried up: he shall spoil the treasure of all pleasant vessels.

14

1 *The destruction of Samaria.* 2 *He exhorteth Israel to turn to God, who requireth praise and thanks.*

1 Samaria shall be desolate: for she hath rebelled against her God: they shall fall by the sword: their infants shall be dashed in pieces, and their women with child shall be ripped.

2 O Israel, [1]return unto the Lord thy God: for thou hast fallen by thine iniquity.

3 Take unto you words, and turn to the Lord, and say unto him, [1]Take away all iniquity, and

---

12:9 [1] Seeing thou wilt not acknowledge my benefits, I will bring thee again to dwell in tents, as in the feast of the Tabernacles, which thou dost now contemn.

12:11 [1] The people thought that no man durst have spoken against Gilead, that holy place, and yet the Prophet saith, that all their religion was but vanity.

12:12 [1] If you boast of your riches and nobility, ye seem to reproach your father, who was a poor fugitive and servant.

12:13 [1] Meaning, Moses, whereby appeareth, that whatsoever they have, it cometh of God's free goodness.

13:1 [1] He showeth the excellency and authority that this tribe had above all the rest.

[2] He made a king of his tribe.

[3] The Ephraimites are not far from destruction, and have lost their authority.

13:2 [1] The false prophets persuaded the idolaters to offer their children after the example of Abraham, and he showeth how they

would exhort one another to the same, and to kiss and worship these calves which were their idols.

13:4 [1] He calleth them to repentance, and reproveth their ingratitude.

13:9 [1] Thy destruction is certain, and my benefits toward thee declare that it cometh not of me: therefore thine own malice, idolatry and vain confidence in men must needs be the cause thereof.

13:10 [1] I am all one, James 1:17.

13:12 [1] It is surely laid up to be punished, as Jer. 17:1.

13:13 [1] But would come out of the womb, that is out of this dangers wherein he is and not to tarry to be stifled.

13:14 [1] Meaning, that no power shall resist God when he will deliver his, but even in death will he give them life.

[2] Because they will not turn to me, I will change my purpose.

14:2 [1] He exhorteth them to repentance to avoid all these plagues, willing them to declare by words their obedience and repentance.

14:3 [1] He showeth them how they ought to confess their sins.

receive *us* graciously: so will we render the calves of our ²lips.

4   Assyria shall ¹not save us, neither will we ride upon horses, neither will we say anymore to the work of our hands, *Ye are* our gods: for in thee the fatherless findeth mercy.

5   ¹I will heal their rebellion: I will love them freely: for mine anger is turned away from him.

6   I will be as the dew unto Israel: he shall grow as the lily and fasten his roots, as *the trees* of Lebanon.

7   His branches shall spread, and his beauty shall be as the olive tree, and his smell as Lebanon.

8   They that dwell under his ¹shadow, shall return: they shall revive *as* the corn, and flourish as the vine: the scent thereof *shall be* as the wine of Lebanon.

9   Ephraim *shall say*, What have I to do anymore with idols? I ¹have heard him, and looked upon him: I am like a green fir tree: upon me is thy fruit found.

10   Who is ¹wise, and he shall understand these things? and prudent, and he shall know them? for the ways of the Lord *are* righteous and the just shall walk in them: but the wicked shall fall therein.

---

² Declaring that this is the true sacrifice, that the faithful can offer, even thanks and praise, Heb. 13:15.
14:4 ¹ We will leave off all vain confidence and pride.
14:5 ¹ He declareth how ready God is to receive them that do repent.
14:8 ¹ Whosoever join themselves to this people, shall be blessed.

14:9 ¹ God showeth how prompt he is to hear his, when they repent, and to offer himself, as a protection and safeguard unto them, as a most sufficient fruit and profit.
14:10 ¹ Signifying, that the true wisdom and knowledge consisteth in this even to rest upon God.

JOEL

1

1 A prophecy against the Jews.   2 He exhorteth the people to prayer and fasting for the misery that was at hand.

1 The word of the Lord that came to Joel the son of Pethuel.

2 Hear ye this, O ¹Elders, and hearken ye all inhabitants of the land, whether ²such a thing hath been in your days, or yet in the days of your fathers.

3 Tell you your children of it, and let your children *show* to their children, and their children, to another generation.

4 That which is left of the palmerworm, hath the grasshopper eaten, and the residue of the grasshopper hath the cankerworm eaten, and the residue of the cankerworm hath the caterpillar eaten.

5 Awake ye ¹drunkards, and weep and howl all ye drinkers of wine, because of the new wine, for it shall be pulled from your mouth.

6 Yea, ¹a nation cometh upon my land, mighty and without number, whose teeth *are like* the teeth of a lion, and he hath the jaws of a great lion.

7 He maketh my vine waste, and pilleth off the bark of my fig tree: he maketh it bare, and casteth it down: the branches thereof are made white.

8 Mourn like a virgin girded with sackcloth, for the ¹husband of her youth.

9 The meat offering and the drink offering is ¹cut off from the house of the Lord: the Priests the Lord's ministers mourn.

10 The field is wasted: the land mourneth: for the corn is destroyed: ¹the new wine is dried up, and the oil is decayed.

11 Be ye ashamed, O husbandmen; howl, O ye vinedressers for the wheat and for the barley, because the harvest of the field is perished.

12 The vine is dried up, and the fig tree is decayed: the pomegranate tree and the palm tree, and the apple tree, *even* all the trees of the field are withered: surely the joy is withered away from the sons of men.

13 ¹Gird yourselves and lament ye Priests: howl ye ministers of the altar: come, *and* lie all night in sackcloth, ye ministers of my God: for the meat offering, and the drink offering is taken away from the house of your God.

14 Sanctify you a fast: call a solemn assembly: gather the Elders, *and* all the inhabitants of the land into the house of the Lord your God, and cry unto the Lord,

15 Alas: for the day, for the ¹day of the Lord is at hand, and it cometh as a destruction from the Almighty.

16 Is not the meat cut off before our eyes? *and* joy, and gladness from the house of our God?

17 The seed is rotten under their clods: the garners are destroyed: the barns are broken down, for the corn is withered.

18 How did the beasts mourn! the herds of cattle pine away, because they have no pasture, and the flocks of sheep are destroyed.

19 O Lord, to thee will I cry: for the fire hath devoured the pastures of the wilderness, and the flame hath burnt up all the trees of the field.

20 The beasts of the field cry also unto thee: for the river of waters are dried up, and the ¹fire hath devoured the pastures of the wilderness.

2

He prophesieth of the coming and cruelty of their enemies.   13 An exhortation to move them to convert.   18 The love of God toward his people.

1 Blow ¹the trumpet in Zion, and shout in mine holy mountain, let all the inhabitants of the land tremble: for the day of the Lord is come: for it *is* at hand.

2 A ¹day of darkness, and of blackness, a day of clouds and obscurity, as the morning spread upon the mountains, *so is* there a ²great people, and a mighty: there was none like it from the beginning, neither shall be anymore after it, unto the years of many generations.

1:2 ¹ Signifying the Princes, the Priests and the governors.

² He calleth the Jews to the consideration of God's judgments, who had now plagued the fruits of the ground for the space of four years, which was for their sins, and to call them to repentance.

1:5 ¹ Meaning, that the occasion of their excess and drunkenness was taken away.

1:6 ¹ This was another plague wherewith God had punished them when he stirred up the Assyrians against them.

1:8 ¹ Mourn grievously, as a woman which hath lost her husband to whom she hath been married in her youth.

1:9 ¹ The tokens of God's wrath did appear in his Temple, insomuch

as God's service was left off.

1:10 ¹ All comfort and substance for nourishment is taken away.

1:13 ¹ He showeth that the only means to avoid God's wrath, and to have all things restored, is unfeigned repentance.

1:15 ¹ We see by these great plagues that utter destruction is at hand.

1:20 ¹ That is, drought.

2:1 ¹ He showeth the great judgments of God, which are at hand, except they repent.

2:2 ¹ Of affliction and trouble.

² Meaning, the Assyrians.

3 A fire devoureth before him, and behind him a flame burneth up: the land *is* as the garden of ¹Eden before him, and behind him a desolate wilderness, so that nothing shall escape him.

4 The beholding of him *is* like the sight of horses, and like the horsemen, so shall they run.

5 Like the noise of chariots in the tops of the mountains shall they leap, like the noise of a flame of fire that devoureth the stubble, *and* as a mighty people prepared to the battle.

6 Before his face shall the people tremble: all faces ¹shall gather blackness.

7 They shall run like strong men, and go up to the wall like men of war, and every man shall go forward in his ways, and they shall not stay in their paths.

8 Neither shall one ¹thrust another, *but* everyone shall walk in his path: and when they fall upon the sword, they shall not be wounded.

9 They shall run to and fro in the city: they shall run upon the wall: they shall clime up upon the houses, *and* enter in at the windows like the thief.

10 The earth shall tremble before him, the heavens shall shake, the ¹sun and the moon shall be dark, and the stars shall withdraw their shining.

11 And the Lord shall ¹utter his voice before his host: for his host is very great: for *he is* strong that doeth his word: ªfor the day of the Lord is great and very terrible, and who can abide it?

12 Therefore also now the Lord saith, Turn you unto me with all your heart, and with fasting, and with weeping, and with mourning,

13 And ¹rent your heart, and not your clothes: and turn unto the Lord your God, for he is gracious and merciful, slow to anger, and of great kindness, and repenteth him of the evil.

14 Who knoweth, *if* he will ¹return and repent and leave a blessing behind him, *even* a meat offering and a drink offering unto the Lord your God?

15 Blow the trumpet in Zion, sanctify a fast, call a solemn assembly.

16 Gather the people, sanctify the congregation: gather the elders: assemble the ¹children, and those

CHAPTER 2
ª Jer. 30:7
Amos 5:18
Zeph. 1:15
ᵇ Ps. 79:10
ᶜ Lev. 26:4
Deut. 11:14

that suck the breasts: let the bridegroom go forth of his chamber, and the bride out of her bride chamber.

17 Let the Priests, the ministers of the Lord, weep between the porch and the altar, and let them say, Spare thy people, O Lord, and give not thine heritage into reproach, that the heathen should rule over them. ᵇWherefore should they say among the people, Where is their God?

18 Then will the Lord be ¹jealous over his land, and spare his people.

19 Yea, the Lord will answer and say unto his people, Behold, I will send you corn and wine, and oil, and you shall be satisfied therewith: and I will no more make you a reproach among the heathen.

20 But I will remove far off from you the ¹Northern *army*, and I will drive him into a land, barren and desolate with his face toward the ²East sea, and his end to the utmost sea, and his stink shall come up, and his corruption shall ascend, because he hath exalted himself to do *this*.

21 Fear not, O land, *but* be glad, and rejoice: for the Lord will do great things.

22 Be not afraid, ye beasts of the field: for the pastures of the wilderness are green for the tree beareth her fruit: the fig tree and the vine do give their force.

23 Be glad then, ye children of Zion, and rejoice in the Lord your God, for he hath given you the rain of ¹righteousness, ᶜand he will cause to come down for you the rain, *even* the *first* rain, and the latter rain in the first *month*.

24 And the barns shall be full of wheat, and the presses shall abound with wine and oil.

25 And I will render you the years that the grasshopper hath eaten, the cankerworm and the caterpillar and the palmerworm, my great host which I sent among you.

26 So you shall eat and be satisfied and praise the name of the Lord your God, that hath dealt marvelously with you: and my people shall never be ashamed.

27 Ye shall also know that I am in the midst of Israel, and that I am the Lord your God and none

---

2:3 ¹ The enemy destroyed our plentiful country, wheresoever he cometh.

2:6 ¹ They shall be pale and black for fear, as Nah. 2:10.

2:8 ¹ For none shall be able to resist them.

2:10 ¹ Read Joel 2:31 and Isa. 13:10; Ezek. 32:7; Joel 3:15; Matt. 24:29.

2:11 ¹ The Lord shall stir up the Assyrians to execute his judgments.

2:13 ¹ Mortify your affections and serve God with pureness of heart, and not with ceremonies.

2:14 ¹ He speaketh this to stir up their slothfulness, and not that he doubted of God's mercies, if they did repent. How God repenteth, read Jer. 18:8.

2:16 ¹ That as all have sinned, so all may show forth signs of their repentance, that men seeing the children which are not free from God's wrath, might be the more lively touched with the consideration of their own sins.

2:18 ¹ If they repent he showeth that God will preserve and defend them with a most ardent affection.

2:20 ¹ That is, the Assyrians your enemies.

² Called the salt sea, or Persian sea: meaning, that though his army were so great that it filled all from this sea to the sea called Mediterranean, yet he would scatter them.

2:23 ¹ That is, such as should come by just measure, and as was wont to be sent when God was reconciled with them.

other, and my people shall never be ashamed.

28 And afterward will I pour ¹out my Spirit upon all flesh: and your sons and your daughters shall prophesy: your old men shall dream ²dreams, *and* your young men shall see visions.

29 And also upon the servants, and upon the maids in those days will I pour my Spirit.

30 And I will show ¹wonders in the heavens and in the earth: blood and fire, and pillars of smoke.

31 The ¹sun shall be turned into darkness, and the moon into blood, before the great and terrible day of the Lord come.

32 But whosoever shall call ¹on the Name of the Lord, shall be saved: for in mount Zion, and in Jerusalem shall be deliverance as the Lord hath said, and in the ²remnant, whom the Lord shall call.

3

Of the judgment of God against the enemies of his people.

1 For behold, in ¹those days and in that time, when I shall bring again the captivity of Judah and Jerusalem,

2 I will also gather all nations, and will bring them down into the ¹valley of Jehoshaphat, and will plead with them there for my people, and for mine heritage Israel: whom they have scattered among the nations, and parted my land.

3 And they have cast lots for my people, and have given the child ¹for the harlot, and sold the girl for wine, that they might drink.

4 Yea, and ¹what have you to do with me, O Tyre and Sidon, and all the coasts of Philistia? will ye render me ²a recompense? and if ye recompense me, swiftly *and* speedily will I render your recompense upon your head:

5 For ye have taken my silver and my gold, and have carried into your temples my goodly *and* pleas-

ant things.

6 The children also of Judah and the children of Jerusalem have you sold unto the Grecians, that ye might send them far from their border.

7 Behold, I will raise them out of the place where ye have sold them, and will render your reward upon your own head.

8 And I will sell your sons and your daughters into the hand of the children of Judah, and they ¹shall send them to the Sabeans, to a people far off, for the Lord hath spoken it.

9 Publish this among the Gentiles: prepare war, wake up the mighty men: let all the men of war draw near *and* come up.

10 ¹Break your plowshares into swords, and your scythes into spears: let the weak say, I am strong.

11 Assemble yourselves, and come all ye heathen, and gather yourselves together round about: there shall the Lord cast down the mighty men.

12 Let the heathen be wakened, and come up to the valley of Jehoshaphat: for there will I sit to judge all the heathen round about.

13 Put in your ¹scythes, for the harvest is ripe, come, get you down, for the winepress is full: yea, the winepresses run over, for their wickedness is great.

14 O multitude, O multitude, *come* into the valley of threshing: for the day of the Lord *is* near in the valley of threshing.

15 The sun and moon shall be darkened, and the stars shall withdraw their light.

16 The Lord also shall roar out of Zion, and utter his voice from Jerusalem, and the heavens and the earth shall shake, but the Lord will be the ¹hope of his people, and the strength of the children of Israel.

17 So shall ye know that I am the Lord your God

2:28 ¹ That is, in greater abundance, and more generally than in times past: and this was fulfilled under Christ, when as God's graces, and his Spirit under the Gospel was abundantly given to the Church, Isa. 44:3; Acts 2:17; John 7:38, 39.

  ² As they had visions and dreams in old time, so shall they now have clearer revelations.

2:30 ¹ He warneth the faithful what terrible things should come, to the intent that they should not look for continual quietness in this world, and yet in all these troubles he would preserve them.

2:31 ¹ The order of nature shall seem to be changed for the horrible afflictions that shall be in the world, Isa. 13:10; Ezek. 32:7; Joel 3:15; Matt. 24:29.

2:32 ¹ God's judgments are for the destruction of the infidels, and to move the godly to call upon the Name of God, who will give them salvation.

  ² Meaning hereby the Gentiles, Rom. 10:13.

3:1 ¹ When I shall deliver my Church, which standeth of the Jews and of the Gentiles.

3:2 ¹ It appeareth that he alludeth to that great victory of

Jehoshaphat, when as God without man's help destroyed the enemies, 2 Chron. 20:26, also he hath respect to this word Jehoshaphat which signifieth pleading or judgment, because God would judge the enemies of his Church, as he did there.

3:3 ¹ That which the enemy gat for the sale of my people, he bestowed upon harlots and drink.

3:4 ¹ He taketh the cause of his Church in hand against the enemy, as though the injury were done to himself.

  ² Have I done you wrong, that ye will render me the like?

3:8 ¹ For afterward God sold them by Nebuchadnezzar and Alexander the great, for the love he bare to his people, and thereby they were comforted, as though the price had been theirs.

3:10 ¹ When I shall execute my judgments against mine enemies, I will cause everyone to be ready, and to prepare their weapons to destroy one another for my Church's sake.

3:13 ¹ Thus he shall encourage the enemies when their wickedness is full ripe, to destroy one another, which he calleth the valley of God's judgment.

3:16 ¹ God assureth his against all trouble, that when he destroyeth his enemies, his children shall be delivered.

dwelling in Zion, mine holy Mountain: then shall Jerusalem be holy, and there shall no strangers go [1]through her anymore.

18 And in that day shall the mountains [1]drop down new wine, and the hills shall flow with milk, and all the rivers of Judah shall run with waters, and a fountain shall come forth of the House of the Lord, and shall water the valley of Shittim.

19 [1]Egypt shall be waste, and Edom shall be a desolate wilderness, for the injuries of the children of Judah, because they have shed innocent blood in their land.

20 But Judah shall dwell forever, and Jerusalem from generation to generation.

21 For I will [1]cleanse their blood, that I have not cleansed, and the Lord will dwell in Zion.

3:17 [1] The strangers shall no more destroy his Church: which if they do, it is the people, which by their sins make the breach for the enemy.
3:18 [1] He promiseth to his Church abundance of graces, read Ezek. 47:1, which should water and comfort the most barren places, Amos 9:13.
3:19 [1] The malicious enemies shall have no part of his graces.
3:21 [1] He had suffered his Church hitherto to lie in their filthiness, but now he promiseth to cleanse them and to make them pure unto him.

AMOS

1 *1 The time of the prophecy of Amos. 3 The word of the Lord against Damascus, 6 The Philistines, Tyre, Idumea, and Ammon.*

1 The words of Amos, who was among the herdsmen at ¹Tekoa, which he saw upon Israel, in the days of Uzziah king of Judah, and in the days of ²Jeroboam the son of Joash king of Israel, two years before the ³earthquake.

2 And he said, The Lord shall roar from Zion, and utter his voice from Jerusalem, and the dwelling places of the shepherds shall perish, and the top ¹of Carmel shall wither.

3 ¶ Thus saith the Lord, For ¹three transgressions of Damascus, and for four, I will not turn to it, because they have ²threshed Gilead with threshing instruments of iron.

4 Therefore will I send a fire into the house of Hazael, and it shall devour the ¹palaces of Ben-Hadad.

5 I will break also the bars of Damascus, and cut off the inhabitant of Bikeath-Aven: and him that holdeth the scepter out of Beth Eden, and the people of Aram shall go into captivity unto ¹Kir, saith the Lord.

6 Thus saith the Lord, For three transgressions of Gaza, and for four, I will not turn to it, because they ¹carried away prisoners the whole captivity to shut them up in Edom.

7 Therefore will I send a fire upon the walls of Gaza, and it shall devour the palaces thereof.

8 And I will cut off the inhabitant from Ashdod, and him that holdeth the scepter from Ashkelon, and turn mine hand to Ekron, and the remnant of the Philistines shall perish, saith the Lord God.

9 ¶ Thus saith the Lord, For three transgressions of Tyre, and for four, I will not turn to it, because they shut the whole captivity in Edom, and have not remembered the ¹brotherly covenant.

10 Therefore will I send a fire upon the walls of Tyre, and it shall devour the palaces thereof.

11 ¶ Thus saith the Lord, For three transgressions of Edom, and for four, I will not turn to it, because he did pursue his brother with the sword, and ¹did cast off all pity, and his anger spoiled him evermore, and his wrath watched him ²[always].

12 Therefore will I send a fire upon Teman, and it shall devour the places of Bozrah.

13 ¶ Thus saith the Lord, For three transgressions of the children of Ammon, and for four, I will not turn to it, because they ¹have ripped up the women with child of Gilead, that they might enlarge their border.

14 Therefore will I kindle a fire in the wall of Rabbah, and it shall devour the palaces thereof, with shouting in the day of battle, *and* with a tempest in the day of the whirlwind.

15 And their king shall go into captivity, he and his princes together, saith the Lord.

2 *Against Moab, Judah, and Israel.*

1 Thus saith the Lord, For three transgressions of Moab, and for four, I will not turn to it, because it burnt the ¹bones of the king of Edom into lime.

2 Therefore will I send a fire upon Moab, and it shall devour the palaces of Kerioth, and Moab shall die with tumult, with shouting, *and* with the sound of a trumpet.

3 And I will cut off the judge out of the midst thereof, and will slay all the princes thereof with

---

1:1 ¹ Which was a town five miles from Jerusalem in Judea, but he prophesied in Israel.

² In his days the kingdom of Israel did most flourish.

³ Which as Josephus writeth, was when Uzziah would have usurped the Priest's office, and therefore was smitten with the leprosy.

1:2 ¹ Whatsoever is fruitful and pleasant in Israel, shall shortly perish.

1:3 ¹ He showeth first that all the people round about should be destroyed for their manifold sins: which are meant by three and four, which make seven, because the Israelites should the more deeply consider God's judgments toward them.

² If the Syrians shall not be spared for committing this cruelty against one city, it is not possible that Israel should escape punishment which hath committed so many and grievous sins against God and man.

1:4 ¹ The antiquity of their buildings shall not avoid my judgments, read Jer. 49:27.

1:5 ¹ Tiglath-Pileser led the Assyrians captive, and brought them to Cyrene, which he calleth here Kir.

1:6 ¹ They joined themselves with the Edomites their enemies, which carried them away captives.

1:9 ¹ For Esau (of whom came the Edomites) and Jacob were brethren, therefore they ought to have admonished them of their brotherly friendship, and not to have provoked them to hatred.

1:11 ¹ Hebrew, *corrupt his compassions.*

² He was a continual enemy unto him.

1:13 ¹ He noteth the great cruelty of the Ammonites, that spared not the women, but most tyrannously tormented them, and yet the Ammonites came of Lot, who was of the household of Abraham.

2:1 ¹ For the Moabites were so cruel against the king of Edom, that they burnt his bones after that he was dead: which declared their barbarous rage, seeing they would revenge themselves of the dead.

him, saith the Lord.

4 ¶ Thus saith the Lord, For three transgressions of Judah, and for four, ¹I will not turn to it, because they have cast away the Law of the Lord, and have not kept his commandments, and their lies caused them to err after the which their fathers have walked.

5 Therefore will I send a fire upon Judah, and it shall devour the palaces of Jerusalem.

6 ¶ Thus saith the Lord, For three transgressions of ¹Israel, and for four, I will not turn to it, because they sold the righteous for silver, and the poor for ²shoes.

7 They gape over the head of the poor, in the ¹dust of the earth, and pervert the ways of the meek: and a man and his father will go in to a maid, to dishonor mine holy Name.

8 And they lie down upon clothes laid to pledge ¹by every altar: and they ²drink the wine of the condemned in the house of their God.

9 Yet destroyed I the ¹Amorite before them, whose height was like the height of the cedars, and he was strong as the oaks: notwithstanding I destroyed his fruit from above, and his root from beneath.

10 Also I brought you up from the land of Egypt, and led you forty years through the wilderness, to possess the land of the Amorite.

11 And I raised up of your sons for Prophets, and of ¹your young men for Nazirites. Is it not even thus, O ye children of Israel, saith the Lord?

12 But ye gave the Nazirites wine to drink, and commanded the Prophets, saying, Prophesy not.

13 Behold, I am ¹pressed under you as a cart is pressed that is full of sheaves.

14 Therefore the flight shall perish from the ¹swift, and the strong shall not strengthen his force, neither shall the mighty save his life.

15 Nor he that handleth the bow shall stand, and he that is swift of foot, shall not escape, neither shall he that rideth the horse, save his life.

16 And he that is of a mighty courage among the strong men, shall flee away naked in that day, saith the Lord.

3

He reproveth the house of Israel of ingratitude. 11 For the which God will punish them.

1 Hear this word that the Lord pronounceth against you, O children of Israel, *even* against the whole family which I brought up from the land of Egypt, saying,

2 You ¹only have I known of all the families of the earth: therefore I will visit you for all your iniquities.

3 Can two walk together except they be ¹agreed?

4 Will a ¹lion roar in the forest, when he hath no prey? or will a lion's whelp cry out of his den, if he hath taken nothing?

5 ¹Can a bird fall in a snare upon the earth, where no fowler is? or will he take up the ²snare from the earth, and have taken nothing at all?

6 Or ¹shall a trumpet be blown in the city, and the people be not afraid? or shall there ²be evil in a city, and the Lord hath not done it?

7 Surely the Lord God will do nothing, but he ¹revealeth his secret unto his servants the Prophets.

8 The lion hath roared: who will not be afraid? the Lord God hath spoken, who can but ¹prophesy?

9 Proclaim in the palaces at ¹Ashdod, and in the palaces in the land of Egypt, and say, Assemble yourselves upon the mountains of Samaria: so behold the great tumults in the midst thereof, and the oppressed in the midst thereof.

10 For they know not to do right, saith the Lord: they store up violence, and robbery ¹in their palaces.

11 Therefore thus saith the Lord God, An adversary

2:4 ¹ Seeing the Gentiles that had not so far knowledge were thus punished, Judah which was so fully instructed of the Lord's will, might not think to escape.

2:6 ¹ If he spare not Judah unto whom his promises were made, much more he will not spare this degenerate kingdom.

² They esteemed most vile bribes more than men's lives.

2:7 ¹ When they have spoiled him and thrown him unto the ground, they gape for his life.

2:8 ¹ Thinking by these ceremonies, that is, by sacrificing, and being near mine altar, they may excuse all their other wickedness.

² They spoil others and offer thereof unto God, thinking that he will dispense with them, when he is made partaker of their iniquity.

2:9 ¹ The destruction of their enemies and his mercy toward them, should have caused their hearts to melt for love toward him.

2:11 ¹ Ye contemned my benefits, and abused my graces, and craftily went about to stop the mouths of my Prophets.

2:13 ¹ You have wearied me with your sins, Isa. 1:14.

2:14 ¹ None shall be delivered by any means.

3:2 ¹ I have only chosen you to be mine among all other people, and yet you have forsaken me.

3:3 ¹ Hereby the Prophet signifieth that he speaketh not of himself, but as God guideth and moveth him, which is called the agreement between God and his Prophets.

3:4 ¹ Will God threaten by his Prophet, except there be some great occasion?

3:5 ¹ Can anything come without God's providence?

² Shall his threatenings be in vain?

3:6 ¹ Shall the Prophets threaten God's judgments and the people not be afraid?

² Doth any adversity come without God's appointment? Isa. 45:7.

3:7 ¹ God dealeth not with the Israelites, as he doeth with other people: for he ever warneth them before of his plagues by his Prophets.

3:8 ¹ Because the people ever murmured against the Prophets, he showeth that God's Spirit moved them so to speak as they did.

3:9 ¹ He calleth the strangers, as the Philistines and Egyptians, to be witness of God's judgments against the Israelites for their cruelty and oppression.

3:10 ¹ The fruit of their cruelty and theft appeareth by their great riches, which they have in their houses.

shall come even round about the country, and shall bring down thy strength from thee, and thy palaces shall be spoiled.

12 Thus saith the Lord, As the shepherd taketh [1]out of the mouth of the lion two legs, or a piece of an ear: so shall the children of Israel be taken out that dwell in Samaria in the corner of a bed: and in [2]Damascus, *as in* a couch.

13 Hear, and testify in the house of Jacob, saith the Lord God, the God of hosts.

14 Surely in the day that I shall visit the transgressions of Israel upon him, I will also visit the altars of Bethel, and the horns of the altar shall be broken off, and fall to the ground.

15 And I will smite the winter house with the summer house, and the houses of ivory shall perish, and the great houses shall be consumed, saith the Lord.

4

Against the governors of Samaria.

1 Hear this word, ye [1]kine of Bashan that are in the mountain of Samaria, which oppress the poor, *and* destroy the needy, and they say to their masters, [2]Bring, and let us drink.

2 The Lord God hath sworn by his holiness, that lo, the days shall come upon you, that he will take you away with [1]thorns, and your posterity with fish-hooks.

3 And ye shall go out at the breaches every *cow* forward: and ye shall cast yourselves out of the palace, saith the Lord.

4 Come to [1]Bethel, and transgress: to Gilgal, and multiply transgression, and bring your sacrifices in the morning, *and* your riches after three [2]years.

5 And offer a thanksgiving [1]of leaven, publish *and* proclaim the free offerings: for this [2]liketh you, O ye children of Israel, saith the Lord God.

6 And therefore have I given you [1]cleanness of teeth in all your cities, and scarceness of bread in all your places, yet have ye not returned unto me, saith the Lord.

7 And also I have withholden the rain from you, when there *were* yet three [1]months to the harvest, and I caused it to rain upon one city, and have not caused it to rain upon another city: one piece was rained upon, and the piece whereupon it rained not, withered.

8 So two *or* three cities wandered unto one city to drink water, but they were [1]not satisfied: yet have ye not returned unto me, saith the Lord.

9 I have smitten you with blasting and mildew: your great gardens and your vineyards, and your fig trees, and your olive trees did the palmerworm devour: yet have ye not returned unto me, saith the Lord.

10 Pestilence have I sent among you after the manner of [1]Egypt: your young men have I slain with the sword, and have taken away your horses: and I have made the stink of your tents to come up even into your nostrils, yet have ye not returned unto me, saith the Lord.

11 I have overthrown you, as God overthrew Sodom and Gomorrah: and ye were as a [1]firebrand plucked out of the burning, yet have ye not returned unto me, saith the Lord.

12 Therefore thus will I do unto thee, O Israel: and because I will do thus unto thee, prepare to [1]meet thy God, O Israel.

13 For lo, he that formeth the mountains, and createth the wind, and declareth unto man what is his thought: which maketh the morning darkness, and walketh upon the high places of the earth, the Lord God of hosts *is* his Name.

5

A lamentation for the captivity of Israel.

1 Hear ye this word, which I lift up upon you, *even* a lamentation of the house of Israel.

2 The [1]virgin Israel is fallen, *and* shall no more rise: she is left upon her land, *and* there *is* none to raise her up.

3 For thus saith the Lord God, The city which went out by a thousand, shall leave [1]an hundred: and that which went forth by an hundred, shall leave ten to the house of Israel.

3:12 [1] When the lion hath satiate his hunger, the shepherd findeth a leg or a rip of an ear, to show that the sheep have been worried.

[2] Where they thought to have had a sure hold, and to have been in safety.

4:1 [1] Thus he calleth the princes and governors, which being overwhelmed with the great abundance of God's benefits, forgot God, and therefore he calleth them by the name of beasts and not of men.

[2] They encourage such as have authority over the people to powle them, so that they may have profit by it.

4:2 [1] He alludeth to fishers, which catch fish by hooks and thorns.

4:4 [1] He speaketh this in contempt of them which resorted to those places, thinking that their great devotion and good intention had been sufficient to have bound God unto them.

[2] Read Deut. 14:28.

4:5 [1] As Lev. 7:13.

[2] You only delight in these outward ceremonies and have none other respect.

4:6 [1] That is, lack of bread and meat.

4:7 [1] I stayed the rain till the fruits of the earth were destroyed with drought, and yet you would not consider it to return to me by repentance.

4:8 [1] They could not find water enough where they had heard say it had rained.

4:10 [1] As I plagued the Egyptians, Exod. 9:10.

4:11 [1] You were almost all consumed, and a few of you wonderfully preserved, 2 Kings 14:26.

4:12 [1] Turn to him by repentance.

5:2 [1] He so calleth them, because they so boasted of themselves or because they were given to wantonness and daintiness.

5:3 [1] Meaning, that the tenth part should scarcely be saved.

4 For thus saith the Lord unto the house of Israel, Seek ye me, and ye shall live.

5 But seek not Bethel, nor enter into ¹Gilgal, and go not to Beersheba: for Gilgal shall go into captivity, and Bethel shall come to nought.

6 Seek the Lord, and ye shall live, lest he break out like fire in the house of Joseph and devour it, and there *be* none to quench it in Bethel.

7 They turn ¹judgment to wormwood, and leave off righteousness in the earth.

8 He ¹maketh Pleiades, and Orion, and he turn-eth the shadow of death into the morning, and he maketh the day dark as night: he calleth the waters of the sea, and poureth them out upon the open earth: the Lord *is* his Name.

9 He strengtheneth the destroyer against the mighty, and the destroyer shall come against the fortress.

10 They have hated him ¹that rebuked in the gate: and they abhorred him that speaketh uprightly.

11 Forasmuch then as your treading *is* upon the poor, and ¹ye take from him burdens of wheat, ye have built houses of hewn stone, but ye shall not dwell in them: ye have planted pleasant vineyards, but ye shall not drink wine of them.

12 For I know your manifold transgressions, and your mighty sins: they afflict the just, they take rewards, and they oppress the poor in the gate.

13 Therefore ¹the prudent shall keep silence in that time, for it is an evil time.

14 Seek good and not evil, that ye may live: and the Lord God of hosts shall be with you, as you have spoken.

15 Hate the evil, and love the good, and establish judgment in the gate: it may be that the Lord God of hosts will be merciful unto the remnant of Joseph.

16 Therefore the Lord God of hosts, the Lord saith thus, Mourning *shall be* in all streets: and they shall say in all the high ways, Alas, alas: and they shall call the ¹husbandman to lamentation, and such as can mourn, to mourning.

17 And in all the vines *shall be* lamentation: for I will pass through thee, saith the Lord.

18 Woe unto you, that ¹desire the day of the Lord: what have you to do with it? the day of the Lord *is* darkness and not light,

19 As if a man did flee from a lion, and a bear met him: or went into the house, and leaned his hand on the wall, and a serpent bit him.

20 Shall not the day of the Lord be darkness, and not light, even darkness and no light in it?

21 I hate *and* abhor your feast days, and I will not smell in your solemn assemblies.

22 Though ye offer me burnt offerings and meat offerings, ¹I will not accept them: neither will I regard the peace offerings of your fat beasts.

23 Take thou away from me the multitude of thy songs (for I will not hear the melody of thy viols.)

24 And let judgment run down as ¹waters, and righteousness as a mighty river.

25 Have ye offered unto me sacrifices and offerings in the wilderness forty years, O house of Israel?

26 But you have born ¹Sikkuth your king, and Chiun your images, *and* the star of your gods which you made to yourselves.

27 Therefore will I cause you to go into captivity beyond Damascus, saith the Lord, whose Name *is* the God of hosts.

6

Against the princes of Israel living in pleasure.

1 Woe to ¹them that are at ease in Zion, and trust in the mountain of Samaria, ²which were famous at the beginning of the nations: and the house of Israel came to them.

2 Go you unto Calneh, and see: and from thence go you to Hamath the great: then go down to Gath of the Philistines: be ¹they better than these

---

5:5 ¹ In those places they worshipped new idols, which aforetime served for the true honor of God: therefore he saith that these shall not save them.

5:7 ¹ Instead of judgment and equity they execute cruelty and oppression.

5:8 ¹ He describeth the power of God, Job 9:9.

5:10 ¹ They hate the Prophets, which reprove them in the open assemblies.

5:11 ¹ Ye take both his money and also his food, wherewith he should live.

5:13 ¹ God will so plague them that they shall not suffer the godly once to open their mouths to admonish them of their faults.

5:16 ¹ So that all degrees shall have matter of lamentation for the great plagues.

5:18 ¹ Thus he speaketh, because the wicked and hypocrites said they were content to abide God's judgments, whereas the godly tremble and fear, Jer. 30:7; Joel 2:2, 11; Zeph. 1:15.

5:22 ¹ Because ye have corrupted my true service, and remain obsti-nate in your vices, Isa. 1:11; Jer. 6:10.

5:24 ¹ Do your duty to God, and to your neighbor, and so ye shall feel his grace plentifully, if you show your abundant affections according to God's word.

5:26 ¹ That idol which you esteemed as your king, and carried about as you did Chiun, in which images you thought that there was a cer-tain divinity.

6:1 ¹ The Prophet threateneth the wealthy, which regarded not God's plagues nor menaces by his Prophets.

² These two cities were famous by their first inhabitants the Canaanites: and seeing beforetime they did nothing avail them that were there born, why should you look that they should save you which were brought in to dwell in other men's pos-sessions?

6:2 ¹ If God have destroyed these excellent cities in three divers kingdoms, as in Babylon, Syria, and of the Philistines, and hath brought their wide borders into a greater straightness than yours yet are, think you to be better, or to escape?

kingdoms? or the border of their land greater than your border,

3 Ye that put far away the [1]evil day, and approach to the seat of iniquity?

4 They lie upon beds of ivory, and stretch themselves upon their beds, and eat the lambs of the flock, and the calves out of the stall.

5 They sing to the sound of the viol: they invent to themselves instruments of music like [1]David.

6 They drink wine in bowls, and anoint themselves with the chief ointments, but no man is [1]sorry for the affliction of Joseph.

7 Therefore now shall they go captive with the first that go captive, and [1]the sorrow of them that stretched themselves, is at hand.

8 [1]The Lord God hath sworn by himself, saith the Lord God of hosts, I abhor [2]the excellency of Jacob, and hate his palaces: therefore will I deliver up the city with all that is therein.

9 And if there remain ten men in one house, they shall die.

10 And his uncle [1]shall take him up and burn him, to carry out the bones out of the house, and shall say unto him, that is by the [2]sides of the house, Is there yet any with thee? And he shall say, None. Then shall he say, [3]Hold thy tongue: for we may not remember the Name of the Lord.

11 For behold, the Lord commandeth, and he will smite the great house with breaches, and the little house with clefts.

12 Shall horses [1]run upon the rock? or will one plow *there* with oxen? for ye have turned judgment into gall, and the fruit of righteousness into [2]wormwood.

13 Yet rejoice in a thing of nought: ye say, Have not we gotten us [1]horns by our own strength?

14 But behold, I will raise up against you a nation, O house of Israel, saith the Lord God of hosts: and they shall afflict you from the entering in of [1]Hamath unto the river of the wilderness.

7 *God showeth certain visions, whereby he signifieth the destruction of the people of Israel.* 10 *The false accusation of Amaziah,* 12 *His crafty counsel.*

1 Thus hath the Lord God showed unto me, and behold, he formed [1]grasshoppers in the beginning of the shooting up of the latter growth: and lo, *it was* in the latter growth [2]after the King's mowing.

2 And when they had made an end of eating the grass of the land, then I said, O Lord God, spare, I beseech thee: who shall raise up Jacob? for he is small.

3 So the Lord [1]repented for this. It shall not be, saith the Lord.

4 ¶ Thus *also* hath the Lord God showed unto me, and behold, the Lord God called to judgment by fire, [1]and it devoured the great deep, and did eat up a part.

5 Then said I, O Lord God, cease, I beseech thee: who shall raise up Jacob? for he is small.

6 So the Lord repented for this. This also shall not be, saith the Lord God.

7 ¶ Thus *again* he showed me, and behold, the Lord stood upon a wall made by line [1]with a line in his hand.

8 And the Lord said unto me, Amos, what seest thou? And I said, A line. Then said the Lord, Behold, I will set a line in the midst of my people Israel, and will pass by them no more.

9 And the high places of Isaac shall be desolate, and the temples of Israel shall be destroyed: and I will rise against the house of Jeroboam with the sword.

10 ¶ [1]Then Amaziah the Priest of Bethel sent to Jeroboam king of Israel, saying, Amos hath conspired against thee in the midst of the house of Israel: the land is not able to bear all his words.

6:3 [1] Ye that continue still in your wickedness, and think that God's plagues are not at hand, but give yourselves to all idleness, wantonness, and riot.

6:5 [1] As he caused divers kinds of instruments to be made to serve God's glory, so these did contend to invent as many to serve their wanton affections and lusts.

6:6 [1] They pitied not their brethren, whereof now many were slain and carried away captive.

6:7 [1] Some read, the joy of them that stretch themselves, shall depart.

6:8 [1] Read Jer. 51:14.

[2] That is, the riches and pomp.

6:10 [1] The destruction shall be so great, that none shall almost be left to bury the dead: and therefore they shall burn them at home, to carry out the burnt ashes with more ease.

[2] That is, to some neighbor that dwelleth round about.

[3] They shall be so astonished at this destruction, that they shall boast no more of the Name of God, and that they are his people: but they shall be dumb when they hear God's Name, and abhor it, as they that are desperate, or reprobate.

6:12 [1] He compareth them to barren rocks, whereupon it is in vain to bestow labor: showing that God's benefits can have no place among them.

[2] Read Amos 5:7.

6:13 [1] That is, power and glory.

6:14 [1] From one corner of the country to another.

7:1 [1] To devour the land: and he alludeth to the invading of the enemies.

[2] After the public commandment for mowing was given: or as some read, when the king's sheep were shorn.

7:3 [1] That is, stayed this plague at my prayer.

7:4 [1] Meaning, that God's indignation was inflamed against the stubbornness of this people.

7:7 [1] Signifying that this should be the last measuring of the people, and that he would defer his judgment no longer.

7:10 [1] That is, when Amos had prophesied that the king should be destroyed: for the wicked Priest more for hatred he bare to the Prophet than for love toward the king, thought this accusation sufficient to condemn him, whereas none other could take place.

11 For thus Amos saith, Jeroboam shall die by the sword, and Israel shall be led away captive out of their own land.

12 Also [1]Amaziah said unto Amos, O thou the Seer, go, flee thou away into the land of Judah, and there eat *thy* bread, and prophesy there.

13 But prophesy no more at Bethel: for it is the king's chapel, and it is the king's court.

14 Then answered Amos, and said to Amaziah, I was no [1]Prophet, neither was I a Prophet's son, but I was an herdsman, and a gatherer of wild figs.

15 And the Lord took me as I followed the flock, and the Lord said unto me, Go prophesy unto my people Israel.

16 Now therefore hear thou the word of the Lord. Thou sayest, Prophesy not against Israel, and speak nothing against the house of Isaac.

17 Therefore thus saith the Lord, [1]Thy wife shall be an harlot in the city, and thy sons and thy daughters shall fall by the sword, and thy land shall be divided by line: and thou shalt die in a polluted land, and Israel shall surely go into captivity forth of his land.

8

1 Against the rulers of Israel.   7 The Lord sweareth.   11 The famine of the word of God.

1 Thus hath the Lord God showed unto me, and behold, a basket of summer fruit.

2 And he said, Amos, what seest thou? And I said, A basket of [1]summer fruit. Then said the Lord unto me, The end is come upon my people of Israel, I will pass by them no more.

3 And the songs of the Temple shall be howlings in that day, saith the Lord God: many dead bodies *shall be* in every place: they shall cast them forth with [1]silence.

4 Hear this, O ye that [1]swallow up the poor, that ye may make the needy of the land to fail,

5 Saying, When will the [1]new month be gone, that we may sell corn? and the Sabbath, that we may set forth wheat, and make [2]the Ephah small and the shekel great, and falsify the weights by deceit?

6 That we may buy the poor for silver, and the needy for shoes: yea, and sell the refuse of the wheat.

7 The Lord hath sworn by the excellency of Jacob, Surely, I will never forget any of their works.

8 Shall not the land tremble for this, and every-one mourn, that dwelleth therein? and it shall rise up wholly as a flood, and it shall be cast out, and [1]drowned as by the flood of Egypt.

9 And in that day, saith the Lord God, I will even cause the [1]Sun to go down at noon: I will darken the earth in the clear day.

10 And I will turn your feasts into mourning: and all your songs into lamentation: and I will bring sackcloth upon all loins, and baldness upon every head: and I will make it as the mourning of an only son, and the end thereof as a bitter day.

11 Behold, the days come, saith the Lord God, that I will send a famine in the Land, not a famine of bread, nor a thirst for water, but of hearing the word of the Lord.

12 And they shall wander from sea to sea, and from the North even unto the East shall they run to and fro to seek the [1]word of the Lord, and shall not find it.

13 In that day shall the fair virgins and the young men perish for thirst.

14 They that swear by the sin [1]of Samaria, and that say, Thy God, O Dan, liveth, and [2]the manner of Beersheba liveth, even they shall fall, and never rise up again.

9

Threatenings against the Temple,   2 And against Israel.   11 The restoring of the Church.

1 I saw the Lord standing upon the [1]Altar, and he said, Smite the lintel of the door, that the posts may shake: and cut them in pieces, *even* the [2]heads of them all, and I will slay the last of them with the

---

7:12 [1] When this instrument of Satan was not able to compass his purpose by the king, he assayed by another practice, that was, to fear the Prophet, that he might depart, and not reprove their idolatry there openly, and so hinder his profit.

7:14 [1] Thus he sheweth by his extraordinary vocation, that God had given him a charge, which he must needs execute.

7:17 [1] Thus God used to approve the authority of his Prophets, by his plagues and judgments against them which were malicious enemies, Jer. 28:12 and 29:21, 25, as this day he doeth against them that persecute the ministers of his Gospel.

8:2 [1] Which signified the ripeness of their sins, and the readiness of God's judgments.

8:3 [1] There shall be none left to mourn for them.

8:4 [1] By staying the sale of food, and necessary things which you have gotten into your own hands, and so cause the poor to spend quickly that little that they have, and at length for necessity to become your slaves.

8:5 [1] When the dearth was once come they were so greedy of gain, that they thought the holy day to be an hindrance unto them.

[2] That is, the measure small, and the price great.

8:8 [1] That is, the inhabitants of the land shall be drowned, as Nile drowneth many when it overfloweth.

8:9 [1] In the midst of their prosperity, I will send great affliction.

8:12 [1] Whereby he sheweth that they shall not only perish in body, but also in soul for lack of God's word, which is the food thereof.

8:14 [1] For the idolaters did use to swear by their idols: which here he calleth their sin, as the Papists yet do by theirs.

[2] That is, the common manner of worshipping, and the service or religion there used.

9:1 [1] Which was at Jerusalem: for he appeared not in the idolatrous places of Israel.

[2] Both the chief of them and also the common people.

sword: he that fleeth of them, shall not flee away: and he that escapeth of them, shall not be delivered.

2 Though they dig into the hell, thence shall mine hand take them: though they climb up to heaven, thence will I bring them down.

3 And though they hide themselves in the top of Carmel, I will search and take them out thence: and though they be hid from my sight in the bottom of the sea, thence will I command the [1]serpent, and he shall bite them.

4 And though they go into captivity before their enemies, thence will I command the sword, and it shall slay them: and I will set mine eyes upon them for evil, and not for good.

5 And the Lord God of hosts shall touch the land, and it shall melt away, and all that dwell therein shall mourn, and it shall rise up wholly like a flood, and shall be drowned as by the flood of Egypt.

6 He buildeth his [1]spheres in the heaven, and hath laid the foundation of his globe of elements in the earth: he calleth the waters of the sea, and poureth them out upon the open earth: the Lord is his Name.

7 Are ye not as the Ethiopians [1]unto me, O children of Israel, saith the Lord? have not I brought up Israel out of the land of Egypt? and the Philistines from [2]Caphtor, and Aram from Kir?

8 Behold, the eyes of the Lord God are upon the sinful kingdom, and I will destroy it clean out of the earth. Nevertheless I will not utterly [1]destroy the house of Jacob, saith the Lord.

9 For lo, I will command and I will sift the house of Israel among all nations, like as corn is sifted in a sieve: yet shall not the [1]least stone fall upon the earth.

10 But all the sinners of my people shall die by the sword, which say, The evil shall not come, nor hasten for us.

11 In that day will I raise up the [1]Tabernacle of David, that is fallen down, and close up the breaches thereof, and I will raise up his ruins, and I will build it, as in the days of old,

12 That they may possess the remnant of [1]Edom, and of all the heathen, because my Name is called upon them, saith the Lord, that doeth this.

13 Behold, the days come, saith the Lord, that the plowman shall [1]touch the mower, and the treader of grapes him that soweth seed: and the mountains shall [2]drop sweet wine, and all the hills shall melt.

14 [1]And I will bring again the captivity of my people of Israel: and they shall build the waste cities, and inhabit them, and they shall plant vineyards, and drink the wine thereof: they shall also make gardens, and eat the fruits of them.

15 And I will plant them upon their land, and they shall no more be pulled up again out of their land which I have given them, saith the Lord thy God.

9:3 [1] He showeth that God will declare himself enemy unto them in all places, and that his elements and all creatures shall be enemies to destroy them.

9:6 [1] He declareth by the wonderful power of God, by the making of the heavens and the elements, that it is not possible for man to escape his judgments when he punisheth.

9:7 [1] Am I more bound to you than to the Ethiopians, or black moors? yet have I bestowed upon you greater benefits.
  [2] Read Jer. 47:4.

9:8 [1] Though he destroy the rebellious multitude, yet he will ever reserve the remnant his Church to call upon his Name.

9:9 [1] Meaning, that none of his should perish in his wrath.

9:11 [1] I will send the Messiah promised, and restore by him the spiritual Israel, Acts 15:16.

9:12 [1] Meaning, that the very enemies as were the Edomites, and others should be joined with the Jews in one society, and body, whereof Christ should be the head.

9:13 [1] Signifying, that there shall be great plenty of all things, so that when one kind of fruit is ripe, another should follow, and every one in course, Lev. 26:5.
  [2] Read Joel 3:18.

9:14 [1] The accomplishment thereof is under Christ, when they are planted in this Church, out of the which they can never be pulled, after they are once grafted therein.

OBADIAH

1

1 The vision of Obadiah. Thus saith the Lord God against Edom, [1]We have heard a rumor from the Lord, and an ambassador is sent among the heathen: arise, and [2]let us rise up against her to battle.

2 Behold, I have made thee small among the heathen: thou art utterly despised.

3 The [1]pride of thine heart hath deceived thee: thou that dwellest in the clefts of the rocks, whose habitation *is* high, that saith in his heart, Who shall bring me down to the ground?

4 Though thou exalt thyself as the eagle, and make thy nest among the stars, thence will I bring thee down, saith the Lord.

5 [1]Came thieves to thee or robbers by night? how wast thou brought to silence? would they not have stolen till they had enough? if the grape gatherers came to thee, would they not leave *some* grapes?

6 How are the things of Esau sought up, *and* his treasures searched?

7 All the men of thy confederacy [1]have driven thee to the borders: the men that were at peace with thee, have deceived thee, *and* prevailed against thee: *they that eat* thy [2]bread, have laid a wound under thee: there is none understanding in him.

8 Shall not I in that day, saith the Lord, even destroy the wise men out of Edom, and understanding from the mount of Esau?

9 And thy strong men, O Teman, shall be afraid, because everyone of the mount of Esau shall be cut off by slaughter.

10 For thy cruelty against thy [1]brother Jacob, shame shall cover thee, and thou shalt be cut off forever.

11 When thou stoodest [1]on the other side, in the day that the strangers carried away his substance, and strangers entered into his gates, and cast lots upon Jerusalem, even thou wast as one of them.

12 But thou shouldest not have beholden the day of thy brother, in the day that he was made [1]a stranger, neither shouldest thou have rejoiced over the children of Judah, in the day of their destruction: thou shouldest not have spoken proudly in the day of affliction.

13 Thou shouldest not have entered into the gate of my people in the day of their destruction, neither shouldest thou have once looked on their affliction in the day of their destruction, nor have laid hands on their substance in the day of their destruction.

14 Neither shouldest thou have stood in the crossways to cut off them, that should escape, neither shouldest thou have shut up the remnant thereof in the day of affliction.

15 For the day [1]of the Lord *is* near, upon all the heathen: as thou hast done, it shall be done to thee: thy reward shall return upon thine head.

16 For as ye have [1]drunk upon mine holy Mountain, *so* shall all the heathen drink continually: yea, they shall drink and swallow up, and they shall be [2]as though they had not been.

17 But upon mount Zion shall be deliverance, and it shall be holy, and the house of Jacob shall possess their possessions,

18 And the house of Jacob shall be [1]a fire, and the house of Joseph a flame, and the house of Esau *as* stubble, and they shall kindle in them and devour them: and there shall be no remnant of the house of Esau: for the Lord hath spoken it.

19 And they shall possess the South side of the

1:1 [1] God hath certainly revealed to his prophets, that he will raise up the heathen to destroy the Edomites, whereof the rumor is now published, Jer. 49:14.

[2] Thus the heathen encourage themselves to rise against Edom.

1:3 [1] Which despisest all others in respect of thyself, and yet art but an handful in comparison of others, and art shut up among the hills as separate from the rest of the world.

1:5 [1] God will so destroy them that he will leave none, though thieves when they come, take but till they have enough, and they that gather grapes, ever leave some behind them, Jer. 49:9.

1:7 [1] They in whom thou didst trust for to have help and friendship of them, shall be thine enemies and destroy thee.

[2] That is, thy familiar friends and guests have by secret practices destroyed thee.

1:10 [1] He showeth the cause why the Edomites were so sharply punished: to wit, because they were enemies to his Church, whom he now comforteth by punishing their enemies.

1:11 [1] When Nebuchadnezzar came against Jerusalem, thou joinedest with him, and hadest part of the spoil, and so didst rejoice when my people, that is, thy brother were afflicted, whereas thou shouldest have pitied and helped thy brother.

1:12 [1] When the Lord deprived them of their former dignity, and gave them to be carried into captivity.

1:15 [1] When he will summon all the heathen, and send them to destroy thee.

1:16 [1] That is, rejoiced and triumphed.

[2] The Edomites shall be utterly destroyed, and yet in despite of all the enemies I will reserve my Church and restore it.

1:18 [1] God attributeth this power, to consume his enemies, to his Church, which power is only proper to himself, as Isa. 10:17; Deut. 4:24; Heb. 12:29.

[1]mount of Esau, and the plain of the Philistines: and they shall possess the fields of Ephraim, and the fields of Samaria, and Benjamin *shall have* Gilead.

20 And the captivity of this host of the children of Israel, which were among the [1]Canaanites, *shall possess*

unto Zarephath, and the captivity of Jerusalem, which is in Sepharad, shall possess the cities of the South.

21 And they [1]that shall save, shall come up to mount Zion to judge the mount of Esau, and the kingdom shall be the Lord's.

1:19 [1] He describeth how the Church shall be enlarged and have great possessions: but this chiefly is accomplished under Christ, when as the faithful are made heirs and lords of all things by him which is their head.

1:20 [1] By the Canaanites, the Jews mean the Dutchmen, and by

Zarephath, France, and by Sepharad, Spain.

1:21 [1] Meaning that God will raise up in his Church such as shall rule and govern for the defense of the same, and destruction of his enemies under Messiah, whom the Prophet calleth here, the Lord and head of this kingdom.

JONAH

1 *3 Jonah fled when he was sent to preach. 4 A tempest ariseth, and he is cast into the sea for his disobedience.*

1 The word of the Lord came ¹also unto Jonah the son of Amittai, saying,

2 Arise, *and* go to ¹Nineveh, that ²great city, and cry against it: for their wickedness is come up before me.

3 But Jonah rose up to ¹flee into Tarshish, from the presence of the Lord, and went down to ²Japho: and he found a ship going to Tarshish: so he paid the fare thereof, and went down into it, that he might go with them unto Tarshish, from the ³presence of the Lord.

4 But the Lord sent out a great wind into the sea, and there was a mighty tempest in the sea, so that the ship was like to be broken.

5 Then the mariners were afraid, and cried every man unto his god, and cast the wares that were in the ship, into the sea, to lighten it of them: but Jonah was gone down ¹into the sides of the ship, and he lay down, and was fast asleep.

6 So the shipmaster came to him, and said unto him, What meanest thou, O sleeper? Arise, call upon thy ¹God, if so be that God will think upon us, that we perish not.

7 And they said everyone to his fellow, Come, and let us cast ¹lots, that we may know for whose cause this evil *is* upon us. So they cast lots, and the lot fell upon Jonah.

8 Then said they unto him, Tell us for whose cause this evil *is* upon us? What is thine occupation? and whence comest thou? which is thy country? and

of what people art thou?

9 And he answered them, I am an Hebrew, and I fear the Lord God of heaven, which hath made the sea, and the dry land.

10 Then were the men exceedingly afraid, and said unto him, Why hast thou done this? (for the men knew that he fled from the presence of the Lord, because he had told them)

11 Then said they unto him, What shall we do unto thee, that the sea may be calm unto us? (for the sea wrought, and was troublous)

12 And he said unto them, Take me, and cast me into the sea: so shall the sea be calm unto you: for I know that for my sake this great tempest *is* upon you.

13 Nevertheless the men rowed to bring it to the land, but they could not: for the sea wrought, and was troublous against them.

14 Wherefore they cried unto the Lord, and said, ¹We beseech thee, O Lord, we beseech thee, let us not perish for this man's life, and lay not upon us innocent blood: for thou, O Lord, hast done as it pleased thee.

15 So they took up Jonah, and cast him into the sea, and the sea ceased from her raging.

16 Then the men ¹feared the Lord exceedingly, and offered a sacrifice unto the Lord, and made vows.

17 Now the Lord had prepared a great fish to swallow up Jonah: and Jonah was in the ¹belly of the fish three days and three nights.

2 *1 Jonah is in the fish's belly. 2 His prayer. 10 He is delivered.*

1:1 ¹ After that he had preached a long time in Israel: and so Ezekiel, after that for a time he had prophesied in Judah, he had visions in Babylon, Ezek. 1:1.

1:2 ¹ For seeing the great obstination of the Israelites, he sent his Prophet to the Gentiles, that they might provoke them to repentance, or at least make them inexcusable: for Nineveh was the chief city of the Assyrians.

² For as authors write, it contained in circuit about eight and forty miles, and had a thousand and five hundred towers, and at this time there were an hundred and twenty thousand children therein, Jonah 4:11.

1:3 ¹ Whereby he declared his weakness, that would not promptly follow the Lord's calling, but gave place to his own reason, which persuaded him that he should nothing at all profit there, seeing he had done so small good among his own people, Jonah 4:2.

² Which was the haven, and port to take shipping thither, called also Joppa.

³ From that vocation whereunto God had called him, and wherein he would have assisted him.

1:5 ¹ As one that would have cast off this care and solicitude by seeking rest and quietness.

1:6 ¹ As they had called on their idols, which declareth that idolaters have no stay nor certainty, but in their troubles seek they cannot tell to whom.

1:7 ¹ Which declareth that the matter was in great extremity and doubt, which thing was God's motion in them, for the trial of the cause: and this may not be done but in matters of great importance.

1:14 ¹ This declareth that the very wicked in their necessities flee unto God for succor and also that they are touched with a certain fear to shed man's blood, whereas they know no manifest sign of wickedness.

1:16 ¹ They were touched with a certain repentance of their life past, and began to worship the true God by whom they saw themselves so wonderfully delivered: but this was done for fear, and not of a pure heart and affection, neither according to God's word.

1:17 ¹ Thus the Lord would chastise his Prophet with a most terrible spectacle of death, and hereby also confirmed him of his favor and support in this his charge which was enjoined him.

1 Then Jonah prayed unto the Lord his God [1]out of the fish's belly,

2 And said, I cried in mine affliction unto the Lord, and he heard me: out of the belly [1]of hell cried I, *and* thou heardest my voice.

3 For thou hadst cast me into the bottom in the midst of the sea, and the floods compassed me about: all thy surges, and all thy waves passed over me.

4 Then I said, I am [1]cast away out of thy sight: yet will I look again toward thine holy Temple.

5 The waters compassed me about unto the soul: the depth closed me round about, and the weeds were wrapped about mine head.

6 I went down to the bottom of the mountains: the earth with her bars was about me forever, yet hast thou brought up my [1]life from the pit, O Lord my God.

7 When my soul fainted within me, I remembered the Lord: and my prayer came unto thee into thine holy Temple.

8 They that wait upon lying [1]vanities, forsake their own [2]mercy.

9 But I will sacrifice unto thee with the voice of thanksgiving, and will pay that that I have vowed: salvation *is* of the Lord.

10 And the Lord spake unto the fish, and it cast out Jonah upon the dry land.

3

1 Jonah is sent again to Ninevah.   5 The repentance of the king of Ninevah.

1 And the word of the Lord came unto [1]Jonah the second time, saying,

2 Arise, go unto Nineveh that great city, and preach unto it the preaching which I bid thee.

3 So Jonah arose, and went to Nineveh according to the word of the Lord: now Nineveh was a [1]great and excellent city of three days journey.

4 And Jonah began to enter into the city a day's [1]journey, and he cried and said, Yet forty days, and Nineveh shall be overthrown.

5 So the people of Nineveh [1]believed God, and proclaimed a fast, and put on sackcloth, from the greatest of them, even to the least of them.

6 For word came unto the king of Nineveh, and he rose from his throne, and he laid his robe from him, and covered him with sackcloth, and sat in ashes.

7 And he proclaimed and said through Nineveh, (by the counsel of the king and his nobles) saying, Let neither man, nor [1]beast, bullock nor sheep taste anything, neither feed nor drink water.

8 But let man and beast put on sackcloth, and [1]cry mightily unto God: yea, let every man turn from his evil way, and from the wickedness that is in their hands.

9 [1]Who can tell *if* God will turn, and repent and turn away from his fierce wrath, that we perish not?

10 And God saw their [1]works that they turned from their evil ways: and [2]God repented of the evil that he had said that he would do unto them, and he did it not.

4

The great goodness of God toward his creatures.

1 Therefore it displeased [1]Jonah exceedingly, and he was angry.

2 And he prayed unto the Lord, and said, I pray thee, O Lord, was not this my saying, when I was yet in my country? therefore I prevented it to flee unto [1]Tarshish: for I knew, that thou art a gracious God, and merciful, slow to anger, and of great kindness, and repentest thee of the evil.

3 Therefore now, O Lord, take, I beseech thee, my life [1]from me: for it is better for me to die than to live.

4 Then said the Lord, Doest thou well to be [1]angry?

2:1 [1] Being now swallowed up of death, and seeing no remedy to escape, his faith brast out unto the Lord, knowing that out of the very hell he was able to deliver him.

2:2 [1] For he was now in the fish's belly as in a grave or place of darkness.

2:4 [1] This declared what his prayer was, and how he labored between hope and despair, considering the neglect of his vocation, and God's judgments for the same: but yet in the end faith got the victory.

2:6 [1] Thou hast delivered me from the belly of the fish and all these dangers, as it were raising me from death to life.

2:8 [1] They that depend upon anything save on God alone.
  [2] They refuse their own felicity, and that goodness which they should else receive of God.

3:1 [1] This is a great declaration of God's mercy, that he receiveth him again, and sendeth him forth as his Prophet, which had before showed so great infirmity.

3:3 [1] Read Jonah 1:2.

3:4 [1] He went forward one day in the city, and preached, and so he continued till the city was converted.

3:5 [1] For he declared that he was a Prophet sent to them from God

to denounce his judgments against them.

3:7 [1] Not that the dumb beasts had sinned or could repent, but that by their example man might be astonished, considering that for his sin the anger of God hanged over all creatures.

3:8 [1] He willed that the men should earnestly call unto God for mercy.

3:9 [1] For partly by the threatening of the Prophet, and partly by the motion of his own conscience, he doubted whether God would show them mercy.

3:10 [1] That is, the fruits of their repentance, which did proceed of faith, which God had planted by the ministry of his Prophet.
  [2] Read Jer. 18:8.

4:1 [1] Because hereby he should be taken as a false prophet, and so the Name of God, which he preached, should be blasphemed.

4:2 [1] Read Jonah 1:3.

4:3 [1] Thus he prayed of grief fearing lest God's Name by this forgiveness might be blasphemed, as though he sent his Prophets forth to denounce his judgments in vain.

4:4 [1] Wilt thou be judge when I do things for my glory, and when I do not?

5　So Jonah went out of the city, and sat on the East side of the city, and there made him a booth, and sat under it in the shadow [1]till he might see what should be done in the city.

6　And the Lord God prepared a [1]gourd, and made it to come up over Jonah, that it might be a shadow over his head, and deliver him from his grief. So Jonah was exceeding glad of the gourd.

7　But God prepared a worm when the morning rose the next day, and it smote the gourd, that it withered.

8　And when the sun did arise, God prepared also a fervent East wind: and the sun beat upon the head of Jonah, that he fainted and wished in his heart to die, and said, It is better for me to die than to live.

9　And God said unto Jonah, Doest thou well to be angry for the gourd? And he said, I do well to be [1]angry unto the death.

10　Then said the Lord, Thou hast had pity on the gourd for the which thou hast not labored, neither madest it grow, which came up in a night, and perished in a night,

11　And should [1]not I spare Nineveh that great city, wherein are sixscore thousand persons, that [2]cannot discern between their right hand and their left hand, and *also* much cattle?

4:5　[1] For he doubted as yet whether God would show them mercy or not, and therefore after forty days he departed out of the city, looking what issue God would send.

4:6　[1] Which was a further means, to cover him from the heat of the sun, as he remained in his booth.

4:9　[1] This declareth the great inconveniences whereinto God's servants do fall when they give place to their own affections, and do not in all things willingly submit themselves to God.

4:11　[1] Thus God mercifully reproveth him which would pity himself, and this gourd, and yet would restrain God to show his compassion to so many thousand people.

[2] Meaning, that they were children and infants.

MICAH

1

1 The word of the Lord, that came unto Micah the ¹Moreshite in the days of Jotham, Ahaz, *and* Hezekiah kings of Judah, which he saw concerning Samaria, and Jerusalem.

2 Hear, ¹all ye people: hearken thou, O earth, and all that therein is, and let the Lord God be witness against you, *even* the Lord from his holy Temple.

3 For behold, the Lord cometh out of his place, and will come ¹down, and tread upon the high places of the earth.

4 And the mountains shall melt under him (so shall the valleys cleave) as wax before the fire, *and* as the waters that are poured downward.

5 For the wickedness of Jacob *is* all this, and for the sins of the house of Israel: what is the wickedness of Jacob? Is not ¹Samaria? and which are the high ²places of Judah? Is not Jerusalem?

6 Therefore I will make Samaria as an heap of the field, *and* for the planting of a vineyard, and I will cause the stones thereof to tumble down into the valley, and I will discover the foundations thereof.

7 And all the graven images thereof shall be broken, and all the ¹gifts thereof shall be burnt with the fire, and all the idols thereof will I destroy: for she gathered it of the hire of an harlot, and they shall return ²to the wages of an harlot.

8 Therefore I will mourn and howl: I will go without clothes, and naked: I will make lamentation like the dragons, and mourning as the ostriches.

9 For her plagues are grievous: for it is come into Judah: *the enemy* is come unto the gate of my people, unto Jerusalem.

10 Declare ye it not at ¹Gath, neither weep ye: for the house of ²Aphrah roll thyself in the dust.

11 Thou that dwellest at ¹Shaphir, go together naked with shame: she that dwelleth at Zaanan, shall not come forth in the mourning of Beth Ezel: *the enemy* shall ²receive of you for his standing.

12 For the inhabitant of Maroth waited for good, but evil came from the Lord unto the ¹gate of Jerusalem.

13 O thou inhabitant of Lachish, bind the chariot to the *beasts* ¹of price: she ²is the beginning of the sin to the daughter of Zion: for the transgressions of Israel were found in thee.

14 Therefore shalt thou give presents to Moresheth ¹Gath: the houses of Achzib *shall be* as a lie to the kings of Israel.

15 Yet will I bring an ¹heir unto thee, O inhabitant of Mareshah, he shall come unto Adullam, ²the glory of Israel.

16 Make thee bald: and shave thee for thy delicate children: enlarge thy baldness as the eagle, for they are gone into captivity from thee.

2

1 Woe unto them that imagine iniquity, and work wickedness upon their beds: ¹when the morning is light they practice it, because their hand ²hath power.

1:1 ¹ Born in Moresheth, a city of Judah.

1:2 ¹ Because of the malice and obstinacy of the people, whom he had so oft exhorted to repentance, he summoneth them to God's judgments, taking all creatures, and God himself to witness, that the preaching of his Prophets, which they have abused, shall be revenged.

1:3 ¹ Meaning hereby, that God will come to judgment against the strong cities and holds.

1:5 ¹ Samaria, which should have been an example to all Israel of true religion and justice, was the puddle, and stews of all idolatry and corruption, and boasted themselves of their father Jacob.

² That is, the idolatry and infection.

1:7 ¹ Which they gathered by evil practices, and thought that their idols had enriched them therewith for their service unto them.

² The gain that came by their idols shall be consumed as a thing of naught: for as the wages or riches of harlots are wickedly gotten, so are they vilely and speedily spent.

1:10 ¹ Lest the Philistines our enemies rejoice at our destruction.

² Which was a city near to Jerusalem, Josh. 18:23, there called Ophrah, and signifieth dust: therefore he willeth them to mourn and roll themselves in the dust, for their dusty city.

1:11 ¹ These were cities whereby the enemy should pass as he came to Judah.

² He shall not depart before he hath overcome you, and so you shall pay for his tarrying.

1:12 ¹ For Rabshakeh had shut up Jerusalem, that they could not send to succor them.

1:13 ¹ To flee away: for Sennacherib laid siege first to that city, and remained therein when he sent his captains and army against Jerusalem.

² Thou first receivedst the idolatry of Jeroboam, and so didst infect Jerusalem.

1:14 ¹ Thou shalt bribe the Philistines thy neighbors, but they shall deceive thee, as well as they of Jerusalem.

1:15 ¹ He prophesieth against his own city: and because it signified an heritage, he saith that God would send an heir to possess it.

² For so they thought themselves for the strength of their city.

2:1 ¹ As soon as they rise, they execute their wicked devices of the night, and according to their power hurt others.

² Hebrew, *is in power.*

2	And they covet fields, and take them by violence, and houses, and take them away: so they oppress a man and his house, *even* man and his heritage.

3	Therefore thus saith the Lord, Behold, against this family have I devised a plague, whereout ye shall not pluck your necks, and ye shall not go *so* proudly, for this time is evil.

4	In that day shall they take up a parable against you, and lament with a doleful lamentation, and say, [1]We be utterly wasted: he hath changed the portion of my people: how hath he taken it away to restore it unto me? he hath divided our fields.

5	Therefore thou shalt have none that shall cast a cord by lot in [1]the congregation of the Lord.

6	[1]They that prophesy, Prophesy ye not. [2]They shall not prophesy to them, neither shall they take shame.

7	O thou that art named of the house of Jacob, is the Spirit of the Lord shortened? [1]are these his works? are not my works good unto him [2]that walketh uprightly?

8	But he that was [1]yesterday my people, is risen up on the other side, *as* against an enemy: they spoil the [2]beautiful garment from them that pass by peaceably, as though they returned from the war.

9	The women of my people have ye cast out from their pleasant houses, *and* from their children have ye taken away [1]my glory continually.

10	Arise and depart, for this is not *your* [1]rest: because it is polluted, it shall destroy *you*, even with a sore destruction.

11	If a man [1]walk in the spirit, and would lie falsely, *saying*, [2]I will prophesy unto thee of wine, and of strong drink, he shall even be the prophet of this people.

12	I will surely gather [1]thee wholly, O Jacob: I will surely gather the remnant of Israel: I will put them together as the sheep of Bozrah, *even* as the flock in the midst of their fold: *the cities* shall be full of brute of the men.

13	The [1]breaker up shall come up before them: they shall break out, and pass by the gate, and go out by it, and their king shall go before them, and the Lord *shall be* [2]upon their heads.

3

1 *Against the tyranny of princes and false prophets.*

1	And I said, Hear, I pray you, O heads of Jacob, and ye princes of the house of Israel: should not ye know [1]judgment?

2	*But* they hate the good, and love the evil: [1]they pluck off their skins from them, and their flesh from their bones.

3	And they eat also the flesh of my people, and flay off their skin from them, and they break their bones, and chop them in pieces, as for the pot, and as flesh within the caldron.

4	Then [1]shall they cry unto the Lord, but he will not hear them: he will even hide his face from them at that time, because they have done wickedly in their works.

5	Thus saith the Lord, Concerning the prophets that deceive my people, and [1]bite them with their teeth, and cry, peace, but if a man put not into their mouths, they prepare war against him.

6	Therefore [1]night shall be unto you for a vision, and darkness *shall be* unto you for a divination, and the Sun shall go down over the prophets, and the day shall be dark over them.

7	Then shall the Seers be ashamed, and the Soothsayers confounded: yea, they shall all cover [1]their lips, for they have none answer of God.

2:4 [1] Thus the Jews lament and say that there is no hope of restitution, seeing their possessions are divided among the enemies.

2:5 [1] Ye shall have no more lands to divide as you had in times past, and as you used to measure them in the Jubilee.

2:6 [1] Thus the people warn the prophets that they speak to them no more, for they cannot abide their threatenings.

[2] God saith that they shall not prophesy, nor receive no more of their rebukes nor taunts.

2:7 [1] Are these your works according to his Law?

[2] Do not the godly find my words comfortable?

2:8 [1] That is, aforetime.

[2] The poor can have no commodity by them, but they spoil them, as though they were enemies.

2:9 [1] That is, their substance and living, which is God's blessing, and as it were part of his glory.

2:10 [1] Jerusalem shall not be your safeguard: but the cause of your destruction.

2:11 [1] That is, show himself to be a Prophet.

[2] He showeth what prophets they delight in, that is, in flatterers, which tell them pleasant tales, and speak of their commodities.

2:12 [1] To destroy thee.

2:13 [1] The enemy shall break their gates and walls, and lead them into Chaldea.

[2] To drive them forward, and to help their enemies.

3:1 [1] That thing which is just and lawful, both to govern my people aright, and also to discharge your own conscience.

3:2 [1] The Prophet condemneth the wicked governors not only of covetousness, theft, and murder, but compareth them to wolves, lions, and most cruel beasts.

3:4 [1] That is, when I shall visit their wickedness: for though I hear the godly before they cry, Isa. 65:24, yet I will not hear these though they cry, Isa. 1:15 and Ezek. 8:18; James 2:13; 1 Pet. 3:11, 12.

3:5 [1] They devour all their substance, and then flatter them, promising that all shall go well, but if one restrain from their bellies, then they invent all ways to mischief.

3:6 [1] As you have loved to walk in darkness, and to prophesy lies, so God shall reward you with gross blindness and ignorance, so that when all others shall see the bright beams of God's graces, ye shall as blind men grope as in the night.

3:7 [1] When God shall discover them to the world, they shall be afraid to speak: for all shall know that they were but false prophets, and did belie the word of God.

8 Yet notwithstanding I am full ¹of power by the Spirit of the Lord, and of judgment, and of strength to declare unto Jacob his transgression, and to Israel his sin.

9 Hear this, I pray you, ye heads of the house of Jacob, and princes of the house of Israel: they abhor judgment, and pervert all equity.

10 They build up Zion with ¹blood, and Jerusalem with iniquity,

11 The heads thereof judge for rewards, and the priests thereof teach for hire, and the prophets thereof prophesy for money: yet will they ¹lean upon the Lord and say, Is not the Lord among us? no evil can come upon us.

12 Therefore shall Zion for your sake be ¹plowed as a field, and Jerusalem shall be an heap, and the mountain of the house, as the high places of the forest.

4 *1 Of the kingdom of Christ, and felicity of his Church.*

1 But in the ¹last days it shall come to pass, that the mountain of the House of the Lord shall be prepared in the top of the mountains, and it shall be exalted above the ²hills, and people shall flow unto it.

2 Yea, many nations shall come and say, Come, and let us go up to the Mountain of the Lord, and to the House of the God of Jacob, and he will ¹teach us his ways, and we will walk in his paths: for the Law shall go forth of Zion, and the word of the Lord from Jerusalem.

3 And he shall judge among many people, and ¹rebuke mighty nations afar off, and they shall break their swords into mattocks, and their spears into ²scythes: nation shall not lift up a sword against nation, neither shall they ³learn to fight anymore.

4 But they shall sit every man under his vine, and under his fig tree, and none shall make them afraid: for the mouth of the Lord of hosts hath spoken it.

5 For all people will walk ¹everyone in the name of his god, and we will walk in the Name of the Lord our God, forever and ever.

6 At the same day saith the Lord, will I gather her that halteth, and I will gather her that is cast out, and her that I have afflicted.

7 And I will make her that halteth, ¹a remnant, and her that was cast far off, a mighty nation, and the Lord shall reign over them in Mount Zion, from henceforth even forever.

8 And thou, O ¹tower of the flock, the stronghold of the daughter Zion, unto thee shall it come, even ²the first dominion, *and* kingdom shall come to the daughter Jerusalem.

9 Now why dost thou cry out with lamentation? *is* ¹there no king in thee? is thy counselor perished? for sorrow hath taken thee, as a woman in travail.

10 Sorrow and mourn, O daughter Zion, like a woman in travail: for now shalt thou go forth of the city, and dwell in the field, and shalt go into Babel, *but* there shalt thou be delivered: there the Lord shall redeem thee from the hand of thine enemies.

11 Now also many nations are gathered against thee, saying, Zion shall be condemned, and our eye shall look upon Zion.

12 But they ¹know not the thoughts of the Lord: they understand not his counsel, for he shall gather them as the sheaves in the barn.

13 Arise and thresh, ¹O daughter Zion: for I will make thine horn iron, and I will make thine hooves brass, and thou shalt break in pieces many people: and I will consecrate their riches unto the Lord: and their substance unto the ruler of the whole world.

5 *1 The destruction of Jerusalem.   2 The excellency of Bethlehem.*

3:8 ¹ The Prophet being assured of his vocation by the Spirit of God, setteth himself alone against all the wicked, showing how God both gave him gifts, ability and knowledge, to discern between good and evil, and also constancy to reprove the sins of the people, and not to flatter them.

3:10 ¹ They build them houses by bribery, which he calleth blood and iniquity.

3:11 ¹ They will say, that they are the people of God, and abuse his Name, as a pretence to cloak their hypocrisy.

3:12 ¹ Read Jer. 26:18.

4:1 ¹ When Christ shall come, and the Temple shall be destroyed.
  ² Read Isa. 2:2.

4:2 ¹ He showeth that there is no true Church, but where as the people are taught by God's pure word.

4:3 ¹ By his corrections and threatenings he will bring the people into subjection which are in the utmost corners of the world.
  ² They shall abstain from all evil doing, and exercise themselves in godliness and in well doing to others.
  ³ Read Isa. 2:4

4:5 ¹ He showeth that the people of God ought to remain constant in their religion, albeit all the world should give themselves to their superstition and idolatry.

4:7 ¹ I will cause that Israel, which is now as one lame and halting, and so almost destroyed, shall live again, and grow into a great people.

4:8 ¹ Meaning, Jerusalem, where the Lord's flock was gathered.
  ² The flourishing state of the kingdom, as it was under David and Solomon, which thing was accomplished to the Church by the coming of Christ.

4:9 ¹ In the mean season he showeth that they should endure great troubles and temptations when thy saw themselves neither to have king nor counsel.

4:12 ¹ He showeth that the faithful ought not to measure God's judgments by the brags and threatenings of the wicked, but thereby are admonished to lift up their hearts to God to call for deliverance.

4:13 ¹ God giveth his Church this victory, so oft as he overcometh their enemies: but the accomplishment thereof shall be at the last coming of Christ.

1 Now assemble thy garrisons, O daughter [1]of garrisons: he hath laid siege against us: they shall smite the judge of Israel with a rod upon the cheek.

2 And thou Bethlehem Ephrathah art [1]little to be among the thousands of Judah, *yet* out of thee shall he come forth unto me, that shall be the ruler in Israel: whose [2]goings forth *have been* from the beginning *and* from everlasting.

3 Therefore will he give them up, until the time that [1]she which shall bear, shall travail: then the remnant of their brethren shall return unto the children of Israel.

4 And he shall [1]stand, and feed in the strength of the Lord, *and* in the majesty of the Name of the Lord his God, and they shall dwell still: for now shall he be magnified unto the ends of the world.

5 And he [1]shall be *our* peace when Assyria shall come into our land: when he shall tread in our palaces, then shall we raise against him seven shepherds, and eight principal men.

6 And they shall destroy [1]Assyria with the sword, and the land of Nimrod with their swords: thus shall he [2]deliver *us* from Assyria, when he cometh into our land, and when he shall tread within our borders.

7 And the [1]remnant of Jacob shall be among many people, as a dew from the Lord, *and* as the showers upon the grass, that waiteth not for man, nor hopeth in the sons of Adam.

8 And the remnant of Jacob shall be among the Gentiles in the midst of many people, as the Lion among the beasts of the forest, *and* as the Lion whelp among the flocks of sheep, who when he goeth through, treadeth down and teareth in pieces, and none can deliver.

9 Thine hand shall be lifted up upon thine adversaries, and all thine enemies shall be cut off.

10 And it shall come to pass in that day, saith the Lord, that I will cut off thine [1]horses out of the midst of thee, and I will destroy thy chariots.

11 And I will cut off the cities of thy land, and overthrow all thy strongholds.

12 And I will cut off thine enchanters out of thine hand: and thou shalt have no more soothsayers.

13 Thine idols also will I cut off, and thine images out of the midst of thee: and thou shalt no more worship the work of thine hands.

14 And I will pluck up thy groves out of the midst of thee: so will I destroy thine enemies.

15 And I will execute a vengeance in *my* wrath and indignation upon the heathen, [1]which they have not heard.

6

An exhortation to the dumb creatures to hear the judgment against Israel being unkind. 6 What manner of sacrifices do please God.

1 Hearken ye now what the Lord saith, Arise thou, *and* contend *before* the [1]mountains, and let the hills hear thy voice.

2 Hear ye, O mountains, the Lord's quarrel, and ye mighty foundations of the earth: for the Lord hath a quarrel against his people, and he will plead with Israel.

3 O my people, what have I done unto thee? or wherein have I grieved thee? testify against me.

4 Surely I [1]brought thee up out of the land of Egypt, and redeemed thee out of the house of servants, and I have sent before thee, Moses, Aaron, and Miriam.

5 O my people, remember now what Balak king of Moab had devised, and what Balaam the son of Beor answered him, from [1]Shittim unto Gilgal, that ye may know the [2]righteousness of the Lord.

6 Wherewith [1]shall I come before the Lord, *and*

5:1 [1] He forewarneth them of the dangers that shall come before they enjoy these comforts, showing that forasmuch as Jerusalem was accustomed with her garrisons to trouble others, the Lord would now cause other garrisons to vex her, and that her rulers should be smitten on the face most contemptuously.

5:2 [1] For so the Jews divided their country that for every thousand there was a chief captain: and because Bethlehem was not able to make a thousand, he calleth it little, but yet God will raise up his captain and governor therein: and thus it is not the least by reason of this benefit, as Matt. 2:6.

[2] He showeth that the coming of Christ and all his ways were appointed of God from all eternity.

5:3 [1] He compareth the Jews to women with child, who for a time should have great sorrows, but at length they should have a comfortable deliverance, John 16:21.

5:4 [1] That is, Christ's kingdom shall be stable and everlasting, and his people as well the Gentiles as the Jews shall dwell in safety.

5:5 [1] This Messiah shall be a sufficient safeguard for us, and though the enemy invade us for a time, yet shall God stir up many which shall be able to deliver us.

5:6 [1] These whom God shall raise up for the deliverance of his Church, shall destroy all the enemies thereof, which are meant here by the Assyrians and Babylonians which were the chief at that time.

[2] By these governors will God deliver us when the enemy cometh into our land.

5:7 [1] This remnant or Church which God shall deliver shall only depend on God's power and defense, as doth the grass of the field, and not on the hope of man.

5:10 [1] I will destroy all things wherein thou puttest thy confidence, as thy vain confidence and idolatry, and so will help thee.

5:15 [1] It shall be so terrible that the like hath not been heard of.

6:1 [1] He took the high mountains and hard rocks to witness against the obstinacy of his people.

6:4 [1] I have not hurt thee, but bestowed infinite benefits upon thee.

6:5 [1] That is, remember my benefits from the beginning how I delivered you from Balaam's curse, and also spared you from Shittim, which was in the plain of Moab, till I brought you into the land promised.

[2] That is, the truth of his promise and his manifold benefits toward you.

6:6 [1] Thus the people by hypocrisy ask how to please God and are content to offer sacrifices, but will not change their lives.

bow myself before the high God? shall I come before him with burnt offerings, *and* with calves of a year old?

7 Will the Lord be pleased with thousands of rams, or with ten thousand rivers of oil? shall I give my [1]firstborn for my transgression, *even* the fruit of my body, for the sin of my soul?

8 He hath showed thee, O man, what is good, and what the Lord requireth of thee: [1]surely to do justly, and to love mercy, and to humble thyself, to walk with thy God.

9 The Lord's voice crieth unto the [1]city, and the man of wisdom shall see thy name: Hear the rod, and who hath appointed it.

10 Are yet the treasures of wickedness in the house of the wicked, and the scant measure, that is abominable?

11 Shall I justify the wicked balances, and the bag of deceitful weights?

12 For the rich men thereof [1]are full of cruelty, and the inhabitants thereof have spoken lies, and their tongue *is* deceitful in their mouth.

13 Therefore also will I make thee sick in smiting thee, *and* in making *thee* desolate, because of thy sins.

14 Thou shalt eat and not be satisfied, and [1]thy casting down *shall be* in the midst of thee, and thou [2]shalt take hold, but shalt not deliver, and that which thou deliverest, will I give up to the sword.

15 Thou shalt sow, but not reap: Thou shalt tread the olives, but thou shalt not anoint thee with oil, and *make* sweet wine, but shall not drink wine.

16 For the [1]statutes of Omri are kept, and all the manner of the house of Ahab, and ye walk in their counsels, that I should make thee waste, and the inhabitants thereof an hissing: therefore ye shall bear the reproach of my people.

7 1 *A complaint for the small number of the righteous.* 4 *The wickedness of those times.* 14 *The prosperity of the Church.*

1 Woe is me, for I am as the [1]Summer gatherings, *and* as the grapes of the vintage: there *is* no cluster to eat: my soul desired the first ripe fruits.

2 The good man is perished out of the earth, and there *is* none righteous among men: [1]they all lie in wait for blood: every man hunteth his brother with a net.

3 To make good for the evil of *their* hands, the prince asked, and the judge *judgeth* for a reward: therefore the [1]great man he speaketh out the corruption of his soul: so [2]they wrapped it up.

4 The best of them *is* as [1]a brier, and the most righteous of them *is sharper* than a thorn-hedge: the day of [2]thy watchmen *and* thy visitation cometh: then shall be their confusion.

5 Trust ye not in a friend, neither put ye confidence in a counselor: keep the doors of thy mouth from her that lieth in thy bosom.

6 For the son revileth the father: the daughter riseth up against her mother, the daughter-in-law against her mother-in-law, *and* a man's enemies *are* the men of his own house.

7 Therefore [1]I will look unto the Lord: I will wait for God my Savior: my God will hear me.

8 Rejoice not against me, [1]O mine enemy: though I fall, I shall arise, when I shall sit in darkness, the Lord *shall be* a light unto me.

9 I will bear the wrath of the Lord, because I have sinned against him, until he plead my cause, and execute judgment for me: *then* will he bring me forth to the light, *and* I shall see his righteousness.

10 Then she that is mine enemy, shall look upon it, and shame shall cover her, which said unto me, Where is the Lord thy God? Mine eyes shall behold

6:7 [1] There is nothing so dear to man, but the hypocrites will offer it unto God, if they think thereby to avoid his anger: but they will never be brought to mortify their own affections, and to give themselves willingly to serve God as he commandeth.
6:8 [1] The Prophet in few words calleth them to the observation of the second Table, to know if they will obey God aright or no, saying that God hath prescribed them to do this.
6:9 [1] Meaning, that when God speaketh to any city or nation, the godly will acknowledge his majesty and consider not the mortal man that bringeth the threatening, but God that sendeth it.
6:12 [1] That is, of Jerusalem.
6:14 [1] Thou shalt be consumed with inward grief and evils.
[2] Meaning, that the city should go about to save her men, as they that lay hold on that which they would preserve.
6:16 [1] You have received all the corruption and idolatry, wherewith the ten tribes were infected under Omri and Ahab his son: and to excuse your doings, you allege the King's authority by his statutes, and also wisdom and policy in so doing, but you shall not escape punishment: but as I have shown you great favor, and taken you for

my people, so shall your plagues be accordingly, Luke 12:47.
7:1 [1] The Prophet taketh upon him the person of the earth, which complaineth that all her fruits are gone, so that none is left: that is, that there is no godly man remaining: for all are given to cruelty and deceit, so that none spareth his own brother.
7:2 [1] He showeth that the prince, the judge, and the rich man are linked together all to do evil, and to cloak the doings one of another.
7:3 [1] That is, the rich man that is able to give money, abstaineth from no wickedness nor injury.
[2] These men agree among themselves and conspire with one consent to do evil.
7:4 [1] They that are of most estimation and are counted most honest among them, are but thorns and briers to prick.
[2] Meaning of the Prophets and governors.
7:7 [1] The Prophet showeth that the only remedy for the godly in desperate evils, is to flee unto God for succor.
7:8 [1] This is spoken in the person of the Church which calleth the malignant Church her enemy.

her: now shall she be trodden down as the mire of the streets.

11 *This is* [1]the day, that thy walls shall be built: this day shall drive far away [2]the decree.

12 In this day also they shall come unto thee from [1]Assyria, and *from* the strong cities, and from the strongholds even unto the river, and from Sea to Sea, and from mountain to mountain.

13 Notwithstanding the land shall be desolate because of them that dwell therein, *and* for the fruits of [1]their inventions.

14 [1]Feed thy people with thy rod, the flock of thine heritage (which dwell solitary in the wood) *as* in the midst of Carmel: let them feed in Bashan and Gilead, as in old time.

15 [1]According to the days of thy coming out of the land of Egypt, will I show unto him marvelous things.

16 The nations shall see, and be confounded for all their power: they shall [1]lay their hand upon their mouth: [2]their ears shall be deaf.

17 They shall [1]lick the dust like a serpent: they shall move out of their holes like worms: they shall be afraid of the Lord our God, and shall fear because of thee.

18 Who is a God like unto thee, that taketh away iniquity, and [1]passeth by the transgression of the remnant of his heritage! He retaineth not his wrath forever, because mercy pleaseth him.

19 He will turn again, *and* have compassion upon us: he will subdue our iniquities, and cast all [1]their sins into the bottom of the sea.

20 Thou wilt perform *thy* [1]truth to Jacob, *and* mercy to Abraham, as thou hast sworn unto our fathers in old time.

7:11 [1] To wit, when God shall show himself a deliverer of his Church, and a destroyer of his enemies.

[2] Meaning, the cruel empire of the Babylonians.

7:12 [1] When the Church shall be restored, they that were enemies afore, shall come out of all the corners of the world unto her, so that neither holds, rivers, seas, nor mountains shall be able to let them.

7:13 [1] Afore this grace appear, he showeth how grievously the hypocrites themselves shall be punished, seeing that the earth itself, which cannot sin shall be made waste because of their wickedness.

7:14 [1] The Prophet prayeth to God to be merciful unto his Church, when they should be scattered abroad as in solitary places in Bab-

ylon, and to be beneficial unto them as in times past.

7:15 [1] God promiseth to be favorable to his people, as he had been afore time.

7:16 [1] They shall be as dumb men, and dare brag no more.

[2] They shall be astonished and afraid to hear men speak, lest they should hear of their destruction.

7:17 [1] They shall fall flat on the ground for fear.

7:18 [1] As though he would not see it, but wink at it.

7:19 [1] Meaning of his elect.

7:20 [1] The Church is assured, that God will declare in effect the truth of his merciful promise, which he had made of old to Abraham, and to all that should apprehend the promise by faith.

NAHUM

1 *Of the destruction of the Assyrians, and of the deliverance of Israel.*

1 The [1]burden of Nineveh. [2]The book of the vision of Nahum the [3]Elkoshite.

2 God *is* [1]jealous, and the Lord revengeth: the Lord revengeth: even the Lord [2]of anger, the Lord will take vengeance on his adversaries, and he reserveth *wrath* for his enemies.

3 The [1]Lord *is* slow to anger, but *he is* great in power, and will not surely clear *the wicked*: the Lord *hath* his way in the whirlwind, and in the storm, and the clouds *are* the dust of his feet.

4 He rebuketh the sea, and drieth it, and he drieth up all the rivers: Bashan is wasted and Carmel, and the flower of Lebanon is wasted.

5 The mountains tremble for him, and the hills melt, and the earth is burnt at his sight, yea the world, and all that dwell therein.

6 [1]Who can stand before his wrath? or who can abide in the fierceness of his wrath? his wrath is poured out like fire, and the rocks are broken by him.

7 The Lord is good [1]*and* as a stronghold in the day of trouble, and he knoweth them that trust in him.

8 But passing over *as* with a flood, he will utterly destroy the [1]place thereof, and darkness shall pursue his enemies.

9 What do ye [1]imagine against the Lord? he will make an utter destruction: affliction shall not rise up the second time.

10 For *he shall come as* unto [1]thorns folden one in another, and as unto drunkards in their drunkenness: they shall be devoured as stubble fully dried.

11 There [1]cometh one out of thee that imagineth evil against the Lord, *even* a wicked counselor.

12 Thus saith the Lord, Though they be [1]quiet, and also many, yet thus shall they be cut off when he shall pass by: though I have afflicted thee, I will afflict thee no more.

13 For now I will break his yoke from thee, and will burst thy bonds in sunder.

14 And the Lord hath given a commandment concerning thee that no more of thy name be [1]sown: out of the house of thy gods will I cut off the graven, and the molten image: I will make it thy grave for thee, for thou art vile.

15 [a]Behold upon the mountains the feet of him that declareth, and publisheth [1]peace: O Judah, keep thy solemn feasts, perform thy vows: for the wicked shall no more pass through thee: he is utterly cut off.

2 *He describeth the victories of the Chaldeans against the Assyrians.*

1 The [1]destroyer is come before thy face: keep the munition: look to the way: make *thy* loins strong: increase *thy* strength mightily.

2 For the Lord hath [1]turned away the glory of Jacob, as the glory of Israel: for the emptiers have emptied them out, and [2]marred their vine branches.

3 The shield of his mighty men is made red, [1]the valiant men are in scarlet: the chariots *shall be as in*

1:1 [1] Read Isa. 13:1.

[2] The vision or revelation, which God commanded Nahum to write concerning the Ninevites.

[3] That is, born in a poor village in the tribe of Simeon.

1:2 [1] Meaning, of his glory.

[2] With his he is but angry for a time, but his anger never assuageth toward the reprobate, though for a time he defer it.

1:3 [1] Thus the wicked would make God's mercy an occasion to sin, but the Prophet willeth them to consider his force and justice.

1:6 [1] If all creatures be at God's commandment, and none is able to resist his wrath, shall man flatter himself, and think by any means to escape, when he provoketh his God to anger?

1:7 [1] Lest the faithful should be discouraged by hearing the power of God, he showeth them that his mercy appertain unto them, and that he hath care over them.

1:8 [1] Signifying, that God will suddenly destroy Nineveh, and the Assyrians, in such sort as they shall lie in perpetual darkness, and never recover their strength again.

1:9 [1] He showeth that the enterprises of the Assyrians against Judah and the Church, were against God, and therefore he would so destroy them at once, that he should not need to return the second time.

1:10 [1] Although the Assyrians think themselves like thorns that prick on all sides, yet the Lord will set fire on them, and as drunken men are not able to stand against any force, so they shall be nothing able to resist him.

1:11 [1] Which may be understood either of Sennacherib, or of the whole body of the people of Nineveh.

1:12 [1] Though they think themselves in most safety, and of greatest strength, yet when God shall pass by, he will destroy them: notwithstanding he comforteth his Church, and promiseth to make an end of punishing them by the Assyrians.

1:14 [1] Meaning, Sennacherib, who should have no more children, but be slain in the house of his gods, 2 Kings 19:36, 37.

1:15 [1] Which peace the Jews should enjoy by the death of Sennacherib.

2:1 [1] That is, Nebuchadnezzar is in readiness to destroy the Assyrians: and the Prophet derideth the enterprises of the Assyrians which prepared to resist him.

2:2 [1] Seeing God hath punished his own people Judah and Israel, he will now punish the enemies by whom he scourged them, read Isa. 10:12.

[2] Signifying, that the Israelites were utterly destroyed.

2:3 [1] Both to fear the enemy, and also that they themselves should not so soon espy blood one of another to discourage them.

the fire *and* flames in the day of his preparation, and [2]the fir trees shall tremble.

4 The chariots shall rage in the streets: they shall run to and fro in the highways: they shall seem like lamps: they shall shoot like the lightning.

5 [1]He shall remember his strong men: they shall stumble as they go: they shall make haste to the walls thereof, and the defense shall be prepared.

6 The gates of the rivers shall be opened, and the palace shall melt.

7 And Huzzab *the Queen* shall be led away captive, and her maids shall lead *her* as with the voice of doves, smiting upon their breasts.

8 But Nineveh is [1]of old like a pool of water: yet they shall flee away. Stand, stand, *shall they cry*: but none shall look back.

9 [1]Spoil ye the silver, spoil the gold: for there is none end of the store *and* glory of all the pleasant vessels.

10 [1]She is empty and void and waste, and the heart melteth, and the knees smite together, and sorrow is in all loins, and the faces [2]of them all gather blackness.

11 Where is the [1]dwelling of the lions, and the pasture of the lion's whelps? where the lion *and* the lioness waked, *and* the lion's whelp, and none made them afraid.

12 The lion did tear in pieces enough for his whelps, and worried for his lioness, and filled his holes with prey, and his dens with spoil.

13 Behold, I *come* unto thee saith the Lord of hosts, and I will burn her chariots in the [1]smoke, and the sword shall devour thy young lions, and I will cut off thy spoil from the earth, and the voice of thy [2]messengers shall no more be heard.

3 1 *Of the fall of Nineveh.*   8 *No power can escape the hand of God.*

1 O bloody city, it is all full of lies *and* robbery: [1]the prey departeth not.

2 The noise of a whip, [1]and the noise of the moving of the wheels, and the beating of the horses, and

the leaping of the chariots.

3 The horseman lifteth up both the bright sword, and the glittering spear, and a multitude *is* slain, and the dead bodies *are* many: there *is* none end of their corpses: they stumble upon their corpses,

4 Because of the multitude of the fornications of the [1]harlot that is beautiful, and is a mistress of witchcraft, and selleth the people through her whoredom, and the nations through her witchcrafts.

5 Behold, *I* come upon thee, saith the Lord of hosts, and will discover thy skirts upon thy face, and will show the nations thy filthiness, and the kingdoms thy shame.

6 And I will cast filth upon thee, and make thee vile, and will set thee as a gazing stock.

7 And it shall come to pass, that all they that look upon thee, shall flee from thee, and say, Nineveh is destroyed, who will have pity upon her? where shall I seek comforters for thee?

8 Art thou better than [1]No, *which was* full of people? that lay in the rivers, and *had* the waters round about it? whose ditch was the sea, *and* her wall *was* from the sea?

9 Ethiopia and Egypt *were* her strength, and there *was* none end: Put and Lubim were [1]her helpers.

10 Yet was she carried away, *and* went into captivity: her young children also were dashed in pieces at the head of all the streets: and they cast lots for her noble men, and all her mighty men were bound in chains.

11 Also thou shalt be drunken: thou shalt hide thyself, and shalt seek help because of the enemy.

12 All thy strong cities *shall be like* fig trees with the first ripe figs: for if they be shaken, they fall into the mouth of the eater.

13 Behold, thy people within thee *are* women: the gates of thy land shall be opened unto thine enemies, *and* the fire shall devour thy bars.

14 Draw thee waters for the siege: fortify thy strongholds: go into the clay, and temper the mortar: make strong brick.

15 There shall the fire devour thee: the sword shall

---

[2] Meaning, their spears should shake and crash together.

2:5 [1] Then the Assyrians shall seek by all means to gather their power, but all things shall fail them.

2:8 [1] The Assyrians will flatter themselves and say, that Nineveh is so ancient that it can never perish, and is as a fishpool, whose waters they that walk on the banks cannot touch, but they shall be scattered, and shall not look back though men would call them.

2:9 [1] God commandeth the enemies to spoil Nineveh, and promiseth them infinite riches and treasures.

2:10 [1] That is, Nineveh, and the men thereof shall be after this sort.
[2] Read Joel 2:6.

2:11 [1] Meaning, Nineveh, whose inhabitants were cruel like the Lions, and given to all oppression, and spared no violence or tyranny

to provide for their wives and children.

2:13 [1] That is, as soon as my wrath beginneth to kindle.
[2] Signifying the heralds, which were accustomed to proclaim war. Some read, of thy gum teeth, wherewith Nineveh was wont to bruise the bones of the poor.

3:1 [1] It never ceaseth to spoil and rob.

3:2 [1] He showeth how the Chaldeans shall haste, and how courageous their horses shall be in beating the ground when they come against the Assyrians.

3:4 [1] He compareth Nineveh to an harlot, which by her beauty and subtlety enticeth young men, and bringeth them to destruction.

3:8 [1] Meaning, Alexandria, which was in league with so many nations, and yet was now destroyed.

3:9 [1] Or, thine.

cut thee off: it shall eat thee up like the ¹locusts, *though* thou be multiplied like the locusts, *and* multiplied like the grasshopper.

16 Thou hast multiplied thy merchants above the stars of heaven: the locust spoileth and flieth away.

17 Thy princes *are* as the grasshoppers, and thy captains as the great grasshoppers which remain in the hedges in the cold day: *but* when the sun ariseth, they flee away, and their place is not known where they are.

18 Thy ¹shepherds do sleep, O king of Assyria: thy strong men lie down: thy people is scattered upon the mountains, and no man gathereth *them*.

19 There is no healing of thy wound: thy plague is grievous: all that hear the brute of thee, shall clap the hands over thee: for upon ¹whom hath not thy malice passed continually?

3:15 ¹ Signifying, that God's judgments should suddenly destroy the Assyrians, as these vermin are with rain or change of weather.

3:18 ¹ Thy princes and counselors.
3:19 ¹ Meaning, that there was no people to whom the Assyrians had not done hurt.

HABAKKUK

1 1 *A complaint against the wicked that persecute the just.*

CHAPTER 1
[a] Zeph. 3:3

1 The burden, which Habakkuk the Prophet did see.

2 O Lord, how long shall I cry, and thou wilt not hear! *even* cry out unto thee [1]for violence, and thou wilt not help!

3 Why dost thou show me iniquity, and cause me to behold sorrow? for spoiling, and violence *are* before me: and there are that raise up strife and contention.

4 Therefore the Law is dissolved, and judgment doth never go forth: for the wicked doth [1]compass about the righteous: therefore [2]wrong judgment proceedeth.

5 Behold among the heathen, and regard, and wonder, *and* marvel: for I will work a work in your days: [1]ye will not believe it, though it be told you.

6 For lo, I raise up the Chaldeans, that bitter and furious nation, which shall go upon the breadth of the land to possess the dwelling places *that are* not theirs.

7 They are terrible and fearful: [1]their judgment, and their dignity shall proceed of themselves.

8 Their horses also are swifter than the leopards, and are more fierce than the wolves in the [a]evening: and their horsemen are many: and their horsemen shall come from far: they shall fly as the eagle hasting to meat.

9 They come all to spoil: for their faces *shall be* an [1]East wind, and they shall gather the captivity [2]as the sand.

10 And they shall mock the Kings, and the princes *shall be* a scorn unto them: they shall deride every stronghold: for they shall gather [1]dust, and take it.

11 Then shall they [1]take a courage, and transgress and do wickedly, *imputing* this their power unto their god.

12 Art not thou of old, O Lord my God, mine holy One? we shall not [1]die: O Lord, thou hast ordained them for judgment, and O God, thou hast established them for correction.

13 *Thou art* of pure eyes, and canst not see evil: thou canst not behold wickedness: wherefore dost thou look upon the transgressors, *and* holdest thy tongue, when the wicked devoureth the man, that is more righteous than he?

14 And makest men as the [1]fishes of the sea, *and* as the creeping things, that have no ruler over them?

15 They take up all with the angle: they catch it in their net, and gather it in their yarn, whereof they rejoice and are glad.

16 Therefore they sacrifice unto their [1]net, and burn incense unto their yarn, because by them their portion *is* fat, and their meat plenteous.

17 Shall they therefore stretch out their net, and not spare continually to slay [1]the nations?

2 1 *A vision.* 5 *Against pride, covetousness, drunkenness, and idolatry.*

1 I will stand upon my [1]watch, and set me upon the tower, and will look and see what he would say unto me, and what I shall answer to him that rebuketh me.

2 And the Lord answered me, and said, Write the vision, and make it plain upon tables, that he may run [1]that readeth it.

3 For the vision *is* yet for an appointed time, but

1:2 [1] The Prophet complaineth unto God, and bewaileth that among the Jews is left none equity and brotherly love: but instead hereof reigneth cruelty, theft, contention and strife.

1:4 [1] To suppress him, if any should show himself zealous of God's cause.

[2] Because the judges which should redress this excess, are as evil as the rest.

1:5 [1] As in times past you would not believe God's word, so shall ye not now believe the strange plagues which are at hand.

1:7 [1] They themselves shall be your judges in this cause, and none shall have authority over them to control them.

1:9 [1] For the Jews most feared this wind, because it destroyed their fruits.

[2] They shall be so many in number.

1:10 [1] They shall cast up mounts against it.

1:11 [1] The Prophet comforteth the faithful that God will also destroy the Babylonians, because they shall abuse this victory, and become proud and insolent, attributing the praise hereof to their idols.

1:12 [1] He assureth the godly of God's protection, showing that the enemy can do no more than God hath appointed, and also that their sins required such a sharp rod.

1:14 [1] So that the great devoureth the small, and the Chaldeans destroy all the world.

1:16 [1] Meaning, that the enemies flatter themselves, and glory in their own force, power and wit.

1:17 [1] Meaning, that they should not.

2:1 [1] I will renounce mine own judgment, and only depend on God to be instructed what I shall answer them that abuse my preaching, and to be armed against all temptations.

2:2 [1] Write it in great letters, that he that runneth may read it.

at the ¹last it shall speak and not lie: though it tarry, wait: for it shall surely come, *and* shall not stay.

4 Behold, ¹he that lifteth up himself, his mind is not upright in him, but the just shall live by his faith,

5 Yea, indeed the proud man *is as* ¹he that transgresseth by wine: therefore shall he not endure, because he hath enlarged his desire as the hell, and is as death, and cannot be satisfied, but gathereth unto him all nations, and heapeth unto him all people.

6 Shall not all these take up a parable against him, and a taunting proverb against him, and say, Ho, he that increaseth *that which is* not his? ¹how long? and he that ladeth himself with thick clay?

7 Shall ¹they not rise up suddenly, that shall bite thee? and awake, that shall stir thee? and thou shalt be their prey?

8 Because thou hast spoiled many nations, all the remnant of the people shall spoil thee, because of men's blood, and for the wrong *done* in the land, in the city, and unto all that dwell therein.

9 Ho, he that coveteth an evil covetousness to his house, that he may set his nest on high, to escape from the power of evil.

10 Thou ¹hast consulted shame to thine own house, by destroying many people, and hast sinned against thine own soul.

11 For the ¹stone shall cry out of the wall, and the beam out of the timber shall answer it.

12 Woe unto him that buildeth a town with blood, and erecteth a city by iniquity.

13 Behold, is it not of the ¹Lord of hosts, that the people shall labor in the very fire? the people shall even weary themselves for very vanity.

14 For the earth shall ¹be filled with the knowledge of the glory of the Lord, as the waters cover the sea.

15 Woe unto him that giveth his neighbor ¹drink: thou joinest thine heat, and makest *him* drunken also, that thou mayest see their privities.

16 Thou art filled with shame ¹for glory: drink thou also, and be made naked: the cup of the Lord's right hand shall be turned unto thee, and shameful spewing *shall be* for thy glory.

17 For the ¹cruelty of Lebanon shall cover thee: so shall the spoil of the beasts, which made them afraid, because of men's blood, and for the wrong *done* in the land, in the city, and unto all that dwell therein.

18 What profiteth the ¹image? for the maker therefore hath made it an image, and a teacher of lies, though he that made it, trust therein, when he maketh dumb idols.

19 Woe unto him that saith to the wood, Awake, *and* to the dumb stone, Rise up, it shall teach thee: ¹behold, it is laid over with gold and silver, and there *is* no breath in it.

20 But the Lord *is* in his holy Temple: let all the earth keep silence before him.

3 2 *A prayer for the faithful.*

1 A prayer of Habakkuk the Prophet for the ¹ignorances.

2 ¹O Lord, I have heard thy voice, *and* was afraid: O Lord, revive thy ²work in the midst of the people, in the midst of the years make it known: in wrath remember mercy.

2:3 ¹ Which contained the destruction of the enemy, and the comfort of the Church: which thing though God execute not according to man's hasty affections, yet the issue of both is certain at his time appointed.

2:4 ¹ To trust in himself, or in any worldly thing, is never to be quiet: for the only rest is to stay upon God by faith, Rom. 1:17; Gal. 3:11; Heb. 10:38.

2:5 ¹ He compareth the proud and covetous man to a drunkard that is without reason and sense, whom God will punish and make him a laughing stock to all the world: and this he speaketh for the comfort of the godly, and against the Chaldeans.

2:6 ¹ Signifying, that all the world shall wish the destruction of tyrants, and that by their oppression and covetousness, they heap upon themselves more heavy burdens: for the more they get, the more are they troubled.

2:7 ¹ That is, the Medes and Persians, that should destroy the Babylonians?

2:10 ¹ Signifying, that the covetous man is the ruin of his own house, when as he thinketh to enrich it by cruelty and oppression.

2:11 ¹ The stones of the house shall cry, and say that they are built of blood, and the wood shall answer and say the same of itself.

2:13 ¹ Meaning, that God will not defer his vengeance long, but will come and destroy all their labors, as though they were consumed with fire.

2:14 ¹ In the destruction of the Babylonians his glory shall appear through all the world.

2:15 ¹ He reproacheth thus the king of Babylon, who as he was drunken with covetousness and cruelty, so he provoked others to the same, and inflamed them by his rage, and so in the end brought them to shame.

2:16 ¹ Whereas thou thoughtest to have glory of these thy doings, they shall turn to thy shame: for thou shalt drink of the same cup with others in thy turn.

2:17 ¹ Because the Babylonians were cruel not only against other nations, but also against the people of God, which is meant by Lebanon and the beasts therein, he showeth that the like cruelty shall be executed against them.

2:18 ¹ He showeth that the Babylonians' gods could nothing avail them, for they were but blocks or stones, read Jer. 10:8.

2:19 ¹ If thou wilt consider what it is, and how that it hath neither breath nor life, but is a dead thing.

3:1 ¹ The Prophet instructeth his people to pray unto God, not only for their great sins but also for such as they had committed of ignorance.

3:2 ¹ Thus the people were afraid when they heard God's threatenings, and prayed.

² That is, the state of thy Church which is now ready to perish, before it come to half a perfect age, which should be under Christ.

3 God cometh from ¹Teman, and the holy One from mount Paran, Selah. His glory covereth the heavens, and the earth is full of his praise,

4 And *his* brightness was as the light: ¹he had horns *coming* out of his hands, *and* there was the hiding of his power.

5 Before him went the pestilence, and burning coals went forth before his feet.

6 He stood and measured the earth: he beheld and dissolved the nations, and the everlasting mountains were broken, *and* the ancient hills did bow: his ¹ways *are* everlasting.

7 ¹For *his* iniquity I saw the tents of Cushan, *and* the curtains of the land of Midian did tremble.

8 Was the Lord angry against the ¹rivers? or was thine anger against the floods? or was thy wrath against the sea, that thou didst ride ²upon thine horses? thy chariots brought salvation.

9 Thy ¹bow was manifestly revealed, *and* the ²oaths of the tribes *were* a sure word, Selah, thou ³didst cleave the earth with rivers.

10 The mountains saw thee, and they trembled: the stream of the water ¹passed by: the deep made a noise, and lifted up his hand on high.

11 The ¹sun *and* moon stood still in *their* habitation: ²at the light of thine arrows they went, *and* at the bright shining of thy spears.

12 Thou trodest down the land in anger, *and* didst thresh the heathen in displeasure.

13 Thou wentest forth for the salvation of thy people, *even* for salvation with thine ¹Anointed: thou hast wounded the head of the house of the wicked, and discoveredst the foundations unto the ²neck, Selah.

14 Thou didst ¹strike through with his own staves the heads of his villages: they came out as a whirlwind to scatter me: their rejoicing *was* as to devour the poor secretly.

15 Thou didst walk in the sea with thine horses upon the heap of great waters.

16 When I ¹heard, my belly trembled: my lips shook at the voice: rottenness entered into my bones, and I trembled in myself, that I might rest in ²the day of trouble: *for* when he cometh up ³unto the people, he shall destroy them.

17 For the fig tree shall not flourish, neither shall fruit *be* in the vines: the labor of the olive shall fail, and the fields shall yield no meat: the sheep shall be cut off from the fold, and there shall be no bullock in the stalls.

18 But I will rejoice in the Lord: I will joy ¹in the God of my salvation.

19 The Lord God *is* my strength: he will make my feet like hinds' *feet*, and he will make me to walk upon mine high places. ¹To the chief singer on Neginoth.

3:3 ¹ Teman and Paran were near Sinai, where the Law was given: whereby is signified that his deliverance was as present now as it was then.

3:4 ¹ Whereby is meant a power that was joined with his brightness, which was hid to the rest of the world, but was revealed in mount Sinai to his people, Ps. 31:16.

3:6 ¹ Signifying, that God hath wonderful means, and ever had a marvelous power when he would deliver his Church.

3:7 ¹ The iniquity of the king of Syria in vexing thy people was made manifest by thy judgment, to the comfort of thy Church, Judg. 5:10, and also of the Midianites, which destroyed themselves, Judg. 7:22.

3:8 ¹ Meaning, that God was not angry with the waters, but that by this means he would destroy his enemies, and deliver his Church.

² And so didst use all the elements as instruments for the destruction of thine enemies.

3:9 ¹ That is, thy power.

² For he had not only made a covenant with Abraham, but renewed it with his posterity.

³ Read Num. 20:11.

3:10 ¹ He alludeth to the red sea and Jordan, which gave passage to God's people, and showed signs of their obedience as it were by the lifting up their hands.

3:11 ¹ As appeareth, Josh. 10:11.

² According to thy commandment, the sun was directed by the weapons of thy people, that fought in thy cause, as though it durst not go forward.

3:13 ¹ Signifying, that there is no salvation, but by Christ.

² From the top to the toe thou hast destroyed the enemies.

3:14 ¹ God destroyed his enemies both great and small with their own weapons, though they were never so fierce against his Church.

3:16 ¹ He returneth to that which he spake in the second verse, and showeth how he was afraid of God's judgments.

² He showeth that the faithful can never have true rest, except they feel before the weight of God's judgments.

³ That is, the enemy, but the godly shall be quiet, knowing that all things shall turn to good unto them.

3:18 ¹ He declareth wherein standeth the comfort and joy of the faithful, though they see never so great afflictions prepared.

3:19 ¹ The chief singer upon the instruments of music, shall have occasion to praise God for this great deliverance of his Church.

ZEPHANIAH

1

4 Threatenings against Judah and Jerusalem, because of their idolatry.

1 The word of the Lord, which came unto Zephaniah the son of Cushi, the son of Gedaliah, the son of Amariah, the son of Hezekiah, in the days of ^aJosiah, the son of ^bAmon king of Judah.

2 I will surely destroy all things from off the land, saith the Lord.

3 I will destroy man and beast: I will destroy the ¹fowls of the heaven, and the fishes of the sea, and ruins *shall be* to the wicked, and I will cut off man from off the land, saith the Lord.

4 I will also stretch out mine hand upon Judah, and upon all the inhabitants of Jerusalem, and I will cut off the remnant of Baal from this place, *and the* name of the ¹Chemarims with the Priests,

5 And them that worship the host of heaven upon the housetops, and them that worship and swear by the Lord, and swear by ¹Milcam.

6 And them that are turned back from the Lord, and those that have not sought the Lord, nor inquired for him.

7 Be still at the presence of the Lord God: for the day of the Lord is at hand: for the Lord hath prepared a sacrifice, *and* hath sanctified his guests.

8 And it shall be in the day of the Lord's sacrifice, that I will visit the princes and the king's children, and all such as are clothed with ¹strange apparel.

9 In the same day also will I visit all those that ¹dance upon the threshold so proudly, which fill their masters' houses by cruelty and deceit.

10 And in that day, saith the Lord, there *shall be* a noise, *and* cry from the ¹fish gate, and an howling from the second *gate*, and a great destruction from the hills.

11 Howl ye inhabitants of ¹the low place: for the company of the merchants is destroyed: all they that bear silver, are cut off.

12 And at that time will I search Jerusalem with ¹lights, and visit the men that are frozen ²in their dregs, and say in their hearts, The Lord will neither do good nor do evil.

13 Therefore their goods shall be spoiled, and their houses waste: ^cthey shall also build houses, but not inhabit *them*, and they shall plant vineyards, but not drink the wine thereof.

14 The great day of the Lord *is* near: it *is* near, and hasteth greatly, *even* the voice of the day of the Lord: ¹the strong man shall cry there bitterly.

15 ^dThat day *is* a day of wrath, a day of trouble and heaviness, a day of destruction and desolation, a day of obscurity and darkness, a day of clouds and blackness,

16 A day of the trumpet and alarm against the strong cities, and against the high towers.

17 And I will bring distress upon men, that they shall walk like blind men, because they have sinned against the Lord, and their blood shall be poured out as dust, and their flesh as the dung.

18 ^eNeither their silver nor their gold shall be able to deliver them in the day of the Lord's wrath, but the ^fwhole land shall be devoured by the fire of his jealousy: for he shall make even a speedy riddance of all them that dwell in the land.

2

1 He moveth to return to God, 5 prophesying destruction against the Philistines, Moabites and others.

1 Gather ¹yourselves, even gather you, O nation not worthy to be loved,

2 Before the decree come forth, *and ye be* as chaff that passeth in a day, *and* before the fierce wrath of the Lord come upon you, *and* before the day of the

CHAPTER 1
^a 2 Kings 22:1
^b 2 Kings 21:19
^c Deut. 28:30
Amos 5:11
^d Jer. 30:7
Joel 2:11
Amos 5:18
^e Ezek. 7:19
^f Zeph. 3:1

1:3 ¹ Not that God was angry with these dumb creatures, but because man was so wicked for whose cause they were created, God maketh them to take part of the punishments with him.

1:4 ¹ Which were an order of superstitious priests appointed to minister in the service of Baal, and were as his peculiar chaplains, read 2 Kings 23:5; Hos. 10:5.

1:5 ¹ He alludeth to their idol Molech which was forbidden, Lev. 20:2, yet they called him, their king, and made him as a god: therefore he here noteth them that will both say they worship God, and yet will swear by idols and serve them: which halting is here condemned, as Ezek. 20:39; 1 Kings 18:21; 2 Kings 17:33.

1:8 ¹ Meaning, the courtiers, which did imitate the strange apparel of other nations to win their favor thereby, and to appear glorious in the eyes of all others, read Ezek. 23:14, 15.

1:9 ¹ He meaneth the servants of the rulers which invade other men's houses, and rejoice and leap for joy, when they can get any prey to please their master withall.

1:10 ¹ Signifying, that all the corners of the city of Jerusalem should be full of trouble.

1:11 ¹ This is meant of the street of the merchants which was lower than the rest of the place about it.

1:12 ¹ So that nothing shall escape me.

² By their prosperity they are hardened in their wickedness.

1:14 ¹ They that trusted in their own strength and contemned the Prophets of God.

2:1 ¹ He exhorteth them to repentance, and willeth them to descend into themselves and gather themselves, lest they be scattered like chaff.

Lord's anger come upon you.

3 Seek ye the Lord all the meek of the earth, which [1]have wrought his judgment: seek righteousness, seek lowliness, if so be that ye may be hid in the day of the Lord's wrath.

4 For [1]Gaza shall be forsaken, and Ashkelon desolate: they shall drive out Ashdod at the noon day, and Ekron shall be rooted up.

5 [Woe] unto the inhabitants of the sea [1]coast. the nation of the Cherethims, the word of the Lord is against you: O Canaan, the land of the Philistines, I will even destroy thee without an inhabitant.

6 And the sea coast shall be dwellings *and* cottages for shepherds and sheepfolds.

7 And *that* coast shall be for the [1]remnant of the house of Judah, to feed thereupon: in the houses of Ashkelon shall they judge toward night: for the Lord their God shall visit them, and turn away their captivity.

8 I have heard the reproach of Moab, and the rebukes of the children of Ammon, whereby they upbraided my people, and [1]magnified themselves against their borders.

9 Therefore, as I live, saith the Lord of hosts, the God of Israel, Surely Moab shall be as Sodom, and the children of Ammon as Gomorrah, *even* the breeding of nettles, and salt pits, and a perpetual desolation, the residue of my folk shall spoil them, and the remnant of my people shall possess them.

10 This shall they have for their pride, because they have reproached, and magnified themselves against the Lord of host's people.

11 The Lord *will be* terrible unto them: [1]for he will consume all the gods of the earth, and every man shall worship him from his place, *even* all the isles of the heathen.

12 Ye Morians also shall be slain by my sword with them.

13 And he will stretch out his hand against the North, and destroy Assyria, and will make Nineveh

CHAPTER 3
[a] Ezek. 22:25,27
  Mic. 3:11
[b] Hab. 1:8

desolate, *and* waste like a wilderness.

14 And flocks shall lie in the midst of her, and all the beasts of the nations, and the [1]pelican and the [2]owl shall abide in the upper posts of it: the voice *of* birds shall sing in the windows, *and* desolations *shall be* upon the posts: for the cedars are uncovered.

15 This is the [1]rejoicing city that dwelt careless, that said in her heart, I am, and there *is* none besides me: how is she made waste, and the lodging of the beasts! everyone that passeth by her shall hiss and wag his hand.

3

4 Against the governors of Jerusalem.   8 Of the calling of all the Gentiles.   13 A comfort to the residue of Israel.

1 Woe to her that is filthy and polluted, to the robbing [1]city.

2 She heard not the voice: she received not correction: she trusted not in the Lord: she drew not near to her God.

3 Her princes within her *are* as roaring [a]lions: her judges *are* as [b]wolves in the evening, *which* [1]leave not the bones till the morrow.

4 Her prophets are light, *and* wicked persons: her priests have polluted the Sanctuary: they have wrested the Law.

5 The [1]just Lord *is* in the midst thereof: he will do none iniquity: every morning doth he bring his judgment to light, he faileth not: but the wicked will not learn to be ashamed.

6 I have [1]cut off the nations: their towers are desolate: I have made their streets waste, that none shall pass by, their cities are destroyed without man, *and* without inhabitant.

7 I said, surely thou wilt fear me: thou wilt receive instruction: so their dwelling should not be destroyed howsoever I visited them, but [1]they rose early, *and* corrupted all their works.

8 Therefore [1]wait ye upon me, saith the Lord, until the day that I rise up to the prey: for I am determined to gather the nations, and that I will

---

2:3 [1] That is, which have lived uprightly and godly according as he prescribeth by his word.
2:4 [1] He comforteth the faithful in that God would change his punishments from them unto the Philistines their enemies and other nations.
2:5 [1] That is, Galilee: by these nations he meaneth the people that dwelt near to the Jews, and instead of friendship were their enemies: therefore he calleth them Canaanites whom the Lord appointed to be slain.
2:7 [1] He showeth why God would destroy their enemies, because their country might be a resting place for his Church.
2:8 [1] These nations presumed to take from the Jews that country which the Lord had given them.
2:11 [1] When he shall deliver his people and destroy their enemies and Idols, his glory shall shine throughout all the world.
2:14 [1] Read Isa. 34:11.

[2] Or, hedgehog.
2:15 [1] Meaning, Nineveh, which rejoicing so much of her strength and prosperity, should be thus made waste, and God's people delivered.
3:1 [1] That is, Jerusalem.
3:3 [1] They are so greedy that they eat up bones and all.
3:5 [1] The wicked thus boasted that God was ever among them, but the Prophet answereth that that cannot excuse their wickedness: for God will not bear with their sins: yet that he did patiently abide and sent his Prophets continually to call them to repentance, but he profited nothing.
3:6 [1] By the destruction of other nations he showeth that the Jews should have learned to fear God.
3:7 [1] They were most earnest and ready to do wickedly.
3:8 [1] Seeing ye will not repent, you shall look for my vengeance as well as other nations.

assemble the kingdoms to pour upon them mine indignation, *even* all my fierce wrath: for all the earth shall be devoured with the fire of my jealousy.

9 Surely [1]then will I turn to the people a pure language, that they may all call upon the name of the Lord to serve him [2]with one consent.

10 From beyond the rivers of Ethiopia, the [1]daughter of my dispersed, praying unto me, shall bring me an offering.

11 In that day shalt thou not be ashamed for [1]all thy works, wherein thou hast transgressed against me: for then will I take away out of the midst of thee them that rejoice of thy pride, and thou shalt no more be proud of mine holy mountain.

12 Then will I leave in the midst of thee an humble and poor people: and they shall trust in the Name of the Lord.

13 The remnant of Israel shall do none iniquity, nor speak lies: neither shall a deceitful tongue be found in their mouth: for they shall be fed and lie down, and none shall make them afraid.

14 Rejoice, O daughter Zion: be ye joyful, O Israel: be glad and rejoice with all *thine* heart, O daughter Jerusalem.

15 The Lord hath taken away thy [1]judgments: he hath cast out thine [2]enemy: the king of Israel, *even* the Lord *is* in the midst of [3]thee: thou shalt see no more evil.

16 In that day it shall be said to Jerusalem, Fear thou not, O Zion, let not thine hands be faint.

17 The Lord thy God in the midst of thee *is* mighty: he will save, he will rejoice over thee with joy: he will quiet himself in [1]his love: he will rejoice over thee with joy.

18 After a certain time will I gather the afflicted that were of thee, *and* them that bare the reproach for [1]it.

19 Behold, at that time I will bruise all that afflict thee, and I will [1]save her that halteth, and gather her that was cast out, and I will get them praise and fame in all the [2]lands of their shame.

20 At that time will I bring you again, and then will I gather you: for I will give you a name and a praise among all people of the earth, when I turn back your captivity before your eyes, saith the Lord.

3:9 [1] Lest any should think then that God's glory should have perished when Judah was destroyed, he showeth that he will publish his grace through all the world.
[2] Hebrew, *with one shoulder*, as Hos. 6:9.
3:10 [1] That is, the Jews shall come as well as the Gentiles: which is to be understood under the time of the Gospel.
3:11 [1] For they shall have full remission of their sins, and the hypocrites which boasted of the Temple, which was also thy pride in times past, shall be taken from thee.
3:15 [1] That is, the punishment for thy sin.

[2] As the Assyrians, Chaldeans, Egyptians and other nations.
[3] To defend thee as by thy sins thou hast put him away, and left thyself naked, as Exod. 32:25.
3:17 [1] Signifying, that God delighteth to show his love and great affection toward his Church.
3:18 [1] That is, them that were had in hatred and reviled for the Church, and because of their religion.
3:19 [1] I will deliver the Church, which now is afflicted, as Mic. 4:6.
[2] As among the Assyrians and Chaldeans which did mock them and put them to shame.

HAGGAI

1

1 The time of the Prophecy of Haggai. 8 An exhortation to build the Temple again.

1 In the second year of king [1]Darius, in the sixth month, the first day of the month, came the word of the Lord (by the ministry of the Prophet Haggai) unto [2]Zerubbabel the son of Shealtiel, a prince of Judah, and to Jehoshua the son of Jehozadak the high Priest, saying,

2 Thus speaketh the Lord of hosts, saying, This people say, the time is not yet come, [1]that the Lord's house should be built.

3 Then came the word of the Lord by the ministry of the Prophet Haggai, saying,

4 Is it time for yourselves to dwell in your [1]ceiled houses, and this house lie waste?

5 Now therefore thus saith the Lord of hosts, Consider your own ways in your hearts.

6 [1]Ye have sown much, and bring in little: ye eat, but ye have not enough: ye drink, but ye are not filled: ye clothe you, but ye be not warm: and he that earneth wages, putteth the wages into a broken bag.

7 Thus saith the Lord of hosts, Consider your own ways in your hearts.

8 Go [1]up to the mountain, and bring wood, and build this House, and [2]I will be favorable in it, and I will [3]be glorified, saith the Lord.

9 Ye looked for much, and lo, *it came* to little: and when ye brought it home, I did blow [1]upon it. And why, saith the Lord of hosts? Because of mine House that is waste, and ye turn every man unto his own house.

10 Therefore the heaven over you stayed itself from dew, and the earth stayed her fruit.

11 And I called for a drought upon the land, and upon the mountains, and upon the corn, and upon the wine, and upon the oil, upon *all* that the ground bringeth forth: both upon men and upon cattle, and upon all the labor of the hands.

12 When Zerubbabel the son of Shealtiel, and Joshua the son of Jehozadak the high Priest, with all the remnant of the people, heard the [1]voice of the Lord their God, and the words of the Prophet Haggai (as the Lord their God had sent him) then the people did fear before the Lord.

13 Then spake Haggai the Lord's messenger in the Lord's message unto the people, saying, I am with you, saith the Lord.

14 And the Lord stirred up [1]the spirit of Zerubbabel the son of Shealtiel, a prince of Judah, and the spirit of Joshua the son of Jehozadak the high Priest, and the spirit of all the remnant of the people, and they came, and did the work in the House of the Lord of hosts their God.

2

He showeth that the glory of the second Temple shall exceed the first.

1 In the four and twentieth day of the sixth month, in the second year of king Darius,

2 In the seventh *month*, in the one and twentieth *day* of the month, came the word of the Lord by the ministry of the Prophet Haggai, saying,

3 Speak now to Zerubbabel the son of Shealtiel prince of Judah, and to Joshua the son of Jehozadak the high Priest, and to the residue of the people, saying,

4 Who is left among you that saw this [1]House in her first glory, and how do you see it now? is it not in your eyes, in comparison of it as nothing?

5 Yet now be of good courage, O Zerubbabel,

1:1 [1] Who was the son of Histaspis and the third king of the Persians, as some think.

[2] Because the building of the Temple began to cease, by reason that the people were discouraged by their enemies: and if these two notable men had need to be stirred up and admonished of their duties, what shall we think of other governors, whose doings are either against God, or very cold in his cause?

1:2 [1] Not that they condemned the building thereof, but they preferred policy and private profit to religion, being content with small beginnings.

1:4 [1] Showing that they sought not only their necessities, but their very pleasures before God's honor.

1:6 [1] Consider the plagues of God upon you for preferring your policies to his religion, and because ye seek not him first of all.

1:8 [1] Meaning, that they should leave off their own commodities, and go forward in the building of God's Temple, and in the setting forth of his religion.

[2] That is, I will hear your prayers according to my promise, 1 Kings 8:21, 29.

[3] That is, my glory shall be set forth by you.

1:9 [1] And so bring it to nothing.

1:12 [1] This declareth that God was the author of the doctrine, and that he was but the minister, as Exod. 14:31; Judg. 7:20; Acts 15:28.

1:14 [1] Which declareth that men are inept and dull to serve the Lord, neither can they obey his word or his messengers, before God reform their hearts, and give them new spirits, John 6:44.

2:4 [1] For the people according as Isa. 30:19 and Ezek. 41:1, had prophesied, thought this Temple should have been more excellent than Solomon's Temple, which was destroyed by the Babylonians, but the Prophets meant the spiritual Temple, The Church of Christ.

saith the Lord, and be of good comfort, O Joshua, son of Jehozadak the high Priest: and be strong, all ye people of the land, saith the Lord, and ¹do it: for I am with you, saith the Lord of hosts.

6 *According* to the word that I covenanted with you, when ye came out of Egypt: so my Spirit shall remain among you, fear ye not.

7 For thus saith the Lord of hosts, ¹Yet a little while, and I will shake the heavens and the earth, and the sea, and the dry land:

8 And I will move all nations, and ¹the desire of all nations shall come, and I will fill this House with glory, saith the Lord of hosts.

9 The ¹silver *is* mine, and the gold *is* mine, saith the Lord of hosts.

10 The glory of this last House shall be greater than the first, saith the Lord of hosts: and in this place will I give ¹peace, saith the Lord of hosts.

11 ¶ In the four and twentieth *day* of the ninth month, in the second year of Darius, came the word of the Lord unto the Prophet Haggai, saying,

12 Thus saith the Lord of hosts, Ask now the Priests *concerning* the Law, and say,

13 If one bear ¹holy flesh in the skirt of his garment, and with his skirt do touch the bread or the pottage, or the wine, or oil, or any meat, shall it be holy? And the Priests answered and said, No.

14 Then said Haggai, If a polluted person touch any of these, shall it be unclean? And the Priests answered, and said, It shall be unclean.

15 Then answered Haggai, and said, So is this people, and so is this nation before me, saith the Lord: and so *are* all the works of their hands, and that which they offer here, is unclean.

16 And now, I pray you, consider in your minds: from this ¹day and afore, *even* afore a stone was laid upon a stone in the Temple of the Lord:

17 ¹Before these things were, when one came to an heap of twenty *measures*, there were but ten: when one came to the winepress, for to draw out fifty *vessels* out of the press, there were but twenty.

18 I smote you with blasting, and with mildew, and with hail, in all the labors of your hands: yet you *turned* not to me, saith the Lord.

19 Consider, I pray you, in your minds, from ¹this day, and afore, from the four and twentieth day of the ninth *month*, even from the day that the foundation of the Lord's Temple was laid: consider it in your minds.

20 Is the ¹seed yet in the barn? as yet the vine, and the fig tree, and the pomegranate, and the olive tree hath not brought forth: from this day will I bless *you*.

21 And again the word of the Lord came unto Haggai in the four and twentieth *day* of the month, saying,

22 Speak to Zerubbabel the prince of Judah, and say, I ¹will shake the heavens and the earth.

23 And I will overthrow the throne of kingdoms, and I will destroy the strength of the ¹kingdoms of the heathen, and I will overthrow the chariots, and those that ride in them, and the horse and the riders shall come down, every one by the sword of his brother.

24 In that day, saith the Lord of hosts, will I take thee, O Zerubbabel my servant, the son of Shealtiel, saith the Lord, and will make thee as a ¹signet: for I have chosen thee, saith the Lord of hosts.

2:5 ¹ That is, go forward in building the Temple.

2:7 ¹ He exhorteth them to patience though see not as yet this Temple so glorious as the Prophets had declared: for this should be accomplished in Christ, by whom all things should be renewed.

2:8 ¹ Meaning, Christ whom all ought to look for and desire: or by desire he may signify all precious things, as riches, and such like.

2:9 ¹ Therefore when his time cometh he can make all the treasures of the world to serve his purpose: but the glory of this second Temple doth not stand in material things, neither can be built.

2:10 ¹ Meaning, all spiritual blessings and felicity purchased by Christ, Phil. 4:7.

2:13 ¹ That is, the flesh of the sacrifices, whereby he signifieth that thing which of itself is good, cannot make another thing so: and therefore they ought not to justify themselves by their sacrifices and ceremonies: but contrary he that is unclean and not pure of heart, doth corrupt those things and make them detestable unto God, which else are good and godly.

2:16 ¹ Consider how God did plague you with famine afore you began to build the Temple.

2:17 ¹ That is, before the building was begun.

2:19 ¹ From the time they began to build the Temple, he promiseth that God would bless them: and albeit as yet the fruit was not come forth, yet in the gathering they should have plenty.

2:20 ¹ He exhorteth them to patience, and to abide till the harvest came, and then they should see God's blessings.

2:22 ¹ I will make a change, and renew all things in Christ, of whom Zerubbabel here is a figure.

2:23 ¹ Hereby he showeth that there shall be no let or hindrance, when God will make this wonderful restitution of his Church.

2:24 ¹ Signifying that his dignity should be most excellent, which thing was accomplished in Christ.

ZECHARIAH

1 *He exhorteth the people to return to the Lord, and to eschew the wickedness of their fathers.* 16 *He signifieth the restitution of Jerusalem and the Temple.*

CHAPTER 1
a Jer. 3:12
Ezek. 18:30
Hos. 14:2
Joel 2:12

1 In the eighth month of the second year of ¹Darius, came the word of the Lord unto ²Zechariah the son of Berechiah, the son of Iddo the Prophet, saying,

2 The Lord hath been ¹sore displeased with your fathers.

3 Therefore say thou unto them, Thus saith the Lord of hosts, ¹Turn ye unto me, saith the Lord of hosts, and I will turn unto you, saith the Lord of hosts.

4 Be ye not as your fathers, unto whom the former ᵃProphets have cried, saying, Thus saith the Lord of hosts, Turn you now from your evil ways, and from your wicked works: but they would not hear, nor hearken unto me, saith the Lord.

5 Your fathers, where ¹are they? and do the Prophets live forever?

6 But did not my words and my statutes, which I commanded by my servants the Prophets, take hold of ¹your fathers? and ²they returned, and said, As the Lord of hosts hath determined to do unto us according to our own ways, and according to our works, so hath he dealt with us.

7 Upon the four and twentieth day of the eleventh month, which is the month ¹Shebat, in the second year of Darius, came the word of the Lord unto Zechariah the son of Berechiah, the son of Iddo

the Prophet, saying,

8 I ¹saw by night, and behold ²a man riding upon a red horse, and he stood among the myrtle trees that were in a bottom, and behind him were there ³red horses speckled and white.

9 Then said I, O my Lord, what are these? And the Angel that talked with me, said unto me, I will show thee what these be.

10 And the man that stood among the myrtle trees, answered and said, These are they whom the Lord hath sent to go through the world.

11 And they answered the Angel of the Lord that stood among the myrtle trees, and said, We have gone through the world: and behold, all the world sitteth still and is at rest.

12 Then the ¹Angel of the Lord answered and said, O Lord of hosts, how long wilt thou be unmerciful to Jerusalem, and to the cities of Judah, with whom thou hast been displeased now these threescore and ten years?

13 And the Lord answered the Angel that talked with me, with good words *and* comfortable words.

14 So the Angel that communed with me, said unto me, Cry thou, and speak, thus saith the Lord of hosts, I am ¹jealous over Jerusalem and Zion with a great zeal,

15 And am greatly angry against the careless heathen: for I was angry but ¹a little, and they helped forward the affliction.

16 Therefore thus saith the Lord, I will return unto Jerusalem with tender mercy: mine house shall be

---

1:1 ¹ Who was the son of Histaspis.

² This was not that Zechariah, whereof is mentioned 2 Chron. 24:20, but had the same name, and is called the son of Berechiah, as he was, because he came of those progenitors, as of Joiada or Berechiah, and Iddo.

1:2 ¹ He speaketh this to fear them with God's judgments, that they should not provoke him as their fathers had done, whom he so grievously punished.

1:3 ¹ Let your fruits declare that you are God's people, and that he hath wrought in you by his Spirit, and mortified you: for else man hath no power to return to God, but God must convert him, as Jer. 31:18; Lam. 5:21; Isa. 21:8 and 31:6 and 45:21.

1:5 ¹ Though your fathers be dead, yet God's judgments in punishing them ought still to be before your eyes: and though the Prophets be dead, yet their doctrine remaineth forever, 2 Pet. 1:15.

1:6 ¹ Seeing ye saw the force of my doctrine in punishing your fathers, why do ye not fear the threatenings contained in the same, and declared by my Prophets?

² As men astonished with my judgments, and not that they were touched with true repentance.

1:7 ¹ Which containeth part of January and part of February.

1:8 ¹ This vision signifieth the restoration of the Church: but as yet it should not appear to man's eyes, which is here meant by the night, by the bottom, and by the myrrh trees which are black, and give a dark shadow, yet he compareth God to a King, who hath his posts and messengers abroad by whom he still worketh his purpose and bringeth his matters to pass.

² Who was the chief among the rest of the horsemen.

³ These signified the divers offices of God's Angels by whom God sometimes punisheth and sometimes comforteth and bringeth forth his works in divers sorts.

1:12 ¹ That is, Christ the mediator prayed for the salvation of his Church, which was now troubled, when all the countries about them were at rest.

1:14 ¹ Though for a time God defer his help and comfort from his Church, yet this declareth that he loveth them still most dearly, as a most merciful father his children, or an husband his wife, and when it is expedient for them, his help is ever ready.

1:15 ¹ In destroying the reprobate, I showed myself but a little angry toward my church, but the enemy would have destroyed them also, and considered not the end of my chastisements.

built in it, saith the Lord of hosts, and a line [1]shall be stretched upon Jerusalem.

17 Cry yet, and speak, Thus saith the Lord of hosts, My cities shall yet [1]be broken with plenty: the Lord shall yet comfort Zion, and shall yet choose Jerusalem.

18 Then lifted I up mine eyes and saw, and behold, [1]four horns.

19 And I said unto the Angel that talked with me, What be these? And he answered me, These are the horns which have scattered Judah, Israel, and Jerusalem.

20 And the Lord showed me four [1]carpenters.

21 Then said I, What come these to do? And he answered, and said, These are the horns, which have scattered Judah, so that a man durst not lift up his head: but these are come to fray them, and to cast out the horns of the Gentiles, which lifted up their horn over the land of Judah to scatter it.

2 The restoring of Jerusalem and Judah.

1 I lifted up mine eyes again, and looked, and behold, a [1]man with a measuring line in his hand.

2 Then said I, Whither goest thou? And he said unto me, To measure Jerusalem, that I may see what is the breadth thereof, and what is the length thereof.

3 And behold, the Angel that talked with me, went forth, and another Angel went out to meet him,

4 And said unto him, Run, speak to this [1]young man, and say, [2]Jerusalem shall be inhabited without walls, for the multitude of men and cattle therein.

5 For I, saith the Lord, will be unto her a wall of [1]fire round about, and will [2]be the glory in the midst of her.

6 Ho, ho, come [1]forth, and flee from the land of the North, saith the Lord: for I have scattered you into the four [2]winds of the heaven, saith the Lord.

7 [1]Save thyself, O Zion, that dwellest with the daughter of Babel.

8 For thus saith the Lord of hosts, After this [1]glory hath he sent me unto the nations, which spoiled you: for he that toucheth you, toucheth the [2]apple of his eye.

9 For behold, I will lift up mine hand [1]upon them: and [2]they shall be a spoil to those that served them, and ye shall know that the Lord of hosts hath [3]sent me.

10 Rejoice and be glad, O daughter Zion: for lo, I come, and will dwell in the midst of thee, saith the Lord.

11 And many nations shall be joined to the Lord in that day, and shall be my people: and I will dwell in the midst of thee, and thou shalt know that the Lord of hosts hath sent me unto thee.

12 And the Lord shall inherit Judah his portion in the holy land, and shall choose Jerusalem again.

13 Let all flesh be still before the Lord: for he is raised up out of his holy place.

3 A prophecy of Christ and of his kingdom.

1 And he showed me Joshua the high Priest, [1]standing before the Angel of the Lord, and [2]Satan stood at his right hand to resist him.

2 And the [1]Lord said unto Satan, The Lord reprove thee, O Satan: even the Lord that hath chosen Jerusalem, reprove thee. Is not this a [2][brand] taken

---

1:16 [1] To measure out the buildings.
1:17 [1] The abundance shall be so great, that the places of store shall not be able to contain these blessings that God will send, but shall even break for fullness.
1:18 [1] Which signified all the enemies of the Church, East, West, North, South.
1:20 [1] These Carpenters or Smiths are God's instruments, which with their mallets and hammers break these hard and strong horns which should overthrow the Church, and declare that none enemy's horn is so strong, but God hath an hammer to break it in pieces.
2:1 [1] This is the Angel who was Christ: for in respect of his office he is ofttimes called an Angel, but in respect of his eternal essence, is God, and so called.
2:4 [1] Meaning, himself Zechariah.
　[2] Signifying the spiritual Jerusalem and Church under Christ, which should be extended by the Gospel through all the world, and should need no material walls, nor trust in any worldly strength, but should be safely preserved and dwell in peace among all their enemies.
2:5 [1] To defend my Church, to fear the enemies and to destroy them if they approach near.
　[2] In me they shall have their full felicity and glory.
2:6 [1] He calleth to them, which partly for fear, and partly for their own case, remained still in captivity, and so preferred their own pri-

vate commodities to the benefits of God promised in his Church.
　[2] As it was I that scattered you, so have I power to restore you.
2:7 [1] By fleeing from Babylon, and coming to the Church.
2:8 [1] Seeing that God had begun to show his grace among you by delivering you, he continueth the same still toward you, and therefore sendeth me his Angel and his Christ to defend you from your enemies, that they shall not hurt you, neither by the way nor at home.
　[2] Ye are so dear unto God, that he can no more suffer your enemies to hurt you, than a man can abide to be thrust in the eye, Ps. 17:8.
2:9 [1] Upon the heathen your enemies.
　[2] They shall be your servants, as you have been theirs.
　[3] This must necessarily be understood of Christ, who being God equal with his Father, was sent as he was Mediator to dwell in his Church and to govern them.
3:1 [1] He prayed to Christ the Mediator for the state of the Church.
　[2] Which declareth that the faithful have not only war with flesh and blood, but with Satan himself and spiritual wickedness, Eph. 6:12.
3:2 [1] That is, Christ speaketh to God as the Mediator of his Church, that he would rebuke Satan: and here he showeth himself to be the continual preserver of his Church.
　[2] Meaning, that Joshua was wonderfully preserved in the captivity, and now Satan sought to afflict and trouble him when he was doing his office.

out of the fire?

3 Now Joshua was clothed with [1]filthy garments, and stood before the Angel.

4 And he answered and spake unto those that stood before him, saying, Take away the [1]filthy garments from him. And unto him he said, Behold, I have [2]caused thine iniquity to depart from thee, and I will clothe thee with change of raiment.

5 And I said, Let them [1]set a fair diadem upon his head. So they set a fair diadem upon his head, and clothed him with garments, and the Angel of the Lord stood by.

6 And the Angel of the Lord testified unto Joshua, saying,

7 Thus saith the Lord of hosts, If thou wilt walk in my ways, and keep my watch, thou shalt also [1]judge mine house, and shalt also keep my [2]courts, and I will give thee place among [3]these that stand by.

8 Hear now, O Joshua the high Priest, thou and thy fellows that sit before thee: for they [1]are monstrous persons: but behold, I will bring forth the [2]Branch my servant.

9 For lo, the [1]stone that I have laid before Joshua: upon one stone shall be seven eyes: behold, I [2]will cut out the graving thereof, saith the Lord of hosts, and I will take [3]away the iniquity of this land in one day.

10 In that day, saith the Lord of hosts, shall ye call every man his neighbor under the [1]vine, and under the fig tree.

4

The vision of the golden candlestick, and the exposition thereof.

1 And the Angel that talked with me, came again and waked me, as a man that is raised out of his sleep,

2 And said unto me, What seest thou? And I said, I have looked, and behold, a [1]candlestick all of gold with a bowl upon the top of it, and his seven lamps therein, and seven [2]pipes to the lamps which were upon the top thereof,

3 And two olive trees over it, one upon the right side of the bowl, and the other upon the left side thereof.

4 So I answered and spake to the Angel that talked with me, saying, What are these my Lord?

5 Then the Angel that talked with me, answered and said unto me, Knowest thou not what these be? And I said, No, my Lord.

6 Then he answered and spake unto me, saying, This is the word of the Lord unto [1]Zerubbabel, saying, Neither by [2]an army nor strength, but by my Spirit, saith the Lord of hosts.

7 Who art thou, O [1]great mountain, before Zerubbabel? *thou shall be* a plain, and [2]he shall bring forth the headstone thereof, with shoutings, *crying,*

3:3 [1] In respect of the glorious garments and precious stones that the Priests did wear before the captivity: and by this contemptible state the Prophet signifieth, that these small beginnings should be made excellent when Christ shall make the full restitution of his Church.

3:4 [1] See verse 3.

[2] He showeth of what apparel he speaketh, which is, when our filthy sins are taken away, and we are clad with God's mercies, which is meant of the spiritual restitution.

3:5 [1] The Prophet prayeth, that besides the raiment, the Priest might also have tyre for his head accordingly, that is, that the dignity of the Priesthood might be perfect: and this was fulfilled in Christ, who was both Priest and King: and here all such are condemned, that can content themselves with any mean reformation in religion, seeing the Prophet desireth the perfection, and obtaineth it.

3:7 [1] That is, have rule and government in my Church, as thy predecessors have had.

[2] Whereby he meaneth to have the whole charge and ministry of the Church.

[3] That is, the Angels, who represented the whole number of the faithful: signifying that all the godly should willingly receive him.

3:8 [1] Because they follow my word, they are contemned in the world, and esteemed as monsters, Isa. 8:18.

[2] That is, Christ, who did so humble himself, that not only he became the servant of God, but also the servant of men: and therefore in him they should have comfort, although in the world they were contemned, Isa. 11:1; Jer. 23:5 and 33:14, 15.

3:9 [1] He showeth that the ministers cannot build, before God lay the first stone, which is Christ, who is full of eyes, both because he

giveth light unto all others, and that all ought to seek light at him, Zech. 4:10.

[2] That is, I will make perfect in all points, as a thing wrought by the hand of GOD.

[3] Though I have punished this land for a time, yet I will even now be pacified, and visit their sins no more.

3:10 [1] Ye shall then live in peace and quietness, that is, in the kingdom of Christ, Isa. 2:2; Mic. 4:4; Hag. 2:10.

4:2 [1] Which was ever in the midst of the Temple, signifying that the graces of God's spirit should shine there in most abundance, and in all perfection.

[2] Which conveyed the oil that dropped from the trees into the lamps, so that the light never failed: and this vision was to confirm the faithful that God had sufficient power in himself to continue his graces, and to bring his promise to pass though he had no help of man.

4:6 [1] Who was a figure of Christ and therefore this doctrine was directed to all the Church who are his body and members.

[2] He showeth that God's power only is sufficient to preserve his Church, though he use not man's help thereunto.

4:7 [1] He compareth the power of the adversaries to a great mountain, who thought the Jews nothing in respect of them, and would have hindered Zerubbabel, who represented Christ, whom the enemies daily labor to let in the building of his spiritual Temple, but all in vain.

[2] Though the enemies think to stay this building, yet Zerubbabel shall lay the highest stone thereof, and bring it to perfection, so that all the godly shall rejoice, and pray unto God that he would continue his grace and favor toward the Temple.

Grace, grace unto it.

8 Moreover, the word of the Lord came unto me, saying,

9 The hands of Zerubbabel have laid the foundation of this house: his hands shall also finish it, and [1]thou shalt know that the Lord of hosts hath sent me unto you.

10 For who hath despised the day of the [1]small things? but they shall rejoice, and shall see the stone of [2]tin in the hand of Zerubbabel: [3]these seven are the eyes of the Lord, which go through the whole world.

11 Then answered I, and said unto him, What are these two olive trees upon the right and upon the left side thereof?

12 And I spake moreover, and said unto him, What be these two olive branches, which through the two golden pipes empty themselves into the gold?

13 And he answered me, and said, Knowest thou not what these be? And I said, No, my Lord.

14 Then said he, These are the two [1]olive branches, that stand with the ruler of the whole earth.

5

1 *The vision of the flying book, signifying the curse of thieves, and such as abuse the Name of God.* 6 *By the vision of the measure is signified the bringing of Judah's afflictions into Babylon.*

1 Then I turned me, and lifted up mine eyes and looked, and behold, a flying book.

2 And he said unto me, What seest thou? And I answered, I see a flying [1]book: the length thereof *is* twenty cubits, and the breadth thereof ten cubits.

3 Then said he unto me, This is the curse that goeth forth over the whole earth: for everyone that [1]stealeth, shall be cut off, *as well* on this [2]side, as on

that: and everyone that [3]sweareth, shall be cut off, *as well* on this side, as on that.

4 I will bring it forth, saith the Lord of hosts, and it shall enter into the house of the thief, and into the house of him that falsely sweareth by my Name: and it shall remain in the midst of his house, and shall consume it, with the timber thereof, and stones thereof.

5 Then the Angel that talked with me, went forth, and said unto me, Lift up now thine eyes, and see what is this that goeth forth.

6 And I said, What is it? And he said, This is an [1]Ephah that goeth forth. He said moreover, This is the [2]sight of them through all the earth.

7 And behold, there was lifted up a [1]talent of lead: and this is a [2]woman that sitteth in the midst of the Ephah.

8 And he said, This is [1]wickedness, and he cast it into the midst of the Ephah, and he cast the weight of lead upon the mouth thereof.

9 Then I lifted mine eyes, and looked: and behold, there came out two [1]women, and the wind *was* in their wings (for they had wings like the wings of a stork) and they lifted up the Ephah between the earth and the heaven.

10 Then said I to the Angel that talked with me, Whither do these bear the Ephah?

11 And he said unto me, To build it an house in the land of Shinar, and it shall be [1]established and set there upon her own place.

6

By the four chariots he describeth the four Monarchies.

1 Again, I turned and lifted up mine eyes, and looked: and behold, there came four [1]chariots out from between [2]two mountains, and the mountains

---

4:9 [1] Meaning, the Prophet, that I am Christ sent of my Father for the building and preservation of my spiritual Temple.

4:10 [1] Signifying, that all were discouraged at the small and poor beginnings of the Temple.

[2] Whereby he signifieth the plummet and line, that is, that Zerubbabel which represented Christ, should go forward with his building to the joy and comfort of the godly, though the world be against him, and though his for a while be discouraged, because they see not things pleasant to the eye.

[3] That is, God hath seven eyes: meaning, a continual providence, so that neither Satan nor any power in the world, can go about to bring anything to pass to hinder his work, Zech. 5:9.

4:14 [1] Which were ever green and full of oil, so that still they poured forth oil into the lamps: signifying, that God will continually maintain and preserve his Church, and endue it still with abundance and perfection of grace.

5:2 [1] Because the Jews had provoked God's plagues by contemning his word, and casting off all judgment and equity, he showeth that God's curses written in this book had justly light both on them and their fathers: but now if they would repent, God would send the same among the Chaldeans their former enemies.

5:3 [1] That is, useth any injury toward his neighbor.

[2] Meaning, wheresoever he be in the world.

[3] He that transgresseth the first table, and serveth not God aright but abuseth God's Name.

5:6 [1] Which was a measure in dry things, containing about ten pottels.

[2] That is, all the wickedness of the ungodly is in God's sight, which he keepeth in a measure, and can shut it or open it at his pleasure.

5:7 [1] To cover the measure.

[2] Which representeth iniquity, as in the next verse.

5:8 [1] Signifying, that Satan should not have such power against the Jews to tempt them, as he had in time past, but that God would shut up iniquity in a measure as in a prison.

5:9 [1] Which declared that God would execute his judgment by the means of the weak and infirm means.

5:11 [1] To remove the iniquity and affliction that came for the same from Judah, to place it forever in Babylon.

6:1 [1] By chariots here, as by horses afore, he meaneth the swift messengers of God to execute and declare his will.

[2] By the brazen mountains he meaneth the external counsel, and providence of God whereby he hath from before all eternity decreed what shall come to pass, and that which neither Satan nor all the world can alter.

were mountains of brass.

2 In the first chariot *were* ¹red horses, and in the second chariot ²black horses,

3 And in the third chariot ¹white horses, and in the fourth chariot, horses of ²divers colors, and reddish.

4 Then I answered, and said unto the Angel that talked with me, What are these, my Lord?

5 And the Angel answered, and said unto me, These are the four ¹spirits of the heaven, which go forth from standing with the Lord of all the earth.

6 That with the black horse went forth into the land of the North, and the white went out after them, and they of divers colors went forth toward the ¹South country.

7 And the ¹reddish went out, and required to go, and pass through the world, and he said, Go, pass through the world. So they went throughout the world.

8 Then cried he upon me, and spake unto me, saying, Behold, these that go toward the North country, have pacified my ¹spirit in the North country.

9 And the word of the Lord came unto me, saying,

10 Take of them of the captivity, *even* of Heldai, and of Tobijah, and Jedaiah, which are come from Babel, and come thou the same day, and go unto the house of ¹Josiah, the son of Zephaniah.

11 Take even silver, and gold, and make crowns, and set *them* upon the ¹head of Joshua, the son of Jehozadak the high Priest,

12 And speak unto him, saying, Thus speaketh the Lord of hosts, and saith, Behold, the man whose name is the ¹Branch, and he shall grow ²up out of his place, and he shall ³build the Temple of the Lord.

13 Even he shall build the Temple of the Lord, and he shall bear the ¹glory, and shall sit and rule upon his throne, and he shall be a Priest upon his throne, and the counsel of peace shall be between ²them both.

14 And the crowns shall be to ¹Helem, and to Tobijah, and to Jedaiah, and to ²Hen the son of Zephaniah, for a ³memorial in the Temple of the Lord.

15 And they that are ¹far off, shall come and build in the Temple of the Lord, and ye shall know, that the Lord of hosts hath sent me unto you. And this shall come to pass, if ye will ²obey the voice of the Lord your God.

7

5 *The true fasting.*   11 *The rebellion of the people is the cause of their affliction.*

1 And in the fourth year of King Darius, the word of the Lord came unto Zechariah in the fourth *day* of the ninth month, even in ¹Chislev,

2 For ¹they had sent unto the House of God Sharezer, and Regem-Melech and their men to pray before the Lord,

3 *And* to speak unto the Priests, which were in the House of the Lord of hosts, and to the Prophets, saying, Should I ¹weep in the fifth month, and ²separate myself as I have done these so many ³years?

4 Then came the word of the Lord of hosts unto me, saying,

6:2 ¹ Which signified the great cruelty and persecution that the Church had endured under divers enemies.

   ² Signifying, that they had endured great afflictions under the Babylonians.

6:3 ¹ These represented their state under the Persians, which restored them to liberty.

   ² Which signified, that God would sometimes give his Church rest, and pour his plagues upon their enemies, as he did in destroying Nineveh and Babylon, and others their enemies.

6:5 ¹ Meaning, all the actions and motions of God's Spirit, which according to his unchangeable counsel he causeth to appear through all the world.

6:6 ¹ That is, toward Egypt, and other countries there about.

6:7 ¹ That is, they of divers colors, which ask […], to signify that Satan hath no power to hurt or afflict, till God gives it him, Job 1:12.

6:8 ¹ By punishing the Chaldeans mine anger ceased, and you were delivered.

6:10 ¹ To receive of him and the other three, money to make the two crowns: which were men of great authority among the Jews, and doubted of the restitution of the kingdom, and of the Priesthood, and hurt others by their example.

6:11 ¹ Because this could not be attributed to anyone according to the Law, therefore it followeth that Joshua must represent the Messiah, who was both Priest and king.

6:12 ¹ Meaning, Christ, of whom Joshua was the figure: for in Greek they were both called Jesus.

   ² That is, of himself without the help of man.

   ³ Which declareth, that none could build this Temple whereof Haggai speaketh, but only Christ: and therefore it was spiritual, and not material, Hag. 2:10.

6:13 ¹ Whereof Joshua had but a shadow.

   ² The two offices of the kingdom, and Priesthood shall be so joined together, that they shall be no more dissevered.

6:14 ¹ Who was also called Heldai.

   ² He was also called Joshiash.

   ³ That they may acknowledge their infirmity, which looked that all things should have been restored incontinently: and of this their infidelity these two crowns shall remain as tokens, Acts 1:16.

6:15 ¹ That is, the Gentiles by the preaching of the Gospel, shall help toward the building of the spiritual Temple.

   ² If ye will believe and remain in the obedience of faith.

7:1 ¹ Which contained part of November and part of December.

7:2 ¹ That is, the rest of the people that remained yet in Chaldea, sent to the Church at Jerusalem, for the resolution of these questions, because these feasts were consented upon by the agreement of the whole Church, the one in the month that the Temple was destroyed, and the other when Gedaliah was slain, Jer. 41:2.

7:3 ¹ By weeping and mourning, appear what exercises they used in their fasting.

   ² That is, prepare myself with all devotion to his fast.

   ³ Which was now since the time the Temple was destroyed.

5 Speak unto all the people of the land, and to the ¹Priests, and say, When ye fasted, and mourned in the fifth and seventh month, even the seventy years, did ye fast unto me? ²do I *approve it*?

6 And when ye did eat, and when ye did drink, did ye not eat¹for yourselves, and drink for yourselves?

7 Should ye not *hear* the words which the Lord ¹hath cried by the ministry of the former Prophets when Jerusalem was inhabited, and in prosperity, and the cities thereof round about her, when the South and the plain was inhabited?

8 And the word of the Lord came unto Zechariah, saying,

9 Thus speaketh the Lord of hosts, saying, ¹Execute true judgment, and show mercy and compassion, every man to his brother,

10 And oppress not the widow, nor the fatherless, the stranger nor the poor, and let none of you imagine evil against his brother in your heart.

11 But they refused to hearken, and ¹pulled away the shoulder, and stopped their ears, that they should not hear.

12 Yea, they made their hearts as an adamant stone, lest they should hear the Law and the words which the Lord of hosts sent in his ¹Spirit by the ministry of the former Prophets: therefore came a great wrath from the Lord of hosts.

13 Therefore it is come to pass, that as he cried, and they would not hear, so they cried, and I would not hear, saith the Lord of hosts.

14 But I scattered them among all the nations, whom they knew not: thus the land was desolate ¹after them, that no man passed through nor returned: for they laid the pleasant land ²waste.

8 2 *Of the return of the people unto Jerusalem, and of the mercy of God toward them.* 16 *Of good works.* 20 *The calling of the Gentiles.*

1 Again the word of the Lord of hosts came *to me*, saying,

2 Thus saith the Lord of hosts, I was ¹jealous for Zion with great jealousy, and I was jealous for her with great wrath.

3 Thus saith the Lord, I will return unto Zion, and will dwell in the midst of Jerusalem: and Jerusalem shall be called a ¹city of truth, and the Mountain of the Lord of hosts, the holy Mountain.

4 Thus saith the Lord of hosts, There shall yet old ¹men and old women dwell in the streets of Jerusalem, and every man with his staff in his hand for very age.

5 And the streets of the city shall be full of boys and girls, playing in the streets thereof.

6 Thus saith the Lord of hosts, Though it be ¹impossible in the eyes of the remnant of this people in these days, should it therefore be impossible in my sight, saith the Lord of hosts?

7 Thus saith the Lord of hosts, Behold, I will deliver my people from the East country, and from the West country.

8 And I will bring them, and they shall ¹dwell in the midst of Jerusalem, and they shall be my people, and I will be their God in truth, and in righteousness.

9 Thus saith the Lord of hosts, Let your ¹hands be strong, ye that hear in these days these words by the mouth of the Prophets, which were in the day, that the foundation of the house of the Lord of hosts was laid, that the Temple might be built.

10 For before these days there was no hire for ¹man, nor any hire for beast, neither was there any

---

7:5 ¹ For there were both of the people, and of the Priests, which doubted as touching this controversy, besides them which as yet remained in Chaldea, and reason of it, as of one of the chief points of their religion.

² For they thought they had deserved toward God because of this fast, which they invented of themselves: and though fasting of itself be good, yet because they thought it a service toward God, and trusted therein, it is here reproved.

7:6 ¹ Did ye not eat and drink for your own commodity and necessity, and so likewise ye did abstain according to your own fantasies, and not after the prescript of my Law.

7:7 ¹ Hereby he condemneth their hypocrisy, which thought by their fasting to please God and by such things as they invented, and in the mean season would not serve him as he had commanded.

7:9 ¹ He showeth that they did not fast with a sincere heart, but for hypocrisy, and that it was not done of a pure religion, because that they lacked these offices of charity, which should have declared that they were godly, Matt. 23:23.

7:11 ¹ And would not carry the Lord's burden, which was sweet and easy, but would bear their own, which was heavy and grievous to the flesh, thinking to merit thereby: which similitude is taken of oxen, which shrink at the yoke, Neh. 9:29.

7:12 ¹ Which declareth that they rebelled not only against the Prophets, but against the Spirit of God that spake in them.

7:14 ¹ That is, after they were called captive.

² By their sins whereby they provoked God's anger.

8:2 ¹ I loved my city with a singular love, so that I could not abide that any should do her any injury.

8:3 ¹ Because she shall be faithful and loyal toward me her husband.

8:4 ¹ Though their enemies did greatly molest and trouble them, yet God would come and dwell among them, and so preserve them so long as nature would suffer them to live, and increase their children in great abundance.

8:6 ¹ He showeth wherein our faith standeth, that is, to believe that God can perform that which he hath promised, though it seem never so impossible to man, Gen. 18:14; Rom. 4:20.

8:8 ¹ So that their return shall not be in vain: for God will accomplish his promise, and their prosperity shall be sure and stable.

8:9 ¹ Let neither respect of your private commodities neither counsel of others, nor fear of enemies discourage you in the going forward with the building of the Temple, but be constant and obey the Prophets, which encourage you thereunto.

8:10 ¹ For God cursed your work, so that neither man nor beast had profit of their labors.

peace to him that went out or came in because of the affliction: for I set all men, everyone against his neighbor.

11 But now, I will not *entreat* the residue of this people as aforetime, saith the Lord of hosts.

12 For the seed *shall be* prosperous: the vine shall give her fruit, and the ground shall give her increase, and the heavens shall give their dew: and I will cause the remnant of this people to possess all these things.

13 And it shall come to pass, that as ye were a curse among the heathen, O house of Judah, and house of Israel, so will I deliver you, and ye shall be a blessing: fear not, *but* let your hands be strong.

14 For thus saith the Lord of hosts, As I thought to punish[1]you, when your fathers provoked me unto wrath, saith the Lord of hosts, and repented not,

15 So again have I determined in these days [1]to do well unto Jerusalem, and to the house of Judah: fear ye not.

16 These are the things that ye shall do, Speak ye every man the truth unto his neighbor: execute judgment truly, and uprightly in your gates,

17 And let none of you imagine evil in your hearts against his neighbor, and love no false oath: for all these are the things that I hate, saith the Lord.

18 And the word of the Lord of hosts came unto me, saying,

19 Thus saith the Lord of hosts, The fast of the fourth *month*, and the fast of the fifth, and the fast of the seventh, and the fast of the [1]tenth, shall be to the house of Judah joy and gladness, and prosperous high feasts: therefore love the truth and peace.

20 Thus saith the Lord of hosts, That there shall yet come [1]people, and the inhabitants of great cities.

21 And they that dwell in one *city*, shall go to another, saying, [a]Up, let us go and pray before the Lord, and seek the Lord of hosts: I will go also.

22 Yea great people and mighty nations shall come

CHAPTER 8
[a] Isa. 2:2
Mic. 4:1

to seek the Lord of hosts in Jerusalem, and to pray before the Lord.

23 Thus saith the Lord of hosts, In those days shall ten men take hold out of all languages of the nations, *even* take hold of the skirt of him that is a Jew, and say, We will go with you: for we have heard that God is with you.

9

The threatenings of the Gentiles.   9 The coming of Christ.

1 The burden of the word of the Lord in the land of [1]Hadrach: and Damascus *shall be* his [2]rest: when the [3]eyes of man, *even* of all the tribes of Israel *shall be* toward the Lord.

2 And Hamath also shall border [1]thereby: Tyre *also* and Sidon, though *they be* [2]very wise.

3 For Tyre did build herself a stronghold, and heaped up silver as the dust, and gold as the mire of the streets.

4 Behold, the Lord will spoil her, and he will smite her [1]power in the sea, and she shall be devoured with fire.

5 Ashkelon shall see it, and fear, and Gaza also shall be very sorrowful, and Ekron: for her countenance shall be ashamed, and the king shall perish from Gaza, and Ashkelon shall not be inhabited.

6 And the [1]stranger shall dwell in Ashdod, and I will cut off the pride of the Philistines.

7 And I will take away his blood out of his mouth, and his abominations from between his [1]teeth: but he that remaineth, even he shall be for our God, and he shall be as a prince in Judah, but [2]Ekron *shall be* as a Jebusite.

8 And I will camp about [1]mine House against the army, against him that passeth by, and against him that returneth, and no oppressor shall come upon them anymore: for now [2]have I seen with mine eyes.

9 Rejoice greatly, O daughter Zion: shout for

8:14 [1] Read Ezek. 18:20.

8:15 [1] Which declareth that man cannot turn to God till he changes man's heart by his spirit, and so begin to do well, which is to pardon his sins and to give him his graces.

8:19 [1] Which fast was appointed when the city was besieged, and was the first fast of these four: and here the Prophet showeth, that if the Jews will repent, and turn wholly to God, they shall have no more occasion to fast, or to show signs of heaviness: for God will send them joy and gladness.

8:20 [1] He declareth the great zeal that God should give the Gentiles to come to his Church, and to join with the Jews in his true religion, which should be in the kingdom of Christ.

9:1 [1] Whereby he meaneth Syria.

[2] God's anger shall abide upon their chief city, and not spare so much as that.

[3] When the Jews shall convert and repent, then God will destroy their enemies.

9:2 [1] That is, by Damascus: meaning, that Hamath or Antioch should

be under the same rod and plague.

[2] He secretly showeth the cause of their destruction, because they deceived all others by their craft and subtlety, which they cloaked with this name of wisdom.

9:4 [1] Though they of Tyre think themselves invincible by reason of the sea that compass them round about, yet they shall not escape God's judgments.

9:6 [1] Meaning, that all should be destroyed, save a very few, that should remain as strangers.

9:7 [1] He promiseth to deliver the Jews when he shall take vengeance on their enemies for their cruelty and wrongs done to them.

[2] As the Jebusites had been destroyed, so should Ekron and all the Philistines.

9:8 [1] He showeth that God's power only shall be sufficient to defend his Church against all adversaries be they never so cruel, or assemble their power never so often.

[2] That is, God hath now seen the great injuries and afflictions wherewith they have been afflicted by their enemies.

joy, O daughter Jerusalem: behold, thy king cometh unto thee: [1]he is just, and saved himself, poor and riding upon an [2]ass, and upon a colt the foal of an ass.

10 And I will cut off the [1]chariots from Ephraim, and the horse from Jerusalem: the bow of the battle shall be broken, and he shall speak peace unto the heathen, and his dominion *shall be* from [2]sea unto sea, and from the [3]River to the end of the land.

11 [1]Thou also *shall be saved* through the blood of thy covenant. I have loosed thy [2]prisoners out of the pit wherein *is* no water.

12 Turn you to the [1]stronghold, ye [2]prisoners of hope: even today do I declare, that I will render the [3]double unto thee.

13 For Judah have I bent as a [1]bow for me: Ephraim's hand have I filled, and I have raised up thy sons, O Zion, against thy sons, O Greece, and have made thee as a giant's sword.

14 And the Lord shall be seen over them, and his arrow shall go forth as the lightning: and the Lord God shall blow the trumpet, and shall come forth with the whirlwinds of the South.

15 The Lord of hosts shall defend them, and they shall devour them, [1]and subdue them with sling stones, and they shall drink, *and* make a noise as through wine, and they shall be filled like bowls, *and* as the horns of the Altar.

16 And the Lord their God shall deliver them in that day as the flock of his people: for *they shall be as*

the [1]stones of the crown lifted up upon his land.

17 For how great is his goodness! and how great is his beauty! corn shall make the young men cheerful, and new wine the maids.

10

1 *The vanity of Idolatry.* 3 *The Lord promiseth to visit and comfort the house of Israel.*

1 Ask you of the [1]Lord rain in the time of the latter rain: *so* shall the Lord make white clouds, and give you showers of rain, *and* to everyone grass in the field.

2 Surely the [1]idols have spoken vanity, and the soothsayers have seen a lie, and the dreamers have told a vain thing: they comfort in vain: therefore [2]they went away as sheep: they were troubled, because there was no shepherd.

3 My wrath was kindled against the shepherds, and I did visit the [1]goats: but the Lord of hosts will visit his flock the house of Judah, and will make them as [2]his beautiful horse in the battle.

4 Out [1]of him shall the corner come forth: out of him the nail, out of him ye bow of battle, *and* out of him every [2]appointer of tribute also.

5 And they shall be as the mighty men, which tread down *their enemies* in the mire of the streets in the battle, and they shall fight, because the Lord *is* with them, and the riders on horses shall be confounded.

6 And I will strengthen the house of Judah, and I will preserve the [1]house of Joseph, and I will bring

---

9:9 [1] That is, he hath righteousness and salvation in himself for the use and commodity of his Church.

[2] Which declareth that they should not look for such a king as should be glorious in the eyes of man, but should be poor, and yet in himself have all power to deliver his: and this is meant of Christ, as Matt. 21:5.

9:10 [1] No power of man or creature shall be able to let this kingdom of Christ, and he shall peaceably govern them by his word.

[2] That is, from the red sea, to the sea, called Syriacum: and by these places which the Jews knew, he meant an infinite space and compass over the whole world.

[3] That is, from Euphrates.

9:11 [1] Meaning, Jerusalem, or the Church which is saved by the blood of Christ whereof the blood of the sacrifices was a figure, and is here called the covenant of the Church, because God made it with his Church: and left it with them for the love that he bare unto them.

[2] God showeth that he will deliver his Church out of all dangers, seem they never so great.

9:12 [1] That is, into the holy land where the city and the Temple are, where God will defend you.

[2] Meaning the faithful, which seemed to be in danger of their enemies on every side, and yet lived in hope that God would restore them to liberty.

[3] That is, double benefits and prosperity, in respect of that which your fathers enjoined from David's time to the captivity.

9:13 [1] I will make Judah and Ephraim, that is, my whole Church, victorious against all enemies, which he here meaneth by the Greecians.

9:15 [1] He promiseth that the Jews shall destroy their enemies, and have abundance and excess of all things, as there is abundance on the altar when the sacrifice is offered: Which things are not to move them to intemperancy, but to sobriety, and a thankful remembrance of God's great liberality.

9:16 [1] The faithful shall be preserved, and reverenced of all, that the very enemies shall be compelled to esteem them: for God's glory shall shine in them, as Josephus declareth of Alexander the great when he met Jadi the high Priest.

10:1 [1] The Prophet reproveth the Jews, because by their own infidelity they put back God's graces promised, and so famine came by God's just judgment: therefore to avoid this plague, he willeth them to turn to God, and to pray in faith to him, and so he will give them abundance.

10:2 [1] He calleth to remembrance God's punishments in times past, because they trusted not in him, but in their idols and sorcerers who ever deceived them.

[2] That is, the Jews went into captivity.

10:3 [1] Meaning, the cruel governors which did oppress the poor sheep, Ezek. 34:16, 17.

[2] He will be merciful to his Church and cherish them as a king or prince doth his best horse which shall be for his own use in war.

10:4 [1] Out of Judah shall the chief governor proceed, who shall be as a corner to uphold the building, and as a nail to fasten it together.

[2] Over their enemies.

10:6 [1] That is, the ten tribes, which should be gathered under Christ to the rest of the Church.

them again, for I pity them: and they shall be as though I had not cast them off: for I am the Lord their God, and will hear them.

7 And they of Ephraim shall be as a giant: and their heart shall rejoice as through wine: yea, their children shall see it, and be glad: *and* their heart shall rejoice in the Lord.

8 I will ¹hiss for them: and gather them: for I have redeemed them: and they shall increase, as they have increased.

9 And I will ¹sow them among the people, and they shall remember me in far countries: and they shall live with their children and ²turn again.

10 I will bring them again also out of the land of Egypt, and gather them out of Assyria: and I will bring them into the land of Gilead, and Lebanon, and *place* shall not be found for them.

11 And he ¹shall go into the sea with affliction, and shall smite the waves in the sea, and all the depths of the river shall dry up: and the pride of Assyria shall be cast down, and the scepter of Egypt shall depart away.

12 And I will strengthen them in the Lord, and they shall walk in his Name, saith the Lord.

11

The destruction of the Temple. 4 *The care of the faithful is committed to Christ.* 7 *A grievous vision against Jerusalem and Judah.*

1 Open thy doors, O ¹Lebanon, and the fire shall devour thy cedars.

2 Howl, ¹fir trees: for the cedar is fallen, because all the mighty are destroyed: howl ye, O oaks of Bashan, for the ²defenced forest is cut down.

3 There *is* the voice of the howling of the shep-

herds: for their ¹glory is destroyed: the voice of the roaring of lion's whelps: for the pride of Jordan is destroyed.

4 Thus saith the Lord my God, Feed the sheep of the ¹slaughter.

5 They that possess them, slay them ¹and sin not: and they that sell them, say, ²Blessed *be* the Lord: for I am rich, and their own shepherds spare them not.

6 Surely I will no more spare those that dwell in the land, saith the Lord: but lo, ¹I will deliver the men every one into his neighbor's hand, and into the hand of his ²king: and they shall smite the land, and out of their hands I will not deliver *them*.

7 For I fed the sheep of slaughter, even the ¹poor of the flock, and I took unto me ²two staves: the one I called Beauty, and the other I called Bands, and I fed the sheep.

8 ¹Three shepherds also I cut off in one month, and my soul loathed ²them, and their soul abhorred me.

9 Then said I, I will not feed you: that that dieth, let it die: and that that perisheth, let it perish: and let the remnant eat, everyone the flesh of his neighbor.

10 And I took my staff, *even* Beauty, and brake it, that I might disannul my covenant, which I had made with all people.

11 And it was broken in that day: and so the ¹poor of the sheep that waited upon me, knew that it was the word of the Lord.

12 And I said unto them, If ye think it good, give *me* ¹my wages: and if no, leave off: so they weighed for my wages thirty *pieces* of silver.

13 And the Lord said unto me, Cast it unto the

10:8 ¹ Whereby he declareth the power of God, who needeth no great preparation when he will deliver his: for with a beck or hiss he can call them from all places suddenly.

10:9 ¹ Though they shall yet be scattered and seem to be lost, yet it shall be profitable unto them: for there they shall come to the knowledge of my Name, which was accomplished under the Gospel, among whom it was first preached.

² Not that they should return into their country, but be gathered and joined in one faith by the doctrine of the Gospel.

10:11 ¹ He alludeth to the deliverance of the people out of Egypt, whereas the Angel smote the floods and rivers.

11:1 ¹ Because the Jews thought themselves so strong by reason of this mountain, that no enemy could come to hurt them, the Prophet showeth that when God sendeth the enemies, it shall show itself ready to receive them.

11:2 ¹ Showing, that if the strong men were destroyed, the weaker were not able to resist.

² Seeing that Lebanon was destroyed, which was the strongest munition, the weaker places could not think to hold out.

11:3 ¹ That is, the renown of Judah and Israel should perish.

11:4 ¹ Which being now destinate to be slain, were delivered as out of the lion's mouth.

11:5 ¹ Their governors destroy them without any remorse of con-

science, or yet thinking that they do evil.

² He noteth the hypocrites, which ever have the Name of God in their mouths, though in their life and doings they deny God, attributing their gain to God's blessings, which cometh of the spoil of their brethren.

11:6 ¹ I will cause one to destroy another.

² Their governors shall execute cruelty over them.

11:7 ¹ That is, the small remnant, whom he thought worthy to show mercy unto.

² God showeth his great benefits toward his people to convince them of greater ingratitude, which would neither be ruled by his most beautiful order of government, neither continue in the bands of brotherly unity, and therefore he breaketh both the one and the other. Some read, for Bands, Destroyers, but in verse 14 the first reading is confirmed.

11:8 ¹ Whereby he showeth his care and diligence that he would suffer them to have no evil rulers, because they should consider his great love.

² Meaning, the people, because they would not acknowledge these great benefits of God.

11:11 ¹ He showeth that the least part ever profit by God's judgments.

11:12 ¹ Besides their ingratitude God accuseth them of malice and wickedness, which did not only forget his benefits, but esteemed them as things of naught.

¹potter: a goodly price, that I was valued at of them. And I took the thirty *pieces* of silver, and cast them to the potter in the house of the Lord.

14 Then brake I mine other staff: *even* the Bands, that I might dissolve the brotherhood between Judah and Israel.

15 And the Lord said unto me, Take to thee yet ¹the instruments of a foolish shepherd.

16 For lo, I will raise up a shepherd in the land, which shall not look for the thing that is lost, nor seek the tender lambs, nor heal that that is hurt, nor feed that that ¹standeth up, but he shall eat flesh of the fat, and tear their claws in pieces.

17 O idol shepherd that leaveth the flock: the sword *shall be* upon his ¹arm, and upon his right eye. His arm shall be clean dried up, and his right eye shall be utterly darkened.

12 *Of the destruction and building again of Jerusalem.*

1 The burden of the word of the Lord upon ¹Israel, saith the Lord, which spread the heavens, and laid the foundation of the earth, and formed the spirit of man within him.

2 Behold, I will make Jerusalem a¹cup of poison unto all the people round about: and also with Judah will he be in the siege against Jerusalem.

3 And in that day will I make Jerusalem an heavy stone for all people: all that lift it up, shall be torn, though all the people of the earth be gathered together against it.

4 In that day, saith the Lord, I will smite every horse with astonishment, and his rider with madness, and I will open mine eyes upon the house of Judah, and will smite every horse of the people with blindness.

5 And the princes of Judah shall say in their hearts, The ¹inhabitants of Jerusalem *shall be* my strength in the Lord of hosts their God.

6 In that day will I make the princes of Judah like coals of fire among the wood, and like a firebrand in the sheaf, and they shall devour all the people round about on the right hand, and on the left: and Jerusalem shall be inhabited again in her own place, *even* in Jerusalem.

7 The Lord also shall preserve the ¹tents of Judah, *as* afore time: therefore the glory of the house of David shall not boast, nor the glory of the inhabitants of Jerusalem against Judah.

8 In that day shall the Lord defend the inhabitants of Jerusalem, and he that is feeble among them, in that day shall be as David: and the house of David *shall be* as God's *house, and* as the Angel of the Lord before them.

9 And in that day will I seek to destroy all the nations that come against Jerusalem.

10 And I will pour upon the house of David, and upon the inhabitants of Jerusalem, the Spirit of ¹grace and of compassion, and they shall look upon me, whom they have ²pierced, and they shall lament for ³him, as one mourneth for *his* only *son*, and be sorry for him as one is sorry for *his* firstborn.

11 In that day shall there be a great mourning in Jerusalem, as the ¹mourning of ²Hadad Rimmon in the valley of Megiddo.

12 And the ¹land shall bewail every family ²apart, the family of the ³house of David apart, and their wives apart: the family of the house of Nathan apart, and their wives apart:

13 The family of the house of Levi apart, and their wives apart: the family of ¹Shemei apart, and their wives apart:

14 All the families that ¹remain, every family apart, and their wives apart.

11:13 ¹ Showing that it was too little to pay his wages, which could scarce suffice to make a few tiles to cover the Temple.

11:15 ¹ Signifying that they should have a certain kind of regiment and outward show of government: but in effect it should be nothing: for they should be wolves, and devouring beasts instead of shepherds.

11:16 ¹ And is in health and sound.

11:17 ¹ By the arms he signifieth strength, as he doth wisdom and judgments by the eye: that is, the plague of God shall take away both thy strength and judgment.

12:1 ¹ That is, the ten tribes, which neglected God's benefit in delivering their brethren, and had rather remain in captivity, than to return home when God called them.

12:2 ¹ Jerusalem shall be defended against all her enemies: so shall God defend all Judah also, and shall destroy the enemies.

12:5 ¹ Every captain, that had many under him afore, shall now think that the small power of Jerusalem shall be sufficient to defend them against all enemies, because the Lord is among them.

12:7 ¹ The people which are now as it were dispersed by the fields, and lie open to their enemies, shall be no less preserved by my power, than if they were under their kings (which is meant by the house of David) or in their defensed cities.

12:10 ¹ They shall have the feeling of my grace by faith, and know that I have compassion on them.

² That is, whom they have continually vexed with their obstinacy, and grieved my Spirit, John 19:37, where it is referred to Christ's body, which here is referred to the Spirit of God.

³ They shall turn to God by true repentance, whom before they had so grievously offended by their ingratitude.

12:11 ¹ They shall lament and repent exceedingly for their offences against God.

² Which was the name of a town and place near to Megiddo where Josiah was slain, 2 Chron. 35:22.

12:12 ¹ That is, in all places where the Jews shall remain.

² Signifying, that this mourning or repentance should not be a vain ceremony: but everyone touched with his own griefs, shall lament.

³ Under these certain families he containeth all the tribes, and showeth that both the Kings and the Priests had by their sins pierced Christ.

12:13 ¹ Called also Simeon.

12:14 ¹ To wit, which were elected by grace, and preserved from the common destruction.

13

1 Of the fountain of grace.   2 Of the clean rid-dance of idolatry.   3 The zeal of the godly against false prophets.

1   In that day there ¹shall be a fountain opened to the house of David, and to the inhabitants of Jerusalem, for sin and for uncleanness.

2   And in that day, saith the Lord of hosts, I will cut off the ¹names of the idols out of the land: and they shall no more be remembered: and I will cause the ²prophets, and the unclean spirit to depart out of the land.

3   And when any shall yet ¹prophesy, his father and his mother that begat him, shall say unto him, Thou shalt not live: for thou speakest lies in the Name of the Lord: and his father and his mother that begat him, ²shall thrust him through, when he prophesieth.

4   And in that day shall the prophets ¹be ashamed everyone of his vision, when he hath prophesied: neither shall they wear a rough garment to deceive.

5   But he shall say, I am no ¹Prophet: I am an husbandman: for man taught me to be an herdsman from my youth up.

6   And one shall say unto him, What are these ¹wounds in thine hands? Then he shall answer, Thus was I wounded in the house of my friends.

7   ¶ Arise, O sword, upon my ¹shepherd, and upon the man, *that is* my fellow, saith the Lord of hosts: smite the shepherd, and the sheep shall be scattered: and I will turn mine hand upon the little ones.

8   And in all the land, saith the Lord, ¹two parts therein shall be cut off, *and* die: but the third shall be left therein.

9   And I will bring that third part through the fire, and will fine them as the silver is fined, and will try them as gold is tried: they shall call on my Name, and I will hear them: I will say, It is my people, and they shall say, The Lord *is* my God.

14

8 Of the doctrine that shall proceed out of the Church, and of the restoration thereof.

1   Behold, the day of the Lord cometh, and thy spoil shall be ¹divided in the midst of thee.

2   For I will gather all nations against Jerusalem to battle, and the city shall be taken, and the houses spoiled, and the women defiled, and half of the city shall go into captivity, and the residue of the people shall not be cut off from the city.

3   Then the Lord shall go forth, and fight against those nations, as when he ¹fought in the day of battle.

4   And his feet shall stand in that day upon the ¹mount of olives, which is before Jerusalem on the Eastside, and the mount of olives shall cleave in the midst thereof: toward the East and toward the West there *shall be* a very great ²valley, and half of the mountain shall remove toward the North, and half of the mountain toward the South.

5   And ye shall flee unto the ¹valley of the mountains: for the valley of the mountains shall reach unto Azal: yea, ye shall flee like as ye fled from the ²earthquake, in the days of Uzziah king of Judah: and the Lord ³my God shall come, and all the Saints with thee.

6   And in that day shall there be no clear light but dark.

13:1 ¹ He showeth what shall be the fruit of their repentance, to wit, remission of sins by the blood of Christ, which shall be a continual running fountain, and purge them from all uncleanness.

13:2 ¹ He promiseth that God will also purge them from all superstition, and that their religion shall be pure.

² Meaning, the false prophets and teachers, who are the corrupters of all religion, whom the Prophet here calleth unclean spirits.

13:3 ¹ That is, when they shall prophesy lies, and make God, who is the author of truth, a cloak thereunto.

² He showeth what zeal the godly shall have under the kingdom of Christ, Deut. 13:6, 9.

13:4 ¹ God shall make them ashamed of their errors and lies, and bring them to repentance, and they shall no more wear Prophet's apparel to make their doctrine seem more holy.

13:5 ¹ They shall confess their former ignorance, and be content to labor for their living.

13:6 ¹ Hereby he showeth that though their parents and friends dealt more gently with them, and put them not to death, yet they would so punish their children, that became false prophets, that the marks and signs should remain forever.

13:7 ¹ The Prophet warneth the Jews, that before this great comfort should come under Christ, there should be an horrible dissipation among the people: for their governors and pastors should be destroyed, and the people should be as scattered sheep: and the Evangelist applieth this to

Christ, because he was the head of all Pastors, Matt. 26:31.

13:8 ¹ The greatest part shall have no portion of these blessings, and yet they that shall enjoy them, shall be tried with great afflictions, so that it shall be known that only God's power and his mercies do preserve them.

14:1 ¹ He armeth the godly against the great tentations that should come, before they enjoyed this prosperous estate promised under Christ, that when these dangers should come, they might know that they were warned of them afore.

14:3 ¹ As your fathers and you have had experience both at the red sea, and at all other times.

14:4 ¹ By this manner of speech the Prophet showeth God's power and care over his Church, and how he will as it were by miracle save it.

² So that out of all the parts of the world, they shall see Jerusalem, which was before hid with this mountain: and this he meaneth of the spiritual Jerusalem the Church.

14:5 ¹ He speaketh of the hypocrites, which could not abide God's presence, but should flee into all places, where they might hide them among the mountains.

² Read Amos 1:1.

³ Because they did not credit the Prophet's words, he turneth to God and comforteth himself in that that he knew that these things should come, and saith, Thou, O God, with thine Angels wilt come to perform this great thing.

7　And there shall be a day (it is known to the Lord) [1]neither day nor night, but about the evening time it shall be light.

8　And in that day shall there [1]waters of life go out from Jerusalem, half of them toward the East sea, and half of them toward the uttermost sea, *and* shall be, both in summer and winter.

9　And the Lord shall be King over all the earth: in that day shall there be one [1]Lord, and his Name shall be one.

10　All the land shall be turned [1]as a plain from Geba to Rimmon, toward the South of Jerusalem, and it shall be lifted up, and inhabited in her place: from Benjamin's gate unto the place of the first gate, unto the corner gate, and from the tower of Hananiel unto the king's winepresses.

11　And men shall dwell in it, and there shall be no more destruction, but Jerusalem shall be safely inhabited.

12　And this shall be the plague wherewith the Lord will smite all people, that have fought against Jerusalem: their flesh shall consume away, though they stand upon their feet, and their eyes shall consume in their holes, and their tongue shall consume in their mouth.

13　But in that day [1]a great tumult of the Lord shall be among them, and everyone shall take [2]the hand of his neighbor, and his hand shall rise up against the hand of his neighbor.

14　And Judah shall fight also against Jerusalem, and the arm of all the heathen shall be gathered round about, with [1]gold and silver, and great abundance of apparel.

15　Yet this shall be the plague of the horse, of the mule, of the camel and of the ass, and of all the beasts that be in these tents at this [1]plague.

16　But it shall come to pass that everyone that is left of all the nations, which came against Jerusalem, shall go up from year to year to worship the King the Lord of hosts, and to keep the feast of Tabernacles.

17　And who so will not come up of *all* the families of the earth unto Jerusalem to worship the King the Lord of hosts, even upon them shall come no rain.

18　And if the family of [1]Egypt go not up, and come not, it shall not *rain* upon them. *This* shall be the plague wherewith the Lord will smite all the heathen, that come not up to keep the feast of tabernacles.

19　This shall be the punishment of Egypt, and the punishment of all the nations that come not up to keep the feast of Tabernacles.

20　In that day shall there be *written* upon the [1]bridles of the horses, The holiness unto the Lord, and the [2]pots in the Lord's house shall be like the bowls before the altar.

21　Yea, every pot in Jerusalem and Judah shall be holy unto the Lord of hosts, [1]and all they that sacrifice, shall come and take of them, and seethe therein: and in that day there shall be no more the Canaanite in the house of the Lord of hosts.

14:7 [1] Signifying, that there should be great troubles in the Church, and that the time hereof is in the Lord's hands, yet at length (which is here meant by the evening) God would send comfort.

14:8 [1] That is, the spiritual graces of God, which should ever continue in most abundance.

14:9 [1] All idolatry and superstition shall be abolished, and there shall be one God, one faith, and one religion.

14:10 [1] This new Jerusalem shall be seen through all the world, and shall excel the first in excellency, wealth, and greatness.

14:13 [1] God will not only raise up war without, but sedition at home to try them.

　[2] To hurt and oppress him.

14:14 [1] The enemies are rich, and therefore shall not come for a prey, but to destroy and shed blood.

14:15 [1] As the men should be destroyed, verse 12.

14:18 [1] By the Egyptians, which were greatest enemies to true religion, he meaneth all the gentiles.

14:20 [1] Signifying, that to what service they were put now (whether to labor, or to serve in war) they were now holy, because the Lord had sanctified them.

　[2] As precious the one as the other, because they shall be sanctified.

14:21 [1] But all shall be pure and clean, and there shall neither be hypocrites, nor any that shall corrupt the true service of God.

MALACHI

1

A complaint against Israel, and chiefly the Priests.

1 The [1]burden of the word of the Lord to Israel by the ministry of Malachi.

2 I have loved you, saith the Lord: yet ye say, [1]Wherein hast thou loved us? Was not Esau Jacob's brother, saith the Lord? Yet I loved Jacob,

3 And I [1,2]hated Esau, and made his mountains waste, and his heritage a wilderness for dragons.

4 Though Edom say, We are impoverished, but we will return and build the desolate places: yet saith the Lord of hosts, They shall build, but I will destroy it, and they shall call them, The border of wickedness, and the people, with whom the Lord is angry forever.

5 And your eyes shall see it, and ye shall say, The Lord will be magnified upon the border of Israel.

6 A son honoreth *his* father, and a servant his master. If then I be a father, where is my honor? and if I be a master, where is my fear, saith the Lord of hosts unto you, [1]O Priests that despise my Name? and ye say, [2]Wherein have we despised thy Name?

7 Ye offer [1]unclean bread upon mine altar: and you say, Wherein have we polluted thee? in that ye say, The table of the Lord is not [2]to be regarded.

8 And if ye offer the blind for sacrifice, it is [1]not evil: and if ye offer the lame and sick, it is not evil: offer it now unto thy princes: will he be content with thee, or accept thy person, saith the Lord of hosts?

9 And now I pray you, [1]pray before God that he may have mercy upon us: this hath been by your means: will he regard [2]your persons, saith the Lord of hosts?

10 Who is there even among you [1]that would shut the doors, and kindle not *fire* on mine altar in vain? I have no pleasure in you, saith the Lord of hosts, neither will I accept an offering at your hand.

11 For from the rising of the sun unto the going down of the same, my Name is [1]great among the Gentiles, and in every place incense shall be offered unto my Name, and a pure offering: for my Name is great among the heathen, saith the Lord of hosts.

12 But ye have polluted it, in that ye say, [1]The table of the Lord *is* polluted, and the fruit thereof *even* his meat is not to be regarded.

13 Ye said also, Behold, *it is* a [1]weariness, and ye have snuffed at it, saith the Lord of hosts, and ye offered that which was torn, and the lame, and the sick: thus ye offered an offering: should I accept this of your hand, saith the Lord?

14 But cursed be the deceiver, which hath in his

1:1 [1] Read Isa. 13:1.

1:2 [1] Which declareth their great ingratitude that did not acknowledge this love, which was so evident, in that he chose Abraham from out of all the world, and next chose Jacob the younger brother of whom they came, and left Esau the elder.

1:3 [1] For beside here the signs of mine hatred appeared even when he was made servant unto his younger brother, being yet in his mother's belly, and also afterward in that he was put from his birthright, yet even now before your eyes the signs hereof are evident, in that that his country lieth waste and he shall never return to inhabit.

[2] Whereas ye my people, whom the enemy hated more than them, are by my grace and love toward you delivered, read Rom. 9:13.

1:6 [1] Besides the rest of the people he condemneth the Priests chiefly, because they should have reproved others for their hypocrisy, and obstinacy against God, and not have hardened them by their example to greater evils.

[2] He noteth their gross hypocrisy, which would not see their faults, but most impudently covered them, and so were blind guides.

1:7 [1] Ye receive all manner offerings for your own greediness, and do not examine whether they be according to my Law, or no.

[2] Not that they said thus, but by their doings they declared no less.

1:8 [1] You make it no fault: whereby he condemneth them, that think it sufficient to serve God partly as he hath commanded, and partly after man's fantasy: and so come not to the pureness of religion, which he requireth, and therefore in reproach he showeth them that a mortal man would not be content to be so served.

1:9 [1] He derideth the Priests who bare the people in hand that they prayed for them, and showeth that they were the occasion, that these evils came upon the people.

[2] Will God consider your office and state, seeing you are so covetous and wicked?

1:10 [1] Because the Levites who kept the doors did not try whether the sacrifices that came in, were according to the Law, God wisheth that they would rather shut the doors, than to receive such as were not perfect.

1:11 [1] God showeth that their ingratitude, and neglect of his true service shall be the cause of the calling of the Gentiles: and here the Prophet that was under the Law, framed his words to the capacity of the people, and by the altar and sacrifice he meaneth the spiritual service of God, which should be under the Gospel, when an end should be made to all these legal ceremonies by Christ's only sacrifice.

1:12 [1] Both the Priests and the people were infected with this error, that they passed not what was offered: for they thought that God was as well content with the lean, as with the fat: but in the mean season they showed not that obedience to God, which he required, and so committed both impiety, and also showed their contempt of God, and covetousness.

1:13 [1] The Priests and people were both weary with serving God, and passed not what manner of sacrifice and service they gave to God: for that which was least profitable, was thought good enough for the Lord.

flock ¹a male, and voweth, and sacrificeth unto the Lord a corrupt thing: for I am a great king, saith the Lord of hosts, and my Name is terrible among the heathen.

2 *1 Threatenings against the Priests, being seducers of the people.*

1 And now, O ye ¹Priests, this commandment is for you.

2 If ye will not hear it, nor consider it in your heart, to give glory ¹unto my Name, saith the Lord of hosts, I will even send a curse upon you, and will curse your ²blessings: yea, I have cursed them already, because ye do not consider it in *your* heart.

3 Behold, I will corrupt ¹your seed, and cast dung upon your faces, *even* the ²dung of your solemn feasts, and you shall be like unto it.

4 And ye shall know, that I have ¹sent this commandment unto you, that my covenant, which I made with Levi, might stand, saith the Lord of hosts.

5 My ¹covenant was with him of life and peace, and I ²gave him fear, and he feared me, and was afraid before ³my Name.

6 The Law of ¹truth was in his mouth, and there was no iniquity found in his lips: he walked with me in peace and equity, and did turn many away from iniquity.

7 For the Priest's ¹lips should preserve knowledge, and they should seek the Law at his mouth: for he is the ²messenger of the Lord of hosts.

8 But ye are gone out of the way: ye have caused many to fall by the Law: ye have broken the covenant of Levi, saith the Lord of hosts.

9 Therefore have I also made you to be despised, and vile before all the people, because ye kept not my ways, but have been partial in the Law.

10 Have we not all one ¹father? hath not one God made us? why do we transgress everyone against his brother, and break the covenant of ²our fathers?

11 Judah hath transgressed, and an abomination is committed in Israel and in Jerusalem: for Israel hath defiled the holiness of the Lord, which he loved, and hath married the ¹daughter of a strange god.

12 The Lord will cut off the man that doeth this: *both* the master and the servant out of the Tabernacle of Jacob, and him that ¹offereth an offering unto the Lord of hosts.

13 And this have ye done again, and ¹covered the altar of the Lord with tears, with weeping and with mourning: because the offering is no more regarded, neither received acceptably at your hands.

14 Yet ye say, ¹Wherein? Because the Lord hath been witness between thee and the wife of thy youth, against whom thou hast transgressed: yet is she thy ²companion, and the wife of thy ³covenant.

15 And did not ¹he make one? yet had he ²abundance of spirit: and wherefore one? because he sought a godly ³seed: therefore keep yourselves in your ⁴spirit, and let none trespass against the wife of his youth.

16 If thou hatest *her*, ¹put her away, saith the Lord God of Israel, yet he covereth ²the injury under his

---

1:14 ¹ That is, hath ability to serve the Lord according to his word, and yet will serve him according to his covetous mind.
2:1 ¹ He speaketh unto them chiefly, but under them he containeth the people also.
2:2 ¹ To serve me according to my word.
² That is, the abundance of God's benefits.
2:3 ¹ Your seed sown shall come to no profit.
² You boast of your holiness, sacrifices and feasts, but they shall turn to your shame and be as vile as dung.
2:4 ¹ The Priests objected against the Prophet that he could not reprove them, but he must speak against the Priesthood, and the office established of God by promise, but he showeth that the office is nothing slandered, when these villains and dung are called by their own names.
2:5 ¹ He showeth what were the two conditions of the covenant made with the tribe of Levi on God's part, that he would give them long life and felicity, and on their part, that they should faithfully serve him according to his word.
² I prescribed Levi a certain Law to serve me.
³ He served me and set forth my glory with all humilitude and submission.
2:6 ¹ He showeth that the Priests ought to have knowledge to instruct others in the word of the Lord.
2:7 ¹ He is as the treasure house of God's word, and ought to give to everyone according to their necessity, and not to reserve it for himself.
² Showing that whosoever doth not declare God's will, is not his

messenger, and Priest.
2:10 ¹ The Prophet accuseth the ingratitude of the Jews toward God and man: for seeing they were all born of one father Abraham, and God had elected them to be his holy people, they ought neither to offend God nor their brethren.
² Whereby they had bound themselves to God to be an holy people.
2:11 ¹ They have joined themselves in marriage with them that are of another religion.
2:12 ¹ That is, the Priest.
2:13 ¹ Yet cause the people to lament, because that God doth not regard their sacrifices, so that they seem to sacrifice in vain.
2:14 ¹ This is another fault, whereof he accuseth them, that is, that they broke the laws of marriage.
² As the one half of thyself.
³ She that was joined to thee by a solemn covenant, and by the invocation of God's name.
2:15 ¹ Did not God make man and woman as one flesh and not many?
² By his power and virtue he could have made many women for one man.
³ Such as should be born in lawful and moderate marriage, wherein is no excess of lusts.
⁴ Contain yourselves within your bounds, and be sober in mind, and bridle your affections.
2:16 ¹ Not that he doth allow divorcement, but of two faults he showeth, which is the less.
² He thinketh it sufficient to keep his wife still, albeit he take others, and so as it were covereth his fault.

garment, saith the Lord of hosts: therefore keep yourselves in your spirit, and transgress not.

17 Ye have [1]wearied the Lord with your words: yet ye say wherein have we wearied him? When ye say, Everyone that doeth [2]evil, is good in the sight of the Lord, and he delighteth in them. Or where is the God of [3]judgment?

3

1 Of the messenger of the Lord, John Baptist, and of Christ's office.

1 Behold, I will send my [1]messenger, and he shall prepare the way before me: and the [2]Lord whom ye seek, shall speedily come to his Temple: even the [3]messenger of the Covenant, whom ye desire: behold, he shall come, saith the Lord of hosts.

2 But who [1]may abide the day of his coming? and who shall endure, when he appeareth? for he is like a purging fire, and like fuller's soap.

3 And he shall sit down to try and fine the silver: he shall even fine the sons of [1]Levi and purify them as gold and silver, that they may bring offerings unto the Lord in righteousness.

4 Then shall the offerings of Judah and Jerusalem be acceptable unto the Lord, as in old time and in the years afore.

5 And I will come near to you to judgment, and I will be a swift witness against the soothsayers, and against the adulterers, and against false swearers, and against those that wrongfully keep back the hireling's wages, and vex the widow, and the fatherless, and oppress the stranger, and fear not me, saith the Lord of hosts.

6 For I am the Lord: I change not, and ye sons of Jacob [1]are not consumed.

7 From the days of your fathers, ye are gone away from mine ordinances, and have not kept them: [1]return unto me, and I will return unto you, saith the Lord of hosts: but ye said, Wherein shall we return?

8 Will a [1]man spoil his gods? yet have ye spoiled me: but ye say, Wherein have we spoiled thee? In [2]tithes and offerings.

9 Ye are cursed with a curse: for ye have spoiled me, even this whole nation.

10 Bring ye all the tithes into the storehouse, that there may be meat in my house, and prove me now herewith, saith the Lord of hosts, if I will not open the windows of heaven unto you, and pour you out a blessing [1]without measure.

11 And I will rebuke the [1]devourer for your sakes, and he shall not destroy the fruit of your ground, neither shall your vine be barren in the field, saith the Lord of hosts.

12 And all nations shall call you blessed: for ye shall be a pleasant land, saith the Lord of hosts.

13 Your words have been stout [1]against me, saith the Lord: yet ye say, What have we spoken against thee?

14 Ye have said, It is in vain to serve God: and what profit is it that we have kept his commandment, and that we walked humbly before the Lord of hosts?

15 Therefore we count the proud blessed: even they that work wickedness, are set up, and they that tempt God, yea, they are [1]delivered.

16 [1]Then spake they that feared the Lord, everyone to his neighbor, and the Lord hearkened and heard it, and a [2]book of remembrance was written before him for them that feared the Lord, and that thought upon his Name.

17 And they shall be to me, saith the Lord of hosts, in that day [1]that I shall do this, for a flock,

---

2:17 [1] Ye murmur against God, because he heard not you as soon as ye called.

[2] In thinking that God favored the wicked, and hath no respect to them that serve him.

[3] Thus they blasphemed God in condemning his power and justice, because he judged not according to their fantasies.

3:1 [1] This is meant of John Baptist, as Christ expoundeth it, Luke 7:27.

[2] Meaning, Messiah, Ps. 40:1, 7; Dan. 9:17, 25.

[3] That is, Christ, by whom the covenant was made and ratified, who is called the Angel or messenger of the covenant, because he reconcileth us to his father and is Lord or king, because he hath the government of his Church.

3:2 [1] He showeth that the hypocrites which wish so much for the Lord's coming will not abide when he draweth near: for he will consume them, and purge his and make them clean.

3:3 [1] He beginneth at the Priests that they might be lights, and shine unto others.

3:6 [1] They murmured against God, because they saw not his help ever present to defend them: and therefore he accuseth them of ingratitude, and showeth that in that they are not daily consumed, it is a token, that he doth still defend them, and so his mercy toward them never changeth.

3:7 [1] Read Zech. 1:3.

3:8 [1] There are none of the heathen so barbarous, that will defraud their gods of their honor, or deal deceitfully with them.

[2] Whereby the service of God should have been maintained, and the Priests and the poor relieved.

3:10 [1] Not having respect how much ye need, but I will give you in all abundance: so that ye shall lack place to put my blessings in.

3:11 [1] Meaning, the caterpillar, and whatsoever destroyeth corn and fruits.

3:13 [1] The Prophet condemneth them of double blasphemy against God: first, in that they said that God had no respect to them that served him, and next, that the wicked were more in his favor than the godly.

3:15 [1] They are not only preferred to honor, but also delivered from dangers.

3:16 [1] After these admonitions of the Prophet, some were lively touched, and encouraged others to fear God.

[2] Both because the thing was strange that some turned to God in that great and universal corruption, and also that this might be an example of God's mercies to all penitent sinners.

3:17 [1] When I shall restore my Church according to my promise, they shall be as mine own proper goods.

and I will ²spare them, as a man spareth his own son that serveth him.

18 Then shall you return, and discern between the righteous and wicked, between him that serveth God, and him that serveth him not.

4

The day of the Lord before the which Elijah should come.

1 For behold, the day cometh that shall ¹burn as an oven, and all the proud, yea, and all that do wickedly, shall be stubble, and the day that cometh, shall burn them up, saith the Lord of hosts, and shall leave them neither root nor branch.

2 But unto you that fear my name, shall the ¹sun of righteousness arise, and health *shall be* under his wings, and ye shall go ²forth and grow up as fat calves.

3 And ye shall tread down the wicked: for they shall be dust under the soles of your feet in the day that I shall do *this*, saith the Lord of hosts.

4 ¹Remember the Law of Moses my servant, which I commanded unto him in Horeb for all Israel with the statutes and judgments.

5 Behold, I will send you ¹Elijah the Prophet before the coming of the great and ²fearful day of the Lord.

6 And he shall ¹turn the heart of the fathers to the children, and the heart of the children to their fathers, lest I come and ²smite the earth with cursing.

3:17 ² That is, forgive their sins, and govern them with my Spirit.
4:1 ¹ He prophesieth of God's judgments against the wicked, who would not receive Christ, when as God should send him for the restoration of his Church.
4:2 ¹ Meaning, Christ, who with his wings or beams of his grace should lighten and comfort his Church, Eph. 5:14, and he is called the sun of righteousness, because in himself he hath all perfection and also the justice of the Father dwelleth in him: whereby he regenerateth us unto righteousness, cleanseth us from the filth of this world, and reformeth us to the image of God.
  ² Ye shall be set at liberty, and increase in the joy of the Spirit, 2 Cor. 3:17.
4:4 ¹ Because the time was come that the Jews should be destitute of Prophets until the time of Christ, because they should with more fervent minds desire his coming, the Prophet exhorteth them to exercise themselves diligently in studying the Law of Moses in the mean season, whereby they might continue in the true religion, and also be armed against all tentations.
4:5 ¹ This Christ expoundeth of John Baptist, Matt. 11:13, 14, who both for his zeal, and restoring of religion, is aptly compared to Elijah.
  ² Which as it is true for the wicked, so doth it waken the godly, and call them to repentance.
4:6 ¹ He showeth wherein John's office should stand: in the turning of men to God, and joining the father and children in one voice of faith: so that the father shall turn to the religion of his son which is converted to Christ, and the son shall embrace the faith of the true fathers, Abraham, Isaac, and Jacob.
  ² The second point of his office was to denounce God's judgments against them that would not receive Christ.

LEVI. SIMEON. RVBEN PETER. ANDREWE. IAMES.

IVDAH. IOHN.

DAN. PHILIP.

NEPHTHALI BARTHOLO.

MATHEW MARC

THE
NEW TESTA-
ment of our Lord IESVS
CHRIST, Translated out of
Greeke by *Theod. Beza* :
With briefe Summaries and expositions vpon the
hard places by the said Authour, *Ioac. Camer.*
and *P. Loseler. Villerius.*
Englished by L. TOMSON.
Together with the Annotations of *Fr. Iunius* vpon
the Reuelation of S. IOHN.

❡ IMPRINTED AT LONDON
by the Deputies of Christopher Barker,
Printer to the Queenes most
Excellent Maiestie.
1599.

GAD. MATHEWE

LVKE. IOHN

ASHER. THOMAS.

ISACAR. IAMES.

IOSEPH. BENIAMIN. MATTHIAS. IVDE.

ZABVLON. SIMON.

THE
New Testament

THE HOLY GOSPEL OF JESUS CHRIST,

ACCORDING TO

MATTHEW

1 *1 That Jesus is that Messiah, the Savior promised to the Fathers. 18 The nativity of Christ.*

1 The [a,1,2]book of the [3]generation of Jesus Christ the son of David, the [4]son of Abraham.

2 [b]Abraham begat Isaac. [c]And Isaac begat Jacob. And [d]Jacob begat Judah and his brethren.

3 [e]And Judah begat Perez, and Zerah of Tamar. And Perez begat Hezron. And Hezron begat Ram.

4 And Ram begat Amminadab. And Amminadab begat Nahshon. And Nahshon begat Salmon.

5 And Salmon begat [f]Boaz of Rahab. And Boaz begat Obed of Ruth. And Obed begat Jesse.

6 And [g]Jesse begat David the King. And David the King begat Solomon of her that was [h]*the wife of* Uriah.

7 And [i]Solomon begat Rehoboam. And Rehoboam begat Abijah. And Abijah begat Asa.

8 And Asa begat Jehoshaphat. And Jehoshaphat begat Joram. And Joram begat Uzziah.

9 And Uzziah begat Jotham. And Jotham begat Ahaz. And Ahaz begat Hezekiah.

10 And [j]Hezekiah begat Manasseh. And Manasseh begat Amon. And Amon begat Josiah.

11 And [k]Josiah begat Jakim. And Jakim [1]begat Jeconiah and his brethren about the time they were carried away to Babylon.

12 And after they were carried away into Babylon, [l]Jeconiah begat Shealtiel. And [m]Shealtiel begat Zerubbabel.

13 And Zerubbabel begat Abiud. And Abiud begat Eliakim. And Eliakim begat Azor.

14 And Azor begat Zadok. And Zadok begat Achim. And Achim begat Eliud.

CHAPTER 1
[a] Luke 3:23
[b] Gen. 21:2
[c] Gen. 25:14
[d] Gen. 29:35
[e] Gen. 38:27
1 Chron. 2:5
Ruth 4:18-19
[f] Ruth 4:21
[g] 1 Sam. 16:1
1 Sam. 17:12
[h] 2 Sam. 12:24
[i] 1 Kings 11:43
2 Chron. 3:10-11
[j] 2 Kings 20:21
2 Chron. 28:11
1 Chron. 3:13-15
[k] 2 Kings 23:34
2 Kings 24:1-6
2 Chron. 36:4-9
[l] 1 Chron. 3:16
[m] 1 Chron. 3:17
Ezra 3:2
Ezra 5:2
[n] Luke 1:27
[o] Deut. 14:1
[p] Luke 1:31
[q] Acts 4:12
[r] Isa. 7:14

15 And Eliud begat Eleazar. And Eleazar begat Matthan. And Matthan begat Jacob.

16 And Jacob begat Joseph the husband of Mary, of whom was born Jesus, that is called Christ.

17 So [1]all the generations from Abraham to David, *are* fourteen generations. And from David until they were carried away into Babylon, fourteen generations: and after they were carried away into Babylon until Christ, fourteen generations.

18 ¶ Now the birth of [1]Jesus Christ was thus, When as his mother Mary was [m]betrothed to Joseph, before they came together, she was found with child of the holy Ghost.

19 Then Joseph her husband being a just man, and not willing to [o]make her a public example, was minded to put her away secretly.

20 But while he thought these things, behold, the Angel of the Lord appeared unto him in a dream, saying, Joseph, the son of David, fear not to [1]take Mary thy [2]wife: for that which is [3]conceived in her, is of the holy Ghost.

21 And she shall bring [1]forth a son, and thou shalt [p]call his name JESUS: for he shall [q,2]save his people from their sins.

22 And all this was done that it might be fulfilled, which is spoken of the Lord by the Prophet, saying,

23 [r]Behold, a [1]virgin shall be with child, and shall bear a son, and they shall call his name Emmanuel, which is by interpretation, God with us.

24 ¶ Then Joseph being raised from sleep, did as the Angel of the Lord had enjoined him, and took his wife.

25 But he knew her not, [1]till she had brought forth

1:1 [1] Jesus Christ came of Abraham of the tribe of Judah, and of the stock of David as God promised.

[2] Rehearsal: As the Hebrews used to speak: as Gen. 5:1, The book of the generations.

[3] Of the ancestors of whom Christ came.

[4] Which Christ is also the son of Abraham.

1:11 [1] That is, the captivity fell in the days of Jakim and Jeconiah: for Jeconiah was born before their carrying away into captivity.

1:17 [1] All those which are reckoned up in this pedigree of David's stock, as they begat one another orderly in their degrees.

1:18 [1] Christ is the true Emmanuel, and therefore, Jesus (that is, Savior) is conceived in the Virgin by the holy Ghost, as it was foretold by the Prophets.

1:20 [1] Receive her at her parents' and kinsfolk's hands.

[2] Which was promised, and made sure to thee to be thy wife.

[3] Of the mother's substance by the holy Ghost.

1:21 [1] Christ is born of the same Virgin which never knew man: and is called Jesus of God himself, by the Angel.

[2] Deliver, and this showeth us the meaning of this name Jesus.

1:23 [1] There is in the Hebrew and Greek text, an article added, to point out the woman, and set her forth plainly: as you would say, that Virgin, or a certain virgin.

1:25 [1] This little word Till, in the Hebrew tongue, giveth us to understand also, that a thing shall not come to pass in time to come: as Michal had no children Till her death day, 2 Sam. 6:23. And in the last Chapter of this Evangelist: Behold, I am with you till the end of the world.

her first born son, and he called his name JESUS.

CHAPTER 2
a Luke 2:6
b Mic. 5:2
John 7:42
c Hos. 11:1
d Jer. 31:15

2

The wise men, who are the firstfruits of the Gentiles, worship Christ. 14 Joseph fled into Egypt with Jesus and his mother. 16 Herod slayeth the children.

1 When *a,*1Jesus then was born at Bethlehem in 2Judea, in the days of Herod the king, behold, there came 3Wise men from the East to Jerusalem,

2 Saying, Where is the King of the Jews that is born? for we have seen his star in the East, and are come to worship him.

3 When king Herod heard *this*, he was 1troubled, and all Jerusalem with him.

4 And gathering together all the 1chief Priests and 2Scribes of the people, he asked of them, where Christ should be born.

5 And they said unto him, At Bethlehem in Judea: for so it is written by the Prophet,

6 *b*And thou Bethlehem in the land of Judah, art not the 1least among the Princes of Judah: for out of thee shall come the governor that 2shall feed my people Israel.

7 Then Herod privily called the Wise men, *and* diligently inquired of them the time of the star that appeared,

8 And sent them to Bethlehem, saying, Go, and search diligently for the babe: and when ye have found him, bring me word again, that I may come also, and worship him.

9 ¶ So when they had heard the king, they departed: and lo, the star which they had seen in the East, went before them, till it came and stood over *the place* where the babe was.

10 And when they saw the star, they rejoiced with an exceeding great joy,

11 And went into the house, and found the babe with Mary his mother, and 1fell down, and worshipped him, and opened their 2treasures, and presented unto him gifts, *even* gold, and frankincense, and myrrh.

12 And after they were 1warned of God in a dream, that they should not go again to Herod, they returned into their country another way.

13 ¶ 1After their departure, behold, the Angel of the Lord appeareth to Joseph in a dream, saying, Arise, and take the babe and his mother, and flee into Egypt, and be there till I bring thee word, for Herod will seek the babe to destroy him.

14 So he arose and took the babe and his mother by night, and departed into Egypt.

15 And was there unto the death of Herod, that it might be fulfilled, which is spoken of the Lord by the *c*Prophet, saying, Out of Egypt have I called my son.

16 ¶ Then Herod, seeing that he was mocked of the Wise men, was exceeding wroth, and sent forth, and slew all the male children that were in Bethlehem, and in all the coasts thereof from two years old and under, according to the time which he had diligently searched out of the Wise men.

17 Then was that fulfilled which is spoken 1by the Prophet Jeremiah, saying,

18 *d*In Ramah was 1a voice heard, mourning, and weeping, and great howling: 2Rachel weeping for her children, and would not be comforted, because they were not.

19 1And when Herod was dead, behold, an Angel of the Lord appeareth in a dream to Joseph in Egypt,

20 Saying, Arise, and take the babe and his mother, and go into the land of Israel: for they are dead which sought the babe's life.

21 Then he arose up, and took the babe and his mother, and came into the land of Israel.

22 But when he heard that Archelaus did reign in Judea instead of his father Herod, he was afraid to go thither: yet after he was warned of God in a dream, he turned aside into the parts of Galilee.

23 And went and dwelt in a city called Nazareth, that it might be fulfilled which was spoken by the Prophets, *which was*, That he should be called a Nazarite.

2:1 1 Christ a poor child, laid down in a crib, and nothing set by of his own people, receiveth notwithstanding a noble witness of his divinity from heaven, and of his kingly estate of strangers: which his own also unwittingly allow of, although they do not acknowledge him.

2 For there was another in the tribe of Zebulun.

3 Wise and learned men: It is a Persian word which they use in good part.

2:3 1 Was much moved, for he was a stranger, and came to the kingdom by force: and the Jews were troubled: for wickedness is mad and raging.

2:4 1 The chief priests, that is, such as were of Aaron's family, which were divided into four and twenty orders, 1 Chron. 14:5 and 2 Chron. 36:14.

2 They that expound the Law to the people, for the Hebrews take this word of another, which signifieth as much as to expound and declare.

2:6 1 Though thou be a small town, yet shalt thou be very famous and notable through the birth of the Messiah, who shall be born in thee.

2 That shall rule and govern: for Kings are fitly called leaders and shepherds of the people.

2:11 1 A kind of humble and lovely reverence.

2 The rich and costly presents, which they brought him.

2:12 1 God warned and told them of it, whereas they asked it not.

2:13 1 Christ being yet scarce born, beginneth to be crucified for us, both in himself, and also in his members.

2:17 1 For God speaketh by the mouth of the Prophets.

2:18 1 A voice of lamenting, weeping, and howling.

2 That is to say, All that compass about Bethlehem: for Rachel Jacob's wife, who died in childbirth, was buried in the way that leadeth to this town, which is also called Ephrathah, because of the fruitfulness of the soil, and plenty of corn.

2:19 1 Christ is brought up in Nazareth, after the death of the tyrant by God's providence: that by the very name of the place, it might plainly appear to the world, that he is the Lord's true Nazarite.

3 *1 John preacheth.   4 His apparel and meat.   5 He baptizeth.   8 The fruits of repentance.   10 The axe at the root of the trees.   12 The fan and the chaff.   13 Christ is baptized.*

1 And *a*,1those days, 2John the Baptist came and preached in the 3wilderness of Judea,

2 And said, 1Repent: for the 2kingdom of heaven is at hand.

3 For this is he of whom it is spoken by the Prophet Isaiah, saying, *b*The voice of him that crieth in the wilderness, Prepare ye the way of the Lord: 1make his paths straight.

4 *c*And this John had his garment of camel's hair, and a girdle of a skin about his loins, his meat was also 1locusts and wild honey.

5 *d*Then went out to him 1Jerusalem and all Judea, and all the region round about Jordan,

6 And they were baptized of him in Jordan, 1confessing their sins.

7 1Now when he saw many of the Pharisees, and of the Sadducees come to his baptism, he said unto them, *e*O generation of vipers, who hath forewarned you to flee from the anger to come?

8 1Bring forth therefore fruit worthy amendment of life,

9 1And 2think not to say 3with yourselves, *f*We have Abraham to *our* father: for I say unto you, that God is able even of these stones to raise up children unto Abraham.

10 And now also is the axe put to the root of the

CHAPTER 3
a Mark 1:4
Luke 3:3
b Isa. 40:3
Mark 1:3
Luke 3:4
John 1:23
c Mark 1:6
d Mark 1:5
Luke 1:7
e Matt. 12:34
f John 8:39
Acts 13:26
g Matt. 7:19
h Mark 1:8
Luke 5:16
John 1:26
Acts 1:5
Acts 2:4
Acts 8:17
Acts 19:4-5
i Mark 1:9
Luke 3:21
j Col. 1:13
2 Pet. 1:17

CHAPTER 4
a Mark 1:12
Luke 4:1

---

trees: *g*therefore every tree which bringeth not forth good fruit, is hewn down, and cast into the fire.

11 *h*,1Indeed I baptize you with water to 2amendment of life, but he that cometh after me is mightier than I, whose shoes I am not worthy to bear, he will baptize you with the holy Ghost, and with fire.

12 1Which hath his fan in his hand, and will 2make clean his floor, and gather his wheat into his garner, but will burn up the chaff with unquenchable fire.

13 ¶ *i*,1Then came Jesus from Galilee to Jordan unto John to be baptized of him.

14 But John earnestly put him back, saying, I have need to be baptized of thee, and comest thou to me?

15 Then Jesus answering, said to him, Let be now: for thus it becometh us to fulfill 1all righteousness. So he suffered him.

16 And Jesus when he was baptized, came straight out of the water. And lo, the heavens were opened unto 1him, and *John* saw the Spirit of God descending like a dove, and [lighting] upon him.

17 1And lo, a voice *came* from heaven, saying, *j*This is my beloved Son, in whom I am 2well pleased.

4 *1 Christ is tempted.   4 He vanquisheth the devil with Scripture.   11 The Angels minister unto him.   12 He preacheth repentance, and that himself is come.   18 The calling of Peter, Andrew.   21 James and John.   24 He preacheth the Gospel, and healeth the diseased.*

1 Then *a*was 1Jesus led aside of the Spirit into the wilderness, to be tempted of the devil.

3:1 1 Not when Joseph went to dwell at Nazareth, but a great while after, about the space of 15 years: for in the 30 year of his age was Jesus baptized of John: therefore by those days is meant, at that time that Jesus remained as yet an inhabitant of the town of Nazareth.

2 John, who through his singular holiness and rare austereness of life caused all men to cast their eyes upon him, prepareth the way for Christ following fast on his heels, as the Prophet Isaiah foretold, and delivereth the sum of the Gospel, which in short space after should be delivered more fully.

3 In a hilly country, which was notwithstanding inhabited, for Zechariah dwelt there, Luke 1:40, and there was Joab's house, 1 Kings 2:34; and besides these, Joshua maketh mention of six towns that were in the wilderness, Josh. 15:62.

3:2 1 The word in the Greek tongue signifieth a changing of our minds and heart from evil to better.

2 The kingdom of Messiah, whose government shall be heavenly, and nothing but heavenly.

3:3 1 Make him a plain and smooth way.

3:4 1 Locusts were a kind of meat which certain of the East people use, which were therefore called devourers of Locusts. . . .

3:5 1 The people of Jerusalem.

3:6 1 Acknowledging that they were saved only by free remission and forgiveness of their sins.

3:7 1 There is nothing that stoppeth up the way of mercy and salvation against us so much as the opinion of our own righteousness doth.

3:8 1 True repentance is an inward thing which hath its seat in the mind and heart.

3:9 1 The faith of the fathers availeth their unbelieving children nothing at all: and yet for all that God playeth not the liar, nor dealeth unfaithfully in his league which he made with the holy fathers.

2 Think not that you have any cause to be proud of Abraham.

3 In your hearts.

3:11 1 We may neither dwell upon the signs which God hath ordained as means to lead us unto our salvation, neither upon them: but we must climb up to the matter itself, that is to say, to Christ, who inwardly worketh that effectually, which is outwardly signified unto us.

2 The outward sign putteth us in mind of this, that we must change our lives and become better, assuring us as by a seal, that we are engrafted into Christ; whereby our old man dieth and the new man riseth up, Rom. 6:4.

3:12 1 The triumphs of the wicked shall end in everlasting torment.

2 Will cleanse it thoroughly, and make a full riddance.

3:13 1 Christ sanctified our baptism in himself.

3:15 1 All such things as it hath appointed us to keep.

3:16 1 To John.

3:17 1 Christ's full consecration and authorizing to the office of mediatorship, is showed by the father's own voice, and a visible sign of the holy Ghost.

2 The Greek word betokeneth a thing of great account, and such as highly pleaseth a man. So then the Father saith, that Christ only is the man whom when he beholdeth, look what opinion he had conceived of us, he layeth it clean aside.

4:1 1 Christ was tempted all manner of ways and still overcometh, that we also through his virtue may overcome.

2 And when he had fasted [1]forty days, and forty nights, he was afterward hungry.

3 Then came to him the tempter, and said, If thou be the Son of God, command that these stones be made bread.

4 But he answering, said, It is written, [b]Man shall not live by bread only, but by every word that proceedeth out of the mouth of God.

5 Then the devil took him up into the holy city, and set him on a [1]pinnacle of the Temple.

6 And said unto him, If thou be the Son of God, cast thyself down, for it is written, [c]that he will give his Angels charge over thee, and with their hands they shall lift thee up, lest at any time thou shouldest dash thy foot against a stone.

7 Jesus said unto him, It is written again, [d]Thou shalt not [1]tempt the Lord thy God.

8 Again the devil took him up into an exceeding high mountain, and showed him all the kingdoms of the world, and the glory of them,

9 And said to him, All these will I give thee, if thou wilt fall down, and worship me.

10 Then said Jesus unto him, Avoid Satan: for it is written, [e]Thou shalt worship the Lord thy God, and him only shalt thou serve.

11 [f]Then the devil left him: and behold, the Angels came, and ministered unto him.

12 ¶ [g][1]And when Jesus had heard that John was committed to prison, he returned into Galilee,

13 And leaving Nazareth, went and dwelt in [1]Capernaum, which is near the sea in the borders of Zebulun and Naphtali,

14 That it might be fulfilled which was spoken by Isaiah the Prophet, saying,

15 [h]The land of Zebulun, and the land of Naphtali by the way of the [1]sea, beyond Jordan, [2]Galilee of the Gentiles:

16 The people which sat in darkness, saw great light: and to them which sat in the region and shadow of death, light is risen up.

17 [i]From that time Jesus began to preach, and to say, Amend your lives: for the kingdom of heaven is at [1]hand.

18 ¶ [1]And Jesus walking by the sea of Galilee saw two brethren, Simon, which was called Peter, and Andrew his brother, casting a net into the sea (for they were fishers.)

19 [j]And he said unto them, Follow me, and I will make you fishers of men.

20 And they straightway leaving the nets, followed him.

21 And when he was gone forth from thence, he saw other two brethren, James the son of Zebedee, and John his brother in a ship with Zebedee their father, mending their nets, and he called them.

22 And they without tarrying, leaving the ship and their father, followed him.

23 So [1]Jesus went about all Galilee, teaching in [2]their [3]Synagogues, and preaching the Gospel of the [4]kingdom, and healing [5]every sickness, and every [6]disease among the people.

24 And his fame spread abroad through all Syria: and they brought unto him all sick people, that were taken with divers diseases, and [1]torments, and them that were possessed with devils, and those which were [2]lunatic, and those that had the [3]palsy: and he healed them.

25 And there followed him great multitudes out of Galilee, and Decapolis, and Jerusalem, and Judea, and from beyond Jordan.

Cross references

[b] Deut. 8:3
[c] Ps. 91:11
[d] Deut. 6:16
[e] Deut. 16:13
Deut. 10:20
[f] Mark 1:13
Luke 4:13
[g] Mark 1:14
Luke 4:14
John 4:43
[h] Isa. 9:1
[i] Mark 1:15
[j] Mark 1:16
1 Cor. 1:27

4:2 [1] Full forty days.

4:5 [1] The battlement wherewith the flat roof of the temple was compassed about, that no man might fall down: as was appointed by the Law, Deut. 22:8.

4:7 [1] Word for word, Thou shalt not go on still in tempting.

4:12 [1] When the Herald's mouth is stopped, the Lord revealeth himself, and bringeth full light into the darkness of this world, preaching free forgiveness of sins to them that repent.

4:13 [1] Which was a town a great deal more famous than Nazareth was.

4:15 [1] Of Tiberias, or because that country bended toward Tyre, which standeth upon the sea that cutteth the midst of the world.

[2] So called, because it bordered upon Tyre and Sidon, and because Solomon gave the king of Tyre twenty cities in that quarter, 1 Kings 9:11.

4:17 [1] Is come to you.

4:18 [1] Christ thinking by time, that he should at length depart from us, even at the beginning of his preaching getteth him disciples after an heavenly sort, men indeed poor, and utterly unlearned, and therefore such as might be least suspected witnesses of the truth of those things which they heard and saw.

4:23 [1] Christ assureth the hearts of the believers of his spiritual and saving virtue, by healing the diseases of the body.

[2] Their, that is, the Galileans'.

[3] Synagogues, the Jews' Churches.

[4] Of Messiah.

[5] Diseases of all kinds, but not every one: that is, as we say, some of every one.

[6] The word signifieth properly the weakness of the stomach: but here it is taken for those diseases which make men faint, and wear away, that have them.

4:24 [1] The word signifieth properly, the stone wherewith gold is tried: and by a borrowed kind of speech is applied to all kinds of examination by torture, when as by rough dealing and torments, we go about to draw out the truth of men, which otherwise they would not confess: and in this place it is taken for those diseases, which put sick men to great woe.

[2] Which at every full Moon, or other changes of the Moon, are shrewdly troubled and diseased.

[3] Weak and feeble men, who have the parts of their body loosed, and so weakened, that they are neither able to gather them up together, nor put them out as they would.

5 1 *Who are blessed.* 13 *The Apostles are the salt and light of the world.* 14 *The city set on an hill.* 15 *The candle.* 16 *Good works.* 19 *The fulfilling of Christ's commandments.* 21 *What killing is.* 23 *Reconciliation is set before sacrifice.* 27 *Adultery.* 29 *The plucking out of the eye.* 30 *Cutting off of the hand.* 31 *The bill of divorcement.* 33 *Not to swear.* 44 *To love our enemies.* 48 *Perfectness.*

1 And when he saw the multitude, he went up into a mountain: and when he was set, his disciples came to him.

2 ¹And he opened his mouth, and taught them, saying,

3 ᵃBlessed *are* the ¹poor in ²spirit, for theirs is the kingdom of heaven.

4 ᵇBlessed *are* they that mourn: for they shall be comforted.

5 ᶜBlessed *are* the meek: for they shall inherit the earth.

6 ᵈBlessed *are* they which hunger and thirst for righteousness: for they shall be filled.

7 Blessed *are* the merciful: for they shall obtain mercy.

8 Blessed *are* the ᵉ,¹pure in heart: for they shall see God.

9 Blessed *are* the peacemakers: for they shall be called the children of God.

10 Blessed *are* theyᶠwhich suffer persecution for righteousness' sake; for theirs is the kingdom of heaven.

11 ᵍBlessed shall ye be when men revile you, and persecute *you,* and say all manner of evil against you for my sake, falsely.

12 Rejoice and be glad, for great is your reward in heaven: for so persecuted they the Prophets which

CHAPTER 5

ᵃ Luke 6:20
ᵇ Isa. 61:2-3
   Luke 6:21
ᶜ Ps. 37:11
ᵈ Isa. 65:13
ᵉ Ps. 24:4
ᶠ 1 Cor. 14:33
   1 Pet. 3:14
ᵍ Acts 5:41
   1 Pet. 4:14
ʰ Mark 9:50
   Luke 14:34
ⁱ Mark 4:21
   Luke 8:16
   Luke 11:33
ʲ 1 Pet. 2:12
ᵏ Luke 16:17
ˡ James 2:10
ᵐ Luke 11:39
ⁿ Exod. 20:13
   Deut. 5:17

were before you.

13 ᵇYe ¹are the salt of the ²earth: but if the salt have lost his savor, wherewith shall it be ³salted? It is thenceforth good for nothing, but to be cast out, and to be trodden under foot of men.

14 Ye are the ¹light of the world. A city that is set on an hill, cannot be hid.

15 ⁱNeither do men light a candle, and put it under a bushel, but on a candlestick, and it giveth light unto all that are in the house.

16 ʲLet your light so shine before men, that they may see your good works, and glorify your father which is in heaven.

17 ¹Think not that I am come to destroy the Law, or the Prophets. I am not come to destroy them, but to ²fulfill them.

18 ᵏFor truly I say unto you, Till heaven and earth perish, one jot or one tittle of the Law shall not escape, till all things be fulfilled.

19 ˡ,¹Whosoever therefore shall break one of these least commandments, and teach men so, he shall be called the ²least in the kingdom of heaven: but whosoever shall observe and teach *them,* the same shall be called great in the kingdom of heaven.

20 For I say unto you, except your righteousness ᵐexceed the *righteousness* of the Scribes and Pharisees, ye shall not enter into the kingdom of heaven.

21 ¹Ye have heard that it was said unto them of the old time, ⁿThou shalt not kill: for whosoever killeth shall be culpable of judgment.

22 But I say unto you, whosoever is angry with his brother unadvisedly, shall be ¹culpable ²of judgment. And whosoever saith unto his brother, Raca, shall be worthy to be punished by the ³Council.

5:2 ¹ Christ teacheth that the greatest joy and felicity is not in the commodities and pleasures of this life, but is laid up in heaven for them that willingly rest in the good will and pleasure of God, and endeavor to profit all men, although they be cruelly vexed, and troubled of the worldlings, because they will not fashion themselves to their manners.

5:3 ¹ Under the name of poverty are all such miseries meant, as are joined with poverty.

² Whose minds and spirits are brought under, and tamed, and obey God.

5:8 ¹ Fitly is this word Pure, joined with the heart, for as a bright and shining resemblance or image may be seen plainly in a clear and pure looking glass, even so doth the face (as it were) of the everlasting God, shine forth, and clear appears in a pure heart.

5:13 ¹ The ministers of the word, especially (unless they will be the most caitiff of all) must needs lead others both by word and deed to this greatest joy and felicity.

² Your doctrine must be very sound and good, for if it be not so, it shall be naught set by, and cast away as a thing unsavory and vain.

³ What shall you have to salt withal? And so are fools in the Latin tongue called saltless, as you would say, men that have no salt, or savor and taste in them.

5:14 ¹ You shine and give light, by being made partakers of the

true light.

5:17 ¹ Christ came not to bring any new way of righteousness and salvation into the world, but to fulfill that in deed which was shadowed by the figures of the Law, by delivering men through grace from the curse of the Law: and moreover to teach the true use of obedience which the Law appointed, and to engrave in our hearts the force of obedience.

² That the prophecies may be accomplished.

5:19 ¹ He beginneth with the true expounding of the Law, and setteth it against the old (but yet false) glosses of the Scribes: So far is he from abolishing the least commandment of his Father.

² He shall have no place in the Church.

5:21 ¹ The true meaning of the first commandment.

5:22 ¹ He speaketh of the judgment of God, and of the difference of sins, and therefore applieth his words to the form of civil judgments, which were then used.

² Of that judgment which was ruled by three men, who had the hearing and deciding of money matters, and such other small causes.

³ By that judgment which stood of 23 Judges, who had the hearing and deciding of weighty affairs and matters of life and death: as the highest Judges of all, were to the number of 71, which had the hearing of most weighty affairs, as the matter of a whole tribe or of an high Priest, or of a false prophet.

And whosoever shall say, Fool, shall be worthy to be punished with [4]hell [5]fire.

23　[1]If then thou bring thy gift to the [2]altar, and there rememberest that thy brother hath ought against thee,

24　Leave there thine offering before the altar, and go thy way: first be reconciled to thy brother, and then come and offer thy gift.

25　[o,1]Agree with thine adversary quickly, while thou art in the way with him, lest thine adversary deliver thee to the Judge, and the Judge deliver thee to the sergeant, and thou be cast into prison.

26　Verily I say unto thee, thou shalt not come out thence, till thou hast [1]paid the utmost farthing.

27　¶ [1]Ye have heard that it was said to them of old time, [p]Thou shalt not commit adultery.

28　But I say unto you, that whosoever looketh on a woman to lust after her, hath committed adultery with her already in his heart.

29　[q]Wherefore if thy [1]right eye cause thee [2]to offend, pluck it out and cast it from thee: for better it is for thee, that one of thy members perish, than that thy whole body should be cast into hell.

30　Also if thy right hand make thee to offend, cut it off, and cast it from thee: for better it is for thee, that one of thy members perish, than that thy whole body should be cast into hell.

31　It hath been said also, [r]Whosoever shall put away his wife, let him give her a bill of divorcement.

32　But I say unto you, whosoever shall put away his wife (except it be for fornication) causeth her to commit adultery: and whosoever shall marry her

that is divorced, committeth adultery.

33　[1]Again, ye have heard that it was said to them of old time, [s]Thou shalt not forswear thyself, but shalt perform thine oaths to the Lord.

34　But I say unto you, Swear not at all, neither by heaven, for it is the throne of God:

35　Nor yet by the earth, for it is his footstool: neither by Jerusalem: for it is the city of the great King.

36　Neither shalt thou swear by thine head, because thou canst not make one hair white or black.

37　[t]But let your communication be [1]Yea, yea: Nay, nay. For whatsoever *is* more than these, cometh of [2]evil.

38　¶ [1]Ye have heard that it hath been said, An [u]eye for an eye, and a tooth for a tooth.

39　But I say unto you, [v]Resist not evil: but whosoever shall smite thee on thy right cheek, turn to him the other also.

40　And if any man will sue thee at the law, and take away thy coat, let him have thy cloak also.

41　And whosoever will compel thee *to go* a mile, go with him twain.

42　[w]Give to him that asketh, and from him that would borrow of thee, turn not away.

43　Ye have heard that it hath been said, [x]Thou shalt love thy neighbor, and hate thine enemy.

44　But I say unto you, [y]Love your enemies: bless them that curse you: do good to them that hate you, [z]and pray for them which hurt you, and persecute you,

45　[a,1]That ye may be the children of your father

Cross references (center column):

[o] Luke 12:58
[p] Exod. 20:14
Rom. 13:9
[q] Matt. 18:8-9
Mark 9:47
[r] Matt. 19:7
Deut. 24:1
Mark 10:4
Luke 16:18
1 Cor. 7:10
[s] Exod. 20:7
Lev. 19:12
Deut. 5:11
[t] James 5:12
[u] Exod. 21:24
Lev. 24:20
Deut. 19:21
[v] Luke 6:29
Rom. 12:17
1 Cor. 6:7
[w] Deut. 15:8
[x] Lev. 19:18
[y] Luke 6:27
[z] Luke 23:34
Acts 7:60
1 Cor. 4:13
[a] Luke 6:35

5:22 [4] Whereas we read here, Hell, it is in the text itself, Gehenna, which is an Hebrew word made of two, and is as much to say, as the Valley of Hinnom, which otherwise the Hebrews called Tophet: it was a place where the Israelites were wont most cruelly to sacrifice their children to false gods, whereupon it was taken for a place appointed to torment the reprobates in Jer. 7:31.

[5] The Jews used four kinds of punishments, before their government was taken away by Herod, hanging, heading, stoning, and burning: this is it that Christ shot at, because burning was the greatest punishment, therefore in that he maketh mention of a judgment, a council, and a fire, he showeth that some sins are worse than other sins, but yet they are all such that we must give account for them, and will be punished for them.

5:23 [1] The covetous Pharisees taught that God was appeased by the sacrifices appointed in the Law, which they themselves devoured. But Christ on the contrary side denieth that God accepteth any man's offering, unless he maketh satisfaction to his brother whom he hath offended: and saith moreover, that these stubborn and stiffnecked despisers of their brethren, shall never escape the wrath and curse of God, before they have made full satisfaction to their brethren.

[2] He applieth all this speech to the state of his time, when as there was an altar standing in Jerusalem, and therefore they are very foolish, that gather hereupon, that we must build altars, and use sacrifices: but they are more fools, which draw that to purgatory, which is

spoken of peacemaking and atonement one with another.

5:25 [1] Cut off all cause for enmity.

5:26 [1] Thou shalt be dealt withall to the utmost extremity.

5:27 [1] He is taken for an adulterer before God, whatsoever he be, that coveteth a woman: and therefore we must keep our eyes chaste, and all the members we have, yea, and we must eschew all occasions which might move us to evil, how dear soever it cost us.

5:29 [1] He nameth the right eye and the right hand, because the parts of the right side of our bodies are the chiefest, and the readiest to commit any wickedness.

[2] Word for word, do cause thee to offend: for sins are stumbling blocks as it were, that is to say, rocks which we are cast upon.

5:33 [1] The meaning of the third commandment against the froward opinion and judgment of the Scribes, which excused by oaths or indirect forms of swearing.

5:37 [1] Whatsoever you vouch, vouch it barely, and whatsoever you deny, deny it barely without any more words.

[2] From an evil conscience, or from the devil.

5:38 [1] He showeth clean contrary to the doctrine of the Scribes, that the sum of the second table must be understood, that we may in no wise render evil for evil, but rather suffer double injury, and do well to them that are our deadly enemies.

5:45 [1] A double reason: the one is taken of relatives, that children must be like their father: the other is taken of comparison, The children of God must be better, than the children of this world.

that is in heaven: for he maketh his sun to arise on the evil and the good, and sendeth rain on the just and unjust.

46 For if ye love them, which love you, what reward shall you have? Do not the Publicans even the same?

47 And if ye be friendly to your brethren only, what singular thing do ye? do not even the [1]Publicans likewise?

48 Ye shall therefore be perfect, as your Father which is in heaven, is perfect.

6

1 Alms. 5 Prayer. 14 Forgiving our brother. 16 Fasting. 19 Our treasure. 20 We must succor the poor. 24 God and riches. 25 Careful seeking for meat and drink, and apparel, forbidden. 33 The kingdom of God and his righteousness.

1 Take heed that ye give not your [1]alms before men to be seen of them, or else ye shall have no [2]reward of your Father which is in heaven.

2 [a]Therefore when thou givest thine alms, thou shalt not make a trumpet to be blown before thee, as the [1]hypocrites do in the Synagogues and in the streets, to be praised of men. Verily I say unto you, they have their reward.

3 But when thou doest thine alms, let not thy left hand know what thy right hand doeth,

4 That thine alms may be in secret, and thy Father that seeth in secret, he will reward thee openly.

5 [1]And when thou prayest, be not as the hypocrites: for they love to stand and pray in the Synagogues, and in the corners of the streets, because they would be seen of men. Verily I say unto you, they have their reward.

6 But when thou prayest, enter into thy chamber: and when thou hast shut thy door, pray unto thy Father which is in secret, and thy Father which seeth in secret, shall reward thee openly.

7 Also when ye pray, use no [1]vain repetitions as the Heathen: for they think to be heard for their

CHAPTER 6
[a] Rom. 2:8
[b] Luke 11:2
[c] Matt. 13:19
[d] Mark 11:25
[e] Luke 12:33
1 Tim. 6:19
[f] Luke 11:34
[g] Luke 16:13

much babbling.

8 Be ye not like them therefore: for your Father knoweth whereof ye have need, before ye ask of him.

9 [1]After this manner therefore pray ye, [b]Our father which art in heaven, hallowed be thy name.

10 Thy kingdom come. Thy will be done even in earth as *it is* in heaven.

11 Give us this day our [1]daily bread.

12 And forgive us our debts, as we also forgive our debtors.

13 And lead us not into temptation, but deliver us [c]from [1]evil: for thine is the kingdom, and the power, and the glory for ever. Amen.

14 [d,1]For if ye do forgive men their trespasses, your heavenly Father will also forgive you.

15 But if ye do not forgive men their trespasses, no more will your father forgive you your trespasses.

16 [1]Moreover, when ye fast, look not sour as the hypocrites: for they [2]disfigure their faces, that they might seem unto men to fast. Verily I say unto you that they have their reward.

17 But when thou fastest, anoint thine head, and wash thy face,

18 That thou seem not unto men to fast, but unto thy Father which is in secret: and thy Father which seeth in secret, will reward thee openly.

19 ¶ [1]Lay not up treasures for yourselves upon the earth, where the moth and canker corrupt, and where thieves dig through and steal.

20 [e]But lay up treasures for yourselves in heaven, where neither the moth nor canker corrupteth, and where thieves neither dig through nor steal.

21 For where your treasure is, there will your heart be also.

22 ¶ [f,1]The light of the body is the eye: if then thine [2]eye be single, thy whole body shall be light.

23 But if thine eye be wicked, then all thy body shall be dark. Wherefore if the light that is in thee, be darkness, how great is that darkness?

24 [g,1]No man can serve [2]two masters: for either

5:47 [1] They that were the toll masters, and had the oversight of tributes and customs: a kind of men that the Jews hated to death, both because they served the Romans in these offices, (whose yokeful bondage they could hardly away withall) and also because these toll masters are for the most part given to covetousness.
6:1 [1] Ambition maketh alms vain.
  [2] This word, Reward, is always taken in the Scriptures for a free recompense, and therefore the schoolmen do fondly set it to be answerable to a deserving, which they call merit.
6:2 [1] Counterfeits, for Hypocrites were players that played a part in a play.
6:5 [1] He reprehendeth two foul faults in prayer, ambition, and vain babbling.
6:7 [1] Long prayers are not condemned, but vain needless, and superstitious.
6:9 [1] A true sum and form of all Christian prayers.
6:11 [1] That, that is meet for our nature for our daily food, or such, as

may suffice our nature and complexion.
6:13 [1] From the Devil, or from all adversity.
6:14 [1] They that forgive wrongs, to them sins are forgiven, but revenge is prepared for them that revenge.
6:16 [1] Against such as hunt after a name of holiness, by fasting.
  [2] They suffer not their first hue to be seen, that is to say, they mar the natural color of their faces, that they may seem lean and palefaced.
6:19 [1] Those men's labors are shown to be vain which pass not for the assured treasure of everlasting life, but spend their lives in scraping together frail and vain riches.
6:22 [1] Men do maliciously and wickedly put out even the little light of nature that is in them.
  [2] The judgment of the mind: that as the body is with the eyes, so our whole life may be ruled with right reason, that is to say, with the Spirit of God wherewith we are lightened.
6:24 [1] God will be worshipped of the whole man.
  [2] Which be at jar together, for if two agree, they are as one.

he shall hate the one, and love the other, or else he shall lean to the one, and despise the other. Ye cannot serve God and [3]riches.

25 [b,1]Therefore I say unto you, be not careful for your life, what ye shall eat, or what ye shall drink: nor yet for your body, what ye shall put on. Is not the life more worth than meat? and the body than raiment?

26 Behold the fowls of the [1]heaven: for they sow not, neither reap, nor carry into the barns, yet your heavenly Father feedeth them. Are ye not much better than they?

27 Which of you by [1]taking care is able to add one cubit unto his stature?

28 And why care ye for raiment? Learn how the Lilies of the field do grow: they [1]are not wearied, neither spin:

29 Yet I say unto you, that even Solomon in all his glory was not arrayed like one of these.

30 Wherefore if God so clothe the grass of the field which is today, and tomorrow is cast into the oven, shall he not do much more unto you, O ye of little faith?

31 Therefore take no thought, saying, What shall we eat? or what shall we drink? or wherewith shall we be clothed?

32 (For after all these things seek the Gentiles) for your heavenly Father knoweth that ye have need of all these things.

33 But seek ye first the kingdom of God, and his righteousness, and all these things shall be ministered unto you.

34 Care not then for the morrow, for the morrow shall care for itself: the day hath enough with his own grief.

7 *1 We may not give judgment of our neighbors,   6 Nor cast that which is holy unto dogs.   13 The broad and strait way.   15 False prophets.   18 The tree and fruit.   24 The house built on a rock,   26 and on the sand.*

1 Judge [1]not, that ye be not judged.

2 For with what [a]judgment ye judge, ye shall be

Marginal references

b Luke 12:22
Phil. 4:6
1 Tim. 6:8
1 Pet. 5:7
Ps. 55:23

CHAPTER 7
a Luke 6:37-38
Rom. 2:1
1 Cor. 4:3
b Mark 4:24
Luke 6:38
c Luke 6:41
d Matt. 21:22
Mark 11:24
Luke 11:9
John 24:13
John 16:23
James 1:5
e Luke 6:31
Job 4:16
f Luke 13:14
g Luke 6:44

judged, and with what [b]measure ye mete, it shall be measured unto you again.

3 And why seest thou the mote, that is in thy brother's eye, and perceivest not the beam that is in thine own eye?

4 [c]Or how sayest thou to thy brother, Suffer me to cast out the mote out of thine eye, and, behold, a beam is in thine own eye?

5 Hypocrite, first cast out that beam out of thine own eye, and then shalt thou see clearly to cast out the mote out of thy brother's eye.

6 ¶ [1]Give ye not that which is holy to dogs, neither cast ye your [2]pearls before swine, lest they tread them under their feet, and turning again, all to rent you.

7 ¶ [d,1]Ask, and it shall be given you: seek, and ye shall find: knock, and it shall be opened unto you.

8 For whosoever asketh, receiveth: and he that seeketh, findeth: and to him that knocketh, it shall be opened.

9 For what man is there among you, which if his son ask him bread, would give him a stone?

10 Or if he ask fish, will he give him a serpent?

11 If ye then, which are evil, can give to your children good gifts, how much more shall your Father which is in heaven, give good things to them that ask him?

12 [e,1]Therefore whatsoever ye would that men should do to you: even so do ye to them: for this is the [2]Law and the Prophets.

13 ¶ [f,1]Enter in at the strait gate: for it is the wide gate, and broad way that leadeth to destruction: and many there be which go in thereat.

14 Because [1]the gate is strait, and the way narrow that leadeth unto life, and few there be that find it.

15 ¶ [1]Beware of false prophets, which come to you in sheep's clothing, but inwardly they are ravening wolves.

16 Ye shall know them by their fruits. [g]Do men gather grapes of thorns? or figs of thistles?

17 So every good tree bringeth forth good fruit, and a corrupt tree bringeth forth evil fruit.

6:24 [3] This word is a Syrian word, and signifieth all things that belong to money.

6:25 [1] The froward carking carefulness for things of this life is corrected in the children of God by an earnest thinking upon the providence of God.

6:26 [1] Of the air, or that live in the air: for in all tongues almost this word Heaven is taken for the air.

6:27 [1] He speaketh of care which is joined with thought of mind, and hath for the most part difficult yoke with it.

6:28 [1] By labor.

7:1 [1] We ought to find fault one with another, but we must beware we do it not without cause, or to seem holier than they, or in hatred of them.

7:6 [1] The stiffnecked and stubborn enemies of the Gospel are

unworthy to have it preached unto them.

[2] A pearl hath his name among the Grecians, for the orient brightness that is in it: and a pearl was in ancient time in great estimation among the Latins: for a pearl that Cleopatra had, was valued at two hundred and fifty thousand crowns, and the word is now borrowed from that, to signify the most precious heavenly doctrine.

7:7 [1] Prayers are a sure refuge in all miseries.

7:12 [1] A rehearsal of the meaning of the second table.

[2] That is to say, the doctrine of the Law and Prophets.

7:13 [1] Example of life must not be taken from a multitude.

7:14 [1] The way is straight and narrow we must pass through this rough way, and suffer and endure, and be thronged, and to enter into life.

7:15 [1] False teachers must be taken heed of, and they are known by false doctrine and evil living.

18 A good tree cannot bring forth evil fruit, neither can a corrupt tree bring forth good fruit.

19 [h]Every tree that bringeth not forth good fruit, is hewn down, and cast into the fire.

20 Therefore by their fruits ye shall know them.

21 ¶ [i]Not everyone that saith unto me, Lord, Lord, shall enter into the kingdom of heaven, [j]but he that doeth my Father's will which is in heaven.

22 [j]Many will say to me in that day, Lord, Lord, have we not by thy [1]Name prophesied, and by thy name cast out devils? and by thy name done many [2]great works?

23 And then will I profess to them, [k,1]I never knew you, [l]depart from me [2]ye that work iniquity.

24 [1]Whosoever then heareth of me these words, [m]and doeth the same, I will liken him to a wise man, which hath builded his house on a rock:

25 And the rain fell, and the floods came, and the winds blew, and beat upon that house, and it fell not: for it was grounded on a rock,

26 But whosoever heareth these my words, and doeth them not, shall be likened unto a foolish man, which hath builded his house upon the sand:

27 And the rain fell, and the floods came, and the winds blew, and beat upon that house, and it fell, and the fall thereof was great.

28 ¶ [n]And it came to pass, when Jesus had ended these words, the people were astonished at his doctrine.

29 For he taught them as one having authority, and not as the Scribes.

8

1 *The Leper cleansed.*   5 *The Centurion's faith.*   11 *The calling of the Gentiles,*   12 *and casting out of the Jews.*   14 *Peter's mother-in-law healed.*   19 *A Scribe desirous to follow Christ.*   23 *The tempest on the sea.*   28 *Two possessed with devils cured.*   32 *The devils go into swine.*

1 Now when he was come down from the mountain, great multitudes followed him.

2 [a,1]And lo, there came a Leper and worshipped him, saying, Master, if thou wilt, thou canst make me clean.

3 And Jesus putting forth his hand, touched

him, saying, I will, be thou clean: and immediately his leprosy was cleansed.

4 Then Jesus said unto him, See thou tell no man, but go, *and* show thyself unto the Priest, and offer the gift that [b]Moses commanded, for a witness to them.

5 ¶ [c,1]When Jesus was entered into Capernaum, there came unto him a Centurion, beseeching him,

6 And said, Master, my servant lieth sick at home of the palsy, and is grievously pained.

7 And Jesus said unto him, I will come and heal him.

8 But the Centurion answered, saying, Master, I am not worthy that thou shouldest come under my roof: but speak the word only, and my servant shall be healed.

9 For I am a man also under the authority *of another*, and have soldiers under me: and I say to one, Go, and he goeth: and to another, Come, and he cometh: and to my servant, Do this, and he doeth it.

10 When Jesus heard *that*, he marveled, and said to them that followed *him*, Verily, I say unto you, I have not found so great faith, even in Israel.

11 But I say unto you, that many shall come from the East and West, and shall [1]sit down with Abraham, and Isaac, and Jacob, in the kingdom of heaven.

12 And the children of the kingdom shall be cast out into [1]utter [d]darkness: there shall be weeping and gnashing of teeth.

13 Then Jesus said unto the Centurion, Go thy way, and as thou hast believed, so be it unto thee. And his servant was healed the same hour.

14 ¶ [e,1]And when Jesus came to Peter's house, he saw his wife's mother laid down, and sick of a fever.

15 And he touched her hand, and the fever left her: so she arose, and ministered unto them.

16 [f]When the Even was come, they brought unto him many that were possessed with devils: and he cast out the spirits with *his* word, and healed [1]all that were sick,

Marginal references

[h] Matt. 3:10
[i] Rom. 2:13
[j] James 1:22
[k] Luke 13:27
[l] Ps. 6:8
[m] Luke 6:47-48
[n] Mark 4:22
  Luke 4:32

CHAPTER 8
[a] Mark 2:40
  Luke 5:12
[b] Lev. 14:3-4
[c] Luke 7:1
[d] Matt. 22:13
[e] Mark 1:29
  Luke 4:38
[f] Mark 1:32
  Luke 4:40

7:21 [1] Even the best gifts that are, are nothing without godliness.

7:22 [1] By Name here, is meant that mighty working power of God, which every man witnesseth that calleth upon him.

[2] Properly powers: Now these excellent works wrought are called Powers, by occasion of these things which they bring to pass, for by them we understand, how mighty the power of God is.

7:23 [1] This is not of ignorance, but because he will cast them away.

[2] You that are given to all kind of wickedness, and seem to make an art of sin.

7:24 [1] True godliness resteth only upon Christ, and therefore always remaineth invincible.

8:2 [1] Christ in healing the leprous with the touching of his hand, showeth that he abhorreth no sinners that come unto him, be they

never so unclean.

8:5 [1] Christ by setting before them the example of the uncircumcised Centurion, and yet of an excellent faith, provoketh the Jews to emulation, and together forewarneth them of their casting off, and the calling of the Gentiles.

8:11 [1] A Metaphor taken of banquets, for they that sit down together are fellows in the banquet.

8:12 [1] Which are without the kingdom: For in the kingdom is light, and without the kingdom darkness.

8:14 [1] Christ, in healing divers diseases, showeth that he was sent of his Father, that in him only we should seek remedy in all our miseries.

8:16 [1] Of all sorts.

17 That it might be fulfilled, which was spoken by ᵍIsaiah the Prophet, saying, He took our infirmities, and bare *our* sicknesses.

18 ¶ ᵇAnd when Jesus saw great multitudes of people about him, he commanded them to go ¹over *the water*.

19 ¹Then came there a certain Scribe, and said unto him, Master, I will follow thee whithersoever thou goest.

20 But Jesus said unto him, The foxes have holes, and the birds of the heaven have ¹nests, but the Son of man hath not whereon to rest his head.

21 ¶ ¹And another of his disciples said unto him, Master, suffer me first to go, and bury my father.

22 But Jesus said unto him, Follow me, and let the dead bury the dead.

23 ¶ ⁱ,¹And when he was entered into the ship, his disciples followed him.

24 And behold, there arose a great tempest in the sea, so that the ship was covered with waves: but he was asleep.

25 Then his disciples came, and awoke him, saying, Master, save us: we perish.

26 And he said unto them, Why are ye fearful, O ye of little faith? Then he arose, and rebuked the winds and the sea: and *so* there was a great calm.

27 And the men marveled, saying, What man is this, that both the winds and the sea obey him?

28 ¶ ʲ,¹And when he was come to the other side into the country of the Gergesenes, there met him two possessed with devils which came out of the graves very fierce, so that no man might go by that way.

29 And behold, they cried out, saying, Jesus the son of God, what have we to do with thee? Art thou come hither to torment us before the time?

30 Now there was ¹afar off from them, a great herd of swine feeding.

31 And the devils besought him, saying, If thou cast us out, suffer us to go into the herd of swine.

32 And he said unto them, Go. So they went out and departed into the herd of swine: and behold,

the whole herd of swine ran headlong into the sea, and died in the water.

33 Then the herdmen fled: and when they were come into the city, they told all things, and what was become of them that were possessed with the devils,

34 And behold, all the city came out to meet Jesus: and when they saw him, they besought him to ¹depart out of their coasts.

9

1 One sick of the palsy, is healed. 5 Remission of sins. 9 Matthew called. 10 Sinners. 17 New wine. 18 The ruler's daughter raised. 20 A woman healed of a bloody issue. 28 Two blind men by faith receive sight. 32 A dumb man possessed is healed. 37 The harvest and workmen.

1 Then he ¹entered into a ship, and passed over, and came into his ²own city.

2 And ᵃlo, they brought to him a man sick of the palsy laid on a bed. And Jesus ¹seeing their faith, said to the sick of the palsy, Son be of good comfort: thy sins are forgiven thee.

3 And behold, certain of the Scribes said with themselves, This man ¹blasphemeth.

4 But when Jesus saw their thoughts, he said, Wherefore think ye evil things in your hearts?

5 For whether is it easier to say, Thy sins are forgiven thee, or to say, Arise, and walk?

6 And that ye may know that the Son of man hath authority in earth to forgive sins (then said he unto the sick of the palsy,) Arise, take up thy bed, and go to thine house.

7 And he arose, and departed to his own house.

8 So when the multitude saw it, they marveled, and glorified God, which had given such authority to men.

9 ¶ ᵇ,¹And as Jesus passed forth from thence, he saw a man sitting at the ²custom, named Matthew, and said to him, Follow me. And he arose, and followed him.

10 And it came to pass, as Jesus sat at meat in *his*

ᵍ Isa. 53:4
1 Pet. 2:24
ᵇ Luke 9:57-58
ⁱ Mark 4:37
Luke 8:23
ʲ Mark 5:1-2
Luke 26:27
CHAPTER 9
ᵃ Mark 2:3
Luke 5:18
ᵇ Mark 2:14
Luke 5:27

8:18 ¹ For Capernaum was situated upon the lake of Tiberias.

8:19 ¹ The true disciples of Christ must prepare themselves to all kind of miseries.

8:20 ¹ Word for word, shades made with boughs.

8:21 ¹ When God requireth our labor, we must leave off all our duty to men.

8:23 ¹ Although Christ seemeth oftentimes to neglect his, even in most extreme danger, yet in time convenient he assuageth all tempests, and bringeth them to the haven.

8:28 ¹ Christ came to deliver me from the miserable thraldom of Satan: but the world had rather lack Christ, than the vilest and least of their commodities.

8:30 ¹ Of an hill, as Mark and Luke witness: Now Gadara as Josephus recordeth, book 17 chapter 13, lived after the order of the Grecians,

and therefore we may not marvel if there were swine there.

8:34 ¹ Where men live as swine, there doth not Christ tarry, but devils.

9:1 ¹ Sins are the causes of our afflictions, and Christ only forgiveth them if we believe.

² Into Capernaum, for as Theophylact saith, Bethlehem brought him forth, Nazareth brought him up, and Capernaum was his dwelling place.

9:2 ¹ Knowing by a manifest sign.

9:3 ¹ To blaspheme, signifieth amongst the divines to speak wickedly: and amongst the more eloquent Grecians, to slander.

9:9 ¹ Christ calleth the humble sinners unto him, but he condemneth the proud hypocrites.

² At the customer's table, where it was received.

house, behold, many Publicans and [1]sinners that came *thither*, sat down at the table with Jesus and his disciples.

11 And when the Pharisees saw that, they said to his disciples, Why eateth your Master with Publicans and sinners?

12 Now when Jesus heard it, he said unto them, The whole need not the Physician, but they that are sick.

13 But go ye and learn what this is, [c]I will have mercy, and not sacrifice: for I am not come to call the righteous, but the [d]sinners to repentance.

14 ¶ [e,1]Then came the disciples of John to him, saying, Why do we and the Pharisees fast oft, and thy disciples fast not?

15 And Jesus said unto them, Can the [1]children of the marriage chamber mourn as long as the bridegroom is with them? But the days will come, when the bridegroom shall be taken from them, and then shall they fast.

16 Moreover, no man pieceth an old garment with a piece of [1]new cloth: for that that should fill it up, taketh away from the garment, and the breach is worse.

17 Neither do they put new wine into old vessels: for then the vessels would break, and the wine would be spilt, and the vessels would perish: but they put new wine into new vessels, and so are both preserved.

18 ¶ [f,1]While he thus spake unto them, behold, there came a certain ruler, and worshipped him, saying, My daughter is now deceased: but come and lay thine hand on her, and she shall live.

19 And Jesus arose and followed him with his disciples.

20 (And behold, a woman which was diseased with an issue of blood twelve years, came behind him, and touched the hem of his garment.

21 For she said in herself, If I may touch but his garment only, I shall be whole.

22 Then Jesus turned him about, and seeing her, did say, Daughter, be of good comfort: thy faith hath made thee whole. And the woman was made whole at that same moment.)

23 [1]Now when Jesus came into the ruler's house, and saw the [2]minstrels and the multitude making

[c] Hos. 6:6
Matt. 12:7
[d] 1 Tim. 1:15
[e] Mark 2:18
Luke 5:33
[f] Mark 5:22
Luke 8:41
[g] Luke 11:14
[b] Matt. 12:24
Mark 3:22
Luke 11:15
[i] Mark 6:6
Luke 13:22
[j] Mark 6:34
[k] Luke 10:2
John 4:35-36

noise,

24 He said unto them, Get you hence: for the maid is not dead, but sleepeth. And they laughed him to scorn.

25 And when the multitude were put forth, he went in and took her by the hand, and the maid arose.

26 And this bruit went throughout all that land.

27 [1]And as Jesus departed thence, two blind men followed him, crying, and saying, O son of David, have mercy upon us.

28 And when he was come into the house, the blind came to him, and Jesus said unto them, Believe ye that I am able to do this? And they said unto him, Yea, Lord.

29 Then touched he their eyes, saying, According to your faith be it unto you.

30 And their eyes were opened, and Jesus gave them great charge, saying, See that no man know it.

31 But when they were departed, they spread abroad his fame throughout all that land.

32 ¶ [g,1]And as they went out, behold, they brought to him a dumb man possessed with a devil.

33 And when the devil was cast out, the dumb spake: then the multitude marveled, saying, The like was never seen in Israel.

34 But the Pharisees said, [h]He casteth out devils, through the prince of devils.

35 ¶ And [i]Jesus went about all cities and towns, teaching in their Synagogues, and preaching the Gospel of the kingdom, and healing every sickness and every disease among the people.

36 [1]But [j]when he saw the multitude, he had compassion upon them, because they were dispersed, and scattered abroad, as sheep having no shepherd.

37 Then said he to his disciples, [k]Surely the harvest is great, but the laborers *are* few.

38 Wherefore pray the Lord of the harvest, that he would [1]send forth laborers into his harvest.

10 1 *The gift of healing given to the Apostles.* 5 *They are sent to preach the Gospel.* 13 *Peace.* 14 *Shaking off the dust.* 18 *Affliction.* 22 *Continuance unto the end.* 23 *Fleeing from persecution.* 28 *Fear.* 29 *Two sparrows.* 30 *Hairs of our head.* 32 *To acknowledge*

9:10 [1] The customers fellows which were placed by the Romans, after that Judea was brought into the form of a province, to gather the customs, and therefore of the rest of the Jews, they were called sinners, that is to say very vile men.

9:14 [1] Against naughty emulation in matters indifferent.

9:15 [1] An Hebrew kind of speech, for they that are admitted into a marriage chamber are as the nearest about the bridegroom.

9:16 [1] Raw, which was never put to the fuller.

9:18 [1] There is no evil so old and incurable, which Christ cannot heal by and by, if he be touched with true faith, but lightly as it were with

the hand.

9:23 [1] Even death itself giveth place to the power of Christ.

[2] It appeareth that they used minstrels at their mournings.

9:27 [1] By healing these two blind, Christ showeth that he is the light of the world.

9:32 [1] An example of that power that Christ hath over the devil.

9:36 [1] Although the ordinary pastors cease, yet Christ hath not cast off the care of his Church.

9:38 [1] Word for word, cast them out: for men are very slow in so holy a work.

Christ. 34 Peace and the sword. 35 Variance. 37 Love of parents. 38 The cross. 39 To lose the life. 40 To receive a Preacher.

1 And *a,1*he called his twelve disciples unto him, and gave them power against unclean spirits, to cast them out, and to heal every sickness, and every disease.

2 Now the names of the twelve Apostles are these. The *1*first *is* Simon called Peter, and Andrew his brother, James *the son* of Zebedee, and John his brother,

3 Philip and Bartholomew: Thomas, and Matthew that Publican: James *the son* of Alphaeus, and Lebbaeus whose surname was Thaddaeus:

4 Simon the Canaanite, and Judas *1*Iscariot, who also betrayed him.

5 These twelve did Jesus send forth, and commanded them, saying, Go not into the way of the Gentiles, and into the cities of the Samaritans enter ye not:

6 But go rather *b*to the lost sheep of the house of Israel.

7 *c,1*And as ye go preach, saying, The kingdom of heaven is at hand.

8 *1*Heal the sick: cleanse the lepers: raise up the dead: cast out the devils. Freely ye have received, freely give.

9 *d,1*Possess *2*not gold, nor silver, nor money in your girdles,

10 Nor a scrip for the journey, neither two coats, neither shoes, nor a staff: *e*for the workman is worthy of his *1*meat.

11 *1*And into *f*whatsoever city or town ye shall come, inquire who is worthy in it, and there abide till ye go thence.

12 And when ye come into an house, salute the same.

13 And if the house be worthy, let your *1*peace come upon it: but if it be not worthy, let your peace return to you.

CHAPTER 10
a Mark 3:13-15
Luke 9:1-2
b Acts 13:46
c Luke 10:9-11
d Mark 6:8-9
Luke 9:3
Luke 22:35
e 1 Tim. 5:15
f Luke 10:8
g Mark 6:11
Luke 9:5
h Acts 13:51
i Luke 10:3
j Mark 13:11
Luke 12:11
k Luke 21:16
l Mark 13:13
m Luke 6:40
John 13:16
John 15:20
n Matt. 12:24
o Mark 4:22
Luke 8:17
Luke 12:1

14 *g*And whosoever shall not receive you, nor hear your words, when ye depart out of that house, or that city, *h*shake off the dust of your feet.

15 Truly I say unto you, it shall be easier for them of the land of Sodom and Gomorrah in the day of judgment, than for that city.

16 ¶ *i,1*Behold, I send you as *2*sheep in the midst of the wolves: be ye therefore wise as serpents, and *3*innocent as doves.

17 But beware of *1*men, for they will deliver you up to the Councils, and will scourge you in their Synagogues.

18 And ye shall be brought to the governors and kings for my sake, in witness to them, and to the Gentiles.

19 *j*But when they deliver you up, take no thought how or what ye shall speak: for it shall be given you in that hour, what ye shall say.

20 For it is not ye that speak, but the spirit of your Father which speaketh in you.

21 And the *k*brother shall betray the brother to death, and the father the son, and the children shall rise against *their* parents, and shall cause them to die.

22 And ye shall be hated of all men for my Name: *l*but he that endureth to the end, he shall be saved.

23 And when they persecute you in this city, flee into another: for verily I say unto you, ye shall not *1*go over *all* the cities of Israel, till the Son of man be come.

24 *m*The disciple is not above his master, nor the servant above his Lord.

25 It is enough for the disciple to be as his master is, and the servant as his Lord. *n*If they have called the master of the house *1*Beelzebub, how much more them of his household?

26 *1*Fear them not therefore: *o*for there is nothing covered, that shall not be disclosed, nor hid, that shall not be known.

27 What I tell you in darkness, that speak ye in light: and what ye hear in the ear, that preach ye on the *1*houses.

10:1 *1* The Apostles are sent to preach the Gospel in Israel.
10:2 *1* Theophylact saith that Peter and Andrew are called the first, because they were first called.
10:4 *1* A man of Kerioth. Now Kerioth was in the tribe of Judah, Josh. 15:25.
10:7 *1* The sum of the Gospel: or preaching of the Apostles.
10:8 *1* Miracles are dependences of the word.
10:9 *1* The ministers of the word must cast away all cares that might hinder them the least wise that might be.
     2 For this journey, to wit, both that nothing might hinder them, and also that they might feel some taste of God's providence: for at their return back, the Lord asketh of them, whether they lacked anything by the way, Luke 22:35.
10:10 *1* God will provide you meat.
10:11 *1* Happy are they that receive the preaching of the Gospel: and unhappy are they, that refuse it.

10:13 *1* It is manner of speech taken from the Hebrews, whereby they meant all kind of happiness.
10:16 *1* Christ showeth how the ministers must behave themselves under the cross.
     2 You shall be in great dangers.
     3 You shall not so much as revenge an injury: and by the mixing of these beasts' natures together, he will not have our wisdom to be malicious, nor our simplicity mad, but a certain form of good nature as exquisitely framed of both of them, as may be.
10:17 *1* For in the cause of religion men are wolves one to another.
10:23 *1* Bring to an end, that is, you shall not have gone through all the cities of Israel, and preached in them.
10:25 *1* It was the idol of the Acronites, which we call the god of flies.
10:26 *1* Truth shall not always be hid.
10:27 *1* Openly, and in the highest places. For the tops of their houses were so made, that they might walk upon them, Acts 10:9.

28 And [1]fear ye not them which kill the body, but are not able to kill the soul: but rather fear him, which is able to destroy both soul and body in hell.

29 Are not two sparrows sold for a [1]farthing, and one of them shall not fall on the ground without your Father?

30 [p]Yea, and all the hairs of your head are numbered.

31 Fear ye not therefore, ye are of more value than many sparrows.

32 [q,1]Whosoever therefore shall confess me before men, him will I confess also before my Father which is in heaven.

33 But whosoever shall deny me before men, him will I also deny before my Father which is in heaven.

34 [r,1]Think not that I am come to send peace into the earth, but the sword.

35 For I am come to set a man at variance against his father, and the daughter against her mother, and the daughter-in-law against her mother-in-law.

36 [s]And a man's enemies *shall be* they of his own household.

37 [t,1]He that loveth father or mother more than me, is not worthy of me. And he that loveth son, or daughter more than me, is not worthy of me.

38 [u]And he that taketh not his cross, and followeth after me, is not worthy of me.

39 [v]He that will find [1]his life, shall lose it: and he that loseth his life for my sake, shall find it.

40 [1]He that receiveth you, receiveth me: and he that receiveth me, receiveth him that sent me.

41 [w,1]He that receiveth a Prophet in [2]the name of a Prophet, shall receive a Prophet's reward: and he that receiveth a righteous man, in the name of a righteous man, shall receive the reward of a righteous man.

42 [x]And whosoever shall give unto one of these [1]little ones to drink a cup of cold water only, in the name of a disciple, verily I say unto you, he shall not lose his reward.

[p] 1 Sam. 14:45 2 Sam. 14:11 Acts 27:34
[q] Mark 8:38 Luke 9:26 Luke 12:8 2 Tim. 2:12
[r] Luke 12:51
[s] Mic. 7:6
[t] Luke 14:26
[u] Matt. 16:24 Mark 8:34 Luke 9:25 Luke 14:27
[v] John 14:25
[w] Luke 10:16 John 13:20
[x] Mark 9:41

CHAPTER 11
[a] Luke 7:18
[b] Isa. 61:1 Luke 4:18
[c] Mal. 3:1 Luke 7:28
[d] Luke 16:16
[e] Mal. 4:5

11

2 John sendeth his disciples to Christ. 7 Christ's testimony of John. 13 The Law and the Prophets. 15 Christ and John. 21 Chorazin, Bethsaida. 25 The Gospel revealed to children. 28 They that are weary and laden.

1 And [1]it came to pass that when Jesus had made an end of [2]commanding his twelve disciples, he departed thence to teach and to preach in [3]their cities.

2 ¶ [a]And when John heard in the prison the works of Christ, he sent two of his disciples, and said unto him,

3 Art thou he that should come, or shall we look for another?

4 And Jesus answering, said unto them, Go, and show John, what things ye hear and see.

5 The blind receive sight, and the halt do walk: the lepers are cleansed, and the deaf hear, the dead are raised up, [b]and the poor receive the Gospel.

6 And blessed is he that shall not be offended in me.

7 [1]And as they departed, Jesus began to speak unto the multitude of John, What went ye out into the wilderness to see? a reed shaken with the wind?

8 But what went ye out to see? A man clothed in soft raiment? Behold they that wear soft clothing, are in kings' houses.

9 But what went ye out to see? A Prophet? Yea, I say unto you, and more than a Prophet.

10 For this is he of whom it is written, [c]Behold, I send my messenger before thy face which shall prepare thy way before thee.

11 Verily I say unto you, Among them which are begotten of women, arose there not a greater than John Baptist, notwithstanding, he that is the least in the [1]kingdom of heaven, is greater than he.

12 And from [d]the time of John Baptist hitherto, the kingdom of God suffereth violence, and the violent take it by force.

13 For all the Prophets and the Law [1]prophesied unto John.

14 And if ye will receive it, this is [e]that Elijah,

10:28 [1] Though tyrants be never so raging and cruel, yet we may not fear them.
10:29 [1] The fourth part of an ounce.
10:32 [1] The necessity and reward of open confessing Christ.
10:34 [1] Civil dissentions follow the preaching of the Gospel.
10:37 [1] Nothing without exception is to be preferred before our duty to God.
10:39 [1] They are said to find their life, which deliver it out of danger: and this is spoken after the opinion of the people which think them clean lost that die, because they think not of the life to come.
10:40 [1] God is both author and revenger of his holy ministry.
10:41 [1] We shall lose nothing that we bestow upon Christ.
[2] As a Prophet.
10:42 [1] Which in the sight of the world are vile and abject.
11:1 [1] Christ showeth by his works, that he is the promised Messiah.
[2] Of instructing them with precepts.
[3] The disciples' cities, that is to say, in Galilee, where many of them were born, Acts 2:7.
11:7 [1] What agreement, and what difference is betwixt the ministry of the Prophets, the preaching of John, and the full light of the Gospel, which Christ hath brought.
11:11 [1] In the new state of the Church where the true glory of God shineth: the persons are not compared together, but the kinds of doctrines, the preaching of John with the law and the Prophets, and again, the most clear preaching of the Gospel with John's.
11:13 [1] They prophesied of things to come, which are now present and clearly and plainly seen.

which was to come.

15 ¶ He that hath ears to hear let him hear.

16 *f,1* But whereunto shall I liken this generation? ²It is like unto little children which sit in the markets, and call unto their fellows,

17 And say, We have piped unto you, and ye have not danced, we have mourned unto you, and ye have not lamented.

18 For John came neither eating nor drinking, and they say, He hath a devil.

19 The Son of men came eating and drinking, and they say, Behold a glutton and a drinker of wine, a friend unto Publicans and sinners: ¹but ²wisdom is justified of her children.

20 ¶ *g,1* Then began he to upbraid the cities, wherein most of his great works were done, because they repented not.

21 Woe *be* to thee Chorazin: Woe *be* to thee Bethsaida: for if the great works which were done in you, had been done in Tyre and Sidon, they had repented long ago in sackcloth and ashes.

22 But I say to you, It shall be easier for Tyre and Sidon at the day of judgment, than for you.

23 And thou Capernaum, which art lifted up unto heaven, shalt be brought down to hell: for if the great works, which have been done in thee, had been done among them of Sodom, they had remained to this day.

24 But I say unto you, that it shall be easier for them of the land of Sodom in the day of judgment, than for thee.

25 *h* At that time Jesus answered and said, I give thee thanks, O Father, Lord of heaven and earth, because thou hast hid these things from the wise, and men of understanding, and hast ¹opened them unto babes.

26 It is ¹so, O Father, because thy ²good pleasure was such.

27 *i,1* All things are given unto me of my Father: and *j* no man knoweth the Son, but the Father: neither knoweth any man the Father, but the Son, and he to whom the Son will reveal *him.*

28 Come unto me, all ye that are weary and lade and I will ease you.

29 Take my yoke on you, and learn of me tha am meek and lowly in heart: and ye shall find *k* re unto your souls.

30 *l* For my yoke is ¹easy, and my burden light.

1 At *a,1* that time Jesus went on a Sabbath da through the corn, and his disciples were an hungere and began to pluck the ears of corn and to eat.

2 And when the Pharisees saw it, they said un him, Behold, thy disciples do *b* that which is not lawf to do upon the Sabbath.

3 But he said unto them, ¹Have ye not read wha David did when he was an hungered, and they th were with him?

4 How he went into the house of God, and di eat the ¹showbread, which was not lawful for hi to eat, neither for them which were with him, b only for the *d* Priests?

5 Or have ye not read in the Law, how that o the Sabbath days the Priests in the Temple *e,1* brea the Sabbath, and are blameless?

6 But I say unto you, that here is one greate than the Temple.

7 Wherefore if ye knew what this is, *f* I will hav mercy and not sacrifice, ye would not have condemne the innocents.

8 For the son of man is Lord, *even* of the Sab bath.

9 *g,1* And he departed thence, and went into thei Synagogue:

10 And behold, there was a man which had *h* hand dried up. And they asked him, saying, Is lawful to heal upon a Sabbath day? that they migh accuse him.

f Luke 7:31
g Luke 10:13
h Luke 10:21
i John 3:35
j John 6:46
k Jer. 6:16
l 1 John 5:3

a Mark 2:23
Luke 6:1
b Deut. 23:25
c 1 Sam. 21:6
d Exod. 29:33
Lev. 8:31
Lev. 24:9
e Num. 28:9
f Hos. 6:6-7
Matt. 9:13
g Mark 3:1
Luke 6:6

11:16 ¹ There are none more stout and stubborn enemies of the Gospel, than they to whom it ought to be most acceptable.

² He blameth the frowardness of this age, by a proverb, in that they could be moved neither with rough, nor gentle dealing.

11:19 ¹ That which the most part refuse, the elect and chosen embrace.

² Wise men do acknowledge the wisdom of the Gospel, when they receive it.

11:20 ¹ The proud reject the Gospel offered unto them, to their great hurt and smart which turneth to the salvation of the simple.

11:25 ¹ Through the ministry of Christ, who only showeth the truth of all things pertaining to God.

11:26 ¹ This word showeth, that he contenteth himself in his father's counsel.

² God's will is the only rule of righteousness.

11:27 ¹ There is no true knowledge of God, nor quietness of min but only in Christ alone.

11:30 ¹ May easily be borne. For his commandments are not griev ous, for all that is born of God overcometh the world, 1 John 5:4.

12:1 ¹ Of the true sanctifying of the Sabbath, and the abrogating of i

12:4 ¹ The Hebrews call it bread of faces, because it stood before th Lord all the weeks upon the golden table appointed to that servic Lev. 24:6.

12:5 ¹ When the Priests do God's service upon the Sabbath day yet they break not the Law: much less doth the Lord of the Sabbat break the Sabbath.

12:9 ¹ The ceremonies of the Law are not against the love of ou neighbor.

11 And he said unto them, What man shall there be among you, that hath a sheep, and if it fall on the Sabbath day into a pit, doth not take it and lift it out?

12 How much more then is a man better than a sheep? therefore, it is lawful to do well on a Sabbath day.

13 Then said he to the man, Stretch forth thine hand. And he stretched it forth, and it was made whole as the other.

14 [1]Then the Pharisees went out, and consulted against him, how they might destroy him.

15 But when Jesus knew it, he departed thence, and great multitudes followed him, and he healed them all,

16 And charged them in threatening wise, that they should not make him known,

17 That it might be fulfilled which was spoken by Isaiah the Prophet, saying,

18 [h]Behold my servant whom I have chosen, my beloved in whom my soul delighteth: I will put my Spirit on him, and he shall show [1]judgment to the Gentiles.

19 He shall not strive, nor cry, neither shall any man hear his voice in the streets.

20 A bruised reed shall he not break, and smoking flax shall he not quench, till he [1]bring forth judgment unto victory.

21 And in his Name shall the Gentiles trust.

22 ¶ [i,1]Then was brought to him one possessed with a devil, both blind and dumb, and he healed him, so that he which was blind and dumb, both spake and saw,

23 And all the people were amazed, and said, Is not this that son of David?

24 But when the Pharisees heard it, they said, [j]This man casteth the devils no otherwise out but through Beelzebub the prince of devils.

25 [1]But Jesus knew their thoughts, and said to them, Every kingdom divided against itself, is brought to naught, and every city or house divided against itself shall not stand.

26 So if Satan cast out Satan, he is divided against himself: how shall then his kingdom endure?

27 Also if I through Beelzebub cast out devils, by whom do your children cast them out? Therefore they shall be your judges.

28 But if I cast out devils by the Spirit of God, then is the kingdom of God come unto you.

29 Else how can a man enter into a strong man's house and spoil his goods, except he first bind the strong man, and then spoil his house?

30 He that is not with me, is against me: and he that gathereth not with me, scattereth.

31 [k]Wherefore I say unto you, Every sin and blasphemy shall be forgiven unto men: but the blasphemy against the holy Ghost shall not be forgiven unto men.

32 And whosoever shall speak a word against the son of man, it shall be forgiven him: [l]but whosoever shall speak against the holy Ghost, it shall not be forgiven him, neither in this world, nor in the world to come.

33 Either make the tree good, and his fruit good: or else make the tree evil, and his fruit evil: for the tree is known by the fruit.

34 [1]O generations of vipers, how can you speak good things, when ye are evil? For of the [l]abundance of the heart the mouth speaketh.

35 A good man out of the good treasure of his heart bringeth forth good things: and an evil man out of an evil treasure, bringeth forth evil things.

36 But I say unto you, that of every [1]idle word that men shall speak, they shall give account thereof at the day of judgment.

37 For by thy words thou shalt be justified, and by thy words thou shalt be condemned.

38 ¶ [m,1]Then answered certain of the Scribes and of the Pharisees, saying, Master, we would see a sign of thee.

39 But he answered and said to them, An evil and [1]adulterous generation seeketh a sign, but no sign shall be given unto it, save that sign of the Prophet Jonah.

40 [n]For as Jonah was three days and three nights in the whale's belly: so shall the son of man be three days and three nights in the heart of the earth.

41 [1]The men of Nineveh shall rise in judgment with this generation, and condemn it: for they [o]repented at the preaching of Jonah: and behold, a greater than

---

[h] Isa. 42:1
[i] Luke 12:14
[j] Matt. 9:34
  Mark 3:22
  Luke 11:15
[k] Mark 3:28-29
  Luke 12:10
  1 John 5:16
[l] Luke 6:45
[m] Matt. 16:1
  Luke 11:29
  1 Cor. 1:22
[n] Jonah 1:17
[o] Jonah 3:5

12:14 [1] How far and in what respect we may give place to the unbridled rage of the wicked.

12:18 [1] By judgment is meant a settled state because Christ was to publish true religion among the Gentiles, and to cast out superstition, which thing wheresoever it is done, the Lord is said to reign and judge there, that is to say, to govern and rule matters.

12:20 [1] He shall pronounce sentence and judgment, maugre the world and Satan, and show himself conqueror over all his enemies.

12:22 [1] A truth be it never so manifest, is subject to the slander of the wicked: yet notwithstanding it ought to be avouched stoutly.

12:25 [1] The kingdom of Christ and the kingdom of the devil cannot consist together.

12:32 [1] Of blasphemy against the holy Ghost.

12:34 [1] Hypocrites at the length betray themselves even by their own mouth.

12:36 [1] Vain and unprofitable trifles which the most part of men spend their lives in.

12:38 [1] Against froward desires of miracles.

12:39 [1] Bastard, which fell from Abraham's faith, or forsook the true worship of God.

12:41 [1] Christ teacheth by the sorrowful example of the Jews, that there are none more miserable than they which put out the light of the Gospel which was kindled in them.

Jonah *is* here.

42 *The Queen of the ¹South shall rise in judgment with this generation, and shall condemn it: for she came from the ²utmost parts of the earth to hear the wisdom of Solomon: and behold, a greater than Solomon *is* here.

43 ¶ ⁹Now when the unclean spirit is gone out of a man, he walketh throughout dry places, seeking rest, and findeth none.

44 Then he saith, I will return into mine house from whence I came: and when he is come, he findeth it empty, swept and garnished.

45 ¶ Then he goeth, and taketh unto him seven other spirits worse than himself, and they enter in, and dwell there: ʳand the end of that man is worse than the beginning. Even so shall it be with this wicked generation.

46 ¶ ¹·ˢWhile he yet spake to the multitude, behold, his mother, and his brethren stood without, desiring to speak with him.

47 Then one said unto him, Behold, thy mother and thy brethren stand without, desiring to speak with thee.

48 But he answered, and said to him that told him, Who is my mother, and who are my brethren?

49 ¹And he stretched forth his hand toward his disciples and said, Behold my mother, and my brethren.

50 For whosoever shall do my Father's will which is in heaven, the same is my brother and sister and mother.

13

1 *The parable of the Sower.   11 and 34 Why Jesus spake in parables.   18 The exposition of the parable.   24 The parable of the tares.   31 Of the mustard seed.   33 Of the leaven.   44 Of the hidden treasure.   45 Of the pearl.   47 Of the draw net cast into the sea.   53 Christ is not received of his countrymen the Nazarites.*

1 The ᵃsame day went Jesus out of the house, and sat by the sea side.

2 ¹And great multitudes resorted unto him, so that he went into a ship, and sat down: and the whole multitude stood on the shore.

3 Then he spake many things to them in parables, saying, Behold, a sower went forth to sow.

4 And as he sowed, some fell by the way side,

---

and the fowls came and devoured them up.

5 And some fell upon stony ground, where they had not much earth, and anon they sprung up, because they had no depth of earth.

6 And when the sun was up, they were parched, and for lack of rooting withered away.

7 And some fell among thorns, and the thorns sprung up, and choked them.

8 And some again fell in good ground, and brought forth fruit, one *corn* an hundredfold, some sixtyfold, and another thirtyfold.

9 He that hath ears to hear, let him hear.

10 ¶ Then the disciples came, and said to him, Why speakest thou to them in parables?

11 ¹And he answered and said unto them, Because it is given unto you to know the secrets of the kingdom of heaven, but to them it is not given.

12 ᵇFor whosoever hath, to him shall be given, and he shall have abundance: but whosoever hath not, from him shall be taken away even that he hath.

13 Therefore speak I to them in parables, because they seeing, do not see: and hearing, they hear not, neither understand.

14 So in them is fulfilled the prophecy of Isaiah, which *prophecy* saith, ᶜBy hearing ye shall hear, and shall not understand, and seeing ye shall see, and shall not perceive.

15 For this people's heart is waxed fat, and their ears are dull of hearing, and with their eyes they have winked, lest they should see with their eyes, and hear with their ears, and should understand with their hearts, and should return, that I might heal them.

16 ¹But blessed *are* your eyes, for they see: and your ears, for they hear.

17 ᵈFor verily I say unto you, that many Prophets, and righteous men have desired to see those things which ye see, and have not seen *them*, and to hear those things which ye hear, and have not heard *them*.

18 ¶ ᵉHear ye therefore the parable of the Sower.

19 Whensoever any man heareth the word of that kingdom, and understandeth it not, that evil one cometh, and catcheth away that which was sown in his ¹heart: and this is he which hath received the seed by the way side.

20 And he that received seed in the stony ground,

ᵖ 1 Kings 10:1
2 Chron. 9:1
ᵠ Luke 11:24
ʳ Heb. 6:4-5
Heb. 10:26
2 Pet. 2:20
ˢ Mark 3:31
Luke 8:20

CHAPTER 13
ᵃ Mark 4:1
Luke 8:4-5
ᵇ Matt. 25:19
ᶜ Isa. 6:9
Mark 4:12
Luke 8:10
John 12:40
Acts 28:26
Rom. 11:8
ᵈ Luke 10:24
ᵉ Mark 4:15
Luke 8:11

12:42 ¹ He meaneth the Queen of Sheba: whose country is South in respect of the land of Israel, 1 Kings 10.
² For Sheba is situated in the utmost coast of . . . Arabia at the mouth of the Arabian Sea.
12:46 ¹ Christ teacheth by his own example, how that all things ought to be set apart in respect of God's glory.
12:49 ¹ None are more near unto us, than they that are of the household of faith.
13:2 ¹ Christ showeth in putting forth this parable of the Sower, that the seed of life which is sown in the world, cometh not on so well in

one as in another, and the reason is, for that men for the most part either do not receive it, or suffer it not to ripen.
13:11 ¹ The gift of understanding and of faith is proper to the elect, and all the rest are blinded through the just judgment of God.
13:16 ¹ The condition of the Church under and since Christ, is better than it was in the time of the Fathers under the Law.
13:19 ¹ Though there be mention made of the heart yet this sowing is referred to hearing without understanding. For whether the seed be received in the heart or no, yet he that soweth, soweth to the heart.

is he which heareth the word, and incontinently with joy receiveth it,

21 Yet hath he no root in himself, and endureth but a season: for as soon as tribulation or persecution cometh because of the word, by and by he is offended.

22 And he that received the seed among thorns, is he that heareth the word: but the care of this world, and the deceitfulness of riches choke the word, and he is made unfruitful.

23 But he that received the seed in the good ground, is he that heareth the word, and understandeth it, which also beareth fruit, and bringeth forth, some an hundredfold, some sixtyfold, and some thirtyfold.

24 ¶ [1]Another parable put he forth unto them, saying, The kingdom of heaven is like unto a man which sowed good seed in his field.

25 But while men slept, there came his enemy and sowed tares among the wheat, and went his way.

26 And when the blade was sprung up, and brought forth fruit, then appeared the tares also.

27 Then came the servants of the householder, and said unto him, Master, sowest thou not good seed in thy field? from whence then hath it tares?

28 And he said unto them, Some envious man hath done this. Then the servants said unto him, Wilt thou then that we go and gather them up?

29 But he said, Nay, lest while ye go about to gather the tares, ye pluck up also with them the wheat.

30 Let both grow together until the harvest, and in time of harvest I will say to the reapers, Gather ye first the tares, and bind them in sheaves to burn them: but gather the wheat into my barn.

31 ¶ [f,1]Another parable he put forth unto them, saying, The kingdom of heaven is like unto a grain of mustard seed, which a man taketh and soweth in his field:

32 Which indeed is the least of all seeds: but when it is grown, it is the greatest among herbs, and it is a tree, so that the birds of heaven come and build in the branches thereof.

33 ¶ [g]Another parable spake he to them, The kingdom of heaven is like unto leaven, which a woman taketh and hideth in three pecks of meal, till all be leavened.

34 ¶ [h]All these things spake Jesus unto the multitude in parables, and without parables spake he

not unto them,

35 That it might be fulfilled, which was spoken by the Prophet, saying, [i]I will open my mouth in parables, and will utter the things which have been kept secret from the foundation of the world.

36 Then sent Jesus the multitude away, and went into the house. And his disciples came unto him, saying, Declare unto us the parable of the tares of that field.

37 [1]Then answered he, and said to them, He that soweth the good seed, is the son of man,

38 And the field is the world, and the good seed are the children of the kingdom, and the tares are the children of that wicked one.

39 And the enemy that soweth them, is the devil, [j]and the harvest is the end of the world, and the reapers be the Angels.

40 As then the tares are gathered and burned in the fire, so shall it be in the end of this world.

41 The Son of man shall send forth his Angels, and they shall gather out of his kingdom all things that offend, and them which do iniquity,

42 And shall cast them into a furnace of fire. There shall be wailing and gnashing of teeth.

43 [k]Then shall the just men shine as the sun in the kingdom of their father. He that hath ears to hear, let him hear.

44 ¶ [1]Again, the kingdom of heaven is like unto a treasure hid in the field, which when a man hath found, he hideth it, and for joy thereof departeth, and selleth all that he hath, and buyeth that field.

45 ¶ Again, the kingdom of heaven is like to a merchant man that seeketh good pearls,

46 Who having found a pearl of great price, went and sold all that he had and bought it.

47 ¶ [1]Again, the kingdom of heaven is like unto a draw net cast into the sea, that gathereth of all kinds of things.

48 Which, when it is full, men draw to land, and sit and gather the good into vessels, and cast the bad away.

49 So shall it be at the end of the world. The Angels shall go forth, and sever the bad from among the just,

50 And shall cast them into a furnace of fire: there shall be wailing and gnashing of teeth.

51 ¶ [1]Jesus said unto them, Understand ye all

13:24 [1] Christ showeth in another parable of the evil seed mixed with the good, that the Church shall never be free and quit from offences, both in doctrine and manners, until the day appointed for the restoring of all things to come, and therefore the faithful have to arm themselves with patience and constancy.
13:31 [1] God beginneth his kingdom with very small beginnings, to the end that by the growing on of it, beside the expectation and hope of all men, his mighty power and working may be the more set forth.
13:37 [1] He expoundeth the former parable of the good and evil seed.
13:44 [1] Few men understand how great the riches of the kingdom of heaven are, and no man can be partaker of them, but he that redeemeth them with the loss of all his goods.
13:47 [1] There are many in the Church, which notwithstanding are not of the Church, and therefore at length shall be cast out: but the full and perfect cleansing of them is deferred to the last day.
13:51 [1] They ought to be diligent, which have not only to be wise for themselves, but to dispense the wisdom of God to others.

these things? They said unto him, Yea, Lord.

52 Then said he unto them, Therefore every Scribe which is taught unto the kingdom of heaven, is like unto an householder, which bringeth forth out of his treasure things both new and old.

53 ¶ And it came to pass, that when Jesus had ended these parables, he departed thence,

54 [l,1]And came into his own country, and taught them in their Synagogue, so that they were astonied, and said, Whence cometh this wisdom and great works unto this man?

55 Is not this the carpenter's son? Is not his mother called Mary, [m]and his brethren James and Joses, and Simon, and Judas?

56 And are not his sisters all with us? Whence then hath he all these things?

57 And they were offended with him. Then Jesus said to them, [n]A Prophet is not without honor, save in his own country, and in his own house.

58 And he did not many great works there, for their unbelief's sake.

14 1 *Herod's judgment of Christ.   3 Wherefore John was bound,   10 and beheaded.   13 Jesus departeth.   18 Of the five loaves, etc.   23 Christ prayeth.   24 The Apostles tossed with the waves.   28 Faith.   30 Peter in jeopardy.   36 The hem of Christ's garment.*

1 At [a,1]that time Herod the Tetrarch heard of the fame of Jesus,

2 And said unto his servants, This is that John Baptist, he is risen again from the dead, and therefore great [1]works are wrought by him.

3 [b]For Herod had taken John, and bound him, and put him in prison for Herodias' sake, his brother Philip's wife.

4 For John said unto him, It is not [c]lawful for thee to have her.

5 And when he would have put him to death, he feared the multitude, because they counted him as a [d]Prophet.

6 But when Herod's birthday was kept, the daughter of Herodias danced before them, and pleased [1]Herod.

7 Wherefore he promised with an oath, that he

would give her whatsoever she would ask.

8 And she being before instructed of her mother, said, Give me here John Baptist's head in a platter.

9 And the king was sorry: nevertheless, because of the oath, and them that sat with him at the table, he commanded it to be given *her*,

10 And sent, and beheaded John in the prison.

11 And his head was brought in a platter, and given to the maid, and she brought it unto her mother.

12 And his disciples came, and took up the body, and buried it, and went and told Jesus.

13 [e]And when Jesus heard it, he departed thence by ship into a desert place apart. And when the multitude had heard it, they followed him on foot out of the cities.

14 [1]And Jesus went forth and saw a great multitude, and was moved with compassion toward them, and he healed their sick.

15 ¶ And when even was come, [f]his disciples came to him, saying, This is a desert place, and the time is already past: let the multitude depart, that they may go into the towns, and buy them vittles.

16 But Jesus said to them, They have no need to go away: give ye them to eat.

17 Then said they unto him, We have here but five loaves, and two fishes.

18 And he said, Bring them hither to me.

19 And he commanded the multitude to sit down on the grass, and took the five loaves, and the two fishes, and looked up to heaven, and blessed, and brake, and gave the loaves to his disciples, and the disciples to the multitude.

20 And they did all eat, and were sufficed, and they took up of the fragments that remained, twelve baskets full.

21 And they that had eaten, were about five thousand men, beside women and little children.

22 ¶ And straightway Jesus compelled his disciples to enter into a ship, and to go over before him, while he sent the multitude away.

23 And as soon as he had sent the multitude away, he went up into a mountain alone to pray: and [g]when the evening was come, he was there alone.

24 [1]And the ship was now in the midst of the sea,

Marginal references:

[l] Mark 6:1 / Luke 4:6
[m] John 6:42
[n] Mark 6:4 / Luke 4:24 / John 4:44

CHAPTER 14
[a] Mark 6:14 / Luke 9:7
[b] Mark 6:17 / Luke 3:19
[c] Lev. 18:16 / Lev. 20:21
[d] Matt. 21:26
[e] Mark 6:32 / Luke 9:10
[f] Mark 6:35 / Luke 9:12 / John 6:5
[g] Mark 6:45-47 / John 6:16-18

Footnotes:

13:54 [1] Men do not only sin of ignorance, but also wittingly and willfully lay stumbling blocks in their own ways, that when God calleth them, they may not obey, and so most plainly destroy and cast away themselves.

14:1 [1] Here is in John an example of an invincible courage, which all faithful Ministers of God's word ought to follow: in Herod, an example of tyrannous vanity, pride and cruelty, and to be short, of a courtly conscience, and of their insufferable slavery, which have once given themselves over to pleasures: in Herodias and her daughter, an example of whore-like wantonness, and womanlike cruelty.

14:2 [1] By works he meaneth that force and power, whereby works are wrought and not the works, as is seen oft before.

14:6 [1] There were three Herods: the first of them was Antipater's son, who is also called Ascalonius, in whose reign Christ was born, and he it was that caused the children to be slain. The second was called Antipas, Magnus his son, whose mother's name was Malthace or Martaca, and this was called Tetrarch, by reason of enlarging his dominion, when Archelaus was banished to Vienna in France. The third was Agrippa, Magnus his nephew by Aristobulus, and he it was that slew James.

14:14 [1] Christ refresheth a great multitude with five loaves and two little fishes, showing thereby, that they shall want nothing, which lay all things aside and seek the kingdom of heaven.

14:24 [1] We must sail even through mighty tempests, and Christ will never forsake us, so that we go whither he hath commanded us.

and was tossed with waves: for it was a contrary wind.

25　And in the ¹fourth watch of the night, Jesus went unto them, walking on the sea.

26　And when his disciples saw him walking on the sea, they were troubled, saying, It is a ¹spirit, and cried out for fear.

27　But straightway Jesus spake unto them, saying, Be of good comfort, It is I: be not afraid.

28　¹Then Peter answered him, and said, Master, if it be thou, bid me come unto thee on the water.

29　And he said, Come. And when Peter was come down out of the ship, he walked on the water to go to Jesus.

30　But when he saw a mighty wind, he was afraid: and as he began to sink, he cried, saying, Master, save me.

31　So immediately Jesus stretched forth his hand, and caught him, and said to him, O thou of little faith, wherefore didst thou doubt.

32　And as soon as they were come into the ship, the wind ceased.

33　Then they that were in the ship, came and worshipped him, saying, Of a truth thou art the Son of God.

34　¶ ᵇAnd when they were come over, they came into the land of ¹Gennesaret.

35　¹And when the men of that place knew him, they sent out into all that country round about, and brought unto him all that were sick,

36　And besought him, that they might touch the hem of his garment only: and as many as touched it were made whole.

15

3 The commandments and traditions of men. 12 Offences. 13 The plant which is rooted up. 14 Blind leading the blind. 18 The heart. 22 The woman of Canaan. 26 The children's bread:

whelps.　28 Faith.　32 4,000 men fed.　36 Thanksgiving.

1　Then ¹came to Jesus the Scribes and Pharisees, which were of Jerusalem, saying,

2　ᵃ Why do thy disciples transgress the tradition of the Elders? for they ¹wash not their hands when they eat bread.

3　¹But he answered and said unto them, Why do ye also transgress the commandment of God by your tradition?

4　ᵇFor God hath commanded, saying, ¹Honor thy father and mother: ᶜand he that curseth father or mother, let him die the death.

5　But ye say, ¹Whosoever shall say to father or mother, By the gift that is *offered* by me, thou mayest have profit,

6　Though he honor not his father, or his mother, *shall be free*: thus have ye made the commandment of God of no ¹authority by your tradition.

7　¹O hypocrites, Isaiah prophesied well of you, saying,

8　ᵈThis people draweth near unto me with their mouth, and honoreth me with the lips, but their heart is far off from me.

9　But in vain they worship me, teaching *for* doctrines, men's precepts.

10　¹Then he called the multitude unto him, and said to them, Hear and understand.

11　ᶜThat which goeth into the mouth, defileth not the man, but that which cometh out of the mouth that defileth the man.

12　¶ Then came his disciples, and said unto him, Perceivest thou not, that the Pharisees are offended in hearing *this* saying?

13　But he answered and said, ᶠEvery plant which mine heavenly Father hath not planted, shall be rooted up.

14　Let them alone, they be the ᵍblind leaders of the blind: and if the blind lead the blind, both shall

ᵇ Mark 6:54

CHAPTER 15
ᵃ Mark 7:1
ᵇ Exod. 20:12
Deut. 5:16
Eph. 6:2
ᶜ Exod. 21:17
Lev. 20:9
Prov. 20:20
ᵈ Isa. 29:13
ᵉ Mark 7:18
ƒ John 15:2
ᵍ Luke 6:39

14:25 ¹ By the fourth watch is meant the time near to day breaking: for in old time they divided the night into four watches, in which they scouted.

14:26 ¹ A spirit, as it is here taken, is that which a man imagineth to himself vainly in his mind, persuading himself that he seeth something, and seeth nothing.

14:28 ¹ By faith we tread under our feet even the tempests themselves, but yet by the virtue of Christ, which helpeth that virtue, which he of his mercy hath given.

14:34 ¹ This Gennesaret was a lake nigh to Capernaum, which is also called the Sea of Galilee, and Tiberias, so that the country itself grew to be called by that name.

14:35 ¹ In that that Christ healeth the sick, we are given to understand that we must seek remedy for spiritual diseases at his hands: and that we are bound not only to run ourselves, but also to bring others to him.

15:1 ¹ None commonly are more bold contemners of God, than they whom God appointeth keepers of his law.

15:2 ¹ Which they received of their ancestors from hand to hand, or their elders allowed, which were the governors of the Church.

15:3 ¹ Their wicked boldness, in corrupting the commandments of God, and that upon the pretence of godliness, and usurping authority to make laws, is here reproved.

15:4 ¹ By honor is meant all kinds of duties which children owe to their parents.

15:5 ¹ The meaning is this: whatsoever I bestow upon the Temple, is to thy profit, for it is as good as if I gave it thee, for (as the Pharisees of our time say) it shall be meritorious for thee: for under this color of religion, they raked all to themselves, as though that he that had given anything to the Temple, had done the duty of a child.

15:6 ¹ You made it of no power and authority as much as lay in you: for otherwise the commandments of God stand fast in the Church of God, in despite of the world and Satan.

15:7 ¹ The same men are condemned for hypocrisy and superstition, because they made the kingdom of God to stand in outward things.

15:10 ¹ Christ teacheth us that hypocrisy of false teachers which deceive our soul, is not to be borne withall, no not in indifferent matters, and there is no reason why their ordinary vocation should blind our eyes: otherwise we are like to perish with them.

fall into the ditch.

15 ¶ [b]Then answered Peter, and said to him, Declare unto us this parable.

16 Then said Jesus, Are ye yet without understanding?

17 Perceive ye not yet, that whatsoever entereth into the mouth, goeth into the belly, and is cast out into the draught?

18 But those things which proceed out of the mouth, come from the heart, and they defile the man.

19 For out of the heart [i]come evil thoughts, murders, adulteries, fornications, thefts, false testimonies, slanders.

20 These are the things which defile the man: but to eat with unwashed hands, defileth not the man.

21 [j]And Jesus went thence, and departed into the [1]coasts of Tyre and Sidon.

22 And behold, a woman a [1]Canaanite came out of the same coasts, and cried, saying unto him, Have mercy on me, O Lord, the son of David: my daughter is miserably vexed with a devil.

23 [1]But he answered her not a word. Then came to him his disciples, and besought him, saying, Send her away, for she crieth after us.

24 But he answered, and said, I am not sent, but unto the [k]lost sheep of the [1]house of Israel.

25 Yet she came, and worshipped him, saying, Lord help me.

26 And he answered, and said, It is not good to take the children's bread, and to cast it to whelps.

27 But she said, Truth, Lord: yet indeed the whelps eat of the crumbs, which fall from their master's table.

28 Then Jesus answered, and said unto her, O woman, great is thy faith: be it to thee, as thou desirest. And her daughter was made whole at that hour.

29 ¶ [l]So Jesus [l]went away from thence, and came near unto the sea of Galilee, and went up in a mountain and sat down there.

[b] Mark 7:10
[i] Gen. 6:5
Gen. 8:21
Mark 7:21
[j] Mark 7:24
[k] Matt. 10:6
[l] Mark 7:31
[m] Isa. 35:5
[n] Mark 8:1

CHAPTER 16
[a] Matt. 12:38
Mark 8:11

30 And great multitudes came unto him, [m]having with them, halt, blind, dumb, [1]maimed, and many others, and cast them down, at Jesus' feet, and he healed them.

31 Insomuch that the multitude wondered, to see the dumb speak, the maimed whole, the halt to go, and the blind to see: and they glorified the God of Israel.

32 [n,1]Then Jesus called his disciples unto him, and said, I have compassion on this multitude, because they have [2]continued with me already three days, and have nothing to eat: and I will not let them depart fasting, lest they faint in the way.

33 And his disciples said unto him, Whence should we get so much bread in the wilderness, as should suffice so great a multitude!

34 And Jesus said unto them, How many loaves have ye? And they said, Seven, and a few little fishes.

35 Then he commandeth the multitude [1]to sit down on the ground.

36 And took the seven loaves, and the fishes, and gave thanks, and brake them, and gave to his disciples, and the disciples to the multitude.

37 And they did all eat, and were sufficed, and they took up of the fragments that remained, seven [1]baskets full.

38 And they that had eaten, were four thousand men, beside women, and little children.

39 Then Jesus sent away the multitude, and took ship, and came into the parts of Magdala.

16

1 The sign of Jonah. 6 The leaven of the Pharisees. 12 for their doctrine. 13 The people's opinion of Christ. 17 Faith cometh of God. 18 The rock. 19 The keys. 21 Christ foreshadoweth his death. 24 The forsaking of ourself, and the cross. 25 To lose the life.

1 Then [a,1]came the Pharisees and Sadducees, and did [2]tempt him, desiring him to show them a sign from heaven.

2 But he answered, and said unto them, When

15:21 [1] Coasts which were near to Tyre and Sidon, that is, in that quarter where Palestine bendeth toward Phoenicia, and the sea of Syria.

15:22 [1] Of the flock of the Canaanites, which dwelled in Phoenicia.

15:23 [1] In that that Christ doth sometimes as it were stop his ears against the prayers of his Saints, he doeth it for his glory and our profit.

15:24 [1] Of the people of Israel, which people was divided into tribes, but all those tribes came of one house.

15:29 [1] Christ ceaseth not to be beneficial even there where he is contemned, and in the midst of wolves he gathered together and fostereth his flock.

15:30 [1] Whose members were weakened with the palsy, or by nature, for afterward it is said, he healed them. Now Christ was wont to heal in this wise, that such members as were weak, he restored to health, and yet he could easily if he had would, have given them

hands and feet and other members which wanted them.

15:32 [1] By doing again this miracle, Christ showeth that he will never be wanting to them that follow him, no not in the wilderness.

[2] Go not from my side.

15:35 [1] Word for word, to lie down backward, as rowers do when in rowing they draw their oars to them.

15:37 [1] A kind of vessel wrought with twigs.

16:1 [1] The wicked which otherwise are at defiance one with another, agree well together against Christ, but do what they can, Christ beareth always the victory, and triumpheth over them.

[2] To try whether he could do that which they desired, but their purpose was naught, for they thought to find some thing in him by that means whereupon they might have just occasion to reprehend him: or else distrust and curiosity moved them so to do, for by such means also is God said to be tempted, that is to say, provoked to anger, as though men would strive with him.

it is evening, ye say, Fair weather, for the sky is red.

3 [b]And in the morning, ye say, Today shall be a tempest: for the sky is red and lowering. O hypocrites, ye can discern the [1]face of the sky, and can ye not discern the signs of the times?

4 [c]The wicked generation, and adulterous seeketh a sign, but there shall no sign be given it, but [1]that sign of the Prophet [d]Jonah: so he left them, and departed.

5 ¶ [1]And when his disciples were come to the other side, they had [e]forgotten to take bread with them.

6 Then Jesus said unto them, Take heed and beware of the leaven of the Pharisees and Sadducees.

7 And they reasoned among themselves, saying, It is because we have brought no bread.

8 But Jesus [1]knowing it, said unto them, O ye of little faith, why reason ye thus among yourselves, because ye have brought no bread?

9 Do ye not yet perceive, neither remember the [1]five loaves, when there were [f]five thousand men, and how many baskets took ye up?

10 Neither the seven loaves when there were [g]four thousand men, and how many baskets took ye up?

11 Why [1]perceive ye not that I [2]said not unto you concerning bread, that ye should beware of the leaven of the Pharisees and Sadducees?

12 Then understood they that he had not said that they should beware of the leaven of bread, but of the doctrine of the Pharisees, and Sadducees.

[b] Luke 12:54
[c] Matt. 12:39
[d] Jonah 1:17
[e] Mark 8:14
  Luke 2:1
[f] Matt. 14:17
  John 6:9
[g] Matt. 15:34
[h] Mark 8:27
  Luke 9:18
[i] Josh. 6:69
[j] John 1:42
[k] John 20:21

13 ¶ [h,1]Now when Jesus came into the coasts of [2]Caesarea Philippi, he asked his disciples, saying, Whom do men say that I, the son of man, am?

14 And they said, Some say, [1]John Baptist: and some, Elijah: and others, Jeremiah, or one of the Prophets.

15 He said unto them, But whom say ye that I am?

16 Then Simon Peter answered, and said, [i]Thou art that Christ, the son of the living God.

17 [1]And Jesus answered, and said to him, Blessed art thou, Simon, the son of Jonah: for [2]flesh and blood hath not revealed it unto thee, but my Father which is in heaven.

18 [1]And I say also unto thee, that thou art [j,2]Peter, and upon this rock I will build my Church: and the [3]gates of hell shall not overcome it.

19 [1]And I [k] will give unto thee the [2]keys of the Kingdom of heaven, and whatsoever thou shalt [3]bind upon earth, shall be bound in heaven: and whatsoever thou shalt loose on earth, shall be loosed in heaven.

20 [1]Then he charged his disciples, that they should tell no man that he was Jesus that Christ.

21 ¶ [1]From that time forth Jesus began to show unto his disciples, that he must go unto Jerusalem, and suffer many things of the [2]Elders, and of the high Priests, and Scribes, and be slain and be raised again the third day.

22 Then Peter [1]took him aside, and began to

16:3 [1] The outward show and countenance as it were of all things, is called in the Hebrews' tongue, a face.
16:4 [1] The article showeth the notableness of the deed.
16:5 [1] False teachers must be taken heed of.
16:8 [1] Not by others, but by virtue of his divinity.
16:9 [1] That five thousand men were filled with so many loaves?
16:11 [1] A demand or question joined with admiration.
  [2] Said, for commanded.
16:13 [1] There are divers judgments and opinions of Christ, notwithstanding he is known of his alone.
  [2] There were two Caesareas, the one called Stratonis upon the sea Mediterranean, which Herod built sumptuously in the honor of Octavius, Josephus, lib. 15. The other was Caesarea Philippi, which Herod the great the Tetrarch's son by Cleopatra built in the honor of Tiberius at the foot of Lebanon, Josephus, lib. 15.
16:14 [1] As Herod thought.
16:17 [1] Faith is of grace, not of nature.
  [2] By this kind of speech is meant man's natural procreation upon the earth, the creature not being destroyed which was made, but deformed through sin: So then this is the meaning: this was not revealed to thee by any understanding of man, but God showed it thee from heaven.
16:18 [1] That is true faith, which confesseth Christ, the virtue whereof is invisible.
  [2] Christ spoke in the Syrian tongue, and therefore used not this descanting betwixt Petros, which signifieth Peter, and Petra, which signifieth a rock, but in both places used this word Cephas: but his mind was that wrote in Greek, by the divers termination to make a

difference between Peter, who is a piece of the building, and Christ the Petra, that is, the rock and foundation: or else he gave his name Peter, because of the confession of his faith, which is the Church's as well as his, as the old fathers witness: For so saith Theophylact, That confession which thou hast made, shall be the foundation of the believers.
  [3] The enemies of the Church are compared to a strong kingdom, and therefore by Gates, are meant cities which are made strong with counsels and fortresses, and this is the meaning, whatsoever Satan can do by counsel or strength. So doth Paul, 2 Cor. 10:4, call them strongholds.
16:19 [1] The authority of the Church is from God.
  [2] A metaphor taken of stewards which carry the keys: and here is set forth the power of the ministers of the word, as Isa. 22:22, and that power is common to all ministers, as Matt. 18:18, and therefore ministers of the Gospel may rightly be called the key of the kingdom of heaven.
  [3] They are bound whose sins are retained, heaven is shut against them, because they received not Christ by faith: on the other side, how happy are they, to whom heaven is open, which embrace Christ, and are delivered by him, and become fellow heirs with him.
16:20 [1] Men must first learn and then teach.
16:21 [1] The minds of men are in time to be prepared and made ready against the stumbling block of persecution.
  [2] It was a name of dignity and not of age, and it is put for them, which were the Judges, which the Hebrews called Sanhedrin.
16:22 [1] Took him by the hand and led him aside, as they used to do, which meant to talk familiarly with one.

rebuke him, saying, Master, pity thyself: this shall not be unto thee.

23 ¹Then he turned back, and said unto Peter, Get thee behind me, ²Satan: thou art an offence unto me, because thou ³understandest not the things that are of God, but the things that are of men.

24 ¹Jesus then said to his disciples, ˡIf any man will follow me, let him forsake himself: and take up his cross, and follow me.

25 For ᵐwhosoever will save his life, shall lose it: and whosoever shall lose his life for my sake, shall ¹find it.

26 ⁿFor what shall it profit a man though he should win the whole world, if he lose his own soul? or what shall a man give for recompense of his soul?

27 For the son of man shall come ¹in the glory of his Father with his Angels, and ᵒthen shall he give to every man according to his deeds.

28 ᵖVerily I say unto you, there be some of them that stand here, which shall not taste of death, till they have seen the Son of man come in his ¹kingdom.

17

2 *The transfiguration of Christ.*   5 *Christ ought to be heard.*   12 *Elijah.*   13 *John Baptist.*   17 *The unbelief of the Apostles.*   20 *The power of faith.*   21 *Prayer and fasting.*   22 *Christ foretelleth his passion.*   24 *He payeth tribute.*

1 And ᵃ,¹,²after six days, Jesus took Peter and James, and John his brother, and brought them up into an high mountain apart,

2 And was ¹transfigured before them: and his face did shine as the Sun, and his clothes were as white as the light.

3 And behold, there appeared unto them Moses, and Elijah, talking with him.

4 Then answered Peter, and said to Jesus, Master, it is good for us to be here: if thou wilt, let us make

here three tabernacles, one for thee, and one for Moses, and one for Elijah.

5 While he yet spake, behold, a bright cloud shadowed them: and behold, there *came* a voice out of the cloud, saying, ᵇ This is ¹that my beloved Son, in whom I am well pleased: hear him.

6 And when the disciples heard that, they ¹fell on their faces, and were sore afraid.

7 Then Jesus came and touched them, and said, Arise, and be not afraid.

8 And when they lifted up their eyes, they saw no man, save Jesus only.

9 ¶ And as they came down from the mountain, Jesus charged them, saying, Show the ¹vision to no man, until the Son of man rise again from the dead.

10 ᶜAnd his disciples asked him, saying, Why then say the Scribes that ᵈ Elijah must first come?

11 And Jesus answered, and said unto them, Certainly Elijah must first come, and restore all things.

12 But I say unto you, that Elijah is come already, and they knew him not, but have done unto him whatsoever they would: likewise shall also the Son of man suffer of them.

13 Then the disciples perceived that he spake unto them of John Baptist.

14 ¶ ᵉ,¹And when they were come to the multitude, there came to him a certain man, and ²fell down at his feet,

15 And said, Master, have pity on my son: for he is ¹lunatic, and is sore vexed: for oft times he falleth into the fire, and oft times into the water.

16 And I brought him to thy disciples, and they could not heal him.

17 Then Jesus answered, and said, O generation faithless, and crooked, how long now shall I be with you! how long now shall I suffer you! bring him hither to me.

Cross-references (center column)

ˡ Matt. 10:38
Mark 8:34
Luke 9:23
Luke 14:27

ᵐ Matt. 10:39
Mark 8:35
Luke 9:24-26
Luke 17:33

ⁿ Job 12:25

ᵒ Ps. 62:12
Rom. 2:6

ᵖ Mark 9:1
Luke 9:27

CHAPTER 17

ᵃ Mark 9:2
Luke 9:28

ᵇ Matt. 3:17
2 Pet. 1:17

ᶜ Mark 9:11-12

ᵈ Mal. 4:5
Matt. 11:14

ᵉ Mark 9:14
Luke 9:38

16:23 ¹ Against a preposterous zeal.

² The Hebrews call him Satan, that is to say, an adversary, whom the Grecians call diabolos, that is to say, slanderer, or tempter: but it is spoken of them, that either of malice, as Judas, John 6:70, or of lightness and pride resist the will of God.

³ By this word we are taught that Peter sinned, through a false persuasion of himself.

16:24 ¹ No men provide worse for themselves, than they that love themselves more than God.

16:25 ¹ Shall gain himself: And this is his meaning, they that deny Christ to save themselves, do not only not gain that which they look for, but also lose the thing they would have kept, that is themselves, which loss is the greatest of all: but as for them that doubt not to die for Christ, it fareth far otherwise with them.

16:27 ¹ Like a King, as Matt. 6:29.

16:28 ¹ By his kingdom is understood the glory of his ascension, and what followeth thereof, Eph. 4:10, or the preaching of the Gospel, Mark 9:1.

17:1 ¹ Christ is in such sort humble in the Gospel, that in the mean season he is Lord both of heaven and earth.

² Luke reckoneth eight days, containing in that number the first and last, and Matthew speaketh but of them that were betwixt them.

17:2 ¹ Changed into another hue.

17:5 ¹ The article or the word, That, severeth Christ from other children. For he is God's natural Son, we by adoption, therefore is called the first begotten among the brethren, because that although he be of right the only Son, yet is he chief among many in that he is the fountain and head of the adoption.

17:6 ¹ Fell down flat on their faces and worshipped him, as Matt. 2:11.

17:9 ¹ Which they saw: otherwise the word, used in this place is properly spoken of that which is seen in a dream.

17:14 ¹ Men are unworthy of Christ his goodness, yet notwithstanding he regardeth them.

² As men that make supplications used to do.

17:15 ¹ They that at certain times of the moon are troubled with the falling sickness, or any other kind of disease: but in this place, we must so take it, that besides the natural disease, he had a devilish frenzy.

18 And Jesus rebuked the devil, and he went out of him: and the child was healed at that hour.

19 ¹Then came the disciples to Jesus apart, and said, Why could not we cast him out?

20 And Jesus said unto them, Because of your unbelief: for ʲverily I say unto you, if ye have faith *as much* as *is a* grain of mustard seed, ye shall say unto this mountain, Remove hence to yonder place, and it shall remove: and nothing shall be impossible unto you.

21 ¹Howbeit this kind goeth not out, but by ²prayer and fasting.

22 ¶ ¹And they ᵍbeing in Galilee, Jesus said unto them, The Son of Man shall be delivered into the hands of men.

23 And they shall kill him, and the third day shall he rise again: and they were very sorry.

24 ¶ ¹And when they were come to Capernaum, they that received poll money, came to Peter, and said, Doth ²not your Master ³pay ⁴poll money?

25 He said, Yes. And when he was come into the house, Jesus prevented him, saying, What thinkest thou, Simon? Of whom do the kings of the earth take tribute, or poll money? of their ¹children, or of strangers?

26 Peter said unto him, Of strangers. Then said Jesus unto him, Then are the children free.

27 Nevertheless, lest we should offend them: go to the sea, and cast in an angle, and take the first fish that cometh up, and when thou hast opened his mouth, thou shalt find a ¹piece of twenty pence: that take, and give it unto them for me and thee.

18 *1 The greatest in the kingdom of God. 5 To receive a little child. 6 To give offence. 7 Offences. 9 The pulling out of the eye. 10 The Angels. 11 The lost sheep. 15 The telling of one his fault. 17 Excommunication. 21 We must always pardon the brother that repenteth. 23 The parable of the king that taketh an account of his servants.*

1 The ᵃsame time the disciples came unto Jesus, saying, Who is the greatest in the kingdom of heaven?

marginal references:
f Luke 17:6
g Matt. 20:17
  Mark 9:3
  Luke 9:44
  Luke 7:24

CHAPTER 18
a Mark 9:34
  Luke 9:46
b Matt. 19:14
  1 Cor. 14:20
c Mark 9:42
  Luke 17:2
d Matt. 5:29-30
  Mark 9:45
e Ps. 34:8
f Luke 19:10
g Luke 15:4
b Lev. 19:7
  Luke 17:3
  James 5:19

2 ¹And Jesus called a ²little child unto him, and set him in the midst of them,

3 And said, Verily I say unto you, except ye be ᵇ,¹converted, and become as little children, ye shall not enter into the kingdom of heaven.

4 Whosoever therefore shall humble himself as this little child, the same is the greatest in the kingdom of heaven.

5 And whosoever shall receive one such little child in my Name, receiveth me.

6 ᶜ,¹But whosoever shall offend one of these little ones which believe in me, it were better for him, that a millstone were hanged about his neck, and that he were drowned in the depth of the sea.

7 ¹Woe be unto the world because of offences, for it must needs be that ²offences shall come, but woe be to that man by whom the offence cometh.

8 ᵈWherefore, if thy hand or thy foot cause thee to ¹offend, cut them off, and cast *them* from thee: it is better for thee to enter into life, halt, or maimed, than having two hands, or two feet, to be cast into everlasting fire.

9 And if thine eye cause thee to offend, pluck it out and cast it from thee: it is better for thee to enter into life with one eye, than having two eyes to be cast into hell fire.

10 ¹See that ye despise not one of these little ones: for I say unto you, that in heaven their ᵉAngels always behold the face of my Father which is in heaven.

11 For ᶠthe Son of man is come to save that which was lost.

12 How think ye? ᵍIf a man have an hundred sheep, and one of them be gone astray, doth he not leave ninety and nine, and go into the mountains, and seek that which is gone astray?

13 And if so be that he find it, verily I say unto you, he rejoiceth more of that sheep, than of the ninety and nine which went not astray:

14 So is it not the will of your Father which is in heaven, that one of these little ones should perish.

15 ¶ ᵇ,¹Moreover, if thy brother trespass against

17:19 ¹ Incredulity and distrust hinder and break the course of God's benefits.
17:21 ¹ The remedy against distrust.
  ² To give us to understand the watchfulness and diligence of earnest prayer, which cannot be without sobriety.
17:22 ¹ Our minds must be prepared more and more against the offence of the cross.
17:24 ¹ In that that Christ doth willingly obey Caesar's edicts, he showeth that civil policy is not taken away by the Gospel.
  ² He denieth not, but he asketh.
  ³ Ought he not to pay?
  ⁴ They that were from twenty years of age to fifty, paid half a shekel of the Sanctuary, Exod. 30:13. This was an Attic didrachma which the Romans exacted, after they had subdued Judea.
17:25 ¹ By children we must not understand subjects which pay tribute, but natural children.

17:27 ¹ The word here used, is stater, which is in value 4 didrachmas; every drachma is about five pence.
18:2 ¹ Humbleness of mind is the right way to preeminence.
  ² A child in years.
18:3 ¹ A kind of speech taken from the Hebrews, and it is as much as, repent.
18:6 ¹ We ought to have great respect to our brethren be they never so base: and he that doeth otherwise, shall be sharply punished.
18:7 ¹ A good man cannot but go through the midst of offences, yet he must cut off all occasion of offences.
  ² Lets and hindrances which stop the course of good works. The Greek word importeth thus much, things which we stumble at.
18:8 ¹ See Matt. 5:29.
18:10 ¹ The weaker that a man is, the greater care we ought to have of his salvation, as God teacheth us by his own example.
18:15 ¹ We must labor for concord, not to revenge injuries.

²thee, go and tell him his fault between thee and him alone: if he hear thee, thou hast won thy brother.

16 But if he hear thee not, take yet with thee one or two, that by the ^{i,1}mouth of two or three witnesses, every word may be ²confirmed.

17 ¹And if he ²refuse to hear them, tell it unto the ³Church: and if he refuse to hear the Church also, let him be unto thee as an ⁴heathen man, and a Publican.

18 Verily I say unto you, ^jWhatsoever ye bind on earth, shall be bound in heaven: and ^kwhatsoever ye loose on earth, shall be loosed in heaven.

19 Again, verily I say unto you, that if two of you shall ¹agree in earth upon anything, whatsoever they shall desire, it shall be given them of my Father which is in heaven.

20 For where two or three are gathered together in my Name, there am I in the midst of them.

21 ¹Then came Peter to him, and said, Master, how oft shall my brother sin against me, and I shall forgive him? ^lunto seven times?

22 Jesus said unto him, I say not to thee, Unto seven times, but, Unto seventy times seven times.

23 Therefore is the kingdom of heaven likened unto a certain King, which would take an account of his servants.

24 And when he had begun to reckon, one was brought unto him, which ought him ¹ten thousand talents.

25 And because he had nothing to pay, his lord commanded him to be sold, and his wife, and *his* children, and all that he had, and *the debt* to be paid.

26 The servant therefore fell down, and ¹worshipped him, saying, Lord, ²refrain thine anger toward me, and I will pay thee all.

27 Then that servant's lord had compassion, and loosed him, and forgave him the debt.

28 But when the servant was departed, he found one of his fellow servants which ought him an hundred

i Deut. 19:15
John 8:17
2 Cor. 13:1
Heb. 10:28

j 1 Cor. 5:4
2 Thess. 3:14

k John 20:24

l Luke 17:4

CHAPTER 19
a Mark 10:1
b Gen. 1:27
c Gen. 2:24
1 Cor. 6:16
Eph. 5:31

pence, and he laid hands on him, and throttled him, saying, Pay me that thou owest.

29 Then his fellow servant fell down at his feet, and besought him, saying, Refrain thine anger toward me, and I will pay thee all.

30 Yet he would not, but went and cast him into prison, till he should pay the debt.

31 And when his *other* fellow servants saw what was done, they were very sorry, and came, and declared unto their lord all that was done.

32 Then his lord called him unto him, and said to him, O evil servant, I forgave thee all that debt, because thou prayedst me.

33 Oughtest not thou also to have had pity on thy fellow servant, even as I had pity on thee?

34 So his lord was wroth, and delivered him to the tormentors, till he should pay all that was due to him.

35 So likewise shall mine heavenly Father do unto you, except ye forgive from your hearts, each one to his brother their trespasses.

19

2 The sick are healed.   3 and 7 A bill of divorcement.   12 Eunuchs.   13 Children brought to Christ.   17 God only good.   The commandments must be kept.   21 A perfect man.   23 A rich man.   26 Salvation cometh of God.   27 To leave all and follow Christ.

1 And ^ait came to pass, that when Jesus had finished these sayings, he ¹departed from Galilee, and came into the coasts of Judea beyond Jordan.

2 And great multitudes followed him, and he healed them there.

3 ¶ ¹Then came unto him the Pharisees tempting him, and saying to him, Is it lawful for a man to ²put away his wife upon every occasion?

4 And he answered and said unto them, Have ye not read, ^bthat he which made *them* at the beginning, made them male and female,

5 And said, ^cFor this cause, shall a man leave

18:15 ² If his offence be such, that thou only knowest thy brother's offence.

18:16 ¹ That is, by the word and witness the mouth is sometime taken for the word or speech, Num. 3:16, and also for a still witness, to wit, when the matter speaketh of itself, as in Matt. 21:16.

   ² Sure and certain.

18:17 ¹ He that contemneth the judgment of the Church, contemneth God.

   ² Word for word, do not vouchsafe to hear, or make as though he did not hear.

   ³ He speaketh not of any kind of policy, but of an Ecclesiastical assembly, for he speaketh afterward of the power of loosing and binding, which belonged to the Church, and he hath regard to the order used in those days, at what time the Elders had the judgment of Church matters in their hands, John 9:22 and 12:42 and 16:2, and used casting out of the Synagogue for a punishment, as we do now excommunication.

   ⁴ Profane, and void of religion: such men, the Jews called Gentiles:

whose company they shunned as they did the Publicans.

18:19 ¹ This word is translated from the body to the mind, for it belongeth properly to song.

18:21 ¹ They shall find God severe and not to be pleased, which do not forgive their brethren, although they have been diversly and grievously injured by them.

18:24 ¹ Here is set down a very great sum of threescore hundred thousand crowns, and a small sum of ten crowns, that the difference may be the greater, for there is no proportion between them.

18:26 ¹ This was a civil reverence which was very usual in the East.

   ² Yield not too much to thine anger against me: so is God called in the Scripture, slow to anger, that is to say, gentle and one that refraineth the storming of his mind, Ps. 86:5, patient and of great mercy.

19:1 ¹ Passed over the water out of Galilee into the borders of Judea.

19:3 ¹ The band of marriage ought not to be broken, unless it be for fornication.

   ² To send her a book of divorcement, see also Matt. 1:19.

father and mother, and ¹cleave unto his wife, and they which were ²two, shall be one flesh?

6 Wherefore they are no more twain, but one flesh. Let not man therefore put asunder that, which God hath ¹coupled together.

7 ¹They said to him, Why did then *d*Moses command to give a bill of divorcement, and to put her away?

8 He said unto them, Moses, ¹because of the hardness of your heart, ²suffered you to put away your wives: but from the beginning it was not so.

9 I say therefore unto you, ᵉthat whosoever shall put away his wife, except it be ¹for whoredom, and marry another, committeth adultery: and whosoever marrieth her which is divorced, doth commit adultery.

10 Then said his disciples to him, If the ¹matter be so between man and wife, it is not good to marry.

11 ¹But he said unto them, All men cannot ²receive this thing, save they to whom it is given.

12 For there are some ¹eunuchs, which were so born of *their* mother's belly: and there be some eunuchs, which be gelded by men: and there be some eunuchs, which have ²gelded themselves for the kingdom of heaven. He that is able to receive *this*, let him receive it.

13 ¶ *f,*¹Then were brought unto him little children, that he should put *his* hands on them, and pray: and the disciples rebuked them.

14 But Jesus said, Suffer little children, and forbid them not to come to me: for of such is the kingdom of heaven.

15 And when he had put his hands on them, he departed thence.

16 ¶ *g,*¹And behold, one came and said unto him, Good Master, what good thing shall I do, that I may have eternal life?

17 And he said unto him, Why called thou me good?

there is none good but one, even God: but if thou wilt enter into life, keep the Commandments.

18 He said unto him, Which? And Jesus said, *h*These, Thou shalt not kill: Thou shalt not commit adultery: Thou shalt not steal: Thou shalt not bear false witness.

19 Honor thy father, and mother: and, Thou shalt love thy neighbor as thyself.

20 The young man said unto him, I have observed all these things from my youth. What lack I yet?

21 Jesus said unto him, If ¹thou wilt be perfect, go, sell that thou hast, and give it to the poor, and thou shalt have treasure in heaven, and come, and follow me.

22 And when the young man heard that saying, he went away sorrowful: for he had great possessions.

23 ¹Then Jesus said unto his disciples, Verily I say unto you, that a rich man shall hardly enter into the kingdom of heaven.

24 And again I say unto you, It is ¹easier for a ²camel to go through the eye of a needle, than for a rich man to enter into the kingdom of God.

25 And when his disciples heard it, they were exceedingly amazed, saying, Who then can be saved?

26 And Jesus beheld them, and said unto them, With men this is impossible, but with God all things are possible.

27 ¶ *i*Then answered Peter, and said to him, Behold, we have forsaken all, and followed thee: what therefore shall we have?

28 ¹And Jesus said unto them, Verily I say to you, that when the Son of man shall sit in the throne of his Majesty, ye which followed me in the ²regeneration, *j*shall sit also upon twelve thrones, and judge the twelve tribes of Israel.

---

d Deut. 24:1
e Matt. 5:32
Mark 10:11
Luke 16:18
1 Cor. 7:11
f Mark 10:13
Luke 18:15
Matt. 18:2
g Mark 10:27
Luke 18:18
h Exod. 20:13
Deut. 5:16
Rom. 13:9
i Mark 10:28
Luke 18:28
j Luke 22:29

19:5 ¹ The Greek word imported to be glued unto, whereby is signified that straight knot, which is between man and wife, as though they were glued together.
² They which were two, become as it were one: and this word flesh is by a figure taken for the whole man, or the body after the manner of the Hebrews.
19:6 ¹ Hath made them yoke fellows, as the marriage itself is by a borrowed kind of speech called a yoke.
19:7 ¹ Because political Laws are constrained to bear with some things, it followeth not by and by that God alloweth them.
19:8 ¹ Being occasioned by reason of the hardness of your hearts.
² By a political law, not by the moral law: for this law is a perpetual law of God's justice, the other boweth and bendeth as the carpenter's Bevel.
19:9 ¹ Therefore in these days the Laws that were made against adulterers were not regarded: for they should have needed no divorcement, if marriage had been cut asunder with punishment by death.
19:10 ¹ If the matter stands so between man and wife, or in marriage.
19:11 ¹ The gift of continency is peculiar, and therefore no man can set a Law to himself of perpetual continency.
² Receive and admit, as by translation we say, that a straight and narrow place is not able to receive many things.

19:12 ¹ The word Eunuch is a general word, and hath divers kinds under it, as gelded men and barren men.
² Which abstain from marriage, and live continently through the gift of God.
19:13 ¹ Infants and little children are contained in the free covenant of God.
19:16 ¹ They neither know themselves nor the Law, that seek to be saved by the Law.
19:21 ¹ The young man did not answer truly in saying that he had kept all the commandments: and therefore he layeth out an example of true charity before him, to show the disease that lay lurking in his mind.
19:23 ¹ Rich men have need of a singular gift of God, to escape out of the snares of Satan.
19:24 ¹ Word for word, it is of less labor.
² Theophylact noteth, that by this word is meant a cable rope, but Caninius allegeth out of the Talmuds that it is a proverb, and the word Camel, signifieth the beast itself.
19:28 ¹ It is not lost, that is neglected for God's sake.
² The regeneration is taken for that day, wherein the elect shall begin to live a new life, that is to say, when they shall enjoy the heavenly inheritance, both in body and soul.

29 And whosoever shall forsake houses, or brethren, or sisters, or father, or mother, or wife, or children, or lands, for my Name's sake, he shall receive an hundredfold more, and shall inherit everlasting life.

30 [k,1]But many that are first, shall be last, and the last *shall be* first.

20

1 *Laborers hired into the vineyard.* 15 *The evil eye.* 17 *He foretelleth his passion.* 20 *Zebedee's sons.* 22 *The cup.* 28 *Christ is our minister.* 30 *Two blind men.*

1 For the kingdom of heaven is like unto a certain [1]householder, which went out at the dawning of the day to hire laborers into his vineyard.

2 And he [1]agreed with the laborers for a penny a day, and sent them into his vineyard.

3 And he went out about the third hour, and saw others standing idle in the marketplace,

4 And said unto them, Go ye also into *my* vineyard, and whatsoever is right, I will give you: and they went their way.

5 Again he went out about the sixth and ninth hour, and did likewise.

6 And he went about the [1]eleventh hour, and found others standing idle, and said unto them, Why stand ye here all the day idle?

7 They said unto him, Because no man hath hired us. He said to them, Go ye also into *my* vineyard, and whatsoever is right, that shall ye receive.

8 ¶ And when even was come, the master of the vineyard said unto his steward, Call the laborers, and give them their hire, beginning at the last, till *thou come* to the first.

9 And they *which were hired* about the eleventh hour, came and received every man a penny.

10 Now when the first came, they supposed that they should receive more, but they likewise received every man a penny.

11 And when they had received it, they murmured against the master of the house,

12 Saying, These last have wrought but one hour, and thou hast made them equal unto us, which have borne the burden and heat of the day.

13 And he answered one of them, saying, Friend, I do thee no wrong: didst thou not agree with me for a penny?

14 Take that which is thine own, and go thy way: I will give unto this last, as much as to thee.

15 Is it not lawful for me to do as I will with mine own? Is thine eye [1]evil, because I am good?

16 [a]So the last shall be first, and the first last: for many are called, but few chosen.

17 [b,1]And Jesus went up to Jerusalem, and took the twelve disciples apart in the way, and said unto them,

18 [1]Behold, we go up to Jerusalem, and the Son of man shall be delivered unto the chief Priests, and unto the Scribes, and they shall condemn him to death,

19 [1]And [c]shall deliver him to the Gentiles, to mock, and to scourge, and to crucify *him*, but the third day he shall rise again.

20 [d,1]Then came to him the mother of Zebedee's children with her sons, worshipping *him*, and desiring a certain thing of him.

21 And he said unto her, What wouldest thou? She said to him, Grant that these my two sons may sit, the one at thy right hand, and the other at thy left hand in thy kingdom.

22 And Jesus answered, and said, Ye know not what ye ask. Are ye able to [1]drink of the cup that I shall drink of, and to be baptized with the [2]baptism that I shall be baptized with? they said to him, We are able.

23 And he said unto them, Ye shall drink indeed of my cup, and shall be baptized with the baptism, that I am baptized with, but to sit at my right hand, and at my left hand, is [1]not mine to give: but it *shall be given* to them for whom it is prepared of my Father.

Marginal references:
[k] Matt. 26:16 / Mark 10:31 / Luke 13:30
CHAPTER 20
[a] Matt. 19:30 / Matt. 22:14 / Mark 10:31 / Luke 13:30
[b] Mark 10:32 / Luke 18:31
[c] John 18:32
[d] Mark 10:35

19:30 [1] To have begun well, and not to continue unto the end, doth not only not profit, but also hurteth very much.

20:1 [1] God is bound to no man, and therefore he calleth whomsoever and whensoever he listeth. This only every man ought to take heed of, and hereupon bestow his whole endeavor, that he go forward and come to the mark without all stopping or staggering, and not curiously to examine other men's doings, or the judgments of God.

20:2 [1] Word for word, fell in time: it is a kind of speech taken from song.

20:6 [1] The last hour: for the day was twelve hours long, and the first hour began at the Sun rising.

20:15 [1] Naught, that is, to say, dost thou envy at my goodness towards them? for the Hebrews by an evil eye, meant envy, because such dispositions appear chiefly in the eyes, as above in Matt. 6:23. It is set to answer the word, single, and is taken there for corrupt: for whereas he said there before, verse 22, If thine eye be single, he

addeth in verse 23, but if thine eye be wicked, or corrupt, the word being the same in that place, as it is here.

20:17 [1] Christ goeth to the cross necessarily, but yet willingly.

20:18 [1] They that least ought, are the greatest persecutors of Christ.

20:19 [1] The ignomy of the cross, is the sure way to the glory of everlasting life.

20:20 [1] The manner of the heavenly kingdom is quite contrary to the earthly kingdom.

20:22 [1] This is spoken by a figure, taking the cup, for that which is contained in the cup. And again the Hebrews understand by this word, Cup, sometime the manner of punishment which is rendered to sin, as Ps. 11:6, or the joy that is given to the faithful, as Ps. 23:5, and sometime a lot or condition, as Ps. 16:5.

[2] This is applied to afflictions, as David commonly useth.

20:23 [1] The almightiness of Christ his divinity is not shut out by this, but it showeth the debasing of himself by taking man's nature upon him.

24 ᶜAnd when the *other* ten heard this, they disdained at the two brethren.

25 Therefore Jesus called them unto him, and said, Ye know that the lords of the Gentiles have [1]domination over them, and they that are great, exercise authority over them.

26 But it shall not be so among you: but whosoever will be great among you, let him be your servant.

27 And whosoever will be chief among you, let him be your servant.

28 ʲEven as the Son of man came not to be served, but to serve, and to give his life for the ransom of many.

29 ¶ ᵍ[1]And as they departed from Jericho, a great multitude followed him.

30 And behold, two blind men, sitting by the way side, when they heard that Jesus passed by, cried, saying, O Lord, the Son of David, have mercy on us.

31 And the multitude rebuked them, because they should hold their peace: but they cried the more, saying, O Lord, the Son of David, have mercy on us.

32 Then Jesus stood still, and [1]called them, and said, What will ye that I should do to you?

33 They said to him, Lord, that our eyes may be opened.

34 And Jesus moved with compassion, touched their eyes, and immediately their eyes received sight, and they followed him.

21

1 Christ rideth on an ass unto Jerusalem.   12 He casteth out the sellers.   13 The house of prayer.   19 The withered fig tree.   25 John's baptism.   28 Who do the will of God.   30 Publicans, Harlots.   33 God's vineyard.   The Jews.   38 The son killed of the husbandmen.   42 The cornerstone.

1 And ᵃ,[1]when they drew near to Jerusalem, and were come to Bethphage, unto the mount of the Olives, then sent Jesus two disciples,

2 Saying to them, Go into the town that is over against you, and anon ye shall find an ass bound, and a colt with her: loose them, and bring them unto me.

Marginal references (center column):

ᵉ Mark 10:41
Luke 22:25
ʲ Phil. 2:7

ᵍ Mark 10:46
Luke 18:35

CHAPTER 21
ᵃ Mark 11:1
Luke 19:29
ᵇ Isa. 62:11
Zech. 9:9
John 12:15
ᶜ Mark 11:11
Luke 19:45
John 2:13
ᵈ Deut. 14:25
ᵉ Isa. 56:6-7
ʲ Jer. 7:11
Mark 11:17
Luke 19:46
ᵍ Ps. 8:2

3 And if any man say ought unto you, say ye, that the Lord hath need of them, and straightway [1]he will let them go.

4 All this was done that it might be fulfilled, which was spoken by the Prophet, saying,

5 ¶ ᵇTell ye the [1]daughter of Zion, Behold, thy King cometh unto thee, meek and sitting upon an ass, and a colt, the foal of an ass used to the yoke.

6 So the disciples went, and did as Jesus had commanded them,

7 And brought the ass and the colt, and put on them their [1]clothes, and set him [2]thereon.

8 And a great multitude spread their garments in the way: and others cut down branches from the trees, and strawed them in the way.

9 Moreover, the people that went before, and they also that followed, cried, saying, [1]Hosanna to the Son of David, [2]Blessed *be* he that cometh in the Name of the Lord, Hosanna *thou which art* in the highest *heavens*.

10 ᶜAnd when he was come into Jerusalem, [1]all the city was moved, saying, Who is this?

11 And the people said, This is Jesus that Prophet of Nazareth in Galilee.

12 ¶ And Jesus went into the Temple of God, and cast out all them ᵈthat sold and bought in the Temple, and overthrew the tables of the moneychangers, and the seats of them that sold doves,

13 And said to them, It is written, ᵉMy house shall be called the house of prayer: but ʲye have made it a den of thieves.

14 Then the blind, and the halt came to him, in the Temple, and he healed them.

15 [1]But when the chief Priests and Scribes saw the marvels that he did, and the children crying in the Temple, and saying, Hosanna to the Son of David, they disdained,

16 And said unto him, Hearest thou what these say? And Jesus said unto them, Yea: read ye never, ᵍBy the mouth of babes and sucklings thou hast [1]made perfect the praise?

17 ¶ [1]So he left them, and went out of the city

Footnotes (bottom):

20:25 [1] Somewhat sharply and roughly.

20:29 [1] Christ by healing these blind men with an only touch, showeth that he is the only light of the world.

20:32 [1] Himself, not by other men's means.

21:1 [1] Christ by his humility triumphing over the pride of this world, ascendeth to true glory by ignomy of the cross.

21:3 [1] He that shall say anything to you, shall let them go, to wit, the ass and the colt.

21:5 [1] The city of Zion. An Hebrew kind of speech, common in the lamentations of Jeremiah.

21:7 [1] Their uppermost garments.

　　[2] Upon their garments, not upon the ass and the colt.

21:9 [1] This was an ancient kind of crying which they used in the feast of Tabernacles, when they carried boughs according as God

commanded, Lev. 23:40. And the word is corruptly made of two, for we should say, Hoshiangna, which is as much to say, as Save I pray thee.

　　[2] Well be it to him that cometh in the name of the Lord, that is to say, whom the Lord hath given us for our king.

21:10 [1] That is, all the men of Jerusalem were moved.

21:15 [1] Such as should be masters of godliness, are they that do most envy the glory of Christ: but in vain.

21:16 [1] Thou hast made most perfect. We read in David, Thou hast established or grounded, and if the matter be considered well, it is all one that the Evangelist saith, for that is stable and sure, which is most perfect.

21:17 [1] Christ doth so forsake the wicked, that yet he hath a consideration and regard of his Church.

unto Bethany, and lodged there.

18 ¹And ʰin the morning, as he returned into the city, he was hungry.

19 And seeing a fig tree in the way, he came to it, and found nothing thereon, but leaves only, and said to it, Never fruit grow on thee henceforward. And anon the fig tree withered.

20 And when his disciples saw it, they marveled, saying, How soon is the fig tree withered!

21 ¹And Jesus answered and said unto them, ⁱVerily I say unto you, if ye have faith, and ²doubt not, ye shall not only do that, *which I have done* to the fig tree, but also if ye say unto this mountain, Take thyself away, and cast thyself into the sea, it shall be done.

22 ʲAnd whatsoever ye shall ask in prayer, if ye believe, ye shall receive it.

23 ¶ ᵏ,¹And when he was come into the Temple, the chief Priests, and the Elders of the people came unto him, as he was teaching, and said, By what ²authority doest thou these things? and who gave thee this authority?

24 Then Jesus answered, and said unto them, I also will ask of you ¹a certain thing, which if ye tell me, I likewise will tell you by what authority I do these things.

25 The ¹baptism of John, whence was it? from ²heaven, or of men? Then they ³reasoned among themselves, saying, If we shall say, From heaven, he will say unto us, Why did ye not then believe him?

26 And if we say, Of men, we fear the multitude, ˡfor all hold John as a Prophet.

27 Then they answered Jesus, and said, We can not tell. And he said unto them, Neither tell I you by what authority I do these things.

28 ¶ ¹But what think ye? A *certain* man had two sons, and came to the elder, and said, Son, go and work today in my vineyard.

29 But he answered, and said, I will not: yet afterward he repented himself, and went.

30 Then came he to the second, and said likewise. And he answered, and said, I will, Sir: yet he went not.

31 Whether of them twain did the will of the father? They said unto him, The first. Jesus said unto them, Verily I say unto you, that the Publicans and the harlots ¹go before you into the kingdom of God.

32 For John came unto you in the ¹way of righteousness, and ye believed him not: but the Publicans and the harlots believed him, and ye though ye saw it, were not moved with repentance afterward, that ye might believe him.

33 ¶ ¹Hear another parable, There was a certain householder, ᵐwhich planted a vineyard, and hedged it round about, and made a winepress therein, and ²built a tower, and let it out to husbandmen, and went into a strange country.

34 And when the time of the fruit drew near, he sent his servants to the husbandmen to receive the fruits thereof.

35 And the husbandmen took his servants and beat one, and killed another, and stoned another.

36 Again he sent other servants, more than the first: and they did the like unto them.

37 But last of all he sent unto them his own son, saying, They will reverence my son.

38 But when the husbandmen saw the son, they said among themselves, ⁿThis is the heir: come, let us kill him, and let us ¹take his inheritance.

39 So they took him, and cast him out of the vineyard, and slew him.

40 When therefore the Lord of the vineyard shall come, what will he do to those husbandmen?

41 They said unto him, He will ¹cruelly destroy those wicked men, and will let out his vineyard unto other husbandmen, which shall deliver him the fruits in their seasons.

42 Jesus said unto them, Read ye never in the Scriptures, ᵒThe stone which the ¹builders refused,

ʰ Mark 21:12
ⁱ Matt. 17:20
ʲ Matt. 7:7
John 15:7
1 John 5:14
ᵏ Mark 11:27-28
Luke 20:1-2
ˡ Matt. 14:5
Mark 6:20
ᵐ Isa. 5:1
Jer. 2:21
Mark 12:1
Luke 20:9
ⁿ Matt. 26:3-4
Matt. 27:1
John 11:53
ᵒ Ps. 118:22
Acts 4:11
Rom. 9:33

21:18 ¹ Hypocrites shall at length have their masks discovered, and their vizards plucked from their faces.
21:21 ¹ How great the force of faith is.
² The Greek word signifieth a sticking or wavering of mind, so that we cannot tell which way to take.
21:23 ¹ Against them which overstepping the doctrine, blind the calling and vocation to an ordinary succession going about by that false pretext, to stop Christ's mouth.
² Or, by what power.
21:24 ¹ One word, that is to say, I will ask you in one word.
21:25 ¹ John his preaching is called by a figure, Baptism, because he preached the baptism of repentance, etc., Mark 1:4; Acts 19:3.
² From God, and so it is plainly seen how these are set one against another.
³ Beat their heads about it and mused, or laid their heads together.

21:28 ¹ It is no new thing to see them to be the worst of all men, which ought to show the way of godliness to others.
21:31 ¹ They make haste to the kingdom of God, and you slack so that at least wise you should have followed their example. Mark then that this word (go before) is improperly taken in this place, whereas no man followeth.
21:32 ¹ Living uprightly, being of a good and honest conversation: For the Hebrews use this word, Way, for life and manners.
21:33 ¹ Those men oftentimes are the cruelest enemies of the Church, to whose fidelity it is committed: But the vocation of God, is neither tied to time, place, nor person.
² Made the place strong: For a tower is the strongest place of a wall.
21:38 ¹ Word for word, let us hold it fast.
21:41 ¹ A kind of proverb, showing what end the wicked are worthy of.
21:42 ¹ Master builders, which are chief builders of the house, that is, of the Church.

the same is ²made the ³head of the corner? ⁴This was the Lord's doing, and it is marvelous in our eyes.

43 Therefore say I unto you, The kingdom of God shall be taken from you, and shall be given to a nation, which shall bring forth the ¹fruits thereof.

44 ^pAnd whosoever shall fall on this stone, he shall be broken: but on whomsoever it shall fall, it will ¹dash him in pieces.

45 And when the chief Priests and Pharisees had heard his parables, they perceived that he spake of them.

46 ¹And they seeking to lay hands on him, feared the people, because they took him as a Prophet.

22 *2 The parable of the marriage. 9 The calling of the Gentiles. 11 The wedding garments, faith. 16 Of Caesar's tribute. 23 They question with Christ touching the resurrection. 32 God is of the living. 36 The greatest commandment. 37 To love God. 39 To love our neighbor. 42 Jesus reasoneth with the Pharisees touching the Messiah.*

1 Then ^{a,1}Jesus answered, and spake unto them again in parables, saying,

2 The kingdom of heaven is like unto a certain king which married his son,

3 And sent forth his servants, to call them that were bidden to the wedding, but they would not come.

4 Again he sent forth other servants, saying, Tell them which are bidden, Behold, I have prepared my dinner: mine oxen and my fatlings are ¹killed, and all things are ready: come unto the marriage.

5 But they made light of it, and went their ways, one to his farm, and another about his merchandise.

6 And the remnant took his servants, and entreated them sharply, and slew them.

Marginal references:
p Isa. 8:14
CHAPTER 22
a Luke 14:16
Rev. 19:9
b Matt. 8:12
Matt. 13:42
Matt. 25:30
c Matt. 20:16
d Mark 12:13
Luke 20:20

7 ¹But when the king heard it, he was wroth, and sent forth his warriors, and destroyed those murderers, and burnt up their city.

8 Then said he to his servants, Truly the ¹wedding is prepared: but they which were bidden, were not worthy.

9 ¹Go ye therefore out into the *high*ways, and as many as ye find, bid them to the marriage.

10 So those servants went out into the highways, and gathered together all that ever they found, both good and ¹bad: so the wedding was furnished with guests.

11 ¹Then the king came in, to see the guests, and saw there a man which had not on a wedding garment.

12 And he said unto him, Friend, how camest thou in hither, and hast not on a wedding garment? And he was ¹speechless.

13 Then said the king to the ¹servants, Bind him hand and foot: take him away, and cast him into utter darkness: ^bthere shall be weeping and gnashing of teeth.

14 ^cFor many are called, but few chosen.

15 ¶ ^dThen went the Pharisees and took counsel how they might ¹tangle him in talk.

16 And they sent unto him their disciples with the ¹Herodians, saying, Master, we know that thou art true, and teachest the way of God ²truly, neither carest for any man: for thou considerest not the ³person of men.

17 ¹Tell us therefore, how thinkest thou? Is it lawful to give ²tribute unto Caesar, or not?

18 But Jesus perceived their wickedness, and said, Why tempt ye me, ye hypocrites?

19 Show me the tribute money. And they brought

---

² Began to be.

³ The chiefest stone in the corner is called the head of the corner, which beareth up the couplings or joints of the whole building.

⁴ That matter (in that the stone which was cast away, is made the head) is the Lord's doing, which we behold and greatly marvel at.

21:43 ¹ They bring forth the fruits of the kingdom of God, which bring forth the fruits of the Spirit, and not of the flesh, Gal. 5.

21:44 ¹ As chaff used to be scattered with the wind, for he useth a word which signifieth properly, to separate the chaff from the corn with winnowing, to scatter it abroad.

21:46 ¹ The wicked can do nothing, but what God will.

22:1 ¹ Not all of the whole company of them that are called by the voice of the Gospel are the true Church before God: for the most part of them had rather follow the commodities of this life: and some do most cruelly persecute those that call them: but they are the true Church, which obey when they are called, such as for the most part they are, whom the world despiseth.

22:4 ¹ The word here used is commonly used in sacrifices, and is by translation used for other feasts also: for feasts and banquets were wont to be begun with sacrifices.

22:7 ¹ A dreadful destruction of them that contemn Christ.

22:8 ¹ The marriage feast.

22:9 ¹ God doth first call us, when we think nothing of it.

22:10 ¹ The general calling offereth the Gospel to all men: but their life is examined that enter in.

22:11 ¹ In the small number which come at the calling, there are some castaways which do not confirm their faith with newness of life.

22:12 ¹ Word for word, haltered, that is to say, he held his peace, as though he had had a bridle or an halter about his neck.

22:13 ¹ To them that served the guests.

22:15 ¹ Snare him in his words or talk. The Greek word is derived of snares which hunters lay.

22:16 ¹ They which with Herod made a new religion patched together of the heathenish and the Jewish religion.

² Truly and sincerely.

³ Thou art not moved with any appearance and outward show.

22:17 ¹ The Christians must obey their Magistrates, although they be wicked and extortioners, but so far forth as the authority that God hath over us may remain safe unto him, and his honor be not diminished.

² The word that is used here, signifieth a valuing and rating of men's substance, according to the proportion whereof they paid tribute in those provinces which were subject to tribute, and it is here taken for the tribute itself.

him a ¹penny.

20 And he said unto them, Whose is this image and superscription?

21 They said unto him, Caesar's. Then said he unto them, ᵉGive therefore to Caesar, the things which are Caesar's, and give unto God, those things which are God's.

22 And when they heard it, they marveled, and left him, and went their way.

23 ¶ ᶠ·¹The same day the Sadducees came to him, (which say that there is no resurrection) and asked him,

24 Saying, Master, ᵍMoses said, If a man die, having no ¹children, his brother shall marry his wife by the right of alliance, and raise up seed unto his brother.

25 Now therefore were with us seven brethren, and the first married a wife, and deceased: and having no issue, left his wife unto his brother.

26 Likewise also the second, and the third, unto the seventh.

27 And last of all the woman died also.

28 Therefore in the resurrection, whose wife shall she be of the seven? for all had her.

29 Then Jesus answered, and said unto them, Ye are deceived, not knowing the Scriptures, nor the power of God.

30 For in the resurrection they neither marry wives, nor wives are bestowed in marriage, but are as the ¹Angels of God in heaven.

31 And concerning the resurrection of the dead, have ye not read what is spoken unto you of God, saying,

32 ʰI am the God of Abraham, and the God of Isaac, and the God of Jacob? God is not the God of the dead, but of the living.

33 And when the multitude heard it, they were astonied at his doctrine.

34 ¶ ⁱ·¹But when the Pharisees had heard, that he had put the Sadducees to silence, they assembled

Column references:
ᵉ Mark 12:17
Luke 20:25
Rom. 13:7
ᶠ Mark 12:18
Luke 20:27
Acts 23:8
ᵍ Deut. 25:5
ʰ Exod. 3:6
Mark 12:27
ⁱ Mark 12:28
ʲ Deut. 6:5
ᵏ Mark 12:31
Rom. 13:9
Gal. 5:14
James 2:8
ˡ Mark 12:35
Luke 10:41
ᵐ Ps. 110:1

CHAPTER 23
ᵃ Neh. 8:4

together.

35 And ¹one of them, *which was* an expounder of the Law, asked him a question, tempting him, and saying,

36 Master, which is the great commandment in the Law?

37 Jesus said to him, ʲThou shalt love the Lord thy God with all thine heart, and with all thy ¹soul, and with all thy mind.

38 This is the first and the great commandment.

39 And the second is like unto this, ᵏThou shalt love thy ¹neighbor as thyself.

40 On these two commandments hangeth the whole Law and the Prophets.

41 ¶ ˡ·¹While the Pharisees were gathered together, Jesus asked them,

42 Saying, What think ye of Christ? ¹whose son is he? They said unto him, David's.

43 He said unto them, How then doth David in spirit, call him Lord, saying,

44 ᵐThe Lord said to my Lord, Sit at my right hand, till I make thine enemies thy footstool?

45 If then David call him Lord, how is he his son?

46 And none could answer him a word, neither durst any from that day forth ask him any more questions.

23

2 *How the Scribes teaching the people the Law of Moses, behave themselves.* 5 *Their Phylacteries, and Fringes.* 7 *Greetings.* 8 *We are brethren.* 9 *The Father.* 10 *The servant.* 13 *To shut the kingdom of heaven.* 14 *To devour widow's houses.* 15 *A Proselyte.* 16 *To swear by the Temple.* 23 *To tithe mint.* 25 *To cleanse the outside of the cup.* 27 *Painted sepulchers.* 33 *Serpents, vipers.* 37 *The Hen.*

1 Then spake Jesus to the multitude, and to his disciples,

2 ¹Saying, The ᵃScribes and the Pharisees ²sit in Moses' seat.

22:19 ¹ Before Matt. 17:24 there is mention made of a didrachma, and here, of a penny, whereas a didrachma is more by the seventh part than a penny: so that there seemeth to be a jar in these two places: but they may easily be recorded thus: The penny was paid to the Romans for tribute according to the proportion they were rated at, the drachma was paid of everyone to the Temple, which also the Romans took to themselves when they had subdued Judea.

22:23 ¹ Christ voucheth the resurrection of the flesh against the Sadducees.

22:24 ¹ Under which name are daughters also comprehended, but yet as touching the family and name of a man, because he that left daughters was in no better case, than if he had left no children at all, (for they were not reckoned in the family) by the name of children are Sons understood.

22:30 ¹ He saith not that they shall be without bodies, for then they should not be men anymore, but they shall be as Angels, for they shall neither marry nor be married.

22:34 ¹ The Gospel doth not abolish the precepts of the Law, but doth rather confirm them.

22:35 ¹ A scribe, so saith Mark 12:28, now what a scribe is, see Matt. 2:4.

22:37 ¹ The Hebrew text readeth, Deut. 6:5, with thine heart, soul, and strength: and in Mark 12:30 and Luke 10:27 we read with soul, heart, strength and thought.

22:39 ¹ Another man.

22:41 ¹ Christ proveth manifestly that he is David's son according to the flesh, but otherwise, David's Lord, and very God.

22:42 ¹ Or, whose stock or family: for the Hebrews call a man's posterity, sons.

23:2 ¹ We ought to hear whatsoever any wicked teachers teach us purely out of the word of God, yet so that we eschew their evil manners.

² Because God appointed the order, therefore the Lord would have his word to be heard even from the mouth of hypocrites and hirelings.

3 [1]All therefore whatsoever they bid you observe, that observe and do: but after their works do not: for they say, and do not.

4 [b,1]For they bind heavy burdens, and grievous to be borne, and lay them on men's shoulders, but they themselves will not move them with *one* of their fingers.

5 [1]All their works they do for to be seen of men: for they make their [2]phylacteries broad, and make long [3]the 'fringes of their garments,

6 [d]And love the chief place at feasts, and to have the chief seats in the [1]assemblies,

7 And greetings in the markets, and to be called of men, Rabbi, [1]Rabbi.

8 [c,1]But be not ye [2]called, Rabbi: for [3]one is your doctor, *to wit*, Christ, and all ye are brethren.

9 And[f]call no man your [1]father upon the earth: for there is but one, your father which is in heaven.

10 Be not called [1]doctors: for one is your doctor, *even* Christ.

11 But he that is greatest among you, let him be your servant.

12 [g]For whosoever [1]will exalt himself, shall be brought low: and whosoever will humble himself, shall be exalted.

13 ¶ [1]Woe therefore *be* unto you, Scribes and Pharisees, [2]hypocrites, because ye shut up the kingdom of heaven before men: for ye yourselves go not in, neither suffer ye them that would [3]enter, to come in.

14 [h,1]Woe *be* unto you, Scribes and Pharisees, hypocrites: for ye devour widows' houses, even [2]under a color of long prayers: wherefore ye shall receive the greater damnation.

15 Woe *be* unto you, Scribes and Pharisees, hypocrites: for ye compass sea and [1]land to make one of your profession: and when he is made, ye make him twofold more the child of hell, than you yourselves.

16 Woe *be* unto you blind guides, which say, Whosoever sweareth by the Temple, it is nothing: but whosoever sweareth by the gold of the Temple, he [1]offendeth.

17 Ye fools and blind, Whether is greater, the gold, or the Temple that [1]sanctifieth the gold?

18 And whosoever sweareth by the altar, it is nothing: but whosoever sweareth by the offering *that is* upon it, offendeth.

19 Ye fools and blind, whether is greater, the offering, or the altar which sanctifieth the offering?

20 Whosoever therefore sweareth by the altar, sweareth by it, and by all things thereon.

21 [i]And whosoever sweareth by the Temple, sweareth by it, and by him that dwelleth therein.

22 [j]And he that sweareth by heaven, sweareth by the [1]throne of God, and by him that sitteth theron.

23 ¶ [k,1]Woe *be* to you, Scribes and Pharisees, hypocrites: for ye tithe mint, and anise, and cummin, and leave the weightier matters of the law, *as* judgment, and mercy and [2]fidelity. These ought ye to have done, and not to have left the other.

24 Ye blind guides, which strain out a gnat, and

[b] Luke 11:46
Acts 15:10

[c] Num. 15:38
Deut. 12:12
Mark 12:38

[d] Luke 11:43
Luke 20:46

[e] James 3:1

[f] Mal. 1:6

[g] Luke 14:11
Luke 18:14

[h] Mark 12:40
Luke 20:47

[i] 1 Kings 8:13
2 Chron. 6:2

[j] Matt. 5:34

[k] Luke 11:42

23:3 [1] Provided always, that they deliver Moses his doctrine which they profess, which thing the Metaphor of the seat showeth, which they occupied as teachers of Moses his learning.

23:4 [1] Hypocrites for the most part are most severe exactors of those things which they themselves chiefly neglect.

23:5 [1] Hypocrites are ambitious.

[2] It was a thread, or ribbon of blue silk in the fringe of a corner, the beholding whereof made them to remember the laws and ordinances of God: and therefore was it called a Phylactery, as ye would say, a keeper, Num. 15:38; Deut. 6:8, which order the Jews afterward abused, as they do nowadays, which hang the St. John's Gospels about their necks: a thing condemned many years ago in the Council of Antioch.

[3] Word for word, Twisted tassels of thread which hung at the nethermost hems of their garments.

23:6 [1] When assemblies and Councils are gathered together.

23:7 [1] This word Rabbi, signifieth one that is above his fellows, and is as good as a number of them: and we may see by the repeating of it, how proud a rule it was. Now they were called Rabbi, which by the laying on of hands were uttered and declared to the world to be wise men.

23:8 [1] Modesty is a singular ornament of God's minsters.

[2] Seek not ambitiously after it: for our Lord doth not forbid us to give the Magistrate and our Masters the honor that is due to them, Augustine de sermone verbi Domine ex, Matt. 11.

[3] He seemeth to allude to a place of Isaiah, chapter 54:13, and Jer. 31:34.

23:9 [1] He shooteth at a fashion which the Jews used, for they called the Rabbis, our fathers.

23:10 [1] It seemeth that the Scribes did very greedily hunt after such titles, whom verse 16 he calleth blind guides.

23:12 [1] He seemeth to allude to the name of the Rabbis, for Rabbi signifieth one that is aloft.

23:13 [1] Hypocrites can abide none to be better than themselves.

[2] Christ when he reproveth any man sharply, uses this word, to give us to understand that there is nothing more detestable than hypocrisy and falsehood in religion.

[3] Which are even at the door.

23:14 [1] It is a common thing among hypocrites, to abuse the pretence of zeal to covetousness and extortion.

[2] Word for word, under a color of long praying. And this word, Even, noteth a double naughtiness in them: the one, that they devoured widows' goods: the other, that they did it under a color of godliness.

23:15 [1] The dry part: now that part of that earth is called dry, which the Lord hath given us to dwell upon.

23:16 [1] Is a debtor. Sins are called in the Syrian tongue, Debts, and it is certain that Christ spake in the Syrian tongue.

23:17 [1] Causeth the gold to be counted holy, which is dedicated to an holy use.

23:22 [1] If heaven be God's throne, then he is no doubt above all this world.

23:23 [1] Hypocrites are careful in trifles, and neglect the greatest things of purpose.

[2] Faithfulness in keeping of promises.

swallow a camel.

25 ¶ [1]Woe *be* to you, [l]Scribes and Pharisees, hypocrites: for ye make clean the utter side of the cup, and of the platter: but within they are full of bribery and excess.

26 Thou blind Pharisee, cleanse first the inside of the cup and platter, that the outside of them may be clean also.

27 Woe *be* to you, Scribes and Pharisees, hypocrites: for ye are like unto whited tombs, which appear beautiful outward, but are within full of dead men's bones, and all filthiness.

28 So are ye also: for outward ye appear righteous unto men, but within ye are full of hypocrisy and iniquity.

29 [m,1]Woe *be* unto you, Scribes and Pharisees, hypocrites: for ye build the tombs of the Prophets, and garnish the sepulchers of the righteous,

30 And say, If we had been in the days of our fathers, we would not have been partners with them in the blood of the Prophets.

31 So then ye be witnesses unto yourselves, that ye are the children of them that murdered the Prophets.

32 [1]Fulfill ye also the measure of your fathers.

33 O serpents, the generation of vipers, how should ye escape the damnation of [1]hell!

34 [1]Wherefore behold, I send unto you Prophets, and wise men, and Scribes, and of them ye shall kill and crucify: and of them shall ye scourge in your Synagogues, and persecute from city to city,

35 [1]That upon you may come all the righteous blood that was shed upon the earth, [n]from the blood of Abel the righteous, unto the blood of Zechariah the son of [2]Berechiah, [o]whom ye slew between the Temple and the altar.

36 Verily I say unto you, all these things shall come upon this generation.

37 [p,1]Jerusalem, Jerusalem, which killest the Prophets, and stonest them which are sent to thee, how often would I have [2]gathered thy children together, as the hen gathered her chickens under her wings,

Marginal references

[l] Luke 12:39
[m] Matt. 5:22
[n] Gen. 4:8
[o] 2 Chron. 24:21
[p] Luke 13:34

CHAPTER 24
[a] Mark 13:1
Luke 21:5-6
[b] Luke 19:44
[c] Eph. 5:6
Col. 2:18
[d] Matt. 10:17
Luke 21:12
John 15:20
John 16:2

and ye would not!

38 Behold, your habitation shall be left unto you desolate.

39 For I say unto you, ye shall not see me henceforth till that ye say, Blessed *is* he that cometh in the Name of the Lord.

24

2 *The destruction of the Temple.* 4 *The signs of Christ's coming.* 12 *Iniquity.* 23 *False Christs.* 29 *The signs of the end of the world.* 31 *The Angels.* 32 *The fig tree.* 37 *The days of Noah.* 42 *We must watch.* 45 *The servant.*

1 And [a]Jesus went out, and departed from the Temple, and his disciples came to him, to show him the building of the Temple.

2 [1]And Jesus said unto them, See ye not all these things? Verily I say unto you, [b]there shall not be here left a stone upon a stone, that shall not be cast down.

3 And as he sat upon the mount of Olives, his disciples came unto him apart, saying, Tell us when these things shall be, and what sign *shall be* of thy coming, and of the end of the world.

4 [1]And Jesus answered, and said unto them, [c]Take heed that no man deceive you.

5 For many shall come in my Name, saying, I am Christ, and shall deceive many.

6 And ye shall hear of wars, and rumors of wars: see that ye be not [c]troubled: for all these things must come to pass, but the [1]end is not yet.

7 For nation shall rise against nation, and realm against realm, and there shall be famine, and pestilence, and earthquakes in [1]divers places.

8 All these are but the beginning of [1]sorrows.

9 [d]Then shall they deliver you up to be afflicted, and shall kill you, and ye shall be hated of all nations for my Name's sake.

10 And then shall many be offended, and shall betray one another, and shall hate one another.

11 And many false prophets shall arise, and shall deceive many.

12 And because iniquity shall be increased, the love of many shall be cold.

23:25 [1] Hypocrites are too much careful of outward things, and the inward they utterly contemn.

23:29 [1] Hypocrites when they go most about to cover their wickedness, then do they by the just judgment of God, shame themselves.

23:32 [1] A proverb used of the Jews, which hath this meaning, Go ye on also and follow your ancestors, that at length your wickedness may come to the full.

23:33 [1] See also Matt. 5:22.

23:34 [1] Hypocrites be cruel.

23:35 [1] The end of them which persecute the Gospel, under the pretence of zeal.

[2] Of Joiada, who was also called Berechiah, that is, blessed of the Lord.

23:37 [1] Where the mercy of God was greatest, there was greatest

wickedness and rebellion, and at length the most sharp judgments of God.

[2] He speaketh of the outward ministry, and as he was promised for the saving of this people, so was he also careful for it, even from the time that the promise was made to Abraham.

24:2 [1] The destruction of the city, and especially of the Temple is foretold.

24:4 [1] The Church shall have a continual conflict with infinite miseries and offences, and that more is, with false prophets, until the day of victory and triumph cometh.

24:6 [1] That is, when those things are fulfilled, yet the end shall not come.

24:7 [1] Everywhere.

24:8 [1] Word for word, of great torments, like unto women in travail.

13 c,1But he that endureth to the end, he shall be saved.

14 And this 1Gospel of the kingdom shall be preached through the whole 2world for a witness unto all nations, and then shall the end come.

15 ¶ 1When ye ftherefore shall see the 2abomination of desolation spoken of by gDaniel the Prophet, set in the holy place (let him that readeth consider it.)

16 Then let them which be in Judea, flee into the mountains.

17 Let him which is on the housetop, not come down to fetch anything out of his house.

18 And he that is in the field, let not him return back to fetch his 1clothes.

19 And woe shall be to them that are with child, and to them that give suck in those days.

20 But pray that your flight be not in the winter, neither on the h,1Sabbath day.

21 For then shall be great tribulation, such as was not from the beginning of the world to this time, nor shall be.

22 And except 1those days should be shortened, there should no 2flesh be saved: but for the elect's sake those days shall be shortened.

23 iThen if any man shall say unto you, Lo, here is Christ, or there, believe it not.

24 For there shall arise false Christs, and false prophets, and 1shall show great signs and wonders, so that if it were possible, they should deceive the very elect.

25 Behold, I have told you before.

26 Wherefore if they shall say unto you, Behold, he is in the desert, go not forth: Behold, he is in the secret places, believe it not.

27 For as the lightning cometh out of the East, and is seen into the West, so shall also the coming of the Son of man be.

28 j,1For wheresoever a dead 2carcass is, thither will the Eagles be gathered together.

29 k,1And immediately after the tribulations of those days shall the sun be darkened, and the moon shall not give her light, and the stars shall fall from heaven, and the powers of heaven shall be shaken.

30 And then shall appear the 1sign of the Son of man in heaven: and then shall all the 2kindreds of the earth 3mourn, land they shall see the Son of man 4come in the clouds of heaven with power and great glory.

31 mAnd he shall send his Angels with a great sound of a trumpet, and they shall gather together his elect, from the 1four winds, and from the one end of the heavens unto the other.

32 1Now learn the parable of the fig tree: when her bough is yet 2tender, and it putteth forth leaves, ye know that summer is near.

33 So likewise ye, when ye see all these things, know that the kingdom of God is near, even at the doors.

34 Verily I say unto you, this 1generation shall not pass, till all these things be done.

35 n,1Heaven and earth shall pass away: but my words shall not pass away.

36 1But of that day and hour knoweth no man, no not the Angels of heaven, but my father only.

37 But as the days of Noah *were*, so likewise shall the coming of the Son of man be.

38 °For as in the days *before* the flood, they did ¹eat and drink, marry, and give in marriage, unto the day that Noah entered into the Ark,

39 And knew nothing, till the flood came, and took them all away, so also shall the coming of the Son of man be.

40 ᵖ·¹Then two shall be in the fields, the one shall be received, and the other shall be refused.

41 ¹Two women shall be grinding at the mill: the one shall be received, and the other shall be refused.

42 ᵠ·¹Watch therefore: for ye know not what hour your master will come.

43 ʳOf this be sure, that if the good man of the house knew at what watch the thief would come, he would surely watch, and not suffer his house to be dug through.

44 Therefore be ye also ready: for in the hour that ye think not, will the Son of man come.

45 ˢWho then is a faithful servant and wise, whom his master hath made ruler over his household, to give them meat in season?

46 Blessed *is* that servant, whom his master when he cometh, shall find so doing.

47 Verily I say unto you, he shall make him ruler over all his goods.

48 But if that evil servant shall say in his heart, My master doth defer his coming,

49 And begin to smite his fellows, and to eat, and to drink with the drunken,

50 That servant's master will come in a day, when he looketh not for him, and in an hour that he is not aware of,

51 And will ¹cut him off, and give him his portion with hypocrites: ᵗthere shall be weeping and gnashing of teeth.

° Luke 17:26
Gen. 7:1
1 Pet. 3:20
ᵖ Luke 17:36
ᵠ Mark 13:35
ʳ Luke 12:39
1 Thess. 5:2
Rev. 16:15
ˢ Luke 12:42
ᵗ Matt. 13:42
Matt. 25:30

CHAPTER 25
ᵃ Matt. 24:42
Mark 13:35
ᵇ Luke 19:12-13

25

1 The virgins looking for the Bridegroom. 13 We must watch. 14 The talents delivered unto the servants. 24 The evil servants. 30 After what sort the last judgment shall be. 41 The cursed.

1 Then ¹the kingdom of heaven shall be likened unto ten virgins, which took their lamps, and ²went forth to meet the bridegroom.

2 And five of them were wise, and five foolish.

3 The foolish took their lamps, but took no oil with them.

4 But the wise took oil in their vessels with their lamps.

5 Now while the bridegroom tarried long, all ¹slumbered and slept.

6 And at midnight there was a cry made, Behold, the bridegroom cometh: go out to meet him.

7 Then all those virgins arose and trimmed their lamps.

8 And the foolish said to the wise, Give us of your oil, for our lamps are out.

9 But the wise answered, saying, *Not so*, lest there will not be enough for us and you: but go ye rather to them that sell, and buy for yourselves.

10 And while they went to buy, the bridegroom came: and they that were ready, went in with him to the wedding, and the gate was shut.

11 Afterwards came also the other virgins, saying, Lord, Lord, open to us.

12 But he answered, and said, Verily I say unto you, I know you not.

13 ᵈWatch therefore: for ye know neither the day, nor the hour, when the son of man will come.

14 ᵇ·¹For the *kingdom of heaven is* as a man that going into a strange country, called his servants, and delivered to them his goods.

15 And unto one he gave five talents, and to another two, and to another one, to every man after his own ¹ability, and straightway went from home.

16 Then he that had received the five talents, went and occupied with them, and gained other

---

24:38 ¹ The word which the Evangelist useth, expresseth the matter more fully than ours doth: for it is a word which is proper to brute beasts: and his meaning is, that in those days men shall be given to their bellies like unto brute beasts: for otherwise it is no fault to eat and drink.

24:40 ¹ Against them that persuade themselves that God will be merciful to all men, and do by that means give over themselves to sin, that they may in the meanwhile live in pleasure void of all care.

24:41 ¹ The Greek women and the Barbarians did grind and bake. (Plutarch, book Problem)

24:42 ¹ An example of the horrible carelessness of men in those things whereof they ought to be most careful.

24:51 ¹ To wit, from the rest, or will cut him into two parts, which was a most cruel kind of punishment, wherewith as Justin Martyr witnesseth, Isaiah the Prophet was executed by the Jews: the like kind of punishment we read of, 1 Sam. 15:33 and Dan. 3:29.

25:1 ¹ We must desire strength at God's hand, which may serve us as a torch while we walk through this darkness, to bring us to our desired end: otherwise if we become slothful and negligent as weary of our pains and travail, we shall be shut out of the doors.

² The pomp of bridals was wont for the most part to be kept in the night seasons, and that by damsels.

25:5 ¹ Their eyes being heavy with sleep.

25:14 ¹ Christ witnesseth that there shall be a long time between his departure to his father, and his coming again to us, but yet notwithstanding that, he will at that day take an account not only of the rebellious and obstinate, how they have bestowed that which they received of him, but also of his household servants, which have not through slothfulness employed those gifts which he bestowed upon them.

25:15 ¹ According to the wisdom and skill in dealing, which was given them.

five talents.

17 Likewise also he that *received* two, he also gained other two.

18 But he that received that one, went and dug it in the earth, and hid his master's money.

19 But after a long season, the master of those servants came, and reckoned with them.

20 Then came he that had received five talents, and brought other five talents, saying, Master, thou deliveredst unto me five talents: behold, I have gained with them other five talents.

21 Then his master said unto him, It is well done good servant and faithful, Thou hast been faithful in little, I will make thee ruler over much: [1]enter into thy master's joy.

22 Also he that had received two talents, came, and said, Master, thou deliveredst unto me two talents: behold, I have gained two other talents more.

23 His master said unto him, It is well done good servant, and faithful, Thou hast been faithful in little, I will make thee ruler over much: enter into thy master's joy.

24 Then he that had received the one talent, came, and said, Master, I knew that thou wast an hard man, which reapest where thou sowedst not, and gatherest where thou strawedst not:

25 I was therefore afraid, and went, and hid thy talent in the earth: behold, thou hast thine own.

26 And his master answered, and said unto him, Thou evil servant, and slothful, thou knewest that I reap where I sowed not, and gather where I strawed not.

27 Thou oughtest therefore to have put my money to the [1]exchangers, and then at my coming should I have received mine own with vantage.

28 Take therefore the talent from him, and give it unto him which hath ten talents.

29 [c]For unto every man that hath, it shall be given, and he shall have abundance, and from him that hath not, even that he hath shall be taken away.

30 Cast therefore that unprofitable servant into utter [d]darkness: there shall be weeping and gnashing of teeth.

31 ¶ [1]And when the Son of man cometh in his glory and all the holy Angels with him, then shall he sit upon the throne of his glory,

32 And before him shall be gathered all nations, and he shall separate them one from another as a shepherd separateth the sheep from the goats.

Margin references:
[c] Matt. 13:12
Mark 4:25
Luke 8:18
Luke 19:26
[d] Matt. 8:12
Matt. 22:13
[e] Isa. 58:7
Ezek. 18:7
[f] Eccl. 7:35
[g] Ps. 6:8
Matt. 7:13
Luke 13:27
[b] Dan. 12:2
John 5:29

CHAPTER 26
[a] Mark 14:1
Luke 22:1

33 And he shall set the sheep on his right hand, and the goats on the left.

34 Then shall the king say to them on his right hand, Come ye [1]blessed of my father: take the inheritance of the kingdom prepared for you from the foundation of the world.

35 [e]For I was an hungered, and ye gave me meat: I thirsted, and ye gave me drink: I was a stranger, and ye took me in unto you.

36 I *was* naked, and ye clothed me: I was [f]sick, and ye visited me: I was in prison, and ye came unto me.

37 Then shall the righteous answer him, saying, Lord, when saw we thee an hungered, and fed thee? or athirst, and gave thee drink?

38 And when saw we thee a stranger, and took thee in unto us? or naked, and clothed thee?

39 Or when saw we thee sick, or in prison, and came unto thee?

40 And the king shall answer, and say unto them, Verily I say unto you, inasmuch as ye have done it unto one of the least of these my brethren, ye have done it to me.

41 Then shall he say to them on the left hand, [g]Depart from me ye cursed, into everlasting fire, which is prepared for the devil and his angels.

42 For I was an hungered, and ye gave me no meat: I thirsted, and ye gave me no drink:

43 I was a stranger, and ye took me not in unto you: I *was* naked, and ye clothed me not: sick, and in prison, and ye visited me not.

44 Then shall they also answer him, saying, Lord, when saw we thee an hungered, or athirst, or a stranger, or naked, or sick, or in prison, and did not minister unto thee?

45 Then shall he answer them, and say, Verily I say unto you, inasmuch as ye did it not to one of the least of these, ye did it not to me.

46 [b]And these shall go into everlasting pain, and the righteous into life eternal.

26

3 *The consultation of the Priests against Christ.* 6 *His feet are anointed.* 15 *Judas selleth him.* 26 *The institution of the supper,* 34 and 36 *Peter's denial: Christ is heavy.* 47 *He is betrayed with a kiss.* 57 *He is led to Caiaphas.* 64 *He confesseth himself to be Christ.* 67 *They spit at him.*

1 And [a,1]it came to pass, when Jesus had finished all these sayings, he said unto his disciples,

---

25:21 [1] Come, and receive the fruit of goodness, now the Lord's joy is doubled, John 15:11, that my joy may remain in you, and your joy be fulfilled.

25:27 [1] Table mates which have their shop bulks or tables set abroad, where they let out money to usury.

25:31 [1] A lively setting forth of the everlasting judgment which is to come.

25:34 [1] Blessed and happy, upon whom my Father hath most abundantly bestowed his benefits.

26:1 [1] Christ witnesseth by his voluntarily going to death, that he will make full satisfaction for the sin of Adam, by his obedience.

2 ¹Ye know that after two days is the Passover, and the Son of man shall be delivered to be crucified.

3 ᵇThen assembled together the chief Priests, and the Scribes, and the Elders of the people into the hall of the high Priest called Caiaphas:

4 And consulted together that they might take Jesus by subtilty, and kill him.

5 But they said, Not on the ¹feast *day*, lest any uproar be among the people.

6 ¶ ᶜ'¹And when Jesus was in Bethany, in the house of Simon the leper,

7 ¹There came unto him a woman, which had a ²box of very costly ointment, and poured it on his head, as he sat at the table.

8 And when his ¹disciples saw it, they had indignation, saying, What needed this ²waste?

9 For this ointment might have been sold for much, and been given to the poor.

10 ¹And Jesus knowing it, said unto them, Why trouble ye the woman? for she hath wrought a good work upon me.

11 ᵈ'¹For ye have the poor always with you, but me shall ye not have always.

12 For ¹in that she poured this ointment on my body, she did it to bury me.

13 Verily I say unto you, wheresoever this Gospel shall be preached throughout all the world, there shall also this that she hath done, be spoken of for a memorial of her.

14 ¶ ᵉThen one of the twelve, called Judas Iscariot, went unto the chief Priests,

Reference column:
ᵇ John 11:47
ᶜ Mark 14:3
  John 11:2
ᵈ Deut. 15:11
ᵉ Mark 14:10
ᶠ Mark 14:12
  Luke 22:7
ᵍ Luke 22:14
ʰ Mark 14:18
  John 13:21
ⁱ Ps. 41:9
ʲ 1 Cor. 11:24

15 And said, What will ye give me, and I will deliver him unto you, and they appointed unto him thirty *pieces* of silver.

16 And from that time, he sought opportunity to betray him.

17 ¶ ᶠ'¹Now ²on the first *day* of the feast of unleavened bread, the disciples came to Jesus, saying unto him, Where wilt thou that we prepare for thee to eat the Passover?

18 And he said, Go ye into the city to such a man, and say to him, The master saith, My time is at hand: I will keep the Passover at thine house with my disciples.

19 And the disciples did as Jesus had given them charge, and made ready the Passover.

20 ᵍSo when the even was come, he ¹sat down with the twelve.

21 And as they did eat, he said, ʰVerily, I say unto you, that one of you shall betray me.

22 And they were exceeding sorrowful, and began every one of them to say unto him, Is it I, Master?

23 And he answered and said, ⁱHe that ¹dippeth his hand with me in the dish, he shall betray me.

24 Surely the Son of man goeth his way, as it is written of him: but woe *be* to that man, by whom the Son of man is betrayed: it had been good for that man, if he had never been born.

25 Then Judas ¹which betrayed him, answered, and said, Is it I, master? He said unto him, Thou hast said it.

26 ¶ ʲ'¹And as they did eat, Jesus took the bread,

26:2 ¹ God himself and not men, appointed the time that Christ should be crucified in.

26:5 ¹ By the word Feast, is meant the whole feast of unleavened bread: the first and eighth day whereof were so holy, that they might do no manner of work therein, though the whole company of the Sanhedrin determined otherwise: And yet it came to pass through God's providence, that Christ suffered at that time, to the end that all the people of Israel might be witnesses of his everlasting sacrifice.

26:6 ¹ By this sudden work of a sinful woman, Christ giveth the guests to understand of his death and burial which was nigh: the favor whereof shall bring life to all sinners which flee unto him. But Judas taketh an occasion hereby to accomplish his wicked purpose and counsel.

26:7 ¹ For these things were done before Christ came to Jerusalem: and yet some think that the Evangelists recite two histories.

² These boxes were of alabaster, which in old time men made hollow to put in ointments: for some write, that alabaster keepeth ointment without corruption, Pliny, book 13, chapter 1.

26:8 ¹ This is a figure called Synecdoche: for it is said but of Judas that he was moved thereat, John 12:4.

² Unprofitable spending.

26:10 ¹ We ought not rashly to condemn that which is not orderly done.

26:11 ¹ Christ, who was once anointed in his own person, must always be anointed in the poor.

26:12 ¹ In that she poured this ointment upon my body, she did it to bury me.

26:17 ¹ Christ verily purposing to bring us into our country out of hand, and so to abrogate the figure of the Law, fulfilleth the Law, neglecting the contrary tradition and custom of the Jews, and there withall showeth that all things shall so come to pass by the ministry of men, that the secret counsel of God shall govern them.

² This was the fourteenth day of the first month: and the first day of unleavened bread should have been the fifteenth, but because this day's evening (which after the manner of the Romans was referred to the day before) did belong by the Jews' manner to the day following, therefore it is called the first day of unleavened bread.

26:20 ¹ Because the Law appointed them to be shod, and have their staffs in their hands, as though they were in haste, thereby it is to be gathered that they sat not down when they did eat the Passover, but stood, for otherwise when they went to meat, they put off their shoes: therefore he speaketh here in this place, not of the Passover, but of the Supper, which was celebrated after that the Passover was solemnly done.

26:23 ¹ That is to say, whom I vouchsafed to come to my table, alluding to the place, Ps. 41:9, which is not so to be understood, as though at the selfsame instant that the Lord spake these words, Judas had had his hand in the dish (for that had been an undoubted token) but it is meant of his tabling and eating with them.

26:25 ¹ Whose head was about nothing then but to betray him.

26:26 ¹ Christ minding forthwith to fulfill the promises of the old covenant, instituteth a new covenant with new figures.

and when he had [2]blessed, he brake it, and gave it to the disciples, and said, Take, eat: [3]this is my body.

27 Also he took the cup, and when he had given thanks, he gave it them, saying, Drink ye [1]all of it.

28 [1]For this is my blood of the [2]new Testament that is shed for many, for the remission of sins.

29 I say unto you that I will not drink henceforth of this fruit of the vine until that day, when I shall drink it new with you in my Father's kingdom.

30 And when they had sung [1]a Psalm, they went out into the mount of Olives.

31 ¶ [1,k]Then said Jesus unto them, All ye shall be offended by me this night: for it is written, I [l]will smite the shepherd, and the sheep of the flock shall be scattered.

32 But [m]after I am risen again, I will go before you into Galilee.

33 But Peter answered, and said unto him, Though that all men should be offended by thee, yet will I never be offended.

34 [n]Jesus said unto him, Verily I say unto thee, that this night, before the cock crow, thou shalt deny me thrice.

35 Peter said unto him, Though I should die with thee, I will in no case deny thee. Likewise also said all the disciples.

36 ¶ [o,1]Then went Jesus with them into a place which is called Gethsemane, and said unto his disciples, Sit ye here, while I go, and pray yonder.

37 And he took unto him Peter, and the two sons of Zebedee, and began to wax sorrowful, and [1]grievously troubled.

38 [1]Then said Jesus unto them, My soul is very

heavy, *even* unto the death: tarry ye here, and watch with me.

39 So he went a little further, and fell on his face, and prayed, saying, O my Father, if it be possible, [1]let this [2]cup pass from me: nevertheless, not as I will, but as thou wilt.

40 [1]After, he came unto the disciples, and found them asleep, and said to Peter, What? could ye not watch with me one hour?

41 Watch, and pray, that ye enter not into temptation: the spirit indeed is ready, but the flesh is weak.

42 Again he went away the second time, and prayed, saying, O my Father, if this cup cannot pass away from me, but that I must drink it, thy will be done.

43 And he came and found them asleep again, for their eyes were heavy.

44 So he left them, and went away again, and prayed the third time, saying the same words.

45 Then came he to his disciples, and said unto them, Sleep henceforth, and take your rest: behold, the hour is at hand, and the Son of man is given into the hands of sinners.

46 [1]Rise, let us go: behold, he is at hand that betrayeth me.

47 [p]And while he yet spake, lo, Judas one of the twelve came, and with him a great multitude with swords and staves, [1]from the high Priests and Elders of the people.

48 Now he that betrayed him, had given them a token, saying, Whomsoever I shall kiss, that is he, lay hold on him.

49 And forthwith he came to Jesus, and said, God save thee, Master, and kissed him.

Marginal refs: k Mark 14:27, John 16:32, John 18:8; l Zech. 13:7; m Mark 14:28, Mark 16:7; n John 13:38, Mark 14:30; o Luke 22:39; p Mark 14:43, Luke 22:47, John 18:3

[2] Mark saith, Had given thanks: and therefore blessing is not a consecrating, with a conjuring kind of murmuring and force of words: and yet the bread and the wine are changed, not in nature, but in quality, for they become undoubted tokens of the body and blood of Christ, not of their own nature or force of words, but by Christ his institution, which must be recited and laid forth, that faith may find what to lay hold on, both in the word and in the elements.

[3] This is a figurative speech, which is called Metonymy: that is to say, the putting of one name for another—so calling the bread his body, which is the sign and sacrament of his body: and yet notwithstanding, it is so a figurative and changed kind of speech, that the faithful do receive Christ indeed with all his gifts (though by a spiritual means) and become one with him.

26:27 [1] Therefore they which took away the cup from the people, did against Christ his institution.

26:28 [1] To wit, this cup or wine, is my blood Sacramentally, as Luke 22:20.

[2] Or covenant, that is to say, whereby the new league and covenant is made, for in making of leagues, they used pouring of wine, and shedding of blood.

26:30 [1] When they had made an end of their solemn singing, which some think was six Psalms, beginning at Ps. 112 to 117.

26:31 [1] Christ being more careful of his disciples, than of himself, forewarneth them of their flight, and putteth them in better comfort.

26:36 [1] Christ having regard to the weakness of his disciples, leaving all the rest in safety, taketh with him but three to be witnesses of his anguish, and goeth of purpose into the place appointed to betray him in.

26:37 [1] The word which he useth, signifieth great sorrow, and marvelous and deadly grief: which thing, as it betokeneth the truth of man's nature, which shunneth death as a thing that entered in against nature, so it showeth that though Christ were void of sin, yet he sustained this horrible punishment, because he felt the wrath of God kindled against us for sins, which he revenged and punished in his person.

26:38 [1] Christ a true man, going about to suffer the punishment which was due unto us, for forsaking of God is forsaken of his own: he hath a terrible conflict with the horror and fear of the curse of God: out of which he escaping as a conqueror, causeth us not to be afraid anymore of death.

26:39 [1] Let it pass me, and not touch me.

[2] That is, which is at hand, and is offered and prepared for me: a kind of speech which the Hebrews use, for the wrath of God, and the punishment he sendeth. See also Matt. 20:22.

26:40 [1] An example of the carelessness of man.

26:46 [1] Christ offereth himself willingly to be taken, that in so obeying willingly, he might make satisfaction for the willful fall of man.

26:47 [1] Sent from the high Priests.

50 ¹Then Jesus said unto him, ²Friend, wherefore art thou come? Then came they, and laid hands on Jesus, and took him.

51 And behold, one of them which were with Jesus, stretched out *his* hand, and drew his sword, and struck a servant of the high Priest, and smote off his ear.

52 ¹Then said Jesus unto him, Put up thy sword into his place: ᑫfor all that ²take the sword, shall perish with the sword.

53 ¹Either thinkest thou, that I cannot now pray to my Father, and he will give me more than twelve legions of Angels?

54 ¹How then should the ʳScriptures be fulfilled, *which say*, that it must be so?

55 The same hour said Jesus to the multitude, Ye be come out as *it were* against a thief, with swords and staves to take me: I sat daily teaching in the Temple among you, and ye took me not.

56 But all this was done, that the Scriptures of the Prophets might be fulfilled. ˢThen all the disciples forsook him, and fled.

57 ¶ ᵗ·¹And they took Jesus, and led him to ²Caiaphas the high Priest, where the Scribes and the Elders were assembled.

58 And Peter followed him afar off unto the high Priest's ¹hall, and went in and sat with the servants to see the end.

59 Now ᵘthe chief Priests and the Elders, and all the whole Council sought false witness against Jesus, to put him to death.

60 But they found none, and though many false witnesses came, yet found they none: but at the last came two false witnesses,

61 And said, This man said, ᵛI can destroy the Temple of God, and build it in three days.

62 Then the chief Priest arose, and said to him, Answerest thou nothing? ¹What is the matter that these men witness against thee?

63 But Jesus held his peace. Then the chief Priest answered, and said to him, I charge thee swear unto

Marginal references:
ᑫ Gen. 9:6
Rev. 13:10
ʳ Isa. 35:10
ˢ Matt. 26:31
ᵗ Mark 14:53
Luke 22:54
John 18:14
ᵘ Mark 14:55
ᵛ John 2:19
ʷ Matt. 16:27
Rom. 14:20
2 Thess. 4:14
ˣ Isa. 30:6
ʸ Mark 14:66
Luke 22:55
John 18:29

us by the living God, to tell us, If thou be that Christ the son of God, *or no*.

64 ʷJesus said to him, Thou hast said it: nevertheless I say unto you, ¹Hereafter shall ye see the Son of man, sitting ²at the right hand of the power *of God*, and come in the ³clouds of the heaven.

65 Then the high Priest ¹rent his clothes, saying, He hath blasphemed, what have we any more need of witnesses: behold, now ye have heard his blasphemy.

66 What think ye? They answered, and said, He is guilty of death.

67 ˣThen spat they in his face, and buffeted him, and others smote him with rods,

68 Saying, Prophesy to us, O Christ, Who is he that smote thee?

69 ¶ ʸ·¹Peter ²sat without in the hall, and a maid came to him, saying, Thou also wast with Jesus of Galilee:

70 But he denied before them all, saying, I wot not what thou sayest.

71 And when he went out into the porch, another *maid* saw him, and said unto them that were there, This man was also with Jesus of Nazareth.

72 And again he denied with an oath, saying, I know not the man.

73 So after a while, came unto him they that stood by, and said unto Peter, Surely thou art also one of them: for even thy speech bewrayeth thee.

74 Then began he to ¹curse *himself*, and to swear, saying, I know not the man. And immediately the cock crew.

75 Then Peter remembered the words of Jesus, which had said unto him, Before the cock crow thou shalt deny me thrice. So he went out, and wept bitterly.

27

2 He is delivered bound to Pilate.   5 Judas hangeth himself.   19 Pilate's wife.   20 Barabbas is asked.   24 Pilate washeth his hands.   29 Christ is crowned with thorns.   34 He is crucified.   40 Reviled.   50 He giveth up the Ghost.   57 He is buried.   62 The soldiers watch him.

26:50 ¹ Christ is taken that we might be delivered.

² Christ reprehendeth Judas tauntingly, and rebuketh him sharply, for he knew well enough for what cause he came.

26:52 ¹ Our vocation must be the rule of our zeal.

² They take the sword to whom the Lord hath not given it, that is to say, they which use the sword, and are not called to it.

26:53 ¹ Christ was taken, because he was willing to be taken.

26:54 ¹ By this questioning he answereth a sly objection, for they might have asked him why he did not in this his great extremity of danger, call to his Father for aid: but to this he answereth by a question.

26:57 ¹ Christ being innocent is condemned of the high Priest for that wickedness whereof we are guilty.

² From Annas to Caiaphas, before whom the multitude was assembled, John 18:13.

26:58 ¹ The word here used, signifieth properly an open large room before an house, as we see in Kings' palaces and noble men's houses: we call it a court, for it is open to the air, and by a figure Synecdoche

is taken for the house itself.

26:62 ¹ How cometh it to pass that these men witness against thee?

26:64 ¹ This word distinguisheth his first coming from the latter.

² Sitting with God in like and equal honor at the right hand of his power, that is, in greatest power: for the right hand signifieth among the Hebrews, that that is mighty and of great power.

³ Clouds of heaven, see also Matt. 24:30.

26:65 ¹ This was an usual matter among the Jews: for so were they bound to do, when they heard any Israelite to blaspheme God, and it was a tradition of their Talmud in the book of the Magistrates, in the title, of the four kinds of death.

26:69 ¹ Peter by the wonderful providence of God appointed to be a witness of all these things, is prepared to the example of singular constancy, by the experience of his own incredulity.

² That is, without the place where the Bishop sat, but not without the house, for afterward he went from thence into the porch.

26:74 ¹ He swore and cursed himself.

1 When the [a]morning was come, all the chief Priests, and the Elders of the people took counsel against Jesus, to put him to death.

2 And led him away bound, and delivered him unto Pontius Pilate the governor.

3 ¶ [1]Then when Judas which betrayed him, saw that he was condemned, he repented himself, and brought again the thirty *pieces* of silver to the chief Priests, and Elders,

4 Saying, I have sinned, betraying the innocent blood. But they said, What is that to us? see thou to it.

5 And when he had cast down the silver *pieces* in the Temple, he [1]departed, and went, [b]and hanged himself.

6 And the chief Priests took the silver *pieces*, and said, It is not lawful for us to put them into the [1]treasure, because it is the price [2]of blood.

7 And they took counsel, and bought with them a potter's field, for the burial of [1]strangers.

8 Wherefore that field is called, ᶜThe field of blood, until this day.

9 (Then was fulfilled that which was spoken by [1]Jeremiah the Prophet, saying, [d,2]And they took thirty silver *pieces*, the price of him that was valued, whom *they* of the children of Israel valued.

10 And they gave them for the potter's field, as the Lord appointed me.)

11 ¶ [e,1]And Jesus stood before the governor, and the governor asked him, saying, Art thou that King of the Jews? Jesus said unto him, Thou sayest it.

12 And when he was accused of the chief Priests, and Elders, he answered nothing.

13 Then said Pilate unto him, Hearest thou not how many things they lay against thee?

14 But he answered him not to one word, insomuch that the governor marveled greatly.

15 [1]Now at the feast the governor was wont to deliver unto the people a prisoner whom they would.

16 And they had then a notable prisoner called

CHAPTER 27
[a] Mark 15:1
Luke 22:66
John 18:28
[b] Acts 1:18
[c] Acts 1:19
[d] Zech. 11:12
[e] Mark 15:2
Luke 23:3
John 18:33
[f] Mark 15:11
Luke 23:18
John 18:40
Acts 3:14
[g] Mark 15:26
John 19:2

Barabbas.

17 When they were then gathered together, Pilate said unto them, Whether will ye that I let loose unto you Barabbas, or Jesus which is called Christ?

18 (For he knew well, that for envy they had delivered him.

19 Also when he was set down upon the judgment seat, his wife sent to him, saying, Have thou nothing to do with that just man: for I have suffered many things this day in a dream by reason of him.)

20 [f]But the chief Priests and the elders had persuaded the people that they should ask Barabbas, and should destroy Jesus.

21 Then the governor answered, and said unto them, Whether of the twain will ye that I let loose unto you? And they said, Barabbas.

22 Pilate said unto them, What shall I do then with Jesus, which is called Christ? They all said to him, Let him be crucified.

23 Then said the governor, But what evil hath he done? Then they cried the more, saying, Let him be crucified.

24 [1]When Pilate saw that he availed nothing, but that more tumult was made, he took water and [2]washed his hands before the multitude, saying, I am innocent of the [3]blood of this just man: look you to it.

25 Then answered all the people, and said, [1]His blood *be* on us, and on our children.

26 Thus let he Barabbas loose unto them, and scourged Jesus, and delivered him to be crucified.

27 ¶ [g]Then the soldiers of the governor took Jesus into the common hall, and gathered about him the whole band,

28 [1]And they stripped him, and [2]put about him a [3]scarlet robe,

29 And platted a crown of thorns, and put it upon his head, and a reed in his right hand, and bowed their knees before him, and mocked him, saying, God save thee, King of the Jews,

---

27:3 [1] An example of the horrible judgment of God, as well against them which sell Christ, as against them which buy Christ.

27:5 [1] Out of men's sights.

27:6 [1] The treasury of the Temple.
[2] Of life and death.

27:7 [1] Strangers and guests, whom the Jews could not abide to be joined unto, no not after they were dead.

27:9 [1] Seeing this prophecy is read in Zech. 11:12, it cannot be denied, but Jeremiah's name crept into the text, either through the Printer's fault, or some other's ignorance: it may be also that it came out of the margin, by reason of the abbreviation of the letters, the one being *iou*, and the other *zou*, which are not much unlike: but in the Syrian text the Prophet's name is not set down at all.
[2] The Evangelist doth not follow the Prophet's words, but his meaning, which he showeth to be fulfilled.

27:11 [1] Christ holdeth his peace when he is accused, that we may not be accused: acknowledging our guiltiness, and therewithall his own innocence.

27:15 [1] Christ is first quitted of the same Judge, before he be condemned, that we might see how the just died for the unjust.

27:24 [1] Christ being quit by the testimony of the Judge himself, is notwithstanding condemned by the same to quit us before God.
[2] It was a manner in old time, when any man was murdered, and in other slaughters, to wash their hands in water, to declare themselves guiltless.
[3] Of the murder; an Hebrew kind of speech.

27:25 [1] If there be any offence committed in slaying him, let us and our posterity smart for it.

27:28 [1] Christ suffereth that reproach which was due to our sins; notwithstanding in the meantime by the secret providence of God, he is entitled King by them which did him that reproach.
[2] They cast a cloak about him, and wrapped it about him, for it lacked sleeves.
[3] John and Mark make mention of a purple robe, which is also a very pleasant red. But these profane and malapert saucy soldiers clad Jesus in this array, to mock him withall, who was indeed a true King.

30 And spitted upon him, and took a reed, and smote him on the head.

31 Thus when they had mocked him, they took the robe from him, and put his own raiment on him, and let him away to crucify him.

32 [h]And as they came out, they found a man of Cyrene, named Simon: him they [1]compelled to bear his cross.

33 [i,1]And when they came unto the place called Golgotha (that is to say, the place of *dead men's* skulls)

34 [1]They gave him vinegar to drink, mingled with gall: and when he had tasted thereof, he would not drink.

35 ¶ [1]And when they had crucified him, they parted his garments, and did cast lots, that it might be fulfilled, which was spoken by the Prophet,[j]They divided my garments among them, and upon my vesture did cast lots.

36 And they sat and watched him there.

37 ¶ [1]They set up also over his head his cause written, THIS IS JESUS THE KING OF THE JEWS.

38 ¶ [1]And there were two thieves crucified with him, one on the right hand, and another on the left.

39 [1]And they that passed by, reviled him, wagging their heads,

40 And saying, [k]Thou that destroyest the Temple, and buildest it in three days, save thyself: if thou be the Son of God, come down from the cross.

41 Likewise also the high Priests mocking him, with the Scribes, and Elders, and Pharisees, said,

42 He saved others, *but* he cannot save himself: if he be the king of Israel, let him now come down from the cross, and we will believe in him.

43 [l]He trusted in God, let him deliver him now, if he will have him: for he said, I am the Son of God.

44 The self same thing also the [1]thieves which

were crucified with him, cast in his teeth.

45 [1]Now from the sixth hour was there darkness over all the land, unto the ninth hour.

46 And about the ninth hour Jesus cried with loud voice, saying, [m]Eli, Eli, lama sabachthani? that is, My God, my God, why hast thou [1]forsaken me?

47 And some of them that stood there, when they heard it, said, This man calleth [1]Elijah.

48 And straightway one of them ran, and took [n]a sponge and filled it with vinegar, and put it on a reed, and gave him to drink.

49 Others said, Let be: let us see if Elijah will come and save him.

50 [1]Then Jesus cried again with a loud voice, and yielded up the ghost.

51 [1]And behold, [o]the [2]veil of the Temple was rent in twain, from the top to the bottom, and the earth did quake, and the stones were cloven.

52 And the [1]graves did open themselves, and many bodies of the Saints, which slept, arose,

53 And came out of the graves after his resurrection, and went into the holy city, and appeared unto many.

54 When the Centurion, and they that were with him, watching Jesus, saw the earth quake, and the things that were done, they feared greatly, saying, Truly this was the Son of God.

55 ¶ And many women were there, beholding him afar off, which had followed Jesus from Galilee, ministering unto him.

56 Among whom was Mary Magdalene, and Mary the mother of James, and Joses, and the mother of Zebedee's sons.

57 ¶ [1,p]And when the even was come, there came a rich man of Arimathea, named Joseph, who had also himself been Jesus' disciple.

58 He went to Pilate, and asked the body of Jesus.

Marginal references:

[h] Mark 15:21 / Luke 23:26
[i] Mark 15:22 / John 19:17
[j] Ps. 22:18 / Mark 15:24
[k] John 2:19
[l] Ps. 22:8
[m] Ps. 22:1
[n] Ps. 69:21
[o] 2 Chron. 3:14
[p] Mark 15:42 / Luke 13:50 / John 19:38

27:32 [1] They compelled Simon to bear his burdensome cross, whereby it appeareth that Jesus was so sore handled before, that he fainted by the way, and was not able to bear his cross throughout: for John writeth that he did bear the cross, to wit, at the beginning.

27:33 [1] He is led out of the city, that we may be brought into the heavenly kingdom.

27:34 [1] Christ found no comfort anywhere, that in him we might be filled with all comfort.

27:35 [1] He is made a curse, that in him we may be blessed: he is spoiled of his garments, that we might be enriched by his nakedness.

27:37 [1] He is pronounced the true Messiah, even of them of whom he is rejected.

27:38 [1] Christ began then to judge the world, when after his judgment he hung betwixt two thieves.

27:39 [1] To make full satisfaction for us, Christ suffereth and overcometh, not only the torments of the body, but also the most horrible torments of the mind.

27:44 [1] This is spoken by the figure Synecdoche, for there was but one of them that did revile him.

27:45 [1] Heaven itself is darkened for very horror, and Jesus crieth out

from the depth of hell, and in the meanwhile he is mocked.

27:46 [1] To wit, in this misery: and this crying out is proper to his humanity, which notwithstanding was void of sin, but yet felt the wrath of God which is due to our sins.

27:47 [1] They allude to Elijah's name, not for want of understanding the tongue, but of a profane impudence and sauciness, and he repeated these words, to the end that this better harping upon the name might be understood.

27:50 [1] Christ after he had overcome other enemies, at length provoked and setteth upon death itself.

27:51 [1] Christ, when he is dead, showeth himself to be God almighty, even his enemies confessing the same.

[2] Which divided the holiest of all.

27:52 [1] That is to say, the stones clave asunder, and the graves did open themselves, to show by this token, that death was overcome: and the resurrection of the dead followed the resurrection of Christ, as appeareth by the next verse following.

27:57 [1] Christ is buried, not privately or by stealth, but by the governor's consent by a famous man, in a place not far distant, in a new sepulcher, so that it cannot be doubted of his death.

Then Pilate commanded the body to be delivered.

59 So Joseph took the body, and wrapped it in a clean linen cloth,

60 And put it in his new tomb, which he had hewn out in a rock, and rolled a great stone to the door of the sepulcher, and departed.

61 And there was Mary Magdalene, and the other Mary, sitting over against the sepulcher.

62 ¶ ¹Now the next day that followed the Preparation *of the Sabbath*, the high Priests and Pharisees assembled to Pilate,

63 And said, Sir, we remember that that deceiver said, while he was yet alive, Within three days I will rise.

64 Command therefore, that the sepulcher be made sure until the third day, lest his Disciples come by night, and steal him away, and say unto the people, He is risen from the dead: so shall the last error be worse than the first.

65 Then Pilate said unto them, Ye have a ¹watch: go, and make it sure, as ye know.

66 And they went, and made the sepulcher sure, with the watch, and sealed the stone.

28

1 The women go to the sepulcher. 2 The Angel. 9 The women see Christ. 18 He sendeth his Apostles to preach.

1 Now ᵃin ¹the ²end of the Sabbath, when the first *day* of the week ³began to dawn, Mary Magdalene, and the other Mary, came to see the sepulcher.

2 And behold, there was a great earthquake: for the Angel of the Lord descended from heaven, and came and rolled back the stone from the door, and sat upon it.

3 And his ¹countenance was like lightning, and his raiment white as snow.

4 And for fear of him, the keepers were astonied, and became as dead men.

5 But the Angel answered, and said to the women, Fear ¹ye not: for I know that ye seek Jesus which was crucified:

CHAPTER 28
ᵃ Mark 16:5
John 20:11
ᵇ Heb. 1:2
Matt. 11:27
John 17:2
ᶜ Mark 16:15
ᵈ John 14:16

6 He is not here, for he is risen, as he said: come, see the place where the Lord was laid,

7 And go quickly, and tell his disciples that he is risen from the dead: and behold, he goeth before you into Galilee: there ye shall see him: lo, I have told you.

8 So they departed quickly from the sepulcher, with fear and great joy, and did run to bring his disciples word.

9 ¹And as they went to tell his disciples, behold, Jesus also met them, saying, God save you. And they came, and took him by the feet, and worshipped him.

10 Then said Jesus unto them, Be not afraid. Go, *and* tell my brethren, that they go into Galilee, and there shall they see me.

11 ¶ ¹Now when they were gone, behold, some of the watch came into the city, and showed unto the high Priests all the things that were done.

12 And they gathered them together with the Elders, and took counsel, and gave large money unto the soldiers,

13 Saying, Say, His disciples came by night, and stole him away while we slept.

14 And if this matter ¹come before the governor to be heard, we will persuade him, and so use the matter that you shall not need to care,

15 So they took the money, and did as they were taught: and this saying is noised among the Jews unto this day.

16 ¶ ¹Then the eleven disciples went into Galilee, into a mountain, where Jesus had appointed them.

17 And when they saw him, they worshipped him: but some doubted.

18 And Jesus came, and spake unto them, saying, ᵇAll power is given unto me, in heaven, and in earth.

19 ᶜ¹Go therefore, and teach all nations, baptizing them ²in the Name of the Father, and the Son, and the holy Ghost,

20 Teaching them to observe all things, whatsoever I have commanded you: and lo, ᵈI am with you ¹alway, until the end of the world, Amen.

27:62 ¹ The keeping of the sepulcher is committed to Christ's own murderers, that there might be no doubt of his resurrection.

27:65 ¹ The soldiers of the garrison, which were appointed to keep the Temple.

28:1 ¹ Christ having put death to flight in the sepulcher, riseth by his own power, as straightway the Angel witnesseth.

² At the going out of the Sabbath, that is, about daybreak after the Roman's count, which reckon the natural day, from the sun rising to the next sun rising: and not as the Hebrews, which count from evening to evening.

³ When the morning after the first day after the Sabbath began to dawn: and that first day is the same, which we now call Sunday or the Lord's day.

28:3 ¹ The beams of his eyes, and by the figure Synecdoche, for the countenance.

28:5 ¹ The word (Ye) is spoken with force to confirm the women,

now that the soldiers were afraid.

28:9 ¹ Christ appeareth himself after his resurrection, and sending the women to his disciples, showeth that he hath not forgotten them.

28:11 ¹ The more the sun shineth, the more are the wicked blinded.

28:14 ¹ For it was to be feared, that it would be brought to the governor's ears.

28:16 ¹ Christ appeareth also to his Disciples, whom he maketh Apostles.

28:19 ¹ The sum of the Apostleship is, the publishing of the doctrine received of Christ throughout all the world, and the ministering of the Sacraments: the efficacy of which things hangeth not of the ministers, but of the Lord.

² Calling upon the name of the Father, the Son, and the holy Ghost.

28:20 ¹ Forever: and this place is meant of the manner of the presence of his spirit, by means whereof he maketh us partakers both of himself and of all his benefits, but is absent from us in body.

THE HOLY GOSPEL OF JESUS CHRIST,

ACCORDING TO

MARK

1

4 John baptizeth.   6 His apparel and meat.   9 Jesus is baptized.   12 He is tempted.   14 He preacheth the Gospel,   21 and   29 he teacheth in the Synagogues.   23 He healeth one that had a devil.   29 Peter's mother-in-law.   32 Many diseased persons.   40 The leper.

1 The beginning of the Gospel of Jesus Christ, the Son of God:

2 ¹As it is written in the ²Prophets, ᵃBehold, ³I send my messenger ⁴before thy face, which shall prepare thy way before thee.

3 ᵇThe voice of him that crieth in the wilderness, *is,* Prepare the way of the Lord: make his paths straight.

4 ᶜ¹John did baptize in the wilderness, and preach the ²baptism of amendment of life, for remission of sins.

5 And all the country of Judea, and they of Jerusalem went out unto him, and were all baptized of him in the river Jordan, confessing their sins.

6 ᵈNow John was clothed with camel's hair, and with a girdle of a skin about his loins: and he did eat ᵉlocusts and wild honey,

7 ᶠ¹And preached, saying, A stronger than I cometh after me, whose shoe's latchet I am not worthy to ²stoop down, and unloose.

8 Truth it is, I have ¹baptized you with water: but he will baptize you with the holy Ghost.

9 ¶ ᵍ¹And it came to pass in those days, that Jesus came from Nazareth, *a city* of Galilee, and was baptized of John in Jordan.

10 ¹And as soon as ²he was come out of the water, *John* saw the heavens cloven in twain, and the holy

CHAPTER 1
ᵃ Mal. 3:1
ᵇ Isa. 40:3
Luke 3:4
John 1:15
ᶜ Matt. 3:1
ᵈ Matt. 3:4
ᵉ Lev. 1:22
ᶠ Matt. 3:11
Luke 3:16
John 1:26
Acts 1:5
Acts 2:4
Acts 2:11
Acts 2:16
Acts 19:4
ᵍ Matt. 3:13
Luke 3:21
John 1:33
ʰ Matt. 4:1
Luke 4:1
Heb. 2:18
ⁱ Matt. 4:12
Luke 4:14
John 4:13
ʲ Matt. 4:18
Luke 5:2
ᵏ Matt. 4:13
Luke 4:32
ˡ Matt. 7:28
Luke 4:32

Ghost descending upon him like a dove.

11 Then there was a voice from heaven, *saying,* Thou art my beloved Son, in whom I am ¹well pleased.

12 ʰ¹And immediately the Spirit ²driveth him into the wilderness,

13 And he was there in the wilderness forty days, and was tempted of Satan: he was also with the wild beasts, and the Angels ministered unto him.

14 ¶ ⁱ¹Now after that John was committed *to prison,* Jesus came into Galilee, preaching the Gospel of the kingdom of God,

15 And saying, The time is fulfilled, and the kingdom of God is at hand: repent and believe the Gospel.

16 ¶ ʲ¹And as he walked by the sea of Galilee, he saw Simon and Andrew his brother, casting a net into the sea (for they were fishers.)

17 Then Jesus said unto them, Follow me, and I will make you to be fishers of men.

18 And straightway they forsook their nets, and followed him.

19 ¹And when he had gone a little further thence, he saw James *the son* of Zebedee, and John his brother, as they were in the ship, mending their nets.

20 And anon he called them: and they left their father Zebedee in the ship with his hired servants, and went their way after him.

21 ¶ So ᵏthey entered into ¹Capernaum: and straightway on the Sabbath day he entered into the Synagogue, and taught.

22 And they were astonied at his doctrine, ˡfor he taught them as one that had authority, and not as

---

1:2 ¹ John goeth before Christ, as it was forespoken by the Prophets.

² This is the figure Metonymy, whereby is meant the books of the Prophets, Malachi and Isaiah.

³ The Prophet useth the present tense, when he speaketh of a thing to come, being as a sure of it, as if he saw it.

⁴ A metaphor taken from the usage of kings, which used to have ushers go before them.

1:4 ¹ The sum of John's doctrine, or rather Christ's, is remission of sins and amendment of life.

² The Jews used many kinds of washings: but here is spoken of a peculiar kind of washing, which hath all the parts of true baptism, amendment of life, and forgiveness of sins.

1:7 ¹ John and all ministers cast their eyes upon Christ the Lord.

² The Evangelist his meaning was to express the condition of the basest servant.

1:8 ¹ He showeth that all the force of baptism proceedeth from Christ, who baptizeth within.

1:9 ¹ Christ doth consecrate our baptism in himself.

1:10 ¹ The vocation of Christ from heaven, as head of the Church.

² John that went down into the water with Christ.

1:11 ¹ See also Matt. 3:17.

1:12 ¹ Christ being tempted overcometh.

² Here is no violent and forcible driving out meant: but the divine power claddeth Christ (who had lived until this time as a private man) with a new person, and prepareth him to the combat that was at hand, and to his ministry.

1:14 ¹ After that John is taken, Christ showeth himself fully.

1:16 ¹ The calling of Simon and Andrew.

1:19 ¹ The calling of James and John.

1:21 ¹ From the city Nazareth.

the Scribes.

23 ¶ [1]And there was in their Synagogue a man [2]in whom was an unclean spirit, and he cried out,

24 Saying, Ah, what have we to do with thee, O [1]Jesus of Nazareth? Art thou come to destroy us? I know thee what thou art, *even* thou [2]holy one of God.

25 And Jesus rebuked him, saying, Hold thy peace, and come out of him.

26 And the unclean spirit [1]tare him, and cried with a loud voice, and came out of him.

27 And they were all amazed, so that they demanded [1]one of another, saying, What thing is this? what new doctrine is this? for he [2]commandeth even the foul spirits with authority, and they obey him.

28 And immediately his fame spread abroad throughout all the region [1]bordering on Galilee.

29 ¶ [m,1]And as soon as they were come out of the Synagogue, they entered into the house of Simon and Andrew, with James and John.

30 And Simon's wife's mother lay sick of a fever, and anon they told him of her.

31 And he came and took her by the hand, and lifted her up, and the fever forsook her by and by, and she ministered unto them.

32 And when even was come, at what time the Sun setteth, they brought to him all that were diseased, and them that were possessed with devils.

33 And the whole city was gathered together at the door.

34 And he healed many that were sick of divers diseases: and he cast out many devils, and [1]suffered not the devils to say that they knew him.

35 And in the morning very early before day, *Jesus* arose and went out into a solitary place, and there prayed.

36 And Simon, and they that were with him, followed carefully after him.

37 And when they had found him, they said unto him, All men seek for thee.

38 Then he said unto them, Let us go into the [1]next towns, that I may preach there also: for I came out

m Matt. 8:14
Luke 4:38

n Matt. 8:2
Luke 5:12

o Lev. 14:4

p Luke 5:15

CHAPTER 2

a Matt. 9:1
Luke 5:28

for that purpose.

39 And he preached in their Synagogues, throughout all Galilee, and cast the devils out.

40 ¶ [n,1]And there came a leper to him, beseeching him, and kneeled down unto him, and said to him, If thou wilt, thou canst make me clean.

41 And Jesus had compassion, and put forth his hand, and touched him, and said to him, I will: be thou clean.

42 And as soon as he had spoken, immediately the leprosy departed from him, and he was made clean.

43 And after he had given him a straight commandment, he sent him away forthwith,

44 [1]And said unto him, See thou say nothing to any man, but get thee hence, and show thyself to the [o,2]Priest, and offer for thy cleansing those things which Moses commanded, for a testimonial unto them.

45 But when he was departed, [p]he began to tell many things, and to publish the matter: so that Jesus could no more openly enter into the city, but was without in desert places: and they came to him from every quarter.

2

3 and 4 *One sick of the palsy, having his sins forgiven him, is healed.* 14 *Matthew is called.* 19 *Fastings and afflictions are foretold.* 23 *The Disciples pluck the ears of corn.* 26 *The showbread.*

1 After [a,1]a few days, he entered into Capernaum again, and it was noised that he was in the [2]house.

2 And anon many gathered together, insomuch, that the [1]places about the door could not receive any more: and he preached the word unto them.

3 And there came unto him, that brought one sick of the palsy, borne of four men.

4 And because they could not come near unto him for the multitude, they uncovered the roof of the house where he was: and when they had broken it open, they [1]let down the [2]bed, wherein the sick of the palsy lay.

5 Now when Jesus saw their faith, he said to the

1:23 [1] He preacheth that doctrine, by which alone Satan is driven out of the world, which also he confirmeth by a miracle.

[2] Word for word, a man in an unclean spirit, that is to say, possessed with an evil spirit.

1:24 [1] He was born in Bethlehem, but through the error of the people, he was called a Nazarene, because he was brought up in Nazareth.

[2] He alludeth to that name that was written in the golden plate which the high Priest wore, Exod. 28:36.

1:26 [1] See also Mark 9:20.

1:27 [1] As men amazed.

[2] By his own authority, or as a Lord.

1:28 [1] Not only into Galilee, but also into the countries bordering upon it.

1:29 [1] By healing of divers diseases, he showeth that he hath

brought true life into the world.

1:34 [1] For it belongeth not to the devils to preach the Gospel, Acts 16:18.

1:38 [1] Villages which were as cities.

1:40 [1] By healing the leprous, he showeth that he came for this cause, to wipe out the sins of the world with his touching.

1:44 [1] He witnesseth that he was not moved with ambition, but with the only desire of his Father's glory, and love toward poor sinners.

[2] All the posterity of Aaron might judge of a leper.

2:1 [1] Christ showeth by healing this man, which was sick of the palsy, that men recover in him through faith only, all their strength which they have lost.

[2] In the house where he used to remain, for he chose Capernaum to dwell in, and left Nazareth.

2:2 [1] Neither the house nor the entry was able to hold them.

sick of the palsy, Son, thy sins are forgiven thee.

6 And there were certain of the Scribes sitting there, and ¹reasoning in their hearts,

7 Why doth this man speak such blasphemies? ᵇwho can forgive sins, but God only?

8 And immediately, when Jesus perceived in his spirit, that thus they reasoned with themselves, he said unto them, Why reason ye these things in your hearts?

9 Whether is it easier to say to the sick of the palsy, Thy sins are forgiven thee? or to say, Arise, take up thy bed, and walk?

10 But that ye may know, that the Son of man hath authority in earth to forgive sins, he said unto the sick of the palsy,

11 I say unto thee, Arise, and take up thy bed, and get thee hence into thine own house.

12 And by and by he arose, and took up his bed, and went forth before them all, insomuch that they were all ¹amazed, and glorified God, saying, We never saw such a thing.

13 ¶¹Then he went forth again toward the sea, and all the people resorted unto him, and he taught them.

14 ᶜAnd as Jesus passed by, he saw ¹Levi *the son of* Alphaeus sit at the receipt of custom, and said unto him, Follow me. And he arose and followed him.

15 ¶ And it came to pass, as Jesus sat at table in his house, many Publicans and sinners sat at table also with Jesus, and his disciples: for there were many that followed him.

16 And when the Scribes and Pharisees saw him eat with the Publicans and sinners, they said unto his disciples, How is it, that he eateth and drinketh with Publicans and sinners?

17 Now when Jesus heard it, he said unto them, The whole have no need of the Physician, but the sick. ᵈI came not to call the righteous, but the sinners to repentance.

18 ᵉˑ¹And the disciples of John, and the Pharisees did fast, and came and said unto him, Why do the disciples of John, and of the Pharisees fast, and thy disciples fast not?

19 And Jesus said unto them, Can the children of the marriage chamber fast, while the bridegroom is with them? as long as they have the bridegroom with them, they cannot fast.

20 But the days will come, when the bridegroom shall be taken from them, and then shall they fast in those days.

21 Also no man soweth a piece of new cloth in an old garment: for else the new piece that filled it up, taketh away *somewhat* from the old, and the breach is worse.

22 Likewise, no man putteth new wine into old vessels: for else the new wine breaketh the vessels, and the wine runneth out, and the vessels are lost; but new wine must be put into new vessels.

23 ¶ ᶠˑ¹And it came to pass as he went through the corn on the ²Sabbath day, that his disciples, as they went on their way, began to pluck the ears of corn.

24 And the Pharisees said unto him, Behold, why do they on the Sabbath day, that which is not lawful?

25 And he said to them, Have ye never read what ᵍDavid did when he had need, and was an hungered, *both* he, and they that were with him?

26 How he went into the house of God, in the days of ¹Abiathar the high Priest, and did eat the Showbread, which were not lawful to eat, but for the ʰPriests, and gave also to them which were with him?

27 And he said unto them, The Sabbath was made for man, and not man for the Sabbath.

28 Wherefore the Son of man is Lord, even of the ¹Sabbath.

3 1 *The withered hand is healed.* 6 *The Pharisees consult with the Herodians.* 10 *Many are healed by touching Christ.* 11 *At his sight the devils fall down before him.* 14 *The twelve Apostles.* 24 *The kingdom divided against itself.* 29 *Blasphemy against the holy Ghost.* 33 *Christ's parents.*

1 And ᵃˑ¹he entered again into the Synagogue, and there was a man which had a ²withered hand.

2 And they watched him, whether he would heal

Cross references (center column):
ᵇ John 14:4 / Isa. 43:25
ᶜ Matt. 9:9 / Luke 5:27
ᵈ 1 Tim. 1:13
ᵉ Matt. 9:14 / Luke 5:33
ᶠ Matt. 12:1
ᵍ 1 Sam. 21:6
ʰ Exod. 29:53 / Lev. 3:31 / Lev. 24:9

CHAPTER 3
ᵃ Matt. 12:9 / Luke 6:6

2:4 ¹ They brake up the upper part of the house, which was plain, and let down the man that was sick of the palsy, into the lower part where Christ preached, for they could not otherwise come into his sight.
² The word signifieth the worst kind of bed, whereupon men used to lay down themselves at noontide, and such other times, to refresh themselves: we call it a couch.
2:6 ¹ In their minds disputing upon that matter, on both sides.
2:12 ¹ Word for word, past themselves, or out of their wits.
2:13 ¹ The Gospel offendeth the proud, and saveth the humble.
2:14 ¹ Matthew's other name.
2:18 ¹ The superstitious and hypocrites do rashly put the sum of godliness in things indifferent, and are here for three causes reprehended. First, for that not considering what every man's strength is able to bear, they rashly make all manner of laws concerning such things, without all discretion.
2:23 ¹ Secondarily, for that they make no difference between the laws which God made concerning the same things, and laws that are made of things which are utterly unlawful.
² Word for word, on the Sabbaths, that is, on the holy days.
2:26 ¹ In 1 Sam. 21:1 he is called Ahimelech and his son Abiathar, but by conference of other places, it is plain, that both of them had two names. See also 1 Chron. 24:6; 2 Sam. 8:17; 2 Sam. 15:29; 1 Kings 2:26; 2 Kings 25:18.
2:28 ¹ Hath the Sabbath day in his power, and may rule as him listeth.
3:1 ¹ Thirdly, for that they preferred the ceremonial Law (which was but an appendant to the moral Law) before the moral Law: whereas contrariwise, they should have learned out of this, the true use of the ceremonial Law.
² That is, unprofitable and dead.

him on the Sabbath day, that they might accuse him.

3　Then he said unto the man which had the withered hand, Arise: *stand forth* in the midst.

4　And he said to them, Is it lawful to do a good deed on the Sabbath day, or to do evil? to save the ¹life, or to kill? but they held their peace.

5　Then he looked round about on them ¹angrily, mourning also for the ²hardness of their hearts, and said to the man, Stretch forth thine hand. And he stretched it out: and his hand was restored, as whole as the other.

6　¶ ¹And the Pharisees departed, and straightway gathered a council with the ²Herodians against him, that they might destroy him.

7　But Jesus avoided with his disciples to the sea: and a great multitude followed him from Galilee, and from Judea,

8　And from Jerusalem, and from Idumea, and ¹beyond Jordan: and they that dwelled about Tyre and Sidon, when they had heard what great things he did, came unto him in great number.

9　And he commanded his disciples, that a little ship should ¹wait for him, because of the multitude, lest they should throng him.

10　For he had healed many, insomuch that they pressed upon him to touch him, as many as had ¹plagues.

11　And when the ¹unclean spirits saw him, they fell down before him, and cried, saying, Thou art the Son of God.

12　And he sharply rebuked them, to the end they should not utter him.

13　¶ ᵇThen he went up into a mountain, and called unto him whom he would, and they came unto him.

14　¹And he ²appointed twelve, that they should be with him, and that he might send them to preach.

15　And that they might have power to heal sicknesses, and to cast out devils:

16　And the first *was* Simon, and he named Simon, Peter,

ᵇ Mark 6:7
Matt. 10:1
Luke 9:1
ᶜ Matt. 9:34
Matt. 12:24
Luke 11:15
ᵈ Matt. 18:31
Luke 12:10
John 5:16
ᵉ Matt. 12:46
Luke 8:19

17　Then James *the son* of Zebedee, and John James' brother (and surnamed them Boanerges, which is, The sons of thunder.)

18　And Andrew, and Philip, and Bartholomew, and Matthew, and Thomas, and James *the son* of Alphaeus, and ¹Thaddaeus, and Simon the Canaanite,

19　And Judas Iscariot, who also betrayed him, and they came ¹home.

20　And the multitude assembled again, so that they could not so much as eat bread.

21　¹And when his ²kinsfolks heard of it, they went out to lay hold on him: for they said that he was beside himself.

22　¶ ᶜAnd the Scribes which came down from Jerusalem, said, He hath Beelzebub, and through the prince of the devils he casteth out devils.

23　But he called them unto him, and said unto them in parables, How can Satan drive out Satan?

24　For if a kingdom be divided against itself, that kingdom cannot stand.

25　Or if a house be divided against itself, that house cannot continue.

26　So if ¹Satan make insurrection against himself, and be divided, he cannot endure, but is at an end.

27　No man can enter into a strong man's house, and take away his goods, except he first bind that strong man, and then spoil his house.

28　¶ ᵈ˒¹Verily I say unto you, all sins shall be forgiven unto the children of men, and blasphemies, wherewith they blaspheme:

29　But he that blasphemeth against the holy Ghost, shall never have forgiveness, but is culpable of eternal damnation.

30　¹Because they said, He had an unclean spirit.

31　¶ ᵉThen came his ¹brethren and mother and stood without, and sent unto him, and called him.

32　And the people sat about him, and they said unto him, Behold, thy mother, and thy brethren seek for thee without.

33　But he answered them, saying, Who is my

3:4 ¹ A figurative speech, by the figure Synecdoche. For this kind of saying, To save the life, is as much, as to save the man.

3:5 ¹ Men, when they have wrong done unto them, are angry, but not without vice, but Christ is angry without vice, neither is he sorry so much for the injury that is done to his own person, as for their wickedness: and therefore he had pity upon them, and for that cause is he said to have mourned.

² As though their heart had been so closed up, and grown together, that wholesome doctrine could prevail no more with them.

3:6 ¹ The more the truth is kept under, the more it cometh out.

² See also Matt. 22:16.

3:8 ¹ Which Josephus calleth stony or rocky.

3:9 ¹ Should always be ready for him.

3:10 ¹ Diseases wherewith God scourgeth men as it were with whips.

3:11 ¹ In them whom they had entered into: or by the figure called Metonymy, for them which were vexed with unclean spirits.

3:14 ¹ The twelve Apostles are set apart to be trained up to the

office of the Apostleship.

² Chose and appointed out twelve to be familiar and conversant with him.

3:18 ¹ Whom Luke also calleth Judas: and for difference's sake, the other Judas is called Iscariot.

3:19 ¹ The disciples whom Christ had taken to be of his train and to live with him, come home to his house, to be with him always after.

3:21 ¹ None are worse enemies of the Gospel, than they that least ought.

² Word for word, they that were of him, that is, his kinfolks: for they that were mad, were brought to their kinsmen.

3:26 ¹ Satan's imps or . . . .

3:28 ¹ They only are without hope of salvation, which do maliciously oppugn Christ, whom they know.

3:30 ¹ These are the words of the Evangelist.

3:31 ¹ Under this name Brother, the Hebrews understand all that are of the same stock and kindred.

mother and my brethren?

34 [1]And he looked round about on them, which sat in compass about him, and said, Behold my mother and my brethren.

35 For whosoever doeth the will of God, he is my brother, my sister, and my mother.

4

4 *The parable of the sower.* 14 *And the meaning thereof.* 18 *Thorns.* 21 *The candle.* 26 *Of him that sowed, and then slept.* 31 *The grain of mustard seed.* 38 *Christ sleepeth in the ship.*

1 And [a]he began again to teach by the [1]seaside, and there gathered unto him a great multitude, so that he entered into a ship, and sat [2]in the sea, and all the people was by the seaside on the land.

2 And he taught them many things in parables, and said unto them in his doctrine,

3 [1]Hearken: Behold, there went out a sower to sow.

4 And it came to pass as he sowed, that some fell by the wayside, and the fowls of the heaven came, and devoured it up.

5 And some fell on stony ground, where it had not much earth, and by and by sprang up, because it had not depth of earth.

6 But as soon as the Sun was up, it was burnt up, and because it had not root, it withered away.

7 And some fell among the thorns, and the thorns grew up, and choked it, so that it gave no fruit.

8 Some again fell in good ground, and did yield fruit that sprung up, and grew, and it brought forth, some thirtyfold, some sixtyfold, and some an hundredfold.

9 Then he said unto them, He that hath ears to hear, let him hear.

10 And when he was [1]alone, they that were [2]about him with the twelve, asked him of the parable.

11 And he said unto them, To you it is given to know the mystery of the kingdom of God: but unto them that are [1]without, all things be done in parables,

12 [b]That they seeing, may see, and not discern: and they hearing, may hear, and not understand, lest at any time they should turn, and their sins should be forgiven them.

[a] Matt. 13:1
Luke 8:4
[b] Isa. 6:9
Matt. 13:14
Luke 8:10
John 12:40
Acts 28:26
Rom. 11:8
[c] 1 Tim. 6:17
[d] Mark 5:15
Luke 8:16
Luke 11:33
[e] Matt. 10:26
Luke 8:17
Luke 12:2
[f] Matt. 7:2
Luke 6:38
[g] Matt. 13:12
Matt. 25:29
Luke 8:18
Luke 19:26

13 Again he said unto them, Perceive ye not this parable? how then should ye understand all *other* parables?

14 The sower soweth the word.

15 And these are they that *receive the seed* by the wayside, in whom the word is sown: but when they have heard it, Satan cometh immediately, and taketh away the word that was sown in their hearts.

16 And likewise they that receive the seed in stony ground, are they, which when they have heard the word, straightway receive it with gladness.

17 Yet have they no root in themselves, and endure but a time: *for* when trouble and persecution ariseth for the word, immediately they be offended.

18 Also they that receive the seed among the thorns, are such as hear the word:

19 But the cares [1]of this world, and the [c]deceitfulness of riches, and the lusts of other things enter in, and choke the word, and it is unfruitful.

20 But they that have received seed in good ground, are they that hear the word, and receive it, and bring forth fruit: one *corn* thirty, another sixty, and some an hundred.

21 ¶ [1]Also he said unto them, [d]Cometh the candle in, to be put under a bushel, or under the bed, and not to be put in a candlestick?

22 [e]For there is nothing hid, that shall not be opened, neither is there a secret, but that it shall come to light.

23 If any man have ears to hear, let him hear.

24 [1]And he said unto them, Take heed what ye hear. [f]With what measure you mete, it shall be measured unto you: and unto you that hear, shall more be given.

25 [g]For unto him that hath, shall it be given, and from him that hath not, shall be taken away even that he hath.

26 ¶ [1]Also he said, So is the kingdom of God, as if a man should cast seed in the ground.

27 And [1]should sleep, and rise up night and day, and the seed should spring and grow up, he [2]not knowing how.

28 For the earth bringeth forth fruit [1]of itself, first the

---

3:34 [1] The spiritual kindred is far otherwise to be accounted of, than the carnal or fleshly.

4:1 [1] Seaside of Tiberias.

[2] In a ship which was launched into the sea.

4:3 [1] The selfsame doctrine of the Gospel is sown everywhere, but it hath not like success indeed through the fault of man, but yet by the just judgment of God.

4:10 [1] Word for word, solitary.

[2] They that followed him at the heels.

4:11 [1] That is to say, to strangers, and such as are none of ours.

4:19 [1] Which pertain to this life.

4:21 [1] Although the light of the Gospel be rejected of the world, yet it ought to be lighted, if it were for no other cause than this, that the

wickedness of the world might be made manifest.

4:24 [1] The more liberally that we communicate such gifts as God hath given us with our brethren, the more bountiful will God be toward us.

4:26 [1] The Lord soweth and reapeth after a manner unknown to men.

4:27 [1] That is, when he hath done sowing, should pass the time both day and night, nothing doubting, but that the seed would spring which groweth both day and night.

[2] It is the part of the ministers, to labor the ground with all diligence, and commend the success to God: for that mighty working whereby the seed cometh to blade and ear, is secret and only known by the fruit.

4:28 [1] By a certain power which moveth itself.

blade, then the ears, after that full corn in the ears.

29 And as soon as the fruit showeth itself, anon he putteth in the sickle, because the harvest is come.

30 ¶ [b,1]He said moreover, Whereunto shall we liken the kingdom of God? or with what comparison shall we compare it?

31 *It is* like a grain of mustard seed, which when it is sown in the earth, is the least of all seeds that be in the earth:

32 But after that it is sown, it groweth up, and is greatest of all herbs, and beareth great branches, so that the fowls of the heaven may build under the shadow of it.

33 And [i]with many such parables he preached the word unto them, [1]as they were able to hear it.

34 And without parables spake he nothing unto them: but he [1]expounded all things to his disciples apart.

35 ¶ [j]Now the same day when even was come, he said unto them, Let us pass over unto the other side.

36 And they left the multitude, and took him as he was in the ship, and there was also with him other little ships.

37 [1]And there arose a great storm of wind, and the waves dashed into the ship, so that it was now full.

38 And he was in the stern asleep on a pillow: and they awoke him, and said to him, Master, carest thou not that we perish?

39 And he arose up, and rebuked the wind, and said unto the sea, Peace, and be still. So the wind ceased, and it was a great calm.

40 Then he said unto them, [1]Why are ye so fearful? how is it that ye have no faith?

41 And they feared exceedingly, and said one to another, Who is this, that both the wind and sea obey him?

5 2 *One possessed is healed.* 7 *The devil acknowledgeth Christ.* 9 *A Legion of devils.* 13 *entered into swine.* 22 *Jairus's daughter.* 25 *A woman is healed of a bloody issue.* 26 *Physicians.* 34 *Faith.* 39 *Sleep.*

1 And [a,1]they came over to the other side of the sea into the country of the [2]Gadarenes.

2 And when he was come out of the ship, there met him incontinently out of the graves, a man [1]which had an unclean spirit:

3 Who had his abiding among the graves, and no man could bind him, no not with chains:

4 Because that when he was often bound with fetters and chains, he plucked the chains asunder, and brake the fetters in pieces, neither could any man tame him.

5 And always both night and day he cried in the mountains, and in the graves, and struck himself with stones.

6 And when he saw Jesus afar off, he ran, and worshipped him,

7 And cried with a loud voice, and said, What have I to do with thee, Jesus the Son of the most High God? I [1]will that thou swear to me by God, that thou torment me not.

8 (For he said unto him, Come out of the man, thou unclean spirit.)

9 And he asked him, What is thy name? and he answered, saying, My name *is* Legion: for we are many.

10 And he [1]prayed him instantly, that he would not send them away out of the country.

11 Now there was there in the [1]mountains a great heard of swine, feeding.

12 And all the devils besought him, saying, Send us into the swine, that we may enter into them.

13 And incontinently Jesus gave them leave. Then the unclean spirits went out and entered into the swine, and the herd ran headlong from the high bank into the [1]sea, (and there were about two thousand swine) and they were choked up in the sea.

14 And the swineherds fled, and told it in the city, and in the country, and they came out to see what it was that was done.

15 And they came to Jesus, and saw him that had been possessed with the devil, and had the legion, sit both clothed, and in his right mind: and they were afraid.

16 And they that saw it, told them, what was done to him that was possessed with the devil, and concerning the swine.

17 Then they began to pray him, that he would depart from their coasts.

18 And when he was come into the ship, he that had been possessed with the devil, prayed him that he might be with him.

b Matt. 13:31 Luke 13:19
i Matt. 8 Matt. 13:34
j Matt. 8:23 Luke 8:22
CHAPTER 5
a Matt. 8:28 Luke 8:16

4:30 [1] God far otherwise than men use, beginneth with the least, and endeth with the greatest.

4:33 [1] According to the capacity of the hearers.

4:34 [1] Word for word, Loosed, as you would say, read them the hard riddles.

4:37 [1] They that sail with Christ, although he seems to sleep never so soundly when they are in danger, yet they are preserved of him in time convenient, being awakened.

4:40 [1] How cometh it to pass that you have no faith?

5:1 [1] Many have the virtue of Christ in admiration, and yet they will not redeem it with the loss of the least thing they have.

[2] See also Matt. 8:30.

5:2 [1] Word for word, in an unclean spirit: now they are said to be in the spirit, because the spirit holdeth them fast locked up, and as it were bound.

5:7 [1] That is, assure me by an oath, that thou wilt not vex me.

5:10 [1] That devil that played the messenger for his fellows.

5:11 [1] This whole country is for the greater part of it very hilly, for the mountains of Galeed run through it.

5:13 [1] Strabo in the sixteenth book saith that in Gadaris there is a standing pool of very naughty water, which if beasts taste of, they shed their hair, nails, or hooves and horns.

19 Howbeit, Jesus would not suffer him, but said unto him, Go thy way home to thy friends, and show them what great things the Lord hath done unto thee, and *how* he hath had compassion on thee.

20 So he departed, and began to publish in Decapolis, what great things Jesus had done unto him: and all men did marvel.

21 ¶ And when Jesus was come over again by ship unto the other side, a great multitude gathered together to him, and he was near unto the sea.

22 [b]And [1]behold, there came one of the rulers of the Synagogue, whose name was Jairus: and when he saw him, he fell down at his feet,

23 And besought him instantly, saying, My little daughter lieth at point of death: *I pray thee* that thou wouldest come and lay thine hands on her, that she may be healed, and live.

24 Then he went with him, and a great multitude followed him and thronged him.

25 ([1]And there was a certain woman, which was diseased with an issue of blood twelve years,

26 And had suffered many things of many physicians, and had spent all that she had, and it availed her nothing, but she became much worse.

27 When she had heard of Jesus, she came in the press behind, and touched his garment.

28 For she said, if I may but touch his clothes, I shall be whole.

29 And straightway the course of her blood was dried up, and she felt in her body, that she was healed of that plague.

30 And immediately when Jesus did know in himself the virtue that went out of him, he turned him round about in the press, and said, Who hath touched my clothes?

31 And his disciples said unto him, Thou seest the multitude throng thee, and sayest thou, Who did touch me?

32 And he looked round about, to see her that had done that.

33 And the woman feared and trembled: for she knew what was done in her, and she came and fell down before him, and told him the whole truth.

34 And he said to her, Daughter, thy faith hath made thee whole: go in peace, and be whole of thy plague.)

35 While he yet spake, there came from the *same* ruler of the Synagogue's house *certain* which said,

[b] Matt. 9:15
Luke 8:41

CHAPTER 6
[a] Matt. 13:54
Luke 4:16

Thy daughter is dead: why diseasest thou the master any further?

36 [1]As soon as Jesus heard that word spoken, he said unto the ruler of the Synagogue, Be not afraid: only believe.

37 And he suffered no man to follow him save Peter and James, and John the brother of James.

38 So he came unto the house of the ruler of the Synagogue, and saw the tumult, and them that wept and wailed greatly.

39 And he went in, and said unto them, Why make ye this trouble, and weep? the child is not dead, but sleepeth.

40 [1]And they laughed him to scorn: but he put them all out, and took the father, and the mother of the child, and them [2]that were with him, and entered in where the child lay,

41 And took the child by the hand, and said unto her, Talitha cumi, which is by interpretation, Maiden, I say unto thee, arise.

42 And straightway the maiden arose, and walked: for she was of the age of twelve years, and they were astonied out of measure.

43 And he charged them straitly that no man should know of it, and commanded to give her meat.

6

3 *Christ preaching in his country, his own condemn him.* 6 *The unbelief of the Nazarites.* 7 *The Apostles are sent.* 13 *They cast out devils: they anoint the sick with oil.* 14 *Herod's opinion of Christ.* 18 *The cause of John's imprisonment.* 22 *Dancing.* 27 *John beheaded,* 29 *buried.* 30 *The Apostles return from preaching.* 34 *Christ teacheth in the desert.* 37 *He feedeth the people with five loaves.* 48 *The Apostles are troubled on the sea.* 56 *The sick that touch Christ's garment, are healed.*

1 And [a,1]he departed thence, and came into his own country, and his disciples followed him.

2 And when the Sabbath was come, he began to teach in the Synagogue, and many that heard him, were astonied, and said, From whence hath this man these things? and what wisdom is this that is given unto him, that even such [1]great works are done by his hands?

3 Is not this that carpenter Mary's son, the brother of James and Joses, and of Judas and Simon? and are not his [1]sisters here with us? And they were

---

5:22 [1] The whole company assembled not disorderly, but in every Synagogue there were certain men which governed the people.

5:25 [1] Jesus being touched with true faith although it be but weak, doth heal us by his virtue.

5:36 [1] Fathers apprehend by faith the promises of life even for their children.

5:40 [1] Such as mock and scorn Christ, are unworthy to be witnesses of his goodness.

[2] The three disciples.

6:1 [1] The faithless world doth no whit at all diminish the virtue of Christ, but wittingly and willingly depriveth itself of the efficacy of it, being offered unto them.

6:2 [1] The word signifieth powers, or virtues, whereby are meant those wonderful works that Christ did, which showed and set forth the virtue and power of his Godhead to all the world, Matt. 7:22.

6:3 [1] After the manner of the Hebrews, who by brethren and sisters, understand all their kinfolks.

offended in him.

4 And Jesus said unto them, A [b]Prophet is not without [1]honor, but in his own country, and among his own kindred, and in his own house.

5 And he [1]could there do no great works, save that he laid his hands upon a few sick folk, and healed *them*.

6 And he marveled at their unbelief, [c]and went about by the towns on every side, teaching.

7 ¶ [d,1]And he called unto him the twelve, and began to send them forth two and two, and gave them power over unclean spirits,

8 [1]And commanded them that they should take nothing for *their* journey, save a staff only: neither scrip, neither bread, neither money in their girdles:

9 But that they should be shod with [e,1]sandals, and that they should not put on [2]two coats,

10 And he said unto them, Wheresoever ye shall enter into an house, [1]there abide till ye depart thence.

11 ¶ [f,1]And whosoever shall not receive you, nor hear you, when ye depart thence, [g]shake off the dust that is under your feet, for a witness unto them. Verily I say unto you, It shall be easier for Sodom, or Gomorrah at the day of Judgment, than for that city.

12 ¶ And they went out, and preached, that *men* should amend their lives.

13 And they cast out many devils: and they [h,1]anointed many that were sick, with oil, and healed *them*.

14 ¶ [i,1]Then King Herod heard *of him* (for his Name was made manifest) and said, John Baptist is risen again from the dead, and therefore great [2]works are wrought by him.

15 Others said, It is Elijah, and some said, It is a Prophet, or as one of [1]those Prophets.

16 [j]So when Herod heard it, he said, It is John whom [1]I beheaded: he is risen from the dead.

17 For Herod himself had sent forth, and had taken John, and bound him in prison for Herodias' sake, which was his brother Philip's wife, because he had married her.

18 For John said unto Herod, [k]It is not lawful for thee to have thy brother's wife.

19 Therefore Herodias [1]laid wait against him: and would have killed him, but she could not:

20 For Herod feared John, knowing that he *was* a just man, and an holy, and reverenced him, and when he heard him, he did many things, and heard him [1]gladly.

21 But the time being convenient, when Herod on his birthday made a banquet to his princes and captains, and chief estates of Galilee:

22 And the daughter [1]of the same Herodias came in, and danced, and pleased Herod, and them that sat at table together, the King said unto the maid, Ask of me what thou wilt, and I will give it thee.

23 And he swore unto her, Whatsoever thou shalt ask of me, I will give it thee, *even* unto the half of my kingdom.

24 [l]So [1]she went forth, and said to her mother, What shall I ask? And she said, John Baptist's head.

25 Then she came in straightway with haste unto the King, and asked, saying, I would that thou shouldest give me even now in a charger the head of John Baptist.

26 Then the King was very sorry: *yet* for his oath's sake, and for their sakes which sat at table with him, he would not refuse her.

27 And immediately the King sent the [1]hangman, and gave charge that his head should be brought in. So he went and beheaded him in the prison,

28 And brought his head in a charger, and gave it to the maid, and the maid gave it to her mother.

29 And when his disciples heard it, they came and took up his body, and put it in a tomb.

30 ¶ [m]And the Apostles gathered themselves together to Jesus, and told him all things, both what they had done, and what they had taught.

31 [1]And he said unto them, Come ye apart into the wilderness, and rest a while: for there were many comers and goers, that they had not leisure to eat.

Cross references (center column):

[b] Matt. 13:57 / Luke 4:24 / John 4:44
[c] Matt. 4:23 / Luke 13:22
[d] Mark 3:14 / Matt. 10:1 / Luke 9:1
[e] Acts 12:3
[f] Matt. 10:14 / Luke 9:5
[g] Acts 13:51 / Acts 18:6
[h] James 5:14
[i] Matt. 14:1 / Luke 9:7
[j] Luke 3:19
[k] Luke 18:16 / Luke 20:21
[l] Matt. 14:8
[m] Luke 9:10

6:4 [1] Not only that hath that honor which of right is due to him taken from him, but also evil spoken of and misreported.

6:5 [1] That is, he would not: for we must needs have faith, if we will receive the works of God.

6:7 [1] The disciples are prepared to that general Apostleship, by a peculiar sending forth.

6:8 [1] Faithful Pastors ought not to have their minds set, no not on things that are necessary for this life, if they may be an hindrance unto them, be it never so little.

6:9 [1] The word signifieth properly women's shoes.
  [2] That is, they should take no change of garments with them, that they might be lighter for this journey, and make more speed.

6:10 [1] That is, change not your inns in this short journey.

6:11 [1] The Lord is a most severe revenger of his servants.

6:13 [1] That oil was a token and a sign of this marvelous virtue: and seeing that the gift of healing is ceased a good while since, the ceremony which is yet retained of some is to no purpose.

6:14 [1] The Gospel confirmeth the godly, and vexeth the wicked.
  [2] This word signifieth Powers, whereby is meant the power of working miracles.

6:15 [1] Of the old Prophets.

6:16 [1] Commanded to be beheaded.

6:19 [1] Sought all means to do him hurt.

6:20 [1] The tyrant was very well content to hear sentence pronounced against him, but the seed fell upon stony places.

6:22 [1] Which the same Herodias had not by Herod Antipas, but by Philip, and Josephus calleth her Salome.

6:24 [1] For women used not to sit at table with men.

6:27 [1] The word signifieth one that beareth a dart, and the king's guard was so called, because they did bear darts.

6:31 [1] Such as follow Christ shall want nothing, no not in the wilderness, but shall have abundance. And how wicked a thing is it, not to look for this transitory life at his hands, who giveth everlasting life?

32 [n]So they went by ship out of the way into a desert place.

33 But the people saw them when they departed, and many knew him, and ran afoot thither out of all cities, and came thither before them, and assembled unto him.

34 [o]Then Jesus went out, and saw a great multitude, and had compassion on them, because they were like sheep which had no shepherd: [p]and he began to teach them many things.

35 [q]And when the day was now far spent, his disciples came unto him, saying, This is a desert place, and now the day is far passed.

36 Let them depart, that they may go into the country and towns about, and buy them bread: for they have nothing to eat.

37 But he answered, and said unto them, Give ye them to eat. And they said unto him, [1]Shall we go, and buy [2]two hundred pennies worth of bread, and give them to eat?

38 [r]Then he said unto them, How many loaves have ye? go and look. And when they knew it, they said, Five, and two fishes.

39 So he commanded them to make them all sit down by [1]companies upon the green grass.

40 Then they sat down by [1]rows, by hundreds, and by fifties.

41 And he took the five loaves, and the two fishes, and looked up to heaven, and gave thanks, and broke the loaves, and gave them to his disciples to set before them, and the two fishes he divided among them all.

42 So they did all eat, and were satisfied.

43 And they took up twelve baskets full of the fragments, and of the fishes.

44 And they that had eaten, were about five thousand men.

45 ¶ [1]And straightway he caused his disciples to go into the ship, and to go before unto the other side unto Bethsaida, while he sent away the people.

[n] Matt. 14:13 Luke 9:20
[o] Matt. 9:36 Matt. 14:14
[p] Luke 9:12
[q] Matt. 14:15
[r] Matt. 14:17 Luke 9:13 John 6:9
[s] Matt. 14:23 John 6:15
[t] Mark 14:34

CHAPTER 7
[a] Matt. 15:2

46 Then as soon as he had sent [1]them away, he departed into a mountain to pray.

47 [s]And when even was come, the ship was in the midst of the sea, and he alone on the land.

48 And he saw them troubled in rowing, (for the wind was contrary unto them) and about the fourth watch of the night, he came unto them, walking upon the sea, and would have passed by them.

49 And when they saw him walking upon the sea, they supposed it had been a spirit, and cried out.

50 For they all saw him, and were sore afraid: but anon he talked with them, and said unto them, Be ye of good comfort: it is I, be not afraid.

51 Then he went up unto them into the ship, and the wind ceased, and they were [1]much more amazed in themselves, and marveled.

52 For they had not [1]considered *the matter* of the loaves, because their hearts were hardened.

53 ¶ [t]And they came over, and went into the land of Gennesaret, and arrived.

54 [1]So when they were come out of the ship, straightway they knew him,

55 And ran about throughout all that region round about, *and* began to carry hither and thither in couches all that were sick, where they heard that he was.

56 And whithersoever he entered into towns, or cities, or villages, they laid their sick in the streets, and prayed him that they might touch at the least the edge of his garment. And as many as touched [1]him, were made whole.

7

2 The Apostles are found fault with, for eating with unwashed hands. 4 The Pharisees' traditions about washings, Hypocrites. 8 Men's traditions more set by than God's. 10 Parents must be honored. 15 The things that do indeed defile a man. 25 The woman of Canaan. 32 The deaf dumb man is healed.

1 Then [a,1]gathered unto him the Pharisees, and certain of the Scribes which came from Jerusalem.

6:37 [1] This declareth that there is an horrible disorder among the people, where the true preaching of God's word wanteth.

[2] Which is about five pounds sterling.

6:39 [1] Word for word, by banquets, after the manner of the Hebrews, who have no distributives, as Mark 6:7. Now he calleth the rows of the sitters, banquets.

6:40 [1] The word signifieth the beds in a garden, and it is word for word, by beds and beds, meaning thereby that they sat down in rows one by another, as beds in a garden.

6:45 [1] The faithful servants of God after their little labor, are subject to great tempest, which Christ doth so moderate being present in power, although absent in body, that he bringeth them to an happy haven, at such time and by such means, as they looked not for: A lively image of the Church tossed to and fro in this world.

6:46 [1] His disciples.

6:51 [1] They were so far from leaving to be amazed, when they knew that it was no spirit, that they were much more astonished than ever they were before, when they saw the wind and the seas obey his commandment.

6:52 [1] Either they perceived not, or had not well considered that miracle of the five loaves, insomuch that that virtue of Christ was no less strange to them, than if they had not been present at that miracle which was done but a little before.

6:54 [1] Christ being rejected in his own country, and arriving upon a sudden amongst them of whom he was not looked for, is received to their profit.

6:56 [1] Or, the hem of the garment.

7:1 [1] None do more resist the wisdom of God, than they that should be wisest, and that upon a zeal of their own traditions: for men do not please themselves more in anything than in superstition, that is to say, in a worship of God fondly devised of themselves.

2 And when they saw some of his disciples [1]eat meat with [2]common hands, (that is to say, unwashen) they complained.

3 (For the Pharisees, and all the Jews, except they wash their hands oft, eat not, [1]holding the traditions of the Elders.

4 And *when they come* from the [1]market, except they wash, they eat not: and many other things there be, which they have taken upon them to observe, *as* the washing of cups, and [2]pots, and of brazen vessels, and of beds.)

5 Then asked him the Pharisees and Scribes, Why [1]walk not thy disciples according to the tradition of the Elders, but eat meat with unwashen hands?

6 [1]Then he answered and said unto them, Surely [b]Isaiah hath prophesied well of you, hypocrites, as it is written, This people honoreth me with lips, but their heart is far away from me.

7 [1]But they worship me in vain, teaching *for* doctrines the commandments of men.

8 [1]For ye lay the Commandments of God apart, and observe the tradition of men, *as* the washing of pots and of cups, and many other such like things ye do.

9 [1]And he said unto them, Well ye reject the commandment of God, that ye may observe your own tradition.

10 For Moses said, [c]Honor thy father and thy mother: and [d]Whosoever shall speak evil of father or mother, let him [1]die the death.

11 But ye say, If a man say to father or mother, Corban, *that is,* By the gift that is *offered* by me, thou mayest have profit, *he shall be free.*

12 So ye suffer him no more to do anything for his father, or his mother.

13 Making the word of God of none authority, by your tradition which ye have ordained: and ye do many such like things.

14 [e]Then he calleth the whole multitude unto him,

and said unto them, Hearken you all unto me, and understand.

15 There is nothing without a man, that can defile him, when it entereth into him: but the things which proceed out of him, are they which defile the man.

16 If any have ears to hear, let him hear.

17 And when he came into an house, *away* from the people, his disciples asked him concerning the parable.

18 And he said unto them, What? are ye without understanding also? Do ye not know that whatsoever thing from without entereth into a man, cannot defile him,

19 Because it entered not into his heart, but into the belly, and goeth out into the draught which is the [1]purging of all meats?

20 Then he said, That which cometh out of man, that defileth man.

21 [f]For from within, *even* out of the heart of men, proceed evil thoughts, adulteries, fornications, murders,

22 Thefts, [1]covetousness, wickedness, deceit, uncleanness, a [2]wicked eye, backbiting, pride, foolishness.

23 All these evil things come from within, and defile a man.

24 ¶ [g,1]And from thence he rose, and went into the [2]borders of Tyre and Sidon, and entered into an house, and would that no man should have known: but he could not be hid.

25 For a certain woman, whose little daughter had an unclean spirit, heard of him, and came, and fell at his feet,

26 (And the woman was a [1]Greek, a [2]Syro-Phoenician by nation) and she besought him that he would cast out the devil out of her daughter.

27 But Jesus said unto her, Let the children first be fed: for it is not good to take the children's bread, and to cast it unto [1]whelps.

[b] Isa. 29:14
[c] Exod. 10:12
Deut. 5:26
Eph. 6:2
[d] Exod. 11:17
Lev. 20:9
Prov. 20:20
[e] Matt. 15:10
[f] Gen. 6:5
Gen. 8:21
[g] Matt. 15:21

7:2 [1] Word for word, eat bread: a kind of speech which the Hebrews use, taking bread for all kinds of food.

[2] For the Pharisees would not eat their meat with unwashed hands, because they thought that their hands were defiled with common handling of things, Matt. 15:11, 12.

7:3 [1] Observing diligently.

7:4 [1] That is to say, from civil affairs and worldly, they go not to meat, unless they wash themselves first.

[2] By these words are understood all kinds of vessels, which are appointed for our daily use.

7:5 [1] Why live they not? a kind of speech taken from the Hebrews: for amongst them, the way is taken for trade of life.

7:6 [1] Hypocrisy is always joined with superstition.

7:7 [1] The more earnest the superstitious are, the more they are mad, in promising themselves God's favor by their deserts.

7:8 [1] The devices of superstitious men do not only not fulfill the Law of God (as they blasphemously persuade themselves) but also do

utterly take it away.

7:9 [1] True Religion, which is clean contrary to superstition, consisteth in spiritual worship: and all enemies of true Religion, although they seem to have taken deep root, shall be plucked up.

7:10 [1] Without hope of pardon, he shall be put to death.

7:19 [1] For that that goeth into the draught, purgeth all meats.

7:22 [1] All kind of craftiness whereby men profit themselves by other men's losses.

[2] Cankered malice.

7:24 [1] That which the proud do reject when it is offered unto them, that same do the modest and humble sinners as it were violently wring out.

[2] Into the uttermost coasts of Palestine, which were next to Tyre and Sidon.

7:26 [1] By profession, profane.

[2] Neighbor or near to Damascus.

7:27 [1] He useth this word Whelps rather than the word Dogs, that he may seem to speak more contumaciously.

28 Then she answered, and said unto him, ¹Truth, Lord: yet indeed the whelps eat under the table of the children's crumbs.

29 Then he said unto her, For this saying go thy way: the devil is gone out of thy daughter.

30 And when she was come home to her house, she found the devil departed, and her daughter lying on the bed.

31 ¶ ¹And he departed again from the coasts of Tyre and Sidon, and came unto the sea of Galilee, through the midst of the coasts of ²Decapolis.

32 And they brought unto him one that was deaf and stammered in his speech, and prayed him to put his hand upon him.

33 Then he took him aside from the multitude, and put his fingers in his ears, and did spit, and touched his tongue.

34 And looking up to heaven, he sighed, and said unto him, Ephphatha, that is, Be opened.

35 And straightway his ears were opened, and the string of his tongue was loosed, and he spake plain.

36 And he commanded them that they should tell no man: but how much soever he forbade them, the more a great deal they published it,

37 And were beyond measure astonied, saying, He hath done all things well: ᵇHe maketh both the deaf to hear, and the dumb to speak.

8

1 The miracle of the seven loaves.   11 The Jews seek signs.   15 To beware of the leaven of the Pharisees.   22 A blind man healed.   27 The people's sundry opinions of Christ.   29 The Apostles acknowledge Christ.   31 He foretelleth his death.   33 Peter, Satan.   35 To save and lose the life.   38 To be ashamed of Christ.

1 In ᵃthose days, when there was a very great multitude, and had nothing to eat, Jesus called his disciples to him, and said unto them,

2 I have compassion on the multitude, because they have now continued with me three days, and have nothing to eat.

3 And if I send them away fasting to their own houses, they would ¹faint by the way: for some of

Marginal references:
ᵇ Gen. 1:31

CHAPTER 8
ᵃ Matt. 15:32
ᵇ Matt. 15:39
ᶜ Matt. 16:1
ᵈ Matt. 16:5
ᵉ John 6:11

them came from far.

4 Then his disciples answered him, Whence can a man satisfy these with bread here in the wilderness?

5 And he asked them, How many loaves have ye? And they said, Seven.

6 Then he commanded the multitude to sit down on the ground: and he took the seven loaves, and gave thanks, brake *them*, and gave to his disciples to set before *them*, and they did set *them* before the people.

7 They had also a few small fishes: and when he had given thanks, he commanded them also to be set before *them*,

8 So they did eat, and were sufficed, and they took up of the broken meat that was left, seven baskets full.

9 (And they that had eaten, were about four thousand) so he sent them away.

10 ¶ ᵇAnd anon he entered into a ship with his disciples, and came into the parts of Dalmanutha.

11 ᶜ¹And the Pharisees ²came forth, and began to dispute with him, seeking of him a sign from heaven, and tempting him.

12 Then he ¹sighed deeply in his spirit, and said, Why doth this generation seek a sign? Verily I say unto you, ²a sign shall not be given unto this generation.

13 ¶ So he left them, and went into the ship again, and departed to the other side.

14 ¶ ᵈAnd they had forgotten to take bread, neither had they in the ship with them, but one loaf.

15 ¹And he charged them, saying, Take heed, and beware of the leaven of the Pharisees, and of the leaven of Herod.

16 ¹And they reasoned among themselves, saying, *It is*, because we have no bread.

17 And when Jesus knew it, he said unto them, Why reason you *thus*, because ye have no bread? perceive ye not yet, neither understand? have ye your hearts yet hardened?

18 Have ye eyes, and see not? and have ye ears, and hear not? and do ye not remember?

19 ᵉWhen I brake the five loaves among five thousand, how many baskets full of broken meat took

---

7:28 ¹ As if she said, it is as thou sayest Lord, for it is enough for the whelps, if they can but gather up the crumbs that are under the table: therefore I crave the crumbs, and not the children's bread.

7:31 ¹ As the Father created us to this life in the beginning in his only Son, so doth he also in him alone renew us unto everlasting life.

    ² It was a little country, and so called of ten cities, which the four governments do run between and compass, Pliny, book 3, chap. 8.

8:3 ¹ Word for word, they will fall in sunder, or be dissolved, for when men fall in a swound, their sinews fall one from another.

8:11 ¹ The stubborn enemies of the doctrine of the Gospel, giving no credit to the miracles already done require new: but Christ being angry with them, doth utterly forsake them.

    ² A common kind of speech, which the Hebrews use, whereby is meant that the Pharisees went from their houses of purpose, to

encounter with him.

8:12 ¹ These sighs came even from the heart root, for the Lord was very much moved with these men's so great infidelity.

    ² Word for word, If a sign be given: It is a cut kind of speech very common among the Hebrews: wherein some such words as these must be understood. Let me be taken for a liar, or some such like. And when they speak out the whole, they say, The Lord do thus and thus by me.

8:15 ¹ We must especially take heed of them which corrupt the word of God, what degree soever they be of, either in the Church, or in civil policy.

8:16 ¹ They that have their minds fixed on earthly things, are utterly blind in heavenly things, although they be never so plainly set forth unto them.

ye up? They said unto him, Twelve.

20 And when I brake seven among four thousand, how many baskets full of the leavings of broken meat took ye up? And they said, Seven.

21 Then he said unto them, ¹How is it that ye understand not?

22 ¹And he came to Bethsaida, and they brought a blind man unto him, and desired him to touch him.

23 Then he took the blind by the hand, and led him out of the town, and spat in his eyes, and put his hands upon him, and asked him, if he saw ought.

24 And he looked up, and said, I ¹see men: for I see them walking like trees.

25 After that, he put his hands again upon his eyes, and made him ¹look again. And he was restored to his sight, and saw every man afar off clearly.

26 ¹And he sent him home to his house, saying, Neither go into the town, nor tell it to any in the town.

27 ¶ ᶠ,¹And Jesus went out, and his disciples into the towns of Caesarea Philippi. And by the way he asked his disciples, saying unto them, Whom do men say that I am?

28 And they answered, Some say, John Baptist: and some, Elijah: and some, one of the Prophets.

29 And he said unto them, But whom say ye that I am? Then Peter answered, and said unto him, Thou art that Christ.

30 ¹And he sharply charged them, that concerning him they should tell no man.

31 ¹Then he began to teach them that the son of man must suffer many things, and should be reproved of the Elders, and of the high Priests, and of the Scribes, and be slain, and within three days rise again.

32 ¹And he spake that thing boldly. Then Peter took him aside, and began to rebuke him.

33 Then he turned back and looked on his disciples, and rebuked Peter, saying, Get thee behind me, Satan: for thou ¹understandest not the things that are of God, but the things that are of men.

34 ¶ ¹And he called the people unto him with

f Matt. 16:13
Luke 9:18
g Matt. 10:38
Matt. 28:24
Luke 9:23
Luke 14:27
h Matt. 10:39
Matt. 16:25
Luke 9:24
Luke 17:33
i Matt. 10:33
Luke 8:26
Luke 12:9

CHAPTER 9
a Matt. 6:28
Luke 9:27
b Matt. 17:1
Luke 9:28

his disciples, and said unto them, ᵍWhosoever will follow me, let him forsake himself, and take up his cross, and follow me.

35 For whosoever will ʰsave his life, shall lose it: but whosoever shall lose his life for my sake and the Gospel's, he shall save it.

36 ¹For what shall it profit a man, though he should win the whole world, if he lose his soul?

37 Or what exchange shall a man give for his soul?

38 ⁱFor whosoever shall be ashamed of me, and of my words among this adulterous and sinful generation, of him shall the Son of man be ashamed also, when he cometh in the glory of his Father with the holy Angels.

9 2 Christ's transfiguration.   7 Christ must be heard.   11 Of Elias and John Baptist.   14 The possessed healed.   23 Faith can do all things.   31 Christ foretelleth his death.   33 Who is greatest among the Apostles.   36 Christ taketh a child in his arms.   42 To offend.   50 Salt. Peace.

1 And ᵃhe said unto them, Verily I say unto you, that there be some of them that stand here, which shall not taste of death till they have seen the ¹kingdom of God come with power.

2 ᵇ,¹And six days after, Jesus taketh unto him Peter, and James, and John, and carrieth them up into an high mountain out of the way alone, and his shape was changed before them.

3 And his raiment did ¹shine, and was very white as snow, so white as no fuller can make upon the earth.

4 And there appeared unto them Elijah with Moses, and they were talking with Jesus.

5 Then Peter answered, and said to Jesus, Master, it is good for us to be here: let us make also three tabernacles, one for thee, and one for Moses, and one for Elijah.

6 Yet he knew not what he said: for they were ¹afraid.

7 And there was a cloud that shadowed them,

8:21 ¹ How cometh it to pass, that you understand not these things which are so plain and evident?

8:22 ¹ A true image of our regeneration, which Christ separating us from the world, worketh and accomplisheth by little and little in us.

8:24 ¹ He perceived some moving of men, when he could not discern their bodies.

8:25 ¹ He commanded him again, to try indeed, whether he could see well or no.

8:26 ¹ Christ will not have his miracles to be separated from his doctrine.

8:27 ¹ Many praise Christ, which yet notwithstanding spoil him of his praise.

8:30 ¹ Christ hath appointed his times to the preaching of the Gospel: and therefore here defers it to a more commodious time, lest sudden haste should rather hinder than further the mystery of his coming.

8:31 ¹ Christ suffered all that he suffered for us, not unwillingly nei-

ther unawares, but foreknowing it, and willingly.

8:32 ¹ None are more mad than they that are wise beside the word of God.

8:33 ¹ This is not godly, but worldly wisdom.

8:34 ¹ The disciples of Christ must bear stoutly what burden soever the Lord layeth upon them, and subdue the affections of the flesh.

8:36 ¹ They are the most foolish of all men which purchase the enjoying of this life with the loss of everlasting bliss.

9:1 ¹ When he shall begin his kingdom through the preaching of the Gospel: that is to say, after the resurrection.

9:2 ¹ The heavenly glory of Christ, which should within a short space be abased upon the cross, is avouched by visible signs, by the presence and talk of Elijah and Moses, and by the voice of the Father himself, before three of his disciples, which are witnesses against whom lieth no exception.

9:3 ¹ Did sparkle as it were.

9:6 ¹ They were beside themselves for fear.

and a voice came out of the cloud, saying, 'This is my beloved Son: hear him.

8   And suddenly they looked round about, and saw no more any man save Jesus only with them.

9   *d,1*And as they came down from the mountain, he charged them, that they should tell no man what they had seen, save when the Son of man were risen from the dead again.

10   So they ¹kept that matter to themselves, and ²demanded one of another, what the rising from the dead again should mean.

11   ¹Also they asked him, saying, Why say the Scribes, that *e*Elijah must first come?

12   And he answered, and said unto them, Elijah verily shall first come, and restore all things: and *f*as it is written of the Son of man, he must suffer many things, and be set at nought.

13   But I say unto you, that Elijah is come, (and they have done unto him whatsoever they would) as it is written of him.

14   ¶ *g,1*And when he came to *his* disciples, he saw a great multitude about them, and the Scribes disputing with them.

15   And straightway all the people, when they beheld him, were amazed, and ran to him, and saluted him.

16   Then he asked the Scribes, What dispute you among yourselves?

17   And one of the company answered, and said, Master, I have brought my son unto thee, which hath a dumb spirit:

18   And wheresoever he taketh him, he ¹teareth him, and he foameth, and gnasheth his teeth, and pineth away: and I spake to thy disciples, that they should cast him out, and they could not.

19   Then he answered him, and said, O faithless generation, how long now shall I be with you! how long now shall I suffer you! Bring him unto me.

20   So they brought him unto him: and as soon as the spirit ¹saw him, he tare him, and he fell down on the ground wallowing and foaming.

21   Then he asked his father, How long time is it since he hath been thus? And he said, Of a child.

22   And oft times he casteth him into the fire, and

c Matt. 3:17
Matt. 27:5
Mark 1:11

d Matt. 17:9
e Mal. 4:5
f Isa. 13:4
g Matt. 17:14
Luke 9:38

h Matt. 17:21
Luke 9:22

i Matt. 18:1
Luke 9:46

into the water to destroy him: but if thou canst do anything, help us, and have compassion upon us.

23   And Jesus said unto him, If thou canst believe it, ¹all things are possible to him that believeth.

24   And straightway the father of the child crying with tears, said, Lord, I believe: help my unbelief.

25   When Jesus saw that the people came running together, he rebuked the unclean spirit, saying unto him, Thou dumb and deaf spirit, I charge thee come out of him, and enter no more into him.

26   ¹Then *the spirit* cried, and rent him sore, and came out, and he was as one dead, insomuch that many said, He is dead.

27   But Jesus took his hand, and lifted him up, and he arose.

28   ¹And when he was come into the house, his disciples asked him secretly, Why could not we cast him out?

29   And he said unto them, This kind can by no other means come forth, but by prayer and fasting.

30   ¶ *b*And they departed thence, and ¹went together through Galilee, and he would not that any should have known it.

31   ¹For he taught his disciples, and said unto them, The Son of man shall be delivered into the hands of men, and they shall kill him, but after that he is killed, he shall rise again the third day.

32   But they understood not that saying, and were afraid to ask him.

33   *i,1*After, he came to Capernaum: and when he was in the ²house, he asked them, What was it that ye disputed among you by the way?

34   And they held their peace: for by the way they reasoned among themselves, who *should be* the chiefest.

35   And he sat down and called the twelve, and said to them, If any man desire to be first, the same shall be last of all, and servant unto all.

36   And he took a little child, and set him in the midst of them, and took him in his arms, and said unto them,

37   Whosoever shall receive one of such little children in my Name, receiveth me: and whosoever receiveth

---

9:9 ¹ The Lord hath appointed his time for the publishing of the Gospel.
9:10 ¹ Even very hardly as it were.
  ² They questioned not together touching the general resurrection which shall be in the latter day, but they understood not what he meant by that which he spake of his own peculiar resurrection.
9:11 ¹ The foolish opinion of the Rabbis is here repelled touching Elijah's coming, which was that either Elijah should rise again from the dead, or that his soul should enter into some other body.
9:14 ¹ Christ showeth by a miracle even to the unworthy, that he is come to bridle the rage of Satan.
9:18 ¹ Vexed him inwardly, as the colic useth to do.
9:20 ¹ So soon as Jesus had looked upon the boy that was brought

unto him, the devil began to rage after his manner.
9:23 ¹ There is nothing but Christ can and will do it, for them that believe in him.
9:26 ¹ The nearer that the virtue of Christ is, the more outrageously doth Satan rage.
9:28 ¹ We have need of faith, and therefore of prayer and fasting, to cast Satan out of his old possession.
9:30 ¹ He and his disciples together.
9:31 ¹ Christ forewarneth us with great diligence, to the end we should not be oppressed with sudden calamities, but the slothfulness of man is wonderful.
9:33 ¹ Only humility doth exalt.
  ² Where he was wont to make his abode.

me, receiveth not [1]me, but him that sent me.

38 ¶ [j,1]Then John answered him, saying, Master, we saw one casting out devils by thy Name, which followeth not us, and we forbade him, because he followeth us not.

39 ¶ [k]But Jesus said, Forbid him not: for there is no man that can do a miracle by my Name, that can lightly speak evil of me.

40 For whosoever is not against us, is on our part.

41 [l]And whosoever shall give you a cup of water to drink for my Name's sake, because ye belong to Christ, verily I say unto you, he shall not lose his reward.

42 [m,1]And whosoever shall offend one of these little ones, that believe in me, it were better for him rather, that a millstone were hanged about his neck, and that he were cast into the sea.

43 [n]Wherefore if thine hand cause thee to offend, cut it off: it is better for thee to enter into life, maimed, than having two hands, to go into hell, into the fire that never shall be quenched,

44 [o]Where their [1]worm dieth not, and the fire never goeth out.

45 Likewise, if thy foot cause thee to offend, cut it off: it is better for thee to go halt into life, than having two feet, to be cast into hell, into the fire that never shall be quenched,

46 Where their worm dieth not, and the fire never goeth out.

47 And if thine eye cause thee to offend, pluck it out: it is better for thee to go into the kingdom of God with one eye, than having two eyes, to be cast into hell fire,

48 Where their worm dieth not, and the fire never goeth out.

49 [1]For every man shall be [2]salted with fire: and [p]every sacrifice shall be salted with salt.

50 [q]Salt is good: but if the salt be unsavory, wherewith shall it be seasoned? have salt in yourselves, and have peace one with another.

10

9 The wife, only for fornication, is to be put away. 13 Little children are brought to Christ. 17 A rich man asketh Jesus, how he may possess eternal life. 28 The

Marginal references
[j] Luke 9:49
[k] 1 Cor. 12:3
[l] Matt. 10:42
[m] Matt. 18:5
Luke 17:1
[n] Matt. 5:29
Matt. 18:8
[o] Isa. 66:24
[p] Lev. 2:13
[q] Matt. 5:13
Luke 14:34

CHAPTER 10
[a] Matt. 19:2
[b] Deut. 24:1
[c] Gen. 2:27
Matt. 9:4
[d] Gen. 2:24
1 Cor. 6:16
Eph. 5:3
[e] 1 Cor. 7:10
[f] Matt. 5:30
Matt. 19:9
Luke 16:18
[g] Matt. 19:13
Luke 13:15

Apostles forsook all things for Christ's sake. 33 Christ foreshoweth his death. 35 Zebedee's sons' request. 46 Blind Bartimaeus healed.

1 And [a]he [1]arose from thence, and went into the coasts of Judea by the far side of Jordan, and the people resorted unto him again, and as he was wont, he taught them again.

2 Then the Pharisees came and asked him, if it were lawful for a man to put away his wife, and tempted him.

3 And he answered, and said unto them, What did [b]Moses command you?

4 And they said, Moses suffered to write a bill of divorcement, and to put her away.

5 [1]Then Jesus answered, and said unto them, For the hardness of your heart he wrote this [2]precept unto you.

6 But at the beginning of the creation [c]God made them male and female:

7 [d]For this cause shall man leave his father and mother, and cleave unto his wife.

8 And they twain shall be one flesh: so that they are no more twain, but one flesh.

9 [e]Therefore, what God hath coupled together, let not man separate.

10 And in the house his disciples asked him again of that matter.

11 And he said unto them, [f]whosoever shall put away his wife and marry another, commiteth adultery [1]against her.

12 And if a woman put away her husband, and be married to another, she commiteth adultery.

13 ¶ [g,1]Then they brought little children to him, that he should touch them, and his disciples rebuked those that brought them.

14 But when Jesus saw it, he was displeased, and said to them, Suffer the little children to come unto me, and forbid them not: for of such is the kingdom of God.

15 Verily I say unto you, Whosoever shall not receive the kingdom of God [1]as a little child, he shall not enter therein.

16 And he took them up in his arms, and put his hands upon them, and blessed them.

9:37 [1] He doth not only receive me, but also him that sent me.

9:38 [1] God who is the author of an ordinary vocation, worketh also extraordinarily so oft as it pleaseth him. But an extraordinary vocation is tried by the doctrine and the effects.

9:42 [1] God is so severe a revenger of offenses, that it is better to suffer any loss, than to be an occasion of offense unto any.

9:44 [1] Their worm which shall be cast into that flame.

9:49 [1] We must be seasoned and powdered by God, both that we may be acceptable sacrifices unto him: and also that we being knit together, may season one another.

[2] That is, shall be consecrated to God, being seasoned with the incorruptible word.

10:1 [1] That is to say, departed and went from thence: for in the

Hebrew tongue, sitting and dwelling are all one, and so are rising and going forth.

10:5 [1] God did never allow those divorces, which the Law did tolerate.

[2] See also Matt. 19. For Moses gave them no commandment to put away their wives, but rather made a good provision for the wives against the stubborn hardness of their husbands.

10:11 [1] Whom he putteth away, for he is an adulterer by keeping company with another.

10:13 [1] God of his goodness comprehendeth in the covenant not only the fathers, but the children also: and therefore he blesseth them.

10:15 [1] We must in malice become children, if we will enter into the kingdom of heaven.

17 ¶ [1]And when he was gone out on the way, there came one [b]running, and kneeled to him, and asked him, Good Master, what shall I do, that I may possess eternal life?

18 Jesus said to him, Why callest thou me good? there is none good but one, even God.

19 Thou knowest the commandments, [i]Thou shalt not commit adultery. Thou shalt not kill. Thou shalt not steal. Thou shalt not bear false witness. Thou shalt [1]hurt no *man*. Honor thy father and mother.

20 Then he answered, and said to him, Master, all these things have I observed from my youth.

21 And Jesus looked upon him, and loved him, and said unto him, One thing is lacking unto thee. Go *and* sell all that thou hast, and give to the poor, and thou shalt have treasure in heaven, and come, follow me, and take up the cross.

22 But he was sad at that saying, and went away sorrowful: for he had great possessions.

23 And Jesus looked round about, and said unto his disciples, How hardly do they that have riches, enter into the kingdom of God!

24 And his disciples were afraid at his words. But Jesus answered again, and said unto them, Children, how hard is it for them that trust in riches, to enter into the kingdom of God!

25 It is easier for a camel to go through the eye of a needle, than for a rich man to enter into the kingdom of God.

26 And they were much more astonied, saying with themselves, Who then can be saved?

27 But Jesus looked upon them, and said, With men *it is* impossible, but not with God: for with God all things are possible.

28 ¶ [j,1]Then Peter began to say unto him, Lo, we have forsaken all, and have followed thee.

29 Jesus answered, and said, Verily I say unto you, there is no man that hath forsaken house, or brethren, or sisters, or father, or mother, or wife, or children, or lands for my sake and the Gospels,

30 But he shall receive an [1]hundredfold, now at this present, houses, and brethren, and sisters, and mothers, and children, and lands [2]with persecutions, and in the world to come, eternal life.

31 [k]But many *that are* first, shall be last, and the last, first.

32 ¶ [l,1]And they were in the way going up to Jerusalem, and Jesus went before them, and they were troubled, and as they followed, they were afraid, and Jesus took the twelve again, and began to tell them what things should come unto him,

33 *Saying,* Behold, we go up to Jerusalem, and the Son of man shall be delivered unto the high Priests, and to the Scribes, and they shall condemn him to death, and shall deliver him to the Gentiles.

34 And they shall mock him, and scourge him, and spit upon him, and kill him: but the third day he shall rise again.

35 ¶ [m,1]Then James and John the sons of Zebedee came unto him, saying, Master, [2]we would that thou shouldest do for us that we desire.

36 And he said unto them, What would ye I should do for you?

37 And they said to him, Grant unto us, that we may sit, one at thy right hand, and the other at thy left hand in thy glory.

38 But Jesus said unto them, Ye know not what ye ask. Can ye drink of the cup that I shall drink of, and be baptized with the baptism that I shall be baptized with?

39 And they said unto him, We can. But Jesus said unto them, Ye shall drink indeed of the cup that I shall drink of, and be baptized with the baptism wherewith I shall be baptized:

40 But to sit at my right hand and at my left, is not mine to give, but *it shall be given* to them for whom it is prepared.

41 And when the ten heard that, they began to disdain at James and John.

42 [1]But Jesus called them unto him, and said to them, [n]Ye know that [2]they which are princes among the Gentiles, have domination over them, and they that be great among them, exercise authority over them.

43 But it shall not be so among you: but whosoever will be great among you, shall be your servant.

44 And whosoever will be chief of you, shall be the servant of all.

45 For even the Son of man came not to be served, but to serve, and to give his life for the ransom of many.

Marginal references:

[b] Matt. 19:16
Luke 18:18
[i] Exod. 20:13
[j] Matt. 19:27
Luke 18:28
[k] Matt. 19:30
Luke 13:30
[l] Matt. 20:17
Luke 18:31
[m] Matt. 20:20
[n] Luke 22:25

10:17 [1] Two things are chiefly to be eschewed of them which earnestly seek eternal life: that is to say, an opinion of their merits or deservings, which is not only understood, but condemned by the due consideration of the Law: and the love of riches, which turneth aside many, from that race wherein they ran with a good courage.

10:19 [1] Neither by force nor deceit, nor any other means whatsoever.

10:28 [1] To neglect all things in comparison of Christ, is a sure way unto eternal life, so that we fall not away by the way.

10:30 [1] An hundredfold as much, if we look to the true use and commodities of this life, so that we measure them after the will of God, and not after the wealth itself, and our greedy desire.

[2] Even in the midst of persecutions.

10:32 [1] The disciples are again prepared to patience, not to be overcome by the foretelling unto them of his death, which was at hand, and therewithal of life which should most certainly follow.

10:35 [1] We must first strive, before we triumph.

[2] We pray thee.

10:42 [1] The Magistrates according to God's appointment, rule over their subjects: but the Pastors are not called to rule, but to serve, according to the example of the Son of God himself, who went before them, for so much as he also was a Minister of his Father's will.

[2] They to whom it is decreed and appointed.

46 ¶ ^{a,1}Then they came to Jericho: and as he went out of Jericho with his disciples, and a great multitude, Bartimaeus the son of Timaeus, a blind man, sat by the wayside, begging.

47 And when he heard that it was Jesus of Nazareth, he began to cry, and to say, Jesus the Son of David, have mercy on me.

48 And many rebuked him, because he should hold his peace: but he cried much more, O Son of David, have mercy on me.

49 Then Jesus stood still, and commanded him to be called: and they called the blind, saying unto him, Be of good comfort: arise, he calleth thee.

50 So he threw away his cloak, and rose, and came to Jesus.

51 And Jesus answered, and said unto him, What wilt thou that I do unto thee? And the blind said unto him, Lord, that I may receive sight.

52 Then Jesus said unto him, Go thy way: thy faith hath saved thee. And by and by he received *his* sight, and followed Jesus in the way.

11

1 Christ entereth into Jerusalem riding on an ass. 13 The fruitless fig tree is cursed. 15 Sellers and buyers are cast out of the Temple. 23 The force of faith. 24 Faith in prayer. 25 The brother's offenses must be pardoned. 27 The Priests ask by what authority he wrought those things that he did. 30 Whence John's baptism was.

1 And ^{a,1}when they came near to Jerusalem, to Bethphage and Bethany unto the mount of Olives, he sent forth two of his disciples,

2 And said unto them, Go your ways into that town that is over against you, and as soon as ye shall enter into it, ye shall find a colt tied, whereon never man sat: loose him, and bring him.

3 And if any man say unto you, Why do ye this? Say that the Lord hath need of him, and straightway he will send him hither.

4 And they went their way, and found a colt, tied by the door without, in a place where two ways met, and they loosed him.

5 Then certain of them, that stood there, said unto them, What do ye loosing the colt?

6 And they said unto them, as Jesus had commanded them: So they let them go.

7 ¶ ^bAnd they brought the colt to Jesus, and cast their garments on him, and he sat upon him.

Marginal references:
Matt. 20:29 / Luke 18:35
CHAPTER 11
a Matt. 21:1 / Luke 18:29
b John 12:24
c Matt. 21:10 / Luke 19:45
d Matt. 21:19
e Isa. 56:7
f Jer. 7:13
g Matt. 21:19

8 And many spread their garments in the way: others cut down branches off the trees, and strawed them in the way.

9 And they that went before, and they that followed, cried, saying, Hosanna; ¹blessed *be* he that cometh in the Name of the Lord.

10 ¹Blessed *be* the kingdom that cometh in the Name of the Lord of our father David: Hosanna, O thou *which art* in the highest *heavens*.

11 ^cSo Jesus entered into Jerusalem, and into the Temple: and when he had looked about on all things, and now it was evening, he went forth unto Bethany with the twelve.

12 ^dAnd on the morrow when they were come out from Bethany, he was hungry.

13 ¹And seeing a fig tree afar off, that had leaves, he went *to see* if he might find anything thereon: but when he came unto it, he found nothing but leaves: for the time of figs was not yet.

14 Then Jesus answered, and said to it, Never man eat fruit of thee hereafter while the world standeth: and his disciples heard it.

15 ¶ ¹And they came to Jerusalem, and Jesus went into the Temple, and began to cast out them that sold and bought in the Temple, and overthrew the tables of the moneychangers, and the seats of them that sold doves.

16 Neither would he suffer that any man should carry a ¹vessel through the Temple.

17 And he taught, saying unto them, Is it not written, ^eMine house shall be ¹called the house of prayer unto all nations? ^fbut you have made it a den of thieves.

18 And the Scribes and high Priests heard it, and sought how to destroy him: for they feared him, because the whole multitude was astonied at his doctrine.

19 But when even was come, *Jesus* went out of the city.

20 ^{g,1}And in the morning as they journeyed together, they saw the fig tree dried up from the roots.

21 Then Peter remembered, and said unto him, Master, behold, the fig tree which thou cursedst, is withered.

22 And Jesus answered, and said unto them, Have ¹the faith of God.

23 For verily I say unto you, that whosoever shall

10:46 ¹ Christ only, being called upon by faith, healeth our blindness.
11:1 ¹ A lively image of the spiritual kingdom of Christ on earth.
11:9 ¹ Well be it to him that cometh to us from God, or that is sent of God.
11:10 ¹ Happy and prosperous.
11:13 ¹ An example of that vengeance which hangeth over the heads of hypocrites.
11:15 ¹ Christ showeth indeed, that he is the true King and high Priest,

and therefore the revenger of the divine service of the Temple.
11:16 ¹ That is, any profane instrument, of which those fellows had a number, that made the court of the Temple a marketplace.
11:17 ¹ Shall openly be so accounted and taken.
11:20 ¹ The force of faith is exceeding great, and charity is ever joined with it.
11:22 ¹ The faith of God is that assured faith and trust which we have in him.

say unto this mountain, Be thou taken away, and cast into the sea, and shall not waver in his heart, but shall believe that those things which he saith, shall come to pass, whatsoever he saith, shall be *done* to him.

24 [b]Therefore I say unto you, Whatsoever ye desire when ye pray, believe that [1]ye shall have it, and it shall be *done* unto you.

25 [i]But when [1]ye shall stand, and pray, forgive, if ye have anything against any man, that your Father also which is in heaven, may forgive you your trespasses.

26 For if you will not forgive, your Father which is in heaven, will not pardon you your trespasses.

27 ¶ [j,1]Then they came again to Jerusalem: and as he walked in the Temple, there came to him the high Priests, and the Scribes, and the Elders,

28 And said unto him, By what authority doest thou these things? and who gave thee this authority, that thou shouldest do these things?

29 Then Jesus answered, and said unto them, I will also ask you a certain thing, and answer ye me, and I will tell you by what authority I do these things.

30 The baptism of John, was it from heaven, or of men? answer me.

31 And they thought with themselves, saying, If we shall say, From heaven, he will say, Why then did ye not believe him?

32 [1]But if we say, Of men, we fear the people: for all men counted John that he was a Prophet indeed.

33 Then they answered, and said unto Jesus, We cannot tell. And Jesus answered, and said unto them, Neither will I tell you by what authority I do these things.

12

Of the vineyard.   10 Christ the stone refused of the Jews.   12 Of tribute to be given to Caesar.   18 The Sadducees denying the resurrection.   28 The first commandment.   31 To love God and the neighbor is better than sacrifices.   36 Christ David's son.   38 To beware of the Scribes and Pharisees.   42 The poor widow.

1 And [1]he began to speak unto them in [2]parables, [a]A *certain* man planted a vineyard, and compassed it with an hedge, and dug a pit for the winepress, and built a tower in it, and let it out to husbandmen, and went into a strange country.

2 [1]And at the time, he sent to the husbandmen

Marginal references

[b] Matt. 7:7
Luke 11:9
[i] Matt. 6:14
[j] Matt. 21:23
Luke 20:1

CHAPTER 12
[a] Isa. 5:1
Jer. 2:2
Matt. 21:33
Luke 20:9
[b] Ps. 118:22
Isa. 28:16
Matt. 21:42
Acts 4:11
Rom. 9:33
1 Pet. 2:8
[c] Matt. 22:15
Luke 20:20
[d] Rom. 13:7

a servant, that he might receive of the husbandmen of the fruit of the vineyard.

3 But they took him, and beat him, and sent him away empty.

4 And again he sent unto them another servant, and at him they cast stones, and brake his head, and sent him away shamefully handled.

5 And again he sent another, and him they slew, and many others, beating some, and killing some.

6 Yet had he one son, his dear beloved: him also he sent the last unto them, saying, They will reverence my son.

7 But the husbandmen said among themselves, This is the heir: come, let us kill him, and the inheritance shall be ours.

8 So they took him, and killed him, and cast him out of the vineyard.

9 What shall then the Lord of the vineyard do? He will come and destroy these husbandmen, and give the vineyard to others.

10 Have ye not read so much as this Scripture, [b]The stone which the builders did refuse, is made the head of the corner.

11 This was done of the Lord, and it is marvelous in our eyes.

12 Then they [1]went about to take him, but they feared the people: for they perceived that he spake that parable against them: therefore they left him, and went their way.

13 ¶ [c,1]And they sent unto him certain of the Pharisees, and of the Herodians, that they might take him in *his* talk.

14 And when they came, they said unto him, Master, we know that thou art true, and carest for no man: for thou [1]considerest not the person of men, but teachest the [2]way of God truly, Is it lawful to give tribute to Caesar, or not?

15 Should we give it, or should we not give it? but he knew their hypocrisy, and said unto them, Why tempt ye me? Bring me a penny, that I may see it.

16 So they brought it, and he said unto them, Whose is this image and superscription? and they said unto him, Caesar's.

17 Then Jesus answered, and said unto them, [d]Give to Caesar the things that are Caesar's, and to God, those that are God's: and they marveled at him.

11:24 [1] Word for word, that you receive it speaking in the time that now is, to show the certainty of the thing and the performance indeed.

11:25 [1] When you shall appear before the altar.

11:27 [1] The Gospel hath been assaulted long time since, under the pretense of an ordinary successsion.

11:32 [1] A reward of an evil conscience to be afraid of those, of whom they should and might have been feared.

12:1 [1] The calling of God is not tied either to place, person, or time, without exception.

[2] This word Parable, which the Evangelists use, doth not only signify a comparing of things together, but also dark speeches and allegories.

12:2 [1] When the fruits of the ground used to be gathered.

12:12 [1] They were greedy and very desirous.

12:13 [1] The Gospel joineth the authority of the Magistrate with the service of God.

12:14 [1] Thou dost not so judge by outward appearance, that the truth is thereby darkened any whit at all.

[2] The way whereby we come to God.

18 ¶ *e,1*Then came the Sadducees unto him, (which say, there is no resurrection) and they asked him, saying,

19 Master, *f*Moses wrote unto us, If any man's brother die, and leave *his* wife, and leave no children, that his brother should take his wife, and raise up seed unto his brother.

20 There were seven brethren, and the first took a wife, and when he died, left no issue.

21 Then the second took her, and he died, neither did he yet leave issue, and the third likewise:

22 So these seven had her, and left no issue: last of all the wife died also.

23 In the resurrection then, when they shall rise again, whose wife shall she be of them? for seven had her to wife.

24 Then Jesus answered, and said unto them, Are ye not therefore deceived, because ye know not the Scriptures, neither the power of God?

25 For when they shall rise again from the dead, neither men marry, nor wives are married, but are as the Angels which are in heaven.

26 And as touching the dead, that they shall rise again, have ye not read in the book of Moses how in the bush God spake unto him, saying, I *g*am the God of Abraham, and the God of Isaac, and the God of Jacob?

27 God is not the God of the dead, but the God of the living. Ye are therefore greatly deceived.

28 ¶ *h,1*Then came one of the Scribes that had heard them disputing together, *and* perceiving that he had answered them well, he asked him, Which is the first commandment of all?

29 Jesus answered him, The first of all the commandments *is*, *i*Hear, Israel, The Lord our God is the only Lord.

30 Thou shalt therefore love the Lord thy God with all thine heart, and with all thy soul, and with all thy mind, and with all thy strength: this is the first commandment.

31 And the second *is* like, that is, *j*Thou shalt love thy neighbor as thyself. There is none other commandment greater than these.

32 Then that Scribe said unto him, Well, Master,

thou hast said the truth, that there is one God, and that there is none but he,

33 And to love him with all the heart, and with all the understanding, and with all the soul, and with all the strength, and to love *his* neighbor as himself, is more than all whole burnt offerings and sacrifices.

34 Then when Jesus saw that he answered discreetly, he said unto him, Thou art not far from the kingdom of God. And no man after that durst ask him any question.

35 ¶ *k,1*And Jesus answered and said teaching in the Temple, How say the Scribes that Christ is the son of David?

36 For David himself said by ¹the holy Ghost, *l*The Lord said to my Lord, Sit at my right hand, till I make thine enemies thy footstool.

37 Then David himself calleth him Lord: by what means is he then his son? and much people heard him gladly.

38 *m,1*Moreover he said unto them in ²his doctrine, Beware of the Scribes which love to go in ³long robes, and *love* salutations in the markets,

39 And the chief seats in the Synagogues, and the first rooms at feasts,

40 Which *n*devour widows' houses, even under a color of long prayers. These shall receive the greater damnation.

41 *o,1*And as Jesus sat over against the treasury, he beheld how the people ²cast money into the treasury, and many rich men cast in much.

42 And there came a certain poor widow, and she threw in two mites, which make a quadrin.

43 Then he called unto him his disciples, and said unto them, Verily I say unto you, that this poor widow hath cast more in, than all they which have cast into the treasury.

44 For they all did cast in of their superfluity: but she of her poverty did cast in all that she had, *even* all her living.

13 *Of the destruction of Jerusalem.　9 Persecutions for the Gospel.　10 The Gospel must be preached to all nations.　26 Of Christ's coming to judgment.　33 We must watch and pray.*

Cross references (center column):

e Matt. 22:23
Luke 20:27
f Deut. 25:5
Matt. 22:24
g Exod. 3:6
Matt. 22:32
h Matt. 22:35
i Deut. 6:4
j Lev. 19:18
Matt. 22:39
Rom. 13:9
Gal. 5:14
James 2:8
k Matt. 22:41
Luke 20:41
l Ps. 110:1
m Mark 23:6
Luke 11:43
Luke 20:43
n Matt. 23:14
Luke 20:47
o Luke 21:1

12:18 ¹ The resurrection of the body is avouched against the foolish ignorance and malice of the Sadducees.

12:28 ¹ Sacrifices and outward worship, never pleased God, unless such necessary duties as we owe to God and our neighbors went afore.

12:35 ¹ Christ proveth his Godhead even out of David himself, of whom he came according to the flesh.

12:36 ¹ Word for word, in the holy Ghost, and there is a great force in this kind of speech, whereby is meant that it was not so much David, as the holy Ghost that spake, who did in a manner possess David.

12:38 ¹ The manners of ministers are not rashly to be followed as

an example.

² While he taught them.

³ The word is a stole, which is a kind of woman's garment, long even down to the heels, and is taken generally, for any garment made for comeliness, but in this place it seemeth to signify that fringed garment mentioned in Deut. 22:11.

12:41 ¹ The doing of our duties, which God alloweth, is not esteemed according to the outward value, but to the inward affects of the heart.

² Money of any kind of metal, as the Romans used, who in the beginning did stamp or coin brass, and after used it for current money.

1 [a]And [1]as he went out of the Temple, one of his disciples said unto him, Master, see what manner stones, and what manner buildings *are here*.

2 [b]Then Jesus answered and said unto him, Seest thou these great buildings? there shall not be left one stone upon a stone, that shall not be thrown down.

3 And as he sat on the mount of Olives, over against the Temple, Peter, and James, and John, and Andrew asked him secretly,

4 Tell us, when shall these things be? and what *shall be* the sign when all these things shall be fulfilled?

5 And Jesus answered them, and began to say, [c]Take heed lest any man deceive you.

6 For many shall come in my Name, saying, I am Christ, and shall deceive many.

7 Furthermore when ye shall hear of wars, and rumors of wars, be ye not troubled, for *such things* must needs be: but the end *shall* not *be* yet.

8 For nation shall rise against nation, and kingdom against kingdom, and there shall be earthquakes in divers quarters, and there shall be famine and troubles: these *are* the beginnings of sorrows.

9 But take ye heed to yourselves: for they shall deliver you up to the Councils, and to the Synagogues: ye shall be beaten, and brought before rulers and kings for my sake, for a [1]testimonial unto them.

10 And the Gospel must first be published among all nations.

11 [d]But when they lead you, and deliver you up, [1]be not careful before hand, [2]neither study what ye shall say: but what is given you at the same time, that speak: for it is not you that speak, but the holy Ghost.

12 Yea, and the brother shall deliver the brother to death, and the father the son, and the children shall rise against their parents, and shall cause them to die.

13 And ye shall be hated of all men [1]for my Name's sake: but whosoever shall endure unto the end, he shall be saved.

14 [e]Moreover, when ye shall see the abomination of desolation (spoken of by [f]Daniel the Prophet) [1]set where it ought not, (let him that readeth, consider it) then let them *that be* in Judea, flee into the mountains.

15 And let him that is upon the house, not come

CHAPTER 13
[d] Matt. 24:1
Luke 21:5
[b] Luke 19:43
[c] Eph. 5:6
2 Thess. 2:3
[d] Matt. 10:19
Luke 12:11
Luke 21:14
[e] Matt. 24:15
Luke 21:20
[f] Dan. 9:27
[g] Matt. 24:23
Luke 17:23
Luke 21:8
[h] Isa. 13:10
Ezek. 52:7
Joel 2:10
Joel 3:15
[i] Matt. 24:31

down into the house, neither enter therein, to fetch anything out of his house.

16 And let him that is in the field, not turn back again to take his garment.

17 Then woe *shall be* to them that are with child, and to them that give suck in those days.

18 Pray therefore that your flight be not in the winter.

19 For [1]those days shall be such tribulation, as was not from the beginning of the creation which God created unto this time, neither shall be.

20 And except that the Lord had shortened those days, no flesh should be saved: but for the elect's sake, which he hath chosen, he hath shortened those days.

21 Then [g]if any man say to you, Lo, here is Christ, or lo, *he is* there, believe it not.

22 For false Christs shall rise, and false prophets, and shall show signs and wonders, to deceive if it were possible the very elect.

23 But take ye heed: behold, I have showed you all things before.

24 ¶ Moreover in those days, after that tribulation, [h]the sun shall wax dark, and the moon shall not give her light,

25 And the stars of heaven shall fall: and the powers which are in heaven, shall shake.

26 And then shall they see the Son of man, coming in the clouds, with great power and glory.

27 [i]And he shall then send his Angels, and shall gather together his elect from the four winds, and from the utmost part of the earth to the utmost part of heaven.

28 Now learn a parable of the fig tree. When her bough is yet tender, and it bringeth forth leaves, ye know that summer *is* near.

29 So in like manner, when ye see these things come to pass, know that *the kingdom of God* is near, *even* at the doors.

30 Verily I say unto you, that this generation shall not pass, till all these things be done.

31 Heaven and earth shall pass away, but my words shall not pass away.

32 [1]But of that day and hour knoweth no man, no, not the Angels which are in heaven, neither the Son himself, but the Father.

13:1 [1] The destruction of the Temple, city, and whole nation is aforetold, and the troubles of the Church, but yet there are annexed many comforts, and last of all, the end of the world is described.
13:9 [1] The hearing of you preaching shall be a most evident witness against them, so that they shall not be able to pretend ignorance.
13:11 [1] We are not forbidden to think beforehand, but pensive carefulness whereby men discourage themselves, which proceedeth from distrust, and want of confidence and sure hope of God's assistance: that carefulness we are willed to beware of, see also Matt. 6:27.
[2] By any kind of artificial and cunning kind of tale what to speak.
13:13 [1] For me.

13:14 [1] When the heathen and profane people shall not only enter into the Temple, and defile both it and the city, but also clean destroy it.
13:19 [1] This is a kind of speech which the Hebrews use, and it hath a great force in it, for it giveth us to understand that in all that time one misery shall so follow upon another, as if the time itself were very misery itself: So the Prophet Amos, 5:20 saith, that the day of the Lord shall be darkness.
13:32 [1] The latter day is not curiouly to be searched for which the Father alone knoweth: but let us rather take heed, that it come not upon us unaware.

33 *Take heed: watch, and pray: for ye know not when the time is.

34 *For the Son of man is* as a man going into a strange country, and leaveth his house, and giveth authority to his servants, and to every man his work, and commandeth the porter to watch.

35 Watch ye therefore, (for ye know not when the master of the house will come, at even, or at midnight, at the cock crowing, or in the dawning,)

36 Lest if he come suddenly, he should find you sleeping.

37 And those things that I say unto you, I say unto all men, Watch.

14

1 *The Priests' conspiracy against Christ.* 3 *The woman pouring oil on Christ's head.* 12 *The preparing of the Passover.* 22 *The institution of the Supper.* 41 *Christ delivered into the hands of men.* 43 *Judas betrayeth him with a kiss.* 53 *Christ is before Caiaphas.* 66 *Peter's denial.*

1 And *ᵃ,¹*two days after followed *the feast of* the Passover, and of unleavened bread: and the high Priests, and Scribes sought how they might take him by craft, and put him to death.

2 But they said, Not in the feast *day*, lest there be any tumult among the people.

3 *ᵇ*And when he was in Bethany in the house of Simon the leper, as he sat at table, there came a woman having a box of ointment of Spikenard, very costly, and she brake the box, and poured it on his head.

4 ¹Therefore some disdained among themselves, and said, To what end is this waste of ointment?

5 For it might have been sold for more than ¹three hundred pence, and been given unto the poor, and they murmured against her.

6 But Jesus said, Let her alone: Why trouble ye her? she hath wrought a good work on me.

7 ¹For ye have the poor with you always, and when ye will ye may do them good, but me ye shall not have always.

8 ¹She hath done that she could: she came aforehand to anoint my body to the burying.

9 Verily I say unto you, wheresoever this Gospel shall be preached throughout the whole world, this also that she hath done, shall be spoken of in remembrance of her.

10 ¶ ᶜ,¹Then Judas Iscariot, one of the twelve, went away unto the high Priests, to betray him unto them.

11 And when they heard it, they were glad, and promised that they would give him money: therefore he sought how he might conveniently betray him.

12 ¶ ᵈ,¹Now the first day of unleavened bread, ²when ³they sacrificed the ⁴Passover, his disciples said unto him, Where wilt thou that we go and prepare, that thou mayest eat the Passover?

13 Then he sent forth two of his disciples, and said unto them, Go ye into the city, and there shall a man meet you bearing a pitcher of water: follow him.

14 And whithersoever he goeth in, say ye to the good man of the house, The master saith, Where is the lodging where I shall eat the Passover with my disciples?

15 And he will show you an ¹upper chamber *which is* large, trimmed and prepared: there make it ready for us.

16 So his disciples went forth, and came to the city, and found as he had said unto them, and made ready the Passover.

17 ¶ And at even he came with the twelve.

18 ᵉ,¹And as they sat at table and did eat, Jesus said, Verily I say unto you, that one of you shall betray me, which eateth with me.

19 Then they began to be sorrowful and to say to him one by one, Is it I? And another, Is it I?

20 And he answered and said unto them, *It is* one of the twelve that ¹dippeth with me in the platter.

21 Truly the Son of man goeth his way, as it is written of him: *ᶠ*but woe *be* to that man, by whom the Son of man is betrayed: it had been good for that man, if he had never been born.

22 ᵍAnd as they did eat, Jesus took the bread, and when he had given thanks, he brake it and gave it to them, and said, Take, eat, this is my body.

23 Also he took the cup, and when he had given

ʲ Matt. 24:23

CHAPTER 14
ᵃ Matt. 26:2
Luke 22:1
ᵇ Matt. 26:6
John 12:2
ᶜ Matt. 26:14
Luke 22:4
ᵈ Matt. 26:17
Luke 2:28
ᵉ Ps. 41:20
Matt. 26:20-23
Luke 22:14
John 13:18-21
ᶠ Acts 1:16
ᵍ Matt. 26:26
1 Cor. 11:24

14:1 ¹ By the will of God, against the counsel of men, it came to pass that Christ should be put to death upon the solemn day of the Passover, that in all respects the truth might agree to the figure.

14:4 ¹ Rash judgments are frustrated before God.

14:5 ¹ Which is about six pounds English.

14:7 ¹ Christ suffered himself to be anointed once or twice for certain considerations: but his will is to be daily anointed in the poor.

14:8 ¹ This woman by the secret instinct of the Spirit, anointing Christ, setteth before men's eyes, his death and burial which were at hand.

14:10 ¹ Covetousness cloaked with a zeal of charity, is an occasion to betray and crucify Christ.

14:12 ¹ Christ being made subject to the Law for us, doth celebrate the Passover according to the Law: and therewithal by a miracle showeth that notwithstanding he in the flesh shall straightway suf-

fer, yet that he is God.

² That is, upon which day, and at the evening of the same day, which was the beginning of the fifteenth, see also Matt. 26:17.

³ They used to sacrifice.

⁴ This is spoken thus, by the figure Metonymy, which is usual in sacraments, and by the Passover is meant the Paschal lamb.

14:15 ¹ The Greek word signifieth that part of the house that is highest from the ground, to what use soever it be put, but because they used to sup in that part of the house, they called it a supping chamber.

14:18 ¹ The figure of the law, which is by and by to be fulfilled, is abrogated: and in place thereof are put figures of the new covenant answerable unto them, which shall continue to the world's end.

14:20 ¹ That useth to eat meat with me.

thanks, gave it to them: and they all drank of it.

24 And he said unto them, This is my blood of that new Testament which is shed for many.

25 Verily I say unto you, I will drink no more of the fruit of the vine until that day, that I drink it new in the kingdom of God.

26 And when they had sung a Psalm, they went out to the mount of Olives.

27 ¶ [h,1]Then Jesus said unto them, All ye shall be offended by me this night: for it is written, [i]I will smite the shepherd, and the sheep shall be scattered.

28 But after that I am risen, I will go into [j]Galilee before you.

29 [1]And Peter said unto him, Although all men should be offended at thee, yet would not I.

30 Then Jesus said unto him, Verily I say unto thee, this day, *even* in this night before the cock crow twice, thou shalt deny me thrice.

31 But he said [1]more earnestly, If I should die with thee, I will not deny thee: likewise also said they all.

32 ¶ [k,1]After, they came into a place named Gethsemane: then he said to his disciples, Sit ye here, till I have prayed.

33 And he took with him Peter, and James, and John, and he began to be troubled, and in great heaviness,

34 And said unto them, My soul is very heavy, *even* unto the death: tarry here, and watch.

35 So he went forward a little, and fell down on the ground, and prayed, that if it were possible, that hour might pass from him,

36 And he said, [1]Abba, Father, all things are possible unto thee: take away this cup from me: nevertheless not that I will, but that thou wilt, *be done.*

37 [1]Then he came, and found them sleeping, and said to Peter, Simon, sleepest thou? couldest not thou watch one hour?

38 ¶ Watch ye, and pray, that ye enter not into temptation: the spirit indeed is ready, but the flesh is weak.

39 And again he went away, and prayed, and spake

b John 16:32
i Zech. 13:7
j Mark 16:7
k Matt. 26:36
  Luke 22:39
l Matt. 26:47
  Luke 22:47
  John 18:3
m Matt. 26:57
  Luke 32:54
  John 18:24

the same words.

40 And he returned, and found them asleep again: for their eyes were heavy: neither knew they what they should answer him.

41 And he came the third time, and said unto them, Sleep henceforth, and take your rest: it is enough: the hour is come: behold, the Son of man is delivered into the hands of sinners.

42 Rise up: let us go: lo, he that betrayeth me, is at hand.

43 [l,1]And immediately while he yet spake, came Judas that was one of the twelve, and with him a great multitude with swords and staves from the high Priests, and Scribes, and Elders.

44 And he that betrayed him, had given them a token, saying, Whomsoever I shall kiss, he it is: take him and lead him away [1]safely.

45 And as soon as he was come, he went straightway to him, and said, Hail Master, and kissed him.

46 Then they laid their hands on him, and took him.

47 And [1]one of them that stood by, drew out a sword, and smote a servant of the high Priest, and cut off his ear.

48 And Jesus answered, and said to them, Ye be come out as against a thief, with swords and with staves, to take me.

49 I was daily with you, teaching in the Temple, and ye took me not: but *this is done* that the Scriptures should be fulfilled.

50 Then they [1]all forsook him, and fled.

51 [1]And there followed him a certain young man, clothed in [2]linen upon his bare *body*, and the young men caught him.

52 But he left his linen cloth, and fled from them naked.

53 [m]So they led Jesus away to the high Priest, and to him came [1]together all the high Priests, and the Elders, and the Scribes.

54 And Peter followed him afar off, even into the

14:27 [1] Christ foretelleth how he shall be forsaken of his, but yet that he will never forsake them.

14:29 [1] Here is set forth in an excellent person, a most sorrowful example of man's rashness and weakness.

14:31 [1] That doubling of words, setteth out more plainly Peter's vehement affirmation.

14:32 [1] Christ suffering for us in that flesh which he took upon him for our sakes, the most horrible terrors of the curse of God, receiveth the cup at his Father's hands, which he being just, doth straightway drink of for the unjust.

14:36 [1] This doubling of the word was used in those days, when their languages were so mixed together: for this word, Abba, is a Syrian word.

14:37 [1] An horrible example of the sluggishness of men, even in the disciples whom Christ had chosen.

14:43 [1] As men did willingly spoil God their Creator of his praise in forsaking and betraying him: so Christ willingly going about to make

satisfaction for this ruin, is forsaken for his own, and betrayed by one of his familiars as a thief, that the punishment might be agreeable to the sin, and we who are very traitors, forsakers, and sacrilegers might be delivered out of the devil's snare.

14:44 [1] So diligently, that he escape not out of your hands.

14:47 [1] That is, Peter.

14:50 [1] All his disciples.

14:51 [1] Under pretence of godliness, all things are lawful to such as do violence against Christ.

[2] Which he cast about him, when he hearing that stir in the night suddenly ran forth: whereby we may understand with how great licentiousness these villains violently set upon him.

14:53 [1] The highest council was assembled, because Christ was accused as a blasphemer and a false prophet: for as for the other crime of treason, it was forged against him by the Priests, to enforce Pilate by that means to condemn him.

hall of the high Priest, and sat with the servants, and warmed *himself* at the fire.

55 [1]And the *n*high Priests, and all the Council sought for witness against Jesus, to put him to death, but found none.

56 For many bare false witness against him, but their witness agreed not together.

57 Then there arose certain, and bare false witness against him, saying,

58 We heard him say, *o*I will destroy this Temple made with hands, and within three days I will build another, made without hands.

59 But their witness yet agreed not together.

60 Then the high Priest stood up amongst them, and asked Jesus, saying, Answerest thou nothing? what is the matter that these bear witness against thee?

61 But he held his peace, and answered nothing. Again the high Priest asked him, and said unto him, Art thou that Christ the son of the [1]Blessed?

62 And Jesus said, I am *he,* *p*and ye shall see the Son of man sit at the right hand of the power of God, and come in the clouds of heaven.

63 Then the high Priest rent his clothes, and said, What have we anymore need of witnesses?

64 Ye have heard the blasphemy: what think ye? And they all condemned him to be worthy of death.

65 [1]And some began to spit at him, and to cover his face, and to beat him with fists, and to say unto him, Prophesy. And the sergeants smote him with *their* rods.

66 *q.*[1]And as Peter was beneath in the hall, there came one of the maids of the high Priest.

67 And when she saw Peter warming *himself,* she looked on him, and said, Thou wast also with Jesus of Nazareth.

68 But he denied it, saying, I know him not, neither wot I what thou sayest. Then he went out into the porch, and the cock crew.

69 *r*Then [1]a maid saw him again, and began to say to them that stood by, This is *one* of them.

70 But he denied it again: and anon after, they that stood by, said again to Peter, Surely thou art *one* of them: for thou art of Galilee, and thy speech is like.

Marginal references

n Matt. 26:59
o John 9:19
p Matt. 24:39
q Matt. 26:69
Luke 22:55
John 18:25
r Matt. 26:71
Luke 22:58
s Matt. 26:75
John 13:38

CHAPTER 15
a Matt. 27:1
Luke 22:66
John 18:19
b Matt. 27:12
Luke 23:3
John 18:35

71 And he began to curse, and swear, *saying,* I know not this man of whom ye speak.

72 *s*Then the second time the cock crew, and Peter remembered the word that Jesus had said unto him, Before the cock crow twice, thou shalt deny me thrice, and weighing that with himself, he wept.

15

1 *Of the things Christ suffered under Pilate.* 11 *Barabbas is preferred before Christ.* 15 *Pilate delivereth Christ to be crucified.* 17 *He is crowned with thorns.* 19 *They spit on him, and mock him.* 21 *Simon of Cyrene carrieth Christ's cross.* 27 *Christ is crucified between two thieves.* 26 *He is railed at.* 37 *He giveth up the ghost.* 43 *Joseph burieth him.*

1 And *a.*[1]anon in the dawning, the high Priests held a Council with the Elders, and the Scribes, and the whole Council, and bound Jesus, and led him away, and [2]delivered him to Pilate.

2 Then Pilate asked him, Art thou the King of the Jews? And he answered, and said unto him, Thou sayest it.

3 And the high Priests accused him of many things.

4 *b*Wherefore Pilate asked him again, saying, Answered thou nothing? behold how many things they witness against thee.

5 But Jesus answered no more at all, so that Pilate marveled.

6 Now at the feast, Pilate [1]did deliver a prisoner unto them, whomsoever they would desire.

7 Then there was one named Barabbas, which was bound with his fellows, that had made insurrection, who in the insurrection had committed murder.

8 And the people cried aloud, and began to desire *that he would do* as he had ever done unto them.

9 Then Pilate answered them, and said, Will ye that I let loose unto you the King of the Jews?

10 For he knew that the high Priests had delivered him of envy.

11 But the high Priests had moved the people *to desire* that he would rather deliver Barabbas unto them.

12 And Pilate answered, and said again unto them, What will ye then that I do *with him,* whom ye call the King of the Jews?

14:55 [1] Christ, who was so innocent that he could not be oppressed, no not by false witnesses, is at the length, for confessing God to be his father, condemned of impiety before the high Priest: that we, who denied God and were indeed wicked, might be quit before God.

14:61 [1] Of God, who is most worthy of all praise?

14:65 [1] Christ suffering all kinds of reproach for our sakes, getteth everlasting glory to them that believe in him.

14:66 [1] An heavy example of the frailness of man, together with a most comfortable example of the mercy of God, who giveth the spirit of repentance and faith to his elect.

14:69 [1] If we compare the Evangelists diligently together, we shall perceive that Peter was known of many through the maiden's report:

yea, and in Luke, when the second denial is spoken of, there is a man-servant mentioned, and not a maid.

15:1 [1] Christ being bound before the judgment seat of an earthly judge, in open assembly is condemned as guilty unto the death of the cross, not for his own sins, (as appeareth by the judge's own words) but for all ours, that we most guilty creatures being delivered from the guiltiness of our sins, might be quitted before the judgment seat of God, even in the open assembly of the Angels.

[2] It was not lawful for them to put any man to death, for all causes of life and death were taken away from them, first by Herod the great, and afterward by the Romans, about forty years before the destruction of the Temple, and therefore they deliver Jesus to Pilate.

15:6 [1] Used Pilate to deliver.

13 And they cried again, Crucify him.

14 Then Pilate said unto them, But what evil hath he done? And they cried the more fervently, Crucify him.

15 So Pilate willing to content the people, loosed them Barabbas, and delivered Jesus, when he had scourged him, that he might be crucified.

16 Then the soldiers led him away into the hall, which is the common hall, and called together the whole band,

17 ¹And clad him with purple, and platted a crown of thorns, and put it about *his head*,

18 And began to salute him, *saying*, Hail, King of the Jews.

19 And they smote him on the head with a reed, and spat upon him, and bowed the knees, *and* did him reverence.

20 And when they had mocked him, they took the purple off him, and put his own clothes on him, and led him out to crucify him.

21 ᶜAnd they ¹compelled one that passed by, *called* Simon of Cyrene (which came out of the country, and was father of Alexander and Rufus) to bear his cross.

22 ᵈ,¹And they brought him to a place named Golgotha, which is by interpretation, the place of *dead mens' skulls*.

23 And they gave him to drink wine mingled with myrrh: but he received it not.

24 ᵉ,¹And when they had crucified him, they parted his garments, casting lots for them, what every man should have.

25 And it was the third hour when they crucified him.

26 And the title of his cause was written above, THAT KING OF THE JEWS.

27 They crucified also with him two thieves, the one on the right hand, and the other on his left.

28 Thus the Scripture was fulfilled, which saith,

*ᶜ Matt. 27:32
Luke 23:26*
*ᵈ Matt. 27:33
Luke 23:33
John 19:17*
ᵉ Luke 23:34
ᶠ Isa. 53:12
ᵍ John 2:19
*ʰ Ps. 22:1
Matt. 27:46*
ⁱ Ps. 69:22
ʲ Luke 8:2
ᵏ Matt. 27:57

ᶠAnd he was counted among the wicked.

29 And they that went by, railed on him, wagging their heads, and saying, ᵍHey, thou that destroyest the Temple, and buildest it in three days,

30 Save thyself, and come down from the cross.

31 Likewise also even the high Priests mocking, said among themselves with the Scribes, He saved other men, himself he cannot save.

32 Let Christ the king of Israel now come down from the cross, that we may see, and believe. They also that were crucified with him, reviled him.

33 ¶ Now when the sixth hour was come, ¹darkness arose over ²all the land until the ninth hour.

34 And at the ¹ninth hour Jesus cried with a loud voice, saying, ʰEloi, Eloi, lama-sabachthani? which is by interpretation, My God, my God, why hast thou forsaken me?

35 And some of them that stood by, when they heard it, said, Behold, he calleth Elijah.

36 And one ran, and filled a ⁱsponge full of vinegar, and put it on a reed, and gave him to drink, saying, Let him alone: let us see if Elijah will come, and take him down.

37 And Jesus cried with a loud voice, and gave up the ghost.

38 And the veil of the Temple was rent in twain, from the top to the bottom.

39 Now when the Centurion, which stood over against him, saw that he thus crying gave up the ghost, he said, Truly this man was the Son of God.

40 ¶ ¹There were also women which beheld afar off, among whom was Mary Magdalene, and Mary the mother of James the less, and of Joses, and Salome,

41 Which also when he was in Galilee, ʲfollowed him, and ministered unto him, and many other women which came up with him unto Jerusalem.

42 ᵏAnd now when the night was come (because it was the day of the preparation that is before the

---

15:17 ¹ Christ going about to take away the sins of men, who went about to usurp the throne of God himself, is condemned as one that hunted after the kingdom, and mocked with a false show of a kingdom, that we on the other side, who shall indeed be eternal kings, might receive the crown of glory at God's own hand.

15:21 ¹ The rage of the wicked hath no measure, but in the mean season, even the weakness of Christ, being in pain under the heavy burden of the cross, doth manifestly show that a lamb is led to be sacrificed.

15:22 ¹ Christ is led out of the walls of the earthly Jerusalem, into a foul place of dead men's carcasses, as a man most unclean, not touching himself, but touching our sins, which were laid upon him, to the end that we being made clean by his blood, might be brought into the heavenly Sanctuary.

15:24 ¹ Christ hangeth naked upon the cross, and as the most wickedest caitiff that ever was, most vilely reproved: that we being clothed with his righteousness, and blessed with his curses, and sanctified by his only oblation, may be taken up into heaven.

15:33 ¹ How angry God was against our sin, which he punished in

our surety, his son, it appeareth by this horrible darkness.

² By this word, land, he meaneth Palestine: so that the strangeness of the wonder, is so much the more set forth in that, that at the feast of the Passover, and in the full moon, when the Sun shined over all the rest of the world and at midday that corner of the world, wherein so wicked an act was committed, was overcovered with most gross darkness.

15:34 ¹ Christ striving mightily with Satan, with sin, and with death, all three armed with the horrible curse of God, grievously tormented in body hanging upon the cross, and in soul plunged in the depth of hell, yet he riddeth himself, crying with a mighty voice: and notwithstanding the wound which he received of death in that that he died, yet by smiting both things above and things beneath, by renting of the veil of the Temple, and by the testimony wrung out of them which murdered him, he showeth evidently unto the rest of his enemies which are as yet obstinate, and mock at him, that he shall be known out of hand to be conqueror and Lord of all.

15:40 ¹ Christ to the great shame of men which forsook the Lord, chose women for his witnesses, which beheld all this whole action.

Sabbath)

43 ¹Joseph of Arimathea, an ¹honorable counselor, which also looked for the kingdom of God, came, and went in ²boldly unto Pilate, and asked the body of Jesus.

44 And Pilate marveled, if he were already dead, and called unto him the Centurion, and asked of him whether he had been any while dead.

45 And when he knew *the truth* of the Centurion, he gave the body to Joseph:

46 Who bought a linen cloth, and took him down, and wrapped him in the linen cloth, and laid him in a tomb that was hewn out of a rock, and rolled a stone unto the door of the sepulcher:

47 And Mary Magdalene, and Mary Joses' *mother*, beheld where he should be laid.

16 1 Of Christ's resurrection. 9 He appeareth to
Mary Magdalene and others. 15 He sendeth his
Apostles to preach. 19 His ascension.

1 And ᵃwhen the Sabbath day was past, Mary Magdalene, and Mary the *mother* of James and Salome, bought sweet ointments, that they might come and anoint him.

2 Therefore early in the morning, the first day of the week, they came unto the sepulcher, when the Sun was now risen.

3 And they said one to another, Who shall roll us away the stone from the door of the sepulcher?

4 And when they ¹looked, they saw that the stone was rolled away (for it was a very great one)

5 ᵇSo they went into the ¹sepulcher, and saw a young man sitting at the right side, clothed in a long white robe: and they were sore troubled.

6 But he said unto them, Be not so troubled: ye seek Jesus of Nazareth, which hath been crucified: he is risen, he is not here: behold the place where they put him.

7 But go your way, and tell his disciples, and

Peter, that he will go before you into Galilee: there shall ye see him, ᶜas he said unto you.

8 And they went out quickly, and fled from the sepulcher: for they trembled, and were amazed: neither said they anything to any man: for they were afraid.

9 ¶ ¹And when Jesus was risen again, early the first day of the week, he appeared first to Mary Magdalene, ᵈout of whom he had cast seven devils:

10 And she went and told them that had been with him, which mourned and wept.

11 And when they heard that he was alive, and had appeared to her, they believed it not.

12 ¶ ᵉ,¹After that, he appeared unto two of them in another form, as they walked and went into the country.

13 And they went and told it to the remnant, neither believed they them.

14 ¶ ᶠ,¹Finally, he appeared unto the eleven as they sat together, and reproached them for their unbelief and hardness of heart, because they believed not them which had seen him, being risen up again.

15 ¹And he said unto them, ᵍGo ye into all the world, and preach the Gospel to ²every creature.

16 He that shall believe and be baptized, shall be saved: ʰbut he that will not believe, shall be damned.

17 And these tokens shall follow them that believe, ⁱIn my Name they shall cast out devils, and ʲshall speak with ¹new tongues,

18 ᵏAnd shall take away serpents, and if they shall drink any deadly thing, it shall not hurt them: ˡthey shall lay their hands on the sick, and they shall recover.

19 ᵐ,¹So after the Lord had spoken unto them, he was received into heaven, and sat at the right hand of God.

20 And they went forth, and preached everywhere. And the ⁿLord wrought with them, and confirmed ¹the word with signs that followed. Amen.

ᶦ Luke 23:50
John 19:38

CHAPTER 16
ᵃ Luke 24:1
John 20:1
ᵇ Matt. 18:1
John 20:12
ᶜ Mark 11:28
Matt. 16:32
ᵈ John 20:16
Luke 8:2
ᵉ Luke 24:13
ᶠ Luke 24:36
John 20:19
ᵍ Matt. 28:19
ʰ John 12:45
ⁱ Acts 16:18
ʲ Acts 2:4
Acts 10:46
ᵏ Acts 28:5
ˡ Acts 28:8
ᵐ Luke 24:51
ⁿ Heb. 2:4

15:43 ¹ A man of great authority, of the counsel of the Sanhedrin, or else taken into counsel by Pilate.

² If we consider what danger Joseph cast himself into, we shall perceive how bold he was.

16:4 ¹ When they cast their eyes toward the sepulchre.

16:5 ¹ Into the cave out where the sepulchre was cut out.

16:9 ¹ Christ himself appeareth to Mary Magdalene to upbraid the disciples' incredulity.

16:12 ¹ Christ appeareth to two other disciples, and at length to the eleven.

16:14 ¹ The Evangelist considered not the order of the time, but the course of his history, which he divided into three parts: The first showeth how he appeared to the women, the second, to his Dis-

ciples, the third, to his Apostles, and therefore he saith, Finally.

16:15 ¹ The Apostles are appointed, and their office is limited unto them, which is to preach that which they heard of him, and to minister the Sacraments, which Christ hath instituted, having besides power to do miracles.

² Not to the Jews only, nor in Judea only, but to all men, and everywhere: and so must all the Apostles do.

16:17 ¹ Strange tongues, such as they knew not before.

16:19 ¹ Christ having accomplished his office on earth, ascendeth into heaven, from whence (the doctrine of his Apostles being confirmed with signs) he will govern his Church, unto the world's end.

16:20 ¹ To wit, the doctrine: therefore doctrine must go before, and signs must follow after.

THE HOLY GOSPEL OF JESUS CHRIST,

ACCORDING TO

LUKE

1 *Luke: Preface   5 Zacharias and Elizabeth.   15 What an one John should be.   20 Zacharias stricken dumb, for his incredulity.   26 The Angel saluteth Mary, and foretelleth Christ's nativity.   39 Mary visited Elizabeth.   46 Mary's song.   68 The song of Zacharias, showing that the promised Christ is come.   76 The office of John.*

CHAPTER 1
a 1 Chron. 24:1
b Exod. 30:7
c Lev. 16:17
d Mal. 4:5
e Matt. 11:14

1   Forasmuch as ¹many have ²taken in hand to set forth the story of those things, whereof we are fully persuaded,

2   ¹As they have delivered them unto us, which from the beginning saw them themselves, and were ministers of the word,

3   It seemed good also to me (¹most noble Theophilus) as soon as I had searched out perfectly all things ²from the beginning, to write unto thee thereof from point to point,

4   That thou mightest ¹acknowledge the certainty of those things whereof thou hast been instructed.

5   In ¹the ²time of ³Herod King of Judea, there *was* a certain Priest named Zacharias, of the *ᵃ,⁴*course of Abijah: and his wife *was* of the daughters of Aaron, and her name *was* Elizabeth.

6   Both were ¹just before God, and ²walked in all the ³commandments and ordinances of the Lord, ⁴without reproof.

7   And they had no child, because that Elizabeth was barren: and both were well stricken in age.

8   And it came to pass, as he executed the Priest's office before God, as his course came in order,

9   ᵇAccording to the custom of the Priest's office, his lot was to burn incense, when he went into the ¹Temple of the Lord.

10   And the whole multitude of the people were without in prayer, ᶜwhile the incense was burning.

11   Then appeared unto him an Angel of the Lord, standing at the right side of the Altar of incense.

12   And when Zacharias saw *him*, he was troubled, and fear fell upon him.

13   But the Angel said unto him, Fear not, Zacharias: for thy prayer is heard, and thy wife Elizabeth shall bear thee a son, and thou shalt call his name John.

14   And thou shalt have joy and gladness, and many shall rejoice at his birth.

15   For he shall be great in the ¹sight of the Lord, and shall neither drink wine, nor ²strong drink: and he shall be filled with the holy Ghost, even from his mother's womb.

16   ᵈAnd many of the children of Israel shall he ¹turn to their Lord God.

17   ᵉFor he shall go ¹before him ²in the spirit and

1:1 ¹ Luke commendeth the witnesses that saw this history.

² Many took it in hand, but did not perform: Luke wrote his Gospel before Matthew and Mark.

1:2 ¹ Luke was not an eyewitness, and therefore it was not he to whom the Lord appeared when Cleopas saw him: and he was taught not only by Paul, but by others of the Apostles also.

1:3 ¹ It is most mighty, and therefore Theophilus was a very honorable man, and in place of great dignity.

² Luke began his Gospel a great deal farther off, than the others did.

1:4 ¹ Have fuller knowledge of those things, which before thou knewest but meanly.

1:5 ¹ John who was another Elijah, and appointed to be herald of Christ, coming of the stock of Aaron, and of two famous and blameless parents, hath showed in his conception, which was against the course of nature, a double miracle, to the end that men should be more readily stirred up to the hearing of his preaching, according to the forewarning of the Prophets.

² Word for word, in the days: so speak the Hebrews, giving us to understand, how short and frail a thing the power of princes is.

³ Herod the great.

⁴ For the posterity of Aaron was divided into courses.

1:6 ¹ The true mark of righteousness is, to be liked and allowed of in the judgment of God.

² Lived, so speak the Hebrews, for our life is as a way, wherein we must walk, until we come to the mark.

³ In all the moral and ceremonial law.

⁴ Whom no man could justly reprove: now so it is, that the fruits of justification are set forth here, and not the cause, which is faith only, and nothing else.

1:9 ¹ The Temple was one, and the Court another, for Zacharias went out of the Court or outward room, where all the people were, and therefore are said to be without, into the temple.

1:15 ¹ So speak the Hebrews when it signified a rare kind of excellency: so is it said of Nimrod, Gen. 10:9. He was a valiant hunter before God.

² Any drink that may make drunken.

1:16 ¹ Shall be a means to bring many to repentance, and turn themselves to the Lord from whom they fell.

1:17 ¹ As they used to go before kings, and when you see them, you know the king is not far off.

² This is spoken by the figure Metonymy, taking the spirit, for the gift of the spirit, as you would say, the cause, for that that cometh of the cause.

power of Elijah, to turn the ³hearts of the fathers to the children, and the disobedient to the ⁴wisdom of the just men, to make ready a people prepared for the Lord.

18 Then Zacharias said unto the Angel, Whereby shall I know this? for I am an old man, and my wife is of a great age.

19 And the Angel answered, and said unto him, I am Gabriel ¹that stand in the presence of God, and am sent to speak unto thee, and to show thee these good tidings.

20 And behold, thou shalt be dumb, and not be able to speak, until the day that these things be done, because thou believest not my words, which shall be fulfilled in their season.

21 Now the people waited for Zacharias, and marveled that he tarried so long in the Temple.

22 And when he came out, he could not speak unto them: then they perceived that he had seen a vision in the Temple: for he made signs unto them, and remained dumb.

23 And it came to pass, when the days of his office were fulfilled, that he departed to his own house.

24 And after those days, his wife Elizabeth conceived, and hid herself five months, saying,

25 Thus hath the Lord dealt with me, in the days wherein he looked on *me*, to take from me my rebuke among men.

26 ¶ ¹And in the sixth month, the Angel Gabriel was sent from God unto a city of Galilee, named Nazareth,

27 ᶠTo a virgin affianced to a man whose name *was* Joseph, of the ¹house of David, and the virgin's name *was* Mary.

28 And the Angel went in unto her, and said, Hail thou *that art* ¹freely beloved: the Lord *is* with thee: ²blessed *art* thou among women.

29 And when she saw *him*, she was ¹troubled at his saying, and thought what manner of salutation that should be.

30 Then the Angel said unto her, Fear not, Mary: for thou hast ¹found favor with God.

31 ᵍFor lo thou shalt conceive in thy womb, and bear a son, ʰand shalt call his Name Jesus.

32 He shall be great, and shall be ¹called the Son of the most High, and the Lord God shall give unto him the throne of his father David.

33 ⁱAnd he shall reign over the house of Jacob forever, and of his kingdom shall be none end.

34 Then said Mary unto the Angel, ¹How shall this be, seeing ²I know not man?

35 And the Angel answered, and said unto her, The holy Ghost ¹shall come upon thee, and the power of the most High shall overshadow thee: therefore also that ²Holy thing which shall be born of thee, shall be ³called the Son of God.

36 And behold, thy ¹cousin, Elizabeth, she hath also conceived a son in her old age: and this is her ²sixth month, which was called barren.

37 For with God shall nothing be impossible.

38 Then Mary said, Behold the servant of the Lord: be it unto me according to thy word. So the Angel departed from her.

39 ¶ ¹And Mary arose in those days, and went into the ²hill *country* with haste to a ³city of Judah,

40 And entered into the house of Zacharias, and saluted Elizabeth.

41 And it came to pass, as Elizabeth heard the

Marginal references:
ᶠ Matt. 1:18
ᵍ Isa. 7:14
ʰ Luke 2:21
  Matt. 1:21
ⁱ Dan. 7:14, 27
  Mic. 4:7

---

³ By this figure Synecdoche, he showeth that he shall take away all kinds of enmities, which used to breed great troubles and turmoils amongst men.

⁴ Wisdom and goodness are two of the chiefest causes which make men to reverence and honor their fathers.

1:19 ¹ That appears, for so the Hebrews use this word (to stand) meaning that they are ready to do his commandment.

1:26 ¹ The Angel serving the Lord which should be born, is sent to the virgin Mary, in whom the Son of the most high promised to David, is conceived by the virtue of the holy Ghost.

1:27 ¹ As much is to be said of Mary, otherwise Christ had not been of the stock, not the son of David.

1:28 ¹ It might be rendered word for word, full of favor and grace, and he showeth straight after, laying out plainly unto us, what that favor is, in that he saith, the Lord is with thee.

² Of God.

1:29 ¹ Moved at the strangeness of the matter.

1:30 ¹ So speak the Hebrews, saying, that men have found favor, which are in favor.

1:32 ¹ He shall be declared so to be, for he was the Son of God from everlasting, but was made manifest in the flesh in his time.

1:34 ¹ The greatness of the matter causeth the Virgin to ask this question, not that she distrusteth any whit at all, for she asketh only of the

manner of the conceiving, so that it is plain she believed all the rest.

² So speak the Hebrews, signifying by this modest kind of speech the company of man and wife together, and this is the meaning of it: how shall this be, forseeing, I shall be Christ his mother, I am very sure. I shall not know any man: for the godly virgin had learned by the Prophets, that the Messiah should be born of a Virgin.

1:35 ¹ That is, the holy Ghost shall cause thee to conceive by his mighty power.

² That pure thing and void of all spot of uncleanness: for it was to take away sin, must needs be void of sin.

³ Declared and showed to the world, to be the Son of God.

1:36 ¹ Though Elizabeth were of the tribe of Levi, yet she might be Mary's cousin: for whereas it was forbidden by the Law, for maidens to be married to men of other tribes, this could not let, but that the Levites might take them wives out of any tribe: for the Levites had no portion allotted them, when the land was divided among the people.

² This is now the sixth month from the time when she conceived.

1:39 ¹ Elizabeth being great with child with John, and Mary with Christ, by the inspiration of the holy Ghost, do rejoice each for other.

² Which is on the South side of Jerusalem.

³ That is to say, Hebron: which was in times past called Kirjath Arba, which was one of the towns, that was given to the Levites, in the tribe of Judah, and is said to be in the mountains of Judah, Josh. 14:15 and 21:11.

salutation of Mary, the babe [1]sprang in her belly, and Elizabeth was filled with the holy Ghost.

42 And she cried with a loud voice, and said, Blessed art thou among women, because [1]the fruit of thy womb is blessed.

43 And whence cometh this to me, that the mother of my Lord should come to me?

44 For lo, as soon as the voice of thy salutation sounded in mine ears, the babe sprang in my belly for joy.

45 And blessed is she that believed: for those things shall be performed, which were told her from the Lord.

46 [1]Then Mary said, My soul magnifieth the Lord,

47 And my spirit rejoiceth in God my Savior.

48 For he hath [1]looked on the [2]poor degree of his servant: for behold, from henceforth shall all ages call me blessed,

49 Because he that is mighty hath done for me great things, and holy is his Name.

50 And his mercy is from generation to generation on them [1]that fear him.

51 [j]He that showed strength with his [1]arm: [k]he hath [2]scattered the proud in the [3]imagination of their hearts.

52 [l]He hath [1]put down the mighty from their seats, and exalted them of [2]low degree.

53 [m]He hath filled the [1]hungry with good things, and sent away the rich empty.

54 [l,n]He hath upholden Israel his servant to be mindful of his mercy,

55 ([o]As he hath [1]spoken to our fathers, to wit, to Abraham and his seed) forever.

56 ¶ And Mary abode with her about three months: after, she returned to her own house.

57 ¶ [1]Now Elizabeth's time was fulfilled, that she

should be delivered, and she brought forth a son.

58 And her neighbors and cousins heard tell how the Lord had showed his great mercy upon her, and they [p]rejoiced with her.

59 And it was so that on the eighth day they came to circumcise the babe, and called him Zacharias, after the name of his father.

60 But his mother answered, and said, Not so, but he shall be called John.

61 And they said unto her, There is none of thy kindred that is named with this name.

62 Then they made signs to his father, how he would have him called.

63 So he asked for writing tablets, and wrote, saying, His name is John, and they marveled all.

64 And his mouth was opened immediately, and his tongue, [1]and he spake and praised God.

65 Then fear came on all them that dwelt near unto them, and all [1]these words were noised abroad throughout all the hill country of Judea.

66 And all they that heard them, [1]laid them up in their hearts, saying, What manner child shall this be! and the [2]hand of the Lord was with him.

67 [1]Then his father Zacharias was filled with the holy Ghost, and prophesied, saying,

68 Blessed be the Lord God of Israel, because he hath [1]visited [q]and [2]redeemed his people,

69 [r]And hath raised up the [1]horn of salvation unto us, in the house of his servant David,

70 [s]As he spake by the mouth of his holy Prophets, which were since the world began, saying,

71 That he would send us deliverance from our enemies, and from the hands of all that hate us,

72 That he might show mercy towards our fathers: and [1]remember his holy covenant,

73 [t]And the oath, which he sware to our father

Cross references

j Isa. 51:9
Ps. 33:10
k Isa. 29:15
l 1 Sam. 2:6
m Ps. 24:10
n Isa. 30:18
Isa. 41:8
Isa. 54:5
Jer. 31:5-20
o Gen. 17:19
Gen. 22:17
Ps. 132:12
p Luke 1:14
q Luke 2:30
Matt. 1:21
r Ps. 131:18
s Jer. 23:6
Jer. 30:10
t Gen. 22:16
Jer. 31:33
Heb. 9:13-17

1:41 [1] This was no ordinary nor usual kind of moving.

1:42 [1] Christ is blessed in respect of his humanity.

1:46 [1] Christ the redeemer of the afflicted, and revenger of the proud, of long time promised to the fathers, is now at length exhibited indeed.

1:48 [1] Hath freely and graciously loved.

[2] Word for word, My baseness, that is, my base estate: so that the Virgin vaunteth not her deserts, but the grace of God.

1:50 [1] To them that live godly and religiously, so speak the Hebrews.

1:51 [1] That is, an heaping up of words more than needed, which the Hebrews use very much, and the arm is taken for strength.

[2] Even as the wind doth the chaff.

[3] He hath scattered them, and the imagination of their hearts; or by and through the imagination of their own hearts: so that their wicked counsel turned to their own destruction.

1:52 [1] The mighty and rich men.

[2] Such as none account is made of, and are vile in men's eyes, which are indeed the poor in spirit, that is, such as challenge nothing to themselves in the sight of God.

1:53 [1] Them that are brought to extreme poverty.

1:54 [1] He hath holpen up Israel with his arm, being clean cast down.

1:55 [1] Promised.

1:57 [1] John's nativity is set out with new miracles.

1:64 [1] was restored to its former state, is read in some copies.

1:65 [1] All this that was said and done.

1:66 [1] Thought upon them diligently and earnestly, and as it were, printed them in their hearts.

[2] That is, the present favor of God, and a singular kind of virtue appeared in him.

1:67 [1] John scarce born, by the authority of the holy Ghost, is appointed to his office.

1:68 [1] That he hath showed himself mindful of his people, insomuch that he came down from heaven himself, to visit us in person, and to redeem us.

[2] Hath paid the ransom, that is to say, the price of our redemption.

1:69 [1] This word Horn in the Hebrew tongue signifieth might, and it is a Metaphor, taken from beasts, that fight with their horns: and by raising up the might of Israel, is meant, that the kingdom of Israel was defended, and the enemies thereof laid on the ground, even then when the strength of Israel seemed to be utterly decayed.

1:72 [1] Declared indeed that he was mindful.

Abraham.

74 *Which was*, that he would grant unto us, that we being delivered out of the hands of our enemies, should serve him without fear,

75 All the days of our life, in "holiness and righteousness [1]before him.

76 And thou, [1]babe, shalt be called the Prophet of the most High: for thou shalt go before the face of the Lord to prepare his ways,

77 *And* to [1]give knowledge of salvation unto his people, by the [2]remission of their sins,

78 Through the tender mercy of our God, whereby "the [1]dayspring from on high hath visited us,

79 To give light to them that sit in darkness, and in the shadow of death, and to guide our feet into the way of [1]peace.

80 And the child grew, and waxed strong in spirit, and was in the wilderness, till the day came that he should show himself unto Israel.

2

Augustus Caesar taxeth all the world.   7 Christ is born.   13 The Angels' Song.   21 Christ is circumcised.   22 Mary purified.   28 Simeon taketh Christ in his arms.   29 His Song.   36 Anna the Prophetess.   40 The child Christ.   46 Jesus disputeth with the doctors.

1 And [1]it came to pass in those days, that there came a decree from Augustus Caesar, that all the [2]world should be [3]taxed.

2 (This first taxing was made when Quirinius was governor of Syria.)

3 Therefore went all to be taxed, every man to his own city.

4 And Joseph also went up from Galilee out of a city called Nazareth, into Judea, unto the [1]city of [a]David, which is called Bethlehem (because he was of the house and lineage of David,)

5 To be taxed with Mary that was given him to wife, which was with child.

6 ¶ And so it was, that while they were there, the days were accomplished that she should be delivered.

" 1 Pet. 1:15
" Zech. 3:8
Zech. 6:12
Mal. 4:2

CHAPTER 2
[a] John 7:42
[b] Gen. 17:12
Lev. 12:3
John 7:22
[c] Luke 1:31
Matt. 1:22

7 And she brought forth her first begotten son, and wrapped him in swaddling clothes, and laid him in a cratch, because there was no room for them in the inn.

8 ¶ [1]And there were in the same country shepherds, [2]abiding in the field, and keeping watch by night over their flock.

9 And lo, the Angel of the Lord [1]came upon them, and the glory of the Lord shone about them, and they were sore afraid.

10 Then the Angel said unto them, Be not afraid: for behold, I bring you glad tidings of great joy, that shall be to all the people,

11 *That is*, that unto you is born this day in the city of David, a Savior, which is Christ the Lord.

12 And this *shall be* a sign to you, Ye shall find the babe swaddled, and laid in a cratch.

13 And straightway there was with the Angel [1]a multitude of heavenly soldiers, praising God, and saying,

14 Glory *be* to God in the high *heavens*, and peace in earth, and toward men [1]good will.

15 And it came to pass when the Angels were gone away from them into heaven, that the shepherds said one to another, Let us go then unto Bethlehem, and see this thing that is come to pass, which the Lord hath showed unto us.

16 So they came with haste, and found both Mary and Joseph and the babe laid in the cratch.

17 And when they had seen it, they published abroad the thing that was told them of that child.

18 And all that heard it, wondered at the things which were told them of the shepherds.

19 But Mary kept all those sayings, and pondered *them* in her heart.

20 And the shepherds returned glorifying and praising God, for all that they had heard and seen, as it was spoken unto them.

21 ¶ [b,1]And when the eight days were accomplished, that they should circumcise the child, his name was then called [c]Jesus, which was named of the Angel,

---

1:75 [1] To God's good liking.
1:76 [1] Though thou be at this present never so little.
1:77 [1] Open the way.
   [2] Forgiveness of sins, is the means whereby God saveth us, Rom. 4:7.
1:78 [1] Or bud, or branch; he alludeth unto the places in Jer. 23:5; Zech. 3:8 and 6:12, and he is called a bud from on high, that is, sent from God unto us, and not as other buds which bud out of the earth.
1:79 [1] Into the way which leadeth us to true happiness.
2:1 [1] Christ the son of God, taking upon him the form of a servant, and making himself of no reputation, is poorly born in a stable: and by the means of Augustus the mightiest prince in the world (thinking nothing less) hath his cradle prepared in Bethlehem, as the Prophets forewarned.
   [2] So far as the Empire of the Romans did stretch.
   [3] That is, the inhabitants of every city should have their names

taken, and their goods rated at a certain value, that the Emperor might understand, how rich every country, city, family, and house was.
2:4 [1] Which David was born, and brought up in.
2:8 [1] The Angels themselves declare to poor shepherds (nothing regarding the pride of the mighty) the Godhead and office of the child lying in the crib.
   [2] Lodging without doors, and open in the air.
2:9 [1] Came suddenly upon them, when they thought of no such matter.
2:13 [1] Whole armies of Angels, which compass the Majesty of God round about, as it were soldiers.
2:14 [1] God's ready, good, infinite, and gracious favor toward men.
2:21 [1] Christ the head of the Church, made subject to the Law, to deliver us from the curse of the Law, (as the Name of Jesus doth well declare) being circumcised, doth ratify and seal in his own flesh, the circumcision of the fathers.

before he was conceived in the womb.

22 ^{d,1}And when the days of ^{2}her purification, after the Law of Moses, were accomplished, they brought him to Jerusalem, to present him to the Lord,

23 (As it is written in the Law of the Lord, ^{e}Every man child that *first* openeth the womb, shall be called holy to the Lord,)

24 And to give an oblation, ^{f}as it is commanded in the Law of the Lord, a pair of turtledoves, or two young pigeons.

25 ^{1}And behold, there was a man in Jerusalem, whose name was Simeon: this man *was* just, and feared God, and waited for the consolation of Israel, and the ^{2}holy Ghost was upon him.

26 And it was declared to him from God by the holy Ghost, that he should not see death, before he had seen that Anointed of the Lord.

27 And he came by *the motion* of the spirit into the Temple, and when the ^{1}parents brought in the babe Jesus, to do for him after the custom of the Law.

28 Then he took him in his arms, and praised God, and said,

29 Lord, now ^{1}lettest thou thy servant depart in peace, according to thy ^{2}word,

30 For ^{1}mine eyes have seen thy ^{2}salvation,

31 Which thou hast prepared ^{1}before the face of all people,

32 A light to be revealed to the Gentiles, and the glory of thy people Israel.

33 And Joseph and his mother marveled at those things, which were spoken touching him.

34 And Simeon blessed them, and said unto Mary his mother, Behold, this *child* is ^{1}appointed for the ^{g,2}fall and rising again of many in Israel, and for a ^{3}sign which shall be spoken against,

35 (Yea and a sword shall ^{1}pierce through thy soul) that the thoughts of many hearts may be opened.

36 ^{1}And there was a Prophetess, one Anna the daughter of Phanuel, of the tribe of Asher, which was of a great age, after she had lived with an husband

^{d} Lev. 12:6
^{e} Exod. 13:2
  Num. 8:16
^{f} Lev. 12:6
^{g} Isa. 8:14
  Rom. 9:32
  1 Pet. 2:8
^{h} Deut. 16:1

seven years from her virginity:

37 And she *was* widow about fourscore, and four years, and went not out of the Temple, but served God with fastings and prayers night and day.

38 She then coming at the same instant upon them, confessed likewise the Lord, and spake of him to all that looked for redemption in Jerusalem.

39 And when they had performed all things, according to the Law of the Lord, they returned into Galilee to their own city Nazareth.

40 And the child grew, and waxed strong in Spirit, ^{1}and was filled with wisdom, and the grace of God was with him.

41 ¶ ^{1}Now his parents went to Jerusalem, every year, ^{h}at the feast of the Passover.

42 And when he was twelve years old, and they were come up to Jerusalem, after the custom of the feast,

43 And had finished the days *thereof*, as they returned, the child Jesus remained in Jerusalem, and Joseph knew not, nor his mother,

44 But they supposing that he had been in the company, went a day's journey, and sought him among *their* kinsfolk, and acquaintances.

45 And when they found him not, they turned back to Jerusalem, and sought him.

46 And it came to pass three days after, that they found him in the Temple, sitting in the midst of the doctors, both hearing them, and asking them questions:

47 And all that heard him, were astonied at his understanding and answers.

48 ^{1}So when they saw him, they were amazed, and his mother said unto him, Son, why hast thou thus dealt with us? behold, thy father and I have sought thee with very heavy hearts.

49 Then said he unto them, How is it that ye sought me? knew ye not that I must go about my Father's business?

50 But they understood not the word that he spake to them.

2:22 ^{1} Christ, upon whom all our sins were laid, being offered to God, according to the Law, doth purify both Mary and us all in himself.

^{2} This is meant, for the fulfilling of the Law: for otherwise the virgin was not defiled, nor unclean, by the birth of this child.

2:25 ^{1} Simeon doth openly in the Temple foretell the deaf, of the coming of Messiah, of the casting out of the greatest part of Israel, and of the calling of the Gentiles.

^{2} He was endued with the gifts of the holy Ghost, and this is spoken by the figure Metonymy.

2:27 ^{1} Joseph and Mary: and so he speaketh, as it was commonly taken.

2:29 ^{1} Lettest me depart out of this life, to be joined to my fathers.

^{2} As thou promised me.

2:30 ^{1} That is, for I have seen with my very eyes: for he saw before in mind, as it is said of Abraham, He saw my day, and rejoiced.

^{2} That, wherein thy salvation is contained.

2:31 ^{1} As a sign set up in an high place, for all men to look upon.

2:34 ^{1} Is appointed and set of God for a mark.

^{2} Fall of the reprobate, which perish through their own default: and for the rising of the elect, unto whom God shall give faith to believe.

^{3} That is, a mark, which all men shall strive earnestly to hit.

2:35 ^{1} Shall wound and grieve most sharply.

2:36 ^{1} Another witness besides Simeon, against whom no exception may be brought, inviting all men to the receiving of the Messiah.

2:40 ^{1} As Christ grew up in age, so the virtue of his Godhead showed itself more and more.

2:41 ^{1} The Scribes and Pharisees are stirred up to hear the wisdom of Christ in his time, by an extraordinary deed.

2:48 ^{1} All duties which we owe to men as they were not to be neglected, so are they according to our vocation, not to be preferred before the glory of God.

51 [1]Then he went down with them, and came to Nazareth, and was subject to them: and his mother kept all these sayings in her heart.

52 And Jesus increased in wisdom, and stature, and in favor with God and men.

3
3 *John exhorteth to repentance.* 15 *His testimony of Christ.* 20 *Herod putteth him in prison.* 21 *Christ is baptized.* 23 *His pedigree.*

1 Now [1]in the fifteenth year of the reign of Tiberius Caesar, Pontius Pilate being governor of Judea, and Herod being Tetrarch of Galilee, and his brother Philip Tetrarch of Iturea, and of the country of Trachonitis, and Lysanias the Tetrarch of Abilene,

2 ([a]When [1]Annas and Caiaphas were the high Priests) the word of God came unto John, the son of Zacharias in the wilderness.

3 [b]And he came into all the coasts about Jordan, preaching the baptism of repentance for the remission of sins,

4 As it is written in the book of the sayings of Isaiah the Prophet, which saith, [c]The voice of him that crieth in the wilderness *is*, Prepare ye the way of the Lord: make his paths straight.

5 Every valley shall be filled, and every mountain and hill shall be brought low, and crooked things shall be made straight, and the rough ways *shall be made* smooth.

6 And all flesh shall see the salvation of God.

7 Then said he to the people that were come out to be baptized of him, [d]O generations of vipers, who hath forewarned you to flee from the wrath to come?

8 Bring forth therefore fruits worthy amendment of life, and begin not to say with yourselves, We have Abraham to *our* Father: for I say unto you, that God is able of these stones to raise up children unto Abraham.

9 Now also is the axe laid unto the root of the trees: therefore every tree which bringeth not forth good fruit, shall be hewn down, and cast into the fire.

10 ¶ Then the people asked him, saying, What shall we do then?

CHAPTER 3
a Acts 4:6
b Matt. 3:2
   Mark 1:4
c Isa. 40:3
   John 1:25
d Matt. 3:7
e James 2:15
   1 John 3:17
f Matt. 3:11
   Mark 1:3
   John 1:26
   Acts 1:5
   Acts 8:4
   Acts 11:16
   Acts 19:4
g Matt. 14:3
   Mark 6:17
b Matt. 3:13
   Mark 1:9
   John 1:32

11 And he answered, and said unto them, [e]He that hath two coats, let him part with him that hath none: and he that hath meat, let him do likewise.

12 Then came there Publicans also to be baptized, and said unto him, Master, what shall we do?

13 And he said unto them, Require no more than that which is [1]appointed unto you.

14 The soldiers likewise demanded of him, saying, And what shall we do? And he said unto them, Do violence to no man, neither accuse any falsely, and be content with your [1]wages.

15 [1]As the people waited, and all men mused in their hearts of John, if he were not that Christ.

16 John answered, and said to them all, [f]Indeed I baptize you with water, but one stronger than I, cometh, whose shoe's latchet I am not worthy to unloose: he will baptize you with the holy Ghost, and with fire.

17 [1]Whose fan *is* in his hand, and he will make clean his floor, and will gather the wheat into his garner, but the chaff will he burn up with fire that never shall be quenched.

18 Thus then exhorting with many other things, he preached unto the people.

19 [g][1]But when Herod the Tetrarch was rebuked of him, for Herodias his brother Philip's wife, and for all the evils which Herod had done,

20 He added yet this above all, that he shut up John in prison.

21 [b][1]Now it came to pass, as all the people were baptized, and that Jesus was baptized and did pray, that the heaven was opened:

22 And the holy Ghost came down in a bodily shape like a dove upon him, and there was a voice from heaven, saying, Thou art my beloved Son: in thee I am well pleased.

23 ¶ [1]And Jesus himself began to be about thirty years of age, being as men supposed the son of Joseph, which was the son of Heli,

24 The son of Matthat, *the son* of Levi, *the son* of Melchi, *the son* of Janna, *the son* of Joseph,

25 The son of Mattathiah, *the son* of Amos, *the son* of Nahum, *the son* of Esli, *the son* of Naggai,

26 The son of Maath, *the son* of Mattathiah, *the*

2:51 [1] Christ very man is made like unto us in all things, except sin.
3:1 [1] John cometh at the time foretold of the Prophets, and layeth the foundation of the Gospel which is exhibited unto us, setting forth the true observing of the Law, and free mercy in Christ, which cometh after him, using also baptism the effectual sign both of regeneration and also of forgiveness of sins.
3:2 [1] Josephus calleth him Ananus.
3:13 [1] Require no more than that sum that is appointed for the tribute money.
3:14 [1] Which was paid them partly in money, and partly in victual.
3:15 [1] If we would rightly, and fruitfully receive the sacraments, we must neither rest in the signs, neither in him that ministereth the signs,

but lift up our eyes to Christ, who is the author of the sacraments, and the giver of that which is represented by the sacraments.
3:17 [1] The Gospel is the fan of the world.
3:19 [1] John's preaching is confirmed with his death.
3:21 [1] Our baptism is sanctified in the head of the Church, and Christ also is pronounced, by the voice of the Father, to be our everlasting King, Priest, and Prophet.
3:23 [1] The stock of Christ, according to the flesh, is brought by order even to Adam, and so to God, that it might appear, that he only it was, whom God promised to Abraham and David, and appointed from everlasting to his Church, which is gathered together of all sorts of men.

son of Semei, *the son of* Joseph, *the son of* Judah,

27 The son of Joannas, *the son of* Rhesa, *the son of* Zerubbabel, *the son of* Shealtiel, *the son of* Neri,

28 The son of Melchi, *the son of* Addi, *the son of* Cosam, *the son of* Elmodam, *the son of* Er,

29 ¶ The son of Jose, *the son of* Eliezer, *the son of* Jorim, *the son of* Matthat, *the son of* Levi,

30 The son of Simeon, *the son of* Judah, *the son of* Joseph, *the son of* Jonan, *the son of* Eliakim,

31 The son of Melea, *the son of* Menan, *the son of* Mattathah, *the son of* Nathan, *the son of* David,

32 The son of Jesse, *the son of* Obed, *the son of* Boaz, *the son of* Salmon, *the son of* Nahshon,

33 The son of Amminadab, *the son of* Ram, *the son of* Hezron, *the son of* Perez, *the son of* Judah,

34 The son of Jacob, *the son of* Isaac, *the son of* Abraham, *the son of* Terah, *the son of* Nahor,

35 The son of Serug, *the son of* Reu, *the son of* Peleg, *the son of* Eber, *the son of* Shelah,

36 The son of Cainan, *the son of* Arphaxad, *the son of* Shem, *the son of* Noah, *the son of* Lamech,

37 The son of Methuselah, *the son of* Enoch, *the son of* Jared, *the son of* Mahalalel, *the son of* Cainan,

38 The son of Enosh, *the son of* Seth, *the son of* Adam, *the son of* God.

4

1 *Of Christ's temptation, and fasting.* 16 *He teacheth in Nazareth to the great admiration of all.* 24 *A Prophet that teacheth in his own country is condemned.* 33 *One possessed of the devil is cured.* 38 *Peter's mother-in-law is healed,* 40 *and divers sick persons are restored to health.* 41 *The devils acknowledge Christ.*

1 And ¹Jesus full of the holy Ghost returned from Jordan, and was led by that Spirit into the wilderness,

2 ªAnd was *there* forty days tempted of the devil, and in those days he did eat nothing, but when they were ended, he afterward was hungry.

3 ¹Then the devil said unto him, If thou be the son of God, command this stone, that it be made bread.

4 But Jesus answered, saying, It is written, ᵇThat man shall not live by bread only, but by every word of God.

5 Then the devil took him up into an high mountain, and showed him all the kingdoms of the world, in the twinkling of an eye.

CHAPTER 4
ª Matt. 4:1
  Mark 1:12
ᵇ Deut. 8:3
  Matt. 4:4
ᶜ Deut. 6:13
  Deut. 10:20
ᵈ Ps. 91:12
ᵉ Deut. 6:16
ᶠ Matt. 13:54
  Mark 6:1
  John 4:43
ᵍ Isa. 61:1

6 And the devil said unto him, All this ¹power will I give thee, and the glory of those *kingdoms*: for that is ²delivered to me: and to whomsoever I will, I give it.

7 If thou therefore wilt worship me, they shall be all ¹thine.

8 But Jesus answered him, and said, Hence from me, Satan: for it is written, ᶜThou shalt worship the Lord thy God, and him alone thou shalt serve.

9 Then he brought him to Jerusalem, and set him on a pinnacle of the Temple, and said unto him, If thou be the Son of God, cast thyself down from hence,

10 For it is written, ᵈThat he will give his Angels charge over thee to keep thee:

11 And with *their* hands they shall lift thee up, lest at anytime thou shouldest dash thy foot against a stone.

12 And Jesus answered, and said unto him, It is said, ᵉThou shalt not tempt the Lord thy God.

13 And when the devil had ended all the temptation, he departed from him for a little season.

14 ¶ And Jesus returned by the power of the spirit into Galilee: and there went a fame of him throughout all the region round about:

15 For he taught in their Synagogues, and was honored of all men.

16 ᶠ¹And he came to Nazareth where he had been brought up, and (as his custom was) went into the Synagogue on the Sabbath day, and stood up to read.

17 And there was delivered unto him the book of the Prophet Isaiah: and when he had ¹opened the book, he found the place, where it was written,

18 ᵍThe Spirit of the Lord is upon me, because he hath anointed me, that I should preach the Gospel to the poor: he hath sent me, that I should heal the brokenhearted, that I should preach deliverance to the captives, and recovering of sight to the blind, that I should set at liberty them that are bruised:

19 And that I should preach the acceptable year of the Lord.

20 And he closed the book, and gave it again to the minister, and sat down: and the eyes of all that were in the Synagogue were fastened on him.

21 Then he began to say unto them, This day is the Scripture fulfilled in your ears.

4:1 ¹ Christ being carried away (as it were out of the world, into the desert) after the fast of forty days, and the overcoming of Satan thrice, coming as it were suddenly from heaven, beginneth his office.

4:3 ¹ Christ being stirred up of Satan, first to distrust in God, secondly to the desire of riches and honor, and lastly to a vain confidence of himself, overcometh him thrice by the word of God.

4:6 ¹ By this word power, are the kingdoms themselves meant, which have the power: and so it is spoken by the figure Metonymy.

² That is surely so, for he is prince of the world yet not absolutely,

and is the sovereign over it, but by sufferance, and way of entreaty, and therefore he saith not true, that he can give it to whom he will.

4:7 ¹ Out of an high place, which had a goodly champion country underneath it, he showed him the situation of all countries.

4:16 ¹ Who Christ is, and wherefore he came, he showeth out of the prophet Isaiah.

4:17 ¹ Their books in those days were rolled up as scrolls upon a ruler: and so Christ unrolled, or unfolded it, which is here called opened.

22 ¹And all ²bare him witness, and ³wondered at the ⁴gracious words, which proceeded out of his mouth, and said, Is not this Joseph's son?

23 Then he said unto them, Ye will surely say unto me this Proverb, Physician, heal thyself: whatsoever we have heard done in Capernaum, do it here likewise in thine own country.

24 And he said, Verily I say unto you, ʰNo Prophet is accepted in his own country.

25 But I tell you of a truth, many widows were in Israel in the days of ⁱElijah, when heaven was shut three years and six months, when great famine was throughout all the ¹land:

26 But unto none of them was Elijah sent, save into Zarephath, a city of Sidon, unto a certain widow.

27 Also many lepers were in Israel, in the time of ʲElisha the Prophet: yet none of them was made clean, saving Naaman the Syrian.

28 ¹Then all that were in the Synagogue, when they heard it, were filled with wrath,

29 And rose up, and thrust him out of the city, and led him unto the edge of the hill, whereon their city was built, to cast him down headlong.

30 But he passed through the midst of them, and went his way,

31 ¶ ᵏAnd came down into Capernaum a city of Galilee, and there taught them on the Sabbath days.

32 ¹And they were astonied at his doctrine: for his word was with authority.

33 ᵐAnd in the Synagogue there was a man which had a spirit of an unclean devil, which cried with a loud voice,

34 ¹Saying, Oh, what have we to do with thee, thou Jesus of Nazareth? art thou come to destroy us? I know who thou art, even the Holy one of God.

35 And Jesus rebuked him, saying, Hold thy peace, and come out of him. Then the devil throwing him in the midst of them, came out of him, and hurt him nothing at all.

36 So fear came on them all, and they spake among themselves, saying, What thing is this: for with authority and power he commandeth the foul spirits, and they come out?

37 And the fame of him spread abroad throughout all the places of the country round about.

38 ¶ ⁿ,¹And he rose up, and came out of the Synagogue, and entered into Simon's house. And Simon's wife's mother was taken with a great fever, and they required him for her.

39 Then he stood over her, and rebuked the fever, and it left her, and immediately she arose, and ministered unto them.

40 Now at the Sun setting, all they that had sick folks of divers diseases, brought them unto him, and he laid his hands on everyone of them, and healed them.

41ᵒ,¹And devils also came out of many, crying, and saying, Thou art that Christ that Son of God: but he rebuked them, and suffered them not to say that they knew him to be that Christ.

42 ¹And when it was day, he departed, and went forth into a desert place, and the people sought him, and came to him, and kept him that he should not depart from them.

43 But he said unto them, Surely I must also preach the kingdom of God to other cities: for therefore am I sent.

44 And he preached in the Synagogues of Galilee.

5 1 Christ teacheth out of the ship. 6 Of the draught of fish. 12 The Leper. 16 Christ prayeth in the desert. 18 One sick of the palsy. 27 Levi the Publican. 34 The fastings and afflictions of the Apostles after Christ's ascension. 36,37,38 Fainthearted and weak disciples are likened to old bottles and worn garments.

1 Then ᵃ,¹it came to pass, as the people ²pressed upon him to hear the word of God, that he stood by the lake of Gennesaret,

2 And saw two ships stand by the lakeside, but the fishermen were gone out of them, and were

Marginal references

ʰ John 4:44
ⁱ 1 Kings 17:9
James 5:17
ʲ 2 Kings 5:14
ᵏ Matt. 4:13
Mark 1:21
ˡ Matt. 7:29
Mark 1:22
ᵐ Mark 1:23
ⁿ Matt. 8:14
Mark 1:30
ᵒ Mark 1:35

CHAPTER 5
ᵃ Matt. 4:18
Mark 1:16

Footnotes

4:22 ¹ Familiarity causeth Christ to be contemned, and therefore he oftentimes goeth to strangers.

² Approved those things, which he spake, with common consent and voice: for the word, witness, signifieth in this place, and many others to allow and approve a thing with open confession.

³ Not only the doctors, but also the common people were present at this conference of the Scriptures: and besides that their mother tongue was used, for else how could the people have wondered? Paul appointed the same order in the Church at Corinth, 1 Cor. 14.

⁴ Words full of the mighty power of God, which appeared in all his doings as well, and allured men marvelously unto him, Ps. 45:2, grace is poured into thy lips.

4:25 ¹ Land of Israel, see Mark 15:38.

4:28 ¹ The more sharply the world is rebuked, the more it rageth openly: but the life of the godly is not simply subject to the pleasure of the wicked.

4:34 ¹ Christ astonisheth not only men, be they never so blockish, but even the demons also, whether they will or no.

4:38 ¹ In that, that Christ healeth the diseases of the body with his word only, he proveth that he is God Almighty, sent for man's salvation.

4:41 ¹ Satan, who is a continual enemy to the truth, ought not to be heard, no not then, when he speaketh the truth.

4:42 ¹ No color of zeal ought to hinder us in the race of our vocation.

5:1 ¹ Christ advertiseth the four disciples, which he had taken unto him, of the office of the Apostleship, which should hereafter be committed unto them.

² Did as it were lie upon him, so desirous they were to see him, and hear him, and therefore he taught them out of a ship.

washing their nets.

3 And he entered into one of the ships, which was Simon's, and required him that he would thrust off a little from the land: and he sat down, and taught the people out of the ship.

4 ¶ Now when he had left speaking, he said unto Simon, Launch out into the deep, and let down your nets to make a draught.

5 Then Simon answered, and said unto him, [1]Master, we have travailed sore all night, and have taken nothing: nevertheless at thy word I will let down the net.

6 And when they had so done, they enclosed a great multitude of fishes, so that their net brake.

7 And they beckoned to their partners, which were in the other ship, that they should come and help them, who came then, and filled both the ships, that they did sink.

8 Now when Simon Peter saw it, he fell down at Jesus knees, saying, Lord, go from me: for I am a sinful man.

9 For he was utterly astonied, and all that were with him, for the draught of fishes which they took.

10 And so was also James and John the sons of Zebedee, which were companions with Simon. Then Jesus said unto Simon, Fear not: from henceforth thou shalt catch men.

11 And when they had brought the ships to land, they forsook all, and followed him.

12 ¶ [b,1]Now it came to pass, as he was in a certain city, behold, there was a man full of leprosy, and when he saw Jesus, he fell on his face, and besought him, saying, Lord, if thou wilt, thou canst make me clean.

13 So he stretched forth his hand, and touched him, saying, I will, be thou clean. And immediately the leprosy departed from him.

14 And he commanded him that he should tell it no man: but Go, saith he, and show thyself to the Priest, and offer for thy cleansing, as [c]Moses hath commanded, for a witness unto them.

15 [1]But so much more went there a fame abroad of him, and great multitudes came together to hear, and to be healed of him of their infirmities.

16 But he kept himself apart in the wilderness, and prayed.

17 ¶ [1]And it came to pass, on a certain day, as he

b Matt. 8:2
Mark 1:40
c Lev. 14:4
d Matt. 9:2
Mark 2:3
e Matt. 9:9
Mark 2:14
f 1 Tim. 1:15
g Matt. 9:14
b Mark 2:18

was teaching, that the Pharisees and doctors of the Law sat by, which were come out of every town of Galilee, and Judea, and Jerusalem, and the power of the Lord [2]was in him, to heal them.

18 [d]Then behold, men brought a man lying in a bed, which was taken with a palsy, and they sought means to bring him in, and to lay him before him.

19 And when they could not find by what way they might bring him in, because of the press, they went up on the house, and let him down through the tiling, bed and all, in the midst before Jesus.

20 And when he saw their faith, he said unto him, Man, thy sins are forgiven thee.

21 Then the Scribes and the Pharisees began to reason, saying, Who is this that speaketh blasphemies? Who can forgive sins, but God only?

22 But when Jesus perceived their reasoning he answered, and said unto them, What reason ye in your hearts?

23 Whether is easier to say, Thy sins are forgiven thee, or to say, Rise and walk?

24 But that ye may know that the Son of man hath authority to forgive sins in earth, (he said unto the sick of the palsy) I say to thee, Arise: take up thy bed, and go into thine house.

25 And immediately he rose up before them, and took up his bed whereon he lay, and departed to his own house, praising God.

26 And they were all amazed, and praised God, and were filled with fear, saying, Doubtless we have seen strange things today.

27 ¶ [e,1]And after that, he went forth and saw a Publican named Levi, sitting at the receipt of custom, and said unto him, Follow me.

28 And he left all, rose up, and followed him.

29 Then Levi made him a great feast in his own house, where there was a great company of Publicans, and of others that sat at table with them.

30 But they that were Scribes and Pharisees among them, murmured against his disciples, saying, Why eat ye and drink ye with Publicans and sinners?

31 Then Jesus answered, and said unto them, They that are whole, need not the Physician, but they that are sick.

32 [f]I came not to call the righteous, but sinners to repentance.

33 [g,h,1]Then they said unto him, Why do the dis-

5:5 [1] The word signifieth him that hath rule over anything.

5:12 [1] Christ by healing the leper with his only touch, and sending him to the Priest, witnesseth that it is he, through whom and by whom, apprehended by faith, all we which are unclean, according to the Law, by the witness of God himself, are pronounced to be pure and clean.

5:15 [1] Christ had rather be famous by his doctrine, than by miracles, and therefore he departeth from them that seek him, as a physician of the body, and not as the author of salvation.

5:17 [1] Christ in healing him that was sick of the palsy, showeth the cause of all diseases, and the remedy.

[2] The mighty power of Christ's Godhead, showed itself in him, at that time.

5:27 [1] The Church is a company of sinners through the grace of Christ repentant, which banquet with him, to the great offence of the proud and envious worldlings.

5:33 [1] It is the point of hypocrites and ignorant men to put an holiness in fasting, and in things indifferent.

ciples of John fast often, and pray, and the *disciples* of the Pharisees also, but thine eat and drink?

34 ¹And he said unto them, Can ye make the children of the wedding chamber to fast, as long as the bridegroom is with them?

35 But the days will come, even when the bridegroom shall be taken away from them: then shall they fast in those days.

36 Again he spake also unto them a parable, No man putteth a piece of a new garment into an old vesture: for then the new renteth it, and the piece *taken* out of the new, agreeth not with the old.

37 Also no man poureth new wine into old vessels: for then the new wine will break the vessels, and it will run out, and the vessels will perish:

38 But new wine must be poured into new vessels: so both are preserved.

39 Also no man that drinketh old wine, straightway desireth new: for he saith, The old is more profitable.

6 1 *The disciples pull the ears of corn on the Sabbath.* 6 *Of him that had a withered hand.* 13 *The election of the Apostles.* 20 *The blessings and curses.* 27 *We must love our enemies.* 46 *With what fruit the word of God is to be heard.*

1 And ᵃ˒¹it came to pass on a second solemn Sabbath, that he went through the corn fields, and his disciples ²plucked the ears of corn, and did eat, and rubbed them in *their* hands.

2 And certain of the Pharisees said unto them, Why do ye that which is not lawful to do on the Sabbath days?

3 Then Jesus answered them, and said, ᵇHave ye not read this, that David did when he himself was an hungered, and they which were with him,

4 How he went into the house of God, and took, and ate the showbread, and gave also to them which were with him, which was not lawful to eat, but for the ᶜPriests only?

5 And he said unto them, The Son of man is Lord also of the Sabbath day.

6 ¶ ᵈ˒¹It came to pass also on another Sabbath, that he entered into the Synagogue, and taught, and

CHAPTER 6

ᵃ Matt. 12:1
Mark 2:23

ᵇ 1 Sam. 21:6

ᶜ Exod. 29:39
Lev. 8:31
Lev. 24:9

ᵈ Matt. 12:19
Mark 3:1

ᵉ Luke 9:1
Matt. 10:1
Mark 13:3
Mark 6:7

ᶠ Matt. 5:3

ᵍ Isa. 65:13

ʰ Isa. 61:3

there was a man, whose right hand was dried up.

7 And the Scribes and Pharisees watched him, whether he would heal on the Sabbath *day*, that they might find an accusation *against* him.

8 But he knew their thoughts, and said to the man which had the withered hand, Arise, and stand up in the midst. And he arose, and stood up.

9 Then said Jesus unto them, I will ask you a question, Whether is it lawful on the Sabbath days to do good, or to do evil? to save life, or to ¹destroy?

10 And he beheld them all in compass, and said unto the man, Stretch forth thine hand. And he did so, and his hand was restored again, as whole as the other.

11 Then they were filled full of madness, and communed one with another, what they might do to Jesus.

12 ¶ And it came to pass in those days, that he went into a mountain to pray, and ¹spent the night in prayer to God.

13 And when it was day, ᵉhe called his disciples, and of them he chose twelve which also he called Apostles:

14 (Simon whom he named also Peter, and Andrew his brother, James and John, Philip and Bartholomew,

15 Matthew and Thomas: James *the son* of Alphaeus, and Simon called Zealous,

16 Judas James' *brother*, and Judas Iscariot, which also was the traitor.)

17 Then he came down with them, and stood in a plain place with the company of his disciples, and a great multitude of people out of all Judea, and Jerusalem, and from the ¹sea coast of Tyre and Sidon, which came to hear him, and to be healed of their diseases:

18 And they that were vexed with foul spirits, and they were healed.

19 And the whole multitude sought to touch him: for there went virtue out of him, and healed them all:

20 ¶ ᶠ˒¹And he lifted up his eyes upon his disciples, and said, Blessed *be* ye poor: for yours is the kingdom of God.

21 ᵍBlessed *are* ye that hunger now: for ye shall be satisfied: ʰblessed *are* ye that weep now: for ye shall

---

5:34 ¹ Laws generally made without any consideration of circumstances, for fasting and other things of like sort, are not only tyrannous, but very hurtful in the Church.

6:1 ¹ Christ showeth against the superstitious, who stick in every trifle, that the Law of the very Sabbath, was not given to be kept without exception: much less that the salvation of man should consist in the outward keeping of it.

  ² Epiphanius noteth well in his treatise, where he confuteth Ebion, that the time, when the disciples plucked the ears of the corn, was in the feast of unleavened bread: Now, whereas in these feasts which were kept many days together, as the feast of Tabernacles, and the Passover, their first day and their last were of like solemnity, Lev. 23. Luke fitly calleth the last day the second Sab-

bath, though Theophylact understandeth it of any other of them, that followed the first.

6:6 ¹ Charity is the rule of all ceremonies.

6:9 ¹ Whoso helpeth not his neighbor when he can, he killeth him.

6:12 ¹ In that, that Christ useth earnest and long prayer, in choosing twelve of his own company, to the office of the Apostleship, he showeth how religiously we ought to behave ourselves in the choice of Ecclesiastical persons.

6:17 ¹ From all the seacoast, which is called Syro-Phoenecia.

6:20 ¹ Christ teacheth against all Philosophers, and especially the Epicureans, that the chiefest felicity of man is laid up in no place here on earth, but in heaven: and that persecution for righteousness' sake, is the right way unto it.

laugh.

22 [i]Blessed are ye when men hate you, and when [1]they separate you, and revile *you*, and put out your name as evil, for the Son of man's sake.

23 Rejoice ye in that day, and [1]be glad: for behold, your reward *is* great in heaven: for after this manner their fathers did to the Prophets:

24 [j]But woe *be* to you *that are* rich: for ye have [1]received your consolation.

25 [k]Woe *be* to you that are full: for ye shall hunger. Woe *be* to you that now laugh: for ye shall wail and weep.

26 Woe *be* to you when all men speak well of you: for so did their fathers to the false prophets.

27 ¶ [l,1]But I say unto you which hear, Love your enemies: do well to them which hate you.

28 Bless them that curse you, and pray for them which hurt you.

29 [m]And unto him that smiteth thee on the *one* cheek, offer also the other, [n]and him that taketh away thy cloak, forbid not *to take thy* coat also.

30 Give to every man that asketh of thee: and of him that taketh away the *things that be* thine, ask them not again.

31 [o]And as ye would that men should do to you, so do ye to them likewise.

32 [p]For if ye love them which love you, [1]what thank shall ye have? for even the sinners love those that love them.

33 And if ye do good for them which do good for you, what thank shall ye have? for even the sinners do the same.

34 [q]And if ye lend to them of whom ye hope to receive, what thank shall ye have? for even the sinners lend to sinners, to receive the like.

35 Wherefore love ye your enemies, and do good, and lend, [1]looking for nothing again, and your reward shall be great, and ye shall be the children of [r]the most High: for he is kind unto the unkind,

and to the evil.

36 Be ye therefore merciful, as your Father also is merciful.

37 ¶ [s,1]Judge not, and ye shall not be judged: condemn not, and ye shall not be condemned: [2]forgive, and ye shall be forgiven.

38 Give, and it shall be given unto you: [t]a good measure, [1]pressed down, shaken together and running over shall men give into your bosom: for with what measure ye mete, with the same shall men mete to you again.

39 [1]And he spake a parable unto them, [u]Can the blind lead the blind? shall they not both fall into the ditch?

40 [v]The disciple is not above the master: but whosoever *will be* a perfect disciple, shall be as his master.

41 ¶ [w,1]And why seest thou a mote in thy brother's eye, and considerest not the beam that is in thine own eye?

42 Either how canst thou say to thy brother, Brother, let me pull out the mote that is in thine eye, when thou seest not the beam that is in thine own eye? Hypocrite, cast out the beam out of thine own eye first, and then shalt thou see perfectly to pull out the mote that is in thy brother's eye.

43 ¶ [x,1]For it is not a good tree that bringeth forth evil fruit: neither an evil tree, that bringeth forth good fruit.

44 [y]For every tree is known by his own fruit: [z]for neither of thorns gather men figs, nor of bushes gather they grapes.

45 A good man out of the good treasure of his heart bringeth forth good; and an evil man out of the evil treasure of his heart bringeth forth evil: for of the abundance of the heart his mouth speaketh.

46 ¶ [a]But why call ye me Lord, Lord, and do not the things that I speak?

47 [1]Whosoever cometh to me, and heareth my

[i] Matt. 5:11
[j] Amos 6:1
[k] Isa. 65:13
[l] Matt. 5:44
[m] Matt. 5:39
[n] 1 Cor. 6:7
[o] Matt. 7:12
[p] Matt. 5:46
[q] Matt. 5:42
   Deut. 15:8
[r] Matt. 5:45
[s] Matt. 7:1
[t] Matt. 7:2
   Mark 4:24
[u] Matt. 15:14
[v] Matt. 10:24
   John 13:16
   John 15:20
[w] Matt. 7:3
[x] Matt. 7:17
[y] Matt. 12:33
[z] Matt. 7:16
[a] Matt. 7:21
   Rom. 2:13
   James 2:21

6:22 [1] Cast you out of their Synagogues, as John expoundeth it, John 16:2, which is the sharpest punishment the Church hath, if so be the Elders judge rightfully, and by the word of God.

6:23 [1] Leaps (as cattle do, which are provender pricked) for exceeding joy.

6:24 [1] That is, you reap now of your riches, all the commodities and blessings you are ever likely to have, and therefore, you have not to look for any other reward, Matt. 6:2.

6:27 [1] Christian charity, which differeth much from the worldly, doth not only not revenge injuries, but comprehended even our most grievous enemies, and that for our Father's sake, which is in heaven: so far is it, from seeking its own profit in doing well.

6:32 [1] What is there in this your work, that is to be accounted of? for if you look to have commodity by loving, seek those commodities, which are commodities indeed: love your enemies, and so you shall show to the world that you look for those commodities, which come from God.

6:35 [1] When you will lend, do it only to benefit and pleasure withall, and not for hope, to receive the principal again.

6:37 [1] Brotherly reprehension must not proceed of curiosity, nor churlishness, nor malice, but they must be just, moderate, and loving.

[2] He speaketh not here of civil judgments, and therefore by the word, forgive, is meant that good nature, which the Christians use in suffering and pardoning wrongs.

6:38 [1] These are borrowed kinds of speeches taken from them which use to measure dry things, as corn and such like, who use a frank kind of dealing therein, and thrust it down and shake it together, and press it and heap it.

6:39 [1] Unskillful reprehenders hurt both themselves and others: for such as the master is, such is the scholar.

6:41 [1] Hypocrites, which are very severe reprehenders of others, are very quick of sight to spy other men's faults, but very blind to see their own.

6:43 [1] He is a good man, not that is skillful to reprehend others, but he that proveth his uprightness in word and deed.

6:47 [1] Affliction doth at the length discern true godliness from false and feigned.

words, and doeth the same, I will show you to whom he is like:

48 He is like a man which built an house, and dug deep, and laid the foundation on a rock: and when the waters arose, the flood beat upon that house, and could not shake it: for it was grounded upon a rock.

49 But he that heareth and doeth not, is like a man that built an house upon the earth without foundation, against which the flood did beat, and it fell by and by: and the fall of that house was great.

7 *1 Of the Centurion's servant.   9 The Centurion's faith.   11 The widow's son raised from death at Nain.   19 John sendeth his disciples to Christ.   33 His peculiar kind of living.   37 The sinful woman washeth Jesus' feet.*

1 When ^{a,1}he had ended all his sayings in the audience of the people, he entered into Capernaum.

2 And a certain Centurion's servant was sick and ready to die, which was dear unto him.

3 And when he heard of Jesus, he sent unto him the Elders of the Jews, beseeching him that he would come, and heal his servant.

4 So they came to Jesus, and besought him instantly, saying that he was worthy that he should do this for him:

5 For he loveth, *said they*, our nation, and he hath built us a Synagogue.

6 Then Jesus went with them: but when he was now not far from the house, the Centurion sent friends to him, saying unto him, Lord, trouble not thyself: for I am not worthy that thou shouldest enter under my roof:

7 Wherefore I thought not myself worthy to come unto thee: but say the word, and my servant shall be whole:

8 For I likewise am a man set under authority, and have under me soldiers, and I say unto one, Go, and he goeth: and to another, Come, and he cometh: and to my servant, Do this, and he doeth it.

9 When Jesus heard these things, he marveled at him, and turned him, and said to the people that followed him, I say unto you, I have not found so great faith, no not in Israel.

10 And when they that were sent, turned back to the house, they found the servant that was sick, whole.

11 ¹And it came to pass the day after, that he went into a city called ²Nain, and many of his disciples went with him, and a great multitude.

CHAPTER 7
ᵃ Matt. 8:5
ᵇ Matt. 3:1

12 Now when he came near to the gate of the city, behold, there was a dead man carried out, *who was* the only begotten son of his mother, which was a widow, and much people of the city was with her.

13 And when the Lord saw her, he had compassion on her, and said unto her, Weep not.

14 And he went and touched the coffin (and they that bare him, stood still) and he said, Young man, I say unto thee, Arise.

15 And he that was dead, sat up, and began to speak, and he delivered him to his mother.

16 Then there came a fear on them all, and they glorified God, saying, A great Prophet is risen among us, and God hath visited his people.

17 And this rumor of him went forth throughout all Judea, and throughout all the region round about.

18 ¹And the disciples of John showed him of all these things.

19 So John called unto him two certain men of his disciples, and sent them to Jesus, saying, Art thou he that should come, or shall we wait for another?

20 And when the men were come unto him, they said, John Baptist hath sent us unto thee, saying, Art thou he that should come, or shall we wait for another?

21 And ¹at that time, he cured many of their sicknesses, and plagues, and of evil spirits, and unto many blind men he gave sight freely.

22 And Jesus answered, and said unto them, Go your ways and show John, what things ye have seen and heard, that the blind see, the halt go, the lepers are cleansed, the deaf hear, the dead are raised, *and* the poor receive the Gospel.

23 And blessed is he, that shall not be offended in me.

24 ¹And when the messengers of John were departed, he began to speak unto the people of John, What went ye out into the wilderness to see? A reed shaken with the wind?

25 But what went ye out to see? A man clothed in soft raiment? behold, they which are gorgeously appareled, and live delicately, are in Kings' courts.

26 But what went ye forth to see? A Prophet? yea, I say to you, and greater than a Prophet.

27 This is he of whom it is written, ᵇBehold, I send my messenger before thy face, which shall prepare thy way before thee.

28 For I say unto you, there is no greater Prophet

7:1 ¹ Christ admonisheth the Jews, by setting before them the example of the Centurion, that for their obstinacy and rebellion, he will go to the Gentiles.

7:11 ¹ Christ avoucheth openly his power over death.

² Nain is the name of a town in Galilee, which was situated on the other side of Kishon, which falleth into the sea of Galilee.

7:18 ¹ John sendeth from the prison his unbelieving disciples, to Christ himself, to be confirmed.

7:21 ¹ When John's disciples came to Christ.

7:24 ¹ That which the Prophets showed long before, John showeth at hand: and Christ himself doth present it daily unto us, in the Gospel, but for the most part in vain, for that many seek nothing else, but foolish toys and vain glory.

than John, among them that are begotten of women: nevertheless, he that is the least in the kingdom of God, is greater than he.

29 Then all the people that heard, and the Publicans [1]justified God, being baptized with the baptism of John.

30 But the Pharisees and the expounders of the Law despised the counsel of God [1]against themselves, and *were* not baptized of him.

31 [c][1]And the Lord said, Whereunto shall I liken the men of this generation? and what thing are they like unto?

32 They are like unto little children sitting in the marketplace, and crying one to another, and saying, We have piped unto you, and ye have not danced: we have mourned to you, and ye have not wept.

33 For John Baptist came neither eating bread, nor drinking wine: and ye say, He hath the devil.

34 The Son of man is come, and eateth, and drinketh: and ye say, Behold, a man *which is* a glutton, and a drinker of wine, a friend of Publicans and sinners:

35 But wisdom is justified of all her children.

36 ¶ [1]And one of the Pharisees desired him that he would eat with him: and he went into the Pharisee's house, and sat down at table.

37 And behold, a woman in the city, which was a sinner, when she knew that Jesus sat at table in the Pharisee's house, she brought a box of ointment.

38 [d]And she stood at his feet behind him weeping, and began to wash his feet with tears, and did wipe them with the hairs of her head, and kissed his feet, and anointed them with the ointment.

39 [1]Now when the Pharisee which bade him, saw it, he spake within himself, saying, If this man were a Prophet, he would surely have known who, and what manner of woman this is which toucheth him: [2]for she is a sinner.

40 [1]And Jesus answered, and said unto him, Simon, I have somewhat to say unto thee. And he said, Master, say on.

41 There was a certain lender which had two debtors: the one ought five hundred pence, and the

[c] Matt. 11:16
[d] Mark 15:42
John 20:11

CHAPTER 8

[a] Mark 16:9

other fifty:

42 When they had nothing to pay, he forgave them both: Which of them therefore, tell *me*, will love him most?

43 Simon answered, and said, I suppose that he to whom he forgave most. And he said unto him, Thou hast truly judged.

44 Then he turned to the woman, and said unto Simon, Seest thou this woman? I entered into thine house, and thou gavest me no water to my feet: but she hath washed my feet with tears, and wiped them with the hairs of her head.

45 Thou gavest me no kiss: but she, since the time I came in, hath not ceased to kiss my feet.

46 Mine head with oil thou didst not anoint: but she hath anointed my feet with ointment.

47 Wherefore I say unto thee, many sins are forgiven her: [1]for she loved much. To whom a little is forgiven, he doth love a little.

48 And he said unto her, Thy sins are forgiven thee.

49 And they that sat at table with him, began to say within themselves, Who is this that even forgiveth sins?

50 And he said to the woman, Thy faith hath saved thee: [1]go in peace.

8 *1 Women that minister unto Christ of their substance.   4 The parable of the sower.   16 The candle.   19 Christ's mother and brethren.   22 He rebuked the winds.   26 Of Legion.   37 The Gadarenes reject Christ.   41 Jairus's daughter healed.   43 The woman delivered from the issue of blood.   52 Weeping for the dead.*

1 And it came to pass afterward, that he himself went through every city and town, preaching and publishing the kingdom of God, and the twelve *were* with him,

2 And certain women, which were healed of evil spirits, and infirmities, *as* [a]Mary which was called Magdalene, out of whom went seven devils,

3 And Joanna the wife of Chuza Herod's steward, and Susanna, and many others which ministered

---

7:29 [1] Said that he was just, good, faithful, and merciful.
7:30 [1] To their own hurt.
7:31 [1] What way soever God followeth in offering us the Gospel, the most part of men procure offences unto themselves: yet notwithstanding some Church is gathered together.
7:36 [1] Proud men deprive themselves of the benefits of the presence of Christ, even then when he is at home with them in their houses; which the humble and base do enjoy.
7:39 [1] Rashness is the fellow of pride.
      [2] The Pharisee respecteth the Law, which holdeth them defiled, that touch the defiled.
7:40 [1] To love Christ, is a sure and perpetual witness of remission of sins.
7:47 [1] That is, saith Theophylact, she hath sheweth her faith

abundantly: and Basil in his sermon of Baptism saith, He that oweth much, hath much forgiven him, that he may love much more: And therefore Christ's saying is so plain by the similitude, that it is a wonder to see the enemies of the truth draw and rack this place so soundly to establish their meritorious works: for the greater sum a man hath forgiven him, the more he loveth him that hath been so gracious to him: And this woman sheweth by duties of love, how great the benefit was she had received: and therefore the charity that is here spoken of, is not to be taken for the cause, but as a sign: for Christ saith not as the Pharisees did, that she was a sinner, but beareth her witness that the sins of her life past are forgiven her.
7:50 [1] He confirmeth the benefit which he had bestowed with a blessing.

unto him of their substance.

4 [b,1]Now when much people were gathered together, and were come unto him out of all cities, he spake by a parable.

5 A sower went out to sow his seed, and as he sowed, some fell by the wayside, and it was trodden under feet, and the fowls of heaven devoured it up.

6 And some fell on the stones, and when it was sprung up, it withered away, because it lacked moistness.

7 And some fell among thorns, and the thorns sprang up with it, and choked it.

8 And some fell on good ground, and sprang up, and bare fruit, an hundredfold. And as he said these things, he cried, He that hath ears to hear, let him hear.

9 Then his disciples asked him, demanding what parable that was.

10 And he said, Unto you it is given to know the [1]secrets of the kingdom of God, but to others in parables, that when [c]they see, they should not see, and when they hear, they should not understand.

11 [d]The parable is this, The seed is the word of God.

12 And they that are beside the way, are they that hear: afterward cometh the devil, and taketh away the word out of their hearts, lest they should believe, and be saved.

13 But they that are on the stones, *are they* which when they have heard, receive the word with joy: but they have no roots: which for a while believe, but in the time of temptation go away.

14 And that which fell among thorns, are they which have heard, and after [1]their departure are choked with cares and with riches, and voluptuous living, and [2]bring forth no fruit.

15 But that *which fell* in good ground, are they which with an [1]honest and good heart hear the word,

Cross references (center column):
[b] Matt. 13:3 / Mark 4:1
[c] Isa. 6:9 / Matt. 13:14 / Mark 4:12 / John 12:40 / Acts 28:26 / Rom. 11:8
[d] Matt. 13:8 / Mark 4:15
[e] Luke 12:33 / Matt. 5:15 / Mark 4:21
[f] Matt. 10:26 / Mark 4:22 / Luke 12:2
[g] Matt. 13:12 / Matt. 25:29 / Mark 4:25 / Luke 19:26
[h] Matt. 12:46 / Mark 3:32
[i] Matt. 8:23 / Mark 4:36
[j] Matt. 8:28 / Mark 5:1

[2]and keep it, and bring forth fruit with patience.

16 ¶ [e,1]No man when he hath lighted a candle, covereth it under a vessel, neither putteth it under the bed, but setteth it on a candlestick, that they that enter in, may see the light.

17 [f]For nothing is secret, that shall not be evident: neither anything hid, that shall not be known, and come to light.

18 [1]Take [2]heed therefore how ye hear: for [g]whosoever hath, to him shall be given: and whosoever hath not, from him shall be taken even that [3]which it seemeth that he hath.

19 ¶ [h,1]Then came to him his mother and his brethren, and could not come near to him for the press.

20 And it was told him *by certain* which said, Thy mother and thy brethren stand without, and would see thee.

21 But he answered, and said unto them, My mother and my brethren are these which hear the word of God, and do it.

22 ¶ [i,1]And it came to pass on a certain day, that he went into a ship with his disciples, and he said unto them, Let us go over unto the other side of the lake. And they launched forth.

23 And as they sailed, he fell [1]asleep, and there came down a storm of wind on the lake, and [2]they were filled with water, and were in jeopardy.

24 Then they went to him, and awoke him, saying, Master, Master, we perish. And he arose, and rebuked the wind, and the waves of water: and they ceased, and it was calm.

25 Then he said unto them, Where is your faith? and they feared, and wondered among themselves, saying, Who is this that commandeth both the winds and water, and they obey him!

26 ¶ [j]So they sailed unto the region of the Gadarenes, which is over against Galilee.

27 [1]And as he went out to land, there met him a

8:4 [1] The selfsame Gospel is sown everywhere, but not with like fruit, and that through the only fault of men themselves.

8:10 [1] Those things are called secret, which may not be uttered: for the word used here, is as much as we say in our tongue, to hold a man's peace.

8:14 [1] That is, so soon as they have heard the word, they go about their business.

[2] They bring not forth perfect and full fruit to the ripening: or, they begin, but they bring not to an end.

8:15 [1] Which seeketh not only to seem such a one, but is so indeed: so that this word, Honest, respecteth the outward life, and the word, good, is referred to the good gifts of the mind.

[2] With much ado: for the devil and the flesh fight against the spirit of God, which is a new guest.

8:16 [1] That that every man hath received in private, he ought to bestow to the use and profit of all men.

8:18 [1] Heavenly gifts are lost with niggardliness, and increase with liberality.

[2] That is, with what minds you come to hear the word, and how you behave yourselves when you have heard it.

[3] Either to himself, or to others, or to both: for there are none so proud, as these fellows, if it were possible to see that, that they cloke: neither are there that deceive the simple more than they do.

8:19 [1] There is no knot of flesh and blood, among men so nigh and strait, as the band which is between Christ, and them who embrace him with a true faith.

8:22 [1] It is expedient for us sometimes to come into extreme danger, as though Christ passed not for us, that we may have a better trial, both of his power, and also of our weakness.

8:23 [1] Jesus fell on sleep: and it appeareth, that he was very fast on sleep, because they called twice before he awoke.

[2] Not the disciples, but the ship.

8:27 [1] Christ showeth, by casting out a Legion of devils by his word only, that his heavenly virtue was appointed to deliver men from the slavery of the devil: but foolish men will not for the most part redeem this so excellent grace freely offered unto them, with the least loss of their pelting pelf.

certain man out of the city, which had devils long time, and he wore no garment, neither abode in house, but in the graves.

28 And when he saw Jesus, he cried out, and fell down before him, and with a loud voice said, What have I to do with thee, Jesus the son of God the most High? I beseech thee torment me not.

29 For he commanded the foul spirit to come out of the man: (for oft times he had caught him: therefore he was bound with chains, and kept in fetters: but he brake the bands, [1]and was carried of the devil into wildernesses.)

30 Then Jesus asked him, saying, What is thy name? and he said, Legion, because many devils were entered into him.

31 And they besought him, that he would not command them to go out into the deep.

32 And there was thereby an herd of many swine feeding on an hill: and the *devils* besought him, that he would suffer them to enter into them. So he suffered them.

33 Then went the devils out of the man, and entered into the swine: and the herd was carried with violence from a steep down place into the lake, and was choked.

34 When the herdsmen saw what was done, they fled: and when they were departed, they told it in the city and in the country.

35 Then they came out to see what was done, and came to Jesus, and found the man, out of whom the devils were departed, sitting at the feet of Jesus, clothed, and in his right mind: and they were afraid.

36 They also which saw it, told them by what means he that was possessed with the devil, was healed.

37 Then the whole multitude of the country about the Gadarenes, besought him that he would depart from them: for they were taken with a great fear: and he went into the ship, and returned.

38 Then the man, out of whom the devils were departed, besought him that he might be with him: but Jesus sent him away, saying,

39 Return into thine own house, and show what great things God hath done to thee. So he went his way, and preached [1]throughout all the city, what great things Jesus had done unto him.

40 ¶ And it came to pass, when Jesus was come again, that the people [1]received him: for they all

k Matt. 9:18
Mark 5:22

waited for him.

41 ¶ [k,1]And behold, there came a man named Jairus, and he was the ruler of the Synagogue, who fell down at Jesus' feet, and besought him that he would come into his house.

42 For he had but a daughter only, about twelve years of age, and she lay a dying (and as he went, the people thronged him.

43 And a woman having an issue of blood, twelve years long, which had spent all her [1]substance upon physicians, and could not be healed of any:

44 When she came behind *him*, she touched the hem of his garment, and immediately her issue of blood stanched.

45 Then Jesus said, Who is it that hath touched me? When every man denied, Peter said and they that were with him, Master, the multitude thrust thee, and tread on thee, and sayest thou, Who hath touched me?

46 And Jesus said, Someone hath touched me: for I perceive that virtue is gone out of me.

47 When the woman saw that she was not hid, she came trembling, and fell down before him, and told him before all the people: for what cause she had touched him, and how she was healed immediately.

48 And he said unto her, Daughter, be of good comfort: thy faith hath saved thee: go in peace.)

49 While he yet spake, there came one from the ruler of the Synagogue's house, which said to him, Thy daughter is dead: disease not the Master.

50 When Jesus heard it, he answered him, saying, Fear not: believe only, and she shall be saved.

51 And when he went into the house, he suffered no man to go in with him, save Peter, and James, and John, and the father and mother of the maid.

52 And all wept, and [1]sorrowed for her: but he said, Weep not: for she is not dead, but sleepeth.

53 And they laughed him to scorn, knowing that she was dead.

54 So he thrust them all out, and took her by the hand, and cried, saying, Maid, arise.

55 And her spirit came again, and she [1]rose straightway: and he commanded to give her meat.

56 Then her parents were astonied: but he commanded them that they should tell no man what was done.

8:29 [1] By force and violence, as a horse when he is spurred.
8:39 [1] To wit, the city of the Gadarenes: and though Mark says that he preached it in Decapolis, they differ not, for Pliny recordeth, lib. 5, chap. 18, that Gadara is a town of Decapolis, so that Decapolis was partly on this side Jordan, and partly on the other side.
8:40 [1] The multitude was glad he was come again, and rejoiced greatly.
8:41 [1] Christ showeth by a double miracle, that he is Lord both of

life and death.
8:43 [1] All that she had to live upon.
8:52 [1] The word signifieth to beat and strike, and is transferred to the mournings and lamentations, that are at burials, at which times men use such kind of behavior.
8:55 [1] The corpse was laid out, and the wench received life, and rose out of the bed, that all the world might see, she was not only restored to life, but also void of all sickness.

9 1 *The Apostles are sent to preach.* 7 *and* 19 *The common people's opinion of Christ.* 12 *Of the five loaves and two fishes.* 20 *The Apostle's confession.* 24 *To lose the life.* 35 *We must hear Christ.* 39 *The possessed of a spirit.* 46 *Strife among the Apostles for the Primacy.* 49 *One casting out devils in Christ's Name.* 52 *The Samaritans will not receive Christ.* 55 *Revenge forbidden.* 57, 59, 61 *Of three that would follow Christ, but on divers conditions.*

1 Then [a,1]called he his twelve disciples together, and gave them power and authority over all devils, and to heal diseases.

2 [b]And he sent them forth to preach the kingdom of God, and to cure the sick.

3 And he said to them, [c]Take nothing to your journey, neither staves, nor scrip, neither bread, nor silver, neither have two coats apiece.

4 And whatsoever house ye enter into, there [1]abide, and thence depart.

5 And how many soever will not receive you, when ye go out of that city, [d]shake off the very dust from your feet for a testimony against them.

6 And they went out, and went through every town preaching the Gospel, and healing everywhere.

7 ¶ [e,1]Now Herod the Tetrarch heard of all that was done by him: and he [2]doubted, because that it was said of some, that John was risen again from the dead:

8 And of some, that Elijah had appeared: and of some, that one of the old Prophets was risen again.

9 Then Herod said, John have I beheaded: who then is this of whom I hear such things? and he desired to see him.

10 ¶ [f,1]And when the Apostles returned, they told him what great things they had done. [g]Then he took them to him, and went aside into a [2]solitary place, *near* to the city called Bethsaida.

11 But when the people knew it, they followed him: and he received them, and spake unto them of the kingdom of God, and healed them that had

CHAPTER 9
[a] Matt. 10:1
Mark 3:13
Mark 6:7
[b] Matt. 10:7
[c] Matt. 10:9
Mark 6:8
[d] Luke 10:11
Matt. 10:14
Mark 6:11
Acts 13:51
[e] Matt. 14:1
Mark 6:14
[f] Mark 6:30
[g] Matt. 14:13
Mark 6:32
[h] Matt. 14:15
Mark 6:35
John 6:5
[i] Matt. 16:13
Mark 8:27
[j] Matt. 17:22
Mark 8:31
[k] Luke 14:27
Matt. 10:38
Matt. 16:24
Mark 8:34
[l] Luke 17:33
Matt. 16:39
Matt. 16:25
John 12:25

need to be healed.

12 [h]And when the day began to wear away, the twelve came, and said unto him, Send the people away, that they may go into the towns and villages round about, and lodge, and get meat: for we are here in a desert place.

13 But he said unto them, Give ye them to eat. And they said, We have no more but five loaves and two fishes, [1]except we should go and buy meat for all this people.

14 For they were about five thousand men. Then he said to his disciples, Cause them to sit down by fifties in a company.

15 And they did so, and caused all to sit down.

16 Then he took the five loaves, and the two fishes, and looked up to heaven, and [1]blessed them, and brake, and gave to the disciples, to set before the people.

17 So they did all eat, and were satisfied: and there was taken up of that remained to them, twelve baskets full of broken meat.

18 ¶ [i,1]And it came to pass, as he was [2]alone praying, his disciples were with him: and he asked them, saying, Whom say the people that I am?

19 They answered, and said, John Baptist: and others say, Elijah: and some say, that one of the old Prophets is risen again.

20 And he said unto them, But whom say ye that I am? Peter answered, and said: That Christ of God.

21 And he warned them and commanded them, that they should tell that to no man,

22 [1]Saying, [j]The Son of man must suffer many things, and be reproved of the Elders, and of the high Priests and Scribes, and be slain, and the third day rise again.

23 ¶ [k]And he said to them all, If any man will come after me, let him deny himself, and take up his cross [1]daily, and follow me.

24 [l]For whosoever will save his life, shall lose it: and whosoever shall lose his life for my sake, the

---

9:1 [1] The twelve Apostles are sent forth at the only commandment of Christ, and furnished with the power of the holy Ghost: both that none of the Israelites might pretend ignorance, and also that they might be better prepared to their general ambassy.

9:4 [1] When you depart out of any city, depart from thence where you first took up your lodging: so that in few words, the Lord forbiddeth them to change their lodgings: for this publishing of the Gospel, was as it were a thorough passage, that none of Judea might pretend ignorance, as though he had not heard that Christ was come.

9:7 [1] So soon as the world heareth tidings of the Gospel, it is divided into divers opinions, and the tyrants especially are afraid.

[2] He stuck as it were fast in the mire.

9:10 [1] They shall lack nothing that follow Christ, no not in the wilderness.

[2] The word signifieth a desert: note this was not in the town Bethsaida, but part of the fields belonging to the town.

9:13 [1] This is unperfectly spoken, and therefore we must understand something, as this, we cannot give them to eat, unless we go and buy, etc.

9:16 [1] He gave God thanks for these loaves and fishes, and withall prayed him to feed this so great a multitude with so small a quantity, and to be short, that this whole banquet might be to the glory of God.

9:18 [1] Although the world be tossed up and down, betwixt divers errors, yet we ought not to contemn the truth, but be so much the more desirous to know it, and be more constant to confess it.

[2] Alone from the people.

9:22 [1] Christ himself attained to the heavenly glory by the cross and invincible patience.

9:23 [1] Even as one day followeth another, so doth one cross follow another, and the cross is by the figure Metonymy, taken for the miseries of this life: for to be hanged, was the sorest and cruelest punishment that was amongst the Jews.

same shall save it.

25 ᵐFor what advantageth it a man, if he win the whole world, and destroy himself, or lose himself?

26 ⁿFor whosoever shall be ashamed of me, and of my words, of him shall the Son of man be ashamed, when he shall come in his glory, and *in the glory* of the Father, and of the holy Angels.

27 ᵒAnd I tell you of a surety, there be some standing here, which shall not taste of death, till they have seen the kingdom of God.

28 ᵖ,¹And it came to pass about an eight days after those words, that he took Peter and John, and James, and went up into a mountain to pray.

29 And as he prayed, the fashion of his countenance was changed, and his garment *was* white and glistered.

30 And behold, two men talked with him, which were Moses and Elijah:

31 Which appeared in glory, and told of his ¹departing, which he should accomplish at Jerusalem.

32 But Peter and they that were with him, were heavy with sleep, and when they awoke, they saw his glory, and the two men standing with him.

33 And it came to pass, as they departed from him, Peter said unto Jesus, Master, it is good for us to be here: let us therefore make three tabernacles, one for thee, and one for Moses, and one for Elijah, and wist not what he said.

34 While he thus spake, there came a cloud and overshadowed them, and they feared when they were entering into the cloud.

35 ᵠAnd there came a voice out of the cloud, saying, This is that my beloved Son, hear him.

36 And when the voice was past, Jesus was found alone: and they kept it close, and told no man in ¹those days any of those things which they had seen.

37 ¶ ¹And it came to pass on the next day, as they came down from the mountain, much people met him.

38 ʳAnd behold, a man of the company cried out, saying, Master, I beseech thee, behold my son: for he is all that I have.

39 And lo, a spirit taketh him, and suddenly he crieth, and he teareth him, that he foameth, and hardly

ᵐ Matt. 16:26
Mark 8:36
ⁿ Luke 12:9
Matt. 10:33
Mark 8:38
2 Tim. 2:12
ᵒ Matt. 16:28
Mark 9:1
ᵖ Matt. 17:2
Mark 9:2
ᵠ 2 Pet. 1:17
ʳ Matt. 17:14
Mark 9:17
ˢ Matt. 17:22
Mark 9:31
ᵗ Matt. 18:1
Mark 9:35
ᵘ Mark 9:38
ᵛ 2 Kings 1:10
2 Kings 12:13

departeth from him, when he hath ¹bruised him.

40 Now I have besought thy disciples to cast him out, but they could not.

41 Then Jesus answered and said, O generation faithless, and crooked, how long now shall I be with you, and suffer you? bring thy son hither.

42 And while he was yet coming, the devil rent him, and tore him: and Jesus rebuked the unclean spirit, and healed the child, and delivered him to his father.

43 ¶ ¹And they were all amazed at the mighty power of God: and while they all wondered at all things which Jesus did, he said unto his disciples,

44 ¹Mark these words diligently: ˢfor it shall come to pass, that the son of man shall be delivered into the hands of men.

45 But they understood not that word: for it was hid from them, *so* that they could not perceive it: and they feared to ask him of that word.

46 ¶ ᵗ,¹Then there arose a disputation among them, which of them should be the greatest.

47 When Jesus saw the thoughts of their hearts, he took a little child, and set him by him,

48 And said unto them, Whosoever receiveth this little child in my Name, receiveth me: and whosoever shall receive me, receiveth him that sent me: for he that is least among you all, he shall be great.

49 ¶ ᵘ,¹And John answered and said, Master, we saw one casting out devils in thy Name, and we forbad him, because he followeth *thee* not with us.

50 Then Jesus said unto him, Forbid ye *him* not: for he that is not against us, is with us.

51 ¶ ¹And it came to pass, when the days were accomplished, that he should be received up, he ²settled himself fully to go to Jerusalem,

52 And sent messengers before him: and they went and entered into a town of the Samaritans, to prepare him *lodging*.

53 But they would not receive him, because his behavior was *as* though he would go to Jerusalem.

54 ¹And when his disciples, James and John saw it, they said, Lord, wilt thou that we command, that fire come down from heaven, and consume them, even as ᵛElijah did?

9:28 ¹ Lest the disciples of Christ should be offended at the debasing himself in his flesh, he teacheth them that it is voluntary, showing therewithall for a space the brightness of his glory.

9:31 ¹ What death he should die in Jerusalem.

9:36 ¹ Until Christ was risen again from the dead.

9:37 ¹ Christ is offended with nothing so much as with incredulity, although he bears with it for a time.

9:39 ¹ As it fareth in the falling sickness.

9:43 ¹ We have no cause to promise ourselves rest and quietness in this world, seeing that they themselves which seemed to fawn upon Christ, do shortly after crucify him.

9:44 ¹ Give diligent ear unto them, and when you have once heard

them, see that you keep them.

9:46 ¹ The end of ambition is ignomy; but the end of modest obedience is glory.

9:49 ¹ Extraordinary things are neither rashly to be allowed, nor condemned.

9:51 ¹ Christ goeth willingly to death.

² Word for word: he hardened his face, that is, he resolved with himself to die, and therefore ventured upon his journey, and cast away all fear of death, and went on.

9:54 ¹ We must take heed of the immoderateness of zeal, and fond imitation, even in good causes, that whatsoever we do, we do it to God's glory, and the profit of our neighbor.

55 But Jesus turned about, and rebuked them, and said, Ye know not of what ¹spirit ye are.

56 For the Son of man is not come to destroy men's lives, but to save them. Then they went to another town.

57 ¶ ¹And it came to pass that as they went in the way, ʷa certain man said unto him, I will follow thee, Lord, whithersoever thou goest.

58 And Jesus said unto him, The foxes have holes, and the birds of the heaven nests, but the Son of man hath not whereon to lay his head.

59 ¹But he said unto another, Follow me. And the same said, Lord, suffer me first to go and bury my father.

60 And Jesus said unto him, Let the dead bury ¹their dead: but go thou, and preach the kingdom of God.

61 ¹Then another said, I will follow thee, Lord: but let me first go bid them farewell, which are at mine house.

62 And Jesus said unto him, No man that putteth his hand to the plough, and looketh back, is apt to the kingdom of God.

10

1 *The seventy disciples.*   10 *The unthankful cities charged with impiety.*   17 *The disciples returning home, are warned to be humble.*   29, 30 *Who is our neighbor.*   38 *Of Martha and her sister Mary.*

1 After ᵃˑ¹these things, the Lord appointed other seventy also, and sent them, two and two before him into every city and place, whither he himself should come.

2 And he said unto them, ᵇThe harvest *is* great, but the laborers *are* few: pray therefore the Lord of the harvest to send forth laborers into his harvest.

3 ᶜˑ¹Go your ways: behold, I send you forth as lambs among wolves.

4 Bear no bag, neither scrip, nor shoes, and ᵈsalute

ʷ Matt. 8:19

CHAPTER 10
ᵃ Matt. 10:1
ᵇ Matt. 9:37
ᶜ Matt. 10:16
ᵈ 2 Kings 4:29
ᵉ Matt. 10:12
   Mark 6:10
ᶠ Deut. 24:14
   Matt. 10:10
   1 Tim. 5:18
ᵍ Matt. 10:11
ʰ Luke 9:5
   Acts 33:51
   Acts 18:6
ⁱ Matt. 11:21
ʲ Matt. 10:40
   John 13:20

¹no man by the way.

5 ᵉAnd into whatsoever house ye enter, first say, Peace *be* to this house.

6 And if ¹the son of peace be there, your peace shall rest upon him, if not, it shall turn to you again.

7 And in that house ¹tarry still, eating and drinking such things as by them *shall be set before you:* ᶠfor the laborer is worthy of his wages. Go not from house to house.

8 ᵍBut into whatsoever city ye shall enter, if they receive you, ¹eat such things as are set before you,

9 And heal the sick that are there, and say unto them, The kingdom of God is come near unto you.

10 ¹But into whatsoever city ye shall enter, if they will not receive you, go your ways out into the streets of the same, and say,

11 Even the very ʰdust, which cleaveth on us of your city, we wipe off against you: notwithstanding know this, that the kingdom of God was come near unto you.

12 For I say to you, that it shall be easier in that day for them of Sodom, than for that city.

13 ⁱWoe *be* to thee, Chorazin: woe *be* to thee, Bethsaida: for if the miracles had been done in Tyre and Sidon, which have been done in you, they had a great while agone repented, sitting in sackcloth and ashes.

14 Therefore it shall be easier for Tyre, and Sidon, at the judgment, than for you.

15 And thou, Capernaum, which art exalted to heaven, shalt be thrust down to hell.

16 ¶ʲHe that heareth you, heareth me: and he that despiseth you, despiseth me: and he that despiseth me, despiseth him that sent me.

17 ¶ ¹And the seventy turned again with joy, saying, Lord, even the devils are subdued to us ²through thy Name.

9:55 ¹ So speak the Hebrews, that is, you know not what will, mind, and counsel you are of: so the gifts of God are called the spirit, because they are given of God's Spirit, and so are they, that are contrary to them, which proceed of the wicked spirit, as the spirit of covetousness, of pride, and madness.

9:57 ¹ Such as follow Christ, must prepare themselves, to suffer all discommodities.

9:59 ¹ The calling of God ought to be preferred, without all controversy before all duties that we owe to men.

9:60 ¹ Who notwithstanding that they live in this frail life of man, yet are strangers from the true life, which is everlasting and heavenly.

9:61 ¹ Such as follow Christ, must at once renounce all worldly cares.

10:1 ¹ The seventy are sent as the second forewarners, of the coming of Christ.

10:3 ¹ The faithful ministers of the word are in this world as lambs among wolves: but if they be diligent to do their duty, he that sent them will also preserve them.

10:4 ¹ This is spoken after the manner of a figure, which men use, when they put down more in words, than is meant: usually among

the Hebrews, when they command a thing to be done speedily without delay, as 2 Kings 4:29: for otherwise courteous and gentle salutations, are points of Christian duty: as for the calling it was but for a season.

10:6 ¹ So speak the Hebrews: that is, he that favoreth the doctrine of peace and embraceth it.

10:7 ¹ Take up your lodging in that house, which ye first enter into, that is, be not careful for commodious lodging, as men do which purpose to stay long in a place: for here is not instituted that solemn preaching of the Gospel, which was used afterward ,when the Churches were settled: but these are sent abroad to all the coasts of Judea, to give them to understand, that the last Jubilee is at hand.

10:8 ¹ Content yourselves with that meat that is set before you.

10:10 ¹ God is a most severe revenger of the ministry of his Gospel.

10:17 ¹ Neither the gift of miracles, neither what else soever excellent gift, but only our election giveth us occasion of true joy: and the only publishing of the Gospel is the destruction of Satan.

² For Christ's disciples used no absolute authority, but wrought such miracles as they did, by calling upon Christ's Name.

18 And he said unto them, I saw Satan, like lightning, ¹fall down from heaven.

19 Behold, I give unto you power to tread on Serpents, and Scorpions, and over all the power of the enemy, and nothing shall ¹hurt you.

20 Nevertheless, in this rejoice not, that the spirits are subdued unto you: but rather rejoice, because your names are written in heaven.

21 ¶ ¹That same hour rejoiced Jesus in the spirit, and said, I confess unto thee, Father, Lord of heaven and earth, that thou hast hid these things from the ²wise and understanding, and hast revealed them to babes: even so, Father, because it so pleased thee. ³

22 ¹All things are given me of my Father: and no man knoweth who the son is, but the Father: neither who the Father is, save the Son, and he to whom the Son will reveal him.

23 ¶ ¹And he turned to his disciples, and said secretly, ᵏBlessed *are* the eyes, which see that ye see.

24 For I tell you that many Prophets and Kings have desired to see those things, which ye see, and have not seen *them*: and to hear those things which ye hear, and have not heard *them*.

25 ¶ ᴸ¹Then behold, ²a certain Lawyer stood up, and tempted him, saying, Master, what shall I do to inherit eternal life?

26 And he said unto him, What is written in the Law? how readest thou?

27 And he answered and said, ᵐThou shalt love thy Lord God with all thine heart, and with all thy soul, and with all thy strength, and with all thy thought, ⁿand thy neighbor as thyself.

28 Then he said unto him, Thou hast answered right: this do, and thou shalt live.

29 ¹But he willing to ²justify himself, said unto Jesus, Who is then my neighbor?

30 And Jesus answered, and said, A certain man went down from Jerusalem to Jericho, and fell among thieves, and they robbed him of his raiment, and wounded him, and departed, leaving him half dead.

31 Now so it fell out, that there came down a certain Priest that same way, and when he saw him, he passed by on the other side.

32 And likewise also a Levite, when he was come

k Matt. 13:16
l Matt. 22:35
  Mark 12:28
m Deut. 6:5
n Lev. 19:18

CHAPTER 11
a Matt. 6:9

near to the place, went and looked *on him*, and passed by on the other side.

33 Then a certain Samaritan, as he journeyed, came near unto him, and when he saw him, he had compassion on him,

34 And went to him, and bound up his wounds and poured in oil and wine, and put him on his own beast, and brought him to an Inn, and made provision for him.

35 And on the morrow when he departed, he took out two pence, and gave them to the host, and said unto him, Take care of him, and whatsoever thou spendest more, when I come again, I will recompense thee.

36 Which now of these three, thinkest thou, was neighbor unto him that fell among the thieves?

37 And he said, He that showed mercy on him. Then said Jesus unto him, Go, and do thou likewise.

38 ¶ ¹Now it came to pass, as they went, that he entered into a certain town, and a certain woman named Martha, received him into her house.

39 And she had a sister called Mary, which also sat at Jesus' feet, and heard his preaching.

40 But Martha was cumbered about much serving, and came to him, and said, Master, dost thou not care that my sister hath left me to serve alone? bid her therefore, that she help me.

41 And Jesus answered, and said unto her, Martha, Martha, thou carest, and art troubled about many things:

42 But one thing is needful, Mary hath chosen the good part, which shall not be taken away from her.

11

1 He teacheth his Apostles to pray.   14 The dumb devil driven out.   27 A woman of the company lifted up her voice.   29 The Jews require signs.   37 He being feasted of the Pharisee, reproveth the outward show of holiness.

1 And so it was, that as he was praying in a certain place, when he ceased, one of his disciples said unto him, Lord, teach us to pray, as John also taught his disciples.

2 ᵃAnd he said unto them, When ye pray, say, ¹Our Father which art in heaven, hallowed be thy Name. Thy kingdom come: Let thy will be done, even in earth, as *it is* in heaven:

10:18 ¹ Paul placeth the devil and his angels, in the air, Eph. 6:12, and he is said to be cast down from thence by force when his power is abolished by the voice of the Gospel.

10:19 ¹ Shall do you wrong.

10:21 ¹ The Church is contemptible, if we behold the outward face of it, but the wisdom of God is not so marvelous, in any thing, as in it.

  ² Of this world.

  ³ Then he turned to his disciples, and said, *Is read in some copies.*

10:22 ¹ Whosoever seeketh the Father without the Son, wandereth out of the way.

10:23 ¹ The difference of the old Testament and the new consisteth in the measure of revelation.

10:25 ¹ Faith doth not take away, but establisheth the doctrine of the Law.

  ² One of them that professed himself to be learned in the rites and laws of Moses.

10:29 ¹ All they are comprehended in the name of our neighbor, by the Law, whomsoever we may help.

  ² That is, to vouch his righteousness, or show, that he was just, that is, void of all faults: and James 5:1 useth the word of justification in this sense.

10:38 ¹ Christ careth not to be entertained delicately, but to be heard diligently, that is it which he especially requireth.

11:2 ¹ A form of true prayer.

3 Our daily bread give us [1]for the day:

4 And forgive us our sins: for even we forgive every man that is indebted to us: And lead us not into temptation: but deliver us from evil.

5 ¶ [1]Moreover he said unto them, Which of you shall have a friend, and shall go to him at midnight, and say unto him, Friend, lend me three loaves?

6 For a friend of mine is come out of the way to me, and I have nothing to set before him:

7 And he within should answer, and say, Trouble me not: the door is now shut, and my children are with me in bed: I cannot rise and give them to thee.

8 I say unto you, Though he would not arise and give him, because he is his friend, yet doubtless because of his [1]importunity, he would rise and give him as many as he needed.

9 [b]And I say unto you, Ask, and it shall be given you: seek, and ye shall find: knock, and it shall be opened unto you.

10 [c]For everyone that asketh, receiveth: and he that seeketh, findeth: and to him that knocketh, it shall be opened.

11 [d]If a son shall ask bread of any of you that is a father, will he give him a stone? or if he ask a fish, will he for a fish give him a serpent?

12 Or if he ask an egg, will he give him a scorpion?

13 If ye then which are evil, can give good gifts unto your children, how much more shall your heavenly Father give the holy Ghost to them that desire him?

14 ¶ [e]Then he cast out a devil which was dumb: and when the devil was gone out, the dumb spake, and the people wondered.

15 [1]But some of them said, [f]He casteth out devils through Beelzebub the chief of the devils.

16 And others tempted him, seeking of him a sign from heaven.

17 [1]But he knew their thoughts, and said unto them, [g]Every kingdom divided against itself, shall be desolate, and an house *divided* against an house, falleth.

18 So if Satan also be divided against himself, how shall his kingdom stand, because ye say that I

[b] Matt. 7:7
Matt. 21:22
Mark 11:24
John 14:13
John 16:23
James 1:5
[c] Matt. 7:8
[d] Matt. 7:9
[e] Matt. 9:32
Matt. 12:22
[f] Matt. 9:34
Matt. 12:24
Mark 3:22
[g] Matt. 12:25
Mark 3:24
[h] Matt. 12:43
[i] Heb. 6:4
2 Pet. 2:20
[j] Matt. 12:38-39
[k] Jonah 1:12
[l] 1 Kings 10:1
2 Chron. 9:1
[m] Jonah 3:5

cast out devils [1]through Beelzebub?

19 If I through Beelzebub cast out devils, by whom do your children cast them out? Therefore shall they be your judges.

20 But if I by the [1]finger of God cast out devils, doubtless the kingdom of God is come unto you.

21 When a strong man armed keepeth his [1]palace, the things that he possesseth, are in peace.

22 But when a stronger than he cometh upon him, and overcometh him: he taketh from him all his armor wherein he trusted, and divideth his spoils.

23 [1]He that is not with me, is against me: and he that gathereth not with me, scattereth.

24 [h,1]When the unclean spirit is gone out of a man, he walketh through dry places, seeking rest: and when he findeth none, he saith, I will return unto mine house whence I came out.

25 And when he cometh, he findeth it swept and garnished.

26 Then goeth he, and taketh to him seven other spirits worse than himself: and they enter in, and dwell there: [i]so the last state of that man is worse than the first.

27 ¶ [1]And it came to pass as he said these things, a certain woman of the company lifted up her voice, and said unto him, Blessed *is* the womb that bare thee, and the paps which thou hast sucked.

28 But he said, Yea, rather blessed *are* they that hear the word of God, and keep it.

29 ¶ [j,1]And when the people were gathered thick together, he began to say, This is a wicked generation: they seek a sign, and there shall no sign be given them, but the sign of [k]Jonah the Prophet.

30 For as Jonah was a sign to the Ninevites: so shall also the son of man be to this generation.

31 [l]The Queen of the South shall rise in judgment, with the men of this generation, and shall condemn them: for she came from the utmost parts of the earth to hear the wisdom of Solomon, and behold, a greater than Solomon is here.

32 The men of Nineveh shall rise in judgment with this generation, and shall condemn it: for they [m]repented at the preaching of Jonah: and behold, a greater than Jonah *is* here.

11:3 [1] That is, as much as is needful for us this day, whereby we are not debarred to have an honest care for the maintenance of our lives; but that carping care, which killeth a number of men, is cut off and restrained.

11:5 [1] We must pray with faith.

11:8 [1] Word for word, impudency: but that impudency which is spoken of here, is not to be found fault withall, but is very commendable before God, for he liketh well of such importunity.

11:15 [1] An example of horrible blindness, and such as cannot be healed, when as upon an evil conscience, and pretended malice, the power of God is blasphemed.

11:17 [1] The true way to know the true Christ, from the false, is this, that the true Christ hath no accord or agreement with Satan: And it

remaineth that after we know him, we acknowledge him.

11:18 [1] By the name and power of Beelzebub.

11:20 [1] That is, by the power of God: so it is said, Exod. 8:19.

11:21 [1] The word signifieth properly an open and void room before an house, and so by translation is taken for noblemen's houses.

11:23 [1] Against indifferent men, and such as love to have a mean, which seek means to reconcile Christ and Satan together.

11:24 [1] He that doth not continue, is in worse case, than he that never began.

11:27 [1] Christ seeketh not praise in himself, but in our salvation.

11:29 [1] They that are fond desireres of miracles, instead of miracles shall receive punishment.

33 ¶ *n,1*No man when he hath lighted a candle, putteth it in a privy place, neither under a bushel: but on a candlestick, that they which come in, may see the light.

34 *o*The light of the body is the eye: therefore when thine eye is single, then is thy whole body light: but if thine eye be evil, then thy body is dark.

35 Take heed therefore, that the light which is in thee, be not darkness.

36 If therefore thy whole body *shall be* light, having no part dark, then shall all be light, even as when a candle doth light thee with the brightness.

37 ¶ *1*And as he spake, a certain Pharisee besought him to dine with him: and he went in, and sat down at the table.

38 And when the Pharisee saw it, he marveled that he had not first washed before dinner.

39 *p*And the Lord said to him, Indeed ye Pharisees make clean the outside of the cup, and of the platter: but the inward part is full of ravening and wickedness.

40 Ye fools, did not he that made that which is without, make that which is within also?

41 Therefore, give alms *1*of those things which you have, and behold, all things shall be clean unto you.

42 *1*But woe *be* to you, Pharisees: for ye *2*tithe the mint and the rue, and *3*all manner herbs, and pass over *4*judgment and the love of God: these ought ye to have done, and not to have left the other undone.

43 *q,1*Woe *be* to you, Pharisees: for ye love the uppermost seats in the Synagogues, and greetings in the markets.

44 *1*Woe *be* to you, Scribes and Pharisees hypocrites: *r*for ye are as graves which appear not, and the men

n Luke 8:16
Matt. 5:15
Mark 4:21

o Matt. 6:22

p Matt. 23:25

q Luke 20:26
Matt. 23:6
Mark 12:38-39

r Matt. 23:27

s Matt. 23:4
Acts 15:10

t Matt. 23:29

u Gen. 4:8

v 2 Chron. 24:21

that walk over them, perceive not.

45 ¶ *1*Then answered one of the Lawyers, and said unto him, Master, thus saying thou puttest us to rebuke also.

46 And he said, Woe *be* to you also, ye Lawyers: *s*for ye lade men with burdens grievous to be borne, and ye yourselves touch not the burdens with one of your fingers.

47 *1*Woe *be* to you: *t*for ye build the sepulchers of the Prophets, and your fathers killed them.

48 Truly *1*ye bear witness, and allow the deeds of your fathers: for they killed them, and ye build their sepulchers.

49 Therefore said the wisdom of God, I will send them Prophets and Apostles, and of them they shall slay, and *1*persecute away,

50 That the blood of all the Prophets, *1*shed from the foundation of the world, may be required of this generation,

51 From the blood of *u*Abel unto the blood of *v*Zechariah, which was slain between the altar and the Temple: verily I say unto you, it shall be required of this generation.

52 *1*Woe *be* to you, Lawyers: for ye have *2*taken away the key of knowledge: ye entered not in yourselves, and them that came in, ye forbade.

53 *1*And as he said these things unto them, the Scribes and Pharisees began to urge him sore, and to *2*provoke him to speak of many things,

54 Laying wait for him, and seeking to catch something of his mouth, whereby they might accuse him.

12

1 *The leaven of the Pharisee.*   5 *Who is to be feared.*   8 *To confess Christ.*   16 *The parable of*

11:33 *1* Our minds are therefore lightened with the knowledge of God, that we should give light unto others, and therefore our chiefest labor ought to be to pray for that light.

11:37 *1* The service of God consisteth not in outward cleanliness, and devised rites or ceremonies, but in the spiritual righteousness of the heart, and charity.

11:41 *1* That is, according to your abilities as who would say, instead of your extortions, which hindered you, that you could not eat cleanly, use charity, and accordingly as your ability shall serve you, be good to the poor, and so shall that, that is within the platter, be sanctified though the platter be unwashed.

11:42 *1* It is the propense of hypocrites, to stand stoutly for little trifles, and let pass greater matters.

2 You decide by God's Law that the tenth part is due to be paid.

3 Of all kind of herbs some, as Augustine expoundeth it in his Enchiridion to Laurence, chap. 99, where he showeth in like sort how that place of Paul, 1 Tim. 2:4, God will have all men to be saved, is to be expoundeth after the same manner.

4 That is to say, that that is right and reason to do: for this word, Judgment, containeth the commandments of the second table, and the other words, The love of God, contain the first.

11:43 *1* Hypocrisy and ambition are commonly joined together.

11:44 *1* Hypocrites deceive men with an outward show.

11:45 *1* Hypocrites are very severe against other men, but think all things lawful to themselves.

11:47 *1* Hypocrites honor those saints when they are dead, whom they most cruelly persecute, when they were alive.

11:48 *1* When you persecute God's servants, like mad men, even as your fathers did, though you color it with a pretence of godliness, yet notwithstanding, in that you beautify the sepulchers of the Prophets, what do you else, but glory in your fathers' cruelty, and set up monuments (as it were) in glory and triumph of it?

11:49 *1* They shall so vex them and trouble them, that at length they shall banish them.

11:50 *1* That you may be called to an account for it, yea, and be punished, for the shedding of that blood of the Prophet.

11:52 *1* They have of long time chiefly hindered the people, from entering into the knowledge of God, which ought to be the doorkeepers of the Church.

2 You have hidden and taken away, so that it cannot be found anywhere.

11:53 *1* The more the world is reprehended, the worse it is, and yet must we not betray the truth.

the rich man whose land was very fertile.   21 Not to care for earthly things.   31 But to seek the kindom of God.   39 The thief in the night.   51 Debate for the Gospel's sake.

1 In ª,¹the meantime, there gathered together ²an innumerable multitude of people, so that they trod one another: and he began to say unto his disciples first, Take heed to yourselves of the leaven of the Pharisees, which is hypocrisy.

2 ᵇFor there is nothing covered, that shall not be revealed: neither hid, that shall not be known.

3 Wherefore whatsoever ye have spoken in darkness, it shall be heard in the light: and that which ye have spoken in the ear, in secret places, shall be preached on the houses.

4 ᶜ,¹And I say unto you, my friends, be not afraid of them that kill the body, and after that are not able to do anymore.

5 But I will ¹forewarn you, whom ye shall fear: fear him which after he hath killed, hath power to cast into hell: yea, I say unto you, him fear.

6 Are not five sparrows bought for two farthings, *and* yet not one of them is forgotten before God?

7 ᵈYea, and all the hairs of your head are numbered: fear not therefore: ye are more of value than many sparrows.

8 ᶜ,¹Also I say unto you, Whosoever shall confess me before men, him shall the Son of man confess also before the Angels of God.

9 But he that shall deny me before men, shall be denied before the Angels of God.

10 ᶠAnd whosoever shall speak a word against the Son of man, it shall be forgiven him: but unto him that shall blaspheme the holy Ghost, it shall not be forgiven.

CHAPTER 12
ª Matt. 16:5
Mark 8:14
ᵇ Matt. 10:26
Mark 4:22
ᶜ Matt. 20:28
ᵈ 1 Sam. 14:45
Acts 27:34
ᵉ Luke 9:26
Matt. 10:32
Mark 8:38
2 Tim. 1:12
ᶠ Matt. 17:31
Mark 3:28
1 John 5:15
ᵍ Matt. 10:19
Mark 13:11
ʰ Matt. 6:25
1 Pet. 5:7
Ps. 55:22

11 ᵍ,¹And when they shall bring you unto the Synagogues, and unto the rulers and Princes, take no thought how, or what thing ye shall answer, or what ye shall speak.

12 For the holy Ghost shall teach you in the same hour, what ye ought to say.

13 ¹And one of the company said unto him, Master, bid my brother divide the inheritance with me.

14 And he said unto him, Man, who made me a judge, or a divider over you?

15 Wherefore he said unto them, Take heed, and beware of ¹covetousness: for though a man have abundance, *yet* his ²life standeth not in his riches.

16 ¹And he put forth a parable unto them, saying, The ²ground of a certain rich man brought forth fruits plenteously.

17 Therefore he ¹thought with himself, saying, What shall I do, because I have no *room* where I may lay up my fruits?

18 And he said, This will I do, I will pull down my barns, and build greater, and therein will I gather all my fruits, and my goods.

19 And I will say to my soul, Soul, thou hast much goods laid up for many years, live at ease, eat, drink, and ¹take thy pastime.

20 But God said unto him, O fool, this night will they fetch away thy soul from thee: then whose shall those things be which thou hast provided?

21 So *is* he that gathereth riches ¹to himself, and is not rich in God.

22 ¹And he spake unto his disciples, Therefore I say unto you, ʰTake no thought for your life, what ye shall eat: neither for your body, what ye shall put on.

---

² They proposed many questions to him, to draw something out of his mouth, which they might traitorously carp at.

12:1 ¹ The faithful teachers of God's word, which are appointed by him for his people, must both take good heed of them, which corrupt the purity of doctrine with goodly glosses, and also take pains through the help of God, to set forth sincere doctrine, openly and without fear.

² Word for word, ten thousands of people, a certain number for an uncertain.

12:4 ¹ Although hypocrites have princes to execute their cruelty, yet there is no cause why we could be afraid of them, the least iota that may be, seeing they can do nothing, but what pleaseth God, and God wills not anything that may be against the salvation of his elect.

12:5 ¹ He warneth them of dangers that presently hang over their heads, for those that come upon the sudden, do make the greater wound.

12:8 ¹ Great is the reward of a constant confession: and horrible is the punishment of the denying of Christ, yea impossible to be called back again shall the punishment be, if upon set purpose, both with mouth and heart we blaspheme a known truth.

12:11 ¹ It is a great and hard conflict to confess the truth, yet he that can do all things, and is almighty, will not be wanting to the weakest which strive and contend in his appointed time.

12:13 ¹ Christ would not for three causes be a judge to divide an inheritance. First, for that he would not foster up and cherish the fleshly opinion that the Jews had of Messiah: Secondly for that he would distinguish the civil governance, from the Ecclesiastical: Thirdly, to teach us to beware of them which abuse the show of the gospel, and also the name of ministers, to their own private commodities.

12:15 ¹ By covetousness is meant, that greedy desire to get, commonly with other men's hurt.

² God is the author and preserver of man's life; goods are not.

12:16 ¹ There are none more mad, than rich men which hang upon their riches.

² Or rather country, for here is set forth a man that possesseth not a piece of ground only, but an whole country, as they do, which join house to house, and field to field, Isa. 5:8.

12:17 ¹ Made his reckoning within himself, which is the property of covetous churls that spend their life in those trifles.

12:19 ¹ Be merry and make good cheer.

12:21 ¹ Caring for no man but for himself, and minding to trust in himself.

12:22 ¹ An earnest thinking upon the providence of God, is a present remedy against the most foolish and pining carefulness of men for this life.

23 The life is more than meat: and the body *more* than the raiment.

24 Consider the ravens: for they neither sow nor reap: which neither have storehouse nor barn, and *yet* God feedeth them: how much more are ye better than fowls?

25 And which of you with taking thought, can add to his stature one cubit?

26 If ye then be not able to do the least thing, why take ye thought for the remnant?

27 Consider the lilies how they grow: they labor not, neither spin they: yet I say unto you, that Solomon himself in all his royalty was not clothed like one of these.

28 If then God so clothe the grass which is today in the field, and tomorrow is cast into the oven, how much more *will he clothe* you, O ye of little faith?

29 Therefore ask not what ye shall eat, or what ye shall drink, neither ¹hang you in suspense.

30 For all such things the people of the world seek for: and your Father knoweth that ye have need of these things.

31 ¹But rather seek ye after the kingdom of God, and all these things shall be cast upon you.

32 ¹Fear not, little flock: for it is your Father's pleasure to give you the kingdom.

33 ¶ ʲ·¹Sell that ye have, and give ²alms: make you bags which wax not old: a treasure that can never fail in heaven, where no thief cometh neither moth corrupteth.

34 For where your treasure is, there will your hearts be also.

35 ¶ ʲ·¹Let your loins be girded about, and your lights burning,

36 And ye yourselves like unto men that wait for their master, when he will return from the wedding, that when he cometh and knocketh, they may open unto him immediately.

37 Blessed *are* those servants, whom the Lord when he cometh shall find waking: verily I say unto you, he will gird himself about, and make them to sit down at table, and will come forth, and serve them.

38 And if he come in the second watch, or come

in the third watch, and shall find them so, blessed are those servants.

39 ᵏNow understand this, that if the good man of the house had known at what hour the thief would have come, he would have watched, and would not have suffered his house to be dug through.

40 ¹Be ye also prepared therefore: for the Son of man will come at an hour when ye think not.

41 Then Peter said unto him, Master, tellest thou this parable unto us, or even to all?

42 And the Lord said, Who is a faithful steward and wise, whom the master shall make ruler over his household, to give them their ¹portion of meat in season?

43 Blessed *is* that servant, whom his master when he cometh, shall find so doing.

44 Of a truth, I say unto you, that he will make him ruler over all that he hath.

45 But if that servant say in his heart, My master doth defer his coming, and shall begin to smite the servants, and maidens, and to eat and drink, and to be drunken,

46 The master of that servant will come in a day when he thinketh not, and at an hour when he is not aware of, and will cut him off, and give him his portion with the unbelievers.

47 ¶ And that servant that knew his master's will, and prepared not himself, neither did according to his will, shall be beaten with many *stripes*.

48 But he that knew it not, and yet did commit things worthy of stripes, shall be beaten with few *stripes*: for unto whomsoever much is given, of him shall be much required, and to whom men much commit, ¹the more of him will they ask.

49 ¶ ¹I am come to put fire on the earth, and what is my desire, if it be already kindled?

50 Notwithstanding I must be baptized with a baptism, and how am I grieved till it be ended?

51 ˡThink ye that I am come to give peace on earth? I tell you, nay, but rather debate.

52 For from henceforth there shall be five in one house divided, three against two, and two against three.

Margin references:

ⁱ Matt. 6:20
ʲ 1 Pet. 1:13
ᵏ Matt. 24:43
  Rev. 26:15
  Rev. 3:3
ˡ Matt. 10:34

12:29 ¹ A Metaphor taken of things that hang in the air, for they that are careful for this worldly life, and hang upon the arm of man, have always wavering and doubtful minds, swaying sometimes this way, and sometimes that way.

12:31 ¹ They shall lack nothing, which are careful for the kingdom of heaven.

12:32 ¹ It is a foolish thing not to look for small things, at his hands, which giveth us freely the greatest things.

12:33 ¹ A godly bountifulness is a ready way to get true riches.

   ² This is the figure Metonymy, for by this word, Alms, is meant that compassion and friendliness of an heart that tendereth the misery and poor estate of man, and showeth forth itself by some gift, and hath the name given it in the Greek tongue, of mercy and compas-

sion: and therefore he is said to give alms, who parteth with some thing to another, and giveth to the poor, showing thereby, that he pitieth their poor estate.

12:35 ¹ The life of the faithful servants of God, in this world is a certain watchful peregrination, having the light of the word going before it.

12:40 ¹ None have more need to watch, than they that have some degree of honor in the household of God.

12:42 ¹ That is, every month such measure of corn as was appointed them.

12:48 ¹ More than of him to whom so much was not given.

12:49 ¹ The Gospel is the only cause of peace between the goodly, and so is it the occasion of great trouble among the wicked.

53 The father shall be divided against the son, and the son against the father: the mother against the daughter, and the daughter against the mother: the mother-in-law against her daughter-in-law, and the daughter-in-law against her mother-in-law.

54 ¶ [m,1]Then said he to the people, When ye see a cloud [2]rise out of the West, straightway ye say, A shower cometh: and so it is.

55 And when *ye see* the South wind blow, ye say, that it will be hot: and it cometh to pass.

56 Hypocrites, ye can discern the face of the earth, and of the sky: but why discern ye not this time?

57 [1]Yea, and why judge ye not of yourselves what is right?

58 ¶ [n]While thou goest with thine adversary to the ruler, as thou art in the way, give diligence in the way, that thou mayest be delivered from him, lest he draw thee to the judge, and the judge deliver thee to the [1]jailer, and the jailer cast thee into prison.

59 I tell thee, thou shalt not depart thence, till thou hast paid the utmost mite.

13

Of the Galileans,   4 and those that were slain under Siloam.   6 The fig tree that bare no fruit.   11 The woman vexed with the spirit of infirmity, that is, with a disease brought on her by Satan, is healed.   19 The parable of the grain of mustard seed.   21 Of leaven.   23 How few shall be saved.   31 Herod that Fox.

1 There [1]were certain men present at the same season, that showed him of the Galileans, whose blood [2]Pilate had mingled with their sacrifices.

2 And Jesus answered, and said unto them, Suppose ye, that these Galileans were greater sinners than all the *other* Galileans, because they have suffered such things?

3 I tell you, nay: but except ye amend your lives, ye shall all likewise perish.

4 Or think you that those eighteen, upon whom the tower in [1]Siloam fell, and slew them, were sinners

[m] Matt. 16:2
[n] Matt. 15:25

above all men that dwell in Jerusalem?

5 I tell you, nay: but except ye amend your lives, ye shall all likewise perish.

6 ¶ [1]He spake also this parable, A certain man had a fig tree, planted in his vineyard: and he came and sought fruit thereon, and found none.

7 Then said he to the dresser of his vineyard, Behold, this three years have I come and sought fruit of this fig tree, and find none: cut it down: why keepeth it also the ground [1]barren?

8 And he answered, and said unto him, Lord, let it alone this year also, till I dig round about it, and dung it.

9 And if it bear fruit, *well*: if not, then after thou shalt cut it down.

10 ¶ [1]And he taught in one of the Synagogues on the Sabbath day.

11 And behold, there was a woman which had a [1]spirit of infirmity eighteen years, and was bowed together, and could not lift up *herself* in any wise.

12 When Jesus saw her, he called her to him, and said to her, Woman, thou art [1]loosed from thy disease.

13 And he laid his hands on her, and immediately she was made straight again, and glorified God.

14 [1]And the [2]ruler of the Synagogue answered with indignation, because that Jesus healed on the Sabbath *day*, and said unto the people, There are six days in which men ought to work: in them therefore come and be healed, and not on the Sabbath day.

15 Then answered him the Lord, and said, Hypocrite, doth not each one of you on the Sabbath *day* loose his ox or his ass from the stall, and lead him away to the water?

16 And ought not this daughter of Abraham, whom Satan had bound, lo, eighteen years, be loosed from this bond on the Sabbath day?

17 And when he said these things, all his adversaries were ashamed: but all the people rejoiced at all the excellent things that were done by him.

12:54 [1] Men which are very quick of sight in earthly things, are blind in those things which pertain to the heavenly life, and that through their own malice.

[2] Which appeareth, and gathereth itself together in that part of the air.

12:57 [1] Men that are blinded with the love of themselves, and therefore are detestable and stubborn, shall bear the reward of their folly.

12:58 [1] To him that had to demand and gather the amerciaments which they were condemned unto that had wrongfully troubled men: moreover, the magistrate's officers make them which are condemned, pay that, that they owe, yea, and oftentimes if they be obstinate, they do not only take the cost and charge of them, but also imprison them.

13:1 [1] We must not rejoice at the just punishment of others, but rather be instructed thereby to repentance.

[2] Pontius Pilate was governor of Judea, almost ten years, and about the fourth year of his government, which might be about the fifteenth year of Tiberius' reign, Christ finished the work of our

redemption by his death.

13:4 [1] To wit, in the place, or river: for Siloam was a small river, from whence the conduits of the city came, whereof John 9:7 and Isa. 8:6, and therefore it was a tower or castle, built upon the conduit side, which fell down suddenly, and killed some.

13:6 [1] Great and longsuffering is the patience of God, but yet so that at length he executed judgment.

13:7 [1] Maketh the ground barren in that part, which otherwise were good for vines.

13:10 [1] Christ came to deliver us from the bands of Satan.

13:11 [1] Troubled with a disease which Satan brought.

13:12 [1] For Satan had the woman bound, as if she had been in chains, insomuch that for eighteen years space she could not hold up her head.

13:14 [1] A lively image of hypocrisy, and reward thereof.

[2] One of the rulers of the Synagogue, for it appeareth by Mark 5:22 and Acts 13:15 that there were many rulers of the Synagogue.

18 ¶ ᵃThen said he, What is the kingdom of God like? or whereto shall I compare it?

19 ¹It is like a grain of mustard seed, which a man took and sowed in his garden, and it grew, and waxed a great tree, and the fowls of the heaven made nests in the branches thereof.

20 ¶ ᵇAnd again he said, Whereunto shall I liken the kingdom of God?

21 It is like leaven, which a woman took, and hid in three pecks of flour, till all was leavened.

22 ¶ ᶜ·¹And he went through all cities and towns, teaching, and journeying towards Jerusalem.

23 Then said one unto him, Lord, *are there few* that shall be saved? And he said unto them,

24 ᵈStrive to enter in at the strait gate: for many, I say unto you, will seek to enter in, and shall not be able.

25 When the good man of the house is risen up, and hath shut to the door, and ye began to stand without, and to knock at the door, saying, Lord, Lord, open to us, and he shall answer and say unto you, I know you not whence ye are,

26 ¹Then shall ye begin to say, We have eaten and drunk in thy presence, and thou hast taught in our streets.

27 ᵉBut he shall say, I tell you, I know you not whence ye are: depart from me, all ye workers of iniquity.

28 ¹There shall be weeping and gnashing of teeth, when ye shall see Abraham, and Isaac, and Jacob, and all the Prophets in the kingdom of God, and yourselves thrust out at doors.

29 Then shall come *many* from the ¹East, and from the West, and from the North, and from the South, and shall sit at Table in the kingdom of God.

30 ᶠAnd behold, there are last, which shall be first, and there are first, which shall be last.

31 ¹The same day there came certain Pharisees, and said unto him, Depart, and go hence: for Herod will kill thee.

CHAPTER 13
ᵃ Matt. 13:31
  Mark 4:31
ᵇ Matt. 13:33
ᶜ Matt. 9:35
  Mark 6:6
ᵈ Matt. 7:13
ᵉ Mark 7:23
  Matt. 25:41
  Ps. 6:8
ᶠ Matt. 19:30
  Matt. 20:16
  Mark 10:31
ᵍ Matt. 23:37

32 Then said he unto them, Go ye and tell that ¹fox, Behold, I cast out devils, and will heal still ²today, and tomorrow, and the third day I shall be ³perfected.

33 ¹Nevertheless I must walk today, and tomorrow, and the day following: for it cannot be that a Prophet should perish out of Jerusalem.

34 ᵍO Jerusalem, Jerusalem, which killest the Prophets, and stonest them that are sent to thee, how often would I have gathered thy children together, as the hen *gathered* her ¹brood under *her* wings, and ye would not.

35 Behold, your house is left unto you desolate: and verily I tell you, ye shall not see me until *the time* come that ye shall say, Blessed *is* he that cometh in the name of the Lord.

14 *The dropsy healed on the Sabbath.* 8 *The chief place: at banquets.* 12 *The poor must be called to our feasts.* 16 *Of those that were bid to the great supper.* 23 *Some compelled to come in.* 28 *One about to build a tower.*

1 And ¹it came to pass that when he was entered into the house of ²one of the chief Pharisees on the Sabbath *day*, to eat bread, they watched him.

2 And behold, there was a certain man before him, which had the dropsy.

3 Then Jesus answering, spake unto the Lawyers and Pharisees, saying, Is it lawful to heal on the Sabbath *day*?

4 And they held their peace. Then he took him, and healed him, and let him go,

5 And answered them, saying, Which of you *shall have* an ass, or an ox fallen into a pit, and will not straightway pull him out on the Sabbath day?

6 And they could not answer him again to those things.

7 ¶ ¹He spake also a parable to the guests, when he marked how they chose out the chief rooms, and said unto them,

8 When thou shalt be bidden of any man to a

13:19 ¹ God beginneth his kingdom with small beginnings, that the unlooked for proceeding of it may better set forth his power.

13:22 ¹ Against them which had rather err with many, than go right with a few, and by that means through their own slowness, are shut out of the kingdom of God.

13:26 ¹ He is in vain in the Church, which is not of the Church, which thing the cleanness of life showeth.

13:28 ¹ The casting off of the Jews, and the calling of the Gentiles is foretold.

13:29 ¹ From all the quarters of the world, and these are four of the chiefest.

13:31 ¹ We must go forward in the case of our calling, through the midst of terrors, whether they be true or fained.

13:32 ¹ That deceitful and treacherous man.

² That is, a small time, and Theophylact saith, it is a proverb: or else, by Today, we may understand the time that now is, and by Tomor-

row, the time to come, meaning thereby all the time of his ministry and office.

³ To wit, when the sacrifice for sin is ended.

13:33 ¹ There are nowhere more cruel enemies of the godly, than they which are within the Sanctuary and Church itself: but God seeth it, and will in his time have an account of it.

13:34 ¹ Word for word, the nest: now the brood of chickens is the nest.

14:1 ¹ The Law of the very Sabbath ought not to hinder the offices of charity.

² Either one of the Elders, whom they called the Sanhedrin, or one of the chiefs of the Synagogue, John 7:48, for this word Pharisee was the name of a sect, though it appears by the whole history that the Pharisees were in great credit.

14:7 ¹ The reward of pride is ignomy and the reward of true modesty is glory.

wedding, set not thyself down in the chiefest place, lest a more honorable man than thou be bidden of him,

9 And he that bade both him and thee, come, and say to thee, Give this man room, and thou then begin with shame to take the lowest room.

10 *But when thou art bidden, go and sit down in the lowest room, that when he that bade thee, cometh, he may say unto thee, Friend, sit up higher: then shalt thou have worship in the presence of them that sit at table with thee.

11 *For whosoever exalteth himself, shall be brought low, and he that humbleth himself, shall be exalted.

12 ¶ ¹Then said he also to him that had bidden him, *When thou makest a dinner or a supper, call not thy friends, nor thy brethren, neither thy kinsmen, nor the rich neighbors, lest they also bid thee again, and a recompense be made thee.

13 But when thou makest a feast, call the poor, the maimed, the lame *and* the blind,

14 And thou shalt be blessed, because they cannot recompense thee: for thou shalt be recompensed at the resurrection of the just.

15 ¶ Now when one of them that sat at table heard these things, he said unto him, Blessed *is* he that eateth bread in the kingdom of God.

16 Then said he to him, *A certain man made a great supper, and bade many,

17 And sent his servant at supper time to say to them that were bidden, Come: for all things are now ready.

18 ¹But they all with ²one *mind* began to make excuse: The first said unto him, I have bought a farm, and I must needs go out and see it: I pray thee have me excused.

19 And another said, I have bought five yoke of oxen, and I go to prove them: I pray thee have me excused.

20 And another said, I have married a wife, and therefore I cannot come.

21 So that servant returned, and showed his master these things. Then was the good man of the house angry, and said to his servant, Go out quickly into the ¹streets and lanes of the city, and bring in

CHAPTER 14
ª Prov. 25:7
ᵇ Luke 28:14
Matt. 23:12
ᶜ Prov. 3:27
Job 4:7
ᵈ Matt. 22:8
Rev. 19:9
ᵉ Matt. 10:47
ᶠ Luke 9:23
Matt. 16:24
Mark 8:34
ᵍ Matt. 5:13
Mark 9:50

hither the poor, and the maimed, and the halt, and the blind.

22 And the servant said, Lord, it is done as thou hast commanded, and yet there is room.

23 Then the master said to the servant, Go out into the highways, and hedges, and compel them to come in, that mine house may be filled.

24 For I say unto you, that none of those men which were bidden, shall taste of my supper.

25 ¹Now there went great multitudes with him, and he turned and said unto them,

26 *If any man come to me, and ¹hate not his father, and mother, and wife, and children, and brethren, and sisters: yea, and his own life also, he cannot be my disciple.

27 *ᶠ,¹And whosoever beareth not his cross, and cometh after me, cannot be my disciple.

28 For which of you minding to build a tower, ¹sitting not down before, and counteth the cost, whether he have sufficient to perform it,

29 Lest that after he hath laid the foundation, and is not able to perform it, all that behold it, begin to mock him,

30 Saying, This man began to build, and was not able to make an end.

31 Or what King going to make war against another King, sitteth not down first, and taketh counsel, whether he be able with ten thousand, to meet him that cometh against him with twenty thousand?

32 Or else while he is yet a great way off, he sendeth an ambassage, and desireth peace.

33 So likewise, whosoever he be of you, that forsaketh not all that he hath, he cannot be my disciple.

34 *ᵍ,¹Salt is good: but if salt have lost his savor, wherewith shall it be salted?

35 It is neither meet for the land, nor yet for the dunghill, but men cast it out. He that hath ears to hear, let him hear.

15

The parable of the lost sheep.   8 Of the groat,   12 And of the prodigal son.

1 Then ¹resorted unto ²him ³all the Publicans and sinners, to hear him.

2 Therefore the Pharisees and Scribes mur-

14:12 ¹ Against them which lavish out their goods either ambitiously, or for hope of recompence, whereas Christian charity respecteth only the glory of God, and the profit of our neighbor.

14:18 ¹ The most part even of them to whom God hath revealed himself are so mad, that such helps as they have received of God, they willingly turn into lets and hindrances.

² As of set purpose, and a thing agreed upon before, for though they allege several causes, yet all of them agree in this, that they have their excuses, that they may not come to supper.

14:21 ¹ Wide and broad quarters.

14:25 ¹ Even those affections, which are of themselves worthy of praise and commendation, must be ruled and ordered, that godli-

ness may have the upper hand and preeminence.

14:26 ¹ If the matter stands between God and him, as Theophylact saith: and therefore these words are not spoken simply, but by comparison.

14:27 ¹ The true followers of Christ must at once build and fight, and therefore be ready and prepared to suffer all kinds of miseries.

14:28 ¹ At home, and casteth all his costs before he begin the work.

14:34 ¹ The disciples of Christ must be wise, both for themselves and for others: otherwise they become the most foolish of all.

15:1 ¹ Or, draw near.

² We must not despair of them, which have gone out of the way, but according to the example of Christ, we must take great pains about them.

³ Some Publicans and sinners came to Christ from all quarters.

mured, saying, He receiveth sinners, and eateth with them.

3 Then spake he this parable to them, saying,

4 "What man of you having an hundred sheep, if he lose one of them, doth not leave ninety and nine in the wilderness, and go after that which is lost, until he find it?

5 And when he hath found it, he layeth it on his shoulders with joy.

6 And when he cometh home, he calleth together his friends and neighbors, saying unto them, Rejoice with me: for I have found my sheep which was lost.

7 I say unto you, that likewise joy shall be in heaven for one sinner that converteth, *more* than for ninety and nine just men, which need none amendment of life.

8 Either what woman having ten groats, if she lose one groat, doth not light a candle, and sweep the house, and seek diligently till she find it?

9 And when she hath found it, she calleth her friends, and neighbors, saying, Rejoice with me: for I have found the groat which I had lost.

10 Likewise I say unto you, there is joy in the presence of the Angels of God, for one sinner that converteth.

11 ¶ [1]He said moreover, A certain man had two sons,

12 And the younger of them said to his father, Father, give me the portion of the goods that falleth to me. So he divided unto them *his* substance.

13 So not many days after, when the younger son had gathered all together, he took his journey into a far country, and there he wasted his goods with riotous living.

14 Now when he had spent all, there arose a great dearth throughout that land, and he began to be in necessity.

15 Then he went and clave to a citizen of that country, and he sent him to his farm, to feed swine.

16 And he would fain have filled his belly with the husks that the swine ate: but no man gave *them* him.

17 [1]Then he came to himself, and said, How many hired servants at my father's have bread enough, and I die for hunger?

18 I will rise and go to my father, and say unto him, Father, I have sinned against [1]heaven, and

CHAPTER 15
[d] Matt. 18:12

before thee,

19 And am no more worthy to be called thy son: make me as one of thine hired servants.

20 So he arose and came to his father, and when he was yet a great way off, his father saw him, and had compassion, and ran and fell on his neck, and kissed him.

21 [1]And the son said unto him, Father, I have sinned against heaven, and before thee, and am no more worthy to be called thy son.

22 Then the father said to his servants, Bring forth the best robe, and put it on him, and put a ring on his hand, and shoes on his feet,

23 And bring the fat calf, and kill him, and let us eat, and be merry:

24 For this my son was dead, and is alive again: and he was lost, but he is found. And they began to be merry.

25 [1]Now the elder brother was in the field, and when he came and drew near to the house, he heard melody, and dancing,

26 And called one of his servants, and asked what those things meant.

27 And he said unto him, Thy brother is come, and thy father hath killed the fat calf, because he hath received him safe and sound.

28 Then he was angry, and would not go in: therefore came his father out, and entreated him.

29 But he answered, and said to his father, Lo, these many years have I done thee service, neither brake I at anytime thy commandment, and yet thou never gavest me a kid that I might make merry with my friends.

30 But when this thy son was come, which hath devoured thy goods with harlots, thou hast for his sake killed the fat calf.

31 And he said unto him, Son thou art ever with me, and all that I have, is thine. It was meet that we should make merry, and be glad: for this thy brother was dead, and is alive again: and he was lost, but he is found.

16

1 *The parable of the steward accused to his master.* 13 *To serve two masters.* 16 *The law and the Prophets.* 19 *Of Dives and Lazarus.*

1 And he said also unto his disciples, [1]There was

15:11 [1] Men by their voluntary falling from God, having spoiled themselves of the benefits which they received of him, cast themselves headlong into infinite calamities: but God of his singular goodness, offering himself freely to them, whom he called to repentance, through the greatness of their misery wherewith they were tamed, doth not only gently receive them, but also enricheth them with far greater gifts, and blesseth them with the chiefest bliss.

15:17 [1] The beginning of repentance is the acknowledging of the mercy of God, which stirreth us to hope well.

15:18 [1] Against God, because he is said to dwell in heaven.

15:21 [1] In true repentance there is a feeling of our sins, joined with sorrow and shame, from whence springeth a confession, after which followeth forgiveness.

15:25 [1] Such as truly fear God, desire to have all men to be their fellows.

16:1 [1] Seeing that men oftentimes purchase friendship to themselves, by other men's costs, it is a shame for us, if with a free and liberal bestowing of the goods which the Lord hath given us to that purpose, we do not please him, nor procure the good will of our neighbors, seeing that by this only means, riches, which are oftentimes occasions of sin, are turned to another end and purpose.

a certain rich man, which had a steward, and he was accused unto him, that he wasted his goods.

2   And he called him, and said unto him, How *is it* that I hear this of thee? Give an account of thy stewardship: for thou mayest be no longer steward.

3   Then the steward said within himself, What shall I do? for my master taketh away from me the stewardship. I cannot dig, *and* to beg I am ashamed.

4   I know what I will do, that when I am put out of the stewardship, they may receive me into their houses.

5   Then called he unto him everyone of his master's debtors, and said unto the first, How much owest thou unto my master?

6   And he said, An hundred measures of oil. And he said to him, Take thy writing, and sit down quickly, and write fifty.

7   Then said he to another, How much owest thou? And he said, An hundred measures of wheat. Then he said to him, Take thy writing and write fourscore.

8   And the Lord commended [1]the unjust steward, because he had done wisely. Wherefore the [2]children of this world are in their generation wiser than the children of light.

9   And I say unto you, Make you friends with the riches [1]of iniquity, that when ye shall want, they may receive you into everlasting [2]habitations.

10   [1]He that is faithful in the least, he is also faithful in much: and he that is unjust in the least, is unjust also in much.

11   If then ye have not been faithful in the wicked riches, who will trust you in the [1]true *treasure?*

12   And if ye have not been faithful in [1]another man's *goods,* who shall give you that which is yours?

CHAPTER 16
[a] Matt. 6:24
[b] Matt. 11:1
[c] Matt. 5:18
[d] Matt. 5:32
Matt. 19:9
1 Cor. 7:11

13   [a,1]No servant can serve two masters: for either he shall hate the one, and love the other: or else he shall lean to the one, and despise the other. Ye cannot serve God and riches.

14   All these things heard the Pharisees also which were covetous, and they scoffed at him.

15   [1]Then he said unto them, Ye are they, which justify yourselves before men: but God knoweth your hearts: for that which is highly esteemed among men, is abomination in the sight of God.

16   [b,1]The Law and the Prophets endured until John: and since that time the kingdom of God is preached, and every man presseth into it.

17   [c]Now it is more easy that heaven and earth should pass away, than that one tittle of the Law should fall.

18   ¶ [d]Whosoever putteth away his wife, and marrieth another, commiteth adultery: and whosoever marrieth her [1]that is put away from her husband, commiteth adultery.

19   ¶ [1]There was a certain rich man, which was clothed in [2]purple and fine linen, and fared well and delicately every day.

20   Also there was a certain beggar named Lazarus, which was laid at his gate full of sores,

21   And desired to be refreshed with the crumbs that fell from the rich man's table: yea, and the dogs came and licked his sores.

22   And it was so that the beggar died, and was carried by the Angels into Abraham's bosom. The rich man also died, and was buried.

23   And being in hell in torments, [1]he lifted up his eyes, and saw Abraham afar off, and Lazarus in his bosom.

24   Then he cried, and said, Father Abraham, have mercy on me, and send Lazarus that he may dip the tip of his finger in water, and cool my tongue: for I

16:8 [1] This parable doth not approve the steward's naughty dealing, for it was very theft: but parables are set forth, to show a thing covertly, and as it were under a figure to represent the truth, though it agree not thoroughly with the matter itself: so that Christ meaneth by this parable to teach us, that worldly men are more heady in the affairs of this world, than the children of God are careful for everlasting life.
[2] Men that are given to this present life, contrary to whom the children of light are set: St. Paul calls those spiritual, and the other carnal.
16:9 [1] This is not spoken of goods that are evil gotten, for God will have our bountifulness to the poor, proceed and come from a good fountain: but he calleth those riches of iniquity, which men use naughtily.
[2] To wit, the poor Christians: for they are the inheritors of these Tabernacles, Theophylact.
16:10 [1] We ought to take heed that for abusing our earthly function and duty, we be not deprived of heavenly gifts: for how can they use spiritual gifts aright, who abuse worldly things?
16:11 [1] That is, heavenly and true riches: which are contrary to worldly and flitting substance.
16:12 [1] In worldly goods, which are called other men's, because they are committed to our credit.

16:13 [1] No man can love God and riches together.
16:15 [1] Our sins are not hidden to God, although they be hidden to men, yea although they be hidden to them whose sins they are.
16:16 [1] The Pharisees despised the excellency of the new Covenant, in respect of the old, being ignorant of the perfect righteousness of the Law, and how false expounders they were of the Law, Christ declareth by the seventh Commandment.
16:18 [1] They that gather by this place, that a man cannot be married again after that he hath put away his wife for adultery, while she liveth, reason fondly: for Christ speaketh of those divorces which the Jews used, of which sort we cannot take the divorcement for adultery, for adulterers were put to death by the law.
16:19 [1] The end of the poverty and misery of the godly, shall be everlasting joy: as the end of riotousness and cruel pride of the rich shall be everlasting misery, without all hope of mercy.
[2] Very gorgeously and sumptuously, for purple garments were costly, and this fine linen which was a kind of linen that came out of Achaia, was as dear as gold.
16:23 [1] Heavenly and spiritual things are expressed, and set forth under colors and resemblances fit for our senses.

am tormented in this flame.

25　But Abraham said, Son, remember that thou in thy lifetime receivedst thy pleasures, and likewise Lazarus pains: now therefore is he comforted, and thou art tormented.

26　Besides all this, between you and us there is a great gulf set, so that they which would go from hence to you, cannot: neither can they come from thence to us.

27　[1]Then he said, I pray thee therefore father, that thou wouldest send him to my father's house,

28　(For I have five brethren) that he may testify unto them, lest they also come into this place of torment.

29　Abraham said unto him, They have Moses and the Prophets: let them hear them.

30　And he said, Nay, father Abraham: but if one came unto them from the dead, they will amend their lives.

31　Then he said unto him, If they hear not Moses and the Prophets, neither will they be persuaded, though one rise from the dead again.

17

1 Offenses.　3 We must forgive him that trespasseth against us.　10 We are unprofitable servants.　11 Of the ten lepers.　20 Of the coming of the kingdom of heaven.　33 False Christs.　36 After what manner Christ's coming shall be.

1　Then said he to his disciples, [a,1]It cannot be avoided, but that offences will come, but woe be to him by whom they come.

2　It is better for him that a great millstone were hanged about his neck, and that he were cast into the sea, then that he should offend one of these little ones.

3　¶ [1]Take heed to yourselves: if thy brother trespass against thee, rebuke him: and if he repent, forgive him.

4　[b]And though he sin against thee seven times in a day, and seven times in a day turn again to thee, saying, it repenteth me, thou shalt forgive him.

5　¶ [1]And the Apostles said unto the Lord, Increase our faith.

CHAPTER 17
[a] Matt. 18:7
Mark 9:42
[b] Matt. 18:28
[c] Matt. 17:20
[d] Lev. 14:2

6　And the Lord said, [c]If ye had faith, as much as is [1]a grain of mustard seed, and should say unto this mulberry tree, Pluck thyself up by the roots, and plant thyself in the sea, it should even obey you.

7　¶ [1]Who is it also of you, that having a servant plowing or feeding cattle, would say unto him by and by, when he were come from the field, Go, and sit down at table,

8　And would not rather say to him, Dress wherewith I may sup, and gird thyself, and serve me, till I have eaten and drunken, and afterward eat thou, and drink thou?

9　Doth he thank that servant, because he did that which was commanded unto him? I trow not.

10　[1]So likewise ye, when ye have done all those things, which are commanded you, say, We are unprofitable servants: we have done that which was our duty to do.

11　¶ [1]And so it was when he went to Jerusalem, that he passed through the midst of Samaria, and Galilee.

12　And as he entered into a certain town, there met him ten men that were lepers, which stood afar off.

13　And they lifted up their voices and said, Jesus, Master, have mercy on us.

14　And when he saw them, he said unto them, [d]Go, show yourselves unto the Priests. And it came to pass, that as they went, they were cleansed.

15　Then one of them, when he saw that he was healed, turned back, and with a loud voice praised God,

16　And fell down on his face at his feet, and gave him thanks: and he was a Samaritan.

17　And Jesus answered, and said, Are there not ten cleansed? but where are the nine?

18　There is none found that returned to give God praise, save this stranger.

19　And he said unto him, Arise, go thy way, thy faith hath saved thee.

20　¶ [1]And when he was demanded of the Pharisees, when the kingdom of God should come, he answered them, and said, The kingdom of God cometh not with [2]observation.

16:27　[1] Seeing that we have a most sure rule to live by, laid forth unto us in the word of God, rashly and vainly do men seek for other revelation.

17:1　[1] The Church is of necessity subject to offences, but the Lord will not suffer them unpunished, if any of the least be offended.

17:3　[1] Our reprehensions must be just, and proceed of love and charity.

17:5　[1] God will never be utterly lacking to the Godly (although he be not so perfectly with them, as they would) even in those difficulties, which cannot be overcome by man's reason.

17:6　[1] If you had no more faith, but the quantity of the grain of mustard seed.

17:7　[1] Seeing that God may challenge unto himself of right, both us and all that is ours, he can be debtor unto us for nothing, although we labor manfully even unto death.

17:10　[1] The most perfect keeping of the Law, which we can perform, deserves no reward.

17:11　[1] Christ doeth well even unto such, as will be unthankful, but the benefits of God profit them only to salvation, which are thankful.

17:20　[1] The kingdom of God is not marked of many, although it be most present before their eyes: because they fondly persuade themselves, that it is joined with outward pomp.

[2] With any outward pomp and show of majesty, to be known by: for there were otherwise many plain and evident tokens, whereby men might have understood, that Christ was the Messiah, whose kingdom was so long looked for: but he speaketh in this place of those signs which the Pharisees dreamed of, which looked for an earthly kingdom of Messiah.

21 Neither shall men say, Lo here, or lo there: for behold, the kingdom of God is ¹within you.

22 ¹And he said unto the disciples, the days will come, when ye shall desire to see ²one of the days of the Son of man, and ye shall not see it.

23 ᵉ˒¹Then they shall say to you, Behold here, or behold there: *but* go not thither, neither follow them.

24 For as the lightning that lighteneth out of the one *part* under heaven, shineth unto the other *part* under heaven, so shall the Son of man be in his day.

25 But first must he suffer many things and be reproved of this generation.

26 ᶠ˒¹And as it was in the days of Noah, so shall it be in the days of the Son of man.

27 They ate, they drank, they married wives, and gave in marriage unto the day that Noah went into the Ark: and the flood came, and destroyed them all.

28 ᵍLikewise also as it was in the days of Lot: They ate, they drank, they bought, they sold, they planted, they built.

29 But in the day that Lot went out of Sodom, it rained fire and brimstone from heaven, and destroyed them all.

30 After these *examples* shall it be in the day when the son of man revealed.

31 ¹At that day he that is upon the house, and his stuff in the house, let him not come down to take it out: and he that is in the field likewise, let him not turn back to that he left behind.

32 ʰRemember Lot's wife.

33 ¹Whosoever will seek to save his soul, shall loose it: and whosoever shall loose it, shall ¹get it life.

34 ʲI tell you, in that night there shall be two in one bed: the one shall be received, and the other shall be left.

35 Two women shall be grinding together, the one shall be taken, and the other shall be left.

36 Two shall be in the field: one shall be received,

Side references:
ᵉ Matt. 24:23
Mark 13:21
ᶠ Gen. 7:5
Matt. 24:38
1 Pet. 3:20
ᵍ Gen. 19:24
ʰ Gen. 19:26
ⁱ Luke 9:24
Matt. 10:39
Mark 8:35
John 12:25
ʲ Matt. 24:41
ᵏ Matt. 24:28

CHAPTER 18
ᵃ Rom. 12:12
1 Thess. 5:17

and another shall be left.

37 ¹And they answered, and said to him, Where, Lord? And he said unto them, ᵏWheresoever the body *is*, thither shall also the eagles be gathered together.

18

2 *The parable of the unrighteous Judge and the widow.* 10 *Of the Pharisee and the Publican.* 15 *Children are of the kingdom of heaven.* 22 *To sell all and give to the poor.* 28 *The Apostles forsake all.* 31 *Christ foretelleth his death.* 35 *The blind man receiveth sight.*

1 And ¹he spake also a parable unto them, *to this end,* that they ᵃought always to pray, and not to ²wax faint,

2 ¹Saying, there was a judge in a certain city, which feared not God, neither reverenced man.

3 And there was a widow in that city, which came unto him, saying, Do me justice against mine adversary.

4 And he would not of a long time: but afterward he said with himself, Though I fear not God, nor reverence man,

5 Yet because this widow troubleth me, I will do her right, lest at the last she come and ¹make me weary.

6 And the Lord said, Hear what the unrighteous judge saith.

7 Now shall not God avenge his elect, which cry day and night unto him, yea, though ¹he suffer long for them?

8 I tell you he will avenge them quickly: but when the Son of man cometh, shall he find faith on the earth?

9 ¶ ¹He spake also this parable unto certain which trusted in themselves that they were just, and despised others.

10 Two men went up into the Temple to pray: the one a Pharisee, and the other a Publican.

17:21 ¹ You look about for Messiah as though he were absent, but he is amongst you in the midst of you.

17:22 ¹ We oftentimes neglect those things when they be present, which we afterward desire when they are gone, but in vain.
² The time will come that you shall seek for the Son of man, with great sorrow of heart, and shall not find him.

17:23 ¹ Christ forewarneth us that false Christs shall come, and that his glory shall suddenly be spread far and wide through the world, after that the ignomy of the cross is put out and extinguished.

17:26 ¹ The world shall be taken unawares with the sudden judgment of God: and therefore the faithful ought to watch continually.

17:31 ¹ We must take good heed, that neither distrust, nor the enticements of this world, nor any respect of friendship hinder us the least that may be.

17:33 ¹ That is, shall save it, so Matthew expoundeth it: for the life that is here spoken of, is everlasting salvation.

17:37 ¹ The only way to continue is to cleave to Christ.

18:1 ¹ God will have us to continue in prayer, not to weary us, but to exercise us, therefore we must so strive with impatience, that long delay cause us not to break off the course of our prayers.
² Yield to afflictions, and adversities, as they do which are out of heart.

18:2 ¹ He doth not compare things that are equal together, but the less with the greater: If a man get his right at a most unrighteous judge's hands, much more shall the prayers of the godly prevail before God.

18:5 ¹ Word for word, beat me down with her blows, and it is a metaphor taken of wrestlers, who beat their adversaries with their fists or clubs: so do they that are importunate beat the judge's ears with their crying out, even as it were with blows.

18:7 ¹ Though he seems slow in revenging the injury done to his.

18:9 ¹ Two things especially make our prayers void and of none effect: confidence of our own righteousness, and the contempt of others: and an humble heart is contrary to both these.

11 ¹The Pharisee stood and prayed thus with himself, O God, I thank thee that I am not as other men, extortioners, unjust, adulterers, or even as this Publican.

12 I fast twice in the week: I give tithe of all that ever I possess.

13 But the Publican standing ¹afar off, would not lift up so much as his eyes to heaven, but smote his breast, saying, O God, be merciful to me a sinner.

14 I tell you, this man departed to his house, justified rather than the other: ᵇfor every man that exalteth himself shall be brought low, and he that humbleth himself shall be exalted.

15 ¶ ⁶¹They brought unto him also babes that he should touch them. ²And when his disciples saw it, they rebuked them.

16 ¹But Jesus ²called them unto him, and said, Suffer the babes to come unto me, and forbid them not: for of such is the kingdom of God.

17 ¹Verily I say unto you, whosoever receiveth not the kingdom of God as a babe, he shall not enter therein.

18 ᵈThen a certain ruler asked him, saying, Good Master, what ought I do, to inherit eternal life?

19 And Jesus said unto him, Why callest thou me good? none is good, save one, *even* God.

20 Thou knowest the commandments, ᶜThou shalt not commit adultery: Thou shalt not kill: Thou shalt not steal: Thou shalt not bear false witness: Honor thy father and thy mother.

21 ¹And he said, All these have I kept from my youth.

22 Now when Jesus heard that, he said unto him, yet lackest thou one thing, Sell all that ever thou hast, and distribute unto the poor, and thou shalt have treasure in heaven, and come follow me.

23 But when he heard those things, he was very heavy: for he was marvelous rich.

24 ¹And when Jesus saw him very sorrowful, he said, With what difficulty shall they that have riches, enter into the kingdom of God!

25 Surely it is easier for a camel to go through a needle's eye, than for a rich man to enter into the

marginal references:
ᵇ Luke 14:11
Matt. 23:12
ᶜ Matt. 19:13
Mark 10:13
ᵈ Matt. 19:16
Mark 10:17
ᵉ Exod. 20:30
ᶠ Matt. 19:27
Mark 10:28
ᵍ Matt. 20:17
Mark 10:32
ʰ Matt. 20:29
Mark 10:46

kingdom of God.

26 Then said they that heard it, And who then shall be saved?

27 And he said, The things which are impossible with men, are possible with God.

28 ¶ ᶠThen Peter said, Lo, we have left all, and have followed thee.

29 ¹And he said unto them, Verily I say unto you, there is no man that hath left house, or parents, or brethren, or wife, or children for the kingdom of God's sake,

30 Which shall not receive much more in this world, and in the world to come life everlasting.

31 ¶ ᵍ¹Then Jesus took unto him the twelve, and said unto them, Behold, we go up to Jerusalem, and all things shall be fulfilled to the Son of man, that are written by the Prophets.

32 For he shall be delivered unto the Gentiles, and shall be mocked, and shall be spiteful entreated, and shall be spitted on.

33 And when they have scourged him, they will put him to death: but the third day he shall rise again.

34 But they understood ¹none of these things, and this saying was hid from them, neither perceived they the things, which were spoken.

35 ¶ ʰ·¹And it came to pass, that as he was come near unto Jericho, a certain blind man sat by the wayside, begging.

36 And when he heard the people pass by, he asked what it meant.

37 And they said unto him, that Jesus of Nazareth passed by.

38 Then he cried, saying, Jesus the Son of David, have mercy on me.

39 ¹And they which went before, rebuked him that he should hold his peace, but he cried much more, O Son of David have mercy on me.

40 And Jesus stood still, and commanded him to be brought unto him. And when he was come near, he asked him,

41 Saying, What wilt thou that I do unto thee? And he said, Lord, that I may receive my sight.

18:11 ¹ Although we confess that whatsoever we have, we have it of God, yet are we despised of God, as proud and arrogant, if we put never so little trust in our own works before God.

18:13 ¹ Far from the Pharisee in a lower place.

18:15 ¹ The children were tender and young, in that they were brought, which appeareth more evidently in that, that they were infants, which is to be marked against them that are enemies to the baptizing of children.

² To judge or think of Christ after the reason of our flesh, is the cause of infinite corruptions.

18:16 ¹ The children also of the faithful are comprehended in the free covenant of God.

² Them that carried the children, whom the disciples drove away.

18:17 ¹ Childlike innocence is an ornament of Christians.

18:21 ¹ The enticement of riches carrieth away many from the right way.

18:24 ¹ To be both rich and godly, is a singular gift of God.

18:29 ¹ They become the richest of all, which refuse not to be poor for Christ's sake.

18:31 ¹ As sure and certain as persecution is, so sure is the glory which remaineth for the conquerors.

18:34 ¹ Hereby we see how ignorant the disciples were.

18:35 ¹ Christ showeth by a visible miracle, that he is the light of the world.

18:39 ¹ The more stops and lets that Satan layeth in our way, even by them which profess Christ's Name, so much the more ought we to go forward.

42 And Jesus said unto him, Receive thy sight: thy faith hath saved thee.

43 Then immediately he received his sight, and followed him, praising God: and all the people, when they saw *this*, gave praise to God.

19

2 Zacchaeus the Publican.   13 Ten pieces of money delivered to servants to occupy withall.   19 Jesus entereth into Jerusalem.   41 He foretelleth the destruction of the ciy with tears.   45 He casteth the sellers out of the Temple.

1 Now ¹when Jesus entered and passed through Jericho,

2 Behold, there was a man named Zacchaeus, which *was* the ¹chief receiver of the tribute, and he was rich.

3 And he sought to see Jesus, who he should be, and could not for the press, because he was of a low stature.

4 Wherefore he ran before, and climbed up into a wild fig tree, that he might see him: for he should come that *way*.

5 And when Jesus came to the place, he looked up, and saw him, and said unto him, Zacchaeus, come down at once: for today I must abide at thine house.

6 Then he came down hastily, and received him joyfully.

7 ¹And when all they saw it, they murmured, saying, that he was gone in to lodge with a sinful man.

8 ¹And Zacchaeus stood forth, and said unto the Lord, Behold, Lord, the half of my goods I give to the poor: and if I have taken from any man by ²forged cavillation, I restore him fourfold.

9 Then Jesus said to him, This day is salvation come unto this house, forasmuch as he is also become the ¹son of Abraham.

10 ªFor the son of man is come to seek, and to save that which was lost.

11 ¹And while they heard these things, he continued and spake a parable, because he was near to

CHAPTER 19
ª Matt. 18:11
ᵇ Matt. 25:14

Jerusalem, and because also they thought that the kingdom of God should shortly appear.

12 He said therefore, ᵇA certain noble man went into a far country, to receive for himself a kingdom, and so to come again.

13 ¹And he called his ten servants, and delivered them ten pieces of money, and said unto them, Occupy till I come.

14 Now his citizens hated him, and sent an ambassage after him, saying, We will not have this man to reign over us.

15 And it came to pass, when he was come again, and had received his kingdom, that he commanded the servants to be called to him, to whom he gave his money, that he might know what every man had gained.

16 Then came the first, saying, Lord, ¹thy piece hath increased ten pieces.

17 And he said unto him, Well, good servant: because thou hast been faithful in a very little thing, take thou authority over ten cities.

18 And the second came, saying, Lord, thy piece hath increased five pieces.

19 And to the same he said, Be thou also *ruler* over five cities.

20 ¹So the other came, and said, Lord, behold thy piece, which I have laid up in a napkin:

21 For I feared thee, because thou art a straight man: thou takest up that thou laidst not down, and reapest that thou didst not sow.

22 Then he said unto him, Of thine own mouth will I judge thee, O evil servant. Thou knewest that I am a straight man, taking up that I laid not down, and reaping that I did not sow.

23 Wherefore then gavest not thou my money into the ¹bank, that at my coming I might have required it with vantage?

24 And he said to them that stood by, Take from him that piece, and give it him that hath ten pieces.

25 (And they said unto him, Lord, he hath ten pieces.)

19:1 ¹ Christ preventeth them with his grace especially which seemed to be furthest from it.

19:2 ¹ The overseer and head of the Publicans which were there together: for the Publicans were divided into companies: as we may gather by many places of Cicero his orations.

19:7 ¹ The world forsaketh the grace of God, and yet is unwilling that it should be bestowed upon others.

19:8 ¹ The example of true repentance, is known by the effect.

  ² By falsely accusing any man: and this agreeth most fitly to the master of the customer's person: for commonly they have this trade among them when they rob and spoil the commonweal, they have nothing in their mouths, but the profit of the commonweal, and under that color they play the thieves, insomuch that if men reprove and go about to redress their robbery, and spoiling, they cry out, the commonwealth is hindered.

19:9 ¹ Beloved of God, one that walketh in the steps of Abraham's faith: and we gather that salvation came to that house, because they

received the blessing as Abraham had, for all of the household were circumcised.

19:11 ¹ We must patiently wait for the judgment of God, which shall be revealed in his time.

19:13 ¹ There are three sorts of men in the Church: the one sort fall from Christ whom they see not; the other, which according to their vocation, bestow the gifts which they have received of God, to his glory with great pains and diligence: the third live idly, and do no good. As for the first, the Lord when he cometh will justly punish them in his time: the other he will bless, according to the pains which they have taken: and as for the slothful and idle persons, he will punish them as the first.

19:16 ¹ This was a piece of money, which the Grecians used, and was in value about an hundred pence, which is about ten crowns.

19:20 ¹ Against them which spend their life idly in deliberating, and otherwise, in contemplation.

19:23 ¹ To the bankers and changers.

26 ⸀For I say unto you, that unto all them that have, it shall be given: and from him that hath not, even that he hath, shall be taken from him.

27 Moreover, those mine enemies, which would not that I should reign over them, bring hither, and slay them before me.

28 ¶ And when he had thus spoken, ¹he went forth before, ascending up to Jerusalem.

29 ᵈ,¹And it came to pass, when he was come near to Bethphage, and Bethany, besides the mount which is called *the mount* of Olives, he sent two of his disciples,

30 Saying, Go ye to the town which is before *you*, wherein as soon as ye are come, ye shall find a colt tied, whereon never man sat: loose him, and bring him *hither*.

31 And if any ask you, why ye loose *him*, thus shall ye say unto him, Because the Lord hath need of him.

32 So they that were sent, went their way, and found it as he had said unto them.

33 And as they were loosing the colt, the owners thereof said unto them, Why loose ye the colt?

34 And they said, The Lord hath need of him.

35 ¶ ᵉSo they brought him to Jesus, and they cast their garments on the colt, and set Jesus thereon.

36 And as he went, they spread their clothes in the way.

37 And when he was now come near to the going down of the mount of Olives, the whole multitude of the disciples began to rejoice, and to praise God with a loud voice, for all the great works that they had seen,

38 Saying, Blessed *be* the King that cometh in the Name of the Lord: peace in heaven, and glory in the highest *places*.

39 ¹Then some of the Pharisees of the company said unto him, Master, rebuke thy disciples.

40 But he answered, and said unto them, I tell you, that if these should hold their peace, the stones would cry.

41 ¶ ᶠ,¹And when he was come near, he beheld the City, and wept for it,

42 ¹Saying, ²O if thou hadst even known ³at the

least in this ⁴thy day those things, which *belong* unto thy ⁵peace! but now are they hid from thine eyes.

43 For the days shall come upon thee, that thine enemies shall cast a trench about thee, and compass thee round, and keep thee in on every side,

44 And shall make thee even with the ground, and thy children which are in thee, and they shall not leave in thee a stone upon a stone, because thou knewest not ¹that season of thy visitation.

45 ¶ ᵍ,¹He went also into the Temple, and began to cast out them that sold therein, and them that bought,

46 Saying unto them, It is written, ʰMine house is the house of prayer, ⁱbut ye have made it a den of thieves.

47 And he taught daily in the Temple. And the high Priests and the Scribes, and the chief of the people sought to destroy him.

48 But they could not find what they might do to him: for all the people hanged upon him when they heard him.

20

4 From whence John's Baptism was. 9 The wickedness of the Priests is noted by the parable of the vineyard and the husbandmen. 21 To give tribute to Caesar. 27 He convinceth the Sadducees denying the resurrection. 41 How Christ is the son of David.

1 And ᵃ,¹it came to pass, that on one of those days, as he taught the people in the Temple, and preached the Gospel, the high Priests and the Scribes came upon him, with the Elders,

2 And spake unto him, saying, Tell us by what authority thou doest these things, or who is he that hath given thee this authority?

3 And he answered, and said unto them, I also will ask you one thing: tell me therefore:

4 The baptism of John, was it from heaven, or of men?

5 And they reasoned within themselves, saying, If we shall say, From heaven, he will say, Why then believed ye him not?

6 But if we shall say, Of men, all the people will stone us: for they be persuaded that John was a

Marginal references

c Luke 8:18
Matt. 13:12
Matt. 25:29
Mark 4:25

d Matt. 21:1
Mark 11:1

e Matt. 21:7
John 12:14

f Luke 21:6
Matt. 24:1
Mark 13:1

g Matt. 21:13

h Mark 11:17

i Isa. 56:7
Jer. 7:11

CHAPTER 20

a Matt. 21:25
Mark 11:27

19:28 ¹ The disciples staggered and stayed at the matter, but Christ goeth on boldly though death were before his eyes.

19:29 ¹ Christ showeth in his own person, that his kingdom is not of this world.

19:39 ¹ When they linger which ought to be the chiefest preachers and setters forth of the kingdom of God, he will raise up others extraordinarily, in despite of them.

19:41 ¹ Christ is not simply delighted with the destruction, no not of the wicked.

19:42 ¹ Christ breaketh off his speech, which showeth partly how he was moved with compassion for the destruction of the city, that was like to ensue: and partly to upbraid them for their treachery and stubbornness against him, such as hath not lightly been heard of.

² At least wise thou, O Jerusalem, to whom this message was properly sent.

³ If after the slaying of so many Prophets, and so oft refusing me the Lord of the Prophets, now especially in this my last coming to thee, thou hadst had any regard to thyself.

⁴ The fit and commodious time is called the day of this city.

⁵ That is, those things wherein thy happiness standeth.

19:44 ¹ That is, this very instant wherein God visited thee.

19:45 ¹ Christ showeth after his entry into Jerusalem by a visible sign, that it is his office enjoined him of his Father to purge the Temple.

20:1 ¹ The Pharisees being overcome with the truth of Christ's doctrine, move a question about his outward calling, and are overcome by the witness of their own conscience.

Prophet.

7 Therefore they answered, that they could not tell whence it *was*.

8 Then Jesus said unto them, Neither tell I you, by what authority I do these things.

9 ¶ [b,1]Then began he to speak to the people this parable, A certain man planted a vineyard, and let it forth to husbandmen: and went into a strange country, for a great time.

10 And at the time convenient he sent a servant to the husbandmen, that they should give him of the fruit of the vineyard: but the husbandmen did beat him, and sent him away empty.

11 Again he sent yet another servant: and they did beat him, and foul entreated him, and sent him away empty.

12 Moreover he sent the third, and him they wounded, and cast out.

13 Then said the Lord of the vineyard, What shall I do? I will send my beloved son: it may be that they will do reverence when they see him.

14 But when the husbandmen saw him, they reasoned with themselves, saying, This is the heir: come, let us kill him, that the inheritance may be ours.

15 So they cast him out of the vineyard, and killed him. What shall the Lord of the vineyard therefore do unto them?

16 He will come and destroy these husbandmen, and will give out his vineyard to others. But when they heard it, they said, God forbid.

17 ¶ And he beheld them, and said, What meaneth this then that is written, [c]The stone that the builders refused, that is made the head of the corner?

18 Whosoever shall fall upon that stone, shall be broken: and on whomsoever it shall fall, it will grind him to powder.

19 Then the high Priests, and the Scribes the same hour went about to lay hands on him (but they feared the people) for they perceived that he had spoken this parable against them.

20 [d,1]And they [2]watched *him*, and sent forth [3]spies, which should feign themselves just men [4]to take him in his talk, and to deliver him unto the power and

b Matt. 21:33
Mark 12:1
Isa. 5:1
Jer. 2:21

c Ps. 118:22
Isa. 28:16
Acts 4:11
Rom. 9:33
1 Pet. 2:8

d Matt. 22:16
Matt. 12:13

e Rom. 13:7

f Matt. 22:23
Mark 12:18

g Deut. 25:5

h Exod. 3:6

[5]authority of the governor.

21 And they asked him, saying, Master, we know that thou sayest, and teachest right, neither dost thou accept [1]any man's person, but teachest the way of God truly.

22 Is it lawful for us to give Caesar tribute or no?

23 But he perceived their [1]craftiness, and said unto them, Why tempt ye me?

24 Show me a penny. Whose image and superscription hath it? They answered, and said, Caesars.

25 Then he said unto them, [e]Give then unto Caesar the things which are Caesar's, and to God those which are God's.

26 And they could not reprove his saying before the people: but they marveled at his answer, and held their peace.

27 [f,1]Then came to him certain of the Sadducees (which deny that there is any resurrection) and they asked him,

28 Saying, Master, [g]Moses wrote unto us, If any man's brother die having a wife, and he die without children, that his brother should take *his* wife, and raise up seed unto his brother.

29 Now there were seven brethren, and the first took a wife, and he died without children.

30 And the second took the wife, and he died childless.

31 Then the third took her: and so likewise the seven died, and left no children.

32 And last of all, the woman died also.

33 Therefore at the resurrection, whose wife of them shall she be? for seven had her to wife.

34 Then Jesus answered, and said unto them, The [1]children of this world marry wives, and are married.

35 But they which shall be counted worthy to enjoy that world, and the resurrection from the dead, neither marry wives, neither are married.

36 For they can die no more, forasmuch as they are equal unto the Angels, and are the sons of God, since they are the [1]children of the resurrection.

37 And that the dead shall rise again, even [h]Moses showed it besides the bush, when he said, The Lord is the God of Abraham, and the God of Isaac, and

---

20:9 [1] It is no new thing to have them the chiefest enemies of Christ and his servants, which are conversant in the very Sanctuary of God's holy place: but at length they shall not escape unpunished.

20:20 [1] The last refuge that false prophets have to destroy the true Prophets, is to lay sedition, and treason to their charge.

[2] A fit time to take him in.

[3] Whom they had deceitfully hired.

[4] That they might take some hold in his talk and thereby forge some false accusation against him.

[5] To put him to death.

20:21 [1] Thou are not moved by favor of any: and by person he meaneth outward circumstances, which if a man have respect unto, he will not judge alike of them that are indeed alike.

20:23 [1] Craftiness is a certain diligence and witness to do evil, gotten by much use and great practice in matters.

20:27 [1] The resurrection of the flesh is avouched against the Sadducees.

20:34 [1] They are called here in this place, the children of this world, which live in this world: and not they, that wholly are given to the world, as before Luke 16:8, which are contrary to the children of light.

20:36 [1] That is, men partakers of the resurrection, for as we say truly, that they shall live indeed, which shall enjoy everlasting bliss, so do they rise indeed, which rise to life, though if this word resurrection, be taken generally, it belongeth also to the wicked which shall rise to condemnation, which is not properly life, but death.

the God of Jacob.

38 For he is not the God of the dead, but of them which live: for all [1]live unto him.

39 Then certain of the Scribes answered, and said, Master, thou hast well said.

40 And after that, durst they not ask him anything at all.

41 ¶ [i,1]Then said he unto them, How say they that Christ is David's son?

42 And David himself saith in the book of the Psalms, [J]The Lord said unto my Lord, Sit at my right hand,

43 Till I shall make thine enemies thy footstool.

44 Seeing David called him Lord, how is he then his son?

45 ¶ Then in the audience of all the people he said unto his disciples,

46 [k,1]Beware of the Scribes, which willingly go in long robes, and love salutations in the markets, and the highest seats in the assemblies, and the chief rooms at feasts:

47 Which devour widow's [1]houses, and in show make long prayers: These shall receive greater damnation.

21

1 *The widow's liberality above her riches.*   5 *Of the time of the destruction of the Temple,*   19 *and Jerusalem.*   25 *The signs going before the last judgment.*

1 And [a,1]as he beheld, he saw the rich men which cast their gifts into the treasury.

2 And he saw also a certain poor widow which cast in thither two mites:

3 And he said, Of a truth I say unto you, that this poor widow hath cast in more than they all.

4 For they all have of their superfluity cast into the offerings of God: but she of her penury hath cast in all the living that she had.

5 [b,1]Now as some spake of the Temple, how it was garnished with goodly stones, and with [2]consecrated things, he said,

6 Are these the things that ye look upon? the days will come wherein a stone shall not be left upon a

[i] Matt. 22:44
Mark 12:35

[J] Ps. 110:1

[k] Luke 11:43
Matt. 23:6
Mark 12:38

CHAPTER 21

[a] Mark 12:42

[b] Luke 19:43
Matt. 24:1
Mark 13:1

[c] Eph. 5:6
2 Thess. 2:3

[d] Matt. 24:7
Mark 13:18

[e] Luke 12:12
Matt. 10:19
Mark 13:11

[f] Matt. 10:30

[g] Dan. 9:27
Matt. 14:15
Mark 13:14

stone, that shall not be thrown down.

7 Then they asked him, saying, Master, but when shall these things be? and what sign *shall* there *be* when these things shall come to pass?

8 [c]And he said, Take heed, that ye be not deceived: for many will come [1]in my Name, saying, I am *Christ*, and the time draweth near: follow ye not them therefore.

9 [1]And when ye hear of wars and seditions, be not afraid: for these things must first come, but the end followeth not by and by.

10 Then said he unto them, Nation shall rise against nation, and kingdom against kingdom,

11 [d]And great earthquakes shall be in divers places, and hunger, and pestilence, and fearful things, and great signs shall there be from heaven.

12 But before all these, they shall lay their hands on you, and persecute *you*, delivering you up to the assemblies, and into prisons, and bring you before Kings and rulers for my Name's sake.

13 And this shall turn to you, for a [1]testimonial.

14 [e]Lay it up therefore in your hearts, that ye cast not beforehand what ye shall answer.

15 For I will give you a mouth, and wisdom where against all your adversaries shall not be able to speak nor resist.

16 Yea, ye shall be betrayed also of your parents and of your brethren, and kinsmen, and friends, and *some* of you shall they put to death.

17 And ye shall be hated of all men for my Name's sake.

18 [f]Yet there shall not one hair of your heads perish.

19 By your patience [1]possess your souls.

20 ¶ [g,1]And when ye see Jerusalem besieged with soldiers, then understand that the desolation thereof is near.

21 Then let them which are in Judea, flee to the mountains: and let them which are in the midst thereof, depart out: and let not them that are in the country, enter therein:

22 For these be the days of vengeance, to fulfill all

20:38 [1] That is, before him: a notable saying, the godly do not die, though they die here on earth.

20:41 [1] Christ is so the son of David according to the flesh, that he is also his Lord (because he is the everlasting son of God) according to the spirit.

20:46 [1] We must avoid the example of the ambitious and covetous pastors.

20:47 [1] This is spoken by the figure Metonymy, houses, for the goods and substance.

21:1 [1] The poor may exceed in bounty and liberality even the richest, according to God's judgment.

21:5 [1] The destruction of the Temple is foretold, that that true spiritual building may be built up, whose head builders must and ought to be circumspect.

[2] There were things that were hanged upon walls and pillars.

21:8 [1] Using my Name.

21:9 [1] The true Temple of God is built up even in the midst of incredible tumults, and most sharp miseries, through invincible patience, so that the end thereof cannot be but most happy.

21:13 [1] This shall be the end of your troubles and afflictions, they shall be witnesses both before God and man, as well of the treacherous and cruel dealing of your enemies, as also of your constancy: A noble saying, that the afflictions of the godly and holy men pertains to the witness of the truth.

21:19 [1] Though you are compassed about on all sides with many miseries, yet notwithstanding be valiant and courageous, and bear out these things manfully.

21:20 [1] The final destruction of the whole city is foretold.

things that are written.

23 But woe *be* to them that be with child, and to them that give suck in those days: for there shall be great distress in this land, and [1]wrath over this people,

24 And they shall fall on the [1]edge of the sword, and shall be led captive into all nations, and Jerusalem shall be trodden under foot of the Gentiles, until the time of the Gentiles be fulfilled.

25 [b,1]Then there shall be signs in the sun, and in the moon, and in the stars, and upon the earth trouble among the nations, with perplexity: the sea and the waters shall roar.

26 [1]And men's hearts shall fail them for fear and for looking after those things which shall come on the world: for the powers of heaven shall be shaken.

27 And then shall they see the Son of man come in a cloud, with power and great glory.

28 And when these things begin to come to pass, then look up, and lift up your heads: [i]for your redemption draweth near.

29 [1]And he spake to them a parable, Behold, the fig tree, and all trees,

30 When they now shoot forth, ye seeing them, know of your own selves, that summer is then near.

31 So likewise ye, when ye see these things come to pass, know ye that the kingdom of God is near.

32 Verily I say unto you, This age shall not pass, till all *these* things be done:

33 Heaven and earth shall pass away, but my words shall not pass away.

34 [j]Take heed to yourselves, lest at any time your hearts be oppressed with surfeiting and drunkenness, and cares of this life, and lest that day come on you at unawares.

35 For as a snare shall it come [1]on all them that dwell on the face of the whole earth.

36 Watch therefore, and pray continually, that ye may be counted worthy to escape all these things that shall come to pass, and that ye may [1]stand before the son of man.

37 ¶ Now in the daytime he taught in the Temple,

Marginal references:
[b] Isa. 13:10
Ezek. 31:7
Matt. 24:29
Mark 13:14
[i] Rom. 8:27
[j] Rom. 13:13

CHAPTER 22
[a] Matt. 26:1-5
Mark 14:10
[b] Matt. 26:14
Mark 14:10
[c] Matt. 26:17
Mark 14:13

and at night he went out, and abode in the mount, that is called the *mount* of Olives.

38 And all the people came in the morning to him, to hear him in the Temple.

22

3 Judas selleth Christ. 7 The Apostles prepare the Passover. 24 They strive who shall be chiefest. 31 Satan desireth them. 35 Christ showeth that they wanted nothing. 42 He prayeth in the mount. 44 He sweateth blood. 50 Malchus's ear cut off and healed. 57, 58, 60 Peter denieth Christ thrice. 63 Christ is mocked and strooken. 69 He confesseth himself to be the Son of God.

1 Now [a]the [1]feast of unleavened bread drew near, which is called the Passover.

2 And the high Priests and Scribes sought how they might kill him: for they feared the people.

3 [b,1]Then entered Satan into Judas, who was called Iscariot, and was of the number of the twelve.

4 And he went his way, and communed with the high Priests and [1]captains, how he might betray him to them.

5 So they were glad, and agreed to give him money.

6 And he consented, and sought opportunity to betray him unto them, when the people were [1]away.

7 ¶ [c,1]Then came the day of unleavened bread, when the Passover [2]must be sacrificed.

8 And he sent Peter and John, saying, Go and prepare us the [1]Passover that we may eat it.

9 And they said to him, Where wilt thou, that we prepare *it?*

10 Then he said unto them, Behold, when ye be entered into the city, there shall a man meet you, bearing a pitcher of water: follow him into the house that he entereth in,

11 And say unto the good man of the house, The Master saith unto thee, Where is the lodging where I shall eat my Passover with my disciples?

12 Then he shall show you a great high chamber trimmed: there make it ready.

13 So they went, and found as he had said unto

21:23 [1] By wrath, those things are meant, which God sendeth when he is displeased.

21:24 [1] Word for word, mouth, for the Hebrews call the edge of a sword the mouth, because the edge biteth.

21:25 [1] When the times are expired, appointed for the salvation of the Gentiles and punishment of the Jews: And so he passeth from the destruction of Jerusalem, to the history of the latter judgment.

21:26 [1] After divers tempests, the Lord will at the length plainly appear to deliver his Church.

21:29 [1] We must be sober and watchful both day and night for the Lord's coming, that we be not taken at unawares.

21:35 [1] On all men wheresoever they be.

21:36 [1] You may so appear that you will abide the countenance and sentence of the Judge without fear.

22:1 [1] Christ is taken upon the day of the Passover, rather by the providence of his Father, than by the will of men.

22:3 [1] God by his wonderful providence, causeth him to be the minister of our salvation, who was the author of our destruction.

22:4 [1] They that had the charge of keeping the Temple, which were none of the Priests and Bishops, as appeareth by verse 52 of this Chapter.

22:6 [1] Without tumult, unwitting to the people which used to follow him: and therefore indeed they watched their time, when they knew he was alone in the garden.

22:7 [1] Christ teacheth his disciples by a manifest miracle, that although he be going to be crucified, yet nothing is hid from him: and therefore that he goeth willingly to death.

[2] By the order appointed by the Law.

22:8 [1] The lamb which was the figure of the Passover: And this is spoken by the figure metonymy, which is very usual in the matter of the Sacraments.

them, and made ready the Passover.

14 ^{d,1}And when the ²hour was come, he sat down, and the twelve Apostles with him.

15 Then he said unto them, I have earnestly desired to eat this Passover with you, before I ¹suffer.

16 For I say unto you, Henceforth I will not eat of it anymore, until it be fulfilleth in the kingdom of God.

17 And he took the cup, and gave thanks, and said, Take this, and divide it among you:

18 For I say unto you, I will not drink of the fruit of the vine, until the kingdom of God be come.

19 ^{e,1}And he took bread, and when he had given thanks, he brake it, and gave to them, saying, This is my body, which is given for you: do this in the remembrance of me.

20 Likewise also after supper *he took* the cup, saying, This ¹cup *is* ²that new Testament in my blood, which is shed for you.

21 ^{f,1}Yet behold, the ²hand of him that betrayeth me, is with me at the table.

22 ¹And truly the Son of man goeth as it is appointed: but woe *be* to that man by whom he is betrayed.

23 Then they began to inquire among themselves which of them it should be, that should do that.

24 ¶ ^{g,1}And there arose also a strife among them, which of them should seem to be the greatest.

25 But he said unto them, The kings of the Gentiles reign over them, and they that bear rule over them, are called ¹bountiful.

26 But ye *shall* not *be* so: but let the greatest among you be as the least: and the chiefest as he that serveth.

27 For who is greater, he that sitteth at table, or

Reference column:
^d Matt. 26:10
Mark 14:17
^e Matt. 26:16
Mark 14:22
1 Cor. 11:24
^f Matt. 26:21
Mark 14:18
Ps. 41:9
^g Matt. 20:25
Mark 10:42
^h Matt. 19:28
ⁱ 1 Pet. 5:8
^j Matt. 26:34
Mark 14:39
John 13:38
^k Matt. 10:9
^l Isa. 63:12
^m Matt. 26:36
Mark 14:32
John 18:1
ⁿ Matt. 26:14
Mark 14:38

he that serveth? is not he that sitteth at table? And I am among you as he that serveth.

28 ¹And ye are they which have continued with me in my tentations.

29 Therefore I appoint unto you a kingdom, as my Father hath appointed unto me,

30 ^hThat ye may eat, and drink at my table, in my kingdom, and sit on seats, and judge the twelve tribes of Israel.

31 ¶ ¹And the Lord said, Simon, Simon, behold, ⁱSatan hath desired you, ²to winnow you as wheat.

32 ¹But I have prayed for thee, that thy faith fail not: therefore when thou art converted, strengthen thy brethren.

33 ^{j,1}And he said unto him: Lord, I am ready to go with thee into prison, and to death.

34 But he said, I tell thee, Peter, the cock shall not crow this day, before thou hast thrice denied that thou knewest me.

35 ¶ And he said unto them, ^kWhen I sent you without bag, and scrip, and shoes, lacked ye anything? And they said, Nothing.

36 ¹Then he said to them, But now he that hath a bag, let him take it, and likewise a scrip: and he that hath none, let him sell his coat, and buy a sword.

37 For I say unto you, That yet the same which is written, must be performed in me, ^lEven with the wicked was he numbered: for doubtless those things which *are written* of me, have an end.

38 And they said, Lord, behold, here are two swords. And he said unto them, It is enough.

39 ¶ ^mAnd he came out, and went (as he was wont) to the mount of Olives: and his disciples also followed him.

40 ^{n,1}And when he came to the place, he said to

22:14 ¹ Christ having ended the Passover according to the order of the Law, forewarneth them that this shall be his last banquet with them, after the manner and necessity of this life.

  ² The evening and twilight, at what time this supper was to be kept.

22:15 ¹ I am put to death.

22:19 ¹ Christ establisheth his new Covenant, and his communicating with us with new signs.

22:20 ¹ Here is a double Metonymy: for first the vessel is taken for that which is contained in the vessel, as the cup, for the wine which is within the cup. Then the wine is called the Covenant or Testament, whereas indeed it is but the sign of the Testament, or rather of the blood of Christ, whereby the Testament was made: neither is it a vain sign, though it be not all one with the thing that it representeth.

  ² This word, *that*, showeth the excellency of the Testament, and answereth to the place of Jeremiah, Chapter 31:31, where the new Testament is promised.

22:21 ¹ Christ showeth again that he goeth to death willingly, although he be not ignorant of Judas's treason.

  ² That is, his practice , so use the Hebrews to speak, 2 Kings 14:19. Is not the hand of Joab in this matter?

22:22 ¹ Although the decree of God's providence comes necessarily to pass, yet it excuseth not the fault of the instruments.

22:24 ¹ The Pastors are not called to rule, but to serve.

22:25 ¹ Have great titles, for so it was the custom to honor Princes with some great titles.

22:28 ¹ Such as are partakers of the afflictions of Christ, shall also be partakers of his kingdom.

22:31 ¹ We must always think upon the wait that Satan layeth for us.

  ² To toss you and scatter you, and also to cast you out.

22:32 ¹ It is through the prayers of Christ, that the elect do never utterly fall away from the faith: and that for this cause, that they should stir up one another.

22:33 ¹ Christ showeth that faith differeth much from a vain security, in setting before us the grievous example of Peter.

22:36 ¹ All this talk is by way of an allegory, as if he said, O my friends and fellow soldiers, you have lived hitherto as it were in peace: but now there is a most sharp battle at hand to be fought, and therefore you must lay all other things aside, and think upon furnishing yourselves in armor. And what this armor is, he showeth by his own example, when he prayed afterward in the garden, and reproved Peter for striking with the sword.

22:40 ¹ Christ hath made death acceptable unto us, by overcoming in our name, all the horrors of death, which had joined with them the curse of God.

them, Pray, lest ye enter into tentation.

41 [1]And he was drawn aside from them about a stone's cast, and kneeled down, and prayed,

42 Saying, Father, If thou wilt, take away this cup from me: nevertheless, not my will, but thine be done.

43 And there appeared an Angel unto him from heaven, comforting him.

44 But being in an [1]agony, he prayed more earnestly: and his sweat was like [2]drops of blood, trickling down to the ground.

45 [1]And he rose up from prayer, and came to *his* disciples, and found them sleeping for heaviness.

46 And he said unto them, Why sleep ye? rise and pray, lest ye enter into tentation.

47 ¶ [o,1]And while he yet spake, behold, a company, and he that was called Judas one of the twelve, went before them, and came near unto Jesus to kiss him.

48 And Jesus said unto him, Judas, betrayest thou the Son of man with a kiss?

49 [1]Now when they which were about him, saw what would follow, they said unto him, Lord, shall we smite with the sword?

50 And one of them smote a servant of the high Priest, and struck off his right ear.

51 Then Jesus answered, and said, Suffer *them* thus far: and he touched his ear, and healed him.

52 [1]Then Jesus said unto the high Priests, and captains of the Temple, and the Elders which were come to him, Be ye come out as unto a thief with swords and staves?

53 When I was daily with you in the Temple, ye stretched not forth the hands against me: but this is your very hour, and the [1]power of darkness.

54 ¶ [p]Then took they him, and led him, and brought him to the high Priest's house. [1]And Peter followed afar off.

55 [q]And when they had kindled a fire in the midst of the hall, and were set down together, Peter also sat down among them.

Marginal references:
[o] Matt. 26:47 / Mark 14:43 / John 18:3
[p] Matt. 26:58
[q] Matt. 26:38,59 / Mark 14:66 / John 18:25
[r] Matt. 26:34 / John 13:38
[s] Matt. 26:67 / Mark 14:65
[t] Matt. 27:1 / Mark 15:1 / John 18:28

56 And a certain maid beheld him as he sat by the fire, and having well looked on him, said, This man was also with him.

57 But he denied him, saying, Woman, I know him not.

58 And after a little while, another man saw him, and said, Thou art also of them. But Peter said, Man, I am not.

59 And about the space of an hour after, a certain other affirmed, saying, Verily, even this man was with him: for he is also a Galilean.

60 And Peter said, Man, I know not what thou sayest. And immediately while he yet spake, the cock crew.

61 Then the Lord turned back, and looked upon Peter: and Peter remembered the word of the Lord, how he had said unto him, [r]Before the cock crow, thou shalt deny me thrice.

62 And Peter went out, and wept bitterly.

63 ¶ [s,1]And the men that held Jesus, mocked him, and struck him.

64 And when they had blindfolded him, they smote him on the face, and asked him, saying, Prophesy who it is that smote thee.

65 And many other things blasphemously spake they against him.

66 [t,1]And as soon as it was day, the Elders of the people, and the high Priests and the Scribes came together, and led him into their Council,

67 Saying, Art thou that Christ? tell us. And he said unto them, If I tell you, ye will not believe it.

68 And if also I ask you, you will not answer me, nor let me go.

69 Hereafter shall the Son of man sit at the right hand of the power of God.

70 Then said they all, Art thou then the Son of God? And he said to them, Ye say, that I am.

71 Then said they, What need we any further witness? for we ourselves have heard it of his own mouth.

22:41 [1] Prayers are a sure succor against the most perilous assaults of our enemies.

22:44 [1] This agony showeth that Christ strove much, and was in great distress: for Christ strove not only with the fears of death, as other men used to do, for so many martyrs might seem more constant than Christ, but with the fearful judgment of his angry Father, which is the fearfullest thing in the world: and the matter was, for that he took the burden of all our sins upon himself.

[2] These do not only show that Christ was true man, but other things also which the goodly have to consider of, wherein redemption of all mankind is contained in the son of God his debasing himself to the state of a servant: such things as no man can sufficiently declare.

22:45 [1] Men are utterly sluggish, even in their greatest dangers until Christ stir them up.

22:47 [1] Christ is willingly betrayed and taken, that by his obedience

he might deliver us which were guilty for the betraying of God's glory.

22:49 [1] That zeal which carrieth us out of the bounds of our vocation, pleaseth not Christ.

22:52 [1] Even the very fear of them which took Christ, proveth partly their evil conscience, and partly also that all these things were done by God's providence.

22:53 [1] The power that was given to darkness, to oppress the light for a season.

22:54 [1] We have to behold in Peter an example both of the fragility of man's nature, and of the singular goodness of God toward his elect.

22:63 [1] Christ bare the shame that was due to our sins.

22:66 [1] Christ is wrongfully condemned of blasphemy before the high Priest's judgment seat, that we might be quit before God from the blasphemy which we deserved.

23 *1 He is accuseth before Pilate. 7 He is sent to Herod. 11 He is mocked. 24 Pilate yieldeth him up to the Jews' request. 27 The women bewail him. 33 He is crucified. 39 One of the thieves revileth him. 43 The other is saved by faith. 45 He dieth. 53 He is buried.*

CHAPTER 23
a Matt. 22:21
Mark 12:17
b Matt. 27:11
Mark 15:2
John 18:33
c Matt. 27:13
Mark 15:14
John 18:34
d Matt. 27:32
Mark 15:21
e Isa. 2:29
Hos. 10:8
Rev. 6:16
f 1 Pet. 4:17

1 Then ¹the whole multitude of them arose, and led him unto Pilate.

2 And they began to accuse him, saying, We have found this man ¹perverting the nation, *a*and forbidding to pay tribute to Caesar, saying, That he is Christ a King.

3 *b*And Pilate asked him, saying, Art thou the King of the Jews? And he answered him, and said, Thou sayest it.

4 Then said Pilate to the high Priests, and to the people, I find no fault in this man.

5 But they were the more fierce, saying, He moveth the people, teaching throughout all Judea, beginning at Galilee, even to this place.

6 ¹Now when Pilate heard of Galilee, he asked whether the man were a Galilean.

7 And when he knew that he was of ¹Herod's jurisdiction, he sent him to Herod, which was also at Jerusalem in those days.

8 And when Herod saw Jesus, he was exceedingly glad: for he was desirous to see him of a long season, because he had heard many things of him, and trusteth to have seen some sign done by him.

9 Then questioned he with him of many things: but he answered him nothing.

10 The high Priests also and Scribes stood forth and accused him vehemently.

11 And Herod with his ¹men of war, despised him, and mocked him, and arrayed him in white, and sent him again to Pilate.

12 ¹And the same day Pilate and Herod were made friends together: for before they were enemies one to another.

13 ¶ ¹Then Pilate called together the high Priests, and the ²rulers, and the people,

14 *c*And said unto them, Ye have brought this man unto me, as one that perverted the people: and

behold, I have examined him before you, and have found no fault in this man, of those things whereof ye accuse him:

15 No, nor yet Herod: for I sent you to him: and lo, nothing worthy of death is done of him.

16 ¹I will therefore chastise him, and let him loose.

17 (For of necessity he must have let one loose unto them at the feast.)

18 Then all the multitude cried at once, saying, Away with him, and deliver unto us Barabbas:

19 Which for a certain insurrection made in the city, and murder, was cast in prison.

20 Then Pilate spake again to them, willing to let Jesus loose.

21 But they cried, saying, Crucify, crucify him.

22 ¹And he said unto them the third time, But what evil hath he done? I find no cause of death in him: I will therefore chastise him, and let him loose.

23 But they were instant with loud voices, and required that he might be crucified: and the voices of them and of the high Priests prevailed.

24 So Pilate gave sentence, that it should be as they required.

25 And he let loose unto them him that for insurrection and murder was cast into prison, whom they desired, and delivered Jesus to do with him what they would.

26 ¶ *d,*¹And as they led him away, they caught one Simon of Cyrene, coming out of the field, and on him they laid the cross, to bear it after Jesus.

27 ¹And there followed him a great multitude of people, and of women, which women bewailed and lamented him.

28 But Jesus turned back unto them, and said, Daughters of Jerusalem, weep not for me, but weep for yourselves, and for your children.

29 For behold, the days will come, when men shall say, Blessed *are* the barren, and the wombs that never bare, and the paps which never gave suck.

30 Then shall they begin to say to the mountains, *e*Fall on us: and to the hills, Cover us.

31 *f*For if they do these things to a ¹green tree,

23:1 ¹ Christ, who is now ready to suffer for the sedition, which we raised in this world, is first of all pronounced guiltless, that it might appear that he suffered not for his own sins (which were none) but for ours.

23:2 ¹ Corrupting the people, and leading them into errors.

23:6 ¹ Christ is a laughingstock to princes, but to their great smart.

23:7 ¹ This was Herod Antipas the Tetrarch, in the time of whose governance, which was almost the space of 22 years, John the Baptist preached and was put to death, and Jesus Christ also died and rose again, and the Apostles began to preach, and divers things were done at Jerusalem almost seven years after Christ's death. This Herod was sent into banishment to Lyons, about the second year of Gaius Caesar.

23:11 ¹ Accompanied with his nobles and soldiers which followed him from Galilee.

23:12 ¹ The hatred of godliness joineth the wicked together.

23:13 ¹ Christ is quit the second time, even of him of whom he is condemned, that it might appear, how he being just, redeemed us which were unjust.

² Those whom the Jews called the Sanhedrin.

23:16 ¹ The wisdom of the flesh, of two evils chooseth the less, but God curseth such counsels.

23:22 ¹ Christ is quit the third time, before he was condemned once, that it might appear, how that our sins were condemned in him.

23:26 ¹ An example of the outrageousness and disorder of the soldiers.

23:27 ¹ The triumph of the wicked hath a most horrible end.

23:31 ¹ As if he said, If they do thus to me that am fruitful, and always flourishing, and who lives forever by reason of my Godhead, what will they do to you, that are unfruitful and void of all lively righteousness?

what shall be done to the dry?

32 ^gAnd there were two others, which were evildoers, led with him to be slain.

33 ¹And when they were come to the place, which is called Calvary, there they crucified him, and the evildoers: one at the right hand, and the other at the left.

34 ¹Then said Jesus, Father, forgive them: for they know not what they do. And they parted his raiment, and cast lots.

35 And the people stood, and beheld: and the rulers mocked him with them, saying, He saved others: let him save himself, if he be that Christ the ¹Chosen of God.

36 The soldiers also mocked him, and came and offered him vinegar,

37 And said, If thou be the King of the Jews, save thyself.

38 ¹And a superscription was also written over him, in Greek letters, and in Latin, and in Hebrew, THIS IS THAT KING OF THE JEWS.

39 ¶ ¹And ²one of the evildoers, which were hanged, railed on him, saying, If thou be that Christ, save thyself and us.

40 But the other answered, and rebuked him, saying, Fearest thou not God, seeing thou art in the same condemnation?

41 We are indeed righteously *here*: for we receive things worthy of that we have done: but this man hath done nothing ¹amiss.

42 And he said unto Jesus, Lord, remember me, when thou comest into thy kingdom.

43 Then Jesus said unto him, Verily I say unto thee, today shalt thou be with me in ¹Paradise.

44 ¶ ¹And it was about the sixth hour: and there was a darkness over all the land, until the ninth hour.

45 ¹And the Sun was darkened, and the veil of

Margin references:
g Matt. 27:38 / Mark 15:27 / John 19:18
h Ps. 31:6
i Matt. 27:57 / Mark 15:43 / John 19:38

the Temple rent through the midst.

46 And Jesus cried with a loud voice, and said, ^hFather, into thine hands I commend my spirit. And when he thus had said, he gave up the ghost.

47 ¶ ¹Now when the Centurion saw what was done, he glorified God, saying, Of a surety this man was just.

48 And all the people that came together to that sight, beholding the things which were done: smote their breasts, and returned.

49 ¹And all his acquaintances stood afar off, and the women that followed him from Galilee, beholding these things.

50 ¶ ^{i,1}And behold, there was a man named Joseph, which was a counselor, a good man and a just.

51 He did not consent to the counsel and deed of them, *which was* of Arimathea, a city of the Jews: who also himself waited for the kingdom of God.

52 He went unto Pilate, and asked the body of Jesus,

53 And took it down, and wrapped it in a linen cloth, and laid it in a tomb hewn out of a rock, wherein was never man yet laid.

54 And that day was the preparation, and the Sabbath ¹drew on.

55 ¹And the women also that followed after, which came with him from Galilee, beheld the sepulcher, and how his body was laid.

56 And they returned and prepared odors, and ointments, and resteth the Sabbath *day* according to the commandment.

24 *The women come to the sepulchre. 9 They report that which they heard of the Angels, unto the Apostles. 13 Christ doth accompany two going to Emmaus. 27 He expoundeth the Scriptures unto them. 39 He offereth himself to his Apostles to be handled. 49 He promiseth the holy Ghost. 51 He is carried up into heaven.*

23:33 ¹ Christ became accursed for us upon the Cross, suffering the punishment which they deserved that would be God's.

23:34 ¹ Christ in praying for his enemies, showeth that he is both the sacrifice and the Priest.

23:35 ¹ Whom God loveth more than all others.

23:38 ¹ Pilate at unawares is made a preacher of the kingdom of Christ.

23:39 ¹ Therefore either we must take that spoken by Synecdoche which Matthew saith, or that both of them mocked Christ. But one of them at length overcome with the great patience of God, brake forth into that confession worthy all memory.

² Christ, in the midst of the humbling of himself upon the cross, showeth indeed that he hath both power of life to save the believers, and of death to revenge the rebellious.

23:41 ¹ More than he ought.

23:43 ¹ God made the visible paradise to the East part of the world: but that which we behold with the eyes of our mind is the place of everlasting joy and salvation through the goodness and mercy of God, a most pleasant rest of the souls of the godly, and most quiet

and joyful dwelling.

23:44 ¹ Christ being even at the point of death, showeth himself to be God almighty, even to the blind.

23:45 ¹ Christ entereth stoutly into the very darkness of death, for to overcome death even within his most secret places.

23:47 ¹ Christ causeth his very enemies to give honorable witness on his side, so oft as it pleaseth him.

23:49 ¹ Christ gathereth together, and defendeth his little flock in the midst of the tormentors.

23:50 ¹ Christ through his famous burial confirmeth the truth both of his death, and resurrection, by the plain and evident witness of Pilate.

23:54 ¹ Word for word, dawning, as now beginning, for the light of the former day drew toward the going down, and that was the day of preparation for the feast which was to be kept the day following.

23:55 ¹ Christ, being set upon by the devil and all his instruments, and being even, in death's mouth, setteth weak women in his foreward, minding straightways to triumph over those terrible enemies without any great endeavor.

1 Now the [a,1]first *day* of the week [2]early in the morning, they came unto the sepulcher, and brought the odors which they had prepared, and certain *women* with them.

2 And they found the stone rolled away from the sepulcher,

3 And went in, but found not the body of the Lord Jesus.

4 And it came to pass, that as they were amazed thereat, behold, two men suddenly stood by them in shining vestures.

5 And as they were afraid, and bowed down their faces to the earth, they said to them, Why seek ye him that liveth, among the dead?

6 He is not here, but is risen: remember [b]how he spake unto you, when he was yet in Galilee,

7 Saying, that the Son of man must be delivered into the hands of sinful men, and be crucified, and the third day rise again.

8 And they remembered his words,

9 [1]And returned from the sepulcher, and told all these things unto the eleven, and to all the remnant.

10 Now it was Mary Magdalene, and Joanna, and Mary the *mother* of James, and other women with them which told these things unto the Apostles.

11 But their words seemed unto them as a feigned thing, neither believed they them.

12 [c,1]Then arose Peter and ran unto the sepulcher, and [2]looked in and saw the linen clothes laid by themselves, and departed wondering in himself at that which was come to pass.

13 ¶ [d,1]And behold two of them went that same day to a town which was from Jerusalem about threescore furlongs, called Emmaus.

14 And they talked together of all these things that were done.

15 And it came to pass, as they communed together, and reasoned, that Jesus himself drew near, and went with them.

16 [1]But their eyes were holden, that they could not know him.

17 And he said unto them, What manner of com-

CHAPTER 24
[a] Mark 16:1
John 20:1
[b] Luke 9:22
Matt. 17:23
Mark 9:31
[c] John 20:6
[d] Mark 16:12

munications are these that ye have one to another as ye walk and are sad?

18 And [1]the one (named Cleopas) answered and said unto him, Art thou only a stranger in Jerusalem, and hast not known the things which are come to pass therein in these days?

19 And he said unto them, What things? And they said unto him, Of Jesus of Nazareth, which was a Prophet, mighty indeed and in word before God, and all people,

20 [1]And how the high Priests, and our rulers delivered him to be condemned to death, and have crucified him.

21 But we trusted that it had been he that should have delivered Israel, and as touching all these things, today is the third day, that they were done.

22 Yea, and certain women among us made us astonied, which came early unto the sepulcher.

23 And when they found not his body, they came, saying, that they had also seen a vision of Angels, which said, that he was alive.

24 Therefore certain of them which were with us, went to the sepulcher, and found it even so as the women had said, but him they saw not.

25 Then he said unto them, O fools and slow of heart to believe all that the Prophets have spoken!

26 Ought not Christ to have suffered these things, and to enter into his glory?

27 And he began at Moses, and at all the Prophets, and interpreted unto them in all the Scriptures the things which were *written* of him.

28 And they drew near unto the town, which they went to, but he made as though he would have gone further.

29 But they constrained him, saying, Abide with us, for it is towards night, and the day is far spent. So he went in to tarry with them.

30 And it came to pass, as he sat at table with them, he took the bread, and blessed, and brake it, and gave it to them.

31 Then their eyes were opened, and they knew him: and he was [1]no more seen of them.

24:1 [1] Poor silly women, even beside their expectation are chosen to be the first witnesses of the resurrection, that there might be no suspicion either of deceit or violence.

[2] Very early as Mark saith: or as John saith, while it was yet dark, that is, when it was yet scarce the dawning of the day.

24:9 [1] The cowardly and dastardly minds of the disciples is upbraided by the stout courage of women, (so wrought by God's great mercy) to show that the kingdom of God consisteth in an extraordinary power.

24:12 [1] Christ useth the incredulity of his disciples, to the fuller setting forth of the truth of his resurrection, lest they should seem to have believed that too lightly, which they preached afterward to all the world.

[2] As it were holding down his head, and bowing his neck, looked diligently in.

24:13 [1] The resurrection is proved by two other witnesses, which saw it, and that it was no forged thing framed of purpose in their own brains, all the circumstances do declare.

24:16 [1] Were held back and stayed, God so appointing it, no doubt: and therefore his body was not invisible, but their eyes were dimmed.

24:18 [1] Some of the old fathers think that the other disciple was this our Evangelist, but Epiphanius writing against the Saturnilians, saith it was Nathanael, but all these are uncertainties.

24:20 [1] It appeareth by the converting of the forewarnings of the Prophets, that all those things are true and certain, which the Evangelists have put down in writing of Christ.

24:31 [1] Suddenly taken away, and therefore we may not imagine that he was there in such a body as could not be seen, but believe indeed that he changed his place.

32 And they said between themselves, Did not our hearts burn within us, while he talked with us by the way, and when he opened to us the Scriptures?

33 And they rose up the same hour, and returned to Jerusalem, and found the eleven gathered together, and them that were with them,

34 Which said, The Lord is risen indeed, and hath appeared to Simon.

35 Then they told what things *were* done in the way, and how he was known of them in ¹breaking of bread.

36 ¶ ᵉ,¹And as they spake these things, Jesus himself stood in the midst of them, and said unto them, Peace *be* to you.

37 But they were abashed and afraid, supposing that they had seen a spirit.

38 Then he said unto them, Why are ye troubled? and wherefore do ¹doubts arise in your hearts?

39 Behold mine hands and my feet: for it is I myself: handle me, and see: for a spirit hath not flesh and bones, as ye see me have.

40 And when he had thus spoken, he showed them *his* hands and feet.

41 And while they yet believed not for joy, and wondered, he said unto them, Have ye here any meat?

42 And they gave him a piece of a broiled fish, and of an honeycomb,

ᵉ Mark 16:14
John 20:19
ᶠ John 15:26
Acts 1:4
ᵍ Mark 16:19
Acts 1:9

43 And he took it, and did eat before them.

44 ¹And he said unto them, These are the words, which I spake unto you while I was yet with you, that all must be fulfilled which are written of me in the Law of Moses, and in the Prophets, and in the Psalms.

45 Then opened he their understanding, that they might understand the Scriptures,

46 And said unto them, Thus is it written, and thus it behooved Christ to suffer, and to rise again from the dead the third day,

47 And that repentance, and remission of sins should be preached in his Name among all nations, ¹beginning at Jerusalem.

48 Now ye are witnesses of these things.

49 And behold, I do send the ᶠpromise of my Father upon you: but tarry ye in the city of Jerusalem, ¹until ye be endued with power from on high.

50 ¹Afterward he lead them out into Bethany, and lifted up his hands, and blessed them.

51 And it came to pass, that as he blessed them, ᵍhe departed from them, and was carried up into heaven.

52 And they worshipped him, and returned to Jerusalem with great joy,

53 And were continually in the Temple, praising, and lauding God. Amen.

24:35 ¹ When he brake bread, which that people used, and as the Jews use yet at this day at the beginning of their meals, and say a prayer.

24:36 ¹ The Lord himself showeth by certain and necessary signs, that he was risen again, and that in the same body which he took upon him.

24:38 ¹ Divers and doubtful thoughts which fall oft into men's heads, when any strange thing falleth out, whereof there is no great likelihood.

24:44 ¹ The preaching of the Gospel, which was promised to the Prophets and performed in his time, is committed unto the Apostles: the sum whereof, is repentance and remission of sins.

24:47 ¹ The Apostles who are the preachers of the Gospel beginning at Jerusalem.

24:49 ¹ Until the holy Ghost comes down from heaven upon you.

24:50 ¹ Christ ascendeth into heaven, and departing bodily from his disciples, filleth their hearts with the holy Ghost.

THE HOLY GOSPEL OF JESUS CHRIST,

ACCORDING TO

JOHN

1 *That Word begotten of God before all worlds, 2 and which was ever with the Father, 14 is made man. 6, 7 For what end John was sent from God. 15 His preaching of Christ's office. 19, 20 The record that he bare given out unto the Priests. 40 The calling of Andrew, 42 of Peter, 43 Philip, 45 and Nathanael.*

CHAPTER 1
a Col. 1:16
b Matt. 3:1
Mark 1:4
Luke 3:2
c Heb. 11:3

1 In ¹the ²beginning ³was ⁴that Word, and that Word was ⁵with God, and that ⁶Word was God.

2 This same was in the beginning with God.

3 ᵃ,¹All ²things were made by it, and ³without it ⁴was made nothing that was made.

4 ¹In it ²was life, and that life was ³the light of men.

5 ¹And that light shineth in the wilderness, and the darkness ²comprehendeth it not.

6 ¶ ᵇ,¹There was a man sent from God, whose name *was* John.

7 *This* same came for a witness, to bear witness of that light, that all men ¹through him might believe.

8 He was not ¹that light, but *was sent* to bear witness of that light.

9 ¹This was ²that true light, which lighteth every man that cometh into the world.

10 ¹He was in the world, and the world was ᶜmade by him: and the world knew him not.

11 He came ¹unto his own, and his own received him not.

12 ¹But as many as received him, to them he gave ²prerogative to be the sons of God, *even* to them that believe in his Name,

13 Which are born not of blood, nor of the ¹will of the flesh, nor of the will of man, but of God.

1:1 ¹ The Son of God is of one, and the selfsame eternity or everlastingness, and of one and the selfsame essence or nature, with the Father.

² From his beginning, as the Evangelist saith, 1 John 1:1, as though he said, that the world began not then to have his being, when God began to make all that was made: for the word was even then when all things that were made, began to be made, and therefore he was before the beginning of all things.

³ Had his being.

⁴ This word, That, pointeth out unto us a peculiar and choice thing above all other, and putteth a difference between this Word, which is the Son of God, and the Laws of God, which otherwise also are called the word of God.

⁵ This word (With) putteth out the distinction of persons to us.

⁶ This word (Word) is the first in order in the sentence, and is that which the learned call (Subjectum:) and this word (God) is the latter in order, and the same which the learned call (Predicatum.)

1:3 ¹ The son of God declareth that same his everlasting Godhead, both by the creating of all things, and also by the preserving of them, and especially by the excellent gifts of reason and understanding, wherewith he that beautified man above all other creatures.

² Paul expoundeth this place, Col. 1:15 and 16.

³ That is, as the Father did work, so did the Son work with him: for he was fellow worker with him.

⁴ Of all those things which were made, nothing was made without him.

1:4 ¹ That is, by him: and it is spoken after the manner of the Hebrews, meaning thereby that by his force and working power all life cometh to the world.

² To wit, even then, when all things are made by him, for else he would have said, Life is in him, and not life was.

³ That force of reason and understanding, which is kindled in our minds to acknowledge him, the author of so great a benefit.

1:5 ¹ The light of men is turned into darkness, but yet so that there is clearness enough to make them without excuse.

² They could not perceive nor reach unto it, to receive any light of it, no, they did not so much as acknowledge him.

1:6 ¹ There is another more full manifestation of the Son of God, to the consideration whereof men are in good time stirred up, even by John's voice, who is as it were the herald of Christ.

1:7 ¹ Through John.

1:8 ¹ That light which we spake of, to wit, Christ, who only can lighten our darkness.

1:9 ¹ When as the Son of God saw, that man did not acknowledge him by his works, although they were endued with understanding (which he had given to them all) he exhibited himself unto his people to be seen of them with their corporal eyes: yet neither so did they acknowledge him, nor receive him.

² Who only and properly deserveth to be called the light, for he shineth of himself and borroweth light of none.

1:10 ¹ That person of the Word, was made manifest even at that time when the world was made.

1:11 ¹ The Word showed himself again, when he came in the flesh.

1:12 ¹ The Son being shut out of the most of his people, and acknowledged but of a few, doth regenerate them by his own virtue and power, and receiveth them into that honor which is common to all the children of God, that is to be the sons of God.

² He vouchsafed to give them this prerogative to take them to be his children.

1:13 ¹ Of that gross and corrupt nature of man, which is throughout the Scriptures set as enemy to the Spirit.

14 ^{d,1}And that Word was made ²flesh, and ³dwelt among us, (and we ^esaw the ⁴glory thereof, ⁵as the glory of the only begotten *Son* of the Father) ⁶full of grace and truth.

15 ¶ ¹John bare witness of him, and cried, saying, This was he of whom I said, He that cometh ²after me, was ³before me: for he was better than I.

16 ^{f,1}And of his fullness have all we received, and ²grace for grace.

17 For the Law was given by Moses, but grace and truth came by Jesus Christ.

18 ^{g,1}No man hath seen God at any time: that only begotten Son, which is in the ²bosom of the Father, he hath ³declared him.

19 ¶ ¹Then this is the record of John, when the Jews sent Priests and Levites from Jerusalem to ask him, Who art thou?

20 And he ¹confessed and ²denied not, and said plainly, I ^ham not that Christ.

21 And they asked him, What then? Art thou Elijah? And he said, ¹I am not. Art thou ²that Prophet?

And he answered, No.

22 Then said they unto him, Who art thou, that we may give an answer to them that sent us? What sayest thou of thyself?

23 He said, I ⁱam the voice of him that crieth in the wilderness, Make straight the way of the Lord, as said the Prophet Isaiah.

24 ¹Now they which were sent, were of the Pharisees.

25 And they asked him, and said unto him, ¹Why baptizest thou then, if thou be not that Christ, neither Elijah, nor that Prophet?

26 John answered them, saying, I baptize with water: but there is one ¹among you, whom ye know not.

27 ^jHe it is that cometh after me, which was before me, whose shoe latchet I am not worthy to unloose.

28 These things were done in Bethabara beyond Jordan, where John did baptize.

29 ¶ ¹The next day John seeth Jesus coming unto him, and saith, Behold ²that Lamb of God, which

Cross references (center column):
d Matt. 1:16
e Matt. 17:2
   2 Pet. 1:17
f Col. 1:19
   Col. 2:9
g 1 Tim. 6:16
   1 John 4:12
h Acts 13:25
i Isa. 40:3
   Matt. 3:3
   Luke 3:4
j Matt. 3:11
   Mark 1:7
   Luke 3:16
   Acts 1:5
   Acts 11:16
   Acts 19:4

1:14 ¹ That Son, who is God from everlasting, took upon him man's nature, that one and the selfsame might be both God and man, which manifestly appeared to many witnesses, that saw him amongst whom he was conversant, and unto whom by sure and undoubted arguments he showed both his natures.

² That is, man: so that the part is taken for the whole, by the figure Synecdoche: for he took upon him all our whole nature, that is to say, a true body, and a true soul.

³ For a season, and when that was ended, he went up into heaven: for the word which he useth, is taken from tents: and yet notwithstanding, his absence from us in body is not such, but that he is always present with us, though not in flesh, yet by the virtue of his Spirit.

⁴ The glory which he speaketh of here, is that manifestation of Christ's majesty, which was as it were laid open before our eyes when the Son of God appeared in flesh.

⁵ This word (as) doth not in this place betoken a likeness, but the truth of the matter, for his meaning is this, that we saw such a glory, as beseemed and was meet for the true and only begotten Son of God, who is Lord and King over all the world.

⁶ He was not only a partaker of grace and truth, but was full of the very substance of grace and truth.

1:15 ¹ John is a faithful witness of the excellency of Christ.

² That is, He before whom I am sent to prepare him the way: so that these words are referred to the time of his calling, and not of his age, for John was six months older than he.

³ This sentence hath in it a turning of the reason as we call it, as who would say, a setting of that first which should be last, and that last which should be first: for in plain speech this it is: He that cometh after me, is better than I am, for he was before me. The like kind of turning the reason we find in Luke 7:47: many sins are forgiven her, because she loved much, which is thus much to say, she loved much, because many sins are forgiven her.

1:16 ¹ Christ is the most plentiful fountain of all goodness, but then he poured out his gifts most bountifully, when he exhibited and showed himself to the world.

² That is grace upon grace, as a man would say graces heaped one upon another.

1:18 ¹ That true knowledge of God proceedeth only from Jesus Christ.

² Who is nearest to his Father, not only in respect of his love towards him, but by the bond of nature, and for that union or oneness that is between them, whereby the Father and the Son are one.

³ Revealed him, and showed him unto us, whereas before he was hid under the shadows of the Law, so that the quickness of the sight of our minds was not able to perceive him: for whosoever seeth him, seeth the Father also.

1:19 ¹ John is neither the Messiah, nor like to any of the other Prophets, but is the herald of Christ, who is now present.

1:20 ¹ He did acknowledge him, and spake of him plainly and openly.

² This repeating of the one and the selfsame thing, though in divers words, is used much of the Hebrews, and it hath great force: for they used to speak one thing twice, to set it out more certainly and plainly.

1:21 ¹ The Jews thought that Elijah should come again before the days of Messiah, and they took the ground of that their opinion out of Mal. 4:5, which place is to be understood of John, Matt. 11:14. And yet John denieth that he is Elijah, answering them indeed according as they meant.

² They inquire of some great Prophet, and not of Christ, for John denied before, that he is Christ, for they thought that some great Prophet should be sent like unto Moses, wresting to that purpose that place of Deut. 18:15, which is to be understood of all the company of the Prophets and ministers, which have been and shall be to the end, and especially of Christ, who is the head of all Prophets.

1:24 ¹ Christ is the author of baptism, and not John: and therefore the force thereof consisteth not in John, who is the minister, but wholly in Christ the Lord.

1:25 ¹ Hereby we may prove that the Jews knew there should be some change in religion under Messiah.

1:26 ¹ Whom all the world seeth not, and is even amongst you.

1:29 ¹ The body and truth of all the sacrifices of the Law, to make satisfaction for the sin of the world, is in Christ.

² This word (That) which is added, hath great force in it, not only to set forth the worthiness of Christ, and so to separate him from the Lamb which was a figure of him, and from all other sacrifices of the Law, but also to bring into our mind the Prophecies of Isaiah and others.

[3]taketh away the [4]sin of the world.

30 This is he of whom I said, After me cometh a man, which was before me: for he was better than I.

31 And [1]I knew him not: but because he should be declared to Israel, therefore am I come, baptizing with water.

32 [1]So John bare record, saying, I beheld, [k]that Spirit come down from heaven, like a dove, and it abode upon him,

33 And I knew him not: but he that sent me to baptize with water, he said unto me, Upon whom thou shalt see that Spirit come down, and tarry still on him, that is he which baptizeth with the holy Ghost.

34 And I saw, and bare record that this is [1]that Son of God.

35 ¶ [1]The next day, John stood again, and two of his disciples.

36 [1]And he beheld Jesus walking by, and said, Behold that Lamb of God.

37 [1]And the two disciples heard him speak, and followed Jesus.

38 Then Jesus turned about, and saw them follow, and said unto them, What seek ye? And they said unto him, Rabbi, (which is to say by interpretation, Master) [1]where dwellest thou?

39 He said unto them, Come, and see. They came and saw where he dwelt, and abode with him that day: for it was about the [1]tenth hour.

40 Andrew, Simon Peter's brother, was one of the two which had heard it of John, and that followed him.

41 The same found his brother Simon first, and said unto him, We have found that Messiah which is by interpretation, that [1]Christ.

42 And he brought him to Jesus. And Jesus beheld him, and said, Thou art Simon the son of Jonah:

[k] Matt. 3:16
Mark 1:10
Luke 3:22
[l] Gen. 49:10
Deut. 18:18
[m] Isa. 4:2
Isa. 40:10
Isa. 45:8
Jer. 25:5
Jer. 33:14
Ezek. 24:43
Ezek. 37:24
Dan. 9:24
[n] Gen. 28:12

thou shalt be called Cephas, which is by interpretation a stone.

43 ¶ The day following, Jesus would go into Galilee, and found Philip, and said unto him, Follow me.

44 Now Philip was of Bethsaida, the city of Andrew and Peter.

45 [l]Philip found Nathanael, and said unto him, We have found him of whom [l]Moses did write in the Law, and the [m]Prophets, Jesus that Son of Joseph, that was of Nazareth.

46 [1]Then Nathanael said unto him, Can there any good thing come out of Nazareth? Philip said to him, Come, and see.

47 [1]Jesus saw Nathanael coming to him, and said of him, Behold indeed an Israelite, in whom is no guile.

48 [1]Nathanael said unto him, Whence knewest thou me? Jesus answered, and said unto him, Before that Philip called thee, when thou wast under the fig tree, I saw thee.

49 Nathanael answered, and said unto him, Rabbi, thou art that Son of God: thou art that King of Israel.

50 Jesus answered, and said unto him, Because I said unto thee, I saw thee under the fig tree, believest thou? thou shalt see greater things than these.

51 And he said unto him, Verily, verily, I say unto you, Hereafter shall ye see heaven open, and the Angels of God [n,1]ascending, and descending upon that Son of man.

2

1 Christ turneth water into Wine, 11 which was the beginning of his miracles. 12 He goeth down to Capernaum: 13 from thence he goeth up to Jerusalem, 15 and casteth the merchandise out of the Temple. 19 He foretelleth that the Temple, that is, his body shall be destroyed of the Jews. 23 Many believe in him, seeing the miracles which he did.

1 And [1]the [2]third day, was there a marriage in

1:29 [3] This word of the present time signifieth a continual act, for the Lamb hath this virtue proper unto him, and forever, to take away the sins of the world.

[4] That is, that root of sins, to wit, our corruption, and so consequently, the fruits of sin, which are commonly called in the plural number sins.

1:31 [1] I never knew him by face before.

1:32 [1] Christ is proved to be the Son of God, by the coming down of the holy Ghost, by the Father's voice, and by John's testimony.

1:34 [1] This word (That) pointeth out unto us some excellent thing, and maketh a difference between Christ and others, whom Moses and the Prophets commonly call the sons of God, or the sons of the most high.

1:35 [1] John gathered disciples, not to himself, but to Christ.

1:36 [1] Christ is set before us to follow not as a vain shadow, but as our Mediator.

1:37 [1] In this first gathering of the disciples we have shown unto us, that the beginning of salvation is from God, who calleth us unto his Son by the ministry of his servants: whom (so preventing us) we must also hear, and follow him home, that being instructed by him, we may also instruct others.

1:38 [1] Where is thy lodging?

1:39 [1] The night grew on.

1:41 [1] That is, anointed, and King after the manner of the Jewish people.

1:45 [1] The good endeavors even of the unlearned, God doth so allow, that he maketh them masters to the learned.

1:46 [1] We must especially take heed of false presumptions, which shut up against us the entrance to Christ.

1:47 [1] Simple uprightness discerneth the true Israelites from the false.

1:48 [1] The end of miracles is to set before us Christ the Almighty, and also the only author of our salvation, that we may apprehend him by faith.

1:51 [1] By these words the power of God is signified which should appear in his ministry by the angels serving him as the head of the Church.

2:1 [1] Christ declaring openly in an assembly by a notable miracle, that he hath power over the nature of things, to feed man's body, leadeth the minds of all men, to his spiritual and saving virtue and power.

[2] After the talk which he had with Nathanael, or after that he departured from John, or after that he came into Galilee.

Cana *a town* of Galilee, and the mother of Jesus was there.

2 And Jesus was called also, and his disciples unto the marriage.

3 [1]Now when the wine failed, the mother of Jesus said unto him, They have no wine.

4 Jesus said unto her, Woman, what have I to do with thee? mine [1]hour is not yet come.

5 His mother said unto the servants, Whatsoever he saith unto you, do it.

6 And there were set there, six [1]waterpots of stone, after the manner of the purifying of the Jews, containing two or three [2]firkins apiece.

7 And Jesus said unto them, Fill the waterpots with water. Then they filled them up to the brim.

8 Then he said unto them, Draw out now, and bear unto the governor of the feast. So they bare it.

9 Now when the governor of the feast had tasted the water that was made wine, (for he knew not whence it was, but the servants, which drew the water, knew) the governor of the feast called the bridegroom,

10 And said unto him, All men at the beginning set forth good wine, and when men have [1]well drunk, then that which is worse: *but* thou hast kept back the good wine until now.

11 This beginning of miracles did Jesus in Cana *a town* of Galilee, and showed forth his glory: and his disciples believed on him.

12 After that, he went down into Capernaum, he and his mother, and his [1]brethren, and his disciples: but they continued not many days there.

13 [1]For the Jews' Passover was at hand. Therefore Jesus went up to Jerusalem.

14 [1]And he found in the Temple those that sold oxen, and sheep, and doves, and changers of money sitting *there*.

15 Then he made a scourge of small cords and

CHAPTER 2
[a] Ps. 69:9
[b] Matt. 26:61
Matt. 27:40
Mark 14:58
Mark 15:29

drove them all out of the Temple with the sheep and oxen, and poured out the changers' money, and overthrew their tables,

16 And said unto them that sold doves, Take these things hence: make not my father's house, an house of merchandise.

17 And his disciples remembered, that it was written, [a]The [1]zeal of thine house hath eaten me up.

18 [1]Then answered the Jews, and said unto him, What [2]sign showest thou unto us, that thou doest these things?

19 Jesus answered, and said unto them, [b]Destroy this Temple, and in three days I will raise it up again.

20 Then said the Jews, Forty and six years was this Temple a building, and wilt thou rear it up in three days?

21 But he spake of the [1]temple of his body.

22 As soon therefore as he was risen from the dead, his disciples remembered that he thus said unto them: and they believed the Scriptures, and the word which Jesus had said.

23 Now when he was at Jerusalem at the Passover in the feast, many believed in his Name, when they saw his miracles which he did.

24 [1]But Jesus did not commit himself unto them, because he knew them all.

25 [1]And had no need that any should testify of man, for he knew what was in man.

3 *1 Christ teacheth Nicodemus the very principles of Christian regeneration. 14 The serpent in the wilderness. 23 John baptizeth, 27 and teacheth his, that he is not Christ.*

1 There [1]was now a man of the Pharisees, named Nicodemus, a [2]ruler of the Jews.

2 This *man* came to Jesus by night, and said unto him, Rabbi, we know that thou art a [1]teacher come from God, for no man could do these miracles that thou doest, [2]except God were with him.

2:3 [1] Christ is careful enough of our salvation, and therefore hath no need of others to put him in mind of it.

2:4 [1] Mine appointed time.

2:6 [1] These were vessels appointed for water, wherein they washed themselves.

[2] Every firkin contained an hundred pounds, at twelve ounces the pound: Whereby we gather that Christ helped them with a thousand and eight hundred pounds of wine.

2:10 [1] Word for word, are drunken. Now this speech, to be drunken, is not always taken in evil part in the Hebrew tongue, but signifieth sometime such store, and plentiful use of wine, as doth not pass measure, as Gen. 43:34.

2:12 [1] That is, his cousins.

2:13 [1] Christ being made subject to the Law for us, satisfieth the Law of the Passover.

2:14 [1] Christ being ordained to purge the Church, doth with great zeal begin his office both of Priest and Prophet.

2:17 [1] Zeal in this place is taken for a wrathful indignation and displeasure of the mind, conceived of some naughty and evil dealing

towards them whom we love well.

2:18 [1] Against them which so bind God to an ordinary calling which they themselves most shamefully abuse, that they will not admit an extraordinary, which God confirmeth from heaven, (and they although in vain would have it extinguished) unless it be sealed with outward and bodily miracles.

[2] With what miracle dost thou confirm it, that we may see that heavenly power and virtue, which giveth thee authority to speak and do thus?

2:21 [1] That is, of his body.

2:24 [1] It is not good crediting them, which stand only upon miracles.

2:25 [1] Christ is the searcher of hearts, and therefore true God.

3:1 [1] There are none sometimes more unlearned, than the learned: but as well the learned as the unlearned must desire wisdom of Christ only.

[2] A man of great estimation, and a ruler amongst the Jews.

3:2 [1] We know that thou art sent from God to teach us.

[2] But he in whom some part of the excellency of God appeareth. And if Nicodemus had known Christ aright, he would not only have said that God was with him, but in him: as Paul doth, 2 Cor. 1:19.

3 [1]Jesus answered and said unto him, Verily verily I say unto thee, Except a man be born again, he cannot [2]see the [3]kingdom of God.

4 Nicodemus said unto him, How [1]can a man be born which is old? can he enter into his mother's womb again, and be born?

5 Jesus answered, Verily, verily I say unto thee, except that a man be born of water and of the Spirit, he cannot enter into the kingdom of God.

6 That which is born of the flesh, is [1]flesh: and that that is born of the Spirit, is spirit.

7 Marvel not that I said to thee, Ye must be born again.

8 The wind bloweth where it [1]listeth, and thou hearest the sound thereof, but canst not tell whence it cometh, and whither it goeth: so is every man that is born of the Spirit.

9 [1]Nicodemus answered, and said unto him, How can these things be?

10 Jesus answered, and said unto him, Art thou a teacher of Israel, and knowest not these things?

11 Verily, verily I say unto thee, We speak that we know, and testify that we have seen: but ye receive not our [1]witness.

12 If when I tell you earthly things, ye believe not, how should ye believe, If I shall tell you of heavenly things?

13 For no [1]man [2]ascendeth up to heaven, but he that had descended from heaven, [3]that Son of man

CHAPTER 3
[a] Num. 31:9
John 12:32
[b] 1 John 4:9
[c] John 1:39
John 12:47
[d] John 1:9
[e] John 4:1

which [4]is in heaven.

14 [a]And as Moses lifted up the serpent in the wilderness, so must that Son of man be lifted up,

15 That whosoever believeth in him, should not perish, but have eternal life.

16 [b,1]For God so loveth the world, that he hath given his only begotten Son, that whosoever believeth [2]in him, should not perish, but have everlasting life.

17 [c,1]For God sent not his Son into the world, that he should [2]condemn the world, but that the [3]world through him might be saved.

18 He that believeth in him, is not condemned: but he that believeth not, is condemned already, because he hath not believed in the Name of that only begotten Son of God.

19 [d,1]And this is the [2]condemnation, that that light came into the world, and men loved darkness rather than that light, because their deeds were evil.

20 For every man that evil doeth, hateth the light, neither cometh to light, lest his deeds should be reproved.

21 But he that [1]doeth truth, cometh to the light, that his deeds might be made manifest, that they are wrought [2]according to God.

22 ¶ After these things came Jesus, and his disciples into the land of Judea, and there tarried with them, and [e]baptized.

23 And John also baptized in Aenon besides Salim, because there was much water there: and they came

---

3:3 [1] The beginning of Christianity consisteth in this, that we know ourselves not only to be corrupt in part, but to be wholly dead in sin: so that our nature hath need to be created anew, as touching the qualities thereof: which can be done by no other virtue, but by the divine and heavenly, whereby we were first created.

[2] That is, go in, or enter, as he expounded himself afterward, verse 5.

[3] The Church: for Christ showeth in this place, how we come to be citizens, and to have ought to do in the city of God.

3:4 [1] How can I that am old, be born again? for he answereth, as if Christ's words belonged to none but to him.

3:6 [1] That is, fleshly, to wit, wholly unclean and under the wrath of God: and therefore this word (Flesh) signifieth the corrupt nature of man: contrary to which is the Spirit, that is, the man ingrafted into Christ through the grace of the holy Ghost, whose nature is everlasting and immortal, though the strife of the flesh remaineth.

3:8 [1] With free and wandering blasts, as it listeth.

3:9 [1] The secret mystery of our regeneration which cannot be comprehended by man's capacity, is perceived by faith, and that in Christ only, because that he is both God on earth, and man in heaven, that is to say, in such sort man, that he is God also, and therefore almighty: and in such sort God, that he is man also, and therefore his power is manifest unto us.

3:11 [1] You handle doubtful things, and such as you have no certain author for, and yet men believe you: but I teach those things that are of a truth and well known, and you believe me not.

3:13 [1] Only Christ can teach us heavenly things for no man ascendeth, etc.

[2] That is, hath any spiritual light and understanding, or ever had, but only that Son of God, which came down to us.

[3] Whereas he is said to have come down from heaven, that must be understood of his Godhead, and of the manner of his conception: for Christ's birth upon the earth was heavenly, and not earthly, for he was conceived by the holy Ghost.

[4] That which is proper to the divinity of Christ, is here spoken of whole Christ, to give us to understand that he is but one person, wherein two natures are united, and this kind of speech men call the communicating of proprieties.

3:16 [1] Nothing else but the free love of the Father, is the beginning of our salvation, and Christ is he in whom our righteousness and salvation is resident: and faith is the instrument or mean whereby we apprehend it, and life everlasting is that which is set before us to apprehend.

[2] It is not all one to believe in a thing, and to believe of a thing, for we may not believe (in anything) save only in God, but we may believe (of anything) whatsoever, this saith Nazianzene in his oration of the Spirit.

3:17 [1] Not Christ, but the despising of Christ doth condemn.

[2] That is, to be the cause of the condemning of the world, for indeed sins are the cause of death, but Christ shall judge the quick and the dead.

[3] Not only the people of the Jews, but whosoever shall believe in him.

3:19 [1] Only wickedness is the cause, why men refuse the light that is offered them.

[2] That is, the cause of condemnation, which sticketh fast in men, unless through God's great benefit they be delivered from it.

3:21 [1] That is, he that leadeth an honest life, and void of all craft and deceit.

[2] That is, with God, God as it were going before.

and were baptized.

24 For John was not yet cast into prison.

25 ¹Then there arose a question between John's disciples and the Jews, about purifying.

26 And they came unto John, and said unto him, Rabbi, he that was with thee beyond Jordan, to whom ᶠthou barest witness, behold, he baptizeth, and all men come to him.

27 John answered, and said, A man ¹can receive nothing, except it be given him from heaven.

28 Ye yourselves are my witnesses, that ᵍI said, I am not that Christ, but that I am sent before him.

29 He that hath the bride, is the bridegroom: but the friend of the bridegroom which standeth and heareth him, rejoiceth greatly, because of the bridegroom's voice. This my joy therefore is fulfilled.

30 He must increase, but I *must* decrease.

31 He that is come from on high, is above all: he that is of the earth, is of the ¹earth, and ²speaketh of the earth: he that is come from heaven, is above all.

32 And what he hath ¹seen and heard, that he testifieth: but ²no man receiveth his testimony.

33 He that hath receiveth his testimony, hath sealed that ʰGod is true.

34 For he whom God hath sent, speaketh the words of God: for God giveth *him* not the Spirit by measure.

35 The Father loveth the Son, and hath ⁱʲgiven all things into his hand.

36 ʲHe that believeth in the Son, hath everlasting life, and he that obeyeth not the Son, shall not ¹see life, but the wrath of God abideth on him.

4

6 *Jesus being weary, asketh drink of the woman of Samaria.   21 He teacheth the true worship.   26 He confesseth that he is the Messiah,   32 His meat.   39 The Samaritans believe in him.   46 He healeth the Ruler's son.*

1 Now ¹when the Lord knew, how the Pharisees had heard, that Jesus made ᵃand baptized more

Side references: ᶠ John 1:34; ᵍ John 1:20; ʰ Rom. 3:4; ⁱ Matt. 11:27; ʲ 1 John 5:10; CHAPTER 4: ᵃ John 3:22; ᵇ Gen. 33:19, Gen. 48:22, John 24:32

disciples than John,

2 (Though Jesus himself baptized not: but his disciples.)

3 He left Judea, and departed again into Galilee.

4 And he must needs go through Samaria.

5 ¹Then came he to a city of Samaria called Sychar, near unto the possession that ᵇJacob gave to his son Joseph.

6 And there was Jacob's Well. Jesus then wearied in the journey, sat ¹thus on the Well: it was about the ²sixth hour.

7 There came a woman of Samaria to draw water. Jesus said unto her, Give me drink.

8 For his disciples were gone away into the city, to buy meat.

9 Then said the woman of Samaria unto him, How is it, that thou being a Jew, askest drink of me, which am a woman of Samaria? For the Jews ¹meddle not with the Samaritans.

10 Jesus answered and said unto her, If thou knewest ¹that gift of God, and who it is that saith to thee, Give me drink, thou wouldest have asked of him, and he would have given thee ²water of life.

11 The woman said unto him, Sir, thou hast nothing to draw with, and the Well is deep: from whence then hast thou that water of life?

12 Art thou greater than our father Jacob, which gave us the Well, and he himself drank thereof, and his sons, and his cattle?

13 Jesus answered, and said unto her, Whosoever drinketh of this water, shall thirst again:

14 But whosoever drinketh of the water that I shall give him, shall never be more athirst: but the water that I shall give him, shall be in him a well of water, springing up into everlasting life.

15 The woman said unto him, Sir, give me of that water, that I may not thirst, neither come hither to draw.

16 Jesus said unto her, Go, call thine husband, and come hither.

3:25 ¹ Satan inflameth the disciples of John with a fond emulation of their master, to hinder the course of the Gospel: but John being mindful of his office, doth not only break off their endeavors, but also taketh occasion thereby to give testimony of Christ, how that in him only the Father hath set forth life everlasting.

3:27 ¹ What mean you to go about to better my state? this is every man's lot and portion that they cannot better themselves one iota.

3:31 ¹ Is nothing else but man, a piece of work and of the slime of the earth.
² Savoreth of nothing but corruption, ignorance, dullness, etc.

3:32 ² That is, very few.

3:35 ¹ Committed them to his power and will.

3:36 ¹ Shall not enjoy.

4:1 ¹ This measure is to be kept in doing of our duty, that neither by fear we be terrified from going forward, neither by rashness procure or pluck dangers upon our heads.

4:5 ¹ Christ leaving the proud Pharisees, communicateth the treasures of everlasting life with a poor sinful woman, and stranger, refelling the gross errors of the Samaritans, and defending the true service of God, which was delivered to the Jews, but yet so, that he calleth both of them back to himself as one whom only all the fathers, and also all the ceremonies of the Law did regard, and had a respect unto.

4:6 ¹ Even as he was weary, or because he was weary.
² It was almost noon.

4:9 ¹ There is no familiarity nor friendship, between the Jews and the Samaritans.

4:10 ¹ By this word (That) we are given to understand, that Christ speaketh of some excellent gift, that is to say, even of himself, whom his Father offered to this woman.
² This everlasting water, that is to say, the exceeding love of God, is called living, or of life, to make a difference between it, and the water that should be drawn out of a well: and these metaphors are very much used of the Jews, Jer. 2:13; Joel 3:18; Zech. 13:11.

17 The woman answered, and said, I have no husband. Jesus said unto her, thou hast well said, I have no husband.

18 For thou hast had five husbands, and he whom thou now hast, is not thine husband: that saidest thou truly.

19 The woman said unto him, Sir, I see that thou art a Prophet.

20 ¹Our fathers worshipped in this ²mountain, and ye say, that in ʿJerusalem is the place where men ought to worship.

21 Jesus said unto her, Woman, believe me, the hour cometh, when ye shall neither in this mountain, nor at Jerusalem worship the Father.

22 Ye worship that which ye ᵈknow not: we worship that which we know: for salvation is of the Jews.

23 But the hour cometh, and now is, when the true worshippers shall worship the Father in ¹Spirit and Truth: for the Father requireth even such to worship him.

24 ʿGod is a ¹Spirit, and they that worship him, must worship him in Spirit and Truth.

25 The woman said unto him, I know well that Messiah shall come, which is called Christ: when he is come, he will tell us all things.

26 Jesus said unto her, I am he, that speak unto thee.

27 ¶ And upon that, came his disciples, and marveled that he talked with a woman: yet no man said unto him, What askest thou? or why talkest thou with her.

28 The woman then left her waterpot, and went her way into the city, and said to the men,

29 Come, see a man which hath told me all things that ever I did: is not he that Christ?

30 Then they went out of the city, and came unto him.

31 ¶ In the meanwhile, the disciples prayed him, saying, Master, eat.

32 ¹But he said unto them, I have meat to eat, that

c Deut. 12:6
d 2 Kings 17:29
e 2 Cor. 3:27
f Matt. 9:37
Luke 10:2
g Matt. 13:57
Mark 6:4
Luke 4:24
b John 2:1, 12

ye know not of.

33 Then said the disciples between themselves, Hath any man brought him meat?

34 Jesus said unto them, My meat is that I may do the will of him that sent me, and finish his work.

35 ¹Say not ye, There are yet four months, and then cometh harvest? Behold, I say unto you, Lift up your eyes, and look on the regions: ᶠfor they are white already unto harvest.

36 ¹And he that reapeth, receiveth reward, and gathered fruit unto life eternal, that both he that soweth, and he that reapeth might rejoice together.

37 For herein is the ¹saying true, that one soweth and another reapeth.

38 I sent you to reap that, whereon ye bestowed no labor: other men labored, and ye are entered into their labors.

39 ¹Now many of the Samaritans of that city believed in him, for the saying of the woman which testified, He hath told me all things that ever I did.

40 Then when the Samaritans were come unto him, they besought him, that he would tarry with them: and he abode there two days.

41 And many more believed because of his own word.

42 And they said unto the woman, Now we believe, not because of thy saying: for we have heard him ourselves, and know that this is indeed that Christ the Savior of the world.

43 ¶ ¹So two days after he departed thence, and went into ²Galilee.

44 For Jesus himself had ᵍtestified, that a Prophet hath none honor in his own country.

45 Then when he was come into Galilee, the Galileans received him, which had seen all the things that he did at Jerusalem at the feast: for they went also to the feast.

46 ¹And Jesus came again into ᵇCana a town of Galilee, where he had made of water wine. And

---

4:20 ¹ All the religion of superstitious people, standeth for the most part, upon two pillars, but very weak, that is to say upon the examples of the fathers perverted, and a foolish opinion of outward things: against which errors we have to set the word and nature of God.

² The name of this mountain is Gerizim, whereupon Sanabaletta the Cushite built a Temple by Alexander of Macedonia's leave, after the victory of Issica, and made there Manasses his son-in-law high priest, Josephus, book 11.

4:23 ¹ This word (Spirit) is to be taken here, as it is set against that commandment, which is called carnal, Heb. 7:16, as the commandment is considered in itself: and so he speaketh of (Truth) not as we set it against a lie, but as we take it in respect of the outward ceremonies of the Law: which did only shadow that which Christ performed indeed.

4:24 ¹ By the word (Spirit) he meaneth the nature of the Godhead, and not the third person in the Trinity.

4:32 ¹ We may have care of our bodies, but yet so, that we prefer willingly and freely the occasion which is offered us to enlarge the

kingdom of God, before all necessities of this life whatsoever.

4:35 ¹ When the spiritual corn is ripe, we must not linger: for so the children of this world would condemn us.

4:36 ¹ The doctrine of the Prophets was as it were a sowing time: and the doctrine of the Gospel, as the harvest, and there is an excellent agreement between them both, and the ministers of them both.

4:37 ¹ That proverb.

4:39 ¹ The Samaritans do most joyfully embrace that which the Jews most stubbornly rejected.

4:43 ¹ The despisers of Christ deprive themselves of his benefit: yet Christ prepareth a place for himself.

² Into the towns and villages of Galilee: for he would not make abode in his country of Nazareth, because they despised him, and where (as the other Evangelists write) the efficacy of his benefits was hindered through their marvelous stiffneckedness.

4:46 ¹ Although Christ be absent in body, yet he worketh mightily in the believers by his word.

there was a certain ²ruler, whose son was sick at Capernaum.

47 When he heard that Jesus was come out of Judea into Galilee, he went unto him, and besought him that he would go down, and heal his son: for he was even ready to die.

48 Then said Jesus unto him, Except ye see signs and wonders, ye will not believe.

49 The ruler said unto him, Sir, go down before my son dies.

50 Jesus said unto him, Go thy way, thy son liveth: and the man believed the word that Jesus had spoken unto him, and went his way.

51 And as he was now going down, his servants met him, saying, Thy son liveth.

52 Then inquired he of them the hour when he began to amend. And they said unto him, Yesterday the seventh hour the fever left him.

53 Then the father knew that it was the same hour in the which Jesus had said unto him, Thy son liveth. And he believed, and all his household.

54 This second miracle did Jesus again, after he was come out of Judea into Galilee.

5 2 One lying at the pool, 5 is healed of Christ on the Sabbath. 10 The Jews that rashly find fault with that his deed, 17 he convinceth with the authority of his Father, 19, 20 He proveth his divine power by many reasons, 45 and with Moses' testimony.

1 After ªthat, there was a feast of the Jews, and Jesus went to Jerusalem.

2 ¹And there is at Jerusalem by the place of the sheep, a ²pool called in Hebrew ³Bethesda, having five porches:

3 In the which lay a great multitude of sick folk, of blind, halt, and withered, waiting for the moving of the water.

4 For an Angel went down at a certain season into the pool, and troubled the water: whosoever then first, after the stirring of the water, stepped in, was made whole of whatsoever disease he had.

5 And a certain man was there, which had been

diseased eight and thirty years.

6 When Jesus saw him lie, and knew that he now long time had been diseased, he said unto him, Wilt thou be made whole?

7 The sick man answered him, Sir, I have no man, when the water is troubled, to put me into the pool: but while I am coming, another steppeth down before me.

8 Jesus said unto him, Rise: take up thy bed, and walk.

9 And immediately the man was made whole, and took up his bed, and walked: and the same day was the Sabbath.

10 ¹The Jews therefore said to him that was made whole, It is the Sabbath day: ᵇit is not lawful for thee to carry thy bed.

11 He answered them, He that made me whole he said unto me, Take up thy bed, and walk.

12 Then asked they him, What man is that which said unto thee, Take up thy bed, and walk?

13 And he that was healed, knew not who it was: for Jesus had conveyed himself away from the multitude that was in that place.

14 And after that, Jesus found him in the Temple, and said unto him, Behold, thou art made whole: sin no more, lest a worse thing come unto thee.

15 ¶ The man departed, and told the Jews that it was Jesus that had made him whole.

16 And therefore the Jews did persecute Jesus, and sought to slay him, because he had done these things on the Sabbath day.

17 ¹But Jesus answered them, My father worketh hitherto, and I work.

18 ꞌTherefore the Jews sought the more to kill him: not only because he had broken the Sabbath: but said also that God was ¹his Father, and made himself equal with God.

19 Then answered Jesus, and said unto them, Verily, verily I say unto you, The Son can do nothing ¹of himself, save that he ²seeth the Father do: for whatsoever things he doeth, the same things doeth the Son ³in like manner.

---

² Some of Herod's courtiers, for though Herod was not a king, but a Tetrarch, yet the lofty name only except, he was a king, or at least the people called him a king.
5:2 ¹ There is no disease so old, which Christ cannot heal.
² Whereof cattle drank, and used to be plunged in; whereof there could not be but great store at Jerusalem.
³ That is to say, the house of pouring out, because great store of water was poured out into that place.
5:10 ¹ True religion is no more cruelly assaulted by any means, than by the pretence of religion itself.
5:17 ¹ The work of God was never the breach of the Sabbath: but the works of Christ are the works of the Father, both because they are one God, and also because the Father doth not work but in the Son.

5:18 ¹ That is, his only and no man's else, which they gather by that, that he saith, (And I work) applying this word (work) to himself, which is proper to God, and therefore maketh himself equal to God.
5:19 ¹ Not only without his Father's authority, but also without his mighty working and power.
² This must be understood of Christ's person, which consisteth of two natures, and not simply of his Godhead: so then he saith that his Father moveth and governeth him in all things, but yet notwithstanding, when he saith he worketh with his Father, he voucheth his Godhead.
³ In like sort, jointly and together. Not for that the Father doeth some things, and then the son worketh after him, and doeth the like, but because the might and power of the Father and the Son do work equally and jointly together.

ª Lev. 23:3 Deut. 16:1
ᵇ Jer. 17:22
ᶜ John 7:19
CHAPTER 5

20 For the Father loveth the Son, and showeth him all things, whatsoever he himself doeth, and he will show him greater works than these, that ye should marvel.

21 [1]For likewise as the Father raiseth up the dead, and quickeneth them, so the Son quickeneth whom he will.

22 For the Father [1]judgeth [2]no man, but hath committed all judgment unto the Son,

23 Because that all men should honor the Son, as they honor the Father: he that honoreth not the Son, the same honoreth not the Father which hath sent him.

24 [1]Verily, verily I say unto you, he that heareth my word, and believeth him that sent me, hath everlasting life, and shall not come into condemnation, but hath passed from death to life.

25 [1]Verily, verily I say unto you, the hour shall come, and now is, when the dead shall hear the voice of the Son of God: and they that hear it shall live.

26 For as the Father hath life in himself, so likewise hath he given to the Son to have life in himself.

27 And hath given him [1]power also to execute judgment, in that he is the [2]Son of man.

28 [1]Marvel not at this: for the hour shall come, in the which all that are in the graves, shall hear his voice.

29 [1]And they shall come [2]forth, [d]that have done good, unto the [3]resurrection of life: but they that have done evil, unto the resurrection of condemnation.

30 [1]I can [2]do nothing of mine own self: [3]as I hear, I judge: and my judgment is just, because I seek not mine own will, but the will of the Father who hath sent me.

31 If I [e]should bear witness of myself, my witness were not [1]true.

32 [f]There is another that beareth witness of me, and I know that the witness, which he beareth of

me, is true.

33 [g][1]Ye sent unto John, and he bore witness unto the truth.

34 But I receive not the record of man: nevertheless these things I say, that ye might be saved.

35 He was a burning and a shining candle: and ye would for [1]a season have rejoiced in his light.

36 But I have greater witness than the witness of John: for the works which the Father hath given me to finish, the same works that I do, bear witness of me, that the Father sent me.

37 And the [h]Father himself, which hath sent me, beareth witness of me. Ye have not heard his voice at any time, [i]neither have ye seen his shape.

38 And his word have you not abiding in you: for whom he hath sent, him ye believed not.

39 [j]Search the Scriptures: for in them ye think to have eternal life, and they are they which testify of me.

40 But ye will not come to me, that ye might have life.

41 I receive not the praise of men.

42 But I know you, that ye have not the [1]love of God in you.

43 I am come in my Father's Name, and ye receive me not: if another shall come in his own name, him will ye receive.

44 How can ye believe, which receive [k]honor one of another, and seek not the honor that cometh of God alone?

45 [1]Do not think that I will accuse you to my Father: there is one that accuseth you, *even* Moses, in whom ye trust.

46 For had ye believed Moses, ye would have believed me: for he [l]wrote of me.

47 But if ye believe not his writings, how shall ye believe my words.

Cross References

[d] Matt. 25:41
[e] John 8:14
[f] Matt. 3:17
[g] John 1:27
[h] Matt. 3:15
   Matt. 17:5
[i] Deut. 4:12
[j] Acts 17:11
[k] John 12:43
[l] Gen. 3:15
   Gen. 22:18
   Gen 49:10
   Deut. 18:15

Footnotes

5:21 [1] The Father maketh no man partaker of everlasting life, but in Christ, in whom only also he is truly worshipped.

5:22 [1] This word (judgeth) is taken by the figure Synecdoche, for all government.

[2] These words are not so to be taken, as though they simply denied that God governeth the world, but as the Jews imagined it, which separate the Father from the Son, whereas indeed, the Father doth not govern the world but only in the person of his Son, being made manifest in the flesh: so saith he afterward, verse 30, that he came not to do his own will: that his doctrine is not his own, John 7:16, that the blind man and his parents sinned not, etc., John 9:3.

5:24 [1] The Father is not worshipped but by his Son's word apprehended by faith, which is the only way that leadeth to eternal life.

5:25 [1] We are all dead in sin and cannot be quickened by any other means, than by the word of Christ apprehended by faith.

5:27 [1] That is, high and sovereign power to rule and govern all things, insomuch that he hath power of life and death.

[2] That is, he shall not only judge the world as he is God, but also as he is man, he received this of his Father to be judge of the world.

5:28 [1] All shall appear before the judgment seat of Christ at length

to be judged.

5:29 [1] Faith and infidelity shall be judged by their fruits.

[2] Of their graves.

[3] To that resurrection which had life everlasting following it: against which is set the resurrection of condemnation: that is, which condemnation followeth.

5:30 [1] The father is the author and approver of all things which Christ doeth.

[2] See verse 22.

[3] As my father directeth me, who dwelleth in me.

5:31 [1] Faithful, that is, worthy to be credited, see John 8:14.

5:33 [1] Christ is declared to be the only Savior by John's voice, and infinite miracles, and by the testimonies of all the Prophets. But the world notwithstanding being addicted to false prophets, and desirous to seem religious, seeth none of all these things.

5:35 [1] A little while.

5:42 [1] Love toward God.

5:45 [1] This denial doth not put away that which is here said, but correcteth it, as if Christ said, the Jews shall have no sorer an accuser than Moses.

6

5 Five thousand are fed with five loaves and two fishes. 15 Christ goeth apart from the people. 17 As his disciples were rowing, 19 he cometh to them walking on the water. 26 He reasoneth of the true 27 and everlasting, 35 bread of life. 42, 52 The Jews murmur, 60 and many of the disciples, 66 depart from him. 69 The Apostles confess him to be the Son of God.

CHAPTER 6
a Lev. 23:7
Deut. 16:2

b Matt. 14:16
Mark 6:37
Luke 9:13

c Matt. 14:25
Mark 6:47

d John 1:32
Mark 3:17
Mark 7:3
John 17:3

1 After these things, Jesus went his way [1]over the sea of Galilee, which is Tiberias.

2 And a great multitude followed him, because they saw his miracles, which he did on them that were diseased.

3 Then Jesus went up into a mountain, and there he sat with his disciples.

4 Now the Passover a *a*feast of the Jews was near.

5 *b*,[1]Then Jesus lift up *his* eyes, and seeing that a great multitude came unto him, he said unto Philip, Whence shall we buy bread, that these might eat?

6 (And this he said to prove him: for he himself knew what he would do.)

7 Philip answered him, Two hundred pennyworth of bread is not sufficient for them, that everyone of them may take a little.

8 Then said unto him one of his disciples, Andrew, Simon Peter's brother,

9 There is a little boy here, which hath five barley loaves, and two fishes: but what are they among so many?

10 And Jesus said, Make the people sit down. (Now there was much grass in that place.) Then the men sat down, in number about five thousand.

11 And Jesus took the bread, and gave thanks, and gave to the disciples, and the disciples to them that were set down: and likewise of the fishes as much as they would.

12 And when they were satisfied, he said unto his disciples, Gather up the broken meat which remaineth, that nothing be lost.

13 Then they gathered it together, and filled twelve baskets with the broken meat of the five barley loaves, which remained unto them that had eaten.

14 Then the men, when they had seen the miracle

that Jesus did, said, This is of a truth that Prophet that should come into the world.

15 [1]When Jesus therefore perceived that they would come, and take him to make him a king, he departed again into a mountain himself alone.

16 ¶ [1]When even was now come, his disciples went down unto the sea,

17 *c*And entered into a ship, and went over the sea, [1]towards Capernaum: and now it was dark, and Jesus was not come to them.

18 And the Sea arose with a great wind that blew.

19 And when they had rowed about five and twenty, or thirty furlongs, they saw Jesus walking on the sea, and drawing near unto the ship: so they were afraid.

20 But he said unto them, It is I: be not afraid.

21 Then [1]willingly they received him into the ship, and the ship was by and by at the land, whither they went.

22 ¶ The day following, the people which stood on the other side of the sea, saw that there was none other ship there, save that one, where into his disciples were entered, and that Jesus went not with his disciples in the ship, but that his disciples were gone alone,

23 And that there came other ships from Tiberias near unto the place where they ate the bread, after the Lord had given thanks.

24 Now when the people saw that Jesus was not there, neither his disciples, they also took shipping, and came to Capernaum, seeking for Jesus.

25 And when they had found him on the other side of the sea, they said unto him, Rabbi, when camest thou hither?

26 [1]Jesus answered them, and said, Verily, verily I say unto you, Ye seek me not, because ye saw the miracles, but because ye ate of the loaves, and were filled.

27 [1]Labor not for the meat which perisheth, but for the meat that endureth unto everlasting life, which the Son of man shall give unto you: for him hath *d*God the Father [2]sealed.

28 Then said they unto him, What shall we do, that we might work the [1]works of God?

6:1 [1] Not that he cut over the lake of Tiberias, but by reason of the large creeks, his sailing made his journey shorter: therefore he is said to have gone over the sea, when as he passed over from one side of the creek to the other.

6:5 [1] They that follow Christ do sometimes hunger, but they are never destitute of help.

6:15 [1] Christ is not only not delighted, but also greatly offended with a preposterous worship.

6:16 [1] The godly are often in peril and danger, but Christ cometh to them in time, even in the midst of the tempests, and bringeth them to the heaven.

6:17 [1] In Mark 6:45 they are willed to go before to Bethsaida, for Bethsaida was in the way to Capernaum.

6:21 [1] They were afraid at the first, but when they knew his voice,

they became new men, and took him willingly into the ship, whom they had shunned and fled from before.

6:26 [1] They that seek the kingdom of heaven lack nothing: notwithstanding the Gospel is not the food of the belly, but of the mind.

6:27 [1] Bestow your labor and pain.

[2] That is, whom God the Father hath distinguished from all other men by planting his own virtue in him, as though he had sealed him with his seal, that he might be a lively pattern and representer of him: and that more is, installed him to this office, to reconcile us men to God, and bring us to everlasting life, which is only proper to Christ.

6:28 [1] Which please God: for they think that everlasting life hangeth upon the condition of fulfilling the Law: therefore Christ calleth them back to faith.

29 ¹Jesus answered, and said unto them, ᶜ'²This is the work of God, that ye believe in him, whom he hath sent.

30 ¹They said therefore unto him, What sign showest thou then, that we may see it, and believe thee? what dost thou work?

31 Our fathers did eat Manna in the desert, as it is ᶠwritten, He gave them bread from heaven to eat.

32 ¹Then Jesus said unto them, Verily, verily I say unto you, Moses gave you not ²that bread from heaven, but my Father giveth you that true bread from heaven.

33 For the bread of God is he which cometh down from heaven, and giveth life unto the world.

34 Then they said unto him, Lord, evermore give us this bread.

35 And Jesus said unto them, I am that bread ¹of life: he that cometh to me, shall not hunger, and he that believeth in me, shall never thirst.

36 But I said unto you, that ye also have seen me, and believe not.

37 ¹All that the Father giveth me, shall come to me: and him that cometh to me, I cast not away.

38 For I came down from heaven, not to do mine ¹own will, but his will which hath sent me.

39 And this is the Father's will which hath sent me, that of all which he hath given me, I should lose nothing, but should raise it up again at the last day.

40 And this is the will of him that sent me, that every man which ¹seeth the Son, and believeth in him, should have everlasting life: and I will raise him up at the last day.

41 ¹The Jews then murmured at him because he said, I am that bread, which is come down from heaven.

42 And they said, ᵍIs not this Jesus that son of Joseph, whose father and mother we know? how then saith he, I came down from heaven?

43 Jesus then answered, and said unto them, Murmur not among yourselves.

44 No man can come to me, except the Father, which hath sent me, draw him: and I will raise him up at the last day.

45 It is written in the ʰ'¹Prophets, And they shall be all ²taught of God. Every man therefore that hath heard, and hath learned of the Father, cometh unto me:

46 ¹Not that any man hath seen the Father, ¹save he which is of God, he hath seen the Father.

47 Verily, verily I say unto you, he that believeth in me, hath everlasting life.

48 ¹I am that bread of life.

49 ʲYour fathers did eat Manna in the wilderness, and are dead.

50 ¹This is that bread, which cometh down from heaven, that he which eateth of it, should not die.

51 ¹I am that ²living bread, which came down from heaven: if any man ³eat of this bread, he shall live forever: and the bread that I will give is my flesh, which I will give for the life of the world.

52 ¹Then the Jews strove among themselves, saying, How can this man give us *his* flesh to eat?

Marginal references:
ᶜ 1 John 3:23
ᶠ Exod. 16:14
Num. 11:7
Ps. 78:25
ᵍ Matt. 13:55
ʰ Isa. 54:13
Jer. 31:13
ⁱ Matt. 11:17
ʲ Exod. 16:15

Footnotes:

6:29 ¹ Men torment themselves in vain, when they go about to please God without faith.

² That is, this is the work that God requireth, that you believe in me, and therefore he calleth them back to faith.

6:30 ¹ The spiritual virtue of Christ is contemned of them which are desirous of earthly miracles.

6:32 ¹ Christ, who is the true and only author and giver of eternal life, was signified unto the fathers, in Manna.

² He denieth that Manna was that true heavenly bread, and saith that he himself is that true bread, because he feedeth unto the true and everlasting life. And as for that, that Paul 1 Cor. 10 calleth Manna spiritual food, it maketh nothing against this place, for he joineth the thing signified with the sign: but in this whole disputation, Christ dealeth with the Jews after their own opinion and conceit of the matter, and they had no further consideration of the Manna, but in that it fed the belly.

6:35 ¹ Which have life, and give life.

6:37 ¹ The gift of faith proceedeth from the free election of the Father in Christ, after which followeth necessarily everlasting life: Therefore faith in Christ Jesus is a sure witness of our election, and therefore of our glorification, which is to come.

6:38 ¹ See John 5:22.

6:40 ¹ Seeing and believing are joined together: for there is another kind of seeing, which is general, which the devils have, for they see: but here he speaketh of that kind of seeing, which is proper to the elect.

6:41 ¹ Flesh cannot perceive spiritual things, and therefore the beginning of our salvation cometh from God, who changeth our nature, so that we being inspired of him, may abide to be instructed and saved by Christ.

6:45 ¹ In the book of the Prophets, for the old Testament was divided by them into three several parts, into the Law the Prophets, and the Holy writ.

² To wit, they shall be children of the Church, for so the Prophet Isaiah expoundeth it, Isa. 54:13, that is to say, ordained to life, Acts 13:48, and therefore the knowledge of the heavenly truth, is the gift and work of God, and standeth not in any power of man.

6:46 ¹ If the son only hath seen the Father, then it is he only that can teach and instruct us truly.

6:48 ¹ The true use of Sacraments, is to ascend from them to the thing itself, that is to Christ: and by the partaking of whom only, we get everlasting life.

6:50 ¹ He pointed out himself when he spake these words.

6:51 ¹ Christ being sent from the Father, is the selfsame unto us for the getting and keeping of everlasting life, that bread and flesh, yea meat and drink are to the use of this transitory life.

² Which giveth life to the world.

³ That is to say, whosoever is partaker of Christ indeed, who is our food.

6:52 ¹ Flesh cannot put a difference between fleshly eating which is done by the help of the teeth, and spiritual eating which consisteth in faith, and therefore is condemneth that which it understandeth not: yet notwithstanding the truth must be preached and taught.

53 Then Jesus said unto them, Verily, verily I say unto you, Except ye eat the flesh of the Son of man, and drink his blood, ye have [1]no life in you.

54 Whosoever [k]eateth my flesh, and drinketh my blood, hath eternal life, and I will raise him up at the last day.

55 For my flesh is meat indeed, and my blood is drink indeed.

56 He that eateth my flesh, and drinketh my blood, dwelleth in me, and I in him.

57 As [1]that living Father hath sent me, so live I by the [2]Father, and he that eateth me, even he shall live by me.

58 This is that bread which came down from heaven: not as your fathers have eaten Manna, and are dead. He that eateth of this bread, shall live forever.

59 These things spake he in the Synagogue, as he taught in Capernaum.

60 [1]Many therefore of his disciples (when they heard this) said, This is an hard saying: who can hear it?

61 But Jesus knowing in himself, that his disciples murmured at this, said unto them, Doth this offend you?

62 *What* then if ye should see that Son of man ascend up [l]where he was before?

63 [1]It is the [2]spirit that quickeneth: the flesh profiteth nothing: the words that I speak unto you, are spirit and life.

64 But there are some of you that believe not: for Jesus knew from the beginning, which they were that believed not, and who should betray him.

65 And he said, Therefore said I unto you, that no man can come unto me, except it be given unto him of my Father.

66 [1]From that time, many of his disciples went back, and walked no more with him.

67 Then said Jesus to the twelve, Will ye also go

k 1 Cor. 11:27
l John 3:13
m Matt. 26:16

CHAPTER 7
a Lev. 13:34
b John 8:20

away?

68 Then Simon Peter answered him, Master, to whom shall we go? thou hast the words of eternal life:

69 And we believe and know that thou art that Christ that Son of the living God.

70 [1]Jesus answered them, Have not I [m]chosen you twelve, and one of you is a devil?

71 Now he spake it of Judas Iscariot the *son* of Simon: for he it was that should betray him, though he was one of the twelve.

7 *2 Christ, after his cousins were gone up to the feast of Tabernacles, 10 goeth thither privily. 12 The people's sundry opinions of him. 14 He teacheth in the Temple. 32 The Priests command to take him. 41 Strife among the multitude about him, 47 and between the Pharisees and the officers that were sent to take him, 50 and Nicodemus.*

1 After these things, Jesus walked in Galilee, and would not walk in Judea: for the Jews sought to kill him.

2 Now the Jews' [a,1]feast of the Tabernacles was at hand.

3 [1]His brethren therefore said unto him, Depart hence, and go into Judea, that thy disciples may see thy works that thou doest.

4 For there is no man that doeth anything secretly, and he himself seeketh to be famous. If thou doest these things, show thyself to the world.

5 For as yet his [1]brethren believed not in him.

6 [1]Then Jesus said unto them, My time is not yet come: but your time is always ready.

7 The world cannot hate you: but me it hateth, because I testify of it, that the works thereof are evil.

8 Go ye up unto this feast: I will not go up yet unto this feast: [b]for my time is not yet fulfilled.

9 ¶ These things he said unto them, and abode still in Galilee.

6:53 [1] If Christ be present, life is present, but when Christ is absent, then is death present.

6:57 [1] In that that Christ is man, he receiveth that power which quickeneth and giveth life to them that are his, of his Father: and he addeth this word (That) to make a difference between him and all other fathers.

[2] Christ his meaning is, that though he be man, yet his flesh can give life, not of the own nature, but because that flesh of his liveth by the Father, that is to say, death suck and draw out of the Father, that power which it hath to give life.

6:60 [1] The reason of man cannot comprehend the uniting of Christ and his members: therefore let it worship and reverence that which is better than itself.

6:63 [1] The flesh of Christ doth therefore quicken us, because that he that is man, is God: which mystery is only comprehended by faith, which is the gift of God, properly only to the elect.

[2] Spirit, that is, that power which floweth from the Godhead, caus-

eth the flesh of Christ, which otherwise were nothing but flesh, but to live in itself, and to give life to us.

6:66 [1] Such is the malice of men, that they take occasion of their own destruction, even of the very doctrine of salvation (unless it be a few, which believe through the singular gift of God.)

6:70 [1] The number of the professors, of Christ is very small, and among them also there be some hypocrites, and worse than all others.

7:2 [1] This feast was so called, because of the booths and tents which they pight of divers kinds of boughs, and sat under them seven days together; all which time the feast lasted.

7:3 [1] The grace of God cometh not by inheritance, but it is a gift that cometh other ways, whereby it cometh to pass, that oftentimes the children of God suffer more affliction by their own kinsfolk than by strangers.

7:5 [1] His kinsfolk: for so use the Hebrews to speak.

7:6 [1] We must not follow the foolish desires of our friends.

10 [1]But as soon as his brethren were gone up, then went he also up unto the feast, not openly, but as it *were* privily.

11 Then the Jews sought him at the feast, and said, Where is he?

12 And much murmuring was there of him among the people. Some said, He is a good man: others said, Nay: but he deceiveth the people.

13 Howbeit no man spake [1]openly of him for fear of the Jews.

14 [1]Now when [2]half the feast was done, Jesus went up into the Temple, and taught.

15 And the Jews marveled, saying, How knoweth this man the Scriptures, seeing that he never learned!

16 [1]Jesus answered them, and said, [2]My doctrine is not mine, but his that sent me.

17 If any man will do his will, he shall know of the doctrine, whether it be of God, or whether I speak of myself.

18 [1]He that speaketh of himself, seeketh his own glory: but he that seeketh his glory that sent him, the same is true, and no unrighteousness is in him.

19 [c,1]Did not Moses give you a Law, and *yet* none of you keepeth the Law? [d]Why go ye about to kill me?

20 The people answered, and said, Thou hast a devil: who goeth about to kill thee?

21 [1]Jesus answered, and said unto them, I have done one work, and ye all marvel.

22 [e]Moses therefore gave unto you circumcision, (not because it is of Moses, but of the [f]fathers) and ye on the Sabbath *day* circumcise a man.

23 If a man on the Sabbath receive circumcision, that the [1]Law of Moses should not be broken, be

ye angry with me, because I have made a man every whit whole on the Sabbath *day?*

24 [g,1]Judge not [2]according to the appearance, but judge righteous judgment.

25 ¶ [1]Then said some of them of Jerusalem, Is not this he whom they go about to kill?

26 And behold, he speaketh openly, and they say nothing to him: do the rulers know indeed that this is indeed that Christ?

27 [1]Howbeit we know this man whence he is: but when that Christ cometh, no man shall know whence he is.

28 ¶ [1]Then cried Jesus in the Temple as he taught, saying, Ye both know me, and know whence I am: yet am I not come of myself, but he that sent me, is true, whom ye know not.

29 But I know him: for I am of him, and he hath sent me.

30 [1]Then they sought to take him, but no man laid hands on him, because his hour was not yet come.

31 Now many of the people believed on him, and said, When that Christ cometh, will he do more miracles than this man hath done?

32 [1]The Pharisees heard that the people murmured these things of him, and the Pharisees, and high Priests sent officers to take him.

33 Then said Jesus unto them, Yet am I a little while with you, and then go I unto him that sent me.

34 [h]Ye shall seek me, and shall not find *me*, and where I am, can ye not come.

35 Then said the Jews among themselves, Whither will he go, that we shall not find him? Will he go unto them that are [1]dispersed among the Greeks,

Marginal references:
c Exod. 24:3
d John 5:12
e Lev. 12:3
f Gen. 17:10
g Deut. 1:16
h John 13:33

7:10 [1] An example of horrible confusion in the very bosom of the Church. The Pastors oppress the people with terrors and fear: the people seek Christ, when he appeareth not: when he offereth himself, they neglect him. Some also that know him condemn him rashly: a very few think well of him, and that in secret.

7:13 [1] Or, boldly and freely: for the chief of the Jews sought nothing so much, as to bury his fame and name.

7:14 [1] Christ striveth with goodness against the wickedness of the world: in the mean season the most part of men take occasion of offense even by that fame, whereby they ought to have been stirred up to embrace Christ.

[2] About the fourth day of the feast.

7:16 [1] Therefore are there few to whom the Gospel favoreth well, because the study of godliness is very rare.

[2] See John 5:22, and he speaketh this after the opinion of the Jews, as if he said, My doctrine is not mine, that is, it is not his whom you take to be a man as others are, and therefore set light by him, but it is his that sent me.

7:18 [1] The true doctrine of salvation differeth from the false in this, that the same setteth forth the glory of God, and this by puffing up of men darkeneth the glory of God.

7:19 [1] None do more confidently boast themselves to be the defenders of the Law of God, than they that do most impudently break it.

7:21 [1] The Sabbath day (which is here set before us for a rule of all

ceremonies) was not appointed to hinder but to further and practice God's works: amongst which the love of our neighbor is the chiefest.

7:23 [1] That is to say, if the law of circumcision which Moses gave, be of so great accompt amongst you, that you doubt not to circumcise upon the Sabbath, do you rightly reprove me for healing a man thoroughly?

7:24 [1] We must judge according to the truth of things, lest the persons of men do turn us and carry us away.

[2] By the show that I make: for I seem to be but an abject and rascal of Galilee, and a carpenter's son, whom no man maketh account of: but mark the matter itself well, and judge the tree by the fruit.

7:25 [1] Many do marvel that the endeavors of the enemies of God have no success: yet in the mean season they do not acknowledge the virtue and power of God.

7:27 [1] Men are very wise to procure stops and stays to themselves.

7:28 [1] The truth of Christ doth not hang upon the judgment of man.

7:30 [1] The wicked cannot do what they list, but what God hath appointed.

7:32 [1] As the kingdom of God increaseth, so increaseth the rage of his enemies, till at length they in vain seek for those blessings absent, which they despised when they were present.

7:35 [1] Word for word, (to the dispersion of the Gentiles or Greeks) and under the name of the Greeks he understandeth the Jews which were dispersed amongst the Gentiles.

and teach the Greeks?

36 What saying is this that he said, Ye shall seek me, and shall not find *me*? and where I am, can ye not come?

37 ¹Now in the ²last *and* ⁱgreat day of the feast, Jesus stood and cried, saying, If any man thirst, let him come unto me, and drink.

38 He that believeth in me,ʲas saith the ¹Scripture, out of his belly shall flow rivers of water of life.

39 (ᵏThis spake he of the Spirit, which they that believed in him, should receive: for the ¹holy Ghost was not yet *given*, because that Jesus was not yet ²glorified.)

40 ¹So many of the people, when they heard this saying, said, ¹Of a truth this is that Prophet:

41 Others said, This is that Christ: and some said, But shall that Christ come out of Galilee?

42 ᵐSaith not the Scripture that that Christ shall come out of the seed of David, and out of the town of Bethlehem, where David was?

43 So was there dissension among the people for him.

44 And some of them would have taken him, but no man laid hands on him.

45 ¹Then came the officers to the high Priests and Pharisees, and they said unto them, Why have ye not brought him?

46 The officers answered, Never man spake like this man.

47 Then answered them the Pharisees, Are ye also deceived?

48 ¹Doth any of the rulers, or of the Pharisees believe in him?

49 But this people, which know not the Law, are cursed,

50 Nicodemus said unto them, (ⁿhe that came to Jesus by night, and was one of them.)

51 Doth our Law judge a man before it hear him, ᵒand know ¹what he hath done?

52 They answered, and said unto him, Art thou also of Galilee? Search and look: for out of Galilee

ⁱ Lev. 23:5
ʲ Deut. 18:15
ᵏ Joel 2:28
Acts 2:17
¹ Deut. 18:15
ᵐ Mic. 5:2
Matt. 2:5
ⁿ John 3:2
ᵒ Deut. 17:8
Deut. 19:15

CHAPTER 8
ᵃ Lev. 20:10
ᵇ Deut. 17:7
ᶜ John 1:5
John 9:5

ariseth no Prophet.

53 ¹And every man went unto his own house.

8 3 *The woman taken in adultery,* 11 *hath her sins forgiven her.* 12 *Christ the light of the world.* 19 *The Pharisees ask where his Father is.* 39 *The sons of Abraham.* 42 *The sons of God,* 44 *The devil the father of lying.* 56 *Abraham saw Christ's day.*

1 And Jesus went unto the mount of Olives,

2 And early in the morning came again into the Temple, and all the people came unto him, and he sat down and taught them.

3 ¹Then the Scribes and the Pharisees brought unto him a woman taken in adultery, and set her in the midst,

4 And said unto him, Master, we found this woman committing adultery even in the very act.

5 ᵃNow Moses in our Law commanded, that such should be stoned: what sayest thou therefore?

6 And this they said to tempt him, that they might have, whereof to accuse him. But Jesus stooped down, and with his finger wrote on the ground,

7 ¹And while they continued asking him, he lifted himself up, and said unto them, ᵇLet him that is among you without sin, cast the first stone at her.

8 And again he stooped down, and wrote on the ground.

9 And when they heard it, being accused by their own conscience, they went out, one by one, beginning at the eldest even to the last: so Jesus was left alone, and the woman standing in the midst.

10 ¹When Jesus had lifted up himself again, and saw no man, but the woman, he said unto her, Woman, where are those thine accusers? hath no man condemned thee?

11 She said, No man, Lord. And Jesus said, Neither do I condemn thee: go and sin no more.

12 ¹Then spake Jesus again unto them, saying, I ᶜam that light of the world: he that followeth me, shall not walk in darkness, but shall have that light

---

7:37 ¹ There are two principles of our salvation: the one is to be thoroughly touched with a true feeling of our extreme poverty: the other to seek in Christ only (whom we catch hold on by faith) the abundance of all good things.
² The last day of the feast of Tabernacles, that as, the eighth day, was as high a day, as the first.
7:38 ¹ This is not read word for word in any place, but it seemeth to be taken out of many places where mention is made of the gifts of the holy Ghost, as Joel 2; Isa. 44, but especially in Isa. 55.
7:39 ¹ What is meant by the holy Ghost, he expressed a little before, speaking of the Spirit which they that believed in him should receive. So that by the name of holy Ghost, are meant the virtues and mighty workings of the holy Ghost.
² That is, those things were not yet seen and perceived, which were to show and set forth the glory of the only begotten.
7:40 ¹ There is contention even in the Church itself about the chief

point of religion: neither hath Christ any more cruel enemies than those that occupy the seat of truth: yet can they not do what they would.
7:45 ¹ God from heaven scorneth such as are his son's enemies.
7:48 ¹ False Pastors are so fond and foolish that they esteem the Church of God according to the multitude and outward show.
7:51 ¹ What he hath committed, who is accused.
7:53 ¹ There is no counsel against the Lord.
8:3 ¹ While the wicked go about to make a snare for good men, they make a snare for themselves.
8:7 ¹ Against hypocrites which are very severe judges against other men, and flatter themselves in their own sins.
8:10 ¹ Christ would not take upon him the civil Magistrates office: he contented himself to bring sinners to faith and repentance.
8:12 ¹ The world which is blind in itself cannot come to have ray light but in Christ only.

of life.

13 ¹The Pharisees therefore said unto him, ²Thou bearest record of thyself: thy record is not true.

14 ᵈJesus answered, and said unto them, ¹Though I bear record of myself, *yet* my record is true: for I know whence I come, and whither I go: but ye cannot tell whence I came, and whither I go.

15 Ye judge after the flesh: I ¹judge no man.

16 And if I also judge, my judgment is true, for I am not alone, but I, and the Father, that sent me.

17 And it is also written in your Law, ᵉthat the testimony of two men is true.

18 ¹I am one that bear witness of myself, and the Father that sent me beareth witness of me.

19 ¹Then said they unto him, Where is that Father of thine? Jesus answered, Ye neither know me, nor the Father of mine. If ye had known me, ye should have known that Father of mine also.

20 These words spake Jesus in the ¹treasury, as he taught in the Temple, and no man laid hands on him: ²for his hour was not yet come.

21 ¹Then said Jesus again unto them, I go my way, and ye shall seek me, and shall die in your sins, Whither I go, can ye not come.

22 Then said the Jews, Will he kill himself, because he saith, Whither I go, can ye not come?

23 And he said unto them, Ye are from beneath, I am from above: ye are of this world, I am not of this world.

24 I said therefore unto you, That ye shall die in your sins: for except ye believe, that I am he, ye shall die in your sins.

25 ¹Then said they unto him, Who art thou? And

ᵈ John 5:31

ᵉ Deut. 17:6
Deut. 19:15
Matt. 18:16
2 Cor. 13:1
Heb. 10:28

ᶠ Rom. 6:20
2 Pet. 2:19

Jesus said unto them, Even ²the same thing that I said unto you from the beginning.

26 ¹I have many things to say, and to judge of you: but he that sent me, is true, and the things that I have heard of him, those speak I to the world.

27 ¹They understood not that he spake to them of the Father.

28 Then said Jesus unto them, When ye have lifted up the Son of man, then shall ye know that I am he, and that I do nothing of myself, but as my Father hath taught me, *so* I spake these things.

29 For he that sent me, is with me: the Father hath not left me alone, because I do always those things that please him.

30 ¶ As he spake these things, many believed in him.

31 ¹Then said Jesus to the Jews which believed in him, If ye continue in my word, ye are verily my disciples,

32 And shall know the truth, and the truth shall ¹make you free.

33 ¹They answered him, We be ²Abraham's seed, and were never bond to any man: why sayest thou then, Ye shall be made free?

34 Jesus answered them, Verily, verily I say unto you, that whosoever committeth sin, is the ᶠservant of sin.

35 And the servant abideth not in the house forever: but the Son abideth forever.

36 If that Son therefore shall make you free, ye shall be free indeed.

37 ¹I know that ye are Abraham's seed, but ye seek to kill me, because my word hath no place in you.

8:13 ¹ Christ is without all exception the best witness of the truth, for he was sent by his Father for that purpose, and was by him approved to the world by infinite miracles.

² Thou bearest witness of thyself which thing by all men's opinion, is naught: and for a man to commend himself is very discommendable.

8:14 ¹ That which he denied afore, John 5:31, must be taken by a manner of granting, for in that place he framed himself somewhat to the humor of his hearers, which acknowledged nothing in Christ but his humanity, and therefore he was content they should set light by his own witness, unless it were otherwise confirmed. But in this place he standeth for the maintenance of his Godhead, and praiseth his Father, who is his witness, and agreeth with him.

8:15 ¹ I do now only teach you, I condemn no man: but yet if I list to do it, I might lawfully do it, for I am not alone, but my Father is with me.

8:18 ¹ The Godhead is plainly distinguished from the manhood, else there were not two witnesses: for the party accused is not taken for a witness.

8:19 ¹ No man can know God, but in Christ only.

8:20 ¹ This was some place appointed for the gathering of the offerings.

² We live and die at the pleasure of God and not of men: Therefore this one thing remaineth that we go forward constantly in our vocation.

8:21 ¹ Because that men do naturally abhor heavenly things, no man can be a fit disciple of Christ, unless the Spirit of God frame him: in the mean season notwithstanding, the world must of necessity perish, because it refuseth the life that is offered unto it.

8:25 ¹ He shall at length know who Christ is, which will diligently hear, what he saith.

² That is, I am Christ, and the savior, for so I told you from the beginning that I was.

8:26 ¹ God is the revenger of Christ's doctrine despised.

8:27 ¹ Even the contempt of Christ maketh for his glory: which thing his enemies shall feel at length to their great smart.

8:31 ¹ The true disciples of Christ continue in his doctrine, that profiting more and more in the knowledge of the truth, they may be delivered from the most grievous burden of sin, into the true liberty of righteousness and life.

8:32 ¹ From the slavery of sin.

8:33 ¹ Some of the multitude, not they that believed: for this is not the speech of men that consent unto him but of men that are against him.

² Born and begotten of Abraham.

8:37 ¹ Our wicked manners declare, that we are plainly born of a devilish nature, But we are changed, and made of the household of God, according to the covenant which he made with Abraham by Christ only, apprehended and laid hold on by faith: which faith is known by a godly and honest life.

38 I speak that which I have seen with my Father: and ye do that which ye have seen with your Father.

39 They answered, and said unto him, Abraham is our father. Jesus said unto them, If ye were Abraham's children, ye would do the works of Abraham.

40 But now ye go about to kill me, a man that have told you the truth, which I have heard of God: this did not Abraham.

41 Ye do the works of your father. Then said they to him, We are not born of fornication: we have one Father, which is God.

42 Therefore Jesus said unto them, If God were your Father, then would ye love me: for I proceeded forth, and came from God, neither came I of myself, but he sent me.

43 Why do ye not understand my ¹talk? because ye cannot hear my word.

44 ⁸Ye are of your father the devil, and the lusts of your father ye will do: he hath been a murderer from the ¹beginning, and ²abode not in the ³truth, because there is no truth in him. When he speaketh a lie, then speaketh he of his ⁴own: for he is a liar, and the ⁵father thereof.

45 And because I tell you the truth, ye believe me not.

46 ¹Which of you can rebuke me of sin? and if I say the truth, why do ye not believe me?

47 ʰHe that is of God heareth God's words: ye therefore hear them not, because ye are not of God.

48 ¹Then answered the Jews, and said unto him, Say we not well that thou art a Samaritan, and hast a devil?

49 Jesus answered, I have not a devil, but I honor my Father, and ye have dishonored me.

50 And I seek not mine own praise: but there is one that ¹seeketh it, and judgeth.

51 ¹Verily, verily I say unto you, If a man keep my word, he shall never ²see death.

52 ¹Then said the Jews to him, Now know we that thou hast a devil. Abraham is dead, and the Prophets: and thou sayest, If a man keep my word, he shall never taste of death.

53 Art thou greater than our father Abraham, which is dead? and the Prophets are dead: whom makest thou thyself?

54 ¹Jesus answered, If I honor myself, mine honor is ²nothing worth: it is my Father that honoreth me, whom ye say, that he is your God.

55 ¹Yet ye have not known him: but I know him, and if I should say I know him not, I should be a liar like unto you: but I know him, and keep his word.

56 ¹Your father Abraham ²rejoiced to see my ³day, and he ⁴saw it, and was glad.

57 Then said the Jews unto him, Thou art not yet fifty years old, and hast thou seen Abraham?

58 Jesus said unto them, Verily, verily I say unto you, before Abraham was, I ¹am.

59 ¹Then took they up stones to cast at him, but Jesus hid himself, and went out of the Temple: And he passed through the midst of them, and so went his way.

9

1 Christ giveth sight on the Sabbath day, to him that was born blind. 13 Whom, after he had long reasoned against the Pharisees, 22, 35 and was cast out of the Synagogue, 36 Christ endueth with the knowledge of the everlasting light.

1 And ¹as Jesus passed by, he saw a man which was blind from his birth.

2 And his disciples asked him, saying, Master,

ᵍ 1 John 3:8
ʰ John 4:6

8:43 ¹ Or, language: as though he said, you do no more understand what I say, than if I spake in a strange and unknown language to you.
8:44 ¹ From the beginning of the world: for as soon as man was made, the devil cast him headlong into death.
² That is, continued not constantly, or remained not.
³ That is, in faithfulness, and uprightness, that is, kept not his creation.
⁴ Even of his own head, and of his own brain or disposition.
⁵ The author thereof.
8:46 ¹ Christ did thoroughly execute the office, that his Father enjoined him.
8:48 ¹ The enemies of Christ make their bravery for a while, but the Father will appear at his time to revenge the reproach that is done unto him in the person of his son.
8:50 ¹ That is, that will revenge both your despising of me, and of him.
8:51 ¹ The only doctrine of the Gospel apprehended by faith, is a sure remedy against death.
² That is, he shall not feel it: for even in the midst of death, the faithful see life.
8:52 ¹ Against them which abuse the glory of the Saints, to darken Christ's glory.
8:54 ¹ There is nothing farther off from all ambition than Christ, but his Father hath set him above all things.
² This is spoken by manner of [a grant]: as if he had said, Be it so, let this report which I give of myself, be of no force: yet there is another that glorifieth me, that is, that honoreth my Name.
8:55 ¹ There is no right knowledge of God, without Christ, neither any right knowledge of Christ without his word.
8:56 ¹ The virtue of Christ showed itself through all former ages in the Fathers, for they saw in the promises, that he should come, and did very joyfully lay hold on him with a lively faith.
² Was very desirous.
³ A day is a space that a man liveth in, or doeth any notable act, or suffereth any great thing.
⁴ With the eyes of faith, Heb. 11:13.
8:58 ¹ Christ as he was God, was before Abraham: and he was the Lamb slain from the beginning of the world.
8:59 ¹ Zeal without knowledge, breaketh out at length into a most open madness: and yet the wicked cannot do what they list.
9:1 ¹ Sin is the beginning even of all bodily diseases, and yet doth it not follow, that God always respecteth their sins, whom he most sharply punisheth.

who did sin, this man, or his parents, that he was born blind?

3 Jesus answered, [1]Neither hath this man sinned, nor his parents, but that the works of God should be showed on him.

4 [1]I must work the works of him that sent me, while it is [2]day: the night cometh when no man can work.

5 As long as I am in the world, [a]I am the light of the world.

6 [1]As soon as he had thus spoken, he spat on the ground, and made clay of the spittle, and anointed the eyes of the blind with the clay,

7 And said unto him, Go wash in the pool of Siloam (which is by interpretation, Sent.) He went his way therefore and washed, and came again seeing.

8 [1]Now the neighbors and they that had seen him before, when he was blind, said, Is not this he that sat and begged?

9 Some said, This is he: and others said, He is like him: but he himself said, I am he.

10 Therefore they said unto him, How were thine eyes [1]opened?

11 He answered, and said, The man that is called Jesus, made clay, and anointed mine eyes, and said unto me, Go to the pool of Siloam and wash. So I went and washed, and received sight.

12 Then they said unto him, Where is he? He said, I cannot tell.

13 ¶ They brought to the Pharisees him that was once blind.

14 And it was the Sabbath *day*, when Jesus made the clay, and opened his eyes.

15 Then again the Pharisees also asked him, how he had received sight. And he said unto them, He laid clay upon mine eyes, and I washed, and do see.

16 [1]Then said some of the Pharisees, This man is not of God, because he keepeth not the Sabbath *day*. Others said, How can a man that is a sinner, do such miracles? and there was a dissension among them.

CHAPTER 9
a John 1:9
John 8:12
John 12:35

17 Then spake they unto the blind again, What sayest thou of him, because he hath opened thine eyes? And he said, He is a Prophet.

18 Then the Jews did not believe him (that he had been blind, and received his sight) until they had called the parents of him that had received sight.

19 And they asked them, saying, Is this your son, whom ye say was born blind? How doth he now see then?

20 His parents answered them, and said, We know that this is our son, and that he was born blind:

21 But by what means he now seeth, we know not: or who hath opened his eyes, can we not tell: he is old enough: ask him: he shall answer for himself.

22 These words spake his parents, because they feared the Jews: for the Jews had ordained already, that if any man did confess that he was Christ, he should be *excommunicated* out of the Synagogue.

23 Therefore said his parents, He is old enough: ask him.

24 Then again called they the man that had been blind, and said unto him, [1]Give glory unto God: we know that this man is a [2]sinner.

25 Then he answered, and said, Whether he be a sinner or no, I cannot tell: one thing I know, that I was blind, and now I see.

26 Then said they to him again, What did he to thee? how opened he thine eyes?

27 He answered them, I have told you already, and ye have not heard it: wherefore would ye hear it again? will ye also be his disciples?

28 [1]Then reviled they him, and said, Be thou his disciple: we be Moses' disciples.

29 We know that God spake with Moses: but this man we know not from whence he is.

30 The man answered, and said unto them, Doubtless, this is a marvelous thing, that ye know not whence he is, and yet he hath opened mine eyes.

31 Now we know that God heareth not sinners: but if any man be a worshipper of God, and doeth

---

9:3 [1] Christ reasoneth here, as his disciples thought, which presuppose that there come no diseases but for sins only: whereupon he answereth that there was another cause of this man's blindness, and that was, that God's his work might be seen.

9:4 [1] The works of Christ are as it were a light, which lighten the darkness of the world.

    [2] By (day) is meant the light, that is, the lightsome, doctrine of the heavenly truth: and by (night) is meant the darkness which cometh by the obscurity of the same doctrine.

9:6 [1] Christ healing the man born blind, by taking the sign of clay, and afterward the sign of the fountain of Siloam (which signifieth Sent) showeth that as he at the beginning made man, so doth he again restore both his body and soul: and yet so, that he himself cometh first of his own accord to heal us.

9:8 [1] A true image of all men, who as they are of nature blind, do neither themselves receive the light that is offered unto them, nor suffer

it in others, and yet make a great ado amongst themselves.

9:10 [1] This is an Hebrew kind of speech, for they call a man's eyes shut, when they cannot receive any light: And therefore they are said to have their eyes opened, which of blind men are made to see.

9:16 [1] Religion is not assaulted by any means more than by pretence of Religion: but the more it is pressed down, the more it riseth up.

9:24 [1] A solemn order, whereby men were constrained in old time to acknowledge their fault before God, as if they should say, Consider thou art before God, who knoweth the whole matter, and therefore see thou reverence his majesty, and do him this honor, rather to confess the whole matter openly, than to lie before him, Josh. 7:19; 1 Sam. 6:5.

    [2] He is called a sinner in the Hebrew tongue, which is a wicked man, and maketh as it were an art of sins.

9:28 [1] Proud wickedness must needs at length break forth, which in vain lieth hid under a zeal of godliness.

his will, him heareth he.

32 Since the world began, was it not heard, that any man opened the eyes of one that was born blind.

33 If this man were not of God, he could have done nothing.

34 They answered, and said unto him, [1]Thou art altogether born in sins, and dost thou teach us? so they cast him out.

35 [1]Jesus heard that they had cast him out: and when he had found him, he said unto him, Dost thou believe in the Son of God?

36 He answered, and said, Who is he, Lord, that I might believe in him?

37 And Jesus said unto him, Both thou hast seen him, and he it is that talketh with thee.

38 Then he said, Lord, I believe, and worshipped him.

39 [1]And Jesus said, I am come unto [2]judgment into this world, that they [3]which see not, might see: and that they [b]which see, might be made blind.

40 And some of the Pharisees which were with him, heard these things, and said unto him, Are we blind also?

41 Jesus said unto them, If ye were blind, ye should not have sin: but now ye say, We see: therefore your sin remaineth.

10

1 Christ proveth that the Pharisees are the evil shepherds, 8 and by many reasons, that himself 11, 14 is the good shepherd: 19 And thereof dissension ariseth. 31 They take up stones, 39 and go about to take him, but he escapeth.

1 Verily, [1]verily I say unto you, He that entereth not in by the door into the sheepfold, but climbeth up another way, he is a thief and a robber.

2 But he that goeth in by the door, is the shepherd

[b] John 3:17
John 12:47

CHAPTER 10

[a] Isa. 40:11
Ezek. 34:23

of the sheep.

3 To him the [1]porter openeth, and the sheep hear his voice, and he calleth his own sheep by name, and leadeth them out.

4 And when he hath sent forth his own sheep, he goeth before them, and the sheep follow him: for they know his voice.

5 And they will not follow a stranger, but they flee from him: for they know not the voice of strangers.

6 This [1]parable spake Jesus unto them: but they understood not what things they were which he spake unto them.

7 Then said Jesus unto them again, Verily, verily I say unto you, I am that door of the sheep.

8 [1]All that [2]ever came before me, are thieves and robbers: but the sheep did not hear them.

9 [1]I am that door: by me if any man enter in, he shall be saved, and shall [2]go in, and go out, and find pasture.

10 The thief cometh not, but for to steal, and to kill, and to destroy: I am come that they might have life, and have it in abundance.

11 [a]I am that good shepherd: that good shepherd giveth his life for his sheep.

12 But an hireling, and he which is not the shepherd, neither the sheep are his own, seeth the wolf coming, and he leaveth the sheep, and fleeth, and the wolf catcheth them, and scattereth the sheep.

13 So the hireling fleeth, because he is an hireling, and careth not for the sheep.

14 I am that good shepherd, and know mine, and am known of mine.

15 As the Father [1]knoweth me, so know I the Father: and I lay down my life for *my* sheep.

16 [1]Other sheep I have also, which are not of this

9:34 [1] Thou art naught even from the cradle, and as we use to say, there is nothing in thee but sin.

9:35 [1] Most happy is their state, which are cast furthest out of the Church of the wicked (which proudly boast themselves of the name of the Church) that Christ may come never to them.

9:39 [1] Christ doth lighten all them by the preaching of the Gospel, which acknowledge their own darkness, but such as seem to themselves to see clearly enough, those he altogether blindeth: of which sort are they oftentimes, which have the highest place in the Church.

[2] With great power and authority, to do what is righteous and just: as if he said, These men take upon them to govern the people of God after their own lusts, as though they saw all things, and no man but they: but I will rule far otherwise than these men do: for whom they account for blind men, them I will lighten, and such as take themselves to be wisest, them will I drown in most gross darkness of ignorance.

[3] In these words (of seeing and not seeing) there is a secret taunting and check to the Pharisees: for they thought all men blind but themselves.

10:1 [1] Seeing that by Christ only we have access to the Father, there are neither other true shepherds, than those which come to Christ themselves, and bring others thither also, neither is any to be thought the true sheepfold, but that which is gathered to Christ.

10:3 [1] In those days they used to have a servant always sitting at the door, and therefore he speaketh after the manner of those days.

10:6 [1] This word (parable) which the Evangelist useth here, signifieth a dark kind of speech, when words are taken from their natural meaning, to signify another thing to us.

10:8 [1] It maketh no matter, how many, neither how old the false teachers there have been.

[2] These large terms must be applied to the matter he speaketh of. And therefore when he calleth himself the door, he calleth all them thieves and robbers which take upon them this name of Door, which none of the Prophets can, for they showed the sheep, that Christ was the door.

10:9 [1] Only Christ is the true Pastor, and that only is the true Church, which acknowledgeth him to be properly their only Pastor: To him are opposite thieves which feed not the sheep, but kill them: and hirelings also, which forsake the flock in time of danger, because they feed it only for their own profit and gains.

[2] That is, shall live safely: so use the Jews to speak, as Deut. 26:6, and yet there is a peculiar alluding to the shepherd's office.

10:15 [1] Loveth me, alloweth me.

10:16 [1] The calling of the Gentiles.

fold: them also must I bring, and they shall hear my voice: and *b*there shall be ²one sheepfold, *and* one shepherd.

17 ¹Therefore doth my Father love me, because *c,*²I lay down my life, that I might take it again.

18 No man taketh it from me, but I lay it down of myself: I have power to lay it down, and have power to take it again: this *d*commandment have I received of my Father.

19 ¶ ¹Then there was a dissension again among the Jews for these sayings.

20 And many of them said, He hath a devil, and is mad: why hear ye him?

21 Others said, These are not the words of him that hath a devil: can the devil open the eyes of the blind?

22 And it was at Jerusalem the *feast of the* ¹Dedication, and it was winter.

23 ¹And Jesus walked in the Temple, in Solomon's porch.

24 Then came the Jews round about him, and said unto him, How long dost thou make us to doubt? If thou be that Christ, tell us plainly.

25 ¹Jesus answered them, I told you, and ye believe not: the works that I do in my Father's Name, they bear witness of me.

26 ¹But ye believe not: ²for ye are not of my sheep, as I said unto you.

27 My sheep hear my voice, and I know them, and they follow me,

28 And I give unto them eternal life, and they shall never perish, neither shall any pluck them out of mine hand.

29 My Father which gave *them* me, is greater than all, and none is able to take them out of my Father's hand.

30 I and my Father are one.

31 *e,*¹Then the Jews again took up stones, to stone him.

b Ezek. 37:22
c Isa. 53:7
d Acts 2:24
e John 8:59
f Ps. 82:6

CHAPTER 11
a John 12:3
Matt. 26:7

32 Jesus answered them, Many good works have I showed you from my ¹Father: for which of these works do ye stone me?

33 The Jews answered him, saying, For the good work we stone thee not, but for blasphemy, and that thou being a man, makest thyself God.

34 Jesus answered them, Is it not written in your Law, ¹I said, Ye are gods?

35 If he called them gods, unto whom the word of God *was given*, and the Scripture cannot be ¹broken,

36 Say ye of him, whom the Father hath sanctified, and sent into the world, Thou blasphemest, because I said, I am the Son of God?

37 If I do not the works of my Father, believe me not.

38 But if I do, then though ye believe not me, *yet* believe the works, that ye may know and believe, that the Father *is* in me, and I in him.

39 ¹Again they went about to take him: but he escaped out of their hands,

40 And went again beyond Jordan, into the place where John first baptized, and there abode.

41 And many resorted unto him, and said, John did no miracle: but all things that John spake of this man, were true.

42 And many believed in him there.

11 *1 Christ, to show that he is,   25 the life and the resurrection,   14 cometh to Lazarus being dead, 17, 34 and buried,   43 and raiseth him up.   47 As the Priests were consulting together,   49 Caiaphas   50 prophecieth that one must die for the people.   56, 57 They command to seek Christ out, and to take him.*

1 And ¹a certain man was sick, *named* Lazarus of Bethany, the ²town of Mary, and her sister Martha.

2 (And it was that *a*Mary which anointed the Lord with ointment, and wiped his feet with her hair, whose brother Lazarus was sick.)

10:16 ² The certain mark of the Catholic Church throughout all the world, which hath one head, that is Christ, the only keeper and only shepherd of it.

10:17 ¹ Christ is by the decree of the Father, the only true shepherd of the true Church, for he willingly gave his life for his sheep, and by his own power rose again to life.

² He speaketh in the time that now is because Christ's whole life was as it were a perpetual death.

10:19 ¹ The Gospel discovereth hypocrisy, and therefore the world must needs rage when it cometh forth.

10:22 ¹ The feast of the Dedication was instituted by Judas Maccabeus and his brethren, after the restoring of God's true religion, by the casting out of Antiochus his garrison, 1 Macc. 4:59.

10:23 ¹ The unbelievers and proud men accuse the Gospel of darkness, which darkness indeed is within themselves.

10:25 ¹ The doctrine of the Gospel is proved from heaven by two witnesses: both by the purity of the doctrine, and by miracles.

10:26 ¹ It is no marvel that there do but a few believe, seeing that all men are by nature untamed beasts: yet notwithstanding God hath his, which he turneth into sheep, and commiteth them unto his Son, and preserveth them against the cruelty of all wild beasts.

² He giveth a reason why they believed not, to wit, because they are none of his sheep.

10:31 ¹ Christ proveth his dignity by divine works.

10:32 ¹ Through my Father's authority and power.

10:35 ¹ Void and of none effect.

10:39 ¹ Christ fleeth danger, not of mistrust, nor for fear of death, nor that he would be idle, but to gather a Church in another place.

11:1 ¹ Christ in restoring the stinking carcass of his friend to life, showeth an example both of his mighty power, and also of his singular good will toward men: which is also an image of the resurrection to come.

² Where his sisters dwelt.

3 Therefore *his* sisters sent unto him, saying, Lord, behold, he whom thou lovest, is sick.

4 When Jesus heard it, he said, This sickness is not unto [1]death, but for the glory of God, that the Son of God might be glorified thereby.

5 ¶ Now Jesus loved Martha and her sister, and Lazarus.

6 [1]And after he had heard that he was sick, yet abode he two days still in the same place where he was.

7 Then after that, said he to his disciples, Let us go into Judea again.

8 [1]The disciples said unto him, Master, the Jews lately sought to [b]stone thee, and dost thou go thither again?

9 Jesus answered, Are there not [1]twelve hours in the day? If a man walk in the day, he stumbleth not, because he seeth the light of this world.

10 But if a man walk in the night, he stumbleth, because there is no light in him.

11 These things spake he, and after, he said unto them, Our friend Lazarus [1]sleepeth: but I go to wake him up.

12 Then said his disciples, Lord, if he sleep, he shall be safe.

13 Howbeit, Jesus spake of his death: but they thought that he had spoken of the natural sleep.

14 Then said Jesus unto them plainly, Lazarus is dead.

15 And I am glad for your sakes, that I was not there, that ye may believe: but let us go unto him.

16 Then said Thomas (which is called Didymus) unto his fellow disciples, Let us also go, that we may die with him.

17 ¶ Then came Jesus, and found that he had lain in the grave four days already.

18 (Now Bethany was near unto Jerusalem, about fifteen furlongs off.)

19 [1]And many of the Jews were come to Martha and Mary to comfort them for their brother.

20 Then Martha, when she heard that Jesus was coming, went to meet him: but Mary sat still in the house.

21 Then said Martha unto Jesus, Lord, if thou hadst been here, my brother had not been dead.

22 But now I know also, that whatsoever thou askest of God, God will give it thee.

[b] John 7:30
John 8:59
John 10:33
[c] John 5:29
Luke 14:14
[d] John 6:35
[e] John 9:6

23 Jesus said unto her, Thy brother shall [1]rise again.

24 Martha said unto him, I know that he shall rise again [c]in the resurrection at the last day.

25 Jesus said unto her, I am the resurrection and the life: [d]he that believeth in me, though he were dead *yet* shall he live.

26 And whosoever liveth, and believeth in me, shall never die: Believest thou this?

27 She said unto him, Yea, Lord, I believe that thou art that Christ that Son of God, which should come into the world.

28 ¶ And when she had so said, she went her way, and called Mary her sister secretly, saying, The Master is come, and calleth for thee.

29 And when she heard it, she arose quickly, and came unto him.

30 For Jesus was not yet come into the town, but was in the place where Martha met him.

31 The Jews then which were with her in the house, and comforted her, when they saw Mary, that she rose up hastily, and went out, followed her, saying, She goeth unto the grave, to weep there.

32 Then when Mary was come where Jesus was, and saw him, she fell down at his feet, saying unto him, Lord, if thou hadst been here, my brother had not been dead.

33 [1]When Jesus therefore saw her weep, and the Jews *also* weep which came with her, he [2]groaned in the spirit, and was troubled in himself,

34 And said, Where have ye laid him? They said unto him, Lord, come and see.

35 *And* Jesus wept.

36 Then said the Jews, behold, how he loved him.

37 And some of them said, [e]Could not he which opened the eyes of the blind, have made also, that this man should not have died?

38 Jesus therefore again groaned in himself, and came to the grave. And it was a cave, and a stone was laid upon it.

39 Jesus said, Take ye away the stone. Martha the sister of him that was dead, said unto him, Lord, he stinketh already for he hath been *dead* four days.

40 Jesus said unto her, Said I not unto thee, that if thou didst believe, thou shouldest see the glory of God?

41 Then they took away the stone *from the place*

11:4 [1] That is to say, sent for the purpose to kill him.

11:6 [1] In that, that God seemeth sometimes to linger in helping of us, he doeth it both for his glory, and for our salvation, as the falling out of the matter in the end, plainly proveth.

11:8 [1] This only is the sure and right way to life, to follow God boldly without fear, who calleth us and shineth before us in the darkness of this world.

11:9 [1] All things are fitly wrought and brought to pass in their season.

11:11 [1] The Jews used a milder kind of speech, and called death a sleep, whereupon in other languages the place of burial where the dead are laid, waiting for the resurrection, is called a sleeping place.

11:19 [1] God who is the maker of nature, doth not condemn natural affections, but showeth that they ought to be examined by the rule of faith.

11:23 [1] That is, shall recover life again.

11:33 [1] Christ took upon him together with our flesh all affections of man (sin only excepted) and amongst them especially mercy and compassion.

[2] These are tokens that he was greatly moved, but yet they were without sin: and these affections are proper to man's nature.

where the dead was laid. And Jesus lifted up his eyes, and said, Father, I thank thee, because thou hast heard me.

42 I know that thou hearest me always, but because of the people that stand by, I said it, that they may believe, that thou hast sent me.

43 As he had spoken these things, he cried with a loud voice, Lazarus, come forth.

44 Then he that was dead, came forth, bound hand and foot with bands, and his face was bound with a napkin. Jesus said unto them, Loose him, and let him go.

45 ¶ Then many of the Jews, which came to Mary, and had seen the things, which Jesus did, believed in him.

46 ¹But some of them went their way to the Pharisees, and told them what things Jesus had done.

47 Then gathered the high Priests, and the Pharisees a ¹council, and said, What shall we do? For this man doeth many miracles.

48 If we let him thus alone, all men will believe in him, and the Romans will come and ¹take away both our place, and the nation.

49 ¹Then one of them *named* Caiaphas, which was the high Priest that same year, said unto them, Ye perceive nothing at all,

50 ¹Nor yet do you consider that it is expedient for us, that one man die for the people, and that the whole nation perish not.

51 ¹This spake he not of himself: but being high Priest that same year, he prophesied that Jesus should die for that nation:

52 And not for that nation only, but that he should gather together in one the children of God, which ¹were scattered.

53 Then from that day forth they consulted together, to put him to death.

54 ¹Jesus therefore walked no more openly among the Jews, but went thence unto a country near to the wilderness, into a city called Ephraim, and there

f John 18:14

CHAPTER 12
a Matt. 26:17
Mark 14:3
b John 13:29

continued with his disciples.

55 ¶ And the Jews' Passover was at hand, and many went out of the country up to Jerusalem before the Passover, to purify themselves.

56 Then sought they for Jesus, and spake among themselves, as they stood in the Temple, What think ye, that he cometh not to the feast?

57 Now both the high Priests and the Pharisees had given a commandment, that if any man knew where he were, he should show it, that they might take him.

12 2 *As Christ is at supper with Lazarus,* 3 *Mary anointeth his feet.* 5 *Judas findeth fault with her.* 7 *Christ defendeth her.* 10 *The Priests would put Lazarus to death.* 12 *As Christ cometh to Jerusalem.* 18 *The people meet him.* 22 *The Greeks desire to see him.* 42 *The chief rulers that believe in him, but for fear do not confess him,* 44 *he exhorteth to faith.*

1 Then ªJesus, six days before the Passover, came to Bethany, where Lazarus was, who died, whom he had raised from the dead.

2 There they made him a supper, and Martha served: but Lazarus was one of them that sat at the table with him.

3 Then took Mary a pound of ointment of Spikenard very costly, and anointed Jesus' feet, and wiped his feet with her hair, and the house was filled with the savor of the ointment.

4 Then said one of his disciples, *even* Judas Iscariot, Simon's *son*, which should betray him:

5 ¹Why was not this ointment sold for three hundred pence, and given to the poor?

6 Now he said thus, not that he cared for the poor, but because he was a thief, and ᵇhad the bag, and bore that which was given.

7 ¹Then said Jesus, Let her alone: against the day of my burying she kept it.

8 For the poor always ye have with you, but me ye shall not have always.

11:46 ¹ The last point of hard and iron-like stubbornness is this, to proclaim open war against God, and yet ceaseth not to make a presence both of godliness and of the profit of the commonwealth.

11:47 ¹ The Jews called the council Sanhedrin: and the word that John useth is Synedri.

11:48 ¹ That is, take away from us by force: for at that time, though the high Priest's authority was greatly lessened and decayed, yet there was some kind of government left among the Jews.

11:49 ¹ The raging and mad company of the false Church, persuade themselves that they cannot be in safety, unless he is taken away, who only upholdeth the Church: And so likewise judgeth the wisdom of the flesh in worldly affairs, which is governed by the spirit of giddiness or madness.

11:51 ¹ Christ doth sometimes so turn the tongues, even of the wicked, that in cursing, they bless.

11:52 ¹ For they were not gathered together in one country, as the

Jews were, but to be gathered from all quarters, from the East to the West.

11:54 ¹ We may give place to the rage of the wicked, when it is expedient so to do, but yet in such sort, that we swerve not from God's vocation.

12:5 ¹ An horrible example in Judas of a mind blinded with covetousness, and yet pretending godliness.

12:7 ¹ This Extraordinary anointing, which was for a sign, is so allowed of God, that he witnesseth how he will not be worshipped with outward pomp, or costly service, but with alms.

12:9 ¹ When the light of the Gospel showeth itself, some are found to be curious, and others (which left ought) to be open enemies: others in a rage honor him, whom they will straightway fall from: and very few do so reverently receive him as they ought: Notwithstanding Christ beginneth his spiritual kingdom in the midst of his enemies.

9 [1]Then much people of the Jews knew that he was there: and they came, not for Jesus' sake only, but that they might see Lazarus also, whom he had raised from the dead.

10 The high Priests therefore consulted, that they might put Lazarus to death also,

11 because that for his sake many of the Jews went away, and believed in Jesus.

12 ¶ [c]On the morrow a great multitude that were come to the feast, when they heard that Jesus should come to Jerusalem,

13 Took branches of palm trees, and went forth to meet him, and cried, Hosanna, Blessed *is* the King of Israel that cometh in the Name of the Lord.

14 And Jesus found a young ass, and sat thereon, as it is written,

15 [d]Fear not, daughter of Zion: behold, thy King cometh sitting on an ass's colt.

16 But his disciples understood not these things at the first: but when Jesus was glorified, then remembered they, that these things were written of him, and that they had done these things unto him.

17 The people therefore that was with him, bare witness that he called Lazarus out of the grave and raised him from the dead.

18 Therefore met him the people also, because they heard that he had done this miracle.

19 [1]And the Pharisees said among themselves, Perceive ye how ye prevail nothing? Behold, the world goeth after him.

20 ¶ Now there were certain Greeks among them that [1]came up to worship at the feast.

21 And they came to Philip, which was of Bethsaida in Galilee, and desired him, saying, Sir, we would see that Jesus.

22 Philip came and told Andrew: and again Andrew and Philip told Jesus.

23 And Jesus answered them, saying, The hour is come, that the Son of man must be glorified.

24 [1]Verily, verily I say unto you, Except the wheat

Cross references (center column):
[c] Matt. 21:8
Mark 11:8
Luke 19:35
[d] Ezek. 9:9
[e] Matt. 10:39
Matt. 16:25
Mark 8:35
Luke 9:24
Luke 17:33
[f] John 17:34
[g] John 3:14
[h] Ps. 89:36
Ps. 110:4
Ps. 117:2
Isa. 40:8
Ezek. 37:25
[i] John 1:9

corn fall into the ground and [2]die, it abideth alone: but if it die, it bringeth forth much fruit.

25 [e]He that loveth his life, shall lose it, and he that hateth his life in this world, shall keep it unto life eternal.

26 [f]If any man serve me, let him follow me: for where I am, there shall my servant be: and if any man serve me, him will my father honor.

27 [1]Now is my soul troubled: and what shall I say? Father, save me from this [2]hour: but therefore came I unto this hour.

28 Father, [1]glorify thy Name. Then came there a voice from heaven, *saying*, I have both glorified it, and will glorify it again.

29 Then said the people that stood by, and heard, that it was a thunder: others said, An Angel spake to him.

30 [1]Jesus answered, and said, This voice came not because of me, but for your sakes.

31 Now is the judgment of this world: now shall the prince of this world be cast out.

32 [g]And I, if I were [1]lift up from the earth, will draw [2]all men unto me.

33 Now this said he, signifying what death he should die.

34 The people answered him, We have heard out of the [h]Law, that that Christ bideth forever: and how sayest thou, that that Son of man must be lift up? Who is that Son of man?

35 [1]Then Jesus said unto them, Yet a little while is [i]the light with you: walk while ye have that light, lest the darkness come upon you: for he that walketh in the dark, knoweth not whither he goeth.

36 While ye have that light, believe in that light, that ye may be the [1]children of the light. These things spake Jesus, and departed, and hid himself from them.

37 ¶ [1]And though he had done so many miracles before them, *yet* believed they not on him,

38 That the saying of Isaiah the Prophet might be

12:19 [1] Even they which go about to oppress Christ, are made instruments of his glory.

12:20 [1] After the solemn custom: the Greeks were first so called by the name of the country of Greece, where they dwelt: but afterward, all that were not of the Jew's religion, but worshipped false gods, and were also called Heathens, were called by this name.

12:24 [1] The death of Christ is as it were a sowing, which seemeth to be a dying to the corn, but indeed is the cause of a far greater harvest: and such as is the condition of the head, so shall it be of the members.

[2] A wheat corn dieth when it is changed by virtue of the ground, and becometh a root of a fruitful blade.

12:27 [1] Whilst Christ went about to suffer all the punishment which is due to our sins, and whilst his divinity did not yet show his might and power so far as this satisfaction might thoroughly wrought, now when he is stricken with the great fear of the curse of God, he crieth out and prayeth , and desireth to be released:

yet notwithstanding he preferreth the will and glory of his Father before all things, whose obedience the Father alloweth even from heaven.

[2] To wit, of death that is now at hand.

12:28 [1] So then the Father's glory is Christ's glory.

12:30 [1] Christ foretelleth to the deaf, the manner of his death, the overcoming of the devil and the world, and in conclusion his triumph.

12:32 [1] Christ used a word, which hath a double meaning: for it signifieth either to lift up, or to rid out of the way, for his meaning was to put them in mind of his death, but the Jews seem to take it another way.

[2] Chrysostom and Theophylact refer this word, All, to all nations: that is, not to the Jews only.

12:35 [1] Unmeasurable is the mercy of God, but an horrible judgment followed, if it be contemned.

12:36 [1] That is, partakers of light.

12:37 [1] Faith is not of nature, but of grace.

fulfilled, that he said, *Lord, who believed our report? and to whom is the ¹arm of the Lord revealed?

39 Therefore could they not believe, because that Isaiah saith again,

40 *He hath blinded their eyes, and hardened their heart, that they should not see with *their* eyes, nor understand with *their* heart, and should be converted, and I should heal them.

41 These things said Isaiah when he saw his glory, and spake of him.

42 ¹Nevertheless, even among the chief rulers, many believed in him: but because of the Pharisees they did not confess him, lest they should be *cast* out of the Synagogue.

43 ¹For they loved the praise of men, more than the praise of God.

44 ¹And Jesus cried, and said, He that believeth in me, believeth ²not in me, but in him that sent me.

45 And he that seeth me, seeth him that sent me.

46 I ᵐam come a light into the world, that whosoever believeth in me, should not abide in darkness.

47 ⁿAnd if any man hear my words, and believe not, I judge him not: for I came not to judge the world, but to save the world.

48 He that refuseth me, and receiveth not my words, hath one that judgeth him: °the word that I have spoken, it shall judge him in the last day.

49 For I have not spoken of myself: but the father which sent me, he gave me a commandment what I should say, and what I should speak.

50 And I know that his commandment is life everlasting: the things therefore that I speak, I speak *them* so as the Father said unto me.

13

4 *Christ rising from supper,* 14 *to command humility to his Apostles, washeth their feet.* 21 *He noteth the traitor Judas,* 26 *with an evident token.* 34 *He commendeth charity.* 37, 38 *He foretelleth Peter of his denial.*

1 Now ᵃ,¹before the feast of the Passover, when Jesus knew that his hour was come, that he should depart out of this world unto the Father, forasmuch as he loved his ²own which were in the world, unto the end he loved them.

2 And when supper was done (and that the devil had now put in the heart of Judas Iscariot, Simon's *son*, to betray him.)

3 Jesus knowing that the Father had given all things into his ¹hands, and that he was come forth from God, and went to God,

4 He ¹riseth from Supper, and layeth aside *his upper* garments, and took a towel, and girded himself.

5 After that, he poured water into a basin, and began to wash the disciples' feet, and to wipe them with the towel, wherewith he was girded.

6 Then came he to Simon Peter, who said to him, Lord, dost thou wash my feet?

7 Jesus answered and said unto him, What I do, thou knowest not now: but thou shalt know it hereafter.

8 Peter said unto him, Thou shalt never wash my feet. Jesus answered him, If I wash thee not, thou shalt have ¹no part with me.

9 Simon Peter said unto him, Lord, not my feet only, but also the hands and the head.

10 Jesus said to him, He that is washed, needeth not, save to wash *his* feet, but is clean every whit: and ye are ᵇclean, but not all.

11 For he knew who should betray him: therefore said he, Ye are not all clean.

12 ¶ So after he had washed their feet, and had taken his garments, and was set down again, he said unto them, Know ye what I have done to you?

13 Ye call me Master, and Lord, and ye say well: for *so* am I.

14 If I then your Lord, and Master, have washed your feet, ye also ought to wash one another's feet.

15 For I have given you an example, that ye should do, even as I have done to you.

16 Verily, verily I say unto you, ᶜThe servant is not greater than his master, neither the ¹ambassador

Cross references (center column)

ʲ Isa. 53:1
Rom. 10:16
k Isa. 6:9
Matt. 13:14
Mark 4:12
Luke 8:10
Acts 28:26
Rom. 11:8
l John 5:44
ᵐ John 3:19
John 9:39
ⁿ John 3:17
° Mark 16:16

CHAPTER 13
ᵃ Matt. 26:2
Mark 14:1
Luke 12:1
ᵇ John 15:3
ᶜ John 15:20
Matt. 10:24
Luke 6:40

12:38 ¹ The arm of the Lord, is the Gospel, which is the power of God to salvation to all that believe: And therefore the arm of the Lord is not revealed to them, whose hearts the Lord hath not opened.

12:42 ¹ Such as believe, are not only few in number, if they be compared with the unbelievers, but also the most of those few (yea and that especially the chiefest) do fear men more than God.

12:44 ¹ The sum of the Gospel, and therefore of salvation, which Christ witnessed in the midst of Jerusalem, by his crying out, is this: to rest upon Christ through faith, as the only Savior appointed and given us of the Father.

² This word Not, doth not take any whit of this from Christ which is here spoken of, but is in way of correction rather, as if he said, He that believeth in me, doth not so much believe in me, as in him that sent me. So is it in Mark 9:37.

13:1 ¹ Christ no less certain of the victory, than of the combat which was at hand, using the sign of washing the feet, doth partly thereby give an example of singular modesty, and his great love toward his Apostles in this notable act, being like very shortly to depart from them: and partly witnesseth unto them, that it is he only which washeth away the filth of his people, and that by little and little, in their time and season.

² Them of his household, that is, his Saints.

13:3 ¹ Into his power.

13:4 ¹ In that he is said to rise, it argueth that there was a space between the ceremonies of the Passover, and this washing of feet, at what time it seemeth that the Supper was instituted.

13:8 ¹ Unless thou suffer me to wash thee, thou shalt have no part in the kingdom of heaven.

13:16 ¹ The word signifieth an Apostle which is anyone that is sent from another.

greater than he that sent him.

17 If ye know these things, blessed are ye if ye do them.

18 ¶ [1]I speak not of you all: I know whom I have chosen: but *it is* that the Scripture might be fulfilled, [d]He that eateth bread with me, hath lift up his heel against me.

19 From henceforth tell I you before it come, that when it is come to pass, ye might believe that I am he.

20 [e]Verily, verily I say unto you, If I send any, he that receiveth him, receiveth me, and he that receiveth me, receiveth him that sent me.

21 When Jesus had said these things, he was troubled in the Spirit, and [1]testified, and said, Verily, verily I say unto you, that one of you shall betray me.

22 [f]Then the disciples looked one on another, doubting of whom he spake.

23 Now there was one of his disciples, which [1]leaned on Jesus' bosom, whom Jesus loved.

24 To him beckoned therefore Simon Peter, that he should ask who it was of whom he spake.

25 He then as he leaned on Jesus' breast, said unto him, Lord, who is it?

26 Jesus answered, He it is, to whom I shall give a sop, when I have dipped it: and he wet a sop, and gave it to Judas Iscariot, Simon's *son*.

27 And after the sop, Satan entered into him. Then said Jesus unto him, That thou doest, do quickly.

28 But none of them that were at table, knew, for what cause he spake it unto him.

29 For some of them thought because Judas had the bag, that Jesus had said unto him, Buy those things that we have need of against the feast: or that he should give something to the poor.

30 As soon then as he had received the sop, he went immediately out, and it was night.

31 ¶ [1]When he was gone out, Jesus said, [2]Now is the

marginal references:
[d] Ps. 41:9
[e] Matt. 10:40
　Luke 10:16
[f] Matt. 26:21
　Mark 14:18
　Luke 22:21
[g] John 7:34
[h] Lev. 19:18
　Matt. 22:39
　John 15:12
　1 John 4:21
[i] Matt. 26:33
　Mark 14:29
　Luke 22:33

son of man glorified, and God is glorified in him.

32 If God be glorified in him, God shall also glorify him in himself, and shall straightway glorify him.

33 [1]Little children, yet a little while am I with you: ye shall seek me, but as I said unto the [g]Jews, Whither I go, can ye not come: also to you say I now.

34 [h]A new commandment give I unto you, that ye love one another: as I have loved you, that ye also love one another.

35 By this shall all men know, that ye are my disciples, if ye have love one to another.

36 [1]Simon Peter said unto him, Lord, whither goest thou? Jesus answered him, Whither I go, thou canst not follow me now: but thou shalt follow me afterward.

37 Peter said unto him, Lord, why can I not follow thee now? [i]I will lay down my life for thy sake.

38 Jesus answered him, Wilt thou lay down thy life for my sake? Verily, verily I say unto thee, The cock shall not crow, till thou have denied me thrice.

14

He comforteth his disciples, 2, 7 declaring his divinity and the fruit of his death, 16 promising the comforter, 17 even the holy Spirit, 26 whose office he setteth out. 27 He promiseth his peace.

1 Let [1]not your heart be troubled: ye believe in God, believe also in me.

2 In my Father's house are many dwelling places: if it were not so, [1]I would have told you: I go to [2]prepare a place for you.

3 [1]And if I go to prepare a place for you, I will [2]come again, and receive you unto myself, that where I am, there may ye be also.

4 [1]And whither I go, ye know, and the way ye know.

5 Thomas said unto him, Lord, we know not whither thou goest: how can we then know the way?

6 Jesus said unto him, I am [1]that Way, and that

13:18 [1] The betraying of Christ was not casual, or a thing that happened by chance, but the Father so ordained the cause of our salvation, to reconcile us unto himself in his Son, and the Son did willingly and voluntarily obey the Father.

13:21 [1] He affirmed it openly, and sealed it.

13:23 [1] John's leaning was such, that sitting down in his bed, his head was toward Jesus' head: so that it was an easy matter for him to touch Jesus' bosom: for it is certain that in old time men used not to sit at the table, but to lie down: on the one side.

13:31 [1] We have to consider the glorifying of Christ in his ignominy.

[2] This verse and the next following, are a most plain and evident testimony of the divinity of Christ.

13:33 [1] The eternal glory shall flow by little and little from the head into the members. But in the meantime, we must take good heed that we pass over the race of this life in brotherly love.

13:36 [1] An heavy example of rash trust and confidence.

14:1 [1] He believeth in God that believeth in Christ, and there is no other way to confirm our minds in greatest distresses.

14:2 [1] That is, if it were not so as I tell you, to wit, unless there were

place enough not only for me, but for you also in my father's house, I would not thus deceive you with a vain hope, but I would have told you so plainly.

[2] All the speech is by way of an allegory, whereby the Lord comforteth his own, declaring unto them his departure into heaven, which is, not to reign there alone, but to go before, and prepare a place for them.

14:3 [1] Christ went not away from us: to the end to forsake us, but rather that he might at length take us up with him into heaven.

[2] These words are to be referred to the whole Church, and therefore the Angels said to the disciples when they were astonished, What stand you gazing up into heaven? This Jesus shall so come as you saw him go up, Acts 1:11, and in all places of the Scripture, the full comfort of the Church is referred to that day when God shall be all in all, and is therefore called the day of redemption.

14:4 [1] Christ only is the way to true and everlasting life, for he it is in whom the Father hath revealed himself.

14:6 [1] This saying showeth unto us both the nature, the will and office of Christ.

Truth, and that Life. No man cometh unto the Father, but by me.

7 ¹If ye had known me, ye should have known my Father also: and from henceforth ye know him, and have seen him.

8 Philip said unto him, Lord, show us *thy* Father, and it sufficeth us.

9 Jesus said unto him, I have been so long time with you, and hast thou not known me, Philip? he that hath seen me, hath seen my Father: how then sayest thou, Show us *thy* Father?

10 ¹Believest thou not, that I am in the Father, and the Father is in me? The words that I speak unto you, I speak not of myself: but the Father that dwelleth in me, he doeth the works.

11 Believe me, that I *am* in the Father, and the Father *is* in me: at the least, believe me for the very works' sake.

12 ¹Verily, verily I say unto you, he that believeth in me, the works that I do, he shall do also, and ²greater than these shall he do: for I go unto my Father.

13 ªAnd whatsoever ye ask in my Name, that will I do, that the Father may be glorified in the Son.

14 If ye shall ask anything in my Name, I will do it.

15 ¹If ye love me, keep my commandments.

16 And I will pray the Father, and he shall give you another Comforter, that he may abide with you forever,

17 *Even* the ¹Spirit of truth, whom the ²world cannot receive, because it seeth him not, neither knoweth him: but ye know him: for he dwelleth with you, and shall be in you.

18 I will not leave you fatherless: *but* I will come to you.

19 Yet a little while, and the world shall see me

CHAPTER 14
ª John 16:23
  Matt. 7:7
  Mark 11:24
  James 1:5
ᵇ John 15:26

no more, but ye shall see me: because I live, ye shall live also.

20 At that day shall ye know that I am ¹in my Father, and you in me, and I in you.

21 He that hath my commandments, and keepeth them: is he that loveth me: and he that loveth me, shall be loved of my Father: and I will love him, and will ¹show mine own self to him.

22 ¹Judas said unto him, (not Iscariot) Lord, what is the cause that thou wilt show thyself unto us, and not unto the world?

23 Jesus answered, and said unto him, If any man love me, he will keep my word, and my Father will love him, and we will come unto him, and will dwell with him.

24 He that ²loveth me not, keepeth not my words, and the word which ye hear, is not mine, but the Father's which sent me.

25 ¹These things have I spoken unto you, being present with you.

26 ᵇBut the Comforter, which is the holy Ghost, whom the Father will send in my Name, he shall teach you all things, and bring all things to your remembrance, which I have told you.

27 ¹Peace I leave with you: my peace I give unto you: not as the world giveth, give I unto you. Let not your heart be troubled, nor fear.

28 ¹Ye have heard how I said unto you, I go away, and will come unto you. If ye loved me, ye would verily rejoice, because I said, I go unto the Father: for the Father ²is greater than I.

29 And now have I spoken unto you, before it come, that when it is come to pass, ye might believe.

30 ¹Hereafter will I not speak many things unto you: for the prince of this world cometh, and hath

---

14:7 ¹ It is plain by this place, that to know God, and to see God, is all one: Now whereas he said before, that no man saw God at any time, that it is to be understood thus, without Christ: or were it not through Christ, no man could ever see, nor saw God at any time: for as Chrysostom saith, the Son is a very short and easy setting forth of the father's nature unto us.

14:10 ¹ The majesty of God showeth itself most evidently, both in Christ's doctrine and deeds.

14:12 ¹ The approving of the virtue of Christ is not included within his own person, but it is spread through the body of his whole Church.

² That is, not I only do them, but I can also give other men power to do greater.

14:15 ¹ He loveth Christ aright, which obeyeth his commandments: and because the same is accompanied with an infinite sort of miseries, although he be absent in body, yet doth he comfort his with the present virtue of the holy Ghost, whom the world despiseth, because it knoweth him not.

14:17 ¹ The holy Ghost is called the Spirit of truth ,of the effect which he worketh, because he inspireth the truth into us, whereas otherwise he hath truth in himself.

² Worldly men.

14:20 ¹ The Son is in the Father after such sort, that he is of one self-same substance with the Father, but he is in his disciples in a certain respect as an aider and helper of them.

14:21 ¹ I will show myself to him, and be known of him, as if he saw me with his eyes: but this showing of himself is not bodily, but spiritually, yet so plain as none can be more.

14:22 ¹ We must not ask why the Gospel is revealed to some rather than to others, but we must rather take heed, that we embrace Christ who is offered unto us, and that we truly love him, that is to say, that we give ourselves wholly to his obedience.

14:25 ¹ It is the office of the holy Ghost to imprint in the midst of the elect in their times and seasons, that which Christ once spake.

14:27 ¹ All true felicity cometh to us by Christ alone.

14:28 ¹ So far is it, that we should be sorry for the departing of Christ, from us according to the flesh, that we should rather rejoice for it, seeing that all the blessing of the members dependeth upon the glorifying of the head.

² This is spoken in that, that he is Mediator, for so the Father is greater than he, inasmuch as the person to whom request is made, is greater than he that maketh the request.

14:30 ¹ Christ goeth to death not unwillingly, but willingly, not as yielding to the devil, but obeying his Father's decree.

²nought in me,

31 But *it is* that the world may know that I love *my* Father: and as the Father hath commanded me, so I do. Arise, let us go hence.

15
1 By the parable of the vine, 2 and the branches, 5, 6 he declareth how the disciples may bear fruit. 12, 17 He commendeth mutual love. 18 He exhorteth them to bear afflictions patiently, 20 by his own example.

1 I ¹am that true vine, and my Father is that husbandman.

2 ªEvery branch that beareth not fruit in me, he taketh away: and everyone that beareth fruit, he purgeth it, that it may bring forth more fruit.

3 ᵇNow are ye clean through the word, which I have spoken unto you.

4 Abide in me, and I in you: as the branch cannot bear fruit of itself, except it abide in the vine, no more can ye, except ye abide in me.

5 I am that vine: ye are the branches: he that abideth in me, and I in him, the same bringeth forth much fruit: for without me can ye do nothing.

6 ᶜIf a man abide not in me, he is cast forth as a branch, and withereth: and men gather them, and cast *them* into the fire, and they burn.

7 ᵈ,¹If ye abide in me, and my words abide in you, ask what ye will, and it shall be done to you.

8 ¹Herein is my Father glorified, that ye bear much fruit, and be made my disciples.

9 ¹As the father hath loved me, so have I loved you: ²continue in that my love.

10 If ye shall keep my commandments, ye shall abide in my love, as I have kept my Father's commandments, and abide in his love.

11 These things have I spoken unto you, that my joy might remain in you, and that your joy might

CHAPTER 15
ª Matt. 15:13
ᵇ John 13:10
ᶜ Col. 2:23
ᵈ 1 John 3:22
ᵉ John 13:34
1 Thess. 4:9
1 John 3:11
1 John 4:21
ᶠ Matt. 28:19
ᵍ John 13:16
Matt. 10:24
ʰ Matt. 24:9
ⁱ John 16:4

be full.

12 ᵉThis is my commandment, that ye love one another, as I have loved you.

13 Greater love than this hath no man, when any man bestoweth his life for his friends.

14 Ye are my friends, if ye do whatsoever I command you.

15 ¹Henceforth call I you not servants: for the servant knoweth not what his master doeth: but I have called you friends: for all things that I have heard of my Father, have I made known to you.

16 ¹Ye ²have not chosen me, but I have chosen you, and ordained you, ᶠthat ye go and bring forth fruits, and that your fruit remain, that whatsoever ye shall ask of the Father in my Name, he may give it you.

17 These things command I you, that ye love one another.

18 ¹If the world hate you, ye know that it hated me before you.

19 If ye were of the world, the world would love his own: but because ye are not of the world, but I have chosen you out of the world, therefore the world hateth you.

20 Remember the word that I said unto you, ᵍThe servant is not greater than his master. ʰIf they have persecuted me, they will persecute you also: if they have kept my word, they will also keep yours.

21 ¹But ⁱall these things will they do unto you for my Name's sake, because they have not known him that sent me.

22 ¹If I had not come and spoken unto them, they should not have had sin: but now have they no cloak for their sin.

23 He that hateth me, hateth my Father also.

24 If I had not done works among them which none other man did, they had not had sin: but now have they both seen, and have hated both me, and

---

² As who would say, Satan will by and by set upon me with all the might he can, but he hath no power over me, neither shall he find any such thing in me as he thinketh he shall.

15:1 ¹ We are of nature dry and fit for nothing but the fire: Therefore that we may live and be fruitful, we must first be grafted into Christ, as it were into a vine by the Father's hand: and then be daily shred with a continual meditation of the word and the cross; otherwise it shall not avail any man at all to have been grafted, unless he cleave fast unto the vine, and so draw juice out of it.

15:7 ¹ He abideth in Christ, which resteth in his doctrine, and therefore bringeth forth good fruit: And the Father will deny such an one nothing.

15:8 ¹ As who would say, Herein shall my Father be glorified, and herein also shall you be my disciples, if you bring forth much fruit.

15:9 ¹ The love of the Father towards the Son, and of the Son towards us, and ours towards God and our neighbor, are joined together with an inseparable knot: and there is nothing more sweet and pleasant than it is. Now this love showeth itself by its effects: a most perfect example whereof, Christ himself exhibited unto us.

² That is, in that love, wherewith I love you: which love is on both

parts.

15:15 ¹ The doctrine of the Gospel (as it is uttered by Christ's own mouth) is a most perfect and absolute declaration of the counsel of God, which pertaineth to our salvation, and is committed unto the Apostles.

15:16 ¹ Christ is the author and preserver of the ministry of the Gospel, even to the world's end, but the ministers have above all things need of prayer and brotherly love.

² This place teacheth us plainly, that our salvation cometh from the only favor and gracious goodness of the everlasting God towards us, and of nothing that we do or can deserve.

15:18 ¹ It ought not only not to fear, but rather confirm the faithful ministers of Christ, when they shall be hated of the world as their Master was.

15:21 ¹ The hatred that the world beareth against Christ, proceedeth of the blockishness of the mind, which notwithstanding is voluntary blind, so that the world can pretend no excuse to cover their fault.

15:22 ¹ As who would say, If I had not come, these men would not have stuck to have said still before God's judgment seat, that they are religious, and void of sin: but seeing I came to them, and they clean refuse me, they can have no cloak for their wickedness.

my Father.

25 But *it is* that the word might be fulfilled, that is written in their ¹Law, ʲThey hated me without a cause.

26 ¹But when that Comforter shall come, ᵏwhom I will send unto you from the Father, *even* the Spirit of truth, which proceedeth of the Father, he shall testify of me.

27 And ye shall witness also, because ye have been with me from the beginning.

16

1 He foretelleth the disciples of persecution.   7 He promiseth the Comforter, and declareth his office.   21 He compareth the affliction of his, to a woman that travaileth with child.

1 These ¹things have I said unto you, that ye should not be offended.

2 They shall excommunicate you: yea the time shall come, that whosoever killeth you, will think that he doeth God service.

3 And these things will they do unto you, because they have not known the Father, nor me.

4 ªBut these things have I told you, that when the hour shall come, ye might remember, that I told you them. And these things said I not unto you from the beginning, because I was with you.

5 But now I go my way to him that sent me, and none of you asketh me, Whither goest thou?

6 But because I have said these things unto you, your hearts are full of sorrow.

7 ¹Yet I tell you the truth, It is expedient for you that I go away: for if I go not away, that Comforter will not come unto you: but if I depart, I will send him unto you,

ʲ Ps. 35:19
ᵏ John 14:26
Luke 24:49

CHAPTER 16
ª John 15:21

8 ¹And when he is come, he will ²reprove the ³world of sin, and of righteousness, and of judgment.

9 Of sin, because they believed not in me:

10 Of ¹righteousness, because I go to my Father, and ye shall see me no more.

11 Of ¹judgment, ²because the prince of this world is judged.

12 ¹I have yet many things to say unto you, but ye cannot bear them now.

13 Howbeit, when he is come which is the spirit of truth, he will lead you into all truth: for he shall not speak of himself, but whatsoever he shall hear, shall he speak, and he will show you the things to come.

14 ¹He shall glorify me: for he shall receive of mine, and shall show it unto you.

15 All things that the Father hath, are mine: therefore said I, that he shall take of mine, and show it unto you.

16 ¹A ²little *while*, and ye shall not see me: and again a little *while*, and ye shall see me: ³for I go to the Father.

17 Then said *some* of his disciples among themselves, What is this that he saith unto us, A little *while*, and ye shall not see me, and again a little *while*, and ye shall see me, and, For I go to the Father.

18 They said therefore, What is this that he saith, A little *while*? we know not what he saith.

19 Now Jesus knew that they would ask him, and said unto them, Do ye inquire among yourselves, of that I said, A little *while*, and ye shall not see me: and again, a little *while*, and ye shall see me?

20 Verily, verily I say unto you, that ye shall weep and lament, and the world shall rejoice, and ye shall

15:25 ¹ Sometime by this word, Law, are meant the five books of Moses, but in this place, the whole Scripture: for the place alleged is in the Psalms.

15:26 ¹ Against the rage of the wicked, we shall stand surely by the inward testimony of the holy Ghost: But the holy Ghost speaketh no otherwise, than he spake by the mouth of the Apostles.

16:1 ¹ The ministers of the Gospel must look for all manner of reproaches, not only of them which are open enemies, but even of them also which seem to be of the same household, and the very pillars of the Church.

16:7 ¹ The absence of Christ, according to the flesh, is profitable to the Church, that we may wholly depend upon his spiritual power.

16:8 ¹ The Spirit of God worketh so mightily by the preaching of the word, that he constraineth the world, will it, nill it, to confess its own unrighteousness, and Christ's righteousness and almightiness.

² He will so reprove the world, that the worldlings shall be able to present no excuse.

³ He respecteth the time that followed his ascension, when as all gainsayers were manifestly reproved through the pouring out of the holy Ghost upon the Church: So that the very enemies of Christ were reproved of sin, in that they were constrained to confess that they were deceived, in that they believed not, and therefore they said to Peter, Acts 2, Men and brethren, what shall we do?

16:10 ¹ Of Christ himself: For when the world shall see, that I have

poured out the holy Ghost, they shall be constrained to confess that I was just, and was not condemned of my Father, when I went out of this world.

16:11 ¹ Of that authority and power, which I have both in heaven and earth.

² That is, because they shall then understand and know indeed, that I have overcome the devil, and do govern the world, when all men shall see, that they set themselves against you in vain, for I will arm you with that heavenly power, whereby you may destroy every high thing which is lifted up against the knowledge of God, 2 Cor. 10:12.

16:12 ¹ The doctrine of the Apostles proceeded from the holy Ghost, and is most perfect.

16:14 ¹ The holy Ghost bringeth no new doctrine, but teacheth that which was uttered by Christ's own mouth, and imprinteth it in our minds.

16:16 ¹ The grace of the holy Ghost is a most lively glass, wherein Christ is truly beholden with the most sharpsighted eyes of faith, and not with the bleared eyes of the flesh: whereby we feel a continual joy even in the midst of sorrows.

² When a little time is once past.

³ For I pass to eternal glory, so that I shall be much more present with you, than I was before: for then you shall feel indeed what I am, and what I am able to do.

sorrow, but your sorrow shall be turned to joy.

21 A woman when she travaileth hath sorrow because her hour is come: but as soon as she is delivered of the child, she remembereth no more the anguish, for joy that a man is born into the world.

22 And ye now therefore are in sorrow: but I will see you again, and your hearts shall rejoice, and your joy shall no man take from you.

23 And in that day shall ye ask me nothing. *b*Verily, verily I say unto you, whatsoever ye shall ask the Father in my Name, he will give it you.

24 Hitherto have ye asked nothing in my Name: ask, and ye shall receive, that your joy may be full.

25 [1]These things have I spoken unto you in parables: but the time will come, when I shall no more speak to you in parables: but I shall show you plainly of the Father.

26 [1]At that day shall ye ask in my Name, and I say not unto you, that I will pray unto the Father for you:

27 For the Father himself loveth you, because ye have loved me, *c*and have believed that I came out from God.

28 I am come out from the Father, and came into the world: again I leave the world, and go to the Father.

29 [1]His disciples said unto him, Lo, now speakest thou plainly, and thou speakest no parable.

30 Now know we that thou knowest all things, and needest not that any man should ask thee. By this we believe, that thou art come out from God.

31 Jesus answered them, Do you believe now?

32 *d*,[1]Behold, the hour cometh, and is already come, that ye shall be scattered every man into his own, and shall leave me alone: But I am not alone:

b John 14:13
Matt. 7:7
Matt. 21:22
Mark 12:24
Luke 11:9
James 1:5
c John 17:8
d Matt. 26:31
Mark 14:27

CHAPTER 17
a Matt. 28:18
b John 16:27

for the Father is with me.

33 [1]These things have I spoken unto you, that [2]in me ye might have peace: in the world ye shall have affliction, but be of good comfort: I have overcome the world.

17 *1 Christ prayeth that his glory together with his Father's may be made manifest. 9 He Prayeth for his Apostles, 20 and for all believers.*

1 These [1]things spake Jesus, and lift up his eyes to heaven, and said, [2]Father, that hour is come: glorify thy Son, that thy Son also may glorify thee,

2 *a*As thou hast given him power *over* [1]all flesh, that he should give eternal life to all them that thou hast given him.

3 And this is life eternal, that they know thee *to be* the [1]only very God, and whom thou hast sent, Jesus Christ.

4 I have glorified thee on the earth: I have finished the work which thou gavest me to do.

5 And now glorify me, thou Father, with thine own self, with the glory which I had with thee before the world was.

6 [1]I have declared thy Name unto the men which thou gavest me out of the world: [2]thine they were, and thou [3]gavest them me, and they have kept thy word.

7 *b*Now they know that all things whatsoever thou hast given me, are of thee.

8 For I have given unto them the words which thou gavest me, and they have received *them*, and have known surely that I came out from thee, and have believed that thou hast sent me.

9 I pray for them: I pray not for the world, but for them which thou hast given me: for they are thine.

16:25 [1] The holy Ghost which was poured upon the Apostles after the Ascension of Christ, instructed both them in all chiefest mysteries and secrets of our salvation, and also by them the Church, and will also instruct it to the end of the world.
16:26 [1] The sum of the worship of God, is the invocation of the Father in the Name of the Son the Mediator, who is already heard for us, for whom he hath abased himself, and is now also glorified.
16:29 [1] Faith and foolish security differ very much.
16:32 [1] Neither the wickedness of the world, neither the weakness of his own can diminish anything of the virtue of Christ.
16:33 [1] The surety and stay of the Church dependeth only upon the victory of Christ.
[2] That in me you might be thoroughly quieted. For by (peace) is meant in this place, that quiet state of mind, which is clean contrary to disquietness and heaviness.
17:1 [1] Jesus Christ the everlasting high Priest being ready straightway to offer up himself, doth by solemn prayers consecrate himself to God the Father as a sacrifice: and us together with himself. Therefore this prayer was from the beginning, is, and shall be to the end of the world, the foundation and ground of the Church of God.
[2] He first declareth, that as he came into the world to the end that the Father might show in him, being apprehended by faith, his glory in sav-

ing his elect, so he applied himself to that only: and therefore desireth of the Father, that he would bless the work which he hath finished.
17:2 [1] Over all men.
17:3 [1] He calleth the Father the only very God, to set him against all false gods, and not to shut out himself and the holy Ghost, For straightway he joineth the knowledge of the Father and the knowledge of himself together, and according to his accustomed manner, setteth forth the whole Godhead in the person of the father: So is the Father alone said to be King, immortal, wise, and dwelling in the light which no man can attain unto, invisible, Rom. 16:17; 1 Tim. 1:17.
17:6 [1] First of all he prayeth for those his disciples, by whom he would have the rest to be gathered together, commendeth them unto the Father, (having once rejected the whole company of the reprobate) because he received them of him into his custody, and for that they embracing his doctrine, shall have so many and so mighty enemies, that there is no way for them to be in safety, but by his help only.
[2] He showeth hereby that everlasting election and choice, which was hidden in the good will and pleasure of God, which is the groundwork of our salvation.
[3] He showeth how the everlasting and hidden purpose of God is declared in Christ, by whom we are justified and sanctified, if we lay hold of him by faith, that at length we may come to the glory of the election.

10 And all mine are thine, and thine are mine, and I am glorified in them.

11 And now am I no more in the world, but these are in the world, and I come to thee. Holy Father, keep them in thy Name, *even* them whom thou hast given me, that they may be [1]one as we *are*.

12 While I was with them in the world, I kept them in thy Name: those that thou gavest me, have I kept, and none of them is lost, but the child of perdition, that the 'Scripture might be fulfilled.

13 And now come I to thee, and these things speak I in the world, that they might have my joy fulfilled in themselves.

14 I have given them thy word, and the world hath hated them, because they are not of the world, as I am not of the world.

15 [1]I pray not that thou shouldest take them out of the world, but that thou keep them from evil.

16 They are not of the world, as I am not of the world.

17 [1]Sanctify them with thy truth: thy word is truth.

18 [1]As thou didst send me into the world, so have I sent them into the world.

19 And for their sakes sanctify I myself, that they also may be sanctified through the [1]truth.

20 [1]I pray not for these alone, but for them also which shall believe in me, through their word,

21 That they all may be one, as thou, O Father, *art* in me, and I in thee: *even* that they may be also one in us, that the world may believe that thou hast sent me.

22 And the glory that thou gavest me, I have given them, that they may be one, as we are one,

23 I in them, and thou in me, that they may be made perfect in one, and that the world may know that thou hast sent me, and hast loved them as thou hast loved me.

24 [d]Father, I will that they which thou hast given me, be with me even where I am, that they may behold that my glory, which thou hast given me: for thou

Marginal references:
c Ps. 109:7
d John 12:26

CHAPTER 18
a Matt. 26:36
Mark 14:32
Luke 22:39
b Matt. 26:47
Mark 14:43
Luke 22:47
c John 17:12

lovedst me before the foundation of the world.

25 O righteous Father, the world also hath not known thee, but I have known thee, and these have known, that thou hast sent me.

26 [1]And I have declared unto them thy Name, and will declare it, that the love wherewith thou hast loved me, may be in them, and I in them.

18

By Christ's power, whom Judas betrayeth, 6 the soldiers are cast down to the ground. 13 Christ is led to Annas, and from him to Caiaphas. 22, 23 His answer to the officer that smote him with a rod. 28 Being delivered to Pilate, 36 he declareth his kingdom.

1 When [1]Jesus had spoken these things, he went forth with his disciples over the brook [a]Kidron, where was a garden, into the which he entered, and his disciples.

2 And Judas which betrayed him knew also the place: for Jesus ofttimes resorted thither with his disciples.

3 [b,1]Judas then, after he had received a band of men and officers of the high Priests, and of the Pharisees, came thither with lanterns and torches, and weapons.

4 [1]Then Jesus, knowing all things that should come unto him, went forth and said unto them, Whom seek ye?

5 They answered him, Jesus of Nazareth. Jesus said unto them, I am he. Now Judas also which betrayed him, stood with them.

6 As soon then as he had said unto them, I am he, they went away backwards, and fell to the ground.

7 Then he asked them again, Whom seek ye? And they said, Jesus of Nazareth.

8 [1]Jesus answered, I said unto you, that I am he: therefore if ye seek me, let these go their way.

9 *This was* that the word might be fulfilled which he spake, 'Of them which thou gavest me, have I lost none.

17:11 [1] He prayeth that his people may peaceably agree and be joined together in one, that as the Godhead is one, so they may be of one mind and one consent together.

17:15 [1] He showeth what manner of deliverance he meaneth: not that they should be in no danger, but that they being preserved from all, might prove by experience that the doctrine of salvation is true, which they received at his mouth to deliver to others.

17:17 [1] That is, make them holy: and that is said to be holy, which is dedicated and made proper to God only.

17:18 [1] He addeth moreover, that the Apostles have a vocation common with him, and therefore that they must be holden up by the selfsame virtue to give up themselves wholly to God, whereby he being first, did consecrate himself to the Father.

17:19 [1] The true and substantial sanctification of Christ, is set against the outward purifyings.

17:20 [1] Secondarily he offereth to God the Father, all his, that is, how many soever shall believe in him by the doctrine of the Apostles: that

as he cleaveth unto the Father receiving from him all fullness, so they being joined with him, may receive life from him, and at length being together beloved in him, may also with him enjoy everlasting glory.

17:26 [1] He communicateth with his by little and little, the knowledge of the Father, which is most full in Christ the Mediator, that they may in him be beloved of the Father, with the selfsame love wherewith he loveth the Son.

18:1 [1] Christ goeth of his own accord into a garden, which his betrayer knew, to be taken: that by his obedience he might take away the sin that entered into the world by one man's rebellion, and that in a garden.

18:3 [1] Christ, who was innocent, was taken as a wicked person, that we which are wicked might be let go as innocent.

18:4 [1] Christ's person (but not his virtue) was bound of the adversaries, when and how he would.

18:8 [1] Christ doth not neglect the office of a good pastor, no not in his greatest danger.

10 ¹Then Simon Peter having a sword, drew it, and smote the high Priest's servant, and cut off his right ear. Now the servants name was Malchus.

11 Then said Jesus unto Peter, Put up thy sword into the sheath: shall I not drink of the cup which *my* Father hath given me?

12 Then the band and the captain, and the officers of the Jews took Jesus, and bound him.

13 ¹And led him away to ᵈAnnas first (for he was father-in-law to Caiaphas, which was the high Priest that same year.)

14 ᵉAnd Caiaphas was he, that gave counsel to the Jews, that it was expedient that one man should die for the people.

15 ¶ ᶠ'¹Now Simon Peter followed Jesus, and another disciple, and that disciple was known of the high Priest: therefore he went in with Jesus into the hall of the high Priest.

16 But Peter stood at the door without. Then went out the other disciple which was known unto the high Priest, and spake to her that kept the door, and brought in Peter.

17 Then said the maid that kept the door, unto Peter, Art not thou also one of this man's disciples? He said, I am not.

18 And the servants and officers stood there, which had made a fire of coals: for it was cold, and they warmed themselves. And Peter also stood among them, and warmed himself.

19 ¶ (¹The high Priest then asked Jesus of his disciples, and of his doctrine,

20 Jesus answered him, I spake openly to the world: I ever taught in the Synagogue and in the Temple, whither the Jews resort continually, and in secret have I said nothing.

21 Why askest thou me? ask them which heard me what I said unto them: behold, they know what I said.

22 When he had spoken these things, one of the officers which stood by, smote Jesus with *his* rod, saying, Answerest thou the high Priest so?

23 Jesus answered him, If I have evil spoken, bear witness of the evil: but if I have well spoken, why

ᵈ Luke 3:2
ᵉ John 11:50
ᶠ Matt. 26:58
  Mark 14:54
  Luke 22:54
ᵍ Matt. 26:57
  Luke 21:54
ʰ Matt. 16:69
  Mark 14:59
  Luke 22:55
ⁱ Matt. 27:2
  Mark 15:1
  Luke 23:1
ʲ Acts 10:28
  Acts 11:3
ᵏ Matt. 20:19
ˡ Matt. 27:11
  Mark 15:2
  Luke 23:3

smitest thou me?

24 ¶ ᵍNow Annas had sent him bound unto Caiaphas the high Priest.)

25 ʰ·¹And Simon Peter stood and warmed himself, and they said unto him, Art not thou also of his disciples? He denied it, and said, I am not.

26 One of the servants of the high Priest, his cousin whose ear Peter smote off, said, Did not I see thee in the garden with him?

27 Peter then denied again, and immediately the cock crew.

28 ⁱ·¹Then led they Jesus from ²Caiaphas into the common hall. Now it was morning, and they themselves went not into the common hall, lest they should be ʲdefiled, but that they might eat the Passover.

29 Pilate then went out unto them, and said, What accusation bring ye against this man?

30 They answered, and said unto him, If he were not an evil doer, we would not have delivered him unto thee.

31 Then said Pilate unto them, Take ye him, and judge him after your own Law. Then the Jews said unto him, ¹It is not lawful for us to put any man to death.

32 *It was* that the word of Jesus ᵏmight be fulfilled which he spake, ˡsignifying what death he should die.

33 ˡSo Pilate entered into the common hall again, and called Jesus, and said unto him, Art thou the king of the Jews?

34 Jesus answered him, Sayest thou that of thyself, or did others tell it thee of me?

35 Pilate answered, Am I a Jew? Thine own nation, and the high Priest have delivered thee unto me. What hast thou done?

36 ¹Jesus answered, My kingdom is not of this world: if my kingdom were of this world, my servants would surely fight, that I should not be delivered to the Jews: but now is my kingdom not from hence.

37 Pilate then said unto him, Art thou a King then? Jesus answered, Thou sayest that I am a King: for this cause am I born, and for this cause came I into the world, that I should bear witness unto the truth: everyone that is of the truth, heareth my voice.

18:10 ¹ We ought to contain the zeal we bear to God, within the bounds of our vocation.

18:13 ¹ Christ is brought before an earthly high Priest to be condemned for our blasphemies, that we might be acquitted of the everlasting high Priest himself.

18:15 ¹ A lively example of the fragility of man even in the best, when they be once left to themselves.

18:19 ¹ Christ defendeth his cause but slenderly, not that he would withdraw himself from death, but to show that he was condemned as an innocent.

18:25 ¹ After that men have once fallen, they cannot only not lift themselves by their own strength, but also they fall more and more into worse, until they be raised up again, by a new virtue

of God.

18:28 ¹ The Son of God is brought before the judgment seat of an earthly and profane man, in whom there is found much less wickedness, than in the princes of the people of God: A lively image of the wrath of God against sin, and therewithal of his great mercy, and least of all, of his most severe judgment against the stubborn contemners of his grace when it is offered unto them.

² From Caiaphas's house.

18:31 ¹ For judgments of life and death were taken from them forty years before the destruction of the temple.

18:32 ¹ For Christ had foretold that he should be crucified.

18:36 ¹ Christ avoucheth his spiritual kingdom, but rejecteth a worldly.

38 ¹Pilate said unto him, ²What is truth? And when he had said that, he went out again unto the Jews, and said unto them, I find in him no cause at all.

39 ᵐBut you have a custom that I should deliver you one loose at the Passover: will ye then that I loose unto you the King of the Jews?

40 ⁿThen ¹cried they all again, saying, Not him, but Barabbas: now this Barabbas was a murderer.

19 Pilate, when Christ was scourged, 2 and crowned with thorns, 4 was desirous to let him loose: 8 but being overcome with the outrage of the Jews, 16 he delivereth him to be crucified. 26 Jesus committeth his mother to the disciple. 30 Having tasted vinegar, he dieth: 34 and being dead, his side is pierced with a spear. 40 He is buried.

1 Then ᵃPilate took Jesus and ¹scourged him.

2 And the soldiers platted a crown of thorns, and put it on his head, and they put on him a purple garment,

3 And said, Hail King of the Jews. And they smote him with *their* rods.

4 ¹Then Pilate went forth again, and said unto them, Behold, I bring him forth to you, that ye may know, that I find no fault in him at all.

5 Then came Jesus forth wearing a crown of thorns, and a purple garment. And *Pilate* said unto them, Behold the man.

6 Then when the high Priests and officers saw him, they cried, saying, ¹Crucify, crucify *him*. Pilate said unto them, Take ye him, and crucify *him*: for I find no fault in him.

7 The Jews answered him, We have a law, and by our law he ought to die, because he made himself the Son of God.

8 ¶¹When Pilate then heard that word, he was the more afraid,

9 And went again into the common hall, and said unto Jesus, Whence art thou? But Jesus gave him none answer.

10 Then said Pilate unto him, Speakest thou not unto me? Knowest thou not that I have power to crucify thee, and have power to loose thee?

ᵐ Matt. 27:15
Mark 15:6
Luke 23:17

ⁿ Acts 3:14

CHAPTER 19
ᵃ Matt. 27:27
Mark 15:16
ᵇ Matt. 27:31
Mark 15:25
Luke 23:26
ᶜ Matt. 27:35
Mark 15:24

11 Jesus answered, Thou couldest have no power at all against me, except it were given thee from above: therefore he that delivered me unto thee, hath the greater sin.

12 From thenceforth Pilate sought to loose him, but the Jews cried, saying, If thou deliver him, thou art not Caesar's friend: *for* whosoever maketh himself a King, speaketh against Caesar.

13 ¶¹When Pilate heard this word, he brought Jesus forth, and sat down in the judgment seat in a place called the pavement, and in Hebrew, ²Gabbatha.

14 And it was the Preparation of the Passover, and about the sixth hour: and he said unto the Jews, Behold your King.

15 But they cried, Away with him, away with him, crucify him. Pilate said unto them, Shall I crucify your King? The high Priests answered, We have no King but Caesar.

16 ¹Then delivered he him unto them, to be crucified. ᵇAnd they took Jesus, and led him away.

17 And he bare his own cross, and came into a place named *of dead men's* skulls, which is called in Hebrew, Golgotha:

18 Where they crucified him, and two other with him, on either side one, and Jesus in the midst.

19 ¶¹And Pilate wrote also a title, and put it on the cross, and it was written, JESUS OF NAZARETH THE KING OF THE JEWS.

20 This title then read many of the Jews: for the place where Jesus was crucified, was near to the city: and it was written in Hebrew, Greek, and Latin.

21 Then said the high Priests of the Jews to Pilate, Write not, The King of the Jews, but that he said, I am the King of the Jews.

22 Pilate answered, What I have written, I have written.

23 ¶¹Then the ʿsoldiers, when they had crucified Jesus, took his garments (and made four parts, to every soldier a part) and *his* coat: and the coat was without seam woven from the top throughout.

24 ¶ Therefore they said one to another, Let us not divide it, but cast lots for it, whose it shall be.

18:38 ¹ It was requisite that Christ should be pronounced innocent, but notwithstanding (in that that he took upon him our person) was to be condemned as a most wicked man.

² He speaketh this disdainfully and scoffingly, and not by way of asking a question.

18:40 ¹ Word for word, made a great and foul voice.

19:1 ¹ The wisdom of the flesh, chooseth of two evils the least, but God curseth that same wisdom.

19:4 ¹ Christ is again acquitted by the same mouth wherewith he is afterward condemned.

19:6 ¹ They will have him crucified, whom by an old custom of theirs, they should have stoned and hanged up as convict of blasphemy: but they desire to have him crucified after the manner of the Romans.

19:8 ¹ Pilate's conscience fighteth for Christ, but straightway it yieldeth, because it is not upholden with the singular virtue of God.

19:13 ¹ Pilate condemneth himself first, with the same mouth wherewith he afterward condemneth Christ.

² Gabbatha signifieth an high place, as judgment seats are.

19:16 ¹ Christ fasteneth Satan, sin and death to the cross.

19:19 ¹ Christ sitting upon the throne of the cross, is openly written everlasting king of all people, with his own hand, whose mouth condemned him for usurping a kingdom.

19:23 ¹ Christ signifieth by the division of his garments amongst the bloody butchers (his coat except, that hath no seam) that it shall come to pass, that he will shortly divide his benefits, and enrich his very enemies throughout the world: but so notwithstanding that the treasure of his Church shall remain whole.

This was that the Scripture might be fulfilled, which saith, ^dThey parted my garments among them, and on my coat did cast lots. So the soldiers did these things indeed.

25 ¶ ¹Then stood by the cross of Jesus his mother, and his mother's sister, Mary *the wife of* Clopas, and Mary Magdalene.

26 And when Jesus saw his mother, and the disciple standing by, whom he loved, he said unto his mother, Woman, behold thy son.

27 Then said he to the disciple, Behold thy mother: and from that hour, the disciple took her home unto him.

28 ¶ ¹After, when Jesus knew that all things were performed, that the ^eScripture might be fulfilled, he said, I thirst.

29 And there was set a ¹vessel full of vinegar: and they filled a sponge with vinegar: and put it about an Hyssop *stalk*, and put it to his mouth.

30 Now when Jesus had received of the vinegar, he said, It is finished, and bowed his head, and gave up the ghost.

31 ¹The Jews then (because it was the Preparation, that the bodies should not remain upon the cross on the Sabbath *day*: for that Sabbath was an high day) besought Pilate that their legs might be broken, and that they might be taken down.

32 Then came the soldiers and brake the legs of the first, and of the other, which was crucified with *Jesus*.

33 But when they came to Jesus, and saw that he was dead already, they brake not his legs.

34 ¹But one of the soldiers with a spear ²pierced his side, and forthwith came there out blood and water.

35 And he that saw it, bare record, and his record is true: and he knoweth that he saith true, that ye might believe it.

36 For these things were done, that the Scripture should be fulfilled, ^fNot a bone of him shall be broken.

37 And again another Scripture saith, ^gThey shall see him whom they have thrust through.

38 ^{h,1}And after these things, Joseph of Arimathea (who was a disciple of Jesus, but secretly for fear of the Jews) besought Pilate that he might take down the body of Jesus. And Pilate gave him license. He came then and took Jesus' body.

39 And there came ⁱalso Nicodemus (which first came to Jesus by night) and brought of myrrh and aloes mingled together about an hundred pounds.

40 Then took they the body of Jesus, and wrapped it in linen clothes with the odors, as the manner of the Jews is to bury.

41 And in that place where Jesus was crucified, was a garden, and in the garden a new sepulcher, wherein was ¹never man yet laid.

42 There then laid they Jesus, because of the Jews' Preparation *day*, for the sepulcher was near.

20

1 *Mary bringeth word that Christ is risen: 3 Peter and John   4 run to see it.   15 Jesus appeareth to Mary,   19 and to the disciples that were together in the house,   25 Thomas, before faithless,   29 now believeth.*

1 Now ^{a,1}the first *day* of the week came Mary Magdalene, early when it was yet dark, unto the sepulcher, and saw the stone taken away from the tomb.

2 Then she ran, and came to Simon Peter, and to the other disciple, whom Jesus loved, and said unto them, They have taken away the Lord out of the sepulcher, and we know not where they have laid him.

3 Peter therefore went forth, and the other disciple, and they came unto the sepulcher.

4 So they ran both together, but the other disciple did outrun Peter, and came first to the sepulcher.

5 And he stooped down, and saw the linen clothes lying: yet went he not in.

6 Then came Simon Peter following him, and went into the sepulcher, and saw the linen clothes lie,

7 And the kerchief that was upon his head, not lying with the linen clothes, but wrapped together in a place by itself.

19:25 ¹ Christ is a perfect example of all righteousness, not only in the keeping of the first, but also of the second table.

19:28 ¹ Christ, when he hath taken the vinegar, yieldeth up the Ghost, drinking up indeed that most bitter and sharp cup of his Father's wrath in our name.

19:29 ¹ Galatinus witnesseth out of the book called Sanhedrin, that the Jews were wont to give them that were executed, vinegar mixed with frankincense to drink, to make their brains somewhat troubled: so charitably the Jews provided for the poor men's consciences which were executed.

19:31 ¹ The body of Christ which was dead for a season (because it so pleased him) is wounded, but the least bone of it is not broken: and such is the state of his mystical body.

19:34 ¹ Christ being dead upon the cross, witnesseth by a double sign, that he only is the true satisfaction, and the true washing for the believers.

² This wound was a most manifest witness of the death of Christ: for the water that issued out by this wound, gave us plainly to understand, that the weapon pierced the very skin that compasseth the heart, which is the vessel that containeth that water, and that being once wounded, that creature which is so pierced and stricken, cannot choose but die.

19:38 ¹ Christ is openly buried, and in a famous place, Pilate writing and suffering it, and that by men which did favor Christ, in such wise, that yet before that day, they never openly followed him: so that by his burial, no man can justly doubt either of his death, or resurrection.

19:41 ¹ That no man might cavil at his resurrection, as though some other that had been buried there, had risen, Theophylact.

20:1 ¹ Mary Magdalene, Peter and John are the first witnesses of the resurrection: and such as cannot justly be suspected, for that they themselves could scarcely be persuaded of it, so far is it off, that they should invent it of set purpose.

8 Then went in also the other disciple, which came first to the sepulcher, and he saw it, and believed.

9 For as yet they knew not the Scripture, That he must rise again from the dead.

10 And the disciples went away again unto their own home.

11 ¶ [b]But Mary stood [1]without at the sepulcher weeping: and as she wept, she bowed herself into the sepulcher,

12 [1]And saw two Angels in [2]white, sitting, the one at the head, and the other at the feet, where the body of Jesus had lain.

13 And they said unto her, Woman, why weepest thou? She said unto them, They have taken away [1]my Lord, and I know not where they have laid him.

14 [1]When she had thus said, she turned herself back, and saw Jesus standing, and knew not that it was Jesus.

15 Jesus saith unto her, Woman, why weepest thou? whom seekest thou? She supposing that he had been the gardener, said unto him, Sir, if thou hast borne him hence, tell me where thou hast laid him, and I will take him away.

16 Jesus saith unto her, Mary. She turned herself, and said unto him, Rabboni, which is to say, Master.

17 [1]Jesus saith unto her, Touch me not: for I am not yet ascended to my Father: but go to my [2]brethren, and say unto them, I ascend unto [3]my Father, and to your Father, and to my God, and your God.

18 Mary Magdalene came and told the disciples that she had seen the Lord, and that he had spoken these things unto her.

19 ¶ [c,1]The same day then at night, which was the first *day* of the week, and when the [2]doors were shut where the disciples were assembled for fear of the Jews, came Jesus and stood in the midst, and said to them, Peace *be* unto you.

20 And when he had so said, he showed unto them *his* hands, and his side. Then were the disciples glad when they had seen the Lord.

[b] Matt. 28:1
Mark 16:5
[c] Mark 16:14
Luke 24:36
1 Cor. 15:5
[d] Matt. 28:18
[e] John 21:25

21 [d]Then said Jesus to them again, Peace *be* unto you: as my Father sent me, so send I you.

22 And when he had said that, he breathed on them, and said unto them, Receive the holy Ghost.

23 [1]Whosoever's sins ye remit, they are remitted unto them: *and* whosoever's sins ye retain, they are retained.

24 ¶ [1]But Thomas one of the twelve, called Didymus, was not with them when Jesus came.

25 The other disciples therefore said unto him, We have seen the Lord: but he said unto them, Except I see in his hands the print of the nails, and put my finger into the print of the nails, and put mine hand into his side, I will not believe it.

26 ¶ And eight days after, again his disciples were within, and Thomas with them. *Then* came Jesus, when the doors were shut, and stood in the midst, and said, Peace *be* unto you.

27 After said he to Thomas, Put thy finger here, and see mine hands, and put forth thine hand, and put it into my side, and be not faithless, but faithful.

28 Then Thomas answered, and said unto him, *Thou art* my Lord, and my God.

29 [1]Jesus said unto him, Thomas, because thou hast seen me, thou believest: blessed *are* they that have not seen, and have believed.

30 [e,1]And many other signs also did Jesus in the presence of his disciples, which are not written in this book.

31 But these things are written that ye might believe, that Jesus is that Christ that Son of God, and that in believing ye might have life through his Name.

21

1 Jesus appeareth to his disciples as they were fishing, 6, 7 whom they know by a miraculous draught of fishes. 15 He committeth the charge of the sheep to Peter, 18 and foretelleth of him the manner of his death.

1 After these things, [1]Jesus showed himself again to his disciples at the sea of Tiberias: and thus

---

20:11 [1] That is, without the cave, which the sepulchre was cut out of.

20:12 [1] Two Angels are made witnesses of the Lord's resurrection.
  [2] In white clothing.

20:13 [1] Many speak as the common people use to speak: for they speak of a dead carcass, as they do of a whole man.

20:14 [1] Jesus witnesseth by his presence, that he is truly risen.

20:17 [1] Christ which is risen, is not to be sought in this world according to the flesh, but in heaven by faith, whither he is gone before us.
  [2] By his brethren he meaneth his disciples: for in the next verse following, it is said, that Mary told his disciples.
  [3] He calleth God his Father because he is his Father naturally in the Godhead, and he saith your Father, because he is our Father by grace, through the adoption of the sons of God: that is, by taking us of his free grace to be his sons, Epiphanius.

20:19 [1] Christ in that that he presented himself before his disciples suddenly through his divine power, when the gates were shut, doth fully assure them both of his resurrection, and also of their Apostleship, inspiring them with the holy Ghost, who is the director of the ministry of the Gospel.
  [2] Either the doors opened to him of their own accord, or the very walls themselves were a passage for him.

20:23 [1] The publishing of the forgiveness of sins by faith in Christ, and the setting forth and denouncing the wrath of God in retaining the sins of the unbelievers, is the sum of the preaching of the Gospel.

20:24 [1] Christ draweth out of the unbelief of Thomas, a certain and sure testimony of his resurrection.

20:29 [1] True faith dependeth upon the mouth of God, and not upon fleshly eyes.

20:30 [1] To believe in Christ, the Son of God, and our only Savior, is the end of the doctrine of the Gospel, and especially of the history of the resurrection.

21:1 [1] In that, that Christ here is not only present, but also eateth with his disciples, he giveth a most full assurance of his resurrection.

showed he *himself*:

2 There were together Simon Peter, and Thomas, which is called Didymus, and Nathanael of Cana in Galilee, and the *sons* of Zebedee, and two others of his disciples.

3 Simon Peter said unto them, I go a fishing. They said unto him, We also will go with thee. They went their way and entered into a ship straightway, and that night caught they nothing.

4 But when the morning was now come, Jesus stood on the shore: nevertheless the disciples knew not that it was Jesus.

5 Jesus then said unto them, Sirs, have ye any meat? They answered him, No.

6 Then he said unto them, Cast out the net on the right side of the ship, and ye shall find. So they cast out, and they were not able at all to draw it, for the multitude of fishes.

7 Therefore said the disciple whom Jesus loved, unto Peter, It is the Lord. When Simon Peter heard that it was the Lord, he girded his ¹coat to him (for he was naked) and cast himself into the sea.

8 But the other disciples came by ship, (for they were not far from land, but about two hundred cubits) and they drew the net with fishes.

9 As soon then as they were come to land, they saw hot coals, and fish laid thereon, and bread.

10 Jesus said unto them, Bring of the fishes, which ye have now caught.

11 Simon Peter stepped forth and drew the net to land full of great fishes, an hundred, fifty and three: and albeit there were so many, yet was not the net broken.

12 Jesus said unto them, Come, *and* dine. And none of the disciples durst ask him, Who art thou? seeing they knew that he was the Lord.

13 Jesus then came and took bread and gave them, and fish likewise.

14 This is now the third time that Jesus showed himself to his disciples, after that he was risen again from the dead.

15 ¶ ¹So when they had dined, Jesus said to

CHAPTER 21
a John 13:23
b John 20:30

Simon Peter, Simon *the son* of Jonah, lovest thou me more than these? He said unto him, Yea, Lord, thou knowest that I love thee. He said unto him, Feed my lambs.

16 He said to him again the second time, Simon *the son* of Jonah, lovest thou me? He said unto him, Yea, Lord, thou knowest that I love thee. He said unto him, Feed my sheep.

17 He said unto him ¹the third time, Simon *the son* of Jonah, lovest thou me? Peter was sorry because he said to him the third time, Lovest thou me? and said unto him, Lord, thou knowest all things: thou knowest that I love thee. Jesus said unto him, Feed my sheep.

18 ¹Verily, verily I say unto thee, When thou wast young, thou ²girdedst thyself, and walkedst whither thou wouldest: but when thou shalt be old, thou shalt stretch forth thine hands, and another shall ³gird thee, and lead thee without thou wouldest ⁴not.

19 And this spake he signifying by what ¹death he should glorify God. And when he had said this, he said to him, Follow me.

20 ¹Then Peter turned about, and saw the disciple whom JESUS loved, following, which had also *a*leaned on his breast at supper, and had said, Lord, which is he that betrayeth thee?

21 When Peter therefore saw him, he said to Jesus, Lord, what shall this man *do?*

22 Jesus said unto him, If I will that he tarry till I come, what is it to thee? follow thou me.

23 Then went this word abroad among the brethren, that this disciple should not die. Yet Jesus said not to him, He shall not die: but if I will that he tarry till I come, what is it to thee?

24 ¹This is that disciple, which testifieth of these things, and wrote these things, and we know that his testimony is true.

25 *b*Now there are also many other things which Jesus did, the which if they should be written every one, I suppose the world could not contain the books that should be written, Amen.

21:7 ¹ It was a linen garment, which could not let his swimming.

21:15 ¹ Peter by his triple confession is restored into his former degree from whence he fell by his triple denial: and therewithal is advertised, that he is indeed a pastor, which showeth his love to Christ in feeding his sheep.

21:17 ¹ It was meet that he that had denied him thrice, should confess him thrice, that Peter might neither doubt of the forgiveness of his so grievous a sin, nor of his restoring to the office of the Apostleship.

21:18 ¹ The violent death of Peter is foretold.

² They that took far journeys, especially in the East country, and in those places [where] the people used long garments, had need to be girded and trussed up.

³ He meant that kind of girding which is used toward captives, when they are bound fast with cords and chains, as who would say, Now thou girdest thyself as thou thinkest best, to go whither thou

listest, but the time will be, when thou shall not gird thee with a girdle, but another shall bind thee with chains, and carry thee whither thou wouldest not.

⁴ Not that Peter suffered ought for the truth of God against his will: for we read that he came with joy and gladness when he returned from the Council where he was whipped: but because this will cometh not from the flesh, but from the gift of the Spirit which is given us from above, therefore he showeth there should be a certain striving and conflict or repugnancy, which also is in us, in all our sufferances as touching the flesh.

21:19 ¹ That is, that Peter should die by a violent death.

21:20 ¹ We must take heed, that while we cast our eyes upon others, we neglect not that which is enjoined us.

21:24 ¹ The history of Christ is true and warily written: not for the curiosity of men, but for the salvation of the godly.

THE

ACTS

OF THE HOLY APOSTLES,

WRITTEN BY LUKE THE EVANGELIST

1 *1 Luke tieth this history to his Gospel. 9 Christ being taken into heaven. 10 The Apostles, 11 being warned by the Angels, 12 to return, 14 and give themselves to prayer. 15 By Peter's motion, 18 into Judas the traitor's place. 26 Matthias is chosen.*

CHAPTER 1
a Luke 24:49
b John 14:25
c Matt. 3:11
Mark 1:8
Luke 3:16
Acts 2:2
Acts 11:16
Acts 19:4
d Acts 2:2
e Luke 24:51

1 I have made the ¹former treatise, O Theophilus, of all that Jesus began to ²do and teach,

2 Until the day that he was taken up, after that he through the holy Ghost, had given commandments unto the Apostles, whom he had chosen:

3 ¹To whom also he presented himself alive after that he had suffered, by many ²infallible tokens, being seen of them by the *space* of forty days, and speaking of those things which *appertained* to the kingdom of God.

4 ᵃAnd when he had ¹gathered *them* together, he commanded them that they should not depart from Jerusalem, but to wait for the promise of the Father, ᵇwhich *said he*, ye have heard of me.

5 ᶜFor John indeed baptized with water, but ye shall be baptized ¹with the holy Ghost within these few days.

6 ¹When they therefore were come together they asked of him, saying, Lord, wilt thou at this time ²restore the kingdom to Israel?

7 And he said unto them, It is not for you to know the times, or the ¹seasons, which the Father hath put in his own power.

8 ᵈBut ye shall receive power of the holy Ghost, when he shall come on you: and ye shall be witnesses unto me both in Jerusalem and in all Judea, and in Samaria, and unto the uttermost part of the earth.

9 ᵉ,¹And when he had spoken these things, while they beheld, he was taken up: for a cloud took him up out of their sight.

10 And while they looked steadfastly toward heaven, as he went, behold, two men stood by them in white apparel.

11 Which also said, Ye men of Galilee, why stand ye gazing into heaven? This Jesus which is taken up ¹from you into heaven, shall so come, as ye have seen him go into heaven.

12 ¶ Then returned they unto Jerusalem from the mount that is called *the mount* of Olives, which is near to Jerusalem, being from it a Sabbath ¹*day's* journey.

13 ¹And when they were ²come in, they went up into an upper chamber, where abode both Peter and James, and John, and Andrew, Philip, and Thomas, Bartholomew, and Matthew, James *the son* of Alphaeus, and Simon Zealot, and Judas James's *brother*.

14 These all ¹continued with ²one accord in ³prayer and supplication with the ⁴women, and Mary the

---

1:1 ¹ A passing over from the history of the Gospel, that is, from the history of the sayings and doings of Christ, unto the acts of the Apostles.

² The acts of Jesus are the miracles and doings which showed his Godhead, and his most perfect holiness and example of his doctrine.

1:3 ¹ Christ did not straightway ascend into heaven after his resurrection: because he would thoroughly prove his resurrection: and with his presence confirm his Apostles in the doctrine, which they had heard.

² He calleth those infallible tokens, which are otherwise [termed] necessary: now in that Christ spake, and walked, and ate, and was felt of many, these are sure signs and tokens that he truly rose again.

1:4 ¹ They were dispersed here and there, but he gathereth them together that they might altogether be witnesses of his resurrection.

1:5 ¹ Either of the Father, or of me: so that either the Father or Christ is set here against John, as the holy Ghost is against the water, as things answerable the one to the other.

1:6 ¹ We must fight before we triumph: and we ought not curiously to search after those things, which God hath not revealed.

² To the old and ancient state.

1:7 ¹ That is, the fit occasions that serve to doing of matters which the Lord hath appointed to bring things to pass in.

1:9 ¹ After that Christ had promised the full virtue of the holy Ghost, wherewith he would govern his Church, although he should be absent in body, he took up his body from us into heavenly tabernacles, there to continue until the latter day of judgment, as the Angels witness.

1:11 ¹ That is, out of your sight.

1:12 ¹ About two miles.

1:13 ¹ Ecclesiastical assemblies to hear the word, and to make common prayer, were first instituted and kept in private houses by the Apostles.

² They went into the house, which the Church hath chosen at that time to be a receipt for the whole assembly.

1:14 ¹ The Greek word signified an invincible constancy, and steadiness.

² It is to good purpose, that this concord is mentioned: for those prayers are most acceptable to God which are made with agreeing minds and wills.

³ The disciples prayed for the sending of the holy Ghost, and also to be delivered from present dangers wherewith they were beset.

⁴ For it was behoovable to have the wives confirmed, who were afterward to be partakers of the dangers with their husbands.

mother of Jesus, and with his [5]brethren.

15 [1]And in those days Peter stood up in the midst of the disciples, and said (now the number of [2]names that were in one place were about an hundred and twenty.)

16 [1]Ye men *and* brethren, this scripture must needs have been fulfilled, Which the [f]holy Ghost by the mouth of David spake before of Judas, which was [g]guide to them that took Jesus.

17 For he was numbered with us, and had obtained fellowship in this ministration.

18 He therefore hath [1]purchased a field with the reward of iniquity: and when [h]he had [2]thrown down himself headlong, he brast asunder in the midst, and all his bowels gushed out.

19 And it is known unto all the inhabitants of Jerusalem, insomuch, that that field is called in their own language, Akel Dama, that is, The field of blood.

20 For it is written in the book of Psalms, [i]Let his habitation be void, and let no man dwell therein: [j]also, Let another take his [1]charge.

21 [1]Wherefore of these men which have companied with us, all the time that the Lord Jesus was [2]conversant among us,

22 Beginning from the baptism of John unto the day that he was taken up [1]from us, must one of them be made a witness with us of his resurrection.

23 [1]And they [2]presented two, Joseph called Bar-

f Ps. 41:9
g John 13:27
h Matt. 27:5
i Ps. 69:26
j Ps. 109:7

sabas, whose surname was Justus, and Matthias.

24 And they prayed, saying, Thou Lord, which knowest the hearts of all men, show whether of these two thou hast chosen,

25 That he may take the [1]room of this ministration and Apostleship, from which Judas hath [2]gone astray, to go to his own place.

26 Then they gave forth their lots: and the lot fell on Matthias, and he was by a common consent counted with the eleven Apostles.

2

1 The Apostles 4 filled with the holy Ghost 8 speak with divers tongues: 12 They are thought to be drunk, 15 but Peter disproveth that. 34 He teacheth that Christ is the Messiah: 37 And seeing the hearers astonied, 38 he exhorteth them to repentance.

1 And [1]when the day of Pentecost was [2]come, they were [3]all with one accord in one place.

2 And suddenly there came a sound from heaven, as of a rushing *and* mighty wind, and it filled all the house where they sat.

3 And there appeared unto them cloven tongues, like fire, and it sat upon each of them.

4 And they were all filled with the holy Ghost, and began to speak with [1]other tongues, as the [2]Spirit gave them utterance.

5 And there were dwelling at Jerusalem Jews, men that feared God, of every nation under heaven.

6 Now when this was noised, the multitude came

---

[5] With his kinfolks.

1:15 [1] Peter is made the mouth and interpreter of the whole company of the Apostles, either by secret revelation of the holy Ghost, or by express judgment of the Congregation.

[2] Because men are commonly billed and enrolled by their names.

1:16 [1] Peter preventeth the offense that might be taken of the falling away of Judas the betrayer, showing that all things which came unto him, were foretold by God.

1:18 [1] Luke considered not Judas's purpose, but that that followed of it, and so we used to say, that a man hath procured himself harm, not that his will and purpose was so, but in respect of that which followed.

[2] The Greek words signify thus much, that Judas fell down flat and was rent in sunder in the middle, with a marvelous huge noise.

1:20 [1] His office and ministry David wrote these words against Doeg the King's herdsman: And these words, Shepherd, Sheep, and Flock, are put over to the Church office and ministry, so that the Church and the offices thereof are called by these names.

1:21 [1] The Apostles deliberate upon nothing, but first they consult and take advisement by God's word: and again they do nothing that concerneth and is behoovable for the whole body of the Congregation, without making the Congregation privy unto it.

[2] Word for word, went in and out, which kind of speech betokeneth as much in the Hebrew tongue, as the exercising of a public and painful office, when they speak of such as are in any public office, Deut. 31:2; 1 Chron. 27:1.

1:22 [1] From our company.

1:23 [1] Apostles must be chosen immediately from God, and therefore after prayers, Matthias is chosen by lot, which is as it were GOD'S

own voice.

[2] Openly, and by the voices of all the whole company.

1:25 [1] That he may be fellow and partaker of this ministry.

[2] Departed from, or fallen from: And it is a Metaphor taken from the way: For callings are signified by the name of ways, with the Hebrews.

2:1 [1] The Apostles being gathered together on a most solemn feast day in one place, that it might evidently appear to all the world, that they had all one office, one Spirit, one faith, are by a double sign from heaven authorized, and anointed with all the most excellent gifts of the holy Ghost and especially with an extraordinary and necessary gift of tongues.

[2] Word for word, was fulfilled: that is, was begun, as Luke 2:21. For the Hebrews say that a day, or a year is fulfilled or ended, when the former days or years are ended, and the other begun, Jer. 25:12. And it shall come to pass, that when seventy years are fulfilled, I will visit, etc. For the Lord did not bring home his people after the seventieth year was ended, but in the seventieth year. Now the day of Pentecost was the fiftieth day after the feast of the Passover.

[3] The twelve Apostles, which were to be the Patriarchs as it were of the Church.

2:4 [1] He calleth them other tongues, which were not the same which the Apostles used commonly, and Mark calleth them new tongues.

[2] Hereby were understood that the Apostles used not now one tongue, and then another by haphazard and at all adventure, or as fantastical men used to do, but with good consideration of their hearers: and to be short, that they spake nothing but as the holy Ghost governed their tongues.

together and were astonied, because that every man heard them speak his own language.

7 And they wondered all, and marveled, saying among themselves, Behold, are not all these which speak, of Galilee?

8 ¹How then hear we every man our own language, wherein we were born?

9 Parthians, and Medes, and Elamites, and the inhabitants of Mesopotamia, and of Judea, and of Cappadocia, of Pontus, and Asia,

10 And of Phrygia, and Pamphylia, of Egypt, and of the parts of Libya, which is beside Cyrene, and strangers of Rome, and ¹Jews, and Proselytes,

11 Cretes, and Arabians: we heard them speak in our own tongues the wonderful *works* of God.

12 ¹They were all then amazed, and doubted, saying one to another, What may this be?

13 And others ¹mocked, and said, They are full of new wine.

14 ¶ But Peter standing with the eleven, ¹lifted up his voice, and said unto them, Ye men of Judea, *and* ye all that inhabit Jerusalem, be this known unto you, and hearken unto my words.

15 For these are not drunken, as ye suppose, since it is but the ¹third hour of the day.

16 But this is that, which was spoken by the ¹Prophet ᵃJoel,

17 ¹And it shall be in the last days, saith God, I will pour out of my Spirit upon ²all ³flesh, and your sons, and your daughters shall prophesy, and your young men shall see visions, and your old men shall

CHAPTER 2
ᵃ Joel 2:28
Isa. 24:3
ᵇ Ps. 16:9

dream dreams.

18 And on my servants, and on mine handmaids I will pour out of my Spirit in those days, and they shall prophesy.

19 And I will show wonders in heaven above, and tokens in the earth beneath, blood, and fire, and the vapors of smoke.

20 The Sun shall be turned into darkness, and the moon into blood, before that great and notable day of the Lord come.

21 ¹And it shall be, that whosoever shall ²call on the Name of the Lord, shall be saved.

22 ¹Ye men of Israel, hear these words, JESUS of Nazareth, a man ²approved of God among you with great works, and wonders, and signs, which God did by him in the midst of you, as ye yourselves also know:

23 Him, *I say*, being delivered by the determinate counsel, and ¹foreknowledge of God, after you had taken, with wicked ²hands you have crucified and ³slain.

24 ¹Whom God hath raised up, and loosed the ²sorrows of death, because it was impossible that he should be holden of it.

25 For David saith concerning him, ᵇI beheld the Lord always before me: for he is at my right hand, that I should not be shaken.

26 Therefore did mine heart rejoice, and my tongue was glad, and moreover also my flesh shall rest in hope,

27 Because thou wilt not ¹leave my soul in grave, neither wilt suffer thine Holy one to see corruption.

28 Thou hast ¹showed me the ways of life, and

2:8 ¹ Not that they spake with one voice, and many languages were heard, but that the Apostles spake with strange tongues: for else the miracle had rather been in the hearers, whereas now it is in the speakers, Nazianzen in his oration of Whitsunday.

2:10 ¹ By Jews, he meaneth them that were both Jews by birth, and Jews by profession of religion though they were born in other places: and they were Proselytes, which were Gentiles born and embraced the Jews' religion.

2:12 ¹ God's word pierceth some so, that it driveth them to seek out the truth, and it doth so choke others, that it forceth them to be witnesses of their own impudency.

2:13 ¹ The word which he useth here, signifieth such a kind of mocking which is reproachful and contumelious: And by this reproachful mocking we see, that there is no miracle so great and excellent, which the wickedness of man dareth not speak evil of.

2:14 ¹ Peter's boldness is to be marked, wherein the grace of the holy Ghost is to be seen, even straight after the beginning.

2:15 ¹ After the sun rising, which may be about seven or eight of the clock with us.

2:16 ¹ There is nothing that can dissolve questions and doubts, but testimonies taken out of the Prophets: for men's reasons may be overturned, but God's voice cannot be overturned.

2:17 ¹ Peter setting the truth of God against the false accusations of men, showeth in himself and in his fellows, that that is fulfilled which Joel spake concerning the full giving of the holy Ghost in the latter days: which grace also is offered to the whole Church, to their certain and undoubted destruction, which do contemn it.

² All without exception, both upon the Jews and Gentiles.

³ That is, men.

2:21 ¹ The chiefest use of all the gifts of the holy Ghost, is to bring men to salvation by faith.

² This word, Call on, signifieth in holy Scriptures, an earnest praying and craving for help at God's hand.

2:22 ¹ Christ being innocent, was by God's providence crucified of wicked men.

² Who is by those works which God wrought by him, so manifestly approved and allowed of, that no man can gainsay him.

2:23 ¹ God's everlasting knowledge going before, which can neither be separated from his determinate counsel, as the Epicureans say, neither yet be the cause of evil: for God in his everlasting and unchangeable counsel, appointed the wicked act of Judas to an excellent end: and God doeth that well which the instruments do ill.

² God's counsel doth not excuse the Jews, whose hands were wicked.

³ The fault is said to be theirs, by whose counsel and egging forward it is done.

2:24 ¹ Christ (as David foretold) did not only rise again, but also was in the grave void of all corruption.

² The dead that was full of sorrow both of body and mind: therefore when death appeared conqueror and victor over those sorrows, Christ is rightly said to have overcome those sorrows of death, when as being dead, he overcame death, to live forever with his Father.

2:27 ¹ Thou wilt not suffer me to remain in grave.

2:28 ¹ Thou hast opened me the way to the true life.

shalt make me full of joy with thy countenance.

29 Men *and* brethren, I may boldly speak unto you of the Patriarch David, 'that he is both dead and buried, and his sepulcher remaineth with us unto this day.

30 Therefore, seeing he was a Prophet, and knew that God had *d,1*sworn with an oath to him, that of the fruit of his loins he would raise up Christ concerning the flesh, to set him upon his throne.

31 He knowing this before, spake of the resurrection of Christ, that 'his soul should not be left in grave, neither his flesh should see corruption.

32 ¹This Jesus hath God raised up, whereof we all are witnesses.

33 Since then that he by the ¹right hand of God hath been exalted, and hath received of his Father the promise of the holy Ghost, he hath shed forth this which ye now see and hear.

34 For David is not ascended into heaven, but he saith, *f*The Lord said to my Lord, Sit at my right hand,

35 Until I make thine enemies thy footstool.

36 Therefore, let all the house of Israel know for a surety, that God hath ¹made him both Lord, and Christ, this Jesus, *I say,* whom ye have crucified.

37 Now when they heard it, they were pricked in their hearts, and said unto Peter and the other Apostles, Men *and* brethren, what shall we do?

38 ¹Then Peter said unto them, Amend your lives, and be baptized every one of you in the Name of Jesus Christ for the remission of sins: and ye shall receive the gift of the holy Ghost.

39 For the¹promise *is made* unto you, and to your children, and to all that are afar off, *even* as many as the Lord our God shall call.

40 ¹And with many other words he besought and exhorted *them,* saying, Save yourselves from this

Marginal references:
c 1 Kings 2:10
Acts 13:36
d Ps. 132:11
e Ps. 16:10
Acts 13:35
f Ps. 110:1

[froward] generation.

41 ¹Then they that gladly received his word, were baptized, and the same day there were added *to the Church* about three thousand souls.

42 ¹And they continued in the Apostles' doctrine, and ²fellowship, and ³breaking of bread, and prayers.

43 ¶ ¹And fear came upon every soul: and many wonders and signs were done by the Apostles.

44 ¹And all that believed, were in one place, and had all things common.

45 And they sold their possessions, and goods, and parted them to all men, as everyone had need.

46 ¹And they continued daily with one accord in the Temple, and breaking bread at home, did eat their meat together with gladness and singleness of heart,

47 Praising God, and had favor with all the people: and the Lord added to the Church from day to day, such as should be saved.

3 *1 Peter goeth into the Temple with John, 2 healeth the cripple. 9 To the people gathered together to see the miracle, 12 he expoundeth the mystery of our salvation through Christ, 14 accusing their ingratitude, 19 and requiring the repentance.*

1 Now ¹Peter and John went up together into the Temple, at the ninth hour of prayer.

2 And a certain man which was a cripple from his mother's womb was carried, whom they laid daily at the gate of the Temple called Beautiful, to ask alms of them that entered into the Temple,

3 Who seeing Peter and John, that they would enter into the Temple, desiring to receive an alms.

4 And Peter earnestly beholding him with John, said, Look on us.

5 And he ¹gave heed unto them, trusting to receive some thing of them.

2:30 ¹ Had sworn solemnly.

2:32 ¹ Peter witnesseth that Jesus Christ is the appointed everlasting King, which he proveth manifestly by the gifts of the holy Ghost,and the testimony of David.

2:33 ¹ Might and power of God.

2:36 ¹ Christ is said to be made, because he was advanced to that dignity: and therefore it is not spoken of his nature, but of his state and dignity.

2:38 ¹ Repentance and remission of sins in Christ, are two principles of the Gospel, and therefore of our salvation: and they are obtained by the promises apprehended by faith, and are ratified in us by Baptism, wherewith is joined the virtue of the holy Ghost.

2:39 ¹ The word that is used here, giveth us to understand that it was a free gift.

2:40 ¹ He is truly joined to the Church which separateth himself from the wicked.

2:41 ¹ A notable example of the virtue of the holy Ghost: but such as are of age, are not baptized before they make confession of their faith.

2:42 ¹ The marks of the true Church of the doctrine of the Apostles, the duties of charity, the pure and simple administration of the Sacra-

ments, and true invocation used of all the faithful.

² Communicating of goods, and all other duties of charity, as is showed afterward.

³ The Jews used thin loaves, and therefore they did rather brake them than cut them: So by breaking of bread, they understood that living together and the banquets which they used to keep. And when they kept their love feasts, they used to celebrate the Lord's Supper, which even in these days began to be corrupted, and Paul amendeth it, 1 Cor. 11.

2:43 ¹ So oft as the Lord thinketh it expedient, he bridleth the rage of strangers that the Church may be planted, and have some refreshing.

2:44 ¹ Charity maketh all things common concerning the use, according as necessity requireth.

2:46 ¹ The faithful came together at the beginning with great fruit, not only to the hearing of the word, but also to meat.

3:1 ¹ Christ in healing a man that was born lame, and well known to all men, both in place and time very famous, by the hands of his Apostles, doth partly confirm them which believed, and partly also calleth others to believe.

3:5 ¹ Both with heart and eyes.

6 Then said Peter, Silver and gold have I none, but such as I have, that give I thee: In the Name of Jesus Christ of Nazareth, rise up and walk.

7 And he took him by the right hand, and lifted *him* up, and immediately his feet and ankle bones received strength.

8 And he leaped up, stood, and walked, and entered with them into the temple, walking and leaping, and praising God.

9 And all the people saw him walk, and praising God.

10 And they knew him, that it was he which sat for the alms at the Beautiful gate of the Temple: and they were amazed, and sore astonied at that which was come unto him.

11 ¶ And as the cripple which was healed, [1]held Peter and John, all the people ran amazed unto them in the porch which is called Solomon's.

12 [1]So when Peter saw it, he answered unto the people, Ye men of Israel, why marvel ye at this? or why look ye so steadfastly on us, as though by our own power or godliness, we had made this man go?

13 The God of Abraham, and Isaac, and Jacob, the [a]God of our fathers hath glorified his Son Jesus, whom ye betrayed, and denied in the presence of Pilate, when he had judged him to be delivered.

14 But ye denied the Holy one and the just, and desired a murderer to be given you,

15 And killed the Lord [1]of life, whom God hath raised from the dead, whereof we are witnesses.

16 And his Name hath made this man sound, whom ye see and know, through faith in his Name: [1]and the faith which is by him, hath given to him this perfect health of his whole body in the presence of you all.

17 [1]And now brethren, I know that through ingnorance ye did it, as *did* also your governors.

CHAPTER 3
[a] Acts 5:30
[b] Deut. 18:15
Acts 7:37
[c] Gen. 12:3
Gal. 3:8

18 But those things, which God before had showed [1]by the mouth of all his Prophets, that Christ should suffer, he hath thus fulfilled.

19 Amend your lives therefore, and turn, that your sins may be put away, when the time of refreshing shall come from the presence of the Lord.

20 And he shall send Jesus Christ, which before was preached unto you.

21 [1]Whom the heaven must contain until the time that all things be restored, which God had spoken by the mouth of all his holy Prophets since the world began.

22 [b]For Moses said unto the Fathers, The Lord your God shall raise up unto you [1]a Prophet, *even* of your brethren, like unto me: ye shall hear him in all things whatsoever he shall say unto you.

23 For it shall be that every person which shall not hear that Prophet, shall be destroyed out of the people.

24 Also all the Prophets [1]from Samuel, and thenceforth as many as have spoken, have likewise foretold of these days.

25 [1]Ye are the [2]children of the Prophets, and of the covenant, which God hath made unto our fathers, saying to Abraham, [c]Even in thy seed shall all the kindreds of the earth be blessed.

26 First unto you hath God [1]raised up his Son Jesus, and him he hath sent to bless you, in turning everyone of you from your iniquities.

4 *1 Peter and John,   3 are taken and brought before the council,   7 and 19 They speak boldly in Christ's cause.   24 The disciples pray unto God.   32 Many sell their possessions.   36 Of whom Barnabas is one.*

1 And [1]as they spake unto the people, the Priests and the [2]Captain of the Temple, and the Sadducees came upon them.

3:11 [1] Either because he loved them, who had healed him: or because he feared that if he once let them go out of his sight, he should be lame again.

3:12 [1] Miracles are appointed to convince the unbelievers, and therefore they do wickedly abuse them, who standeth amazed either at the miracles themselves, or at the instruments and means which it pleaseth God to use, take an occasion to establish idolatry and superstition by that, which God hath provided for the knowledge of his true worship, that is, Christianity.

3:15 [1] Who hath life in himself, and giveth life to others.

3:16 [1] Because he believed on him being raised from the dead, whose Name he heard of by us.

3:17 [1] It is best of all to receive Christ so soon as he is offered unto us: but such as have neglected so great a benefit through man's weakness, have yet repentance for a means. As for the ignominy of the cross, we have to set against that, the decree and purpose of God, foretold by the Prophets, of Christ, how that first of all he should be crucified here upon earth, and then he should appear from heaven the judge and restorer of all things, that all believers might be saved, and all unbelievers utterly perish.

3:18 [1] Though there were many Prophets, yet he speaketh but of one mouth, to show unto us the consent and agreement of the Prophets.

3:21 [1] Or, be taken up into heaven.

3:22 [1] This promise was of an excellent and singular Prophet.

3:24 [1] At what time the kingdom of Israel was established.

3:25 [1] The Jews that believe are the first begotten in the kingdom of God.

[2] For whom the Prophets were specially appointed.

3:26 [1] Given to the world, or raised from the dead, and advanced to his kingdom.

4:1 [1] None are commonly more diligent or bolder enemies of the Church, than such as profess themselves to be head builders: but the more they rage, the more constantly the faithful servants of God do continue.

[2] The Jews had certain garrisons for the guard and safety of the Temple and holy things, Matt. 26:65. These garrisons had a Captain, such as Eleazarus Ananias, the high Priest's son was, in the time of the war that was in Judea, being a very impudent and proud young man, Josephus, lib. 2, of the taking of Judea.

2 Taking it grievously that they taught the people, and preached in Jesus' *Name* the resurrection from the dead.

3 And they laid hands on them, and put them in hold, until the next day, for it was now eventide.

4 Howbeit many of them which heard the word, believed, and the [1]number of the men was about five thousand.

5 ¶ And it came to pass on the morrow, that their [1]rulers, and Elders, and Scribes, were gathered together at Jerusalem,

6 And Annas the chief Priest, and Caiaphas, and John, and Alexander, and as many as were of the [1]kindred of the high Priest.

7 [1]And when they had set them before them, they asked, By what power, or in what [2]Name have ye done this?

8 Then Peter full of the holy Ghost, said unto them, Ye rulers of the people, and Elders of Israel,

9 [1]For as much as we this day are examined, of the good deed *done* to the impotent man, *to wit*, by what means he is made whole,

10 [1]Be it known unto you all, and to all the people of Israel, that by the Name of Jesus Christ of Nazareth, whom ye have crucified, whom God raised again from the dead, *even* by him doth this man stand here before you, whole.

11 *a*This is the stone cast aside of you builders, which is become the head of the corner.

12 Neither is there salvation in any other: for among men there is [1]given none other [2]Name [3]under heaven, whereby we must be saved.

13 [1]Now when they saw the boldness of Peter and John, and understood that they were unlearned men

CHAPTER 4
a Ps. 118:12
Isa. 28:16
Matt. 21:42
Mark 12:10
Luke 21:17
Rom. 9:33
1 Pet. 2:7

and without [2]knowledge, they marveled, and knew them, that they had been with Jesus:

14 And beholding also the man which was healed standing with them, they had nothing to say against it.

15 Then they commanded them to go aside out of the Council, and [1]conferred among themselves,

16 [1]Saying, What shall we do to these men? for surely a manifest sign is done by them, *and it is* openly known to all them that dwell in Jerusalem: and we cannot deny it.

17 But that it be noised no farther among the people, let us threaten and charge them, that they speak henceforth to no man in this Name.

18 So they called them, and commanded them, that in no wise they should speak or teach in the Name of Jesus.

19 [1]But Peter and John answered unto them, and said, Whether it be right in the sight of God, to obey you rather than God, judge ye.

20 For we cannot but speak the things which we have seen and heard.

21 [1]So they threatened them, and let them go, and found nothing how to punish them, because of the people: for all men praised God for that which was done.

22 For the man was above forty years old, on whom this miracle of healing was showed.

23 [1]Then as soon as they were let go, they came to their fellows, and showed all that the high Priests and Elders had said unto them.

24 [1]And when they heard it, they lifted up their voices to God with one accord, and said, O Lord, thou art the God which had made the heaven, and

---

4:4 [1] While they thought to diminish the number, they increased them.

4:5 [1] These were they that made the Sanhedrin, which were all of the tribe of Judah, until Herod used that cruelty against David's stock.

4:6 [1] Of whom the high Priests were wont to be chosen and made, the execution of the yearly office being now changed them.

4:7 [1] Against such as brag of a succession of persons, without a succession of doctrine, and by that means beat down the true ministers of the word, so far forth as they are able.

[2] By what authority.

4:9 [1] Wolves which succeed true pastors plead their own cause, and not God's neither the Churches'.

4:10 [1] He is indeed a true Shepherd, that teacheth his sheep to hang upon Christ only, as upon one that is not dead, but hath conquered death, and hath all rule in his own hand.

4:12 [1] Of God.

[2] There is no other man, or no other power and authority whatsoever: which kind of speech being usual among the Jews, rose upon this, that when we are in danger, we call upon them at whose hands we look for help.

[3] Anywhere: and this setteth forth unto us the largeness of Christ's kingdom.

4:13 [1] The good liberty and boldness of the servants of God doeth

yet thus much good that such as lay hid under a vizard of zeal, do at length bewray themselves to be indeed wicked men.

[2] The word used here, is Idiot, which being spoken in comparison had to a Magistrate, betokeneth a private man, but when we speak of sciences and studies, it signifieth one that is unlearned: and in accompt of honor and estimation it importeth one of base degree, and no estimation.

4:15 [1] Laid their heads together.

4:16 [1] He that flattereth himself in ignorance, cometh at length to do open wickedness, and that against his own conscience.

4:19 [1] We must so obey men to whom we are subject, that especially and before all things we obey God.

4:21 [1] So far off are the wicked from doing what they list, that contrariwise God useth even that to the setting forth of his glory, which he giveth them leave to do.

4:23 [1] The Apostles communicate their troubles with the Congregation.

4:24 [1] We ought neither to be afraid of the threatenings of our enemies, neither yet foolishly condemn their rage and madness against us: but we have to set against their force and malice, an earnest thinking upon the power and good will of God (both which we do manifestly behold in Christ) and so flee to the aid and succor of our Father.

the earth, the sea, and all things that are in them.

25 Which by the mouth of thy servant David hast said, [b]Why did the Gentiles rage, and the people imagine vain things?

26 The kings of the earth assembled, and the rulers came together against the Lord, and against his Christ.

27 For doubtless, against thine holy Son Jesus, whom thou hadst anointed, both Herod and Pontius Pilate, with the Gentiles and the [1]people of Israel gathered themselves together.

28 To [1]do whatsoever [2]thine hand, and thy counsel had determined before to be done.

29 And now, O Lord, behold their threatenings, and grant unto thy servants with all boldness to speak thy word,

30 So that thou stretch forth thine hand that healing, and signs, and wonders may be done by the Name of thine holy Son Jesus.

31 [1]And when as they had prayed, the place was shaken where they were assembled together, and they were all filled with the holy Ghost, and they spake the word of God boldly.

32 [1]And the multitude of them that believed, were of [2]one heart, and of one soul: neither any of them said, that anything of that which he possessed, was his own, but they had all things [c]common.

33 And with great power gave the Apostles witness of the resurrection of the Lord Jesus: and great grace was upon them all.

34 [1]Neither was there any among them, that lacked: for as many as were possessors of lands or houses, sold them, and brought the price of the things that were sold,

35 And laid it down at the Apostles' feet, and it was distributed unto every man, according as he had need.

36 Also Joses which was called of the Apostles, Barnabas (that is by interpretation, the son of consolation) being a Levite, and of the country of

[b] Ps. 2:1
[c] Acts 2:44

Cyprus,

37 Where as he had land, sold it, and brought the money, and laid it down at the Apostles' feet.

5 1 Ananias for his deceit in keeping back part of price, 5 falleth down dead, 10 and likewise Sapphira his wife. 12 Through divers the Apostles' miracles, 14 the faith is increased. 18 The Apostles that were imprisoned, 19 are delivered by an Angel, 26 and being before the Synod of the Priests, 36 through Gamaliel's counsel they are kept alive, 40 and beaten: 41 They glorify God.

1 But [a]a certain man named Ananias, with Sapphira his wife, sold a possession,

2 And [1]kept away part of the price, his wife also being of counsel, and brought a certain part, and laid it down at the Apostles' feet.

3 Then said Peter, Ananias, why hath Satan [1]filled thine heart, that thou shouldest [2]lie unto the holy Ghost, and keep away part of the price of this possession?

4 While it remained, appertained it not unto thee? and after it was sold, was it not in thine own power? how is it that thou hast [1]conceived this thing in thine heart? thou hast not lied unto men, but unto God.

5 Now when Ananias heard these words, he fell down, and gave up the ghost. Then great fear came on all them that heard these things.

6 And the young men rose up, and took him up, and carried him out, and buried him.

7 And it came to pass about the space of three hours after, that his wife came in, ignorant of that which was done.

8 And Peter said unto her, Tell me, sold ye the land for so much? And she said, Yea, for so much.

9 Then Peter said unto her, Why have ye agreed together, to [1]tempt the Spirit of the Lord? behold, the feet of them which have buried thine husband, are at the [2]door, and shall carry thee out.

10 Then she fell down straightway at his feet, and

4:27 [1] Although the people of Israel was but one people, yet the plural number is here used, not so much for the twelve tribes, every one of which made a people, as for the great multitude of them, as though many nations had assembled themselves together, as Judg. 5:14.

4:28 [1] The wicked execute God's counsel, though they think nothing of it, but they are not therefore without fault.

[2] Thou hadst determined of thine absolute authority and power.

4:31 [1] God witnesseth to his Church by a visible sign, that it is he that will establish it by shaking the powers both of heaven and earth.

4:32 [1] An example of the true Church, wherein there is consent as well in doctrine as in charity one towards another: And the Pastors deliver true doctrine both sincerely, and constantly.

[2] They agreed both in counsel, will, and purposes.

4:34 [1] True charity helpeth the necessity of the poor with its own loss: but so, that all things be done well and orderly.

5:1 [1] Luke showeth by contrary examples, how great a sin hypocrisy is, especially in them which under a false pretence and cloak of zeal would seem to shine and be chief in the Church.

5:2 [1] Craftily took away.

5:3 [1] Fully possessed.

[2] For when they had appointed that farm or possession for the Church, they stuck not at it to keep away a part of the price, as though they had had to do with men, and not with God, and therefore he saith afterward that they tempted God.

5:4 [1] Hereby is declared an advised and purposed deceit, and the fault of the man in admitting the devil's suggestions.

5:9 [1] Look how oft men do things with an evil conscience; so oft they pronounce sentence against themselves, and as much as in them lieth, provoke God to anger, as of set purpose, minding to try whether he be just and almighty or no.

[2] Are at hand.

yielded up the ghost: and the young men came in, and found her dead, and carried her out, and buried her by her husband.

11 ¹And great fear came on all the Church, and on as many as heard these things.

12 Thus by the hands of the Apostles were many signs and wonders showed among the people (and they were all with one accord in Solomon's porch.

13 And of the other durst no man join himself to them: nevertheless the people ¹magnified them.

14 Also the number of them that believed in the Lord, both of men and women, grew more and more)

15 Insomuch that they brought the sick into the streets, and laid them on beds and couches, that at the leastway the shadow of Peter, when he came by, might shadow some of them.

16 There came also a multitude out of the cities round about unto Jerusalem, bringing sick folks, and them which were vexed with unclean spirits, who were all healed.

17 ¶ ¹Then the chief Priest rose up, and all they that were with him (which was the ²sect of the Sadducees) and were full of indignation,

18 And laid hands on the Apostles, and put them in the common prison.

19 ¹But the Angel of the Lord by night opened the prison doors, and brought them forth, and said,

20 ¹Go your way, and stand in the Temple, and speak to the people, all the ²words of this life.

21 ¹So when they heard it, they entered into the Temple early in the morning, and taught. And the chief Priest came, and they that were with him, and called the Council together, and all the Elders of the children of Israel, and sent to the prison, to cause them to be brought.

22 But when the officers came, and found them not in the prison, they returned and told it,

23 Saying, Certainly we found the prison shut

CHAPTER 5
ᵃ Acts 3:13

as sure as was possible, and the keepers standing without, before the doors: but when we had opened, we found no man within.

24 Then when the *chief* Priest and the captain of the Temple, and the high Priests heard these things, they doubted of them, whereunto this would grow.

25 ¹Then came one and showed them, saying, Behold, the men that ye put in prison, are standing in the Temple, and teach the people.

26 ¹Then went the captain with the officers, and brought them without violence (for they feared the people, lest they should have been stoned.)

27 And when they had brought them, they set them before the Council, and the chief Priest asked them,

28 ¹Saying, Did we not straightly command you, that ye should not teach in this name? and behold, ye have filled Jerusalem with your doctrine, and ye would ²bring this man's blood upon us.

29 ¹Then Peter and the Apostles answered, and said, We ought rather to obey God than men.

30 ¹The ᵃGod of our fathers hath raised up Jesus whom ye slew, and hanged on a tree.

31 Him hath God lifted up with his right hand, to be a Prince and a Savior, to give repentance to Israel, and forgiveness of sins.

32 ¹And we are his witnesses concerning these things which we say: yea, and the holy Ghost, whom God hath given to them that obey him.

33 Now when they heard it, they ¹brast for anger, and consulted to slay them.

34 ¹Then stood there up in the Council a certain Pharisee named Gamaliel, a doctor of the Law, honored of all the people, and commanded to put the Apostles forth a little space,

35 And said unto them, Men of Israel, take heed to yourselves, what ye intend to do touching these men.

5:11 ¹ The Lord by his marvelous virtue bridleth some, that they may not hurt the Church: other some he awe and fear: and other some he allureth unto him.

5:13 ¹ Highly praised them.

5:17 ¹ The more that the Church increaseth, the more increaseth the rage of Satan, and therefore they proceed from threatenings, to prisoning.

² The word which is used here, is Heresy, which signifieth a choice, and so is taken for a right form of learning, or faction, or study and course of life, which the Latins call a sect: at the first this word was indifferently used, but at length, it came to be taken only in evil part, whereupon came the name of Heretic, which is taken for one that goeth astray from sound and wholesome doctrine after such sort, that he setteth light by the judgment of God and his Church, and continueth in his opinion, and breaketh the peace of the Church.

5:19 ¹ Angels are made servants of the servants of God.

5:20 ¹ God doth therefore deliver his, that they may more stoutly provoke his enemies.

² Words, whereby the way unto life is showed.

5:21 ¹ God mocketh his enemies' attempts from above.

5:25 ¹ The more openly that Christ's virtue showeth itself, the more increaseth the madness of his enemies which conspire against him.

5:26 ¹ Tyrants which fear not God, are constrained to fear his servants.

5:28 ¹ It is the property of tyrants to set out their own commandments as right and reason, be they never so wicked.

² Make us guilty of murdering, that man whom yet they will not vouchsafe to name.

5:29 ¹ We ought to obey no man, but so far forth as obeying him, we may obey God.

5:30 ¹ Christ is appointed and indeed declareth Prince and preserver of his Church in despite of his enemies.

5:32 ¹ It is not sufficient for us that there is a right end, but we must also according to our vocation go on forward till we come unto it.

5:33 ¹ This reckoneth that they were in a most vehement rage, and marvelously disquieted in mind, for it is a borrowed kind of speech taken from them which are harrishly cut in sunder with a saw.

5:34 ¹ Christ findeth defenders of his cause even in the very routs of his enemies, so oft as he thinketh it needful.

36 ¹For before these times, rose up Theudas ²boasting himself, to whom resorted a number of men, about a four hundred, who was slain: and they all which obeyed him were scattered, and brought to naught.

37 After this man, arose up Judas of Galilee, in the days of the tribute, and drew away much people after him: he also perished, and all that obeyed him, were scattered abroad.

38 And now I say unto you, ¹Refrain yourselves from these men, and let them alone: for if this counsel, or this work be of ²men, it will come to naught:

39 But if it be of God, ye cannot destroy it, lest ye be found even fighters against God.

40 And to him they agreed, and called the Apostles: and when they had beaten them, they commanded that they should not speak in the Name of Jesus, and let them go.

41 ¹So they departed from the Council, rejoicing, that they were counted worthy to suffer rebuke for his Name.

42 And daily in the ¹Temple, and from house to house they ceased not to teach, and preach Jesus Christ.

6 1 The Apostles, 3 appoint the office of Deaconship, 5 to seven chosen men: 8 Of whom Stephen, full of faith, is one: 12 He is taken, 13 and accused as a transgressor of Moses' Law.

1 And ¹in those days, as the number of the disciples grew, there arose a murmuring of the ²Grecians towards the Hebrews, because their widows were neglected in the ³daily ministering.

CHAPTER 6
ᵃ Acts 21:8

2 ¹Then the twelve called the multitude of the disciples together, and said, It is not ²meet that we should leave the word of God to serve the ³tables.

3 ¹Wherefore brethren, look you out among you seven men of honest report, and full of the holy Ghost, and of wisdom, which we may appoint to this business.

4 And we will give ourselves continually to prayer, and to the ministration of the word.

5 And the saying pleased the whole multitude: and they chose Stephen a man full of faith and of the holy Ghost, and ᵃPhilip, and Prochorus, and Nicanor, and Timon, and Parmenas, and Nicolas a Proselyte of Antioch,

6 ¹Which they set before the Apostles: and they prayed, and ²laid their hands on them.

7 ¹And the word of God increased, and the number of the disciples was multiplied in Jerusalem greatly, and a great company of the Priests were obedient to the ²faith.

8 ¶ ¹Now Stephen full of faith and ²power, did great wonders and miracles among the people.

9 ¹Then there arose certain of the ²Synagogue, which are called Libertines, and Cyrenians, and of Alexandria, and of them of Cilicia, and of Asia, and disputed with Stephen.

10 ¹But they were not able to resist the wisdom, and the Spirit by the which he spake.

11 Then they suborned men, which said, We have heard him speak blasphemous words against Moses, and God.

5:36 ¹ In matters of religion we must take good heed that we attempt nothing under a color of zeal, beside our vocation.
² To be of some fame.
5:38 ¹ He dissuadeth his fellows from murdering the Apostles, neither doth he think it good to refer the matter to the Roman Magistrate, for the Jews could abide nothing worse, than to have the tyranny of the Romans confirmed.
² If it be counterfeit and devised.
5:41 ¹ The Apostles, accustomed to suffer and bear words, are at length inured to bear stripes, yet so, that by that means they become stronger.
5:42 ¹ Both publicly and privately.
6:1 ¹ When Satan has assailed the Church without, and that to small purpose and in vain, he assaileth it within, with civil dissension and strife betwixt themselves: but the Apostles take occasion thereby to set order in the Church.
² Of their parts which of Grecians became religious Jews.
³ In the bestowing of alms according to their necessity.
6:2 ¹ The office of preaching the word and dispensing the goods of the Church, are different one from another, and not rashly to be joined together, as the Apostles do here institute: And the Apostles do not choose so much as the Deacons without the consent of the Church.
² It is such a matter, as we may in no wise accept of it.
³ Banquets though by the name of tables, other offices are also meant, which are annexed to it, such as pertain to the care of the poor.
6:3 ¹ In choosing of Deacons (and much more of Ministers) there must be examination both of their learning and manners of life.
6:6 ¹ The ancient Church did with laying on of hands, as it were consecrate to the Lord, such as were lawfully elected.
² This ceremony of laying on of hands came from the Jews, who used this order both in public affairs, and offering of sacrifices, and also in private prayers and blessings, as appeareth Gen. 28, and the Church observed this ceremony, 1 Tim. 5:22; Acts 8:17, but here is no mention made either of cream, or shaving, or raising, or crossing, etc.
6:7 ¹ An happy end of temptation.
² This is the figure Metonymy, meaning by faith, the doctrine of the Gospel which engendereth faith.
6:8 ¹ God exerciseth his Church first with evil words and slanders, then with imprisonments, afterward with scourgings, and by these means prepareth it in such sort, that at length he causeth it to encounter with Satan and the world, even to bloodshed and death, and that with good success.
² Excellent and singular gifts.
6:9 ¹ Schools and Universities were of old time addicted to false pastors, and were the instruments of Satan to blow abroad and defend false doctrines.
² Of the company and College as it were.
6:10 ¹ False teachers, because they will not be overcome, flee from disputations to manifest and open slandering and false accusations.

12 ¹Thus they moved the people and the Elders, and the Scribes: and running upon him, caught him, and brought him to the Council,

13 ¹And set forth false witnesses, which said, This man ceaseth not to speak blasphemous words against this holy place, and the Law.

14 For we have heard him say, that this Jesus of Nazareth shall destroy this place, and shall change the ordinances which Moses gave us.

15 And as all that sat in the Council looked steadfastly on him, they ¹saw his face as *it had been* the face of an Angel.

7

1 Stephen pleading his cause, showeth that God chose the Fathers, 20 before Moses was born, 42 and before the Temple was built: 44 And that all outward ceremonies were ordained according to the heavenly Pattern. 54 The Jews gnashing their teeth, 59 stone him.

1 Then ¹said the chief Priest, Are these things so?

2 ¹And he said, Ye men, brethren, and Fathers, hearken, ᵃThat God of ²glory appeared unto our father Abraham, while he was in ³Mesopotamia, before he dwelt in Haran,

3 And said unto him, Come out of thy country, and from thy kindred, and come into the land which I shall show thee.

4 Then came he out of the land of the Chaldeans, and dwelt in Haran. And after that his father was dead, *God* brought him from thence into this land, wherein ye now dwell,

5 And he gave him none inheritance in it, ¹no not the breadth of a foot: yet he ²promised that he would give it to him for a possession, and to his seed after him, when as yet he had no child.

6 But God spake thus, that his ᵇseed should be a sojourner in a strange land: and that they should

Marginal references
- CHAPTER 7
- ᵃ Gen. 12:4
- ᵇ Gen. 15:13
- ᶜ Gen. 17:9
- ᵈ Gen. 21:3
- ᵉ Gen. 25:14
- ᶠ Gen. 29:33, Gen. 30:5, Gen. 35:23
- ᵍ Gen. 37:18
- ʰ Gen. 41:37
- ⁱ Gen. 42:1
- ʲ Gen. 45:4
- ᵏ Gen. 46:5
- ˡ Gen. 49:33
- ᵐ Gen. 23:16
- ⁿ Exod. 1:7

keep it in bondage, and entreat it evil ¹four hundred years.

7 But the nation to whom they shall be in bondage, will I judge, saith God: and after that, they shall come forth and serve me in this place.

8 ᶜHe gave him also the covenant of circumcision: and to *Abraham* begat ᵈIsaac, and circumcised him the eighth day: and Isaac *begat* ᵉJacob, and Jacob the twelve ᶠPatriarchs.

9 ¹And the Patriarchs moved with envy, sold ᵍJoseph into Egypt: but God was ²with him,

10 And delivered him out of all his afflictions, and ʰgave him ¹favor and wisdom in the sight of Pharaoh king of Egypt, who made him governor over Egypt, and *over* his whole house.

11 ¶ Then came there a famine over all the land of Egypt and Canaan, and great affliction, that our fathers found no sustenance.

12 But when ⁱJacob heard that there was corn in Egypt, he sent our fathers first:

13 ʲAnd at the second time Joseph was known of his brethren, and Joseph's kindred was made known unto Pharaoh.

14 Then sent Joseph and caused his father to be brought, and all his kindred, even threescore and fifteen souls.

15 So ᵏJacob went down into Egypt, and he ˡdied, and our fathers,

16 And were ¹removed into Shechem, and were put in the sepulcher, that Abraham had bought ᵐfor money of the sons of Hamor, *son* of Shechem.

17 But when the time of the promise drew near, which God had sworn to Abraham, the people ⁿgrew and multiplied in Egypt,

18 Till another King arose, which knew not Joseph.

6:12 ¹ The first bloody persecution of the Church of Christ began and sprang from a Council of Priests by the suggestion of the University doctors.

6:13 ¹ An example of cavillers or false accusers, which gather false conclusions of things that are well uttered and spoken.

6:15 ¹ Hereby it appeareth that Stephen had an excellent and goodly countenance, having a quiet and settled mind, a good conscience, and sure persuasion that his cause was just: for seeing he was to speak before the people, God beautified his countenance, to the end that with the very beholding of him, the Jews' minds might be pierced and amazed.

7:1 ¹ Stephen is admitted to plead his cause, but to this end and purpose, that under a cloak, and color of Law, he might be condemned.

7:2 ¹ Stephen witnesseth unto the Jews, that he acknowledgeth the true fathers, and the only true God: and showeth moreover, that they are more ancient than the Temple, with all that service appointed by the Law, and therefore they ought to lay another foundation of true religion, that is to say, the free covenant that God made with the fathers.

² That mighty God full of glory and majesty.

³ When he saith afterward, verse 4, that Abraham came out of Chaldea, it is evident that Mesopotamia contained Chaldea which

was near unto it, and bordering upon it, and so writeth Plinius, book 6, chap. 27.

7:5 ¹ Not so much ground as to set his foot upon.

² The promise of the possession was certain and belonged to Abraham, though his posterity enjoyed it a great while after his death: and this is the figure Synecdoche.

7:6 ¹ There are reckoned four hundred years, from the beginning of Abraham's progeny, which was at the birth of Isaac: and four hundred and thirty years which are spoken of by Paul, Gal. 3:17, from the time that Abraham and his father departed together out of Ur of the Chaldeans.

7:9 ¹ Stephen reckoneth up diligently the horrible mischiefs of some of the Fathers, to teach the Jews that they ought not rashly to rest in the authority or examples of the Fathers.

² By this kind of speech, is meant the peculiar favor that God showeth men: for he seemeth to be away from them, whom he helpeth not, and on the other side, he is with them whom he delivereth out of whatsoever great troubles.

7:10 ¹ Gave him favor in Pharaoh's sight for his wisdom.

7:16 ¹ The Patriarchs the sons of Jacob, though there be mention made of no more than Joseph, Josh. 24:32.

19 The same [1]dealt subtly with our kindred, and evil entreated our fathers, and made them to cast out their young children, that they should not remain alive.

20 [o]The same time was Moses born and was [1]acceptable unto God: which was nourished up in his father's house three months.

21 And when he was cast out, Pharaoh's daughter took him up, and nourished him for her own son.

22 And Moses was learned in all the wisdom of the Egyptians, and was mighty in words and in deeds.

23 Now when he was full forty years old, it came into his heart to visit his brethren, the children of Israel.

24 [p]And when he saw one *of them* suffer wrong, he defended him, and avenged his quarrel that had the harm done to him, and smote the Egyptian.

25 For he supposed his brethren would have understood, that God by his hand should give them deliverance: but they understood it not.

26 [q]And the next day, he showed himself unto them as they strove, and would have set them at one again, saying, Sirs, ye are brethren: why do ye wrong one to another?

27 But he that did his neighbor wrong, thrust him away, saying, Who made thee a prince, and a judge over us?

28 Wilt thou kill me, as thou didst the Egyptian yesterday?

29 Then fled Moses at that saying, and was a stranger in the land of Midian, where he begat two sons.

30 And when forty years were expired, there appeared to him in the [r]wilderness of mount Sinai, an [1]Angel of the Lord in a flame of fire, in a bush.

31 And when Moses saw it, he wondered at the sight: and as he drew near to consider it, the voice of the Lord came unto him, *saying,*

32 I am the God of thy fathers, the God of Abraham, and the God of Isaac, and the God of Jacob. Then Moses trembled, and durst not behold it.

33 Then the Lord said to him, Put off thy shoes from thy feet: for the place where thou standest, is holy ground.

[o] Exod. 2:2
[p] Exod. 2:11
[q] Exod. 2:13
[r] Exod. 3:2
[s] Exod. 7–10; 13–14
[t] Exod. 16:1–3
[u] Deut. 18:15 Acts 3:22
[v] Exod. 19:2
[w] Exod. 32:1
[x] Amos 5:25
[y] Exod. 25:40 Heb. 8:5
[z] Josh. 3:14

34 I have seen, I have seen the affliction of my people, which is in Egypt, and I have heard their groaning, and am come down to deliver them: and now come, and I will send thee into Egypt.

35 This Moses whom they forsook, saying, Who made thee a prince and a judge? the same God sent for a prince, and a deliverer by the [1]hand of the Angel which appeared to him in the bush.

36 He [s]brought them out, doing wonders, and miracles in the land of Egypt, and in the Red Sea, and in the wilderness [t]forty years.

37 [1]This is that Moses, which said unto the children of Israel, [u]A Prophet shall the Lord your God raise up unto you, *even* of your brethren, like unto me: him shall ye hear.

38 [v]This is he that was in the Congregation, in the wilderness with the Angel, which spake to him in mount Sinai, and with our fathers, who received the lively oracles to give unto us.

39 To whom our fathers would not obey, but refused, and in their hearts turned back again into Egypt,

40 Saying unto Aaron, [w]Make us gods that may go before us: for we know not what is become of this Moses that brought us out of the land of Egypt.

41 And they made a [1]calf in those days, and offered sacrifice unto the idol, and rejoiced in the works of their own hands.

42 Then God turned himself away, and [1]gave them up to serve the [2]host of heaven, as it is written in the book of the Prophets, [x]O house of Israel, have ye offered to me slain beasts and sacrifices by the space of forty years in the wilderness?

43 And ye [1]took up the Tabernacle of Moloch, and the star of your god Remphan, figures, which ye made to worship them: therefore I will carry you away beyond Babylon.

44 [1]Our fathers had the Tabernacle of [2]witness in the wilderness, as he had appointed, speaking unto [y]Moses, that he should make it according to the fashion that he had seen.

45 [z]Which *tabernacle* also our fathers [1]received, and brought in with Jesus into the [2]possession of the Gentiles, which God drove out [3]before our fathers,

7:19 [1] He devised a subtle invention against our stock, in that he commanded all the males to be cast out.

7:20 [1] That child was born through God's merciful goodness and favor, to be of a goodly and fair countenance.

7:30 [1] Now he calleth the Son of God an Angel, for he is the Angel of great counsel, and therefore, straightway after he showeth him, saying to Moses, I am that God of thy Fathers, etc.

7:35 [1] By the power.

7:37 [1] He acknowledgeth Moses for the lawgiver, but so that he proveth by his own witness, that the Law had respect to a more perfect thing, that is to say, to the prophetic office which tended to Christ, the head of all Prophets.

7:41 [1] This was the superstition of the Egyptians' idolatry: for they worshipped Apis a strange and marvelous calf, and made goodly images of Kine, Herodias, lib. 2.

7:42 [1] Being destitute and void of his Spirit, he gave them up to Satan, and wicked lusts to worship stars.

[2] By the host of heaven, here he meaneth not the Angels, but the moon and sun and other stars.

7:43 [1] You took it upon your shoulders and carried it.

7:44 [1] Moses indeed erected a Tabernacle, but that was to call them back to that form which he had seen in the mountain.

[2] That is, of the covenant.

7:45 [1] Delivered from hand to hand.

unto the days of David:

46 ᵃWho found favor before God, and desired that he might find a tabernacle for the God of Jacob.

47 ᵇ,¹But Solomon built him an house.

48 Howbeit the most High ᶜdwelleth not in temples made with hands, as saith the Prophet,

49 ᵈHeaven is my throne, and earth is my footstool: what house will ye build for me, saith the Lord? or what place is it that I should rest in?

50 Hath not mine hand made all these things?

51 ᵉ,¹Ye stiff-necked and of ²uncircumcised hearts and ears, ye have always resisted the holy Ghost: as your fathers did, so do you.

52 Which of the Prophets have not your fathers persecuted? and they have slain them, which showed before of the coming of that Just, of whom ye are now the betrayers and murderers,

53 ᶠWhich have received the law by the ¹ordinance of Angels, and have not kept it.

54 ¹But when they heard these things, their hearts brast for anger, and they gnashed at him with their teeth.

55 ¹But he being full of the holy Ghost, looked steadfastly into heaven, and saw the glory of God, and Jesus ²standing at the right hand of God,

56 And said, Behold, I see the heavens open, and the Son of man standing at the right hand of God.

57 ¹Then they gave a shout with a loud voice, and stopped their ears, and ²ran upon him violently all at once,

58 And cast him out of the city, and stoned him: and the ¹witnesses laid down their clothes at a young

man's feet, named Saul.

59 And they stoned Stephen, who called on God, and said, Lord Jesus receive my spirit.

60 ¹And he kneeled down, and cried with a loud voice, Lord, ²lay not this sin to their charge. And when he had thus spoken, he ³slept.

8 2 The godly make lamentation for Stephen. 3 Saul maketh havoc of the Church. 5 Philip preacheth Christ at Samaria. 9 Simon Magus, 13 his covetousness reproved. 26 Philip 27 cometh to the Ethiopian Eunuch, 38 and baptizeth him.

1 And ¹Saul consented to his death. And at that time, there was a great persecution against the Church which was at Jerusalem, and they were all scattered abroad throughout the regions of Judea and of Samaria, except the Apostles.

2 ¹Then certain men fearing God, ²carried Stephen among them, to be buried, and made great lamentation for him.

3 ¹But Saul made havoc of the Church, and entered into every house, and drew out both men and women, and put them into prison.

4 Therefore they that were scattered abroad, went to and fro preaching the word.

5 ¶ ¹Then came Philip into the city of Samaria, and preached Christ unto them.

6 And the people gave heed unto those things which Philip spake, with one accord, hearing and seeing the miracles which he did.

7 For unclean spirits crying with a loud voice, came out of many that were possessed of them: and many taken with palsies, and that halted, were healed.

a 2 Sam. 7:2 Ps. 132:5
b 1 Chron. 17:12 1 Kings 6:1
c Acts 17:24
d Isa. 66:1
e Jer. 9:26 Ezek. 44:9
f Exod. 19:16 Gal. 3:19

² By the figure Metonymy, for the countries which the Gentiles possessed.

³ God drove them out, that they should yield up the possession of those countries to our fathers, when they entered into the land.

7:47 ¹ Solomon built a Temple, according to God's commandment, but not with any such condition, that the Majesty of God should be enclosed therein.

7:51 ¹ Stephen moved with the zeal of God, at length judgeth his own judges.

² They are of uncircumcised hearts, which lie drowned still in the sins of nature, and stick fast in them: for otherwise all the Jews were circumcised as touching the flesh, and therefore there were two kinds of circumcision, Rom. 2:28.

7:53 ¹ By the ministry of Angels.

7:54 ¹ The more Satan is pressed, the more he brasteth out into an open rage.

7:55 ¹ The nearer that the Martyrs approach to death, the nearer they beholding Christ, do rise up even into heaven.

² Ready to confirm him in the confession of the truth, and to receive him to him.

7:57 ¹ The zeal of hypocrites and superstitious people, breaketh out at length into most open madness.

² This was done in a rage and fury: for at that time the Jews could

put no man to death by law, as they confess before Pilate, saying that it was not lawful for them to put any man to death, and therefore it is reported by Josephus, lib. 20, that Ananus a Sadducee slew James the brother of the Lord, and for so doing, was accused before Albinus the President of the country.

7:58 ¹ It was appointed by the Law, that the witnesses should cast the first stones, Deut. 17:7.

7:60 ¹ Faith and charity never forsake the true servants of God, even to the last breath.

² The word which he useth here noteth out such a kind of imputing or laying to one's charge, as remaineth firm, and steady forever, never to be remitted.

³ See 1 Thess. 4:13.

8:1 ¹ Christ useth the rage of his enemies to the spreading forth and enlarging of his kingdom.

8:2 ¹ The godly mourn for Stephen after his death, and bury him, showing therein an example of singular faith and charity: but no man prayeth to him.

² Amongst all the duties of charity which the godly use, there is no mention made of shrining up of relics.

8:3 ¹ The dispersion or scattering abroad of the faithful, is the joining together of Churches.

8:5 ¹ Philip, who was before a Deacon in Jerusalem, is made of God extraordinarily an Evangelist.

8　And there was great joy in that city.

9　¹And there was before in the city, a certain man called Simon, which used ²witchcraft, and ³bewitched the people of Samaria, saying that he himself was some great man,

10　To whom they gave heed from the least to the greatest, saying, This man is that great power of God.

11　And they gave heed unto him, because that of long time he had bewitched them with sorceries.

12　But as soon as they believed Philip, which preached the things that concerned the kingdom of God, and the Name of Jesus Christ, they were baptized both men and women.

13　¹Then Simon himself believed also, and was baptized, and continued with Philip, and wondered, when he saw the signs and great miracles which were done.

14　¶ ¹Now when the Apostles, which were at Jerusalem, heard say, that Samaria had received the word of God, they sent unto them Peter and John.

15　Which when they were come down, prayed for them, that they might receive the ¹holy Ghost.

16　(For as yet he was fallen down on none of them, but they were baptized only in the Name of the Lord Jesus.)

17　Then laid they their hands on them, and they received the holy Ghost.

18　¹And when Simon saw that through laying on of the Apostles' hands the holy Ghost was given, he offered them money,

19　Saying, Give me also this power, that on whomsoever I lay the hands, he may receive the holy Ghost.

20　¹Then said Peter unto him, Thy money perish with thee, because thou thinkest that the gift of God may be obtained with money.

CHAPTER 8
ª Isa. 53:7

21　Thou hast neither part nor fellowship in this ¹business: for thine heart is not ²right in the sight of God.

22　¹Repent therefore of this thy wickedness, and pray God, that if it be possible, the thought of thine heart may be forgiven thee.

23　For I see that thou art in the ¹gall of bitterness, and in the ²bond of iniquity.

24　Then answered Simon, and said, Pray ye to the Lord for me, that none of these things which ye have spoken, come upon me.

25　¶ So they, when they had testified and preached the word of the Lord, returned to Jerusalem, and preached the Gospel in many towns of the Samaritans.

26　¹Then the Angel of the Lord spake unto Philip, saying, Arise, and go toward the South unto the way that goeth down from Jerusalem unto Gaza, which is waste.

27　And he arose and went on: and behold, a certain Eunuch of Ethiopia, Candace the Queen of the Ethiopians' ¹chief Governor, who had the rule of all her treasure, and came to Jerusalem to worship.

28　And as he returned sitting in his chariot, he read Isaiah the Prophet.

29　Then the Spirit said unto Philip, Go near and join thyself to yonder chariot.

30　And Philip ran thither, and heard him read the Prophet Isaiah, and said, But understandest thou what thou readest?

31　And he said, How can I, except I had ¹a guide? And he desired Philip, that he would come up and sit with him.

32　¹Now the place of the Scripture which he read, was this, ªHe was lead as a sheep to the slaughter: and like a lamb dumb before his shearer, so opened he not his mouth.

8:9　¹ Christ overcometh Satan so oft as he listeth, and carrieth him about as it were in a triumph in the sight of them, whom he deceived and bewitched.

　² The word which is used in this place was at the first taken in good part, and is borrowed out of the Persians' language, who call their wise men by that name, but afterward it was taken in evil part.

　³ He had so allured the Samaritans with his witchcrafts, that as blind and mad harebrains they were wholly addicted to him.

8:13　¹ The wicked and the very reprobate are constrained oftentimes to taste of the good gift of God, but they cast it up again forthwith.

8:14　¹ Peter not chief, but as an ambassador sent from the whole company of the Apostles, and John his companion according to the authority which was committed unto them, confirm and build up the Churches of Samaria, whose foundation had been laid afore by Philip.

8:15　¹ Those excellent gifts, which are necessary, especially for them that were to be appointed rulers and governors of the Church.

8:18　¹ Ambition and covetousness do at length pluck the hypocrites out of their dens.

8:20　¹ They are the successors of Simon Magus, and not of Simon Peter, which either buy or sell holy things.

8:21　¹ In this doctrine which I preach.

　² Is not upright in deed, and without dissembling.

8:22　¹ We must hope well even of the vilest sinners, so long and so far forth as we may.

8:23　¹ He calleth the inward malice of the heart, and that venomous and devilish wickedness wherewith this Magician was wholly replenished, the gall of bitterness: and he is said to be in the gall as though he were wholly overwhelmed with gall, and buried in it.

　² Entangled in the bonds of iniquity.

8:26　¹ Christ who calleth freely whom he listeth, doth now use Philip who thought on no such matter, to instruct and baptize the Eunuch at unawares, and by this means extendeth the limits of his kingdom even into Ethiopia.

8:27　¹ A man of great wealth and authority with Candaces: Now this word Candaces is a common name to all the Queens of Ethiopia.

8:31　¹ To show me the way how to understand it.

8:32　¹ Those things which seem most to come by chance or fortune (as men term it) are governed by the secret providence of God.

33 In his ¹humility his judgment hath been exalted: but who shall declare his ²generation? for his life is taken from the earth.

34 Then the Eunuch answered Philip, and said, I pray thee, of whom speaketh the Prophet this? of himself, or of some other man?

35 Then Philip opened his mouth, and began at the same Scripture, and preached unto him Jesus.

36 And as they went on their way, they came unto a certain water, and the Eunuch said, See, here is water: what doth let me to be baptized?

37 ¹And Philip said unto him, If thou believest with all thine heart, thou mayest. Then he answered, and said, ²I believe that that Jesus Christ is that Son of God.

38 Then he commanded the chariot to stand still: and they went down both into the water, both Philip and the Eunuch, and he baptized him.

39 And as soon as they were come up out of the water, the Spirit of the Lord caught away Philip, that the Eunuch saw him no more: so he went on his way rejoicing.

40 But Philip was found at Azotus, and he walked to and fro preaching in all the cities, till he came to Caesarea.

9 2 Saul going towards Damascus, 4 is stricken down to the ground of the Lord: 10 Ananias is sent 18 to baptize him. 23 The laying away of the Jews, 25 he escapeth, being let down through the wall. 33 Peter cureth Aeneas of the palsy, 36 and by him Tabitha being dead, 40 is restored to life.

1 And ᵃ,¹Saul yet ²breathing out threatenings and slaughter against the disciples of the Lord, went unto the high Priest,

2 And desired of him letters to Damascus to the Synagogues, that if he found any that were of that ¹way, (either men or women) he might bring them bound unto Jerusalem.

CHAPTER 9
ᵃ Rom. 9:3
Gal. 1:13
ᵇ Acts 22:6
1 Cor. 15:8

3 Now as he journeyed, it came to pass that as he was come near to Damascus, ᵇsuddenly there shined round about him a light from heaven.

4 And he fell to the earth, and heard a voice saying to him, Saul, Saul, why persecutest thou me?

5 And he said, Who art thou, Lord? And the Lord said, I am Jesus whom thou persecutest: it is ¹hard for thee to kick against pricks.

6 He then both trembling and astonied, said, Lord, what wilt thou that I do? And the Lord said unto him, Arise, and go into the city, and it shall be told thee what thou shalt do.

7 The men also which journeyed with him, ¹stood amazed, hearing his ²voice, but seeing no man.

8 And Saul arose from the ground, and opened his eyes, but saw no man. Then led they him by the hand, and brought him into Damascus,

9 Where he was three days without sight, and neither ate nor drank.

10 And there was a certain disciple at Damascus named Ananias, and to him said the Lord in a vision, Ananias. And he said, Behold, I am here Lord.

11 Then the Lord said unto him, Arise, and go into the street which is called Straight, and seek in the house of Judas after one called Saul of ¹Tarsus: for behold, he prayeth.

12 (And he saw in a vision a man named Ananias coming in to him, and putting his hands on him, that he might receive his sight.)

13 Then Ananias answered, Lord, I have heard by many of this man, how much evil he hath done to thy saints at Jerusalem.

14 Moreover here he hath authority of the high Priests, to bind all that call on thy Name.

15 Then the Lord said unto him, Go thy way: for he is a ¹chosen vessel unto me, to bear my Name before the Gentiles, and Kings, and the children of Israel.

16 For I will ¹show him, how many things he must

8:33 ¹ The Hebrew text readeth it thus, Out of a narrow strait, and out of judgment was he taken: whereby the narrow strait, he meaneth the grave and the very bands of death, and by judgment, the punishment which was laid upon him, and the miserable state which Christ took upon him for our sakes, in bearing his Father's wrath.
² How long his age shall last: for Christ having once risen from the dead, dieth no more, Rom. 6:9.
8:37 ¹ Profession of faith is requisite in baptizing of them which are of years, and therefore it is evident that we are not then first ingrafted into Christ, when we are baptized, but being already ingrafted are then confirmed.
² The sum of the confession which is necessary for baptism.
9:1 ¹ Saul (who is also Paul) persecuting Christ most cruelly, who did as it were flee before him, falleth into his hands, and is overcome: and with a singular example of the goodness of God, instead of punishment which he justly deserved for his cruelty, is not only received to favor, but is also even by the mouth of God appointed an Apostle,

and is confirmed by the ministry and witness of Ananias.
² This is a token that Saul's stomach boiled and cast out great threatenings to murder the disciples.
9:2 ¹ Any trade of life which a man taketh himself unto, the Jews call a way.
9:5 ¹ This is a proverb which is spoken of them that through their own stubbornness hurt themselves.
9:7 ¹ Stood still and could not go one step forward, but abode amazed as if they had been very stones.
² They heard Paul's voice: for afterwards it is said in flattering, that they heard not his voice that speak: as beneath, Acts 22:9. But others go about to set these places at one which seem to be at ajar, after this sort, to wit, that they heard a sound of a voice, but no perfect voice.
9:11 ¹ Tarsus was a city of Cilicia near unto Anchiala, which two cities Sardanapalus is said to have built in one day.
9:15 ¹ To bear my name in.
9:16 ¹ I will show him plainly.

suffer for my Name's sake.

17 Then Ananias went his way, and entered into [1]that house, and put his hands on him, and saith, Brother Saul, the Lord hath sent me (*even* Jesus that appeared unto thee in the way as thou camest) that thou mightest receive thy sight, and be filled with the holy Ghost.

18 And immediately there fell from his eyes as *it had been* scales, and suddenly he received sight, and arose, and was baptized,

19 And received meat, and was strengthened. So was Saul certain days with the disciples which were at Damascus.

20 [1]And straightway he preached Christ in the Synagogues, that he was that Son of God.

21 So that all that heard him were amazed, and said, Is not this he, that made havoc of them which called on this Name in Jerusalem, and came hither for that intent, that he should bring them bound unto the high Priests?

22 [1]But Saul increased the more in strength, and confounded the Jews which dwelt at Damascus, [2]confirming that this was that Christ.

23 [1]And after that many days were fulfilled, the Jews took counsel to kill him,

24 But their laying await was known of Saul: now they 'watched the gates day and night, that they might kill him.

25 [1]Then the disciples took him by night, and put him through the wall, and let him down by a rope in a basket.

26 [1]And when Saul was come to Jerusalem, he assayed to join himself with the disciples: but they were all afraid of him, and believed not that he was a disciple.

27 But Barnabas took him, and brought him to the Apostles, and declared to them, how he had seen the Lord in the way, and that he had spoken unto him, and how he had spoken boldly at Damascus

c 2 Cor. 11:31

in the Name of Jesus.

28 [1]And he was conversant [2]with them at Jerusalem,

29 And spake boldly in the Name of the Lord Jesus, and spake and disputed against the [1]Grecians: but they went about to slay him.

30 [1]But when the brethren knew it, they brought him to Caesarea, and sent him forth to Tarsus.

31 [1]Then had the Churches rest through all Judea, and Galilee, and Samaria, and were [2]edified, and walked in the fear of the Lord, and were multiplied by the comfort of the holy Ghost.

32 [1]And it came to pass, as Peter walked throughout all *quarters*, he came also to the saints which dwelt at Lydda.

33 And there he found a certain man named Aeneas, which had kept his couch eight years, and was sick of the palsy.

34 Then said Peter unto him, Aeneas, Jesus Christ maketh thee whole: arise and truss thy couch together. And he arose immediately.

35 And all that dwelt at [1]Lydda and Sharon, saw him, and turned to the Lord.

36 [1]There was also at Joppa a certain *woman*, a disciple named Tabitha (which by interpretation is called Dorcas) she was full of good works and alms which she did.

37 And it came to pass in those days, that she was sick and died: and when they had washed her, they laid her in an upper chamber.

38 Now forasmuch as Lydda was near to Joppa, and the disciples had heard that Peter was there, they sent unto him two men, desiring that he would not delay to come unto them.

39 Then Peter arose and came with them: and when he was come, they brought him into the upper chamber, where all the widows stood by him weeping, and showing the coats and garments, which Dorcas made, while she was with them.

9:17 [1] Into Judas's house.

9:20 [1] Paul beginneth straightways to execute the office which was enjoined him, never consulting with flesh and blood.

9:22 [1] Paul striveth not with his own authority alone, but with the testimonies of the Prophets.

[2] By conferring places of the Scripture together, as cunning craftsman do, when they make up anything, they use to gather all parts together, to make them agree fitly one with another.

9:23 [1] Paul, who was before a persecutor, hath now persecution laid before himself, but yet afar off.

9:25 [1] We are not forbidden to avoid and eschew the dangers and conspiracies that the enemies of God lay for us, so that we swerve not from our vocation.

9:26 [1] In ancient times no man was rashly or lightly received into the number of and amongst the sheep of Christ, much less to be a pastor.

9:28 [1] The constant servants of God must look for danger after danger: yet God watcheth for them.

[2] With Peter and James, for he saith that he saw none of the Apostles but them, Gal. 1:18-19.

9:29 [1] See Acts 6:1.

9:30 [1] The ministers of the word may change their place, by the advice and counsel of the congregation and Church.

9:31 [1] The end of persecution is the building of the Church, so that we will patiently wait for the Lord.

[2] This is a borrowed kind of speech, which signifieth establishment and increase.

9:32 [1] Peter's Apostleship is confirmed by healing of the man that was sick of the palsy.

9:35 [1] Lydda was a city of Palestine, and Sharon a Champion country and a place of good pasturage between Caesarea of Palestine and the mountain Tabor, and the lake of Gennesaret, which extendeth itself in great length beyond Joppa.

9:36 [1] Peter declareth evidently by raising up a dead body through the Name of Christ, that he preacheth the glad tidings of life.

40 But Peter put them all forth, and kneeled down, and prayed, and turned him to the body, and said, Tabitha, arise. And she opened her eyes, and when she saw Peter, sat up.

41 Then he gave her the hand and lifted her up, and called the Saints and widows, and restored her alive.

42 And it was known throughout all Joppa, and many believed in the Lord.

43 And it came to pass, that he tarried many days in Joppa with one Simon a Tanner.

10

1 Cornelius   4 at the Angel's commandment,   5 sendeth for Peter.   11 Who also by a vision,   15, 20 is taught not to despise the Gentiles.   34 He preacheth the Gospel to Cornelius and his household.   45 Who having received the holy Ghost,   47 are baptized.

1 Furthermore ¹there was a certain man in Caesarea called Cornelius, a captain of the band called the Italian *band,*

2 A ¹devout man, and one that feared God with ²all his household, which gave much alms to the people, and prayed God continually.

3 He saw in a vision evidently (about the ninth hour of the day) an Angel of God coming in to him, and saying unto him, Cornelius.

4 But when he looked on him, he was afraid, and said, ¹What is it, Lord? and he said unto him, Thy prayers and thine alms are ²come up into ³remembrance before God.

5 Now therefore send men to Joppa, and call for Simon, whose surname is Peter.

6 He lodgeth with one Simon a Tanner, whose house is by the sea side: he shall tell thee what thou oughtest to do.

7 And when the Angel which spake unto Cornelius, was departed, he called two of his servants, and a soldier that feared God, one of them that waited on him,

8 And told them all things, and sent them to Joppa.

9 On the morrow as they went on their journey, and drew near unto the city, Peter went up upon the house to pray, about the sixth hour.

10 Then waxed he an hungered, and would have eaten: but while they made *something* ready, he fell into a ¹trance.

11 And he saw heaven opened, and a certain vessel come down unto him, as *it had been* a great sheet, knit at the ¹four corners, and was let down to the earth.

12 Wherein were ¹all manner of ²four footed beasts of the earth, and wild beasts and ³creeping things, and fowls of the heaven.

13 And there came a voice to him, Arise, Peter: kill, and eat.

14 ¹But Peter said, Not so, Lord: for I have never eaten anything that is polluted, or unclean.

15 And the voice *spake* unto him again the second time, The things that God hath purified, ¹pollute thou not.

16 This was so done thrice: and the vessel was drawn up again into heaven.

17 ¶ Now while Peter doubted in himself what this vision which he had seen, meant, behold, the men which were sent from Cornelius, had inquired for Simon's house, and stood at the gate,

18 And called, and asked, whether Simon, which was surnamed Peter, were lodged there.

19 And while Peter thought on the vision, the Spirit said unto him, Behold, three men seek thee.

20 Arise therefore, and get thee down, and go with them, and doubt nothing: For I have sent them.

21 ¶ Then Peter went down to the men, which were sent unto him from Cornelius, and said, Behold, I am he whom ye seek: what is the cause wherefore ye are come?

22 And they said, Cornelius the captain, a just man, and one that feareth God, and of good report among all the nation of the Jews, was warned from heaven by an holy Angel to send for thee into his house, and to hear thy words.

10:1 ¹ Peter consecrateth the firstfruits of the Gentiles to God by the means of two miracles.

10:2 ¹ So that he worshipped one God, and was no idolater, and neither could be void of faith in Christ, because he was a devout man but as yet he knew not that he was come.

² This is a great commendation to this man, that he labored to have all his household and familiar friends and acquaintances to be religious and godly.

10:4 ¹ What wilt thou with me, Lord? for he settleth himself to hear.

² This is a borrowed kind of speech, which the Hebrews use very much, taken from sacrifices, and applied to prayers: for it is said of whole burnt sacrifices, that the smoke and savor of them goeth up into God's nostrils: so do our prayers as a sweet-smelling sacrifice which the Lord taketh great pleasure in.

³ That is, insomuch that they will not suffer God as it were, to for-

get thee: for so doth the Scripture use oftentimes to prattle with us as nurses do with little children, when they frame their tongues to speak.

10:10 ¹ For though Peter stand not amazed as one that is tongue tied, but talketh with God, and is instructed in his mysteries, yet his mind was far otherwise than it was wont to be, but shortly returned to the old bent.

10:11 ¹ So that it seemed to be a foursquare sheet.

10:12 ¹ Here is this word (All) which is general, plainly put for an indefinite and uncertain, that is to say, for some of all sorts, not for all of every sort.

² That is, such as were meet for men's use.

³ What is meant by the creeping things, see Lev. 11.

10:14 ¹ Peter profiteth daily in the knowledge of the benefit of Christ, yea, after that he had received the holy Ghost.

10:15 ¹ Do not thou hold them as unprofitable.

23 Then called he them in, and lodged them: and the next day, Peter went forth with them, and certain brethren from Joppa accompanied him.

24 ¶ And the day after, they entered into Caesarea. Now Cornelius waited for them, and had called together his kinsmen, and special friends.

25 ¹And it came to pass as Peter came in, that Cornelius met him, and fell down at his feet, and worshipped him.

26 But Peter took him up, saying, Stand up: for even I myself am a man.

27 And as he talked with him, he came in, and found many that were come together.

28 And he said unto them, Ye know that it is an unlawful thing for a man that is a Jew, to company, or come unto one of another nation: but God hath showed me, that I should not call any man polluted, or unclean.

29 Therefore came I unto you without saying nay, when I was sent for. I ask therefore, for what intent have ye sent for me?

30 Then Cornelius said, Four days ago, about ¹this hour, I fasted, and at the ninth hour I prayed in mine house, and behold, a man stood before me in bright clothing,

31 ¹And said, Cornelius, thy prayer is heard, and thine alms are had in remembrance in the sight of God.

32 ¹Send therefore to Joppa, and call for Simon, whose surname is Peter (he is lodged in the house of Simon a Tanner by the Seaside) who when he cometh, shall speak unto thee.

33 Then sent I for thee immediately, and thou hast well done to come. Now therefore are we all here present before God to hear all things that are commanded thee of God.

34 ¹Then Peter opened *his* mouth, and said, Of a truth

CHAPTER 10
ᵃ Deut. 10:17
2 Chron. 19:7
Job 34:19
Rom. 2:11
Gal. 2:6
Eph. 6:9
Col. 3:25
1 Pet. 1:17
ᵇ Luke 4:14
ᶜ Jer. 31:34
Mic. 7:18
Acts 15:9

I perceive, that ᵃ²God is no [respecter] of persons.

35 But in every nation he that ¹feareth him, and worketh righteousness, is accepted with him.

36 Ye ¹know the word which God hath sent to the children of Israel, preaching peace by Jesus Christ, which is Lord of all:

37 ¹*Even* the word which came through all Judea, ᵇbeginning in Galilee, after the Baptism which John preached:

38 *To wit*, how God ¹anointed Jesus of Nazareth with the holy Ghost, and with power: who went about doing good, and healing all that were oppressed of the devil: for God was with him.

39 And we are witnesses of all things which he did both in the land of the Jews, and in Jerusalem, whom they slew, hanging him on a tree.

40 Him God raised up the third day, and caused that he was showed openly:

41 Not to all the people, but unto the witnesses ¹chosen before of God, *even* to us which did eat and drink with him, after he arose from the dead.

42 And he commanded us to preach unto the people, and to testify, that it is he that is ordained of God a judge of quick and dead.

43 To him also give all the ᶜProphets witness, that through his Name all that believe in him, shall receive remission of sins.

44 ¹While Peter yet spake these words, the holy Ghost fell on all them which heard the word.

45 So they of the circumcision, which believed, were astonied, as many as came with Peter, because that on the Gentiles also was poured out the gift of the holy Ghost.

46 For they heard them speak with tongues, and magnify God. Then answered Peter,

47 ¹Can any man forbid water, that these should

10:25 ¹ Religious adoration or worship agreeth only to God: but civil worship is given to the Ministers of the word, although not without danger.

10:30 ¹ He meaneth not the selfsame hour, but the like, that is, about nine of the clock the other day, as it was then nine when he spake to Peter.

10:31 ¹ Cornelius's faith showeth forth itself by prayer and charity.

10:32 ¹ As faith cometh by hearing, so is it nourished and groweth up by the same.

10:34 ¹ Distinction of nations is taken away by the coming of Christ: And it is evidently seen by faith and righteousness, who is agreeable to him, or whom he accepteth.

² That God judgeth not after the outward appearance.

10:35 ¹ By the fear of God, the Hebrews understand the whole service of God: whereby we perceive that Cornelius was not void of faith, no more than they were which lived before Christ's time: and therefore they deal foolishly, which build preparative works and free will upon this place.

10:36 ¹ God gave the Israelites to understand, that whosoever liveth godly, is acceptable to God, of what nation soever he be, for he preached peace to men through Jesus Christ, who is Lord not of one

nation only, that is, of the Jews, but of all.

10:37 ¹ The sum of the Gospel (which shall be made manifest at the latter day when Christ himself shall sit as judge both of the quick and the dead) is this, that Christ promised to the Fathers, and exhibited in his time with the mighty power of God, (which was by all means showed) and at length crucified to reconcile us to God, did rise again the third day, that whosoever believeth in him should be saved through the remission of sins.

10:38 ¹ This style is taken from an old custom of the Jews, who used to anoint their Kings and Priests, whereupon it grew, to call them anointed, upon whom God bestowed gifts and virtues.

10:41 ¹ This choosing of the Apostles is properly given to God: for though God be president in the lawful election of ministers, yet there is in this place a secret opposition and setting of God's choosing, and men voice the one against the other, for the Apostles are immediately appointed of God, and the Church Ministers by means.

10:44 ¹ The Spirit of God sealeth that in the heart of the hearers, which the minister of the word speaketh by the commandment of God, as it appeareth by the effects.

10:47 ¹ Baptism doth not sanctify or make them holy which receive it, but sealeth up and confirmeth their sanctification.

not be baptized, which have received the holy Ghost, as well as we?

48 So he commanded them to be baptized in the Name of the Lord. Then prayed they him to tarry certain days.

11 *2 Peter being accused for going to the Gentiles, 5 defendeth himself. 22 Barnabas is sent to Antioch, 26 where the disciples are called Christians: 28 and there Agabus foretelleth a famine to come.*

1 Now [1]the Apostles and the brethren that were in Judea, heard, that the Gentiles had also received the word of God.

2 And when Peter was come up to Jerusalem, they of the circumcision contended against him,

3 Saying, Thou wentest into men uncircumcised, and hast eaten with them.

4 Then Peter began, and expounded *the thing* in order to them, saying,

5 I was in the city of Joppa, praying, and in a trance I saw *this* vision, A certain vessel coming down as *it had been* a great sheet, let down from heaven by the four corners, and it came to me,

6 Toward the which when I had fastened mine eyes, I considered, and saw four footed beasts of the earth, and wild beasts, and creeping things, and fowls of the heaven.

7 Also I heard a voice, saying unto me, Arise, Peter: slay and eat.

8 And I said, God forbid, Lord: for nothing polluted or unclean hath at anytime entered into my mouth.

9 But the voice answered me the second time from heaven, The things that God hath purified, pollute thou not.

10 And this was done three times, and all were taken up again into heaven.

11 Then behold, immediately there were three men already come unto the house where I was, sent from Caesarea unto me.

12 And the Spirit said unto me, that I should go with them, without doubting: moreover these six brethren came with me, and we entered into the man's house.

13 And he showed us, how he had seen an Angel in his house, which stood and said to him, Send men to Joppa, and call for Simon, whose surname is Peter.

14 He shall speak words unto thee, whereby both

CHAPTER 11
a Acts 2:4
b Acts 1:5
Acts 19:4
Matt. 3:11
Mark 1:8
Luke 3:16
John 1:26
c Acts 8:1

thou and all thine house shall be saved.

15 And as I began to speak, the holy Ghost fell on them, *a*even as upon us at the beginning.

16 Then I remembered the word of the Lord, how he said, *b*John baptized with water, but ye shall be baptized with the holy Ghost.

17 For as much then as God gave them a like gift, as *he did* unto us, when we believed in the Lord Jesus Christ, who was I, that I could let God?

18 [1]When they heard these things, they held their peace, and glorified God, saying, Then hath God also to the Gentiles granted repentance unto life.

19 ¶ [1]And they which were [c]scattered abroad because of the affliction that arose about Stephen, went throughout till they came unto Phonicia and Cyprus, and [2]Antioch, preaching the word to no man, but unto the Jews only.

20 [1]Now some of them were men of Cyprus and of Cyrene, which when they were come into Antioch, spake unto the Grecians, and preached the Lord Jesus.

21 And the hand of the Lord was with them, so that a great number believed and turned unto the Lord.

22 [1]Then tidings of those things came unto the ears of the Church, which was in Jerusalem, and they sent forth Barnabas, that he should go unto Antioch.

23 Who when he was come and had seen the grace of God, was glad, and exhorted all, that with purpose of heart they would continue in the Lord.

24 For he was a good man, and full of the holy Ghost, and faith and much people joined themselves unto the Lord.

25 ¶ [1]Then departed Barnabas to Tarsus to seek Paul:

26 And when he had found him, he brought him unto Antioch: and it came to pass that a whole year they were conversant with the Church, and taught much people, insomuch that the disciples were first called Christians in Antioch.

27 [1]In those days also came Prophets from Jerusalem unto Antioch.

28 And there stood up one of them named Agabus, and signified by the Spirit, that there should be great famine throughout all the world, which also came to pass under Claudius Caesar.

29 [1]Then the disciples every man according to his

11:1 [1] Peter being without cause reprehended of the unskillful and ignorant, doth not object that he ought not to be judged of any, but openly giveth an account of his doing.

11:18 [1] Such as ask a question of the truth which they know not, ought to be quietly heard, and must also quietly yield to the declaration thereof.

11:19 [1] The scattering abroad of the Church of Jerusalem is the cause of the gathering together of many other Churches.

[2] He speaketh of Antioch which was in Syria and bordered upon Cilicia.

11:20 [1] The Church of Antioch, the new Jerusalem of the Gentiles was extraordinarily called.

11:22 [1] The Apostles do not rashly condemn an extraordinary vocation, but yet they judge it by the effects.

11:25 [1] There was no contention amongst the Apostles either of usurping, or of holding places and degrees.

11:27 [1] God doth so wrap up his Church with the wicked, in his scourges and plagues which he sendeth upon the earth, that notwithstanding he provideth for it conveniently.

11:29 [1] All Congregations or Churches make one body.

ability, purposed to send ²succor unto the brethren which dwelt in Judea.

30 Which thing they also did, and sent it to the Elders by the hand of Barnabas and Saul.

12

Herod killeth James with the sword,   4 And imprisoneth Peter,   8 whom the Angel delivereth.   20 Herod being offended with them of Tyrus,   21 is pacified: 22 And taking the honor due to God, to himself,   23 he is eaten with worms , and so dieth.

1 Now ¹about that time, ²Herod the king stretched forth *his* hand to vex certain of the Church,

2 And he ¹killed James the brother of John with the sword.

3 ¹And when he saw that it pleased the Jews, he proceeded further, to take Peter also (then were the days of unleavened bread.)

4 ¹And when he had caught him, he put him in prison, and delivered him to four quaternions of soldiers to be kept, intending after the Passover to bring him forth to the people.

5 ¹So Peter was kept in prison, but earnest prayer was made of the Church unto God for him.

6 And when Herod would have brought him out unto the people, the same night slept Peter between two soldiers, bound with two chains, and the keepers before the door, kept the prison.

7 ªAnd behold the Angel of the Lord came upon them, and a light shined in the ¹house, and he smote Peter on the side, and raised him up, saying, Arise quickly. And his chains fell off from *his* hands.

8 And the Angel said unto him, Gird thyself, and bind on thy sandals. And so he did. Then he said unto him, Cast thy garment about thee, and follow me.

9 So *Peter* came out and followed him, and knew not that it was true, which was done by the Angel, but thought he had seen a vision.

10 Now when they were past the first and the second watch, they came unto the iron gate that leadeth unto

CHAPTER 12
ª Acts 5:19

the city, which opened to them by its own accord, and they went out, and passed through one street, and by and by the Angel departed from him.

11 ¶ And when Peter was come to himself, he said, Now I know for a truth, that the Lord hath sent his Angel, and hath delivered me out of the hand of Herod, and from all the waiting for of the people of the Jews.

12 ¹And as he considered *the thing*, he came to the house of Mary, the mother of John, whose surname was Mark, where many were gathered together, and prayed.

13 ¹And when Peter knocked at the entry door, a maid ²came forth to hearken, named Rhoda,

14 But when she knew Peter's voice, she opened not the entry *door* for gladness, but ran in, and told how Peter stood before the entry.

15 But they said unto her, Thou art mad. Yet she affirmed it constantly, that it was so. Then said they, It is his Angel.

16 But Peter continued knocking, and when they had opened it, and saw him, they were astonied.

17 ¹And he beckoned unto them with the hand, to hold their peace, and told them how the Lord had brought him out of the prison. And he said, Go show these things unto James and to the brethren: and he departed and went into another place.

18 ¶ ¹Now as soon as it was day, there was no small trouble among the soldiers, what was become of Peter.

19 And when Herod had sought for him, and found him not, he examined the keepers, and commanded them to be led to be punished. And he went down from Judea to Caesarea, and *there* abode.

20 ¹Then Herod was angry with them of Tyre and Sidon, but they came all with one accord unto him, and persuaded Blastus the King's Chamberlain, and they desired peace, because their country was nourished by the King's *land*.

21 And upon a day appointed, Herod arrayed

11:29 ² That is, that thereof the Deacons might succor the poor: for it behooved to have all these things done orderly, and decently, and therefore it is said, that they sent these things to the Elders, that is, to the governors of the Church.

12:1 ¹ God giveth his Church a truce, but for a little time.

² This name Herod was common to all them that came of the stock of Herod Ascalonites, whose surname was Magnus: but he that is spoken of here, was nephew to Herod the great son to Aristobulus, and father to that Agrippa who is spoken of afterward.

12:2 ¹ Violently, his cause being not once heard.

12:3 ¹ It is an old fashion of tyrants to procure the favor of the wicked, with the blood of the godly.

12:4 ¹ The tyrants and wicked make a gallows for themselves, even then when they do most according to their own will and fantasy.

12:5 ¹ The prayers of the godly overturn the counsel of tyrants,

obtain Angels of God, break the prison, unloose chains, put Satan to flight and preserve the Church.

12:7 ¹ In the prison.

12:12 ¹ Holy meeting in the night as well of men as women (when they cannot be suffered in the day time) are allowable by the example of the Apostles.

12:13 ¹ We obtain more of God, than we dare well hope for.

² Out of the place where they were assembled, but not out of the house.

12:17 ¹ We may sometimes give place to the rage of the wicked, but yet so that our diligence which ought to be used in God's business, be not a whit slackened.

12:18 ¹ Evil counsel falleth out in the end to the hurt of the devisers of it.

12:20 ¹ A miserable and shameful example of the end of the enemies of the Church.

himself in royal apparel, and sat on the judgment seat, and made an oration unto them.

22 [1]And the people gave a shout, *saying*, The voice of God, and not of man.

23 [1]But immediately the Angel of the Lord smote him, because he [2]gave not glory unto God, so that he was eaten of worms, and gave up the ghost.

24 [1]And the [2]word of God grew, and multiplied.

25 So Barnabas and Saul returned from Jerusalem, when they had fulfilled their office, and took with them John, whose surname was Mark.

13

2 The holy Ghost commandeth that Paul and Barnabas be separated unto him. 6 At Paphos, 8 Elymas the sorcerer 11 is stricken blind: 14 From whence being come to Antioch, 17 They preach the Gospel, 45 the Jews vehemently withstanding them.

1 There [1]were also in the Church that was at Antioch, certain Prophets and teachers, as Barnabas, and Simeon called Niger, and Lucius of Cyrene, and Manaen (which had been brought up with [2]Herod the Tetrarch) and Saul.

2 Now as they [1]ministered to the Lord, and fasted, the holy Ghost said, Separate me Barnabas and Saul, for the work whereunto I have [2]called them.

3 [1]Then fasted they and prayed, and laid their hands on them, and let them go.

4 [1]And they after they were sent forth of the holy Ghost, came down unto [2]Seleucia, and from thence they sailed to Cyprus.

5 And when they were at Salamis, they preached the word of God in the Synagogues of the Jews: and they had also John to *their* minister.

6 So when they had gone throughout the isle unto Paphos, they found a certain sorcerer, a false prophet, being a Jew, named Bar-Jesus,

7 Which was with the Deputy Sergius Paulus, a prudent man. He called unto him Barnabas and Saul, and desired to hear the word of God.

8 [1]But Elymas the sorcerer, (for so is his name by interpretation) withstood them, and sought to turn away the Deputy from the faith.

9 Then Saul (which also *is called* Paul) being full of the holy Ghost, set his eyes on him,

10 [1]And said, O full of all subtlety and all [2]mischief, the child of the devil, *and* enemy of all righteousness, wilt thou not cease to pervert the straight ways of the Lord?

11 Now therefore behold, the [1]hand of the Lord *is* upon thee, and thou shalt be blind, and not see the sun for a season. And immediately there fell on him a mist and a darkness, and he went about, seeking some to lead him by the hand.

12 Then the Deputy when he saw what was done, believed, and was astonied at the doctrine of the Lord.

13 [1]Now when Paul and they that were with him were departed by ship from Paphos, they came to Perga *a city* of Pamphylia: then John departed from them, and returned to Jerusalem.

14 But when they departed from Perga, they came to Antioch *a city* of [1]Pisidia, and went into the Synagogue on the Sabbath day, and sat down.

15 [1]And after the lecture of the Law and Prophets, the rulers of the Synagogue sent unto them, saying, Ye men and brethren, if ye [2]have any word of

---

12:22 [1] The flattery of the people, maketh fools fain.

12:23 [1] God resisteth the proud.

[2] Josephus recordeth, that this king did not repress those flatterers' tongues, and therefore at his death he complained and cried out of their vanity.

12:24 [1] Tyrants build up the Church by plucking it down.

[2] They that heard the word of God.

13:1 [1] Paul with Barnabas is again the second time appointed Apostle of the Gentiles, not of man, neither by man, but by an extraordinary commandment of the holy Ghost.

[2] The same was Antipas, which put John Baptist to death.

13:2 [1] While they were busy doing their office, that is, as Chrysostom expoundeth it, while they were preaching.

[2] The Lord is said to call (whereof this word (calling) cometh, which is usual in the Church) when he causeth that to be, which was not, whether you refer it to the matter itself or to any quality or thing about the matter: and it groweth of this, because when things begin to be, then they have some name: as God's mighty power is also declared thereby, who spake the word, and things were made.

13:3 [1] Fast, and solemn prayers were used before the laying on of hands.

13:4 [1] Paul and his companions do at the first bring Cyprus to the subjection and obedience of Christ.

[2] Seleucia was a city of Cilicia, so called of Seleucus one of Alexander's successors.

13:8 [1] The devil maketh the conquest of Christ more glorious, in that that he setteth himself against him.

13:10 [1] The sorcerer which was stricken of Paul with a corporal punishment (although extraordinarily) showeth an example to lawful magistrates, how they ought to punish them which wickedly and obstinately hinder the course of the Gospel.

[2] He noteth out such a fault, as whoso hath it, runneth headlong and with great desire to all kinds of wickedness with the least motion in the world.

13:11 [1] His power which he showeth in striking and beating down his enemies.

13:13 [1] An example in one and the selfsame company both of singular constancy, and also of great weakness.

13:14 [1] This putteth a difference betwixt it, and Antioch which was in Syria.

13:15 [1] In the Synagogue of the Jews (according to the pattern whereof Christian Congregations were instituted) first the Scriptures were read, then such as were learned were licensed by the rulers of the Synagogue to speak and expound.

[2] Word for word, If there be any word in you: and this is a kind of speech taken from the Hebrews, whereby is meant, that the gifts of God's grace are in us, as it were in treasure houses, and that they are not ours, but God's: In like sort saith David, Thou hast put a new song in my mouth, Ps. 40:1.

exhortation for the people, say on.

16 [1]Then Paul stood up and beckoned with the hand, and said, Men of Israel, and ye that fear God, hearken.

17 The God of this people of Israel chose our fathers, and [1]exalted the people when they dwelt in the land of [a]Egypt, and with an [b,2]high arm brought them out thereof.

18 And about the time [c]of forty years, suffered he their manners in the wilderness.

19 And he destroyed seven nations in the land of Canaan, and [d]divided their land to them by lot.

20 Then afterward he gave unto them [e]Judges about [1]four hundred and fifty years, unto *the time of* Samuel the Prophet.

21 So after that, they desired a [f]King, and God gave unto them [g]Saul, the son of Cis, a man of the tribe of Benjamin, *by the space of* [1]forty years.

22 And after he had taken him away, he raised up [h]David to be their King, of whom he witnessed, saying, I have found David *the son* of Jesse, a man after mine own heart, which will do all things that I will.

23 [1]Of this man's seed hath God [i]according to *his* promise raised up to Israel, the Savior Jesus:

24 When [j]John had first preached [1]before his coming the baptism of repentance to all the people of Israel.

25 And when John had fulfilled *his* course, he said, [k]Whom ye think that I am, I am not he: but behold, there cometh one after me, whose shoe of *his* feet I am not worthy to loose.

26 [1]Ye men and brethren, children of the generation of Abraham, and whosoever among you feareth God, to you is the word of this salvation sent.

CHAPTER 13
[a] Exod. 1:9
[b] Exod. 13:14
[c] Exod. 16:1
[d] Josh. 14:1
[e] Judg. 3:9
[f] 1 Sam. 8:5
[g] 1 Sam. 9:15 1 Sam. 10:1
[h] 1 Sam. 16:13
[i] Ps. 89:21 Isa. 11:1
[j] Mal. 3:1 Matt. 3:2 Mark 1:2 Luke 3:2
[k] Matt. 3:11 Mark 1:7 John 1:20
[l] Matt. 27:22 Mark 15:13 Luke 23:20 John 19:6
[m] Matt. 28:2 Mark 16:6 Luke 24:6 John 20:19
[n] Ps. 2:7 Heb. 1:5 Heb. 5:5
[o] Isa. 55:3
[p] Ps. 16:11 Acts 2:31
[q] 1 Kings 2:10 Acts 2:29

27 [1]For the inhabitants of Jerusalem, and their rulers, because they knew him not, nor yet the words of the Prophets, which are read every Sabbath *day*, they have fulfilled them in condemning him.

28 And though they found no cause of death *in him*, [l]yet desired they Pilate to kill him.

29 And when they had fulfilled all things that were written of him, they took him down from the tree, and put him in a sepulcher.

30 [1]But God [m]raised him up from the dead.

31 And he was seen many days of them, which came up with him from Galilee to Jerusalem, which are his witnesses unto the people.

32 And we declare unto you, that touching the promise made unto the fathers,

33 God hath fulfilled it unto us their children, in that he [1]raised up Jesus, [2]even as it is written in the second Psalm, [n]Thou art my Son: this day have I begotten thee.

34 Now as concerning that he raised him up from the dead, no more to return to corruption, he hath said thus, [o]I will give you the holy things of David, [1]which are faithful.

35 [1]Wherefore he saith also in another place, [p]Thou wilt not suffer thine holy one to see corruption.

36 Howbeit, David after he had served his time by the counsel of God, he [q]slept, and was laid with his fathers, and saw corruption.

37 But he whom God raised up, saw no corruption.

38 [1]Be it known unto you therefore, men *and* brethren, that through this man is preached unto you the forgiveness of sins.

39 And from [1]all things, from which ye could not be justified by the Law of Moses, by him everyone

13:16 [1] God bestowed many peculiar benefits upon his chosen Israel, but this especially, that he promised them the everlasting redeemer.

13:17 [1] Advanced and brought to honor.

[2] Openly and with [much] force, breaking in pieces the enemies of his people.

13:20 [1] There were from the birth of Isaac unto the destruction of the Canaanites under the governance of Joshua four hundred and seven and forty years, and therefore he addeth in this place, this word, About, for there want three years, but the Apostle useth the whole greater number.

13:21 [1] In this space of forty years must the time of Samuel be reckoned with the days of Saul: for the kingdom did as it were swallow up his government.

13:23 [1] He proveth by the witness of John, that Jesus is that Savior which should come of David.

13:24 [1] John as an Herald, did not show Christ's coming afar off as the other Prophets did, but hard at hand, and entered on his journey.

13:26 [1] Christ was promised and sent properly to the Jews.

13:27 [1] All things came to pass to Christ, which the Prophets foretold of Messiah: so that hereby also it appeareth that he is the true and only Savior: and yet notwithstanding they are not to be excused which did not only not receive him, but also persecute him most cruelly although he was innocent.

13:30 [1] We must set the glory of the resurrection against the shame of the cross, and grave. And the resurrection is proved as well by witnesses which saw it, as by the testimonies of the Prophets.

13:33 [1] For then he appeared plainly and manifestly as that only Son of God, when as he left off his weakness, and came out of the grave, having conquered death.

[2] If Christ had tarried in death, he had not been the true Son of God, neither had the covenant, which was made with David, been sure.

13:34 [1] The Greeks call those holy things, which the Hebrews call gracious bounties: and they are called David's bounties in the passive signification, because God bestowed them upon David: Moreover, they are termed faithful, after the manner of speech which the Hebrews use, who terms those things faithful, which are steady and sure such as never alter nor change.

13:35 [1] The Lord was so in grave, that he felt no corruption.

13:38 [1] Christ was sent to give them free remission of sins, which were condemned by the Law.

13:39 [1] Whereas the ceremonies of the Law could not absolve you from your sins, this man doth absolve you, if you lay hold on him by faith.

that believeth, is justified.

40 [1]Beware therefore lest that come upon you, which is spoken of in the Prophets,

41 [r]Behold, ye despisers, and wonder, and vanish away: for I work a work in your days, a work which ye shall not believe, if a man would declare it you.

42 ¶ [1]And when they were come out of the Synagogue of the Jews, the Gentiles besought, that they would preach these words to them the next Sabbath day.

43 Now when the congregation was dissolved, many of the Jews and [1]Proselytes that feared God, followed Paul and Barnabas, which spake unto them, and exhorted them to continue in the grace of God.

44 And the next Sabbath day came almost the whole city together, to hear the word of God.

45 [1]But when the Jews saw the people, they were full of envy, and spake against those things, which were spoken of Paul, contrarying them, and railing on them.

46 [1]Then Paul and Barnabas spake boldly, and said, It was necessary that the word of God should first have been spoken unto you: but seeing ye put it from you, and [2]judge yourselves unworthy of everlasting life, lo, we turn to the Gentiles.

47 For so hath the Lord commanded us, saying, [s]I have made thee a light of the Gentiles, that thou shouldest be the salvation unto the end of the world.

48 And when the Gentiles heard it, they were glad, and glorified the word of the Lord: and as many as were [1]ordained unto eternal life, believed.

49 Thus the word of the Lord was published throughout the whole country.

50 [1]But the Jews stirred certain [2]devout and honorable women, and the chief men of the city, and raised persecution against Paul and Barnabas, and expelled them out of their coasts.

[r] Hab. 1:5
[s] Isa. 49:6
[t] Matt. 20:14
Mark 6:11
Luke 9:5
Acts 18:6

51 [1]But they [t]shook off the dust of their feet against them, and came unto Iconium.

52 And the disciples were filled with joy, and with the holy Ghost.

14

1 Paul and Barnabas   5 are persecuted at Iconium: 6 At Lystra Paul   10 healeth a cripple: 13 They are about to do sacrifice unto them,   18 but they forbid it.   19 Paul by the persuasion of certain Jews, is stoned: 23 From thence passing through divers Churches,   26 they return to Antioch.

1 And [1]it came to pass in [2]Iconium, that they went both together into the Synagogue of the Jews, and so spake, that a great multitude both of the Jews and of the Grecians believed.

2 And the [1]unbelieving Jews stirred up, and corrupted the minds of the Gentiles against the brethren.

3 [1]So therefore they abode there a long time, and spake boldly in the Lord, which gave testimony unto the word of his grace, and caused signs and wonders to be done by their hands.

4 But the multitude of the city was divided: and some were with the Jews, and some with the Apostles.

5 And when there was an assault made both of the Gentiles, and of the Jews with their rulers, to do them violence, and to stone them,

6 They were ware of it, and [1]fled unto Lystra, and Derbe, cities of Lycaonia, and unto the region round about,

7 And there preached the Gospel.

8 ¶ [1]Now there sat a certain man at Lystra, impotent in his feet, which was a cripple from his mother's womb, who had never walked.

9 He heard Paul speak: who beholding him and perceiving that he had faith to be healed,

10 Said with a loud voice, Stand upright on thy

13:40 [1] The benefits of God turn to the utter undoing of them that contemn them.

13:42 [1] The Gentiles go before the Jews into the kingdom of heaven.

13:43 [1] Which had forsaken their heathenish religion, and embraced the religion set forth by Moses.

13:45 [1] The favor of one selfsame Gospel is unto the reprobate and unbelievers, death, and to the elect and such as believe, life.

13:46 [1] The Gospel is published to the Gentiles by the express commandment of God.

[2] By this your doing you do as it were, pronounce sentence against yourselves, and judge yourselves.

13:48 [1] Therefore either all were not appointed to everlasting life, or else all should have believed: but because that is not so, it followeth, that some certain were ordained, and therefore God did not only foreknow, but also foreordain, that neither faith nor the effects of faith should be the cause of his ordaining or appointment, but his ordaining the cause of faith.

13:50 [1] Such is the craft and subtlety of the enemies of the Gospel,

that they abuse the simplicity of some which are not altogether evil men, to execute their cruelty.

[2] Such as embraced Moses' Law.

13:51 [1] The wickedness of the world cannot let God to gather his Church together, and to foster and cherish it, when it is gathered together.

14:1 [1] We ought to be no less constant in preaching of the Gospel, than the perverseness of the wicked is obstinate in persecuting of it.

[2] Iconium was a city of Lycaonia.

14:2 [1] Which obeyed not the doctrine.

14:3 [1] We ought not to leave our places and give place to threatenings, neither to open rage, but when there is no other remedy, and that not for our own quietness' sake, but that the Gospel of Christ may be spread further abroad.

14:6 [1] It is lawful sometimes to flee dangers, in time convenient.

14:8 [1] It is an old subtlety of the devil, either to cause the faithful servants of God to be banished at once, or to be worshipped for idols: and that chiefly taking occasion by miracles wrought by them.

feet. And he leaped up, and walked.

11 Then when the people saw what Paul had done, they lifted up their voices, saying in the speech of Lycaonia, Gods are come down to us in the likeness of men.

12 And they called Barnabas, Jupiter: and Paul Mercurius, because he was the chief speaker.

13 Then Jupiter's Priest, which was before their city, brought bulls with garlands unto the ¹gates, and would have sacrificed with the people.

14 But when the Apostles, Barnabas and Paul heard it, they rent their clothes, and ran in among the people, crying,

15 ¹And saying, O men, why do ye these things? We are even men subject to the ²like passions that ye be, and preach unto you, that ye should turn from these ³vain things unto the living God, ᵃwhich made heaven and earth, and the sea, and all things that in them are:

16 ¹Who in times past ᵇ,²suffered all the Gentiles to walk in their own ways.

17 Nevertheless, he left not himself without witness, in that he did good *and* gave us rain from heaven, and fruitful seasons, filling our hearts with food, and gladness.

18 And speaking these things, scarce appeased they the multitude, that they had not sacrificed unto them.

19 ¹Then there came certain Jews from Antioch and Iconium, which when they had persuaded the people, ᶜstoned Paul, and drew him out of the city, supposing he had been dead.

20 Howbeit, as the disciples stood round about him, he arose up, and came into the city, and the next day he departed with Barnabas to Derbe.

21 ¹And after they had preached the glad tidings of the Gospel to that city, and had taught many, they returned to Lystra, and to Iconium, and to

CHAPTER 14
ᵃ Gen. 1:1
Ps. 146:5
Rev. 14:7
ᵇ Ps. 81:13
Rom. 1:24
ᶜ 2 Cor. 11:25
ᵈ Acts 13:3

Antioch.

22 ¹Confirming the disciples hearts, and exhorting them to continue in the faith, *affirming* that we must through many afflictions enter into the kingdom of God.

23 ¹And when they had ordained them Elders by election in every Church, and prayed, and fasted, they commended them to the Lord in whom they believed.

24 ¹Thus they went throughout Pisidia, and came to Pamphylia.

25 And when they had preached the word in Perga, they came down to ¹Attalia,

26 And thence sailed to ¹Antioch, ᵈfrom whence they had been commended unto the grace of God, to the work, which they had fulfilled.

27 And when they were come and had gathered the Church together, they rehearsed all the things that God had done by them, and how he had opened the door of faith unto the Gentiles.

28 So there they abode a long time with the disciples.

15 *1 Certain go about to bring in circumcision at Antioch: 6 About which matter the Apostles consult: 19 and what must be done 23 they declare by letters. 36 Paul and Barnabas 39 are at great variance.*

1 Then ¹came down ²certain from Judea, and taught the brethren, *saying*, Except ye be circumcised after the manner of Moses, ye cannot be saved.

2 ¹And when there was great dissension, and disputation by Paul and Barnabas against them, they ordained that Paul and Barnabas, and certain others of them, should go up to Jerusalem unto the Apostles and Elders about this question.

3 Thus ¹being brought forth by the Church, they passed through Phoenicia and Samaria, declaring the

---

14:13 ¹ Of the house where Paul and Barnabas were.

14:15 ¹ That is also called idolatry, which giveth to creatures, be they never so holy and excellent, that which is proper to the only one God, that is invocation or calling upon.

² Men, as ye are, and partakers of the selfsame nature of man as you.

³ He calleth idols vain things, after the manner of the Hebrews.

14:16 ¹ Custom, be it never so old, doth not excuse the idolaters.

² Suffered them to live as they listed, prescribing and appointing them no kind of religion.

14:19 ¹ The devil when he is brought to the last cast, at length rageth openly, but in vain, even then when he seemeth to have the upper hand.

14:21 ¹ We must go forward in our vocation through a thousand deaths.

14:22 ¹ It is the office of the ministers, not only to teach, but also to confirm them that are taught, and prepare them to the cross.

14:23 ¹ The Apostles committed the Churches which they had planted, to proper and peculiar Pastors, which they made not rashly,

but with prayers and fastings going before: neither did they thrust them upon Churches through bribery or lordly superiority, but chose and placed them by the voice of the congregation.

14:24 ¹ Paul and Barnabas having made an end of their peregrination, and being returned to Antioch, do render an account to the Congregation or Church.

14:25 ¹ Attalia was a sea city of Pamphylia, near to Lycia.

14:26 ¹ Antioch of Syria.

15:1 ¹ The Church is at length troubled with dissension within itself, and the trouble riseth of the proud and stubborn wits of certain evil men: The first strife was concerning the office of Christ, whether we be saved by his only righteousness apprehended by faith, or we have need also to observe the Law.

² Epiphanius is of opinion that this was Cerinthus.

15:2 ¹ Meetings of Congregations were instituted to suppress heresies, whereunto certain were sent by common consent in the name of all.

15:3 ¹ Courteously and lovingly brought on their way by the Church, that is, by certain appointed by the Church.

conversion of the Gentiles, and they brought great joy unto all the brethren.

4 And when they were come to Jerusalem, they were received of the Church, and of the Apostles and Elders, and they declared what things God had done by them.

5 But *said they*, certain of the sect of the Pharisees, which did believe, rose up, saying that it was needful to circumcise them, and to command *them* to keep the Law of Moses.

6 [1]Then the Apostles and Elders came together to look to this matter.

7 And when there had been great disputation, Peter rose up, and said unto them, [a,1]Ye men *and* brethren, ye know that a [2]good while ago, among us God chose out *me*, that the Gentiles by my mouth should hear the word of the Gospel, and believe.

8 And God which knoweth the hearts, bare them witness, in giving unto them the holy Ghost even as *he did* unto us.

9 And he put no [1]difference between us and them, after that [b,2]by faith he had purified their hearts.

10 [1]Now therefore, why [2]tempt ye God, to [c]lay a yoke on the disciples' necks, which neither our fathers, nor we were able to bear?

11 But we believe, through the grace of the Lord Jesus Christ to be saved, even as they *do*.

12 [1]Then all the multitude kept silence, and heard Barnabas and Paul, which told what signs and wonders God had done among the Gentiles by them.

13 And when they held their peace, [1]James answered, saying, Men *and* brethren, hearken unto me.

14 [1]Simeon hath declared, how God first did visit the Gentiles, to take *of them* a people unto his Name.

CHAPTER 15
[a] Acts 10:20
Acts 11:13
[b] Acts 10:43
1 Cor. 1:2
[c] Matt. 23:4
[d] Amos 9:11

15 And to this agree the words of the Prophets, as it is written,

16 [d]After this I will return, and will build again the Tabernacle of David, which is fallen down, and the ruins thereof will I build again, and I will set it up.

17 That the residue of men might seek after the Lord, and all the Gentiles upon whom my Name is called, saith the Lord which doeth all these things.

18 From the beginning of the world, God [1]knoweth all his works.

19 [1]Wherefore my sentence is, that we trouble not them of the Gentiles that are turned to God,

20 But that we send unto them, that they abstain themselves from [1]filthiness of idols, and fornication, and that is strangled, and from blood.

21 For Moses of old time hath in every city them that preach him, seeing he is read in the Synagogues every Sabbath *day*.

22 [1]Then it seemed good to the Apostles and Elders with the whole Church to send chosen men of their own company to Antioch with Paul and Barnabas: *to wit*, Judas whose surname was Barsabas, and Silas, which were chief men among the brethren,

23 And wrote letters by them after this manner, THE APOSTLES, and the Elders, and the brethren, Unto the brethren which are of the Gentiles in Antioch, and in Syria, and in Cilicia, send greeting.

24 [1]Forasmuch as we have heard, that certain which [2]went out from us, have troubled you with words, and [3]cumbered your minds, saying, Ye must be circumcised and keep the Law: to whom we gave no such commandment,

25 It seemed therefore good to us, when we were come together with one accord, to [send] chosen men

15:6 [1] The matter is first handled, both parts being heard in the assembly of the Apostles and ancients, and after is communicated with the people.
15:7 [1] God himself in calling of the Gentiles which are uncircumcised, did teach that our salvation doth consist in faith without the worship appointed by the Law.
[2] Word for word, of old time, that is, even from the first time that we were commanded to preach the Gospel, and straightways after that the holy Ghost came down upon us.
15:9 [1] He put no difference between us and them, as touching the benefit of his free favor.
[2] Christ pronounceth them Blessed, which are pure of heart: and here we are plainly taught that men are made such by faith.
15:10 [1] Peter passing from the Ceremonies to the Law itself in general, showeth that none could be saved, if salvation were to be sought for by the Law, and not by grace only in Jesus Christ; because that no man could ever fulfil the Law, neither Patriarch, nor Apostle.
[2] Why tempt ye God, as though he could not save by faith?
15:12 [1] A true pattern of a lawful Council, where God's truth only reigneth.
15:13 [1] The son of Alphaeus, who is called the Lord's brother.
15:14 [1] James confirmeth the calling of the Gentiles, out of the word

of God, therein agreeing to Peter.
15:18 [1] And therefore nothing cometh to pass by fortune, but by God's appointment.
15:19 [1] In matters indifferent we may so far bear with the weakness of our brethren, as they may have time to be instructed.
15:20 [1] From sacrifices or from feasts which were kept in idols' Temples.
15:22 [1] In a lawful Synod, neither they which are appointed and chosen Judges, appoint and determine anything tyrannously or upon a lordliness, neither doth the common multitude set themselves tumultuously against them, which sit as Judges by the word of God: as the like order also is held in publishing and ratifying those things which have been so determined and agreed upon.
15:24 [1] The Council of Jerusalem concludeth, that they trouble men's consciences, which teach us to seek salvation in any other means than in Christ only, apprehended by faith, from whence soever they come, and whomsoever they pretend to be author of their vocation.
[2] From our congregation.
[3] A borrowed kind of speech taken of them which pull down that that was built up: and it is a very usual metaphor in the Scriptures: to say the Church is built, for, the Church is planted and stablished.

unto you, with our beloved Barnabas and Paul.

26 Men that have ¹given up their lives for the Name of our Lord Jesus Christ.

27 We have therefore sent Judas and Silas, which shall also tell you the same things by mouth.

28 ¹For it seemed good to the ²holy Ghost, and ³to us, to lay no more burden upon you, than these ⁴necessary things.

29 ¹*That is*, that ye abstain from things offered to idols, and blood, and that that is strangled, and from fornication: from which if ye keep yourselves, ye shall do well. Fare ye well.

30 ¹Now when they were departed, they came to Antioch, and after that they had assembled the multitude, they delivered the Epistle,

31 And when they had read it, they rejoiced for the consolation.

32 And Judas and Silas being Prophets, exhorted the brethren with many words, and strengthened them.

33 And after they had tarried there a space, they were let go in ¹peace of the brethren unto the Apostles.

34 Notwithstanding Silas thought good to abide there still.

35 Paul also and Barnabas continued in Antioch, teaching and preaching with many others the word of the Lord.

36 ¶ ¹But after certain days, Paul said unto Barnabas, Let us return and visit our brethren in every city, where we have preached the word of the Lord, *and see* how they do.

37 ¹And Barnabas counseled to take with them John, called Mark.

38 But Paul thought it not meet to take him unto

CHAPTER 16
ᵃ Rom. 16:21
Phil. 2:19
1 Thess. 3:2

their company, which departed from them from Pamphylia, and went not with them to the work.

39 ¹Then were they so ²stirred, that they departed asunder one from the other, so that Barnabas took Mark, and sailed unto Cyprus.

40 And Paul chose Silas and departed, being commended of the brethren unto the grace of God.

41 And he went through Syria and Cilicia, establishing the Churches.

16

1 Paul having circumcised Timothy, 12 being at Philippi, 14 instructed Lydia in the faith. 16 The spirit of divination, 18 is by him cast out: 20 and for that cause 22 they are whipped, 24 and imprisoned. 26 Through an earthquake, 27 the prison doors are opened. 31, 32 The Gaoler receiveth the faith.

1 Then ¹came he to Derbe and to Lystra: and behold, a certain disciple was there, named ᵃTimothy, a woman's son, which was a ²Jewess and believed, but his father was a Grecian,

2 Of whom the brethren which were at Lystra and Iconium, ¹reported well.

3 ¹Therefore Paul would that he should go forth with him, and took and circumcised him, because of the Jews, which were in those quarters: for they knew all that his father was a Grecian.

4 ¹And as they went through the cities, they delivered them ²the decrees to keep, ordained of the Apostles and Elders which were at Jerusalem.

5 And so were the Churches established in the faith, [and] increased in number daily.

6 ¶ ¹Now when they had gone throughout Phrygia, and the region of Galatia, they were ²forbidden of the holy Ghost, to preach the word in Asia.

7 Then came they to Mysia, and sought to go

15:26 ¹ Have greatly hazarded their lives.

15:28 ¹ That is, a lawful Council, which the holy Ghost ruleth.

² First they made mention of the holy Ghost, that it may not seem to be any man's work.

³ Not that men have any authority of themselves, but to show the faithfulness that they used in their ministry and labor.

⁴ This was no precise necessity, but in respect of the state of that time, that the Gentiles and the Jews might more peaceably live together with less occasion of quarrel.

15:29 ¹ Charity is required even in things indifferent.

15:30 ¹ It is requisite for all people to know certainly what to hold in matters of faith and religion, and not that the Church by ignorance and knowing nothing, should depend upon the pleasure of a few.

15:33 ¹ This is an Hebrew kind of speech, which is as much to say, as the brethren wished them all prosperous success, and the Church dismissed them with good leave.

15:36 ¹ Congregations or Churches do easily degenerate, unless they be diligently seen unto, and therefore went these Apostles to oversee such as they had planted, and for this cause also Synods were instituted and appointed.

15:37 ¹ A lamentable example of discord between excellent men and very great friends, yet not for profane or their private affairs, neither yet for doctrine.

15:39 ¹ God useth the faults of his servants to the profit and building of his Church, yet we have to take heed, even in the best matters that we pass not measure in our heat.

² They were in great heat: but herein we have to consider the force of God's counsel: for by this means it came to pass, that the doctrine of the Gospel was exercised in many places.

16:1 ¹ Paul himself doth not receive Timothy into the ministry without sufficient testimony, and allowance of the brethren.

² Paul in his latter Epistle to Timothy, commendeth the godliness of Timothy's mother and grandmother.

16:2 ¹ Both for his godliness and honesty.

16:3 ¹ Timothy is circumcised, not simply for any necessity, but in respect of the time only to win the Jews.

16:4 ¹ Charity is to be observed in things indifferent so that regard be had both of the weak, and the quietness of the Church.

² These decrees which he spake of in the former chapter.

16:6 ¹ God appointeth certain and determinate times to open and set forth his truth, that both the election and the calling may proceed of grace.

² He showeth not why they were forbidden, but only that they were forbidden, teaching us to obey and not to inquire.

into Bithynia: but the Spirit suffered them not.

8 Therefore they passed through Mysia, and came down to Troas,

9 [1]Where a vision appeared to Paul in the night. There stood a man of Macedonia, and prayed him, saying, Come into Macedonia, and help us.

10 [1]And after he had seen the vision, immediately we prepared to go into Macedonia, being assured that the Lord had called us to preach the Gospel unto them.

11 Then went we forth from Troas, and with a straight course came to Samothrace, and the next day to Neapolis.

12 ¶ And from thence to Philippi, which is the chief city in the parts of Macedonia, and whose inhabitants came from Rome to dwell there: and we were in that city abiding certain days.

13 [1]And on the Sabbath day we went out of the city, besides a river, where they were wont to [2]pray: and we sat down, and spake unto the women, which were come together.

14 [1]And a certain woman named Lydia, a seller of purple, of the city of the Thyatirians, which worshipped God, heard us: whose heart the Lord opened, that she attended unto the things, which Paul spake.

15 [1]And when she was baptized, and her household, she besought us, saying, If ye have judged me to be faithful to the Lord, come into mine house, and abide there: and she constrained us.

16 [1]And it came to pass that as we went to prayer, a certain maid having a spirit [2]of divination, met us, which gat her masters much vantage with divining.

17 She followed Paul and us, and cried, saying, These men are the servants of the most high God, which show unto you the way of salvation.

18 And this did she [1]many days: but Paul being grieved, turned about, and said to the spirit, I command thee in the Name of Jesus Christ, that thou come out of her. And he came out the same hour.

19 [1]Now when her masters saw that the hope of their gain was gone, they caught Paul and Silas, and drew them into the marketplace unto the Magistrates.

20 [1]And brought them to the governors, saying, These men which are Jews trouble our city,

21 [1]And preach ordinances, which are not lawful for us to receive, neither to observe, seeing we are Romans.

22 [1]The people also rose up together against them, and the governors rent their clothes, and commanded them to be beaten with rods.

23 And when they had beaten them sore, they cast them into prison, commanding the Gaoler to keep them surely,

24 Who having received such commandment, cast them into the inner prison, and made their feet [1]fast in the stocks.

25 [1]Now at midnight Paul and Silas prayed, and sung Psalms unto God: and the prisoners heard them.

26 And suddenly there was a great earthquake, so that the foundation of the prison was shaken: and by and by all the doors opened, and every man's bands were loosed.

27 [1]Then the keeper of the prison waked out of his sleep, and when he saw the prison doors open, he drew out his sword and would have killed himself, supposing the prisoners had been fled.

28 [1]But Paul cried with a loud voice, saying, Do thyself no harm: for we all are here.

29 Then he called for a light, and leaped in, and came trembling, and fell down before Paul and Silas.

30 And brought them out, and said, Sirs, what must I do to be saved?

31 And they said, Believe in the Lord Jesus Christ, and thou shalt be saved, and thine household.

32 And they preached unto him the word of the Lord, and to all that were in the house.

16:9 [1] They are the ministers of the Gospel, by whom he helpeth such as were like to perish.

16:10 [1] The Saints did not easily believe every vision.

16:13 [1] God beginneth his kingdom in Macedonia by the conversion of a woman, and so showeth that there is no [exception] of persons in the Gospel.

[2] Where they were wont to assemble themselves.

16:14 [1] The Lord only openeth the heart to hear the word which is preached.

16:15 [1] An example of a godly housewife.

16:16 [1] Satan transformeth himself into an Angel of light, and coveteth to enter by undermining, but Paul openly letteth him, and casteth him out.

[2] This is a proper note of Apollo, which was wont to give answers to them that asked him.

16:18 [1] Paul made no haste to this miracle, for he did all things as he was led by the Spirit.

16:19 [1] Covetousness of lucre and gain is an occasion of persecuting the truth. In the mean season, God sparing Timothy, calleth Paul and Silas as the stronger, to battle.

16:20 [1] Covetousness pretendeth a desire of common peace and godliness.

16:21 [1] It is an argument of the devil, to urge the authority of ancestors without any distinction.

16:22 [1] An Example of evil Magistrates to obey the fury and rage of the people.

16:24 [1] Because he would be more sure of them, he set them fast in the stocks.

16:25 [1] The prayers of the godly do shake both heaven and earth.

16:27 [1] The merciful Lord, so oft as he listeth, draweth men to life, even through the midst of death, and whereas justly they deserved great punishment, he showeth them great mercy.

16:28 [1] In means which are especially extraordinary, we ought not to move our foot forward, unless that God goes before us.

33 ¹Afterward he took them the same hour of the night, and washed *their* stripes, and was baptized with all that belonged unto him straightway.

34 And when he had brought them into his house, he set meat before them, and rejoiced that he with all his household believed in God.

35 ¹And when it was day, the governors sent the sergeants, saying, Let those men go.

36 Then the keeper of the prison told these words unto Paul, *saying*, The governors have sent to loose you: now therefore get you hence, and go in peace.

37 ¹Then said Paul unto them, After that they have beaten us openly uncondemned, which are Romans, they have cast us into prison, and now would they put us out privily? nay verily: but let them come and bring us out.

38 ¹And the sergeants told these words unto the governors, who feared when they heard that they were Romans.

39 Then came they and prayed them, and brought them out, and desired them to depart out of the city.

40 ¹And they went out of the prison, and entered into *the house of* Lydia: and when they had seen the brethren, they comforted them, and departed.

17 1 Paul at Thessalonica   3 preaching Christ,   6, 7 is entertained of Jason: 10 He is sent to Berea: 15 from thence coming to Athens,   19 in Mars' street   23 he preacheth the living God to them unknown,   34 and so many are converted unto Christ.

1 Now ¹as they passed through Amphipolis, and Apollonia, they came to Thessalonica, where was a Synagogue of the Jews.

2 And Paul, as his manner was, went in unto them, and three Sabbath *days* disputed with them by the Scriptures,

3 ¹Opening, and alleging that Christ must have suffered, and risen again from the dead, and this is Jesus Christ, whom *said he*, I preach to you.

4 And some of them believed, and joined in company with Paul and Silas: also of the Grecians that feared God a great multitude, and of the chief women not a few.

5 ¹But the Jews which believed not, moved with envy, took unto them certain ²vagabonds *and* wicked fellows, and when they had assembled the multitude, they made a tumult in the city, and made assault against the house of Jason, and sought to bring them out to the people.

6 But when they found them not, they drew Jason and certain brethren unto the heads of the city, crying, These are they which have subverted the state of the ¹world, and here they are,

7 Whom Jason hath received, and these all do against the decrees of Caesar, saying, that there is another King one Jesus.

8 Then they troubled the people, and the heads of the city, when they heard these things.

9 Notwithstanding when they had received sufficient ¹assurance of Jason and of the others, they let them go.

10 ¹And the brethren immediately sent away Paul and Silas by night unto Berea, which when they were come thither, entered into the Synagogue of the Jews.

11 ¹These were also more ²noble men than they which were at Thessalonica, which received the word with all readiness, and searched the Scriptures daily, whether those things were so.

12 Therefore many of them believed, and of honest women, which were Grecians, and men not a few.

13 ¶ ¹But when the Jews of Thessalonica knew, that the word of God was also preached of Paul at Berea, they came thither also, and moved the people.

14 ¹But by and by the brethren sent away Paul to

16:33 ¹ God with one selfsame hand woundeth and healeth, when it pleaseth him.

16:35 ¹ Shame and confusion is in process of time, the reward of wicked and unjust Magistrates.

16:37 ¹ We must not render injury for injury, and yet notwithstanding it is lawful for us to use such helps as God giveth us, to bridle the outrageousness of the wicked, that they hurt not others in like sort.

16:38 ¹ The wicked are not moved with the fear of God, but with the fear of men: and by that means also God provideth for his, when it is needful.

16:40 ¹ We may eschew dangers, so that we never neglect our duty.

17:1 ¹ The casting out of Silas and Paul, was the saving of many others.

17:3 ¹ Christ is therefore the Mediator, because he was crucified and rose again: much less is he to be rejected, because the cross is ignominious.

17:5 ¹ Although the zeal of the unfaithful seems never so goodly, yet at length it is found to have neither truth nor equity: But yet the wicked cannot do what they list, for even among themselves God stirreth up some, whose help he useth to the deliverance of his.

² Certain companions which do nothing but walk the streets, wicked men, to be hired for every man's money, to do any mischief, such as we commonly call the rascals and very sinks and dunghill knaves of all towns and cities.

17:6 ¹ Into what country and place soever they come, they cause sedition and tumult.

17:9 ¹ When Jason had put them in good assurance that they should appear.

17:10 ¹ That is indeed the wisdom of the Spirit, which always setteth the glory of God before itself as a mark whereunto it directeth itself, and never swerveth from it.

17:11 ¹ The Lord setteth out in one moment, and in one people, divers examples of his unsearchable wisdom, to cause them to fear him.

² He compareth the Jews, with the Jews.

17:13 ¹ Satan hath his, who are zealous for him, and that even such, as least of all ought.

17:14 ¹ There is neither counsel, nor fury, nor madness, against the Lord.

go as *it were* to the sea: but Silas and Timothy abode there still.

15 [1]And they that did conduct Paul, [2]brought him unto Athens: and when they had received a commandment unto Silas and Timothy that they should come to him at once, they departed.

16 ¶ [1]Now while Paul waited for them at Athens, his spirit was [2]stirred in him, when he saw the city subject to [3]idolatry.

17 Therefore he disputeth in the Synagogue with the Jews, and with them that were religious, and in the market daily with [1]whomsoever he met.

18 [1]Then certain Philosophers of the Epicureans, and of the Stoics, disputed with him, and some said, What will this [2]babbler say? Others *said*, He seemeth to be a setter forth of strange gods (because he preached unto them Jesus, and the resurrection.)

19 And they took him, and brought him into [1]Mars' street, saying, May we not know, what this new doctrine, whereof thou speakest, is?

20 For thou bringest certain strange things unto our ears: we would know therefore what these things mean.

21 [1]For all the Athenians and strangers which dwelt there, gave themselves to nothing else, but either to tell, or to hear some news.

22 [1]Then Paul stood in the midst of Mars' street, and said, Ye men of Athens, I perceive that in all things ye are too [2]superstitious.

23 For as I passed by, and beheld your [1]devotions, I found an altar wherein was written, UNTO THE

CHAPTER 17
[a] Acts 7:48
[b] Ps. 50:8
[c] Isa. 40:19

[2]UNKNOWN GOD. Whom ye then ignorantly worship, him show I unto you.

24 [1]God that made the world, and all things that are therein, seeing that he is Lord of heaven and earth, [a]dwelleth not in temples made with hands.

25 [b]Neither is worshipped with men's hands, as though he needed anything, seeing he giveth to all life and breath and all things,

26 [1]And hath made of [2]one blood all mankind, to dwell on all the face of the earth, and hath assigned the seasons which were ordained before, and the bounds of their habitation,

27 That they should seek the Lord, if so be they might have [1]groped after him, and found *him*, though doubtless he be not far from every one of us.

28 For in him we live, and move, and have our being, as also certain of your own Poets have said: For we are also his generation.

29 'Forasmuch then, as we are the generation of God, we ought not to think that the Godhead is like unto gold, or silver, or stone [1]graven by art and the invention of man.

30 [1]And the time of this ignorance God regarded not: but now he admonisheth all men everywhere to repent.

31 Because he hath appointed a day in the which he will judge the world in righteousness, by that man whom he hath appointed, *whereof* he hath given an [1]assurance to all men, in that he hath raised him from the dead.

17:15 [1] The sheep of Christ do also watch for their pastor's health and safety, but yet in the Lord.

[2] It is not for nought that the Jews of Berea were so commended, for they brought Paul safe from Macedonia to Athens, and there is in distance betwixt those two, all Thessalia, and Boeotia, and Attica.

17:16 [1] In comparing the wisdom of God with man's wisdom, men scoff and mock at that which they understand not: And God useth the curiosity of fools to gather together his elect.

[2] He could not forbear.

[3] Slavishly given to Idolatry: Pausanias writeth that there were more Idols in Athens, than in all Greece, yea they had altars dedicated to Shame, and Fame, and Lust, whom they made goddesses.

17:17 [1] Whomsoever Paul met with, that would suffer him to talk with him, he reasoned with him, so thoroughly did he burn with the zeal of God's glory.

17:18 [1] Two sects especially of the Philosophers do set themselves against Christ: the Epicureans, which make a mock and scoff at all religions, and the Stoics, which determine upon matters of religion according to their own brains.

[2] Word for word, seed gatherer: a borrowed kind of speech taken of birds which spoil corn, and is applied to them which without all art bluster out such knowledge as they have gotten by hearing this man and that man.

17:19 [1] This was a place called as you would say, Mars hill, where the judges sat which were called Areopagus, upon weighty affairs, which in old time arraigned Socrates, and afterward condemned him of impiety.

17:21 [1] The wisdom of man is vanity.

17:22 [1] The idolaters themselves minister most strong and forcible arguments against their own superstition.

[2] To stand in too peevish and servile a fear of your gods.

17:23 [1] Whatsoever men worship for religion's sake, that we call devotion.

[2] Pausanias in his Atticis, maketh mention of the altar which the Athenians had dedicated to unknown gods: and Laertius in his Epimenides maketh mention of an altar that had no name entitled.

17:24 [1] It is a most foolish and vain thing to compare the Creator with the creature, to limit him within a place, which can be comprehended in no place, and to think to allure him with gifts, of whom all men have received all things whatsoever they have: And these are the fountains of all idolatry.

17:26 [1] God is wonderful in all his works, but especially in the work of man: not that we should stand amazed at his works, but that we should lift up our eyes to the workman.

[2] Of one stock and one beginning.

17:27 [1] For as blind men we could not seek out God, but only by groping wise, before the true light came and lightened the world.

17:29 [1] Which stuff, as gold, silver, stones, are customably graven as a man's wit can devise, for men will not worship that gross stuff as it is, unless by some art it have gotten some shape upon it.

17:30 [1] The oldness of the error doth not excuse them that err, but it commendeth and setteth forth the patience of God: who notwithstanding will be a just judge to such as contemn him.

17:31 [1] By declaring Christ to be the judge of the world through the resurrection from the dead.

32 ¹Now when they had heard of the resurrection from the dead, some mocked, and others said, We will hear thee again of this thing.

33 And so Paul departed from among them.

34 Howbeit certain men clave unto Paul, and believed: among whom was also Dionysius Areopagite, and a woman named Damaris, and others with them.

18

As Paul at Corinth   6 taught the Gentiles,   9 the Lord comforteth him.   12 He is accused before Gallio,   16 but in vain: 18 From thence he saileth to Syria,   19 and so to Ephesus.   23 At Galatia and Phrygia he strengtheneth the disciples.   24 Apollos being more perfectly instructed by Aquila,   28 preacheth Christ with great efficacy.

1 After ¹these things, Paul departed from Athens, and came to Corinth,

2 And found a certain Jew named ᵃAquila, born in Pontus, lately come from Italy, and his wife Priscilla (because that ¹Claudius had commanded all Jews to depart from Rome) and he came unto them.

3 And because he was of the same craft, he abode with them and wrought (for their craft was to make tents.)

4 ¹And he disputed in the Synagogue every Sabbath day, and ²exhorted the Jews, and the Grecians.

5 Now when Silas and Timothy were come from Macedonia, Paul, ¹forced in spirit, testified to the Jews that Jesus was the Christ.

6 ¹And when they resisted and blasphemed, he ᵇshook his raiment, and said unto them, Your ²blood be upon your own head: I am clean: from henceforth will I go unto the Gentiles.

7 So he departed thence, and entered into a certain man's house, named Justus, a worshipper of God, whose house joined hard to the Synagogue.

CHAPTER 18
ᵃ Rom. 16:3
ᵇ Acts 13:51
Matt. 10:14
ᶜ 1 Cor. 1:14
ᵈ Num. 16:18
Acts 21:24

8 And ᶜCrispus the chief ruler of the Synagogue, believed in the Lord with all his household: and many of the Corinthians hearing it, believed and were baptized.

9 ¹Then said the Lord to Paul in the night by a vision, Fear not, but speak, and hold not thy peace.

10 For I am with thee, and no man shall lay hands on thee to hurt thee: for I have much people in this city.

11 So he ¹continued there a year and six months, and taught the word of God among them.

12 ¶ ¹Now when Gallio was deputy of ²Achaia, the Jews arose with one accord against Paul, and brought him to the judgment seat,

13 Saying, This fellow persuadeth men to worship God otherwise than the Law appointeth.

14 And as Paul was about to open his mouth, Gallio said unto the Jews, If it were a matter of wrong, or an evil deed, O ye Jews, I would according to ¹reason maintain you.

15 But if it be a question of ¹words and ²names, and of your Law, look ye to it yourselves: for I will be no judge of those things.

16 And he drove them from the judgment seat.

17 Then took all the Grecians Sosthenes the chief ruler of the Synagogue, and beat him before the judgment seat: but Gallio cared nothing for those things.

18 ¹But when Paul had tarried there yet a good while, he took leave of the brethren, and sailed into Syria, (and with him Priscilla and Aquila) after that ²he had shorn his head in ³Cenchrea: for he had made a ᵈvow.

19 Then he came to Ephesus, and left them there: but he entered into the Synagogue and disputed with the Jews.

17:32 ¹ Men, to show forth their vanity, are diversely affected and moved with one selfsame Gospel, which notwithstanding ceaseth not to be effectual in the elect.

18:1 ¹ The true ministers are so far from seeking their own profit, that they do willingly depart from their right, rather than the course of the Gospel should be hindered in the least wise that might be.

18:2 ¹ Suetonius recordeth that Rome banished the Jews, because they were always at disquiet, and that by Christ's means.

18:4 ¹ The truth ought always to be freely uttered, yet notwithstanding the doctrine may be so moderated, as occasion of the profit that the people take thereby, shall require.

² Exhorted so that he persuaded, and so the word signifieth.

18:5 ¹ Was very much grieved in mind: whereby is signified the great earnestness of his mind, which was greatly moved: for Paul was so zealous, that he clean forgot himself, and with a wonderful courage gave himself to preach Christ.

18:6 ¹ Although we have assayed all means possible, and yet in vain, we must not leave off from our work, but forsake the rebellious, and go to them that be more obedient.

² This is a kind of speech taken from the Hebrews, whereby he meaneth that the Jews are cause of their own destruction: and as

for him, that he is without fault in forsaking them and going to other nations.

18:9 ¹ God doth avouch and maintain the constancy of his servants.

18:11 ¹ Word for word, sat, whereupon they in former time, took the name of their Bishop's seat: but Paul sat, that is, continued teaching the word of God: and this kind of seat belongeth nothing to them which never saw their seats with a mind to teach in them.

18:12 ¹ The wicked are never weary of evil doing, but the Lord mocketh their endeavors marvelously.

² That is, of Greece, yet the Romans did not call him Deputy of Greece, but of Achaia, because the Romans brought the Greeks into subjection by the Achaians, which in those days were Princes of Greece, as Pausanias recordeth.

18:14 ¹ As much as in right I could.

18:15 ¹ As if a man have not spoken well, as the case of your religion standeth.

² For this profane man thinketh that the controversy of religion, is but a brawl about words, and for no matter of substance.

18:18 ¹ Paul is made all to all, to win all to Christ.

² That is, Paul.

³ Cenchrea was an haven of the Corinthians.

20 ¹Who desired him to tarry a longer time with them: but he would not consent,

21 But bade them farewell, saying, I must needs keep this feast that cometh, in Jerusalem: but I will return again unto you, ᵉ·¹if God will. So he sailed from Ephesus.

22 ¶ And when he came down to Caesarea, he went up *to Jerusalem*: and when he had saluted the Church, he went down unto Antioch.

23 Now when he had tarried *there* a while, he departed, and went through the country of Galatia and Phrygia by order, strengthening all the disciples.

24 ¹And a certain Jew named ʲApollos, born at Alexandria, came to Ephesus, an eloquent man, and ²mighty in the Scriptures.

25 The same was instructed in the way of the Lord, and he spake fervently in the Spirit, and taught diligently the things of the Lord, and knew but the baptism of John only.

26 And he began to speak boldly in the Synagogue. Whom when ᵍAquila and Priscilla had heard, they took him unto them, and expounded unto him the ¹way of God more perfectly.

27 And when he was minded to go into Achaia, the brethren exhorting him, wrote to the disciples to receive him: and after he was come thither, he helped them much which had believed through ¹grace.

28 For mightily he confuted publicly the Jews, with great vehemency, showing by the Scriptures, that Jesus was that Christ.

19 *Certain disciples at Ephesus, 3 having only received John's baptism, 2 and know not the visible gifts of the holy Ghost, wherewith God had beautified his Son's kingdom, 5 are baptized in the Name of Jesus. 13 The Jewish exorcists 16 are beaten of the devil. 19 Conjuring books are burnt. 24 Demetrius 29 raiseth sedition against Paul.*

1 And ¹it came to pass, while Apollos was at Corinth, that Paul when he passed through the upper coasts, came to Ephesus, and found certain disciples,

2 And said unto them, Have ye received the ¹holy Ghost since ye believed? And they said unto him, We have not so much as heard whether there be an holy Ghost.

3 ¹And he said unto them, Unto ²what were ye then baptized? And they said, Unto ³John's baptism.

4 Then said Paul, ᵃJohn verily baptized with the baptism of repentance, saying unto the people, that they should believe in him, which should come after him, that is, in Christ Jesus.

5 And when they heard it, they were baptized in the Name of the Lord Jesus.

6 So Paul laid his hands upon them, and the holy Ghost came on them, and they spake the tongues, and prophesied.

7 And all the men were about twelve.

8 ¶ Moreover he went into the Synagogue, and spake boldly for the space of three months, disputing and exhorting to the things that *appertain* to the kingdom of God.

9 ¹But when certain were hardened, and disobeyed, speaking evil of the ²way *of God* before the multitude, he departed from them, and separated the disciples, and disputed daily in the school of one ³Tyrannus.

10 And this was done by the space of two years, so that all they which dwelt in Asia, heard the word of the Lord Jesus, both Jews and Grecians.

11 And God wrought no small miracles by the hands of Paul,

12 So that from his body were brought unto the sick, kerchiefs, or handkerchiefs, and the diseases departed from them, and the evil spirits went out of them.

13 ¹Then certain of the vagabond Jews, ²exorcists took in hand to name over them which had evil spirits, the name of the Lord Jesus, saying, We adjure you by Jesus, whom Paul preacheth.

14 (And there were certain sons of Sceva a Jew,

Cross references (margin):
ᵉ 1 Cor. 4:19
James 4:15
ᶠ 1 Cor. 1:12
ᵍ Rom. 16:3

CHAPTER 19
ᵃ Acts 1:5
Acts 2:2
Acts 11:16
Matt. 3:11
Mark 1:8
Luke 3:16
John 1:26

18:20 ¹ The Apostles were carried about not by the will of man, but by the leading of the holy Ghost.

18:21 ¹ So we should promise nothing without this clause, for we know not what the day following will bring forth.

18:24 ¹ Apollos, a godly and learned man, refuseth not to profit in the school of a base and abject handicraftsman, and also of a woman: and so becometh an excellent minister of the Church.

² Very well instructed in the knowledge of the Scriptures.

18:26 ¹ The way that leadeth to God.

18:27 ¹ Through God's gracious favor, or by those excellent gifts which God hath bestowed upon him.

19:1 ¹ Paul being nothing offended at the rudeness of the Ephesians, planted a Church among them.

19:2 ¹ Those excellent gifts of the holy Ghost, which were in those days in the Church.

19:3 ¹ John did only begin to instruct the disciples whom Christ should make perfect.

² In what doctrine then are you taught and instructed?

³ To be baptized into John's baptism, is to profess the doctrine which John preached and sealed with his baptism.

19:9 ¹ For a man to separate himself and others from infidels which are utterly desperate, it is not to divide the Church, but rather to unite it and make it one.

² By this word Way, the Hebrews understand any kind of life, and here it is taken for Christianity.

³ This was a man's proper name.

19:13 ¹ Satan is constrained to give witness against himself.

² So were they called which cast out devils by conjuring them in the Name of God: and in the beginning of the Church, they which had the gift of working miracles, and laid their hands on them that were possessed with devils, were also so called.

the Priest, *about* seven which did this.)

15　And the evil spirit answered, and said, Jesus I acknowledge, and Paul I know: but who are ye?

16　And the man in whom the evil spirit was, ran on them, and overcame them, and ¹prevailed against them, so that they fled out of that house, naked and wounded.

17　And this was known to all the Jews and Grecians also which dwelt at Ephesus, and fear came on them all, and the Name of the Lord Jesus was magnified,

18　¹And many that believed, came and ²confessed, and showed their works.

19　Many also of them which used curious arts, brought their books, and burned them before all men: and they counted the price of them, and found it ¹fifty thousand *pieces* of silver.

20　So the word of God grew mightily, and prevailed.

21　¶ ¹Now when these things were accomplished, Paul purposed by the ²Spirit to pass through Macedonia and Achaia, and to go to Jerusalem, saying, After I have been there, I must also see Rome.

22　So sent he into Macedonia two of them that ministered unto him, Timothy, and Erastus, *but* he remained in Asia for a season.

23　¹And the same time there arose no small trouble about that way.

24　For a certain man named Demetrius a silversmith, which made silver ¹temples of Diana, brought great gains unto the craftsmen,

25　Whom he called together, with the workmen of like things, and said, Sirs, ye know that by this craft we have our goods:

26　Moreover ye see and hear, that not alone at Ephesus, but almost throughout all Asia this Paul hath persuaded, and turned away much people, saying, That they be not Gods which are made with hands.

27　So that not only this thing is dangerous unto us, that this our ¹portion shall be reproved, but also

ᵇ Rom. 16:23
1 Cor. 1:14
ᶜ Col. 4:10

that the temple of the great goddess Diana should be nothing esteemed, and that it would come to pass that her magnificence, which all Asia and the world worshippeth, should be destroyed.

28　Now when they heard it, they were full of wrath, and cried out, saying, Great *is* Diana of the Ephesians.

29　And the whole city was full of confusion, and they rushed into the common place with one assent, and caught ᵇGaius, and ᶜAristarchus, men of Macedonia, and Paul's companions of his journey.

30　And when Paul would have entered in unto the people, the disciples suffered him not.

31　¹Certain also of the chief of Asia, which were his friends, sent unto him, desiring him that he would not present himself in the Common place.

32　Some therefore cried one thing, and some another: for the assembly was out of order, and the more part knew not wherefore they were come together.

33　And *some* of the company drew forth Alexander, the Jews thrusting him forwards. Alexander then beckoned with the hand, and would have excused the matter to the people.

34　¹But when they knew that he was a Jew, there arose a shout almost for the space of two hours, of all men, crying, Great *is* Diana of the Ephesians.

35　¹Then the town clerk when he had stayed the people, said, Ye men of Ephesus, what man is it that knoweth not how that the city of the Ephesians is a worshipper of the great goddess Diana, and of *the image*, which ²came down from Jupiter?

36　Seeing then that no man can speak against these things, ye ought to be appeased, and to do nothing rashly.

37　For ye have brought hither these men, which have neither committed sacrilege, neither do blaspheme your goddess.

38　Wherefore, if Demetrius and the craftsmen which are with him, have a ¹matter against any man, the ²law is open, and there are ³Deputies: let them

19:16 ¹ He prevailed against them, though they strove never so much.
19:18 ¹ Conjuring and sorcery is condemned by open testimony, and by the authority of the Apostle.
　² Confessed their errors, and detested them openly, being terrified with the fear of the judgment of God: and what is this to ear shrift?
19:19 ¹ They that make the least value of it, reckon it to be about eight hundred pounds English.
19:21 ¹ Paul is never weary.
　² By the motion of God's Spirit: therefore we may not say that Paul ran hand over head to death, but as the Spirit of God led him.
19:23 ¹ Gain cloaked with a show of religion is the very cause wherefore idolatry is stoutly and stubbornly defended.
19:24 ¹ These were certain counterfeit temples with Diana's picture in them which they bought that worshipped her.
19:27 ¹ As if he said, If Paul go on thus as he hath begun to confute the opinion which men have of Diana's image, all this our gain will

come to nought.
19:31 ¹ There ought to be in all Christians and especially in the Ministers, an invincible constancy, which may not by any storms or assaults be overcome, which notwithstanding must suffer itself modestly to be governed by wisdom.
19:34 ¹ Instead of reason, the idolaters are sufficiently contented with their own madness and outcries, and those are the greatest defenses that they have.
19:35 ¹ An example of a political man who redeemeth peace and quietness with lies, which Paul would never have done.
　² The Ephesians believed superstitiously, that the image of Diana came down from heaven to them.
19:38 ¹ Have ought to accuse any man of.
　² For there are certain days appointed for civil causes and matters of judgment, and the Deputies sit.
　³ By the Deputies are meant also the Deputies' Substitutes, that is, such as did sit for them.

accuse one another.

39 But if ye inquire anything concerning other matters, it may be determined in a ¹lawful assembly.

40 For we are even in jeopardy to be accused of this day's sedition, forasmuch as there is no cause, whereby we may give a reason of this concourse of people.

41 And when he had thus spoken, he let the assembly depart.

20

1 Paul appointed to go to Macedonia. 7 In Troas preaching until midnight, 9 Eutychus fell down dead out of a window, 10 he raised him to life: 15 At Miletus, 17 Having called the Elders of Ephesus together, 23 he declareth what things shall come upon himself, 28 and others.

1 Now ¹after the tumult was appeased, Paul called the disciples unto him, and embraced them, and departed to go into Macedonia.

2 And when he had gone through those parts, and had exhorted them with ¹many words, he came into Greece.

3 ¹And having tarried *there* three months, because the Jews laid wait for him, as he was about to sail into Syria, he purposed to return through Macedonia.

4 And there accompanied him into Asia, Sopater of Berea, and of them of Thessalonica, Aristarchus, and Secundus, and Gaius of Derbe, and Timothy, and of them of Asia, Tychicus, and Trophimus.

5 These went before, and tarried us at Troas.

6 And we sailed forth from Philippi, after the days of unleavened bread, and came unto them to Troas in five days, where we abode seven days.

7 ¹And the ²first day of the week, the disciples being come together to break bread, Paul preached unto them, ready to depart on the morrow, and continued the preaching unto midnight.

8 ¹And there were many lights in an upper chamber, where they were gathered together.

9 And there sat in a window a certain young man, named Eutychus, fallen into a dead sleep: and as Paul was long preaching, he overcome with sleep, fell down from the third loft, and was taken up dead.

10 But Paul went down, and laid himself upon him, and embraced him, saying, Trouble not yourselves: for his life is in him.

11 Then when *Paul* was come up again, and had broken bread, and eaten, having spoken a long while till the dawning of the day, he so departed.

12 And they brought the boy alive, and they were not a little comforted.

13 ¶ Then we went before to ship, and sailed unto *the city* Assos, that we might receive Paul there: for so had he appointed, and would himself go afoot.

14 Now when he was come unto us to Assos, and we had received him, we came to Mitylene.

15 And we sailed thence, and came the next day over against Chios, and the next day we arrived at Samos, and tarried at Trogyllium: the next day we came to Miletus.

16 ¹For Paul had determined to sail by Ephesus, because he would not spend the time in Asia: for he hasted to be, if he could possible, at Jerusalem, at the day of Pentecost.

17 ¶ Wherefore from ¹Miletus, he sent to Ephesus, and called the Elders of the Church.

18 ¹Who when they were come to him, he said unto them, Ye know from the first day that I came into Asia, after what manner I have been with you at all seasons,

19 Serving the Lord with all modesty, and with many tears, and temptations, which came unto me by the layings await of the Jews,

20 And how I kept ¹back nothing that was profitable, but have showed you, and taught you openly and throughout every house.

21 Witnessing both to the Jews, and to the Grecians the repentance toward God, and faith toward our Lord Jesus Christ.

22 ¹And now behold, I go ²bound in the Spirit

19:39 ¹ He speaketh of a lawful assembly, not only to except against the disordered hurly-burly of the people, but also against all meeting and coming together which was not by order: for there were certain days appointed to call the people together in.

20:1 ¹ Paul departed from Ephesus by the consent of the Church, not to be idle or at rest, but to take pains in another place.

20:2 ¹ For after so great trouble there was need of a long exhortation.

20:3 ¹ A froward zeal is the guider and instructor to murders: and we are not debarred by the wisdom of God to prevent the endeavors of wicked men.

20:7 ¹ Assemblies in the nighttime cannot be justly condemned, neither ought, when the cause is good.

² Word for word, the first day of the Sabbath, that is upon the Lord's day: so that by this place, and by 1 Cor. 16:2, it is not amiss gathered, that in those days the Christians were wont to assemble themselves solemnly together upon that day.

20:8 ¹ The devil minding to trouble the Church with a great offense, giveth Paul a singular occasion to confirm the Gospel.

20:16 ¹ Paul an earnest and diligent follower of Christ, making haste to his bonds without any ceasing or stopping in his race, doth first of all as it were make his testament, wherein he giveth an account of his former life, defendeth the doctrine which he taught, and exhorteth the Pastors of the Church to persevere and go forward with continuance in their office.

20:17 ¹ According as the situation of these places is set forth, that distance between Ephesus and Miletus was about 400 furlongs, which maketh almost fifty Dutch miles.

20:18 ¹ A lively image of a true pastor.

20:20 ¹ I refrained not to speak, neither dissembled in any respect whatsoever, either for fear or lucre's sake.

20:22 ¹ He testifieth that he goeth to his bonds by the commandment of God.

² He calleth that motion of the holy Ghost, which forced him to take his journey to Jerusalem, the bond of the Sprit, whom he followed with all his heart.

unto Jerusalem, and know not what things shall come unto me there,

23 Save that the holy Ghost witnesseth in every city, saying, that bonds and afflictions abide me.

24 But I pass not at all, neither is my life dear unto myself, so that I may fulfill my course with joy, and the ministration which I have received of the Lord Jesus, to testify the Gospel of the grace of God.

25 And now behold, I know that henceforth ye all, through whom I have gone preaching the kingdom of God, shall see my face no more.

26 Wherefore I take you to record this day, that I am ¹pure from the blood of all men.

27 ¹For I have kept nothing back, but have showed you all the counsel of God.

28 Take heed therefore unto yourselves, and to all the flock, whereof the holy Ghost hath made you Overseers to ¹feed the Church of God which ²he hath purchased with ³that his own blood.

29 ¹For I know this, that after my departing shall grievous wolves enter in among you, not sparing the flock.

30 Moreover of your own selves shall men arise speaking perverse things, to ¹draw disciples after them.

31 Therefore watch, and remember, that by *the space* of three years I ceased not to warn everyone, both night and day with tears.

32 ¹And now brethren, I commend you to God, and to the word of his grace, which is able to build further, and to give you an ²inheritance, among all them, which are sanctified.

33 ¹I have coveted no man's silver, nor gold, nor apparel.

34 Yea, ye know, that these hands have ministered unto my ªnecessities, and to them that were with me.

35 I have showed you all things, how that so laboring, ye ought to ¹support the weak, and to remember the words of the Lord Jesus, how that he said, It is

CHAPTER 20
ᵈ 1 Cor. 4:12
1 Thess. 2:9
2 Thess. 3:8

CHAPTER 21
ᵈ Acts 6:5

a blessed thing to give, rather than to receive.

36 And when he had thus spoken, he kneeled down, and prayed with them all.

37 ¹Then they wept all abundantly, and fell on Paul's neck, and kissed him,

38 Being chiefly sorry for the words which he spake, That they should see his face no more. And they accompanied him unto the ship.

21

1 Paul goeth toward Jerusalem: 8 at Caesarea he talketh with Philip the Evangelist: 10 Agabus foretelleth him of his bonds. 17 After he came to Jerusalem, 26 and into the Temple, 27 The Jews laid hands on him: 32 Lysias the captain taketh him from them.

1 And ¹as we launched forth, and were departed from them, we came with a straight course unto Cos, and the day following unto the Rhodes, and from thence unto Patara.

2 And we found a ship that went over unto Phoenicia, and went aboard, and set forth.

3 And when we had discovered Cyprus, we left it on the left hand, and sailed toward Syria, and arrived at Tyre: for there the ship unladed the burden.

4 And when we had found disciples, we tarried there seven days. And they told Paul through the ¹Spirit, that he should not go up to Jerusalem.

5 But when the days were ended, we departed and went our way, and they all accompanied us with *their* wives and children, even out of the city: and we kneeled down on the shore, prayed.

6 Then when we had embraced one another, we took ship, and they returned home.

7 And when we had ended the course from Tyre, we arrived at Ptolemais, and saluted the brethren, and abode with them one day.

8 And the next day, Paul and we that were with him, departed, and came unto Caesarea: and we entered into the house of ªPhilip the Evangelist, which was one of the ¹seven *Deacons*, and abode with him.

20:26 ¹ If you do perish, yet there shall be no fault in me, see Acts 18:6.
20:27 ¹ The doctrine of the Apostles is most perfect and absolute.
20:28 ¹ To keep it, to feed it, and govern it.
² A notable sentence for Christ's Godhead: which showeth plainly in his person, how that by reason of the joining together of the two natures in his own person, that which is proper to one is spoken of the other being taken in the derivative, and not in the primitive: which in old time the godly fathers termed a communicating or fellowship of proprieties, that is to say, a making common of that to two, which belongeth but to one.
³ This word, That showeth the excellency of this blood.
20:29 ¹ A prophecy of pastors that should straightway degenerate into wolves against such as boast and brag only of a succession of persons.
20:30 ¹ This is a great misery, to want the presence of such a shepherd, but greater to have wolves enter in.
20:32 ¹ The power of God, and his free promises revealed in his

word, are the props and upholders of the ministry of the Gospel.
² As children, and therefore of free love and good will.
20:33 ¹ Pastors must before all things beware of covetousness.
20:35 ¹ As it were by reaching out the hand to them, which otherwise are apt to slip and fall away, and so to stay them.
20:37 ¹ The Gospel doth not take away natural affections, but ruleth and bridleth them in good order.
21:1 ¹ Not only men simply, but even our friends, and such as are endued with the Spirit of God, do sometimes go about to hinder the course of our vocation: but it is our part to go forward without all stopping or staggering, after that we are sure of our calling from God.
21:4 ¹ They foretold through the Spirit what danger hanged over Paul's head, and this they did as Prophets: but of a fleshly affection they frayed him from going to Jerusalem.
21:8 ¹ He speaketh of the seven Deacons which he mentioned before, Acts 6.

9 Now he had four daughters, virgins, which did ¹prophesy.

ᵇ Acts 18:18
Num. 6:18

10 And as we tarried there many days, there came a certain Prophet from Judea, named Agabus.

11 And when he was come unto us, he took Paul's girdle, and bound his own hands and feet, and said, Thus saith the holy Ghost, So shall the Jews at Jerusalem bind the man that owneth this girdle, and shall deliver him into the hands of the Gentiles.

12 And when we had heard these things, both we and others of the same place besought him that he would not go up to Jerusalem.

13 Then Paul answered, and said, What do ye weeping and breaking mine heart? For I am ready not to be bound only, but also to die at Jerusalem for the Name of the Lord Jesus.

14 ¹So when he would not be persuaded, we ceased, saying, The will of the Lord be done.

15 And after those days we trussed up our fardels, and went up to Jerusalem.

16 There went with us also *certain* of the disciples of Caesarea, and brought with them one Mnason of Cyprus, an old disciple, with whom we should lodge.

17 And when we were come to Jerusalem, the brethren received us gladly.

18 And the next day Paul went in with us unto James: and all the Elders were there assembled.

19 ¹And when he had embraced them, he told by order all things, that God had wrought among the Gentiles by his ministration.

20 ¹So when they heard it, they glorified God, and said unto him, Thou seest, brother, how many thousand Jews there are which believe, and they are all zealous of the Law:

21 Now they are informed of thee, that thou teachest all the Jews, which are among the Gentiles, to forsake Moses, and sayest that they ought not to circumcise their sons, neither to live *after* the customs.

22 What is then *to be done?* the multitude must needs come together: for they shall hear that thou art come.

23 Do therefore this that we say to thee. We have four men, which have made a vow,

24 Them take, and ¹purify thyself with them, and ²contribute with them, that they may ᵇshave their heads: and all shall know, that those things, whereof they have been informed concerning thee, are nothing, but that thou thyself also walkest and keepest the Law.

25 For as touching the Gentiles, which believe, we have written, and determined that they observe no such thing, but that they keep themselves from things offered to idols, and from blood, and from that that is strangled, and from fornication.

26 Then Paul took the men, and the next day was purified with them, and entered into the Temple, ¹declaring the accomplishment of the days of the purification, until that an offering should be offered for everyone of them.

27 ¹And when the seven days were almost ended, the Jews which were of Asia (when they saw him in the Temple) moved all the people, and laid hands on him,

28 Crying, Men of Israel, help: this is the man that teacheth all men everywhere against the people, and the Law, and this place: moreover, he hath brought Grecians into the Temple, and hath polluted this holy place.

29 For they had seen before Trophimus an Ephesian with him in the city, whom they supposed that Paul had brought into the Temple.

30 Then all the city was moved, and the people ran together: and they took Paul, and drew him out of the Temple, and forthwith the doors were shut.

31 ¹But as they went about to kill him, tidings came unto the chief captain of the band, that all Jerusalem was on an uproar.

32 Who immediately took soldiers and Centurions, and ran down unto them: and when they saw the chief captain and the soldiers, they left beating of Paul.

33 Then the chief Captain came near and took him, and commanded him to be bound with two chains, and demanded who he was, and what he had done.

34 And one cried this, another that, among the people. So when he could not know the certainty for the tumult, he commanded him to be led into the castle.

35 And when he came unto the grieces, it was so

21:9 ¹ They had a peculiar gift of foretelling things to come.

21:14 ¹ The will of God bridleth all affections in them which earnestly seek the glory of God.

21:19 ¹ God is to be praised, who is the Author of all good sayings and deeds.

21:20 ¹ In things indifferent (of which sort were not the traditions of the Pharisees, but the ceremonies of the Law, until such time as Christian liberty was more fully revealed to the Jews) charity willeth us to conform or apply ourselves willingly so far as we may, to our brethren which do not stubbornly, and maliciously, resist the truth, but are not thoroughly instructed especially if the question be of a whole multitude.

21:24 ¹ That is, consecrate thyself: for he speaketh not here of the

unclean, but of such as were subject to the vow of the Nazarites.
² That it may be known, that thou wast not only present at the vow, but also a chief man in it: and therefore it is said afterwards, that Paul declared the days of purification: for although the charges for the Nazarites' offerings were appointed, yet they might add somewhat unto them, Num. 6:21.

21:26 ¹ The Priests were to be advertised of the accomplishment of the days of the purification, because there were sacrifices to be offered the same day that their vow was ended.

21:27 ¹ A preposterous zeal is the cause of great confusion, and great mischiefs.

21:31 ¹ God findeth some even amongst the wicked and profane themselves, to hinder the endeavors of the rest.

that he was borne of the soldiers, for the violence of the people.

36 For the multitude of the people followed after, crying, Away with him.

37 And as Paul should have been led into the castle, he said unto the chief captain, May I speak unto thee? Who said, Canst thou *speak* Greek?

38 Art not thou the [1]Egyptian who before these days raised a sedition, and led out into the wilderness four thousand men that were murderers?

39 Then Paul said, Doubtless, I am a man which am a Jew, and citizen of Tarsus, a famous city of Cilicia, and I beseech thee, suffer me to speak unto the people.

40 And when he had given him license, Paul stood on the grieces, and beckoned with the hand unto the people, and when there was made great silence, he spake unto them in the Hebrew tongue, saying,

22

1 Paul yieldeth a reason of his faith,   22 and the Jews heard him awhile: 23 But so soon as they cried out,   24 He is commanded to be scourged and examined,   27 and so declareth that he is citizen of Rome.

1 Ye men, brethren and fathers, hear my defense now towards you.

2 (And when they heard that he spake in the Hebrew tongue to them, they kept the more silence, and he said,)

3 [1]I am verily a man, *which am* a Jew, born in Tarsus in Cilicia, but brought up in this city at the [2]feet of Gamaliel, and instructed according to the perfect manner of the Law of the fathers, and was zealous toward God, as ye all are this day.

4 And I persecuted this way unto the death, binding and delivering into prison both men and women.

5 As also the chief Priest doth bear me witness, and all the company of the Elders: of whom also I received letters unto the brethren, and went to Damascus to bring them which were there, bound unto Jerusalem, that they might be punished.

6 ¶ And so it was, as I journeyed, and was come near unto Damascus about noon, that suddenly there shone from heaven a great light round about me.

7 So I fell unto the earth, and heard a voice, saying unto me, Saul, Saul, why persecutest thou me?

8 Then I answered, Who art thou, Lord? And he said to me, I am Jesus of Nazareth, whom thou persecutest.

9 Moreover they that were with me, saw indeed a light and were afraid: but they heard not the voice of him that spake unto me.

10 Then I said, What shall I do, Lord? And the Lord said unto me, Arise, and go into Damascus: and there it shall be told thee of all things, which are appointed for thee to do.

11 So when I could not see for the glory of that light, I was led by the hand of them that were with me, and came into Damascus.

12 And one Ananias a godly man, as pertaining to the Law, having good report of all the Jews which dwelt there,

13 Came unto me, and stood, and said unto me, Brother Saul, receive thy sight: and that same hour I looked upon him.

14 And he said, The God of our fathers hath appointed thee, that thou shouldest know his will, and shouldest see that Just one, and shouldest hear the voice of his mouth.

15 For thou shalt be his witness unto all men, of the things which thou hast seen and heard.

16 Now therefore why tarriest thou? Arise, and be baptized, and wash away thy sins, in calling on the Name of the Lord.

17 ¶ And it came to pass, that when I was come again to Jerusalem, and prayed in the Temple, I was in a trance,

18 And saw him, saying unto me, Make haste, and get thee quickly out of Jerusalem: for they will not receive thy witness concerning me.

19 Then I said, Lord, they know that I prisoned, and beat in every Synagogue them that believed in thee.

20 And when the blood of thy martyr Stephen was shed, I also stood by, and consented unto his death, and kept the clothes of them that [1]slew him.

21 Then he said unto me, Depart: for I will send thee far hence unto the Gentiles.

22 ¶ [1]And they heard him unto this word, *but* then they lifted up their voices, and said, Away with such a fellow from the earth: for it is not meet that he should live.

23 And as they [1]cried and cast off their clothes, and threw dust into the air,

24 [1]The chief captain commanded him to be led

21:38 [1] Touching this Egyptian which assembled thirty thousand men, read Josephus, book 2, chap. 12.

22:3 [1] Paul making a short declaration of his former life, proveth both his vocation and doctrine to be of God.

[2] That is, his daily hearer: the reason of this speech is this: for that they which teach, sit commonly in the higher place speaking to their scholars which sit upon forms beneath: and therefore he saith, at the feet of Gamaliel.

22:20 [1] This is properly spoken: for Stephen was murdered of a sort

of cutthroats, not by order of justice, but by open force: for at that time the Jews could not put any man to death by Law.

22:22 [1] Stout and stubborn pride will neither itself embrace the truth, neither suffer others to receive it.

22:23 [1] The description of a seditious hurly-burly, and of an harebrained and mad multitude.

22:24 [1] The wisdom of the flesh doth not consider what is just, but what is profitable, and therewithall measure the profit, according as it appeareth presently.

into the castle, and bade that he should be scourged, and examined, that he might know wherefore they cried so on him.

25 [1]And as they bound him with thongs, Paul said unto the Centurion that stood by, Is it lawful for you to scourge one that is a Roman, and not condemned?

26 Now when the Centurion heard it, he went, and told the chief captain, saying, Take heed what thou doest: for this man is a Roman.

27 Then the chief captain came, and said to him, Tell me, art thou a Roman? And he said, Yea.

28 And the chief captain answered, With a great sum obtained I this freedom. Then Paul said, But I was so born.

29 Then straightway they departed from him, which should have examined him: and the chief captain also was afraid, after he knew that he was a [1]Roman, and that he had bound him.

30 On the next day, because he would have known the certainty wherefore he was accused of the Jews, he loosed him from *his* bonds, and commanded the high Priests and all their Council to come *together*: and he brought Paul, and set him before them.

23

1 As Paul pleadeth his cause,   2 Ananias commandeth them to smite him.   7 Dissension among his accusers.   11 God encourageth him.   14 The Jews laying wait for Paul,   17 is declared unto the chief captain.   24 He sendeth him to Felix the Governor.

1 And [1]Paul beheld earnestly the Council, and said, Men *and* brethren, I have in all good conscience served God until this day.

2 [1]Then the high Priest Ananias commanded them that stood by, to smite him on the mouth.

3 [1]Then said Paul to him, God [2]will smite thee, thou [3]whited wall: for thou sittest to judge me according to the Law, and [4]transgressing the Law,

CHAPTER 23
a Exod. 22:27
b Acts 14:22
  Phil. 3:5
c Matt. 22:23

commandest thou me to be smitten?

4 And they that stood by, said, Revilest thou God's high Priest?

5 [1]Then said Paul, I knew not brethren, that he was the high Priest: for it is written, [a]Thou shalt not speak evil of the ruler of thy people.

6 [1]But when Paul perceived that the one part were of the Sadducees, and the other of the Pharisees, he cried in the Council, Men *and* brethren, [b]I am a Pharisee, the son of a Pharisee: I am accused of the hope and resurrection of the dead.

7 [1]And when he had said this, there was a dissension between the Pharisees and the Sadducees, so that the multitude was divided.

8 [c,1]For the Sadducees say that there is no resurrection, neither [2]Angel, nor spirit: but the Pharisees confess both.

9 [1]Then there was a great cry: and the [2]Scribes of the Pharisees' part rose up, and strove, saying, We find none evil in this man: but if a spirit or an Angel hath spoken to him, let us not fight against God.

10 [1]And when there was a great dissension, the chief captain, fearing lest Paul should have been pulled in pieces of them, commanded the soldiers to go down, and take him from among them, and to bring him into the castle.

11 Now the night following, the Lord stood by him, and said, Be of good courage, Paul, for as thou hast testified of me in Jerusalem, so must thou bear witness also at Rome.

12 [1]And when the day was come, certain of the Jews made an assembly, and bound themselves [2]with a curse, saying, that they would neither eat nor drink till they had killed Paul.

13 And they were more than forty, which had made this conspiracy.

14 And they came to the chief Priests and Elders, and said, We have bound ourselves with a solemn curse, that we will eat nothing, until we have slain

---

22:25 [1] There is no cause why we may not use those lawful means which God giveth us, to repel, or put away an injury.

22:29 [1] Not by Nation, but by the law of his city.

23:1 [1] Paul against the false accusations of his enemies, setteth a good conscience, for proof whereof, he repeateth the whole course of his life.

23:2 [1] Hypocrites are constrained at length to betray themselves by their intemperance.

23:3 [1] It is lawful for us to complain of injuries, and to summon the wicked to the judgment seat of God, so that we do it without hatred, and with a quiet and peaceable mind.

[2] It appeareth plainly by the Greek plural, that Paul did not curse the high Priest, but only pronounce the punishment of God against him.

[3] This is a vehement and sharp speech, but yet not reproachful: For the godly may speak roundly, and yet be void of the bitter affection of a sharp and angry mind.

[4] For the Law commandeth the judge to hear the person that is accused patiently, and to pronounce the sentence advisedly.

23:5 [1] We must willingly and from the heart give honor to Magistrates, although they be tyrants.

23:6 [1] We may lawfully sometimes set the wicked together by the ears, that they may leave off to assault us, so that it be with no hindrance of the truth.

23:7 [1] The concord of the wicked is weak although they conspire together to oppress the truth.

23:8 [1] It is an old heresy of the Sadducees, to deny the substance of Angels and souls, and therewithall the resurrection of the dead.

[2] Natures that want bodies.

23:9 [1] The Lord when it pleaseth him, findeth defenders of his cause, even amongst his enemies.

[2] The Scribes' office was a public office, and the name of the Pharisees was the name of a sect.

23:10 [1] God will not forsake his to the end.

23:12 [1] Such as are carried away with a foolish zeal, think that they may lie and murder, and do whatsoever mischief they list.

[2] They cursing and banning themselves, promised.

Paul.

15 Now therefore, [1]ye and the Council, signify to the chief captain, that he bring him forth unto you tomorrow, as though you would know something more perfectly of him, and we, or ever he come near will be ready to kill him.

16 But when Paul's sister's son heard of their laying await, he went, and entered into the castle, and told Paul.

17 [1]And Paul called one of the Centurions unto him, and said, Take this young man hence unto the chief captain: for he hath a certain thing to show him.

18 So he took him, and brought him to the chief captain, and said, Paul the prisoner called me unto him, and prayed me to bring this young man unto thee, which hath something to say unto thee.

19 Then the chief captain took him by the hand, and went apart with him alone, and asked him, What hast thou to show me?

20 And he said, The Jews have conspired to desire thee, that thou wouldest bring forth Paul tomorrow into the Council, as though they would inquire somewhat of him more perfectly:

21 But let them not persuade thee: for there lie in wait for him of them, more than forty men, which have bound themselves with a curse, that they will neither eat nor drink, till they have killed him: and now are they ready, and wait for thy promise.

22 [1]The chief captain then let the young man depart, after he had charged him to utter it to no man, that he had [2]showed him these things.

23 And he called unto him two certain Centurions, saying, Make ready two hundred soldiers, that they may go to Caesarea, and horsemen threescore and ten, and two hundred with darts, at the third hour of the night:

24 And let them make ready an horse, that Paul being set on, may be brought safe unto Felix the governor.

25 And he wrote an Epistle in this manner:

26 [1]Claudius Lysias unto the most noble governor Felix sendeth greeting.

27 As this man was taken of the Jews, and should have been killed of them, I came upon them with a garrison, and rescued him, perceiving that he was a Roman.

28 And when I would have known the cause

wherefore they accused him, I brought him forth into their Council.

29 There I perceived that he was accused of questions of their Law, but had no crime worthy of death, or of bonds.

30 And when it was showed me, how that the Jews laid wait for the man, I sent him straightway to thee, and commanded his accusers to speak before thee the things that they had against him. Farewell.

31 Then the soldiers as it was commanded them, took Paul, and brought him by night to Antipatris,

32 And the next day, they left the horsemen to go with him, and returned into the Castle.

33 Now when they came to Caesarea, they delivered the Epistle to the governor, and presented Paul also unto him.

34 So when the Governor had read it, he asked of what province he was: and when he understood that he was of Cilicia,

35 I will hear thee, said he, when thine accusers also are come, and commanded him to be kept in Herod's judgment hall.

24

2 Tertullus accuseth Paul: 10 He answereth for himself: 21 He preacheth Christ to the governor and his wife. 26 Felix hopeth, but in vain, to receive a bribe, 27 who going from his office, leaveth Paul in prison.

1 Now [1]after five days, Ananias the high Priest came down with the Elders, and *with* Tertullus a certain orator, which appeared before the governor against Paul.

2 And when he was called forth, Tertullus began to accuse *him*, saying, Seeing that we have obtained great quietness [1]through thee, and that many [2]worthy things are done unto this nation through thy providence,

3 We acknowledge it wholly, and in all places, most noble Felix, with all thanks.

4 But that I be not tedious unto thee, I pray thee, that thou wouldest hear us of thy courtesy a few words.

5 Certainly we have found this man a [1]pestilent fellow, and a mover of sedition among all the Jews throughout the world, and a [2]chief maintainer of the sect of the [3]Nazarenes:

23:15 [1] Ye and the Senate requiring the same to be done, lest that the Tribune should think that it was demanded of him at some private man's suit.

23:17 [1] The wisdom of the Spirit must be joined with simplicity.

23:22 [1] There is no counsel against the Lord and his servants.

  [2] Greek, that thou hast showed these things to me.

23:26 [1] Lysias is suddenly made by the Lord Paul's patron.

24:1 [1] Hypocrites, when they cannot do what they would do by force and deceit, at length they go about to compass it by a show of Law.

24:2 [1] Felix ruled that province with great cruelty and covetousness,

and yet Josephus recordeth that he did many worthy things, as that he took Eleazar the captain of certain cutthroats, and put that deceiving wretch the Egyptian to flight, which caused great troubles in Judea.

  [2] He useth a word which the Stoics defined to be a perfect duty and behavior.

24:5 [1] Word for word, a plague.

  [2] As you would say, a ringleader, or ensign bearer.

  [3] So they called the Christians scoffingly of the town's name where they thought that Christ was born, whereupon it came that Julian the Apostate called him Galilean.

6 And hath gone about to pollute the Temple: therefore we took him, and would have judged him according to our Law:

7 But the chief captain Lysias came upon us, and with great violence took him out of our hands,

8 Commanding his accusers to come to thee: of whom thou mayest (if thou wilt inquire) know all these things whereof we accuse him.

9 And the Jews likewise [1]affirmed, saying that it was so.

10 [1]Then Paul, after that the governor had beckoned unto him that he should speak, answered, I do the more gladly answer for myself, forasmuch as I know that [2]thou hast been oft many years a judge unto this nation,

11 Seeing that thou mayest know, that there are but twelve days since I came up to worship in Jerusalem.

12 And they neither found me in the Temple, disputing with any man, neither making uproar among the people, neither in the Synagogues, nor in the city.

13 Neither can they [1]prove the things, whereof they now accuse me.

14 [1]But this I confess unto thee, that after the way (which they call [2]heresy) so worship I the God of my fathers, believing all things which are written in the Law and the Prophets,

15 And have hope towards God, that the resurrection of the dead, which they themselves look for also, shall be both of just and unjust.

16 And herein I endeavor myself to have always a clear conscience toward God and toward men.

17 [1]Now after many years, I came and brought alms to my nation and offerings,

18 At [1]what time, certain Jews of [2]Asia found me purified in the Temple, neither with multitude, nor with tumult.

19 Who ought to have been present before thee, and accuse *me*, if they had ought against me.

20 Or let these themselves say, if they have found any unjust thing in me, while I stood in the [1]Council,

21 Except *it be* for this one voice, that I cried standing among them, Of the resurrection of the dead am I accused of you this day.

22 [1]Now when Felix heard these things, he deferred them, and said, When I shall more [2]perfectly know the things which concern this way, by the coming of Lysias the chief Captain, I will decide your matter.

23 [1]Then he commanded a Centurion to keep Paul, and that he should have ease, and that he should forbid none of his acquaintance to minister unto him, or to come unto him.

24 ¶ And after certain days, came Felix with his wife [1]Drusilla, which was a Jewess, *and* he called forth Paul, and heard him of the faith in Christ.

25 And as he disputed of righteousness and temperance, and of the judgment to come, Felix trembled, and answered, Go thy way for this time, and when I have convenient time, I will call for thee.

26 He hoped also that money should have been given him of Paul, that he might loose him: wherefore he sent for him the oftener, and communed with him.

27 [1]When two years were expired, Porcius Festus came into Felix's room, and Felix willing to [2]get favor of the Jews, left Paul bound.

25 *1 Festus succeeding Felix, 6 commandeth Paul to be brought forth. 11 Paul appealeth unto Caesar. 14 Festus openeth Paul's matter to king Agrippa, 23 and*

24:9 [1] Confirmed Tertullus's saying.
24:10 [1] Tertullus by the devil's rhetoric beginneth with flattery, maketh an end with lies: but Paul using heavenly eloquence, and but a simple beginning casteth off from himself the crime of sedition, wherewith he was burdened, with a simple denial.
[2] Paul pleaded his cause two years before Felix departed out of the province, Acts 27, but he had governed Trachonite, and Batanea, and Galavnite, before that Claudius made him governor of Judea: Josephus in the *History of the Jewish War*, lib. 2, chap. 11.
24:13 [1] They cannot lay forth before thee and prove by good reasons.
24:14 [1] Paul goeth in the cause of Religion from a state conjectural to a state of quality not only not denying that objected against him, but also proving it to be true, to be heavenly and from God, and to be the oldest of all religions.
[2] Here this word, Heresy, or sect, is taken in good part.
24:17 [1] Paul in conclusion telleth the thing which was done, truly, which Tertullus had before divers ways corrupted.
24:18 [1] And while I was busy about those things.
[2] Hereby it appeareth that these of Asia were Saul's enemies, and those that stirred up the people against him.
24:20 [1] Whither the Tribune brought me.

24:22 [1] The Judge suspendeth his sentence, because the matter is doubtful.
[2] Felix could not judge whether he had done wickedly in the matters of his religion or no, until he had better understanding of that way which Paul professed: and as for other matters touching the sedition, he thinketh good to defer it till he hears Lysias, and therefore he gave Paul somewhat more liberty.
24:23 [1] God is a most faithful keeper of his servants, and the force of the truth is wonderful, even amongst men which are otherwise profane.
24:24 [1] This Drusilla was Agrippa's sister, of whom Luke speaketh afterward, a very harlot and licentious woman, and being the wife of Azizus king of the Emesens, who was circumcised, departed from him, and went to Felix, the brother of one Pallas, who was sometime Nero's bondman.
24:27 [1] In a naughty mind that is guilty to itself, although, sometimes there be some show of equity, yet by and by, it will be extinguished: but in the mean season we have need to patience, and that continual.
[2] For whereas he had behaved himself very wickedly in the province, had it not been for favor of his brother Pallas, he should have died for it: so that we may gather hereby why he would have pleasured the Jews.

bringeth him before him,   27 that he may understand his cause.

1 When ¹Festus was then come into the province, after three days he went up from Caesarea unto Jerusalem.

2 Then the high Priest, and the chief of the Jews appeared before him against Paul: and they besought him,

3 And desired favor against him, that he would send for him to Jerusalem: and they laid wait to kill him by the way.

4 But Festus answered, that Paul should be kept at Caesarea, and that he himself would shortly depart thither.

5 Let them therefore, said he, which among you are able, come down with us: and if there be any wickedness in the man, let them accuse him.

6 ¶ ¹Now when he had tarried among them no more than ten days, he went down to Caesarea, and the next day sat in the judgment seat, and commanded Paul to be brought.

7 And when he was come, the Jews which were come from Jerusalem, stood about him and laid many and grievous complaints against Paul, whereof ¹they could make no plain proof,

8 Forasmuch as he answered, that he had neither offended anything against the law of the Jews, neither against the temple, nor against Caesar.

9 ¹Yet Festus willing to get favor of the Jews, answered Paul and said, Wilt thou go up to Jerusalem, and there be judged of these things before me?

10 Then said Paul, I stand at Caesar's judgment seat, where I ought to be judged: to the Jews I have done no wrong, as thou very well knowest.

11 For if I have done wrong, or committed anything worthy of death, I refuse not to die: but if there be none of these things, whereof they accuse me, no man, to pleasure them, can deliver me to them: I appeal unto Caesar.

12 Then when Festus had spoken with the Council, he answered, Hast thou appealed unto Caesar? unto Caesar shalt thou go.

13 ¶ ¹And after certain days, King ²Agrippa and Bernice came down to Caesarea to salute Festus.

14 And when they had remained there many days, Festus declared Paul's cause unto the king, saying, There is a certain man left in prison by Felix,

15 Of whom when I came to Jerusalem, the high Priests and Elders of the Jews informed me, and desired to have judgment against him.

16 To whom I answered, that it is not the manner of the Romans for favor to ¹deliver any man to the death, before that he which is accused, have the accusers before him, and have place to defend himself, concerning the crime.

17 Therefore when they were come hither, without delay the day following I sat on the judgment seat, and commanded the man to be brought forth.

18 Against whom when the accusers stood up, they brought no crime of such things as I supposed:

19 ¹But had certain questions against him of their own ²superstitions, and of one Jesus which was dead, whom Paul affirmed to be alive.

20 And because I doubted of such manner of question, I asked him whether he would go to Jerusalem, and there be judged of these things.

21 But because he appealed to be reserved to the examination of Augustus, I commanded him to be kept, till I might send him to Caesar.

22 ¹Then Agrippa said unto Festus, I would also hear the man myself. Tomorrow, said he, thou shalt hear him.

23 And on the morrow when Agrippa was come, and Bernice with great ¹pomp, and were entered into the Common hall with the chief captains and chief men of the city, at Festus's commandment Paul was brought forth.

24 And Festus said, King Agrippa, and all men which are present with us, ye see this man, about whom all the multitude of the Jews have called upon me, both at Jerusalem, and here, crying, that he ought not to live any longer.

25 Yet have I found nothing worthy of death, that he hath committed: nevertheless, seeing that he hath appealed to Augustus, I have determined to send him.

25:1 ¹ Satan's Ministers are subtle and diligent in seeking all occasions: but God who watcheth for his, hindereth all their counsels easily.
25:6 ¹ We may repel an injury justly, but not with injury.
25:7 ¹ They could not prove them certainly and with undoubted reasons.
25:9 ¹ God doth not only turn away the counsel of the wicked, but also turneth it upon their own heads.
25:13 ¹ Festus thinking no such thing, even before kings, bringing to light the wickedness of the Jews, and Paul's innocence, doth marvelously confirm the Church of God.
² This Agrippa was Agrippa's son, whose death Luke spake of before, and Bernice was his sister.
25:16 ¹ The Romans used not to deliver any man to be punished before, etc.
25:19 ¹ The profane and wicked take an occasion to condemn the true doctrine by reason of private controversies and contentions of men betwixt themselves: but the truth nevertheless abideth in the mean season safe and sure.
² This profane man calleth the Jews' religion, superstition, and that before king Agrippa, but no marvel: for the rulers of provinces by reason of the majesty of the empire of Rome, used to prefer themselves before kings.
25:22 ¹ That is fulfilled in Paul, which the Lord before had told to Ananias of him, Acts 9:15.
25:23 ¹ Gorgeously like a Prince.

26 Of whom I have no certain thing to write unto my [1]lord: wherefore I have brought him forth unto you, and especially unto thee, King Agrippa, that after examination had, I might have somewhat to write.

27 For me thinketh it unreasonable to send a prisoner, and not to show the causes which are *laid* against him.

26

2 Paul in the presence of Agrippa, 4 declareth his life from his childhood, 16 and his calling, 21 with such efficacy of words 28 that almost he persuaded him to Christianity. 30 But he and his company depart doing nothing in Paul's matter.

1 Then Agrippa said unto Paul, Thou art permitted to speak for thyself. So Paul stretched forth the hand, and answered for himself.

2 [1]I think myself happy, King Agrippa, because I shall answer this day before thee of all the things whereof I am accused of the Jews:

3 Chiefly, because thou hast knowledge of all customs, and questions which are among the Jews: wherefore I beseech thee to hear me patiently.

4 [1]As touching my life from *my* childhood, and what it was from the beginning among mine own nation at Jerusalem, know all the Jews,

5 Which [1]knew me heretofore, even from my [2]Elders (if they would testify) that after the [3]most straight sect of our religion, I lived a Pharisee.

6 [1]And now I stand and am accused for the hope of the promise made of God unto our fathers.

7 Whereunto our twelve tribes instantly serving *God* day and night, hope to come: for the which hope's sake, O King Agrippa, I am accused of the Jews.

8 [1]Why should it be thought a thing incredible unto you, that God should raise again the dead?

9 I also verily thought in myself, that I ought to do many contrary things against the Name of Jesus of Nazareth.

10 [a]Which thing I also did in Jerusalem: for many of the Saints I shut up in prison, having received authority of the High Priests, and when they were

CHAPTER 26
[a] Acts 8:3
[b] Acts 9:2
[c] Acts 9:22, 26
Acts 13:4
[d] Acts 21:30

put to death, I gave *my* [1]sentence.

11 And I punished them throughout all the Synagogues, and [1]compelled them to blaspheme and being more mad against them, I persecuted them, even unto strange cities.

12 At which time, even as I went to [b]Damascus with authority, and commission from the high Priests,

13 At midday, O king, I saw in the way a light from heaven passing the brightness of the sun, shine round about me, and them which went with me.

14 So when we were all fallen to the earth, I heard a voice speaking unto me, and saying in the Hebrew tongue, Saul, Saul, why persecutest thou me? It is hard for thee to kick against pricks.

15 Then I said, Who art thou, Lord? And he said, I am Jesus whom thou persecutest.

16 But rise and stand up on thy feet: for I have appeared unto thee for this purpose to appoint thee a minister and a witness, both of the things which thou hast seen, and of the things in the which I will appear unto thee,

17 Delivering thee from this people, and from the Gentiles, unto whom now I send thee,

18 [1]To open their eyes, that they may turn from darkness to light, and from the power of Satan unto God, that they may receive forgiveness of sins, and inheritance among them, which are sanctified by faith in me.

19 [1]Wherefore, King Agrippa, I was not disobedient unto the heavenly vision,

20 [c]But showed first unto them of Damascus, and at Jerusalem, and throughout all the coasts of Judea, and *then* to the Gentiles, that they should repent and turn to God, and do works worthy amendment of life.

21 For this cause the Jews caught me in the [d]Temple, and went about to kill me.

22 [1]Nevertheless, I obtained help of God, and continue unto this day, witnessing both to [2]small and to great, saying none other things, than those which the Prophets and Moses did say should come,

23 *To wit*, that Christ should [1]suffer, and that he

25:26 [1] To Augustus. Good Princes refused this name at the first, to wit, to be called Lords, but afterwards they admitted it, as we read of Traianus.
26:2 [1] To have a skillful judge, is a great and singular gift of God.
26:4 [1] Paul divideth the history of his life into two times: for the first [he] calleth his adversaries witnesses: for the latter, the fathers and prophets.
26:5 [1] What I was, and where, and how I lived.
[2] That my parents were Pharisees.
[3] The sect of the Pharisees was the most exquisite amongst all the sects of the Jews, for it was better than all the rest.
26:6 [1] There are three chief and principal witnesses of true doctrine, God, the true Fathers, and the consent of the Church.
26:8 [1] He proveth the resurrection of the dead, first by the power

of God, then by the resurrection of Christ: whereof he is a sufficient witness.
26:10 [1] I consented to, and allowed of their doing: for he was not a judge.
26:11 [1] By extreme punishment.
26:18 [1] The end of the Gospel is to save them which are brought to the knowledge of Christ, and are justified and sanctified in him being laid hold on by faith.
26:19 [1] Paul allegeth God to be author of the office of his Apostleship, and his grace as a witness.
26:22 [1] Christ is the end of the Law and the Prophets.
[2] To everyone.
26:23 [1] That Christ should not be such a king as the Jews dreamed of, but one appointed to bear our miseries, and the punishment of our sins.

should be the ²first that should rise from the dead, and should show ³light unto this people, and to the Gentiles.

24 ¹And as he thus answered for himself, Festus said with a loud voice, Paul, thou art beside thyself, much learning doth make thee mad.

25 But he said, I am not mad, O noble Festus, but I speak the words of truth, and soberness.

26 For the king knoweth of these things, before whom also I speak boldly: for I am persuaded that none of these things are hidden from him: for this thing was [not] done in a ¹corner.

27 ¹O King Agrippa, believest thou the Prophets? I know that thou believest.

28 Then Agrippa said unto Paul, Almost thou persuadest me to become a Christian.

29 Then Paul said, ¹I would to God that [not] only thou, but also all that hear me today, were both almost, and altogether such as I am, except these bonds.

30 ¹And when he had thus spoken, the king rose up, and the governor, and Bernice, and they that sat with them.

31 And when they were gone apart, they talked between themselves, saying, This man doeth nothing worthy of death, nor of bonds.

32 Then said Agrippa unto Festus, This man might have been loosed, if he had not appealed unto Caesar.

27

1 Paul   7, 9 foretelleth the peril of the voyage,   11 but he is not believed.   14 They are tossed to and fro with the tempest,   22, 41 and suffer shipwreck: 34 Yet all safe and sound   44 escape to land.

1 Now ¹when it was concluded, that we should sail into Italy, they delivered both Paul, and certain other prisoners unto a Centurion, named Julius, of the band of Augustus.

2 And ªwe entered into a ship of Adramyttium, purposing to sail by the coasts of Asia, and launched forth, and had Aristarchus of Macedonia, a Thes-

CHAPTER 27
ª 2 Cor. 11:15

salonian, with us.

3 And the next day we arrived at Sidon: and Julius courteously entreated Paul, and gave him liberty to go unto his friends, that they might refresh him.

4 And from thence we launched, and sailed hard by Cyprus, because the winds were contrary.

5 Then sailed we over the sea by Cilicia, and Pamphilia, and came to Myra, a city in Lycia.

6 And there the Centurion found a ship of Alexandria, sailing into Italy, and put us therein.

7 And when we had sailed slowly many days, and scarce were come against Cnidus, because the wind suffered us not, we sailed hard by Candia, near to ¹Salmone,

8 And with much ado sailed beyond it, and came unto a certain place called the Fair Havens, near unto the which was the city Lasea.

9 ¹So when much time was spent, and sailing was now jeopardous, because also the ²Fast was now passed, Paul exhorted them,

10 And said unto them, Sirs, I see that this voyage will be with hurt, and much damage, not of the lading and ship only, but also of our lives.

11 ¹Nevertheless the Centurion believed rather the governor and the master of the ship, than those things which were spoken of Paul.

12 And because the haven was not commodious to winter in, many took counsel to depart thence, if by any means they might attain to Phoenix, there to winter, which is an haven of Crete, and lieth toward the Southwest and by West, and Northwest and by West.

13 And when the Southern wind blew softly, they supposing to attain their purpose, loosed nearer, and sailed by Crete.

14 But anon after, there arose by ¹it a stormy wind called ²Euroclydon.

15 And when the ship was caught, and could not resist the wind, we let her go, and were carried away.

16 And we ran under a little Isle named Clauda,

26:23 ² The first of them which are raised from the dead.
³ Life, yea, and that a most blessed life which shall be endless: and this is set against darkness, which almost in all tongues signifieth sometimes death, and sometimes misery and calamity.
26:24 ¹ The wisdom of God is madness to fools, yet notwithstanding we must boldly avouch the truth.
26:26 ¹ Secretly, and privately.
26:27 ¹ Paul as it were forgetting himself that he stood a prisoner to defend his cause, he forgetteth not the office of his Apostleship.
26:29 ¹ I would to God that not only almost, but thoroughly and altogether both thou and all that hear me this day, might be made as I am, my bonds only except.
26:30 ¹ Paul is solemnly quit, and yet not dismissed.
27:1 ¹ Paul with many other prisoners, and through the midst of many deaths, is brought to Rome, but yet by God's own hand as it

were, and set forth and commended unto the world with many singular testimonies.
27:7 ¹ Which was an high hill of Candia.
27:9 ¹ God's providence taketh not away the causes which God useth as means, but rather ordereth and disposeth their right use even then when he openeth an extraordinary issue.
² This is meant of the Jews' fast, which they keep in the feast of expiation, as we read Lev. 23:27, which fell in the seventh month which we call October, and is not good for navigation, or sailing.
27:11 ¹ Men cast themselves willingly into an infinite sort of dangers, when they choose to follow their own wisdom, rather than God speaking by the mouth of his servants.
27:14 ¹ By Candia, from whose shore our ship was driven by that means.
² Northeast wind.

and had much ado to get the boat.

17 Which they took up and used all help, undergirding the ship, fearing lest they should have fallen into Syrtis, and they strake sail, and so were carried.

18 [1]The next day when we were tossed with an exceeding tempest, they lightened the ship.

19 And the third day we cast out with our own hands the tackling of the ship.

20 And when neither sun nor stars in many days appeared, and no small tempest lay upon us, all hope that we should be saved, was then taken away.

21 [1]But after long abstinence, Paul stood forth in the midst of them, and said, Sirs, ye should have hearkened to me, and not have loosed from Candia: so should ye have gained this hurt and loss.

22 But now I exhort you to be of good courage: for there shall be no loss of any man's life among you, save of the ship only.

23 For there stood by me this night the Angel of God, whose I am, and whom I serve.

24 Saying, Fear not, Paul: for thou must be brought before Caesar: and lo, God hath given unto thee freely, all that sail with thee.

25 [1]Wherefore, Sirs, be of good courage: for I believe God, that it shall be so as it hath been told me.

26 Howbeit, we must be cast into a certain Island.

27 [1]And when the fourteenth night was come, as we were carried to and fro in the [2]Adriatic *sea* about midnight, the shipmen deemed that some country [3]approached unto them.

28 And sounded, and found it twenty fathoms: and when they had gone a little further, they sounded again, and found fifteen fathoms.

29 Then fearing lest they should have fallen into some rough places, they cast four anchors out of the stern, and wished that the day were come.

30 [1]Now as the mariners were about to flee out of the ship, and had let down the boat into the sea

under a color as though they would have cast anchors out of the foreship.

31 [1]Paul said unto the Centurion and the soldiers, Except these abide in the ship, ye cannot be safe.

32 Then the soldiers cut off the ropes of the boat, and let it fall away.

33 [1]And when it began to be day, Paul exhorted them all to take meat, saying, This is the fourteenth day that ye have tarried, and continued fasting, receiving nothing:

34 Wherefore I exhort you to take meat: for this is for your safeguard: for there shall not an [1]hair fall from the head of any of you.

35 And when he had thus spoken, he took bread, and gave thanks to God in presence of them all, and brake it, and began to eat.

36 Then were they all of good courage, and they also took meat.

37 Now we were in the ship in all two hundred threescore and sixteen souls.

38 And when they had eaten enough, they lightened the ship, and cast out the wheat into the sea.

39 [1]And when it was day, they knew not the country, but they spied a certain [2]creek with a bank, into the which they were minded (if it were possible) to thrust in the ship.

40 So when they had taken up the anchors, they committed *the ship* unto the sea, and loosed the rudder bonds, and hoisted up the main sail to the wind, and drew to the shore.

41 And when they fell into a place, where [1]two seas met, they thrust in the ship: and the forepart stuck fast, and could not be moved, but the hinder part was broken with the violence of the waves.

42 [1]Then the soldiers' counsel was to kill the prisoners, lest any of them, when he had swam out, should flee away.

43 [1]But the Centurion willing to save Paul, stayed them from *this* counsel, and commanded that they that could swim, should cast themselves first into the sea, and go out to land:

27:18 [1] The end proveth that none provide worse for themselves, than they which commit themselves to be governed only by their own wisdom.

27:21 [1] God spareth the wicked for a time, for his elect and chosen's sake.

27:25 [1] The promise is made effectual through faith.

27:27 [1] We attain and come to the promised and sure salvation through the midst of tempests and death itself.

[2] For Ptolemy writeth, that the Adriatic Sea beateth upon the East shore of Cilicia.

[3] That they drew near to some country.

27:30 [1] There is none so foul an act, whereupon distrust and an evil conscience do not enforce men.

27:31 [1] Although the performing of God's promises doth not simply depend upon second causes, yet they make themselves unworthy of

God's bountifulness, which do not embrace those means which God offereth them, either upon rashness or distrust.

27:33 [1] When the world trembleth, the faithful alone be not only quiet, but confirm others by their example.

27:34 [1] This is a proverb which the Hebrews use, whereby is meant, that they shall be safe, and not one of them perish.

27:39 [1] Then are tempests most of all to be feared and looked for, when the port or haven is nearest.

[2] A creek is a sea within land, as the Adriatic Sea, and the Persian Sea.

27:41 [1] So is Isthmus called, because the sea toucheth it on both sides.

27:42 [1] There is nowhere more unfaithfulness and unthankfulness than in unbelievers.

27:43 [1] God findeth even amongst his enemies them whose help he useth to preserve his.

44 ¹And the others, some on boards, and some on certain *pieces* of the ship: and so it came to pass, that they came all safe to land.

28

2 The Barbarians' courtesy towards Paul and his company.   3 A viper on Paul's hand: 6 He shaketh it off without harm: 8 Publius   9 and others are by him healed.   11 They depart from Malta,   16 and come to Rome.   17 Paul openeth to the Jews,   20 the cause of his coming: 22 He preacheth Jesus   30 two years.

1   And when they were come safe, then they knew that the Isle was called ¹Malta.

2   And the Barbarians showed us no little kindness, for they kindled a fire, and received us everyone, because of the present shower, and because of the cold.

3   ¹And when Paul had gathered a number of sticks, and laid them on the fire, there came a viper out of the heat, and leaped on his hand.

4   ¹Now when the Barbarians saw the worm hang on his hand, they said among themselves, This man surely is a murderer, whom, though he hath escaped the sea, yet ²Vengeance hath not suffered to live.

5   But he shook off the worm into the fire, and felt no harm.

6   Howbeit they waited when he should have ¹swollen, or fallen down dead suddenly: ²but after they had looked a great while, and saw no inconvenience come to him, they changed their minds, and said, That he was a God.

7   ¹In the same quarters, the chief man of the Isle (whose name was Publius) had possessions: the same received us, and lodged us three days courteously.

8   And so it was, that the father of Publius lay sick of the fever, and of a bloody flix: to whom Paul entered in, and when he prayed, he laid *his* hands on him, and healed him.

9   ¹When this then was done, others also in the Isle, which had diseases, came to him, and were healed,

10   ¹Which also did us great honor: and when we departed, they laded us with things necessary.

11   ¶ ¹Now after three months we departed in a ship of Alexandria, which had wintered in the Isle, whose ²badge was Castor and Pollux.

12   And when we arrived at Syracuse, we tarried *there* three days.

13   And from thence we set a compass, and came to Rhegium: and after one day, the South wind blew, and we came the second day to Puteoli:

14   ¹Where we found brethren, and were desired to tarry with them seven days, and so we went toward Rome.

15   ¶ ¹And from thence when the brethren heard of us, they came to meet us at the ²Market of Appius, and at the three taverns, whom when Paul saw, he thanked God, and waxed bold.

16   So when we came to Rome, the Centurion delivered the prisoners to the general Captain: but Paul was suffered to dwell by ¹himself with a soldier that kept him.

17   ¹And the third day after, Paul calleth the chief of the Jews together, and when they were come, he said unto them, Men *and* brethren, though I have committed nothing against the people, or Laws of the fathers, *yet* was I delivered prisoner from Jerusalem into the hands of the Romans.

18   Who when they had examined me, would have let me go, because there was no cause of death in me.

19   ¹But when the Jews spake contrary, I was constrained to appeal unto Caesar, not because I had ought to accuse my nation of.

20   For this cause therefore have I called for you to see *you*, and to speak with *you*: for that hope of Israel's sake, I am bound with this chain.

21   Then they said unto him, We neither received letters out of Judea concerning thee, neither came any of the brethren that showed or spake any evil

---

27:44 ¹ The goodness of God overcometh man's malice.
28:1 ¹ That is it which at this day we call Malta.
28:3 ¹ The godly are sure to have danger upon danger, but they have always a glorious issue.
28:4 ¹ Although adversity be the punishment of sin, yet seeing that God in punishing of men doth not always respect sin, they judge rashly, which either do not wait for the end, or do judge and esteem of men according to prosperity or adversity.
   ² Right and reason.
28:6 ¹ The Greek word signifieth, to be inflamed, or to swell: moreover Dioscorides in book 6, chap. 38, witnesseth, that the biting of a viper causeth a swelling of the body, and so saith Nicander, in his remedies against poisons.
   ² There is nothing more unconstant, every way, than they which are ignorant of true religion.
28:7 ¹ It never yet repented any man, that received the servant of God, were he never so miserable and poor.
28:9 ¹ Although Paul were a captive, yet the virtue of God was not

captive.
28:10 ¹ God doeth well to strangers for his children's sake.
28:11 ¹ Idols do not defile the Saints, which do in no wise consent unto them.
   ² So they used to deck the forepart of their ships, whereupon the ships were called by such names.
28:14 ¹ God boweth and bendeth the hearts even of profane men, as it pleaseth him to favor his.
28:15 ¹ God never suffereth his to be afflicted above their strength.
   ² Appius way, was a pavement made by Appius the blind with the help of his soldiers, long and broad, and running out toward the sea, and there were three taverns in it.
28:16 ¹ Not in a common prison, but in a house which he hired for himself.
28:17 ¹ Paul in every place remembereth himself to be an Apostle.
28:19 ¹ We may use the means which God giveth us, but so that we seek the glory of God, and not ourselves.

of thee.

22 But we will hear of thee what thou thinkest: for as concerning this sect, we know that everywhere it is spoken against.

23 ¹And when they had appointed him a day, there came many unto him into *his* lodging, to whom he expounded, ²testifying the kingdom of God, and persuading them those things that concern Jesus, both out of the Law of Moses, and out of the Prophets, from morning to night.

24 ¹And some were [persuaded] with the things which were spoken, and some believed not.

25 Therefore when they agreed not among themselves, they departed, after that Paul had spoken one word, *to wit*, Well spake the holy Ghost by Isaiah the Prophet unto our fathers,

26 ¹Saying, "Go unto this people, and say, By hearing ye shall hear, and shall not understand, and

CHAPTER 28
ᵃ Isa. 6:9
Matt. 13:14
Mark 14:12
Luke 8:10
John 12:40
Rom. 11:8

seeing ye shall see, and not perceive.

27 For the heart of this people is waxed fat, and their ears are dull of hearing, and with their eyes have they ¹winked, lest they should see with *their* eyes, and hear with *their* ears, and understand with *their* hearts, and should return that I might heal them.

28 ¹Be it known therefore unto you, that this salvation of God is sent to the Gentiles, and they shall hear it.

29 ¹And when he had said these things, the Jews departed, and had great reasoning among themselves.

30 ¹And Paul remained two years full in an house hired for himself, and received all that came in unto him,

31 Preaching the kingdom of God, and teaching those things which concern the Lord Jesus Christ, with all boldness of speech, without let.

28:23 ¹ The law and the Gospel agree well together.
   ² By good reasons, and proved that the kingdom of God foretold them by the Prophets, was come.
28:24 ¹ The Gospel is a savor of life to them that believe, and a savor of death to them that be disobedient.
28:26 ¹ The unbelievers do willingly resist the truth, and yet not by chance.

28:27 ¹ They made as though they saw not that which they saw against their wills: yea they did see, but they would not see.
28:28 ¹ The unbelief of the reprobate and castaways cannot cause the truth of God to be of none effect.
28:29 ¹ Not the Gospel, but the contempt of the Gospel is the cause of strife and debate.
28:30 ¹ The word of God cannot be bound.

THE EPISTLE OF THE APOSTLE
PAUL TO THE
ROMANS

1 1 *He first showeth on what authority his Apostleship standeth.* 15 *Then he commendeth the Gospel,* 16 *by which God setteth out his power to those that are saved,* 17 *by faith,* 21 *but were guilty of wicked unthankfulness to God:* 26 *For which his wrath was worthily powered on them,* 29 *so that they ran headlong to all kinds of sin.*

1 PAUL ¹a ²,³servant of JESUS Christ called *to be* an ⁴Apostle, ᵃ,⁵put apart *to preach* the Gospel of God,

2 (Which he had promised afore by his Prophets in the holy Scriptures)

3 ¹Concerning his ²Son Jesus Christ our Lord (which was ³made of the seed of David ⁴according to the flesh,

4 And ¹declared ²mightily *to be* the Son of God, touching the Spirit of sanctification by the resurrection from the dead)

5 ¹By whom we have received ²grace and Apostleship (that ³obedience might be given unto the faith) for his name ⁴among all the Gentiles,

6 Among whom ye be also the ¹called of Jesus Christ:

7 To all *you* that be at Rome beloved of God,

CHAPTER 1
ᵃ Acts 13:1

called *to be* Saints: ¹Grace *be* with you, and peace from God our Father, and *from* the Lord Jesus Christ.

8 ¹First I thank my God through Jesus Christ for you all, because your faith is ²published throughout the ³whole world.

9 For God is my witness (whom I serve in my ¹spirit in the ²Gospel of his Son) that without ceasing I make mention of you.

10 Always in my prayers, beseeching that by some means, one time or other I might have a prosperous journey by the will of God, to come unto you.

11 For I long to see you, that I might bestow among you some spiritual gift, that you might be strengthened:

12 That is, that ¹I might be comforted together with you, through *our* mutual faith, both yours and mine.

13 Now my brethren, I would that ye should not be ignorant, how that I have oftentimes purposed to come unto you (but have been let hitherto) that I might have some fruit also among you, as I *have* among the other Gentiles.

14 I am debtor both to the Grecians, and to the Barbarians, both to the wise men and to the unwise.

1:1 ¹ The first part of the Epistle containing a most profitable preface unto verse 16.

² He moving the Romans to give diligent ear unto him in that he showeth that he cometh not in his own name, but as God's messenger unto the Gentiles, entreateth with them of the weightiest matter, that is promised long since by God, by many fit witnesses, and now at length performed indeed.

³ A Minister, for this word servant, is not taken in this place, as set against this word, Freeman, but declareth his ministry and office.

⁴ Whereas he said before in a general term, that he was a minister, now he cometh to a more special name, and saith that he is an Apostle, and that he took not upon him this office of his own lead, but being called of God, and therefore in this his writing to the Romans, doeth nothing but his duty.

⁵ Appointed of God to preach the Gospel.

1:3 ¹ By declaring the sum of the doctrine of the Gospel, he stirreth up the Romans to good consideration of the matter whereof he entreateth: So then he showeth that Christ (who is the very substance and sum of the Gospel) is the only son of God the Father, who as touching his humanity, is made of the seed of David, but touching his divine and spiritual nature, whereby he sanctified himself, is begotten of the Father from everlasting, as by his mighty resurrection manifestly appeareth.

² This is a plain testimony of the person of Christ, that he is but one,

and of his two natures, and their properties.

³ Which took flesh of the virgin, David's daughter.

⁴ As he is man: for this word Flesh, by the figure Synecdoche, is taken for man.

1:4 ¹ Showed and made manifest.

² The divine and mighty power is set against the weakness of the flesh, for that overcame death.

1:5 ¹ Of whom.

² This marvelous liberal and gracious gift, which is given me, the least of all the Saints, to preach, etc., Eph. 3:8.

³ That men through faith might obey God.

⁴ For his Name's sake.

1:6 ¹ Which through God's goodness, are Christ's.

1:7 ¹ God's free good will: by peace, the Hebrews mean a prosperous success in all things.

1:8 ¹ He procureth their favorable patience, in that he reckoneth up their true commendation, and his true Apostolic good will toward them, confirmed by taking God himself to witness.

² Because your faith is such, that it is commended in all Churches.

³ In all Churches.

1:9 ¹ Very willingly and with all my heart.

² In preaching his Son.

1:12 ¹ Though Paul were never so excellent, yet by teaching the Church, he might be instructed by it.

15 Therefore, as much as in me is, I am ready to preach the Gospel to you also that are at [1]Rome.

16 For I am not ashamed of the Gospel of Christ: [1]for it is the [2]power of God unto salvation to everyone that believeth, to the Jew first, and also to the [3]Grecian.

17 [1]For by it the righteousness of God is revealed from [2]faith to faith: [3]as it is written, [b]The just shall live by faith.

18 [1]For the wrath of God is revealed from heaven against [2]all ungodliness, and unrighteousness of men, which withhold the [3]truth in unrighteousness.

19 [1]Forasmuch as that, which may be known of God, is manifest in [2]them, for God hath showed it unto them.

20 For the invisible things of him, that is, his eternal power and Godhead, are seen by the creation of the world, being [1]considered in *his* works, to the intent that they should be without excuse:

21 Because that when they knew God, they [1]glorified him not as God, neither were thankful, but became [2]vain in their thoughts, and their foolish heart was full of darkness.

22 When they [1]professed themselves to be wise, they became fools.

23 For they turned the glory of the [1]incorruptible God to the similitude of the image of a corruptible man, and of birds, and four footed beasts, and of creeping things.

24 [1]Wherefore [2]also God [3]gave them up to their

[b] Hab. 2:4

hearts lusts, unto uncleanness, to defile their own bodies between themselves:

25 Which turned the truth of God unto a lie, and worshipped and served the creature, forsaking the Creator which is blessed forever, Amen.

26 For this cause God gave them up to vile affections: for even their women did change the natural use into that which is against nature.

27 And likewise also the men left the natural use of the woman, and burned in their lust one toward another, and man with man wrought filthiness, and received in themselves such [1]recompense of their error, as was meet.

28 [1]For as they regarded not to acknowledge God, *even so* God delivered them up unto a [2]reprobate mind, to do those things which are not convenient,

29 Being full of all unrighteousness, fornication, wickedness, covetousness, maliciousness, full of envy, of murder, of debate, of deceit, taking all things in the evil part, whisperers,

30 Backbiters, haters of God, doers of wrong, proud, boasters, inventors of evil things, disobedient to parents, without understanding, [1]covenant breakers, without natural affection, such as can never be appeased, merciless.

31 Which men, though they knew the [1]Law of God, how that they which commit such things are worthy of death, *yet* not only do the same, but also [2]favor them that do them.

1:15 [1] He meaneth all them that dwelt in Rome, though some of them were not Romans, see the end of the epistle.

1:16 [1] The second part of the Epistle unto the beginning of Chap. 9. Now the whole end and purpose of the disputation is this: that is to say: to show that there is but one way to attain unto salvation (which is set forth unto us of God in the Gospel, without any difference of nations) and that is Jesus Christ apprehended by faith.

[2] God's mighty and effectual instrument to save men by.

[3] When this word Grecian, is set against this word Jew, then doth it signify a Gentile.

1:17 [1] The confirmation of the former proposition: we are taught in the Gospel that we are justified before God by faith which increaseth daily: and therefore also saved.

[2] From faith which increaseth daily.

[3] The proof as well of the first as the second proposition, out of Habakkuk, who attributeth and giveth unto faith both justice and life before God.

1:18 [1] Another confirmation of that principal question: All men being considered in themselves or without Christ, are guilty both of [ungodliness], and also unrighteousness, and therefore are subject to condemnation: Therefore must they needs seek righteousness in some other.

[2] Against all kinds of ungodliness.

[3] By truth, Paul meaneth all the light that is left in man since his fall, not as though they being led thereby were able to come into favor with God, but that their own reason might condemn them of wickedness both against God and man.

1:19 [1] Their ungodliness he proveth hereby, that although all men have a most clear and evident glass wherein to behold the everlasting and almighty nature of God, even in his creatures, yet have they fallen away from those principles to most foolish and sound devices of their own brains, in consituting and appointing the service of God.

[2] In their hearts.

1:20 [1] Thou seest not God, and yet thou acknowledgest him as God by his works, Cicero.

1:21 [1] They did not honor him with that honor, and service, which was meet for his everlasting power and Godhead.

[2] As if he said, became so mad of themselves.

1:22 [1] Or thought themselves.

1:23 [1] For the true God they took another.

1:24 [1] The unrighteousness of men he setteth forth first, in this, that even against nature following their lusts, they defiled themselves one with another, by the just judgment of God.

[2] The contempt of religion, is the fountain of all mischief.

[3] As a just judge.

1:27 [1] A meet reward for their deserts.

1:28 [1] He proveth the unrighteousness of man by a large rehearsal of many kinds of wickedness, from which (if not from all, yet at the least from many of them) no man is altogether free.

[2] Into a mad and froward mind, whereby it cometh to pass, that the conscience being once put out, and having almost no more remorse of sin, men run headlong into all kinds of mischief.

1:30 [1] Unmindful of their covenants and bargains.

1:31 [1] By the Law of God he meaneth that which the Philosophers called the Law of nature, and the Lawyers themselves termed the Law of nations.

[2] Are fellows and partakers with them in their wickedness, and besides that, commend them which do amiss.

2 *1 He bringeth all before the judgment seat of God. 12 The excuse the Gentiles might pretend, 14 of ignorance, he taketh quite away. 17 He urgeth the Jews with the written Law, 23 in which they boasted. 27 And so maketh both Jew and Gentile alike.*

CHAPTER 2
a James 5:3
b Ps. 62:12
Matt. 16:27
Rev. 22:12

1 Therefore ¹thou art inexcusable, O man, whosoever thou art that condemnest: for in that thou condemnest another, thou condemnest thyself: for thou that condemnest, doest the same things.

2 But we ¹know that the judgment of God is according to ²truth, against them which commit such things.

3 And thinkest thou this, O thou man, that condemnest them which do such things, and doest the same, that thou shalt escape the judgment of God?

4 ¹Or despisest thou the riches of his bountifulness, and patience, and long sufferance, not knowing that the bountifulness of God leadeth thee to repentance?

5 But thou, after thine hardness, and heart that cannot repent, *a*,¹heapest up as a treasure unto thyself wrath against the day of wrath, and of the declaration of the just judgment of God,

6 *b*,¹Who will reward every man according to his works:

7 *That is*, to them which through patience in well doing, seek ¹glory, and honor, and immortality, everlasting life:

8 But unto them that are contentious, and disobey the ¹truth, and obey unrighteousness, *shall be* ²indignation and wrath.

9 Tribulation and anguish *shall be* upon the soul of every man that doeth evil: of the Jew first, and *also* of the Grecian.

10 But to every man that doeth good, *shall be* glory, and honor, and peace: to the Jew first, and *also* to the Grecian.

11 For there is ¹no respect of persons with God.

12 ¹For as many as have sinned without the Law, shall perish also without the Law: and as many as have sinned in the Law, shall be judged by the Law,

13 ¹(For the hearers of the Law *are* not righteous before God: but the doers of the Law shall be ²justified.

14 ¹For when the Gentiles which have ²not the Law, do by ³nature the things *contained* in the Law, they having not the Law, are a Law unto themselves,

15 Which show the effect of the Law ¹written in their hearts, their conscience also bearing witness and their thoughts accusing one another, or excusing.)

16 ¹At the day when God shall judge the secrets of men by Jesus Christ, according to ²my Gospel.

17 ¶ ¹Behold, thou art called a Jew, and restest in the Law, and gloriest in God,

18 And knowest *his* will, and ¹,²triest the things that dissent from it, in that thou art instructed by

---

2:1 ¹ He convinceth them which would seem to be exempt out of the number of other men, because they reprehend other men's faults, and saith that they are least of all to be excused, for if they were well and narrowly searched (as God surely doth) they themselves would be found guilty in those things which they reprehend, and punish in others: so that in condemning others they pronounce sentence against themselves.

2:2 ¹ Paul allegeth no places of Scripture, for he reasoneth generally against all men: but he bringeth such reasons as every man is persuaded of in his mind, so that the devil himself is not able to pluck them clean out.

² Considering and judging things aright, and not by any outward show.

2:4 ¹ A vehement and grievous crying out against them that please themselves, because they see more than others do, and yet are no whit better than others are.

2:5 ¹ Whilst thou givest thyself to pleasures, thinking to increase thy goods, thou shalt find God's wrath.

2:6 ¹ The ground of the former disputation, That both the Jews and Gentiles have together need of righteousness.

2:7 ¹ Glory which followeth good works, which he layeth not out before us, as though there were any that could attain to salvation by his own strength, but, by laying this condition of salvation before us, which no man can perform, to bring men to Christ, who alone justified the believers, as he himself concludeth, Rom. 2:21-22, following.

2:8 ¹ By truth, he meaneth that knowledge which we have of nature.

² God's indignation against sinners, which shall quickly be kindled.

2:11 ¹ God doth not measure men either by their blood, or by their country, either to receive them, or to cast them away.

2:12 ¹ He applieth that general accusation of mankind particularly both to the Gentiles, and to the Jews.

2:13 ¹ He preventeth an objection which might be made by the Jews, whom the Law doth not excuse, but condemns, because that not the hearing of the Law, but the keeping of the Law doth justify.

² Shall be pronounced just before God's judgment seat: which is true indeed, if any such could be found that had fulfilled the law: but seeing Abraham was not justified by the Law, but by faith, it followeth that no man can be justified by works.

2:14 ¹ He preventeth an objection which might be made by the Gentiles, who although they have not the Law of Moses, yet they have no reason whereby they may excuse their wickedness in that they have somewhat written in their hearts instead of a Law, as men that forbid, and punish some things as wicked, and command and commend other some as good.

² Not simply, but in comparison of the Jews.

³ Command honest things, and forbid dishonest.

2:15 ¹ This knowledge is a natural knowledge.

2:16 ¹ God deferreth many judgments, which notwithstanding he will execute at their convenient time by Jesus Christ, with a most straight examination, not only of words and deeds, but of thoughts also, be they never so hidden or secret.

² As this my doctrine witnesseth, which I am appointed to preach.

2:17 ¹ He proveth by the testimony of David, and the other Prophets, that God bestowed greatest benefits upon the Jews, in giving them also the Law, but that they are the most unthankful and unkindest of all men.

2:18 ¹ Canst try and discern what things swerve from God's will.

² Or allowest the things that are excellent.

the Law:

19 And persuadest thyself that thou art a guide of the blind, a light of them which *are* in darkness,

20 An instructor of them which lack discretion, a teacher of the unlearned, which hast the [1]form of knowledge, and of the truth in the [2]law.

21 Thou therefore, which teachest another, teachest thou not thyself? thou that preachest, A man should not steal, dost thou steal?

22 Thou that sayest, A man should not commit adultery, dost thou commit adultery? thou that abhorrest idols, committest thou sacrilege?

23 Thou that gloriest in the Law, through breaking the Law, dishonorest thou God?

24 For the Name of God is blasphemed among the Gentiles through you, [c]as it is written.

25 [1]For circumcision verily is profitable, if thou do the Law: but if thou be a transgressor of the Law, thy circumcision is made uncircumcision.

26 Therefore [1]if the uncircumcision keep the ordinances of the Law, shall not his [2]uncircumcision be counted for circumcision?

27 And shall not [1]uncircumcision which is by nature (if it keep the Law) condemn thee which by the [2]letter and circumcision *art* a transgressor of the Law?

28 For he is not a Jew, which is one [1]outward: neither is that circumcision, which is outward in the flesh:

29 But he is a Jew which is one within, and the

[c] Isa. 52:5
Ezek. 36:20

circumcision *is* of the heart, in the [1]spirit, not in the letter, whose praise is not of men, but of God.

3 *1 He giveth the Jews some   2 preferment, for the covenant's sake,   4 but yet such, as wholly dependeth on God's mercy.   9 That both Jews and Gentiles are sinners,   11 he proveth by Scriptures: 19 and showing the use of the Law,   28 he concludeth that we are justified by faith.*

1 What [1]is then the preferment of the Jew? or what is the profit of circumcision?

2 Much every manner of way: for [1]chiefly, because unto them were of credit committed the [2]oracles of God.

3 For what, though some did not [1]believe? shall their unbelief make the [2]faith of God without effect?

4 God forbid: yea, let God be true, and every man a liar, as it is written, That thou mightest be [1]justified in thy words, and overcome, [2]when thou art judged.

5 [1]Now if our [2]unrighteousness commend the righteousness of God, what shall we say? is God unrighteous which punisheth? (I speak as [3]a man.)

6 God forbid: (else how shall God judge the world?)

7 [1]For if the [2]verity of God hath more abounded through my lie unto his glory, why am I yet condemned as a sinner?

8 And (as we are blamed, and as some affirm, that we say) why do we not evil, that good may come *thereof*? whose damnation is just.

2:20 [1] The way to teach and frame others in the knowledge of the truth.

[2] As though he said, that the Jews under a color of an outward serving of God, challenged all to themselves, when as indeed, they did nothing less than observe the Law.

2:25 [1] He precisely preventeth their objection, which set an holiness in circumcision, and the outward observation of the Law: So that he showeth that the outward circumcision, if it be separated from the inward, doth not only not justify, but also condemns them that are indeed circumcised, of whom requireth that, which is signifieth, that is to say, cleanness of the heart and the whole life, according to the commandment of the Law, so that if there be a man uncircumcised according to the flesh, who is circumcised in heart, he is far better and more to be more accounted of, than any Jew that is circumcised according to the flesh only.

2:26 [1] This is the figure Metonymy, for, if the uncircumcised.

[2] The state and condition of the uncircumcised.

2:27 [1] He which is uncircumcised by nature and blood.

[2] Paul useth oftentimes to set the letter against the Spirit: but in this place, the circumcision which is according to the letter, is the cutting off of the foreskin, but the circumcision of the Spirit, is the circumcision of the heart, that is to say, the spiritual end of the ceremony, is true holiness and righteousness whereby the people of God is known from profane and heathenish men.

2:28 [1] By the outward ceremony only.

2:29 [1] Whose force is inward, and in the heart.

3:1 [1] The first meeting with, or preventing an objection of the Jews: what then, have the Jews no more preferment than the Gentiles? yes,

that have they, saith the Apostle, on God's behalf: for he committed the tables of the covenant to them, so that the unbelief of a few, cannot cause the whole nation without exception to be cast away of God, who is true, and who also useth their unworthiness to commend and set forth his goodness.

3:2 [1] The Jews' state and condition was chiefest.

[2] Words.

3:3 [1] Break the covenant.

[2] The faith that God gave.

3:4 [1] That thy justice might be plainly seen.

[2] Forasmuch as thou showest forth an evident token of thy righteousness, constancy and faith, by preserving him who had broken his covenant.

3:5 [1] Another prevention, issuing out of the former answer: that the justice of God is in such sort commended and set forth by our unrighteousness, that therefore God forgetteth not that he is the judge of the world, and therefore a most severe revenger of unrighteousness.

[2] Treachery, and all the fruits thereof.

[3] Therefore I speak not these words in mine own person, as though I thought so, but this is the talk of man's wisdom, which is not subject to the will of God.

3:7 [1] A third objection which addeth somewhat to the former, If sins do turn to the glory of God, they are not only not to be punished, but we ought rather to give ourselves to them: which blasphemy Paul contending himself to curse and detest, pronounceth just punishment against such blasphemers.

[2] The truth and constancy.

9 ¹What then? are we more excellent? No, in no wise: for we have already proved, that all, both Jews and Gentiles are ²under sin,

10 As it is written, ᵃThere is none righteous no not one.

11 There is none that understandeth: there is none that seeketh God.

12 They have all gone out of the way: they have been made altogether unprofitable: there is none that doeth good, no not one.

13 ᵇTheir throat is an open sepulcher: they have used their tongues to deceit: ᶜthe poison of asps is under their lips.

14 ᵈWhose mouth is full of cursing and bitterness.

15 ᵉTheir feet are swift to shed blood.

16 Destruction and calamity are in their ways:

17 And the ¹way of peace they have not known.

18 ᶠThe fear of God is not before their eyes.

19 ¹Now we know that whatsoever the ²law saith, it saith it to them which are under the law, that ³every mouth may be stopped, and all the world be ⁴subject to the judgment of God.

CHAPTER 3
ᵃ Ps. 14:1-3
   Ps. 53:1-3
ᵇ Ps. 5:10
ᶜ Ps. 140:3
ᵈ Ps. 10:7
ᵉ Isa. 59:7
ᶠ Ps. 36:1

20 Therefore by the ¹works of the Law shall no ²flesh be ³justified in his ⁴sight: for by the Law cometh the knowledge of sin.

21 ¹But now is the righteousness of God made manifest without the Law, having witness of the Law, and of the Prophets,

22 ¹To wit, the righteousness of God by the faith of ²Jesus Christ, unto all, and upon all that believe.

23 For there is no difference: for all have sinned, and are deprived of the ¹glory of God,

24 ¹And are justified ²freely by his grace, through the redemption that is in Christ Jesus,

25 ¹Whom God hath set forth to be a reconciliation through faith in his ²blood to declare his righteousness, by the forgiveness of the sins that ³are passed,

26 Through the ¹patience of God, to show at ²this time his righteousness, that he might be ³just, and a ⁴justifier of him which is of the ⁵faith of Jesus.

27 ¹Where is then the rejoicing? It is excluded. By what ²Law? of works? Nay: but by the Law of faith.

28 Therefore we conclude, that a man is justified by faith, without the works of the Law.

3:9 ¹ Another answer to the first objection: that the Jews, if they be considered in themselves, are no better than other men are: as it has been long since pronounced by the mouth of the Prophets.

² Are guilty of sin.

3:17 ¹ An innocent and peaceable life.

3:19 ¹ He proveth that this grievous accusation which is uttered by David and Isaiah, doth properly concern the Jews.

² The law of Moses.

³ A conclusion of all the former disputation, from verse 8 of the first Chapter. Therefore saith the Apostle, No man can hope to be justified by any Law, whether it be that general Law, or the particular Law of Moses, and therefore to be saved: seeing it appeareth (as we have already proved) by comparing the Law and man's life together, that all men are sinners, and therefore worthy of condemnation in the sight of God.

⁴ Be found guilty before God.

3:20 ¹ By that that the Law can by us be performed.

² Flesh is here taken for man, as in many other places, and furthermore hath here a greater force: for it is put to show the contrariety betwixt God and man: as if you would say, Man who is nothing else but a piece of flesh defiled with sin, and God who is most pure and most perfect in himself.

³ Absolved before the judgment seat of God.

⁴ A secret setting of the righteousness which is before men, be they never so just, against the justice which can stand before God: now there is no righteousness can stand before God, but the righteousness of Christ only.

3:21 ¹ Therefore saith the Apostle, Lest that men should perish, God doth now exhibit that, which he promised of old, that is to say, a way whereby we may be justified and saved before him without the Law.

3:22 ¹ The matter, as it were of this righteousness, is Christ Jesus apprehended by faith, and for this end offered to all people, as without him all people are shut out from the kingdom of God.

² Which we give to Jesus Christ, or which resteth upon him.

3:23 ¹ By the Glory of God, is meant that mark which we all shoot at, that is, everlasting life, which standeth in that we are made partakers of the glory of God.

3:24 ¹ Therefore this righteousness touching us, is altogether freely given, for it standeth upon those things which we have not done ourselves, but such as Christ hath suffered for our sakes, to deliver us from sin.

² Of his free gift, and mere liberality.

3:25 ¹ God then is the author of that free justification, because it pleaseth him: and Christ is he, which suffered punishment for our sins, and in whom we have remission of them: and the means whereby we apprehend Christ, is faith. To be short, the end is the setting forth of the goodness of God, that by this means it may appear, that he is merciful indeed, and constant in his promises, as he that freely, and of mere grace justifieth the believers.

² This name of Blood, calleth us back to the figure of the old sacrifices, the truth and substance of which sacrifices is in Christ.

³ Of those sins which we committed when we were his enemies.

3:26 ¹ Through his patience, and suffering nature.

² To wit, when Paul wrote this.

³ That he might be found exceeding true and faithful.

⁴ Making him just, and without blame by imputing Christ's righteousness unto him.

⁵ Of the number of them which by faith lay hold upon Christ: contrary to whom, are they which look to be saved by circumcision, that is, by the Law.

3:27 ¹ An argument to prove this conclusion, that we are justified by faith without works, taken from the end of Justification. The end of Justification is the glory of God alone: therefore we are justified by faith without works: for if we were justified either by our own works only, or partly by faith, and partly by works, the glory of this justification should not be wholly given to God.

² By what doctrine? now the doctrine of works hath [this] condition joined with it, If thou doest: and the doctrine of faith hath this condition, If thou believest.

29 ¹*God*, is he the God of the ²Jews only, and not of the Gentiles also? Yes, even of the Gentiles also.

30 For it is one God, who shall justify ¹circumcision of faith, and uncircumcision through faith.

31 ¹Do we then make the Law of ²none effect through faith? God forbid: yea, we ³establish the Law.

4 *1 He proveth that which he said before of faith, by the example of Abraham, 3, 6 and the testimony of the Scripture: and ten times in the Chapter he beateth upon this word, Imputation.*

1 What ¹shall we say then, that Abraham our father hath found concerning the ²flesh?

2 ¹For if Abraham were justified by works, he hath wherein to rejoice, but not with God.

3 ¹For what saith the Scripture? Abraham believed God, and it was counted to him for righteousness.

4 ¹Now to him that ²worketh, the wages is not ³counted by favor, but by debt:

5 But to him that worketh not, but believeth in him that ¹justifieth the ungodly, his faith is counted for righteousness.

6 ¹Even as David declareth the blessedness of the man, unto whom God imputeth righteousness

without works, *saying*,

7 Blessed *are* they whose iniquities are forgiven, and whose sins are covered.

8 Blessed *is* the man to whom the Lord imputeth not sin.

9 ¹*Came* this ²blessedness then upon the circumcision *only*, or upon the uncircumcision also? For we say, that faith was imputed unto Abraham for righteousness.

10 ¹How was it then imputed? when he was circumcised, or uncircumcised? not when he was circumcised, but when he was uncircumcised.

11 ¹After, he received the ²sign of circumcision, *as* the ³seal of the righteousness of the faith which he had, when he was uncircumcised, ⁴that he should be the father of all them that believe, not being circumcised, that righteousness might be imputed to them also.

12 ¹And the father of circumcision, not unto them only which are of the circumcision, but unto them also that walk in the steps of the faith of our father Abraham *which he had* when he was uncircumcised.

13 ¹For the promise that he should be the ²heir of the world, was not *given* to Abraham, or to his seed, through the ³Law, but through the righteousness of faith.

3:29 ¹ Another argument of an absurdity: if justification depended upon the Law of Moses, then should God be a Savior to the Jews only. Again: if he should save the Jews after one sort, and the Gentiles after another, he should not be one and like himself. Therefore he will justify both of them after one selfsame manner, that is to say, by faith. Moreover, this argument must be joined to that which followeth next, that this conclusion may be firm and evident.

² God is said to be their God, after the manner of the Scripture, whom he loveth and tendereth.

3:30 ¹ The circumcised.

3:31 ¹ The taking away of an objection: yet it is not the Law taken away therefore, but is rather established, as it shall be declared in [its] proper place.

² Vain, void, to no purpose, and of no force.

³ We make it effectual and strong.

4:1 ¹ A new argument of great weight, taken from the example of Abraham the father of all believers: And this is the proposition: if Abraham be considered in himself by his works, he hath deserved nothing wherein to rejoice with God.

² By works, as appeareth in the next verse.

4:2 ¹ A preventing of an objection: Abraham may well rejoice and extol himself amongst men, but not with God.

4:3 ¹ A confirmation of the proposition: Abraham was justified by imputation of faith, therefore freely without any respect of his works.

4:4 ¹ The first proof of the confirmation, taken of contraries: to him that deserveth anything by his labor, the wages is not counted by favor, but by debt: but to him that hath done nothing, but believeth in him which promiseth freely, faith is imputed.

² To him that hath deserved anything by his work.

³ Is not reckoned nor given him.

4:5 ¹ That maketh him which is wicked in himself, just in Christ.

4:6 ¹ Another proof of the same confirmation: David putteth blessedness in free pardon of sins, therefore justification also.

4:9 ¹ A new proposition: that this manner of justification belongeth both to uncircumcised, and also to the circumcised, as is declared in the person of Abraham.

² This saying of David, wherein he pronounceth them blessed.

4:10 ¹ He proveth that it belongeth to the uncircumcised (for there was no doubt of the circumcised) in this sort: Abraham was justified in uncircumcision, therefore this justification belongeth also to the uncircumcised. Nay, it does not appertain to the circumcised in respect of the circumcision, much less are the uncircumcised shut out for their uncircumcision.

4:11 ¹ A preventing of an objection: why then was Abraham circumcised, if he were already justified? That the gift of righteousness (saith he) might be confirmed in him.

² Circumcision, which is a sign: as we say, the Sacrament of Baptism, for Baptism which is a Sacrament.

³ Circumcision was called before a sign, in respect of the outward ceremony: now Paul showeth the force and substance of that sign, that is, to what end it is used, to wit, not only to signify, but also to seal up the righteousness of faith, whereby we come to possess Christ himself: for the holy Ghost worketh that inwardly indeed, which the Sacraments being joined with the word, do represent.

⁴ An applying of the example of Abraham to the uncircumcised believers, whose father also he maketh Abraham.

4:12 ¹ An applying of the same example, to the circumcised believers, whose father Abraham is, but yet by faith.

4:13 ¹ A reason why the seed of Abraham is to be esteemed by faith, because that Abraham himself through faith was made partaker of that promise, whereby he was made the father of all nations.

² That all the nations of the world should be his children: or by the world may be understood the land of Canaan.

³ For works that he had done, or upon this condition that he should fulfill the Law.

14 [1]For if they which are of the [2]Law, *be* heirs, faith is made void, and the promise is made of none effect.

15 [1]For the Law causeth wrath: for where no Law is, there *is* no transgression.

16 [1]Therefore *it is* by faith, that *it might come* by grace, and the promise might be sure to all the [2]seed, [3]not to that only which is of the Law: but also to that which is of the faith of Abraham who is the father of us all,

17 (As it is written, I have made thee a [1]father of many nations) *even* before [2]God whom he believed, who [3]quickeneth the dead, and [4]calleth those things which be not, as though they were.

18 [1]Which *Abraham* above hope, believed under hope, that he should be the father of many nations: according to that which was spoken *to him*, So shall thy seed be.

19 And he [1]not weak in the faith, considered not his own body, which was now [2]dead, being almost an hundred years old, neither the deadness of Sarah's womb.

20 Neither did he doubt of the promise of God through unbelief, but was strengthened in the faith, and gave [1]glory to God,

21 Being [1]fully assured that he which had promised,

CHAPTER 5
a Eph. 2:18
b James 1:2

was also able to do it.

22 And therefore it was imputed to him for righteousness.

23 [1]Now is it not written for him only, that it was imputed to him for righteousness,

24 But also for us, to whom it shall be imputed *for righteousness*, which believe in him that raised up Jesus our Lord from the dead,

25 Who was delivered *to death* for our [1]sins, and is risen again for our justification.

5 *1 He amplifieth   2 Christ's righteousness, which is laid hold on by faith,   5 who was given for the weak,   8 and sinful.   14 He compareth Christ with Adam.   17 Death with Life,   20 and the Law with Grace.*

1 Then being [1]justified by faith, we have peace toward God through our Lord Jesus Christ.

2 [a][1]By whom also through faith we have [2]had this access into this grace [3]wherein we [4]stand, [5]and [6]rejoice under the hope of the glory of God.

3 [1]Neither *that* only, but also we [b]rejoice in tribulations, [2]knowing that tribulation bringeth forth patience.

4 And patience experience, and experience hope.

5 [1]And hope maketh not ashamed, because the

4:14 [1] A double confirmation of that reason: the one is, that the promise cannot be apprehended by the Law, and therefore it should be frustrated: the other, that the condition of faith should be joined in vain to that promise which should be apprehended by works.

[2] If they be heirs which have fulfilled the Law.

4:15 [1] A reason of the first confirmation, why the promise cannot be apprehended by the Law: because that the Law doth not reconcile God and us, but rather denounceth his anger against us, forsomuch as no man can observe it.

4:16 [1] The conclusion of this argument. The salvation and justification of all the posterity of Abraham (that is, of the Church which is gathered together of all people) proceedeth of faith, which layeth hold on the promise made unto Abraham, and which promise Abraham himself first of all laid hold on.

[2] To all the believers.

[3] That is to say, not only of them which believe and are also circumcised according to the Law, but of them also which without circumcision, and in respect of faith only, are counted amongst the children of Abraham.

4:17 [1] This fatherhood is spiritual, depending only upon the virtue of God, who made the promise.

[2] Before God, that is, by a spiritual kindred, which had place before God, and maketh us acceptable to God.

[3] Who restored to life.

[4] With whom these things are already, which as yet are not in deed, as he that can with a word make what he will of nothing.

4:18 [1] A description of true faith, wholly resting in the power of God, and his good will, set forth in the example of Abraham.

4:19 [1] Very strong and constant.

[2] Void of strength, and unmeet to get children.

4:20 [1] Acknowledged and praised God, as most gracious and true.

4:21 [1] A description of true faith.

4:23 [1] The rule of justification is always one, both in Abraham and

in all the faithful: that is to say, faith in God, who after that there was made a full satisfaction for our sins in Christ our mediator, raised him from the dead, that we also being justified, might be saved in him.

4:25 [1] To pay the ransom for our sins.

5:1 [1] Another argument taken of the effects: we are justified with that, which truly appeaseth our conscience before God but faith in Christ doth appease our conscience, and not the Law, as it was before said, therefore by faith we are justified, and not by the Law.

5:2 [1] Whereas quietness of conscience is attributed to faith, it is to be referred to Christ, who is the giver of faith itself, and in whom faith itself is effectual.

[2] We must here know, that we have yet still this same effect of faith.

[3] By which grace, that is, by which gracious love and good will, or that state whereunto we are graciously taken.

[4] We stand steadfast.

[5] A preventing of an objection against them which beholding the daily miseries and calamities of the Church, think that the Christians dream, when they brag of their felicity: to whom the Apostle answereth, that their felicity is laid up under hope of another place: which hope is so certain and sure, that they do not less rejoice for that happiness, than if they did presently enjoy it.

[6] Our minds are not only quiet and settled, but also we are marvelously glad and conceive great joy for that heavenly inheritance which waiteth for us.

5:3 [1] Tribulation itself giveth us divers and sundry ways occasion to rejoice, much less doth it make us miserable.

[2] Afflictions accustom us to patience, and patience assureth us of the goodness of God, and this experience confirmeth, and fostereth our hope, which never deceiveth us.

5:5 [1] The ground of hope is an assured testimony of the conscience, by the gift of the holy Ghost, that we are beloved of God, and this is nothing else but that which we call faith: whereof it followeth, that through faith our consciences are quieted.

[2]love of God is shed abroad in our hearts by the holy Ghost, which is given unto us.

6 [1]For Christ, when we were yet of no strength, at *his* [2]time died for the ʿungodly.

7 [1]Doubtless one will scarce die [2]for a righteous man: but yet for a good man it may be that one dare die.

8 But God [1]setteth out his love towards us, seeing that while we were yet [2]sinners, Christ died for us.

9 Much more then, being now justified by his blood, we shall be saved from [1]wrath through him.

10 For if when we were enemies, we were reconciled to God by the death of his Son, much more being reconciled, we shall be saved by his life,

11 [1]And not only *so*, but we also rejoice in God through our Lord Jesus Christ, by whom we have now received the atonement.

12 [1]Wherefore, as by [2]one man [3]sin entered into the world, and death by sin, and so death went over all men: [4]in whom all men have sinned.

13 [1]For unto the [2]time of the Law was sin in the

ᶜ Heb. 9:15
1 Pet. 3:18

world, but sin is not [3]imputed, while there is no law.

14 [1]But death reigned from Adam to Moses, even over [2]them also that sinned not after the like [3]manner of the transgression of Adam, [4]which was the figure of him that was to come.

15 [1]But yet the gift is not so as is the offense: for if through the offense of [2]that one, many be dead, much more the grace of God, and the gift by grace, which is by one man Jesus Christ, hath abounded unto many.

16 [1]Neither is the gift *so*, as *that which entered in* by one that sinned: for the fault *came* of one *offense* unto condemnation: but the gift *is* of many offenses to [2]justification.

17 [1]For if by the offense of one, death reigned through one, much more shall they which receive that abundance of grace, and of that gift of that righteousness, [2]reign in life through one, *that is*, Jesus Christ.

18 [1]Likewise then, as by the offense of one, the *fault came* on all men to condemnation, so by the

---

[2] Wherewith he loveth us.

5:6 [1] A sure comfort in adversity, that our peace and quietness of conscience be not troubled: for he that so loved them that were of no strength, and while they were yet sinners, that he died for them, how can he neglect them being now sanctified and living in him?

[2] In time fit and convenient, which the father hath appointed.

5:7 [1] An amplifying of the love of God towards us, so that we cannot doubt of it, who delivereth Christ to death for the unjust, and for them of whom he could receive no commodity, and (that more is) for his very enemies. How can it be then that Christ being now alive, should not save them from destruction, whom by his death he justifieth and reconcileth?

[2] In the stead of some just man.

5:8 [1] He setteth out his love unto us, that in the midst of our afflictions we may know assuredly, he will be present with us.

[2] While sin reigned in us.

5:9 [1] From affliction and destruction.

5:11 [1] He now passeth over to the other part of justification, which consisteth in the free imputation of the obedience of Christ: so that to the remission of sins there is added moreover and besides, the gift of Christ's righteousness imputed or put upon us by faith, which swalloweth up that unrighteousness which flowed from Adam into us, and all the fruits thereof: so that in Christ we do not only cease to be unjust, but we begin also to be just.

5:12 [1] From Adam, in whom all have sinned, both guiltiness and death (which is the punishment of the guiltiness) came upon all.

[2] By Adam, who is compared with Christ, like to him in this, that both of them make those who are theirs, partakers of that they have into: but they are unlike in this, that Adam deriveth sin into them that are his, even of nature, and that to death: but Christ maketh them that are his, partakers of his righteousness by grace, and that unto life.

[3] By sin is meant that disease which is ours by inheritance, and men commonly call it original sin: for so he useth to call that sin in the singular number, whereas, if he speaks of the fruits of it, he useth the plural number, calling them sins.

[4] That is, in Adam.

5:13 [1] That this is so, that both guiltiness and death began not after the giving and transgressing of Moses' Law, it appeareth manifestly

by that, that men died before that Law was given: for in that they died, sin, which is the cause of death, was then: and in such sort, that it was also imputeth: whereupon it followeth that there was then some Law, the breach whereof was the cause of death.

[2] Even from Adam to Moses.

[3] Where there is no Law made, no man is punished as faulty and guilty.

5:14 [1] But that this Law was not that universal Law, and that death did not proceed from any actual sin of everyone particularly, it appeareth hereby, that the very infants which neither could ever know nor transgress that natural Law, are notwithstanding dead as well as Adam.

[2] Our infants.

[3] Not after that sort as they sin that are of more years, following their lusts: but yet the whole posterity was corrupt in Adam, when as he wittingly and willingly sinned.

[4] Now the first Adam answereth the latter, who is Christ, as it is afterward declared.

5:15 [1] Adam and Christ are compared together in this respect, that both of them do give and yield to theirs, that which is their own: but herein first they differ, that Adam by nature hath spread his fault to the destruction of many, but Christ's obedience hath by grace overflowed many.

[2] That is, Adam.

5:16 [1] Another inequality consisteth in this, that by Adam's one offense men are made guilty, but the righteousness of Christ imputed unto us freely, doth not only absolve us from that one fault, but from all others.

[2] To the sentence of absolution, whereby we are quit, and pronounced righteous.

5:17 [1] The third difference is, that the righteousness of Christ being imputed unto us by grace, is of greater power to bring life, than the offense of Adam is to addict his posterity to death.

[2] Be partakers of true and everlasting life.

5:18 [1] Therefore to be short, as by one man's offense, the guiltiness came on all men, to make them subject to death: so on the contrary side, the righteousness of Christ, which by God's mercy is imputed to all believers, justifieth them, that they may become partakers of everlasting life.

justifying of one, *the benefit abounded* toward all men to the ²justification of life.

19 ¹For as by one man's ²disobedience ³many were made sinners, so by that obedience of that one, shall many also be made righteous.

20 ¹Moreover, the Law ²entered thereupon, that the offense should abound: nevertheless, where sin abounded, *there* grace ³abounded much more:

21 That as sin had reigned unto death, so might grace also reign by righteousness unto eternal life through Jesus Christ our Lord.

6

1 He cometh to sanctification, without which, that no man putteth on Christ's righteousness, he proveth   4 by an argument taken of Baptism,   12 and thereupon exhorteth to holiness of life,   16 briefly making mention of the Law transgressed.

1 What ¹shall we say then? Shall we continue still in ²sin, that grace may abound? God forbid.

2 ¹How shall we, that are ²dead to sin, live yet therein?

3 ¹Know ye not, that ªall we which have been baptized into ²Jesus Christ, have been baptized into

CHAPTER 6
ª Gal. 3:27
ᵇ Col. 2:12
ᶜ Eph. 4:23
Col. 3:3
Heb. 12:1
1 Pet. 2:1
ᵈ 1 Cor. 6:14
2 Tim. 2:11

his death?

4 ᵇWe are buried then with him by baptism into his death, that like as Christ was raised up from the dead ¹to the glory of the Father, so ²we also should ᶜwalk in newness of life.

5 ᵈ·¹For if we be planted with him to the ²similitude of his death, even so shall we ³be *to the similitude* of his resurrection,

6 Knowing this, that our ¹old man is crucified with ²him, that the body of ³sin might be destroyed, that henceforth we should not ⁴serve sin,

7 ¹For he that is dead, is freed from sin.

8 Wherefore, if we be dead with Christ, we believe that we shall live also with him,

9 Knowing that Christ being raised from the dead, dieth no more: death hath no more dominion over him.

10 For in that he died, he died ¹once to sin: but in that he liveth, he liveth to ²God.

11 Likewise think ye also, that ye are dead to sin, but are alive to God in Jesus Christ our Lord.

12 ¹Let not sin ²reign therefore in your mortal body, that ye should obey it in the lusts thereof:

5:18 ² Not only because our sins are forgiven us, but also because the righteousness of Christ is imputed unto us.

5:19 ¹ The ground of this whole comparison is this, that these two men are set as two stocks or roots, so that out of the one, sin by nature, out of the other, righteousness by grace doth spring forth upon others.

² So then, sin entered not into us only by following the steps of our forefather, but we take corruption of him by inheritance.

³ This word, Many, is set against this word, A few.

5:20 ¹ A preventing of an objection: why then did the Law of Moses enter thereupon? that men might be so much the more guilty, and the benefit of God in Christ Jesus be so much the more glorious.

² Beside that disease which all men were infected withall by being defiled with one man's sin, the Law entered.

³ Grace was poured so plentifully from heaven, that it did not only countervail sin, but above measure passed it.

6:1 ¹ He passeth now to another benefit of Christ, which is called sanctification or regeneration.

² In that corruption: for though the guiltiness of sin be not imputed to us, yet the corruption remaineth still in us: the which Sanctification that followeth Justification killeth by little and little.

6:2 ¹ The benefits of Justification and Sanctification, are always joined together inseparably, and both of them proceed from Christ, by the grace of God: Now sanctification is the abolishing of sin, that is, of our natural corruption, into whose place succeedeth the cleanness and pureness of nature reformed.

² They are said of Paul to be dead to sin, which are in such sort made partakers of the virtue of Christ, that that natural corruption is dead in them, that is, the force of it is put out, and it bringeth not forth his bitter fruits: and on the other side, they are said to live to sin, which are in the flesh, that is, whom the spirit of God hath not delivered from the slavery of the corruption of nature.

6:3 ¹ There are three parts of this Sanctification, to wit, the dead of the old man or sin, his burial, and the resurrection of the new man, descending into us from the virtue of the death, burial, and resurrection of Christ, of which benefit our baptism is the sign and pledge.

² To the end that growing up in one with him, we should receive his strength to quench sin in us, and to make us new men.

6:4 ¹ That Christ himself being discharged of his infirmity and weakness, might live in glory with God forever.

² And we which are his members rise for this end, that being made partakers of the selfsame virtue, we should begin to lead a new life, as though we were already in heaven.

6:5 ¹ The death of sin and the life of righteousness, or our ingrafting into Christ, and growing up into one with him, cannot be separated by any means, neither in death nor life, whereby it followeth, that no man is sanctified, which lived still to sin, and therefore is no man made partaker of Christ by faith, which repenteth not, and turneth not from his wickedness: for as he said before, the Law is not subverted, but established by faith.

² Insomuch as by the means of the strength which cometh from him to us, we so die to sin as he is dead.

³ For we become every day more perfect than others: for we shall never be perfectly sanctified, as long as we live here.

6:6 ¹ All our whole nature, as we are conceived and born into this world with sin, which is called old, partly by comparing that old Adam with Christ, and partly also in respect of the deformation of our corrupt nature, which we change with a new.

² Our corrupt nature is attributed to Christ, not in deed, but by imputation.

³ That naughtiness which sticketh fast in us.

⁴ The end of sanctification which we shoot at, and shall at length come to, to wit when God shall be all in all.

6:7 ¹ He proveth it by the effects of death, using a comparison of Christ the head with his members.

6:10 ¹ Once for all.

² With God.

6:12 ¹ An exhortation to contend and strive with corruption and all the effects thereof.

² By reigning, Saint Paul meaneth that chiefest and high rule, which no man striveth against, and if any do, yet it is in vain.

13 Neither ¹give ye your ²members, *as* ³weapons of unrighteousness unto sin: but give yourselves unto God, as they that are alive from the dead, and *give* your members *as* weapons of righteousness unto God.

14 ¹For sin shall not have dominion over you: for ye are not under the Law, but under grace.

15 ¹What then? shall we sin, because we are not under the Law, but under grace? God forbid.

16 ᶜKnow ye not, that to whomsoever ye give yourselves as servants to obey, his servants ye are to whom ye obey, whether it be of sin unto death, or of obedience unto righteousness?

17 ¹But God *be* thanked, that ye have been the servants of sin, but ye have obeyed from the heart unto the ²form of the doctrine, whereunto ye were delivered.

18 Being then made free from sin, ye are made the servants of righteousness.

19 I speak after the manner of man, because of the infirmity of your flesh: for as ye have given your members servants to uncleanness and to iniquity, to *commit* iniquity, so now give your members servants unto righteousness in holiness.

20 For when ye were the servants of sin, ye were ¹freed from righteousness.

21 ¹What fruit had ye then in those things, whereof ye are now ashamed? For the ²end of those things *is* death.

22 But now being freed from sin, and made servants unto God, ye have your fruit in holiness, and

ᶜ John 1:34 2 Pet. 2:19

CHAPTER 7

ᵃ 1 Cor. 7:32
ᵇ Matt. 5:32

the end, everlasting life.

23 ¹For the wages of sin is death: but the gift of God *is* eternal life, through Jesus Christ our Lord.

7 *1 He declareth what it is, to be no more under the Law, 2 by an example taken of the Law of marriage, 7, 12 And lest the Law should seem faulty, 14 he proveth, that our sin is the cause, 2, 5 that the same is an occasion of death, 17 which was given us unto life. 21 He setteth out the battle between the flesh and the spirit.*

1 Know ¹ye not, brethren, (for I speak to them that know the Law) that the Law hath dominion over a man as long as he liveth?

2 ᵃFor the woman which is in subjection to a man, is bound by the Law to the man, while he liveth: but if the man be dead, she is delivered from the Law of the man.

3 So then, if while the man liveth, she taketh another man, she shall be ¹called an ᵇadulteress: but if the man be dead, she is free from the Law, so that she is not an adulteress, though she take another man.

4 ¹So ye, my brethren, are dead also to the Law by the ²body of Christ, that ye should be unto another, *even* unto him that is raised up from the dead, that we should bring forth ³fruit unto ⁴God.

5 ¹For when we ²were in the flesh, the ³affections of sins, which were by the ⁴law, had ⁵force in our members, to bring forth fruit unto death,

6 But now we are delivered from the Law, he

6:13 ¹ To sin, as to a Lord or tyrant.
² Your mind and all the powers of it.
³ As instruments to commit wickedness withall.
6:14 ¹ He granteth that sin is not yet so dead in us that it is utterly extinct: but he promised victory to them that contend manfully, because we have the grace of God given us which worketh so, that the Law is not now in us the power and instrument of sin.
6:15 ¹ To be under the law and under sin, signify all one, in respect of them which are not sanctified, as on the contrary side, to be under grace and righteousness, agree to them that are regenerate. Now these are contraries, so that one cannot agree with the other: Therefore let righteousness expel sin.
6:17 ¹ By nature we are slaves to sin, and free from righteousness, but by the grace of God we are made servants to righteousness, and therefore free from sin.
² This kind of speech hath a force in it: for he meaneth thereby that the doctrine of the Gospel is like a certain mold which we are cast into to be framed and fashioned like unto it.
6:20 ¹ Righteousness had no rule over you.
6:21 ¹ An exhortation to the study of righteousness and hatred of sin, the contrary ends of both, being set down before us.
² The reward or payment.
6:23 ¹ Death is the punishment due to sin, but we are sanctified freely, unto life everlasting.
7:1 ¹ By propounding the similitude of a marriage, he compareth the state of man both before and after regeneration together. The law of matrimony, saith he, is this, that so long as the husband liveth, the marriage abideth in force, but if he be dead, the woman may

marry again.
7:3 ¹ That is, she shall be an adulteress, by the consent and judgment of all men.
7:4 ¹ An application of the similitude thus. So, saith he, doth it fare with us: for now we are joined to the spirit as it were to the second husband, by whom we must bring forth new children: we are dead in respect of the first husband, but in respect of the latter we are as it were raised from the dead.
² That is, in the body of Christ, to give us to understand how straight and near that fellowship is betwixt Christ and his members.
³ He calleth the children, which the wife hath by her husband, fruit.
⁴ Which are acceptable to God.
7:5 ¹ A declaration of the former saying: for the concupiscences (saith he) which the law stirred up in us, were in us as it were an husband, of whom we brought forth very deadly and cursed children. But now since that husband is dead, and so consequently being delivered from the force of that killing law, we have passed into the governance of the spirit, so that we bring forth now, not those rotten and dead, but lively children.
² When we were in the state of the first marriage, which he calleth in the next verse following the oldness of the letter.
³ The motions that egged us to sin, which show their force even in our minds.
⁴ He saith not, of the law, but by the law, because they spring of sin which dwelleth within us, and take occasion to work thus in us, by reason of the restraint that the law maketh, not that the fault is in the law, but in ourselves.
⁵ Wrought their strength.

¹being dead ²in whom we were ³holden, that we should serve in ⁴newness of Spirit, and not in the oldness of the ⁵letter.

7 ¹What shall we say then? *Is* the Law sin? God forbid. Nay, I knew not sin, but by the Law: for I had not known ²lust, except the Law had said, ᶜThou shalt not lust.

8 But sin took an occasion by the commandment, and wrought in me all manner of concupiscence: for without the Law sin *is* ¹dead.

9 ¹For I once was alive, without the ²law: but when the commandment ³came, sin revived,

10 But I ¹died: and the same commandment which was *ordained* unto life, was found *to be* unto me unto death.

11 For sin took occasion by the commandment, and deceived me, and thereby slew *me*.

ᶜ Exod. 20:17
Deut. 5:21
ᵈ 1 Tim. 1:8

12 ¹Wherefore the Law *is* ᵈholy, and that ²commandment *is* holy, and just, and good.

13 ¹Was that then which is good, ²made death unto me? God forbid: but sin, that it might ³appear sin, wrought death in me by that which is good, that sin might be ⁴out of measure sinful by the commandment.

14 ¹For we know that the Law is spiritual, but I am carnal, sold under sin.

15 ¹For I ²allow not that which I do: for what I ³would, that do I not: but what I hate, that do I.

16 If I do then that which I would not, I consent to the Law, that *it is* good.

17 Now then, it is no more I, that do it, but ¹sin that dwelleth in me.

18 ¹For I know, that in me, that is, in my flesh, dwelleth no good thing: for to will is present with me: but I find ²no means to perform that which is

---

7:6 ¹ As if he said, The bond which bound us, is dead, and vanished away, insomuch, that sin which held us, hath not now wherewith to hold us.

² For this husband is within us.

³ Satan is an unjust possessor, for he brought us in bondage of sin and himself deceitfully: and yet notwithstanding so long as we are sinners, we sin willingly.

⁴ As becometh them, which after the death of their old husband are joined to the spirit: as whom the spirit of God hath made new men.

⁵ By the letter he meaneth the law, in respect of that old condition: for before that our will be framed by the holy Ghost, the law speaketh but to deaf men, and therefore it is dumb and dead to us, as touching the fulfilling of it.

7:7 ¹ An objection: what then? are the law and sin all one, and do they agree together? nay, saith he: Sin is reproved and condemned by the law. But because sin cannot abide to be reproved, and was not in a manner felt until it was provoked and stirred up by the law, it taketh occasion thereby to be more outrageous, and yet by no fault of the law.

² By the word, Lust, in this place he meaneth not evil lusts themselves, but the fountain from whence they spring: for the very heathen philosophers themselves condemned wicked lusts, though somewhat darkly, but as for the fountain of them, they could not so much as suspect it, and yet it is the very seat of the natural and unclean spot and filth.

7:8 ¹ Though sin be in us, yet it is not known for sin, neither doth it so rage, as it rageth after that the law is known.

7:9 ¹ He setteth himself before us for an example, in whom all men may behold, first what they are of nature before they earnestly think upon the law of God: to wit, blockish, and ready to sin and wickedness, without all true sense and feeling of sin, then what manner of persons they become, when their conscience is reproved by the testimony of the law, to wit, stubborn, and more inflamed with the desire of sin, than ever they were before.

² When I knew not the law, then me thought I lived in deed: for my conscience never troubled me, because it knew not my disease.

³ When I began to understand the commandment.

7:10 ¹ In sin, or by sin.

7:12 ¹ The conclusion: That the law of itself is holy, but all the fault is in us which abuse the law.

² Touching not coveting.

7:13 ¹ The proposition: That the Law is not the cause of death, but our corrupt nature, being therewith not only discovered, but also

stirred up, and took occasion thereby to rebel, as which, the more that things are forbidden it, the more it desireth them, and from hence cometh guiltiness, and occasion of death.

² Beareth it the blame of my death?

³ That sin might show itself to be sin, and bewray itself to be that, which is in deed.

⁴ As evil as it could, showing all the venom it could.

7:14 ¹ The cause of this matter, is this: Because that the Law requireth a heavenly pureness, but men, such as they be born, are bondslaves of corruption, which they willingly serve.

7:15 ¹ He setteth himself, being regenerate, before us, for an example, in whom may easily appear the strife of the Spirit and the flesh, and therefore of the Law of God, and our wickedness. For since that the Law in a man not regenerate bringeth forth death only, therefore in him it may easily be accused: but seeing that in a man which is regenerate, it bringeth forth good fruit, it doth better appear that evil actions proceed not from the Law, but from sin, that is, from our corrupt nature: And therefore the Apostle teacheth also, what the true use of the Law is, in reproving sin in the regenerate, unto the end of the chapter, as a little before (to wit, from the seventh verse unto this fifteenth) he declared the use of it in them which are not regenerate.

² The deeds of my life, saith he, answer not, nay they are contrary to my will: Therefore by the consent of my will with the Law, and repugnancy with the deeds of my life, it appeareth evidently, that the Law and a right ruled do persuade one thing, but corruption which hath her seat also in the regenerate, another thing.

³ It is to be noted, that one selfsame man is said to will and not to will, in divers respects: to wit, he is said to will, in that, that he is regenerate by grace: and not to will, in that, that he is not regenerate, or in that, that he is such an one as he was born. But because the part which is regenerate, at length becometh conqueror, therefore Paul sustaining the part of the regenerate, speaketh in such sort as if the corruption which sinneth willingly, were something without a man: although afterward he granteth that this evil is in his flesh, or in his members.

7:17 ¹ That natural corruption, which cleaveth fast even to them that are regenerate, and not clean conquered.

7:18 ¹ This vice, or sin, or law of sin, doth wholly possess those men which are not regenerate, and hindereth them or holdeth them back that are regenerate.

² This doth indeed agree to that man, whom the grace of God hath made a new man: for where the Spirit is not, how can there be any strife there.

good,

19 For I do not the good thing, which I would, but the evil, which I would not, that do I.

20 Now if I do that I would not, it is no more I that do it, but the sin that dwelleth in me.

21 ¹I find then that when I would do good, I am thus yoked, that evil is present with me.

22 For I delight in the Law of God, concerning the ¹inner man.

23 But I see another Law in my members, rebelling against the law of my ¹mind, and leading me captive unto the law of sin, which is in my members.

24 ¹O ²wretched man that I am, who shall deliver me from the body of this death!

25 I ¹thank God through Jesus Christ our Lord. Then I ²myself in my mind serve the Law of God, but in my flesh the law of sin.

8 *1 He concludeth that there is no condemnation to them, who are grafted in Christ through his Spirit, 3 howsoever they be as yet burdened with sins: 9 For they live through that Spirit, 14 Whose testimony, 15 driveth away all fear, 28 and relieveth our present miseries.*

1 Now ¹then there *is* no condemnation to them that are in Christ Jesus, which ²walk not after the ³flesh, but after the Spirit.

2 ¹For the ²Law of the Spirit of ³life *which is* in ⁴Christ Jesus, hath ⁵freed me from the Law of sin and of death.

3 ¹For (that that was ²impossible to the Law, inasmuch as it was weak, because of the ³flesh) God sending his own Son, in the similitude of ⁴sinful flesh, and for ⁵sin, ⁶condemned sin in the flesh,

4 That that ¹righteousness of the Law might be fulfilled ²in us, which walk not after the flesh, but

---

7:21 ¹ The conclusion: As the Law of God exhorteth to goodness, so doth the Law of sin (that is, the corruption wherein we are born) force us to wickedness: but the Spirit, that is, our mind, in that that it is regenerate, consenteth with the Law of God: but the flesh, that is, the whole natural man, is bondslave to the Law of sin. Therefore to be short, wickedness and death are not of the Law, but of sin, which reigneth in them that are not regenerate: for they neither will, nor do good, but will, and do evil: But in them that are regenerate, it striveth against the Spirit or law of the mind, so that they cannot either live so well as they would, or be so void of sin as they would.

7:22 ¹ The inner man, and the new man are all one, and are answerable and set as contrary to the old man: neither doth this word, Inner man, signify man's mind and reason, and the old man, the powers that are under them, as the Philosophers imagine, but by the outward man is meant whatsoever is either without or within a man, from top to toe, so long as that man is not born anew by the grace of God.

7:23 ¹ The law of the mind in this place, is not to be understood of the mind as it is naturally, and as our mind is from our birth, but of the mind which is renewed by the Spirit of God.

7:24 ¹ It is a miserable thing to be yet in part subject to sin, which of its own nature maketh us guilty of death: but we must cry to the Lord, who will by death itself at length make us conquerors as we are already conquerors in Christ.

² Wearied with miserable and continual conflict.

7:25 ¹ He recovereth himself, and showeth us that he resteth only in Christ.

² This is the true perfection of them that are born anew, to confess that they are imperfect.

8:1 ¹ A conclusion of all the former disputation from Rom 1:16 even to this place: Seeing that we being justified by faith in Christ, do obtain remission of sins and imputation of righteousness, and are also sanctified, it followeth hereof, that they that are grafted into Christ by faith, are out of all fear of condemnation.

² The fruits of the Spirit, or effects of sanctification, which is begun in us, do not ingraft us into Christ, but do declare that we are grafted into him.

³ Follow not the flesh for their guide: for he is not said to live after the flesh, that hath the holy Ghost for his guide, though sometimes he step away.

8:2 ¹ A preventing of an objection: seeing that the virtue of the spirit which is in us, is so weak, how may we gather thereby, that there is no condemnation to them that have that virtue? because saith he, that

virtue of the quickening spirit which is so weak in us, is most perfect and most mighty in Christ, and being imputed unto us which believe, causeth us to be so accounted of, as though there were no relics of corruption, and death in us. Therefore hitherto Paul disputed of remission of sins, and imputation of fulfilling the Law, and also of sanctification which is begun in us: but now he speaketh of the perfect imputation of Christ's manhood, which part was necessarily required to the full appeasing of our consciences: for our sins are defaced by the blood of Christ, and the guiltiness of our corruption is covered with the imputation of Christ's obedience: and the corruption itself (which the Apostle calleth sinful sin) is healed in us by little and little, by the gift of sanctification, but yet it lacketh besides that another remedy, to wit, the perfect sanctification of Christ's own flesh, which also is to us imputed.

² The power and authority of the spirit, against which is set the tyranny of sin.

³ Which mortifieth the old man, and quickeneth the new man.

⁴ To wit, absolutely and perfectly.

⁵ For Christ's sanctification being imputed unto us, perfecteth our sanctification which is begun in us.

8:3 ¹ He useth no argument here, but expoundeth the mystery of sanctification, which is imputed unto us: for because, that the virtue of the law was not such (and that by reason of the corruption of our nature) that it could make man pure and perfect: and for that it rather kindled the disease of sin, than did put it out and extinguish it, therefore God clothed his Son with flesh like unto our sinful flesh, wherein he utterly abolished our corruption, that being accounted thoroughly pure and without fault in him apprehended and laid hold on by faith, we might be found to have fully that singular perfection which the Law requireth, and therefore that there might be no condemnation in us.

² Which is not proper to the Law, but cometh by our fault.

³ In man not born anew, whose disease the law could not heal it.

⁴ Of man's nature which was corrupt through sin, until he sanctified it.

⁵ To abolish sin in our flesh.

⁶ Showed that sin hath no right in us.

8:4 ¹ The very substance of the law of God might be fulfilled, or that same which the law requireth, that we may be found just before God: for if with our justification there be joined that sanctification which is imputed to us, we are just, according to the perfect form which the Lord requireth.

² He returneth to that which he said, that the sanctification which is begun in us, is a sure testimony of our ingrafting into Christ, which is a most plentiful fruit of a godly and honest life.

after the Spirit.

5 ¹For they that are after the ²flesh, savor the things of the flesh: but they that are after the Spirit, the things of the Spirit.

6 ¹For the wisdom of the flesh *is* death: but the wisdom of the Spirit *is* life and peace,

7 ¹Because the wisdom of the flesh *is* enmity against God: ²for it is not subject to the Law of God, neither indeed can be.

8 ¹So then they that are in the flesh, cannot please God.

9 ¹Now ye are not in the flesh, but in the Spirit, because the spirit of God dwelleth in you: but if any man hath not the Spirit of Christ, the same is not his.

10 ¹And if Christ be in you, the ²body is dead, because of sin: but the Spirit *is* life for righteousness sake.

11 ¹But if the Spirit of him that raised up Jesus from the dead, dwell in you, he that raised up Christ from the dead, shall also quicken your mortal bodies, by his Spirit that ²dwelleth in you.

12 ¹Therefore brethren, we are debtors not to the flesh, to live after the flesh:

13 ¹For if ye live after the flesh, ye shall die: but if ye mortify the deeds of the body by the Spirit, ye shall live.

14 ¹For as many as are led by the Spirit of God, they are the sons of God.

15 ¹For ye have not received the ²Spirit of bondage, to ³fear again: but ye have received the Spirit of ⁴adoption, whereby we cry, Abba, Father.

16 The same Spirit beareth witness with our spirit, that we are the children of God.

17 ¹If *we be* children, *we are* also ²heirs, even the heirs of God, and heirs annexed with Christ: ³if so be that we suffer with him, that we may also be glorified with him.

18 ¹For I ²count that the afflictions of this present time *are* not worthy of the glory, which shall be showed unto us.

19 ¹For the fervent desire of the ²creature waiteth

8:5 ¹ A reason why to walk after the flesh, agreeth not to them which are grafted in Christ, but to walk after the spirit agreeth and is meet for them: because, saith he, that they which are after the flesh, savor the things of the flesh, but they that are after the spirit, the things of the spirit.

² They that live as the flesh leadeth them.

8:6 ¹ He proveth the consequent: because that whatsoever the flesh savoreth, that engendereth death: and whatsoever the spirit savoreth, that tendeth to joy and life everlasting.

8:7 ¹ A reason and proof, why the wisdom of the flesh is death: because, saith he, it is the enemy of God.

² A reason why the wisdom of the flesh is enemy to God: because it neither will neither can be subject to him. And by flesh he meaneth a man not regenerate.

8:8 ¹ The conclusion: therefore they that walk after the flesh, cannot please God: whereby it followeth, that they are not ingrafted into Christ.

8:9 ¹ He cometh to the others, to wit, to them which walk after the spirit, of whom we have to understand contrary things to the former: and first of all he defineth what it is to be in the spirit, or to be sanctified: to wit, to have the spirit of God dwelling in us; then he declareth, that sanctification is so joined and knit to our grafting in Christ, that it can by no means be separated.

8:10 ¹ He confirmeth the faithful against the relics of flesh and sin, granting that they are yet (as appeareth by the corruption which is in them) touching one of their parts (which he calleth the body, that is to say, a lump) which is not yet purged from the earthly filthiness in death: but therewithall willing them to doubt nothing of the happy success of their combat, because that even the little spark of the Spirit, (that is, of the grace of regeneration) which appeareth to be in them by the fruits of righteousness, is the seed of life.

² The flesh, or all that which as yet sticketh fast in the clefts of sin, and death.

8:11 ¹ A confirmation of the former sentence. You have the selfsame Spirit, which Christ hath: Therefore at length it shall die the same in you, that it did in Christ, to wit, when all infirmities being utterly laid aside, and death overcome, it shall clothe you with heavenly glory.

² By the virtue and power of it, which showed the same might first in our head, and daily worketh in his members.

8:12 ¹ An exhortation to oppress the flesh daily more and more by the virtue of the Spirit of regeneration, because (saith he) you are debtors unto God, forsomuch as you have received so many benefits of him.

8:13 ¹ Another reason of the profit that ensueth: for such as strive and fight valiantly, shall have everlasting life.

8:14 ¹ A confirmation of this reason: they be the children of God, which are governed by his Spirit, therefore shall they have life everlasting.

8:15 ¹ He declareth and expoundeth by the way, in these two verses, by what right this name, to be called the children of God, is given to the believers: because saith he, they have received the grace of the Gospel, wherein God showeth himself, not (as before in the publishing of the Law) terrible and fearful, but a most benign and loving father in Christ, so that with great boldness we call him Father, that holy Ghost sealing this adoption in our hearts by faith.

² By the Spirit is meant the holy Ghost, whom we are said to receive, when he worketh in our minds.

³ Which fear is stirred up in our minds, by the preaching of the Law.

⁴ Which sealeth our adoption in our minds, and therefore openeth our mouths.

8:17 ¹ A proof of the consequent of the confirmation: because that he which is the Son of God, doth enjoy God with Christ.

² Partakers of our father's goods, and that freely, because we are children by adoption.

³ Now Paul teacheth by what way the sons of God do come to that felicity, to wit, by the cross, as Christ himself did: and therewithall openeth unto them fountains of comfort: as first, that we have Christ a companion and fellow of our afflictions: secondly, that we shall be also his followers in that everlasting glory.

8:18 ¹ Thirdly that this glory which we look for, doth a thousand parts surmount the misery of our afflictions.

² All being well considered, I gather.

8:19 ¹ Fourthly, he plainly teacheth us that we shall certainly be renewed from that confusion and horrible deformation of the whole world, which cannot be continual, as it was not at the beginning: But as it had a beginning by the sin of man, for whom it was made by the ordinance of God, so shall it at length be restored with the elect.

² All this world.

when the sons of God shall be revealed,

20 Because the creature is subject to ¹vanity, not of its ²own will, but by reason ³of him, which hath subdued it under ⁴hope,

21 Because the creature also shall be delivered from the ¹bondage of corruption into the glorious liberty of the sons of God.

22 For we know that every creature groaneth with us also, and ¹travaileth in pain together unto this present.

23 ¹And not only *the creature*, but we also which have the firstfruits of the Spirit, even we do sigh in ²ourselves, waiting for the adoption, *even* ³,ᵃthe redemption of our body.

24 ¹For we are saved by hope: but ²hope that is seen, is not hope: for how can a man hope for that which he seeth?

25 But if we hope for that we see not, we do with patience abide for it.

26 ¹Likewise the Spirit also ²helpeth our infirmities: for we know not what to pray as we ought: but the Spirit itself maketh ³request for us with sighs, which cannot be expressed.

27 But he that searcheth the hearts, knoweth what is the ¹meaning of the Spirit: for he maketh request for the Saints, ²according to *the will of* God.

CHAPTER 8
ᵃ Luke 21:28
ᵇ Ps. 44:22

28 ¹Also we know that ²all things work together for the best unto them that love God, even to them that are called of *his* ³purpose.

29 For those which he knew before, he also predestinated to be made like to the image of his Son, that he might be the firstborn among many brethren.

30 Moreover, whom he ¹predestinated, them also he called, and whom he called, them also he justified, and whom he justified, them he also glorified.

31 ¹What shall we then say to these things? If God be on our side, who *can be* against us?

32 Who spared not his own Son, but gave him for us all *to death*, how shall he not with him ¹give us all things also?

33 ¹Who shall lay anything to the charge of God's chosen? *it is* ²God that justifieth.

34 Who shall condemn? *it is* Christ which is dead: yea, or rather, which is risen again, who is also at the right hand of God, and maketh request also for us.

35 Who shall separate us from the love of ¹Christ? shall tribulation or anguish, or persecution, or famine, or nakedness, or peril, or sword?

36 As it is written, ᵇFor thy sake are we killed all day long: we are counted as sheep for the slaughter:

37 ¹Nevertheless, in all these things we are more than conquerors through him that loved us.

8:20 ¹ Is subject to a vanishing and flitting state.

² Not by their natural inclination.

³ That they should obey the Creator's commandment, whom it pleased to show by their fickle estate, how greatly he was displeased with man.

⁴ God would not make the world subject to everlasting curse, for the sin of man, but gave it hope that it should be restored.

8:21 ¹ From the corruption which they are now subject to, they shall be delivered and changed into that blessed state of incorruption, which shall be revealed when the sons of God shall be advanced to glory.

8:22 ¹ By this word is meant, not only exceeding sorrow, but also the fruit that followeth of it.

8:23 ¹ Fifthly, if the rest of the world looks for a restoring, groaning as it were for it, and that not in vain, let it not grieve us also to sigh, yea, let us be more certainly persuaded of our redemption to come, forasmuch as we have the firstfruits of the Spirit.

² Even from the bottom of our hearts.

³ That last restoring, which shall be the accomplishment of our adoption.

8:24 ¹ Sixthly, hope is necessarily joined with faith: seeing then that we believe those things, which we are not yet in possession of, and hope respected not the thing that is present, we must therefore hope and patiently wait for that which we believe shall come to pass.

² This is spoken by the figure Metonymy: Hope, for that which is hoped for.

8:26 ¹ Seventhly, There is no cause why we should faint under the burden of afflictions, seeing that prayers minister unto us a most sure help, which cannot be frustrated, seeing they proceed from the spirit of God which dwelleth in us.

² Beareth our burden, as it were that we faint not under it.

³ Provoketh us to prayers, and telleth us as it were within, what we shall say, and how we shall groan.

8:27 ¹ What sobs and sighs proceed from the instinct of his Spirit.

² Because he teacheth the godly to pray according to God's will.

8:28 ¹ Eighthly, we are not afflicted, either by chance or to our harm, but by God's providence for our great profit, who as he chose us from the beginning, so hath he predestined us to be made like to the image of his Son: and therefore will bring us in his time, being called and justified, to glory, by the cross.

² Not only afflictions, but whatsoever else.

³ He calleth that, Purpose, which God hath from everlasting appointed with himself according to his good will and pleasure.

8:30 ¹ He useth the time past, for the time present, as the Hebrews use, who sometimes set down the thing that is to come, by the time that is past, to signify the certainty of it: and he hath also regard to God's continual working.

8:31 ¹ Ninethly, we have no cause to fear that the Lord will not give us whatsoever is profitable for us, seeing that he hath not spared his own Son to save us.

8:32 ¹ Give us freely.

8:33 ¹ A most glorious and comfortable conclusion of the whole second part of this Epistle, that is, of the treatise of justification. There are no accusers that we have need to be afraid of before God, seeing that God himself absolveth us as just: and therefore much less need we to fear damnation, seeing that we rest upon the death and resurrection, the almighty power and defense of Jesus Christ. Therefore what can there be so weighty in this life, or of so great force and power, that might seize us, as though we might fall from the love of God, wherewith he loveth us in Christ: Surely nothing. Seeing that it is in itself most constant and sure, and also in us being confirmed by steadfast faith.

² Who pronounceth us not only guiltless, but also perfectly just in his Son.

8:35 ¹ Wherewith Christ loveth us.

8:37 ¹ We are not only not overcome with so great and many miseries and calamities, but also more than conquerors in all of them.

38 For I am persuaded that neither death, nor life, nor Angels, nor principalities, nor powers, nor things present, nor things to come,

39 Nor height, nor depth, nor any other creature, shall be able to separate us from the love of God, which is in Christ Jesus our Lord.

9

1 He answereth an objection, that might be brought on the Jews' behalf, 7 and telleth of two sorts of Abraham's children, 15 and that God worketh all things in this matter according to his will, 20 even as the potter doth. 24, 30 He proveth as well the calling of the Gentiles, 31 as also the rejecting of the Jews, 25, 27 by the testimony of the Prophets.

1 I say [1]the truth in Christ, I lie not, my conscience bearing me witness in the holy Ghost,

2 That I have great heaviness, and continual sorrow in mine heart.

3 For I would wish myself to be [1]separate from Christ, for my brethren that are my kinsmen according to the [2]flesh,

4 Which are the Israelites, to whom *pertaineth* the adoption, and the [1]glory, and the [a,2]Covenants, and the giving of the [3]Law, and the [4]service *of God*, and the [5]promises.

CHAPTER 9
a Rom. 2:17
   Eph. 2:12
b Rom. 2:28
c Gen. 21:12
   Heb. 11:18
d Gal. 4:28
e Gen. 18:10
f Gen. 25:21
g Gen. 25:23
h Mal. 1:2

5 Of whom *are* the fathers, and of whom concerning the flesh, Christ *came*, who is [1]God over all, blessed forever, Amen.

6 [b,1]Notwithstanding it cannot be that the word of God should take none effect: for all they are not [2]Israel, which are of Israel:

7 Neither *are they* all children, because they are the seed of Abraham: [c,1]but, In [2]Isaac shall thy seed be called:

8 [1]That is, they which are the children of the [2]flesh, are not the children of God: but the [d]children of the [3]promise, are counted for the seed.

9 [1]For this is a word of promise, [e]In this same time will I come, and Sarah shall have a son.

10 [1]Neither *he* only *felt this*, but also [f]Rebecca, when she had conceived by one, *even* by our father Isaac.

11 For ere *the children* were born, and when they had neither done good nor evil (that the [1]purpose of God might [2]remain according to election, not by works, but by him that calleth.)

12 [1]It was said unto her, [g]The Elder shall serve the younger.

13 As it is written, [h]I have loved Jacob, and have hated Esau.

9:1 [1] The third part of this Epistle, even to the twelfth Chapter, wherein Paul ascendeth to the higher causes of faith: and first of all because he purposed to speak much of the casting off of the Jews, he useth an insinuation, declaring by a double or triple oath, and by witnessing of his great desire towards their salvation, his singular love towards them, and therewithall granting unto them all their prerogatives.

9:3 [1] The Apostle loved his brethren so entirely, that if it have been possible he would have been ready to have redeemed the casting away of the Israelites, with the loss of his own soul forever: for this word separate, betokeneth as much in this place.

[2] Being brethren by flesh, as of one nation and country.

9:4 [1] The ark of the covenant, which was a token of God's presence.

[2] The tables of the covenant: and this is spoken by the figure Metonymy.

[3] Of the judicial Law.

[4] The ceremonial Law.

[5] Which were made to Abraham and to his posterity.

9:5 [1] A most manifest testimony of the Godhead and divinity of Christ.

9:6 [1] He entereth into the handling of predestination by a kind of preventing an objection: How may it be, that Israel is cast off, but that therewithall we must also make the covenant which God made with Abraham and his seed, frustrate and void? He answereth therefore, that God's word is true, although that Israel be cast off: for the election of the people of Israel is so general and common, that notwithstanding the same, God chooseth by his secret counsel, such as it pleaseth him. So then this is the proposition and state of this Treatise: The grace of salvation is offered generally in such sort, that notwithstanding it, the efficacy thereof pertaineth only to the elect.

[2] Israel in the first place, is taken for Jacob: and in the second, for the Israelites.

9:7 [1] The first proof is taken from the example of Abraham's own house, wherein Isaac only was counted the son, and that by God's ordinance: although that Ishmael also was born of Abraham, and circumcised before Isaac.

[2] Isaac shall be thy true and natural son, and therefore heir of thy blessing.

9:8 [1] A general application of the former proof or example.

[2] Which are born of Abraham by the course of nature.

[3] Which are born by virtue of the promise.

9:9 [1] A reason of that application: Because that Isaac was born by the virtue of the promise, and therefore he was not chosen, nay he was not at all, but by the free will of God: whereby it followeth that the promise is the fountain of predestination, and not the flesh from which promise the particular election proceedeth: that is, that the elect be born elect: and not that they be first born and then afterward elected, in respect of God who doth predestinate.

9:10 [1] Another forcible proof, taken from the example of Esau and Jacob, which were both born of the same Isaac, which was the son of promise, of one mother, and at one birth, and not at divers as Ishmael and Isaac were: and yet notwithstanding, Esau being cast off, only Jacob was chosen: and that before their birth, that neither any goodness of Jacob's might be thought to be the cause of his election, neither any wickedness of Esau, of his casting away.

9:11 [1] God's decree, which proceedeth of his mere good will, whereby it pleased him to choose one, and refuse the other.

[2] Paul saith not, *might be made*, but *being made, might remain*. Therefore they are deceived which make foreseen faith the cause of election, and foreknown infidelity, the cause of reprobation.

9:12 [1] He proveth the casting away of Esau by that, that he was made servant to his brother: and proveth the choosing of Jacob by that that he was made Lord of his brother, although his brother were the first begotten. And lest that any man might take this saying of God, and refer it to external things, the Apostle showeth out of Malachi, who is a good interpreter of Moses, that the servitude of Esau was joined with the hatred of God, and the Lordship of Jacob with the love of God.

14 [1]What shall we say then? Is there [2]unrighteousness with God? God forbid.

15 [1]For he saith to Moses, [i]I will [2]have mercy on him, to whom I will show mercy: and will have [3]compassion on him, on who I will have compassion.

16 [1]So then *it is* not in him that [2]willeth, nor in him that runneth, but in God that showeth mercy.

17 [1]For the [2]Scripture saith unto Pharaoh, [j]For this same purpose have [3]I stirred thee up, that I might [4]show my power in thee, and that my Name might

[i] Exod. 33:19
[j] Exod. 9:16
[k] Isa. 45:9
[l] Jer. 18:6

be declared throughout all the earth.

18 [1]Therefore he hath mercy on whom he [2]will, and whom he will he hardeneth.

19 [1]Thou wilt say then unto me, Why doth he yet complain? for who hath resisted his will?

20 [1]But, O man, who art thou which pleadest against God? [2]shall the [k]thing [3]formed say to him that formed it, Why hast thou made me thus?

21 [l.1]Hath not the potter power of the clay to make of the same lump one [2]vessel to [3]honor, and another unto [4]dishonor?

9:14 [1] The first objection: If God doth love or hate upon no consideration of worthiness or unworthiness, then [is] he unjust, because he may love them which are unworthy, and hate them that are worthy. The Apostle detesteth this blasphemy, and afterward answereth it severally, point by point.

[2] Man's will knoweth no other causes of love or hatred, but those that are in the persons, and thereupon this objection riseth.

9:15 [1] He answereth first touching them which are chosen to salvation. in choosing of whom, he denieth that God may seem unjust, although he choose and predestinate to salvation, them that are not yet born, without any respect of worthiness: because he bringeth not the chosen to the appointed end, but by the means of his mercy, which is a cause next under predestination. Now mercy presupposeth misery, and again misery presupposeth sin or voluntary corruption of mankind, and corruption presupposeth a pure and perfect creation. Moreover mercy is showed by her degrees: to wit, by calling, by faith, by justification and sanctification, so that at length we come to glorification, as the Apostle will show afterward. Now all these things, orderly following the purpose of God, do clearly prove that he can by no means seem unjust in loving and saving his.

[2] I will be merciful and favorable to whom I list to be favorable.

[3] I will have compassion on whomsoever I list to have compassion.

9:16 [1] The conclusion of the answer: Therefore God is not unjust in choosing and saving of his free goodness, such as it pleaseth him: as he also answered Moses, when he prayed for all the people.

[2] By will, he meaneth the thought and endeavor of heart, and by running, good works: to neither of which he giveth the praise, but only to the mercy of God.

9:17 [1] Now he answereth concerning the reprobate or them whom God hateth being not yet born, and hath appointed to destruction, without any respect of unworthiness. And first of all he proveth this to be true, by alleging the testimony of God himself touching Pharaoh, whom he stirred up to this purpose, that he might be glorified in his hardening and just punishing.

[2] God so speaketh unto Pharaoh in the Scripture, or, the Scripture bringeth in God, so speaking to Pharaoh, Exodus 9:16.

[3] Brought thee into this world.

[4] Secondly, he bringeth the end of God's counsel, to show that there is no unrighteousness in him. Now this chiefest end, is not properly and simply the destruction of the wicked, but God's glory which appeareth in their rightful punishment.

9:18 [1] A conclusion of the full answer to the first objection: therefore seeing that God doth not save them whom he freely chose according to his good will and pleasure, but by justifying and sanctifying them by his grace, his counsel in saving them cannot seem unjust. And again, there is not injustice in the everlasting counsel of God touching the destruction of them whom he listeth to destroy, for that he hardeneth before he destroyeth: Therefore the third answer for the maintenance of God's justice is the everlasting counsel of reprobation, consisteth in this word

Hardening: which notwithstanding he concealed in the former verse, because the History of Pharaoh was well known. But the force of the word is great: for Hardening, which is set against Mercy, presupposeth the same things that mercy did, to wit, a voluntary corruption, wherein the reprobate are hardened: and again corruption presupposeth a perfect state of creation. Moreover, this hardening also is voluntary, for God so hardeneth being offended with corruption, that he useth their own will whom he hardeneth, to the executing of that judgment. Then follow the fruits of Hardening, to wit, unbelief and sin, which are the true and proper causes of the condemnation of the reprobate. Why doth he then appoint to destruction? because he will: why doth he harden? because they are corrupt: why doth he condemn? because they are sinners. Where is then unrighteousness? Nay, if he should destroy all after this same sort, to whom should he do injury?

[2] Whom it pleased him to appoint, to show his favor upon.

9:19 [1] Another objection but only for the reprobate, rising upon the former answer. If God do appoint to everlasting destruction, such as he listeth, and if that cannot be hindered notwithstanded that he hath once decreed, how doth he justly condemn them, which perish by his will?

9:20 [1] The Apostle doth not answer that it is not God's will, or that God doth not either reject or elect according to his pleasure, which thing the wicked call blasphemy, but he rather granteth, his adversary both the antecedents, to wit, that it is God's will, and that it must of necessity so fall out, yet he denieth that God is therefore to be thought an unjust revenger of the wicked: for seeing it appeareth by manifest proof that this is the will of God and his doing, what impudency is it for man, which is but dust and ashes to dispute with God, and as it were to call him into judgment? Now if any man say that the doubt is not so dissolved and answered, I answer, that there is no surer demonstration in any matter, because it is grounded upon this principle, That the will of God is the rule of righteousness.

[2] An amplification of the former answer, taken from a comparison, whereby also it appeareth that God's determined counsel is set of Paul the highest of all causes, so that it dependeth not upon any respect of second causes, but doth rather frame and direct them.

[3] This similitude agreeth very fitly in the first creation of mankind.

9:21 [1] Alluding to the creation of Adam, he compareth mankind not yet made (but in the Creator's mind) to a lump of clay: whereof afterward God made and doth daily make, according as he purposed from everlasting both such as should be elect, and such as should be reprobate, as also this word, making, declareth.

[2] Whereas in the objection propounded, mention was only made of vessels to dishonor: yet he speaketh of the other also in this answer, for that he proveth the Creator to be just in either of them, as the rule of contraries doth require.

[3] To honest uses.

[4] Seeing then, that in the name of dishonor, the ignomy of everlasting death is signified, they speak with Paul, which say, that some are made of God to most just destruction: and they [that] are offended with this kind of speech bewray their own folly.

22 [1]*What* and if God would, to show his wrath, and to make his power known, suffer with long patience the [2]vessels of wrath, prepared to [3]destruction?

23 And that he might declare the [1]riches of his glory upon the vessels of mercy, which he hath prepared unto glory?

24 [1]Even us whom he hath called, not of the [2]Jews only, but also of the Gentiles.

25 [1]As he saith also in Hosea, [m]I will call them, My people, which were not my people: and her, Beloved, which was not beloved.

26 And it shall be in the place where it was said unto them, [n]Ye are not my people, that there they shall be called, The children of the living God.

27 [1]Also Isaiah crieth concerning Israel, [o]Though the number of the children of Israel were as the sand of the sea, *yet* shall *but* a remnant be saved.

28 For he will make his account, and gather it into a [1]short sum with righteousness: for the Lord will make a short count in the earth.

29 [p]And as Isaiah said before, Except the Lord of [1]hosts had left us a [2]seed, we had been made as Sodom, and had been like to Gomorrah.

30 [1]What shall we say then? That the Gentiles which followed [2]not righteousness, have attained unto righteousness, even the righteousness which is of faith.

31 [1]But Israel which followed the Law of righteousness, could not attain unto the Law of righteousness.

32 Wherefore? Because *they sought it* not by faith, but as *it were* by the [1]works of the Law: for they have stumbled at the stumbling stone,

33 As it is written, [q]Behold, I lay in Zion a stumbling stone, and a rock to make men fall: and everyone that believeth in him, shall not be ashamed.

Marginal references:
[m] Hos. 2:23; 1 Pet. 2:10
[n] Hos. 1:10
[o] Isa. 20:21
[p] Isa. 1:9
[q] Ps. 118:22; Isa. 8:14; Isa. 28:16; 1 Pet. 2:6

CHAPTER 10
[a] Gal. 3:24

10

1 He handleth the effects of election,   3 that some refuse, and some embrace.   4 Christ, who is the end of the Law.   15 He showeth that Moses foretold the calling of the Gentiles,   20 and Isaiah the hardening of the Jews.

1 Brethren, [1]mine hearts desire and prayer to God for Israel is, that they might be saved.

2 For I bear them record that they have the zeal of God, but not according to knowledge.

3 [1]For they, [2]being ignorant of the righteousness of God, and going about to [3]establish their own righteousness, have not submitted themselves to the righteousness of God.

4 [a,1]For Christ *is* the [2]end of the Law for righteousness unto [3]everyone that believeth.

9:22 [1] The second answer is this, that God, moreover and besides that he doth justly decree whatsoever he doth decree, useth that moderation in executing of his decrees, as declareth his singular lenity even in the reprobate in that, that he suffereth them a long time, and permitteth them to enjoy many and singular benefits, until at length he justly condemns them: and that to good end and purpose, to wit, to show himself to be an enemy and revenger of wickedness, that it may appear what power he is of by these severe judgments, and finally by comparison of contraries to set forth indeed, how great his mercy is towards the elect.

[2] By vessels, the Hebrews understand all kinds of instruments.

[3] Therefore again, we may say with Paul that some men are made of God the Creator to destruction.

9:23 [1] The unmeasurable and marvelous greatness.

9:24 [1] Having established the doctrine of the eternal predestination of God on both parts: that is, as well of the reprobate, as of the elect, he cometh now to show the use of it, teaching us that we ought not to seek the testimony of it in the secret counsel of God, but by the vocation which is made manifest and set forth in the Church, propounding unto us the example of the Jews and Gentiles, that the doctrine may be better perceived.

[2] He saith not that all and every one of the Jews are called, but some of the Jews, and some of the Gentiles.

9:25 [1] Our vocation or calling is free and of grace, even as our predestination is: and therefore there is no cause why either our own unworthiness, or the unworthiness of our ancestors should cause us to think that we are not the elect and chosen of God, if we be called of him, and so embrace through faith the salvation that is offered us.

9:27 [1] Contrariwise, Neither any outward general calling, neither any worthiness of our ancestors is a sufficient witness of election, unless by faith and belief we answer God's calling: which thing came to pass in the Jews, as the Lord had forewarned.

9:28 [1] God purposeth to bring the unkind and unthankful people to an extreme fewness.

9:29 [1] Armies, by which word the chiefest power that is, is given to God.

[2] Even a very few.

9:30 [1] The declaration and manifestation of our election, is our calling apprehended by faith, as it came to pass in the Gentiles.

[2] So then, the Gentiles had no works to prepare and procure God's mercy beforehand: and as for that, that the Gentiles attained to that which they sought not for, the mercy of God is to be thanked for it: and in that the Jews attained not that which they sought after, they can thank none for it but themselves, because they sought it not aright.

9:31 [1] The pride of men is the cause that they condemn vocation, so that the cause of their damnation need not to be sought for any other where but in themselves.

9:32 [1] Seeking to come by righteousness, they followed the Law of righteousness.

10:1 [1] Purposing to set forth in the Jews an example of marvelous obstinacy, he useth an insinuation.

10:3 [1] The first entrance into the vocation unto salvation, is to renounce our own righteousness: the next is, to embrace that righteousness by faith, which God freely offereth us the Gospel.

[2] The ignorance of the Law which we ought to know, excuseth none before God, especially it excuseth not them that are of his household.

[3] Ignorance hath always pride joined with it.

10:4 [1] The proof: The Law itself hath respect unto Christ, that such as believe in him should be saved. Therefore the calling to salvation by the works of the law is vain and foolish, but Christ is offered for salvation to every believer.

[2] The end of the Law is to justify them that keep the Law: but seeing we do not observe the Law through the fault of our flesh, we attain not unto this end: but Christ salveth this disease, for he fulfilled the Law for us.

[3] Not only to the Jews, but also to the Gentiles.

5 [1]For Moses *thus* describeth the righteousness which is of the Law, [b]That the man which doeth these things, shall live thereby.

6 But the righteousness which is of faith, speaketh on this wise, [c,1]Say not in thine heart, Who shall ascend into heaven? (that is to bring Christ from above.)

7 Or, Who shall descend into the deep? (that is to bring Christ again from the dead.)

8 [1]But what saith it? [d]The [2]word is near thee, *even* in thy mouth, and in thine heart. This is the word of faith which we preach.

9 [1]For if thou shalt [2]confess with thy mouth the Lord Jesus, and shalt believe in thine heart, that [3]God raised him up from the dead, thou shalt be saved:

10 For with the heart man [1]believeth unto righteousness, and with the mouth man confesseth to salvation.

11 [1]For the Scripture saith, [e]Whosoever [2]believeth in him, shall not be ashamed.

12 For there is no difference between the Jew and the Grecian: for he that is Lord over all, is rich unto all that call on him.

13 [f,1]For whosoever shall call upon the Name of the Lord, shall be saved.

14 But how shall they call on him, in whom they have not believed? [1]and how shall they believe in him, of whom they have not heard? and how shall they hear without a preacher?

15 And how shall they preach, except they be sent? as it is written, [g]How beautiful are the feet of them which bring glad tidings of peace, and bring glad tidings of good things!

16 [1]But they have not [2]all obeyed the Gospel: for Isaiah saith, [h]Lord, who hath believed our report?

17 [1]Then faith *is* by hearing, and hearing by the [2]word of God.

18 [1]But I demand, Have they not heard? [i]No doubt their sound went out through all the earth, and their words into the ends of the world.

19 [1]But I demand, Did not Israel know *God*? First Moses saith, [j]I will provoke you to envy by a [2]nation that is not my *nation*, and by a foolish *nation* I will anger you.

20 [k]And Isaiah is [1]bold, and saith, I was found of them that sought me not, and have been made manifest to them that asked not after me.

21 And unto Israel he saith, All the day long have I stretched forth mine hand unto a disobedient, and gainsaying people.

11   1 *Lest the casting off of the Jews should be limited according to the outward appearance,*   4 *he showeth*

Cross references:
[b] Lev. 18:5, Ezek. 20:11, Gal. 3:12
[c] Deut. 30:12
[d] Deut. 30:14
[e] Isa. 28:16
[f] Joel 2:32
[g] Isa. 52:7, Nah. 1:15
[h] Isa. 53:1, John 12:38
[i] Ps. 19:3
[j] Deut. 32:21
[k] Isa. 65:1

10:5 [1] That the Law regardeth and tendeth to Christ, that is a manifest proof, for that is propoundeth such a condition, as can be and is fulfilled of none but Christ only: which being imputed unto us by faith, our conscience is quieted, so that now no man can ask, Who can ascend up into heaven, or bring us from hell, seeing the Gospel teacheth that both of these is done by Christ, and that for their sakes, which with true faith embrace him which calleth them.

10:6 [1] Think not with thyself, as men that are staggering use to do.

10:8 [1] Vocation cometh by the word preached.

[2] By the word, Moses understood the Law which the Lord published with his own voice: and Paul applied it to the preaching of the Gospel which was the perfection of the Law.

10:9 [1] That is indeed true faith which is settled not only in the head, but also in the heart of man, whereof also we give testimony, by our outward life, and which tendeth to Christ as to our alone and only Savior, even as he setteth forth himself in his word.

[2] If thou profess plainly, sincerely, and openly, that thou takest Jesus only to be thy Lord and Savior.

[3] The Father, who is said to have raised the Son from the dead: and this is not spoken to shut out the divinity of the Son, but to set forth the Father's counsel touching our redemption in the resurrection of the Son.

10:10 [1] Faith is said to justify, and furthermore seeing the confession of the mouth is an effect of faith, and confession is the way to come to salvation, it followeth that faith is also said to save.

10:11 [1] Now he proveth the other part which he propounded afore in the fourth verse, to wit, that Christ calleth whomsoever he listeth without any difference, and this he confirmeth by a double testimony.

[2] To believe in God is to yield and consent to God's promise of our salvation by Christ, and that not only in general, but when we know that the promises pertain to us whereupon riseth a sure trust.

10:13 [1] True calling upon the Name of God is the testimony of true faith, and true faith of true vocation or calling, and true calling, of true election.

10:14 [1] That is, true faith which seeketh God in his word, and preached according as God hath appointed in the Church.

10:16 [1] Wheresover faith is, there is also the word, but not contrariwise, wheresoever the word is, there is faith also: for many refuse and reject the word.

[2] He speaketh this because of the Jews.

10:17 [1] A conclusion of the former gradation: we must ascend from faith, to our vocation, as by our vocation we came to the testimony of our election.

[2] By God's Commandment.

10:18 [1] An objection: If calling be a testimony of election, were not the Jews called? why should I not … that, saith the Apostle, seeing that there is no nation which hath not been called? much less can I say, that the Jews were not called.

10:19 [1] The defender and maintainer of the Jews' cause goeth on still to ask, whether the Jews also knew not God which called them. Isaiah (saith the Apostle) denieth it: and witnesseth that the Gospel was translated from them to the Gentiles, because the Jews neglected it. And therewithall the Apostle teacheth, that that outward and universal calling, which is set forth by the creation of the world, sufficeth not to the knowledge of God: yea, and that the particular also which is by the word of God, is of itself of small or no efficacy, unless it be apprehended or laid hold on by faith, by the gift of God: otherwise by unbelief it is made unprofitable, and that by the only fault of man, who can pretend no ignorance.

[2] He calleth all profane people, a nation that is no nation, that they are not said to live but to die, which are appointed for everlasting condemnation.

10:20 [1] Speaketh without fear.

that Elijah was in times past decieved: 16 and that, seeing they have an holy root, 23 many of them likewise shall be holy. 18, 24 He exhorteth the Gentiles to be humble, 33 and crieth out, that God's judgments are unsearchable.

1 I Demand then, [1]Hath God cast away his people? God forbid: for [2]I also am an Israelite, of the seed of Abraham, of the tribe of Benjamin.

2 [1]God hath not cast away his people which he [2]knew before. [3]Know ye not what the Scripture saith of Elijah, how he communeth with God against Israel, saying,

3 [a]Lord, they have killed thy Prophets, and dug down thine Altars: and I am left alone, and they seek my life?

4 But what saith the answer of God to him? [b]I have [1]reserved unto myself seven thousand men, which have not bowed the knee to [2]Baal.

5 Even so then, at this present time is there a remnant according to the [1]election of grace.

6 [1]And if *it be* of grace, it is [2]no more of works: or else were grace no more grace: but if it be of works, it is no more grace: or else were work no more work.

CHAPTER 11
[a] 1 Kings 19:10
[b] 1 Kings 19:18
[c] Isa. 6:9
   Isa. 29:10
   Matt. 13:14
   John 12:40
   Acts 28:26
[d] Ps. 69:23

7 What then? Israel hath not obtained that he sought: but the election hath obtained it, and the rest have been [1]hardened,

8 [1]According as it is written, 'God hath given them the spirit of [2]slumber: eyes that they [3]should not see, and ears that they should not hear unto this day.

9 And David saith, [d,1]Let their table be made a snare, and a net, and a stumbling block, even for a recompense unto them.

10 Let their eyes be darkened that they see not, and bow down their back always.

11 [1]I demand then, Have they stumbled, that they should fall? God forbid: but through their fall, salvation *cometh* unto the Gentiles, to provoke them to follow them.

12 Wherefore if the fall of them *be* the [1]riches of the world, and the diminishing of them the riches of the Gentiles, how much more shall their [2]abundance *be*?

13 [1]For *in that* I speak to you Gentiles, inasmuch as I am the Apostle of the Gentiles, I [2]magnify mine

---

11:1 [1] Now the Apostle showeth how this doctrine is to be applied to others, abiding still in his propounded cause. Therefore he teacheth us that all the Jews in particular are not cast away, and therefore we ought not to pronounce rashly of private persons, whether they be of the number of the elect or not.

[2] The first proof, I am a Jew, and yet elected, therefore we may and ought fully to resolve upon our election, as hath been before said: but of another man's we cannot be so certainly resolved, and yet ours may cause us to hope well of others.

11:2 [1] The second proof: Because that God is faithful in his league or Covenant, although men be unfaithful: So then seeing that God hath said, that he will be the God of his unto a thousand generations, we must take heed, that we think not that the whole race and offspring is cast off, by reason of the unbelief of a few, but rather, that we hope well of every member of the Church, because of God's league and Covenant.

[2] Which he loved and chose from everlasting.

[3] The third proof, taken from the answer that was made to Elijah: even then also, when there appeared openly to the face of the world no elect, yet God knew his elect and chosen, and of them also good store and number. Whereupon this also is concluded, that we ought not rashly to pronounce of any man as of a reprobate, seeing that the Church is oftentimes brought to that state, that even the most watchful and sharp-sighted pastors think it to be clean extinct and put out.

11:4 [1] He speaketh of remnants and reserved people which were chosen from everlasting, and not of remnants that should be chosen afterward: for they are not chosen, because they were not idolaters, but therefore they were not idolaters, because they were chosen and elect.

[2] Baal signifieth as much as Master or patron, or one in whose power another is, which name the idolaters at this day give their idols, naming them patrons, and patronesses or Ladies.

11:5 [1] The election of grace, is not whereby men chose grace, but whereby God chose us of his grace and goodness.

11:6 [1] Although that all be not elect and chosen, yet let them that

are elected, remember that they are freely chosen, and let them that stubbornly refuse the grace and free mercy of God, impute it unto themselves.

[2] This saying beateth down flat to the ground all the doctrine of all kinds and manner of works, whereby our justifiers of themselves do teach, that works are either wholly or partly the cause of our justification.

11:7 [1] See Mark 3:5.

11:8 [1] And yet this hardness of heart cometh not but by God's just decree and judgment, and yet without fault, whom as he so punisheth the unthankful by taking from them all sense and perseverance and by doubling their darkness, that the benefits of God which are offered unto them, do redound to their just destruction.

[2] A very dead sleep which taketh away all sense.

[3] That is, eyes unjust to see.

11:9 [1] As unhappy birds are enticed to death by that which is their sustenance, so did that only thing turn to the Jews' destruction, out of which they sought life, to wit, the Law of God, for the preposterous zeal whereof they refused the Gospel.

11:11 [1] God appointed this casting out of the Jews, that it might be an occasion to call the Gentiles: and again might turn this calling of the Gentiles, to be an occasion to restore the Jews, to wit, that they being inflamed and provoked by emulation of the Gentiles, might themselves at length embrace the Gospel. And hereby we may learn, that the severity of God serveth as well for the setting forth of his glory as his mercy doth, and also that God prepares himself a way to mercy, by his severity, so that we ought not rashly to despair of any man, nor proudly triumph over other men, but rather provoke them to an holy emulation, that God may be glorified in them also.

11:12 [1] By riches he meaneth the knowledge of the Gospel to everlasting life: and by the world, all nations dispersed throughout the whole world.

[2] Of the Jews, when the whole nation without exception shall come to Christ.

11:13 [1] He witnesseth by his own example, that he goeth before all others in this behalf.

[2] I make noble and famous.

office,

14 *To try* if by any means I might provoke them of my flesh to follow them, and might save some of them.

15 For if the casting away of them *be* the reconciling of the world, what *shall* the receiving *be*, [1]but life from the dead?

16 [1]For if the [2]firstfruits *be* holy, so *is* the whole lump: and if the [3]root be holy, so *are* the branches.

17 [c,1]And though some of the branches be broken off, and thou being a wild Olive tree, wast grafted in [2]for them, and made [3]partaker of the root and fatness of the Olive tree:

18 [1]Boast not thyself against the branches: and if thou boast thyself, thou bearest not the root, but the root thee.

19 Thou wilt say then, The branches are broken off, that I might be grafted in.

20 Well: through unbelief they are broken off, and thou standest by faith: be not high-minded, but [1]fear.

21 For if God spared not the [1]natural branches, *take heed*, lest he also spare not thee.

[e] Jer. 11:6
[f] Isa. 59:20
[g] Isa. 27:9

22 [1]Behold therefore the [2]bountifulness, and severity of God: toward them which have fallen, severity: but toward thee, bountifulness, if thou continue in *his* [3]bountifulness: or else thou shalt also be cut off.

23 [1]And they also, if they abide not still in unbelief, shall be grafted in: for God is able to graft them in again.

24 For if thou wast cut out of the Olive tree, which was wild by [1]nature, and was grafted contrary to nature in a [2]right Olive tree, how much more shall they that are by nature, be grafted in their own Olive tree?

25 [1]For I would not, brethren, that ye should be ignorant of this secret (lest ye should be arrogant in [2]yourselves) that partly obstinacy is come to Israel, until the fullness of the Gentiles be [3]come in.

26 And so all Israel shall be saved, as it is written, [f]The deliverer shall come out of Zion, and shall turn away the ungodliness from Jacob.

27 And this is my covenant to them, [g]When I shall take away their sins.

28 [1]As concerning the [2]Gospel, *they are* enemies for your sakes: but as touching the [3]election, they

---

11:15 [1] It shall come to pass that when the Jews come to the Gospel, the world shall as it were come quicken again, and rise from death to life.

11:16 [1] The nation of the Jews being considered in their stock and root, that is, in Abraham, is holy, although that many of the branches be cut off. Therefore in judging of our brethren, we must not stick in their unworthiness, to think that they are at once all cast off, but we ought to consider the root of the Covenant, and rather go back to their ancestors which were faithful, that we may know that the blessing of the Covenant resteth in some of their posterity, as we also find proof hereof in ourselves.

[2] He alludeth to the firstfruits of the loaves by the offering whereof all the whole crop of corn was sanctified, and they might vie the rest of the year following with good conscience.

[3] Abraham.

11:17 [1] There is no cause why the Gentiles which have obtained mercy, should triumph over the Jews which condemn the grace of God, seeing they are grafted into the Jews' ancestors. But let them rather take heed that that also be not found in them which is worthily condemned in the Jews. And hereof also this general doctrine may be gathered and taken, that we ought to be studious of God's glory, even in respect of our neighbors: so far ought we to be from bragging and glorying, for that, that we are preferred before others by a singular grace.

[2] In place of those boughs which are broken off.

[3] It is against the common course of husbandry, that the barren juice of the imp is changed with the juice of the good tree.

11:18 [1] We may rejoice in the Lord, but so that we despise not the Jews, whom we ought rather to provoke to that good striving with us.

11:20 [1] See that thou stand in awe of God modestly and carefully.

11:21 [1] He calleth them natural, not because they had any holiness of nature, but because they were born of them, whom the Lord set apart for himself from, other nations, by his league and covenant which he freely made with them.

11:22 [1] Seeing the matter itself declareth that election cometh not by inheritance (although the fault be in men, and not in God, why the blessing of God is not perpetual) we must take good heed, that that be not found in ourselves, which we think blameworthy in others, for the election is sure, but they that are truly elect and ingrafted, are not proud in themselves with contempt of others, but with due reverence to God, and love towards their neighbor, run to the mark which is set before them.

[2] The tender and loving heart.

[3] In that state which God's bountifulness hath advanced thee unto: and we must mark here, that he speaketh not of the election of every private man, which remaineth steadfast forever, but of the election of the whole nation.

11:23 [1] Many are now for a season cut off, that is, are without the root, which in their time shall be grafted in: and again there are a great sort, which after a sort, and touching the outward show, seem to be ingrafted, which notwithstanding through their own fault afterward are cut off and clean cast away: which thing is especially to be considered in nations and peoples, as in the Gentiles and Jews.

11:24 [1] Understand nature, not as it was first made, but as it was corrupted in Adam, and so derived from him to his posterity.

[2] Into the people of the Jews which God had sanctified of his mere grace: and he speaketh of the whole nation, not of every one part.

11:25 [1] The blindness of the Jews is neither so universal that the Lord hath no elect in that nation, neither shall it be continual: for there shall be a time wherein they also (as the Prophets have forewarned) shall effectually embrace that which they do now so stubbornly for the most part reject and refuse.

[2] That ye be not proud within yourselves.

[3] Into the Church.

11:28 [1] Again, that he may join the Jews and Gentiles together as it were in one body, and especially may teach what duty the Gentiles owe to the Jews, he beateth this into their heads, that the nation of the Jews is not utterly cast off without hope of recovery.

[2] Forasmuch as they received it not.

[3] In that, that God respecteth not what they deserve, but what he promised to Abraham.

are beloved for the fathers' sakes.

29 ¹For the gifts and calling of God are without repentance.

30 ¹For even as ye in times past have not believed God, yet have now obtained mercy through their unbelief:

31 Even so now have they not believed by the mercy *showed* unto you, that they also may obtain mercy.

32 For God hath shut up ¹all in unbelief, that he might have mercy on all.

33 ¹O the deepness of the riches, both of the wisdom, and knowledge of God! how unsearchable are his ²judgments, and his ³ways past finding out!

34 ᵇ,¹For who hath known the mind of the Lord? or who was his counselor?

35 Or who hath given unto him ¹first, and he shall be recompensed?

36 For of him, and through him, and for ¹him are all things: to him *be* glory forever. Amen.

ᵇ Job 41:2
Isa. 40:13
1 Cor. 2:16

CHAPTER 12
ᵃ Eph. 5:17
1 Thess. 4:3
ᵇ 1 Cor. 12:11
Eph. 4:7

12

1 He exhorteth   2 to that worship which is acceptable to God,   9 to love unfained,   14, 20 even towards our enemies.

1 I Beseech ¹you therefore brethren, ²by the mercies of God, that ye ³give up your ⁴bodies a ⁵living sacrifice, holy, acceptable unto God, *which is* your ⁶reasonable serving of God.

2 ¹And fashion not yourselves like unto this world, but be ye changed by the renewing of your ²mind, that ye may ᵃprove what that good, and acceptable and perfect will of God is.

3 ¹For I ²say through the grace that is given unto me, to everyone that is among you, that no man ³presume to understand above that which is meet to understand, but that he understand according to ⁴sobriety, as God hath dealt to every man the ᵇmeasure of ⁵faith.

4 ¹For as we have many members in one body, and all members have not one office,

5 So we being many, are one body in Christ, and every one, one anothers members.

11:29 ¹ The reason or proof: because the covenant made with that nation of life everlasting, cannot be frustrate and vain.

11:30 ¹ Another reason, because that although that they which are hardened, are worthily punished, yet hath not this stubbornness of the Jews so come to pass properly for an hatred to that nation, but that an entry might as it were be opened to bring in the Gentiles, and afterward the Jews being inflamed with emulation of this mercy which is showed to the Gentiles, might themselves also be partakers of the same benefit, and so it might appear that both Jews and Gentiles are saved, only by the free mercy and grace of God, which could not have been so manifest, if at the beginning, God had brought all together into the Church, or if he had saved the nation of the Jews without this interruption.

11:32 ¹ Both Jews and Gentiles.

11:33 ¹ The Apostle crieth not as astonished with this wonderful wisdom of God, which he teacheth us, ought to be religiously reverenced, and not curiously and profanely to be searched beyond the compass of that that God hath revealed unto us.

² The course that he holdeth in governing all things both generally and particularly.

³ The order of his counsels and doings.

11:34 ¹ He bridleth three manner of ways, the wicked boldness of man: First, because that God is above all, most wise, and therefore it is very absurd, and plainly godless to measure him by our folly. Moreover, because he is debtor to no man, and therefore no man can complain of injury done unto him. Thirdly, because all things are made for his glory, and therefore we must refer all things to his glory, much less may we contend and debate the matter with him.

11:35 ¹ This saying overthroweth the doctrine of foreseen works and merits.

11:36 ¹ To wit, for God, to whose glory all things are referred, not only things that were made, but especially his new works which he worketh in his elect.

12:1 ¹ The fourth part of this Epistle, which after the finishing of the chief points of Christian doctrine, consisteth in declaring of precepts of Christian life. And first of all he giveth general precepts and grounds: the chiefest whereof is this that every man consecrate himself wholly to the spiritual service of God, and do as it were sacrifice

himself, trusting to the grace of God.

² By this preface he showeth that God's glory is the utmost end of all our doings.

³ In times past the sacrifices were presented before the altar, but now the altar is everywhere.

⁴ Yourselves: in times past, other bodies than our own, now our own must be offered.

⁵ In times past, dead sacrifices were offered, but now we must offer such as have the spirit of life in them.

⁶ Spiritual.

12:2 ¹ The second precept is this, That we take not other men's opinions or manners for a rule of life, but that we wholly renouncing this world, set before us as our mark, the will of God, as it is manifested and opened unto us in his word.

² Why then there is no place left for reason, which the heathen Philosophers place as a Queen in a Castle, nor for man's free will, which the Popish Schoolmen dream on, if the mind must be renewed. See Eph. 1:18 and 2:5 and 4:17 and Col. 1:21.

12:3 ¹ Thirdly he admonisheth us very earnestly, that every man keep himself within the bounds of his vocation, and that every man be wise according to the measure of grace that God hath given him.

² I charge.

³ That he please not himself too much, as they do, which persuade themselves they know more than indeed they do.

⁴ We will be sober if we take not that upon us, which we have not, and if we brag not of that we have.

⁵ By faith he meaneth the knowledge of God in Christ, and the gifts which the holy Ghost poureth upon the faithful.

12:4 ¹ There is a double reason of the precept going afore: the one is because God hath not committed everything to be done of every man: and therefore, he doeth backwardly, and not only unprofitably, but also to the great disprofit of others, wearieth himself and others, which passeth the bounds of his vocation: the other is, for that this diversity and inequality of vocations and gifts, redoundeth to our commodity seeing that the same is therefore instituted and appointed, that we should be bound one to another. Whereupon it followeth that no man ought to be grieved thereat, seeing that the use of every private gift is common.

6 *,1Seeing then that we have gifts that are divers, according to the grace that is given unto us, whether *we have* prophecy, *let us prophesy* according to the 2portion of faith.

7 Or an office, *let us wait* on the office: or he that 1teacheth, on teaching:

8 Or he that 1exhorteth, on exhortation: he that 2distributeth, *let him do it* dwith simplicity: he that 3ruleth, with diligence: he that 4showeth mercy, with cheerfulness.

9 1*Let* love *be* without dissimulation. *Abhor that which is evil, and cleave unto that which is good.

10 fBe affectioned to love one another with brotherly love. In giving honor, go one before another.

11 Not slothful to do service, fervent in spirit 1serving the Lord,

12 1Rejoicing in hope, patient in tribulation, gcontinuing in prayer.

13 b,1Distributing unto the 2necessities of the Saints: igiving yourselves to hospitality.

14 jBless them which persecute you: bless, *I say,* and curse not.

15 Rejoice with them that rejoice, and weep with them that weep.

16 Be like affectioned one towards another: kbe not high-minded: but make yourselves equal to them of the 1lower sort: be not 2wise in yourselves.

17 lRecompense to no man evil for evil: procure things honest in the sight of all men.

18 mIf it be possible, as much as in you is, have peace with all men.

19 Dearly beloved, navenge not yourselves, but give place unto wrath: for it is written, oVengeance is mine: I will repay, saith the Lord.

20 pTherefore if thine enemy hunger, feed him: if he thirst, give him drink: for in so doing thou shalt heap 1coals of fire on his head.

21 Be not overcome of evil, but overcome evil with goodness.

13 *1 He willeth that we submit ourselves to Magistrates: 8 To love our neighbor: 13 To love uprightly, 14 and to put on Christ.*

1 Let a,1every 2soul be subject unto the higher 3powers: 4for there is no power but of God: and the powers that be, are 5ordained of God.

2 Whosoever therefore resisteth the power, resisteth the ordinance of God: and they that resist, shall receive to themselves condemnation.

3 1For Magistrates are not to be feared *for* good works, but *for* evil. 2Wilt thou then be without fear

Cross-references (center column):
c 1 Pet. 4:10
d Matt. 6:2 / 2 Cor. 9:7
e Amos 5:15
f Eph. 4:2 / 1 Pet. 2:17
g 1 Pet. 5:8
h Luke 18:1 / 1 Cor. 16:1
i Heb. 13:2 / 1 Pet. 4:13
j Matt. 5:44
k Prov. 3:7 / Isa. 5:21
l Prov. 20:22 / Matt. 5:39 / 2 Cor. 8:11 / 1 Pet. 3:9
m Heb. 12:14
n Eccl. 2:18 / Matt. 5:39
o Deut. 32:35 / Heb. 10:30
p Prov. 24:22

CHAPTER 13
a Titus 3:1 / 1 Pet. 2:13

12:6 1 That which he spake before in general, he applieth particularly to the holy functions, wherein men offend with greater danger. And he divideth them into two sorts, to wit, into Prophets, and Deacons, and again he divideth the Prophets into doctors, and Pastors. And of Deacons he maketh three sorts: to wit, the one to be such as are (as it were) treasurers of the Church coffers, whom he calleth properly Deacons: the other to be the governors of discipline, who are called Seniors or Elders: the third to be such as properly served in the help of the poor, of which sort the company of widows were.

2 That every man observe the measure of that which is revealed unto him.

12:7 1 Whose office only is to expound the Scriptures.

12:8 1 Who in other places is called the Pastor.

2 To wit, the alms, that he distribute them faithfully, and without respect of person.

3 The Elders of the Church.

4 They that are busied about tending on the poor, must do it with cheerfulness, lest they add sorrow to sorrow.

12:9 1 Now he cometh to the duties of the second Table, which he deriveth from charity, which is as it were the fountain of them all. And he defineth Christian charity by sincerity, hatred of evil, earnest study of good things, good affection to help our neighbor, and whose final end is, the glory of God.

12:11 1 This piece is well put in, for it maketh difference between Christian duties, and Philosophical duties.

12:12 1 He reckoneth up divers other virtues together with their effects, to wit, hope, patience in tribulation, equanimity, continuance in prayer, liberality towards the saints, hospitality, moderation of mind, even in helping our enemies, a selfsame feeling with others as well in adversity as prosperity, modesty, endeavor to maintain honest concord so nigh as we may with all men, which cannot be extinguished by any man's injuries.

12:13 1 A true rule of charity, when we are no less touched with other men's wants, than with our own, and having that feeling, help them as much as we can.

2 Not upon pleasure, and needless duties, but upon necessary uses.

12:16 1 There is nothing that doth so much break concord as ambition, when as every man loatheth a base estate, and seeketh ambitiously to be aloft.

2 Be not puffed up, with opinion of your own wisdom.

12:20 1 After this sort doth Solomon point out the wrath of God which hangeth over a man.

13:1 1 Now he showeth severally, what subjects owe to their Magistrates, to wit, obedience: From which he showeth that no man is free: and in such sort that it is not only due to the highest Magistrate himself, but also even to the basest, which hath any office under him.

2 Yea, though an Apostle, though an Evangelist, though a Prophet: Chrysostom. Therefore the tyranny of the Pope over all kingdoms must down to the ground.

3 A reason taken of the nature of the thing itself: For to what purpose are they placed in higher degree, but that the inferior should be subject unto them?

4 Another argument of great force: Because God is author of this order: so that such as are rebels ought to know, that they make war with God himself: wherefore they cannot but purchase to themselves great misery and calamity.

5 Be distributed: for some are greater, some smaller.

13:3 1 The third argument taken from the end wherefore they were made, which is most profitable: for that God by this means preserveth the good and bridleth the wicked: by which words the Magistrates themselves are put in mind of that duty which they owe to their subjects.

2 An excellent way to bear this yoke, not only without grief, but also with great profit.

of the power? do well: so shalt thou have praise of the same.

4 For he is the minister of God for thy wealth: [1]but if thou do evil, fear: for he beareth not the sword for nought: for he is the minister of God to [2]take vengeance on him that doeth evil.

5 [1]Wherefore ye must be subject, not because of wrath only, but [2]also for conscience sake.

6 [1]For, for this cause ye pay also tribute: for they are God's ministers, applying themselves for the same thing.

7 [b]Give to all men therefore their duty: tribute, to whom ye owe tribute: custom, to whom custom: fear, to whom [1]fear: honor, to whom ye owe [2]honor.

8 [1]Owe nothing to any man, but to love one another: [2]for he that loveth another, hath fulfilled the [3]Law.

9 For this, [c]Thou shalt not commit adultery, Thou shalt not kill, Thou shalt not steal, Thou shalt not bear false witness, Thou shalt not covet: and if there be any other commandment, it is [1]briefly comprehended in this saying, even in this, [d]Thou shalt love thy neighbor as thyself.

10 Love doeth not evil to his neighbor: therefore is love the [e]fulfilling of the Law.

11 [1]And that, considering the season, that it is

b Matt. 22:11
c Exod. 20:14
  Deut. 5:18
d Lev. 19:11
  Matt. 21:39
  Mark 12:31
  Gal. 5:14
  James 1:8
e 1 Tim. 1:1
f Luke 21:34
g Gal. 5:16
  1 Pet. 2:11

CHAPTER 14
a James 4:12

now time that we should arise from sleep: for now is our salvation nearer, than when we believed it.

12 The night is past, and the day is [1]at hand, let us therefore cast away the works [2]of darkness, and let us put on the armor of light,

13 So that we walk honestly, as in the day: not in [f]gluttony, and drunkenness, neither in chambering and wantonness, nor in strife and envying.

14 [g]But [1]put ye on the Lord JESUS CHRIST, and take no thought for the flesh, to fulfill the lust of it.

14 1 He willeth that we so deal with the weak in faith, 2, 5 that through our fault they be not offended. 10 And on the other side he commandeth them not rashly to judge of the stronger: 19 That within the bounds of edification 20 and charity. 22 Christian liberty may conflict.

1 Him [1]that is weak in the faith, [2]receive unto you, but not for [3]controversies of disputations.

2 [1]One [2]believeth that he may eat of all things: and another, which is weak, eateth herbs.

3 [1]Let not him that eateth, despise him that eateth not: and let not him which eateth not, condemn him that eateth: for [2]God hath received him.

4 [a,1]Who art thou that condemnest another man's servant? he standeth or falleth to his own master:

13:4 [1] God hath armed the Magistrate even with a revenging sword.
[2] By whom God revengeth the wicked.
13:5 [1] The conclusion: We must obey the magistrate, not only for fear of punishment, but much more because that (although the Magistrate have no power over the conscience of man, yet seeing he is God's minister) he cannot be resisteth by any good conscience.
[2] So far as lawfully we may: for if unlawful things be commanded us, we must answer as Peter teacheth us, It is better to obey God than men.
13:6 [1] He reckoneth up the chiefest things wherein consisteth the obedience of subjects.
13:7 [1] Obedience, and that from the heart.
[2] Reverence, (which as reason is) we must give to the Magistrate.
13:8 [1] He showeth how very few judgments need to be executed, to wit, if we so order our life, as no man may justly require anything of us, besides that only that we owe one to another, by the perpetual law of charity.
[2] He commendeth charity, as an abridgement of the whole Law.
[3] He hath not only done one commandment, but performed generally that which the Law commandeth.
13:9 [1] For the whole Law commandeth nothing else, but that we love God and our neighbor. But seeing Paul speaketh here of the duties we owe one to another, we must restrain this word, Law to the second Table.
13:11 [1] An application taken of the circumstance of the time: which also itself putteth us in mind of our duty, seeing this remaineth after that the darkness of ignorance and wicked affections by the knowledge of God's truth be driven out of us, that we order our life according to that certain and sure rule of all righteousness and honesty, being fully grounded upon the virtue of the Spirit of Christ.
13:12 [1] In other places we are said to be in the light, but yet so, that it appeareth not as yet what we are, for as yet we see but as it were in the twilight.
[2] That kind of life, which they lead, that flee the light.

13:14 [1] To put on Christ, is to possess Christ, to have him in us, and us in him.
14:1 [1] Now he showeth how we ought to behave ourselves toward our brethren in matters and things indifferent, offending in the use of them, not of malices or damnable superstition, but for lack of knowledge of the benefit of Christ. And thus he teacheth that they are to be instructed gently and patiently, and so that we apply ourselves to their ignorance in such matters according to the rule of charity.
[2] Do not for a matter or thing that is indifferent, and such as you may do or not do, shun his company, but take him to you.
[3] To make him by your doubtful and uncertain disputations go away more in doubt than he came, or start back with a troubled conscience.
14:2 [1] He propoundeth for an example, the difference of meats, which some thought was necessarily to be observed as a thing prescribed by the Law (not knowing that it was taken away) whereas on the contrary side, such as had profited in the knowledge of the Gospel, knew well that this schoolmastership of the Law was abolished.
[2] Knows by faith.
14:3 [1] In such a matter, saith the Apostle, Let neither them which know their liberty, proudly despise their weaker brother, neither let the unlearned crabbedly or frowardly condemn that, that they understand not.
[2] The first reason: Because that seeing both he that eateth and he that eateth not, is notwithstanding the member of Christ, neither he which eateth not, can justly be condemned, neither he which eateth be justly condemned: Now the first proposition is declared in the sixth verse following.
14:4 [1] Another reason which hangeth upon the former: why the ruder and more unlearned ought not to be contemned of the more skillful, as men without hope of salvation: Because, saith the Apostle, he is ignorant today, may be endued tomorrow with further knowledge, so that he also may stand sure: Therefore it belongeth to God, and not unto man, to pronounce the sentence of condemnation.

yea, he shall be established: for God is able to make him stand.

5 ¹This man esteemeth one day above another day, and another man counteth every day alike: ²let ³every man be fully persuaded in his mind.

6 ¹He that ²observeth the day, observeth it to the Lord: and he that observeth not the day, observeth it not to the ³Lord. He that ⁴eateth, eateth to the Lord: ⁵for he giveth God thanks: and he that eateth ⁶not, eateth not to the Lord, and giveth God thanks.

7 ¹For none of us liveth to ²himself, neither doth any die to himself.

8 For whether we live, we live unto the Lord: or whether we die, we die unto the Lord: whether we live therefore, or die, we are the Lords.

9 For Christ therefore died and rose again, and revived, that he might be Lord both of the dead and the quick.

10 ¹But why dost thou condemn thy brother? or

b 2 Cor. 1:10
c Isa. 45:23
Phil. 2:10
d 1 Cor. 8:11

why dost thou despise thy brother? ᵇfor we shall all appear before the judgment seat of Christ.

11 For it is written, ¹I ᶜlive, saith the Lord, and every knee shall bow to me, and all tongues shall ²confess unto God.

12 So then everyone of us shall give accounts of himself to God.

13 ¹Let us not therefore judge one another anymore: but use *your* judgment rather in ²this that no man put an occasion to fall, or a stumbling block before *his* brother.

14 ¹I know, and am persuaded through the ²Lord Jesus, that there is nothing unclean of ³itself: but unto him that judgeth anything to be unclean, to him *it is* unclean.

15 But if thy brother be grieved for the meat, now walkest thou not charitably: ᵈ,¹destroy not him with thy meat, for whom ²Christ died.

14:5 ¹ Another example of the difference of days according to the law.

² He setteth against this contempt, and hasty or rash judgments, a continual desire to profit, that the strong may be certainly persuaded of their liberty, of what manner and sort it is, and how they ought to use it: and again the weak may daily profit, lest either they abuse the gift of God, or these please themselves in their infirmity.

³ That he may say in his conscience, that he knoweth and is persuaded by Jesus Christ, that nothing is unclean of itself, and this persuasion must be grounded upon the word of God.

14:6 ¹ A reason taken from the nature of indifferent things, which a man may with good conscience do and omit: for seeing that the difference of days and meats was appointed by God, how could they, which as yet understood not the abrogating of the Law, and yet otherwise acknowledged Christ as their Savior, with good conscience neglect that which they knew was commanded of God? And on the contrary side, they that knew the benefit of Christ in this behalf, did with good conscience neither observe days nor meats. Therefore saith the Apostle, verse 10, Let not the strong condemn the weak for these things, seeing that the weak brethren are brethren notwithstanding. Now if any man would draw this doctrine to these our times and ages, let them know that the Apostle speaketh of such things indifferent, as they which thought them not to be indifferent, had a ground in the Law, and were deceived by simple ignorance: and not of malice (for to such the Apostles yielded not, no not for a moment) nor superstition, but of a religious fear of God.

² Observeth precisely.

³ God shall judge whether he do well or no: And therefore you should rather strive about this, how every one of you will be allowed of God, than to think upon other men's doings.

⁴ He that maketh no difference of meats.

⁵ So the Apostle showeth that he speaketh of the faithful, both strong and weak. But what if we have to do with infidels? Then must we here take heed of two things, as also is declared in the Epistle to the Corinthians. The one is, that we count not their superstitions among things indifferent, as they did which sat down to meat in Idols' Temples: the other is, that then also when the matter is indifferent (as to buy a thing offered to idols, in the butcher's shambles, and to eat it at home in a private banquet) we wound not the conscience of our weak brother.

⁶ He that toucheth not meats which he taketh to be unclean by the Law.

14:7 ¹ We must not stick, saith he, in the meat itself, but in the use of the meat, so that he is justly to be reprehended that liveth so, that he casteth not his eyes upon God. For both our life and our death is dedicated to him, and for this cause Christ hath properly died, and not simply, that we might eat this meat or that.

² Hath respect to himself only, which the Hebrews utter after this sort, Doeth well to his own soul.

14:10 ¹ The conclusion: we must leave to God his right: and therefore in matters, which according as the conscience if affected, are either good or evil, the strong must not despise their weak brethren, much less condemn them. But this consequent cannot be taken of equal force in the contrary, to wit, that the weak should not judge the strong, because the weak do not know, that they which do not observe a day, and eat, observe it not to the Lord, and eat to the Lord, as the strong men know, that the weak which observe a day and eat not, observe the day to the Lord, and eat not to the Lord.

14:11 ¹ This is a form of an oath, proper to God only, for he and none but he liveth, and hath his being of himself.

² Shall acknowledge me from God.

14:13 ¹ After that he hath concluded what is not to be done, he showeth what is to be done: to wit, we must take heed that we do not utterly cast down with abusing our liberty, our brother who is not yet strong.

² He rebuketh by this way, these malicious judgers of others, which occupy their heads about nothing, but to find fault with their brethren's life, whereas they should rather bestow their wits upon this, that they do not with their disdainfulness either cast their brethren clean down, or give them some offense.

14:14 ¹ The preventing of an objection: It is true that the schoolmastership of the Law is taken away by the benefit of Christ, to such as know it, but yet notwithstanding we have to consider in the use of this liberty what is expedient, that we may have regard of our weak brother, seeing that our liberty is not lost thereby.

² By the Spirit of the Lord Jesus, or by the Lord Jesus, who I am sure brake down the wall at his coming.

³ By nature.

14:15 ¹ It is the part of a cruel mind to make more account of meat, than of our brother's salvation. Which thing they do, that presume to eat with offense of any brother, and so give him occasion to go back from the Gospel.

² Another argument: We must follow Christ's example: who was so far from destroying the weak with meat, that he gave his life for them.

16 ¹Cause not your commodity to be evil spoken of.

17 ¹For the kingdom of God, is not meat nor drink, but righteousness, and peace, and joy in the holy Ghost.

18 For whosoever in ¹these things serveth Christ, is acceptable unto God, and is approved of men.

19 ¹Let us then follow those things which concern peace, and wherewith one may edify another.

20 Destroy not the work of God for meat's sake: ᶜall things indeed are pure: but *it is* evil for the man which eateth with offense.

21 ꜰ*It is* good neither to eat flesh, nor to drink wine, nor anything whereby thy brother stumbleth, or is offended, or made weak.

22 ¹Hast thou ²faith? have it with thyself before God: blessed *is* he that condemneth not himself in that thing which he ³alloweth.

23 For he that ¹doubteth, is condemned if he eat, because *he eateth* not of faith: and whatsoever is not of faith, is sin.

15

1 The stronger must employ their strength to strengthen the weak. 5 By Christ's example, 7 who received 8 not only the Jews, 10 but also the Gentiles. 15 The cause why he wrote this Epistle.

1 We ¹which are strong, ought to bear the infirmities of the weak, and not to ²please ourselves.

2 *Therefore* let every man please his neighbor in that that is ¹good to edification.

Marginal references:
ᵉ Titus 1:15
ꜰ 2 Cor. 8:13

CHAPTER 15
ᵃ Ps. 69:10
ᵇ 1 Cor. 1:10
ᶜ Ps. 18:50
ᵈ Deut. 32:43
ᵉ Ps. 117:1
ꜰ Isa. 11:10

3 ¹For Christ also would not please himself, but as it is written, ᵃThe rebukes of them which rebuke thee, fell on me.

4 ¹For whatsoever things are written ²aforetime, are written for our learning, that we through patience, and comfort of the ³Scriptures might have hope.

5 ¹Now the God of patience and consolation give you that ye be ᵇlike-minded one towards another, according to Christ Jesus,

6 That ye with one mind, *and* with one mouth may praise God, even the Father of our Lord Jesus Christ.

7 Wherefore receive ye one another, as Christ also ¹received us to the glory of God.

8 ¹Now I say, that Jesus Christ was a minister of the ²circumcision, for the ³truth of God, to confirm the promises *made* unto the fathers.

9 ¹And let the Gentiles praise God, for *his* mercy, as it is written, ᶜFor this cause I will ²confess thee among the Gentiles, and sing unto thy Name.

10 And again he saith, ᵈRejoice, ye Gentiles with his people.

11 And again, ᵉPraise the Lord, all ye Gentiles, and laud ye him all people together.

12 And again Isaiah saith, ꜰThere shall be a root of Jesse, and he that shall rise to reign over the Gentiles, in him shall the Gentiles trust.

13 ¹Now the God of ²hope fill you with ³all joy,

14:16 ¹ Another argument: for that by this means the liberty of the Gospel is evil spoken of, as though it openeth the way to attempt any thing whatsoever, and boldeneth us to all things.

14:17 ¹ A general reason, and the ground of all the other arguments: The kingdom of heaven consisteth not in these outward things, but in the study of righteousness, and peace, and comfort of the holy Ghost.

14:18 ¹ He that liveth peaceably, and doeth righteously, through the holy Ghost.

14:19 ¹ A general conclusion: The use of this liberty, yea and our whole life, ought to be referred to the edifying of one another, insomuch that we esteem that thing unlawful by reason of the offense of our brother, which is of itself pure and lawful.

14:22 ¹ He giveth a double warning in these matters, one, which pertaineth to the strong, that he which hath obtained a sure knowledge of this liberty, keep that treasure to the end he may use it wisely and profitably as hath been said: the other which respecteth the weak, that they do nothing rashly by other men's example with a wavering conscience, for that cannot be done without sin, whereof we are not persuaded by the word of God, that he liketh, and approveth it.

² He showed before verse 14 what he meaneth by faith, to wit, for a man to be certain and out of doubt in matters and things indifferent.

³ Embraceth.

14:23 ¹ Reasoneth with himself.

15:1 ¹ Now the Apostle reasoneth generally of tolerating or bearing with the weak by all means, so far forth as may be for their profit.

² And despise others.

15:2 ¹ For his profit and edification.

15:3 ¹ A confirmation taken of the example of Christ, who suffered all things to bring not only the weak, but also his most cruel enemies, overcoming them with patience, to his Father.

15:4 ¹ The preventing of an objection: Such things as are cited out of the examples of the ancients, are propounded unto us to this end and purpose, that according to the example of our Fathers, we should in patience and hope bear one with another.

² By Moses and the Prophets.

³ The Scriptures are said to teach and comfort, because God useth them to teach and comfort his people withall.

15:5 ¹ We must take an example of patience, of God that both the weak and the strong serving God with a mutual consent, may bring one another to God, as Christ also received us unto himself, although we were never so unworthy.

15:7 ¹ He did not disdain us, but received us of his own accord, to make us partakers of God's glory.

15:8 ¹ An applying of the example of Christ to the Jews, whom he vouchsafed this honor for the promises which he made unto their fathers, although they were never so unworthy, that he executed the office of a minister amongst them with marvelous patience. Therefore much less ought the Gentiles despise them for certain faults, whom the Son of God so much esteemed.

² Of the circumcised Jews, for as long as he lived, he never went out of their quarters.

³ That God might be seen to be true.

15:9 ¹ An applying of the same to the Gentiles, whom also the Lord of his incomprehensible goodness had regard of, so that they are not to be condemned of the Jews as strangers.

² I will openly profess, and set forth thy Name.

15:13 ¹ He sealeth up as it were all the former treatise with prayers, wishing all that to be given them of the Lord, that he had commanded them.

² In whom we hope.

³ Abundantly and plentifully.

and peace in believing, that ye may abound in hope, through the power of the holy Ghost.

14 ¹And I myself also am persuaded of you, my brethren, that ²ye also are full of goodness, and filled with all knowledge, and are able to admonish one another.

15 Nevertheless, brethren, I have somewhat boldly after a sort written unto you, as one that putteth you in remembrance, through the grace that is given me of God,

16 That I should be the minister of Jesus Christ toward the Gentiles, ministering the Gospel of God, that the ¹offering up of the Gentiles might be acceptable, being sanctified by the holy Ghost.

17 ¹I have therefore whereof I may rejoice in Christ Jesus in those things which *pertain* to God.

18 For I dare not speak of anything, which ¹Christ hath not wrought by me, *to make* the Gentiles obedient in word and deed,

19 With the ¹power of signs and wonders, by the power of the spirit of God: so that from Jerusalem, and round about unto Illyricum, I have caused to abound the Gospel of Christ.

20 Yea, so I enforced myself to preach the Gospel, not where Christ was named, lest I should have built on another man's foundation.

21 But as it is written, ᵍTo whom he was not spoken of, they shall see *him*, and they that heard not, shall understand *him*.

22 ʰ'¹Therefore also I have been oft let to come unto you:

23 But now seeing I have no more place in these quarters, and also have ⁱbeen desirous many years agone to come unto you,

g Isa. 52:15
h Rom. 1:11
i 1 Thess. 2:17
j 1 Cor. 6:21

24 When I shall take my journey into Spain, I will come to you: for I trust to see you in my journey, and to be brought on my way thitherward by you, after that I have been somewhat filled with your *company*.

25 But now go I to Jerusalem, to ¹minister unto the Saints.

26 For it hath pleased them of Macedonia and Achaia, to make a certain distribution unto the poor Saints which are at Jerusalem.

27 ¹For it hath pleased them, and their debtors are they: ʲfor if the Gentiles be made partakers of their spiritual things, their duty is also to ²minister unto them in carnal things.

28 When I have therefore performed this, and have ¹sealed them this ²fruit, I will pass by you into Spain.

29 ¹And I know when I come, that I shall come to you with abundance of the blessing of the Gospel of Christ.

30 Also brethren, I beseech you for our Lord Jesus Christ's sake, and for the ¹love of the spirit, that ye would strive with me by prayers to God for me,

31 That I may be delivered from them which are disobedient in Judea, and that my service which I have to do at Jerusalem, may be accepted of the Saints,

32 That I may come unto you with joy by the will of God, and may with you be refreshed.

33 Thus the God of peace *be* with you all. Amen.

16 *1 He commendeth Phoebe. 3 He sendeth greeting to many. 17 And warneth to beware of them which are the causes of division.*

1 I ¹Commend unto you Phoebe our sister, which is a servant of the Church of Cenchrea:

2 That ye receive her in the ¹Lord, as it becometh

15:14 ¹ The conclusion of the Epistle, wherein he first excuseth himself, that he hath written somewhat at large unto them, rather to warn them, than to teach them, and that of necessity, by reason of his vocation, which bindeth him peculiarly to the Gentiles.

² Of your own accord, and of yourselves.

15:16 ¹ By the offering up of the Gentiles, he meaneth the Gentiles themselves, whom he offered to God as a sacrifice.

15:17 ¹ He commendeth his Apostleship highly by the effects, but yet so that moreover and besides that he speaketh all things truly, he giveth all the glory to God as the only author: and doth not properly respect himself, but this rather: that men might less doubt of the truth of the doctrine which he propoundeth unto them.

15:18 ¹ Christ was so with me in all things, and by all means, that if I would never so fain, yet I cannot say, what he hath done by me to bring the Gentiles to obey the Gospel.

15:19 ¹ In the first place this word, Power, signifieth the force, and working of the wonders in piercing men's minds: and in the latter, it signifieth God's mighty power which was the worker of those wonders.

15:22 ¹ He writeth at large to the Romans, and that familiarly, his singular good will towards them, and the state of his affairs, but so, that he swerveth not an iota from the end of Apostolical doctrine: for he declareth nothing but that which appertaineth to his office, and is godly: and commending by a little digression as it were, the liberal-

ity of the Churches of Macedonia, he provoketh them modestly to follow their godly deed.

15:25 ¹ Doing, his duty for the Saints, to carry them that money which was gathered for their use.

15:27 ¹ Alms are voluntary, but yet such as we owe by the law of charity.

² To serve the turns.

15:28 ¹ Performed it faithfully, and sealed it as it were with my ring.

² This money which was gathered for the use of the poor: which alms is very fitly called fruit.

15:29 ¹ He promiseth them through the blessing of God, not to come empty unto them: and requiring of them the duty of prayers, he showeth what thing we ought chiefly to rest upon in all difficulties and adversities.

15:30 ¹ For that mutual communion, wherewith the holy Ghost hath tied our hearts and minds together.

16:1 ¹ Having made an end of the whole disputation, he cometh now to familiar commendations and salutations, and that to good consideration and purpose, to wit, that the Romans might know, who are most to be honored and made account of amongst them, and also whom they ought to set before them to follow: and therefore he attributeth unto every of them peculiar and singular testimonies.

16:2 ¹ For Christ's sake, which is proper to the Christians, for the heathen Philosophers have resemblances of the same virtues.

Saints, and that ye assist her in whatsoever business she needeth of your aid: for she hath given hospitality unto many, and to me also.

3 Greet *Priscilla, and Aquila, my fellow helpers in Christ Jesus.

4 (Which have for my life laid down their own neck. Unto whom not I only give thanks, but also all the Churches of the Gentiles.)

5 Likewise *greet* the [1]Church that is in their house. Salute my beloved Epaenetus, which is the [2]firstfruits of Achaia in Christ.

6 Greet Mary which bestowed much labor on us.

7 Salute Andronicus and Junia my cousins and fellow prisoners, which are notable among the Apostles, and were in [1]Christ before me.

8 Greet Amplias my beloved in the Lord.

9 Salute Urbanus our fellow helper in Christ, and Stachys my beloved.

10 Salute Apelles approved in Christ. Salute them which are of Aristobulus' *friends*.

11 Salute Herodion my kinsman. Greet them which are of the *friends* of Narcissus which are in the Lord.

12 Salute Tryphena and Tryphosa, which *women* labor in the Lord. Salute the beloved Persis, which *woman* hath labored much in the Lord.

13 Salute Rufus chosen in the Lord, and his mother and mine.

14 Greet Asyncritus, Phlegon, Hermas, Patrobas, Mercurius, and the brethren which are with them.

15 Salute Philologus and Julia, Nereus, and his sister, and Olympas and all the Saints which are with them.

16 Salute one another with an *holy [1]kiss. The Churches of Christ salute you.

CHAPTER 16
a Acts 18:3
b 1 Cor. 16:20
2 Cor. 13:2
1 Pet. 5:14
c 2 John 10
d Acts 16:1
Phil. 2:29
e Eph. 3:20
f Eph. 3:9
Col. 2:26
2 Tim. 1:10
Titus 1:2

17 ¶ [1]Now I beseech you brethren, [2]mark them diligently which cause division and offenses, contrary to the doctrine which ye have learned, and *avoid them.

18 For they that are such, serve not the Lord Jesus Christ but their own bellies, and with [1]fair speech and flattering deceive the hearts of the simple.

19 [1]For your obedience is come abroad among all: I am glad therefore of you: but yet I would have you [2]wise unto that which is good, and [3]simple concerning evil.

20 [1]The God of peace shall tread Satan under your feet shortly. The grace of our Lord Jesus Christ *be* with you.

21 [d,1]Timothy my helper, and Lucius and Jason, and Sosipater my kinsmen, salute you.

22 I Tertius, which [1]wrote out this Epistle, salute you in the Lord.

23 Gaius mine host, and of the whole Church saluteth you. Erastus the steward of the city saluteth you, and Quartus a brother.

24 [1]The grace of our Lord Jesus Christ *be* with you all, Amen.

25 [e,1]To him now that is of power to establish you according to my Gospel, and preaching of Jesus Christ, *f*by the revelation of the [2]mystery, which was kept secret since the world began:

26 (But now is opened, and [1]published among all nations by the Scriptures of the Prophets, at the commandment of the everlasting God for the obedience of faith.)

27 To God, *I say*, only wise, be praise through Jesus Christ for ever. Amen.

Written to the Romans from Corinth, *and sent* by Phoebe, servant of the Church which is at Cenchrea.

16:5 [1] The company of the faithful, for in so great a city as that was, there were divers companies.

[2] For he was the first of Achaia that believed in Christ: and this kind of speech is an allusion to the ceremonies of the Law.

16:7 [1] Ingrafted by faith.

16:16 [1] He calleth that an holy kiss, which proceedeth from an heart that is full of that holy love: now this is to be referred to the manner used in those days.

16:17 [1] As by namely describing them, which were worthy of commendation, he sufficiently declared when they ought to hear and follow, so doth he now point out unto them whom they ought to take heed of, yet he nameth them not, for that it was not needful.

[2] Warily and diligently, as though you should scout out for your enemies in a watch tower.

16:18 [1] The word which he useth, signifieth a promising which performeth nothing, and if thou hearest any such, thou mayest assure thyself that he that promiseth thee is more careful of thy matters, than of his own.

16:19 [1] Simplicity must be joined with wisdom.

[2] Furnished with the knowledge of the truth, and wisdom, that you may embrace good things, and eschew evil, beware of the deceits and snares of false prophets, and resist them openly: and this

place doth plainly destroy the Papists' faith of credit, whereas they maintain it to be sufficient for one man to believe as another man believeth, without further knowledge, or examination what the matter is, or what ground it hath: using these daily speeches, We believe as our fathers believed, and we believe as the Church believeth.

[3] As men that know no way to deceive, much less to deceive in deed.

16:20 [1] We must fight, with a certain hope of victory.

16:21 [1] He annexeth salutations, partly to renew mutual friendship, and partly to the end that this Epistle might be of some weight with the Romans, having the confirmation of so many that subscribed unto it.

16:22 [1] Wrote it as Paul uttered it.

16:24 [1] Now taking his leave of them this third time, he wisheth that unto them, whereupon dependeth all the force of the former doctrine.

16:25 [1] He setteth forth the power and wisdom of God with great thanksgiving, which especially appears in the Gospel, and maketh mention also of the calling of the Gentiles to confirm the Romans in the hope of this salvation.

[2] That secret and hidden thing, that is to say, the calling of the Gentiles.

16:26 [1] Offered and exhibited to all nations to be known.

THE FIRST EPISTLE OF PAUL

TO THE

CORINTHIANS

1 *After the salutation,* 10 *which in effect is an exhortation.* 12 *He reprehendeth the Corinthians' sects and divisions,* 17 *and calleth them from pride to humility:* 20 *For overthrowing all worldly wisdom.* 23, 25 *he advanceth only the preaching of the cross.*

1 Paul ¹called *to be* an ²Apostle of Jesus Christ, through the will of God, and *our* brother ³Sosthenes,

2 ¹Unto the Church of God, which is at Corinth, to them that are *ᵃ*²sanctified in ³Christ Jesus, *ᵇ*Saints by ⁴calling, *ᶜ*with all that ⁵call on the Name of our Lord Jesus Christ in every place, both their *Lord,* and ours:

3 ¹Grace *be* with you, and peace from God our Father, and *from* the Lord Jesus Christ.

4 ¹I thank my God always on your behalf for the grace of God, which is given you in Jesus Christ.

5 That in all things ye are made rich in him ¹in

CHAPTER 1
ᵃ Acts 15:9
1 Thess. 4:7
ᵇ Rom. 1:7
Eph. 1:1
Col. 1:22
1 Tim. 1:9
Titus 2:3
ᶜ 2 Tim. 1:21
ᵈ Titus 2:11
ᵉ 1 Thess. 3:13
1 Thess. 5:23
ᶠ 1 Thess. 5:24

²all kind of speech, and in all knowledge:

6 ¹As the testimony of Jesus Christ hath been ²confirmed in you:

7 So that ye are not destitute of any gift: *ᵈ*,¹waiting for the ²appearing of our Lord Jesus Christ.

8 *ᵉ*,¹Who shall also confirm you unto the end, that ye may be ²blameless in the day of our Lord Jesus Christ.

9 *ᶠ*God is ¹faithful, by whom ye are called unto the fellowship of his son Jesus Christ our Lord.

10 ¹Now I beseech you, brethren, by the Name of our Lord Jesus Christ, that ²ye all speak one thing, and that there be no dissensions among you: but be ye ³knit together in one mind, and in one judgment.

11 ¹For it hath been declared unto me, my brethren, of you by them that are of the house of Chloe, that

---

1:1 ¹ The inscription of the Epistle, wherein he chiefly goeth about to procure the good will of the Corinthians towards him, yet notwithstanding so, that always he letteth them to wit, that he is the servant of God, and not of men.

² If he be an Apostle, then he must be heard, although he sometimes reprehend them sharply, seeing he hath not his own cause in hand, but is a messenger that bringeth the commandments of Christ.

³ He joineth Sosthenes with himself, that this doctrine might be confirmed by two witnesses.

1:2 ¹ It is a Church of God, although it hath great faults in it, so that it obey them which admonish it.

² A true definition of the Catholic Church, which is one.

³ The father sanctifieth us, that is to say, separateth us from the wicked, in giving us to his Son, that he may be in us, and we in him.

⁴ Whom God of his gracious goodness and mere love hath separated for himself: or whom God hath called to holiness: the first of these two expositions showeth from whence our sanctification cometh, and the second showeth to what end it tendeth.

⁵ He is said properly to call on God, who crieth unto the Lord when he is in danger, and craveth help at his hands: and by the figure Synecdoche it is taken for all the service of God: and therefore to call upon Christ's Name, is to acknowledge and take him for very God.

1:3 ¹ The foundation and the life of the Church, is Christ Jesus given of the Father.

1:4 ¹ Going about to condemn many vices, he beginneth with a true commendation of their virtues, lest he might seem after to descend to chiding being moved with malice or envy: yet so, that he referreth all to God as the author of them, and that in Christ. That the Corinthians might be more ashamed to profane and abuse the holy gifts of God.

1:5 ¹ He toucheth that by name, which they most abused.

² Seeing that while we live here, we know but in part and prophesy in part, this word (All) must be refrained to the present state of

the faithful: and by speech he meaneth not a vain kind of babbling, but the gift of holy eloquence, which the Corinthians abused.

1:6 ¹ He showeth that the true use of these gifts consisteth herein that the mighty power of Christ might thereby be set forth in them, that hereafter it might evidently appear how wickedly they abused them to glory and ambition.

² By those excellent gifts of the holy Ghost.

1:7 ¹ He saith by the way, that there is no cause why they should please themselves so much in those gifts which they had received, seeing that those were nothing in comparison of them which are to be looked for.

² He speaketh of the last coming of Christ.

1:8 ¹ He testifieth that he hopeth well of them hereafter, that they may more patiently abide his reprehension afterward. And yet together therewithall showeth, that as well the beginning as the accomplishing of our salvation is only the work of God.

² He calleth them blameless, not whom man never found fault with, but with whom no man can justly find fault, that is to say, them which are in Christ Jesus, in whom there is no condemnation. See Luke 1:6.

1:9 ¹ True and constant, who doth not only call us, but giveth us the gift of perseverance also.

1:10 ¹ Having made an end of the preface, he cometh to the matter itself, beginning with the most grave obtestation, as though they should hear Christ himself speaking and not Paul.

² The first part of this Epistle, wherein his purpose is to call back the Corinthians to brotherly concord, and to take away all occasion of discord. So then this first part concerneth the taking away of schisms. Now a schism is when men which otherwise agree and consent together in doctrine, do yet separate themselves one from another.

³ Knit together, as a body that consisteth of all his parts fitly knit together.

1:11 ¹ He beginneth his reprehension and chiding by taking away of

there are contentions among you.

12 Now [1]this I say, that every one of you saith, I am Paul's, and I am [g]Apollos's, and I am Cephas's and I am Christ's.

13 [1]Is Christ divided? was [2]Paul crucified for you? either were ye [3]baptized into the name of Paul?

14 [1]I thank God, that I baptized none of you, but [h]Crispus, and Gaius,

15 Lest any should say, that I had baptized into mine own name.

16 I baptized also the household of Stephanas: furthermore know I not, whether I baptized any other.

17 [1]For CHRIST sent me not to baptize, but to

Marginal references:
g Acts 18:24
h Acts 18:8
i 1 Cor. 2:13
2 Pet. 1:16
j Rom. 1:16
k Isa. 29:14

preach the Gospel, [2]not with [i,3]wisdom of words, lest the [4]cross of Christ should be made of none effect.

18 For that [1]preaching of the cross is to them that perish, foolishness: but unto us, which are saved, it is the [j,2]power of God.

19 [1]For it is written, [k]I will destroy the wisdom of the wise, and will cast away the understanding of the prudent.

20 Where is the wise? where is the [1]Scribe? where is the [2]disputer of this world? hath not God made the wisdom of this world foolishness?

21 [1]For seeing the [2]world by wisdom knew not God in the [3]wisdom of GOD, [4]it pleased God by the

---

an objection: for that be understood by good witnesses, that there were many factions among them. And therewithall he openeth the cause of dissensions, because that some did hang on one doctor, some on another, and some were so addicted to themselves, that they neglected all doctors and teachers, calling themselves the disciples of Christ only, shutting forth their teachers.

1:12 [1] The matter I would say to you, is this.

1:13 [1] The first reason why schisms ought to be eschewed: because Christ formeth by that means, to be divided and torn in pieces, who cannot be the head of two divers and disagreeing bodies, being himself one.

[2] Another reason: Because they cannot without great injury to God so hang of men as of Christ: which thing no doubt they do, which allow whatsoever some man speaketh, even for his person's sake: as these men allowed one selfsame Gospel being uttered of one man, and did loathe it being uttered of another man. So that these factions were called by the names of their teachers. Now Paul setteth down his own name not only to grieve no man, but also to showeth it he pleadeth not his own cause.

[3] The third reason taken of the form and end of Baptism, wherein we make a promise to Christ, calling on also the Name of the Father and the holy Ghost. Therefore although a man does not fall from the doctrine of Christ, yet if he hang upon some certain teachers, and despise others, he forsaketh Christ: for if he hold Christ his only master, he would hear him, teaching by whomsoever.

1:14 [1] He protesteth that he speaketh so much the more boldly of these things, because that through God's providence he is void of all suspicion of challenging disciples unto himself, and taking them from others. Whereby we may understand that not the scholars only, but the teachers also are here reprehended, which gathered themselves flocks apart.

1:17 [1] The taking away of an objection: that he gave not himself to baptize many amongst them: not for the contempt of Baptism, but because he was chiefly occupied in delivering the doctrine, and committed them that received his doctrine to others to be baptized, whereof he had store. And so he declared sufficiently how far he was from all ambition: whereas on the other side they whom he reprehendeth, as though they gathered disciples unto themselves and not to Christ, bragged most ambitiously of numbers, which they had baptized.

[2] Now he turneth himself to the doctors themselves, which pleased themselves in brave and ambitious eloquence, to the end that they might draw more disciples after them. He confesseth plainly that he was unlike unto them, opposing gravely as it became an Apostle, his example against their perverse judgments: So that this is another place of this Epistle, touching the observing of a godly simplicity, both in words and sentences in teaching the Gospel.

[3] With eloquence: which Paul casteth off from him not only, as not

necessary, but also as flat contrary to the office of his Apostleship: and yet had Paul his kind of eloquence, but it was heavenly, not of man, and void of painted words.

[4] The reason why he used not the pomp of words and painted speech: because it was God's will to bring the world to his obedience by that way, whereby the most idiots amongst men might understand, that this work was done of God himself without the art of man. Therefore as salvation is set forth unto us in the Gospel by the cross of Christ, then which nothing is more contemptible, and more far from life, so God would have the manner of the preaching of the cross most different from those means, with which men do use to draw and entice others, either to hear or believe: therefore it pleased him by a certain kind of most wise folly, to triumph over the most foolish wisdom of the world, as he had said before by Isaiah: that he would. And hereby this we may gather, that both those doctors which were puffed up with ambitious eloquence, and also their hearers strayed far away from the end and mark of their vocation.

1:18 [1] The preaching of Christ crucified, or the kinds of speech which we use.

[2] It is that wherein he declareth his marvelous power in saving his elect, which would not so evidently appear, if it hanged upon any help of man: for so man might attribute that to himself, which is proper only to the cross of Christ.

1:19 [1] The Apostle proveth that this ought not only not to seem strange, seeing that it was foretold so long before, but declareth further, that God is wont to punish the pride of the world in such sort, which so pleaseth itself in its own wisdom: and therefore that that is vain, yea a thing of nothing, and such as God rejecteth as unprofitable, which they so carefully labored for, and made so great account of.

1:20 [1] Where art thou, O thou learned fellow, and thou that spendeth thy days in turning thy books?

[2] Thou that spendeth all thy time in seeking out the secret things of this world, and in expounding all hard questions: and thus triumpheth he against all the men of this world, for there was not one of them that could so much as dream upon this secret and hidden mystery.

1:21 [1] He showeth that the pride of men was worthily punished of GOD, because they would not behold God, as meet was they should; in the most clear glass of the wisdom of the world, which is the workmanship of the world.

[2] By the world he meaneth all men which are not born anew, but remain as they were, when they were first born.

[3] In the workmanship of this world, which hath the marvelous wisdom of God engraved in it, so that every man may behold it.

[4] The goodness of God is wonderful, for while he goeth about to punish the pride of the world, he is very provident and careful, for the salvation of it, and teacheth men to become fools, that they may be wise to God.

⁵foolishness of preaching to save them that believe:

22 ¹ʼ¹Seeing also that the Jews require a sign, and the Grecians seek after wisdom.

23 But we preach Christ crucified: unto the Jews, even a stumbling block, and unto the Grecians, foolishness:

24 But unto them which are called, both of the Jews and Grecians, *we preach* Christ, the power of God, and the wisdom of God.

25 For the foolishness of God is wiser than men, and the weakness of God is stronger than men.

26 ¹For brethren, you see your ²calling, how that not many wise men ³after the flesh, not many mighty, not many noble *are called.*

27 But God hath chosen the foolish things of the world to confound the wise, and God hath chosen the weak things of the world, to confound the mighty things,

28 And vile things of the world, and things which are despised, hath God chosen, and things which ¹are not, to bring to ²nought things that are.

29 That no ¹flesh should rejoice in his presence.

30 But ye are ¹of him in Christ Jesus, ²who of

ᶠ Matt. 12:38
ᵐ Jer. 9:24
2 Cor. 10:17

CHAPTER 2
ᵃ 1 Cor. 1:17
ᵇ Acts 18:1
ᶜ 1 Cor. 1:17
2 Pet. 1:16

God is made unto us wisdom and righteousness, and sanctification, and redemption.

31 That, according as it is written, ᵐ,¹He that rejoiceth, let him rejoice in the Lord.

2 *1 He setteth down a platform of his preaching,   4 which was base in respect of man's wisdom,   7, 13 but noble in respect of the spiritual power and efficacy.   14 And so concludeth that flesh and blood cannot rightly judge thereof.*

1 And ¹I, brethren, when I came to you, came not with ᵃexcellency of words, or of wisdom, showing unto you the ²testimony of God.

2 For I ¹esteemed not to know any thing among you, save Jesus Christ, and him crucified.

3 ᵇAnd I was among you in ¹weakness, and in fear, and in much trembling.

4 Neither *stood* my word, and my preaching in the ᶜenticing speech of man's wisdom, ¹but in plain ²evidence of the Spirit and of power.

5 ¹That your faith should not be in the wisdom of men, but in the power of God.

6 ¹And we speak wisdom among them that are

---

⁵ So calleth the preaching of the Gospel as the enemies supposed it: but in the mean season he taunteth them very sharply, who had rather charge God with folly, than acknowledge their own and crave pardon for it.

1:22 ¹ A declaration of that which he said that the preaching of the Gospel, is foolish. It is foolish, saith he, to them whom God had not endued with new light, that is to say, to all men, being considered in themselves: for the Jews require miracles, and the Greeks arguments, which they may comprehend by their wit and wisdom: and therefore they do not only not believe the Gospel, but also they mock at it. Notwithstanding in this foolish preaching, there is the great virtue and wisdom of God, but such as those only which are called, do perceive. God showing most plainly, that even then when mad men think him most foolish, he is far wiser than they are: and that he surmounteth all their might and power, when he useth most vile and abject things, as it hath appeared in the fruit of the preaching of the Gospel.

1:26 ¹ A confirmation taken of those things which came to pass at Corinth, where the Church especially consisted of the basest and common people, insomuch that the philosophers of Greece were driven to shame, when they saw that they could do nothing with their wisdom and eloquence, in comparison of the Apostles, whom notwithstanding they called idiots and unlearned. And herewithall doth he beat down their pride, for God did not prefer them before those noble and wise men because they should be proud, but that they might be constrained even whether they would or not, to rejoice in the Lord, by whose mercy, although they were, the most abject of all, they had obtained in Christ, both this wisdom, and all things necessary to salvation.

² What way the Lord hath taken in calling you.

³ After that kind of wisdom which men make account of, as though there were none else: who because they are carnal, know not spiritual wisdom.

1:28 ¹ Which in man's judgment are almost nothing.

² To show that they are vain and unprofitable, and nothing worth, see Rom. 3:31.

1:29 ¹ Flesh is oft as we see, taken for the whole man: and he ruleth this word flesh, very fitly, to set the weak and miserable condition of man with the majesty of God, one against the other.

1:30 ¹ Whom he cast down before, now he lifteth up, yea, higher then all men: yet so, that he showeth them all their worthiness is without themselves, that is, standeth in Christ, and that of God.

² He teacheth that especially and above all things, the Gospel ought not to be contemned, seeing it containeth the chiefst things that are to be desired, to wit, true wisdom, the true way to obtain righteousness, the true way to live honestly and godly, the true deliverance from all miseries and calamities.

1:31 ¹ Let man yield all to God and give him thanks: and so by this place is man's free will beaten down, which the Papist so dream of.

2:1 ¹ He returneth to 1 Cor. 1:17, that is to say, to his own example: confessing that he used not amongst them either excellency of words, or enticing speech of man's wisdom, but with great simplicity of speech, both knew and preached Jesus Christ crucified, humble and abject, as touching the flesh.

² The Gospel.

2:2 ¹ I purposed not to profess any other knowledge, but the knowledge of Christ and him crucified.

2:3 ¹ He setteth weakness, against excellency of words, and therefore joineth with it fear and trembling, which are the companions of true modesty, not such fear and trembling as terrify the conscience, but such as are contrary to vanity and pride.

2:4 ¹ He turneth that now to the commendation of his ministry, which he had granted to his adversaries: for his virtue and power which they knew well enough, was so much the more excellent, because it had no worldly help joined with it.

² By plain evidence he meaneth such a proof, as is made by certain and necessary reasons.

2:5 ¹ And he telleth the Corinthians, that he did it for their great profit, because they might thereby know manifestly, that the Gospel was from heaven. Therefore he privately rebuketh them, because that in seeking vain ostentation, they willingly deprived themselves of the greatest help of their faith.

2:6 ¹ Another argument taken of the nature of the thing, that is, of the Gospel, which is true wisdom, but known to them only which are desirous of perfection: and is unsavory to them which otherwise excel in the world, but yet vainly and frailly.

²perfect: not the wisdom of this world, neither of the ³princes of this world, which come to nought.

7 ¹But we speak the wisdom of God in a ²mystery, *even* the hid *wisdom*, ³which God had determined before the world, unto our glory.

8 ¹Which none of the princes of this world hath known: for had they known it, they would not have crucified the ²Lord of glory.

9 ¹But as it is written, ᵈThe things which eye hath not seen, neither ear hath heard, neither came into ²man's heart, *are*, which God hath prepared for them that love him.

10 ¹But God hath revealed *them* unto us by his Spirit: for the spirit ²searcheth all things, yea, the deep things of God.

11 ¹For what man knoweth the things of a man, save

the ²spirit of a man, which is in him? even so the things of God knoweth no man, but the Spirit of God.

12 Now we have receiveth not the ¹spirit of the world, but the Spirit, which is of God, ²that we might ³know the things that are given to us of God.

13 ¹Which things also we speak, not in the ᶜwords which man's wisdom teacheth, but which the holy Ghost teacheth, ²comparing spiritual things with spiritual things.

14 ¹But the ²natural man perceiveth not the things of the Spirit of God: for they are foolishness unto him, neither can he know *them*, because they are ³spiritually discerned.

15 ¹But he that is spiritual, ²discerneth all things: yet ³he himself is judged of ⁴no man.

16 ᶠ¹For who hath known the mind of the Lord,

Reference column:
ᵈ Isa. 64:4
ᵉ 1 Cor. 1:17
2 Pet. 1:16
ᶠ Isa 40:13
Rom. 11:34

2:6 ² Those are called perfect here, not which had gotten perfection already, but such as tend to it, as Phil. 3:15, so that perfect, is set against weak.

³ They that are wiser, richer, or mightier than other men are.

2:7 ¹ He showeth the cause why this wisdom cannot be perceived of those excellent worldly writes: to wit, because indeed it is so deep that they cannot attain unto it.

² Which men could not so much as dream of.

³ He taketh away an objection: if it be so hard, when and how is it known? God, saith he, determined with himself from the beginning, that which his purpose was to bring forth at this time out of his secrets for the salvation of men.

2:8 ¹ He taketh away another objection: why then, how cometh it to pass, that this wisdom was so rejected of men of highest authority, that they crucified Christ himself? Paul answereth: because they knew not Christ such as he was.

² That mighty God, full of true majesty and glory: Now this place hath in it a most evident proof of the divinity of Christ, and of his joining of the two natures in one, which hath this in it, that that which is proper to the manhood alone, is vouched of the Godhead joined with the manhood: which kind of speech is called of the old fathers, a making common of things belonging to someone, with other to whom they do not belong.

2:9 ¹ Another objection: But how could it be that those witty men could not perceive this wisdom? Paul answereth: Because we preach those things which pass all man's understanding.

² Man cannot so much as think of them, much less conceive them with his senses.

2:10 ¹ A question: if it surmount the capacity of men, how can it be understood of any man, or how can you declare and preach it? by a peculiar lightening by God's Spirit, wherewith whosoever is inspired, he can enter even to the very secrets of God.

² There is nothing so secret and hidden in God, but the Spirit of God peereth into it.

2:11 ¹ He setteth that forth by a similitude, which he spake of the inspiration of the Spirit. As the force of man's wit searcheth out things pertaining to man, so doth our mind by that power of the holy Ghost, understand heavenly things.

² The mind of man, which is endued with ableness to understand and judge.

2:12 ¹ The Spirit which we have received, doth not teach us things of this world, but lifteth us up to God, and this place teacheth us against the Papists, what faith is, from whence it cometh, and what force it is of.

² That which he spake generally, he restraineth now to those

things which God hath opened unto us of our salvation in Christ: lest that any man should separate the Spirit from the preaching of the word and Christ: or should think that those fantastical men are governed by the Spirit of God, which wandering besides the word, thrust upon us their vain imaginations for the secrets of God.

³ This word (know) is taken here in his proper sense, for true knowledge, which the Spirit of God worketh in us.

2:13 ¹ Now he returneth to his purpose, and concludeth the argument which he began verse 6, and it is thus: the words must be applied to the matter, and the matter must be set forth with words which are meet and convenient for it: now this wisdom is spiritual and not of man, and therefore it must be delivered by a spiritual kind of teaching, and not by enticing words of man's eloquence, that the simple, and yet wonderful majesty of the holy Ghost may therein appear.

² Applying the words unto the matter, to wit, that as we teach spiritual things, so [must] our kind of teaching be spiritual.

2:14 ¹ Again he preventeth an offence or stumbling block: how cometh it to pass that so few allow these things? This is not to be marveled at, sayeth the Apostle, seeing that men in their natural powers (as they termed them) are not endued with that faculty, whereby spiritual things are discerned (which faculty cometh another way) and therefore they accompt spiritual wisdom as folly: and it is as if he should say, It is no marvel that blind men cannot judge of colors, seeing that they lack the light of their eyes, and therefore light is to them as darkness.

² The man that hath no further light of understanding than that which he brought with him, even from his mother's womb, as Jude defineth it, Jude 19.

³ By the virtue of the holy Ghost.

2:15 ¹ He amplifieth the matter by contraries.

² Understandeth and discerneth.

³ The wisdom of the flesh, saith Paul, determined nothing certainly, no not in its own affairs, much less can it discern strange, that is, spiritual things. But the Spirit of God, wherewith spiritual men are endued, can be deceived by no means, and therefore be reproved of no man.

⁴ Of no man: for when the Prophets are judged of the Prophets, it is the Spirit that judges, and not the man.

2:16 ¹ A reason of the former saying: for he is called spiritual, which hath learned that by the virtue of the Spirit, which Christ hath taught us. Now if that which we have learned of that Master, could be reproved of any man, he must needs be wiser than God: whereupon it followeth, that they are not only foolish, but also wicked, which think that they can devise something that is either more perfect, or that they can teach the wisdom of God a better way than they knew or taught, which undoubtedly, were endued with God's Spirit.

that he might ²instruct him? But we have the ³mind of Christ.

CHAPTER 3
ᵃ Ps. 62:12
Gal. 6:5

3 *1 He yieldeth a reason why he preached small matters unto them: 4 He showeth how they ought to esteem of Ministers: 6 The minister's office. 10 A true form of edifying. 16 He warneth the Corinthians, that they be not drawn away to profane things, 18 through the proud wisdom of the flesh.*

1 And ¹I could not speak unto you, brethren, as unto spiritual men, but as unto ²carnal, *even* as unto babes in Christ.

2 I gave you milk to drink, and not ¹meat: for ye were not yet ²able *to bear it*, neither yet now are ye able.

3 For ye are yet carnal: for whereas *there is* among you envying, and strife, and divisions, are ye not carnal, and walk as ¹men?

4 For when one saith, I am Paul's, and another, I am Apollos's, are ye not carnal?

5 ¹Who is Paul then? and who is Apollos, but the ministers by whom ye believed, and as the Lord gave to every man?

6 ¹I have planted, Apollos watered, but God gave the increase.

7 So then, neither is he that planteth anything, neither he that watereth, but God that giveth the increase.

8 And he that planteth, and he that watereth, are one, ᵃand every man shall receive his wages, according to his labor.

9 For we together are God's ¹laborers: ye are God's husbandry, *and* God's building.

10 According to the grace of God given to me, as a skillful master builder, I have laid the foundation, and another buildeth thereon: ¹but let every man take heed how he buildeth upon it.

11 ¹For other foundation can no man lay, than that which is laid, which is Jesus Christ.

12 ¹And if any man build on this foundation, gold, silver, precious stones, timber, hay, *or* stubble,

---

² Lay his head to his, and teach him what he should do.

³ We are endued with the Spirit of Christ, who openeth unto us those secrets, which by all other means are unsearchable, and also all truth whatsoever.

3:1 ¹ Having declared the worthiness of heavenly wisdom, and of the Gospel, and having generally condemned the blindness of man's mind, now at length he applieth it particularly to the Corinthians, calling them carnal, that is, such in whom as yet the flesh prevaileth against the spirit. And he bringeth a double testimony of it: first, for that he had proved them to be such, insomuch that he dealt with them no otherwise than with ignorant men, and such as are almost babes in the doctrine of godliness; and secondly, because they showed indeed by these dissensions, which sprang up by reason of the ignorance of the virtue of the Spirit, and heavenly wisdom, that they had profited very little or nothing.

² He calleth them carnal, which are as yet ignorant, and therefore to express it the better, he termeth them babes.

3:2 ¹ Substantial meat, or strong meat.

² To be fed by me with substantial meat: therefore as the Corinthians grew up in age, so the Apostle nourished them by teaching first with milk, then with strong meat, which difference was only but in the manner of teaching.

3:3 ¹ By the square and compass of man's wit and judgment.

3:5 ¹ After that he hath sufficiently reprehended ambitious teachers, and their foolish esteemers, now he showeth how the true ministers are to be esteemed, that we attribute not unto them, more or less than we ought to do. Therefore he teacheth us, that they are they by whom we are brought to faith and salvation, but yet as the ministers of God, and such as do nothing of themselves, but God so working by them as it pleaseth him to furnish them with his gifts. Therefore we have not to mark or consider what minister it is that speaketh, but what is spoken: and we must depend only upon him which speaketh by his servants.

3:6 ¹ He beautifieth the former sentence, with two similitudes: first comparing the company of the faithful, to a field which God maketh fruitful, when it is sowed and watered through the labor of his servants: next, by comparing it to a house, which indeed the Lord buildeth, but by the hands of his workmen, some of whom, he useth in

laying the foundation, others in building of it up. Now, both these similitudes tend to this purpose, to show that all things are wholly accomplished by God's only authority and might, so that we must only have an eye to him. Moreover, although that God useth some in the better part of the work, we must not therefore contemn others, in respect of them, and much less may we divide, or set them apart, (as these factious men did) seeing that all of them labor in God's business, and in such sort, that they serve to finish one selfsame work, although by a divers manner of working, insomuch that they need one another's help.

3:9 ¹ Serving under him: Now they which serve under another, do nothing by their own strength, but as it is given them by grace, which grace maketh them fit to that service. See 1 Cor. 15:10; 2 Cor. 3:6, and all the increase that cometh by their labor, doth so proceed from God, that no part of the praise of it may be given to the under servant.

3:10 ¹ Now he speaketh to the teachers themselves, who succeeded him in the Church of Corinth, and in their person, to all that were after or shall be Pastors of Congregations, seeing that they succeed into the labor of the Apostles, which were planters and chief builders. Therefore he warneth them first, that they persuade not themselves that they may build after their own fantasy, that is, that they may propound and set forth anything in the Church, either in matter, or in kind of teaching, different from the Apostles which were the chief builders.

3:11 ¹ Moreover, he showeth what this foundation is, to wit, Christ Jesus, from which they may not turn away one iota in the building up of this building.

3:12 ¹ Thirdly, he showeth that they must take heed that the upper part of the building be answerable to the foundation, that is, that admonitions, exhortations, and whatsoever pertaineth to the edifying of the flock, be answerable to the doctrine of Christ, as well in matter as in form: which doctrine is compared to gold, silver, and precious stones: of which matter, Isaiah also and John in the Revelation build the heavenly Jerusalem. And to these are opposite, wood, hay, stubble, that is to say, curious and vain questions or decrees: and besides to be short, all that kind of teaching which serveth to ostentation. For false doctrines, whereof he speaketh not here, are not said properly to be built upon this foundation, unless peradventure in show only.

13 ¹Every man's work shall be made manifest: for the day shall declare it, because it shall be revealed by the fire: and the fire shall try every man's work of what sort it is.

14 If any man's work, that he hath built upon, abide, he shall receive wages.

15 If any man's work burn, he shall lose, but ¹he shall be saved himself: nevertheless yet as it were by the fire.

16 ᵇ,¹Know ye not that ye are the Temple of God, and that the Spirit of God dwelleth in you?

17 If any man ¹destroy the Temple of God, him shall God destroy: for the Temple of God is holy, which ye are.

18 ¹Let no man deceive himself: If any man among you seem to be wise in this world, let him be a fool, that he may be wise.

19 For the wisdom of this world is foolishness with God: for it is written, ᶜHe ¹catcheth the wise in their own craftiness.

20 ᵈAnd again, The Lord knoweth that the thoughts

ᵇ 1 Cor. 6:19
2 Cor. 6:16
ᶜ Job 5:13
ᵈ Ps. 44:11

of the wise be vain.

21 ¹Therefore let no man ²rejoice in men: for all things are ³yours.

22 Whether it be Paul, or Apollos, or Cephas, or the ¹world, or life, or death, whether they be things present, or things to come, *even* all are yours,

23 And ye Christ's, and Christ God's.

4 1 Bringing in the definition of a true Apostle, 7 he showeth that humility ought rather to be an honor than a shame unto him. 9 He bringeth in proof, whereby it may evidently appear, 10 that he neither had care of glory, 11 nor of his belly. 17 He commendeth Timothy.

1 Let ¹a ²man so think of us, as of the ministers of Christ, and disposers of the secrets of God:

2 ¹And as for the rest, it is required of the disposers, that every man be found faithful.

3 ¹As touching me, I pass very little to be judged of you, ²or of man's ³judgment: no, ⁴I judge not mine own self.

4 For I know nothing by myself, yet am I not

3:13 ¹ He testifieth, as indeed the truth is, that all are not good builders, no not some of them which stand upon this one and only foundation: but howsoever this work of evil builders, saith he, stand for a season, yet shall it not always deceive, because that the light of the truth appearing at length, as day shall dissolve this darkness, and show what it is. And as that stuff is tried by the fire, whether it be good or not, so will God in his time by the touch of his Spirit and word, try all buildings, and so shall it come to pass, that such as be found pure and sound, shall still continue so, to the praise of the workman; but they that are otherwise, shall be consumed, and vanish away, and so shall the workman be frustrated of the hope of his labor, which pleased himself in a thing of nought.
3:15 ¹ He taketh not away hope of salvation from the unskillful and foolish builders, which hold fast the foundation, of which sort were those Rhetoricians rather than pastors of Corinth: but he addeth an exception, that they must notwithstanding suffer this trial of their work, and also abide the loss of their vain labors.
3:16 ¹ Continuing still in the metaphor of a building, he teacheth us that this ambition is not only vain, but also sacrilegious: For he saith that the Church is as it were the Temple of God, which God hath as it were consecrated unto himself by his Spirit. Then turning himself to these ambitious men: he showeth that they profane the Temple of God, because those vain arts wherein they please themselves so much, are as he teacheth, so many pollutions of the holy doctrine of God, and the purity of the Church. Which wickedness shall not be suffered unpunished.
3:17 ¹ Defileth it, and maketh it unclean, being holy: and surely they do defile it, by Paul's judgment, which by fleshly eloquence defile the purity of the Gospel.
3:18 ¹ He concludeth by the contrary, that they profess pure wisdom in the Church of God, which refuse and cast away all those vanities of men, and if they be mocked of the world, it is sufficient for them that they be wise according to the wisdom of God, and as he will have them to be wise.
3:19 ¹ Be they never so crafty, yet the Lord will take them when he shall discover their treachery.
3:21 ¹ He returneth to the proposition of verse 2, first warning the hearers, that henceforward they esteem not as lords, those whom

God hath appointed to be ministers, and not lords of their salvation, which thing they do, that depend upon men, and not upon God, that speaketh by them.
² Please himself.
³ Helps, appointeth for your benefit.
3:22 ¹ He passeth from the persons to the things themselves, that his argument may be more forcible, yea, he ascendeth from Christ to the Father, to show us that we rest ourselves no not in Christ himself, in that that he is man, but because he carrieth us up even to the Father, as Christ witnesseth of himself everywhere, that he was sent of his Father, that by this band we may be all knit with God himself.
4:1 ¹ He concludeth the duty of the hearers towards their ministers: that they esteem them not as lords: and yet notwithstanding, that they give ear unto them, as to them that are sent from Christ, sent I say to this end and purpose, that they may receive as it were at their hands, the treasure of salvation which is drawn out of the secrets of God.
² Every man.
4:2 ¹ Last of all, he warneth the ministers that they also behave themselves not as lords, but as faithful servants, because they must render an account of their stewardship unto God.
4:3 ¹ Because in reprehending others, he set himself for an example, he useth a preoccupation or preventing of an objection, and using the gratuity of an Apostle, he showeth that he careth not for the contrary judgments that they have of him, in that they esteemed him as a vile person, because he did not set forth himself as they did. And he bringeth good reasons why he was nothing moved with the judgments which they had of him.
² First, because that that which men judge in these cases of their own brains, is no more to be accounted of, than when the unlearned do judge of wisdom.
³ Word for word, Day, after the manner of speech of the Cilicians.
⁴ Secondly, saith he, how can you judge how much or how little I am to be accounted of, seeing that I myself which know myself better than you do, and which dare profess that I have walked in my vocation with a good conscience, dare not yet notwithstanding challenge anything to myself: for I know that I am not unblameable, all this notwithstanding: much less therefore should I please myself as you do.

thereby justified: but he that judgeth me, is the ¹Lord.

5 ¹Therefore ªjudge nothing before the time, until the Lord come, who will lighten things that are hid in darkness, and make the counsels of the hearts manifest: and then shall every man have ²praise of God.

6 ¹Now these things, brethren, I have figuratively applied unto mine own self and Apollos, for your sakes, that ye might learn ²by us, that no man presume above that which is written, that one swell not against another for any man's cause.

7 ¹For who separateth thee? and what hast thou, that thou hast not received? if thou hast received it, why rejoicest thou, as though ²thou hadst not received it?

8 ¹Now ye are full: now ye are made rich: ye reign as kings without us, and would to God ye did reign, that we also might reign with you.

9 For I think that God hath set forth us the last Apostles, as men appointed to death, for we are made a ¹gassing stock unto the world, and to the Angels, and to men.

10 We *are* fools for Christ's sake, and ye *are* wise in Christ: we *are* weak, and ye *are* strong: ye *are* honorable, and we *are* despised.

11 Unto this hour we both hunger, and thirst, and are naked, and are buffeted, and have no certain dwelling place,

12 ᵇAnd labor, working with our own hands: we are reviled, and *yet* we bless: we are persecuted, *and* suffer it.

CHAPTER 4
ª Matt. 7:1
ᵇ Acts 20:34
1 Thess. 2:9
2 Thess. 3:8
ᶜ Matt. 5:44
Luke 23:34
Acts 7:60
ᵈ Acts 19:21
James 4:15

13 ᶜWe are evil spoken of, and we pray: we are made as the ¹filth of the world, the offscouring of all things, unto this time.

14 ¹I write not these things to shame you, but as my beloved children I admonish you.

15 For though ye have ten thousand instructors in Christ, yet *have ye* not many fathers: for in Christ Jesus I have begotten you through the Gospel.

16 Wherefore, I pray you, be followers of me.

17 For this cause have I sent unto you Timothy, which is my beloved son, and faithful in the Lord, which shall put you in remembrance of my ¹ways in Christ as I teach everywhere in every Church.

18 ¹Some are puffed up as though I would not come unto you.

19 But I will come to you shortly, ᵈif the Lord will, and I will know, not the ¹words of them which are puffed up, but the power.

20 For the kingdom of God *is* not in word, but in power.

21 ¹What will ye? shall I come unto you with a rod, or in love, and in the ²spirit of meekness?

5 1 *That they have winked at him who committed incest with his mother-in-law,* 2, 6 *he showeth should cause them rather to be ashamed, than to rejoice:* 10 *Such kind of wickedness is to be punished with excommunication,* 12 *lest others be infected with it.*

1 It ¹is heard certainly *that there is* fornication among you: and such fornication as is not once named among the Gentiles, that one should have his father's wife.

4:4 ¹ I permit myself to the Lord's judgment.
4:5 ¹ A third reason proceeding of a conclusion as it were, out of the former reasons. It is God's office, to esteem every man according to his value, because he knoweth the secrets of the heart, which men for the most part are ignorant of. Therefore this judgment pertaineth not to you.
² One could not be praised above the rest, but the other should be blamed: and he mentioneth praise rather than dispraise, for that the beginning of this sore was this, that they gave more to some men than meet was.
4:6 ¹ Having rejected their judgment, he setteth forth himself again as a singular example of modesty, as one which concealing in this Epistle those factious teacher's names, doubted not to put down his own name and Apollos' in their place, and took upon him, as it were, their shame: so far was he from preferring himself to any.
² By our example, which chose rather to take other men's faults upon us, than to carpe any by name.
4:7 ¹ He showeth a good means to bridle pride: first, if thou consider how rightly thou exemptest thyself out of the number of others, seeing thou art a man thyself: again, if thou consider that although thou have something more than other men have, yet thou hast it not but by God's bountifulness. And what wise man is he that will brag of another's goodness, and that against God?
² There is nothing then in us of nature, that is worthy of commendation: but all that we have, we have it of grace, which the Pelagians

and half Pelagians will not confess.
4:8 ¹ He descendeth to a most grave mock, to cause these ambitious men to blush even against their wills.
4:9 ¹ He that will take a right view how like Paul and the Pope are, who lyingly boasteth that he is his successor, let him compare the delicates of the Popish court with Saint Paul's state, as we see it here.
4:13 ¹ Such as by sweeping is gathered together.
4:14 ¹ Moderating the sharpness of his mock, he putteth them in mind to remember of whom they were begotten in Christ, and that they should not doubt to follow him for an example, although he seem vile according to the outward show, in respect of others, yet mighty by the efficacy of God's Spirit, as they had trial thereof in themselves.
4:17 ¹ What way and rule I follow everywhere in teaching the Churches.
4:18 ¹ Last of all he descendeth also to Apostolic threatenings, but yet chiding them as a father, lest by their disorder he be constrained to come to punish some among them.
4:19 ¹ By words, he meaneth their painted and colored kind of eloquence, against which he setteth the virtue of the Spirit.
4:21 ¹ A passing over to another part of this Epistle, wherein he reprehended more sharply a very heinous offence, showing the use of ecclesiastical correction.
² Meekly affected towards you.
5:1 ¹ They are greatly to be reprehended which by suffering of wickedness, set forth the Church of God to be mocked and scorned as the infidels.

2 [1]And ye are puffed up, and have not rather sorrowed, that he which hath done this deed, might be put from among you.

3 [1]For I verily as absent in body, but present in [2]spirit, have determined already as though I were present, that he that hath thus done this thing,

4 When ye are gathered together, and my spirit, in the [1]Name of our Lord Jesus Christ, that such one, I say, [2]by the power of our Lord Jesus Christ,

5 [1]Be [2]delivered unto Satan, for the [3]destruction of the flesh, that the spirit may be saved in the day of the Lord Jesus.

6 [1]Your rejoicing [2]is not good: know ye not that a little leaven leaveneth the whole lump?

7 [1]Purge out therefore the old leaven, that ye may be a new [2]lump, as ye are unleavened: for Christ our [3]Passover is sacrificed for us.

8 Therefore let us keep the [1]feast, not with old leaven, neither in the leaven of maliciousness and wickedness: but with the unleavened bread of sincerity and truth.

9 [1]I wrote unto you in an Epistle, that ye should not company together with fornicators,

10 And not [1]altogether with the fornicators of this world, or with the covetous, or with extortioners, or with idolaters: for then ye must go out of the world.

11 But now I have written unto you, that ye company not together: if any that is called a brother, be a fornicator, or covetous, or an idolater, or a railer, or a drunkard, or an extortioner, with such one eat not.

12 [1]For what have I to do to judge them also which are without? do ye not judge them that are within?

13 But God judgeth them that are without. Put away therefore from among yourselves that wicked man.

6

1 He inveigheth against their contention in law matters, 6 wherewith they vexed one another under judges that were infidels, to the reproach of the Gospel, 9 and then sharply threateneth fornicators.

1 Dare [1,2]any of you, having business against another, be judged [3]under the unjust, [4]and not under the Saints?

2 [1]Do ye not know that the Saints shall judge the

5:2 [1] There are none more proud, than they that least know themselves.

5:3 [1] Excommunication ought not to be committed to one man's power, but must be done by the authority of the whole Congregation, after that the matter is diligently examined.

[2] In mind, thought, and will.

5:4 [1] Calling upon Christ his Name.

[2] There is no doubt but that judgment is ratified in heaven, wherein Christ himself sitteth as Judge.

5:5 [1] The excommunicate is delivered to the power of Satan, in that, that he is cast out of the house of God.

[2] What it is to be delivered to Satan, the Lord himself declareth when he saith, Let him be unto thee as an Heathen and Publican, Matt 18:17, that is to say, to be disfranchised, and put out of the right and liberty of the city of Christ, which is the Church, without which Satan is lord and master.

[3] The end of excommunication is not to cast away the excommunicate, that he should utterly perish, but that he may be saved, to wit, that by this means his flesh may be tamed, that he may learn to live to the Spirit.

5:6 [1] Another end of excommunication is, that others be not infected, and therefore it must of necessity be retained in the Church, that the one be not infected by the other.

[2] Is naught, and not grounded upon good reason, as though you were excellent, and yet there is such wickedness found amongst you.

5:7 [1] By alluding to the ceremony of the Passover, he exhorteth them to cast out that unclean person from amongst them. In times past, saith he, it was not lawful for them which did celebrate the Passover, to eat leavened bread: insomuch that he was holden as unclean and unworthy to eat the Passover, whosoever had but tasted of leaven. Now our whole life must be as it were the feast of unleavened bread, wherein all they that are partakers of that immaculate Lamb which is slain, must cast out both of themselves, and also out of their houses and Congregations all impurity.

[2] By lump he meaneth the whole body of the Church, every member whereof must be unleavened bread, that is, be renewed in spirit, by plucking away the old corruption.

[3] The Lamb of our Passover.

5:8 [1] Let us lead our whole life, as it were a continual feast, honestly and uprightly.

5:9 [1] Now he speaketh more generally; and that which he spake before of the incestuous person, he showeth that it pertaineth to others, which are known to be wicked, and such as through their naughty life are a slander to the Church, which ought also by lawful order be cast out of the community of the Church. And making mention of eating meat, either he meaneth those feasts of love whereat the Supper of the Lord was received, or else their common usage and manner of life which is rightly to be taken, lest any man should think that either matrimony were broken by excommunication, or such duties hindered and cut off thereby, as we owe one to another: children to their parents, subjects to their rulers, servants to their masters, and neighbor to neighbor, to win one another to God.

5:10 [1] If you should utterly abstain from such men's company, you should go out of the world: therefore I speak of them which are in the very bosom of the Church, which must be called home by discipline, and not of them which are without, with whom we must labor by all means possible, to bring them to Christ.

5:12 [1] Such as are false brethren, ought to be cast out of the Congregation: as for them which are without, they must be left to the judgment of God.

6:1 [1] The third question is of civil judgments: Whether it be lawful for one faithful to draw another faithful before the judgment seat of an infidel? He answereth that it is not lawful, for offense sake, for it is not evil of itself.

[2] As if he said, Are ye become so impudent, that you are not ashamed to make the Gospel a laughingstock to profane men?

[3] Before the unjust.

[4] He addeth that he doth not forbid that one neighbor may go to law with another, if need so require, but yet under holy judges.

6:2 [1] He gathereth by a comparison that the faithful cannot seek to infidels to be judged, without great injury done to the Saints, seeing that God himself will make the Saints judges of the world, and of the devils, with his Son Christ: much more ought they to judge these light and small causes: which may be by equity, and good conscience, determineth.

world? If the world then shall be judged by you, are ye unworthy to judge the smallest matters?

3　Know ye not that we shall judge the Angels? how much more things that pertain to this life?

4　[1]If then ye have [2]judgments of things pertaining to this life, set them up which are [3]least esteemed in the Church.

5　[1]I speak it to your shame. Is it so that there is not a wise man among you? no, not one, that can judge between his brethren?

6　But a brother goeth to law with a brother, and that under the infidels.

7　[1]Now therefore there is altogether [2]infirmity in you, that ye go to law one with another: [a,3]why rather suffer ye not wrong? why rather sustain ye not harm?

8　[b]Nay, ye yourselves do wrong, and do harm, and that to your brethren.

9　Know ye not that the unrighteous shall not inherit the kingdom of God? [1]Be not deceived: neither fornicators, nor idolaters, nor adulterers, nor wantons, nor buggerers,

CHAPTER 6
[a] Matt. 5:39
Luke 6:29
Rom. 12:19
[b] 1 Thess. 4:6
[c] Titus 3:3
[d] 1 Cor. 10:23
[e] Rom. 6:5

10　Nor thieves, nor covetous, nor drunkards, nor railers, nor extortioners shall inherit the kingdom of God.

11　And such were [c]some of you: but ye are washed, but ye are sanctified, but ye are justified, in the [1]Name of the Lord Jesus, and by the Spirit of our God.

12　¶ [d,1,2]All things are lawful unto me, but all things are not profitable. I may do all things, but I will not be brought under the [3]power of any thing.

13　[1]Meats are ordained for the belly, and the belly for the meats: but God shall destroy both it, and them. Now the body is not for fornication, but for the Lord, and the Lord for the body.

14　And God hath also raised up the Lord, and [e]shall raise us up by his power.

15　[1]Know ye not, that your bodies are the members of Christ? shall I then take the members of Christ, and make them the members of an harlot? God forbid.

16　[1]Do ye not know, that he which coupleth himself

6:4 [1] The conclusion, wherein he prescribeth a remedy for this mischief: to wit, if they end their private affairs betwixt themselves by chosen arbiters out of the Church: for which matter and purpose, the least of you, saith he, is sufficient. Therefore he condemneth not judgment seats, but showeth what is expedient for the circumstance of the time, and that without any diminishing of the right of the magistrate: for he speaketh not of judgments which are practiced between the faithful and the infidels, neither of public judgments, but of controversies which may be ended by private arbiters.

[2] Courts and places of judgments.

[3] Even the most abject among you.

6:5 [1] He applieth the general proposition to a particular, always calling them back to this, to take away from them that false opinion of their own excellency, from whence all these mischiefs sprang.

6:7 [1] Now he goeth further also, and although by granting them private arbiters out of the Congregation of the faithful, he doth not simply condemn, but rather establish private judgments, so that they be exercised without offense, yet he showeth that if they were such as they ought to be, and as it were to be wished, they should not need to use that remedy neither.

[2] A weakness of mind which is said to be in them that suffer themselves to be overcome of their lusts, and it is a fault that squareth greatly from temperance and moderation, so that he nippeth them which could not put up an injury done unto them.

[3] This pertaineth chiefly to the other part of the reprehension, to wit, that they went to law even under infidels, whereas they should rather have suffered any loss, than to have given that offense. But yet this is generally true, that we ought rather depart from our right, than try the uttermost of the Law hastily, and upon an affection to revenge an injury. But the Corinthians cared for neither, and therefore he saith that they must repent, unless they will be shut out of the inheritance of God.

6:9 [1] Now he prepareth himself to pass over to the fourth treatise of this Epistle, which concerneth matters indifferent: debating this matter first, how men may well use women or not: which question hath three branches, fornication, matrimony, and a single life. As for fornication, he utterly condemneth it. And marriage he commandeth to some, as a good and necessary remedy for them, to others he leaveth it free: And

others some he dissuadeth from it, not as unlawful, but as discommodious, and that not without exception. As for singleness of life (under which also I comprehend virginity) he enjoineth it to no man: yet he persuadeth men unto it, but not for itself, but for another respect, neither all men nor without exception. And being about to speak against fornication, he beginneth with a general reprehension of those vices, wherewith that rich and riotous city most abounded: warning and teaching them earnestly, that repentance is unseparably joined with forgiveness of sins, and sanctification with justification.

6:11 [1] In Jesus.

6:12 [1] Secondly, he showeth that the Corinthians do simply offend in matters indifferent. First, because they abused them: next, because they used indifferent things, without any discretion, seeing the use of them ought to be brought to the rule of charity: and that he doth not use them aright, which immoderately abuseth them, and so becometh a slave unto them.

[2] Whatever: but this general word must be restrained to things that are indifferent.

[3] He is in subjection to things that are indifferent, whatsoever he be that thinketh he may not be without them, which is a flattering kind of slavery under a color of liberty, which sealeth upon such men.

6:13 [1] Secondarily, because they counted many things for indifferent which were of themselves unlawful, as fornication, which they numbered amongst mere natural and lawful desires, as well as meat and drink: Therefore the Apostle showeth, that they are utterly unlike: for meats, saith he, were made for the necessary use of man's life, which is not perpetual. For both meats, and all this manner of nourishing are quickly abolished. But we must not so think of the uncleanness of fornication, for which the body is not made, but on the contrary side is ordained to pureness, as appeareth by this, that is consecrated to Christ, even as Christ also is given us of his Father, to quicken our bodies with that virtue wherewith he also rose again.

6:15 [1] A declaration of the former argument by contraries, and the applying of it.

6:16 [1] A proof of the same argument: a harlot and Christ are clean contrary, so are the flesh and the Spirit: therefore he that is one with an harlot (which is done by carnal copulation of their bodies) cannot be one with Christ, which unity is pure and spiritual.

with an harlot, is one body? *f*for ²two, saith he, shall be one flesh.

17 But he that is joined unto the Lord, is one spirit.

18 ¹Flee fornication: every sin that a man doeth, is without the body: but he that commiteth fornication, sinneth against his own body.

19 ¹Know ye not, that *g*your body is the temple of the holy Ghost, *which is* in you, whom ye have of God? and ²ye are not your own.

20 *h*For ye are bought for a price: therefore glorify God in your body, and in your spirit: for they are God's.

7 *Entreating here of marriage,   4 which is a remedy against fornication,   10 and may not be broken, 18, 20 he willeth every man to live contented with his lot. 25 He showeth what the end of virginity should be,   35 and who ought to marry.*

1 Now ¹concerning the things ²whereof ye wrote unto me, It *were* ³good for a man not to touch a woman.

2 Nevertheless, to avoid fornication, let every man have his wife, and let every woman have her own husband.

3 *d,*¹Let the husband give unto the wife ²due benevolence, and likewise also the wife unto the husband.

4 ¹The wife hath not the power of her own body,

but the husband: and likewise also the husband hath not the power of his own body, but the wife.

5 Defraud not one another, ¹except *it be* with consent for a time, that ye may ²give yourselves to fasting and prayer, and again come together, that Satan tempt you not for your incontinency.

6 ¹But I speak this by permission, not by commandment.

7 For I ¹would that all men were even as I myself *am:* but every man hath his proper gift of God, one after this manner, and another after that.

8 ¹Therefore I say unto the ²unmarried, and unto the widows, It is good for them if they abide even as I *do.*

9 But if they cannot abstain, let them marry: for it is better to marry than to ¹burn.

10 *b,*¹And unto the married I command, not I, but the Lord, Let not the wife depart from her husband.

11 But and if she depart, let her remain unmarried, or be reconciled unto her husband, and let not the husband put away *his* wife.

12 ¹But to the remnant I speak, *and* not the Lord, If any brother have a wife that believeth not, if she be content to dwell with him, let him not forsake her.

13 And the woman which hath an husband that believeth not, if he be content to dwell with her, let her not forsake him.

Marginal references:
f Gen. 2:24
Matt. 19:5
Mark 10:8
Eph. 5:31
g 1 Cor. 3:17
2 Cor. 6:16
h 1 Cor. 7:13
1 Pet. 1:18

CHAPTER 7
a 1 Pet. 3:7
b Matt. 5:32
Matt. 19:9
Mark 10:11-12
Luke 16:18

6:16 ² Moses doth not speak these words of fornication, but of marriage: but seeing that fornication is the corrupting of marriage, and both of them is a carnal and fleshly copulation, we cannot say that the Apostle abuseth his testimony. Again, Moses hath not this word (Two) but it is very well expresseth both here and in Matt. 29:5, because he speaketh only but of man and wife: whereupon the opinion of them that vouch it to be lawful to have many wives, is beaten down: for he that companieth with many, is sundered as it were into many parts.

6:18 ¹ Another argument why fornication is to be eschewed, because it defileth the body with a peculiar kind of filthiness.

6:19 ¹ The third argument: Because a fornicator is sacrilegious, for that our bodies are consecrate to God.

² The fourth argument: Because we are not our own men, to give ourselves to any other, much less to Satan and the flesh, seeing that God himself hath bought us, and that with a great price, to the end that both in body and soul, we should serve to his glory.

7:1 ¹ He teacheth concerning marriage, that although a single life hath his commodities, which he will declare afterwards, yet that marriage is necessary for the avoiding of fornication: but so that neither one man may have many wives, or any wife many husbands.

² Touching those matters whereof you wrote unto me.

³ Commodious, and (as we say) expedient. For marriage bringeth many griefs with it, and that by reason of the corruption of our first estate.

7:3 ¹ Secondly, he showeth that the parties married, must with singular affection entirely love one the other.

² This word (due) containeth all kind of benevolence, though he speak more of one sort than of the other, in that that followeth.

7:4 ¹ Thirdly, he warneth them that they are each in other's power, as touching the body, so that they may not defraud one another.

7:5 ¹ He addeth an exception: unless the one abstain from the other by mutual consent, that they may the better give themselves to prayer, wherein notwithstanding, he warneth them to consider what is expedient, lest by this long breaking off as it were from marriage, they bestirred up to incontinency.

² Do nothing else.

7:6 ¹ Fifthly, he teacheth that marriage is not simply necessary for all men, but for them which have not the gift of continency, and this gift is by a peculiar grace of God.

7:7 ¹ I wish.

7:8 ¹ Sixthly, he giveth the selfsame admonition touching the second marriage, to wit, that a single life is to be allowed, but for such as have the gift of continency: otherwise they ought to marry again, that their conscience may be at peace.

² This whole place is flat against them which condemn second marriages.

7:9 ¹ So to burn with lust, that either the will yieldeth to the temptation, or else we cannot call upon God with a quiet conscience.

7:10 ¹ Seventhly, he forbiddeth contentions and the publishing of divorces (for he speaketh not here of the fault of whoredom, which was then dealt even by the law of the Romans also) whereby he affirmeth that the hand of marriage is not dissolved, and that from Christ's mouth.

7:12 ¹ Eighthly, he affirmeth that those marriages which are already contracted between a faithful and an unfaithful or infidel, are firm, so that the faithful may not forsake the unfaithful.

14 ¹For the unbelieving husband is ²sanctified to the ³wife, and the unbelieving wife is sanctified to the ⁴husband, else were your children unclean: but now are they ⁵holy.

15 ¹But if the unbelieving depart, let him depart: a brother or a sister is not in subjection in ²such things: ³but God hath called us in peace.

16 For what knowest thou, O wife, whether thou shalt save thine husband? Or what knowest thou, O man, whether thou shalt save thy wife?

17 ¹But as God hath distributeth to every man, as the Lord ²hath called every one, so let him walk: and so ordain I in all Churches.

18 ¹Is any man called being circumcised? let him not ²gather *his uncircumcision*: is any called uncircumcised? let him not be circumcised.

19 Circumcision is nothing, and uncircumcision is nothing, but the keeping of the commandments of God.

20 ᶜLet every man abide in the same vocation wherein he was called.

c 1 Tim. 6:1
d 1 Cor. 6:20
1 Pet. 18:19

21 Art thou called *being* a servant? ¹care not for it: but if yet thou mayest be free, use it rather.

22 For he that is called in the ¹Lord, *being* a servant, is the Lord's freeman: likewise also he that is called *being* free, is Christ's servant.

23 ᵈ,¹Ye are bought with a price: be not the servants of men.

24 ¹Brethren, let every man, wherein he was called, therein abide with ²God.

25 ¹Now concerning virgins, I have no commandment of the Lord: but I give mine ²advise, as ³one that hath obtained mercy of the Lord to be faithful.

26 I suppose then ¹this to be good for the ²present necessity: *I mean* that it is good for a man so to be.

27 Art thou bound unto a wife? seek not to be loosed: art thou loosed from a wife? seek not a wife.

28 But if thou takest a wife, thou sinnest not: and if a virgin marry, she sinneth not: nevertheless, such shall have trouble in the ¹flesh: but I ²spare you.

29 And this I say, brethren, because the time is

7:14 ¹ He answereth an objection: But the faithful is defiled by the society of the unfaithful. The Apostle denieth that, and proveth that the faithful man with good conscience may use the vessel of his unfaithful wife, by this that their children which are born of them, are accounted holy (that is, contained within the promise) for it is said to all the faithful, I will be thy God, and the God of thy seed.

² The godliness of the wife is of more force, to cause their coupling together to be accounted holy, than the infidelity of the husband is, to profane the marriage.

³ The infidel is not sanctified or made holy in his own person, but in respect of his wife, he is sanctified to her.

⁴ To the faithful husband.

⁵ This place destroyeth the opinion of them that would not have children to be baptized, and their opinion also, that make baptism the very cause of salvation. For the children of the faithful are holy, by virtue of the covenant, even before Baptism, and baptism is added as the seal of that holiness.

7:15 ¹ He answereth to a question: what if the unfaithful forsake the faithful? then is the faithful free, saith he, because he is forsaken of the unfaithful.

² When any such thing falleth out.

³ Lest any man upon pretence of this liberty should give occasion to the unfaithful to depart, he giveth to understand, that marriage contracted with an infidel, ought peaceably to be kept, that if it be possible the infidel may be won to the faith.

7:17 ¹ Taking occasion by that which he said of the bondage and liberty of matrimony, he digresseth to a general doctrine concerning the outward state and condition of man's life, as Circumcision and uncircumcision, servitude and liberty: warning every man generally to live with a contented mind in the Lord, what state or condition forever he be in, because that those outward things, as to be circumcised or uncircumcised, to be bond or free, are not of the substance (as they term it) of the kingdom of heaven.

² Hath bound him to a certain kind of life.

7:18 ¹ Notwithstanding he giveth us to understand, that in these examples all are not like sort: because that circumcision is not simply of itself to be desired, but such as are bound may desire to be free. Therefore herein only they are equal, that the kingdom of God consisteth

not in them, and therefore these are no hindrance to obey God.

² He is said to gather his uncircumcision, who by the help of a Chirurgeon recovereth an upper skin: which is done by the drawing the skin with an instrument, to make it to cover the nut. Celsus in book 7, chapter 25.

7:21 ¹ As though this calling were too unworthy a calling for Christ.

7:22 ¹ He that is in state of a servant, and is called to be a Christian.

7:23 ¹ He showeth the reason of the unlikeness, because that he that desireth to be circumcised, maketh himself subject to man's tradition, and not to God. And this may be much more understood of superstitions, which some do foolishly accompt for things indifferent.

7:24 ¹ A repetition of the general doctrine.

² So purely and from the heart, that your doings may be approved before God.

7:25 ¹ He enjoineth virginity to no man, yet he persuadeth and praiseth it for another respect, to wit, both for the necessity of the present time, because the faithful could scarce abide in any place, and use the commodities of this present life, and therefore such as were not troubled with families, might be the readier: and also for the cares of this life, which marriage draweth with it necessity, so that they cannot but have their minds distracteth: and this hath place in women especially.

² The circumstances considered, this I counsel you.

³ It is I that speak this which I am minded to speak: and the truth is, I am a man, but yet worthy credit, for I have obtained of the Lord to be such an one.

7:26 ¹ To remain a virgin.

² For the necessity which the Saints are daily subject unto, who are continually tossed up and down, so that their estate may seem most unfit for marriage, were it not that the weakness of the flesh enforced them to it.

7:28 ¹ By the (flesh) he understandeth what things forever belong to this present life, for marriage bringeth with it many discommodities: so that he bendeth more to a sole life, not because it is a service more agreeable to God than marriage is, but for those discommodities, which (if it were possible) he would wish all men to be void of, that they might give themselves to God only.

² I would your weakness were provided for.

short, hereafter that both they which have wives, be as though they had none:

30 And they that ¹weep, as though they wept not: and they that rejoice, as though they rejoiced not: and they that buy, as though they possessed not:

31 And they that use this ¹world, as though they used it not: for the ²fashion of this world goeth away.

32 And I would have you without care. The unmarried careth for things of the Lord, how he may please the Lord.

33 But he that is married, ¹careth for the things of the world, how he may please *his* wife.

34 There is difference also between a virgin and a wife: the unmarried woman careth for the things of the Lord, that she may be holy, both in body and in ¹spirit: but she that is married, careth for the things of the world, how she may please her husband.

35 And this I speak for your own ¹commodity, not to tangle you in a snare, but that *ye follow* that which is honest, and that ye may cleave fast unto the Lord without separation.

36 ¹But if any man think that it is uncomely for his virgin, if she pass the flower of *her* age, and need so require, let him do what he will, he ²sinneth not: let them be married.

37 Nevertheless, he that standeth firm in his ¹heart, that he hath no ²need, but hath power over his own

e Rom. 7:1
f 1 Thess. 4:8

will, and hath so decreed in his heart, that he will keep his virgin, he doeth well.

38 So then he that giveth her to marriage, doeth well, but he that giveth her not to marriage, doeth ¹better.

39 ¹The wife is bound by the ²law, as long as her husband *e*liveth: but if her husband be dead, she is at liberty to marry with whom she will, only in the ³Lord.

40 But she is more blessed, if she so abide in my judgment: *f*and I think that I have also the Spirit of God.

8 *1 From this place unto the end of the tenth Chapter, he willeth them not to be at the Gentiles' profane banquets. 13 He restraineth the abuse of Christian liberty, 11 and showeth that knowledge must be tempered with charity.*

1 And as ¹touching things sacrificed unto idols, we know that we ²all have knowledge: knowledge ³puffeth up, but love ⁴edifieth.

2 Now, if any man think that he knoweth anything, he knoweth nothing, yet as he ought to know.

3 But if any man love God, the same is known of him.

4 ¹Concerning therefore the eating of things sacrificed unto ²idols, we know that an idol *is* ³nothing in the world, and that there *is* none other God but one.

7:29 ¹ For we are now in the latter end of the world.

7:30 ¹ By weeping, the Hebrews understand all adversity, and be joy, all prosperity.

7:31 ¹ Those things which God giveth us here.

² The guise, the shape, and fashion: whereby he showeth us, that there is nothing in this world that continueth.

7:33 ¹ They that are married, have their wits drawn hither and thither, and therefore if any man have the gift of continency, it is more commodious for him to live alone: but they that are married may care for the things of the Lord also, Clement, Strom. 3.

7:34 ¹ Mind.

7:35 ¹ He meaneth that he will enforce no man either to marry or not to marry, but to show them barely what kind of life is most commodious.

7:36 ¹ Now he turneth himself to the Parents, in whose power and authority their children are, warning them that according to the former doctrine they consider what is meet and convenient for their children, that they neither deprive them of the necessary remedy against incontinency, nor constrain them to marriage, whereas neither their will doth lead them, nor any necessity urgeth them. And again he praiseth virginity, but of itself, and not in all.

² He doeth well: for so he expoundeth it verse 38.

7:37 ¹ Resolved with himself.

² That the weakness of his daughter enforceth him not, or any other matter, that that he may safely keep her a virgin still.

7:38 ¹ Provideth more commodiously for his children, and that not simply, but by reason of such conditions as are before mentioned.

7:39 ¹ That which he spake of a widower, he speaketh now of a widow, to wit, that she may marry again, so that she do it in the fear of God: and yet he dissembleth not, but saith, that if she remain still a widow, she shall be void of many cares.

² By the law of marriage.

³ Religiously, and in the fear of God.

8:1 ¹ He entereth to entreat of another kind of things indifferent, to wit, of things offered to idols, or the use or flesh so offered and sacrificed. And first of all he removeth all those things which the Corinthians pretended in using things offered to idols without any respect. First of all they affirmed that this difference of meats was for unskillful men, but as for them, they knew well enough the benefit of Christ, which causeth all these things to be clean to them that are clean. Be it so saith Paul: be it that we are all sufficiently instructed in the knowledge of Christ. I say notwithstanding that we must not simply rest in this knowledge. The reason is that unless our knowledge be tempered with charity, it doth not only not avail, but also doeth much hurt, because it is the mystery of pride: nay, it doth not so much as discern the name of godly knowledge, if it be separate from the love of God and therefore from the love of our neighbor.

² This general word is to be abridged as appeareth verse 7, for there is a kind of taunt in it, as we may perceive by the next verse.

³ Ministereth occasion of vanity and pride, because it is void of charity.

⁴ Instructed our neighbor.

8:4 ¹ The application of that answer to things offered to idols: I grant, saith he that an idol is indeed a vain imagination, and that there is but one God and Lord, herefore that meat cannot be made holy or profane by the idol: but it followeth not therefore that a man may without respect use those meats as any other.

² This word (idol) in this place is taken for an image which is made to present some godhead, that worship might be given unto it: whereupon came the word (idolatry) that is to say, Image service.

³ It is a vain dream.

5 For though there be that are called gods, whether in heaven, or in earth (as there be many gods, and many lords.)

6 Yet unto us there *is* but one God, *which is* that Father, [1]of whom are all things, and we [2]in him, and [a,3]one Lord Jesus Christ, [4]by whom *are* all things, and we by him.

7 [1]But every man hath not that knowledge: for [2]many having [3]conscience of the idol, until this hour, eat as a thing sacrificed unto the idol, and so their conscience being weak, is defiled.

8 [1]But meat maketh us not acceptable to God, for neither if we eat, have we the more: neither if we eat not, have we the less.

9 But take heed lest by any means this power of yours be an occasion of falling, to them that are weak.

10 [1]For if any man see thee which hast knowledge, sit at table in the idols' temple, shall not the conscience of him which is weak, be boldened, to eat those things which are sacrificed to idols?

CHAPTER 8
[a] John 13:13
1 Cor. 12:3
[b] Rom. 14:15
[c] Rom. 14:21

11 [1]And through thy knowledge shall the [b]weak brother perish, for whom Christ died.

12 [1]Now when ye sin so against the brethren, and wound their weak conscience, ye sin against Christ.

13 [c,1]Wherefore if meat offend my brother, I will eat no flesh while the world standeth, that I may not offend my brother.

9 *1 He declareth, that from the liberty which the Lord gave him, 15 he willingly abstained, 18, 22 lest in things indifferent he should offend any. 24 He showeth that our life is like unto a race.*

1 Am [1]I not an Apostle? am I not free? [2]have I not seen Jesus Christ our Lord? are ye not my work [3]in the Lord?

2 If I be not an Apostle unto others, yet doubtless I am unto you: for ye are the [1]seal of mine Apostleship in the Lord.

3 [1]My defense to him that [2]examine me, is this,

8:6 [1] When the Father is distinguished from the Son, He is named the beginning of all things.

[2] We have our being in him.

[3] But as the Father is called Lord, so is the Son, God therefore this word (One) doth not respect the persons, but the natures.

[4] This word (By) doth not signify the instrumental cause, but the efficient: For the Father and the Son work together, which is not so to be taken, that we make two causes, seeing they have both but one nature though they be distinct persons.

8:7 [1] The reason why that followeth not, is this: because there are many men which do not know that which you know. Now the judgments of outward things depend not only upon your conscience, but upon the conscience of them that behold you, and therefore your actions must be applied not only to your knowledge, but also to the ignorance of your brethren.

[2] An applying of the reason, There are many which cannot eat of things offered to idols, but with a wavering conscience, because they think them to be unclean: therefore if by thy example they enterprise to do that which inwardly they thinketh displeaseth God, their conscience is defiled with this eating, and thou hast been the occasion of this mischief.

[3] By conscience of the idol, he meaneth the secret judgment that they had within themselves, whereby they thought all things unclean, that were offered to idols, and therefore they could not use them with good conscience. For this force hath conscience, that if it be good, it maketh things indifferent good, and if it be evil, it maketh them evil.

8:8 [1] A preventing of an objection: Why then, shall we therefore be deprived of our liberty? Nay saith the Apostle, you shall lose no part of Christianity although you abstain for your brethren's sake, as also if you receive the meat, it maketh you no whit the more holy, for our commendation before God consisteth not in meats: but to use our liberty with offense of our brethren, is an abuse of liberty, the true use whereof is clean contrary, to wit, so to use it, as in using of it we have consideration of our weak brethren.

8:10 [1] Another plainer explication of the same reason, propounding the example of the sitting down at the table in the idol's temple, which thing the Corinthians did evil accompt of among things indifferent, because it is simply forbidden for the circumstance of the place, although offense do cease, as it shall be declared in his place.

8:11 [1] An amplification of the argument taken both of comparison and contraries: Thou wretched man, saith he, pleasing thyself with thy knowledge which indeed is none (for if thou haddest true knowledge, thou wouldest not sit down to meat in idol's temple) wilt thou destroy thy brother, hardening his weak conscience by this example to do evil, for whose salvation Christ himself has died?

8:12 [1] Another amplification: Such offending of our weak brethren redoundeth unto Christ, and therefore let not these men think that they have to do only with their brethren.

8:13 [1] The conclusion, which Paul conceiveth in his own person, that he might not seem to exact that of others, which he will not be first subject unto himself. I had rather (saith he) abstain forever from all kind of flesh, than give occasion of sin to any of my brethren, much less would I refuse in any certain place or time for my brother's sake not to eat flesh offered to idols.

9:1 [1] Before he proceedeth any further in his proposed manner of things offered to idols he would show the cause of all this mischief, and also take it away: to wit, that the Corinthians thought themselves not bound to depart from an iota of their liberty for any man's pleasure. Therefore he propoundeth himself for an example and that in a matter almost necessary. And yet he speaketh generally of both, but first of his own person. If (saith he) you allege for yourselves that you are free, and therefore will use your liberty, am I not also free, seeing I am an Apostle?

[2] He proveth his Apostleship by the effects, in that that he was appointed of Christ himself, and the authority of his function was sufficiently confirmed to him amongst them by their conversion. And all these things he setteth before their eyes, to make them ashamed for that they would not in the least wise that might be, debase themselves, for the weak's sake, whereas the Apostle himself did all that he could to win them to God when they were utterly reprobate and without God.

[3] By the Lord.

9:2 [1] As a seal whereby it appeareth sufficiently that God is the author of my Apostleship.

9:3 [1] He addeth this by the way, as if he would say, So far it is off, that you may doubt of my Apostleship, that I use it to refute them which call it into controversy, by opposing those things which the Lord hath done by me amongst you.

[2] Which like Judges examine me and my doings.

4 ¹Have we not power to ²eat and to drink?

5 Or have we not power to lead about a wife being a ¹sister, as well as the rest of the Apostles, and as the brethren of the Lord, and Cephas?

6 Or I only and Barnabas, have not we power ¹not to work?

7 ¹Who ²goeth a warfare any time at his own cost? who planteth a vineyard, and eateth not of the fruit thereof? or who feedeth a flock, and eateth not of the milk of the flock?

8 ¹Say I these things ²according to man? saith not the Law the same also?

9 For it is written in the Law of Moses, *Thou shalt not muzzle the mouth of the ox that treadeth out the corn: doth God take care for ¹oxen?

10 Either saith he it not altogether for our sakes? For our sakes no doubt it is written, that he which eareth, should ear in hope, and that he that thresheth in hope, should be partaker of his hope.

11 *b,1*If we have sown unto you spiritual things, *is it* a great thing if we reap your carnal things?

12 ¹If others with you be partakers of *this* ²power, *are* not we rather? nevertheless, we have not used this power: but suffer all things, that we should not hinder the Gospel of Christ.

13 ¹Do ye not know, that they which minister about the ᶜholy things, eat of the ²things of the Temple? and they which wait at the altar, are ³partakers with the altar?

CHAPTER 9
ᵃ Deut. 25:4
1 Tim. 5:18
ᵇ Rom. 15:27
ᶜ Deut. 18:1
ᵈ Acts 16:3
Gal. 2:3

14 So also hath the Lord ordained, that they which preach the Gospel, should live ¹of the Gospel.

15 But I have used none of these things: ¹neither wrote I these things, that it should be so done unto me: for it were better for me to die, than that any man should make my rejoicing vain.

16 For though I preach the Gospel, I have nothing to rejoice of: for necessity is laid upon me, and woe is unto me, if I preach not the Gospel.

17 For if I do it willingly, I have a reward, but if I do it against my will, *notwithstanding* the dispensation is committed unto me.

18 What is my reward then? verily that when I preach the Gospel, I make the Gospel of Christ ¹free, that I abuse not mine authority in the Gospel.

19 For though I be free from all men, yet have I made myself servant unto all men, that I may win the more.

20 ᵈAnd unto the Jews, I become as a Jew, that I may win the Jews: to them that are under the ¹Law, as *though I were* under the Law, that I may win them that are under the Law:

21 To them that are without Law, as *though I were* without Law, (when I am not without Law as pertaining to God, but *am* in the Law through Christ) that I may win them that are without Law:

22 To the weak I become as weak, that I may win the weak: I am made all things to ¹all men, that I might by all means save some.

9:4 ¹ Now touching the matter itself, he saith, Seeing that I am free, and truly an Apostle, why may not I (I say not, eat of all things offered to idols) but be maintained by my labors, yea and keep my wife also, as the residue of the apostles lawfully do, as by name, John and James, the Lord's cousins, and Peter himself?

² Upon the expense of the Church?

9:5 ¹ One that is a Christian and a true believer?

9:6 ¹ Not to live by the work of our hands?

9:7 ¹ That he may not seem to burden the Apostles, he showeth that it is just that they do, by an argument of comparison, seeing that soldiers live by their wages, and husbandmen by the fruits of their labors, and shepherds by that that cometh of their flocks.

² Useth to go a warfare?

9:8 ¹ Secondly he bringeth forth the authority of God's institution by an argument of comparison.

² Have I no better ground than the common custom of men?

9:9 ¹ Was it God's proper drift to provide for oxen, when he made this Law? for otherwise there is not the smallest thing in the world, but God hath a care of it.

9:11 ¹ An assumption of the arguments with an amplification, for neither in so doing do we require a reward meet for our deserts.

9:12 ¹ Another argument of great force: others are nourished amongst you, therefore it was lawful for me, yea rather for me than any other: and yet I refused it, and had rather still suffer any discommodity, than the Gospel of Christ should be hindered.

² The word signifieth a right and interest, whereby he giveth us to understand that the ministers of the word must of right and duty be found of the Church.

9:13 ¹ Last of all he bringeth forth the express Law concerning the

nourishing of the Levites, which privilege notwithstanding he will not use.

² This is spoken by the figure Metonymy, for, of those things that are offered in the temple.

³ Are partakers with the altar in dividing the sacrifice.

9:14 ¹ Because they preach the Gospel. It followed by this place, that Paul gat no living, neither would have any other man get, by any commodity of masses, or any other such superstitious trumperies.

9:15 ¹ He taketh away occasion of suspicion by the way, that it might not be thought that he wrote this as though he challenged his wages that was not paid him. Nay saith him, I had rather die, than not continue in this purpose to preach the Gospel freely. For I am bound to preach the Gospel, seeing that the Lord hath enjoined me this office: but unless I do it willingly and for the love of God, nothing is to be allowed that I do. If I had rather that the Gospel should be evil spoken of, than that I should not require my wages, then would it appear that I took these pains not so much for the Gospel's sake, as for my gains and advantages. But I say, this were not to use, but abuse my right and liberty. Therefore not only in this thing, but also in all others (as much as I could) I am made all things to all men, that I might win them to Christ, and might together with them be won to Christ.

9:18 ¹ By taking nothing of them to whom I preach it.

9:20 ¹ The word (Law) in this place, must be restrained to the ceremonial Law.

9:22 ¹ In matters that are indifferent, which may be done or not done with a good conscience: as if he said, I changed myself into all fashions, that by all means, I might save some.

23 And this I do for the Gospel's sake, that I might be partaker thereof with ¹you.

24 ¹Know ye not, that they which run in a race, run all, yet one receiveth the prize? so run that ye may obtain.

25 And every man that proveth masteries, ¹abstaineth from all things: and they *do it* to obtain a corruptible crown: but we for an incorruptible.

26 I therefore so run, not as uncertainly: so fight I, not as one that beateth the air.

27 But I beat down my ¹body, and bring it into subjection, lest by any means after that I have preached to others, I myself should be ²reproved.

10

1 If God spared not the Jews, neither will he spare those who are of like condition, 3, 4 touching the outward signs of his grace. 14 That it is absurd, that such should be partakers of the table of the devils, who are partakers of the Lord's Supper. 24 To have consideration of our neighbor in things indifferent.

1 Moreover, ¹brethren, I would not that ye should be ignorant, that all our ²fathers were under ᵃthat cloud, and all passed through that ᵇsea,

2 ¹And were all ²baptized unto ³Moses, in that cloud, and in that sea,

CHAPTER 10
ᵃ Exod. 13:21
Num. 9:19
ᵇ Exod. 14:22
ᶜ Exod. 16:15
ᵈ Exod. 17:6
Num. 20:19
Num. 21:16
ᵉ Num. 26:65
ᶠ Num. 11:4
Num. 26:64
Ps. 106:14
ᵍ Exod. 32:6
ʰ Num. 25:9
ⁱ Num. 21:6
Ps. 106:14
ʲ Num. 14:37
Judg. 3:24

3 ᶜAnd did all eat the ¹same spiritual ²meat,

4 ᵈAnd did all drink the same spiritual drink (for they drank of the spiritual Rock that ¹followed them: and the Rock was ²Christ.)

5 But with many of them God was not pleased: for they were ᵉoverthrown in the wilderness.

6 ¹Now these things are our ²examples, to the intent that we should not lust after evil things ᶠas they also lusted.

7 Neither be ye idolaters as *were* some of them, as it is written, ᵍThe people sat down to eat and drink, and rose up to play.

8 Neither let us commit fornication, as some of them committed fornication, and fell in one ʰday three and twenty thousand.

9 Neither let us tempt ¹Christ, as some of them also tempted him, and ⁱwere destroyed of serpents.

10 Neither murmur ye, as some of them ʲalso murmured, and were destroyed of the destroyer.

11 Now all these things came unto them for examples, and were written to admonish us, upon whom the ¹ends of the world are come.

12 ¹Wherefore, let him that thinketh he standeth, take heed lest he fall.

13 There hath no temptation taken you, but such

9:23 ¹ That both I and they to whom I preach the Gospel, may receive fruit by the Gospel.

9:24 ¹ He bringeth in another cause of this mischief, to wit, that they were given to gluttony, for there were solemn banquets of sacrifices, and the riot of the Priests was always too much celebrated and kept. Therefore it was hard for them which were accustomed to righteousness, especially when they pretended the liberty of the Gospel, to be restrained from these banquets: but contrarywise, the Apostle calleth them by a pleasant similitude, and also by his own example, to sobriety and mortification of the flesh, showing that they cannot be fit to run or wrestle (as then the games of Isthmians were) which pamper up their bodies, and therefore affirming that they can have no reward, unless they take another course and trade of life.

9:25 ¹ Useth a most exquisite diet.

9:27 ¹ The old man which striveth against the spirit.

² This word (Reproved) is not set as contrary to the word (Elect) but as contrary to the word (Approved) when we see one by experience not to be such an one as he ought to be.

10:1 ¹ He setteth out that which he said, laying before them an example of the horrible judgment of God against them which had in effect the selfsame pledges, of the same adoption and salvation that we have: and yet notwithstanding when they gave themselves to idols' feasts, perished in the wilderness, being horribly and manifoldly punished. Now, moreover and besides that these things are fitly spoken against them which frequented idols' feasts, the same also seems to be alleged to this end and purpose, because many men are thus minded, that those things are not of such great weight, that God will be angry with them if they use them, so that they frequent Christian assemblies and be baptized, and receive the Communion, and confess Christ.

² Paul speaketh thus in respect of the covenant, and not in respect of the persons, saving in general.

10:2 ¹ In effect the Sacrament of the old fathers were all one with ours, for they respected Christ only who offered himself unto them

in divers shadows.

² All of them were baptized with the outward sign, but not in deed, wherewith God cannot be charged, but they themselves.

³ Moses being their guide.

10:3 ¹ The same that we do.

² Manna, which was a spiritual meat to the believers, which in faith lay hold upon Christ who is the true meat.

10:4 ¹ Of the river and running Rock, which followed the people.

² Did sacramentally signify Christ, so that together with the sign, there was the thing signified, and the truth itself: for God doth not offer a bare sign, but the thing signifieth by the sign, together with it which is to be received with faith.

10:6 ¹ An amplifying of the example against them which are carried away with their lusts beyond the bounds which God has measured out. For this is the beginning of all evil, as of idolatry (which hath gluttony a companion unto it) fornication, rebelling against Christ, murmuring, and such like, which God punished most sharply in that old people, to the end that we which succeed them, and have a more full declaration of the will of God, might by that means take better heed.

² Some read figures: which signified our sacraments: for circumcision was to the Jews a seal of righteousness, and to us a lively pattern of Baptism, and so in the other Sacraments.

10:9 ¹ To tempt Christ, is to provoke him to a combat as it were which those men do, who abuse the knowledge that he hath given them, and make it to serve for a cloak for their lusts and wickedness.

10:11 ¹ This our age is called the end, for it is the shutting up of all ages.

10:12 ¹ In conclusion, he descendeth to the Corinthians themselves, warning them that they please not themselves, but rather that they prevent the subtleties of Satan. Yet he useth an insinuation, and comforteth them, that he may not seem to make them altogether like to those wicked idolaters and contemners of Christ, which perished in the wilderness.

as appertaineth to ¹man: and God is faithful, which will not suffer you to be tempted above that you be able, but will even ²give the issue with the temptation, that ye may be able to bear it.

14 Wherefore my beloved, flee from idolatry.

15 ¹I speak as unto them which have understanding: judge ye what I say.

16 The cup of ¹blessing which we bless, is it not the ²communion of the blood of Christ? The bread which we break, is it not the communion of the body of Christ?

17 For we that are many, are one bread and one body, because we all are partakers of one bread.

18 Behold Israel, *which is* after the ¹flesh: are not they which eat of the sacrifices ²partakers of the Altar?

19 What say I then? that the idol is anything? or that that which is sacrificed to idols, is anything?

20 *Nay*, but that the things which the Gentiles sacrifice, they sacrifice to devils, and not unto God: and I would not that ye should have ¹fellowship with the devils.

21 Ye cannot drink the cup of the Lord, and the ¹cup of the devils. Ye cannot be partakers of the Lord's table, and of the table of the devils.

22 Do we provoke the Lord to anger? are we stronger than he?

k 1 Cor. 6:12
l Ps. 24:1
m Col. 3:17

23 *k,1,2*All things are lawful for me, but all things are not expedient: all things are lawful for me, but all things edify not.

24 Let no man seek his own, but every man another's wealth.

25 ¹Whatsoever is sold in the ²shambles, eat ye, and ask no question for conscience sake.

26 *l*For the earth *is* the Lord's, and ¹all that therein is.

27 If any of them which believe not, call you *to a feast*, and if ye will go, whatsoever is set before you, eat, asking no question for conscience sake.

28 But if any man say unto you, This is sacrificed unto idols, eat it not, because of him that showed it, and for the conscience (for the earth *is* the Lord's, and all that therein is.)

29 And the conscience, I say, not thine, but of that other: ¹for why should my liberty be condemned of another man's conscience?

30 For if I through *God's* ¹benefit be partaker, why am I evil spoken of, for that wherefore I give thanks?

31 *m,1*Whether therefore ye eat, or drink, or whatsoever ye do, do all to the glory of God.

32 Give none offence, neither to the Jews, nor to the Grecians, nor to the Church of God:

33 Even as I please all men in all things, not seek-

10:13 ¹ Which cometh of weakness.

² He that would have you tempted for your profit's sake, will give you an issue to escape out of the temptation.

10:15 ¹ Now returning to those idols' feasts, that he may not seem to dally at all, first he promiseth that he will use no other reasons than such as they knew very well themselves. And he useth an induction borrowed of the agreement that is the things themselves. The holy banquets of the Christians are pledges, first of all of the community that they have with Christ, and next, one with another. The Israelites also do ratify in the sacrifices, their mutual conjunction in one selfsame religion: therefore so do the idolaters also join themselves with their idols or devils rather (for idols are nothing) in those solemn banquets, whereupon it followeth, that that table is a table of devils, and therefore you must eschew it: for you cannot be partakers of the Lord and of idols together, much less may such banquets be accounted for things indifferent. Will ye then strive with God? and if you do, think you that you shall get the upper hand?

10:16 ¹ Of thanksgiving: whereupon, that holy banquet was called Eucharist, that is, a thanksgiving.

² A most effectual pledge and note of our knitting together with Christ, and ingrafting to him.

10:18 ¹ That is, as yet observe their ceremonies.

² Are consenting and guilty, both of that worship and sacrifice.

10:20 ¹ Have anything to do with the devils, or enter into that society which is begun on the devil's name.

10:21 ¹ The heathen and profane people were wont to shut up and make an end of their feasts which they kept to the honor of their gods, in offering meat offerings and drink offerings to them, with banquets and feastings.

10:23 ¹ Coming to another kind of things offered to idols, he repeateth that general rule, that in the use of things indifferent we ought

to have consideration not of ourselves only, but of our neighbors, and therefore these are many things which of themselves are lawful, which may be evil done of us, because of offense to our neighbor.

² See 1 Cor. 6:13.

10:25 ¹ An applying of the rule to the present matter: Whatsoever is sold in the shambles, you may indifferently buy it as it were at the Lord's hand, and eat it either at home with the faithful, or being called home to the unfaithful, to wit, in a private banquet: but yet with this exception, unless any man is present which is weak, whose conscience may be offended, by setting meats offered to idols before them: for then you ought to have consideration of their weakness.

² The flesh that was sacrificed, was used to be sold in the shambles, and the price returned to the priests.

10:26 ¹ All those things whereof it is full.

10:29 ¹ A reason: for we must take heed that our liberty be not evil spoken of, and that the benefit of God which we ought to use with thanksgiving be not changed into impiety, and that through our fault, if we choose rather to offend the conscience of the weak, than to yield a little of our liberty in a matter of no importance, and so give occasion to the weak to judge in such sort of us, and of Christian liberty. And the Apostle taketh these things upon his own person, that the Corinthians may have so much the less occasion to oppose anything against him.

10:30 ¹ If I may through God's benefits eat this meat, or that meat, why should I through my fault, cause that benefit of God to turn to my blame?

10:31 ¹ The conclusion: We must order our lives in such sort, that we seek not ourselves, but God's glory, and so the salvation of as many as we may, wherein the Apostle flicketh not to propound himself to the Corinthians (even his own flock) as an example, but so that he calleth them back to Christ, unto whom he himself hath regard.

ing mine own profit, but *the profit* of many, that they might be saved.

11 1 *He blameth the Corinthians for that in their holy assemblies,* 4 *men do pray having their heads covered,* 6 *and women bareheaded: and because their meetings tended to evil,* 21 *who mingled profane banquets with the holy Supper of the Lord,* 23 *which he required to be celebrated according to Christ's institution.*

1 Be ªye followers of me, even as I am of Christ:

2 ¹Now brethren, I commend you, that ye remember all my things, and keep the ordinances, as I delivered them to you.

3 ¹But I will that ye know, that Christ is the ᵇhead of every man: and the man is the woman's head: and God is ²Christ's head.

4 Every ²man praying or prophesying having *anything* on *his* head, dishonoreth his head.

5 ¹But every woman that prayeth or prophesieth bareheaded, dishonoreth her head: ²for it is even one very thing, as though she were shaven.

6 Therefore if the woman be not covered, let her also be shorn: and if it be shame for a woman to be

CHAPTER 11
ª 2 Thess. 3:9
ᵇ Eph. 5:23
ᶜ Gen. 1:26
Gen. 5:1
Gen. 9:6
Col. 3:10
ᵈ Gen. 2:22

shorn or shaven, let her be covered.

7 ¹For a man ought not to cover *his* head: forasmuch as he is the ᶜimage and glory of God: but the woman is the glory of the man.

8 ¹For the man is not of the woman, but the woman of the man.

9 ᵈ'¹For the man was not created for the woman's sake: but the woman for the man's sake.

10 ¹Therefore ought the woman to have ²power on *her* head, because of the ³Angels.

11 ¹Nevertheless, neither is the man without the woman, neither the woman without the man ²in the Lord.

12 For as the woman is of the man, so is the man also by the woman: but all things are of God.

13 ¹Judge in yourselves, Is it comely that a woman pray unto God uncovered?

14 Doth not nature itself teach you, that if a man have long hair, it is a shame unto him?

15 But if a woman have long hair, it is a praise unto her: for her hair is given her for a ¹covering.

16 ¹But if any man list to be contentious, we have no such custom, neither the Churches of God.

17 ¶ ¹Now in this that I declare, I praise *you* not,

11:2 ¹ The fifth treatise of this epistle concerning the right ordering of public assemblies, containing three points, to wit, of the comely apparel of men and women, of the order of the Lord's supper, and of the right use of spiritual gifts. But going about to reprehend certain things, he beginneth notwithstanding with a general praise of them, calling those particular laws of comeliness and honesty, which belong to the ecclesiastical policy, traditions: which afterward they called Canons.

11:3 ¹ He setteth down God, in Christ our mediator, for the end and mark not only of doctrine, but also of ecclesiastical comeliness. Then applying it to the question proposed, touching the comely apparel both of men and women in public assemblies, he declareth that the woman is one degree beneath the man by the ordinance of God, and that the man is so subject to Christ, that the glory of God ought to appear in him for the preeminence of the sex.
² In that, that Christ is our mediator.

11:4 ¹ Hereof he gathereth that if men do either pray or preach in public assemblies having their heads covered (which was then a sign of subjection) they did as it were spoil themselves of their dignity, against God's ordinance.
² It appeareth that this was a political law serving only for the circumstances of the time that Paul lived in, by this reason, because in these our days for a man to speak bareheaded in an assembly, is a sign of subjection.

11:5 ¹ And in like sort he concludeth, that women which show themselves in public and ecclesiastical assemblies without the sign and token of their subjection, that is to say, uncovered, shame themselves.
² The first argument taken from the common sense of man, forsomuch as nature teacheth women, that it is dishonest for them to come abroad bareheaded, seeing that she hath given them thick and long hair, which they do so diligently trim and deck, that they can in no wise abide to have it shaven.

11:7 ¹ The taking away of an objection: Have not men also hair given

to them? I grant, saith the Apostle, but there is another matter in it: For man was made to this end and purpose, that the glory of God should appear in his rule and authority: but the woman was made, that by profession of her obedience, she might more honor her husband.

11:8 ¹ He proveth the inequality of the woman, by that, that the man is the matter whereof woman was first made.

11:9 ¹ Secondly, by that, that the woman was made for man, and not the man for the woman's sake.

11:10 ¹ The conclusion: Women must be covered, to show by this external sign their subjection.
² A covering which is a token of subjection.
³ What this meaneth, I do not yet understand.

11:11 ¹ A digression which the Apostle useth, lest that which he spake of the superior tie of men, and the lower degrees of women in consideration of the policy of the Church, should be so taken as though there were no measure of this inequality. Therefore he teacheth that men have in such sort the preeminence, that God made them not alone, but women also: and woman was so made of man, that men also are born by the means of women, and this ought to put them in mind to observe the degree of every sex, in such sort that mutual conjunction may be cherished.
² By the Lord.

11:13 ¹ He urgeth the argument taken from the common sense of nature.

11:15 ¹ To be a covering for her, and such a covering as should procure another.

11:16 ¹ Against such as are stubbornly contentious we have to oppose this, that the Churches of God are not contentious.

11:17 ¹ He passeth now to the next treatise concerning the right administration of the Lord's Supper. And the Apostle useth this sharper preface that the Corinthians might understand, that whereas they observed generally the Apostle's commandments, yet they foully neglected them in a matter of greatest importance.

that ye come together, not with profit, but with hurt.

18 [1]For first of all, when ye come together in the Church, I hear that there are dissensions among you: and I believe it *to be true* in some part.

19 [1]For there must be heresies even among you, that they which are [2]approved among you, might be known.

20 When ye come together therefore into one place, *this* is [1]not to eat the Lord's Supper.

21 For every man when they should eat, taketh his own supper [1]afore, and one is hungry, and another is drunken.

22 [1]Have ye not houses to eat and to drink in? despise ye the Church of God, and shame them that have not? what shall I say to you? shall I praise you in this? I praise you not.

23 [1]For I have received of the Lord that which I also have delivered unto you, *to wit,* That the Lord Jesus in the night when he was betrayed, took bread.

24 [c]And when he had given thanks, he brake it, and said, Take, eat: this is my body, which is [1]broken for you: this do ye in remembrance of me.

25 After the same manner also *he took* the cup, when he had supped, saying, This cup is the New Testament in my blood: this do as oft as ye drink it, in remembrance of me.

26 For as often as ye shall eat this bread, and drink

[c] Matt. 25:26
Mark 14:21
Luke 22:19
[f] 1 Cor. 13:5

this cup, ye show the Lord's death till he come.

27 [1]Wherefore, whosoever shall eat this bread, and drink the cup of the Lord [2]unworthily, shall be guilty of the body and blood of the Lord.

28 [f,1]Let [2]every man therefore examine himself, and so let them eat of this bread, and drink of this cup.

29 For he that eateth and drinketh unworthily, eateth and drinketh his own damnation, *because* he [1]discerneth not the Lord's body.

30 [1]For this cause many *are* weak, and sick among you, and many sleep.

31 For if we would [1]judge ourselves, we should not be judged.

32 But when we are judged, we are chastened of the Lord, because we should not be condemned with the world.

33 [1]Wherefore, my brethren, when ye come together to eat, tarry one for another.

34 [1]And if any man be hungry, let him eat at home, that ye come not together unto condemnation. [2]Other things will I set in order when I come.

12

1 *To draw away the Corinthians from contention and pride, he showeth that spiritual gifts are therefore diversely bestowed,* 7 *that the same being jointly to each other employed,* 12 *we may grow up together into one body of Christ in such equal proportion and measure,* 20 *as the members of man's body do.*

11:18 [1] To celebrate the Lord's Supper aright, it is required that there be not only consent of doctrine, but also of affections, that it be not profaned.

11:19 [1] Although that schisms and heresies proceed from the devil, are evil, and yet they come not by chance, nor without cause, and they turn to the profit of the elect.

[2] Whom experience hath taught to be of sound Religion and godliness.

11:20 [1] This is an usual kind of speech, whereby the Apostle denieth that flatly, which many did not well.

11:21 [1] Eateth his meat and tarrieth not till other come.

11:22 [1] The Apostle thinketh it good to take away the love feasts, for their abuse, although they had been a long time, and with commendation used in Churches, and were appointed and instituted by the Apostles.

11:23 [1] We must take a true form of keeping the Lord's Supper, out of the institution of it, the parts whereof are these, touching the Pastors, to show forth the Lord's death, by preaching his word: to bless the bread and the wine by calling upon the name of God, and together with prayers to declare the institution thereof, and finally to deliver the bread broken to be eaten, and the cup received to be drunk with thanksgiving. And touching the flock, that every man examine himself, that is to say, to prove both his knowledge, and also faith and repentance: to show forth the Lord's death, that is, in true faith to yield unto his word and institution: and last of all, to take the bread at the Minister's hand, and to eat it and to drink the wine, and give God thanks: This was Paul's and the Apostles' manner of ministering.

11:24 [1] This word (Broken) noteth out unto us Christ his manner

of death, for although his legs were not broken, as the thieves legs were, yet was his body very sore tormented, and torn, and bruised.

11:27 [1] Whoever contemn the holy Sacrament: that is, use them not aright, are guilty not of the bread and wine, but of the thing itself, that is of Christ, and shall be grievously punished for it.

[2] Otherwise then meet is such mysteries should be handled.

11:28 [1] The examination of a man's self, is of necessity required in the Supper and therefore they ought not to be admitted unto it, which cannot examine themselves: as children, furious and mad men, also such as either have no knowledge of Christ, or not sufficient, although they profess Christian Religion: and others such like.

[2] This place beateth down the faith of credit, or unwrapped faith, which the Papists maintain.

11:29 [1] He is said to discern the Lord's body, that hath consideration of the worthiness of it, and therefore cometh to eat of this meat with great reverence.

11:30 [1] The profaning of the body and blood of the Lord in his mysteries is sharply punished of him, and therefore such a mischief ought diligently to be prevented by judging and correcting of a man's self.

11:31 [1] Try and examine ourselves, by faith and repentance, separating yourselves from the wicked.

11:33 [1] The Supper of the Lord is a common action of the whole Church, and therefore there is no place, for private suppers.

11:34 [1] The Supper of the Lord was instituted not to feed the belly but to feed the soul with the communion of Christ, and therefore it ought to be separate from common banquets.

[2] Such things as pertain to order, as place, time, form of prayers, and other such like, the Apostle took order for in Congregations according to the consideration of times, places and persons.

1 Now ¹concerning spiritual *gifts*, brethren, I would not have you ²ignorant.

2 ¹Ye know that ye were ²Gentiles, and were carried away unto the dumb idols, as ye were led.

3 ¹Wherefore I declare unto you, that no man ªspeaking by the spirit of God, calleth Jesus ᵇ'²execrable: also no man can say that Jesus is the Lord, but by the holy Ghost.

4 ¹Now there are diversities of gifts, but the ²same Spirit.

5 And there are diversities of administrations, but the same Lord.

6 And there are diversities of ¹operations, but God is the same which worketh all in all.

7 But the manifestation of the Spirit is ¹given to every man, to ²profit withal.

8 ¹For to one is given by the Spirit the word of ²wisdom: and to another the word of knowledge, by the same Spirit:

9 And to another *is given* faith by the same Spirit: and to another the gifts of healing, by the

CHAPTER 12
ᵈ Mark 9:31
ᵇ John 13:15
1 Cor. 8:6
Phil. 2:11
ᶜ Rom. 12:3
Eph. 4:7

same Spirit:

10 And to another the ¹operations of great works: and to another, ²prophecy: and to another, the ³discerning of spirits: and to another, diversities of tongues: and to another, the interpretation of tongues.

11 ʿAnd all these things worketh one and the selfsame Spirit, distributing to every man severally ¹as he will.

12 ¹For as the body is one, and hath many members, and all the members of the body, which is one, though they be many, *yet* are *but* one body: ²even so is ³Christ.

13 For by one Spirit are we all baptized into ¹one body, whether *we be* Jews, or Grecians, whether *we be* bond, or free, and have been all made to ²drink into one Spirit.

14 ¹For the body also is not one member, but many.

15 ¹If the foot would say, Because I am not the hand, I am not of the body, is it therefore not of the body?

12:1 ¹ Now he entereth into the third part of this treatise, touching the right use of spiritual gifts, wherein he giveth the Corinthians plainly to understand that they abused them: for they that excelled, bragged ambitiously of them, and so robbed God of the praise of his gifts: and having no consideration of their brethren abused to a vain ostentation, and so robbed the Church of the use of those gifts. On the other side, the inferior sort envied the better, and went about to make a departure, so that all that body was as it were scattered and rent in pieces. So then he going about to remedy these abuses, willeth them first to consider diligently, that they have not these gifts of themselves, but from the free grace and liberality of God, to whose glory they ought to bestow them all.

² Ignorant to what purpose those gifts are given you.

12:2 ¹ He proveth the same by comparing their former state with that wherein they were at this time endued with those excellent gifts.

² As touching God's service and the Covenant, mere strangers.

12:3 ¹ The conclusion: Know you therefore, that you cannot so much as move your lips to honor Christ withall, but by the grace of the holy Ghost.

² Doth curse him, only any means whatsoever diminish his glory.

12:4 ¹ In the second place, he layeth another foundation, to wit, that these gifts are divers, as the functions also are divers, and their offices divers, but that one selfsame Spirit Lord and God is the giver of all these gifts, and that to one end, to wit, for the profit of all.

² The Spirit is plainly distinguished from the gifts.

12:6 ¹ So Paul endeth that inward force which cometh from the holy Ghost, and maketh men fit to wonderful things.

12:7 ¹ The holy Ghost openeth and showeth himself freely in giving of these gifts.

² To the use and benefit of the Church.

12:8 ¹ He declareth this manifold diversity, and reckoneth up the chiefest gifts, beating that into their heads, which he said before, to wit, that all these things proceeded from one selfsame Spirit.

² Wisdom is a most excellent gift, very requisite, not only for them which teach, but also for them that exhort and comfort, which thing is proper to the Pastor's office, as the word of knowledge agreeth to the Doctors.

12:10 ¹ By operation he meaneth those great workings of God's

mighty power, which pass and excel amongst his miracles, as the delivery of his people Israel by the hand of Moses: that which he did by Elijah against the Priests of Baal, in sending down fire from heaven to consume his sacrifice: and that which he did by Peter in the matter of Ananias and Sapphira.

² Foretelling of things to come.

³ Whereby false prophets are known from true, wherein Peter passed Philip in discovering Simon Magus, Acts 8:20.

12:11 ¹ He addeth moreover something else, to wit, that although these gifts are unequal, yet they are most wisely divided, because the will of the Spirit of God is the rule of this distribution.

12:12 ¹ He setteth forth his former saying by a similitude taken from the body: This saith he, is manifestly seen in the body, whose members are divers, but yet so knit together, that they make but one body.

² The applying of the similitude. So must we also think, saith he, of the mystical body of Christ: for all we that believe, whether we be Jews or Gentiles, are by one selfsame Baptism joined together with our head, that by that means, there may be framed one body compact of many members: and we have drunk one selfsame spirit, that is to say, a spiritual feeling, perseverance and motion common to us all, out of one cup.

³ Christ joined together with his Church.

12:13 ¹ To become one body with Christ.

² By one quickening drink of the Lord's blood, we are made partakers of his only Spirit.

12:14 ¹ He amplifieth that which followed of the similitudes, as if he should say, The unity of the body is not only not left by this diversity of members, but also it could not be a body, if it did not consist of many, and those were divers members.

12:15 ¹ Now he buildeth his doctrine upon the foundations which he had laid: and first of all he continueth in his purposed similitude, and afterward he goeth to the matter barely and simply. And first of all he speaketh unto them which would have separated themselves from those whom they envied, because they had not such excellent gifts as they: now this is, saith he, as if the foot should say it were not of the body, because it is not the hand: or the ear, because it is not the eye. Therefore all parts ought rather to defend the unity of the body, being coupled together to serve one the other.

16 And if the ear would say, Because I am not the eye, I am not of the body, is it therefore not of the body?

17 ¹If the whole body *were* an eye, where *were* the hearing? If the whole *were* hearing, where *were* the smelling?

18 But now hath God disposed the members every one of them in the body at his own pleasure.

19 For if they were all one member, where *were* the body?

20 But now *are* there many members, yet but one body.

21 ¹And the eye cannot say unto the hand, I have no need of thee: nor the head again to the feet, I have no need of you.

22 Yea, much rather those members of the body, which seem to be ¹more feeble, are necessary.

23 And upon those *members* of the body, which we think most unhonest, put we more ¹honesty on: and our uncomely *parts* have more comeliness on.

24 For our comely *parts* need it not: but God hath tempered the body together: and hath given the more honor to that *part* which lacked,

25 Lest there should be any division in the body: but that the members should have the same ¹care one for another.

26 ¹Therefore if one member suffer, all suffer with it: if one member be had in honor, all the members

rejoice with it.

27 Now ye are the body of Christ, and members for *your* ¹part.

28 ᵈAnd God hath ordained some in the Church: as first Apostles, secondly Prophets, thirdly teachers, then them that do miracles: after that, the gifts of healing, ¹helpers, ²governors, diversity of tongues.

29 Are all Apostles? are all Prophets? are all teachers?

30 Are all doers of miracles? have all the gifts of healing? do all speak with tongues? do all interpret?

31 ¹But desire you the best gifts, and I will yet show you a more excellent way.

13 *1 He showeth that there are gifts so excellent, which in God's sight are not corrupt, if Charity be away: 4 and therefore he digresseth unto the commendation of it.*

1 Though ¹I speak with the tongues of men and ²Angels, and have not love, I am *as* sounding brass, or a ³tinkling cymbal.

2 And though I had the *gift* of prophecy, and knew all secrets and all knowledge, yea, if I had all ¹faith, so that I could remove ᵃmountains, and had not love, I were nothing.

3 And though I feed the poor with all my goods, and though I give my body, that I be burned, and have not love, it profiteth me nothing.

4 ¹Love ²suffereth long: it is bountiful: love envieth

ᵈ Eph. 4:11

CHAPTER 13
ᵃ Matt. 17:20

12:17 ¹ Again, speaking to them, he showeth them that if that should come to pass which they desire, to wit, that all should be equal one to another, there would follow a destruction of the whole body, yea, and of themselves: for it could not be a body, unless it were made of many members knit together, and divers one from another. And that no man might find fault with this division as unequal, he addeth that God himself hath coupled all these together. Therefore all must remain coupled together, that the body may remain in safety.

12:21 ¹ Now on the other side, he speaketh unto them which were endued with more excellent gifts, willing them not to despise the inferiors as unprofitable, and as though they served to no use: for God, saith he, hath in such sort tempered this inequality, that the more excellent and beautiful members can in no wise lack the more abject and such as we are ashamed of, and that they should have more care to see unto them, and to cover them: that by this means the necessity which is on both parts, might keep the whole body in peace and concord: that although if each part be considered apart, they are of divers degrees and conditions, yet because they are joined together, they have a community both in commodities and discommodities.

12:22 ¹ Of the smallest and vilest offices, and therefore finally accounted of, of the rest.

12:23 ¹ We more carefully cover them.

12:25 ¹ Should bestow their operations and offices to the profit and preservation of the whole body.

12:26 ¹ Now he applieth the same doctrine to the Corinthians without any allegory, warning them that seeing there are divers functions and divers gifts, it is their duty, not to offend one against another, either by envy or ambition, but rather that they being joined together in love and charity one with another, every one of them bestow to the profit of all, that which he hath received, according as

his ministry doth require.

12:27 ¹ For all churches wheresoever they are dispersed through the whole world, are divers members of one body.

12:28 ¹ The offices of Deacons.

² He setteth forth the order of Elders, which were the maintainers of the Church's discipline.

12:31 ¹ He teacheth them that are ambitious and envious, a certain holy ambition and envy, to wit, if they give themselves to the best gifts, and such as are most profitable to the Church, and so if they contend to excel one another in love, which surpasseth all other gifts.

13:1 ¹ He reasoneth first of Charity, the excellency whereof he first showeth by this, that without it, all other gifts are as nothing before God which thing he proveth partly by an induction, and partly also by an argument taken of the end, wherefor those gifts are given. to what purpose are those gifts, but to God's glory, and the profit of the Church, as is before proved? so that those gifts, without Charity, have no right use.

² A very earnest kind of amplifying a matter, as if he said, If there were any tongues of Angels, and I had them, and did not use them to the benefit of my neighbor, it were nothing else but a vain and prattling type of babbling.

³ That giveth a rude and no certain sound.

13:2 ¹ By faith, he meaneth the gift of doing miracles, and not that faith which justified, which cannot be void of Charity as the other may.

13:4 ¹ He describeth the force and nature of charity, partly by a comparison of contraries, and partly by the effects of itself: whereby the Corinthians may understand, both how profitable it is in the Church, and how necessary and also how far they are from it: and therefore how vainly and without cause they are proud.

² Word for word deferreth wrath.

not: love doth not boast itself: it is not puffed up:

5 It doth ¹no uncomely thing: it seeketh not her own thing: it is not provoked to anger: it thinketh no evil:

6 It rejoiceth not in iniquity, but ¹rejoiceth in the truth:

7 It suffereth all things: it believeth all things: it hopeth all things: it endureth all things.

8 ¹Love doth never fall away, though that prophesyings be abolished, or the tongues cease, or ²knowledge vanish away.

9 ¹For we know in ²part, and we prophesy in part.

10 But when that which is perfect, is come, then that which is in part shall be abolished.

11 ¹When I was a child, I spake as a child: I understood as a child, I thought as a child: but when I became a man, I put away childish things.

12 ¹For ²now we see through a glass darkly: but then *shall we see* face to face. Now I know in part:

but then shall I know even as I am known.

13 ¹And now abideth faith, hope *and* love, *even* these three: but the chiefest of these *is* love.

14 *1 He commendeth the gifts of prophecying: 7 and by a similitude taken of musical instruments,   12 he teacheth the true use of interpreting the Scriptures: 17 he taketh away the abuse: 34 And forbiddeth women to speak in the Congregation.*

1 Follow ¹after love, and covet spiritual *gifts*, and rather that ye may ²prophesy.

2 ¹For he that speaketh a *strange* ²tongue, speaketh not unto men, but unto God: for no man heareth *him*: howbeit in the ³spirit he speaketh secret things.

3 But he that prophesieth, speaketh unto men to ¹edifying, and to exhortation, and to comfort.

4 He that speaketh *strange* language, edifieth himself: but he that prophesieth, edifieth the ¹Church.

5 I would that ye all spake *strange* languages, but rather that ye prophesied: for greater is he that

---

13:5 ¹ It is not contumelious.

13:6 ¹ Rejoice that righteousness in the righteous. For the Hebrews mean by truth, righteousness.

13:8 ¹ Again he commendeth the excellency of charity, in that that it shall never be abolished in the Saints, whereas the other gifts which are necessary for the building up of the Church, so long as we live here, shall have no place in the world to come.

² The way to get knowledge by prophesying.

13:9 ¹ The reason: Because we are now in the state, that we have need to learn daily, and therefore we have need of those helps, to wit, of the gift of tongues, and knowledge, and also of those that teach them. But to what purpose serve they then, when we have obtained and gotten the full knowledge of God, which serve now but for them which are imperfect, and go by degrees to perfection?

² We learn imperfectly.

13:11 ¹ He setteth forth that that he said, by an excellent similitude, comparing this life to our infancy or childhood, wherein we stagger and stammer rather than speak, and think and understand but childish things, and therefore have need of such things as may form and frame our tongue and mind: But when we become men, to what purpose should we desire that stammering, those childish toys, and such like things, whereby our childhood is framed by little and little?

13:12 ¹ The applying of the similitude of our childhood to this present life, wherein we darkly behold heavenly things, according to the small measure of light which is given us, through the understanding of tongues, and hearing the teachers and ministers of the Church: of our man's age and strength, to that heavenly and eternal life, wherein when we behold God himself present, and are lightened with his full and perfect light, to what purpose should we desire the voice of man, and those worldly things which are most imperfect? But yet then, shall all the Saints be knit both with God, and between themselves with most fervent love, and therefore charity shall not be abolished, but perfected, although it shall not be showeth forth and entertained by such manner of duties as peculiarly and only belong to the infirmity of this life.

² All this must be understood by comparison.

13:13 ¹ The conclusion: As if the Apostle should say, Such therefore shall be our condition then: but now we have three things, and they remain sure if we be Christ's as without which true religion cannot

consist, to wit, faith, hope, and charity. And among these, charity is the chiefest, because it ceaseth not in the life to come as the rest do, but is perfected and accomplished. For seeing that faith and hope tend to things which are promised, and are to come, when we have presently gotten them, to what purpose should we have faith and hope? but yet there at length shall we truly and perfectly love both God, and one another.

14:1 ¹ He inferreth now that, that he spake before: Therefore seeing charity is the chiefest of all, before all things set it before you as chief and principal: and so esteem those things as most excellent: which profit the greater part of men: (as prophecy that is to say, the gifts of teaching and applying the doctrine, which was contemned in respect of other gifts, although it be chiefest and most necessary for the Church) and not those which for a show seem to be marvelous as the gifts of tongues, when a man was suddenly endued with the knowledge of many tongues, which made men greatly amazed, and yet of itself was not greatly to any use, unless there were an interpreter.

² What prophecy is, he showeth in the third verse.

14:2 ¹ He reprehendeth their perverse judgment touching the gift of tongues. For why was it given? to wit, to the intent that the mysteries of God might be the better known to a greater sort. Thereby it is evident that Prophecy, whereunto the gift of tongues ought to serve, is better than this: and therefore the Corinthians did judge amiss, in that they made more account of the gift of tongues, than of prophesying: because forsooth the gift of tongues was a thing more to be bragged of. And hereupon followed another abuse of the gift of tongues, in that the Corinthians used tongues in the Congregation, without an interpreter. Which thing although it might be done to some profit of him, that spake them, yet he corrupted the right use of that gift, because there came thereby no profit to the hearers: and common assemblies were instituted and appointed not for any private man's commodity, but for the profit of the whole company.

² A strange language, which no man can understand without an interpreter.

³ By that inspiration which he has received of the Spirit, which notwithstanding he abuseth, when he speaketh mysteries which none of the company can understand.

14:3 ¹ Which may further men in the study of godliness.

14:4 ¹ The company.

prophesieth, than he that speaketh *diverse* tongues, except he expound it, that the Church may receive edification.

6 And now, brethren, if I come unto you speaking *diverse* tongues, what shall I profit you, except I speak to you, either by revelation, or by knowledge, or by prophesying, or by doctrine?

7 [1]Moreover things without life which give a sound, whether *it be* a pipe or an harp, except they make a distinction in the sounds, how shall it be known what is piped or harped?

8 And also if the trumpet give an uncertain sound, who shall prepare himself to battle?

9 So likewise you, by the tongue, except ye utter words that have [1]signification, how shall it be understood what is spoken? for ye shall speak in the air.

10 [1]There are so many kinds of voices (as it cometh to pass) in the world, and none of them is dumb.

11 Except I know then the power of the voice, I shall be unto him that speaketh a Barbarian, and he that [1]speaketh, shall be a Barbarian unto me.

12 [1]Even so, forasmuch as ye covet spiritual *gifts*, seek that ye may excel unto the edifying of the Church.

13 Wherefore, let him that speaketh a *strange* tongue, [1]pray that he may interpret.

14 [1]For [2]if I pray in a *strange* tongue, my [3]spirit prayeth: but mine understanding is [4]without fruit.

CHAPTER 14
[a] Matt. 28:3
[b] Isa. 28:11

15 What is it then? I will pray with the spirit, but I will pray with the [1]understanding also: I will sing with the spirit: but I will sing with the understanding also.

16 [1]Else, when thou blessest with the [2]spirit, how shall he that [3]occupieth the room of the unlearned, say [4]Amen, at thy giving of thanks, seeing he knowest not what thou sayest?

17 For thou verily givest thanks well, but the other is not edified.

18 [1]I thank my God, I speak languages more than ye all.

19 Yet had I rather in the Church to speak [1]five words with mine understanding, that I might also instruct others, than ten thousand words in a *strange* tongue.

20 [1]Brethren, be not [a]children in understanding, but as concerning maliciousness be children, but in understanding be of a ripe age.

21 In the [1]Law it is written, [b]By men of other tongues, and by other languages will I speak unto this people: yet so shall they not hear me, saith the Lord.

22 [1]Wherefore *strange* tongues are for a sign, not to them that believe, but to them that believe not: but prophesying *serveth* not for them that believe not, but for them which believe.

23 [1]If therefore, when the whole Church is come together in one, and all speak *strange* tongues, there come in they that are [2]unlearned, or they which believe

---

14:7 [1] He setteth forth that which he said, by a similitude, which he borroweth and taketh from instruments of music, which although they speak not perfectly, yet they are distinguished by their sounds, that they may be the better used.

14:9 [1] That do fitly utter the matter itself.

14:10 [1] He proveth that interpretation is necessarily to be joined with the gift of tongues, by the manifold variety of languages, insomuch that if one speak to another without an interpreter, it is as if he spake not.

14:11 [1] As the Papists in all their sermons and they that ambitiously pour out some Hebrew or Greek words in the Pulpit before the unlearned people, thereby to get them a name of vain learning.

14:12 [1] The conclusion: if they will excel in those spiritual gifts, as it is meet, they must seek the profit of the Church, and therefore they must not use gift of tongues, unless there is an interpreter to expound the strange and unknown tongue, whether it be himself that speaketh, or another interpreter.

14:13 [1] Pray for the gift of interpretation.

14:14 [1] A reason: Because it is not sufficient for us to speak so in the Congregation, that we ourselves do worship God in spirit, that is, according to the gift that we have received, but we must also be understood of the company, lest that be unprofitable to others which we have spoken.

[2] If I pray, when the church is assembled together, in a strange tongue.

[3] The gift and inspiration which the spirit giveth me, doeth his part, but only to myself.

[4] No fruit cometh to the Church by my prayers.

14:15 [1] So that I may be understood of others, and may instruct others.

14:16 [1] Another reason: Seeing that the whole Congregation must agree to him that speaketh, and also witness this agreement, how shall they give their assent or agreement which know not what is spoken?

[2] Only without all consideration of the hearers.

[3] He that sitteth as a private man.

[4] So then one uttered the prayers, and all the company answered, Amen.

14:18 [1] He propoundeth himself for an example, both that they may be ashamed of their foolish ambition, and also that he may eschew all suspicion of envy.

14:19 [1] A very few words.

14:20 [1] Now he reproveth them freely for their childish folly, which see not how this gift of tongues which was given to the profit of the Church, is turned by their ambition into an instrument of cursing, seeing that this same also is contained amongst the punishments wherewith God punished the stubbornness of his people, that he dispersed them amongst strangers whose language they understood not.

14:21 [1] By the Law he understandeth all the whole Scripture.

14:22 [1] The conclusion: Therefore the gift of tongues serveth to punish the unfaithful and unbelievers, unless it be referred to prophecy (that is to say, to the interpretation of Scripture) and that that which is spoken, be by the means understood of the hearers.

14:23 [1] Another argument: The gift of tongues without prophecy is not only unprofitable to the faithful: but also doth very much hurt as well to them as to the unfaithful which should be won in the public assemblies. For by this means it cometh to pass, that the faithful seem to others to be mad, much less can the unfaithful be instructed thereby.

[2] See Acts 4:13.

not, will they not say, that ye are out of your wits?

24 But if all prophesy, and there come in one that believeth not, or one unlearned, he is rebuked of all men, and is judged of all,

25 And so are the secrets of his heart made manifest, and so he will fall down on his face and worship God, and say plainly that God is in you indeed.

26 ¹What is to be *done* then, brethren? when ye come together, *according as* every one of you hath a Psalm, *or* hath doctrine, *or* hath a tongue, *or* hath revelation, *or* hath interpretation, let all things be done unto edifying.

27 ¹If any man speak a *strange* tongue, *let it be* by two, or at the most, by three, and that by course, and let one interpret.

28 But if there be no interpreter, let him keep silence in the Church, *which speaketh languages*, and let him speak to himself, and to God.

29 ¹Let the Prophets speak, two or three, and let the others judge.

30 And if anything be revealed to another that sitteth by, let the first hold his peace.

31 For ye may all prophesy one by one, that all may learn, and all may have comfort.

32 And the ¹spirits of the Prophets are subject to the Prophets.

33 For God is not *the author* of confusion, but of peace, as *we see* in all the Churches of the Saints.

34 ᶜ·¹Let your women keep silence in the Churches: for it is not permitted unto them to speak: but *they ought* to be subject, as also ᵈthe Law saith.

35 And if they will learn anything, let them ask their husbands at home: for it is a shame for women to speak in the Church.

36 ¹Came the word of God out from you? either

ᶜ 1 Tim. 2:12
ᵈ Gen. 3:16

CHAPTER 15
ᵃ Gal. 1:11
ᵇ Isa. 53:5
1 Pet. 2:24
ᶜ Jonah 2:1
ᵈ John 20:19

came it unto you only?

37 If any man think himself to be a Prophet, or ¹spiritual, let him acknowledge, that the things that I write unto you, are the commandments of the Lord.

38 ¹And if any man be ignorant, let him be ignorant.

39 ¹Wherefore, brethren, covet to prophesy, and forbid not to speak languages.

40 Let all things be done honestly, and by order.

15

1 *The Gospel that Paul preached.* 3 *The death and resurrection of Christ.* 8 *Paul saw Christ.* 9 *He had persecuted that Church, whereof afterward he was made a minister.* 12 *Christ first rose again, and we all shall rise by him.* 26 *The last enemy, death.* 29 *To be baptized for dead.* 32 *At Ephesus Paul fought with beasts.* 35 *How the dead are raised.* 45 *The first Adam. The last Adam,* 47 *The first and second man.* 51 *We shall all be changed, we shall not all sleep.* 55 *Death's sting.* 57 *Victory.* 58 *Constancy and steadfastness.*

1 Moreover ᵃ·¹brethren, I declare unto you the Gospel which I preached unto you, which ye have also received, and wherein ye ²continue,

2 And whereby ye are saved, if ye keep in memory, after what manner I preached it unto you, ¹except ye have believed in vain.

3 For first of all, I delivered unto you that which I received, how that Christ died for our sins, according to the ᵇScriptures,

4 And that he was buried, and that he arose the third day, according to the ᶜScriptures,

5 ᵈAnd that he was seen of Cephas, then of the ¹twelve.

14:26 ¹ The conclusion: The edifying of the Congregation is a rule and square of the right use of all spiritual gifts.

14:27 ¹ The manner how to use the gift of tongues. It may be lawful for one or two, or at the most three, to use the gift of tongues, one after another in an assembly, so that there be some to expound the same: but if there are none to expound, let him that hath that gift, speak to himself alone.

14:29 ¹ The manner of prophesying: Let two or three propound, and let the other judge of that that is propoundeth, whether it be agreeable to the word of God or no: If in this examination the Lord give any man nought to speak, let them give him leave to speak. Let every man be admitted to prophesy, severally and in his order, so far forth as it is required for the edifying of the Church. Let them be content to be subject to each other's judgment.

14:32 ¹ The doctrine which the Prophets bring which are inspired with God's Spirit.

14:34 ¹ Women are commanded to be silent in public assemblies, and they are commanded to ask of their husbands at home.

14:36 ¹ A general conclusion of the treatise of the right use of spiritual gifts in assemblies: with a sharp reprehension, lest the Corinthians might alone seem to themselves to be wise.

14:37 ¹ Skillful in knowing and judging spiritual things.

14:38 ¹ The Church ought not to care for such as be stubbornly ignorant, and will not abide to be taught, but to go forward notwithstanding in those things which are right.

14:39 ¹ Prophecy ought simply to be retained and kept in Congregations, the gift of tongues is not to be forbidden, but all things must be done orderly.

15:1 ¹ The sixth treatise of this Epistle, concerning the resurrection: and he useth a transition, or passing over from one matter to another, showing first that he bringeth no new thing, to the end that the Corinthians might understand that they had begun to swerve from the right course: and next that he goeth not about to entreat of a trifling matter, but of another chief point of the Gospel, which if it be taken away, their faith must needs come to nought. And so at the length he beginneth this treatise at Christ's resurrection, which is the ground and foundation of ours, and confirmeth it first by the testimony of the Scriptures, and by the witness of the Apostles, and of more than five hundred brethren, and last of all his own.

² In the profession whereof you continue yet.

15:2 ¹ Which is very absurd, and cannot be, but that they believe, must reap the fruit of faith.

15:5 ¹ Of those twelve picked and chosen Apostles, which were commonly called twelve, though Judas was put out of the number.

6 After that, he was seen of more than five hundred brethren at [1]once: whereof many remain unto this present, and some also are asleep.

7 After that, he was seen of James: then of all the Apostles.

8 [e,1]And last of all he was seen also of me, as of one born out of due time.

9 [f]For I am the least of the Apostles, which am not meet to be called an Apostle, because I persecuted the Church of God.

10 [g]But by the grace of God I am that I am: and his grace which is in me, was not in vain: but I labored more abundantly than they all: yet not I, but the grace of God which is with me.

11 Wherefore, whether it were I, or they, so we preach, and so have ye believed.

12 ¶ [1]Now if it be preached, that Christ is risen from the dead, how say some among you, that there is no resurrection of the dead?

13 [1]For if there be no resurrection of the dead, then is Christ not risen:

14 [1]And if Christ be not risen, then is our preaching vain, and your faith is also vain.

[e] Acts 9:5
[f] Eph. 3:8
[g] Eph. 3:7
[h] Col. 1:18
Rev. 1:5
[i] 1 Thess. 4:13

15 And we are found also false witnesses of God: for we have testified of God, that he hath raised up Christ: whom he hath not raised up, if so be the dead be not raised.

16 [1]For if the dead be not raised, then is Christ not raised.

17 And if Christ be not raised, your faith is vain: [1]ye are [2]yet in your sins.

18 [1]And so they which are asleep in Christ, are perished.

19 [1]If in this life only we have hope in Christ, we are of all men the most miserable.

20 [1]But now is Christ risen from the dead, [2]and was made the [h,3]firstfruits of them that slept.

21 [1]For since by man came death, by man came also the resurrection of the dead.

22 For as in Adam all die, even so in Christ shall all be [1]made alive.

23 [1]But every man in his [i]own order: the firstfruits is Christ, afterward, they that are of Christ, at his coming shall rise again.

24 [1]Then shall be the [2]end, when he hath delivered up the kingdom to God, even the Father, when he hath

---

15:6 [1] Not fewer all times, but together and at one instant.

15:8 [1] He maintaineth by the way, the authority of his Apostleship, which was requisite to be in good credit among the Corinthians, that this Epistle might be of force and weight amongst them. In the mean season he compareth himself to such sort after a certain divine art with certain others, that he maketh himself inferior to them all.

15:12 [1] The first argument to prove that there is a resurrection from the dead: Christ is risen again, therefore the dead shall rise again.

15:13 [1] The second by an absurdity, If there is no resurrection of the dead, then is not Christ risen again.

15:14 [1] The proof of that absurdity by other absurdities: If Christ be not risen again, the preaching of the Gospel is in vain, and the credit that you gave unto it is vain, and we are liars.

15:16 [1] He repeateth the same argument taken of an absurdity, purposing to show how faith is in vain if the resurrection of Christ be taken away.

15:17 [1] First, seeing death is the punishment of sin, in vain should we believe that our sins were forgiven us, if they remain: but they do remain, if Christ rose not from death.

[2] They are yet in their sins, which are not sanctified, nor have obtained remission of their sins.

15:18 [1] Secondly, unless that this be certain that Christ rose again, all they which died in Christ, are perished. So then what profit cometh of faith?

15:19 [1] The third argument, which is also taken from an absurdity: for unless there be another life, wherein such as trust and believe in Christ shall be blessed, they were the most miserable of all creatures, because in this life they are the most miserable.

15:20 [1] A conclusion of the former argument: Therefore Christ is risen again.

[2] He putteth the last conclusion for the first proposition of the argument that followeth. Christ is risen again, Therefore shall we the faithful (for of them he speaketh) rise again: Then followeth the first reason of this consequent: for Christ is set forth unto us, to be considered of, not as a private man apart and by himself, but as the firstfruits: And he taketh that which was known, to all men, to wit, that the whole heap is sanctified in the firstfruits.

[3] He alludeth to the firstfruits of corn, the offering whereof sanctified the rest of the fruits.

15:21 [1] Another confirmation of the same consequent: for Christ is to be considered as opposite to Adam, that as from one man Adam, sin came over all, so from one man Christ, life cometh unto all: that is to say, that all the faithful, as they die, because by nature they were born of Adam, so because in Christ they are made the children of God by grace, they are quickened and restored to life by him.

15:22 [1] Shall rise by the virtue of Christ.

15:23 [1] He doeth two things together: for he showeth that the resurrection is in such sort common to Christ with all his members, that notwithstanding he far passeth them, both in time (for he was the first that rose again from the dead) and also in honor, because that from him and in him is all our life and glory. Then by this occasion he passeth in the next argument.

15:24 [1] The fourth argument, wherewith also he confirmeth the others, hath a most sure ground, to wit, because that God must reign. And this is the manner of his reign, that the Father will be showed to be King in his Son who was made man, to whom all things are made subject (the promiser only except) to the end that the Father may afterward triumph in his Son the conqueror. And he maketh two parts of this reign and dominion of the Son, wherein the Father's glory consisteth: to wit, the overcoming of his enemies (whereof some must be deprived of all power, as Satan and all the wicked, be they never so proud and mighty, and others must be utterly abolished as death) and a plain and full delivery of the godly from all enemies, that by this means God may fully set forth the body of the Church, cleaving fast to their head Christ, his kingdom and glory as a king in his subjects. Moreover he putteth the first degree of this kingdom in the resurrection of the Son, who is the head: and the perfection, in the full conjunction of the members with the head, which shall be in the latter day. Now all these tend to this purpose, to show that unless the dead do rise again, neither the Father can be King above all, neither Christ be Lord of all: for neither should the power of Satan and death be overcome, nor the glory of God be full in his Son, nor his Son in his members.

[2] The shutting up and finishing of all things.

put down ³all rule, and all authority and power.

25 For he must reign ʲtill he hath put all his enemies ¹under his feet.

26 The ¹last enemy that shall be destroyed, *is* death.

27 ᵏFor he hath put down all things under his feet. (And when he saith that all things are subdued *to him*, it is manifest that he is excepted, which did put down all things under him.)

28 And when all things shall be subdued unto him, ¹then shall the Son also himself be subject unto him, that did subdue all things under him, that ²God may be all in all.

29 ¹Else what shall they do which are baptized ²for dead? if the dead rise not at all, why are they then baptized for dead?

30 ¹Why are we also in jeopardy every hour?

31 By your ¹rejoicing which I have in Christ Jesus our Lord, I die daily.

32 ¹If I have fought with beasts at Ephesus ²after the manner of men, what advantageth it me, if the dead be not raised up? ¹,³let us ⁴eat and drink: for tomorrow we shall die.

ʲ Ps. 110:1
Acts 2:34
Heb. 1:13
Heb. 10:13

ᵏ Ps. 8:6
Heb. 2:8

ˡ Isa. 22:13

33 ¹Be not deceived: evil speakings corrupt good manners.

34 Awake to *live* righteously, and sin not: for some have not the knowledge of God, I speak this to your shame.

35 ¹But some man will say, How are the dead raised up? and with what body come they forth?

36 ¹O fool, that which thou sowest, is not quickened, except it die.

37 And that which thou sowest, thou sowest not that body that shall be, but bare corn as it falleth, of wheat, or of some other.

38 ¹But God giveth it a body at his pleasure, even to every seed his own body.

39 All flesh *is* not the same flesh, but there is one flesh of men, and another flesh of beasts, and another of fishes, and another of birds:

40 There *are* also heavenly bodies, and earthly bodies: but the glory of the heavenly *is* one, and *the glory* of the earthly *is* another.

41 There is another glory of the sun, and another glory of the moon, and another glory of the stars:

---

³ All his enemies which shall be spoiled of all the power they have.

15:25 ¹ Christ is considered here, as he appeared in the form of a servant, in which respect he ruleth the Church as head, and that because this power was given him of his Father.

15:26 ¹ The shutting up of the argument, which is taken from the whole to the part: for if all his enemies shall be put under his feet, then must it needs be that death also shall be subdued under him.

15:28 ¹ Not because the Son was not subject to his Father before, but because his body, that is to say, the Church which is here in distress, and not yet wholly partaker of his glory, is not yet fully perfect, and also because the bodies of the saints which be in the graves shall not be glorified until the resurrection: but Christ as he is God, hath us subject to him as his Father hath, but as he is Priest, he is subject to his father together with us. Augustine, book 1, chap. 8, of the Trinity.

² By this high kind of speech, is set forth an incomprehensible glory which floweth from God, and shall fill all of us, as we are joined together with our head, but yet so, that our head shall always reserve his preeminence.

15:29 ¹ The fifth argument taken of the end of Baptism, to wit, because that they which are baptized, are baptized for dead, that is to say, that they may have a remedy against death because that Baptism is a token of regeneration.

² They that are baptized, to this end and purpose, that death may be put out in them, or to rise again from the dead, whereof baptism is a seal.

15:30 ¹ The sixth argument: Unless there be a resurrection of the dead, why should the Apostles so daily cast themselves into danger of so many deaths?

15:31 ¹ As though he said, I die daily, as all the miseries I suffer can well witness, which I may truly boast of, that I have suffered amongst you.

15:32 ¹ The taking away of an objection: but thou Paul, didst ambitiously, as commonly men are wont to do, when thou didst fight

with beasts at Ephesus: That is very like, saith Paul, for what could that advantage me, were it not for the glory of eternal life which I hope for?

² Not upon any godly motion, nor casting mine eyes upon God, but carried away with vain glory, or a certain headiness.

³ The seventh argument which dependeth upon the last: if there be no resurrection of the dead, why do we give ourselves to anything else, save to eating and drinking?

⁴ These are speeches that Epicureans use.

15:33 ¹ The conclusion with a sharp exhortation, that they take heed of the naughty company of certain: from whence he showeth that this mischief sprang: warning them to be wise with sobriety unto righteousness.

15:35 ¹ Now that he hath proved the resurrection, he discovereth their doltishness, in that they scoffingly demanded, how it could be that the dead should rise again, and if they did rise again, they asked mockingly, what manner of bodies they should have. Therefore he sendeth these fellows which seemed to themselves to be marvelous wise and witty, to be instructed of poor rude husbandmen.

15:36 ¹ Thou mightest have learned either of these, saith Paul, by daily experience: for seeds are sown, and rot, and yet notwithstanding so far it is off, that they perish, that contrariwise they grow up far more beautiful: and whereas they are sown naked and dry, they spring up green from death by the virtue of God: and doth it seem incredible to thee that our bodies should rise from corruption, and that endued with a far more excellent quality?

15:38 ¹ We see a diversity both in one and the selfsame thing which hath now one form and then another, and yet keepeth its own kind, as it is evident in a grain which is sown bare, but springeth up far after another sort: and also in divers kinds of one selfsame sort, as amongst beasts: and also among things of divers sorts, as the heavenly bodies and the earthly bodies: which also differ very much one from another. Therefore there is no cause why we should reject either the resurrection of the bodies, or changing of them into a better state, as a thing impossible, or strange.

for one star differeth from *another* star in glory.

42 ¹So also *is* the resurrection of the dead. *The* body is ²sown in corruption, *and* is raised in incorruption.

43 It is sown in ¹dishonor, *and* is raised in glory: it is sown in weakness, *and* is raised in ²power.

44 ¹It is sown a natural body, *and* is raised a spiritual body: there is a natural body, *and* there is a spiritual body.

45 ¹As it is also written, The ²first man ᵐAdam was made a living soul: and the last Adam *was made* a ³quickening spirit.

46 ¹Howbeit that *was* not first which is spiritual: but that *which is* natural, and afterward that *which is* spiritual.

47 The first man *is* of the earth, ¹earthly: the second man *is* the Lord from ²heaven.

48 ¹As *is* the earthly, such *are* they that are earthly: and as *is* the heavenly, such *are* they also that are heavenly.

49 And as we have born the ¹image of the earthly, so shall we bear the image of the heavenly.

50 ¹This say I, brethren, that ²flesh and blood cannot inherit the kingdom of God, neither doth corruption inherit incorruption.

51 ¹Behold, I show you a ²secret thing, We shall

ᵐ Gen. 2:7
ⁿ Matt. 24:31
1 Thess. 4:16
ᵒ Hos. 13:14
Heb. 2:4
ᵖ 1 John 5:5

not all sleep, but we shall all be changed,

52 In ¹a moment, in the twinkling of an eye at the last ⁿtrumpet: for the trumpet shall blow, and the dead shall be raised up incorruptible, and we shall be changed.

53 For this corruptible must put on incorruption: and this mortal *must* put on immortality.

54 So when this corruptible hath put on incorruption, and this mortal hath put on immortality, then shall be brought to pass the saying, that is written, ᵒDeath is swallowed up into victory.

55 O death where *is* thy sting? O grave where *is* thy victory?

56 The sting of death *is* sin: and the strength of sin *is* the Law.

57 ᵖBut thanks *be* unto God, which hath given us victory through our Lord Jesus Christ.

58 ¹Therefore my beloved brethren, be ye steadfast, unmovable, abundant always in the work of the Lord, forasmuch as ye know that your labor is not in vain in the ²Lord.

16

1 He exhorteth them to help the poor brethren of Jerusalem: 10 Then he commendeth Timothy, 13 and so with a friendly exhortation, 19 and commendations, endeth the Epistle.

15:42 ¹ He maketh three manner of qualities of the bodies being raised: Incorruption, to wit, because they shall be sound, and altogether of a nature that cannot be corrupt: Glory, because they shall be adorned with beauty and honor: Power, because they shall continue everlasting without meat, drink, and all other helps, without which this frail life cannot keep itself from corruption.

² Is buried, and man is hid as seed in the ground.

15:43 ¹ Void of honor, void of glory, and beauty.

² Freed from the former weakness, whereas it is subject to such alteration and change, that it cannot maintain itself without meat and drink, and such otherlike helps.

15:44 ¹ He showeth perfectly in one word, this change of the quality of the body by the resurrection, when he saith, that of a natural body, it shall become a spiritual body, which two qualities being clean different, the one from the other, he straightway expoundeth and setteth forth diligently.

15:45 ¹ That is called a natural body, which is quickened and maintained by a living soul only, such as Adam was, of whom all we are born naturally: and that is said to be a spiritual, which together with the soul is quickened with a far more excellent virtue: to wit, with the Spirit of God, which descendeth from Christ the second Adam unto us.

² Adam is called the first man, because he is the root as it were from which we spring: and Christ is the latter man: because he is the beginning of all them that are spiritual, and in him we are all comprehended.

³ Christ is called a Spirit, by reason of that most excellent nature, that is to say, God who dwelleth in him bodily, as Adam is called a living soul, by reason of the soul which is the best part in him.

15:46 ¹ Secondly he willeth the order of this double state or quality to be observed, that the natural was first, Adam being created of the clay of the earth: and the spiritual followed and came upon

it, to wit, when the Lord being sent from heaven, endued our flesh which was prepared and made fit for him, with the fulness of the Godhead.

15:47 ¹ Wallowing in dirt, and wholly given to an earthly nature.

² The Lord is said to come down from heaven by that kind of speech, whereby that which is proper to one is touched of another.

15:48 ¹ He applieth both the earthly naturalness of Adam (if I may so say) to our bodies, so long as they are naturally conversant on earth, to wit, in this life, and in the grave: and also the spirituality of Christ to the same our bodies, after that they are risen again: and he saith, that that goeth before and this shall follow.

15:49 ¹ Not a vain and false image, but such an one as had the truth with it indeed.

15:50 ¹ The conclusion: We cannot be partakers of the glory of God, unless we put off all that gross and filthy nature of our bodies subject to corruption, that the same body may be adorned with incorruptible glory.

² Flesh and blood are taken here for a living body, which cannot attain to incorruption, unless it put off corruption.

15:51 ¹ He goeth further, declaring that it shall come to pass that they which shall be found alive in the latterday, shall not descend into that corruption of the grave, but shall be renewed with a sudden change, which change is very requisite: and that the certain enjoying of the benefit and victory of Christ, is deferred unto that latter time.

² A thing that hath been hid, and never known hitherto, and therefore worthy that you give good care unto it.

15:52 ¹ He showeth us that the time shall be very short.

15:58 ¹ An exhortation taken from the profit that ensueth, that seeing they understand that the glory of the other life is laid up for faithful workmen, they continue and stand fast in the truth of the doctrine of the resurrection of the dead.

² Through the Lord's help and goodness working in us.

1 Concerning [1]the gathering for the Saints, as I have ordained in the Churches of Galatia, so do ye also.

2 Every [1]first *day* of the week, let every one of you put aside by himself, and lay up as *God* hath [2]prospered him, that then there be no gatherings when I come.

3 And when I am come, whomsoever ye shall allow by [1]letters, them will I send to bring your liberality unto Jerusalem.

4 [1]And if it be meet that I go also, they shall go with me.

5 Now I will come unto you, after I have gone through Macedonia (for I will pass through Macedonia.)

6 And it may be that I will abide, yea, or winter with you, that ye may bring me on my way, whithersoever I go.

7 For I will not see you now in my passage, but I trust to abide a while with you, if the Lord permit.

8 And I will tarry at Ephesus until Pentecost.

9 For a great door and [1]effectual is opened unto me, and there are many adversaries.

10 ¶ Now if Timothy come, see that he be [1]without fear with you: for he worketh the work of the Lord, even as I *do*.

11 Let no man therefore despise him: but convey him forth [1]in peace, that he may come unto me: for I looked for him with the brethren.

12 As touching *our* brother Apollos, I greatly desired him to come unto you with the brethren: but

CHAPTER 16
a Rom. 16:16
1 Cor. 3:2
1 Pet. 3:14

his mind was not at all to come at this time: howbeit he will come when he shall have convenient time.

13 ¶ Watch ye: stand fast in the faith: quit you like men, *and* be strong.

14 Let all your things be done in love.

15 Now brethren, I beseech you (ye know the house of [1]Stephanas, that it is the firstfruits of Achaia, and that they have [2]given themselves to minister unto the Saints.)

16 That ye be [1]obedient even unto such, and to all that help with us and labor.

17 I am glad of the coming of Stephanas, and Fortunatus, and Achaicus: for they have supplied the want of you.

18 For they have comforted my [1]spirit and yours: [2]acknowledge therefore such men.

19 The Churches of Asia salute you: Aquila and Priscilla with the Church that is in their house, salute you greatly in the Lord.

20 All the brethren greet you. Greet ye one another with an *a*holy kiss.

21 The salutation of *me* Paul with mine own hand.

22 If any man love not the Lord Jesus Christ, let him be had in execration [1]maran-atha.

23 The grace of our Lord Jesus Christ *be* with you.

24 My love *be* with you all in Christ Jesus, Amen.

The first *Epistle* to the Corinthians,
written from Philippi, *and sent* by Stephanas,
and Fortunatus, and Achaicus, and Timothy.

16:1 [1] Collections in old time were made by the Apostles appointment the first day of the week, on which day the manner was then to assemble themselves.
16:2 [1] Which in times past was called Sunday, but now is called the Lord's day.
  [2] That every man bestow, according to the ability that God hath blessed him with.
16:3 [1] Which you shall give them to carry.
16:4 [1] The residue of the Epistle is spent in writing of familiar matters, yet so that all things be referred to his purposed mark, that is to say, to the glory of God, and the edifying of the Corinthians.
16:9 [1] Very fit and convenient to do great things by.
16:10 [1] Without any just occasion of fear.

16:11 [1] Safe and sound, and that with all kinds of courtesy.
16:15 [1] Stephanas is the name of a man and not of a woman.
  [2] Given themselves wholly to the ministry.
16:16 [1] That you honor and reverence them, be obedient to them and be content to be ruled by them, as meet as you should, seeing they have bestowed themselves, and their goods to help you withall.
16:18 [1] Mine heart.
  [2] Take them for such men as they are indeed.
16:22 [1] By these words, are betokened the [secret] kind of curse and excommunication that was amongst the Jews: and the words are as much as to say, as our Lord cometh: So that his meaning may be this, Let him be accursed even to the coming of the Lord, that is to say, to his death's day, even for ever.

THE SECOND EPISTLE OF PAUL

TO THE

CORINTHIANS

1 *1 He beginneth with the praise of afflictions, 8 declaring what he hath suffered in Asia, 10 and how happily God assisted him. 17 He saith it was not upon any lightness, that he came not, according to his promise.*

1 PAUL ¹an Apostle of JESUS Christ, by the will of God, and *our* brother Timothy, to the Church of God, which is at Corinth, with all the Saints, which are in all Achaia:

2 Grace *be* with you, and peace from God, our Father, and *from* the Lord Jesus Christ.

3 *a,1,2*Blessed *be* God, even the Father of our Lord Jesus Christ, the Father of ³mercies, and the God of all comfort,

4 Which comforteth us in all our tribulation, ¹that we may be able to comfort them which are in any affliction by the comfort wherewith we ourselves are comforted of God.

5 For as the ¹sufferings of Christ abound in us, so our consolation aboundeth through Christ.

6 ¹And whether we be afflicted, *it is* for your consolation and salvation, which is ²wrought in the enduring of the same sufferings, which we also

suffer: or whether we be comforted, *it is* for your consolation and salvation.

7 And our hope is steadfast concerning you, in as much as we know, that as ye are partakers of the sufferings, so *shall ye be* also of the consolation.

8 ¹For brethren, we would not have you ignorant of our affliction, which came unto us in Asia, how we were pressed out of measure passing strength, so that we altogether ²doubted even of life.

9 Yea, we received the sentence of death in ¹ourselves, because we should not rest in ourselves, but in God, which raised the dead.

10 Who delivered us from so ¹great a death, and doth deliver *us*: in whom we trust, that yet hereafter he will deliver *us*.

11 *b,1*So that ye labor together in prayer for us, ²that for the gift *bestowed* upon us for many, thanks may be given by many persons for us.

12 ¹For our rejoicing is this, the testimony of our conscience, that in simplicity and godly ²pureness, *and* not in fleshly wisdom, but by the ³grace of God we have had our conversation in the world, and most

---

1:1 ¹ See the declaration of such salutations in the former Epistles.

1:3 ¹ He beginneth after his manner with thanksgiving, which notwithstanding (otherwise than he was wont) he applieth to himself: beginning his Epistle with the setting forth of the dignity of his Apostleship, constrained (as it should seem) by their importunity, which took an occasion to despise him by reason of his miseries. But he answereth that he is not so afflicted, but that his comforts do exceed his afflictions, showing the ground of them, even the mercy of God the Father in Jesus Christ.

² To him be praise and glory given.

³ Most merciful.

1:4 ¹ The Lord doth comfort us to this end and purpose, that we may so much the more surely comfort others.

1:5 ¹ The miseries which we suffer for Christ, or which Christ suffereth in us.

1:6 ¹ He denieth that either his afflictions wherewith he was often afflicted, or the consolations which he received of God, may justly be despised, seeing that the Corinthians both might and ought to take great occasion to be confirmed by either of them.

² Although salvation be given us freely, yet because there is a way appointed us wherewith we must come to it, which is the race of an innocent and upright life, which we must run, therefore we are said to work our salvation, Philippians 2:12. And because it is God only that of his free good will worketh all things in us, therefore is he said to work the salvation in us by those selfsame things by which we

must pass to everlasting life, after that we have once overcome all encumbrances.

1:8 ¹ He witnesseth that he is not only not ashamed of his afflictions, but that he desireth also to have all men know the greatness of them, and also his delivery from them, although it be not yet perfect.

² I know not at all what to do, neither did I see by man's help which way to save my life.

1:9 ¹ I was resolved within myself to die.

1:10 ¹ From these great dangers.

1:11 ¹ That he may not seem to boast himself, he attributeth all to God, and therewith also confesseth that he attributeth much to the prayers of the faithful.

² The end of the afflictions of the Saints, is the glory of God, and therefore they ought to be precious unto us.

1:12 ¹ Secondly he putteth away another slander, to wit, that he was a light man, and such a one as was not lightly to be credited, seeing that he promised to come unto them, and came not. And first he speaks of the simplicity of his mind, and sincerity, which they know both by his voice when he was present, and they ought to acknowledge it also in his letters, being absent: and moreover he protesteth that he will never be otherwise.

² With clearness, and holy and true plainness of mind, as God himself can witness.

³ Trusting to that very wisdom, which God of his free goodness hath given me from heaven.

of all to youwards.

13 For we write ¹none other things unto you, than that ye read or else that ye acknowledge, and I trust ye shall acknowledge unto the ²end.

14 Even as ye have acknowledged us partly, that we are your ¹rejoicing, even as ye are ours, in the ²day of *our* Lord Jesus.

15 And in this confidence was I minded first to come unto you, that ye might have had a ¹double grace,

16 And to pass by you into Macedonia, and to come again out of Macedonia, unto you, and to be led forth toward Judea of you.

17 ¹When I therefore was thus minded, did I use lightness? or mind I those things which I mind, according to the ²flesh, that with me should be, ³Yea, yea, and Nay, nay?

18 ¹Yea, God is ²faithful, that our word toward you, was not Yea, and Nay?

19 ¹For the Son of God Jesus Christ, who was preached among you by us, *that is*, by me, and Silvanus, and Timothy, ²was not Yea, and Nay: but in ³him it was Yea.

20 ¹For all the promises of God in him *are* Yea, and are in ²him Amen, unto the glory of God through ³us.

21 ¹And it is God which established us with you in Christ, and hath anointed us.

22 Who hath also sealed us, and hath given the ¹earnest of the Spirit in our hearts.

23 ¹Now, I call God for a record unto my ²soul, that to spare you, I came not as yet unto Corinth.

24 ¹Not that we have dominion over your faith, but we are helpers of your ²joy: for by faith ye stand.

2

1 He excuseth his not coming unto them, 2 and privily reprehendeth them: 4 He showeth that such is his affection towards them, 5 that he never rejoiceth but when they are merry. 6 Perceiving the adulterer (whom he commanded to be delivered up to Satan) to repent, he requesteth that they forgive him. 13 He mentioneth his going into Macedonia.

1 But I determined thus in myself, that I would not come again to you in ¹heaviness.

2 For if I make you sorry, who is he then that should make me glad, but the same which is made sorry by me?

3 And I wrote this same thing unto you, lest when I came, I should take heaviness of them of whom I ought to rejoice: this ¹confidence have I in you all, that my joy is the *joy* of you all.

4 For in great affliction, and anguish of heart I wrote unto you with many tears: not that ye should be made sorry, but that ye might perceive the love which I have, specially unto you.

5 ¹And if any hath caused sorrow, the same hath

1:13 ¹ He saith he writeth barely and simply: for he that writeth in colored sort, is rightly said to write otherwise than we read: and this he saith the Corinthians shall know and like of very well.

² Perfectly.

1:14 ¹ Paul's rejoicing in the Lord was, that he had won the Corinthians: and they themselves rejoiced that such an Apostle was their instructor, and taught them so purely and sincerely.

² When he shall sit as judge.

1:15 ¹ Another benefit.

1:17 ¹ He putteth away their slander and false report by denying it, and first of all in that divers went about to persuade the Corinthians, that in the preaching of the Gospel, Paul agreed not to himself: for this was the matter and the case.

² As men do, which will rashly promise anything, and change their purpose at every turning of an hand.

³ That I should say and unsay a thing?

1:18 ¹ He calleth God to witness, and for judge of his constancy in preaching and teaching one selfsame Gospel.

² True, and of whose faithfulness it [were] horrible wickedness to doubt.

1:19 ¹ He joineth also with himself, his fellows as witnesses, with whom he fully consented in teaching one selfsame thing, to wit, one selfsame Christ.

² Was not divers and wavering.

³ That is in God.

1:20 ¹ Last of all he declareth the sum of his doctrine, to wit, that all the promises of salvation are sure and ratified in Christ.

² Christ is set also forth to exhibit and fulfill them all most assuredly, and without all doubt.

³ Through our ministry.

1:21 ¹ He attributeth the praise of this constancy, only to the grace of God, through the holy Ghost, and therewithall concludeth that they cannot doubt of his faith, and his fellows, without doing injury to the Spirit of God, seeing that they themselves do know all this to be true.

1:22 ¹ An earnest, is, whatsoever is given to confirm a promise.

1:23 ¹ Now coming to the matter, he sweareth, that he did not only, not lightly alter his purpose of coming to them, but rather that he came not unto them for this cause, that he might not be constrained to deal more sharply, with them being present, than he would.

² Against myself and to the danger of mine own life.

1:24 ¹ He removeth all suspicion of arrogance, declaring that he speaketh not as a Lord unto them, but as a servant, appointed of God to comfort them.

² He setteth the joy and peace of conscience, which God is author of, against tyrannous fear, and therewithall showeth the end of the Gospel.

2:1 ¹ Causing grief amongst you, which he should have done if he had come to them before they had repented them.

2:3 ¹ For I trusted that you would take that out of the way forewith, which you knew I was discontented with, considering how you are persuaded that my joy is your joy.

2:5 ¹ He passeth to another part of this Epistle: which notwithstanding is put amongst the first, whereunto he returneth afterward, and he handleth the releasing and unloosing of the incestuous person, because he seemed to have given sufficient testimony of his repentance: showing the true use of excommunication, to wit, that it proceed not of hatred, but of love, and so ends lest if we keep no measure, we serve Satan the devil.

not made [2]me sorry, but [3]partly (lest I should more [4]charge *him*) you all.

6   It is sufficient unto the same man, that he was rebuked of many.

7   So that now contrariwise ye ought rather to [1]forgive *him*, and comfort *him*, lest the same should be swallowed up with overmuch heaviness.

8   Wherefore, I pray you, that you would [1]confirm your love towards him.

9   For this cause also did I write: that I might know the proof of you, whether ye would be obedient in all things.

10   To whom ye forgive anything, I *forgive* also: for verily if I forgave anything, to whom I forgave it, for your sakes *forgave I it* in the [1]sight of Christ,

11   Lest Satan should circumvent us: for we are not ignorant of his [1]enterprises.

12   ¶ [1]Furthermore, when I came to Troas *to preach* Christ's Gospel, and a door was opened unto me of the Lord,

13   I had no rest in my spirit, because I found not Titus my brother, but took my leave of them, and went away into Macedonia.

14   Now thanks *be* unto God, which always maketh us to triumph in Christ, and maketh manifest the [1]savor of his knowledge by us in every place.

15   [1]For we are unto God the sweet savor of Christ, in them that are saved, and in them which perish.

16   To the one *we are* the savor of death, unto death,

CHAPTER 2
[d] 2 Cor. 4:2

and to the other the savor of life, unto life: [1]and who is sufficient for these things?

17   [a]For we are not as many, which make [1]merchandise of the word of God: but as of sincerity, but as of God in the sight of God speak we in Christ.

3 *1 He desireth no other commendation,   3 than their continuing in the faith.   6 He is a minister not of the letter, but of the Spirit.   8 He showeth the difference of the Law, and the Gospel,   13 that the brightness of the Law doth rather dim the sight than lighten it: 18 But the Gospel doth make manifest God's countenance unto us.*

1   Do we begin to praise ourselves again? or need we as some others, Epistles of recommendation unto you, or *letters* of recommendation from you?

2   Ye are our epistle, written in our hearts, which is understood and read of all men,

3   In that ye are [1]manifest, to be the Epistle of Christ, [2]ministered by us, and written, not with ink, but with the Spirit of the [3]living God, [4]not in tables of stone, but in fleshly tables of the heart.

4   And such [1]trust have we through Christ to God:

5   Not that we are sufficient of ourselves, to think anything, as of ourselves: but our [1]sufficiency *is* of God,

6   [1]Who also hath made us able ministers of the New Testament, not of the [2]letter, but of the Spirit: for the letter killeth, but the Spirit giveth life.

2:5 [2] As if he said, All that sorrow is so clean wiped away, as though he had never felt it.

[3] As for me (saith Paul) I have no more to do with him.

[4] Lest I should overcharge him, who is burdened enough of himself, which I would be glad were taken from him.

2:7 [1] That whereas before you punished him sharply, you would now forgive him.

2:8 [1] That at my entreaty, you would declare by the consent of the whole Church, that you take him again for a brother.

2:10 [1] Truly and from the heart.

2:11 [1] Of his mischievous counsel and devilish will.

2:12 [1] He returneth to the confirmation of his Apostleship, and bringeth forth the testimonies, both of his labor, and also of God's blessing.

2:14 [1] He alludeth to the anointing of the Priests, and the incense of the sacrifices.

2:15 [1] He denieth that ought should be taken away from the dignity of his Apostleship, because they saw evidently that it was not received with like success in every place, nay rather very many rejected and detested him, seeing that he preacheth Christ, not only as a Savior of them that believe, but also as a Judge of them that condemn him.

2:16 [1] Again, he putteth away all suspicion of arrogance, attributing all things that he did, to the virtue of God, whom he serveth sincerely, and without all dishonest affection: whereof he maketh them witnesses even to verse 6 of the next chapter.

2:17 [1] We do not handle it craftily and covetously, or less sincerely than we ought: and he useth a metaphor which is taken from hucksters, which used to play the false harlots with whatsoever cometh

into their hands.

3:3 [1] The Apostle frameth his speech wisely, that by little and little he may come from the commendation of the person, to the matter itself.

[2] Which I took pains to write as it were.

[3] By the way he setteth the virtue of God, against the ink wherewith Epistles are commonly written, to show that it was wrought by God.

[4] He alludeth by the way, to the comparison of the outward ministry of the Priesthood of Levi, with the ministry of the Gospel, and the Apostolic ministry, which he handleth afterward more fully.

3:4 [1] This boldness we show, and thus gloriously may we boast of the worthiness and fruit of our ministry.

3:5 [1] In that we are fit and meet to make other men partakers of so great a grace.

3:6 [1] He amplifieth his ministry and his fellows: that is to say, the ministry of the Gospel, comparing it with the ministry of the Law, which he considereth in the person of Moses, by whom the Law was given: against whom he setteth Christ the author of the Gospel. Now this comparison is taken from the very substance of the ministry. The Law is as it were a writing of itself dead, and without efficacy: but the Gospel, or new covenant, is as it were the very virtue of God itself, in renewing, justifying, and saving men. The Law propoundeth death, accusing all men of unrighteousness: The Gospel offereth and giveth righteousness and life. The governance of the Law served for a time to the promise: The Gospel remaineth to the end of the world. Therefore what is the glory of that in comparison of the majesty of this?

[2] Not of the Law, but of the Gospel.

7　If then the ministration of death *written* with letters [1]and engraven in stones, was [2]glorious, so that the children of Israel could not behold the face of Moses, for the glory of his countenance (which *glory* is gone away.)

8　How shall not the [1]ministration of the Spirit be more glorious?

9　For if the ministry of condemnation *was* glorious, much more doth the ministration of [1]righteousness exceed in glory.

10　For even that which was glorified, was not glorified in this point, *that is*, as touching the exceeding glory.

11　For if that they should be [1]abolished, *was* glorious, much more shall that which remaineth be glorious.

12　[1]Seeing then that we have such trust, we use great boldness of speech.

13　[a,1]And *we are* not as Moses, *which* put a veil upon his face, that the children of Israel should not look unto the [2]end of that which should be abolished.

14　Therefore their minds are hardened: for until this day remaineth the same covering untaken away in the reading of the old Testament, which *veil* in Christ is put away.

15　But even unto this day, when Moses is read, the veil is laid over their hearts.

CHAPTER 3
[a] Exod. 34:34
[b] Job 4:14

16　Nevertheless when their *heart* shall be turned to the Lord, the veil shall be taken away.

17　Now the [1]Lord is the [b]Spirit, and where the Spirit of the Lord *is*, there *is* liberty.

18　[1]But we all behold as in a mirror the glory of the Lord with open face, and are changed into the same image, from glory to glory, as by the Spirit of the Lord.

4　*1 He showeth that he hath so labored in preaching the Gospel, 4 That such are even blinded of Satan, who do not perceive the brightness thereof, 7 that the same is carried in earthen vessels, 10 who are subject to many miseries: 16 and therefore he exhorteth them by his own example to be courageous, 17 and condemn this present life.*

1　Therefore, [1]seeing that we have this ministry, as we have received mercy, we [2]faint not:

2　But have cast from us the [1]cloaks of shame, and walk not in craftiness, neither handle we the word of God [2]deceitfully: but in declaration of the truth we approve ourselves to every man's conscience in the sight of God.

3　[1]If the Gospel be then hid, it is hid to them that are lost.

4　In whom the god of this world hath blinded the minds, *that is*, of the infidels, that the [1]light of the glorious Gospel of Christ, which is the [2]image of God, should not shine unto them.

3:7 [1] Imprinted and engraven: so that by this place we may plainly perceive, that the Apostle speaketh not of the ceremonies of the Law, but even of the ten commandments.

[2] This word Glory, betokeneth a brightness, and a majesty, which was bodily in Moses, but spiritually in Christ.

3:8 [1] Whereby God offereth, yea and giveth the Spirit, not as a dead thing, but a quickening Spirit, working life.

3:9 [1] To wit, of Christ, which being imputed to us as our own, we are not only not condemned, but also we are crowned as righteous.

3:11 [1] The Law, yea, and the ten commandments themselves, together with Moses, is abolished, if we consider the ministry of Moses apart by itself.

3:12 [1] He showeth wherein standeth this glory of the preaching of the Gospel, to wit, in that that it setteth forth plainly and evidently, that which the Law showeth darkly, for it sent them that heard it to be healed of Christ, which was to come, after it had wounded them.

3:13 [1] He expoundeth by the way the allegory of Moses' covering, which was a token of the darkness and weakness that is in men, which were rather dulled by the bright shining of the Law, then lightened, which covering was taken away by the coming of Christ, who lighteneth the hearts, and turneth them to the Lord, that we may be brought from the slavery of this blindness, and set in the liberty of the light, by the virtue of Christ's Spirit.

[2] Into the very bottom of Moses' ministry.

3:17 [1] Christ is that spirit which taketh away that covering, by working in our hearts, whereunto also the Law itself called us, though in vain, because it speaketh to dead men, until the spirit quickeneth us.

3:18 [1] Going forwards in the allegory of the covering, he compareth the Gospel to a glass, which although it be most bright and

sparkling, yet doth it not only not dazzle their eyes, which look in it, as the law doth, but also transformeth them with its beams, so that they also be partakers of the glory and shining of it, to lighten others: as Christ said unto his, You are the light of the world, whereas he himself was the only light. We are also commanded in another place, to shine as candles before the world, because we are partakers of God's Spirit. But Paul speaketh here properly, of the ministers of the Gospel, as it appeareth both by that that goeth before, and that that cometh after, and that, setting them his own example and his fellows.

4:1 [1] Now he plainly witnesseth that both he and his fellows (through the mercy of God) do their vocation and duty uprightly and sincerely, neglecting all dangers.

[2] Though we are broken in pieces with miseries and calamities, yet we yield not.

4:2 [1] Subtlety, and all kinds of deceit, which men hunt after, as it were dens and lurking holes, to cover their shameless dealings withall.

[2] This is it that in the former Chapter he called, making merchandise of the word of God.

4:3 [1] An objection: Many hear the Gospel, and yet are no more lightened thereby than by the preaching of the Law. He answereth, The fault is in the men themselves, whose eyes Satan plucketh out, who ruleth in this world. And yet notwithstanding doth he and his fellows set forth the most clear light of the Gospel to be seen and beholden, seeing that Christ whom only they preach, is he in whom only God will be known, and as it were seen.

4:4 [1] The light of plain and lightsome preaching, which telleth forth the glory of Christ.

[2] In whom the Father setteth forth himself to be seen and beholden.

5 ¹For we preach not ourselves, but Christ Jesus the Lord, and ourselves your servants for ²Jesus' sake.

6 For God ᵃ'¹that commanded the light to shine out of darkness, *is he* which hath shined in our hearts, to give the ²light of the knowledge of the glory of God in the face of Jesus Christ.

7 ¹But we have this treasure in earthen vessels, ²that the excellency of that power might be of God, and not of us.

8 We are afflicted on every side, yet *are we* not in distress: we are in doubt, but yet we despair not.

9 *We are* persecuted, but not forsaken: cast down, but we perish not.

10 ¹Everywhere we bear about in our body the ²dying of the Lord Jesus, that the life of Jesus might also be made manifest in our bodies.

11 For we which ¹live, are always delivered unto death for Jesus' sake, that the life also of Jesus might be made manifest in our ²mortal flesh.

12 ¹So then death worketh in us, and life in you.

13 ¹And because we have the same ²spirit of faith, according as it is written, ᵇI believed, and therefore have I spoken, we also believe, and therefore speak,

14 Knowing that he which hath raised up the

CHAPTER 4
ᵃ Gen. 1:3
ᵇ Ps. 116:10

Lord Jesus, shall raise us up also by Jesus, and shall set us with you.

15 ¹For all things are for your sakes, ²that that most plenteous grace by the thanksgiving of many, may redound to the praise of God.

16 Therefore we faint not, ¹but though our outward man perish, yet the inward man is ²renewed daily.

17 For our ¹light affliction which is but for a moment, causeth unto us a far most excellent *and* an eternal weight of ²glory:

18 While we look not on the things which are seen, but on the things which are not seen for the things which are seen, *are* temporal: but the things which are not seen, *are* eternal.

5 *1 He continueth in the same argument, 5 touching the certain hope of salvation 7 through faith, 12 not to praise himself, 14 seeing he hath God and his Church before his eyes, 17 and esteemeth nothing, but newness of life in Christ.*

1 For ¹we know that if our earthly house of this tabernacle be destroyed, we have a building *given* of God, *that is,* an house not made with hands, *but* eternal in the heavens.

2 For therefore we sigh, desiring to be ¹clothed

4:5 ¹ He removeth according to his accustomed manner, all suspicion of ambition: avouching that he teacheth faithfully, but as a servant, and witnessing that all this light which he and his fellows give to others, proceedeth from the Lord.

² To preach this selfsame Jesus to you.

4:6 ¹ Which made only with his word.

² That being lightened of God, we should in like sort give that light to others.

4:7 ¹ He taketh away a stumbling block, by which was darkened, amongst some, the bright shining of the ministry of the Gospel, to wit, because the Apostles were the most miserable of all men, Paul answereth that he and his fellows are as it were earthen vessels, but yet there is in them a most precious treasure.

² He bringeth marvelous reasons, why the Lord doth so afflict his chiefest servants, to the end saith he that all men may perceive that they stand not by any man's virtue, but by the singular virtue of God, in that they die a thousand times, but never perish.

4:10 ¹ An amplification of the former sentence, wherein he compareth his afflictions to a daily death, and the virtue of the Spirit of God in Christ, to life, which oppresseth that death.

² So Paul calleth that miserable estate and condition, that the faithful, but especially the minsters, are in.

4:11 ¹ Which live, that life, to wit, by the Spirit of Christ, amongst so many and so great miseries.

² Subject to that miserable condition.

4:12 ¹ A very cunning conclusion: as if he would say, Therefore to be short, we die, that you may live by our death, for that they ventured into all those dangers for the building of the Church's sake, and they ceased not to confirm all the faithful with the examples of their patience.

4:13 ¹ He declareth the former sentence, showing that he and his fellows die in a sort to purchase life to others, but yet notwithstanding they are partakers of the same life with them: because they them-

selves do first believe that, which they propound to others to believe, to wit, that they also shall be saved together with them in Christ.

² The same faith by the inspiration of the same Spirit.

4:15 ¹ He showeth how this constancy is preserved in them, to wit, because they respect God's glory, and the salvation of the Churches committed unto them.

² When it shall please God to deliver me, and restore me to you, that exceeding benefit which shall be poured upon me, shall in like sort redound to the glory of God, by the thanksgiving of many.

4:16 ¹ He addeth as it were a triumphant song, how that he is outwardly afflicted, but inwardly he profiteth daily: and passeth not at all for all the miseries that may be sustained in this life, in comparison of that most constant and eternal glory.

² Gathereth new strength, that the outward man be not overcome with the miseries which come freshly one upon the neck of another, being maintained and upholden with the strength of the inward man.

4:17 ¹ Afflictions are not called light, as though they were light of themselves, but because they pass away quickly, when as indeed our whole life is of no long continuance.

² Which remaineth forever firm and stable, and can never be shaken.

5:1 ¹ Taking occasion by the former comparison, he compareth this miserable body, as it is in this life, to a frail and brickle tabernacle, against which he setteth the heavenly Tabernacle, so terming that sure and everlasting condition of this same body glorified in heaven, insomuch, saith he, that we are not only not addicted to this tabernacle, but also do with sobs and sighs desire rather that tabernacle. And so this place also concerning the glory to come, is put within the treatise of the dignity of the ministry, as the other was, whereof we spake in the beginning of the second Chapter.

5:2 ¹ He calleth the glory of immortality, which we shall be as it were clothed with, a garment.

with our house, which is from [2]heaven.

3 [1]Because that if we be clothed, we shall not be found [a]naked.

4 For indeed we that are in this tabernacle, sigh and are burdened because we would not be unclothed, but would be clothed upon, that mortality might be swallowed up of life.

5 And he that hath [1]created us for this thing, is God, who also hath given unto us the earnest of the Spirit.

6 [1]Therefore we are always [2]bold, though we know that while we are at home in the body, we are absent from the Lord.

7 (For we walk by [1]faith, and not by sight.)

8 Nevertheless, we are [1]bold, and love rather to remove out of the body, and to dwell with the Lord.

9 Wherefore also we [1]covet, that both dwelling at home, and removing from home, we may be acceptable to him.

10 [b,1]For we must all [2]appear before the judgment seat of Christ, that every man may receive the things which are done in his body, according to that he hath

CHAPTER 5
[a] Rev. 16:15
[b] Rom. 14:10

done, whether it be good or evil.

11 [1]Knowing therefore that [2]terror of the Lord, we persuade men, and we are made manifest unto God, and I trust also that we are made manifest in your consciences.

12 [1]For we praise not ourselves again unto you, but give you an occasion to rejoice of us that ye may have to answer against them, which rejoice in the [2]face, and not in the heart.

13 [1]For whether we be out of our wit, we are it to God: or whether we be in our right mind, we are it unto you.

14 [1]For that love of Christ [2]constraineth us,

15 Because we thus judge, that if [1]one be dead for all, then were all dead, and he died for all, that they which live, should not henceforth [2]live unto themselves, but unto him which died for them, and rose again.

16 [1]Wherefore, henceforth know we no man after the flesh, [2]yea though we had known Christ after the flesh, yet not henceforth know we him no more.

17 [1]Therefore if any man be in Christ, let him be a

---

[2] Heavenly, not that the substance of it is heavenly, but for the glory of it.

5:3 [1] An exposition of the former saying: We do not without cause, desire to be clad with the heavenly house, that is, with that everlasting and immortal glory, as with a garment: for when we depart hence, we shall not remain naked, having once cast off the covering of this body, but we shall take our bodies again, which shall put on as it were another garment besides: and therefore we sigh not for the weariness of this life, but for the desire of a better life. Neither is this desire in vain, for we are made to that life, the pledge whereof we have, even the Spirit of adoption.

5:5 [1] He meaneth that first creation, to give us to understand, that our bodies were made to this end, that they should be clothed with heavenly immortality.

5:6 [1] He inferreth upon that sentence which went next before, thus, Therefore, seeing that we know by the Spirit, that we are strangers so long as we are here, we patiently suffer this tarriance (for we are now so with God, that we behold him but by faith, and are therefore now absent from him) but so that we aspire and have a longing always to him: therefore also we behave ourselves so, that we may be acceptable to him, both while we live here, and when we go from hence to him.

[2] He calleth them (bold) which are always resolved with a quiet and settled mind to suffer what dangers soever, nothing doubting, but their end shall be happy.

5:7 [1] Faith of those things which we hope for, and not having God presently in our view.

5:8 [1] And yet we are in such sort bold and do so pass on our pilgrimage with a valiant and quiet mind, that yet notwithstanding, we had rather depart hence to the Lord.

5:9 [1] And seeing it is so, we strive to live so, that both in this our pilgrimage here we may please him, and that at length we may be received home to him.

5:10 [1] That no man might think it to pertain to all, which he spoke of that heavenly glory, he addeth, that every one shall first render an account of his pilgrimage, after that he is departed from hence.

[2] We must all appear personally, and inquiry shall be made of us,

that all may see, how we have lived.

5:11 [1] Now he passeth over, and taking occasion of the former sentence, returneth to 4:16, confirming his own sincerity and his fellows'.

[2] That terrible judgment.

5:12 [1] He removeth all suspicion of pride, by a new reason, because it is behoovable, not for his part, but for theirs, that his Apostleship be counted sincere against the vain ostentation of a few others.

[2] In outward disguising, and that colored show of man's wisdom and eloquence, and not in true godliness, which is sealed in the heart.

5:13 [1] The meaning is: Even when I am mad (as some men think of me) while I seem as a fool to boast myself, I do it for your profit, no less than when I preach the Gospel simply unto you.

5:14 [1] He goeth forward in putting away all suspicion of desire of estimation and boasting: for the love of Christ, saith he, compelleth us hereunto, that seeing he died for us all, which were dead when as we lived to ourselves (that is, while we were yet given to these earthly affections) we in like sort should consecrate our whole life which we have received of him, to him (to wit) being endued with the holy Ghost to this end and purpose, that we should meditate upon nothing but that which is heavenly.

[2] Possesseth us wholly.

5:15 [1] He speaketh here of sanctification, whereby it cometh to pass that Christ liveth in us.

[2] See Romans, chapters 6 and 7.

5:16 [1] He showeth what it is, not to live to ourselves, but to Christ, to wit, to know no man according to the flesh, that is to say, to be so conversant amongst men, as not to care for those worldly and carnal things, as they do which respect a man's stock, his country, form, glory, riches, and such like, wherein men commonly dote, and weary themselves.

[2] An amplification: This is, saith he, so true, that we do not now think carnally of Christ himself, who hath now left the world, and therefore must be considered of us spiritually.

5:17 [1] An exhortation for every man which is renewed with the spirit of Christ, to meditate heavenly things, and not earthly.

²new creature. ʿOld things are passed away: behold, all things are become new.

18 ¹And all things *are* of God, which hath reconciled us unto himself by Jesus Christ, and hath given unto us the ministry of reconciliation.

19 For God was in Christ, and reconciled the world to himself, not imputing their sins unto them, and hath ¹committed to us the word of reconciliation.

20 Now then are we ambassadors for Christ: as though God did beseech *you* through us, we pray you in Christ's stead, that ye be reconciled to God.

21 For he hath made him *to be* ¹sin for us, which ²knew no sin, that we should be made the ³righteousness of God in him.

6 *1 He exhorteth them to lead their lives as it becometh Christians,   5 neither to be dismayed in tribulations,   9 nor puffed up with glory: 14 to avoid all uncleanness,   16 considering that they are the temples of the living God.*

1 So ¹we therefore as workers together beseech *you*, that ye receive not the grace of God in vain.

2 ¹For he saith, ʿI have heard thee in a time ²accepted, and in the day of salvation have I succored thee: behold now the accepted time, behold now the day of salvation.

3 ¹We give no occasion of offence in anything,

ʿIsa. 43:19
Rev. 21:5

CHAPTER 6
ᵈIsa. 49:8
ᵇ1 Cor. 4:1

that *our* ministry should not be reprehended.

4 But in all things we ¹approve ourselves as ᵇthe ministers of God, ²in much patience, in afflictions, in necessities, in distresses,

5 In stripes, in prisons, in ¹tumults, in labors,

6 ¹By watchings, by fastings, by purity, by knowledge, by long suffering, by kindness, by the holy Ghost, by love unfeigned,

7 By the ¹word of truth, by the ²power of God, by the ³armor of righteousness on the right hand, and on the left,

8 By honor, and dishonor, by evil report, and good report, as deceivers, and *yet* true:

9 As unknown, and *yet* known: as dying, and behold, we live, as chastened, and *yet* not killed:

10 As sorrowing, and *yet* always rejoicing: as poor, and *yet* making many rich: as having nothing, and *yet* possessing all things.

11 ¹O Corinthians, our mouth is ²open unto you, our heart is made large.

12 Ye are not ¹kept strait in us, but ye are kept strait in your own ²bowels.

13 Now for the same recompense, I speak as to *my* children, Be you also enlarged.

14 ¹Be not unequally yoked with the infidels: for what fellowship hath righteousness with unrigh-

---

5:17 ² As a thing made anew of God, for though a man be not newly created when God giveth him the spirit of regeneration, but only his qualities are changed, yet notwithstanding it pleased the holy Ghost to speak so, to teach us, that we must attribute all things to the glory of God: not that we are as stocks or blocks: but because God creates in us, both the will to will well, and the power to do well.

5:18 ¹ He commendeth the excellency of the ministry of the Gospel, both by the authority of God himself, who is the author of that ministry, and also by the excellency of the doctrine of it: for it announceth atonement with God, by free forgiveness of our sins, and justification offered unto us in Christ, and that so lovingly and liberally, that God himself doth after a sort pray men by the mouth of his ministers, to have consideration of themselves, and not to despise so great a benefit. And when he so saith, he plainly reprehendeth them which falsely challenged to themselves the name of pastors.

5:19 ¹ Used our labor and travail.

5:21 ¹ A sinner, not in himself, but by imputation of the guilt of all our sins to him.

² Who was clean void of sin.

³ Righteous before God, and that with righteousness which is not essential to us, but being essential in Christ, God imputeth it to us through faith.

6:1 ¹ Men do not only need the ministry of the Gospel, before they have received grace, that they may be partakers of it, but also after they have received grace, that they may continue in it.

6:2 ¹ In that that grace is offered, it is of the grace of God, who hath appointed times and seasons to all things, that we may take occasion when it is offered.

² Which I of my free mercy and love towards you, … appointed, at which time God poured out that his marvelous love upon us.

6:3 ¹ He showeth the Corinthians a pattern of a true minister, in his own example, and Timothy and Silvanus, to the end, that (as he pur-

posed from the beginning) he might procure authority to himself and his like.

6:4 ¹ Declare and show indeed.

² He first of all reckoneth up those things which are neither always in the ministers, nor without exception, unless it be according to the affection of the mind, patience only except, which also is one of the virtues which ought to be always in a good minister.

6:5 ¹ In tossing to and fro, finding no place of rest and quietness.

6:6 ¹ Secondly, he reckoneth up such virtues as are necessary, and ought always to be in them, and whereby as by good armor, all lets and hindrances may be overcome.

6:7 ¹ Preaching of the Gospel.

² Power to work miracles, and to bring under the wicked.

³ Uprightness.

6:11 ¹ Going about to rebuke them, he saith first, that he dealeth with them sincerely and with an open and plain heart, and therewithall complaineth that they do not the like in loving again their Father.

² The opening of the mouth and heart, betokeneth a most earnest affection in him that speaketh, as it fareth commonly with them that are in some great joy.

6:12 ¹ You are in mine heart, as in an house, and that no narrow or strait house, for I have opened my whole heart to you, but you are inwardly straitlaced to me-ward.

² After the manner of the Hebrews, he calleth those tender affections which rest in the heart, bowels.

6:14 ¹ Now he rebuked them boldly, for that they became fellows with infidels in outward idolatry, as though it were a thing indifferent. And this is the fourth part of this Epistle, the conclusion whereof is, that such as the Lord has vouchsafed the name of his children, must keep themselves pure, not only in mind, but also in body, that they may wholly be holy unto the Lord.

teousness? and what communion hath light with darkness?

15 And what concord hath Christ with Belial? or what [1]part hath the believer with the infidel?

16 And what agreement hath the Temple of God with idols? [c]for ye are the Temple of the [1]living God: as God hath said, [d]I will [2]dwell among them, and walk there: and I will be their God, and they shall be my people.

17 [e]Wherefore come out from among them, and separate yourselves, saith the Lord, and touch none unclean thing, and I will receive you.

18 [f]And I will be a Father unto you, and ye shall be my sons and daughters, saith the Lord Almighty.

[c] 1 Cor. 3:16
1 Cor. 6:19
[d] Lev. 26:11
[e] Isa. 52:11
[f] Jer. 31:1

7 *1 Lest by overmuch urging them he should dismay their tender minds, 2 he proveth that all that he said, 4 proceeded of the great good will he bare unto them: 8 and therefore they should not be offended, that he made them sorry, 10 and brought them to repentance not to be repented of.*

1 Seeing then we have these promises, dearly beloved, let us cleanse ourselves from all filthiness of the [1]flesh and spirit, and finish *our* sanctification in the fear of God.

2 [1,2]Receive us: we have done wrong to no man: we have corrupted no man: we have defrauded no man.

3 I speak it not to *your* [1]condemnation: for I have said before, that ye are in our hearts, to die and live together.

4 I use great boldness of speech toward you: I rejoice greatly in you: I am filled with comfort, and am exceeding joyous in all our tribulation.

5 For when we were come into Macedonia, our flesh had no rest, but we were troubled on every side, fightings without, and terrors within.

6 But God, that comforteth the [1]abject, comforted us at the [2]coming of Titus:

7 And not by his coming only, but also by the consolation wherewith he was comforted of you,

when he told us your great desire, your mourning, your fervent mind to me-ward, so that I rejoiced much more.

8 [1]For though I made you sorry with a letter, I repent not, though I did repent: for I perceive that the same Epistle made you sorry, though *it were* but for a season.

9 I now rejoice, not that ye were sorry, but that ye sorrowed to [1]repentance: for ye sorrowed godly, so that in nothing ye were hurt by us.

10 For [1]godly sorrow causeth repentance unto salvation, not to be repented of: but the worldly sorrow causeth death.

11 For behold, this thing that ye have been godly sorry, what great care hath it wrought in you: yea, what clearing of yourselves: yea, *what* indignation: yea, *what* fear: yea, *how* great desire: yea, *what* a zeal: yea, *what* revenge: in all things ye have showed yourselves, that ye are pure in this matter.

12 Wherefore, though I wrote unto you, I did not it for his cause that had done the wrong, neither for his cause that had the injury, but that our care toward you in the [1]sight of God might appear unto you.

13 Therefore we were comforted, because ye were comforted: but rather we rejoiced much more for the joy of Titus, because his spirit was refreshed by you all.

14 For if that I have boasted anything to him of you, I have not been ashamed: but as I have spoken unto you all things in truth, even so our boasting unto Titus was true.

15 And his inward affection is more abundant toward you, when he remembereth the obedience of you all, *and* how with fear and trembling ye received him.

16 I rejoice *therefore* that I may put my confidence in you in all things.

8 *1 He exhorteth them by the example of the Macedonians, 9 and also even of Christ himself, 14 to be*

6:15 [1] What can there be between them?

6:16 [1] He setteth the living God against idols.

[2] God dwelleth with us, because Christ is become God with us.

7:1 [1] Both of body and soul, that by this means the sanctification may be perfect, consisting in both the parts thereof.

7:2 [1] He returneth again from that admonition to his own person, opposing the testimonies both of his faithfulness and also of his continual good will towards them.

[2] Let me have some place amongst you, that I may teach you.

7:3 [1] To condemn you of unkindness or treachery.

7:6 [1] Whose hearts are cast down, and are very far spent.

[2] With those things which Titus told me of you at his coming, to wit, how fruitfully you read over my letters, moreover and besides that, I am exceedingly refreshed with his presence.

7:8 [1] An objection: But thou hast handled us roughly. The Apostle answereth that he used not this toughness without grief. And he

addeth moreover, that he is also glad now that he drove them to that sorrow, although it was against his will, since it was so profitable unto them: for there is a sorrow not only praiseworthy, but also necessary, to wit, whereby repentance groweth by certain degrees, for the which repentance he praiseth them highly. And this is the fifth part of this Epistle.

7:9 [1] Insomuch that that sorrow did you much good toward the amending of your lewdness and sins.

7:10 [1] Godly sorrow is when we are not terrified with the fear of punishment, but because we feel we have offended God our most merciful Father: contrary to this, there is another sorrow, that only feareth punishment, or when a man is vexed for the loss of some worldly goods: the fruit of the first, repentance, and the fruit of the second, is desperation, unless the Lord helps speedily.

7:12 [1] It was not colored nor counterfeit, but such as I dare stand to before God.

liberal towards the saints: · *16 for which purpose, he showeth that Titus,* *18 and another brother came unto them.*

CHAPTER 8
a Exod. 16:18
b Rom. 12:17

1   We [1]do you also to wit, brethren, of the [2]grace of God bestowed upon the Churches of Macedonia.

2   Because in [1]great trial of affliction their joy abounded, and their most extreme poverty abounded unto their rich liberality.

3   For to *their* power (I bear record) yea, and beyond their power they were [1]willing.

4   And prayed us with great instance that we would receive the [1]grace, and fellowship of the ministering which is toward the Saints.

5   [1]And *this they did*, not as we looked for: but gave their own selves, first to the Lord, and *after* unto us by the will of God,

6   That we should exhort Titus, that as he had begun, so he would also accomplish the same grace among you also.

7   Therefore, as ye abound in everything, in faith and word, and knowledge, and in all diligence, and in your love towards us, *even so see* that ye abound in this grace also.

8   [1]This say I not by commandment, but because of the [2]diligence of others: therefore prove I the [3]naturalness of your love.

9   [1]For ye know the grace of our Lord Jesus Christ, that he being rich, for your sakes became poor, that ye through his poverty might be made rich.

10   [1]And I show *my* mind herein: for this is expedient for you, which have begun not to do only, but also to [2]will, a year ago.

11   Now therefore perform to do it also, that as *there was* a readiness to will, even so ye may perform it of that which ye have.

12   [1]For if there be first a willing mind, it is accepted according to that a man hath, and not according to that he hath not.

13   [1]Neither *is it* that other men should be eased and you grieved: But upon [2]like condition, at this time your abundance *supplieth* their lack:

14   That also their abundance may be for your lack, that there may be equality.

15   As it is written, [a]He that *gathered* much, had nothing over, and he that *gathered* little, had not the less.

16   [1]And thanks *be* unto God, which had put in the heart of Titus the same care for you.

17   Because he accepted the exhortation, yea, he was so careful that of his own accord he went unto you.

18   And we have sent also with him the brother, whose praise *is* [1]in the Gospel throughout all the Churches.

19   (And not so only, but is also chosen of the Churches to be a fellow in our journey, concerning this [1]grace that is ministered by us unto the glory of the same Lord, and *declaration* of your prompt mind.)

20   Avoiding this, that no man should blame us in this [1]abundance that is ministered by us,

21   [b]Providing for honest things, not only before the Lord, but also before men.

22   And we have sent with them our brother, whom we have ofttimes proved to be diligent in many things, but now much more diligent, for the great confidence, which *I have* in you.

23   Whether *any do inquire* of Titus, *he is* my fellow and helper to you-ward: or of our [1]brethren, they are messengers of the Churches, *and* the [2]glory of

---

8:1 [1] The sixth part of this epistle containing divers exhortations to stir up the Corinthians to liberality, wherewith the poverty of the Church of Jerusalem might be holpen in time convenient. And first of all he setteth out before them the example of the Churches of Macedonia, which otherwise were brought by great misery to extreme poverty, to the end that they should follow them.

  [2] The benefit that God bestowed upon the Churches.

8:2 [1] For those manifold afflictions wherewith the Lord tried them, did not only not quail their joyful readiness, but also made it much more excellent, and famous.

8:3 [1] Of their own accord they were liberal.

8:4 [1] He calleth that, Grace, that other men would have called a burden. And this verse is to be expounded by the sixth verse.

8:5 [1] He amplifieth the forwardness of the Macedonians, in this, that they also desired Paul to stir up the Corinthians to accomplish the giving of alms, by sending again of Titus unto them.

8:8 [1] Thirdly he warneth them that they deceive not their expectation which they have conceived of them.

  [2] At the request of the Macedonians.

  [3] Then appeareth the naturalness of our love, when as in deed and that frankly and freely we help our brethren, even for Christ's sake.

8:9 [1] The fourth argument taken from the example of Christ.

8:10 [1] He taketh good heed that he seem not to wrest it out of them by constraint, for unless it be voluntary, God doth not accept it.

  [2] Not only to do, but also to do willingly: for he noteth out a ready willingness without any enforcement by any other men; much less came it of ambition and vainglory.

8:12 [1] Against such as use to excuse themselves, because they are not rich, as though it were only proper to rich men to help the poor.

8:13 [1] Christian liberality is mutual, that proportion may be observed.

  [2] That like as now in your abundance you help others, which are poor, with some part of your goods, so should others in like sort bestow some of theirs upon you.

8:16 [1] He commendeth Titus and his two companions for many causes, both that their credit might not be suspected, as though he had sent them slyly to spoil the Churches, and also that they might be so much the readier to contribute.

8:18 [1] In the preaching of the Gospel.

8:19 [1] These alms which are bestowed for the relief of the Church of Jerusalem.

8:20 [1] In this plentiful liberality of the Churches, which is committed to our trust.

8:23 [1] Titus's two companions.

  [2] By whom the glory of Christ is set forth.

Christ.

24 Wherefore show toward them, and before the [1]Churches the proof of your love, and of the rejoicing that we have of you.

9
1 Why, albeit he think well of their ready wills, 3 yet earnestly exhorteth them, 4 he yieldeth a reason: 6 He compareth alms to seed sowing, 10 which God doth repay with great gain.

1 For [1]as touching the ministering to the Saints, it is superfluous for me to write unto you.

2 For I know your readiness of mind, whereof I boast myself of you unto them of Macedonia, *and say*, that Achaia was prepared a year ago, and your zeal hath provoked many.

3 Now have I sent the brethren, lest our rejoicing over you should be in vain in this behalf, that ye (as I have said) be ready.

4 Lest if they of Macedonia come with me, and find you unprepared, we (that we may not say, you) should be ashamed in this my [1]constant boasting.

5 Wherefore, I thought it necessary to exhort the brethren to come before unto you; and to finish your benevolence appointed afore, that it might be ready, *and come* as of benevolence, and not as of [1]niggardliness.

6 [1]This yet *remember*, that he which soweth sparingly, shall reap also sparingly, and he that soweth liberally, shall reap also liberally.

7 As every man [1]wisheth in his heart, *so let him give*, not [a,2]grudgingly, or of [3]necessity: for God loveth

a cheerful giver.

8 And God is able to make all [1]grace to abound toward you, that ye always having all sufficiency in all things, may abound in [2]every good work,

9 ([b]As it is written, He hath sparsed abroad and hath given to the poor: his benevolence remaineth for [1]ever.

10 Also he that findeth seed to the sower, will minister likewise bread for food, and multiply your seed, and increase the [1]fruits of your benevolence.)

11 That on all parts ye may be made rich unto all liberality, which causeth through us thanksgiving unto God.

12 [1]For the ministration of this service not only supplieth the necessities of the Saints, but also abundantly causeth many to give thanks to God,

13 (Which by the [1]experiment of this ministration praise God for your [2]voluntary submission to the Gospel of Christ, and for your liberal distribution to them, and to all men.)

14 And in their prayer for you, to long after you greatly, for the abundant grace of God in you.

15 [1]Thanks therefore *be* unto God for his unspeakable gift.

10
2 He showeth with what confidence, 4 with what weapons, 6 and with what revenge he is armed against the cavillations of the wicked, 7 and that, when he is present, his deeds have no less power, 11 than his words have force when he is absent.

1 Now [1]I Paul myself beseech you by the meek-

8:24 [1] All Churches shall be witnesses of this your godly dealing, in whose presence you are, for so much as you see the messengers whom they have chosen by all their consents, and sent them unto you.

9:1 [1] He wisely meeteth with the suspicion which the Corinthians might conceive, as though the Apostle in urging them so carefully, should doubt of their good will. Therefore he witnesseth that he doeth it not to teach them that they ought to help the Saints, seeing that he had become surety for them to the Macedonians, but only to stir them up which were running of themselves to the end that all things might both be in a better readiness, and also be more plentiful.

9:4 [1] The word which he useth, signifieth such a stayedness and settledness of mind, as cannot be moved with any terror or fear.

9:5 [1] As from covetous men.

9:6 [1] Alms must be given neither niggardly, nor with a loathful mind, or hardly: But as frank and free alms is compared to a sowing which hath a most plentiful harvest of most abundant blessing following it.

9:7 [1] Determineth and appointeth freely with himself.

[2] With a sparing and niggardly heart.

[3] Against his will, as loath to be evil reported of.

9:8 [1] All God's bountiful liberality.

[2] To help others by all means possible, in doing them good in their necessities.

9:9 [1] Is everlasting: Now David speaketh of a man that feareth God, and loveth his neighbor, who shall never want (saith he) to give to others.

9:10 [1] There is none so good an inheritance to the godly, as bountifulness is.

9:12 [1] Another excellent and double fruit of liberality towards the Saints, is this: that it giveth occasion to praise God, and that our faith is also thereby made manifest.

9:13 [1] By this proof of your liberality in this helping and succoring of them.

[2] In showing with one consent, that you acknowledge that only Gospel which you have willingly submitted yourselves unto, declaring thereby, that you agree with the Church of Jerusalem.

9:15 [1] Lest by his great commendation and praise, the Corinthians should be puffed up, he shutteth up this exhortation, with this exclamation.

10:1 [1] He returneth to the defense of his Apostleship, but so that he useth this authority therein: for he warneth them earnestly and gravely, using also terrible threatenings to show themselves such as are apt to be instructed. And he refelleth certain proud men which made no better accompt of him, than of a bragging Thraso, in that he used to be sharp against them when he was absent, because they saw no great majesty in him after the manner of men, and besides, had proved his lenity, notwithstanding that in his absence, he had written to them sharply. Therefore first of all he professeth that he was gentle and moderate, but after the example of Christ: but if they continue, still to despise his gentleness, he protesteth unto them that he will show indeed how far they are deceived, which make that accompt of the office of an Apostle, that they do of worldly offices, that is, according to the outward appearance.

ness, and ²gentleness of Christ, which when I am present among you *am* base, but am bold toward you being absent:

2 And *this* I require you, that I need not to be bold when I am present, with that same confidence, wherewith I think to be bold against some, which esteem us as though we walked ¹according to the flesh.

3 ¹Nevertheless, though we walk in the flesh, yet we do not war after the flesh.

4 (For the weapons of our warfare are not ¹carnal, but mighty through ²God, to cast down holds.)

5 Casting down the imaginations, and every high thing that is exalted against the knowledge of God, ¹and bringing into captivity every thought to the obedience of Christ,

6 And having ready the vengeance against all disobedience, when your obedience is fulfilled.

7 ¹Look ye on things after the ²appearance? If any man trust in himself that he is Christ's, let him consider this again of ³himself, that as he is Christ's, even so *are* we Christ's.

8 For though I should boast somewhat more of our authority, which the Lord hath given us for edification, and not for your destruction, I should have no shame.

9 *This I say,* that I may not seem as *it were* to fear you with letters.

10 For the letters, saith ¹he, are sore and strong, but his bodily presence is weak, and his speech is of no value.

11 Let such one think this, that such as we are in word by letters, when we are absent, such *will we be*

CHAPTER 10
a Eph. 4:7
b Jer. 9:24
1 Cor. 1:31

also in deed, when we are present.

12 ¹For we ²dare not make ourselves of the number, or to compare ourselves to them, which praise themselves: but they understand not that they measure themselves with ³themselves, and ⁴compare themselves with themselves.

13 But we will not rejoice of things, which are not within *our* ¹measure, *ᵇ*but according to the measure of the line, whereof God hath distributed unto us a measure to attain even unto you.

14 For we stretch not ourselves beyond *our* measure, as though we had not attained unto you: for even to you also have we come *in preaching* the Gospel of Christ,

15 Not boasting of things which are ¹without *our* measure: *that is,* of other men's labors: and we hope, when your faith shall increase, to be magnified by you according to your line abundantly,

16 And to preach the Gospel in those *regions* which *are* beyond you: not to rejoice in ¹another man's line: *that is,* in the things that are prepared already.

17 *ᵇ*¹But let him that rejoiceth, rejoice in the Lord.

18 For he that praiseth himself, is not allowed, but he whom the Lord praiseth.

11

2 He testifieth that for the great loves sake he beareth to the Corinthians, he is compelled 5 to utter his *own praises:* 9 *and that he bestowed his labor on them without any reward,* 13 *that the false apostles should not surpass him in anything,* 22 *whom he far excelled in those things which are praiseworthy indeed.*

1 Would ¹to God, ye could suffer a little my

10:1 ² That nature which is inclined to mercy, rather than to rigor of justice.

10:2 ¹ As though I had no other aid and help than that which outwardly I seem to have: and therefore Paul setteth his flesh, that is, his weak condition and state, against his spiritual and Apostolic dignity.

10:3 ¹ Secondly he witnesseth, that although he be like unto other men, yet he cometh furnished with that strength, which no holds of man can match, whether they resist by craft and deceit, or by force and might, because he warrioreth with divine weapons.

10:4 ¹ Are not such as men get them authority withall one of another, and do great acts.

² Stand upon that infinite power of God.

10:5 ¹ An amplification of this spiritual virtue, which in such sort conquereth the enemies be they never so crafty and mighty, that it bringeth some of them by repentance unto Christ, and justly revengeth others, that are stubbornly obstinate, separating them from the others which suffer themselves to be ruled.

10:7 ¹ He beateth into their heads that same matter, with great weight of words and sentences.

² Do ye judge of things according to the outward show.

³ Not being told of it by me.

10:10 ¹ He noteth out someone that was the seeds man of this speech.

10:12 ¹ Being constrained to refel the foolish brags of certain ambitious men, he witnesseth, that they are able to bring nothing, but that they falsely persuade themselves of themselves: and as for him-

self, although he brags of excellent things, yet he will not pass the bounds which God hath measured him out, according whereunto he came even unto them in preaching the Gospel of Christ, and trusteth that he shall go further, when they have so profited that he shall not need to tarry any longer amongst them to instruct them. And hereunto is added an amplification, in that he never succeeded other men in their labors.

² This is spoken after a taunting sort.

³ Upon a vain persuasion that they have of themselves, they take upon them they care not what.

⁴ They condemn all others, and measure all their doings only by themselves.

10:13 ¹ Of those things which God hath not measured to me.

10:15 ¹ As though God had divided the whole world among the Apostles, to be husbanded.

10:16 ¹ In countries which other men have prepared and husbanded with the preaching of the Gospel.

10:17 ¹ He somewhat mitigateth that which he spake of himself and therewith also prepareth the Corinthians to hear other things, witnessing that he seeketh nothing else but to approve himself to God, whose glory he only seeketh.

11:1 ¹ He granteth that after a sort he playeth the fool in this vaunting of things, but he addeth that he doeth it against his will, for their profit because he seeth them deceived by certain vain and crafty men, through the craft and subtlety of Satan.

foolishness, and indeed, ye suffer me.

2   For I am jealous over you, with ¹godly jealousy: for I have prepared you for one husband, to ²present you *as* a pure virgin to Christ:

3   But I fear lest as the ªserpent beguiled Eve through his subtlety, so your minds should be ¹corrupt from the simplicity that is in ²Christ:

4   ¹For if he that cometh, preacheth ²another Jesus whom we have not preached: or if ye receive another spirit whom ye have not received: either another Gospel which ye have not received, ye might well have suffered *him*.

5   Verily I suppose that I was not inferior to the very chief Apostles.

6   ¹And though *I be* ²rude in speaking, yet *I am* not *so* in knowledge, but among you we have been made manifest to the uttermost, in all things.

7   ¹Have I committed an offence, because I abased myself, that ye might be exalted, and because I preached to you the Gospel of God freely?

8   I robbed other Churches, and took wages *of them* to do you service.

9   And when I was present with you, and had need, ᵇI was not slothful to the hindrance of any man: for that which was lacking unto me, the brethren which came from Macedonia, supplied, and in all things I kept, ¹and will keep myself, that I should not be grievous unto you.

10   The ¹truth of Christ is in me, that this rejoicing

CHAPTER 11
ª Gen. 3:4
ᵇ 2 Cor. 12:13

shall not be ²shut up against me in the regions of Achaia.

11   Wherefore? because I love you not? God knoweth.

12   But what I do, that will I do, that I may cut away occasion from them which desire occasion, that they might be found like unto us in that wherein they ¹rejoice.

13   ¹For such false apostles are deceitful workers, and transform themselves into the Apostles of Christ.

14   And no marvel: for Satan himself is transformed into an Angel of ¹light.

15   Therefore it is no great thing, though his ministers transform themselves, as though *they were* the ministers of righteousness, whose end shall be according to their works.

16   ¹I say again, Let no man think that I am foolish, or else take me even as a fool, that I also may boast myself a little.

17   That I speak, I speak it not after the Lord: but as *it were* foolishly, in this *my* great boasting.

18   Seeing that many rejoice after [the] flesh, I will rejoice also.

19   For ye suffer fools gladly, because that ye are wise.

20   ¹For ye suffer, even if a man bring you into bondage, if a man devour *you*, if a man take *your* goods, if a man exalt himself, if a man smite you on the face.

11:2 ¹ He speaketh as a woer, but yet as one that seeketh them not for himself, but for God.

² To marry you together.

11:3 ¹ This place is to be marked against them which loathe that plain and pure simplicity of the Scriptures, in comparison of the colors and paintings of man's eloquence.

² Which is meet for them that are in Christ.

11:4 ¹ He showeth that they deceive themselves, if they look to receive of any other man, either a more excellent Gospel, or more excellent gifts of the holy Ghost.

² A more perfect doctrine of Jesus Christ.

11:6 ¹ He refuteth the slanders of those Thrasoes. I grant, saith he, that I am not so eloquent an Orator, but yet they cannot take away the knowledge of the Gospel from me, whereof you have had good proof, and that every manner of way.

² Paul lacked not the kind of eloquence which is meet for a man, and fit for the Gospel, but he willingly wanted that painted kind of speech, which too many nowadays hunt after and follow.

11:7 ¹ Another slander, to wit, that he was a rascal, and lived by the labor of his own hands. But herein, saith the Apostle, what can you lay against me, but that I was content to take any pains for your sakes, and when I lacked, to travail for my living with mine own hands in part, and partly also when poverty constrained me, I chose rather otherwise to seek my sustenance, than to be any burden to you, although I preached the Gospel unto you?

11:9 ¹ An amplification: so far is he from being ashamed of this act, that he hath also resolved with himself to do no otherwise hereafter amongst them, to the intent that it may always be truly said, that he taught in Achaia for nothing: not that he disdaineth the Corinthians,

but that these Thrasoes may never find the occasion which they have already sought for, and he in the mean season may set something before them to follow, that at length they may truly say, that they are like to Paul.

11:10 ¹ This is a form of an oath, as if he said, let me not be thought to have any truth in me.

² Shall be always open to me.

11:12 ¹ Paul's adversaries sought all occasions they could, to be equal to him. And therefore seeing they had rather eat up the Corinthians, than preach to them for nothing, they sought another occasion, to wit, to make Paul to take something: which thing if he had done, then hoped they by that means to be equal to him: for they made such a show of zeal and knowledge, and set it forth with such a glossing kind of eloquence, that some of them even despised Paul: but he showeth that all this is nothing but colors and painting.

11:13 ¹ Now at length he pointeth out these fellows in their colors, forewarning that it will come to pass, that they will at length betray themselves, what countenance soever they make of zeal that they have to God's glory.

11:14 ¹ By light is meant the heavenly glory, whereof the Angels are partakers.

11:16 ¹ He goeth forward boldly, and using a vehement Irony of kind of taunting, desireth the Corinthians to pardon him, if for a time he contend as a fool before them being wise, with those jolly fellows touching those eternal things, to wit, touching his stock, his ancestors and valiant acts.

11:20 ¹ Before he cometh to the matter, he toucheth the Corinthians, who persuading themselves to very wise men, did not mark in the mean season that those false apostles abused their simplicity for advantage.

21 I speak as concerning the [1]reproach: as though that we had been [2]weak: but wherein any man is bold (I speak foolishly) I am bold also.

22 They are Hebrews, [c]so am I: they are Israelites, so am I: they are the seed of Abraham, so am I.

23 They are the ministers of Christ (I speak as a fool) I am [1]more: in labors more abundant: in stripes above measure: in prison more plenteously: in [2]death oft.

24 Of the Jews [1]five times received I forty *stripes* save one.

25 I was [1]thrice [d]beaten with rods: I was [e]once stoned: I suffered thrice [f]shipwreck: night and day have I been in the deep sea.

26 In journeying *I was* often, in perils of waters, in perils of robbers, in perils of mine own nation, in perils among the Gentiles, in perils in the city, in perils in wilderness, in perils in the sea, in perils among false brethren,

27 In weariness and [1]painfulness, in watching often, in hunger and thirst, in fastings often, in cold and in nakedness.

28 [1]Beside the things which are outward, I am cumbered daily, *and have* the care of all the Churches.

29 Who is weak, and I am not weak? Who is offended, and I burn not?

30 [1]If I must needs rejoice, I will rejoice of mine infirmities.

31 The God, even the Father of our Lord Jesus Christ, which is blessed for evermore, knoweth that I lie not.

c Phil. 3:5
d Acts 16:23
e Acts 14:19
f Acts 27:14
g Acts 9:24

32 In [g]Damascus the governor of the people under King Aretas, laid watch in the city of the Damascenes, and would have caught me.

33 But at a window was I let down in a basket through the wall, and escaped his hands.

12

1 He doth even unwillingly make rehearsal, 3 of the heavenly visions, 4 that were revealed unto him, 6 for which though he might indeed glory, yet he will not, 10 being privy of his own infirmities: 11 but they drive him to this kind of folly, 20 in that they give ear to certain vainglorious persons, who draw them from Christ.

1 It [1]is not expedient for me no doubt to rejoice: for I will come to visions and revelations of the Lord.

2 I know a man [1]in Christ above fourteen years ago, (whether *he were* in the body, I cannot tell, or out of the body, I cannot tell: God knoweth) which was taken up into the [2]third heaven.

3 And I know such a man (whether in the body, or out of the body, I cannot tell: God knoweth.)

4 How that he was taken up into [1]Paradise, and heard words which [2]cannot be spoken, which are not [3]possible for man to utter.

5 [1]Of such a man will I rejoice: of myself will I not rejoice, except it be of mine infirmities.

6 For though I would rejoice, I should not be a fool, for I will say the truth: but I refrain, lest any man should think of me above that he seeth in me, or that he heareth of me.

7 [1]And lest I should be exalted out of measure

11:21 [1] As if he said, in respect of that reproach which they do unto you (I speak it) which surely is as evil as if they did beat you.

[2] Paul is called weak, in that he seemeth to the Corinthians a vile and abject man, a beggarly artificer, a most wretched and miserable idiot, whereas notwithstanding therein God's mighty power was made manifest.

11:23 [1] Paul being honorable indeed, defendeth his ministry openly, not for his own sake, but because he saw his doctrine come into hazard.

[2] In danger of present death.

11:24 [1] He alludeth to that that is written, Deut. 25:3, and moreover this place showeth us, that Paul suffered many things which Luke passed over.

11:25 [1] Of the Roman Magistrates.

11:27 [1] Painfulness is a troublesome sickness, as when a man who is weary and would rest, he is constrained to fall to new labor.

11:28 [1] He addeth this in conclusion further, that the Corinthians might be ashamed to despise him, upon whose care almost all Churches depended, as it was plainly seen by experience.

11:30 [1] He turneth that against the adversaries, which they objected against him: as if he should say, They allege my calamities, to take away my authority from me: but if I would boast myself, I would take no better argument: and God himself is my witness that I devise and forge nothing.

12:1 [1] He goeth forward in his purpose, and because those bragging mates boasted of revelations, he reckoneth up those things

which lift him up above the common capacity of men: but he useth a preface, and excuseth himself advisedly.

12:2 [1] I speak this in Christ, that is, be it spoken without vainglory, for I seek nothing but Christ Jesus only.

[2] Into the highest heaven: for we need not to dispute subtly upon the word (Third) but yet this place is to be marked against them which would make heaven to [be] everywhere.

12:4 [1] So the Grecians name that which we call a park, that is to say, a place where trees are planted, and wild beasts kept, by which name they that translated the old Testament out of the Hebrew into Greek, called the garden Eden, whereunto Adam was put straight after his creation, as a most delicate and pleasant place. And hereunto grew it, that that blessed seat of the glory of God is called by that name.

[2] Which no man is able to utter.

[3] Which the Saints themselves are not by any means able to express, because it is God himself. Thus doth Clement Alexandria expound this place, Strom. 5.

12:5 [1] To remove all suspicion of ambition he witnesseth that he braggeth not of those things as his own, but as out of himself, and yet notwithstanding faineth nothing, lest by this occasion other men should attribute more unto him than indeed he is: and therefore he had rather glory in his miseries.

12:7 [1] An excellent doctrine: why God will have even his best servants to be vexed of Satan and by all kinds of temptations, to wit, lest they should be too much puffed up, and also that they may be made perfect by that continual exercise.

through the abundance of revelations, there was given unto me a ²prick in the flesh, the messenger of ³Satan to buffet me, because I should not be exalted out of measure.

8   For this thing I besought the Lord ¹thrice, that it might depart from me.

9   And he said unto me, My grace is sufficient for thee: for my power is made perfect through weakness. ¹Very gladly therefore will I rejoice rather in mine infirmities, that the power of Christ may ²dwell in me.

10   Therefore I take ¹pleasure in infirmities, in reproaches, in necessities, in persecutions, in anguish for Christ's sake: for when I am weak, then am I strong.

11   I was a fool to boast myself: ye have compelled me: ¹for I ought to have been commended of you: for in nothing was I inferior unto the very chief Apostles, though I be nothing.

12   The ¹signs of an Apostle were wrought among you with all patience, with signs, and wonders and great works.

13   For what is it, wherein ye were inferiors unto other Churches, ᵃexcept that I have not been ¹slothful to your hindrance? forgive me this wrong.

14   Behold, the third time I am ready to come unto you, and yet will I not be slothful to your hindrance: for I seek not yours, but you: for the children ought not to lay up for the fathers, but the fathers for the children.

15   And I will most gladly bestow, and will be bestowed for your souls: though the more I love you, the less I am loved.

16   ¹But be it that I charged you not: yet for as much as I was crafty, I took you with guile.

CHAPTER 12
ᵃ 2 Cor. 11:9

CHAPTER 13
ᵃ Deut. 19:17
Matt. 18:16
John 8:17
Heb. 10:28

17   Did I pill you by any of them whom I sent unto you?

18   I have desired Titus, and with him I have sent a brother: did Titus pill you of any things? walked we not in the selfsame spirit? walked we not in the same steps?

19   ¹Again, think ye that we excuse ourselves unto you? we speak before God in ²Christ. But we do all things, dearly beloved, for your edifying.

20   ¹For I fear lest when I come, I shall not find you such as I would: and that I shall be found unto you such as ye would not: and lest there be strife, envying, wrath, contentions, backbitings, whisperings, swellings, and discord.

21   I fear lest when I come again, my God abase me among you, and I shall bewail many of them which have sinned already, and have not repented of the uncleanness, and fornication, and wantonness which they have committed.

13

1 Coming the third time,   2 he denounceth the sharper vengeance toward them,   4 who have a perfect trial of the power of Christ in his Apostleship: 7 At length he prayeth for their repentance,   11 And wisheth them prosperity.

1   Lo this is the third time that I come unto you. ᵃIn the mouth of two or three witnesses shall every word stand.

2   I told you before, and tell you before: as though I had been present the second time, so write I now being absent to them, which heretofore have sinned, and to all others, that if I come again, I will not spare,

3   ¹Seeing that ye seek experience of Christ, that speaketh in me, which toward you is not weak, but

---

² He meaneth concupiscence, that sticketh fast in us, as it were a prick, insomuch that it constrained Paul himself being regenerate, to cry out, I do not that good that I would, etc. And he calleth it a prick, by a borrowed kind of speech taken from thorns, or stumps, which are very dangerous and hurtful for the feet, if a man walks through woods that are cut down.

³ Which setteth those lusts on fire.

12:8 ¹ Oft.

12:9 ¹ He concludeth, that he will only see his miseries against the vain brags of the false apostles, and therewith also excuseth himself, for that by their importunity, he was constrained to speak so much of these things as he did: to wit, because that if his Apostleship were subverted his doctrine must needs fall.

² That I might feel the virtue of Christ more and more: For the weaker that our tabernacles are, the more doth Christ's virtue appear in them.

12:10 ¹ I do not only take them patiently and with a good heart, but also I take great pleasure in them.

12:11 ¹ Again he maketh the Corinthians witnesses of those things whereby God had sealed his Apostleship amongst them, and again he desireth by certain arguments, how far he is from all covetous-

ness, and also how he is affectioned towards them.

12:12 ¹ The arguments whereby it may well appear, that I am indeed an Apostle of Jesus Christ.

12:13 ¹ I was not slothful in getting my living with mine own hands, that I might not be burdensome to you.

12:16 ¹ He putteth away another most grievous slander, to wit, that he did subtly and by others, make his gain and profit of them.

12:19 ¹ He concludeth, that he writeth not these things unto them, as though he needed to defend himself, for he is guilty of nothing: but because it is behoovable for them to doubt nothing of his fidelity who instructed them.

² As it becometh him to speak truly and sincerely, that professeth himself to be in Christ, that is to say, to be a Christian.

12:20 ¹ Having confirmed his authority unto them, he rebuketh them sharply, and threateneth them also like an Apostle, showing that he will not spare them hereafter, unless they repent, seeing that this is the third time that he hath warned them.

13:3 ¹ A most sharp reprehension, for that, while they despise the Apostle's admonitions, they tempt Christ's own patience: and also while they condemn him as wretched and miserable, they lay nothing herein against him, which is not common to him with Christ.

is [2]mighty in you.

4 For though he was crucified concerning [1]*his* infirmity, yet liveth he through the power of God. And we no doubt are weak in him, but we shall live with him, through the power of God toward you.

5 [b,1]Prove yourselves whether ye are in the faith: examine yourselves: know ye not your own selves, how that Jesus Christ is in you, except ye be reprobates?

6 [1]But I trust that ye shall know that we are not reprobates.

7 Now I pray unto God that ye do none evil, not that we should seem approved, but that ye should do that which is honest: though we be as [1]reprobates.

8 For we cannot *do* anything against the truth, but for the truth.

[b] 1 Cor. 11:28
[c] 1 Cor. 16:20

9 For we are glad when we are weak, and that ye are strong: this also we wish for, *even* your [1]perfection.

10 Therefore write I these things being absent, lest when I am present, I should use sharpness, according to the power which the Lord hath given me, to edification, and not to destruction.

11 [1]Finally brethren, fare ye well: be perfect: be of good comfort: be of one mind: live in peace, and the God of love and peace shall be with you.

12 [1]Greet one another with an 'holy kiss. All the Saints salute you.

13 The grace of our Lord Jesus Christ, and the love of God, and the communion of the holy Ghost be with you all, Amen.

¶ The second *Epistle* to the Corinthians, written from Philippi, a city in Macedonia, *and sent* by Titus and Lucas.

13:3 [2] And will be most mighty to be revenged of you, when need shall be.

13:4 [1] As touching that base form of a servant which he took upon him when he abased himself.

13:5 [1] He confirmeth that which he spake of the virtue of God appearing in his ministry, and he gathereth by the mutual relation between the people's faith and the minister's preaching, that they must either reverence his Apostleship, upon whose doctrine their faith is grounded, or they must condemn themselves of infidelity, and must confess themselves not to be of Christ's body.

13:6 [1] He mitigateth that sharpness, trusting that they will show

themselves towards their faithful Apostle, apt and willingly to be taught: adding this moreover, that he passeth not for his own fame and estimation, so that he may serve to their salvation, which is the only mark that he shooteth at.

13:7 [1] In men's judgment.

13:9 [1] That all things may be in good order amongst you, and the members of the Church restored into their place, which have been shaken and out of place.

13:11 [1] A brief exhortation, but yet such an one as comprehendeth all the parts of a Christian man's life.

13:12 [1] He saluteth them familiarly, and in conclusion wisheth well unto them.

THE EPISTLE OF THE APOSTLE PAUL TO THE

GALATIANS

1 *1 Straight after the salutation, 6 He reprehendeth the Galatians for revolting, 9 from his Gospel, 15 which he received from God, 17 before he had communicated with any of the Apostles.*

CHAPTER 1
a Titus 1:3
b Luke 1:74
c 1 Cor. 15:1
d Acts 9:8

1 Paul [1]an Apostle (not [2]of men, neither by [3]man, [a]but by [4]Jesus Christ, and God the Father which hath raised him from the dead.)

2 And all the brethren which are with me unto the Churches of Galatia:

3 Grace *be* with you, and peace from God the Father, and *from* our Lord Jesus Christ,

4 [1]Which gave himself for our sins, that he might deliver us [b]from this present evil [2]world according to the will of God even our Father,

5 To whom *be* glory forever and ever, Amen.

6 [1]I marvel that ye are so soon [2]removed away unto another Gospel, from him that had called you in the grace of Christ,

7 [1]Which is not another *Gospel,* save that there be some which trouble you, and intend to [2]pervert the Gospel of Christ.

8 But though that we, or an Angel from heaven preach unto you otherwise than that which we have preached unto you, let him be [1]accursed.

9 As we said before, so say I now again, If any man preach unto you otherwise than that ye have received, let him be accursed.

10 [1]For now preach I [2]man's *doctrine,* or God's? or go I about to please men? for if I should yet please men, I were not the servant of Christ.

11 [c,1]Now I certify you, brethren, that the Gospel which was preached of me, was not after man.

12 For neither received I it of man, neither was I taught it, but by the [1]revelation of Jesus Christ.

13 [1]For ye have heard of my conversation in time past, in the Jewish religion, how that [d]I persecuted

---

1:1 [1] A salutation comprehending in few words, the sum of the Apostle's doctrine, and also besides straightway from the beginning, showing the gravity meet for the authority of an Apostle, which he had to maintain against the false apostles.

[2] He showeth who is the author of the minister generally: for herein the whole ministry agreeth, that whether they be Apostles, or Shepherds, or Doctors, they are appointed of God.

[3] He toucheth the instrumental cause: for this is a peculiar prerogative to the Apostles, to be called immediately from Christ.

[4] Christ no doubt is man, but he is God also, and head of the Church, and in this respect to be exempted out of the number of men.

1:4 [1] The sum of the true Gospel is this, that Christ by his only offering, saveth us being chosen out from the world, by the free decree of God the Father.

[2] Out of that [most] corrupt state which is without Christ.

1:6 [1] The first part of the Epistle wherein he witnesseth that he is an Apostle, nothing inferior to those chief disciples of Christ, and wholly agreeing with them, whose names the false apostles did abuse. And he beginneth with chiding, reproving them of lightness for that they have ear so easily unto them which perverted them and drew them away to a new Gospel.

[2] He useth the passive voice, to cast the fault upon the false apostles, and he useth the time that now is, to give them to understand, that it was not already done, but in doing.

1:7 [1] He warneth them in time to remember that there are not many Gospels, and therefore whatsoever these false apostles pretend which had the Law, Moses and the Fathers in their mouths, yet they are in deed so many corruptions of the true Gospel, insomuch that he himself, yea, and the very Angels themselves, (and therefore much more these false apostles) ought to be holden accursed, if they

go about to change the least iota that may be in the Gospel, that he delivered to them before.

[2] For there is nothing more contrary to faith or free justification, than justification by the Law, or by our deserving.

1:8 [1] See Rom. 9:3.

1:10 [1] A confirmation taken both from the nature of the doctrine itself, and also from that manner which he useth in teaching: for neither saith he, did I teach those things which pleased men as these men do which put part of salvation in external things, and works of the Law, neither went I about to procure any man's favor. And therefore the matter itself showeth that that doctrine which I delivered unto you, is heavenly.

[2] He toucheth the false apostles who had nothing but men in their mouths, and he, though he would derogate nothing from the Apostles, preacheth God and not men.

1:11 [1] A second argument to prove that this doctrine is heavenly, because he had it from heaven, from Jesus Christ himself, without any man's help, wherein he excelleth them whom Christ taught here on earth after the manner of men.

1:12 [1] This place is to be understood of an extraordinary revelation, for otherwise the Son alone revealed his Gospel by his Spirit, although by the ministry of men, which Paul shutteth out here.

1:13 [1] He proveth that he was extraordinarily taught of Christ himself, by the history of his former life, which the Galatians themselves know well enough: for saith he, it is well known in what school I was brought up, even from a child, to wit, amongst the deadly enemies of the Gospel. And no man may cavil and say that I was a scholar of the Pharisees in name only and not in deed, no man is ignorant, how that I excelled in Pharisaism, and was suddenly made of a Pharisee, an Apostle of the Gentiles, so that I had no space to be instructed of men.

the Church of God extremely, and wasted it,

14 And profited in the Jewish religion above many of my companions of mine own nation, and was much more zealous of the ¹traditions of my fathers.

15 But when it pleased God (which had ¹separated me from my mother's womb, and called *me* by his grace.)

16 To reveal his Son ¹in me, that I should preach him ᵉamong the Gentiles immediately, ²I communicated not with ³flesh and blood:

17 Neither came I again to Jerusalem to them which were Apostles before me, but I went into Arabia, and turned again unto Damascus.

18 Then after three years I came again to Jerusalem, to visit Peter, and abode with him fifteen days.

19 And none other of the Apostles saw I, save James the Lord's brother.

20 Now the things which I write unto you, behold, I *witness* ¹before God, that I lie not.

21 After that, I went into the coasts of Syria and Cilicia: for I was unknown by face unto the Churches of Judea which were in Christ.

22 But they had heard only *some say*, He which persecuted us in time past, now preacheth the ¹faith which before he destroyed.

23 And they glorified God for me.

2 1 *That the Apostles did nothing disagree from his Gospel,* 3 *he declareth by the example of Titus being uncircumcised,* 11 *and also by his . . . the same against Peter's dissimulation.* 17 *And so he passeth to the handling of our free justification by Christ, etc.*

ᵉ Eph. 3:8

CHAPTER 2
ᵈ Deut. 10:17
2 Chron. 19:7
Job 34:19
Acts 10:34
Rom. 2:11
Eph. 6:9
Col. 3:25
1 Pet. 1:17

1 Then ¹fourteen years after, I went up again to Jerusalem with Barnabas, and took with me Titus also.

2 And I went up by revelation, and declared unto them that Gospel which I preach among the Gentiles, but particularly to them that were the chief, lest by any means I should run, or had run ¹in vain:

3 But neither yet Titus which was with me, though he were a Grecian, was compelled to be circumcised,

4 To wit, for the ¹false brethren which were craftily sent in, and crept in privily to spy out our liberty which we have in Christ Jesus, that they might bring us into bondage.

5 To whom we gave not place by ¹subjection for an hour, that the ²truth of the Gospel might continue with ³you.

6 But by them which seemed to be great, *I was not taught* (whatsoever they were in time passed, I am nothing the better: ᵃGod accepteth no man's person) for they that are the chief, did add nothing to me *above that I had.*

7 But contrariwise, when they saw that the Gospel over the ¹uncircumcision was committed unto me, as *the Gospel* over the circumcision was unto Peter:

8 (For he that was mighty by Peter in the Apostleship over the circumcision, was also mighty by me toward the Gentiles.)

9 And when James, and Cephas, and John, knew of the grace that was given unto me, which are ¹counted to be pillars, they gave to me and to Barnabas the right ²hands of fellowship, that we *should preach* unto the Gentiles, and they unto the circumcision,

---

1:14 ¹ He calleth them the traditions of his Fathers, because he was not only a Pharisee himself, but also had a Pharisee to his father.

1:15 ¹ He speaketh of God's everlasting predestination, whereby he appointed him to be an Apostle, whereof he maketh three degrees, the everlasting counsel of God, his appointing from his mother's womb, and his calling: here is no mention at all, we see, of works foreseen.

1:16 ¹ To me, and this is a kind of speech which the Hebrews use, whereby this is given us to understand, that this gift cometh from God.

² Because it might be objected, that indeed he was called of Christ in the way, but afterwards was instructed of the Apostles and others, whose names (as I said before) the false apostles abused to destroy his Apostleship, as though he delivered another Gospel than the true Apostles did, and as though he were not of their number, which are to be credited without exception: therefore Paul answereth, that he began straightway after his calling to preach the Gospel at Damascus and in Arabia, and was not from that time in Jerusalem but only fifteen days, where he saw only Peter and James, and afterwards, he began to teach in Syria and Cilicia, with the consent and approbation of the Churches of the Jews, which knew him only by name, so far off was it, that he was there instructed of men.

³ With any man in the world.

1:20 ¹ This is a kind of an oath.

1:22 ¹ The doctrine of faith.

2:1 ¹ Now he showeth how he agreeth with the Apostles with

whom he granteth that he conferred touching his Gospel which he taught among the Gentiles, fourteen years after his conversion, and they allowed it in such sort, that they constrained not his fellow Titus to be circumcised, although some tormented themselves therein, which traitorously laid wait against him, but in vain: neither did they add the least iota that might be to the doctrine which he had preached, but contrariwise they gave to him and Barnabas the right hands of fellowship and acknowledged them as Apostles appointed of the Lord to the Gentiles.

2:2 ¹ Unfruitfully, for as touching his doctrine, Paul doubted not of it, but because there were certain reports cast abroad of him, that he was of another opinion than the rest of the Apostles were, which thing might have hindered the course of the Gospel, therefore he labored to remedy this sore.

2:4 ¹ Which by deceit, and counterfeit holiness crept in amongst the faithful.

2:5 ¹ By submitting ourselves to them, and betraying our own liberty.

² The true and sincere doctrine of the Gospel, which remained safe from being corrupt with any of these men's false doctrines.

³ Under the Galatians' name, he understandeth all nations.

2:7 ¹ Among the Gentiles, as Peter had to preach it among the Jews.

2:9 ¹ Whom alone and only, these men count for pillars of the Church, and whose name they abuse to deceive you.

² They gave us their hand in token that we agreed wholly in the doctrine of the Gospel.

10 *Warning* only that we should remember the poor: which thing also I was diligent to do.

11 ¶ And when Peter was come to Antioch, I withstood him to his ¹face: for he was to be condemned.

12 ¹For before that certain came from James, he ate with the Gentiles: but when they were come, he withdrew and separated himself, fearing them which were of the circumcision.

13 And the other Jews played the hypocrites likewise with him, insomuch that Barnabas was ¹led away with them by that their hypocrisy.

14 But when I saw, that they went not the ¹right way to the ²truth of the Gospel, I said unto Peter before all men, If thou being a Jew, livest as the Gentiles, and not like the Jews, why ³constrainest thou the Gentiles to do like the Jews?

15 ¹We *which are* Jews ²by nature, and not ³sinners of the Gentiles,

16 Know that a man is not justified by the works of the Law, but by the faith ¹of Jesus Christ, even we, *I say*, have believed in Jesus Christ, that we might be justified by the faith of Christ, and not by the works of the Law, because that by the works of the Law, ²no

b Rom. 3:19

flesh shall be justified.

17 ᵇ,¹If then while ²we seek to be made righteous by Christ, we ourselves are found sinners, is Christ therefore the minister of sin? God forbid.

18 For if I build again the things that I have destroyed, I make myself a trespasser.

19 For I through the Law am dead to the ¹Law, that I might live unto God.

20 I am crucified with Christ, but I live, *yet* not ¹I anymore, but Christ liveth in me: and in that I now live in the ²flesh, I live by the faith in the Son of God, who hath loved me, and given himself for me.

21 ¹I do not abrogate the grace of God: for if righteousness *be* by the Law, then Christ died without a ²cause.

3 *1 He rebuketh them, for suffering themselves to be drawn from the grace of free justification in Christ, most lively set out unto them. 6 He bringeth in Abraham's example, 10 declaring the effects, 21 and causes of the giving of the Law.*

1 ¹O foolish Galatians, who hath bewitched you, that ye should not obey the truth, to whom Jesus Christ before was described in your ²sight,

---

2:11 ¹ Before all men.

2:12 ¹ Another most vehement proof of his Apostleship, and also of that doctrine, which he had delivered concerning free justification by faith only because that for this thing only he reprehended Peter at Antioch, who offended herein, in that for a few Jews' sakes which came from Jerusalem he played the Jew, and offended the Gentiles which had believed.

2:13 ¹ By example rather than by judgment.

2:14 ¹ Word for word, with a right foot which he setteth against halting and dissembling which is backward.

² He calleth the truth of the Gospel both the doctrine itself, and also the use of doctrine, which we call the practice.

³ He saith they were constrained, which played the Jews by Peter's example.

2:15 ¹ The second part of this Epistle, the state whereof is this: we are justified by faith in Christ Jesus without the works of the Law: which thing he propoundeth in such sort, that first of all he meeteth with an objection, (for I also saith he am a Jew, that no man may say against me, that I am an enemy to the Law) and afterward, he confirmeth it by the express witness of David.

² Although we be Jews, yet we preach justification by faith because we know undoubtedly, that no man can be justified by the Law.

³ So the Jews called the Gentiles, because they were strangers from God's covenant.

2:16 ¹ In Jesus Christ.

² No man, and in this word (flesh) there is a great vehemence, whereby is meant that the nature of man is utterly corrupt.

2:17 ¹ Before he goeth any further, he meeteth with their objection, which abhorred this doctrine of free justification by faith, because say they, men are by this means withdrawn from the study of good works. And in this sort is the objection, If sinners should be justified through Christ by faith without the Law Christ should approve sinners, and should as it were exhort them thereunto by his ministry. Paul answereth that this consequence is false, because that Christ

destroyeth sin in the believers: For so saith he do men flee unto Christ, through the terror and fear of the Law that being quit from the curse of the Law and justified, they may be saved by him, that together therewithall, he beginneth in them by little and little, that strength and power of his which destroyeth sin: to the end that this old man being abolished by the virtue of Christ crucified, Christ may live in them, and they may consecrate themselves to God. Therefore if any man give himself to sin after he hath received the Gospel, let him not accuse Christ nor the Gospel, but himself, for that he destroyeth the work of God in himself.

² He goeth from justification to sanctification, which is another benefit we receive by Christ, if we lay hold on him by faith.

2:19 ¹ The Law that terrifieth the conscience, bringeth us to Christ, and he only causeth us to die to the Law indeed, because that by making us righteous, he taketh away from us the terror of conscience, and by sanctifying us, causeth through the mortifying of lust in us, that it cannot take such occasion to sin by the restraint which the Law maketh, as it did before, Rom. 7:10-11.

2:20 ¹ The same that I was before.

² In this mortal body.

2:21 ¹ The second argument taken of an absurdity: If men may be justified by the Law, then was it not necessary for Christ to die.

² For there was no cause why he should do so.

3:1 ¹ The third reason or argument taken of those gifts of the holy Ghost, wherewith they were endued from heaven after they had heard and believed the Gospel by Paul's ministry: which seeing they were so evident to all men's eyes, that they were as it were lively images, wherein they might behold the truth of the doctrine of the Gospel, no less than if they had beheld with their eyes Christ himself crucified, in whose only death they ought to have their trust, he marvelleth how it could be that they could be so bewitched by the false apostles.

² Christ was laid before you, so notably and so plainly, that you had his lively image as it were represented before your eyes, as if he had been crucified before you.

and among you crucified?

2 This only would I learn of you, Received ye the ¹Spirit by the works of the Law, or by the hearing of ²faith *preached?*

3 ¹Are ye so foolish, that after ye have begun in the Spirit, ye would now be made perfect by the ²flesh?

4 ¹Have ye suffered so many things in vain? if so be it be even in vain.

5 ¹He therefore that ministereth to you the Spirit, and worketh miracles among you, *doeth he it* through the works of the Law, or by the hearing of faith *preached?*

6 ¹*Yea rather* as ²Abraham believed God, and it was ᵃimputed to him for righteousness.

7 ¹Know ye therefore, that they which are of faith, the same are the children of Abraham.

8 ¹For the Scripture foreseeing, that God would justify the Gentiles through faith, preached before the Gospel unto Abraham, *saying,* ᵇ,²In thee shall all

CHAPTER 3
ᵃ Gen. 15:6
Rom. 4:3
James 2:23
ᵇ Gen. 12:3
Acts 3:25
ᶜ Deut. 27:26
ᵈ Hab. 2:4
Rom. 1:17
Heb. 10:10
ᵉ Lev. 18:5
ᶠ Lev. 21:13
ᵍ Heb. 9:17

the Gentiles be ³blessed.

9 ¹So then they which be of faith, are blessed with ²faithful Abraham.

10 ¹For as many as are of the works of the Law, are under the curse: ²For it is written, 'Cursed is every man that continueth not in all things, which are written in the book of the Law, to do them.

11 ¹And that no man is justified by the Law in the sight of God, it is evident: ᵈfor the just shall live by faith.

12 ¹And the Law is not of faith: but ᵉthe man that shall do those things, shall live in them.

13 ¹Christ hath redeemed us from the curse of the Law, made a curse for us, (²for it is written, ᶠ,³Cursed is everyone that hangeth on tree.)

14 ¹That the blessing of Abraham might come on the Gentiles through Christ Jesus, that we might receive the promise of the Spirit through faith.

15 ¹Brethren, I speak as ²men do: ᵍthough it be

3:2 ¹ Those spiritual graces and gifts, which were a seal as it were to the Galatians, that the Gospel which was preached to them was true.

² Of the doctrine of faith.

3:3 ¹ The fourth argument mixed with [the former] and it is double, If the Law is to be joined with faith, this were not to go forward, but backward, seeing that those spiritual gifts which were bestowed upon you, are more excellent than any that could proceed from yourselves. And moreover, it should follow, that the Law is better than Christ, because it should perfect and bring to end that which Christ began only.

² By the (flesh) he meaneth the ceremonies of the Law, against which he setteth the Spirit, that is, the spiritual working of the Gospel.

3:4 ¹ An exhortation by manner of upbraiding, that they do not in vain suffer so many conflicts.

3:5 ¹ He repeateth the third argument which was taken of the effects, because he had interlaced certain other arguments by the way.

3:6 ¹ The first argument which is of great force, and hath three grounds, The first, That Abraham was justified by faith, to wit, by free imputation of righteousness according to the promise apprehended by faith, as Moses doth most plainly witness.

² See Rom. 4.

3:7 ¹ The second, that the sons of Abraham must be esteemed and accounted of by faith.

3:8 ¹ The third, that all people that believe, are without exception, comprehended in the promise of the blessing.

² A proof of the first and second grounds, out of the words of Moses.

³ Blessing in this place, signifieth the free promise by faith.

3:9 ¹ The conclusion of the fifth argument: Therefore as Abraham is blessed by faith, so are all his children (that is to say, all the Gentiles that believe) blessed, that is to say, freely justified.

² With faithful Abraham, and not by faithful Abraham, to give us to understand that the blessing cometh not from Abraham, but from him, by whom Abraham and all his posterity is blessed.

3:10 ¹ The sixth argument, the conclusion whereof is also in the former verse taken of contraries, thus, They are accursed which are of the works of the Law, that is to say, which value their [righteousness] by the performance of the Law. Therefore they are blessed which are of faith, that is, they which have righteousness by faith.

² A proof of the former sentence or proposition: and the proposition of this argument is this: Cursed is he that fulfilleth not the whole Law.

3:11 ¹ The second proposition with the conclusion: But no man ful-

filleth the Law. Therefore no man is justified by the works of the Law, or else, which seek righteousness by the works of the Law. And there is annexed also this manner of proof of the second proposition, to wit, Righteousness and life are attributed to faith, Therefore no man fulfilleth the Law.

3:12 ¹ Here is a reason shown of the former consequence: Because the law promiseth life to all that keep it, and therefore if it be kept, it justifieth and giveth life. But the Scripture attributing righteousness and life to faith, taketh it from the Law, seeing that faith justifieth by imputation, and the Law by the performing of the work.

3:13 ¹ A preventing of an objection: How then can they be blessed, whom the Law pronounceth to be accursed? Because Christ sustained the curse which the Law laid upon us, that we might be quit from it.

² A proof of the answer by the testimony of Moses.

³ Christ was accursed for us, because he bare the curse that was due to us, to make us partakers of his righteousness.

3:14 ¹ A conclusion of all that was said before in the handling of the fifth and sixth reasons, to wit, that both the Gentiles are made partakers of the free blessing of Abraham in Christ, and also that the Jews themselves, of whose number the Apostle counteth himself to be, cannot obtain that promised grace of the Gospel, which he calleth the Spirit, but only by faith. And the Apostle doth severally apply the conclusion, both to the one and the other, preparing himself a way, to the next argument, whereby he declareth, that the one only seed of Abraham, which is made of all peoples can no otherwise be joined and grow up together, but by faith in Christ.

3:15 ¹ He putteth forth two general [rules] before the next argument, which is the seventh in order: That one is, that it is not lawful to break covenants and contracts which are justly made and according to Law amongst men, neither may any thing be added unto them: The other is, that God did so make a covenant with Abraham, that he would gather together his children which consist both of Jews and Gentiles into one body (as appeareth by that which hath been said before.) For he did not say, that he would be the God of Abraham and of his seeds, (which things notwithstanding should have been said, if he had many and divers seeds, as the Gentiles apart and the Jews apart,) but that he would be the God of Abraham, and of his seed, as of one.

² I will use an example which is common among you, that you may be ashamed you give not so much to God's covenants, as you do to man's.

but a man's covenant, when it is [3]confirmed, *yet no* man doth abrogate it, or addeth anything thereto,

16 Now to Abraham and his seed were the promises made. He saith not, and to the seeds, as *speaking* of many: but, And to thy seed, as of one, [1]which is [2]Christ.

17 [1]And this I say, that the covenant that was confirmed afore of God [2]in respect of Christ, the [3]Law which was four hundred and thirty years after, cannot disannul, that it should make the promise of none effect.

18 [1]For if the [2]inheritance *be* of the Law, *it is* no more by the promise, but God gave it freely unto Abraham by promise.

19 [1]Wherefore then *serveth* the Law? It was added because of the [2]transgressions, [3]till the seed came, unto the which the promise was made: [4]and it was [5]ordained by [6]Angels in the hand of a Mediator.

[h] Rom. 3:9

20 Now a Mediator is not a *Mediator* of one: [1]but God is one.

21 [1]*Is* the Law then against the promises of God? God forbid: For if there had been a Law given which could have given life, surely righteousness should have been by the Law.

22 But the [1]Scripture hath [h]concluded [2]all under sin, that the [3]promise by the faith of Jesus Christ should be given to them that believe.

23 [1]But before faith came, we were kept under the Law, *as under* a garrison, and shut up unto [2]that faith, which should afterward be revealed.

24 Wherefore the Law was our schoolmaster *to bring us* to Christ, that we might be made righteous by faith.

25 But after that faith is come, we are no longer under a schoolmaster.

26 [1]For ye are all the sons of God by faith, in

---

[3] Authentical, as we call it.

3:16 [1] He putteth forth the sum of the seventh argument, to wit, that both the Jews and the Gentiles grow together into one body of the seed of Abraham, in Christ only, so that all are one in Christ, as it is afterward declared, verse 21.

[2] Paul speaketh not of Christ's person, but of two peoples, which grew together in one, in Christ.

3:17 [1] The eighth argument taken of comparison, thus: If a man's covenant (being authentical) be firm and strong, much more God's covenant. Therefore the Law was not given to abrogate the promise made to Abraham, which had respect to Christ, that is to say, the end whereof did hang of Christ.

[2] Which tendeth to Christ.

[3] An enlarging of that argument, thus: Moreover and besides that the promise is of itself firm and strong, it was also confirmed with the prescription of long time, to wit, of 430 years, so that it could in no wise be broken.

3:18 [1] An objection: We grant that the promise was not abrogated by the covenant of the Law, and therefore we join the Law with the promise. Nay, saith the Apostle, these two cannot stand together, to wit, that the inheritance should both be given by the Law and also by promise, for the promise is free: whereby it followeth, that the Law was not given to justify, for by that means the promise should be broken.

[2] By this word (inheritance) is meant the right of the seed, which is, that God should be our God, that is to say, that by virtue of the covenant that was made with faithful Abraham, we that be faithful, might by that means be blessed of God as well as he.

3:19 [1] An objection which riseth of the former answer: If the inheritance be not by the Law (at the least in part) then why was the Law given, after that the promise was made? Therefore saith the Apostle, to reprove men of sin, and so teach them to look unto Christ, in whom at length that promise of saving all people together should be fulfilled, and not that the Law was given to justify men.

[2] That men might understand, by discovering of their sins, by the only grace of God, which he revealed to Abraham, and that in Christ.

[3] Until the partition wall was broken down, and that full seed sprang up, framed of two peoples, both of Jews and Gentiles: for by this word Seed, we may not understand, Christ alone by himself, but coupled and joined together with his body.

[4] A confirmation of the former answer taken from the manner and form of giving the Law: for it was given by Angels, striking a great

terror into all, and by Moses a Mediator coming between. Now they that are one, need no Mediator, but they that are twain at the least, and that are at variance one with another. Therefore the Law itself and the Mediator, were witnesses of the wrath of God, and not that God would by this means reconcile men to himself, and abolish the promise, or add the Law unto the promise.

[5] Commanded and given, or proclaimed.

[6] By the service and ministry.

3:20 [1] A taking away of an objection, lest any man might say, that sometimes by consent of the parties which have made a covenant, something is added to the covenant, or the former covenants are broken. This, saith the Apostle, cometh to pass in God, who is always one, and the selfsame, and like himself.

3:21 [1] The conclusion uttered by a manner of asking a question, and it is the same that was uttered before, verse 17, but proceeding of another rule: so that the argument is new, and is this: God is always like unto himself: Therefore the Law was not given to abolish the promises. But it should abolish them if it gave life, for by that means it should justify, and therefore it should abolish that justification which was promised to Abraham and to his seed by faith. Nay it was rather given to bring to light the guiltiness of all men, to the end that all believers fleeing to Christ promised, might be freely justified in him.

3:22 [1] By this word, Scripture, he meaneth the Law.

[2] All men, and whatsoever cometh from man.

[3] In every one of these words, there lieth an argument against the merits of works, for all these words, promise, faith, Christ, might be given, to believers, are against merits, and not one of them can stand with deserving works.

3:23 [1] Now there followeth another handling of the second part of this Epistle: the state whereof is this: Although the Law (that is, the whole government of God's house according to the Law) [does] not justify, is it therefore to be abolished, seeing that Abraham himself was circumcised, and his posterity held still the use of Moses' Law? Paul affirmeth that it ought to be abolished, because it was instituted for that end and purpose, that is should be as it were a schoolmaster and keeper to the people of God, until the promise appeared in deed, that is to say, Christ, and the Gospel manifestly published with great efficacy of the Spirit.

[2] The cause why we were kept under the Law, is set down here.

3:26 [1] Because age changeth not the condition of servants, he addeth that we are free by condition, and therefore, seeing we are out of our childhood, we have no more need of a keeper and Schoolmaster.

Christ Jesus.

27 [1]For all ye that are [2]baptized into Christ, have [3]put on Christ.

28 There is neither Jew nor Grecian: there is neither bond nor free: there is neither male nor female: for ye are all [1]one in Christ Jesus.

29 And if *ye be* Christ's, then are ye Abraham's seed, and heirs by promise.

4

1 Being delivered from the bondage of the Law, 4 by Christ's coming, who is the end thereof, 9 it is very absurd to slide back to beggarly ceremonies: 13 He calleth them again therefore to the purity of the doctrine of the Gospel, 21 confirming his discourse with a fine allegory.

1 Then [1]I say, that the heir as long as he is a child, differeth nothing from a servant, though he be Lord of all,

2 But is under tutors and governors, [1]until the time appointed of the Father.

3 Even so we, when we were children, were in bondage under the [1]rudiments of the world.

4 [1]But when the [2]fullness of time was come, God sent forth his Son made of a [3]woman, *and* made

CHAPTER 4
a Rom. 8:15

under the Law,

5 That he might redeem them which were under the Law, that we *a*might receive the [1]adoption of the sons.

6 [1]And because ye are sons, God hath [2]sent forth the [3]Spirit of his Son into your hearts, which crieth, Abba, Father.

7 Wherefore, thou art no more a [1]servant, but a son: now if *thou be* a son, *thou art* also the [2]heir of God through Christ.

8 [1]But even then, when ye knew not God, ye did service unto them, which by nature are not gods:

9 But now seeing ye know God, yea, rather are known of God, how turn ye again unto impotent and [1]beggarly rudiments, whereunto *as* from the beginning ye will be in bondage [2]again?

10 Ye observe days, and months, and times, and years.

11 I am in fear of you, lest I have bestowed on you labor in vain.

12 [1]Be ye as I (for I am even as you) brethren, I beseech you: ye have not hurt me at all.

13 And ye know, how through [1]infirmity of the

3:27 [1] Using a general particle, lest the Jews at the least should not think themselves bound with the band of the Law, he pronounceth that Baptism is common to all believers, because it is a pledge of our delivery in Christ, as well to the Jews as to the Grecians, that by this means all may be truly one in Christ, that is to say, that promised seed to Abraham and inheritors of everlasting life.

[2] He setteth Baptism secretly against circumcision, which the false apostles so much bragged of.

[3] The Church must put on Christ, as it were a garment, and be covered with him, that it may be thoroughly holy, and without blame.

3:28 [1] You are all as one: and so in this great knot and conjunction signified.

4:1 [1] He declareth that by another double similitude, which he said before concerning the keeper and schoolmaster. For he saith, that the Law, (that is, the whole government of God's house according to the Law) was as it were a tutor or overseer appointed for a time, until such time as that protection and overseeing which was but for a time, being ended, we should at length come to be at our own liberty, and should live as children, and not as servants. Moreover, he showeth by the way, that that governance of the Law, was as it were an ABC, and as certain principles in comparison of the doctrine of the Gospel.

4:2 [1] This is added, because he that is always under a tutor or governor, may hardly be counted a freeman.

4:3 [1] The Law is called rudiments, because that by the Law God instructed his Church as it were by rudiments, and afterward poured out his holy Spirit most plentifully in the time of the Gospel.

4:4 [1] He uttereth and declareth many things at once, to wit, that this tutorship was ended at his time, that curious men may leave to ask, why that schoolmastership lasted so long. And moreover, that we are not sons by nature, but by adoption, and that in that Son of God, who therefore took upon him our flesh, that we might be made his brethren.

[2] The time is said to be full, when all parts of it are past and ended, and therefore Christ could not have come either sooner or later.

[3] He calleth Mary a woman, in respect of the sex, and not as the word is used in a contrary sense to a virgin still.

4:5 [1] The adoption of the sons of God, is from everlasting, but is revealed and showed in the time appointed for it.

4:6 [1] He showeth that we are in such sort free and set at liberty, that in the mean season we must be governed by the Spirit of Christ, which reigning in our hearts, may teach us the true service of the Father. But this is not to serve, but rather to enjoy true liberality, as it cometh sons and heirs.

[2] By that that followeth he gathereth that that went before: for if we have his spirit, we are his sons, and if we are his sons, then are we free.

[3] The holy Ghost, who is both of the Father and of the Son: but there is a peculiar reason why he is called the Spirit of the Son, to wit, because the holy Ghost sealeth up our adoption in Christ, and maketh us a full assurance of it.

4:7 [1] The word, servant, is not taken here for one that liveth in sin, which is proper to the infidels, but for one that is yet under the ceremonies of the Law, which is proper to the Jews.

[2] Partaker of this blessing.

4:8 [1] He applieth the former doctrine to the Galatians, with a peculiar reprehension: for in comparison of them, the Jews might have pretended some excuse as men that were born and brought up in that service of the Law. But seeing the Galatians were taken and called out of idolatry to Christian liberty: what pretence might they have to go back to those impotent and beggarly rudiments?

4:9 [1] They are called impotent and beggarly ceremonies, being considered apart by themselves without Christ: and again, for that by that means they gave good testimony that they were beggars in Christ, when as notwithstanding, for men, to fall back from Christ to ceremonies, is nothing else, but to cast away riches, and to follow beggarly.

[2] By going backward.

4:12 [1] He mitigateth and qualifieth those things wherein he might have seemed to have spoken somewhat sharply, very artificially and divinely, declaring his good will towards them in such sort, that the Galatians could not but either be utterly desperate when they read these things, or acknowledge their own lightness with tears, and desire pardon.

4:13 [1] Many afflictions.

flesh, I preached the Gospel unto you at the first.

14 And the [1]trial of me which was in my flesh, ye despised not, neither abhorred: but ye received me as an Angel of God, *yea*, as [2]Christ Jesus.

15 [1]What was then your felicity? for I bear you record, that if it had been possible, ye would have plucked out your own eyes, and have given them unto me.

16 Am I therefore become your enemy, because I tell you the truth?

17 They are jealous over you [1]amiss: yea, they would exclude you, [2]that ye should altogether love them.

18 But it is a good thing to love [1]earnestly always in a good thing, and not only when I am present with you,

19 My little children, of whom I travail in birth again, until Christ be formed in you.

20 And I would I were with you now, that I might [1]change my voice: for I am in doubt of you.

21 [1]Tell me, ye that [2]will be under the Law, do ye not hear the Law?

22 For it is written, that Abraham had two sons, [b]one by a servant, and [c]one by a free woman.

23 But he which was of the servant, was born after

the [1]flesh: and he which was of the free woman, *was* born by [2]promise.

24 By the which things another thing is meant: for [1]these *mothers* are the [2]two Testaments, the one which is Hagar of mount [3]Sinai, which gendereth unto bondage.

25 (For Hagar *or* Sinai is a mountain in Arabia, and it [1]answered to Jerusalem which now is) and [2]she is in bondage with her children.

26 But Jerusalem, which is [1]above, is free: which is the mother of us all.

27 [1]For it is written, [d]Rejoice thou barren that bearest no children: break forth, and cry, thou that travailest not: for the [2]desolate hath many more children, than she which hath an husband.

28 [e]Therefore, brethren, we are after the [1]manner of Isaac, children of the [2]promise.

29 But as then he that was born after the [1]flesh, persecuted him that *was born* after the [2]Spirit, even so *it is* now.

30 But what saith the Scripture? [f]Put out the servant and her son: for the son of the servant shall not be heir with the son of the free woman.

31 [1]Then brethren, we are not children of the servant, but of the free woman.

[b] Gen. 16:15
[c] Gen. 21:1
[d] Isa. 54:1
[e] Rom. 8:9
[f] Gen. 21:10

4:14 [1] Those daily troubles wherewith the Lord tried me amongst you.

[2] For my ministry's sake.

4:15 [1] What a talk was there abroad in the world amongst men, how happy you were?

4:17 [1] For they are jealous over you for their own commodity.

[2] That they may convey all your love from me to themselves.

4:18 [1] He setteth his own true and good love, which he earnestly bent towards them, against the naughty vicious love of the false apostles.

4:20 [1] Use other words among you.

4:21 [1] Because the false apostles always urged this, that unless the Gentiles were circumcised, Christ could profit them nothing at all, and this dissension of them which believed of the circumcision against them which believed the uncircumcision, was full of offense: the Apostle, after divers arguments whereby he hath refuted their error, bringeth forth an allegory, wherein he saith the holy Ghost did shadow not unto us, all these mysteries: to wit, that it should come to pass, that two sorts of sons should have Abraham a father common to them both, but not with like success: for as Abraham begat Ishmael, by the common course of nature, of Hagar his bondmaid and a stranger, and begat Isaac of Sarah a free woman by the virtue of the promise and by grace only, and the first was not only not heir, but also persecuted the heir: So there are two covenants, and as it were two sons born to Abraham of those two covenants, as it were of two mothers. The one was made in Sinai, without the land of promise according to which covenant Abraham's children according to the flesh were begotten: to wit, the Jews which seek righteousness by that covenant, that is, by the Law: but they are not heirs, nay they shall at length be cast out of the house, as they that persecute the true heirs. The other was made in that high Jerusalem or in Zion (to wit, by the sacrifice of Christ) which begetteth children of promise, to wit, believers by the virtue of the holy Ghost which children (as

Abraham) do rest themselves in the free promise, and they only by the right of children shall be partakers of the father's inheritance, and those servants shall be shut out.

[2] That desire so greatly.

4:23 [1] As all men are, and by the common course of nature.

[2] By virtue of the promise, which Abraham laid hold on for himself and his true seed, for otherwise Abraham and Sarah were past begetting and bearing children.

4:24 [1] These do represent and shadow forth.

[2] They are called two covenants, one of the old Testament, and another of the New: which were not two indeed, but in respect of the times, and the diversity of the government.

[3] He maketh mention of Sinai, because that covenant was made in that mountain, of which mountain Hagar was a shadow.

4:25 [1] Look how the case standeth betwixt Hagar and her children, even so standeth it between Jerusalem and hers.

[2] That is, Sinai.

4:26 [1] Which is excellent, and of great account.

4:27 [1] He showeth that in this allegory, he hath followed the steps of Isaiah, who foretold that the Church should be made and consist of the children of barren Sarah, that is to say, of them which only spiritually should be made Abraham's children by faith, rather than of fruitful Hagar, even then foreshowing the casting off of the Jews, and calling of the Gentiles.

[2] She that is destroyed and wasted.

4:28 [1] After the manner of Isaac who is the first begotten of the heavenly Jerusalem, as Israel is of the slavish Synagogue.

[2] That seed, unto which the promise belongeth.

4:29 [1] By the common course of nature.

[2] By the virtue of God's promise and after a spiritual manner.

4:31 [1] The conclusion of the former allegory, that we by no means procure and call back again the slavery of the Law, seeing that the children of the bondmaid shall not be heirs.

5   *1 Having declared that we came of the free woman, he showeth the price of that freedom,*   *13 and how we should use the same,*   *16 that we may obey the Spirit,*   *19 and resist the flesh.*

1   Stand fast therefore in the liberty wherewith Christ hath made us free, and be not entangled again with the yoke of bondage.

2   *a,1*Behold, I Paul say unto you, that if ye be *2*circumcised, Christ shall profit you nothing.

3   For I testify again to every man, which is circumcised, that he is bound to keep the whole Law.

4   Ye are *b,1*abolished from Christ: whosoever are *2*justified by the Law, ye are fallen from grace.

5   *1*For we through the *2*Spirit wait for the hope of righteousness through faith.

6   *1*For in Jesus Christ neither circumcision availeth anything, neither *2*uncircumcision, *3*but *4*faith which worketh by love.

7   *1*Ye did run well: who did let you, that ye did not obey the truth?

8   *1It is* not the persuasion of *2*him that calleth you.

9   *c,1*A little leaven doth leaven the whole lump.

CHAPTER 5
a Acts 15:1
b 1 Cor. 1:17
c 1 Cor. 5:6
d Lev. 19:18
Matt. 22:39
Mark 12:31
Rom. 13:9
James 2:8
e Rom. 13:14
1 Pet. 2:11

10   *1*I have trust in you through the Lord, that ye will be none otherwise minded: but he that troubleth you, shall bear *his* condemnation, whosoever he be.

11   *1*And brethren, if I yet preach circumcision, why do I yet suffer persecution? Then is the slander of the cross abolished.

12   *1*Would to God they were even cut off which do *2*disquiet you.

13   For brethren, ye have been called unto liberty: *1*only use not *your* liberty as an occasion unto the flesh, but by love serve one another.

14   *1*For *2*all the Law is fulfilled in one word, which is this, *d*Thou shalt love thy neighbor as thyself.

15   *1*If ye bite and devour one another, take heed lest ye be consumed one of another.

16   *1*Then I say, *e*Walk in the Spirit, and ye shall not fulfill the lusts of the flesh.

17   For the *1*flesh lusteth against the Spirit, and the Spirit against the flesh: and these are contrary one to another, so that ye cannot do the same things that ye would.

18   And if ye be led by the Spirit, ye are not under the Law.

5:2 *1* Another obtestation wherein he plainly witnesseth that justification of works, and justification of faith cannot stand together, because no man can be justified by the Law, but he that doth fully and perfectly fulfill it. And he taketh the example of circumcision, because it was the ground of all the service of the Law, and was chiefly urged of the false Apostles.

2 Circumcision is in other places called the seal of righteousness, but here we must have consideration of the circumstance of the Baptism come in place of circumcision. And moreover Paul reasoneth according to the opinion that his enemies had of it, which made circumcision a piece of their salvation.

5:4 *1* That is, as he himself expoundeth it afterwards, ye are fallen from grace.

2 That is, seek to be justified by the Law, for in deed no man is justified by the Law.

5:5 *1* He privily compareth the new people with the old: for it is certain that they also did ground all their hope of justification and life in faith and not in circumcision, but so, that their faith was wrapped in the external and ceremonial worship: but our faith is bare and content with spiritual worship.

2 Through the Spirit, which engendereth faith.

5:6 *1* He addeth a reason for that now circumcision is abolished, seeing that Christ is exhibited unto us with full plenty of spiritual circumcision.

2 He maketh mention also of uncircumcision, lest the Gentiles should please themselves in it, as the Jews do in circumcision.

3 The taking away of an objection: If all that worship of the Law be taken away, wherein then shall we exercise ourselves? In charity, saith Paul: for faith, whereof we speak, cannot be idle, nay it bringeth forth daily fruits of charity.

4 So is true faith distinguished from counterfeit faith: for charity is not joined to faith as a fellow cause, to help forward our justification with faith.

5:7 *1* Again he chideth the Galatians, but with an admiration, and therewithall a praise of their former race, to the end that he may make them more ashamed.

5:8 *1* He playeth the part of an Apostle with them, and useth his authority, denying that that doctrine can come from God which is contrary to his.

2 Of God.

5:9 *1* He addeth this, that he may not seem to contend upon a trifle, warning them diligently (by a similitude which he borroweth of leaven, as Christ himself also did) not to suffer the purity of the Apostolical doctrine, to be infected with the least corruption that may be.

5:10 *1* He mitigateth the former reprehension, casting the fault upon the false Apostles, against whom he denounceth the horrible judgment of God.

5:11 *1* He willeth them to consider how that he seeketh not his own profit in this matter, seeing that he could eschew the hatred of men, if he would join Judaism with Christianity.

5:12 *1* An example of a true Pastor inflamed with the zeal of God's glory and love of his flock.

2 For they that preach the Law, cause men's consciences always to tremble.

5:13 *1* The third part of this Epistle, showing that the right use of Christian liberty consisteth in this, that being delivered from the slavery of sin and the flesh, and being obedient to the Spirit, we should serve unto one another's salvation through love.

5:14 *1* He propoundeth the love of our neighbor, as a mark whereunto all Christians ought to refer all their actions, and thereunto he citeth the testimony of the Law.

2 This particle (All) must be restrained to the second table.

5:15 *1* An exhortation to the duties of charity, by the profit that ensueth thereof, because that no men provide worse for themselves, than they that hate one another.

5:16 *1* He acknowledgeth the great weakness of the godly, for that they are but in part regenerate: but he willeth them to remember that they are endued with the Spirit of God, which hath delivered them from the slavery of sin, and so of the Law so far forth as it is the virtue of sin, that they should not give themselves to lusts.

5:17 *1* For the flesh dwelleth even in the regenerate man, but the Spirit reigneth although not without great strife, as is largely set forth, Rom. 7.

19 ¹Moreover the works of the flesh are manifest, which are adultery, fornication, uncleanness, wantonness,

20 Idolatry, witchcraft, hatred, debate, emulations, wrath, contentions, seditions, heresies,

21 Envy, murders, drunkenness, gluttony, and such like, whereof I tell you before, as I also have told you before, that they which do such things, shall not inherit the kingdom of God.

22 But the ¹fruit of the Spirit is love, joy, peace, longsuffering, gentleness, goodness, faith,

23 Meekness, temperancy: ¹against such there is no law.

24 For they that are Christ's, have crucified the flesh with the affections and the lusts.

25 If we ¹live in the Spirit, let us also walk in the Spirit.

26 ¹Let us not be desirous of vainglory, provoking one another, envying one another.

6 *1 Now he entreateth particularly of charity toward such as offend, 6 toward the Minsters of the word, 10 and those that are of the household of faith: 12 Not like unto such who have a counterfeit zeal of the Law, 13 glorying in the mangling of the flesh, 14 and not in the cross of Christ.*

1 Brethren, ¹If a man be ²suddenly taken in any

CHAPTER 6
ᵃ 1 Cor. 3:18
ᵇ 1 Cor. 9:7
ᶜ 2 Thess. 3:13

offense, ye which are ³spiritual, ⁴restore such one with the ⁵spirit of meekness, ⁶considering thyself, lest thou also be tempted.

2 ¹Bear ye one another's burden, and so fulfill the ²Law of Christ.

3 For if any man seem to himself, that he is somewhat, when he is nothing, he deceiveth himself in his imagination.

4 But let every man prove his own work: and then shall he have rejoicing in himself only and not in another.

5 ᵃ,¹For every man shall bear his own burden.

6 ¹Let him that is taught in the word, make him that hath taught him, partaker of ²all *his* ᵇgoods.

7 ¹Be not deceived: God is not mocked: for whatsoever a man soweth, that shall he also reap.

8 For he that soweth to his ¹flesh, shall of the flesh reap corruption: but he that soweth to the spirit, shall of the spirit reap life everlasting.

9 ᶜ,¹Let us not therefore be weary of well doing: for in due season we shall reap, if we faint not.

10 ¹While we have therefore time, let us do good unto all men, but especially unto them, which are of the household of faith.

11 ¶ ¹Ye see how large a letter I have written unto you with mine own hand.

5:19 ¹ He setteth out that particularly, which he spake generally, reckoning up some chief effects of the flesh, and opposing them to the fruits of the Spirit, that no man may pretend ignorance.

5:22 ¹ Therefore, they are not the fruits of free will, but so far forth as our will is made free by grace.

5:23 ¹ Lest that any man should object, that Paul played the Sophister, as one who urging the Spirit, urgeth nothing but that which the Law commandeth, he showeth that he requireth not that liberal and outward obedience, but spiritual, which proceedeth not from the Law, but from the Spirit of Christ, which doth beget us again, and must and ought to be the ruler and guider of life.

5:25 ¹ If we be indeed endued with the quickening Spirit, which causeth us to die to sin, and live to God, let us show it in our deeds, that is, by holiness of life.

5:26 ¹ He addeth peculiar exhortations according as he knew the Galatians subject to divers vices: and first of all he warneth them to take heed of ambition, which vice hath two fellows, backbiting and envy, out of which two it cannot be but many contentions must needs arise.

6:1 ¹ He condemneth importunate rigor, because that brotherly reprehensions ought to be moderated and tempered by the spirit of meekness.

² Through the malice of the flesh and the devil.

³ Which are upholden by the virtue of God's Spirit.

⁴ Labor to fill up that that is wanting in him.

⁵ This is a kind of speech which the Hebrews use, giving to understand thereby, that all good gifts come from God.

⁶ He toucheth the fore: for they commonly are most severe judges, which forget their own infirmities.

6:2 ¹ He showeth that this is the end of reprehensions, to raise up our brother which is fallen, and not proudly to oppress him. Therefore everyone must seek to have commendation of his own life by approving of himself, and not by reprehending others.

² Christ, in plain and flat words, calleth the commandment of charity, his commandment.

6:5 ¹ A reason wherefore men ought to have the greatest eye upon themselves, because that every man shall be judged before God according to his own life, and not by comparing himself with other men.

6:6 ¹ It is meet that masters should be sound by their scholars, so far forth as they are able.

² Of whatsoever he hath, according to his ability.

6:7 ¹ He commendeth liberality towards the poor, and first of all chideth them which were not ashamed to pretend this and that, and all because they would not help their neighbors, as though they could deceive God: and afterward compareth alms to a spiritual sowing, which shall have a most plentiful harvest, so that it shall be very profitable: and compareth covetous niggardliness to a carnal sowing, whereof nothing can be gathered but such things as fade away, and perish by and by.

6:8 ¹ To the commodities of this present life.

6:9 ¹ Against such as are liberal at the beginning, but continue not, because the harvest seemeth to be deferred very long, as though the seed time and the harvest were at one instant.

6:10 ¹ They that are of the household of faith, that is, such as are joined with us in the profession of one selfsame religion, ought to be preferred before all others, yet so notwithstanding that our liberality extends to all.

6:11 ¹ The fourth and last part of the Epistle, wherein he returneth to his principal end and purpose: to wit, that the Galatians should not suffer themselves to be led out of the way by the false apostles: and he pointeth out those false apostles in their colors, reproving them of ambition, as men that do not that which they do, for any affection and zeal they have to the Law, but only for this purpose, that they may purchase themselves favor amongst their own sort, by the circumcision of the Galatians.

12 As many as desire to make a [1]fair show in the [2]flesh, they constrain you to be circumcised, only because they would not suffer persecution for the [3]cross of Christ.

13 For they themselves which are circumcised keep not the Law, but desire to have you circumcised, that they might rejoice in [1]your flesh.

14 [1]But God forbid that I should [2]rejoice, but in the cross of our Lord Jesus Christ, whereby the world is crucified unto me, and I unto the world.

15 For in Christ Jesus neither circumcision availeth anything, nor uncircumcision, but a new creature.

16 And as many as walk according to this rule, peace *shall be* upon them, and mercy, and upon the [1]Israel of God.

17 [1]From henceforth let no man put me to business: for I bear, in my body the [2]marks of the [3]Lord Jesus.

18 [1]Brethren, the grace of our Lord Jesus Christ *be* with your [2]spirit, Amen.

¶ Unto the Galatians written from Rome.

6:12 [1] He setteth a far show against the truth.

[2] In keeping of ceremonies.

[3] For the preaching of him that was crucified.

6:13 [1] That they have entangled you in Judaism, and yet he harpeth on the form of circumcision.

6:14 [1] He sticketh not to compare himself with them, showing that on the contrary part he rejoiceth in those afflictions which he suffereth for Christ's sake, and as he is despised of the world, so doth he in like sort esteem the world as naught: which is the true circumcision of a true Israelite.

[2] When Paul useth this word in good sense of part, it signifieth to rest a man's self wholly in a thing, and to content himself therewith.

6:16 [1] Upon the true Israel, whose praise is of God and not of men,

Rom. 2:19.

6:17 [1] Continuing still in the same metaphor, he opposeth his miseries and the marks of those stripes which he bare for Christ's sake, against the scar of the outward circumcision, as a true mark of his Apostleship.

[2] Marks which are burnt into a man's flesh, as they used in old times, to mark their servants that had run away from them.

[3] For it importeth much, whose marks we bear: for the cause maketh the Martyr, and not the punishment.

6:18 [1] Taking his farewell of them, he wisheth them grace, and the Spirit against the deceits of the false apostles, who labored to beat those outward things into their brains.

[2] With your minds and hearts.

THE EPISTLE OF
PAUL TO THE
EPHESIANS

1 *1 After the salutation,* *4 he entreateth of the free election of God,* *5 and adoption.* *7, 13 from whence man's salvation floweth, as from the true and natural fountain: and because so high a mystery cannot be understood,* *16 he prayeth that the full,* *20 knowledge of Christ, may by God be reavealed unto the Ephesians.*

CHAPTER 1
a 1 Cor. 1:2
b 1 Cor. 1:3
1 Pet. 1:3

1　Paul [1]an Apostle of Jesus Christ by the will of God, to the [a]Saints, which are at Ephesus, and to the [2]faithful in Christ Jesus:

2　Grace *be* with you, and peace from God our Father, and *from* the Lord Jesus Christ.

3　[b,1]Blessed *be* God, [2]and the Father of our Lord Jesus Christ, [3]which hath blessed us, with [4]all spiritual blessing in [5]heavenly things in [6]Christ,

4　[1]As he hath chosen us in [2]him, before the foundation of the world, [3]that we [4]should [5]be holy, and without blame [6]before him in love:

5　[1]Who hath predestinated us, to be adopted through Jesus Christ [2]in himself, according to the good pleasure of his will.

6　[1]To the [2]praise of the glory of his grace, [3]wherewith he hath made us freely accepted in *his* beloved.

7　[1]By whom we have redemption through his blood, *even* the forgiveness of sins, according to his rich grace:

8　[1,2]Whereby he hath been abundant toward us in [3]all wisdom and understanding,

9　And hath opened unto us the [1]mystery of his will [2]according to his good pleasure, which he hath purposed in him,

---

1:1 [1] The inscription and salutation, whereof we have spoken in the former Epistles.

[2] This is the definition of the Saints, showing what they are.

1:3 [1] The first part of the Epistle, wherein he handleth all the parts of our salvation, propounding the example of the Ephesians, and using divers exhortations, and beginning after his manner with thanksgiving.

[2] The efficient cause of our salvation is God, not considered confusedly and generally, but as the father of our Lord Jesus Christ.

[3] The next final cause, and in respect of us, is our salvation, all things being bestowed upon us which are necessary to our salvation, which kind of blessings is heavenly and proper to the elect.

[4] With all kind of gracious and bountiful goodness which is heavenly indeed, and from God only.

[5] Which God our Father gave us from his high throne from above: or because the Saints have those gifts bestowed on them, which belong properly to the citizens of heaven.

[6] The matter of our salvation is Christ, in whom only we are endued with spiritual blessing and unto salvation.

1:4 [1] He declareth the efficient cause, or by what means God the Father saveth us in his Son: Because saith he, he chose us from everlasting in his Son.

[2] To be adopted in him.

[3] He expoundeth the next final cause, which he maketh double, to wit, sanctification and justification, whereof he will speak hereafter. And hereby also two things are to be noted, to wit, that holiness of life cannot be separated from the grace of election: and again what pureness forever is in us, is the gift of God, who hath freely of his mercy chosen us.

[4] Then God did not choose us, because we were, or otherwise should have been holy, but to the end we should be holy.

[5] Being clothed with Christ's righteousness.

[6] Truly and sincerely.

1:5 [1] Another plainer exposition of the efficient cause, and also of eternal election, whereby God is saith to have chosen us in Christ, to wit, because it pleased him to appoint us out when we were not yet born, whom he would make to be his children by Jesus Christ: so that there is no reason here of our election to be sought, but in the free mercy of God, neither is faith which God foresaw, the cause of predestination, but the effect.

[2] God respecteth nothing, either that present is, or that is to come, but himself only.

1:6 [1] The uttermost and chiefest final cause is the glory of God the Father, who saveth us freely in his Son.

[2] That as his bountiful goodness deserveth all praise, so also it should be set forth and published.

[3] Another final cause more near, is our justification, while that he freely accounteth us for just in his Son.

1:7 [1] An expounding of the material cause, how we are made acceptable to God in Christ, for it is he only, whose sacrifice by the mercy of God is imputed unto us, for the forgiveness of sin.

1:8 [1] Now he cometh at length to the formal cause, that is to say, to vocation or preaching of the Gospel, whereby God executeth that eternal counsel of our free reconciliation and salvation in Christ. And putting in place of the Gospel all wisdom and understanding, he showeth how excellent it is.

[2] By which gracious goodness and bountifulness.

[3] In perfect and sound wisdom.

1:9 [1] For unless the Lord had opened unto us that mystery, we could never have so much as dreamed of it ourselves.

[2] Not only the election, but also the vocation proceedeth of meer grace.

10 ¹That in the dispensation of the fullness of the times, he might ²gather together in one all things, both which are in heaven, and which are in earth, *even* in Christ:

11 ¹In whom also we are chosen when we were predestinated according to the purpose of him, which worketh ²all things after the counsel of his own will,

12 That we, which ¹first trusted in Christ, should be unto the praise of his glory:

13 ¹In whom also ye *have trusted*, after that ye heard the ²word of truth, *even* the Gospel of your salvation, wherein also after that ye believed, ye were ³sealed with the holy ⁴Spirit of promise,

14 Which is the earnest of our inheritance, for the ¹redemption of that liberty purchased unto the praise of his glory.

15 ¹Therefore also after that I heard of the faith, which ye have in the Lord Jesus, and love toward all the Saints,

16 I cease not to give thanks for you, making mention of you in my prayers,

ᶜ Eph. 3:7
Col. 2:12

17 ¹That the God of our Lord Jesus Christ, that Father of ²glory, might give unto you the Spirit of wisdom, and revelation through the ³knowledge of him,

18 That the eyes of your understanding may be lightened, that ye may know what the ¹hope is of his calling, and what the riches of his glorious inheritance *is* in the Saints,

19 ¹And what is the exceeding greatness of his power toward us, which believe, ᶜaccording to the working of his mighty power,

20 ¹Which he wrought in Christ, when he raised him from the dead, and set him at his ²right hand in the heavenly *places,*

21 Far above all principality, and power, and might, and domination, and every ¹Name, that is named, not in this world only, but also in that that is to come,

22 ¹And hath made all things subject under his feet, and hath given him over all things *to be* the ²head to the Church,

23 Which is his body, *even* the ¹fullness of him that filleth all in all things.

1:10 ¹ The Father exhibiteth and gave Christ, who is the head of all the elect unto the world, at that time which was convenient, according as he most wisely disposed all times from everlasting. And Christ is he in whom all the elect from the beginning of the world, (otherwise wandering and separated from God) are gathered together: of which some were then in heaven when he came into the earth, (to wit, such as by faith in him to come, were gathered together) and others being found upon the earth, were gathered together of him, and the rest are daily gathered together.

² The faithful are said to be gathered together in Christ, because they are joined together with him through faith, and become as it were one man.

1:11 ¹ He applieth severally the benefit of vocation to the believing Jews, going back to the very fountain, that even they also may not attribute their salvation neither to themselves, nor to their stock, nor to any other thing, but to the only grace and mercy of God, both because they were called, and also because they were first called.

² All things are attributed to the grace of God without exception, and yet for all that, we are not stocks, for he giveth us grace both to will and to be able to do those things that are good, Phil. 2:13.

1:12 ¹ He speaketh of the Jews.

1:13 ¹ Now he maketh the Ephesians (or rather all the Gentiles) equal to the Jews, because that notwithstanding they came last, yet being called by the same Gospel, they embraced it by faith, and were sealed up with the same spirit, which is the pledge of election, until the inheritance itself be seen, that in them also also the glory of God might shine forth, and be manifested.

² That word which is truth indeed, because it cometh from God.

³ This is a borrowed kind of speech taken of a seal, which being put to any thing, maketh a difference between those things that are authentical, and others that are not.

⁴ With that Spirit, which bringeth not the Law, but the promise of free adoption.

1:14 ¹ Full and perfect.

1:15 ¹ He returneth to the former gratulation, concluding two things together of those things that went before: the first is, that all good things come to us from God the Father in Christ, and by Christ, that for

them he may be praised of us. The second is that all those things (which he bringeth to two heads, to wit, faith and charity) are increased in us by certain degrees, so that we must desire increase of his grace from whom we have the beginning, and of whom we hope for the end.

1:17 ¹ The causes of faith are God the Father lightening our minds with his holy spirit, that we may embrace Christ opened unto us in the Gospel, to the obtaining of everlasting life, and the setting forth of God's glory.

² Full of majesty.

³ For it is not enough for us to have known God once, but we must know him every day more and more.

1:18 ¹ What blessings they are which he calleth you to hope for whom he calleth to Christ.

1:19 ¹ The excellency of faith is declared by the effects, because the mighty power of God is set forth and shown therein.

1:20 ¹ The Apostle willeth us to behold in our most glorious Christ with the eye of faith, that most excellent power and glory of God, whereof all the faithful are partakers, although it be as yet very dark in us, by reason of the ignominy of the cross and the weakness of the flesh.

² To be set on God's right hand, is to be partaker of the sovereignty which he hath over all creatures.

1:21 ¹ Everything whatsoever it be, or above all things be they of never such power or excellency.

1:22 ¹ That we should not think that that excellent glory of Christ is a thing wherewith we have nought to do, he witnesseth, that he was appointed of God the Father the head of all the Church, and therefore the body must be joined to his head, which otherwise should be a maimed thing without the members: which notwithstanding is not of necessity (seeing that the Church is rather quickeneth and sustained by the only virtue of Christ, so far off is it, that he needeth the fullness thereof) but of the infinite goodwill and pleasure of God, who vouchsafeth to join us to his Son.

² Insomuch that there is nothing but is subject to him.

1:23 ¹ For the love of Christ is so great toward the Church, that though he do fully satisfy all with all things, yet he esteemeth himself but a maimed and unperfect head, unless he have the Church joined to him as his body.

2 1 *The better to set out the grace of Christ, he useth a comparison, calling them to mind,* 5 *that they were altogether castaways and aliants,* 8 *that they are saved by grace,* 13 *and brought near,* 16 *by reconciliation through Christ,* 17 *published by the Gospel.*

CHAPTER 2
a Col. 2:13
b Rom. 9:4

1 And *a,1*you *hath he quickened,* that were *2*dead in *3*trespasses and sins,

2 *1*Wherein, in times past ye walked, *2*according to the course of this world, *and* *3*after the prince that ruleth in the air, even the spirit, that now *4*worketh in the *5*children of disobedience,

3 *1*Among whom we also had our conversation in time past in the lusts of our *2*flesh, in fulfilling the will of the flesh, and of the mind, and *3*were by nature the *4*children of wrath, as well as *5*others.

4 *1*But God which is rich in mercy, through his great love wherewith he loved us,

5 Even when we were dead by sins, hath quickened us together in Christ, *by whose* grace ye are saved,

6 And hath raised us up *1*together, and made us sit together in the heavenly *places* in Christ Jesus,

7 That he might show in the ages to come the exceeding riches of his grace through his kindness toward us in Christ Jesus.

8 For by *1*grace are ye saved through faith, and that not of yourselves: *it is* the gift of God,

9 *1*Not of works, lest any man should boast himself.

10 For we are *1*his workmanship created in Christ Jesus unto good works, which God hath ordained, that we should walk in them.

11 *1*Wherefore remember that ye being in time past Gentiles in the flesh, *and* *2*called uncircumcision of them, which are *3*called circumcision in the flesh, made with hands,

12 That ye were, *I say,* at that time *1*without Christ, and were *2*aliens from the commonwealth of Israel, and were *b*strangers from the covenants of promise, and had no hope, and *were* without God in the world.

13 *1*But now in Christ Jesus, ye which once were far off, are made near by the blood of Christ.

14 *1*For he is our peace, which hath made of both one, and hath broken the stop of the partition

---

2:1 *1* He declareth again the greatness of God's good will, by comparing that miserable state wherein we are born, with that dignity whereunto we are advanced by God the Father in Christ. So he describeth that condition in such sort, that he saith, that touching spiritual motions we are not only born half dead, but wholly and altogether dead.

2 See Rom. 6:2. So then he calleth them dead, which are not regenerate: for as the immortality of them which are damned, is no life, so this knitting together of body and soul is properly no life, but death in them which are not ruled by the Spirit of God.

3 He showeth the cause of death, to wit, sins.

2:2 *1* He proveth by the effects that all were spiritually dead.

2 He proveth this evil to be universal, insomuch as all are slaves of Satan.

3 At the pleasure of the prince.

4 Men are therefore slaves to Satan, because they are willingly rebellious against God.

5 They are called the children of disobedience, which are given to disobedience.

2:3 *1* After that he hath severally condemned the Gentiles, he confesseth that the Jews, amongst whom he numbereth himself, are not a whit better.

2 By the name of flesh in the first place, he meaneth the whole man, which he divideth into two parts: into the flesh, which is the part that the Philosophers term without reason, and into the thought, which they call reasonable: so that he leaveth nothing in man half dead, but concludeth that the whole man is of nature the son of wrath.

3 The conclusion: All men are born subject to the wrath and curse of God.

4 Men are said to be children of wrath passively, that is to say, guilty of everlasting death by the judgment of God, who is angry with them.

5 Profane people which knew not God.

2:4 *1* Now hereof followeth another member of the comparison, declaring our excellency, to wit, that by the virtue of Christ we are delivered from that death, and made partakers of eternal life, to the end that at length we may reign with him. And by divers and sundry means he beateth this into their heads, that the efficient cause of this benefit is the free mercy of God: and Christ himself is the material cause: and faith is the instrument which also is the free gift of God: and the end is God's glory.

2:6 *1* To wit, as he addeth afterward in Christ, for as yet this is not fulfilled in us, but only in our head, by whose spirit we have begun to die to sin, and live to God, until that work be fully brought to an end: but yet the hope is certain, for we are as sure of that we look for: as we are of that we have received already.

2:8 *1* So then, Grace, that is to say, the gift of God, and faith, do stand one with another, to which two these are contrary, To be saved by ourselves, or by our works. Therefore what mean they which would join together things of so contrary nature?

2:9 *1* He taketh away expressly and namely from our works the praise of justification, seeing that the good works themselves are the effects of grace in us.

2:10 *1* He speaketh here of grace, and not of nature: therefore be the works never so good, look what they are, they are it of grace.

2:11 *1* Applying the former doctrine to the Gentiles, he showeth that they were not only as the Jews, by nature, but also after an especial sort, strangers and without God: and therefore they ought so much the rather remember that same so great a benefit of God.

2 You were called no otherwise than Gentiles, that all the world might witness of your uncleanness.

3 Of the Jews which were known from you by the mark of circumcision, the mark of the covenant.

2:12 *1* He beginneth first with Christ, who was the end of all the promises.

2 You had no right or title, to the common wealth of Israel.

2:13 *1* Christ is the only bond of the Jews and Gentiles, whereby they be reconciled to God.

2:14 *1* As by the ceremonies and worship appointed by the Law, the Jews were divided from the Gentiles, so now Christ, having broken down the partition wall, joineth them both together, both in himself, and betwixt themselves, and to God. Whereby it followeth, that whosoever established the ceremonies of the Law, maketh the grace of Christ void and of none effect.

wall,

15 'In abrogating through his flesh the hatred, *that is*, the Law of commandments *which standeth* in ordinances, for to make of twain one new man in himself, *so* making peace,

16 And that he might reconcile both unto God in 'one body by *his* cross, and 2slay hatred thereby,

17 'And came, and preached peace to you which were afar off, and to them that were near.

18 For 'through him we both have an entrance unto the Father by one Spirit.

19 'Now therefore ye are no more strangers and foreigners: but citizens with the Saints, and of the household of God.

20 'And are built upon the foundation of the Apostles and Prophets, Jesus Christ himself being the 2chief cornerstone,

21 In whom all the building 'coupled together, groweth unto an holy Temple in the Lord.

22 In whom ye also are built together to be the habitation of God by the Spirit.

3 *1 He declareth that therefore he suffered many things of the Jews, 3 because he preached the mystery touching the salvation of the Gentiles, 8 at God's commandment. 13 After he desired the Ephesians not to faint for his afflictions. 14 And for this cause he prayeth unto God, 18 that they may understand the great love of Christ.*

1 For 'this cause, I Paul *am* the 2prisoner of Jesus Christ for you Gentiles.

2 If ye have heard of the dispensation of the grace of God, which is given me to youward,

c Col. 2:14

3 *That is*, that God by revelation hath showed this mystery unto me (as I wrote above in few words,

4 Whereby when ye read, ye may know mine understanding in the mystery of Christ)

5 Which in 'other ages was not opened unto the sons of men, as it is now revealed unto his holy Apostles and Prophets by the Spirit,

6 That the Gentiles should be inheritors also, and of the same body, and partakers of his promise in Christ by the Gospel,

7 Whereof I am made a minister by the gift of the grace of God given unto me through the effectual working of his power.

8 Even unto me the least of all Saints is this grace given, that I should preach among the Gentiles, the unsearchable riches of Christ,

9 And to make clear unto all men what the fellowship of the mystery is, which from the beginning of the world hath been hid in God, who hath created all things by Jesus Christ,

10 'To the intent, that now unto principalities and powers in heavenly *places*, might be known by the Church the 2manifold wisdom of God,

11 According to the 'eternal purpose, which he wrought in Christ Jesus our Lord:

12 By whom we have boldness and entrance with confidence, by faith in him.

13 Wherefore I desire that ye faint not at my tribulations for your sakes, which is your glory.

14 'For this cause I bow my knees unto the Father of our Lord Jesus Christ,

15 (Of whom is named the whole 'family in heaven

2:16 ¹ He alludeth to the sacrifices of the Law, which represented that true and only sacrifice.
² For he destroyed death by death, and fastened it as it were to the cross.
2:17 ¹ The preaching of the Gospel is an effectual instrument of this grace, common as well to the Jews as to the Gentiles.
2:18 ¹ Christ is the gate as it were, by whom we come to the Father, and the holy Ghost is as it were our lodes man who leadeth us.
2:19 ¹ The conclusion: The Gentiles are taken into the fellowship of salvation. And he describeth the excellency of the Church, calling it the city and house of God.
2:20 ¹ The Lord committed the doctrine of salvation, first to the Prophets, and then to the Apostles, the end whereof and matter as it were and substance, is Christ. Therefore that is indeed the true and Catholic Church, which is builded upon Christ by the Prophets and Apostles, as a spiritual temple consecrated to God.
² That is, the head of the building, for the foundations are as it were the heads of the buildings.
2:21 ¹ So that God is the workman not only of the foundation, but also of the whole building.
3:1 ¹ He maintaineth his Apostleship against the offense of the cross, whereon also he taketh an argument to confirm himself, affirming that he was not only appointed an Apostle by the mercy of God, but was also particularly appointed to the Gentiles, to call them on every side to salvation: because God had so determined it from the

beginning, although he deferred a great while the manifestation of that his counsel.
² These words, The prisoner of Jesus Christ, are taken passively, that is to say I Paul am cast into prison for maintaining the glory of Christ.
3:5 ¹ He meaneth not that none knew the calling of the Gentiles before, but because very few knew of it, and they that did know it, as the Prophets, had it revealed unto them very darkly, and under figures.
3:10 ¹ The unlooked for calling of the Gentiles, was as it were a glass to the heavenly Angels, wherin they might behold the marvellous wisdom of God.
² God never had but one way only, to save men by: but it had divers fashions and forms.
3:11 ¹ Which was before all beginnings.
3:14 ¹ He teacheth by his own example, that the efficacy of the doctrine dependeth upon the grace of God, and therefore we ought to join prayers with the preaching and hearing of the word: which are needful not only to them which are younglings in religion, but even to the oldest also, that they growing up more and more by faith in Christ, being confirmed with all spiritual gifts, may be grounded and rooted in the knowledge of that immeasurable love, wherewith God the Father hath loved us in Christ, seeing that the whole family, whereof part is already received into heaven, and part is yet here on earth, dependeth upon that adoption of the heavenly Father, in his only Son.
3:15 ¹ All that whole people which hath but one household Father, and that is the Church which is adopted in Christ.

and in earth)

16 That he might grant you according to the ¹riches of his glory, that ye may be strengthened by his Spirit in the ²inner man,

17 That Christ may dwell in your hearts by faith:

18 That ye, being rooted and grounded in ¹love, may be able to comprehend with all Saints, ²what is the breadth, and length, and depth, and height:

19 And to know the ¹love of Christ, which ²passeth knowledge, that ye may be filled with all ³fullness of God.

20 ¹Unto him therefore that is able to do exceeding abundantly above all that we ask or think, according to the power that worketh in us,

21 Be praise in the Church by Christ Jesus, throughout all generations forever, Amen.

4 *These three last Chapters contain precepts of manners. 1 He exhorteth them to mutual love. 7 Sundry gifts are therefore bestowed of God, 16 that the Church may be built up. 18 He calleth them from the vanity of infidels, 25 from lying, 29 and from filthy talk.*

1 I therefore, ¹being prisoner in the Lord, pray you that ye walk worthy of the ²vocation whereunto ye are called,

2 ¹With all humbleness of mind, and meekness, with ²long suffering, supporting one another through love,

3 ¹Endeavoring to keep the unity of the Spirit in the bond of peace.

4 ¹There is one body, and one Spirit, even as ye are called in one hope of your vocation.

5 There is one Lord, one Faith, one Baptism.

6 One God and Father of all, which is ¹above all, and ²through all, and ³in you all.

7 ¹But unto every one of us is given grace according to the measure of the ²gift of Christ.

8 Wherefore he saith, When he ascended upon high, he led ¹captivity captive, and gave gifts unto men.

9 (Now, in that he ascended, what is it but that he had also descended first into the ¹lowest parts of the earth?

10 He that descended, is even the same that ascended, far above all heavens, that he might ¹fill ²all things.)

11 ¹He therefore gave some to be ²Apostles, and some ³Prophets, and some ⁴Evangelists, and some ⁵Pastors, and Teachers,

12 ¹For the repairing of the Saints, for the work of the ministry, and for the edification of the ²body

3:16 ¹ According to the greatness of his mercy.
² See Rom. 7:22.
3:18 ¹ Wherewith God loveth us, which is the root of our election.
² How perfect that work of Christ is in every part.
3:19 ¹ Which God hath showeth us in Christ.
² Which passeth all the capacity of man's wit, to comprehend it fully in his mind: for otherwise who so hath the Spirit of God, perceiveth so much (according to the measure that God hath given him) as is sufficient to salvation.
³ So that we have abundantly in us, whatsoever things are required to make us perfect with God.
3:20 ¹ He breaketh forth into a thanksgiving, whereby the Ephesians also may be confirmed to hope for anything of God.
4:1 ¹ Another part of the Epistle containing precepts of Christian life, the sum whereof is this, that every man behave himself as it is meet for so excellent grace of God.
² By this is meant the general calling of the faithful, which is this, to be holy, as our God is holy.
4:2 ¹ Secondly, he commendeth meekness of the mind, which is shown forth by bearing one with another.
² See Matt. 18:25.
4:3 ¹ Thirdly, he requireth perfect agreement, but yet such as is knit with the band of the holy Ghost.
4:4 ¹ An argument of great weight, for an earnest entertaining of brotherly love and charity one with another, because we are made one body as it were of one God, and Father, by one Spirit, worshipping one Lord with one faith, and consecrated to him with one Baptism, and hope for one selfsame glory, whereunto we are called. Therefore whosoever breaketh charity, breaketh all these things asunder.
4:6 ¹ Who only hath the chief authority over the Church.
² Who only poureth forth his providence, through all the members of the Church.

³ Who only is joined together with us in Christ.
4:7 ¹ He teacheth us, that we indeed are all one body, and that all good gifts proceed from Christ only, who reigneth in heaven having mightily conquered all his enemies (from whence he heapeth all gifts upon his Church:) but yet notwithstanding these gifts are diversely and sundry ways divided according to his will and pleasure, and therefore every man ought to be content with that measure that God hath given him, and to bestow it to the common profit of the whole body.
² Which Christ hath given.
4:8 ¹ A multitude of captives.
4:9 ¹ Down to the earth, which is the lowest part of the world.
4:10 ¹ Fill with his gifts.
² The Church.
4:11 ¹ First of all he reckoneth up the Ecclesiastical functions, which are partly extraordinary and for a season, as Apostles, Prophets, Evangelists, and partly ordinary and perpetual, as Pastors and Doctors.
² The Apostles were those twelve, unto whom Paul was afterward added, whose office was to plant Churches throughout all the world.
³ The Prophet's office was one of the chiefest, which were men of marvellous wisdom, and some of them could foretell things to come.
⁴ These the Apostles used as fellows in the execution of their office, being not able to answer all places themselves.
⁵ Pastors are they which govern the Church, and Teachers are they which govern the Schools.
4:12 ¹ He showeth the end of Ecclesiastical functions, to wit, that by the ministry of men all the Saints may so grow up together, that they may make one mystical body of Christ.
² The Church.

of Christ,

13 [1]Till we all meet together (in the [2]unity of faith and that acknowledging of the Son of God) unto a perfect man, *and* unto the measure of the [3]age the fullness of Christ,

14 [1]That we henceforth be no more children, [2]wavering and carried about with every wind of doctrine, by the [3]deceit of men, and with craftiness, whereby they lay in [4]wait to deceive.

15 [1]But let us follow the truth in love, and in all things, grow up into him, which is the head, *that is*, Christ.

16 By whom all the body being coupled and knit together by every joint, for the furniture *thereof* (according to the [1]effectual power, *which is* in the measure of every part) receiveth [2]increase of the body, unto the edifying of itself in [3]love.

17 [1]This I say therefore and testify in the Lord, that ye henceforth walk not as [a]other Gentiles walk, in [2]vanity of their mind.

18 Having their understanding darkened, and

CHAPTER 4

[a] Rom. 1:21
[b] Col. 3:8

being strangers from the [1]life of God through the ignorance that is in them, because of the hardness of their heart:

19 Which being [1]past feeling, have given themselves unto wantonness, to work all uncleanness, *even* with [2]greediness.

20 [1]But ye have not so learned Christ,

21 If so be ye have heard him, and have been taught by him, [1]as the truth is in Jesus,

22 [b]*That is*, that ye cast off, concerning the conversation in time past, [1]that old man, which is corrupt through the deceivable lusts,

23 And be renewed in the [1]spirit of your mind,

24 And put on the new man, which [1]after God is created unto [2]righteousness, and [3]true holiness.

25 [1]Wherefore cast off lying, and speak every man truth unto his neighbor: for we are members one of another.

26 [1]Be [2]angry, but sin not: let not the sun go down [3]upon your wrath,

27 Neither give place to the devil.

4:13 [1] The use of this ministry is perpetual so long as we are in this world, that is, until that time that having put off the flesh, and thoroughly and perfectly agreeing betwixt ourselves, we shall be joined with Christ our head. Which thing is done by that knowledge of the Son of God increasing in us, and he himself by little and little growing up in us until we come to be a perfect man, which shall be in the world to come, when God shall be all in all.

[2] In that most near conjunction which is knit and fastened together by faith.

[3] Christ is said to grow up to full age, not in himself, but in us.

4:14 [1] Betwixt our childhood (that is to say, a very weak state, while as we do yet altogether waiver) and our perfect age, which we shall have at length in another world, there is a mean, to wit, our youth, and steady going forward to perfection.

[2] He compareth them which rest not themselves upon the word of God, to little boats which are tossed hither and thither with the doctrines of men, as it were with contrary winds, and therewithall forewarneth them that it cometh to pass not only by the lightness of man's brain, but also by the craftiness of certain, which make as it were an art of it.

[3] With those uncertain chances which toss men to and fro.

[4] By the deceit of those men which are very well practised in deceiving of others.

4:15 [1] By earnest affection of the truth and love, we grow up into Christ: for he (being effectual by the ministry of his word, which as the vital spirit doth so quicken the whole body, that it nourisheth all the limbs thereof according to the measure and proportion of each one) quickeneth and cherisheth his Church, which consisteth of divers functions, as of divers members, and preserveth the proportion of every one. And thereof it followeth that neither this body can live without Christ, neither can any man grow up spiritually, which separateth himself from the other members.

4:16 [1] Of Christ, who in manner of the soul, quickeneth all the members.

[2] Such increase as is meet the body should have.

[3] Charity is the knitting of the limbs together.

4:17 [1] He descendeth to the fruits of Christian doctrine, and reasoneth first upon the principles of manners and actions, setting down a most grave comparison between the children of God, and

them which are not regenerate. For in these men, all the powers of the mind are corrupted and their mind is given to vanity, and their senses are darkened with most gross mistiness, and their affections are so accustomed by little and little to wickedness, that at length they run headlong into all uncleanness, being utterly destitute of all judgment.

[2] If the noblest parts of the soul be corrupt, what is man but corruption only?

4:18 [1] Whereby God liveth in them.

4:19 [1] Void of all judgment.

[2] They strove to pass one another as though there had been some gain to be gotten by it.

4:20 [1] Here followeth the contrary part touching men which are regenerate by the true and lively knowledge of Christ, which have other principles of their doings far different, to wit, holy and honest desires, and a mind clean changed by the virtue of the holy Ghost, from whence proceed also like effects, as a just and holy life indeed.

4:21 [1] As they have learned which acknowledge Christ indeed, and in good earnest.

4:22 [1] Yourselves.

4:23 [1] Where there ought to have been the greatest force of reason, there is the greatest corruption of all which wasteth all things.

4:24 [1] After the image of God.

[2] The effect and end of the new creation.

[3] Not fained nor counterfeit.

4:25 [1] He commendeth severally certain peculiar Christian virtues, and first of all he requireth truth (that is to say, sincere manners) condemning all deceit and dissembling, because we are born one for another.

4:26 [1] He teacheth us to bridle our anger in such sort, that although it be not, yet that it break not out, and that it be straightway quenched before we sleep, lest Satan taking occasion to give us evil counsel through the wicked counselor, destroy us.

[2] If it so fall out, that you be angry, yet sin not: that is, bridle your anger, and do not wickedly put that in execution, which you have wickedly conceived.

[3] Let not the night come upon you in your anger, that is, make atonement quickly for all matters.

28 [1]Let him that stole, steal no more: but let him rather labor, and work with his hands the thing which is [2]good, that he may have to give unto him that needeth.

29 [1]Let no [2]corrupt communication proceed out of your mouths: but that which is good to the use of edifying, that it may minister [3]grace unto the hearers.

30 [1]And grieve not the holy Spirit of God, by whom ye are sealed unto the day of redemption.

31 Let all bitterness, and anger, and wrath, crying, and evil speaking be put away from you, with all maliciousness.

32 Be ye courteous one to another, and tender hearted, freely forgiving one another, [1]even as God for Christ's sake, freely forgave you.

5 *3 Lest, in those vices which he reprehended, they should set light by his admonitions, 5 he terrifieth them by denouncing severe judgment, 8 and stirreth them forward: 15 Then he defendeth from general lessons of manners, 22 to the particular duties of wives, 25 and husbands.*

1 Be ye therefore followers of God, as dear children,

2 [a]And walk in love, even as Christ hath loved us, and hath given himself for us, *to be* an offering and a sacrifice of a sweet smelling savor to God.

3 [b,1]But fornication, and all uncleanness, or covetousness, let it not be once named among you, as it becometh Saints,

4 Neither filthiness, neither foolish talking,

CHAPTER 5
[a] John 13:14
John 15:12
[b] Eph. 4:29
Col. 3:5
1 Thess. 2:17
[c] Matt. 24:4
Mark 13:5
Luke 21:8
2 Thess. 2:3
[d] Col. 4:5
[e] Rom. 12:2
1 Thess. 4:3

neither [1]jesting, which are things not comely, but rather giving of thanks.

5 [1]For this ye know, that no whoremonger, neither unclean person, nor covetous person, which is an [2]idolater, hath any inheritance in the kingdom of Christ, and of God.

6 [c]Let no man deceive you with vain words: for, for such things cometh the wrath of God upon the children of disobedience.

7 [1]Be not therefore companions with them.

8 For ye were once darkness, but are now [1]light in the Lord: walk as children of light.

9 (For the fruit of the [1]Spirit *is* in all goodness, and righteousness, and truth.)

10 Approving that which is pleasing to the Lord.

11 And have no fellowship with the unfruitful works of darkness, but even [1]reprove them rather.

12 For it is shame even to speak of the things which are done of them in secret.

13 But all things when they are reproved of the light, are manifest: for it is light that maketh all things manifest.

14 Wherefore [1]he saith, Awake thou that sleepest, and stand up from the [2]dead, and Christ shall give thee light.

15 [1]Take heed therefore that ye walk circumspectly, not as fools, but as [d]wise,

16 [1]Redeeming the season: for the [2]days are evil.

17 [e]Wherefore, be ye not unwise, but understand what the will of the Lord is.

4:28 [1] He descendeth from the heart to the hands condemning theft: and because that men which give themselves to this wickedness use to pretend poverty, he showeth that labor is a good remedy against poverty, which God blesseth in such sort that they which labor have always some overplus to help others so far is it from this, that they are constrained to steal other men's goods.

[2] By laboring in things that are holy, and profitable to his neighbor.

4:29 [1] He bridleth the tongue also, teaching us so to temper our talk, that our hearer's mind be not only not destroyed, but also instructed.

[2] Word for word, rotten.

[3] By grace he meaneth that, whereby men may profit to the going on forward godliness and love.

4:30 [1] A general precept against all excess of affections which dwell in the part of the mind, which they call, Angry, and he setteth against them the contrary means. And useth a most vehement preface, how we ought to take heed that we grieve not the holy Spirit of God through our immoderateness and intemperance, who dwelleth in us to this end, to moderate all our affections.

4:32 [1] An argument taken from the example of Christ, most grave and vehement, both for pardoning of those injuries which have been done unto us by our greatest enemies, and much more for having consideration of the miserable, and using moderation and gentle behavior towards all men.

5:3 [1] Now he cometh to another kind of affections, which is in that part of the mind, which men call covetous or desirous: and he reprehended fornication, covetousness, and jesting, very sharply.

5:4 [1] Jests which men cast one at another: that no lightness be seen, nor evil example given, nor any offense moved by evil words

or backbiting.

5:5 [1] Because these sins are such that the most part of men count them not for sins, he awaketh the godly, to the end they should so much the more take heed to themselves from them, as most hurtful plagues.

[2] A bondslave to idolatry, for the covetous man thinketh that his life standeth in his goods.

5:7 [1] Because we are not so ready to anything as to follow evil examples, therefore the Apostle warneth the godly to remember always that the others are but as it were darkness, and that they themselves are as it were light. And therefore the others commit all villany (as men are wont in the dark) but they ought not only not to follow their examples, but also (as the property of the light is) reprove their darkness, and to walk so (having Christ that true light going before them) as it becometh wise men.

5:8 [1] The faithful are called light, both because they have the true light in them which lighteneth them, and also because they give light to others, insomuch, that their honest conversation reproveth the life of wicked men.

5:9 [1] By whose force we are made light in the Lord.

5:11 [1] Make them open to all the world, by your good life.

5:14 [1] The Scripture, or God in the Scripture.

[2] He speaketh of the death of sin.

5:15 [1] The worse and more corrupt that the manners of this world are, the more watchful ought we to be against all occasions, and respect nothing but the will of God.

5:16 [1] This is a metaphor taken from the merchants: who prefer the least profit that may be, before all their pleasures.

[2] The times are troublesome and sharp.

18 [1]And be not drunk with wine, wherein is [2]excess: but be fulfilled with the Spirit,

19 Speaking unto yourselves in Psalms, and hymns, and spiritual songs, singing and making melody to the Lord in your [1]hearts,

20 Giving thanks always for all things unto God even the Father, in the Name of our Lord Jesus Christ,

21 [1]Submitting yourselves one to another in the fear of God.

22 ¶[f,1]Wives, submit yourselves unto your husbands, [2]as unto the Lord.

23 [g,1]For the husband is the wife's head, even as Christ is the head of the Church, [2]and the same is the Savior of *his* body.

24 [1]Therefore as the Church is in subjection to Christ, even so *let* the wives *be* to their husbands in everything.

25 ¶[h,1]Husbands, love your wives, even as Christ loved the Church, and gave himself for it,

26 [1]That he might [2]sanctify it, and cleanse it by the washing of water through the [3]word,

27 That he might make it unto himself a glorious Church, [1]not having spot or wrinkle, or any such thing: but that it should be holy and without blame.

28 [1]So ought men to love their wives, as their own bodies: he that loveth his wife, loveth himself.

29 For no man ever yet hated his [1]own flesh, but nourished and cherisheth it, even as the Lord *doth* the Church.

30 For we are members of his body, [1]of his flesh, and of his bones.

31 [i]For this cause shall a man leave father and mother, and shall [1]cleave to his wife, and they twain shall be one flesh.

32 [1]This is a great secret, but I speak concerning Christ, and concerning the Church.

33 [1]Therefore everyone of you, *do ye so*: let everyone love his wife, even as himself, and *let* the wife *see* that she fear her husband.

6 *1 He showeth the duties of children,   5 servants,   9 and masters: 10 Then he speaketh of the fierce battle that the faithful have,   12 and what weapons we must use in the same: 21 In the end he commendeth Tychicus.*

1 Children, [a,1]obey your parents [2]in the [3]Lord: [4]for this is right.

2 [b,1]Honor thy father and mother ([2]which is the first commandment with [3]promise)

Marginal references:
[f] Col. 3:18
Titus 2:5
1 Pet. 3:1
[g] 1 Cor. 11:3
[h] Col. 3:19
[i] Gen. 2:14
Mark 10:7
1 Cor. 6:16

CHAPTER 6
[a] Col. 3:20
[b] Exod. 20:12
Deut. 5:16
Matt. 15:4
Mark 7:10

5:18 [1] He setteth the sober and holy assemblies of the faithful, against the dissolute bankers of the unfaithful, in which the praises of the only Lord must ring, be it in prosperity or adversity.

[2] All kind of riot, joined with all manner of filthiness and shamefulness.

5:19 [1] With an earnest affection of the heart, and not with the tongue only.

5:21 [1] A short repetition of the end whereunto all things ought to be referred, to serve one another for God's sake.

5:22 [1] Now he descendeth to a family, dividing orderly all the parts of a family. And he saith that the duty of wives consisteth herein, to be obedient to their husbands.

[2] The first argument, for they cannot be disobedient to their husbands, but they must resist God also, who is the author of this subjection.

5:23 [1] A declaration of the former saying: Because God hath made the man head of the woman in matrimony, as Christ is the head of the Church.

[2] Another argument: Because the good estate of the wife dependeth of the man, so that this submission is not only just, but also very profitable: as also the salvation of the Church is of Christ, although far otherwise.

5:24 [1] The conclusion of the wives' duty towards their husbands.

5:25 [1] The husbands' duty towards their wives, is to love them as themselves, of which love, the love of Christ toward his Church is a lively pattern.

5:26 [1] Because many men pretend the infirmities of their wives to excuse their own hardness and cruelty, the Apostle willeth us to mark what manner of Church Christ gat, when he joined it to himself, and how he doth not only not loathe all her filth and uncleanness, but ceaseth not to wipe the same away with his cleanness, until he have wholly purged it.

[2] Make it holy.

[3] Through the promise of free justification and sanctification in Christ, received by faith.

5:27 [1] The Church, as it is considered in itself, shall not be without wrinkle, before it come to the mark it shooteth at: for while it is in this life, it runneth in a race: but if it be considered in Christ, it is clean and without wrinkle.

5:28 [1] Another argument: Every man loveth himself, even of nature: therefore he striveth against nature that loveth not his wife: he proveth the consequent, first by the mystical knitting of Christ and the Church together, and then by the ordinance of God, who saith, that man and wife are as one, that is, not to be divided.

5:29 [1] His own body.

5:30 [1] He alludeth to the making of the woman, which signifieth our coupling together with Christ, which is wrought by faith, but is sealed by the Sacrament of the Supper.

5:31 [1] See Matt. 19:5

5:32 [1] That no man might dream of natural conjunction or knitting of Christ and his Church together (such as the husbands and the wives is) he showeth that it is secret, to wit, spiritual and such as far differeth from the common capacity of man: as which consisteth by the virtue of the Spirit, and not of the flesh by faith, and by no natural band.

5:33 [1] The conclusion both of the husband's duty toward his wife, and of the wife's toward her husband.

6:1 [1] He cometh to another part of a family, and showeth that the duty of the children toward their parents, consisteth in obedience unto them.

[2] The first argument: because God hath so appointed: whereupon it followeth also, that children are so far forth bound to obey their parents, as they may not swerve from the true worship of God.

[3] For the Lord is author of all fatherhood, and therefore we must yield such obedience as he will have us.

[4] The second argument: because this obedience is most just.

6:2 [1] A proof of the first argument.

[2] The third argument, taken of the profit that ensueth thereby: because the Lord vouchsafed this commandment amongst the rest, of a special blessing.

[3] With a special promise: for otherwise the second commandment hath a promise of mercy to a thousand generations, but that promise is general.

3 That it may be well with thee, and that thou mayest live long on earth.

4 ¹And ye, fathers, provoke not your children to wrath: but bring them up in instruction and ²information of the Lord.

5 ᶜ¹Servants, be obedient unto them that are *your* masters, ²according to the flesh, with ³fear and trembling in singleness of your hearts, as unto Christ,

6 Not with service to the eye, as men pleasers, but as the servants of Christ, ¹doing the will of God from the heart.

7 With good will, serving the ¹Lord, and not men.

8 ¹And know ye that whatsoever good thing any man doeth, that same shall he receive of the Lord, whether *he be* bond or free,

9 ¹And ye masters, do the same things unto them, putting away threatening: and know that even your master also is in heaven, neither is there ᵈ²respect of person with him.

10 ¶ ¹Finally, my brethren, be strong in the Lord, and in the power of his might.

11 Put on the whole armor of God, that ye may be able to stand against the assaults of the devil.

12 ¹For we wrestle not against flesh and ²blood, but against ᵉ³principalities, against powers, *and* against the worldly governors, *the princes* of the darkness of this world, against spiritual wickedness, *which are* in the high places.

13 ¹For this cause take unto you the whole armor of God, that ye may be able to resist in the ²evil day,

Col. 3:22
Titus 2:9
1 Pet. 2:18

ᵈ *Deut. 10:17*
2 Chron. 16:7
Job 34:19
Acts 10:34
Rom. 2:11
Gal. 2:6
Col. 3:25
1 Pet. 1:17

ᵉ *Eph. 2:2*

and having finished all things, stand fast.

14 Stand therefore, and your loins girded about with verity, and having on the breastplate of righteousness,

15 And your feet shod with the ¹preparation of the Gospel of peace.

16 Above all, take the shield of Faith, wherewith ye may quench all the fiery darts of the wicked,

17 And take the helmet of Salvation, and the sword of the Spirit, which is the word of God.

18 And pray always with all manner prayer and supplication in the ¹spirit: and watch thereunto with all perseverance and supplication for all Saints,

19 And for me, that utterance may be given unto me, that I may open my mouth boldly to publish the secret of the Gospel,

20 Whereof I am the ambassador in bonds, that therein I may speak boldly, as I ought to speak.

21 ¶ ¹But that ye may also know mine affairs, *and* what I do, Tychicus *my* dear brother and faithful minister in the Lord, shall show you of all things.

22 Whom I have sent unto you for the same purpose, that ye might know mine affairs, and that he might comfort your hearts.

23 Peace *be* with the brethren, and love with faith from God the Father, and *from* the Lord Jesus Christ.

24 Grace *be* with all them which love our Lord Jesus Christ, to *their* ¹immortality, Amen.

¶ Written from Rome unto the Ephesians, *and sent* by Tychicus.

6:4 ¹ It is the duty of fathers to use their fatherly authority moderately, and to God's glory.

² Such information and precepts, as being taken out of God's book are holy and acceptable to him.

6:5 ¹ Now he ascendeth to the third part of a family, to wit, to the duty both of the masters and of the servants. And he showeth that the duty of servants consisteth in a hearty love and reverence to their master.

² He mitigateth the sharpness of service, in that they are spiritually free, notwithstanding the same, and yet that spiritual freedom taketh not away corporal service, insomuch that they cannot be Christ's, unless they serve their masters willingly and faithfully, so far forth as they may with safe conscience.

³ With careful reverence: for slavish fear is not allowable, much less in Christian servants.

6:6 ¹ To cut off occasion of all pretences, he teacheth us that it is God's will that some are either born or made servants, and therefore they must respect God's will, although their service be never so hard.

6:7 ¹ Being moved with a reverence so Godward, as though ye served God himself.

6:8 ¹ Although they serve unkind and cruel masters, yet the obedience of servants is no less acceptable to God, than the obedience of them that are free.

6:9 ¹ It is the duty of masters to use the authority that they have over their servants modestly, and holily, seeing that they in another respect have a common master, which is in heaven, who will judge both the bond and the free.

² Either of freedom or bondage.

6:10 ¹ He concludeth the other part of this Epistle with a grave

exhortation, that all be ready, and fight constantly, trusting to spiritual weapons, until their enemies be clean put to flight. And first of all, he warneth us to take the armor of God, whereby only our enemy may be dispatched.

6:12 ¹ Secondly he declareth that our chiefest and mightiest enemies are invisible, that we may not think that our chiefest conflict is with men.

² Against men, which are of a frail and brittle nature, against which are set spiritual subtleties, more mighty than the other by a thousand parts.

³ He giveth these names to the evil angels, reason of the effects which they work: not that they are able to do the same of themselves, but because God giveth them the bridle.

6:13 ¹ He showeth that these enemies are put to flight with the only armor of God, to wit, with uprightness of conscience, a godly and holy life, knowledge of the Gospel, faith, and to be short, with the word of God, and using daily earnest prayer for the health of the Church, and especially, for the constance of the true, godly, and valiant ministers of the word.

² See Eph. 5:16.

6:15 ¹ That the preparation of the Gospel may be as it were shoes to you: and it is very fitly called the Gospel of peace, for that, seeing we have to go to God through most dangerous ranks of enemies, this may encourage us to go on manfully, in that we know by the doctrine of the Gospel, that we take our journey to God, who is at peace with us.

6:18 ¹ That holy prayers may proceed from the holy Spirit.

6:21 ¹ A familiar and very amiable declaration of his state, together with a solemn prayer, wherewith Paul is wont to end his Epistles.

6:24 ¹ To life everlasting.

THE EPISTLE OF
PAUL TO THE
PHILIPPIANS

1 *3 Having testified his godly and tender affection towards the Philippians, 12 he entreateth of himself and his bands: 22 And pricketh them forward by his own example, 27 and exhorteth them to unity, 28 and patience.*

1 Paul [1]and Timothy the servants of JESUS CHRIST, to all the Saints in Christ Jesus, which are at Philippi, with the [2]Bishops, and Deacons:

2 Grace *be* with you, and peace from God our Father, and *from* the Lord Jesus Christ:

3 I thank my God, *having* you in perfect memory,

4 (Always in all my prayers for all you, praying with gladness)

5 Because of the [1]fellowship which ye have in the Gospel, from the [2]first day unto now.

6 And I am persuaded of this same thing, that he that hath begun *this* good work in you, will perform it until the [1]day of Jesus Christ,

7 As it becometh me so to judge of you all, because I have you in remembrance, that both in my [1]bands, and in *my* defense, and confirmation of the Gospel you all were partakers of my [2]grace.

8 [1]For God is my record, how I long after you all from the very heart root in Jesus Christ.

9 [1]And this I pray that your love may abound yet more and more in knowledge, and in all judgment,

10 That ye may allow those things which are best, that ye may be pure, and without offense, until the day of Christ,

11 Filled with the [1]fruits of righteousness, which are by Jesus Christ unto the glory and praise of God.

12 ¶ [1]I would ye understood, brethren, that the things which *have come* unto me, are turned rather to the furthering of the Gospel,

13 So that my bands [1]in Christ are famous throughout all the [2]judgment hall, and in all other *places*.

14 Insomuch that many of the brethren in the Lord are boldened through my bands, and dare more frankly speak the [1]Word.

15 Some preach Christ even through envy and strife, and some also of good will.

16 The one part preacheth Christ of contention, *and* not [1]purely, supposing to add more affliction to my bands.

17 But the others of love, knowing that I am set for the defense of the Gospel.

18 [1]What then: yet Christ is preached all manner ways, whether *it be* under a [2]pretence, or sincerely: and I therein joy: yea, and will joy.

19 For I know that this shall turn to my salvation through your prayer, and by the help of the Spirit

---

1:1 [1] The mark whereat he shooteth in this Epistle, is to confirm the Philippians by all means possible, not only not to faint, but also to go forward. And first of all, he commendeth their former doings, to exhort them to go forward: which thing he sayeth, he hopeth fully they will do, and that by the testimony of their lively charity, but in the mean season he referreth all things to the grace of God.

[2] By the Bishops are meant both the Pastors, which have the dispensation of the word and the Elders, that govern: and by Deacons are meant those that were stewards of the treasury of the Church and had to look unto the poor.

1:5 [1] Because that you also are made partakers of the Gospel.

[2] Ever since I knew you.

1:6 [1] The Spirit of God will not forsake you unto the very latter end, until your mortal bodies shall appear before the judgment of Christ, to be glorified.

1:7 [1] A true proof of a true knitting together with Christ.

[2] He calleth his bands, grace, as though he had received some singular benefit.

1:8 [1] He declareth his good will towards them, therewithal showing by what means chiefly they may be confirmed, to wit, by continual prayer.

1:9 [1] He showeth what thing we ought chiefly desire, to wit, first of

all, that we may increase in the true knowledge of God (so that we may be able to discern things that differ one from another) and also in charity, that even to the end we may give ourselves to good works indeed, to the glory of God by Jesus Christ.

1:11 [1] If righteousness be the tree, and good works the fruits, then must the papists needs be deceived, when they say that works are the cause of righteousness.

1:12 [1] He preventeth the offense that might come by his persecution, whereby divers took occasion to disgrace his Apostleship. To whom he answereth, that God hath blesseth his imprisonment in such wise, that he is by that means become more famous, and the dignity of the Gospel by this occasion is greatly enlarged, although not with like affection in all men, yet indeed.

1:13 [1] For Christ's sake.

[2] In the Emperor's court.

1:14 [1] The Gospel is called the Word, to set forth the excellence of it.

1:16 [1] Not with a pure mind: for otherwise their doctrine was pure.

1:18 [1] He showeth by setting forth his own example, that the end of our affliction is true joy: and that through the virtue of the Spirit of Christ, which he giveth to them that ask it.

[2] Under a goodly color and show: for they made Christ a cloak for their ambition and envy.

of Jesus Christ,

20 [1]As I fervently look for, and hope, that in nothing I shall be ashamed, but that with all confidence, as always, so now Christ shall be magnified in my body, whether *it be* by life or by death.

21 For Christ *is* to me both in life and in death advantage.

22 [1]And whether to live in the [2]flesh *were* profitable for me, and what to choose I know not.

23 For I am distressed between both, desiring to be loosed and to be with Christ, which is best of all.

24 Nevertheless, to abide in the flesh, *is* more needful for you.

25 And this am I sure of, that I shall abide, and with you all continue, for your furtherance and joy of *your* faith,

26 That ye may more abundantly rejoice in JESUS CHRIST for me, by my coming to you again.

27 [1]Only let your conversation be as it becometh the Gospel of Christ, that whether I come and see you, or else be absent, I may hear of your matters, that ye [2]continue in one spirit, *and* in one mind, fighting together through the faith of the Gospel.

28 [1]And in nothing fear your adversaries, which is to them a token of perdition, and to you of salvation, and that of God.

29 [1]For unto you it is given for Christ, that not only ye should believe in him, but also suffer for his sake,

30 [1]Having the same fight, which ye saw in me, and now hear *to be* in me.

2

[1] He exhorteth them above all things, 3 to humility, 6 and that by the example of Christ. 19 He promiseth to send Timothy shortly unto them, 26 and excuseth the long tarrying of Epaphroditus.

1 [1]If *there be* therefore any consolation in [2]Christ, if any comfort of love, if any fellowship of the Spirit, if any [3]compassion and mercy,

2 Fulfill my joy, that ye be like minded, having the [1]same love, being of one accord, and of one judgment,

3 That nothing *be done* through contention or vainglory, but that in meekness of mind every man esteem others better than himself.

4 Look not every man on his own things, but every man also on the things of other men.

5 [1]Let the same mind be in you that was even in Christ Jesus,

6 Who being in the [1]form of God, [2]thought it no robbery to be [3]equal with God:

7 But he made himself of [1]no reputation, and took on him the [2]form of a servant, and was made like unto men, and was found in shape as a man.

8 He humbled himself, and became obedient unto the death, even the death of the cross.

9 [1]Wherefore God hath also highly exalted him, and given him a [2]name above every name.

10 That at the Name of Jesus should [1]every knee bow, *both* of things in heaven, and things in earth, and things under the earth.

11 And that [1]every tongue should confess that Jesus Christ *is* the Lord, unto the glory of God the Father.

1:20 [1] We must continue even to the end, with great confidence, having nothing before our eyes but Christ's glory only, whether we live or die.
1:22 [1] An example of a true shepherd, who maketh more acount how he may profit his sheep, than he doth of any commodity of his own whatsoever.
  [2] To live in this mortal body.
1:27 [1] Having set down those things before, in manner of a Preface, he descendeth now to exhortations, warning them first of all, to consent both in doctrine and mind, and afterward, that being thus knit together with those common bands, they continue through the strength of faith to bear all adversity in such sort, that they admit nothing unworthy the profession of the Gospel.
  [2] The word signifieth, to stand fast, and it is proper to wrestlers, that stand fast, and shrink not a foot.
1:28 [1] We ought not to be discouraged, but rather encouraged by the persecutions which the enemies of the Gospel imagine and practice against us: seeing that they are certain witnesses from God himself, both of our salvation, and of the destruction of the wicked.
1:29 [1] He proveth that his saying, that persecution is a token of our salvation, because it is a gift of God to suffer for Christ, which gift he bestoweth upon his own, as he doth the gift of faith.
1:30 [1] Now he showeth for what purpose he made mention of his afflictions.
2:1 [1] A most earnest request to remove all those things, whereby that great and special consent and agreement is commonly broken, to wit, contention and pride, whereby it cometh to pass, that they separate themselves one from another.
  [2] Any Christian comfort.
  [3] If any feeling of inward love.
2:2 [1] Like love.
2:5 [1] He setteth before them a most perfect example of all modesty and sweet conversation, Christ Jesus, whom we ought to follow with all our might: who abased himself so far for our sakes, although he be above all, that he took upon him the form of a servant, to wit, our flesh willingly, subject to all infirmities, even to the death of the cross.
2:6 [1] Such as God himself is, and therefore God, for there is none in all parts like to God, but God himself.
  [2] Christ, that glorious and everlasting God, knew that he might rightfully and lawfully not appear in the base flesh of man, but remain with majesty meet for God: yet he chose rather to debase himself.
  [3] If the Son be equal to the Father, then is there of necessity an equality, which Arrius, that Heretic, denieth: and if the Son be compared with the Father, then is there a distinction of persons, which Sabellius, that heretic, denieth.
2:7 [1] He brought himself from all things, as it were to nothing.
  [2] By taking our manhood upon him.
2:9 [1] He showeth the most glorious event of Christ's submission, to teach us, that modesty is the true way to true praise and glory.
  [2] Dignity and renown, and the matter with it.
2:10 [1] All creatures shall at length be subject to Christ.
2:11 [1] Every nation.

12 [1]Wherefore my beloved, as ye have always obeyed me, not as in my presence only, but now much more in mine absence, so [2]make an end of your own salvation with fear and trembling.

13 [1]For it is God which worketh in you both [2]the will and the deed, even of his good pleasure.

14 [1]Do all things without [a]murmuring and reasonings,

15 [1]That ye may be blameless, and pure, and the sons of God without rebuke in the midst of a naughty and crooked nation, among whom ye shine as [b]lights in the world,

16 Holding forth the [1]word of life, [2]that I may rejoice in the day of Christ, that I have not run in vain, neither have labored in vain.

17 Yea, and though I be offered up upon the [1]sacrifice, and service of your faith, I am glad, and rejoice with you all.

18 For the same cause also be ye glad, and rejoice with me.

19 [1]And I trust in the Lord Jesus, to send [c]Timothy shortly unto you, that I also may be of [2]good comfort, when I know your state.

20 For I have no man like-minded, who will faithfully care for your matters.

21 [d]For [1]all seek their own, and not that which is Jesus Christ's.

22 But ye know the proof of him, that as a son with the father, he hath served with me in the Gospel.

23 Him therefore I hope to send as soon as I know how it will go with me,

CHAPTER 2
[a] 1 Pet. 4:9
[b] Matt. 5:14
[c] Acts 16:1
[d] 1 Cor. 10:24

24 And I trust in the Lord, that I also myself shall come shortly.

25 But I supposed it necessary to send my brother Epaphroditus unto you my companion in labor, and fellow soldier, even your messenger, and he that ministered unto me such things as I wanted.

26 For he longed after all you, and was full of heaviness, because ye had heard that he had been sick.

27 And no doubt he was sick, very near unto death: but God had mercy on him, and not on him only, but on me also, lest I should have sorrow upon sorrow.

28 I sent him therefore the more diligently, that when ye should see him again, ye might rejoice, and I might be the less sorrowful.

29 Receive him therefore in the Lord with all gladness, and make much of such:

30 Because that for the [1]work of Christ he was near unto death, and regarded not his life, to fulfill that service which was lacking on your part toward me.

3

2 He refuteth the vain boastings of the false apostles, 7 and setteth Christ against them. 10 He setteth out the force and nature of faith, 15 that laying all things aside, they may be partakers of the Cross of Christ, 18 the enemies whereof, he noteth out.

1 Moreover, [1]my brethren, rejoice in the Lord. [2]It grieveth me not to write the [3]same things to you, and for you it is a sure thing.

2 Beware of dogs: beware of evil workers: beware of the [1]concision.

3 [1]For we are the circumcision, which worship

2:12 [1] The conclusion: We must go on to salvation with humility and submission, by the way of our vocation.

[2] He is said to make an end of his salvation, which runneth in the race of righteousness.

2:13 [1] A most sure and grounded argument against pride, for that we have nothing in us praiseworthy but it cometh of the free gift of God, and is without us, for we have no ability or power, so much as to will well (much less to do well) but only of the free mercy of God.

[2] Why then, we are not stocks, but yet we do not will well of nature, but only because God hath made of our naughty will a good will.

2:14 [1] He describeth modesty by the contrary effects of pride, teaching us, that it is far both from all malicious, and close or inward hatred and also from open contentions and brawlings.

2:15 [1] To be short, he requireth a life without fault, and pure, that being lightened with the word of God, they may shine in the darkness of this world.

2:16 [1] The Gospel is called the word of life, because of the effects which it worketh.

[2] Again he pricketh them forward, setting before them his true Apostolic care that he had of them, comforting them moreover, to the end they should not be sorry for the greatness of his afflictions, no not although he should die to make perfect their oblation with his blood, as it were with a drink offering.

2:17 [1] As if he said, I brought you Philippians to Christ, my desire is that you present yourselves a lively sacrifice to him, and then shall it not grieve me to be offered up as a drink offering, to accomplish this your spiritual offering.

2:19 [1] Moreover he confirmeth their minds both by sending back Epaphroditus unto them, whose fidelity towards them, and great pains in helping him, he commendeth: and also promising to send Timothy shortly unto them, by whose presence they shall receive great commodity, and hoping also to come himself shortly unto them, if God wills.

[2] May be confirmed in my joy of mind.

2:21 [1] The most part.

2:30 [1] He calleth it here the work of Christ, to visit Christ, being poor and in bands in the person of Paul.

3:1 [1] A conclusion of those things which have been before said, to wit, that they go forward cheerfully in the Lord.

[2] A preface to the next admonition that followeth, to take good heed and beware of false apostles, which join Circumcision with Christ, (that is to say, justification by works, with free justification by faith) and beat into men's heads the ceremonies which are abolished: for true exercises of godliness and charity. And he calleth them dogs as profane barkers, and evil workmen, because they neglected true works and did not teach the true use of them. To be short, he calleth them Concision, because in urging Circumcision, they cut off themselves and others from the Church.

[3] Which you have oftentimes heard of me.

3:2 [1] He alludeth to Circumcision, of the name whereof while they boasted, they cut asunder the Church.

3:3 [1] He showeth that we ought to use true circumcision, to wit, the circumcision of the heart, that cutting off all wicked affections by the virtue of Christ, we may serve God in purity of life.

God in the spirit, and rejoice in Christ Jesus, and have no confidence [2]in the flesh:

4 [1]Though I might also have confidence in the flesh. If any other man thinketh that he hath whereof he might trust in the flesh, much more I,

5 Circumcised the eighth day, of the kindred of Israel, of the tribe of Benjamin, [a]an Hebrew of the Hebrews, [b]by the Law a Pharisee.

6 Concerning zeal, I persecuted the Church: touching the righteousness which is in the Law, I was unrebukeable.

7 But the things that were [1]vantage unto me, the same I counted loss for Christ's sake.

8 Yea, doubtless I think [1]all things but loss for the excellent knowledge sake of Christ Jesus my Lord, for whom I have counted all things loss, and do judge *them* to be dung, that I might [2]win Christ,

9 And might be found in [1]him, *that is*, [2]not having mine own righteousness, which is of the Law, but that which is through the faith of Christ, *even the* righteousness which is of God through faith,

10 [1]That I may [2]know him, and the virtue of his resurrection, and the [3]fellowship of his afflictions, and be made conformable unto his death,

11 If by any means I might attain unto the [1]resurrection of the dead:

12 Not as though I had already attained *to it*, either were already perfect: but I follow, if that I may comprehend *that* for whose sake also I am [1]comprehended of Christ Jesus.

CHAPTER 3
a 2 Cor. 11:22
b Acts 23:6
c Rom. 16:17
d 1 Cor. 1:7
Titus 2:13

13 Brethren, I count not myself, that I have attained *to it*, but one thing I *do*: I forget that which is behind, and endeavor myself unto that which is before,

14 And follow hard toward the mark, for the prize of the high calling of God in Christ Jesus.

15 [1]Let us therefore as many as be [2]perfect, be thus minded: and if ye be otherwise minded, God shall reveal even the same unto you.

16 Nevertheless, *in that* whereunto we are come, let us proceed by one rule, that we may mind one thing.

17 Brethren, be followers of me, and look on them, which walk so, as ye have us for an example.

18 [c,1] For many walk, of whom I have told you often, and now tell you weeping, *that they are* the enemies of the cross of Christ:

19 Whose [1]end *is* damnation, whose God *is their* belly, and *whose* [2]glory *is* to their shame, which mind earthly things.

20 [1]But our conversation is in heaven, from whence also we look for the [d]Savior, *even* the Lord Jesus Christ,

21 Who shall change our vile body, that it may be fashioned like unto his glorious body, according to the working, whereby he is able even to subdue all things unto himself.

4 1 *From particular exhortations,* 4 *he cometh to general.* 10 *He saith that he took such joy in their readiness to liberality,* 12 *that he will patiently bear the want.*

1 Therefore, [1]my brethren, beloved and longed for, *my* joy and my [2]crown, so continue in the [3]Lord,

---

[2] In outward things, which pertain nothing to the soul.
3:4 [1] He doubteth not to prefer himself even according to the flesh, before those perverse hote urgers of the Law, that all men may know that he doth with good judgment of mind, lightly esteem all those outward things: forsomuch as he lacketh nothing which hath Christ, nay, the confidence of our works cannot stand with the free justification in Christ by faith.
3:7 [1] Which is accounted for vantage.
3:8 [1] He shutteth out all works, as well those that go before, as those that come after faith.
   [2] That in their place I might get Christ, and of a poor man become rich: so far off am I from losing anything.
3:9 [1] In Christ: for they that are found without Christ, are subject to condemnation.
   [2] That is, to be in Christ, to be found not in a man's own righteousness, but clothed with the righteousness of Christ imputed to him.
3:10 [1] This is the end of righteousness by faith touching us, that by the virtue of his resurrection we may scape from death.
   [2] That I may feel him indeed, and have a trial of him.
   [3] The way to that eternal salvation is to follow Christ's steps, by afflictions and persecutions, until we come to Christ himself, who is our mark whereat we shoot, and receive that reward whereunto God calleth us in him. And the Apostle setteth these true exercises of godliness against those vain ceremonies of the Law, wherein the false apostles put the sum of godliness.
3:11 [1] To life everlasting, which followeth the resurrection of the Saints.
3:12 [1] For we run not, but so far forth, as we are laid hold on of Christ, that is, as God giveth us strength, and showeth us the way.

3:15 [1] The conclusion of this exhortation standing upon three members: The one is, that such as have profited in the truth of this doctrine, should continue in it. The second is, that if there be any which are yet ignorant and understand not these things, and doubt of the abolishing of the Law, they should cause no trouble, and should be gently born withall, until they also be instructed of the Lord. The third is, that they esteem the false apostles by their fruits: wherein he doubteth not to set forth himself for an example.
   [2] He said before that he was not perfect. So that in this place he calleth them perfect, which have somewhat profited in the knowledge of Christ and the Gospel, whom he setteth against the rude and ignorant, as he expoundeth himself in the next verse following.
3:18 [1] He painteth out the false apostles in their colors, not upon malice or ambition, but with sorrow and tears, to wit, because that being enemies of the Gospel (for that is joined with affliction) they regard nothing else, but the commodities of this life: that is to say, that flowing in peace, and quietness, and all worldly pleasures, they may live in great estimation amongst men, whose miserable end he forewarned them of.
3:19 [1] Reward.
   [2] Which they hunt after at men's hands.
3:20 [1] He setteth against these fellows, true pastors which neglect earthly things, and aspire to heaven only, where they know, that even in their bodies they shall be clothed with that eternal glory, by the virtue of God.
4:1 [1] A rehearsal of the conclusion: That they manfully continue, until they have gotten the victory, trusting to the Lord's strength.
   [2] My honor.
   [3] In that concord, whereof the Lord is the band.

ye beloved.

2 ¹I pray Euodia, and beseech Syntyche, that they be of one accord in the Lord.

3 Yea, and I beseech thee, faithful yokefellow, help those *women*, which labored with me in the Gospel, with Clement also, and with other my fellow laborers, whose names *are* in the ᵃ·¹book of life.

4 ¹Rejoice in the ²Lord always, again I say, rejoice.

5 ¹Let your ²patient mind be known unto all men. ³The Lord *is* at hand.

6 ¹Be nothing careful, but in all things let your requests be showed unto God in prayer and supplication with ²giving of thanks.

7 And the ¹peace of God which passeth all understanding, shall preserve your ²hearts and minds in Christ Jesus.

8 ¹Furthermore, brethren, whatsoever things are true, whatsoever things ²*are* honest, whatsoever things *are* just, whatsoever things *are* pure, whatsoever things *are* worthy love, whatsoever things *are* of good report, if there *be* any virtue, or if there *be* any praise, think on these things.

9 Which ye have both learned and received, and heard, and seen in me: those things do, and the God of peace shall be with you.

10 ¹Now I rejoice also in the Lord greatly, that now at the last your care for me springeth afresh, wherein notwithstanding ye were careful, but ye lacked opportunity.

11 I speak not because of ¹want: for I have learned in whatsoever state I am, therewith to be content.

CHAPTER 4
ᵃ Rev. 3:5
Rev. 10:8
Rev. 21:27

12 And I can be ¹abased, and I can abound: everywhere in all things I am ²instructed, both to be full, and to be hungry, and to abound, and to have want.

13 I am able to *do* all things through the help of Christ, which strengtheneth me.

14 Notwithstanding ye have well done, that ye did communicate to mine affliction.

15 ¹And ye Philippians know also that in the ²beginning of the Gospel, when I departed from Macedonia, no Church communicated with me, concerning the matter of giving and receiving, but ye only.

16 For even *when I was* in Thessalonica, ye sent once, and afterward again for my necessity.

17 ¹Not that I desire a gift: but I desire the fruit which may further your reckoning.

18 Now I have received all, and have plenty: I was even filled, after that I had received of Epaphroditus that which *came* from you, an ¹odor that smelleth sweet, a sacrifice acceptable and pleasant to God.

19 And my God shall fulfill all your necessities through his riches with glory in Jesus Christ.

20 Unto God even our Father *be* praise for evermore, Amen.

21 Salute all the Saints in Christ Jesus. The brethren, which are with me, greet you.

22 All the Saints salute you, and most of all they which are of ¹Caesar's household.

23 The grace of our Lord Jesus Christ *be* with you all, Amen.

¶Written to the Philippians from Rome, *and sent* by Epaphroditus.

4:2 ¹ He also calleth on some by name, partly, because they needed private exhortation, and partly also to stir up others, to be more prompt and ready.

4:3 ¹ God is said after the manner of men, to have a book, wherein the names of his elect are written, to whom he will give everlasting life. Ezekiel calleth it the writing of the house of Israel, and the secret of the Lord, Ezek. 13:9.

4:4 ¹ He addeth particular exhortations: and the first is, that the joy of the Philippians be not hindered by any afflictions that the wicked imagine and work against them.

² So is the joy of the world distinguisheth from our joy.

4:5 ¹ The second is not taking all things in good part, they behave themselves moderately with all men.

² Your quiet and settled mind.

³ The taking away of an objection: We must not be disquieted through impatience, seeing that God is at hand to give us remedy in time against all our miseries.

4:6 ¹ The third is, that we be not too careful for anything, but with sure confidence give God thanks, and crave of him whatsoever we have need of, that with a quiet conscience we may wholly and with all our hearts submit ourselves to him.

² So David began very oft with tears, but ended with thanksgiving.

4:7 ¹ That great quietness of mind, which God only giveth in Christ.

² He divideth the mind into the heart, that is, into that part which is the seat of the will and affections, and into the higher part, whereby we understand and reason of matters.

4:8 ¹ A general conclusion, that as they have been taught both in word and example, so they frame their lives to the rule of all holiness and righteousness.

² Whatsoever things are such as do beautify and set you out with a holy gravity.

4:10 ¹ He witnesseth that their liberality was acceptable to him, wherewith they did help him in his extreme poverty: but yet so moderating his words, that he might declare himself void of all suspicion of dishonesty, and that he hath a mind contented both with prosperity and adversity, and to be short, that he reposeth himself in the only will of God.

4:11 ¹ As though I passed for my want.

4:12 ¹ He useth a general word, and yet he speaketh but of one kind of cross, which is poverty, for commonly poverty bringeth all kinds of discommodity with it.

² This is a metaphor taken from holy things or sacrifices, for our life is like a sacrifice.

4:15 ¹ He witnesseth that he remembereth also their former benefits, and again putteth away sinistrous suspicion of immoderate desire, in that that he received nought of any else.

² At that beginning when I preached the Gospel amongst you.

4:17 ¹ He witnesseth again, that he alloweth well of their benefit not so much for his own sake as for theirs, because they gave it not so much to him, as they offered it to God as a sacrifice, whereof the Lord himself will not be forgetful.

4:18 ¹ He alludeth to the sweet smelling savors that were offered in the old Law.

4:22 ¹ Such as belong to the Emperor Nero.

THE EPISTLE OF
PAUL TO THE
COLOSSIANS

1 *1 After the salutation, 4 he praiseth them the more, to make them attentive unto him. 7 He reporteth the testimony of the doctrine which they heard of Epaphras. 13 He magnifieth God's grace towards them, 20 and showeth that all the parts of our salvation consist in Christ alone.*

1 Paul an Apostle of Jesus Christ, by the ¹will of God, and Timothy *our* brother,

2 To them which are at ¹Colosse, Saints and faithful brethren in Christ: Grace *be* with you, and peace from God our Father, and *from* the Lord Jesus Christ.

3 ¹We give thanks to God even the ²Father of our Lord Jesus Christ, always praying for you:

4 Since we heard of your faith in Christ Jesus, and of *your* love toward all Saints.

5 For the ¹hope's sake, which is laid up for you in heaven, whereof ye have heard before by the word of truth, *which is* the Gospel,

6 Which is come unto you, even as *it is* unto all the world, and is fruitful as *it is* also among you from the day that ye heard and truly knew the grace of God,

7 As ye also learned of Epaphras our dear fellow servant, which is for you a faithful minister of Christ:

CHAPTER 1
ᵃ Matt. 3:17
Matt. 17:5
2 Pet. 1:17
ᵇ Heb. 1:3
ᶜ John 1:3

8 ¹Who hath also declared unto us your love in the ²Spirit.

9 For this cause we also, since the day we heard *of it*, cease not to pray for you, and to desire that ye might be fulfilled with knowledge of ¹his will in all wisdom, and spiritual understanding.

10 That ye might walk worthy of the Lord, and please *him* in all things, being fruitful in all good works, and increasing in the knowledge of God,

11 ¹Strengthened with all might through his glorious power, unto all patience, and longsuffering with ²joyfulness,

12 ¹Giving thanks unto the ²Father, which hath made us meet to be partakers of the inheritance of the Saints in ³light,

13 Who hath delivered us from the power of darkness, and hath translated us into the kingdom ᵈof his dear Son,

14 ¹In whom we have redemption through his blood, *that is*, the forgiveness of sins.

15 ¹Who is the ᵇimage of the invisible God, ²the first begotten of every creature.

16 'For by him were all things created which are in heaven, and which are in earth, things visible and invisible: whether *they be* ¹Thrones, or Dominions,

---

1:1 ¹ By the free bountifulness of God.

1:2 ¹ Colosse is situated in Phrygia, not far from Hierapolis and Laodicea, on that side that they bend toward Lycia and Pamphylia.

1:3 ¹ He commendeth the doctrine that was delivered them by Epaphras, and their readiness in receiving it.

² We cannot otherwise consider of God to our salvation, but as he is Christ's Father, in whom we are adopted.

1:5 ¹ For the glory that is hoped for.

1:8 ¹ He declareth his good will towards them, telling them that they must not still remain at one stay but go on further both in the knowledge of the Gospel, and also in the true use of it.

² Your spiritual love, or your love which cometh from the Spirit.

1:9 ¹ God's will.

1:11 ¹ The gift of continuance is not of us, but it proceedeth from the virtue of God, which he doth freely give us.

² It must not be unwilling, and as it were drawn out of us by force, but proceed from a merry and joyful mind.

1:12 ¹ Having ended the preface, he goeth to the matter itself, that is to say, to an excellent description (although it be but short) of whole Christianity, which is fitly divided into three treatises: for first of all he expoundeth the true doctrine, according to the order of the causes, beginning from this verse to the 24. And from thence he beginneth

to apply the same to the Colossians with divers exhortations to verse 6 of the second Chapter. And last of all in the third place even to the third Chapter, he refuteth the corruption of true doctrine.

² The efficient cause of our salvation is the only mercy of God the Father, who maketh us meet to be partakers of eternal life, delivering us from the darkness wherein we were born, and bringing us to the light of the knowledge of the glory of his Son.

³ In that glorious and heavenly kingdom.

1:14 ¹ The matter itself of our salvation, is Christ the Son of God, who hath obtained remission of sins for us by the offering up of himself.

1:15 ¹ A lively description of the person of Christ, whereby we understand that in him only, God showeth himself to be seen: who was begotten of the Father before anything was made, that is, from everlasting, by whom also all things that are made, were made without any exception, by whom also they do consist, and whose glory they serve.

² Begotten before anything was made: and therefore the everlasting Son of the everlasting Father.

1:16 ¹ He setteth forth the Angels with glorious names, that by the comparison of most excellent spirits we may understand how far passing the excellence of Christ, in whom only we have to content ourselves, and let go all Angels.

or Principalities, or Powers, all things were created by him, and for him.

17 And he is before all things, and in him all things consist.

18 [1]And he is the head of the body of the Church: he is the beginning, [d]and the [2]first begotten of the dead, that in all things he might have the preeminence.

19 [e]For it pleased the Father, that in him should [1]all fullness dwell.

20 [1]And through peace made by that blood of that his cross, to reconcile to himself through him, through him, I say, [2]all things, both which are in earth, and which are in heaven.

21 [1]And you which were in times past strangers and enemies, because your minds were set in evil works, hath [2]he now also reconciled,

22 In that body of his [1]flesh through death, to make you holy and unblameable, and without fault in his sight.

23 [1]If ye continue, grounded and established in the faith, and be not moved away from the hope of the Gospel, whereof ye have heard, and which hath been preached to [2]every creature, which is under heaven, [3]whereof I Paul am a minister.

24 Now rejoice I in my sufferings [1]for you, and

fulfill the [2]rest of the afflictions of Christ in my flesh, for his body's sake, which is the Church,

25 [1]Whereof I am a minister, according to the dispensation of God, which is given me unto youward, to fulfill the word of God,

26 [f]Which is the mystery hid since the world began, and from all ages, but now is made manifest to his [1]Saints,

27 To whom God [1]would make known what is the riches of his glorious mystery among the Gentiles, which riches is Christ in you, the hope of glory,

28 [1]Whom we preach, admonishing every man, and teaching every man in [2]all wisdom, that we may present every man perfect in Christ Jesus.

29 Whereunto I also labor and strive, according to his working which worketh in me mightily.

2

4 He condemneth, as vain, whatsoever is without Christ, 11 entreating specially of circumcision, 16 of abstinence from meats, 18 and of worshipping of Angels. 20 That we are delivered from the traditions of the Law through Christ.

1 For I [1]would ye knew what great fighting I have for your sakes, and for them of Laodicea, and for as many as have not seen my [2]person in the flesh.

2 [1]That [2]their hearts might be comforted, and

Margin references:
[d] Rev. 1:5 / 1 Cor. 15:20
[e] John 1:14 / Col. 2:9
[f] Rom. 16:25 / Eph. 3:9 / 2 Tim. 1:10 / Titus 1:2 / 1 Pet. 1:20

1:18 [1] Having gloriously declared the excellent dignity of the person of Christ, he describeth his office and function, to wit, that he is that same to the Church, that the head is to the body, that is to say, the prince and governor of it, and the very beginning of true life, as who rising first from death, he is the Author of eternal life, so that he is above all, in whom only there is most plentiful abundance of all good things, which is poured out upon the Church.

[2] Who so rose again that he shall die no more, and who raiseth others from death to life by his power.

1:19 [1] Most plentiful abundance of all things pertaining to God.

1:20 [1] Now he teacheth how Christ executed that office which his Father joined him, to wit, by suffering the death of the cross (which was joined with the curse of God) according to his decree, that by this sacrifice he might reconcile his Father all men as well them which believed in him to come, and were already under this hope gathered into heaven, as them which should upon the earth believe in him afterwards. And thus is justification described of the Apostle, which is one and the chiefest part of the benefit of Christ.

[2] The whole Church.

1:21 [1] Sanctification is another work of God in us by Christ, in that that he restored us (which hated God extremely, and were wholly and willingly given to sin) to his gracious favor, in such sort, that he therewithall purifieth us with his holy Spirit, and consecrateth us to righteousness.

[2] The Son.

1:22 [1] In that fleshly body, to give us to understand that his body was not a fantastical body, but a true body.

1:23 [1] This second treatise of this part of the Epistle, wherein he exhorteth the Colossians not to suffer themselves by any means to be moved from this doctrine, showing and declaring that there is nowhere any other true Gospel.

[2] To all men: whereby we learn that the Gospel was not shut up within the corners of Judea alone.

[3] He purchased authority to this doctrine by his Apostleship, and

taketh a most sure proof thereof, of his afflictions which he suffereth for Christ's Name to instruct the Churches with these examples of patience.

1:24 [1] For your profit and commodity.

[2] The afflictions of the Church are said to be Christ's afflictions, by reason of that fellowship and knitting together, that the body and the head have the one with the other, not that there is any more need to have the Church redeemed, but that Christ showeth his power in the daily weakness of his, and that for the comfort of the whole body.

1:25 [1] He bringeth another proof of his Apostleship, to wit, that God is the author of it, by whom also he was appointed peculiarly Apostle of the Gentiles, to the end that by this means, that same might be fulfilled by him, which the Prophets foretold of the calling of the Gentiles.

1:26 [1] Whom he chose to sanctify unto himself in Christ: moreover he sayeth that the mystery of our redemption was hidden since the world began, except it were revealed unto a few, who also were taught it extraordinarily.

1:27 [1] This Paul bridleth the curiosity of men.

1:28 [1] He protesteth that he doth faithfully execute his Apostleship in every place, bringing men unto Christ only, through the Lord's plentiful blessings of his labors.

[2] Perfect and sound wisdom, which is perfect in itself, and shall in the end make them perfect that follow it.

2:1 [1] The taking away of an objection, in that that he visited not the Colossians, nor the Laodiceans, he did it not of any negligence but is so much the more careful for them.

[2] Me present in body.

2:2 [1] He concludeth shortly the sum of the former doctrine, to wit, that the whole sum of true wisdom and most secret knowledge of God, consisteth in Christ only, and that this is the use of it touching men, that they being knit together in love, rest themselves happily in the knowledge of so great a goodness, until they come fully to enjoy it.

[2] Whom he never saw.

they knit together in love, and in all riches of the ³full assurance of understanding, to know the mystery of God, even the Father, and of Christ:

3   In whom are hid all the treasures of ¹wisdom and knowledge.

4   ¹And this I say, lest any man should beguile you with ²enticing words:

5   ªFor though I be absent in the flesh, yet am I with you in the spirit, rejoicing and beholding your ¹order, and your ²steadfast faith in Christ.

6   As ye have therefore ¹received Christ Jesus the Lord, *so* walk in him.

7   Rooted and built in him, and established in the faith, as ye have been taught, abounding therein with thanksgiving:

8   ¹Beware lest there be any man that ²spoil you through philosophy, and vain deceit, ³through the traditions of men, ⁴according to the ⁵rudiments of the world, ⁶and not after Christ.

9   ¹For ²in him ³dwelleth ⁴all the fullness of the

CHAPTER 2

ª 1 Cor. 5:3
ᵇ Rom. 2:29
ᶜ Rom. 6:4
  Eph. 1:19
ᵈ Eph. 2:1
ᵉ Eph. 2:15

Godhead ⁵bodily.

10   And ye are complete in him, which is the head of all principality and power.

11   ¹In whom also ye are circumcised with ᵇcircumcision made without hands, by putting off the ²sinful body of the flesh, through the circumcision of Christ,

12   ¹In that ye are ᶜ,²buried with ³him through baptism, ⁴in whom ye are also raised up together through the faith of the operation of ⁵God, which raised him from the dead.

13   ᵈ,¹And you which were dead in sins, ²and in the uncircumcision of your flesh, hath he quickened together with him, forgiving you all *your* trespasses,

14   ¹And putting out the ᵉ,²handwriting of ordinances that was against us, which was contrary to us, he even took it out of the way, and fastened it upon the cross,

15   And hath spoiled the ¹Principalities, and Powers, and hath ²made a show of them openly, and hath triumphed over them in the ³same *cross*.

16   ¹Let no man therefore condemn you in meat

---

³ Of that understanding, which bringeth forth certain and undoubted persuasion in our minds.

2:3 ¹ There is no true wisdom without Christ.

2:4 ¹ A passing over to the treatise following against the corruptions of Christianity.

² With a framed kind of talk made to persuade.

2:5 ¹ The manner of your Ecclesiastical discipline.

² Doctrine.

2:6 ¹ So then Christ hangeth not upon men's traditions.

2:8 ¹ He bringeth all corruptions to three kinds: The first is that, which resteth of vain and curious speculations, and yet beareth a show of a certain subtle wisdom.

² This is a word of war, and it is as much as to drive or carry away a spoil or booty.

³ The second which is manifestly superstitious and vain, and standeth only upon custom and fained inspirations.

⁴ The third kind was of them which joined the rudiments of the world, (that is to say, the ceremonies of the Law) with the Gospel.

⁵ Principles and rulers, wherewith God ruled his Church, as it were under a schoolmaster.

⁶ A general confutation of all corruptions is this, that that must needs be a false religion, which addeth anything to Christ.

2:9 ¹ A reason: Because only Christ God and man, is most perfect, and passeth far above all things, so that whosoever hath him, may require nothing more.

² By these words, is showed a distinction of the natures.

³ This word (Dwelleth) noteth out unto us the joining together of those natures, so that of God and Man, is one Christ.

⁴ These words set down most perfect Godhead to be in Christ.

⁵ The knitting together of God and man, is substantial and essential.

2:11 ¹ Now he dealeth perfectly against the third kind, that is to say, against them which urged the Jewish religion: and first of all, he denieth that we have need of the Circumcision of the flesh, seeing that without it we are circumcised within, by the virtue of Christ.

² These many words are used to show what the old man is, whom Paul in other places calleth the body of sin.

2:12 ¹ The taking away of an objection: we need not so much as the eternal sign which our fathers had, seeing that our baptism is a most effectual pledge and witness, of that inward restoring and renewing.

² See Rom. 6:4.

³ So then all the force of the matter cometh not from the very deed done, that is to say, it is not the dipping of us into the water by a Minister that maketh us to be buried with Christ, as the Papists say, that even for the very act's sake, we become verily Christians, but it cometh from the virtue of Christ, for the Apostle addeth the resurrection of Christ and faith.

⁴ One end of Baptism is the death and burial of the old man, and that by the mighty power of God only, whose virtue we lay hold on by faith, in the death and resurrection of Christ.

⁵ Through faith which cometh from God.

2:13 ¹ Another end of Baptism is, that we which were dead in sin, might obtain free remission of sins and eternal life through faith in Christ who died for us.

² A new argument which lieth in these few words, and it is thus: Uncircumcision was no hindrance to you, why you being justified in Christ should not obtain life therefore you need not circumcision to the argument of salvation.

2:14 ¹ He speaketh now more generally against the whole service of the Law, and showeth by two reasons that it is abolished: First, to what purpose should he that hath obtained remission of all his sins in Christ require those helps of the Law? Secondly, because that if a man do rightly consider those rites, he shall find that they were so many testimonies of our guiltiness, whereby we manifestly witnessed as it were by our own handwriting that we deserved damnation. Therefore did Christ put out that handwriting by his coming and fastening it to the cross, triumphed over all our enemies, were they never so mighty. Therefore to what end and purpose should we now use those ceremonies, as though we were still guilty of sin, and subject to the tyranny of our enemies?

² Abolishing the rites and ceremonies.

2:15 ¹ Satan and his angels.

² As a conqueror made by a show of those captives, and put them to shame.

³ The cross was as a chariot of triumph. No conqueror could have triumphed so gloriously in his chariot, as Christ did upon the cross.

2:16 ¹ The conclusion: wherein also he nameth certain kinds, as the difference of days and meats, and proveth by a new argument that we are not bond unto them: to wit, because those things were shadows of Christ to come but we possess him now exhibited unto us.

and drink, or in respect of an holy day, or of the new moon, or of the Sabbath *days,*

17 Which are *but* a shadow of things to come: but the [1]body is in Christ.

18 [1]Let no man at his pleasure bear rule over you by [2]humbleness of mind, and worshipping of Angels, [3]advancing himself in those things which he never saw, [4,5]rashly puffed up with his fleshly mind,

19 [1]And holdeth not the [2]head, whereof all the body furnished and knit together by joints and bands, increaseth with the increasing of [3]God.

20 [1]Wherefore if ye *be* dead with Christ from the ordinances of the world, why, [2]as though ye lived in the world, are ye burdened with traditions?

21 [1]*As,* Touch not, Taste not, Handle not.

22 [1]Which all perish with the using, [2]*and are* after the commandments and doctrines of men.

23 [1]Which things have indeed a show of [2]wisdom, in [3]voluntary religion and humbleness of mind, and in [4]not sparing the body, which are things of no value, *since they pertain* to the [5]filling of the flesh.

3 *1 Against earthly exercises, which the false apostles urged, 2 he setteth heavenly: 5 and beginneth with the mortifying of the flesh, 8 whence he draweth particular exhortations, 18 and particular duties which depend on each man's calling.*

1 If [1]ye then [2]be [3]risen with Christ, [4]seek those things which are above, where Christ sitteth at the right hand of God.

2 Set your affections on things which are above, *and* not on things which are on the [1]earth.

2:17 [1] The body as a thing of substance and pith, he setteth against shadows.

2:18 [1] He disputeth against the first kind of corruptions, and setteth down the worshipping of Angels for an example: which kind of false religion he confuteth, first this way: because that they which being in such a worship, attribute that unto themselves which is proper only to God, to wit, authority to bind men's consciences with religion, although they seem to bring in these things by humbleness of mind.

[2] By a foolish humbleness of mind: for otherwise humbleness is a virtue. For these Angel worshippers blamed such of pride, as would go straight to God, and use no other under means besides Christ.

[3] Secondly, because they rashly thrust upon them for oracles, those things which they neither saw nor heard, but devised of themselves.

[4] Thirdly, because these things have no other ground, whereupon they are built, but only the opinion of men, which please themselves without all measure in their own duties.

[5] Without reason.

2:19 [1] The fourth argument, which is of great weight, because they spoil Christ of his dignity, who only is sufficient both to nourish, and also to increase his whole body.

[2] Christ.

[3] With the increasing which cometh from God.

2:20 [1] Now last of all he fighteth against the second kind of corruptions, that is to say, against mere superstitions, invented of men, which partly deceive the simplicity of some with their craftiness, and partly with very foolish superstitions, and to be laughed at: as when godliness, remission of sins, or any such like virtue is put in some certain kind of meat and such like things, which the inventors of such rites themselves understand not, because indeed it is not. And he useth an argument taken of comparison. If by the death of Christ who establisheth a new covenant with his blood, you be delivered from those external rites wherewith it pleased the Lord to prepare the world, as it were by certain rudiments to that full knowledge of true religion, why would ye be burdened with traditions, I wrote not what, as though ye were citizens of this world, that is to say, as though ye depended upon this life, and earthly things? Now this is the cause why before verse 8 he followed another order than he doth in the confutation: because he showeth thereby what degrees false religions came into the world, to wit, beginning first by curious speculations of the wise after which in process of time succeeded gross superstition, against which mischiefs the Lord set at length that service of the Law, which some abused in like sort: but in the confutation he began with the abolishing of the Law service, that

he might show by comparison, that those false services ought much more to be taken away.

[2] As though your felicity stood in these earthly things, and the kingdom of God were not rather spiritual.

2:21 [1] An imitation in the person of these superstitious men, rightly expressing their nature and use of speech.

2:22 [1] Another argument: The spiritual and inward kingdom of God cannot consist in these outward things, and such as perish with the using.

[2] The third argument: Because God is not the author of these traditions, and therefore they do not bind the conscience.

2:23 [1] The taking away of an objection. These things have a goodly show, because men by this means, seem to worship God with a good mind and humble themselves, and neglect the body, which the most part of men curiously pamper up and cherish: but yet notwithstanding the things themselves are of no value, for so much as they pertain not to things that are spiritual and everlasting, but to the nourishment of the flesh.

[2] Which seem indeed to be some exquisite thing, and so wise devices as though they came from heaven.

[3] Hence sprang the works of supererogation, as the Papists term them, that is to say, needless works, as though men performed more than is commanded them, which was the beginning and the very ground whereon Monks' merits were brought in.

[4] A lively description of Monkery.

[5] Seeing they stand in meat and drink, wherein the kingdom of God doth not stand.

3:1 [1] Another part of this Epistle, wherein he taketh occasion by the reason of those vain exercises, to show the duty of a Christian life: which is an ordinary thing with him after he hath once set down the doctrine itself.

[2] Our renewing or new birth, which is wrought in us by being partakers of the resurrection of Christ, is the fountain of all holiness, out of which sundry arms or rivers do afterwards flow.

[3] For if we be partakers of Christ, we are carried as it were into another life, where we shall need neither meat nor drink, for we shall be like unto the Angels.

[4] The end and mark which all the duties of Christian life shoot at, is to enter into the kingdom of heaven, and to give ourselves to those things which lead us thither, that is to true godliness, and not to those outward and corporal things.

3:2 [1] So he calleth that show of religion, which he spake of in the former Chapter.

3 [1]For ye are dead, [2]and your life is hid with Christ in God.

4 When Christ which is our life, shall appear, then shall ye also appear with him in glory.

5 [a,1]Mortify therefore your [2]members which are on the earth, fornication, uncleanness, the inordinate affection, evil concupiscence, and covetousness which is idolatry.

6 For the which things' sake the wrath of God [1]cometh on the children of disobedience.

7 Wherein ye also walked once, when ye lived in them.

8 But now put ye away even all these things, wrath, anger, maliciousness, cursed speaking, filthy speaking, out of your mouth.

9 Lie not one to another: [1]seeing that ye have put off the old man with his works,

10 And have put on the new, [1]which is renewed in [2]knowledge after the image of him that created him,

11 [1]Where is neither Grecian nor Jew, circumcision nor uncircumcision, Barbarian, Scythian, bond, free: But Christ is all, and in all things.

12 Now therefore as the elect of God, holy and beloved, [1]put on the [2]bowels of mercies, kindness, humbleness of mind, meekness, longsuffering:

CHAPTER 3
[a] Eph. 5:3
[b] 1 Cor. 10:31
[c] Eph. 5:22
[d] 1 Pet. 3:1
[e] Eph. 6:1
[f] Eph. 6:5
Titus 2:9
1 Pet. 2:8

13 Forbearing one another, and forgiving one another, if any man have a quarrel to another: even as Christ forgave, even so do ye.

14 And above all these things put on love, which is the [1]bond of perfectness.

15 And let the peace of God [1]rule in your hearts, to the which ye are called in [2]one body, and be ye thankful:

16 Let the word of Christ dwell in you plenteously in all wisdom, teaching and admonishing your own selves, in [1]Psalms, and hymns, and spiritual songs, singing with a grace in your hearts to the Lord,

17 [b]And whatsoever ye shall do, in word or deed, do all in the [1]Name of the Lord Jesus, giving thanks to God even the Father by him.

18 ¶ [c,1]Wives, submit yourselves unto your husbands, as it is [2]comely in the Lord.

19 [d,1]Husbands, love your wives, and be not bitter unto them.

20 ¶ [e,1]Children, obey your parents in [2]all things: for that is well pleasing unto the Lord.

21 [1]Fathers, provoke not your children to anger, lest they be discouraged.

22 ¶ [f,1]Servants, be obedient unto them that are your masters according to the flesh, in all things, not with eye service as men pleasers, but in singleness

3:3 [1] A reason taken of the efficient causes and others: you are dead as touching the flesh, that is, touching the old nature which seeketh after all transitory things, and on the other side, you have begun to live according to the Spirit, therefore give yourselves to spiritual and heavenly, and not to carnal and earthly things.

[2] The taking away of an objection: while we are yet in this world, we are subject to many miseries of this life, so that the life that is in us, is as it were hidden: yet notwithstanding we have the beginnings of life and glory, the accomplishment whereof which lieth now in Christ's and in God's hand, shall be assuredly and manifestly performed in that glorious coming of the Lord.

3:5 [1] Let not your dead nature be any more effectual in you, but let your living nature be effectual. Now the force of nature is known by the motions. Therefore let the affections of the flesh die in you, and let the contrary motions which are spiritual, live. And he reckoneth up a great long scroll of vices, and their contrary virtues.

[2] The motions and lusts that are in us, are in this place very properly called members, because that the reason and will of man corrupted, doth use them as the body doth his members.

3:6 [1] Useth to come.

3:9 [1] A definition of our new birth taken of the parts thereof, which are the putting off of the old man, that is to say, of the wickedness which is in us by nature, and the restoring, and repairing of the new man, that is to say, of pureness which is given us by grace: but both of them are but begun in us in this present life, and by certain degrees finished: the one dying in us by little and little, and the other coming to the perfection of another life, by little and little.

3:10 [1] Newness of life consisteth in knowledge, which transformeth man to the image of God his maker, that is to say, to the sincerity and pureness of the whole soul.

[2] He speaketh of an effectual knowledge.

3:11 [1] He telleth them again, that the Gospel doth not respect those external things, but true justification and sanctification in Christ only, which have many fruits, as he reckoneth them up here: But commendeth two things especially, to wit, godly concord, and continual study of God's word.

3:12 [1] So put on, that you never put off.

[2] Those most tender affections of exceeding compassion.

3:14 [1] Which bindeth and knitteth together all the duties that pass from man to man.

3:15 [1] Rule and govern all things.

[2] You are joined together into one body through God's goodness, that you might help one another as fellow members.

3:16 [1] By Psalms he meaneth all godly songs, which were written upon divers occasions, and by hymns, all such as contain the praise of God, and by spiritual songs, other more peculiar and artificious songs which were also in praise of God, but they were made fuller of music.

3:17 [1] Call upon the name of Christ, when you do it, or, do it to Christ's praise and glory.

3:18 [1] He goeth from precepts which concern the whole civil life of man, to precepts pertaining to every man's family, and requireth of wives, subjection in the Lord.

[2] For those wives do not well, that do not set God in Christ before them in their love, but this Philosophy knoweth not.

3:19 [1] He requireth of husbands, that they love their wives, and use them gently.

3:20 [1] He requireth of children, that according to God's Commandment they be obedient to their parents.

[2] In the Lord, and so is it expounded, Eph. 5:19.

3:21 [1] Of parents, that they be gentle towards their children.

3:22 [1] Of servants that fearing God himself to whom their obedience is acceptable, they reverently, faithfully, and from the heart, obey their masters.

of heart, fearing God.

23 And whatsoever ye do, do it heartily, as to the Lord, and not to men,

24 Knowing that of the Lord ye shall receive the [1]reward of the inheritance: for ye serve the Lord Christ.

25 [1]But he that doeth wrong, shall receive for the wrong that he hath done: and there is no respect of persons.

4

2 He returneth to general exhortations, 3 touching prayer and gracious speech, 7 and so endeth with greetings and commendations.

1 Ye masters, do unto your servants, that which is just and equal, knowing that ye also have a master in heaven.

2 [a,1,2]Continue in prayer, and watch in the same with thanksgiving,

3 [b,1]Praying also for us, that God may open unto us the [2]door of utterance, to speak the mystery of Christ: wherefore I am also in bonds,

4 That I may utter it, as it becometh me to speak.

5 ¶ [c,1]Walk [2]wisely toward them that are without, and redeem the [3]season.

6 [1]Let your speech *be* [2]gracious always, and powdered with [3]salt, that ye may know how to answer every man.

7 ¶ Tychicus *our* beloved brother and faithful minister, and fellow servant in the Lord, shall declare unto you my whole state:

8 Whom I have sent unto you for the same purpose that he might know your state, and might

CHAPTER 4
[a] Luke 18:1
1 Thess. 5:17
[b] Eph. 6:18
2 Thess. 3:1
[c] Eph. 5:15
[d] 2 Tim. 4:11

comfort your hearts,

9 With Onesimus a faithful and a beloved brother, who is one of you. They shall show you of all things here.

10 Aristarchus my prison fellow saluteth you, and Marcus, Barnabas's cousin (touching whom ye received commandments: If he come unto you, receive him.)

11 And Jesus which is called Justus, which are of the circumcision. These [1]only are my work-fellows unto the [2]kingdom of God, which have been unto my consolation.

12 Epaphras the servant of Christ, which is one of you, saluteth you, and always striveth for you in prayers, that ye may stand perfect, and full in all the will of God.

13 For I bear him record, that he hath a great zeal for you, and for them of Laodicea, and them of Hierapolis,

14 [d]Luke the beloved physician greeteth you, and Demas.

15 Salute the brethren which are of Laodicea, and Nymphas, and the Church which is in his house.

16 And when this Epistle is read of you, cause that it be read in the Church of the Laodiceans also, and that ye likewise read the Epistle *written* from Laodicea,

17 And say to Archippus, Take heed to the ministry, that thou hast received in the Lord, that thou fulfill it.

18 The salutation by the hand of me Paul. Remember my bands. Grace *be* with you, Amen.

¶ Written from Rome to the Colossians, *and sent* by Tychicus, and Onesimus.

3:24 [1] For that that you shall have duly obeyed your masters, the time shall come, that you shall be made sons of servants, and then shall you know this of a surety, which shall be when you are made partakers of the heavenly inheritance.

3:25 [1] He requireth of masters that being mindful how that they themselves also shall render an account before that heavenly Lord and Master, which will revenge wrongful doings without any respect of masters or servants, they show themselves just and upright with equity, unto their servants.

4:2 [1] He addeth certain general exhortations and at length endeth his Epistle with divers familiar and godly salutations.

[2] Prayers must be continual and earnest.

4:3 [1] Such as minister the word, must especially be commended to the prayers of the Church.

[2] An open and free mouth to preach the Gospel.

4:5 [1] In all parts of our life, we ought to have good consideration even of them which are without the Church.

[2] Advisedly and circumspectly.

[3] Seek occasion to win them, although you lose of your own by it.

4:6 [1] Our speech and talk must be applied to the profit of the hearers.

[2] Framed to the profit of your neighbor.

[3] Against this is set filthy communication, as Eph. 4:29.

4:11 [1] Why then, Peter was not at that time at Rome.

[2] In the Gospel.

THE FIRST EPISTLE OF
PAUL TO THE
THESSALONIANS

1 *1 He therefore beginneth with thanksgiving, 4 to put them in mind that whatsoever was praiseworthy in them, it came of God's goodness: 7 and that they are ensamples unto others.*

1 Paul, and Silvanus, and Timothy, unto the Church of the Thessalonians, *which is* in God the Father, and in the Lord Jesus Christ: Grace *be* with you, and peace from God our Father, and *from* the Lord Jesus Christ.

2 [1]We give God thanks always for you all, making mention of you in our prayers.

3 [1]Without ceasing, remembering your effectual faith, and diligent love, and the patience of *your* hope in our Lord Jesus Christ, in the sight of God, even our Father,

4 Knowing, beloved brethren, that ye are [1]elect of God.

5 [1]For our Gospel was not unto you in word only, but also in power, and in the holy Ghost, and in [2]much assurance, as ye know after what manner we were among you for your sakes.

6 [1]And ye became followers of us, and of the Lord, and received the word in much affliction, with [2]joy of the holy Ghost,

7 So that ye were as ensamples to all that believe in Macedonia and in Achaia.

a Acts 16:12

8 For from you sounded out the word of the Lord, not in Macedonia and in Achaia only: but your faith also which is toward God, spread abroad in all quarters, that we need not to speak anything.

9 For [1]they themselves show of us what manner of entering in we had unto you, [2]and how ye turned to God from idols, to serve the living and true God.

10 And to look for his son from heaven, whom he raised from the dead, *even* Jesus which delivereth us from [1]that wrath to come.

2 *1 He declareth how faithfully he preacheth the Gospel unto them, 5 seeking neither gain, 6 nor praise of men: 10 and he proveth the same by their own testimony: 14 that they did courageously bear persecution of their countrymen: 17 that he desireth very much to see them.*

1 For [1]ye yourselves know, brethren, that our entrance in unto you was not in vain,

2 [1]But even after that we had suffered before, and were shamefully entreated at [a]Philippi, (as ye know) we were bold in [2]our God, to speak unto you the Gospel of God, with much striving.

3 [1]For our exhortation was not by deceit, nor [2]by uncleanness, nor by guile.

1:2 [1] An example of a right Christian rejoicing:whereby also we learn, that such as have great gifts in them are in two sorts bridled, to wit, if they consider that they have received all from God, and that continuance must be desired at his hands, whereunto also the whole Epistle exhorteth the Thessalonians.

1:3 [1] He commendeth them for three special gifts, effectual faith, continual love, and patient hope: to the end they might be ashamed being endued with such excellent gifts, not to continue in God's election.

1:4 [1] Word for word, that your election is of God.

1:5 [1] Another reason why they ought in no wise start back but continue to the end, because they cannot doubt of his doctrine which hath been so many ways confirmed unto them, even from heaven as they themselves did well know.

[2] Paul showeth by two things, that there followed very great fruits of his preaching, to wit, by these gifts of the holy Ghost, and that certain assurance which was thoroughly settled in their minds, as appeared by their willing bearing of the cross.

1:6 [1] Another reason: Because even to that day, they embraced the Gospel with great cheerfulness, insomuch that they were an example to all their neighbors: so that it should be more shame for them to faint in the mid-race.

[2] With joy which cometh from the holy Ghost.

1:9 [1] All the believers.

[2] It is no true conversion to forsake idols, unless a man therewithall worship the true and living God in Christ the only redeemer.

1:10 [1] This word (That) is not put here without cause: and by (wrath) is meant that revenge and punishment, wherewith the Lord will judge the world at length in his terrible wrath.

2:1 [1] That which he touched before shortly concerning his Apostleship, he handleth now more at large, and to that end and purpose which we spake of.

2:2 [1] The virtues of a true Pastor are freely, and without fear to preach the Gospel, even in the midst of dangers.

[2] Through God his gracious help.

2:3 [1] To teach pure doctrine faithfully and with a pure heart.

[2] By any wicked and naughty kind of dealing.

4 ¹But as we were ²allowed of God, that the Gospel should be committed *unto us*, so we speak, not as they that please men, but God, which ³approveth our hearts:

5 Neither yet did we ever use flattering words, as ye know, nor colored covetousness, God *is* record.

6 ¹Neither sought we praise of men, neither of you, nor of others, when we might have been ²chargeable, as the Apostles of Christ.

7 But we were ¹gentle among you, even as a nurse cherisheth her children.

8 ¹Thus being affectioned toward you, our good will was to have dealt unto you, not the Gospel of God only, but also our own souls, because ye were dear unto us.

9 ¹For ye remember, brethren, ᵇour labor and travail: for we labored day and night, because we would not be chargeable unto any of you, and preached unto you the Gospel of God.

10 ¹Ye *are* witnesses, and God *also*, how holily, and justly, and unblameably we behaved ourselves among you that believe.

11 ¹As ye know how that we exhorted you, and comforted, and besought every one of you, (as a father his children,)

12 ¹That ye ᶜwould walk worthy of God, who hath called you unto his kingdom and glory.

13 ¹For this cause also thank we God without ceasing, that when ye received the word of God, which ye heard of us, ye received it not as the word

ᵇ Acts 20:34
1 Cor. 4:12
2 Thess. 3:8

ᶜ Eph. 4:1
Phil. 1:27
Col. 1:10

of men, but as it is indeed the word of God, which also worketh in you that believe.

14 ¹For brethren, ye are become followers of the Churches of God, which in Judea are in ²Christ Jesus, because ye have also suffered the same things of your own ³country men, even as they *have* of the Jews,

15 ¹Who both killed the Lord Jesus and their own Prophets, and have persecuted us away, ²and God they please not, and are contrary to ³all men,

16 And forbid us to preach unto the Gentiles, that they might be saved, to ¹fulfill their sins always: for the ²wrath *of God* is come on them to the utmost.

17 ¹Forasmuch, brethren, as we ²were kept from you for a season, concerning sight, but not in the heart, we enforced the more to see your face with great desire.

18 Therefore we would have come unto you (I Paul, at least once or twice) but Satan hindered us.

19 For what is our hope or joy, or crown of rejoicing? are not even you it in the presence of our Lord Jesus Christ at his coming?

20 Yea, ye are our glory and joy.

3 *1 To show his affection towards them, he sendeth Timothy unto them: 6 He is so moved by the report of their prosperous state, 9 that he cannot give sufficient thanks, 11 and therefore he breaketh out into prayer.*

1 Wherefore since we could no longer forbear, we thought it good to remain at Athens alone,

2:4 ¹ To approve his conscience to God, being free from all flattery and covetousness.

² Seeing there is this difference between the judgments of God and the judgments of men, that when men choose, they respect the qualities of those things which stand before them, but God findeth the reason of his counsel only in himself, it followeth, that seeing we are not able to think a good thought, that whomsoever he first chooseth to those holy callings, he maketh them able, and doth not find them able. And therefore in that we are allowed of God, it hangeth upon his mercy.

³ Which liketh and alloweth them.

2:6 ¹ To submit himself even to the basest, to win them, and to eschew all pride.

² When I might lawfully have lived upon the expenses of the Church.

2:7 ¹ We were not rough, but easy, and gentle, as a nurse that is neither ambitious nor covetous, but taketh all pains as patiently, as if she were a mother.

2:8 ¹ To have the flock that is committed unto him in more estimation than his own life.

2:9 ¹ To depart with his own rights rather than to be chargeable to his sheep.

2:10 ¹ To excel others in example of godly life.

2:11 ¹ To exhort and comfort with a fatherly mind and affection.

2:12 ¹ To exhort all men diligently and earnestly to lead a godly life.

2:13 ¹ Having approved his ministry, he commendeth again (to that end and purpose that I spake of) the cheerfulness of the Thessalonians, which was answerable to his diligence in preaching, and their

manly patience.

2:14 ¹ He confirmeth them in their afflictions which they suffered of their own people, because they were afflicted of their own countrymen: which came as well (saith he) to the Churches of the Jews, as to them: and therefore they ought to take it in good part.

² Which Christ hath gathered together.

³ Even of them which are of the same country, and the same town that you are of.

2:15 ¹ He preventeth an offense which might be taken, for that the Jews especially above all others persecuted the Gospel. That is no new thing, sayeth he, seeing they slew Christ himself and his Prophets, and have banished me also.

² He foretelleth the utter destruction of the Jews, lest any man should be moved by their rebellion.

³ For the Jews would neither enter into the kingdom of God themselves, nor suffer others to enter in.

2:16 ¹ Until the wickedness of theirs which they have by inheritance as it were of their fathers, be grown so great that the measure of their iniquity being filled, God may come forth to wrath.

² The judgments of God being angry, which indeed appeared shortly after in the destruction of the city of Jerusalem, whither many resorted even out of divers provinces, when it was besieged.

2:17 ¹ He meeteth with an objection, why he came not to them straightway being in so great misery, I desired oftentimes (saith he) and it lay not in me, but Satan hindered my endeavors, and therefore I sent Timothy my faithful companion unto you, because you are most dear to me.

² Were kept asunder from you, and as it were orphans.

2 ^aAnd have sent Timothy our brother and minister of God, and our labor fellow in the Gospel of Christ, to establish you, and to comfort you touching your faith,

3 That no man should be moved with these afflictions: ¹for ye yourselves know, that we are appointed thereunto.

4 For verily when we were with you, we told you before that we should suffer tribulations, even as it came to pass, and ye know it.

5 Even for this cause, when I could no longer forbear, I sent *him* that I might know of your faith, lest the tempter had tempted you in any sort, and that our labor had been in vain.

6 ¹But now lately when Timothy came from you unto us, and brought us good tidings of your faith and love, and that ye have good remembrance of us always, desiring to see us, as we also *do* you,

7 Therefore brethren, we had consolation in you, in all our affliction and necessity through your faith.

8 For now are we ¹alive, if ye stand fast in the Lord.

9 For what thanks can we recompense to God again for you, for all the joy wherewith we rejoice for your sakes before our God,

10 Night and day, ^bpraying exceedingly, that we might see your face, and might ¹accomplish that which is lacking in your faith?

11 Now God himself, even our Father, and our Lord Jesus Christ, guide our journey unto you.

12 ¹And the Lord increase you, and make you abound in love one toward another, and toward all men, even as we *do* toward you:

13 ^cTo make your hearts stable and unblameable in holiness before God even our Father, at the coming of our Lord Jesus Christ with all his Saints.

CHAPTER 3
^a Acts 16:1
^b Rom. 1:10
Rom. 15:23
^c 1 Thess. 5:23
1 Cor. 1:8

CHAPTER 4
^a Rom. 12:2
Eph. 5:17
^b 1 Cor. 6:8
^c 1 Cor. 1:2
^d John 13:43
John 15:11
1 John 2:8
1 John 4:22

4 1 *He exhorteth them* 3 *to holiness,* 9 *and brotherly love.* 13 *He forbiddeth them to sorrow after to manner of infidels.* 15 *He setteth out the history of our resurrection.*

1 And ¹furthermore we beseech you, brethren, and exhort you in the Lord Jesus, that ye ²increase more and more, as ye have received of us, how ye ought to walk, and to please God.

2 For ye know what commandments we gave you by the Lord Jesus.

3 ^{a,1}For this is the will of God *even* your ²sanctification, *and* that ye should abstain from fornication,

4 ¹That everyone of you should know, how to possess his vessel in holiness and honor,

5 ¹And not in the lust of concupiscence, even as the Gentiles which know not God:

6 ^{b,1}That no man oppress or defraud his brother in any matter: for the Lord *is* avenger of all such things, as we also have told you beforetime, and testified.

7 ^cFor God hath not called us unto uncleanness, but unto holiness.

8 He therefore that ¹despiseth *these things*, despiseth not man, but God who hath even given you his holy Spirit.

9 ¹But as touching brotherly love, ye need not that I write unto you: ^dfor ye are taught of God to love one another.

10 Yea, and that thing verily ye do unto all the brethren, which are throughout all Macedonia: but we beseech you brethren, that ye increase more and more,

11 ¹And that ye study to be quiet, and to meddle with your own business, ²and to work with your own hands, as we commanded you.

12 That ye may behave yourselves honestly toward them that are without, and that nothing be lacking unto you.

3:3 ¹ The will of God, who calleth his on this condition, to bring them to glory by affliction is a most sure remedy against all affliction.

3:6 ¹ Because they have hitherto gone so well forward, he exhorteth them again to make an end of the rest of the journey, seeing that therein also they shall do him their Apostle a great pleasure.

3:8 ¹ For now you cannot otherwise think me safe and in good case, unless you go forward in religion and faith.

3:10 ¹ Paul was constrained through the importunate dealing of the enemies to leave the building which he had scarce begun: And for that cause he had left Silas and Timothy in Macedonia, and when Timothy came to Athens to him, he sent him back again straightway. So that he desireth to see the Thessalonians, that he may thereby thoroughly accomplish their faith and religion, that was as yet imperfect.

3:12 ¹ Another part of the Epistle, wherein he speaketh of the duties of a Christian life. And he showeth that the perfection of a Christian life consisteth in two things, to wit, in charity toward all men, and inward purity of the heart, the accomplishment whereof notwithstanding is deferred to the next coming of Christ, who will then perfect his work by the same grace, wherewith he began it in us.

4:1 ¹ Divers exhortations, the ground whereof is this, to be mindful

of those things, which they have heard of the Apostle.

² That ye labor to excel more and more, and daily pass yourselves.

4:3 ¹ This is the sum of those things, which he delivered them, to dedicate themselves wholly to God. And he condemneth plainly all filthiness through lust, because it is altogether contrary to the will of God.

² See John 19:17.

4:4 ¹ Another reason, because it defileth the body.

4:5 ¹ The third, because the Saints are discerned from them which know not God, by honesty and purity.

4:6 ¹ Secondly, he reprehendeth all violent oppression and immoderate desire, and showeth most severely as the Prophet of God, that God will revenge such wickedness.

4:8 ¹ These commandments which I gave you.

4:9 ¹ Thirdly, he requireth a ready mind to all manner of lovingkindness, and exhorteth them to profit more and more in that virtue.

4:11 ¹ He condemneth unquiet brains, and such as are curious in matters which appertain not unto them.

² He rebuketh idleness and slothfulness, which vices whosoever are given unto, fall into other wickedness, to the great offense of the Church.

13 ¶ ¹I would not brethren, have you ignorant ²concerning them ³which are asleep, that ye sorrow not even as others which have no hope.

14 ¹For if we believe that Jesus is dead, and is risen, even so them which sleep in ²Jesus, will God ³bring with him.

15 ¹For this say we unto you by the ²word of the Lord, that ³we which live, and are remaining in the coming of the Lord, shall not prevent them which sleep.

16 For the Lord himself shall descend from heaven with a ¹shout, *and* with the voice of the Archangel, and ᶜwith the trumpet of God: and the dead in Christ shall rise first:

17 Then shall we which live and remain, be ¹caught up with them also in the clouds, to meet the Lord in the air: and so shall we ever be with the Lord.

18 Wherefore, comfort yourselves one another with these words.

ᶜ 1 Cor. 15:52

CHAPTER 5
ᵈ Isa. 59:17
Eph. 6:17

5

1 Condemning the curious searching for the seasons of Christ's coming, *6 he warneth them to be ready daily to receive him:* *11 And so giveth them sundry good lessons.*

1 But ¹of the times and ²seasons, brethren, ye have no need that I write unto you.

2 For ye yourselves know perfectly, that the day of the Lord shall come, even as a thief in the night.

3 For when they shall say, Peace and safety, then shall come upon them sudden destruction, as the travail upon a woman with child, and they shall not escape.

4 ¹But ye, brethren, are not in darkness, that that day shall come on you, as *it were* a thief.

5 Ye are all the children of light, and the children of the day: we are not of the night, neither of darkness.

6 Therefore let us not sleep as do others, but let us watch and be sober.

7 For they that sleep, sleep in the night, and they that be drunken, are drunken in the night.

8 ¹But let us which are of the day, be sober, ᵈputting on the breastplate of faith and love, and the hope of salvation for an helmet.

9 ¹For God hath not appointed us unto wrath, but to obtain salvation by the means of our Lord Jesus Christ.

10 ¹Which died for us, that whether we wake or sleep, we should live together with him.

11 ¹Wherefore exhort one another, and edify one another, even as ye do.

12 ¹Now we beseech you brethren, that ye ²acknowledge them which labor among you, and are over you in the ³Lord, and admonish you.

13 That ye have them in singular love for ¹their work's sake. ²Be at peace among yourselves.

4:13 ¹ The third part of the Epistle, which is interlaced among the former exhortations (which he returneth unto afterward) wherein he speaketh of mourning for the dead, and the manner of the resurrection, and of the latter day.

² We must take heed that we do not immoderately bewail the dead, that is, as they used to do which think that they are utterly perished.

³ A confirmation: for death is but a sleep of the body (for he speaketh of the faithful) until the Lord cometh.

4:14 ¹ A reason of the confirmation, for seeing that the head is risen, the members also shall rise, and that by the virtue of God.

² They die in Christ, which continue in faith, whereby they are grafted into Christ, even to the last gasp.

³ Will call their bodies out of their graves, and join their souls to them again.

4:15 ¹ The manner of the resurrection shall be thus: The bodies of the dead shall be as it were raised out of sleep, at the sound of the trumpet of God, Christ himself shall descend from heaven. The Saints (for he speaketh properly of them) which shall then be found alive together with the dead which shall rise, shall be taken up into the clouds to meet the Lord, and shall be in perpetual glory with him.

² In the Name of the Lord, as though he himself speaks unto you.

³ He speaketh of these things, as though he should be one of them whom the Lord shall find alive at his coming, because that time is uncertain, and therefore every one of us ought to be in such a readiness, as if the Lord were coming at every moment.

4:16 ¹ The word which the Apostle useth here, signifieth properly that encouragement which mariners use to one another, when they altogether with one shout put forth their oars and row together.

4:17 ¹ Suddenly and in the twinkling of an eye.

5:1 ¹ The day that God hath appointed for his judgment, we know not. But this is sure that it shall come upon men when they look for nothing less.

² See Acts 1:7.

5:4 ¹ Returning to exhortations he warneth us which are lightened with the knowledge of God, that it is our duty not to live securely in deliciousness, lest we be suddenly taken in a dead sleep in pleasures, and contrarywise to have an eye to the Lord, and not suffer ourselves to be oppressed with the cares of this world, for that is meet for the darkness of the night, and this for the light.

5:8 ¹ We must fight with faith and hope, much less ought we lie carelessly snorting.

5:9 ¹ He pricketh us forward by seeing most certain hope of victory before us.

5:10 ¹ The death of Christ is a pledge of our victory, for therefore he died, that we might be partakers of his life or virtue, yea even while we live here.

5:11 ¹ We must not only watch ourselves, but we are also bound to stir up and to confirm one another.

5:12 ¹ We must have great consideration of them which are appointed to the ministry of the word, and government of the Church by God, and do their duty.

² That you acknowledge and take them for such as they are, that is to say, men worthy to be greatly accounted of among you.

³ In those things which pertain to God's service: so is the Ecclesiastical function distinguished from civil authority, and true shepherds from wolves.

5:13 ¹ So then, where this cause ceaseth, there must the honor cease.

² This maintenance of mutual concord, is especially to be looked unto.

14 [1]We desire you, brethren, admonish them that are [2]out of order: comfort the feebleminded: bear with the weak: be patient toward all men.

15 [b,1]See that none recompense evil for evil unto any man: but ever follow that which is good, both toward yourselves, and toward all men.

16 [1]Rejoice evermore.

17 [c]Pray continually.

18 In all things, give thanks, for this is the [1]will of God in Christ Jesus toward you.

19 [1]Quench not the Spirit.

20 Despise not [1]prophesying.

21 Try all things, and keep that which is good.

22 [1]Abstain from all [2]appearance of evil.

[b] Prov. 17:13
Prov. 20:22
Matt. 5:39
Rom. 12:17
1 Pet. 3:9
[c] Luke 18:1
[d] 1 Cor. 1:9

23 Now the very God of peace [1]sanctify you throughout: and I pray God that your whole spirit and soul and body, may be kept blameless unto the coming of our Lord Jesus Christ.

24 [d,1,2]Faithful is he which calleth you, which will also [3]do it.

25 [1]Brethren, pray for us.

26 Greet all the brethren with an holy kiss.

27 I charge you in the Lord, that this Epistle be read unto all the brethren the Saints.

28 The grace of our Lord Jesus Christ be with you, Amen.

¶ The first Epistle unto the Thessalonians
written from Athens.

5:14 [1] We must have consideration of every man, and as the disease is, so must the remedy be used.

[2] That keep not their rank or standing.

5:15 [1] Charity ought not to be overcome with any injuries.

5:16 [1] A quiet and appeased mind, is nourisheth with continual prayers, respecting the will of God.

5:18 [1] An acceptable thing to God and such as he liketh well of.

5:19 [1] The sparks of the Spirit of God that are kindled in us, are nourished by daily hearing the word of God: but true doctrine must be diligently distinguished from false.

5:20 [1] The expounding of the word of God.

5:22 [1] A general conclusion, that we waiting for the coming of Christ, do give ourselves to pureness both in mind, will, and body, through the grace and strength of the Spirit of God.

[2] Whatsoever hath but the very show of evil, abstain from it.

5:23 [1] Separate you from the world, and make you holy to himself through his spirit, in Christ in whom only you shall attain unto that true peace.

5:24 [1] The good will and power of God is a sure confirmation against all difficulties, whereof we have a sure witness in our vocation.

[2] Always one and ever like himself, who performeth in deed whatsoever he promiseth: and an effectual calling is nothing else but a right declaring and true setting forth of God's will: and therefore the salvation of the elect is safe and sure.

[3] Who will also make you perfect.

5:25 [1] The last part of the Epistle, wherein with most weighty charge, he commendeth both himself and this Epistle unto them.

THE SECOND EPISTLE OF
PAUL TO THE
THESSALONIANS

1 *3 He commendeth the increase of faith and charity, 4 and the patience of the Thessalonians: 6 And describing God's vengeance against such as oppress the godly, 10 he teacheth the godly to wait for the last judgment.*

1 Paul and Silvanus, and Timothy, unto the Church of the Thessalonians, *which is* in God our Father, and in the Lord Jesus Christ:

2 Grace *be* with you, and peace from God our Father, and *from* the Lord Jesus Christ.

3 [a],1 We ought to thank God always for you, brethren, as it is meet, because that your faith [2]groweth exceedingly, and the love of every one of you toward another, aboundeth,

4 So that we ourselves rejoice of you in the Churches of God, because of your patience and faith in all your persecutions and tribulations that ye suffer.

5 [b],1 *Which is* a manifest token of the righteous judgment of God, that ye may be counted worthy of the kingdom of God, for the which ye also suffer.

6 [1]For it is a righteous thing with God, to recompense tribulation to them that trouble you,

7 And to you which are troubled, rest [1]with us, [c],2 when the Lord Jesus shall show himself from heaven with his mighty Angels,

CHAPTER 1
[a] 1 Thess. 1:2
[b] Jude 6
[c] 1 Thess. 4:16

8 In flaming fire, rendering vengeance unto them, [1]that do not know God, and which obey not unto the Gospel of our Lord Jesus Christ,

9 Which shall be punished with everlasting perdition from the presence of the Lord, and from the glory of his power,

10 When he shall come to be glorified in his Saints, and to be made marvelous in all them that believe ([1]because our testimony toward you was believed) in that day.

11 [1]Wherefore, we also pray always for you, that our God may make you worthy of [2]this calling, and fulfill [3]all the good pleasure of *his* goodness, and the [4]work of faith with power.

12 That the Name of our Lord Jesus Christ may be glorified in you, and ye in him, according to the grace of our God, and of the Lord Jesus Christ.

2 *2 He showeth that the day of the Lord shall not come, till there be a departure from the faith, 3 and that Antichrist be revealed, 8 whose destruction he setteth out, 15 and thereupon exhorteth to constancy.*

1 Now [1]we beseech you, brethren, by the coming of our Lord Jesus Christ, and by our [2]assembling unto him,

---

1:3 [1] The first part of the Epistle, wherein he rejoiceth that through the grace of God, they have manfully sustained all the assaults of their enemies, wherein he confirmeth them moreover showing with what gifts they must chiefly fight, to wit, with faith and charity, which must daily increase.

[2] That whereas it grew us before, it doth also receive some increase every day more and more.

1:5 [1] He openeth the fountain of all true comfort, to wit, that in afflictions, which we suffer of the wicked for righteousness sake, we may behold as it were in a glass the testimony of that judgment to come, and the end therefore most acceptable to us, and most sharp to his enemies.

1:6 [1] A proof: God is just, therefore he will worthily punish the unjust, and will do away the miseries of his people.

1:7 [1] He confirmeth them also by the way, by this means, that the condition both of this present state and the state to come, is common to him with them.

[2] A most glorious description of the second coming of Christ, to be set against all the miseries of the godly, and the triumphs of the wicked.

1:8 [1] There is no knowledge of God unto salvation, without the Gospel of Christ.

1:10 [1] The children of God shall be counted by the faith which they

have in the Gospel, which is preached unto them by the Apostles.

1:11 [1] Seeing that we have the mark set before us, it remaineth that we go unto it. And we go to it, by certain degrees of causes: first by the free love and good pleasure of God, by virtue whereof all other inferior causes work: from thence proceedeth the free calling to Christ, and from calling, faith, whereupon followeth both the glorifying of Christ in us, and us in Christ.

[2] By (calling) he meaneth not the very act of calling, but that selfsame thing whereunto we are called, which is the glory of that heavenly kingdom.

[3] Which he determined long since, only upon his gracious and merciful goodness toward you.

[4] So then, faith is an excellent work of God in us: and we see here plainly that the Apostle leaveth nothing to free will, to make it checkmate with God's working therein, as the Papists dream.

2:1 [1] The second part of the Epistle, containing an excellent prophecy of the state of the Church, which shall be from the Apostles' times unto the latter day of judgment.

[2] If we think earnestly upon that immeasurable glory, which we shall be partakers of with Christ, it will be an excellent remedy for us against wavering, and impatience, so that neither the glistering of the world shall allure us, nor the dreadful sight of the cross dismay us.

2 ¹That ye be not suddenly moved from *your* mind, nor troubled neither by ²spirit, nor by ³word, nor by ⁴letter, as *it were* from us, as though the day of Christ were at hand.

3 Let no man deceive you by any means: ¹for *that day shall not come*, except there come a departing first, and that ²that man of sin be disclosed, *even* the son of perdition.

4 Which is an adversary, and ¹exalteth himself against all that is called God, or that is worshipped: ²so that he doth sit as God in the Temple of God, showing himself that he is God.

5 ¹Remember ye not, that when I was yet with you, I told you these things?

6 And now ye know ¹what withholdeth, that he might be revealed in his time.

7 ¹For the mystery of iniquity doth already work: ²only he which now ³withholdeth, *shall let* till he be taken out of the way.

8 ¹And then shall ²that wicked man be revealed, ᵃwhom the Lord shall ³consume with the ⁴Spirit of his mouth, and shall abolish with the brightness of his coming,

9 ¹*Even him* whose coming is by the effectual working of Satan, with all power, and signs, and ²lying wonders,

10 And in all deceivableness of unrighteousness, among them that perish, because they received not the love of the truth, that they might be saved.

11 And therefore God shall send them ¹strong delusion, that they should believe lies,

12 That all they might be damned which believed not the truth, but ¹had pleasure in unrighteousness.

13 ¹But we ought to give thanks always to God for you, brethren beloved of the Lord, because that God hath from the beginning chosen you to salvation, through ²sanctification of the Spirit, and the ³faith of truth,

14 Whereunto he called you by our ¹Gospel, to obtain the glory of our Lord Jesus Christ.

15 ¹Therefore, brethren, stand fast and keep the instructions, which ye have been taught, either by word, or by our Epistle.

16 Now the same Jesus Christ our Lord, and our God, even the Father, which hath loved us, and hath given us everlasting consolation and good hope through grace,

17 Comfort your hearts, and stablish you in every word and good work.

3 1 He desireth them to further the preaching of the Gospel with their prayers, 6 and to withdraw themselves

---

2:2 ¹ We must take heed of false prophets, especially in this matter, which go about to deceive, and that for the most part, after three sorts: for either they brag of fained prophetical revelations, or they bring conjectures and reasons of their own, or use counterfeit writings.

² By dreams and fables, which men pretend to be spiritual revelations.

³ Either by word of mouth, or by books written.

⁴ Either by forged letters, or falsely glossed upon.

2:3 ¹ The Apostle foretelleth that before the coming of the Lord, there shall be a throne set up clean contrary to Christ's glory, wherein that wicked man shall sit, and transfer all things that appertain to God, to himself, and many shall fall away from God to him.

² By speaking of one, he pointed out the body of the tyrannous and persecuting Church.

2:4 ¹ All men know who he is that saith he can shut up heaven and open it at his pleasure, and took upon him to be Lord and master above all Kings and Princes, before whom Kings and Princes fall down and worship, honoring that Antichrist as a god.

² He foretelleth that Antichrist, (that is, whosoever he be that shall occupy that seat that falleth away from God) shall not reign without the Church, but in the very bosom of the Church.

2:5 ¹ This prophecy was continually declared to the Ancient Church, but it was neglected of them that followed.

2:6 ¹ What hindereth and stayeth.

2:7 ¹ Even in the Apostles' time the first foundations of the Apostolical seat were laid, but yet so, that they deceived men.

² He foretelleth that when the empire of Rome is taken away, the seat that falleth away from God shall succeed and shall hold his place, as the old writers, Tertullian, Chrysostomes and Jerome do expound it.

³ He which is now in authority and ruleth all, to wit, the Roman Empire.

2:8 ¹ That wickedness shall at length be detected by the word of the Lord, and utterly be abolished by Christ's coming.

² Word for word, that lawless fellow: that is to say, he that shall tread God's law clean underfoot.

³ Bring to nought.

⁴ With his word: for the true Ministers of the word are as a mouth, whereby the Lord breatheth out that mighty and everlasting word, which shall break his enemies in sunder, as it were an iron rod.

2:9 ¹ He foretelleth that Satan will bestow all his might and power, and use all false miracles that he can to establish that seat, and that with great success, because the wickedness of the world doeth so deserve it: yet so, that only the unfaithful shall perish through his deceit.

² Which are partly false, and partly wrought to establish a falsehood.

2:11 ¹ A most mighty working to deceive them.

2:12 ¹ They liked lies so well, that they had pleasure in them which is the greatest madness that may be.

2:13 ¹ The elect shall stand steadfast and safe from all these mischiefs. Now election is known by these testimonies: Faith is gathered by sanctification: faith, by that that we accord unto the truth: truth by calling through the preaching of the Gospel: from whence we come at length to a certain hope of glorification.

² To sanctify you.

³ Faith which layeth hold not upon lies, but upon the truth of God, which is the Gospel.

2:14 ¹ By our preaching.

2:15 ¹ The conclusion remaineth then, that we continue in the doctrine which was delivered unto us by the mouth and writings of the Apostles, through the free good will of God, which comforteth us with an invincible hope, and also in all godliness our whole life long.

from those, who through idleness,   11 and curiosity pervert good order: 14 Whom he excludeth from the company of the faithful.

1   Furthermore, [1]brethren, [a]pray for us, that the word of the Lord may have free passage and be glorified, even as *it is* with you.

2   And that we may be delivered from [1]unreasonable and evil men: [2]for all men have not faith.

3   But the Lord is faithful, which will stablish you, and keep you from [1]evil.

4   [1]And we are persuaded of you through the Lord, that ye both do, and will do the things which we warn you of.

5   [1]And the Lord guide your hearts to the love of God, and the waiting for of Christ.

6   [1]We warn you, brethren, in the Name of our Lord Jesus Christ, that ye withdraw yourselves from every brother that walked inordinately, and not after the instruction, which he received of us.

7   [1]For ye yourselves know, [b]how ye ought to follow us: [c]for we behaved not ourselves inordinately among you,

8   Neither took we bread of any man for nought: but we wrought with labor and travail night and day, because we would not be chargeable to any of you.

9   Not because we have not authority, but that

CHAPTER 3
[a] Eph. 6:19
Col. 4:3
[b] 1 Cor. 11:1
[c] 1 Thess. 4:11

we might make ourselves an ensample unto you to follow us.

10   For even when we were with you, this we warned you of, that if there were any, which would not work, that he should not [1]eat.

11   For we hear, that there are some which walk among [1]you inordinately, and work not at all, [2]but are busybodies.

12   [1]Therefore them that are such, we warn and exhort by our Lord Jesus Christ, that they work with quietness, and eat their own bread.

13   [1]And ye, brethren, be not weary in well doing.

14   [1]If any man obey not this our saying in this letter, note him, and have no [2]company with him, [3]that he may be ashamed.

15   [1]Yet count him not as an enemy, but admonish him as a brother.

16   [1]Now the Lord himself of peace give you peace always by all means. The Lord *be* with you all.

17   [1]The salutation of me Paul, with mine own hand, which is the token in every Epistle: so I write,

18   The grace of our Lord Jesus Christ *be* with you all, Amen.

¶ The second *Epistle* to the Thessalonians, written from Athens.

3:1 [1] He addeth now consequently according to his manner, divers admonitions: The first of them is, that they make prayers for the increase and free passage of the Gospel, and for the safety of the faithful ministers of the same.
3:2 [1] Which have no care of their duty.
[2] It is no marvel that the Gospel is hated of so many, seeing that faith is a rare gift of God. Notwithstanding, the Church shall never be destroyed by the multitude of the wicked, because it is grounded and stayed upon the faithful promise of God.
3:3 [1] From Satan's snares, or from evil.
3:4 [1] The second admonition is, that they follow always the doctrine of the Apostles as a rule for their life.
3:5 [1] Thirdly, he diligently and earnestly admonisheth them of two things which are given us by the only grace of God, to wit, of charity, and a watchful mind to the coming of Christ.
3:6 [1] Fourthly, he saith, that idle and lazy persons ought not to be relieved of the Church, nay, that they are not to be suffered.
3:7 [1] Lest he might seem to deal harshly with them, he setteth forth himself as an example, who besides his travail in preaching labored with his hands, which he saith he was not simply bound to do.
3:10 [1] What shall we do then with those idle bellied Monks, and sacrificing Priests? A Monk (saith Socrates, book 8, of his Tripartite history) which worketh not with hands, is like a thief.
3:11 [1] How great a fault idleness is, he declareth by that that God created no man in vain or to no purpose, neither is there any unto

whom he hath not allotted as it were a certain standing and room. Whereupon it followeth, that the order which God hath appointed, is troubled by the idle, yea, broken, which is great sin and wickedness.
[2] He reprehendeth a vice which is joined with the former, whereupon follow an infinite sort of mischiefs: to wit, that there are none more busy in other men's matters than they which neglect their own.
3:12 [1] The Lord commandeth, and the Apostles pray in the name of Christ, first that no men be idle, and next, that every man do quietly and carefully see to do his duty in that office and calling wherein the Lord hath placed him.
3:13 [1] We must take heed that some men's unworthiness cause us not to be slacker in well doing.
3:14 [1] Excommunication is a punishment for the obstinate.
[2] We must have no familiarity nor fellowship with the excommunicate.
[3] The end of the excommunication is not the destruction, but the salvation of the sinner, that at least through shame he may be driven in repentance.
3:15 [1] We must so eschew familiarity with the excommunicate, that we diligently seek all occasions and means that may be to bring them again into the right way.
3:16 [1] Prayers are the seals of all exhortations.
3:17 [1] The Apostle subscribeth his letters with his own hand, that false letters might not be brought and put in place of true.

THE FIRST EPISTLE OF
PAUL TO
TIMOTHY

1 *Setting forth a perfect pattern of a true Pastor, whose office especially consisteth in teaching,* 4 *he warneth him that vain questions set apart, he teach those things,* 5 *which further charity and faith:* 12 *and that his authority be not condemned,* 14 *he showeth what an one he is made through the grace of God.*

1 Paul ¹an Apostle of Jesus Christ, by the ²commandment of God our Savior, and of *our* Lord Jesus Christ our hope,

2 Unto Timothy *my* natural son in the faith: Grace, ¹mercy, *and* peace from God our Father, and *from* Christ Jesus our Lord.

3 ¹As I besought thee to abide still in Ephesus, when I departed into Macedonia, *so do*, that thou mayest warn some, that they teach none other doctrine,

4 ¹Neither that they give heed to fables and ²genealogies *which are* endless, which breed questions rather than godly edifying which is by faith.

5 *ᵃ,*¹ For the end of the ²commandment is ³love out of a pure heart, and of a good conscience, and

of faith unfeigned.

6 ¹From the which things some have erred, and have turned unto vain jangling.

7 ¹They would be doctors of the Law, and yet understand not what they speak, neither whereof they affirm.

8 ¹And we know, that the Law is good, if a man use it lawfully.

9 ¹Knowing this, that the Law is not given unto a ²righteous man, but unto the lawless and disobedient, to the ungodly, and to ³sinners, to the unholy, and to the profane, to murderers of fathers and mothers, to manslayers,

10 To whoremongers, to buggerers, to menstealers, to liars, to the perjured, and if there be any other thing that is contrary to wholesome doctrine,

11 ¹*Which is* according to the glorious Gospel of the blessed God, ²which is committed unto me.

12 ¹Therefore I thank him which hath made me ²strong, *that is,* Christ Jesus our Lord: for he counted me faithful, and put me in *his* service:

1:1 ¹ First of all, he avoucheth his own free vocation, and also Timothy's, that the one might be confirmed by the other: and therewithal he declareth the sum of the Apostolical doctrine, to wit, the mercy of God in Christ Jesus apprehended by faith, the end whereof is yet hoped for.

² Or, ordinance.

1:2 ¹ There is as much difference betwixt mercy and grace, as is betwixt the effect, and the cause: For grace is that free good will of God, whereby he chose us in Christ, and mercy is that free justification which followeth it.

1:3 ¹ This whole Epistle consisteth in admonitions, wherein all the duties of a faithful Pastor are lively set out. And the first admonition is this, that no innovation be made either in the Apostle's doctrine itself, or in the manner of teaching it.

1:4 ¹ The doctrine is corrupted not only by false opinions, but also by vain and curious speculations: the declaration and utterance whereof can nothing help our faith.

² He noteth out one kind of vain question.

1:5 ¹ The second admonition is, that the right use and practice of the doctrine must be joined with the doctrine. And that consisteth in pure charity, and a good conscience, and true faith.

² Of the Law.

³ There is neither love without a good conscience, nor a good conscience without faith, nor faith without the word of God.

1:6 ¹ That which he spake before generally of vain and curious controversies, he applieth to them, which pretending a zeal of the Law,

dwelled upon outward things, and never made an end of babbling of foolish trifles.

1:7 ¹ There are none more unlearned, and more impudent in usurping the name of holiness, than foolish sophistical babblers.

1:8 ¹ The taking away of an objection. He condemneth not the Law, but requireth the right use and practice of it.

1:9 ¹ He indeed escapeth the curse of the Law, and therefore doth not abhor it, who fleeing and eschewing those things which the Law condemneth, giveth himself with all his heart to observe it: and not he that maketh a vain babbling of outward and curious matters.

² And such a one is he, whom the Lord hath endued with true doctrine, and with the holy Ghost.

³ To such as make an art as it were of sinning.

1:11 ¹ He setteth against fond and vain babbling, not only the Law, but the Gospel also, which condemneth not, but greatly commendeth the wholesome doctrine contained in the commandments of God, and therefore he calleth it a glorious Gospel, and the Gospel of the blessed God, the virtue whereof these babblers knew not.

² A reason why neither any other Gospel is to be taught than he hath taught in the Church, neither after any other sort, because there is no other Gospel besides that which God committed to him.

1:12 ¹ He maintaineth of necessity his Apostleship against some that did carp at his former life, debasing himself, even to hell, to advance Christ's only mercy, wherewith he abolished all those his former doings.

² Which gave me strength, not only when I had no will to do well, but also when I was wholly given to evil.

13 When before I was a ¹blasphemer, and a persecutor, and an oppressor: but I was received to mercy: for I did it ignorantly through unbelief.

14 But the grace of our Lord was exceeding abundant ¹with faith and love, which is in Christ Jesus.

15 ¹This *is* a ²true saying, and by all means worthy to be received, that *ᵇ*Christ Jesus came into the world to save sinners, of whom I am chief.

16 Notwithstanding for this cause was I received to mercy, that Jesus Christ should first show on me all long suffering unto the ensample of them, which shall in time to come believe in him unto eternal life.

17 ¹Now unto the king everlasting, immortal, invisible, unto God ²only wise, *be* honor, *and* glory, for ever, and ever, Amen.

18 ¹This commandment commit I unto thee, son Timothy, according to the prophecies, which went before upon thee, that thou ²by them shouldest fight a good fight,

19 Having ¹faith and a good conscience, ²which some have put away, and as concerning faith, have made shipwreck.

20 Of whom is Hymenaeus, and Alexander, *ᶜ*¹whom I have ²delivered unto Satan, that they might ³learn

ᵇ Matt. 4:13
Mark 2:17

ᶜ 1 Cor. 5:5

CHAPTER 2
ᵈ 2 Tim. 1:11

not to blaspheme.

2 *He exhorteth them to make public prayers for all men, 4, 5 and that for two causes, 8 and therefore he willeth all men in all places to pray, 9 and declareth in what apparel, 11 and with what modesty, women ought to behave themselves in holy assemblies.*

1 I ¹Exhort therefore, that first of all supplications, prayers, intercessions, *and* giving of thanks be made for all men,

2 For Kings, and for all that are in authority, ¹that we may lead a quiet and a peaceable life, in all godliness, and ²honesty.

3 For this is good and acceptable in the sight of God our Savior,

4 ¹Who will that all men shall be saved, and come unto the acknowledging of the truth.

5 ¹For there is one God, and one Mediator between God and man, *which is* the ²man Christ Jesus,

6 Who gave himself a ransom for all men, ¹*to be* that testimony in due time,

7 *ᵈ*Whereunto I am ordained a preacher and an Apostle (I speak the truth in Christ, and lie not) *even* a teacher of the Gentiles in ¹faith and verity.

8 ¹I will therefore that the men pray, everywhere

1:13 ¹ These are the preparative works which Paul braggeth of.

1:14 ¹ He proveth this change by the effects, for that, that he that was a profane man, is become a believer: and he that did most outrageously persecute Christ, burneth now in love towards him.

1:15 ¹ He turneth the reproach of the adversaries upon their own head, showing that this singular example of the goodness of God, redoundeth to the commodity of the whole Church.

² Worthy to be believed.

1:17 ¹ He breaketh out into an exclamation, even for very zeal of mind, for that he cannot satisfy himself in amplifying the grace of God.

² See John 17:3.

1:18 ¹ The conclusion of both the former fatherly admonitions, to wit, that Timothy striving manfully against all lets, being called to the ministry according to many prophecies which went before of him, should both maintain the doctrine which he had received, and keep also a good conscience.

² By the help of them.

1:19 ¹ Wholesome and sound doctrine.

² Whosoever keep not a good conscience, do lose also by little and little the gift of understanding: which he proveth by two most lamentable examples.

1:20 ¹ Such as fall from God, and his religion, are not to be suffered in the Church, but rather ought to be excommunicated.

² Cast out of the Church, and so delivered them to Satan.

³ That by their smart they might learn what it is to blaspheme.

2:1 ¹ Having dispatched those things which pertain to doctrine, he speaketh now in the second place of the other part of the ministry of the word, to wit, of public prayers. And first of all declaring this question, for whom we ought to pray: he teacheth that we must pray for all men, and especially for all manner of magistrates, which thing was at that time somewhat doubted of, seeing that kings, yea and the most part of magistrates were at that time enemies of the Church.

2:2 ¹ An argument taken of the end: to wit, because that magistrates

are appointed to this end, that men might peaceably and quietly live in all godliness and honesty, and therefore must we commend them especially to God, that they may faithfully execute so necessary an office.

² This word containeth all kind of duty, which is to be used amongst men in all their affairs.

2:3 ¹ Another argument, why Churches or Congregations ought to pray for all men, without any difference of nation, kind, age, or order: to wit, because the Lord by calling of all sorts, yea, sometimes those that are greatest enemies to the Gospel, will have his Church gathered together after this sort, and therefore prayers to be made for all.

2:5 ¹ God would not else be manifested to be the only God of all men, unless he would show his goodness in saving of all sorts of men: neither should Christ be seen to be the only mediator between God and all sorts of men, by having taken upon him that nature of man which is common to all men, unless he had satisfied for all sorts of men, and made intercession for all.

² Christ Jesus which was made man.

2:6 ¹ A confirmation, because that even to the Gentiles in the secret of salvation now opened and made manifest the Apostle himself being appointed properly to this office, which he doth faithfully and sincerely execute.

2:7 ¹ Faithfully and sincerely: and by faith he meaneth wholesome and sound doctrine, and by truth, an upright and sincere handling of it.

2:8 ¹ He hath spoken of the persons for whom we must pray: and now he teacheth that the difference of places is taken away: for in times past, one only nation, and in one certain place, came together to public service: but now Churches or Congregations are gathered together everywhere (orderly and decently) and men come together to serve God publicly with common prayer, neither must we strive for the nation or for the purification of the body, or for the place, but for the mind, to have it clean from all offense, and full of sure trust and confidence.

[2]lifting up pure hands without [3]wrath, or [4]doubting.

9   [b,1]Likewise also the women, that they array themselves in comely apparel, with shamefastness and modesty, not with braided hair, or gold, or pearls, or costly apparel,

10   But (as becometh women that profess the fear of God) with good works.

11   Let the woman learn in silence with all subjection.

12   [c]I permit not a woman to teach, [1]neither to usurp authority over the man, but to be in silence.

13   [1]For [d]Adam was first formed, then Eve.

14   [e,1]And Adam was not [2]deceived, but the woman was deceived, and was in the transgression.

15   [1]Notwithstanding, through bearing of children she shall be saved, if they continue in faith, and love, and holiness with modesty.

3   *2 He setteth out Bishops,   8 and Christian deacons with their wives,   12 children and family,   15 he calleth the Church the house of God.*

1   This [1]is a true saying, [2]If any man [3]desire the office of a Bishop, he desireth a worthy work.

2   [a]A Bishop therefore must be unreproveable, the husband of one [1]wife, watching, temperate, modest, harborous, apt to teach,

3   Not [1]given to wine, no striker, not given to filthy lucre, but gentle, no fighter, not covetous.

4   One that can rule his own house honestly, having children under obedience with all honesty.

5   For if any cannot rule his own house, how shall he care for the Church of God?

6   He may not be a young scholar, lest he being puffed up fall into the [1]condemnation of the devil.

7   He must also be well reported of, even of them which are without, lest he fall into rebuke, and the snare of the devil.

8   [1]Likewise *must* [2]Deacons *be* grave, not double tongued, not given unto much wine, neither to filthy lucre,

9   [b]Having the [1]mystery of the faith in pure conscience.

10   And let them first be proved, then let them minister, if they be found blameless.

11   [1]Likewise their wives *must be* honest, not evil speakers, *but* sober, *and* faithful in all things.

12   [1]Let the Deacons be the husbands of one wife, and such as can rule their children well, and their own households.

13   For they that have ministered well, get themselves a good [1]decree, and [2]great liberty in the faith, which is in Christ Jesus.

14   [1]These things write I unto thee, trusting to come very shortly unto thee.

15   But if I tarry long, that thou mayest yet know, how thou oughtest to behave thyself in the [1]house

---

Marginal references:
[b] 1 Pet. 3:3
[c] 1 Cor. 14:34
[d] Gen. 1:27 / Gen. 27:21
[e] Gen. 3:6

CHAPTER 3
[a] Titus 2:6
[b] 1 Tim. 1:19

---

[2] He putteth the sign for the thing itself, the lifting up of hands, for the calling upon God.

[3] Without these griefs and offenses of the mind, which hinder us from calling upon God with a good conscience.

[4] Doubting which is against faith, James 1:6.

2:9 [1] Thirdly he appointeth women to learn in the public assemblies with silence and modesty, being comely appareled without any riot or excess in their apparel.

2:12 [1] The first argument, why it is not lawful for women to teach in the Congregation, because by this means they should be placed above men, for they should be their masters: which is against God's ordinance.

2:13 [1] He proveth this ordinance of God, whereby the woman is subject to man, first by that, that God made the woman after man, for man's sake.

2:14 [1] Then because that after sin God enjoined the woman this punishment, for that the man was deceived by her.

[2] Adam was deceived, but through his wife's means, and therefore she is worthily for this cause subject to her husband, and ought to be.

2:15 [1] He addeth a comfort by the way, that their subjection hindereth not but that women may be saved as well as men, if they behave themselves in those burdens of marriage holily and modestly, with faith and charity.

3:1 [1] Having dispatched the treatise, as well of doctrine and of the manner of handling of it, as also of public prayer, he now in the third place cometh to the persons themselves, speaking first of Pastors and afterward of Deacons, and he useth a preface, that the Church may know that these be certain and sure rulers.

[2] A Bishopric or the ministry of the word is not an idle dignity, but a work and that an excellent work: and therefore a Bishop must be furnished with many virtues both at home and abroad. Wherefore it

be requisite before he be chosen, to examine well his learning, his gifts, and ableness, and his life.

[3] He speaketh not here of ambitious seeking, than the which there cannot be a worse fault in the Church, but general of the mind, and disposition of man, framed and disposed to help and edify the Church of God, when and wheresoever it shall please the Lord.

3:2 [1] Therefore he that shutteth out married men from the office of Bishops, only because they are married, is Antichrist.

3:3 [1] A common tippler, and one that will sit by it.

3:6 [1] Lest by reason that he is advanced to that degree, he take occasion to be proud, which will undo him, and so he fall into the same condemnation that the devil himself is fallen into.

3:8 [1] Likewise the Deacons must first be proved that there may be a good trial of their honesty, truth, sobriety, mind, void of covetousness, that they are well instructed in the doctrine of faith, and to be short, of their good conscience and integrity.

[2] These are they that had to see to the poor.

3:9 [1] The doctrine of the Gospel, which is a mystery indeed: for flesh and blood do not reveal it.

3:11 [1] Regard must be had also to the Pastors' and Deacons' wives.

3:12 [1] They that have more wives than one at one time, must neither be called to be ministers, nor to be Deacons.

3:13 [1] Honor and estimation.

[2] Bold and assured confidence without fear.

3:14 [1] Paul purposing to add many peculiar things pertaining to the daily office of a Pastor, speaketh first a word or two concerning his coming to Timothy, that he would be so much the more careful, lest at his coming he might be reproved of negligence.

3:15 [1] The Pastor hath always to think, how that he is occupied in the house of the living God, wherein the treasure of the truth is kept.

of God, which is the Church of the living God, the ²pillar and ground of truth.

16 ¹And without controversy, great is the mystery of godliness, *which is*, God is manifested in the flesh, ²justified in the Spirit, seen of Angels, preached unto the Gentiles, believed on in the world, *and* received up in glory.

4 *1 He condemneth as well false doctrine, 3 of marriage and the choice of meats, 7 as also profane fables: 8 and commendeth the godly exercise, 13 and the daily reading of the Scriptures.*

1 Now ¹the Spirit speaketh evidently, that in the latter times some shall depart from the ²faith, and shall give heed unto spirits of error, and doctrines of devils,

2 ¹Which speak lies through ²hypocrisy, and have their ³consciences burned with an hot iron,

3 ¹Forbidding to marry, *and commanding* to abstain from meats ²which God hath created ³to be received ⁴with giving thanks of them which believe and know the truth.

4 ¹For every creature of God *is* good, and nothing *ought* to be refused, if it be received with thanksgiving.

5 ¹For it is ²sanctified by the ³word of God, and prayer.

6 ¹If thou put the brethren in remembrance of these things, thou shalt be a good minister of Jesus Christ, which hast been nourished up in the words of faith, and of good doctrine which thou hast continually ²followed.

7 ¹But cast away profane, and old wives' fables, ²and exercise thyself unto ³godliness.

8 ¹For bodily exercise profiteth little: but godliness is profitable unto all things, which hath the promise of the life present, and of that that is to come.

9 ¹This *is* a true saying, and by all means worthy to be received.

10 For therefore we labor and are rebuked, because we trust in the living God, which is the Savior of all men, specially of those that believe.

11 These things warn and teach.

3:15 ² To wit, in respect of men: for the Church resteth upon that cornerstone, Christ, and is the preserver of the truth, but not the mother.

3:16 ¹ There is nothing more excellent than this truth, whereof the Church is the keeper and preserver here amongst men, the ministry of the word being appointed to that end and purpose: for it teacheth us the greatest matters that may be thought of, to wit, that God is become visible in the person of Christ by taking our nature upon him, whose Majesty notwithstanding in so great weakness was manifested many ways, insomuch that the sight of it pierced the very Angels: and to conclude, he being preached unto the Gentiles was received of them, and is now placed above in glory unspeakable.

² The power of the Godhead showeth itself so marvelously in that weak flesh of Christ, that though he were a weak man, yet all the world knoweth he was, and is God.

4:1 ¹ He setteth against that true doctrine, false opinions, which he foretelleth that certain which shall fall away from God and his religion, shall bring in by the suggestion of Satan, and so that a great number shall give ear to them.

² From the true doctrine of God.

4:2 ¹ Although heretics counterfeit holiness never so much, yet they have no conscience.

² For they will as it were practice the art of disguised persons and players, that we may not think they will lie lurking in some one corner, or keep any resemblance of shamefastness.

³ Whose conscience waxed so hard, that there grew an hard fleshiness over it, and so became to have a canker on it, and now at length required of very necessity to be burned with an hot iron.

4:3 ¹ He setteth down two kinds of this false doctrine, to wit, the Law of sole life, and difference of meats.

² He proveth that he justly called such doctrines devilish, first, because the teachers of them make laws of things which are not their own: for have they created the meats?

³ Secondly, because they overthrow with their decrees, the end wherefore they were created of God, to wit, that we should use them.

⁴ Thirdly, for that by this means they rob God of his glory, who will be honored in the use of them. And herewithal the Apostle declareth that we must use the liberality of God soberly, and with a good

conscience.

4:4 ¹ He setteth an Apostolical rule, for taking away the difference of meats, against that false doctrine.

4:5 ¹ He useth God's benefits rightly, which acknowledge the giver of them by his word, and calleth upon him.

² It is so made pure and holy in respect of us, so that we may use it with a good conscience, as received at the Lord's hand.

³ We confess and acknowledge that God is the maker and giver of those creatures which we use. Secondly, that we are of the number of those, who through Christ's benefit have recovered that right over all creatures, which Adam lost by his fall. Thirdly, by our prayers we crave of the Lord, that we may use those meats with a good conscience, which we receive at his hands. Fourthly, we make an end of our eating and drinking, with thanksgiving and prayer: and so are our meats sanctified to us.

4:6 ¹ The conclusion with an exhortation to Timothy, to propound these things diligently to the Churches, which he had sucked of the Apostle, even in a manner from the teat.

² Never departing from the side of it.

4:7 ¹ He setteth again true doctrine not only against that false and apostatical doctrine, but also against all vain and curious subtleties.

² It is not only requisite that the minister of the word be sound in doctrine, but also that his life be godly and religious.

³ In the true serving of God.

4:8 ¹ Godliness consisteth in spiritual exercise, and not in outward austereness of life, which though it be something to be accounteth of, if it be rightly used, yet is it in no wise comparable with godliness: For it profiteth not of itself, but through the benefit of another, but this hath the promise both of the life present, and of that that is to come.

4:9 ¹ He goeth a little from his matter, and showeth that they which give themselves to godliness, although they are afflicted and reproached, are notwithstanding not to be counted miserable as other men are, because they are not afflicted for that cause that other men are, and the end of them both is far different one from the other. For how can God forsake his, which is bountiful even towards his enemies? And he willeth that this doctrine be well beaten into their heads.

12 ¹Let no man despise thy youth, but be unto them that believe, an ensample, in word, in conversation, in love, in spirit, in faith *and* in pureness.

13 ¹Till I come, give attendance to reading, to exhortation, *and* to doctrine.

14 Despise not the gift that is in thee, which was given thee by prophecy with the laying on of the hands of the company of the Eldership.

15 These things exercise, *and* give thyself unto them, that it may be seen how thou profitest among all men.

16 Take heed unto thyself, and unto learning: continue therein: for in doing this thou shalt both ¹save thyself, and them that hear thee.

5 1 *Having set down a manner how to rebuke all degrees.* 5 *He entreateth of widows, who then were chosen for the service of the Church:* 17 *Then he cometh to Elders,* 23 *and speaketh somewhat touching the health of the body.*

1 Rebuke ¹not an elder, but exhort him as a father, *and* the younger men as brethren,

2 The elder women as mothers, the younger as sisters, with all pureness.

3 ¹,²Honor widows, which are widows indeed.

4 ¹But if any widow have children or nephews let them learn first to show godliness ²toward their own house, and ³to recompense their kindred: ⁴for that is an honest thing, and acceptable before God.

5 ¹And she that is a widow indeed and left alone, trusteth in God, and continueth in supplications and prayers night and day.

6 ¹But she that liveth in pleasure, is dead, while she liveth.

7 These things therefore warn *them* of, that they may be blameless.

8 If there be any that provideth not for his own, and namely for them of his household, he denieth the faith, and is worse than an infidel.

9 ¹Let not a widow be taken into the number under threescore years old, that hath been the wife of ²one husband.

10 And well reported of for good works: if she have nourished her children, if she have lodged the strangers, if she have ¹washed the Saints' feet, if she have ministered unto them which were in adversity, if she were continually given unto every good work.

11 ¹But ²refuse the younger widows: for when they have begun to wax wanton against Christ, they will marry.

12 Having damnation, because they have broken the first faith.

13 ¹And likewise also being idle they learn to go about from house to house: yea *they are* not only idle, but also prattlers and busybodies, speaking things which are not comely.

14 ¹I will therefore that the younger women marry, and bear children, and govern the house, *and* give none occasion to the adversary to speak evil.

15 For certain are already turned back after Satan.

16 ¹If any faithful man or faithful woman have widows, let them minister unto them, and let not the Church be charged, that there may be sufficient for them that are widows indeed.

4:12 ¹ Now he returneth to that exhortation, showing which are the virtues of a Pastor, whereby he may come to be reverenced, although he be but young, to wit, such speech and life as are witnesses of charity, zeal, faith, and purity, but here is no mention made of the crosier staff, ring, cloak, and such other foolish and childish toys.

4:13 ¹ The private exercise of Pastors, is continual reading of the Scriptures, whence out they may draw matter of wholesome doctrine and exhortation, both to themselves and to others.

4:16 ¹ Faith is by hearing, and hearing by preaching: and therefore the ministers of the word are so said to save themselves and others, for that in them the Lord hath put the word of reconciliation.

5:1 ¹ Of keeping measure in private reprehensions according to the degrees of ages and kinds.

5:3 ¹ The Apostle giveth these rules touching the care of widows.

² Have care of those widows which have need of help.

5:4 ¹ Widows' children and nephews must take care for their parents, according to their ability.

² The first reason, because that, that which they bestow upon theirs, they bestow it upon themselves.

³ Another, because nature itself teacheth us to recompense our parents.

⁴ The third: because this dutifulness pleaseth God.

5:5 ¹ The second rule: Let the church have care of such as are widows indeed, that is to say, such as are poor and destitute of help of

their own friends, and live godly and religiously.

5:6 ¹ The third rule: Let widows that live in pleasure, and neglect the care of their own family, be holden and accompted as fallers away from God and his religion, and worse than very infidels.

5:9 ¹ The fourth rule: Let none under threescore years old, be taken into the number of widows, to serve the Congregations or Churches, and such as are free from all reproach of unchastity, and are well reported of for their diligence, charity, and integrity.

² That hath had no more husbands, but one at one time.

5:10 ¹ This is spoken in respect of the manner of those countries.

5:11 ¹ The first reason why younger widows are not to be admitted to this ministry, to wit, because for the lightness of their age, they will at length shake off the burden that Christ hath laid upon them, and think rather upon marrying again: and so will forsake the ministry whereunto they had bound themselves.

² Take them not into the college of widows.

5:13 ¹ Another reason: because they are for the most part prattlers and busybodies, and gadders up and down, neglecting their charge and duty.

5:14 ¹ The fifth rule: Let younger widows marry and govern their houses godly.

5:16 ¹ The sixth rule: Let the faithful help their widows at their own charges as much as they can, and let not the Congregation be burdened with these expenses.

17 ¶ ¹The Elders that rule well, let them be had in ²double honor, ³specially they which labor in the word and doctrine.

18 For the Scripture saith, ᵃThou shalt not muzzle the mouth of the ox that treadeth out the corn: and, ᵇThe laborer is worthy of his wages.

19 ¹Against an Elder receive none accusation, but under two or three witnesses.

20 ¹Them that sin, rebuke openly, that the rest also may fear.

21 ¶ ᶜ,¹I charge *thee* before God and the Lord Jesus Christ, and the elect Angels, that thou observe these things, without preferring one to another, and do nothing partially.

22 ¹Lay hands ²suddenly on no man, neither be partaker of other men's sins; keep thyself pure.

23 ¹Drink no longer water, but use a little wine for thy stomach's sake, and thine often infirmities.

24 ¹Some men's sins are open before hand, and go before unto judgment: but some men's follow after.

25 ¹Likewise also the good works are manifest before hand, and they that are otherwise, cannot be hid.

CHAPTER 5
ᵃ Deut. 25:4
  1 Cor. 9:9
ᵇ Matt. 10:10
  Luke 10:7
ᶜ 1 Tim. 6:13

6

1 He showeth the duty of servants: 10 and what a mischievous evil covetousness is: 13 and having spoken somewhat of rich men, he once again forbiddeth Timothy, 20 to cumber himself with vain babblings.

1 Let ¹as many servants as are under the yoke, count their masters worthy of all honor, ²that the Name of God, and *his* doctrine be not evil spoken of.

2 ¹And they which have believing masters, let them not despise them, because they are brethren, but rather do service, because they are faithful, and beloved, and ²partakers of the benefit. ³These things teach and exhort.

3 ¹If any man teach otherwise, and consenteth not to the wholesome words of our Lord Jesus Christ, and to the doctrine which is according to godliness,

4 He is puffed up and knoweth nothing, but doteth about questions and ¹strive of words, whereof cometh envy, strife, railings, evil surmisings,

5 Froward ¹disputations of men of corrupt minds and destitute of the truth, which think that gain is godliness: from such separate thyself.

6 ¹But godliness is great gain, if a man be content with that he hath.

5:17 ¹ Now he giveth rules, and showeth how he ought to behave himself with the Elders, that is to say, with the Pastors and such as have the governance in the discipline of the Church, which is president of their company. The first rule: Let the Church or Congregation see unto this especially, as God himself hath commanded, that the Elders that do their duty well, be honestly maintained.

² We must be more careful for them, than for the rest.

³ There were two kinds of Elders, the one attended upon the government only, and looked to the manners of the Congregation; the other did beside that, attend upon preaching and prayers, to and for the Congregation.

5:19 ¹ The second rule: Let no accusation be admitted against an Elder, but under two or three witnesses.

5:20 ¹ The third rule: Let the Elders so convicted be rebuked openly, that they may be an example to others.

5:21 ¹ The fourth rule: Let sincerity be used without any prejudice or respect of persons in Ecclesiastical proceedings, (especially against the Elders) because God himself is there present, and the Lord Jesus Christ with a multitude of Angels.

5:22 ¹ The [fifth] rule: Let the minister lay hands suddenly on no man. Let him not be faulty herein either by favoring any man's folly, or perverse affection: If ought be done otherwise than well of his fellows, let him keep his conscience pure.

² As much as in thee lieth do not rashly admit any whatsoever, to any Ecclesiastical function.

5:23 ¹ The sixth rule: Let the Elders have indifferent consideration of their health, in the manner of their diet.

5:24 ¹ Because hypocrites sometimes creep into the ministry although there be never so great diligence used, the Apostle willeth the Pastors not to be troubled therefore, or slack any whit of their diligence in trying and examining, because the Lord hath appointed a time to discover the faults of such men, and it is our parts to take heed that we offend not therein.

5:25 ¹ Another comfort belonging to them, which sometimes are slandered and misreported of.

6:1 ¹ He addeth also rules for the servants' duty towards their masters: whereupon no doubt there were many questions then moved by them which took occasion by the Gospel to trouble the common state. And this is the first rule: Let servants that are come to the faith, and have infidels to their masters, serve them notwithstanding with great fidelity.

² The reason: lest God should seem by the Doctrine of the Gospel to stir up men to rebellion and all wickedness.

6:2 ¹ The second rule: Let not servants that are come to the faith, and have also masters of the same profession and religion, abuse the name of brotherhood, but let them so much the rather obey them.

² Let this be sufficient, that as touching those things which pertain to everlasting life, they are partakers of the same good will and love of God, as their masters themselves are.

³ A general conclusion, that these things ought not only to be simply taught, but must with exhortations be diligently beaten into their heads.

6:3 ¹ He condemneth severely, and excommunicateth or casteth out of the Church as proud men, such as content not themselves with Christ's doctrine, (that is to say, the doctrine of godliness) but weary both themselves and others in vain questions, (for all other things are vain) because they content not themselves in Christ's doctrine: and as lying deceivers, because they savor or sound of nothing but vanity: as mad men, because they trouble themselves so much in matters of nothing: as mischievous plagues, for that they cause great contentions, and corrupt men's minds and judgment: to be short, as profane and wicked, because they abuse the precious name of godliness and religion to filthy lucre.

6:4 ¹ Striving about words, and not about matter: and by words he meaneth all those things which have no pith in them, and whereby we can reap no profit.

6:5 ¹ Such as we see in those shameless schools of Popery, which are nothing else but vain babbling and prating.

6:6 ¹ He turneth away fitly the name of gain and lucre, confessing that godliness is great gain, but far after another sort, to wit, because it bringeth true sufficience.

7 ¹For we brought nothing into the world, *and* it is certain, that we can carry nothing out.

8 Therefore when we have food and raiment, let us therewith be content.

9 ¹For they that will be rich, fall into tentation and snares, and into many foolish and noisome lusts, which drown men in perdition and destruction.

10 For the desire of money is the root of all evil, which while some lusted after they erred from the faith, and ¹pierced themselves through with many sorrows.

11 ¹But thou, O ²man of God, flee these things, and follow after righteousness, godliness, faith, love, patience, *and* meekness.

12 Fight the good fight of faith: lay hold of eternal life, whereunto thou art also called, and hast professed a good profession before many witnesses.

13 *a,*¹I charge thee in the sight of God, who quickeneth all things, and before Jesus Christ, which under Pontius Pilate *b*witnessed a good confession.

14 That thou keep *this* commandment without spot, and unrebukeable, until the appearing of our Lord Jesus Christ,

CHAPTER 6
a 1 Tim. 5:21
b Matt. 27:11
    John 18:37
c 2 Thess. 1:11
    Rev. 17:14
    Rev. 19:10
d John 1:18
e Mark 4:19
    Luke 12:15
f Matt. 6:2

15 Which in due time he shall show, that is *c,*¹ blessed and Prince only, the King of kings and Lord of lords.

16 Who only hath immortality, and dwelleth in the light that none can attain unto, *d*whom never man saw, neither can see, unto whom *be* honor and power everlasting, Amen.

17 ¹Charge them that are rich in ²this world, that they be not high minded, and that they *e*trust not in uncertain riches, but in the ³living God, (which giveth us abundantly all things to enjoy.)

18 That they do good, *and* be rich in good works, *and* be ready to distribute, and communicate,

19 *f,*¹Laying up in store for themselves a good foundation against the time to come, that they may obtain eternal life.

20 ¹O Timothy, keep that which is committed unto thee, and avoid profane *and* vain babblings, and oppositions of science falsely so called,

21 Which while some ¹profess, they have erred concerning the faith. Grace *be* with thee, Amen.

¶The first *Epistle* to Timothy, written from Laodicea, which is the chiefest city of Phrygia Pacatiana.

6:7 ¹ He mocketh their folly, which do so greedily gape after frail things, that they can in no wise be satisfied, and yet notwithstanding they cannot enjoy that excess.

6:9 ¹ He frayeth Timothy from covetousness after another sort, to wit, because it draweth with it an infinite sort of lusts, and those very hurtful, wherewith covetous men do torment themselves so far forth, that in the end they cast away from them their faith and salvation.

6:10 ¹ Sorrow and grief do as it were pierce through the mind of man, and are the harvest and true fruits of covetousness.

6:11 ¹ A peculiar exhortation to divers virtues, wherewith it behooveth the Pastors especially to be furnished.

² Whom the Spirit of God ruleth.

6:13 ¹ A most earnest request and charge, to observe and keep all the premises faithfully, with our eyes set upon the coming of Jesus Christ, whose glory we have to set against the vain glistering of this world, and his power, against all the terrors of the wicked.

6:15 ¹ He heapeth many words together, to one purpose: whereby he voucheth the power of God, which if we stick fast unto, we shall not be moved out of our standings.

6:17 ¹ He addeth for an overplus as it were a sharp admonition to the rich, that they chiefly take heed of two mischiefs, to wit, of pride, and deceitful hope, against which he setteth three excellent virtues, hope in the living God, liberality towards their neighbor, and gentle conditions.

² In things pertaining to this life, with whom those men are compared which are rich in good works.

³ Who only is, and that everlasting: for he setteth the frail nature of riches against God.

6:19 ¹ The praise of liberality by the effects thereof: because it is a sure testimony of the Spirit of God which dwelleth in us, and therefore of the salvation that shall be given us.

6:20 ¹ He rehearseth the chiefest of all the former exhortations, which ought to be deeply imprinted in the minds of all ministers of the word, to wit, that they eschew all vain babblings of sophistry and continue in the simplicity of sincere doctrine.

6:21 ¹ Not only in word, but also in countenance and gesture: to be short, while their behavior was such that even when they held their peace, they would make men believe their heads were occupied about nothing but high and weighty matters, even then they erred concerning the faith.

THE SECOND EPISTLE OF
PAUL TO
TIMOTHY

1

3 He commendeth Timothy's faith, 6 and exhorteth him to go on faithfully in the charge committed unto him: 8 and that neither for his bonds, 15 nor the revolting of others, he faint. 11 He triumpheth of his Apostleship. 14 He willeth him to have care of the thing committed unto him, 16 and praiseth Onesiphorus.

1 Paul an Apostle of Jesus Christ by the will of God, [1]according to the promise of life which is in Christ Jesus,

2 To Timothy *my* beloved son: Grace, mercy *and* peace from God the Father, and *from* Jesus Christ our Lord.

3 [1]I thank God, [a]whom I serve from *mine* [2]elders with pure conscience, that without ceasing I have remembrance of thee in my prayers night and day.

4 Desiring to see thee, mindful of thy tears, that I may be filled with joy:

5 When I call to remembrance the unfeigned faith that is in thee, which dwelt first in thy grandmother Lois, and in thy mother Eunice, and am assured that *it dwelleth* in thee also.

6 [1]Wherefore, I put thee in remembrance that

CHAPTER 1
[a] Acts 22:3
[b] 1 Cor. 1:2
[c] Titus 3:5
[d] Rom. 16:25
Eph. 1:4
Col. 1:26
Titus 1:2
[e] 1 Tim. 2:7

thou [2]stir up the gift of God which is in thee, by the putting on of mine hands.

7 For God hath not given to us the Spirit of [1]fear, but of power, and of love, and of a sound mind.

8 [1]Be not therefore ashamed of the testimony of our Lord, neither of me [2]his prisoner: but be partaker of the afflictions of the [3]Gospel according to the [4]power of God,

9 [1]Who hath saved us, and called us with an [b]holy calling, not according to our [c]works, but according to his own purpose and grace, which was [2]given to us through Christ Jesus [3]before the [d]world was,

10 But is now made manifest by that appearing of our Savior Jesus Christ, who hath abolished death, and hath brought life and immortality unto [1]light through the Gospel.

11 [e,1]Whereunto I am appointed a preacher, and Apostle, and a teacher of the Gentiles.

12 [1]For the which cause I also suffer these things, [2]but I am not ashamed: for I know whom I have believed, and I am persuaded that he is able to keep that which I have committed to him against that

---

1:1 [1] Sent of God to preach that life which he promised in Christ Jesus.

1:3 [1] The chiefest mark that he shooteth at in this Epistle, is to confirm Timothy to continue constantly and manfully even to the end, setting first before him the great good will he beareth him, and then reckoning up the excellent gifts which God would as it were have to be by inheritance in Timothy, and his ancestors, which might so much the more make him bound to God.

[2] From Abraham, Isaac and Jacob: for he speaketh not of Pharisaism, but of Christianism.

1:6 [1] He warneth us to set the invincible power of the Spirit, which God hath given us, against those storms which may and do come upon us.

[2] The gift of God is as it were a certain lively flame kindled in our hearts, which the flesh and the devil go about to put out: and therefore we on the contrary side must labor as much as we can to foster and keep it burning.

1:7 [1] To pierce us through, and terrify us, as men whom the Lord will destroy.

1:8 [1] He proveth that the ignomiy or shame of the cross is not only not to be ashamed of, but also that it is glorious and most honorable: first, because the Gospel wherefore the godly are afflicted, is the testimony of Christ: and secondly, because at length the great virtue and power of God appeareth in them.

[2] For his sake.

[3] The Gospel after a sort is said to be afflicted in them that preach it.

[4] Through the power of God.

1:9 [1] He showeth with how great benefits God hath bound us to maintain boldly and constantly his glory which is joined with our salvation, and reckoneth up the causes of our salvation, to wit, that free and eternal purpose of God to save us in Christ which was to come, whereby it should come to pass, that we should at length be freely called of God by the preaching of the Gospel, to Christ the destroyer of death and author of immortality.

[2] He sayeth that that grace was given us from everlasting, unto which we were predestinate from everlasting. So that the doctrine of foreseen faith and foreseen works, is clean contrary to the doctrine which preached and teacheth the grace of God.

[3] Before that course of years, which hath run on ever since the beginning of the world.

1:10 [1] Hath caused life and immortality to appear.

1:11 [1] That is, the Gospel which the Apostle preached.

1:12 [1] He confirmeth his Apostleship by a strange argument, to wit, because the world could not abide it, and therefore it persecuted him that preached it.

[2] By setting his own example before us, he showeth us how it may be, that we shall not be ashamed of the cross of Christ, to wit, if we be sure that God both can and will keep the salvation which he hath as it were laid up in store by himself for us against that day.

day.

13 ¹Keep the true pattern of the wholesome words, which thou hast heard of me in faith and love which is in Christ Jesus.

14 ¹That worthy thing, which was committed to thee, keep ²through the holy Ghost, which dwelleth in us.

15 ¹This thou knowest, that all they which are in Asia, be turned from me: of which sort are Phygellus and Hermogenes.

16 The Lord give mercy unto the house of Onesiphorus: for he oft refreshed me, and was not ashamed of my chain,

17 But when he was at Rome, he sought me out very diligently, and found me.

18 The Lord grant unto him, that he may find mercy with the Lord at that day, and in how many things he hath ministered unto me at Ephesus, thou knowest very well.

2 2 *The better to set out perseverance in the Christian warfare,* 3 *he taketh similitudes,* 4 *from soldiers,* 6 *and from husbandmen.* 10 *He sheweth that his bonds are for the profit of the Saints:* 15 *Then he warneth Timothy to divide the word of truth aright,* 17 *to beware of the examples of the wicked,* 22 *and to do all things modestly.*

1 Thou ¹therefore, my son, be strong in the grace that is in Christ Jesus.

2 And what things thou hast heard of me, by ¹many witnesses, the same deliver to faithful men,

CHAPTER 2
ᵃ Rom. 6:5
ᵇ Matt. 10:33
Mark 8:38
ᶜ Rom. 3:3
Rom. 9:6

which shall be able to teach others also.

3 ¹Thou therefore suffer affliction as a good soldier of Jesus Christ.

4 No man that warreth, entangleth himself with the affairs of ¹*this* life, because he would please him that hath chosen him to be a soldier.

5 ¹And if any man also strive for a mastery, he is not crowned, except he strive as he ought to do.

6 ¹The husbandman must labor before he receive the fruits.

7 ¹Consider what I say: and the Lord give thee understanding in all things.

8 ¹Remember that Jesus Christ, *made* of the seed of David, was raised again from the dead according to my Gospel,

9 ¹Wherein I suffer trouble as an evil doer, even unto bonds: but the word of God is not bound.

10 Therefore I suffer all things for the elect's sake, that they might also obtain the salvation which is in Christ Jesus, with eternal glory.

11 ¹*It* is a true saying, For if we be ᵃ·²dead together *with him:* we also shall live together *with him.*

12 If we suffer, we shall also reign together *with him:* ᵇif we deny *him,* he also will deny us.

13 If ᶜwe believe not, *yet* abideth he faithful: he cannot deny himself.

14 Of these things put them in remembrance, and ¹protest before the Lord, that they strive not about words, which is to no profit, *but* to the perverting of the hearers.

1:13 ¹ He sheweth wherein he ought to be most constant, to wit, both in the doctrine itself, the abridgment whereof is faith and charity, and next in the manner of teaching it, a lively pattern and shape whereof Timothy knew in the Apostle.

1:14 ¹ An amplification, taken of the dignity of so great a benefit committed of the ministers.

² The taking away of an objection. It is a hard thing to do it, but the Spirit of God is mighty, who hath inwardly endued us with his virtue.

1:15 ¹ He preventeth an offense which arose by the means of certain that fell from God and the religion, and uttereth also their names, that they might be known of all men. But he setteth against them the singular faith of one man, that one only good example might counterpoise and weigh down all evil examples.

2:1 ¹ The conclusion of the former exhortation, which hath also added unto it a declaration how that they do not keep that worthy thing that is committed unto them which keep it to themselves, but they rather which do most freely communicate it with others, to the end that many may be partakers of it, without any man's loss or hindrance.

2:2 ¹ When many were by, which can bear witness of these things.

2:3 ¹ Another admonition: That the ministry of the word is a spiritual warfare, which no man can so travail in, that he may please his captain, unless he forgo and part with all hindrances which might draw him away from it.

2:4 ¹ With affairs of household, or other things that belong to other ordinary businesses.

2:5 ¹ The third admonition: The ministry is like to a game or justing, wherein men strive for the victory, and no man is crowned unless he

strive according to the laws which are prescribed, be they never so hard and painful.

2:6 ¹ Another similitude tending to the same end: no man may look for the harvest, unless he first take pains to plow and sow his ground.

2:7 ¹ All these things cannot be understood, and much less practiced, unless we ask of God and he gives us understanding.

2:8 ¹ He confirmeth plainly two principles of our faith, which are always assaulted of heretics, the one whereof (to wit, that Christ is the true Messiah made man of the seed of David) is the ground of our salvation: and the other is the highest part of it, to wit, that he is risen again from the dead.

2:9 ¹ The taking away of an objection: Truth it is, that he is kept in prison, as an evildoer, yet there is no cause, why therefore some should go about to derogate credit from his Gospel, seeing that notwithstanding God did bless his ministry, nay rather, that example of this his captivity and patience did sundry ways confirm the Church in the hope of a better life.

2:11 ¹ The fourth admonition: we ought not to contend upon words and questions, which are not only unprofitable, but also for the most part hurtful: but rather upon this, how we may frame ourselves to all manner of patience, and to die also with Christ (that is to say, for Christ's Name) because that is the plain way to the most glorious life: as contrariwise the falling away of men can diminish no part of the truth of God, although by such means, they procure most certain destruction to themselves.

² If we be afflicted with Christ, and for Christ's sake.

2:14 ¹ Call God to witness, or as a Judge: as Moses, Joshua, Samuel, and Paul himself did, Acts 20.

15 ¹Study to show thyself approved unto God a workman that needeth not to be ashamed, dividing the word of truth ²aright.

16 ¹Stay profane, and vain babblings: ²for they shall increase unto more ungodliness.

17 And their word shall fret as a canker: of which sort is Hymenaeus and Philetus.

18 Which as concerning the truth have erred from the mark, saying that the resurrection is past already, and do destroy the faith of certain.

19 ¹But the foundation of God remaineth sure, and hath this seal, The Lord knoweth who are his: and, Let everyone that ²calleth on the Name of Christ, depart from iniquity.

20 ¹Notwithstanding in a great house are not only vessels of gold and of silver, but also of wood and of earth, ᵈand some for honor, and some unto dishonor.

21 If any man therefore ¹purge himself from these, he shall be a vessel unto honor, sanctified, and meet for the Lord, and prepared unto every good work.

22 ¹Flee also from the lusts of youth, and follow after righteousness, faith, love, and ²peace, with them that ᶜcall on the Lord with pure heart,

23 ʃAnd put away foolish and unlearned questions, knowing that they engender strife.

24 But the servant of the Lord must not strive, but *must* be gentle toward all men, apt to teach, ¹suffering the evil,

25 Instructing them with meekness that are ¹contrary minded, *proving* if God at any time will give them repentance, that they may acknowledge

Side notes:
ᵈ Rom. 9:21
ᵉ 1 Cor. 1:2
ʃ 1 Tim. 1:4
1 Tim. 4:7
Titus 3:9

CHAPTER 3
ᵃ 1 Tim. 4:1
2 Pet. 3:3
Jude 18
ᵇ Exod. 7:11

the truth,

26 And come to amendment out of that snare of the devil, of whom they are taken prisoners, to *do* his will.

CHAPTER 3

1 He foretelleth the dangerous times that are to ensue: 9 but with the certain hope of victory, 10 he encourageth him to the combat, 14 setting out especially the trial of sound doctrine.

1 This ¹know also, that in the ᵃlast days shall come perilous times.

2 For men shall be lovers of their own selves, covetous, boasters, proud, cursed speakers, disobedient to parents, unthankful, ¹unholy,

3 Without natural affection, truce breakers, false accusers, intemperate, fierce, no lovers at all of them which are good,

4 Traitors, heady, high-minded, lovers of pleasures more than lovers of God,

5 Having a show of godliness, but have denied the power thereof: ¹turn away therefore from such.

6 For of this sort are they which creep into houses, and lead captive simple women laden with sins, and led with divers lusts,

7 *Which women are* ever learning, and are never able to come to the acknowledging of the truth.

8 ᵇAnd as Jannes and Jambres withstood Moses, so do these also resist the truth, men of corrupt minds, reprobate concerning the faith.

9 ¹But they shall prevail no longer: for their madness shall be evident unto all men, as theirs also was.

2:15 ¹ The fifth admonition: A minister must not be an idle disputer, but a faithful steward in dividing aright the word of truth, insomuch that he must stop the mouths of other vain babblers.

² By adding nothing to it, neither overslipping anything, neither mangling it, nor renting it in sunder, nor wresting of it: but marking diligently what his hearers are able to hear, and what is fit to edifying.

2:16 ¹ Mark and watch, and see they creep not on further.

² He discovereth the subtlety of Satan, who beginning with these principles draweth us by little and little to ungodliness through the means of that wicked and profane babbling, still creeping on: which he proveth by the horrible example of them that taught that, the resurrection was already past.

2:19 ¹ A digression: wherein he salveth that offense that rose by their falling away: showing first, that the elect are out of all danger of any such falling away: secondly, that they are known to God and not to us: and therefore it is no marvel if we count hypocrites oftentimes for true brethren: but we must take heed that we be not like them, but rather that we be indeed, such as we are said to be.

² That serveth and worshippeth him, and is as it were named of him, a faithful man or Christian.

2:20 ¹ The taking away of an objection: it is no dishonor to the good man of the house, that he hath not in a great house all vessels of one sort and for one service, but we must look to this, that we be found vessels prepared to honor.

2:21 ¹ By these words is meant the execution of the matter, and not the cause: for in that we purge ourselves, it is not to be attributeth to any free will that is in us, but to God, who freely and wholly worketh in us a good and an effectual will.

2:22 ¹ Returning to the matter from whence he digressed, verse 16, he warneth him to exercise himself in weighty matters, and such as pertain to godliness.

² The sixth admonition: We must above all things eschew all bitterness of mind both in teaching all men, and also in calling them back which have gone out of the way.

2:24 ¹ To win them through our patient bearing with them, but not to please them or excuse them in their wickedness.

2:25 ¹ He meaneth such as do not yet see the truth.

3:1 ¹ The seventh admonition: we may not hope for any Church in this world without corruption: but there shall be rather great abundance of most wicked men, even in the very bosom of the Church, which notwithstanding shall make a show and countenance of great holiness and charity.

3:2 ¹ Which make no account, either of right or honesty.

3:5 ¹ We must not dally with such men as resist the truth not of simple ignorance, but of a perverse mind, (which thing appeareth by their fruits which he painteth out here lively) but we must rather turn away from them.

3:9 ¹ He addeth a comfort: The Lord will at length pluck off all their vizards.

10 ¶ [1]But thou hast [2]fully known my doctrine, manner of living, purpose, faith, longsuffering, love, patience,

11 Persecutions, *and* afflictions which came unto me at [1]Antioch, at Iconium, and at Lystra, which persecutions I suffered: but from them all the Lord delivered me.

12 Yea, and all that will live godly in Christ Jesus, shall suffer persecution.

13 But the evil men and deceivers shall wax [1]worse and worse, deceiving, and being deceived.

14 But continue thou in the things which thou hast learned, and which are committed unto thee, knowing of whom thou hast learned *them:*

15 And that thou hast known the holy Scriptures of a child, which are able to make thee wise unto salvation, through the faith which is in Christ Jesus.

16 [c,1]For the whole Scripture *is* given by inspiration of God, and *is* profitable to teach, to convince, to correct, *and* to instruct in righteousness,

17 That the [1]man of God may be absolute, being made perfect unto all good works.

4

1 He chargeth him to preach the Gospel with all diligence,   3 in that so miserable a time: 6 that his death is hard at hand,   8 yet so, that as a conqueror he maketh haste to a glorious triumph.   10 He sheweth the cause why he sendeth for Timothy,   11 even by reason of his present state.

1 I [1]Charge *thee* therefore before God, and *before* the Lord Jesus Christ, which shall judge the quick and dead at that his appearing, and in his kingdom,

2 Preach the word: be instant, in season, and out of season: improve, rebuke, exhort with all longsuffering and doctrine.

3 [1]For the time will come when they will not

c 2 Pet. 1:20

CHAPTER 4
d Col. 4:10,14

suffer wholesome doctrine: but having their ears itching, shall after their own lusts get them an heap of teachers,

4 And shall turn their ears from the truth, and shall be given unto [1]fables.

5 [1]But watch thou in all things: suffer adversity: do the work of an Evangelist: [2]cause thy ministry to be thoroughly liked of.

6 [1]For I am now ready to be [2]offered, and the time of my departing is at hand.

7 I have fought a good fight, and have finished my course: I have kept the faith.

8 *For* henceforth is laid up for me the crown of righteousness, which the Lord the righteous Judge shall give me at that day: and not to me only, but unto all them also that love that his appearing.

9 [1]Make speed to come unto me at once:

10 For Demas hath forsaken me, and hath [1]embraced this present world, and is departed unto Thessalonica. Crescens *is gone* to Galatia, Titus unto Dalmatia.

11 [d]Only Luke is with me. Take Mark and bring him with thee: for he is profitable unto me to minister.

12 And Tychicus have I sent to Ephesus.

13 The cloak that I left at Troas with Carpus, when thou comest, bring with thee, and the books, but specially the parchments.

14 Alexander the coppersmith hath done me much evil: the Lord reward him according to his works.

15 Of whom be thou ware also: for he withstood our preaching sore.

16 At my first answering no man assisted me, but all forsook me: *I pray God,* that it may not be laid to their charge.

17 Notwithstanding the Lord assisted me, and strengthened me, that by me the preaching might be fully believed, and that all the Gentiles should

---

3:10 [1] That we be not deceived by such hypocrites, we must set before us the virtues of the holy servants of God, and we must not be afraid of persecution, which they suffered willingly, and which always followeth true godliness. But we must especially hold fast the doctrine of the Apostles, the sum whereof is this, that we are saved through faith in Christ Jesus.

[2] Thou knowest thoroughly, not only what I taught and did, but also how I was minded and disposed.

3:11 [1] Which is in Pisidia.

3:13 [1] Their wickedness shall daily increase.

3:16 [1] The eighth admonition, which is most precious: A Pastor must be wise by the word of God only: wherein we have perfectly delivered unto us, whatsoever pertaineth either to discern, know and establish true opinions, and to confute false, and furthermore, to correct evil manners, and to frame good.

3:17 [1] The Prophets and expounders of God's will, are properly and peculiarly called, Men of God.

4:1 [1] The principal and chief of all admonitions, being therefore proposed with a most earnest charge, is this: That the word of God be propounded with a certain holy importunity, as necessity requireth:

but so, that a good and true ground of the doctrine be laid, and the vehemency be tempered with all holy meekness.

4:3 [1] Faithful Pastors in times past took all occasions they could, because men were very prompt and ready to return to their fables.

4:4 [1] To false and unprofitable doctrines, which the world is now so bewitched withal, that it had rather the open light of the truth were utterly put out, when it would come out of darkness.

4:5 [1] The wickedness and falling away of the world, ought to cause faithful ministers to be so much the more careful.

[2] Prove and show by good and substantial proof, that thou art the true minister of God.

4:6 [1] He foretelleth his death to be at hand, and setteth before them an excellent example, both of invincible constancy and sure hope.

[2] To be offered for a drink offering: and he alludeth to the pouring out of blood or wine which was used in sacrifices.

4:9 [1] The last part of the Epistle, setting forth grievous complaints against certain, and examples of singular godliness in every place, and of a mind never wearied.

4:10 [1] Contented himself with this world.

hear: and I was delivered out of the mouth of the [1]lion.

18 And the Lord will deliver me from every [1]evil work, and will preserve me unto his [2]heavenly kingdom: to whom *be* praise for ever and ever, Amen.

19 Salute Prisca and Aquila, and the [b]household of Onesiphorus.

20 Erastus abode at Corinth: Trophimus I left at Miletus sick.

b 2 Tim. 1:16

21 Make speed to come before winter. Eubulus greeteth thee, and Pudens, and Linus, and Claudia, and all the brethren.

22 The Lord Jesus Christ *be* with thy Spirit. Grace *be* with you, Amen.

¶ The second *Epistle* written from Rome unto Timothy, the first Bishop elected of the Church of Ephesus, when Paul was presented the second time before the Emperor Nero.

4:17 [1] Of Nero.
4:18 [1] Preserve me pure from committing anything unworthy my Apostleship.
[2] To make me partaker of his kingdom.

THE EPISTLE OF
PAUL TO
TITUS

1 *6 He showeth what kind of men ought to be chosen Ministers: 10 how vain babblers' mouths should be stopped: 12 and through this occasion he toucheth the nature of the Cretans, 14 and the Jews, who put boldness in outward things.*

1 Paul [1]a [2]servant of God, and an Apostle of Jesus Christ, according to the faith of God's [3]elect, [4]and the acknowledging of the truth, which is according unto godliness.

2 Unto the [1]hope of eternal life, which God that cannot lie, hath [2]promised before the [a,3]world began:

3 [1]But hath made his word manifest in due time through the preaching, which is [b]committed unto me according to the commandment of God our [2]Savior:

4 [1]To Titus *my* natural son according to the common faith, [2]Grace, mercy, *and* peace from God the Father, and *from* the Lord Jesus Christ our Savior.

5 [1]For this cause left I thee in Crete, that thou shouldest continue to redress the things that remain, and shouldest ordain Elders in every city as I ap-

6 [1]If any be unreproveable, the husband of one wife, having faithful children, which are not slandered of riot, neither are [1]disobedient.

7 [1]For a Bishop must be unreproveable, as God's [2]steward, not [3]froward, not angry, not given to wine, no striker, not given to filthy lucre,

8 But harberous, one that loveth goodness, [1]wise, righteous, holy, temperate,

9 [1]Holding fast that faithful word according to doctrine, [2]that he also may be able to exhort with wholesome doctrine, and convince them that say against it.

10 [1]For there are many disobedient and vain talkers and deceivers of minds, chiefly they of the [2]Circumcision,

11 Whose mouths must be stopped, which subvert whole houses, teaching things which they ought not, for filthy lucre's sake.

12 [1]One of themselves, *even* one of their own Prophets said, The Cretans *are* always liars, evil beasts, slow bellies.

CHAPTER 1
a Rom. 16:25
Eph. 3:9
Col. 1:26
2 Tim. 1:9
1 Pet. 1:20
b Gal. 1:1
c 1 Tim. 3:2

1:1 [1] He voucheth his Apostleship, (not for Titus, but for the Cretans' sake) both by the testimony of his outward calling, and by his consent wherein he agreeth with all the elect from the beginning of the world.

[2] Minister, as Christ himself, in that that he was a minister and head of the Prophets, is called a servant, Isa. 43:10.

[3] Of those whom God hath chosen.

[4] The faith wherein all the elect consent, is the true and sincere knowledge of God, tending to this end, that worshipping God aright that they at length obtain life everlasting according to the promise of God, who is true, which promise was exhibited to Christ in due time according to his eternal purpose.

1:2 [1] Hope is the end of faith.

[2] Freely, and of his mere liberality.

[3] See 2 Tim. 1:9.

1:3 [1] This truth is no other where to be sought, but in the preaching of the Apostle.

[2] This word (Savior) doth not only signify a preserver of life, but also a giver of life.

1:4 [1] The Apostle moveth the Cretans to hear Titus, by setting forth his consent and agreement with him in the faith, and therewithal showeth by what special note we may distinguish true ministers from false.

[2] There is but one way of salvation, common both to the Pastor and the flock.

1:5 [1] The first admonition, to ordain Elders in every city.

1:6 [1] This word is proper to horses and oxen, which will not abide the yoke.

1:7 [1] The second admonition, what faults pastors (whom he comprehended afore under the word Elders) ought to be void of, and what virtues they ought to have.

[2] Whom the Lord hath appointed steward of his gifts.

[3] Not hard conditioned, and evil to please.

1:8 [1] Circumspect, of a sound judgment, and of a singular example of moderation.

1:9 [1] The third admonition: The Pastor must hold fast that doctrine, which the Apostles delivered, and pertaineth to salvation, leaving all curious and vain matters.

[2] The fourth admonition: To apply the knowledge of true doctrine unto use, which consisteth in two things, to wit, in governing them which show themselves apt to learn, and confuting the obstinate.

1:10 [1] An applying of the general proposition to a particular: The Cretans above all others need sharp reprehensions: both because their minds are naturally given to lies and slothfulness, and also because of certain covetous Jews, which under a color of godliness joined partly certain vain traditions, and partly old ceremonies with the Gospel.

[2] Of the Jews, or rather of those Jews, which went about to join Christ and the Law together.

1:12 [1] Epimenides, who was counted a Prophet amongst them. Look upon Laertius and Cicero in his first book of Divination.

13 This witness is true: wherefore convince them ¹sharply, that they may be sound in the faith.

14 And not taking heed to ᵈJewish fables and commandments of men, that turn away from the truth.

15 ¹Unto the pure ᵉare all things pure, but unto them that are defiled, and unbelieving, is nothing pure, but even their ²minds and consciences are defiled.

16 They profess that they know God, but by works they deny him, and are abominable and disobedient, and unto every good work reprobate.

2

2 He setteth out the duties of sundry persons and states, 6 and willeth him to instruct the Church in manners. 11 He draweth an argument from the end of our redemption, 12 which is, that we live godly and uprightly.

1 But ¹speak thou the things which become wholesome doctrine,

2 ¹That the elder men be watchful, grave, temperate, sound in the faith, in love, and in patience:

3 The elder women likewise, that they be in such behavior as becometh holiness, not false accusers, not subject to much wine, but teachers of honest things.

4 That they may instruct the young women to be sober minded, that they love their husbands, that they love their children,

5 That they be temperate, chaste, ¹keeping at home, good and ᵃsubject unto their husbands, that the word of God be not evil spoken of.

6 Exhort young men likewise, that they be sober minded.

7 ¹In all things show thyself an example of good works with uncorrupt doctrine, with ²gravity, integrity,

ᵈ 1 Tim. 1:4
ᵉ Rom. 14:20

CHAPTER 2
ᵃ Eph. 5:23
ᵇ Eph. 6:5
Col. 3:22
1 Pet. 2:18
ᶜ 1 Cor. 1:2
Col. 1:22

CHAPTER 3
ᵃ Rom. 15:1
1 Pet. 2:13
ᵇ 1 Cor. 6:11

8 And with the wholesome word, which cannot be condemned, that he which withstandeth, may be ashamed, having nothing concerning you to speak evil of.

9 ᵇ·¹Let servants be subject to their masters, and please them in all ²things, not answering again,

10 Neither pickers, but that they show all good faithfulness, that they may adorn the doctrine of God our Savior in all things.

11 ᶜ·¹For that grace of God, that bringeth salvation unto all men, hath appeared,

12 And teacheth us, that we should deny ungodliness and ¹worldly lusts, and that we should live soberly and righteously, and godly in this present world,

13 ¹Looking for that blessed hope, and appearing of that glory of that mighty God, and of our Savior Jesus Christ.

14 Who gave himself for us, that he might redeem us from all iniquity, and purge us to be a ¹peculiar people unto himself, zealous of good works.

15 These things speak, and exhort, and convince with all ¹authority. See that no man despise thee.

3

1 He willeth that all generally be put in mind to reverence such as be in authority: 3 That they remember their former life, and attribute all justification unto grace. 9 And if any brabbler withstand these things, 10 he willeth that he be rejected.

1 Put ¹them in remembrance that they ᵃbe subject to the principalities and powers, and that they be obedient, and ready to every good work.

2 That they speak evil of no man, that they be no fighters, but soft, showing all meekness unto all men.

3 ᵇ·¹For we ourselves also were in times past unwise, disobedient, deceived, serving the lusts and

---

1:13 ¹ Roughly and plainly, and go not about the bush with them.
1:15 ¹ He showeth in few words, that purity consisteth not in any external worship, and that that is according to the old Law, (as in difference of meats, and washing, and other such things which are abolished) but in the mind and conscience: and whosoever teach otherwise, know not what is true religion indeed, and also are nothing less than that they would seem to be.
² If our minds and conscience be unclean, what cleanness is there in us before regeneration?
2:1 ¹ The fifth admonition: The doctrine must not only be generally pure, but also be applied to all ages and orders of men, according to the diversity of circumstances.
2:2 ¹ What are the chiefest virtues for old and young, both men and women: and how they ought to be stirred up unto them continually.
2:5 ¹ No gadders up and down.
2:7 ¹ The sixth admonition: That both the Pastor's life and doctrine must be sound.
² Not such a gravity as may drive men from coming to the minister, but such as may cause them to come in most reverent and honest sort.
2:9 ¹ The seventh admonition, of servants' duty toward their masters.

² Which may be done without offense to God.
2:11 ¹ The eighth admonition belonging to all the godly, that seeing God calleth all men to the Gospel, and Christ hath so justified us, that he hath also sanctified us, we must all of us give ourselves to true godliness and righteousness, setting before us a sure hope of that immeasurable glory: which thing must in such sort be beaten into their heads, that the gainsayers also must be reproved, by the authority of the mighty God.
2:12 ¹ Lusts of the flesh, which belong to the present state of this life and world.
2:13 ¹ Christ is here most plainly called that mighty God, and his appearance and coming is called by the figure Metonymy, our hope.
2:14 ¹ As it were a thing peculiarly laid up for himself.
2:15 ¹ With all authority possible.
3:1 ¹ He declareth particularly and severally, that which he said before generally, noting out certain chief and principal duties, which men owe to men, and especially subjects to their magistrates.
3:3 ¹ He confirmeth again the former exhortation, by propounding the free benefit of our regeneration, the pledge whereof is our Baptism.

divers pleasures, living in maliciousness and envy, hateful, *and* hating one another.

4 But when that bountifulness and that love of God our Savior toward man appeared,

5 ᶜNot by the works of ¹righteousness, which we had done, but according to his mercy he saved us, by the washing of the new birth, and the renewing of the ²holy Ghost,

6 Which he shed on us abundantly, through Jesus Christ our Savior,

7 That we, being justified by his grace, should be made heirs according to the hope of eternal life.

8 ¹This is a true saying, and these things I will thou shouldest affirm, that they which have believed God, might be careful to show forth ²good works. These things are good and profitable unto men.

9 ᵈBut stay foolish questions, and genealogies, and contentions, and brawlings about the Law: for

ᶜ 2 Tim. 1:9
ᵈ 1 Tim. 1:4
1 Tim. 4:7
2 Tim. 2:23

they are unprofitable and vain.

10 ¹Reject him that is an heretic, after once or twice admonition,

11 Knowing that he that is such, is perverted, and sinneth, being damned of his own self.

12 ¹When I shall send Artemas unto thee, or Tychicus, be diligent to come to me unto Nicopolis: for I have determined there to winter.

13 Bring Zenas the expounder of the Law, and Apollos on their journey diligently, that they lack nothing.

14 And let ours also learn to show forth good works for necessary uses, that they be not unfruitful.

15 All that are with me, salute thee. Greet them that love us in the faith. Grace *be* with you all. Amen.

¶ To Titus, elect the first Bishop of the Church of the Cretans, written from Nicopolis in Macedonia.

3:5 ¹ Word for word, of works which are done in righteousness: and this place doth fully refute the doctrine of merits.

² Which the virtue of the holy Ghost worketh.

3:8 ¹ Again with great earnestness he beateth into our heads, how that we ought to give ourselves, to true godliness, and eschew all vain questions, which serve to nothing but to move strife and debate.

² Give themselves earnestly unto good works.

3:10 ¹ The ministers of the word must at once cast off heretics, that is, such as stubbornly and seditiously disquiet the Church, and will give no ear to Ecclesiastical admonitions.

3:12 ¹ Least of all, he writeth a word or two of private matters and commendeth certain men.

THE EPISTLE OF
PAUL TO
PHILEMON

1 *Paul handling a base and small matter, yet according to his manner mounteth aloft unto God.* 8 *Sending again to Philemon his vagabond and thievish servant, he entreateth pardon for him, and very gravely preacheth of Christian equity.*

1 Paul a prisoner of Jesus Christ, and *our* brother Timothy, unto Philemon our dear friend, and fellow helper,

2 And to *our* dear sister Apphia, and to Archippus our fellow soldier, and to the Church that is in thine house:

3 Grace *be* with you, and peace from God our Father, and *from* the Lord Jesus Christ.

4 I *a*give thanks to my God, making mention always of thee in my prayers,

5 (When I hear of thy love and faith, which thou hast toward the Lord Jesus, and toward all Saints.)

6 That the [1]fellowship of thy faith may be made effectual, and that whatsoever good thing is in you through Christ Jesus, may be [2]known.

7 For we have great joy and consolation in thy love, because by thee, brother, the Saints [1]bowels are comforted.

8 Wherefore, though I be very bold in Christ to command thee that which is convenient,

9 [1]*Yet* for love's sake I rather beseech thee, though I be as I am, even Paul aged, and even now a prisoner for Jesus Christ.

10 I beseech thee for my son *b*Onesimus, whom I have begotten in my bonds,

11 Which in times past was to thee unprofitable, but now profitable both to thee and to me.

12 Whom I have sent again: thou therefore receive him, that is mine own [1]bowels,

13 Whom I would have received with me, that in thy stead he might have ministered unto me in the bonds of the Gospel.

14 But without thy mind would I do nothing, that thy benefit should not be as it were of [1]necessity, but willingly.

15 It may be that he therefore [1]departed for [2]a season, that thou shouldest receive him forever,

16 Not now as a servant, but above a servant, *even as* a brother beloved, specially to me: how much more then unto thee, both in the [1]flesh and in the Lord?

17 If therefore thou count our things common, receive him as myself.

18 If he hath hurt thee, or oweth thee ought, that put on my accounts.

19 I Paul have written *this* with mine own hand: I will recompense it, albeit I do not say to thee, that thou owest moreover unto me even thine own self.

20 [1]Yea, brother, let me obtain this pleasure of thee in the Lord: comfort my bowels in the Lord.

21 Trusting in thine obedience, I wrote unto thee knowing that thou wilt do even more than I say,

22 Moreover also prepare me lodging: for I trust through your prayers I shall be freely given unto you.

23 There salute thee Epaphras my fellow prisoner in Christ Jesus,

24 Mark, Aristarchus, Demas *and* Luke, my fellow helpers.

25 The grace of our Lord Jesus Christ *be* with your spirit, Amen.

¶ Written from Rome to Philemon, *and sent* by Onesimus a servant.

1:6 [1] By fellowship of faith, he meaneth those duties of charity which are bestowed upon the Saints, and flow forth of an effectual faith.

[2] That by this means all men may perceive how rich you are in Christ, to wit, in faith, charity, and all bountifulness.

1:7 [1] Because thou didst so dutifully and cheerfully refresh the Saints, that they conceived inwardly a marvelous joy: for by this word (Bowels) is meant not only the inward feeling of wants and miseries that men have one of another's state, but also that joy and comfort which entereth into the very bowels, as though the heart were refreshed and comforted.

1:9 [1] An example of a Christian exercise and commendation for another man.

1:12 [1] As mine own son, and as if I had begotten him of mine own body.

1:14 [1] That thou mightest not seem to have lent me thy servant upon constraint, but willingly.

1:15 [1] Thus he assuageth the harder kind of speech, which is to say, he ran away.

[2] For a little time.

1:16 [1] Because he is thy servant, as other servants are, and because he is the Lord's servant, so that thou must needs love him both for the Lord's sake, and for thine own sake.

1:20 [1] Good brother let me obtain this benefit at thine hand.

THE EPISTLE TO THE

HEBREWS

The drift and end of this Epistle, is to show that Jesus Christ the Son of God both God and man, is that true eternal and only Prophet, King, and high Priest, that was shadowed by the figures of the old Law, and is now indeed exhibited: of whom the whole Church ought to be taught, governed and sanctified.

CHAPTER 1
a Col. 1:15
b Ps. 2:7
Heb. 5:5
c 2 Sam. 7:14
d Ps. 97:7
e Ps. 104:4
f Ps. 55:7
g Ps. 102:25

1 *2 To show that the doctrine which Christ brought, is most excellent, in that it is the knitting up of all prophecies, 4 he advanceth him above the Angels: 10 And proveth by divers testimonies of the Scripture, that he far passeth all others.*

1 At ¹sundry times and in divers manners God spake in the old time to *our* fathers by the Prophets: in these ²last days he hath spoken unto us by his ³Son,

2 ¹Whom he hath made ²heir of all things, by whom also he made the ³worlds,

3 ᵃWho being the ¹brightness of the glory, and the engraved form of his ²person, and ³bearing up all things by his mighty word: ⁴hath by himself purged our sins: and ⁵sitteth at the right hand of the Majesty in the highest places,

4 ¹And is made so much more excellent than the Angels, inasmuch as he hath obtained a more excellent ²Name than they.

5 ¹For unto which of the Angels said he at any time, ᵇThou art my Son, ²this day begat I thee? and again, I ᶜwill be his Father, and he shall be my Son:

6 And ¹again, when he bringeth in *his* first begotten Son into the world, he saith, ᵈAnd let all the Angels of God worship him.

7 And of the Angels he saith, ᵉHe maketh the spirits his ¹messengers, and his ministers a flame ²of fire.

8 But unto the Son *he saith,* ᶠO God, thy ¹throne *is* forever ²and ever: the scepter of thy kingdom *is* a ³scepter of righteousness.

9 Thou hast loved righteousness and ¹hated iniquity. Wherefore God, *even* thy God, hath ²anointed thee with the oil of gladness, above thy ³fellows.

10 And, ᵍThou, Lord, in the beginning hast ¹established the earth, and the heavens are the works of thine hands.

11 They shall perish, but thou dost remain, and they all shall wax old as doth a garment,

12 And as a vesture shalt thou fold them up, and they shall be changed: but thou art the same, and thy years shall not fail.

13 Unto which also of the Angels said he at any

1:1 ¹ The first part of the general proposition of this Epistle: the Son of God is indeed that Prophet or teacher, which hath actually now performed that that God after a sort and in shadows signified by his Prophets, and hath fully opened his Father's will to the world.

² So that the former declaration made by the Prophets was not full, and nothing must be added to this latter.

³ Which one Son is God and man.

1:2 ¹ The second part of the same proposition: The same Son is appointed by the Father to be our King and Lord, by whom also he made all things, and in whom only he setteth forth his glory, yea and himself also to be beholden of us, who beareth up and sustaineth all things by his will and pleasure.

² Possessor and equal compartner of all things with the Father.

³ That is, whatsoever hath been at any time, is, or shall be.

1:3 ¹ He in whom that glory and Majesty of the Father shineth, who is otherwise infinite, and cannot be beholden.

² His father's person.

³ Sustaineth, defendeth and cherisheth.

⁴ The third part of the same proposition. The same Son executed the office of the high Priest in offering up himself, and is our only and most mighty Mediator in heaven.

⁵ This showeth that the savor of that his sacrifice is not only most acceptable to the Father, but also is everlasting, and furthermore how far this high Priest passeth all the other high Priests.

1:4 ¹ Before he cometh to declare the office of Christ, he setteth forth the excellency of his person, and first of all he showeth him so to be man, that therewithal he is God also.

² Dignity and honor.

1:5 ¹ He proveth and confirmeth the dignity of Christ manifested in the flesh by these six evident testimonies, whereby it appeareth that he far passeth all Angels, insomuch that he is called both Son, and God, in verses 5, 6, 7, 10, 13.

² The Father begat the Son from everlasting, but that everlasting generation was made manifest and represented to the world in his time, and therefore he addeth this word (Today.)

1:6 ¹ The Lord was not content to have spoken it once, but repeateth it in another place.

1:7 ¹ Cherub, Ps 18:11.

² Seraph, Isa. 6:2.

1:8 ¹ The throne is proper to the Prince, and not to the servant.

² For everlasting, for this doubling of the word increaseth the signification of it beyond all measure.

³ The government of thy kingdom is righteous.

1:9 ¹ This kind of rehearsing in which the Jews use contraries, hath great force in it.

² In that, that the word became flesh, by pouring the holy Ghost upon him without measure.

³ For he is the head and we are his members.

1:10 ¹ Madest the earth firm and sure.

time, [b]Sit at my right hand, till I make thine enemies thy footstool?

14 Are they not all [1]ministering spirits, sent forth to minister, for their sakes which shall be heirs of salvation?

2 *1 Thereof he inferreth, that good heed must be given to Christ's doctrine: 9 And he setteth him out unto us even as our brother in our flesh, that we may with a good will yield up ourselves wholly unto him.*

1 Wherefore [1]we ought diligently to give heed to the things which [2]we have heard, lest at any time we [3]run out.

2 For if the [1]word spoken by Angels was steadfast, and every transgression, and disobedience received a just recompense of reward,

3 How shall we escape if we neglect so great salvation, [1]which at the first began to be preached by the Lord, and *afterward* was confirmed unto us by [2]them that heard him.

4 [a]God bearing witness thereto, both with [1]signs and wonders, and with divers miracles, and gifts of

[column reference notes]
[b] Ps. 110:1
1 Cor. 15:25
Heb. 10:12,13

CHAPTER 2
[a] Mark 16:20
[b] Ps. 8:6
[c] 1 Cor. 15:27
[d] Phil. 2:8

the holy Ghost, according to his own will?

5 [1]For he hath not put in subjection unto the Angels the [2]world to come, whereof we speak.

6 [b]But [b]one in a certain place witnessed, saying, [2]What is man, that thou shouldest be mindful of him? or the [3]son of man, that thou wouldest consider him?

7 Thou [1]madest him a little inferior to the Angels: thou crownedst him with [2]glory and honor, and hast set him above the works of thine hands.

8 [c]Thou hast put all things in subjection under his feet. And in that he hath put all things in subjection under him, he left nothing that should not be subject unto him. [1]But we yet see not all things subdued unto him,

9 [1]But we [2]see Jesus crowned with glory and honor, [d]which was made little [3]inferior to the Angels, [4]through the [5]suffering of death, that by God's grace he might [6]taste death for [7]all men.

10 [1]For it became [2]him, for whom *are* all these things, and by whom *are* all these things, [3]seeing that he brought many children unto glory, [4]that

---

1:14 [1] By that name by which we commonly call Princes' messengers, he here calleth the spirits.
2:1 [1] Now as it were pausing with himself and showing to what end and purpose all these things were spoken, to wit, to understand by the excellency of Christ above all creatures, that his doctrine, majesty and Priesthood is most perfect, he useth an exhortation taken from a comparison.
[2] He maketh himself an hearer.
[3] They are said to let the word run out, which hold it not fast when they have heard it.
2:2 [1] The Law which appointed punishment for the offenders: and which Paul saith was given by Angels, Gal. 3:19, and Stephen, Acts 7:53.
2:3 [1] If the breach and trangression of the word spoken by Angels was not suffered unpunished, much less shall it be lawful for us to neglect the Gospel which the Lord of Angels preached, and was confirmed by the voice of the Apostles, and with so many signs and wonders from heaven, and especially with so great and mighty working of the holy Ghost.
[2] By the Apostles.
2:4 [1] This is the true end of miracles. Now they are called signs, because they appear one thing, and represent another: and they are called wonders, because they represent some strange and unaccustomed things and virtues, because they give us a glimpse of God's mighty power.
2:5 [1] If it were an heinous matter to contemn the Angels which are but servants, much more heinous is it to contemn that most mighty King of the restored world.
[2] The world to come, whereof Christ is Father, Isa. 9:6, or the Church, which as a new world, was to be gathered together by the Gospel.
2:6 [1] He showeth that the use of this kingly dignity consisteth herein, that men might not only [in] Christ recover that dignity which they have lost, but also might be through him advanced above all things, which dignity of men David describeth most excellently.
[2] What is there in man that thou shouldest have so great regard of him, and do him that honor?
[3] He calleth all the citizens of that heavenly kingdom as they are considered in themselves, before that God giveth them the liberty of that city in Christ, Man, and Son of man.
2:7 [1] This is the first honor of the citizens of the world to come, that

they are next [to] the Angels.
[2] For they shall be in very great honor, when they shall be partakers of the kingdom. And he speaketh of the thing that shall be, as though it were already, because it is so certain.
2:8 [1] An objection: But where is this so great rule and dominion?
2:9 [1] The answer: this is already fulfilled in Jesus Christ our head, who was for a time for our sakes inferior to the Angels, being made man: but now is advanced into most high glory.
[2] By his virtue and power which appeareth manifestly in the Church.
[3] Who abased himself for a season, and took upon him the position of a servant.
[4] He showeth the cause of this subjection, to wit, to taste of death for our sakes, that so doing the part of a redeemer, he might not only be our Prophet and King, but also our high Priest.
[5] That he might die.
[6] Feel death.
[7] Herein consisteth the force of the argument: for we could not at length be glorified with him, unless he was abased for us even all the faithful. And by this occasion the Apostle cometh to the other part of the declaration of Christ's person, wherein he proveth him to be in such sort God, and he is also man.
2:10 [1] He proveth moreover by other arguments, why it behooveth the Son of God who is true God (as he proveth a little before) to become man notwithstanding, subject to all miseries, sin only except.
[2] God.
[3] First of all, because the Father, to whose glory all these things are to be referred, purposed to bring many sons unto glory. And how could he have men for his sons, unless his only begotten Son had become brother to men?
[4] Secondly, The Father determined to bring those sons to glory, to wit, out of that ignominy wherein they lay before. Therefore the Son should not have been seen plainly to be made man, unless he had been made like unto other men, that he might come to glory in the selfsame way, by which he should bring others: yea rather, it became him which was Prince of the salvation of others, to be consecrated above others, through those afflictions, Prophet, King, and Priest, which are the parts of that principality for the salvation of others.

he should consecrate the [5]Prince of their salvation through afflictions.

11 [1]For he that [2]sanctifieth, and they which are sanctified, *are* all of [3]one: wherefore he is not ashamed to call them brethren,

12 [1]Saying, ‹I will declare thy Name unto my brethren: in the midst of the Church will I sing praises to thee.

13 [1]And again, ‹I will put my [2]trust in him. And again, [g][3]Behold, here am I, and the children which God hath given me.

14 Forasmuch then as the children are [1]partakers of flesh and blood, he also himself likewise took part with them, that he might destroy [h]through death, him that had the [2]power of death, that is, the [3]devil,

15 And that he might deliver all them, which for fear of [1]death were all their lifetime subject to bondage.

16 [1]For he in no sort took on *him* the [2]Angels' *nature*, but he took on *him* the [3]seed of Abraham.

17 [1]Wherefore in [2]all things it behooved him to be made like unto his brethren, that he might

e Ps. 22:25
f Ps. 18:2
g Isa. 1:18
h Hos. 13:14
1 Cor. 15:55

CHAPTER 3

a Num. 12:7

be [3]merciful, and a [4]faithful high Priest in things concerning God, that he might make reconciliation for the sins of the people.

18 For in that he suffered, and was [1]tempted, he is able to succor them that are tempted.

3 *1 Now he showeth how far inferior Moses is to Christ, 5, 6 even so much as the servant to the Master: and so he bringeth in certain exhortations and threatenings taken out of David,   8 against such as either stubbornly resist,   12 or else are very slow to obey.*

1 Therefore, [1]holy brethren, partakers of the heavenly vocation, consider the [2]Apostle and high Priest of our [3]profession Christ Jesus:

2 [1]Who was faithful to him that hath [2]appointed him, [3]even as [a]Moses *was* in all his house.

3 [1]For this man is counted worthy of more glory than Moses, inasmuch as he which hath builded the house, hath more honor than the house.

4 For every house is builded of some man, and he that hath built all things, *is* God.

[5] The Chieftain, who as he is chiefest in dignity, so is he the first begotten from among the dead, amongst many brethren.

2:11 [1] The ground of both the former arguments: for neither should we be sons through him, neither could he be consecrated through afflictions, unless he hath been made man like unto us. But because this Sonhood dependeth not upon nature only, for no man is accompted the son of God, unless that besides that he is a son of a man, he be also Christ's brother, (which is by sanctification, that is, by becoming one with Christ, who sanctifieth us through faith) therefore the Apostle maketh mention of the sanctifier, to wit, of Christ, and of them that are sanctified, to wit, of all the faithful, whom therefore Christ vouchsafeth to call brethren.

[2] He useth the time that now is, to show us that we are yet still going on, and increasing in this sanctification, and by sanctification he meaneth our separation from the rest of the world, our cleansing from sin, and our dedication wholly unto God, all which Christ alone worketh in us.

[3] One, of one selfsame nature of man.

2:12 [1] That which he taught before of the incarnation of the sanctifier, he applieth to the prophetical office.

2:13 [1] He applieth the same to the kingly power of Christ in delivering his from the power of the devil and death.

[2] I will commit myself to him, and to his defense.

[3] This Isaiah speaketh of himself and his disciples, but betokening thereby all ministers, as also his disciples signify the whole Church. And therefore seeing Christ is the head of the Prophets and ministers, these words are more rightly verified of him, than of Isaiah.

2:14 [1] Are made of flesh and blood which is a frail and brittle nature.

[2] The devil is said to have the power of death, because he is the author of sin: and from sin cometh death, and for this cause he eggeth us daily to sin.

[3] He speaketh of one as of the Prince, joining to him secretly all his angels.

2:15 [1] By (death) thou must understand here that death which is joined with the wrath of God, as it must needs be, if it be without Christ, then there can be nothing devised more miserable.

2:16 [1] He expoundeth those words of flesh and blood, showing that Christ is true man, and not by turning his divine nature, but by taking

on man's nature. And he nameth Abraham, respecting the promises made to Abraham in this behalf.

[2] The nature of Angels.

[3] The very nature of man.

2:17 [1] He applieth the same to the Priesthood, for which he should not have benefit, unless he had become man, and that like unto us in all things, sin only except.

[2] Not only as touching nature, but qualities also.

[3] That he might be truly touched with the feeling of our miseries.

[4] Doing his office sincerely.

2:18 [1] Was tried and egged to wickedness by the devil.

3:1 [1] Having laid the foundation, that is to say, declared and proved both the natures of one selfsame Christ, he giveth him three offices, to wit, the office of a Prophet, king, and Priest: and as touching the office of teaching and governing, compareth them with Moses and Joshua, unto verse 14 of the next Chapter, and with Aaron touching the Priesthood. And he propoundeth that which he purposeth to speak of, with a most grave exhortation, that all our faith may tend to Christ, as to the only everlasting teacher, governor, and high Priest.

[2] The Ambassador or messenger, as Rom. 1:5, he is called the minister of circumcision.

[3] Of the doctrine of the Gospel which we profess.

3:2 [1] He confirmeth this exhortation with two reasons, first of all because Christ Jesus was appointed such an one of God: secondly, because he thoroughly executed the offices that his Father enjoined him.

[2] Apostle and high Priest.

[3] Now he cometh to the comparison with Moses, and he maketh them like one to the other in this, that they were both appointed rulers over God's house, and executed faithfully their office: but by and by after he showeth that there is great unlikeness in that similitude.

3:3 [1] The first comparison: The builder of the house is better than the house itself, therefore is Christ better than Moses. The reason of the consequent is this: because the builder of this house is God, which cannot be attributed to Moses: and therefore Moses was not properly the builder, but a part of the house: but Christ as Lord and God, made all this house.

5 [1]Now Moses verily was faithful in all his house, as a servant, for a witness of the things which should be spoken after.

6 But Christ *is* as the Son, over his own house, [1]whose [2]house we are, if we hold fast that [3]confidence and that rejoicing of that hope unto the end.

7 Wherefore, as the holy Ghost saith, [b]Today if ye [1]shall hear his voice,

8 Harden not your hearts, as in the [1]provocation, according to the day of the temptation in the wilderness,

9 Where your fathers tempted me, proved me, and saw my works forty years long.

10 Wherefore I was grieved with that generation, and said, They [1]err ever in *their* heart, neither have they known my ways.

11 Therefore I swear in my wrath, If they shall enter into my rest.

12 [1]Take heed brethren, lest at any time there be in any of you an evil heart, and unfaithful, to depart away from the living God.

13 But exhort one another daily, [1]while it is called today, lest any of you be hardened through the deceitfulness of sin.

14 [1]For we are made partakers of Christ, if we keep sure unto the end that [2]beginning, wherewith we are upholden,

15 [1]So long as it is said, Today if ye hear his voice, harden not your hearts, as in the provocation.

16 For some when they heard, provoked him to anger: howbeit, not all that came out of Egypt by Moses.

b Ps. 95:8
Heb. 4:7
c Num. 14:37

CHAPTER 4
a Ps. 95:11
b Gen. 2:2
Deut. 5:14

17 But with whom was he displeased forty years? Was he not displeased with them that sinned, [c]whose carcasses fell in the wilderness?

18 And to whom swear he that they should not enter into his rest, but unto them that obeyed not?

19 So we see that they could not enter in, because of unbelief.

4 *1 He joineth exhortation with threatening, lest they, even as their fathers were be deprived of the rest offered unto them,　11 but that they endeavor to enter into it.　14 And so he beginneth to entreat of Christ's Priesthood.*

1 Let us fear therefore, lest at any time by forsaking the promise of entering into his rest, any of you should seem to be deprived.

2 [1]For unto us was the Gospel preached as also unto them: but the word that they heard, profited not them, because it was not [2]mixed with faith in those that heard it.

3 [1]For we which have believed, do enter into rest, as he said *to the other*, [a]As I have sworn in my wrath, If they shall enter into my rest: although the works were finished from the foundation of the world.

4 For he spake in a certain place of the seventh day on this wise, [b]And God did rest the seventh day from all his works.

5 And in this place again, If they shall enter into my rest.

6 Seeing therefore it remaineth that some must enter thereinto, and they to whom it was first preached, entered not therein for unbelief's sake:

7 Again he appointed in David a certain day, by

3:5 [1] Another comparison: Moses was a faithful servant in this house, that is, in the Church, seeing the Lord that was to come, but Christ ruleth and governeth his house as Lord.

3:6 [1] He applieth the former doctrine to this end, exhorting all men by the words of David to hear the Son himself speak, and to give full credit to his words, seeing that otherwise they cannot enter into that eternal rest.

[2] To wit, Christ's.

[3] He calleth that excellent effect of faith (whereby we cry, Abba, that is, Father) confidence, and to confidence he joineth hope.

3:7 [1] So that God was to speak once again after Moses.

3:8 [1] In the day that they vexed the Lord, or strove with him.

3:10 [1] They are brutish and mad.

3:12 [1] Now weighing the words of David, he showeth first by this word, *Today* that we must not neglect the occasion while we have it: for that word is not to be restrained to David's time, but it comprehendeth all the time wherein God calleth us.

3:13 [1] While today lasteth, that is to say, so long as the Gospel is offered to us.

3:14 [1] Now he considereth these words, *If you hear his voice*, etc., showing that they are spoken and meant of the hearing of faith, against which he setteth hardening through unbelief.

[2] That beginning of trust and confidence: and after the manner of the Hebrews, he calleth that beginning, which is chiefest.

3:15 [1] So long as this voice soundeth out.

4:2 [1] By these words, *His voice*, he showeth that David meant the preaching of Christ, who was then also preached, for Moses and the Prophets respected none other.

[2] He compareth the preaching of the Gospel to drink, which being drunk, that is to say, heard, profiteth nothing, unless it be tempered with faith.

4:3 [1] Lest any man should object, that those words were meant of the Land of Canaan, and of Moses'doctrine, and therefore cannot well be drawn to Christ, and to eternal life, the Apostle showeth that there are two manner of rests spoken of in the Scriptures: the one, of the seventh day, wherein God is said to have rested from all his works: the other is said to be that same, whereinto Joshua led the people: but this rest is not the last rest whereto we are called and that he proveth by two reasons. For seeing that David so long time after, speaking to the people which were then placed in the land of Canaan, useth these words, *Today*, and threateneth them still that they shall not enter into the rest of God, which refuseth then the voice of God that sounded in their ears, we must needs say that he meant another time than the time of Moses, and another rest than the rest of the land of Canaan: And that is, that everlasting rest, wherein we begin to live to God, after that the race of this life ceaseth: as God resteth the seventh day from those his works, that is to say, from making the world. Moreover, the Apostle therewithal signifieth that the way to this rest, which Moses and the land of Canaan and all that order of the Law did shadow, is opened in the Gospel only.

Today, after so long a time, saying, as it is said, 'This day, if ye hear his voice, harden not your hearts.

8 For if 'Jesus had given them rest, then would he not after this have spoken of another day.

9 There remaineth therefore a rest to the people of God.

10 'For he that is entered into his rest, hath also ceased from his own works, as God *did* from his.

11 'Let us study therefore to enter into that rest, lest 'any man fall after the same example of disobedience.

12 'For the 'word of God *is* 'lively, and mighty in operation, and sharper than any two edged sword, and entereth through, even unto the dividing asunder of the 'soul and the 'spirit, and of the joints, and the marrow, and is a discerner of the thoughts, and the intents of the heart.

13 Neither is there any creature, which is not manifest in 'his sight: but all things *are* naked and open unto his eyes, with whom we have to do.

14 'Seeing then that we have a great high Priest, which is entered into heaven, *even* Jesus the Son of God, let us 'hold fast our profession.

15 'For we have not an high Priest, which cannot be touched with the feeling of our infirmities, but was in all things tempted in like sort, *yet* without sin.

16 Let us therefore go boldly unto the throne of grace, that we may receive mercy, and find grace to

c Heb. 3:7

CHAPTER 5
a 1 Chron. 13:10
1 Chron. 23:13

b Ps. 2:7
Heb. 1:5

c Ps. 110:4
Heb. 7:17

help in time of need.

5

1 First he showeth the duty of the high Priest: 5 Secondly, that Christ is appointed of God to be our high Priest, 7 and that he hath fulfilled all things belonging thereunto.

1 For 'every high Priest is taken from among men, and is ordained for men, in things pertaining to God, 'that he may offer both 'gifts and 'sacrifices for sins.

2 Which is 'able sufficiently to have compassion 'on them that are ignorant, and that are out of the way, because that he also is 'compassed with infirmity,

3 And for the same sake he is bound to offer for sins, as well for his own part, as for the peoples.

4 *a,*'And no man taketh this honor unto himself, but he that is called of God, as *was* Aaron.

5 So likewise Christ took not to himself this honor to be made the high Priest, but he that said unto him, *b*'Thou art my son, this day begat I thee, *gave it him.*

6 As he also in another place speaketh, 'Thou art a Priest forever, after the 'order of Melchizedek,

7 'Who in the 'days of his flesh did offer up prayers and supplications, with strong crying and tears unto him, that was able to 'save him from death, and was also heard in that which he feared.

8 And though he were the Son, yet 'learned he

4:8 ¹ He speaketh of Joshua the son of Nun: and as the land of Canaan was a figure of our true rest, so was Joshua a figure of Christ.
4:10 ¹ As God rested the seventh day, so must we rest from our works, that is, from such as proceed from our corrupt nature.
4:11 ¹ He returneth to an exhortation.
 ² Lest any man become a like example of infidelity.
4:12 ¹ An amplification taken from the nature of the word of God, the power whereof is such, that it entereth even to the deepest and most inward and secret parts of the heart, wounding them deadly that are stubborn, and plainly quickening the believers.
 ² The doctrine of God which is preached both in the Law and in the Gospel.
 ³ He calleth the word of God lively by reason of the effects it worketh in them, to whom it is preached.
 ⁴ He calleth that the soul, which hath the affections resident in it.
 ⁵ By the spirit he meaneth that nobelest part which is called the mind.
4:13 ¹ In God's sight.
4:14 ¹ Now he entereth into the comparison of Christ's Priesthood with Aaron's, and declareth even in the very beginning the marvelous excellency of this Priesthood, calling him the Son of God and placing him in the seat of God in heaven, plainly and evidently setting him against Aaron's Priests, and the transitory tabernacle: which comparisons he setteth forth afterward more at large.
 ² And let it not go out of your hands.
4:15 ¹ Lest he might seem by this great glory of our high Priest, to stay and stop us from going unto him, he addeth straightways after, that he is notwithstanding our brother indeed, (as he proved it also before) and that he accounteth all our miseries, as his own, to call us boldly to him.

5:1 ¹ The first part of the first comparison of Christ's high Priesthood, with Aaron's: Other high Priests are taken from among men, and are called after the order of men.
 ² The first part of the second comparison, Others as weak: are made high Priests, to the end that feeling the same infirmity in themselves which is in all the rest of the people, they should in their own and the people's name offer gifts and sacrifices, which are witnesses of common faith, and repentance.
 ³ Offering of things without life.
 ⁴ Beasts which were killed, but especially in the sacrifices for sins and offenses.
5:2 ¹ Fit and meet.
 ² On them that are sinful: for in the Hebrew tongue, under ignorance and error is every sin meant, even that sin that is voluntary.
 ³ For that he himself beareth about with him a nature subject to the same discommodities and vices.
5:4 ¹ The third comparison which is whole: The others are called of God, and so was Christ, but in another order than Aaron: for Christ is called the Son, begotten of God, and a Priest forever after the order of Melchizedek.
5:6 ¹ After the likeness or manner as it is afterward declared, Heb. 7:15.
5:7 ¹ The other part of the second comparison: Christ being exceedingly afflicted and exceedingly merciful, asked not for his sins, for he had none, but for his fear, and obtained his request, and offered himself for all his.
 ² While he lived here with us in our weak and frail nature.
 ³ To deliver him from death.
5:8 ¹ He learned indeed what it is to have a Father, whom a man must obey.

obedience, by the things which he suffered.

9 ¹And being ²consecrated, was made the author of eternal salvation unto all them that obey him:

10 And is called of God an high Priest after the order of Melchizedek.

11 ¹Of whom we have many things to say, which are hard to be uttered, because ye are dull of hearing.

12 ¹For when as concerning the time ye ought to be teachers, yet have ye need again that we teach you what *are* the first principles of the word of God: and are become such as have need of milk, and not of strong meat.

13 For everyone that useth milk, is inexpert in the ¹word of righteousness: for he is a babe.

14 But strong meat belongeth to them that are of age, which through long custom have their ¹wits exercised, to discern both good and evil.

6 *1 He briefly toucheth the childish slothfulness of the Hebrews, 4 and terrifieth them with severe threatenings: 7 He stirreth them up to endeavor in time to go forward: 9 He hopeth well of them: 13 He allegeth Abraham's example: 17 and compareth faith that taketh hold on the word, 19 unto an anchor.*

1 Therefore, leaving the doctrine of the ¹beginning of Christ, let us be led forward unto perfection, ²not laying again the foundation of repentance from dead works, and of faith toward God,

2 Of the doctrine of baptisms, and laying on of hands, and of the resurrection from the dead, and of eternal judgment.

3 And this will we do if God permit.

CHAPTER 6
ª Heb. 10:26
Matt. 12:45
2 Pet. 1:10
ᵇ Gen. 12:2
Gen. 17:1
Gen. 22:17

4 ª,¹ For it is ²impossible that they which were once lightened, and have ³tasted of the heavenly gift, and were made partakers of the holy Ghost,

5 And have tasted of the good word of God, and of the powers of the world to come,

6 If they fall away, should be renewed again by repentance: seeing they ¹crucify again to themselves the Son of God, and make a mock of him.

7 ¹For the earth which drinketh in the rain that cometh oft upon it, and bringeth forth herbs meet for them by whom it is dressed, receiveth blessing of God.

8 But that which beareth thorns and briars, *is* reproved, and is near unto cursing, whose end *is* to be burned.

9 ¹But beloved, we have persuaded ourselves better things of you, and such as accompany salvation, though we thus speak.

10 ¹For God *is* not unrighteous, that he should forget your work, and labor of love, which ye showed toward his Name, in that ye have ministered unto the Saints, and *yet* minister.

11 And we desire that every one of you show the same diligence, to the full assurance of hope unto the end,

12 ¹That ye be not slothful, but followers of them, which through faith and patience, inherit the promises.

13 ¹For when God made the promise to Abraham, because he had no greater to swear by, he swore by himself,

14 Saying, ᵇSurely I will ¹abundantly bless thee, and multiply thee marvelously.

15 And so after that he had tarried patiently, he

5:9 ¹ The other part of the first comparison: Christ was consecrate of God the Father as the author of our salvation, and an high Priest forever, and therefore he is so a man that notwithstanding he is far above all men.

² See Heb. 2:10.

5:11 ¹ A digression, until he comes to the beginning of the seventh chapter: wherein he partly holdeth the Hebrews in the diligent consideration of those things which he hath said, and partly prepareth them to the understanding of those things whereof he will speak.

5:12 ¹ An example of an Apostolic chiding.

5:13 ¹ In the word that teacheth righteousness.

5:14 ¹ All their power whereby they understand and judge.

6:1 ¹ The first principles of Christian religion, which we call the Catechism.

² Certain principles of a Catechism, which comprehend the sum of the doctrine of the Gospel, were given in few words and briefly to the rude and ignorant, to wit, the profession of repentance and faith in God: the articles of which doctrine, were demanded of them which were not as yet received members of the Church, at the days appointed for Baptism: and of the children of the faithful which were baptized in their infancy: when hands were laid upon them. And of those articles, two are by name recited: the resurrection of the flesh, and the eternal judgment.

6:4 ¹ He addeth a vehemency to his exhortation, and a most sharp

threatening of the certain destruction that shall come to them which fall from God and his religion.

² He speaketh of a general backsliding, and such as do altogether fall away from the faith, and not of sins which are committed through the frailty of man against the first and the second table.

³ We must mark the force of this word, for it is one thing to believe as Lydia did, whose heart God opened, Acts 16:13, and another thing to have some taste.

6:6 ¹ As men that hate Christ, and as though they crucified him again make him a mocking stock to all the world, and that to their own destruction, as Julian the Apostate or backslider did.

6:7 ¹ He setteth forth the former threatening with a similitude.

6:9 ¹ He mitigateth and assuageth all that sharpness, hoping better of them to whom he writeth.

6:10 ¹ He praiseth them for their charity, thereby encouraging them to go forward, and to hold out to the end.

6:12 ¹ He showeth what virtues chiefly they have need of to go forward constantly, and also to profit: to wit, of charity, and patience: and lest any man should object and say, that these things are impossible to be done, he willeth them to set before themselves the examples of their ancestors, and to follow them.

6:13 ¹ Another prick to prick them forward: Because the hope of the inheritance is certain, if we continue to the end, for God hath not only promised it, but also promised it with an oath.

6:14 ¹ I will heap up benefits most plentifully upon thee.

enjoyed the promise.

16 For men verily swear by him that is greater *than themselves*, and an oath for confirmation is among them an end of all strife.

17 So God, willing more ¹abundantly to show unto the heirs of promise the stableness of his counsel, bound himself by an oath,

18 That by two immutable things, wherein it is impossible that God should lie, we might have strong consolation, which have our refuge to lay hold upon that hope that is set before us,

19 ¹Which *hope* we have, as an anchor of the soul, but sure and steadfast, and it entereth into that which is within the veil.

20 ¹Whither the forerunner is for us entered in, *even* Jesus that is made an high Priest forever after the order of Melchizedek.

7 *1 He hath hitherto stirred them up, to mark diligently what things are to be considered in Melchizedek, 15 wherein he is like unto Christ. 20 Wherefore the Law should give place to the Gospel.*

1 For this ¹Melchizedek ª*was* King of Salem, the Priest of the most high God, who met Abraham, as he returned from the slaughter of the Kings, and ²blessed him:

2 To whom also Abraham gave the tithe of all things: who first is by interpretation King of righteousness: after that, *he is* also King of Salem, that is, King of peace,

CHAPTER 7
ª Gen. 14:18
ᵇ Num. 18:21

3 ¹Without father, without mother, without kindred, and hath neither beginning of *his* days, neither end of life: but is likened unto the Son of God, and continueth a Priest forever.

4 ¹Now consider how great this man *was*, unto whom even the Patriarch Abraham gave the tithe of the spoils.

5 For verily they which are the children of Levi, which receive the office of the Priesthood, have a ᵇcommandment to take, according to the Law, tithes of the people (that is, of their brethren) though they ¹came out of the loins of Abraham.

6 But he whose kindred is not counted among them, received tithes of Abraham, and blessed him that had the promises.

7 And ¹without all contradiction the less is blessed of the greater.

8 And here men that die, receive tithes: but there he *receiveth them*, of whom it is witnessed, that he liveth.

9 ¹And to say as the thing is, Levi also which receiveth tithes, payeth tithes in Abraham.

10 For he was yet in the loins of his father *Abraham*, when Melchizedek met him.

11 ¹If therefore ²perfection had been by the Priesthood of the Levites (for under it the Law was established to the people) what needed it furthermore, that another Priest should rise after the order of Melchizedek, and not to be called after the order of Aaron?

12 ¹For if the Priesthood be changed, then of necessity must there be a change of the ²Law.

6:17 ¹ More than was needful, were it not for the wickedness of men which believe not God, no though he swear.

6:19 ¹ He likeneth hope to an anchor: because that even as an anchor being cast into the bottom of the sea, stayeth the whole ship, so doth hope also enter even into the very secret places of heaven. And he maketh mention of the Sanctuary, alluding to the old tabernacle, and by this means returneth to the comparisons of the Priesthood of Christ with the Levitical.

6:20 ¹ He repeateth David's words, wherein all those comparisons whereof he hath before made mention, are signified, as he declareth in all the next chapter.

7:1 ¹ Declaring those words, *According to the order of Melchizedek*, whereupon that comparison standeth of the Priesthood of Christ with the Levitical: first Melchizedek himself is considered as the figure of Christ, and these are the hands of that comparison, Melchizedek was a King and a Priest: and such an one indeed is Christ alone. He was a King of peace and righteousness: such an one indeed is Christ alone.

² With a solemn and Priestly blessing.

7:3 ¹ Another figure: Melchizedek set before us to be considered as one without beginning and without ending, for neither his father, nor his mother, nor his ancestors, nor his death are written of: and such an one indeed is the Son of God, to wit, an everlasting Priest: as he is God, without mother wonderfully begotten: as he is man, without father wonderfully conceived.

7:4 ¹ Another figure: Melchizedek in consideration of his Priesthood was above Abraham, for he took tenths of him, and blessed him as a Priest: Such an one indeed is Christ, upon whom dependeth even Abraham's sanctification, and all the believers, and whom all men

ought to worship and reverence as the author of all.

7:5 ¹ Were begotten by Abraham.

7:7 ¹ He speaketh of the public blessing which the Priests used.

7:9 ¹ A double amplification: The first, that Melchizedek took the tenths, as one immortal (to wit, in respect, that he is the figure of Christ, for his death is in no place made mention of, and David setteth him forth as an everlasting Priest) but the Levitical Priests, as mortal men, for they succeed one another: the second, that Levi himself was tithed in Abraham by Melchizedek. Therefore the Priesthood of Melchizedek (that is, Christ's who is pronounced to be an everlasting Priest according to his order) is more excellent than the Levitical.

7:11 ¹ The third treatise of this Epistle, wherein after he hath proved Christ to be a King, a Prophet, and a Priest, he now handleth distinctly the condition and excellency of all these offices, showing that all these were but shadows in all other, but in Christ they are true and perfect. And he beginneth with the Priesthood, wherewith also the former treatise ended, that by this means all the parts and members of this disputation, may better hang together. And first of all he proveth that the Levitical Priesthood was imperfect because another Priest is promised a long time after according to another order, that is to say, of another manner of rule and fashion.

² If the priesthood of Levi could have made any man perfect.

7:12 ¹ He showeth how that by the institution of the new Priesthood, not only the imperfection of the Priesthood of Levi was declared, but also that it was changed for this: for these two cannot stand together, because that first appointment of the tribe of Levi, did shut forth the tribe of Judah, and made it also inferior to Levi: and this latter doth place the Priesthood in the tribe of Judah.

² Of the institution of Aaron.

13 For he of whom these things are spoken, pertaineth unto another tribe, whereof no man ¹served at the altar.

14 For it is evident, that our Lord sprung out of Judah, concerning the which tribe Moses spake nothing, touching the Priesthood.

15 ¹And it is yet a more evident thing, because that after the similitude of Melchizedek, there is risen up another Priest,

16 ¹Which is not made *Priest* after the ²Law of the carnal commandment, but after the power of the endless life.

17 For he testifieth *thus*, Thou art a Priest forever, after the order of Melchizedek.

18 ¹For the ²commandment that went afore, is disannulled, because of the weakness thereof, and unprofitableness.

19 For the Law made nothing perfect, but the bringing in of a better hope *made perfect*, whereby we draw near unto God.

20 ¹And forasmuch as it is not without an oath (for these are made Priests without an oath:

21 But this *is made* with an oath by him that said unto him, *ᵈ*The Lord hath sworn, and will not repent, Thou art a Priest forever, after the order of Melchizedek.)

22 By so much is Jesus made a surety of a better Testament.

23 ¹And among them many were made Priests,

ᶜ Ps. 110:4
Heb. 5:6
ᵈ Ps. 110:4
ᵉ Lev. 16:11

because they were not suffered to endure, by the reason of death.

24 But this man, because he endureth ever, hath a Priesthood, which ¹cannot pass from one to another.

25 Wherefore, he is ¹able also perfectly to save them that come unto God by him, seeing he ever liveth, to make intercession for them.

26 ¹For such an high Priest it became us to have, *which is* holy, harmless, undefiled, separate from sinners, and made higher than the heavens:

27 Which needeth not daily as those high Priests to offer up sacrifice, ᶜfirst for his own sins, and then for the peoples: ¹for ²that did he ³once, when he offered up himself.

28 For the Law maketh men high Priests, which have infirmity: but the ¹word of the oath ²that ³was since the Law, *maketh* the Son, who is consecrated for evermore.

8 *1 To prove more certainly that the ceremonies of the Law are abrogated, 5 he showeth that they were appointed to serve the heavenly pattern. 8 He bringeth in the place of Jeremiah, 13 to prove the amendment of the old covenant.*

1 Now ¹of the things which we have spoken, *this is* the sum, that we have such an high Priest, that sitteth at the right hand of the throne of the Majesty in heavens,

2 ¹And *is* a minister of the ²Sanctuary, ³and of

7:13 ¹ Had anything to do about the altar.

7:15 ¹ Lest any man might object, that the Priesthood indeed was translated from Levi to Judah, but yet notwithstanding the same remaineth still, he both weigheth and expoundeth these words of David, *forever, according to the order of Melchizedek*, whereby also a divers institution of priesthood is well perceived.

7:16 ¹ He proveth the diversity and excellency of the institution of Melchizedek's Priesthood, by this, that the priesthood of the Law did stand upon an outward and bodily anointing: but the sacrifice of Melchizedek is set out to be everlasting and more spiritual.

² Not after the ordination, which commandeth frail and transitory things, as was done in Aaron's consecration, and all that whole Priesthood.

7:18 ¹ Again, that no man might object that the last Priesthood was added to make a perfect one, by the coupling of them both together, he proveth that the first was abrogated by the latter as unprofitable, and that by the nature of them both. For how could those corporal and transitory things sanctify us, either of themselves, or being joined with another?

² The ceremonial law.

7:20 ¹ Another argument whereby he proveth that the Priesthood of Christ is better than the Priesthood of Levi, because his was established with an oath, but theirs was not so.

7:23 ¹ Another argument tending to the same purpose. The Levitical Priests (as mortal men) could not be everlasting, but Christ as he is everlasting, so hath he also an everlasting Priesthood making most effectual intercession for them which by him come unto God.

7:24 ¹ Which cannot pass away.

7:25 ¹ He is fit and meet.

7:26 ¹ Another argument: There are required in an high Priest inno-

cency, and perfect pureness, which may separate him from sinners, for whom he offereth. But the Levitical high Priests shall not be found to be such, for they offer first for their own sins: But Christ only is such a one; and therefore the true and only high Priest.

7:27 ¹ Another argument which notwithstanding he handleth afterward: The Levitical Priests offered sacrifice after sacrifice, first for themselves, and then for the people. But Christ offered not for himself, but for others, not sacrifices, but himself, not oftentimes, but once. And this ought not to seem strange; saith he, forsomuch as they are weak, but this man is consecrated an everlasting Priest, and that by an oath.

² That sacrifice which he offered.

³ It was so done, that it needeth not to be repeated or offered again anymore.

7:28 ¹ The commandment of God which was bound with an oath.

² Another argument taken of the time: former things are taken away by the latter.

³ Exhibited.

8:1 ¹ He briefly repeateth that, whereunto all these things are to be referred, to wit, we have a far other high Priest than those Levitical high Priests are, even such an one as sitteth at the right hand of the most high God in heaven.

8:2 ¹ They of Levi were high Priests in an earthly sanctuary, but Christ is in the heavenly.

² Of heaven.

³ They of Levi exercised their Priesthood in a frail tabernacle, but Christ beareth about with him a far other tabernacle, to wit, his body which God himself made to be everlasting, as it shall afterward be declared, Heb. 9:11.

that [4]true Tabernacle which the Lord pitched, and not man.

3 [1]For every high Priest is ordained to offer both gifts and sacrifices: wherefore it was of necessity, that this man should have somewhat also to offer.

4 [1]For he were not a Priest, if he were on the earth, seeing there are Priests that according to the Law offer gifts,

5 Who serve unto the pattern and shadow of heavenly things, as Moses was warned by God when he was about to finish the Tabernacle. [a]See, said he, that thou make all things according to the pattern, showed to thee in the mount.

6 [1]But now our high Priest hath obtained a more excellent office, inasmuch as he is the Mediator of a better Testament, which is established upon better promises.

7 [1]For if that first Testament had been unblameable, no place should have been sought for the second.

8 For in rebuking them he saith, [b]Behold, the days will come, saith the Lord, when I shall make with the [1]house of Israel, and with the house of Judah a new Testament:

9 Not like the Testament that I made with their fathers, in the day that I took them by the hand, to lead them out of the land of Egypt: for they continued not in my Testament, and I regarded them not, saith the Lord.

10 For this is the Testament that I will make with the house of Israel, After those days, saith the Lord, I will put my Laws in their mind, and in their heart I will write them, and I will be their God, and they shall be my people.

11 And they shall not teach every man his neighbor, and every man his brother, saying, Know the Lord:

CHAPTER 8
[a] Exod. 15:40
Acts 7:44

[b] Jer. 31:31-34
Rom. 11:17
Heb. 10:16

CHAPTER 9
[a] Num. 7:10
[b] 1 Kings 8:9
2 Chron. 5:10
[c] Exod. 21:22
[d] Exod. 30:10
Lev. 16:2

for all shall know me, from the least of them to the greatest of them.

12 For I will be merciful to their unrighteousness, and I will remember their sins and their iniquities no more.

13 [1]In that he saith a new Testament, he hath abrogated the old: now that which is disannulled and waxed old, is ready to vanish away.

9 2 Comparing the form of the Tabernacle, 10 and the ceremonies of the Law, 11 unto the truth set out in Christ, 15 he concludeth that now there is no more need of another Priest, 24 because Christ himself had fulfilled these duties under the new covenant.

1 Then [1]the first Testament had also ordinances of religion, and a [2]worldly Sanctuary,

2 For the first Tabernacle was made, wherein was the candlestick, and the table, and the showbread, which Tabernacle is called the Holy places.

3 And after the [1]second veil was the Tabernacle, which is called the [2]Holiest of all,

4 Which had the golden censer, and the Ark of the Testament overlaid round about with gold, wherein the golden pot, which had Manna, was, and [a]Aaron's rod that had budded, and the [b]tables of the Testament.

5 [c]And over the Ark were the glorious Cherubims, shadowing the [1]mercy seat: of which things we will not now speak particularly.

6 [1]Now when these things were thus ordained, the Priest went always into the first Tabernacle, and accomplished the service.

7 But into the second went the [d]high Priest alone, once every year, not without blood which he offered for himself, and for the [1]ignorances of the people.

---

[4] Of his body.

8:3 [1] He bringeth a reason why it must needs be that Christ should have a body (which he calleth a tabernacle which the Lord pight and not man) to wit, that he might have what to offer: for otherwise he could not be an high Priest. And the selfsame body is both the tabernacle and the sacrifice.

8:4 [1] He giveth a reason why he said that our high Priest is in the heavenly sanctuary and not in the earthly: because, saith he, if he were now on the earth, he could not minister in the earthly sanctuary, seeing there are yet Levitical Priests, which are appointed for him, that is to say, to be patterns of that perfect example. And to what purpose should the patterns serve when the true and original example is present.

8:6 [1] He entereth into the comparison of the old and transitory Testament or covenant being but for a time, whereof the Levitical Priests were mediators with the new the everlasting Mediator whereof is Christ, to show that this is not only better than that in all respects, but also that that was abrogated by this.

8:7 [1] He proveth by the testimony of Jeremiah, that there is a second Testament or covenant, and therefore that the first was not perfect.

8:8 [1] He calleth it an house, as it were one family of the whole

kingdom: for whereas the kingdom of David was divided into two factions, the Prophet giveth us to understand that through the new Testament they shall be joined together again in one.

8:13 [1] The conclusion: Therefore by the latter and the new, the first and old is taken away, for it could not be called new if it differed not from the old. And again that same is at length taken away: which is subject to corruption, and therefore imperfect.

9:1 [1] A division of the first Tabernacle which he calleth worldly, that is to say, transitory and earthly into two parts, to wit, into the holy places and the Holiest of all.

[2] An earthy and a flitting.

9:3 [1] He calleth it the second veil, not because there were two veils, but because it was behind the Sanctuary or the first Tabernacle.

[2] The holiest Sanctuary.

9:5 [1] The Hebrews call the cover of the Ark of the covenant, the mercy seat, whom both the Greeks and we follow.

9:6 [1] Now he cometh to the sacrifices which he divideth into those daily sacrifices, and that yearly and solemn sacrifice, with the which the high Priest only, but once every year entering into the Holiest of all with blood, offered for himself and the people.

9:7 [1] For the sins. See Heb. 5:2.

8 ¹Whereby the holy Ghost this signified, that the way into the Holiest of all was not yet opened, while as yet the first tabernacle was standing,

9 ¹Which was a figure ²for that present time, wherein were offered gifts and sacrifices that could not make holy, concerning the conscience, him that did the service,

10 ¹Which only stood in meats and drinks, and divers washings, and carnal rites, ²which were enjoined, until the time of reformation.

11 ¹But Christ being come an high Priest of good things to come, ²by a ³greater and a more perfect Tabernacle, not made with hands, that is, not of this building,

12 ¹Neither by the blood of ²goats and calves: but by his own blood entered he in once unto the holy place, and obtained eternal redemption *for us.*

13 *ᵉ,¹*For if the blood of bulls and of goats, and the ashes of an heifer, sprinkling them that are unclean, sanctifieth as touching the ²purifying of the flesh,

ᵉ Lev. 16:14
Num. 19:4
ᶠ 1 Pet. 1:19
1 John 1:7
Rev. 1:5
ᵍ Luke 1:74
ʰ Rom. 5:6
1 Pet. 3:18
ⁱ Gal. 3:15

14 How much more shall the *ᶠ*blood of Christ which through the eternal Spirit offered himself without fault to God, *ᵍ*purge your conscience from ¹dead works, to serve the living God?

15 ¹And for this cause is he the Mediator of the new Testament, that through *ʰ*death which was for the redemption of the transgressions *that were* in the former Testament, they which were called, might receive the promise of eternal inheritance.

16 ¹For where a Testament *is,* there must be the death of him that made the Testament.

17 ¹For the Testament is confirmed when men are dead: for it is yet of no force as long as he that made it, is alive.

18 ¹Wherefore, neither was the first ordained without blood.

19 For when Moses had spoken every precept to the people, ¹according to the Law, he took the blood of calves and of goats, with water and purple wool and hyssop, and ²sprinkled both the book, and all

---

9:8 ¹ Of that yearly rite and ceremony he gathereth that the way was not by such sacrifices opened into heaven, which was shadowed by the Holiest of all. For why did the high Priest alone enter in thither, shutting out all other, and that to offer sacrifices there both for himself and for others, and after did shut the Holiest of all again?

9:9 ¹ An objection: If the way were not opened into heaven by those sacrifices (that is to say, If the worshippers were not purged by them) why then were those ceremonies used? to wit, that men might be called back to that spiritual example, that is to say, to Christ, who should correct all those things at his coming.

² For that time that that figure had to last.

9:10 ¹ Another reason why they could not make clean the conscience of the worshipper, to wit, because they were outward and carnal or corporal things.

² For they were as you would say a burden, from which Christ delivered us.

9:11 ¹ Now he entereth into the declaration of the figures, and first of all comparing the Levitical high Priest with Christ, (that is to say, the figure with the thing itself) he attributeth to Christ the administration of good things to come, that is, everlasting, which those carnal things had respect unto.

² Another comparison of the first corruptible Tabernacle with the latter (that is to say, with the human nature of Christ) which is the true incorruptible Temple of God, whereinto which the Son of GOD entered, as the Levitical high Priests into the other which was frail and transitory.

³ By a more excellent and better.

9:12 ¹ Another comparison of the blood of sacrifices with Christ. The Levitical high Priests entering by their holy places into the Sanctuary, offered corruptible blood for one year only: but Christ entering into that holy body of his, entered by it into heaven itself, offering his own most pure blood for an everlasting redemption: For one selfsame Christ answereth both to the high Priest, and the Tabernacle, and the sacrifices, and offering themselves, as the truth to the figures, so that Christ is both the high Priest, and Tabernacle, and Sacrifice, yea, all these both truly, and forever.

² For in this yearly sacrifice of reconciliation, there were two kinds of sacrifices, the one a goat, the other a heifer, or calf.

9:13 ¹ If the outward sprinkling of blood and ashes of beasts, was a

true and effectual sign of purifying and cleansing, how much more shall the thing itself and the truth being present, which in times past was shadowed by those external Sacraments, that is to say, his blood which is in such sort man's blood, that is also the blood of the Son of God, and therefore hath an everlasting virtue of purifying and cleansing, does it?

² He considereth the signs apart, being separate from the thing itself.

9:14 ¹ From sins which proceed from death, and bring forth nothing but death.

9:15 ¹ The conclusion of the former argument: therefore seeing the blood of beasts did not purge sins, the new Testament which was before time promised, whereunto those outward things had respect, is now indeed established, by the virtue whereof all transgressions might be taken away, and heaven indeed opened unto us: whereof it followeth that Christ shed his blood also for the Fathers: For he was shadowed by those old ceremonies, otherwise, unless they had served to represent him, they had been nothing at all profitable. Therefore this Testament is called the latter, not concerning the virtue of it, (that is to say, remission of sins) but in respect of that time, wherein the thing itself was finished, that is to say, wherein Christ was indeed exhibited to the world, and fulfilled all things which were necessary to our salvation.

9:16 ¹ A reason why the Testament must be established by the death of the Mediator, because this Testament hath the condition of a Testament or gift, which is made effectual by death, and therefore that it might be effectual, it must needs be that he that made the Testament, should die.

9:18 ¹ There must be a proportion between those things which purify, and those which are purified: Under the Law all those figures were earthly, the Tabernacle, the book, the vessels, the sacrifices, although they were the figures of heavenly things. Therefore it was requisite that all those should be purified with some matter and ceremony of the same nature, to wit, with the blood of beasts, with water, wool, hyssop. But under Christ all things are heavenly, an heavenly tabernacle, an heavenly sacrifice, an heavenly people, an heavenly doctrine, and heaven itself is set open before us for an eternal habitation. Therefore all these things are sanctified in like sort, to wit, with the everlasting offering of the quickening blood of Christ.

9:19 ¹ As the Lord had commanded.

² He useth to sprinkle.

the people,

20 ^{j}Saying, This is the blood of the Testament, which God hath appointed unto you.

21 Moreover, he sprinkled likewise the Tabernacle with blood also, and all the ministering vessels,

22 And almost all things are by the Law purged with blood, and without shedding of blood is no remission.

23 It was then necessary, that the ^{1}similitudes of heavenly things should be purified with such things: but the heavenly things themselves *are purified* with better sacrifices than are these.

24 ^{1}For Christ is not entered into the holy places that are made with hands, which are similitudes of the true *Sanctuary*: but *is entered* into very heaven, to appear now in the sight of God for us,

25 ^{1}Not that he should offer himself often, as the high Priest entered into the Holy place every year with others' blood,

26 ^{1}(For then must he have often suffered since the foundation of the world) but now in the ^{2}end of the world hath he been made manifest, once to put away ^{3}sin by the sacrifice of himself.

27 And as it is appointed unto men that they shall ^{1}once die, and after that *cometh* the judgment:

28 So ^{k}Christ was once offered to take away the sins of ^{1}many, ^{2}and unto them that look for him, shall he appear the second time without sin unto salvation.

^{j} Exod. 24:8
^{k} Rom. 5:8
1 Pet. 3:18

CHAPTER 10
^{a} Ps. 40:7

10

1 *He proveth that the sacrifices of the Law were imperfect,* 2 *because they were yearly renewed.* 5 *But that the sacrifice of Christ is one, and perpetual,* 6 *he proveth by David's testimony:* 19 *Then he addeth an exhortation,* 29 *and severely threateneth them that reject the grace of Christ.* 36 *In the end he praiseth patience,* 38 *that cometh of faith.*

1 For ^{1}the law having the shadow of good things to ^{2}come, and not the very image of the things, can never with those sacrifices, which they offer year by year continually, sanctify the comers thereunto.

2 For would they not then have ceased to have been offered, because that the offerers once purged, should have had no more conscience of sins?

3 But in those *sacrifices* there *is* a remembrance again of sins every year.

4 For it is impossible that the blood of bulls and goats should take away sins.

5 ^{1}Wherefore when he ^{2}cometh into the world, he saith, ^{a}Sacrifice and offering thou wouldest not: but a ^{3}body hast thou ordained me.

6 In burnt offerings, and sin offerings thou hast had no pleasure.

7 Then I said, Lo, I come (in the beginning of the book it is written of me) that I should do thy will, O God.

8 Above, when he said, Sacrifice and offering, and burnt offerings, and sin offerings, thou wouldest not have, neither hadst pleasure *therein* (which are

---

9:23 ^{1} The similitudes of heavenly things were earthly, and therefore they were to be set forth with earthly things, as with the blood of beasts, and wool, and hyssop. But under Christ all things are heavenly, and therefore they could not but be sanctified with the offering of his lively blood.

9:24 ^{1} Another double comparison: the Levitical high Priest entered into the Sanctuary, which was made indeed by the commandment of God, but yet with men's hands, that it might be a pattern of another more excellent, to wit, of the heavenly place. But Christ entered even into heaven itself. Again, he appeared before the Ark, but Christ before God the Father himself.

9:25 ^{1} Another double comparison: the Levitical high Priest offered other blood, but Christ offered his own: he every year once iterated his offering: Christ offering himself but once, abolished sin altogether, both of the former ages and of the ages to come.

9:26 ^{1} An argument to prove that Christ's offering ought not to be repeated: Seeing that sins were to be purged from the beginning of the world, and it is proved that sins cannot be purged, but by the only blood of Christ: he must needs have died oftentimes since the beginning of the world. But a man can die but once: therefore Christ's oblation which was once done in the latter days, neither could nor can be repeated. Seeing then it is so, surely the virtue of it extendeth both to sins that were before, and to sins that are after his coming.

^{2} In the latter days.

^{3} That whole root of sin.

9:27 ^{1} He speaketh of the natural state and condition of man: For as for Lazarus and certain others that died twice, that was no usual thing but extraordinary, and for them that shall be changed, their changing is a kind of death, 1 Cor. 15:51.

9:28 ^{1} Thus the general promise is restrained to the elect only: and

we have to seek the testimony of our election: not in the secret counsel of God, but in the effects that our faith worketh, and so we must climb up from the lowest step to the highest, there to find such comfort as is most certain, and shall never be moved.

^{2} Shortly by the way he setteth out Christ as Judge, partly to terrify them, which do not rest themselves in the only oblation of Christ once made, and partly to keep the faithful in their duty, that they will go not back.

10:1 ^{1} He preventeth a privy objection. Why then were those sacrifices offered? The Apostle answereth first touching that yearly sacrifice which was the solemnest of all, wherein (saith he) there was made every year a remembrance again of all former sins. Therefore that sacrifice had no power to sanctify: for to what purpose should those sins which are purged be repeated again, and wherefore should new sins come to be repeated every year, if those sacrifices did abolish sin?

^{2} Of things which are everlasting, which were promised to the Fathers, and exhibited in Christ.

10:5 ^{1} A conclusion following of those things that went before, and comprehending also the other sacrifices. Seeing that the sacrifices of the Law could not do it, therefore Christ speaking of himself as of our high Priest manifested in the flesh, witnesseth evidently that God resteth not in the sacrifices, but in the obedience of his Son our high Priest, in which obedience he offered up himself once to his Father for us.

^{2} The Son of God is said to come into the world, when he was made man.

^{3} It is word for word in the Hebrew text, Thou hast pierced mine ears through, that is, thou hast made me obedient, and willing to hear.

offered by the Law.)

9 Then said he, Lo, I come to do thy will, O God, he taketh away the [1]first, that he may stablish the second.

10 By the which will we are sanctified, *even* by the offering of the body of Jesus Christ once *made*.

11 [1]And every Priest [2]standeth daily ministering, and ofttimes offereth one manner of offering, which can never take away sins:

12 But this man after he had offered one sacrifice for sins, [b]sitteth forever at the right hand of God,

13 [1]And from henceforth tarrieth, [c]till his enemies be made his footstool.

14 For with one offering hath he consecrated forever them that are sanctified.

15 [1]For the holy Ghost also beareth us record: for after that he had said before,

16 [d]This *is* the Testament that I will make unto them after those days, saith the Lord, I will put my Laws in their heart, and in their minds I will write them.

17 And their sins and iniquities will I remember [1]no more.

18 Now where remission of these things *is*, there *is* no more offering for [1]sin.

19 [1]Seeing therefore, brethren, that by the blood of Jesus we may be bold to enter into the Holy place,

20 By the new and living way, which he hath

[b] Heb. 1:13
Ps. 110:1
1 Cor. 15:25
[c] Heb. 1:13
[d] Jer. 31:33
Rom. 11:27
Heb. 8:8
[e] Heb. 6:4
[f] Deut. 19:15
Matt. 18:16
John 8:17
2 Cor. 13:1
[g] Deut. 32:35
Rom. 12:19

prepared for us, through the veil, that is, his [1]flesh:

21 *And seeing we have* an high Priest, *which is* over the house of God,

22 [1]Let us draw near with a [2]true heart in assurance of faith, our [3]hearts being pure from an evil conscience,

23 And washed in our bodies with [1]pure water, let us keep the profession of our hope, without wavering, (for *he is* faithful that promised.)

24 And let us consider one another, to provoke unto love, and to good works,

25 Not forsaking the fellowship that we have among ourselves, as the manner of some *is*: but let us exhort *one another*, [1]and that so much the more, because ye see that the day draweth near.

26 [e]For if we sin [1]willingly after that we have received and acknowledged that truth, there remaineth no more sacrifice for sins,

27 But a fearful looking for of judgment, and violent fire, which shall devour the [1]adversaries.

28 [1]He that despiseth Moses' Law, dieth without mercy [f]under two, or three witnesses:

29 Of how much sorer punishment suppose ye shall he be worthy, which treadeth under foot the Son of God, and counteth the blood of the Testament as an unholy thing, wherewith he was sanctified, and doeth despite the Spirit of grace?

30 [1]For we know him that hath said, [g]Vengeance

10:9 [1] That is the sacrifices, to establish the second, that is, the will of God.

10:11 [1] A conclusion, with the other part of the comparison. The Levitical high Priest repeateth the same sacrifices daily in his sanctuary: whereupon which it followeth that neither those sacrifices, neither those offerings, neither those high Priests could take away sins. But Christ, having offered one sacrifice once for the sins of all men, and having sanctified his own forever, sitteth at the right hand of the Father, having all power in his hands.

[2] At the altar.

10:13 [1] He preventeth a privy objection, to wit, that yet notwithstanding we are subject to sin and death, whereunto the Apostle answereth, that the full efficacy of Christ's virtue hath not yet showed itself, but shall at length appear when he will at once put to flight all his enemies, with whom as yet we strive.

10:15 [1] Although there do yet remain in us relics of sin, yet the work of our sanctification which is to be perfected, hangeth upon the selfsame sacrifice which never shall be repeated: and that the Apostle proveth by alledging again the testimonies of Jeremiah, thus, Sin is taken away by the new Testament, seeing the Lord saith that it shall come to pass, that according to the form of it, he will no more remember our sins: Therefore we need now no purging sacrifice to take away that which is already taken away, but we must rather take pains, that we may now through faith be partakers of that sacrifice.

10:17 [1] Why then, where is the fire of Purgatory, and that Popish distinction of the fault and the punishment?

10:18 [1] He said well, for sin: for there remaineth another offering, to wit, of thanksgiving.

10:19 [1] The sum of the former treatise: We are not shut out now of the holy place, as the Fathers were, but we have an entrance into the true holy place (that is, into heaven) seeing that we are purged with the blood not of beasts, but of Jesus. Neither as in times past, doth the high Priest shut us out by setting the veil against us, but through the veil, which is his flesh, he hath brought us into heaven itself, being present with us, so that we have now truly an high Priest, which is over the house of God.

10:20 [1] So Christ's flesh showeth us the Godhead as it were under a veil, for otherwise we were not able to abide the brightness of it.

10:22 [1] A most grave exhortation, wherein which he showeth how that sacrifice of Christ may be applied to us: to wit, by faith, which also he describeth, by the consequence, to wit, by sanctification of the Spirit, which causeth us surely to hope in God, and to procure by all means possible one another's salvation, through the love that is in us one toward another.

[2] With no double and counterfeit heart, but with such an heart as is truly and indeed given to God.

[3] This is it which the Lord saith, Be ye holy, for I am holy.

10:23 [1] With the grace of the holy Ghost.

10:25 [1] Having mentioned the last coming of Christ, he stirreth up the godly to the meditation of an holy life, and cites the faithless fallers from God, to the fearful judgment seat of the judge, because they wickedly rejected him in whom only salvation consisteth.

10:26 [1] Without any cause or occasion, or show of occasion.

10:27 [1] For it is another matter to sin through the frailty of man's nature, and another thing to proclaim war as it were to God as to an enemy.

10:28 [1] If the breach of the Law of Moses was punished by death, how much more worthy death is it to fall away from Christ?

10:30 [1] The reason of all these things is, because God is a revenger of such as despise him: otherwise he should not rightly govern his Church. Now there is nothing more horrible then the wrath of the living God.

belongeth unto me: I will recompense, saith the Lord. And again, The Lord shall [2]judge his people.

31 It is a fearful thing to fall into the hands of the living God.

32 [1]Now call to remembrance the days that are passed, in the which, after ye had received light ye endured a great fight in afflictions,

33 Partly while ye were made a [1]gazing stock both by reproaches and afflictions, and partly while ye became [2]companions of them which were so tossed to and fro.

34 For both ye sorrowed with me for my bonds, and suffered with joy the spoiling of your goods, knowing in yourselves how that ye have in heaven a better, and an enduring [1]substance.

35 Cast not away therefore your confidence which hath great recompense of reward.

36 For ye have need of patience, that after ye have done the will of God, ye might receive the promise.

37 For yet a very [1]little while, and he that shall come, will come, and will not tarry.

38 [b,1]Now the just shall live by faith: but if *any* withdraw himself, my soul shall have no pleasure in him.

39 But we are not they which withdraw ourselves unto perdition, but *follow* faith unto the conservation of the soul.

11

1 He declareth in the whole Chapter, that the Fathers, which from the beginning of the world were approved of God, attained salvation no other way than by faith, that the Jews may know that by the same only, they are knit unto the Fathers in an holy union.

1 Now [1]faith is the grounds of things which are hoped for, and the evidence of things which are not seen.

2 [1]For by it *our* [2]elders were well reported of.

[b] Hab. 2:4
Rom. 1:17
Gal. 3:11

CHAPTER 11
[a] Gen. 1:1
John 1:10
[b] Gen. 4:4
[c] Matt. 23:35
[d] Gen. 5:25
[e] Gen. 6:13
[f] Gen. 12:4
[g] Gen. 17:19
Gen. 21:2

3 [a,1]Through faith we understand that the world was ordained by the word of God, so that the things which we [2]see, are not made of things which did appear.

4 [1]By faith Abel [b]offered unto God a greater sacrifice than Cain, by [c]the which he obtained witness that he was righteous, God testifying of his gifts: by the which *faith* also he being dead, yet speaketh.

5 [1]By faith was [d]Enoch translated, that he should not [2]see death: neither was he found: for God had translated him: for before he was translated, he was reported of, that he had pleased God.

6 But without faith it is impossible to please *him*: for he that cometh to God, must believe that *God* is, and that he is a [1]rewarder of them that seek him.

7 [1]By faith [e]Noah being warned of God of the things which were as yet not seen, moved with reverence, prepared the Ark to the saving of his household, through the which *Ark* he condemned the world, and was made heir of the righteousness, which is by faith.

8 [1]By faith [f]Abraham, when he was called, obeyed *God*, to go out into a place, which he should afterward receive for inheritance, and he went out, not knowing whither he went.

9 By faith he abode in the land of promise, as in a strange country, as one that dwelt in tents with Isaac and Jacob heirs with him of the same promise.

10 For he looked for a city having a [1]foundation, whose builder and maker *is* God.

11 Through faith [g]Sarah also received strength to conceive seed, and was delivered of a child when she was past age, because she judged him faithful which had promised.

12 And therefore sprang thereof one, even of one which was [1]dead, *so many* as the stars of the sky in multitude, and as the sand of the sea shore which is innumerable.

13 All these died in [1]faith, and received not the

---

[2] Rule or govern.

10:32 [1] As he terrified the fallers away from God so doth he now comfort them that are constant and stand strongly setting before them the success of their former fights, so stirring them up to a sure hope of a full and ready victory.

10:33 [1] You were brought forth to be ashamed.

[2] In taking their miseries, to be your miseries.

10:34 [1] Goods and riches.

10:37 [1] He will come within this very little while.

10:38 [1] He commendeth the excellency of a sure faith by the effect, because it is the only way to life, which sentence he setteth forth and amplifieth by setting the contrary against it.

11:1 [1] An excellent description of faith by the effects, because it representeth things which are but yet in hope, and setteth as it were before our eyes things that are invisible.

11:2 [1] He showeth that the Fathers ought to be accounted of, by this virtue.

[2] That is, those Fathers of whom we came: and whose authority

and example ought to move us very much.

11:3 [1] He showeth the propriety of faith, by setting unto us most piked examples of such as from the beginning of the world excelled in the Church.

[2] So that the world which we see, was not made of any matter that appeared or was before, but of nothing.

11:4 [1] Abel.

11:5 [1] Enoch.

[2] That he should not die.

11:6 [1] This reward is not referred to our merits, but to the free promise, as Paul teacheth in Abraham the father of all the faithful, Rom. 4:4.

11:7 [1] Noah.

11:8 [1] Abraham and Sarah.

11:10 [1] This foundation is set against their tabernacle.

11:12 [1] As unlikely to bear children, as if she had been stark dead.

11:13 [1] In faith, which they had while they lived, and followed them even to their grave.

²promises, but saw them afar off, and believed *them*, and ³received *them* thankfully, and confessed that they were strangers and pilgrims on the earth.

14 For they that say such things, declare plainly, that they seek a country.

15 And if they had been mindful of that *country*, from whence they came out, they had leisure to have returned.

16 But now they desire a better, that is an heavenly: wherefore God is not ashamed of them to be called their God: for he hath prepared for them a city.

17 By faith *b*Abraham offered up Isaac, when he was ¹tried, and he that had received the ²promises, offered his only begotten son.

18 (To whom it was said, ¹In Isaac shall thy seed be called.)

19 For he considered that God was able to raise *him* up even from the dead: from ¹whence he received him also after ²a sort.

20 ¹By faith *j*Isaac blessed Jacob and Esau, concerning things to come.

21 ¹By faith *k*Jacob when he was a dying, blessed both the sons of Joseph, and *l*leaning on the end of his staff, worshipped God.

22 ¹By faith *m*Joseph when he died, made mention of the departing of the children of Israel, and gave commandment of his bones.

23 *n*,¹ By faith Moses when he was born, was hid three months of his parents, because they saw he was a proper child, neither ²feared they the king's *o*commandment.

24 By faith *p*Moses when he was come to age, refused to be called the son of Pharaoh's daughter,

25 And chose rather to suffer adversity with the people of God, than to enjoy the ¹pleasures of sin for a season,

26 Esteeming the rebuke of Christ greater riches, than the treasures of Egypt: for he had respect unto

the recompense of the reward.

27 By faith he forsook Egypt, and feared not the fierceness of the king: for he endured, as he that saw him which is invisible.

28 Through faith he ordained the *q*Passover and the effusion of blood, lest he that destroyed the first born, should touch them.

29 ¹By faith they *r*passed through the red sea as by dry land, which when the Egyptians had assayed to do, they were swallowed up.

30 ¹By faith the *s*walls of Jericho fell down after they were compassed about seven days.

31 ¹By faith the ²harlot *t*Rahab perished not with them which obeyed not, when *u*she had received the spies ³peaceably.

32 ¹And what shall I more say? for the time would be too short for me to tell of *v*Gideon, of *w*Barak, and of *x*Samson, and of *y*Jephthah, also of David, and Samuel, and of the Prophets:

33 Which through faith subdued kingdoms, wrought righteousness, obtained the ¹promises, stopped the mouths of lions,

34 Quenched the violence of fire, escaped the edge of the sword, of weak were made strong, waxed valiant in battle, turned to flight the armies of the aliens.

35 The ¹women received their dead raised to life: others also were ²racked, and would not be delivered, that they might receive a better resurrection.

36 And others have been tried by mockings and scourgings, yea, moreover by bonds, and imprisonment.

37 They were stoned, they were hewn asunder, they were tempted, they were slain with the sword, they wandered up and down in ¹sheep's skins, and in goats' skins, being destitute, afflicted, *and* tormented:

38 Whom the world was not worthy of: they wandered in wildernesses and mountains, and dens, and caves of the earth.

39 ¹And these all through faith obtained good

b Gen. 22:10
i Gen. 21:12 Rom. 9:7
j Gen. 27:28,39
k Gen. 48:15
l Gen. 47:31
m Gen. 50:25
n Exod. 2:2 Acts 7:22
o Exod. 1:16
p Exod. 2:11
q Exod. 12:27
r Exod. 14:21
s Josh. 6:20
t Josh. 6:23
u Josh. 2:1
v Judg. 6:11
w Judg. 4:6
x Judg. 13:24
y Judg. 11:1 Judg. 12:7

11:13 ² This is the figure Metonymy, for the things promised.

³ For the Patriarchs were wont when they received the promises, to profess their religion, by building of altars, and calling on the name of the Lord.

11:17 ¹ Tried of the Lord.

² Although the promises of life were made in that only begotten Son Isaac, yet he appointed him to die, and so against hope he believed in hope.

11:19 ¹ From which death.

² For there was not the true and very death of Isaac, but as it were the death, by means whereof he seemed also as it were to have risen again.

11:20 ¹ Isaac.

11:21 ¹ Jacob.

11:22 ¹ Joseph.

11:23 ¹ Moses.

² They were not afraid to bring him up.

11:25 ¹ Such pleasures as he could not enjoy, but he must needs provoke God's wrath against him.

11:29 ¹ The red sea.

11:30 ¹ Jericho.

11:31 ¹ Rahab.

² A notable example of God's goodness.

³ Courteously and friendly, so that she did not only not hurt them, but also kept them safe.

11:32 ¹ Gideon, Barak and other Judges and Prophets.

11:33 ¹ The fruit of the promises.

11:35 ¹ He seemeth to mean the story of that woman of Zarephath, whose son Elijah raised again from death, and the Shunammite, whose son Elisha restored to his mother.

² He meaneth that persecution which Antiochus wrought.

11:37 ¹ In vile and rough clothing, so were the saints brought to extreme poverty, and constrained to live like beasts in wildernesses.

11:39 ¹ An amplification taken of the circumstance of the time: their faith is so much the more to be marveled at, by how much the promises of things to come were more dark, yet at length were indeed exhibited to us, so that their faith and ours is as one, as is also their consecration and ours.

report, and received [2]not the promise,

40 God providing a better thing for us, that they [1]without us should not be made perfect.

12

1 He doth not only by the examples of the Fathers before recited, exhort them to patience and constancy, 3 but also by the example of Christ. 11 That the chastenings of God cannot be rightly judged by the outward sense of our flesh.

1 Wherefore, [a,1]let us also, seeing that we are compassed with so great a cloud of witnesses, cast away everything that presseth down, and the sin that [2]hangeth so fast on: let us run with patience the race that is set before us,

2 [1,2]Looking unto Jesus the author and finisher of our faith, who for the [3]joy that was set before him, endured the cross, and despised the shame, and is set at the right hand of the throne of God.

3 [1]Consider therefore him that endureth such speaking against of sinners, lest ye should be wearied and faint in your minds.

4 [1]Ye have not yet resisted unto blood, striving against sin.

5 [1]And ye have forgotten the consolation, which speaketh unto you as unto children, [b]My son, despise not the chastening of the Lord, neither faint when thou art rebuked of him.

6 For whom the Lord loveth, he chasteneth: and he scourgeth every son that he receiveth.

7 If ye endure chastening, God offered himself unto you as unto sons: for what son is it whom the

CHAPTER 12

[a] Rom. 6:4
Col. 3:8
Eph. 4:24
1 Pet. 2:1
[b] Prov. 3:11
[c] Rom. 12:18
[d] Gen. 25:33
[e] Gen. 27:38
[f] Exod. 19:16

father chasteneth not?

8 If therefore ye be without correction, whereof all are partakers, then are ye bastards, and not sons.

9 [1]Moreover we have had the fathers of our bodies which corrected us, and we gave them reverence: should we not much rather be in subjection unto the father of spirits, that we might live?

10 [1]For they verily for a few days chastened us after their own pleasure, but he *chastened us* for our profit, that we might be partakers of his holiness.

11 Now no chastising for the present seemeth to be joyous, but grievous: but afterward, it bringeth the quiet fruit of righteousness, unto them which are thereby exercised.

12 [1]Wherefore lift up *your* hands which [2]hang down, and *your* weak knees,

13 And make [1]straight steps unto your feet, lest that which *is* halting, be turned out of the way, but let it rather be healed.

14 [c,1]Follow peace with all men, and holiness, without the which no man shall see the Lord.

15 [1]Take heed, that no man fall away from the grace of God: let no [2]root of bitterness spring up and trouble *you*, lest thereby many be defiled.

16 [1]Let there be no fornicator, or profane person as [d]Esau, which for one portion of meat sold his birthright.

17 [e]For ye know how that afterward also when he would have inherited the blessing, he was rejected: for he found no [1]place to repentance, though he sought *that blessing* with tears.

18 [1]For ye are not come unto the [f]mount that might

---

[2] But saw Christ afar off.

11:40 [1] For their salvation did hang upon Christ, who was exhibited in our days.

12:1 [1] An applying of the former examples, whereby we ought to be stirred up to run the whole race, casting away all stops and impediments.

[2] For sin besiegeth us on all sides, so that we cannot escape out.

12:2 [1] He setteth before us, as the mark of this race, Jesus himself our captain, who willingly overcame all the roughness of the same way.

[2] As it were upon the mark of our faith.

[3] Whereas he had all kind of blessedness in his hand and power, yet suffered willingly the ignomy of the cross.

12:3 [1] An amplification taken of the circumstance of the person, and the things themselves, which he compareth betwixt themselves: for how great is Jesus in comparison of us, and how far more grievous things did he suffer than we?

12:4 [1] He taketh an argument of the profit which cometh to us by God's chastisements, unless we be in fault. First of all because sin, or that rebellious wickedness of our flesh, is by this means turned.

12:5 [1] Secondly, because they are testimony of his fatherly good will toward us, insomuch that they show themselves to be bastards, which cannot abide to be chastened of God.

12:9 [1] Thirdly, if all men yield this right to fathers, to whom next after God we owe this life, that they may rightfully correct their children, shall we not be much more subject to that our Father, who is the Author of the spiritual and everlasting life?

12:10 [1] An amplification of the same argument: Those fathers have corrected us after their fancy, for some frail and transitory profit: but God chasteneth and instructeth us for our singular profit, to make us partakers of his holiness: which thing although these our senses do not presently perceive, yet the end of the matter proveth it.

12:12 [1] The conclusion, we must go forward courageously and keep always a right course, and (as far forth as we may) without any staggering or stumbling.

[2] The description of a man that is out of heart and clean discouraged.

12:13 [1] Keep a right course, and so, that you show example of good life for others to follow.

12:14 [1] We must live in peace, and holiness with all men.

12:15 [1] We must study to edify one another, both in doctrine and example of life.

[2] That no heresy, or backsliding be an offense.

12:16 [1] We must eschew fornication, and a profane mind, that is, such a mind, as giveth not to God his due honor, which wickedness how severely God will at length punish, the horrible example of Esau teacheth us.

12:17 [1] There was no place left for his repentance: and it appeareth by the effects, what his repentance was, for when he was gone out of his father's sight, he threatened his brother to kill him.

12:18 [1] Now he applieth the same exhortation, to the Prophetical and kingly office of Christ compared with Moses, after this sort, If the majesty of the Law was so great, how great think you that the glory of Christ and the Gospel is? And this comparison he declareth also particularly.

be [2]touched, nor unto burning fire, nor to blackness and darkness, and tempest,

19 Neither unto the sound of a trumpet, and the voice of words, which they that heard it, excused themselves, [g]that the word should not be spoken to them any more.

20 (For they were not able to abide that which was commanded, [h]yea, though a beast touch the mountain, it shall be stoned, or thrust through with a dart:

21 And so terrible was the [1]sight which appeared, that Moses said, I fear and quake.)

22 But ye are come unto the mount Sion, and to the city of the living God, the celestial Jerusalem, and to the company of innumerable Angels.

23 And to the assembly and congregation of the first born, which are written in heaven, and to God the judge of all, and to the spirits of just and [1]perfect men,

24 And to Jesus the Mediator of the new Testament, and to the blood of sprinkling that speaketh better things than that of Abel.

25 [1]See that ye despise not him that speaketh: for if they escaped not which refused him, that spake on earth: much more shall we *not escape*, if we turn away from him that *speaketh* from heaven.

26 [1]Whose voice then shook the earth, and now hath declared, saying, [i]Yet [2]once more will I shake, not the earth only, but also heaven.

27 And this *word*, Yet once more, signifieth the removing of those things which are shaken, as of things which are made *with hands*, that the things which are not shaken, may remain.

28 [1]Wherefore seeing we receive a kingdom, which

[g] Exod. 20:19
[h] Exod. 19:12
[i] Hag. 2:7
[j] Deut. 4:24

CHAPTER 13
[a] Rom. 12:10
[b] 1 Pet. 4:9
[c] Gen. 18:3
    Gen. 19:3
[d] Josh. 1:5
[e] Ps. 118:6

cannot be shaken, let us have grace whereby we may so serve God, that we may please him with [2]reverence and [3]fear.

29 For [j]even our God *is* a consuming fire.

13

1 He giveth good lessons not only for manners,   7 but also for doctrine.

1 Let [a,1]brotherly love continue.

2 [b]Be not forgetful to entertain strangers: for thereby some have [c]received Angels into their houses unawares.

3 Remember them that are in bonds, as though ye were bound with them: and them that are in affliction, as [1]if ye were also *afflicted* in the body.

4 [1]Marriage *is* honorable among all, and the bed undefiled: but whoremongers and adulterers God will judge.

5 [1]Let your conversation be without covetousness, and be content with those things that ye have, for [2]he hath said,

6 [d]I will not fail thee, neither forsake thee:

7 So that we may boldly say, [e]The Lord *is* mine helper, neither will I fear what [1]man can do unto me.

8 [1]Remember them which have the oversight of you, which have declared unto you the word of God: whose faith follow, considering what hath been the end of their conversation. [2]Jesus Christ yesterday, and today, the same also *is* forever.

9 Be not carried about with divers *and* strange doctrines: [1]for it is a good thing that the heart be stablished with grace, *and* not with [2]meats, which have not profited them that have been [3]occupied therein.

12:18 [2] Which might be touched with hands, which was of a gross and earthly matter.

12:21 [1] The shape and form which he saw, which was no counterfeit and forged shape, but a true one.

12:23 [1] So he calleth them that are taken up into heaven, although one part of them sleep in the earth.

12:25 [1] The applying of the former comparison, If it were not lawful to contemn his word which spake on the earth, how much less his voice which is from heaven?

12:26 [1] He compareth the steadfast majesty of the Gospel, wherewith the whole world was shaken, and even the very frame of heaven was as it were astonished, with the small and vanishing sound of the governance by the Law.

[2] It appeareth evidently in this that the Prophet speaketh of the calling of the Gentiles, that these words must be referred to the kingdom of Christ.

12:28 [1] A general exhortation to live reverently and religiously under the most happy subjection of so mighty a king, who as he blesseth his most mightily, so doth he most severely revenge the rebellious. And this is the sum of a Christian life, respecting the first table.

[2] By reverence is meant that honest shamefastness which keepeth them in their duties.

[3] Religious and godly fear.

13:1 [1] He cometh to the second table, the sum whereof is charity, especially toward strangers and such as are afflicted.

13:3 [1] Be so much touched, as if their misery were yours.

13:4 [1] He commendeth chaste matrimony in all sorts of men, and threateneth utter destruction from God, against whoremongers and adulterers.

13:5 [1] Covetousness is condemned, against which is set a contented mind with that which the Lord hath given.

[2] Even the Lord himself.

13:7 [1] He setteth man against God.

13:8 [1] We have to set before us the examples of valiant Captains, whom we ought diligently to follow.

[2] He repeateth the sum of the doctrine, to wit, the only ground of all precepts of manners, and that is this: That we ought to quiet and content ourselves in Christ only: for there was yet never any man saved without the knowledge of him, neither is at this day saved, neither shall be saved hereafter.

13:9 [1] He toucheth them which mixed an external worship, and especially the difference of meats, with the Gospel, which doctrine he plainly condemneth as clean repugnant to the benefit of Christ.

[2] By this one kind which concerneth the difference of clean and unclean meats, we have to understand all the ceremonial worship.

[3] Which observed the difference of them superstitiously.

10 ¹We have an ²altar, whereof they have no authority to eat, which ³serve in the Tabernacle.

11 ʲFor the bodies of those beasts whose blood is brought into the holy place by the high Priest for sin, are burnt without the camp.

12 Therefore even Jesus, that he might sanctify the people with his own blood, suffered without the gate.

13 ¹Let us go forth to him therefore out of the camp, bearing his reproach.

14 ᵍFor here have we no continuing city: but we seek one to come.

15 ¹Let us therefore by him offer the sacrifice of praise always to God, that is, the ʰfruit of the lips, which confess his Name.

16 To do good, and to distribute forget not: for with such sacrifices God is pleased.

17 ¹Obey them that have the oversight of you, and submit yourselves: for they watch for your souls, as they that must give accounts, that they may do it with joy, and not with grief: for that is unprofitable for you.

f Lev. 4:11
Lev. 6:30
Lev. 16:17
g Mic. 2:10
h Hos. 14:3

18 ¹Pray for us, for we are assured that we have a good conscience in all things, desiring to live honestly.

19 And I desire you somewhat the more earnestly, that ye so do, that I may be restored to you more quickly.

20 The God of peace that brought again from the dead our Lord Jesus, the great shepherd of the sheep, through the blood of the everlasting Covenant,

21 Make you ¹perfect in all good works, to do his will, ²working in you that which is pleasant in his sight through Jesus Christ, to whom *be* praise forever and ever, Amen.

22 I beseech you also, brethren, suffer the words of exhortation: for I have written unto you in few words.

23 Know that our brother Timothy is delivered, with whom (if he come shortly) I will see you.

24 Salute all them that have the oversight of you, and all the Saints. They of Italy salute you.

25 Grace *be* with you all, Amen.

¶ Written to the Hebrews from Italy,
and sent by Timothy.

13:10 ¹ He refuteth their error by an apt and fit comparison. They which in times past served the Tabernacle, did not eat of the sacrifices whose blood was brought for sin into the holy place by the high Priest. Moreover these sacrifices did represent Christ our offering. Therefore they cannot be partakers of him which serve the Tabernacle, that is, such as stand in the service of the Law: but let not us be ashamed to follow him out of Jerusalem, from whence he was cast out and suffered: for in this also Christ, who is the truth, answereth that figure, in that he suffered without the gate.
² By the Altar, he meaneth the offering.
³ Whereof they cannot be partakers which stubbornly retain the rites of the Law.
13:13 ¹ He goeth on further in this comparison, and showeth that this also signified unto us, that the godly followers of Christ must as it were go out of the world, bearing his cross.

13:15 ¹ Now that those corporal sacrifices are taken away, he teacheth us that the true sacrifices of confession remain, which consist partly in giving of thanks, and partly in liberality, with which sacrifices indeed God is now delighted.
13:17 ¹ We must obey the warnings and admonitions of our Ministers and Elders, which watch for the salvation of the souls which are committed unto them.
13:18 ¹ The last part of this Epistle, wherein he commendeth his ministry to the Hebrews, and wisheth them continuance and increase of graces from the Lord: and excuseth himself in that he hath used but few words to comfort them, having spent the Epistle in disputing: and saluteth certain brethren familiarly and friendly.
13:21 ¹ Make you fit or meet.
² Hence cometh that saying of the Fathers, that God crowneth his works in us.

THE ¹GENERAL EPISTLE OF

JAMES

1 *4 He entreateth of patience, 6 of faith, 10 and of lowliness of mind in rich men. 13 That tentations come not of God for our evil, 17 because he is the author of all goodness. 21 In what manner the word of life must be received.*

CHAPTER 1
ª Rom. 5:3
ᵇ Matt. 7:7
Luke 11:9
Mark 11:24
John 14:13
John 16:23
ᶜ Isa. 40:6
1 Pet. 2:24
ᵈ Job 5:17

1 James a servant of God, and of the Lord Jesus Christ, to the twelve Tribes, which are ¹scattered abroad, salutation.

2 ¹My brethren, ²count it exceeding joy, ³when ye fall into divers tentations,

3 ª,¹Knowing that the ²trying of your faith bringeth forth patience,

4 ¹And let patience have *her* perfect work, that ye may be perfect and entire, lacking nothing.

5 ¹If any of you lack ²wisdom, let him ask of God, which giveth to all men liberally, and reproacheth no man, and it shall be given him.

6 ᵇBut let him ask in faith, and ¹waver not: ²for he that wavereth, is like a wave of the sea, tossed of the wind, and carried away.

7 Neither let that man think that he shall receive anything of the Lord.

8 A double minded man *is* unstable in ¹all his ways.

9 ¹Let the brother of ²low degree rejoice in that he is exalted:

10 ¹Again, he that is ²rich, in that he is made low: ³for as the flower of the grass, shall he ᶜvanish away.

11 For *as when* the sun riseth with heat, then the grass withereth, and his flower falleth away, and the goodly shape of it perisheth: even so shall the rich man wither away in *all* his ¹ways.

12 ¹,ᵈBlessed *is* the man, that endureth ²tentation: for when he is tried, he shall receive the crown of life, which the Lord hath promised to them that love him.

13 ¹Let no man say when he is ²tempted, I am tempted of God: ³for God cannot be tempted with

---

Title ¹ That is, written to no one man, city or country, but to all the Jews generally, being now dispersed.

1:1 ¹ To all the believing Jews, of what Tribe soever they be, and are dispersed through the whole world.

1:2 ¹ The first place or part touching comfort in afflictions, wherein we ought not be cast down and be fainthearted, but rather rejoice and be glad.

² Seeing their condition was miserable in that scattering abroad, he doth well to begin as he doth.

³ The first argument, because our faith is tried through afflictions: which ought to be most pure, for so it is behoovable for us.

1:3 ¹ The second, Because patience, far passing and most excellent virtue, is by this means engendered in us.

² That wherewith your faith is tried, to wit, those manifold temptations.

1:4 ¹ The third argument propounded in manner of an exhortation, that true and continual patience may be discerned from fained and for a time. The cross is as it were the instrument wherewith God doth polish and [re]fine us. Therefore the work and effect of afflictions, is the perfecting of us in Christ.

1:5 ¹ An answer to a privy objection: It is easily said, but it is not so easily done. He answereth that we need in this case a far other manner of wisdom, than the wisdom of man, to judge those things best for us, which are most contrary to the flesh: but yet we shall easily obtain this gift of wisdom, if we ask it rightly, that is, with a sure confidence of God, who is most bountiful and liberal.

² By wisdom he meaneth the knowledge of that doctrine whereof mention was made before, to wit, wherefore we are afflicted of God, and what fruit we have to reap of affliction.

1:6 ¹ Why then what need other Mediator?

² A digression or going aside from his matter, against prayers which are conceived with a doubting mind, whereas we have a certain promise of God, and this is that second part of the Epistle.

1:8 ¹ In all his thoughts and his deeds.

1:9 ¹ He returneth to his purpose, repeating the proposition, which is, that we must rejoice in the cross, for it doth not press us down, but exalt us.

² Who is afflicted with poverty, or contempt, or with any kind of calamity.

1:10 ¹ Before he concludeth, he giveth a doctrine contrary to the former: to wit, how we ought to use prosperity, which is plenty of all things: to wit, so that no man therefore please himself, but be so much the more void of pride.

² Who hath all things at his will.

³ An argument taken of the very nature of the things themselves, for that they are most vain and uncertain.

1:11 ¹ Whatsoever he either purposeth in his mind, or doeth.

1:12 ¹ The conclusion: Therefore we must patiently bear the cross: and he addeth a fourth argument, which comprehendeth the sum of all the former, to wit, because we come by this way to the crown of life, but yet of grace according to the promise.

² Affliction whereby the Lord trieth him.

1:13 ¹ The third part of this Epistle, wherein he descendeth from outward tentations, that is, from afflictions, whereby God trieth us, to inward, that is, to those lusts whereby we are stirred up to do evil. The sum is this: Every man is the author of these temptations to himself, and not God: for we bear about in our bosoms that wicked corruption, which taketh occasions by what means soever, to stir up evil motions in us, whence out at length proceed wicked doing, and in conclusion followeth death the just reward of them.

² When he is provoked to do evil.

³ Here is a reason showed, why God cannot be the author of evil doing in us, because he desireth not evil.

evil, neither tempteth he any man.

14 But every man is tempted, when he is drawn away by his own concupiscence, and is enticed.

15 Then when lust hath conceived, it bringeth forth ¹sin, and sin when it is finished, bringeth forth death.

16 ¹Err not my dear brethren.

17 Every good giving and every perfect gift is from above, and cometh down from the ¹Father of lights, with whom is no variableness, neither ²shadow of turning.

18 ¹Of his own ²will begat he us with the word of truth, that we should be as the ³firstfruits of his creatures.

19 Wherefore my dear brethren, let every man be swift to hear, slow to speak, *and* slow to wrath.

20 For the wrath of man doth not accomplish the ¹righteousness of God.

21 Wherefore lay apart all filthiness, and superfluity of maliciousness, *and* receive with ¹meekness the word that is grafted in you, which is able to save your souls.

22 ⸵¹And be ye doers of the word, and not hearers only, ²deceiving your own selves.

23 ¹For if any hear the word, and do it not, he is like unto a man, that beholdeth his ²natural face in a glass.

24 For when he hath considered himself, he goeth his way, and forgetteth immediately what manner of one he was.

25 But who so looketh in the perfect law of liberty,

e Matt. 7:21
Rom. 2:13

CHAPTER 2
d Lev. 9:15
Deut. 1:17
Deut. 16:29
Prov. 24:23

and continueth *therein*, he not being a forgetful hearer, but a doer of the work, shall be blessed in his ¹deed.

26 ¹If any man among you seem religious, and refraineth not his tongue, but deceiveth his ²own heart, this man's religion *is* vain.

27 ¹Pure religion and undefiled before God, even the Father, is this, to ²visit the fatherless, and widows in their adversity, *and* to keep himself unspotted of the world.

2 *1 He sayeth, that to have respect of persons is not agreeable to Christ's faith, 14 which to profess in words is not enough, unless 15 we show it also in deeds of mercy and charity, 21 after the example of Abraham.*

1 My ¹brethren, have not the faith of our ²glorious Lord Jesus Christ ⸵in respect of persons.

2 For if there come into your company a man with a gold ring, and in goodly apparel, and there come in also a poor man in vile raiment,

3 And ye have a respect to him that weareth the gay clothing; and say unto him, Sit thou here in a ¹goodly place, and say unto the poor, Stand thou there, or sit here under my footstool,

4 Are ye not partial in ¹your selves, and are become Judges of evil thoughts?

5 ¹Hearken my beloved brethren, hath not God chosen the ²poor of this world, *that they should be* rich in faith, and heirs of the kingdom which he

---

1:15 ¹ By sin is meant in this place actual sin.

1:16 ¹ Another reason taken of contraries: God is the author of all goodness, and so, that he is always like himself; how then can he be thought to be author of evil?

1:17 ¹ From him who is the fountain and author of all goodness.

² He goeth on in the metaphor: for the sun by his manifold and sundry kinds of turning, maketh hours, days, months, years, light and darkness.

1:18 ¹ The fourth part concerning the excellency and fruit of the word of God. The sum is this: we must hear the word of God most carefully and diligently, seeing it is the seed, wherewith God of his free favor and love hath begotten us unto himself, picking us out of the number of his creatures. And the Apostle condemneth two faults, which do greatly trouble us in this matter, to wit, for that we so please ourselves, that we had rather speak ourselves than hear God speaking: yea, we snuff and are angry when we are reprehended: against which faults, he setteth a peaceable and quiet mind, and such an one as is desirous of purity.

² This is it which Paul calleth gracious favor, and good will, which is the fountain of our salvation.

³ As it were an holy kind of offering, taken out of the residue of man.

1:20 ¹ That which God appointeth.

1:21 ¹ By meekness, he meaneth modesty, and whatsoever is contrary to an haughty and proud stomach.

1:22 ¹ Another admonition. Therefore is God's word heard, that we may frame our lives according to the prescript thereof.

² He addeth reasons, and those most weighty: first, because they that do otherwise, do very much hurt themselves.

1:23 ¹ Secondly, because they lose the chiefest use of God's word, which correct not by it the faults that they know.

² He alludeth to that natural spot, to which is contrary that purity whereunto we are born again, the lively image whereof we behold in the Law.

1:25 ¹ Behaving himself so: for works do show faith.

1:26 ¹ The third admonition: The word of God prescribeth a rule not only to do well, but also to speak well.

² The fountain of all brabbling, and cursed speaking, and sauciness, is this, that men know not themselves.

1:27 ¹ The fourth: the true service of God standeth in charity toward our neighbors (especially such as need others' help, as the fatherless and widows), and purity of life.

² To have a care of them, and to help them as much as we can.

2:1 ¹ The fifth: Charity which proceedeth from a true faith, cannot stand with the accepting of persons: which he proveth plainly by setting forth their example, who with the reproach or disdain of the poor, honor the rich.

² For if we knew what Christ's glory is, and esteemed it as we ought to do, there would not be such respect of persons as there is.

2:3 ¹ In a worshipful and honorable place.

2:4 ¹ Have ye not (which you ought not to do) by this means with yourselves judged one man to be preferred before another?

2:5 ¹ He showeth that they are perverse and naughty Judges, which prefer the rich before the poor, by that that God on the contrary side preferreth the poor, whom he hath enriched with true riches, before the rich.

² The needy and wretched, and (if we measure it after the opinion of the world) the veriest abjects of all men.

promised to them that love him?

6　But ye have despised the poor. [1]Do not the rich oppress you by tyranny, and do they not draw you before the judgment seats?

7　Do not they blaspheme the worthy Name after which ye be [1]named?

8　[1]But if ye fulfill the [2]royal Law according to the Scripture, *which saith*, Thou shalt love thy neighbor as thyself, ye do well.

9　But if ye regard the persons, ye commit sin, and are rebuked of the Law, as transgressors.

10　[1]For whosoever shall keep the whole Law, *and* yet faileth in one *point*, he is guilty of [2]all.

11　[1]For he that said, Thou shalt not commit adultery, said also, Thou shalt not kill. Now though thou doest none adultery, yet if thou killest, thou art a transgressor of the Law.

12　[1]So speak ye, and so do, as they that shall be judgeth by the Law of liberty.

13　For there shall be condemnation merciless to him that showeth not [1]mercy, and mercy rejoiceth against condemnation.

14　[1]What availeth it my brethren, though a man saith, he hath faith, when he hath no works? can that faith save him?

15　[1]For if a brother or a sister be naked and des-

[b] Gen. 22:10
[c] Gen. 15:6
Rom. 4:3
Gal. 3:6

titute of daily food,

16　And one of you say unto them, Depart in peace: warm yourselves, and fill your bellies, notwithstanding ye give them not those things, which are needful to the body, what helpeth it?

17　Even so the faith, if it have no works, is dead in itself.

18　But [1]some man might say, Thou hast the faith, and I have works: show me thy faith out of thy works, and I will show thee my faith by my works.

19　[1]Thou believest that there is one God: thou doest well: the devils also believe it, and tremble.

20　[1]But wilt thou understand, O thou vain man, that the faith *which is* without works, is dead?

21　Was not Abraham our father [1]justified through works, [b]when he offered Isaac his son upon the altar?

22　Seest thou not that the faith [1]wrought with his works? and through the works was the faith made [2]perfect.

23　And the Scripture was [1]fulfilled which saith, [c]Abraham believed God, and it was imputed unto him for righteousness: and he was called the friend of God.

24　[1]Ye see then how that of works a man is [2]justified, and not of [3]faith only.

2:6 [1] Secondly, he proveth them to be mad men: for that the rich men are rather to be holden execrable and cursed, considering that they persecute the Church, and blaspheme Christ: for he speaketh of wicked and profane rich men, such as the most part of them have been always, against whom he setteth the poor and abject.

2:7 [1] Word for word, which is called upon of you.

2:8 [1] The conclusion: Charity which God prescribeth cannot agree with the accepting of persons, seeing that we must walk in the King's highway.

[2] The Law is said to be royal and like the King's highway, for that it is plain and without turnings, and that the Law calleth everyone our neighbor, without respect, whom we may help by any kind of duty.

2:10 [1] A new argument to prove the same conclusion: They do not love their neighbors, which neglect some, and ambitiously honor others: for he doth not obey God, which cutteth off from the commandments of God that that is not so commodious for him, nay he is rather guilty generally for the breach of the whole Law, although he observe the residue.

[2] Not that all sins are equal, but because he that breaketh one tittle of the Law, offendeth the majesty of the Lawgiver.

2:11 [1] A proof: because the Lawmaker is always one and the self-same, and the body of the Law cannot be divided.

2:12 [1] The conclusion of the whole treatise: we are upon this condition delivered from the curse of the Law by the mercy of God, that in like sort we should maintain and cherish charity and goodwill one towards another, and whoso doth not so, shall not taste of the grace of God.

2:13 [1] He that is hard and currish against his neighbor, or else helpeth him not, he shall find God an hard and rough Judge to himself-ward.

2:14 [1] The fifth place which hangeth very well with the former trea-

tise, touching a true and lively faith. And the proposition of this place is this: faith which bringeth not forth works, is not that faith whereby we are justified, but an image of faith: or else this, they are not justified by faith, which show not the effects of faith.

2:15 [1] The first reason taken of a similitude: If a man say to one that is hungry, Fill thy belly, and yet giveth him nothing, this shall not be true charity: so if a man say he believeth, and bringeth forth no works of his faith, this shall not be a true faith, but a certain dead thing set out with the name of faith, whereof no man hath to brag, unless he will openly incur reprehension, seeing that the cause is understood by the effects.

2:18 [1] Nay, thus may every man beat down the pride.

2:19 [1] Another reason taken of an absurdity: If such a faith were the true faith whereby we are justified, the devils should be justified: for they have that, but yet notwithstanding they tremble, and are not justified therefore, neither is that faith a true faith.

2:20 [1] The third reason from the example of Abraham, who no doubt had a true faith: but he in offering his son, showed himself to have that faith which was not void of works, and therefore he received a true testimony when it was said, that faith was imputed to him for righteousness.

2:21 [1] Was he not by his works known and found to be justified? for he speaketh not here of the causes of justification, but by what effects we may know that a man is justified.

2:22 [1] Was effectual and fruitful with good works.

[2] That the faith was declared to be a true faith, and that by works.

2:23 [1] Then was the Scripture fulfilled, when it appeared plainly, how truly it was written of Abraham.

2:24 [1] The conclusion: he is only justified that hath that faith which hath works following it.

[2] Is proved to be just.

[3] Of that dead and fruitless faith which you boast of.

25 [1]Likewise also was not [d]Rahab the harlot justified through works, when she had received the messengers, and sent them out another way?

26 [1]For as the body without the spirit is dead, even so the faith without works is dead.

3 *2 To show that a Christian man must govern his tongue with the bridle of faith and charity, 6 he declareth the commodities and mischiefs that ensue thereof: 15 and how much man's wisdom 17 differeth from heavenly.*

1 My [1]brethren, be not many masters, [2]knowing that we [3]shall receive the greater condemnation.

2 For in many things we [1]sin all. [2]If any man sin not in word, he is a perfect man, and able to bridle all the body.

3 [1]Behold, we put bits into the horses' mouths, that they should obey us, and we turn about all their body.

4 Behold also the ships, which though they be so great, and are driven of fierce winds, yet are they turned about with a very small rudder, whithersoever the governor listeth.

5 Even so the tongue is a little member, and boasteth of great things: [1]behold, how great a thing a little fire kindleth.

6 And the tongue is fire, *yea,* a [1]world of wickedness: so is the tongue set among our members, that it defileth the whole body, and [2]setteth on fire the course of nature, and it is set on fire of hell.

7 For the whole nature of beasts, and of birds, and of creeping things, and things of the sea is tamed, and hath been tamed of the nature of man.

d Josh. 2:1

8 But the tongue can no man tame. *It is* an unruly evil, full of deadly poison.

9 [1]Therewith bless we God even the Father, and therewith curse we men, which are made after the [2]similitude of God.

10 [1]Out of one mouth proceedeth blessing and cursing: my brethren, these things ought not so to be.

11 Doth a fountain send forth at one place sweet *water* and bitter?

12 Can the fig tree, my brethren, bring forth olives, either a vine figs? so can no fountain make both salt water and sweet.

13 [1]Who is a wise man and endued with knowledge among you? let him show by good conversation his works in meekness of wisdom.

14 But if ye have bitter envying and strife in your hearts, rejoice not, neither be liars against the truth.

15 This wisdom descendeth not from above, but *is* earthly, sensual, and devilish.

16 For where envying and strife *is,* there *is* sedition, and all manner of evil works.

17 But the wisdom that *is* from above, is first pure, then peaceable, gentle, easy to be entreated, full of [1]mercy and good fruits, without judging, and without hypocrisy.

18 [1]And the fruit of righteousness is sown in peace, of them that make peace.

4 *1 He reckoneth up the mischiefs that proceed of the works of the flesh. 7 He exhorteth to humility, 8 and to purge the heart 3 from pride, 10 backbiting, 14 and the forgetfulness of our own infirmity.*

2:25 [1] A fourth reason taken from a like example of Rahab the harlot, who also proved by her works that she was justified by a true faith.

2:26 [1] The conclusion repeated again: faith which bringeth not forth fruits and works, is not faith, but a dead carcass.

3:1 [1] The sixth part or place: Let no man usurp (as most men ambitiously do) authority to judge and censure others righteously.

[2] A reason: Because they provoke God's severity against themselves, which do so curiously and rigorously condemn others, being themselves guilty and faulty.

[3] Unless we surcease from this masterlike and proud finding fault with others.

3:2 [1] Or, stumble.

[2] The seventh place, touching the bridling of the tongue, joined with the former, so that it is manifest that there is no man which may not justly be found fault withal, seeing it is a rare virtue to bridle the tongue.

3:3 [1] He showeth by two similitudes the one taken from the bridles of horses, the other from the rudders of ships, how great matters may be brought to pass by the good moderation of the tongue.

3:5 [1] On the contrary part he showeth how great discommodities arise by the intemperance of the tongue, throughout the whole world, to the end that men may so much the more diligently give themselves to moderate it.

3:6 [1] An heap of all mischiefs.

[2] It is able to set the whole world on fire.

3:9 [1] Amongst other faults of the tongue, the Apostle chiefly reproveth backbiting and speaking evil of our neighbors, even in them especially which otherwise will seem godly and religious.

[2] He denieth by two reasons, that God can be praised by that man, that useth cursed speaking, or to backbite: first because man is the image of God, which whosoever reverenceth not doth not honor God himself.

3:10 [1] Secondly, because the order of nature which God hath set in things, will not suffer things that are so contrary the one to the other, to stand the one with the other.

3:13 [1] The eighth part which hangeth with the former, touching meekness of mind, against which he setteth envy and a contentious mind. And in the beginning he stoppeth the mouth of the chief fountain of all these mischiefs, to wit, a false persuasion of wisdom, whereas notwithstanding there is no true wisdom, but that is heavenly, and frameth our minds to all kinds of true moderation and simplicity.

3:17 [1] He setteth mercy against the fierce and cruel nature of man, and showeth that heavenly wisdom bringeth forth good fruits, for he that is heavenly wise, referreth all things to God's glory, and the profit of his neighbor.

3:18 [1] Because the world persuadeth itself that they are miserable which live peaceably and simply, on the contrary side the Apostle pronounceth that they shall at the length reap the harvest of peaceable righteousness.

1 From ¹whence *are* wars and contentions among you? are they not hence, *even* of your pleasures, that fight in your members?

2 Ye lust, and have not: ye envy, and desire immoderately, and cannot obtain: ye fight, and war, and get nothing, ¹because ye ask not.

3 Ye ask, and receive not, because ye ask amiss, that ye might lay the same on your pleasures.

4 ¹Ye adulterers and adulteresses, know ye not that the amity of the world is the enmity of God? Whosoever therefore will be a friend of the world, maketh himself the enemy of God.

5 ¹Do ye think that the Scripture saith in vain, The spirit that dwelleth in us, lusteth after envy?

6 But *the* Scripture offereth more grace, *and* therefore saith, ᵃGod resisteth the proud, and giveth grace to the humble.

7 ᵇ·¹Submit yourselves to God: resist the devil, and he will flee from you.

8 Draw near to God, and he will draw near to you. Cleanse your hands, ye sinners, and purge your hearts, ye double minded.

9 ¹Suffer afflictions, and sorrow ye, and weep: let your laughter be turned into mourning, and *your* joy into ²heaviness.

10 ᶜCast down yourselves before the Lord, and he will lift you up.

11 ¹Speak not evil one of another, brethren. He that speaketh evil of his brother, or he that condemneth his brother, speaketh evil of the Law, and condemneth the Law: and if thou condemnest the Law, thou art not an observer of the Law, but a judge.

12 There is one Lawgiver, which is able to save,

CHAPTER 4
ᵃ Prov. 3:34
1 Pet. 5:5
ᵇ Eph. 4:27
ᶜ 1 Pet. 5:6
ᵈ Rom. 14:4
ᵉ 1 Cor. 4:19

and to destroy, ᵈWho art thou that judgest another man?

13 ¹Go to now, ye that say, Today or tomorrow we will go into such a city, and continue there a year, and buy and sell, and get gain,

14 (And yet ye cannot tell what *shall be* tomorrow. For what is your life? It is even a vapor that appeareth for a little time, and afterward vanisheth away.)

15 For that ye ought to say, ᵉIf the Lord will, and if we live, we will do this or that.

16 But now ye rejoice in your boastings: all such rejoicing is evil.

17 ¹Therefore to him that knoweth how to do well, and doeth it not, to him it is sin.

5 1 *He threateneth the rich with God's severe judgment, for their pride,* 7 *that the poor hearing the miserable end of the rich,* 8 *may patiently bear afflictions,* 11 *as Job did,* 14 *even in their distresses.*

1 Go ¹to now, ye rich men: weep, and howl for your miseries that shall come upon you.

2 Your riches are corrupt, and your garments are moth eaten.

3 Your gold and silver is cankered, and the rust of them shall be a witness against you, and shall eat your flesh, as *it were* fire. Ye have heaped up treasure for the last days.

4 Behold, the hire of the laborers, which have reaped your fields (which is of you kept back by fraud) crieth, and the cries of them which have reaped, are entered into the ¹ears of the Lord of hosts.

5 Ye have lived in pleasure on the earth, and in

4:1 ¹ He goeth on forward in the same argument, condemning certain other causes of wars and contentions, to wit, unbridled pleasures and immoderate lusts, by their effects, for so much as the Lord doth worthily make them void, so that they bring nothing else to them in whom they are but incurable torments.

4:2 ¹ He reprehendeth them by name, which are not ashamed to go about to make God the minister and helper of their lusts and pleasures, in asking things which either are of themselves unlawful, or being lawful, ask them to wicked purposes and uses.

4:4 ¹ Another reason why such unbridled lusts and pleasures are utterly to be condemned, to wit, because that he that giveth himself to the world, divorceth himself from God, and breaketh the band of that holy and spiritual marriage.

4:5 ¹ The taking away of an objection: Indeed our minds run headlong into these vices, but we ought so much the more diligently take heed of them: which care and study shall not be in vain, seeing that God resists the stubborn, and giveth that grace to the modest and humble that surmounteth all those vices.

4:7 ¹ The conclusion: We must set the contrary virtues against those vices, and therefore whereas we obeyed the suggestions of the devil, we must submit our minds to God, and resist the devil, with a certain and assured hope of victory: To be short, we must employ ourselves to come near unto God by purity and sincerity of life.

4:9 ¹ He goeth on in the same comparison of contraries, and setteth against those profane joys with an earnest sorrow of mind, and

against pride and arrogance, holy modesty.

² By this word the Greeks meant an heaviness joined with shamefastness, which is to be seen in a cast down countenance, and settled as it were upon the ground.

4:11 ¹ He reprehended most sharply another double mischief of pride: the one is in that the proud and arrogant will have other men to live according to their will and pleasure and therefore they do most arrogantly condemn whatsoever pleaseth them not: which thing cannot be done without great injury to our only Lawmaker, for by this means his Laws are found fault withal, as not circumspectly enough written, and men challenge that unto themselves which properly belongeth to God alone, in that they lay a Law upon men's consciences.

4:13 ¹ The other fault is this: that men do so confidently determine upon these and those matters and businesses, as though that every moment of their life did not depend of God.

4:17 ¹ The conclusion of all the former treatise: The knowledge of the will of God doth not only nothing at all profit, unless the life be answerable unto it, but also maketh the sins far more grievous.

5:1 ¹ He denounceth utter destruction to the wicked and profane rich men, and such as are drowned in their riotousness, mocking at their foolish confidence when as there is nothing indeed more vain than such things.

5:4 ¹ The Lord who is more mighty than ye are, hath heard them.

wantonness. Ye have [1]nourished your hearts, as in a [2]day of slaughter.

6 Ye have condemned, *and* have killed the just, and he hath not resisted you.

7 [1]Be patient therefore, brethren, unto the coming of the Lord. [2]Behold, the husbandman waiteth for the precious fruit of the earth, and hath long patience for it, until he receive the former, and the latter rain.

8 Be ye also patient therefore, and settle your hearts: for the coming of the Lord draweth near.

9 [1,2]Grudge not one against another, brethren, lest ye be condemned: [3]behold, the judge standeth before the door.

10 [1]Take, my brethren, the Prophets for an example of suffering adversity, and of long patience, which have spoken in the name of the Lord.

11 Behold, we count them blessed which endure. Ye have heard of the patience of Job, and have known what [1]end the Lord *made*. For the Lord is very pitiful and merciful.

12 [1]But before all things, my brethren, [a]swear not, neither by heaven, nor by earth, nor by any other oath: but let [2]your yea, be yea, and *your* nay, nay, lest ye fall into condemnation.

CHAPTER 5
[a] Matt. 5:34
[b] Mark 6:13
[c] 1 Kings 17:1
1 Kings 18:45
Luke 4:25
[d] Matt. 8:15

13 [1]Is any among you afflicted? Let him pray. Is any merry? Let him sing.

14 [1]Is any sick among you? Let him call for the Elders of the Church, and let them pray for him, and anoint him with [b,2]oil in the [3]Name of the Lord.

15 And the prayer of faith shall save the sick, and the Lord shall raise him up: and if he have committed [1]sins, they shall be forgiven him.

16 [1]Acknowledge your faults one to another, and pray one for another, that ye may be healed: [2]for the prayer of a righteous man availeth much, if it be fervent.

17 'Elijah was a man subject to like passions as we are, and he prayed earnestly that it might not rain, and it rained not on the earth for three years and six months.

18 And he prayed again: and the heaven gave rain, and the earth brought forth her fruit.

19 [1]Brethren, [d]If any of you hath erred from the truth, and some man hath [2]converted him,

20 Let him know that he which hath converted the sinner from going astray out of his way, shall save a soul from death, and shall hide a multitude of sins.

5:5 [1] Ye have pampered up yourselves.

[2] The Hebrews call a day that is appointed to solemn banqueting, a day of slaughter or feasting.

5:7 [1] He applieth that to the poor, which he spake against the rich, warning them to wait for the Lord's coming patiently, who will revenge the injuries which the rich men do them.

[2] The taking away of an objection: Although his coming serve to linger, yet at the least we must follow the husbandmen, who do patiently wait for the times that are proper for the fruits of the earth. And again, God will not defer the least iota of the time that he hath appointed.

5:9 [1] He commendeth Christian patience, so that whereas others through impatience use to accuse one another, the faithful on the contrary side complain not, although they receive injury.

[2] By grudging, he meaneth a certain inward complaining which betokeneth impatience.

[3] The conclusion: The Lord is at the door, who will defend his own, and revenge his enemies, and therefore we need not to trouble ourselves.

5:10 [1] Because most men are wont to object, that it is good to repel injuries by what means soever, he setteth against that, the examples of the Fathers, whose patience had a most happy end, because God as a most bountiful Father, never forsaketh his.

5:11 [1] What end the Lord gave.

5:12 [1] Because even the best men sometimes through impatience break out into oaths sometimes lesser, sometimes greater, the Apostle warneth us to detest such wickedness, and to accustom our tongues to simple and true talk.

[2] That that you have to say or affirm, speak or affirm it simply, and without an oath: and that that you will deny, deny it simply and flatly.

5:13 [1] He showeth the best remedy against all afflictions, to wit, prayers which have their place both in sorrow and joy.

5:14 [1] He showeth peculiarly, to what physicians especially we must go, when we are diseased, to wit, to the prayers of the Elders, which then also could cure the body, (for so much as the gift of healing was then in force) and take away the chiefest cause of sickness and diseases, by obtaining for the sick through their prayers and exhortations, remission of sins.

[2] This was a sign of the gift of healing: and now seeing we have the gift no more, the sign is no longer necessary.

[3] By calling on the Name of the Lord.

5:15 [1] He hath reason in making mention of sins, for diseases are for the most part sent because of sins.

5:16 [1] Because God pardoneth their sins which confess and acknowledge them, and not theirs which justify themselves, therefore the Apostle addeth, that we ought freely to confer one with another touching those inward diseases, that we may help one another with our prayers.

[2] He commendeth prayers by the effects that come of them, that all men may understand that there is nothing more effectual than they are, so that they proceed from a pure mind.

5:19 [1] The taking away of an objection: All reprehensions are not condemned, seeing that on the contrary part there is nothing more acceptable to God, than to call into the way a brother that was wandering out of the way.

[2] Hath called him back from his way.

THE FIRST EPISTLE GENERAL OF

PETER

1 *1 He extolleth God's mercy showed in Christ, which we lay hold on by faith, and possess through hope: 10 whereof the Prophets foretold. 13 He exhorteth 15 to renounce the world, 23 and their former life, and so wholly yield themselves to God.*

1 PETER an Apostle of JESUS CHRIST, to the strangers that dwell here and there throughout Pontus, Galatia, Cappadocia, Asia and Bithynia,

2 ¹Elect according to the ²foreknowledge of God the Father unto ³sanctification of the Spirit, through obedience and sprinkling of the blood of Jesus Christ: Grace and peace be multiplied unto you.

3 Blessed *be* God, even the Father of our Lord Jesus Christ, which according to his abundant mercy hath begotten us again unto a ¹lively hope by the resurrection of Jesus Christ from the dead,

4 To an inheritance immortal and undefiled, and that withereth not, reserved in heaven for us,

5 ¹Which are kept by the power of God through faith unto salvation, which is prepared to be showed in the ²last time.

6 Wherein ye rejoice, though now for a season (if need require) ye are in heaviness, through manifold tentations,

7 That the trial of your faith, being much more precious than gold that perisheth (though it be tried with fire) might be found unto *your* praise, and honor and glory at the ¹appearing of Jesus Christ:

8 Whom ye have not seen, and yet love *him*, in whom now, though ye see him not, yet do you believe, and rejoice with [joy] unspeakable and glorious,

9 Receiving the ¹end of your faith, *even* the salvation of *your* souls.

10 ¹Of the which salvation the Prophets have inquired and searched, which prophesied of the grace that should come unto you,

11 Searching when or what time the Spirit which testified before of Christ which was in them, should declare the sufferings *that should come* unto Christ, and the glory that should follow.

12 Unto whom it was revealed, that not unto themselves, but unto us they should minister the things, which are showed unto you by them which have preached unto you the Gospel by the holy Ghost ¹sent down from heaven, the which things the Angels desire to behold.

13 ¹Wherefore ²gird up the loins of your mind:

1:2 ¹ Peter purposing to speak of the duties of a Christian life, reasoneth first of the principles and beginning of all Christian actions, rising far higher than nature, and carrying us also far above the same. For he showeth that we which are otherwise of nature sinners, were through the free mercy of God the Father first chosen from everlasting: then according to that everlasting decree were by a certain second creation made his sons in Christ his only begotten, by whose Spirit we are inwardly changed, and by whose blood we also are reconciled, to the end, that as Christ himself rose again from the dead, we also might be received into that same heavenly and everlasting glory.

² Or according to the purpose of God, who never altereth nor changeth the same.

³ That being set apart from the rest of the wicked world, through the working of the holy Ghost, they should be consecrate to God, Eph. 1:5.

1:3 ¹ Everlasting hope.

1:5 ¹ Now he showeth by what way we come unto that glory, to wit, through all kinds of afflictions, wherein notwithstanding faith maketh us so secure, that we are not only not overcome with sorrow, but also through the beholding of God himself (who otherwise is invisible) with the eyes of faith are unspeakably joyful: because all such things, as they are but for a time, so are they not applied unto us to destroy us, but as it were by fire to purge us, and to make us perfect, that at the length we may obtain salvation.

² This is that time which Daniel calleth the time of the end, when as that great restoring of all things shall be, which all creatures look for. Rom. 8:19.

1:7 ¹ He speaketh of the second coming of Christ.

1:9 ¹ Or, reward.

1:10 ¹ He putteth a difference between true faith, that is to say, that faith which only hath an eye to the doctrine of the Prophets and Apostles, and false faith: Afterward he maketh two degrees of one and the selfsame faith, according to the manner of the divers revelations, when as indeed it is but one only faith: Thirdly, he saith, that the preaching of the Apostles is the fulfilling of the preaching of the Prophets, although the latter end of it be as yet looked for of the very Angels.

1:12 ¹ He alludeth to the prophecy of Joel, which was exhibited upon the day of Pentecost, in the Apostles, as it were in the firstfruits of the holy Ghost, which this same our Peter declareth, Acts 2:6.

1:13 ¹ He goeth from faith to hope, which is indeed a companion that cannot be sundered from faith: and he useth an argument taken of comparison: We ought not to be wearied in looking for so excellent a thing, which the very Angels wait for with great desire.

² This is a borrowed speech, taken of a common usage amongst them: for by reason that they wore long garments, they could not travel unless they girded up themselves: and hence it is that Christ said, Let your loins be girded up.

be sober, [3]and trust [4]perfectly on that grace [5]that is brought unto you, [6]in the revelation of Jesus Christ,

14 [1]As obedient children, not fashioned yourselves unto the former lusts of your ignorance:

15 But as he which hath called you, is holy, so be ye holy in [a]all manner of conversation,

16 [1]Because it is written, [b]Be ye holy, for I am holy.

17 [1]And if ye [2]call him Father, which without [c]respect of person judgeth according to every man's work, pass the time of your dwelling here in fear.

18 [1]Knowing that ye were not redeemed with corruptible things, as silver and gold, from your vain conversation, received by the traditions of the fathers,

19 [d]But with the precious blood of Christ, as of a Lamb undefiled, and without spot.

20 [1]Which was [e]ordained before the [2]foundation of the world, but was declared in the last times for your sakes,

21 Which by his means do believe in God that raised him from the dead, and gave him glory, that your faith and hope might be in God.

22 [1]Having purified your souls in obeying the truth through the Spirit, to [f]love brotherly without feigning, love one another with a pure heart fervently:

23 Being born anew, not of mortal seed, but of immortal, by the word of God, who liveth and endureth forever.

24 [1]For all [g.2]flesh is as grass, and all the glory of man is as the flower of grass. The grass withereth, and the flower falleth away.

25 [1]But the word of the Lord endureth forever: and this is the word which is preached among you.

CHAPTER 2

He exhorteth the newborn in faith, to lead their lives answerable to the same: 6 and lest their faith should stagger, he bringeth in that which was foretold touching Christ. 11 Then he willeth them to be obedient to Magistrates, 21 and that they patiently bear adversity after Christ's example.

1 Wherefore, [a.1]laying aside all maliciousness, and all guile, and dissimulation, and envy, and all evil speaking,

2 [1]As [2]newborn babes desire that sincere milk of the word, that ye may grow thereby,

Cross-references

CHAPTER 1
a Luke 1:75
b Lev. 11:44
Lev. 19:2
Lev. 20:7
c Deut. 10:17
Rom. 2:11
Gal. 2:6
d 1 Cor. 6:20
1 Cor. 7:13
Heb. 9:14
1 John 1:7
Rev. 1:5
e Rom. 16:25
Eph. 3:9
Col. 1:26
2 Tim. 1:10
Titus 1:2
f 1 Pet. 2:17
Rom. 2:10
Eph. 4:2
g Isa. 40:6
James 1:10

CHAPTER 2
a Rom. 6:4
Eph. 4:23
Col. 3:8
Heb. 12:1

Footnotes

[3] He setteth forth very briefly, what manner of hope ours ought to be, to wit, continual, until we enjoy the thing we hope for: then, what we have to hope for, to wit, grace (that is, free salvation) revealed to us in the Gospel, and not that, that men do rashly and fondly promise to themselves.

[4] Soundly and sincerely.

[5] An argument to stir up our minds, seeing that God doth not wait till we seek him, but causeth so great a benefit to be brought even unto us.

[6] He setteth out the end of faith, lest any man should promise himself, either sooner or later that full salvation, to wit, the later coming of Christ: and therewithal warneth us, not to measure the dignity of the Gospel according to the present state, seeing that that which we are now, is not yet revealed.

1:14 [1] He passeth from faith and hope, to the fruits of them both, which are understood in the name of obedience: And it consisteth in two things, in renouncing our lusts, and living godly: which lusts have their beginning of that blindness wherein all men are born: but holiness proceedeth from the grace and favor of GOD, which adopteth us, and therefore regenerateth us, that the father and the children may be of one disposition.

1:16 [1] He showeth that sanctification doth necessarily follow adoption.

1:17 [1] As before he distinguished true faith and hope from false, so doth he now obedience, setting the quick and sharp sight of God, against an outward mask, and earnest reverence against vain severity.

[2] If you will be called the sons of that Father.

1:18 [1] An exhortation, wherein he setteth forth the excellency and greatness of the benefit of God the Father, in sanctifying us by the death of his own Son. And he partly setteth the purifyings of the Law against the thing itself, that is, against the blood of Christ, and partly also men's traditions which he condemneth as utterly vain and superstitious, be they never so old and ancient.

1:20 [1] The taking away of an objection: what was done to the world before that Christ was sent into the world? was there no holiness before, and was there no Church? The Apostle answereth, that Christ was ordained and appointed to redeem and deliver mankind, before that mankind was: much less was there any Church without him before his coming into the flesh: yet we are happiest above the rest, to whom Christ was exhibited indeed, in this that he having suffered and overcome death for us, doth now most effectually work in us by the virtue of his Spirit, to create in us faith, hope, and charity.

[2] From everlasting.

1:22 [1] He commendeth the practice of obedience, that is, charity: earnestly beating into their heads again, that he speaketh not of any common charity, and such as proceedeth from that our corrupt nature, but of that whose beginning is the Spirit of God, which purifieth our souls through the word laid hold on by faith, and engendereth also in us a spiritually and everlasting life, as God is most pure and truly living.

1:24 [1] A reason why we have need of this heavenly generation, to wit, because that men, be their glory never so great, are of nature void of all true and sound goodness.

[2] The word (flesh) showeth the weakness of our nature, which is chiefly to be considered in the flesh itself.

1:25 [1] Again, lest any man should seek that spiritual force and virtue in fained imaginations, the Apostle calleth us back to the word of God: teaching us furthermore, that there is no other word of the Lord to be looked for, than this which is preached, in which only we must trust.

2:1 [1] Having laid for the foundation the Spirit of God effectually working by the word, and having built thereupon three virtues which are the grounds of all Christian actions, to wit, faith, hope, and charity: now he proceedeth to a general exhortation, the first member whereof is, that we flee all show, both of secret and also open malice.

2:2 [1] The second is, that being newly begotten and born of the new seed of the incorrupt word drawing and sucking greedily the same word as milk, we should more and more as it were grow up in that spiritual life. And he calleth it, Sincere, not only because it is a most pure thing, but also that we should take heed of them which corrupt it.

[2] As becometh new men.

3 [1]Because ye [2]have tasted that the Lord *is* bountiful.

4 [1]To whom coming as unto a living stone, disallowed of men, but chosen of God *and* precious,

5 Ye also as lively stones, be made a spiritual house, [1]an holy [b]Priesthood to offer up spiritual sacrifices acceptable to God by Jesus Christ.

6 [1]Wherefore also it is contained in the Scripture, [c]Behold, I put in Zion a chief cornerstone, elect and precious, and he that believeth therein, shall not be ashamed.

7 [1]Unto you therefore which believe, it is precious: but unto them which be disobedient, the [d]stone which the builders disallowed, the same is made the head of the corner,

8 And a [e]stone to stumble at, and a rock of offence, even *to them* which stumble at the word, being disobedient, unto the which thing they were even ordained.

9 [1]But ye are a chosen generation, a royal [f]Priesthood, an holy nation, a people set at liberty, that ye should show forth the virtues of him that hath called you out of darkness into his marvelous light,

10 [g]Which in time past were not a people, yet *are* now the people of God: which in time past were not under mercy, but now have obtained mercy.

11 [1]Dearly beloved, [2]I beseech you, as strangers and pilgrims, [h,3]abstain from fleshly lusts [4]which fight against the soul,

12 [i,1] And have your conversation honest among the Gentiles, that they which speak evil of you as of evil doers, [2]may by *your* good [j]works which they shall see, glorify God in the day of [3]visitation.

13 [k,1] Therefore submit yourselves unto [2]all manner ordinance of man [3]for the Lord's sake, [4]whether it be unto the King, as unto the superior,

---

b Rev. 1:6
c Isa. 28:16
  Rom. 9:33
d Ps. 118:21
  Matt. 21:41
  Acts 4:11
e Isa. 8:14
  Rom. 9:33
f Exod. 19:6
g Hos. 2:23
  Rom. 9:25
h Rom. 13:14
  Gal. 5:16
i 1 Pet. 3:16
j Matt. 5:16
k Rom. 13:1

2:3 [1] He commendeth that spiritual nourishment for the sweetness and profit of it.

[2] Or, do taste.

2:4 [1] He goeth on forward in the same exhortation, and useth another kind of borrowed speech, alluding to the Temple. Therefore he saith, that the company of the faithful is as it were a certain holy and spiritual building, built of lively stones, the foundation whereof is Christ, as a lively stone sustaining all that are joined unto him with his living virtue, and knitting them together with himself, although this so great a treasure be neglected of men.

2:5 [1] Going forward in the same similitude, he compareth us now to Priests placed to this end in that spiritual temple, that we should serve him with spiritual worship, that is, with holiness and righteousness: but as the temple, so is the Priesthood built upon Christ, in whom only all our spiritual offerings are accepted.

2:6 [1] He proveth it by the testimony of the Prophet Isaiah.

2:7 [1] By setting the most blessed condition of the believers, and the most miserable of the rebellious one against another, he pricketh forward the believers, and triumpheth over the others: and also preventeth an offense which ariseth hereof, that none do more resist this doctrine of the Gospel, than they which are chiefest amongst the people of God, as were at that time that Peter wrote these things, the Priests and Elders, and Scribes. Therefore he answereth first of all that there is no cause why any man should be astonished at this their stubbornness, as though it were a strange matter, seeing that we have been forewarned so long before, that it should so come to pass: and moreover, that it pleased God to create and make certain to this selfsame purpose, that the Son of God might be glorified in their just condemnation. Thirdly, for that the glory of Christ is hereby set forth greatly, whereas notwithstanding Christ remaineth the sure head of his Church, and they that stumble at him, cast down and overthrow themselves, and not Christ. Fourthly, although they be created to this end and purpose, yet their fall and decay is not to be attributeth to God, but to their own obstinate stubbornness which cometh between God's decree, and the execution thereof or their condemnation, and is the true and proper cause of their destruction.

2:9 [1] The contrary member, to wit, he describeth the singular excellency of the elect: and also lest any man should doubt whether he be chosen or not, the Apostle calleth us back to the effectual calling, that is, to the voice of the Gospel sounding both in our ears and minds by the outward preaching and Sacraments, whereby we may certainly understand that everlasting decree of our salvation, (which otherwise is most secret and hidden) and that through the only mercy of God, who freely chooseth and calleth us. Therefore this only remaineth, sayeth he, that by all means possible we set forth so great goodness of the most mighty God.

2:11 [1] He returneth to that general exhortation.

[2] A reason why we ought to live holily, to wit, because we are citizens of heaven, and therefore we ought to live according to the Laws not of this world, which is most corrupt, but of the heavenly city, although we be strangers in the world.

[3] Another argument: The children of God live not according to the flesh, that is, according to that corrupt nature, but according to the spirit. Therefore fleshly motions ought not to bear rule in us.

[4] The third argument: for although those lusts flatter us, yet they cease not to fight against our salvation.

2:12 [1] The fourth argument, taken of the profit of so doing: for by this means also we provide for our good name and estimation, whilest we compel them at length to change their minds, which speak evil of us.

[2] The fifth argument, which also is of great force: Because the glory of God is greatly set forth by that means, whilst by example of our honest life, even the most profane men are brought unto God, and submit themselves unto him.

[3] When God shall also have mercy on them.

2:13 [1] That which he spoke generally, he now expoundeth by parts, describing severally every man's duty. And first of all he speaketh of obedience which is due both to the Laws, and also to the Magistrates both higher and lower.

[2] By ordinance, is meant the framing and ordering of civil government: which he calleth ordinance of man, not because man invented it, but because it is proper to men.

[3] The first argument: because the Lord is the author and revenger of this policy of men, that is, which is set amongst men: and therefore the true servants of the Lord must above all others be diligent observers of this order.

[4] He preventeth a cavil which is made by some, that say they will obey Kings and the higher magistrates, and yet contemn their ministers: as though their ministers were not armed with their authority which sent them.

14 Or unto governors, as unto them that are sent of him, [1]for the punishment of evil doers, and for the praise of them that do well.

15 [1]For so is the will of God, that by well doing ye may put to silence the ignorance of the foolish men.

16 As free, and not as having the liberty for a cloak of maliciousness, but as the servants of God.

17 [1,2]Honor all men: [l]love [3]brotherly fellowship: fear God: honor the King.

18 [m,1]Servants, be subject to your masters with all fear, not only to the good and courteous, but also to the froward.

19 [n,1]For this is thankworthy, if a man for [2]conscience toward God endure grief, suffering wrongly.

20 For what praise is it, if when ye be buffeted for your faults, ye take it patiently? but and if when ye do well, ye suffer *wrong* and take it patiently, this is acceptable to God.

21 [1]For hereunto ye are called: for Christ also suffered for you, leaving you an [2]example that ye should follow his steps,

22 [o]Who did no sin, neither was there guile found in his mouth.

23 Who when he was reviled, reviled not again: when he suffered, he threatened not, but [1]committed it to him [2]that judgeth righteously.

[l] 1 Pet. 1:12
Rom. 12:10
[m] Eph. 5:6
Col. 3:22
[n] 2 Cor. 7:10
[o] Isa. 53:9
1 John 3:5
[p] Isa. 53:5
Matt. 8:17

CHAPTER 3
[a] Col. 3:18
Eph. 5:22
[b] 1 Tim. 2:9

24 [p,1]Who his own self bare our sins in his body on the tree, that we being dead to sin, should live in righteousness: by whose stripes ye were healed.

25 For ye were as sheep going astray: but are now returned unto the Shepherd and Bishop of your souls.

3 *1 That Christian women should not contemn their husbands, though they be infidels.   6 He bringeth in examples of godly Women.   8 General exhortations,   14 patiently to bear persecutions,   15 and boldly to yield a reason of their faith.   18 Christ's example.*

1 Likewise [a,1]let the wives be subject to their husbands, [2]that even they which obey not the word, may without the word be won by the conversation of the wives.

2 While they behold your pure conversation which is with fear:

3 [b,1]Whose appareling let it not be that outward, with braided hair, and gold put about, or in putting on of apparel:

4 But let it be the [1]hidden man of the heart, *which consisteth* in the incorruption of a meek and quiet spirit, which is [2]before God a thing much set by.

5 [1]For even after this manner in time past did the holy women, which trusted in God, tire themselves, and were subject to their husbands.

2:14 [1] The second argument taken of the end of this order, which is not only most profitable, but also very necessary: seeing that by this means virtue is rewarded, and vice punished: wherein the quietness and happiness of this life consisteth.

2:15 [1] He declareth the first argument more amply, showing that Christian liberty doth amongst all things least, or not at all consist herein, to wit, to cast off the bridle of Laws, (as at that time some altogether unskillful in the kingdom of God reported) but rather in this, that living holily according to the will of God, we should make manifest to all men, that the Gospel is not a cloak for sin and wickedness, seeing we are in such sort free, that yet we are still the servants of God, and not of sin.

2:17 [1] He divideth the civil life of man, by occasion of those things of which he spake into two general parts: to wit, into those duties which private men owe to private men, and especially the faithful to the faithful, and into that subjection whereby inferiors are bound to their superiors: but so, that Kings be not made equal to God, seeing that fear is due to God, and honor to Kings.

[2] Be charitable and dutiful towards all men.

[3] The assembly and fellowship of the brethren, as Zech. 11:14.

2:18 [1] He goeth to the duty of servants towards their masters, which he describeth with these bounds, that servants submit themselves willingly and not by constraint, not only to the good and courteous, but also to the froward and sharp masters.

2:19 [1] The taking away of an objection: Indeed the condition of servants is hard, especially if they have froward masters: but this their subjection shall be so much the more acceptable to God, if his will prevails more with servants, than the masters' injuries.

[2] Because he maketh a conscience of it to offered God, by whose good will and appointment, he knoweth this burden is laid upon him.

2:21 [1] He mitigateth the grievousness of servitude, while he

showeth plainly that Christ died also for servants, that they should bear so much the more patiently this inequality betwixt men which are of one selfsame nature, moreover setting before them Christ that Lord of Lords for an ensample, he signifieth that they cannot but seem too delicate, which show themselves more grieved in bearing of injuries, than Christ himself who was most just, and most sharply of all afflicted, and yet was most patient.

[2] A borrowed kind of speech taken of painters and schoolmasters.

2:23 [1] He showeth them a remedy against injuries, to wit, that they commend their cause to God, by the ensample of Christ.

[2] He seemeth now to turn his speech to masters, which have also themselves a master and judge in heaven: who will justly revenge the injuries that are done to servants without any respect of persons.

2:24 [1] He calleth the servants back from the consideration of the injuries which they are constrained to bear, to think upon the greatness, and the end of the benefit received of Christ.

3:1 [1] In the third place he setteth forth the wives' duty to their husbands, commanding them to be obedient.

[2] He speaketh namely of them which had husbands that were not Christians, which ought so much the more be subject to their husbands, that by their honest and chaste conversation they may give them to the Lord.

3:3 [1] He condemneth the riot and excess of women and setteth forth their true appareling such as is precious before God: to wit, the inward and incorruptible which consisteth in a meek and quiet spirit.

3:4 [1] Who hath his seat fastened in the heart: so that the hid man is set against the outward decking of the body.

[2] Precious indeed, and so taken of God.

3:5 [1] An argument taken of the example of women, and especially of Sarah who was the mother of all believers.

6 As Sarah obeyed Abraham, and 'called him Sir: whose daughters ye are, while ye do well, ¹not being afraid of any terror.

7 ᵈ,¹Likewise ye husbands, ²dwell with them as men of ³knowledge, ⁴giving ⁵honor unto the woman, as unto the weaker ⁶vessel, ⁷even as they which are heirs together of the ⁸grace of life, ⁹that your prayers be not interrupted.

8 ¹Finally, be ye all of one mind: one suffer with another: love as brethren: be pitiful, be courteous.

9 ᵉ,¹Not rendering evil for evil, neither rebuke for rebuke: but contrariwise bless, ²knowing that ye are thereunto called, that ye should be heirs of blessing.

10 ᶠ,¹For if any man long after life, and to ²see good days, let him refrain his tongue from evil, and his lips that they speak no guile.

11 ᵍLet him eschew evil and do good: let him seek peace and follow after it.

12 For the eyes of the Lord are over the righteous, and his ears are open unto their prayers: and the ¹face of the Lord is against them that do evil.

13 ¹And who is it that will harm you, if ye follow that which is good?

14 ʰNotwithstanding blessed are ye, if ye suffer for righteousness' sake. ¹Yea, ʲfear not their ²fear, neither be troubled.

15 But ¹sanctify the Lord God in your hearts, ²and be ready always to give an answer to every man that asketh you a reason of the hope that is in you, with meekness and reverence.

16 Having a good conscience, that when they speak evil of you as of evil doers, they may be ashamed which slander your good conversation in Christ.

17 ¹For it is better (if the will of God be so) that ye suffer for well doing, than for evil doing.

18 ʲ,¹For Christ also hath once suffered for sins,

ᶜ Gen. 18:12
ᵈ 1 Cor. 7:3
ᵉ Prov. 17:13
  Prov. 20:21
  Matt. 5:39
  Rom. 12:17
  1 Thess. 5:15
ᶠ Ps. 34:13
ᵍ Isa. 1:16
ʰ Matt. 5:10
ⁱ Isa. 8:12,13
ʲ Rom. 5:6
  Heb. 9:15

3:6 ¹ Because women are of nature fearful, he giveth them to understand, that he requireth of them that subjection, which is not wrung out of them either by force or fear.

3:7 ¹ He teacheth husbands also their duties, to wit, that the more understanding and wisdom they have, the more wisely and circumspectly they behave themselves.

² Do all the duties of wedlock.

³ The more wisdom the husband hath, the more circumspectly he must behave himself in bearing those commodities, which through the woman's weakness ofttimes cause trouble both to the husband and the wife.

⁴ The second argument, because the wife notwithstanding that she is weaker by nature than the man, is an excellent instrument of the man made to far most excellent uses: whereupon it followeth that she is not therefore to be neglected because she is weak, but on the contrary part she ought to be so much the more cared for.

⁵ Having an honest care of her.

⁶ The woman is called a vessel after the manner of the Hebrews, because the husband useth her as his fellow and helper to live faithfully before God.

⁷ The third argument: for that they are equal in that which is the chiefest (that is to say, in the benefit of eternal life) which otherwise are unequal as touching the governance and conversation at home, and therefore they are not to be despised although they be weak.

⁸ Of that gracious and free benefit whereby we have everlasting life given us.

⁹ The fourth argument: All brawlings and chidings must be eschewed, because they hinder prayers and the whole service of God whereunto both the husband and wife are equally called.

3:8 ¹ He returneth to common exhortations and commendeth concord and whatsoever things pertain to the maintenance of peace and mutual love.

3:9 ¹ We must not only not recompense injury for injury, but we must also recompense them with benefits.

² An argument taken of comparison: Seeing that we ourselves are called of God whom we offend so often, to so great a benefit (so far is he from revenging the injuries which we do unto him) shall we rather make ourselves unworthy of so great bountifulness, than forgive one

another's faults? And from this verse to the end of the chapter, there is a digression or going from the matter he is in hand with, to exhort us valiantly to bear afflictions.

3:10 ¹ A secret objection: But this our patience shall be nothing else but a fleshing and hardening of the wicked in their wickedness, to make them to set upon us more boldly, and to destroy us. (Nay saith the Apostle by the words of David) to live without doing hurt, and to follow after peace when it fleeth away, is the way to the happy and quiet peace. And if so be any man be afflicted for doing justly, the Lord maketh all things, and will in his time deliver the godly, which cry unto him, and will destroy the wicked.

² Lead a blessed and happy life.

3:12 ¹ This word (Face) after the manner of the Hebrews, is taken for (anger.)

3:13 ¹ The second argument: when the wicked are provoked, they are more wayward: therefore they must rather be overcome with good turns: And if they cannot be gotten by that means also, yet notwithstanding we shall be blessed, if we suffer for righteousness' sake.

3:14 ¹ A most certain counsel in afflictions, be they never so terrible, to be of a constant mind, and to stand fast. But how shall we attain unto it? If we sanctify God in our minds and hearts, that is to say, if we rest upon him, as one that is Almighty, that loveth mankind, that is good and true indeed.

² Be not dismayed as they are.

3:15 ¹ Give him all praise and glory, and hang only on him.

² He will have us when we are afflicted for righteousness' sake, to be careful not for redeeming of our life, either with denying, or renouncing the truth, or with like violence, or any such means: but rather to give an account of our faith boldly, and yet with a meek spirit, and full to godly reverence, that the enemies may not have anything justly to object, but may rather be ashamed of themselves.

3:17 ¹ A reason which standeth upon two general rules of Christianity, which notwithstanding all men allow not of. The one is, if we must needs suffer afflictions, it is better to suffer wrongfully than rightfully: the other is this, because we are so afflicted, not by hap, but by the will of our God.

3:18 ¹ A proof of either of the rules, by the example of Christ himself our chief pattern who was afflicted, not for his own sins (which were none) but for ours, and that according to his Father's decree.

²the just for the unjust, ³that he might bring us to God, ⁴and was put to death concerning the ⁵flesh, but was quickened by the spirit.

19 ¹By ²the which he also went, and preached unto the ³spirits that *are* in prison.

20 Which were in time passed disobedient, when ¹once the long suffering of God abode in the days of ᵏNoah, while the Ark was preparing, wherein few, that is, eight ²souls were saved in the water.

21 ¹Whereof the baptism *that* now *is*, answering that figure, (*which is* not a putting away of the filth of the flesh, but a confident demanding with a good conscience maketh to ²God) saveth us also ³by the resurrection of Jesus Christ.

22 Which is at the right hand of God, gone into heaven, to whom the Angels, and Powers, and might are subject.

4 *1 He bringeth in Christ's example, and applieth it, 6 to the mortifying of the flesh, especially commending Charity: 12 And so entreateth of patience. 19 That it is necessary*

ᵏ Gen. 6:14
Matt. 24:33
Luke 17:26

CHAPTER 4
ᵃ Eph. 4:22
ᵇ Prov. 10:12

that correction begin at the Church.

1 Forasmuch ¹then as Christ hath suffered for us in the flesh, arm yourselves likewise with the same mind, *which is*, that he which hath suffered in the flesh, hath ceased from sin,

2 That he hence forward should live (as much time as ¹remaineth in the flesh) not after the lusts of men, but after the will of God.

3 ᵃ,¹For it is sufficient for us that we have spent the time past of the life, after the lust ²of the Gentiles walking in wantonness, lusts, drunkenness, in gluttony, drinkings, and in abominable idolatries.

4 ¹Wherein it seemeth to them ²strange, that ye run not with them unto the same excess of riot: *therefore* speak they evil *of you.*

5 Which shall give account to him, that is ready to judge quick and dead.

6 ¹For unto this purpose was the Gospel preached also unto the dead, that they might be condemned according to men in the flesh, but might live according to God in the spirit.

² An argument taken of comparison: Christ the just suffered for us that are unjust, and shall it grieve us who are unjust to suffer for the just's cause?

³ Another argument being partly taken of things coupled together, to wit, because Christ bringeth us to his Father that same way that he went himself, and partly from the cause efficient: to wit, because Christ is not only set before us for an example to follow, but also he holdeth us up by his virtue in all the difficulties of this life, until he bring us to his Father.

⁴ Another argument taken of the happy end of these afflictions, wherein also Christ goeth before us both in example and virtues, as one who suffered most grievous torments even unto death, although but in one part only of him, to wit, in the flesh or man's nature, but yet became conqueror by virtue of his divinity.

⁵ As touching his manhood, for his body was dead, and his soul felt the sorrows of death.

3:19 ¹ A secret objection: Christ indeed might do this, but what is that to us? yet (saith the Apostle) for Christ hath showed forth this virtue in all ages both to the preservation of the godly, were they never so few and miserable, and to revenge the rebellion of his enemies, as it appeareth by the history of the flood: for Christ is he which in those days (when God through his patience appointed a time of repentance to the world) was present not in corporal presence, but by his divine virtue, preaching repentance even by the mouth of Noah himself who then prepared the Ark, to those disobedient spirits which are now in prison waiting for the full recompence of their rebellion, and saved those few (that is, eight only persons) in the water.

² By the virtue of which Spirit, that is to say of the divinity: therefore this word, Spirit, cannot in this place be taken for the soul, unless we say, that Christ was raised up again, and quickened by the virute of his soul.

³ He calleth them Spirits, in respect of his time, not in respect of the time that they were in the flesh.

3:20 ¹ This word (once) showeth that there was a furthermost day appointed, and if that were once past, there should be no more.

² Men.

3:21 ¹ A proportional applying of the former example to the times

which followed the coming of Christ: for that preservation of Noah in the waters was a figure of our Baptism, not as though that material water of Baptism saveth us, as those waters which bare up the Ark saved Noah, but because Christ with his inward virtue, which the outward Baptism shadoweth, preserveth us being washed, so that we may call upon God with a good conscience.

² The conscience being sanctified may freely call upon God.

³ That selfsame virtue, whereby Christ rose again, and now being carried into heaven, hath received all power, doth at this day defend and preserve us.

4:1 ¹ Having ended his digression and sliding from his matter, now he returneth to the exhortation which he brake off, taking occasion by that which he said touching the death, and resurrection of Christ, so defining our sanctification, that to be sanctified, is all one as to suffer in the flesh, that is to say: to leave off from our wickedness and viciousness: and to rise again to God, that is to say, to be renewed, by the virtue of the holy Ghost, that we may lead the rest of our life which remaineth, after the will of God.

4:2 ¹ So much of this present life as remaineth yet to be passed over.

4:3 ¹ By putting us in mind of the dishonesty of our former life led in the filth of sin, he calleth us to earnest repentance.

² Wickedly and licentiously after the manner of the Gentiles.

4:4 ¹ That we be not moved with the enemies' perverse and slanderous judgments of us, we have to set against them that last judgment of God which remaineth for them, for none, whether they be then found living, or were dead before, shall escape it.

² They think it a new and strange matter.

4:6 ¹ A digression because he made mention of the last general judgement. And he preventeth an objection, that seeing Christ came very lately, they may seem to be excusable which died before. But this the Apostle denieth, for (saith he) this selfsame Gospel was preached unto them also: (for he speaketh unto the Jews) and that to the same end that I now preach it unto you, to wit, that the flesh being abolished and put away (that is to say, that wicked and naughty corruption which reigneth in men) they should suffer themselves to be governed by the virtue of the Spirit of God.

7 [1]Now the end of all things is at hand. Be ye therefore sober, and watching in prayer.

8 [1]But above all things have fervent love among you: [b]for love shall cover the multitude of sins.

9 [1]Be ye [c]harberous one to another, without grudging.

10 [1,d]Let every man as he hath received the gift, minister the same one to another, [2]as good disposers of the manifold grace of God.

11 [1]If any man speak, *let him speak* as the words of God. If any man minister, *let him do it* as of the ability which God ministereth, that God in all things may be glorified through Jesus Christ, to whom is praise and dominion forever, and ever, Amen.

12 [1]Dearly beloved, think it not [2]strange [3]concerning the fiery trial, which is among you to prove you as though some strange thing were come unto you.

13 [1]But rejoice, inasmuch as ye are partakers of Christ's sufferings, that when his glory shall appear, ye may be glad and rejoice.

14 [e,1]If ye be railed upon for the Name of Christ, blessed *are* ye: for the [2]spirit of glory and of God resteth upon you: *which* on their part is evil spoken of, but on your part is glorified.

[c] Rom. 12:13
Heb. 13:2
[d] Rom. 12:6
Phil 2:14
[e] Matt. 10
[f] Prov. 2:31

15 [1]But let none of you suffer as a murderer, or *as* a thief, or an evil doer, or as a busybody in other men's matters.

16 But if *any man suffer* as a Christian, let him not be ashamed: but let him glorify God in this behalf.

17 [1]For the time *is come* that judgment must begin at the house of God. [2]If it first *begin* at us, what shall the end be of them which obey not the Gospel of God?

18 [f]And if the righteous scarcely be saved, where shall the ungodly and the sinner appear?

19 [1]Wherefore let them that suffer according to the will of God, commit their souls *to him* in well doing, as unto a faithful Creator.

5 1 He warneth the Elders not to usurp authority over the Church, 5 willing the younger sort to be willing to be taught, and to be modest, 8 to be sober and watchful to resist the cruel adversary.

1 The [1]Elders which are among you, [2]I beseech which am also an Elder, and a witness of the sufferings of Christ, and also a partaker of the glory that shall be revealed,

---

4:7 [1] He returneth to his purpose, using an argument taken from the circumstance of the time, because the last end is at hand, and therefore we must so much the more diligently watch and pray with true sobriety of mind.

4:8 [1] He commendeth charity of one toward another, because it doth as it were bury a multitude of sins, and therefore preserveth and maintaineth peace and concord: for they that love one another, do easily forgive one another their offense.

4:9 [1] Of all the duties of charity, he commendeth one, namely, which was at that time most necessary, to wit, hospitality, which he will have to be voluntary and most courteous and bountiful.

4:10 [1] He showeth the use of charity, to wit, that every man bestow that gift which he hath received to the profit of his neighbor.

[2] A reason, because that what gift soever we have we have received it of God upon this condition, to be his disposers and stewards.

4:11 [1] He reckoneth up two kinds of these gifts as chief, to wit, the office of teaching in the Church, and the other Ecclesiastical functions, wherein two things specially are to be observed, to wit, that the pure word of God be taught, and whatsoever is done, be referred to the glory of God the Father, in Christ, as to the proper mark.

4:12 [1] Because the cross is joined with the sincere profession of Religion, the Apostle fitly repeateth that which he touched before, warning us not to be troubled at persecutions and afflictions, as a new and strange thing.

[2] As though some new thing had befallen you, which you never thought of before.

[3] The first reason: Because the Lord meaneth not to consume us with this fire (as it were) but to purge us of our dross, and make us perfect.

4:13 [1] Another reason: Because the afflictions of the godly and the wicked differ very much, and chiefly in three points. First, because the godly communicate with Christ in their afflictions, and therefore shall in their time be partakers also of his glory.

4:14 [1] Secondly, because that although the infidels think far other-

wise, who in afflicting the godly, blaspheme God, yet the godly in that they are so railed upon, are honored of God with the true spiritual glory, and their adoption sealed in them by the Spirit of God.

[2] By Spirit he meaneth the gifts of the Spirit.

4:15 [1] The third difference: for the godly are not afflicted for their evil doings, but for righteousness' sake as Christians: whereby it cometh to pass that the cross, seeing it is a testimony unto them of faith and righteousness, ministereth unto them not an occasion of sorrow, but of unspeakable joy: now the Apostle propoundeth the third difference under the form of an exhortation.

4:17 [1] The third reason because the Lord of all the world being especially careful for them of his household, doth therefore chastise them first of all, yet so that he keepeth a measure in his greatest severity: And as he hath always used to do heretofore, so doth he now specially when as he exhibited himself in person to his Church.

[2] Lest the godly should be offended and stumble at that vain shadow of felicity of the wicked, as though God were not the governor of the world, for that the wicked are in good case, and the godly in evil, the Apostle teacheth by an argument of a comparison of them together, that God who spareth not his own, but nurtureth them under the cross, will at length in his time handle the rebellious and wicked far otherwise, whom he hath appointed to utter destruction.

4:19 [1] The conclusion: Seeing the godly are not afflicted by chance, but by the will of God, they ought not to despair, but go forward, notwithstanding in the way of holiness and well doing, commending themselves to God their faithful Creator, that is to say, their Father.

5:1 [1] He describeth peculiarly the office of the Elders, that is to say, of them that have the care of the Church.

[2] He useth a preface touching the circumstance of his own person: to wit, that he as their companion, communeth with them not of matters which he knoweth not, but wherein he is as well experienced as any, and propoundeth unto them no other condition but that which he himself hath sustained before, and doth still take the same pains, and also hath one selfsame hope together with them.

2 [1,2]Feed the [3]flock of God, [4]which dependeth upon you, [5]caring for it not by constraint, but willingly: not for filthy lucre, but of a ready mind:

3 Not as though ye were Lords over *God's* [1]heritage, but that ye may be examples to the flock.

4 [1]And when that chief Shepherd shall appear, ye shall receive an incorruptible crown of glory.

5 [1]Likewise ye younger submit yourselves unto the Elders, and submit yourselves every man, one to another: [a]deck yourselves inwardly in lowliness of mind: [2]for [b]God resisteth the proud, and giveth grace to the humble.

6 Humble [c]yourselves therefore [1]under the mighty hand of God, that he may exalt you in due time.

7 [d]Cast all your care on him: for he careth for you.

8 [1]Be sober, and watch: for [e]your adversary the devil as a roaring lion walketh about, seeking whom

CHAPTER 5
[a] Rom. 12:10
[b] James 4:6
[c] James 4:10
[d] Ps. 55:23
Matt. 6:25
Luke 12:22
[e] Luke 22:31
[f] Rom. 16:16
1 Cor. 16:20
2 Cor. 13:11

he may devour:

9 Whom resist steadfast in the faith, [1]knowing that the same afflictions are accomplished in your [2]brethren which are in the world.

10 [1]And the God of all grace, which hath called us unto his eternal glory by Christ Jesus, after that ye have suffered a little, make you perfect, confirm, strengthen, and establish *you*.

11 To him *be* glory and dominion forever and ever, Amen.

12 [1]By Silvanus a faithful brother unto you, as I suppose, have I written briefly, exhorting and testifying how that this is the true grace of God, wherein ye stand.

13 [1]The Church that is at [2]Babylon elected together with you, saluteth you, and Mark my son.

14 Greet ye one another with the [f]kiss of love. Peace *be* with you all which are in Christ Jesus, Amen.

5:2 [1] The first rule: He that is a shepherd, let him feed the flock.
[2] He saith not, Offer for the quick and dead, and sing patched shreds in a strange tongue, but (Feed.)
[3] The second: Let the shepherd consider, that the flock is not his, but God's.
[4] The third: Let not the shepherds invade other men's flocks, but let them feed that which God hath committed unto them.
[5] Let the shepherds govern the Church with the word and example of godly and unblamable life, not by constraint but willingly, not for filthy lucre, but of a ready mind, not as Lords over God's portion and heritage, but as his ministers.
5:3 [1] Which is the Christian people.
5:4 [1] That the shepherds' minds be not overcome either with the wickedness of men, or their cruelty, he warneth them to cast their eyes continually upon that chief Shepherd, and the crown which is laid up for them in heaven.
5:5 [1] He commendeth many peculiar Christian virtues, and especially modesty: which admonition all of us stand in need of, but especially the younger sort, by reason of the outwardness and pride of that age.
[2] Because pride seemeth to many, to be the way unto the glory of this life, the Apostle witnesseth on the contrary side, that ignominy and shame is the reward of pride, and glory the reward of modesty.

5:6 [1] Because those proud and lofty spirits threaten the modest and humble, the Apostle warneth us to set the power of God against the vanity of proud men, and to hang wholly upon his providence.
5:8 [1] The cruelty of Satan, who seeketh by all means to devour us, is overcome by watchfulness and faith.
5:9 [1] The persecutions which Satan stirreth up are neither new nor proper to any one man, but from old and ancient time common to the whole Church, and therefore we must suffer that patiently wherein we have such and so many fellows of our conflicts and combats.
[2] Amongst your brethren which are dispersed throughout the world.
5:10 [1] He sealeth up as it were with a seal the former exhortation with a solemn prayer, again willing them to ask increase of strength at his hands of whom they had the beginning, and hope to have the accomplishment, to wit, of God the Father in Jesus Christ in whom we are sure of the glory of eternal life.
5:12 [1] Continuance and perseverance in the doctrine of the Apostles, is the only ground and foundation of Christian strength: Now the sum of the Apostles' doctrine, is salvation freely given of God.
5:13 [1] Familiar salutations.
[2] In that famous city of Assyria, where Peter the Apostle of the circumcision then was.

THE SECOND EPISTLE GENERAL OF

PETER

1 *3 Having spoken of the bountifulness of God,   5 and of the virtues of faith.   6 He exhorteth them to holiness of life.   12 And that his counsel may be the more effectual.   14 He showeth that his death is at hand,   16 and that himself did see the power of Christ, which he opened unto them.*

1   Simon ¹Peter a servant and an Apostle of Jesus Christ, to you which have obtained like precious faith with us by the ²righteousness of our God and Savior Jesus Christ.

2   Grace and peace be multiplied to you, ¹through the acknowledging of God, and of Jesus Christ our Lord,

3   ¹According as his ²divine power hath given unto us all things that *pertain* unto ³life and godliness, through the ⁴acknowledging of him that hath called us unto glory and virtue.

4   ¹Whereby most great and precious promises are given unto us, that by them ye should be partakers of the ²divine nature, in that ye flee the corruption, which is in the ³world through ⁴lust.

5   ¹Therefore give even all diligence thereunto: ²join moreover virtue with your faith: and with virtue, knowledge:

6   ¹And with knowledge, temperance: and with temperance, patience: and with patience, godliness:

7   And with godliness, brotherly kindness: and with brotherly kindness, love.

8   ¹For if these things be among you, and abound, they will make you that ye neither shall be idle, nor unfruitful in the acknowledging of our Lord Jesus Christ:

9   For he that hath not these things, is blind, and ¹cannot see far off, and hath forgotten that he was purged from his old sins.

10   ¹Wherefore, brethren, give rather diligence to make your calling and election sure: for if ye do these things, ye shall never fall.

11   For by this means an entering shall be ministered unto you abundantly into the everlasting kingdom of our Lord and Savior Jesus Christ.

12   ¹Wherefore, I will not be negligent to put you always in remembrance of these things, though that ye have knowledge, and be established in the present truth.

1:1 ¹ A salutation wherein he giveth them to understand that he dealeth with them as Christ's ambassador, and otherwise agreeth with them in one selfsame faith which is grounded upon the righteousness of Jesus Christ our God and Savior.

² In that God standing to his promises, showed himself faithful, and therefore just unto us.

1:2 ¹ Faith is the acknowledging of God and Christ, from whence all our blessedness issueth and showed.

1:3 ¹ Christ setteth forth himself to us plainly in the Gospel, and that by his only power, and giveth us all things which are requisite both to eternal life, wherein he hath appointed to glorify us, and also to godliness, in that he doth furnish us with true virtue.

² He speaketh of Christ, whom he maketh God, and the only Savior.

³ Unto salvation.

⁴ This is the sum of true Religion, to be led by Christ to the Father, as it were by the hand.

1:4 ¹ An explication of the former sentence, declaring the causes of so great benefits, to wit, God and his free promise, from whence all these benefits proceed, I say, these most excellent benefits, whereby we are delivered from the corruption of the world, (that is, from the wicked lusts which we carry about us) and are made, after a sort, like unto God himself.

² By the divine nature, he meaneth not the substance of the Godhead, but the partaking of these qualities whereby the image of God is restored in us.

³ In men.

⁴ For lust is the fear of corruption, and hath his fear even in our very bowels and inmost parts.

1:5 ¹ Having laid the foundation (that is, having declared the causes of our salvation and especially of our sanctification) now he beginneth to exhort us to give our minds wholly to the true use of this grace. And he beginneth with faith without which nothing can please God, and he warneth us to have it full fraught with virtue (that is to say) with good and godly manners, being joined with the knowledge of God's will, without which there is neither faith neither any true virtue.

² Supply also, and support or aid.

1:6 ¹ He reckoneth up certain and other principal virtues, whereof some pertain to the first Table of the Law, others to the last.

1:8 ¹ As those fruits do spring from the true knowledge of Christ, so in like sort the knowledge itself is fostered, and groweth by bringing forth such fruits, insomuch that he that is unfruitful did either never know the true light, or hath forgotten the gift of sanctification which he hath received.

1:9 ¹ He that hath not an effectual knowledge of God in him, is blind as touching the kingdom of God, for he cannot see things that are afar off, that is to say, heavenly things.

1:10 ¹ The conclusion: Therefore seeing our calling and election is approved by those fruits, and is confirmed in us, and moreover seeing this is the only way to the everlasting kingdom of Christ, it remaineth that we cast our minds wholly that way.

1:12 ¹ An amplifying of the conclusion joined with a modest excuse, wherein he declareth his love towards them, and foretelleth them of his death, which is at hand.

13 For I think it meet as long as I am in this [1]tabernacle, to stir you up by putting you in remembrance,

14 Seeing I know that the time is at hand that I must lay down this my tabernacle, even as our Lord Jesus Christ hath [a]showed me.

15 [b]I will endeavor therefore always, that ye also may be able to have remembrance of these things after my departing.

16 [c,1]For we followed not deceivable fables, when we opened unto you the power, and coming of our Lord Jesus Christ, but with our eyes we saw his majesty:

17 For he received of God the Father honor and glory, when there came such a voice to him from that excellent Glory, [d]This is my beloved Son, in whom I am well pleased.

18 And this voice we heard when it came from heaven being with him in the holy mount.

19 [1]We have also a most sure word of the Prophets, [2]to the which ye do well that ye take heed, as unto a light that shineth in a dark place, until the [3]day dawns, and the [4]day star arise in your hearts.

20 [c,1]So that ye first know this, that no prophecy of the [2]Scripture is of any [3]private interpretation:

21 For the prophecy came not in old time by the will of man: but [1]holy men of God spake as they were [2]moved by the holy Ghost.

2 *1 He foretelleth them of false teachers,　13 whose wicked sleights and destruction he declareth.　12 He*

CHAPTER 1
[a] John 21:18
[b] 1 Cor. 1:17
[c] 1 Cor. 2:1
[d] Matt. 17:5
[e] 2 Tim. 3:16

CHAPTER 2
[a] Job 4:18
Jude 6
[b] Gen. 7:1
[c] Gen. 19:13,14

compareth them to bruit beasts,　17 and to wells without water,　20 because they seek to withdraw men from God to their old filthiness.

1 But [1]there were false prophets also among the [2]people, even as there shall be false teachers among you: which privily shall bring in damnable heresies, even denying the Lord that hath bought them, and bring upon themselves swift damnation.

2 [1]And many shall follow their destructions, by whom the way of truth shall be evil spoken of.

3 [1]And through covetousness shall they with feigned words make [2]merchandise of you, [3]whose condemnation long since resteth not, and their destruction slumbereth not.

4 For if God spared not the [a]Angels that had sinned, but cast them down into [1]hell, and delivered them into [2]chains of darkness, to be kept unto damnation:

5 Neither hath spared the [1]old world, but saved [b]Noah the eighth *person* a [2]preacher of righteousness, and brought in the Flood upon the world of the ungodly,

6 And [c]turned the cities of Sodom and Gomorrah into ashes, condemned them and overthrew them, and made them an ensample unto them that after should live ungodly,

7 And delivered just Lot vexed with the uncleanly conversation of the wicked:

8 (For he being righteous, and dwelling among them, in [1]seeing and hearing, [2]vexed his righteous soul from day to day with their unlawful deeds.)

1:13 [1] In this body.

1:16 [1] Another amplification taken both of the great certainty and also excellency of this doctrine, as whereof our Lord Jesus Christ the Son of God is author, whose glory the Apostle himself both saw and heard.

1:19 [1] The truth of the Gospel is hereby also manifest, in that it agreeth wholly with the foretellings of the Prophets.

[2] The doctrine of the Apostles doth not shut out the doctrine of the Prophets, for they confirm each other by each other's testimonies, but the Prophets were as candles which gave light unto the blind, until the brightness of the Gospel began to shine.

[3] A more full and open knowledge than was under the shadows of the Law.

[4] That clearer doctrine of the Gospel.

1:20 [1] The Prophets are to be read, but so that we ask of God the gift of interpretation: for he that is the author of the writings of the Prophets, is also the interpreter of them.

[2] He joineth the Scripture and prophecy together to distinguish true prophecies from false.

[3] For all interpretation cometh from God.

1:21 [1] The godly interpreters and messengers.

[2] Inspired of God: and these their motions were in very good order, and not such as were the motions of the profane soothsayers, and foretellers of things to come.

2:1 [1] As in times past there were two kinds of Prophets, the one true, the other false, so Peter fortelleth them that there shall be some true and some false teachers in the Church, insomuch that Christ himself shall be denied by some, who notwithstanding shall call him

redeemer.

[2] Under the Law, while the state and policy of the Jews was yet standing.

2:2 [1] There shall not only be heresies, but also many followers of them.

2:3 [1] Covetousness for the most part is a companion of heresy, and maketh merchandise even of souls.

[2] They will abuse you, and sell you as they sell cattle in a Fair.

[3] A comfort for the godly: God who cast the Angels that fell away from him headlong into the darkness of hell, at length to be judged, and who destroyed the old world with the flood, and preserved Noah the eight person, and who burned Sodom, and saved Lot, will deliver his elect from these errors, and will utterly destroy those unrighteous.

2:4 [1] So the Greeks called the deep dungeon under the earth, which should be appointed to torment the souls of the wicked in.

[2] Bound them with darkness as it were with chains: and by darkness, he meaneth that most miserable state of life, that is full of horror.

2:5 [1] Which was before the Flood: not that God made a new world, but because the world seemed new.

[2] For he ceased not for the space of an hundred and twenty years to warn the wicked both by word and deed, what wrath of God hanged over their heads.

2:8 [1] Which way soever he looked and turned his ears.

[2] He had a troubled soul, and being vehemently grieved, lived a painful life.

9 The Lord ¹knoweth to deliver the godly out of tentation, and to reserve the unjust unto the day of judgment under punishment:

10 ¹And chiefly them that walk after the flesh, in the lust of uncleanness, and despise government, *which are* bold, and stand in their own conceit, and fear not to speak evil of them that are in ²dignity.

11 Whereas the Angels which are greater both in power and might, give not railing judgment against them before the Lord.

12 ¹But these as natural brute beasts, led with sensuality and ²made to be taken, and destroyed, speak evil of those things which they know not, and shall perish through their own ³corruption.

13 And shall receive the wages of unrighteousness, as they which count it pleasure daily to live deliciously. ¹Spots *they are* and blots, delighting themselves in their deceivings, ²in feasting with you.

14 ¹Having eyes full of adultery, and that cannot cease to sin, beguiling unstable souls, they have hearts exercised with covetousness, *they are* the children of curse:

15 Which forsaking the right way, have gone astray following the way of ᵈBalaam, *the son* of Beor, which loved the wages of unrighteousness.

16 But he was rebuked for his iniquity: *for* the dumb beast speaking with man's voice forbade the foolishness of the Prophet.

17 ᵉ˒¹These are ²wells without water, *and* clouds carried about with a tempest, to whom the ³black darkness is reserved forever.

18 For in speaking ¹swelling words of vanity, they ²beguile with wantonness through the lusts of the

Marginal references:
ᵈ Num. 22:23
ᵉ Jude 12
ᶠ John 8:34
   Rom. 6:20
ᵍ Matt. 12:45
   Heb. 6:4
ʰ Prov. 16:11

flesh them that were ³clean escaped from them which are wrapped in error,

19 Promising unto them liberty, and are themselves the ᶠservants of corruption: for of whomsoever a man is overcome, even unto the same is he in bondage.

20 ᵍ˒¹ For if they, after they have escaped from the filthiness of the world, through the acknowledging of the Lord, and of the Savior Jesus Christ, are yet tangled again therein, and overcome, the latter end is worse with them than the beginning.

21 For it had been better for them not to have acknowledged the way of righteousness, than after they have acknowledged it, to turn from the holy commandment given unto them.

22 But it is come unto them according to the true proverb, ʰThe dog is returned to his own vomit: and the sow that was washed, to the wallowing in the mire.

3 *1 He showeth that he writeth the same things again. 2 Because they must often be stirred up, 3 because dangers hang over their heads through certain mockers. 8 Therefore he warneth the godly that they do not after the judgment of the flesh, 12 appoint the day of the Lord, 14 but that they think it always at hand, 15 in which doctrine he showeth that Paul agreeth with him.*

1 This ¹second Epistle I now write unto you, beloved, wherewith I stir up, and warn your pure minds,

2 To call to remembrance the words, which were told before of the holy Prophets, and also the commandment of us the Apostles of the Lord and Savior.

2:9 ¹ Hath been long practiced in saving and delivering the righteous.

2:10 ¹ He goeth to another sort of corrupt men, which notwithstanding are within the bosom of the Church, which are wickedly given, and do seditiously speak evil of the authority of Magistrates, (which the Angels themselves that minister before God, do not dispraise) A true and lively description of the Romish Clergy (as they call it.)

² Princes and great men, be they never so high in authority.

2:12 ¹ A lively painting out of the same persons, wherein they are compared to beasts, which are made to snare themselves to destruction, while they give themselves to fill their bellies: For there is no greater ignorance than is in these men, although they most impudently find fault with those things which they know not: and it shall come to pass that they shall destroy themselves as beasts, with those pleasures wherewith they are delighted, and dishonor and defile the company of the godly.

² Made to this end, to be a prey to others: so do these men willingly cast themselves into Satan's snares.

³ Their own wicked manners shall bring them to destruction.

2:13 ¹ Or, little rocks.

² When as by being amongst the Christians in the holy banquets which the Church keepeth, they would seem by that means to be true members of the Church, yet they are indeed but blots on the

Church.

2:14 ¹ He condemneth those men, as showing even in their behavior and countenance an immeasurable lust, as making merchandise of the souls of light persons, as men exercised in all the crafts of covetousness, to be short, as men that sell themselves for money to curse the Sons of God after Balaam's example, whom the dumb beast reproved.

2:17 ¹ Another note whereby they may be well known what manner of men they are, because they have inwardly nothing but either utterly vain or very hurtful, although they make a show of some great goodness: but they shall not escape unpunished for it, because under pretence of false liberty, they draw men into most miserable slavery of sin.

² Which boast of knowledge, and have nothing in them.

³ Most gross darkness.

2:18 ¹ They deceive men with vain and swelling words.

² They take them as fishes are taken with the hook.

³ Unfeignedly and indeed clean departed from Idolatry.

2:20 ¹ It were better never to have known the way of righteousness, than to turn back from it to the old filthiness: and men that do so are compared to dogs and swine.

3:1 ¹ The remedy against those wicked enemies both of true doctrine and holiness, is to be sought for by the continual meditation of the writings of the Prophets and Apostles.

3 *,1This first understand, that there shall come in the last days, 2mockers, which will walk after their lusts,

4 1And say, Where is the promise of his coming? for since the Fathers died, all things continue alike from the beginning of the creation.

5 1For this they willingly know not, that the heavens were of old, and the 2earth that was of the water, and by the water, by the word of God.

6 1Wherefore the world that then was, perished, overflowed with the 2water.

7 1But the heavens and earth, which are now, are kept by the same word in store, and reserved unto fire against the day of condemnation, and of the destruction of ungodly men.

8 1Dearly beloved, be not ignorant of this one thing, that one day is with the Lord, bas a thousand years, and a thousand years as one day.

9 1The Lord of that promise is not slack (as some men count slackness) 2but is patient toward us, and cwould have no man to perish, but would all men to come to repentance.

10 1But the day dof the Lord will come as a thief in the night, in the which the heavens shall pass away with a 2noise, and the elements shall melt with heat, and the earth with the works that are therein shall be burnt up.

11 1Seeing therefore that all these things must be dissolved, what manner persons ought ye to be in holy conversation and godliness,

12 Looking for, and 1hasting unto the coming of that day of God, by the which the heavens being on fire, shall be dissolved, and the elements shall melt with heat?

13 But we look for enew heavens, and a new earth, according to his promise, 1wherein dwelleth righteousness.

14 Wherefore, beloved, seeing that ye look for such things, be diligent that ye may be found of him in 1peace, without spot and blameless.

15 fAnd suppose that the long suffering of our Lord is salvation, 1even as our beloved brother Paul according to the wisdom given unto him wrote to you.

16 As one that in all his Epistles speaketh of these things: 1among the 2which, some things are hard to be understood, which they that are unlearned and unstable, wrest, as they do also other Scriptures unto their own destruction.

17 Ye therefore beloved, seeing ye know these things before, beware, lest ye be also plucked away with the error of the wicked, and fall from your own steadfastness.

18 But grow in grace, and in the knowledge of our Lord and Savior Jesus Christ: to him be glory both now and for evermore. Amen.

CHAPTER 3
a 1 Tim. 4:1
1 Tim. 3:1
Jude 18
b Ps. 90:4
c Ezek. 8:32
Ezek. 33:11
1 Tim. 2:4
d Matt. 24:44
1 Thess. 5:2
Rev. 3:3
Rev. 16:15
e Isa. 65:17
Isa. 66:22
Rev. 21:1
f Rom. 2:4

3:3 1 He voucheth the second coming of Christ against the Epicureans by name.

2 Monstrous men, who will seem wise by their contempt of God, and wicked boldness.

3:4 1 The reason which these mockers pretend because the course of nature is all one as it was from the beginning: therefore the world is from everlasting, and shall be forever.

3:5 1 He setteth against them the creation of heaven and earth by the word of God, which these men are willingly ignorant of.

2 Which appeared when the waters were gathered together into one place.

3:6 1 Secondly, he setteth against them the universal flood which was the destruction, as it were of the whole world.

2 For the waters returning into their former place this world, that is to say, this beauty of the earth which we see, and all living creatures which live upon the earth perished.

3:7 1 Thirdly, he pronounceth that it shall not be harder for God to burn heaven and earth with fire in that day which is appointed for the destruction of the wicked, (which thing he will also do) than it was for him in times past to make them with his only word and afterward to overwhelm them with water.

3:8 1 The taking away of an objection: in that he seemeth to defer this judgment a long season, in respect of us it is true, but not before God with whom there is no time either long or short.

3:9 1 The Lord will surely come, because he hath promised: and that neither sooner nor later than he hath promised.

2 A reason why the latter day cometh not out of hand, because God doth patiently wait till the elect are brought to repentance, that none of them may perish.

3:10 1 A very short description of the least distinction of the world, but in such sort as nothing could be spoken more gravely.

2 With the violence as it were of a hissing storm.

3:11 1 An exhortation to purity of life, setting before us that horrible judgment of God both to bridle our wantonness, and also to comfort us, so that we be found watching and ready to meet him at his coming.

3:12 1 He requireth patience of us, yet such patience as is not slothful.

3:13 1 In which heavens.

3:14 1 That you may try to your profit, how gentle and peaceable he is.

3:15 1 Paul's Epistles are allowed by the express testimony of Peter.

3:16 1There be certain of these things obscure and dark, whereof the unlearned take occasion to overthrow some men that stand not fast, wrestling the testimonies of the Scripture to their own destruction. But this is the remedy against such deceit, to labor that we may daily more and more grow up and increase in the knowledge of Christ.

2 That is to say, among the which things: for he disputeth not here whether Paul's Epistles be plain or dark, but saith, that amongst those things which Paul hath written of his Epistles, and Peter himself in these two of his own, there are some things which cannot be easily understood, and therefore are of some drawn to their own destruction: and this he saith to make us more attentive and diligent, and not remove us from the reading of holy things, for to what end should they have written vain speculations?

THE FIRST EPISTLE GENERAL OF

JOHN

1

1 He testifieth that he bringeth the eternal word, wherein is life, 5 and light. 9 God will be merciful unto the faithful, if groaning under the burden of their sins, they learn to flee unto his mercy.

1 That [1]which was from the beginning, which we have [2]heard, which we have seen with these our eyes, which we have looked upon, and these hands of ours have handled of that [3]word of life,

2 (For that life was made manifest, and we have seen it, and bear witness, and [1]show unto you that eternal life, which was with the Father, and was made manifest unto us.)

3 That *I say*, which we have seen and heard declare we unto you, [1]that ye may also have fellowship with us, and that our fellowship also may be with the Father and with his Son Jesus Christ.

4 And these things write I unto you, that your joy may be full.

5 [1]This then is the message, which we have heard of him, and declare unto you, that God [a]is light, and in him is no darkness.

CHAPTER 1
[a] John 8:12
[b] Heb. 9:28
1 Pet. 1:19
Rev. 1:5
[c] 1 Kings 8:46
2 Chron. 6:36
Prov. 20:9

6 If we say that we have fellowship with him, and walk in darkness, we lie, and do not truly.

7 But if we walk in the [1]light as he is in the light, we have fellowship one with another, [2]and the [b]blood of Jesus Christ his Son cleanseth us from all sin.

8 [c,1] If we say that we have no sin, we [2]deceive ourselves, and [3]truth is not in us.

9 [1]If we acknowledge our sins, he is [2]faithful and just, to [3]forgive us our sins, and to cleanse us from all unrighteousness.

10 [1]If we say, we have not sinned, we make him [2]a liar, and his [3]word is not in us.

2

1 He declareth that Christ is our mediator and advocate, 3 and showeth that the knowledge of God consisteth in holiness of life, 12 which appertaineth to all sorts, 14 that depend on Christ alone: 15 Then having exhorteth them to contemn the world, 18 he giveth warning that Antichrists be avoided, 24 and that the known truth be stood unto.

1 My [1]little children, these things write I unto you, that ye sin not: and if any man sin, we have an

---

1:1 [1] He beginneth with the description of the person of Christ, whom he maketh one and not two: and him both God from everlasting (for he was with the Father from the beginning, and is that eternal life) and also made true man, whom John himself and his companions, both heard and beheld, and handled.

[2] I heard him speak, I saw him myself with mine eyes, I handled with mine hands him that is very God, being made very man, and not I alone, but others also that were with me.

[3] That same everlasting word, by whom all things are made, and in whom only there is life.

1:2 [1] Being sent by him: and that doctrine is rightly said to be showed, for no man could so much as have thought of it, if it had not been thus showed.

1:3 [1] The use of this doctrine is this, that all of us being coupled and joined together with Christ by faith, might become the Sons of God, in which thing only consisteth all happiness.

1:5 [1] Now he entereth into a question, whereby we may understand that we are joined together with Christ, to wit, if we be governed with his light, which is perceived by the ordering of our life. And thus he reasoneth, God is in himself most pure light, therefore he agreeth with them, which are lightsome, but with them which are of the darksome he hath no fellowship.

1:7 [1] God is said to be light of his own nature, and to be in light, that is to say, in that everlasting infinite blessedness: and we are said to walk in light, in that the beams of that light do shine unto us in the world.

[2] A digression or going from the matter he is in with, to the remission of sins: for this our sanctification which walk in the light, is a testimony of our joining and knitting together, with Christ: but because this our light is very dark, we must needs obtain another benefit in Christ,

to wit, that our sins may be forgiven us being sprinkled with his blood: and this in conclusion is the prop and stay of our salvation.

1:8 [1] There is none but needeth this benefit, because there is none that is not a sinner.

[2] This place doth fully refute that perfectness, and works of supererogation which the Papists dream of.

[3] So then John speaketh not thus for modesty's sake, as some say, but because it is so indeed.

1:9 [1] Therefore the beginning of salvation is to acknowledge our wickedness, and to require pardon from him who freely forgiveth all sins, because he hath promised so to do, and he is faithful and just.

[2] So then our salvation hangeth upon the free promise of God, who because he is faithful and just, will perform that which he hath promised.

[3] Where are then our merits? for this is our true felicity.

1:10 [1] A rehearsal of the former sentence: wherein he condemned all of sin without exception, insomuch that if any man persuade himself otherwise, he doth as much as in him lieth, make the word of God himself vain and to no purpose, yea he maketh God a liar, for to what end either in times past needed sacrifices or now Christ and the Gospel, if we be not sinners?

[2] They do not only deceive themselves, but also are blasphemous against God.

[3] His doctrine shall have no place in us, that is, in our hearts.

2:1 [1] It followeth not hereof that we must give our wicked nature the bridle, or sin so much the more freely, because our sins are cleansed away by the blood of Christ but we must rather so much more diligently resist sin. And yet we must not despair because of our weakness, for we have an Advocate and a purger, Christ Jesus the just, and therefore acceptable unto his father.

²Advocate with the Father, Jesus Christ, the Just.

2 And he is the ¹reconciliation for our sins: and not for ours only, but also for *the sins* of the ²whole world.

3 ¹And hereby we are sure that we ²know him, ³if we keep his commandments.

4 ¹He that saith, I know him, and keepeth not his commandments, is a liar, and the truth is not in him.

5 ¹But he that keepeth his word, in him is the ²love of God perfect indeed: hereby we know that we are in ³him.

6 ¹He that saith he remaineth in him, ought even so to walk as he hath walked.

7 ¹Brethren, I write no new commandment unto you, but an old commandment, which ye have had from the beginning: this old commandment is that word, which ye have heard from the beginning.

8 ¹Again, a new commandment I write unto you, that ²which is true in him: and also in you: for the darkness is past, and that true light now shineth.

9 ¹He that saith that he is in that light, and hateth his brother, is in darkness, until this time.

10 ᵃHe that loveth his brother, abideth in that light, and there is no occasion of evil in him.

11 But he that hateth his brother, is in darkness, and walketh in darkness, and knoweth not whither he goeth, because that darkness hath blinded his eyes.

12 ¹Little children, ²I write unto you, because your sins are forgiven you for his ³Name's sake.

13 ¹I write unto you, fathers, because ye have known him that is from the beginning. ²I write unto you, young men, because ye have overcome that wicked one. ³I write unto you, little children, because ye have known the Father.

14 ¹I have written unto you fathers, because ye have known him that is from the beginning. I have written unto you, young men, because ye are strong, and the word of God abideth in you, and ye have overcome that wicked one.

15 ¹Love not this ²world, neither the things that are in this world. If any man love this world, the ³love of the Father is not in him.

16 For all that is in this world, (*as* the lust of the flesh, the lust of the eyes, and the pride of life) is not

---

² In that he nameth Christ he shutteth forth all other.

2:2 ¹ Reconciliation and intercession go together, to give us to understand that he is both advocate and high Priest.

² For men of all sorts, of all ages and all places, so that this benefit belongeth not to the Jews only, of whom he speaketh, as appeareth 1 John 2:7, but also to other nations.

2:3 ¹ He returneth to the testimony of our conjunction with God, to wit, to sanctification, declaring what it is to walk in the light, to wit, to keep God's commandments whereby it followeth that holiness doth not consist in those things which men have devised, neither in a vain profession of the Gospel.

² This must be understood of such a knowledge, as hath faith with it, and not of a common knowledge.

³ For the tree is known by the fruit.

2:4 ¹ Holiness, that is, a life ordered according to the prescript of God's commandments how weak soever they be, is of necessity joined with faith, that is, with the true knowledge of the Father in the Son.

2:5 ¹ He that keepeth God's commandments loveth God indeed. He that loveth God, is in God, or is joined together with God. Therefore he that keepeth his commandments, is in him.

² Wherewith we love God.

³ He meaneth our conjunction with Christ.

2:6 ¹ He that is one with Christ must needs live his life, that is, must walk in his steps.

2:7 ¹ The Apostle going about to expound the commandment of charity one toward another, telleth first, that when he urgeth holiness bringeth no new trade of life (as they use to do which devise traditions, one after another) but putteth them in mind of the same Law which God gave in the beginning, to wit, by Moses, at that time that God began to give Laws to his people.

2:8 ¹ He addeth that the doctrine indeed is old, but it is now after a sort new both in respect of Christ, and also of us: in whom he through the Gospel, engraveth his Law effectually, not in tables of stone, but in our minds.

² Which thing (to wit, that the doctrine is new of which I write unto you) is true in him and in you.

2:9 ¹ Now he cometh to the second Table, that is, to charity one towards another, and denieth that that man hath true light in him, or is indeed regenerate and the son of God, which hateth his brother: and such an one wandereth miserably in darkness, brag he of never so great knowledge of God, for that wittingly and willingly he casteth himself headlong into hell.

2:12 ¹ He returneth again from sanctification to remission of sins, because that free reconciliation in Christ is the ground of our salvation, whereupon afterwards sanctification must be built as upon a foundation.

² Therefore I write unto you, because you are of their number whom God hath reconciled to himself.

³ For his own sake: And in that he nameth Christ, he shutteth out all others, whether they be in heaven or earth.

2:13 ¹ He showeth that this doctrine agreeth to all ages, and first of all speaking to old men, he showeth that Christ and his doctrine are passing ancient, and therefore they be delighted with old things, nothing ought to be more acceptable unto them.

² He advertiseth young men, if they be desirous to show their strength that they have a most glorious combat set here before them, to wit, Satan the worst enemies, who must be overcome: willing them to be as sure of the victory as if they had already gotten it.

³ Finally, he showeth to children, that true Father, from whom they have to look for all good things, is set forth unto them in the Gospel.

2:14 ¹ He addeth afterward in like order, as many exhortations, as if he should say, Remember your fathers: as I wrote even now, that the everlasting Son of God is revealed to us. Remember ye young men, that that strength whereby I said that you put Satan to flight, is given you by the word of God, which dwelleth in you.

2:15 ¹ The world which is full of wicked desires, lusts or pleasures, and pride, is utterly hated of our heavenly Father. Therefore the Father and the world cannot be loved together: and this admonition is very necessary for green and flourishing youth.

² He speaketh of the world, as it agreeth not with the will of God, for otherwise God is said to love the world with an infinite love, John 3:16, that is to say, those whom he chose out of the world.

³ Wherewith the Father is loved.

of the Father, but is of this world.

17 [1]And this world passeth away, and the lust thereof: but he that fulfilleth the will of God, abideth ever.

18 [1,2]Little children, [3]it is the last time, [4]and as ye have heard that Antichrist shall come, even now there are many Antichrists: whereby we know that it is the last time.

19 [1]They went out from us, but they were not of us: for if they had been of us, [2]they should have continued with us. [3]But this cometh to pass, that it might appear, that they are not all of us.

20 [1]But ye have an [2]ointment from that [3]Holy one, and know all things.

21 [1]I have not written unto you, because ye know not the truth: but because ye know it, and that no lie is of the truth.

22 [1]Who is a liar, but he that denieth that Jesus is [2]that Christ? the same is that Antichrist that denieth the Father and the Son.

23 [1]Whosoever denieth the Son, the same hath not the Father.

24 [1]Let therefore abide in you that same which ye have heard from the beginning. If that which ye have heard from the beginning, shall remain in you, ye shall also continue in the Son, and in the Father.

25 And this is the promise that he hath promised us, even that eternal life.

26 [1]These things have I written unto you, concerning them that deceive you.

27 But that [1]anointing which ye received of him, dwelleth in you: and ye [2]need not that any man teach you: but as the same [3]anointing teacheth you of all things, and it is true and is not lying, and as it taught you, ye shall abide in him.

28 [1]And now, little children, abide in him, that when he shall appear, we may be bold, and not be ashamed before him, at his coming.

29 [1]If ye know that he is righteous, know ye that he which doeth righteously, is born of him.

3 *1 Setting down the inestimable glory of this that we are God's sons, 7 he showeth that newness of life must be testifieth by good works, whereof charity is a manifest token. 19 Of faith, 22 and praying unto God.*

1 Behold, [1,2]what love the Father hath given to

2:17 [1] He showeth how much better it is to obey the Father's will, than the lusts of the world, by both their natures and unlike event.
2:18 [1] Now he turneth himself to little children, which notwithstanding are well instructed in the sum of religion, and willeth them by divers reasons to shake off slothfulness, which is too too familiar with that age.

[2] He useth this word (little) not because he speaketh to children, but to allure them the more by using such sweet words.

[3] First, because the last time is at hand, so that the matter suffereth no delay.

[4] Secondly because Antichrists, that is, such as fall from God, are already come, even as they heard that they should come. And it was very requisite to warn that unheedy and wariless age of that danger.
2:19 [1] A digression against certain offenses and stumbling blocks, whereat that rude age especially might stumble and be shaken. Therefore that they should not be terrified with the soul falling back of certain, first he maketh plain unto them, that although such as fall from God and his religion, had place in the Church, yet they were never of the Church, because the Church is the company of the elect which cannot perish, and therefore cannot fall from Christ.

[2] So then the elect can never fall from grace.

[3] Secondly, he showeth that these things fall out to the profit of the Church, that hypocrites may be plainly known.
2:20 [1] Thirdly, he comforteth them to make them stand fast, insomuch as they are anointed by the holy Ghost with the true knowledge of salvation.

[2] The grace of the holy Ghost, and this is a borrowed kind of speech taken from the anointings used in the Law.

[3] From Christ who is peculiarly called holy.
2:21 [1] The taking away of an objection. He wrote not these things as to men which are ignorant of religion, but rather as to them which do well know the truth, yet so far forth that they are able to discern truth from falsehood.
2:22 [1] He showeth now plainly the false doctrine of the Antichrists, to wit, that either they fight against the person of Christ, or his office or

both together, and at once. And they that do so do in vain boast and brag of God, for that in denying the Son the Father also is denied.

[2] Is the true Messiah.
2:23 [1] They then are deceived themselves, and also do deceive others, which say that the Turks and other infidels worship the same God that we do.
2:24 [1] The whole preaching of the Prophets and Apostles is contrary to that doctrine: Therefore it is utterly to be cast away and this wholly to be holden and kept, which leadeth us to seek eternal life in the free promise, that is to say, in Christ alone, who is given to us of the Father.
2:26 [1] The same Spirit which endueth the elect with the knowledge of the truth, and sanctifieth them, giveth them therewithal the gift of perseverance, to continue to the end.
2:27 [1] The Spirit which you have received of Christ, and which hath led you into all truth.

[2] You are not ignorant of these things, and therefore I teach them not as things that were never heard of, but call them to your remembrance as things which you do know.

[3] He commendeth both the doctrine which they had embraced, and also highly praiseth their faith and the diligence of such as taught them, yet so, that he taketh nothing from the honor due to the holy Ghost.
2:28 [1] The conclusion both of the whole exhortation, and also of the former treatise.
2:29 [1] A passing over to the treatise following, which tendeth to the same purpose, but yet is more ample, and handleth the same matter after another order: for before he taught us to go up from the effects to the cause, and in this that followeth, he goeth down from the causes to the effects. And this is the sum of the argument: God is the fountain of all righteousness: and therefore they that give themselves to righteousness, are known to be born of him, because they resemble God the Father.
3:1 [1] He beginneth to declare this agreement between the Father and the Son at the highest cause, to wit, at that free love of God towards us, wherewith he so loveth us, that he also adopteth us to be his children.

[2] What a gift of how great love.

us, that we should be [3]called the sons of God: [4]For this cause this world knoweth you not, because it knoweth not him.

2 [1]Dearly beloved, now are we the sons of God, but yet it is not made manifest what we shall be: and we know that when he shall be made manifest: we shall be [2]like him: for we shall see him [3]as he is.

3 [1]And every man that hath this hope in him purgeth himself, even [2]as he is pure.

4 [1]Whosoever [2]committeth sin, transgresseth also the Law: for [3]sin is the transgression of the Law.

5 [1]And ye know that he was made manifest, that he might [a]take away our sins, and in him is no sin.

6 Whosoever abideth in him, sinneth not: whosoever [1]sinneth, hath not seen him, neither hath known him.

7 [1]Little children, let no man deceive you, he that doeth righteousness, is righteous, as he is righteous.

8 [1]He that [b]committeth sin, is of the [2]devil: for the devil [3]sinneth from the [4]beginning: for this purpose was made manifest that Son of God, that he might

CHAPTER 3
[a] Isa. 53:6,9
2 Pet. 2:22,24
[b] John 8:44
[c] John 13:34
John 15:12
[d] Gen. 4:8
[e] 1 John 2:10
Lev. 9:17

loose the works of the devil.

9 Whosoever is born of God sinneth not: for his [1]seed remaineth in him, neither can he sin, because he is born of God.

10 [1]In this are the children of God known, and the children of the devil: whosoever doeth not righteousness, is not of God, [2]neither he that loveth not his brother.

11 [1]For this is the message that ye heard from the beginning, that [c]we should love one another,

12 [1]Not as [d,2]Cain *which* was of that wicked one, and slew his brother: [3]and wherefore slew he him? because his own works were evil, and his brother's good.

13 Marvel not my brethren, though this world hate you.

14 [1]We know that we are [2]translated from death unto life, because we love the brethren: [e]he that loveth not *his* brother, abideth in death.

15 [1]Whosoever hateth his brother, is a manslayer: and ye know that no manslayer hath eternal life abiding in him.

---

[3] That we should be the sons of God, and so that all the world may perceive we are so.

[4] Before he declareth this adoption, he saith two things: the one, that this so great a dignity is not to be esteemed, according to the judgment of the flesh, because it is unknown to the world, for the world knoweth not God the Father himself.

3:2 [1] The other: This dignity is not fully made manifest to ourselves, much less to strangers, but we are sure of the accomplishment of it, insomuch that we shall be like to the Son of God himself, and shall enjoy his sight indeed, such as he is now: but yet notwithstanding this is deferred until his next coming.

[2] Like, but not equal.

[3] For now we see as in a glass, 1 Cor. 13:12.

3:3 [1] Now he describeth this adoption, (the glory whereof as yet consisteth in hope) by the effect, to wit, because that whosoever is made the Son of God, endeavoreth to resemble the Father in purity.

[2] This word signifieth a likeness, but not in equality.

3:4 [1] The rule of this purity can from no whence else be taken but from the Law of God, the transgression whereof is that which is called sin.

[2] Giveth not himself to pureness.

[3] A short definition of sin.

3:5 [1] An argument taken from the material cause of our salvation: Christ in himself is most pure, and he came to take away our sins, by sanctifying us with the holy Ghost. Therefore, whosoever is truly partaker of Christ doth not give himself to sin: and so contrariwise he that giveth himself to sin knoweth not Christ.

3:6 [1] He is said to sin, that giveth not himself to pureness, and in him sin reigneth, but sin is said to dwell in the faithful, and not to reign in them.

3:7 [1] Another argument of things coupled together: He that liveth justly, is just, and resembleth Christ that is just, and by that is known to be the son of God.

3:8 [1] An argument taken of contraries: the devil is the author of sin, and therefore he is of the devil, or is ruled by the inspiration of the devil that serve sin: and if he be the devil's son, then is he not God's son: for the devil and God are so contrary the one to the other,

that even the Son of God was sent to destroy the works of the devil. Therefore on the contrary side, whosoever resists sin, is the Son of God, being born again of his spirit as of new seed, insomuch that of necessity he is now delivered from the slavery of sin.

[2] Resembleth the devil, as the child doth the father, and is governed by his spirit.

[3] He saith not sinned, but sinneth, for he did nothing else but sin.

[4] From the very beginning of the world.

3:9 [1] The holy Ghost is so called of the effect he worketh, because by his virtue and mighty working, as it were by seed, we are made new men.

3:10 [1] The conclusion, by a wicked life they are known which are governed by the spirit of the Devil, and by a pure life, which are God's children.

[2] He beginneth to commend charity towards the brethren, as another mark of the Sons of God.

3:11 [1] The first reason, taken of the authority of God, which giveth the commandment.

3:12 [1] An amplification, taken of the contrary example of Cain, which slew his brother.

[2] He bringeth forth a very fit and very old example, wherein we may behold both the nature of the sons of God, and of the sons of the devil, and what state and condition remaineth for us in this world: and what shall be the end of both at length.

[3] A short digression: Let us not marvel that we are hated by the world for doing our duty, for such was the condition of Abel who was a just person: and who would not rather be like him than Cain?

3:14 [1] The second reason: Because charity is a testimony that we are translated from death to life: and therefore hatred towards the brethren is a testimony of death, and whosoever nourished it, doth as it were foster death in his bosom.

[2] Love is a token that we are translated from death to life, for as such as by the effects the cause is known.

3:15 [1] A confirmation: Whosoever is a murderer, is in eternal death, who so hateth his brother, is a murderer, therefore he is in death. And thereupon followeth the contrary. He that loveth his brother, hath passed to life, for indeed we are born dead.

16 *f,1*Hereby have we perceived love, that he laid down his life for us: therefore we ought also to lay down *our* lives for the brethren.

17 *g,1*And whosoever hath this *²*world's good, and seeth his brother have need, and *³*shutteth up his compassion from him, how dwelleth the love of God in him?

18 *¹*My little children, let us not love in word, neither in tongue *only*, but in deed and in truth.

19 *¹*For thereby we know that we are of the truth, *²*and shall before him assure our hearts.

20 For *¹*if our hearts condemn us, God is greater than our heart, and knoweth all things.

21 *¹*Beloved, if our heart condemn us not, then have we boldness toward God.

22 *h,1*And whatsoever we ask, we receive of him, because we keep his commandments, and do those things which are pleasing in his sight.

23 *¹*This is then his commandment, that we believe in the Name of his Son Jesus Christ, and love one another, as he gave commandment.

24 *j*For he that keepeth his commandments, dwelleth in him, and he in him: and hereby we know that he abideth in us, *even* by that *¹*Spirit which he hath given us.

f John 15:13
Eph. 5:2
g Luke 3:11
b Matt. 21:22
John 15:7
John 16:25
1 John 5:14
i John 6:23
John 17:3
j John 13:34
John 15:10

CHAPTER 4
d John 8:47

4

1 Having spoken somewhat touching the trying of spirits: 4 For some speak after the world,   5 and some after God.   7 He returneth to charity,   11, 19 and by the example of God he exhorteth to brotherly love.

1 Dearly *¹*beloved, believe not every *²*spirit, but try the spirits whether they are of God: for many false Prophets are gone out into the world.

2 *¹*Hereby shall ye know the Spirit of God, *²*Every spirit which confesseth that *³*Jesus Christ is come in the *⁴*flesh is of God.

3 And every spirit that confesseth not that Jesus Christ is come in the flesh, is not of God: but this is the *spirit* of Antichrist, of whom ye have heard, how that he should come, and now already he is in this world.

4 *¹*Little children, ye are of God, and have overcome them: for greater is he that is in you, than that that is in this world.

5 *¹*They are of this world, therefore spake they of this world, and this world heareth them.

6 *¹*We are of God, *ᵈ*he that knoweth God, heareth us: he that is not of God heareth us not. Hereby know we the *²*Spirit of truth, and the spirit of error.

7 *¹*Beloved, let us love one another: *²*for love

3:16 *¹* Now he showeth how far Christian charity extendeth, even so far, that according to the example of Christ, every man forget himself, to provide for and help his brethren.

3:17 *¹* He reasoneth by comparison: For if we are bound even to give our life for our neighbors, how much more are we bound to help our brothers' necessity with our goods and substance?

² Wherewith this life is sustained.

³ Openeth not his heart to him, nor helpeth him willingly and cheerfully.

3:18 *¹* Christian charity standeth not in words, but in deed, and proceedeth from a sincere affection.

3:19 *¹* He commendeth charity by a triple effect: for first of all, by it we know that we are indeed the sons of God, as he showeth before.

² Therefore it cometh that we have a quiet conscience, as on the contrary side he that thinketh that he hath God for a judge, because he is guilty to himself, either he is never or else very rare quiet: for God hath a far quicker sight than we, and judgeth more severely.

3:20 *¹* If an evil conscience convinceth us, much more ought the judgments of God contemn us, who knoweth our hearts better than we ourselves do.

3:21 *¹* A third effect also riseth out of the former, that in these miseries we are sure to be heard, because we are the sons of God, as we understand by the grace of sanctification which is proper to the elect.

3:22 *¹* The conclusion: That faith in Christ, and love one towards another, are things joined together, and therefore the outward testimonies of sanctification must and do answer that inward testimony of the Spirit given unto us.

3:24 *¹* He meaneth the Spirit of sanctification whereby we are born anew, and live unto God.

4:1 *¹* Taking occasion by the name of the Spirit, lest love and charity should be separated from the worship of God, which chiefly dependeth of his true knowledge, he returneth to that which he spake in the second Chapter touching the taking heed of Antichrists. And he will

have us here to take heed of two things, the one is, that seeing there be many false prophets, we do not lightly give credit to every man: the other is, that because many men teach false things, we should not therefore believe any. We must then observe a mean, that we may be able to discern the Spirit of God, which are altogether to be followed from impure spirits which are to be eschewed.

² This is spoken by the figure Metonymy, and it is as if he had said, Believe not everyone that saith that he hath a gift of the holy Ghost to do the office of a Prophet.

4:2 *¹* He giveth a certain and perpetual rule to know the doctrine of Antichrist by, to wit, if either the divine or human nature of Christ, or the true uniting of them together be denied: or if the least jot that may be, be derogate from his office who is our only King, Prophet, and everlasting high Priest.

² He speaketh simply of the doctrine, and not of the person.

³ The true Messiah.

⁴ Is true man.

4:4 *¹* He comforteth the elect with a most sure hope of victory: but yet so, that he teacheth them that they fight not with their own virtue, but with the virtue and power of God.

4:5 *¹* He bringeth a reason: why the world receiveth these teachers more willingly than the true: to wit, because they breathe out nothing but that which is worldly: which is another note also to know the doctrine of Antichrist by.

4:6 *¹* He testifieth unto them that his doctrine and the doctrine of his fellows, is the assured word of God, which of necessity we have boldly to set against all the mouths of the whole world, and thereby discern the truth from falsehood.

² True Prophets against whom are set false Prophets, that is, such as err themselves, and lead others into error.

4:7 *¹* He returneth to the commending of brotherly love and charity.

² The first reason: Because it is a very divine thing: and therefore very meet for the sons of God: so that whosoever is void of it, cannot be said to know God aright.

cometh of God, and everyone that loveth is born of God, and knoweth God.

8　He that loveth not, knoweth not God, [1]for God is [2]love.

9　[b]Herein was that love of God made manifest amongst us, because God sent that his only begotten Son into this world, that we might live through him.

10　Herein is that love, not that we loved God, but that he loved us, and sent his Son *to be* a reconciliation for our sins.

11　[1]Beloved, if God so loved us, we ought also to love one another.

12　[c,1]No man hath seen God at any time. If we love one another, God dwelleth in us, and his love is [2]perfect in us.

13　Hereby know we, that we dwell in him, and he in us: because he hath given us of his Spirit.

14　[1]And we have seen, and do testify, that the Father sent the Son *to be* the Savior of the world.

15　Whosoever [1]confesseth that Jesus is the Son of God, in him dwelleth God, and he in God.

16　And we have known, and believed the love that God hath in us, [1]God is love, and he that dwelleth in love, dwelleth in God, and God in him.

17　[1]Herein is that love perfect in us, that we should have boldness in the day of judgment: for [2]as he is, even so are we in this world.

18　There is no [1]fear in love, but perfect love casteth out fear: for fear hath painfulness: and he that feareth, is not perfect in love.

19　[1]We love him, because he loved us first.

20　[1]If any man say, I love God, and hate his brother, he is a liar: [2]for how can he that loveth not his brother whom he hath seen, love God whom he hath not seen?

21　[d,1]And this commandment have we of him, that he that loveth God, should love his brother also.

[b] John 3:16
[c] John 1:18
1 Tim. 6:16
[d] John 13:34
John 15:12

5 *1 He showeth that brotherly love and faith are things inseparable: 10 And that there is no faith towards God, but by believing in Christ: 14 Hence proceedeth calling upon God with assurance: 16 and also that our prayers be available for our brethren.*

1　Whosoever [1]believeth that Jesus is that [2]Christ, is born of God: and everyone that loveth him, which begat, loveth [3]him also which is begotten of him.

2　[1]In this we know that we love the children of God, when we love God, and keep his [2]commandments.

4:8 [1] A confirmation: For it is the nature of God to love men, whereof we have a most manifest proof above all others: in that that of his only free and infinite goodwill towards us his enemies, he delivered unto death not a common man, but his own Son, yea, his only begotten Son, to the end that we being reconciled through his blood, might be made partakers of his everlasting glory.

[2] In that he called God, Love he saith more than if he had said that he loveth us infinitely.

4:11 [1] Another reason by comparison: if God so loved us, shall not we his children love one another.

4:12 [1] A third reason: Because God is invisible, therefore by this effect of his Spirit, to wit, by charity, he is understood, yea, and to be not out of us, but joined with us, and in us, in whom he is so effectually working.

[2] Is surely in us, in deed and in truth.

4:14 [1] He underlayeth this charity with another foundation, to wit, faith in Jesus, which joineth us indeed with him, even as charity witnesseth that we are joined with him. Furthermore he testifieth of Christ, as who had seen him with his eyes.

4:15 [1] With such a confession as cometh from true faith and is accompanied with love, so that there be an agreement of all things.

4:16 [1] A fourth reason: God is the fountain and wellspring of charity, yea, charity itself: therefore whosoever abideth in it, hath God with him.

4:17 [1] Again (as a little before) he commendeth love, for that seeing that by our agreement with God in this thing, we have a certain testimony of our adoption, it cometh thereby to pass, that without fear we look for that latter day of judgment, so that trembling and that torment of conscience is cast out by this love.

[2] This signifieth all likeness, not equality.

4:18 [1] If we understand by love, that we are in God, and God in us, that we are sons, and that we know God, and that everlasting life is in us: he concludeth aright that we may well gather peace and quietness thereby.

4:19 [1] Lest any man should think that that peace of conscience proceedeth from our love as from the cause, he goeth back to the fountain, to wit, to the free love, wherewith God loveth us although we deserved and do deserve his wrath. And hereof springeth another double charity, which both are tokens and witnesses of that first, to wit, that, wherewith we love God who loved us first, and then for his sake our neighbors also.

4:20 [1] As he showed that the love of our neighbor cannot be separate from the love wherewith God loveth us, because this last engendereth the other: so he denieth that the other kind of love wherewith we love God, can be separate from the love of our neighbor: whereof it followeth, that they lie impudently which say they worship God, and yet regard not their neighbor.

[2] The first reason taken of comparison, why we cannot hate our neighbor and love God, to wit, because that he that cannot love his brother, whom he seeth, how can he love God whom he seeth not?

4:21 [1] A second reason, why God cannot be hated and our neighbor loved, because the selfsame Lawmaker commanded both to love him and our neighbor.

5:1 [1] He goeth on forward in the same argument, showing how both those loves come into us from the love wherewith God loveth us, to wit, by Jesus our Mediator laid hold on by faith, in whom we are made the children of God, and do love the Father of whom we are begotten and also our brethren which are begotten with us.

[2] Is the true Messiah.

[3] By one he meaneth all the faithful.

5:2 [1] The love of our neighbor doth so hang upon the love wherewith we love God, that this last must needs go before the first, whereof it followeth, that that is not to be called love when men agree together to do evil, neither that, when as in loving our neighbors, we respect not God's commandments.

[2] There is no love where there is no true doctrine.

3 [1]For this is the love of God, that we keep his commandments: [2]and his [a]commandments are not [3]burdenous.

4 [1]For all that is born of God, overcometh this world: [2]and this is that victory that [3]hath overcome this world *even* our [4]faith.

5 [b,1]Who is it that overcometh this world, but he which believeth that Jesus is that Son of God?

6 [1]This is that Jesus Christ that came by water and blood: [2]not by water only, but by water and blood: and it is that [3]Spirit that beareth witness: for that Spirit is truth.

7 For there are three, which bear record in heaven, the Father, the [1]Word, and the holy Ghost: and these three are [2]one.

8 And there are three, which bear record in the earth, the Spirit, and the Water and the Blood: and these three agree in one.

9 [1]If we receive the witness of men, the witness of God is greater: for [2]this is the witness of God, which he testified of his Son.

CHAPTER 5
[a] Matt. 11:30
[b] 1 Cor.15:57
[c] John 3:16
[d] 1 John 3:22

10 [c,1]He that believeth in that Son of God, hath the witness in himself: he that believeth not God, hath made him a liar, because he believed not the record, that God witnessed of that his Son.

11 [1]And this is that record, *to wit*, that God hath given unto us eternal life, and this life is in that his Son.

12 He that hath that Son, hath that life: and he that hath not that Son of God, hath not that life.

13 [1]These things have I written unto you, that believe in the name of that Son of God, that ye may know that ye have eternal life, and that ye may believe in the Name of that Son of God.

14 [1]And this is that assurance that we have in him, [d]that if we ask anything according to his will, he heareth us.

15 And if we know that he heareth us, whatsoever we ask, we know that we have the petitions, that we have desired of him.

5:3 [1] The reason: for to love God is to keep his commandments, which being so, and seeing that both the loves are commanded of one and the selfsame lawmaker (as he taught before) it followeth also that we do not love our neighbor, when we break God's commandments.

[2] Because experience teacheth us that there is no ability in our flesh, neither yet will to perform God's commandments, therefore lest the Apostle should seem, by so often putting them in mind of the keeping of the commandments of God, to require things that are impossible, he pronounceth that the commandments of God are not in such sort grievous or burdensome, that we can be oppressed with the burden of them.

[3] To them that are regenerate, that is to say, born anew, which are led by the Spirit of God, and are through grace delivered from the curse of the Law.

5:4 [1] A reason: Because by regeneration we have gotten strength to overcome the world, that is to say, whatsoever striveth against the commandments of God.

[2] He declareth what that strength is, to wit, Faith.

[3] He useth the time that is past to give us to understanding, that although we be in the battle, yet undoubtedly we shall be conquerors, and are most certain of the victory.

[4] Which is the instrumental cause, and as a mean and hand whereby we lay hold on him who indeed doth perform this, that is, hath and doth overcome the world, Even Christ Jesus.

5:5 [1] Moreover he declareth two things, the one what true faith is, to wit, that which resteth upon Jesus Christ the Son of God alone: whereupon followeth the other, to wit, that this strength is not proper to faith, but by faith as an instrument is drawn from Jesus Christ the Son of God.

5:6 [1] He proveth the excellency of Christ, in whom only all things are given us by six witnesses, three heavenly, and three earthly, which wholly and fully agree together. The heavenly witnesses are: the Father who sent the Son, the word itself which became flesh, and the holy Ghost. The earthly witnesses are, water, (that is, our sanctification) blood, (that is, our justification) the Spirit, (that is, acknowledge of God the Father in Christ by faith through the testimony of the holy Ghost.)

[2] He warneth us not to separate water from blood, (that is, sanctification from justification, or righteousness begun, from righteousness imputed) for we stand not upon sanctification but so far forth as it is a witness of Christ's righteousness imputed unto us: and although this imputation of Christ's righteousness be never separated from sanctification, yet it is only the matter of our salvation.

[3] Our spirit, which is the third witness, testifies that the holy Ghost is truth; that is to say, that that is true which he telleth us, to wit, that we are the sons of God.

5:7 [1] See John 8:13, 14.

[2] Agree in one.

5:9 [1] He showeth by an Argument of comparison, of what great weight the heavenly testimony is, that the Father hath given of the Son, unto whom agreeth both the Son himself and the holy Ghost.

[2] I conclude this aright: for that testimony which I said is given in heaven, cometh from God, who so setteth forth his Son.

5:10 [1] He proveth the sureness of the earthly witnesses by every man's conscience, having that testimony in itself, which conscience he saith cannot be deceived, because it consenteth the heavenly testimony, which the Father giveth of the Son: For otherwise the Father must needs be a liar, if the conscience, which accordeth and assenteth to the Father should lie.

5:11 [1] Now at length he showeth what this testimony is, that is confirmed with so many witnesses: to wit, that life or everlasting felicity, is the mere, and only gift of God, which is in the Son, and proceedeth from him unto us, which by faith are joined with him, so that without him life is nowhere to be found.

5:13 [1] The conclusion of the Epistle wherein he showeth first of all, that even they which already believe, do stand in deed of this doctrine, to the end that they may grow more and more in faith, that is to say, to the end that they may be daily more and more certified of their salvation in Christ through faith.

5:14 [1] Because we do not yet in effect obtain that which we hope for, the Apostle joineth invocation or prayer with faith, which he will have to proceed from faith, and moreover to be conceived in such sort, that nothing be asked but that which is agreeable to the will of God: and such prayers cannot be vain.

16 ¹If any man see his brother sin a sin that is not unto death, let him ²ask, and he shall give him life for them that sin not unto death. ʿThere is a sin unto death, I say not that thou shouldest pray for it.

17 ¹All unrighteousness is sin, but there is a sin not unto death.

18 ¹We know that whosoever is born of God, sinneth not: but he that is begotten of God keepeth himself, and that wicked one toucheth him not.

ᶜ Matt. 12:31
Mark 3:29
ᶠ Luke 24:45

19 ¹We know that we are of God, and this whole world lieth in wickedness.

20 But we know that that Son of God is ᶠcome, and hath given us a mind to know him, which is true, and we are in him that is true, *that is,* in that his Son Jesus Christ, the same is that very ¹God, and that eternal life.

21 ¹Little children, keep yourselves from idols, Amen.

5:16 ¹ We have to make prayers not only for ourselves, but also for our brethren which do sin, that their sins be not unto them, to death: and yet he excepteth that sin, which is never forgiven, or the sin against the holy Ghost, that is to say, an universal and willful falling away from the known truth of the Gospel.

² This is as much as if he said, Let him desire the Lord to forgive him, and he will forgive him being so desired.

5:17 ¹ The taking away of an objection: Indeed all iniquity is comprehended under the name of sin, but yet we must not despair therefore, because every sin is not deadly, and without hope of remedy.

5:18 ¹ A reason why not all, nay rather why no sin is mortal to some: to wit, because they be born of God, that is to say, made the sons of

God in Christ, and being endued with his Spirit, they do not serve sin, neither are deadly wounded of Satan.

5:19 ¹ Every man must particularly apply to himself the general promises, that we may certainly persuade ourselves, that whereas all the world is by nature lost, we are freely made the sons of God, by the sending of Jesus Christ his Son unto us, of whom we are lightened with the knowledge of the true God, and everlasting life.

5:20 ¹ The divinity of Christ is most plainly proved by this place.

5:21 ¹ He expresseth a plain precept of taking heed of idols: which he setteth against the only true God, that with this seal as it were he might seal up all the former doctrine.

THE SECOND EPISTLE OF

JOHN

1 *This Epistle is written to a woman of great renown, 4 who brought up her children in the fear of God: 6 he exhorteth her to continue in Christian charity, 7 that she accompany not with Antichrists, 10 but avoid them.*

CHAPTER 1
a John 15:12
b Rom. 16:17

1 The Elder to the [1]elect [2]Lady, and her children, [3]whom I love in the truth: and not I only, but also all that have known the truth,

2 For the truth's sake which dwelleth in us, and shall be with us forever:

3 Grace be with you, mercy and peace from God the Father, and from the Lord Jesus Christ the Son of the Father, with [1]truth and love.

4 [1]I rejoiced greatly, that I found of thy children walking in [2]truth, as we have received a commandment of the Father.

5 And now beseech I thee, Lady, (not as writing a new commandment unto thee, but the same which we had from the beginning) that we [a]love one another.

6 And this is that love that we should walk after his commandments. This commandment is, that as ye have heard from the beginning, ye should walk in it.

7 [1]For many deceivers are entered into this world, which confess not that Jesus Christ is come in the flesh. He that is such one, is a deceiver and an Antichrist.

8 [1,2]Look to yourselves, that we lose not the things, which we have done, but that we may receive a full reward.

9 Whosoever transgresseth, and abideth not in the doctrine of Christ, hath not God. He that continueth in the doctrine of Christ, he hath both the Father and the Son.

10 [1]If there come any unto you, and bring not this doctrine, [b]receive him not to house, neither bid him Godspeed.

11 For he that biddeth him Godspeed, is partaker of his evil deeds. Although I had many things to write unto you, yet would I not *write* with paper and ink: but I trust to come unto you, and speak mouth to mouth, that our joy may be full.

12 The sons of thine elect sister greet thee, Amen.

1:1 [1] This is no proper name, but to be taken as the word soundeth, that is to say to the worthy and noble Lady.

[2] Excellent and honorable Dame.

[3] The bond of Christian conjunction or linking together, is the true and constant profession of the truth.

1:3 [1] With true knowledge, which hath always love joined with it, and following it.

1:4 [1] This true profession consisteth both in love one toward another which the Lord hath commanded, and also especially in wholesome and sound doctrine, which also is delivered unto us: for the commandment of God is a sound and sure foundation both of the rule of manners and of doctrine, and these cannot be separated the one from the other.

[2] According as the truth directeth them.

1:7 [1] Antichrists fighting against the person and office of Christ, were already crept into the Church in the time of the Apostles.

1:8 [1] He that maketh shipwreck of doctrine, loseth all.

[2] Beware and take good heed.

1:10 [1] We ought to have nothing to do with them that defend perverse doctrine.

THE THIRD EPISTLE OF

JOHN

1 *He commendeth Gaius for hospitality,   9 and reprehendeth Diotrephes for vainglory: 10 he exhorteth Gaius to continue in well doing: 12 and in the end commendeth Demetrius.*

1   The [1]Elder unto the beloved Gaius whom I love in the truth.

2   Beloved, I wish chiefly that thou prosperedst and faredst well as thy soul prospereth.

3   For I rejoiceth greatly when the brethren came and testified of the truth that is in thee, how thou walkest in the truth.

4   I have no greater joy than [1]these, *that is*, to hear that my sons walk in verity.

5   Beloved, thou doest [1]faithfully, whatsoever thou doest to the brethren, and to strangers,

6   Which bore witness of thy love before the Churches, Whom if thou [1]bringest on their journey as it seemeth according to God, thou shalt do well,

7   Because that for his Name's sake they went forth, and took nothing of the Gentiles.

8   We therefore ought to receive such, that we might be [1]helpers to the truth.

9   [1]I wrote unto the Church, but Diotrephes which loveth to have the preeminence among them, receiveth us not.

10   Wherefore if I come, I will call to your remembrance his deeds which he doeth, prattling against us with malicious words, and not therewith content, neither he himself receiveth the brethren, but forbiddeth them that would, and thrusteth them out of the Church.

11   Beloved, follow not that which is evil, but that which is good: he that doeth well is of God: but he that doeth evil, hath not [1]seen God.

12   Demetrius hath good report of all men, and of the truth itself: yea, and we ourselves bear record, and ye know that our record is true.

13   I have many things to write: but I will not with ink and pen write unto thee:

14   For I trust I shall shortly see thee, and we shall speak mouth to mouth. Peace *be* with thee. The friends salute thee. Greet thy friends by name.

1:1 [1] An example of a Christian gratulation.
1:4 [1] Than these joys.
1:5 [1] As becometh a believer and a Christian.
1:6 [1] He commendeth to Gaius either those selfsame men whom he had entertained before, returning now again to him about the affairs of the Church, or else some other which had like business.
1:8 [1] That we ourselves may help somewhat to the preaching of the truth.
1:9 [1] Ambition and covetousness, two pestilent plagues (especially in them which have any Ecclesiastical function) are condemned in Diotrephes' person.
1:11 [1] Hath not known God.

THE GENERAL EPISTLE OF

JUDE

1

3 He warneth the godly to take heed of such men, 4 that make the grace of God a cloak for their wantonness: 5 and that they shall not escape unpunished, for the contempt of that grace, 6, 7 he proveth by three examples: 14 and allegeth the prophecy of Enoch: 20 Finally he showeth the godly a means to overthrow all the snares of those deceivers.

CHAPTER 1
a 2 Pet. 2:1
b Num. 14:37
c 2 Pet. 2:4
d Gen. 19:24
e Gen. 4:8
f Num. 22:21
2 Pet. 2:15
g Num. 16:1

1 Jude a servant of Jesus Christ, and ¹brother of James, to them which are called and sanctified ²of God the Father, and ³reserved to Jesus Christ:

2 Mercy unto you, and peace and love be multiplied.

3 ¹Beloved, when I gave all diligence to write unto you of the ²common salvation, it was needful for me to write unto you, to exhort you, that ye should earnestly ³contend for *the maintenance* of the faith, which was ⁴once given unto the Saints.

4 ¹For there are certain men crept in, which were before of old ordained to this condemnation: ²ungodly men *they are*, which turn the grace of our God into wantonness, and *ᵈ*deny God the only Lord, and our Lord Jesus Christ.

5 ¹I will therefore put you in remembrance, forasmuch as ye once knew this, how that the Lord, after that he had delivered the people out of Egypt, *ᵇ*destroyed them afterward which believed not.

6 ¹The *ᶜ*Angels also which kept not their first estate, but left their own habitation, he hath reserved in everlasting chains under darkness unto the judgment of the great day.

7 As *ᵈ*Sodom and Gomorrah, and the cities about them, which in like manner as they did, ¹committed fornication, and followed ²strange flesh, are set forth for an example, and suffer the vengeance of eternal fire.

8 Likewise notwithstanding these ¹sleepers also defile the flesh, ²and despise ³government, and speak evil of them that are in authority.

9 ¹Yet Michael the Archangel, when he strove against the devil, and disputed about the body of Moses, durst not blame him with cursed speaking, but said, The Lord rebuke thee.

10 ¹But these speak evil of those things, which they know not: and whatsoever things they know naturally as beasts, which are without reason, in those things they corrupt themselves.

11 ¹Woe *be* unto them: for they have followed the way ᶜof Cain, and are cast away by the deceit ᶠof Balaam's wages, and perish in the gainsaying ᵍof Korah.

12 ¹These are rocks in your ²feasts of charity,

1:1 ¹ This is put to make a difference between him and Judas Iscariot.

² By God the Father.

³ Set apart by the everlasting counsel of God, to be delivered to Christ to be kept.

1:3 ¹ The end and mark whereat he shooteth in this Epistle is that he confirmeth the godly against certain wicked men, both in wholesome doctrine and good manners.

² Of those things that pertain to the salvation of all of us.

³ That ye should defend the faith by all the might you can, both by true doctrine and good example of life.

⁴ Which was once so given, that it may never be changed.

1:4 ¹ It is by God's providence and not by chance, that many wicked men creep into the Church.

² He condemneth this first in them, that they take a pretense or occasion to wax wanton, by the grace of God: which cannot be, but the chief empire of Christ must be abrogated, in that such men give up themselves to Satan: as at this time the sect of the Anabaptists doth, which they call Libertines.

1:5 ¹ He setteth forth the horrible punishment of them which have abuseth the grace of God to follow their own lusts.

1:6 ¹ The fall of the Angels was most sincerely punished, how much more then will the Lord punish wicked and faithless men?

1:7 ¹ Following the steps of Sodom and Gomorrah.

² Thus he covertly setteth forth their horrible and monstrous lusts.

1:8 ¹ Which are so blockish and void of reason as if all their senses and wits were in a most dead sleep.

² Another most pernicious doctrine of theirs, in that they take away the authority of Magistrates, and speak evil of them, as at this day the Anabaptists do.

³ It is a greater matter to despise government, than the governors, that is to say, the matter itself, than the persons.

1:9 ¹ An argument of comparison, Michael one of the chiefest Angels, was content to deliver Satan, although as most cursed enemy, to the judgment of God to be punished: and these perverse men are not ashamed to speak evil of the powers which are ordained of God.

1:10 ¹ The conclusion. These men are in a double fault, to wit, both for their rash folly in condemning some, and for their impudent and shameless contempt of that knowledge, which when they had gotten, yet notwithstanding they lived as brute beasts, serving their bellies.

1:11 ¹ He foretelleth their destruction, because they resemble or show forth Cain's shameless malice, Balaam's filthy covetousness, and to be short, Korah's seditious and ambitious head.

1:12 ¹ He rebuketh most sharply with many other notes and marks, both their dishonesty or filthiness, and their sauciness, but especially their vain bravery of words, and most vain pride, joining herewithal a most grave and heavy threatening out of a most ancient prophecy of Enoch touching the judgment to come.

² The feasts of charity were certain banquets, which the brethren that were members of the Church kept altogether, as Tertullian setteth them forth in his Apology, Chap. 3:9.

when they feast with you, without [3]all fear, feeding themselves: [h]clouds *they are* without water, carried about of winds, corrupt trees *and* without fruit, twice dead, *and* plucked up by the roots.

13 *They are* the raging waves of the sea, foaming out their own shames: *they are* wandering stars, to whom is reserved the [1]blackness of darkness forever.

14 And Enoch also the seventh from Adam, prophesied of such, saying, [i]Behold, the Lord [1]cometh with thousands of his Saints,

15 To give judgment against all men, and to rebuke all the ungodly among them of all their wicked deeds, which they have ungodly committed, and of all their cruel speakings, which wicked sinners have spoken against him.

16 These are murmurers, complainers, walking after their own lusts: [j]whose mouths speak proud things, having men's persons in admiration, because of advantage.

17 [1]But, ye beloved, remember the words which were spoken before of the Apostles of our Lord

[h] 2 Pet. 2:17
[i] Rev. 1:7
[j] Ps. 17:10
[k] 1 Tim. 4:1
2 Tim. 3:1
2 Pet. 3:3

Jesus Christ:

18 How that they told you that there should be mockers [k]in the last time, which should walk after their own ungodly lusts.

19 [1]These are they that separate themselves from others, natural, having not the Spirit.

20 But, ye beloved, edify yourselves in your most holy faith, praying in the holy Ghost.

21 And keep yourselves in the love of God, looking for the mercy of our Lord Jesus Christ, unto eternal life.

22 [1]And have compassion of some, in putting difference:

23 And others save with [1]fear, pulling them out of the fire, and hate even that [2]garment which is spotted by the flesh.

24 [1]Now unto him that is able to keep you that ye fall not, and to present you faultless before the presence of his glory with joy,

25 *That is*, to God only wise, our Savior *be* glory, and majesty, and dominion, and power, both now and forever, Amen.

1:12 [3] Impudently, without all reverence either to God or man.
1:13 [1] Most gross darkness.
1:14 [1] The present time for the time to come.
1:17 [1] The rising up of such monsters was spoken of before, that we should not be troubled at the newness of the matter.
1:19 [1] It is the property of Antichrists to separate themselves from the godly, because they are not governed by the Spirit of God: and contrariwise it is the property of Christians to edify one another through godly prayers both in faith and also in love until the mercy of Christ appears to their full salvation.
1:22 [1] Among them which wander and go astray, the godly have to

use this choice, that they handle some of them gently, and that others some being even in the very flame, they endeavor to save with severe and sharp instruction of the present danger: yet so, that they do in such sort abhor the wicked and dishonest, that they eschew even the least contagion that may be.
1:23 [1] By fearing them, and holding them back with godly severity.
    [2] An amplification taken from the forbidden things of the Law which did defile.
1:24 [1] He commendeth them to the grace of God, declaring sufficiently that it is God only that can give us that constancy which he requireth of us.

THE

REVELATION

OF SAINT JOHN THE APOSTLE

1 *2 He declareth what kind of doctrine is here handled, 8 even his that is the beginning and ending. 12 Then the mystery of the seven Candlesticks and stars, 20 is expounded.*

1 The [1,2]Revelation of [3]Jesus Christ, which God gave unto him, to show unto his servants things which must shortly be done: which he sent, and showed by his Angel unto his servant John,

2 Who bare record of the word of God, and of the testimony of Jesus Christ, and of all things that he saw.

3 Blessed *is he* that readeth, and they that hear the words of this prophecy, and keep those things which are written therein: for the time is at hand.

4 [1]John to the seven Churches which are in Asia, Grace *be* with you, and peace [2]from him, [3]Which [a]is,

CHAPTER 1
[a] Exod. 3:14
[b] Ps. 89:38
[c] 1 Cor. 15:21
Col. 1:18
[d] Heb. 9:14
1 Pet. 1:29
1 John 1:9
[e] 1 Pet. 2:5
[f] Isa. 3:14
Matt. 24:30
Jude 14
[g] Rev. 21:6
Rev. 22:13

and Which was, and Which is to come, and from [4]the [5]seven Spirits which are before his Throne,

5 And from Jesus Christ [1]which is that [b]faithful witness, *and* [c]that first begotten of the dead, and that Prince of the Kings of the earth, unto him that loved us, and washed us from our sins in his [d]blood,

6 And made us [e]Kings and Priests unto God even his Father, to him, *I say, be* glory, and dominion for evermore, Amen.

7 Behold, he cometh with [f]clouds, and every [1]eye shall see him: yea, even they which pierced him through: and all kindreds of the earth shall wail before him, Even so, Amen.

8 [1]I [g]am [2]Alpha and Omega, the beginning and the ending, saith the Lord, Which is, and Which

---

1:1 [1] This Chapter hath two principal parts, the title or inscription, which standeth instead of an exordium: and a narration going before the whole prophecy of this book: The inscription is double, general and particular. The general containeth the kind of prophecy, the author, and, matter, instruments, and manner of communicating the same, in the first verse: the most religious faithfulness of the Apostle as public witness, verse 2. And the use of communicating the same taken from the promise of God, and from the circumstance of the time, the third verse.

[2] An opening of a secret and hid thing.

[3] Which the Son opened to us out of his Father's bosom by Angels.

1:4 [1] This is the particular or singular inscription wherein salutation is written unto certain Churches by name, which represent the Church Catholic: and the certainty and the truth of the same is declared, from the Author thereof, unto the eighth verse.

[2] That is, from God the Father, eternal, immortal, immutable: whose unchangeableness S. John declareth by a form of speech which is undeclined. For there is no incongruity in this place, where, of necessity the words must be attempted unto the mysteries, not the mysteries corrupted or impaired by the word.

[3] By these three times, Is, Was and shall be, is signified this word Jehovah, which is the proper name of God.

[4] That is, from the holy Ghost which proceedeth from the Father and the Son. This Spirit is one in person according to his subsistence: but in communication of his virtue, and in demonstration of his divine works in those seven Churches, doth so perfectly manifest himself, as if there were many Spirits, every one perfectly working in his own Church, wherefore after Rev. 5:6, they are called the seven horns and seven eyes of the Lamb, as much to say, as his most absolute power and wisdom: and Rev. 3:1. Christ is said to have there seven Spirits of God, and Rev. 4:5, it is said, that seven lamps do burn before his throne, which also are those seven Spirits of God. That this place ought to be so understood, it is thus proved. For first grace and peace

is asked by prayer of this Spirit, which is a divine work, and an action incommunicable, in respect of the most high Deity. Secondly, he is placed between the Father and the Son, as set in the same degree of dignity and operation with them. Besides he is before the throne as of the same substance with the Father and the Son: as the seven eyes and seven horns of the Lamb. Moreover, these spirits are never said to adore God, as all other things are. Finally, that is the power whereby the Lamb opened the book, and loosed the seven seals thereof when none could be found amongst all creatures by whom the book might be opened, Rev. 5. Of these things long ago, Master John Luide of Oxford wrote learnedly unto me. Now the holy Ghost is set in order of words before Christ, because there was in that which followeth, a long process of speech to be used concerning Christ.

[5] These are the seven spirits, which are, afterward, Rev. 5:6, called the horns and eyes of the Lamb, and are now made as a guard waiting upon God.

1:5 [1] A most ample and grave commendation of Christ, first from his offices the Priesthood and kingdoms, secondly from his benefits, as his love toward us, and washing us with his blood, in this verse, and communication of his kingdom and Priesthood with us: thirdly from his eternal glory and power, which always is to be celebrated of us, verse 6. Finally from the accomplishment of all things once to be effected by him, at his second coming, what time he shall openly destroy the wicked, and comfort the godly in the truth, verse 7.

1:7 [1] All men.

1:8 [1] A confirmation of the salutation aforegoing, taken from the words of God himself: in which he avoucheth his operation in every single creature, the immutable eternity that is in himself, and his omnipotence in all things: and concludeth in the unity of his own essence, that Trinity of persons, which was before spoken of.

[2] I am he before whom there is nothing, yea, by whom everything that is made, was made and shall remain though all they should perish.

was, and Which is to come, *even* the Almighty.

9　[1]I John even your brother and companion in tribulation, and in the kingdom and patience of Jesus Christ, was in the [2]Isle called Patmos, for the word of God, and for the witnessing of Jesus Christ.

10　And I was *ravished* in [1]spirit on the [2]Lord's day, and heard behind me a great voice, as it had been of a trumpet,

11　Saying, I am Alpha and Omega, that first and that last: and that which thou seest write in a book, and send it unto the seven Churches which are in Asia, unto Ephesus, and unto Smyrna, and unto Pergamos, and unto Thyatira, and unto Sardis, and unto Philadelphia, and unto Laodicea.

12　[1]Then I turned back to [2]see the voice that spake with me: [3]and when I was turned, I saw seven golden candlesticks,

13　And in the midst of the seven candlesticks, one like unto the son of man, clothed with a garment down to the feet, and girded about the paps with a golden girdle.

14　His head and hairs *were* white as white wool, and as snow, and his eyes *were* as a flame of fire,

15　And his feet like unto fine brass burning as in a

[*h* Isa. 41:4]

furnace: and his voice as the sound of many waters.

16　And he had in his right hand seven stars: and out of his mouth went a sharp two edged sword, and his face *shone* as the sun shineth in his strength.

17　[1]And when I saw him, I fell at his feet as dead: [2]then he laid his right hand upon me, saying unto me, Fear not: [3]I am that [*h*]first and that last,

18　And am alive, but I was dead: and behold, I am alive for evermore, Amen: and I have the keys of hell and of death.

19　[1]Write these things which thou hast seen, and the things which are, and the things which shall come hereafter.

20　[1]The mystery of the seven stars which thou sawest in my right hand, and the seven golden candlesticks, *is this*, The seven stars are the [2]Angels of the seven Churches: and the seven candlesticks which thou sawest, are the seven Churches.

2　*1 John is commanded to write those things which the Lord knew necessary to the Churches of Ephesus.　8 Of the Smyrnians,　12 of Pergamos,　18 and of Thyatira, as that they keep those things which they received of the Apostles.*

1　[1]Unto the Angel of the Church of Ephesus

1:9 [1] The narration opening the way to the declaring of the authority and calling of Saint John the Evangelist in this singular Revelation, and to procure faith, and credit unto this prophecy. This is the second part of this Chapter consisting of a proposition and an exposition. The proposition showeth, first who was called unto this Revelation, in what place, and how occupied, verse 9. Then at what time and by what means, namely, by the spirit and the word, and that on the Lord's day, which day ever since the resurrection of Christ, was consecrated for Christians unto the religion of the Sabbath: that is to say, to be a day of rest, verse 10. Thirdly, who is the author that calleth him, and what is the sum of his calling.

[2] Patmos is one of the isles of Sporas whither John was banished as some write.

1:10 [1] This is that holy ravishment expressed, wherewith the prophets were ravished, and being as it were carried out of the world were conversant with God, and so Ezekiel saith often that he was carried from place to place of the Lord's Spirit and that the Spirit of the Lord fell upon him.

[2] He calleth it the Lord's day, which Paul calleth the first day of the week, 1 Cor. 16:2.

1:12 [1] The exposition, declaring the third and last point of the proposition (for the other points are evident of themselves) wherein is spoken first of the author of his calling unto verse 17. Secondly of the calling itself unto the end of the Chap. And first of all the occasion is noted in this verse, in that S. John turned himself towards the vision: after is set down the description of the author in the verses following, Rev. 1:13–16.

[2] To see him whose voice I had heard.

[3] The description of the Author, which is Christ: by the candlesticks that standeth about him, that is the Churches that stand before him, and depend upon his direction, in this verse: by his properties, that he is one furnished with wisdom and dexterity to the achieving of great things, verse 13, and ancient gravity and most excellent sight of the eye, verse 14, with strength invincible and with a mighty word, verse 15. By his operations, that he ruleth the ministry of his servants in the Church, giveth the effect thereunto by the sword of his word,

and enlightening all things with his countenance, doth most mightily provide for everyone by his divine providence, verse 16.

1:17 [1] A religious fear that goeth before the calling of the Saints, and their full confirmation to take upon them the vocation of God.

[2] A divine confirmation is this calling partly by sign and partly by word of power.

[3] A most elegant description of this calling contained in three things, which are necessary unto a just vocation: first the authority of him that calleth, for that he is the beginning and end of all things, in this verse, for that he is eternal and omnipotent, verse 18. Secondly, the sum of this prophetical calling, and revelation, verse 19. Lastly a declaration of those persons unto whom this prophecy is by the commandment of God directed in the description thereof, verse 20.

1:19 [1] The sum of this prophecy, that the Apostle must write whatsoever he should see, adding nothing, nor taking away anything, as verse 2. Hereof there are two parts: one is a narration of those things which are, that is, which then were at that time contained in the second and third Chapters, the other part is of those things which were to come, contained in the rest of this book.

1:20 [1] That is, the things which [were] mystical, signified by the particulars of the vision beforegoing.

[2] By the Angels he meaneth the Ministers of the Church.

2:1 [1] The former part of this book is comprised in a narration of those things which then were as S. John taught us, Rev. 1:19, it belongeth wholly to instruction and in these next two Chapters, containeth seven places according to the number and condition of those Churches which were named before, Rev. 1:11, figured verse 12, distributed most aptly into their Pastors and flocks, verse 20, which verse of that Chap. is as it were a passage unto the first part. Every one of the seven places hath three principal members, an Exordium taken from the person of the Author: a Proposition, in which is praise and commendation of that which is good, reprehension of that which is evil: an instruction containing either an exhortation alone, or withal a dissuasion opposite unto it, and a conclusion stirring unto attention by divine promises. And this first place is unto the Pastors of the Church of Ephesus.

write, [2]These things saith he that holdeth the seven stars in his right hand, and walketh in the midst of the seven golden candlesticks.

2 [1]I know thy works, and thy labor, and thy patience, and how thou canst not bear with them which are evil, and hast examined them which say they are Apostles, and are not, and hast found them liars.

3 And thou wast burdened, and hast patience, and for my Name's sake hast labored, and hast not fainted.

4 Nevertheless, I have *somewhat* [1]against thee, because thou hast left thy first love.

5 Remember therefore from whence thou art fallen, and repent and do the first works: or else I will come against thee shortly, and will remove thy candlestick out of his place, except thou amend.

6 But this thou hast that thou hatest the works of the Nicolaitans, which I also hate.

7 [1]Let him that hath an ear hear what the Spirit saith unto the Churches: To him that overcometh, will I give to eat of the tree of life which is in [2]the midst of the [3]Paradise of God.

8 ¶ [1]And unto the Angel of the Church of the [2]Smyrnians write, These things saith he that is first and last, which was dead and is alive.

9 [1]I know thy works and tribulation, and poverty (but thou art rich) and *I know* the blasphemy of them, which say they are Jews, and are not, but *are* the Synagogue of Satan.

10 Fear none of those things, which thou shalt

CHAPTER 2
[a] Num. 24:14
Num. 25:1

suffer: behold, it shall come to pass, that the devil shall cast some of you into prison, that ye may be tried, and ye shall have [1]tribulation ten days: be thou faithful unto the death, and I will give thee the crown of life.

11 [1]Let him that hath an ear hear what the Spirit saith unto the Churches. He that overcometh shall not be hurt [2]of the second death.

12 [1]And to the Angel of the Church, which is at [2]Pergamos write, Thus saith he which hath that sharp sword with two edges.

13 [1]I know thy works, and where thou dwellest, *even* where Satan's throne is, and thou keepest my Name, and hast not denied my faith, even in [2]those days when Antipas my faithful martyr was slain among you, where Satan dwelleth.

14 But I have a few things against thee, because thou hast there them that maintain the doctrine of [a]Balaam, which taught Balak to put a stumbling block before the children of Israel, that they should [1]eat of things sacrificed unto idols, and commit fornication.

15 Even so hast thou them that maintain the doctrine of the [1]Nicolaitans, which thing I hate.

16 Repent thyself, or else I will come unto thee shortly, and will fight against them with the sword of my mouth.

17 [1]Let him that hath an ear, hear what the spirit saith unto the Churches. To him that overcometh, will I give to eat [2]of the [3]Manna that is hid, and will give him

---

2:1 [2] The exordium wherein are contained the special praises of Christ Jesus the Author of this prophecy, out of verses 16 and 13 of the first Chapter.

2:2 [1] The proposition, first condemning the Pastor of this Church, verses 2, 3, then reproving him, verse 4, after informing him and withal threatening that he will translate the Church to another place, verse 5. This commutation or threat Christ mitigateth by a kind of correction, calling to mind the particular virtue and piety of the Church, which God never leaveth without recompense, verse 6. Concerning the Nicolaitans see after upon verse 11.

2:4 [1] To deal with thee for.

2:7 [1] The conclusion, containing a commandment of attention and a promise of everlasting life, shadowed out in a figure of which, Gen. 2:9.
 [2] That is, in Paradise after the manner of the Hebrew phrase.
 [3] Thus Christ speaketh as the Mediator.

2:8 [1] The second place is unto the Pastors of the Church of the Smyrnians. The exordium is taken out of verses 17 and 18 of the first Chap.
 [2] Smyrna was one of the cities of Ionia in Asia.

2:9 [1] The proposition of praise is in this verse and of exhortation joined with promise, is in the next verse.

2:10 [1] That is, of ten years. For so commonly both in this book and in Daniel, years are signified by the name of days: that God thereby might declare, that the space of time is appointed by him, and the same very short. Now because Saint John wrote this book in the end of Domitian the Emperor his reign, as Justin and Ireneus do witness, it is altogether necessary that this should be referred unto that persecution which was done by the authority of the Emperor Trajan: who began to make havoc of the Christian Church in the tenth year of his reign, as the His-

toriographers do write: and his bloody persecution continued until Adrian the Emperor had succeeded in his place: the space of which time is precisely ten years, which are here mentioned.

2:11 [1] The conclusions as verse 7.
 [2] See Rev. 20:6.

2:12 [1] The third place is unto the Pastors of Pergamos. The Exordium is taken out of verse 16 of the first Chapter.
 [2] Pergamos was the name of a famous city in old time in Asia, where the Kings of the Attalians were always resident.

2:13 [1] The proposition of praise is in this verse, of reprehension in the two following, and of exhortation joined with a conditional threat, verse 16. Now this Antipas was the Angel or minister of the Church of Pergamos, as Aretas writeth.
 [2] The faith of them of Pergamos is so much the more highly commended because they remained constant even in the very heat of persecution.

2:14 [1] That which is here spoken of things offered to idols, is meant of the same kind which Paul speaketh of, 1 Cor. 10:13.

2:15 [1] Which follow the footsteps of Balaam, and such as are abandoned unto all filthiness, as he showed in the verse foregoing, and is here signified by a note of similitude. And thus also must the next verse be understood. For this matter especially Ireneus must be consulted withal.

2:17 [1] The conclusion, standing of exhortation as before, and of promise.
 [2] He alludeth to that sermon which we read of John 6, and to the place we find, Ps. 105:40.
 [3] Aretas writeth, that such a stone was wont to be given to wrestlers at games, or else that such stones did in old times witness the quitting of a man.

a [4,5]white stone, and in the stone a new [6]name written, which no man knoweth, saving he that receiveth it.

18 ¶ And unto [1]the Angel of the Church which is at Thyatira write, These things saith the Son of God, which hath his eyes like unto a flame of fire, and his feet like fine brass.

19 I know [1]thy works and thy love, and [2]service and faith, and thy patience, and thy works, and that they are more at the last, than at the first.

20 Notwithstanding, I have a few things against thee, that thou sufferest the woman Jezebel which calleth herself a prophetess, to teach and to deceive my servants, to make them commit [1]fornication and to eat meat sacrificed unto idols.

21 And I gave her space to repent of her fornication, and she repented not.

22 Behold, I will cast her into a bed, and them that commit fornication with her, into great affliction, except they repent them of their works.

23 And I will kill her children with death, and all the Churches shall know that I am he which [b]search the reins and hearts: and I will give unto every one of you according unto your works.

24 And unto you I say, the rest of them of Thyatira, As many as have not this learning, neither have known the [1]deepness of Satan (as they speak) I will [2]put upon you none other burden,

25 But that which ye have already, hold fast till I come.

26 [1]For he that overcometh and keepeth my words

unto the end, to him will I give [2]power over nations.

27 [c]And he shall rule them with a rod of iron: and as the vessels of a potter, shall they be broken:

28 Even as I received of my Father, so will I give him [1]the morning Star.

29 Let him that hath an ear, hear what the Spirit saith to the Churches.

3 1 The first Epistle sent to the Pastors of the Church of Sardis, 7 of Philadelphia, 14 And of the Laodiceans, 16 that they be not lukewarm, 20 but endeavor to further God's glory.

1 [1]And write unto the Angel of the Church which is at [2]Sardis, These things saith he that hath the seven Spirits of God, and the seven stars, [3]I know thy works: for thou hast a [4]name that thou livest, but thou art dead.

2 Be awake, and strengthen the things which remain, that are [1]ready to die: for I have not found thy work perfect before God.

3 Remember therefore, how thou hast received and heard, and hold fast and repent. [a]If therefore thou wilt not watch, I will come on thee as a thief, and thou shalt not know what hour I will come upon thee.

4 Notwithstanding thou hast a few names yet in Sardis, [1]which have not defiled their garments: and they shall walk with me in [2]white: for they are [3]worthy.

5 He [1]that overcometh, shall be clothed in white array, and I will not put out his Name out of the [b]book of life, but I will confess his name before my Father, and before his Angels.

6 Let him that hath an ear, hear what the Spirit

Marginal references:

[b] 1 Sam. 16:7
Ps. 7:10
Jer. 11:20
Jer. 17:10

[c] Ps. 2:9

CHAPTER 3

[a] Rev. 16:15
1 Thess. 5:2
2 Pet. 3:10

[b] Rev. 20:12
Rev. 21:27
Phil. 5:3

2:17 [4] The bread of life, invisible, spiritual, and heavenly, which is kept secretly with God, from before all eternity.

[5] Which is a sign and witness of forgiveness and remission of sins, of righteousness and true holiness, and of purity uncorrupted, after that the old man is killed.

[6] A sign and testimony of newness of life in righteousness and true holiness, by putting on the new man, whom none doth inwardly know, save the spirit of man which is in himself, the praise whereof is not of man, but of God, Rom. 2:28.

2:18 [1] The fourth place is unto the Pastors of Thyatira. The exordium is taken out of verses 14 and 15 of the first Chapter.

2:19 [1] The proposition of praise is in this verse: of reprehension, for they tolerated with them, the doctrine of ungodliness and unrighteousness, is verse 20, the authors whereof though they were called back of God, yet repented not verse 21, whereunto is added a most heavy threatening, verses 22 and 23, of a conditional promise, and of exhortation to hold fast the truth, is in the two verses following.

[2] So he calleth those offices of charity which are done to the saints.

2:20 [1] By Fornication, is often in the Scripture idolatry meant.

2:24 [1] He pointeth out the bragging of certain men, which boasted of their deep, that is, plentiful and common knowledge, which notwithstanding is devilish.

[2] I will speak no worse thing against you, being content to have showed you what I require to be in you.

2:26 [1] The conclusion, wherein Christ assureth unto his servants the communion of his Kingdom and glory, in this verse and the next following, and commandeth an holy attention in the last verse.

[2] That is, I will make him a King by communion with me, and my fellow heir, as it is promised, Matt. 19:28 and 25:34; Rom. 8:17 and 1 Cor. 6:3; Eph. 2:6 and 1 Tim. 2:12.

2:28 [1] The brightness of greatest glory and honor nearest approaching unto the light of Christ, who is the Son of righteousness, and our head, Matt. 4.

3:1 [1] The fifth place is unto the Pastors of Sardis. The exordium is taken out of verses 4 and 16 of the first Chap.

[2] Sardis is the name of a most flourishing and famous City, where the Kings of Lydia kept their courts.

[3] The proposition of reproof is in this verse: of exhortation joined with a threatening in the two verses that follow, and of qualification by way of correction unto the comfort of the good which yet remained there, verse 4.

[4] Thou art said to live, but art dead indeed.

3:2 [1] Other things, whose state is such, that they are now going, and unless they be confirmed, will perish forthwith.

3:4 [1] That is, who have with all religion guarded themselves from sin and moral contagion, even from the very show of evil, as S. Jude exhorteth, verse 23.

[2] Pure from all spot and shining with glory. So it is to be understood always hereafter as in the next verse.

[3] They are meet and fit, to wit, because they are justified in Christ, as they have truly showed it: for he is righteous that worketh righteousness: but so, as the tree bringeth forth fruit. See Rom. 8:18.

3:5 [1] The conclusion standing upon a promise and a commandment as before.

saith unto the Churches.

7 ¶ [1]And write unto the Angel of the Church which is of Philadelphia, These things saith he that is Holy, and True, which hath the [2]key of David, which openeth and no man shutteth, and shutteth and no man openeth.

8 [1]I know thy works: behold I have set before thee an open door, and no man can shut it: for thou hast a little strength and hast kept my word, and hast not denied my Name.

9 Behold, I will make them [1]of the Synagogue of Satan, which call themselves Jews, and are not, but do lie: behold, *I say*, I will make them that they shall come [2]and worship before thy feet, and shall know that I have loved thee.

10 Because thou hast [1]kept the word of my patience, therefore I will deliver thee from the hour of tentation, which will come upon all the world, to try them that dwell upon the earth.

11 Behold, I come shortly: hold that which thou hast, that no man take thy crown.

12 [1]Him that overcometh, will I make a pillar in the Temple of my God, and he shall go no more out: [2]and I will write upon him the Name of my God, and the name of the city of my God, *which is* the new Jerusalem, which cometh down out of heaven from my God, and *I will write upon him* my new Name.

13 Let him that hath an ear, hear what the Spirit saith unto the Churches.

14 [1]And unto the Angel of the Church of the Laodiceans write, These things saith [2]Amen, the

[c] Prov. 3:12
Heb. 22:5

faithful and true witness, that [3]beginning of the creatures of God.

15 [1]I know thy works, that thou art neither cold nor hot: I would thou werest cold or hot.

16 Therefore because thou art lukewarm, and neither cold nor hot, it will come to pass, that I shall spew thee out of my mouth.

17 For thou sayest, I am rich, and increased with goods, and have need of nothing, and knowest not how thou art wretched and miserable, [1]and poor, and blind, and naked.

18 I counsel thee to buy of me gold tried by the fire, that thou mayest be made rich: and white raiment, that thou mayest be clothed, and that thy filthy nakedness do not appear: and anoint thine eyes with eye salve, that thou mayest see.

19 As many as I love, [c]I rebuke and chasten: be [1]zealous therefore and amend.

20 Behold, I stand at the door, and knock, [1]If any man hear my voice, and open the door, I will come in unto him, and will sup with him, and he with me.

21 [1]To him that overcometh, will I grant to sit with me in my throne, even as I overcame, and sit with my Father in his throne.

22 Let him that hath an ear, hear what the Spirit saith unto the Churches.

4   1 *Another vision containing the glory of God's Majesty: 3 which is magnified of the four beasts, 10 and the four and twenty Elders.*

1 After [1]this I looked, and behold, a door was

3:7 [1] The sixth place is unto the Pastors of Philadelphia. The exordium is taken out of verse 18 of the first chapter.

[2] All power of rule in commanding and forbidding, delivering and punishing. And the house of David is the Church, and the continual promise of David's Kingdom belongeth to Christ.

3:8 [1] The proposition of praise is in this verse, of promises, to bring home again them that wander, verse 9, and to preserve the godly, verse 10, and of exhortation, verse 11.

3:9 [1] I will bring them to that case.

[2] That is, fall down and worship either thee civilly, or Christ religiously at thy feet (and thus I had rather take it) whether here in the Church (which seemeth more proper to the argument of this place) or there in the world to come. For Christ verily shall fulfill his word.

3:10 [1] Because thou hast been patient and constant, as I would my servants should be.

3:12 [1] The conclusion, which containeth a promise and a commandment.

[2] That is, the new man shall be turned after his Father, Mother, and head Christ.

3:14 [1] The seventh place is unto the pastors of the Church of Laodicea. The exordium is taken out of verse 15 of the first chapter.

[2] Amen soundeth as much in the Hebrew tongue, as Truly, or Truth itself.

[3] Of whom all things that are made, have their beginning.

3:15 [1] The proposition of reproof is in this verse, whereunto is adjoined a threatening, verse 16, with a confirmation declaring the same, verse 17, and of exhortation unto faith and repentance, verses

18, 19, whereunto is added a conditional promise, verse 20.

3:17 [1] The spiritual misery of men is metaphorically expressed in three points: unto which are matched as correspondent those remedies which are offered, verse 18.

3:19 [1] Zeal is set against them which are neither hot nor cold.

3:20 [1] This must be taken after the manner of an allegory, as John 14:23.

3:21 [1] The conclusion, consisting of a promise, as Rev. 2:26, and of an exhortation. Hitherto hath been the first part of the book of the Apocalypse.

4:1 [1] Hereafter followeth the second part of this book, altogether prophetical, foretelling those things which were to come, as was said before, Rev. 1:19. This is divided into two histories: one common unto the whole world, unto Chapter 9: and another singular of the Church of God, thence unto chapter 22. And these histories are said to be described in several books, Rev. 5:1 and 10:2. Now this verse is as it were a passage from the former part unto this second: where it is said, that the heaven was opened, that is, that heavenly things were unlocked, and that a voice as of a trumpet sounded in heaven to stir up the Apostle, and call him to the understanding of things to come. The first history hath two parts: one the causes of things done, and of this whole Revelation, in that and the next chapter. Another of the acts done, in the next 4 chapters. The principal causes according to the distinction of persons in the vanity of divine essence, and according to the economy or dispensation thereof, are two. One the beginning, which none can approach unto, that is, God the Father, of whom is spoken in this chapter. The other, the Son, who is the mean cause, easy to be approached unto us, in respect that he is God and man in one person: of whom, Rev. 5.

open in heaven, and the first voice which I heard, was as it were of a trumpet talking with me, saying, Come up hither, and I will show thee things which must be done hereafter.

2 And [1]immediately I was *ravished* [2]in the spirit, [3]and behold, a throne was set in heaven, and one sat upon the throne.

3 [1]And he that sat, was to look upon, like unto a Jasper stone, and a sardine, and there *was* a rainbow round about the throne, in sight like to an emerald.

4 [1]And round about the throne *were* four and twenty seats, and upon the seats I saw four and twenty Elders sitting, clothed in white raiment, and had on their heads crowns of gold.

5 [1]And out of the throne proceeded lightnings, and thunderings and voices, and there were seven lamps of fire burning before the throne, which are the seven spirits of God.

6 [1]And before the throne there *was* a Sea of glass like unto crystal: and in the midst of the throne, and round about the throne *were* four beasts, full of eyes before and behind.

7 And the first beast *was* like a lion, and the

CHAPTER 4
[a] Rev. 5:12

second beast like a calf, and the third beast had a face as a man, and the fourth beast *was* like a flying Eagle.

8 And the [1]four beasts had each one of them six wings about him, and they were full of eyes within, and they ceased not [2]day nor night, saying, Holy, holy, holy, Lord God Almighty, Which was, and which is, and which is to come.

9 And when those beasts [1]gave glory, and honor, and thanks to him that sat on the throne, which liveth forever and ever,

10 [1]The four and twenty Elders fell down before him that sat on the throne, and worshipped him that liveth for evermore, and cast their crowns before the throne, saying,

11 [1]Thou art [a]worthy, O Lord, [2]to receive glory, and honor, and power: for thou hast created all things, and for thy will's sake they are, and have been created.

5 *1 The book sealed with seven seals, 3 which none could open. 6 That Lamb of God, 9 is thought worthy to open, 12 even by the consent of all the company of heaven.*

1 [1]And I saw in the [2]right hand of him that sat upon the throne, [3]a book written within, and on the

---

4:2 [1] The manner of revelation, as before, 1:10.

[2] See Rev. 1:12.

[3] A description of God the Father, and of his glory in the heavens, framed unto the manner of men, by his office, nature, company, attending, effect, instruments and events that follow afterwards. In this verse, he is presented in office a judge, as Abraham said, Gen. 18, which is declared by his throne, as an ensign of judgment, and his sitting thereupon.

4:3 [1] By his nature, in that he is the Father, most glorious in his own person, and with his glory overshining all other things.

4:4 [1] By the company attending about him in that, as that most high Judge, he is accompanied with the most honorable attendance of Prophets and Apostles, both of the old and new Church, whom Christ hath made to be Priests and Kings, Rev. 1:6 and 5:10.

4:5 [1] By effects, in that most mightily he speaketh all things by his voice and word, as Ps. 29:3, and with the light of his spirit and providence peruseth and passes through all.

4:6 [1] By instruments used, in that he both hath a most ready treasury, and as it were a workhouse excellently furnished with all things, unto the executing of his will, which things flow from his commandment, as is repeated, Rev.15:2. And hath also the Angels most ready administers of his counsels and pleasure unto all parts of the world, continually watching (in this verse) working by reason otherwise than the instruments, without life last mentioned, courageous as lions, mighty as bulls, wise as men, swift as eagles, verse 7, most apt unto all purposes, as furnished with wings on every part, most piercing of sight, and finally pure and perfect Spirits, always in continual motion, verse 8.

4:8 [1] Every beast had six wings.

[2] By events, in that for all the causes before mentioned God is glorified both of Angels, as holy, Judge, omnipotent, eternal and immutable, verse 8, and also after their example he is glorified of holy men (verse 9) in sign and in speech, verses 10, 11.

4:9 [1] God is said to have glory, honor, kingdom, and such like given unto him, when we godly and reverently set forth that which is properly and only his.

4:10 [1] Three signs of divine honor given unto God, prostration or falling down, adoration and casting their crowns before God, in which the godly, though made kings by Christ, do willingly empty themselves of all glory, moved with a religious respect for the majesty of God.

4:11 [1] The sum of their speech: that all glory must be given unto God: the reason, because he is the eternal beginning of all things, from whose only will they have their being and are governed: and finally in all respects are that which they are.

[2] That is, that thou shouldest challenge the same to thyself alone. But as for us, we are unworthy, that even by thy goodness we should be made partakers of this glory. And hitherto hath been handled the principal cause unapproachable, which is God.

5:1 [1] A passing unto the second principal cause, which is the Son of God, God and man, the mediator of all, as the eternal word of God the Father manifested in the flesh. This chapter hath two parts: one that prepareth the way unto the Revelation, by rehearsal of the occasions that did occur in the first four verses. Another, the history of the Revelation of Christ, thence unto the end of the chapter.

[2] That is, in the very right hand of God.

[3] Here are showed the occasions for which this principal cause, and this Revelation was also necessary: the same are three, the first a present vision of the book of the counsels of God, concerning the government of this whole world, which book is said to be laid up with the Father as it were in his hand: but shut and unknown unto all creatures, in this verse. The second is a religious desire of the Angels of God to understand the mysteries of this book, verse 2, whereof see 1 Pet. 1:12. The third is a lamentation of Saint John and all the godly, moved by the same desire, verse 4, when they saw that it was a thing impossible for any creature to effect: which is declared in the third verse.

backside sealed with seven seals.

2 And I saw a strong Angel which preached with a loud voice, Who is worthy to open the book, and to loose the seals thereof?

3 ¹And no man in heaven nor in earth, neither under the earth, was able to open the book, neither to look thereon.

4 Then I wept much, because no man was found worthy to open, and to read the book, neither to look thereon.

5 ¹And one of the Elders said unto me, Weep not: behold, that ᵃʹ²Lion which is of the tribe of Judah, that root of David, hath obtained to open the book, and to loose the seven seals thereof.

6 Then I beheld, and lo, ¹in the midst of the throne, and of the four beasts, and in the midst of the Elders stood a Lamb, as though he had been killed, which had seven horns, and seven eyes, which are the seven spirits of God, sent into all the world.

7 ¹And he came, and took the book out of the right hand of him that sat upon the throne.

8 ¹And when he hath taken the book, the four beasts, and the four and twenty Elders fell down before the Lamb, having every one ²harps and golden vials full of odors, which are the ³prayers of the Saints,

9 And they sung a ¹new ²song, saying, ³Thou

CHAPTER 5
ᵃ Gen. 49:6
ᵇ Rev. 1:6
1 Pet. 2:9
ᶜ Dan. 7:10

art worthy to take the book, and to open the seals thereof, because thou wast killed, and hast redeemed us to God by thy blood out of every kindred, and tongue, and people, and nation.

10 And hast made us unto our God ᵇKings, and Priests, and we shall reign on the earth.

11 ¹Then I beheld, and I heard the voice of many Angels round about the throne, and *about* the beasts and the Elders, ²and there were ᶜʹ³ten thousand times ten thousand, and thousand thousands,

12 Saying with a loud voice, Worthy is the Lamb that was killed, to ¹receive power, and riches, and wisdom, and strength, and honor, and glory, and praise.

13 ¹And all the creatures which are in heaven, and on the earth, and under the earth, and in the sea, and all that are in them, heard I saying, Praise, and honor, and glory, and power *be* unto him, that sitteth upon the throne, and unto the Lamb for evermore.

14 ¹And the four beasts said, Amen, and the four and twenty Elders fell down and worshipped him that liveth for evermore.

6 1 *The Lamb openeth the first seal of the book.* 3 *The second,* 5 *the third,* 7 *the fourth,* 9 *the fifth,* 12 *and the sixth, and then arise murders, famine, pestilence, outcries of Saints, earthquakes, and divers strange sights in heaven.*

5:3 ¹ Thus neither of them that are in heaven, nor of them which are in the earth, etc. And this I like better. Now this enumeration of parts is sufficient to the denying of the whole. For of the creatures one sort is in heaven above the earth: another in the earth: and another under the earth in the sea, as is after declared, verse 13.

5:5 ¹ The second part of this chapter, in which is set down the Revelation of the Son, as before was said. This part containeth first an history of the manner how God prepared S. John to understand this Revelation in this verse. Secondly, the Revelation of the Son himself unto verse 7. Thirdly, the accidents of this Revelation, in the rest of this chapter. The manner now, is here described in two sorts, one from without him, by speech in this verse. Another within, by opening the eyes of S. John (which before were held) that he might see, in the verse following.

² That is, the most mighty and most approved Prince: according to the use of the Hebrew speech.

5:6 ¹ The sum of this Revelation: Christ the mediator taketh and openeth the book, verses 6, 7. Therefore in his Revelation is described the person of Christ, in this verse. His fact, in the next verse. The person is thus described, Christ, the mediator between God, Angels and men, as the eternal word of God, and our redeemer: as the Lamb of God, standing as slain, and making intercession for us by the virtue and merit of his everlasting sacrifice, is armed with the Spirit of God, in his own person, that is, with the power and wisdom of God essentially unto the government of this whole world.

5:7 ¹ The fact of Christ the Mediator, that he cometh unto the throne of the Father, of which Rev. 4, and taketh the book out of his hand to open it. For that he opened it, it is first expressed, Rev. 6:1, etc.

5:8 ¹ Now follow in the end the accidents of the Revelation last spo-

ken of that all the holy Angels, and men did sing unto him: both the chief, verses 9, 10, and common order of Angels, verses 11, 12, and of all things created, verse 13, the princes of both sorts agreeing thereunto, verse 14.

² The symbols or signs of praise, sweet in savor, and acceptable unto God. See Rev. 8:3.

³ See Rev. 9:3.

5:9 ¹ No common song.

² That is composed according to the present matter: the Lamb having received the book, as it were with his feet, and opened it with his horns, as is said in the Canticles.

³ The song of the Nobles or Princes standing by the throne, consisting of a publication of the praise of Christ, and a confirmation of the same from his benefits, both which we have received of himself (as are the suffering of his death, our redemption upon the cross by his blood in this verse: and our communion with him in Kingdom and Priesthood, which long ago he hath granted unto us with himself) and which we hereafter hope to obtain, as our kingdom to come in Christ, in the verse following.

5:11 ¹ The consent of the common order of Angels, answering in melody unto their Princes that stood by the throne.

² A number finite, but almost infinite for one infinite indeed, as Dan. 7:10.

³ By this is meant a great number.

5:12 ¹ To have all praise given to him, as to the mightiest and wisest, etc.

5:13 ¹ The consent of all the common multitude of the creatures.

5:14 ¹ A confirmation of the praise beforegoing, from the contestation of the Nobles, expressed in word and signs, as once or twice before this.

1 [1]After I beheld when the Lamb had opened one of the seals, and I heard one of the four beasts say, as *it were* the noise of thunder, Come and see.

2 Therefore [1]I beheld, and lo, there *was* a white horse, and he that sat on him, had a bow, and a crown was given unto him, and he went forth conquering that he might overcome.

3 And [1]when he had opened the second seal, I heard the second beast say, Come and see.

4 And there went out another horse, *that was* red, and power was given to him that sat thereon to take peace from the earth, and that they should kill one another, and there was given unto him a great sword.

5 [1]And when he had opened the third seal, I heard the third beast say, Come and see. Then I beheld, and lo, a black horse, and he that sat on him, had balances in his hand.

6 And I heard a voice in the midst of the four beasts say, A [1]measure of wheat for a penny, and three measures of barley for a penny, [2]and oil, and wine hurt thou not.

7 [1]And when he had opened the fourth seal, I heard the voice of the fourth beast say, Come and see.

8 And I looked, and behold, a pale horse, and his name that sat on him was Death, and Hell followed after him, and power was given unto them over the fourth part of the earth, to kill with sword, and with hunger, and with death, and with beasts of the earth.

9 [1]And when he had opened the fifth seal, I saw under the altar the souls of them that were killed for the word of God, and for the testimony which they maintained.

10 And they cried with a loud voice, saying, How long, Lord, which art holy and true! dost not thou judge and avenge our blood on them, that dwell on the earth?

11 And long [1]white robes were given unto every one, and it was said unto them, that they should rest for a little season until their fellow servants, and their brethren that should be killed even as they were, were [2]fulfilled.

12 [1]And I beheld when he had opened the sixth seal, and lo, there was a great earthquake, and the Sun was as black as [2]sackcloth of hair, and the Moon was like blood.

13 And the stars of heaven fell unto the earth, as a fig-tree casteth her green figs, when it is shaken of a mighty wind.

14 And heaven departed away, as a scroll, when it

6:1 [1] This is the second part of this first history (which I said was common and of the whole world) of the works of God in the government of all things. Of this part there are generally 3 members, the foresignifying, the caution, and the execution of all the evils which God poureth out upon this world, which hath most hardly deserved of him. The foresignifying is set down in this chapter, the caution for preserving the Church, is in the next chapter, and the execution is described, Rev. 8:9. In every part of the foresignifying, there are three branches: the several and express calling of S. John, to prepare himself to take knowledge of the things that were to be showed unto him in the opening of the seals: the sign and the word expounding the sign: And albeit the express calling of S. John, be used only in four of the signs, yet the same is also to be understood in the rest that follow. The author of the foresignifying is the Lamb, as that word of the Father made the Mediator, opening the seals of the book. The instruments are the Angels in most of the visions, who expound the sign and words thereof. Now this first verse containeth an express calling of S. John to mark the opinion of the first seal.

6:2 [1] The first sign joined with declaration, is that God for the sins, and horrible rebellion of the world, will invade the same: and first of all as afar off, with his darts of pestilence most suddenly, mightily, and gloriously, bear down the same as judge, and triumph over it as conqueror.

6:3 [1] The second sign joined with words of declaration (after the express calling of S. John as before) is that God being provoked unto wrath by the obstinacy and hardheartedness of the world not repenting for the former plague, as setting upon the same hand, will kindle the fire of debate amongst men, and will destroy the inhabitants of this world, one by the sword of another.

6:5 [1] The third sign with declaration, is that God will destroy the world with famine, withdrawing all provision: which is by the figure Synecdoche comprehended in wheat, barley, wine and oil.

6:6 [1] Hereby is signified what great scarcity of corn there was, for the word here used is a kind of measure of dry things, which is in quantity but the eighth part of a bushel, which was an ordinary portion to be given servants for their stint of meat for one day.

[2] I had rather distinguish and read the words thus, *and the wine and the oil thou shalt not deal unjustly*. In this sense likewise the wine and the oil shall be sold a very little for a penny. Thou shalt not deal unjustly, namely, when thou shalt measure out a very little for a great price: so is the place evident: otherwise that is most true, which the wise man saith, that whoso withholdeth the corn shall be cursed of the people, Prov. 11:26.

6:7 [1] The fourth sign joined with words of declaration, is, that God will addict the fourth part of the world indifferently, unto death and hell, or the grave by all those means at once, by which before severally and in order he had recalled their minds unto amendment. Unto these are also added the wild and cruel beasts of the earth, out of Lev. 26:22. Thus doth God according to his wisdom dispense the treasures of his power, justly towards all, mercifully towards the good, and with patience or longsufferance towards his enemies.

6:9 [1] The fifth sign is that the holy martyrs which are under the altar, whereby they are sanctified, that is, received into the trust and tuition of Christ (into whose hands they are committed) shall cry out for the justice of God, in an holy zeal to advance his kingdom and not of any private perturbation of the mind, in this and the next verse, and that God will, in deed, sign and word comfort them, verse 11.

6:11 [1] As before 3:4.

[2] Until their number be fulfilled.

6:12 [1] The sixth sign, the narration whereof hath two parts, the sign, and the event. The sign is, that the earth, heaven, and the things that are in them for the horror of the sins of the world upon those most heavy foretellings of God, and complaints of the Saints shall be shaken most vehemently, trembling in horrible manner, and losing their light in this verse: falling from on high, verse 13, withdrawing themselves and flying away for the greatness of the trouble, verse 14. So boldly do all creatures depend upon the will of God, and content themselves in his glory.

[2] So they called in old time those woven works that were of hair.

is rolled, and every mountain and isle were moved out of their places.

15 ¹And the kings of the earth, and the great men, and the rich men, and the chief captains, and the mighty men, and every bondman, and every free man, hid themselves in dens, and among the rocks of the mountains,

16 And said to the mountains and rocks, ¹ᵃFall on us, and hide us from the presence of him that sitteth on the throne, and from the wrath of the Lamb.

17 For the great day of his wrath is come, and who can stand?

7 1 The Angels coming to hurt the earth,   3 are stayed until the elect of the Lord,   5 of all tribes were sealed.   13 Such as suffered persecution for Christ's sake,   16 have great felicity,   17 and joy.

1 And ¹after that, I saw four Angels stand on the ²four corners of the earth, holding the four winds of the earth, that the winds should not blow on the earth, neither on the sea, ³neither on any tree.

2 ¹And I saw ²another Angel come up from the East, which had the seal of the living God, and he cried with a loud voice to the four Angels to whom power was given to hurt the earth, and the sea, saying,

3 Hurt ye not the earth, neither the sea, neither

CHAPTER 6
ᵃ Isa. 2:19
Hos. 10:8
Luke 23:30

the trees, till we have sealed the servants of our God in their foreheads.

4 And I heard the number of them, which were sealed, and there were sealed ¹an hundred and four and forty thousand of all the tribes of the children of Israel.

5 Out of the tribe of Judah were sealed twelve thousand. Of the tribe of Reuben were sealed twelve thousand. Of the tribe of Gad were sealed twelve thousand.

6 Of the tribe of Asher were sealed twelve thousand. Of the tribe of Naphtali were sealed twelve thousand. Of the tribe of Manasseh were sealed twelve thousand.

7 Of the tribe of Simeon were sealed twelve thousand. ¹Of the tribe of ²Levi were sealed twelve thousand. Of the tribe of Issachar were sealed twelve thousand. Of the tribe of Zebulun were sealed twelve thousand.

8 Of the tribe of ¹Joseph were sealed twelve thousand. Of the tribe of Benjamin were sealed twelve thousand.

9 After these things I beheld, and lo, a great multitude, ¹which no man could number, of all nations and kindreds, and people, and tongues ²stood before the throne, and before the Lamb, clothed with

6:15 ¹ The event of the sign aforegoing: that there is no man that shall not be astonished at that general commotion, fly away for fear and hide himself in this verse, and wish unto himself most bitter death for exceeding horror of the wrath of God, and of the Lamb, at which before he was astonished. Now this perplexity is not of the godly, but of the wicked, whose portion is in this life, as the Psalmist speaketh, Ps. 17:14. Not that sorrow which is according unto God, which worketh repentance unto salvation, whereof a man shall never repent him, but that worldly sorrow that bringeth death, 2 Cor. 7:9, as their wishings do declare: for this history is of the whole world, severed from the history of the Church, as I have showed before, Rev. 4:1.

6:16 ¹ These are words of such as despair of their escape: of which despair there are two arguments, the presence of God and the Lamb provoked to wrath against the world in this verse, and the conscience of their own weakness, whereby men feel that they are no way able to stand in the day of the wrath of God, verse 17, as it is said, Isa. 14:27.

7:1 ¹ The second member of this part, is a preventing of danger as we distinguished the same before, Chap. 6:1, that is of the caution whereby God took care before hand and provided for his that after the example of the Israelites of old, Exod. 8:13, the faithful might be exempted from the plagues of this wicked world. This whole place is a certain interlocution and bringing in for this whole chapter by occasion of the prediction and argument of the sixth seal. For first that evil is prevented in the elect unto verse 9. Then thanks are given by the elect for that cause, verses 10, 11, 12. Lastly, the accomplishment of the thing is set forth unto the end of the chapter. The first verse is a transition speaking of the Angels which keep these inferior parts from all evil, until God do command. For (as it is excellently figured by Ezek. 11:12) their faces and their wings are reached upwards, continually waiting upon and beholding the countenance of God for their direction: and every [one] of them goeth into that part that is right before his face, whithesoever the Spirit shall go, they go, they step not out of the way, that is, they depart not so

much as a foot breadth from the path commanded them of God.

² On the four quarters or coasts of the earth.

³ That is, neither into the air, into which the tops of trees are advanced.

7:2 ¹ Now God provideth against the danger of his elect by commandment, verses 2 and 3, and by sign or figure, both for those of the nation of the Jews, thence unto verse 8, and also of the Gentiles, verse 9.

² Not only another, or differing in number from the common Angels of God, but also in essence, office, and operation excelling all Angels: that is, Christ Jesus the eternal Angel or word of God, and mediator of the covenant. So hereafter Rev. 8:3 and 10:1, 5.

7:4 ¹ That is, of the Jews a number certain in itself before God, and such as may be numbered of us: for which cause also the same is here set down as certain. But of the elect which are of the Gentiles, the number indeed is in itself certain with God, but of us not possibly to be numbered, as God, Gen. 15:5, and often elsewhere, and Isaiah figured most excellently, Isa. 49 and 60. This therefore is spoken with respect, when a certain number is put for one uncertain. Confer this with verse 6.

7:7 ¹ Here the tribe of Levi is reckoned up in common with the rest, because all the Israelites were equally made Priests with them in Christ by his Priesthood, Rev. 1:6, and 5:10, and Rom. 12:1, and 1 Pet. 2:9. The name of Dan is not mentioned because the Danites long before forsaking the worship of God, were fallen away from the fellowship of God's people unto the part of the Gentiles, which evil many ages before Jacob foresaw, Gen. 49:18, for which cause also there is no mention made of this tribe in the first book of the Chronicles.

² He skipped Dan, and reckoneth Levi.

7:8 ¹ Of Ephraim, who was Joseph's other son, and had the birthright given him, whereof he is called Joseph.

7:9 ¹ See before upon verse 4.

² As Priests, Kings and glorious conquerors by martyrdom: which things are noted by their proper signs in this verse.

long white robes, and palms in their hands.

10 [1]And they cried with a loud voice, saying, Salvation *cometh* of our God, that sitteth upon the throne, and of the Lamb.

11 And all the Angels stood round about the throne, and *about* the Elders, and the four beasts, and they fell before the throne on their faces, and worshipped God,

12 Saying, Amen, Praise and glory, and wisdom, and thanks, and honor, and power, and might, *be* unto our God for evermore, Amen.

13 [1]And one of the Elders spake, saying unto me, What are these which are arrayed in long white robes? and whence came they?

14 And I said unto him, Lord, thou knowest. And he said unto me, These are they which came out of great tribulation, and have washed their long robes, and have made their long robes white in the blood of the Lamb.

15 Therefore are they in the presence of the throne of God, and serve him [1]day and night in his Temple, and he that sitteth on the throne will dwell [2]among them.

16 [a]They shall hunger no more, neither thirst anymore, neither shall the sun light on them, neither

CHAPTER 7
[a] Isa. 49:10
[b] Isa. 25:8
Rev. 11:4

any heat.

17 For the Lamb, which is in the midst of the throne, shall govern them, and shall lead them unto the lively fountains of waters, and [b]God shall wipe away all tears from their eyes.

8 1 *After the opening of the seventh seal,* 3 *the Saints' prayers are offered up with odors.* 6 *The seven Angels come forth with trumpets.* 7 *The four first blow, and fire falleth on the earth,* 8 *the sea is turned into blood,* 10, 11 *the waters wax bitter.* 12 *and the stars are darkened.*

1 [1]And when he had opened the seventh seal, there was silence in heaven about half an hour.

2 [1]And I saw the seven Angels, which [2]stood before God, and to them were given seven trumpets.

3 [1]Then another Angel came and stood before the Altar, having a golden censer, and much odors was given unto him, that he should offer with the prayers of all Saints upon the golden Altar, which is before the throne.

4 And the smoke of the odors with the prayers of the Saints, [1]went up before God, out of the Angel's hand.

5 And the Angel took the censer, and filled it with fire of the Altar, and cast it into the earth, and

---

7:10 [1] The praise of God celebrated first by the holy men, in this verse, then by the heavenly Angels in the two verses following.

7:13 [1] A passage over unto the expounding of the vision, of which the Angel inquireth of S. John to stir him up withal, in this verse and John in the form of speech, both acknowledgeth his own ignorance, attributing knowledge unto the Angel, and also in most modest manner requesteth the expounding of the vision.

7:14 [1] The exposition of the vision, wherein the Angel telleth first the acts of the Saints, that is, their sufferings and work of faith in Christ Jesus, in this verse. Secondly their glory, both present, which consisteth in two things, that they minister unto God, and that God protecteth them, verse 15, and to come, in their perfect deliverance from all annoyances, verse 16, and in participation of all good things which even the memory of former evils shall never be able to diminish, verse 17. The cause efficient, and which containeth all these things is only one, the Lamb of God, the Lord, the Mediator, and the Savior Christ Jesus.

7:15 [1] He alludeth to the Levites, which served day and night, for else there is no night in heaven.

[2] Or, upon them, whereby is meant God's defense and protection, as it were towards them, who are as safe, as men in the Lord's tent.

8:1 [1] He returneth to the history of the seals of the book, which the Lamb openeth. The seventh seal is the next foresignification, and a precise commandment of the execution of the most heavy judgments of God upon this wicked world: which foresignification being understood by the seal, all things in heaven are silent, and in horror thorough admiration until commandment of execution be severally given of God unto the ministers of his wrath. So he passeth unto the third member of which I spake before in Rev. 6:1, which is of the execution of those evils wherewith God most justly determined to afflict the world.

8:2 [1] Now followeth the third branch of the common history, as

even now I said: which is the execution of the judgments of God upon the world. This is first generally prepared unto verse 6, then by several parts expoundeth according to the order of those that administered the same unto the end of the Chap. following. Unto the preparation of this execution are declared these things: first, who were the administers and instruments thereof in this verse. Secondly, what is the work both of the Prince of Angels giving order for this execution, thence unto verse 5, and of his administers in verse 6. The administers of the execution are said to be seven Angels: their instruments, trumpets, whereby they should as it were sound the alarm at the commandment of God. They are propounded seven in number, because it pleased God not at once to pour out his wrath upon the rebellious world, but at divers times, and by piecemeal, and in slow order, and as with an unwilling mind to exercise his judgments upon his creatures, so long called upon both by word and signs if happily they had learned to repent.

[2] Which appear before him as his ministers.

8:3 [1] This is the great Emperor, the Lord Jesus Christ our King and Savior: who both maketh intercession to God the Father for the Saints, filling the heavenly Sanctuary with most sweet odor, and offering up their prayers, as the Calves and burnt sacrifices of their lips, in this verse: in such sort as every one of them (so powerful is that sweet savor of Christ, and the efficacy of his sacrifice) are held in reconcilement with God and themselves made most acceptable unto him, verse 4. And then also out of his treasury, and from the same sanctuary poureth forth upon the world the fire of his wrath, adding also divine tokens thereto: and by that means (as of old the Heralds of Rome were wont to do) he proclaimeth war against the rebellious world.

8:4 [1] Our prayers are nothing worth, unless that true and sweet savor of that only oblation be especially and before all things with them, that is to say, unless we being first of all justified through faith in his Son, be acceptable unto him.

there were voices, and thunderings, and lightnings, and earthquake.

6 ¹Then the seven Angels, which had the seven trumpets, prepared themselves to blow the trumpets.

7 ¹So the first Angel blew the trumpet, and there was hail and fire mingled with blood, and they were cast into the earth, and the third part of trees was burnt, and all green grass was burnt.

8 ¹And the second Angel blew the trumpet, and as *it were* a great mountain, burning with fire, was cast into the sea, and the third part of the sea became blood.

9 And the third part of the creatures, which were in the sea, and had life, died, and the third part of ships were destroyed.

10 ¹Then the third Angel blew the trumpet, and there fell a great star from heaven, burning like a torch, and it fell into the third part of the rivers, and into the fountains of waters.

11 And the name of the star is called ¹wormwood: therefore the third part of the waters became wormwood, and many men died of the waters, because they were made bitter.

12 ¹And the fourth Angel blew the trumpet, and the third part of the sun was smitten, and the third part of the moon, and the third part of the stars, so that the third part of them was darkened: and the day *was smitten*, that the third part of it could not shine, and likewise the night.

13 ¹And I beheld, and heard one Angel flying through the midst of heaven, saying with a loud voice, Woe, woe, woe to the inhabitants of the earth, because of the sounds to come of the trumpet of the three Angels, which were yet to blow the trumpets.

9

1 *The fifth Angel bloweth his trumpet,* 3 *and spoiling locusts come out.* 13 *The sixth Angel bloweth,* 16 *and bringeth forth horsemen,* 20 *to destroy mankind.*

1 And the ¹fifth Angel blew the trumpet, and I saw a ²star fall from heaven unto the earth, ³and to him was given the key of the ⁴bottomless pit.

2 ¹And he opened the bottomless pit, and there arose the smoke of the pit, the smoke of a great furnace, and the sun, and the air were darkened by the smoke of the pit.

3 ¹And there came out of the smoke Locusts upon the earth, and unto them was given power, as the scorpions of the earth have power.

8:6 ¹ This is the work of the administers. The Angels the administers of Christ, only by sounding trumpet and voice (for they are only as Heralds) do effectual call forth the instruments of the wrath of God, through his power. Hitherto have been things general. Now followeth the narration of things particular, which the Angels fix in number wrought in their order set out in verse 19 of the next chap., and is concluded with the declaration of the event which followed upon these things done in the world, and in chapters 10 and 11.
8:7 ¹ The first execution at the sound of the first Angel upon the earth, that is, the inhabitants of the earth (by Metonymy) and upon all the fruits thereof: as the comparing of this verse with the second member of verse 9 doth not obscurely declare.
8:8 ¹ The second execution, upon the sea in this verse and all things that are there in the next verse.
8:10 ¹ The third execution upon the floods and fountains, that is, upon all fresh waters, in this verse: the effect whereof is, that many are destroyed with the bitterness of waters, in the verse following.
8:11 ¹ This is spoken by Metaphor of the name of a most bitter herb, and commonly known, unless perhaps a man following those that note the derivation of words had rather expound it adjectively, for that which by reason or bitterness cannot be drunk, or which maketh the liquor into which is poured more bitter than that any man can drink the same.
8:12 ¹ The fourth execution upon these lightsome bodies of heaven, which minister unto this inferior world.
8:13 ¹ A lamentable prediction or foretelling of those parts of the divine execution which are yet behind: which also is a passage unto the argument of the next Chapter. Of all these things in a manner Christ himself expressly foretold in Luke 12:24, and they are common plagues generally denounced, without particular note of time.
9:1 ¹ The first execution upon the wicked men inhabiting the earth (as a little before the Angel said) wrought by the infernal powers, is declared in this place unto the eleventh verse. And after the sixth execution thence unto the nineteenth verse. And lastly ʼis showed the common event that followed the former execution in the world, in the two last verses.
² That is, that the Angel of God glittering with glory, as a star fell down from heaven. Whether thou take him for Christ, who hath the keys of hell himself, and by Princely authority, Rev. 1:18, or whether for some inferior Angel, who hath the same key permitted unto him, and occupieth it ministerially, or by office of his ministry, here, and Rev. 21, so the word *falling,* is taken, Gen. 14:10, and 24:64, and Heb. 6:6.
³ The key was given to his star. For those powers of wickedness are thrust down into hell, and bound with chains of darkness: and are there kept unto damnation, unless God for a time do let them loose, 2 Pet. 2:4; Jude 1:6, and of this book, Rev. 20:20, the history of which chapter hath agreement of time with this present chapter.
⁴ By the bottomless pit, he meaneth the deepest darkness of hell.
9:2 ¹ Unto this is added, the smoke of the hellish and infernal spirits, all dark, and darkening all things in heaven and in earth. The spiritual darknesses are the causes of all disorder and confusion. For the devil at a time certain (whereof the fifth verse) sent these darknesses into his kingdom, that he might at once and with one impression overthrow all things, and pervert if it were possible the elect themselves. By this darkness all spiritual light, both active as of the Sun, and passive, as of the air which is lightened by the Sun, is taken away: and this is that which goeth before the spirits: it followeth of the spirits themselves.
9:3 ¹ A description of the malignant spirits invading the world, taken from their nature, power, form and order. From their nature, for that they are like unto certain locusts, in quickenness, subtlety, hurtfulness, number, and such like in this verse. From their power, for that they are as the scorpions of the earth, of a secret force to do hurt. For our battle is not here with flesh and blood, but with powers, etc., Eph. 6:12. This place of the power of the Devils generally noted in this verse, is particularly declared afterwards in the three next verses.

4 ¹And it was commanded them that they should not hurt the grass of the earth, neither any green thing, neither any tree: but only those men which have not the seal of God in their foreheads.

5 And to them was commanded that they should not kill them, but that they should be vexed five months, and that their pain should be as the pain that cometh of a scorpion, when he hath stung a man.

6 ᵃTherefore in those days shall men seek death, and shall not find it, and shall desire to die, and death shall flee from them.

7 ¹And the form of the locusts *was* like unto horses prepared unto the battle, and on their heads *were* as *it were* crowns, like unto gold, and their faces *were* like the faces of men.

8 And they had hair as the hair of women, and their teeth were as the teeth of lions.

CHAPTER 9
ᵃ Rev. 6:16
Isa. 2:19
Hos. 10:8

9 And they had habergeons, like unto habergeons of iron, and the sound of their wings *was* like the sound of chariots when many horses run unto battle.

10 And they had tails like unto scorpions, and there were stings in their tails, and their power was to hurt men five months.

11 ¹And they have a king over them, which is the Angel of the bottomless pit, whose name in Hebrew *is* Abaddon, and in Greek he is named Apollyon, *that is, destroying.*

12 ¹One woe is past, *and* behold, yet two woes come after this.

13 ¶ ¹Then the sixth Angel blew the trumpet, ²and I heard a voice from the ³four horns of the golden altar, which is before God,

14 Saying to the sixth Angel, which had the

9:4 ¹ Here that power of the devils is particularly described according to their actions and effects of the same. Their actions are said to be bounded by the counsel of God: both because they hurt not all men, but only the reprobate (for the godly and elect, in whom there is any part of a better life, God guardeth by his decree) whom Christ shall not have sealed, in this verse: and also because they neither had all power not at all times, no not over those that are their own, but limited in manner and time, by the prescript of God, verse 5. So their power to afflict the godly, is none, and for the wicked is limited in act and in effect by the will of God: for the manner was prescribed unto them that they should not slay, but torment the wretched world. The time is for five months or for an hundred and fifty days, that is, for so many years in which the devils have indeed mightily perverted all things in the world: and yet without that public and unpunished license of killing, which afterward they usurped when the sixth Angel had blown his trumpet, as shall be said upon verse 13. Now this space is to be accounted from the end of that thousand years mentioned, Rev. 20:3, and that is from the Popedom of that Gregory the seventh, a most monstrous Necromancer, who before was called Hildebrandus Senensis: for this man being made altogether of impiety and wickedness, as a slave of the devil, whom he served, was the most wicked firebrand of the world: he excommunicated the Emperor Henry the fourth: went about by all manner of treachery to set up and put down empires and kingdoms as liked himself: and doubted not to set Rodolph the Swedon over the Empire instead of Henry before named, sending unto him a Crown with this verse annexed unto it: *Petra dedit Petro, Petrus diadema Rodolpho:* that is, The Rock to Peter gave the crown, and Peter Rodolph doth renown. Finally, he so finely bestirred himself in his affairs, as he miserably set all Christendom on fire, and conveyed over unto his successors the burning brand of the same: who enraged with like ambition, never ceased to nourish that flame, and to enkindle it more and more: whereby Cities, Commonwealths, and whole kingdoms set together by the ears amongst themselves by most expert cut-throats, came to ruin, whiles they miserably wounded one another. This term of an hundred and fifty years, taketh end in the time of Gregory the ninth, or *Hugolinus Anagniensis* (as he was before called) who caused to be compiled by one Raimond his chaplain and confessor, the body of Decretals, and by sufferance of the Kings and Princes to be published in the Christian world, and established for a law. For by this sleight at length the Popes arrogated unto themselves license to kill whom they would, whiles others were unawares: and without fear established a butchery out of many of the wicked Canons of the

Decretals, which the trumpet of the fifth Angel had expressly forbidden, and had hindered until this time. The effects of the bloody actions are declared upon the sixth verse: that the miserable world languishing in so great calamities, should willingly run together unto death, and prefer the same before life, by reason of the grievousness of the miseries that oppressed them.

9:7 ¹ The form of these hellish spirits and administers, is shadowed out by signs and visible figures in this sort: that they are very expert and swift: that wheresoever they are in the world, the kingdom of theirs: that they manage all their affairs with cunning and skill, in this verse, that making show of mildness and tender affection to draw on men withal, they most impudently rage in all mischief: that they are most mighty to do hurt, Verse 8, that they are freed from being hurt of any man, as armed with the color of religion, and sacred authority of privilege, that they fill all things with horror, Verse 9, that they are fraudulent: that they are venomous and extremely noisome, though their power be limited, Verse 10. All which things are properly in the infernal powers, and communicated by them unto their ministers and vassals.

9:11 ¹ The order of the powers of maliciousness: that they are subject to one infernal King, whom thou mayest call in English, The Destroyer: who driveth the whole world both Jews and Gentiles into the destruction that belongeth unto himself. And I cannot tell whether this name belongeth unto the Etymological interpretation of Hildebrand, by a figure often used in the holy Scripture: which albeit it may otherwise be turned of the Germans (as the sense of compound words is commonly ambiguous) yet in very deed it signifieth as much as if thou shouldest call him the firebrand, that is, he that setteth on fire those that be faithful unto him.

9:12 ¹ A passage unto the next point, and the history of the time following.

9:13 ¹ The sixth execution done upon the world by the tyrannical powers thereof working in the four parts of the earth, that is in most cruel manner executing their tyrannous dominion through the whole world, and killing the miserable people without punishment, which before was not lawful for them to do in that sort, as I showed upon the fourth verse. This narration has two parts: a commandment from God, in verse 14, and execution of the commandment, in the verse following.

² The commandment given by Christ himself, who is governor over all.

³ He alludeth to the altar of incense, which stood in the Court which the Priests were in, over against the Ark of the Covenant, having a veil betwixt them.

trumpet, [1]Loose the four Angels, which are bound in the great river Euphrates.

15 [1]And the four Angels were loosed, which were prepared at an hour, at a day, at a month, and at a year to slay the third part of men.

16 And the number of horsemen of war were twenty thousand times ten thousand: for I heard the number of them.

17 And thus I saw the horses in a vision, and them that sat on them, having fiery habergeons, and of hyacinth, and of brimstone, and the heads of the horses were as the heads of lions, and out of their mouths went forth fire, and smoke, and brimstone.

18 Of these three was the third part of men killed, *that is*, of the fire, and of the smoke, and of the brimstone, which came out of their mouths.

19 For their power is in their mouths, and in their tails: [1]for their tails were like unto serpents, and had heads wherewith they hurt.

20 [1]And the remnant of the men which were not killed by these plagues, repented not of the works

b Ps. 115:4
Ps. 135:25

of their hands that they should not worship devils, and [b]idols of gold, and of silver, and of brass, and of stone, and of wood, which neither can see, neither hear, nor go.

21 Also they repented not of their murder, and of their sorcery, neither of their fornication, nor of their theft.

10

Another Angel appeareth with a cloud, 2 holding a book open, 3 and crieth out. 8 A voice from heaven commandeth John to take the book. 10 He eateth it.

1 And [1]I saw [2]another mighty Angel come down from heaven, clothed with a cloud, and the rainbow upon his head, and his face was as the sun, and his feet as pillars of fire.

2 And he had in his hand a [1]little book open, and he put his right foot upon the sea, and *his* left on the earth,

3 And cried with a loud voice, as when a lion roareth: and when he had cried, seven thunders uttered their voices.

9:14 [1] As if he should have said, These hitherto have been so bound by the power of God, that they could not freely run upon all men as themselves lusted, but were stayed and restrained at that great flood of Euphrates, that is, in their spiritual Babylon (for this is a Paraphrase of the spiritual Babylon by the limits of the spiritual Babylon long since overthrown) that they might not commit those horrible slaughters which they long breathed after. Now go to: let loose those four Angels, that is, administers of the wrath of God, in that number that is convenient to the slaughtering of the four quarters of the world: stir them up and give them the bridle, that rushing of that Babylon of theirs, which is the seat of the wicked ones, they may fly upon all the world, therein to rage, and most licentiously to exercise their tyranny, as God hath ordained. This was done when Gregory the ninth by public authority established for law his own Decretals, by which he might freely lay trains for the life of simple men. For who is it that seeth not that the laws Decretal most of them are as snares to catch souls withal? Since that time (O good God!) how great slaughters have there been? how great massacres? All histories are full of them: and this our age aboundeth with most horrible and monstrous examples of the same.

9:15 [1] The execution of the commandment is in two points: one, that those butchers are let loose, that out of their tower of the spiritual Babylon they might with fury run abroad through all the world, as well the thief of that crew which are most prompt unto all assays, in this verse: as their multitudes, both most copious, of which a number certain is named for a number infinite, Verse 16, and in themselves by all means fully furnished to hide and to hurt, Verse 17, as being armed with fire, smoke and brimstone, as appeareth in the color of their armor, which dazzleth the eyes of all men: and have the strength of Lions to hurt withal, from which (as out of their mouth) the fiery, smoky, and stinking darts of the Pope are shot out, Verse 18. The other point is, that these butchers have effected the commandment of God by fraud and violence, in the two verses following.

9:19 [1] That is, they [are] harmful every way: on what part soever thou put thine hand unto them or they touch thee, they do hurt. So the former are called Scorpions, Verse 3.

9:20 [1] Now remaineth the event (as I said upon the first verse) which followed of so many and so grievous judgments in the most wicked world: namely an impenitent affirmation of the ungodly in their impiety and unrighteousness, though they feel themselves most vehemently pressed

with the hand of God: for their obstinate ungodliness is showed in this verse: and their unrighteousness in the verse following. Hitherto hath been the general history of things to be done universal in the whole world: which because it doth not so much belong to the Church of Christ, is therefore not so expressly distinguished by certainty of time and other circumstances, but is woven, as they say with a slight hand. Also there is none other cause why the history of the seventh Angel is passed over in this place, than for that the same more properly appertaineth unto the history of the Church. But this is more diligently set out according to the time thereof, Rev. 11 and 16, as shall appear upon those places.

10:1 [1] Now Saint John passeth unto the other Prophetical history, which is of the Church of God, as I showed that this book should be distinguished, Rev. 4:1. This story reacheth hence unto the two and twentieth Chapter. And this whole Chapter is but a transition from the common history of the world unto that which is particular of the Church. There are in this transition or passage, two preparatives as it were, unto this Church story comprised in this whole Chapter. One is the authority of Christ revealing his mysteries, and calling his servants unto the seventh verse. The other is Saint John's calling, proper unto this place, and prepared from before unto the end of this chapter. Authority is given unto this Revelation by these things: First, by the appearing from heaven in this habit and countenance, strong, ready, glorious, surveying all things by his providence and governing them by his omnipotence, the first verse. Secondly, that he brought not by chance, but out of a book, this open Revelation, set forth unto the eye, to signify the same unto the sea, and land, as the Lord over all, the second Verse. Thirdly, that he offered the same not whispering or muttering in a corner (as false prophets do) but crying out with a loud voice unto them which sleep, and with a lionish and terrible noise roused the secure: the very thunders themselves giving testimony thereunto, the third Verse. Lastly, for that he confirmed all by an oath, Verses 5, 6, 7.

[2] Christ Jesus, see the seventh Chapter and the second verse.

10:2 [1] Namely, a special book of the affairs of God's Church. For the book that containeth things belonging [unto] the whole world, is said to be kept with the Creator, the fifth Chapter and the first verse, but the book of the Church, with the Redeemer: and out of this book is taken the rest of the history of this Apocalypse.

4 ¹And when the seven thunders had uttered their voices, I was about to write: but I heard a voice from heaven, saying unto me, ²Seal up those things which the seven thunders have spoken, and write them not.

5 And the Angel which I saw stand upon the sea, and upon the earth, ¹lift up his hand to heaven,

6 And sware by him that liveth for evermore, which created heaven, and the things that therein are, and the earth, and the things that therein are, and the sea, and the things that therein are, ¹that ²time should be no more.

7 But in the days of the ¹voice of the seventh Angel, when he shall begin to blow the trumpet, even the mystery of God shall be finished, as he hath declared to his servants the Prophets.

8 ¹And the voice which I heard from heaven, spake unto me again, and said, Go, and take the little book which is open in the hand of the Angel, which standeth upon the sea, and upon the earth.

9 So I went unto the Angel, and said to him, Give me the little book. And he said unto me, Take it, and eat it up, and it shall make thy belly bitter, but it shall be in thy mouth as sweet as honey.

10 Then I took the little book out of the Angel's hand, and ate it up, and it was in my mouth as sweet as honey: but when I had eaten it, my belly was bitter.

11 ¹And he said unto me, Thou must prophesy again among the people and nations, and tongues, and to many Kings.

11

1 *The temple is commanded to be measured.* 3 *The Lord stirred up two witnesses,* 7 *whom the beast murdereth,* 9 *and no man burieth them.* 11 *God raiseth them to life,* 12 *and calleth them up to heaven,* 13 *the wicked are terrified,* 15 *by the trumpet of the seventh Angel the resurrection,* 18 *and judgment is described.*

1 ¹Then was given me a reed like unto a rod, and the Angel stood by, saying, Rise and ²mete Temple of God, and the Altar, and them that worship therein.

10:4 ¹ A godly care is laudable, but must be joined with knowledge. Therefore nothing is to be taken in hand, but by calling: which must be expected and waiting for of the godly.

² Keep them close.

10:5 ¹ This was a gesture used of one that sweareth, which men do nowadays use.

10:6 ¹ Neither time itself, nor the things that are in time: but that the world to come is at hand which is altogether of eternity and beyond all times.

² There shall never be anymore time.

10:7 ¹ Whereof Rev. 11:15 and 16:17.

10:8 ¹ The other part of this Chapter, concerning the particular calling of Saint John to the receiving of the prophecy following which is enjoined him, first by sign in three verses, then in plain words in the last verse. Unto the setting forth of the sign belong these things: That Saint John is taught from heaven to demand the book of the Prophecy in this verse: for these motions and desires God doth inspire: that demanding the book, he is charged to take it in a figurative manner, the use whereof also is expounded, the ninth verse, (as in the second Chapter of Ezekiel and the ninth verse) whence this similitude is borrowed: lastly, for that Saint John at the commandment of Christ took the book, and found by experience that the same as proceeding from Christ was most sweet, but in that it foretelleth the afflictions of the Church it was most bitter unto his spirit.

10:11 ¹ A simple and plain declaration of the sign before going, witnessing the divine calling of S. John, and laying upon him the necessity thereof.

11:1 ¹ The authority of the intended revelation being declared, together with the necessity of that calling, which was particularly imposed upon Saint John: hereafter followeth the history of the estate of Christ's Church both conflicting or warfaring, and overcoming in Christ. For both the true Church of Christ is said to fight against that which is falsely so called over the which Antichrist ruleth. Christ Jesus overthrowing Antichrist by the spirit of his mouth: and Christ is said to overcome most gloriously until he shall slay the Antichrist by the appearance of his coming, as the Apostle excellently teacheth, 2 Thess. 2:8. So this history hath two parts. One of the state of the Church conflicting with temptations, until Chapter 16. The other of the state of the same Church obtaining victory, thence unto Chapter 20. The first part hath two members most conveniently distributed into their times, whereof the first containeth an history of the Christian Church for 1260 years, what time the Gospel of Christ was as it were taken up from amongst men into heaven: the second containeth an history of the same Church unto the victory perfected. And these two members are briefly, though distinctly propounded in this Chapter, but are both of them more at large discussed after in due order. For we understand the state of the Church conflicting out of Chapters 12 and 13 and of the same growing out of afflictions out of Chapters 14, 15 and 16. Neither did Saint John at unawares join together the history of these two times in this Chapter, because here is spoken of prophecy, which all confess to be one just and innumerable in the Church, and which Christ commanded to be continual. The history of the former time reacheth unto verse 14: the latter is set down in the rest of this Chapter. In the former are showed these things: the calling of the servants of God in 4 verses: the conflicts which the faithful must undergo in their calling, for Christ and his Church, thence unto verse 10, and their resurrection and receiving up into heaven unto verse 14. In the calling of the servants of God are mentioned two things: the begetting and setting of the Church in two verses, and the education thereof in two verses. The begetting of the Church is here commended unto S. John by sign and by speech: the sign is a measuring rod, and the speech a commandment to measure the Temple of God, that is, to reduce the same unto a new form: because the Gentiles are already entered into the Temple of Jerusalem, and shall shortly defile and overthrow the same utterly.

² Either that of Jerusalem which was a figure of the Church of Christ, or that heavenly Example, whereof verse 19, but the first liketh me better and the things following do agree thereunto. The sense therefore is, Thou seest all things in God's house almost from the passion of Christ to be disordered: and that not only the city of Jerusalem but also the court of the Temple is trampled underfoot by the nations, and by profane men whether Jews or strangers: and that only the Temple, that is, the body of the Temple, with the Altar, and a small company of good men which truly worship God, do now remain, whom God doth sanctify and confirm by his presence. Measure therefore this, even this true Church, or rather the true type of the true Church, omitting the rest and so describe all things from me that the true Church of Christ may be as it were a very little center, and the Church of Antichrist as the circle of the center, every way in length and breadth compassing about the same, that by way of prophecy thou mayest so declare openly, that the state of the Temple of God and the faithful which worship him, that is, of the Church, is much more straight than the Church of Antichrist.

2 ¹But the ²Court which is without the Temple ³cast out, and mete it not: for it is given unto the ⁴Gentiles, and the holy city shall they tread under foot, ⁵two and forty Months.

3 But ¹I will give power unto my two witnesses and they shall ²prophesy a thousand two hundred and threescore days, clothed in sackcloth.

4 These ¹are two olive trees, and two candlesticks, standing before the God of the earth.

5 ¹And if any man will hurt them, fire proceedeth out of their mouths and devoureth their enemies: for if any man would hurt them, thus must he be killed.

6 These have power to shut heaven, that it rain not in the days of their prophesying, and have power over waters to turn them into blood, and to smite the earth with all manner plagues, as often as they will.

7 ¹And when they have ²finished their testimony, ³the beast that cometh out of the bottomless pit, shall make war against them, and shall ⁴overcome them, and kill them,

8 And their corpses shall lie in the ¹streets of the

11:2 ¹ As if he should say, it belongeth nothing unto them to judge those which are without, 1 Cor. 5:12, which be innumerable: look unto those of the household only, or unto the house of the living God.

² He speaketh of the outward court, which was called the peoples court, because all men might come into that.

³ That is counted to be cast out, which in measuring is refused as profane.

⁴ To profane persons wicked and unbelievers, adversaries unto the Church.

⁵ Or a thousand and two hundred and threescore days as is said in the next verse: that is a thousand two hundred and threescore years, a day for a year as often in Ezekiel and Daniel, which thing I noted before, 2:10. The beginning of these thousand two hundred and threescore years, we account from the passion of Christ, whereby (the partition wall being broken down) we were made of two one, Eph. 2:14. I say one flock under one Shepherd, John 10:16 and the end of these years precisely falleth into the Popedom of Boniface the eighth who a little before the end of the year of Christ a thousand two hundred ninety four, entered the Popedom of Rome, in the feast of S. Lucie (as *Bergomensis* saith) having put in prison his predecessor *Coelestinus*, whom by fraud, under color of oracle, he deceived: for which cause, that well said of him, *Intravit ut vulpes, regnavit ut leo, mortuus est ut canis.* That is, he entered like a fox, reigned like a lion, and died like a dog. For if from a thousand two hundred ninety four years thou shalt take the age of Christ which he lived on the earth, thou shalt find there remaineth 1260 years, which are mentioned in this place and many others.

11:3 ¹ I had rather translate it *illud* than *illam*, the Temple than the city: for God saith, I will give that Temple, and commit it unto my two witnesses, that is unto the Ministers of the word, who are few indeed, weak and contemptible: but yet two, that is, of such a number as one of them may help another, and one confirm the testimony of another unto all men, that from the mouth of two or three witnesses every word may be made good amongst men, 2 Cor. 13:1.

² They shall exercise their office enjoined by me by the space of those thousand two hundred and sixty years, in the midst of afflictions though never so lamentable which is figuratively showed by the mourning garment.

11:4 ¹ That is, the ordinary and perpetual instruments of spiritual grace, peace and light in my Church, which God by his only power preserved in this Temple. See Zech. 4:3.

11:5 ¹ The power and efficacy of the holy ministry, and which is truly Evangelical, is declared both in earth and in heaven, protecting the administers thereof, and destroying the enemies in this verse, virtue indeed divine most mightily showing itself forth in heaven, earth and the sea, verse 6, as it described, 2 Cor. 10:4, according to the promise of Christ, Mark 16:17. And this is the second place (as I said before) of the combats which the servants of God must needs undergo in the executing of their calling, and of the things that follow the same combats. In the combats or conflicts are these things: to overcome, in these two verses: to be overcome and killed, verse 7. After the slaughter follow these things, that the carcasses of the godly are laid abroad, verse 8 being unburied, are made a matter of scorn together of cursing and bitter execrations, verse 9, and that therefore gratulations are publicly and privately made, verse 10.

11:7 ¹ That is, when they have spent those thousand two hundred and sixty years, mentioned verses 2 and 3, in publishing their testimony according to their office.

² When they have done their message.

³ Of which after Rev. 13. That beast is the Roman Empire, made long ago of civil, Ecclesiastical: the chief head whereof was then Boniface the eighth, as I said before: who lifted up himself in so great arrogancy (saith the author of *Falsciculus temporum*) that he called himself Lord of the whole world, as well in temporal causes as in spiritual: There is an extant of that matter, written by the same Boniface most arrogantly, shall I say, or most wickedly, *ca. unam sanctam, extra de majoritate & obedientia*, and in the sixth of the Decretals (which is from the same author) many things are found of the same argument.

⁴ He shall persecute most cruelly the holy men, and put them to death, and shall wound and pierce through with cursings both their names and writings. And that this was done to very many godly men by Boniface and others, the histories do declare, especially since the time that the odious and condemned name amongst the multitude first of the brethren Waldenses or Lugdunenses, then also of the Fratricels, was pretended, that good men might with more approbation be massacred.

11:8 ¹ That is, openly at Rome: where at that time was a most great concourse of people, the year of Jubilee being then first ordained by Boniface unto the same end, in the year of Christ a thousand three hundred, example whereof is read, Rev. 1. *Extra, de penitentys & remissionibus*. So by one act he committed double injury against Christ, both abolishing his truth by the restoring of the type of the Jubilee, and triumphing over his members by most wicked superstitions. O religious heart! Now that we should understand the things of Rome, Saint John himself is the author, both after in the seventeenth Chapter almost throughout, and also in the circumscription now next following, when he saith, it is that great City (as Rev. 17; 18 he calleth it) and is spiritually termed Sodom and Egypt: that spiritually (for that must here again be repeated from before) Christ was there crucified. For the two first appellations signify spiritual wickednesses: the latter signifieth the show and pretence of good, that is, of Christian and sound religion. Sodom signifieth most licentious impiety and injustice: Egypt most cruel persecution of the people of God: and Jerusalem signifieth the most confident glorying of that city, as it were in true religion, being yet full of falsehood and ungodliness. Now who is ignorant that these things do rather, and more agree unto Rome than unto any other city? The commendations of the City of Rome for many years past are publicly notorious, which are not for me to gather. This only I will say that he long since did very well see what Rome is, who taking his leave thereof, used these verses:

great city, which ²spiritually is called Sodom and Egypt, ³where our Lord also was crucified.

9 And they of the people and kindreds, and tongues, and Gentiles, shall see their corpses ¹three days and an half, and shall not suffer their carcasses to be put in graves.

10 And they that dwell upon the earth, ¹shall rejoice over them and be glad, and shall send gifts one to another, for these two Prophets ²vexed them that dwelt on the earth.

11 ¹But after ²three days and an half, ³the spirit of life *coming* from God, shall enter into them, and they ⁴shall stand up upon their feet: and great fear shall come upon them which saw them.

12 And they shall hear a great voice from heaven, saying unto them, ¹Come up hither: And they shall ascend up to heaven in a cloud, ²and their enemies shall see them.

13 ¹And the same hour shall there be a great earthquake, and the tenth part of the city shall fall, and in the earthquake shall be slain in number seven

thousand: and the remnant were sore feared, ²and ³gave glory to God of heaven.

14 ¹The second woe is past, *and* behold, the third woe will come anon.

15 ¹And the seventh Angel blew the trumpet, and there were great voices in heaven, saying, ²The kingdoms of the world are our Lord's, and his Christ's, and he shall reign for evermore.

16 ¹Then the four and twenty Elders, which sat before God on their seats, fell upon their faces and worshipped God.

17 Saying, We give thee thanks, Lord God Almighty, Which art, and which wast, and which art to come: for thou hast received thy great might, and hast obtained thy kingdom.

18 ¹And the Gentiles were angry, and thy wrath is come, and the time of the dead, that they should be judged, and that thou shouldest give reward unto thy servants the Prophets, and to thy Saints, and to them that fear thy Name, to small and great, and shouldest destroy them, which destroy the earth.

Roma vale, vidi, Satis est vidisse: revertar,
    Quumleno, meretrix, scurra, cinadus ero.
Now farewell Rome, I have thee seen: It was enough to see:
    I will return when as I mean, bawd, harlot knave to be.
11:8 ² After a most secret kind of meaning and understanding.
³ Namely in his members, as also he said unto Saul, Acts 9:5.
11:9 ¹ That is, for three years and a half for so many years Boniface lived after his Jubilee as Bergomensis witnesseth.
11:10 ¹ So much the more shall they by this occasion exercise the jollity of their Jubilee.
² The gospel of Christ, in the affliction of the world, and the ministry thereof, the savor of death unto death to those that perish, 2 Cor. 2:16.
11:11 ¹ The third place as noted I before, is of the rising again of the Prophets from the dead, and their carrying up into heaven. For their resurrection is showed in this verse: their calling and lifting up into heaven, in the verse following.
² That is, what time God shall destroy that wicked Boniface.
³ That is, the Prophets of God shall in a sort rise again, not the same in person (as they say) but in spirit, that is in the power and efficacy of their ministry, which S. John expressed before verses 5 and 6. And so the prophecy that is spoken of Elijah, is interpreted by the Angel to be understood of John the Baptist, Luke 1:17. For the same Boniface himself, who sought to kill and destroy them, was by the fire of God's mouth (which the holy ministry showeth and exhibiteth) devoured and died miserably in prison, by the endeavor of Satra Columensis, and Nogaretus a french knight, whom Philip the fair King of France sent into Italy but with a small power.
⁴ That is, the most grievous heat of afflictions and persecution shall stay for a while, for the great amaze that shall arise upon that sudden and unlooked for judgment of God.
11:12 ¹ They were called by God into heaven and taken out of this malignant world, into the heavenly Church, which also lieth hidden here in the earth, to exercise their calling secretly: as of whom this wretched world was unworthy, Heb. 11:38. For the Church of the wicked is by comparison called the earth or the world: and the Church of the godly heaven. So in ancient time amongst the godly Israelites: so amongst the Jews in the days of Manasseh and other

Kings, when the earth refused the heirs of heaven, we read that they lay hidden as heaven in the earth.
² Yet could they not hinder the secret ones of the Lord (as the Psalmist called them, Ps 83:4) but they that went on forward in his work.
11:13 ¹ Bergomensis saith, in the year of our Lord 1301, this year a blazing star foretelling great calamity to come, appeared in heaven, in which year upon the feast of S. Andrew, so great an earthquake arose, as never before: which also continuing, by times, for many days, overthrew many stately houses. This saith he of the year next following the Jubilee: which S. John so many ages before, expressed word for word.
² They were indeed broken with present astonishment of mind, but did not earnestly repent as they ought to have done.
³ Glorified God by confessing his name.
11:14 ¹ He passeth unto the second history: which is the second part of this Chapter. S. John calleth these the second and third woes, having respect unto Rev. 9:12.
11:15 ¹ Of whose sounding the trumpet Christ expressly foretold, Rev. 10:7, and this is the second part of this Chapter, containing a general history of the Christian Church, from the time of Boniface 8 unto the consummation of the victory declared by voice from heaven. In this history there are three branches: a preparation by the sound of the Angels trumpet: a narration by the voice of heavenly Angels and Elders: and a confirmation by sign.
² The narration hath two parts: an acclamation of the heavenly creatures, in this verse, and both an adoration by all the Elders, verse 16, and also a most ample thanksgiving, verses 17, 18. The sense of the acclamation is, Now the Lord is entered on his kingdom, and hath restored his Church, in which most mightily recovered from the profanation of the Gentiles, he may glorify himself. Namely, that which the Lord ordained when first he ordained his Church, that the faith of the Saints doth now behold as accomplished.
11:16 ¹ As before, 7:11. This giving of thanks is altogether of the same content with the words going before.
11:18 ¹ A speech of the Hebrew language, as much to say, as Gentiles being angry thine inflamed wrath came upon them and showed itself from heaven, occasioned by their anger and fury.

19 Then the Temple of God was ¹opened in heaven, and there was seen in the Temple the Ark of his covenant: and there were lightnings, and voices, and thunderings, and earthquake, and much hail.

12

1 A woman   2 appeareth travailing with child,   4 whose child the dragon would devour,   7 but Michael overcometh him   9 and casteth him out,   13 and the more he is cast down and vanquished, the more fiercely he exercised his subtleties.

1   And ¹there appeared a great wonder in heaven: ²A woman clothed with the Sun, and the Moon was under her feet, and upon her head a crown of twelve Stars.

2   And ¹she was with child, and cried travailing in birth, and was pained ready to be delivered.

3   And there appeared another wonder in heaven: ¹for behold, a great red dragon having ²seven heads, and ten ³horns, and seven crowns upon his heads:

4   ¹And his tail drew the third part of the stars of heaven, and cast them to the earth. And the dragon ²stood before the woman, which was ready to be delivered, ³to devour her child, when she had brought it forth.

5   ¹So she brought forth a man ²child, which should rule all nations with a rod of iron: and that her child was taken up unto God and to his throne.

6   ¹And the woman fled into the wilderness, where she hath a place prepared of God, that ²they should feed her there a thousand, two hundred and

---

11:19 ¹ This is the confirmation of the next prophecy before going by signs exhibited in heaven, and that of two sorts, whereof some are visible, as the passing away of the heaven, the opening of the Temple, the Ark of the covenant appearing in the Temple, and testifying the glorious presence of God, and the lightning: others apprehended by ear and such dull senses which bear witness in heaven and in earth to the truth of the judgments of God.

12:1 ¹ Hitherto hath been the general prophecy comprehended in 2 parts, as I showed upon Rev. 11. Now shall be declared the first part of this prophecy, in this and the next chapter and the latter part in chapters 14, 15 and 16. Unto the first part, which is of the conflicting or militant Church belong 2 things. The beginning and the progress of the same in conflicts and Christian combats. Of which two, the beginning or upspring of the Church is described in this Chap. and the progress thereof in the Chap. following. The beginning of the Christian Church, we define to be from the first moment of her the conception of Christ, until the time wherein this Church was as it were weaned and taken away from the breast or milk of her Mother: which is the time when the Church of the Jews with their city and Temple was overthrown by the judgment of God. So we have in this chapter the story of 60 years and upwards. The parts of this chapter are three. The first is, the history of the conception and bearing in womb, in 4 verses. The second, an history of the birth from verse 5 unto verse 12. The third is, of the woman that had brought forth,unto the end of the chapter. And these several parts have every one their conflicts. Therefore in that first part are two things contained, one, the conception and bearing in womb in two verses: and another of the lying in wait of the Dragon against that should be brought forth, in the next 2 verses. In the first point are these things, the description of the mother, verse 1, and the dolors of childbirth, verse 2, all showed unto John from heaven.

² A type of the true and holy Church, which then was in the nation of the Jews. This Church (as is the state of the holy Church Catholic) did in itself shine about with glory given of God, trod under feet mutability and changeableness, and possessed the kingdom of heaven as the heir thereof.

12:2 ¹ For this is that barren woman that brought not forth, of which Isa. 45:1, and Gal. 4:27, she cried out for good cause, and was tormented at that time, when in the judgment of all she seemed near unto death, and in means ready to give up the ghost by reason of her weakness and poverty.

12:3 ¹ That is the devil or Satan (as is declared verse 9,) mighty, angry, and full of wrath.

² Thereby to withstand those seven Churches spoken of, that is the Catholic Church, and that with kingly furniture and tyrannical magnificence: signified by the crowns set upon his heads, and if the same

without controversy belonged unto him by proper right: as also he boasted unto Christ, Matt. 4:9. See after, upon Rev. 13:1.

³ More than are the horns of the Lamb, or than the Churches are: so well furnished doth the tyrant brag himself to be, unto all manner of mischief.

12:4 ¹ After the description of Satan followeth this action, that is, his battle offered unto the Church partly to that which is visible wherein the wheat is mingled with the chaff, and the good fish with that which is evil: a good part thereof, though in appearance it shined as the Stars shine in heaven, he is said to thrust down out of heaven and to pervert: for if it were possible he would pervert even the elect, Matt. 24:24, and partly to the elect members of the holy Catholic Church in the second part of this verse. Many therefore of the members of this visible Church (saith S. John) he overthrew and triumphed upon them.

² He withstood that elect Church of the Jews which was now ready to bring forth the Christian Church, and watched for that she should bring forth. For the whole Church, and whole body is compared unto a woman: and a part of the Church unto that which is brought forth as we have noted at large upon, Cant. 7:6.

³ Christ mystical (as they call him) that is the whole Church, consisting of the person of Christ as the head, and of the body united thereunto by the Spirit, so is the name of Christ taken, 1 Cor. 12:12.

12:5 ¹ The second history of the Church delivered of child: in which first the consideration of the child born, and of the Mother is described in 2 verses: secondly the battle of the Dragon against the young child, and the victory obtained against him 3 verses following: last of all is sung a song of victory, unto verse 12. Now S. John in consideration of the child born, noteth two things: for he describeth him, and his station or place in this verse.

² That is, Christ the head of the Church (the beginning, root and foundation whereof is the same Christ) endowed with kingly power, and taken up into heaven out of the jaws of Satan (who as a serpent did bite him upon the cross) that sitting upon the celestial throne he might reign over all.

12:6 ¹ The Church of Christ which was of the Jews, after his assumption into heaven, hid itself in the world as in a wilderness, trusting in the only defense of God, as witnesseth S. Luke in the Acts of the Apostles.

² Namely the Apostles, and servants of God ordained to feed with the word of life, the Church collected both of the Jews and Gentiles, unless that any man will take the word *alerent* impersonally after the use of the Hebrews instead, of *aleretur*, but I like the first better. For he hath respect unto those two Prophets, of whom Rev. 11:3, as for the meaning of the 1260 days, look the same place.

threescore days.

7 And there was a battle in heaven, [1]Michael and his Angels, fought against the dragon, and the dragon fought and his angels.

8 [1]But they prevailed not, neither was their [2]place found anymore in heaven.

9 And the great dragon that old serpent, called the devil and Satan, was cast out, which deceiveth all the world: he was *even* cast into the earth, and his angels were cast out with him.

10 Then I heard a loud voice in heaven, saying, [1]Now is salvation, and strength, and the kingdom of our God, and the power of his Christ: for the accuser of our brethren is cast down, which accused them before our God day and night.

11 But they overcame him by that blood of that Lamb, and by that word of their testimony, and they [1]loved not their lives unto the death.

12 Therefore rejoice, ye heavens, and ye that dwell in them. Woe to the inhabitants of the earth, and of the sea: for the devil is come down unto you, which hath great wrath, knowing that he hath but a short time.

13 And when [1]the dragon saw that he was cast unto the earth, he persecuted the woman which had brought forth the man *child*.

14 [1]But to the woman were given two wings of a great Eagle, that she might fly into the wilderness, into her [2]place where she is nourished for a [3]time, and times, and half a time, from the presence of the serpent.

15 [1]And the serpent cast out of his mouth water after the woman, like a flood, that he might cause her to be carried away of the flood,

16 [1]But the earth helped the woman, and the earth opened her mouth, and swallowed up the flood, which the dragon had cast out of his mouth.

17 [1]Then the dragon was wroth with the woman, and went and made war with the remnant of her seed, which keep the commandments of God, and have the testimony of Jesus Christ.

18 [1]And I stood on the sea sand.

12:7 [1] Christ is the Prince of Angels, and head of the Church, who beareth that iron rod, the fifth verse. See the notes upon Daniel, Dan. 12:1. In this verse a description of the battle and of the victory in the two verses following. The Psalmist had respect unto this battle, Ps. 68:9, and Paul, Eph. 4:1 and Col. 2:15.

12:8 [1] The description of the victory, by denying of the thing in this verse, and by affirming the contrary in the next verse. As that Satan gained nothing in heaven but was by the power of God thrown down into the world, whereof he is the prince, Christ himself and his elected members standing still by the throne of God.

[2] They were cast out, so that they were never seen anymore in heaven.

12:10 [1] The song of victory or triumph containing first, a proposition of the glory of God and of Christ showed in that victory: secondly, it containeth a reason of the same proposition taken from the effects, as that the enemy is overcome in battle in this verse, and that the godly are made conquerors (and more than conquerors, Rom. 8:37) verse 11. Thirdly, a conclusion wherein is an exhortation unto the Angels, and the Saints, and unto the world, a prophecy of great misery, and of destruction procured by the devil against mankind, lest himself should shortly be miserable alone, verse 12.

12:11 [1] He is said in the Hebrew tongue, to love his life that esteemeth nothing more precious than his life: and on the other side, he is said not to love his life, who doubteth not to hazard it, wheresoever need requireth.

12:13 [1] The third part: an history of the woman delivered, consisting of two members, the second battle of Satan against the Christian Church of the Jewish nation, in four verses: and the battle intended against the seed thereof, that is against the Church of the Gentiles, which is called holy, by reason of the Gospel of Christ in the two last verses.

12:14 [1] That is, being strengthened with divine power: and taught by oracle, she fled swiftly from the assault of the devil, and from the common destruction of Jerusalem, and went into a solitary City beyond Jordan called Pella, as Eusebius telleth in the first Chapter of the third book of his Ecclesiastical history, which place God had commanded her by Revelation.

[2] Into that place where God had appointed her.

[3] That is, for three years and a half: so the same speech is taken, Dan. 7:15. This space of time is reckoned in manner from that last and most grievous rebellion of the Jews, unto the destruction of the city and Temple, for their destrution or falling away, began in the twelfth year of Nero, before the beginning whereof, many foresigns and predictions were showed from heaven, as Josephus writeth, lib. 7, chap. 12, and Hegesippus, lib. 5, chap. 44, amongst which this is very memorable, that in the feast of Pentecost, not only a great sound and noise was heard in the Temple, but also a great voice was heard of many out of the Sanctuary which cried out to all, Let us depart hence. Now three years and a half after this defection was begun of the Jews, and those wonders happened, the City was taken by force, the Temple overthrown, and the place forsaken of God: and this compass of time Saint John noted in this place.

12:15 [1] That is, he inflamed the Romans and the nations, that they persecuting the Jewish people with cruel arms might by the same occasion invade the Church of Christ, now departed from Jerusalem and out of Judea. For it is an usual thing in Scripture that the raging tumults of the nations, should be compared unto waters.

12:16 [1] That is, there was offered in their place other Jews, unto the Romans and nations raging against that people: and it came to pass thereby that the Church of God was saved whole from that violence, that most raging flood of persecution which the Dragon vomited out being altogether spent in the destruction of those other Jews.

12:17 [1] Being set on fire by this means, he began to be more mad, and because he perceived that his purpose against the Christian Church of the Jewish remnant was come to nought, he resolved to fall upon her seed, that is, the Church gathered also by God of the Gentiles, and the holy members of the same. And this is that other branch, as I said upon verse 13, in which the purpose of Satan is showed, verse 17, and his attempt, verse 18.

12:18 [1] That is, a most mighty tempest, that he rushed upon the whole world (whose prince he is) to raise the floods and provoke the nations, that they might with their furious bellows toss up and down, drive here and there, and finally destroy the Church of Christ with the holy members of the same. But the providence of God resisted his attempt, that he might favor the Church of the Gentiles, yet tender and as it were green. The rest of the story of the Dragon is excellently prosecuted by the Apostle S. John hereafter in the twentieth chapter. For here the Dragon endeavoring to do mischief, was by God cast into prison.

13

1 The beast with many heads is described   12 which draweth the most part of the world to idolatry.   13 The other beast rising out of the earth,   15 giveth power unto him.

1 And I ¹saw a beast rise ²out of the sea, having seven heads, and ³ten horns, and upon his horns *were* ten crowns, and ⁴upon his head ⁵the name of blasphemy.

2 And the beast which I saw was ¹like a leopard, and his feet like a bear, and his mouth as the mouth of a Lion: ²and the dragon gave him his power and his throne, and great authority.

3 ¹And I saw one of his heads as *it were* wounded to death, but his deadly wound was healed, and all the world wondered *and* followed the beast.

4 And they worshipped the dragon which gave power unto the beast, and they worshipped the beast, saying, Who is like unto the beast! who is able to war with him!

13:1 ¹ The Apostle having declared the springing up of the Christian Church and the state of the Church from which ours taketh her beginning, doth now pass unto the story of the progress thereof, as I showed in the entrance of the former Chapter. And this history of the progress of the Church, and the battles thereof, is set down in this Chapter, but distinctly in two parts, one is of the civil Roman Empire, unto the tenth verse. Another of the body Ecclesiastical or prophetical, thence unto the end of the chapter. In the former part are showed these things: First the state of that Empire, in four verses: then the acts thereof in three verses: after the effect, which is exceeding great glory, verse 8. And last of all is commended the use: and the instruction of the godly against the evils that shall come from the same, verses 9, 10. The history of the state containeth a most ample description of the beast, first entire, verses 1, 2, and then restored after hurt, verses 3, 4.

² On the sand whereof stood the devil practicing new tempests against the Church, in the verse next beforegoing: what time the Empire of Rome was endangered by domestical dissensions, and was mightily tossed, having ever and anon new heads, and new Emperors. See in the seventeenth chapter and the eighth verse.

³ Having the same instruments of power, providence, and most expert government which the Dragon is said to have had in Rev. 12:3.

⁴ We read in chapter 12 and third verse, that the Dragon had seven crowns set upon seven heads: because the thief announceth himself to be proper Lord and Prince of the world: but this beast is said to have ten crowns set upon several, not heads, but horns: because the beast is beholden for all unto the Dragon, verse 2, and doth not otherwise reign them by law of subjection given by him, namely that he employ his horns against the Church of God. The speech is taken from the ancient custom and form of dealing in such case: by which they that were absolute kings did wear the diadem upon their heads: but their vassals and such as reigned by grace from them, wore the same upon their hoods: for so they might commodiously lay down their diadems when they came into the presence of their Sovereigns: as also their Elders are said, when they adored God which sat upon the throne, to have cast down their crowns before him, chap. 4, verse 10.

⁵ Contrary to that which God of old commanded should be written in the head piece of the high Priest, that is, *Sanctitas Jehova*, Holiness unto the Lord. The name of blasphemy imposed by the Dragon, is (as I think) that which S. Paul saith in chapter 2 of his 2 Epistle to the Thessalonians, verse 4. *He sitteth as God, and boasteth himself to be God.* For this name of blasphemy both the Roman Emperors did then challenge unto themselves, as Suetonius and Dion do report of Caligula and Domitian: and after them the Popes of Rome did with full mouth profess the same of themselves, when they challenged unto themselves sovereignty in holy things: of which kind of sayings the sixth book of the Decretals, the Clementines, and the Extravagants, are very full. For these men were not content with that which Anglicus wrote in his *Poetria* (the beginning whereof is, *Papa stupor mundi*. The Pope is the wonder of the world. *Nec Deus es, nec homo, sed neuter es inter utrunque.* Thou art not God, nay art thou man, but neuter mixed of both: as the gloss witnesseth upon the sixth book: but they were bold to take unto themselves the very name of God, and to accept it given of other: according as almost an hundred and twenty years since, there was made for Sixtus the fourth, when he should first enter into Rome in his dignity Papal, a Pageant of triumph, and cunningly fixed upon the gate of the city he should enter at, having written upon it this blasphemous verse:

> *Oraclo vocis mundi moderaris habenas,*
>   *Et merito in terris crederis esse deus.*

> By oracle of thine own voice the world thou governest all,
>   And worthily a God on earth, men think, and do thee call.

These and six hundred the like who can impute unto that modesty whereby good men of old would have themselves called the servants of the servants of God, verily either this is a name of blasphemy, or there is none at all.

13:2 ¹ Swift as the Leopard, easily clasping all things, as the bear doth with his foot, and tearing and devouring all things with the mouth as doth the Lion.

² That is, he lent the same unto the beast to use, when he perceived that himself could not escape, but must needs be taken by the hand of the Angel, and cast into the bottomless pit, Rev. 20, yet did not he abandon the same utterly from himself, but that he might use it as long as he could.

13:3 ¹ This is the other place that pertaineth to the description of the beast of Rome: that besides that natural dignity and amplitude of the Roman Empire, which was shadowed in the two former verses, there was added this also as miraculous, that one head was wounded as it were unto death, and was healed again, as from heaven, in the sight of all men. This head was Nero the Emperor, in whom the race of the Caesars fell from imperial dignity, and the government of the Commonwealth was translated unto others: in whose hands the Empire was so cured and recovered unto health, as he seemed unto all so much the more deeply rooted and grounded fast, than ever before. And hence followed those effects, which are next spoken of: First an admiration of certain power, as it were sacred and divine sustaining the Empire and governing it: Secondly the obedience and submission of the whole earth in this verse: Thirdly, the adoration of the Dragon, and most wicked worshipping of Devils, confirmed by the Roman Emperors: Lastly, the adoration of the beast himself, who grew into so great estimation, as that both the name and worship of a God was given unto him, the fourth verse. Now there were two causes which brought in the minds of men this religion: the show of excellency, which bringeth with it reverence: and the show of power invincible, which bringeth fear. Who is like (say they) unto the beast? Who shall be able to fight with him?

5 ¹And there was given unto him a mouth, that spake great things and blasphemies, and power was given unto him, ²to do two and forty months.

6 And he opened his mouth unto blasphemy against God, to blaspheme his Name, ¹and his tabernacle, ²and them that dwell in heaven.

7 And it was given unto him to make war with the Saints, and to overcome them, and power was given him over every kindred, and tongue, and nation.

8 Therefore all that dwell upon the earth, shall worship him, ¹whose names are not written in the book of life of that Lamb, which was slain from the

CHAPTER 13
*Gen. 9:6
Matt. 26:52

beginning of the world.

9 ¹If any man have an ear let him hear.

10 If any lead into captivity, he shall go into captivity: *if any kill with a sword, he must be killed by a sword: here is the patience and the faith of the Saints.

11 ¹And I beheld, another beast coming out of the earth, ²which had two horns like the Lamb, but he spake like the dragon.

12 ¹And he did all that the first beast could do before him, and he caused the earth and them which dwell therein, ²to worship the first beast whose deadly wound was healed.

13 ¹And he did great wonders, so that he made

13:5 ¹ The second member containing an history of the acts of the beast, as I said verse 1. The history of them is concluded in two points, the beginning and the manner of them. The beginning is the gift of the Dragon, who put and inspired into the beast both his impiety against God and his eminity and injustice against all men, especially against the godly and those that were of the household of faith, the fifth verse. The manner of the acts or actions done, is of two sorts both impious in mind, and blasphemous in speech against God, his Church and the godly, verse six, and also most cruel and injurious in deeds, even such as were done of most raging enemies and of most insolent and proud conquerors, the seventh verse.

² Namely his actions and manner of dealing. As concerning those two and forty months, I have spoken of them before in the twelfth Chapter and second verse.

13:6 ¹ That is, the holy Church, the true house of the living God.

² That is, the godly in several who hid themselves from his cruelty. For this bloody beast surcharged those holy souls most falsely with innumerable accusations for the Name of Christ, as we read in Justin Martyr, Tertullian, Arnobius, Minutius, Eusebius, Augustine, and others: which example the latter times followed most diligently in destroying the flock of Christ and we in our own memory have found by experience to our incredible grief. Concerning heaven, see the eleventh Chapter and twelfth verse.

13:8 ¹ That is, such as are not from everlasting elect in Christ Jesus. For this is that Lamb slain, of which the fifth Chapter, verse six. These words I do with Aretas distinguish in this manner: *Whose names are not written even from the laying of the foundation of the world, in the book of life, of the Lamb slain.* And this distinction is confirmed by a like place hereafter, Rev. 17:8.

13:9 ¹ The conclusion of this speech of the first beast, consisting of two parts, An exhortation to attentive audience in this verse: and a foretelling, which partly containeth threatenings against the wicked, and partly comforts for those which in patience and faith shalt wait for that glorious coming of our Lord and Savior Christ, the tenth verse.

13:11 ¹ The second member of the vision, concerning the ecclesiastical dominion, which in Rome succeeded that which was politic, and is in the power of the corporation of false Prophets, and of the forgers of false doctrine. Wherefore the same body or corporation is called of S. John by the name of false prophet, Rev. 6:13, 19 and 20. The form of this beast is first described in this verse, then his acts, in the verses following, and the whole speech is concluded in the last verse. This beast is by his breed a Son of the earth (as they say) obscurely born, and by little and little creeping up out of his abject estate.

² That is, in show he resembled the Lamb (for what is more mild or more humble than to be the servant of the servants of God) but in deed he played the part of the Dragon, and of the Wolf, Matt. 7:15. For even Satan changeth himself into an Angel of light, 2 Cor. 11:14,

and what should his honest disciples and servants do?

13:12 ¹ The history of the acts of this beast containeth in sum three things, hypocrisy, the witness of miracles and tyranny: of which the first is noted in this verse, the second in the 3 verses following: the third in the sixteenth and seventeenth verses. His hypocrisy is most full of leasing, whereby he abuseth both the former beast and the whole world: in that albeit he hath by his cunning, as it were by lime made of the former beast a most miserable … or anatomy, usurped all his authority unto himself and most impudently exerciseth the same in the sight and view of him: yet he carrieth himself so, as if he honored him with most high honor, and did in very truth cause him to be honored of all men.

² For unto this beast of Rome, which of civil Empire is made an Ecclesiastical hierarchy, are given divine honors, and divine authority so far as he is believed to be above the Scriptures, which the gloss upon the Decretals declareth by this devilish verse,

Articulos solvit, synodumque facit generalem,

That is,

He changeth the Articles of faith, and giveth authority
to general Counsels.

Which is spoken of the Papal power. So the beast is by birth, foundation, feat, and finally substance, one: only the Pope hath altered the form and manner thereof being himself the head both of that tyrannical Empire, and also of the false Prophets, for the Empire hath he taken unto himself, and thereunto hath added this cunning device. Now these words, *whose deadly wound was cured* are put here for distinction sake, as also sometimes afterwards: that even at that time the godly readers of this prophecy might by this sign be brought to see the things as present: as if it were said, that they might adore this very Empire that now is, whose head we have seen in our own memory to have been cut off, and to be cured again.

13:13 ¹ The second point of the things done by the beast, is the credit of great wonders or miracles, appertaining to the strength of this impiety: of which signs some were given from above, as it is said, that fire was sent down from heaven by false sorcery, in this verse. Others were showed here below in the sight of the beast to establish idolatry, and deceive souls, which part S. John setteth forth beginning (as they say) at that which is last, in this manner: First the effect is declared in these words, *He deceiveth the inhabitants of the earth,* Secondly the common manner of working in two sorts, one of miracles. *For the signs that were given him to do in the presence of the beasts:* the other of the words added to the signs, and teaching the idolatry confirmed by those signs, *Saying unto the inhabitants of the earth, that they should make an image unto the beasts which,* etc. Thirdly, a special manner is declared: *That is given unto him to put life into the image of the beast:* and that such a kind of quickening, that the same both speaketh by answer unto those that ask counsel of it, and also pronounceth death against all those that do not obey nor worship it: all which things oftentimes by false miracles through the procurement and inspiration of the Devil,

fire to come down from heaven on the earth, in the sight of men.

14 And deceived them that dwell on the earth by the signs which were permitted to him to do in the sight of the beast, saying to them that dwell on the earth, that they should make the [1]image of the [2]beast, which had the wound of a sword, and did live.

15 [1]And it was permitted to him to give a [2]spirit unto the image of the beast, so that the image of the beast should speak, and should cause that as many

as would not worship the image of the beast should be killed.

16 [1]And he made all, both small and great, rich and poor, free and bond, to receive [2]a [3]mark in their right hand or in their foreheads.

17 And that no man might [1]buy or sell, save he that had the [2]mark or the name of the beast or the number of his name.

18 [1]Here is wisdom. Let him that hath wit, count the number of the beast: for it is the [2]number of

---

have been effected and wrought in images. The histories of the Papists are full of examples of such miracles, the most of them feigned, many also done by the devil in images: as of old in the serpent, Gen. 3:1. By which examples is confirmed, not the authority of the beast, but the truth of God, and of these prophecies.

13:14 [1] That is, images by *enallage* or change of the number: for the worship of them ever since the second Council of Nice, hath been ordained in the Church by public credit, and authority contrary unto the Law of God.

[2] In the Greek the word is in the Dative case, as much to say, as unto the worship, honor and obeying of the beast: for by this maintenance of images this Pseudoprophetical beast doth mightily profit the beast of Rome, of whom long ago he received them. Wherefore the same is hereafter very fitly called the image of the beast, for that images have their beginning from the beast, and have their form or manner from the will of the beast, and have their end and use fixed in the profit and commodity of the beast.

13:15 [1] And of this miracle of the images of the beast (that is, which the beast hath ordained to establish idolatry) which miraculously speak and give judgment, or rather marvelously, by the fraud of the false prophets, the Papists books are full fraughted.

[2] To give life as Jannes and Jambres imitated the wonders that Moses wrought.

13:16 [1] The third place, is a most wicked and most insolent tyranny as was said before, usurped over the persons of men in this verse: and over their goods and actions, in the next verse. For he is said, both to bring upon all persons a tyrannous servitude, that as bondslaves they might serve the beast: and also to exercise over all their goods and actions, a peddler-like abuse of indulgences and dispensations (as they term them) amongst their friends, and against others to use most violent interdictions, and to shoot out cursings, even in natural and civil, private and public contracts, wherein all good faith ought to have place.

[2] That is, their Chrism, by which in the Sacrament (as they call it) of Confirmation, they make servile unto themselves, the persons and doings of men, signing them in their forehead and hands: and as for the sign left by Christ (of which Rev. 7:3) and the holy Sacrament of Baptism they make as void. For whom Christ hath joined unto himself by Baptism, this beast maketh challenge unto them by her greasy Chrism, which he doubteth not to prefer over Baptism, both in authority and efficacy.

[3] The mark of the name of the beast.

13:17 [1] That is, have any traffic or intercourse with men, but they only those which have this anointing and consecration of Clearkely tonsure, as they call it. Read Gratian *de Consecratione, distinct. s. c. omnes, cap. Spiritus, etc.* of these matters.

[2] Here the false Prophets do require three things, which are set down in the order of their greatness, a character, a name and the number of the name. The meaning is, that man that hath not first their anointing and clerical tonsure or shaving: secondly holy orders, by reserving whereof is communicated the same of the beast: or finally hath not attained

that high degree of Pontifical knowledge, and of the Law (as they call it) Canonical, and hath not as it were made up in account and cast the number of the mysteries thereof: for in these things consisteth the number of that name of the beast. And this is excellently set forth in the next verse.

13:18 [1] That is in this number of the beast consisteth that Popish wisdom, which unto them seemeth the greatest of all others. In these words S. John expoundeth that saying which went before of the number of the beast, what it hath above his mark or acconisance and his name. These things, saith S. John, the mark and the name of the beast, do easily happen unto any man: but to have the number of the beast, is wisdom: that is, only the wise and such as have understanding, can come by that number for they must be most illuminated doctors that attain thereunto, as the words following do declare.

[2] How great and of what denomination this number of the beast is, by which the beast accounted his wisdom, S. John declareth in these words. Dost thou demand how great it is? it is so great, that it occupieth the whole man: he is always learning, and never cometh to the knowledge thereof: he must be a man indeed that doth attain unto it. Askest thou of what denomination it is? verily it standeth of six throughout and perfectly ariseth of all the parts thereof in their several denominations (as they term them) it standeth of six by units, tens, hundreds, etc. so as there is no one part in the learning and order Pontifical, which is not either referred unto the head, and as it were the top thereof, or contained in the same: so fitly do all things in this hierarchy agree one with another, and with their head. Therefore that cruel beast Boniface the eighth doth commend by the number of six those Decretals which he perfected, in the proem of the sixth book. *Which book* (saith he) *being to be added unto five other books of the same volume of Decretals, we thought good to name Sextum the sixth: that the same volume by addition thereof containing a senary, or the number of six books (which is a number perfect) may yield a perfect form of managing all things, and perfect discipline of behavior.* Here therefore is the number of the beast, who poureth from himself all his parts and bringeth them all back again unto himself by his discipline in most wise and cunning manner. If any man desire more of this, let him read the gloss upon that place. I am not ignorant that other interpretations are brought upon this place: but I thought it my duty, with the good favor of all and without the offense of any, to propound mine opinion in this point. And for this cause especially, for that it seemed unto me neither profitable, nor like to be true, that the number of the beast, or of the name of the beast should be taken as the common sort of interpreters do take it. For this number of the beast teacheth, giveth out, imprinteth, as a public mark of such as be his, and esteemeth that mark above all others as the mark of those whom he loveth best. Now those other expositions seem rather to be far removed from this property and condition of that number: whether you respect the name *Latinus* or *Titan*, or another. For these the beast doth not teach, nor give forth nor imprint, but most diligently forbiddeth to be taught, and audaciously denieth: he approveth not these, but reproveth them: and hateth them that think so of this number, with an hatred, greater than that of *Vatinius*.

a man, and his number is six hundred threescore and six.

CHAPTER 14
a Ps. 14:5,6
b Acts 14:15
c Isa. 21:9
Jer. 51:8
Rev. 18:2

14

1 The Lamb standeth on mount Zion: 4 with his chaste worshippers. 6 One Angel preacheth the Gospel. 8 Another foretelleth the fall of Babylon: 9 the third warneth that the beast be avoided. 13 A voice from heaven pronounceth them happy who die in the Lord. 16 The Lord's sickle thrust into the harvest, 18 and into the vintage.

1 Then I looked, and lo, a Lamb [1]stood on mount Zion, and with him an [2]hundred forty and four thousand, having his Father's [3]Name written in their foreheads.

2 And I heard a voice from heaven as the sound of many waters, and as the sound of a great thunder: and I heard the voice of harpers, harping with their harps.

3 And they sung as *it were* a new song before the throne, and before the four beasts, and the Elders: and no man could learn that song, but the hundred, forty and four thousand, which were bought from the earth.

4 These are they which are not defiled with women: for they are virgins: these follow the Lamb whithersoever he goeth: these are bought from men, being the firstfruits unto God, and unto the Lamb.

5 And in their mouths was found no guile: for they are without spot before the throne of God.

6 ¶ [1]Then I saw [2]another Angel fly in the midst of heaven, having an everlasting Gospel to preach unto them that dwell on the earth, and to every nation and kindred, and tongue, and people,

7 [1,a]Saying with a loud voice, Fear God, and give glory to him: for the hour of his judgment is come: and worship him that made [b]heaven and earth, and the sea and the fountains of waters.

8 And there followed another Angel, saying, [c]Babylon that great city is fallen, it is fallen: for she made all nations to drink of the wine of the [1]wrath of her fornication.

9 ¶ And the third Angel followed them, saying with a loud voice, [1]If any man worship the beast and his image, and receive his mark in his forehead, or on his hand,

10 The same shall drink of the wine of the wrath

14:1 [1] The history of the Church of Christ being finished for more than a thousand and three hundred years, at which time Boniface the eighth lived as before hath been said, there remaineth the rest of the history of the conflicting or militant Church, from thence unto the time of the last victory in three chapters. For first of all, as the foundation of the whole history, is described the standing of the lamb with his army and retinue in five verses, after his worthy acts which he hath done, and yet doth in most mighty manner, whilst he overthroweth Antichrist with the spirit of his mouth, in the rest of this chapter, and in the two following. Unto the description of the Lamb, are propounded three things: his situation, place and attendance: for the rest are expounded in the former visions, especially upon the fifth chapter.

[2] As ready girt to do his office (as Acts 6:56) in the midst of the Church which aforetime mount Zion did prefigure.

[3] As before 7:2. This retinue of the Lamb is described first by divine mark (as before 7:2) in this verse. Then by divine occupation, in that all and every one in his retinue most vehemently and sweetly (verse 2) do glorify the Lamb with a special song before God and his elect Angels: which song flesh and blood cannot hear, nor understand, verse 3. Lastly by their deeds done before, and their sanctification in that they were virgins, pure from spiritual and bodily fornication that is, from impiety and unrighteousness, that they followed the Lamb as a guide unto all goodness, and cleaved unto him that they are holy unto him as of grace redeemed by him: that in truth and in simplicity of Christ, they have exercised all these things, sanctimony of life, the direction of the Lamb, a thankful remembrance of the redemption by him: finally (to conclude in a word) that they are blameless before the Lord, verses 4, 5.

14:6 [1] The other part (as I said in the first verse) is of the acts of the Lamb, the manner whereof is delivered in two sorts, of his speech, and of his facts. His speeches are set forth unto verse 13 of this chapter, and his facts unto chapter 16. In the speech of the Lamb, which is the word of the Gospel, are taught in this place, these things: The service of the godly consisting inwardly of reverence towards God, and outwardly of the glorifying of him: the visible sign of which is

adoration, verse 7. The overthrowing of wicked Babylon, verse 8, and the fall of every one of the ungodly which worship the beast, verses 9, 10, 11. Finally, the state of the holy servants of God both present, verse 11, and to come, most blessed, according to the promise of God, verse 15.

[2] This Angel is a type or figure of the good and faithful servants of God, whom God especially from that time of Boniface the eighth, hath raised up to the publishing of the Gospel of Christ, both by preaching and by writing. So God first, near unto the time of the same Boniface, used Peter Cassiodorus an Italian: after, Arnold *de villa nova*, a Frenchman, then Occam, Dante, Petrarch, after that *Johannes de rupe casa*, a Franciscan: after again, John Wycliff an Englishman, and so continually one or another unto the restoring of the truth and enlarging of his Church.

14:7 [1] That is, Babylon is destroyed by the sentence and judgment of God: the execution whereof S. John described, chap. 18. And this voice of the ministers of Christ hath continued since the time that Babylon (which is Rome) hath by deliberate counsel and manifest malice oppugned the light of the Gospel offered from God.

14:8 [1] Of her fornication, whereby God was provoked to wrath.

14:9 [1] That is, shall not worship God alone, but shall transfer his divine honor unto this beast, whether he doeth it with his heart or counterfeiting in show. For he (saith Christ) that denieth me before men, him will I deny before my Father, and his Angels, Matt. 10:32. And this is that voice of the holy ministry; which at this time is very much used of the holy and faithful servants of God. For having now sufficiently found out the public obstinacy of Babylon they labor not any longer to thunder out as against the same but to save some particular members by terror (as S. Jude speaketh) and to pluck them out of the public flame, or else by a vehement commiseration of their state to lead them away, they set before them eternal death, into which they rush unawares, unless in good time they return unto God, but the godly which are of their own flock, they exhort unto patience, obedience, and faith in the Lord Jesus, and charge them to give light by their good example, of good life unto others.

of God, yea, of the pure wine, which is poured into the cup of his wrath, and he shall be tormented in fire and brimstone before the holy Angels, and before the Lamb.

11 And the smoke of their torment shall ascend evermore: and they shall have no rest day nor night, which worship the beast and his name.

12 [1]Here is the patience of Saints: here are they that keep the commandments of God, and the faith of Jesus.

13 Then I heard a voice from heaven, saying unto me, Write, The dead which die [1]in the Lord, are fully blessed. Even so saith the Spirit: for they rest from their labors, and their [2]works follow them.

14 ¶ [1]And I looked, and behold, [2]a white cloud, and upon the cloud one sitting like unto the Son of man, [3]having on his head a golden crown, and in his hand a [4]sharp sickle.

15 [1]And another Angel came out of the Temple, crying with a loud voice to him that sat on the cloud, [d]Thrust in thy sickle and reap, for the time is come to reap: for the [e]harvest of the earth is ripe.

[d] Joel 3:13
[e] Matt. 13:39

16 And he that sat on the cloud, thrust in his sickle on the earth, and the earth was reaped.

17 [1]Then another Angel came out of the Temple, which is in heaven, having also a sharp sickle.

18 And another Angel came out from the altar, which had power over fire, and cried with a loud cry to him that had the sharp sickle, and said, Thrust in thy sharp sickle, and gather the clusters of the vineyard of the earth: for her grapes are ripe.

19 And the Angel thrust in his sharp sickle on the earth, and cut down the vines of the vineyard of the earth, and cast them into that great winepress of the wrath of God.

20 And the winepress was trodden without the city, [1]and blood came out of the winepress, unto the horse bridles, by the space of a thousand and six hundred furlongs.

15 1 The seven Angels having the seven last plagues. 3 They that conquered the beast praise God. 6 To the seven Angels, 7 seven vials full of God's wrath are delivered.

14:12 [1] The patience, sanctification and justification by faith: the consequence whereof are rest, felicity, and glory eternal, in the heavenly fellowship of God and his Angels.

14:13 [1] That is for the Lord.

[2] By works, is meant the reward which followeth good works.

14:14 [1] The second part of this Chapter, as I said, verse 1. Of the acts and doings of Christ in overthrowing of Antichrist and his Church by the Spirit of his divine mouth: seeing that having been called back by word both publicly and privately unto his duty, and admonished of his most certain ruin: he yet ceaseth not to maintain and protect his own adherents, that they may do him service: and to afflict the godly with most barbarous persecutions. Of those things which Christ doeth, there are two kinds: one common or general in the rest of this chapter, another particular against that savage and rebellious beast and his worshippers in chapters 15 and 16. That common kind, is the calamity of wars spread abroad through the whole earth, and filling all things with blood, and that without respect of any person. This is figured or shadowed out in two types, of the harvest and vintage. Since the time that the light of the Gospel began to shine out, and since prophecy or preaching by the grace of God was raised up again, how horrible wars have been kindled in the world? how much human flesh hath been thrown to the earth by this divine reaping? how much blood (alas for woe) hath overflown for these hundred years almost? all history do cry out, and this our age (if ever before) is now in horror, by reason of the rage of the sickle which Antichrist calleth for. In this place is the first type, that is of the harvest.

[2] Declaring his fierceness by his color, like unto that which is in the white or milk circle of heaven.

[3] As one that shall reign from God, and occupy place of Christ in this miserable execution.

[4] That is, a most fit and commodious instrument of Execution, destroyed all by hewing and thrusting through, for who may stand against God?

14:15 [1] Christ giveth a commandment in this verse. And the Angel executeth in the next verse.

14:17 [1] The other type (as I said, verse14) is the vintage: the manner whereof is one with that which went before, if thou except this, that

the grape gathering is more exact in seeking out everything, than is the harvest labor. This is therefore a more grievous judgment, both because it succeedeth the other, and because it is understood to be executed with great diligence.

14:20 [1] That is, it overflowed very deep, and very far and wide: the speech is by hyperbole or excessive, to signify the greatness of the slaughter. And these be those pleasant fruits forsooth, of the contempt of Christ, and desiring of Antichrist rather than him, which the miserable, mad, and blind world doth at this time reap.

15:1 [1] This is that other place of the acts of Christ, as I noted before, 14:14. Now therefore is showed a singular work of the judgment of God belonging to the overthrow of Antichrist and his forces of which divine work the preparation is described in this Chapter and the execution in the next. The preparation is first set down generally and in type in this verse: and is after particularly set forth in the rest of the Chapter.

[2] Of which Rev. 8:9, in pouring forth in the plagues of the world: for even these plagues do for the most part agree with those.

15:2 [1] There are two parts of the narration: one the confession of the Saints glorifying God, when they saw that preparation of the judgments of God, unto verse 4: another the vocation, instruction, and confirmation of those instruments which God hath ordained for the execution of his judgments, in 4 other verses.

[2] This part of the vision alludeth unto the sea or large vessel of brass in which the Priests washed themselves in the entrance of the Temple: for in the entrance of the heavenly Temple (as it is called, verse 5) is said to have been a sea of glass, most lightsome and clear, unto the commodity of choice mixed with fire, that is, as containing the treasury of the judgments of God, which he bringeth forth and dispenseth according to his own pleasure: for out of the former, the Priests were cleansed of old and out of this the ungodly are destroyed now, Rev. 4:6.

[3] That is, the Godly martyrs of Christ, who shall not give place even in miracles unto that beast: of these, see before, Rev. 13:17 and 14:9, 10.

[4] Glorified God, from the particular observation of the weapons and instruments of God's wrath, floating in the sea of glass.

1 And ¹I saw another sign in heaven, great and marvelous, seven ²Angels having the seven last plagues: for by them is fulfilled the wrath of God.

2 ¹And I saw ²as *it were* a glassy sea, mingled with fire, and ³them that had gotten victory of the beast, and of his image, and of his mark, and of the number of his name, ⁴stand at the glassy sea, having the harps of God,

3 And they sung ¹the song of Moses the ²servant of God, and the song of the Lamb, saying, ³Great and marvelous *are* thy works, Lord God Almighty: just and true *are* thy *ᵃ,*⁴ways, King of Saints.

4 ᵇWho shall not fear thee, O Lord, and glorify thy name! for thou only *art* holy, and all nations shall come and worship before thee: for thy judgments are made manifest.

5 ¹And after that, I looked, and behold, the Temple of the tabernacle of Testimony was open in heaven.

6 And the seven Angels came out of the Temple, which had the ¹seven plagues, clothed in ²pure and bright linen, and having their breasts ³girded with golden girdles.

7 And therefore ¹four beasts gave unto the seven Angels seven golden vials full of the wrath of God which lived for evermore.

CHAPTER 15
ᵃ Ps. 145:17
ᵇ Jer. 10:7

8 And the temple was full of the smoke of the glory of God and of his power, and ¹no man was able to enter into the Temple, till the seven plagues of the seven Angels were fulfilled.

16 2 And 17 the Angels pour out the seven vials of God's wrath given unto them, and so divers plagues arise in the world, 18 to terrify the wicked, 19 and the inhabitants of the great city.

1 And ¹I heard a great voice out of the Temple, saying to the seven Angels, Go your ways, and pour out the *seven* vials of the wrath of God upon the earth.

2 ¹And the first went and poured out his vial upon the earth: and there fell a noisome and a grievous sore upon the men which had the ²mark of the beast, and upon them which worshipped his image.

3 ¹And the second Angel poured out his vial upon the sea, and it ²became as the blood of a dead man: and every living thing died in the sea.

4 ¹And the third Angel poured out his vial upon the rivers and fountains of waters, and they became blood.

5 And I heard the Angel of the waters say, Lord, thou art just, which art, and which wast: and Holy, because thou hast judged these things.

15:3 ¹ That song of triumph which is Exod. 15:2.

² So is Moses called for honor's sake, as it is set forth, Deut. 34:10.

³ This song hath two parts, one a confession, but particular in this verse, and general, in the beginning of the next verse: another, a narration of causes belonging to the confession, whereof one kind is eternal in itself, and most present unto the godly in that God is both holy, and alone God, another kind is future and to come, in that the elect taken out of the Gentiles (that is, out of the wicked ones and unbelieving: as Rev. 11:2) were to be brought unto the same state of happiness by the magnificence of the judgment of God, in the next verse.

⁴ Thy doings.

15:5 ¹ The second part of the narration (as was [noted,] verse 2) wherein first the authority of the whole argument and matter thereof is figured by a forerunning type of a temple opened in heaven, as Rev. 11:19, namely that all those things are divine and of God, that proceed from thence, in this verse. Secondly, the administers or executors, come forth out of the Temple, verse 6. Thirdly, they are furnished with instruments of the judgments of God, and weapons fit for the manner of the same judgments, verse 7. Finally they are confirmed by testimony of the visible glory of God, in the last verse. A like testimony whereunto was exhibited of old in the Law, Exod. 40:34.

15:6 ¹ That is, commandments to inflict those seven plagues. Here is the figure called Metonymy.

² Which was in old time a sign of the kingly or princely dignity.

³ That is, girding was a sign of diligence, and the girdle of gold was a sign of sincerity and trustiness in taking in charge the commandments of God.

15:7 ¹ Of these before, Rev. 4:7.

15:8 ¹ None of those seven Angels might resume, till he had performed fully the charge committed unto him according to the decree of God.

16:1 ¹ In the former Chapter was set down the preparation unto the work of God: here is delivered the execution thereof. And in this discourse of the execution, is a general commandment, in this verse, then a particular recital in order of the execution done by every of the seven Angels, in the rest of the chapter. This special execution against Antichrist and his crew, doth in manner agree unto that which was generally done upon the whole world, Rev. 8 and 9, and belongeth (if my conjecture fail me not) unto the same time. Yet herein they do differ one from another, that this was particularly effected upon the Princes and ringleaders of the wickedness of the world, the other generally against the whole world being wicked. And therefore these judgments are figured more grievous than those.

16:2 ¹ The history of the first Angel, whose plague upon the earth, is described almost in the same words with that sixth plague of the Egyptians, Exod. 9:9. But it doth signify a spiritual ulcer, and that torture or butchery of conscience seared with an hot iron, which accuseth the ungodly within and both by truth of the word (the light whereof God hath now so long showed forth) and by bitterness stirreth up and forceth out the sword of God's wrath.

² See Rev. 13:16

16:3 ¹ The history of the second Angel who troubleth and molesteth the seas, that he may stir up the conscience of men sleeping in their wickedness. See Rev. 8:8.

² It was turned into rotten and filthy blood, such as is in dead bodies.

16:4 ¹ The history of the third Angel striking the rivers, in this verse who proclaiming the justice of God, commendeth the same by a most grave comparison of the sins of men with the punishment of God: which is common to this place and that which went before. Wherefore also this praising is attributed to the Angel of the waters, a name common to the second and third Angels according as both of them are said to be sent against the waters, albeit, the one of the sea the other of the rivers, in two verses.

6 For they shed the blood of the Saints, and Prophets, and therefore hast thou given them blood to drink: for they are worthy.

7 ¹And I heard another out of the Sanctuary say, Even so, Lord God almighty, true and righteous are thy judgments.

8 ¹And the fourth Angel poured out his vial on the sun, and it was given to him to torment men with heat of fire,

9 And men boiled in great heat, and blasphemed the Name of God, which hath power over these plagues, and they repented not to give him glory.

10 ¹And the fifth Angel poured out his vial upon the throne of the beast, and the kingdom waxed dark, and they gnawed their tongues for sorrow.

11 And blasphemed the God of heaven for their pains, and for their sores, and repented not of their works.

12 ¹And the sixth Angel poured out his vial upon

CHAPTER 16
ᵃ Matt. 24:43
Mark 14:16
Mark 15:13
Luke 12:39

the great river ²Euphrates, and the ³water thereof dried up, ⁴that the way of the Kings of the East should be prepared.

13 And I saw ¹three unclean spirits ²like frogs come out of the mouth of that ³dragon, and out of the mouth of that ⁴beast, and out of the mouth of that ⁵false prophet.

14 For they are the spirits of devils, working miracles, to go unto the kings of the earth, and of the whole world, to gather them to the battle of that great day of God Almighty.

15 ¹(ᵃBehold I come as a thief. Blessed *is* he that watcheth, and keepeth his garments, lest he walk naked, and men see his filthiness.)

16 ¹And they gathered them together into a place called in Hebrew, ²Armageddon.

17 ¹And the seventh Angel poured out his vial into the ²air: and there came a loud voice out of the Temple of heaven from ³the throne, saying,

---

16:7 ¹ A confirmation of the praise before going, out of the sanctuary of God, whether immediately by Christ, or by some of his Angels, for Christ also is called another Angel, Rev. 3:8; 7:2; 12:1.

16:8 ¹ The history of the fourth Angel, who throweth the plague upon the heaven and upon the Sun, of which Luke 21:26 the effects whereof are noted two. The one peculiar, that it shall scorch men with heat, in this verse. The other proceeding accidentally from the former, that their fury shall so much the more be enraged against God in the next verse, when yet (O wonderful mercy and patience of God) all other creatures are first stricken often and grievously by the hand of God before mankind by whom he is provoked: as the things beforegoing [do] declare.

16:10 ¹ The story of the first Angel, who striketh the kingdom of the beast with two plagues abroad with darkness, within which biles and dolors most grievous, throughout his whole kingdom, that thereby he might wound the conscience of the wicked, and punish that most perverse obstinacy of the idolaters, whereof arose perturbation, and thence a furious indignation and desperate madness, raging against God and hurtful unto itself.

16:12 ¹ The story of the sixth Angel, divided into his act, and the event thereof. The act is, that the Angel did cast out of his mouth the plague of a most glowing heat, wherewith even the greatest floods, and which most were wont to swell and overflow (as Euphrates) were dried up by the counsel of God in this verse. The event is, that the mere madness wherewith the wicked are enraged, that they may scorn the judgments of God, and abuse them furiously to serve their own turn, and to the executing of their own wicked outrage.

² The bound of the spiritual Babylon, and to the fortresses of the same, Rev. 9:14.

³ So the Church of the ungodly, and kingdom of the beast is said to be left naked, all the defenses whereof, in which they put their trust being taken away from it.

⁴ That is, that even they which dwell further off, may with more commodity make haste unto that sacrifice which the Lord hath appointed.

16:13 ¹ That is, every of them bent their whole force, and conspired that by wonders, word and work, they might bring into the same destruction all Kings, Princes and Potentates of the world, cursedly bewitched of them by their spirits, and teachers of the vanity and impurity of the beast that committed fornication with the kings of the earth. And this is a right description of our times.

² Croaking with all importunity, and continually day and night pro-

voking and calling forth to arms, as the trumpets, and furies of wars: as is declared in the next verse.

³ That is, the devil, as Rev. 11:3

⁴ Whereof Rev. 13:1.

⁵ That is, of that other beast, of which Rev. 13:11, for so he is called also Rev. 19:20 and 20:10.

16:15 ¹ A parenthesis for admonition in which God warneth his holy servants who rest in the expectation of Christ, always to address their minds unto his coming, and to look unto themselves, that they be not shamefully made naked and circumvented of these unclean spirits, and so they be miserable unprepared at the coming of their Lord.

16:16 ¹ Namely the Angel, who holily according to the commandment of God was to do sacrifice: notwithstanding that those impure spirits do the same wickedly as servants not unto God, but unto that beast that hath seven heads.

² That is, (to say nothing of other expositions) the mountain itself, or mountain places of Megiddo. Now it is certain by the holy Scripture, that Megiddo is a city and territory in the tribe of Manasseh, bordering upon Issachar and Asher, and was made famous by that lamentable overthrow of king Josiah, whereof 2 Kings 23:30; 2 Chron. 37:22; Zech. 12:11. In this mountain country God saith by figure and type, that the kings of the peoples which serve the beast shall meet together: because the Gentiles did always cast that lamentable overthrow in the teeth of the Church of the Jews unto their great reproach: and therefore were persuaded that that place should be most fortunate unto them (as they speak) and unfortunate unto the godly: but God here pronounceth, that that reproach of the Church, and confidence of the ungodly shall by himself be taken away, in the selfsame places where the nations persuaded themselves, they should mightily exult and triumph against God and his Church.

16:17 ¹ The story of the seventh Angel unto the end of the chapter, in which first is showed by figure and speech, the argument of this plague, in this verse: and then is declared the execution thereof in the verses following.

² From whence he might move the heaven above and the earth beneath.

³ That is, from him that sitteth on the throne, by the figure called Metonymy.

[4]It is done.

18 [1]And there were voices, and thunderings, and lightnings, and there was a great earthquake, such as was not since men were upon the earth, even so mighty an earthquake.

19 [1]And the great city was divided into three parts: and the cities of the nations [2]fell: and that great [3]Babylon came in remembrance before God, [b]to give unto her the cup of the wine of the fierceness of his wrath.

20 And every isle fled away, and the mountains [1]were not [2]found.

21 [1]And there fell a great hail, like [2]talents out of heaven upon the men, and men blasphemed God, because of the plague of the hail: for the plague thereof was exceeding great.

17
1 *That great whore is described,* 2 *with whom the Kings of the earth committed fornication.* 6 *She is drunken with the blood of Saints.* 7 *The mystery of the woman, and the beast that carried her, expounded.* 11 *Their destruction.* 14 *The Lamb's victory.*

b Jer. 25:15

1 Then [1]there came one of the seven Angels, which had the seven vials, and talked with me, saying unto me, Come: I will show [2]thee the [3]damnation of the great whore that sitteth upon many waters,

2 With whom have committed fornication the kings of the earth, and the inhabitants of the earth are drunken with the wine of her fornication.

3 [1]So he carried me away into the wilderness in the Spirit, and I saw a woman sit upon a [2]scarlet colored beast, full of names of blasphemy, which had seven heads, and ten horns.

4 And [1]the woman was arrayed [2]in purple and scarlet, and gilded with gold, and precious stones, and pearls, [3]and had a cup of gold in her hand full of abomination, and filthiness of her fornication.

5 [1]And in her forehead *was* a name written, A mystery, [2]that great Babylon that mother of whoredoms, and abominations of the earth.

6 [1]And I saw the woman drunken with the blood of Saints, and with the blood of the Martyrs

---

16:17 [4] That is, Babylon is undone, as is showed verse 16 and in the Chapters following. For the first onset (as I might say) of this denunciation, is described in this Chapter: and the last containing a perfect victory is described in those that follow.

16:18 [1] Now is declared the execution (as is said in verse 27) and the things that shall last come to pass in heaven and in earth, before the overthrow of the beast of Babylon: both generally, verse 18, and particularly in the cursed city, and such as have any familiarity therewith, in the 3 last verses.

16:19 [1] That seat or standing place of Antichrist.

[2] Of all such as cleave unto Antichrist, and fight against Christ.

[3] That harlot, of whom in the Chapter next following. Now this phrase *to come into remembrance* is after the common use of the Hebrew speech, but borrowed from men, attributed unto God.

16:20 [1] That is, were seen no more, or were no more extant. A borrowed Hebraism.

[2] Appeared not, which the Hebrews utter after this sort, were not, Gen. 5:24.

16:21 [1] The manner of the particular execution, most evidently testifying the wrath of God by the original and greatness thereof: the event whereof is the same with that which is, Rev. 9:12, and that which hath been mentioned in this Chapter, from the execution of the fourth Angel hitherto, that is to say, an incorrigible pertinency of the world in their rebellion, and an heart that cannot repent, verses 9 and 11.

[2] As it were about the weight of a talent was threescore pound, that is, six hundred groats, whereby is signified a marvelous and strange kind of weight.

17:1 [1] The state of the Church militant being declared, now followeth the state of the Church overcoming and getting victory, as I showed before in the beginning of chapter 10. The state is set forth in 4 chapters. As in the place beforegoing I noted, that in that history the order of time was not always exactly observed, so the same is to be understood in this history, that it is distinguished according to the persons of which it treateth, and that in the several stories of the persons is severly observed in the time thereof. For first is delivered the story of Babylon destroyed, in this and the next chap. (for this Babylon out of all doubt shall perish before the 2 beasts and the Dragon). Secondly is delivered the destruction of both the two beasts, chap. 19. And lastly of

the Dragon, chap. 20, in the story of the spiritual Babylon are distinctly set forth the state thereof in this chap. and the overthrow done from God, chap. 18. In this verse and that which followeth is a transition or passage unto the first argument, consisting of a particular calling of the Prophet (as often heretofore) and a general proposition.

[2] That is the damnable harlot, by a figure of speech called *hypallage*. For S. John as yet had not seen her. Although another interpretation may be borne, yet I like this better.

[3] The sentence that is pronounced against this harlot.

17:3 [1] Henceforth is propounded the type of Babylon, and the state thereof in 4 verses. After a declaration of the type, in the rest of this chap., in the type are described two things, the beast (of whom chap. 13), in verse 3, and the woman that sitteth upon the beast, verses 4, 5, 6. The beast in process of time hath gotten somewhat more than was expressed in the former vision. First in that it is not read before that he was appareled in scarlet, a robe imperial and of triumph. Secondly, in that this is full of names of blasphemy: the other carried the name of blasphemy only in his head. So God did teach that this beast is much increased in impiety and injustice and doth in this last age, triumph in both these more insolently and proudly than ever before.

[2] A scarlet color, that is, with a red and purple garment: and surely it was not without cause that the Romish clergy were so much delighted with this color.

17:4 [1] That harlot, the spiritual Babylon, which is Rome. She is described by her attire, profession and deeds.

[2] In attire most glorious, triumphant, most rich, and most gorgeous.

[3] In profession, the nourisher of all, in this verse, and teaching her mysteries unto all, verse 5, setting forth all things most magnificently: but indeed most pernicious besotting miserable men with her cup, and bringing upon them a deadly giddiness.

17:5 [1] Deceiving with the title of religion, and public inscription of mystery: which the beast in times past did not bear.

[2] An exposition: in which S. John declareth what manner of woman this is.

17:6 [1] In manner of deeds: She is red with blood, and sheddeth it most licentiously, and therefore is colored with the blood of the Saints, as on the contrary part. Christ is set forth imbrued with the blood of his enemies; Isa. 3:1.

of JESUS: and when I saw her, [2]I wondered with great marvel.

7 [1]Then the Angel said unto me, Wherefore marvelest thou? I will show thee the mystery of that woman, and of that beast that beareth her, which hath seven heads and ten horns.

8 [1]The beast that thou hast seen, [2]was and is not, and [3]shall ascend out of the bottomless pit, and shall go into perdition, and they that dwell on the earth, shall wonder (whose names are not written in the book of life from the foundation of the world) [4]when they behold the beast that was, and is not, and yet is.

9 [1]Here is the mind that hath wisdom, The [2]seven heads [3]are seven mountains, whereon the woman sitteth: [4]they are also seven Kings.

10 [1]Five are fallen, [2]and one is, [3]and another is not yet come: and when he cometh, he must continue a short space.

11 [1]And the beast that was, and is not, is even

17:6 [2] A passage unto the second part of this chapter, by occasion given of S. John, as the words of the Angel do show, in the next verse.

17:7 [1] The second part or place, as I said, verse 1. The narration of the vision, promised in this verse, and delivered in the verse following. Now there is delivered first a narration of the beast and his story, unto verse 14. After, of the harlot, unto the end of the chap.

17:8 [1] The story of the beast hath a triple description of him. The first is a distinction of this beast from all that ever hath been at any time: which distinction is contained in this verse: The second is a delineation or painting out of the beast by things present, by which he might even at that time be known of the godly, and this delineation is according to his heads, verses 2, 10, 11. The third is an historical foretelling of things to come, and to be done by him: and these are ascribed unto his horns, verses 12, 13, 14. This beast is that Empire of Rome, of which I spake, chap. 13:11, according to the mutations and changes whereof which then had already happened, the holy Ghost hath distinguished and set out the same. The Apostle distinguisheth this beast from all others in these words. *The beast which thou sawest, was and is not.* For so I expound the words of the Apostle for evidence's sake as I will further declare in the notes following.

[2] The meaning is, that beast which thou sawest before (Rev. 13:1) and which yet thou hast now seen, was, (I say was) even from Julius Caesar in respect of beginning, rising up, station, glory, dominion, manner and stock, from the house of Julius: and yet is not now the same, if thou look unto the house and stock for the dominion of this family was translated unto another, after the death of Nero from the other unto a third, from a third unto a fourth, and so forth was varied and altered by innumerable changes. Finally, the Empire is one, as it were one beast: but exceedingly varied by kindreds, families, and persons. It was therefore (saith S. John) in the kindred or house of Julius: and now it is not in that kindred, but translated unto another.

[3] As if he should say, Also the same that is, shall shortly not be: but shall ascend out of the depth, or out of the sea (as was said, Rev. 13:1) that is, shall be a new stock from amongst the nations without difference, and shall in the same state go unto destruction or ruin, and perish: and so shall successively new Princes or Emperors come and go, arise and fall, the body of the beast remaining still, but tossed with so many and often alterations, as no man can but marvel that this beast was able to stand and hold out, in so many mutations. Verily no Empire that ever was tossed with so many changes, and as it were with so many tempests of the sea, ever continued so long.

[4] That is as many as have not learned the providence of God, according to the faith of the Saints, shall marvel at these grievous and often changes when they shall consider, the selfsame beast, which is the Roman Empire, to have been, not to be, and to be and still molested with perpetual mutation, and yet in the same to stand and continue. This in mine opinion is the most simple exposition of this place, and confirmed by the event of the things themselves. Although by the last change also, by which the Empire, that before was civil became Ecclesiastical, is not obscurely signified by these words: of which two, the first exercised cruelty upon the bodies of the saints: the other also upon their souls: the first by human order and policy, the other under the color of the law of God,

and of Religion, raged and imbrued itself with the blood of the godly.

17:9 [1] An exhortation preparing unto audience, by the same argument, with that of Christ: *He that hath ears to hear, let him hear.* Wherefore, for mine own part, I had rather read in this place, *Let there be here a mind, etc.* So the Angel passeth fully unto the second place of this description.

[2] *Very children know what that seven hilled city is, which is so much spoken of, and whereof Virgil thus reporteth,* And compasseth seven towers in one wall: *that city it is, which when John wrote these things had rule over the kings of the earth: It was and is not, and yet it remaineth this day, but it is declining to destruction.*

[3] This is the painting out of the beast by things present (as I said before) whereby S. John endeavored to describe the same, that he might both be known of the godly in that age, and be further observed and marked of posterity afterwards. This delineation hath one type, that is, his heads, but a double description or application of the type: one permanent from the nature of itself, the other changeable, by the working of men. The description permanent, is by the seven hills, in this verse, the other that fleeteth, is from the seven kings, verses 10, 11. And here it is worthy to be observed, that one type hath sometimes two or more applications, as seemeth good unto the holy Ghost to express either one thing by divers types, or divers things by one type. So I noted before, of the seven spirits, Rev. 1:4. Now this woman that sitteth upon seven hills, is the city of Rome, called in times past of the Greeks, … i. of seven tops or crests, and of Varro, *septiceps,* i. of her seven heads (as here) of seven heads, and of others, *septicollis,* i. standing upon seven hills.

[4] The beginning of these Kings or Emperors is almost the same with the beginning of the Church of Christ, which I showed before, Rev. 11:1. Namely from the year 35, after the passion of Christ, what time the Temple and Church of the Jews was overthrown. In which year it came to pass by the providence of God that that saying *The beast was and is not,* was fulfilled before that the destruction of the Jews immediately following came to pass. That was the year from the building of the city of Rome, 109, from which year S. John both numbered the Emperors which hitherto hath been, when he wrote these things, and foretelleth two others next to come: and that with this purpose, that when this particular prediction of foretelling of things to come, should take effect the truth of all other predictions in the Church might be the more confirmed. Which sign God of old mentioned this in the Law, Deut. 18, and Jeremiah confirmeth, Jer. 28:8.

17:10 [1] Whose names are these: the first, *Servius Sulpicius Galba,* who was the seventh Emperor of the people of Rome, the second *Marcus Salvius Otho,* the third *Aulus Vitellius,* the fourth, *Titus Flavius Vespasianus,* the fifth, *Titus Vespasianus* his son of his own name.

[2] *Flavius Domitian* son of the first *Vespasian.* For in the latter end of his days S. John wrote these things, as witnesseth Irenaus, *Lib. 5 adversus hareses.*

[3] *Nerua.* The Empire being now translated from the family of *Flavius.* This man reigned only one year, four months, and nine days, as the history writers do tell.

17:11 [1] This is spoken by the figure synecdoche, as much to say as that head of the beast which was and is not, because it is cut off, and Nerua

²the eighth, and is ³one of the seven, and ⁴all go into destruction.

12 ¹And the ten horns which thou sawest, are ²ten kings, which yet have not received a kingdom, but shall receive power, as Kings ³at one hour with the beast.

13 ¹These have one mind, and shall give their power and authority unto the beast.

14 These shall fight with the ¹Lamb, and the Lamb shall overcome them: ᵃfor he is Lord of Lords, and King of Kings: and they that are on his side, called, and chosen, and faithful.

15 ¹And he said unto me, The waters which thou sawest, where the whore sitteth, ²are people, and multitudes, and nations, and tongues.

16 And the ten ¹horns which thou sawest upon the beast, are they that shall hate the whore, and shall make her desolate, and naked, and shall eat her flesh, and burn her with fire.

CHAPTER 17
ᵃ Rev. 19:16
1 Tim. 6:15

CHAPTER 18
ᵃ Rev. 14:8
Isa. 21:9
Jer. 51:8

17 ¹For God hath put in their hearts to fulfill his will, and to do with one consent for to give their kingdom unto the beast, until the words of God be fulfilled.

18 And that woman which thou sawest, is that ¹great city which reigned over the kings of the earth.

18 2 The horrible destruction of Babylon set out. 11, 16, 18 The merchants of the earth, who were enriched with the pomp and luxuriousness of it, weep and wail: 20 but all the elect rejoice for that just vengeance of God.

1 ¹And after these things, I saw another ²Angel come down from heaven, having great power, so that the earth was lightened with his glory,

2 And he cried out mightily with a loud voice, ¹saying, ᵃIt is fallen, it is fallen, Babylon that great city, and is become the habitation of devils, and the hold of all foul spirits, and a cage of every unclean and hateful bird.

in so short time extinguished. How many heads there were, so many beasts there seemed to be in one. See the like speech in Rev. 13.3

² Nerua Traianus, who himself in divers respects is called here the seventh and the eighth.

³ Though in number and order of succession he be the eighth, yet he is reckoned together with one of these heads, because Nerua and he were one head. For this man obtained authority together with Nerua, and was Consul with him, when Nerua left his life.

⁴ Namely, to molest with persecutions the Churches of Christ, as the histories do accord, and I have briefly noted, Rev. 2:10.

17:12 ¹ The third place of this description as I said, verse 18, is a prophetical prediction of things to come which the beast should do, as in the words following S. John doth not obscurely signify, saying, which have not yet received the kingdom, etc. For there is an Antithesis or opposition between these kings, and those that went before. And first the persons are described, in this verse, then their deeds in the two verses following.

² That is, arising with their kingdoms out of the Roman beast: at such time as that political Empire began by the craft of the Popes greatly to fall.

³ Namely, with the second beast whom we called before a false prophet, which beast, ascending out of the earth got unto himself all the authority and power of the first beast, and exerciseth the same before his face, as was said, Rev. 14:11, 12. For when the political Empire of the West began to bow downwards, there both arose those ten kings, and the second beast took the opportunity offered to usurp unto himself all the power of the former beast. These kings long ago, many have numbered and described to be ten and a great part of the events plainly testifieth the same in this our age.

17:13 ¹ That is, by consent and agreement, that they may conspire with the beast, and depend upon his beck. Their story is divided into three parts, counsels, acts, and events. The counselors some of them consist in communicating of judgments and affections: and some in communicating of power, which they are said to have given unto this beast in this verse.

17:14 ¹ With Christ and his Church, as the reason following doth declare, and here are mentioned the facts and the events which followed for Christ's sake, and for the grace of God the Father towards those that are called, elected, and are his faithful ones in Christ.

17:15 ¹ This is the other member of the narration as I said verse 7, belonging unto the harlot, showed in the vision, verse 3. In this history of the harlot, these 3 things are distinctly propounded, what is

her magnificence in this verse, what is her fall, and by whom it shall happen unto her, in the two verses following: and lastly, who that harlot is, in the last verse. This place which by order of nature should have been the first, is therefore made the last, because it was more fit to be joined with the next Chap.

² That is, as unconstant and variable as the waters. Upon this foundation sitteth this harlot as Queen, a vain person upon that which is vain.

17:16 ¹ The ten Kings as verse 12. The accomplishment of this fact and event, is daily increased in this our age by the singular providence and most mighty government of God. Wherefore the facts are propounded in this verse, and the cause of them in the verses following.

17:17 ¹ A reason rendered from the chief efficient cause, which is the providence of God, by which alone S. John by inversion of order affirmeth to have come to pass, both that the Kings should execute upon the harlot, that which pleased God, and which he declared in the verse next beforegoing: and also that by one consent and counsel, they should give their kingdom unto the beast, etc., verses 13, 14. For as these being blinded have before depended upon the beck of the beast that lifteth up the harlot, so it is said that afterward it shall come to pass, that they shall turn back, and shall fall away from her when their hearts shall be turned into better state by the grace and mercy of God.

17:18 ¹ That is, Rome that great City, or only City (as Justinian calleth it) the King and head whereof was then the Emperor, but now the Pope, since that the condition of the beast was changed.

18:1 ¹ The second place (as I said before, 17:1) of the history of Babylon, is of the woeful fall and ruin of that whore of Babylon. This historical prediction concerning her, is threefold. The first a plain and simple foretelling of her ruin in three verses, the second a figurative prediction by the circumstances, thence, unto verse 20. The third, a confirmation of the same by sign or wonder, unto the end of the Chapter.

² Either Christ the eternal word of God the Father (as often elsewhere) or a created Angel, and one deputed unto this service: but thoroughly furnished with greatness of power, and with light of glory, as the ensign of power.

18:2 ¹ The prediction or foretelling of her ruin, containing both the fall of Babylon, in this verse, and the cause thereof uttered by way of allegory concerning her spiritual and carnal wickedness, that is, her most great impiety and injustice, in the next verse: her fall is first simply declared by the Angel: and then the greatness thereof is showed here by the events, when he saith it shall be the seat and habitation of devils, of wild beasts and of cursed souls, as of old, Isa. 13:21, and often elsewhere.

3 For all nations have drunken of the wine of the wrath of her fornication, and the kings of the earth have committed fornication with her, and the merchants of the earth are waxed rich of the abundance of her pleasures.

4 [1]And I heard another voice from heaven say, [2]Go out of her, my people, that ye be not [3]partakers of her sins, and that ye receive not of her plagues:

5 For her sins are [1]come up into heaven, and God hath remembered her iniquities.

6 [1]Reward her, even as she hath rewarded you, and give her double according to her works: *and* in the cup that she hath filled to you, fill her the double.

7 Inasmuch as she glorified herself, and lived in pleasure, so much give ye to her torment and sorrow: for she saith [1]in her heart, I sit being a queen, and am [2]no widow, and shall [3]see no mourning.

8 Therefore shall her plagues come at [1]one day, death, and sorrow, and famine, and she shall be burnt with fire: for that God which condemneth her, is a strong Lord,

9 And the [1]kings of the earth shall bewail her, and lament for her, which have committed fornication, and lived in pleasure with her, when they shall see that smoke of that her burning,

10 And shall stand afar off for fear of her torment, saying, Alas, alas, that great city Babylon, that mighty city: for in one hour is thy judgment come.

11 [1]And the merchants of the earth shall weep and wail over her: for no man buyeth their ware anymore.

12 The ware of gold, and silver, and of precious stone, and of pearls, and of fine linen, and of purple, and of silk, and of scarlet, and of all manner of Thynewood, and of all vessels of ivory, and of all vessels of most precious wood, and of brass, and of iron, and of marble,

13 And of cinnamon, and odors, and ointments, and frankincense, and wine, and oil, and fine flour, and wheat, and beasts, and sheep, and horses, and chariots, and servants, and souls of men.

14 ([1]And the [2]apples that thy soul lusted after, are departed from thee, and all things which were fat and excellent, are departed from thee, and thou shalt find them no more.)

15 The merchants of these things which were waxed rich, shall stand afar off from her, for fear of her torment, weeping and wailing.

16 And saying, Alas, alas, that great city, that was clothed in fine linen and purple, and scarlet, and gilded with gold, and precious stones, and pearls.

17 [1]For in one hour so great riches are come to desolation. And every shipmaster, and all the people that occupy ships and shipmen, and whosoever traffic on the sea, shall stand afar off.

18 And cry, when they see that smoke of that her burning, saying, What *city was* like unto this great city?

19 And they shall cast dust on their heads, and cry, weeping, and wailing, and say, Alas, alas that great city, wherein were made rich all that had ships on the sea by her coastlines: for in one hour she is made desolate.

20 [1]O heaven, rejoice of her, and ye holy Apostles

18:4 [1] The second prediction, which is of the circumstances of the ruin of Babylon: of these there are two kinds: one going before it: as that beforehand the godly are delivered unto the ninth verse: the other following upon her ruin, namely the lamentation of the wicked and rejoicing of the godly, unto the twentieth verse.

[2] Two circumstances going before the ruin, are commanded in this place: one is, that the godly depart out of Babylon: as I mentioned, chapter 12, to have been done in time past, before the destruction of Jerusalem: this charge is given here, and in the next verse. The other is, that every one of them occupy themselves in their own place, in executing the judgment of God, as it was commanded the Levites of old, Exod. 32:27, and that they sanctify their hands unto the Lord, verses 6, 7, 8.

[3] Of his commandment there are two causes to avoid the contagion of sin, and to shun the participation of those punishments that belong thereunto.

18:5 [1] He useth a word which signifieth the following of sins one after another, and rising one another in such sort, that they grew at length to such an heap that they came up even to heaven.

18:6 [1] The provocation of the godly, and the commandment of executing the judgments of God, stand upon three causes which are here expressed: the unjust wickedness of the whore of Babylon, in this verse her cursed pride opposing itself against God, which is the fountain of all evil actions, verse 7, and her most just damnation by the sentence of God, verse 8.

18:7 [1] With herself.

[2] I am full of people and mighty.

[3] I shall taste of none.

18:8 [1] Shortly and at one instant.

18:9 [1] The circumstances following the fall of Babylon, or the consequences thereof (as I distinguished them, verse 4) are two. Namely the lamentation of the wicked unto verse 19: and the rejoicing of the godly, verse 20. This most sorrowful lamentation, according to the person of them that lament, hath three members, the first whereof is the mourning of the kings and mighty men of the earth, in two verses. The second is the lamentation of the merchants that traffic by land thence unto verse 16. The third is the wailing of those that merchandise by sea, verses 16, 17, 18. In every [one] of these the cause and manner of their mourning is described in order, according to the condition of those [that] mourn, with observation of that which best agreeth unto them.

18:11 [1] The lamentation of those that trade by land, as I distinguished immediately before.

18:14 [1] An apostrophe, or turning of the speech by imitation, used for more vehemence, as if those merchants, after the manner of mourners should in passionate speech speak unto Babylon, though now utterly fallen and overthrown. So Isa. 12:9, and in many other places.

[2] By this is meant that season which is next before the fall of the leaf, at what season fruits ripen, and the word signifieth such fruits as are longed for.

18:17 [1] The manner of mourning used by them that trade by sea.

18:20 [1] The other consequent unto the other ruin of Babylon, is the exultation or rejoicing of the godly in heaven and in earth, as was noted, verse 9.

and Prophets: for God hath punished her, to be revenged on her for your sakes.

21 ¹Then a mighty Angel took up a stone, like a great millstone, *b*and cast it into the sea, saying, With such violence shall that great city Babylon be cast and shall be found no more.

22 ¹And the voice of harpers, and musicians and of pipers, and trumpeters shall be heard no more in thee, and no craftsman, of whosoever craft *he be*, shall be found anymore in thee: and the sound of a millstone shall be heard no more in thee.

23 And the light of a candle shall shine no more in thee: and the voice of the bridegroom and of the bride shall be heard no more in thee: for thy merchants were the great men of the earth: and with thine enchantment were deceived all nations.

24 And in her was found the ¹blood of the Prophets ²and of the Saints, and of all that were slain upon the earth.

19

1 The heavenly company praise God for avenging the blood of his servants on the whore. 9 They are written blessed, that are called to the Lamb's supper. 10 The Angel will not be worshipped. 11 That mighty King of Kings appeareth from heaven. 19 The battle, 20 wherein the beast is taken, and cast into the burning lake.

1 And ¹after these things I heard a great voice of a great multitude in heaven, saying, ²,³Hallelujah, salvation, and glory, and honor, and power *be* to the

b Jer. 51:63

CHAPTER 19
a Matt. 22:2
b Rev. 22:8

Lord our God.

2 For true and righteous *are* his judgments: for he hath condemned the great whore which did corrupt the earth with her fornication, and hath avenged the blood of his servants *shed* by her hand.

3 And again they said, ¹Hallelujah: and that her smoke rose up for evermore.

4 And the four and twenty Elders, and the four beasts fell down, and worshipped God that sat on the throne, saying, Amen, Hallelujah.

5 ¹Then a voice came out of the ²throne, saying, Praise our God, all ye his servants, and ye that fear him, both small and great.

6 And I heard ¹like a voice of a great multitude, and as the voice of many waters, and as the voice of strong thunderings, saying, Hallelujah: for the Lord that God that Almighty one hath reigned.

7 Let us be glad and rejoice, and give glory to him: for the marriage of the Lamb is come, and his wife hath made ¹herself ready.

8 And to her was granted, that she should be arrayed with ¹pure fine linen and shining, for the fine ²linen is the ³righteousness of Saints.

9 ¹Then he said unto me, Write, *a*Blessed *are* they which are called unto the Lamb's supper. And he said unto me, These words of God are true.

10 ¹And I fell before his feet, *b*to worship him, but he said unto me, See thou do it not: I am thy fellow servant, and one of thy brethren, which have the

---

18:21 ¹ The third prediction, as I said verse 1, standing of a sign, and the interpretation thereof: the interpretation thereof is in 2 sorts, first by a simple propounding of the thing itself, in this verse, and then by declaration of the events in the verses following.

18:22 ¹ The events are two, the one of them opposite unto the other for amplification sake. There shall be, saith he, in Babylon no mirth nor joy at all, in this and the next verse, but all heavy and lamentable things from the bloody slaughters of the righteous and the vengeance of God coming upon it for the same.

18:24 ¹ That is shed by bloody massacres, and calling for vengeance.
² That is, proved and found out, as if God had appointed a just inquiry, concerning the impiety, unnaturalness and injustice of those men.

19:1 ¹ This chapter hath in sum two parts, one transitory or of passage unto the things that follow unto verse 10, another historical of the victory of Christ gotten against both the beasts unto the end of the chapter, which I said was the second history of this argument, Rev. 17:1. The transition hath two places, one of praising God for the overthrow done unto Babylon in 4 verses, and another likewise of praise, and Prophetical, for the coming of Christ unto his kingdom, and his most royal marriage with his Church, thence unto the tenth verse. The former praise has three branches, distinguished after the ancient manner of those that sing: … , that is, an invitation or provokement in 2 verses, … , a response or answer in the third verse, and … , a close or joining together in harmony: all which I thought good of purpose to distinguish in this place, lest any man should with Porphyrius, or other like dogs, object to Saint John of the heavenly Church, a childish and idle repetition of speech.
² Praise the Lord.
³ The proposition of praise with exhortation in this verse, and the

cause thereof, in the next verse.

19:3 ¹ The song of the Antiphony or response, containing an amplification of the praise of God, from the perpetual and most certain testimony of his divine judgment as was done at Sodom and Gomorrah, Gen. 19.

19:5 ¹ The second place of praise as I said verse 1, which first is commanded from God in this verse: and then is in most ample manner pronounced of the creatures, both because they see that kingdom of Christ to come, which most they desire, verse 6, also because they see that the Church is called forth to be brought home: into the house of her husband by holy marriage unto the fellowship of his kingdom, verses 7, 8. Wherefore S. John is commanded to write in a book the Epiphonema , or acclamation joined with a divine testimony, verse 9.
² Out of the temple from God, as Rev. 11:19.

19:6 ¹ Without the Temple in heaven.

19:7 ¹ Namely unto that holy marriage both herself in person in this verse and also furnished of her spouse with marriage gifts princely and divine is adorned and prepared in the next verse.

19:8 ¹ As an ensign of Kingly and priestly dignity: which dignity Christ bestoweth upon us, Rev. 1:6.
² This is a gift given by the husband for marriage sake and a most choice ornament, which Christ bestoweth upon us, as upon his spouse.
³ Good works which are lively testimonies of faith.

19:9 ¹ Namely the Angel, as appeareth by the next verse.

19:10 ¹ The particular history of this verse is brought in by occasion, and as it were besides the purpose, that Saint John might make a public example of his own infirmity, and of the modest sanctimony of the Angel, who hath renounced for himself the divine honors, and recalled all the servants of God, unto the worship of him alone: as also Rev. 22:8.

²testimony of Jesus, Worship God: for the testimony of ³Jesus is the Spirit of prophecy.

11 ¹And I saw ²heaven open, and behold a white horse, and he that sat upon him was called faithful and true, and he judgeth and fighteth righteously.

12 And his eyes *were* as a flame of fire, and on his head *were* many crowns: and he had a name written, that no man knew but himself.

13 And he was clothed with a garment dipped in blood, and his name is called, THE WORD OF GOD.

14 ¹And the hosts which were in heaven, followed him upon white horses, clothed with fine linen white and pure.

15 ¹And out of his mouth went out a sharp sword, that with it he should smite the heathen: for he shall ʿrule them with a rod of iron, for he it is that treadeth the winepress of the fierceness and wrath of Almighty God.

16 ¹And he hath upon his garment, and upon his thigh, a name written, ᵈTHE KING OF KINGS AND LORD OF LORDS.

17 ¹And I saw an Angel stand in the ²sun who cried with a loud voice, saying, to all the fowls that did fly by ³the midst of heaven, come, and gather yourselves together unto the supper of the great God,

18 That ye may eat the flesh of kings, and the flesh

ᶜ Ps. 2:9
ᵈ Rev. 17:14
1 Tim. 6:15

of high captains, and the flesh of mighty men, and the flesh of horses, and of them that sit on them, and the flesh of all freemen, and bondmen, and of small and great.

19 ¹And I saw the beast, and the kings of the earth, and their hosts gathered together to make battle against him that sat on the horse, and against his army.

20 But the beast ¹was taken, and with him ²that false Prophet that wrought miracles before him, whereby he deceived them that received the beast's mark, and them that worshipped his image. These both were alive cast into a lake of fire burning with brimstone.

21 And the remnant were slain with the sword of him that sitteth upon the horse, which cometh out of his mouth, and all the fowls were filled full with their flesh.

20 1 *The Angel* 2 *bindeth Satan for a thousand years.* 8 *Being loosed, he stirreth up Gog and Magog, that is, privy and open enemies against the Saints,* 11 *but the vengeance of the Lord cutting off their insolency.* 12 *The books are opened, by which the dead are judged.*

1 And ¹I saw an Angel come down from heaven, having the key ²of the bottomless pit, and a great chain in his hand.

2 And he took the dragon that old serpent, which is the devil and Satan, and he bound him ¹a thousand

---

19:10 ² Which are commanded to bear witness of Jesus.

³ For Jesus is the mark that all the prophecies shoot at.

19:11 ¹ The second place of this Chapter (as I said verse 1) is of the victory gotten by Christ against both the beasts: in which first Christ is described as one ready to fight, unto verse 16, then is showed the battle to be begun, thence unto verse 18: lastly is set forth the victory unto the end of the Chapter. In this place do shine most excellent properties of Christ as our heavenly Judge and revenger, according to his person, company, effects, and names.

² Properties belonging to his person, that he is heavenly, judge, faithful, true, just, in this verse, searching out all things ruling over all, to be searched out of none, verse 12, the trumpet, and the very essential word of God, verse 13.

19:14 ¹ The company or retinue of Christ, holy, innumerable, heavenly, judicial, royal and pure.

19:15 ¹ The effects of Christ prepared unto battle, that with his mouth he striketh the Gentiles, ruleth and destroyeth.

19:16 ¹ The name agreeing unto Christ according to the former properties, expressed after the manner of the Hebrews.

19:17 ¹ The second member as I said, verse 11. A reproachful calling forth of his enemies unto battle: in which not themselves (for why should they be called forth of the king of the world, or provoked being his subjects? for that is not comely) but in their hearing, the birds of the air are called to eat their carcasses.

² That is, openly, and in sight of all, as Num. 25:4 and 2 Sam. 12:11.

³ That is, through this inferior heaven, and which is nearer unto us: a Hebrew phrase.

19:19 ¹ The third member (as was said, verse 11) of the victory obtained by Christ. Unto this apppertaineth two things: his bucking with the beast and his forces in this verse: and the event most magnificent, described after the manner of men, in the verses following. All these things are plain.

19:20 ¹ Namely, that beast with seven heads, of which before, Rev. 13:1 and 17:3.

² That is, that beast with two heads, of which Rev. 13:11. See also Rev. 16:14.

20:1 ¹ Now followeth the third place of the prophetical history, which is of the victory whereby Christ overcame the dragon, as I note, Rev. 7:1. This place must necessarily be joined with the end of chapter 12 and be applied unto the just understanding thereof. This chapter hath two parts, one of the dragon overcome, unto verse 10, the other of the resurrection and last judgment unto the end of the chapter. The history of the dragon is double: First of the first victory after which he was bound by Christ unto verse 6. The second is of the last victory, whereby he has thrown down into everlasting punishment, thence unto verse 10. This first history happened in the first time of the Christian Church, when the dragon thrown down from heaven by Christ, went about to molest the new birth of the Church in the earth, Rev. 12:17, 18. For which cause I gave warning, that this story of the Dragon must be annexed unto that place.

² That is of hell, whither God threw down the Angels which had sinned, and bound them in chains of darkness to be kept unto damnation, 2 Pet. 2:4; Jude 6.

20:2 ¹ The first whereof (continuing this history with the end of chapter 12) is the 36 year from the passion of Christ, when the Church of the Jews being overthrown, Satan assayed to invade the Christian Church gathered of the Gentiles, and to destroy part of her seed, Rev. 12:17. The thousandth year falleth precisely upon the times of that wicked Hildebrand, who was called Gregory the seventh a most damnable Necromancer and sorcerer, whom Satan used as an instrument when he was loosed out of bonds, thenceforth to annoy the Saints of God with most cruel persecutions, and the whole world with dissentions, and most bloody wars: as Benno the Cardinal reporteth at large. This is the first victory gotten over the dragon in the earth.

years:

3 And cast him into the bottomless pit, and he shut him up, and sealed *the door* upon him, that he should deceive the people [1]no more till the thousand years were fulfilled: for after that he must be loosed for [2]a little season.

4 [1]And I saw [2,3]seats: and they sat upon them, and judgment was given unto them, and *I saw* the souls of them that were [4]beheaded for the witness of Jesus, and for the word of God, and which [5]did not worship the beast, neither his image, neither had taken his mark upon their foreheads or on their hands: and they lived, and reigned with Christ a thousand years.

5 [1]But the rest of the dead men [2]shall not live again, until the thousand years be finished: this is the first resurrection.

6 Blessed and holy is he, that hath part in the first resurrection: *for* on such the [1]second death hath no power: but they shall be the Priests of God and of Christ, [2]and shall reign with him a thousand years.

7 [1]And when the [2]thousand years are expired, Satan shall be loosed out of his prison,

8 [1]And shall go out to deceive the people, which

are in the four quarters of the earth: *even* [a]Gog and Magog, to gather them together to battle, whose number *is* as the sand of the Sea.

9 And they went up into the [1]plain of the earth, and they compassed the tents of the Saints about, and the beloved city: but [2]fire came down from God out of heaven, and devoured them.

10 [1]And the devil that deceived them, was cast into a lake of fire and brimstone, where that beast and that false prophet *are*, and shall be tormented even day and night for evermore.

11 [1]And I saw a great [2]white throne, and one that sat on it, [3]from whose face fled away both the earth and heaven, and their place was no more found.

12 And I saw the dead, both great and small stand before [1]God: and the [2]books were opened, and [b]another book was opened, which is *the book* [3]of life, and the dead were judged of those things, which were written in the books, according to their works.

13 [1]And the sea gave up her dead, which were in her, and death and hell delivered up the dead, which were in them: and they were judged every man according to their works.

20:3 [1] Namely, with that public and violent deceit which he attempted before, Chapter 12, and which after a thousand years (alack for woe) he most mightily procured in the Christian world.

[2] Which being once expired, the second battle and victory shall be, of which verses 7, 8.

20:4 [1] A description of the common state of the Church of Christ in earth in that space of a thousand years, for which the devil was in bonds: in which first the authority, life, and common honor of the godly, is declared, verse 4. Secondly, newness of life is preached unto others by the Gospel, after that space, verse 5. Finally, he concludeth with promises, verse 6.

[2] For judgment was committed to them, as to members joined to the head, not [that] Christ's office was given over [to] them.

[3] This was a type of the authority of the good and faithful servants of God in the Church, taken from the manner of men.

[4] Of the Martyrs, which suffered in those first times.

[5] Of the Martyrs which suffered after that both the beasts were now risen up, Chapter 13, for these three things are expounded.

20:5 [1] Whoever shall lie dead in sin, and not know the truth of God.

[2] They shall not be renewed with that newness of the life by the enlightening of the Gospel of the glory of Christ. For this is the first resurrection, by which the souls of the godly do rise from their death. In the second resurrection their bodies shall rise again.

20:6 [1] That whereby both body and soul, that is, the whole man is addicted and delivered unto eternal death. So Rev. 2:11.

[2] A return unto the intended history, by resuming the words which are in the end of the fourth verse.

20:7 [1] The second history, of the latter victory of Christ, as was said verse 1. In which are summarily described the work, overthrow and eternal punishment of Satan.

[2] Of which I spake, verse 2. Then therefore shall be given unto him liberty to rage against the Church, and to molest the Saints for the sins of men: unto whom the faithful shall have associated themselves more than was meet, tasting with them of their impurity of doctrine

and life.

20:8 [1] The work or act of Satan (which is the first member as I distinguished in the verse beforegoing) to deceive the whole world, even unto the uttermost nations thereof: to arm them against the people of God, in this verse, and to besiege and oppress the Church, with his whole strength, in the verse following.

20:9 [1] As if he said insomuch that the whole face of the earth, how great soever it is was filled.

[2] The wrath of God, consuming the adversaries, and overthrowing all their enterprises, Heb. 10:27. And this is the second member mentioned, verse 7, the overthrow of Satan.

20:10 [1] The third member, eternal destruction against those that are overcome: as I noted in the same place.

20:11 [1] The second part of this Chapter, in which is described the judge, in this verse, and the last judgment in the verse following.

[2] That is, a tribunal seat most Princelike and glorious: for so doth the Greek word also signify.

[3] That is, Christ, before whom when he cometh unto judgment, heaven and earth shall perish for the greatness of his majesty, 2 Pet. 3:7, 10, etc.

20:12 [1] That is, Christ the judge, 2 Cor. 5:10.

[2] As it were, our books of reckoning or accompts: that is, the testimony of our conscience, and of our works, which by no means can be avoided. This is spoken after the manner of men.

[3] The book of the eternal decree of God, in which God the Father hath elected in Christ according to the good pleasure of his will, those that shall be heirs of life. This also is spoken according to the manner of men.

20:13 [1] This is a prevention or an answer to an objection: for happily some man will say, but they are dead, whom the sea, death and the grave hath consumed, how shall they appear before the judge? S. John answereth by resurrection from death, whereunto all things (however repugnant) shall minister and serve at the commandment of God, as Dan. 12.

14 ¹And death, and hell were cast into the lake of fire: this is the second death.

15 And whosoever was not found written in the book of life, was cast into the lake of fire.

21 2 *He describeth new Jerusalem descending from heaven,* 6 *The bride the Lamb's wife,* 12 *and the glorious building of the city,* 19 *garnished with precious stones,* 22 *whose Temple the Lamb is.*

1 And ¹I saw ᵃa new heaven, and a new earth: for the ᵇfirst heaven, and the first earth were passed away, and there was no more sea.

2 ¹And I John saw the holy city new Jerusalem come down from God out of heaven, prepared as a bride trimmed for her husband.

3 ¹And I heard a great voice out of heaven, saying, Behold, the Tabernacle of God *is* with men, and he will dwell with them: and they shall be his people, and God himself shall be their God with them.

4 ᶜAnd God shall wipe away all tears from their eyes, and there shall be no more death, neither sorrow, neither crying, neither shall there be anymore pain: for the first things are passed.

5 ¹And he that sat upon the throne, said, ᵈBehold, I make all things new, and he said unto me, Write: for these things are faithful and true.

6 And he said unto me, ᵉ,¹It is done, I am Alpha

CHAPTER 21
ᵃ Isa. 65:17
Isa. 66:22
ᵇ 2 Pet. 3:13
ᶜ Rev. 7:17
Isa. 15:8
ᵈ Isa. 43:19
2 Cor. 5:17
ᵉ Rev. 1:8
Rev. 22:13

and Omega, the beginning and the end: I will give to him that is athirst, of the well of the water of life freely.

7 He that overcometh, shall inherit all things, and I will be his God, and he shall be my Son.

8 But the fearful and unbelieving, and the abominable and murderers, and whoremongers, and sorcerers, and idolaters, and all liars shall have their ¹part in the lake which burneth with fire and brimstone, which is the second death.

9 ¹And there came unto me one of the seven Angels, which had the seven vials full of the seven last plagues, and talked with me, saying, Come: I will show thee the bride the Lamb's wife.

10 And he carried me away in the spirit to a great and ¹an high mountain, and he showed me ²that great city, that holy Jerusalem, descending out of heaven from God,

11 Having the glory of God, and her shining was like unto a stone most precious, as a jasper stone clear as crystal,

12 ¹And had a great wall and high, and had ²twelve gates, and at the gates ³twelve Angels, and the names written which are the twelve tribes of the children of Israel.

13 On the East part *there were* three gates, *and* on the North side three gates, on the South side three gates, *and* on the West side three gates.

20:14 ¹ The last enemy which is death shall be abolished by Christ (that he may no more make any attempt against us), 1 Cor. 15:16, and death shall feed upon the reprobate in hell for evermore, according to the righteous judgment of God, in the next verse.

21:1 ¹ Now followeth the second part of the history prophetical (as I said, Rev. 1 and 11:1) of the future estate of the Church in heaven after the last judgment, unto the fifth verse of the next chapter, in this are two things briefly declareth. The station, seat, or place thereof, verse 1. Then her state and condition in the verses following. Before the state of the Church described, is set down the state of the whole world, that there shall be a new heaven, and a new earth, as Isa. 65:17 and 66:12 and 2 Pet. 3:13, and this is the seat or place of the Church, in which righteousness shall dwell.

21:2 ¹ The state of this glorious Church is first described generally, unto verse 8 and then specially and by parts, in the verses following. The general description consisteth in a vision showed afar off, verse 2, and in speech spoken from heaven. In the general these things are common that the Church is holy, new, the workmanship of God, heavenly, most glorious, the spouse of Christ, and partaker of this glory in this verse.

21:3 ¹ The Church is described by the speech first of an Angel, in two verses, then of God himself in 4 verses. The Angel's speech describeth the glory of the Church by the most familiar cohabitation of God therewith, by communication of all manner [of] good things according to the covenant, in this verse: and by removing or putting far away of all evil things in the verse following.

21:5 ¹ In the speech of God himself describing the Church, is first a certain exordium, or entrance, verse 5. Then followeth a magnificent description of the Church, by the present and future good things of the same in 3 verses following. In the exordium God challengeth to

himself the restoring of all the creatures of which verse 1 and witnesseth the calling of S. John unto the writing of these things, in this verse.

21:6 ¹ The description of the Church is of three sorts, by the abolishing of old things: by the being of present things in God, that is of things eternal and by the communication of all good things with the godly, verse 6. If so be they shall strive manfully, verse 7. But the reprobate are excluded from thence, verse 8.

21:8 ¹ Their lot, and inheritance as it were.

21:9 ¹ A transition unto the particular describing of the heavenly Church by the express calling of Saint John in this verse, and his rapting up by the Spirit, in confirmation of the truth of God in the verse following.

21:10 ¹ He meaneth the place and stately seat of the Church, shadowed out in a mountain.

² A type of that Church which is one, ample, or Catholic, holy celestial, built of God, in this verse: and glorious in the verse following. This type propounded generally, is after particularly declared, verse 12, etc.

21:12 ¹ A particular description (as I noted, verse 2) of the celestial Church. First, by the essential parts of the same, under the similitude of a city to verse 12. Secondly, from foreign accidents, unto the end of the chapter. Thirdly, by the effects, in the beginning of the next chapter, the essential parts are noted the matter and the form in the whole work: of these the superficies and foundation of the wall are entire parts (as they use to be called) which parts are first described in figure, unto verse 14 and afterward more exactly.

² According to the number of the tribes, of which chap. 7. For here the outward part is attributed unto the old Testament, and the foundation of the new Testament.

³ He meaneth the Prophets, who are the messengers of God, and watchmen of the Church.

14 And the wall of the city had ¹twelve foundations, and in them the names of the Lamb's twelve Apostles.

15 ¹And he that walked with me, had a golden reed, to measure the city withal, and the gates thereof, and the wall thereof.

16 ¹And the city lay ²foursquare, and the length is as large as the breadth of it, and he measured the city with the reed, twelve thousand furlongs: and the length, and the breadth, and the height of it are equal.

17 And he measured the wall thereof an hundred forty and four cubits, by the measure of man, that is, of the ¹Angel.

18 ¹And the building of the wall of it was of jasper: and the city was pure gold, like unto clear glass.

19 And the foundations of the wall of the city were garnished with all manner of precious stones: the first foundation *was* jasper: the second of Sapphire: the third of a Chalcedony: the fourth of an Emerald:

20 The fifth of a Sardonyx: the sixth of a Sardius: the seventh of a Chrysolite: the eight of a Beryl: the ninth of a Topaz: the tenth of a Chrysoprase: the eleventh of a Jacinth: the twelfth an Amethyst.

21 And the twelve gates *were* twelve pearls, and every gate *is* of one pearl, and the ¹street of the city *is* pure gold, as shining glass.

22 And I saw no Temple therein: for the Lord God Almighty and the Lamb are the Temple of it.

23 *f,1*And their city hath no need of the Sun, neither of the Moon to shine in it: for the glory of God did light it: and the Lamb is the light of it.

24 *g*And the people which are saved, shall walk in the light of it: and the kings of the earth shall bring their glory and honor unto it.

25 *h*And the gates of it shall not be shut by day: for there shall be no night there.

26 And the glory and honor of the Gentiles shall be brought unto it.

27 And there shall enter into it none unclean thing, neither whatsoever worketh abomination or lies: but they which are written in the Lamb's ¹book of life.

CHAPTER 22

1 The river of water of life is showed, 2 and the tree of life: 6, 7 Then followeth the conclusion of this prophecy, 8 where John declareth, that the things herein contained are most true. 13 And now the third time repeateth these words, All things come from him, who is the beginning and the end.

1 And ¹he showed me a pure river of water of life, clear as crystal, proceeding out of the throne of God, and of the Lamb.

2 In the midst of the street of it, and of either side of the river was the tree of life, which bare twelve manner of fruits, and gave fruit every month: and the leaves of the tree *served* to heal the nations with.

3 And there shall be no more curse, but the throne of God and of the Lamb shall be in it, and his servants shall serve him.

4 And they shall see his face, and his Name shall be in their foreheads.

5 *a*And there shall be no night there, and they need no candle, neither light of the Sun: for the Lord God giveth them light, and they shall reign for evermore.

6 ¹And he said unto me, These words are faithful and true: and the Lord God of the holy Prophets sent his Angel to show unto his servants the things which must shortly be fulfilled.

7 Behold, I come shortly. Blessed *is* he that keepeth

f Isa. 10:19 *g* Isa. 60:3 *h* Isa. 60:11 *i* Rev. 2:3 Rev. 20:12 Phil. 4:3 CHAPTER 22 *a* Isa. 60:19

21:14 ¹ That is, foundation stones, according to the number of the gates, as is showed verse 19.
21:15 ¹ A transition unto a more exquisite description of the parts of the Church, by finding out the measure of the same by the Angel that measured them.
21:16 ¹ The measure and form most equal, in 2 verses.
² A foursquared figure hath equal sides, and outright corners, and therefore the Greeks call by this name those things that are steady, and of continuance and perfect.
21:17 ¹ He addeth this, because the Angel had the shape of a man.
21:18 ¹ The matter most precious and glittering which the presence of God maketh most glorious.
21:21 ¹ By street, he meaneth the broadest place of the city.
21:23 ¹ The second form of particular description (as I said, verse 12) from foreign and outward accidents: which are these, Light from God himself, in this verse, glory from men, verse 24, perfect security from all harm, verse 25. Finally such truth and incorruption of glory (verse 26) as can bear and abide with it, nothing that is inglorious, the last verse.
22:1 ¹ Here is absolved and finished the description of the celestial Church (as I showed before, Rev. 21:12) by the effects in 5 verses, and then this book is concluded in the rest of the chapter. The effects proceeding from God, who dwelleth in the Church are these: the everlasting grace of God in this verse, the eternal living of the godly,

as Rev. 2:7, the eternal fruits which the godly bring forth unto God, themselves and others, verse 2, freedom and immunity from all evil, God himself taking pleasure in his servants and they likewise in their God, verse 3. The beholding and sight of God, and sealing of the faithful from all eternity, verse 4, the light of God, and an everlasting kingdom and glory, verse 5.
22:6 ¹ The whole book is concluded and made up by a confirmation, and a salutation. The confirmation hath three places: The words of the Angel unto verse 15, the words of Christ: verses 16, 17, and the obtestation made by S. John from divine authority, thence unto verse 20. By speech of the Angel this prophecy is confirmed unto verse 8 and then he speaketh of the use of this book in the verses following. The prophecy is first confirmed by the Angel from the nature thereof, that it is faithful and true. Secondly from the nature of the efficient cause, both principal which is God, and instrumental, which is the Angel in this verse. Thirdly from the promises of God concerning his coming to effect all these things, and concerning our salvation, verse 7. Fourthly, from the testification of S. John himself, verse 8. The rest of the speech of the angel tending to the same and S. John interrupted or brake off by his unadvised act of worshipping him, in the same verse which the Angel forbidding, teacheth him that adoration must be given not to him, but only to God, as for himself, that he is of such nature and office, as he may not be adored: which thing also was in like manner done, Rev. 16:10.

the words of the prophecy of this book.

8 And I am John, which saw and heard these things: and when I had heard and seen, [b]I fell down to worship before the feet of the Angel which showed me these things.

9 But he said unto me, See thou *do it* not: for I am thy fellow servant, and of thy brethren the Prophets, and of them which keep the words of this book: worship God.

10 [1]And he said unto me, [2]Seal not the words of the prophecy of this book: for the time is at hand.

11 [1]He that is unjust, let him be unjust still: and he which is filthy, let him be filthy still: and he that is righteous, let him be righteous still: and he that is holy, let him be holy still.

12 [1]And behold, I come shortly, and my reward is with me, [c]to give to every man according as his work shall be.

13 I am [d]Alpha and Omega, the beginning and the end, the first and the last.

14 Blessed *are* they, that do his Commandments, [1]that their right may be in the tree of Life, and may enter in through the gates into the City.

15 For without *shall be* dogs and enchanters, and whoremongers, and murderers, and idolaters, and whosoever loveth or maketh lies.

16 [1]I Jesus have sent mine Angel, to testify unto you these things in the Churches: I am the root and the generation of David, and the bright morning star.

17 And the Spirit and the bride say, Come. And let him that heareth say, Come: and let him that is athirst, come: and [e]let whosoever will, take of the water of life freely.

18 [1]For I protest unto every man that heareth the words of the prophecy of this book, If any man shall add unto these things, God shall add unto him the plagues that are written in this book.

19 And if any man shall diminish of the words of the book of this prophecy, God shall take away his part out of the book of life, and out of the holy City, and from those things which are written in this book.

20 [1]He which testifieth these things, saith, Surely I come quickly, Amen. Even so, come Lord Jesus.

21 [1]The grace of our Lord Jesus Christ *be* with you all, AMEN.

THE END

[b] Rev. 19:10
[c] Rom. 2:6
[d] Rev. 1:8
   Rev. 21:6
   Isa. 41:44
   Isa. 34:6
[e] Isa. 55:1

22:10 [1] The Angel returneth unto his former speech: in which he teacheth the use of this book, both towards ourselves, in this and the next verse and in respect of God for declaration of his truth, thence unto verse 15.

[2] That is, propound this prophecy openly unto all, and conceal no part of it. The contrary whereunto is commanded, Isa. 8:6 and Dan. 8:26.

22:11 [1] An objection prevented. But there will be some that will abuse this occasion unto evil, and will wrest this Scripture unto their own destruction, as Peter saith. What then saith the Angel, the mysteries of God must not therefore be concealed, which it hath pleased him to communicate unto us. Let them be hurtful unto others, let such be more and more vile in themselves, whom this Scripture doth not please: yet others shall be further conformed thereby unto righteousness and true holiness. The care and reformation of these may not be neglected, because of the voluntary and malicious offense of others.

22:12 [1] The second place belonging unto the use of this book, as I said, verse 10. Also (saith God by the Angel) though there should be no use of this book unto men: yet it shall be of this use unto me, that it is a witness of my truth unto my glory, who will come shortly to give and execute just judgment, in this verse: who have taught that all these things have their being in me, in verse 13, and have denounced blessedness unto my servants in the Church, verse 14, and reprobation unto the ungodly, verse 15.

22:14 [1] The blessedness of the godly set down by their title and interest thereunto: and their fruit in the same.

22:16 [1] The second place of confirmation, as I said, is the speech of Christ, ratifying the vocation of S. John, and the authority of his calling and testimony, both from the condition of his own person being God and man, in whom all the promises of God are Yea and Amen, 2 Cor. 1:20: and also from the testification of other persons, by the acclamation of the holy Ghost, who here is as it were an honorable assistant of the marriage of the Church as the spouse: and of every of the godly as members: and finally from the thing present, that of their own knowledge and accord they are called forth unto the participation of the good things of God, verse 17.

22:18 [1] The obtestation of Saint John (which is the third place of the confirmation, as was noted, verse 6) joined with a curse of execration, to preserve the truth of this book entire and uncorrupted, in two verses.

22:20 [1] A divine confirmation or sealing of the obtestation: first from Christ avouching the same, and denouncing his coming against all those that shall put their sacrilegious hands hereunto: then from Saint John himself, who by a most holy prayer calleth Christ to take vengeance of them.

22:21 [1] The salutation Apostolical, which is the other place of the conclusion, as I said, verse 6, and is the end of almost every Epistle: which we wish unto the Church, and to all the holy and elect members thereof in Christ Jesus our Lord, until his coming to judgment, *Come Lord Jesus*, and do it. Amen, again, Amen.

A FORM OF PRAYER TO BE USED
IN PRIVATE HOUSES EVERY
MORNING & EVENING

Morning Prayer.

Almighty God and most merciful father, we do not present ourselves here before thy Majesty, trusting in our own merits or worthiness, but in thy manifold mercies, which hast proved to hear our prayers and grant our requests, which we shall make to thee in the name of thy beloved Son Jesus Christ our Lord, who also hath commanded us to assemble ourselves together in his name, with full assurance, that he will not only be amongst us, but also be our mediator and advocate to thy Majesty, that we may obtain all things which shall seem expedient to thy blessed will, for our necessities. Therefore we beseech thee sweet Father, to turn thy loving countenance towards us, and impute not unto us our manifold sins and offenses, whereby we most justly deserve thy wrath and sharp punishment, but rather receive us to thy mercy, for Jesus Christ's sake, accepting his death and passion as a just recompense for all our offenses, in whom only thou art pleased, and through whom thou canst not be offended with us. And seeing that of thy great mercy we have quietly passed this night: Grant (O heavenly Father) that we may bestow this day wholly in thy service, so that all our thoughts, words, and deeds, may redound to the glory of thy name and good ensample of all men, who seeing our good works, may glorify thee our heavenly Father. And forasmuch as of thy mere favor and love, thou hast not only created us to thine own similitude and likeness, but also hast chosen us to be heirs with thy dear son Jesus Christ, of that immortal kingdom, which thou preparedst for us before the beginning of the world: we beseech thee to increase our faith and knowledge, and to lighten our hearts with thy holy spirit, that we may in the meantime live in godly conversation and integrity of life, knowing that Idolaters, adulterers, covetous men, contentious persons, drunkards, gluttons and suchlike, shall not inherit the kingdom of God.

And because thou hast commanded us to pray one for another, we do not only make request (O Lord) for ourselves, and for them that thou hast already called to the true understanding of thy heavenly will, but for all people and nations of the world, who as they know by thy wonderful works, that thou art God over all, so they may be instructed by thy holy spirit, to believe in thee, their only Savior and Redeemer, but forasmuch as they cannot believe, except they hear, nor cannot hear but by preaching, and none can preach, except he be sent: therefore (O Lord) raise up faithful distributors of thy mysteries, who setting apart all worldly respects, may both in their life and doctrine only seek thy glory. Continually confound Satan, Antichrist, with all hirelings, whom thou hast already cast off into a reprobate sense, that they may not by sects, schisms, heresies, and errors, disquiet thy little flock. And because, O Lord, we be fallen into the latter days and dangerous times, wherein ignorance hath gotten the upper hand, and Satan by his Ministers seeks by all means to quench the light of thy Gospel: we beseech thee to maintain thy cause against those ravening Wolves and strengthen all thy servants, whom they keep in prison and bondage. Let not thy long suffering be an occasion, either to increase their tyranny, or to discourage thy children: neither yet let our sins and wickedness, be an hindrance to thy mercies, but with speed (O Lord) consider their great misery. For thy people Israel many times by their sin provoked thine anger and thou punishedst them by thy just judgment, yet though their sins were never so grievous, if they once returned from their iniquity, thou receivedst them to mercy. We therefore most wretched sinners bewail our manifold sins, and earnestly repent us of our former wickedness, and ungodly behavior towards thee: and whereas we cannot of ourselves purchase thy pardon, yet we humbly beseech thee for Jesus Christ's sake, to show thy mercy upon us, and receive us again to thy favor: Grant us dear Father these our requests, and all other things necessary for us, and thy whole Church, according to thy promise in Jesus Christ our Lord. In whose name we beseech thee, as he hath taught us, saying: Our Father which art in heaven, ect.

Evening Prayer.

O Lord God, Father everlasting, and full of pity, we acknowledge and confess, that we be not worthy to lift up our eyes to heaven, much less to present ourselves before thy Majesty, with confidence that thou wilt hear our prayers, and grant our requests: if we consider our own deservings: for our consciences do accuse us, and our sins do witness against us, and we know that thou art an upright Judge, which dost not justify the sinners and wicked men, but punisheth the faults of all such as transgress thy commandments: yet most merciful Father, since it hath pleased thee to command us to call on thee in all our troubles and adversities, promising even then to help us, when we feel ourselves, (as it were) swallowed up of death and desperation, we utterly renounce all worldly confidence, and fly to thy sovereign bounty as our only stay and refuge: beseeching thee not to call to remembrance our manifold sins and wickedness, whereby we continually provoke thy wrath and indignation against us, neither our negligence and unkindness, which have neither worthily esteemed, nor in our lives sufficiently expressed the sweet comfort of thy Gospel revealed unto us, but rather to accept the death and obedience of thy Son Jesus Christ, who by offering up his body in sacrifice once for all hath made a sufficient recompense for all our sins. Have mercy therefore upon us, O Lord, and forgive us our offenses. Teach us by thy holy Spirit, that we may rightly weigh them, and earnestly repent for the same. And so much the rather, O Lord, because that the reprobate and such as thou hast forsaken, cannot praise thee, nor call upon thy name, but the repenting heart, the sorrowful mind, the conscience oppressed, hungering and thirsting for thy grace, shall ever set forth thy praise and glory.

And albeit we be but worms and dust, yet thou art our Creator, and we be the work of thine hands: yea, thou art our Father, and we thy Children: thou art our Shepherd, and we thy flock: thou art our Redeemer, and we thy people whom thou hast bought: thou art our God, and we thine inheritance. Correct us not therefore in thine anger (O Lord) neither according to our deserts punish us, but mercifully chastise us with a fatherly affection, that all the world may know at what time soever a sinner doth repent him of his sin from the bottom of his heart, thou wilt put away all his wickedness out of thy remembrance, as thou hast promised by thy holy Prophet.

Finally, forasmuch as it hath pleased thee to make the night for man to rest in, as thou hast ordained him the day to travail in, grant O dear Father, that we may continually watch for the time that our Lord Jesus Christ shall appear for our deliverance out of this mortal life, and in the mean season, that we be not overcome by any fantasies, dreams, or other temptations, may fully set our minds upon thee, love thee, fear thee, and rest in thee. Furthermore, that our sleep be not excessive or overmuch, after the insatiable desires of our flesh, but only sufficient to content our weak nature, that we may be the better disposed to live in all godly conversation, to the glory of the holy Name, and profit of our brethren. So be it.

A godly prayer to be said at all times.

Honor and praise be given to thee, O Lord God Almighty, most dear Father of heaven, for all thy mercies and loving-kindnesses showed unto us, in that it hath pleased thy gracious goodness, freely and of thine own accord to elect and choose us to salvation before the beginning of the world: And even like continual thanks be given to thee, for creating us after thine own image, for redeeming us with the precious blood of thy dear Son, when we were utterly lost: for sanctifying us with thy holy Spirit in the revelation and knowledge of thy word: for helping and succoring us in all our needs and necessities, for saving us from all dangers of body and soul, for comforting us so fatherly in all our tribulations and persecutions, for sparing us so long, and giving us so large a time of repentance. These benefits O most merciful Father, like as we acknowledge to have received them of thy only goodness, even so we beseech thee for thy dear Son Jesus Christ's sake, grant us always thy holy Spirit, whereby we may continually grow in thankfulness towards thee, to be led into all truth, and comforted in all adversities. O Lord strengthen our faith, kindle it more in ferventness and love towards thee, and our neighbors for thy sake: suffer us not (most dear Father) to receive thy word any more in vain: but grant us always the assistance of thy grace and holy Spirit, that in heart, word, and deed, we may sanctify and do worship to thy name, help to amplify and increase thy kingdom, and whatsoever thou sendest, we may be hardly well content with thy good pleasure and will. Let us not lack the thing, O Father, without the which we cannot serve thee: but bless thou so all the works of our hands, that we may have sufficient, and not be chargeable but rather helpful unto others. Be merciful O Lord to our offenses, and seeing our debt is great which thou hast forgiven in Jesus Christ, make us to love thee and our neighbors so much the more: be thou our Father, Captain, and defender in all temptations: hold thou us by thy merciful hand, that we may be delivered from all inconveniences, and end our lives in the sanctifying and honoring of thy holy name, through Jesus Christ our Lord and only Savior.

Let thy mighty hand and outstretched arm (O Lord) be still our defense, thy mercy and loving-kindness in Jesus Christ thy dear Son our salvation, thy true and holy word our instruction, thy grace and holy Spirit our comfort and consolation unto the end and in the end. So be it.

O Lord increase our faith.

A Confession for all estates and times.

O Eternal God and most merciful Father, we confess and acknowledge here before thy divine Majesty, that we are miserable sinners, conceived and born in sin and iniquity, so that in us there is no goodness. For the flesh evermore rebelleth against the spirit, whereby we continually transgress thy holy precepts and commandments: and so purchase to ourselves through thy just judgment, death and damnation. Notwithstanding (O heavenly Father) forasmuch as we are displeased with ourselves for the sins that we have committed against thee, and do unfeignedly repent us of the same, we most humbly beseech thee for Jesus Christ's sake to show thy mercy upon us, to forgive us all our sins, and increase thy holy Spirit in us, that we acknowledging from the bottom of our hearts, our own unrighteousness, may from henceforth not only mortify our sinful lusts and affections, but also bring forth such fruits as may be agreeable to thy most blessed will, not for the worthiness thereof, but for the merits of thy dearly beloved Son Jesus Christ our only Savior, whom thou hast already given an oblation and offering for our sins, and for whose sake we are certainly persuaded that thou wilt deny us nothing that we shall ask in his name, according to thy will. For thy Spirit doth assure our consciences, that thou art our merciful Father, and so lovest us thy children through him, that nothing is able to remove thy heavenly grace and favor from us. To thee therefore (O Father) with the Son, and the holy Ghost, be all honor and glory world without end. Amen.

A prayer to be said before a man begin his work.

O Lord God most merciful Father and Savior, seeing it hath pleased thee to command us to travail, that we may relieve our need, we beseech thee of thy grace so to bless our labors, that thy blessing may extend unto us, without the which we are not able to continue, and that this great favor may be a witness unto us of thy bountifulness and assistance, so that thereby we may know the fatherly care that thou hast over us.

Moreover (O Lord) we beseech thee that thou wouldest strengthen us with thy holy Spirit, that we may faithfully travail in our estate and vocation, without fraud or deceit, and that we may endeavor ourselves to follow thine holy ordinance, rather than to seek to satisfy our greedy affections or desire to gain.

And if it please thee (O Lord) to prosper our labor, give us a mind also to help them that need, according to that ability that thou of thy mercy shalt give us: And knowing that all good things come of thee, grant that we may humble ourselves to our neighbors, and not by any means lift ourselves above them which have not received so liberal a portion as of thy mercy thou hast given unto us. And if it please thee to try and exercise us by greater poverty and need than our flesh would desire, that thou wouldest yet (O Lord) grant us grace to know that thou wilt nourish us continually, through thy bountiful liberality, that we be not so tempted, that we fall into distrust, but that we may patiently wait till

thou fill us, not only with corporal graces and benefits, but chiefly with thine heavenly and spiritual treasures, to the intent we may always have more ample occasion to give thee thanks, and wholly to rest upon thy mercies. Hear us O Lord of mercy, through Jesus Christ thy Son our Lord, Amen.

A prayer for the whole estate of Christ's Church.

Almighty God and most merciful Father, we humbly submit ourselves and fall down before thy majesty, beseeching thee from the bottom of our hearts, that this seed of thy word now sown amongst us, may take such deep root, that neither the burning heat of persecution cause it to wither, neither the thorny cares of this life choke it, but that as seed sown in a good ground, it may bring forth thirty, sixty, and an hundredfold, as thy heavenly wisdom hath appointed. And because we have need continually to crave many things at thy hands, we humbly beseech thee (O heavenly Father) to grant us thy holy Spirit, to direct our petitions, that they may proceed from such a fervent mind, as may be agreeable to thy most holy will, and seeing that our infirmity is able to do nothing without thy help, and that thou art not ignorant with how many and great temptations we poor wretches are on every side enclosed and compassed, let thy strength (O Lord) sustain our weakness, that we being defended with the force of thy grace, may be safely preserved against all assaults of Satan, who goeth about continually like a roaring Lion, seeking to devour us. Increase our faith (O merciful Father) that we do not swerve at any time from thy heavenly word, but augment in us hope and love, with a careful keeping of all thy commandments, that no hardness of heart, no hypocrisy, no concupiscence of the eyes, nor enticements of the world do draw us away from thy obedience. And seeing we live now in these most perilous times, let thy fatherly providence defend us against the violence of our enemies, which seek all means to oppress thy truth.

Furthermore, forasmuch as by thy holy Apostle we be taught to make our prayers and supplications for all men: We pray not only for ourselves here present, but beseech thee also to reduce all such as be yet ignorant from the miserable captivity of blindness and error, to the pure understanding and knowledge of thy truth, that we all with one accord and unity of mind may worship thee our only God and Savior. And that all Pastors, Shepherds, and Ministers, to whom thou hast committed the dispensation of thy holy word, and charge of thy chosen people, may both in their life and doctrine be found faithful, setting only before their eyes thy glory, and that by them all poor sheep which wander and go astray, may be gathered and brought home to thy fold.

Moreover, because the hearts of Rulers are in thy

hands, we beseech thee to direct and govern the hearts of all Kings, Princes, and Magistrates, to whom thou hast committed the sword: Especially (O Lord) according to our bounden duty, we beseech thee to maintain and increase the Honorable estate of the King's Majesty, and all his most noble Counselors and Magistrates, with all the spiritual Pastors and Ministers, and all the whole body of this commonweal. Let thy fatherly favor so preserve them, and thy holy spirit so govern their hearts, that they may in such sort execute their office, that thy religion may be purely maintained, manners reformed, and sin punished, according to the precise rule of thy holy word: and for that we be all members of the mystical body of Jesus Christ, we make our requests unto thee (O Heavenly Father) for all such as are afflicted with any kind of cross or tribulation: as war, plague, famine, sickness, poverty, imprisonment, persecution, banishment, or any other kind of thy rods, whether it be calamity of body, or vexation of mind, that it would please thee to give them patience and constancy, till thou send them full deliverance out of all their troubles. Root out from hence, O Lord, all ravening Wolves, which to fill their bellies, seek to destroy thy flock. And show thy great mercies upon those our brethren in other countries, which are persecuted, cast into prison, and daily condemned for the testimony of thy truth. And although they be utterly destitute of all man's aid, yet let thy sweet comfort never depart from them, but so inflame their hearts with thy holy spirit, that they may boldly and cheerfully abide such trial as thy godly wisdom shall appoint: So that at length as well by their death, as by their life, the kingdom of thy dear Son Jesus Christ, may increase and shine through all the world. In whose name we make our humble petitions unto thee, as he hath taught us.

Our father, ect.

A prayer against the Devil and his manifold tentations, made by S. Augustine.

There wanted a tempter, and thou wast the cause that he was wanting: there wanted time and place, and thou wast the cause: that they wanted. The tempter was present, and there wanted neither place nor time, but thou heldest me back that I should not consent.

The tempter came full of darkness as he is, and thou didst harden me that I might despise him. The tempter came armed and strongly, but to the intent he should not overcome me, thou didst restrain him and strengthen me. The tempter came transformed into an Angel of light, and to the intent he should not deceive me, thou didst rebuke him, and to the intent I should know him, thou didst enlighten me. For he is the great red dragon the old serpent, called the Devil and Satan, which hath seven heads and ten horns, whom thou hast created to take his

pleasure in this huge and broad sea, wherein there creep living wights innumerable, and beasts great and small, that is to say, divers sorts of fiends which practiceth nothing else day and night, but goeth about seeking whom he may devour, except thou resist him O Lord Jesus. For it is that old dragon which draweth down the third part of the stars of heaven with his raise, and casteth them to the ground, which with his venom poisoneth the waters of the earth, that as many men as drink of them, may die, which trampleth upon gold, as if it were mire, and is of opinion that Jordan shall run into his mouth and which is made of such a mold that he feareth no man: And who shall save us from his chaps, O Lord Jesus? who shall pluck us out of his mouth, saving thou O Lord, who hast broken the head of this great Dragon? Help us Lord, spread out thy wings over us O Lord, that we may flee under them from the face of this Dragon that pursueth us: and fence thou us from his horns with thy shield: For this is his continual endeavor, this is his only desire to devour the souls that thou hast created. And therefore we cry unto thee O God, deliver us from our daily adversary, who whether we sleep or wake, whether we eat or drink, or whether we be doing of any thing else presseth upon us by all kind of means, assaulting us day and night with trains and policies, and shooting his venomous arrows at us, sometimes openly, and sometimes privily to slay our souls. And yet such is our great madness O Lord, that whereas we see the dragon continually in a readiness to devour us with open mouth, we nevertheless do sleep, and rejoice in our own slothfulness, as though we were out of his danger, who desireth nothing else but to destroy us. Our mischievous enemy to the intent to kill us, watcheth continually and never sleepeth, and yet will not we awake from sleep to save ourselves. Behold he hath pitched infinite snares before our feet, and filled all our ways with sundry traps to catch our souls. And who can escape O Lord Jesus, so many and great dangers? He hath laid snares for us in our riches, in our poverty, in our meat, in our drink, in our pleasures, in our sleep, and in our waking. He hath set snares for us in our words, and our works in all our life. But thou, O Lord, deliver us from the net of the fowler, and from hard words that we may give praise to thee, saying: Blessed be the Lord who hath not given us to be a prey for their teeth: our soul is delivered as a sparrow out of the fowler's net, the net is broken and we have escaped.

The Confession of the Christian faith.

I believe and confess my Lord God, eternal, infinite, immeasurable, incomprehensible, and invisible, one in substance, and three in person, Father, Son, and holy Ghost, who by his almighty power and wisdom, hath not only of nothing created heaven and earth, and all things therein contained, and man after his own image, that he might in him be glorified, but also by his fatherly providence governeth, maintaineth, and preserveth the same, according to the purpose of his will.

I believe also and confess Jesus Christ the only Savior and Messiah, who being equal with God, made himself of no reputation, but took on him the shape of a servant, and became man, in all things like unto us, except sin, to assure us of mercy and forgiveness: for when through our Father Adam's transgression, we were become children of perdition, there was no means to bring us from the yoke of sin and damnation, but only Jesus Christ our Lord, Who giving us that by grace, which was by nature his, made us through faith the children of God, who when that fullness of time was come, was conceived by the power of the holy Ghost, born of the Virgin, Mary (according to the flesh) and preached in earth the Gospel of Salvation, till at length by tyranny of the Priests, he was guiltlessly condemned under Pontius Pilate, the President of Jury, and most slanderously hanged on the Cross between two thieves, as a notorious trespasser, where taking upon him the punishment of our sins, he delivered us from the curse of the law.

And forasmuch as he being only God, could not feel death, neither being only man, could overcome death, he joined both together, and suffered his humanity to be punished with most cruel death, feeling in himself the anger and severe judgment of God, even as he had been in extreme torments of hell, and therefore cried with a loud voice, My God, my God, why hast thou forsaken me? Thus of his mercy: without compulsion, he offered up himself as the only sacrifice to purge the sins of all the world, so that all other sacrifices for sin, are blasphemous and derogate from the sufficiency hereof, which death, albeit it did sufficiently reconcile us to God, yet the Scriptures commonly do attribute our regeneration to his resurrection, For as by rising again from the grave, the third day he conquered death, even so the victory of our faith standeth in his resurrection: and therefore without the one, we cannot feel the benefits of the other. For as by his death sin was taken away, so our righteousness was restored by his resurrection. And because he would accomplish all things, and take possession for us in his kingdom, he ascended into heaven, to enlarge the same kingdom, by the abundant power of his spirit, by whom we are most assured of his continual intercession towards God the Father for us.

And although he be in heaven as touching his corporal presence, where the Father hath now set him at his right hand, committing unto him the administration of all things, as well in heaven above, as in earth beneath: yet is he present with us his members, even to the end of the world, in preserving and governing us with his effectual power and grace: who when all things are fulfilled, which God hath spoken by the mouth of all his Prophets, since the world began, will come in the same visible form, in the which he ascended, with an unspeakable Majesty, power, and company, to separate the Lambs from the Goats, the elect from the reprobate: So that none, whether he be alive then, or dead before, shall escape his judgment.

Moreover, I believe and confess the holy Ghost, God equal with the Father, and the Son, who regenerateth and sanctifieth us, ruleth and guideth us unto all truth, persuading most assuredly in our consciences that we be the children of God, brethren to Jesus Christ, and fellow heirs with him of life everlasting: yet notwithstanding it is not sufficient to believe that God is omnipotent and merciful, that Christ hath made satisfaction, or that the holy Ghost hath his power and effect, except we do apply the same benefits to us which are God's elect.

I believe therefore and confess one holy Church, which as members of Jesus Christ, the only head thereof, consent in faith, hope, and charity, using the gifts of God, whether they be temporal or spiritual, to the profit and furtherance of the same, which Church is not seen to man's eye, but only known to God, who of the lost sons of Adam, hath ordained some as vessels of wrath to damnation, and hath chosen others as vessels of his mercy to be saved: the which in due time he calleth to integrity of life, and godly conversation, to make them a glorious Church in himself.

But that Church which is visible, and seen to the eye, hath three tokens and marks whereby it may be known. First, the word of God contained in the old and new Testament, which as it is above the authority of the same Church, and only sufficient to instruct us in all things concerning salvation: so it is left for all degrees of men, to read and understand. For without this word, neither Church, Counsel, nor decree, can establish any point touching salvation: The second is, the holy Sacraments, to wit, of Baptism, and the Lord's Supper, which Sacraments Christ hath left unto us, as holy signs and seals of God's promises. For as by Baptism once received, is signified, that we (as well Infants as others of age and discretion) being strangers from God by original sin, are received into his family and congregation, with full assurance, that although this root of sin lie hid in us, yet to the Elect it shall not be imputed: So the Supper declareth that God as a most provident Father, doth not only feed our bodies, but also spiritually nourisheth our souls with the graces and benefits of Jesus Christ, (which the Scripture calleth eating of his flesh, and drinking of his blood) neither must we in the administration of these Sacraments, follow man's fantasy, but as Christ himself hath ordained, so must they be administered, and by such as by ordinary vocation are thereunto called. Therefore whosoever reserveth and worshippeth these Sacraments, or contrariwise contemneth them in time and place, procureth to himself damnation.

The third mark of this Church, is Ecclesiastical Discipline, which standeth in admonition and correction of faults. The final end whereof is Excommunication, by the consent of the Church determined, if the offender be obstinate: And besides this Ecclesiastical Discipline, I acknowledge to belong to his Church, a politic Magistrate, that ministereth to every man justice, defending the good and punishing the evil. To whom we must render honor and obedience in all things which are not contrary to the word of God. And as Moses, Hezekiah, Josiah, and other good rulers, purged the Church of God from superstition and idolatry, so the defense of Christ's Church apperteineth, to Christian Magistrates, against all Idolaters and Heretics, as Papists, Anabaptists, with such like limbs of Antichrist, to root out all doctrine of Devils and men, as the Mass, Purgatory, Limbus patrum, prayers to Saints, and for the dead, free-will, distinction of meats, apparel, and days, vows of single life, presence at Idol service, man's merits with such like, which draw us from the society of Christ's church, wherein standeth only remission of sins purchased by Christ's blood to all them that believe, they be Jews or Gentiles, and lead us to vain confidence in creatures and trust in our own imaginations, the punishment whereof although God

oftentimes deferreth in this life, yet after the general resurrection, when our souls and bodies shall rise again to immortality, they shall be damned to unquenchable fire, and then we which have forsaken all man's wisdom, to cleave unto Christ, shall hear the joyful voice, Come ye blessed of my father, inherit the Kingdom prepared for you from the beginning of the world: and so shall go triumphing with him in body and soul to remain everlastingly in glory, where we shall see God face to face, and shall no more need to instruct one another, we shall all know him from the highest to the lowest. To whom with the Son and the holy Ghost, be all praise, honor and glory now and ever. So be it.

FINIS.

The preceding prayers, from the 1599 Geneva Bible (the source copy for this edition), has been itself updated in accordance with standards we employed with the full Bible text and its annotations, as explained in the Preface.

—*Editor*

GLOSSARY

WORD	MEANING	SAMPLE LOCATION
abalienate	to estrange, to withdraw	Numbers 36:5 (notes)
accompt	obsolete spelling of "account" with the same pronunciation	1 Corinthians 2:14 (notes)
acconisance	a distinguishing mark or emblem	Revelation 13:18 (notes)
admiration	wonder	Revelation 8:1 (notes)
advertiseth	reveals to	Luke 5:1 (notes)
affianced	betrothed	Luke 1:27
Agnus deis	a cake of wax, stamped with a lamb bearing a cross or flag, that has been blessed by the Pope	Genesis 35:4 (notes)
ague	fever	Leviticus 26:16
allowed of	accepted	Luke 1:6 (notes)
Almuggim	almug or algum tree	1 Kings 10:11
ambassage	embassy; a mission of diplomats headed by an ambassador	Luke 14:32
ambassy	mission	Luke 9:1 (notes)
ambries	plural of ambry, dialect, pantry	Exodus 8:3 (notes)
amend	improve	John 4:52
amerciaments	fines	Luke 12:58 (notes)
anon	immediately	Matthew 13:5
apostatical	apostate	1 Timothy 4:7 (notes)
approbation	commendation or praise	1 Kings 22:17 (notes)

WORD	MEANING	SAMPLE LOCATION
appurtenances	the things that pertain to it	Exodus 40 introduction
artificers	skilled craftsmen	1 Chronicles 4:14 (notes)
artificially	artfully, cunningly	Galatians 4:12 (notes)
asps	cobras	Job 20:14
assayed	endeavored	Acts 9:26
assuageth	diminishes	Philemon 1:15
astonied	filled with consternation or dismay	Matthew 28:4
avarice	covetousness	Proverbs 1:12 (notes)
back	a shallow vat or tub used chiefly by brewers	Isaiah 2:20
baite	a place to stop for food and rest when traveling	Genesis 35:16 (notes)
bakemeats	pastries or pies	Genesis 40:17
beeves	plural of beef, or cow	Leviticus 1:2
besoms	brooms made from bunches of twigs, for sweeping	Exodus 27:3
besotting	making drunk	Revelation 17:4 (notes)
bewail	mourn	2 Chronicles 35 introduction
bier	archaic, a framework for carrying	1 Samuel 3:31
bleared	blurred, dimmed	John 16:16 (notes)
blockish	stupid	Luke 4:34 (notes)
bolled	swollen; podded	Exodus 9:31
botches	swellings on the skin, boils or sores	Exodus 9 introduction
bounches	camel's humps	Isaiah 30:6
bowings	bends, or arches	Leviticus 11:21 (notes)

WORD	MEANING	SAMPLE LOCATION
brainpan	braincase, the cranium enclosing the brain	Judges 9:53
brast	burst	Acts 1:18
brickle	brittle	2 Corinthians 5:1 (notes)
brigandine	body armor	1 Kings 22:34
bruit	noise, news	Matthew 9:26
Budeus	French scholar on ancient currency: "De Asse" was his major work	II Chronicles 9:15 (notes)
buggerers	people who practice sodomy or unnatural sexual relations	1 Corinthians 6:9
business	rebuke, tongue-lashing	Galatians 6:17
caitiff	despicable person	Mark 15:24
calumnies	slander	Psalm 57:4 (notes)
Candia	Crete	Acts 27:7 (notes)
canker	rust	Matthew 6:19
cankered	malignant, polluted	Mark 7:22 (notes)
carp	to find fault or complain querulously	1 Timothy 1:12 (notes)
carrions	putrefying flesh	Leviticus 14:41 (notes)
cauls	This word (Heb. shebisim), denotes network caps to contain the hair, worn by females. Others explain it as meaning "wreaths worn round the forehead, reaching from one ear to the other."	Isaiah 3:18
cavil	to raise trivial and frivolous objection	1 Peter 2:13 (notes)
cavillers	frivolous objectors	Acts 6:13 (notes)

WORD	MEANING	SAMPLE LOCATION
ceil (verb)	to overlay the inner roof of (obsolete)	2 Chronicles 3:5
challenge	claims	Luke 1:52 (notes)
chambering	lewd behavior	Romans 13:13
chapiters	capitals, as on a column	1 Kings 7:16
chapmen	peddlers	Nehemiah 13:20
chaws (n)	jaws, teeth	Proverbs 30:14
chemarims	"black ones"; idolatrous priests; Gentile priests	2 Kings 23:5 (notes)
chirurgeon	old form of "surgeon"	1 Corinthians 7:18
chode	past tense of chide, as in chided	Genesis 31:36
Chrism	consecrated oil used in Greek and Latin churches	Revelation 13:16 (notes)
churls	surly men	Luke 12:17 (notes)
clave	past tense of cleave, to unite with	Luke 15:15
cockatrice	a serpent hatched from a cock's egg and having the power to kill by its glance.	Proverbs 23:32
cockle	weeds	Job 31:40
coffer	a strong box	1 Samuel 6:8
collops	a slice of meat, fried or not	Job 15:27
colloquintida	same as colocynth, a cathartic drug from a kind of cucumber	2 Kings 4:39 (notes)
commodity	a reward	Luke 6:32 (notes)
commonweal	archaic for commonwealth, the common good or welfare	Proverbs 28:2 (notes)
compass	accomplish	Acts 24:1 (notes)

WORD	MEANING	SAMPLE LOCATION
comprehendeth	extends to, includes	Luke 6:27 (notes)
concision	archaic, cutting off	Philippians 3:2
coney	rock hyrax	Deuteronomy 14:7
confuted	proved to be false; refuted	Acts 18:28
contemn	to view or treat with contempt; scorn; despise	Deuteronomy 8:10 (notes)
contemner	one who despises, or one who is guilty of contempt of court; views or treats with contempt	Deuteronomy 17 introduction
contumaciously	reproachfully	Mark 7:27
contumelious	insolently abusive and humiliating	Acts 2:13 (notes)
could not let	was an exception	Luke 1:36 (notes)
counterpoise	counterbalance	2 Timothy 1:15 (notes)
countervail	equal, match	Romans 5:21 (notes)
crabbedly	harshly, ill-naturedly	Romans 14:3 (notes)
cratch	manger	Luke 2:7
crisping pin	a device used for making hair curly or wavy	Isaiah 3:22
cumber	trouble, harrass	1 Timothy 6
currish	ignoble	James 2:13 (notes)
customably	customarily	Acts 17:29 (notes)
customer's person	tax gatherers	Luke 19:8 (notes)
dam	a female parent; mother	Leviticus 22:27
deflower	deprive of virginity; take away the prime beauty of	Exodus 21:8 (notes)
delices	delicacies, delights	II Chronicles 4:5 (notes)

WORD	MEANING	SAMPLE LOCATION
derogate	detract, cause to seem inferior	1 John 4:2 (notes)
deserts	what they deserve	Mark 7:7 (notes)
despite (noun)	a looking down with contempt	Psalm 6:7
despite (verb)	archaic, to treat with contempt	Deuteronomy 22:5 (notes)
discommodities	inconveniences	Hebrews 5:2 (notes)
disease	disturb	Luke 8:49
diseasest thou	do you trouble	Mark 5:36
dissembling	the concealing of hypocritical motives	Acts 8:21 (notes)
divers (adj)	various, diverse	Hebrews 1:1
doctor	master, teacher	Matthew 23:8
doltishness	stupidity	1 Corinthians 15:35 (notes)
door cheek	a side-post of a door	Exodus 12:23
draught	that which is taken in a net by drawing	Luke 5:4
draw and rack	distort and misinterpret	Luke 7:47 (notes)
drove	a group of animals driven or moving in a body	Leviticus 3:1
ear	hear	Acts 19:18 (notes)
eareth	plows, tills the soil	1 Corinthians 9:10
ebenum	tropical tree having hard, dark-colored wood; ebony	2 Chronicles 2:8 (notes)
eftsoons	again; anew; a second time	Psalm 89:9 (notes)
emerods	hemorrhoids; representations of them in gold, as used for charms	1 Samuel 5:6

WORD	MEANING	SAMPLE LOCATION
endue	provide, endow	Psalm 72:1 (notes)
engines	anything used to effect a purpose; a device, contrivance, wile (obsolete)	2 Chronicles 26:15
ensample	example	1 Peter 2:21, 23 (notes)
envious	emulous, desiring to copy	Matthew 13:28
epiphonema	an exclamation; a phrase or reflection added as a finishing touch	Revelation 19:5 (notes)
ere	before	Exodus 32:1
eschewed	avoided	1 Corinthians 1:13 (notes)
exception	objection	Luke 2:36 (notes)
excommunicate	accursed	1 Chronicles 2:7
execrable	detestable; deserving to be denounced; wretched	1 Corinthians 12:3
fain	gladly, rather; more inclined to	Romans 15:18 (notes)
fained	feigned; counterfeit	Ephesians 4:24 (notes)
familiars (noun)	members of a household; companions	2 Kings 10:11
fancy	imagination	Hebrews 12:10 (notes)
fardels	packs	Acts 21:15
farther off	earlier	Luke 1:3 (notes)
fet	obs. form of "fetch"	Judges 18:18
fitches	probably the nutmeg tree	Isaiah 28:25, 27
flattering	soothing, beguiling	Acts 9:7 (notes)
flay (verb)	to strip off the skin or surface of	2 Chronicles 35:11
flitting	fleeting or temporary	Hebrews 9:1 (notes)

WORD	MEANING	SAMPLE LOCATION
flix	an old form of flux, a discharge	Acts 28:8
fond	indulgent	John 7:48 (notes)
foresignify	to show beforehand; to typify	Revelation 6:1 (notes)
forsooth	in truth	1 Corinthians 14:2 (notes)
fraughted	filled	Revelation 13:15 (notes)
fray	frighten away	Acts 21:4 (notes)
fructify	to bear fruit	2 Chronicles 30:10 (notes)
furlong	unit of distance equal to 220 yards	John 6:19
gadders	people who are on the go to little purpose	1 Timothy 5:13 (notes)
gage	collateral, security deposit	1 Samuel 17:18 (notes)
gainsay	deny, contradict	Acts 2:22 (notes)
gaoler	jailer	Acts 16:23
gassing	talking idly	1 Corinthians 4:9
gat	archaic past tense of get	Ephesians 5:26 (notes)
gendereth	engenders, produces	Galatians 4:24
gins	traps, snares	Psalm 140:5
glede	any of several birds of prey	Deuteronomy 14:13
glistering	glittering	2 Thessalonians 2:1 (notes)
glossed	masked the true nature of; false or willfully misleading interpretation of a text	2 Thessalonians 2:2 (notes)
goodly glosses	smooth speech	Luke 12:1 (notes)
goshawk	a short-winged hawk, once used for hunting wild geese and other fowl	Leviticus 11:13

WORD	MEANING	SAMPLE LOCATION
gradation	position attained	Romans 10:17 (notes)
gratulation	congratulation, greeting	3 John 1
greaves	armor for the leg below the knee	1 Samuel 17:6 (notes)
grieces	stairs	Acts 21:35
groat	an old British coin worth four pennies	Revelation 16:21 (notes)
grudge (verb)	grumble, complain	Exodus 17 introduction
gryphon	a European vulture	Leviticus 11:13 (notes)
habergeon	a short medieval jacket of mail	Exodus 28:32
halt	lame	Matthew 15:30
hap	chance	1 Peter 3:17 (notes)
harborous	hospitable	1 Timothy 3:2
harrow	farm implement with sharp teeth or upright disks	1 Chronicles 20:3
hart	deer	Deuteronomy 12:15
helve	handle of a tool or weapon	Deuteronomy 19:5
hoary	gray or white, as with age	Psalm 147:16
holpen	helped	Matthew 12 introduction
hote	past participle of "hight," archaic for named or being called	Philippians 3:4 (notes)
hypallage	an interchange of two elements in a phrase or sentence from a more logical to a less logical relationship	Revelation 17:1 (notes)
ignominy	disgrace	Hebrews 2:10 (notes)
Iim	probably hyenas	Isaiah 13:22

WORD	MEANING	SAMPLE LOCATION
imbrued	soaked	Revelation 17:6 (notes)
impostume	abscess	Leviticus 13:18 (notes)
incontinently	straightway, immediately	Matthew 13:20
	or, without restraint or limit	Ezra 6:8
incredulity	skepticism; lack of belief	Deuteronomy 1 introduction
indite	to dictate	Jeremiah 36:4 (notes)
insinuation	archaic, to creep, to ingratiate oneself	Romans 10:1
instant (adj)	importunate, urgent	2 Kings 2:17
inured	accustomed to accepting something undesirable	Acts 5:41 (notes)
Isthmians	of or relating to the Isthmus of Corinth in Greece or the games held there in ancient times	1 Corinthians 9:24 (notes)
jakes	privy; small building used for a toilet	2 Kings 10:27
jangling	talking idly, quarreling	1 Timothy 1:6
justing	jousting	2 Timothy 2:5 (notes)
kine	plural of cow	Acts 7:41 (notes)
knops	ornamental knobs	1 Kings 6:18
laded	loaded, or carried	Nehemiah 4:17
lap	flap, the lobe of an ear	Leviticus 8:23
lapwing	a crested Old World plover noted for its slow irregular flapping flight and shrill wailing cry	Deuteronomy 14:18
lawns	a light cotton or linen fabric of very fine weave	Isaiah 3:23
leisure	opportunity	Hebrews 11:15

WORD	MEANING	SAMPLE LOCATION
lenity	mercifulness, clemency	Romans 9:22 (notes)
let (verb)	resist; hinder	Acts 11:17
lets (noun)	obstructions	Luke 14:18 (notes)
liberality	generosity	Psalm 11:25
ligure	precious stone, probably the jacinth	Exodus 39:12 (notes)
lime	a sticky substance; something that ensnares	Revelation 13:12 (notes)
liquor	grease, or liquid	Leviticus 7:10 (notes)
listeth	pleaseth	Mark 2:28 (notes)
Locrian	of Locris in Greece, or its people	Leviticus 19:29 (notes)
lodes	support	Ephesians 2:18 (notes)
lodging without doors	living outside	Luke 2:8 (notes)
lucre	money, profit, gain	Acts 16:19 (notes)
magnifical	archaic for magnificent	1 Chronicles 22:5
malediction	curse	1 Kings 14:11 (notes)
mallows	any of the plants of the genus Malva, with downy leaves and disklike fruits	Job 30:4 (notes)
marvelous	archaic for astonishing, beyond belief	Judges 13:18 (notes)
matrix	womb	Numbers 3:12
mattock	a digging tool with a flat blade set at right angles to the handle.	Isaiah 2:4
maugre	in spite of	Matthew 12:20 (notes)
maw	opening through which food is taken; mouth; stomach	Leviticus 1:16

WORD	MEANING	SAMPLE LOCATION
mean	intermediary	Revelation 4:1 (notes)
meanly	partially	Luke 1:4 (notes)
meet	appropriate, precisely adapted to a particular situation, need, or circumstance	Luke 14:35
meres	pools, lakes	Deuteronomy 8:7 (notes)
mete (v)	measure	Luke 6:38
milch kine	milk cows	1 Samuel 6:7
milt	spleen	2 Samuel 2:23 (notes)
miter	a turban; a high head-dress, split on top, worn by archbishops and bishops, and by some abbots	Exodus 28:4
monkery	monasticism	Colossians 2:23 (notes)
Moor	Ethiopian	Jeremiah 13:23
moraine	alternate spelling of *murrain*: a pestilence or plague, especially affecting domestic animals	Exodus 9:3
mortises	holes or grooves	Exodus 26:19 (notes)
mow	grimace	Psalm 22:7
mufflers	light and tremulous veils	Isaiah 3:21
munitions	defense or ammunition	1 Kings 9:19 (notes)
nether	lower	Exodus 19:17
niggard	miser	Proverbs 11:24 (notes)
niggardliness	stinginess	Luke 8:18 (notes)
nigh and strait	intimate and upright	Luke 8:19 (notes)
nothing less	nothing of it	Luke 2:1 (notes)

WORD	MEANING	SAMPLE LOCATION
nothing regarding	not at all regarding	Luke 2:8 (notes)
oblation	sacrifice, offering	Hebrews 9:26 (notes)
obtestation	testimony	1 Corinthians 1:10 (notes)
offscouring	outcast	1 Corinthians 4:13
Ohim	probably owls	Isaiah 13:21
oppugn	fight against	Mark 3:28 (notes)
order	manner for doing things	Luke 4:22 (notes)
ordinary	a meal served as a fixed portion or share	Genesis 47:22
ouches	obsolete for clasps; brooches	Exodus 39:13
particle	clause or article of a composition or document	Galatians 3:27 (notes)
parti-colored	having different colors, esp. having a predominant color broken by patches of other color(s).	Genesis 30:35
pate	head	Psalm 7:16
peevish	foolish	Acts 17:22 (notes)
pelting pelf	paltry riches	Luke 8:27 (notes)
penury	severe poverty	Luke 21:4
peradventure	perhaps, possibly	Genesis 16:2 (notes)
peregrination	journey, travel trip	Luke 12:35 (notes)
pertinence	relevance; the state of being pertinent	Exodus 12:9
pight	pitched, set	Hebrews 8:3 (notes)
piked	pointed, peaked	Hebrews 11:3 (notes)
pill	*vb.* to plunder	Job 24:9 (notes)
pilled	peeled	Genesis 30:37

WORD	MEANING	SAMPLE LOCATION
pismire	an ant	Proverbs 6:6 (notes)
pith	core; importance	Colossians 2:17 (notes)
plagues	afflictions	Luke 7:21
plaint	complaint	1 Samuel 6:18 (notes)
pommels	knobs	1 Kings 7:16 (notes)
Porphyrio	any bird of the purple coot genus	Leviticus 11:18 (notes)
porphyry	a very hard, variegated rock, of a purple and white color	Esther 1:6
postern	back	2 Kings 25:4 (notes)
potsherd	a broken piece of pottery	Job 2:8
pottle	container holding ½ gallon	Exodus 16:16 (notes)
powle	cheat, or impoverish	Proverbs 21:7 (notes)
powling	gambling or betting, cheating	Job 15:34 (notes)
prattlers	babblers	1 Timothy 5:13 (notes)
prayedst	begged	Matthew 18:32
preace, prease	obs. for press, to exert a pushing force upon, to go forward; a crowd	Leviticus 21:17
premisses	the things stated beforehand	1 Timothy 6:13 (notes)
preparative	introductory	1 Timothy 1:13 (notes)
press	crowd	Luke 8:19
prevented	anticipated	Matthew 17:25
privily	privately	John 7:10
privities	arch. for something kept private	Leviticus 16:4 (notes)
privy	familiar	Hebrews 10:1 (notes)
prodigality	reckless extravagance	2 Kings 4:1 (notes)

WORD	MEANING	SAMPLE LOCATION
proem	preliminary comment, preface	Revelation 13:18 (notes)
propense	leaning or inclining toward; disposed	Luke 11:42 (notes)
propitiatory	an atoning sacrifice	Exodus 25:17 (notes)
provender	dry feed for domestic animals, or food, victuals	Genesis 24:25
purgation	act of clearing from guilt	Leviticus 14:2 (notes)
purtenances	entrails	Exodus 12:9
quail	slacken, subdue	2 Corinthians 8:2 (notes)
quaternions	a set or group of four	Acts 12:4
quick	living, alive	1 Peter 4:5
quite (quit)	acquitted, released from penalty	Exodus 21:19
racks	framework for holding fodder for livestock	2 Chronicles 32:28 (notes)
rapine	plundering	Psalm 76:4 (notes)
rapting up	carrying away	Revelation 21:9
rebecks	a medieval instrument of the viol class shaped like a mandolin	1 Samuel 18:6
receipt	receptacle; place to gather	Acts 1:13 (notes)
refection	refreshment of mind, spirit, or body; esp. nourishment	Genesis 14:18 (notes)
refelleth	rejects, repulses	2 Corinthians 10:1 (notes)
refelling	disputing, disproving	John 4:5 (notes)
reins	controlling or guiding power; *archaic* the kidneys, esp. as formerly supposed seat of emotion: the loins	Revelation 2:23

WORD	MEANING	SAMPLE LOCATION
rent (v)	tear apart	Matthew 7:6
rent (n)	probably a rope	Isaiah 3:24
repine	to lament, to grudge	Job 37:20 (notes)
reprehension	judgments	Luke 6:37 (notes)
requite	repay	1 Samuel 25:21
rigor	severity	Job 32:2 (notes)
rosen	archaic for rosin	Genesis 37:25 (notes)
roule	archaic for the verb roll	Genesis 43:18 (notes)
routs	throngs, crowds	Acts 5:34 (notes)
rudiments	basic principles, elements	Galatians 4:3
runagates	vagabonds, runaways	Judges 12:4
sackbut	old instrument with slide like a trombone	Daniel 3:5
sallets	helmet with neck guard	Jeremiah 46:4
salveth	preserved unhurt, quiet, assuage	Romans 10:4 (notes)
sardine	a sardius stone	Revelation 4:3
schism	division	1 Corinthians 1:10 (notes)
scrip	small bag, wallet	Matthew 10:10
scurf	dandruff	Leviticus 13:13 (notes)
seethe	to boil	2 Kings 4:38
senary	of, based on, or characterized by six	Revelation 13:18 (notes)
separate	exclude	Luke 6:22
shalm	a wind instrument, supposed to have resembled either the clarinet or the oboe in form	Psalm 98:6

WORD	MEANING	SAMPLE LOCATION
shambles	butcher's market stall; slaughterhouse	1 Corinthians 10:25
shamefastness	being shamefaced	1 Timothy 4:2 (notes)
sheepcote	sheepfold	1 Samuel 24:4
shred	pruned	John 15:1 (notes)
shrift	prescribed penance; absolution; confession; a confessional	Acts 19:18 (notes)
similitude	likeness	Numbers 12:8
sinistrous	archaic for sinister	Philippians 4:15 (notes)
sirrah	implying inferiority in the person addressed	Ruth 4:1 (notes)
skriking	wailing	Isaiah 15:8
slop	a loose outer garment	Isaiah 3:20
sod	archaic for "seethed" meaning boiled; or soaked	2 Kings 6:29
sop	piece of food dipped or steeped in liquid	John 13:26
Sophister	an intentionally fallacious reasoner	Galatians 5:23 (notes)
sophistical	plausible but fallacious	1 Timothy 1:7 (notes)
sorer	more severe	John 5:45 (notes)
staggie	stagnant, still, or calm	Genesis 41:2 (notes)
stanched	stopped	Luke 8:44
stint	allowance or share	Revelation 6:5 (notes)
stock	family	Luke 1:5 (notes)
stops (noun)	snares	Luke 18:39 (notes)
strait	narrow, small, difficult, stressful	Matthew 7:13

WORD	MEANING	SAMPLE LOCATION
straitly	strictly, rigorously	Mark 5:43
strake	past tense of strike	Acts 27:17
strakes	streaks	Genesis 30:37
strawed	spread, scattered	Matthew 21:9
suborned	induced to commit perjury	Acts 6:11
succor	relief, aid, help	2 Samuel 17:19 (notes)
suffer (verb)	allow	Esther 3:8
sufferance	permission	Luke 4:6 (notes)
supererogation	the act of performing more than is required by duty, obligation or need	1 John 1:8 (notes)
surcease	cease, discontinue	James 3:1 (notes)
surfeiting	indulging in excess	Luke 21:34
swinge	to punish with blows; thrash; beat	Psalm 1:4 (notes)
swound	archaic for swoon	Mark 8:3 (notes)
table	an engraved slab or tablet bearing an inscription or a device.	Proverbs 7:3
taboret, tabret	small drum	2 Kings 23:10 (notes)
taches	fastenings, clasps	Exodus 35:11
tale (noun)	count, total	Exodus 5:18
tentation	old form of temptation	James 1:13 (notes)
therewithal	besides	1 Timothy 1:1 (notes)
thraldom	slavery; bondage	Psalm 136:11 (notes)
Thraso	braggart soldier in the comedy *Eunuchus* by Terence, 1564; braggard	2 Corinthians 10:1 (notes)

WORD	MEANING	SAMPLE LOCATION
Thynewood	thyine, a tree supposed to be sandarach	Revelation 18:12
tippler	one that drinks liquor continuously and in small amounts	1 Timothy 3:3 (notes)
tire, tyre (noun)	ornament for the head or hair	Isaiah 3:18
tire (verb)	to adorn (the hair) with an ornament	2 Kings 9:30
tow	coarse broken flax or hemp fiber prepared for spinning.	Isaiah 1:31
transom	horizontal crossbar	Exodus 12:22 (notes)
travaileth	labors hard, as in childbirth	John 16:21
treacle	a medicinal compound used against poison	Genesis 37:25 (notes)
trow	believe, think	Luke 17:9
trumperies	tawdry fineries	1 Corinthians 9:14 (notes)
truss	bundle	Acts 9:34
tunicle	a little tunic; an ecclesiastical vestment worn by a sub-deacon or a bishop at mass	Exodus 29:5
usury	archaic for interest	Deuteronomy 23:20
utter	outer	Matthew 23:25
verily	truly	John 3:3
victualler	keeper of a tavern	Judges 11:1 (notes)
vie	contend, wager, match	Romans 11:16 (notes)
vittles	victuals; food usable by people; provisions	Exodus 12:39
vizards	masks, disguises	2 Timothy 3:9 (notes)
wantons	lewd, lacivious persons	1 Corinthians 6:9

WORD	MEANING	SAMPLE LOCATION
-ward	(suffix) directed toward, situated in the direction of	Exodus 25:20
ware	archaic for "aware"	Leviticus 5:2
wench	young girl	Luke 8:55 (notes)
whelps	dogs	Matthew 15:26
Whitsuntide	the week beginning with Whitsunday, lit. "White Sunday" probably from the custom of wearing white robes by those newly baptized at this season; Pentecost	Exodus 23:16 (notes)
wist	knew	Luke 9:33
withies	flexible slender twigs or branches	Judges 16:7 (notes)
wont	accustomed	1 Corinthians 1:19
woof	the threads that run crosswise in a woven fabric, at right angles to the warp threads	Judges 16:13
wot	know	Matthew 26:70
wrest	gain with difficulty, force	John 1:21 (notes)
wroth	wrathful; stormy	Esther 2:21
wrought	worked	Joshua 9:4

THE NINETY-FIVE THESES

by Martin Luther

Out of love for the truth and from desire to elucidate it, the Reverend Father Martin Luther, Master of Arts and Sacred Theology, and ordinary lecturer therein at Wittenberg, intends to defend the following statements and to dispute on them in that place. Therefore he asks that those who cannot be present and dispute with him orally shall do so in their absence by letter. In the name of our Lord Jesus Christ, Amen.

1. When our Lord and Master Jesus Christ said, "Repent" (Mt 4:17), he willed the entire life of believers to be one of repentance.

2. This word cannot be understood as referring to the sacrament of penance, that is, confession and satisfaction, as administered by the clergy.

3. Yet it does not mean solely inner repentance; such inner repentance is worthless unless it produces various outward mortifications of the flesh.

4. The penalty of sin remains as long as the hatred of self (that is, true inner repentance), namely till our entrance into the kingdom of heaven.

5. The pope neither desires nor is able to remit any penalties except those imposed by his own authority or that of the canons.

6. The pope cannot remit any guilt, except by declaring and showing that it has been remitted by God; or, to be sure, by remitting guilt in cases reserved to his judgment. If his right to grant remission in these cases were disregarded, the guilt would certainly remain unforgiven.

7. God remits guilt to no one unless at the same time he humbles him in all things and makes him submissive to the vicar, the priest.

8. The penitential canons are imposed only on the living, and, according to the canons themselves, nothing should be imposed on the dying.

9. Therefore the Holy Spirit through the pope is kind to us insofar as the pope in his decrees always makes exception of the article of death and of necessity.

10. Those priests act ignorantly and wickedly who, in the case of the dying, reserve canonical penalties for purgatory.

11. Those tares of changing the canonical penalty to the penalty of purgatory were evidently sown while the bishops slept (Mt 13:25).

12. In former times canonical penalties were imposed, not after, but before absolution, as tests of true contrition.

13. The dying are freed by death from all penalties, are already dead as far as the canon laws are concerned, and have a right to be released from them.

14. Imperfect piety or love on the part of the dying person necessarily brings with it great fear; and the smaller the love, the greater the fear.

15. This fear or horror is sufficient in itself, to say nothing of other things, to constitute the penalty of purgatory, since it is very near to the horror of despair.

16. Hell, purgatory, and heaven seem to differ

the same as despair, fear, and assurance of salvation.

17. It seems as though for the souls in purgatory fear should necessarily decrease and love increase.

18. Furthermore, it does not seem proved, either by reason or by Scripture, that souls in purgatory are outside the state of merit, that is, unable to grow in love.

19. Nor does it seem proved that souls in purgatory, at least not all of them, are certain and assured of their own salvation, even if we ourselves may be entirely certain of it.

20. Therefore the pope, when he uses the words "plenary remission of all penalties," does not actually mean "all penalties," but only those imposed by himself.

21. Thus those indulgence preachers are in error who say that a man is absolved from every penalty and saved by papal indulgences.

22. As a matter of fact, the pope remits to souls in purgatory no penalty which, according to canon law, they should have paid in this life.

23. If remission of all penalties whatsoever could be granted to anyone at all, certainly it would be granted only to the most perfect, that is, to very few.

24. For this reason most people are necessarily deceived by that indiscriminate and high-sounding promise of release from penalty.

25. That power which the pope has in general over purgatory corresponds to the power which any bishop or curate has in a particular way in his own diocese and parish.

26. The pope does very well when he grants remission to souls in purgatory, not by the power of the keys, which he does not have, but by way of intercession for them.

27. They preach only human doctrines who say that as soon as the money clinks into the money chest, the soul flies out of purgatory.

28. It is certain that when money clinks in the money chest, greed and avarice can be increased; but when the church intercedes, the result is in the hands of God alone.

29. Who knows whether all souls in purgatory wish to be redeemed, since we have exceptions in St. Severinus and St. Paschal, as related in a legend.

30. No one is sure of the integrity of his own contrition, much less of having received plenary remission.

31. The man who actually buys indulgences is as rare as he who is really penitent; indeed, he is exceedingly rare.

32. Those who believe that they can be certain of their salvation because they have indulgence letters will be eternally damned, together with their teachers.

33. Men must especially be on guard against those who say that the pope's pardons are that inestimable gift of God by which man is reconciled to him.

34. For the graces of indulgences are concerned only with the penalties of sacramental satisfaction established by man.

35. They who teach that contrition is not necessary on the part of those who intend to buy souls out of purgatory or to buy confessional privileges preach unchristian doctrine.

36. Any truly repentant Christian has a right to full remission of penalty and guilt, even without indulgence letters.

37. Any true Christian, whether living or dead, participates in all the blessings of Christ and the church; and this is granted him by God, even without indulgence letters.

38. Nevertheless, papal remission and blessing are by no means to be disregarded, for they are, as I have said (Thesis 6), the proclamation of the divine remission.

39. It is very difficult, even for the most learned theologians, at one and the same time to commend to the people the bounty of indulgences and the need of true contrition.

40. A Christian who is truly contrite seeks and loves to pay penalties for his sins; the bounty of indulgences, however, relaxes penalties and causes men to hate them—at least it furnishes occasion for hating them.

41. Papal indulgences must be preached with caution, lest people erroneously think that they are preferable to other good works of love.

42. Christians are to be taught that the pope does not intend that the buying of indulgences should in any way be compared with works of mercy.

43. Christians are to be taught that he who gives to the poor or lends to the needy does a better deed than he who buys indulgences.

44. Because love grows by works of love, man thereby becomes better. Man does not, however, become better by means of indulgences but is merely freed from penalties.

45. Christians are to be taught that he who sees a needy man and passes him by, yet gives his money for indulgences, does not buy papal indulgences but God's wrath.

46. Christians are to be taught that, unless they have more than they need, they must reserve enough for their family needs and by no means squander it on indulgences.

47. Christians are to be taught that the buying of indulgences is a matter of free choice, not commanded.

48. Christians are to be taught that the pope, in granting indulgences, needs and thus desires their devout prayer more than their money.

49. Christians are to be taught that papal indulgences are useful only if they do not put their trust in them, but very harmful if they lose their fear of God because of them.

50. Christians are to be taught that if the pope knew the exactions of the indulgence preachers, he would rather that the basilica of St. Peter were burned to ashes than built up with the skin, flesh, and bones of his sheep.

51. Christians are to be taught that the pope would and should wish to give of his own money, even though he had to sell the basilica of St. Peter, to many of those from whom certain hawkers of indulgences cajole money.

52. It is vain to trust in salvation by indulgence letters, even though the indulgence commissary, or even the pope, were to offer his soul as security.

53. They are the enemies of Christ and the pope who forbid altogether the preaching of the Word of God in some churches in order that indulgences may be preached in others.

54. Injury is done to the Word of God when, in the same sermon, an equal or larger amount of time is devoted to indulgences than to the Word.

55. It is certainly the pope's sentiment that if indulgences, which are a very insignificant thing, are celebrated with one bell, one procession, and one ceremony, then the gospel, which is the very greatest thing, should be preached with a hundred bells, a hundred processions, a hundred ceremonies.

56. The true treasures of the church, out of which the pope distributes indulgences, are

not sufficiently discussed or known among the people of Christ.

57. That indulgences are not temporal treasures is certainly clear, for many indulgence sellers do not distribute them freely but only gather them.

58. Nor are they the merits of Christ and the saints, for, even without the pope, the latter always work grace for the inner man, and the cross, death, and hell for the outer man.

59. St. Lawrence said that the poor of the church were the treasures of the church, but he spoke according to the usage of the word in his own time.

60. Without want of consideration we say that the keys of the church, given by the merits of Christ, are that treasure.

61. For it is clear that the pope's power is of itself sufficient for the remission of penalties and cases reserved by himself.

62. The true treasure of the church is the most holy gospel of the glory and grace of God.

63. But this treasure is naturally most odious, for it makes the first to be last (Mt. 20:16).

64. On the other hand, the treasure of indulgences is naturally most acceptable, for it makes the last to be first.

65. Therefore the treasures of the gospel are nets with which one formerly fished for men of wealth.

66. The treasures of indulgences are nets with which one now fishes for the wealth of men.

67. The indulgences which the demagogues acclaim as the greatest graces are actually understood to be such only insofar as they promote gain.

68. They are nevertheless in truth the most insignificant graces when compared with the grace of God and the piety of the cross.

69. Bishops and curates are bound to admit the commissaries of papal indulgences with all reverence.

70. But they are much more bound to strain their eyes and ears lest these men preach their own dreams instead of what the pope has commissioned.

71. Let him who speaks against the truth concerning papal indulgences be anathema and accursed.

72. But let him who guards against the lust and license of the indulgence preachers be blessed.

73. Just as the pope justly thunders against those who by any means whatever contrive harm to the sale of indulgences.

74. Much more does he intend to thunder against those who use indulgences as a pretext to contrive harm to holy love and truth.

75. To consider papal indulgences so great that they could absolve a man even if he had done the impossible and had violated the mother of God is madness.

76. We say on the contrary that papal indulgences cannot remove the very least of venial sins as far as guilt is concerned.

77. To say that even St. Peter if he were now pope, could not grant greater graces is blasphemy against St. Peter and the pope.

78. We say on the contrary that even the present pope, or any pope whatsoever, has greater graces at his disposal, that is, the gospel, spiritual powers, gifts of healing, etc., as it is written. (1 Co 12[:28])

79. To say that the cross emblazoned with the papal coat of arms, and set up by the indulgence preachers is equal in worth to the cross of Christ is blasphemy.

80. The bishops, curates, and theologians who permit such talk to be spread among the people will have to answer for this.

81. This unbridled preaching of indulgences makes it difficult even for learned men to rescue the reverence which is due the pope from slander or from the shrewd questions of the laity.

82. Such as: "Why does not the pope empty purgatory for the sake of holy love and the dire need of the souls that are there if he redeems an infinite number of souls for the sake of miserable money with which to build a church?" The former reason would be most just; the latter is most trivial.

83. Again, "Why are funeral and anniversary masses for the dead continued and why does he not return or permit the withdrawal of the endowments founded for them, since it is wrong to pray for the redeemed?"

84. Again, "What is this new piety of God and the pope that for a consideration of money they permit a man who is impious and their enemy to buy out of purgatory the pious soul of a friend of God and do not rather, because of the need of that pious and beloved soul, free it for pure love's sake?"

85. Again, "Why are the penitential canons, long since abrogated and dead in actual fact and through disuse, now satisfied by the granting of indulgences as though they were still alive and in force?"

86. Again, "Why does not the pope, whose wealth is today greater than the wealth of the richest Crassus, build this one basilica of St. Peter with his own money rather than with the money of poor believers?"

87. Again, "What does the pope remit or grant to those who by perfect contrition already have a right to full remission and blessings?"

88. Again, "What greater blessing could come to the church than if the pope were to bestow these remissions and blessings on every believer a hundred times a day, as he now does but once?"

89. "Since the pope seeks the salvation of souls rather than money by his indulgences, why does he suspend the indulgences and pardons previously granted when they have equal efficacy?"

90. To repress these very sharp arguments of the laity by force alone, and not to resolve them by giving reasons, is to expose the church and the pope to the ridicule of their enemies and to make Christians unhappy.

91. If, therefore, indulgences were preached according to the spirit and intention of the pope, all these doubts would be readily resolved. Indeed, they would not exist.

92. Away, then, with all those prophets who say to the people of Christ, "Peace, peace," and there is no peace! (Jer 6:14)

93. Blessed be all those prophets who say to the people of Christ, "Cross, cross," and there is no cross!

94. Christians should be exhorted to be diligent in following Christ, their Head, through penalties, death and hell.

95. And thus be confident of entering into heaven through many tribulations rather than through the false security of peace (Acts 14:22).

THE AUGSBURG CONFESSION

by Philip Melanchthon

PREFACE TO THE EMPEROR CHARLES V

Most Invincible Emperor, Caesar Augustus, Most Clement Lord: Inasmuch as Your Imperial Majesty has summoned a Diet of the Empire here at Augsburg to deliberate concerning measures against the Turk, that most atrocious, hereditary, and ancient enemy of the Christian name and religion, in what way, namely, effectually to withstand his furor and assaults by strong and lasting military provision; and then also concerning dissensions in the matter of our holy religion and Christian Faith, that in this matter of religion the opinions and judgments of the parties might be heard in each other's presence; and considered and weighed among ourselves in mutual charity, leniency, and kindness, in order that, after the removal and correction of such things as have been treated and understood in a different manner in the writings on either side, these matters may be settled and brought back to one simple truth and Christian concord, that for the future one pure and true religion may be embraced and maintained by us, that as we all are under one Christ and do battle under Him, so we may be able also to live in unity and concord in the one Christian Church.

And inasmuch as we, the undersigned Elector and Princes, with others joined with us, have been called to the aforesaid Diet the same as the other Electors, Princes, and Estates, in obedient compliance with the Imperial mandate, we have promptly come to Augsburg, and—what we do not mean to say as boasting—we were among the first to be here.

Accordingly, since even here at Augsburg at the very beginning of the Diet, Your Imperial Majesty caused to be proposed to the Electors, Princes, and other Estates of the Empire, amongst other things, that the several Estates of the Empire, on the strength of the Imperial edict, should set forth and submit their opinions and judgments in the German and the Latin language, and since on the ensuing Wednesday, answer was given to Your Imperial Majesty, after due deliberation, that we would submit the Articles of our Confession for our side on next Wednesday, therefore, in obedience to Your Imperial Majesty's wishes, we offer, in this matter of religion, the Confession of our preachers and of ourselves, showing what manner of doctrine from the Holy Scriptures and the pure Word of God has been up to this time set forth in our lands, dukedoms, dominions, and cities, and taught in our churches.

And if the other Electors, Princes, and Estates. of the Empire will, according to the said Imperial proposition, present similar writings, to wit, in Latin and German, giving their opinions in this matter of religion, we, with the Princes and friends aforesaid, here before Your Imperial Majesty, our most clement Lord are prepared to confer amicably concerning all possible ways and means, in order that we may come together, as far as this may be honorably done, and, the matter between us on both sides being peacefully discussed without offensive strife, the dissension, by God's help, may be done away and brought back to one true accordant religion; for as we all are under one Christ and do battle under Him, we ought to confess the one Christ, after the tenor of Your Imperial Majesty's edict, and everything ought to be conducted according to the truth of God; and this it is what, with most fervent prayers, we entreat of God.

However, as regards the rest of the Electors, Princes, and Estates, who constitute the other part, if no progress should be made, nor some result be attained by this treatment of the cause of religion after the manner in which Your Imperial Majesty has wisely held that it should be dealt with and treated namely, by such mutual presentation of writings and calm conferring together among ourselves, we at least leave with you a clear testimony, that we here in no wise are holding back from anything that could bring about Christian concord,—such as could be effected with God and a good conscience,—as also Your Imperial Majesty and, next, the other Electors and Estates of the Empire, and all who are moved by sincere love and zeal for religion, and who will give an impartial hearing to this matter, will graciously deign to take notice and to understand this from this Confession of ours and of our associates.

Your Imperial Majesty also, not only once but often, graciously signified to the Electors Princes, and Estates of the Empire, and at the Diet of Spires held A. D. 1526, according to the form of Your Imperial instruction and commission given and prescribed, caused it to be stated and publicly proclaimed that Your Majesty, in dealing with this matter of religion, for certain reasons which were alleged in Your Majesty's name, was not willing to decide and could not determine anything, but that Your Majesty would diligently use Your Majesty's office with the Roman Pontiff for the convening of a General Council. The same matter was thus publicly set forth at greater length a year ago at the last Diet which met at Spires. There Your Imperial Majesty, through His Highness Ferdinand, King of Bohemia and Hungary, our friend and clement Lord, as well as through the Orator and Imperial Commissioners caused this, among other things, to be submitted: that Your Imperial Majesty had taken notice of; and pondered, the resolution of Your Majesty's Representative in the Empire, and of the President and Imperial Counselors, and the Legates from other Estates convened at

Ratisbon, concerning the calling of a Council, and that your Imperial Majesty also judged it to be expedient to convene a Council; and that Your Imperial Majesty did not doubt the Roman Pontiff could be induced to hold a General Council, because the matters to be adjusted between Your Imperial Majesty and the Roman Pontiff were nearing agreement and Christian reconciliation; therefore Your Imperial Majesty himself signified that he would endeavor to secure the said Chief Pontiff's consent for convening, together with your Imperial Majesty such General Council, to be published as soon as possible by letters that were to be sent out.

If the outcome, therefore, should be such that the differences between us and the other parties in the matter of religion should not be amicably and in charity settled, then here, before Your Imperial Majesty we make the offer in all obedience, in addition to what we have already done, that we will all appear and defend our cause in such a general, free Christian Council, for the convening of which there has always been accordant action and agreement of votes in all the Imperial Diets held during Your Majesty's reign, on the part of the Electors, Princes, and other Estates of the Empire. To the assembly of this General Council, and at the same time to Your Imperial Majesty, we have, even before this, in due manner and form of law, addressed ourselves and made appeal in this matter, by far the greatest and gravest. To this appeal, both to Your Imperial Majesty and to a Council, we still adhere; neither do we intend nor would it be possible for us, to relinquish it by this or any other document, unless the matter between us and the other side, according to the tenor of the latest Imperial citation should be amicably and charitably settled, allayed, and brought to Christian concord; and regarding this we even here solemnly and publicly testify.

Article I:
Of God

Our Churches, with common consent, do teach that the decree of the Council of Nicaea concerning the Unity of the Divine Essence and concerning the Three Persons, is true and to be believed without any doubting; that is to say, there is one Divine Essence which is called and which is God: eternal, without body, without parts, of infinite power, wisdom, and goodness, the Maker and Preserver of all things, visible and invisible; and yet there are three Persons, of the same essence and power, who also are coeternal, the Father the Son, and the Holy Ghost. And the term "person" they use as the Fathers have used it, to signify, not a part or quality in another, but that which subsists of itself.

They condemn all heresies which have sprung up against this article, as the Manichaeans, who assumed two principles, one Good and the other Evil- also the Valentinians, Arians, Eunomians, Mohammedans, and all such. They condemn also the Samosatenes, old and new, who, contending that there is but one Person, sophistically and impiously argue that the Word and the Holy Ghost are not distinct Persons, but that "Word" signifies a spoken word, and "Spirit" signifies motion created in things.

Article II:
Of Original Sin

Also they teach that since the fall of Adam all men begotten in the natural way are born with sin, that is, without the fear of God, without trust in God, and with concupiscence; and that this disease, or vice of origin, is truly sin, even now condemning and bringing eternal death upon those not born again through Baptism and the Holy Ghost.

They Condemn the Pelagians and others who deny that original depravity is sin, and who, to obscure the glory of Christ's merit and benefits, argue that man can be justified before God by his own strength and reason.

Article III:
Of the Son of God

Also they teach that the Word, that is, the Son of God, did assume the human nature in the womb of the blessed Virgin Mary, so that there are two natures, the divine and the human, inseparably enjoined in one Person, one Christ, true God and true man, who was born of the Virgin Mary, truly suffered, was crucified, dead, and buried, that He might reconcile the Father unto us, and be a sacrifice, not only for original guilt, but also for all actual sins of men

He also descended into hell, and truly rose again the third day; afterward He ascended into heaven that He might sit on the right hand of the Father, and forever reign and have dominion over all creatures, and sanctify them that believe in Him, by sending the Holy Ghost into their hearts, to rule, comfort, and quicken them, and to defend them against the devil and the power of sin.

The same Christ shall openly come again to judge the quick and the dead, etc., according to the Apostles' Creed.

Article IV:
Of Justification

Also they teach that men cannot be justified before God by their own strength, merits, or works, but are freely justified for Christ's sake, through faith, when they believe that they are received into favor, and that their sins are forgiven for Christ's sake, who, by His death, has made satisfaction for our sins. This faith God imputes for righteousness in His sight. Rom. 3 and 4.

Article V:
Of the Ministry

That we may obtain this faith, the Ministry of Teaching the Gospel and administering the Sacraments was instituted. For through the Word and Sacraments, as through instruments, the Holy Ghost is given, who works faith; where and when it pleases God, in them that hear the Gospel, to wit, that God, not for our own merits, but for Christ's sake, justifies those who believe that they are received into grace for Christ's sake.

They condemn the Anabaptists and others who think that the Holy Ghost comes to men without the external Word, through their own preparations and works.

ARTICLE VI:
OF NEW OBEDIENCE

Also they teach that this faith is bound to bring forth good fruits, and that it is necessary to do good works commanded by God, because of God's will, but that we should not rely on those works to merit justification before God. For remission of sins and justification is apprehended by faith, as also the voice of Christ attests: When ye shall have done all these things, say: We are unprofitable servants. Luke 17, 10. The same is also taught by the Fathers. For Ambrose says: It is ordained of God that he who believes in Christ is saved, freely receiving remission of sins, without works, by faith alone.

ARTICLE VII:
OF THE CHURCH

Also they teach that one holy Church is to continue forever. The Church is the congregation of saints, in which the Gospel is rightly taught and the Sacraments are rightly administered.

And to the true unity of the Church it is enough to agree concerning the doctrine of the Gospel and the administration of the Sacraments. Nor is it necessary that human traditions, that is, rites or ceremonies, instituted by men, should be everywhere alike. As Paul says: One faith, one Baptism, one God and Father of all, etc. Eph. 4, 5. 6.

ARTICLE VIII:
WHAT THE CHURCH IS

Although the Church properly is the congregation of saints and true believers, nev-

ertheless, since in this life many hypocrites and evil persons are mingled therewith, it is lawful to use Sacraments administered by evil men, according to the saying of Christ: The Scribes and the Pharisees sit in Moses' seat, etc. Matt. 23, 2. Both the Sacraments and Word are effectual by reason of the institution and commandment of Christ, notwithstanding they be administered by evil men.

They condemn the Donatists, and such like, who denied it to be lawful to use the ministry of evil men in the Church, and who thought the ministry of evil men to be unprofitable and of none effect.

ARTICLE IX:
OF BAPTISM

Of Baptism they teach that it is necessary to salvation, and that through Baptism is offered the grace of God, and that children are to be baptized who, being offered to God through Baptism are received into God's grace.

They condemn the Anabaptists, who reject the baptism of children, and say that children are saved without Baptism.

ARTICLE X:
OF THE LORD'S SUPPER

Of the Supper of the Lord they teach that the Body and Blood of Christ are truly present, and are distributed to those who eat the Supper of the Lord; and they reject those that teach otherwise.

ARTICLE XI:
OF CONFESSION

Of Confession they teach that Private Absolution ought to be retained in the churches, although in confession an enumeration of all sins is not necessary. For it is impossible according to the Psalm: Who can understand his errors? Ps. 19, 12.

ARTICLE XII:
OF REPENTANCE

Of Repentance they teach that for those who have fallen after Baptism there is remission of sins whenever they are converted and that the Church ought to impart absolution to those thus returning to repentance. Now, repentance consists properly of these two parts: One is contrition, that is, terrors smiting the conscience through the knowledge of sin; the other is faith, which is born of the Gospel, or of absolution, and believes that for Christ's sake, sins are forgiven, comforts the conscience, and delivers it from terrors. Then good works are bound to follow, which are the fruits of repentance.

They condemn the Anabaptists, who deny that those once justified can lose the Holy Ghost. Also those who contend that some may attain to such perfection in this life that they cannot sin.

The Novatians also are condemned, who would not absolve such as had fallen after Baptism, though they returned to repentance.

They also are rejected who do not teach that remission of sins comes through faith but command us to merit grace through satisfactions of our own.

ARTICLE XIII:
OF THE USE OF THE SACRAMENTS

Of the Use of the Sacraments they teach that the Sacraments were ordained, not only to be marks of profession among men, but rather to be signs and testimonies of the will of God toward us, instituted to awaken and confirm faith in those who use them. Wherefore we must so use the Sacraments that faith be added to believe the promises which are offered and set forth through the Sacraments.

They therefore condemn those who teach that the Sacraments justify by the outward act, and who do not teach that, in the use of the Sacraments, faith which believes that sins are forgiven, is required.

ARTICLE XIV:
OF ECCLESIASTICAL ORDER

Of Ecclesiastical Order they teach that no one should publicly teach in the Church or administer the Sacraments unless he be regularly called.

ARTICLE XV:
OF ECCLESIASTICAL USAGES

Of Usages in the Church they teach that those ought to be observed which may be observed without sin, and which are profitable unto tranquillity and good order in the Church, as particular holy-days, festivals, and the like.

Nevertheless, concerning such things men are admonished that consciences are not to be burdened, as though such observance was necessary to salvation.

They are admonished also that human traditions instituted to propitiate God, to merit grace, and to make satisfaction for sins, are opposed to the Gospel and the doctrine of faith. Wherefore vows and traditions concerning meats and days, etc., instituted to merit grace and to make satisfaction for sins, are useless and contrary to the Gospel.

ARTICLE XVI:
OF CIVIL AFFAIRS

Of Civil Affairs they teach that lawful civil ordinances are good works of God, and that it is right for Christians to bear civil office, to sit as judges, to judge matters by the Imperial and other existing laws, to award just punishments, to engage in just wars, to serve as soldiers, to make legal contracts, to hold property, to make oath when required by the magistrates, to marry a wife, to be given in marriage.

They condemn the Anabaptists who forbid these civil offices to Christians.

They condemn also those who do not place evangelical perfection in the fear of God and in faith, but in forsaking civil offices, for the Gospel teaches an eternal righteousness of the heart. Meanwhile, it does not destroy the State or the family, but very much requires that they be preserved as ordinances of God, and that charity be practiced in such ordinances. Therefore, Christians are necessarily bound to obey their own magistrates and laws save only when commanded to sin; for then they ought to obey God rather than men. Acts 5, 29.

ARTICLE XVII:
OF CHRIST'S RETURN TO JUDGMENT

Also they teach that at the Consummation of the World Christ will appear for judgment and will raise up all the dead; He will give to the godly and elect eternal life and everlasting joys, but ungodly men and the devils He will condemn to be tormented without end.

They condemn the Anabaptists, who think that there will be an end to the punishments of condemned men and devils.

They condemn also others who are now spreading certain Jewish opinions, that before the resurrection of the dead the godly shall take possession of the kingdom of the world, the ungodly being everywhere suppressed.

ARTICLE XVIII:
OF FREE WILL

Of Free Will they teach that man's will has some liberty to choose civil righteousness, and to work things subject to reason. But it has no power, without the Holy Ghost, to work the righteousness of God, that is, spiritual righteousness; since the natural man receiveth not the things of the Spirit of God, 1 Cor. 2,14; but this righteousness is wrought in the heart when the Holy Ghost is received through the Word. These things are said in as many words by Augustine in his Hypognosticon, Book III: We grant that all men have a free will, free, inasmuch as it has the judgment of reason; not that it is thereby capable, without God, either to begin, or, at least, to complete aught in things pertaining to God, but only in works of this life, whether good or evil. "Good" I call those works which spring from the good in nature, such as, willing to labor in the field, to eat and drink, to have a friend, to clothe oneself, to build a house, to marry a wife, to raise cattle, to learn divers useful arts, or whatsoever good pertains to this life. For all of these things are not without dependence on the providence of God; yea, of Him and through Him they are and have their being. "Evil" I call such works as willing to worship an idol, to commit murder, etc.

They condemn the Pelagians and others, who teach that without the Holy Ghost, by the power of nature alone, we are able to love God above all things; also to do the commandments of God as touching "the substance of the act." For, although nature is able in a manner to do the outward work, (for it is able to keep the hands from theft and murder,) yet it cannot produce the inward motions, such as the fear of God, trust in God, chastity, patience, etc.

ARTICLE XIX:
OF THE CAUSE OF SIN

Of the Cause of Sin they teach that, although God does create and preserve nature, yet the cause of sin is the will of the wicked, that is, of the devil and ungodly men; which will, unaided of God, turns itself from God, as Christ says John 8, 44: When he speaketh a lie, he speaketh of his own.

ARTICLE XX:
OF GOOD WORKS

Our teachers are falsely accused of forbidding good Works. For their published writings on the Ten Commandments, and others of like import, bear witness that they have taught to good purpose concerning all estates and duties of life, as to what estates of life and what works in every calling be pleasing to God. Concerning these things preachers heretofore taught but little, and urged only childish and needless works, as particular holy-days, particular fasts, brotherhoods, pilgrimages, services in honor of saints, the use of rosaries, monasticism, and such like. Since our adversaries have been admonished of these things, they are now unlearning them, and do not preach these unprofitable works as heretofore. Besides, they begin to mention faith, of which there was heretofore marvelous silence. They teach that we are justified not by works only, but they conjoin faith and works, and say that we are justified by faith and works. This doctrine is more tolerable than the former one, and can afford more consolation than their old doctrine.

Forasmuch, therefore, as the doctrine concerning faith, which ought to be the chief one in the Church, has lain so long unknown, as all must needs grant that there was the deepest silence in their sermons concerning the righteousness of faith, while only the doctrine of works was treated in the churches, our teachers have instructed the churches concerning faith as follows: --

First, that our works cannot reconcile God or merit forgiveness of sins, grace, and justification, but that we obtain this only by faith when we believe that we are received into favor for Christs sake, who alone has been set forth the Mediator and Propitiation, 1 Tim. 2, 6, in order that the Father may be reconciled through Him. Whoever, therefore, trusts that by works he merits grace, despises the merit and grace of Christ, and seeks a way to God without Christ, by human strength, although Christ has said of Himself: I am the Way, the Truth, and the Life. John 14, 6.

This doctrine concerning faith is everywhere treated by Paul, Eph. 2, 8: By grace are ye saved through faith; and that not of yourselves; it is the gift of God, not of works, etc.

And lest any one should craftily say that a new interpretation of Paul has been devised by us, this entire matter is supported by the testimonies of the Fathers. For Augustine, in many volumes, defends grace and the righteousness of faith, over against the merits of works. And Ambrose, in his De Vocatione Gentium, and elsewhere, teaches to like effect. For in his De Vocatione Gentium he says as follows: Redemption by the blood of Christ would become of little value, neither would the preeminence of man's works be superseded by the mercy of God, if justification, which is

wrought through grace, were due to the merits going before, so as to be, not the free gift of a donor, but the reward due to the laborer.

But, although this doctrine is despised by the inexperienced, nevertheless God-fearing and anxious consciences find by experience that it brings the greatest consolation, because consciences cannot be set at rest through any works, but only by faith, when they take the sure ground that for Christ's sake they have a reconciled God. As Paul teaches Rom. 5, 1: Being justified by faith, we have peace with God. This whole doctrine is to be referred to that conflict of the terrified conscience, neither can it be understood apart from that conflict. Therefore inexperienced and profane men judge ill concerning this matter, who dream that Christian righteousness is nothing but civil and philosophical righteousness.

Heretofore consciences were plagued with the doctrine of works, they did not hear the consolation from the Gospel. Some persons were driven by conscience into the desert, into monasteries hoping there to merit grace by a monastic life. Some also devised other works whereby to merit grace and make satisfaction for sins. Hence there was very great need to treat of, and renew, this doctrine of faith in Christ, to the end that anxious consciences should not be without consolation but that they might know that grace and forgiveness of sins and justification are apprehended by faith in Christ.

Men are also admonished that here the term "faith" does not signify merely the knowledge of the history, such as is in the ungodly and in the devil, but signifies a faith which believes, not merely the history, but also the effect of the history—namely, this Article: the forgiveness of sins, to wit, that we have grace, righteousness, and forgiveness of sins through Christ.

Now he that knows that he has a Father gracious to him through Christ, truly knows God; he knows also that God cares for him, and calls upon God; in a word, he is not without God, as the heathen. For devils and the ungodly are not able to believe this Article:

the forgiveness of sins. Hence, they hate God as an enemy, call not upon Him, and expect no good from Him. Augustine also admonishes his readers concerning the word "faith," and teaches that the term "faith" is accepted in the Scriptures not for knowledge such as is in the ungodly but for confidence which consoles and encourages the terrified mind.

Furthermore, it is taught on our part that it is necessary to do good works, not that we should trust to merit grace by them, but because it is the will of God. It is only by faith that forgiveness of sins is apprehended, and that, for nothing. And because through faith the Holy Ghost is received, hearts are renewed and endowed with new affections, so as to be able to bring forth good works. For Ambrose says: Faith is the mother of a good will and right doing. For man's powers without the Holy Ghost are full of ungodly affections, and are too weak to do works which are good in God's sight. Besides, they are in the power of the devil who impels men to divers sins, to ungodly opinions, to open crimes. This we may see in the philosophers, who, although they endeavored to live an honest life could not succeed, but were defiled with many open crimes. Such is the feebleness of man when he is without faith and without the Holy Ghost, and governs himself only by human strength.

Hence it may be readily seen that this doctrine is not to be charged with prohibiting good works, but rather the more to be commended, because it shows how we are enabled to do good works. For without faith human nature can in no wise do the works of the First or of the Second Commandment. Without faith it does not call upon God, nor expect anything from God, nor bear the cross, but seeks, and trusts in, man's help. And thus, when there is no faith and trust in God all manner of lusts and human devices rule in the heart. Wherefore Christ said, John 16,6: Without Me ye can do nothing; and the Church sings:

Lacking Thy divine favor,
There is nothing found in man,
Naught in him is harmless.

ARTICLE XXI:
OF THE WORSHIP OF THE SAINTS

Of the Worship of Saints they teach that the memory of saints may be set before us, that we may follow their faith and good works, according to our calling, as the Emperor may follow the example of David in making war to drive away the Turk from his country; For both are kings. But the Scripture teaches not the invocation of saints or to ask help of saints, since it sets before us the one Christ as the Mediator, Propitiation, High Priest, and Intercessor. He is to be prayed to, and has promised that He will hear our prayer; and this worship He approves above all, to wit, that in all afflictions He be called upon, 1 John 2, 1: If any man sin, we have an Advocate with the Father, etc.

This is about the Sum of our Doctrine, in which, as can be seen, there is nothing that varies from the Scriptures, or from the Church Catholic, or from the Church of Rome as known from its writers. This being the case, they judge harshly who insist that our teachers be regarded as heretics. There is, however, disagreement on certain Abuses, which have crept into the Church without rightful authority. And even in these, if there were some difference, there should be proper lenity on the part of bishops to bear with us by reason of the Confession which we have now reviewed; because even the Canons are not so severe as to demand the same rites everywhere, neither, at any time, have the rites of all churches been the same; although, among us, in large part, the ancient rites are diligently observed. For it is a false and malicious charge that all the ceremonies, all the things instituted of old, are abolished in our churches. But it has been a common complaint that some abuses were connected with the ordinary rites. These, inasmuch as they could not be approved with a good conscience, have been to some extent corrected.

[*ARTICLES IN WHICH ARE REVIEWED THE ABUSES WHICH HAVE BEEN CORRECTED*]

Inasmuch, then, as our churches dissent in no article of the faith from the Church Catholic, but only omit some abuses which are new, and which have been erroneously accepted by the corruption of the times, contrary to the intent of the Canons, we pray that Your Imperial Majesty would graciously hear both what has been changed, and what were the reasons why the people were not compelled to observe those abuses against their conscience. Nor should Your Imperial Majesty believe those who, in order to excite the hatred of men against our part, disseminate strange slanders among the people. Having thus excited the minds of good men, they have first given occasion to this controversy, and now endeavor, by the same arts, to increase the discord. For Your Imperial Majesty will undoubtedly find that the form of doctrine and of ceremonies with us is not so intolerable as these ungodly and malicious men represent. Besides, the truth cannot be gathered from common rumors or the revilings of enemies. But it can readily be judged that nothing would serve better to maintain the dignity of ceremonies, and to nourish reverence and pious devotion among the people than if the ceremonies were observed rightly in the churches.

ARTICLE XXII:
OF BOTH KINDS IN THE SACRAMENT

To the laity are given Both Kinds in the Sacrament of the Lord's Supper, because this usage has the commandment of the Lord in Matt. 26, 27: Drink ye all of it, where Christ has manifestly commanded concerning the cup that all should drink.

And lest any man should craftily say that this refers only to priests, Paul in 1 Cor. 11,27 recites an example from which it appears that the whole congregation did use both kinds. And this usage has long remained in the Church, nor is it known when, or by whose authority, it was changed; although Cardinal Cusanus mentions the time when it was approved. Cyprian in some places testifies that the blood was given to the people. The same

is testified by Jerome, who says: The priests administer the Eucharist, and distribute the blood of Christ to the people. Indeed, Pope Gelasius commands that the Sacrament be not divided (dist. II., De Consecratione, cap. Comperimus). Only custom, not so ancient, has it otherwise. But it is evident that any custom introduced against the commandments of God is not to be allowed, as the Canons witness (dist. III., cap. Veritate, and the following chapters). But this custom has been received, not only against the Scripture, but also against the old Canons and the example of the Church. Therefore, if any preferred to use both kinds of the Sacrament, they ought not to have been compelled with offense to their consciences to do otherwise. And because the division of the Sacrament does not agree with the ordinance of Christ, we are accustomed to omit the procession, which hitherto has been in use.

ARTICLE XXIII:
OF THE MARRIAGE OF PRIESTS

There has been common complaint concerning the examples of priests who were not chaste. For that reason also Pope Pius is reported to have said that there were certain causes why marriage was taken away from priests, but that there were far weightier ones why it ought to be given back; for so Platina writes. Since, therefore, our priests were desirous to avoid these open scandals, they married wives, and taught that it was lawful for them to contract matrimony. First, because Paul says, 1 Cor. 7, 2. 9: To avoid fornication, let every man have his own wife. Also: It is better to marry than to burn. Secondly Christ says, Matt. 19,11: All men cannot receive this saying, where He teaches that not all men are fit to lead a single life; for God created man for procreation, Gen. 1, 28. Nor is it in man's power, without a singular gift and work of God, to alter this creation. [For it is manifest, and many have confessed that no good, honest, chaste life, no Christian, sincere, upright conduct has resulted (from the attempt), but a horrible, fearful unrest and torment of conscience has been felt by many until the end.] Therefore, those who are not fit to lead a single life ought to contract matrimony. For no man's law, no vow, can annul the commandment and ordinance of God. For these reasons the priests teach that it is lawful for them to marry wives.

It is also evident that in the ancient Church priests were married men. For Paul says, 1 Tim. 3, 2, that a bishop should be chosen who is the husband of one wife. And in Germany, four hundred years ago for the first time, the priests were violently compelled to lead a single life, who indeed offered such resistance that the Archbishop of Mayence, when about to publish the Pope's decree concerning this matter, was almost killed in the tumult raised by the enraged priests. And so harsh was the dealing in the matter that not only were marriages forbidden for the future, but also existing marriages were torn asunder, contrary to all laws, divine and human, contrary even to the Canons themselves, made not only by the Popes, but by most celebrated Synods. [Moreover, many God-fearing and intelligent people in high station are known frequently to have expressed misgivings that such enforced celibacy and depriving men of marriage (which God Himself has instituted and left free to men) has never produced any good results, but has brought on many great and evil vices and much iniquity.]

Seeing also that, as the world is aging, man's nature is gradually growing weaker, it is well to guard that no more vices steal into Germany.

Furthermore, God ordained marriage to be a help against human infirmity. The Canons themselves say that the old rigor ought now and then, in the latter times, to be relaxed because of the weakness of men; which it is to be wished were done also in this matter. And it is to be expected that the churches shall at some time lack pastors if marriage is any longer forbidden.

But while the commandment of God is in force, while the custom of the Church is well known, while impure celibacy causes many

scandals, adulteries, and other crimes deserving the punishments of just magistrates, yet it is a marvelous thing that in nothing is more cruelty exercised than against the marriage of priests. God has given commandment to honor marriage. By the laws of all well-ordered commonwealths, even among the heathen, marriage is most highly honored. But now men, and that, priests, are cruelly put to death, contrary to the intent of the Canons, for no other cause than marriage. Paul, in 1 Tim. 4,3, calls that a doctrine of devils which forbids marriage. This may now be readily understood when the law against marriage is maintained by such penalties.

But as no law of man can annul the commandment of God, so neither can it be done by any vow. Accordingly, Cyprian also advises that women who do not keep the chastity they have promised should marry. His words are these (Book I, Epistle XI): But if they be unwilling or unable to persevere, it is better for them to marry than to fall into the fire by their lusts; they should certainly give no offense to their brethren and sisters.

And even the Canons show some leniency toward those who have taken vows before the proper age, as heretofore has generally been the ease.

Article XXIV: Of the Mass

Falsely are our churches accused of abolishing the Mass; for the Mass is retained among us, and celebrated with the highest reverence. Nearly all the usual ceremonies are also preserved, save that the parts sung in Latin are interspersed here and there with German hymns, which have been added to teach the people. For ceremonies are needed to this end alone that the unlearned be taught [what they need to know of Christ]. And not only has Paul commanded to use in the church a language understood by the people 1 Cor. 14,2. 9, but it has also been so ordained by man's law. The people are accustomed to partake of the Sacrament together, if any be fit for it, and this also increases the reverence and devotion of public worship. For none are admitted except they be first examined. The people are also advised concerning the dignity and use of the Sacrament, how great consolation it brings anxious consciences, that they may learn to believe God, and to expect and ask of Him all that is good. [In this connection they are also instructed regarding other and false teachings on the Sacrament.] This worship pleases God; such use of the Sacrament nourishes true devotion toward God. It does not, therefore, appear that the Mass is more devoutly celebrated among our adversaries than among us.

But it is evident that for a long time this also has been the public and most grievous complaint of all good men that Masses have been basely profaned and applied to purposes of lucre. For it is not unknown how far this abuse obtains in all the churches by what manner of men Masses are said only for fees or stipends, and how many celebrate them contrary to the Canons. But Paul severely threatens those who deal unworthily with the Eucharist when he says, 1 Cor. 11, 27: Whosoever shall eat this bread, and drink this cup of the Lord, unworthily, shall be guilty of the body and blood of the Lord. When, therefore our priests were admonished concerning this sin, Private Masses were discontinued among us, as scarcely any Private Masses were celebrated except for lucre's sake.

Neither were the bishops ignorant of these abuses, and if they had corrected them in time, there would now be less dissension. Heretofore, by their own connivance, they suffered many corruptions to creep into the Church. Now, when it is too late, they begin to complain of the troubles of the Church, while this disturbance has been occasioned simply by those abuses which were so manifest that they could be borne no longer. There have been great dissensions concerning the Mass, concerning the Sacrament. Perhaps the world is being punished for such long-continued profanations of the Mass as have been tolerated in the churches for so many centuries by the very men who were both able and in duty bound to correct them. For in the Ten Commandments it is written, Ex. 20, 7: The Lord will not hold him guiltless that taketh His name in vain. But since the world began, nothing that God ever ordained seems to have been so abused for filthy lucre as the Mass.

There was also added the opinion which infinitely increased Private Masses, namely that Christ, by His passion, had made satisfaction for original sin, and instituted the Mass wherein an offering should be made for daily sins, venial and mortal. From this has arisen the common opinion that the Mass takes away the sins of the living and the dead by the outward act. Then they began to dispute whether one Mass said for many were worth as much as special Masses for individuals, and this brought forth that infinite multitude of Masses. [With this work men wished to obtain from God all that they needed, and in the mean time faith in Christ and the true worship were forgotten.]

Concerning these opinions our teachers have given warning that they depart from the Holy Scriptures and diminish the glory of the passion of Christ. For Christ's passion was an oblation and satisfaction, not for original guilt only, but also for all other sins, as it is written to the Hebrews, 10, 10: We are sanctified through the offering of Jesus Christ once for all. Also, 10, 14: By one offering He hath perfected forever them that are sanctified. [It is an unheard-of innovation in the Church to teach that Christ by His death made satisfaction only for original sin and not likewise for all other sin. Accordingly it is hoped that everybody will understand that this error has not been reproved without due reason.]

Scripture also teaches that we are justified before God through faith in Christ, when we believe that our sins are forgiven for Christ's sake. Now if the Mass take away the sins of the living and the dead by the outward act, justification comes of the work of Masses, and not of faith, which Scripture does not allow. But Christ commands us, Luke 22, 19:

This do in remembrance of Me; therefore the Mass was instituted that the faith of those who use the Sacrament should remember what benefits it receives through Christ, and cheer and comfort the anxious conscience. For to remember Christ is to remember His benefits, and to realize that they are truly offered unto us. Nor is it enough only to remember the history; for this also the Jews and the ungodly can remember. Wherefore the Mass is to be used to this end, that there the Sacrament [Communion] may be administered to them that have need of consolation; as Ambrose says: Because I always sin, I am always bound to take the medicine. [Therefore this Sacrament requires faith, and is used in vain without faith.]

Now, forasmuch as the Mass is such a giving of the Sacrament, we hold one communion every holy-day, and, if any desire the Sacrament, also on other days, when it is given to such as ask for it. And this custom is not new in the Church; for the Fathers before Gregory make no mention of any private Mass, but of the common Mass [the Communion] they speak very much. Chrysostom says that the priest stands daily at the altar, inviting some to the Communion and keeping back others. And it appears from the ancient Canons that some one celebrated the Mass from whom all the other presbyters and deacons received the body of the Lord; for thus the words of the Nicene Canon say: Let the deacons, according to their order, receive the Holy Communion after the presbyters, from the bishop or from a presbyter. And Paul, 1 Cor. 11, 33, commands concerning the Communion: Tarry one for another, so that there may be a common participation.

Forasmuch, therefore, as the Mass with us has the example of the Church, taken from the Scripture and the Fathers, we are confident that it cannot be disapproved, especially since public ceremonies, for the most part like those hitherto in use, are retained; only the number of Masses differs, which, because of very great and manifest abuses doubtless might be profitably reduced. For in olden times, even in churches most frequented, the Mass was not celebrated every day, as the Tripartite History (Book 9, chap. 33) testifies: Again in Alexandria, every Wednesday and Friday the Scriptures are read, and the doctors expound them, and all things are done, except the solemn rite of Communion.

ARTICLE XXV: OF CONFESSION

Confession in the churches is not abolished among us; for it is not usual to give the body of the Lord, except to them that have been previously examined and absolved. And the people are most carefully taught concerning faith in the absolution, about which formerly there was profound silence. Our people are taught that they should highly prize the absolution, as being the voice of God, and pronounced by God's command. The power of the Keys is set forth in its beauty and they are reminded what great consolation it brings to anxious consciences, also, that God requires faith to believe such absolution as a voice sounding from heaven, and that such faith in Christ truly obtains and receives the forgiveness of sins. Aforetime satisfactions were immoderately extolled; of faith and the merit of Christ and the righteousness of faith no mention was made; wherefore, on this point, our churches are by no means to be blamed. For this even our adversaries must needs concede to us that the doctrine concerning repentance has been most diligently treated and laid open by our teachers.

But of Confession they teach that an enumeration of sins is not necessary, and that consciences be not burdened with anxiety to enumerate all sins, for it is impossible to recount all sins, as the Psalm testifies, 19,13: Who can understand his errors? Also Jeremiah, 17,9: The heart is deceitful; who can know it; But if no sins were forgiven, except those that are recounted, consciences could never find peace; for very many sins they neither see nor can remember. The ancient writers also testify that an enumeration is not necessary. For in the Decrees, Chrysostom is quoted, who says thus: I say not to you that you should disclose yourself in public, nor that you accuse yourself before others, but I would have you obey the prophet who says: "Disclose thy self before God." Therefore confess your sins before God, the true Judge, with prayer. Tell your errors, not with the tongue, but with the memory of your conscience, etc. And the Gloss (Of Repentance, Distinct. V, Cap. Consideret) admits that Confession is of human right only [not commanded by Scripture, but ordained by the Church]. Nevertheless, on account of the great benefit of absolution, and because it is otherwise useful to the conscience, Confession is retained among us.

ARTICLE XXVI:
OF THE DISTINCTION OF MEATS

It has been the general persuasion, not of the people alone, but also of those teaching in the churches, that making Distinctions of Meats, and like traditions of men, are works profitable to merit grace, and able to make satisfactions for sins. And that the world so thought, appears from this, that new ceremonies, new orders, new holy-days, and new fastings were daily instituted, and the teachers in the churches did exact these works as a service necessary to merit grace, and did greatly terrify men's consciences, if they should omit any of these things. From this persuasion concerning traditions much detriment has resulted in the Church.

First, the doctrine of grace and of the righteousness of faith has been obscured by it, which is the chief part of the Gospel, and ought to stand out as the most prominent in the Church, in order that the merit of Christ may be well known, and faith, which believes that sins are forgiven for Christ's sake be exalted far above works. Wherefore Paul also lays the greatest stress on this article, putting aside the Law and human traditions, in order to show that Christian righteousness is something else than such works, to wit, the faith which believes that sins are freely forgiven for Christ's sake. But this doctrine of Paul has been almost wholly smothered by traditions, which have produced an opinion that, by making distinctions in meats and like services, we must merit grace and righteousness. In treating of repentance, there was no mention made of faith; only those works of satisfaction were set forth; in these the entire repentance seemed to consist.

Secondly, these traditions have obscured the commandments of God, because traditions were placed far above the commandments of God. Christianity was thought to consist wholly in the observance of certain holy-days, rites, fasts, and vestures. These observances had won for themselves the exalted title of being the spiritual life and the perfect life. Meanwhile the commandments of God, according to each one's calling, were without honor namely, that the father brought up his offspring, that the mother bore children, that the prince governed the commonwealth,—these were accounted works that were worldly and imperfect, and far below those glittering observances. And this error greatly tormented devout consciences, which grieved that they were held in an imperfect state of life, as in marriage, in the office of magistrate; or in other civil ministrations; on the other hand, they admired the monks and such like, and falsely imagined that the observances of such men were more acceptable to God.

Thirdly, traditions brought great danger to consciences; for it was impossible to keep all traditions, and yet men judged these observances to be necessary acts of worship. Gerson writes that many fell into despair, and that some even took their own lives, because they felt that they were not able to satisfy the traditions, and they had all the while not heard any consolation of the righteousness of faith and grace. We see that the summists and theologians gather the traditions, and seek mitigations whereby to ease consciences, and yet they do not sufficiently unfetter, but sometimes entangle, consciences even more. And with the gathering of these traditions, the schools and sermons have been so much occupied that they have had no leisure to touch upon Scripture, and to seek the more profitable doctrine of faith, of the cross, of hope, of the dignity of civil affairs of consolation of sorely tried consciences. Hence Gerson and some other theologians have grievously complained that by these strivings concerning traditions they were prevented from giving attention to a better kind of doctrine. Augustine also forbids that men's consciences should be burdened with such observances, and prudently advises Januarius that he must know that they are to be observed as things indifferent; for such are his words.

Wherefore our teachers must not be looked upon as having taken up this matter rashly or from hatred of the bishops, as some falsely suspect. There was great need to warn the churches of these errors, which had arisen from misunderstanding the traditions. For the Gospel compels us to insist in the churches upon the doctrine of grace, and of the righteousness of faith; which, however, cannot be understood, if men think that they merit grace by observances of their own choice.

Thus, therefore, they have taught that by the observance of human traditions we cannot merit grace or be justified, and hence we must not think such observances necessary acts of worship. They add hereunto testimonies of Scripture. Christ, Matt. 15, 3, defends the Apostles who had not observed the usual tradition, which, however, evidently pertains to a matter not unlawful, but indifferent, and to have a certain affinity with the purifications of the Law, and says, 9: In vain do they worship Me with the commandments of men. He, therefore, does not exact an unprofitable service. Shortly after He adds: Not that which goeth into the mouth defileth a man. So also Paul, Rom. 14, 17: The kingdom of God is not meat and drink. Col. 2, 16: Let no man, therefore, judge you in meat, or in drink, or in respect of an holy-day, or of the Sabbath-day; also: If ye be dead with Christ from the rudiments of the world, why, as though living in the world, are ye subject to ordinances: Touch not, taste not, handle not! And Peter

says, Acts 15, 10: Why tempt ye God to put a yoke upon the neck of the disciples, which neither our fathers nor we were able to bear? But we believe that through the grace of the Lord Jesus Christ we shall be saved, even as they. Here Peter forbids to burden the consciences with many rites, either of Moses or of others. And in 1 Tim. 4,1.3 Paul calls the prohibition of meats a doctrine of devils; for it is against the Gospel to institute or to do such works that by them we may merit grace, or as though Christianity could not exist without such service of God.

Here our adversaries object that our teachers are opposed to discipline and mortification of the flesh, as Jovinian. But the contrary may be learned from the writings of our teachers. For they have always taught concerning the cross that it behooves Christians to bear afflictions. This is the true, earnest, and unfeigned mortification, to wit, to be exercised with divers afflictions, and to be crucified with Christ.

Moreover, they teach that every Christian ought to train and subdue himself with bodily restraints, or bodily exercises and labors that neither satiety nor slothfulness tempt him to sin, but not that we may merit grace or make satisfaction for sins by such exercises. And such external discipline ought to be urged at all times, not only on a few and set days. So Christ commands, Luke 21, 34: Take heed lest your hearts be overcharged with surfeiting; also Matt. 17, 21: This kind goeth not out but by prayer and fasting. Paul also says, 1 Cor. 9, 27: I keep under my body and bring it into subjection. Here he clearly shows that he was keeping under his body, not to merit forgiveness of sins by that discipline, but to have his body in subjection and fitted for spiritual things, and for the discharge of duty according to his calling. Therefore, we do not condemn fasting in itself, but the traditions which prescribe certain days and certain meats, with peril of conscience, as though such works were a necessary service.

Nevertheless, very many traditions are kept on our part, which conduce to good order in the Church, as the Order of Lessons in the

Mass and the chief holy-days. But, at the same time, men are warned that such observances do not justify before God, and that in such things it should not be made sin if they be omitted without offense. Such liberty in human rites was not unknown to the Fathers. For in the East they kept Easter at another time than at Rome, and when, on account of this diversity, the Romans accused the Eastern Church of schism, they were admonished by others that such usages need not be alike everywhere. And Irenaeus says: Diversity concerning fasting does not destroy the harmony of faith; as also Pope Gregory intimates in Dist. XII, that such diversity does not violate the unity of the Church. And in the Tripartite History, Book 9, many examples of dissimilar rites are gathered, and the following statement is made: It was not the mind of the Apostles to enact rules concerning holy-days, but to preach godliness and a holy life [, to teach faith and love].

ARTICLE XXVII:
OF MONASTIC VOWS

What is taught on our part concerning Monastic Vows, will be better understood if it be remembered what has been the state of the monasteries, and how many things were daily done in those very monasteries, contrary to the Canons. In Augustine's time they were free associations. Afterward, when discipline was corrupted, vows were everywhere added for the purpose of restoring discipline, as in a carefully planned prison.

Gradually, many other observances were added besides vows. And these fetters were laid upon many before the lawful age, contrary to the Canons.

Many also entered into this kind of life through ignorance, being unable to judge their own strength, though they were of sufficient age. Being thus ensnared, they were compelled to remain, even though some could have been freed by the kind provision of the Canons. And this was more the case in convents of women than of monks, although more consideration should have been shown the weaker sex. This rigor displeased many good men before this time, who saw that young men and maidens were thrown into convents for a living. They saw what unfortunate results came of this procedure, and what scandals were created, what snares were cast upon consciences! They were grieved that the authority of the Canons in so momentous a matter was utterly set aside and despised. To these evils was added such a persuasion concerning vows as, it is well known, in former times displeased even those monks who were more considerate. They taught that vows were equal to Baptism; they taught that by this kind of life they merited forgiveness of sins and justification before God. Yea, they added that the monastic life not only merited righteousness before God but even greater things, because it kept not only the precepts, but also the so-called "evangelical counsels."

Thus they made men believe that the profession of monasticism was far better than Baptism, and that the monastic life was more meritorious than that of magistrates, than the life of pastors, and such like, who serve their calling in accordance with God's commands, without any man-made services. None of these things can be denied; for they appear in their own books. [Moreover, a person who has been thus ensnared and has entered a monastery learns little of Christ.]

What, then, came to pass in the monasteries? Aforetime they were schools of theology and other branches, profitable to the Church; and thence pastors and bishops were obtained. Now it is another thing. It is needless to rehearse what is known to all. Aforetime they came together to learn; now they feign that it is a kind of life instituted to merit grace and righteousness; yea, they preach that it is a state of perfection, and they put it far above all other kinds of life ordained of God. These things we have rehearsed without odious exaggeration, to the end that the doctrine of our teachers on this point might be better understood.

First, concerning such as contract matrimony, they teach on our part that it is lawful for all men who are not fitted for single life to contract matrimony, because vows cannot annul the ordinance and commandment of God. But the commandment of God is 1 Cor. 7, 2: To avoid fornication, let every man have his own wife. Nor is it the commandment only, but also the creation and ordinance of God, which forces those to marry who are not excepted by a singular work of God, according to the text Gen. 2, 18: It is not good that the man should be alone. Therefore they do not sin who obey this commandment and ordinance of God.

What objection can be raised to this? Let men extol the obligation of a vow as much as they list, yet shall they not bring to pass that the vow annuls the commandment of God. The Canons teach that the right of the superior is excepted in every vow; [that vows are not binding against the decision of the Pope;] much less, therefore, are these vows of force which are against the commandments of God.

Now, if the obligation of vows could not be changed for any cause whatever, the Roman Pontiffs could never have given dispensation for it is not lawful for man to annul an obligation which is simply divine. But the Roman Pontiffs have prudently judged that leniency is to be observed in this obligation, and therefore we read that many times they have dispensed from vows. The case of the King of Aragon who was called back from the monastery is well known, and there are also examples in our own times. [Now, if dispensations have been granted for the sake of securing temporal interests, it is much more proper that they be granted on account of the distress of souls.]

In the second place, why do our adversaries exaggerate the obligation or effect of a vow when, at the same time, they have not a word to say of the nature of the vow itself, that it ought to be in a thing possible, that it ought to be free, and chosen spontaneously and deliberately? But it is not unknown to what extent perpetual chastity is in the power of man. And how few are there who have taken the vow spontaneously and deliberately! Young maidens and men, before they are

able to judge, are persuaded, and sometimes even compelled, to take the vow. Wherefore it is not fair to insist so rigorously on the obligation, since it is granted by all that it is against the nature of a vow to take it without spontaneous and deliberate action.

Most canonical laws rescind vows made before the age of fifteen; for before that age there does not seem sufficient judgment in a person to decide concerning a perpetual life. Another Canon, granting more to the weakness of man, adds a few years; for it forbids a vow to be made before the age of eighteen. But which of these two Canons shall we follow? The most part have an excuse for leaving the monasteries, because most of them have taken the vows before they reached these ages.

Finally, even though the violation of a vow might be censured, yet it seems not forthwith to follow that the marriages of such persons must be dissolved. For Augustine denies that they ought to be dissolved (XXVII. Quaest. I, Cap. Nuptiarum), and his authority is not lightly to be esteemed, although other men afterwards thought otherwise.

But although it appears that God's command concerning marriage delivers very many from their vows, yet our teachers introduce also another argument concerning vows to show that they are void. For every service of God, ordained and chosen of men without the commandment of God to merit justification and grace, is wicked, as Christ says Matt. 16, 9: In vain do they worship Me with the commandments of men. And Paul teaches everywhere that righteousness is not to be sought from our own observances and acts of worship, devised by men, but that it comes by faith to those who believe that they are received by God into grace for Christ's sake.

But it is evident that monks have taught that services of man's making satisfy for sins and merit grace and justification. What else is this than to detract from the glory of Christ and to obscure and deny the righteousness of faith? It follows, therefore, that the vows thus commonly taken have been wicked services, and, consequently, are void. For a wicked vow, taken against the commandment of God, is not valid; for (as the Canon says) no vow ought to bind men to wickedness.

Paul says, Gal. 5,4: Christ is become of no effect unto you, whosoever of you are justified by the Law, ye are fallen from grace. To those, therefore, who want to be justified by their vows Christ is made of no effect, and they fall from grace. For also these who ascribe justification to vows ascribe to their own works that which properly belongs to the glory of Christ.

Nor can it be denied, indeed, that the monks have taught that, by their vows and observances, they were justified, and merited forgiveness of sins, yea, they invented still greater absurdities, saying that they could give others a share in their works. If any one should be inclined to enlarge on these things with evil intent, how many things could he bring together whereof even the monks are now ashamed! Over and above this, they persuaded men that services of man's making were a state of Christian perfection. And is not this assigning justification to works? It is no light offense in the Church to set forth to the people a service devised by men, without the commandment of God, and to teach that such service justifies men. For the righteousness of faith, which chiefly ought to be taught in the Church, is obscured when these wonderful angelic forms of worship, with their show of poverty, humility, and celibacy, are east before the eyes of men.

Furthermore, the precepts of God and the true service of God are obscured when men hear that only monks are in a state of perfection. For Christian perfection is to fear God from the heart, and yet to conceive great faith, and to trust that for Christ's sake we have a God who has been reconciled, to ask of God, and assuredly to expect His aid in all things that, according to our calling, are to be done; and meanwhile, to be diligent in outward good works, and to serve our calling. In these things consist the true perfection and the true service of God. It does not consist in celibacy, or in begging, or in vile apparel.

But the people conceive many pernicious opinions from the false commendations of monastic life. They hear celibacy praised above measure; therefore they lead their married life with offense to their consciences. They hear that only beggars are perfect; therefore they keep their possessions and do business with offense to their consciences. They hear that it is an evangelical counsel not to seek revenge; therefore some in private life are not afraid to take revenge, for they hear that it is but a counsel, and not a commandment. Others judge that the Christian cannot properly hold a civil office or be a magistrate.

There are on record examples of men who, forsaking marriage and the administration of the Commonwealth, have hid themselves in monasteries. This they called fleeing from the world, and seeking a kind of life which would be more pleasing to God. Neither did they see that God ought to be served in those commandments which He Himself has given and not in commandments devised by men. A good and perfect kind of life is that which has for it the commandment of God. It is necessary to admonish men of these things.

And before these times, Gerson rebukes this error of the monks concerning perfection, and testifies that in his day it was a new saying that the monastic life is a state of perfection.

So many wicked opinions are inherent in the vows, namely, that they justify, that they constitute Christian perfection, that they keep the counsels and commandments, that they have works of supererogation. All these things, since they are false and empty, make vows null and void.

Article XXVIII:
Of Ecclesiastical Power

There has been great controversy concerning the Power of Bishops, in which some have awkwardly confounded the power of the Church and the power of the sword. And from this confusion very great wars and tumults have resulted, while the Pontiffs, emboldened by the power of the Keys, not only have instituted new services and burdened consciences with reservation of cases and ruthless excommunications, but have also undertaken to transfer the kingdoms of this world, and to take the Empire from the Emperor. These wrongs have long since been rebuked in the Church by learned and godly men. Therefore our teachers, for the comforting of men's consciences, were constrained to show the difference between the power of the Church and the power of the sword, and taught that both of them, because of God's commandment, are to be held in reverence and honor, as the chief blessings of God on earth.

But this is their opinion, that the power of the Keys, or the power of the bishops, according to the Gospel, is a power or commandment of God, to preach the Gospel, to remit and retain sins, and to administer Sacraments. For with this commandment Christ sends forth His Apostles, John 20, 21 sqq.: As My Father hath sent Me, even so send I you. Receive ye the Holy Ghost. Whosoever sins ye remit, they are remitted unto them; and whosoever sins ye retain, they are retained. Mark 16, 15: Go preach the Gospel to every creature.

This power is exercised only by teaching or preaching the Gospel and administering the Sacraments, according to their calling either to many or to individuals. For thereby are granted, not bodily, but eternal things, as eternal righteousness, the Holy Ghost, eternal life. These things cannot come but by the ministry of the Word and the Sacraments, as Paul says, Rom. 1, 16: The Gospel is the power of God unto salvation to every one that believeth. Therefore, since the power of the Church grants eternal things, and is exercised only by the ministry of the Word, it does not interfere with civil government; no more than the art of singing interferes with civil government. For civil government deals with other things than does the Gospel. The civil rulers defend not minds, but bodies and bodily things against manifest injuries, and restrain men with the sword and bodily punishments in order to preserve civil justice and peace.

Therefore the power of the Church and the civil power must not be confounded. The power of the Church has its own commission to teach the Gospel and to administer the Sacraments. Let it not break into the office of another; Let it not transfer the kingdoms of this world; let it not abrogate the laws of civil rulers; let it not abolish lawful obedience; let it not interfere with judgments concerning civil ordinances or contracts; let it not prescribe laws to civil rulers concerning the form of the Commonwealth. As Christ says, John 18, 33: My kingdom is not of this world; also Luke 12, 14: Who made Me a judge or a divider over you? Paul also says, Phil. 3, 20: Our citizenship is in heaven; 2 Cor. 10, 4: The weapons of our warfare are not carnal, but mighty through God to the casting down of imaginations.

After this manner our teachers discriminate between the duties of both these powers, and command that both be honored and acknowledged as gifts and blessings of God.

If bishops have any power of the sword, that power they have, not as bishops, by the commission of the Gospel, but by human law having received it of kings and emperors for the civil administration of what is theirs. This, however, is another office than the ministry of the Gospel.

When, therefore, the question is concerning the jurisdiction of bishops, civil authority must be distinguished from ecclesiastical jurisdiction. Again, according to the Gospel or, as they say, by divine right, there belongs to the bishops as bishops, that is, to those to whom has been committed the ministry of the Word and the Sacraments, no jurisdiction except to forgive sins, to judge doctrine, to reject doctrines contrary to the Gospel, and to exclude from the communion of the Church wicked men, whose wickedness is known, and this without human force, simply by the Word. Herein the congregations of necessity and by divine right must obey them, according to Luke 10, 16: He that heareth you heareth Me. But when they teach or ordain anything against the Gospel, then the congregations have a commandment of God prohibiting obedience, Matt. 7, 15: Beware of false prophets; Gal. 1, 8: Though an angel from heaven preach any other gospel, let him be accursed; 2 Cor. 13, 8: We can do nothing against the truth, but for the truth. Also: The power which the Lord hath given me to edification, and not to destruction. So, also, the Canonical Laws command (II. Q. VII. Cap., Sacerdotes, and Cap. Oves). And Augustine (Contra Petiliani Epistolam): Neither must we submit to Catholic bishops if they chance to err, or hold anything contrary to the Canonical Scriptures of God.

If they have any other power or jurisdiction, in hearing and judging certain cases, as of matrimony or of tithes, etc., they have it by human right, in which matters princes are bound, even against their will, when the ordinaries fail, to dispense justice to their subjects for the maintenance of peace.

Moreover, it is disputed whether bishops or pastors have the right to introduce ceremonies in the Church, and to make laws concerning meats, holy-days and grades, that is, orders of ministers, etc. They that give this right to the bishops refer to this testimony John 16, 12. 13: I have yet many things to say unto you, but ye cannot bear them now. Howbeit when He, the Spirit of Truth, is come, He will guide you into all truth. They also refer to the example of the Apostles, who commanded to abstain from blood and from things strangled, Acts 15, 29. They refer to the Sabbath-day as having been changed into the Lord's Day, contrary to the Decalog, as it seems. Neither is there any example whereof they make more than concerning the changing of the Sabbath-day. Great, say they, is the power of the Church, since it has dispensed with one of the Ten Commandments!

But concerning this question it is taught on our part (as has been shown above) that bishops have no power to decree anything against the Gospel. The Canonical Laws teach the same thing (Dist. IX) . Now, it is against Scripture to establish or require the observance of any traditions, to the end that by such observance we may make satisfaction

for sins, or merit grace and righteousness. For the glory of Christ's merit suffers injury when, by such observances, we undertake to merit justification. But it is manifest that, by such belief, traditions have almost infinitely multiplied in the Church, the doctrine concerning faith and the righteousness of faith being meanwhile suppressed. For gradually more holy-days were made, fasts appointed, new ceremonies and services in honor of saints instituted, because the authors of such things thought that by these works they were meriting grace. Thus in times past the Penitential Canons increased, whereof we still see some traces in the satisfactions.

Again, the authors of traditions do contrary to the command of God when they find matters of sin in foods, in days, and like things, and burden the Church with bondage of the law, as if there ought to be among Christians, in order to merit justification a service like the Levitical, the arrangement of which God had committed to the Apostles and bishops. For thus some of them write; and the Pontiffs in some measure seem to be misled by the example of the law of Moses. Hence are such burdens, as that they make it mortal sin, even without offense to others, to do manual labor on holy-days, a mortal sin to omit the Canonical Hours, that certain foods defile the conscience that fastings are works which appease God that sin in a reserved case cannot be forgiven but by the authority of him who reserved it; whereas the Canons themselves speak only of the reserving of the ecclesiastical penalty, and not of the reserving of the guilt.

Whence have the bishops the right to lay these traditions upon the Church for the ensnaring of consciences, when Peter, Acts 15, 10, forbids to put a yoke upon the neck of the disciples, and Paul says, 2 Cor. 13, 10, that the power given him was to edification not to destruction? Why, therefore, do they increase sins by these traditions?

But there are clear testimonies which prohibit the making of such traditions, as though they merited grace or were necessary to salvation. Paul says, Col. 2, 16-23: Let no man judge you in meat, or in drink, or in respect of an holy-day, or of the new moon, or of the Sabbath-days. If ye be dead with Christ from the rudiments of the world, why, as though living in the world, are ye subject to ordinances (touch not; taste not; handle not, which all are to perish with the using) after the commandments and doctrines of men! which things have indeed a show of wisdom. Also in Titus 1, 14 he openly forbids traditions: Not giving heed to Jewish fables and commandments of men that turn from the truth.

And Christ, Matt. 15, 14. 13, says of those who require traditions: Let them alone; they be blind leaders of the blind; and He rejects such services: Every plant which My heavenly Father hath not planted shall be plucked up.

If bishops have the right to burden churches with infinite traditions, and to ensnare consciences, why does Scripture so often prohibit to make, and to listen to, traditions? Why does it call them "doctrines of devils"? 1 Tim. 4, 1. Did the Holy Ghost in vain forewarn of these things?

Since, therefore, ordinances instituted as things necessary, or with an opinion of meriting grace, are contrary to the Gospel, it follows that it is not lawful for any bishop to institute or exact such services. For it is necessary that the doctrine of Christian liberty be preserved in the churches, namely, that the bondage of the Law is not necessary to justification, as it is written in the Epistle to the Galatians, 5, 1: Be not entangled again with the yoke of bondage. It is necessary that the chief article of the Gospel be preserved, to wit, that we obtain grace freely by faith in Christ, and not for certain observances or acts of worship devised by men.

What, then, are we to think of the Sunday and like rites in the house of God? To this we answer that it is lawful for bishops or pastors to make ordinances that things be done orderly in the Church, not that thereby we should merit grace or make satisfaction for sins, or that consciences be bound to judge

them necessary services, and to think that it is a sin to break them without offense to others. So Paul ordains, 1 Cor. 11, 5, that women should cover their heads in the congregation, 1 Cor. 14, 30, that interpreters be heard in order in the church, etc.

It is proper that the churches should keep such ordinances for the sake of love and tranquillity, so far that one do not offend another, that all things be done in the churches in order, and without confusion, 1 Cor. 14, 40; comp. Phil. 2, 14; but so that consciences be not burdened to think that they are necessary to salvation, or to judge that they sin when they break them without offense to others; as no one will say that a woman sins who goes out in public with her head uncovered provided only that no offense be given.

Of this kind is the observance of the Lord's Day, Easter, Pentecost, and like holy-days and rites. For those who judge that by the authority of the Church the observance of the Lord's Day instead of the Sabbath-day was ordained as a thing necessary, do greatly err. Scripture has abrogated the Sabbath-day; for it teaches that, since the Gospel has been revealed, all the ceremonies of Moses can be omitted. And yet, because it was necessary to appoint a certain day, that the people might know when they ought to come together, it appears that the Church designated the Lord's Day for this purpose; and this day seems to have been chosen all the more for this additional reason, that men might have an example of Christian liberty, and might know that the keeping neither of the Sabbath nor of any other day is necessary.

There are monstrous disputations concerning the changing of the law, the ceremonies of the new law, the changing of the Sabbath-day, which all have sprung from the false belief that there must needs be in the Church a service like to the Levitical, and that Christ had given commission to the Apostles and bishops to devise new ceremonies as necessary to salvation. These errors crept into the Church when the righteousness of faith was not taught clearly enough. Some dispute that the keeping of the Lord's Day is not indeed of divine right, but in a manner so. They prescribe concerning holy-days, how far it is lawful to work. What else are such disputations than snares of consciences? For although they endeavor to modify the traditions, yet the mitigation can never be perceived as long as the opinion remains that they are necessary, which must needs remain where the righteousness of faith and Christian liberty are not known.

The Apostles commanded Acts 15, 20 to abstain from blood. Who does now observe it? And yet they that do it not sin not; for not even the Apostles themselves wanted to burden consciences with such bondage; but they forbade it for a time, to avoid offense. For in this decree we must perpetually consider what the aim of the Gospel is.

Scarcely any Canons are kept with exactness, and from day to day many go out of use even among those who are the most zealous advocates of traditions. Neither can due regard be paid to consciences unless this mitigation be observed, that we know that the Canons are kept without holding them to be necessary, and that no harm is done consciences, even though traditions go out of use.

But the bishops might easily retain the lawful obedience of the people if they would not insist upon the observance of such traditions as cannot be kept with a good conscience. Now they command celibacy; they admit none unless they swear that they will not teach the pure doctrine of the Gospel. The churches do not ask that the bishops should restore concord at the expense of their honor; which, nevertheless, it would be proper for good pastors to do. They ask only that they would release unjust burdens which are new and have been received contrary to the custom of the Church Catholic. It may be that in the beginning there were plausible reasons for some of these ordinances; and yet they are not adapted to later times. It is also evident that some were adopted through erroneous conceptions. Therefore it would be befitting the clemency of the Pontiffs to mitigate them now, because such a modification does not shake the unity of the Church. For many human traditions have been changed in process of time, as the Canons themselves show. But if it be impossible to obtain a mitigation of such observances as cannot be kept without sin, we are bound to follow the apostolic rule, Acts 5, 29, which commands us to obey God rather than men.

Peter, 1 Pet. 5, 3, forbids bishops to be lords, and to rule over the churches. It is not our design now to wrest the government from the bishops, but this one thing is asked, namely, that they allow the Gospel to be purely taught, and that they relax some few observances which cannot be kept without sin. But if they make no concession, it is for them to see how they shall give account to God for furnishing, by their obstinacy, a cause for schism.

Conclusion

These are the chief articles which seem to be in controversy. For although we might have spoken of more abuses, yet, to avoid undue length, we have set forth the chief points, from which the rest may be readily judged. There have been great complaints concerning indulgences, pilgrimages, and the abuse of excommunications. The parishes have been vexed in many ways by the dealers in indulgences. There were endless contentions between the pastors and the monks concerning the parochial right, confessions, burials, sermons on extraordinary occasions, and innumerable other things. Issues of this sort we have passed over so that the chief points in this matter, having been briefly set forth, might be the more readily understood. Nor has anything been here said or adduced to the reproach of any one. Only those things have been recounted whereof we thought that it was necessary to speak, in order that it might be understood that in doctrine and ceremonies nothing has been received on our part against Scripture or the Church Catholic. For it is manifest that we have taken most diligent care that no new and ungodly doctrine should creep into our churches.

The above articles we desire to present in accordance with the edict of Your Imperial Majesty, in order to exhibit our Confession and let men see a summary of the doctrine of our teachers. If there is anything that any one might desire in this Confession, we are ready, God willing, to present ampler information according to the Scriptures.

Your Imperial Majesty's faithful subjects:

John, Duke of Saxony, Elector.
George, Margrave of Brandenburg.
Ernest, Duke of Lueneberg.
Philip, Landgrave of Hesse.
John Frederick, Duke of Saxony.
Francis, Duke of Lueneburg.
Wolfgang, Prince of Anhalt.
Senate and Magistracy of Nuremburg.
Senate of Reutlingen.

THE SMALL CATECHISM

by Martin Luther

I. THE TEN COMMANDMENTS:
THE SIMPLE WAY A FATHER SHOULD PRESENT THEM TO HIS HOUSEHOLD

A. THE FIRST COMMANDMENT
YOU MUST NOT HAVE OTHER GODS.

Q. What does this mean?

A. We must fear, love, and trust God more than anything else.

B. THE SECOND COMMANDMENT
YOU MUST NOT MISUSE YOUR GOD'S NAME.

Q. What does this mean?

A. We must fear and love God, so that we will not use His name to curse, swear, cast a spell, lie or deceive, but will use it to call upon Him, pray to Him, praise Him and thank Him in all times of trouble.

C. THE THIRD COMMANDMENT
YOU MUST KEEP THE SABBATH HOLY.

Q. What does this mean?

A. We must fear and love God, so that we will not look down on preaching or God's Word, but consider it holy, listen to it willingly, and learn it.

D. THE FOURTH COMMANDMENT
YOU MUST HONOR YOUR FATHER AND MOTHER. [SO THAT THINGS WILL GO WELL FOR YOU AND YOU WILL LIVE LONG ON EARTH].

Q. What does this mean?

A. We must fear and love God, so that we will neither look down on our parents or superiors nor irritate them, but will honor them, serve them, obey them, love them and value them.

E. THE FIFTH COMMANDMENT
YOU MUST NOT KILL.

Q. What does this mean?

A. We must fear and love God, so that we will neither harm nor hurt our neighbor's body, but help him and care for him when he is ill.

F. THE SIXTH COMMANDMENT
YOU MUST NOT COMMIT ADULTERY.

Q. What does this mean?

A. We must fear and love God, so that our words and actions will be clean and decent and so that everyone will love and honor their spouses.

G. The Seventh Commandment
You must not steal.

Q. What does this mean?

A. We must fear and love God, so that we will neither take our neighbor's money or property, nor acquire it by fraud or by selling him poorly made products, but will help him improve and protect his property and career.

H. The Eighth Commandment
You must not tell lies about your neighbor.

Q. What does this mean?

A. We must fear and love God, so that we will not deceive by lying, betraying, slandering or ruining our neighbor's reputation, but will defend him, say good things about him, and see the best side of everything he does.

I. The Ninth Commandment
You must not desire your neighbor's house.

Q. What does this mean?

A. We must fear and love God, so that we will not attempt to trick our neighbor out of his inheritance or house, take it by pretending to have a right to it, etc. but help him to keep & improve it.

J. The Tenth Commandment
You must not desire your neighbor's wife, servant, maid, animals or anything that belongs to him.

Q. What does this mean?

A. We must fear and love God, so that we will not release his cattle, take his employees from him or seduce his wife, but urge them to stay and do what they ought to do.

K. The Conclusion to the Commandments

Q. What does God say to us about all these commandments?

A. This is what He says: "I am the Lord Your God. I am a jealous God. I plague the grandchildren and great-grandchildren of those who hate me with their ancestor's sin. But I make whole those who love me for a thousand generations."

Q. What does it mean?

A. God threatens to punish everyone who breaks these commandments. We should be afraid of His anger because of this and not violate such commandments. But He promises grace and all good things to those who keep such commandments. Because of this, we, too, should love Him, trust Him, and willingly do what His commandments require.

II. The Creed:
The Simple Way a Father Should Present it to His Household

A. The First Article: On Creation
I believe in God the Almighty Father, Creator of Heaven and Earth.

Q. What does this mean?

A. I believe that God created me, along with all creatures. He gave to me: body and soul, eyes, ears and all the other parts of my body, my mind and all my senses and preserves them as well. He gives me clothing and shoes, food and drink, house and land, wife and children, fields, animals and all I own. Every day He abundantly provides everything I need to nourish this body and life. He protects me against all danger, shields and defends me from all evil. He does all this because of His pure, fatherly and divine goodness and His mercy, not because I've earned it or desrved it. For all of this, I must thank Him, praise Him, serve Him and obey Him. Yes, this is true!

B. The Second Article: On Redemption
And in Jesus Christ, His only Son, our Lord, Who was conceived by the Holy Spirit, born of the Virgin Mary, suffered under Pontius Pilate, was crucified, died and was buried, descended to Hell, on the third day rose again from the dead, ascended to Heaven and sat down at the right hand of God the Almighty Father. From there He will come to judge the living and the dead.

Q. What does this mean?

A. I believe that Jesus Christ is truly God, born of the Father in eternity and also truly man, born of the Virgin Mary. He is my Lord! He redeemed me, a lost and condemned person, bought and won me from all sins, death and the authority of the Devil. It did not cost Him gold or silver, but His holy, precious blood, His innocent body—His death! Because of this, I am His very own, will live under Him in His kingdom and serve Him righteously, innocently and blessedly forever, just as He is risen from death, lives and reigns forever. Yes, this is true.

C. The Third Article: On Becoming Holy
I believe in the Holy Spirit, the holy Christian Church, the community of the saints, the forgiveness of sins, the resurrection of the body, and an everlasting life. Amen.

Q. What does this mean?

A. I believe that I cannot come to my Lord Jesus Christ by my own intelligence or power. But the Holy Spirit call me by the Gospel, enlightened me with His gifts, made me holy and kept me in the true faith, just as He calls, gathers together, enlightens and makes holy the whole Church on earth and keeps it with Jesus in the one, true faith. In this Church, He generously forgives each day every sin committed by me and by every believer. On the last day, He will raise me and all the dead from the grave. He will give eternal life to me and to all who believe in Christ. Yes, this is true!

III. THE OUR FATHER
THE SIMPLE WAY A FATHER SHOULD PRESENT IT TO HIS HOUSEHOLD

A. INTRODUCTION
OUR FATHER, WHO IS IN HEAVEN.

Q. What does this mean?

A. In this introduction, God invites us to believe that He is our real Father and we are His real children, so that we will pray with trust and complete confidence, in the same way beloved children approach their beloved Father with their requests.

B. THE FIRST REQUEST
MAY YOUR NAME BE HOLY.

Q. What does this mean?

A. Of course, God's name is holy in and of itself, but by this request, we pray that He will make it holy among us, too.

Q. How does this take place?

A. When God's Word is taught clearly and purely, and when we live holy lives as God's children based upon it. Help us, Heavenly Father, to do this! But anyone who teaches and lives by something other than God's Word defiles God's name among us. Protect us from this, Heavenly Father!

C. THE SECOND REQUEST
YOUR KINGDOM COME.

Q. What does this mean?

A. Truly God's Kingdom comes by itself, without our prayer. But we pray in this request that it come to us as well.

Q. How does this happen?

A. When the Heavenly Father gives us His Holy Spirit, so that we believe His holy Word by His grace and live godly lives here in this age and there in eternal life.

D. THE THIRD REQUEST
MAY YOUR WILL BE ACCOMPLISHED, AS IT IS HEAVEN, SO MAY IT BE ON EARTH.

Q. What does this mean?

A. Truly, God's good and gracious will is accomplished without our prayer. But we pray in this request that is be accomplished among us as well.

Q. How does this happen?

A. When God destroys and interferes with every evil will and all evil advice, which will not allow God's Kingdom to come, such as the Devil's will, the world's will and will of our bodily desires. It also happens when God strengthens us by faith and by His Word and keeps living by them faithfully until the end of our lives. This is His will, good and full of grace.

E. The Fourth Request

GIVE US OUR DAILY BREAD TODAY.

Q. What does this mean?

A. Truly, God gives daily bread to evil people, even without our prayer. But we pray in this request that He will help us realize this and receive our daily bread with thanksgiving.

Q. What does "Daily Bread" mean?

A. Everything that nourishes our body and meets its needs, such as: Food, drink, clothing, shoes, house, yard, fields, cattle, money, possessions, a devout spouse, devout children, devout employees, devout and faithful rulers, good government, good weather, peace, health, discipline, honor, good friends, faithful neighbors and other things like these.

F. The Fifth Request

AND FORGIVE OUR GUILT, AS WE FORGIVE THOSE GUILTY OF SINNING AGAINST US.

Q. What does this mean?

A. We pray in this request that our Heavenly Father will neither pay attention to our sins nor refuse requests such as these because of our sins and because we are neither worthy nor deserve the things for which we pray. Yet He wants to give them all to us by His grace, because many times each day we sin and truly deserve only punishment. Because God does this, we will, of course, want to forgive from our hearts and willingly do good to those who sin against us.

G. The Sixth Request

AND LEAD US NOT INTO TEMPTATION.

Q. What does this mean?

A. God tempts no one, of course, but we pray in this request that God will protect us and save us, so that the Devil, the world and our bodily desires will neither deceive us nor seduce us into heresy, despair or other serious shame or vice, and so that we will win and be victorious in the end, even if they attack us.

H. The Seventh Request

BUT SET US FREE FROM THE EVIL ONE.

Q. What does this mean?

A. We pray in this request, as a summary, that our Father in Heaven will save us from every kind of evil that threatens body, soul, property and honor. We pray that when at last our final hour has come, He will grant us a blessed death, and, in His grace, bring us to Himself from this valley of tears.

I. Amen.

Q. What does this mean?

A. That I should be certain that such prayers are acceptable to the Father in Heaven and will be granted, that He Himself has commanded us to pray in this way and that He promises to answer us. Amen. Amen. This means: Yes, yes it will happen this way.

IV: THE SACRAMENT OF HOLY BAPTISM:
THE SIMPLE WAY A FATHER SHOULD PRESENT IT TO HIS HOUSEHOLD

Q. What is Baptism?

A. Baptism is not just plain water, but it is water contained within God's command and united with God's Word.

Q. Which Word of God is this?

A. The one which our Lord Christ spoke in the last chapter of Matthew:

> "Go into all the world, teaching all heathen nations, and baptizing them in the name of the Father, the Son and of the Holy Spirit."

Q. What does Baptism give? What good is it?

A. It gives the forgiveness of sins, redeems from death and the Devil, gives eternal salvation to all who believe this, just as God's words and promises declare.

Q. What are these words and promises of God?

A. Our Lord Christ spoke one of them in the last chapter of Mark:

> "Whoever believes and is baptized will be saved; but whoever does not believe will be damned."

Q. How can water do such great things?

A. Water doesn't make these things happen, of course. It is God's Word, which is with and in the water. Because, without God's Word, the water is plain water and not baptism. But with God's Word it is a Baptism, a grace-filled water of life, a bath of new birth in the Holy Spirit, as St. Paul said to Titus in the third chapter:

> "Through this bath of rebirth and renewal of the Holy Spirit, which He poured out on us abundantly through Jesus Christ, our Savior, that we, justified by the same grace are made heirs according to the hope of eternal life. This is a faithful saying."

Q. What is the meaning of such a water Baptism?

A. It means that the old Adam in us should be drowned by daily sorrow and repentance, and die with all sins and evil lusts, and, in turn, a new person daily come forth and rise from death again. He will live forever before God in righteousness and purity.

Q. Where is this written?

A. St. Paul says to the Romans in chapter six:

> "We are buried with Christ through Baptism into death, so that, in the same way Christ is risen from the dead by the glory of the Father, thus also must we walk in a new life."

V. Confession
How One Should Teach the Uneducated to Confess

Q. What is confession?

A. Confession has two parts:

First, a person admits his sin

Second, a person receives absolution or forgiveness from the confessor, as if from God Himself, without doubting it, but believing firmly that his sins are forgiven by God in Heaven through it.

Q. Which sins should people confess?

A. When speaking to God, we should plead guilty to all sins, even those we don't know about, just as we do in the "Our Father," but when speaking to the confessor, only the sins we know about, which we know about and feel in our hearts.

Q. Which are these?

A. Consider here your place in life according to the Ten Commandments. Are you a father? A mother? A son? A daughter? A husband? A wife? A servant? Are you disobedient, unfaithful or lazy? Have you hurt anyone with your words or actions? Have you stolen, neglected your duty, let things go or injured someone?

VI. The Sacrament of the Altar:
The Simple Way a Father Should Present it to his Household

Q. What is the Sacrament of the Altar?

A. It is the true body and blood of our Lord Jesus Christ under bread and wine for us Christians to eat and to drink, established by Christ Himself.

Q. Where is that written?

A. The holy apostles Matthew, Mark and Luke and St. Paul write this:

"Our Lord Jesus Christ, in the night on which He was betrayed, took bread, gave thanks, broke it, gave it to His disciples and said: 'Take! Eat! This is My body, which is given for you. Do this to remember Me!' In the same way He also took the cup after supper, gave thanks, gave it to them, and said: 'Take and drink from it, all of you! This cup is the New Testament in my blood, which is shed for you to forgive sins. This do, as often as you drink it, to remember Me!'"

Q. What good does this eating and drinking do?

A. These words tell us: "Given for you" and "Shed for you to forgive sins." Namely, that the forgiveness of sins, life and salvation are given to us through these words in the sacrament. Because, where sins are forgiven, there is life and salvation as well.

Q. How can physical eating and drinking do such great things?

Of course, eating and drinking do not do these things. These words, written here, do them: "given for you" and "shed for you to forgive sins." These words, along with physical eating and drinking are the important part of the sacrament. Anyone who believes these words has what they say and what they record, namely, the forgiveness of sins.

Q. Who, then, receives such a sacrament in a worthy way?

A. Of course, fasting and other physical preparations are excellent disciplines for the body. But anyone who believes these words, "Given for you," and "Shed for you to forgive sins," is really worthy and well prepared. But whoever doubts or does not believe these words is not worthy and is unprepared, because the words, "for you" demand a heart that fully believes.

APPENDIX 1: DEVOTIONS
HOW A FATHER SHOULD TEACH HIS HOUSEHOLD TO CONDUCT MORNING AND EVENING DEVOTIONS.

MORNING DEVOTIONS

As soon as you get out of bed in the morning, you should bless yourself with the sign of the Holy Cross and say:

May the will of God, the Father, the Son and the Holy Spirit be done! Amen.

Then, kneeling or standing, say the creed and pray the Lord's Prayer. If you wish, you may then pray this little prayer as well:

My Heavenly Father, I thank You, through Jesus Christ, Your beloved Son, that You kept me safe from all evil and danger last night. Save me, I pray, today as well, from every evil and sin, so that all I do and the way that I live will please you. I put myself in your care, body and soul and all that I have. Let Your holy Angels be with me, so that the evil enemy will not gain power over me. Amen.

After that, with joy go about your work and perhaps sing a song inspired by the Ten Commandments or your own thoughts.

THE EVENING DEVOTIONS

When you go to bed in the evening, you should bless yourself with the sign of the Holy Cross and say:

May the will of God, the Father, the Son and the Holy Spirit be done! Amen.

Then, kneeling or standing, say the creed and pray the Lord's Prayer. If you wish, then you may pray this little prayer as well:

My Heavenly Father, I thank You, through Jesus Christ, Your beloved Son, that You have protected me, by Your grace. Forgive, I pray, all my sins and the evil I have done. Protect me, by Your grace, tonight. I put myself in your care, body and soul and all that I have. Let Your holy angels be with me, so that the evil enemy will not gain power over me. Amen. After this, go to sleep immediately with joy.

HOW A FATHER SHOULD TEACH HIS HOUSEHOLD
TO SAY GRACE AND RETURN THANKS AT MEALS:

The children and servants should come to the table modestly and with folded hands and say:

All eyes look to you, O Lord, and You give everyone food at the right time. You open Your generous hands and satisfy the hunger of all living things with what they desire.

Note: "What they desire" means that all animals get so much to eat, that they are happy and cheerful. Because, worry and greed interferes with such desires.

After this, pray the Lord's Prayer and the following prayer:

Lord God, Heavenly Father, bless us and these gifts, which we receive from Your generous hand, through Jesus Christ, our Lord. Amen.